MARTIN'S

ANNUAL CRIMINAL CODE

2020

CANADA LAW BOOK

MARTIN'S
ANNUAL CRIMINAL CODE
2020

With Annotations by

MARIE HENEIN, LL.B., LL.M.

In Memory and Acknowledgement of his valued contributions from 1997 to 2015:
The Honourable Mr. Justice
MARC ROSENBERG

In Memory and Acknowledgement of his valued contributions from 1978 to 2014:
EDWARD L. GREENSPAN, Q.C.

THOMSON REUTERS®

A cataloguing record for this publication is available from Library and Archives Canada

ISBN: 978-0-7798-9071-2; 978-0-7798-9072-9 (judicial);
978-0-7798-9073-6 (police); 978-0-7798-9074-3 (student)

Printed in the United States by Thomson Reuters

THOMSON REUTERS®

THOMSON REUTERS CANADA, A DIVISION OF THOMSON REUTERS CANADA LIMITED

One Corporate Plaza
2075 Kennedy Road
Toronto, ON
M1T 3V4

Customer Support
1-416-609-3800 (Toronto & International)
1-800-387-5164 (Toll Free Canada & U.S.)
Fax 1-416-298-5082 (Toronto)
Fax 1-877-750-9041 (Toll Free Canada Only)
Email CustomerSupport.LegalTaxCanada@TR.com

TABLE OF CONTENTS

IN MEMORY OF
The Honourable Justice Marc Rosenberg
(1950-2015)

It is with great sadness that we commemorate the passing of The Honourable Justice Marc Rosenberg.

Justice Rosenberg was a highly regarded appellate advocate, judge and one of our greatest legal minds. His tireless commitment to legal judicial education, both nationally and internationally, was a great contribution. The Honourable Justice Rosenberg was a long-standing co-author and co-editor of *Martin's Annual Criminal Code*, *Martin's Criminal Code (Counsel Edition)*, *Martin's Related Criminal Statutes*, *Martin's Ontario Criminal Practice*, *Martin's Pocket Criminal Code*, *Martin's Online Criminal Code*, the *Dominion Law Reports* and the *Canadian Criminal Cases*.

It was a great honour to work with him and be the beneficiary, like so many in his profession, of his knowledge, compassion and great wisdom. He will be greatly missed.

Marie Henein

IN MEMORY OF
The Honourable Justice Marc Rosenberg
(1950-2015)

It is with great sadness that we commemorate the passing of The Honourable Justice Marc Rosenberg.

Justice Rosenberg was a highly regarded appellate advocate, judge and one of our greatest legal minds. His tireless commitment to legal judicial education, both nationally and internationally, was a great contribution. The Honourable Justice Rosenberg was a long-standing co-author and co-editor of *Martin's Annual Criminal Code*, *Martin's Criminal Code* (*Counsel Edition*), *Martin's Related Criminal Statutes*, *Martin's Ontario Criminal Practice*, *Martin's Pocket Criminal Code*, *Martin's Online Criminal Code*, the *Dominion Law Reports* and the *Canadian Criminal Cases*.

It was a great honour to work with him and be the beneficiary, like so many in his profession, of his knowledge, compassion and great wisdom. He will be greatly missed.

Marie Henein

IN MEMORY OF
Edward L. Greenspan, Q.C.
(1944-2014)

It is with great sadness that we acknowledge the passing of Edward L. Greenspan, Q.C., one of the most celebrated criminal defence lawyers in Canada.

A tireless and passionate advocate, speaker and writer, Mr. Greenspan was a long-standing co-author of *Martin's Annual Criminal Code*, *Martin's Criminal Code (Counsel Edition)*, *Martin's Related Criminal Statutes*, *Martin's Ontario Criminal Practice*, *Martin's Pocket Criminal Code*, *Martin's Online Criminal Code*, *Canadian Charter of Rights Annotated*, and *Dubin Lectures on Advocacy 1998-2002*. He was, in addition, on the Editorial Boards for the *Canadian Criminal Cases* law report series from 1972 and the *Weekly Criminal Bulletin* from 1976.

It was a privilege and a pleasure to work with him on these career-long projects that he cared so deeply about. We are filled with great sadness at the loss of our colleague and dear friend.

Marc Rosenberg
Marie Henein

PREFACE

This edition of *Martin's Annual Criminal Code* contains the annotated *Criminal Code*, the *Canada Evidence Act*, the *Controlled Drugs and Substances Act*, the *Crimes Against Humanity and War Crimes Act*, the *Youth Criminal Justice Act* and excerpts from the *Constitution Act*.

This edition has been updated to include all statutory amendments up to April 26, 2019. The text of any amendments which have not been brought into force are printed in shaded boxes. As always, Thomson Reuters Canada will provide subscribers with free legislative supplements, as necessary, posted on the website at www.carswell.com. In addition, subscribers will receive annotated print supplements with the legislative developments enhanced with the latest case law developments. Subscribers may also register to receive the *Martin's Annual Criminal Code* e-notes service. The e-notes service will alert subscribers via email when a legislative amendment has been made to their edition and provide them with a direct link to the website. To register for this service, visit www.carswell.com or contact Customer Support at CustomerSupport.LegalTax-Canada@TR.com/email, or call 1-416-609-3800, toll free 1-800-387-5164.

For your convenience we have again included the *Regulations Prescribing Certain Firearms and Other Weapons, Components and Parts of Weapons, Accessories, Cartridge Magazines, and Projectiles as Prohibited or Restricted*, SOR/98-462 following s. 84 of the *Criminal Code*, *Regulations Prescribing Public Officers*, SOR/98-466 following s. 117.07 of the Code, and the *Order Declaring an Amnesty Period (2014)*, SOR/2014-56 following s. 117.14 of the Code. The texts of these regulations are found in shaded boxes. The complete text of the *Firearms Act*, S.C. 1994-95, c. 39, can be found in the 2018-2019 edition of *Martin's Related Criminal Statutes*.

With respect to statutory amendments enacted since the last edition, on December 13, 2018, the *Act to amend the Criminal Code and the Department of Justice Act and to make consequential amendments to another Act*, S.C. 2018, c. 29 (former Bill C-51) was given Royal Assent. In addition to amending and repealing obsolete provisions, the Act made modifications to the regime under ss. 276 and 278 of the *Criminal Code*, which governs the admission of prior sexual history evidence and the production and use of third party records in sexual offence prosecutions. Notably, s. 276 has expanded to define sexual activity as including any communication made for a sexual purpose or whose content is of a sexual nature: see subsec. (4). In addition, s. 278.92 now dictates that any "records" (as defined by s. 278.2) in the possession of the defence cannot be adduced by the defence without an application under this provision and a consideration of the factors set out in s. 278.92(3).

Substantial amendments have also been made to the drinking and driving provisions. On December 18, 2018, ss. 249 through to 261 were repealed and replaced by Part VIII.1, which is titled "Offences Relating to Conveyances" and contains a new substantive and procedural scheme governing these offences (see ss. 320.11 to 320.4). These amendments include an increase of certain maximum and minimum penalties and the modernization of offences and procedures relating to impaired driving. The amendments to the *Criminal Code* provisions dealing with drug-impaired driving include the creation of new criminal offences for driving with a blood-drug concentration equal to or higher than a permitted level and the establishment of an officer's power to demand a sample of bodily substances from a driver suspected of having a drug in his or her body. Perhaps most notably, the scheme enacts a new police power to demand a breath test from a motorist without having formed any individualized suspicion in respect of that motorist: s. 320.27(2).

Finally, on October 17, 2018 the *Cannabis Act*, S.C. 2018, c. 1, came into force, providing legal access to cannabis under strict regulations.

This edition contains annotations of all relevant decisions reported to April 10, 2019. In addition, unreported decisions of particular significance, which have come to our attention prior to April 10, 2019, are also included. Where there is a large volume of case law under a section, headings are included to make the annotations more accessible. The annotations under the Charter of Rights sections are of general application. Cases dealing with a specific provision (of the *Criminal Code*, for example) are noted under that section.

The practice initiated in the very first edition of *Martin's Criminal Code* (1955) of including cross-references has been continued in this edition in order to assist the user in locating related provisions. A synopsis of most sections is also included, along with the cross-references and annotations.

This edition contains the Offence Grid, which is based upon charts prepared by the Provincial Judges' Association of British Columbia. We wish to acknowledge the kind offer of the Association to permit us to include these charts in this edition of Martin's.

Particular thanks to Matthew Gourlay for his research and assistance in the preparation of this edition.

We are grateful to Sue Rose of Thomson Reuters Canada for her able assistance in the preparation of this edition.

MARIE HENEIN, LL.B., LL.M.

Toronto, Ontario
May, 2019

CRIMINAL CODE CONCORDANCE

This Table sets out all sections of the *Criminal Code*, R.S.C. 1970, c. C-34, as amended to December, 1988, and the corresponding numbering in R.S.C. 1985, c. C-46, as amended to April 26, 2019. References to subsections, paragraphs and subparagraphs appear only when the numbering has been changed in the R.S.C. 1985 Code. The numbers listed under the heading "R.S.C. 1985" reflect the numbering scheme set out in the main volumes of the Revised Statutes of Canada, 1985, the First, Second, Third and Fourth Supplements and amendments.

Locate the number under the heading R.S.C. 1970, c. C-34, and cross-refer to the number that appears in the opposite column under the heading R.S.C. 1985, c. C-46. Where a case cites provisions from the 1970 Code, consult the R.S.C. 1985 column for the corresponding 1985 Code section numbers. Where contemporary cases cite the 1985 Code, consult the R.S.C. 1970 column for the corresponding 1970 Code numbers.

Note: Users should bear in mind, however, that the Concordance is not a citator and has been assembled only as a guide to the numbering of the 1985 Code.

R.S.C. 1970, c. C-34	R.S.C. 1985, c. C-46
1	1
2	2
—	2 "associated personnel" [en. 2001, c. 41, s. 2(2)]
—	2 "common-law partner" [en. 2000, c. 12, s. 91]
—	2 "criminal organization" [en. 1997, c. 23, s. 1]
—	2 "criminal organization offence" [en. 1997, c. 23, s. 1]
—	2 "environment" [en. 2013, c. 13, s. 2(2)]
—	2 "government or public facility" [en. 2001, c. 41, s. 2(2)]
—	2 "justice system participant" [en. 2001, c. 41, s. 2(2)]
—	2 "nuclear facility" [en. 2013, c. 13, s. 2(2)]
—	2 "nuclear material" [en. 2013, c. 13, s. 2(2)]
—	2 "offence-related property" [en. 1997, c. 23, s. 1]
—	2 "magistrate" [rep. R.S.C. 1985, c. 27 (1st Supp.), s. 2(4)]
2 "peace officer"	2 "peace officer"
2(d.1)	2(e)
2(e)	2(f)
2(f)	2(g)
—	2 "radioactive material" [en. 2013, c. 13, s. 2(2)]
—	2 "street racing" [en. 2006, c. 14, s. 1; rep. 2018, c. 21, s. 12]
2 "superior court of criminal jurisdiction"	2 "superior court of criminal jurisdiction"
—	2 "terrorism offence" [en. 2001, c. 41, s. 2(2)]
—	2 "terrorist activity" [en. 2001, c. 41, s. 2(2)]
—	2 "terrorist group" [en. 2001, c. 41, s. 2(2)]
—	2 "United Nations operation" [en. 2001, c. 41, s. 2(2)]
—	2 "United Nations personnel" [en. 2001, c. 41, s. 2(2)]
—	2 "valuable mineral" [en. 1999, c. 5, s. 1]
2(d)	2(e)
2(e)	2(d)
2(f)	2(f)
2(g)	2(g)
—	2.1 [en. 2009, c. 22, s. 1]
—	2.2 [en. 2015, c. 13, s. 4]
2.1	3
—	3 (3.71) to (3.75) [en. 2001, c. 41, s. 126(2)]

R.S.C. 1970, c. C-34	R.S.C. 1985, c. C-46
—	3.1 [en. 2002, c. 13, s. 2]
Part I	Part I
3	4
3(1)	repealed
3(2)	4(1)
3(3)	4(2)
3(4)	4(3)
3(5)	4(4)
3(6)	4(5)
3(7)	4(6)
3(8)	4(7)
—	4(8) [en. 2014, c. 31, s. 2]
4	5
5	6
6	7
6(1.1)	7(2)
—	7(2.01)-(2.02) [en. 2005, c. 40, s. 2]
—	7(2.21) [en. 2013, c. 13, s. 3(1)]
6(1.2)	7(3)
6(1.3)	7(3.1)
6(1.4)	7(3.2) [rep. 2013, c. 13, s. 3(2)]
6(1.5)	7(3.3) [rep. 2013, c. 13, s. 3(2)]
6(1.6)	7(3.4) [rep. 2013, c. 13, s. 3(2)]
6(1.7)	7(3.5) [rep. 2013, c. 13, s. 3(2)]
6(1.8)	7(3.6) [rep. 2013, c. 13, s. 3(2)]
6(1.9)	7(3.7)
6(1.91)	7(3.71)
6(1.92)	7(3.72)
6(1.93)	7(3.73)
6(1.94)	7(3.74)
6(1.95)	7(3.75)
6(1.96)	7(3.76)
6(1.97)	7(3.77)
6(2)	7(4)
—	7(4.2) [rep. 2002, c. 13, s. 3(2)]
6(3)	7(5)
6(3.1)	7(5.1)
6(4)	7(6)
6(5)	7(7)
6(6)	7(8)
6(7)	7(9)
6(8)	7(10)
6(9)	7(11)
7	8

R.S.C. 1970, c. C-34	R.S.C. 1985, c. C-46
7(1)(a)	8(1)(b)
7(1)(b)	8(1)(a)
8	9
9	10
10	11
11	12
12	13
13	repealed
14-33	14-33
—	25.1 to 25.4 [en. 2001, c. 32, s. 2]
—	27.1 [en. 2004, c. 12, s. 2]
—	33.1 [en. 1995, c. 32, s. 1]
34	34
35	35
36-42	36-42 [rep. 2012, c. 9, s. 2]
43	43
44	44 [rep. 2001, c. 26, s. 294]
45	45
Part II	Part II
46-55	46-55
—	49 [rep. 2018, c. 29, s. 1]
56	repealed
57	56
—	56.1 [en. 2009, c. 28, s. 1]
58	57
59	58
60	59
61	60
62	61
63	62
64	63
65	64
66	65 [renumbered as (1) and (2) en. 2013, c. 15, s. 2]
67	66 [renumbered as (1) and (2) en. 2013, c. 15, s. 3]
68	67
69	68
70	69
71	70
72	71 [rep. 2018, c. 29, s. 4]
73	72
74	73
75	74
76	75

R.S.C. 1970, c. C-34	R.S.C. 1985, c. C-46
76.1	76
76.2	77
76.3	78
—	78.1 [en 1993, c. 7, s. 4]
77	79
78	80
79	81
80	82
—	82.1 [en. 1997, c. 23, s. 2]
—	82.2 [en. 2013, c. 13, s. 5]
—	82.3 [en. 2013, c. 13, s. 5]
—	82.4 [en. 2013, c. 13, s. 5]
—	82.5 [en. 2013, c. 13, s. 5]
—	82.6 [en. 2013, c. 13, s. 5]
—	82.7 [en. 2013, c. 13, s. 5]
81	83
—	Part II.1 (ss. 83.01 to 83.33) [en. 2001, c. 41, s. 4]
—	83.181 [en. 2013, c. 9, c. 6]
—	83.191 [en. 2013, c. 9, c. 7]
—	83.201 [en. 2013, c. 9, c. 8]
—	83.202 [en. 2013, c. 9, c. 8]
—	83.221 [en. 2015, c. 20, c. 16]
—	83.222 [en. 2015, c. 20, c. 16]
—	83.223 [en. 2015, c. 20, c. 16]
—	83.231 [en. 2004, c. 15, s. 32]
—	83.3(7.1), (7.2), (8.1), (11.1) and (11.2) [en. 2015, c. 20, c. 17]
Part II.1	Part III (replaced 1995, c. 39, s. 139)
82	—
83	—
84	—
85	—
86	—
87	—
88	—

R.S.C. 1970, c. C-34	R.S.C. 1985, c. C-46
—	—
89	—
—	—
90	—
91	—
92	—
93	—
—	—
94	—
95	—
96	—
97	—
98	—
98(11) "appeal court"	—
98(11)(a)	—
98(11)(b)	—
98(11)(b.1)	—
98(11)(c)	—
98(11)(d)	—
98(11)(e)	—
98(11)(f)	—
99	—
100	—
101	—
102	—
103	—
104	—
104 [1976-77, c. 53, s. 47(3)]	—
104(3)	—
104(4)	—
104(5)	—
104(6)	—
104(7)	—
104(8)	—
104(9)	—
104(10)	—
104(11)	—
104(12)	—
105	—
106	—
106.1	—
106.2	—
—	—
106.3	—
106.4	—
106.5	—
106.6	—
106.7	—
106.8	—
106.9	—
—	84
—	85

R.S.C. 1970, c. C-34	R.S.C. 1985, c. C-46
—	86
—	87
—	88
—	89
—	90
—	91
—	92
—	93
—	94
—	95
—	96
—	97 [not yet in force]
—	98
—	99
—	100
—	101
—	102
—	103
—	104
—	105
—	106
—	107
—	108
—	109
—	109(1)(*c.1*) [en. 2018, c. 16, s. 208]
—	110
—	110(2.1) [en. 2015, c. 27, s. 31]
—	110.1 [en. 2015, c. 27, s. 32]
—	111
—	112
—	113
—	114
—	115
—	116
—	117
—	117.01
—	117.011
—	117.02
—	117.03
—	117.04
—	117.05
—	117.06
—	117.07
—	117.08
—	117.09
—	117.1
—	117.11
—	117.12
—	117.13
—	117.14
—	117.15

R.S.C. 1970, c. C-34	R.S.C. 1985, c. C-46
—	117.15(3) and (4) [en. 2015, c. 27, s. 34]
Part III	Part IV
107	118
108	119
109	120
110	121
—	121.1 [en. 2014, c. 23, s. 3]
111	122
112	123
113	124
114	125
115	126
116	127
117	128
118	129
119	130
—	130.1 [en. 2014, c. 10, s. 1]
120	131
121	132
122	133
122.1	134
123	135 [rep. R.S.C. 1985, c. 27 (1st Supp.), s. 17]
124	136
125	137
126	138
127	139
128	140
129	141
130	142
131	143 [rep. 2018, c. 29, s. 8]
132	144
133	145
—	145(5.1) [en. 1997, c. 18, s. 3(2)]
133(7)	145(7) [rep. R.S.C. 1985, c. 27 (1st Supp.), s. 20(2)]
134	146
135	147
136	148
137	149
Part IV	Part V
138	150
139	150.1
—	150.1(2.3) [en. 2015, c. 29, s. 6]
140	151

R.S.C. 1970, c. C-34	R.S.C. 1985, c. C-46
141	152
142-145	repealed
146	153
—	153(1.1) and (1.2) [en. 2005, c. 32, s. 4(2)]
—	153.1 [en. 1998, c. 9, s. 2]
—	153.1(2.1), (2.2) [en. 2018, c. 29, s. 10(1)]
147	154 [rep. R.S.C. 1985, c. 19 (3rd Supp.), s. 1]
148 and 149	repealed
150	155
151-153	156-158 [rep. R.S.C. 1985, c. 19 (3rd Supp.), s. 2]
154	159
155	160
156	repealed
157 and 158	161 and 162 [rep. R.S.C. 1985, c. 19 (3rd Supp.), s. 4]
—	161 [en. 1993, c. 45, s. 1]
—	161(1.1) [en. 2005, c. 32, s. 5(2)]
—	162 [en. 2005, c. 32, s. 6]
—	162.1 [en. 2014, c. 31, s. 3]
—	162.2 [en. 2014, c. 31, s. 3]
159	163
159(6)	163(6) [rep. 1993, c. 46, s. 1(2)]
—	163(7) [rep. 2018, c. 29, s. 11(4)]
—	163.1 [en. 1993, c. 46, s. 2]
—	163.1(4.1) and (4.2) [en. 2002, c. 13, s. 5(3)]
160	164
160(8) "court"	164(8) "court"
—	164(8) "crime comic" [rep. 2018, c. 29, s. 12(3)]
160(8)(a)	164(8)(a)
160(8)(a.1)	164(8)(b)
160(8)(b)	164(8)(c)
160(8)(c)	164(8)(d)
—	164.1 [en. 2002, c. 13, s. 7]

R.S.C. 1970, c. C-34	R.S.C. 1985, c. C-46
—	164.2 [en. 2002, c. 13, s. 7]
—	164.3 [en. 2002, c. 13, s. 7]
161	165 [rep. 2018, c. 29, s. 13]
162	166 [rep. 1994, c. 44, s. 9]
163	167
164	168
165	169
166	170
167	171
168	172
168(2)	172(2) [rep. R.S.C. 1985, c. 19 (3rd Supp.), s. 6]
—	172.1 [en. 2002, c. 13, s. 8]
169	173
170	174
171	175
172	176
173	177
174	178 [rep. 2018, c. 29, s. 14]
175	179
175(1)(a) to (c)	repealed
175(1)(d)	179(1)(a)
175(1)(e)	179(1)(b)
175(2)	179(2)
175(3)	repealed
176	180
177	181
178	182
Part IV.1	Part VI
178.1	183
—	183.1 [en. 1993, c. 40, s. 2]
178.11	184
—	184(2)(e) [en. 2004, c. 12, s. 4(1)]
178.11(3)	184(3) [rep. 1993, c. 40, s. 3(3); re-en. 2004, c. 12, s. 4(2)]
—	184.1 [en. 1993, c. 40, s. 4]
—	184.2 [en. 1993, c. 40, s. 4]
—	184.2(5) [en. 2014, c. 31, s. 8]
—	184.3 [en. 1993, c. 40, s. 4]
—	184.4 [en. 1993, c. 40, s. 4]

R.S.C. 1970, c. C-34	R.S.C. 1985, c. C-46
—	184.5 [en. 1993, c. 40, s. 4]
—	184.6 [en. 1993, c. 40, s. 4]
178.12	185
178.12(1)(e.1)	185(1)(f)
178.12(1)(f)	185(1)(g)
178.12(1)(g)	185(1)(h)
—	185(1.1) [en. 1997, c. 23, s. 4]
178.13	186
—	186(1.1) [en. 1997, c. 23, s. 5]
178.13(1.1)	186(2)
178.13(1.2)	186(3)
178.13(2)	186(4)
178.13(2.1)	186(5)
—	186(5.1) [en. 1999, c. 5, s. 5]
—	186(5.2) [en. 1999, c. 5, s. 5]
178.13(3)	186(6)
178.13(4)	186(7)
—	186(8) [en. 2014, c. 31, s. 9]
—	186.1 [en. 1997, c. 23, s. 6]
178.14	187
—	187(8) [en. 2014, c. 31, s. 10]
178.15	188
178.15(3)	188(3) [rep. 1993, c. 40, s. 8(3)]
178.15(4)(a), (b)	188(4)(a), (b)
178.15(4)(b.1)	188(4)(e.1)
178.15(4)(c)	188(4)(f.1)
178.15(4)(c.1)	188(4)(d)
178.15(4)(c.2)	188(4)(c)
178.15(4)(d)	188(4)(e)
178.15(4)(e)	188(4)(f)
178.15(4)(f)	188(4)(g)
178.15(4)(g)	188(4)(h)
—	188(6) [en. 2014, c. 31, s. 11]
—	188.1 [en. 1993, c. 40, s. 9]
—	188.2 [en. 1993, c. 40, s. 9]
178.16	189
178.16(1)-(3)	189(1)-(3) [rep. 1993, c. 40, s. 10(1)]
178.16(3.1)	189(4) [rep. 1993, c. 40, s. 10(1)]
178.16(4)	189(5)
178.16(5)	189(6)

R.S.C. 1970, c. C-34	R.S.C. 1985, c. C-46
178.17	190
178.18	191
178.19	192
178.2	193
—	193(2)(d)(iii) [en. 2004, c. 12, s. 5]
—	193.1 [en. 1993, c. 40, s. 12]
178.21	194
178.22	195
178.22(2)(g.1)	195(2)(h)
178.22(2)(h)	195(2)(i)
178.22(2)(i)	195(2)(j)
178.22(2)(j)	195(2)(k)
178.22(2)(k)	195(2)(l)
178.22(2)(l)	195(2)(m)
178.22(2)(m)	195(2)(n)
—	195(2.1) [en. 2013, c. 8, s. 5(3)]
178.23	196
178.23(2)	—
178.23(3)	196(2)
178.23(4)	196(3)
178.23(5)	196(4)
—	196(5) [en. 1997, c. 23, s. 7]
—	196.1 [en. 2013, c. 8, s. 6]
Part V	Part VII
179	197
180	198 [rep. 2018, c. 29, s. 16]
181	199
182 and 183	repealed
184	200 [rep. R.S.C. 1985, c. 27 (1st Supp.), s. 30]
185	201
186	202
187	203
188	204
188(6.1)	204(7)
188(6.2)	204(8)
188(6.3)	204(8.1)
188(7)	204(9)
188(7.1)	204(9.1)
188(8)	204(10)
188.1	205 [rep. R.S.C. 1985, c. 52 (1st Supp.), s. 1]
189	206
190	207
—	207(4.1) [en. 2014, c. 39, s. 171]

R.S.C. 1970, c. C-34	R.S.C. 1985, c. C-46
—	207.1 [en. 1999, c. 5, s. 7]
—	207.1(4.01) [en. 2018, c. 29, s. 17(2)]
191	208 [rep. R.S.C. 1985, c. 27 (1st Supp.), s. 32]
192	209
193	210
194	211
195	212 [rep., with heading, 2014, c. 25, s. 13]
—	212(5) [rep. 1999, c. 5, s. 8]
195.1	213
—	213(1.1) [en. 2014, c. 25, s. 15(3)]
Part VI	Part VIII
196	214
—	214 "aircraft" [rep. 2018, c. 21, s. 13]
—	214 "operate" [rep. 2018, c. 21, s. 13]
—	214 "vessel" [rep. 2018, c. 21, s. 13]
197	215
198	216
199	217
200	218
201	repealed
202	219
203	220
204	221
205	222
206	223
207	224
208	225
209	226
210	227 [rep. 1999, c. 5, s. 9(1); re-en. 2016, c. 3, s. 2]
211	228
212	229
213	230
214	231
214(6)	231(6) [rep. R.S.C. 1985, c. 27 (1st Supp.), s. 35]
—	231(6.01) [en. 2001, c. 41, s. 9]
—	231(6.1) [en. 1997, c. 23, s. 8]

R.S.C. 1970, c. C-34	R.S.C. 1985, c. C-46
—	231(6.2) [en. 2001, c. 32, s. 9(2)]
215	232
216	233
217	234
218	235
219	236
220	237
221	238
222	239
223	240
224	241
—	241.1 [en. 2016, c. 3, s. 3]
—	241.2 [en. 2016, c. 3, s. 3]
—	241.3 [en. 2016, c. 3, s. 3]
—	241.31 [en. 2016, c. 3, s. 4]
—	241.4 [en. 2016, c. 3, s. 3]
225	repealed
226	242
227	243
228	244 [en. 1995, c. 39, s. 144]
—	244.1 [en. 1995, c. 39, s. 144]
—	244.2 [en. 2009, c. 22, s. 8]
229	245
—	245(2) and (3) [en. 2016, c. 3, s. 6]
230	246
231	247
232	248
233	249 [(and heading) rep. 2018, c. 21, s. 14]
—	249.1 [en. 2000, c. 2, s. 1; rep. 2018, c. 21, s. 14]
—	249.2 [en. 2006, c. 14, s. 2; rep. 2018, c. 21, s. 14]
—	249.3 [en. 2006, c. 14, s. 2; rep. 2018, c. 21, s. 14]
—	249.4 [en. 2006, c. 14, s. 2; rep. 2018, c. 21, s. 14]
234	250 [rep. 2018, c. 21, s. 14]
235	251 [rep. 2018, c. 21, s. 14]

R.S.C. 1970, c. C-34	R.S.C. 1985, c. C-46
236	252 [rep. 2018, c. 21, s. 14]
237	253 [rep. 2018, c. 21, s. 14]
—	253.1 [en. 2018, c. 21, s. 2; rep. 2018, c. 21, s. 14]
238	254 [rep. 2018, c. 21, s. 14]
—	254.01 [en. 2018, c. 21, s. 4; rep. 2018, c. 21, s. 14]
—	254.1 [en. 2008, c. 6, s. 20; rep. 2018, c. 21, s. 14]
239	255 [rep. 2018, c. 21, s. 14]
—	255.1 [en. 1999, c. 32, s. 4; rep. 2018, c. 21, s. 14]
240	256 [rep. 2018, c. 21, s. 14]
240.1	257 [rep. 2018, c. 21, s. 14]
241	258 [rep. 2018, c. 21, s. 14]
—	258.1 [en. 2008, c. 6, s. 25; rep. 2018, c. 21, s. 14]
242	259 [rep. 2018, c. 21, s. 14]
243	260 [rep. 2018, c. 21, s. 14]
243.1	261 [rep. 2018, c. 21, s. 14]
243.2	262
243.3	263
243 [*old provision*]	264 [rep. R.S.C. 1985, c. 27 (1st Supp.), s. 37]
—	264 [en. 1993, c. 45, s. 2]
243.4	264.1
244	265
245	266
245.1	267
245.2	268
245.3	269
—	269.01 [en. 2015, c. 1, s. 1]
245.4	269.1
246	270
—	270.01 [en. 2009, c. 22, s. 9]
—	270.02 [en. 2009, c. 22, s. 9]

R.S.C. 1970, c. C-34	R.S.C. 1985, c. C-46
—	270.03 [en. 2015, c. 34, s. 2]
—	270.1 [en. 2002, c. 13, s. 11]
246.1	271
246.1(2)	271(2) [rep. R.S.C. 1985, c. 19 (3rd Supp.), s. 10]
246.2	272
246.3	273
—	273.1 [en. 1992, c. 38, s. 1]
—	273.1(1.1), (1.2) [en. 2018, c. 29, s. 19(1)]
—	273.2 [en. 1992, c. 38, s. 1]
—	273.3 [en. 1992, c. 38, s. 1]
246.4	274
246.5	275
246.6	276
—	276(4) [en. 2018, c. 29, s. 21(3)]
—	276.1-276.5 [en. 1992, c. 38, s. 2; rep. 2018, c. 29, s. 22]
246.7	277
246.8	278
—	278.1 to 278.91 [en. 1997, c. 30, s. 1]
—	278.92-278.97 [en. 2018, c. 29, s. 25]
247	279
—	279(3) [rep. 2018, c. 29, s. 26]
—	279(1.21) [en. 2013, c. 32, s. 1]
—	279.01 [en. 2005, c. 43, s. 3]
—	279.02 [en. 2005, c. 43, s. 3]
—	279.03 [en. 2005, c. 43, s. 3]
—	279.04 [en. 2005, c. 43, s. 3]
247.1	279.1
—	279.1(3) [rep. 2018, c. 29, s. 27]
248	repealed
249	280
250	281
250.1	282
250.2	283
250.3	284

R.S.C. 1970, c. C-34	R.S.C. 1985, c. C-46
250.4	285
250.5	286
—	286.1 [en. 2014, c. 25, s. 20]
—	286.2 [en. 2014, c. 25, s. 20]
—	286.3 [en. 2014, c. 25, s. 20]
—	286.4 [en. 2014, c. 25, s. 20]
—	286.5 [en. 2014, c. 25, s. 20]
251	287
251(6) "Minister of Health"	287(6) "Minister of Health"
251(6)(a)	287(6)(a)
251(6)(a.1)	287(6)(d)
251(6)(b)	287(6)(c)
251(6)(c)	287(6)(b)
251(6)(d)	287(6)(e)
252	288 [rep. 2018, c. 29, s. 28]
253	289 [rep. R.S.C. 1985, c. 27 (1st Supp.), s. 41]
254	290
255	291
256	292
257	293
—	293.1 [en. 2015, c. 29, s. 9]
—	293.2 [en. 2015, c. 29, s. 9]
258	294
259	295
260	296 [(and heading) rep. 2018, c. 29, s. 30]
261	297
262	298
263	299
264	300
265	301
266	302
267	303
268	304
269	305
270	306
271	307
272	308
273	309
274	310
275	311
276	312
277	313
278	314
279	315
280	316
281	317
281.1	318
281.2	319
281.3	320
281.3(8) "court"	320(8) "court"
281.3(8)(a)	320(8)(a)
281.3(8)(a.1)	320(8)(b)
281.3(8)(b)	320(8)(c)
281.3(8)(c)	320(8)(d)
—	320.1 [en. 2001, c. 41, s. 10]
—	Part VIII.1 [en. 2018, c. 21, s. 15]
—	320.11 [en. 2018, c. 21, s. 15]
—	320.12 [en. 2018, c. 21, s. 15]
—	320.13 [en. 2018, c. 21, s. 15]
—	320.14 [en. 2018, c. 21, s. 15]
—	320.15 [en. 2018, c. 21, s. 15]
—	320.16 [en. 2018, c. 21, s. 15]
—	320.17 [en. 2018, c. 21, s. 15]
—	320.18 [en. 2018, c. 21, s. 15]
—	320.19 [en. 2018, c. 21, s. 15]
—	320.2 [en. 2018, c. 21, s. 15]
—	320.21 [en. 2018, c. 21, s. 15]
—	320.22 [en. 2018, c. 21, s. 15]
—	320.23 [en. 2018, c. 21, s. 15]
—	320.24 [en. 2018, c. 21, s. 15]
—	320.25 [en. 2018, c. 21, s. 15]
—	320.26 [en. 2018, c. 21, s. 15]
—	320.27 [en. 2018, c. 21, s. 15]
—	320.28 [en. 2018, c. 21, s. 15]
—	320.29 [en. 2018, c. 21, s. 15]
—	320.3 [en. 2018, c. 21, s. 15]

R.S.C. 1970, c. C-34	R.S.C. 1985, c. C-46
—	320.31 [en. 2018, c. 21, s. 15]
—	320.32 [en. 2018, c. 21, s. 15]
—	320.33 [en. 2018, c. 21, s. 15]
—	320.34 [en. 2018, c. 21, s. 15]
—	320.35 [en. 2018, c. 21, s. 15]
—	320.36 [en. 2018, c. 21, s. 15]
—	320.37 [en. 2018, c. 21, s. 15]
—	320.38 [en. 2018, c. 21, s. 15]
—	320.39 [en. 2018, c. 21, s. 15]
—	320.4 [en. 2018, c. 21, s. 15]
Part VII	Part IX
282	321
283	322
284	323
285	324
286	325
287	326 [rep. 2014, c. 31, s. 14(2)]
287.1	327
288	328
289	329 [rep. 2000, c. 12, s. 94]
290	330
291	331
292	332
293	333
—	333.1 [en. 2010, c. 14, s. 3]
294	334
295	335
—	335(1.1) [en. 1997, c. 18, s. 15]
296	336
297	337 [rep. 2018, c. 29, s. 33]
298	338
298(1.1)	338(2)
298(2)	338(3)
298(3)	338(4)
299	339
300	340
301	341
301.1	342
—	342(3) [en. 1997, c. 18, s. 16(2)]

R.S.C. 1970, c. C-34	R.S.C. 1985, c. C-46
—	342(4) [en. 1997, c. 18, s. 16(2)]
—	342.01 [en. 1997, c. 18, s. 17]
301.2	342.1
—	342.1(1)(*d*) [en. 1997, c. 18, s. 18(1)]
—	342.1(2) "computer data" [en. 2014, c. 31, s. 16(4)]
—	342.1(2) "computer password" [en. 1997, c. 18, s. 18(2)]
—	342.1(2) "traffic" [en. 1997, c. 18, s. 18(2)]
—	342.2 [en. 1997, c. 18, s. 19]
—	342.2(4) [en. 2014, c. 31, s. 17(2)]
302	343
303	344
304	345
305	346
305.1	347
—	347.1 [en. 2007, c. 9, s. 2]
306	348
—	348.1 [en. 2002, c. 13, s. 15]
306(3)	repealed
306(4)	348(3)
307	349
308	350
309	351
310	352
311	353
—	353(1.1) [en. 1997, c. 18, s. 22(1)]
—	353(2.1) [en. 1997, c. 18, s. 22(2)]
—	353.1 [en. 2010, c. 14, s. 4]
312	354
—	354(4) [en. 1997, c. 18, s. 23]
313	355
—	355.1 [en. 2010, c. 14, s. 5]
—	355.2 [en. 2010, c. 14, s. 5]
—	355.3 [en. 2010, c. 14, s. 5]

R.S.C. 1970, c. C-34	R.S.C. 1985, c. C-46
—	355.4 [en. 2010, c. 14, s. 5]
—	355.5 [en. 2010, c. 14, s. 5]
314	356
315	357
316	358
317	359 [rep. 2018, c. 29, s. 40]
318	360 [rep. 2018, c. 29, s. 40]
319	361
320	362
321	363
322	364
323	365 [rep. 2018, c. 29, s. 41]
324	366
—	366(5) [en. 2009, c. 28, s. 7]
325	367
—	367(2) [rep. 1994, c. 44, s. 24]
326	368
—	368(1)(*c*) [en. 1997, c. 18, s. 25]
—	368(1)(*d*) [en. 1997, c. 18, s. 25]
—	368(1.1) [en. 2009, c. 28, s. 8]
—	368.1 [en. 2009, c. 28, s. 9]
—	368.2 [en. 2009, c. 28, s. 9]
327	369
328	370 [rep. 2018, c. 29, s. 42]
329	371 [rep. 2018, c. 29, s. 42
330	372
331	373 [rep. R.S.C. 1985, c. 27 (1st Supp.), s. 53]
332	374
333	375
334	376
335	377
336	378
Part VIII	Part X
337	379
338	380
—	380(1.1) [en. 2011, c. 6, s. 2]
—	380.1 [en. 2004, c. 3, s. 3]

R.S.C. 1970, c. C-34	R.S.C. 1985, c. C-46
—	380.01(1.1) [en. 2011, c. 6, s. 3(5)]
—	380.2 [en. 2011, c. 6, s. 4]
—	380.3 [en. 2011, c. 6, s. 4; rep. 2015, c. 13, s. 11]
—	380.4 [en. 2011, c. 6, s. 4; rep. 2015, c. 13, s. 11]
339	381
340	382
341	383
342	384
343	385
344	386
345	387
346	388
347	389
348	390
349	391
350	392
351	393
352	394
—	394.1 [en. 1999, c. 5, s. 10]
353	395
354	396
355	397
356	398
357	399
358	400
359	401
360	402 [rep. 2018, c. 29, s. 44]
—	402.1 [en. 2009, c. 28, s. 10]
—	402.2 [en. 2009, c. 28, s. 10]
361	403
362	404
363	405
364	406
365	407
366	408
367	409
368	410
369	411
370	412
371	413 [rep. 2018, c. 29, s. 47]
372	414
373	415
374	416

R.S.C. 1970, c. C-34	R.S.C. 1985, c. C-46
375	417
376	418
377	419
378	420
379	421
380	422
381	423
—	423.1 [en. 2001, c. 32, s. 11]
—	423.1(2) [rep. 2015, c. 13, s. 12(2)]
381.1	424
—	424.1 [en. 2001, c. 41, s. 11]
382	425
383	426
384	427 [(and heading) rep. 2018, c. 29, s. 50]
Part IX	Part XI
385	428
386	429
387	430
—	430(4.1) [en. 2001, c. 41, s. 12]
—	430(4.11) [en. 2014, c. 9, s. 1]
—	430(4.2) [en. 2005, c. 40, s. 3]
387.1	431
—	431.1 [en. 2001, c. 41, s. 13]
—	431.2 [en. 2001, c. 41, s. 13]
388	432 [rep. R.S.C. 1985, c. 27 (1st Supp.), s. 58]
389	433
390	434
—	434.1 [en. 1990, c. 15, s. 1]
391	435
392	436
—	436.1 [en. 1990, c. 15, s. 1]
393	437
394	438
395	439
396	440
397	441
398	442
399	443
400	444 [rep. 2018, c. 29, s. 52]
401	445

R.S.C. 1970, c. C-34	R.S.C. 1985, c. C-46
—	445.01 [en. 2015, c. 34, s. 3]
—	445.1 [en. 2008, c. 12, s. 1]
402	446
403	447
—	447.1 [en. 2008, c. 12, s. 1]
404 and 405	repealed
Part X	Part XII
406	448
407	449
408	450
409	451
410	452
411	453
412	454
413	455
414	456
415	457
416	458
417	459
418	460
419	461
—	461(4) [en. 2018, c. 21, s. 17]
420	462
Part X.1	Part XII.1 [rep. 2018, c. 16, s. 211]
420.1	462.1 [rep. 2018, c. 16, s. 211]
420.2	462.2 [rep. 2018, c. 16, s. 211]
Part X.1	Part XII.2
420.1	462.3
—	462.3 "designated drug offence" [rep. 1996, c. 19, s. 68(1)]
—	462.3 "designated substance offence" [rep. 2001, c. 32, s. 12(3)]
—	462.3 "designated offence" [en. 2001, c. 32, s. 12(6)]
—	462.3 "enterprise crime offence" [rep. 2001, c. 32, s. 12(2)]
—	462.3(2)-(4) [en. 2001, c. 32, s. 12(7)]
420.11	462.31

R.S.C. 1970, c. C-34	R.S.C. 1985, c. C-46
—	462.31(3) [en. 1997, c. 18, s. 28(2)]
420.12	462.32
—	462.32(4.1) [en. 2001, c. 41, s. 14(2)]
420.13	462.33
—	462.33(2)(*e*) [en. 1997, c. 18, s. 30(1)]
—	462.33(3.01) [en. 1997, c. 18, s. 30(3)]
—	462.331 [en. 2001, c. 32, s. 16]
420.14	462.34
—	462.34(5.1) [en. 1997, c. 18, s. 31(2)]
—	462.34(5.2) [en. 1997, c. 18, s. 31(2)]
—	462.341 [en. 1997, c. 18, s. 32]
420.15	462.35
420.16	462.36
420.17	462.37
—	462.37(2.01)-(2.07) [en. 2005, c. 44, s. 6]
—	462.37(2.02)(*c*) [en. 2018, c. 16, s. 214]
—	462.37(2.1) [en. 2001, c. 32, s. 19]
—	462.371 [en. 1997, c. 18, s. 34]
420.18	462.38
—	462.38(2.1) [en. 2001, c. 32, s. 20(3)]
420.19	462.39
420.2	462.4
420.21	462.41
420.22	462.42
420.23	462.43
—	462.43(2) [en. 2001, c. 32, s. 24]
420.24	462.44
420.25	462.45
420.26	462.46
420.27	462.47
420.28	462.48
—	462.48(1)(*a*.1) [en. 2018, c. 16, s. 215]
—	462.48(1)(*c*) [en. 1997, c. 23, s. 10]

R.S.C. 1970, c. C-34	R.S.C. 1985, c. C-46
420.29	462.49
420.3	462.5
Part XI	Part XIII
421	463
422	464
423	465
423(1)(c)	repealed
423(1)(d)	465(1)(c)
423(1)(e)	465(1)(d)
423(2)	465(2) [rep. R.S.C. 1985, c. 27 (1st Supp.), s. 61(3)]
424	466
425	467
—	467.1 [en. 1997, c. 23, s. 11]
—	467.11 to 467.14 [en. 2001, c. 32, s. 27]
—	467.111 [en. 2014, c. 17, s. 9]
—	467.2 [en. 1997, c. 23, s. 11]
Part XII	Part XIV
426	468
427	469
428	470
429	471
429.1	472 [rep. R.S.C. 1985, c. 27 (1st Supp.), s. 63]
430	473
431	474
431.1	475
432	476
433	477
—	477.1 [rep. 1996, c. 31, s. 8]
—	477.2 [en. 1990, c. 44, s. 15]
—	477.3 [en. 1990, c. 44, s. 15]
—	477.4 [en. 1990, c. 44, s. 15]
434	478
435	479
436	480
437	481
—	481.1 [en. 1996, c. 31, s. 72]
—	481.2 [en. 1996, c. 31, s. 72]
—	481.3 [en. 1996, c. 31, s. 72]
438	482
438(1.1)	482(2)

R.S.C. 1970, c. C-34	R.S.C. 1985, c. C-46
438(2)	482(3)
438(3)	not consolidated
438(4)	482(4)
438(5)	482(5)
—	482.1 [en. 2002, c. 13, s. 18]
Part XIII	Part XV
439	483
440	484
440.1	485
—	485(1.1) [en. 1997, c. 18, s. 40]
440.2	485.1
441	repealed
442	486
—	486(1.5) [en. 2001, c. 32, s. 29(1)]
442(2.1)	486(2.1)
442(2.2)	486(2.2)
442(3)	486(3)
442(3.1) [re-en. 1987, c. 24, s. 14(1)]; 1988, c. 30, s. 1	486(4)
442(4)	486(5)
442(5)	486(6) [rep. R.S.C. 1985, c. 19 (3rd Supp.), s. 14(2)]
—	486.1 to 486.6 [en. 2005, c. 32, s. 15]
—	486.2(7) and (8) [rep. 2015, c. 13, s. 15]
—	486.31 [en. 2015, c. 13, s. 17]
—	486.5(2.1) [en. 2015, c. 13, s. 19(1)]
—	486.7 [en. 2015, c. 20, s. 22]
443	487
—	487(1)(*c*.1) [en. 1997, c. 23, s. 12]
—	487(2.1) [en. 1997, c. 18, s. 40]
—	487(2.2) [en. 1997, c. 18, s. 40]
—	487.01 [en. 1993, c. 40, s. 15]
—	487.01(5.1) [en. 1997, c. 23, s. 13]
—	487.01(5.2) [en. 1997, c. 23, s. 13]
—	487.01(7) [en. 1997, c. 18, s. 49(2)]
—	487.018 to 487.0199 [en. 2014, c. 31, s. 20]
—	487.02 [en. 1993, c. 40, s. 15]
—	487.021 [en. 2014, c. 31, s. 20]
—	487.03 [en. 1993, c. 40, s. 15]
—	487.04 [en. 1995, c. 27, s. 1]
—	487.04 "secondary designated offence" (*a*.1) [en. 2018, c. 16, s. 216]
—	487.04 "secondary designated offence" (*c*)(iv) [rep. 2018, c. 21, s. 18(1)]
—	487.04 "secondary designated offence" (*c*)(viii.2) [en. 2018, c. 21, s. 18(2)]
—	487.04 "secondary designated offence" (*d*.1), (*d*.2) [en. 2018, c. 21, s. 18(3)]
—	487.05(3) [en. 1997, c. 18, s. 44]
—	487.051 to 487.058 [en. 1998, c. 37, s. 17]
—	487.06 to 487.09 [en. 1995, c. 27, s. 1]
—	487.071 [en. 1998, c. 7, s. 20]
—	487.091 [en. 1998, c. 37, s. 23]
—	487.092 [en. 1997, c. 18, s. 45; renum. 1998, c. 37, s. 23]
443.1	487.1
—	487.11 [en. 1997, c. 18, s. 46]
443.2	487.2
—	487.2(2) [rep. 2005, c. 32, s. 16(2)]
—	487.3 [en. 1997, c. 23, s. 14]
444	488
—	488.01 [en. 2017, c. 22, s. 3]
—	488.02 [en. 2017, c. 22, s. 3]
444.1	488.1
445	489
445.1	489.1

R.S.C. 1970, c. C-34	R.S.C. 1985, c. C-46
446	490
—	490(1.1) [en. 2001, c. 41, s. 18; rep. 2001, c. 41, s. 130(7.1)]
—	490(3.1) [en. 1997, c. 18, s. 50(1)]
—	490(18) [en. 1997, c. 18, s. 50(4)]
—	490.01 [en. 1997, c. 18, s. 5; am. 1999, c. 5, s. 17]
—	490.011 to 490.032 [en. 2004, c. 10, c. 20]
—	490.016(3) [en. 2007, c. 5, s. 16(2)]
—	490.017(2) [en. 2007, c. 5, s. 17]
—	490.023(1.1) [en. 2007, c. 5, s. 23]
—	490.027(3) [en. 2007, c. 5, s. 25(2)]
—	490.02901 to 490.02915 [en. 2010, c. 17, s. 19]
—	490.03111 [en. 2007, c. 5, s. 29]
—	490.0312 [en. 2010, c. 17, s. 23]
—	490.1 to 490.9 [en. 1997, c. 23, s. 15]
—	490.2(4.1) [en. 2001, c. 32, s. 31(4)]
—	490.41 [en. 2001, c. 32, s. 33]
—	490.8(3.1) [en. 2001, c. 32, s. 35(2)]
—	490.81 [en. 2001, c. 32, s. 36]
446.1	491
446.2	491.1
446.3	491.2
447	492
—	492.1 [en. 1993, c. 40, s. 18]
—	492.1(5) [en. 1999, c. 5, s. 18(2)]
—	492.2 [en. 1993, c. 40, s. 18]
Part XIV	Part XVI
448	493
449	494
—	494(4) [en. 2012, c. 9, s. 3(2)]
450	495
451	496

R.S.C. 1970, c. C-34	R.S.C. 1985, c. C-46
452	497
453	498
453.1	499
—	499(2)(*e*) to (*g*) [en. 1997, c. 18, s. 53(1)]
—	499(4) [en. 1997, c. 18, s. 53(2)]
453.2	500 [rep. 1999, c. 25, s. 6]
453.3	501
453.4	502
454	503
454(1.1)	503(2)
—	503(2.1)(*e*) to (*g*) [en. 1997, c. 18, s. 55(1)]
—	503(2.3) [en. 1997, c. 18, s. 55(2)]
454(2)	503(3)
454(2.1)	503(3.1)
454(3)	503(4)
454(4)	503(5)
455	504
455.1	505
455.2	506
455.3	507
—	507.1 [en. 2002, c. 13, s. 22]
455.4	508
—	508.1 [en. 1997, c. 18, s. 56]
455.5	509
455.6	510
456	511
—	511(3) [en. 1997, c. 18, s. 57]
—	511(4) [en. 1997, c. 18, s. 57]
456.1	512
456.2	513
456.3	514
457	515
457(2)(c.1)	515(2)(d)
457(2)(d)	515(2)(e)
457(2.1)	515(2.1)
457(3)	515(3)
457(4)	515(4)
—	515(4.1)(*b*.1) [en. 2001, c. 32, s. 37(1)]
—	515(4.1)(*b*.2) [en. 2018, c. 16, s. 218]
—	515(4.3) [en. 2001, c. 41, s. 19(3)]

R.S.C. 1970, c. C-34	R.S.C. 1985, c. C-46
457(5)	515(5)
457(5.1)	515(6)
457(5.2)	515(7)
457(5.3)	515(8)
457(6)	515(9)
—	515(9.1) [en. 2009, c. 29, s. 2]
457(7)	515(10)
457(8)	515(11)
—	515(13) and (14) [en. 2015, c. 13, s. 20]
—	515.1 [en. 1997, c. 18, s. 60]
457.1	516
—	516(2) [en. 1999, c. 5, s. 22]
457.2	517
—	517(3) [rep. 2005, c. 32, s. 17(2)]
457.3	518
457.4	519
457.5	520
457.6	521
457.7	522
457.7(2.1)	522(3)
457.7(2.2)	522(4)
457.7(3)	522(5)
457.7(4)	522(6)
457.8	523
—	523(1.2) [en. 2011, c. 16, s. 2(1)]
458	524
458(4.1)	524(5)
458(4.2)	524(6)
458(4.3)	524(7)
458(5)	524(8)
458(5.1)	524(9)
458(6)	524(10)
458(7)	524(11)
458(8)	524(12)
458(9)	524(13)
459	525
459.1	526
460	527
461	528
462	529 [rep. 1994, c. 44, s. 52]
—	529 to 529.5 [en. 1997, c. 39, s. 2]
Part XIV.1	Part XVII
462.1	530
—	530.01 [en. 2008, c. 18, s. 19]
462.11	530.1
—	530.2 [en. 2008, c. 18, s. 21]
462.2	531
462.3	532
462.4	533
—	534 [rep. 1997, c. 18, s. 63]
Part XV	Part XVIII
463	535
464	536
—	536.1 [en. 1999, c. 3, s. 35]
—	536.2 [en. 2002, c. 13, s. 27]
—	536.3 [en. 2002, c. 13, s. 27]
—	536.4 [en. 2002, c. 13, s. 27]
—	536.5 [en. 2002, c. 13, s. 27]
465	537
465(1)(a)	repealed
465(1)(b)	537(1)(a)
465(1)(c)	537(1)(b)
465(1)(d)	537(1)(c)
465(1)(e)	537(1)(d)
465(1)(f)	537(1)(e)
465(1)(g)	repealed
465(1)(h)	537(1)(f)
465(1)(i)	537(1)(g)
465(1)(j)	537(1)(h)
465(1)(k)	537(1)(i)
—	537(1)(j.1) [en. 2002, c. 13, s. 28]
—	537(1)(*k*) [en. 1997, c. 18, s. 64(1)]
—	537(1.1) [en. 2002, c. 13, s. 28]
—	537(2) [en. 1997, c. 18, s. 64(2)] [*new provision*]
466	538
467	539
—	539(4) [rep. 2005, c. 32, s. 18(2)]
468	540
469	541
470	542
—	542(3) [rep. 2005, c. 32, s. 19(2)]
471	543
471.1	544
472	545
473	546
474	547

R.S.C. 1970, c. C-34	R.S.C. 1985, c. C-46
474.1	547.1
475	548
476	549
477	550
478	551
479 — 481	repealed
—	Part XVIII.1 [en. 2011, c. 16, s. 4]
—	551.1 [en. 2011, c. 16, s. 4]
—	551.2 [en. 2011, c. 16, s. 4]
—	551.3 [en. 2011, c. 16, s. 4]
—	551.4 [en. 2011, c. 16, s. 4]
—	551.5 [en. 2011, c. 16, s. 4]
—	551.6 [en. 2011, c. 16, s. 4]
—	551.7 [en. 2011, c. 16, s. 4]
Part XVI	Part XIX
482	552
482 "judge"	552 "judge"
482(b)	552(b)
482(c.1)	552(d)
482(d)	552(g)
482(e)	552(e)
482(f)	552(h)
482(g)	552(f)
482(h)	552(i)
482 "magistrate"	552 "magistrate" [rep. R.S.C. 1985, c. 27 (1st Supp.), s. 103(2)]
483	553
—	553(*c*)(viii.1) [en. 1997, c. 18, s. 66]
—	553(*c*)(x) [en. 1997, c. 19, s. 72]
—	553(*c*)(xi) [en. 1997, c. 19, c. 72; rep. 2018, c. 16, s. 219]
484	554
484(2)-(4)	554(2)-(4) [rep. R.S.C. 1985, c. 27 (1st Supp.), s. 105]
—	554(2) [en. 1999, c. 3, s. 38]
485	555
—	555.1 [en. 1999, c. 3, s. 39]
486	556
487	557
488	558
489	559
490	560
490(5)	560(5) [rep. R.S.C. 1985, c. 27 (1st Supp.), s. 109(2)]
491	561
—	561.1 [en. 1999, c. 3, s. 43]
492	562
—	562.1 [en. 1999, c. 3, s. 44]
493	563
—	563.1 [en. 1999, c. 3, s. 45]
494	564 [rep. R.S.C. 1985, c. 27 (1st Supp.), s. 110]
495	565
—	565(1.1) [en. 1999, c. 3, s. 46]
496	566
—	566.1 [en. 1999, c. 3, s. 47]
497	567
—	567.1 [en. 1999, c. 3, s. 48]
498	568
499	569 [rep. R.S.C. 1985, c. 27 (1st Supp.), s. 111]
—	569 [en. 1999, c. 3, s. 49]
500	570
501	571
502	572
503	573 [rep. R.S.C. 1985, c. 27 (1st Supp.), s. 113]
—	Part XIX.1
—	573 [en. 1999, c. 3, s. 50]
—	573.1 [en. 1999, c. 3, s. 50]
—	573.2 [en. 1999, c. 3, s. 50]
Part XVII	Part XX
504	574
505	575 [rep. R.S.C. 1985, c. 27 (1st Supp.), s. 113]
506	576
507	577
507.1	578

R.S.C. 1970, c. C-34	R.S.C. 1985, c. C-46
508	579
—	579.01 [en. 2002, c. 13, s. 47]
—	579.1 [en. 1994, c. 44, s. 60]
509	580
510	581
511	582
512	583
513	584
514	585
515	586
516	587
517	588
518	589
519	590
520	591
—	591(4.1) [en. 2011, c. 16, s. 5]
521	592
522	593
523-525	594-596 [rep. R.S.C. 1985, c. 27 (1st Supp.), s. 120]
526	597
—	597(4) [en. 1997, c. 18, s. 68]
—	597(5) [en. 1997, c. 18, s. 68]
526.1	598
527	599
527(1.1)	599(2) [rep. R.S.C. 1985, c. 1 (4th Supp.), s. 16]
527(2)	599(3)
527(3)	599(4)
527(4)	599(5)
528	600
529	601
530	602
531	603
532	604 [rep. 1997, c. 18, s. 69]
533	605
534	606
—	606(1.1), (1.2) and (5) [en. 2002, c. 13, s. 49(1)]
—	606(4.1), (4.2), (4.3) and (4.4) [en. 2015, c. 13, s. 21]
535	607
535(6)	607(6)
536	608
537	609

R.S.C. 1970, c. C-34	R.S.C. 1985, c. C-46
538	610
539	611
540	612
541	613
542	614
543	615
543(2.1)	615(3)
543(3)	615(4)
543(4)	615(5)
543(5)	615(6)
543(6)	615(7)
543(7)	615(8)
543(8)	615(9)
544	616
545	617
546	618
547	619
548	620
549	621
550	622
551	623
552	624
553	625
553.1	625.1
554	626
—	626.1 [en. 2002, c. 13, s. 51]
555	627 [en. 1998, c. 9, s. 4]
556	repealed
557 [rep. 1985, c. 19, s. 129]	628 [rep. R.S.C. 1985, c. 27 (1st Supp.) s. 129]
558	629
559	630
560	631
—	631(2.2) [en. 2011, c. 16, s. 7]
561	632
562	633
563	634
—	634(2.01) [en. 2011, c. 16, s. 8]
—	634(2.1) [en. 2002, c. 13, s. 54(2)]
564	635
565	636 [rep. 1992, c. 41, s. 2]
566	637 [rep. 1992, c. 41, s. 2]
567	638
—	638(3) and (4) [rep. 1997, c. 18, s. 74]
568	639

R.S.C. 1970, c. C-34	R.S.C. 1985, c. C-46
569	640
570	641
571	642
—	642.1 [en. 2002, c. 13, s. 57]
572	643
—	643(1.1) [en. 2002, c. 13, s. 58]
573	644
—	644(1.1) [en. 1997, c. 18, s. 75]
574	645
575	646
576	647
576.1	648
—	648(3) [rep. 2005, c. 32, s. 21(2)]
576.2	649
577	650
—	650(1.2) [en. 1997, c. 18, s. 77]
—	650.01 [en. 2002, c. 13, s. 61]
—	650.02 [en. 2002, c. 13, s. 61]
—	650.1 [en. 1997, c. 18, s. 78]
578	651
579	652
—	652.1 [en. 2011, c. 16, s. 13]
580	653
—	653.1 [en. 2011, c. 16, s. 14]
581	654
582	655
583	656
584	657
584.1	657.1
—	657.1(2)(c.1) [en. 1997, c. 18, s. 79]
—	657.2 [en. 1997, c. 18, s. 80]
—	657.3 [en. 1997, c. 18, s. 80]
—	657.3(3) to (7) [en. 2002, c. 13, s. 62]
585	658
586	659 [rep. R.S.C. 1985, c. 19 (3rd Supp.), s. 15]
—	659 [en. 1993, c. 45, s. 9]
587	660
588	661

R.S.C. 1970, c. C-34	R.S.C. 1985, c. C-46
589	662
590	663
591	664
592	665 [rep. 1995, c. 22, s. 3]
593	666
594	667
594(3.1)	667(4)
594(4)	667(5)
595	668 [rep. 1995, c. 22, s. 4]
596	669 [rep. 1995, c. 22, s. 4]
597	669.1
597.1	669.2
—	669.3 [en. 1994, c. 44, s. 66]
598	670
599	671
600	672
—	Part XX.1
—	672.1-672.95 [en. 1991, c. 43, s. 4]
—	672.1(2) [en. 2005, c. 22, s. 1(3)]
—	672.121 [en. 2005, c. 22, s. 3]
—	672.16(1.1) and (1.2) [en. 2005, c. 22, s. 7(2)]
—	672.191 [en. 1997, c. 18, s. 81]
—	672.21(3)(c) [rep. 2005, c. 22, s. 12]
—	672.24(2) and (3) [en. 1997, c. 18, s. 82]
—	672.33(1.1) [en. 2005, c. 22, s. 13]
—	672.38(3) [en. 1997, c. 18, s. 83]
—	672.45(1.1) [en. 2005, c. 22, s. 14]
—	672.47(4) and (5) [en. 2014, c. 6, s. 6(2)]
—	672.5(5.1) [en. 2005, c. 22, s. 16(1)]
—	672.5(5.2) [en. 2014, c. 6, s. 7(2)]
—	672.5(8.1) and (8.2) [en. 1997, c. 18, s. 84(1)]
—	672.5(13) [en. 1997, c. 18, s. 84(2)]

R.S.C. 1970, c. C-34	R.S.C. 1985, c. C-46
—	672.5(13.1) and (13.2) [en. 2005, c. 22, s. 16(2)]
—	672.5(13.3) [en. 2014, c. 6, s. 7(3)]
—	672.5(15.1), (15.2) and (15.3) [en. 2005, c. 22, s. 16(3)]
—	672.501 [en. 2005, c. 22, s. 17]
—	672.54 [en. 1999, c. 25, s. 12]
—	672.5401 [en. 2014, c. 6, s. 10]
—	672.541 [en. 2014, c. 6, s. 10]
—	672.542 [en. 2014, c. 6, s. 10]
—	672.55(2) [rep. 2005, c. 22, s. 22]
—	672.56(1.1) [en. 2014, c. 6, s. 11(2)]
—	672.64-672.66 and heading [rep. 2005, c. 22, s. 24]
—	672.64 [re-en. 2014, c. 6, s. 12]
—	672.79 [rep. 2005, c. 22, s. 26]
—	672.8 [rep. 2005, c. 22, s. 25]
—	672.83(2) [rep. 2005, c. 22, s. 29]
—	672.84 [rep. 2005, c. 22, s. 30; re-en. 2014, c. 6, s. 16]
—	Schedule to Part XXI [rep. 2005, c. 22, s. 37]
—	672.851 [en. 2005, c. 22, s. 33]
—	672.852 [en. 2005, c. 22, s. 33]
Part XVIII	Part XXI
601	673
—	673 "sentence" (*d*) [en. 1996, c. 19, s. 74]
—	673 "sentence" (*e*) [en. 2018, c. 16, s. 220]
602	674
603	675
—	675(1.1) [en. 1997, c. 18, s. 92(1)]
603(1.1)	675(2)
—	675(2.1) [en. 1997, c. 18, s. 92(2)]
—	675(2.3) [en. 2011, c. 5, s. 2]
603(2)	675(3)
603(3)	675(4)
604	repealed
605	676
—	676(1.1) [en. 1997, c. 18, s. 93(2)]
—	676(6) [en. 2011, c. 5, s. 3]
—	676.1 [en. 1997, c. 18, s. 94]
606	677
607	678
607.1	678.1
608	679
—	679(7.1) [en. 1997, c. 18, s. 95]
608.1	680
608.2	681
609	682
610	683
—	683(2.1) amd (2.2) [en. 2002, c. 13, s. 68]
—	683(5)(*e*) [en. 1997, c. 18, s. 97(2)]
—	683(5.1) [en. 2008, c. 18, s. 29(1)]
—	683(7) [en. 2008, c. 18, s. 29(2)]
611	684
612	685
613	686
—	686(5.1) [en. 1997, c. 18, s. 98]
614	687
615	688
—	688(2.1) [en. 2002, c. 13, s. 68]
616	689
617	690 [rep. 2002, c. 13, s. 70]
618	691
619	repealed
620	692
621	693
622	694
622.1	694.1
622.2	694.2
623	695

R.S.C. 1970, c. C-34	R.S.C. 1985, c. C-46
—	695(2) [rep. 1999, c. 3, s. 27]
624	696
—	Part XXI.1 [en. 2002, c. 13, s. 71]
625	697
626	698
627	699
—	699(5.1) [en. 1997, c. 30, s. 2]
—	699(7) [en. 1997, c. 30, s. 2]
628	700
—	700.1 [en. 1999, c. 18, s. 94]
629	701
—	701.1 [en. 1997, c. 18, s. 100]
630	702
631	703
631.1	703.1
631.2	703.2
632	704
633	705
634	706
635	707
636	708
—	708.1 [en. 1997, c. 18, s. 101]
637	709
638	710
639	711
640	712
640(3)	712(3) [rep. R.S.C. 1985, c. 27 (1st Supp.), s. 153(2)]
641	713
—	713.1 [en. 1994, c. 44, s. 76]
642	714
—	714.1 [en. 1999, c. 18, s. 95]
—	714.2 [en. 1999, c. 18, s. 95]
—	714.3 [en. 1999, c. 18, s. 95]
—	714.4 [en. 1999, c. 18, s. 95]
—	714.5 [en. 1999, c. 18, s. 95]
—	714.6 [en. 1999, c. 18, s. 95]
—	714.7 [en. 1999, c. 18, s. 95]

R.S.C. 1970, c. C-34	R.S.C. 1985, c. C-46
—	714.8 [en. 1999, c. 18, s. 95]
643	715
643.1	715.1
—	715.2 [en. 1998, c. 9, s. 8]
—	Part XXII.1 [en. 2018, c. 12, s. 404]
—	715.3 [en. 2018, c. 12, s. 404]
—	715.31 [en. 2018, c. 12, s. 404]
—	715.32 [en. 2018, c. 12, s. 404]
—	715.33 [en. 2018, c. 12, s. 404]
—	715.34 [en. 2018, c. 12, s. 404]
—	715.35 [en. 2018, c. 12, s. 404]
—	715.36 [en. 2018, c. 12, s. 404]
—	715.37 [en. 2018, c. 12, s. 404]
—	715.38 [en. 2018, c. 12, s. 404]
—	715.39 [en. 2018, c. 12, s. 404]
—	715.4 [en. 2018, c. 12, s. 404]
—	715.41 [en. 2018, c. 12, s. 404]
—	715.42 [en. 2018, c. 12, s. 404]
—	715.43 [en. 2018, c. 12, s. 404]
Part XX	Part XXIII
ss. 644 to 686	ss. 716 to 751.1, as amended. *Please note: this Part was replaced as a whole by 1995, c. 22, s. 6. For in force information, see the list of amendments to the Code starting on page CC/1.
—	718.01 [en. 2005, c. 32, s. 24]
—	718.02 [en. 2009, c. 22, s. 18]
—	718.03 [en. 2015, c. 34, s. 4]
—	718.3(5), (6) and (7) [en. 2015, c. 23, s. 17]

R.S.C. 1970, c. C-34	R.S.C. 1985, c. C-46
—	720(2) [en. 2008, c. 18, s. 35]
—	722.1 [rep. 1999, c. 25, s. 18]
—	722.2 [en. 1999, c. 25, s. 18]
—	722.2(3), (4) and (5) [en. 2015, c. 13, s. 26]
—	729.1 [en. 2011, c. 7, s. 2]
—	731(3.1) [en. 1997, c. 17, s. 1]
—	732(6) [en. 2008, c. 18, s. 37]
—	732.1 [en. 1995, c. 22, s. 6]
—	732.1(2.1), (2.2) [en. 2014, c. 21, s. 2]
—	732.1(7)-(12) [en. 2011, c. 7, s. 3(2)]
—	732.11 [en. 2011, c. 7, s. 4]
—	737
—	737.1 [en. 2015, c. 13, s. 29]
—	738(1)(d) [en. 2009, c. 28, s. 11]
—	739.1 [en. 2015, c. 13, s. 30]
—	742.3(1.1), (1.2), (1.3) [en. 2014, c. 21, s. 3]
—	742.3(4) [en. 2008, c. 18, s. 40]
—	742.3(5)-(10) [en. 2011, c. 7, s. 5(2)]
—	742.31 [en. 2011, c. 7, s. 6]
—	743.21 [en. 2008, c. 28, s. 42]
—	743.4 [rep. 2002, c. 1, s. 184]
—	743.6(1.1) [en. 1997, c. 23, s. 18]
—	743.6(1.2) [en. 2001, c. 41, s. 21]
—	745.1
—	745.01 [en. 1999, c. 25, s. 21]
—	745.01(2) [en. 2011, c. 2, s. 2]
—	745.2
—	745.21 [en. 2011, c. 5, s. 4]
—	745.3
—	745.4
—	745.5
—	745.51 [en. 2011, c. 5, s. 5]
—	745.6
—	745.6 (2.1) to (2.8) [en. 2011, c. 2, s. 3]
—	745.61
—	745.62
—	745.63
—	745.64
Part XXI	Part XXIV
—	747 to 747.8 and heading [rep. 2005, c. 22, s. 39]
687	752
—	752 "designated offence" [en. 2008, c. 6, ss. 40, 61]
—	752 "long-term supervision" [en. 2008, c. 6, s. 40]
—	752 "primary designated offence" [en. 2008, c. 6, s. 40]
—	752.01 [en. 2008, c. 6, s. 41]
—	752.1 [en. 1997, c. 17, s. 4]
688	753
—	753(1.1) [en. 2008, c. 6, s. 42(2)]
—	753(4.1) [en. 1997, c. 17, s. 4]
—	753(4.2) [en. 2008, c. 6, s. 42(4)]
—	753(6) [rep. 2008, c. 6, s. 42(5)]
—	753.01 [en. 2008, c. 6, s. 43]
—	753.02 [en. 2008, c. 6, s. 43]
—	753.1 [en. 1997, c. 17, s. 4]
—	753.1(4), (5) [rep. 2008, c. 6, s. 44(2)]
—	753.2 [en. 1997, c. 17, s. 4]
—	753.3 [en. 1997, c. 17, s. 4]
—	753.4 [en. 1997, c. 17, s. 4]
689	754

R.S.C. 1970, c. C-34	R.S.C. 1985, c. C-46
690	755 [rep. 1997, c. 17, s. 5; re-en. 2008, c. 6, s. 49]
691	756 [rep. 1997, c. 17, s. 5]
692	757
693	758
694	759
—	759(1.1) [en. 1997, c. 17, s. 6]
—	759(3.1) [en. 1997, c. 17, s. 6]
—	759(3.2) [en. 1997, c. 17, s. 6]
—	759(4.1) [en. 1997, c. 17, s. 6]
—	759(4.2) [en. 1997, c. 17, s. 6]
695	760
695.1	761
Part XXII	Part XXV
696	762
697	763
698	764
699	765
700	766
701	767
701.1	767.1
702	768
703	769
704	770
705	771
706	772
707	773
Part XXIII	Part XXVI
708	774
—	774.1 [en. 2002, c. 13, s. 77]
709	775
710	776
711	777
712	778
713	779
714	780
715	781
716	782
717	783
718	repealed
719	784
Part XXIV	Part XXVII
720	785
—	785 "sentence" (*d*) [en. 1997, c. 19, s. 76]
—	785 "sentence" (*e*) [en. 2018, c. 16, s. 223]
721	786
722	787
723	788
724	789
725	790
725(3) and (4)	790(3) and (4) [rep. R.S.C. 1985, c. 27 (1st Supp.), s. 172]
725(5)	repealed
726	791 [rep. R.S.C. 1985, c. 27 (1st Supp.), s. 173]
727	repealed
728	792 [rep. R.S.C. 1985, c. 27 (1st Supp.), s. 174]
729	793 [rep. R.S.C. 1985, c. 27 (1st Supp.), s. 175]
730	794
—	794(2) [rep. 2018, c. 29, s. 68]
731	795
732	796 [rep. R.S.C. 1985, c. 27 (1st Supp.), s. 176]
732.1	797 [rep. R.S.C. 1985, c. 27 (1st Supp.), s. 176]
733	798
734	799
735	800
—	800(2.1) [en. 1997, c. 18, s. 111]
736	801
736(4) and (5)	801(4) and (5) [rep. R.S.C. 1985, c. 27 (1st Supp.), s. 177(2)]
737	802
—	802.1 [en. 2002, c. 13, s. 79]
738	803
738(2)	repealed
738(3)	803(2)
738(3.1)	803(3)
739	804
740	805 [rep. R.S.C. 1985, c. 27 (1st Supp.), s. 179]
741	806
742	807
743	808

R.S.C. 1970, c. C-34	R.S.C. 1985, c. C-46
744	809
745	810
—	810(3.01), (3.02) [en. 2011, c. 7, s. 7]
—	810.01 [en. 1997, c. 23, s. 19]
—	810.01(3.1), (4.1) [en. 2009, c. 22, s. 19]
—	810.011 [en. 2015, c. 20, s. 25]
—	810.02 [en. 2015, c. 29, s. 11]
—	810.1 [en. 1993, c. 45, s. 11]
—	810.1(3.01) to (3.05) [en. 2008, c. 6, ss. 52, 62]
—	810.1(3.1) [en. 1997, c. 18, s. 113(2)]
—	810.2 [en. 1997, c. 17, s. 9]
—	810.2(3.1) [en. 2008, c. 6, s. 53(1)]
—	810.2(4.1) [en. 2008, c. 6, s. 53(2)]
—	810.21 [en. 2015, c. 20, s. 26]
—	810.22 [en. 2015, c. 20, s. 26]
—	810.3 [en. 2011, c. 7, s. 11]
—	810.4 [en. 2011, c. 7, s. 11]
746	811
—	811.1 [en. 2011, c. 7, s. 12]
747	812
747 "appeal court"	812 "appeal court"
747(a)	812(1)(f)
747(b)	812(1)(g)
747(c)	812(1)(c)
747(d)	812(1)(b)
747(e)	812(1)(a)
747(f)	812(1)(d)
747(g)	repealed
747(h)	812(1)(e) [rep. 1992, c. 51, s. 43(2)]
747(i)	812(1)(h)
—	812(1)(i) [en. 1999, c. 3, s. 55]
—	812(2) [en. 1999, c. 3, s. 55]
748	813
749	814

R.S.C. 1970, c. C-34	R.S.C. 1985, c. C-46
750	815
751	repealed
752	816
752.1	817
752.2	818
752.3	819
753	820
754	821
755	822
755.1	823
756	824
757	825
758	826
759	827
760	828
761	829
—	829(2) [en. 1999, c. 3, s. 56]
762	830
763	831
764	832
765	833
766	834
767	835
768	836
769	837
770	838
771	839
—	839(1.1) [en. 1999, c. 3, s. 57]
772	840
Part XXV	Part XXVIII [replaced 2002, c. 13, s. 84]
773	841 [replaced 2002, c. 13, s. 84]
773(3)	841(3)
—	842 to 849 [en. 2002, c. 13, s. 84]
Forms 1 and 2	Forms 1 and 2
Form 3	Form 3 [rep. R.S.C. 1985, c. 27 (1st Supp.), s. 184(2)]
Forms 4 to 5.2	Forms 4 to 5.2
—	Forms 5.01 to 5.09 [en. 1998, c. 37, s. 24]
—	Forms 5.001 to 5.0091 [en. 2014, c. 31, s. 26]
—	Form 5.041 [en. 2005, c. 25, s. 12; 2007, c. 22, s. 23]

R.S.C. 1970, c. C-34	R.S.C. 1985, c. C-46
—	Form 5.061 [en. 2005, c. 25, s. 12; 2007, c. 22, s. 23]
Form 5.3	Form 5.3
Forms 6 and 7	Forms 6 and 7
Form 8	Form 7.1 [en. 1997, c. 39, s. 3]
—	Form 8
Form 8.1	Form 9
Form 8.2	Form 10
Form 8.3	Form 11
—	Form 11.1 [en. 1994, c. 44, s. 84]
Form 9	Form 12
Form 9.1	Form 13
Form 9.2	Form 14
Form 10	Form 15
Form 11	Form 16
—	Form 16.1 [en. 1997, c. 30, s. 3]
Form 12	Form 17
Form 13	Form 18
Form 14	Form 19
Form 15	repealed
Form 16	Form 20
Form 17	repealed
Form 18	Form 21
Form 19	Form 22
Form 20	Form 23
Form 21	Form 24
Form 22	Form 25
Form 23	Form 26
Form 24	Form 27
Form 25	Form 28
—	Form 28.1 [en. 2000, c. 10, s. 24; rep. 2007, c. 22, s. 26]
Form 25.1	Form 29
Form 26	Form 30
Form 27	Form 31
Form 28	Form 32

R.S.C. 1970, c. C-34	R.S.C. 1985, c. C-46
Form 29	Form 33
Form 30	Form 34
—	Form 34.1 [en. 2011, c. 6, s. 5]
—	Form 34.2 [en. 2015, c. 13, s. 35]
—	Form 34.3 [en. 2015, c. 13, s. 35]
Form 31	Form 35
Form 32	Form 36
Form 33	Form 37
Form 34	Form 38
Form 35	Form 39
Form 36	Form 40
Form 37	Form 41
Form 38	Form 42
Form 39	Form 43
Forms 40 and 41	repealed
Form 42	Form 44
Form 43	Form 45
Form 44	Form 46
Form 45	Form 47
774	repealed
—	Form 48 [en. 1991, c. 43, s. 8]
—	Form 48.1 [en. 2005, c. 22, s. 40]
—	Form 48.2 [en. 2015, c. 13, s. 36]
—	Form 49 [en. 1991, c. 43, s. 8]
—	Form 50 [en. 1991, c. 43, s. 8]
—	Form 51 [en. 1991, c. 43, s. 8; rep. 2005, c. 22, s. 41; en. 2011, c. 7, s. 13]
—	Form 52 [en. 2004, c. 10, s. 21]
—	Form 53 [en. 2004, c. 10, s. 2]
—	Form 54 [en. 2010, c. 17, s. 27]

TABLE OF CASES

References are to section numbers of the *Criminal Code* except where preceded by one of the following:

CE Canada Evidence Act
CH Canadian Charter of Rights and Freedoms
CD Controlled Drugs and Substances Act
WC Crimes Against Humanity and War Crimes Act
YC Youth Criminal Justice Act

Sections

Sections

Sections

Sections

Sections

Sections

Sections

Sections

Sections

Sections

Sections

Sections

Sections

Sections

Sections

Sections

Sections

Sections

Sections

Sections

Sections
Lowry and Lepper, R. v., [1974] S.C.R. 195, 6 C.C.C. (2d) 531, affg 2 C.C.C. (2d) 39, 13 C.R.N.S. 332 *sub nom.* R. v. Lowry (Man. C.A.) .... 686, (CH)2
Loyer and Blouin, R. v., [1978] 2 S.C.R. 631, 40 C.C.C. (2d) 291 613
Lubovac, R. v. (1989), 52 C.C.C. (3d) 551, 101 A.R. 119 (C.A.), leave to appeal to S.C.C. refused 53 C.C.C. (3d) vii, 105 A.R. 254*n* 183
Lucas, R. v. (1983), 6 C.C.C. (3d) 147, 150 D.L.R. (3d) 118 (N.S.C.A.) .... (CH)11
Lucas, R. v. (1983), 9 C.C.C. (3d) 71 (Ont. C.A.), leave to appeal to S.C.C. refused C.C.C. *loc. cit.*, 52 N.R. 399*n* 606
Lucas, R. v. (1987), 34 C.C.C. (3d) 28 (Que. C.A.) 268
Lucas, R. v. (1995), 129 Sask. R. 53, 31 C.R.R. (2d) 92 *sub nom.* Lucas v. Saskatchewan (Minister of Justice) (Q.B.) 301
Lucas, R. v. (2014), 313 C.C.C. (3d) 159, 121 O.R. (3d) 303 (C.A.), leave to appeal to S.C.C. refused, 2015 CarswellOnt 639, 2015 CarswellOnt 638, leave to appeal to S.C.C. refused [2014] S.C.C.A. No. 460 .... 186, 487.01, 650, (CE)37
Lucas, R. v., [1998] 1 S.C.R. 439, 123 C.C.C. (3d) 97 .... 298, 299, 300, (CH)2
Luckett, R. v., [1980] 1 S.C.R. 1140, 50 C.C.C. (2d) 489.......................... 343, 662
Ludacka, R. v. (1996), 105 C.C.C. (3d) 565, 46 C.R. (4th) 184 (Ont. C.A.) 167
Ludlow, R. v. (1999), 136 C.C.C. (3d) 460, 27 C.R. (5th) 46 (B.C.C.A.).................. 145
Ludwig, R. v. (2018), 367 C.C.C. (3d) 341, 51 C.R. (7th) 99 (Ont. C.A.) 433
Luedecke, R. v. (2008), 236 C.C.C. (3d) 317, 61 C.R. (6th) 139 (Ont. C.A.)........ 16, 686
Luis, R. v. (1989), 50 C.C.C. (3d) 398 (Ont. H.C.J.) 473, 606
Lukacko, R. v. (2002), 164 C.C.C. (3d) 550, 1 C.R. (6th) 309 (Ont. C.A.)...........(CE)30
Luke, R. v. (1994), 87 C.C.C. (3d) 121, 28 C.R. (4th) 93 (Ont. C.A.), leave to appeal to S.C.C. refused 92 C.C.C. (3d) vi, 23 C.R.R. (2d) 384*n* .... (CH)11
Lumen Inc. v. Canada (Attorney General) (1997), 119 C.C.C. (3d) 91, 10 C.R. (5th) 246 (Que. C.A.), leave to appeal to S.C.C. refused 119 C.C.C. (3d) vi, 152 D.L.R. (4th) vi.......................... 462.42
Lund, R. v. (2008), 440 A.R. 362, 70 M.V.R. (5th) 43 (C.A. [In Chambers]) .... (CH)10
Lundgard, R. v. (1991), 63 C.C.C. (3d) 368, [1991] 4 W.W.R. 259 (Alta. C.A.), leave to appeal to S.C.C. refused 61 C.C.C. (3d) vi, 127 A.R. 391*n* 441
Lunn, R. v. (1990), 61 C.C.C. (3d) 193, 26 M.V.R. (2d) 209 (B.C.C.A.).................. 256
Lupyrypa, R. v. (2011), 270 C.C.C. (3d) 571, 45 Alta. L.R. (5th) 348 (C.A.) 508.1
Luther, R. v. (1971), 5 C.C.C. (2d) 354, 16 C.R.N.S. 14 (Ont. C.A.) 718.2
Lutoslawski, R. v. (2010), 258 C.C.C. (3d) 1, 326 D.L.R. (4th) 637 (Ont. C.A.), affd [2010] 3 S.C.R. 60, 262 C.C.C. (3d) 1.......................... 273.1
Luxton, R. v., [1990] 2 S.C.R. 711, 58 C.C.C. (3d) 449...................... 231, 745, (CH)7, (CH)9, (CH)12
Luz, R. v. (1988), 5 O.R. (3d) 52 (H.C.J.) 2
Lyall, R. v. (1974), 18 C.C.C. (2d) 381, [1974] 6 W.W.R. 479 (B.C.C.A.)............... 732
Lynch, R. v. (1982), 69 C.C.C. (2d) 88, 38 Nfld. & P.E.I.R. 267 (Nfld. C.A.) 253
Lyons, R. v. (1979), 52 C.C.C. (2d) 113 (B.C. Co. Ct.) 186
Lyons, R. v. (1981), 64 C.C.C. (2d) 73 (Ont. H.C.J.), leave to appeal to S.C.C. refused 55 N.R. 75*n* 487
Lyons, R. v., [1984] 2 S.C.R. 633, 15 C.C.C. (3d) 417, affg 69 C.C.C. (2d) 318, 140 D.L.R. (3d) 223 (B.C.C.A.) 25, 186
Lyons, R. v., [1987] 2 S.C.R. 309, 37 C.C.C. (3d) 1 .... 753, 754, 755, (CH)1, (CH)7, (CH)9, (CH)11, (CH)12
Lyver, R. v. (2007), 229 C.C.C. (3d) 535, 425 A.R. 320 (C.A.).......................... 742.1
M. (A.), R. v. (1996), 30 O.R. 313, 92 O.A.C. 381 (C.A.).......................... 684
M. (A.), R. v. (2011), 271 C.C.C. (3d) 201, 95 W.C.B. (2d) 677 (Ont. C.J.)......... (YC)42
M. (A.), R. v., [2008] 1 S.C.R. 569, 230 C.C.C. (3d) 377 .... (CH)8
M. (A.M.), R. v. (2003), 181 C.C.C. (3d) 532, 180 Man. R. (2d) 239 (C.A.) .... (YC)48
M. (B.), R. v. (1999), 139 C.C.C. (3d) 480, 28 C.R. (5th) 129 (Ont. C.A.), leave to appeal to S.C.C. refused 144 C.C.C. (3d) vi, 185 D.L.R. (4th) vii .... (YC)25
M. (C.), R. v. (1992), 75 C.C.C. (3d) 556, 15 C.R. (4th) 368 (Ont. Ct. (Gen. Div.)), affd 98 C.C.C. (3d) 481, 41 C.R. (4th) 134 (C.A.).......................... 159
M. (C.A.), R. v., [1996] 1 S.C.R. 500, 105 C.C.C. (3d) 327................ 687, 718.2, 718.3

Sections

Sections

Sections

Sections

Sections

Sections

Sections

Sections

Sections

Sections

Sections

Sections

Sections

Sections

Sections

Sections

Tzimopoulos, R. v. (1986), 29 C.C.C. (3d) 304, 54 C.R. (3d) 1 (Ont. C.A.), leave to appeal to S.C.C. refused 54 C.R. (3d) xxvii, 27 C.R.R. 296 475
U. (D.A.), R. v. (2008), 239 C.C.C. (3d) 409, 270 N.S.R. (2d) 67 (S.C.) ....(CE)12, (YC)82
U. (F.J.), R. v., [1995] 3 S.C.R. 764, 101 C.C.C. (3d) 97, affg 90 C.C.C. (3d) 541, 32 C.R. (4th) 378 (Ont. C.A.) ....(CE)9
UFCW, Local 1518 v. KMart Canada Ltd., [1999] 2 S.C.R. 1083, 176 D.L.R. (4th) 607...(CH)2
Ubhi, R. v. (1994), 27 C.R. (4th) 332, 65 W.A.C. 248 (B.C.C.A.), leave to appeal to S.C.C. refused 31 C.R. (4th) 405, 5 M.V.R. (3d) 249*n* 219
Ullrich, R. v. (1991), 69 C.C.C. (3d) 473, 19 W.A.C. 304 (B.C.C.A.).................. (CE)9
Ulrich, R. v. (1977), 38 C.C.C. (2d) 1, [1978] 1 W.W.R. 422 (Alta. S.C.) 485, 540, 541, 655
Underwood, R. v., [1998] 1 S.C.R. 77, 121 C.C.C. (3d) 117 ....(CE)12
Ungaro, R. v., [1950] S.C.R. 430, 96 C.C.C. 245 354
United Nurses of Alberta v. Alberta (Attorney General), [1992] 1 S.C.R. 901, 71 C.C.C. (3d) 225, affg 54 C.C.C. (3d) 1, 66 D.L.R. (4th) 385 (Alta. C.A.)............9
United States of America v. Allard, [1987] 1 S.C.R. 564, 33 C.C.C. (3d) 501 .... (CH)7
United States of America v. Amhaz (2001), 159 C.C.C. (3d) 570, 90 C.R.R. (2d) 177 (B.C.S.C.) 517
United States of America v. Burns, [2001] 1 S.C.R. 283, 151 C.C.C. (3d) 97 ....(CH)7
United States of America v. Cotroni, [1989] 1 S.C.R. 1469, 48 C.C.C. (3d) 193 ..... (CH)6
United States of America v. Desfosses, [1997] 2 S.C.R. 326, 115 C.C.C. (3d) 257 784
United States of America v. Dynar, [1997] 2 S.C.R. 462, 115 C.C.C. (3d) 481 ..... 24, 465
United States of America v. Kwok, [2001] 1 S.C.R. 616, 152 C.C.C. (3d) 225 ...... (CH)6, (CH)7
United States of America v. Leon, [1996] 1 S.C.R. 888, 105 C.C.C. (3d) 385, affg 96 C.C.C. (3d) 568, 77 O.A.C. 313 (C.A.)...(CH)7
United States of America v. M. (D.J.) (2001), 156 C.C.C. (3d) 276, 50 W.C.B. (2d) 469 (Ont. S.C.J.), leave to appeal to S.C.C. refused 158 C.C.C. (3d) vi, 163 O.A.C. 396*n*..487.3
United States of America v. New (2017), 140 W.C.B. (2d) 154, 2017 BCCA 249 (B.C.C.A.), leave to appeal to S.C.C. refused Robert New v. Canada (Minister of Justice), 2018 CarswellBC 712...(CE)30
United States of America v. Sheppard, [1977] 2 S.C.R. 1067, 30 C.C.C. (2d) 424 ....548, 650
United States of America v. Shulman, [2001] 1 S.C.R. 616, 152 C.C.C. (3d) 294.... (CH)7
United States of America v. Smith (1984), 10 C.C.C. (3d) 540, 38 C.R. (3d) 228 (Ont. C.A.), leave to appeal to S.C.C. refused 4 O.A.C. 239*n*, 55 N.R. 395*n* ....(CH)7
United States of America v. Tsioubris, [2001] 1 S.C.R. 613, 152 C.C.C. (3d) 292... (CH)7
United States of America v. Wakeling, [2014] 3 S.C.R. 549, 318 C.C.C. (3d) 134...193
United States of America v. Zschiegner (2001), 154 C.C.C. (3d) 547, 194 N.S.R. (2d) 30 (C.A.) 734.6
United States v. Fafalios (2012), 284 C.C.C. (3d) 432, 110 O.R. (3d) 641 *sub nom.* Canada (Attorney General) v. Fafalios (Ont. C.A.)................................ 674
United States v. Potts, 297 F. 2d 68 (1961) (6th Cir.)..2
Unnamed Person, R. v. (1985), 22 C.C.C. (3d) 284, 10 O.A.C. 305 (C.A.) 486.4
Untinen, R. v. (2017), 355 C.C.C. (3d) 371, 141 W.C.B. (2d) 471, 2017 BCCA 320, 2017 CarswellBC 2482 (B.C.C.A.), leave to appeal to S.C.C. refused Raymond John Untinen v. Her Majesty the Queen (2018), [2017] S.C.C.A. No. 485, 2018 CarswellBC 1194 ....715.1
Urbanovich and Brown, R. v. (1985), 19 C.C.C. (3d) 43, 31 Man. R. (2d) 268 (C.A.).. 721
Urizar, R. c. (2013), 99 C.R. (6th) 370 (C.A. Que.) 279.011
Urton, R. v., [1974] 5 W.W.R. 476 (Sask. C.A.) 720
Ururyar, R. v. (2016), 132 W.C.B. (2d) 445, [2016] O.J. No. 4293 (S.C.J.).............. 679

Sections

Sections

Sections

THE CRIMINAL CODE

R.S.C. 1985, Chap. C-46

Amended R.S.C. 1985, c. 11 (1st Supp.); proclaimed in force December 12, 1988

Amended R.S.C. 1985, c. 27 (1st Supp.); originally proclaimed in force as follows: ss. 1 to 35, 37 to 93, 96 to 126, 128 to 186, 188 and 203 to 208 proclaimed in force December 4, 1985; parts of s. 36 enacting ss. 249 to 253, 254(1), (3) to (6), 255(1) to (4) and 256 to 261 with the exception of s. 258(1)(*c*)(i) and (*g*)(iii)(A) of the *Criminal Code* proclaimed in force December 4, 1985; s. 258(1)(*c*)(i) and (*g*)(iii)(A) to come into force on proclamation (repealed before coming into force 2008, c. 20, s. 3); part of s. 36 enacting s. 254(2) of the *Criminal Code* proclaimed in force December 4, 1985 in each of the provinces; part of s. 36 enacting s. 255(5) of the *Criminal Code* proclaimed in force December 4, 1985 in New Brunswick, Manitoba, Prince Edward Island, Alberta, Saskatchewan, Yukon Territory and Northwest Territories, proclaimed in force January 1, 1988 in Nova Scotia, and to come into force on proclamation in the remaining provinces; s. 94 in force June 20, 1985 in New Brunswick, Manitoba, Ontario, Yukon Territory, Northwest Territories, proclaimed in force September 1, 1987 in Nova Scotia, P.E.I. and Saskatchewan and with respect to indictable offences in Saskatchewan, into force on proclamation in the remaining provinces; and s. 127 proclaimed in force September 1, 1988

Amended R.S.C. 1985, c. 31 (1st Supp.), s. 61; proclaimed in force December 12, 1988

Amended R.S.C. 1985, c. 47 (1st Supp.); proclaimed in force December 12, 1988

Amended R.S.C. 1985, c. 51 (1st Supp.); in force December 12, 1988

Amended R.S.C. 1985, c. 52 (1st Supp.); proclaimed in force December 12, 1988

Amended R.S.C. 1985, c. 1 (2nd Supp.), s. 213; proclaimed in force December 12, 1988

Amended R.S.C. 1985, c. 24 (2nd Supp.), ss. 45 to 47; proclaimed in force December 12, 1988

Amended R.S.C. 1985, c. 27 (2nd Supp.), s. 10, Sch. item 6(1) to (16); proclaimed in force December 12, 1988 (but see s. 11)

Amended R.S.C. 1985, c. 35 (2nd Supp.), s. 34; proclaimed in force December 12, 1988

Amended R.S.C. 1985, c. 10 (3rd Supp.); proclaimed in force May 1, 1989

Amended R.S.C. 1985, c. 19 (3rd Supp.), ss. 1 to 16; proclaimed in force May 1, 1989 (but see s. 19)

Amended R.S.C. 1985, c. 30 (3rd Supp.), ss. 1 and 2; proclaimed in force May 1, 1989

Amended R.S.C. 1985, c. 34 (3rd Supp.), ss. 9 to 13; proclaimed in force May 1, 1989

Amended R.S.C. 1985, c. 1 (4th Supp.), ss. 13 to 17; originally in force February 4, 1988

Amended R.S.C. 1985, c. 23 (4th Supp.); originally ss. 1 to 3 and 7 proclaimed in force October 1, 1988, ss. 4, 5 and that part of s. 6 which enacts s. 727.9 proclaimed in force July 31, 1989, s. 8 proclaimed in force November 1, 1989; that part of s. 6 which enacts ss. 725 to 727.8 repealed by 1995, c. 22, s. 11 (in force September 3, 1996)

Amended R.S.C. 1985, c. 29 (4th Supp.), s. 17; proclaimed in force November 1, 1989

Amended R.S.C. 1985, c. 30 (4th Supp.), s. 45; proclaimed in force November 1, 1989

Amended R.S.C. 1985, c. 31 (4th Supp.), ss. 94 to 97; s. 96 proclaimed in force September 15, 1988, s. 97 proclaimed in force February 1, 1989, remainder in force as noted

Amended R.S.C. 1985, c. 32 (4th Supp.), ss. 55 to 62; proclaimed in force November 1, 1989
Amended R.S.C. 1985, c. 40 (4th Supp.), s. 2; proclaimed in force November 1, 1989
Amended R.S.C. 1985, c. 42 (4th Supp.), ss. 1 to 8; proclaimed in force November 1, 1989
Amended R.S.C. 1985, c. 50 (4th Supp.); proclaimed in force November 1, 1989
Amended 1989, c. 2, s. 1; in force June 29, 1989
Amended 1990, c. 15; brought into force July 1, 1990 by SI/90-83, *Can. Gaz., Part II*, July 4, 1990
Amended 1990, c. 16, ss. 2 to 7; brought into force July 1, 1990 by SI/90-90, *Can. Gaz., Part II*, July 18, 1990 (but see s. 24)
Amended 1990, c. 17, ss. 7 to 15; brought into force September 1, 1990 by SI/90-106, *Can. Gaz., Part II*, August 29, 1990 (but see s. 45)
Amended 1990, c. 44, s. 15; brought into force February 4, 1991 by SI/91-18, *Can. Gaz., Part II*, February 13, 1991 (but see s. 20)
Amended 1991, c. 1, s. 28; in force January 17, 1991
Amended 1991, c. 4; in force January 17, 1991
Amended 1991, c. 28, ss. 6 to 12; brought into force October 3, 1991 by SI/91-136, *Can. Gaz., Part II*, October 23, 1991
Amended 1991, c. 40, ss. 1 to 20, 21(2) and 22 to 41; s. 28 brought into force March 26, 1992, remainder, except ss. 3, 5(1) and (2), 8, 10(1), 14, 18, 19(1) to (7), 20, 22, 23, 39, 40 and 42, brought into force August 1, 1992 by SI/92-138, *Can. Gaz., Part II*, July 29, 1992, *however*, by SI/92-144, *Can. Gaz., Part II*, August 12, 1992, s. 2(3) and that part of s. 2(6) which enacts s. 84(1.2) are brought into force July 27, 1992; ss. 5(1) and (2), 10(1), 23(1), (2), (3), (5) and 42 brought into force October 1, 1992; that part of s. 3 which enacts s. 86(3), ss. 14, 18, 19(1), (2), (5) to (7), 20, 22, 23(4), 39 (except s. 39(4)(*a*)) and 40 in force January 1, 1993; s. 19(3) and (4) were to come into force July 1, 1993 (see SI/92-156) but amended by P.C. 1993-1446, so that s. 19(3) and (4) came into force January 1, 1994 (see SI/94-7), s. 106(2)(*c*) as enacted by s. 19(3) in force (*a*), in Alberta, British Columbia, Ontario, Prince Edward Island, Quebec and the Yukon Territory on January 1, 1994, and (*b*), in Manitoba, New Brunswick, Newfoundland, Nova Scotia and Saskatchewan on April 1, 1994, however, the coming into force in Saskatchewan was deferred to September 1, 1994, the coming into force in the Northwest Territories was repealed by SI/98-80, *Can. Gaz., Part II*, July 8, 1998; the order bringing ss. 8 and 39(4)(*a*) into force on January 1, 1993 was amended so that s. 8 now in force as of January 1, 1995 and s. 39(4)(*a*) is to come into force on some future, unspecified date; that part of s. 3 which enacts s. 86(2) to come into force by order of the Governor in Council; however, s. 86(2) as enacted by s. 3 repealed by 1995, c. 39, s. 163 (brought into force December 1, 1998 by SI/98-93, *Can. Gaz., Part II*, September 30, 1998 (in force date amended by SI/98-95, *Can. Gaz., Part II*, September 30, 1998)); s. 34 repealed by 1995, c. 39, s. 162 (brought into force December 1, 1998 by SI/98-93, *Can. Gaz., Part II*, September 30, 1998 (in force date amended by SI/98-95, *Can. Gaz., Part II*, September 30, 1998)); s. 105(4) of the *Criminal Code* as enacted by s. 39(4) repealed by 1995, c. 39, s. 164 (brought into force December 1, 1998 by SI/98-93, *Can. Gaz., Part II*, September 30, 1998 (in force date amended by SI/98-95, *Can. Gaz., Part II*, September 30, 1998))
Amended 1991, c. 43, ss. 1 to 10; brought into force, except that part of s. 4 which enacts ss. 672.64 to 672.66, ss. 5, 6 and 10(8), February 4, 1992 by SI/92-9, *Can. Gaz., Part II*, February 12, 1992; ss. 5 and 6 repealed by 1995, c. 22, s. 12 (in force September 3, 1996); that part of s. 4 which enacts ss. 672.64 to 672.66 and 10(8) to come into force by order of the Governor in Council (repealed before coming into force by 2005, c. 22, ss. 24, 43(3) (in force January 2, 2006))
Amended 1992, c. 1, ss. 58 and 59; in force February 28, 1992
Amended 1992, c. 11, ss. 14 to 17; in force May 15, 1992

Amended 1992, c. 20, ss. 199 to 204, 215, 216, 228 and 229; brought into force, except s. 204, November 1, 1992; s. 204 repealed by 1995, c. 42, s. 61 (in force January 24, 1996)
Amended 1992, c. 21, s. 9; brought into force June 30, 1992 by SI/92-126, *Can. Gaz., Part II*, July 15, 1992
Amended 1992, c. 22, s. 12; brought into force July 24, 1992 by SI/92-134, *Can. Gaz., Part II*, July 29, 1992
Amended 1992, c. 27, s. 90(1)(*i*); brought into force November 30, 1992
Amended 1992, c. 38; brought into force August 15, 1992 by SI/92-136, *Can. Gaz., Part II*, July 29, 1992
Amended 1992, c. 41; in force July 23, 1992 (but see s. 7)
Amended 1992, c. 47, ss. 68 to 72; brought into force August 1, 1996 by SI/96-56, *Can. Gaz., Part II*, July 1, 1996
Amended 1992, c. 51, ss. 32 to 43; brought into force January 30, 1993
Amended 1993, c. 7; brought into force September 1, 1993
Amended 1993, c. 25, ss. 93 to 95; s. 93 deemed in force January 1, 1993; ss. 94 and 95 in force June 10, 1993
Amended 1993, c. 28, Sch. III, ss. 25 to 37; however, s. 27 repealed by 1995, c. 39, s. 192 and s. 35 replaced by 1998, c. 15, s. 20 (in force June 11, 1998); in force April 1, 1999; however, ss. 25(2), 28, 29, 31, 32, 34, 35.1 to 36 repealed 1999, c. 3, s. 12 (in force March 11, 1999)
Amended 1993, c. 34, s. 59(1); in force on the day after the day on which 1993, c. 34, s. 142 is brought into force (1993, c. 34, s. 59(1) in force December 15, 1994)
Amended 1993, c. 37, ss. 21 and 32; brought into force September 1, 1993
Amended 1993, c. 40, ss. 1 to 18; brought into force August 1, 1993
Amended 1993, c. 45, ss. 1 to 14 and 16 to 19; brought into force August 1, 1993 by SI/94-137
Amended 1993, c. 46, ss. 1 to 5; brought into force August 1, 1993
Amended 1994, c. 12, s. 1; brought into force July 1, 1994
Amended 1994, c. 13, s. 7(1)(*b*); in force May 12, 1994
Amended 1994, c. 38, ss. 14 and 25(1)(*g*); brought into force January 12, 1995 by SI/95-9, *Can. Gaz., Part II*, January 25, 1995
Amended 1994, c. 44, ss. 1 to 84 and 103; brought into force, except ss. 8(2), 39 to 43 and 84, February 15, 1995; ss. 8(2), 39 to 43 and 84 brought into force April 1, 1995
Amended 1995, c. 5, s. 25(1)(*g*); brought into force May 13, 1995 by SI/95-65, *Can. Gaz., Part II*, May 31, 1995
Amended 1995, c. 19, ss. 37 to 41; brought into force December 1, 1995 by SI/95-116, *Can. Gaz., Part II*, November 29, 1995
Amended 1995, c. 22, ss. 1 to 12, 14, 15, 18 to 24 and 26; brought into force September 3, 1996 by SI/96-79, *Can. Gaz., Part II*, August 21, 1996, except that part of s. 6 that enacts ss. 718.3(5) and 747 to 747.8 (to come into force by order of the Governor in Council (that part of s. 6 that enacts s. 718.3(5) repealed before coming into force by 1999, c. 5, s. 30 (in force July 1, 1999); that part of s. 6 that enacts ss. 747-747.8 repealed before coming into force by 2005, c. 22, s. 39 (in force January 2, 2006); s. 7(2) repealed before conditions were satisfied by 2005, c. 22, s. 44 (in force January 2, 2006)); that part of s. 6 that enacted ss. 745.6 to 745.64 re-enacted 1996, c. 34, s. 2(2); brought into force January 9, 1997 by SI/97-12, *Can. Gaz., Part II*, January 22, 1997
Amended 1995, c. 27, ss. 1 and 3; in force July 13, 1995
Amended 1995, c. 29, ss. 39 and 40; brought into force November 1, 1995 by SI/95-115, *Can. Gaz., Part II*, November 15, 1995
Amended 1995, c. 32, s. 1; brought into force September 15, 1995 by SI/95-101, *Can. Gaz., Part II*, September 20, 1995

Amended 1995, c. 39, ss. 138 to 157, 163, 164, 188(*a*) and (*b*), 189(*e*) and 190; that part of s. 139 which replaces s. 85 and ss. 141 to 150 brought into force January 1, 1996, by SI/96-2, *Can. Gaz., Part II*, January 10, 1996; ss. 138, 139 (except to the extent that it replaces ss. 85 and 97 of the *Criminal Code*), 140, 151 to 157, 163, 164, 188(*a*) and (*b*), 189(*e*), 190 brought into force December 1, 1998 by SI/98-93, *Can. Gaz., Part II*, September 30, 1998 (in force date amended by SI/98-95, *Can. Gaz., Part II*, September 30, 1998); that part of s. 139 which replaces s. 97 to come into force by order of the Governor in Council; however, repealed before coming into force

Amended 1995, c. 42, ss. 73 to 76, 86 and 87; brought into force January 24, 1996 by SI/96-10, *Can. Gaz., Part II*, February 7, 1996 (see ss. 86 and 87)

Amended 1996, c. 7, s. 38; brought into force July 31, 1996 by SI/96-57, Can. Gaz., Part II, July 10, 1996

Amended 1996, c. 8, s. 32(1)(*d*); brought into force July 12, 1996 by SI/96-69, *Can. Gaz., Part II*, July 24, 1996

Amended 1996, c. 16, s. 60(1)(*d*); brought into force July 12, 1996 by SI/96-67, *Can. Gaz., Part II*, July 24, 1996

Amended 1996, c. 19, ss. 65 to 76 and 93.3; ss. 65 to 76 brought into force May 14, 1997 by SI/97-47, *Can. Gaz., Part II*, May 14, 1997; s. 93.3 in force December 1, 1998 as provided by that section

Amended 1996, c. 31, ss. 67 to 72; brought into force January 31, 1997 by SI/97-21, *Can. Gaz., Part II*, February 5, 1997

Amended 1996, c. 34, ss. 1 and 2(2); s. 2(2) in force January 1, 1997; s. 1 to come into force by order of the Governor in Council (repealed before coming into force 2008, c. 20, s. 3)

Amended 1997, c. 16, s. 2; brought into force May 26, 1997 by SI/97-66, *Can. Gaz., Part II*

Amended 1997, c. 17, ss. 1 to 10; brought into force August 1, 1997 by SI/97-84, *Can. Gaz., Part II*, July 23, 1997

Amended 1997, c. 18, ss. 1 to 115; ss. 107.1 and 139.1 in force May 2, 1997 by SI/97-60, *Can. Gaz., Part II*, May 14, 1997; ss. 1, 23, 27 to 39, 99, 100, 109 and 140 in force May 14, 1997 by SI/97-62, *Can. Gaz., Part II*, May 28, 1997; ss. 2 to 22, 24 to 26, 40 to 98, 101 to 105, 108, 110 to 115 and 141 in force June 16, 1997 by SI/97-68, *Can. Gaz., Part II*, June 25, 1997; ss. 106 and 107 to come into force by order of the Governor in Council (repealed before coming into force 2008, c. 20, s. 3)

Amended 1997, c. 23, ss. 1 to 20 and 26; ss. 1 to 20 in force May 2, 1997 by SI/97-61, *Can. Gaz., Part II*, May 14, 1997; s. 26 brought into force December 1, 1998

Amended 1997, c. 30; brought into force May 12, 1997 by SI/97-63, *Can. Gaz., Part II*, May 28, 1997

Amended 1997, c. 39, ss. 1 to 3; in force December 18, 1997

Amended 1998, c. 7, ss. 2, 3; brought into force May 1, 2000 by SI/2000-25, *Can. Gaz., Part II*, April 26, 2000

Amended 1998, c. 9, ss. 2 to 8; brought into force June 30, 1998 by SI/98-79, *Can. Gaz., Part II*, June 24, 1998

Amended 1998, c. 30, ss. 14(*d*) and 16 (and see ss. 10 and 11); brought into force April 19, 1999 by SI/99-37, *Can. Gaz., Part II*, April 28, 1999

Amended 1998, c. 34, ss. 8, 9 and 11; ss. 8 and 9 brought into force February 14, 1999 by SI/99-13, *Can. Gaz., Part II*, March 3, 1999; s. 11 in force September 1, 1999 (as provided by s. 11)

Amended 1998, c. 35, ss. 119 to 121; brought into force September 1, 1999 by SI/99-75, *Can. Gaz., Part II*, July 21, 1999

Amended 1998, c. 37, ss. 15 to 24; brought into force June 30, 2000 by SI/2000-60, *Can. Gaz., Part II*, July 19, 2000

Amended 1999, c. 2, s. 47; brought into force March 18, 1999 by SI/99-25, *Can. Gaz.*, *Part II*, March 31, 1999
Amended 1999, c. 3, ss. 12, 25 to 58; s. 12 in force March 11, 1999; ss. 25 to 58 in force April 1, 1999
Amended 1999, c. 5, ss. 1 to 47; s. 9 in force March 11, 1999; s. 51 in force July 1, 1999 (as provided by 1999, c. 5, s. 51); s. 52 in force March 18, 1999 (as provided by 1999, c. 5, s. 52); ss. 6 and 7 brought into force March 15, 1999 by para. (*a*) of SI/99-24, *Can. Gaz.*, *Part II*, March 31, 1999; ss. 1 to 5, 8, 10 to 24, 26 to 28 and 43 to 47 brought into force May 1, 1999 by para. (*b*) of SI/99-24, *Can. Gaz.*, *Part II*, March 31, 1999; ss. 25 and 29 to 42 brought into force July 1, 1999 by para. (*c*) of SI/99-24, *Can. Gaz.*, *Part II*, March 31, 1999
Amended 1999, c. 17, s. 120; brought into force November 1, 1999 by SI/99-111, *Can. Gaz.*, *Part II*, October 13, 1999
Amended 1999, c. 18, ss. 92 to 95; in force June 17, 1999
Amended 1999, c. 25, ss. 1 to 27, 30, 31(3) and (5); ss. 1 to 27, 31(3) and (5) brought into force December 1, 1999 by SI/99-135, *Can. Gaz.*, *Part II*, December 8, 1999; s. 30 brought into force May 1, 2000 as provided by s. 30; (s. 29(2) repealed before conditions were satisfied by 2005, c. 22, s. 46 (in force January 2, 2006))
Amended 1999, c. 28, ss. 155 and 156; brought into force June 28, 1999 by SI/99-70, *Can. Gaz.*, *Part II*, July 7, 1999
Amended 1999, c. 31, ss. 67 to 69; in force June 17, 1999
Amended 1999, c. 32, ss. 1 to 6; brought into force July 1, 1999 by SI/99-73, *Can. Gaz.*, *Part II*, July 21, 1999
Amended 1999, c. 33, s. 346; brought into force March 31, 2000 by SI/2000-15, *Can. Gaz.*, *Part II*, March 29, 2000
Amended 1999, c. 35, s. 11; brought into force May 1, 2000 by SI/2000-27, *Can. Gaz.*, *Part II*, April 26, 2000
Amended 2000, c. 1, s. 9; brought into force August 1, 2000 by SI/2000-73, *Can. Gaz.*, *Part II*, August 16, 2000
Amended 2000, c. 2, ss. 1 to 3; in force March 30, 2000
Amended 2000, c. 10, ss. 13 to 24; brought into force June 30, 2000 by SI/2000-61, *Can. Gaz.*, *Part II*, July 19, 2000
Amended 2000, c. 12, ss. 91 to 95; brought into force July 31, 2000 by SI/2000-76, *Can. Gaz.*, *Part II*, August 16, 2000
Amended 2000, c. 17, s. 89; brought into force October 28, 2001 by SI/2001-88, *Can. Gaz.*, *Part II*, September 12, 2001
Amended 2000, c. 24, ss. 42 to 46; brought into force October 23, 2000 by SI/2000-95, *Can. Gaz.*, *Part II*, November 8, 2000 (however, s. 43 later replaced 2001, c. 34, s. 36, in force December 18, 2001)
Amended 2000, c. 25, ss. 2 to 4; brought into force March 15, 2001 by SI/2001-42, *Can. Gaz.*, *Part II*, March 28, 2001
Amended 2001, c. 26, s. 294; brought into force July 1, 2007 by SI/2007-65, *Can. Gaz.*, *Part II*, June 27, 2007
Amended 2001, c. 27, ss. 244 to 247; ss. 244, 246 and 247 brought into force June 28, 2002 by paras. (*f*) and (*g*) of SI/2002-97, *Can. Gaz.*, *Part II*, June 14, 2002 (however, s. 246 since repealed 2001, c. 32, s. 81(3)(*d*) in force June 28, 2002 as provided by the section); s. 245 to come into force by order of the Governor in Council (repealed before coming into force 2004, c. 15, s. 110)
Amended 2001, c. 32, ss. 1(1) to (5), 2, 4 to 8, 9(1), 10, 11, 12(1) to (4), (6), (7), 13 to 30, 31(1), (2), (4), 32 to 42, 45 and 46; ss. 1(1) to (5), 4 to 8, 9(1), 10, 11, 16, 24, 27 to 30, 31(1), (2), (4), 32 to 42, 45 and 46 brought into force January 7, 2002 by para. (*a*) of SI/

2002-17, *Can. Gaz.*, *Part II*, January 16, 2002; ss. 2, 12(1) to (4), (6), (7), 13 to 15, 17 to 23, 25 and 26 brought into force February 1, 2002 by part (*b*) of SI/2002-17, *Can. Gaz.*, *Part II*, January 16, 2002

Amended 2001, c. 37, s. 1; in force December 18, 2001

Amended 2001, c. 41, ss. 2 to 23, 31 to 34, 80, 126(2), (3), 130(7.1), 131(2), 133(2), (5), (8) to (11), (13), (14) to (19), (21) and 143; ss. 80, 133(21) in force December 18, 2001; ss. 2 to 23, 31 to 34 brought into force December 24, 2001 by SI/2002-16; s. 131(2) in force December 24, 2001 (as provided by this section); ss. 130(7.1), 133(2), (5), (8) to (10), (13) to (19) in force January 7, 2002 (as provided by these sections); s. 133(11) in force February 1, 2002 (as provided by this section); s. 126(2), (3) in force June 28, 2002 (as provided by these sections); s. 143 in force July 2, 2003 (as provided by this section)

Amended 2002, c. 1, ss. 175 to 177, 179 and 181 to 186 brought into force April 1, 2003 by SI/2002-91, *Can. Gaz.*, *Part II*, June 19, 2002

Amended 2002, c. 7, ss. 137 to 150 brought into force April 1, 2003 by SI/2003-48, *Can. Gaz.*, *Part II*, April 9, 2003

Amended 2002, c. 13, ss. 2 to 4, 5(2), (3), (4), 6 to 15 and 17 to 85; ss. 2 to 4, 5(2), (3), (4), 6 to 15, 17 to 23, 47, 50 to 58, 60, 61, 63 to 65, 67 to 69, 73 to 78, 80 to 86 brought into force July 23, 2002 by para. (*b*) of SI/2002-106, *Can. Gaz.*, *Part II*, July 31, 2002; ss. 49 and 62 brought into force September 23, 2002 by para. (*c*) of SI/2002-106, *Can. Gaz.*, *Part II*, July 31, 2002; ss. 66, 70, 71 brought into force November 25, 2002 by para. (*d*) of SI/2002-106, *Can. Gaz.*, *Part II*, July 31, 2002; ss. 24 to 46, 48, 59 and 72 brought into force June 1, 2004 as provided by para. (*b*) of SI/2003-182, *Can. Gaz.*, *Part II*, December 3, 2003; s. 79 brought into force July 23, 2003 by para. (*b*) of SI/2003-127, *Can. Gaz.*, *Part II*, July 2, 2003

Amended 2002, c. 22, ss. 324 to 327 and 409(2)(*b*); s. 409(2)(*b*) in force June 13, 2002 as provided by this section; ss. 324 to 327 brought into force July 1, 2003 by SI/2003-47, *Can. Gaz.*, *Part II*, April 9, 2003 [Note: ss. 326 and 327 since repealed by 2002, c. 22, s. 409(2)(*a*) and (6) as provided in the section, in force June 13, 2002.]

Amended 2003, c. 8, ss. 2 to 8; s. 2(1) brought into force May 30, 2003 by SI/2003-114, *Can. Gaz.*, *Part II*, June 18, 2003; ss. 2(2) and 3 to 7 brought into force August 15, 2003 by SI/2003-144, *Can. Gaz.*, August 27, 2003; s. 8 to come into force by order of the Governor in Council (repealed before coming into force 2012, c. 1, s. 47)

Amended 2003, c. 21, ss. 1 to 21; brought into force March 31, 2004 by SI/2004-22, *Can. Gaz.*, *Part II*, February 25, 2004; s. 22 in force June 1, 2004, as provided by that section

Amended 2003, c. 22, s. 224(*z*.23), brought into force April 6, 2005 by SI/2005-24, *Can. Gaz.*, *Part II*, April 6, 2005

Amended 2004, c. 3, ss. 1 to 8; ss. 2 to 8 brought into force September 15, 2004 by SI/2004-119, *Can. Gaz.*, *Part II*, September 22, 2004; s. 1 brought into force September 15, 2005 by SI/2005-60, *Can. Gaz.*, *Part II*, June 29, 2005

Amended 2004, c. 10, ss. 20 and 21 brought into force December 15, 2004 by SI/2004-157, *Can. Gaz.*, *Part II*, December 15, 2004

Amended 2004, c. 12, ss. 1 to 7 and 9 to 17; ss. 1 to 7 and 9 to 16 in force on Royal Assent, April 22, 2004; s. 17 brought into force October 1, 2004 by SI/2004-131, *Can. Gaz.*, *Part II*, October 20, 2004

Amended 2004, c. 14, ss. 1 and 2, in force on Royal Assent, April 29, 2004

Amended 2004, c. 15, ss. 32 and 108; brought into force December 1, 2004 by SI/2004-158, *Can. Gaz.*, *Part II*, December 15, 2004

Amended 2005, c. 10, ss. 18 to 25 and 34(1)(*f*), brought into force April 4, 2005 by SI/2005-29, *Can. Gaz.*, *Part II*, April 20, 2005

Amended 2005, c. 22, ss. 1 to 8, 10 to 26, 27(2), 28 to 34, 36 to 41 and 64(2); ss. 1 to 7, 10, 11, 33 and 40 brought into force June 30, 2005 by para. (*a*) of SI/2005-56, *Can. Gaz.*,

Part II, June 15, 2005; ss. 8, 12 to 26, 27(2), 28 to 32, 34, 36 to 39 and 41, brought into force January 2, 2006 by para. (*b*) of SI/2005-56, *Can. Gaz.*, *Part II*, June 15, 2005; s. 64(2) in force January 2, 2006 as provided by the section

Amended 2005, c. 25, ss. 1 and 3 to 13; s. 5 in force on Royal Assent, May 19, 2005; ss. 1, 3, 4 and 6 to 13 brought into force January 1, 2008 by SI/2007-108, *Can. Gaz.*, *Part II*, December 12, 2007

Amended 2005, c. 32, ss. 1 to 7, 8(2) to (5) and 9 to 25; ss. 1 to 7, 8(2) to (5), 9 to 12, 24 and 25 brought into force November 1, 2005 by para. (*a*) of SI/2005-104, *Can. Gaz.*, *Part II*, November 16, 2005; ss. 13 to 23 brought into force January 2, 2006 by para. (*b*) of SI/2005-104, *Can. Gaz.*, *Part II*, November 16, 2005

Amended 2005, c. 38, ss. 58, 138(*e*) and 140(*b*); brought into force December 12, 2005 by SI/2005-119, *Can. Gaz.*, *Part II*, December 14, 2005

Amended 2005, c. 40, ss. 1 to 3 and 7; ss. 1 to 3 in force November 24, 2005; s. 7 in force November 24, 2005 as provided by the section

Amended 2005, c. 43, ss. 1 to 7 and 8(3); ss. 1 to 7 in force November 25, 2005; s. 8(3) in force November 25, 2005 as provided by the section

Amended 2005, c. 44, ss. 1, 3 to 12; in force November 25, 2005

Amended 2006, c. 9, s. 246; brought into force March 1, 2007 by SI/2007-15, *Can. Gaz.*, *Part II*, February 21, 2007

Amended 2006, c. 14, ss. 1, 2, 3(2) and (3), and 4 to 7, in force on Royal Assent, December 14, 2006

Amended 2007, c. 5, ss. 11 to 20, 21(2), 22 to 29, 30(2), (3) and 31; brought into force September 12, 2008 by SI/2008-93, *Can. Gaz.*, *Part II*, September 4, 2008

Amended 2007, c. 9, ss. 1 and 2; in force on Royal Assent, May 3, 2007

Amended 2007, c. 12, ss. 1 and 2; in force December 1, 2007, as provided by s. 2 (received Royal Assent May 31, 2007)

Amended 2007, c. 13, ss. 1 to 11; in force on Royal Assent, May 31, 2007

Amended 2007, c. 20, s. 1; in force on Royal Assent, June 22, 2007

Amended 2007, c. 22, ss. 2 to 4, 7 to 26; ss. 2 to 4, 8(2) to (5), 9, 11(1), 13(1), 18, 19, 20(1) to (3), 21, 23 and 25 in force June 22, 2007; ss. 7, 8(1), 10, 11(2) to (4), 12, 13(2), 14 to 17, 20(4), 22, 24 and 26 brought into force January 1, 2008 by SI/2007-108, *Can. Gaz.*, *Part II*, December 12, 2007

Amended 2007, c. 28, s. 1; in force on Royal Assent, June 22, 2007

Amended 2008, c. 6, ss. 2 to 44, 45(1), (2), 46, 47, 48(1) and 49 to 54; ss. 2 to 17, 28 to 38 and 54 brought into force May 1, 2008 by SI/2008-34, *Can. Gaz.*, *Part II*, April 2, 2008; remainder brought into force July 2, 2008, by SI/2008-34, *Can. Gaz.*, *Part II*, April 2, 2008

Amended 2008, c. 12, s. 1; in force on Royal Assent, April 17, 2008

Amended 2008, c. 18, ss. 1 to 26, and 28 to 45.2; ss. 1 to 6, 9 to 17, 22 to 26, 28, 30 to 34, 36, 41, 43, 45 and 45.2 in force on Royal Assent, May 29, 2008; remainder in force October 1, 2008 by SI/2008-71, *Can. Gaz.*, *Part II*, June 25, 2008

Amended 2009, c. 2, s. 442; in force March 12, 2010 by s. 444 of the Act

Amended 2009, c. 22, ss. 1 to 19; brought into force October 2, 2009 by SI/2009-92, *Can. Gaz.*, *Part II*, September 30, 2009

Amended 2009, c. 28, ss. 1 to 11; brought into force January 8, 2010 by SI/2009-120, *Can. Gaz.*, *Part II*, December 23, 2009

Amended 2009, c. 29, ss. 2 to 5; brought into force February 22, 2010 by SI/2010-9, *Can. Gaz.*, *Part II*, February 17, 2010

Amended 2010, c. 3, ss. 1 to 8; in force June 29, 2010

Amended 2010, c. 14, ss. 2 to 11; brought into force April 29, 2011 by SI/2011-23, *Can. Gaz.*, *Part II*, April 13, 2011

Amended 2010, c. 17, ss. 2 to 27; brought into force April 15, 2011 by SI/2011-35, April 13, 2011
Amended 2010, c. 19, s. 1; brought into force November 30, 2011 by SI/2011-99, *Can. Gaz.*, *Part II*, December 7, 2011
Amended 2010, c. 20, s. 1; in force on Royal Assent, December 15, 2010
Amended 2011, c. 2, ss. 2 to 5; brought into force December 2, 2011 by SI/2011-108, *Can. Gaz.*, *Part II*, December 21, 2011
Amended 2011, c. 5, ss. 2 to 5; brought into force December 2, 2011 by SI/2011-107, *Can. Gaz.*, *Part II*, December 21, 2011
Amended 2011, c. 6, ss. 2 to 5; brought into force November 1, 2011 by SI/2011-82, *Can. Gaz.*, *Part II*, October 12, 2011
Amended 2011, c. 7, ss. 2 to 13; brought into force March 31, 2015 by SI/2014-105, *Can. Gaz.*, *Part II*, December 31, 2014
Amended 2011, c. 16, ss. 2, and 4 to 16; ss. 2, 4 to 6, 7(2) and (4), 10, 11 and 14 to 16 brought into force August 15, 2011 by SI/2011-62, *Can. Gaz.*, *Part II*, August 17, 2011; remainder bought into force October 24, 2011 by SI/2011-62, *Can. Gaz.*, *Part II*, August 17, 2011
Amended 2012, c. 1, ss. 10 to 38, 47, 141(2) and (3), 143 to 146, 160(c), 200; s. 32(2), 141(2) and (3), 143 to 146 in force March 13, 2012; s. 147 brought into force June 13, 2012 by SI/2012-40 *Can. Gaz.*, *Part II*, June 20, 2012; ss. 10 to 31 and 35 to 38 brought into force August 9, 2012 by SI/2012-48, *Can. Gaz.*, *Part II*, July 4, 2012; ss. 32(1), 33 and 47 brought into force November 6, 2012 by SI/2012-48, *Can. Gaz.*, *Part II*, July 4, 2012; s. 34 brought into force November 20, 2012 by SI/2012-48, *Can. Gaz.*, *Part II*, July 4, 2012; s. 200 brought into force October 23, 2012 by SI/2012/48, *Can. Gaz.*, *Part II*, July 4, 2012; s. 160(c) brought into force February 28, 2013 by SI/2013-13, *Can. Gaz.*, *Part II*, February 27, 2013
Amended 2012, c. 6, ss. 2 to 8; brought into force April 5, 2012 by SI/2012-28, *Can. Gaz.*, *Part II*, April 25, 2012
Amended 2012, c. 9, ss. 2 and 3; brought into force March 11, 2013, by SI/2013-5, *Can. Gaz.*, *Part II*, September 12, 2012
Amended 2012, c. 15, ss. 1 and 2; in force on Royal Assent, June 28, 2012
Amended 2012, c. 19, s. 371; brought into force August 20, 2012 by *Can. Gaz.*, *Part II*, SI/2012-68, September 12, 2012
Amended 2012, c. 29, s. 2; brought into force January 13, 2013
Amended 2013, c. 8, ss. 2 to 6; s. 5 in force September 27, 2013; remainder in force March 27, 2013
Amended 2013, c. 9, ss. 2, 3(2) and 4 to 16; in force July 15, 2013 by SI/2013-67, *Can. Gaz.*, *Part II*, June 19, 2013
Amended 2013, c. 11, ss. 2 to 4; brought into force October 24, 2013 by SI/2013-112, *Can. Gaz.*, *Part II*, October 23, 2013
Amended 2013, c. 13, ss. 2 to 9; brought into force November 1, 2013 by SI/2013-108, *Can. Gaz.*, *Part II*, October 9, 2013
Amended 2013, c. 15, ss. 2 and 3; in force on Royal Assent, June 19, 2013
Amended 2013, c. 19, s. 1; in force on Royal Assent, June 19, 2013
Amended 2013, c. 32, s. 1; in force June 26, 2013
Amended 2013, c. 40, s. 174; in force on Royal Assent, December 12, 2013
Amended 2014, c. 6, ss. 2 to 20; in force July 11, 2014, three months after Royal Assent, April 11, 2014
Amended 2014, c. 9, s. 1; in force on Royal Assent, June 19, 2014
Amended 2014, c. 10, s. 1; in force on Royal Assent, June 19, 2014
Amended 2014, c. 17, ss. 1 to 16; in force on Royal Assent, June 19, 2014

Amended 2014, c. 20, s. 366(1); brought into force June 17, 2019 by SI/2018-100, *Can. Gaz., Part II*, November 14, 2018

Amended 2014, c. 21, ss. 1 to 4; in force September 19, 2014

Amended 2014, c. 23, ss. 2 and 3; brought into force April 10, 2015 by SI/2015-26, *Can. Gaz., Part II*, April 8, 2015

Amended 2014, c. 25, ss. 2 to 33, 46(2) to (7) and 48(5) and (6); ss. 2 to 33 in force December 6, 2014; s. 46(2) to (7) in force March 9, 2015; s. 48(5) and (6) in force July 23, 2015

Amended 2014, c. 31, ss. 2 to 13, 14(2), 15 to 26; in force March 9, 2015

Amended 2014, c. 32, s. 59 in force on Royal Assent, December 9, 2014

Amended 2014, c. 39, s. 171 in force on Royal Assent, December 16, 2014

Amended 2015, c. 1, s. 1; in force on Royal Assent, February 25, 2015

Amended 2015, c. 3, ss. 44 to 59; in force on Royal Assent, February 26, 2015

Amended 2015, c. 13, ss. 3 to 36; in force July 23, 2015, 90 days after Royal Assent, April 23, 2015; ss. 5(1), 18(3) repealed 2014, c. 25, s. 48(3), (8)

Amended 2015, c. 16, ss. 1, 3, 4; to come into force by order of the Governor in Council

Amended 2015, c. 20, ss. 15-28, 34(2)-(4), 35, 38; ss. 15(1), 16, 19-23, 35 in force on Royal Assent, June 18, 2015; ss. 15(2), 17, 18, 24, 25-28 in force July 18, 2015, 30 days after Royal Assent, June 18, 2015; s. 27(2) repealed 2015, c. 20, s. 37(3); s. 38 in force July 23, 2015

Amended 2015, c. 23, ss. 2-19, 30, 31, 33; ss. 2-19, 33 brought into force July 17, 2015 by SI/2015-68, *Can. Gaz., Part II*, July 17, 2015; ss. 30, 31; to come into force by order of the Governor in Council

Amended 2015, c. 27, ss. 18-34; in force on Royal Assent, June 18, 2015

Amended 2015, c. 29, ss. 6-12; brought into force July 17, 2015 by SI/2015-67, *Can. Gaz., Part II*, July 17, 2015

Amended 2015, c. 34; in force on Royal Assent, June 23, 2015

Amended 2016, c. 3, ss. 1 to 6; ss. 1 to 3 and 6 in force June 17, 2016; ss. 4 and 5 in force June 17, 2017

Amended 2017, c. 7, ss. 54, 56, 58, 59(1), 60(1), 61, 64-68; ss. 56 in force on Royal Assent, May 18, 2017; ss. 54, 58, 59(1), 60(1), 61, 64-68 brought into force June 21, 2018 by SI/2018-46, *Can. Gaz., Part II*, July 11, 2018

Amended 2017, c. 13, ss. 3, 4; in force on Royal Assent, June 19, 2017

Amended 2017, c. 22, s. 3; in force on Royal Assent, October 18, 2017

Amended 2017, c. 23, ss. 1, 2; in force on Royal Assent and conditions satisfied, December 12, 2017

Amended 2017, c. 27, ss. 61, 62; to come into force by order of the Governor in Council

Amended 2017, c. 33, s. 255; brought into into force October 1, 2018 by SI/2018-83, *Can. Gaz., Part II*, September 5, 2018

Amended 2018, c. 11, ss. 27 to 29; in force on Royal Assent, June 21, 2018

Amended 2018, c. 12, ss. 114, 403 to 405; ss. 403 to 405 in force September 19, 2018; s. 114 in force October 17, 2018

Amended 2018, c. 16, ss. 190, 207 to 225; ss. 207 to 224 in force October 17, 2018; if Bill C-28, introduced in the 1st session of the 42nd Parliament and entitled *An Act to amend the Criminal Code (victim surcharge)*, receives royal assent, then, on the first day on which both subsec. 2(1) of that Act and s. 222 of 2018, c. 16 are in force, s. 190 will come into force; s. 225 to come into force on the first day on which both of *An Act to amend the Criminal Code (exploitation and trafficking in persons)*, 2015, c. 16, s. 4 and 2018, c. 16, s. 214 are in force

Amended 2018, c. 21, ss. 1 to 9, 12 to 23, 25 to 31; ss. 1 to 9 in force on Royal Assent, June 21, 2018; ss. 12 to 31 in force December 18, 2018

Amended 2018, c. 26, s. 23; to come into force by order of the Governor in Council
Amended 2018, c. 27, ss. 28 and 686; in force on Royal Assent, December 13, 2018
Amended 2018, c. 29, ss. 1 to 72; in force on Royal Assent, December 13, 2018

An Act respecting the Criminal Law

SHORT TITLE

SHORT TITLE.

1. This Act may be cited as the *Criminal Code*. R.S., c. C-34, s. 1.

INTERPRETATION

DEFINITIONS / "Act" / "Associated personnel" / "Attorney General" / "Bank-note" / "Bodily harm" / "Canadian Forces" / "Cattle" / "Clerk of the court" / "Common-law partner" / "Complainant" / "Counsel" / "Count" / "Court of appeal" / "Court of criminal jurisdiction" / "Criminal organization" / "Criminal organization offence" / "Day" / "Document of title to goods" / "Document of title to lands" / "Dwelling-house" / "Every one", "person", "owner" / "Explosive substance" / "Firearm" / "Government or public facility" / "Her Majesty's Forces" / "Highway" / "Indictment" / "Internationally protected person" / "Justice" / "Justice system participant" / "Mental disorder" / "Military" / "Military law" / "Motor vehicle" / "Municipality" / "Newly-born child" / "Night" / "Offence-related property" / "Offender" / "Offensive weapon" / "Organization" / "Peace officer" / "Prison" / "Property" / "Prosecutor" / "Provincial court judge" / "Public department" / "Public officer" / "Public stores" / "Railway equipment" / "Representative" / "Senior officer" / "Serious offence" / "Steal" / "Street racing" / "Superior court of criminal jurisdiction" / "Territorial division" / "Terrorism offence" / "Terrorist activity" / "Terrorist group" / "Testamentary Instrument" / "Trustee" / "Unfit to stand trial" / "United Nations operation" / "United Nations personnel" / "Valuable mineral" / "Valuable security" / "Victim" / "Weapon" / "Wreck" / "Writing".

2. In this Act,

"Act" includes

(*a*) an Act of Parliament,
(*b*) an Act of the legislature of the former Province of Canada,
(*c*) an Act of the legislature of a province, and
(*d*) an Act or ordinance of the legislature of a province, territory or place in force at the time that province, territory or place became a province of Canada;

"associated personnel" means persons who are

(*a*) assigned by a government or an intergovernmental organization with the agreement of the competent organ of the United Nations,
(*b*) engaged by the Secretary-General of the United Nations, by a specialized agency of the United Nations or by the International Atomic Energy Agency, or
(*c*) deployed by a humanitarian non-governmental organization or agency under an agreement with the Secretary-General of the United Nations, by a specialized agency of the United Nations or by the International Atomic Energy Agency,

to carry out activities in support of the fulfilment of the mandate of a United Nations operation;

"Attorney General"

(*a*) subject to paragraphs (*b*.1) to (*g*), with respect to proceedings to which this Act applies, means the Attorney General or Solicitor General of the province in which those proceedings are taken and includes his or her lawful deputy,

(*b*) with respect to Yukon, the Northwest Territories and Nunavut, or with respect to proceedings commenced at the instance of the Government of Canada and conducted by or on behalf of that Government in respect of a contravention of, a conspiracy or attempt to contravene, or counselling the contravention of, any Act of Parliament other than this Act or any regulation made under such an Act, means the Attorney General of Canada and includes his or her lawful deputy,

(*b*.1) with respect to proceedings in relation to an offence under subsection 7(2.01), means either the Attorney General of Canada or the Attorney General or Solicitor General of the province in which those proceedings are taken and includes the lawful deputy of any of them,

(*c*) with respect to proceedings in relation to a terrorism offence or to an offence under section 57, 58, 83.12, 424.1 or 431.1 or in relation to an offence against a member of United Nations personnel or associated personnel under section 235, 236, 266, 267, 268, 269, 269.1, 271, 272, 273, 279 or 279.1, means either the Attorney General of Canada or the Attorney General or Solicitor General of the province in which those proceedings are taken and includes the lawful deputy of any of them,

(*d*) with respect to proceedings in relation to an offence referred to in subsection 7(3.71), or in relation to an offence referred to in paragraph (*a*) of the definition "terrorist activity" in subsection 83.01(1) if the act or omission was committed outside Canada but is deemed under any of subsections 7(2), (2.1) to (2.21), (3), (3.1), (3.72) and (3.73) to have been committed in Canada, means either the Attorney General of Canada or the Attorney General or Solicitor General of the province in which those proceedings are taken and includes his or her lawful deputy,

(*e*) with respect to proceedings in relation to an offence where the act or omission constituting the offence

(i) constitutes a terrorist activity referred to in paragraph (*b*) of the definition "terrorist activity" in subsection 83.01(1), and

(ii) was committed outside Canada but is deemed by virtue of subsection 7(3.74) or (3.75) to have been committed in Canada,

means either the Attorney General of Canada or the Attorney General or Solicitor General of the province in which those proceedings are taken and includes the lawful deputy of any of them,

(*f*) with respect to proceedings under section 83.13, 83.14, 83.222, 83.223, 83.28, 83.29 or 83.3, means either the Attorney General of Canada or the Attorney General or Solicitor General of the province in which those proceedings are taken and includes the lawful deputy of any of them, and

(*g*) with respect to proceedings in relation to an offence referred to in sections 121.1, 380, 382, 382.1 and 400, means either the Attorney General of Canada or the Attorney General or Solicitor General of the province in which those proceedings are taken and includes the lawful deputy of any of them;

Note: Subparagraph (*b*)(i) of the definition "Attorney General" had been replaced by 2002, c. 7, s. 137(1); however, before it came into force, the definition was replaced by 2001, c. 41, s. 2, and as such, there was no longer a subpara. (*b*)(i).

"bank-note" includes any negotiable instrument

(*a*) issued by or on behalf of a person carrying on the business of banking in or out of Canada, and

(*b*) issued under the authority of Parliament or under the lawful authority of the government of a state other than Canada,

intended to be used as money or as the equivalent of money, immediately on issue or at some time subsequent thereto, and includes bank bills and bank post bills;

"bodily harm" means any hurt or injury to a person that interferes with the health or comfort of the person and that is more than merely transient or trifling in nature;

"Canadian Forces" means the armed forces of Her Majesty raised by Canada;

"cattle" means neat cattle or an animal of the bovine species by whatever technical or familiar name it is known, and includes any horse, mule, ass, pig, sheep or goat;

"clerk of the court" includes a person, by whatever name or title he may be designated, who from time to time performs the duties of a clerk of the court;

"common-law partner", in relation to an individual, means a person who is cohabiting with the individual in a conjugal relationship, having so cohabited for a period of at least one year;

"complainant" means the victim of an alleged offence;

"counsel" means a barrister or solicitor, in respect of the matters or things that barristers and solicitors, respectively, are authorized by the law of a province to do or perform in relation to legal proceedings;

"count" means a charge in an information or indictment;

"court of appeal" means, in all provinces, the Court of Appeal;

"court of criminal jurisdiction" means

(*a*) a court of general or quarter sessions of the peace, when presided over by a superior court judge,

(*a*.1) in the Province of Quebec, the Court of Quebec, the municipal court of Montreal and the municipal court of Quebec,

(*b*) a provincial court judge or judge acting under Part XIX, and

(*c*) in the Province of Ontario, the Ontario Court of Justice;

"criminal organization" has the same meaning as in subsection 467.1(1);

"criminal organization offence" means

(*a*) an offence under section 467.11, 467.111, 467.12 or 467.13, or a serious offence committed for the benefit of, at the direction of, or in association with, a criminal organization, or

(*b*) a conspiracy or an attempt to commit, being an accessory after the fact in relation to, or any counselling in relation to, an offence referred to in paragraph (*a*);

"day" means the period between six o'clock in the forenoon and nine o'clock in the afternoon of the same day;

"document of title to goods" includes a bought and sold note, bill of lading, warrant, certificate or order for the delivery or transfer of goods or any other valuable thing, and any other document used in the ordinary course of business as evidence of the possession or control of goods, authorizing or purporting to authorize, by endorsement or by delivery, the person in possession of the document to transfer or receive any goods thereby represented or therein mentioned or referred to;

"document of title to lands" includes any writing that is or contains evidence of the title, or any part of the title, to real property or to any interest in real property, and any notarial or registrar's copy thereof and any duplicate instrument, memorial, certificate or document authorized or required by any law in force in any part of Canada with respect to registration of titles that relates to title to real property or to any interest in real property;

"dwelling-house" means the whole or any part of a building or structure that is kept or occupied as a permanent or temporary residence, and includes

(*a*) a building within the curtilage of a dwelling-house that is connected to it by a doorway or by a covered and enclosed passageway, and

(*b*) a unit that is designed to be mobile and to be used as a permanent or temporary residence and that is being used as such a residence;

"environment" means the components of the Earth and includes

(*a*) air, land and water,

(*b*) all layers of the atmosphere,

(*c*) all organic and inorganic matter and living organisms, and

(*d*) the interacting natural systems that include components referred to in paragraphs (*a*) to (*c*);

"every one", "person" and "owner", and similar expressions, include Her Majesty and an organization;

"explosive substance" includes

(*a*) anything intended to be used to make an explosive substance,

(*b*) anything, or any part thereof, used or intended to be used, or adapted to cause, or to aid in causing an explosion in or with an explosive substance, and

(*c*) an incendiary grenade, fire bomb, molotov cocktail or other similar incendiary substance or device and a delaying mechanism or other thing intended for use in connection with such a substance or device;

"feeble-minded person" [*Repealed*, 1991, c. 43, s. 9.]

"firearm" means a barrelled weapon from which any shot, bullet or other projectile can be discharged and that is capable of causing serious bodily injury or death to a person, and includes any frame or receiver of such a barrelled weapon and anything that can be adapted for use as a firearm;

"government or public facility" means a facility or conveyance, whether permanent or temporary, that is used or occupied in connection with their official duties by representatives of a state, members of a government, members of a legislature, members of the judiciary, or officials or employees of a state or of any other public authority or public entity, or by officials or employees of an intergovernmental organization;

"Her Majesty's Forces" means the naval, army and air forces of Her Majesty wherever raised, and includes the Canadian Forces;

"highway" means a road to which the public has the right of access, and includes bridges over which or tunnels through which a road passes;

"indictment" includes

(*a*) information or a count therein,

(*b*) a plea, replication or other pleading, and

(*c*) any record;

"internationally protected person" means

(*a*) a head of state, including any member of a collegial body that performs the functions of a head of state under the constitution of the state concerned, a head of a government or a minister of foreign affairs, whenever that person is in a state other than the state in which he holds that position or office,

(*b*) a member of the family of a person described in paragraph (*a*) who accompanies that person in a state other than the state in which that person holds that position or office,

(*c*) a representative or an official of a state or an official or agent of an international organization of an intergovernmental character who, at the time when and at the place where an offence referred to in subsection 7(3) is

committed against his person or any property referred to in section 431 that is used by him, is entitled, pursuant to international law, to special protection from any attack on his person, freedom or dignity, or

(*d*) a member of the family of a representative, official or agent described in paragraph (*c*) who forms part of his household, if the representative, official or agent, at the time when and at the place where any offence referred to in subsection 7(3) is committed against the member of his family or any property referred to in section 431 that is used by that member, is entitled, pursuant to international law, to special protection from any attack on his person, freedom or dignity;

"justice" means a justice of the peace or a provincial court judge, and includes two or more justices where two or more justices are, by law, required to act or, by law, act or have jurisdiction;

"justice system participant" means

(*a*) a member of the Senate, of the House of Commons, of a legislative assembly or of a municipal council, and

(*b*) a person who plays a role in the administration of criminal justice, including

(i) the Minister of Public Safety and Emergency Preparedness and a Minister responsible for policing in a province,

(ii) a prosecutor, a lawyer, a member of the Chambre des notaires du Québec and an officer of a court,

(iii) a judge and a justice,

(iv) a juror and a person who is summoned as a juror,

(v) an informant, a prospective witness, a witness under subpoena and a witness who has testified,

(vi) a peace officer within the meaning of any of paragraphs (*b*), (*c*), (*d*), (*e*) and (*g*) of the definition "peace officer",

(vii) a civilian employee of a police force,

(viii) a person employed in the administration of a court,

(viii.1) a public officer within the meaning of subsection 25.1(1) and a person acting at the direction of such an officer,

(ix) an employee of the Canada Revenue Agency who is involved in the investigation of an offence under an Act of Parliament,

(ix.1) an employee of the Canada Border Services Agency who is involved in the investigation of an offence under an Act of Parliament,

(x) an employee of a federal or provincial correctional service, a parole supervisor and any other person who is involved in the administration of a sentence under the supervision of such a correctional service and a person who conducts disciplinary hearings under the *Corrections and Conditional Release Act*, and

(xi) an employee and a member of the Parole Board of Canada and of a provincial parole board; and

(*c*) a person who plays a role in respect of proceedings involving

(i) security information,

(ii) criminal intelligence information,

(iii) information that would endanger the safety of any person if it were disclosed,

(iv) information that is obtained in confidence from a source in Canada, the government of a foreign state, an international organization of states or an institution of such a government or international organization, or

(v) potentially injurious information or sensitive information as those terms are defined in section 38 of the *Canada Evidence Act*;

"magistrate" [*Repealed*, R.S.C. 1985, c. 27 (1st Supp.), s. 2(4).]

"mental disorder" means a disease of the mind;

"military" shall be construed as relating to all or any of the Canadian Forces;

"military law" includes all laws, regulations or orders relating to the Canadian Forces;

"motor vehicle" means a vehicle that is drawn, propelled or driven by any means other than muscular power, but does not include railway equipment;

"municipality" includes the corporation of a city, town, village, county, township, parish or other territorial or local division of a province, the inhabitants of which are incorporated or are entitled to hold property collectively for a public purpose;

"newly-born child" means a person under the age of one year;

"night" means the period between nine o'clock in the afternoon and six o'clock in the forenoon of the following day;

"nuclear facility" means

(*a*) any nuclear reactor, including a reactor installed on a vessel, vehicle, aircraft or space object for use as an energy source in order to propel the vessel, vehicle, aircraft or space object or for any other purpose, and

(*b*) any plant or conveyance used for the production, storage, processing or transport of nuclear material or radioactive material;

"nuclear material" means

(*a*) plutonium, except plutonium with an isotopic concentration of plutonium-238 that is greater than 80%,

(*b*) uranium-233,

(*c*) uranium containing uranium-233 or uranium-235 or both in an amount such that the abundance ratio of the sum of those isotopes to the isotope uranium-238 is greater than 0.72%,

(*d*) uranium with an isotopic concentration equal to that occurring in nature, except uranium in the form of ore or ore-residue, and

(*e*) any substance containing any material described in paragraphs (*a*) to (*d*);

"offence-related property" means any property, within or outside Canada,

(*a*) by means or in respect of which an indictable offence under this Act or the *Corruption of Foreign Public Officials Act* is committed,

(*b*) that is used in any manner in connection with the commission of such an offence, or

(*c*) that is intended to be used for committing such an offence;

"offender" means a person who has been determined by a court to be guilty of an offence, whether on acceptance of a plea of guilty or on a finding of guilt;

"offensive weapon" has the same meaning as "weapon";

"organization" means

(*a*) a public body, body corporate, society, company, firm, partnership, trade union or municipality, or

(*b*) an association of persons that

(i) is created for a common purpose,

(ii) has an operational structure, and

(iii) holds itself out to the public as an association of persons;

"peace officer" includes

(*a*) a mayor, warden, reeve, sheriff, deputy sheriff, sheriff's officer and justice of the peace,

(*b*) a member of the Correctional Service of Canada who is designated as a peace officer pursuant to Part I of the *Corrections and Conditional Release Act*, and a warden, deputy warden, instructor, keeper, jailer, guard and any other officer or permanent employee of a prison other than a penitentiary as defined in Part I of the *Corrections and Conditional Release Act*,

(*c*) a police officer, police constable, bailiff, constable, or other person employed for the preservation and maintenance of the public peace or for the service or execution of civil process,

(*c*.1) a designated officer as defined in section 2 of the *Integrated Cross-border Law Enforcement Operations Act*, when

(i) participating in an integrated cross-border operation, as defined in section 2 of that Act, or

(ii) engaging in an activity incidental to such an operation, including travel for the purpose of participating in the operation and appearances in court arising from the operation;

(*d*) an officer within the meaning of the *Customs Act*, the *Excise Act* or the *Excise Act, 2001*, or a person having the powers of such an officer, when performing any duty in the administration of any of those Acts,

(*d*.1) an officer authorized under subsection 138(1) of the *Immigration and Refugee Protection Act*,

(*e*) a person designated as a fishery guardian under the *Fisheries Act* when performing any duties or functions under that Act and a person designated as a fishery officer under the *Fisheries Act* when performing any duties or functions under that Act or the *Coastal Fisheries Protection Act*,

(*f*) the pilot in command of an aircraft

(i) registered in Canada under regulations made under the *Aeronautics Act*, or

(ii) leased without crew and operated by a person who is qualified under regulations made under the *Aeronautics Act* to be registered as owner of an aircraft registered in Canada under those regulations,

while the aircraft is in flight, and

(*g*) officers and non-commissioned members of the Canadian Forces who are

(i) appointed for the purposes of section 156 of the *National Defence Act*, or

(ii) employed on duties that the Governor in Council, in regulations made under the *National Defence Act* for the purposes of this paragraph, has prescribed to be of such a kind as to necessitate that the officers and non-commissioned members performing them have the powers of peace officers;

"prison" includes a penitentiary, common jail, public or reformatory prison, lock-up, guard-room or other place in which persons who are charged with or convicted of offences are usually kept in custody;

"property" includes

(*a*) real and personal property of every description and deeds and instruments relating to or evidencing the title or right to property, or giving a right to recover or receive money or goods,

(*b*) property originally in the possession or under the control of any person, and any property into or for which it has been converted or exchanged and anything acquired at any time by the conversion or exchange, and

(*c*) any postal card, postage stamp or other stamp issued or prepared for issue under the authority of Parliament or the legislature of a province for the payment to the Crown or a corporate body of any fee, rate or duty, whether or not it is in the possession of the Crown or of any person;

"prosecutor" means the Attorney General or, where the Attorney General does not intervene, means the person who institutes proceedings to which this Act applies, and includes counsel acting on behalf of either of them;

"provincial court judge" means a person appointed or authorized to act by or pursuant to an Act of the legislature of a province, by whatever title that person may be designated, who has the power and authority of two or more justices of the peace and includes the lawful deputy of that person;

"public department" means a department of the Government of Canada or a branch thereof or a board, commission, corporation or other body that is an agent of Her Majesty in right of Canada;

"public officer" includes

(*a*) an officer of customs or excise,

(*b*) an officer of the Canadian Forces,

(*c*) an officer of the Royal Canadian Mounted Police, and

(*d*) any officer while the officer is engaged in enforcing the laws of Canada relating to revenue, customs, excise, trade or navigation;

"public stores" includes any personal property that is under the care, supervision, administration or control of a public department or of any person in the service of a public department;

"radioactive material" means any material that emits one or more types of ionizing radiation, such as alpha or beta particles, neutrons and gamma rays, and that is capable of, owing to its radiological or fissile properties, causing death, serious bodily harm or substantial damage to property or the environment;

"railway equipment" means

(*a*) any machine that is constructed for movement exclusively on lines of railway, whether or not the machine is capable of independent motion, or

(*b*) any vehicle that is constructed for movement both on and off lines of railway while the adaptations of that vehicle for movement on lines of railway are in use;

"representative", in respect of an organization, means a director, partner, employee, member, agent or contractor of the organization;

"senior officer" means a representative who plays an important role in the establishment of an organization's policies or is responsible for managing an important aspect of the organization's activities and, in the case of a body corporate, includes a director, its chief executive officer and its chief financial officer;

"serious offence" has the same meaning as in subsection 467.1(1);

"steal" means to commit theft;

"street racing" [*Repealed*, 2018, c. 21, s. 12.]

"superior court of criminal jurisdiction" means

(*a*) in the Province of Ontario, the Court of Appeal or the Superior Court of Justice,

(*b*) in the Province of Quebec, the Superior Court,

(*c*) in the Provinces of Nova Scotia, British Columbia and Prince Edward Island, the Court of Appeal or the Supreme Court,

(*d*) in the Provinces of New Brunswick, Manitoba, Saskatchewan and Alberta, the Court of Appeal or the Court of Queen's Bench,

(*e*) in the Province of Newfoundland and Labrador, Yukon and the Northwest Territories, the Supreme Court, and

(*f*) in Nunavut, the Nunavut Court of Justice;

(*g*) [*Repealed*, 2015, c. 3, s. 44(3)]

(*h*) [*Repealed*, 2015, c. 3, s. 44(3)]

"territorial division" includes any province, county, union of counties, township, city, town, parish or other judicial division or place to which the context applies;

"terrorism offence" means

(*a*) an offence under any of sections 83.02 to 83.04 or 83.18 to 83.23,

(*b*) an indictable offence under this or any other Act of Parliament committed for the benefit of, at the direction of or in association with a terrorist group,

(*c*) an indictable offence under this or any other Act of Parliament where the act or omission constituting the offence also constitutes a terrorist activity, or

(*d*) a conspiracy or an attempt to commit, or being an accessory after the fact in relation to, or any counselling in relation to, an offence referred to in paragraph (*a*), (*b*) or (*c*);

"terrorist activity" has the same meaning as in subsection 83.01(1);

"terrorist group" has the same meaning as in subsection 83.01(1);

"testamentary instrument" includes any will, codicil or other testamentary writing or appointment, during the life of the testator whose testamentary disposition it purports to be and after his death, whether it relates to real or personal property or to both;

"trustee" means a person who is declared by any Act to be a trustee or is, by the law of the province, a trustee, and without restricting the generality of the foregoing, includes a trustee on an express trust created by deed, will or instrument in writing, or by parol;

"unfit to stand trial" means unable on account of mental disorder to conduct a defence at any stage of the proceedings before a verdict is rendered or to instruct counsel to do so, and, in particular, unable on account of mental disorder to

(*a*) understand the nature or object of the proceedings,

(*b*) understand the possible consequences of the proceedings, or

(*c*) communicate with counsel;

"United Nations operation" means an operation that is established by the competent organ of the United Nations in accordance with the Charter of the United Nations and is conducted under United Nations authority and control, if the operation is for the purpose of maintaining or restoring international peace and security or if the Security Council or the General Assembly of the United Nations has declared, for the purposes of the Convention on the Safety of United Nations and Associated Personnel, that there exists an exceptional risk to the safety of the personnel participating in the operation. It does not include an operation authorized by the Security Council as an enforcement action under Chapter VII of the Charter of the United Nations in which any of the personnel are engaged as combatants against organized armed forces and to which the law of international armed conflict applies;

"United Nations personnel" means

(*a*) persons who are engaged or deployed by the Secretary-General of the United Nations as members of the military, police or civilian components of a United Nations operation, or

(*b*) any other officials or experts who are on mission of the United Nations or one of its specialized agencies or the International Atomic Energy Agency and who are present in an official capacity in the area where a United Nations operation is conducted;

"valuable mineral" means a mineral of a value of at least $100 per kilogram, and includes precious metals, diamonds and other gemstones and any rock or ore that contains those minerals;

"valuable security" includes

(*a*) an order, exchequer acquittance or other security that entitles or evidences the title of any person

(i) to a share or interest in a public stock or fund or in any fund of a body corporate, company or society, or

(ii) to a deposit in a financial institution,

(*b*) any debenture, deed, bond, bill, note, warrant, order or other security for money or for payment of money,

(*c*) a document of title to lands or goods wherever situated,

(*d*) a stamp or writing that secures or evidences title to or an interest in a chattel personal, or that evidences delivery of a chattel personal, and

(*e*) a release, receipt, discharge or other instrument evidencing payment of money;

"victim" means a person against whom an offence has been committed, or is alleged to have been committed, who has suffered, or is alleged to have suffered, physical or emotional harm, property damage or economic loss as the result of the commission or alleged commission of the offence and includes, for the purposes of sections 672.5, 722 and 745.63, a person who has suffered physical or emotional harm, property damage or economic loss as the result of the commission of an offence against any other person;

"weapon" means any thing used, designed to be used or intended for use

(*a*) in causing death or injury to any person, or

(*b*) for the purpose of threatening or intimidating any person

and, without restricting the generality of the foregoing, includes a firearm and, for the purposes of sections 88, 267 and 272, any thing used, designed to be used or intended for use in binding or tying up a person against their will;

"wreck" includes the cargo, stores and tackle of a vessel and all parts of a vessel separated from the vessel, and the property of persons who belong to, are on board or have quitted a vessel that is wrecked, stranded or in distress at any place in Canada;

"writing" includes a document of any kind and any mode in which, and any material on which, words or figures, whether at length or abridged, are written, printed or otherwise expressed, or a map or plan is inscribed. R.S., c. C-34, s. 2; 1972, c. 13, s. 2, c. 17, s. 2; 1973-74, c. 17, s. 9; 1974-75-76, c. 19, ss. 1, 2, c. 48, s. 24, c. 93, s. 2; 1976-77, c. 35, s. 21; 1978-79, c. 11, s. 10; 1980-81-82-83, c. 125, s. 1; R.S.C. 1985, c. 11 (1st Supp.), s. 2, c. 27 (1st Supp.), s. 2, c. 31 (1st Supp.), s. 61; c. 1 (2nd Supp.), s. 213(4), c. 27 (2nd Supp.), s. 10, c. 35 (2nd Supp.), s. 34; c. 32 (4th Supp.), s. 55; c. 40 (4th Supp.), s. 2; 1990, c. 17, s. 7; 1991, c. 1, s. 28; 1991, c. 43, ss. 1, 9; 1991, c. 40, s. 1; 1992, c. 20, s. 216; 1992, c. 51, s. 32; 1993, c. 28, Sch. III, s. 25(1), (2) (repealed by 1999, c. 3, s. 12); 1994, c. 44, s. 2; 1995, c. 29, ss. 39, 40, c. 39, s. 138; 1997, c. 23, s. 1; 1998, c. 30, s. 14(*d*); 1999, c. 3, ss. 12, 25; c. 5, s. 1; c. 25, s. 1; c. 28, s. 155; 2000, c. 12, s. 91; 2001, c. 32, s. 1; 2001, c. 41, s. 2 and 131(2); 2002, c. 7, s. 137(2); 2002, c. 22, s. 324; 2003, c. 21, s. 1; 2004, c. 3, s. 1; 2005, c. 10, s. 34(1)(*f*)(i); 2005, c. 38, s. 58; 2005, c. 40, ss 1 and 7; 2006, c. 14, s. 1; 2007, c. 13, s. 1; 2012, c. 1, s. 160(*c*)(i); 2012, c. 19, s. 371; 2013, c. 13, s. 2; 2014, c. 17, s. 1; 2014, c. 23, s. 2; 2014, c. 25, s. 2; 2015, c. 3, s. 44; 2015, c. 13, s. 3; c. 20, s. 15; 2018, c. 21, s. 12.

CROSS-REFERENCES

In addition to the definitions set out in this section which are applicable to the *Criminal Code* as a whole, certain provisions contain their own definitions of particular words or phrases. Some Parts of the *Criminal Code* also contain definition sections as follows: Part III, firearms and other offensive weapons, s. 84; Part IV, offences against the administration of law and justice; Part V, sexual offences, public morals and disorderly conduct, s. 150; Part VI, invasion of privacy, s. 183; Part VII, disorderly houses, gaming and betting, s. 197; Part VIII, offences against the person and reputation, ss. 214, 254; Part IX, offences against rights of property, s. 321; Part X, fraudulent transactions relating to contracts and trade, s. 379; Part XI, wilful and forbidden acts in respect of certain property, s. 428; Part XII, offences relating to currency, s. 448; Part XII.1, instruments and literature for illicit drug use, s. 462.1; Part XII.2, proceeds of crime, s. 462.3; Part XVI, compelling appearance of accused before a justice and interim release, s. 493; Part XIX, indictable offences — trial without jury, s. 552; Part XXI, appeals — indictable offences, s. 673; Part XXIII, punishment, fines, forfeitures, costs and restitution of property, s. 716; Part XXIV, dangerous and long-term offenders, s. 752; Part XXV, effect and enforcement of recognizances, s. 762; Part XXVII, summary convictions, s. 785.

Refer also to Part XX.1 of the *Criminal Code* containing definitions for the following: accused, assessment, chairperson, court, justice, dual status offender, hospital, medical practitioner, party, placement decision, prescribed, Review Board and verdict of not criminally responsible on account of mental disorder, s. 672.1; protected statements, s. 672.21; psychosurgery, s. 672.61(2); electro-convulsive therapy, s. 672.61(2); Minister, s. 672.68(1).

Reference should also be made to the *Interpretation Act*, R.S.C. 1985, c. I-21, which, pursuant to s. 3(1) of that Act, applies to every federal enactment, "unless a contrary intention appears". That Act, in addition to codifying certain rules of interpretation, also defines certain terms in s. 35. Other federal enactments may also contain definitions of words or phrases which are applicable to the *Criminal Code* by virtue of s. 4(4) of the Code and s. 15(2) of the *Interpretation Act* which provides that, "where an enactment contains an interpretation section or provision, it shall be read and construed . . . as being applicable to all other enactments relating to the same subject-matter unless a contrary intention appears". Throughout the *Criminal Code* in the note of related sections, an attempt has been made to identify these related sections in other enactments.

ANNOTATIONS

"Attorney General" / *also see definition of prosecutor, infra* – It is clear that Parliament may constitutionally vest exclusive jurisdiction in the Attorney General of Canada to prosecute offences which do not depend for their validity on s. 91(27) of the *Constitution Act, 1867*: *R. v. Hauser*, [1979] 1 S.C.R. 984, 46 C.C.C. (2d) 481 (5:2). It would also seem that Parliament may vest prosecutorial authority in the federal Attorney General under this section even where the offence depends for its validity on the criminal law power in s. 91(27): *Canada (Attorney General) v. Canadian National Transportation, Ltd.; Canada (Attorney General) v. Canadian Pacific Transport Co.*, [1983] 2 S.C.R. 206, 7 C.C.C. (3d) 449 (the court splitting 4:3 on the issue) with respect to the *Combines Investigation Act*, R.S.C. 1970, c. C-23; and *R. v. Wetmore*, [1983] 2 S.C.R. 161, 7 C.C.C. (3d) 507 (6:1) with respect to the *Food and Drugs Act*, R.S.C. 1970, c. F-27.

Where the Attorney General of Canada does not intervene in a prosecution, such as for an offence under the *Fisheries Act*, R.S.C. 1970, c. F-14, then counsel for the provincial Attorney General may conduct the prosecution: *R. v. Sacobie and Paul* (1979), 51 C.C.C. (2d) 430, 28 N.B.R. (2d) 288 (C.A.), affd [1983] 1 S.C.R. 241, 1 C.C.C. (3d) 446*n* (7:0).

It was open to the Crown Attorney by letter to appoint a federal prosecutor as an *ad hoc* counsel or agent for the provincial Attorney General to prosecute an offence under the *Criminal Code* which was jointly charged with an offence under the former *Narcotic Control Act*: *R. v. Luz* (1988), 5 O.R. (3d) 52 (H.C.J.).

Proceedings under the former *Narcotic Control Act* are commenced at the instance of the Government of Canada if charges are laid pursuant to agreed procedures which confer general authority on officers of a municipal police force to institute or commence proceedings on behalf of the Government of Canada. It is not necessary that counsel for the Attorney General of Canada be consulted specifically with respect to each particular charge or that there be specific authority to lay that charge: *R. v. King* (1987), 40 C.C.C. (3d) 359 (Ont. C.A.).

Reference should also be made to s. 467.2 respecting the authority of the Attorney General of Canada to conduct proceedings in respect of a criminal organization offence where the offence arises out of contravention of an Act of Parliament other than the *Criminal Code*.

"bank-note" – Most offences relating to currency are found in Part XII which also defines certain terms in s. 448. Under s. 35(1) of the *Interpretation Act*, R.S.C. 1985, c. I-21, "bank" means a bank to which the *Bank Act*, R.S.C. 1985, c. B-1, applies.

"Canadian Forces" – Note definition of "peace officer" in this section. Reference may also be made to *National Defence Act*, R.S.C. 1985, c. N-5.

"cattle" – The principal offences relating to injury to cattle and other animals are in ss. 444 to 447.

An information charging the accused with wilfully killing a "heifer" properly charged the offence contrary to s. 444 of wilfully killing "cattle", heifer" being the familiar name for a young cow: *R. v. Allen* (1974), 17 C.C.C. (2d) 549 (N.B.C.A.).

"clerk of the court" – The definition of this position is wide enough to include a person describing himself as a deputy clerk: *Ex p. Leclerc* (1972), 7 C.C.C. (2d) 346 (Que. Q.B.).

"counsel" – In light of this definition, reference must be made to the applicable provincial legislation which will define the matters which barristers and solicitors are required to do. Note also s. 10(*b*) of the *Charter of Rights and Freedoms* giving a person arrested or detained the right to "counsel".

"day" – "Day" as defined in this section refers to "day" as distinguished from "night" and has no application to provisions which, for example, require that a notice be served within seven clear days: *R. ex rel. McLearn v. Meagher* (1956), 117 C.C.C. 198 (N.S.S.C.). Thus, this definition would apply where there is a requirement that a certain act be done "by day" as in execution of a search warrant in s. 488. For other definitions relating to periods of time, see *Interpretation Act*, R.S.C. 1985, c. I-21, s. 35: "local time", "month", "standard time", s. 37: "year". As to calculation of time periods, see ss. 26, 27, 28 and 29 of the *Interpretation Act*, especially s. 27 relating to calculation of number of days where the time is expressed in terms of "clear days" or "at least" a number of days.

"dwelling-house" – A motel unit is a dwelling-house: *R. v. Henderson*, [1975] 1 W.W.R. 360 (B.C. Prov. Ct.).

"Curtilage" is not a term of normal usage in Canada, but has been extensively considered in the United States because of the Fourth Amendment protection against unreasonable search and seizure. In *United States v. Potts*, 297 F. 2d 68 (6th Cir. 1961), curtilage was defined to include all buildings in close proximity to a dwelling, which are continually used for carrying on domestic employment; or such place as is necessary and convenient to a dwelling and is habitually used for family purposes.

Detached buildings on an accused's property fall outside "dwelling-house": *R. v. M. (N.)* (2007), 223 C.C.C. (3d) 417 (Ont. S.C.J.).

Explosive substance – The definition is met whether or not a device functions properly and "explodes": *R. v. A. (K.D.S.)* (2010), 253 C.C.C. (3d) 556 (N.B.C.A.).

Liability of the Crown and Crown corporations – In determining the liability of the Crown or a Crown corporation for alleged criminal acts, reference must be made to s. 17 of the *Interpretation Act*, R.S.C. 1985, c. I-21, which provides that, "No enactment is binding on Her Majesty or affects Her Majesty or Her Majesty's rights or prerogatives in any manner, except as mentioned or referred to in the enactment."

The definitions of "person" and "every one" in this section were held to apply to the C.B.C. which was charged with broadcasting an obscene film contrary to s. 163, although the corporation, as a Crown corporation, is an agent of Her Majesty. It is only when the C.B.C. is lawfully executing the powers entrusted to it by the *Broadcasting Act*, R.S.C. 1985, c. B-9, that it is deemed to be a Crown agent and entitled to Crown immunity. When the corporation exercises its powers in a manner inconsistent with the purposes of the *Broadcasting Act*, it steps outside its agency role: *R. v. Canadian Broadcasting Corporation*, [1983] 1 S.C.R. 339, 3 C.C.C. (3d) 1 (7:0).

The Crown was held to be immune from prosecution under the former *Combines Investigation Act*. This immunity also extends to Crown corporations who are agents of the Crown for all their purposes, acting within their authorized purposes: *R. v. Eldorado Nuclear Ltd.-Eldorado Nucleaire Ltée; R. v. Uranium Canada Ltd.-Uranium Canada Ltée*, [1983] 2 S.C.R. 551, 8 C.C.C. (3d) 449 (5:2).

Where, from an examination of the statute as a whole, it is apparent that Parliament's intention was that the Crown be bound then, notwithstanding the Crown is not expressly referred to, it will be bound by the statute. Thus it was apparent from the provisions of the *Criminal Code* with respect to costs in summary conviction appeal matters that both the Crown and the defendant were to be treated equally with respect to costs and accordingly the court had power to award costs against the Crown in summary conviction appeals notwithstanding the applicable provisions of the *Criminal Code* did not expressly mention the Crown: *R. v. Ouellette*, [1980] 1 S.C.R. 568, 52 C.C.C. (2d) 336.

"explosive substance" – The principle provisions relating to liability for the handling of explosives are found in ss. 79 to 82.1.

"firearm" – This definition includes not only a barrelled weapon that is actually capable of causing serious bodily injury or death, but also anything that has the potential of becoming a firearm through an adaptation. The acceptable amount of adaptation, and the time required therefor, for something still to remain within the definition is dependent upon the nature of the offence where the definition is involved. The purpose of each section must be identified and the amount, nature and time spent for adaptation determined so as to give effect to Parliament's intention when enacting the particular section: *R. v. Covin and Covin*, [1983] 1 S.C.R. 725, 8 C.C.C. (3d) 240 (5:0).

There is no burden on the Crown to negative what theoretically might be a defence, that the pistol was not a firearm in the sense that it was incapable of firing bullets or missiles, but has no foundation in the evidence. "If there is evidence on the record either *viva voce* or based upon an examination of the exhibit itself from which it can be reasonably inferred that the alleged firearm is, because of some physical defect or inadequacy, incapable of being fired then, depending on the circumstances, it might be that it is something less than a firearm": *R. v. Marchesani*, [1970] 1 C.C.C. 350 (Ont. H.C.J.) at p. 351.

An inoperative handgun can constitute a firearm if it can be converted into an operating weapon in a relatively short period of time and with relative ease: *R. v. Sinclair* (2005), 207 C.C.C. (3d) 80 (Alta. C.A.).

Barrelled objects that meet the definition of "firearm" in s. 2 need not also meet the definition of "weapon" in paras. (*a*) or (*b*) to be deemed firearms and hence weapons for the various weapons offences in the Code. Therefore, a handgun that fires BBs propelled by compressed air is a weapon for these purposes: *R. v. Dunn* (2013), 305 C.C.C. (3d) 372 (Ont. C.A.), affirmed [2014] S.C.J. No. 69 (S.C.C.).

However, a pellet gun lacking a magazine and a CO2 canister was held not to qualify as a firearm: *R. v. Crawford* (2015), 322 C.C.C. (3d) 528 (Alta. C.A.).

"highway" – A road in a company town, owned by the company but which the public have a *de facto* right to use, was held to constitute a highway for the purposes of the intimidation offence in s. 423: *R. v. Stockley* (1977), 36 C.C.C. (2d) 387 (Nfld. C.A.).

A logging road, however, built and maintained by the company which controls access to the road by means of a permit system, is not a highway: *R. v. Sahonovitch* (1969), 69 W.W.R. 674 (B.C.S.C.).

"indictment" – See definition of "count" above. As to provisions respecting sufficiency of indictments and informations, see ss. 581 to 601.

"mental disorder" – The definition of "mental disorder" as a disease of the mind clearly imports the terminology used to define insanity under the previous provisions of s. 16. Therefore, see the notes under s. 16.

"military" and "military law" – See definition of "Canadian Forces" above. Reference may also be made to *National Defence Act*, R.S.C. 1985, c. N-5, and the regulations made thereunder, especially the Queen's Regulations.

"motor vehicle" – This definition contemplates a kind of vehicle, not whether the vehicle is actually operable or effectively functionable: *R. v. Saunders*, [1967] 3 C.C.C. 278, [1967] S.C.R. 284. Thus, an automobile which is out of gas is still a motor vehicle: *R. v. Lloyd*, [1988] 4 W.W.R. 423, 66 Sask. R. 100 (C.A.).

"night" – See notes under "day", *supra*.

"offence-related property" – This term extends to proceeds of sale of offence-related property: *Scotia Mortgage Corp. v. Leung* (2007), 221 C.C.C. (3d) 505 (B.C.C.A.), leave to appeal to S.C.C. refused 223 C.C.C. (3d) vi.

"offensive weapon" – See notes under "weapon", *infra.*

"peace officer" / *municipal enforcement officers* – A municipal by-law enforcement officer was not entitled to enforce the provisions of the *Criminal Code: R. v. Laramee* (1972), 9 C.C.C. (2d) 433 (N.W.T. Mag. Ct.). Folld: *R. v. Wright*, [1973] 6 W.W.R. 687 (Sask. D.C.).

In *R. v. Jones and Huber* (1975), 30 C.R.N.S. 127, [1975] 5 W.W.R. 97 (Y.T. Mag. Ct.), it was held that an animal control officer appointed under a municipal by-law enacted pursuant to the Municipal Ordinance, R.O.Y.T. 1971, c. M-12, is a peace officer within the Code as is a poundkeeper appointed under a municipal by-law: *R. v. Moore*, [1983] 5 W.W.R. 176, 21 Man. R. (2d) 77 (Co. Ct.).

First Nations constables appointed pursuant to the *Police Services Act* (Ont.) are peace officers within the meaning of this section: *R. v. Stephens* (1995), 102 C.C.C. (3d) 416 (Ont. C.A.).

Bailiff refers to a Crown-appointed officer or court and does not include a person employed by a private bailiff company: *R. v. Burns* (2002), 170 C.C.C. (3d) 288 (Man. C.A).

Territorial limits – A peace officer is limited territorially by the authority which appoints him: *R. v. Soucy* (1975), 23 C.C.C. (2d) 561 (N.B.S.C. App. Div.).

Military Police – A military police officer is not a peace officer within the meaning of para. (*g*)(i) when exercising authority over persons not subject to the Code of Service Discipline. He is, however, a peace officer within the meaning of para. (*g*)(ii) if the circumstances fall within s. 22.01(2) of the Queen's Regulations which sets out duties of a kind as to necessitate the officers and members performing them to have the powers of peace officers, including duties performed as a result of established military action or practice related to the maintenance of law and order, protection of property and persons, and the arrest or custody of persons. This would include the detection and arrest of an impaired driver and making of a breathalyzer demand after the driver, a civilian, was stopped, albeit on a public highway, for breach of a traffic regulation on an armed forces base: *R. v. Nolan*, [1987] 1 S.C.R. 1212, 34 C.C.C. (3d) 289 (7:0).

A military police officer, appointed pursuant to s. 156 of the *National Defence Act*, R.S.C. 1985, c. N-5, is a peace officer within the meaning of this section when exercising authority over a person, such as a regular member of the armed forces, who is subject to the Code of Service Discipline even where the offence was committed by that person off a military establishment: *R. v. Courchene* (1989), 52 C.C.C. (3d) 375 (Ont. C.A.).

Game wardens and wildlife enforcement officers – A wildlife officer appointed under the *Wildlife Act*, 1979 (Sask.), c. W-13.1 is a peace officer: *R. v. Rutt* (1981), 59 C.C.C. (2d) 147 (Sask. C.A.), as is a game warden appointed under the *Fish and Wildlife Act*, 1980 (N.B.), c. F-14: *R. v. Rushton* (1981), 62 C.C.C. (2d) 403 (N.B.C.A.); and a conservation officer appointed under the *Game and Fish Act*, R.S.O. 1970, c. 186; *R. v. Renz* (1972), 10 C.C.C. (2d) 250 (Ont. C.A.).

Band constable / Indian reserve – A band constable on an Indian reserve appointed as a special constable to enforce certain provisions of the *Indian Act*, such as s. 97 which involves drunkenness on the reserve, is a person "employed for the preservation and maintenance of the public peace" and thus within the definition of "peace officer": *R. v. Whiskeyjack and Whiskeyjack* (1984), 17 C.C.C. (3d) 245 (Alta. C.A.).

First Nations Constables are "peace officers" within the meaning of this section and are empowered to discharge their duties outside the reserve in relation to the First Nations communities they were primarily employed to serve: *R. v. Decorte*, [2005] 1 S.C.R. 133, 192 C.C.C. (3d) 441.

in flight – This term is defined in s. 7(8).

"prison" – This definition would override the narrower definition of "prison" in the *Prisons and Reformatories Act*, R.S.C. 1985, c. P-20. The term "penitentiary" is defined in s. 2 of the *Corrections and Conditional Release Act*, S.C. 1992, c. 20.

"property" – A promissory note falls within this definition and is also "anything" capable of being stolen within the meaning of s. 322: *R. v. Cinq-Mars* (1989), 51 C.C.C. (3d) 248 (Que. C.A.).

"prosecutor" – Notwithstanding the accused elects trial by provincial court judge, where the offence charged is an indictable offence he is tried under the provisions of Part XIX and it is the definition of "prosecutor" in this section which applies rather than the definition in Part XXVII. Accordingly, a police officer who is neither the informant nor counsel may not conduct the prosecution: *R. v. Edmunds*, [1981] 1 S.C.R. 233, 58 C.C.C. (2d) 485 (4:1).

However, a police officer, as agent of the Attorney General, may communicate to the court the Attorney General's decision as to whether or not to proceed by indictment on a Crown option offence and the officer is not at that stage a prosecutor: *R. v. Parsons* (1984), 14 C.C.C. (3d) 490 (Nfld. C.A.), leave to appeal to S.C.C. refused 51 Nfld. & P.E.I.R. 90*n*, 57 N.R. 77*n*.

Absent flagrant impropriety, the Attorney General has the right to intervene in any private prosecution: *R. v. Kowalski* (1990), 57 C.C.C. (3d) 168 (Alta. Prov. Ct.).

Prosecutors on indictable offences need to be legally trained: *Alberta (Attorney General) v. Edmonton Police Service* (2017), 344 C.C.C. (3d) 357 (Alta. Q.B.).

"public officer" – This definition is not exhaustive and therefore an officer who reports to a provincial or municipal government such as a municipally appointed agricultural inspector is a public officer for the purposes of the offence contrary to s. 129 of the *Criminal Code: R. v. Cartier; R. v. Libert* (1978), 43 C.C.C. (2d) 553 (Que. S.C.).

Also see definition in s. 35 of the *Interpretation Act*, R.S.C. 1985, c. I-21.

"unfit to stand trial" – The definition of "unfit to stand trial" statutorily entrenches the extensive case law in the area. Any individual who is unable to understand either the nature or object of the proceedings, the possible consequences or to communicate with counsel as a result of a mental disorder is rendered "unfit to stand trial". The terminology provides clarification of the conflicting case-law by requiring the issue of fitness to be raised solely in the context of a mental disorder and at any stage in the proceedings prior to the rendering of a verdict. Reference should also be made to ss. 672.22 to 672.33 relating to the trial of the issue of fitness.

"valuable security" – A travellers cheque is a valuable security, its value being the amount paid for it by the owner: *R. v. Pennell*, [1966] 1 C.C.C. 258 (B.C.C.A); *R. v. Zinck* (1986), 32 C.C.C. (3d) 150 (N.B.C.A.).

"weapon" – A firearm will always fall within the definition of weapon. It is not necessary to prove that the accused used it or intended to use it for causing death or injury or for a purpose of threatening or intimidation: *R. v. Felawka*, [1993] 4 S.C.R. 199, 85 C.C.C. (3d) 248.

Barrelled objects that meet the definition of "firearm" in s. 2 need not also meet the definition of "weapon" in paras. (*a*) or (*b*) to be deemed firearms and hence weapons for the various weapons offences in the Code. Therefore, a handgun that fires BBs propelled by compressed air is a weapon for these purposes: *R. v. Dunn* (2013), 305 C.C.C. (3d) 372 (Ont. C.A.), affd [2014] 3 S.C.R. 490.

The expression "injury" in para. (*a*) of the definition is not synonymous with "bodily harm". In contrast to the design, the use or the intended use of an object to threaten or intimidate in para. (*b*), when an object is actually used in causing death or injury, there is no requirement that the object be used "for the purpose" of killing or injuring, but merely "in causing" death or injury. When an accused sexually assaults the complainant, by using force against her without her consent, and causes her injuries by the use of such force which includes forcible penetration with an object (here a dildo), that object falls squarely within this definition being an object used in causing injury, thereby constituting a weapon: *R. v. Lamy*, [2002] 1 S.C.R. 860, 162 C.C.C. (3d) 353.

FURTHER DEFINITIONS — FIREARMS.

2.1 In this Act, "ammunition", "antique firearm", "automatic firearm", "cartridge magazine", "cross-bow", "handgun", "imitation firearm", "prohibited ammunition", "prohibited device", "prohibited firearm", "prohibited weapon", "replica firearm", "restricted firearm" and "restricted weapon", as well as "authorization", "licence" and "registration certificate" when used in relation to those words and expressions, have the same meaning as in subsection 84(1). 2009, c. 22, s. 1.

ACTING ON VICTIM'S BEHALF / Exception.

2.2 (1) For the purposes of sections 606, 672.5, 715.37, 722, 737.1 and 745.63, any of the following individuals may act on the victim's behalf if the victim is dead or incapable of acting on their own behalf:

(*a*) the victim's spouse, or if the victim is dead, their spouse at the time of death;
(*b*) the victim's common-law partner, or if the victim is dead, their common-law partner at the time of death;
(*c*) a relative or dependant of the victim;
(*d*) an individual who has in law or fact custody, or is responsible for the care or support, of the victim; and
(*e*) an individual who has in law or fact custody, or is responsible for the care or support, of a dependant of the victim.

(2) An individual is not entitled to act on a victim's behalf if the individual is an accused in relation to the offence or alleged offence that resulted in the victim suffering harm or loss or is an individual who is found guilty of that offence or who is found not criminally responsible on account of mental disorder or unfit to stand trial in respect of that offence. 2015, c. 13, s. 4; 2018, c. 12, s. 403.

DESCRIPTIVE CROSS-REFERENCES.

3. Where, in any provision of this Act, a reference to another provision of this Act or a provision of any other Act is followed by words in parenthesis that are or purport to be descriptive of the subject-matter of the provision referred to, the words in parenthesis form no part of the provision in which they occur but shall be deemed to have been inserted for convenience of reference only. 1976-77, c. 53, s. 2.

CROSS-REFERENCES

Other rules of interpretation may be found in the *Interpretation Act*, R.S.C. 1985, c. I-21. See especially s. 14 relating to marginal notes and historical references.

SYNOPSIS

This section is designed to avoid confusion arising from the use of *descriptive cross-references* within sections. It states that such words, which appear in parentheses, are not intended to have any interpretative value and are solely added for ease of cross-reference. (For an example of a descriptive cross-reference, see s. 183 – definition section within the "wiretap" section of the *Criminal Code*.)

EFFECT OF JUDICIAL ACTS.

3.1 Unless otherwise provided or ordered, anything done by a court, justice or judge is effective from the moment it is done, whether or not it is reduced to writing. 2002, c. 13, s. 2.

CROSS-REFERENCES
With respect to commencement of sentence, see s. 719.

Part I / GENERAL

POSTCARD A CHATTEL, VALUE / Value of valuable security / Possession / Expressions taken from other Acts / Sexual intercourse / Proof of notifications and service of documents / Proof of service in accordance with provincial laws / Attendance for examination / Means of telecommunication.

4. (1) For the purposes of this Act, a postal card or stamp referred to in paragraph (*c*) of the definition "property" in section 2 shall be deemed to be a chattel and to be equal in value to the amount of the postage, rate or duty expressed on its face.

(2) For the purposes of this Act, the following rules apply for the purpose of determining the value of a valuable security where value is material:

(*a*) where the valuable security is one mentioned in paragraph (*a*) or (*b*) of the definition "valuable security" in section 2, the value is the value of the share, interest, deposit or unpaid money, as the case may be, that is secured by the valuable security;

(*b*) where the valuable security is one mentioned in paragraph (*c*) or (*d*) of the definition "valuable security" in section 2, the value is the value of the lands, goods, chattel personal or interest in the chattel personal, as the case may be; and

(*c*) where the valuable security is one mentioned in paragraph (*e*) of the definition "valuable security" in section 2, the value is the amount of money that has been paid.

(3) For the purposes of this Act,

(*a*) a person has anything in possession when he has it in his personal possession or knowingly

(i) has it in the actual possession or custody of another person, or

(ii) has it in any place, whether or not that place belongs to or is occupied by him, for the use or benefit of himself or of another person; and

(*b*) where one of two or more persons, with the knowledge and consent of the rest, has anything in his custody or possession, it shall be deemed to be in the custody and possession of each and all of them.

(4) Where an offence that is dealt with in this Act relates to a subject that is dealt with in another Act, the words and expressions used in this Act with respect to that offence have, subject to this Act, the meaning assigned to them in that other Act.

(5) For the purposes of this Act, sexual intercourse is complete on penetration to even the slightest degree, notwithstanding that seed is not emitted.

(6) For the purposes of this Act, the service of documents and the giving or sending of any notice may be proved

(*a*) by oral evidence given under oath by, or by the affidavit or solemn declaration of, the person claiming to have served, given or sent it; or

(*b*) in the case of a peace officer, by a statement in writing certifying that the document was served or the notice was given or sent by the peace officer, and such a statement is deemed to be a statement made under oath.

(6.1) Despite subsection (6), the service of documents may be proved in accordance with the laws of a province relating to offences created by the laws of that province.

(7) Despite subsection (6) or (6.1), the court may require the person who appears to have signed an affidavit, a solemn declaration or a statement in accordance with that subsection to appear before it for examination or cross-examination in respect of the issue of proof of service or of the giving or sending of any notice.

(8) For greater certainty, for the purposes of this Act, if the elements of an offence contain an explicit or implicit element of communication without specifying the means of communication, the communication may also be made by a means of telecommunication. R.S., c. C-34, s. 3; 1980-81-82-83, c. 125, s. 2; R.S.C. 1985, c. 27 (1st Supp.), s. 3; 1994, c. 44, s. 3; 1997, c. 18, s. 2; 2008, c. 18, s. 1; 2014, c. 31, s. 2.

CROSS-REFERENCES

Subsection (1) – "property" is defined in s. 2.

Subsection (2) – "valuable security" is defined in s. 2.

Subsection (3) – The definition of possession in this subsection is applicable to all offences. However, s. 358 enacts a special provision relating to possession for the purposes of ss. 342, 354 and 356(1)(*b*). Also note the rule in s. 588 respecting deemed ownership of property.

Subsection (4) – Also see similar rule in s. 15(2) of the *Interpretation Act*, R.S.C. 1985, c. I-21, and note under s. 2, *supra*.

Subsection (5) – With the gradual amendment to the sexual offences, sexual intercourse as an element of an offence is now rare. However, it is still relevant to the incest offence in s. 156.

Subsections (6), (7) – As to service of subpoena, see ss. 509(2) and 701.

As to service of summons, see s. 509.

Note: This section formerly provided the formula for determining when a person gained a certain age. Resort must now be had to s. 30 of the *Interpretation Act*, R.S.C. 1985, c. I-21. The effect of that provision is that, for example, a person attains the age of 16 years on the day of the anniversary of her birthday rather than the following day as was the effect of the former Code provision.

SYNOPSIS

This section contains several general statements of criminal law. The first two subsections provide interpretative assistance in determining the value to be ascribed to "postal cards or stamps" and "valuable security" if the value is material. The former phrase is part of the s. 2 definition of "property" and the latter is a defined term in the same section.

Subsection (3) deals with the often contentious subject of what constitutes "possession". Determining when an accused is in possession of an item arises in many types of property offences and is also pivotal in many drug cases. The first definition states that *personal possession includes actual possession or knowingly* having an item in the possession of another *with* some measure of *control* over the item. The possessor must *know* the *nature of the item*. It does not matter if the accused owns or occupies the place where the goods are as long as the elements of knowledge and control are satisfied and the goods are for the benefit of the accused or another.

Subsection (4) provides that interpretive assistance may be gained from referring to other Acts which deal with the same subject, unless the *Criminal Code* modifies the meaning otherwise applicable.

Subsection (5) was created to avoid technical arguments about what amount of penile penetration constitutes sexual intercourse.

Subsections (6), (6.1) and (7) set out simple methods of proving service of a document and notice, and permit a court to order the person who did the service to testify, if necessary.

Subsection (8) sets out a general rule that, if an offence contains an element of communication, it is deemed to include telecommunication.

ANNOTATIONS

Subsection (3) / personal possession – To constitute possession for purposes of the criminal law, in a case of manual handling of the object, there must also be knowledge of what that thing is; and both these elements must be co-existent with some act of control (outside public duty): *R. v. Beaver*, [1957] S.C.R. 531, 118 C.C.C. 129.

There can exist circumstances where there is no possession in law notwithstanding there is a right of control with knowledge of the presence and character of the thing if there is no intent to exercise control over it, as where the accused manually handles the thing to destroy it or turn it over to the police: *R. v. Christie* (1978), 41 C.C.C. (2d) 282, 21 N.B.R. (2d) 261 (App. Div.).

Whether or not the inference of possession from the presence of fingerprints on the contraband can be drawn is not subject to a hard and fast rule. It is a question of fact which depends on all of the circumstances of the case and all of the evidence adduced: *R. v. Lepage*, [1995] 1 S.C.R. 654, 95 C.C.C. (3d) 385.

Constructive possession – Constructive possession is complete where the accused: (i) has knowledge of the character of the object; (ii) knowingly puts or keeps the object in a particular place whether or not that place belongs to him; and (iii) intends to have the object in the particular place for his use or benefit or that of another person: *R. v. Morelli*, [2010] 1 S.C.R. 253, 252 C.C.C. (3d) 273.

In dealing with virtual objects, such as computer images, the mere fact that an image has been accessed by or displayed in a Web browser does not, without more, constitute possession. Previous access and the possibility of again accessing a website that contains digital images, located on a distant server over which the viewer has no control, do not constitute, either alone or together, constructive possession. Furthermore, the automatic caching of a file to the hard drive does not, without more, constitute possession. The cached file might be a place over which the computer user has control but, in order to establish possession, it is necessary to satisfy the *mens rea* or fault requirement as well by showing that the file was knowingly stored and retained through the cache: *R. v. Morelli, supra*.

In *R. v. Terrence*, [1983] 1 S.C.R. 357, 4 C.C.C. (3d) 193 (7:0), the court held that for para. (*b*) to apply there must be evidence of a measure of control on the part of the accused. In upholding the acquittal of the accused, a passenger in the stolen motor vehicle, the court noted that there was no such evidence and no evidence that he was a party to the offence of the person actually in possession (the driver) pursuant to s. 21.

The requisite element of control can be found in the fact that the contraband was in the accused's room and she had the right to grant or withhold her consent to the contraband being stored there: *R. v. Chambers* (1985), 20 C.C.C. (3d) 440 (Ont. C.A.).

Innocent possession – This doctrine applies to circumstances in which the accused exercises control over the contraband, but with the absence of intent to exercise control beyond that needed to destroy it or otherwise put it permanently beyond one's control: *R. v. Chalk* (2007), 227 C.C.C. (3d) 141 (Ont. C.A.); *R. v. Farmer* (2014), 318 C.C.C. (3d) 322 (Ont. C.A.).

Application – The definition of "possession" in this subsection is applicable to all proceedings under the *Criminal Code* and is not limited to possession offences. Possession of certain articles may link the accused to pieces of evidence in respect of a crime, such as robbery, in which their possession is not, otherwise, a material element: *R. v. Lovis*, [1975] 2 S.C.R. 294, 17 C.C.C. (2d) 481, 47 D.L.R. (3d) 732 (8:0).

An accused may be found in possession as a party by virtue of s. 21. The accused's liability is not confined to this subsection: *R. v. Zanini*, [1967] S.C.R. 715, [1968] 2 C.C.C. 1 (5:0).

Subsection (5) – When intercourse "complete": "for the purposes of [s. 4(5)] of the Code sexual intercourse is complete upon the penetration of the labia, either labia majora or labia minora, no matter how little, even though the hymen is never touched nor is there any penetration of the vagina": *R. v. Johns* (1956), 116 C.C.C. 200, 25 C.R. 153, 20 W.W.R. 92 (B.C. Co. Ct.).

Subsection (6) – A certificate of analysis under s. 258 is a document within the meaning of this section and therefore proof of service may be made by way of affidavit: *R. v. Spreen* (1987), 40 C.C.C. (3d) 190, 8 M.V.R. (2d) 148, 82 A.R. 318 (C.A.).

CANADIAN FORCES NOT AFFECTED.

5. Nothing in this Act affects any law relating to the government of the Canadian Forces. R.S., c. C-34, s. 4.

CROSS-REFERENCES

The terms "Canadian Forces", "Her Majesty's Forces", "military" and "military law" are defined in s. 2. In addition, in certain circumstances, members of the armed forces come within the definition of "peace officer" in s. 2 and officers of the Canadian Forces are within the definition of "public officer" in s. 2. As to offences involving the military, see ss. 46, 50, 52, 53, 62, 269.1, 419, 420. As to immunity of armed forces personnel from firearms and weapons provisions, see ss. 92, 98.

SYNOPSIS

This section states that the *Criminal Code* does not affect other laws relating to the *Canadian Forces.* The *National Defence Act* and its regulations set out a full Code of Service Discipline and it also provides that a breach of an offence under the *Criminal Code* may be tried by court martial. However, neither this section of the *Criminal Code* nor the *National Defence Act* exempt members of the armed forces from trial by a civilian court for a *Criminal Code* offence committed in Canada.

PRESUMPTION OF INNOCENCE / Offences outside Canada / Definition of "enactment".

6. (1) Where an enactment creates an offence and authorizes a punishment to be imposed in respect of that offence,

(*a*) a person shall be deemed not to be guilty of the offence until he is convicted or discharged under section 730 of the offence; and

(*b*) a person who is convicted or discharged under section 730 of the offence is not liable to any punishment in respect thereof other than the punishment prescribed by this Act or by the enactment that creates the offence.

(2) Subject to this Act or any other Act of Parliament, no person shall be convicted or discharged under section 730 of an offence committed outside Canada.

(3) In this section, "enactment" means

(*a*) an Act of Parliament, or

(*b*) an Act of the legislature of a province that creates an offence to which Part XXVII applies,

or any regulation made thereunder. R.S., c. C-34, s. 5; R.S.C. 1985, c. 27 (1st Supp.), s. 4; 1995, c. 22, s. 10.

CROSS-REFERENCES

Subsection (1) – As to presumption of innocence, see s. 11(*d*) of the *Canadian Charter of Rights and Freedoms.*

Subsection (2) – For offences committed on territorial sea or inland waters of Canada, see s. 477. As to definition of territorial sea, see *Territorial Sea and Fishing Zones Act*, R.S.C. 1985, c. T-8.

Those sections providing for trial in Canada of offences committed outside Canada are as follows: s. 7(1), offence committed on Canadian aircraft; s. 7(2), hijacking and offences relating to aircraft where accused found in Canada; s. 7(3), certain offences against internationally protected person committed on Canadian aircraft or ships, by Canadian citizen or against internationally protected person performing duties on behalf of Canada; s. 7(3.1), hostage taking in certain circumstances; s. 7(3.2) to (3.6), offences involving nuclear material; s. 7(3.7), torture; s. 7(3.71) to (3.77), war crimes and crimes against humanity; s. 7(4), indictable offences by employee within meaning of *Public Service Employment Act*; s. 57, passport offences; s. 58, offences in relation to certificate of citizenship or naturalization; s. 74, piracy; s. 75, piratical acts; s. 290, bigamy; s. 342, possession in Canada of credit card obtained by crime outside Canada; s. 354, possession in Canada of goods obtained by crime outside Canada; s. 357, bringing into Canada property obtained by crime; s. 462.31, laundering proceeds of offences committed outside Canada; s. 465(1)(*a*), conspiracy to commit murder outside Canada; s. 465(4), conspiracy outside Canada to commit offence inside Canada.

SYNOPSIS

Subsection (1)(*a*) provides a legislative statement of the *presumption of innocence*, first articulated in the common law and now enshrined in the *Canadian Charter of Rights and Freedoms*. If the accused is convicted, or found guilty and discharged under s. 736, subsec. (1)(*b*) states that the only punishment which can be imposed is that set out in the enactment creating the offence. The enactment, as defined in subsec. (3), may be either the *Criminal Code*, another federal statute or a provincial statute creating a summary conviction offence.

Subsection (2) states the rule limiting the *territorial application* of Canadian criminal law to those offences committed in Canada, unless Canadian jurisdiction is specifically extended by federal law. For an example of such a provision, see s. 7. If the relevant legislation does not extend jurisdiction, it will be necessary to show that there is a *real and substantial link* between the offence and Canada.

ANNOTATIONS

Subsection (1)(*a*) – In *R. v. Negridge* (1980), 54 C.C.C. (2d) 304, 17 C.R. (3d) 14 (Ont. C.A.), reference was made to this subsection when the Court held that an accused was not liable to the increased minimum penalties for a second or subsequent "offence" when the second or subsequent offence was committed before the earlier conviction although after the commission of the offence that led to the earlier conviction.

Subsection (1)(*b*) – Where the offence with which the accused was charged has been repealed and new offences created which would apply to the accused's conduct, had it occurred after enactment of these new offences, then the accused is entitled to the benefit of the lesser maximum punishment prescribed for the new offences. This results not from s. 11(*i*) of the *Charter of Rights and Freedoms* but s. 44(*c*) of the *Interpretation Act*, R.S.C. 1985, c. I-21: *R. v. B.(J.W.)* (1989), 51 C.C.C. (3d) 35 (P.E.I.S.C.).

Subsection (2) – All that is necessary to make an offence subject to the jurisdiction of Canadian courts is that a significant portion of the activities constituting that offence take place in Canada. It is sufficient that there is a real and substantial link between the offence and this country. For this purpose, the court must take into account all relevant facts that take place in Canada that may legitimately give this country an interest in prosecuting the offence. The court must then consider whether there is anything in those facts that offends international comity and it may be that the outer limits of the test of a real and substantial link are coterminous with the requirements of international comity. Where the evidence with respect to charges of fraud and conspiracy was that the fraudulent inducements were made by persons in Canada, albeit over the telephone, to residents of the United States, and that some of the proceeds found their way back to Canada, then the charges were properly tried in Canada: *R. v. Libman*, [1985] 2 S.C.R. 178, 21 C.C.C. (3d) 206 (7:0).

Whether there is a "real and substantial link" to Canada is assessed having regard to the circumstances and the importance of the elements of the offence linked to Canada, the relevant facts which arose in Canada and the harmful consequences which were caused or which could have been caused in Canada. In this case, the victim had suffered the injury in another country, but had died in Canada. In addition, the harmful consequences of the offence occurred in Canada as both the victim, the accused and their families were resident in

Canada. The accused's interest in being tried in Canada is also a relevant factor in determining whether Canadian courts have jurisdiction: *R. v. Ouellette* (1998), 126 C.C.C. (3d) 219 (Que. S.C.).

A Canadian court has the jurisdiction to try an accused for breach of a probation order even if the breaching acts occurred in a foreign country. There is no rule of international law depriving a judge of jurisdiction to make a probation order binding on the conduct of a probationer abroad. There was a "real and substantial link" between the commission of the offence and Canada where the accused and his companion had travelled from Canada abroad where he assaulted her: *R. v. Greco* (2001), 159 C.C.C. (3d) 146 (Ont. C.A.), leave to appeal to S.C.C. refused [2002] 2 S.C.R. vi, 162 C.C.C. (3d) vi.

See also *R. v. Rattray* (2008), 229 C.C.C. (3d) 496 (Ont. C.A.), to the same effect in respect of an extra-territorial breach of a recognizance.

In *Chowdhury v. Canada* (2014), 309 C.C.C. (3d) 447 (Ont. S.C.J.), the court applied the above principles to hold that Canada lacked territorial jurisdiction to try a foreign national who had never been to Canada for offences under the *Corruption of Foreign Public Officials Act*, S.C. 1998, c. 34.

OFFENCES COMMITTED ON AIRCRAFT / Idem / Offences in relation to cultural property / Definition of "Convention" / Offences against fixed platforms or international maritime navigation / Offences against fixed platforms or navigation in the internal waters or territorial sea of another state / Nuclear terrorism offence committed outside Canada / Space Station — Canadian crew members / Space Station — crew members of Partner States / Proceedings by Attorney General of Canada / Consent of Attorney General of Canada / Definitions / Offence against internationally protected person / Offence of hostage taking / Jurisdiction / Offence against United Nations or associated personnel / Offence involving explosive or other lethal device / Offence relating to financing of terrorism / Terrorism offence committed outside Canada / Terrorist activity committed outside Canada / Offences by Public Service employees / Offence in relation to sexual offences against children / Offence in relation to trafficking in persons / Consent of Attorney General / Jurisdiction / Appearance of accused at trial / Where previously tried outside Canada / If accused not Canadian citizen / Definition of "flight" and "in flight" / Definition of "in service" / Certificate as evidence / Idem.

7. (1) Notwithstanding anything in this Act or any other Act, every one who

(*a*) on or in respect of an aircraft

(i) registered in Canada under regulations made under the *Aeronautics Act*, or

(ii) leased without crew and operated by a person who is qualified under regulations made under the *Aeronautics Act* to be registered as owner of an aircraft registered in Canada under those regulations,

while the aircraft is in flight, or

(*b*) on any aircraft, while the aircraft is in flight if the flight terminated in Canada,

commits an act or omission in or outside Canada that if committed in Canada would be an offence punishable by indictment shall be deemed to have committed that act or omission in Canada.

(2) Notwithstanding this Act or any other Act, every one who

(*a*) on an aircraft, while the aircraft is in flight, commits an act or omission outside Canada that if committed in Canada or on an aircraft registered in Canada under regulations made under the *Aeronautics Act* would be an offence against section 76 or paragraph 77(*a*),

(*b*) in relation to an aircraft in service, commits an act or omission outside Canada that if committed in Canada would be an offence against any of paragraphs 77(*c*), (*d*) or (*g*),

(*c*) in relation to an air navigation facility used in international air navigation, commits an act or omission outside Canada that if committed in Canada would be an offence against paragraph 77(*e*),

(*d*) at or in relation to an airport serving international civil aviation, commits an act or omission outside Canada that if committed in Canada would be an offence against paragraph 77(*b*) or (*f*), or

(*e*) commits an act or omission outside Canada that if committed in Canada would constitute a conspiracy or an attempt to commit an offence referred to in this subsection, or being an accessory after the fact or counselling in relation to such an offence,

shall be deemed to have committed that act or omission in Canada if the person is, after the commission thereof, present in Canada.

(2.01) Despite anything in this Act or any other Act, a person who commits an act or omission outside Canada that if committed in Canada would constitute an offence under section 322, 341, 344, 380, 430 or 434 in relation to cultural property as defined in Article 1 of the Convention, or a conspiracy or an attempt to commit such an offence, or being an accessory after the fact or counselling in relation to such an offence, is deemed to have committed that act or omission in Canada if the person

(*a*) is a Canadian citizen;

(*b*) is not a citizen of any state and ordinarily resides in Canada; or

(*c*) is a permanent resident within the meaning of subsection 2(1) of the *Immigration and Refugee Protection Act* and is, after the commission of the act or omission, present in Canada.

(2.02) For the purpose of subsection (2.01), "Convention" means the Convention for the Protection of Cultural Property in the Event of Armed Conflict, done at The Hague on May 14, 1954. Article 1 of the Convention is set out in the schedule to the *Cultural Property Export and Import Act*.

(2.1) Notwithstanding anything in this Act or any other Act, every one who commits an act or omission outside Canada against or on board a fixed platform attached to the continental shelf of any state or against or on board a ship navigating or scheduled to navigate beyong the territorial sea of any state, that if committed in Canada would constitute an offence against, a conspiracy or an attempt to commit an offence against, or being an accessory after the fact or counselling in relation to an offence against, section 78.1, shall be deemed to commit that act or omission in Canada if it is committed

(*a*) against or on board a fixed platform attached to the continental shelf of Canada;

(*b*) against or on board a ship registered or licensed, or for which an identification number has been issued, pursuant to any Act of Parliament;

(*c*) by a Canadian citizen;

(*d*) by a person who is not a citizen of any state and who ordinarily resides in Canada;

(*e*) by a person who is, after the commission of the offence, present in Canada;

(*f*) in such a way as to seize, injure or kill, or threaten to injure or kill, a Canadian citizen; or

(*g*) in an attempt to compel the Government of Canada to do or refrain from doing any act.

(2.2) Notwithstanding anything in this Act or any other Act, every one who commits an act or omission outside Canada against or on board a fixed platform not attached to the continental shelf of any state or against or on board a ship not navigating or scheduled to navigate beyond the territorial sea of any state, that if committed in Canada would constitute an offence against, a conspiracy or an attempt to commit an offence against, or being an accessory after the fact or counselling in relation to an offence against, section 78.1, shall be deemed to commit that act or omission in Canada

CR. CODE

(*a*) if it is committed as described in any of paragraphs (2.1)(*b*) to (*g*); and
(*b*) if the offender is found in the territory of a state, other than the state in which the act or omission was committed, that is
(i) a party to the Convention for the Suppression of Unlawful Acts against the Safety of Maritime Navigation, done at Rome on March 10, 1988, in respect of an offence committed against or on board a ship, or
(ii) a party to the Protocol for the Suppression of Unlawful Acts against the Safety of Fixed Platforms Located on the Continental Shelf, done at Rome on March 10, 1988, in respect of an offence committed against or on board a fixed platform.

(2.21) Despite anything in this Act or anyother Act, everyone who commits an act or omission outside Canada that if committed in Canada would constitute an offence under any of sections 82.3 to 82.6, or a conspiracy or attempt to commit such an offence, or being an accessory after the fact or counselling in relation to such an offence, is deemed to have committed that act or omission in Canada if
(*a*) the act or omission is committed on a ship that is registered or licensed, or for which an identification number has been issued, under any Act of Parliament;
(*b*) the act or omission is committed on an aircraft that
(i) is registered in Canada under regulations made under the *Aeronautics Act*, or
(ii) is leased without crew and operated by a person who is qualified under regulations made under the *Aeronautics Act* to be registered as owner of an aircraft in Canada under those regulations;
(*c*) the person who commits the act or omission is a Canadian citizen; or
(*d*) the person who commits the act or omission is, after the commission of the act or omission, present in Canada.

(2.3) Despite anything in this Act or any other Act, a Canadian crew member who, during a space flight, commits an act or omission outside Canada that if committed in Canada would constitute an indictable offence is deemed to have committed that act or omission in Canada, if that act or omission is committed
(*a*) on, or in relation to, a flight element of the Space Station; or
(*b*) on any means of transportation to or from the Space Station.

(2.31) Despite anything in this Act or any other Act, a crew member of a Partner State who commits an act or omission outside Canada during a space flight on, or in relation to, a flight element of the Space Station or on any means of transportation to and from the Space Station that if committed in Canada would constitute an indictable offence is deemed to have committed that act or omission in Canada, if that act or omission
(*a*) threatens the life or security of a Canadian crew member; or
(*b*) is committed on or in relation to, or damages, a flight element provided by Canada.

(2.32) Despite the definition "Attorney General" in section 2, the Attorney General of Canada may conduct proceedings in relation to an offence referred to in subsection (2.3) or (2.31). For that purpose, the Attorney General of Canada may exercise all the powers and perform all the duties and functions assigned to the Attorney General by or under this Act.

(2.33) No proceedings in relation to an offence referred to in subsection (2.3) or (2.31) may be instituted without the consent of the Attorney General of Canada.

(2.34) The definitions in this subsection apply in this subsection and in subsections (2.3) and (2.31).

"Agreement" has the same meaning as in section 2 of the *Civil International Space Station Agreement Implementation Act*.

"Canadian crew member" means a crew member of the Space Station who is

(*a*) a Canadian citizen; or

(*b*) a citizen of a foreign state, other than a Partner State, who is authorized by Canada to act as a crew member for a space flight on, or in relation to a flight element.

"crew member of a Partner State" means a crew member of the Space Station who is

(*a*) a citizen of a Partner State; or

(*b*) a citizen of a state, other than that Partner State, who is authorized by that Partner State to act as a crew member for a space flight on, or in relation to, a flight element.

"flight element" means a Space Station element provided by Canada or by a Partner State under the Agreement and under any memorandum of understanding or other implementing arrangement entered into to carry out the Agreement.

"Partner State" means a State, other than Canada, who contracted to enter into the Agreement and for which the Agreement has entered into force in accordance with article 25 of the Agreement.

"space flight" means the period that begins with the launching of a crew member of the Space Station, continues during their stay in orbit and ends with their landing on earth.

"Space Station" means the civil international Space Station that is a multi-use facility in low-earth orbit, with flight elements and dedicated ground elements provided by, or on behalf of, the Partner States.

(3) Notwithstanding anything in this Act or any other Act, every one who, outside Canada, commits an act or omission against the person of an internationally protected person or against any property referred to in section 431 used by that person that, if committed in Canada, would be an offence against any of sections 235, 236, 266, 267, 268, 269, 269.1, 271, 272, 273, 279, 279.1, 280 to 283, 424 and 431 is deemed to commit that act or omission in Canada if

(*a*) the act or omission is committed on a ship that is registered or licensed, or for which an identification number has been issued, pursuant to any Act of Parliament;

(*b*) the act or omission is committed on an aircraft

(i) registered in Canada under regulations made under the *Aeronautics Act*, or

(ii) leased without crew and operated by a person who is qualified under regulations made under the *Aeronautics Act* to be registered as owner of an aircraft in Canada under those regulations;

(*c*) the person who commits the act or omission is a Canadian citizen or is, after the act or omission has been committed, present in Canada; or

(*d*) the act or omission is against

(i) a person who enjoys the status of an internationally protected person by virtue of the functions that person performs on behalf of Canada, or

(ii) a member of the family of a person described in subparagraph (i) who qualifies under paragraph (*b*) or (*d*) of the definition "internationally protected person" in section 2.

(3.1) Notwithstanding anything in this Act or any other Act, every one who, outside Canada, commits an act or omission that if committed in Canada would be an offence against section 279.1 shall be deemed to commit that act or omission in Canada if

(*a*) the act or omission is committed on a ship that is registered or licensed, or for which an identification number has been issued, pursuant to any Act of Parliament;

(*b*) the act or omission is committed on an aircraft

(i) registered in Canada under regulations made under the *Aeronautics Act*, or

(ii) leased without crew and operated by a person who is qualified under regulations made under the *Aeronautics Act* to be registered as owner of an aircraft in Canada under such regulations;

(*c*) the person who commits the act or omission

(i) is a Canadian citizen, or

(ii) is not a citizen of any state and ordinarily resides in Canada;

(*d*) the act or omission is committed with intent to induce Her Majesty in right of Canada or of a province to commit or cause to be committed any act or omission;

(*e*) a person taken hostage by the act or omission is a Canadian citizen; or

(*f*) the person who commits the act or omission is, after the commission thereof, present in Canada.

(3.2) [*Repealed*, 2013, c. 13, s. 3(2).]

(3.3) [*Repealed*, 2013, c. 13, s. 3(2).]

(3.4) [*Repealed*, 2013, c. 13, s. 3(2).]

(3.5) [*Repealed*, 2013, c. 13, s. 3(2).]

(3.6) [*Repealed*, 2013, c. 13, s. 3(2).]

(3.7) Notwithstanding anything in this Act or any other Act, every one who, outside Canada, commits an act or omission that, if committed in Canada, would constitute an offence against, a conspiracy or an attempt to commit an offence against, being an accessory after the fact in relation to an offence against, or any counselling in relation to an offence against, section 269.1 shall be deemed to commit that act or omission in Canada if

(*a*) the act or omission is committed on a ship that is registered or licensed, or for which an identification number has been issued, pursuant to any Act of Parliament;

(*b*) the act or omission is committed on an aircraft

(i) registered in Canada under regulations made under the *Aeronautics Act*, or

(ii) leased without crew and operated by a person who is qualified under regulations made under the *Aeronautics Act* to be registered as owner of an aircraft in Canada under those regulations;

(*c*) the person who commits the act or omission is a Canadian citizen;

(*d*) the complainant is a Canadian citizen; or

(*e*) the person who commits the act or omission is, after the commission thereof, present in Canada.

(3.71) Notwithstanding anything in this Act or any other Act, every one who, outside Canada, commits an act or omission against a member of United Nations personnel or associated personnel or against property referred to in section 431.1 that, if committed in Canada, would constitute an offence against, a conspiracy or an attempt to commit an offence against, or being an accessory after the fact or counselling in relation to an offence against, section 235, 236, 266, 267, 268, 269, 269.1, 271, 272, 273, 279, 279.1, 424.1 or 431.1 is deemed to commit that act or omission in Canada if

(*a*) the act or omission is committed on a ship that is registered or licensed, or for which an identification number has been issued, under an Act of Parliament;

(*b*) the act or omission is committed on an aircraft

(i) registered in Canada under regulations made under the *Aeronautics Act*, or

(ii) leased without crew and operated by a person who is qualified under regulations made under the *Aeronautics Act* to be registered as owner of an aircraft in Canada under those regulations;

(*c*) the person who commits the act or omission

(i) is a Canadian citizen, or

(ii) is not a citizen of any state and ordinarily resides in Canada;

(*d*) the person who commits the act or omission is, after the commission of the act or omission, present in Canada;
(*e*) the act or omission is committed against a Canadian citizen; or
(*f*) the act or omission is committed with intent to compel the Government of Canada or of a province to do or refrain from doing any act.

(3.72) Notwithstanding anything in this Act or any other Act, every one who, outside Canada, commits an act or omission that, if committed in Canada, would constitute an offence against, a conspiracy or an attempt to commit an offence against, or being an accessory after the fact or counselling in relation to an offence against, section 431.2 is deemed to commit that act or omission in Canada if
(*a*) the act or omission is committed on a ship that is registered or licensed, or for which an identification number has been issued, under any Act of Parliament;
(*b*) the act or omission is committed on an aircraft
(i) registered in Canada under regulations made under the *Aeronautics Act*,
(ii) leased without crew and operated by a person who is qualified under regulations made under the *Aeronautics Act* to be registered as owner of an aircraft in Canada under those regulations, or
(iii) operated for or on behalf of the Government of Canada;
(*c*) the person who commits the act or omission
(i) is a Canadian citizen, or
(ii) is not a citizen of any state and ordinarily resides in Canada;
(*d*) the person who commits the act or omission is, after the commission of the act or omission, present in Canada;
(*e*) the act or omission is committed against a Canadian citizen;
(*f*) the act or omission is committed with intent to compel the Government of Canada or of a province to do or refrain from doing any act; or
(*g*) the act or omission is committed against a Canadian government or public facility located outside Canada.

(3.73) Notwithstanding anything in this Act or any other Act, every one who, outside Canada, commits an act or omission that, if committed in Canada, would constitute an offence against, a conspiracy or an attempt to commit an offence against, or being an accessory after the fact or counselling in relation to an offence against, section 83.02 is deemed to commit the act or omission in Canada if
(*a*) the act or omission is committed on a ship that is registered or licensed, or for which an identification number has been issued, under an Act of Parliament;
(*b*) the act or omission is committed on an aircraft
(i) registered in Canada under regulations made under the *Aeronautics Act*, or
(ii) leased without crew and operated by a person who is qualified under regulations made under the *Aeronautics Act* to be registered as the owner of an aircraft in Canada under those regulations;
(*c*) the person who commits the act or omission
(i) is a Canadian citizen, or
(ii) is not a citizen of any state and ordinarily resides in Canada;
(*d*) the person who commits the act or omission is, after its commission, present in Canada;
(*e*) the act or omission is committed for the purpose of committing an act or omission referred to in paragraph 83.02(*a*) or (*b*) in order to compel the Government of Canada or of a province to do or refrain from doing any act;
(*f*) the act or omission is committed for the purpose of committing an act or omission referred to in paragraph 83.02(*a*) or (*b*) against a Canadian government or public facility located outside Canada; or
(*g*) the act or omission is committed for the purpose of committing an act or omission referred to in paragraph 83.02(*a*) or (*b*) in Canada or against a Canadian citizen.

(3.74) Notwithstanding anything in this Act or any other Act, every one who commits an act or omission outside Canada that, if committed in Canada, would be a terrorism offence, other than an offence under section 83.02 or an offence referred to in paragraph (*a*) of the definition "terrorist activity" in subsection 83.01(1), is deemed to have committed that act or omission in Canada if the person

(*a*) is a Canadian citizen;

(*b*) is not a citizen of any state and ordinarily resides in Canada; or

(*c*) is a permanent resident within the meaning of subsection 2(1) of the *Immigration and Refugee Protection Act* and is, after the commission of the act or omission, present in Canada.

(3.75) Notwithstanding anything in this Act or any other Act, every one who commits an act or omission outside Canada that, if committed in Canada, would be an indictable offence and would also constitute a terrorist activity referred to in paragraph (*b*) of the definition "terrorist activity" in subsection 83.01(1) is deemed to commit that act or omission in Canada if

(*a*) the act or omission is committed against a Canadian citizen;

(*b*) the act or omission is committed against a Canadian government or public facility located outside Canada; or

(*c*) the act or omission is committed with intent to compel the Government of Canada or of a province to do or refrain from doing any act.

(3.76) [*Repealed*, 2000, c. 24, s. 42.]

(3.77) [*Repealed*, 2000, c. 24, s. 42.]

(4) Every one who, while employed as an employee within the meaning of the *Public Service Employment Act* in a place outside Canada, commits an act or omission in that place that is an offence under the laws of that place and that, if committed in Canada, would be an offence punishable by indictment shall be deemed to have committed that act or omission in Canada.

(4.1) Notwithstanding anything in this Act or any other Act, every one who, outside Canada, commits an act or omission that if committed in Canada would be an offence against section 151, 152, 153, 155 or 159, subsection 160(2) or (3), section 163.1, 170, 171, 171.1, 172.1, 172.2 or 173 or subsection 286.1(2) shall be deemed to commit that act or omission in Canada if the person who commits the act or omission is a Canadian citizen or a permanent resident within the meaning of subsection 2(1) of the *Immigration and Refugee Protection Act*.

(4.11) Notwithstanding anything in this Act or any other Act, every one who, outside Canada, commits an act or omission that if committed in Canada would be an offence against section 279.01, 279.011, 279.02 or 279.03 shall be deemed to commit that act or omission in Canada if the person who commits the act or omission is a Canadian citizen or a permanent resident within the meaning of subsection 2(1) of the *Immigration and Refugee Protection Act*.

(4.2) [*Repealed*, 2002, c. 13, s. 3(2).]

(4.3) Proceedings with respect to an act or omission deemed to have been committed in Canada under subsection (4.1) may only be instituted with the consent of the Attorney General.

(5) Where a person is alleged to have committed an act or omission that is an offence by virtue of this section, proceedings in respect of that offence may, whether or not that person is in Canada, be commenced in any territorial division in Canada and the accused may be tried and punished in respect of that offence in the same manner as if the offence had been committed in that territorial division.

(5.1) For greater certainty, the provisions of this Act relating to

(*a*) requirements that an accused appear at and be present during proceedings, and
(*b*) the exceptions to those requirements,

apply to proceedings commenced in any territorial division pursuant to subsection (5).

(6) If a person is alleged to have committed an act or omission that is an offence by virtue of this section and that person has been tried and dealt with outside Canada in respect of the offence in such a manner that, if that person had been tried and dealt with in Canada, they would be able to plead *autrefois acquit, autrefois convict*, pardon or an expungement order under the *Expungement of Historically Unjust Convictions Act*, that person shall be deemed to have been so tried and dealt with in Canada.

(7) If the accused is not a Canadian citizen, no proceedings in respect of which courts have jurisdiction by virtue of this section shall be continued unless the consent of the Attorney General of Canada is obtained not later than eight days after the proceedings are commenced.

(8) For the purposes of this section, of the definition "peace officer" in section 2 and of sections 27.1, 76 and 77, "flight" means the act of flying or moving through the air and an aircraft is deemed to be in flight from the time when all external doors are closed following embarkation until the later of

(*a*) the time at which any such door is opened for the purpose of disembarkation, and

(*b*) where the aircraft makes a forced landing in circumstances in which the owner or operator thereof or a person acting on behalf of either of them is not in control of the aircraft, the time at which control of the aircraft is restored to the owner or operator thereof or a person acting on behalf of either of them.

(9) For the purposes of this section and section 77, an aircraft shall be deemed to be in service from the time when pre-flight preparation of the aircraft by ground personnel or the crew thereof begins for a specific flight until

(*a*) the flight is cancelled before the aircraft is in flight,
(*b*) twenty-four hours after the aircraft, having commenced the flight, lands, or
(*c*) the aircraft, having commenced the flight, ceases to be in flight,

whichever is the latest.

(10) In any proceedings under this Act, a certificate purporting to have been issued by or under the authority of the Minister of Foreign Affairs is admissible in evidence without proof of the signature or authority of the person appearing to have signed it and, in the absence of evidence to the contrary, is proof of the facts it states that are relevant to the question of whether any person is a member of United Nations personnel, a member of associated personnel or a person who is entitled under international law to protection from attack or threat of attack against his or her person, freedom or dignity.

(11) A certificate purporting to have been issued by or under the authority of the Minister of Foreign Affairs stating

(*a*) that at a certain time any state was engaged in an armed conflict against Canada or was allied with Canada in an armed conflict,

(*b*) that at a certain time any convention, treaty or other international agreement was or was not in force and that Canada was or was not a party thereto, or

(*c*) that Canada agreed or did not agree to accept and apply the provisions of any convention, treaty or other international agreement in an armed conflict in which Canada was involved,

is admissible in evidence in any proceedings without proof of the signature or authority of the person appearing to have issued it, and is proof of the facts so stated. R.S., c. C-34, s. 6; 1972, c. 13, s. 3; 1974-75-76, c. 93, s. 3; 1980-81-82-83, c. 125, s. 3; R.S.C. 1985, c. 27 (1st Supp.), s. 5; R.S.C. 1985, c. 10 (3rd Supp.), s. 1, c. 30 (3rd Supp.), s. 1; 1992, c. 1, s. 58; 1993, c. 7, s. 1; 1995, c. 5, s. 25; 1997, c. 16, s. 1; 1999, c. 35, s. 11; 2000, c. 24, s. 42;

2001, c. 41, ss. 3, 126(1) and (2); 2002, c. 13, s. 3; 2004, c. 12, s. 1; 2005, c. 40, s. 2; 2012, c. 1, s. 10; 2012, c. 15, s. 1; 2013, c. 9, s. 2; 2013, c. 13, s. 3; 2014, c. 25, s. 3; 2018, c. 11, s. 27.

CROSS-REFERENCES

This section deals with some, but not all, of the circumstances where offences may be tried in Canada although the act may have been committed outside Canada. Thus, see note of related sections under s. 6, *supra*. As to other terms referred to in this section, see the following s. 2, definitions of "Attorney General", "internationally protected person", "United Nations personnel", "associated personnel", "terrorism offence", "territorial division"; *Citizenship Act*, R.S.C. 1985, c. C-29, definition of Canadian citizen; s. 465, definition and punishment of conspiracy; s. 24, definition of attempt; s. 463, punishment for attempt; s. 23, definition of accessory after fact; s. 463, punishment of accessory after fact; s. 22, definition of counselling; s. 464, punishment of counselling; s. 21, parties generally; s. 2, definition of "territorial divisions"; Part XVI, commencement of proceedings and compelling appearance; ss. 607 to 610, *autrefois* pleas, especially limitation on plea of *autrefois* in s. 607(6). As to place of trial, see ss. 481.1 to 481.3.

Although "ship" and "fixed platform" are not defined in this section, reference may be made to the definition of those terms in s. 78.1. For war crimes and crimes against humanity, now see *Crimes Against Humanity and War Crimes Act*, S.C. 2000, c. 24.

SYNOPSIS

This section extends Canadian criminal law jurisdiction to cover a number of offences which often have international law implications such as air piracy, offences against diplomats, terrorist offences, protection of nuclear material and torture. A number of the offences referred to in this section, such as torture (s. 269.1), crimes against internationally protected persons (s. 431), and terrorism offences (Part II.1), were created to fulfil Canada's obligations under international treaties aimed at preventing and suppressing certain types of offences.

Section 7 permits such offences to be tried in Canada as if the offence had occurred here. The bulk of the section contains definitions and deeming provisions to facilitate the trial within Canada of these offences when they have occurred largely or entirely outside Canada.

Subsections (2.3) to (2.34) extend Canadian jurisdiction to offences committed in some circumstances in relation to the International Space Station. No proceedings in relation to such offences may be instituted without the consent of the Attorney General of Canada. Subsections (3) to (3.75) extend Canadian jurisdiction to offences committed in the defined circumstances relating to *inter alia* internationally protected persons, United Nations personnel and terrorism offences.

Subsection (4) extends Canadian jurisdiction to permit the trial in Canada of offences committed outside Canada by *public service employees*, while so employed, as long as the conduct would be an indictable offence if it had occurred here. Subsections (4.1) to (4.3) allow for the trial of certain sexual offences when committed outside Canada by Canadian citizens or permanent residents.

To preserve defences otherwise available if the accused had been tried elsewhere, s. 7(6) makes the *special pleas* of *autrefois acquit, convict* and pardon applicable. This means that, if an accused had previously been tried and acquitted, convicted or pardoned elsewhere in connection with the same conduct which led to the Canadian prosecution, the accused could rely on the special plea as if the prior trial had been in Canada.

Section 7(7) prevents the institution of proceedings under this section against *non-citizens without the consent* of the federal Attorney General.

Subsection (4.1) does not violate s. 7 of the *Charter of Rights and Freedoms* as evidence obtained through extra-territorial investigations may be excluded if its admission would render the trial unfair: *R. v. Klassen* (2008), 240 C.C.C. (3d) 328 (B.C.S.C.).

APPLICATION TO TERRITORIES / Application of criminal law of England / Common law principles continued.

8. (1) The provisions of this Act apply throughout Canada except

(*a*) in Yukon, in so far as they are inconsistent with the *Yukon Act*;

(*b*) in the Northwest Territories, in so far as they are inconsistent with the *Northwest Territories Act*, and

(*c*) in Nunavut, in so far as they are inconsistent with the *Nunavut Act*.

(2) The criminal law of England that was in force in a province immediately before April 1, 1955 continues in force in the province except as altered, varied, modified or affected by this Act or any other Act of the Parliament of Canada.

(3) Every rule and principle of the common law that renders any circumstance a justification or excuse for an act or a defence to a charge continues in force and applies in respect of proceedings for an offence under this Act or any other Act of Parliament except in so far as they are altered by or are inconsistent with this Act or any other Act of Parliament. R.S., c. C-34, s. 7; 1993, c. 28, Sch. III, s. 26; 2002, c. 7, s. 138.

CROSS-REFERENCES

Subsection (1) – Definition of "Attorney General" for the Territories is the Attorney General of Canada pursuant to s. 2.

Subsections (2), (3) – The combined effect of this section and s. 9 is to abolish criminal liability, except as provided in a Canadian statute. The only common law crime which has been preserved is contempt of court. On the other hand, this section preserves any common law defence, except as it may be inconsistent with a statutory provision. The purpose of preserving the criminal law of England was to provide for gaps in procedure or rules of evidence not provided for in the *Criminal Code*. However, it should be noted that it is the criminal law of England which was in force in the province in 1955 and this varies somewhat between provinces because of the different dates of reception of the law of England. [See 1955 *Martin's* at p. 34.] As far as procedure, this can have little practical effect since the *Criminal Code*, to a large extent, codifies the procedure and renders obsolete the criminal procedure in England. On the other hand, very recently it was held in *R. v. Jacobson*, noted under s. 672, *infra*, that a trial judge had jurisdiction to exercise the common law power to arrest judgment where it was discovered after conviction, but prior to sentence, that the accused had been convicted of an offence unknown to law. As regards the rules of evidence, these are largely a creature of common law which is declared by the various courts in Canada from time to time. The most important effect of this section is to preserve the common law defences and excuses. These, of course, are not tied to any date and will continue to evolve with the common law. Thus, the Supreme Court of Canada has recognized a common law "defence" of entrapment although, as noted below, the House of Lords has clearly rejected such a defence.

Many defences and excuses of general application have been at least partially codified as follows: s. 15, obedience to *de facto* law; s. 16, insanity; ss. 17, 18, compulsion by threats; s. 19, ignorance of the law is no excuse; s. 25, use of force in administration or enforcement of law; s. 27, use of force to prevent commission of certain offences; s. 28, execution of warrant; ss. 30, 31, detention or arrest for breach of peace; s. 32, use of force to suppress riot; s. 33.1, intoxication; ss. 34, 35, 37, self-defence; s. 37, use of force to defend person under accused's protection; ss. 38 to 42, defence of property; s. 43, correction of child or pupil; s. 44, use of force by ship's master; s. 45, reasonable surgical operation.

As to the so-called *Kienapple* defence, see notes under ss. 12 and 613, *infra*. As to double jeopardy, including *res judicata* and *issue estoppel*, see notes under s. 613, *infra*. The pleas of *autrefois* are dealt with in ss. 607 to 610. As to abuse of process, see notes under s. 579. As to mistake of fact and mistake of law, see notes under s. 19, *infra*.

SYNOPSIS

This section explains where within Canada the *Criminal Code* applies and its relationship to the common law. Section 8(1) makes the *Criminal Code* applicable throughout Canada except that, in the Yukon, Northwest Territories and Nunavut, it has no effect if it is inconsistent with the Acts creating those jurisdictions.

Section 8(2) permits the English criminal law which was in force before the major *1953-54 Criminal Code* revision came into force to continue, *except* as changed by the *Criminal Code* or other federal legislation.

The key aspect of this section is s. 8(3) which retains all common law defences, excuses and justifications, except as altered by or to the extent that they are inconsistent with the *Criminal Code* or other federal enactments. It is under this provision that defences such as necessity, due diligence, intoxication, mistake of fact and entrapment have remained an uncodified part of our criminal law. Recently, s. 7 of the Charter has also been used to interpret the scope of these defences.

ANNOTATIONS

Necessity defence – The common law defence of necessity is preserved by s. 8(3): *R. v. Morgentaler*, [1976] 1 S.C.R. 616, 20 C.C.C. (2d) 449.

In *R. v. Perka*, [1984] 2 S.C.R. 232, 14 C.C.C. (3d) 385 (5:0), Dickson J., for the majority, set out the elements of the necessity defence as follows:

(1) necessity is an excuse rather than a justification and operates by virtue of this subsection;

(2) the criterion is the moral involuntariness of the wrongful action;

(3) this involuntariness is measured on the basis of society's expectation of appropriate and normal resistance to pressure;

(4) negligence or involvement in criminal or immoral activity does not disentitle the actor to the excuse of necessity;

(5) actions or circumstances which indicate that the wrongful deed was not truly involuntary do disentitle;

(6) the existence of a reasonable legal alternative similarly disentitles; to be involuntary the act must be inevitable, unavoidable and afford no reasonable opportunity for an alternative course of action that does not involve a breach of the law;

(7) the defence only applies in circumstances of imminent risk where the action was taken to avoid a direct and immediate peril;

(8) the defence cannot excuse the infliction of a greater harm so as to allow the actor to avert a lesser evil; and

(9) where the accused places before the court sufficient evidence to raise the issue, the onus is on the Crown to meet it beyond a reasonable doubt.

There are three elements to the defence of necessity: (1) imminent peril or danger; (2) the absence of a reasonable legal alternative; and (3) proportionality between the harm inflicted and the harm avoided. The first two elements must be evaluated on a modified objective standard that involves an objective evaluation that takes into account the situation and characteristics of the particular accused person. The proportionality requirement must be assessed on an objective standard: *R. v. Latimer*, [2001] 1 S.C.R. 3, 150 C.C.C. (3d) 129.

The defence of necessity was not made out to a charge of "over 80" contrary to s. 253 where the accused, although believing an attacker was pursuing her, was not in immediate danger and had other options available besides getting into her car and driving away. Her act of driving while intoxicated was not realistically unavoidable: *R. v. Berriman* (1987), 62 Nfld. & P.E.I.R. 239, 45 M.V.R. 165 (Nfld. C.A.).

The common law defence of necessity was not available to accused charged with contempt of court as result of their violation of a court order against interfering with the operation of an abortion services clinic. The defence of necessity is only available to those whose wrongful acts are committed under pressure which no reasonable person could withstand. The accused's genuine belief that abortion is immoral could not change the fact that it could not be said that no reasonable person could withstand the pressure to defy the court order: *R. v. Bridges* (1989), 48 C.C.C. (3d) 535, 61 D.L.R. (4th) 126 (B.C.S.C.), affd (1990), 62 C.C.C. (3d) 455, 78 D.L.R. (4th) 529 (B.C.C.A.).

Entrapment defence – In *R. v. Mack*, [1988] 2 S.C.R. 903, 44 C.C.C. (3d) 513 (7:0), the court laid down both the elements of the entrapment defence and the procedure to be followed. The important holdings may be summarized as follows:

1. Entrapment arises either when the authorities provide an opportunity to persons to commit an offence without reasonable suspicion or acting *mala fides* for dubious motives unrelated to the investigation and repression of crime or, having a reasonable suspicion or acting in the course of a *bona fide* inquiry, they go beyond providing an opportunity and induce the commission of an offence;
2. As regards the latter form of entrapment the court should consider whether an average person in the position of the accused would have been induced to commit the offence;
3. As far as possible an objective assessment is to be made of the conduct of the police and their agents;
4. The pre-disposition of the accused is relevant only in considering whether the authorities were justified in providing the accused an opportunity to commit the offence;
5. In considering whether the police have used means which go further than providing an opportunity the court will consider a number of factors such as the following:
   (a) the type of crime being investigated and the availability of other investigative techniques;
   (b) whether an average person with both the strengths and weaknesses in the position of the accused would be induced into the commission of a crime;
   (c) the persistence and number of attempts made by the police;
   (d) the type of inducement used by the police including deceit, fraud, trickery or reward;
   (e) the timing of the police conduct;
   (f) whether the police conduct involved an exploitation of human characteristics such as friendship;
   (g) whether the police appear to have exploited a particular vulnerability of a person such as mental handicap or substance addiction;
   (h) the proportionality between the police involvement as compared to the accused;
   (i) the existence of any threats implied or expressed made to the accused by the police or their agents; and
   (j) whether the police conduct is directed at undermining other constitutional values;
6. The entrapment issue is to be tried by the judge after the Crown has proved beyond a reasonable doubt that the accused is guilty;
7. In a jury case the jury determines guilt or innocence and then the judge determines the entrapment issue;
8. The burden of proof of entrapment is on the accused on a balance of probabilities and while he need not show that the police conduct shocks the community the defence will only be made out in the clearest of cases;
9. Where the defence is made out the appropriate remedy is a stay of proceedings, not an acquittal.

In *R. v. Barnes*, [1991] 1 S.C.R. 449, 63 C.C.C. (3d) 1 (8:1), the court considered the defence of entrapment based on the fact that the officer was not engaged in a *bona fide* inquiry, but rather so-called "random virtue testing". While the basic rule is that the police may only present the opportunity to commit a particular crime to an individual who arouses a suspicion of involvement in that crime, there is an exception when the police undertake a *bona fide* investigation directed in an area where it is reasonably suspected that criminal activity is occurring. When such location is defined with sufficient precision, the police may present any person associated with the area with the opportunity to commit the particular offence. Random virtue testing only arises when an officer presents a person with the opportunity to commit an offence without a reasonable suspicion that the person is already engaged in a particular activity or that the physical location with which the person is associated is a place where the particular criminal activity is likely occurring. In this case, the court approved an investigation which included offering to persons anywhere within a six-block pedestrian mall the opportunity to sell drugs to an undercover officer. The mall as a whole was responsible for a substantial number of the drug offences in the city.

Where the police, pursuant to a "dial-a-dope" operation, had obtained the accused's cell phone number from a contact list compiled from tips received from various sources, the defence of entrapment was available. Although the police were operating *bona fides* to the extent that they were conducting their operation with the genuine goal of pursuing serious crime and without ulterior motive, they overstepped their bound by proceeding with only a mere suspicion and the hope that their unknown targets would provide the additional support which was a necessary precursor to the invitation to traffic drugs: *R. v. Swan* (2009), 244 C.C.C. (3d) 108, 65 C.R. (6th) 240 (B.C.C.A.).

Entrapment may be made out where the police provided the accused an opportunity to commit an offence and did so without reasonable suspicion. Merely asking an accused "Can you hook me up" with drugs does not make out the defence: *R. v. Imoro* (2010), 251 C.C.C. (3d) 131, 72 C.R. (6th) 292 (Ont. C.A.), affd [2010] 3 S.C.R. 62, 263 C.C.C. (3d) 296.

The defence of entrapment is available to an accused who had no contact with the undercover officer, if the officer was at the time engaged in impermissible random virtue testing: *R. v. Kenyon* (1990), 61 C.C.C. (3d) 538 (B.C.C.A.).

Due diligence defence – In *R. v. Sault Ste. Marie (City)*, [1978] 2 S.C.R. 1299, 40 C.C.C. (2d) 353 (9:0), the court in considering provincial pollution legislation held that there are three categories of offences created by statute distinguished as follows: (1) full *mens rea* offences requiring proof by the prosecution of a positive state of mind such as intent, knowledge or recklessness; (2) strict liability offences in which there is no necessity for the prosecution to prove *mens rea* but which leave it open to the accused to avoid liability by proving that he took all reasonable care; and (3) offences of absolute liability where it is not open to the accused to exculpate himself by showing that he was free of fault. Offences which are criminal in the true sense fall in the first category. "Public welfare offences" are *prima facie* in the second category unless the statute includes the words such as "wilfully" evidencing an intent that the offence be placed in the first category. Offences in the third category would be those in respect of which the legislature has made it clear that guilt would follow proof merely of the proscribed act.

Shifting the burden to the defendant, charged with a regulatory offence, to prove on a balance of probabilities that it acted with due diligence is a reasonable limit on the guarantee to the presumption of innocence: *R. v. Wholesale Travel Group Inc.*, [1991] 3 S.C.R. 154, 67 C.C.C. (3d) 193.

Intoxication defence – See notes under s. 33.1.

Alibi Defence – Where the accused fails to disclose the alibi defence to the Crown in advance of the trial, the trier of fact may draw an adverse inference when weighing the alibi evidence heard at trial. Improper disclosure can, however, only weaken alibi evidence, but cannot exclude the alibi. The alibi need not be disclosed at the time of arrest or at the first possible opportunity. It is sufficient if it was disclosed at a time and in a manner which would permit a meaningful investigation. Furthermore, there is no requirement that the alibi be disclosed by the accused himself: *R. v. Cleghorn*, [1995] 3 S.C.R. 175, 100 C.C.C. (3d) 393 (3:2).

An alibi which is disbelieved does not have any evidentiary value whereas an alibi which is proven to be false can be evidence of consciousness of guilt. If the evidence adduced by the Crown is capable of supporting the inference that an accused concocted a false alibi, an alibi notice professing an intention to advance that alibi at trial would be relevant in that it would tend to support the inference of consciousness of guilt. Before this inference is available, however, there must be evidence from which a reasonable jury could infer that the alibi was deliberately fabricated and that the accused was a party to that fabrication. Mere rejection of an alibi as untruthful or unreliable does not constitute affirmative evidence of guilt: *R. v. Witter* (1996), 105 C.C.C. (3d) 44, 27 O.R. (3d) 579 (C.A.). See also *R. v. Carey* (1996), 113 C.C.C. (3d) 74 (Que. C.A.).

Where the issue had been raised by the testimony of the accused and the rebuttal evidence went to the context and essential fabric of the alibi defence, the Crown was entitled to adduce rebuttal evidence that, contrary to the accused's testimony, the accused had not disclosed his alibi to the witness: *R. v. Lawes*, [1997] 3 S.C.R. 694, 119 C.C.C. (3d) 289, affg 119 C.C.C. (3d) 289 at p. 290 (Alta. C.A.).

CRIMINAL OFFENCES TO BE UNDER LAW OF CANADA.

9. Notwithstanding anything in this Act or any other Act, no person shall be convicted or discharged under section 730

(*a*) of an offence at common law,

(*b*) of an offence under an Act of the Parliament of England, or of Great Britain, or of the United Kingdom of Great Britain and Ireland, or

(*c*) of an offence under an Act or ordinance in force in any province, territory or place before that province, territory or place became a province of Canada,

but nothing in this section affects the power, jurisdiction or authority that a court, judge, justice or provincial court judge had, immediately before April 1, 1955, to impose punishment for contempt of court. R.S., c. C-34, s. 8; R.S.C. 1985, c. 27 (1st Supp.), s. 6; 1995, c. 22, s. 10.

CROSS-REFERENCES

Rights of appeal from finding of contempt of court and from sentence are set out in s. 10. The notes under s. 10 deal with procedural issues relating to contempt of court.

As noted under s. 8, the only common law offence for which a person may now be convicted is the offence of criminal contempt of court. This is not to say that contempt of court is wholly a common law offence. Certain aspects of contempt of court have been codified as offences or the court's power to deal with the misconduct has been codified, thus see: ss. 119, 120, offences relating to bribery of judicial officers; s. 127, disobeying lawful order of court; ss. 131 to 137, perjury and related offences; s. 139, attempt to obstruct justice; s. 484, preserving order in court; s. 545, witness at preliminary inquiry refusing to be sworn or testify; s. 605(2), failing to comply with order respecting testing of exhibits; ss. 648 to 649, offences relating to juries; s. 708, witness failing to attend.

SYNOPSIS

This section prohibits prosecution for common law offences, offences under British law or the law in force in the provinces before they joined Canada. The only exception is the retention of the common law power of judges to punish for contempt of court.

The common law offence of contempt of court can be divided into two broad categories of civil and criminal contempt. The former lies essentially in disobeying the order of a court or a judgment in civil proceedings. However, as the case of *Poje v. A.-G. B.C.*, [1953] 1 S.C.R. 516, illustrates, even disobedience of a civil injunction can amount to criminal contempt if the conduct of the accused in disobeying the order amounts to a public challenge to the court's authority. In general, criminal contempt can be described as conduct likely to obstruct the administration of justice or to bring discredit onto the administration of justice. As a common law crime, contempt of court suffers from lack of clarity of definition of procedure and of the elements of the offence. Criminal contempt can, however, be subdivided into two types, contempt in the face of the court [*in facie*], for example, disruption of the proceedings in the courtroom, failure of counsel to attend court as required, or refusal of a witness to be sworn or to answer questions, and contempt out of the face of the court [*ex facie*].

The most troublesome aspect of criminal contempt is contempt out of the face of the court. It involves essentially three different types of conduct: (1) breach of the *sub judice* rule, *e.g.*, publication of material likely to interfere with the fair trial of the case; (2) obstruction of justice, *e.g.*, interfering with a witness or a juror; and (3) scandalizing the court, *i.e.*, criticism of a court or a judge. While the elements of these three types of contempt are not well-defined, it is suggested that case law supports the following propositions:

Breach of the *sub judice* rule – Until recently, this has been considered a strict liability offence if not virtually an absolute liability offence, the offence being described as requiring proof only that the words were calculated to interfere with the course of justice in the sense that they had that tendency. It was not necessary to find either that the words were intended to have that effect or that they did in fact interfere with the course of justice. Moreover, liability has been attributed to persons such as the editor or publisher on a vicarious basis, if they were responsible for the publication of the newspaper, for example, even if they had no prior knowledge of the contemptuous remarks. It is not sufficient, however, that there be a mere possibility of interference with the due administration of justice, the conduct must present a real risk to the due administration of justice. [A somewhat lesser standard adopted by the House of Lords in the *Times Newspapers* case, [1974] A.C. 273, probably does not represent the law in Canada.] It is suggested that, in light of the *Charter of Rights and Freedoms* and in particular the fundamental justice guarantee in s. 7 as interpreted by the Supreme Court of Canada in *Reference re Section 94(2) of the Motor Vehicle Act (B.C.)*, [1985] 2 S.C.R. 486, 23 C.C.C. (3d) 289, it can no longer be confidently stated that liability can be imposed on a vicarious basis or that no intent to interfere with the administration of justice is required. At least the accused should probably be able to defend the case by demonstrating that they were without fault, perhaps through the exercise of due diligence or was operating under an honest (and perhaps reasonable) mistake of fact. Finally, it would seem that a contempt can be made out even if there was no real risk of interference in the due administration of justice by the particular publication, if the accused intended to produce such prejudice. Perhaps such conduct is more accurately described as an attempt but the cases do not make any such distinction.

Obstruction of justice – The elements of this offence are similar to those for breach of the *sub judice* rule, and, in fact, the former may be considered simply a special example of this form of contempt which has been described as anything done that is calculated to obstruct or interfere with the due course of justice or the lawful process of the courts. Again "calculated" does not mean intended but merely "fixed, suited, apt". In *B.C.G.E.U. v. British Columbia (Attorney General)*, [1988] 2 S.C.R. 214, 44 C.C.C. (3d) 289, Chief Justice Dickson adopted the following list of acts which could fall into this category: victimizing jurors, witnesses and other persons; obstructing person officially connected with court or its process; interference with person under the special protective jurisdiction of the court; breach of duty by persons officially connected with the court or its process; forging; altering or abusing the process of the court; divulging the confidences of the jury-room; preventing access by the public to courts of law, service of process in the precinct of the court and disclosing the identity of witnesses. Again, the Charter may have implications for the *mens rea* of the offence, bearing in mind, however, that it could be argued that some limits on Charter guarantees may be upheld under s. 1 because of the close connection of this form of contempt to the fundamental principle of the rule of law.

Scandalizing the court – This is the one form of contempt which does not bear a clear, direct relationship to the administration of justice. It has been defined as any act done or writing published, calculated to bring a court into contempt or lower its authority. Thus, conduct which could have no possible effect on any particular case may nevertheless come within this definition. The difficulty with this form of contempt has always been to distinguish between contemptuous comment and fair criticism of the courts and the judiciary. The basis for this form of contempt lies in the assumption that public confidence in the administration of justice would be undermined by comments that tend to lower the authority of the court.

Perhaps the clearest examples of this form of contempt would be comments attributing improper motives to a court or allegations of corruption, partiality and attempts to pervert the course of justice by a judge. It is equally clear that reasonable argument or expostulation offered against any judicial act as contrary to law or the public good is not contempt. [*Re Duncan*, [1958] S.C.R. 41]. The impact of the *Charter of Rights and Freedoms* has been felt in relation to this form of contempt, a majority of the Ontario Court of Appeal holding in *R. v. Kopyto, infra* that, as presently framed, contempt by scandalizing the court is not a reasonable limit on the guarantee to freedom of expression. The defect in the common law definition appeared to lie in the fact that there was no requirement of proof of any real danger, present or future, to the fair and effective administration of justice. Interestingly, the dissenting members of the court would be prepared to uphold the constitutionality of this form of contempt because, in their view, it required proof of an intent to bring the administration of justice into disrepute and truth would be a defence. Further, the *actus reus* of the offence requires proof that, by reason of the statement, there was a serious risk that the administration of justice would be interfered with.

ANNOTATIONS

Grounds for finding contempt of court / Violation of court orders – An unincorporated union is capable of being found in criminal contempt of court for violation of a court order. The fact that criminal contempt is not codified does not result in a violation of ss. 7 or 11(*a*) or (*g*) of the Charter. To establish criminal contempt, the Crown must prove beyond a reasonable doubt that the accused defied or disobeyed a court order in a public way (the *actus reus*), with intent, knowledge or recklessness as to the fact that the public disobedience will tend to depreciate the authority of the court (the *mens rea*). The necessary *mens rea* may however be inferred from the circumstances and since an open and public defiance of a court order will tend to depreciate the authority of the court, when it is clear that the accused must have known her act of defiance would be public, it may be inferred that she was at least reckless as to whether the authority of the court would be brought into contempt. While publicity is required for the offence, a civil contempt is not converted to a criminal contempt merely because it attracts publicity, but rather because it constitutes a public act of defiance of the court in circumstances where the accused knew, intended or was reckless as to the fact that the act would publicly bring the court into contempt. While it would seem that a judge entertaining a motion for contempt of an order made by a judge of the court, as opposed to an inferior tribunal, would not have the power to go behind the order. The validity of the order is not an issue on the contempt hearing. Unless the order has been set aside for want of jurisdiction, the judge hearing the motion on criminal contempt must accept it as valid: *U.N.A. v. Alberta (Attorney General)*, [1992] 1 S.C.R. 901, 71 C.C.C. (3d) 225 (4:3).

The accused were properly found in contempt of court for their flagrant disobedience of an injunction. While the accused sought to argue that the injunction was overbroad and infringed their rights under the Charter, the injunction was valid until set aside and the accused had taken no steps to challenge the injunction: *Everywoman's Health Centre Society (1988) v. Bridges* (1990), 62 C.C.C. (3d) 455, 78 D.L.R. (4th) 529 (B.C.C.A.), supp. reasons 54 B.C.L.R. (2d) 294 (C.A.). Also see: *R. v. Toth* (1991), 63 C.C.C. (3d) 273 (B.C.C.A.), leave to appeal to S.C.C. refused 7 W.A.C. 23*n*, 136 N.R. 404*n*.

The defence of necessity was not available to accused charged with violating a court injunction prohibiting obstruction of logging crews. The necessity defence cannot operate to excuse conduct which has been specifically enjoined. An application to the court, which could be heard on short notice, would have determined whether the circumstances were sufficient to engage the defence of necessity. In addition, the defence of necessity can never operate to avoid a peril that is lawfully authorized by the law. Similarly, s. 27 of the *Criminal Code* was not available. Section 27 does not contemplate the justification of force or other conduct which the court has already specifically enjoined: *MacMillan Bloedel Ltd. v. Simpson* (1994), 89 C.C.C. (3d) 217, 113 D.L.R. (4th) 368 (B.C.C.A.), leave to appeal to S.C.C. refused 23 C.R.R. (2d) 192*n* (Pulker app'n granted).

An allegation of contempt of court is criminal, or at least *quasi*-criminal, in character and therefore the elements of the offence must be proved beyond a reasonable doubt. Where the allegation is based on failure to comply with a court order, there must be proof of knowledge of the order alleged to have been breached. Service of a court order on the solicitor for a Minister of the Crown did not fix the Minister with actual knowledge in the absence of evidence from which that knowledge could be inferred as where there were circumstances which reveal a special reason for bringing the order to the Minister's attention. Further, the Minister could not be held liable for contempt of court on the basis of the doctrine of vicarious liability, delegation or the identification theory: *Bhatnager v. Canada (Minister of Employment and Immigration)*, [1990] 2 S.C.R. 217, 71 D.L.R. (4th) 84 (9:0).

Even though the conduct may involve a breach of the criminal law, contempt will remain civil where the conduct falls short of public defiance: *Wightman v. Walmsley* (1997), 117 C.C.C. (3d) 470, [1998] 4 W.W.R. 459 (B.C.C.A.).

Interference with access to courts – Any action to prevent, impede or obstruct access to the courts runs counter to the rule of law and constitutes a criminal contempt of court: *N.A.P.E. v. Newfoundland (Attorney General)*, [1988] 2 S.C.R. 204, 44 C.C.C. (3d) 186 (6:0); *B.C.G.E.U. v. British Columbia (Attorney General)*, [1988] 2 S.C.R. 214, 44 C.C.C. (3d) 289 (6:0).

Scandalizing the court – In determining contempt scandalizing a court or judge it is not the effect that the author intended his article to have but the effect the article itself was calculated to have: *R. v. Murphy*, [1969] 4 C.C.C. 147, 6 C.R.N.S. 353 (N.B.S.C. App. Div.).

It is *prima facie* legitimate to criticize a judge's conduct in a particular case or to criticize any particular decision given by the courts if done without casting any aspersions on the motives of a judge or court, and without abuse: *R. v. Dalke* (1981), 59 C.C.C. (2d) 477, 21 C.R. (3d) 380 (B.C.S.C.).

It was held in *R. v. Kopyto* (1987), 39 C.C.C. (3d) 1, 61 C.R. (3d) 209 (Ont. C.A.) (3:2), that the offence of contempt of court by scandalizing the court, as presently understood, is unconstitutional by reason of the guarantee of freedom of expression in s. 2(*b*) of the Charter. It would seem, however, that if the offence were redefined to require proof that the accused's remarks created a real, significant, and present or imminent danger to the fair and effective administration of justice then the offence might be valid. The dissenting members of the court held that properly understood the offence did not violate s. 2(*b*) but that the Crown would have to prove an intention to bring the administration of justice into disrepute and that by reason of the statement made there was a serious risk that the administration of justice would be interfered with. As well, truth would be a defence.

It was held in *R. v. Edmonton Sun Publishing Ltd.* (1981), 62 C.C.C. (2d) 318 (Alta. Q.B.), that for the court to find that an editorial cartoon concerning a court case was a contempt of court it must be proved that it tended to obstruct or defeat the administration of justice or that it showed disrespect of the court process or that it tended to bring the court into disrespect.

Publicity – In *R. v. Carocchia* (1973), 15 C.C.C. (2d) 175, 43 D.L.R. (3d) 427 (Que. C.A.), the publication of a police press release which was of such a nature as to influence the result of a non-jury criminal case was held to be an interference of the administration of justice and a contempt of court.

A broadcaster was properly found in contempt of court for broadcasting during the accused's trial details of other criminal conduct by the accused, even though in the end the same information was placed before the jury through evidence called during the defence. The issue in every case is whether there has been a real risk of prejudice to the course of justice, not simply to the accused. Thus, substantial interference with the trial process by causing undue delay and expense or by creating an appearance of substantial unfairness at any stage of the proceedings may result in a conviction for contempt, regardless of prejudice to the accused. Finally, it was also not improper for the trial judge to base the amount of the fine on the costs thrown away as a result of contempt: *R. v. CHEK TV Ltd.* (1987), 33 C.C.C. (3d) 24, 30 B.C.L.R. (2d) 36 (C.A.).

The public's vital interest in knowing the facts as protected by freedom of expression, including freedom of the press in s. 2(*b*) of the Charter, will be assessed differently in the context of an accused who is in custody awaiting trial than it will be where a dangerous suspect is at large and public assistance may be required to apprehend the suspect. Publication of the criminal record of an accused who is not at large and who does not constitute a danger to the community is *prima facie* a contempt of court: *Alberta (Attorney General) v. Interwest Publications Ltd.* (1990), 58 C.C.C. (3d) 114, 73 D.L.R. (4th) 83 (Alta. Q.B.).

Although a contempt of court charge brought as a result of violation of the *sub judice* rule infringes a publisher's freedom of expression as guaranteed by s. 2(*b*) of the Charter of Rights, the *sub judice* is a reasonable limit on freedom of expression, being required to ensure the fair trial of the accused. Contempt of court will lie only where there is proof of either a clear intent to influence the fair trial of an accused or where the publication presents a real risk that the article will prejudice the fair hearing of the accused, and the *sub judice* rule only delays publication until completion of the trial: *R. v. Robinson-Blackmore Printing & Publishing Co.* (1989), 47 C.C.C. (3d) 366, 73 Nfld. & P.E.I.R. 46 (Nfld. S.C.).

The test for publication contempt is whether having regard to all the circumstances, including the effectiveness of alternative means, the court is satisfied beyond a reasonable doubt that the publication created a real and substantial risk to the administration of justice. This test does not violate ss. 2(*b*) or 7 of the Charter as it is neither void for vagueness nor an unconstitutional limit on the freedom of the press: *R. v. Edmonton Sun* (2003), 170 C.C.C. (3d) 455 (Alta. C.A.).

The *actus reus* of contempt is made out where a publication impairs the right of an accused to a fair trial or the publication otherwise deprecates the authority of the court: *R. v. Edmonton Sun, supra.*

While publication contempt requires proof of a real risk of prejudice, the enactment of the Charter has not changed the *mens rea* for publication contempt, which is the intention to publish words that, on an objective basis, are calculated to interfere with the course of justice: *R. v. CHBC Television* (1999), 132 C.C.C. (3d) 390, 23 C.R. (5th) 135 (B.C.C.A.).

Publication of a summary of the evidence given on the preliminary issue of the accused's fitness to stand trial, in violation of the trial judge's order that it not be published was held to constitute contempt of court: *R. v. Southam Press (Ontario) Ltd.* (1976), 31 C.C.C. (2d) 205 (Ont. C.A.).

Counsel's failure to attend court – In *R. v. Hill* (1976), 33 C.C.C. (2d) 60, 73 D.L.R. (3d) 621 (B.C.C.A.), affg 25 C.C.C. (2d) 348, 62 D.L.R. (3d) 692 (Co. Ct.), it was held that conduct, in this case by a lawyer, which is calculated to delay, disrupt and bring the judicial process into contempt will constitute criminal contempt and it need not be further proved that the accused intended to disrupt, hinder or delay the course of justice.

In considering whether or not a lawyer is guilty of contempt the court must consider the apology tendered by the lawyer at the contempt hearing: *R. v. Kopyto* (1981), 60 C.C.C. (2d) 85, 21 C.R. (3d) 276 (Ont. C.A.), leave to appeal to S.C.C. refused 38 N.R. 540*n*.

However, the lawyer's apology did not negative his contempt where his conduct in failing to appear at court showed a serious indifference to his obligation to the court and to his client and when he again failed to attend court on the following day as directed by the judge: *R. v. Anders* (1982), 67 C.C.C. (2d) 138, 136 D.L.R. (3d) 316 (Ont. C.A.).

The *actus reus* of criminal contempt is conduct which seriously interferes with, or obstructs, the administration of justice or would cause a serious risk of that occurring. While the failure, of a lawyer who has undertaken to appear in court, to attend is capable of constituting contempt, the court should consider the consequences of failing to appear. Conduct that had little or no effect on the administration of justice could not support a conviction for contempt. The *mens rea* of contempt requires proof of deliberate or intentional conduct, or indifference akin to recklessness: *R. v. Glasner* (1994), 93 C.C.C. (3d) 226, 119 D.L.R. (4th) 113, 19 O.R. (3d) 739 (C.A.).

Before an absent lawyer may be found in contempt he must first be brought before the court and given the right to make full answer and defence which at a minimum requires that he be given notice that he is facing a charge of contempt of court: *R. v. Pinx* (1979), 50 C.C.C. (2d) 65, 105 D.L.R. (3d) 143 (Man. C.A.).

While the deliberate failure of counsel who has undertaken to represent an accused to appear when the case is called, or even failure to attend in circumstances showing indifference, may constitute contempt of court, failure to attend due to mere inadvertence even if due to negligence, but falling short of indifference, does not necessarily constitute contempt of court: *R. v. Jones* (1978), 42 C.C.C. (2d) 192 (Ont. C.A.).

Counsel withdrawing from case – In contempt proceedings against a lawyer a distinction must be drawn between the lawyer who deliberately frustrates the due carrying on of court proceedings by the wilful act of non-attendance, an act which may constitute contempt of court, and the act of a lawyer who impulsively reacts to an adverse ruling by the court by attempting to withdraw, which is at worst an error of judgment: *R. v. Swartz* (1977), 34 C.C.C. (2d) 477, [1977] 2 W.W.R. 751 (Man. C.A.).

A trial judge has no right in law to order counsel to continue in the defence of an accused after counsel has advised that he has decided that he will no longer represent the accused. While the judge may urge counsel to reconsider and to try to reconcile any differences with his client, should counsel stand firm then he cannot properly be cited for contempt for refusing to comply with an order by the trial judge that he continue to act: *Leask v. Cronin* (1985), 18 C.C.C. (3d) 315, [1985] 3 W.W.R. 152 (B.C.S.C.).

Conduct of counsel in court – Language by a lawyer attributing dishonourable or disgraceful conduct to the judge trying a case and suggesting that the judge acted dishonestly, is capable of constituting contempt of court: *R. v. Doz* (1985), 19 C.C.C. (3d) 434 (Alta. C.A.), revd on other grounds [1987] 2 S.C.R. 463, 38 C.C.C. (3d) 479, 55 Alta. L.R. (2d) 289.

There is a distinction between conduct by a barrister which though open to censure is merely discourteous and conduct which constitutes contempt of court: *R. v. Fox* (1976), 30 C.C.C. (2d) 330, 70 D.L.R. (3d) 577 (Ont. C.A.).

Mere discourtesy or use of uncomplimentary remarks to the court is not always to be taken as contempt. On the other hand where there has been a proper question put to counsel by the presiding judge the repeated refusal by counsel to answer the question will normally constitute contempt: *R. v. Barker* (1980), 53 C.C.C. (2d) 322, [1980] 4 W.W.R. 202 (Alta. C.A.).

A charge of contempt of court, arising out of a lawyer's submissions in the course of a trial, requires proof of a serious, real imminent risk of obstruction of the administration of justice. It must be shown that he had a dishonest intention or acted in bad faith in that he intentionally discredited or attempted to discredit the administration of justice: *R. v. Bertrand* (1989), 49 C.C.C. (3d) 397, 70 C.R. (3d) 362 (Que. S.C.).

Conduct of other persons in court – Words or actions directed at other persons besides the judge such as jurors, counsel or other officers of the court may also be regarded as contempt where such words or acts interfere or tend to interfere with the administration of justice. Thus, in *R. v. Paul* (1978), 44 C.C.C. (2d) 257, 6 C.R. (3d) 272 (Ont. C.A.), it was held (2:1) that the deliberately false allegation in open court by an unrepresented accused that the charges laid against him were the work of a "corrupt" Crown Attorney, constituted contempt of court. The decision of the Court of Appeal was affirmed, [1980] 2 S.C.R. 169, 52 C.C.C. (2d) 331, 15 C.R. (3d) 219 (5:0), where it was held that the trial judge did not err in dealing with the contempt summarily rather than requiring the Crown Attorney to take the matter to the Attorney General.

An accused's voluntary act in consuming a large quantity of alcohol shortly before his trial well-knowing the effect this would have on him and which would result in the court being unable to proceed with the trial constitutes contempt of court notwithstanding the accused did not intend to obstruct the course of justice: *R. v. Perkins* (1980), 51 C.C.C. (2d) 369, [1980] 4 W.W.R. 763 (B.C.C.A.).

It was held by the majority in *R. v. Flamand* (1980), 57 C.C.C. (2d) 366 (Que. C.A.), that remarks by an accused to the trial judge that he was not fit to try the case because the judge's son was a police officer and that he (the accused) no longer had confidence in the judge constituted contempt of court being deliberately calculated to bring the trial judge into contempt, lower his authority, cast discredit on the administration of justice and impede its normal course. Mayrand J.A. dissenting would have quashed the conviction on the basis that an expressed lack of confidence in a judge, if a genuinely held belief, even if not justified on a rational basis, does not constitute contempt of court. His Lordship also considered the summary manner in which the proceedings were conducted by the trial judge deprived the accused of an opportunity to present a full and complete defence. On further appeal [1982] 1 S.C.R. 337, 65 C.C.C. (2d) 192*n*, 42 N.R. 87 (7:0), the dissenting judgment of Mayrand J.A. was approved and the conviction quashed.

Abusive language by an accused attributing gross insensitivity to the trial judge could be viewed as calculated to lower his authority and thus capable of constituting contempt of court: *R. v. Martin* (1985), 19 C.C.C. (3d) 248, 15 C.R.R. 231 (Ont. C.A.).

Conduct outside of court – Notwithstanding the accused's conduct may also have constituted the offence of attempting to obstruct justice contrary to s. 139 [R.S.C. 1985], the Crown may proceed by way of contempt of court: *R. v. Vermette*, [1987] 1 S.C.R. 577, 32 C.C.C. (3d) 519, 57 C.R. (3d) 340 (4:0).

Refusal of witness to be sworn or answer questions – On an appeal from conviction for contempt of court in the face of the court based on a refusal to answer a question in a criminal case if it is not shown that the question was relevant then the conviction cannot stand. However, at the trial itself it is the judge not the witness who must decide whether or not the question is relevant and a witness who disagrees with the judge's ruling on relevancy nevertheless must abide by it or risk being cited for contempt. On the other hand where the witness objects to the question the trial judge ought to inquire into and determine its relevancy: *R. v. Fields* (1986), 28 C.C.C. (3d) 353, 53 C.R. (3d) 260, 56 O.R. (2d) 213 (C.A.).

APPEAL / Idem / Part XXI applies.

10. (1) Where a court, judge, justice or provincial court judge summarily convicts a person for a contempt of court committed in the face of the court and imposes punishment in respect thereof, that person may appeal

(*a*) from the conviction; or

(*b*) against the punishment imposed.

(2) Where a court or judge summarily convicts a person for a contempt of court not committed in the face of the court and punishment is imposed in respect thereof, that person may appeal

(*a*) from the conviction; or

(*b*) against the punishment imposed.

(3) An appeal under this section lies to the court of appeal of the province in which the proceedings take place, and, for the purposes of this section, the provisions of Part XXI apply, with such modifications as the circumstances require. R.S., c. C-34, s. 9; 1972, c. 13, s. 4.

CROSS-REFERENCES

Section 9 preserves the common law power to punish for contempt and the notes under that section relate to the grounds of contempt of court. The notes under this section relate to procedural issues, including rights of appeal. Procedure on appeal and powers of the Court of Appeal, in appeals from summary contempt proceedings, is governed by Part XXI: procedure on appeal by indictment [notwithstanding the contempt finding was made in the course of a summary conviction proceeding]. This section would not apply to an accused convicted in summary conviction proceedings of a summary conviction offence such as the offence in s. 648 of publishing proceedings in the absence of the jury.

SYNOPSIS

This section creates the right to have an appeal from a conviction for contempt of court heard in accordance with the procedure for appeals in cases which have proceeded by indictment, even if the conviction for contempt of court was summary. The appeal is to be heard by the provincial court of appeal, with such modifications to the procedure on appeals from convictions on indictable offences as may be necessary.

The forms of contempt of court are discussed in a comment under s. 9, *supra*. This comment is meant to draw attention to certain procedural problems. It is first necessary to distinguish between contempt in the face of the court [*in facie*], for example, disruption of the proceedings in the courtroom, failure of counsel to attend court as required, or refusal of a witness to be sworn or to answer questions; and contempt out of the face of the court [*ex facie*], such as interference with a witness, or publication of material calculated to interfere with the fair trial of an accused. The distinction is important because, while a superior court can punish both types of contempt, an inferior court can only punish contempts committed in the face of the court. The line between the two types of contempt can be exceedingly fine. Consider the failure of counsel to appear at a criminal trial as required. While the act of non-appearance is committed in the face of the court, the reasons why counsel failed to attend court may be, and usually would be, completely outside the personal knowledge of the presiding judge. Nevertheless, since the decision in *R. v. McKeown*, [1971] S.C.R. 446, there can be little doubt that this conduct constitutes contempt *in facie* and is punishable by the presiding judge.

A second problem concerns the procedure by which the contempt is initiated. For contempt *in facie*, it would seem that no particular form of notice is required and even verbal notice to a person disrupting the proceedings would be sufficient, provided the alleged contemnor is sufficiently advised of the act said to constitute contempt. On the other hand, the presiding judge can leave it to some other party such as the Attorney General to initiate proceedings through some more formal process. Where the contempt is out of the face of the court and thus triable only by the superior court, some form of written notice would ordinarily be required to secure the person's attendance. The usual notice is by way of originating notice of motion served upon the alleged contemnor and returnable in the superior court and is referred to as the summary procedure. However, it would also seem that a more formal process is available by preferring a direct indictment in the superior court. This latter form of process has fallen almost entirely into disuse, but the Supreme Court of Canada in *R. v. Vermette, infra*, recognized that it was still available.

It seems clear that the *Charter of Rights and Freedoms* applies to the trial of the contempt charge whether *ex facie* or *in facie* and that, unless very unusual circumstances arise, the person must be given a reasonable opportunity to prepare a defence and to consult counsel. Further, it would seem that proof of contempt must be made out on the criminal standard and the accused would have the right to call witnesses, be represented by counsel if he wished and the right not to be compelled to be a witness. Authority is unanimous that the constitutional right to jury trial does not apply. On the other hand, it may be that, where the unusual direct indictment procedure were resorted to, the trial would have to be by jury, which was the manner of trying such contempts before use of the summary process was widely resorted to. A particular concern relates to the constitutional guarantee to trial by an independent and impartial tribunal. Some forms of contempt *in facie* involve insulting or abusive behaviour towards the presiding judge. Once the judge has restored order, which may include removal of the person from the court and citing the person for contempt, it is probably best that the actual contempt be tried by some other judge in order to preserve the appearance of fairness. It should be noted, however, that, in light of *R. v. Doz*, [1987] 2

S.C.R. 463, 38 C.C.C. (3d) 479, 82 A.R. 394, one judge of an inferior court has no jurisdiction to try a contempt committed in the face of the court of another inferior court judge. Accordingly, if fairness requires that the inferior court judge not deal with the contempt himself then the proceedings for contempt of court would have to be taken in the superior court.

ANNOTATIONS

Contempt of court: Procedure / Jurisdiction of courts to try contempt of court – At common law, superior courts have an inherent and exclusive jurisdiction to punish for contempt not committed in the face of the court while inferior courts have only a limited inherent jurisdiction to punish for contempt in the face of court. Inferior courts which are not courts of record have no power to punish for contempt unless such power is conferred by statute. Violation of an order of the Quebec Police Commission prohibiting publication of the photograph of a witness is contempt out of the face of the court and therefore punishable only by the superior court: *Canadian Broadcasting Corp. v. Cordeau,* [1979] 2 S.C.R. 618, 48 C.C.C. (2d) 289, 101 D.L.R. (3d) 24 (9:0).

A judge presiding at a preliminary hearing has no power to punish summarily for contempt of court a witness who refuses to answer relevant questions without reasonable excuse. The power of the judge is limited to the procedure under s. 545: *R. v. Bubley* (1976), 32 C.C.C. (2d) 79, [1976] 6 W.W.R. 179 (Alta. S.C. App. Div.).

Section 484 of this Act, however, gives the judge power to commit for contempt in the face of court in order to preserve order in his court-room: *R. v. Barker* (1980), 53 C.C.C. (2d) 322, [1980] 4 W.W.R. 202 (Alta. C.A.).

A provincial court judge exercising the jurisdiction to try an indictable offence under Part XIX does have an inherent jurisdiction to punish for contempt committed in the face of the court, such as the wilful refusal of a witness to testify: *R. v. Dunning* (1979), 50 C.C.C. (2d) 296 (Ont. C.A.); *R. v. Layne* (1984), 14 C.C.C. (3d) 149, [1984] 6 W.W.R. 108 (B.C.S.C.). *Contra*: *R. v. Heer* (1982), 68 C.C.C. (2d) 333, 38 B.C.L.R. 176 (S.C.).

Similarly a provincial court judge presiding at a trial of an accused for a summary conviction offence under Part XXVII constitutes a court of record and has power to punish for contempt of court committed in the face of the court, such as the refusal of a witness to answer relevant questions: *R. v. Fields* (1986), 28 C.C.C. (3d) 353, 53 C.R. (3d) 260, 56 O.R. (2d) 213 (C.A.).

It was held in *R. v. Vaillancourt*, [1981] 1 S.C.R. 69, 58 C.C.C. (2d) 31, 19 C.R. (3d) 178 (5:0), that a judge presiding in the criminal courts has power to punish summarily as a contempt in the face of the court the refusal of a juvenile witness to testify. It was held that such a contempt is not a delinquency which could only be tried under the former *Juvenile Delinquents Act* but rather was the exercise of the court's inherent power which is preserved by this section. It would seem that in light of s. 15(3) of the *Youth Criminal Justice Act* this jurisdiction in the ordinary courts is retained but the Youth Court also has jurisdiction to try the contempt. In either case the penalty is determined by the provisions of the *Youth Criminal Justice Act* (see s. 15(4) of that Act).

Initiation of contempt proceedings – Although rarely employed, procedure by indictment for punishment of contempt *ex facie* is preserved by this section. However, the offence is triable only by the superior court and the provisions of Part IX do not apply to the trial of such offence so as to permit the accused to elect trial by provincial court judge. Finally, it would seem that where an indictment for criminal contempt is employed it would have to be by direct indictment to the superior court: *R. v. Vermette*, [1987] 1 S.C.R. 577, 32 C.C.C. (3d) 519, 57 C.R. (3d) 340 (4:0).

Even where the court initiates summary procedure for contempt out of the face of the court, in a matter of interference with the administration of justice the Attorney General has the responsibility to present the evidence and if he chooses not to adduce any evidence on the show cause hearing then the charge should be dismissed: *R. v. Hamel and Lesage* (1978), 9 C.R. (3d) 214 (Que. C.A.).

Criminal contempt proceedings may be brought at the instance of an individual: *Letourneau-Belanger v. Société de Publication Merlin Ltée*, [1969] 4 C.C.C. 313, 6 C.R.N.S. 308 (Que. Q.B., App. Side) or any interested party: *R. v. Froese (No. 1)* (1979), 50 C.C.C. (2d) 105, [1980] 1 W.W.R. 667 (B.C.S.C.).

The initiation of the summary process by way of an originating notice of motion for a contempt *ex facie curiae* is appropriate where the accused has broadcast inflammatory and prejudicial material at the opening of a criminal trial. Further, the hearing of the contempt motion may then be properly adjourned until the conclusion of the criminal trial so as not to further prejudice that trial. In the interim should there be any repetition of the contempt the currency of the notice of motion ensures that the accused can be immediately controlled: *R. v. Froese and British Columbia Television Broadcasting System Ltd. (No. 3)* (1980), 54 C.C.C. (2d) 315, 18 C.R. (3d) 75 *sub nom. R. v. Bengert; R. v. Froese and British Columbia Television Broadcasting System Ltd. (No. 3)* (B.C.C.A.).

In *Cotroni v. Quebec Police Commission and Brunet*, [1978] 1 S.C.R. 1048, 38 C.C.C. (2d) 56, a conviction for contempt of the Commissioners was quashed because of the vagueness of the charge. It was held that where testimony is false in its entirety, a charge of perjury, and consequently of contempt, is specific enough if it simply states that. However, where as in this case the objection is not to the testimony as a whole, the charge must specify which part of the testimony is complained of. Where the complaint is the evasiveness of some of the witnesses' answers it was necessary to specify what was considered evasive.

Procedure on trial of contempt – As developed at common law, the summary procedure for dealing with the contempt of a witness refusing to testify at a criminal trial, does not offend the principles guaranteed by s. 7 or s. 11. Those principles include the right to be presumed innocent until proven guilty beyond a reasonable doubt, to be informed without unreasonable delay of the specific offence with which he is charged, to have counsel, to have a reasonable time to prepare a defence, to call witnesses and not to be compelled to give evidence. He also has the right to be tried by an independent and impartial tribunal and where the contempt alleged consists of insolent or contemptuous behaviour or other disorderly conduct or behaviour which reflects adversely upon the character, integrity or reputation of the initiating judge, the charge should be tried by another judge. However, there may be very exceptional cases where the circumstances are so compelling and the need for action on the part of the presiding judge so urgent to preserve the order and protect the authority of the court that some limitation on such rights, particularly with respect to time, may be justified: *R. v. Cohn* (1984), 15 C.C.C. (3d) 150, 42 C.R. (3d) 1 (Ont. C.A.), leave to appeal to S.C.C. refused [1985] 1 S.C.R. vii, 9 O.A.C. 160, 58 N.R. 160*n*.

However, the fact that the witness was the last witness for the Crown was not such a compelling circumstance as required infringement of the accused's rights, particularly an opportunity to consult counsel and prepare the defence to a charge of contempt for refusing to testify. The major inducement to a recalcitrant witness to give evidence is the knowledge that his actions may constitute contempt of court, and if found in contempt he may be sentenced to a substantial term of imprisonment. In those cases where a witness refuses to be sworn or to testify, the trial judge is always in a position to threaten that he will cite the proposed witness for contempt and to warn him that if he is found in contempt he may be sentenced to imprisonment. If, however, after repeated appearances and repeated warnings, the witness still refuses to testify it is most unlikely that a finding of contempt by the trial judge would induce such witness to testify. Once he has been sentenced, there is no longer any effective inducement as the court cannot vary a sentence once it is imposed: *R. v. Ayres* (1984), 15 C.C.C. (3d) 208, 42 C.R. (3d) 33 (Ont. C.A.).

While *instanter* summary contempt procedures may be justified in some exceptional cases, in most circumstances, natural justice requires the usual steps of putting the witness on notice that he or she must show cause why they should not be found in contempt of court, followed by an adjournment which need be no longer than that required to offer the witness an opportunity to be advised by counsel and, if he or she chooses, to be represented by counsel. In addition, upon a finding of contempt, there should be an opportunity to have representations made as to the appropriate sentence: *R. v. K. (B.)*, [1995] 4 S.C.R. 186, 102 C.C.C. (3d) 18, 43 C.R. (4th) 123.

A contempt citation is not a finding of contempt but rather notice to the accused that he has been contemptuous and would have to show cause why he should not be held in contempt. Contempt may be dealt with two ways: the ordinary procedure which provides the same procedural guarantees of a criminal trial, or the summary procedure which allows a judge to avoid the formalities of a criminal trial, even *instanter*, in some cases. The summary procedure can only be justified where it is urgent and imperative to act immediately. Other than in exceptional circumstances where the *instanter* summary proceeding is justified, the power to punish summarily is subject to the requirements of natural justice. While citing for contempt may take place at any time, including in the presence of the jury, conviction and sentence where it is not urgent and imperative to act immediately is an error of law that is reviewable by the appellate court. In some cases, it may be appropriate to convict an accused of contempt of court *instanter* in the presence of the jury, but in so doing, the trial judge must ensure that the jury is not given the impression that the judge is making a determination as to the credibility of the accused. Accordingly, in this case the accused's refusal to answer questions constituted contempt of court but the circumstances did not justify recourse to the *instanter* proceedings: *R. v. Arradi* (2003), 173 C.C.C. (3d) 1, 9 C.R. (6th) 207, 224 D.L.R. (4th) 301 (S.C.C.).

A person cited for civil contempt who is liable to be imprisoned for up to one year cannot be compelled to testify at the contempt proceedings: *Vidéotron Ltée v. Industries Microlec Produits Electroniques Inc.*, [1992] 2 S.C.R. 1065, 76 C.C.C. (3d) 289, 96 D.L.R. (4th) 376.

Proceedings for contempt of court arising out of abusive remarks by the accused to the trial judge after he convicted her, having made adverse findings of credibility, ought not to have been tried by that same judge. In the circumstances, the accused could have a reasonable apprehension of bias and her rights under s. 11(*d*) of the Charter were infringed: *R. v. Martin* (1985), 19 C.C.C. (3d) 248 (Ont. C.A.).

Where there are contradicted facts relating to matters essential to a decision as to whether or not a party is in contempt of court, those facts cannot be found by an assessment of the credibility of deponents of affidavits who have not been seen or heard by the trier of fact: *R. v. Jetco Manufacturing Ltd. and Alexander* (1987), 31 C.C.C. (3d) 171, 57 O.R. (2d) 776 (C.A.).

While the same sentencing provisions are available in respect of the offence of contempt, the victim fine surcharge pursuant to s. 737 of the *Criminal Code*, however, has no application as it does not apply to common law offences: *R. v. Puddester* (2003), 174 C.C.C. (3d) 453, 226 Nfld. & P.E.I.R. 1 *sub nom. R. v. Puddister* (Nfld. C.A.).

Right to jury trial – A witness cited for contempt of court is "charged with an offence" within the meaning of s. 11 of the *Charter of Rights and Freedoms* and therefore is entitled to the rights guaranteed by that section as well as to fundamental justice under s. 7. However, the summary procedure is not an unconstitutional derogation from the right to a jury trial as guaranteed by s. 11(*f*) since the offender is subject only to a punishment of less than five years' imprisonment: *R. v. Cohn* (1984), 15 C.C.C. (3d) 150, 42 C.R. (3d) 1 (Ont. C.A.); *R. v. Robinson-Blackmore Printing & Publishing Co.* (1989), 47 C.C.C. (3d) 366, 73 Nfld. & P.E.I.R. 46 (Nfld. S.C.). Similarly: *MacMillan Bloedel Ltd. v. Simpson* (1994), 89 C.C.C. (3d) 217 (B.C.C.A.).

A person before the superior court on a summary motion to have him cited for contempt is not "charged with an offence" within the meaning of s. 11(*f*) of the *Canadian Charter of Rights and Freedoms* so as to have the benefit of a jury trial as guaranteed by that provision: *Quebec (Attorney General) v. Laurendeau* (1982), 3 C.C.C. (3d) 250 (Que. S.C.); *Manitoba (Attorney General) v. Groupe Quebecor Inc.* (1987), 37 C.C.C. (3d) 421 (Man. C.A.).

The summary procedure for trying contempt of court is a reasonable limitation on the right to a jury trial as provided for in s. 11(*f*) of the Charter: *R. v. Layne, supra.*

Appeal – Where the trial judge made an order for costs against defence counsel personally, there was a right of appeal. The jurisdiction to impose such a penalty could only be consequent upon a finding of contempt and therefore, the trial judge was effectively exercising contempt powers: *R. v. McCullough* (1995), 24 O.R. (3d) 239, 82 O.A.C. 63 (C.A.). [Also, now see s. 676.1.]

CIVIL REMEDY NOT SUSPENDED.

11. No civil remedy for an act or omission is suspended or affected by reason that the act or omission is a criminal offence. R.S., c. C-34, s. 10.

SYNOPSIS

This section states that parties may pursue civil remedies notwithstanding the fact that the same act or omission giving rise to the civil proceeding is also a criminal offence. Courts retain their inherent jurisdiction to protect their process and may, in an exceptional case, stay the civil proceedings until the conclusion of the criminal trial, to protect the accused's right to a fair trial.

ANNOTATIONS

In *British Acceptance Corporation Ltd. v. Belzberg* (1962), 36 D.L.R. (2d) 587, 39 C.R. 72 (Alta. S.C.), it was held that there was no general principle in Canada preventing the simultaneous trial of criminal and civil proceedings. A stay may be granted for either of the proceedings if simultaneous action would be vexatious but that is entirely discretionary.

Concurrent criminal and civil proceedings against a person is not in itself an exceptional cause for staying the latter proceedings: *Stickney v. Trusz* (1973), 16 C.C.C. (2d) 25, 25 C.R.N.S. 257 (Ont. H.C.J.), affd 17 C.C.C. (2d) 478*n*, 28 C.R.N.S. 125 (Div. Ct.), affd 17 C.C.C. (2d) 480*n*, 46 D.L.R. (3d) 82*n* (C.A.).

OFFENCE PUNISHABLE UNDER MORE THAN ONE ACT.

12. Where an act or omission is an offence under more than one Act of Parliament, whether punishable by indictment or on summary conviction, a person who does the act or makes the omission is, unless a contrary intention appears, subject to proceedings under any of those Acts, but is not liable to be punished more than once for the same offence. R.S., c. C-34, s. 11.

CROSS-REFERENCES

As to an *autrefois* plea, see ss. 7(6), 607 to 610 of the Code and s. 11(*h*) of the *Charter of Rights and Freedoms.* As to the abuse of process generally, see notes following s. 579. As to the common law rule precluding multiple convictions for same *delict*, the "*Kienapple*" rule and common law principles of *res judicata* and issue estoppel, see notes following s. 613.

SYNOPSIS

This provision *prevents* the *punishment* of an accused *more than once* for the same conduct where such conduct is an offence under more than one Act of Parliament. However, Parliament can make specific exceptions to this general rule (see, for example, s. 85).

ANNOTATIONS

This section does not modify the scope of *res judicata* which precludes multiple convictions for the same delict, although the matter is the basis of two separate offences: *R. v. Kienapple*,

[1975] 1 S.C.R. 729, 15 C.C.C. (2d) 524, 26 C.R.N.S. 1 (5:4) Folld: *Dore v. Canada (Attorney General) (No. 2)*, [1975] 1 S.C.R. 756, 17 C.C.C. (2d) 359, 27 C.R.N.S. (8:1).

Also see notes under s. 613, *infra*.

CHILD UNDER TWELVE.

13. No person shall be convicted of an offence in respect of an act or omission on his part while that person was under the age of twelve years. R.S., c. C-34, s. 12; 1980-81-82-83, c. 110, s. 72.

CROSS-REFERENCES

Note that s. 23.1 provides that an accused may be convicted as a party, or accessory after the fact under ss. 21 to 23, notwithstanding that the person whom the accused aids or abets, counsels or procures or receives, comforts or assists, cannot be convicted of the offence.

Trial of offences committed by young persons aged 12 to 17 years is governed by the *Youth Criminal Justice Act*.

A person's age is determined by s. 30 of the *Interpretation Act*, R.S.C. 1985, c. I-21.

SYNOPSIS

No child under 12 years of age may be held criminally accountable. The age of 12 represents a relatively recent increase from the common law rule which established age seven as the start of accountability. Below this age, provincial child welfare legislation may apply to children who are involved in criminal activity.

ANNOTATIONS

The reference to age in this section is to chronological age not "mental age". Thus, this section does not bar the trial of a mentally retarded adult, nor do such proceedings violate s. 15 of the Charter: *R. v. Sawchuk* (1991), 66 C.C.C. (3d) 255, [1991] 5 W.W.R. 381, 6 W.A.C. 311 (Man. C.A.), leave to appeal to S.C.C. refused 67 C.C.C. (3d) vi, 137 N.R. 385*n*.

CONSENT TO DEATH.

14. No person is entitled to consent to have death inflicted on them, and such consent does not affect the criminal responsibility of any person who inflicts death on the person who gave consent. R.S., c. C-34, s. 14, 2016, c. 3, s. 1.

CROSS-REFERENCES

For the offences of murder and manslaughter see ss. 222 to 240. The offence of counselling or aiding suicide is set out in s. 241.

SYNOPSIS

This section states that *no* one has the *right to consent* to have death inflicted on him. In addition, if a person causes the death of another, the consent of the deceased does not provide the person who caused the death a defence to criminal responsibility.

ANNOTATIONS

Notwithstanding this section, in the case of a genuine suicide pact, the surviving party should have a defence to murder. This defence will only be available when the parties are in such a mental state that they have formed a common and irrevocable intent to commit suicide together simultaneously and by the same act where the risk of death is identical and equal for both. The survivor may, however, be liable to be convicted of the offence contrary to s. 241: *R. v. Gagnon* (1993), 84 C.C.C. (3d) 143, 24 C.R. (4th) 369, [1993] R.J.Q. 1716 (C.A.).

CR. CODE

OBEDIENCE TO *DE FACTO* LAW.

15. No person shall be convicted of an offence in respect of an act or omission in obedience to the laws for the time being made and enforced by persons in *de facto* possession of the sovereign power in and over the place where the act or omission occurs. R.S., c. C-34, s. 15.

CROSS-REFERENCES

This provision does not apply to trials of war crimes and crimes against humanity: *Crimes Against Humanity and War Crimes Act*, s. 13. Note also the provisions of s. 269.1(3) which limit the availability of the defence of obedience to superior orders, etc., to the offence of torture. This provision is of quite limited application and provisions similar to it were originally enacted in England to protect persons serving the King *de facto* who might turn out to be on the wrong side of a civil war, and to make it clear that it was not treason to the successful claimant to the throne to have faithfully served the then reigning monarch.

In present times, a more relevant defence may be the emerging defence of officially induced error noted under s. 19, *infra*.

SYNOPSIS

This provision states that obedience to the laws, for the time being, made and enforced by those who are *de facto* in possession of the sovereign power in and over the place where the acts or omissions occur will prevent a conviction – unless a specific exception is made in the provision creating the offence.

ANNOTATIONS

This section does not afford a defence to a movie theatre, that, in compliance with provincial legislation, received approval for public showing of a film later alleged by the Crown to be obscene: *R. v. Daylight Theatre Company Ltd.* (1973), 13 C.C.C. (2d) 524, 41 D.L.R. (3d) 236 (Sask. C.A.). Folld: *R. v. McFall* (1975), 26 C.C.C. (2d) 181 (B.C.C.A.), although evidence of the provincial censor as to why he approved the film is relevant to the issue of whether in fact the film was obscene. Similarly, on a charge of distributing obscene publications, this section has no application notwithstanding the offending publications were first cleared through customs: *R. v. 294555 Ontario Ltd.* (1978), 39 C.C.C. (2d) 352, 61 D.L.R. (4th) 85, 69 O.R. (2d) 557 (C.A.).

DEFENCE OF MENTAL DISORDER / Presumption / Burden of proof.

16. (1) No person is criminally responsible for an act committed or an omission made while suffering from a mental disorder that rendered the person incapable of appreciating the nature and quality of the act or omission or of knowing that it was wrong.

(2) Every person is presumed not to suffer from a mental disorder so as to be exempt from criminal responsibility by virtue of subsection (1), until the contrary is proved on the balance of probabilities.

(3) The burden of proof that an accused was suffering from a mental disorder so as to be exempt from criminal responsibility is on the party that raises the issue. R.S. c. C-34, s. 16; 1991, c. 43, s. 2.

CROSS-REFERENCES

This section deals with the defence of mental disorder. Where that defence is made out, the trier of fact is required to deliver a verdict of not criminally responsible on account of mental disorder: s. 672.34. As to the disposition hearing subsequent to a verdict of not criminally responsible on account of mental disorder or unfit to stand trial, see. ss. 672.45 to 672.52. As to dispositions by a court or review board, see ss. 672.54 to 672.63. As to review of dispositions, see ss. 672.81 to 672.85. As to remand for assessment, see ss. 672.11 to 672.2. As to trial of issue of fitness to stand trial, see ss. 672.22 to 672.33. As to review boards, see ss. 672.38 to 672.44. As to dual status offender, see ss. 672.67 to 672.71. As to appeals, see ss. 672.72 to 672.8. As to interprovincial transfers, see ss. 672.86 to 672.89. As to application of Part XX.1 to young offenders, see s. 141 of the *Youth Criminal Justice Act*. Mental disorder is defined in s. 2. The report of an expert may be admitted under s. 657.3.

SYNOPSIS

These provisions are effectively identical to the previous s. 16 except for terminology which replaces the concept of insanity with the phraseology "mental disorder". The new terminology, however, still codifies the common law test of insanity, now termed mental disorder. Subsection (1) sets out the long-standing principle of criminal law that no person who committed an offence while suffering a mental disorder may be convicted. Subsection (1) also restates, with one significant modification, the common law rule developed in nineteenth century England in the *McNaughten* case. This is a legal and not a medical test although expert psychiatric and psychological evidence is almost invariably used to assist in making the determination. Subsection (2) sets out the presumption of sanity until the contrary is proven on the balance of probabilities and subsec. (3) requires the party raising the issue of mental disorder to bear the burden of proof.

The first arm of the test is that the accused is proved to be suffering from a mental disorder which replaces the concepts of "natural imbecility" and "disease of the mind" contained in the prior definition of insanity. These principles, however, are incorporated by virtue of the generic term "mental disorder". To be found to be suffering from a mental disorder, the accused must meet one of two tests: the mental disorder must have rendered them incapable (1) of appreciating the nature and quality of the act or omission or (2) of knowing that an act or omission is wrong.

Subsection (3) of the previous legislation which stated that a person "who has specific delusions, but is in other respects sane, shall not be acquitted on the ground of insanity unless the delusions caused that person to believe in the existence of a state of things that, if it existed, would have justified or excused the act or omission of that person" is now subsumed under the definition of "mental disorder" contained in subsec. (1). Consequently, a person who suffers from a delusion to the point where it renders them incapable of appreciating the nature and quality of the act or omission or of knowing that it was wrong will be characterized as suffering from a "mental disorder".

Subsections (2) and (3) of the new provisions speak to the presumption of sanity and the burden of proof on the balance of probability which must be borne by the party raising the issue.

ANNOTATIONS

Note: Many of the cases below were decided under the predecessor legislation. The two significant changes to the legislation are to replace the term "insane" with the term "not criminally responsible" and to replace the term "state of natural imbecility or has disease of the mind" with the term "mental disorder". However, "mental disorder" is defined in s. 2 as meaning a "disease of the mind" and so it is believed that much of the case-law decided under the predecessor legislation is applicable to the new provision.

Constitutional considerations – While the reverse onus infringes the presumption of innocence protected by s. 11(*d*) of the Charter, it is justified under s. 1: *R. v. Chaulk*, [1990] 3 S.C.R. 1303, 62 C.C.C. (3d) 193. Subsequent legal developments were not sufficient to justify lower courts in revisiting that conclusion on justification: *R. v. Ejigu* (2016), 340 C.C.C. (3d) 53 (B.C.S.C.).

General – In determining whether an accused has met the evidential burden necessary to leave the issue with the jury, the trial judge must assume the truth of the evidence that tends to support the defence and leave questions of reliability, credibility and weight to be determined by the jury. In this case, the trial judge erred in refusing to leave the defence of mental disorder on the basis that the defence psychiatrist's opinion had been based on facts recounted by the accused, that the evidence was contradicted by other psychiatrists and that the accused's testimony contained significant inconsistencies. It is not necessary that the relevant evidence be believed in order for the defence to succeed, as an accused is entitled to be acquitted on the basis of exculpatory evidence that the jury does not reject but either accepts or about which it is undecided: *R. v. Fontaine*, [2004] 1 S.C.R. 702, 183 C.C.C. (3d) 1, 18 C.R. (6th) 203.

A malfunctioning of the mind exclusively from the voluntary consumption of drugs is not a disease of the mind in the legal sense, since it is not a product of the individual's inherent psychological make-up but rather voluntary activity: *R. v. Bouchard-Lebrun*, [2011] 3 S.C.R. 575, 275 C.C.C. (3d) 145.

Meaning of "disease of the mind" – The term "disease of the mind" is a legal concept and it is therefore a question of law for the trial judge what mental conditions are included within the term. Any malfunctioning of the mind, or mental disturbance having its source primarily in some subjective condition or weakness internal to the accused (whether fully understood or not), may be a disease of the mind if it prevents the accused from knowing what he is doing, but transient disturbances of consciousness due to certain specific external factors do not fall within the concept. In particular, the ordinary stresses and disappointments of life, though they may bring about malfunctioning of the mind such as a dissociative state, do not constitute an external cause constituting an explanation for a malfunctioning of the mind which takes it out of the category of a disease of the mind and could not form the basis of a defence of non-insane automatism: *R. v. Rabey* (1977), 37 C.C.C. (2d) 461, 79 D.L.R. (3d) 414 (Ont. C.A.), affd [1980] 2 S.C.R. 513, 54 C.C.C. (2d) 1, 15 C.R. (3d) 225 (4:3). [Also see *R. v. Stone*, *infra*, under "Automatism".]

The term "disease of the mind" embraces any illness, disorder or abnormal condition which impairs the human mind and its functioning, excluding, however, self-induced states caused by alcohol or drugs, as well as transitory mental states such as hysteria or concussion. Thus personality disorders may constitute disease of the mind. The word "appreciates" imports a requirement beyond mere knowledge of the physical quality of the act and requires a capacity to apprehend the nature of the act and its consequences: *R. v. Cooper*, [1980] 1 S.C.R. 1149, 51 C.C.C. (2d) 129, 13 C.R. (3d) 97 and 18 C.R. (3d) 138 (5:2), where the decisions of the Ontario Court of Appeal in *R. v. Rabey, supra*, and *R. v. Simpson* (1977), 35 C.C.C. (2d) 337, 77 D.L.R. (3d) 507, were referred to with approval.

The syndrome known as delirium tremens, brought about by prolonged and chronic, albeit voluntary, consumption of alcohol, is a "disease of the mind". Delirium tremens is not self-induced in the way of drunkenness, but is the supervening result of abuse of alcohol over an extended period of time: *R. v. Malcolm* (1989), 50 C.C.C. (3d) 172 (Man. C.A.).

"Mental disorder" includes mental retardation: *R. v. R. (M.S.)* (1996), 112 C.C.C. (3d) 406 (Ont. Ct. (Gen. Div.)).

A mental disorder may still constitute a disease of the mind even if it is not prone to recur. "Disease of the mind" includes any medically recognized mental disorder or mental illness that could render a person incapable of appreciating the nature and quality of his act, or of knowing that it is wrong, save for transient mental disturbances caused by external factors such as violence or drugs: *R. v. Oakley* (1986), 24 C.C.C. (3d) 351 (Ont. C.A.).

Automatism – The determination of whether non-insane [more properly non-mental disorder] automatism should be left to the jury involves a two-step procedure. The trial judge must first determine whether the accused has satisfied the evidentiary burden for the defence of automatism and then whether the condition alleged by the accused is mental disorder or non-mental disorder automatism. Since the law presumes that people act voluntarily, the accused bears the legal burden of proving involuntariness by reason of automatism on a balance of probabilities. Accordingly, to meet the evidentiary burden, the accused must satisfy the trial judge that there is evidence upon which a properly instructed jury could find that the accused acted involuntarily on a balance of probabilities. To meet this burden the accused must claim that he acted involuntarily at the relevant time and this assertion must be confirmed by expert psychiatric evidence. With respect to automatism alleged to have been caused by a psychological blow, the defence will generally have to provide evidence of a trigger equivalent to a "shock" to satisfy the evidentiary burden. Other evidence that should be considered is the accused's appearance at the time, a history of similar involuntary conduct and whether there was a motive for the crime. If the crime is explicable without reference to the alleged automatism, this will generally tell against the existence of automatism. Assuming the defence can meet the first step, the judge must then consider the question of mixed law and fact as to whether the condition the accused claims to have suffered from satisfied the legal test for disease of the mind. In making this determination the trial judge starts from the proposition that the condition the accused claims to have suffered from is a disease of the mind and that therefore only the defence of mental disorder under this section should be put to the jury. In making the mental disorder determination the trial judge should consider a number of factors. One factor is the internal cause factor, namely, that the defence of non-mental disorder automatism is limited to cases involving triggers that a normal person, similarly situated, would find extremely shocking. Involuntariness caused by any less severe shock or mere stress is presumed to be triggered by a factor internal to the accused and thus a disease of the mind. Another factor is whether the accused presents a recurring danger to the public. If so, this favours a finding that a mental disorder is involved. In considering this factor the judge will take into account the accused's psychiatric history and the likelihood that the trigger will recur. There may as well be other policy factors: *R. v. Stone*, [1999] 2 S.C.R. 290, 134 C.C.C. (3d) 353. As to the burden on the accused to read sufficient evidence to require that the automatism defence be left to the jury, also see *R. v. Fontaine*, *supra*.

In charging the jury on non-mental disorder automatism, the trial judge should thoroughly review the serious policy factors that surround automatism including concerns about feignability and the repute of the administration of justice. The judge should also refer specifically to evidence relevant to the issue of involuntariness: *R. v. Stone*, *supra*.

Where the accused is in a state of automatism to which a disease of the mind is a contributing factor then his defence is insanity, not non-insane automatism, even if there were other factors such as consumption of alcohol and a physical illness which were contributing factors: *R. v. Revelle* (1979), 48 C.C.C. (2d) 267 (Ont. C.A.), affd [1981] 1 S.C.R. 576, 61 C.C.C. (2d) 575 (9:0).

Except in the rarest of cases, the trial judge should not leave both mental disorder and non-mental disorder automatism with the jury: *R. v. Alexander* (2015), 330 C.C.C. (3d) 417 (B.C.C.A.), leave to appeal to S.C.C. refused [2016] S.C.C.A. No. 40.

Automatism is not a defence but rather a denial of the commission of the *actus reus* of the crime. A person who is unable to decide whether to perform an act and unable to control the performance of the act cannot be said to have committed the act. If an accused's automatism is rooted in a mental disorder, the accused should be found not criminally responsible on account of mental disorder rather than acquitted. Such a finding would require a post-verdict disposition hearing before either the trial judge or review board. The distinction between non-mental disorder automatism and mental disorder automatism depends on whether the automatistic state is the product of a mental disorder as defined within s. 2 of the *Criminal Code*. In deciding whether to characterize the automatism as "mental disorder" or "non-mental disorder", the trial judge has to assess the danger that the accused's condition poses to the public, including not only the risk of further violence while in an automatistic state, but also the risk of recurrence of the factors or events that triggered that state. In this case, the hereditary nature of the parasomnia and the accused's history of sexomania were particularly relevant to the likelihood of the recurrence of triggering circumstances, which support the characterization of the accused's condition as a mental disorder: *R. v. Luedecke* (2008), 236 C.C.C. (3d) 317 (Ont. C.A.).

Meaning of "appreciating" and "knowing" – In using the two words "appreciating" and "knowing", Parliament clearly intended that different tests be used. The verb "know" has a positive connotation requiring a base awareness while "appreciate" involves a further step of analysis of knowledge or experience: *R. v. Barnier*, [1980] 1 S.C.R. 1124, 51 C.C.C. (2d) 193 (7:0), affg 37 C.C.C. (2d) 508 (B.C.C.A.). And see: *R. v. Baltzer* (1979), 27 C.C.C. (2d) 118 (N.S.S.C. App. Div.), and *R. v. Simpson, infra*.

Appreciation of the nature and quality of the act refers to an incapacity by reason of disease of the mind to appreciate the physical consequences of the act. Thus, an accused could not rely on this branch of the insanity defence where he was aware that he was killing the victim and knew that killing was a crime, although he believed that the victim was "Satan" and that in killing the deceased he was acting on divine orders. On the other hand, an accused, who by reason of disease of the mind was acting under such a delusion, would be entitled to a finding of insanity on the basis that he did not know the act was wrong in view of the expanded definition given the term "wrong" in *R. v. Chaulk, infra: R. v. Landry*, [1991] 1 S.C.R. 99, 62 C.C.C. (3d) 117 (7:0).

An accused's personal sense of justifiability is never sufficient to ground the defence. Rather, the accused's mental disorder must also render him or her incapable of knowing that the act in question is morally wrong as measured against societal standards, and therefore incapable of making the choice to act in accordance with those standards: *R. v. Campione* (2015), 321 C.C.C. (3d) 63 (Ont. C.A.).

Although personality disorders or psychopathic personalities are capable of constituting a disease of the mind the defence of insanity is not made out where the accused has the necessary understanding of the nature, character and consequences of the act, but merely lacks appropriate feelings for the victim or lacks feelings of remorse or guilt for what he has done, even though such lack of feeling stems from disease of the mind: *R. v. Simpson* (1977), 35 C.C.C. (2d) 337 (Ont. C.A.).

This part of the judgment in *R. v. Simpson, supra*, was approved in *R. v. Kjeldsen*, [1981] 2 S.C.R. 617, 64 C.C.C. (2d) 161 (9:0).

A delusion which renders the accused incapable of appreciating that the penal sanctions attaching to the commission of the crime are applicable to him does not render him incapable of appreciating the nature and quality of the act within the meaning of this section so as to give rise to the insanity defence. While the concept of appreciating the nature and quality of an act requires an understanding of the consequences of the act, this refers to the physical consequences of the act: *R. v. Abbey*, [1982] 2 S.C.R. 24, 68 C.C.C. (2d) 394 (9:0).

This provision has no application where the accused understands society's views as to what is right and wrong but because of a delusion chooses to act in contravention of society's view: *R. v. W. (J.M.)* (1998), 123 C.C.C. (3d) 245 (B.C.C.A.).

In *R. v. Wolfson*, [1965] 3 C.C.C. 304 (Alta. S.C. App. Div.), it was held that evidence of an irresistible impulse is not, by itself, enough to support a finding of insanity under this section.

Meaning of "wrong" – The term "wrong" in subsec. (2) means "morally wrong" and not simply "legally wrong". The court must determine whether the accused, because of a disease of the mind, was rendered incapable of knowing that the act committed was something that he ought not to have done. Thus, the inquiry cannot terminate with the discovery that the accused knew that the act was contrary to the formal law. A person may know that the act was contrary to law and yet, by reason of a disease of the mind, be incapable of knowing that the act is morally wrong in the circumstances according to the moral standards of society: *R. v. Chaulk*, [1990] 3 S.C.R. 1303, 62 C.C.C. (3d) 193.

The inquiry under this section focuses not on a general capacity to know right from wrong, but rather on the ability to know that a particular act was wrong in the cirumstances. The accused must not only possess the intellectual ability to know right from wrong in an abstract sense but must possess the ability to apply that knowledge in a rational way to the alleged criminal act. The crux of the inquiry is whether the accused lacks the capacity to rationally decide whether the act is right or wrong and hence to make a rational choice of whether to do it or not. The accused would not be criminally responsible where, by reason of delusions, he perceives an act which is wrong as right or justifiable, and the disordered condition of his mind deprives the accused of the ability to rationally evaluate what he is doing. It is not necessary to show that, if the delusions were true, a specific defence such as self-defence would also apply: *R. v. Oommen*, [1994] 2 S.C.R. 507, 91 C.C.C. (3d) 8.

Mental illness short of insanity – Our *Criminal Code* does not recognize the defence of diminished responsibility and even though the accused may have been ill at the time of the offence he is technically sane if he was able to distinguish between right and wrong: *R. v. Chartrand*, [1977] 1 S.C.R. 314, 26 C.C.C. (2d) 417 (8:0).

Nevertheless where the accused is charged with an offence which requires proof of a specific intent, evidence that the accused was suffering from mental illness or mental disorder, though falling short of proof of insanity, may negative the requisite specific intent, as in the case of murder reduce the charge to manslaughter: *R. v. Baltzer, supra*. And to the same effect: *R. v. Hilton* (1977), 34 C.C.C. (2d) 206 (Ont. C.A.); *R. v. Meloche* (1975), 34 C.C.C. (2d) 184 (Que. C.A.); *R. v. Lechasseur* (1977), 38 C.C.C. (2d) 319 (Que. C.A.); *R. v. Browning* (1976), 34 C.C.C. (2d) 200 (Ont. C.A.); *R. v. Leblanc* (1991), 4 C.R. (4th) 98, [1991] R.J.Q. 686 (C.A.); *R. v. Wright* (1979), 48 C.C.C. (2d) 334, 11 C.R. (3d) 257 (Alta. S.C. App. Div.), leave to appeal to S.C.C. refused 48 C.C.C. (2d) 334*n*; *R. v. Bailey* (1996), 111 C.C.C. (3d) 122, 133 W.A.C. 105 (B.C.C.A.).

Where evidence is adduced in support of a defence of insanity to a charge of first degree murder, the jury is to be directed to first consider that defence. If that defence fails, then the jury should consider all the evidence in the case, including relevant evidence which was adduced in support of the insanity defence to determine whether the accused had the relevant intent for murder and, if so, whether the killing was planned and deliberate: *R. v. Allard* (1990), 57 C.C.C. (3d) 397, 78 C.R. (3d) 228 (Que. C.A.).

Procedure – Where the accused seeks to introduce evidence to support a defence of automatism, whether insane or non-insane automatism, a *voir dire* should not be resorted to where the evidence is relevant and not subject to rejection on any recognized legal ground. The evidence should be led before the jury and at the end of the case it will be for the trial judge to instruct the jury whether there is any evidence which will support the particular defence: *R. v. Sproule* (1975), 26 C.C.C. (2d) 92 (Ont. C.A.).

The accused may raise the defence of insanity at any time during the trial and in fact may raise the defence after the trier of fact has found the accused guilty but prior to conviction. If, during the course of the trial, prior to the finding of guilt, evidence is led which does not satisfy the trier of fact of insanity under this section, such evidence may nevertheless be considered on the issue of whether the accused had the requisite *mens rea*: *R. v. Swain*, [1991] 1 S.C.R. 933, 63 C.C.C. (3d) 481 (6:1).

Section 650(3) which gives the accused the right "after the close of the case for the prosecution" to make full answer and defence must apply to evidence given by way of rebuttal as well as to that given during the Crown's case in chief. Accordingly, it was held in *R. v. Ewert* (1989), 52 C.C.C. (3d) 280 (B.C.C.A.), that the rules regarding the permissible scope of surrebuttal must be applied liberally in favour of the accused, where the accused relied on the defence of insanity and evidence to rebut that defence was first given by the Crown in rebuttal.

Where the trial judge is of the view that there is no evidence to support the defence of insanity, he should so inform counsel prior to their making their jury addresses: *R. v. Charest* (1990), 57 C.C.C. (3d) 312 (Que. C.A.).

Even where the Crown has notice that the accused intends to rely on the insanity defence as provided in this section, the Crown need not adduce evidence in chief to challenge that defence. The Crown was therefore properly permitted to adduce its evidence with respect to sanity in rebuttal. The accused suffered no prejudice as he was given the opportunity for surrebuttal: *R. v. Chaulk, supra*.

Expert evidence – The placing of the crucial question of the accused's state of mind to the expert witness, while ordinarily framed as a hypothetical question may, if the facts are uncontradicted be put in direct form. This discretion of the trial judge was confirmed in *R. v. Bleta*, [1964] S.C.R. 561, [1965] 1 C.C.C. 1 (5:0), *per* Ritchie J., at p. 6 C.C.C., p. 198 C.R.: "Provided that the questions are so phrased as to make clear what the evidence is on which an expert is being asked to found his conclusion, the failure of counsel to put such questions in hypothetical form does not of itself make the answers inadmissible. It is within the competence of the trial judge in any case to insist upon the foundation for the expert opinion being laid by way of hypothetical question if he feels this to be the best way in which he can be assured of the matter being fully understood by the jury, but this does not, in my opinion, mean that the judge is necessarily precluded in the exercise of his discretion in the conduct of the trial from permitting the expert's answer to go before the jury if the nature and foundation of his opinion has been clearly indicated by other means."

While an expert opinion based on second-hand evidence is admissible, if relevant, the facts asserted in this second-hand evidence are not admissible for their truth. Thus, while medical experts are entitled to take into consideration all possible information in forming their opinions, "this in no way removes from the party tendering such evidence the obligation of establishing, through properly admissible evidence, the factual basis on which such opinions are based." *R. v. Abbey, supra.*

Provided there is some admissible evidence to establish the foundation for the expert opinion, a trial judge cannot subsequently instruct the jury to completely ignore the testimony. Where the factual basis of an expert opinion is a mixture of admissible and second-hand (hearsay) evidence the duty of the trial judge is to caution the jury that the weight attributable to the expert testimony is directly related to the amount and quality of admissible evidence on which the opinion depends: *R. v. Lavallee*, [1990] 1 S.C.R. 852, 55 C.C.C. (3d) 97 (7:0). See also *R. v. Skrzydlewski* (1995), 103 C.C.C. (3d) 467 (Ont. C.A.).

On the other hand, not all "second-hand" evidence is hearsay and thus, statements of a preposterous nature by an accused may be relevant to the issue of insanity and may be original evidence on that issue. For example, utterances by the accused manifesting a delusion or hallucination are not used to prove any fact asserted in them, but as circumstantial evidence to support an inference that the accused suffers from delusions or hallucinations. While such statements may be feigned, whether they indicate an actual mental state must be determined by the court, usually with the assistance of experts: *R. v. Kirkby* (1985), 21 C.C.C. (3d) 31 (Ont. C.A.), leave to appeal to S.C.C. refused [1986] 2 S.C.R. vii.

An expert may be cross-examined to determine what the expert considered relevant, whether there are matters relevant that were not considered and whether the expert might have arrived at his conclusion as a result of considerations irrelevant to his particular expertise. Since an expert cannot take into account facts that are not subject to his professional expert assessment, he cannot be cross-examined and asked to take such facts into account. Further, it is not open to the cross-examiner or examiner to put as a fact or even a hypothetical fact, that which is not and will not become part of the case as admissible evidence: *R. v. Howard*, [1989] 1 S.C.R. 1337, 48 C.C.C. (3d) 38 (3:1).

Where counsel requires the services of an expert in order to assist him in preparing the defence, communications between the accused and the expert are covered by solicitor-client privilege. There is no requirement that counsel be present during the examination. Where defence counsel, however, subsequently calls the expert, he may be required to disclose his communications with the accused. This is because the accused, by calling as a witness in his defence a psychiatrist, whose opinion was based at least in part on what the accused has confided in him, thereby waived privilege: *R. v. Perron* (1990), 54 C.C.C. (3d) 108 (Que. C.A.).

Where statements by the accused are adduced through cross-examination of defence experts or through examination of experts retained by the Crown solely for their bearing on the expert opinion and not as evidence of their truth on which the jury could act independently, then no issue of voluntariness arises: *R. v. Stevenson* (1990), 58 C.C.C. (3d) 464 (Ont. C.A.).

Also see notes under s. 150.1 re expert evidence.

Confession of "insane" accused – While the correct test for admissibility of the confession of an insane accused may be framed *per R. v. Ward*, [1979] 2 S.C.R. 30, 44 C.C.C. (2d) 498, as to whether it represents the "operating mind" of the accused, this is not the only word formula for testing the admissibility of an insane accused's statements to the police. Thus in *R. v. Nagotcha*, [1980] 1 S.C.R. 714, 51 C.C.C. (2d) 353 (9:0), the trial judge's ruling admitting the statements was upheld where he found that the accused, who at the time of the making of the statements was a paranoid schizophrenic and unfit to stand trial, was not "so devoid of rationality and understanding, or so replete with psychotic delusions that his uttered words could not be fairly be said to be his statements at all". Also see: *R. v. Whittle*, [1994] 2 S.C.R. 914, 92 C.C.C. (3d) 11, noted under s. 10 of the Charter, *infra.*

Adverse inference from failure to submit to examination – Where the accused relies on the defence of insanity, although he is not required to submit to psychiatric examination by a psychiatrist retained by the Crown, evidence of such refusal is admissible and an inference adverse to the accused may be drawn from such refusal: *R. v. Sweeney (No. 2)* (1977), 35 C.C.C. (2d) 245 (Ont. C.A.).

Further, the drawing of the adverse inference does not infringe the accused's right to fundamental justice under s. 7 of the Charter: *R. v. Worth* (1995), 98 C.C.C. (3d) 133 (Ont. C.A.), leave to appeal to S.C.C. refused 109 C.C.C. (3d) vi, application for extension of time granted per S.C.C. bull. 11/08/96, pp. 1877-8.

The defence decision to permit access to the accused by a Crown psychiatrist is imbued with a use limitation restricted by the character of the disclosure impelled by the principle that an accused, who raises an issue of diminished intent or mental disorder and refuses to see a Crown psychiatrist, may suffer an adverse inference. The Crown may not lead evidence from its psychiatrist in-chief to prove the identity of the accused by virtue of statements made by the accused during the interview: *R. v. Brunczlik* (1995), 103 C.C.C. (3d) 131 (Ont. Ct. (Gen. Div.)).

Where the accused, who relied on a defence of lack of specific intent, relied upon the evidence of psychiatrists retained by the defence, it was open to the Crown to adduce evidence that the accused refused to discuss details of the offence with a psychiatrist who examined the accused on behalf of the Crown. This evidence was admissible to explain why the Crown's expert's evidence may not have been as complete as that of the defence experts. The trial judge ought however to have instructed the jury that, in not discussing the circumstances of the offence, the accused was exercising his right to remain silent and that no inference of guilt could be drawn against him on this account: *R. v. Stevenson, supra.*

Right of Crown to adduce evidence of insanity – The Crown may lead evidence of insanity only in two circumstances: (1) where the accused's own defence, in the opinion of the trial judge, has somehow put the accused's mental capacity for criminal intent in issue, in which case the trial judge will be entitled to charge on the insanity defence; and (2) after the trier of fact had concluded that the accused was otherwise guilty of the offence charged. Where the Crown is required to adduce its evidence only after the accused has been found guilty, then the jury should be instructed that the Crown does so only because this is what the law requires, not because the Crown has chosen to conduct its case in this manner: *R. v. Swain, supra.*

COMPULSION BY THREATS.

17. A person who commits an offence under compulsion by threats of immediate death or bodily harm from a person who is present when the offence is committed is excused for committing the offence if the person believes that the threats will be carried out and if the person is not a party to a conspiracy or association whereby the person is subject

to compulsion, but this section does not apply where the offence that is committed is high treason or treason, murder, piracy, attempted murder, sexual assault, sexual assault with a weapon, threats to a third party or causing bodily harm, aggravated sexual assault, forcible abduction, hostage taking, robbery, assault with a weapon or causing bodily harm, aggravated assault, unlawfully causing bodily harm, arson or an offence under sections 280 to 283 (abduction and detention of young persons). R.S., c. C-34, s. 17; 1974-75-76, c. 105, s. 29; 1980-81-82-83, c. 125, s. 4; R.S.C. 1985, c. 27 (1st Supp.), s. 40(2).

CROSS-REFERENCES

The offences excepted from the defence created by this section are defined in the following sections: ss. 46, 47, high treason or treason; ss. 229, 230, murder; s. 74, piracy; s. 239, attempted murder; ss. 271 to 273, sexual assault; s. 279(2), forcible abduction; s. 279.1, hostage taking; s. 343, robbery; s. 267(*a*), assault with weapon; s. 267(*b*), assault causing bodily harm; s. 268, aggravated assault; s. 269, unlawfully causing bodily harm; s. 433, arson.

SYNOPSIS

Subject to the application of the Charter (see *R. v. Ruzic*, *infra*), this section defines the scope of the defence of *duress* as it affects those who personally commit an offence. For reasons of public policy many *serious offences involving personal violence* (*e.g.*, murder, sexual assault) or threats to public safety (*e.g.*, arson, high treason) are exempted from the operation of this section and therefore duress will afford *no defence* to a *principal* charged with the listed offences. Cases have held that a *party may rely* on the defence of duress, notwithstanding that they were a party to one of the exempted offences listed in s. 17.

ANNOTATIONS

Constitutional Considerations – The requirements of immediacy (threat of immediate death or bodily harm) and presence (threat from a person who is present when the offence is committed) infringe s. 7 of the *Canadian Charter of Rights and Freedoms* and must be struck down as unconstitutional. It would seem that an accused, even a principal offender, may rely upon the common law defence of duress: *R. v. Ruzic*, [2001] 1 S.C.R. 687, 153 C.C.C. (3d) 1.

The exclusion of robbery and assault with a weapon from the statutory defence of duress is contrary to s. 7 of the Charter because it does not comply with the requirement of moral voluntariness recognized in *Ruzic*, *supra*. By way of remedy, the court severed the words "robbery" and "assault with a weapon" from s. 17: *R. v. Allen* (2014), 318 C.C.C. (3d) 335 (Sask. Q.B.).

In *R. v. Aravena* (2015), 323 C.C.C. (3d) 54 (Ont. C.A.), leave to appeal to S.C.C. refused 2016 CarswellOnt 5410, the constitutionality of the murder exception to the duress defence in s. 17 was not before the court. However, as a result of its analysis of the common law defence as applied to parties, the court observed that, subject to any s. 1 argument the Crown might advance justifying the exception as it applies to perpetrators, the exception must be found unconstitutional.

However, see *R. v. Willis* (2016), 344 C.C.C. (3d) 443 (Man. C.A.), leave to appeal to S.C.C. refused 2017 CarswellMan 192, in which the court expressly rejected *Aravena*, holding that s. 17 is consistent with the principles of fundamental justice because it can never be proportionate to take another life to avoid a mere threat to one's own.

Elements of statutory defence – The statutory defence of duress applies to principals and the common law to parties. Nonetheless, both forms share the following common elements: there must be an explicit or implicit threat of present or future death or bodily harm (this threat can be directed at the accused or a third party); the accused must reasonably believe that the threat will be carried out; there must be no safe avenue of escape, evaluated on a modified objective standard; there must be a close temporal connection between the threat and the harm threatened; there must be proportionality between the harm threatened and the harm inflicted by the accused, also evaluated on a modified objective standard; and the accused cannot be a party to a conspiracy or association whereby he or she is subject to compulsion and actually knew that threats and coercion to commit an offence were a possible result of this criminal activity, conspiracy or association: *R. v. Ryan*, [2013] 1 S.C.R. 14, 290 C.C.C. (3d) 477.

There was no evidence to support a defence of duress to a charge of perjury where the accused could have informed the police of the threats he received prior to testifying and thus obtained police protection. A threat of death, from which the accused could have easily escaped and that he could have rendered unenforceable when he gave his evidence, does not give rise to the defence under this section: *R. v. Hebert*, [1989] 1 S.C.R. 233, 49 C.C.C. (3d) 59, affg 3 Q.A.C. 251, C.C.C. *loc. cit.* (C.A.).

The defence of duress to a charge of perjury was rejected where although the persons who threatened the accused were present in court at the time the false testimony was given the accused had the opportunity to seek official protection: *R. v. Falkenberg* (1973), 13 C.C.C. (2d) 562 (Ont. Co. Ct.), revd on other grounds 16 C.C.C. (2d) 525 (C.A.). *Cf. R. v. Hudson and Taylor* (1971), 56 Cr. App. R. 1 (C.A.).

The offence of "forcible abduction" is not the equivalent of kidnapping. The latter offence is defined by s. 279 and therefore this section does offer a defence to a person charged with kidnapping. However, a threat that the accused's own children would be kidnapped and taken to another country is not a threat of death of grievous bodily harm so as to give the accused a defence under this section: *R. v. Robins* (1982), 66 C.C.C. (2d) 550 (Que. C.A.).

Availability of common law defence – The common law defence of duress is available to a party to an offence such as murder or robbery. While that defence, if made out, excuses the commission of the offence, the existence of threats does not negate the *mens rea* of the party: *R. v. Hibbert*, [1995] 2 S.C.R. 973, 99 C.C.C. (3d) 193; *R. v. Paquette*, [1977] 2 S.C.R. 189, 30 C.C.C. (2d) 417.

The common law defence remains available to persons charged as parties to murder. Duress is an excuse, not a justification. The availability of the defence cannot be settled by giving automatic priority to the right to life of the victim over that of an accused. Instead, the right to life of the victim must be factored into the proportionality assessment as part of the broader moral involuntariness inquiry: *R. v. Aravena* (2015), 323 C.C.C. (3d) 54 (Ont. C.A.), leave to appeal to S.C.C. refused 2016 CarswellOnt 5410.

The common law defence of duress is similar to the defence of necessity and, like necessity, can only be invoked where there is no legal way out of the situation of duress the accused faces. Accordingly, the defence is unavailable if a safe avenue of escape was available to the accused. The question of whether or not a safe avenue of escape existed is to be determined according to an objective standard. When considering the perceptions of a reasonable person, however, the personal circumstances of the accused are relevant and important and should be taken into account: *R. v. Hibbert, supra.*

Where the accused relies upon the common law defence of duress, the trial judge should instruct the jury on *inter alia* the need for a close temporal connection between the threat and the harm threatened. The jury should also be instructed on the need for the application of an objective-subjective assessment of whether there was an obvious safe avenue of escape. However, the law does not require an accused to seek the official protection of the police in all cases before the defence can succeed. The objective requirement must take into consideration the special circumstances where the accused found herself as well as her perception of them. Once the duress defence has been raised and there is some evidence to support it, the burden is on the Crown to show beyond a reasonable doubt that the accused did not act under duress: *R. v. Ruzic, supra.*

While threat of death or serious physical injury is necessary that threat may be express or implied, provided that where an implied threat is relied upon to constitute duress there must be evidence from the acts, conduct or words of the person alleged to have made the threat which could reasonably be construed as a threat of the required kind. *R. v. Mena* (1987), 34 C.C.C. (3d) 304 (Ont. C.A.).

The proviso in this section that the defence is unavailable where the accused was party to a conspiracy whereby he was subject to compulsion also exists at common law and therefore participation in such a conspiracy would similarly prevent an accused from relying on the common law duress defence: *R. v. Logan* (1988), 46 C.C.C. (3d) 354 (Ont. C.A.), affd on other grounds [1990] 2 S.C.R. 731, 58 C.C.C. (3d) 391.

The defence of duress is unavailable where the accused voluntarily joined a criminal organization that he knew might pressure him to engage in criminal acts: *R. v. Li* (2002), 162 C.C.C. (3d) 360 (Ont. C.A.).

The defence of duress is only available when a person commits an offence while under compulsion of a threat made for the purpose of compelling him or her to commit the offence. Accordingly, duress was not available to a battered spouse who tried to hire a hit man to kill her abusive husband: *R. v. Ryan* (2013), 290 C.C.C. (3d) 477 (S.C.C.).

COMPULSION OF SPOUSE.

18. No presumption arises that a married person who commits an offence does so under compulsion by reason only that the offence is committed in the presence of the spouse of that married person. R.S., c. C-34, s. 18; 1980-81-82-83, c. 125, s. 4.

CROSS-REFERENCES

The defence of compulsion by threats is found in s. 17.

SYNOPSIS

At common law there was an outdated presumption that a woman who committed an offence in the presence of her husband was presumed to have been coerced by him. This section abolishes this presumption.

ANNOTATIONS

This section has abolished the antiquated common law defence of marital coercion: *R. v. Robins* (1982), 66 C.C.C. (2d) 550 (Que. C.A.).

IGNORANCE OF THE LAW.

19. Ignorance of the law by a person who commits an offence is not an excuse for committing that offence. R.S., c. C-34, s. 19.

CROSS-REFERENCES

Notwithstanding the apparent breadth of this section, certain offences by their definition allow for a colour of right defence which would include at least mistake as to the civil law, for example: s. 322, theft; s. 429, mischief and arson; s. 72, forcible entry.

SYNOPSIS

This provision codifies the common law rule that *ignorance of the law is no excuse* for the commission of a criminal offence. This section does not affect the common law defence of mistake of fact which is preserved by s. 8. In addition, there may be a defence of officially induced error if an accused relies upon incorrect legal advice from governmental officials but the scope of this defence remains uncertain.

ANNOTATIONS

Ignorance of the law – By virtue of this section, ignorance, whether of the existence of the law or of its meaning, scope or application, is no defence. Thus, an accused's ignorance that a certain drug had been added to [former] Sch. H to the *Food and Drugs Act*, R.S.C. 1985, c. F-27, by regulation which was published in the *Canada Gazette,* was no defence to a charge of trafficking in that drug contrary to [former] s. 48(1) of that Act: *R. v. Molis*, [1980] 2 S.C.R. 356, 55 C.C.C. (2d) 558 (7:0).

Where, on the trial for a provincial offence, the only possible defence an accused can put forward is his ignorance of the fact that his licence had been suspended by the provisions of the provincial statute, which constitutes a mistake of law and is therefore not available as a defence, the accused is effectively denied the defence of due diligence. In those circumstances, the offence must be characterized as absolute liability: *R. v. Pontes*, [1995] 3 S.C.R. 44, 100 C.C.C. (3d) 353.

Officially induced error – By virtue of this section an accused's honest belief based on reasonable inquiries of customs authorities that certain gambling devices were legal in Canada is no defence to a charge contrary to s. 202(1)(*b*) of the *Criminal Code*: *R. v. Potter* (1978), 39 C.C.C. (2d) 538 (P.E.I.S.C.).

However, in *R. v. MacDougall*, [1982] 2 S.C.R. 605, 1 C.C.C. (3d) 65 (7:0), the court in dealing with a provincial offence referred to this section as "no more than a codification of the common law rule" and applicable to the provincial prosecution. Ritchie J., for the court then continued: "It is not difficult to envisage a situation in which an offence could be committed under mistake of law arising because of, and therefore induced by, "officially induced error' and if there was evidence in the present case to support such a situation existing it might well be an appropriate vehicle for applying the reasoning adopted by Mr. Justice Macdonald". Macdonald J.A. had held at 60 C.C.C. (2d) 137, 46 N.S.R. (2d) 47 (C.A.), that officially induced error was a defence to the charge, in this case driving while suspended contrary to the *Motor Vehicle Act*, R.S.N.S. 1967, c. 191.

In *R. v. Cancoil Thermal Corp. and Parkinson* (1986), 27 C.C.C. (3d) 295, 52 C.R. (3d) 188 (Ont. C.A.), the court considered officially induced error as a defence to a provincial offence. It was held that the defence is available as a defence to a "regulatory" offence where the accused reasonably relied upon the erroneous legal opinion or advice of an official who is responsible for the administration or enforcement of the particular law.

An accused must demonstrate the objective reasonableness of the advice given and the reliance on the advice. The issue must be considered from the perspective of a reasonable person in a situation similar to that of the accused: *Lévis (City) v. Tétreault; Lévis (City) v. 2629-4470 Québec Inc.*, [2006] 1 S.C.R. 420, 207 C.C.C. (3d) 1.

Mistake of fact – Unless the statute otherwise provides, as in s. 150.1, a mistake of fact is made out if the belief is honestly, *i.e.*, genuinely held. The reasonableness or unreasonableness of the belief is merely evidence from which the trier of fact may determine whether the mistake was genuine: *R. v. Pappajohn*, [1980] 2 S.C.R. 120, 52 C.C.C. (2d) 481; *R. v. Rees*, [1956] 2 S.C.R. 640, 115 C.C.C. 1.

Closely related to the defence of mistake of fact is the concept of wilful blindness. The doctrine of wilful blindness is "justified by the accused's fault in deliberately failing to inquire when he knows there is reason for inquiry" and the defence of mistake will not be available if the accused's mistake or ignorance falls within this doctrine: *R. v. Sansregret*, [1985] 1 S.C.R. 570, 18 C.C.C. (3d) 223.

Where, on the facts as he believed them to be, the accused was in fact committing a more serious offence than the offence with which he is charged then he is properly convicted of the offence, the *actus reus*, of which he committed: *R. v. Ladue*, [1965] 4 C.C.C. 264 (Y.T.C.A.).

Mistake of fact is available as a defence where the belief under which the accused claimed to have acted involved both fact and law. Mistakes of mixed fact and law were, for the purpose of the defence, considered mistakes of fact and not in conflict with this provision: *R. v. Manuel* (2008), 231 C.C.C. (3d) 468 (B.C.C.A.), leave to appeal to S.C.C. refused 233 C.C.C. (3d) vi.

A mistaken belief as to the type of narcotic being imported would not be a defence, but a mere belief by the accused that he was importing something illegal would not be sufficient *mens rea*: *R. v. Blondin* (1970), 2 C.C.C. (2d) 118 (B.C.C.A.).

On the other hand, the accused's mistake as to the nature of the drug in his possession is no defence provided that the drug is proscribed either by the [former] *Food and Drugs Act* or *Narcotic Control Act*: *R. v. Couture* (1976), 33 C.C.C. (2d) 74 (Ont. C.A.); *R. v. Futa* (1976), 31 C.C.C. (2d) 568 (B.C.C.A.).

It has been held that a provision of the Code [former s. 146, now repealed], which removed the defence of mistake of fact, was to that extent inconsistent with s. 7 of the *Charter of Rights and Freedoms* and that part of the provision was struck out: *R. v. Nguyen*, [1990] 2 S.C.R. 906, 59 C.C.C. (3d) 161 (5:2) [noted under the Charter, s. 7].

CERTAIN ACTS ON HOLIDAYS VALID.

20. A warrant or summons that is authorized by this Act or an appearance notice, promise to appear, undertaking or recognizance issued, given or entered into in accordance with Part XVI, XXI or XXVII may be issued, executed, given or entered into, as the case may be, on a holiday. R.S., c. C-34, s. 20; c. 2 (2nd Supp.), s. 2.

CROSS-REFERENCES

Definition of "holiday", see s. 35 of the *Interpretation Act*, R.S.C. 1985, c. I-21. Where the time limited for doing of a thing expires or falls on a holiday, the thing may be done on the day next following that is not a holiday . . . s. 26 of the *Interpretation Act*. The jury's verdict may be taken on Sunday or on a holiday, see s. 654.

SYNOPSIS

Warrants, summons and other forms of process created by the *Criminal Code* (*e.g.*, a promise to appear) may be validly issued, given or entered into on holidays. This section reverses a common law rule that prohibited the issuance and execution of process on holidays.

Parties to Offences

PARTIES TO OFFENCE / Common intention.

21. (1) Every one is a party to an offence who

(*a*) actually commits it;

(*b*) does or omits to do anything for the purpose of aiding any person to commit it; or

(*c*) abets any person in committing it.

(2) Where two or more persons form an intention in common to carry out an unlawful purpose and to assist each other therein and any one of them, in carrying out the common purpose, commits an offence, each of them who knew or ought to have known that the commission of the offence would be a probable consequence of carrying out the common purpose is a party to that offence. R.S., c. C-34, s. 21.

CROSS-REFERENCES

This section defines the liability of a person for the offence actually committed by the principal. Pursuant to s. 22, an accused is also rendered liable for offences committed by a person whom he counselled to commit an offence. Liability of an organization as a party to an offence is defined in ss. 22.1 and 22.2. A series of related provisions concern other forms of liability as follows: ss. 23, 463, accessory after the fact; ss. 24, 463, attempt; s. 465, conspiracy; s. 464, counselling offence not committed; s. 23.1, as to liability of party notwithstanding person who actually commits offence cannot be convicted.

Certain provisions deal specifically with the liability of a secondary party. For example: s. 46, treason; s. 50, failing to report treason or high treason; s. 54, assisting Canada Forces deserters; s. 56, assisting R.C.M.P. deserters; s. 129(*b*), failing to assist peace officer; s. 146, assisting escape; s. 147, permitting rescue of prisoner; s. 148, assisting prisoner of war; s. 160(2), compelling person to commit bestiality; s. 167, assisting in immoral performance; ss. 170, 171, procuring or permitting sexual activity of minors; s. 201, gaming house offences; s. 210, bawdy house offences; s. 212, procuring; s. 240, accessory after the fact to murder; s. 241, counselling or aiding suicide; s. 272, party to sexual assault.

SYNOPSIS

Section 21 sets out the *liability of principals and parties* to an offence.

Section 21(1)(*a*) holds an accused liable for the role as principal (or perpetrator) if the accused personally committed that offence.

Section 21(1)(*b*) makes an accused liable as a party for acts or omissions which are done *for the purpose* of aiding a principal to commit an offence. It is not sufficient that the acts had the effect of aiding in the commission of the offence – the purpose must be proven.

Section 21(1)(*c*) makes an accused liable as a party to the offence if that accused *abetted* the principal. Abetting simply means encouraging. Merely being present is not enough, unless presence is accompanied by such additional factors as the prior knowledge that the principal was going to commit the offence.

Section 21(2) extends the liability of the principal and parties beyond the wrongful act originally intended. It encompasses other offences which are committed while carrying out the original intention if the additional offence is a *probable consequence* of carrying out the original *unlawful purpose*. The key to establishing liability for the party is proving that the accused foresaw that the resulting offence was a probable consequence of carrying out the unlawful purpose agreed to. The phrase, referring to the liability of a party, "or ought to have known" has been the subject of attack under the *Canadian Charter of Rights and Freedoms*. See the notes below under heading "Application of Charter of Rights".

ANNOTATIONS

Subsection (1) / *Liability of party generally* – Mere presence at the scene of an offence is not sufficient to ground liability under this subsection. There must be more: encouragement of the principal; an act which facilitates the commission of the offence; or an act which tends to prevent or hinder interference with accomplishment of the criminal act. Passive acquiescence is not sufficient. Presence at the scene of an offence can be evidence of aiding and abetting only if accompanied by other factors such as prior knowledge of the principal's intention to commit the offence or attendance for the purpose of encouragement: *R. v. Dunlop and Sylvester*, [1979] 2 S.C.R. 881, 47 C.C.C. (2d) 93 (4:3). And see the earlier apellate court decisions in *R. v. Salajko*, [1970] 1 C.C.C. 352 (Ont. C.A.); *R. v. Clow* (1975), 25 C.C.C. (2d) 97, 8 Nfld. & P.E.I.R. 96 (P.E.I.S.C.), and *R. v. Black*, [1970] 4 C.C.C. 251, 10 C.R.N.S. 17 (B.C.C.A.).

Where there is evidence that the offence was committed by one or more persons then it is appropriate to direct the jury as to the application of this section even on the trial of a single accused and although the identity of the other person is unknown as is the precise part played by each person. However, where there is no evidence to support the proposition that more than one person was involved then it is misdirection to charge the jury on this section: *R. v. Sparrow* (1979), 51 C.C.C. (2d) 443 (Ont. C.A.); *R. v. Isaac*, [1984] 1 S.C.R. 74, 9 C.C.C. (3d) 289 (7:0); *R. v. Thatcher*, [1987] 1 S.C.R. 652, 32 C.C.C. (3d) 481 (7:0).

The words "actually commits it" in subsec. (1)(*a*) include the case of an accused who commits an offence by means of an innocent agent: *R. v. Berryman* (1990), 57 C.C.C. (3d) 375 (B.C.C.A.).

To render a person liable as a party to attempted murder under this subsection, it is not sufficient that it be shown merely that the accused knew the principal offender intended to commit some act of violence. While the party need not necessarily have knowledge of the details of the specific crime committed by the principal, he must have some knowledge of the essential nature of the offence committed by the principal. Thus, on a charge of attempted murder, the accused must know of the principal's intention to kill: *R. v. Adams* (1989), 49 C.C.C. (3d) 100 (Ont. C.A.).

The *actus reus* of aiding or abetting is doing or omitting to do something that assists or encourages the perpetrator to commit the offence. The concepts of aiding and abetting are distinct. Aiding means to assist or help the actor. To abet includes encouraging, instigating, promoting or procuring the crime to be committed. The *mens rea* reflected in "purpose" under para. (*b*) is synonymous with intention. The Crown must prove that the accused intended to assist the principal in the commission of the offence. However, the accused need not have desired that the offence be successfully committed. In order to have the intention to assist in the commission of an offence, the aider must know that the perpetrator intends to commit the crime although he or she does not need to know precisely how it will be committed. *R. v. Kirkness*, [1990] 3 S.C.R. 74, should not be read as requiring that the aider and abettor of a murder have the same *mens rea* as the actual killer. It is sufficient that, armed with the knowledge of the perpetrator's intention to commit the crime, the accused acts with the intention of assisting the perpetrator in its commission. Willful blindness can substitute for actual knowledge whenever knowledge is a component of *mens rea*. The doctrine of willful blindness imputes knowledge to an accused whose suspicion is aroused to the point where he or she sees the need for further inquiries but deliberately chooses not to make those inquiries. This is distinct from recklessness and involves no departure from the subjective inquiry into the accused's state of mind. Willful blindness is not simply a failure to inquire but deliberate ignorance: *R. v. Briscoe*, [2010] 1 S.C.R. 411, 253 C.C.C. (3d) 140.

A person may be convicted of manslaughter who aids and abets another in the offence of murder, where a reasonable person in all the circumstances would have appreciated that bodily harm was the foreseeable consequence of the dangerous act which was being undertaken; *R. v. Jackson*, [1993] 4 S.C.R. 573, 86 C.C.C. (3d) 385.

The term "for the purpose of" is essentially synonymous with "intention" and does not require proof that the accused also desired the commission of the offence: *R. v. Hibbert*, [1995] 2 S.C.R. 973, 99 C.C.C. (3d) 193.

The charge "or omitted to do anything which assisted the rape" is incorrect, it should be "or omitted to do anything for the purpose of aiding such person to commit the rape": *R. v. Cosgrove* (1975), 29 C.C.C. (2d) 169 (Ont. C.A.), leave to appeal to S.C.C. refused February 21, 1977.

A failure to act where there is a legal duty to do so can constitute an act of aiding and abetting. Any act or omission that occurs before or during the commission of the crime and which somehow and to some extent furthers, facilitates, promotes, assists or encourages the perpetrator in the commission of the crime will suffice, irrespective of any causative role in the commission of the crime: *R. v. Dooley* (2009), 249 C.C.C. (3d) 449 (Ont. C.A.), leave to appeal to S.C.C. refused [2010] 2 S.C.R. vi, 258 C.C.C. (3d) iv.

Self-induced intoxication is a defence to a charge of a general intent offence where the accused's liability depends on his being a party under para. (*b*) or para. (*c*): *R. v. Fraser* (1984), 13 C.C.C. (3d) 292 (B.C.C.A.).

The *mens rea* required is proof of actual knowledge or willful blindness but does not include recklessness: *R. v. Roach* (2004), 192 C.C.C. (3d) 557 (Ont. C.A.).

Abetting – "Abets" means to encourage and while it is common to speak of "aiding and abetting", the two concepts are not the same and either activity constitutes a sufficient basis of liability: *R. v. Meston* (1975), 28 C.C.C. (2d) 497 (Ont. C.A.).

Although subsec. (1)(*c*) does not provide that the words or actions must be for the purpose of abetting the person nevertheless the Crown must prove that the accused intended that the words or acts would encourage the principal: *R. v. Curran* (1977), 38 C.C.C. (2d) 151 (Alta. S.C. App. Div.), motion for leave to appeal to S.C.C. dismissed 20 N.R. 180*n*.

An accused who is present at the scene of the offence and who carries out no act to aid or encourage the commission of the offence may, nevertheless, be convicted as a party, if his purpose in failing to act was to aid in the commission of the offence and the accused was under a duty to act. Thus, a police officer who was the officer in charge of the lock-up could be convicted as a party to an assault committed by another officer on a prisoner. The accused was under a statutory and common law duty to protect the prisoner and his failure to act to prevent the assault may be found to have encouraged the commission of the offence: *R. v. Nixon* (1990), 57 C.C.C. (3d) 97 (B.C.C.A.).

Involvement of party undetermined – This section precludes a requirement of jury unanimity as to the particular nature of the accused's participation in the offence, whether he personally committed the offence or aided or abetted someone else to commit the offence: *R. v. Thatcher*, [1987] 1 S.C.R. 652, 32 C.C.C. (3d) 481.

Where, on a charge of murder, evidence shows that the accused acted in concert pursuant to a common motive, there is no requirement that the jury be instructed that if it could not decide which of the accused had administered the fatal beating to the deceased then all must be acquitted. In such circumstances, it is open to the jury to convict all accused as aiders or abettors although the extent of individual participation in the violence is unclear: *R. v. Wood* (1989), 51 C.C.C. (3d) 201 (Ont. C.A.).

Two persons may both be actual committers of an offence even though each has not performed every act which constitutes the *actus reus* of the offence. Where co-perpetrators engaged in a deadly assault, the Crown is not required to prove which attacker struck the fatal blow. For the purpose of subsec. (1)(*a*), agreement to carry out a common purpose is not necessary. The issue is whether there was an indication of common participation. In this case, where the death occurred in the context of a swarming of two individuals, it did not matter that each attacker did not lay a hand on each person assaulted: *R. v. Ball* (2011), 267 C.C.C. (3d) 532 (B.C.C.A.), leave to appeal to S.C.C. refused November 24, 2011.

Liability as a party to a conspiracy is limited to cases where the accused aids or abets the initial formation of the agreement, or aids or abets a new member to join a pre-existing agreement. Aiding or abetting the furtherance of the unlawful object does not establish aiding or abetting the principal with any element of the offence of conspiracy, and thus cannot ground party liability for conspiracy. However, where a person, with knowledge of a conspiracy, does or omits to do something for the purpose of furthering the unlawful object, with the knowledge and consent of one or more of the existing conspirators, this provides powerful circumstantial evidence from which membership in the conspiracy can be inferred: *R. v. F. (J.)*, [2013] 1 S.C.R. 565, 293 C.C.C. (3d) 377. See also: *R. v. Trieu* (2008), 429 A.R. 200 (C.A.). The broader approach to party liability proposed in *R. v. McNamara (No. 1)* (1981), 56 C.C.C. (2d) 193 (Ont. C.A.), affd [1985] 1 S.C.R. 662, *sub nom. Canadian Dredge & Dock Co. v. R.*, 19 C.C.C. (3d) 1, must now be read in light of *R. v. F. (J.)*, *supra*.

Relationship to corporate liability – The fact that the acts of an individual accused were at law those of his corporation, which was also charged, for the purpose of imposing liability on the corporation, does not prevent the conviction of the individual accused either as a principal or as a party under this subsection: *R. v. Fell* (1981), 64 C.C.C. (2d) 456, 131 D.L.R. (3d) 105 (Ont. C.A.).

Subsection (2) / *Application of Charter of Rights* – If the offence with which the accused is charged is one of the few for which s. 7 of the Charter requires a minimum degree of *mens rea,* then Parliament is precluded from providing for the conviction of a party to that offence on the basis of a degree of *mens rea* below the constitutionally required minimum. Thus, since it has been determined that as a constitutional requirement no one can be convicted of murder unless the Crown proves that the person had subjective foresight of the death of the victim, then a party cannot be convicted on the basis of any lesser *mens rea*. Similarly, the constitutionally required minimum for attempted murder is subjective foresight of the consequences and so the party to a charge of attempted murder cannot be convicted on any lesser *mens rea*. To the extent that subsec. (2) would allow for the conviction of a party to the offence of attempted murder or murder on the basis of objective foresight, it is of no force and effect. Accordingly, the words "or ought to have known" in subsec. (2) must be declared inoperative in such a case: *R. v. Logan*, [1990] 2 S.C.R. 731, 58 C.C.C. (3d) 391; *R. v. Rodney*, [1990] 2 S.C.R. 687, 58 C.C.C. (3d) 408.

Since there is no constitutional requirement of foresight of death for the offence of manslaughter, liability for that offence may be based on objective liability and the words "or ought to have known" are operative: *R. v. Jackson* (1991), 68 C.C.C. (3d) 385 (Ont. C.A.), affd [1993] 4 S.C.R. 573, 86 C.C.C. (3d) 385. *Contra*: *R. v. Haché* (2007), 227 C.C.C. (3d) 162 (N.B.C.A.).

Application of subsection generally – This subsection has no application where the unlawful purpose is the same as the offence charged. This subsection covers the case where, in the absence of aiding and abetting, a person may become a party to an offence committed by another which he knew or ought to have known was a probable consequence of carrying out the unlawful purpose: *R. v. Simpson and Ochs*, [1988] 1 S.C.R. 3, 38 C.C.C. (3d) 481.

This subsection may be resorted to on a possession charge. The liability of the accused is not confined to s. 4(3): *R. v. Zanini*, [1967] S.C.R. 715, [1968] 2 C.C.C. 1 (5:0), where it was also held that an accused may be convicted as a party to the offence committed by his companions notwithstanding the charge against them had been withdrawn.

In a "gang rape" situation it was held that the trial judge erred in leaving this subsection to the jury where there was no evidence that the accused, although present at the scene, were part of a plan to lure the victim there as part of the motorcycle gang's initiation rites: *R. v. Dunlop and Sylvester*, [1979] 2 S.C.R. 881, 47 C.C.C. (2d) 93 (4:3).

The expression "intention in common" means only that the party and principal must have in mind the same unlawful purpose and does not require proof of a mutuality of motives and desires between them: *R. v. Hibbert*, [1995] 2 S.C.R. 973, 99 C.C.C. (3d) 193.

Where three accused were charged with a murder committed in the course of a robbery, the judge was required to make clear to the jury that guilt could only be found under this section if each accused had actual foresight or knowledge that another accused would stab the deceased with intent to kill in carrying out the robbery: *R. v. Laliberty* (1997), 117 C.C.C. (3d) 97 (Ont. C.A.).

This provision is applicable to render a party guilty of second degree murder where the common unlawful purpose is assault and the accused knew that murder would be a probable consequence of carrying out that assault: *R. v. Rochon* (2003), 173 C.C.C. (3d) 321 (Ont. C.A.), leave to appeal to S.C.C. refused [2004] 3 S.C.R. xii, 188 C.C.C. (3d) vi; *R. v. Young* (2009), 246 C.C.C. (3d) 417 (Ont. C.A.), leave to appeal to S.C.C. refused 251 C.C.C. (3d) vii.

Liability of party for offence committed by principal – In *R. v. Jackson*, [1993] 4 S.C.R. 573, 86 C.C.C. (3d) 385, the court held that the wording of this subsection did not preclude the conviction of the party of manslaughter although the principal offender was convicted of murder. If the accused party did not foresee the probability of murder by the principal offender, but a reasonable person in all the circumstances would have foreseen at least a risk of harm to another as a result of carrying out the common intention, the party could be found guilty of manslaughter. Liability of manslaughter under this subsection does not depend upon proof that a reasonable person would have foreseen the risk of death. [Note: The holding that the party could be convicted of a different offence than the principal appears to have been based, in part, on the theory that the words "the offence" and "that offence" in subsec. (2) refer not only to the actual offence committed by the principal offender but encompass all included offences. The court had no occasion to consider the reverse situation where it is sought to render the party liable for a more serious offence than the principal. On this latter issue, see the earlier decision in *R. v. Hebert* (1986), 51 C.R. (3d) 264, 68 N.B.R. (2d) 379

(C.A.), leave to appeal to S.C.C. refused 76 N.B.R. (2d) 360*n*, 72 N.R. 79*n*, holding that where the principal was convicted of manslaughter the party could not be convicted of murder under this subsection.]

Liability for first degree murder under s. 231(5) can be made out pursuant to s. 21(2). While liability for first degree murder under s. 231(5) is premised on active participation in the murder, that liability flows from the participant's acts, not any additional mental element. Provided the participant's conduct was a substantial cause of the death and the other elements of s. 231(5) are made out including liability for murder and the underlying crime, the accused can be found guilty of murder as a party. Liability under s. 231(5) would also flow if the party, while not intending to kill the victim, knew that the principal offender would probably commit murder in carrying out the unlawful purpose. The participation by the party is the same whether the party intended to kill or merely knew that the principal offender would probably commit murder: *R. v. Ferrari* (2012), 287 C.C.C. (3d) 503 (Ont. C.A.).

An accused's conviction as a party to first degree murder where the principal was only convicted of second degree murder does not violate s. 7 of the *Charter of Rights and Freedoms*: *R. v. Huard* (2013), 302 C.C.C. (3d) 469 (Ont. C.A.), leave to appeal to S.C.C. refused 2014 CarswellOnt 4229.

Abandonment – For the defence of abandonment there must be evidence of timely and reasonable unequivocal notice by the accused to his co-accused of his intention to abandon the common criminal purposes before the crime was committed: *R. v. Miller and Cockriell*, [1977] 2 S.C.R. 680, 31 C.C.C. (2d) 177 (9:0).

Under either s. 21(1) or (2), the defence of abandonment requires: (1) an intention to abandon or withdraw from the unlawful purpose; (2) timely communication of abandonment or withdrawal from the person in question to those who wished to continue; (3) the communication served unequivocal notice upon those who wished to continue; and (4) that the accused took reasonable steps in the circumstances either to neutralize or otherwise cancel out the effects of his participation or to prevent the commission of the offence. There will be circumstances in which timely and unequivocal communication by the accused of his intention to abandon the unlawful purpose will be sufficient to neutralize the effects of his participation in the crime. But there will be other circumstances, primarily where a person has aided in the commission of the offence, in which it is hard to see how timely communication to the principal offender of the person's intention to withdraw from the unlawful purpose would, on its own, be considered reasonable and sufficient: *R. c. Gauthier*, [2013] 2 S.C.R. 403, 298 C.C.C. (3d) 277.

The accused was charged with another with murder. The evidence indicated that the co-accused sexually assaulted the victim after he and the accused broke into her house, and then the co-accused strangled and suffocated the victim. In the course of the strangulation the accused told the co-accused to stop as he would kill her. This statement to the co-accused constituted timely notice that the co-accused was from that point on acting on his own and that the accused was not a party to the strangulation and suffocation. Thus even if the accused could be considered a party to the earlier sexual assault by the time of the attempted strangulation he had clearly resiled from any agreement or arrangement with the co-accused and was not party to the suffocation of the victim: *R. v. Kirkness*, [1990] 3 S.C.R. 74, 60 C.C.C. (3d) 97 (5:2).

Evidence – In *R. v. Vetrovec; R. v. Gaja*, [1982] 1 S.C.R. 811, 67 C.C.C. (2d) 1 (9:0) (affirming *R. v. Vetrovec* (1980), 58 C.C.C. (2d) 537 (B.C.C.A.)), the Supreme Court of Canada had occasion to re-examine the question of the mandatory accomplice warning. The court held that it is no longer a rule of law that a trial judge must direct the jury that it is dangerous to act on the uncorroborated evidence of an accomplice. An accomplice is to be treated like any other witness testifying at a criminal trial and the judge's conduct if he chooses to give his opinion, is governed by the general rules. Thus a judge may properly consider that he should instruct the jury that in the circumstances the jury should, as a matter of prudence, look for evidence which confirms the story of such a witness. A clear and sharp warning to attract the attention of the juror to the risks of adopting, without more, the evidence of the witness, may be appropriate. The judge may, as well, properly illustrate from the evidence the kind of evidence which might be drawn upon by the juror in confirmation of the witness' testimony or some important part thereof. This common sense approach applies to other kinds of witnesses such as a disreputable witness of demonstrated moral lack or other situations where corroboration was required at common law. It does not of course apply where corroboration is required by statute as in s. 133.

In providing a *Vetrovec* warning, the court should draw the attention of the jury to the testimonial evidence requiring special scrutiny, explain why this evidence is subject to special scrutiny, caution the jury that it is dangerous to convict on unconfirmed evidence of this sort though the jury is entitled to do so if satisfied that the evidence is true, and instruct the jury that, in determining the veracity of the suspect evidence, it should look for evidence from another source tending to show that the untrustworthy witness is telling the truth as to the guilt of the accused. Not all evidence presented at trial is capable of confirming the testimony of an impugned witness. The attribute of independence defines the kind of evidence that is capable of constituting confirmation. Where evidence is tainted by connection to the *Vetrovec* witness, it cannot serve to confirm his or her testimony. While individual items of confirmatory evidence need not implicate the accused, when looked at in the context of the case as a whole, the items of confirmatory evidence should give comfort to the jury that the witness can be trusted in his assertion that the accused is the person who committed the offence. Confirmatory evidence must be capable of restoring the trier's faith in the relevant aspects of the witness' evidence. Accordingly, where the only issue in dispute is whether the accused committed the offence, the trier must be comforted that the impugned witness is telling the truth in that regard before convicting on the strength of the witness' evidence: *R. v. Khela*, [2009] 1 S.C.R. 104, 238 C.C.C. (3d) 489.

There is no requirement that the jury be instructed to make separate and distinct assessments of an accomplice's credibility as it related to each accused, as it is inevitable that the assessment of the overall credibility of the accomplice would be influenced by the totality of the evidence heard at trial, including that relating solely to one accused: *R. v. Rojas*, [2008] 3 S.C.R. 111, 236 C.C.C. (3d) 153.

Independent evidence to be confirmatory does not have to implicate the accused. The evidence should, however, be capable of restoring the trier's faith in the relevant aspects of the witness's evidence, although not necessarily a disputed aspect of the witness's evidence. Where a particular risk attaches to one critical element of the evidence of a disreputable witness, the trier of fact must be satisfied that the potentially unreliable evidence of the witness can be relied upon as truthful in that regard. Such a risk may arise where there is any basis in the record for suggesting that the unsupported evidence of an accomplice, though evidently truthful as to his own participation in the offence charged, is for any reason subject to particular caution as regards his implication of the accused: *R. v. Kehler*, [2004] 1 S.C.R. 328, 181 C.C.C. (3d) 1.

The trial judge has a discretion to determine whether the evidence of any witness is for some reason untrustworthy to such an extent that a warning to the jury is necessary. However, if a warning is given regarding a particular witness it is not the case that the trial judge must always go on to point out in detail evidence which is capable of corroborating that witnesses testimony. While an instruction of that nature may be given in tandem with the clear sharp warning, it is not a requirement in all cases. The extent to which the trial judge should refer to potentially corroborative evidence depends upon the circumstances of the case, although it is not required, nor would it be appropriate, that the potentially corroborative evidence be reviewed exhaustively: *R. v. Bevan*, [1993] 2 S.C.R. 599, 82 C.C.C. (3d) 310.

Also see *R. v. Brooks*, [2000] 1 S.C.R. 237, 141 C.C.C. (3d) 321, holding that the prosecutorial use of jailhouse informants generally calls for special caution. Whether a warning should be given for a particular witness depends upon the credibility of the witness and the importance of the evidence to the Crown's case. In this case, a majority of the court held that a *Vetrovec* warning should have been given in relation to the two informants to whom the accused allegedly confessed. (A different majority upheld the accused's conviction although no warning had been given.)

Collusion among "*Vetrovec*" witnesses does not necessarily prevent the evidence of one such witness from confirming the evidence of another. Whether the witness's evidence is so tainted by collusion that it loses its required independence and cannot reasonably be used as confirmation is a matter for the jury to decide: *R. v. Magno* (2015), 321 C.C.C. (3d) 554 (Ont. C.A.), leave to appeal to S.C.C. refused 2015 CarswellOnt 10830.

The so-called co-conspirators exception to the hearsay rule that acts or declarations done in furtherance of a common criminal design are admissible against all the parties thereto applies in all situations where one person is talking or acting on behalf of another and not just when the charge is one of conspiracy: *R. v. Koufis*, [1941] S.C.R. 481, 76 C.C.C. 161.

PERSON COUNSELLING OFFENCE / Idem / Definition of "counsel".

22. (1) Where a person counsels another person to be a party to an offence and that other person is afterwards a party to that offence, the person who counselled is a party to that offence, notwithstanding that the offence was committed in a way different from that which was counselled.

(2) Every one who counsels another person to be a party to an offence is a party to every offence that the other commits in consequence of the counselling that the person who counselled knew or ought to have known was likely to be committed in consequence of the counselling.

(3) For the purposes of this Act, "counsel" includes procure, solicit or incite. R.S., c. C-34, s. 22; R.S.C. 1985, c. 27 (1st Supp.), s. 7(1).

CROSS-REFERENCES

Section 464, where the offence counselled is not committed; s. 23.1, as to liability of accused notwithstanding, person counselled cannot be convicted of the offence; s. 53(*b*), inciting mutiny; s. 56(*a*), counselling R.C.M.P. member to desert or go absent without leave; s. 62(1)(*c*), counselling disloyalty, mutiny, etc., of member of military forces. As to terrorism offences, see s. 83.01(1), definition of "terrorist activity".

SYNOPSIS

This section, like s. 21, defines when a person is party to an offence as a result of counselling commission of an offence.

Subsection (3) provides a non-exhaustive definition of *counsel* stating that it includes procure, solicit or incite.

Subsection (1) requires proof that the person who was *counselled* by the accused *actually was a party to* the offence counselled. If that is established, the accused is a *party* to that offence, even if it is committed in a different way than that suggested by the accused.

Subsection (2) applies when the person counselled commits an additional offence as a consequence of committing the offence originally counselled by the accused. It must be shown that the accused (counsellor) *knew or ought to have known* that the additional offence was the consequence of counselling the original offence. If the liability of the counselled accused for the additional offence is based on proof of a subjective mental element, it is doubtful that the phrase "or ought to have known" can be relied upon as a basis of liability, as it would impose liability for an objective intent upon the counsellor, which would likely be a violation of the accused's rights under ss. 7 and 11(*d*) of the Charter.

ANNOTATIONS

The *mens rea* for counseling a specific offence is the same whether or not the offence counseled is actually committed. The requisite mental element requires that the counselor intend the commission of the offence counseled be committed or that the result of his conduct was that the offence would actually be committed. Recklessness is insufficient as it may attach liability to instances of counseling that are casual or accidental: *R. v. Janeteas* (2003), 172 C.C.C. (3d) 97, 11 C.R. (6th) 330 (Ont. C.A.).

The offence of counseling to commit the offence of inciting genocide or hatred requires that the statements, viewed objectively, actively promote, advocate, or encourage the commission of the offence described in them. The criminal act will be made out where the statements are likely to incite and are made with a view to inciting the commission of the offence. An intention to bring about the criminal result, in that the counselor intended the commission of the offence, will satisfy the requisite *mens rea* for the offence of counseling: *Mugesera v. Canada (Minister of Citizenship and Immigration)*, [2005] 2 S.C.R. 100, 197 C.C.C. (3d) 233.

OFFENCES OF NEGLIGENCE / Organizations.

22.1 In respect of an offence that requires the prosecution to prove negligence, an organization is a party to the offence if

(*a*) acting within the scope of their authority

(i) one of its representatives is a party to the offence, or

(ii) two or more of its representatives engage in conduct, whether by act or omission, such that, if it had been the conduct of only one representative, that representative would have been a party to the offence; and

(*b*) the senior officer who is responsible for the aspect of the organization's activities that is relevant to the offence departs — or the senior officers, collectively, depart — markedly from the standard of care that, in the circumstances, could reasonably be expected to prevent a representative of the organization from being a party to the offence. 2003, c. 21, s. 2.

CROSS-REFERENCES

The terms "organization", "representative" and "senior officer" are defined in s. 2. Section 22.2 defines the liability of an organization as a party to the offence where the offence requires proof of fault other than negligence. Section 21 sets out the liability of a party to an offence.

SYNOPSIS

This section defines the liability of an organization as a party to an offence, where the offence is one that only requires proof of negligence. The prosecution must prove two elements to render the organization liable for the negligence of a representative of the organization. The first element, in effect, requires proof that a representative or representatives acting within the scope of their authority were parties to the offence, which would be determined in accordance with normal party liability principles, for example, as set out in s. 21. Second, there must be proof that a senior officer who is responsible for the aspect of the organization's activities that is relevant to the offence departs markedly from the standard of care that could reasonably be expected to prevent the representative from being a party to the offence.

ANNOTATIONS

Note: The following case was decided before the enactment of this section and s. 22.2 and therefore must be applied with care to cases involving liability of organizations.

In *R. v. Sault Ste. Marie (City)*, [1978] 2 S.C.R. 1299, 40 C.C.C. (2d) 353, Dickson J., for the court, considered the issue of corporate responsibility with respect to a strict liability offence for which proof of due diligence would be a defence. Dickson J. pointed out that, where an employer is charged in respect of an act committed by an employee acting in the course of employment, the question will be whether the act took place without the accused's direction or approval, thus negating wilful involvement of the accused, and whether the accused exercised all reasonable care by establishing a proper system to prevent commission of the offence and by taking reasonable steps to ensure the effective operation of the system. The availability of the defence to a corporation will depend on whether such due diligence was taken by those who are the directing mind and will of the corporation, whose acts are therefore in law the acts of the corporation itself.

OTHER OFFENCES / Organizations.

22.2 In respect of an offence that requires the prosecution to prove fault — other than negligence — an organization is a party to the offence if, with the intent at least in part to benefit the organization, one of its senior officers

(*a*) acting within the scope of their authority, is a party to the offence;

(*b*) having the mental state required to be a party to the offence and acting within the scope of their authority, directs the work of other representatives of the organization so that they do the act or make the omission specified in the offence; or

(*c*) knowing that a representative of the organization is or is about to be a party to the offence, does not take all reasonable measures to stop them from being a party to the offence. 2003, c. 21, s. 2.

CROSS-REFERENCES

The terms "organization", "representative" and "senior officer" are defined in s. 2. Section 22.1 defines the liability of an organization as a party to the offence where the offence only requires proof of negligence. Section 21 sets out the liability of a party to an offence.

SYNOPSIS

This section defines the liability of an organization as a party to an offence, where the offence is one that requires proof of fault other than negligence. The prosecution must prove that one of the senior officers at least had the intent in part to benefit the organization. In addition, the prosecution must prove one of three alternatives bases for liability: one of the senior officer acting within the scope of their authority was a party to the office; the senior officer had the *mens rea* for the offence, was acting within the scope of authority and directed the work of other representatives to perform the *actus reus* of the offence; or the senior officer did not take reasonable measures to stop the commission of the offence by a representative.

ANNOTATIONS

Note: The following cases were decided before the enactment of this section and s. 22.2 and therefore must be applied with care to cases involving liability of organizations.

In the case of true criminal offences requiring proof of *mens rea*, liability is attributed to the corporate accused through the identification theory of liability. This theory produces the element of *mens rea* in the corporate entity. The theory establishes the identity between the directing mind and the corporation that results in the corporation being found guilty for the act of the natural person, the employee. The identity of the directing mind and the corporation coincide and the corporation is liable so long as the actions of the directing mind are performed by the manager within the sector of operation assigned to him by the corporation. The sector may be functional or geographic or may embrace the entire undertaking of the corporation. The act in question must be done by the directing force of the company when carrying out his assigned function in the corporation. Acts of the ego of a corporation taken within the assigned managerial area may give rise to corporate criminal responsibility whether or not there is formal delegation; whether or not there is awareness of the activity in the board of directors or the officers of the company, and whether or not there is express prohibition from the board of directors. The identity doctrine merges the board of directors, the managing director, the superintendent, the manager or anyone else to whom the board of directors has delegated the governing executive authority of the corporation, and the conduct of any of the merged entities is thereby attributed to the corporation. Accordingly, a corporation may have more than one directing mind. However, the outer limit of the delegation doctrine is reached and exceeded when the directing mind ceases completely to act, in fact or in substance, in the interests of the corporation. The identification doctrine, accordingly, only operates where the Crown demonstrates that the action taken by the directing mind was within the field of operation assigned to him, was not totally in fraud of the corporation and was by design or result partly for the benefit of the company: *R. v. Canadian Dredge & Dock Co.*, [1985] 1 S.C.R. 662, 19 C.C.C. (3d) 1 (8:0). Also see "*Rhone*" *(The) v.* "*Peter A.B. Widener*" *(The)*, [1993] 1 S.C.R. 497, 101 D.L.R. (4th) 188.

ACCESSORY AFTER THE FACT.

23. (1) An accessory after the fact to an offence is one who, knowing that a person has been a party to the offence, receives, comforts or assists that person for the purpose of enabling that person to escape. R.S., c. C-34, s. 23; 1974-75-76, c. 66, s. 7; 2000, c. 12, s. 92.

(2) [*Repealed*, 2000, c. 12, s. 92.]

CROSS-REFERENCES

The punishment and classification of the offence of accessory after the fact is found in s. 463, except for accessory after the fact to murder, see s. 240. The effect of s. 463 is that the accessory's liability depends on the nature of the offence to which he or she is an accessory. For example, an accessory after the fact to the indictable offence of robbery which has a maximum punishment of life imprisonment is by virtue of s. 463(*a*) guilty of an indictable offence and liable to imprisonment for 14 years. The mode of trial will be determined by the nature of the offence. For example, an accessory after the fact to robbery will have an election under s. 536(2). Certain offences are, however, within the absolute jurisdiction of a provincial court judge pursuant to s. 553(*b*). For example, accessory after the fact to theft of goods of a value not exceeding one thousand dollars where the prosecution elects to proceed by way of indictment is pursuant to s. 553(*b*) within the absolute jurisdiction of a provincial court judge. Note as well that, by virtue of s. 469(*b*), the offences of accessory after the fact to high treason, treason or murder may be tried only by the superior court of criminal jurisdiction (defined in s. 2).

Section 23.1, liability of accessory after the fact although person assisted cannot be convicted.

Section 592, indictment of accessory after the fact, whether or not the principal has been indicted, convicted or is amenable to justice. Under s. 657.2(2), where an accused is charged with being an accessory after the fact, evidence of the conviction or discharge of another person of the offence is admissible against the accused and, in the absence of evidence to the contrary, is proof that the offence was committed.

Section 54, specific offence for assisting, harbouring, etc., deserter or absentee without leave from Canadian Forces and s. 56(*b*), deserter or absentee without leave of member of R.C.M.P. As to terrorism offences, see s. 83.01(1), definition of "terrorist activity".

SYNOPSIS

It is an offence under this section to be an *accessory* after the commission of a crime.

The *actus reus* of the offence is described as *receiving, comforting or assisting* another after that person has committed an offence. The mental element requires that the accused *knew that the person assisted* has been a party to an offence and that the acts were done *for the purpose* of assisting that person to escape. Proof that the acts had the effect of assisting the party to the prior offence to escape is not sufficient.

ANNOTATIONS

Elements of offence – Mere failure to disclose the fact that an offence has been committed in his presence does not make the accused an accessory after the fact: *R. v. Dumont* (1921), 37 C.C.C. 166, 64 D.L.R. 128 (Ont. C.A.); nor does the mere failure to aid in the apprehension of the principal: *R. v. Young* (1950), 98 C.C.C. 195, 10 C.R. 142 (Que. C.A.).

The charge must allege the commission of a specific offence and the Crown must prove that the alleged accessory knew that the person assisted was a party to that offence. This burden will be met if it is proven that the accused had actual knowledge of the offence committed or actual suspicion combined with a conscious decision not to make inquiries which could confirm that suspicion. Where the accused chooses to make no inquiries, speculation as to what the accused would have learned if the inquiries had been made is irrelevant to the determination of the blameworthiness of that accused's state of mind: *R. v. Duong* (1998), 124 C.C.C. (3d) 392, 15 C.R. (5th) 209 (Ont. C.A.).

Trial of accessory after the fact although no conviction of principal offender – In *R. v. S. (F.J.)* (1997), 115 C.C.C. (3d) 450, 159 N.S.R. (2d) 285 (C.A.), affd [1998] 1 S.C.R. 88, 121 C.C.C. (3d) 223, 165 N.S.R. (2d) 160, Jones J.A., for the court, held that in light of ss. 23.1 and 592, it is not necessary to convict a principal in order to convict an accessory. Further, while the language does not refer to the acquittal of the principal, the words, "whether or not the principal or any other party to the offence has been indicted or convicted", in s. 592, are broad enough to encompass the acquittal of the principal. On appeal by the accused, the Supreme Court of Canada, "substantially for the reasons of Jones J.A.", dismissed the appeal. This would appear to overrule the earlier decision in *R. v. Vinette*, [1975] 2 S.C.R. 222, 19 C.C.C. (2d) 1, 50 D.L.R. (3d) 697, where the court held that an accessory after the fact may not be tried or tender a valid plea of guilty until the principal is convicted, so that if the latter is acquitted, the accessory must of necessity be discharged.

The decision in *R. v. S. (F.J.), supra*, would also appear to confirm the correctness of these earlier decisions: In *R. v. Anderson* (1980), 57 C.C.C. (2d) 255, 26 A.R. 172 (C.A.), leave to appeal to S.C.C. refused 28 A.R. 498*n*, 35 N.R. 356*n*, the court held that an accessory after the fact can be convicted, notwithstanding there is no evidence the principal was convicted, if the Crown proves that the principal committed the offence. Further, in tendering such proof, any evidence that is admissible against the principal is admissible against the accessory. A similar conclusion was reached in *R. v. McAvoy* (1981), 60 C.C.C. (2d) 95, 21 C.R. (3d) 305 (Ont. C.A.). Similarly, in *R. v. Camponi* (1993), 82 C.C.C. (3d) 506, 22 C.R. (4th) 348 (B.C.C.A.), it was held that, especially in light of s. 23.1, the accessory could be convicted although the charge against the principal offender has been stayed.

WHERE ONE PARTY CANNOT BE CONVICTED.

23.1 For greater certainty, sections 21 to 23 apply in respect of an accused notwithstanding the fact that the person whom the accused aids or abets, counsels or procures or receives, comforts or assists cannot be convicted of the offence. R.S.C. 1985, c. 24 (2nd Supp.), s. 45.

CROSS-REFERENCES

Section 592, indictment of accessory after the fact, whether or not the principal has been indicted, convicted or is amenable to justice.

SYNOPSIS

This section has been recently added to the *Criminal Code* to clarify that an accused may be convicted under ss. 21 to 23 even if the principal whom the accused aids, abets, counsels or in relation to whose offence the accused is an accessory after the fact cannot be convicted. Examples of circumstances under which the other accused may not be convicted would be if the person is under 12 years or is not guilty by reason of insanity.

ANNOTATIONS

An accessory after the fact may be convicted even if the principal is acquitted: *R. v. S. (F.J.)* (1997), 115 C.C.C. (3d) 450, 159 N.S.R. (2d) 285 (C.A.), affd [1998] 1 S.C.R. 88, 121 C.C.C. (3d) 223, 165 N.S.R. (2d) 160.

ATTEMPTS / Question of law.

24. (1) Every one who, having an intent to commit an offence, does or omits to do anything for the purpose of carrying out his intention is guilty of an attempt to commit the offence whether or not it was possible under the circumstances to commit the offence.

(2) The question whether an act or omission by a person who has an intent to commit an offence is or is not mere preparation to commit the offence, and too remote to constitute an attempt to commit the offence, is a question of law. R.S., c. C-34, s. 24.

CROSS-REFERENCES

The punishment and classification of the offence of attempt is found in s. 463, except for certain offences such as attempted murder, see s. 239 and certain terrorist offences, see s. 83.01(1), definition of "terrorist activity". Certain other substantive offences resemble attempts such as treason and high treason, s. 46, 47; mutiny, s. 53; attempt to influence municipal official, s. 123; bribery of judicial officers, members of Parliament or the legislature, s. 119; bribery of other officers, s. 120; obstruct justice, s. 139. These provisions set out the classification and punishment for the offence. The effect of s. 463 for other attempt offences is that the accused's liability depends on the nature of the offence which he attempted to commit. For example, robbery has a maximum punishment of life imprisonment and, thus, by virtue of s. 463(*a*), a person convicted of attempted robbery is guilty of an indictable offence and liable to imprisonment for 14 years. The mode of trial will be determined by the nature of the offence. For example, an accused charged with attempted robbery will have an election under s. 536(2). Certain offences are, however, within the absolute jurisdiction of a provincial court judge pursuant to s. 553(*b*). For example, attempted theft of goods of a value not exceeding one thousand dollars where the prosecution elects to proceed by way of indictment is pursuant to s. 553(*b*) within the absolute jurisdiction of a provincial court judge. Note as well that, by virtue of s. 469(*d*), an attempt to commit the offences in ss. 47, 49, 51, 53, 61, 74, and 75 may be tried only by the superior court of criminal jurisdiction (defined in s. 2). Thus, attempted murder is not within the exclusive jurisdiction of the superior court of criminal jurisdiction and the accused has his election as to mode of trial pursuant to s. 536(2). The offence described by s. 119 which includes attempt to obtain a bribe (subsec. (1)(*a*)(iii)) where the accused is the holder of a judicial office, can only be tried by the superior court of criminal jurisdiction by virtue of s. 469(*c*).

Sections 660 and 661 make provision for conviction of an accused for attempt where the full offence is charged, and conviction of the accused for the attempt charged although the full offence is proved.

SYNOPSIS

This section creates liability for attempting to commit an offence regardless of whether it was factually possible to commit.

Subsection (1) sets out that it must be proven that the accused intended to commit an offence and did or attempted to do anything for the purpose of committing that offence. The *mens rea* for the offence of attempt will vary with the mental element required to commit the full offence attempted.

A vexing aspect of this section is determining whether the acts of the accused have progressed beyond mere preparation to commit the offence to an attempt to commit it. It is not necessary to show that the accused's acts were unlawful. Subsection (2) states that whether the acts done by an accused proven to have the requisite *mens rea*, constitutes an attempt or mere preparation is a question of law and is therefore to be determined by a judge. However, it is no defence, if the acts were done with intention, that the offence could not be committed only because the would-be victim of the offence (for example in a case of fraud or public mischief) was not deceived by the acts.

ANNOTATIONS

Distinction between preparation and attempt – In *R. v. Cline* (1956), 115 C.C.C. 18, 24 C.R. 58 (Ont. C.A.), the court substituted a conviction of an attempt to commit the offence charged. The court said that there can be no general test to distinguish attempt from preparation, but laid down the following propositions:

1. There must be both *mens rea* and an *actus reus* to constitute a criminal attempt, but the criminality of misconduct lay mainly in the intention of the accused.
2. Evidence of similar acts done by the accused before the offence with which he is charged, and also afterwards, if not too remote in time, was admissible to establish a pattern of conduct from which the court might properly find *mens rea*.
3. Such evidence might be advanced in the case for the prosecution without waiting for the defence to raise a specific issue.
4. It was not essential that the *actus reus* be a crime or a tort or even a moral wrong or social mischief.
5. The *actus reus* must be more than mere preparation to commit a crime.
6. But when the preparation was fully complete and ended, the next step done by the accused for the purpose and with the intention of committing a specific crime constituted an *actus reus* sufficient in law to establish a criminal attempt to commit that crime.

Where the accused's intention is otherwise proved, acts which on the face are equivocal may none the less be sufficiently proximate to constitute an attempt. However, where there is no such extrinsic evidence as to the accused's intent acts which on the face are equivocal may be insufficient to show the acts were done with intent to commit the crime charged: *R. v. Sorrell and Bondett* (1978), 41 C.C.C. (2d) 9 (Ont. C.A.).

No satisfactory general criterion can be formulated for drawing a line between preparation and attempt. The application of the distinction to the facts of a particular case must be left to common-sense judgment. The distinction is essentially a qualitative one, involving the relationship between the nature and quality of the act in question and the nature of the complete offence, although consideration must necessarily be given, in making that qualitative distinction, to the relative proximity of the act in question to what would have been the completed offence, in terms of time, location and acts under the control of the accused remaining to be accomplished. While relative proximity may give an act which might otherwise appear to be mere preparation the quality of an attempt, an act which on its face is an act of commission, does not lose its quality as the *actus reus* of attempt because further acts were required or because a significant period of time may have to elapse before the completion of the offence: *R. v. Deutsch*, [1986] 2 S.C.R. 2, 27 C.C.C. (3d) 385 (5:0). See also *R. v. Root* (2008), 241 C.C.C. (3d) 125 (Ont. C.A.), leave to appeal to S.C.C. refused 247 C.C.C. (3d) vi.

"Impossible" attempt – Canadian law does not recognize the distinction between legal impossibility and factual impossibility. Subsection (1) draws no distinction between attempts to do the possible but by inadequate means, attempts to do the physically impossible, and attempts to do something that turns out to be impossible following completion. All are varieties of attempts to do the factually impossible and all are crimes. Only attempts to commit imaginary crimes fall outside the scope of this subsection: *United States of America v. Dynar*, [1997] 2 S.C.R. 462, 115 C.C.C. (3d) 481.

It is no bar to a conviction for an attempt that the acts went beyond mere preparation and were fully carried out although in circumstances which did not amount to the full offence, as on a charge of fraud where proof of the full offence failed because the "victim" was not in fact deceived by the accused's act: *R. v. Detering*, [1982] 2 S.C.R. 583, 70 C.C.C. (2d) 321 (7:0).

Attempting to conspire to commit a substantive offence is not a crime in Canadian law: *R. v. Déry*, [2006] 2 S.C.R. 669, 213 C.C.C. (3d) 289.

Protection of Persons Administering and Enforcing the Law

PROTECTION OF PERSONS ACTING UNDER AUTHORITY / Idem / When not protected / When protected / Power in case of escape from penitentiary.

25. (1) Every one who is required or authorized by law to do anything in the administration or enforcement of the law

- **(*a*) as a private person,**
- **(*b*) as a peace officer or public officer,**
- **(*c*) in aid of a peace officer or public officer, or**
- **(*d*) by virtue of his office,**

is, if he acts on reasonable grounds, justified in doing what he is required or authorized to do and in using as much force as is necessary for that purpose.

(2) Where a person is required or authorized by law to execute a process or to carry out a sentence, that person or any person who assists him is, if that person acts in good faith, justified in executing the process or in carrying out the sentence notwithstanding that the process or sentence is defective or that it was issued or imposed without jurisdiction or in excess of jurisdiction.

(3) Subject to subsections (4) and (5), a person is not justified for the purposes of subsection (1) in using force that is intended or is likely to cause death or grievous bodily harm unless the person believes on reasonable grounds that it is necessary for the self-preservation of the person or the preservation of any one under that person's protection from death or grievous bodily harm.

(4) A peace officer, and every person lawfully assisting the peace officer, is justified in using force that is intended or is likely to cause death or grievous bodily harm to a person to be arrested, if

- **(*a*) the peace officer is proceeding lawfully to arrest, with or without warrant, the person to be arrested;**
- **(*b*) the offence for which the person is to be arrested is one for which that person may be arrested without warrant;**
- **(*c*) the person to be arrested takes flight to avoid arrest;**
- **(*d*) the peace officer or other person using the force believes on reasonable grounds that the force is necessary for the purpose of protecting the peace officer, the person lawfully assisting the peace officer or any other person from imminent or future death or grievous bodily harm; and**
- **(*e*) the flight cannot be prevented by reasonable means in a less violent manner.**

(5) A peace officer is justified in using force that is intended or is likely to cause death or grievous bodily harm against an inmate who is escaping from a penitentiary within the meaning of subsection 2(1) of the *Corrections and Conditional Release Act*, if

(*a*) **the peace officer believes on reasonable grounds that any of the inmates of the penitentiary poses a threat of death or grievous bodily harm to the peace officer or any other person; and**

(*b*) **the escape cannot be prevented by reasonable means in a less violent manner. R.S., c. C-34, s. 25; 1994, c. 12, s. 1.**

CROSS-REFERENCES

Definition of "peace officer" and "public officer", s. 2.

As to power of arrest by private citizen, see s. 494, and peace officer, s. 495.

The following provisions also define circumstances where a person is required or authorized to use force: s. 27, use of force to prevent commission of certain offences; s. 30, use of force to prevent breach of peace; s. 31, arrest by peace officer of person in breach of peace; s. 32, 33, use of force to suppress riot; ss. 34, 35, 37, self-defence; s. 37, defence of persons under protection; ss. 38 to 42, defence of property; s. 43, use of force by way of correction; s. 44, use of force by master of ship.

Also see the following: s. 25.1, defence to commission of certain offences by public officer where authorized by a competent authority; s. 26, liability of person for excessive force; s. 28, protection of persons executing and assisting in execution of warrant; s. 29, also note requirement that person have possession of the warrant or other process; s. 45, protection from liability for surgical operations.

Section 31 of the *Interpretation Act*, R.S.C. 1985, c. I-21, gives persons, authorized to exercise a power to do or enforce the doing of any act or thing, ancillary powers necessary to do the act or thing. Section 31 has, however, been strictly construed where the statutory power would encroach on the common law rights of the property owner. Thus, a former provision of the *Criminal Code*, which authorized police officers to seize firearms in certain circumstances, did not imply the right to enter and search private property: *R. v. Colet*, [1981] 1 S.C.R. 2, 57 C.C.C. (2d) 105, 19 C.R. (3d) 84. However, compare *R. v. Lyons*, [1984] 2 S.C.R. 633, 15 C.C.C. (3d) 417, where reference was made to s. 31 as confirmation that the authority to intercept private communications included the power to enter private premises to install the electronic device where such entry was necessary to implement the authorization granted under Part VI. Section 24 of the *Interpretation Act* provides for the exercise of powers by a successor in office. Also see *Crimes Against Humanity and War Crimes Act*, s. 14.

SYNOPSIS

This section establishes protection from liability for certain persons acting under authority.

Subsection (1) provides justification for the actions of any of the persons listed in paras. (*a*) to (*d*), if the additional requirements of the subsection are met. The person must be either *required or authorized by law* to do anything in relation to the *administration* or *enforcement* of the law. The requirement or authorization may be found in either statute or common law. In addition, it must be shown that the specified person acted on *reasonable grounds* and used *only as much force as was necessary* to achieve that purpose. If the actions of the person exceed the scope of activities authorized or required by law or the force used was more than that which was necessary to achieve that protected purpose, this subsection will not apply to exclude liability. However, to understand the scope of the provision as it applies to peace officers, it must be read together with subsecs. (3) and (4).

Subsection (2) protects a person acting *in good faith* who was executing process or carrying out a sentence, if authorized or required to do so. This protection will apply, even if the sentence or the process is determined to have been defective or without effect for any of the reasons noted in the subsection. The protection also extends to those who assist the authorized person in carrying out these functions.

Subsection (3) both provides an exception to the scope of protection conferred by the section and is itself subject to an exception in subsecs. (4) and (5). It limits the type of harm which may be inflicted under the protection of the section, by excluding the use of force *intended to or likely to cause death* or *grievous bodily harm unless the person believes, on reasonable grounds*, that such force must be used to protect himself or a person under his protection from death or grievous bodily harm. The application of the subsection is to take account of the circumstances in which the force is used and it is not required that a person in such a situation weigh the force used with precision. The phrase "grievous bodily harm" has been held to mean serious hurt or pain.

Subsection (4) permits a peace officer and persons lawfully assisting the officer to use force, that is intended or likely to cause death or grievous bodily harm, to prevent flight from a lawful arrest provided that the conditions in the subsection are met. Those conditions include that the arrest is lawful, the offence is one for which the person can be arrested without a warrant, the flight cannot be prevented by reasonable means in a less violent manner and the peace officer or person assisting believes on reasonable grounds that the force is necessary for the purpose of protecting the peace officer, the person assisting the officer or any other person from "imminent or future death or grievous bodily harm".

Subsection (5) is a special provision permitting use of force that is intended or likely to cause death or grievous bodily harm to prevent an escape from a penitentiary. However, the officer must believe on reasonable grounds that any of the inmates poses a threat of death or grievous bodily harm to the officer or any other person and the escape cannot be prevented by reasonable means in a less violent manner.

ANNOTATIONS

Use of force in enforcement or administration of law – An analysis of the justification of a peace officer's apprehension of a citizen who he has been informed was going to commit a crime is found in *Kennedy v. Tomlinson* (1959), 126 C.C.C. 175 (Ont. C.A.).

The exemption from liability under subsec. (1) has no application to negligent conduct: *Green v. Lawrence* (1998), 127 C.C.C. (3d) 416 (Man. C.A.).

This provision protects against civil liability for reasonable mistakes of fact but not for mistakes of law. Accordingly, the police were not protected from a claim for trespass in entering the plaintiff's home to execute a warrantless arrest. Subsec. (2) has no application because this was not a case in which the law or process under which the officers were operating was later found to be defective: *Hudson v. Brantford Police Services Board* (2001), 158 C.C.C. (3d) 390 (Ont. C.A.).

However, in *Tymkin v. Ewatski* (2014), 306 C.C.C. (3d) 24 (Man. C.A.), leave to appeal to S.C.C. refused 2014 CarswellMan 301, a police officer entering a dwelling house without a warrant to effect an arrest was entitled to the protection of subsec. (2) because the officer sought and obtained consent to enter from a person with ostensible authority to grant it.

This section does not permit a police officer to use as much force as necessary to generally carry out the lawful execution of his duty. Thus, while an officer has a duty to investigate crimes and question citizens, this section does not give him the right to detain the person or to use force for that purpose short of arrest: *R. v. O'Donnell; R. v. Cluett* (1982), 3 C.C.C. (3d) 333 (N.S.C.A.), reversed, with respect to *Cluett*, on other grounds [1985] 2 S.C.R. 216, 21 C.C.C. (3d) 318 (7:0).

In the absence of a specific statutory exemption, a police officer, pursuing a person suspected of committing a criminal offence, is not insulated from liability for the offence of failing to stop at a stop sign contrary to the *Highway Traffic Act* (Ont.). Assuming that this section could apply, the issue is not whether the officer was required or authorized by law to apprehend the suspect but, rather, whether he was required or authorized by law to drive through the stop sign without stopping. There is no common law authority in a constable which would give him immunity wider than that provided by this section: *R. v. Brennan* (1989), 52 C.C.C. (3d) 366 (Ont. C.A.).

While a search warrant authorizes a search of the premises for the items referred to in the warrant, the existence of the warrant does not determine whether the officers acted reasonably in the manner in which they executed the warrant. In a civil action, the officers had to prove on a balance of probabilities that it was reasonable, in the circumstances, to execute the warrant in the aggressive manner that they did in this case. The bald statement by one of the officers that he believed the occupants might be armed was not sufficient to meet this onus, there being no evidence to allow the trial judge to evaluate the objective reasonableness of the officer's belief. As the information to obtain the warrant was sealed, the police defendants should have applied under s. 487.3 to lift the sealing order if they needed this material to make out the defence under this section: *Crampton v. Walton* (2005), 194 C.C.C. (3d) 207 (Alta. C.A.).

A peace officer's honest belief in the legality of his conduct must be founded on reasonable grounds. This provision was applicable, therefore, where a peace officer forcibly returned a prisoner to his cell due to the prisoner's refusal to sign a property release form. The officer honestly believed that he had the authority to detain the complainant as a result of the applicability of operation procedures of the prison: *R. v. Devereaux* (1996), 112 C.C.C. (3d) 243 (Nfld. C.A.).

Subsection (2) – In *R. v. Finta*, [1994] 1 S.C.R. 701, 88 C.C.C. (3d) 417, the court considered this subsection in the context of a prosecution for war crimes under now repealed provisions of this Act. The court held that the defence under this subsection is distinct from the defence of obedience to or in conformity with the law in force at the time and in the place of commission of the offence and was therefore available to a person charged with war crimes or crimes against humanity. Unless the law was manifestly illegal, the police officer must obey and implement that law and, if it turns out that the officer has followed an illegal order, he may plead the defence under this subsection just as a military officer may properly put forth the defence of obedience to superior orders under certain limited conditions. However, an officer acting pursuant to a manifestly unlawful order or law would not be able to defend his actions on the grounds they were justified under this subsection. The holding in *Finta* must now be read with care when applied to prosecutions for war crimes and crimes against humanity having regard to the codification of the defence of obedience to superior orders in s. 14 of the *Crimes Against Humanity and War Crimes Act*.

Subsection (3) – The use of force is to be judged on a subjective-objective basis. Police actions should not be judged against a standard of perfection. Regard must be had to the circumstances as they existed at the time that the force was used: *R. v. Nasogaluak*, [2010] 1 S.C.R. 206, 251 C.C.C. (3d) 293.

The words "grievous bodily harm" in subsec. (3) mean serious hurt or pain. Moreover, in determining the availability of the defence under this section the jury must be directed to have regard to the circumstances as they existed at the time the force was used, keeping in mind that the officer could not be expected to measure the force used with exactitude: *R. v. Bottrell* (1981), 60 C.C.C. (2d) 211 (B.C.C.A.).

Use of force where person takes flight / subsec. (4) – **Note:** The case noted below was decided under the predecessor to this section which allowed the use of as much force as necessary to prevent the escape, unless the escape could not be prevented by reasonable means in a less violent manner.

A peace officer who had lawful authority to arrest a person in one province under s. 495 and is in fresh pursuit of that person retains for the purposes of subsec. (4) his status of a peace officer even where the pursuit takes him into an adjoining province: *R. v. Roberge*, [1983] 1 S.C.R. 312, 4 C.C.C. (3d) 304 (7:0).

DEFINITIONS / "Competent authority" / "Public officer" / "Senior official" / Principle / Designation of public officers / Condition — civilian oversight / Declaration as evidence / Considerations / Designation of senior officials / Emergency designation / Conditions / Justification for acts or omissions / Requirements for certain acts / Person acting at direction of public officer / Limitation / Protection, defences and immunities unaffected / Compliance with requirements / Exception — *Controlled Drugs and Substances Act* and *Cannabis Act*.

25.1 (1) The following definitions apply in this section and sections 25.2 to 25.4.

"competent authority" means, with respect to a public officer or a senior official,

(*a*) in the case of a member of the Royal Canadian Mounted Police, the Minister of Public Safety and Emergency Preparedness, personally;

(*b*) in the case of a member of a police service constituted under the laws of a province, the Minister responsible for policing in the province, personally; and

(*c*) in the case of any other public officer or senior official, the Minister who has responsibility for the Act of Parliament that the officer or official has the power to enforce, personally.

"public officer" means a peace officer, or a public officer who has the powers of a peace officer under an Act of Parliament.

"senior official" means a senior official who is responsible for law enforcement and who is designated under subsection (5).

(2) It is in the public interest to ensure that public officers may effectively carry out their law enforcement duties in accordance with the rule of law and, to that end, to expressly recognize in law a justification for public officers and other persons acting at their direction to commit acts or omissions that would otherwise constitute offences.

(3) A competent authority may designate public officers for the purposes of this section and sections 25.2 to 25.4.

(3.1) A competent authority referred to in paragraph (*a*) or (*b*) of the definition of that term in subsection (1) may not designate any public officer under subsection (3) unless there is a public authority composed of persons who are not peace officers that may review the public officer's conduct.

(3.2) The Governor in Council or the lieutenant governor in council of a province, as the case may be, may designate a person or body as a public authority for the purposes of subsection (3.1), and that designation is conclusive evidence that the person or body is a public authority described in that subsection.

(4) The competent authority shall make designations under subsection (3) on the advice of a senior official and shall consider the nature of the duties performed by the public officer in relation to law enforcement generally, rather than in relation to any particular investigation or enforcement activity.

(5) A competent authority may designate senior officials for the purposes of this section and sections 25.2 to 25.4.

(6) A senior official may designate a public officer for the purposes of this section and sections 25.2 to 25.4 for a period of not more than 48 hours if the senior official is of the opinion that

(*a*) by reason of exigent circumstances, it is not feasible for the competent authority to designate a public officer under subsection (3); and

(*b*) in the circumstances of the case, the public officer would be justified in committing an act or omission that would otherwise constitute an offence.

The senior official shall without delay notify the competent authority of the designation.

(7) A designation under subsection (3) or (6) may be made subject to conditions, including conditions limiting

(*a*) the duration of the designation;

(*b*) the nature of the conduct in the investigation of which a public officer may be justified in committing, or directing another person to commit, acts or omissions that would otherwise constitute an offence; and

(*c*) the acts or omissions that would otherwise constitute an offence and that a public officer may be justified in committing or directing another person to commit.

(8) A public officer is justified in committing an act or omission — or in directing the commission of an act or omission under subsection (10) — that would otherwise constitute an offence if the public officer

(*a*) is engaged in the investigation of an offence under, or the enforcement of, an Act of Parliament or in the investigation of criminal activity;

(*b*) is designated under subsection (3) or (6); and

(*c*) believes on reasonable grounds that the commission of the act or omission, as compared to the nature of the offence or criminal activity being investigated, is reasonable and proportional in the circumstances, having regard to such matters as the nature of the act or omission, the nature of the investigation and the reasonable availability of other means for carrying out the public officer's law enforcement duties.

(9) No public officer is justified in committing an act or omission that would otherwise constitute an offence and that would be likely to result in loss of or serious damage to property, or in directing the commission of an act or omission under subsection (10), unless, in addition to meeting the conditions set out in paragraphs (8)(*a*) to (*c*), he or she

(*a*) is personally authorized in writing to commit the act or omission — or direct its commission — by a senior official who believes on reasonable grounds that committing the act or omission, as compared to the nature of the offence or criminal activity being investigated, is reasonable and proportional in the circumstances, having regard to such matters as the nature of the act or omission, the nature of the investigation and the reasonable availability of other means for carrying out the public officer's law enforcement duties; or

(*b*) believes on reasonable grounds that the grounds for obtaining an authorization under paragraph (*a*) exist but it is not feasible in the circumstances to obtain the authorization and that the act or omission is necessary to

(i) preserve the life or safety of any person,

(ii) prevent the compromise of the identity of a public officer acting in an undercover capacity, of a confidential informant or of a person acting covertly under the direction and control of a public officer, or

(iii) prevent the imminent loss or destruction of evidence of an indictable offence.

(10) A person who commits an act or omission that would otherwise constitute an offence is justified in committing it if

(*a*) a public officer directs him or her to commit that act or omission and the person believes on reasonable grounds that the public officer has the authority to give that direction; and

(*b*) he or she believes on reasonable grounds that the commission of that act or omission is for the purpose of assisting the public officer in the public officer's law enforcement duties.

(11) Nothing in this section justifies

(*a*) the intentional or criminally negligent causing of death or bodily harm to another person;

(*b*) the wilful attempt in any manner to obstruct, pervert or defeat the course of justice; or

(*c*) conduct that would violate the sexual integrity of an individual.

(12) Nothing in this section affects the protection, defences and immunities of peace officers and other persons recognized under the law of Canada.

(13) Nothing in this section relieves a public officer of criminal liability for failing to comply with any other requirements that govern the collection of evidence.

(14) Nothing in this section justifies a public officer or a person acting at his or her direction in committing an act or omission — or a public officer in directing the commission of an act or omission — that constitutes an offence under a provision of

Part I of the *Controlled Drugs and Substances Act* or of the regulations made under it or a provision of Division 1 of Part 1 of the *Cannabis Act*. 2001, c. 32, s. 2; 2005, c. 10, s. 34(1)(*f*)(ii); 2018, c. 16, s. 207.

CROSS-REFERENCES

"Peace officer" is defined in s. 2. Section 25 sets out the circumstances where the use of force is justified. Also see: s. 26, respecting use of excessive force; s. 27, use of force to prevent commission of offence; ss. 30 and 31 preventing and arrest for breach of the peace. Under s. 25.2 every public officer who commits or directs commission of an act or omission under subsec. (9) must file a written report as soon as feasible. Section 25.3 provides for publication of an annual report by a competent authority concerning the use of this section. Section 25.4 provides for the notification of any person whose property was lost or seriously damaged as a result of acts or omissions undertaken in accordance with subsec. (9). By its terms, this section does not apply to offences committed by public officers under Part I of the *Controlled Drugs and Substances Act*. However, s. 55(2) and (2.1) of the *Controlled Drugs and Substances Act* and the *Controlled Drugs and Substances Act (Police Enforcement) Regulations*, SOR/97-234 provide a similar defence.

ANNOTATIONS

In *R. v. Campbell*, [1999] 1 S.C.R. 565, 133 C.C.C. (3d) 257, 24 C.R. (5th) 365, *sub nom. R. v. Shirose*, the court considered whether an illegal "reverse sting operation" conducted in the course of a drug investigation would amount to an abuse of process and thus entitle an accused caught up in such an investigation to a stay of proceedings. That investigation was carried out before the enactment of this provision. The decision will still be of assistance where the police conduct an investigation involving commission of crimes without proper designation under this section. Authorization for the type of investigation undertaken in that case would now be governed by ss. 55(2) and (2.1) of the *Controlled Drugs and Substances Act* and the regulations made thereunder, especially *Controlled Drugs and Substances Act (Police Enforcement) Regulations*, SOR/97-234.

This provision provides a legislated exemption from the application of the rule of law. While police must comply with its requirements in order to avail themselves of the exemption, failure to comply does not necessarily entitle the accused to a stay of proceedings: *R. v. Lising* (2010), 337 C.C.C. (3d) 91 (B.C.C.A.).

The exemption provisions are constitutionally valid. Simply because a police officer or agent might make a wrong call with respect to the proportionality test in subsec. (8)(*c*) does not mean that the legislation is vague or overbroad: *R. v. Lising*, *supra*.

PUBLIC OFFICER TO FILE REPORT.

25.2 Every public officer who commits an act or omission — or directs the commission by another person of an act or omission — under paragraph 25.1(9)(*a*) or (*b*) shall, as soon as is feasible after the commission of the act or omission, file a written report with the appropriate senior official describing the act or omission. 2001, c. 32, s. 2.

CROSS-REFERENCES

"Public officer" and "senior official" are defined in s. 25.1.

ANNUAL REPORT / Limitation.

25.3 (1) Every competent authority shall publish or otherwise make available to the public an annual report for the previous year that includes, in respect of public officers and senior officials designated by the competent authority,

(*a*) the number of designations made under subsection 25.1(6) by the senior officials;

(*b*) the number of authorizations made under paragraph 25.1(9)(*a*) by the senior officials;

(*c*) the number of times that acts and omissions were committed in accordance with paragraph 25.1(9)(*b*) by the public officers;

(*d*) the nature of the conduct being investigated when the designations referred to in paragraph (*a*) or the authorizations referred to in paragraph (*b*) were made or when the acts or omissions referred to in paragraph (*c*) were committed; and

(*e*) the nature of the acts or omissions committed under the designations referred to in paragraph (*a*), under the authorizations referred to in paragraph (*b*) and in the manner described in paragraph (*c*).

(2) The annual report shall not contain any information the disclosure of which would

(*a*) compromise or hinder an ongoing investigation of an offence under an Act of Parliament;

(*b*) compromise the identity of a public officer acting in an undercover capacity, of a confidential informant or of a person acting covertly under the direction and control of a public officer;

(*c*) endanger the life or safety of any person;

(*d*) prejudice a legal proceeding; or

(*e*) otherwise be contrary to the public interest. 2001, c. 32, s. 2.

CROSS-REFERENCES

"Competent authority", "public officer" and "senior official" are defined in s. 25.1.

WRITTEN NOTIFICATION TO BE GIVEN / Limitation.

25.4 (1) When a public officer commits an act or omission — or directs the commission by another person of an act or omission — under paragraph 25.1(9)(*a*) or (*b*), the senior official with whom the public officer files a written report under section 25.2 shall, as soon as is feasible after the report is filed, and no later than one year after the commission of the act or omission, notify in writing any person whose property was lost or seriously damaged as a result of the act or omission.

(2) The competent authority may authorize the senior official not to notify the person under subsection (1) until the competent authority is of the opinion that notification would not

(*a*) compromise or hinder an ongoing investigation of an offence under an Act of Parliament;

(*b*) compromise the identity of a public officer acting in an undercover capacity, of a confidential informant or of a person acting covertly under the direction and control of a public officer;

(*c*) endanger the life or safety of any person;

(*d*) prejudice a legal proceeding; or

(*e*) otherwise be contrary to the public interest. 2001, c. 32, s. 2.

Transitional provision

2001, c. 32, s. 46.1 provides as follows:

46.1 Within three years after this section comes into force, a review of sections 25.1 to 25.4 of the *Criminal Code* and their operation shall be undertaken by any committee of the Senate, of the House of Commons or of both Houses of Parliament that is designated or established for that purpose.

CROSS-REFERENCES

"Competent authority", "public officer" and "senior official" are defined in s. 25.1.

EXCESSIVE FORCE.

26. Every one who is authorized by law to use force is criminally responsible for any excess thereof according to the nature and quality of the act that constitutes the excess. R.S., c. C-34, s. 26.

CROSS-REFERENCES

A number of provisions authorize the use of force in carrying out duties under the law, to prevent commission of offences or in defence of oneself or others, such as the following: s. 25, use of force by person required or authorized by law to do anything in the administration or enforcement of the law [*e.g.*, to effect an arrest under s. 494 or s. 495]; s. 27, use of force to prevent commission of certain offences; s. 30, use of force to prevent breach of peace; s. 31, arrest by peace officer of person in breach of peace; ss. 32, 33, use of force to suppress riot; ss. 34, 35, 37, self-defence; s. 37, defence of persons under protection; ss. 38 to 42, defence of property; s. 43, use of force by way of correction; s. 44, use of force by master of ship. Also see s. 25.1 authorizing commission of certain otherwise illegal acts by designated public officers.

SYNOPSIS

This section imposes criminal liability for the use of force in excess of that authorized by law. Thus, it has been held that if one exceeds the force permitted by s. 27 or the force permitted as self-defence under s. 34, the excess force which results in death will be murder and not considered reduced to manslaughter.

ANNOTATIONS

It now seems clear as a result of a series of cases in the Supreme Court of Canada: *R. v. Gee*, [1982] 2 S.C.R. 286, 68 C.C.C. (2d) 516, 29 C.R. (3d) 347, *R. v. Faid*, [1983] 1 S.C.R. 265, 2 C.C.C. (3d) 513, 33 C.R. (3d) 1, *R. v. Brisson*, [1982] 2 S.C.R. 227, 69 C.C.C. (2d) 97, 29 C.R. (3d) 289, and *R. v. Reilly*, [1984] 2 S.C.R. 396, 15 C.C.C. (3d) 1, 42 C.R. (3d) 154 (6:0), that there does not exist in Canada a qualified defence of excessive force in self-defence or in preventing the commission of an offence which would have the effect of reducing murder to manslaughter. If the accused has used excessive force so that the defence provided by s. 34 or s. 27 is not available, then absent any other defence, the accused is liable to be convicted of murder. The evidence led in self-defence may however support a defence of provocation or negative the specific intent for murder in which case the proper verdict would be manslaughter.

In *R. v. Bayard* (1988), 29 B.C.L.R. (2d) 366, 92 N.R. 376 (C.A.), the majority of the court ordered a new trial on a Crown appeal from the accused's acquittal on murder and conviction for manslaughter on the basis, *inter alia*, that the trial judge had misdirected the jury as to the effect of excessive force in self defence. Lambert J.A., dissenting, was of the view that the impugned instructions related solely to s. 34(1) which could not apply if the accused had the intent for murder. If, however, he did not have the intent to kill and used no more force than necessary, then, pursuant to that subsection, the accused would be acquitted. If, however, he did use more force than was necessary then, in fact, the verdict should be manslaughter. On appeal by the accused to the Supreme Court of Canada, [1989] 1 S.C.R. 425, 70 C.R. (3d) 95, [1989] 5 W.W.R. 121, the appeal was allowed and the accused's conviction for manslaughter restored substantially for the dissenting reasons of Lambert J.A.

USE OF FORCE TO PREVENT COMMISSION OF OFFENCE.

27. Every one is justified in using as much force as is reasonably necessary

(*a*) to prevent the commission of an offence

(i) for which, if it were committed, the person who committed it might be arrested without warrant, and

(ii) that would be likely to cause immediate and serious injury to the person or property of anyone; or

(*b*) to prevent anything being done that, on reasonable grounds, he believes would, if it were done, be an offence mentioned in paragraph (*a*). R.S., c. C-34, s. 27.

CROSS-REFERENCES

In most cases, the determination of whether or not the person, "might be arrested without warrant", will be determined by reference to ss. 494 and 495 which authorizes warrantless arrest by anyone and by a peace officer, respectively. The most important power is that provided by s. 494(1)(*a*) which authorizes the arrest of a person found committing an indictable offence. Virtually all offences which would be likely to cause immediate and serious injury to person or property will constitute indictable offences, bearing in mind that even Crown-option offences are deemed to be indictable offences by s. 34(1)(*a*) of the *Interpretation Act*, R.S.C. 1985, c. I-21.

In many circumstances, the use of force will be authorized not only by this section but the self-defence and defence of property provisions set out in ss. 34 to 42.

Section 26 renders the person liable for any excessive use of force. The use of force to prevent commission of an offence on aircraft in flight in Canadian airspace or in respect of any aircraft registered in Canada is found in s. 27.1.

SYNOPSIS

This section provides authorization for the use of force to prevent the commission of specified types of offences or to prevent anything that might lead to the commission of such offences.

Section 27(*a*) permits the use of such *force* by *any one* as is *reasonably necessary* to *prevent the commission of certain types of offences* under the circumstances outlined in s. 27(*a*)(i) and (ii). This paragraph may be applied to any person, as contrasted with provisions such as s. 28 which can be relied upon only by a person authorized to execute process. In addition, it should be noted that the amount of force used will be judged by an objective standard as denoted by the term "reasonably necessary". Section 27(*a*)(i) limits the type of offence to those for which a person may be arrested without warrant. The criteria in s. 27(*a*)(ii) must also be met, namely that the offence, if committed, would be *likely* to cause *immediate* and *serious* injury to either a person or property. Again, it should be noted that the likelihood of the result is to be judged on an objective basis and the harm feared must be immediate and serious.

Section 27(*b*) permits an element of the accused's subjective beliefs to be incorporated but only if those beliefs are *reasonable* on an objective basis.

ANNOTATIONS

A personal assault against the accused does not trigger the application of this provision: *R. v. Hebert*, [1996] 2 S.C.R. 272, 107 C.C.C. (3d) 42, 135 D.L.R. (4th) 577.

USE OF FORCE ON BOARD AN AIRCRAFT / Application of this section.

27.1 (1) Every person on an aircraft in flight is justified in using as much force as is reasonably necessary to prevent the commission of an offence against this Act or another Act of Parliament that the person believes on reasonable grounds, if it were committed, would be likely to cause immediate and serious injury to the aircraft or to any person or property therein.

(2) This section applies in respect of any aircraft in flight in Canadian airspace and in respect of any aircraft registered in Canada in accordance with the regulations made under the *Aeronautics Act* in flight outside Canadian airspace. 2004, c. 12, s. 2.

CROSS-REFERENCES
"Flight" is defined in s. 7(8). The general defence of use of force to prevent commission of an offence is found in s. 27.

ARREST OF WRONG PERSON / Person assisting.

28. (1) Where a person who is authorized to execute a warrant to arrest believes, in good faith and on reasonable grounds, that the person whom he arrests is the person named in the warrant, he is protected from criminal responsibility in respect thereof to the same extent as if that person were the person named in the warrant.

(2) Where a person is authorized to execute a warrant to arrest,

(*a*) every one who, being called on to assist him, believes that the person in whose arrest he is called on to assist is the person named in the warrant, and

(*b*) every keeper of a prison who is required to receive and detain a person who he believes has been arrested under the warrant,

is protected from criminal responsibility in respect thereof to the same extent as if that person were the person named in the warrant. R.S., c. C-34, s. 28.

CROSS-REFERENCES
This provision, in and of itself, does not authorize the use of force but merely deals with the case of mistake in execution of the warrant. The use of force to arrest is dealt with primarily under s. 25 and see notes under that section. Section 29 requires the person executing a warrant to have it with him where feasible and prescribes other duties. In addition, s. 10 of the *Canadian Charter of Rights and Freedoms* requires a police officer to inform the arrestee of the reason for the arrest and of his right to counsel. See notes under s. 10 of the Charter, *infra*. As to where an arrest warrant may be exercised, see ss. 514, 703 and 528. An accused who was illegally arrested and in the course of the arrest killed the person attempting to effect the arrest, may, in some circumstances, have a defence of provocation under s. 232(4) or self-defence under s. 34. The offence of resisting or obstructing a peace officer, public officer, or person in the lawful execution of process is found in s. 129. The offences of assault with intent to resist arrest and assault of an officer in the execution of duty are in s. 270. The offence of misconduct by officers executing process is found in s. 128.

SYNOPSIS

Section 28 creates a limited exemption from criminal liability for persons who are *authorized* to execute arrest warrants and mistakenly arrest the wrong person or keep such wrongfully arrested person in custody.

It must be shown that the mistake of identity was made *in good faith and on reasonable grounds*.

Section 28(2) provides protection for those who *assist the person making the mistaken arrest* or *detain* such wrongfully arrested person on the same basis as if the person arrested was the person sought. As with s. 28(1), the person making the arrest must have been authorized to execute an arrest warrant. Section 28(2)(*a*) deals with the person who assists in the arrest after being *called upon to do so*. The assistant must believe that the person whom he is asked to help arrest is the person sought. This is a much lower standard of belief than that applied in s. 28(1); it need not be based on reasonable and probable grounds. Section 28(2)(*b*) protects the keeper of a prison, if the keeper has a subjective belief that the person he is asked to detain has been arrested under a warrant.

DUTY OF PERSON ARRESTING / Notice / Failure to comply.

29. (1) It is the duty of every one who executes a process or warrant to have it with him, where it is feasible to do so, and to produce it when requested to do so.

(2) It is the duty of every one who arrests a person, whether with or without a warrant, to give notice to that person, where it is feasible to do so, of

(*a*) the process or warrant under which he makes the arrest; or

(*b*) the reason for the arrest.

(3) Failure to comply with subsection (1) or (2) does not of itself deprive a person who executes a process or warrant, or a person who makes an arrest, or those who assist them, of protection from criminal responsibility. R.S., c. C-34, s. 29.

CROSS-REFERENCES

Subsection (1) – This provision, in and of itself, does not authorize the use of force. The use of force to arrest is dealt with primarily under s. 25 and see notes under that section. Section 28 deals with the case of mistake in execution of an arrest warrant. As to where an arrest warrant may be exercised, see ss. 514, 703 and 528. As to execution of a search warrant, see s. 487, search warrant; s. 487.1, tele-warrants; s. 488, time of execution; s. 488.1, execution of warrant at lawyer's office; s. 489, seizure of other items; s. 462.32, proceeds of crime. As to search warrants for weapons etc., see s. 103. An accused who was illegally arrested and, in the course of the arrest, killed the person attempting to effect the arrest may, in some circumstances, have a defence of provocation under s. 232(4) or self-defence under s. 34. The offence of misconduct by officers executing process is found in s. 128.

Subsection (2) – In addition to the duties prescribed by this subsection, s. 10 of the Charter requires a police officer to inform the arrestee of the reason for the arrest and of his right to counsel. See notes under s. 10 of the Charter, *infra*. The power of arrest is also circumscribed by other provisions of the Charter, see especially notes under s. 9 of the Charter. Arrest without warrant is authorized by a number of sections: s. 31, breach of the peace; s. 33, arrest of rioters; s. 117.02, arrest for weapons offences; s. 199(2), arrest of inmates of disorderly house; s. 494, arrest by any person for certain criminal offences; s. 495, arrest by peace officer for criminal offences; s. 524(2), arrest by peace officer of accused on interim release. The offence of resisting or obstructing a peace officer, public officer, or person in the lawful execution of process is found in s. 129. The offences of assault with intent to resist arrest and assault of an officer in the execution of duty are in s. 270.

SYNOPSIS

This section outlines the duties imposed upon those who execute process or make an arrest, and states the effect of non-compliance with the section.

Section 29(1) states that it is the duty of a person *executing a process or warrant* to have a copy of such document with him. In addition, such document must be shown if a request is made to see it. Both requirements apply only if it is *feasible* to comply with them.

Section 29(2) sets out the *duty of a person making an arrest* with or without warrant. The requirements are that the person being arrested is to be told of the process or warrant permitting the arrest *or* the reason for the arrest. As with s. 29(1), the duties apply only *when feasible*. These duties are supplemented by the requirements in s. 10 of the Charter.

Section 29(3) spells out that *non-compliance* with either of the foregoing subsections does not *by itself* deprive the person making the arrest, executing process, or those who assist such persons, of the protection from criminal responsibility conferred elsewhere under the *Criminal Code* (see, for example, s. 28).

ANNOTATIONS

Subsection (1) – A search is not presumptively unreasonable because the initial team first entering did not have the warrant. The purpose of the provision is to allow the occupant to know why the search is being carried out, to allow an assessment of his or her legal position and to know that there is a color of authority for the search making forcible resistance improper. This requirement is met if the warrant is in the possession of at least one member of the team executing the warrant: *R. v. Cornell*, [2010] 2 S.C.R. 142, 258 C.C.C. (3d) 429.

An officer executing a search warrant is required to have the warrant with her. Where, however, the officer forgot to bring the warrant through inadvertence and the accused consented to the search commencing while the warrant was being brought to his home, then it was not shown that the search was unlawful: *R. v. B. (J.E.)* (1989), 52 C.C.C. (3d) 224 (N.S.C.A.).

The failure to produce a search warrant when requested in relation to the search of a dwelling house constitutes a breach of s. 8 of the *Canadian Charter of Rights and Freedoms*: *R. v. Bohn* (2000), 145 C.C.C. (3d) 320, 33 C.R. (5th) 265 (B.C.C.A.).

The failure to comply with this provision does not, by itself, give rise to a breach of s. 8 of the Charter: *R. v. Patrick* (2007), 227 C.C.C. (3d) 525 (Alta. C.A.), affd 242 C.C.C. (3d) 158 (S.C.C.).

Subsection (2) – The provisions of this subsection are to be read disjunctively, so that when an arrest is being made without possession of a warrant, but pursuant thereto, the duty of the arresting officer is fully discharged by telling the arrested person that the reason for his arrest is the existence of an outstanding warrant. The arresting officer is under no duty to obtain the warrant or ascertain its contents to tell the accused: *R. v. Gamracy*, [1974] S.C.R. 640, 12 C.C.C. (2d) 209 (3:2), where Ritchie J., writing the major decision also held that the leading British case in this area, *Christie v. Leachinsky*, [1947] 1 All E.R. 567 (H.L.), was of no assistance in interpreting s. 29.

PREVENTING BREACH OF PEACE.

30. Every one who witnesses a breach of the peace is justified in interfering to prevent the continuance or renewal thereof and may detain any person who commits or is about to join in or to renew the breach of the peace, for the purpose of giving him into the custody of a peace officer, if he uses no more force than is reasonably necessary to prevent the continuance or renewal of the breach of the peace or than is reasonably proportioned to the danger to be apprehended from the continuance or renewal of the breach of the peace. R.S., c. C-34, s. 30.

CROSS-REFERENCES

Section 31 authorizes a peace officer to receive into custody a person detained under this section. This section does not itself create an offence, however, a provincial court judge would appear to still have a common law power to bind a person over to keep the peace. See notes under s. 810, *infra*. There are also other provisions of the *Criminal Code* which may apply to conduct amounting to breach of the peace. See s. 49, breach of the peace in presence of Her Majesty; s. 175, causing a disturbance. A breach of the peace may escalate into an unlawful assembly or a riot, in which case see ss. 32, 33 and 63 to 69.

SYNOPSIS

This section empowers *anyone who witnesses a breach of the peace* to do a number of things, including using force, to stop it or prevent its continuation or renewal.

A person described above may *detain another* who *is committing* such a breach or *is about to*, if the *purpose* of the detention is to turn the person over to a peace officer. In addition, it must be shown on an objective standard, *either* that the *force used did not exceed that required* to prevent the continuation of the breach of the peace, or its renewal, *or* that it is *proportionate to the danger feared* from such activity.

ARREST FOR BREACH OF PEACE / Giving person in charge.

31. (1) Every peace officer who witnesses a breach of the peace and every one who lawfully assists the peace officer is justified in arresting any person whom he finds

committing the breach of the peace or who, on reasonable grounds, he believes is about to join in or renew the breach of the peace.

(2) Every peace officer is justified in receiving into custody any person who is given into his charge as having been a party to a breach of the peace by one who has, or who on reasonable grounds the peace officer believes has, witnessed the breach of the peace. R.S., c. C-34, s. 31.

CROSS-REFERENCES

"Peace officer" is defined in s. 2. Section 30 authorizes a citizen to detain a person for breach of the peace. Neither this section nor s. 30 create an offence, however, a provincial court judge would appear to still have a common law power to bind a person over to keep the peace. See notes under s. 810, *infra*. There are also other provisions of the *Criminal Code* which may apply to conduct amounting to breach of the peace. See s. 49, breach of the peace in presence of Her Majesty; s. 175, causing a disturbance. A breach of the peace may escalate into an unlawful assembly or a riot, in which case see ss. 32, 33 and 63 to 69. As to use of force in effecting an arrest, see s. 25 and notes thereunder. As to duty of peace officer when effecting an arrest, see s. 29. The offence of resisting or obstructing a peace officer is found in s. 129. The offences of assault with intent to resist arrest and assault of an officer in the execution of duty are in s. 270.

SYNOPSIS

Section 31 empowers peace officers to arrest and detain persons involved in a breach of the peace.

Section 31(1) applies only to peace officers and anyone *lawfully assisting* a peace officer. It is a requirement that the officer *witness* the breach of the peace. The subsection authorizes the arrest of a person committing the breach *or* a person the officer believes is about to join or renew the breach. In the latter circumstance, it must be shown that the officer's belief was based on *reasonable grounds*. This objective requirement modifies the standard to be applied to the officer's beliefs.

Section 31(2) justifies a peace officer in receiving into custody anyone who has been detained by another who either has witnessed that person commit a breach of the peace or the officer believes has witnessed the breach. In the latter case, it must be shown that the officer had *reasonable grounds for the belief* that the person who turned over the suspect witnessed the breach.

ANNOTATIONS

Subsection (1) – In *Blanchard v. Galbraith* (1966), 10 Crim. L.Q. 122 (Man. Q.B.), the plaintiff claimed damages for false imprisonment when in a belligerent and defiant manner he accepted gaol on being given the alternative of returning to his hotel room by an R.C.M.P. constable who was endeavouring to disperse a group of loiterers outside a location that was a known town trouble spot. Hall J. dismissed the action with costs for the defendant R.C.M.P. officers, holding that it was the plain duty of peace officers to act in anticipation of, and thereby prevent breaches of the peace, and the plaintiff's refusal by inviting arrest amounted to obstruction in the discharge of the arresting officer's duty.

Although there is no offence in Canada of breach of the peace, this section does give the police officer a power to arrest anyone for breach of the peace and resisting such an arrest may be the basis for a charge under s. 129. This section is a form of preventive remedy either through arrest for not more than 24 hours or a peace bond at common law: *R. v. Lefebvre* (1982), 1 C.C.C. (3d) 241 (B.C. Co. Ct.), affd 15 C.C.C. (3d) 503 (B.C.C.A.). See also *R. v. Januska* (1996), 106 C.C.C. (3d) 183 (Ont. Ct. (Gen. Div.)).

Although this subsection is confined to breaches of the peace that have actually taken place, there is a common law power for a peace officer to arrest without a warrant where the officer honestly and reasonably believes that such a breach will be committed in the immediate future: *Hayes v. Thompson* (1985), 18 C.C.C. (3d) 254, 44 C.R. (3d) 316 (B.C.C.A.).

The police were justified in making an arrest under this subsection where the accused persisted in interfering with attempts by the officers to shut down a noisy house party. The officers were engaged in the preservation of the peace arising from the continuance of the large and noisy party: *R. v. Khatchadorian* (1998), 127 C.C.C. (3d) 565, 178 W.A.C. 264 (B.C.C.A.).

Subsection (2) – The word "justified" in subsec. (2) gives lawful sanction to the actions of an officer who receives into his custody any person who is given into his charge as having been a party to a breach of the peace by a person who he reasonably believes has witnessed a breach of the peace. The officer is then in the execution of his duty and an accused may be convicted of the offence under s. 129(*a*) if he resists this officer notwithstanding his acquittal on the charge for which he was originally arrested: *R. v. Biron*, [1976] S.C.R. 56, 23 C.C.C. (2d) 513 (5:3).

Suppression of Riots

USE OF FORCE TO SUPPRESS RIOT / Person bound by military law / Obeying order of peace officer / Apprehension of serious mischief / Question of law.

32. (1) Every peace officer is justified in using or in ordering the use of as much force as the peace officer believes, in good faith and on reasonable grounds,

(*a*) is necessary to suppress a riot; and

(*b*) is not excessive, having regard to the danger to be apprehended from the continuance of the riot.

(2) Every one who is bound by military law to obey the command of his superior officer is justified in obeying any command given by his superior officer for the suppression of a riot unless the order is manifestly unlawful.

(3) Every one is justified in obeying an order of a peace officer to use force to suppress a riot if

(*a*) he acts in good faith; and

(*b*) the order is not manifestly unlawful.

(4) Every one who, in good faith and on reasonable grounds, believes that serious mischief will result from a riot before it is possible to secure the attendance of a peace officer is justified in using as much force as he believes in good faith and on reasonable grounds,

(*a*) is necessary to suppress the riot; and

(*b*) is not excessive, having regard to the danger to be apprehended from the continuance of the riot.

(5) For the purposes of this section, the question whether an order is manifestly unlawful or not is a question of law. R.S., c. C-34, s. 32.

CROSS-REFERENCES

"Peace officer" and "military law" are defined by s. 2. Section 33 sets out the duties of peace officers and others, where rioters do not disperse after a proclamation has been read under s. 67 or an offence committed under s. 68. The offence of resisting or obstructing a peace officer is found in s. 129. The offences of assault with intent to resist arrest and assault of an officer in the execution of duty are in s. 270. Section 26 makes a person liable for excessive force. Also see s. 25 as to use of force generally in acting to enforce the law.

SYNOPSIS

This section and s. 33 have the combined effect of protecting specified categories of persons who seek to suppress a riot.

Section 32(1) applies only to peace officers. It justifies the use of force, or ordering others to use it to suppress a riot. The officer will be protected if he had both *good faith* and *reasonable grounds* for believing that the other requirements of the subsection were met. They are that the force used was necessary to suppress a riot *and* that it was *not excessive* considering the *danger* perceived if the riot continued.

Section 32(2) applies to those who are bound by *military law* to obey the orders of a superior officer. It justifies obeying an order by such superior to suppress a riot. However, the protection is removed if the order was *manifestly unlawful*.

Section 32(3) justifies the actions of *anyone obeying the orders of a peace officer* to suppress a riot, if the other conditions of the section are met. It must be shown that the person obeying the order acts in good faith. In addition, the subsection limits protection to those circumstances in which the order of the peace officer is not manifestly unlawful.

Section 32(5) states that the determination of whether an order was manifestly unlawful is a question of law.

Section 32(4) permits a person to act to suppress a riot under certain stringent conditions. It must be shown that the person believes *in good faith and on reasonable grounds* that a peace officer cannot be brought to the scene in time to prevent *serious mischief* from a riot. The remaining requirements of this subsection are the same as those imposed upon peace officers under s. 32(1).

ANNOTATIONS

It was held in *Hebert v. Martin*, [1931] S.C.R. 145, 54 C.C.C. 257, that the taking of life can only be justified by the necessity to disperse a riotous crowd which is dangerous unless dispersed and a police officer was not liable civilly for the death of a person when he had good reason to fear danger to his own life.

The defence under subsec. (1) is made out where the peace officer: (1) believed that the force used was necessary to suppress the riot; (2) believed that the force used was not excessive having regard to the danger to be apprehended from the continuance of the riot; (3) had reasonable grounds for the belief that the force used was necessary to suppress the riot; and (4) had reasonable grounds for the belief that the force was not excessive having regard to the danger apprehended from the continuance of the riot. The determination of "reasonable grounds" requires a consideration of the peace officer's training, experience and the orders of the day. It is not an element of the defence that the person injured by the use of force unlawfully assaulted the police officer or anyone else: *Berntt v. Vancouver (City)* (1999), 135 C.C.C. (3d) 353, 174 D.L.R. (4th) 403, supplementary reasons 139 C.C.C. (3d) 139, 179 D.L.R. (4th) 380 (B.C.C.A.).

DUTY OF OFFICERS IF RIOTERS DO NOT DISPERSE / Protection of officers / Section not restrictive.

33. (1) Where the proclamation referred to in section 67 has been made or an offence against paragraph 68(*a*) or (*b*) has been committed, it is the duty of a peace officer and of a person who is lawfully required by him to assist, to disperse or to arrest persons who do not comply with the proclamation.

(2) No civil or criminal proceedings lie against a peace officer or a person who is lawfully required by a peace officer to assist him in respect of any death or injury that by reason of resistance is caused as a result of the performance by the peace officer or that person of a duty that is imposed by subsection (1).

(3) Nothing in this section limits or affects any powers, duties or functions that are conferred or imposed by this Act with respect to the suppression of riots. R.S., c. C-34, s. 33.

CROSS-REFERENCES

"Peace officer" is defined in s. 2. This section is complementary to ss. 67 to 69 which deal with providing for the reading of a proclamation to disperse a riotous assembly. The unlawful assembly offences and riot offences are found in ss. 63 to 66. Section 32 authorizes the use of force to suppress a riot. The offence of resisting or obstructing a peace officer is found in s. 129. The offences of assault with intent to resist arrest and assault of an officer in the execution of duty are in s. 270. Section 26 makes a person liable for excessive force. Also see s. 25 as to use of force generally in acting to enforce the law.

SYNOPSIS

Section 33 states the duties of peace officers and those lawfully required to assist them if a crowd fails to disperse following the reading of the proclamation under s. 67 of the *Criminal Code* (the "riot act") or if an offence under s. 68 is committed (which relates to the prevention of or interference with the reading of the "riot act" or the failure to disperse after it is read). In addition, subsec. (3) explicitly provides that this section does not limit any powers conferred elsewhere in the *Criminal Code* in relation to the suppression of riots.

Section 33(1) imposes a duty upon peace officers or those lawfully required to assist them to disperse or arrest those who fail to disperse after the proclamation is read or an offence under s. 68 is committed.

Section 33(2) protects persons carrying out the duties imposed by subsec. (1) from civil or criminal liability if death or injury results from the resistance to the carrying out of those duties.

Self-induced Intoxication

WHEN DEFENCE NOT AVAILABLE / Criminal fault by reason of intoxication / Application.

33.1 (1) It is not a defence to an offence referred to in subsection (3) that the accused, by reason of self-induced intoxication, lacked the general intent or the voluntariness required to commit the offence, where the accused departed markedly from the standard of care as described in subsection (2).

(2) For the purposes of this section, a person departs markedly from the standard of reasonable care generally recognized in Canadian society and is thereby criminally at fault where the person, while in a state of self-induced intoxication that renders the person unaware of, or incapable of consciously controlling, their behaviour, voluntarily or involuntarily interferes or threatens to interfere with the bodily integrity of another person.

(3) This section applies in respect of an offence under this Act or any other Act of Parliament that includes as an element an assault or any other interference or threat of interference by a person with the bodily integrity of another person. 1995, c. 32, s. 1.

CROSS-REFERENCES

For notes on other defences generally, see s. 8. For intoxication as a defence to murder, see s. 229. While the term "bodily integrity" is not defined in this Act, reference might be made to *R. v. McCraw*, [1991] 3 S.C.R. 72, 66 C.C.C. (3d) 517, 7 C.R. (4th) 314, where the court considered the term "serious bodily harm" in the former s. 264.1, and held that the phrase includes any hurt or injury, whether physical or psychological, that interferes in a substantial way with the physical or psychological integrity, health or well-being of the complainant.

SYNOPSIS

This section was enacted in response to the decision of the Supreme Court of Canada in *R. v. Daviault*, [1994] 3 S.C.R. 63, 93 C.C.C. (3d) 21, 33 C.R. (4th) 165, noted below, where the court held that self-induced intoxication can be a defence to a general intent offence, including an offence involving assault, such as sexual assault. This section now places limits on the defence. The defence recognized in *Daviault* will not be available for any of the offences referred to in subsec. (3) if the accused departed markedly from the standard of care described in subsec. (2). The effect of subsec. (2) is to deem a certain level of fault in an accused who departs markedly from the standard of care set out in that subsection. Subsection (3) would probably include most of the personal injury offences since even a threat of interference with the complainant's bodily integrity is sufficient to trigger the limits set down in this section.

ANNOTATIONS

Classification of general and specific intent offences – The analysis starts with determining the mental element of the offence by way of statutory interpretation. The next question is whether the crime is one of general or specific intent. There are two main considerations: the importance of the mental element and the social policy underlying the offence. The importance of the mental element refers to the complexity of the thought and reasoning processes that are required. For general intent offences, the mental element simply relates to the performance of the illegal act. These crimes involve such minimal mental acuity that intoxication short of automatism could not deprive the accused of the low level of intent required. In contrast, specific intent offences involve a heightened mental element which may take the form of an ulterior purpose or may entail actual knowledge of circumstances or consequences. When this analysis fails to yield a clear answer, one should turn to policy considerations. This assessment will generally focus on whether alcohol consumption is habitually associated with the crime in question. If it is, then allowing an accused to rely on intoxication as a defence is likely inappropriate: *R. v. Tatton*, [2015], 2 S.C.R. 574, 323 C.C.C. (3d) 166.

Intoxication defence (specific intent offences) – The rules in *D.P.P. v. Beard*, [1920] A.C. 479, 14 Cr. App. R. 159 (H.L.), violate ss. 7 and 11(*d*) of the Charter because they limit the defence of intoxication to the capacity of an accused to form the specific intent. Before a trial judge charges a jury on the issue of intoxication, the judge must be satisfied that the effect of the intoxication was such that it might have impaired the accused's foresight of consequences sufficient to raise a reasonable doubt. Once this threshold test is met, the judge must make clear to the jury that the issue is whether the Crown has satisfied them beyond a reasonable doubt that the accused had the requisite intent. In most circumstances, a one-step charge which omits any reference to "capacity" or "capability" and focuses the jury on the question of "intent in fact" is appropriate. Consequently, the jury must consider whether the accused possessed the requisite specific intent having regard to the evidence of intoxication, along with all of the other evidence in the case. In certain cases, however, in light of the facts of the case and/or the admission of expert evidence, a two-step charge may be appropriate. In this case, the jury is charged both with regard to the capacity to form the requisite intent and with regard to the need to determine in all of the circumstances whether the requisite intent was in fact formed by the accused. In these circumstances, the jury might be instructed that their overall duty is to determine whether or not the accused possessed the requisite intent for the crime. If, on the basis of the expert evidence, the jury is left with a reasonable doubt as to whether, as a result of the consumption of the alcohol, the accused had the capacity to form the requisite intent, that ends the inquiry and the accused must be acquitted of the offence and consideration must then be given to any included lesser offences. If the jury is not left with a reasonable doubt as a result of the expert evidence as to the capacity to form the intent, they must consider and take into account all the surrounding circumstances and the evidence pertaining to those circumstances in determining whether or not the accused possessed the requisite intent for the offence. Furthermore, the presumption that a person intends the natural consequences of their act refers only to a common-sense and logical inference that the jury can, but is not compelled, to make. Where there is some evidence of intoxication, the trial judge must link the instructions on intoxication with the instruction on the common-sense inference so that the jury is specifically instructed that evidence of intoxication can rebut the inference: *R. v. Robinson*, [1996] 1 S.C.R. 683, 105 C.C.C. (3d) 97. See also *R. v. McMaster*, [1996] 1 S.C.R. 740, 105 C.C.C. (3d) 193; and *R. v. Seymour*, [1996] 2 S.C.R. 252, 106 C.C.C. (3d) 520.

The threshold for putting the intoxication defence to the jury on a charge of murder must be evidence sufficient to permit a reasonable inference that the accused did not in fact foresee those consequences. The defence of intoxication is available in circumstances in which evidence falls short of establishing that the accused lacked capacity to form the intent but may still leave the jury with a reasonable doubt that when the offence was committed, the accused in fact foresaw the likelihood of death: *R. v. Lemky*, [1996] 1 S.C.R. 757, 105 C.C.C. (3d) 137.

Where the accused not only understood the nature and quality of his or her acts and knew that they were wrong but had formed the specific intent required for the offence, the fact that, by reason of consumption of drugs, he or she had entered a psychotic state which had caused a loss of self-control or an irresistible impulse, did not constitute a defence of self-induced intoxication: *R. v. Courville* (1982), 2 C.C.C. (3d) 118 (Ont. C.A.), affd [1985] 1 S.C.R. 847, 19 C.C.C. (3d) 97 (7:0).

Intoxication defence (general intent offences) – Extreme drunkenness inducing a state akin to insanity or automatism is a defence to a general intent offence. However, the burden is on the accused to prove the defence on a balance of probabilities and the accused's testimony would have to be supported by expert evidence: *R. v. Daviault*, [1994] 3 S.C.R. 63, 93 C.C.C. (3d) 21. [Note: this case was decided prior to the enactment of this section and, thus, while its holding may apply to certain other general intent offences, this section now limits the availability of the drunkenness defence for the offence considered by the court in *Daviault*, *i.e.*, sexual assault.]

The Crown need not prove that the substance was illegal, that the accused knew precisely what the substance was, or that the accused's purpose in taking the substance was to experience its effects. Voluntary intoxication means the consuming of a substance where the person knew or had reasonable grounds for believing such might cause him to be impaired. The accused need not contemplate the extent of the intoxication or intend a certain level of intoxication. The test for self-induced intoxication requires that the accused voluntarily consumed a substance which he knew or ought to have known was an intoxicant, and the risk of becoming intoxicated was or should have been within his contemplation: *R. v. Chaulk* (2007), 223 C.C.C. (3d) 174 (N.S.C.A.).

Application of subsec. (1) – This section did not apply where the Crown failed to prove that the intoxication was self-induced in the sense that the accused intended to become intoxicated, either by voluntarily ingesting a substance knowing or having reasonable grounds to know it might be dangerous, or by recklessly ingesting the substance, in this case, prescription medication: *R. v. Vickberg* (1998), 16 C.R. (5th) 164 (B.C.S.C.).

Constitutional considerations – Section 7 of the Charter does not require that the intoxication defence be available for all offences and, thus, it was open to Parliament to create an offence such as impaired care or control as defined in s. 253 for which intoxication is no defence: *R. v. Penno*, [1990] 2 S.C.R. 865, 59 C.C.C. (3d) 344.

There is conflicting jurisprudence on whether this section unjustifiably limits the accused's rights under ss. 7 and 11(*d*) of the Charter. The provision has been held to be unconstitutional in *R. v. Dunn*, [1999] O.J. No. 5452; *R. v. Fleming*, 2010 ONSC 8022; and *R. v. McCaw*, 2018 ONSC 3464. It has been upheld as a reasonable limit in *R. v. Vickberg*, [1998] B.C.J. No. 1034; *R. v. Decaire*, [1998] O.J. No. 6339 (Gen. Div.); *R. v. Dow* (2010), 261 C.C.C. (3d) 399 (C.S. Que.); and *R. v. Chan* (2018), 365 C.C.C. (3d) 376 (Ont. S.C.J.).

Defence of Person

DEFENCE — USE OR THREAT OF FORCE / Factors / No defence.

34. (1) A person is not guilty of an offence if

(*a*) they believe on reasonable grounds that force is being used against them or another person or that a threat of force is being made against them or another person;

(*b*) the act that constitutes the offence is committed for the purpose of defending or protecting themselves or the other person from that use or threat of force; and

(*c*) the act committed is reasonable in the circumstances.

(2) In determining whether the act committed is reasonable in the circumstances, the court shall consider the relevant circumstances of the person, the other parties and the act, including, but not limited to, the following factors:

(*a*) the nature of the force or threat;

(*b*) the extent to which the use of force was imminent and whether there were other means available to respond to the potential use of force;

(*c*) the person's role in the incident;

(*d*) whether any party to the incident used or threatened to use a weapon;

(*e*) the size, age, gender and physical capabilities of the parties to the incident;

(*f*) the nature, duration and history of any relationship between the parties to the incident, including any prior use or threat of force and the nature of that force or threat;

(*f*.1) any history of interaction or communication between the parties to the incident;

(*g*) the nature and proportionality of the person's response to the use or threat of force; and

(*h*) whether the act committed was in response to a use or threat of force that the person knew was lawful.

(3) Subsection (1) does not apply if the force is used or threatened by another person for the purpose of doing something that they are required or authorized by law to do in the administration or enforcement of the law, unless the person who commits the act that constitutes the offence believes on reasonable grounds that the other person is acting unlawfully. R.S., c. C-34, s. 34; 2012, c. 9, s. 2.

CROSS-REFERENCES

The defence of property is dealt with in s. 35. As to use of force in administration or enforcement of the law, see s. 25.

SYNOPSIS

This section codifies the defence of use of force in defence of one's self or another person. It replaces a number of sections that had created a complex web of overlapping and confusing provisions. For ease of reference, the person using the force in self-defence is referred to here as the accused. Under this section, the accused is justified in acting in defence of themselves or another person if the following three basic conditions are met: (1) they must believe on reasonable grounds that force is being used against them or another person or that a threat of force is being used against them or another person; (2) the accused's act is committed for the purpose of defending or protecting themselves or the other person from that use or threat of force; and (3) the accused's act was reasonable in the circumstances. Note that, unlike the predecessor sections, the use of force in defence of another is not limited to a person under the accused's protection. However, a factor to be considered in subsec. (2) is the nature of the relationship between the parties to the incident (para. (*f*)).

As under the predecessor provisions, this section incorporates a subjective and objective test. The accused's belief lies at the core of the defence but that belief in the need to resort to force must be based on reasonable grounds and the justifiable amount of force must be reasonable. Subsection (2) is of great importance because it contains a list of non-exhaustive factors that the trier of fact must consider in determining whether the amount of force was reasonable. Unlike the predecessor sections, this section does not explicitly distinguish between deadly force and other types of force in defence. The issue is whether the resort to this amount of force was reasonable in the circumstances. Subsection (2) avoids hard and fast rules such as a duty to retreat before responding with use of force or that the force used be proportionate to the attack defended against. But the subsection does incorporate common sense considerations such as the availability of other means (para. (*b*)) in measuring the reasonableness of the need to resort to force and the amount of force and the need to take into account proportionality (para. (*g*)). Similarly, the section does not expressly distinguish between cases where the resort to force in defence was provoked and unprovoked by the accused. But, subsec. (2) does require the trier of fact to consider the accused's role in the incident (para. (*c*)) and the history of the interaction or communication between the parties to the incident (para. (*f*.1)).

Finally, subsec. (3) incorporates an important limit on the use of the defence under this section. The defence is not available if the victim used force or the threat of force for the purpose of doing something that they are required or authorized by law to do in the administration or enforcement of the law, unless the accused believed on reasonable grounds that the victim was acting unlawfully.

ANNOTATIONS

Editors' Note: We have removed most of the annotations from ss. 34 to 42 which previously dealt with self-defence and related defences. The remaining annotations, although decided under the predecessor sections, were thought to be of some assistance but they must be read with considerable care given the wholesale revisions of the provisions of the Code dealing with the justifiable use of force in defence of person or property.

Application of new provisions – The dominant view is that the amendments to the self-defence provisions effected a substantive change in the law and should be applied purely prospectively: *R. v. Evans* (2015), 321 C.C.C. (3d) 130 (B.C.C.A.); *R. v. Bengy* (2015), 325 C.C.C. (3d) 22 (Ont. C.A.); *R. v. Carriere* (2013), [2014] 1 W.W.R. 117 (Alta. Q.B.). Other cases have held that the provisions should apply retrospectively to charges pre-dating enactment of the new provisions: *R. v. Pandurevic* (2013), 298 C.C.C. (3d) 504 (Ont. S.C.J.); *R. v. Paskimin* (2014), 440 Sask. R. 152 (Q.B.). Still others have held that a judge sitting alone should give the accused the benefit of both regimes: *R. v. Parker* (2013), 107 W.C.B. (2d) 10, [2013] O.J. No. 1755 (C.J.); *R. v. Rothgordt* (2014), 114 W.C.B. (2d) 623, [2014] B.C.J. No. 1398 (S.C.).

Subsection (1) – The issue is not whether the accused was, in fact, unlawfully assaulted but rather whether she reasonably believed in the circumstances that she was being unlawfully assaulted. Further, there is no requirement that the danger be imminent. The imminence of apprehended danger is only one factor that the jury should weigh in determining whether the accused had a reasonable apprehension of danger and a reasonable belief that she could not extricate herself otherwise than by killing the attacker: *R. v. Pétel*, [1994] 1 S.C.R. 3, 87 C.C.C. (3d) 97. Also see *R. v. Nelson* (1992), 71 C.C.C. (3d) 449 (Ont. C.A.); and *R. v. Proulx* (1998), 127 C.C.C. (3d) 511 (B.C.C.A.).

While a trial judge has a duty to put to the jury any defence for which there is an air of reality, the judge also has a duty not to put defences for which there is no air of reality. A defence possesses an air of reality if a properly instructed jury acting reasonably could acquit the accused on the basis of the defence. In applying the air of reality test, a trial judge considers the totality of the evidence, and assumes the evidence relied upon by the accused to be true. The evidential foundation can be indicated by evidence emanating from the examination-in-chief or cross-examination of the accused, of defence witnesses, or of Crown witnesses. It can also rest upon the factual circumstances of the case or from any other evidential source on the record. There is no requirement that the evidence be adduced by the accused. This requires an assessment of whether the evidence relied upon is reasonably capable of supporting the inferences required for the defence to succeed: *R. v. Cinous*, [2002] 2 S.C.R. 3, 162 C.C.C. (3d) 129.

The air of reality test applies to affirmative defences such as self-defence, but it is never the function of the trial judge in a jury trial to assess the evidence and make a determination that the Crown has proven one or more of the essential elements of the offence and direct the jury accordingly. It does not matter how obvious the judge may believe the answer to be or that the judge may be of the view that any other conclusion would be perverse. The trial judge may give an opinion on the matter but never a direction: *R. v. Gunning*, [2005] 1 S.C.R. 627, 196 C.C.C. (3d) 123.

Subsection (2) – To avail himself of this defence, the accused is not necessarily required to retreat and certainly when he is in his own home is not required to retreat and give up his home to his adversary: *R. v. Deegan* (1979), 49 C.C.C. (2d) 417 (Alta. C.A.). Similarly, in *R. v. Docherty* (2012), 292 C.C.C. (3d) 465, the Ontario Court of Appeal held that the jury was not entitled to consider whether the accused could have retreated from his own home in the face of an attack by the deceased.

A person need not be reduced to a state of frenzy in resisting the attack before self-defence is available to him as a defence to a charge of assault: *R. v. Antley* (1963), [1964] 2 C.C.C. 142 (Ont. C.A.).

Subsection (3) – Where physical resistance is offered to an illegal search by peace officers this defence will lie: *R. v. Larlham*, [1971] 4 W.W.R. 304 (B.C.C.A.).

Evidence to support self-defence – Expert psychiatric evidence as to the "battered wife syndrome" was admissible where the accused relied upon the defence under former subsec. (2), which justified the use of deadly force in certain circumstances. Such evidence, relating to the ability of the accused to perceive danger from the deceased, went to the issue of whether she reasonably apprehended death or grievous bodily harm, on the occasion in question, from a threat by the deceased to kill the accused at some later time. While subsec. (2) does not actually stipulate that the accused apprehend imminent danger before acting in self-defence, there is an assumption that it is inherently unreasonable to apprehend death or grievous bodily harm unless and until the physical assault is actually in progress, at which point the victim can reasonably gauge the requisite amount of force needed to repel the attack and act accordingly. Expert testimony can cast doubt on these assumptions as they applied in the context of the battered wife's efforts to repel an assault. Such evidence can explain the heightened sensitivity of a battered woman to her partner's acts. The issue is not what an outsider would have reasonably perceived but what the accused reasonably perceived given her situation and experience. The expert evidence would also be of assistance to the jury on the issue of whether the accused believed on reasonable grounds that it was not otherwise possible to preserve herself from death or grievous bodily harm. The question the jury must ask itself is whether, given the history, circumstances and perception of the accused, her belief that she could not preserve herself from being killed by the deceased later that night except by killing the spouse first was reasonable. This evidence would explain, for example, why the accused could not flee: *R. v. Lavallee*, [1990] 1 S.C.R. 852, 55 C.C.C. (3d) 97 (7:0). See also *R. v. McConnell*, [1996] 1 S.C.R. 1075, affg the dissenting judgment of Conrad J.A. (1995), 169 A.R. 321 (C.A.).

An unlawful assault includes an honest but reasonable mistake as to the existence of an assault. To the extent that expert evidence respecting battered woman syndrome may assist a jury in assessing the reasonableness of an accused's perception, it is relevant to the issue of unlawful assault. A jury must be charged that evidence regarding battered woman syndrome is relevant to the issue of self-defence in respect of the following: why an abused woman might remain in an abusive relationship; the nature and extent of the violence that may exist in an abusive relationship; the accused's ability to perceive danger from her abuser; and whether the accused believed on reasonable grounds that she could not otherwise preserve herself from death or grievous bodily harm: *R. v. M. (M.A.)*, [1998] 1 S.C.R. 123, 121 C.C.C. (3d) 456.

On the trial of a charge of murder where the accused relies on self-defence, evidence of the deceased's character or disposition for violence is admissible to show the probability of the deceased having been the aggressor and to support the accused's evidence that he was attacked by the deceased. This disposition may be evidenced by proof of specific acts of violence unknown to the accused at the time of the incident, by evidence of reputation and by psychiatric evidence, if the question falls within the proper sphere of expert evidence. However, to be admissible, the specific acts of violence unknown to the accused must have sufficient probative value that they will legitimately and reasonably assist the jury and there must exist some other appreciable evidence of the deceased's aggression on the occasion in question. This latter evidence may emanate from the accused himself: *R. v. Scopelliti* (1981), 63 C.C.C. (2d) 481 (Ont. C.A.).

In assessing the admissibility of prior acts of violence by the deceased, its prejudicial impact in arousing feelings of hostility towards the deceased must be weighed against its probative value within the context of affording a fair trial to the accused. On the other hand, where the evidence was of acts of violence against the accused and her relatives, it was no objection to admission that some of these acts had taken place sometime in the past. Even prior acts of destruction of property can be admitted in proper circumstances where, as here, in light of the deceased's history of violence, it would not be unreasonable for the accused to fear that anger directed for the moment towards property would be expanded to assaults upon the person. Further, in light of defence counsel's statement that the evidence was essential for the defence of self-defence to which the accused would be testifying, it may be elicited by counsel through cross-examination of Crown witnesses: *R. v. Ryan* (1989), 49 C.C.C. (3d) 490 (Nfld. C.A.).

The mere fact that the accused raised the defence of self-defence in his evidence, here evidence that the deceased pointed a gun at him, did not permit the Crown to lead evidence of the deceased's peaceable character in rebuttal: *R. v. Dejong* (1998), 125 C.C.C. (3d) 302 (B.C.C.A.).

The evidence of the prior acts of violence unknown to the accused must have sufficient probative value for the purpose for which it is tendered to justify its admission. Evidence which is logically relevant may still be excluded because of the costs or risks associated with its admission: *R. v. Yaeck* (1991), 68 C.C.C. (3d) 545 (Ont. C.A.), leave to appeal to S.C.C. refused [1992] 1 S.C.R. xii, 71 C.C.C. (3d) vii.

Defence of Property

DEFENCE — PROPERTY / No defence / No defence.

35. (1) A person is not guilty of an offence if

(*a*) they either believe on reasonable grounds that they are in peaceable possession of property or are acting under the authority of, or lawfully assisting, a person whom they believe on reasonable grounds is in peaceable possession of property;

(*b*) they believe on reasonable grounds that another person

(i) is about to enter, is entering or has entered the property without being entitled by law to do so,

(ii) is about to take the property, is doing so or has just done so, or

(iii) is about to damage or destroy the property, or make it inoperative, or is doing so;

(*c*) the act that constitutes the offence is committed for the purpose of

(i) preventing the other person from entering the property, or removing that person from the property, or

(ii) preventing the other person from taking, damaging or destroying the property or from making it inoperative, or retaking the property from that person; and

(*d*) the act committed is reasonable in the circumstances.

(2) Subsection (1) does not apply if the person who believes on reasonable grounds that they are, or who is believed on reasonable grounds to be, in peaceable possession of the property does not have a claim of right to it and the other person is entitled to its possession by law.

(3) Subsection (1) does not apply if the other person is doing something that they are required or authorized by law to do in the administration or enforcement of the law, unless the person who commits the act that constitutes the offence believes on reasonable grounds that the other person is acting unlawfully. R.S.C. 1970, c. C-34, s. 35; 2012, c. 9, s. 2.

CROSS-REFERENCES

The defence of use of force to protect persons is dealt with in s. 34. As to use of force in administration or enforcement of the law, see s. 25.

SYNOPSIS

This section codifies the defence of use of force in defence of property. It replaces a number of sections that had created a complex web of overlapping and confusing provisions. The section also avoids terms such as trespasser and trespassing. While the former provisions dealt separately with real and personal property, this section deals with both types of property. Subsection (1) sets out four essential requirements. For the sake of convenience, the person seeking to avail themselves of the defence will be referred to as the accused. First, the accused must believe that they are in peaceable possession of the property or they are acting under the authority of, or lawfully assisting, the person who they believe is in peaceable possession. The belief must be on reasonable grounds. Second, the accused must believe on reasonable grounds that the other person is entering or has entered the property without being entitled by law, is about to take the property, is doing so, or has just done so or is about to damage or destroy the property or make it inoperative or is doing so. Third, the act constituting the offence must be committed for the purpose of prevent the other person from entering the property or removing the person from the property or preventing the other person from taking, damaging, or destroying the property or from making it inoperative, or retaking the property from that person. Finally, the act committed by the accused must be reasonable in the circumstances.

Under subsec. (2), the defence in this section is not available if the accused does not have a claim of right and the other person is entitled to possession by law. The defence is also not available if victim is doing something that they are required or authorized by law to do in the administration or enforcement of the law, unless the accused believes on reasonable grounds that the victim is acting unlawfully.

ANNOTATIONS

Editors' Note: We have removed most of the annotations from ss. 34 to 42 which previously dealt with self-defence, related defences and defence of property. The remaining annotations, although decided under the predecessor sections, were thought to be of some assistance but they must be read with considerable care give the wholesale revisions of the provisions of the Code dealing with the justifiable use of force in defence of person or property.

While the firing of a gun at a person to prevent him from taking movable property may not be justified, the mere pointing of the firearm to scare the person off may, depending on the circumstances, be justified: *R. v. Weare* (1983), 4 C.C.C. (3d) 494 (N.S.C.A.).

A private licensed bailiff may re-acquire possession of movable property for his principal peacefully, but he cannot oppose resistance by another person entitled by law to its possession: *R. v. Doucette* (1960), 129 C.C.C. 102 (Ont. C.A.).

"Claim of right" includes an honest although mistaken belief in entitlement to the property, even though the mistake of fact is based on an error of law or fact: *R. v. Lei* (1997), 120 C.C.C. (3d) 441 (Man. C.A.), leave to appeal to S.C.C. refused (1998), 123 C.C.C. vi, *sub nom. R. v. Kwan.*

On a prosecution for obstructing a peace officer in the execution of his duty arising out of an attempt by the accused to prevent the warrantless entry of the officer into the accused's home, the onus of establishing justification is a severe one. Where the Crown failed to establish either a statutory or common law right of entry, the accused was entitled to resist the entry by force: *R. v. Kephart* (1988), 44 C.C.C. (3d) 97 (Alta. C.A.).

36. [*Repealed*, 2012, c. 9, s. 2.]

37. [*Repealed*, 2012, c. 9, s. 2.]

38. [*Repealed*, 2012, c. 9, s. 2.]

39. [*Repealed*, 2012, c. 9, s. 2.]

40. [*Repealed*, 2012, c. 9, s. 2.]

41. [*Repealed*, 2012, c. 9, s. 2.]

42. [*Repealed*, 2012, c. 9, s. 2.]

Protection of Persons in Authority

CORRECTION OF CHILD BY FORCE.

43. Every schoolteacher, parent or person standing in the place of a parent is justified in using force by way of correction toward a pupil or child, as the case may be, who is under his care, if the force does not exceed what is reasonable under the circumstances. R.S., c. C-34, s. 43.

CROSS-REFERENCES

The terms "schoolteacher", "child", "pupil" and "parent" are not defined, but case-law has provided meaning to those terms. See especially *R. v. Ogg-Moss*, and *R. v. Nixon, infra.* As to liability for excessive force, see s. 26.

SYNOPSIS

This section justifies the use of *force* by certain persons *to correct a child or pupil.*

The persons who may rely upon this section are *schoolteachers, parents or those standing in the place of a parent*. The child or pupil must be *under the care of the person using the force*, and the force must be applied for the *purpose of correcting the child.* Thus, if the child is too young to learn from the correction or is incapable due to mental disability, the use of force will not be justified by s. 43. The force applied cannot exceed what is *reasonable* in the circumstances. This would appear to be an objective standard, although the reference to "in the circumstances" permits some element of subjectivity to be considered.

ANNOTATIONS

This provision does not violate ss. 7, 12, or 15 of the *Canadian Charter of Rights and Freedoms* due to vagueness or overbreadth: *Canadian Foundation for Children, Youth, and the Law v. Canada (Attorney General)*, [2004] 1 S.C.R. 76, 180 C.C.C. (3d) 353.

The person applying the force must have intended it to be for educative or corrective purposes and the child must be capable of benefiting from the correction. "Reasonable under the circumstances" requires the application of an objective test in the context and in light of all of the circumstances of the case. The gravity of the precipitating event is not a relevant consideration. Only minor corrective force of a transitory and trifling nature is exempt from criminal sanction. The provision does not apply to children under two or teenagers as they are not capable of benefiting from such correction. Similarly, children suffering from a disability or as a result of some other contextual factor may not be capable of learning from the force and in such circumstances, the force cannot be said to be corrective. Degrading, inhuman or harmful conduct is not protected. Discipline by the use of objects or blows or slaps to the head is unreasonable. Teachers may reasonably apply force to remove a child from a classroom or secure compliance with instructions but not merely as corporal punishment. Conduct stemming from the caregiver's frustration, loss of temper or abusive personality is not reasonable: *Canadian Foundation for Children, Youth, and the Law v. Canada (Attorney General), supra.*

A mentally retarded adult at a residential centre is neither a "child" nor a "pupil" within the meaning of this section. A "pupil" is limited to a child taking instruction. Further, a mental retardation counsellor at such a centre is not a person standing in the place of a parent, having only temporary care of the adult, not being responsible for the adult's pecuniary needs and by express direction not the delegate of the Minister for the purpose of using force for correction. As well, such counsellor having functions related to personal care of the patient rather than *teaching was not a "schoolteacher"*: *R. v. Ogg-Moss*, [1984] 2 S.C.R. 173, 14 C.C.C. (3d) 116 (5:0); *R. v. Nixon*, [1984] 2 S.C.R. 197, 14 C.C.C. (3d) 257 (5:0).

A babysitter in charge of a child is a person standing in the place of a parent for the purpose of this section: *R. v. Murphy* (1996), 108 C.C.C. (3d) 414 (B.C.C.A.).

In determining whether the force used was reasonable under the circumstances the court must consider the customs of the contemporary Canadian community, not the customs of the accused's former country where corporal punishment may have greater acceptance: *R. v. Baptiste and Baptiste* (1980), 61 C.C.C. (2d) 438 (Ont. Prov. Ct.).

Religious beliefs cannot be used to expand the constitutionally accepted scope of this provision: *R. v. Poulin* (2002), 169 C.C.C. (3d) 378 (P.E.I.S.C.T.D.).

The trial judge erred by stating that the spanking should not have gone on to the point that an onlooker called police. This wrongly applied a subjective standard that effectively delegated the determination of reasonableness to the onlooker: *R. v. S. (S.)* (2011), 277 C.C.C. (3d) 169 (N.B.C.A.).

44. [*Repealed*, 2001, c. 26, s. 294.]

SURGICAL OPERATIONS.

45. Every one is protected from criminal responsibility for performing a surgical operation on any person for the benefit of that person if

(*a*) the operation is performed with reasonable care and skill; and

(*b*) it is reasonable to perform the operation, having regard to the state of health of the person at the time the operation is performed and to all the circumstances of the case. R.S., c. C-34, s. 45.

CROSS-REFERENCES

As to duty to use reasonable knowledge, skill and care in administering surgical care, see s. 216. This section is complementary to the criminal negligence provisions in ss. 219 to 221.

SYNOPSIS

This section sets forth the circumstances in which a person performing surgery for the benefit of a patient is protected from criminal responsibility. They are where: (1) the surgery was done with reasonable care and skill; and (2) it was demonstrably reasonable to perform the operation. In assessing whether these circumstances existed, the relevant factors are the state of the patient's health when the surgery was performed and all other circumstances of the case.

ANNOTATIONS

The conduct of a physician in stopping the respiratory support treatment of his patient, at the freely given and informed request of the patient so that nature may take its course, is not unreasonable within the meaning of this section and would not attract criminal liability: *Nancy B. v. Hôtel-Dieu de Québec* (1992), 69 C.C.C. (3d) 450 (Que. S.C.).

Part II / OFFENCES AGAINST PUBLIC ORDER

Treason and other Offences against the Queen's Authority and Person

HIGH TREASON / Treason / Canadian citizen / Overt act.

46. (1) Every one commits high treason who, in Canada,

(*a*) kills or attempts to kill Her Majesty, or does her any bodily harm tending to death or destruction, maims or wounds her, or imprisons or restrains her;

(*b*) levies war against Canada or does any act preparatory thereto; or

(*c*) assists an enemy at war with Canada, or any armed forces against whom Canadian Forces are engaged in hostilities, whether or not a state of war exists between Canada and the country whose forces they are.

(2) Every one commits treason who, in Canada,

(*a*) uses force or violence for the purpose of overthrowing the government of Canada or a province;

(*b*) without lawful authority, communicates or makes available to an agent of a state other than Canada, military or scientific information or any sketch, plan, model, article, note or document of a military or scientific character that he knows or ought to know may be used by that state for a purpose prejudicial to the safety or defence of Canada;

(*c*) conspires with any person to commit high treason or to do anything mentioned in paragraph (*a*);

(*d*) forms an intention to do anything that is high treason or that is mentioned in paragraph (*a*) and manifests that intention by an overt act; or

(*e*) conspires with any person to do anything mentioned in paragraph (*b*) or forms an intention to do anything mentioned in paragraph (*b*) and manifests that intention by an overt act.

(3) Notwithstanding subsection (1) or (2), a Canadian citizen or a person who owes allegiance to Her Majesty in right of Canada,

(*a*) commits high treason if, while in or out of Canada, he does anything mentioned in subsection (1); or

(*b*) commits treason if, while in or out of Canada, he does anything mentioned in subsection (2).

(4) Where it is treason to conspire with any person, the act of conspiring is an overt act of treason. R.S., c. C-34, s. 46; 1974-75-76, c. 105, s. 2.

CROSS-REFERENCES

Punishment for high treason, see ss. 47(1), 745(*a*). Punishment for treason, see s. 47(2). Limitation period for treason, see s. 48. Limitation as to admission of evidence of overt acts in treason trials, see s. 55. Section 581(4) requires that every overt act that is to be relied on shall be stated in the indictment and by s. 601(9) the indictment may not be amended so as to add to the overt acts. Indictments in case of high treason, see s. 582. Section 604 enacts special provisions for delivery of the indictment, list of witnesses and jury panel to the accused prior to trial of treason or high treason, with some exceptions, as, for example, the offence described by subsec. (1)(*a*). Unavailability of defence of compulsion by threats, see s. 17. The offences in this section are triable only by the superior court of criminal jurisdiction (defined in s. 2) by virtue of ss. 468 and 469. By virtue of s. 522, only a judge of the superior court of criminal jurisdiction may release an accused charged with this offence. This offence may be the basis for constructive murder under s. 230 and the basis for an application for an authorization to intercept private communications by reason of s. 183.

Related offences: s. 49, acts intended to alarm Her Majesty or cause her bodily harm; s. 50(1)(*a*), assisting enemy alien; s. 51, intimidating Parliament or legislature; s. 52, sabotage; s. 53, inciting mutiny; s. 54, assisting deserter from Canadian Forces; s. 56, assisting deserter from R.C.M.P. It is also an offence to fail to report the fact that a person is about to commit treason or high treason, s. 50(1)(*b*). Reference should also be made to the *Official Secrets Act*, R.S.C. 1985, c. O-5.

SYNOPSIS

This section creates the offences of treason and high treason. It also prohibits certain activities by persons outside of Canada.

The elements of high treason are set out in s. 46(1). It includes specified violent actions against the Queen, levying war (or preparing to do so) against Canada or assisting an enemy at war with Canada or whose armed forces are engaged in hostilities with our armed forces.

The offence of treason is created by s. 46(2). Section 46(2)(*a*) states that treason is committed if a person uses force to overthrow the government of Canada or of a province. Section 46(2)(*d*) provides that if a person forms the intention to commit the acts described in s. 46(1)(*a*) and shows that intention by doing an overt act, this is also the full offence of treason. It is also treason to conspire to do the acts described in s. 46(1)(*a*) or to conspire to commit high treason.

An alternative basis for liability is found in s. 46(2)(*b*), stemming from making available any of a specified class of documents to a foreign agent or state which the accused *knows or ought to know* could be used for a purpose prejudicial to the *safety or defence of Canada*. This paragraph specifies that the accused must have no lawful authority for communicating or making available such material. A conspiracy to do so or the intention to do so if accompanied by an overt act constitutes treason under s. 46(2)(*e*).

Section 46(4) provides that conspiring is an overt act of treason in circumstances in which it is treason to conspire with another person.

Section 46(3) imposes liability for either high treason or treason, as the case may be, upon Canadians or those who owe allegiance to Her Majesty in right of Canada for doing the things *inside or outside of Canada* described in s. 46(1) or (2).

PUNISHMENT FOR HIGH TREASON / Punishment for treason / Corroboration / Minimum punishment.

47. (1) Every one who commits high treason is guilty of an indictable offence and shall be sentenced to imprisonment for life.

(2) Every one who commits treason is guilty of an indictable offence and liable

(*a*) to be sentenced to imprisonment for life if he is guilty of an offence under paragraph 46(2)(*a*), (*c*) or (*d*);

(*b*) to be sentenced to imprisonment for life if he is guilty of an offence under paragraph 46(2)(*b*) or (*e*) committed while a state of war exists between Canada and another country; or

(*c*) to be sentenced to imprisonment for a term not exceeding fourteen years if he is guilty of an offence under paragraph 46(2)(*b*) or (*e*) committed while no state of war exists between Canada and another country.

(3) No person shall be convicted of high treason or treason on the evidence of only one witness, unless the evidence of that witness is corroborated in a material particular by evidence that implicates the accused.

(4) For the purposes of Part XXIII, the sentence of imprisonment for life prescribed by subsection (1) is a minimum punishment. R.S., c. C-34, s. 47; 1974-75-76, c. 105, s. 2.

CROSS-REFERENCES

Definition of treason and high treason, see s. 46. Punishment for high treason, parole ineligibility, see s. 745(*a*).

Limitation period in treason, see s. 48; Limitation as to admission of evidence of overt acts in treason trials, see s. 55. Section 581(4) requires that every overt act that is to be relied on shall be stated in the indictment and, by s. 601(9), the indictment may not be amended so as to add to the overt acts. Indictments in case of high treason, see s. 582. Unavailability of defence of compulsion by threats, see s. 17. Trial of these offences is by the superior court of criminal jurisdiction (defined in s. 2) by virtue of ss. 468 and 469. By virtue of s. 522, only a judge of the superior court of criminal jurisdiction may release an accused charged with these offences. This offence may be the basis for constructive murder under s. 230 and the basis for an application for an authorization to intercept private communications by reason of s. 183.

SYNOPSIS

This section sets out the punishment for high treason and treason as well as providing for an evidentiary rule applicable to such cases.

The *punishment for high treason is life imprisonment* and this is the *minimum* mandatory punishment. Subsection (2) defines a number of different circumstances under which the sentence for treason varies from 14 years to life.

Section 47(3) provides that no one may be convicted of either offence on the evidence of a sole witness unless that evidence is corroborated in a material particular by evidence implicating the accused.

ANNOTATIONS

In *R. v. B.(G.)*, [1990] 2 S.C.R. 3, 56 C.C.C. (3d) 161 (5:0), the court considered the effect of now repealed s. 586, which provided that no person shall be convicted on the unsworn evidence of a child "unless the evidence of the child is corroborated in a material particular by evidence that implicates the accused". The wording is thus almost identical to subsec. (3) of this section. It was there held that the requirement that the corroborating evidence implicate the accused requires only that the evidence confirm in some material particular the story of the witness giving the evidence which required corroboration. The confirming evidence need not also itself implicate the accused.

LIMITATION / Information for treasonable words.

48. (1) No proceedings for an offence of treason as defined by paragraph 46(2)(*a*) shall be commenced more than three years after the time when the offence is alleged to have been committed.

(2) No proceedings shall be commenced under section 47 in respect of an overt act of treason expressed or declared by open and considered speech unless

(*a*) an information setting out the overt act and the words by which it was expressed or declared is laid under oath before a justice within six days after the time when the words are alleged to have been spoken; and
(*b*) a warrant for the arrest of the accused is issued within ten days after the time when the information is laid. R.S., c. C-34, s. 48; 1974-75-76, c. 105, s. 29.

CROSS-REFERENCES
The term "year" is defined in s. 37 of the *Interpretation Act*, R.S.C. 1985, c. I-21, and, by reason of that definition, calculation of the three year period would be pursuant to s. 28 of the same Act as a number of months. Calculation of the periods of time set out in subsec. (2) is pursuant to the rules in s. 27 of the *Interpretation Act*. In particular, subsec. (5) which provides that where anything is to be done "within" a time after a specified day, the time does not include that day. Also see s. 26 for when time limited expires on a holiday (defined in s. 35 of the same Act). For other provisions relating to treason, see notes under ss. 46 and 47.

SYNOPSIS
This section imposes certain time limits within which prosecutions for particular types of treason may be commenced.

Section 48(1) states that a three-year time-limit applies from the date of the offence if the allegation is based upon the use of force to overthrow the government of Canada or of a province (s. 46(2)(*a*)).

Section 48(2) requires that in order for a prosecution on an allegation of treason based on words spoken in open speech to proceed, the information must be placed before a justice within six days of the words being said and a warrant for the arrest of the accused issued within 10 days thereafter. The information alleging the offence must specify the words which are said to constitute treason.

Prohibited Acts

49. [*Repealed*, 2018, c. 29, s. 1.]

ASSISTING ALIEN ENEMY TO LEAVE CANADA, OR OMITTING TO PREVENT TREASON / Punishment.

50. (1) Every one commits an offence who
(*a*) incites or wilfully assists a subject of
(i) a state that is at war with Canada, or
(ii) a state against whose forces Canadian Forces are engaged in hostilities, whether or not a state of war exists between Canada and the state whose forces they are,
to leave Canada without the consent of the Crown, unless the accused establishes that assistance to the state referred to in subparagraph (i) or the forces of the state referred to in subparagraph (ii), as the case may be, was not intended thereby; or
(*b*) knowing that a person is about to commit high treason or treason does not, with all reasonable dispatch, inform a justice of the peace or other peace officer thereof or make other reasonable efforts to prevent that person from committing high treason or treason.

(2) Every one who commits an offence under subsection (1) is guilty of an indictable offence and liable to imprisonment for a term not exceeding fourteen years. R.S., c. C-34, s. 50; 1974-75-76, c. 105, s. 29.

CROSS-REFERENCES

The terms "Canadian forces", "justice" and "peace officer" are defined in s. 2. Treason and high treason are defined in s. 46. Limitation on admission of evidence of overt acts, see s. 55. The accused has an election as to mode of trial pursuant to s. 536(2). Release of the accused pending trial is governed by s. 515. Section 581(4) requires that every overt act that is to be relied on shall be stated in the indictment and, by s. 601(9), the indictment may not be amended so as to add to the overt acts. Section 7(11) provides for admission of a certificate of the Secretary of State for External Affairs stating that, at a certain time, any state was engaged in an armed conflict against Canada. The term "wilfully" does not have a fixed meaning and must take its meaning from the context. Generally speaking, however, it connotes an intention to bring about a proscribed consequence. See: *R. v. Buzzanga and Durocher* (1979), 49 C.C.C. (2d) 369 (Ont. C.A.).

SYNOPSIS

This section sets out the indictable offences of assisting an enemy alien to leave Canada or omitting to prevent treason. Both offences are punishable by a maximum sentence of 14 years imprisonment.

The offence created by s. 50(1)(*a*) is committed by either *inciting or wilfully assisting* a person who is a subject of a country with whom Canada is at war or with whom our armed forces are engaged in hostilities (regardless of whether war has been declared) to leave Canada. It must be shown that the accused did not have the consent of the Crown for the impugned actions or incitement. The accused may rely upon the defence that there was no intention to assist the foreign government or forces but the *onus is upon the accused* to establish that no such intention existed.

Section 50(1)(*b*) creates one of the few offences in the *Criminal Code* in which liability is established by an omission to report to the authorities the *knowledge that another is about to commit* an offence. The offence is based on the omission of the accused to advise a justice of the peace or peace officer that another person is about to commit *treason or high treason* or to make other reasonable efforts to prevent the commission of either offence.

INTIMIDATING PARLIAMENT OR LEGISLATURE.

51. Every one who does an act of violence in order to intimidate Parliament or the legislature of a province is guilty of an indictable offence and liable to imprisonment for a term not exceeding fourteen years. R.S., c. C-34, s. 51.

CROSS-REFERENCES

Limitation on admission of evidence of overt acts, see s. 55. Section 581(4) requires that every overt act that is to be relied on shall be stated in the indictment and, by s. 601(9), the indictment may not be amended so as to add to the overt acts. This offence is triable only by the superior court of criminal jurisdiction (defined in s. 2) pursuant to ss. 468 and 469. By virtue of s. 522, only a judge of the superior court of criminal jurisdiction may release an accused charged with this offence. This offence may be the basis for an application for an authorization to intercept private communications by reason of s. 183.

SYNOPSIS

This section spells out the indictable offence of intimidating Parliament or a provincial legislature. It must be shown that the accused did an act of violence with the *intention* of creating such intimidation. The maximum sentence upon conviction is 14 years.

SABOTAGE / Definition of "prohibited act" / Saving / Idem.

52. (1) Every one who does a prohibited act for a purpose prejudicial to

(*a*) the safety, security or defence of Canada, or

(*b*) the safety or security of the naval, army or air forces of any state other than Canada that are lawfully present in Canada,

is guilty of an indictable offence and liable to imprisonment for a term not exceeding ten years.

(2) In this section, "prohibited act" means an act or omission that

(*a*) impairs the efficiency or impedes the working of any vessel, vehicle, aircraft, machinery, apparatus or other thing; or

(*b*) causes property, by whomever it may be owned, to be lost, damaged or destroyed.

(3) No person does a prohibited act within the meaning of this section by reason only that

(*a*) he stops work as a result of the failure of his employer and himself to agree on any matter relating to his employment;

(*b*) he stops work as a result of the failure of his employer and a bargaining agent acting on his behalf to agree on any matter relating to his employment; or

(*c*) he stops work as a result of his taking part in a combination of workmen or employees for their own reasonable protection as workmen or employees.

(4) No person does a prohibited act within the meaning of this section by reason only that he attends at or near or approaches a dwelling-house or place for the purpose only of obtaining or communicating information. R.S., c. C-34, s. 52.

CROSS-REFERENCES

"Dwelling-house" is defined in s. 2.

Limitation on admission of evidence of overt acts, see s. 55. Section 581(4) requires that every overt act that is to be relied on shall be stated in the indictment. Note, however, that unlike, for example, on the trial of an offence under s. 53, s. 601(9), which provides that the indictment may not be amended so as to add to the overt acts, does not apply to the trial of this offence. The accused has an election as to mode of trial pursuant to s. 536(2). Release of the accused pending trial is governed by s. 515. This offence may be the basis for an application for an authorization to intercept private communications by reason of s. 183 or a warrant to conduct video surveillance under s. 487.01(5).

SYNOPSIS

This section creates the indictable offence of sabotage and provides exceptions from liability for certain acts or omissions.

The offence is set out in s. 52(1) and consists of doing one of the *prohibited acts* specified in subsec. (2) *for a purpose prejudicial* to the safety, security or defence of the nation, or to the armed forces of another nation which are lawfully within Canada. The maximum sentence for this offence is 10 years.

Subsections (3) and (4) set out the exceptions to the application of this section. Subsection (3) details a number of reasons why an accused may have stopped work (relating primarily to labour disputes and safety concerns) and provides that *these actions alone* do not constitute a prohibited act (see subsec. (2)). Subsection (4) exempts those who go near a place or house *for the purpose only* of obtaining or communicating information.

INCITING TO MUTINY.

53. Every one who

(*a*) attempts, for a traitorous or mutinous purpose, to seduce a member of the Canadian Forces from his duty and allegiance to Her Majesty, or

(*b*) attempts to incite or to induce a member of the Canadian Forces to commit a traitorous or mutinous act,

is guilty of an indictable offence and liable to imprisonment for a term not exceeding fourteen years. R.S., c. C-34, s. 53.

CROSS-REFERENCES

"Canadian Forces" is defined in s. 2. Attempt is defined in s. 24.

Limitation on admission of evidence of overt acts, see s. 55. Section 581(4) requires that every overt act that is to be relied on shall be stated in the indictment and, by s. 601(9), the indictment may not be amended so as to add to the overt acts. This offence is triable only by the superior court of criminal jurisdiction (defined in s. 2) pursuant to ss. 468 and 469. By virtue of s. 522, only a judge of the superior court of criminal jurisdiction may release an accused charged with this offence. Other provisions also deal with offences concerning the military, see, for example, s. 54, assisting deserter; s. 62, offences in relation to military forces; ss. 419, 420, offences in relation to military uniforms and certificates and military stores.

Reference should also be made to the *National Defence Act*, R.S.C. 1985, c. N-5.

SYNOPSIS

This section prohibits attempting to *incite* members of the armed forces *to mutiny*. Paragraph (*a*) requires proof that the accused had a *traitorous or mutinous purpose* for attempting to seduce a member of the forces from his duty and allegiance to the Queen. Paragraph (*b*) prohibits the accused from attempting to induce or incite a member of the armed forces to a mutinous or traitorous act. In neither case is it necessary to show that the attempt was successful. The maximum sentence upon conviction for this indictable offence is 14 years.

ASSISTING DESERTER.

54. Every one who aids, assists, harbours or conceals a person who he knows is a deserter or absentee without leave from the Canadian Forces is guilty of an offence punishable on summary conviction, but no proceedings shall be instituted under this section without the consent of the Attorney General of Canada. R.S., c. C-34, s. 54.

CROSS-REFERENCES

"Canadian Forces" and "Attorney General" are defined in s. 2. As to consent of Attorney General, see s. 583(*h*). Trial of this offence is by a summary conviction court pursuant to Part XXVII. The punishment for this offence is set out in s. 787. The limitation period is set out in s. 786(2). Release pending trial is governed by s. 515, although the accused is eligible for release by a peace officer or the officer in charge, pursuant to ss. 496, 497 and 498. Other provisions also deal with offences concerning the military, see for example: s. 53, inciting to mutiny; s. 62, offences in relation to military forces; ss. 419, 420, offences in relation to military uniforms and certificates and military stores and s. 120, bribery of public officer [note *officers* of the Canadian Forces are within the definition of public officer in s. 2]; s. 122, breach of trust by official; s. 129(*a*), obstructing public officer; s. 129(*b*), refusing to aid public officer; s. 399, false return by public officer.

SYNOPSIS

Section 54 creates an offence punishable on summary conviction for *aiding, assisting, harbouring,* or *concealing* a *deserter* or person who is absent without leave from the armed forces. The accused *must know the status* of the forces member. The federal Attorney General must consent to the commencement of any prosecution under this section.

EVIDENCE OF OVERT ACTS.

55. In proceedings for an offence against any provision in section 47 or sections 50 to 53, evidence of an overt act is not admissible unless that overt act is set out in the

indictment or unless the evidence is otherwise relevant as tending to prove an overt act that is set out in the indictment. R.S., c. C-34, s. 55; 2018, c. 29, s. 2.

CROSS-REFERENCES

Section 581(4) also requires that every overt act that is to be relied on shall be stated in the indictment and except in the case of the offence of sabotage under s. 52, by s. 601(9), the indictment may not be amended so as to add to the overt acts.

SYNOPSIS

This section sets out a rule of criminal procedure which imposes particular requirements upon the wording of an indictment in prosecutions under ss. 47 and 50 to 53. The indictment (which includes an information pursuant to s. 2) must specify the overt act alleged in order for such evidence to be received against the accused. This section mirrors the contents of s. 581(3), in that the substance of the overt act alleged in prosecutions under the aforementioned sections must be specified in the indictment. However, if the evidence is otherwise relevant as tending to prove an overt act alleged in the indictment it may be admitted.

OFFENCES IN RELATION TO MEMBERS OF R.C.M.P.

56. Every one who wilfully

(*a*) persuades or counsels a member of the Royal Canadian Mounted Police to desert or absent himself without leave,

(*b*) aids, assists, harbours or conceals a member of the Royal Canadian Mounted Police who he knows is a deserter or absentee without leave, or

(*c*) aids or assists a member of the Royal Canadian Mounted Police to desert or absent himself without leave, knowing that the member is about to desert or absent himself without leave,

is guilty of an offence punishable on summary conviction. R.S., c. C-34, s. 57; R.S.C. 1985, c. 27 (1st Supp.), s. 8.

CROSS-REFERENCES

"Counsel" is defined in s. 22(3). Trial of this offence is by a summary conviction court pursuant to Part XXVII. The punishment for this offence is set out in s. 787. The limitation period is set out in s. 786(2). Release pending trial is governed by s. 515 although the accused is eligible for release by a peace officer or the officer in charge pursuant to ss. 496, 497 and 498. Other provisions also deal with offences concerning the R.C.M.P., see for example: s. 120, bribery of public officer [note *officers* of the R.C.M.P. are within the definition of public officer in s. 2]; s. 122, breach of trust by official; s. 129(*a*), obstructing public officer; s. 129(*b*), refusing to aid public officer; s. 399, false return by public officer.

SYNOPSIS

Section 56 creates a number of summary conviction offences in relation to members of the R.C.M.P. who are deserters or unlawfully absent without leave. The section specifies a number of prohibited activities which may occur prior to the action by the member or after the member has deserted or is absent without leave. The actions must be done *wilfully* and the assistance be given to the member about to improperly leave the force must be done either *with the knowledge* that the member of the force *is about to desert* or be absent without leave (s. 56(*c*)), or *knowing* that the member has already done so (s. 56(*b*)). It is also an offence to counsel to persuade a member to desert or to be absent without leave. It is not necessary to prove that the accused succeeded in convincing the member to leave the force improperly.

Official Documents

IDENTITY DOCUMENTS / For greater certainty / Definition of "identity document" / Punishment.

56.1 (1) Every person commits an offence who, without lawful excuse, procures to be made, possesses, transfers, sells or offers for sale an identity document that relates or purports to relate, in whole or in part, to another person.

(2) For greater certainty, subsection (1) does not prohibit an act that is carried out

(*a*) in good faith, in the ordinary course of the person's business or employment or in the exercise of the duties of their office;

(*b*) for genealogical purposes;

(*c*) with the consent of the person to whom the identity document relates or of a person authorized to consent on behalf of the person to whom the document relates, or of the entity that issued the identity document; or

(*d*) for a legitimate purpose related to the administration of justice.

(3) For the purposes of this section, "identity document" means a Social Insurance Number card, a driver's licence, a health insurance card, a birth certificate, a death certificate, a passport as defined in subsection 57(5), a document that simplifies the process of entry into Canada, a certificate of citizenship, a document indicating immigration status in Canada, a certificate of Indian status or an employee identity card that bears the employee's photograph and signature, or any similar document, issued or purported to be issued by a department or agency of the federal government or of a provincial or foreign government.

(4) Every person who commits an offence under subsection (1)

(*a*) is guilty of an indictable offence and liable to imprisonment for a term of not more than five years; or

(*b*) is guilty of an offence punishable on summary conviction. 2009, c. 28, s. 1.

CROSS-REFERENCES

Related offences are: s. 57, offences in relation to passports; s. 130, personating a peace officer; s. 340, destroying identity documents; s. 342, unauthorized use of credit cards; s. 342.01, possession of instrument for copying credit cards; s. 362, obtaining by false pretences; s. 367, forgery; s. 368, use and trafficking in a forged document; s. 368.1, possession of instruments for purpose of committing forgery; s. 374, drawing a false document; s. 380, fraud; ss. 402.1-403, identity theft and fraud; s. 404, personation at an examination.

SYNOPSIS

This section, part of Bill S-4, a comprehensive scheme for dealing with identity theft and related offences, makes it an offence, without lawful excuse, to procure to be made, possess, transfer, sell or offer for sale identity documents as defined in subsec. (3) that relate or purport to relate, in whole or in part, to another person. For greater certainty, subsec. (2) makes clear that certain activities do not come within the offence, such as a person who creates such documents as part of their ordinary business or employment, or has the consent of the other person, or for a legitimate purpose related to the administration of justice.

FORGERY OF OR UTTERING FORGED PASSPORT / False statement in relation to passport / Possession of forged passport, etc. / Special provisions applicable / Definition of "passport" / Jurisdiction / Appearance of accused at trial.

57. (1) Every one who, while in or out of Canada,

(*a*) forges a passport, or

(*b*) knowing that a passport is forged

(i) uses, deals with or acts on it, or

(ii) causes or attempts to cause any person to use, deal with, or act on it, as if the passport were genuine,

is guilty of an indictable offence and liable to imprisonment for a term not exceeding fourteen years.

(2) Every one who, while in or out of Canada, for the purpose of procuring a passport for himself or any other person or for the purpose of procuring any material alteration or addition to any such passport, makes a written or an oral statement that he knows is false or misleading

(*a*) is guilty of an indictable offence and liable to imprisonment for a term not exceeding two years; or

(*b*) is guilty of an offence punishable on summary conviction.

(3) Every person who, without lawful excuse, has in their possession a forged passport or a passport in respect of which an offence under subsection (2) has been committed is guilty of an indictable offence and liable to imprisonment for a term of not more than five years.

(4) For the purposes of proceedings under this section,

(*a*) the place where a passport was forged is not material; and

(*b*) the definition "false document" in section 321, and section 366, apply with such modifications as the circumstances require.

(5) In this section, "passport" has the same meaning as in section 2 of the *Canadian Passport Order*.

(6) Where a person is alleged to have committed, while out of Canada, an offence under this section, proceedings in respect of that offence may, whether or not that person is in Canada, be commenced in any territorial division in Canada and the accused may be tried and punished in respect of that offence in the same manner as if the offence had been committed in that territorial division.

(7) For greater certainty, the provisions of this Act relating to

(*a*) requirements that an accused appear at and be present during proceedings, and

(*b*) the exceptions to those requirements,

apply to proceedings commenced in any territorial division pursuant to subsection (6). R.S., c. C-34, s. 58; R.S.C. 1985, c. 27 (1st Supp.), s. 9; 1994, c. 44, s. 4; 1995, c. 5, s. 25; 2013, c. 19, s. 1; 2018, c. 29, s. 3.

CROSS-REFERENCES

The general offence of forgery is set out in ss. 366 and 367 and of uttering in s. 368. For the offences prescribed by subsec. (1) and (3) the accused has an election as to mode of trial pursuant to s. 536(2). For the offence prescribed by subsec. (2), where the prosecution proceeds by way of summary conviction, then the trial is conducted by a summary conviction court pursuant to Part XXVII. The punishment for the offence is then as set out in s. 787 and the limitation period is set out in s. 786(2). Where the prosecution proceeds by way of indictment, then the accused has an election as to mode of trial pursuant to s. 536(2). In any event, release pending trial is governed by s. 515, except that, for the offence in subsec. (2), the accused is eligible for release by a peace officer or the officer in charge pursuant to ss. 496, 497 and 498 and, in the case of the offence in subsec. (3), by the officer in charge pursuant to s. 498. The reference in subsec. (7) to requirements as to presence of the accused is to s. 650. The term "territorial division" is defined in s. 2. The offences in this section may be the basis for an application for an authorization to intercept private communications by reason of s. 183.

The related offence of fraudulent use of a certificate of citizenship and similar documents is found in s. 58. Reference may also be made to the personation offence in s. 403.

SYNOPSIS

This section creates offences relating to the creation of forged passports and their subsequent use or possession.

Section 57(5) provides a definition of passport for the purpose of this section. Section 57(4)(*b*) provides that the definitions of "false document" in ss. 321 and 366 apply to this section with whatever modifications are required. Section 57(6) extends the normal concept of jurisdiction to facilitate prosecution in any territorial division of Canada for an offence under this section which was committed outside the country. Section 57(7) provides that provisions which normally govern when the accused must be present at trial (and when there are exceptions to that rule) apply to any prosecution brought using the special jurisdictional provisions in s. 57(6). The section states that it does not matter where the passport was forged (s. 57(4)(*a*)).

Section 57(1) creates an indictable offence punishable by a maximum of 14 years if the accused *forges the passport personally* or for specified acts relating to either using, dealing with it or acts on it personally or causes another to do so when the accused *knows* that it is forged. The subsection applies regardless of whether these acts occur in Canada.

Section 57(2) creates an offence which turns on the accused making *false or misleading statements* in connection with passports. It must be shown that these statements were made *for the purpose* of either obtaining a passport initially or getting one altered or added to in some *material* way. This offence states that the accused may be in or out of Canada when the statements are made. This offence may be tried by summary conviction proceeding or by way of indictment. If prosecuted by indictment the maximum sentence is two years.

Section 57(3) makes it an offence to possess a passport resulting from the commission of the offence described in subsec. (2). This is an indictable offence punishable by a maximum sentence of five years. The accused may rely upon a lawful excuse but must prove such excuse. As with all burdens placed upon the accused, this provision is likely to attract scrutiny under the *Canadian Charter of Rights and Freedoms*.

ANNOTATIONS

An accused may be convicted of the offence under subsec. (1)(*a*) where she caused another person to actually make the false passport, although the other person was unaware that the statements provided by the accused were false. While the accused could not be convicted of aiding or abetting the other person, who committed no offence, she could be convicted as a principal by application of the common law doctrine of innocent agent, a doctrine preserved in s. 21(1)(*a*): *R. v. Berryman* (1990), 57 C.C.C. (3d) 375 (B.C.C.A.).

An accused could be convicted of the offences under both subsec. (1)(*a*) and subsec. (2), although both charges arose out of the same circumstances. The elements of the two offences are quite different and, in this case, there were other acts beside the providing of the false statements which were instrumental in the forging of the passport: *R. v. Berryman, supra.*

FRAUDULENT USE OF CERTIFICATE OF CITIZENSHIP / Definition of "certificate of citizenship" and "certificate of naturalization".

58. (1) Every one who, while in or out of Canada,

(*a*) uses a certificate of citizenship or a certificate of naturalization for a fraudulent purpose, or

(*b*) being a person to whom a certificate of citizenship or a certificate of naturalization has been granted, knowingly parts with the possession of that certificate with intent that it should be used for a fraudulent purpose,

is guilty of an indictable offence and liable to imprisonment for a term not exceeding two years.

(2) In this section, "certificate of citizenship" and "certificate of naturalization", respectively, mean a certificate of citizenship and a certificate of naturalization as defined by the *Citizenship Act*. R.S., c. C-34, s. 59; 1974-75-76, c. 108, s. 41.

CROSS-REFERENCES

The accused has an election as to mode of trial pursuant to s. 536(2). Release pending trial is governed by s. 515, except that the accused is eligible for release by the officer in charge pursuant to s. 498.

The related offences of forgery of or uttering a forged passport are found in s. 57. Reference may also be made to the personation offence in s. 403.

SYNOPSIS

This section creates the indictable offence of *fraudulently using* a certificate of naturalization or citizenship. It also prohibits *parting with* a certificate of citizenship or naturalization, *knowing and intending* that it will be used fraudulently. The offence is committed whether the improper activities involving these certificates occur inside or outside Canada. The certificates referred to in the section are to be given the meaning set out in the *Citizenship Act*. The maximum sentence for this offence is two years.

Sedition

SEDITIOUS WORDS / Seditious libel / Seditious conspiracy / Seditious intention.

59. (1) Seditious words are words that express a seditious intention.

(2) A seditious libel is a libel that expresses a seditious intention.

(3) A seditious conspiracy is an agreement between two or more persons to carry out a seditious intention.

(4) Without limiting the generality of the meaning of the expression "seditious intention", every one shall be presumed to have a seditious intention who

(*a*) teaches or advocates, or

(*b*) publishes or circulates any writing that advocates,

the use, without the authority of law, of force as a means of accomplishing a governmental change within Canada. R.S., c. C-34, s. 60.

CROSS-REFERENCES

Defence of good faith, see s. 60.

Punishment for sedition, see s. 61.

Special provisions for indictment of seditious libel and for proof of the libel, see s. 584. The sedition offences are triable only by the superior court of criminal jurisdiction (defined in s. 2) by virtue of ss. 468 and 469. By virtue of s. 522, only a judge of the superior court of criminal jurisdiction may release an accused charged with this offence. The offences in this section may be the basis for an application for an authorization to intercept private communications by reason of s. 183. The offence of blasphemous libel is in s. 296, of defamatory libel in ss. 297 to 317 and advocating genocide and hate propaganda in ss. 318 to 320.

SYNOPSIS

This section sets out the essential elements of offences relating to sedition which are created in s. 61. Section 59(4) provides two examples of what is *presumed to demonstrate a seditious intention*, but it is expressly stated that this subsection is not intended to exhaustively define what is encompassed by the phrase *seditious intention*. This presumption may be subject to attack under the *Canadian Charter of Rights and Freedoms*. The heart of the examples given in this subsection is advocating, without legal authority, the use of *force to achieve governmental change within Canada*.

Section 59(1) to (3) defines what is meant by seditious words, seditious libel and seditious conspiracy, all of which have, as the cornerstone, the concept of expressing or agreeing to carry out a seditious intention.

ANNOTATIONS

The leading case on this section is *R. v. Boucher*, [1951] S.C.R. 265, 99 C.C.C. 1 (after rehearing ordered from 96 C.C.C. 48) decided under s. 133 of the 1927 Code which was essentially worded the same as this section. The court was divided on whether a "seditious intention" required proof in all cases of an intention to incite acts of violence or public disorder. Kerwin, Rand, Kellock and Estey JJ. were of the view that it did. Taschereau, Cartwright, Fauteux and (*semble*) Locke JJ. were of the view that it did in all cases except those related to the administration of justice which required only proof of an intention to bring the administration of justice into hatred or contempt or incite disaffection against it. Rinfret C.J.C. did not come to a firm conclusion on the matter but merely pointed out that the advocating of force was not the only instance in which there could be a "seditious intention".

EXCEPTION.

60. Notwithstanding subsection 59(4), no person shall be deemed to have a seditious intention by reason only that he intends, in good faith,

(*a*) to show that Her Majesty has been misled or mistaken in her measures;

(*b*) to point out errors or defects in

(i) the government or constitution of Canada or a province,

(ii) Parliament or the legislature of a province, or

(iii) the administration of justice in Canada;

(*c*) to procure, by lawful means, the alteration of any matter of government in Canada; or

(*d*) to point out, for the purpose of removal, matters that produce or tend to produce feelings of hostility and ill-will between different classes of persons in Canada. R.S., c. C-34, s. 61.

CROSS-REFERENCES

The sedition offences are defined in s. 59.

Punishment for sedition offences is in s. 61.

The sedition offences are triable only by the superior court of criminal jurisdiction (defined in s. 2) by virtue of ss. 468 and 469. By virtue of s. 522 only a judge of the superior court of criminal jurisdiction may release an accused charged with this offence. The sedition offences may be the basis for an application for an authorization to intercept private communications by reason of s. 183.

SYNOPSIS

This section sets out several specific exceptions protecting what might otherwise be said to come within the phrase *seditious intention* as expressed in s. 59(4). The focus of the exceptions is to permit legitimate criticism of the Queen or government policies or to procure change in the government by lawful means. In addition, s. 60(*d*) permits a person to point out matters which may produce ill will among the people of Canada if this is done with the intention of their removal.

PUNISHMENT OF SEDITIOUS OFFENCES.

61. Every one who

(*a*) speaks seditious words,

(*b*) publishes a seditious libel, or

(*c*) is a party to a seditious conspiracy,

is guilty of an indictable offence and liable to imprisonment for a term not exceeding fourteen years. R.S., c. C-34, s. 62.

CROSS-REFERENCES

The sedition offences are defined in s. 59. Note the good faith exception in s. 60.

Special provision for indictment of seditious libel, see s. 584.

Special provisions for indictment of seditious libel and for proof of the libel, see s. 584.

The sedition offences are triable only by the superior court of criminal jurisdiction (defined in s. 2) by virtue of ss. 468 and 469. By virtue of s. 522, only a judge of the superior court of criminal jurisdiction may release an accused charged with this offence. The offences referred to in this section may be the basis for an application for an authorization to intercept private communications by reason of s. 183.

SYNOPSIS

This section creates indictable offences relating to sedition and provides for a maximum sentence upon conviction of 14 years. The gravamen of these offences is expressing a seditious intention, either through speaking words evincing such intention or publishing such words. The third offence also involves seditious intention and prohibits conspiring to carry out this intention.

OFFENCES IN RELATION TO MILITARY FORCES / Definition of "member of a force".

62. (1) Every one who wilfully

(*a*) interferes with, impairs or influences the loyalty or discipline of a member of a force,

(*b*) publishes, edits, issues, circulates or distributes a writing that advises, counsels or urges insubordination, disloyalty, mutiny or refusal of duty by a member of a force, or

(*c*) advises, counsels, urges or in any manner causes insubordination, disloyalty, mutiny or refusal of duty by a member of a force,

is guilty of an indictable offence and liable to imprisonment for a term not exceeding five years.

(2) In this section, "member of a force" means a member of

(*a*) the Canadian Forces; or

(*b*) the naval, army or air forces of a state other than Canada that are lawfully present in Canada. R.S., c. C-34, s. 63.

CROSS-REFERENCES

"Canadian Forces" is defined in s. 2. "Counsels" is defined in s. 22(3). The term "wilfully" does not have a fixed meaning and must take its meaning from the context. Generally speaking, however, it connotes an intention to bring about a proscribed consequence. See: *R. v. Buzzanga and Durocher* (1979), 49 C.C.C. (2d) 369 (Ont. C.A.). The accused has an election as to mode of trial pursuant to s. 536(2). Release pending trial is governed by s. 515 except that the accused is eligible for release by the officer in charge pursuant to s. 498.

Other provisions also deal with offences concerning the military, see, for example, s. 53, inciting to mutiny; s. 54, assisting deserter; ss. 419, 420, offences in relation to military uniforms and certificates and military stores.

Reference should also be made to the *National Defence Act*, R.S.C. 1985, c. N-5.

SYNOPSIS

This section prohibits activity designed to create disloyalty, insubordination, mutiny or refusal of duty by military forces in Canada. Subsection (2) expands the section to apply to both Canadian forces and the armed forces of any other nation which are lawfully present in Canada. Section 62(1)(*a*) spells out a variety of activities which are prohibited, including interfering with the loyalty or discipline of a member of the forces. Section 62(1)(*b*) focuses on participation in activities such as the publication, circulation and distribution of written material advocating such insubordination, disloyalty, mutiny or refusal of duty. Section 62(1)(*c*) prohibits urging, counselling, *or in any way causing* the same range of improper activities by a member of a force as is set out in s. 62(1)(*b*).

The maximum sentence for this indictable offence is five years.

Unlawful Assemblies and Riots

UNLAWFUL ASSEMBLY / Lawful assembly becoming unlawful / Exception.

63. (1) An unlawful assembly is an assembly of three or more persons who, with intent to carry out any common purpose, assemble in such a manner or so conduct themselves when they are assembled as to cause persons in the neighbourhood of the assembly to fear, on reasonable grounds, that they

(*a*) will disturb the peace tumultuously; or

(*b*) will by that assembly needlessly and without reasonable cause provoke other persons to disturb the peace tumultuously.

(2) Persons who are lawfully assembled may become an unlawful assembly if they conduct themselves with a common purpose in a manner that would have made the assembly unlawful if they had assembled in that manner for that purpose.

(3) Persons are not unlawfully assembled by reason only that they are assembled to protect the dwelling-house of any one of them against persons who are threatening to break and enter it for the purpose of committing an indictable offence therein. R.S., c. C-34, s. 64.

CROSS-REFERENCES

Arrest powers for breach of the peace, see ss. 30, 31.

Being a member of an unlawful assembly is a summary conviction offence pursuant to s. 66. The trial is conducted by a summary conviction court pursuant to Part XXVII. The punishment for the offence is then as set out in s. 787 and the limitation period is set out in s. 786(2).

Related provisions concerning riots, including procedure for reading of proclamation to disperse rioters and offences relating to riots, see ss. 64, 65, 67, 68, 69. Use of force to suppress a riot and the duty of officers to disperse rioters, see ss. 32 and 33. The offence of causing a disturbance is in s. 175.

SYNOPSIS

Section 63 sets out what constitutes an *unlawful assembly*, and also provides for certain exceptions. Stripped to its essentials, s. 63(1) requires that three or more persons be involved, and that they assemble in a way, or behave in such a way after assembling, that causes others in the neighbourhood to be afraid that the assembly will either disturb the peace tumultuously or provoke others to do so. Tumultuous means chaotic, disorderly, clamourous or uproarious. It must be shown that the assembly has gathered together *with the intention to carry out a common purpose*, and that the *fears* of those in the area of the assembly are *based on reasonable grounds*. If the offence lies under s. 63(1)(*b*) (provoking others), the accused have the defence of reasonable cause.

Simplified, s. 63(2) provides that any assembly, which was initially lawful may become an unlawful assembly if the people assembled conduct themselves in a manner which would have brought them within s. 63(1), had they done so at the outset of the assembly. Again, it must be shown that there was a common purpose for the assembly under this paragraph.

Subsection (3) exempts persons from criminal liability if they have assembled for the *purpose of protecting the dwelling house* of any of those assembled from others who wish to break and enter this dwelling with the intention of committing therein an indictable offence.

ANNOTATIONS

Subsection (1)(*a*) does not violate ss. 2(*b*), (*c*), (*d*) or 7 of the Charter: *R. v. Lecompte* (2000), 149 C.C.C. (3d) 185 (Que. C.A.), leave to appeal to S.C.C. refused 151 C.C.C. (3d) vi.

An individual member of an assembly is not guilty if he is unaware that the other individuals assembled for the purpose of disturbing the peace or that some individuals conducted themselves in the neighbourhood of the assembly in a manner as to cause fear, on reasonable grounds, that they will disturb the peace tumultuously: *R. v. Lecompte, supra.*

A grievance against the authorities does not provide a legal right to occupy a roadway, which is a public highway over which all members of the public are entitled to traverse: *R. v. Thomas* (1971), 2 C.C.C. (2d) 514 (B.C. Co. Ct.).

Provided that the accused is part of the assembly which has become unlawful through the conduct of its members then it is no defence that he was passively acquiescent: *R. v. Paulger and Les* (1982), 18 C.C.C. (3d) 78 (B.C. Co. Ct.).

RIOT.

64. A riot is an unlawful assembly that has begun to disturb the peace tumultuously. R.S., c. C-34, s. 65.

CROSS-REFERENCES

Section 63, definition of "unlawful assembly"; s. 65, punishment of rioters; s. 67, procedure for reading of proclamation to disperse rioters; s. 68, offences relating to reading of proclamation; s. 69, offence for failure of peace officer to suppress riot; ss. 32 and 33, use of force to suppress a riot and the duty of officers to disperse rioters.

ANNOTATIONS

It is essential to proof of a riot that there be actual or threatened force and violence, in addition to public disorder, confusion and uproar. Moreover, even if a tumultuous disturbance of the peace breaks out during an assembly, the accused must be shown first to have taken some part in that disturbance in one way or another. In addition, the requirement that the persons in the neighbourhood of the assembly fear "on reasonable grounds" that the members of the assembly will disturb the peace tumultuously requires that these grounds be manifest to any reasonable person within the assembly. What is required is at least objective foresight of the consequences set out in s. 63. Finally, the accused must be shown not only to have acted as a participant, but also to have intended to take part in the riot or to have been so reckless as to have acted as if he did so intend. The offence therefore requires proof of a guilty intent, does not impose absolute liability and therefore does not violate s. 7 of the Charter: *R. v. Brien* (1993), 86 C.C.C. (3d) 550 (N.W.T.S.C.).

A tumultuous disturbance requires an air or atmosphere of actual or constructive force of violence. This provision does not violate s. 7 of the Charter as it is neither vague nor overbroad: *R. v. Berntt* (1997), 120 C.C.C. (3d) 344 (B.C.C.A.).

PUNISHMENT OF RIOTER / Concealment of identity.

65. (1) Every one who takes part in a riot is guilty of an indictable offence and liable to imprisonment for a term not exceeding two years.

(2) Every person who commits an offence under subsection (1) while wearing a mask or other disguise to conceal their identity without lawful excuse is guilty of an indictable offence and liable to imprisonment for a term not exceeding 10 years. R.S., c. C-34, s. 66; 2013, c. 15, s. 2.

CROSS-REFERENCES

Definition of "riot", see s. 64. The accused has an election as to mode of trial pursuant to s. 536(2). Release pending trial is governed by s. 515 except that the accused is eligible for release by the officer in charge pursuant to s. 498. Conviction for this offence may, in certain circumstances, attract imposition of an order prohibiting possession of firearms, ammunition or explosive substance under s. 110. Procedure for reading of proclamation to disperse rioters, see s. 67 and offences relating to reading of proclamation, see s. 68. Offence for failure of peace officer to suppress riot, see s. 69. Use of force to suppress a riot and the duty of officers to disperse rioters, see ss. 32 and 33.

PUNISHMENT FOR UNLAWFUL ASSEMBLY / Concealment of identity.

66. Every one who is a member of an unlawful assembly is guilty of an offence punishable on summary conviction.

(2) Every person who commits an offence under subsection (1) while wearing a mask or other disguise to conceal their identity without lawful excuse is guilty of

- **(*a*) an indictable offence and liable to imprisonment for a term not exceeding five years; or**
- **(*b*) an offence punishable on summary conviction. R.S., c. C-34, s. 67; 2013, c. 15, s. 3.**

CROSS-REFERENCES

Definition of "unlawful assembly", see s. 63. The trial is conducted by a summary conviction court pursuant to Part XXVII. The punishment for the offence is set out in s. 787 and the limitation period is set out in s. 786(2). Release pending trial is governed by s. 515, except that the accused is eligible for release by a peace officer or the officer in charge pursuant to ss. 496, 497 and 498. Arrest powers for breach of the peace, see ss. 30, 31. Related provisions concerning riots, including procedure for reading of proclamation to disperse rioters and offences relating to riots, see ss. 64, 65, 67, 68, 69. Use of force to suppress a riot and the duty of officers to disperse rioters, see ss. 32 and 33. The offence of causing a disturbance is in s. 175.

ANNOTATIONS

This provision does not violate ss. 2(*b*), (*c*), (*d*) or 7 of the Charter: *R. v. Lecompte* (2000), 149 C.C.C. (3d) 185 (Que. C.A.), leave to appeal to S.C.C. refused 151 C.C.C. (3d) vi.

The actions of only a few members can turn the assembly into an unlawful one as defined in s. 63 and thereby render all members of the assembly liable to be convicted of the offence under this section: *R. v. Kalyn* (1980), 52 C.C.C. (2d) 378 (Sask. Prov. Ct.).

READING PROCLAMATION.

67. A person who is

- **(*a*) a justice, mayor or sheriff, or the lawful deputy of a mayor or sheriff,**
- **(*b*) a warden or deputy warden of a prison, or**
- **(*c*) the institutional head of a penitentiary, as those expressions are defined in subsection 2(1) of the *Corrections and Conditional Release Act*, or that person's deputy,**

who receives notice that, at any place within the jurisdiction of the person, twelve or more persons are unlawfully and riotously assembled together shall go to that place and, after approaching as near as is safe, if the person is satisfied that a riot is in progress, shall command silence and thereupon make or cause to be made in a loud voice a proclamation in the following words or to the like effect:

Her Majesty the Queen charges and commands all persons being assembled immediately to disperse and peaceably to depart to their habitations or to their lawful business on the pain of being guilty of an offence for which, on conviction, they may be sentenced to imprisonment for life. GOD SAVE THE QUEEN. R.S., c. C-34, s. 68; 1994, c. 44, s. 5.

CROSS-REFERENCES

Definition of "justice", see s. 2. Definition of riot, see s. 64. The definition of sheriff or mayor will be found in the relevant provincial legislation. A justice, sheriff and mayor are peace officers as defined by s. 2. Offences of obstructing a peace officer, see s. 129 and assaulting a peace officer in execution of duty, see s. 270. The offence of taking part in a riot is in s. 65. Punishment of offences in relation to reading of proclamation, see s. 68. Offence by peace officer in failing to suppress riot, see s. 69. Use of force to suppress a riot and the duty of officers to disperse rioters, see ss. 32 and 33.

SYNOPSIS

Section 67 provides for what is commonly referred to as "*reading the riot act*" by a justice, mayor or sheriff (or lawful deputy of the latter two officials) or the head of a prison or penitentiary. The prerequisites for reading the proclamation are that there be *12 or more people* who are unlawfully and riotously assembled and that the official is satisfied that a riot is in progress. The official must then command silence, and shall read, or cause another to read, the "riot act" in a loud voice from as close to those assembled as is safe. The precise words set out in the *Criminal Code* need not be used, so long as the words are "of like effect".

ANNOTATIONS

The trial judge erred in instructing Crown witnesses to omit reference to imprisonment "for life" when testifying about the proclamation, as the evidence did not convey the same message as the proclamation referred to in this provision: *R. v. Thorne* (2004), 192 C.C.C. (3d) 424, 27 C.R. (6th) 366 (N.B.C.A.).

OFFENCES RELATED TO PROCLAMATION.

68. Every one is guilty of an indictable offence and liable to imprisonment for life who

(*a*) opposes, hinders or assaults, wilfully and with force, a person who begins to make or is about to begin to make or is making the proclamation referred to in section 67 so that it is not made;

(*b*) does not peaceably disperse and depart from a place where the proclamation referred to in section 67 is made within thirty minutes after it is made; or

(*c*) does not depart from a place within thirty minutes when he has reasonable grounds to believe that the proclamation referred to in section 67 would have been made in that place if some person had not opposed, hindered or assaulted, wilfully and with force, a person who would have made it. R.S., c. C-34, s. 69.

CROSS-REFERENCES

Procedure for reading proclamation, see s. 67 and cross-references noted under that section. The accused has an election as to mode of trial pursuant to s. 536(2). Release pending trial is governed by s. 515. Conviction for these offences will, in certain circumstances, require imposition of an order prohibiting possession of firearms, ammunition or explosive substance under s. 109.

SYNOPSIS

Section 68 creates a number of indictable offences which flow from the reading of the "riot act" pursuant to s. 67, or an effort to do so. The maximum punishment for these offences is imprisonment for life.

Section 68(*a*) sets out a number of different means of obstructing the efforts of the person who is about to begin, or who has begun, to read the "riot act". The actions of the accused must prevent the completion or the reading of the proclamation. There is no intention specified in the paragraph beyond the intention to do the specified acts *wilfully and with force* to thwart the reading of the proclamation.

Section 68(*b*) makes it an offence not to leave the location where the "riot act" was read and to disperse peacefully within 30 minutes of it being read.

Section 68(*c*) imposes liability for failing to depart and disperse in similar terms to that described in para. (*b*) if the accused had *reasonable grounds to believe* that the proclamation, although not read, would have been, had the official not been thwarted from doing so.

NEGLECT BY PEACE OFFICER.

69. A peace officer who receives notice that there is a riot within his jurisdiction and, without reasonable excuse, fails to take all reasonable steps to suppress the riot is guilty of an indictable offence and liable to imprisonment for a term not exceeding two years. R.S., c. C-34, s. 70.

CROSS-REFERENCES

"Peace officer" is defined in s. 2. Definition of "riot", see s. 64. Procedure for reading proclamation to disperse rioters, see s. 67 and see cross-references noted under that section. Use of force to suppress a riot and the duty of officers to disperse rioters, see ss. 32 and 33. The accused has an election as to mode of trial pursuant to s. 536(2). Release pending trial is governed by s. 515 except that the accused is eligible for release by the officer in charge pursuant to s. 498.

SYNOPSIS

This section creates an offence applicable *only to peace officers* who fail to take all reasonable steps to suppress a riot. It must be shown that the peace officer had notice of the riot within the officer's jurisdiction, and that there was no reasonable excuse for the failure to take steps. This is an indictable offence with a maximum sentence of two years.

ANNOTATIONS

An action against a police officer for damages as the result of the killing of a person taking part in a riot by the officer was dismissed where the officer was found to be acting lawfully within the scope of his duty imposed by this section and s. 32: *Herbert v. Martin*, [1931] S.C.R. 145, 54 C.C.C. 257.

Unlawful Drilling

ORDERS BY GOVERNOR IN COUNCIL / General or special order / Punishment.

70. (1) The Governor in Council may, by proclamation, make orders

- **(*a*) to prohibit assemblies, without lawful authority, of persons for the purpose**
  - **(i) of training or drilling themselves,**
  - **(ii) of being trained or drilled to the use of arms, or**
  - **(iii) of practising military exercises; or**
- **(*b*) to prohibit persons when assembled for any purpose from training or drilling themselves or from being trained or drilled.**

(2) An order that is made under subsection (1) may be general or may be made applicable to particular places, districts or assemblies to be specified in the order.

(3) Every one who contravenes an order made under this section is guilty of an indictable offence and liable to imprisonment for a term not exceeding five years. R.S., c. C-34, s. 71.

CROSS-REFERENCES

"Proclamation" is defined in s. 35 of the *Interpretation Act*, R.S.C. 1985, c. I-21, and procedure for issuing proclamations in s. 18 of that Act. Publication of proclamations is governed by the *Statutory Instruments Act*, R.S.C. 1985, c. S-22.

The accused has an election as to mode of trial pursuant to s. 536(2).

Release pending trial is governed by s. 515 except that the accused is eligible for release by the officer in charge pursuant to s. 498.

SYNOPSIS

Section 70 authorizes the Governor in Council (Cabinet) to make orders which prohibit various types of assemblies for the purpose of activities such as the training or drilling of groups, practising military exercises or arms training. The section only applies if the assembly is without lawful authority. It also prohibits persons who are assembled *for any purpose* from undertaking any of the prohibited activities.

Subsection (2) states that an order made under s. 70(1) may be general or made specifically applicable at a particular area, assembly and so on. One example of the latter would be an order prohibiting a particular private paramilitary training school from being run within Canada.

If the accused contravenes an order proclaimed under s. 70(1), s. 70(3) makes this an indictable offence punishable by up to five years' imprisonment. Basic principles of criminal responsibility (and s. 7 of the *Canadian Charter of Rights and Freedoms*) would require that there be proof that the accused knew of the existence of the relevant order.

Duels

71. [*Repealed*, 2018, c. 29, s. 4.]

Forcible Entry and Detainer

FORCIBLE ENTRY / Matters not material / Forcible detainer / Questions of law.

72. (1) A person commits forcible entry when that person enters real property that is in the actual and peaceable possession of another in a manner that is likely to cause a breach of the peace or reasonable apprehension of a breach of the peace.

(1.1) For the purposes of subsection (1), it is immaterial whether or not a person is entitled to enter the real property or whether or not that person has any intention of taking possession of the real property.

(2) A person commits forcible detainer when, being in actual possession of real property without colour of right, he detains it in a manner that is likely to cause a breach of the peace or reasonable apprehension of a breach of the peace, against a person who is entitled by law to possession of it.

(3) The questions whether a person is in actual and peaceable possession or is in actual possession without colour of right are questions of law. R.S., c. C-34, s. 73; R.S.C. 1985, c. 27 (1st Supp.), s. 10.

CROSS-REFERENCES

Punishment for this offence is prescribed by s. 73 and see cross-references under that section as to mode of trial. There are a number of related provisions as follows: ss. 30 and 31, arrest and detention for breach of the peace; s. 40, defence of dwelling against person forcibly breaking or entering dwelling house; ss. 41 and 42, defence of real property.

The offence of break and enter with intent to commit an indictable offence is defined by s. 348. The term "colour of right" is not defined, but likely embraces an honest, although mistaken, belief of entitlement to the property although the mistake is based on a mistake of law or fact. [See discussion of colour of right in relation to theft in *R. v. Howson*, [1966] 3 C.C.C. 348 (Ont. C.A.).]

SYNOPSIS

Section 72 sets out what constitutes forcible entry or detainer.

Section 72(1) states that *forcible entry* requires proof that the accused entered real property that was actually peacefully possessed by another. It must be further shown that the accused did so in a manner that is *likely to produce either a breach of the peace* or a *reasonable apprehension* of a breach of the peace. Section 72(1.1) provides the clarification that it is irrelevant whether the accused is entitled to enter the property or whether the accused intends to try to take possession of it. Section 72(3) specifies that the issue of whether a person is in actual and peaceable possession is a question of law.

Section 72(2) spells out what comprises *forcible detainer*. It focuses upon the *improper retention of real property* by an accused who does *not have a colour of right* for doing so against the person who has a lawful right to possess this property. The accused must be in actual possession of the real property. It must be shown that the manner of detaining the property is likely to cause a breach of the peace or the reasonable apprehension of this occurring. Subsection (3) provides that the question of whether the accused is in actual possession without colour of right is a question of law. This means that the judge will determine these issues.

ANNOTATIONS

Forcible entry requires taking possession in the sense of some interference with the peaceable possession of the person in actual possession of the real property at the time of entry. The possession must be done in a manner likely to cause a breach of the peace or a reasonable apprehension of a breach of the peace. The breach or apprehended breach must flow from the manner in which possession of the real property is taken, not from the subsequent events. Accordingly, where the accused, while being pursued by the police, was allowed into the home of an acquaintance, there was no interference with peaceable possession and no actual or apprehended breach of the peace. *R. v. D. (J.)* (2002), 171 C.C.C. (3d) 188 (Ont. C.A.).

PUNISHMENT.

73. Every person who commits forcible entry or forcible detainer is guilty of

(*a*) an offence punishable on summary conviction; or

(*b*) an indictable offence and liable to imprisonment for a term not exceeding two years. R.S., c. C-34, s. 74; R.S.C. 1985, c. 27 (1st Supp.), s. 11; 1992, c. 1, s. 58.

CROSS-REFERENCES

Where the prosecution proceeds by way of summary conviction, the trial is conducted by a summary conviction court pursuant to Part XXVII. The punishment for the offence is then as set out in s. 787 and the limitation period is set out in s. 786(2). Where the prosecution proceeds by way of indictment, then the accused has an election as to mode of trial pursuant to s. 536(2), except that the accused is eligible for release by the peace officer and officer in charge pursuant to ss. 496, 497 and 498. Conviction for this offence may in some circumstances attract imposition of an order prohibiting possession of firearms, ammunition or explosive substance under s. 110.

SYNOPSIS

This section sets out the punishment for offences committed under s. 72 (forcible entry or detainer). The offence may be prosecuted by way of summary conviction or by indictment. In the latter case, the maximum sentence is two years' imprisonment.

Piracy

PIRACY BY LAW OF NATIONS / Punishment.

74. (1) Every one commits piracy who does any act that, by the law of nations, is piracy.

(2) Every one who commits piracy while in or out of Canada is guilty of an indictable offence and liable to imprisonment for life. R.S., c. C-34, s. 75; 1974-75-76, c. 105, s. 3.

CROSS-REFERENCES

There is no definition of piracy in the *Criminal Code*, apparently because there was no internationally recognized definition of piracy when the Code was first enacted. In their text, *Canadian Criminal Law, International and Transnation Aspects* (Butterworths, 1981), Williams and Castel suggest that the 1958 Geneva Convention on the High Seas, to which Canada is not a party, is generally declaratory of established principles relating to piracy. Articles 15 and 16 of that Convention are as follows:

> Article 15
>
> Piracy consists of any of the following acts:
>
> (1) Any illegal acts of violence, detention or any act of depredation, committed for private ends by the crew or the passengers of a private ship or a private aircraft, and directed:
>
> (*a*) On the high seas, against another ship or aircraft, or against persons or property on board such ship or aircraft;
>
> (*b*) Against a ship, aircraft, persons or property in a place outside the jurisdiction of any state;
>
> (2) Any act of voluntary participation in the operation of a ship or of an aircraft with knowledge of facts making it a pirate ship or aircraft;
>
> (3) Any act of inciting or of intentionally facilitating an act described in sub-paragraph 1 or sub-paragraph 2 of this article.
>
> Article 16
>
> The acts of piracy, as defined in Article 15, committed by a warship, government ship or government aircraft whose crew has mutinied and taken control of the ship or aircraft are assimilated to acts committed by a private ship.

As to unavailability of defence of compulsion by threats, see s. 17. The offence in this section is triable only by the superior court of criminal jurisdiction (defined in s. 2) by virtue of ss. 468 and 469. By virtue of s. 522, only a judge of the superior court of criminal jurisdiction may release an accused charged with this offence. Where the offence is committed on the territorial sea or on internal waters, see s. 477. Conviction for this offence will require imposition of an order prohibiting possession of firearms, ammunition or explosive substance under s. 109.

SYNOPSIS

Section 74 makes it an indictable offence to commit any act which is defined by the law of nations as *piracy*.

Subsection (2) provides for a maximum sentence of imprisonment for life regardless of whether the act of piracy takes place in or out of Canada.

PIRATICAL ACTS.

75. Every one who, while in or out of Canada,

(*a*) steals a Canadian ship,

(*b*) steals or without lawful authority throws overboard, damages or destroys anything that is part of the cargo, supplies or fittings in a Canadian ship,

(*c*) does or attempts to do a mutinous act on a Canadian ship, or

(*d*) counsels a person to do anything mentioned in paragraph (*a*), (*b*) or (*c*),

CR. CODE

is guilty of an indictable offence and liable to imprisonment for a term not exceeding fourteen years. R.S., c. C-34, s. 76; R.S.C. 1985, c. 27 (1st Supp.), s. 7(3).

CROSS-REFERENCES

"Counsels" is defined in s. 22(3). "Steal" is defined in s. 2 as theft. Theft is defined in s. 322. Inciting to mutiny is also an offence under s. 53.

The offences in this section are triable only by the superior court of criminal jurisdiction (defined in s. 2) by virtue of ss. 468 and 469. By virtue of s. 522, only a judge of the superior court of criminal jurisdiction may release an accused charged with this offence. Where the offence is committed on the territorial sea or on internal waters, see s. 477. Conviction for this offence may, in some circumstances, require imposition of an order prohibiting possession of firearms, ammunition or explosive substance under s. 109.

SYNOPSIS

This indictable offence deals with *piracy*, but is limited to such acts committed in relation to a *Canadian ship*. The maximum sentence upon conviction for any of the offences created by this section is 14 years.

Paragraph (*a*) prohibits stealing a Canadian ship. Paragraph (*b*) prohibits, *without lawful authority*, throwing anything overboard, stealing, or damaging either the cargo of the ship or any part of supplies or fittings of the ship. Paragraph (*c*) states that doing or attempting to do a mutinous act on a Canadian ship is an offence. Finally, para. (*d*) makes it an offence to counsel any one to do any of the acts in the aforementioned paragraphs.

Offences against Air or Maritime Safety **1993, c. 7, s. 2.**

HIJACKING.

76. Every one who, unlawfully, by force or threat thereof, or by any other form of intimidation, seizes or exercises control of an aircraft with intent

(*a*) to cause any person on board the aircraft to be confined or imprisoned against his will,

(*b*) to cause any person on board the aircraft to be transported against his will to any place other than the next scheduled place of landing of the aircraft,

(*c*) to hold any person on board the aircraft for ransom or to service against his will, or

(*d*) to cause the aircraft to deviate in a material respect from its flight plan,

is guilty of an indictable offence and liable to imprisonment for life. 1972, c. 13, s. 6.

CROSS-REFERENCES

Definition of "flight", see s. 7(8).

This offence, if committed outside Canada, is deemed to have been committed in Canada where the accused is found in Canada (s. 7(2)). As to place of trial, see s. 7(5). Availability of plea of *autrefois*, see s. 7(6). Requirement of consent of Attorney General of Canada where offence committed outside Canada and accused is not a Canadian citizen, see s. 7(7). As to territorial jurisdiction where offence committed in Canada, see s. 476(*d*). The accused has an election as to mode of trial pursuant to s. 536(2). Release pending trial is governed by s. 515. This offence may be the basis for first degree murder under s. 231(5)(*a*), and the basis for an application for an authorization to intercept private communications by reason of s. 183 or a warrant to conduct video surveillance under s. 487.01(5). Conviction for this offence will require imposition of an order prohibiting possession of firearms, ammunition or explosive substance under s. 109.

SYNOPSIS

Section 76 prohibits, as an indictable offence, hijacking of aircraft and provides that a person is liable to life imprisonment upon conviction.

It must be shown that the accused acted unlawfully and used either *force or the threat* thereof, or any other form of intimidation *with the intention* of procuring one of the results described in paras. (*a*) to (*d*). Briefly stated, the prohibited acts relate to confining any one against their will on a plane, holding such persons for ransom, transporting any person on a plane against their will, or causing a plane to be diverted from its scheduled flight plan. Also prohibited is forcing any person on the plane from serving against their will.

ENDANGERING SAFETY OF AIRCRAFT OR AIRPORT.

77. Every one who

- **(*a*) on board an aircraft in flight, commits an act of violence against a person that is likely to endanger the safety of the aircraft,**
- **(*b*) using a weapon, commits an act of violence against a person at an airport serving international civil aviation that causes or is likely to cause serious injury or death and that endangers or is likely to endanger safety at the airport,**
- **(*c*) causes damage to an aircraft in service that renders the aircraft incapable of flight or that is likely to endanger the safety of the aircraft in flight,**
- **(*d*) places or causes to be placed on board an aircraft in service anything that is likely to cause damage to the aircraft, that will render it incapable of flight or that is likely to endanger the safety of the aircraft in flight,**
- **(*e*) causes damage to or interferes with the operation of any air navigation facility where the damage or interference is likely to endanger the safety of an aircraft in flight,**
- **(*f*) using a weapon, substance or device, destroys or causes serious damage to the facilities of an airport serving international civil aviation or to any aircraft not in service located there, or causes disruption of services of the airport, that endangers or is likely to endanger safety at the airport, or**
- **(*g*) endangers the safety of an aircraft in flight by communicating to any other person any information that the person knows to be false,**

is guilty of an indictable offence and liable to imprisonment for life. 1972, c. 13, s. 6; 1993, c. 7, s. 3.

CROSS-REFERENCES

Definition of "flight", see s. 7(8). Aircraft deemed to be in service, see s. 7(9). Assault is defined in s. 265.

This offence, if committed outside Canada, is deemed to have been committed in Canada where the accused is found in Canada (s. 7(2)). As to place of trial, see s. 7(5). Availability of plea of *autrefois*, see s. 7(6). Requirement of consent of Attorney General of Canada where offence committed outside Canada and accused is not a Canadian citizen, see s. 7(7). As to territorial jurisdiction where offence committed in Canada, see s. 476(*d*). The accused has an election as to mode of trial pursuant to s. 536(2). Release pending trial is governed by s. 515. This offence may be the basis for an application for an authorization to intercept private communications by reason of s. 183. Conviction for this offence may in some circumstances require imposition of an order prohibiting possession of firearms, ammunition or explosive substance under s. 109.

SYNOPSIS

Section 77 creates five indictable offences relating to endangering aircraft safety while in flight or rendering an aircraft incapable of flight. Upon conviction under s. 77, a person is liable to imprisonment for life.

Paragraphs (*a*) and (*e*) involve actions by the accused *during flight*. The former makes it an offence to commit an assault that is *likely to endanger* the safety of the aircraft. Paragraph (*e*) imposes criminal liability upon any one who *communicates* any information to another that the *accused knows is false* and *endangers the safety* of the aircraft. Note that, unlike the other paragraphs in this section, para. (*e*) requires actual danger to result from the accused's action.

Paragraphs (*b*) and (*c*) prohibit activities which either result in damage to the aircraft so that it is *likely to endanger the safety* of the aircraft or make it incapable of flight. Paragraph (*d*) prohibits interference with air navigation facilities which is likely to endanger aircraft in flight. The doing of an action specified in one of these paragraphs which has the likelihood of producing the endangerment is sufficient to make out the offence.

OFFENSIVE WEAPONS AND EXPLOSIVE SUBSTANCES / Definition of "civil aircraft".

78. (1) Every one, other than a peace officer engaged in the execution of his duty, who takes on board a civil aircraft an offensive weapon or any explosive substance

(*a*) without the consent of the owner or operator of the aircraft or of a person duly authorized by either of them to consent thereto, or

(*b*) with the consent referred to in paragraph (*a*) but without complying with all terms and conditions on which the consent was given,

is guilty of an indictable offence and liable to imprisonment for a term not exceeding fourteen years.

(2) For the purposes of this section, "civil aircraft" means all aircraft other than aircraft operated by the Canadian Forces, a police force in Canada or persons engaged in the administration or enforcement of the *Customs Act*, the *Excise Act* or the *Excise Act, 2001*. 1972, c. 13, s. 6; R.S.C. 1985, c. 1 (2nd Supp.), s. 213(3); 2002, c. 22, s. 325.

CROSS-REFERENCES

Definitions of "Canadian Forces", "peace officers", "offensive weapon", "explosive substance", see s. 2.

Pursuant to s. 7(1), offences, whether inside or outside Canada, in relation to aircraft registered in Canada, or on any aircraft in flight, if the flight terminates in Canada, are deemed to be committed in Canada. Requirement of consent of Attorney General of Canada where proceedings instituted under s. 7 and accused is not a Canadian citizen, see s. 7(7). As to territorial jurisdiction where offence committed in Canada, see s. 476(*d*). The accused has an election as to mode of trial pursuant to s. 536(2). Release pending trial is governed by s. 515. This offence may be the basis for an application for an authorization to intercept private communications by reason of s. 183. Conviction for this offence may attract the imposition of an order prohibiting possession of firearms, ammunition or explosive substance under s. 109.

SYNOPSIS

This section makes it an indictable offence, subject to a number of exceptions, to take an *offensive weapon or explosive device on board a civilian aircraft*. Subsection (2) provides a definition of "civil aircraft".

Peace officers, engaged in the lawful execution of their duty, are exempted from the operation of the section. Also exempt are persons who have the consent of the owner or operator of the aircraft or a duly authorized representative of either. If conditions are imposed as part of such an agreement, it is still an offence to take explosives or offensive weapons on the aircraft *unless the accused acts in compliance with all of the terms and conditions imposed* upon the consent. The maximum sentence for an offence under this section is 14 years.

SEIZING CONTROL OF SHIP OR FIXED PLATFORM / Endangering safety of ship or fixed platform / False communication / Threats causing death or injury/ Definitions / "fixed platform" / "ship".

78.1 (1) Every one who seizes or exercises control over a ship or fixed platform by force or threat of force or by any other form of intimidation is guilty of an indictable offence and liable to imprisonment for life.

(2) Every one who

(*a*) commits an act of violence against a person on board a ship or fixed platform,

(*b*) destroys or causes damage to a ship or its cargo or to a fixed platform,

(*c*) destroys or causes serious damage to or interferes with the operation of any maritime navigational facility, or

(*d*) places or causes to be placed on board a ship or fixed platform anything that is likely to cause damage to the ship or its cargo or to the fixed platform,

where that act is likely to endanger the safe navigation of a ship or the safety of a fixed platform, is guilty of an indictable offence and liable to imprisonment for life.

(3) Every one who communicates information that endangers the safe navigation of a ship, knowing the information to be false, is guilty of an indictable offence and liable to imprisonment for life.

(4) Every one who threatens to commit an offence under paragraph (2)(*a*), (*b*) or (*c*) in order to compel a person to do or refrain from doing any act, where the threat is likely to endanger the safe navigation of a ship or the safety of a fixed platform, is guilty of an indictable offence and liable to imprisonment for life.

(5) In this section,

"fixed platform" means an artificial island or a marine installation or structure that is permanently attached to the seabed for the purpose of exploration or exploitation of resources or for other economic purposes;

"ship" means every description of vessel not permanently attached to the seabed, other than a warship, a ship being used as a naval auxiliary or for customs or police purposes or a ship that has been withdrawn from navigation or is laid up; 1993, c. 7, s. 4.

CROSS-REFERENCES

Section 7(2.2), (2.3), (3.5) and (3.7) deems certain offences to have been committed in Canada where they were committed on board a fixed platform or a ship in the circumstances set out in those subsections. Reference should be made to ss. 477 to 477.2, which set out special rules for Canadian courts assuming jurisdiction over certain offences committed in the exclusive economic zone of Canada, the continental shelf of Canada and on a ship. Section 477.3 sets out powers of arrest, entry, search or seizure or other powers of investigation in relation to such offences. Section 477.4 provides for proof by way of certificate of certain jurisdictional facts. Where a firearm is used in relation to these offences, the accused may be liable to be convicted of the offence under s. 85. The accused may also be liable to the mandatory firearm prohibition in s. 109. This offence may be the basis for an application for an authorization to intercept private communications by reason of s. 183.

The related offences of interfering with marine signals are found in s. 439.

SYNOPSIS

This section creates a number of offences in relation to a ship or fixed platform as defined in subsec. (5). While this section creates the offences, jurisdiction to try the offences will be determined in accordance with the rules set out in s. 7 and ss. 477 to 477.2. Subsection (1) creates an offence similar to the offence of hijacking aircraft. Subsection (2) creates offences where the acts of the accused endanger the safe navigation of a ship or the safety of a fixed platform. Subsection (3) makes it an offence to knowingly communicate false information that endangers the safe navigation of a ship. Subsection (4) makes it an offence to threaten to commit one of the offences set out in subsec. (2)(*a*) to (*c*) to compel a person to do or refrain from doing any act, where the threat is likely to endanger the safe navigation of a ship or the safety of the fixed platform. All offences are indictable offences for which the maximum penalty is life imprisonment.

Dangerous Materials and Devices **2013, c. 13, s. 4.**

DUTY OF CARE RE EXPLOSIVE.

79. Every one who has an explosive substance in his possession or under his care or control is under a legal duty to use reasonable care to prevent bodily harm or death to persons or damage to property by that explosive substance. R.S., c. C-34, s. 77.

CROSS-REFERENCES

Definition of "explosive substance", see s. 2. Definition of "possession", see s. 4(3).

Offences for breach of duty of care re explosives, see s. 80. Note that it would seem the criminal negligence offences would also apply, see ss. 219, 220, 221.

Other offences in relation to explosives: s. 78 (take explosives aboard civil aircraft); s. 81 (using explosive); s. 82 (unlawful possession of explosives).

Although "bodily harm" is not defined in this Part, reference might be made to the definition of that term in the assault section, s. 2.

SYNOPSIS

Section 79 imposes a legal duty upon anyone, who has possession, care or control over an *explosive substance*, to use *reasonable care to prevent bodily harm, death or property damage* arising from the substance.

BREACH OF DUTY.

80. Every one who, being under a legal duty within the meaning of section 79, fails without lawful excuse to perform that duty, is guilty of an indictable offence and, if as a result an explosion of an explosive substance occurs that

(*a*) causes death or is likely to cause death to any person, is liable to imprisonment for life; or

(*b*) causes bodily harm or damage to property or is likely to cause bodily harm or damage to property, is liable to imprisonment for a term not exceeding fourteen years. R.S., c. C-34, s. 78.

CROSS-REFERENCES

Definition of "explosive substance", see s. 2. Although "bodily harm" is not defined for this Part, reference might be made to s. 2. The accused has an election as to mode of trial pursuant to s. 536(2). Release pending trial is governed by s. 515. This offence may be the basis for an application for an authorization to intercept private communications by reason of s. 183. Conviction for this offence may, in some circumstances, require imposition of an order prohibiting possession of firearms, ammunition or explosive substance under s. 109.

Other offences in relation to explosives: s. 78 (taking explosives aboard civil aircraft); s. 81 (using explosives); s. 82 (unlawful possession).

SYNOPSIS

Section 80 makes it an indictable offence for anyone upon whom a legal duty regarding explosives was imposed by the terms of s. 79 to breach that duty. It provides for punishment upon conviction which varies depending on the harm which was likely to result or did result from the failure of the accused to perform that duty. Note that there must be an actual explosion for this section to come into operation. The accused may rely upon a lawful excuse for the failure.

If death resulted or was likely to result, the accused is liable to life imprisonment. For lesser potential or actual harm, the punishment is a maximum of 14 years.

ANNOTATIONS

This section does not contain an included offence of failing to discharge the duty to take reasonable care under s. 79 when no explosion results: *R. v. Yanover and Gerol* (1985), 20 C.C.C. (3d) 300 (Ont. C.A.).

USING EXPLOSIVES / Punishment.

81. (1) Every one commits an offence who

(*a*) does anything with intent to cause an explosion of an explosive substance that is likely to cause serious bodily harm or death to persons or is likely to cause serious damage to property;

(*b*) with intent to do bodily harm to any person

(i) causes an explosive substance to explode,

(ii) sends or delivers to a person or causes a person to take or receive an explosive substance or any other dangerous substance or thing, or

(iii) places or throws anywhere or at or on a person a corrosive fluid, explosive substance or any other dangerous substance or thing;

(*c*) with intent to destroy or damage property without lawful excuse, places or throws an explosive substance anywhere; or

(*d*) makes or has in his possession or has under his care or control any explosive substance with intent thereby

(i) to endanger life or to cause serious damage to property, or

(ii) to enable another person to endanger life or to cause serious damage to property.

(2) Every one who commits an offence under subsection (1) is guilty of an indictable offence and liable

(*a*) for an offence under paragraph (1)(*a*) or (*b*), to imprisonment for life; or

(*b*) for an offence under paragraph (1)(*c*) or (*d*), to imprisonment for a term not exceeding fourteen years. R.S., c. C-34, s. 79.

CROSS-REFERENCES

Definition of "explosive substance", see s. 2. Definition of possession, see s. 4(3).

The accused has an election as to mode of trial pursuant to s. 536(2). Release pending trial is governed by s. 515. This offence may be the basis for an application for an authorization to intercept private communications by reason of s. 183 and a warrant to conduct video surveillance by reason of s. 487.01(5). Conviction for this offence may, in some circumstances, require imposition of an order prohibiting possession of firearms, ammunition or explosive substance under s. 109. Under s. 231(6.1) murder is first degree murder where death is caused while committing or attempting to commit this offence for the benefit etc. of a "criminal organization".

Other offences in relation to explosives: s. 78 (taking explosive aboard civil aircraft); s. 80 (breach of duty of care in relation to explosives); s. 82 (possession without lawful excuse); s. 431.2 (placing explosives in place of public use, government or public facility or public transportation system).

SYNOPSIS

This section makes certain actions relating to dangerous substances into indictable offences and provides for the punishment of such actions.

Section 81(1)(*a*) and (*b*) prohibit actions done which may result in bodily harm to another or, in the case of para. (*a*), either bodily harm or serious damage to property. Violations of either paragraph carry a maximum sentence of life imprisonment. Section 81(1)(*a*) requires that the accused did the action with the intention of causing the explosion of an explosive device. Section 81(1)(*b*) requires that the accused intended to cause bodily harm to another by doing one of the things specified in subparas. (i) to (iii). Note that para. (*a*) requires the *likelihood* of *serious* bodily harm or death, but not the *intent* to cause such harm. On the other hand, para. (*b*) requires the intent to harm but no likelihood that such harm result.

Section 81(1)(*c*) makes it an offence to place or throw an explosive device. However, it must be shown that the accused did the act with the intention of damaging or destroying property without lawful excuse.

Section 81(1)(*d*) relates to the possession, care or control over such a device. To make out the offence under this paragraph, it must be shown that the accused had the intention by the possession, etc., of the device to either endanger life, cause serious property damage or to enable another to do so.

The maximum sentence for offences under s. 81(1)(*c*) and (*d*) is 14 years.

ANNOTATIONS

A conspiracy to violate subsec. (1)(*a*) may be based on possession of explosives where the requisite intent is shown, notwithstanding the existence of the specific possession offence in subsec. (1)(*d*): *R. v. Musitano* (1985), 24 C.C.C. (3d) 65 (Ont. C.A.).

POSSESSION OF EXPLOSIVE / Possession in association with criminal organization.

82. (1) Every person who, without lawful excuse, makes or has in their possession or under their care or control any explosive substance is guilty of an indictable offence and liable to imprisonment for a term of not more than five years.

(2) Every person who, without lawful excuse, makes or has in their possession or under their care or control any explosive substance for the benefit of, at the direction of or in association with a criminal organization is guilty of an indictable offence and liable to imprisonment for a term of not more than 14 years. R.S., c. C-34, s. 80; R.S.C. 1985, c. 27 (1st Supp.), s. 12; 1997, c. 23, s. 2; 2018, c. 29, s. 5.

CROSS-REFERENCES

Definition of "explosive substance" and "criminal organization", see s. 2. Definition of possession, see s. 4(3).

The accused has an election as to mode of trial pursuant to s. 536(2). Release pending trial is governed by s. 515. This offence may be the basis for an application for an authorization to intercept private communications by reason of s. 183.

Other offences in relation to explosives: s. 78 (taking explosive aboard civil aircraft); s. 80 (breach of duty of care in relation to explosives); s. 81 (using explosives).

SYNOPSIS

This section makes it an indictable offence to make, possess or have care or control of an *explosive substance*. The section permits the accused to rely upon a lawful excuse, but places the onus on the accused to establish it. The punishment upon conviction for this offence is a maximum of five years, except if the possession is for the benefit etc., of a criminal organization, in which case the maximum is 14 years and any sentence is to be served consecutively pursuant to s. 82.1.

ANNOTATIONS

The burden imposed on the accused by this section does not apply until the Crown proves beyond a reasonable doubt that the accused had possession of the explosives: *R. v. Mongeau* (1957), 25 C.R. 195 (Que. C.A.).

An accused can be guilty of possession of an explosive substance even if the device he built did not in fact explode when tested by the police. The words "explosive device" are broad enough to encompass devices that fail to function as intended: *R. v. A. (K.D.S.)* (2010), 253 C.C.C. (3d) 556 (N.B.C.A.).

SENTENCES TO BE SERVED CONSECUTIVELY

82.1 A sentence imposed on a person for an offence under subsection 82(2) shall be served consecutively to any other punishment imposed on the person for an offence arising out of the same event or series of events and to any other sentence to which the person is subject at the time the sentence is imposed on the person for an offence under subsection 82(2). 1997, c. 23, s. 2.

DEFINITION OF "DEVICE".

82.2 For the purposes of sections 82.3 to 82.5, "device" means any of the following:

(*a*) a nuclear explosive device;

(*b*) a device that disperses radioactive material;

(*c*) a device that emits ionizing radiation and that is capable of causing death, serious bodily harm or substantial damage to property or the environment;

(*d*) a device that emits ionizing radiation and that is capable of causing death, serious bodily harm or substantial damage to property or the environment. 2013, c. 13, s. 5.

CROSS-REFERENCES

The terms "environment", "nuclear facility", "nuclear material" and "radioactive material" are defined in s. 2. Section 7(2.21) allows for the prosecution in Canada of the offences in ss. 82.3 to 82.6, or a conspiracy or attempt to commit, accessory after the fact or counselling those offences although the acts or omissions were committed outside Canada if the conditions in s. 7(2.21)(*a*), (*b*), (*c*) or (*d*) are met. The definition of "terrorist activity" in s. 83.01 encompasses the offences referred to in s. 7(2.21) that implement the international instruments referred to in s. 83.01(1)(*a*)(v).

SYNOPSIS

The offences in ss. 82.3 to 82.6 were added to this Act to implement the amendments to the Convention on the Physical Protection of Nuclear Material and the International Convention for the Suppression of Acts of Nuclear Terrorism. This section defines "device" for the purpose of ss. 82.3 to 82.5. These three offences are all punishable by life imprisonment. The s. 82.3 offence deals with making a device or possessing, using or otherwise dealing with nuclear material, radioactive material or a device with intent to cause death, serious bodily harm or substantial damage to property or the environment. The section also creates offences in relation to acts against a nuclear facility. Section 82.4 in effect creates offences where nuclear material, radioactive material or a device are used for purposes of extortion. The section makes it an offence to use or alter nuclear material, radioactive material or a device to compel a person, government or international organization to do or refrain from doing any act. The section also makes it an offence to commit an act against a nuclear facility or an act that causes serious interference with or serious disruption of the facility's operation. Section 82.5 makes it an offence to commit an indictable offence with intent to obtain nuclear material, radioactive material or a device or to obtain access to a nuclear facility. Under s.

82.6, a threat to commit any of the offences under ss. 82.3 to 82.5 is itself an offence punishable by 14 years' imprisonment.

Section 82.7 confirms that these offences are not committed where the acts are committed during an armed conflict in accordance with customary or conventional international law or to activities undertaken by military forces in the circumstances set out in that section.

POSSESSION, ETC., OF NUCLEAR MATERIAL, RADIOACTIVE MATERIAL OR DEVICE.

82.3 Everyone who, with intent to cause death, serious bodily harm or substantial damage to property or the environment, makes a device or possesses, uses, transfers, exports, imports, alters or disposes of nuclear material, radioactive material or a device or commits an act against a nuclear facility or an act that causes serious interference with or serious disruption of its operations, is guilty of an indictable offence and liable to imprisonment for life. 2013, c. 13, s. 5.

CROSS-REFERENCES

See CROSS-REFERENCES under s. 82.2.

SYNOPSIS

See SYNOPSIS under s. 82.2.

USE OR ALTERATION OF NUCLEAR MATERIAL, RADIOACTIVE MATERIAL OR DEVICE.

82.4 Everyone who, with intent to compel a person, government or international organization to do or refrain from doing any act, uses or alters nuclear material, radioactive material or a device or commits an act against a nuclear facility or an act that causes serious interference with or serious disruption of its operations, is guilty of an indictable offence and liable to imprisonment for life. 2013, c. 13, s. 5.

CROSS-REFERENCES

See CROSS-REFERENCES under s. 82.2.

SYNOPSIS

See SYNOPSIS under s. 82.2.

COMMISSION OF INDICTABLE OFFENCE TO OBTAIN NUCLEAR MATERIAL, ETC.

82.5 Everyone who commits an indictable offence under this or any other Act of Parliament, with intent to obtain nuclear material, radioactive material or a device or to obtain access to a nuclear facility, is guilty of an indictable offence and is liable to imprisonment for life. 2013, c. 13, s. 5.

CROSS-REFERENCES

See CROSS-REFERENCES under s. 82.2.

SYNOPSIS

See SYNOPSIS under s. 82.2.

THREATS.

82.6 Everyone who threatens to commit an offence under any of sections 82.3 to 82.5 is guilty of an indictable offence and is liable to imprisonment for a term of not more than 14 years. 2013, c. 13, s. 5.

CROSS-REFERENCES
See CROSS-REFERENCES under s. 82.2.

SYNOPSIS
See SYNOPSIS under s. 82.2.

ARMED FORCES.

82.7 For greater certainty, sections 82.3 to 82.6 do not apply to an act that is committed during an armed conflict and that, at the time and in the place of its commission, is in accordance with customary international law or conventional international law applicable to the conflict, or to activities undertaken by military forces of a state in the exercise of their official duties, to the extent that those activities are governed by other rules of international law. 2013, c. 13, s. 5.

CROSS-REFERENCES
See CROSS-REFERENCES under s. 82.2.

SYNOPSIS
See SYNOPSIS under s. 82.2.

Prize Fights

ENGAGING IN PRIZE FIGHT / Definition of "prize fight".

83. (1) Every one who

(*a*) engages as a principal in a prize fight,

(*b*) advises, encourages or promotes a prize fight, or

(*c*) is present at a prize fight as an aid, second, surgeon, umpire, backer or reporter,

is guilty of an offence punishable on summary conviction.

(2) In this section, "prize fight" means an encounter or fight with fists, hands or feet between two persons who have met for that purpose by previous arrangement made by or for them, but does not include

(*a*) a contest between amateur athletes in a combative sport with fists, hands or feet held in a province if the sport is on the programme of the International Olympic Committee or the International Paralympic Committee and, in the case where the province's lieutenant governor in council or any other person or body specified by him or her requires it, the contest is held with their permission;

(*b*) a contest between amateur athletes in a combative sport with fists, hands or feet held in a province if the sport has been designated by the province's lieutenant governor in council or by any other person or body specified by him or her and, in the case where the lieutenant governor in council or other specified person or body requires it, the contest is held with their permission;

(*c*) a contest between amateur athletes in a combative sport with fists, hands or feet held in a province with the permission of the province's lieutenant governor in council or any other person or body specified by him or her; and

(*d*) a boxing contest or mixed martial arts contest held in a province with the permission or under the authority of an athletic board, commission or similar body established by or under the authority of the province's legislature for the control of sport within the province. R.S., c. C-34, s. 81; R.S.C. 1985, c. 27 (1st Supp.), s. 186; 2013, c. 19, s. 1.

CROSS-REFERENCES

The trial of this offence is conducted by a summary conviction court pursuant to Part XXVII. The punishment for the offence is set out in s. 787 and the limitation period is set out in s. 786(2). Release pending trial is determined by s. 515, although the accused is eligible for release by a peace officer under ss. 496, 497 or by the officer in charge under s. 498.

SYNOPSIS

This section prohibits *prize fights* as defined by s. 83(2). The definition is tailored to exclude sanctioned bouts and amateur boxing if the match meets one of the criteria in subsec. (2).

This summary conviction offence may be committed by being one of the pugilists, advising or encouraging others to fight or by promoting the fight. The presence of certain persons is also an offence if the person is there to act in one of the specific capacities which are prohibited, including that of surgeon, second, reporter, umpire, aid or backer.

Part II.1 / TERRORISM

Note: Part II.1 (ss. 83.01 to 83.33) enacted by 2001, c. 41, s. 4 (in force January 17, 2002).

Interpretation

DEFINITIONS / For greater certainty / For greater certainty / Facilitation.

83.01 (1) The following definitions apply in this Part.

"Canadian" means a Canadian citizen, a permanent resident within the meaning of subsection 2(1) of the *Immigration and Refugee Protection Act* or a body corporate incorporated and continued under the laws of Canada or a province.

"entity" means a person, group, trust, partnership or fund or an unincorporated association or organization.

"listed entity" means an entity on a list established by the Governor in Council under section 83.05.

"terrorist activity" means

(*a*) an act or omission that is committed in or outside Canada and that, if committed in Canada, is one of the following offences:

(i) the offences referred to in subsection 7(2) that implement the Convention for the Suppression of Unlawful Seizure of Aircraft, signed at The Hague on December 16, 1970,

(ii) the offences referred to in subsection 7(2) that implement the Convention for the Suppression of Unlawful Acts against the Safety of Civil Aviation, signed at Montreal on September 23, 1971,

(iii) the offences referred to in subsection 7(3) that implement the Convention on the Prevention and Punishment of Crimes against Internationally Protected Persons, including Diplomatic Agents, adopted by the General Assembly of the United Nations on December 14, 1973,

(iv) the offences referred to in subsection 7(3.1) that implement the International Convention against the Taking of Hostages, adopted by the General Assembly of the United Nations on December 17, 1979,

(v) the offences referred to in subsection 7(2.21) that implement the Convention on the Physical Protection of Nuclear Material, done at Vienna and New York on March 3, 1980, as amended by the Amendment to the Convention on the Physical Protection of Nuclear Material, done at Vienna on July 8, 2005 and the International Convention for the Suppression of Acts of Nuclear Terrorism, done at New York on September 14, 2005,

(vi) the offences referred to in subsection 7(2) that implement the Protocol for the Suppression of Unlawful Acts of Violence at Airports Serving International Civil Aviation, supplementary to the Convention for the Suppression of Unlawful Acts against the Safety of Civil Aviation, signed at Montreal on February 24, 1988,

(vii) the offences referred to in subsection 7(2.1) that implement the Convention for the Suppression of Unlawful Acts against the Safety of Maritime Navigation, done at Rome on March 10, 1988,

(viii) the offences referred to in subsection 7(2.1) or (2.2) that implement the Protocol for the Suppression of Unlawful Acts against the Safety of Fixed Platforms Located on the Continental Shelf, done at Rome on March 10, 1988,

(ix) the offences referred to in subsection 7(3.72) that implement the International Convention for the Suppression of Terrorist Bombings, adopted by the General Assembly of the United Nations on December 15, 1997, and

(x) the offences referred to in subsection 7(3.73) that implement the International Convention for the Suppression of the Financing of Terrorism, adopted by the General Assembly of the United Nations on December 9, 1999, or

(*b*) an act or omission, in or outside Canada,

(i) that is committed

(A) in whole or in part for a political, religious or ideological purpose, objective or cause, and

(B) in whole or in part with the intention of intimidating the public, or a segment of the public, with regard to its security, including its economic security, or compelling a person, a government or a domestic or an international organization to do or to refrain from doing any act, whether the public or the person, government or organization is inside or outside Canada, and

(ii) that intentionally

(A) causes death or serious bodily harm to a person by the use of violence,

(B) endangers a person's life,

(C) causes a serious risk to the health or safety of the public or any segment of the public,

(D) causes substantial property damage, whether to public or private property, if causing such damage is likely to result in the conduct or harm referred to in any of clauses (A) to (C), or

(E) causes serious interference with or serious disruption of an essential service, facility or system, whether public or private, other than as a result of advocacy, protest, dissent or stoppage of work that is not intended to result in the conduct or harm referred to in any of clauses (A) to (C),

and includes a conspiracy, attempt or threat to commit any such act or omission, or being an accessory after the fact or counselling in relation to any such act or omission, but, for greater certainty, does not include an act or omission that is committed during an armed conflict and that, at the time and in the place of its commission, is in accordance with customary international law or conventional international law

applicable to the conflict, or the activities undertaken by military forces of a state in the exercise of their official duties, to the extent that those activities are governed by other rules of international law.

"terrorist group" means

(*a*) an entity that has as one of its purposes or activities facilitating or carrying out any terrorist activity, or

(*b*) a listed entity,

and includes an association of such entities.

(1.1) For greater certainty, the expression of a political, religious or ideological thought, belief or opinion does not come within paragraph (*b*) of the definition "terrorist activity" in subsection (1) unless it constitutes an act or omission that satisfies the criteria of that paragraph.

(1.2) For greater certainty, a suicide bombing is an act that comes within paragraph (*a*) or (*b*) of the definition "terrorist activity" in subsection (1) if it satisfies the criteria of that paragraph.

(2) For the purposes of this Part, facilitation shall be construed in accordance with subsection 83.19(2). 2001, c. 41, ss. 4, 126(3); 2010, c. 19, s. 1; 2013, c. 13, s. 6.

CROSS-REFERENCES

Expanded jurisdiction to try offences committed outside Canada that, if committed in Canada would be an indictable offence and would also constitute terrorist activity as defined in para. (*b*) of the definition of terrorist activity in this section, is set out in s. 7(3.75). As to the place of trial in such circumstances, see s. 7(5); procuring attendance of accused, see s. 7(5.1); defences of *autrefois acquit* and *autrefois convict* and pardon, see s. 7(6); consent of the Attorney General of Canada for trial in such cases of non-citizens, see s. 7(7).

ANNOTATIONS

The "motive clause" in s. 83.01(1)(*b*)(i)(A) does not infringe freedom of expression under s. 2(*b*) of the Charter. While the activities targeted by the terrorism offences are in a sense expressive activities, most of the conduct caught by the provisions concerns acts or threats of violence, which are excluded from the scope of the s. 2(*b*) guarantee. Further, it is impossible to infer, without evidence, that the motive clause will have a chilling effect on the exercise of s. 2 freedoms: *R. v. Khawaja* (2012), 290 C.C.C. (3d) 361 (S.C.C.), affg 273 C.C.C. (3d) 415 (Ont. C.A.).

The mental component of the definition of "terrorist activity" has three components: (i) the act or omission must be done with the intention of bringing about one of the consequences described in sub-paras. (A) through (E); (ii) the act or omission must be done with the further intention of bringing about one of the consequences described in subsec. (1)(*b*)(i)(B), namely the intimidation of the public or a segment of the public with respect to its security or compelling a person, government or domestic or international organization to do or refrain from doing any act; and (iii) the act must be done for political, religious or ideological purpose, objective or cause: *R. v. Khawaja*, *supra*.

Financing of Terrorism

PROVIDING OR COLLECTING PROPERTY FOR CERTAIN ACTIVITIES.

83.02 Every one who, directly or indirectly, wilfully and without lawful justification or excuse, provides or collects property intending that it be used or knowing that it will be used, in whole or in part, in order to carry out

(*a*) an act or omission that constitutes an offence referred to in subparagraphs (*a*)(i) to (ix) of the definition of "terrorist activity" in subsection 83.01(1), or

(*b*) any other act or omission intended to cause death or serious bodily harm to a civilian or to any other person not taking an active part in the hostilities in a situation of armed conflict, if the purpose of that act or omission, by its nature or context, is to intimidate the public, or to compel a government or an international organization to do or refrain from doing any act,

is guilty of an indictable offence and is liable to imprisonment for a term of not more than 10 years. 2001, c. 41, s. 4.

CROSS-REFERENCES

Expanded jurisdiction to try offences committed outside Canada that, if committed in Canada would be an offence under this section or a conspiracy, an attempt, being an accessory after or counselling the offence under this section, is set out in s. 7(3.73). As to the place of trial in such circumstances, see s. 7(5); procuring attendance of accused, see s. 7(5.1); defences of *autrefois acquit* and *autrefois convict* and pardon, see s. 7(6); consent of the Attorney General of Canada for trial in such cases of non-citizens, see s. 7(7).

The offence under this section cannot be commenced without the consent of the Attorney General, s. 83.24.

Procedure for freezing terrorist property, see ss. 83.08 to 83.17.

Proceedings may be commenced at instance of Government of Canada and conducted by Attorney General of Canada where the offence was alleged to have occurred outside the province in which the proceedings are commenced, whether or not proceedings have previously been commenced elsewhere in Canada and whether or not the person is in Canada, s. 83.25.

The sentence imposed under this section is to be served consecutively to any other punishment in accordance with s. 83.26. As to parole ineligibility, see s. 743.6(1.2).

A wiretap authorization may be obtained for the offence under this section in accordance with Part VI. Special provisions apply to such authorizations, thus see ss. 185(1.1)(*c*), 186(1.1)(*c*), 186.1(*c*).

Special protections for victims or witnesses in proceedings against an accused for this offence are set out in s. 486. See ss. 37 to 39 of the *Canada Evidence Act*, respecting Crown privilege and disclosure of information injurious to national security, national defence and foreign relations.

PROVIDING, MAKING AVAILABLE, ETC., PROPERTY OR SERVICES FOR TERRORIST PURPOSES.

83.03 Every one who, directly or indirectly, collects property, provides or invites a person to provide, or makes available property or financial or other related services

(*a*) intending that they be used, or knowing that they will be used, in whole or in part, for the purpose of facilitating or carrying out any terrorist activity, or for the purpose of benefiting any person who is facilitating or carrying out such an activity, or

(*b*) knowing that, in whole or part, they will be used by or will benefit a terrorist group,

is guilty of an indictable offence and is liable to imprisonment for a term of not more than 10 years. 2001, c. 41, s. 4.

CROSS-REFERENCES

Expanded jurisdiction to try offences committed outside Canada that, if committed in Canada would be an offence under this section, is set out in s. 7(3.74). As to the place of trial in such circumstances, see s. 7(5); procuring attendance of accused, see s. 7(5.1); defences of *autrefois acquit* and *autrefois convict* and pardon, see s. 7(6); consent of the Attorney General of Canada for trial in such cases of non-citizens, see s. 7(7).

"Terrorist activity" and "terrorist group" are defined in s. 83.01. Section 83.05 sets out the process for listing entities, which then fall within the definition of terrorist group. Procedure for freezing terrorist property, see ss. 83.08 to 83.17.

The offence under this section cannot be commenced without the consent of the Attorney General, s. 83.24

Proceedings may be commenced at instance of Government of Canada and conducted by Attorney General of Canada where the offence was alleged to have occurred outside the province in which the proceedings are commenced, whether or not proceedings have previously been commenced elsewhere in Canada and whether or not the person is in Canada, s. 83.25.

The sentence imposed under this section is to be served consecutively to any other punishment in accordance with s. 83.26. As to parole ineligibility, see s. 743.6(1.2).

A wiretap authorization may be obtained for the offence under this section in accordance with Part VI. Special provisions apply to such authorizations, thus see ss. 185(1.1)(*c*), 186(1.1)(*c*), 186.1(*c*).

Special protections for victims or witnesses in proceedings against an accused for this offence are set out in s. 486. See ss. 37 to 39 of the *Canada Evidence Act*, respecting Crown privilege and disclosure of information injurious to national security, national defence and foreign relations.

USING OR POSSESSING PROPERTY FOR TERRORIST PURPOSES.

83.04 Every one who

(*a*) uses property, directly or indirectly, in whole or in part, for the purpose of facilitating or carrying out a terrorist activity, or

(*b*) possesses property intending that it be used or knowing that it will be used, directly or indirectly, in whole or in part, for the purpose of facilitating or carrying out a terrorist activity,

is guilty of an indictable offence and is liable to imprisonment for a term of not more than 10 years. 2001, c. 41, s. 4.

CROSS-REFERENCES

Expanded jurisdiction to try offences committed outside Canada that, if committed in Canada would be an offence under this section, is set out in s. 7(3.74). As to the place of trial in such circumstances, see s. 7(5); procuring attendance of accused, see s. 7(5.1); defences of *autrefois acquit* and *autrefois convict* and pardon, see s. 7(6); consent of the Attorney General of Canada for trial in such cases of non-citizens, see s. 7(7).

"Terrorist activity" is defined in s. 83.01.

Procedure for freezing terrorist property, see ss. 83.08 to 83.17.

The offence under this section cannot be commenced without the consent of the Attorney General, s. 83.24

Proceedings may be commenced at instance of Government of Canada and conducted by Attorney General of Canada where the offence was alleged to have occurred outside the province in which the proceedings are commenced, whether or not proceedings have previously been commenced elsewhere in Canada and whether or not the person is in Canada, s. 83.25.

The sentence imposed under this section is to be served consecutively to any other punishment in accordance with s. 83.26. As to parole ineligibility, see s. 743.6(1.2).

A wiretap authorization may be obtained for the offence under this section in accordance with Part VI. Special provisions apply to such authorizations, thus see ss. 185(1.1)(*c*), 186(1.1)(*c*), 186.1(*c*).

Special protections for victims or witnesses in proceedings against an accused for this offence are set out in s. 486. See ss. 37 to 39 of the *Canada Evidence Act*, respecting Crown privilege and disclosure of information injurious to national security, national defence and foreign relations.

List of Entities

ESTABLISHMENT OF LIST / Recommendation / Application to Minister / Deeming / Notice of the decision to the applicant / Judicial review / Reference / Evidence / Publication / New application / Review of list / Completion of review / Definition of "judge".

83.05 (1) The Governor in Council may, by regulation, establish a list on which the Governor in Council may place any entity if, on the recommendation of the Minister of Public Safety and Emergency Preparedness, the Governor in Council is satisfied that there are reasonable grounds to believe that

- **(*a*) the entity has knowingly carried out, attempted to carry out, participated in or facilitated a terrorist activity; or**
- **(*b*) the entity is knowingly acting on behalf of, at the direction of or in association with an entity referred to in paragraph (*a*).**

(1.1) The Minister may make a recommendation referred to in subsection (1) only if he or she has reasonable grounds to believe that the entity to which the recommendation relates is an entity referred to in paragraph (1)(*a*) or (*b*).

(2) On application in writing by a listed entity, the Minister shall decide whether there are reasonable grounds to recommend to the Governor in Council that the applicant no longer be a listed entity.

(3) If the Minister does not make a decision on the application referred to in subsection (2) within 60 days after receipt of the application, he or she is deemed to have decided to recommend that the applicant remain a listed entity.

(4) The Minister shall give notice without delay to the applicant of any decision taken or deemed to have been taken respecting the application referred to in subsection (2).

(5) Within 60 days after the receipt of the notice of the decision referred to in subsection (4), the applicant may apply to a judge for judicial review of the decision.

(6) When an application is made under subsection (5), the judge shall, without delay

- **(*a*) examine, in private, any security or criminal intelligence reports considered in listing the applicant and hear any other evidence or information that may be presented by or on behalf of the Minister and may, at his or her request, hear all or part of that evidence or information in the absence of the applicant and any counsel representing the applicant, if the judge is of the opinion that the disclosure of the information would injure national security or endanger the safety of any person;**
- **(*b*) provide the applicant with a statement summarizing the information available to the judge so as to enable the applicant to be reasonably informed of the reasons for the decision, without disclosing any information the disclosure of which would, in the judge's opinion, injure national security or endanger the safety of any person;**
- **(*c*) provide the applicant with a reasonable opportunity to be heard; and**
- **(*d*) determine whether the decision is reasonable on the basis of the information available to the judge and, if found not to be reasonable, order that the applicant no longer be a listed entity.**

(6.1) The judge may receive into evidence anything that, in the opinion of the judge, is reliable and appropriate, even if it would not otherwise be admissible under Canadian law, and may base his or her decision on that evidence.

(7) The Minister shall cause to be published, without delay, in the *Canada Gazette* notice of a final order of a court that the applicant no longer be a listed entity.

(8) A listed entity may not make another application under subsection (2), except if there has been a material change in its circumstances since the time when the entity made its last application or if the Minister has completed the review under subsection (9).

(9) Two years after the establishment of the list referred to in subsection (1), and every two years after that, the Minister shall review the list to determine whether there are still reasonable grounds, as set out in subsection (1), for an entity to be a listed entity and make a recommendation to the Governor in Council as to whether the entity should remain a listed entity. The review does not affect the validity of the list.

(10) The Minister shall complete the review as soon as possible and in any event, no later than 120 days after its commencement. After completing the review, he or she shall cause to be published, without delay, in the *Canada Gazette* notice that the review has been completed.

(11) In this section, "judge" means the Chief Justice of the Federal Court or a judge of the Trial Division of that Court designated by the Chief Justice. 2001, c. 41, s. 4; 2005, c. 10, ss. 18 and 34(1)(*f*)(iii).

CROSS-REFERENCES

"Terrorist activity" is defined in s. 83.01. Once an entity becomes a listed entity under this section it falls within the definition of "terrorist group" in s. 83.01. Specific offences relating to terrorist groups include collecting, providing, making available, etc. property or services for use or benefit of a terrorist group, s. 83.03. As to freezing property of terrorist groups see ss. 83.08, 83.1, 83.12; freezing property of listed entity, see s. 83.11, 83.12. As to forfeiture of property owned controlled by or on behalf of terrorist group, see ss. 83.13 to 83.17. Offence of participating in activity of terrorist group, s. 83.18; committing offence for terrorist group, s. 83.2; instructing persons to carry out activity for benefit etc. of terrorist group, s. 83.21; harbouring or concealing persons known to have or likely to commit terrorist activity, s. 83.24.

Special provision for receiving foreign confidential information, see s. 83.06. Also see generally ss. 37 to 39 of the *Canada Evidence Act*, respecting Crown privilege and disclosure of information injurious to national security, national defence and foreign relations.

Under s. 83.07, an entity may apply to the Solicitor General of Canada for a certificate stating that it is not a listed entity.

ADMISSION OF FOREIGN INFORMATION OBTAINED IN CONFIDENCE / Return of information / Use of information.

83.06 (1) For the purposes of subsection 83.05(6), in private and in the absence of the applicant or any counsel representing it,

(*a*) the Minister of Public Safety and Emergency Preparedness may make an application to the judge for the admission of information obtained in confidence from a government, an institution or an agency of a foreign state, from an international organization of states or from an institution or an agency of an international organization of states; and

(*b*) the judge shall examine the information and provide counsel representing the Minister with a reasonable opportunity to be heard as to whether the information is relevant but should not be disclosed to the applicant or any counsel representing it because the disclosure would injure national security or endanger the safety of any person.

(2) The information shall be returned to counsel representing the Minister and shall not be considered by the judge in making the determination under paragraph 83.05(6)(*d*), if

(*a*) the judge determines that the information is not relevant;

(*b*) the judge determines that the information is relevant but should be summarized in the statement to be provided under paragraph 83.05(6)(*b*); or

(*c*) the Minister withdraws the application.

(3) If the judge decides that the information is relevant but that its disclosure would injure national security or endanger the safety of persons, the information shall not be disclosed in the statement mentioned in paragraph 83.05(6)(*b*), but the judge may base the determination under paragraph 83.05(6)(*d*) on it. 2001, c. 41, s. 4; 2005, c. 10, s. 19.

CROSS-REFERENCES
See cross-references under s. 83.05.

MISTAKEN IDENTITY / Issuance of certificate.

83.07 (1) An entity claiming not to be a listed entity may apply to the Minister of Public Safety and Emergency Preparedness for a certificate stating that it is not a listed entity.

(2) The Minister shall, within 15 days after receiving the application, issue a certificate if he or she is satisfied that the applicant is not a listed entity. 2001, c. 41, s. 4; 2005, c. 10, s. 20.

CROSS-REFERENCES
"Listed entity" is defined in s. 83.01 as an entity listed in accordance with s. 83.05. For other cross-references, see s. 83.05.

Freezing of Property

FREEZING OF PROPERTY / No civil liability.

83.08 (1) No person in Canada and no Canadian outside Canada shall knowingly

(*a*) deal directly or indirectly in any property that is owned or controlled by or on behalf of a terrorist group;

(*b*) enter into or facilitate, directly or indirectly, any transaction in respect of property referred to in paragraph (*a*); or

(*c*) provide any financial or other related services in respect of property referred to in paragraph (*a*) to, for the benefit of or at the direction of a terrorist group.

(2) A person who acts reasonably in taking, or omitting to take, measures to comply with subsection (1) shall not be liable in any civil action arising from having taken or omitted to take the measures, if they took all reasonable steps to satisfy themselves that the relevant property was owned or controlled by or on behalf of a terrorist group. 2001, c. 41, s. 4; 2013, c. 9, s. 3(2).

CROSS-REFERENCES
"Terrorist group" and "Canadian" are defined in s. 83.01. In accordance with s. 83.09 the Solicitor General of Canada or a person designated by the Solicitor General may exempt persons from activity otherwise prohibited by this section. Contravention of this section is an offence under s. 83.12. As to procedures for seizure and forfeiture of property owned or controlled by or on behalf of a terrorist group, see ss. 83.13 to 83.17.

EXEMPTIONS / Ministerial authorization / Existing equities maintained / Third party involvement.

83.09 (1) The Minister of Public Safety and Emergency Preparedness, or a person designated by him or her, may authorize any person in Canada or any Canadian outside Canada to carry out a specified activity or transaction that is prohibited by section 83.08, or a class of such activities or transactions.

(2) The Minister, or a person designated by him or her, may make the authorization subject to any terms and conditions that are required in their opinion and may amend, suspend, revoke or reinstate it.

(3) All secured and unsecured rights and interests in the frozen property that are held by persons, other than terrorist groups or their agents, are entitled to the same ranking that they would have been entitled to had the property not been frozen.

(4) If a person has obtained an authorization under subsection (1), any other person involved in carrying out the activity or transaction, or class of activities or transactions, to which the authorization relates is not subject to sections 83.08, 83.1 and 83.11 if the terms or conditions of the authorization that are imposed under subsection (2), if any, are met. 2001, c. 41, s. 4; 2005, c. 10, s. 21.

CROSS-REFERENCES

"Terrorist group" is defined in s. 83.01. Under s. 83.11, certain entities, such as banks, have additional obligations to determine whether they are in possession or control of property owned or controlled by or on behalf of listed entities (see ss. 83.01 and 83.05).

DISCLOSURE / Immunity.

83.1 (1) Every person in Canada and every Canadian outside Canada shall disclose without delay to the Commissioner of the Royal Canadian Mounted Police or to the Director of the Canadian Security Intelligence Service

- **(*a*) the existence of property in their possession or control that they know is owned or controlled by or on behalf of a terrorist group; and**
- **(*b*) information about a transaction or proposed transaction in respect of property referred to in paragraph (*a*).**

(2) No criminal or civil proceedings lie against a person for disclosure made in good faith under subsection (1). 2001, c. 41, s. 4; 2013, c. 9, s. 4.

CROSS-REFERENCES

"Terrorist group" and "Canadian" are defined in s. 83.01. Contravention of this section is an offence under s. 83.12. As to procedures for seizure and forfeiture of property owned or controlled by or on behalf of a terrorist group, see ss. 83.13 to 83.17.

AUDIT / Monthly report / Immunity / Regulations.

83.11 (1) The following entities must determine on a continuing basis whether they are in possession or control of property owned or controlled by or on behalf of a listed entity:

- **(*a*) authorized foreign banks within the meaning of section 2 of the *Bank Act* in respect of their business in Canada, or banks to which that Act applies;**
- **(*b*) cooperative credit societies, savings and credit unions and caisses populaires regulated by a provincial Act and associations regulated by the *Cooperative Credit Associations Act*;**
- **(*c*) foreign companies within the meaning of subsection 2(1) of the *Insurance Companies Act* in respect of their insurance business in Canada;**
- **(*c*.1) companies, provincial companies and societies within the meaning of subsection 2(1) of the *Insurance Companies Act*;**
- **(*c*.2) fraternal benefit societies regulated by a provincial Act in respect of their insurance activities, and insurance companies and other entities engaged in the business of insuring risks that are regulated by a provincial Act;**
- **(*d*) companies to which the *Trust and Loan Companies Act* applies;**

(*e*) trust companies regulated by a provincial Act;

(*f*) loan companies regulated by a provincial Act; and

(*g*) entities authorized under provincial legislation to engage in the business of dealing in securities, or to provide portfolio management or investment counselling services.

(2) Subject to the regulations, every entity referred to in paragraphs (1)(*a*) to (*g*) must report, within the period specified by regulation or, if no period is specified, monthly, to the principal agency or body that supervises or regulates it under federal or provincial law either

(*a*) that it is not in possession or control of any property referred to in subsection (1), or

(*b*) that it is in possession or control of such property, in which case it must also report the number of persons, contracts or accounts involved and the total value of the property.

(3) No criminal or civil proceedings lie against a person for making a report in good faith under subsection (2).

(4) The Governor in Council may make regulations

(*a*) excluding any entity or class of entities from the requirement to make a report referred to in subsection (2), and specifying the conditions of exclusion; and

(*b*) specifying a period for the purposes of subsection (2). 2001, c. 41, s. 4.

CROSS-REFERENCES

"Listed entity" is defined in s. 83.01 as an entity listed in accordance with s. 83.05. Contravention of this section is an offence under s. 83.12. As to procedures for seizure and forfeiture of property owned or controlled by or on behalf of a terrorist group, see ss. 83.13 to 83.17.

OFFENCES — FREEZING OF PROPERTY, DISCLOSURE OR AUDIT / No contravention.

83.12 (1) Every one who contravenes any of sections 83.08, 83.1 and 83.11 is guilty of an offence and liable

(*a*) on summary conviction, to a fine of not more than $100,000 or to imprisonment for a term of not more than one year, or to both; or

(*b*) on conviction on indictment, to imprisonment for a term of not more than 10 years. 2001, c. 41, s. 4; 2013, c. 9, c. 5.

(2) [*Repealed*, 2013, c. 9, s. 5.]

CROSS-REFERENCES

Proceedings for an offence under this section cannot be commenced without the consent of the Attorney General, s. 83.24.

Proceedings may be commenced at instance of Government of Canada and conducted by Attorney General of Canada where the offence was alleged to have occurred outside the province in which the proceedings are commenced, whether or not proceedings have previously been commenced elsewhere in Canada and whether or not the person is in Canada, s. 83.25.

As to procedures for seizure and forfeiture of property owned or controlled by or on behalf of a terrorist group, see ss. 83.13 to 83.17.

See ss. 37 to 39 of the *Canada Evidence Act*, respecting Crown privilege and disclosure of information injurious to national security, national defence and foreign relations.

CR. CODE

Seizure and Restraint of Property

SEIZURE AND RESTRAINT OF ASSETS / Contents of application / Appointment of manager / Appointment of Minister of Public Works and Government Services / Power to manage / Application for destruction order / Notice / Manner of giving notice / Destruction order / Forfeiture order / When management order ceases to have effect / For greater certainty / Application to vary / Procedure / Procedure.

83.13 (1) Where a judge of the Federal Court, on an *ex parte* application by the Attorney General, after examining the application in private, is satisfied that there are reasonable grounds to believe that there is in any building, receptacle or place any property in respect of which an order of forfeiture may be made under subsection 83.14(5), the judge may issue

(*a*) if the property is situated in Canada, a warrant authorizing a person named therein or a peace officer to search the building, receptacle or place for that property and to seize that property and any other property in respect of which that person or peace officer believes, on reasonable grounds, that an order of forfeiture may be made under that subsection; or

(*b*) if the property is situated in or outside Canada, a restraint order prohibiting any person from disposing of, or otherwise dealing with any interest in, that property other than as may be specified in the order.

(1.1) An affidavit in support of an application under subsection (1) may be sworn on information and belief, and, notwithstanding the *Federal Court Rules, 1998*, no adverse inference shall be drawn from a failure to provide evidence of persons having personal knowledge of material facts.

(2) On an application under subsection (1), at the request of the Attorney General, if a judge is of the opinion that the circumstances so require, the judge may

(*a*) appoint a person to take control of, and to manage or otherwise deal with, all or part of the property in accordance with the directions of the judge; and

(*b*) require any person having possession of that property to give possession of the property to the person appointed under paragraph (*a*).

(3) When the Attorney General of Canada so requests, a judge appointing a person under subsection (2) shall appoint the Minister of Public Works and Government Services.

(4) The power to manage or otherwise deal with property under subsection (2) includes

(*a*) the power to make an interlocutory sale of perishable or rapidly depreciating property;

(*b*) the power to destroy, in accordance with subsections (5) to (8), property that has little or no value; and

(*c*) the power to have property, other than real property or a conveyance, forfeited to Her Majesty in accordance with subsection (8.1).

(5) Before a person who is appointed to manage property destroys property that has little or no value, they shall apply to a judge of the Federal Court for a destruction order.

(6) Before making a destruction order, a judge shall require notice in accordance with subsection (7) to be given to and may hear any person who, in the judge's opinion, appears to have a valid interest in the property.

(7) A notice shall

(*a*) be given in the manner that the judge directs or that may be specified in the rules of the Federal Court; and

(*b*) specify the effective period of the notice that the judge considers reasonable or that may be set out in the rules of the Federal Court.

(8) A judge shall order that the property be destroyed if they are satisfied that the property has little or no financial or other value.

(8.1) On application by a person who is appointed to manage the property, a judge of the Federal Court shall order that the property, other than real property or a conveyance, be forfeited to Her Majesty to be disposed of or otherwise dealt with in accordance with the law if

(*a*) a notice is given or published in the manner that the judge directs or that may be specified in the rules of the Federal Court;

(*b*) the notice specifies a period of 60 days during which a person may make an application to the judge asserting their interest in the property; and

(*c*) during that period, no one makes such an application.

(9) A management order ceases to have effect when the property that is the subject of the management order is returned in accordance with the law, destroyed or forfeited to Her Majesty.

(9.1) Before making a destruction order, a judge shall require notice in accordance with subsection (7) to be given to and may hear any person who, in the judge's opinion, appears to have a valid interest in the property.

(10) The Attorney General may at any time apply to a judge of the Federal Court to cancel or vary an order or warrant made under this section, other than an appointment made under subsection (3).

(11) Subsections 462.32(4) and (6), sections 462.34 to 462.35 and 462.4, subsections 487(3) and (4) and section 488 apply, with such modifications as the circumstances require, to a warrant issued under paragraph (1)(*a*).

(12) Subsections 462.33(4) and (6) to (11) and sections 462.34 to 462.35 and 462.4 apply, with such modifications as the circumstances require, to an order issued under paragraph (1)(*b*). 2001, c. 41, s. 4; 2017, c. 7, s. 54.

CROSS-REFERENCES

"Attorney General" is defined in s. 2. Sections 462.42(6), 462.43 and 462.46 (which deal with disposal of seized property) apply with necessary modifications to property subject to a warrant or restraint order issued under this section, see s. 83.15. An appeal from an order under this section presumably lies to the Federal Court of Appeal under s. 27 of the *Federal Courts Act*.

Forfeiture of Property

APPLICATION FOR ORDER OF FORFEITURE / Contents of application / Respondents / Notice / Granting of forfeiture order / Use of proceeds / Regulations / Order refusing forfeiture / Notice / Third party interests / Dwelling-house / Motion to vary or set aside / No extension of time.

83.14 (1) The Attorney General may make an application to a judge of the Federal Court for an order of forfeiture in respect of

(*a*) property owned or controlled by or on behalf of a terrorist group; or

(*b*) property that has been or will be used, in whole or in part, to facilitate or carry out a terrorist activity.

(2) An affidavit in support of an application by the Attorney General under subsection (1) may be sworn on information and belief, and, notwithstanding the *Federal Court Rules, 1998*, no adverse inference shall be drawn from a failure to provide evidence of persons having personal knowledge of material facts.

(3) The Attorney General is required to name as a respondent to an application under subsection (1) only those persons who are known to own or control the property that is the subject of the application.

(4) The Attorney General shall give notice of an application under subsection (1) to named respondents in such a manner as the judge directs or as provided in the rules of the Federal Court.

(5) If a judge is satisfied on a balance of probabilities that property is property referred to in paragraph (1)(*a*) or (*b*), the judge shall order that the property be forfeited to Her Majesty to be disposed of as the Attorney General directs or otherwise dealt with in accordance with the law.

(5.1) Any proceeds that arise from the disposal of property under subsection (5) may be used to compensate victims of terrorist activities and to fund anti-terrorist initiatives in accordance with any regulations made by the Governor in Council under subsection (5.2).

(5.2) The Governor in Council may make regulations for the purposes of specifying how the proceeds referred to in subsection (5.1) are to be distributed.

(6) Where a judge refuses an application under subsection (1) in respect of any property, the judge shall make an order that describes the property and declares that it is not property referred to in that subsection.

(7) On an application under subsection (1), a judge may require notice to be given to any person who, in the opinion of the Court, appears to have an interest in the property, and any such person shall be entitled to be added as a respondent to the application.

(8) If a judge is satisfied that a person referred to in subsection (7) has an interest in property that is subject to an application, has exercised reasonable care to ensure that the property would not be used to facilitate or carry out a terrorist activity, and is not a member of a terrorist group, the judge shall order that the interest is not affected by the forfeiture. Such an order shall declare the nature and extent of the interest in question.

(9) Where all or part of property that is the subject of an application under subsection (1) is a dwelling-house, the judge shall also consider

- **(*a*) the impact of an order of forfeiture on any member of the immediate family of the person who owns or controls the dwelling-house, if the dwelling-house was the member's principal residence at the time the dwelling-house was ordered restrained or at the time the forfeiture application was made and continues to be the member's principal residence; and**
- **(*b*) whether the member appears innocent of any complicity or collusion in the terrorist activity.**

(10) A person who claims an interest in property that was forfeited and who did not receive notice under subsection (7) may bring a motion to the Federal Court to vary or set aside an order made under subsection (5) not later than 60 days after the day on which the forfeiture order was made.

(11) The Court may not extend the period set out in subsection (10). 2001, c. 41, s. 4.

CROSS-REFERENCES

"Attorney General" is defined in s. 2. "Terrorist activity" and "terrorist group" are defined in s. 83.01. Sections 462.42(6), 462.43 and 462.46 (which deal with disposal of seized property) apply with necessary modifications to property ordered forfeited under this section, see s. 83.15. The property is to be preserved pending any appeal from an order made under this section, see s. 83.16. Section 83.16(2) incorporates with necessary modifications the provisions in s. 462.34 to an appeal from refusal to make a forfeiture order. The provisions of this Part do not affect other provisions under this Act order other federal legislation relating to forfeiture of property (s. 83.17).

Thus, for example see Part XX.2. An appeal from an order under this section presumably lies to the Federal Court of Appeal under s. 27 of the *Federal Courts Act*.

DISPOSITION OF PROPERTY.

83.15 Subsection 462.42(6) and sections 462.43 and 462.46 apply, with such modifications as the circumstances require, to property subject to a warrant or restraint order issued under subsection 83.13(1) or ordered forfeited under subsection 83.14(5). 2001, c. 41, s. 4.

INTERIM PRESERVATION RIGHTS / Appeal of refusal to grant order.

83.16 (1) Pending any appeal of an order made under section 83.14, property restrained under an order issued under section 83.13 shall continue to be restrained, property seized under a warrant issued under that section shall continue to be detained, and any person appointed to manage, control or otherwise deal with that property under that section shall continue in that capacity.

(2) Section 462.34 applies, with such modifications as the circumstances require, to an appeal taken in respect of a refusal to grant an order under subsection 83.14(5). 2001, c. 41, s. 4.

CROSS-REFERENCES

Presumably, the appeal referred to in this section is an appeal taken to the Federal Court of Appeal in accordance with s. 27 of the *Federal Courts Act*.

OTHER FORFEITURE PROVISIONS UNAFFECTED / Priority for restitution to victims of crime.

83.17 (1) This Part does not affect the operation of any other provision of this or any other Act of Parliament respecting the forfeiture of property.

(2) Property is subject to forfeiture under subsection 83.14(5) only to the extent that it is not required to satisfy the operation of any other provision of this or any other Act of Parliament respecting restitution to, or compensation of, persons affected by the commission of offences. 2001, c. 41, s. 4.

Participating, Facilitating, Instructing and Harbouring

PARTICIPATION IN ACTIVITY OF TERRORIST GROUP / Prosecution / Meaning of participating or contributing / Factors.

83.18 (1) Every one who knowingly participates in or contributes to, directly or indirectly, any activity of a terrorist group for the purpose of enhancing the ability of any terrorist group to facilitate or carry out a terrorist activity is guilty of an indictable offence and liable to imprisonment for a term not exceeding ten years.

(2) An offence may be committed under subsection (1) whether or not

(*a*) a terrorist group actually facilitates or carries out a terrorist activity;

(*b*) the participation or contribution of the accused actually enhances the ability of a terrorist group to facilitate or carry out a terrorist activity; or

(*c*) the accused knows the specific nature of any terrorist activity that may be facilitated or carried out by a terrorist group.

(3) Participating in or contributing to an activity of a terrorist group includes

(*a*) providing, receiving or recruiting a person to receive training;

(*b*) providing or offering to provide a skill or an expertise for the benefit of, at the direction of or in association with a terrorist group;

(*c*) recruiting a person in order to facilitate or commit
(i) a terrorism offence, or
(ii) an act or omission outside Canada that, if committed in Canada, would be a terrorism offence;
(*d*) entering or remaining in any country for the benefit of, at the direction of or in association with a terrorist group; and
(*e*) making oneself, in response to instructions from any of the persons who constitute a terrorist group, available to facilitate or commit
(i) a terrorism offence, or
(ii) an act or omission outside Canada that, if committed in Canada, would be a terrorism offence.

(4) In determining whether an accused participates in or contributes to any activity of a terrorist group, the court may consider, among other factors, whether the accused
(*a*) uses a name, word, symbol or other representation that identifies, or is associated with, the terrorist group;
(*b*) frequently associates with any of the persons who constitute the terrorist group;
(*c*) receives any benefit from the terrorist group; or
(*d*) repeatedly engages in activities at the instruction of any of the persons who constitute the terrorist group. 2001, c. 41, s. 4.

CROSS-REFERENCES

"Terrorist activity" and "terrorist group" are defined in s. 83.01. "Terrorism offence" is defined in s. 2. Expanded jurisdiction to try offences committed outside Canada that, if committed in Canada would be an offence under this section, is set out in s. 7(3.74). As to the place of trial in such circumstances, see s. 7(5); procuring attendance of accused, see s. 7(5.1); defences of *autrefois acquit* and *autrefois convict* and pardon, see s. 7(6); consent of the Attorney General of Canada for trial in such cases of non-citizens, see s. 7(7).

The offence under this section cannot be commenced without the consent of the Attorney General, s. 83.24.

Proceedings may be commenced at instance of Government of Canada and conducted by Attorney General of Canada where the offence was alleged to have occurred outside the province in which the proceedings are commenced, whether or not proceedings have previously been commenced elsewhere in Canada and whether or not the person is in Canada, s. 83.25.

The sentence imposed under this section is to be served consecutively to any other punishment in accordance with s. 83.26. As to parole ineligibility, see s. 743.6(1.2).

As to freezing of assets of terrorist groups, see ss. 83.08 to 83.12 and seizure and forfeiture of terrorist property, see ss. 83.13 to 83.17. Offences relating to terrorist property, see ss. 83.01 to 83.04.

A wiretap authorization may be obtained for the offence under this section in accordance with Part VI. Special provisions apply to such authorizations, thus see ss. 185(1.1)(*c*), 186(1.1)(*c*), 186.1(*c*).

Special protections for victims or witnesses in proceedings against an accused for this offence are set out in s. 486. See ss. 37 to 39 of the *Canada Evidence Act*, respecting Crown privilege and disclosure of information injurious to national security, national defence and foreign relations.

ANNOTATIONS

This provision is not overbroad and does not violate s. 7 of the Charter. A purposive interpretation of the *actus reus* and *mens rea* excludes convictions for: (1) innocent or socially useful conduct that is undertaken absent any intent to enhance the abilities of a terrorist group to facilitate or carry out a terrorist activity; and (2) conduct that a reasonable person would not view as capable of materially enhancing the abilities of a terrorist group to facilitate or carry out a terrorist activity. To convict under s. 83.18, a judge must be satisfied beyond a reasonable doubt that the accused specifically intended to enhance the ability of a terrorist group to facilitate or carry out a terrorist activity: *R. v. Khawaja* (2012), 290 C.C.C. (3d) 361 (S.C.C.), affg 273 C.C.C. (3d) 415 (Ont. C.A.).

The Crown is not required to prove that the accused's conduct actually enhanced the terrorist group's ability to do anything, only that it created a risk of harm beyond *de minimis*: *R. v. Ansari* (2015), 330 C.C.C. (3d) 105 (S.C.C.).

LEAVING CANADA TO PARTICIPATE IN ACTIVITY OF TERRORIST GROUP.

83.181 Everyone who leaves or attempts to leave Canada, or goes or attempts to go on board a conveyance with the intent to leave Canada, for the purpose of committing an act or omission outside Canada that, if committed in Canada, would be an offence under subsection 83.18(1) is guilty of an indictable offence and liable to imprisonment for a term of not more than 10 years. 2013, c. 9, c. 6.

CROSS-REFERENCES

"Terrorism offence" is defined in s. 2. Expanded jurisdiction to try offences committed outside Canada that, if committed in Canada would be an offence under this section, is set out in s. 7(3.74). As to the place of trial in such circumstances, see s. 7(5); procuring attendance of accused, see s. 7(5.1); defences of *autrefois acquit* and *autrefois convict* and pardon, see s. 7(6); consent of the Attorney General of Canada for trial in such cases of non-citizens, see s. 7(7).

The offence under this section cannot be commenced without the consent of the Attorney General, s. 83.24.

Proceedings may be commenced at instance of Government of Canada and conducted by Attorney General of Canada where the offence was alleged to have occurred outside the province in which the proceedings are commenced, whether or not proceedings have previously been commenced elsewhere in Canada and whether or not the person is in Canada, s. 83.25.

The sentence imposed under this section is to be served consecutively to any other punishment in accordance with s. 83.26. As to parole ineligibility, see s. 743.6(1.2).

As to freezing of assets of terrorist groups, see ss. 83.08 to 83.12 and seizure and forfeiture of terrorist property, see ss. 83.13 to 83.17. Offences relating to terrorist property, see ss. 83.01 to 83.04.

A wiretap authorization may be obtained for the offence under this section in accordance with Part VI. Special provisions apply to such authorizations, thus see ss. 185(1.1)(*c*), 186(1.1)(*c*), 186.1(*c*).

Special protections for victims or witnesses in proceedings against an accused for this offence are set out in s. 486. See ss. 37 to 39 of the *Canada Evidence Act*, respecting Crown privilege and disclosure of information injurious to national security, national defence and foreign relations.

FACILITATING TERRORIST ACTIVITY / Facilitation.

83.19 (1) Every one who knowingly facilitates a terrorist activity is guilty of an indictable offence and liable to imprisonment for a term not exceeding fourteen years.

(2) For the purposes of this Part, a terrorist activity is facilitated whether or not

(*a*) the facilitator knows that a particular terrorist activity is facilitated;

(*b*) any particular terrorist activity was foreseen or planned at the time it was facilitated; or

(*c*) any terrorist activity was actually carried out. 2001, c. 41, s. 4.

CROSS-REFERENCES

"Terrorist activity" is defined in s. 83.01. Expanded jurisdiction to try offences committed outside Canada that, if committed in Canada would be an offence under this section, is set out in s. 7(3.74). As to the place of trial in such circumstances, see s. 7(5); procuring attendance of accused, see s. 7(5.1); defences of *autrefois acquit* and *autrefois convict* and pardon, see s. 7(6); consent of the Attorney General of Canada for trial in such cases of non-citizens, see s. 7(7).

The offence under this section cannot be commenced without the consent of the Attorney General, s. 83.24

Proceedings may be commenced at instance of Government of Canada and conducted by Attorney General of Canada where the offence was alleged to have occurred outside the province in which the proceedings are commenced, whether or not proceedings have previously been commenced elsewhere in Canada and whether or not the person is in Canada, s. 83.25.

The sentence imposed under this section is to be served consecutively to any other punishment in accordance with s. 83.26. As to parole ineligibility, see s. 743.6(1.2).

As to freezing of assets of terrorist groups, see ss. 83.08 to 83.12 and seizure and forfeiture of terrorist property, see ss. 83.13 to 83.17. Offences relating to terrorist property, see ss. 83.01 to 83.04.

A wiretap authorization may be obtained for the offence under this section in accordance with Part VI. Special provisions apply to such authorizations, thus see ss. 185(1.1)(*c*), 186(1.1)(*c*), 186.1(*c*).

Special protections for victims or witnesses in proceedings against an accused for this offence are set out in s. 486. See ss. 37 to 39 of the *Canada Evidence Act*, respecting Crown privilege and disclosure of information injurious to national security, national defence and foreign relations.

ANNOTATIONS

The fault requirement of the offence in this section is consistent with s. 7 of the *Canadian Charter of Rights and Freedoms*: *R. v. Khawaja* (2006), 214 C.C.C. (3d) 399, 42 C.R. (6th) 348 (Ont. S.C.J.), leave to appeal to S.C.C. refused [2007] 1 S.C.R. x, 216 C.C.C. (3d) vi.

LEAVING CANADA TO FACILITATE TERRORIST ACTIVITY.

83.191 Everyone who leaves or attempts to leave Canada, or goes or attempts to go on board a conveyance with the intent to leave Canada, for the purpose of committing an act or omission outside Canada that, if committed in Canada, would be an offence under subsection 83.19(1) is guilty of an indictable offence and liable to imprisonment for a term of not more than 14 years. 2013, c. 9, s. 7.

CROSS-REFERENCES

"Terrorism offence" is defined in s. 2. Expanded jurisdiction to try offences committed outside Canada that, if committed in Canada would be an offence under this section, is set out in s. 7(3.74). As to the place of trial in such circumstances, see s. 7(5); procuring attendance of accused, see s. 7(5.1); defences of *autrefois acquit* and *autrefois convict* and pardon, see s. 7(6); consent of the Attorney General of Canada for trial in such cases of non-citizens, see s. 7(7).

The offence under this section cannot be commenced without the consent of the Attorney General, s. 83.24.

Proceedings may be commenced at instance of Government of Canada and conducted by Attorney General of Canada where the offence was alleged to have occurred outside the province in which the proceedings are commenced, whether or not proceedings have previously been commenced elsewhere in Canada and whether or not the person is in Canada, s. 83.25.

The sentence imposed under this section is to be served consecutively to any other punishment in accordance with s. 83.26. As to parole ineligibility, see s. 743.6(1.2).

As to freezing of assets of terrorist groups, see ss. 83.08 to 83.12 and seizure and forfeiture of terrorist property, see ss. 83.13 to 83.17. Offences relating to terrorist property, see ss. 83.01 to 83.04.

A wiretap authorization may be obtained for the offence under this section in accordance with Part VI. Special provisions apply to such authorizations, thus see ss. 185(1.1)(*c*), 186(1.1)(*c*), 186.1(*c*).

Special protections for victims or witnesses in proceedings against an accused for this offence are set out in s. 486. See ss. 37 to 39 of the *Canada Evidence Act*, respecting Crown privilege and disclosure of information injurious to national security, national defence and foreign relations.

COMMISSION OF OFFENCE FOR TERRORIST GROUP.

83.2 Every one who commits an indictable offence under this or any other Act of Parliament for the benefit of, at the direction of or in association with a terrorist group is guilty of an indictable offence and liable to imprisonment for life. 2001, c. 41, s. 4.

CROSS-REFERENCES

"Terrorist group" is defined in s. 83.01. Expanded jurisdiction to try offences committed outside Canada that, if committed in Canada would be an offence under this section, is set out in s. 7(3.74). As to the place of trial in such circumstances, see s. 7(5); procuring attendance of accused, see s. 7(5.1); defences of *autrefois acquit* and *autrefois convict* and pardon, see s. 7(6); consent of the Attorney General of Canada for trial in such cases of non-citizens, see s. 7(7).

The offence under this section cannot be commenced without the consent of the Attorney General, s. 83.24

Proceedings may be commenced at instance of Government of Canada and conducted by Attorney General of Canada where the offence was alleged to have occurred outside the province in which the proceedings are commenced, whether or not proceedings have previously been commenced elsewhere in Canada and whether or not the person is in Canada, s. 83.25.

The sentence imposed under this section is to be served consecutively to any other punishment in accordance with s. 83.26. As to parole ineligibility, see s. 743.6(1.2).

As to freezing of assets of terrorist groups, see ss. 83.08 to 83.12 and seizure and forfeiture of terrorist property, see ss. 83.13 to 83.17. Offences relating to terrorist property, see ss. 83.01 to 83.04.

A wiretap authorization may be obtained for the offence under this section in accordance with Part VI. Special provisions apply to such authorizations, thus see ss. 185(1.1)(*c*), 186(1.1)(*c*), 186.1(*c*).

Special provisions for protecting witnesses on trials of this offence are set out in s. 486. See ss. 37 to 39 of the *Canada Evidence Act*, respecting Crown privilege and disclosure of information injurious to national security, national defence and foreign relations.

A person who commits an indictable offence alone in pursuit of a personal terrorist agenda is not captured by this provision: *R. v. Ali* (2018), 361 C.C.C. (3d) 350 (Ont. S.C.J.).

LEAVING CANADA TO COMMIT OFFENCE FOR TERRORIST GROUP.

83.201 Everyone who leaves or attempts to leave Canada, or goes or attempts to go on board a conveyance with the intent to leave Canada, for the purpose of committing an act or omission outside Canada that, if committed in Canada, would be an indictable offence under this or any other Act of Parliament for the benefit of, at the direction of or in association with a terrorist group is guilty of an indictable offence and liable to imprisonment for a term of not more than 14 years. 2013, c. 9, s. 8.

CROSS-REFERENCES

"Terrorism offence" is defined in s. 2. Expanded jurisdiction to try offences committed outside Canada that, if committed in Canada would be an offence under this section, is set out in s. 7(3.74). As to the place of trial in such circumstances, see s. 7(5); procuring attendance of accused, see s. 7(5.1); defences of *autrefois acquit* and *autrefois convict* and pardon, see s. 7(6); consent of the Attorney General of Canada for trial in such cases of non-citizens, see s. 7(7).

The offence under this section cannot be commenced without the consent of the Attorney General, s. 83.24.

Proceedings may be commenced at instance of Government of Canada and conducted by Attorney General of Canada where the offence was alleged to have occurred outside the province in which the proceedings are commenced, whether or not proceedings have previously been commenced elsewhere in Canada and whether or not the person is in Canada, s. 83.25.

The sentence imposed under this section is to be served consecutively to any other punishment in accordance with s. 83.26. As to parole ineligibility, see s. 743.6(1.2).

As to freezing of assets of terrorist groups, see ss. 83.08 to 83.12 and seizure and forfeiture of terrorist property, see ss. 83.13 to 83.17. Offences relating to terrorist property, see ss. 83.01 to 83.04.

A wiretap authorization may be obtained for the offence under this section in accordance with Part VI. Special provisions apply to such authorizations, thus see ss. 185(1.1)(*c*), 186(1.1)(*c*), 186.1(*c*).

Special protections for victims or witnesses in proceedings against an accused for this offence are set out in s. 486. See ss. 37 to 39 of the *Canada Evidence Act*, respecting Crown privilege and disclosure of information injurious to national security, national defence and foreign relations.

LEAVING CANADA TO COMMIT OFFENCE THAT IS TERRORIST ACTIVITY.

83.202 Everyone who leaves or attempts to leave Canada, or goes or attempts to go on board a conveyance with the intent to leave Canada, for the purpose of committing an act or omission outside Canada that, if committed in Canada, would be an indictable offence under this or any other Act of Parliament if the act or omission constituting the offence also constitutes a terrorist activity is guilty of an indictable offence and liable to imprisonment for a term of not more than 14 years. 2013, c. 9, s. 8.

CROSS-REFERENCES

"Terrorism offence" is defined in s. 2. Expanded jurisdiction to try offences committed outside Canada that, if committed in Canada would be an offence under this section, is set out in s. 7(3.74). As to the place of trial in such circumstances, see s. 7(5); procuring attendance of accused, see s. 7(5.1); defences of *autrefois acquit* and *autrefois convict* and pardon, see s. 7(6); consent of the Attorney General of Canada for trial in such cases of non-citizens, see s. 7(7).

The offence under this section cannot be commenced without the consent of the Attorney General, s. 83.24.

Proceedings may be commenced at instance of Government of Canada and conducted by Attorney General of Canada where the offence was alleged to have occurred outside the province in which the proceedings are commenced, whether or not proceedings have previously been commenced elsewhere in Canada and whether or not the person is in Canada, s. 83.25.

The sentence imposed under this section is to be served consecutively to any other punishment in accordance with s. 83.26. As to parole ineligibility, see s. 743.6(1.2).

As to freezing of assets of terrorist groups, see ss. 83.08 to 83.12 and seizure and forfeiture of terrorist property, see ss. 83.13 to 83.17. Offences relating to terrorist property, see ss. 83.01 to 83.04.

A wiretap authorization may be obtained for the offence under this section in accordance with Part VI. Special provisions apply to such authorizations, thus see ss. 185(1.1)(*c*), 186(1.1)(*c*), 186.1(*c*)

Special protections for victims or witnesses in proceedings against an accused for this offence are set out in s. 486. See ss. 37 to 39 of the *Canada Evidence Act*, respecting Crown privilege and disclosure of information injurious to national security, national defence and foreign relations.

INSTRUCTING TO CARRY OUT ACTIVITY FOR TERRORIST GROUP / Prosecution.

83.21 (1) Every person who knowingly instructs, directly or indirectly, any person to carry out any activity for the benefit of, at the direction of or in association with a terrorist group, for the purpose of enhancing the ability of any terrorist group to facilitate or carry out a terrorist activity, is guilty of an indictable offence and liable to imprisonment for life.

(2) An offence may be committed under subsection (1) whether or not

- **(*a*) the activity that the accused instructs to be carried out is actually carried out;**
- **(*b*) the accused instructs a particular person to carry out the activity referred to in paragraph (*a*);**

(*c*) the accused knows the identity of the person whom the accused instructs to carry out the activity referred to in paragraph (*a*);

(*d*) the person whom the accused instructs to carry out the activity referred to in paragraph (*a*) knows that it is to be carried out for the benefit of, at the direction of or in association with a terrorist group;

(*e*) a terrorist group actually facilitates or carries out a terrorist activity;

(*f*) the activity referred to in paragraph (*a*) actually enhances the ability of a terrorist group to facilitate or carry out a terrorist activity; or

(*g*) the accused knows the specific nature of any terrorist activity that may be facilitated or carried out by a terrorist group. 2001, c. 41, s. 4.

CROSS-REFERENCES

"Terrorist activity" and "terrorist group" are defined in s. 83.01. Expanded jurisdiction to try offences committed outside Canada that, if committed in Canada would be an offence under this section, is set out in s. 7(3.74). As to the place of trial in such circumstances, see s. 7(5); procuring attendance of accused, see s. 7(5.1); defences of *autrefois acquit* and *autrefois convict* and pardon, see s. 7(6); consent of the Attorney General of Canada for trial in such cases of non-citizens, see s. 7(7).

The offence under this section cannot be commenced without the consent of the Attorney General, s. 83.24.

Proceedings may be commenced at instance of Government of Canada and conducted by Attorney General of Canada where the offence was alleged to have occurred outside the province in which the proceedings are commenced, whether or not proceedings have previously been commenced elsewhere in Canada and whether or not the person is in Canada, s. 83.25.

The sentence imposed under this section is to be served consecutively to any other punishment in accordance with s. 83.26. As to parole ineligibility, see s. 743.6(1.2).

As to freezing of assets of terrorist groups, see ss. 83.08 to 83.12 and seizure and forfeiture of terrorist property, see ss. 83.13 to 83.17. Offences relating to terrorist property, see ss. 83.01 to 83.04.

A wiretap authorization may be obtained for the offence under this section in accordance with Part VI. Special provisions apply to such authorizations, thus see ss. 185(1.1)(*c*), 186(1.1)(*c*), 186.1(*c*).

Special protections for victims or witnesses in proceedings against an accused for this offence are set out in s. 486. See ss. 37 to 39 of the *Canada Evidence Act*, respecting Crown privilege and disclosure of information injurious to national security, national defence and foreign relations.

ANNOTATIONS

The fault requirement of the offence in this section is consistent with s. 7 of the *Canadian Charter of Rights and Freedoms*: *R. v. Khawaja* (2006), 214 C.C.C. (3d) 399 (Ont. S.C.J.), leave to appeal to S.C.C. refused [2007] 1 S.C.R. x, 216 C.C.C. (3d) vi.

INSTRUCTING TO CARRY OUT TERRORIST ACTIVITY / Prosecution.

83.22 (1) Every person who knowingly instructs, directly or indirectly, any person to carry out a terrorist activity is guilty of an indictable offence and liable to imprisonment for life.

(2) An offence may be committed under subsection (1) whether or not

(*a*) the terrorist activity is actually carried out;

(*b*) the accused instructs a particular person to carry out the terrorist activity;

(*c*) the accused knows the identity of the person whom the accused instructs to carry out the terrorist activity; or

(*d*) the person whom the accused instructs to carry out the terrorist activity knows that it is a terrorist activity. 2001, c. 41, s. 4.

CROSS-REFERENCES

"Terrorist activity" is defined in s. 83.01. Expanded jurisdiction to try offences committed outside Canada that, if committed in Canada would be an offence under this section, is set out in s. 7(3.74). As to the place of trial in such circumstances, see s. 7(5); procuring attendance of accused, see s. 7(5.1); defences of *autrefois acquit* and *autrefois convict* and pardon, see s. 7(6); consent of the Attorney General of Canada for trial in such cases of non-citizens, see s. 7(7).

The offence under this section cannot be commenced without the consent of the Attorney General, s. 83.24

Proceedings may be commenced at instance of Government of Canada and conducted by Attorney General of Canada where the offence was alleged to have occurred outside the province in which the proceedings are commenced, whether or not proceedings have previously been commenced elsewhere in Canada and whether or not the person is in Canada, s. 83.25.

The sentence imposed under this section is to be served consecutively to any other punishment in accordance with s. 83.26. As to parole ineligibility, see s. 743.6(1.2).

As to freezing of assets of terrorist groups, see ss. 83.08 to 83.12 and seizure and forfeiture of terrorist property, see ss. 83.13 to 83.17. Offences relating to terrorist property, see ss. 83.01 to 83.04.

A wiretap authorization may be obtained for the offence under this section in accordance with Part VI. Special provisions apply to such authorizations, thus see ss. 185(1.1)(*c*), 186(1.1)(*c*), 186.1(*c*).

Special protections for victims or witnesses in proceedings against an accused for this offence are set out in s. 486. See ss. 37 to 39 of the *Canada Evidence Act*, respecting Crown privilege and disclosure of information injurious to national security, national defence and foreign relations.

ADVOCATING OR PROMOTING COMMISSION OF TERRORISM OFFENCES / Definitions.

83.221 (1) Every person who, by communicating statements, knowingly advocates or promotes the commission of terrorism offences in general — other than an offence under this section — while knowing that any of those offences will be committed or being reckless as to whether any of those offences may be committed, as a result of such communication, is guilty of an indictable offence and is liable to imprisonment for a term of not more than five years.

(2) The following definitions apply in this section.

"communicating" has the same meaning as in subsection 319(7).

"statements" has the same meaning as in subsection 319(7). 2015, c. 20, s. 16.

CROSS-REFERENCES

"Terrorism offence" is defined in s. 2. Expanded jurisdiction to try offences committed outside Canada that, if committed in Canada, would be an offence under this section, is set out in s. 7(3.74). As to the place of trial in such circumstances, see s. 7(5); procuring attendance of accused, see s. 7(5.1); defences of *autrefois acquit* and *autrefois convict* and pardon, see s. 7(6); consent of Attorney General for trial in such cases of non-citizens, see s. 7(7).

The offence under this section cannot be commenced without the consent of the Attorney General, s. 83.24.

Proceedings may be commenced at the instance of the Government of Canada and conducted by the Attorney General of Canada where the offence was alleged to have occurred outside the province in which the proceedings are commenced, whether or not proceedings have previously been commenced elsewhere in Canada and whether or not the person is in Canada, s. 83.25.

The sentence imposed under this section is to be served consecutively to any other punishment in accordance with s. 83.26. As to parole ineligibility, see s. 743.6(1.2.).

As to freezing of assets of terrorist groups, see ss. 83.08 to 83.12 and seizure and forfeiture of terrorist property, see ss. 83.13 to 83.17.

A wiretap authorization may be obtained for the offence under this section in accordance with Part VI. Special provisions apply to such authorizations, thus see ss. 185(1.1)(*c*), 186(1.1)(*c*), and 186(1)(*c*).

Special protections for victims or witnesses in proceedings against an accused for this offence are set out in s. 486. See ss. 37 to 39 of the *Canada Evidence Act*, respecting Crown privilege and disclosure of information injurious to national security, national defence and foreign relations.

WARRANT OF SEIZURE / Summons to occupier / Owner and author may appear / Order of forfeiture / Disposal of matter / Appeal / Consent / Definitions.

83.222 (1) A judge who is satisfied by information on oath that there are reasonable grounds to believe that any publication, copies of which are kept for sale or distribution in premises within the court's jurisdiction, is terrorist propaganda may issue a warrant authorizing seizure of the copies.

(2) Within seven days after the day on which the warrant is issued, the judge shall issue a summons to the premises' occupier requiring the occupier to appear before the court and to show cause why the matter seized should not be forfeited to Her Majesty.

(3) The owner and the author of the matter seized and alleged to be terrorist propaganda may appear and be represented before the court in order to oppose the making of an order for the forfeiture of the matter.

(4) If the court is satisfied, on a balance of probabilities, that the publication is terrorist propaganda, it may make an order declaring that the matter be forfeited to Her Majesty, for disposal as the Attorney General may direct.

(5) If the court is not satisfied that the publication is terrorist propaganda, it may order that the matter be restored to the person from whom it was seized without delay after the time for final appeal has expired.

(6) An appeal lies from an order made under subsection (4) or (5) by any person who appeared before the court, on any ground of appeal that involves a question of law or fact alone, or a question of mixed law and fact, as if it were an appeal against conviction or against a judgment or verdict of acquittal, as the case may be, on a question of law alone under Part XXI, and sections 673 to 696 apply with any modifications that the circumstances require.

(7) No proceeding under this section shall be instituted without the Attorney General's consent.

(8) The following definitions apply in this section.

"court" has the same meaning as in subsection 320(8).

"judge" has the same meaning as in subsection 320(8).

"terrorist propaganda" means any writing, sign, visible representation or audio recording that advocates or promotes the commission of terrorism offences in general — other than an offence under subsection 83.221(1) — or counsels the commission of a terrorism offence. 2015, c. 20, s. 16.

CROSS-REFERENCES

A similar procedure for *in rem* seizure of proscribed materials is provided by s. 164.1 (child pornography) and s. 320 (hate propaganda).

Section 83.223 provides for an *in rem* proceeding to shut down terrorist propaganda sites on a computer system.

"Attorney General" is defined in s. 2.

ORDER TO COMPUTER SYSTEM'S CUSTODIAN / Notice to person who posted material / Person who posted material may appear / Non-appearance / Order of deletion / Destruction of electronic copy / Return of material / Appeal / Consent / When order takes effect / Definitions.

83.223 (1) If a judge is satisfied by information on oath that there are reasonable grounds to believe that there is material — that is terrorist propaganda or computer data that makes terrorist propaganda available — stored on and made available to the public through a computer system that is within the court's jurisdiction, the judge may order the computer system's custodian to

(*a*) give an electronic copy of the material to the court;

(*b*) ensure that the material is no longer stored on and made available through the computer system; and

(*c*) provide the information that is necessary to identify and locate the person who posted the material.

(2) Within a reasonable time after receiving the information referred to in paragraph (1)(*c*), the judge shall cause notice to be given to the person who posted the material, giving that person the opportunity to appear and be represented before the court and to show cause why the material should not be deleted. If the person cannot be identified or located or does not reside in Canada, the judge may order the computer system's custodian to post the text of the notice at the location where the material was previously stored and made available, until the time set for the appearance.

(3) The person who posted the material may appear and be represented before the court in order to oppose the making of an order under subsection (5).

(4) If the person who posted the material does not appear before the court, the court may proceed to hear and determine the proceedings in the absence of the person as fully and effectually as if the person had appeared.

(5) If the court is satisfied, on a balance of probabilities, that the material is available to the public and is terrorist propaganda or computer data that makes terrorist propaganda available, it may order the computer system's custodian to delete the material.

(6) When the court makes the order for the deletion of the material, it may order the destruction of the electronic copy in the court's possession.

(7) If the court is not satisfied that the material is available to the public and is terrorist propaganda or computer data that makes terrorist propaganda available, the court shall order that the electronic copy be returned to the computer system's custodian and terminate the order under paragraph (1)(*b*).

(8) An appeal lies from an order made under subsection (5) or (6) by any person who appeared before the court, on any ground of appeal that involves a question of law or fact alone, or a question of mixed law and fact, as if it were an appeal against conviction or against a judgment or verdict of acquittal, as the case may be, on a question of law alone under Part XXI, and sections 673 to 696 apply with any modifications that the circumstances require.

(9) No proceeding under this section shall be instituted without the Attorney General's consent.

(10) No order made under any of subsections (5) to (7) takes effect until the time for final appeal has expired.

(11) The following definitions apply in this section.

"computer data" has the same meaning as in subsection 342.1(2).

"computer system" has the same meaning as in subsection 342.1(2).

"court" has the same meaning as in subsection 320(8).

"data" [Repealed 2015, c. 20, s. 35(d).]

"judge" has the same meaning as in subsection 320(8).

"terrorist propaganda" has the same meaning as in subsection 83.222(8). 2015, c. 20, ss. 16, 35.

CROSS-REFERENCES

A similar *in rem* procedure for shutting down sites on a computer system is provided by s. 164.1 (child pornography).

Section 83.222 provides a procedure for the seizure of terrorist propaganda and *in rem* forfeiture proceedings.

"Attorney General" is defined in s. 2.

CONCEALING PERSON WHO CARRIED OUT TERRORIST ACTIVITY / Concealing person who is likely to carry out terrorist activity.

83.23 (1) Everyone who knowingly harbours or conceals any person whom they know to be a person who has carried out a terrorist activity, for the purpose of enabling the person to facilitate or carry out any terrorist activity, is guilty of an indictable offence and liable to imprisonment

(*a*) for a term of not more than 14 years, if the person who is harboured or concealed carried out a terrorist activity that is a terrorism offence for which that person is liable to imprisonment for life; and

(*b*) for a term of not more than 10 years, if the person who is harboured or concealed carried out a terrorist activity that is a terrorism offence for which that person is liable to any other punishment.

(2) Everyone who knowingly harbours or conceals any person whom they know to be a person who is likely to carry out a terrorist activity, for the purpose of enabling the person to facilitate or carry out any terrorist activity, is guilty of an indictable offence and liable to imprisonment for a term of not more than 10 years. 2001, c. 41, s. 4; 2013, c. 9, s. 9.

CROSS-REFERENCES

"Terrorist activity" is defined in s. 83.01. Expanded jurisdiction to try offences committed outside Canada that, if committed in Canada would be an offence under this section, is set out in s. 7(3.74). As to the place of trial in such circumstances, see s. 7(5); procuring attendance of accused, see s. 7(5.1); defences of *autrefois acquit* and *autrefois convict* and pardon, see s. 7(6); consent of the Attorney General of Canada for trial in such cases of non-citizens, see s. 7(7).

The offence under this section cannot be commenced without the consent of the Attorney General, s. 83.24.

Proceedings may be commenced at instance of Government of Canada and conducted by Attorney General of Canada where the offence was alleged to have occurred outside the province in which the proceedings are commenced, whether or not proceedings have previously been commenced elsewhere in Canada and whether or not the person is in Canada, s. 83.25.

The sentence imposed under this section is to be served consecutively to any other punishment in accordance with s. 83.26. As to parole ineligibility, see s. 743.6(1.2).

As to freezing of assets of terrorist groups, see ss. 83.08 to 83.12 and seizure and forfeiture of terrorist property, see ss. 83.13 to 83.17. Offences relating to terrorist property, see ss. 83.01 to 83.04.

A wiretap authorization may be obtained for the offence under this section in accordance with Part VI. Special provisions apply to such authorizations, thus see ss. 185(1.1)(*c*), 186(1.1)(*c*), 186.1(*c*).

Special protections for victims or witnesses in proceedings against an accused for this offence are set out in s. 486. See ss. 37 to 39 of the *Canada Evidence Act*, respecting Crown privilege and disclosure of information injurious to national security, national defence and foreign relations.

Hoax Regarding Terrorist Activity

HOAX — TERRORIST ACTIVITY / Punishment / Causing bodily harm / Causing death.

83.231 (1) Every one commits an offence who, without lawful excuse and with intent to cause any person to fear death, bodily harm, substantial damage to property or serious interference with the lawful use or operation of property,

(*a*) conveys or causes or procures to be conveyed information that, in all the circumstances, is likely to cause a reasonable apprehension that terrorist activity is occurring or will occur, without believing the information to be true; or

(*b*) commits an act that, in all the circumstances, is likely to cause a reasonable apprehension that terrorist activity is occurring or will occur, without believing that such activity is occurring or will occur.

(2) Every one who commits an offence under subsection (1) is guilty of

(*a*) an indictable offence and liable to imprisonment for a term not exceeding five years; or

(*b*) an offence punishable on summary conviction.

(3) Every one who commits an offence under subsection (1) and thereby causes bodily harm to any other person is guilty of

(*a*) an indictable offence and liable to imprisonment for a term not exceeding ten years; or

(*b*) an offence punishable on summary conviction and liable to imprisonment for a term not exceeding eighteen months.

(4) Every one who commits an offence under subsection (1) and thereby causes the death of any other person is guilty of an indictable offence and liable to imprisonment for life. 2004, c. 15, s. 32.

CROSS-REFERENCES

"Bodily harm" is defined in s. 2. "Terrorist activity" is defined in s. 83.01.

SYNOPSIS

This section creates two types of offences relating to terrorist activity hoaxes. The offence defined in subsec. (1)(*a*) is committed where the person without lawful excuse and with intent to cause a person to fear death, bodily harm, substantial damage to property or serious interference with the lawful use or operation of property conveys, causes or procures to be conveyed information that is likely to cause a reasonable apprehension that terrorist activity is occurring or will occur, without believing the information is true. The subsec. (1)(*b*) offence has a similar intent but is based on the commission by the accused of an act that is likely to cause a reasonable apprehension of terrorist activity. The penalty imposed depends on the consequences of the offence as set out in subsecs. (2), (3) and (4).

Proceedings and Aggravated Punishment

ATTORNEY GENERAL'S CONSENT.

83.24 Proceedings in respect of a terrorism offence or an offence under section 83.12 shall not be commenced without the consent of the Attorney General. 2001, c. 41, s. 4.

CROSS-REFERENCES

"Attorney General" and "terrorism offence" are defined in s. 2.

JURISDICTION / Trial and punishment.

83.25 (1) Where a person is alleged to have committed a terrorism offence or an offence under section 83.12, proceedings in respect of that offence may, whether or not that person is in Canada, be commenced at the instance of the Government of Canada and conducted by the Attorney General of Canada or counsel acting on his or her behalf in any territorial division in Canada, if the offence is alleged to have occurred outside the province in which the proceedings are commenced, whether or not proceedings have previously been commenced elsewhere in Canada.

(2) An accused may be tried and punished in respect of an offence referred to in subsection (1) in the same manner as if the offence had been committed in the territorial division where the proceeding is conducted. 2001, c. 41, s. 4.

CROSS-REFERENCES

"Territorial division" is defined in s. 2. For special provisions respecting territorial jurisdiction for offences under this Part committed outside Canada see ss. 7(3.73) to (3.75).

SENTENCES TO BE SERVED CONSECUTIVELY.

83.26 A sentence, other than one of life imprisonment, imposed on a person for an offence under any of sections 83.02 to 83.04 and 83.18 to 83.23 shall be served consecutively to

(*a*) any other punishment imposed on the person, other than a sentence of life imprisonment, for an offence arising out of the same event or series of events; and

(*b*) any other sentence, other than one of life imprisonment, to which the person is subject at the time the sentence is imposed on the person for an offence under any of those sections. 2001, c. 41, s. 4.

ANNOTATIONS

This provision does not oust the application of the totality principle in sentencing for terrorism offences. The fact that sentences of over 20 years may be imposed more often in terrorism cases is not inconsistent with the totality principle. It merely attests to the particular gravity of terrorist offences and the moral culpability of those who commit them. Denunciation and deterrence, both specific and general, are inevitably important principles in the sentencing of terrorism offences: *R. v. Khawaja* (2012), 290 C.C.C. (3d) 361 (S.C.C.), affg 273 C.C.C. (3d) 415 (Ont. C.A.).

PUNISHMENT FOR TERRORIST ACTIVITY / Offender must be notified.

83.27 (1) Notwithstanding anything in this Act, a person convicted of an indictable offence, other than an offence for which a sentence of imprisonment for life is imposed as a minimum punishment, where the act or omission constituting the offence also constitutes a terrorist activity, is liable to imprisonment for life.

(2) Subsection (1) does not apply unless the prosecutor satisfies the court that the offender, before making a plea, was notified that the application of that subsection would be sought. 2001, c. 41, s. 4.

CROSS-REFERENCES

"Terrorist activity" is defined in s. 83.01. For proof of notice, see s. 4(6), (7).

Investigative Hearing

DEFINITION OF "JUDGE" / Order for gathering information /Attorney General's consent / Making of order / Contents of order / Execution of order / Variation of order / Obligation to answer questions and produce things / Judge to rule / No person excused from complying with subsection (8) / Right to counsel / Order for custody of thing.

83.28 (1) In this section and section 83.29, "judge" means a provincial court judge or a judge of a superior court of criminal jurisdiction.

(2) Subject to subsection (3), a peace officer may, for the purposes of an investigation of a terrorism offence, apply ex parte to a judge for an order for the gathering of information.

(3) A peace officer may make an application under subsection (2) only if the Attorney General's prior consent was obtained.

(4) The judge to whom the application is made may make an order for the gathering of information if they are satisfied that the Attorney General's consent was obtained as required by subsection (3), and

(*a*) that there are reasonable grounds to believe that

(i) a terrorism offence has been committed,

(ii) information concerning the offence, or information that may reveal the whereabouts of a person suspected by the peace officer of having committed the offence, is likely to be obtained as a result of the order, and

(iii) reasonable attempts have been made to obtain the information referred to in subparagraph (ii) by other means; or

(*b*) that

(i) there are reasonable grounds to believe that a terrorism offence will be committed,

(ii) there are reasonable grounds to believe that a person has direct and material information that relates to the offence referred to in subparagraph (i), or that may reveal the whereabouts of an individual who the peace officer suspects may commit the offence referred to in that subparagraph, and

(iii) reasonable attempts have been made to obtain the information referred to in subparagraph (ii) by other means.

(5) An order made under subsection (4) shall order the examination, on oath or not, of the person named in the order and require the person to attend at the place fixed by the judge, or by the judge designated under paragraph (*b*), as the case may be, for the examination and to remain in attendance until excused by the presiding judge, and may

(*a*) order the person to bring to the examination any thing in their possession or control, and produce it to the presiding judge;

(*b*) designate another judge as the judge before whom the examination is to take place; and

(*c*) include any other terms or conditions that the judge considers desirable, including terms or conditions for the protection of the interests of the person named in the order and of third parties or for the protection of any ongoing investigation.

(6) The order may be executed anywhere in Canada.

(7) The judge who made the order, or another judge of the same court, may vary its terms and conditions.

(8) A person named in an order made under subsection (4) shall answer questions put to them by the Attorney General or the Attorney General's agent, and shall produce to the presiding judge things that the person was ordered to bring, but may refuse if

answering a question or producing a thing would disclose information that is protected by any law relating to privilege or to disclosure of information.

(9) The presiding judge shall rule on any objection or other issue relating to a refusal to answer a question or to produce a thing.

(10) No person shall be excused from answering a question or producing a thing under subsection (8) on the ground that the answer or thing may tend to incriminate them or subject them to any proceeding or penalty, but

- **(*a*) no answer given or thing produced under subsection (8) shall be used or received against the person in any criminal proceedings against them, other than a prosecution under section 132 or 136; and**
- **(*b*) no evidence derived from the evidence obtained from the person shall be used or received against the person in any criminal proceedings against them, other than a prosecution under section 132 or 136.**

(11) A person has the right to retain and instruct counsel at any stage of the proceedings.

(12) The presiding judge, if satisfied that any thing produced during the course of the examination will likely be relevant to the investigation of any terrorism offence, may order that the thing be given into the custody of the peace officer or someone acting on the peace officer's behalf. 2001, c. 41, s. 4; 2013, c. 9, s. 10.

CROSS-REFERENCES

"Attorney General", "peace officer", "provincial court judge", "superior court of criminal jurisdiction", and "terrorism offence" are defined in s. 2. A judge may issue a warrant for the arrest of the person named in the order if the circumstances set out in s. 83.29.

The Attorney General of Canada is to report to Parliament on the operation of this section annually in accordance with s. 83.31. This provision is subject to the "sunset provision" in s. 83.32.

ANNOTATIONS

Note: The cases noted below were decided before the repeal and re-enactment of this section, which came into force on July 15, 2013. The section was re-enacted in almost identical terms.

This provision does not violate ss. 7 or 11(*d*) of the Charter: *R. v. Bagri*, [2004] 2 S.C.R. 248, 184 C.C.C. (3d) 449.

This provision is procedural and accordingly, applies retrospectively to incidents that occurred prior to its enactment: *R. v. Bagri, supra.*

The purpose of this legislation is the prosecution and prevention of terrorism offences. The role of counsel for the named person should be broadly defined to include objections not only on the specified grounds based on the application of law related to non-disclosure of information or privilege, but also objections on the basis of abusive or irrelevant questioning. The investigative hearing is governed by Part I of the *Canada Evidence Act* which affords the named person the protections of spousal privilege, procedures concerning cross-examination of adverse witnesses and cross-examination in relation to prior statements. In addition, the common rule of relevance applies to the hearing. The boundaries of relevance will be dictated in large measure by the supporting materials for the s. 83.28 order for the gathering of information, as well as by the investigatory nature of the proceeding. While the nature of the proceeding may increase the scope of allowable questioning, it must be kept within reasonable bounds by the judicial nature of the investigative hearing and all of the procedural protections that the oversight of a judge implies: *R. v. Bagri, supra.*

Subsection (10) provides both use and derivative use immunity. The protection in para. (*b*) provides absolute derivative use immunity such that evidence derived from the evidence provided at the judicial investigative hearing may not be presented in evidence against the witness in another prosecution, even if the Crown is able to establish, on a balance of probabilities, that it would have inevitably discovered the same evidence through alternative means. These procedural safeguards must be extended to extradition and deportation proceedings. Where there is the potential for the use by the state of the evidence gathered in deportation or extradition proceedings against the named person, the hearing judge must make and, if necessary, vary the terms of an order to properly provide use and derivative use immunity in extradition or deportation proceedings: *R. v. Bagri, supra.*

ARREST WARRANT / Execution of warrant / Person to be brought before judge / Application of section 707.

83.29 (1) The judge who made the order under subsection 83.28(4), or another judge of the same court, may issue a warrant for the arrest of the person named in the order if the judge is satisfied, on an information in writing and under oath, that the person

- **(*a*) is evading service of the order;**
- **(*b*) is about to abscond; or**
- **(*c*) did not attend the examination, or did not remain in attendance, as required by the order.**

(2) The warrant may be executed at any place in Canada by any peace officer having jurisdiction in that place.

(3) A peace officer who arrests a person in the execution of the warrant shall, without delay, bring the person, or cause them to be brought, before the judge who issued the warrant or another judge of the same court. The judge in question may, to ensure compliance with the order, order that the person be detained in custody or released on recognizance, with or without sureties.

(4) Section 707 applies, with any necessary modifications, to persons detained in custody under this section. 2001, c. 41, s. 4; 2013, c. 9, s. 10.

CROSS-REFERENCES

The Attorney General of Canada is to report to Parliament on the operation of this section annually in accordance with s. 83.31. This provision is subject to the "sunset provision" in s. 83.32.

Recognizance with Conditions

ATTORNEY GENERAL'S CONSENT / Terrorist activity / Appearance / Arrest without warrant / Duty of peace officer / When person to be taken before judge / How person dealt with / Adjournment under subparagraph (7)(*b*)(ii) / Adjournment under paragraph (7.1)(*b*) / Hearing before judge / Duration extended / Refusal to enter into recognizance / Conditions — firearms / Surrender, etc. / Condition — passport / Condition — specified geographic area / Reasons / Variance of conditions / Other provisions to apply.

83.3 (1) The Attorney General's consent is required before a peace officer may lay an information under subsection (2).

(2) Subject to subsection (1), a peace officer may lay an information before a provincial court judge if the peace officer

- **(*a*) believes on reasonable grounds that a terrorist activity may be carried out; and**
- **(*b*) suspects on reasonable grounds that the imposition of a recognizance with conditions on a person, or the arrest of a person, is likely to prevent the carrying out of the terrorist activity.**

(3) The judge who receives the information may cause the person to appear before any provincial court judge.

(4) Despite subsections (2) and (3), a peace officer may arrest a person without a warrant and cause the person to be detained in custody, in order to bring them before a provincial court judge in accordance with subsection (6), if

(*a*) either

(i) the grounds for laying an information referred to in paragraphs (2)(*a*) and (*b*) exist but, by reason of exigent circumstances, it would be impracticable to lay an information under subsection (2), or

(ii) an information has been laid under subsection (2) and a summons has been issued; and

(*b*) the peace officer suspects on reasonable grounds that the detention of the person in custody is likely to prevent a terrorist activity.

(5) If a peace officer arrests a person without a warrant in the circumstance described in subparagraph (4)(*a*)(i), the peace officer shall, within the time prescribed by paragraph (6)(*a*) or (*b*),

(*a*) lay an information in accordance with subsection (2); or

(*b*) release the person.

(6) Unless a peace officer, or an officer in charge as defined in Part XVI, is satisfied that a person should be released from custody unconditionally before their appearance before a provincial court judge in accordance with the rules in paragraph (*a*) or (*b*), and so releases the person, the person detained in custody shall be taken before a provincial court judge in accordance with the following rules:

(*a*) if a provincial court judge is available within 24 hours after the person has been arrested, the person shall be taken before a provincial court judge without unreasonable delay and in any event within that period; and

(*b*) if a provincial court judge is not available within 24 hours after the person has been arrested, the person shall be taken before a provincial court judge as soon as feasible.

(7) When a person is taken before a provincial court judge under subsection (6),

(*a*) if an information has not been laid under subsection (2), the judge shall order that the person be released; or

(*b*) if an information has been laid under subsection (2),

(i) the judge shall order that the person be released unless the peace officer who laid the information shows cause why the person's detention in custody is justified on one or more of the following grounds:

(A) the detention is necessary to ensure the person's appearance before a provincial court judge in order to be dealt with in accordance with subsection (8),

(B) the detention is necessary for the protection or safety of the public, including any witness, having regard to all the circumstances including

(I) the likelihood that, if the person is released from custody, a terrorist activity will be carried out, and

(II) any substantial likelihood that the person will, if released from custody, interfere with the administration of justice, and

(C) the detention is necessary to maintain confidence in the administration of justice, having regard to all the circumstances, including the apparent strength of the peace officer's grounds under subsection (2), and the gravity of any terrorist activity that may be carried out, and

(ii) the judge may adjourn the matter for a hearing under subsection (8) but, if the person is not released under subparagraph (i), the adjournment may not exceed 48 hours.

(7.1) If a judge has adjourned the matter under subparagraph (7)(*b*)(ii) and the person remains in custody at the end of the period of adjournment, the person shall be taken before a provincial court judge who

(*a*) shall order that the person be released unless a peace officer shows cause why the person's detention in custody is justified on one or more of the grounds set out in clauses (7)(*b*)(i)(A) to (C) and satisfies the judge that the investigation in relation to which the person is detained is being conducted diligently and expeditiously; and

(*b*) may adjourn the matter for a hearing under subsection (8) but, if the person is not released under paragraph (*a*), the adjournment may not exceed 48 hours.

(7.2) If a judge has adjourned the matter under paragraph (7.1)(*b*) and the person remains in custody at the end of the period of adjournment, the person shall be taken before a provincial court judge who

(*a*) shall order that the person be released unless a peace officer shows cause why the person's detention in custody is justified on one or more of the grounds set out in clauses (7)(*b*)(i)(A) to (C) and satisfies the judge that the investigation in relation to which the person is detained is being conducted diligently and expeditiously; and

(*b*) may adjourn the matter for a hearing under subsection (8) but, if the person is not released under paragraph (*a*), the adjournment may not exceed 48 hours.

(8) The judge before whom the person appears in accordance with subsection (3)

(*a*) may, if the judge is satisfied by the evidence adduced that the peace officer has reasonable grounds for the suspicion, order that the person enter into a recognizance, with or without sureties, to keep the peace and be of good behaviour for a period of not more than 12 months and to comply with any other reasonable conditions prescribed in the recognizance, including the conditions set out in subsections (10), (11.1) and (11.2), that the judge considers desirable for preventing the carrying out of a terrorist activity; and

(*b*) if the person was not released under subparagraph (7)(*b*)(i) or paragraph (7.1)(*a*) or (7.2)(*a*), shall order that the person be released, subject to the recognizance, if any, ordered under paragraph (*a*).

(8.1) However, if the judge is also satisfied that the person was convicted previously of a terrorism offence, the judge may order that the person enter into the recognizance for a period of not more than two years.

(9) The judge may commit the person to prison for a term not exceeding 12 months if the person fails or refuses to enter into the recognizance.

(10) Before making an order under paragraph (8)(*a*), the judge shall consider whether it is desirable, in the interests of the safety of the person or of any other person, to include as a condition of the recognizance that the person be prohibited from possessing any firearm, crossbow, prohibited weapon, restricted weapon, prohibited device, ammunition, prohibited ammunition or explosive substance, or all of those things, for any period specified in the recognizance, and if the judge decides that it is so desirable, they shall add the condition to the recognizance.

(11) If the judge adds the condition described in subsection (10) to a recognizance, they shall specify in it the manner and method by which

(*a*) the things referred to in that subsection that are in the person's possession shall be surrendered, disposed of, detained, stored or dealt with; and

(*b*) the authorizations, licences and registration certificates that are held by the person shall be surrendered.

(11.1) The judge shall consider whether it is desirable, to prevent the carrying out of a terrorist activity, to include in the recognizance a condition that the person deposit, in the specified manner, any passport or other travel document issued in their name that is in their possession or control. If the judge decides that it is desirable, the judge shall add the condition to the recognizance and specify the period during which it applies.

(11.2) The judge shall consider whether it is desirable, to prevent the carrying out of a terrorist activity, to include in the recognizance a condition that the person remain within a specified geographic area unless written permission to leave that area is obtained from the judge or any individual designated by the judge. If the judge decides that it is desirable, the judge shall add the condition to the recognizance and specify the period during which it applies.

(12) If the judge does not add a condition described in subsection (10), (11.1) or (11.2) to a recognizance, the judge shall include in the record a statement of the reasons for not adding it.

(13) The judge, or any other judge of the same court, may, on application of the peace officer, the Attorney General or the person, vary the conditions fixed in the recognizance.

(14) Subsections 810(4) and (5) apply, with any necessary modifications, to proceedings under this section. 2001, c. 41, s. 4; 2013, c. 9, s. 10; 2015, c. 20, s. 17.

CROSS-REFERENCES

"Attorney General", "peace officer", "provincial court judge" and "terrorism offence" are defined in s. 2.

"Terrorist activity" is defined in s. 83.01.

With respect to the grounds for detention in subsec. (7)(*b*)(i)(A) to (C), reference should be had to the analogous grounds in s. 515(10)(*a*) to (*c*) and the case law developed thereunder.

The Attorney General of Canada is to report to Parliament on the operation of this section annually in accordance with s. 83.31. This section is subject to the "sunset provision" in s. 83.32.

ANNUAL REPORT (SECTIONS 83.28 AND 83.29) / Attorney General's opinion / Annual report (section 83.3) / Annual report (section 83.3) / Opinions / Limitation.

83.31 (1) The Attorney General of Canada shall prepare and cause to be laid before Parliament and the Attorney General of every province shall publish or otherwise make available to the public an annual report for the previous year on the operation of sections 83.28 and 83.29 that includes

- **(*a*) the number of consents to make an application that were sought, and the number that were obtained, by virtue of subsections 83.28(2) and (3);**
- **(*b*) the number of orders for the gathering of information that were made under subsection 83.28(4); and**
- **(*c*) the number of arrests that were made with a warrant issued under section 83.29.**

(1.1) The Attorney General of Canada shall include in the annual report under subsection (1) his or her opinion, supported by reasons, on whether the operation of sections 83.28 and 83.29 should be extended.

(2) The Attorney General of Canada shall prepare and cause to be laid before Parliament and the Attorney General of every province shall publish or otherwise make available to the public an annual report for the previous year on the operation of section 83.3 that includes

- **(*a*) the number of consents to lay an information that were sought, and the number that were obtained, by virtue of subsections 83.3(1) and (2);**
- **(*b*) the number of cases in which a summons or a warrant of arrest was issued for the purposes of subsection 83.3(3);**
- **(*c*) the number of cases in which a person was not released under subsection 83.3(7), (7.1) or (7.2) pending a hearing;**
- **(*d*) the number of cases in which an order to enter into a recognizance was made under paragraph 83.3(8)(*a*), and the types of conditions that were imposed;**

(*e*) the number of times that a person failed or refused to enter into a recognizance, and the term of imprisonment imposed under subsection 83.3(9) in each case; and

(*f*) the number of cases in which the conditions fixed in a recognizance were varied under subsection 83.3(13).

(3) The Minister of Public Safety and Emergency Preparedness shall prepare and cause to be laid before Parliament and the Minister responsible for policing in every province shall publish or otherwise make available to the public an annual report for the previous year on the operation of section 83.3 that includes

(*a*) the number of arrests without warrant that were made under subsection 83.3(4) and the period of the arrested person's detention in custody in each case; and

(*b*) the number of cases in which a person was arrested without warrant under subsection 83.3(4) and was released

(i) by a peace officer under paragraph 83.3(5)(*b*), or

(ii) by a judge under paragraph 83.3(7)(*a*), (7.1)(*a*) or (7.2)(*a*).

(3.1) The Attorney General of Canada and the Minister of Public Safety and Emergency Preparedness shall include in their annual reports under subsections (2) and (3), respectively, their opinion, supported by reasons, on whether the operation of section 83.3 should be extended.

(4) The annual report shall not contain any information the disclosure of which would

(*a*) compromise or hinder an ongoing investigation of an offence under an Act of Parliament;

(*b*) endanger the life or safety of any person;

(*c*) prejudice a legal proceeding; or

(*d*) otherwise be contrary to the public interest. 2001, c. 41, s. 4; 2005, c. 10, s. 35(1)(*f*)(iv); 2013, c. 9, s. 11; 2015, c. 20, s. 18.

SUNSET PROVISION / Review / Report / Order in Council / Rules / Subsequent extensions / Definition of "sitting day of Parliament".

83.32 (1) Sections 83.28, 83.29 and 83.3 cease to have effect at the end of the 15th sitting day of Parliament after the fifth anniversary of the coming into force of this subsection unless, before the end of that day, the operation of those sections is extended by resolution — whose text is established under subsection (2) — passed by both Houses of Parliament in accordance with the rules set out in subsection (3).

(1.1) A comprehensive review of sections 83.28, 83.29 and 83.3 and their operation shall be undertaken by any committee of the Senate, of the House of Commons or of both Houses of Parliament that may be designated or established by the Senate or the House of Commons, or by both Houses of Parliament, as the case may be, for that purpose.

(1.2) The committee referred to in subsection (1.1) shall, within a year after a review is undertaken under that subsection or within any further time that may be authorized by the Senate, the House of Commons or both Houses of Parliament, as the case may be, submit a report on the review to Parliament, including its recommendation with respect to extending the operation of section 83.28, 83.29 or 83.3.

(2) The Governor in Council may, by order, establish the text of a resolution that provides for the extension of the operation of section 83.28, 83.29 or 83.3 and that specifies the period of the extension, which may not exceed five years from the first day on which the resolution has been passed by both Houses of Parliament.

(3) A motion for the adoption of the resolution may be debated in both Houses of Parliament but may not be amended. At the conclusion of the debate, the Speaker of the House of Parliament shall immediately put every question necessary to determine whether or not the motion is concurred in.

(4) The operation of section 83.28, 83.29 or 83.3 may be further extended in accordance with the procedure set out in this section, but the reference to "the fifth anniversary of the coming into force of this subsection" in subsection (1) is to be read as a reference to "the expiry of the most recent extension under this section".

(5) In subsection (1), "sitting day of Parliament" means a day on which both Houses of Parliament sit. 2001, c. 41, s. 4; 2013, c. 9, s. 12.

TRANSITIONAL PROVISION — SECTIONS 83.28 AND 83.29 / Transitional provision — section 83.3.

83.33 (1) In the event that sections 83.28 and 83.29 cease to have effect in accordance with section 83.32, proceedings commenced under those sections shall be completed if the hearing before the judge of the application made under subsection 83.28(2) began before those sections ceased to have effect.

(2) In the event that section 83.3 ceases to have effect in accordance with section 83.32, a person detained in custody under section 83.3 shall be released when that section ceases to have effect, except that subsections 83.3(7) to (14) continue to apply to a person who was taken before a judge under subsection 83.3(6) before section 83.3 ceased to have effect. 2001, c. 41, s. 4; 2013, c. 9, s. 13.

Part III / FIREARMS AND OTHER WEAPONS

Note: Part III (ss. 84, 86 to 96, 98 to 117) replaced 1995, c. 39, s. 139 (brought into force December 1, 1998) (s. 85 in force January 1, 1996) (s. 97 in force January 1, 2003):

Interpretation

DEFINITIONS / "Ammunition" / "Antique firearm" / "Authorization" / "Automatic firearm" / "Cartridge magazine" / "Chief firearms officer" / "Commissioner of firearms" / "Cross-bow" / "Export" / "Firearms officer" / "Handgun" / "Imitation firearm" / "Import" / "Licence" / "Non-restricted firearm" / "Prescribed" / "Prohibited ammunition" / "Prohibited device" / "Prohibited firearm" / "Prohibited weapon" / "Prohibition order" / "Registrar" / "Registration certificate" / "Replica firearm" / "Restricted firearm" / "Restricted weapon" / "Superior court" / "Transfer" / Barrel length / Certain weapons deemed not to be firearms / Exception / antique firearms / Meaning of "holder" / Subsequent offences / Sequence of convictions only.

84. (1) In this Part,

"ammunition" means a cartridge containing a projectile designed to be discharged from a firearm and, without restricting the generality of the foregoing, includes a caseless cartridge and a shot shell;

"antique firearm" means

- **(*a*) any firearm manufactured before 1898 that was not designed to discharge rim-fire or centre-fire ammunition and that has not been redesigned to discharge such ammunition, or**
- **(*b*) any firearm that is prescribed to be an antique firearm;**

"authorization" means an authorization issued under the *Firearms Act*;

"automatic firearm" means a firearm that is capable of, or assembled or designed and manufactured with the capability of, discharging projectiles in rapid succession during one pressure of the trigger;

"cartridge magazine" means a device or container from which ammunition may be fed into the firing chamber of a firearm;

"chief firearms officer" means a chief firearms officer as defined in subsection 2(1) of the *Firearms Act*;

"Commissioner of Firearms" means the Commissioner of Firearms appointed under section 81.1 of the *Firearms Act*.

"cross-bow" means a device with a bow and a bowstring mounted on a stock that is designed to propel an arrow, a bolt, a quarrel or any similar projectile on a trajectory guided by a barrel or groove and that is capable of causing serious bodily injury or death to a person;

"export" means export from Canada and, for greater certainty, includes the exportation of goods from Canada that are imported into Canada and shipped in transit through Canada;

"firearms officer" means a firearms officer as defined in subsection 2(1) of the *Firearms Act*;

"handgun" means a firearm that is designed, altered or intended to be aimed and fired by the action of one hand, whether or not it has been redesigned or subsequently altered to be aimed and fired by the action of both hands;

"imitation firearm" means any thing that imitates a firearm, and includes a replica firearm;

"import" means import into Canada and, for greater certainty, includes the importation of goods into Canada that are shipped in transit through Canada and exported from Canada;

"licence" means a licence issued under the *Firearms Act*;

"non-restricted firearm" means

(*a*) a firearm that is neither a prohibited firearm nor a restricted firearm, or

(*b*) a firearm that is prescribed to be a non-restricted firearm;

"prescribed" means prescribed by the regulations;

"prohibited ammunition" means ammunition, or a projectile of any kind, that is prescribed to be prohibited ammunition;

"prohibited device" means

(*a*) any component or part of a weapon, or any accessory for use with a weapon, that is prescribed to be a prohibited device,

(*b*) a handgun barrel that is equal to or less than 105 mm in length, but does not include any such handgun barrel that is prescribed, where the handgun barrel is for use in international sporting competitions governed by the rules of the International Shooting Union,

(*c*) a device or contrivance designed or intended to muffle or stop the sound or report of a firearm,

(*d*) a cartridge magazine that is prescribed to be a prohibited device, or

(*e*) a replica firearm;

"prohibited firearm" means

(*a*) a handgun that

(i) has a barrel equal to or less than 105 mm in length, or

(ii) is designed or adapted to discharge a 25 or 32 calibre cartridge,

but does not include any such handgun that is prescribed, where the handgun is for use in international sporting competitions governed by the rules of the International Shooting Union,

(*b*) a firearm that is adapted from a rifle or shotgun, whether by sawing, cutting or any other alteration, and that, as so adapted,

(i) is less than 660 mm in length, or

(ii) is 660 mm or greater in length and has a barrel less than 457 mm in length,

(*c*) an automatic firearm, whether or not it has been altered to discharge only one projectile with one pressure of the trigger, or

(*d*) any firearm that is prescribed to be a prohibited firearm;

"prohibited weapon" means

(*a*) a knife that has a blade that opens automatically by gravity or centrifugal force or by hand pressure applied to a button, spring or other device in or attached to the handle of the knife, or

(*b*) any weapon, other than a firearm, that is prescribed to be a prohibited weapon;

"prohibition order" means an order made under this Act or any other Act of Parliament prohibiting a person from possessing any firearm, cross-bow, prohibited weapon, restricted weapon, prohibited device, ammunition, prohibited ammunition or explosive substance, or all such things;

"Registrar" means the Registrar of Firearms appointed under section 82 of the *Firearms Act*;

"registration certificate" means a registration certificate issued under the *Firearms Act*;

"replica firearm" means any device that is designed or intended to exactly resemble, or to resemble with near precision, a firearm, and that itself is not a firearm, but does not include any such device that is designed or intended to exactly resemble, or to resemble with near precision, an antique firearm;

"restricted firearm" means

(*a*) a handgun that is not a prohibited firearm,

(*b*) a firearm that

(i) is not a prohibited firearm,

(ii) has a barrel less than 470 mm in length, and

(iii) is capable of discharging centre-fire ammunition in a semi-automatic manner,

(*c*) a firearm that is designed or adapted to be fired when reduced to a length of less than 660 mm by folding, telescoping or otherwise, or

(*d*) a firearm of any other kind that is prescribed to be a restricted firearm;

"restricted weapon" means any weapon, other than a firearm, that is prescribed to be a restricted weapon;

"superior court" means

(*a*) in Ontario, the Superior Court of Justice, sitting in the region, district or county or group of counties where the relevant adjudication was made,

(*b*) in Quebec, the Superior Court,

(*c*) in New Brunswick, Manitoba, Saskatchewan and Alberta, the Court of Queen's Bench,

(*d*) in Nova Scotia, British Columbia, Prince Edward Island and a territory, the Supreme Court, and

(*e*) in Newfoundland and Labrador, the Trial Division of the Supreme Court;

"transfer" means sell, provide, barter, give, lend, rent, send, transport, ship, distribute or deliver.

(2) For the purposes of this Part, the length of a barrel of a firearm is

(*a*) in the case of a revolver, the distance from the muzzle of the barrel to the breach end immediately in front of the cylinder, and

(*b*) in any other case, the distance from the muzzle of the barrel to and including the chamber,

but does not include the length of any component, part or accessory including any component, part or accessory designed or intended to suppress the muzzle flash or reduce recoil.

(3) For the purposes of sections 91 to 95, 99 to 101, 103 to 107 and 117.03 of this Act and the provisions of the *Firearms Act*, the following weapons are deemed not to be firearms:

(*a*) any antique firearm;

(*b*) any device that is

(i) designed exclusively for signalling, for notifying of distress, for firing blank cartridges or for firing stud cartridges, explosive-driven rivets or other industrial projectiles, and

(ii) intended by the person in possession of it to be used exclusively for the purpose for which it is designed;

(*c*) any shooting device that is

(i) designed exclusively for the slaughtering of domestic animals, the tranquilizing of animals or the discharging of projectiles with lines attached to them, and

(ii) intended by the person in possession of it to be used exclusively for the purpose for which it is designed; and

(*d*) any other barrelled weapon, where it is proved that the weapon is not designed or adapted to discharge

(i) a shot, bullet or other projectile at a muzzle velocity exceeding 152.4 m per second or at a muzzle energy exceeding 5.7 Joules, or

(ii) a shot, bullet or other projectile that is designed or adapted to attain a velocity exceeding 152.4 m per second or an energy exceeding 5.7 Joules.

(3.1) Notwithstanding subsection (3), an antique firearm is a firearm for the purposes of regulations made under paragraph 117(*h*) of the *Firearms Act* and subsection 86(2) of this Act.

(4) For the purposes of this Part, a person is the holder of

(*a*) an authorization or a licence if the authorization or licence has been issued to the person and the person continues to hold it; and

(*b*) a registration certificate for a firearm if

(i) the registration certificate has been issued to the person and the person continues to hold it, or

(ii) the person possesses the registration certificate with the permission of its lawful holder.

(5) In determining, for the purpose of subsection 85(3), 95(2), 99(2), 100(2) or 103(2), whether a convicted person has committed a second or subsequent offence, if the person was earlier convicted of any of the following offences, that offence is to be considered as an earlier offence:

(*a*) an offence under section 85, 95, 96, 98, 98.1, 99, 100, 102 or 103 or subsection 117.01(1);

(*b*) an offence under section 244 or 244.2; or

(*c*) an offence under section 220, 236, 239, 272 or 273, subsection 279(1) or section 279.1, 344 or 346 if a firearm was used in the commission of the offence.

However, an earlier offence shall not be taken into account if 10 years have elapsed between the day on which the person was convicted of the earlier offence and the day on which the person was convicted of the offence for which sentence is being imposed, not taking into account any time in custody.

(6) For the purposes of subsection (5), the only question to be considered is the sequence of convictions and no consideration shall be given to the sequence of commission of offences or whether any offence occurred before or after any conviction. 1995, c. 39, s. 139; 1998, c. 30, s. 16; 2003, c. 8, s. 2; 2008, c. 6, s. 2; 2009, c. 22, s. 2; 2015, c. 3, s. 45; 2015, c. 27, s. 18.

CROSS-REFERENCES
"Firearm" and "weapon" are defined in s. 2. Section 117.15 gives the Governor in Council power to make regulations prescribing anything that may be prescribed under this part, for example prohibited and restricted firearms and weapons, provided those things are not reasonably for use for hunting and sporting purposes.

SYNOPSIS

Subsection (1) sets out the definitions for use in this part and certain other specified sections of the Code. In particular, these definitions apply to ss. 491 [forfeiture of weapons and ammunition], 515(4.1), (4.11) [condition of release pending trial prohibiting possession of weapons], 810(3.1), (3.11) [condition of peace bond prohibiting possession of weapons]. Subsection (2) determines the length of the barrel of a firearm for the purposes of the definitions of prohibited devices and firearms and restricted firearms. Subsection (3) deems certain types of weapons not to be firearms for the purposes of provisions of this part dealing with firearms, except that pursuant to subsec. (3) antique firearms are still deemed to be firearms for certain purposes. Subsection (4) defines who is the "holder" of an authorization or licence or a firearm registration certificate. Subsection (5) defines what are earlier offences of the purpose of determining if the offender is liable to the increased punishment in ss. 85, 95, 99, 100 and 103, by reason of having committed a second or subsequent offence. Subsection (6) provides that the sequence of convictions is the only relevant consideration, not the sequence in which the offences were committed.

ANNOTATIONS

Note: Some of the following cases were decided under the predecessor legislation but were thought to be of some assistance in applying these provisions.

"Antique firearm" – The trial judge erred by acquitting the accused on the basis that the evidence had not established that the firearm was manufactured after 1898, without going on to consider whether the firearm was designed to discharge rim-fire or centre-fire ammunition: *R. v. Kennedy* (2016), 334 C.C.C. (3d) 68 (Man. C.A.).

"Automatic firearm" – It was held, considering the slightly different definition of prohibited weapon under the former legislation, that firearms that in their original condition were capable of firing bullets in rapid succession during one pressure of the trigger and of being converted to fire automatically, by use of hand tools and without replacement of any part in about 10 minutes, fell within the definition: *R. v. Barnes* (1996), 104 C.C.C. (3d) 374, 27 O.R. (3d) 626 (C.A.).

"Handgun" – It was held, considering the slightly different definition of restricted weapon under the former legislation, that a pistol, although lacking a magazine when found in the possession of the accused, comes within this definition, notwithstanding that in this state two hands would be required to fire. Once the magazine was loaded, it could be fired with one hand and was thus "designed" to be aimed and fired by the action of one hand: *R. v. Watkins and Graber* (1987), 33 C.C.C. (3d) 465 (B.C.C.A.).

"Prohibited weapon" – A knife may come within para. (*a*) whether or not it comes within the ordinary meaning of weapon and whether or not it was designed to be used as a prohibited weapon if in fact its blade, through wear and tear or alteration, can be fully opened for use by applying centrifugal force or gravity to the blade. It is the capability and not the design of the knife that determines whether or not it is a prohibited weapon. The words "any knife that has a blade that opens automatically by . .. centrifugal force" should be interpreted as meaning one that opens by means of a centrifugal force applied to the blade and not to the handle. The word "open" in the definition means open with the capacity for use as a weapon. Any knife which, when held in a position where the handle is above the blade and the blade drops open at or about a 90-degree angle to the handle and by gravity continues to open fully, available for use, when the handle is placed in a vertical position or when centrifugal force is applied to a partially opened blade, is a knife having a blade that opens automatically by gravity or centrifugal force and is therefore a prohibited weapon: *R. v. Richard and Walker* (1981), 63 C.C.C. (2d) 333, 24 C.R. (3d) 373 (N.B.C.A.).

A knife that will only open by holding the blade and applying centrifugal force to the handle is not within the definition. However, a knife although not originally so designed, which through long use opens by application of centrifugal force to the blade, is a prohibited weapon: *R. v. Archer* (1983), 6 C.C.C. (3d) 129 (Ont. C.A.).

The fact that an additional manual operation had to be performed before the knife, a so-called "butterfly knife", was in a position to be opened automatically by centrifugal force, and that some skill was required to perform the operation, did not prevent the knife from being a prohibited weapon: *R. v. Vaughan*, [1991] 3 S.C.R. 691, 69 C.C.C. (3d) 576*n* (5:0).

In *R. v. Vokac* (1978), 42 C.C.C. (2d) 201, [1978] 5 W.W.R. 397 (B.C.C.A.), it was held that where the prohibited weapon was defined under [former] Prohibited Weapons Order No. 1, SOR/74-297 [now see Part 3 of the Regulation], as "any device designed to be used for the purpose of injuring, immobilizing or otherwise incapacitating any person by the discharge therefrom of . . . (b) any liquid, spray, powder or other substance that is capable of injuring, immobilizing or otherwise incapacitating any person", the label on the spray canister was admissible as proof of the purpose for which it was designed although the label could not prove the capability of the spray. This latter element was proved by *viva voce* evidence of a police officer who experimented with the spray seized from the accused.

In order to constitute a prohibited weapon it was held not to be sufficient that the device falls within the description set out in a Prohibited Weapons Order. The device must also come within the definition of "weapon" in s. 2: *R. v. Murray* (1985), 24 C.C.C. (3d) 568, 7 O.A.C. 127 (C.A.). *Contra: R. v. K. (A.)* (1991), 68 C.C.C. (3d) 135, 9 C.R. (4th) 269 (B.C.C.A.), leave to appeal to S.C.C. refused 70 C.C.C. (3d) vi, 17 W.A.C. 79*n*, where it was held that the word "weapon" in [former] para. (*e*) [now para. (*b*)] should be given a broader meaning than as defined in s. 2 to encompass any article or device that can on occasion be used to inflict injury, harm or death to a person whether used offensively or defensively. Thus, in the absence of a challenge to the power of the Governor in Council to designate the device as a prohibited weapon on the basis that it does not fall within this normal everyday meaning of weapon, a prohibited weapon under s. 84 is simply what the Governor in Council has declared [now prescribed] to be a prohibited weapon.

If the accused knew he possessed an object that met the description of brass knuckles prescribed under subsec. (1) (whether or not he knew it was prescribed by regulation to be a "prohibited weapon"), then he possessed an object that was "designed to be used" as a weapon within the meaning of s. 2. The amendment to s. 2 has removed the concern of the court in *K.(A.)*, *supra*, that the interpretation of s. 84(1)(*e*) in *Murray*, *supra*, imposed a completely subjective element: *R. v. Strong* (2012), 288 C.C.C. (3d) 357 (B.C.C.A.).

"Cartridge magazine" – An accused was convicted of an offence for possessing several magazine casings with a 30-round capacity. His argument that he intended to alter the casings in order to bring them within the requirement that magazines have no more than a 5-round capacity was rejected. Even though an expert testified that the casings would require the installation of a number of parts before they could be functional as magazines, the court concluded that they were prohibited devices because they were capable of becoming operable with the addition of readily available parts: *R. v. Cancade* (2011), 270 C.C.C. (3d) 536 (B.C.C.A.).

Exemptions (subsec. (3)) – This provision had no application where the accused stole a starter pistol knowing that the purchaser intended to drill out the gun to accommodate the firing of live ammunition: *R. v. Goswami* (2002), 164 C.C.C. (3d) 378 (Ont. C.A.).

REGULATIONS PRESCRIBING CERTAIN FIREARMS AND OTHER WEAPONS, COMPONENTS AND PARTS OF WEAPONS, ACCESSORIES, CARTRIDGE MAGAZINES, AMMUNITION AND PROJECTILES AS PROHIBITED, RESTRICTED OR NON-RESTRICTED

Interpretation

1. In these Regulations, "semi-automatic", in respect of a firearm, means a firearm that is equipped with a mechanism that, following the discharge of a cartridge, automatically operates to complete any part of the reloading cycle necessary to prepare for the discharge of the next cartridge.

Prescription

2. The firearms listed in Part 1 of the schedule are prohibited firearms for the purposes of paragraph (*d*) of the definition "prohibited firearm" in subsection 84(1) of the *Criminal Code*.

3. The firearms listed in Part 2 of the schedule are restricted firearms for the purposes of paragraph (*d*) of the definition "restricted firearm" in subsection 84(1) of the *Criminal Code*, except for those firearms that are prohibited firearms within the meaning of paragraph (*b*) or (*c*) of the definition "prohibited firearm" in that subsection.

3.1 The firearms listed in Part 2.1 of the schedule that have a barrel that is less than 470 mm in length, and firearms listed in items 3, 4, 6, 7, 9 and 10 of that Part that do not have a barrel, are restricted firearms for the purposes of paragraph (*d*) of the definition "restricted firearm" in subsection 84(1) of the *Criminal Code*, except for those firearms that

(a) discharge projectiles in rapid succession during one pressure of the trigger; or

(b) are prohibited firearms within the meaning of paragraph (*b*) of the definition "prohibited firearm" in subsection 84(1) of the *Criminal Code*.

3.2 The firearms listed in Part 2.1 of the schedule that have a barrel that is at least 470 mm in length, and the firearms listed in items 1, 2, 5, 8 and 11 to 15 of that Part that do not have a barrel, are non-restricted firearms for the purposes of paragraph (*b*) of the definition "non-restricted firearm" in subsection 84(1) of the *Criminal Code*, except for those firearms that

(a) discharge projectiles in rapid succession during one pressure of the trigger; or

(b) are prohibited firearms within the meaning of paragraph (*b*) of the definition "prohibited firearm" in subsection 84(1) of the *Criminal Code*.

4. The weapons listed in Part 3 of the schedule are prohibited weapons for the purposes of paragraph (*b*) of the definition "prohibited weapon" in subsection 84(1) of the *Criminal Code*.

5. The components and parts of weapons, accessories, and cartridge magazines listed in Part 4 of the schedule are prohibited devices for the purposes of paragraphs (*a*) and (*d*) of the definition "prohibited device" in subsection 84(1) of the *Criminal Code*.

6. The ammunition and projectiles listed in Part 5 of the schedule are prohibited ammunition for the purposes of the definition "prohibited ammunition" in subsection 84(1) of the *Criminal Code*.

Coming into Force

7. These Regulations come into force on December 1, 1998.

Schedule

(Sections 2 to 6)

PART 1
Prohibited Firearms

Former Prohibited Weapons Order, No. 3

1. Any firearm capable of discharging a dart or other object carrying an electrical current or substance, including the firearm of the design commonly known as the Taser Public Defender and any variant or modified version of it.

Former Prohibited Weapons Order, No. 8

2. The firearm known as the SSS-1 Stinger and any similar firearm designed or of a size to fit in the palm of the hand.

Former Prohibited Weapons Order, No. 11

3. The firearm of the design commonly known as the Franchi SPAS 12 shotgun, and any variant or modified version of it, including the Franchi LAW 12 shotgun.

4. The firearm of the design commonly known as the Striker shotgun, and any variant or modified version of it, including the Striker 12 shotgun and the Streetsweeper shotgun.

5. The firearm of the design commonly known as the USAS-12 Auto Shotgun, and any variant or modified version of it.

6. The firearm of the design commonly known as the Franchi SPAS-15 shotgun, and any variant or modified version of it.

7. The firearms of the designs commonly known as the Benelli M1 Super 90 shotgun and the Benelli M3 Super 90 shotgun, and any variants or modified versions of them, with the exception of the

(a) M1 Super 90 Field;
(b) M1 Super 90 Sporting Special;
(c) Montefeltro Super 90;
(d) Montefeltro Super 90 Standard Hunter;
(e) Montefeltro Super 90 Left Hand;
(f) Montefeltro Super 90 Turkey;
(g) Montefeltro Super 90 Uplander;
(h) Montefeltro Super 90 Slug;
(i) Montefeltro Super 90 20 Gauge;
(j) Black Eagle;
(k) Black Eagle Limited Edition;
(l) Black Eagle Competition;
(m) Black Eagle Slug Gun;
(n) Super Black Eagle; and
(o) Super Black Eagle Custom Slug.

8. The firearms of the designs commonly known as the Bernardelli B4 shotgun and the Bernardelli B4/B shotgun, and any variants or modified versions of them.

9. The firearm of the design commonly known as the American 180 Auto Carbine, and any variant or modified version of it, including the AM-180 Auto Carbine and the Illinois Arms Company Model 180 Auto Carbine.

10. The firearms of the designs commonly known as the Barrett "Light Fifty" Model 82A1 rifle and the Barrett Model 90 rifle, and any variants or modified versions of them.

11. The firearm of the design commonly known as the Calico M-900 rifle, and any variant or modified version of it, including the M-951 carbine, M-100 carbine and M-105 carbine.

12. The firearm of the design commonly known as the Iver Johnson AMAC long-range rifle, and any variant or modified version of it.

13. The firearm of the design commonly known as the McMillan M87 rifle, and any variant or modified version of it, including the McMillan M87R rifle and the McMillan M88 carbine.

14. The firearms of the designs commonly known as the Pauza Specialties P50 rifle and P50 carbine, and any variants or modified versions of them.

15. The firearm of the design commonly known as the Encom MK-IV carbine, and any variant or modified version of it.

16. The firearms of the designs commonly known as the Encore MP-9 and MP-45 carbines, and any variants or modified versions of them.

17. The firearm of the design commonly known as the FAMAS rifle, and any variant or modified version of it, including the MAS 223, FAMAS Export, FAMAS Civil and Mitchell MAS/22.

18. The firearm of the design commonly known as the Feather AT-9 Semi-Auto Carbine, and any variant or modified version of it, including the Feather AT-22 Auto Carbine.

19. The firearm of the design commonly known as the Federal XC-450 Auto Rifle, and any variant or modified version of it, including the Federal XC-900 rifle and Federal XC-220 rifle.

20. The firearm of the design commonly known as the Gepard long-range sniper rifle, and any variant or modified version of it.

21. The firearm of the design commonly known as the Heckler and Koch (HK) Model G11 rifle, and any variant or modified version of it.

22. The firearm of the design commonly known as the Research Armament Industries (RAI) Model 500 rifle, and any variant or modified version of it.

23. The firearm of the design commonly known as the Spectre Auto Carbine, and any variant or modified version of it.

24. The firearm of the design commonly known as the US Arms PMAI "Assault" 22 rifle, and any variant or modified version of it.

25. The firearm of the design commonly known as the Weaver Arms Nighthawk Carbine, and any variant or modified version of it.

26. The firearm of the design commonly known as the A.A. Arms AR9 Semi-Automatic Rifle, and any variant or modified version of it.

27. The firearms of the designs commonly known as the Claridge HI-TEC c. LEC-9 and ZLEC-9 carbines, and any variants or modified versions of them.

28. The firearm of the design commonly known as the Kimel Industries AR-9 rifle or carbine, and any variant or modified version of it.

29. The firearm of the design commonly known as the Grendel R-31 Auto Carbine, and any variant or modified version of it.

30. The firearms of the designs commonly known as the Maadi Griffin Rifle and the Maadi Griffin Carbine, and any variants or modified versions of them.

31. The firearm of the design commonly known as the AA Arms Model AR-9 carbine, and any variant or modified version of it.

32. The firearm of the design commonly known as the Bushmaster Auto Pistol, and any variant or modified version of it.

33. The firearm of the design commonly known as the Calico M-950 Auto Pistol, and any variant or modified version of it, including the M-110 pistol.

34. The firearm of the design commonly known as the Encom MK-IV assault pistol, and any variant or modified version of it.

35. The firearms of the designs commonly known as the Encom MP-9 and MP-45 assault pistols, and any variants or modified versions of them, including the Encom MP-9 and MP-45 mini pistols.

36. The firearm of the design commonly known as the Federal XP-450 Auto Pistol, and any variant or modified version of it, including the XP-900 Auto Pistol.

37. The firearm of the design commonly known as the Heckler and Koch (HK) SP89 Auto Pistol, and any variant or modified version of it.

38. The firearm of the design commonly known as the Intratec Tec-9 Auto Pistol, and any variant or modified version of it, including the Tec-9S, Tec-9M, Tec-9MS, and any semi-automatic variants of them, including the Tec-DC9, Tec-DC9M, Tec-9A, Tec-Scorpion, Tec-22T and Tec-22TN.

39. The firearms of the designs commonly known as the Iver Johnson Enforcer Model 3000 Auto Pistol and the Iver Johnson Plainfield Super Enforcer Carbine, and any variants or modified versions of them.

40. The firearm of the design commonly known as the Skorpion Auto Pistol, and any variant or modified version of it.

41. The firearm of the design commonly known as the Spectre Auto Pistol, and any variant or modified version of it.

42. The firearm of the design commonly known as the Sterling Mk 7 pistol, and any variant or modified version of it, including the Sterling Mk 7 C4 and Sterling Mk 7 C8.

43. The firearm of the design commonly known as the Universal Enforcer Model 3000 Auto Carbine, and any variant or modified version of it, including the Universal Enforcer Model 3010N, Model 3015G, Model 3020TRB and Model 3025TCO Carbines.

44. The firearm of the design commonly known as the US Arms PMAIP "Assault" 22 pistol, and any variant or modified version of it.

45. The firearm of the design commonly known as the Goncz High-Tech Long Pistol, and any variant or modified version of it, including the Claridge Hi-Tec models s. L, T, ZL-9 and ZT-9 pistols.

46. The firearm of the design commonly known as the Leader Mark 5 Auto Pistol, and any variant or modified version of it.

47. The firearm of the design commonly known as the OA-93 assault pistol, and any variant or modified version of it.

48. The firearm of the design commonly known as the A.A. Arms AP9 Auto Pistol, and any variant or modified version of it.

49. The firearm of the design commonly known as the Patriot pistol, and any variant or modified version of it.

50. The firearm of the design commonly known as the XM 231S pistol, and any variant or modified version of it, including the A1, A2 and A3 Flattop pistols.

51. The firearm of the design commonly known as the AA Arms Model AP-9 pistol, and any variant or modified version of it, including the Target AP-9 and the Mini AP-9 pistols.

52. The firearm of the design commonly known as the Kimel Industries AP-9 pistol, and any variant or modified version of it.

53. The firearms of the designs commonly known as the Grendel P-30, P-30 M, P-30 L and P-31 pistols, and any variants or modified versions of them.

54. The firearms of the designs commonly known as the Claridge HI-TEC ZL-9, HI-TEC S. HI-TEC L, HI-TEC T, HI-TEC ZT-9 and HI-TEC ZL-9 pistols, and any variants or modified versions of them.

55. The firearm of the design commonly known as the Steyr SPP Assault Pistol, and any variant or modified version of it.

56. The firearm of the design commonly known as the Maadi Griffin Pistol, and any variant or modified version of it.

57. The firearm of the design commonly known as the Interdynamics KG-99 Assault Pistol, and any variant or modified version of it.

Former Prohibited Weapons Order, No. 12

58. The firearm of the design commonly known as the Sterling Mk 6 Carbine, and any variant or modified version of it.

59. The firearm of the design commonly known as the Steyr AUG rifle, and any variant or modified version of it.

60. The firearm of the design commonly known as the UZI carbine, and any variant or modified version of it, including the UZI Model A carbine and the Mini-UZI carbine.

61. The firearms of the designs commonly known as the Ingram M10 and M11 pistols, and any variants or modified versions of them, including the Cobray M10 and M11 pistols, the RPB M10, M11, SM10 and SM11 pistols and the SWD M10, M11, SM10 and SM11 pistols.

62. The firearm of the design commonly known as the Partisan Avenger Auto Pistol, and any variant or modified version of it.

63. The firearm of the design commonly known as the UZI pistol, and any variant or modified version of it, including the Micro-UZI pistol.

Former Prohibited Weapons Order, No. 13

64. The firearm of the design commonly known as the AK-47 rifle, and any variant or modified version of it except for the Valmet Hunter, the Valmet Hunter Auto and the Valmet M78 rifles, but including the

(a) AK-74;
(b) AK Hunter;
(c) AKM;
(d) AKM-63;
(e) AKS-56S;
(f) AKS-56S-1;
(g) AKS-56S-2;
(h) AKS-74;
(i) AKS-84S-1;
(j) AMD-65;
(k) AR Model .223;
(l) Dragunov;
(m) Galil;
(n) KKMPi69;
(o) M60;
(p) M62;
(q) M70B1;
(r) M70AB2;
(s) M76;

(t) M77B1;
(u) M78;
(v) M80;
(w) M80A;
(x) MAK90;
(y) MPiK;
(z) MPiKM;
(z.1) MPiKMS-72;
(z.2) MPiKS;
(z.3) PKM;
(z.4) PKM-DGN-60;
(z.5) PMKM;
(z.6) RPK;
(z.7) RPK-74;
(z.8) RPK-87S;
(z.9) Type 56;
(z.10) Type 56-1;
(z.11) Type 56-2;
(z.12) Type 56-3;
(z.13) Type 56-4;
(z.14) Type 68;
(z.15) Type 79;
(z.16) American Arms AKY39;
(z.17) American Arms AKF39;
(z.18) American Arms AKC47;
(z.19) American Arms AKF47;
(z.20) MAM70WS762;
(z.21) MAM70FS762;
(z.22) Mitchell AK-22;
(z.23) Mitchell AK-47;
(z.24) Mitchell Heavy Barrel AK-47;
(z.25) Norinco 84S;
(z.26) Norinco 84S AK;
(z.27) Norinco 56;
(z.28) Norinco 56-1;
(z.29) Norinco 56-2;
(z.30) Norinco 56-3;
(z.31) Norinco 56-4;
(z.32) Poly Technologies Inc. AK-47/S;
(z.33) Poly Technologies Inc. AKS-47/S;
(z.34) Poly Technologies Inc. AKS-762;
(z.35) Valmet M76;
(z.36) Valmet M76 carbine;
(z.37) Valmet M78/A2;
(z.38) Valmet M78 (NATO) LMG;
(z.39) Valmet M82; and
(z.40) Valmet M82 Bullpup.

65. The firearm of the design commonly known as the Armalite AR-180 Spotter carbine, and any variant or modified version of it.

66. The firearm of the design commonly known as the Beretta AR70 assault rifle, and any variant or modified version of it.

67. The firearm of the design commonly known as the BM 59 rifle, and any variant or modified version of it, including

(a) the Beretta

(i) BM 59,
(ii) BM 59R,
(iii) BM 59GL,
(iv) BM 59D,
(v) BM 59 Mk E,
(vi) BM 59 Mk I,
(vii) BM 59 Mk Ital,
(viii) BM 59 Mk II,
(ix) BM 59 Mk III,
(x) BM 59 Mk Ital TA,
(xi) BM 59 Mk Ital Para,
(xii) BM 59 Mk Ital TP, and
(xiii) BM 60CB; and
(b) the Springfield Armory
(i) BM 59 Alpine,
(ii) BM 59 Alpine Paratrooper, and
(iii) BM 59 Nigerian Mk IV.

68. The firearm of the design commonly known as the Bushmaster Auto Rifle, and any variant or modified version of it.

69. The firearm of the design commonly known as the Cetme Sport Auto Rifle, and any variant or modified version of it.

70. The firearm of the design commonly known as the Daewoo K1 rifle, and any variant or modified version of it, including the Daewoo K1A1, K2, Max 1, Max 2, AR-100, AR 110C, MAXI-II and KC-20.

71. The firearm of the design commonly known as the Demro TAC-1M carbine, and any variant or modified version of it, including the Demro XF-7 Wasp Carbine.

72. The firearm of the design commonly known as the Eagle Apache Carbine, and any variant or modified version of it.

73. The firearm of the design commonly known as the FN-FNC rifle, and any variant or modified version of it, including the FNC Auto Rifle, FNC Auto Paratrooper, FNC-11, FNC-22 and FNC-33.

74. The firearm of the design commonly known as the FN-FAL (FN-LAR) rifle, and any variant or modified version of it, including the FN 308 Model 44, FN-FAL (FN-LAR) Competition Auto, FN-FAL (FN-LAR) Heavy Barrel 308 Match, FN-FAL (FN-LAR) Paratrooper 308 Match 50-64 and FN 308 Model 50-63.

75. The firearm of the design commonly known as the G3 rifle, and any variant or modified version of it, including the Heckler and Koch

(a) HK 91;
(b) HK 91A2;
(c) HK 91A3;
(d) HK G3 A3;
(e) HK G3 A3 ZF;
(f) HK G3 A4;
(g) HK G3 SG/1; and
(h) HK PSG1.

76. The firearm of the design commonly known as the Galil assault rifle, and any variant or modified version of it, including the AP-84, Galil ARM, Galil AR, Galil SAR, Galil 332 and Mitchell Galil/22 Auto Rifle.

77. The firearm of the design commonly known as the Goncz High-Tech Carbine, and any variant or modified version of it.

78. The firearm of the design commonly known as the Heckler and Koch HK 33 rifle, and any variant or modified version of it, including the

(a) HK 33A2;
(b) HK 33A3;
(c) HK 33KA1;
(d) HK 93;
(e) HK 93A2; and
(f) HK 93A3.

79. The firearm of the design commonly known as the J & R Eng M-68 carbine, and any variant or modified version of it, including the PJK M-68 and the Wilkinson Terry carbine.

80. The firearm of the design commonly known as the Leader Mark Series Auto Rifle, and any variant or modified version of it.

81. The firearms of the designs commonly known as the MP5 submachine gun and MP5 carbine, and any variants or modified versions of them, including the Heckler and Koch

(a) HK MP5;
(b) HK MP5A2;
(c) HK MP5A3;
(d) HK MP5K;
(e) HK MP5SD;
(f) HK MP5SD1;
(g) HK MP5SD2;
(h) HK MP5SD3;
(i) HK 94;
(j) HK 94A2; and
(k) HK 94A3.

82. The firearm of the design commonly known as the PE57 rifle, and any variant or modified version of it.

83. The firearms of the designs commonly known as the SG-550 rifle and SG-551 carbine, and any variants or modified versions of them.

84. The firearm of the design commonly known as the SIG AMT rifle, and any variant or modified version of it.

85. The firearm of the design commonly known as the Springfield Armory SAR-48 rifle, and any variant or modified version of it, including the SAR-48 Bush, SAR-48 Heavy Barrel, SAR-48 Para and SAR-48 Model 22.

86. The firearm of the design commonly known as the Thompson submachine gun, and any variant or modified version of it, including the

(a) Thompson Model 1921;
(b) Thompson Model 1927;
(c) Thompson Model 1928;
(d) Thompson Model M1;
(e) Auto-Ordnance M27A-1;
(f) Auto-Ordnance M27A-1 Deluxe;
(g) Auto-Ordnance M1927A-3;
(h) Auto-Ordnance M1927A-5;
(i) Auto-Ordnance Thompson M1;
(j) Commando Arms Mk I;
(k) Commando Arms Mk II;
(l) Commando Arms Mk III;
(m) Commando Arms Mk 9; and
(n) Commando Arms Mk 45.

PART 2
Restricted Firearms

Former Restricted Weapons Order

1. The firearms of the designs commonly known as the High Standard Model 10, Series A shotgun and the High Standard Model 10, Series B shotgun, and any variants or modified versions of them.

2. The firearm of the design commonly known as the M-16 rifle, and any variant or modified version of it, including the

(a) Colt AR-15;
(b) Colt AR-15 SPI;
(c) Colt AR-15 Sporter;
(d) Colt AR-15 Collapsible Stock Model;
(e) Colt AR-15 A2;
(f) Colt AR-15 A2 Carbine;
(g) Colt AR-15 A2 Government Model Rifle;
(h) Colt AR-15 A2 Government Model Target Rifle;
(i) Colt AR-15 A2 Government Model Carbine;
(j) Colt AR-15 A2 Sporter II;
(k) Colt AR-15 A2 H-BAR;
(l) Colt AR-15 A2 Delta H-BAR;
(m) Colt AR-15 A2 Delta H-BAR Match;
(n) Colt AR-15 9mm Carbine;
(o) Armalite AR-15;
(p) AAI M15;
(q) AP74;
(r) EAC J-15;
(s) PWA Commando;
(t) SGW XM15A;
(u) SGW CAR-AR;
(v) SWD AR-15; and
(w) any 22-calibre rimfire variant, including the
(i) Mitchell M-16A-1/22,
(ii) Mitchell M-16/22,
(iii) Mitchell CAR-15/22, and
(iv) AP74 Auto Rifle.

PART 2.1
Firearms for the Purpose of Sections 3.1 and 3.2M

1. Ceská Zbrojovka (CZ) Model CZ858 Tactical-2P rifle
2. Ceská Zbrojovka (CZ) Model CZ858 Tactical-2V rifle
3. Ceská Zbrojovka (CZ) Model CZ858 Tactical-4P rifle
4. Ceská Zbrojovka (CZ) Model CZ858 Tactical-4V rifle
5. SAN Swiss Arms Model Classic Green rifle
6. SAN Swiss Arms Model Classic Green carbine
7. SAN Swiss Arms Model Classic Green CQB rifle
8. SAN Swiss Arms Model Black Special rifle
9. SAN Swiss Arms Model Black Special carbine

10. SAN Swiss Arms Model Black Special CQB rifle
11. SAN Swiss Arms Model Black Special Target rifle
12. SAN Swiss Arms Model Blue Star rifle
13. SAN Swiss Arms Model Heavy Metal rifle
14. SAN Swiss Arms Model Red Devil rifle
15. SAN Swiss Arms Model Swiss Arms Edition rifle

PART 3
Prohibited Weapons

Former Prohibited Weapons Order, No. 1

1. Any device designed to be used for the purpose of injuring, immobilizing or otherwise incapacitating any person by the discharge therefrom of

(a) tear gas, Mace or other gas; or
(b) any liquid, spray, powder or other substance that is capable of injuring, immobilizing or otherwise incapacitating any person.

Former Prohibited Weapons Order, No. 2

2. Any instrument or device commonly known as "nunchaku", being hard non-flexible sticks, clubs, pipes, or rods linked by a length or lengths of rope, cord, wire or chain, and any similar instrument or device.

3. Any instrument or device commonly known as "shuriken", being a hard non-flexible plate having three or more radiating points with one or more sharp edges in the shape of a polygon, trefoil, cross, star, diamond or other geometrical shape, and any similar instrument or device.

4. Any instrument or device commonly known as "manrikigusari" or "kusari", being hexagonal or other geometrically shaped hard weights or hand grips linked by a length or lengths of rope, cord, wire or chain, and any similar instrument or device.

5. Any finger ring that has one or more blades or sharp objects that are capable of being projected from the surface of the ring.

Former Prohibited Weapons Order, No. 3

6. Any device that is designed to be capable of injuring, immobilizing or incapacitating a person or an animal by discharging an electrical charge produced by means of the amplification or accumulation of the electrical current generated by a battery, where the device is designed or altered so that the electrical charge may be discharged when the device is of a length of less than 480 mm, and any similar device.

7. A crossbow or similar device that

(a) is designed or altered to be aimed and fired by the action of one hand, whether or not it has been redesigned or subsequently altered to be aimed and fired by the action of both hands; or
(b) has a length not exceeding 500 mm.

Former Prohibited Weapons Order, No. 4

8. The device known as the "Constant Companion", being a belt containing a blade capable of being withdrawn from the belt, with the buckle of the belt forming a handle for the blade, and any similar device.

9. Any knife commonly known as a "push-dagger" that is designed in such a fashion that the handle is placed perpendicular to the main cutting edge of the blade and any other similar device other than the aboriginal "ulu" knife.

10. Any device having a length of less than 30 cm and resembling an innocuous object but designed to conceal a knife or blade, including the device commonly known as the "knife-comb", being a comb with the handle of the comb forming a handle for the knife, and any similar device.

Former Prohibited Weapons Order, No. 5

11. The device commonly known as a "Spiked Wristband", being a wristband to which a spike or blade is affixed, and any similar device.

Former Prohibited Weapons Order, No. 6

12. The device commonly known as "Yaqua Blowgun", being a tube or pipe designed for the purpose of shooting arrows or darts by the breath, and any similar device.

Former Prohibited Weapons Order, No. 7

13. The device commonly known as a "Kiyoga Baton" or "Steel Cobra" and any similar device consisting of a manually triggered telescoping spring-loaded steel whip terminated in a heavy calibre striking tip.

14. The device commonly known as a "Morning Star" and any similar device consisting of a ball of metal or other heavy material, studded with spikes and connected to a handle by a length of chain, rope or other flexible material.

Former Prohibited Weapons Order, No. 8

15. The device known as "Brass Knuckles" and any similar device consisting of a band of metal with one or more finger holes designed to fit over the fingers of the hand.

PART 4
Prohibited Devices

Former Prohibited Weapons Order, No. 9

1. Any electrical or mechanical device that is designed or adapted to operate the trigger mechanism of a semi-automatic firearm for the purpose of causing the firearm to discharge cartridges in rapid succession.

2. Any rifle, shotgun or carbine stock of the type known as the "bull-pup" design, being a stock that, when combined with a firearm, reduces the overall length of the firearm such that a substantial part of the reloading action or the magazine-well is located behind the trigger of the firearm when it is held in the normal firing position.

Former Cartridge Magazine Control Regulations

3. (1) Any cartridge magazine

(a) that is capable of containing more than five cartridges of the type for which the magazine was originally designed and that is designed or manufactured for use in

(i) a semi-automatic handgun that is not commonly available in Canada,

(ii) a semi-automatic firearm other than a semi-automatic handgun,

(iii) an automatic firearm whether or not it has been altered to discharge only one projectile with one pressure of the trigger,

(iv) the firearms of the designs commonly known as the Ingram M10 and M11 pistols, and any variants or modified versions of them, including the Cobray M10 and M11 pistols, the RPB M10, M11 and SM11 pistols and the SWD M10, M11, SM10 and SM11 pistols,

(v) the firearm of the design commonly known as the Partisan Avenger Auto Pistol, and any variant or modified version of it, or

(vi) the firearm of the design commonly known as the UZI pistol, and any variant or modified version of it, including the Micro-UZI pistol; or

(b) that is capable of containing more than 10 cartridges of the type for which the magazine was originally designed and that is designed or manufactured for use in a semi-automatic handgun that is commonly available in Canada.

(2) Paragraph (1)(*a*) does not include any cartridge magazine that

(a) was originally designed or manufactured for use in a firearm that

(i) is chambered for, or designed to use, rimfire cartridges,

(ii) is a rifle of the type commonly known as the "Lee Enfield" rifle, where the magazine is capable of containing not more than 10 cartridges of the type for which the magazine was originally designed, or

(iii) is commonly known as the U.S. Rifle M1 (Garand) including the Beretta M1 Garand rifle, the Breda M1 Garand rifle and the Springfield Armoury M1 Garand rifle;

(b) is not a reproduction and was originally designed or manufactured for use in a firearm that

(i) is commonly known as the Charlton Rifle,

(ii) is commonly known as the Farquhar-Hill Rifle, or

(iii) is commonly known as the Huot Automatic Rifle;

(c) is of the "drum" type, is not a reproduction and was originally designed or manufactured for use in a firearm commonly known as

(i) the .303 in. Lewis Mark 1 machine-gun, or any variant or modified version of it, including the Lewis Mark ⋆, Mark 2, Mark 2⋆, Mark 3, Mark 4, Lewis SS and .30 in. Savage-Lewis,

(ii) the .303 in. Vickers Mark 1 machine-gun, or any variant or modified version of it, including the Mark 1⋆, Mark 2, Mark 2⋆, Mark 3, Mark 4, Mark 4B, Mark 5, Mark 6, Mark 6⋆ and Mark 7, or

(iii) the Bren Light machine-gun, or any variant or modified version of it, including the Mark 1, Mark 2, Mark 2/1, Mark 3 and Mark 4;

(d) is of the "metallic-strip" type, is not a reproduction and was originally designed or manufactured for use in conjunction with the firearm known as the Hotchkiss machine-gun, Model 1895 or Model 1897, or any variant or modified version of it, including the Hotchkiss machine-gun, Model 1900, Model 1909, Model 1914 and Model 1917, and the Hotchkiss machine-gun (Enfield), Number 2, Mark 1 and Mark 1⋆;

(e) is of the "saddle-drum" type (doppeltrommel or satteltrommel), is not a reproduction and was originally designed or manufactured for use in the automatic firearms known as the MG-13, MG-15, MG-17, MG-34, T6-200 or T6-220, or any variant or modified version of it; or

(f) is of the "belt" type consisting of a fabric or metal belt, is not a reproduction and was originally designed or manufactured for the purpose of feeding cartridges into a automatic firearm of a type that was in existence before 1945.

(3) Paragraph (1)(b) does not include any cartridge magazine that

(a) is of the "snail-drum" type (schneckentrommel) that was originally designed or manufactured for use in a firearm that is a handgun known as the Parabellum-Pistol, System Borchardt-Luger, Model 1900, or "Luger", or any variant or modified version of it, including the Model 1902, Model 1904 (Marine), Model 1904/06 (Marine), Model 1904/08 (Marine), Model 1906, Model 1908 and Model 1908 (Artillery) pistols;

(b) was originally designed or manufactured for use in a firearm that is a semi-automatic handgun, where the magazine was manufactured before 1910;

(c) was originally designed or manufactured as an integral part of the firearm known as the Mauser Selbstladepistole C/96 ("broomhandle"), or any variant or modified version of it, including the Model 1895, Model 1896, Model 1902, Model 1905, Model 1912, Model 1915, Model 1930, Model 1931, M711 and M712; or

(d) was originally designed or manufactured for use in the semi-automatic firearm that is a handgun known as the Webley and Scott Self-Loading Pistol, Model 1912 or Model 1915.

(4) A cartridge magazine described in subsection (1) that has been altered or re-manufactured so that it is not capable of containing more than five or ten cartridges, as the case may be, of the type for which it was originally designed is not a prohibited device as prescribed by that subsection if the modification to the magazine cannot be easily removed and the magazine cannot be easily further altered so that it is so capable of containing more than five or ten cartridges, as the case may be.

(5) For the purposes of subsection (4), altering or re-manufacturing a cartridge magazine includes

(a) the indentation of its casing by forging, casting, swaging or impressing;

(b) in the case of a cartridge magazine with a steel or aluminum casing, the insertion and attachment of a plug, sleeve, rod, pin, flange or similar device, made of steel or aluminum, as the case may be, or of a similar material, to the inner surface of its casing by welding, brazing or any other similar method; or

(c) in the case of a cartridge magazine with a casing made of a material other than steel or aluminum, the attachment of a plug, sleeve, rod, pin, flange or similar device, made of steel or of a material similar to that of the magazine casing, to the inner surface of its casing by welding, brazing or any other similar method or by applying a permanent adhesive substance, such as a cement or an epoxy or other glue.

PART 5
Prohibited Ammunition

Former Prohibited Weapons Order, No. 10

1. Any cartridge that is capable of being discharged from a commonly available semi-automatic handgun or revolver and that is manufactured or assembled with a projectile that is designed, manufactured or altered so as to be capable of penetrating body armour, including KTW, THV and 5.7 x 28 mm P-90 cartridges.

2. Any projectile that is designed, manufactured or altered to ignite on impact, where the projectile is designed for use in or in conjunction with a cartridge and does not exceed 15 mm in diameter.

3. Any projectile that is designed, manufactured or altered so as to explode on impact, where the projectile is designed for use in or in conjunction with a cartridge and does not exceed 15 mm in diameter.

4. Any cartridge that is capable of being discharged from a shotgun and that contains projectiles known as "fléchettes" or any similar projectiles. **SOR/98-462; SOR/98-472; SOR/2015-213.**

Use Offences

USING FIREARM IN COMMISSION OF OFFENCE / Using imitation firearm in commission of offence / Punishment / Sentences to be served consecutively.

85. (1) Every person commits an offence who uses a firearm, whether or not the person causes or means to cause bodily harm to any person as a result of using the firearm,

(*a*) while committing an indictable offence, other than an offence under section 220 (criminal negligence causing death), 236 (manslaughter), 239 (attempted murder), 244 (discharging firearm with intent), 244.2 (discharging firearm — recklessness), 272 (sexual assault with a weapon) or 273 (aggravated sexual assault), subsection 279(1) (kidnapping) or section 279.1 (hostage taking), 344 (robbery) or 346 (extortion);

(*b*) while attempting to commit an indictable offence; or

(*c*) during flight after committing or attempting to commit an indictable offence.

(2) Every person commits an offence who uses an imitation firearm

(*a*) while committing an indictable offence,

(*b*) while attempting to commit an indictable offence, or

(*c*) during flight after committing or attempting to commit an indictable offence,

whether or not the person causes or means to cause bodily harm to any person as a result of using the imitation firearm.

(3) Every person who commits an offence under subsection (1) or (2) is guilty of an indictable offence and liable

(*a*) in the case of a first offence, except as provided in paragraph (*b*), to imprisonment for a term not exceeding fourteen years and to a minimum punishment of imprisonment for a term of one year; and

(*b*) in the case of a second or subsequent offence, to imprisonment for a term not exceeding 14 years and to a minimum punishment of imprisonment for a term of three years.

(*c*) [*Repealed*, 2008, c. 6, s. 3(2).]

(4) A sentence imposed on a person for an offence under subsection (1) or (2) shall be served consecutively to any other punishment imposed on the person for an offence arising out of the same event or series of events and to any other sentence to which the person is subject at the time the sentence is imposed on the person for an offence under subsection (1) or (2). R.S., c. C-34, s. 83; 1976-77, c. 53, s. 3; 1995, c. 39, s. 139; 2003, c. 8, s. 3; 2008, c. 6, s. 3; 2009, c. 22, s. 3.

CROSS-REFERENCES

"Firearm" is defined in s. 2. "Imitation firearm" is defined in s. 84.

A person convicted of this offence is subject to the mandatory prohibition order prescribed by s. 109.

An accused charged with this offence may elect his mode of trial pursuant to s. 536(2) and release pending trial is determined by s. 515.

Note provision for forfeiture of weapons used in commission of an offence in s. 491.

The prosecutor must give notice under s. 727 where it seeks the greater punishment pursuant to subsec. (3)(*c*).

Upon conviction, the accused is liable to the mandatory prohibition order under s. 109.

For the purpose of determining whether a person has committed a second or subsequent offence, see s. 84(5) and (6).

SYNOPSIS

This offence was created by Parliament for the purpose of imposing an additional punishment upon those accused who use firearms or imitation firearms while committing or fleeing from the commission of indictable offences (or the attempt to do either). It is important to note that s. 85(1)(a) does not apply in respect of certain indictable offences which already impose an additional penalty for the use of a firearm during the commission of the offence. It is not necessary that the accused intend to harm anyone with the firearm nor that it be proven to be loaded at the time it is used. There were several early challenges to the constitutional validity of the preceding s. 85 alleging violations of ss. 11(*h*) and 7 of the Charter. These efforts were unsuccessful but may need to be re-assessed as the case law continues to evolve, setting out the constitutionally permissible minimum level of intention in the criminal law.

This section carries a maximum punishment of 14 years' imprisonment and a minimum period of imprisonment upon a first conviction of one year, and upon a second (or subsequent) conviction of three years. For the purpose of determining whether a person has committed a second or subsequent offence, see s. 84(5) and (6). Subsection (4) requires that the sentence for this offence must be consecutive to any other sentence imposed in connection with the same events.

ANNOTATIONS

Underlying offences which may found liability – An accused may be convicted of attempted robbery, specified as an attempt to commit the offence under s. 343(*d*), and the offence under this section. Further, conviction of both offences does not violate the principles of fundamental justice as guaranteed by s. 7 of the *Canadian Charter of Rights and Freedoms*: *R. v. Krug*, [1985] 2 S.C.R. 255, 21 C.C.C. (3d) 193 (7:0).

An accused cannot be convicted of the offence under this section where the "indictable offence" referred to in subsec. (1) by its definition in the Code required the use of a firearm as a constituent element of the offence, for example, pointing a firearm under s. 86(1): *R. v. Langevin* (1979), 47 C.C.C. (2d) 138 (Ont. C.A.); *R. v. Krug, supra*.

An accused may also be convicted of this offence and the offence of possession of a weapon for a purpose dangerous to the public peace contrary to s. 87 where the evidence showed that the accused discharged the firearm: *R. v. Yurkiv* (1980), 18 C.R. (3d) 287 (Ont. C.A.).

An accused may be convicted of this offence and aggravated assault contrary to s. 268: *R. v. Switzer* (1987), 32 C.C.C. (3d) 303 (Alta. C.A.); *R. v. Osbourne* (1994), 94 C.C.C. (3d) 435 (Ont. C.A.); *R. v. Griffin* (1996), 111 C.C.C. (3d) 567 (B.C.C.A.).

A conviction under s. 88(1) for possession of a weapon for a purpose dangerous to the public peace cannot constitute the predicate indictable offence necessary for a conviction under this section: *R. v. Andrade* (2015), 326 C.C.C. (3d) 507 (Ont. C.A.), leave to appeal to S.C.C. refused 2016 CarswellOnt 5734.

Requirement of conviction for underlying offence – To render the accused guilty of the offence under this section, there must be a distinct conviction for the underlying indictable offence and not merely a finding of fact that the accused had committed an indictable offence in the course of which he used a firearm. Further, the count charging the offence under this section should clearly indicate the offence during which the accused allegedly used the firearm: *R. v. Pringle*, [1989] 1 S.C.R. 1645, 48 C.C.C. (3d) 449 (5:0).

Proof of "use" of firearm – A person may be convicted of this offence although he does not use the firearm himself but is merely a party to the offence by virtue of s. 21: *R. v. McGuigan*, [1982] 1 S.C.R. 284, 66 C.C.C. (2d) 97.

An offender "uses" a firearm where, to facilitate the commission of an offence or escape, the offender reveals by words or conduct the actual presence or immediate availability of the firearm. The weapon must be in the physical possession of the offender or readily at hand. In this case, although the weapon was not seen by the victims, the offenders repeatedly referred to a firearm in their physical possession or readily at hand during the break and enter, such that the firearm was "used" within the meaning of this provision: *R. v. Steele*, [2007] 3 S.C.R. 3, 221 C.C.C. (3d) 14.

The use of the firearm must be connected to the commission of an indictable offence for which a conviction has been entered. If it were otherwise, an accused could be convicted under s. 85 for conduct that is merely coincidental to the commission of the indictable offence. This would open the door for prohibited convictions under s. 85 based on uncharged conduct or charges that do not result in conviction: *R. v. Andrade, supra.*

Neither the Charter nor the "*Kienapple*" rule against multiple convictions bar a conviction under this provision where the predicate offence is accosting someone while "openly wearing or carrying a weapon" under s. 265(1)(*c*). For a conviction to be registered under the use firearm provisions of s. 85(1), it is simply necessary to prove that the accused did something beyond what is required to establish the predicate offence. The element of "use" is an additional and distinguishing element from that required for a conviction for assault under s. 265(1)(*c*): *R. v. Meszaros* (2013), 309 C.C.C. (3d) 392 (Ont. C.A.).

The one-year minimum sentence imposed by subsec. (3)(*a*) does not constitute cruel and unusual punishment within the meaning of s. 12 of the Charter: *R. v. Meszaros, supra.*

A separate offence contrary to this section is committed by the accused each time he uses a firearm in the commission of a separate indictable offence notwithstanding the indictable offences take place within a short time of each other and involve the same firearm: *R. v. Woods* (1982), 65 C.C.C. (2d) 554 (Ont. C.A.).

Meaning of "firearm" – To constitute a firearm within the meaning of this section, whatever is used on the scene of the crime must be proven by the Crown as capable either at the outset or through adaptation or assembly of being loaded and fired so as to have the potential for causing serious bodily harm during the commission of the offence or during the flight after the commission of that main offence. An operable but unloaded revolver or air pistol is a firearm because it is capable, during the commission of the offence when loaded and fired, of causing bodily injury. There is no requirement that the Crown prove that the accused was in possession of ammunition. If, however, the weapon is inoperable, then it is a firearm if, given the nature of the repairs or modifications required and the availability of parts on the scene, whatever was used could, during the commission of the offence, have been adapted by an ordinary person or by the accused, if possessing special skills, so as to be capable of firing and of causing serious injury: *R. v. Covin and Covin*, [1983] 1 S.C.R. 725, 8 C.C.C. (3d) 240 (5:0).

Thus, a pistol which lacked the magazine was a firearm for the purposes of this section, although without the magazine the safety disconnector was also engaged. The Crown is not required to prove that the accused at the time of the offence was in possession of ammunition and any of the paraphernalia, including the magazine, by which the ammunition is loaded into the weapon: *R. v. Watkins and Graver* (1987), 33 C.C.C. (3d) 465 (B.C.C.A.).

The Crown may prove that the weapon used is a "firearm" by establishing that the weapon was fired during the offence; adducing expert evidence that the weapon was operable at the time of the offence and capable of causing bodily injury or death, or where the weapon is not available for examination, calling a witness who is knowledgeable about guns and may be able to satisfy the court that the weapon was an operable firearm: *R. v. Osiowy* (1997), 113 C.C.C. (3d) 117 (Alta. C.A.).

Meaning of "imitation" – Imitation firearm includes a real firearm. Imitation may be read to include an object that appears to be a firearm whether or not that object is in fact a firearm: *R. v. Scott* (2000), 145 C.C.C. (3d) 52 (B.C.C.A.), affd [2001] 3 S.C.R. 425, 159 C.C.C. (3d) 319.

Imposition of sentence – It was held in *R. v. MacLean* (1979), 49 C.C.C. (2d) 552 (N.S.S.C. App. Div.); *R. v. Goforth* (1986), 24 C.C.C. (3d) 573 (B.C.C.A.); *R. v. Cochrane* (1994), 88 C.C.C. (3d) 570 (B.C.C.A.); *R. v. Herrell* (1994), 88 C.C.C. (3d) 412 (Ont. C.A.), that in view of the language of subsec. (2) where the accused is convicted of several offences under subsec. (1) the sentences imposed for those offences must not only be consecutive to the indictable offence but consecutive to each other. The court in *R. v. MacLean* did not appear to consider the further question whether where all convictions for the offence under subsec. (1) occur after the commission of the last offence the three-year minimum rather than the one-year minimum applies to all but the first conviction under this section. In *R. v. Boucher*, [1986] 1 S.C.R. 750 (5:0), the court in a brief judgment indicated that it essentially agreed with the interpretation of this section by the Court of Appeal in *R. v. MacLean, supra*.

The mandatory minimum of one consecutive year does not violate s. 12 of the *Canadian Charter of Rights and Freedoms*: *R. v. Stewart* (2010), 253 C.C.C. (3d) 301 (B.C.C.A.).

Former subsec. (1)(*d*) [now subsec. (3)(*b*)] applies even where the accused did not actually use the firearm himself in the prior non-s. 85 offence and was merely a party to its use: *R. v. Nicholson*, [1981] 2 S.C.R. 600, 64 C.C.C. (2d) 116, 24 C.R. (3d) 284 (7:0).

Notwithstanding the wording of subsec. (2), the sentence for the offence under this section cannot be made consecutive to a life sentence: *R. v. Cochrane* (1994), 88 C.C.C. (3d) 570, 67 W.A.C. 315 (B.C.C.A.).

The totality principle is considered in determining the fitness for the underlying offence only and should not take into account the consequences of adding the required consecutive sentence to the sentence for the underlying offence: *R. v. Brewer* (1999), 141 C.C.C. (3d) 290, 182 Nfld. & P.E.I.R. 14 (Nfld. C.A.).

Where it was unclear whether the nature of an object used in the commission of a robbery was a firearm, an imitation firearm or an offensive weapon, the trial judge should have convicted on the offence not carrying a mandatory consecutive sentence and stayed the charge of use of a firearm in the commission of an indictable offence: *R. v. Delage* (2001), 154 C.C.C. (3d) 85 (Que. C.A.), remanded to the Que. C.A. [2002] 1 S.C.R. ix.

Constitutional considerations – The minimum one-year consecutive sentences mandated by the combination of subsecs. (3)(*a*) and (4) do not infringe the s. 12 Charter guarantee against cruel and unusual punishment: *R. v. Al-Isawi* (2017), 348 C.C.C. (3d) 524 (B.C.C.A.).

CARELESS USE OF FIREARM, ETC. / Contravention of storage regulations, etc. / Punishment.

86. (1) Every person commits an offence who, without lawful excuse, uses, carries, handles, ships, transports or stores a firearm, a prohibited weapon, a restricted weapon, a prohibited device or any ammunition or prohibited ammunition in a careless manner or without reasonable precautions for the safety of other persons.

(2) Every person commits an offence who contravenes a regulation made under paragraph 117(*h*) of the *Firearms Act* respecting the storage, handling, transportation, shipping, display, advertising and mail-order sales of firearms and restricted weapons.

(3) Every person who commits an offence under subsection (1) or (2)

(*a*) is guilty of an indictable offence and liable to imprisonment

(i) in the case of a first offence, for a term not exceeding two years, and

(ii) in the case of a second or subsequent offence, for a term not exceeding five years; or

(*b*) is guilty of an offence punishable on summary conviction. 1995, c. 39, s. 139.

CROSS-REFERENCES

"Firearm" and "weapon" are defined in s. 2. "Prohibited weapon", "restricted weapon", "prohibited device", "ammunition" and "prohibited ammunition" are defined in s. 84(1). Section 117.13 allows for the admission into evidence of a certificate of an analyst who has examined the weapon, prohibited device, ammunition, prohibited ammunition, explosive substance, or any part or component of such a thing.

Where the prosecution seeks the higher penalty prescribed by subsec. (3)(*a*)(ii), it must comply with the provisions of s. 727. Section 667 provides one method of proof of the prior conviction. Note that no reference to the prior conviction may be made in the indictment, by virtue of s. 664.

Where the prosecution elects to proceed by way of summary conviction, then the trial of this offence is conducted by a summary conviction court pursuant to Part XXVII. The punishment for the offence is then as set out in s. 787 and the limitation period is set out in s. 786(2). In either case, release pending trial is determined by s. 515, although the accused is eligible for release by a peace officer under ss. 496, 497 or by the officer in charge under s. 498.

A person found guilty of the offences in this section is liable to the discretionary prohibition order prescribed by s. 110, unless the accused was prohibited from possessing weapons or other regulated items at the time of the offence, in which case the mandatory prohibition order in s. 109 applies.

Note provision for forfeiture of weapons used in commission of an offence in s. 491.

SYNOPSIS

This section creates two offences: subsec. (1) relates to the careless storage, use etc. of a firearm, prohibited weapon, restricted weapon, prohibited device or ammunition or prohibited ammunition; subsec. (2) deals with breach of regulations.

Subsection (1) requires that it be proven that the care used to deal with the weapon fell below the reasonable standard of care required to ensure that no person is endangered by the firearm, weapon etc. In addition, it must be shown that there is no lawful excuse for the apparent carelessness. Case law has established that the offence is proven if only a single person is endangered, notwithstanding the use of the words "other persons" in the section.

Subsection (2) makes it an offence to breach *Firearms Act* regulations on storage, handling, transportation, shipping, display, advertising and mail-order sales of firearms and restricted weapons.

Subsection (3) sets out the penalty for these offences. Note the increased maximum punishment in the case of a second or subsequent offence.

ANNOTATIONS

Subsection (1) – This offence requires proof of conduct showing a marked departure from the standard of care of a reasonably prudent person in the circumstances. So interpreted this provision does not violate s. 7 of the *Canadian Charter of Rights and Freedoms*. This offence can also constitute the underlying or predicate offence for the unlawful act of manslaughter: *R. v. Gosset*, [1993] 3 S.C.R. 76, 83 C.C.C. (3d) 494, 23 C.R. (4th) 280; *R. v. Finlay*, [1993] 3 S.C.R. 103, 83 C.C.C. (3d) 513, 23 C.R. (4th) 321.

The offence of use of a firearm in a careless manner was made out where the accused intentionally discharged a firearm over the head of another hunter in order to scare him: *R. v. Zimmer* (1981), 60 C.C.C. (2d) 190 (B.C.C.A.).

The offence under this subsection is not included in the offence of pointing a firearm under [now] s. 87: *R. v. Morrison* (1991), 66 C.C.C. (3d) 257, 7 W.A.C. 73 (B.C.C.A.).

In a series of cases, the Supreme Court of Canada had occasion to explore the fault element in cases of so-called "penal negligence" apparently as distinguished from criminal negligence. Careless use of a firearm would be one of these offences. In *R. v. Creighton*, [1993] 3 S.C.R. 3, 83 C.C.C. (3d) 346, 23 C.R. (4th) 189, McLachlin J., writing for a majority of the court, suggested the following approach to proof of such offences. The first question is whether the *actus reus* is established. This requires that the negligence constitute a marked departure from the standards of a reasonable person in all the circumstances of the case. The next question is whether the *mens rea* is established. Normally the *mens rea* for objective foresight of risk of harm is inferred from the facts. The standard is that of the reasonable person in the circumstances of the accused. The normal inference that a person who committed a manifestly dangerous act failed to direct their mind to the risk and the need to take care may be negated by evidence raising a reasonable doubt as to the incapacity to appreciate the risk. Short of incapacity, personal factors are not relevant whether those factors might indicate, for example, either a lack of experience or a special experience. Also see: *R. v. Naglik*, [1993] 3 S.C.R. 122, 83 C.C.C. (3d) 526, 23 C.R. (4th) 335; *R. v. Finlay, supra*; and *R. v. Gosset, supra*.

A finding of careless storage cannot be based upon the personal opinion of a police officer. Where existing regulations dealing with the storage of firearms and ammunition were not relevant, as in the instant case, it was incumbent upon the Crown to adduce expert evidence to establish that the storage of the firearms and ammunition was careless: *R. v. Halliday* (1995), 100 C.C.C. (3d) 574, 82 O.A.C. 150 (C.A.), leave to appeal to S.C.C. refused 103 C.C.C. (3d) vi, 93 O.A.C. 79*n*. In considering carelessness, the federal firearm storage regulations are relevant in determining the appropriate standard for those who are transporting or storing guns: *R. v. Blanchard* (1994), 103 C.C.C. (3d) 360 (Y.T. Terr. Ct.).

There is no requirement under this section that the accused plan a long-term or permanent storage. The accused having deposited a loaded .357 Magnum in an ill-planned temporary hiding spot was guilty of the careless storage offence under subsec. (1). While a short interruption in the use or handling of firearms would still constitute use or handling rather that storage, in this case the accused took steps to put away and hide his weapons such that the proper characterization of his actions was that he stored them, albeit temporarily, rather than continue his use and handling of the firearms in plain view of the police. Similarly, the temporary placing of the two loaded handguns inside a locked safe in violation of the regulations constituted the offence under subsec. (2): *R. v. Carlos*, [2002] 2 S.C.R. 411, 163 C.C.C. (3d) 449, 1 C.R. (6th) 1.

The defence under s. 41 (defence of property) is available on a charge under subsec. (1) and thus to the offence of unlawful act manslaughter where the unlawful act relied upon by the Crown is the offence under subsec. (1): *R. v. Gunning*, [2005] 1 S.C.R. 627, 196 C.C.C. (3d) 123, 29 C.R. (6th) 17.

Subsection (2) – It was held under the predecessor to subsec. (2) that the Crown need only prove beyond a reasonable doubt that the accused stored firearms in a manner contrary to the regulations and need not prove that the accused was negligent. The defence may raise a reasonable doubt with respect to mistake of fact or by raising the defence of due diligence in complying with the regulation. The provision did not violate s. 7 of the *Canadian Charter of Rights and Freedoms*: *R. v. Smillie* (1998), 129 C.C.C. (3d) 414, 20 C.R. (5th) 179 (B.C.C.A.).

This provision creates an offence of strict liability: *R. v. Porter* (2004), 193 C.C.C. (3d) 254 (B.C.S.C.), affd 221 C.C.C. (3d) 309 (B.C.C.A.), leave to appeal to S.C.C. refused [2007] 2 S.C.R. vii, 374 N.R. 393*n*.

Risk is not an essential element in the *mens rea* required under this provision: *R. v. Porter, supra* (B.C.C.A.).

Editor's Note: Regulations respecting the *Storage, Display, Transportation and Handling of Firearms by Individuals Regulations*, SOR/98-209, enacted under the *Firearms Act*, may be found in *Martin's Related Criminal Statutes*.

POINTING A FIREARM / Punishment.

87. (1) Every person commits an offence who, without lawful excuse, points a firearm at another person, whether the firearm is loaded or unloaded.

(2) Every person who commits an offence under subsection (1)

(*a*) is guilty of an indictable offence and liable to imprisonment for a term not exceeding five years; or

(b) is guilty of an offence punishable on summary conviction. 1995, c. 39, s. 139.

CROSS-REFERENCES

"Firearm" is defined in s. 2. Where the prosecution elects to proceed by way of summary conviction then the trial of this offence is conducted by a summary conviction court pursuant to Part XXVII. The punishment for the offence is then as set out in s. 787 and the limitation period is set out in s. 786(2). In either case, release pending trial is determined by s. 515, although the accused is eligible for release by a peace officer under ss. 496, 497 or by the officer in charge under s. 498.

A person found guilty of the offences in this section is liable to the discretionary prohibition order prescribed by s. 110, unless the accused was prohibited from possessing weapons or other regulated items at the time of the offence, in which case the mandatory prohibition order in s. 109 applies.

Note mandatory forfeiture of weapons used in commission of an offence in s. 491.

SYNOPSIS

This section creates the offence of pointing a firearm at another person without lawful excuse. The offence is committed whether or not the firearm was loaded.

ANNOTATIONS

The offence created by this section is one of general intent for the purpose of the self-induced intoxication defence: *R. v. Kelly* (1984), 13 C.C.C. (3d) 203, 50 Nfld. & P.E.I.R. 106 (Nfld. Dist. Ct.).

Possession Offences

POSSESSION OF WEAPON FOR DANGEROUS PURPOSE / Punishment.

88. (1) Every person commits an offence who carries or possesses a weapon, an imitation of a weapon, a prohibited device or any ammunition or prohibited ammunition for a purpose dangerous to the public peace or for the purpose of committing an offence.

(2) Every person who commits an offence under subsection (1)

(*a*) is guilty of an indictable offence and liable to imprisonment for a term not exceeding ten years; or

(*b*) is guilty of an offence punishable on summary conviction. 1995, c. 39, s. 139.

CROSS-REFERENCES

"Weapon" is defined in s. 2. "Prohibited device", "ammunition" and "prohibited ammunition" are defined in s. 84(1). "Possession" is defined in s. 4(3). Section 117.13 allows for the admission into evidence of a certificate of an analyst who has examined the weapon, prohibited device, ammunition, prohibited ammunition, explosive substance, or any part or component of such a thing.

An accused charged with this offence may elect the mode of trial pursuant to s. 536(2) where the Crown proceeds by way of indictment. Where the prosecution elects to proceed by way of summary conviction then the trial of this offence is conducted by a summary conviction court pursuant to Part XXVII. The punishment for the offence is then as set out in s. 787 and the limitation period is set out in s. 786(2). In either case, release pending trial is determined by s. 515, although the accused is eligible for release by a peace officer under ss. 496, 497 or by the officer in charge under s. 498.

A person found guilty of the offences in this section is liable to the discretionary prohibition order prescribed by s. 110, unless the accused was prohibited from possessing weapons or other regulated items at the time of the offence, in which case the mandatory prohibition order in s. 109 applies.

Note mandatory forfeiture of weapons used in commission of an offence in s. 491.

SYNOPSIS

The crucial element in this offence is the purpose for which the accused has the weapon. Merely using the weapon in a way which is in fact dangerous will not make out the charge unless it is proven that this was the accused's purpose for possessing the weapon or other specified thing. All circumstances surrounding the possession of the weapon, or specified thing including its use, if any, will be considered to determine the accused's purpose.

ANNOTATIONS

Note: The following cases were decided under the predecessor to this section which while similarly worded applied only to weapons and imitations of weapons.

Elements of offence – The offence contrary to this section requires proof of possession and proof that the purpose of that possession was one dangerous to the public peace. There must, at some time, be a meeting of these two elements and generally the purpose will have been formed prior to the taking of possession and will continue as possession is taken. However, the elements of the offence must be distinguished from the evidentiary problems which can arise as demonstrated by cases such as *R. v. Proverbs, infra*, where the proof of the unlawful purpose is only through the actual use of the weapon. In this case, *R. v. Cassidy*, [1989] 2 S.C.R. 345, 50 C.C.C. (3d) 193, 71 C.R. (3d) 350 (7:0), the court held that it did not have to determine whether the accused could never be convicted if the actual use was the only evidence of the purpose since there was evidence adduced of formation of the unlawful purpose prior to use of the weapon.

The purpose for which the accused had possession of the weapon must be determined at an instant of time that precedes its use. The use of the weapon in a manner dangerous to the public peace does not constitute the offence although the formation of the unlawful purpose may be inferred from the circumstances in which the weapon was used. Thus, if the accused, in fear of harm to himself in his own home loaded, on the sudden, a weapon that he had not had for a purpose dangerous to the public peace and only intended to use it to defend himself in the event that his premises were broken into, unaware that it was the police seeking entry to execute a warrant, the offence was not made out: *R. v. Proverbs* (1983), 9 C.C.C. (3d) 249, 2 O.A.C. 98 (C.A.).

Relevance of self-defence – The subjective purpose, *i.e.*, self-defence, of a person carrying an offensive weapon is only a factor that should be considered in determining whether an offence has been committed. Therefore, notwithstanding the explanation given by the possessor of the weapon, the trial judge may still convict if the other circumstances in the evidence prove a purpose dangerous to the public peace: *R. v. Nelson* (1972), 8 C.C.C. (2d) 29, [1972] 3 O.R. 174 (C.A.) (4:1).

This section does not prohibit persons arming themselves for self-protection and, in the absence of other circumstances, the offence under this section is not committed if the accused carries for self-defence a weapon that is an appropriate instrument with which to repel, in a lawful manner, the type of attack reasonably apprehended and if the accused is competent to handle the weapon and likely to use it responsibly: *R. v. Sulland* (1982), 2 C.C.C. (3d) 68, 41 B.C.L.R. 167 (C.A.).

Meaning of "weapon" – A broken beer bottle was held to be a weapon so as to support a conviction under this section: *R. v. Allan* (1971), 4 C.C.C. (2d) 521, 4 N.B.R. (2d) 6 (Q.B.). As also was sulphuric acid where the accused intended to inflict injury, albeit to himself in a suicide attempt. The further element of the purpose dangerous to the public peace was established where the accused exposed others to danger, namely those whom he knew would attempt to frustrate his suicide: *R. v. Dugan* (1974), 21 C.C.C. (2d) 45 (Ont. Prov. Ct.). Similarly, *R. v. Pelly*, [1980] 1 W.W.R. 120 (Sask. Prov. Ct.).

Proof of offence – The possession by the accused of weapons in his own home does not preclude a finding of a purpose dangerous to the public peace: *R. v. Stavroff*, [1980] 1 S.C.R. 411, 101 D.L.R. (3d) 193, 48 C.C.C. (2d) 353 (7:0).

CARRYING WEAPON WHILE ATTENDING PUBLIC MEETING / Punishment.

89. (1) Every person commits an offence who, without lawful excuse, carries a weapon, a prohibited device or any ammunition or prohibited ammunition while the person is attending or is on the way to attend a public meeting.

(2) Every person who commits an offence under subsection (1) is guilty of an offence punishable on summary conviction. 1995, c. 39, s. 139.

CROSS-REFERENCES

"Weapon" is defined in s. 2. "Prohibited device", "ammunition" and "prohibited ammunition" are defined in s. 84(1).

The trial of this offence is conducted by a summary conviction court pursuant to Part XXVII. The punishment for the offence is set out in s. 787 and the limitation period is set out in s. 786(2). Release pending trial is determined by s. 515, although the accused is eligible for release by a peace officer under ss. 496, 497 or by the officer in charge under s. 498.

Under s. 117.11, the onus is on the accused to prove that he or she is the holder of a licence, authorization or registration certificate. Section 117.12 provides for admission into evidence of copies of such documents and the evidentiary value of the original and copies. Section 117.13 allows for the admission into evidence of a certificate of an analyst who has examined the weapon, prohibited device, ammunition, prohibited ammunition, explosive substance, or any part or component of such a thing.

A person found guilty of the offences in this section is liable to the discretionary prohibition order prescribed by s. 110, unless the accused was prohibited from possessing weapons or other regulated items at the time of the offence, in which case the mandatory prohibition order in s. 109 applies.

Note mandatory forfeiture of weapons used in commission of an offence in s. 491.

SYNOPSIS

This section focuses on the circumstances under which the accused carries a weapon, prohibited device, ammunition or prohibited ammunition. If the accused has it while attending or on the way to a public meeting, the accused is guilty unless there is a lawful excuse for the possession of the weapon. An example of such an excuse would be that the accused is a peace officer armed in the line of duty (see s. 117.07). No additional intention, such as the intention to use the weapon, is required.

CARRYING CONCEALED WEAPON / Punishment.

90. (1) Every person commits an offence who carries a weapon, a prohibited device or any prohibited ammunition concealed, unless the person is authorized under the *Firearms Act* to carry it concealed.

(2) Every person who commits an offence under subsection (1)

(*a*) is guilty of an indictable offence and liable to imprisonment for a term not exceeding five years; or

(*b*) is guilty of an offence punishable on summary conviction. 1995, c. 39, s. 139.

CROSS-REFERENCES

"Weapon" is defined in s. 2. "Prohibited device" and "prohibited ammunition" are defined in s. 84(1). Under s. 117.11, the onus is on the accused to prove that he or she is the holder of a licence, authorization or registration certificate. Section 117.12 provides for admission into evidence of copies of such documents and the evidentiary value of the original and copies. Section 117.13 allows for the admission into evidence of a certificate of an analyst who has examined the weapon, prohibited device, ammunition, prohibited ammunition, explosive substance, or any part or component of such a thing.

An accused charged with this offence may elect the mode of trial pursuant to s. 536(2) where the Crown proceeds by way of indictment. Where the prosecution elects to proceed by way of summary conviction then the trial of this offence is conducted by a summary conviction court pursuant to Part XXVII. The punishment for the offence is then as set out in s. 787 and the limitation period is set out in s. 786(2).

A person found guilty of the offences in this section is liable to the discretionary prohibition order prescribed by s. 110, unless the accused was prohibited from possessing weapons or other regulated items at the time of the offence, in which case the mandatory prohibition order in s. 109 applies.

Note mandatory forfeiture of weapons used in commission of an offence in s. 491.

SYNOPSIS

The intentional concealment of a weapon, prohibited device or prohibited ammunition is the central element of this offence. The weapon may be concealed on the accused's person or in a vehicle under the control of the accused. A defence is provided if the person is authorized under the *Firearms Act* to carry it concealed.

ANNOTATIONS

Note: The following cases were decided under the predecessor to this section which while similarly worded applied only to weapons.

Meaning of "carries" – A person carries a weapon if it is in an automobile of which he has care and control and it was not necessary that the accused have the weapon on his person: *R. v. Hanabury* (1970), 1 C.C.C. (3d) 438, 13 C.R.N.S. 378 (P.E.I.S.C.).

Meaning of "concealed" – To prove concealment it must be established that the accused took steps to hide an object that he knew to be a weapon so that it would not be observed or come to the notice of others. On the other hand, a gun that is carried in a gun case will not be considered concealed. In most cases the gun carrying case will resemble the firearm itself so that it cannot be considered to be hidden. Wrapping a firearm in a blanket or canvass and securing it with a rope as required by some provincial regulations should also not be considered to be concealing the weapon. In most cases the wrapped weapon will still resemble a firearm and not be considered to be concealed. Finally placing of a firearm in a locked trunk in a locked and unattended vehicle in compliance with federal regulations must be considered an exception to the carrying a concealed weapon offence: *R. v. Felawka*, [1993] 4 S.C.R. 199 , 85 C.C.C. (3d) 248, 25 C.R. (4th) 70.

Meaning of "weapon" – In the absence of evidence to the contrary, the concealment of certain objects such as a handgun, switch-blade knife or brass knuckles fall within this provision because the unlawful purpose of the object may be assumed or implied. Where the object could be used for a peaceful purpose, such as a hunting knife or steak knife, the prosecution must establish that the object is being concealed for an unlawful purpose in that the object was intended to be used as a weapon: *R. v. Constantine* (1996), 46 C.R. (4th) 105, 137 Nfld. & P.E.I.R. 85 (Nfld. C.A.).

UNAUTHORIZED POSSESSION OF FIREARM / Unauthorized possession of prohibited weapon or restricted weapon / Punishment / Exceptions / Borrowed firearm for sustenance.

91. (1) Subject to subsection (4), every person commits an offence who possesses a prohibited firearm, a restricted firearm or a non-restricted firearm without being the holder of

(*a*) a licence under which the person may possess it; and

(*b*) in the case of a prohibited firearm or a restricted firearm, a registration certificate for it.

(2) Subject to subsection (4), every person commits an offence who possesses a prohibited weapon, a restricted weapon, a prohibited device, other than a replica firearm, or any prohibited ammunition, without being the holder of a licence under which the person may possess it.

(3) Every person who commits an offence under subsection (1) or (2)

(*a*) is guilty of an indictable offence and liable to imprisonment for a term not exceeding five years; or

(*b*) is guilty of an offence punishable on summary conviction.

(4) Subsections (1) and (2) do not apply to

(*a*) a person who possesses a prohibited firearm, a restricted firearm, a non-restricted firearm, a prohibited weapon, a restricted weapon, a prohibited device or any prohibited ammunition while the person is under the direct and immediate supervision of a person who may lawfully possess it, for the purpose of using it in a manner in which the supervising person may lawfully use it; or

(*b*) a person who comes into possession of a prohibited firearm, a restricted firearm, a non-restricted firearm, a prohibited weapon, a restricted weapon, a prohibited device or any prohibited ammunition by the operation of law and who, within a reasonable period after acquiring possession of it,

(i) lawfully disposes of it, or

(ii) obtains a licence under which the person may possess it and, in the case of a prohibited firearm or a restricted firearm, a registration certificate for it.

1995, c. 39, s. 139; 2008, c. 6, s. 4; 2012, c. 6, s. 2; 2015, c. 27, s. 19.

(5) [*Repealed*, 2012, c. 1, s. 2(3).]

CROSS-REFERENCES

"Firearm" is defined in s. 2. "Possession" is defined in s. 4(3). "Prohibited firearm", "restricted firearm", "non-restricted firearm", "prohibited weapon", "restricted weapon", "prohibited device", "replica firearm", "prohibited ammunition", "licence" and "registration certificate" are defined in s. 84(1).

An accused charged with this offence may elect the mode of trial pursuant to s. 536(2) where the Crown proceeds by way of indictment. Where the prosecution elects to proceed by way of summary conviction, then the trial of this offence is conducted by a summary conviction court pursuant to Part XXVII. The punishment for the offence is then as set out in s. 787 and the limitation period is set out in s. 786(2).

A person found guilty of the offences in this section is liable to the discretionary prohibition order prescribed by s. 110, unless the accused was prohibited from possessing weapons or other regulated items at the time of the offence, in which case the mandatory prohibition order in s. 109 applies.

Note mandatory forfeiture of weapons used in commission of an offence in s. 491.

Under s. 117.11, the onus is on the accused to prove that he or she is the holder of a licence, authorization or registration certificate. Section 117.12 provides for admission into evidence of copies of such documents and the evidentiary value of the original and copies. Section 117.13 allows for the admission into evidence of a certificate of an analyst who has examined the weapon, prohibited device, ammunition, prohibited ammunition, explosive substance, or any part or component of such a thing.

Section 92 creates the related offence of possession of prohibited firearm, restricted firearm, non-restricted firearm, prohibited weapon, restricted weapon, prohibited device and prohibited ammunition knowing its possession is unauthorized.

Sections 117.07 to 117.09 exempt certain persons such as police officers from the operation of this section, provided that the person is not subject to a prohibition order (see s. 117.1).

SYNOPSIS

This section creates two offences relating to the simple possession of firearms and other weapons. Under subsec. (1), it is an offence to have possession of a firearm without a licence and, in the case of prohibited and restricted firearms, a registration certificate. Subsection (2) creates the similar offence of possession of a prohibited weapon, restricted weapon, prohibited device, or prohibited ammunition without being the holder of a licence. By virtue of subsec. (4)(*a*), no offence is committed if the person is under the direct and immediate supervision of someone who is authorized to have the weapon, provided that they are using the weapon in a manner in which the supervising person is authorized. Under subsec. (4)(*b*), the offence does not apply to a person who comes into possession by operation of law and who, within a reasonable time, lawfully disposes of it or obtains a licence and registration certificate, if necessary.

ANNOTATIONS

Constitutional considerations – The licensing and registration provisions of the *Firearms Act* are *intra vires* Parliament even to the extent that they regulate the ownership of an ordinary firearm: *Reference re: Firearms Act (Canada)* (1998), 128 C.C.C. (3d) 225, 164 D.L.R. (4th) 513 (Alta. C.A.), affd [2000] 1 S.C.R. 783, 144 C.C.C. (3d) 385.

Note: The following annotations were decided under the previous legislation.

Elements of offence/*mens rea* – *Mens rea* is an element of this offence and where the prohibited weapon is a knife "that opens automatically by gravity or centrifugal force" as defined in [now] para. (*a*) of the definition "prohibited weapon" in s. 84(1), ignorance by the accused that the knife possessed this quality is a defence to a charge under this section: *R. v. Phillips* (1978), 44 C.C.C. (2d) 548 (Ont. C.A.).

The requisite *mens rea* is supplied by either knowledge or recklessness with respect to the characteristics of the knife which, in fact, make it a prohibited weapon: *R. v. Archer* (1983), 6 C.C.C. (3d) 129 (Ont. C.A.).

However, in *R. v. Richard* (1981), 63 C.C.C. (2d) 333, 24 C.R. (3d) 373 (N.B.C.A.), it was held that the offence was one of strict liability but it was open to the accused to avoid liability by proof that he did not know that the blade would open by the application of centrifugal force to the blade.

Provided the accused was aware of the characteristics that make the weapon a prohibited weapon, it is no defence that he was unaware that such a weapon was prohibited. The accused's mistake is one of law: *R. v. Baxter* (1982), 6 C.C.C. (3d) 447 (Alta. C.A.). Similarly, *R. v. Williams* (1988), 44 C.C.C. (3d) 58 (Y.T. Terr. Ct.).

Exemption for possession by operation of law – The exemption in former s. 91(4)(*c*) [now subsec. (4)(*b*)] did not apply to police officers who did not have registration certificates and took possession of restricted weapons at the scene of an investigation with the intention of keeping the weapons for themselves. The officers had attended at the scene of a suicide and, at the insistence of a relative of the deceased, had removed all the firearms from the home. The officers treated the firearms as gifts and only turned them in to the police when their superior learned of the "gift". The term "by operation of law" refers to a situation where the person, from the outset, was justified in acquiring the weapon without first having obtained a certificate: *R. v. Bibeau* (1990), 61 C.C.C. (3d) 339, 1 C.R. (4th) 397 (Que. C.A.).

POSSESSION OF FIREARM KNOWING ITS POSSESSION IS UNAUTHORIZED / Possession of prohibited weapon, device or ammunition knowing its possession is unauthorized / Punishment / Exceptions / Borrowed firearm for sustenance / Evidence for previous conviction.

92. (1) Subject to subsection (4), every person commits an offence who possesses a prohibited firearm, a restricted firearm or a non-restricted firearm knowing that the person is not the holder of

(*a*) a licence under which the person may possess it; and

(*b*) in the case of a prohibited firearm or a restricted firearm, a registration certificate for it.

(2) Subject to subsection (4), every person commits an offence who possesses a prohibited weapon, a restricted weapon, a prohibited device, other than a replica firearm, or any prohibited ammunition knowing that the person is not the holder of a licence under which the person may possess it.

(3) Every person who commits an offence under subsection (1) or (2) is guilty of an indictable offence and liable

(*a*) in the case of a first offence, to imprisonment for a term not exceeding ten years;

(*b*) in the case of a second offence, to imprisonment for a term not exceeding ten years and to a minimum punishment of imprisonment for a term of one year; and

(*c*) in the case of a third or subsequent offence, to imprisonment for a term not exceeding ten years and to a minimum punishment of imprisonment for a term of two years less a day.

(4) Subsections (1) and (2) do not apply to

(*a*) a person who possesses a prohibited firearm, a restricted firearm, a non-restricted firearm, a prohibited weapon, a restricted weapon, a prohibited device or any prohibited ammunition while the person is under the direct and immediate supervision of a person who may lawfully possess it, for the purpose of using it in a manner in which the supervising person may lawfully use it; or

(*b*) a person who comes into possession of a prohibited firearm, a restricted firearm, a non-restricted firearm, a prohibited weapon, a restricted weapon, a prohibited device or any prohibited ammunition by the operation of law and who, within a reasonable period after acquiring possession of it,

(i) lawfully disposes of it, or

(ii) obtains a licence under which the person may possess it and, in the case of a prohibited firearm or a restricted firearm, a registration certificate for it. 1995, c. 39, s. 139; 2008, c. 6, s. 5; 2012, c. 6, s. 3; 2015, c. 27, s. 20.

(5) and (6) [*Repealed*, 2012, c. 6, s. 3(3).]

CROSS-REFERENCES

"Firearm" is defined in s. 2. "Possession" is defined in s. 4(3). "Prohibited firearm", "restricted firearm", "non-restricted firearm", "prohibited weapon", "restricted weapon", "prohibited device", "prohibited firearm", "restricted firearm", "replica firearm", "prohibited ammunition", "licence" and "registration certificate" are defined in s. 84(1). Section 117.12 provides for admission into evidence of copies of any licence, registration certificate or authorization and the evidentiary value of the original and copies of such documents. Section 117.13 allows for the admission into evidence of a certificate of an analyst who has examined the weapon, prohibited device, ammunition, prohibited ammunition, explosive substance, or any part or component of such a thing.

Where the prosecution seeks the higher penalty prescribed by subsec. (3)(*b*) or (*c*), it must comply with the provisions of s. 727. Section 667 provides one method of proof of the prior conviction. Note that no reference to the prior conviction may be made in the indictment, by virtue of s. 664. A person found guilty of the offences in this section is liable to the discretionary prohibition order prescribed by s. 110, unless the accused was prohibited from possessing weapons or other regulated items at the time of the offence, in which case the mandatory prohibition order in s. 109 applies.

Note mandatory forfeiture of weapons used in commission of an offence in s. 491.

Section 91 creates the related offence of simple unauthorized possession of a firearm, prohibited weapon, restricted weapon, prohibited device and prohibited ammunition. Sections 117.07 to 117.09 exempt certain persons such as police officers from the operation of this section, provided that the person is not subject to a prohibition order (see s. 117.1).

SYNOPSIS

This section creates two offences relating to the possession of firearms and other weapons. Under subsec. (1), it is an offence to have possession of a prohibited firearm, restricted firearm, or non-restricted firearm knowing that one is not the holder of a licence or, in the case of prohibited and restricted firearms, a registration certificate. Subsection (2) creates the similar offence of possession of a prohibited weapon, restricted weapon, prohibited device, or prohibited ammunition knowing one is not the holder of a licence. By virtue of subsec. (4)(*a*), no offence is committed if the person is under the direct and immediate supervision of someone who is authorized to have the weapon, provided that they are using the weapon in a manner in which the supervising person is authorized. Under subsec. (4)(*b*), the offence does not apply to a person who comes into possession by operation of law and who, within a reasonable time, lawfully disposes of it or obtains a licence and registration certificate, if necessary.

ANNOTATIONS

Constitutional considerations – The licensing and registration provisions of the *Firearms Act* are *intra vires* Parliament even to the extent that they regulate the ownership of an ordinary firearm: *Reference re: Firearms Act (Canada)* (1998), 128 C.C.C. (3d) 225, 19 C.R. (5th) 63 (Alta. C.A.), affd [2000] 1 S.C.R. 783, 144 C.C.C. (3d) 385.

Exemption for possession by operation of law – The exemption in former s. 91(4)(*c*) [now subsec. (4)(*b*)] did not apply to police officers who did not have registration certificates and took possession of restricted weapons at the scene of an investigation with the intention of keeping the weapons for themselves. The officers had attended at the scene of a suicide and, at the insistence of a relative of the deceased, had removed all the firearms from the home. The officers treated the firearms as gifts and only turned them in to the police when their superior learned of the "gift". The term "by operation of law" refers to a situation where the person, from the outset, was justified in acquiring the weapon without first having obtained a certificate: *R. v. Bibeau* (1990), 61 C.C.C. (3d) 339, 1 C.R. (4th) 397 (Que. C.A.).

POSSESSION AT UNAUTHORIZED PLACE / Punishment / Exception.

93. (1) Subject to subsection (3), every person commits an offence who, being the holder of an authorization or a licence under which the person may possess a prohibited firearm, a restricted firearm, a non-restricted firearm, a prohibited weapon, a restricted weapon, a prohibited device or prohibited ammunition, possesses them at a place that is

(*a*) indicated on the authorization or licence as being a place where the person may not possess it;

(*b*) other than a place indicated on the authorization or licence as being a place where the person may possess it; or

(*c*) other than a place where it may be possessed under the *Firearms Act*.

(2) Every person who commits an offence under subsection (1)

(*a*) is guilty of an indictable offence and liable to imprisonment for a term not exceeding five years; or

(*b*) is guilty of an offence punishable on summary conviction.

(3) Subsection (1) does not apply to a person who possesses a replica firearm. 1995, c. 39, s. 139; 2008, c. 6, s. 6; 2015, c. 27, s. 21.

CROSS-REFERENCES

"Firearm" is defined in s. 2. "Prohibited firearm", "restricted firearm", "non-restricted firearm", "prohibited weapon", "restricted weapon", "prohibited device", "replica firearm", "prohibited ammunition", "licence" and "authorization" are defined in s. 84(1). "Possession" is defined in s. 4(3).

An accused charged with this offence may elect the mode of trial pursuant to s. 536(2) where the Crown proceeds by way of indictment. Where the prosecution elects to proceed by way of summary conviction then the trial of this offence is conducted by a summary conviction court pursuant to Part XXVII. The punishment for the offence is then as set out in s. 787 and the limitation period is set out in s. 786(2).

A person found guilty of the offences in this section is liable to the discretionary prohibition order prescribed by s. 110, unless the accused was prohibited from possessing weapons or other regulated items at the time of the offence, in which case the mandatory prohibition order in s. 109 applies.

Note mandatory forfeiture of weapons used in commission of an offence in s. 491.

Under s. 117.11, the onus is on the accused to prove that he or she is the holder of a licence, authorization or registration certificate. Section 117.12 provides for admission into evidence of copies of such documents and the evidentiary value of the original and copies. Section 117.13 allows for the admission into evidence of a certificate of an analyst who has examined the weapon, prohibited device, ammunition, prohibited ammunition, explosive substance, or any part or component of such a thing. Section 98 of the Code and ss. 120 to 135 of the *Firearms Act* provide transitional provisions relating to registration and licensing.

The related offence of unauthorized possession of a weapon in a motor vehicle is in s. 94.

SYNOPSIS

Subsection (1) creates an offence relating to the possession of a prohibited firearm, restricted firearm, non-restricted firearm, prohibited weapon, restricted weapon, prohibited device, or prohibited ammunition in places not authorized by the authorization or licence or in a place where they may not be possessed under the *Firearms Act*. The offence may be committed in three different ways: (1) possession in a place prohibited by the authorization or licence; (2) possession in a place other than the places permitted by the authorization or licence; or (3) possession in a place where it may not be possessed under the *Firearms Act*. Section 98 allows for a transitional period for licences and registration of firearms. The offence under this section does not apply to a replica of a firearm [subsec. (3)].

UNAUTHORIZED POSSESSION IN MOTOR VEHICLE / Punishment / Exception / Exception.

94. (1) Subject to subsections (3) and (4), every person commits an offence who is an occupant of a motor vehicle in which the person knows there is a prohibited firearm, a restricted firearm, a non-restricted firearm, a prohibited weapon, a restricted weapon, a prohibited device, other than a replica firearm, or any prohibited ammunition, unless

(*a*) in the case of a prohibited firearm, a restricted firearm or a non-restricted firearm,

(i) the person or any other occupant of the motor vehicle is the holder of

(A) a licence under which the person or other occupant may possess the firearm, and

(B) in the case of a prohibited firearm or a restricted firearm, an authorization and a registration certificate for it,

(ii) the person had reasonable grounds to believe that any other occupant of the motor vehicle was the holder of

(A) a licence under which that other occupant may possess the firearm, and

(B) in the case of a prohibited firearm or a restricted firearm, an authorization and a registration certificate for it, or

(iii) the person had reasonable grounds to believe that any other occupant of the motor vehicle was a person who could not be convicted of an offence under this Act by reason of sections 117.07 to 117.1 or any other Act of Parliament; and

(*b*) in the case of a prohibited weapon, a restricted weapon, a prohibited device or any prohibited ammunition,

(i) the person or any other occupant of the motor vehicle is the holder of an authorization or a licence under which the person or other occupant may transport the prohibited weapon, restricted weapon, prohibited device or prohibited ammunition, or

(ii) the person had reasonable grounds to believe that any other occupant of the motor vehicle was

(A) the holder of an authorization or a licence under which the other occupant may transport the prohibited weapon, restricted weapon, prohibited device or prohibited ammunition, or

(B) a person who could not be convicted of an offence under this Act by reason of sections 117.07 to 117.1 or any other Act of Parliament.

(2) Every person who commits an offence under subsection (1)

(*a*) is guilty of an indictable offence and liable to imprisonment for a term not exceeding ten years; or

(*b*) is guilty of an offence punishable on summary conviction.

(3) Subsection (1) does not apply to an occupant of a motor vehicle who, on becoming aware of the presence of the firearm, weapon, device or ammunition in the motor vehicle, attempted to leave the motor vehicle, to the extent that it was feasible to do so, or actually left the motor vehicle.

(4) Subsection (1) does not apply to an occupant of a motor vehicle when the occupant or any other occupant of the motor vehicle is a person who came into possession of the firearm, weapon, device or ammunition by the operation of law. 1995, c. 39, s. 139; 2008, c. 6, s. 7; 2012, c. 6, s. 4; 2015, c. 27, s. 22.

(5) [*Repealed*, 2012, c. 6, s. 4(3).]

CROSS-REFERENCES

"Firearm" and "motor vehicle" are defined in s. 2. "Possession" is defined in s. 4(3). "Prohibited firearm", "restricted firearm", "non-restricted firearm", "prohibited weapon", "restricted weapon", "prohibited device", "prohibited firearm", "restricted firearm", "replica firearm", "prohibited ammunition", "licence", "registration certificate" and "authorization" are defined in s. 84(1).

An accused charged with this offence may elect the mode of trial pursuant to s. 536(2) where the Crown proceeds by way of indictment. Where the prosecution elects to proceed by way of summary conviction, then the trial of this offence is conducted by a summary conviction court pursuant to Part XXVII. The punishment for the offence is then as set out in s. 787 and the limitation period is set out in s. 786(2).

A person found guilty of the offences in this section is liable to the discretionary prohibition order prescribed by s. 110, unless the accused was prohibited from possessing weapons or other regulated items at the time of the offence, in which case the mandatory prohibition order in s. 109 applies. Sections 117.07 to 117.09 exempt certain persons such as police officers from the operation of this section, provided that the person is not subject to a prohibition order (see s. 117.1).

Note mandatory forfeiture of weapons used in commission of an offence in s. 491.

Section 117.13 allows for the admission into evidence of a certificate of an analyst who has examined the weapon, prohibited device, ammunition, prohibited ammunition, explosive substance, or any part of component of such a thing.

The related offence of unauthorized possession of a weapon in an unauthorized place is in s. 93.

SYNOPSIS

This somewhat complex provision in essence makes it an offence to be an occupant in a motor vehicle knowing that possession of the weapon in that place is not authorized. The scheme of the section is to make it an offence to be an occupant of a motor vehicle knowing that there is a prohibited firearm, restricted firearm, non-restricted firearm, prohibited weapon, restricted weapon, prohibited device, other than a replica firearm, or prohibited ammunition in the motor vehicle. Subsection (1)(*a*) and (*b*) then provide for exemptions from liability if some person in the vehicle is entitled to possess and transport the weapon and, in the case of a prohibited or restricted firearm, the person has a registration certificate. The accused will also be exempt from liability if he or she had "reasonable grounds" to believe that another occupant had the requisite authorization, licence or registration certificate. Subsection (3) also creates a type of due diligence defence for an occupant who attempts to leave the vehicle when he or she learned of the presence of the weapon. Subsection (4) provides a defence for an occupant who came into possession of the weapon by operation of law.

POSSESSION OF PROHIBITED OR RESTRICTED FIREARM WITH AMMUNITION / Punishment / Exception.

95. (1) Subject to subsection (3), every person commits an offence who, in any place, possesses a loaded prohibited firearm or restricted firearm, or an unloaded prohibited firearm or restricted firearm together with readily accessible ammunition that is capable of being discharged in the firearm, without being the holder of

(*a*) an authorization or a licence under which the person may possess the firearm in that place; and

(*b*) the registration certificate for the firearm.

(2) Every person who commits an offence under subsection (1)

(*a*) is guilty of an indictable offence and liable to imprisonment for a term not exceeding 10 years and to a minimum punishment of imprisonment for a term of

(i) in the case of a first offence, three years, and

(ii) in the case of a second or subsequent offence, five years; or

(*b*) is guilty of an offence punishable on summary conviction and liable to imprisonment for a term not exceeding one year.

(3) Subsection (1) does not apply to a person who is using the firearm under the direct and immediate supervision of another person who is lawfully entitled to possess it and is using the firearm in a manner in which that other person may lawfully use it. 1995, c. 39, s. 139; 2008, c. 6, s. 8; 2012, c. 6, s. 5.

CROSS-REFERENCES

"Possession" is defined in s. 4(3). "Prohibited firearm", "restricted firearm", "ammunition", "licence", "registration certificate" and "authorization" are defined in s. 84(1).

An accused charged with this offence may elect the mode of trial pursuant to s. 536(2) where the Crown proceeds by way of indictment. Where the prosecution elects to proceed by way of summary conviction then the trial of this offence is conducted by a summary conviction court pursuant to Part XXVII. The maximum punishment for the offence is then one year imprisonment, rather than the punishment as set out in s. 787, and the limitation period is set out in s. 786(2). A person convicted of this offence is subject to the mandatory prohibition orders provided for in s. 109. For the purpose of determining whether a person has committed a second or subsequent offence, see s. 84(5) and (6).

Section 117.13 allows for the admission into evidence of a certificate of an analyst who has examined the weapon, prohibited device, ammunition, prohibited ammunition, explosive substance, or any part or component of such a thing.

SYNOPSIS

This section creates an offence to have a prohibited or restricted firearm that is either loaded or together with readily accessible ammunition capable of being discharged in that firearm, unless the person has an authorization or a licence that allows possession of the firearm at that particular place and a registration certificate for that firearm. By virtue of subsec. (3), no offence is committed if the person is under the direct and immediate supervision of someone who is authorized to have the weapon provided that they are using the weapon in a manner that the supervising person is authorized.

ANNOTATIONS

The *mens rea* is satisfied where the accused had knowledge that he was in possession of a loaded firearm. Knowledge of the length of the handgun's barrel is immaterial to the *mens rea*: *R. v. Williams* (2009), 244 C.C.C. (3d) 138 (Ont. C.A.).

This section creates two offences: possession of a loaded firearm and possession of an unloaded firearm with readily accessible ammunition. The latter is *not* a lesser included offence of the former: *R. v. Wong* (2012), 289 C.C.C. (3d) 38 (Ont. C.A.).

The Crown is not required to prove that the accused knew his possession and acquisition licence and authorization to transport the firearm did not extend to the place where he unlawfully had it in his possession. Ignorance of the law is no excuse. Knowledge that one possesses a loaded restricted firearm, together with an intention to possess the loaded firearm in that place, is enough: *R. v. MacDonald*, [2014] 1 S.C.R. 37, 303 C.C.C. (3d) 113.

The three-year mandatory minimum sentence for a first offender violates s. 12 of the Charter and cannot be justified under s. 1: *R. v. Nur*, [2015] 1 S.C.R. 773, 322 C.C.C. (3d) 149.

The five-year mandatory minimum sentence for a repeat offender also violates s. 12 of the Charter and cannot be justified under s. 1: *R. v. Nur, supra*.

See also *R. v. Adamo* (2013), 300 C.C.C. (3d) 515 (Man. Q.B.), holding that the mandatory minimum sentences violate ss. 7 and 12, as well as s. 15 of the Charter on the ground that it perpetuated and worsened the accused's disadvantage arising from his mental disability.

POSSESSION OF WEAPON OBTAINED BY COMMISSION OF OFFENCE / Punishment / Exception.

96. (1) Subject to subsection (3), every person commits an offence who possesses a firearm, a prohibited weapon, a restricted weapon, a prohibited device or any prohibited ammunition that the person knows was obtained by the commission in Canada of an offence or by an act or omission anywhere that, if it had occurred in Canada, would have constituted an offence.

(2) Every person who commits an offence under subsection (1)

- **(*a*) is guilty of an indictable offence and liable to imprisonment for a term not exceeding ten years and to a minimum punishment of imprisonment for a term of one year; or**
- **(*b*) is guilty of an offence punishable on summary conviction and liable to imprisonment for a term not exceeding one year.**

(3) Subsection (1) does not apply to a person who comes into possession of anything referred to in that subsection by the operation of law and who lawfully disposes of it within a reasonable period after acquiring possession of it. 1995, c. 39, s. 139.

CROSS-REFERENCES

"Firearm" is defined in s. 2. "Possession" is defined in s. 4(3). "Prohibited weapon", "restricted weapon", "prohibited device" and "prohibited ammunition" are defined in s. 84(1). An accused charged with this offence may elect the mode of trial pursuant to s. 536(2) where the Crown proceeds by way of indictment. Where the prosecution elects to proceed by way of summary conviction then the trial of this offence is conducted by a summary conviction court pursuant to Part XXVII. The maximum punishment for the offence is then one year imprisonment, rather than the punishment as set out in s. 787, and the limitation period is set out in s. 786(2).

A person found guilty of the offences in this section is liable to the discretionary prohibition order prescribed by s. 110, unless the accused was prohibited from possessing weapons or other regulated items at the time of the offence, in which case the mandatory prohibition order in s. 109 applies.

Note mandatory forfeiture of weapons used in commission of an offence in s. 491.

Section 117.13 allows for the admission into evidence of a certificate of an analyst who has examined the weapon, prohibited device, ammunition, prohibited ammunition, explosive substance, or any part or component of such a thing.

An authorization to intercept private communications may be obtained in relation to an offence under this section by virtue of ss. 183 and 186.

The related offence of possession of property obtained by crime is found in s. 354.

SYNOPSIS

This offence is similar to the offence of property obtained by crime under s. 354, except that this offence relates specifically to firearms, prohibited weapons, restricted weapons, prohibited devices and prohibited ammunition. As with the offence under s. 354, the prosecution must prove that the accused had possession of the item with knowledge that it had been obtained by the commission in Canada of an offence or by an act of omission anywhere that, if it had occurred in Canada, would have constituted an offence. Subsection (3) provides a defence for a person who comes into possession of the item by operation of law and who lawfully disposes of it within a reasonable period.

ANNOTATIONS

Note: The following cases were decided under s. 354 and may be of assistance in applying this section.

Doctrine of recent possession – The most recent review of the elements of the "doctrine" of recent possession that, in part, permits the trier of fact to infer the requisite guilty knowledge from possession of recently stolen goods is found in *R. v. Kowlyk*, [1988] 2 S.C.R. 59, 43 C.C.C. (3d) 1 (4:1). Those elements, as set out in that case and distilled from the various decisions as approved in *Kowlyk*, may be summarized as follows:

1. No adverse inference may be drawn against an accused from the fact of possession alone unless it was recent: *R. v. Graham*, [1974] S.C.R. 206, 7 C.C.C. (2d) 93;
2. If a pre-trial explanation of such possession were given by the accused, and if it possessed that degree of contemporaneity with the possession making evidence of it admissible, no adverse inference could be drawn on the basis of recent possession alone if the explanation were one which could reasonably be true: *R. v. Graham, supra*;
3. Where the accused does not testify, a jury instruction as to the inference arising from unexplained possession does not constitute a "comment" within the meaning of s. 4(6) of the *Canada Evidence Act: R. v. Newton*, [1977] 1 S.C.R. 399, 28 C.C.C. (2d) 286;

4. Where an explanation which could reasonably be true is given for the possession, no inference of guilt on the basis of recent possession alone may be drawn, even if the trier of fact is not satisfied as to the truth of the explanation and thus, to obtain a conviction in the face of such an explanation, the prosecution must establish by other evidence the guilt of the accused beyond a reasonable doubt.

In *Saieva v. Canada*, [1982] 1 S.C.R. 897, 68 C.C.C. (2d) 97 (7:0), the court, in considering whether possession was sufficiently "recent" to entitle reliance on the doctrine of recent possession, approved the statement in *R. v. Killam* (1973), 12 C.C.C. (2d) 114 (B.C.C.A.), that the criteria to be used are the nature of the object, "its rareness, the readiness in which it can, and is likely to, pass from hand to hand, the ease of its identification and the likelihood of transferability".

For other notes on recent possession, see s. 354.

Proof that goods obtained by crime – An admission by the accused is admissible for its truth, even if the admission itself contains hearsay, provided that the accused indicates a belief in the acceptance of the truth of the hearsay statement. If, however, the accused merely reports a hearsay statement without either adopting it or indicating a belief in its truth then the statement is not admissible for the truth of its contents. Thus, out of court statements by an accused, charged with the offence under this section, that he did not know the origin of the goods but his friend had stolen the goods and he knew they were "hot", made in circumstances indicating he believed the statements were true, were admissible not only to prove guilty knowledge but that, in fact, the goods were stolen: *R. v. Streu*, [1989] 1 S.C.R. 1521, 48 C.C.C. (3d) 321 (5:0).

Constitutional considerations – Application of the doctrine of recent possession does not offend the guarantees in s. 11(*c*) and (*d*) of the *Canadian Charter of Rights and Freedoms*: *R. v. Russell* (1983), 4 C.C.C. (3d) 460 (N.S.S.C.A.D.).

97. [Enacted 1995, c. 39, s. 139; however, repealed before coming into force]

BREAKING AND ENTERING TO STEAL FIREARM / Definitions of "break" and "place" / Entrance / Punishment.

98. (1) Every person commits an offence who

(*a*) breaks and enters a place with intent to steal a firearm located in it;

(*b*) breaks and enters a place and steals a firearm located in it; or

(*c*) breaks out of a place after

(i) stealing a firearm located in it, or

(ii) entering the place with intent to steal a firearm located in it.

(2) In this section, "break" has the same meaning as in section 321, and "place" means any building or structure — or part of one — and any motor vehicle, vessel, aircraft, railway vehicle, container or trailer.

(3) For the purposes of this section,

(*a*) a person enters as soon as any part of his or her body or any part of an instrument that he or she uses is within any thing that is being entered; and

(*b*) a person is deemed to have broken and entered if he or she

(i) obtained entrance by a threat or an artifice or by collusion with a person within, or

(ii) entered without lawful justification or excuse by a permanent or temporary opening.

(4) Every person who commits an offence under subsection (1) is guilty of an indictable offence and liable to imprisonment for life. 1995, c. 39, s. 139, 2008, c. 6, s. 9.

CROSS-REFERENCES

"Firearm" and "steal" are defined in s. 2. The other break and enter offences are defined in s. 348. Section 350 enacts a deeming provision similar to subsec. (3) of this section. Section 98.1 creates a specific robbery offence where the object of the robbery is a firearm. Section 662(6) provides that a person charged with the offence under subsec. (1)(*b*), may be convicted of the offence under subsec. (1)(*a*), where the evidence does not prove the former offence but does prove the latter. Being unlawfully in a dwelling house is an offence under s. 349. Possession of break-in instruments is an offence under s. 351(1). Defence of property is dealt with in ss. 38 to 42. Section 494 gives the owner of property or person in possession and persons authorized by them a power to arrest, without warrant, a person found committing a criminal offence on or in relation to that property. This offence may be the basis for an application for an authorization to intercept private communications by reason of s. 183.

Pursuant to s. 348.1, if a person is convicted of the offence under this section in relation to a dwelling-house, it is an aggravating factor in sentencing that the dwelling-house was occupied at the time and the offender knew or was reckless as to whether the dwelling-house was occupied and used violence or threats of violence to a person or property.

SYNOPSIS

This section creates offences that are virtually identical to the offences in s. 348 of the *Criminal Code* except that the target of the break and enter is theft of a firearm. Unlike s. 348, this section does not distinguish between places as far as penalty; the offender is liable to life imprisonment even though the premises are not a dwelling-house.

ANNOTATIONS

Note: For notes on the meaning of break and enter and the application of the deeming provision in subsec. (3), see ss. 348 and 350.

ROBBERY TO STEAL FIREARM.

98.1 Every person who commits a robbery within the meaning of section 343 with intent to steal a firearm or in the course of which he or she steals a firearm commits an indictable offence and is liable to imprisonment for life. 2008, c. 6, s. 9.

CROSS-REFERENCES

"Firearm" is defined in s. 2. The similar break and enter offence, where the object of the theft is a firearm, is created by s. 98. This offence may be the basis for an application for an authorization to intercept private communications by reason of s. 183.

Trafficking Offences

WEAPONS TRAFFICKING / Punishment — firearm / Punishment — other cases.

99. (1) Every person commits an offence who

(*a*) manufactures or transfers, whether or not for consideration, or

(*b*) offers to do anything referred to in paragraph (*a*) in respect of

a prohibited firearm, a restricted firearm, a non-restricted firearm, a prohibited weapon, a restricted weapon, a prohibited device, any ammunition or any prohibited ammunition knowing that the person is not authorized to do so under the *Firearms Act* or any other Act of Parliament or any regulations made under any Act of Parliament.

(2) Every person who commits an offence under subsection (1) when the object in question is a prohibited firearm, a restricted firearm, a non-restricted firearm, a prohibited device, any ammunition or any prohibited ammunition is guilty of an

indictable offence and liable to imprisonment for a term not exceeding 10 years and to a minimum punishment of imprisonment for a term of

(*a*) in the case of a first offence, three years; and

(*b*) in the case of a second or subsequent offence, five years.

(3) In any other case, a person who commits an offence under subsection (1) is guilty of an indictable offence and liable to imprisonment for a term not exceeding 10 years and to a minimum punishment of imprisonment for a term of one year. 1995, c. 39, s. 139; 2008, c. 6, s. 10; 2015, c. 27, s. 23.

CROSS-REFERENCES

"Firearm" is defined in s. 2. "Prohibited firearm", "restricted firearm", "non-restricted firearm", "prohibited weapon", "restricted weapon", "prohibited device", "ammunition", "prohibited ammunition" and "transfer" are defined in s. 84(1). The accused may elect the mode of trial pursuant to s. 536(2). A person convicted of this offence is subject to the mandatory prohibition order under s. 109. For the purpose of determining whether a person has committed a second or subsequent offence, see s. 84(5) and (6).

Note mandatory forfeiture of weapons used in commission of an offence in s. 491.

Section 117.13 allows for the admission into evidence of a certificate of an analyst who has examined the weapon, prohibited device, ammunition, prohibited ammunition, explosive substance, or any part of component of such a thing.

An authorization to intercept private communications may be obtained in relation to an offence under this section by virtue of ss. 183 and 186.

Section 101 creates the related offence of unauthorized transfer of weapons and s. 100 creates the offence of possession of weapons for the purpose of trafficking. Section 104 creates the offence of unauthorized importing and exporting of weapons. Section 105 creates the offence of smuggling weapons into and out of Canada.

SYNOPSIS

This section creates the offence of trafficking in weapons. This offence requires proof that the accused knew that he or she was not authorized to manufacture or transfer, or offer to do so, under the *Firearms Act* or regulations or any other federal legislation or regulations.

Subsection (2) creates a special penalty regime where the offence is committed in relation to a prohibited firearm, restricted firearm, non-restricted firearm, prohibited device, any ammunition or any prohibited ammunition. The maximum penalty is 10 years and the minimum punishment for a first offence is three years and is five years for a second or subsequent offence, as determined in accordance with the rules set out in s. 84(5) and (6). In any other case, the minimum punishment is one year.

ANNOTATIONS

Trafficking by offer requires that the offer be put forward in a serious manner and that the accused intends for the offer to be taken as genuine. It was an error not to instruct the jury to this effect: *R. v. Duncan* (2015), 332 C.C.C. (3d) 347 (Ont. C.A.).

POSSESSION FOR PURPOSE OF WEAPONS TRAFFICKING / Punishment — firearm / Punishment — other cases.

100. (1) Every person commits an offence who possesses a prohibited firearm, a restricted firearm, a non-restricted firearm, a prohibited weapon, a restricted weapon, a prohibited device, any ammunition or any prohibited ammunition for the purpose of

(*a*) transferring it, whether or not for consideration, or

(*b*) offering to transfer it,

knowing that the person is not authorized to transfer it under the *Firearms Act* or any other Act of Parliament or any regulations made under any Act of Parliament.

(2) Every person who commits an offence under subsection (1) when the object in question is a prohibited firearm, a restricted firearm, a non-restricted firearm, a prohibited device, any ammunition or any prohibited ammunition is guilty of an indictable offence and liable to imprisonment for a term not exceeding 10 years and to a minimum punishment of imprisonment for a term of

(*a*) in the case of a first offence, three years; and

(*b*) in the case of a second or subsequent offence, five years.

(3) In any other case, a person who commits an offence under subsection (1) is guilty of an indictable offence and liable to imprisonment for a term not exceeding 10 years and to a minimum punishment of imprisonment for a term of one year. 1995, c. 39, s. 139; 2008, c. 6, s. 11; 2015, c. 27, s. 24.

CROSS-REFERENCES

"Firearm" is defined in s. 2. "Possession" is defined in s. 4(3). "Prohibited firearm", "restricted firearm", "non-restricted firearm", "prohibited weapon", "restricted weapon", "prohibited device", "ammunition", "prohibited ammunition" and "transfer" are defined in s. 84(1). The accused may elect the mode of trial pursuant to s. 536(2). A person convicted of this offence is subject to the mandatory prohibition order under s. 109. For the purpose of determining whether a person has committed a second or subsequent offence, see s. 84(5) and (6).

Note mandatory forfeiture of weapons used in commission of an offence in s. 491.

Section 117.13 allows for the admission into evidence of a certificate of an analyst who has examined the weapon, prohibited device, ammunition, prohibited ammunition, explosive substance, or any part or component of such a thing.

An authorization to intercept private communications may be obtained in relation to an offence under this section by virtue of ss. 183 and 186.

Section 99 creates the related offence of trafficking in weapons and s. 101 creates the basic offence of unauthorized transfer of weapons. Section 104 creates the offence of unauthorized importing and exporting of weapons. Section 105 creates the offence of smuggling weapons into and out of Canada.

SYNOPSIS

This section creates the offence of possession of weapons for the purpose of trafficking in weapons. This offence requires proof that the accused had possession of the prohibited firearm, restricted firearm, non-restricted firearm, prohibited weapon, restricted weapon, prohibited device, ammunition or prohibited ammunition for the purpose of transferring it, or offering to do so, knowing that he or she was not authorized to transfer it under the *Firearms Act* or regulations or any other federal legislation or regulations.

Subsection (2) creates a special penalty regime where the offence is committed in relation to a prohibited firearm, restricted firearm, non-restricted firearm, prohibited device, any ammunition or any prohibited ammunition. The maximum penalty is 10 years and the minimum punishment for a first offence is three years and is five years for a second or subsequent offence, as determined in accordance with the rules set out in s. 84(5) and (6). In any other case, the minimum punishment is one year.

ANNOTATIONS

This provision does not apply to the mere movement of a firearm from one place to another. A contextual reading of s. 100 and the related provisions reveals that Parliament intended to reserve the stiffest penalties for transfers that amount to weapons trafficking, not for the mere movement of a firearm from place to place. Since the trial judge did not find that the accused was in possession of the gun for the purpose of transferring it to another person, the s. 100(1) conviction cannot stand. There are other provisions, such as s. 86(2) that capture conduct falling short of trafficking: *R. v. Grant* (2009), 245 C.C.C. (3d) 1 (S.C.C.).

TRANSFER WITHOUT AUTHORITY / Punishment.

101. (1) Every person commits an offence who transfers a prohibited firearm, a restricted firearm, a non-restricted firearm, a prohibited weapon, a restricted weapon, a prohibited device, any ammunition or any prohibited ammunition to any person otherwise than under the authority of the *Firearms Act* or any other Act of Parliament or any regulations made under an Act of Parliament.

(2) Every person who commits an offence under subsection (1)

(*a*) is guilty of an indictable offence and liable to imprisonment for a term not exceeding five years; or

(*b*) is guilty of an offence punishable on summary conviction. 1995, c. 39, s. 139; 2015, c. 27, s. 25.

CROSS-REFERENCES

"Firearm" is defined in s. 2. "Prohibited firearm", "restricted firearm", "non-restricted firearm", "prohibited weapon", "restricted weapon", "prohibited device", "ammunition", "prohibited ammunition" and "transfer" are defined in s. 84(1). An accused charged with this offence may elect the mode of trial pursuant to s. 536(2) where the Crown proceeds by way of indictment. Where the prosecution elects to proceed by way of summary conviction then the trial of this offence is conducted by a summary conviction court pursuant to Part XXVII. The punishment for the offence is then as set out in s. 787 and the limitation period is set out in s. 786(2). In either case, release pending trial is determined by s. 515, although the accused is eligible for release by a peace officer under ss. 496, 497 or by the officer in charge under s. 498.

A person found guilty of the offences in this section is liable to the discretionary prohibition order prescribed by s. 110, unless the accused was prohibited from possessing weapons or other regulated items at the time of the offence, in which case the mandatory prohibition order in s. 109 applies.

Note mandatory forfeiture of weapons used in commission of an offence in s. 491.

Under s. 117.11, where any question arises as to whether a person is the holder of an authorization, a licence or a registration certificate, the onus is on the accused to prove that the person is the holder of the authorization, licence or registration certificate. Section 117.12 provides for admission into evidence of copies of such documents and the evidentiary value of the original and copies. Section 117.13 allows for the admission into evidence of a certificate of an analyst who has examined the weapon, prohibited device, ammunition, prohibited ammunition, explosive substance, or any part or component of such a thing.

Section 99 creates the related offence of trafficking in weapons and s. 100 creates the offence of possession of weapons for the purpose of trafficking.

SYNOPSIS

This section makes it an offence to transfer a prohibited firearm, restricted firearm, non-restricted firearm, prohibited weapon, restricted weapon, prohibited device, ammunition and prohibited ammunition to any person except under the authority of the *Firearms Act* or regulations or any other federal legislation or regulations. "Transfer" is broadly defined in s. 84(1) to mean "sell, provide, barter, give, lend, rent, send, transport, ship, distribute or deliver".

ANNOTATIONS

The Crown must prove that the accused knew, was wilfully blind to or reckless as to the fact that the recipient of the ammunition was unlicensed: *R. v. Hault* (2004), 201 C.C.C. (3d) 375 (Alta. Q.B.).

CR. CODE

Assembling Offence

MAKING AUTOMATIC FIREARM / Punishment.

102. (1) Every person commits an offence who, without lawful excuse, alters a firearm so that it is capable of, or manufactures or assembles any firearm that is capable of, discharging projectiles in rapid succession during one pressure of the trigger.

(2) Every person who commits an offence under subsection (1)

(*a*) is guilty of an indictable offence and liable to imprisonment for a term not exceeding ten years and to a minimum punishment of imprisonment for a term of one year; or

(*b*) is guilty of an offence punishable on summary conviction and liable to imprisonment for a term not exceeding one year. 1995, c. 39, s. 139.

CROSS-REFERENCES

"Firearm" is defined in s. 2. "Automatic firearm" is defined in s. 84(1). An accused charged with this offence may elect the mode of trial pursuant to s. 536(2) where the Crown proceeds by way of indictment. Where the prosecution elects to proceed by way of summary conviction then the trial of this offence is conducted by a summary conviction court pursuant to Part XXVII. The maximum punishment for the offence is then one year imprisonment, rather than the punishment as set out in s. 787, and the limitation period is set out in s. 786(2). Where the Crown proceeds by indictment, this offence carries a minimum punishment of one year imprisonment. A person convicted of this offence is subject to the mandatory prohibition order under s. 109.

Note mandatory forfeiture of weapons used in commission of an offence in s. 491.

Section 117.13 allows for the admission into evidence of a certificate of an analyst who has examined the weapon, prohibited device, ammunition, prohibited ammunition, explosive substance, or any part or component of such a thing.

An authorization to intercept private communications may be obtained in relation to an offence under this section by virtue of ss. 183 and 186.

SYNOPSIS

This offence, in effect, prohibits, without lawful excuse, the alteration of a firearm into an automatic firearm. It also prohibits, without lawful excuse, the manufacture or assembly of such firearms. Note the minimum punishment of one year imprisonment where the Crown proceeds by way of indictment.

Export and Import Offences

IMPORTING OR EXPORTING KNOWING IT IS UNAUTHORIZED / Punishment — firearm / Punishment — other cases / Attorney General of Canada may act.

103. (1) Every person commits an offence who imports or exports

(*a*) a prohibited firearm, a restricted firearm, a non-restricted firearm, a prohibited weapon, a restricted weapon, a prohibited device or any prohibited ammunition, or

(*b*) any component or part designed exclusively for use in the manufacture of or assembly into an automatic firearm,

knowing that the person is not authorized to do so under the *Firearms Act* or any other Act of Parliament or any regulations made under an Act of Parliament.

(2) Every person who commits an offence under subsection (1) when the object in question is a prohibited firearm, a restricted firearm, a non-restricted firearm, a prohibited device or any prohibited ammunition is guilty of an indictable offence and

liable to imprisonment for a term not exceeding 10 years and to a minimum punishment of imprisonment for a term of

(*a*) in the case of a first offence, three years; and

(*b*) in the case of a second or subsequent offence, five years.

(2.1) In any other case, a person who commits an offence under subsection (1) is guilty of an indictable offence and liable to imprisonment for a term not exceeding 10 years and to a minimum punishment of imprisonment for a term of one year.

(3) Any proceedings in respect of an offence under subsection (1) may be commenced at the instance of the Government of Canada and conducted by or on behalf of that government. 1995, c. 39, s. 139; 2008, c. 6, s. 12; 2015, c. 27, s. 26.

CROSS-REFERENCES

"Firearm" is defined in s. 2. "Prohibited firearm", "restricted firearm", "non-restricted firearm", "prohibited weapon", "restricted weapon", "prohibited device", "automatic firearm", "prohibited ammunition", "import" and "export" are defined in s. 84(1). The accused may elect the mode of trial pursuant to s. 536(2). A person convicted of this offence is subject to the mandatory prohibition order under s. 109. For the purpose of determining whether a person has committed a second or subsequent offence, see s. 84(5) and (6).

Section 117.13 allows for the admission into evidence of a certificate of an analyst who has examined the weapon, prohibited device, ammunition, prohibited ammunition, explosive substance, or any part or component of such a thing.

An authorization to intercept private communications may be obtained in relation to an offence under this section by virtue of ss. 183 and 186. The related offence of simple unauthorized importing or exporting of weapons is found in s. 104.

SYNOPSIS

This section makes it an offence to import or export a prohibited firearm, restricted firearm, non-restricted firearm, prohibited weapon, restricted weapon, prohibited device or any prohibited ammunition, or any component or part designed exclusively for use in the manufacture of or assembly into an automatic firearm knowing that one is not authorized to do so under the authority of the *Firearms Act* and regulations or some other federal legislation or regulations. If prosecuted by indictment, the offence carries a minimum punishment of one year imprisonment. Offences under this section may be prosecuted at the instance of the federal government.

Subsection (2) creates a special penalty regime where the offence is committed in relation to a prohibited firearm, restricted firearm, non-restricted firearm, prohibited device, or any prohibited ammunition. The maximum penalty is 10 years and the minimum punishment for a first offence is three years and is five years for a second or subsequent offence, as determined in accordance with the rules set out in s. 84(5) and (6). In any other case, the minimum punishment is one year.

UNAUTHORIZED IMPORTING OR EXPORTING / Punishment / Attorney General of Canada may act.

104. (1) Every person commits an offence who imports or exports

(*a*) a prohibited firearm, a restricted firearm, a non-restricted firearm, a prohibited weapon, a restricted weapon, a prohibited device or any prohibited ammunition, or

(*b*) any component or part designed exclusively for use in the manufacture of or assembly into an automatice firearm,

otherwise than under the authority of the *Firearms Act* or any other Act of Parliament or any regulations made under an Act of Parliament.

(2) Every person who commits an offence under subsection (1)

(*a*) **is guilty of an indictable offence and liable to imprisonment for a term not exceeding five years; or**

(*b*) **is guilty of an offence punishable on summary conviction.**

(3) Any proceedings in respect of an offence under subsection (1) may be commenced at the instance of the Government of Canada and conducted by or on behalf of that government. 1995, c. 39, s. 139; 2015, c. 27, s. 27.

CROSS-REFERENCES

"Firearm" is defined in s. 2. "Prohibited firearm", "restricted firearm", "non-restricted firearm", "prohibited weapon", "restricted weapon", "prohibited device", "automatic firearm", "prohibited ammunition", "import" and "export" are defined in s. 84(1). An accused charged with this offence may elect the mode of trial pursuant to s. 536(2) where the Crown proceeds by way of indictment. Where the prosecution elects to proceed by way of summary conviction then the trial of this offence is conducted by a summary conviction court pursuant to Part XXVII. The punishment for the offence is then as set out in s. 787 and the limitation period is set out in s. 786(2).

A person found guilty of the offences in this section is liable to the discretionary prohibition order prescribed by s. 110, unless the accused was prohibited from possessing weapons or other regulated items at the time of the offence, in which case the mandatory prohibition order in s. 109 applies.

Note mandatory forfeiture of weapons used in commission of an offence in s. 491.

Under s. 117.11, where any question arises as to whether a person is the holder of an authorization, a licence or a registration certificate, the onus is on the accused to prove that the person is the holder of the authorization, licence or registration certificate. Section 117.12 provides for admission into evidence of copies of such documents and the evidentiary value of the original and copies. Section 117.13 allows for the admission into evidence of a certificate of an analyst who has examined the weapon, prohibited device, ammunition, prohibited ammunition, explosive substance, or any part of component of such a thing.

An authorization to intercept private communications may be obtained in relation to an offence under this section by virtue of ss. 183 and 186.

The related offence of smuggling weapons is found in s. 104. Unauthorized transfer of weapons is an offence under s. 101, and trafficking in weapons is an offence under s. 99.

SYNOPSIS

This section makes it an offence to import or export a prohibited firearm, restricted firearm, non-restricted firearm, prohibited weapon, restricted weapon, prohibited device or any prohibited ammunition, or any component or part designed exclusively for use in the manufacture of or assembly into an automatic firearm otherwise than under the authority of the *Firearms Act* and regulations or some other federal legislation or regulations. Offences under this section may be prosecuted at the instance of the federal government.

Offences relating to Lost, Destroyed or Defaced Weapons, etc.

LOSING OR FINDING / Punishment.

105. (1) Every person commits an offence who

(*a*) **having lost a prohibited firearm, a restricted firearm, a non-restricted firearm, a prohibited weapon, a restricted weapon, a prohibited device, any prohibited ammunition, an authorization, a licence or a registration certificate, or having had it stolen from the person's possession, does not with reasonable despatch report the loss to a peace officer, to a firearms officer or a chief firearms officer; or**

(*b*) **on finding a prohibited firearm, a restricted firearm, a non-restricted firearm, a prohibited weapon, a restricted weapon, a prohibited device or any**

prohibited ammunition that the person has reasonable grounds to believe has been lost or abandoned, does not with reasonable despatch deliver it to a peace officer, a firearms officer or a chief firearms officer or report the finding to a peace officer, a firearms officer or a chief firearms officer.

(2) Every person who commits an offence under subsection (1)

(*a*) is guilty of an indictable offence and liable to imprisonment for a term not exceeding five years; or

(*b*) is guilty of an offence punishable on summary conviction. 1995, c. 39, s. 139; 2015, c. 27, s. 28.

CROSS-REFERENCES

"Firearm" and "peace officer" are defined in s. 2. "Prohibited firearm", "restricted firearm", "non-restricted firearm", "prohibited weapon", "restricted weapon", "prohibited device", "prohibited ammunition", "firearms officer", "chief firearms officer, "licence", "registration certificate" and "authorization" are defined in s. 84(1). An accused charged with this offence may elect the mode of trial pursuant to s. 536(2) where the Crown proceeds by way of indictment. Where the prosecution elects to proceed by way of summary conviction then the trial of this offence is conducted by a summary conviction court pursuant to Part XXVII. The punishment for the offence is then as set out in s. 787 and the limitation period is set out in s. 786(2). A person found guilty of the offences in this section is liable to the discretionary prohibition order prescribed by s. 110, unless the accused was prohibited from possessing weapons or other regulated items at the time of the offence, in which case the mandatory prohibition order in s. 109 applies.

Note mandatory forfeiture of weapons used in commission of an offence in s. 491.

Under s. 117.11, where any question arises as to whether a person is the holder of an authorization, a licence or a registration certificate, the onus is on the accused to prove that the person is the holder of the authorization, licence or registration certificate. Section 117.12 provides for admission into evidence of copies of such documents and the evidentiary value of the original and copies. Section 117.13 allows for the admission into evidence of a certificate of an analyst who has examined the weapon, prohibited device, ammunition, prohibited ammunition, explosive substance, or any part or component of such a thing.

The related offence of failing to report the destruction of weapons is found in s. 106. It is also an offence under s. 107 to make a false report concerning the loss or theft of a weapon or an authorization, licence or registration certificate.

SYNOPSIS

This section creates two offences of omission concerning firearms, weapons and documents. Under subsec. (1)(*a*), it is an offence to fail with reasonable despatch to report the loss or theft of a prohibited firearm, restricted firearm, non-restricted firearm, prohibited weapon, restricted weapon, prohibited device, any prohibited ammunition, an authorization, a licence or a registration certificate. Similarly, it is an offence under subsec. (1)(*b*) to fail to report or deliver with reasonable despatch any prohibited firearm, restricted firearm, non-restricted firearm, prohibited weapon, restricted weapon, prohibited device, or any prohibited ammunition that the person reasonably believes to have been abandoned or lost. The report or delivery, as the case may be, is to be made to a peace officer, firearms officer or chief firearms officer.

DESTROYING / Punishment.

106. (1) Every person commits an offence who

(*a*) after destroying any prohibited firearm, restricted firearm, prohibited weapon, restricted weapon, prohibited device or prohibited ammunition, or

(*b*) on becoming aware of the destruction of any prohibited firearm, restricted firearm, prohibited weapon, restricted weapon, prohibited device or prohibited ammunition that was in the person's possession before its destruction,

does not with reasonable despatch report the destruction to a peace officer, firearms officer or chief firearms officer.

(2) Every person who commits an offence under subsection (1)

(*a*) is guilty of an indictable offence and liable to imprisonment for a term not exceeding five years; or

(*b*) is guilty of an offence punishable on summary conviction. 1995, c. 39, s. 139; 2012, c. 6, s. 6.

CROSS-REFERENCES

"Firearm" and "peace officer" are defined in s. 2. "Possession" is defined in s. 4(3). "Prohibited weapon", "restricted weapon", "prohibited device", "prohibited ammunition", "restricted firearm", "prohibited firearm", "firearms officer", "chief firearms officer", "licence", "registration certificate" and "authorization" are defined in s. 84(1). An accused charged with this offence may elect the mode of trial pursuant to s. 536(2) where the Crown proceeds by way of indictment. Where the prosecution elects to proceed by way of summary conviction then the trial of this offence is conducted by a summary conviction court pursuant to Part XXVII. The punishment for the offence is then as set out in s. 787 and the limitation period is set out in s. 786(2). A person found guilty of the offences in this section is liable to the discretionary prohibition order prescribed by s. 110, unless the accused was prohibited from possessing weapons or other regulated items at the time of the offence, in which case the mandatory prohibition order in s. 109 applies.

Note mandatory forfeiture of weapons used in commission of an offence in s. 491.

Section 117.13 allows for the admission into evidence of a certificate of an analyst who has examined the weapon, prohibited device, ammunition, prohibited ammunition, explosive substance, or any part or component of such a thing.

The related offence of failing to report the loss or theft of weapons is found in s. 105. It is also an offence under s. 107 to make a false report concerning the destruction of weapons.

SYNOPSIS

This section makes it an offence to fail with reasonable despatch to report destroying any prohibited or restricted firearm, prohibited weapon, restricted weapon, prohibited device, and any prohibited ammunition. It is also an offence to fail to report the destruction of such items that were in the person's possession before their destruction on becoming aware of the destruction. The report may be made to a peace officer, firearms officer or chief firearms officer.

FALSE STATEMENTS / Punishment / Definition of "report" or "statement".

107. (1) Every person commits an offence who knowingly makes, before a peace officer, firearms officer or chief firearms officer, a false report or statement concerning the loss, theft or destruction of a prohibited firearm, a restricted firearm, a non-restricted firearm, a prohibited weapon, a restricted weapon, a prohibited device, any prohibited ammunition, an authorization, a licence or a registration certificate.

(2) Every person who commits an offence under subsection (1)

(*a*) is guilty of an indictable offence and liable to imprisonment for a term not exceeding five years; or

(*b*) is guilty of an offence punishable on summary conviction.

(3) In this section, "report" or "statement" means an assertion of fact, opinion, belief or knowledge, whether material or not and whether admissible or not. 1995, c. 39, s. 139; 2015, c. 27, s. 29.

CROSS-REFERENCES

"Firearm" and "peace officer" are defined in s. 2. "Possession" is defined in s. 4(3). "Prohibited firearm", "restricted firearm", "non-restricted firearm", "prohibited weapon", "restricted weapon", "prohibited device", "prohibited ammunition", "firearms officer", "chief firearms officer", "licence", "registration certificate" and "authorization" are defined in s. 84(1). An accused charged with this offence may elect the mode of trial pursuant to s. 536(2) where the Crown proceeds by way of indictment. Where the prosecution elects to proceed by way of summary conviction then the trial of this offence is conducted by a summary conviction court pursuant to Part XXVII. The punishment for the offence is then as set out in s. 787 and the limitation period is set out in s. 786(2).

The offence of failing to report the loss or theft of weapons and documents is found in s. 105. The offence of failing to report the destruction of weapons is found in s. 106. There are a number of related offences under the *Firearms Act*. See, for example, s. 106 of that Act, which makes it an offence to provide false information for the purpose of obtaining a licence, registration certificate or authorization.

SYNOPSIS

This section creates the offence of knowingly making a false report or statement about the loss, theft or destruction of a prohibited firearm, restricted firearm, non-restricted firearm, prohibited weapon, restricted weapon, prohibited device, any prohibited ammunition, authorization, licence or registration certificate. The terms "report" and "statement" are defined in subsec. (3).

TAMPERING WITH SERIAL NUMBER / Punishment / Exception / Evidence.

108. (1) Every person commits an offence who, without lawful excuse,

(*a*) alters, defaces or removes a serial number on a firearm; or

(*b*) possesses a firearm knowing that the serial number on it has been altered, defaced or removed.

(2) Every person who commits an offence under subsection (1)

(*a*) is guilty of an indictable offence and liable to imprisonment for a term not exceeding five years; or

(*b*) is guilty of an offence punishable on summary conviction.

(3) No person is guilty of an offence under paragraph (1)(*b*) by reason only of possessing a prohibited firearm or restricted firearm the serial number on which has been altered, defaced or removed, if that serial number has been replaced and a registration certificate in respect of the firearm has been issued setting out a new serial number for the firearm.

(4) In proceedings for an offence under subsection (1), evidence that a person possesses a firearm the serial number on which has been wholly or partially obliterated otherwise than through normal use over time is, in the absence of evidence to the contrary, proof that the person possesses the firearm knowing that the serial number on it has been altered, defaced or removed. 1995, c. 39, s. 139; 2012, c. 6, s. 7; 2018, c. 29, s. 6.

CROSS-REFERENCES

"Firearm" is defined in s. 2. "Possession" is defined in s. 4(3). "Registration certificate", "restricted firearm" and "prohibited firearm" are defined in s. 84(1). An accused charged with this offence may elect the mode of trial pursuant to s. 536(2) where the Crown proceeds by way of indictment. Where the prosecution elects to proceed by way of summary conviction, then the trial of this offence is conducted by a summary conviction court pursuant to Part XXVII. The punishment for the offence is then as set out in s. 787 and the limitation period is set out in s. 786(2). A person found guilty of the offences in this section is liable to the discretionary prohibition order prescribed by s. 110, unless the accused was prohibited from possessing weapons or other regulated items at the time of the offence, in which case the mandatory prohibition order in s. 109 applies.

Note mandatory forfeiture of weapons used in commission of an offence in s. 491.

CR. CODE

SYNOPSIS

It is an offence under this section to, without lawful excuse, alter, deface or remove a firearm's serial number or to possess a firearm knowing that the serial number has been altered, defaced or removed. The onus is on the accused to show a lawful excuse. Subsection (3) provides a defence where the serial number on a restricted or prohibited firearm has been replaced and a registration certificate has been issued setting out the new serial number. Under subsec. (4), evidence that the accused possesses a firearm, the serial number on which has been wholly or partially obliterated otherwise than through normal use over time, is, in the absence of evidence to the contrary, proof that the accused knew that the serial number had been altered, defaced or removed.

Prohibition Orders

MANDATORY PROHIBITION ORDER / Duration of prohibition order — first offence / Duration of prohibition order — subsequent offences / Definition of "release from imprisonment" / Application of ss. 113 to 117.

109. (1) Where a person is convicted, or discharged under section 730, of

(*a*) an indictable offence in the commission of which violence against a person was used, threatened or attempted and for which the person may be sentenced to imprisonment for ten years or more,

(*a*.1) an indictable offence in the commission of which violence was used, threatened or attempted against

(i) the person's current or former intimate partner,

(ii) a child or parent of the person or of anyone referred to in subparagraph (i), or

(iii) any person who resides with the person or with anyone referred to in subparagraph (i) or (ii),

(*b*) an offence under subsection 85(1) (using firearm in commission of offence), subsection 85(2) (using imitation firearm in commission of offence), 95(1) (possession of prohibited or restricted firearm with ammunition), 99(1) (weapons trafficking), 100(1) (possession for purpose of weapons trafficking), 102(1) (making automatic firearm), 103(1) (importing or exporting knowing it is unauthorized) or section 264 (criminal harassment),

(*c*) an offence relating to the contravention of subsection 5(1) or (2), 6(1) or (2) or 7(1) of the *Controlled Drugs and Substances Act*,

(*c*.1) an offence relating to the contravention of subsection 9(1) or (2), 10(1) or (2), 11(1) or (2), 12(1), (4), (5), (6) or (7), 13(1) or 14(1) of the *Cannabis Act*, or

(*d*) an offence that involves, or the subject-matter of which is, a firearm, a cross-bow, a prohibited weapon, a restricted weapon, a prohibited device, any ammunition, any prohibited ammunition or an explosive substance and, at the time of the offence, the person was prohibited by any order made under this Act or any other Act of Parliament from possessing any such thing,

the court that sentences the person or directs that the person be discharged, as the case may be, shall, in addition to any other punishment that may be imposed for that offence or any other condition prescribed in the order of discharge, make an order prohibiting the person from possessing any firearm, cross-bow, prohibited weapon, restricted weapon, prohibited device, ammunition, prohibited ammunition and explosive substance during the period specified in the order as determined in accordance with subsection (2) or (3), as the case may be.

(2) An order made under subsection (1) shall, in the case of a first conviction for or discharge from the offence to which the order relates, prohibit the person from posssessing

(*a*) any firearm, other than a prohibited firearm or restricted firearm, and any cross-bow, restricted weapon, ammunition and explosive substance during the period that

(i) begins on the day on which the order is made, and

(ii) ends not earlier than ten years after the person's release from imprisonment after conviction for the offence or, if the person is not then imprisoned or subject to imprisonment, after the person's conviction for or discharge from the offence; and

(*b*) any prohibited firearm, restricted firearm, prohibited weapon, prohibited device and prohibited ammunition for life.

(3) An order made under subsection (1) shall, in any case other than a case described in subsection (2), prohibit the person from possessing any firearm, cross-bow, restricted weapon, ammunition and explosive substance for life.

(4) In subparagraph (2)(*a*)(ii), "release from imprisonment" means release from confinement by reason of expiration of sentence, commencement of statutory release or grant of parole.

(5) Sections 113 to 117 apply in respect of every order made under subsection (1). 1995, c. 39, ss. 139, 188(*a*), 190(*d*); 1996, c. 19, s. 65.1; 2003, c. 8, s. 4; 2015, c. 27, s. 30; 2018, c. 16, s. 208.

CROSS-REFERENCES

"Intimate partner" is defined in s. 110.1. "Firearm", " explosive substance" and "weapon" are defined in s. 2. "Prohibition order", "prohibited weapon", "restricted weapon", "prohibited device", "cross-bow", "ammunition" and "prohibited ammunition" are defined in s. 84(1). Possession is defined in s. 4(3). This is one of four provisions in this part that mandate or permit the imposition of orders prohibiting the possession of weapons and other articles such as explosive substances. There are, as well, other provisions of the Code authorizing various forms of prohibition orders. Thus see: s. 110 [discretionary prohibition order upon conviction of certain offences]; s. 111 [preventative prohibition order]; s. 117.05 [preventative prohibition order after seizure]; s. 515(4.1) [condition of bail]; s. 732.1 [condition of probation]; and s. 742.3 [conditional sentence], ss. 810(3.1), 810.01(5), 810.2(5) [condition of recognizance (peace bond)]. A prohibition order shall also be made under subsecs. 51(1) and (2) of the *Youth Criminal Justice Act*.

Section 117.01 creates the offences of possessing a firearm, cross-bow, prohibited weapon, restricted weapon, prohibited device, ammunition, prohibited ammunition or explosive substance while prohibited from doing so and wilfully failing to surrender an authorization, licence or registration certificate when the person was required to surrender it by any order made under the Code.

Under s. 113, the judge may lift the prohibition order for sustenance or employment purposes. Section 114 permits the court that makes a prohibition order to order the person to surrender anything the possession of which is prohibited by the order and every authorization, licence and registration certificate relating to anything the possession of which is prohibited by the order. The person must be given a reasonable time to comply with the order and during that period the offence under s. 117.01 does not apply. Under s. 115, unless the prohibition order specifies otherwise, everything the possession of which is prohibited by the order is forfeited to the Crown. However, on application under s. 117, the judge may order the return of articles to the person who is lawfully entitled to possess it provided that the owner had no reasonable grounds to believe that the thing would or might be used in the commission of the offence in respect of which the prohibition order was made. Pursuant to s. 116, every authorization, licence and registration certificate relating to anything the possession of which is prohibited by a prohibition order and issued to a person against whom the prohibition order is made is, on the commencement of the prohibition order, revoked, or amended, as the case may be, to the extent of the prohibitions in the order. Section 117.011 allows for an application to a provincial court judge for a limitation on access order against a person who is an associate of, or cohabits with, a person subject to a prohibition order.

Section 89 of the *Firearms Act* requires a court that makes, varies or revokes a prohibition order to have the chief firearms officer informed of the order or its variation or revocation.

An order made under this section falls within the definition of "sentence" in s. 673 and therefore may be appealed as a sentence appeal under Part XXI.

SYNOPSIS

This section sets out the circumstances in which a prohibition order relating to weapons and other articles such as ammunition and explosive substances is mandatory. The order is mandatory in four circumstances: subsec. (1)(*a*), an indictable offence in the commission of which violence against a person was used, threatened or attempted and for which the person may be sentenced to imprisonment for 10 years or more; para. (*a*.1), an indictable offence in the commission of which violence is used, threatened or attempted against a current or former intimate partner, child or parent of a current or former intimate partner, or any person residing with any such individuals; paras. (*b*) and (*c*), an offence under certain specified offences in this part, under s. 264 [criminal harrassment] and under certain provisions of the *Controlled Drugs and Substances Act*; and para. (*d*), an offence that involves, or the subject-matter of which is, a firearm, a cross-bow, a prohibited weapon, a restricted weapon, a prohibited device, any ammunition, any prohibited ammunition or an explosive substance and, at the time of the offence, the person was prohibited by any order made under the Code any other Act of Parliament from possessing any such thing. Where the circumstances do not fit within one of these categories, reference should be made to s. 110.

The section envisages two types of orders. The offender will be subject to a lifetime prohibition in relation to prohibited firearms, restricted firearms, prohibited weapons, prohibited devices and prohibited ammunition. The offender will be subject to a 10-year prohibition with respect to other firearms, restricted weapons, cross-bows, ammunition and explosive substances in the case of a first offence to which the order relates. For second and subsequent offences the order for these articles is for life. As to other conditions that may be included in the order, see ss. 113 to 116. The 10-year period is calculated in accordance with subsec. (4) from the date the offender is released from confinement after conviction for the offence or the date of the conviction or discharge if no term of imprisonment is imposed.

ANNOTATIONS

Note: Some of the following cases were decided under the predecessor legislation but were thought to be of some assistance in applying this section.

Constitutional Considerations – The mandatory firearms prohibition under subsec. (1)(*c*) for a conviction for the production of cannabis does not violate s. 12 of the *Canadian Charter of Rights and Freedoms* as the provision has a legitimate connection to s. 7 offences pursuant to the *Controlled Drugs and Substances Act*: *R. v. Wiles* (2005), 203 C.C.C. (3d) 161 (S.C.C.).

Circumstances in which order must be made – An order was to be made under former s. 100(1) [similar to present subsec. (1)(*a*)] whether or not a firearm was used in the commission of the offence: *R. v. Savard* (1979), 55 C.C.C. (2d) 286 (Que. C.A.); *R. v. Broome* (1981), 63 C.C.C. (2d) 426 (Ont. C.A.).

Further, the order must be made even where the commission of violence is not an essential element of the offence (as in break and enter with intent to commit an indictable offence under s. 348), it being sufficient that violence occurred in a manner which was closely related to the commission of the offence: *R. v. Howard* (1981), 60 C.C.C. (2d) 344 (B.C.C.A.).

Sex with a child always involves a violent assault notwithstanding that, in this case, other than pleading with the child, the accused did not use any other form of coercion or force. No other form of violence or threat is required where a child's sexual integrity has been compromised: *R. v. Bossé* (2005), 201 C.C.C. (3d) 77 (N.B.C.A.).

The phrase "against a person" refers to a person other than the accused and thus this subsection does not apply where the offence arises out of a suicide attempt and violence was not used against any other person: *R. v. Vandermeulen* (1986), 33 C.C.C. (3d) 286 (B.C.C.A.).

In ordering a weapons prohibition, reasons should be given specifying clearly the weapons to which the prohibition extends, whether the basis of a prohibition for life is under subsec. (2)(*b*) or (3) and, if the prohibition is under subsec. (3), the court must be satisfied that the notice to the accused has been given by the Crown. The failure to provide reasons constitutes an error of law: *R. v. Friesen* (2004), 192 C.C.C. (3d) 67 (Man. C.A.).

The prohibition under subsec. (1) is mandatory, notwithstanding the prosecutor's failure to apply for an order: *R. v. Goguen* (2006), 208 C.C.C. (3d) 181 (N.B.C.A.).

Making of order where previous conviction – The mandatory prohibition is to be imposed even where the previous conviction for an offence, in the commission of which violence was used, threatened or attempted was registered prior to the proclamation of the section: *R. v. Keays* (1983), 10 C.C.C. (3d) 229 (Ont. C.A.).

Where the Crown seeks the longer prohibition for a subsequent conviction, it must give notice as required by former s. 665 [now s. 727]: *R. v. Jobb* (1988), 43 C.C.C. (3d) 476 (Sask. C.A.); *R. v. Ellis* (2001), 143 O.A.C. 43 (C.A.).

DISCRETIONARY PROHIBITION ORDER / Duration of prohibition order / Exception / Reasons / Definition of "release from imprisonment" / Application of ss. 113 to 117.

110. (1) Where a person is convicted, or discharged under section 730, of

(*a*) an offence, other than an offence referred to in any of paragraphs 109(1)(*a*) to (*c*.1), in the commission of which violence against a person was used, threatened or attempted, or

(*b*) an offence that involves, or the subject-matter of which is, a firearm, a cross-bow, a prohibited weapon, a restricted weapon, a prohibited device, ammunition, prohibited ammunition or an explosive substance and, at the time of the offence, the person was not prohibited by any order made under this Act or any other Act of Parliament from possessing any such thing,

the court that sentences the person or directs that the person be discharged, as the case may be, shall, in addition to any other punishment that may be imposed for that offence or any other condition prescribed in the order of discharge, consider whether it is desirable, in the interests of the safety of the person or of any other person, to make an order prohibiting the person from possessing any firearm, cross-bow, prohibited weapon, restricted weapon, prohibited device, ammunition, prohibited ammunition or explosive substance, or all such things, and where the court decides that it is so desirable, the court shall so order.

(2) An order made under subsection (1) against a person begins on the day on which the order is made and ends not later than ten years after the person's release from imprisonment after conviction for the offence to which the order relates or, if the person is not then imprisoned or subject to imprisonment, after the person's conviction for or discharge from the offence.

(2.1) Despite subsection (2), an order made under subsection (1) may be imposed for life or for any shorter duration if, in the commission of the offence, violence was used, threatened or attempted against

(*a*) the person's current or former intimate partner;

(*b*) a child or parent of the person or of anyone referred to in paragraph (*a*); or

(*c*) any person who resides with the person or with anyone referred to in paragraph (*a*) or (*b*).

(3) Where the court does not make an order under subsection (1), or where the court does make such an order but does not prohibit the possession of everything referred to in that subsection, the court shall include in the record a statement of the court's reasons for not doing so.

(4) In subsection (2), "release from imprisonment" means release from confinement by reason of expiration of sentence, commencement of statutory release or grant of parole.

(5) Sections 113 to 117 apply in respect of every order made under subsection (1). 1995, c. 39, ss. 139, 190(*e*); 2015, c. 27, s. 31; 2018, c. 16, s. 209.

CROSS-REFERENCES

"Intimate partner" is defined in s. 110.1. "Firearm", "explosive substance" and "weapon" are defined in s. 2. "Prohibition order", "prohibited weapon", "restricted weapon", "prohibited device", "cross-bow", "ammunition" and "prohibited ammunition" are defined in s. 84(1). Possession is defined in s. 4(3). This is one of four provisions in this part that mandate or permit the imposition of orders prohibiting the possession of weapons and other articles such as explosive substances. There are, as well, other provisions of the Code authorizing various forms of prohibition orders. Thus see: s. 109 (mandatory prohibition order upon conviction of certain offences); s. 111 (preventative prohibition order); s. 117.05 (preventative prohibition order after seizure); s. 515(4.1) (condition of bail); s. 732.1 (condition of probation); s. 742.3 (conditional sentence), ss. 810(3.1), 810.01(5), 810.2(5) (condition of recognizance (peace bond)). A prohibition order may also be made under subsecs. 51(3) and (4) of the *Youth Criminal Justice Act*.

Section 117.01 creates the offences of possessing a firearm, cross-bow, prohibited weapon, restricted weapon, prohibited device, ammunition, prohibited ammunition or explosive substance while prohibited from doing so and wilfully failing to surrender an authorization, licence or registration certificate when the person was required to surrender it by any order made under the Code. Under s. 113, the judge may lift the prohibition order for sustenance or employment purposes. Section 114 permits the court that makes a prohibition order to require the person to surrender anything the possession of which is prohibited by the order and every authorization, licence and registration certificate relating to anything the possession of which is prohibited by the order. The person must be given a reasonable time to comply with the order and during that period the offence under s. 117.01 does not apply. Under s. 115, unless the prohibition order specifies otherwise, everything the possession of which is prohibited by the order is forfeited to the Crown. However, on application under s. 117, the judge may order the return of articles to the person who is lawfully entitled to possess it provided that the owner had no reasonable grounds to believe that the thing would or might be used in the commission of the offence in respect of which the prohibition order was made. Pursuant to s. 116, every authorization, licence and registration certificate relating to anything the possession of which is prohibited by a prohibition order and issued to a person against whom the prohibition order is made is, on the commencement of the prohibition order, revoked, or amended, as the case may be, to the extent of the prohibitions in the order. Section 117.011 allows for an application to a provincial court judge for a limitation on access order against a person who is an associate of, or cohabits with, a person subject to a prohibition order.

Section 89 of the *Firearms Act* requires a court that makes, varies or revokes a prohibition order to have the chief firearms officer informed of the order or its variation or revocation.

An order made under this section falls within the definition of "sentence" in ss. 673 and 785 and therefore may be appealed as a sentence appeal under Part XXI [indictable offence] or Part XXVII [summary conviction offence], as the case may be.

SYNOPSIS

This section gives a court a discretion to impose a prohibition against possession of firearms, weapons and other articles such as explosive substances where the accused has been convicted or discharged of an offence in circumstances not covered by the mandatory order under s. 109. Unlike s. 109, which involves a blanket order, the order under this section may prohibit the person from possessing any firearm, cross-bow, prohibited weapon, restricted weapon, prohibited device, ammunition, prohibited ammunition or explosive substance, or all such things. The maximum length of the order is 10 years calculated from the date of the conviction or discharge or the date from which the person was released from confinement as defined in subsec. (4), except in the case of an order made in the circumstances described in s. 110(2.1) (violence used, threatened or attempted against an intimate partner or relation thereof), which may be imposed for life. As to other conditions that may be included in the order, see ss. 113 to 116.

The prerequisite for making the prohibition order is the determination that the order is desirable in the interests of the safety of the offender or any other person. Where the court does not make the order or does not make a blanket order, the court must include reasons in the record.

ANNOTATIONS

This provision does not require actual violence or force and could operate where violence was merely threatened. In this case, breaching a no contact term of a recognizance could constitute an implied threat of violence: *R. v. Samery* (2007), 219 C.C.C. (3d) 435 (Ont. S.C.J.).

Before a weapons prohibition is imposed under this section, there must be some evidence of a safety concern. In some cases, the nature of the offence itself will be sufficient to raise a safety concern and justify a discretionary prohibition: *R. v. Wauer* (2014), 315 C.C.C. (3d) 170 (Alta. C.A.).

Sentencing principles such as proportionality apply to weapons prohibition orders: *R. v. Levesque* (2010), 264 C.C.C. (3d) 531 (P.E.I.C.A.).

DEFINITION OF "INTIMATE PARTNER".

110.1 In sections 109 and 110, "intimate partner" includes a spouse, a common-law partner and a dating partner. 2015, c. 27, s. 32.

CROSS-REFERENCES

"Common-law partner" is defined in s. 2.

APPLICATION FOR PROHIBITION ORDER / Date for hearing and notice / Hearing of application / Where hearing may proceed *ex parte* / Prohibition order / Reasons / Application of ss. 113 to 117 / Appeal by person or Attorney General / Appeal by Attorney General / Application of Part XXVII to appeals / Definition of "provincial court judge".

111. (1) A peace officer, firearms officer or chief firearms officer may apply to a provincial court judge for an order prohibiting a person from possessing any firearm, cross-bow, prohibited weapon, restricted weapon, prohibited device, ammunition, prohibited ammunition or explosive substance, or all such things, where the peace officer, firearms officer or chief firearms officer believes on reasonable grounds that it is not desirable in the interests of the safety of the person against whom the order is sought or of any other person that the person against whom the order is sought should possess any such thing.

(2) On receipt of an application made under subsection (1), the provincial court judge shall fix a date for the hearing of the application and direct that notice of the hearing be given, in such manner as the provincial court judge may specify, to the person against whom the order is sought.

(3) Subject to subsection (4), at the hearing of an application made under subsection (1), the provincial court judge shall hear all relevant evidence presented by or on behalf of the applicant and the person against whom the order is sought.

(4) A provincial court judge may proceed *ex parte* to hear and determine an application made under subsection (1) in the absence of the person against whom the order is sought in the same circumstances as those in which a summary conviction court may, under Part XXVII, proceed with a trial in the absence of the defendant.

(5) Where, at the conclusion of a hearing of an application made under subsection (1), the provincial court judge is satisfied that the circumstances referred to in that subsection exist, the provincial court judge shall make an order prohibiting the person from possessing any firearm, cross-bow, prohibited weapon, restricted weapon, prohibited device, ammunition, prohibited ammunition or explosive substance, or all such things, for such period, not exceeding five years, as is specified in the order, beginning on the day on which the order is made.

(6) Where a provincial court judge does not make an order under subsection (1), or where a provincial court judge does make such an order but does not prohibit the possession of everything referred to in that subsection, the provincial court judge shall include in the record a statement of the court's reasons.

(7) Sections 113 to 117 apply in respect of every order made under subsection (5).

(8) Where a provincial court judge makes an order under subsection (5), the person to whom the order relates, or the Attorney General, may appeal to the superior court against the order.

(9) Where a provincial court judge does not make an order under subsection (5), the Attorney General may appeal to the superior court against the decision not to make an order.

(10) The provisions of Part XXVII, except sections 785 to 812, 816 to 819 and 829 to 838, apply in respect of an appeal made under subsection (8) or (9), with such modifications as the circumstances require and as if each reference in that Part to the appeal court were a reference to the superior court.

(11) In this section and sections 112, 117.011 and 117.012, "provincial court judge" means a provincial court judge having jurisdiction in the territorial division where the person against whom the application for an order was brought resides. 1995, c. 39, s. 139.

CROSS-REFERENCES

"Attorney General", "firearm", "explosive substance", "peace officer" and "weapon" are defined in s. 2. "Superior court", "chief firearms officer", "prohibition order", "prohibited weapon", "restricted weapon", "prohibited device", "cross-bow", "ammunition" and "prohibited ammunition" are defined in s. 84(1). "Possession" is defined in s. 4(3). This is one of four provisions in this part that mandate or permit the imposition of orders prohibiting the possession of weapons and other articles such as explosive substances. There are, as well, other provisions of the Code authorizing various forms of prohibition orders. Thus see: s. 109 [mandatory prohibition order upon conviction of certain offences]; s. 110 [discretionary prohibition order upon conviction of certain offences]; s. 117.05 [preventative prohibition order after seizure]; s. 515(4.1) [condition of bail]; s. 732.1 [condition of probation]; s. 742.3 [conditional sentence], ss. 810(3.1), 810.01(5), 810.2(5) [condition of recognizance (peace bond)]. A prohibition order is also available under s. 51 of the *Youth Criminal Justice Act*.

Section 117.01 creates the offences of possessing a firearm, cross-bow, prohibited weapon, restricted weapon, prohibited device, ammunition, prohibited ammunition or explosive substance while prohibited from doing so and wilfully failing to surrender an authorization, licence or registration certificate when the person was required to surrender it by any order made under the Code. Under s. 113, the judge may lift the prohibition order for sustenance or employment purposes. Section 114 permits the court that makes a prohibition order to require the person to surrender anything the possession of which is prohibited by the order and every authorization, licence and registration certificate relating to anything the possession of which is prohibited by the order. The person must be given a reasonable time to comply with the order and during that period the offence under s. 117.01 does not apply. Under s. 115, unless the prohibition order specifies otherwise, everything the possession of which is prohibited by the order is forfeited to the Crown. However, on application under s. 117, the judge may order the return of articles to the person who is lawfully entitled to possess it. Pursuant to s. 116, every authorization, licence and registration certificate relating to anything the possession of which is prohibited by a prohibition order and issued to a person against whom the prohibition order is made is, on the commencement of the prohibition order, revoked, or amended, as the case may be, to the extent of the prohibitions in the order. Section 117.011 allows for an application to a provincial court judge for a limitation on access order against a person who is an associate of, or cohabits with, a person subject to a prohibition order.

As to the circumstances in which the judge can proceed *ex parte*, see s. 803(2).

Section 89 of the *Firearms Act* requires a court that makes, varies or revokes a prohibition order to have the chief firearms officer informed of the order or its variation or revocation.

Under s. 112, a provincial court judge may revoke an order made under subsec. (5).

SYNOPSIS

This section allows a peace officer, firearms officer or chief firearms officer to apply to a provincial court judge for a preventative prohibition order, *i.e.*, where the person has not committed an offence that would allow or require a prohibition order under either of s. 109 or s. 110. The grounds for making the application under subsec. (1) and the making of the order under subsec. (5) are that there are reasonable grounds to believe that it is not desirable in the interests of the safety of the person against whom the order is sought or of any other person that the person against whom the order is sought should possess any firearm, cross-bow, prohibited weapon, restricted weapon, prohibited device, ammunition, prohibited ammunition or explosive substance, or all such things. The maximum period of the order is five years. Subsection (2) requires the provincial court judge to fix a date for hearing the application and the manner in which the person is to be given notice of the hearing. The judge is to hear all relevant evidence adduced by the parties and may proceed *ex parte* if the same circumstances exist that would have permitted a judge to have proceeded with a summary conviction trial in the absence of the defendant. Where the judge does not make the order requested, or does not make a blanket order prohibiting possession of all the things referred to in subsec. (1), the judge must include reasons in the record. As to other conditions that may be included in the order, see ss. 113 to 116.

The decision of the judge may be appealed by the person against whom the order was made or the Attorney General to the superior court in accordance with the summary conviction appeal procedure in Part XXVII.

ANNOTATIONS

Note: Some of the following cases were decided under the predecessor to this section but may be of assistance in applying this section.

It was held that the predecessor legislation is *intra vires* Parliament: *R. v. Motiuk* (1981), 60 C.C.C. (2d) 161, 127 D.L.R. (3d) 146 (B.C.S.C.); *R. v. Anderson* (1981), 59 C.C.C. (2d) 439 (Ont. Co. Ct.), leave to appeal refused 1 C.C.C. (3d) 267 (Ont. C.A.).

The scheme of the pre-emptive prohibition is that a peace officer, acting on reasonable grounds, may apply to a provincial court judge for an order prohibiting a particular person from possessing a firearm. The peace officer is not required to act solely on the basis of evidence that would be admissible at trial. At the subsequent hearing, the provincial court judge must be satisfied that there are reasonable grounds to believe that it is not desirable, in the interests of the safety of the person or of others, that the subject of the prohibition application should possess a firearm. The provincial court judge thus confirms the existence of the reasonable grounds that led the peace officer to launch the application. It was not intended that the judge strictly applies the rules of evidence. Rather, the judge must simply be satisfied that the peace officer had reasonable grounds to believe as he did, that is, that there was an objective basis for the reasonable grounds on which the peace officer acted. Accordingly, hearsay evidence is admissible at a firearm prohibition hearing under this section. Frailties in the evidence are a matter of weight. In considering what weight to attach to hearsay evidence, the judge should take into account the explanation, if any, for not making the best evidence available. Further, the Crown bears the burden of proof and, in considering the weight of the evidence, a judge must scrutinize the evidence to ensure that it is credible and trustworthy: *R. v. Zeolkowski*, [1989] 1 S.C.R. 1378, 50 C.C.C. (3d) 566, 69 C.R. (3d) 281 (5:0).

A judge conducting a hearing under this provision is not limited to considering only the three criteria set out in s. 5(2) of the *Firearms Act*, S.C. 1995, c. 39: *Christiansen (Re)* (2006), 208 C.C.C. (3d) 154 (B.C.C.A.).

REVOCATION OF PROHIBITION ORDER UNDER S. 111(5).

112. A provincial court judge may, on application by the person against whom an order is made under subsection 111(5), revoke the order if satisfied that the circumstances for which it was made have ceased to exist. 1995, c. 39, s. 139.

CROSS-REFERENCES

"Provincial court judge" is defined in s. 111. Section 111(5) allows a provincial court judge to make a preventative prohibition order for a period not exceeding five years where the judge is satisfied that there are reasonable grounds to believe that it is not desirable in the interests of the safety of the person against whom the order is sought or of any other person that the person against whom the order is sought should possess any firearm, cross-bow, prohibited weapon, restricted weapon, prohibited device, ammunition, prohibited ammunition or explosive substance, or all such things. Section 89 of the *Firearms Act* requires a court that makes, varies or revokes a prohibition order to have the chief firearms officer informed of the order or its variation or revocation.

LIFTING OF PROHIBITION ORDER FOR SUSTENANCE OR EMPLOYMENT / Factors / Effect of order / When order can be made / Meaning of "competent authority".

113. (1) Where a person who is or will be a person against whom a prohibition order is made establishes to the satisfaction of a competent authority that

(*a*) the person needs a firearm or restricted weapon to hunt or trap in order to sustain the person or the person's family, or

(*b*) a prohibition order against the person would constitute a virtual prohibition against employment in the only vocation open to the person,

the competent authority may, notwithstanding that the person is or will be subject to a prohibition order, make an order authorizing a chief firearms officer or the Registrar to issue, in accordance with such terms and conditions as the competent authority considers appropriate, an authorization, a licence or a registration certificate, as the case may be, to the person for sustenance or employment purposes.

(2) A competent authority may make an order under subsection (1) only after taking the following factors into account:

(*a*) the criminal record, if any, of the person;

(*b*) the nature and circumstances of the offence, if any, in respect of which the prohibition order was or will be made; and

(*c*) the safety of the person and of other persons.

(3) Where an order is made under subsection (1),

(*a*) an authorization, a licence or a registration certificate may not be denied to the person in respect of whom the order was made solely on the basis of a prohibition order against the person or the commission of an offence in respect of which a prohibition order was made against the person; and

(*b*) an authorization and a licence may, for the duration of the order, be issued to the person in respect of whom the order was made only for sustenance or employment purposes and, where the order sets out terms and conditions, only in accordance with those terms and conditions, but, for greater certainty, the

authorization or licence may also be subject to terms and conditions set by the chief firearms officer that are not inconsistent with the purpose for which it is issued and any terms and conditions set out in the order.

(4) For greater certainty, an order under subsection (1) may be made during proceedings for an order under subsection 109(1), 110(1), 111(5), 117.05(4) or 515(2), paragraph 732.1(3)(*d*) or subsection 810(3).

(5) In this section, "competent authority" means the competent authority that made or has jurisdiction to make the prohibition order. 1995, c. 39, ss. 139, 190(*f*).

CROSS-REFERENCES

"Firearm" is defined in s. 2. "Possession" is defined in s. 4(3). "Prohibition order", "restricted weapon", "Registrar", "chief firearms officer, "licence", "registration certificate" and "authorization" are defined in s. 84(1).

SYNOPSIS

This section permits the justice or judge who made or had jurisdiction to make a prohibition order to lift the prohibition order for the purposes of sustenance hunting and trapping or for employment where the prohibition order would constitute a virtual prohibition against employment in the only vocation open to the person. The entire order is not lifted, rather the Registrar and chief firearms officer are required to issue an authorization, licence or registration certificate, as the case may be, for the purposes specified in the order and on the conditions and terms specified by the court. However, the chief firearms officer may also impose terms and conditions not inconsistent with the purpose for which the authorization or licence was issued. The order may only be made after the court has taken into account the person's criminal record, the nature and circumstances of the offence, if any, that led to the prohibition order and the safety of that person or any other person. While subsec. (4) specifies "for greater certainty" that an order may be made under this section during proceedings for a prohibition order under certain specified provisions, the term "prohibition order" is broadly defined in s. 84(1), and thus this section likely applies to other weapons prohibition orders made under the Code.

REQUIREMENT TO SURRENDER.

114. A competent authority that makes a prohibition order against a person may, in the order, require the person to surrender to a peace officer, a firearms officer or a chief firearms officer

- **(*a*) any thing the possession of which is prohibited by the order that is in the possession of the person on the commencement of the order, and**
- **(*b*) every authorization, licence and registration certificate relating to any thing the possession of which is prohibited by the order that is held by the person on the commencement of the order,**

and where the competent authority does so, it shall specify in the order a reasonable period for surrendering such things and documents and during which section 117.01 does not apply to that person. 1995, c. 39, s. 139.

CROSS-REFERENCES

"Peace officer" is defined in s. 2. "Prohibition order, "firearms officer", "chief firearms officer, "licence", "registration certificate" and "authorization" are defined in s. 84(1). "Competent authority" is defined in s. 113(5). Section 117.01 creates the offences of possessing a firearm, cross-bow, prohibited weapon, restricted weapon, prohibited device, ammunition, prohibited ammunition or explosive substance while prohibited from doing so and wilfully failing to surrender an authorization, licence or registration certificate when the person was required to surrender it by any order made under the Code. A person may be prohibited from possessing weapons under several sections of the Code including: s. 109 [mandatory prohibition order upon conviction of certain offences]; s. 110 [discretionary prohibition order upon conviction of certain offences]; s. 111 [preventative prohibition order]; s. 117.05 [preventative prohibition order after seizure]; s. 515(4.1) [condition of bail]; s. 732.1 [condition of probation]; s. 742.3 [conditional sentence], ss. 810(3.1), 810.01(5), 810.2(5) [condition of recognizance (peace bond)]. A prohibition order is also available under s. 51 of the *Youth Criminal Justice Act*.

SYNOPSIS

This section allows the "competent authority", which could include a justice or judge, that makes a prohibition order to include conditions requiring the surrender of anything the possession of which is prohibited by the order and to surrender any authorization, licence or registration certificate relating to any such thing. The order is to give the person a reasonable period for surrendering such things and documents and no offence contrary to s. 117.01 is committed during that time. Prohibition order is broadly defined in s. 84(1), and thus would include not only orders made under this part but orders under ss. 515(4.1), 732.1, 810(3.1) and 810.2(5).

FORFEITURE / Disposal.

115. (1) Unless a prohibition order against a person specifies otherwise, every thing the possession of which is prohibited by the order that, on the commencement of the order, is in the possession of the person is forfeited to Her Majesty.

(1.1) Subsection (1) does not apply in respect of an order made under section 515.

(2) Every thing forfeited to Her Majesty under subsection (1) shall be disposed of or otherwise dealt with as the Attorney General directs. 1995, c. 39, s. 139; 2003, c. 8, s. 5.

CROSS-REFERENCES

"Prohibition order" is defined in s. 84(1). "Attorney General" is defined in s. 2.

ANNOTATIONS

While a term of probation made under s. 732.1(3)(*d*) of the Code was a prohibition order for the purpose of this section and s. 84, this provision did not apply as the accused could not be said to be in possession of the firearms at the commencement of the order as they were in the possession of the police. The appropriate procedure is for the Crown to seek a forfeiture order under s. 491: *Roggie v. Ontario* (2012), 293 C.C.C. (3d) 46 (Ont. C.A.).

AUTHORIZATIONS REVOKED OR AMENDED / Duration of revocation or amendment — orders under s. 115.

116. (1) Subject to subsection (2), every authorization, licence and registration certificate relating to any thing the possession of which is prohibited by a prohibition order and issued to a person against whom the prohibition order is made is, on the commencement of the prohibition order, revoked, or amended, as the case may be, to the extent of the prohibitions in the order.

(2) An authorization, a licence and a registration certificate relating to a thing the possession of which is prohibited by an order made under section 515 is revoked, or amended, as the case may be, only in respect of the period during which the order is in force. 1995, c. 39, s. 139; 2003, c. 8, s. 6.

CROSS-REFERENCES

"Authorization", "licence", "registration certificate" and "prohibition order" are defined in s. 84(1). Possession is defined in s. 4(3). Failure to surrender a licence, registration certificate or authorization that is revoked is an offence contrary to s. 114 of the *Firearms Act*.

SYNOPSIS

This section deems any authorization, licence or registration certificate relating to anything the possession of which is prohibited by a prohibition order and issued to a person against whom the prohibition order is made, is to be revoked, or amended, as the case may be, to the extent of the prohibitions in the order.

RETURN TO OWNER.

117. Where the competent authority that makes a prohibition order or that would have had jurisdiction to make the order is, on application for an order under this section, satisfied that a person, other than the person against whom a prohibition order was or will be made,

- **(*a*) is the owner of any thing that is or may be forfeited to Her Majesty under subsection 115(1) and is lawfully entitled to possess it, and**
- **(*b*) in the case of a prohibition order under subsection 109(1) or 110(1), had no reasonable grounds to believe that the thing would or might be used in the commission of the offence in respect of which the prohibition order was made,**

the competent authority shall order that the thing be returned to the owner or the proceeds of any sale of the thing be paid to that owner or, if the thing was destroyed, that an amount equal to the value of the thing be paid to the owner. 1995, c. 39, s. 139.

CROSS-REFERENCES

"Prohibition order" is defined in s. 84(1).

SYNOPSIS

The true owner of articles subject to a prohibition order may apply to a judge or justice who made a prohibition order, or who would have had jurisdiction to make the order for return of the articles. The applicant cannot be the person against whom the order was made and must show that he or she is the owner and is lawfully entitled to possess it. Further, in the case of the prohibition orders made under ss. 109 and 110 as a result of the commission of an offence, the applicant must show that he or she had no reasonable grounds to believe that the article would or might be used in the commission of the offence. If the article has been sold, the owner is entitled to the proceeds of the sale. If it has been destroyed, the owner is entitled to an amount equal to its value.

POSSESSION CONTRARY TO ORDER / Failure to surrender authorization, etc. / Punishment / Exception.

117.01 (1) Subject to subsection (4), every person commits an offence who possesses a firearm, a cross-bow, a prohibited weapon, a restricted weapon, a prohibited device, any ammunition, any prohibited ammunition or an explosive substance while the person is prohibited from doing so by any order made under this Act or any other Act of Parliament.

(2) Every person commits an offence who wilfully fails to surrender to a peace officer, a firearms officer or a chief firearms officer any authorization, licence or registration certificate held by the person when the person is required to do so by any order made under this Act or any other Act of Parliament.

(3) Every person who commits an offence under subsection (1) or (2)

- **(*a*) is guilty of an indictable offence and liable to imprisonment for a term not exceeding ten years; or**
- **(*b*) is guilty of an offence punishable on summary conviction.**

(4) Subsection (1) does not apply to a person who possessed a firearm in accordance with an authorization or licence issued to the person as the result of an order made under subsection 113(1). 1995, c. 39, s. 139.

CROSS-REFERENCES

"Firearm", "explosive substance" and "peace officer" are defined in s. 2. "Possession" is defined in s. 4(3). "Prohibited weapon", "restricted weapon", "prohibited device", "prohibited ammunition", "cross-bow", "firearms officer", "chief firearms officer, "licence", "registration certificate" and "authorization" are defined in s. 84(1). "Provincial court judge" is defined in s. 2. An accused charged with this offence may elect the mode of trial pursuant to s. 536(2) where the Crown proceeds by way of indictment. Where the prosecution elects to proceed by way of summary conviction then the trial of this offence is conducted by a summary conviction court pursuant to Part XXVII. The punishment for the offence is then as set out in s. 787 and the limitation period is set out in s. 786(2). Weapons that are the subject-matter of the offence must be forfeited pursuant to s. 491. An accused convicted of the offence under subsec. (2) is subject to the mandatory prohibition order under s. 109.

A person may be prohibited from possessing weapons under several sections of the Code including: s. 109 [mandatory prohibition order upon conviction of certain offences]; s. 110 [discretionary prohibition order upon conviction of certain offences]; s. 111 [preventative prohibition order]; s. 117.05 [preventative prohibition order after seizure]; s. 515(4.1) [condition of bail]; s. 732.1 [condition of probation]; s. 742.3 [conditional sentence]; and ss. 810(3.1), 810.01(5), 810.2(5) [condition of recognizance (peace bond)]. A prohibition order is also available under s. 51 of the *Youth Criminal Justice Act*. Section 114 permits the court that makes a prohibition order to require the person to surrender anything the possession of which is prohibited by the order and every authorization, licence and registration certificate relating to anything the possession of which is prohibited by the order. The person must be given a reasonable time to comply with the order and during that period this section does not apply. Section 113 allows the court to lift the prohibition order for sustenance or employment purposes. The related offence of failing to surrender a licence, authorization or registration certificate that has been revoked is found in s. 114 of the *Firearms Act*.

SYNOPSIS

This section creates two offences to deal with persons who fail to comply with the terms of a prohibition order made under the Code or other federal legislation. Subsection (1) makes it an offence to possess any firearm, cross-bow, prohibited weapon, restricted weapon, prohibited device, ammunition, prohibited ammunition or explosive substance while prohibited from doing so. No offence is committed under this subsection if the person has possession of a firearm in accordance with an authorization or licence issued pursuant to an order made under s. 113 for sustenance or employment purposes. Subsection (2) makes it an offence to wilfully fail to surrender an authorization, licence or registration certificate when the person was required to surrender it by any order made under the Code (such as s. 114) or other federal legislation.

ANNOTATIONS

In the absence of evidence of present operability through firing, by virtue of missing or broken parts or modifications, expert evidence is required to establish that the gun is a firearm: *R. v. Stacey* (2009), 249 C.C.C. (3d) 389, 292 Nfld. & P.E.I.R. 140 (Nfld. & Lab. C.A.).

Limitations on Access

APPLICATION FOR ORDER / Date for hearing and notice / Hearing of application / Where hearing may proceed *ex parte* / Order / Terms and conditions / Appeal by person or Attorney General / Appeal by Attorney General / Application of Part XXVII to appeals.

117.011 (1) A peace officer, firearms officer or chief firearms officer may apply to a provincial court judge for an order under this section where the peace officer, firearms officer or chief firearms officer believes on reasonable grounds that

(*a*) the person against whom the order is sought cohabits with, or is an associate of, another person who is prohibited by any order made under this Act or any other Act of Parliament from possessing any firearm, cross-bow, prohibited weapon, restricted weapon, prohibited device, ammunition, prohibited ammunition or explosive substance, or all such things; and

(*b*) the other person would or might have access to any such thing that is in the possession of the person against whom the order is sought.

(2) On receipt of an application made under subsection (1), the provincial court judge shall fix a date for the hearing of the application and direct that notice of the hearing be given, in such manner as the provincial court judge may specify, to the person against whom the order is sought.

(3) Subject to subsection (4), at the hearing of an application made under subsection (1), the provincial court judge shall hear all relevant evidence presented by or on behalf of the applicant and the person against whom the order is sought.

(4) A provincial court judge may proceed *ex parte* to hear and determine an application made under subsection (1) in the absence of the person against whom the order is sought in the same circumstances as those in which a summary conviction court may, under Part XXVII, proceed with a trial in the absence of the defendant.

(5) Where, at the conclusion of a hearing of an application made under subsection (1), the provincial court judge is satisfied that the circumstances referred to in that subsection exist, the provincial court judge shall make an order in respect of the person against whom the order was sought imposing such terms and conditions on the person's use and possession of anything referred to in subsection (1) as the provincial court judge considers appropriate.

(6) In determining terms and conditions under subsection (5), the provincial court judge shall impose terms and conditions that are the least intrusive as possible, bearing in mind the purpose of the order.

(7) Where a provincial court judge makes an order under subsection (5), the person to whom the order relates, or the Attorney General, may appeal to the superior court against the order.

(8) Where a provincial court judge does not make an order under subsection (5), the Attorney General may appeal to the superior court against the decision not to make an order.

(9) The provisions of Part XXVII, except sections 785 to 812, 816 to 819 and 829 to 838, apply in respect of an appeal made under subsection (7) or (8), with such modifications as the circumstances require and as if each reference in that Part to the appeal court were a reference to the superior court. 1995, c. 39, s. 139.

CROSS-REFERENCES

"Attorney General", "firearm", "explosive substance", "peace officer" and "weapon" are defined in s. 2. "Superior court", "chief firearms officer", "prohibition order", "prohibited weapon", "restricted weapon", "prohibited device", "cross-bow", "ammunition" and "prohibited ammunition" are defined in s. 84(1). Possession is defined in s. 4(3). This section should be read with the provisions of the Code that permit a court to make a prohibition order. Thus see: s. 109 [mandatory prohibition order upon conviction of certain offences]; s. 110 [discretionary prohibition order upon conviction of certain offences]; s. 111 [preventative prohibition order]; s. 117.05 [preventative prohibition order after seizure]; s. 515(4.1) [condition of bail]; s. 732.1 [condition of probation]; s. 742.3 [conditional sentence]; and ss. 810(3.1), 810.01(5), 810.2(5) [condition of recognizance (peace bond)]. A prohibition order is also available under s. 51 of the *Youth Criminal Justice Act*.

Under s. 117.012, a provincial court judge may revoke an order made under subsec. (5).

SYNOPSIS

This section allows a peace officer, firearms officer or chief firearms officer to apply to a provincial court judge for a limitation on access order, *i.e.*, where the respondent cohabits or associates with a person who is subject to a prohibition order. The grounds for making the application under subsec. (1) and the making of the order under subsec. (5) are that there are reasonable grounds to believe that the person against whom the order is sought, cohabits with, or is an associate of, another person who is prohibited by any order made under the Code or any other Act of Parliament from possessing any firearm, cross-bow, prohibited weapon, restricted weapon, prohibited device, ammunition, prohibited ammunition or explosive substance, or all such things, and that the other person would or might have access to any such thing that is in the possession of the person against whom the order is sought. Subsection (2) requires the provincial court judge to fix a date for hearing the application and the manner in which the person is to be given notice of the hearing. The judge is to hear all relevant evidence adduced by the parties and may proceed *ex parte* if the same circumstances exist that would have permitted a judge to have proceeded with a summary conviction trial in the absence of the defendant.

If the judge decides to make the order, he or she shall impose terms and conditions on the respondent's use and possession of his weapons and other things referred to in subsec. (1). The judge is required by subsec. (6) to impose the least intrusive terms and conditions.

The decision of the judge may be appealed by the person against whom the order was made, or by the Attorney General, to the superior court in accordance with the summary conviction appeal procedure in Part XXVII.

REVOCATION OF ORDER UNDER S. 117.011.

117.012 A provincial court judge may, on application by the person against whom an order is made under subsection 117.011(5), revoke the order if satisfied that the circumstances for which it was made have ceased to exist. 1995, c. 39, s. 139.

CROSS-REFERENCES

"Provincial court judge" is defined in s. 111.

SYNOPSIS

This section allows a person who has been the subject of a limitation on access order to apply to have the order revoked. The judge may revoke the order if the circumstances have changed, in that the circumstances for which the order was originally made under s. 117.011 have ceased to exist. This is not an appeal section. An appeal of s. 117.011 must be taken to the superior court in accordance with s. 117.011(7).

Search and Seizure

SEARCH AND SEIZURE WITHOUT WARRANT WHERE OFFENCE COMMITTED / Disposition of seized things.

117.02 (1) Where a peace officer believes on reasonable grounds

(a) that a weapon, an imitation firearm, a prohibited device, any ammunition, any prohibited ammunition or an explosive substance was used in the commission of an offence, or

(b) that an offence is being committed, or has been committed, under any provision of this Act that involves, or the subject-matter of which is, a firearm, an imitation firearm, a cross-bow, a prohibited weapon, a restricted weapon, a prohibited device, ammunition, prohibited ammunition or an explosive substance,

and evidence of the offence is likely to be found on a person, in a vehicle or in any place or premises other than a dwelling-house, the peace officer may, where the conditions for obtaining a warrant exist but, by reason of exigent circumstances, it would not be practicable to obtain a warrant, search, without warrant, the person, vehicle, place or premises, and seize any thing by means of or in relation to which that peace officer believes on reasonable grounds the offence is being committed or has been committed.

(2) Any thing seized pursuant to subsection (1) shall be dealt with in accordance with sections 490 and 491. 1995, c. 39, s. 139.

CROSS-REFERENCES

The terms "imitation firearm", "prohibited weapon", "restricted weapon", "prohibited device", "cross-bow", "ammunition" and "prohibited ammunition" are defined in s. 84(1). "Dwelling house", "peace officer", "explosive substance", "weapon" and "firearm" are defined in s. 2. Search of a dwelling house would have to be pursuant to a warrant as authorized by s. 487 or s. 487.1. Section 117.04 provides for the issuance of a search warrant or for a warrantless search where there are grounds for believing that it is not desirable in the interests of safety for a person to have possession, custody or control of a firearm, offensive weapon, ammunition or explosive substance. Seizure of weapons and other regulated articles is also authorized in certain circumstances under s. 117.03. Reference should also be made to s. 8 of the *Canadian Charter of Rights and Freedoms*. A person searched pursuant to this section would be detained within the meaning of s. 10 of the Charter and, therefore, see the notes under that section. Use of force in enforcement of the law is principally dealt with in s. 25. Obstructing a peace officer in the execution of his or her duty is an offence under s. 129 and assaulting a peace officer in the execution of his or her duty is an offence under s. 270.

SYNOPSIS

This section authorizes a search without warrant of persons, vehicles or places, other than dwelling houses, in two different circumstances where the peace officer has reasonable grounds to believe: subsec. (1)(*a*), that a weapon, an imitation firearm, a prohibited device, any ammunition, any prohibited ammunition or an explosive substance was used in the commission of an offence; and subsec. (1)(*b*), an offence is being committed, or has been committed under the Code that involves, or the subject-matter of which is, a firearm, an imitation firearm, a cross-bow, a prohibited weapon, a restricted weapon, a prohibited device, ammunition, prohibited ammunition or an explosive substance. This section applies if the peace officer has reasonable grounds to believe that evidence of the offence is likely to be found but exigent circumstances make the obtaining of a warrant impracticable.

Subsection (2) states that the usual procedures making a return before a justice after the search and the restitution or forfeiture of property seized apply to this type of search.

ANNOTATIONS

This provision does not require reasonable grounds to make an arrest but merely requires a reasonable belief that an offence has been committed and that the evidence is likely to be found in the search: *R. v. V. (T.A.)* (2001), 48 C.R. (5th) 366, (Alta. C.A.).

SEIZURE ON FAILURE TO PRODUCE AUTHORIZATION / Return of seized thing on production of authorization / Forfeiture of seized thing.

117.03 (1) Despite section 117.02, a peace officer who finds

(*a*) a person in possession of a prohibited firearm, a restricted firearm or a non-restricted firearm who fails, on demand, to produce, for inspection by the peace officer, an authorization or a licence under which the person may lawfully possess the firearm and, in the case of a prohibited firearm or a restricted firearm, a registration certificate for it, or

(*b*) a person in possession of a prohibited weapon, a restricted weapon, a prohibited device or any prohibited ammunition who fails, on demand, to produce, for inspection by the peace officer, an authorization or a licence under which the person may lawfully possess it,

may seize the firearm, prohibited weapon, restricted weapon, prohibited device or prohibited ammunition unless its possession by the person in the circumstances in which it is found is authorized by any provision of this Part, or the person is under the direct and immediate supervision of another person who may lawfully possess it.

(2) If a person from whom any thing is seized under subsection (1) claims the thing within 14 days after the seizure and produces for inspection by the peace officer by whom it was seized, or any other peace officer having custody of it,

(*a*) a licence under which the person is lawfully entitled to possess it, and

(*b*) in the case of a prohibited firearm or a restricted firearm, an authorization and registration certificate for it,

the thing shall without delay be returned to that person.

(3) Where any thing seized pursuant to subsection (1) is not claimed and returned as and when provided by subsection (2), a peace officer shall forthwith take the thing before a provincial court judge, who may, after affording the person from whom it was seized or its owner, if known, an opportunity to establish that the person is lawfully entitled to possess it, declare it to be forefeited to Her Majesty, to be disposed of or otherwise dealt with as the Attorney General directs. 1995, c. 39, s. 139; 2012, c. 6, s. 8; 2015, c. 27, s. 33.

CROSS-REFERENCES

"Attorney General", "firearm", "provincial court judge" and "peace officer" are defined in s. 2. "Possession" is defined in s. 4(3). "Authorization", "licence", "registration certificate", "restricted firearm", "prohibited firearm", "non-restricted firearm", "prohibited weapon", "restricted weapon", "prohibited device" and "prohibited ammunition" are defined in s. 84(1). This section deals only with seizure. Other provisions under this part and in the Code, as well as the common law, provide for the search of persons and places. See, in particular, s. 117.02, which provides for a warrantless search and seizure power. As well, s. 117.04 provides for the issuance of a search warrant or for a warrantless search where there are grounds for believing that it is not desirable in the interests of safety for a person to have possession, custody or control of a weapon and other articles. Reference should also be made to s. 8 of the *Canadian Charter of Rights and Freedoms.*

SYNOPSIS

This provision permits the warrantless seizure of certain types of weapons, firearms and other regulated items where the person fails to produce the authorization, licence or registration certificate that allows the person to lawfully possess the article upon demand, unless possession of the article in the circumstances in which it is found is authorized under this part, or the person is under the direct and immediate supervision of another person who may lawfully possess it. Subsection (2) requires the return of the article if the requisite authorization, licence or registration certificate is produced within 14 days after the seizure.

If the weapon or firearm is not returned pursuant to subsec. (2), the police shall bring the article to a provincial court judge for forfeiture. The person from whom the article is seized, or the owner of the weapon, has the opportunity to establish that he or she had lawful possession of the weapon.

APPLICATION FOR WARRANT TO SEARCH AND SEIZE / Search and seizure without warrant / Return to justice / Authorizations, etc., revoked.

117.04 (1) Where, pursuant to an application made by a peace officer with respect to any person, a justice is satisfied by information on oath that there are reasonable grounds to believe that the person possesses a weapon, a prohibited device, ammunition, prohibited ammunition or an explosive substance in a building, receptacle or place and that it is not desirable in the interests of the safety of the person, or of any other person, for the person to possess the weapon, prohibited device, ammunition, prohibited ammunition or explosive substance, the justice may issue a warrant authorizing a peace officer to search the building, receptacle or place and seize any such thing, and any authorization, licence or registration certificate relating to any such thing, that is held by or in the possession of the person.

(2) Where, with respect to any person, a peace officer is satisfied that there are reasonable grounds to believe that it is not desirable, in the interests of the safety of the person or any other person, for the person to possess any weapon, prohibited device, ammunition, prohibited ammunition or explosive substance, the peace officer may, where the grounds for obtaining a warrant under subsection (1) exist but, by reason of a possible danger to the safety of that person or any other person, it would not be practicable to obtain a warrant, search for and seize any such thing, and any authorization, licence or registration certificate relating to any such thing, that is held by or in the possession of the person.

(3) A peace officer who executes a warrant referred to in subsection (1) or who conducts a search without a warrant under subsection (2) shall forthwith make a return to the justice who issued the warrant or, if no warrant was issued, to a justice who might otherwise have issued a warrant, showing

(*a*) in the case of an execution of a warrant, the things or documents, if any, seized and the date of execution of the warrant; and

(*b*) in the case of a search conducted without a warrant, the grounds on which it was concluded that the peace officer was entitled to conduct the search, and the things or documents, if any, seized.

(4) Where a peace officer who seizes any thing under subsection (1) or (2) is unable at the time of the seizure to seize an authorization or a licence under which the person from whom the thing was seized may possess the thing and, in the case of a seized firearm, a registration certificate for the firearm, every authorization, licence and registration certificate held by the person is, as at the time of the seizure, revoked. 1995, c. 39, s. 139; 2004, c. 12, s. 3.

CROSS-REFERENCES

"Firearm", "explosive substance", "justice", "weapon" and "peace officer" are defined in s. 2. "Possession" is defined in s. 4(3). "Prohibited device", "ammunition", "prohibited ammunition", "licence", "registration certificate" and "authorization" are defined in s. 84(1). As to other cross-references respecting seizure of weapons and other regulated articles, see s. 117.02. Failing to surrender a licence, authorization or registration certificate that has been revoked is an offence under s. 114 of the *Firearms Act*. Application for the disposition of the seized things is made under s. 117.05. If no application is made, the things are dealt with under s. 117.06.

SYNOPSIS

This section deals primarily with the issuance of a warrant to seize firearms, etc., and the procedure for the disposition of the things so seized. Subsection (1) permits a peace officer to make an application to a justice for a warrant to search for and seize any weapon, prohibited device, ammunition, prohibited ammunition or explosive substance, and any authorization, licence or registration certificate relating to any such thing that is held by or in the possession of the person. It must be shown that there are reasonable grounds to believe that the weapon, prohibited device, ammunition, prohibited ammunition or explosive substance is in the place to be searched and that it is against the interests of the safety of the person in possession, control or custody of the weapons, etc., or any other person, for such possession to continue. Subsection (2) permits a warrantless search and seizure by a peace officer in the same circumstances as subsec. (1), if it is impractical, for reasons of safety, to obtain a warrant.

Subsection (3) requires a return to the justice after a seizure is made under either subsec. (1) or (2). If the search is made without warrant, the officer must also set out the grounds upon which the search was made and why the seizure of the objects is justified. Subsection (4) deems any licence, authorization and registration certificate relating to seized articles and which could not be seized at the time of the search to be revoked.

ANNOTATIONS

Note: The following case was decided under the predecessor legislation but may be of assistance in applying this provisions.

Subsection (1) – The bare, unsupported allegation that the persons were members of a motorcycle gang shown to be involved in violent criminal activity was not a sufficient basis for the issuance of a search warrant under this section. On the other hand, it may be that if it were shown that the persons wore the gang "colours" or insignia and thus were identified with the gang then there would be a basis for issuing the warrant: *R. v. Conrad* (1989), 51 C.C.C. (3d) 311, 72 C.R. (3d) 364 (Alta. C.A.).

Subsection (2) – It was impracticable to obtain a warrant because of a possible danger to the safety of the accused, notwithstanding that she was detained in a psychiatric facility under the authority of a Form 1. The accused could have been released from the hospital at any time. The police are not required to speculate upon the timing of the release from hospital before seizing the firearms without a warrant: *R. v. Peacock-McDonald* (2007), 218 C.C.C. (3d) 257, 46 C.R. (6th) 163 (Ont. C.A.).

APPLICATION FOR DISPOSITION / *Ex parte* hearing / Hearing of application / Forfeiture and prohibition order on finding / Reasons / Application of ss. 113 to 117 / Appeal by person / Appeal by Attorney General / Application of part XXVII to appeals.

117.05 (1) Where any thing or document has been seized under subsection 117.04(1) or (2), the justice who issued the warrant authorizing the seizure or, if no warrant was issued, a justice who might otherwise have issued a warrant, shall, on application for an order for the disposition of the thing or document so seized made by a peace officer within thirty days after the date of execution of the warrant or of the seizure without a warrant, as the case may be, fix a date for the hearing of the application and direct that notice of the hearing be given to such persons or in such manner as the justice may specify.

(2) A justice may proceed *ex parte* to hear and determine an application made under subsection (1) in the absence of the person from whom the thing or document was seized in the same circumstances as those in which a summary conviction court may, under Part XXVII, proceed with a trial in the absence of the defendant.

(3) At the hearing of an application made under subsection (1), the justice shall hear all relevant evidence, including evidence respecting the value of the thing in respect of which the application was made.

(4) Where, following the hearing of an application made under subsection (1), the justice finds that it is not desirable in the interests of the safety of the person from

whom the thing was seized or of any other person that the person should possess any weapon, prohibited device, ammunition, prohibited ammunition and explosive substance, or any such thing, the justice shall

(*a*) order that any thing seized be forfeited to Her Majesty or be otherwise disposed of; and

(*b*) where the justice is satisfied that the circumstances warrant such an action, order that the possession by that person of any weapon, prohibited device, ammunition, prohibited ammunition and explosive substance, or of any such thing, be prohibited during any period, not exceeding five years, that is specified in the order, beginning on the making of the order.

(5) Where a justice does not make an order under subsection (4), or where a justice does make such an order but does not prohibit the possession of all of the things referred to in that subsection, the justice shall include in the record a statement of the justice's reasons.

(6) Sections 113 to 117 apply in respect of every order made under subsection (4).

(7) Where a justice makes an order under subsection (4) in respect of a person, or in respect of any thing that was seized from a person, the person may appeal to the superior court against the order.

(8) Where a justice does not make a finding as described in subsection (4) following the hearing of an application under subsection (1), or makes the finding but does not make an order to the effect described in paragraph (4)(*b*), the Attorney General may appeal to the superior court against the failure to make the finding or to make an order to the effect so described.

(9) The provisions of Part XXVII, except sections 785 to 812, 816 to 819 and 829 to 838, apply in respect of an appeal made under subsection (7) or (8) with such modifications as the circumstances require and as if each reference in that Part to the appeal court were a reference to the superior court. 1995, c. 39, s. 139.

CROSS-REFERENCES

"Justice", "peace officer", "weapon", "explosive substance" and "Attorney General" are defined in s. 2. "Superior court", "prohibited device", "ammunition" and "prohibited ammunition" are defined in s. 84(1).

This is one of several provisions in this part and in the Code that authorize the making of a prohibition order. Thus see: s. 109 [mandatory prohibition order upon conviction of certain offences]; s. 110 [discretionary prohibition order upon conviction of certain offences]; s. 111 [preventative prohibition order]; s. 515(4.1) [condition of bail]; s. 732.1 [condition of probation]; s. 742.3 [conditional sentence]; and ss. 810(3.1), 810.01(5), 810.2(5) [condition of recognizance (peace bond)]. A prohibition order is also available under s. 51 of the *Youth Criminal Justice Act*.

Section 117.01 creates the offences of possessing a firearm, cross-bow, prohibited weapon, restricted weapon, prohibited device, ammunition, prohibited ammunition or explosive substance while prohibited from doing so and wilfully failing to surrender an authorization, licence or registration certificate when the person was required to surrender it by any order made under the Code. Under s. 113, the judge may lift the prohibition order for sustenance or employment purposes. Section 114 permits the court that makes a prohibition order to require the person to surrender anything the possession of which is prohibited by the order and every authorization, licence and registration certificate relating to anything the possession of which is prohibited by the order. The person must be given a reasonable time to comply with the order and during that period the offence under s. 117.01 does not apply. Under s. 115, unless the prohibition order specifies otherwise, everything the possession of which is prohibited by the order is forfeited to the Crown. However, on application under s. 117, the judge may order the return of articles to the person who is lawfully entitled to possess it. Pursuant to s. 116, every authorization, licence and registration certificate relating to anything the possession of which is prohibited by a prohibition order and issued to a person against whom the prohibition order is made is, on the commencement of the prohibition order, revoked, or amended, as the case may be, to the extent of the prohibitions in the order. Section 117.011 allows for an application to a provincial court judge for a limitation on access order against a person who is an associate of, or cohabits with, a person subject to a prohibition order.

Section 89 of the *Firearms Act* requires a court that makes, varies or revokes a prohibition order to have the chief firearms officer informed of the order or its variation or revocation.

This section sets out the procedure for disposition of items seized for public safety concerns under s. 117.04. Where no application is made under this section or the justice does not find that the seized things should be forfeited, they are dealt with in accordance with s. 117.06. As to the circumstances in which the judge can proceed *ex parte*, see s. 803(2).

SYNOPSIS

This section sets out the procedure for dealing with things seized either with or without warrant for public safety reasons under s. 117.04. The section contemplates two types of orders based on a finding that it is not desirable in the interests of safety that the person should possess any weapon, prohibited device, ammunition, prohibited ammunition or explosive substance, namely: subsec. (4)(*a*), forfeiture of the things seized; and subsec. (4)(*b*), an order prohibiting the person from possessing any weapon, prohibited device, ammunition, prohibited ammunition or explosive substance. The peace officer is required to make an application for an order under this section within 30 days of the seizure. The justice will then fix a date for the hearing and direct notice be given to persons and in the manner as the justice specifies. The judge is to hear all relevant evidence adduced by the parties and may proceed *ex parte* if the same circumstances exist that would have permitted a judge to have proceeded with a summary conviction trial in the absence of the defendant. Where the justice does not make the order requested, or does not make a blanket order prohibiting possession of all the things referred to in subsec. (4), the justice must include reasons in the record. The maximum period of the prohibition order is five years. As to other conditions that may be included in the order, see ss. 113 to 116.

The decision of the justice may be appealed by the person against whom the order was made or the Attorney General to the superior court in accordance with the summary conviction appeal procedure in Part XXVII.

ANNOTATIONS

It was held, considering the predecessor to this section [former s. 103(4)] that the warrant having been quashed, it was not open to the Crown to proceed with a disposition hearing and the firearms must be returned to their owners: *R. v. Merchant*, (1991), 64 C.C.C. (3d) 316 (Alta. C.A.).

As to the conduct of the hearing, see *R. v. Zeolkowski*, [1989] 1 S.C.R. 1378, 50 C.C.C. (3d) 566, noted under s. 111.

The public safety assessment under subsec. (4) is to be made from the perspective of the present day, not the time of the events giving rise to the application: *R. v. Douglas* (2013), 304 C.C.C. (3d) 318 (Ont. C.J.).

WHERE NO FINDING OR APPLICATION / Restoration of authorizations.

117.06 (1) Any thing or document seized pursuant to subsection 117.04(1) or (2) shall be returned to the person from whom it was seized if

- **(*a*) no application is made under subsection 117.05(1) within thirty days after the date of execution of the warrant or of the seizure without a warrant, as the case may be; or**
- **(*b*) an application is made under subsection 117.05(1) within the period referred to in paragraph (*a*), and the justice does not make a finding as described in subsection 117.05(4).**

(2) Where, pursuant to subsection (1), any thing is returned to the person from whom it was seized and an authorization, a licence or a registration certificate, as the case may be, is revoked pursuant to subsection 117.04(4), the justice referred to in paragraph (1)(*b*) may order that the revocation be reversed and that the authorization, licence or registration certificate be restored. 1995, c. 39, s. 139.

CROSS-REFERENCES

"Authorization", "licence" and "registration certificate" are defined in s. 84(1).

SYNOPSIS

Where no application is made under s. 117.05 following a seizure under s. 117.04, the things or documents are to be returned to the person from whom they were seized. They are also to be returned if an application is made but the judge does not find that it is not desirable in the interests of the safety of the person from whom the thing was seized or of any other person that the person should possess any weapon, prohibited device, ammunition, prohibited ammunition and explosive substance, or any such thing. In the latter case, the judge may also reverse the revocation of any licence, authorization or registration certificate and order that the documents be restored.

Exempted Persons

PUBLIC OFFICERS / Definition of "public officer".

117.07 (1) Notwithstanding any other provision of this Act, but subject to section 117.1, no public officer is guilty of an offence under this Act or the *Firearms Act* by reason only that the public officer

(*a*) possesses a firearm, a prohibited weapon, a restricted weapon, a prohibited device, any prohibited ammunition or an explosive substance in the course of or for the purpose of the public officer's duties or employment;

(*b*) manufactures or transfers, or offers to manufacture or transfer, a firearm, a prohibited weapon, a restricted weapon, a prohibited device, any ammunition or any prohibited ammunition in the course of the public officer's duties or employment;

(*c*) exports or imports a firearm, a prohibited weapon, a restricted weapon, a prohibited device or any prohibited ammunition in the course of the public officer's duties or employment;

(*d*) exports or imports a component or part designed exclusively for use in the manufacture of or assembly into an automatic firearm in the course of the public officer's duties or employment;

(*e*) in the course of the public officer's duties or employment, alters a firearm so that it is capable of, or manufactures or assembles any firearm with intent to produce a firearm that is capable of, discharging projectiles in rapid succession during one pressure of the trigger;

(*f*) fails to report the loss, theft or finding of any firearm, prohibited weapon, restricted weapon, prohibited device, ammunition, prohibited ammunition or explosive substance that occurs in the course of the public officer's duties or employment or the destruction of any such thing in the course of the public officer's duties or employment; or

(*g*) alters a serial number on a firearm in the course of the public officer's duties or employment.

(2) In this section, "public officer" means

(*a*) a peace officer;

(*b*) a member of the Canadian Forces or of the armed forces of a state other than Canada who is attached or seconded to any of the Canadian forces;

(*c*) an operator of a museum established by the Chief of the Defence Staff or a person employed in any such museum;

(*d*) a member of a cadet organization under the control and supervision of the Canadian Forces;

(*e*) a person training to become a police officer or a peace officer under the control and supervision of

(i) a police force, or

(ii) a police academy or similar institution designated by the Attorney General of Canada or the lieutenant governor in council of a province;

(*f*) a member of a visiting force, within the meaning of section 2 of the *Visiting Forces Act*, who is authorized under paragraph 14(*a*) of that Act to possess and carry explosives, ammunition and firearms;

(*g*) a person, or member of a class of persons, employed in the federal public administration or by the government of a province or municipality who is prescribed to be a public officer; or

(*h*) the Commissioner of Firearms, the Registrar, a chief firearms officer, any firearms officer and any person designated under section 100 of the *Firearms Act*. 1995, c. 39, s. 139; 2003, c. 8, s. 7; c. 22, s. 224(*z*.23).

CROSS-REFERENCES

"Peace officer", "Canadian forces", "firearm" and "weapon" are defined in s. 2. "Possession" is defined in s. 4(3). "Prohibited weapon", "restricted weapon", "prohibited device", "ammunition", "prohibited ammunition", "import", "export", "transfer", "automatic firearm", "chief firearms officer" and "firearms officer" are defined in s. 84(1).

Pursuant to s. 117.1, the exemption in this section does not apply where the person is subject to a prohibition order and the person acts contrary to the order or to an authorization or a licence issued under the authority of a sustenance or hunting order made under s. 113. Section 117.08 exempts persons who supply the weapons and other regulated items to police forces, the Canadian Forces and visiting forces.

SYNOPSIS

This section acts as an exception to liability otherwise triggered by the offences under the Code or the *Firearms Act*. Subsections (1) and (2) exempt wide categories of law enforcement and armed forces personnel acting in the course of their duties or employment.

Note: Section 117.071 enacted, to come after s. 117.07, 2017, c. 27, s. 61 (to come into force by order of the Governor in Council):

Preclearance officers

117.071 Despite any other provision of this Act, but subject to section 117.1, no "preclearance officer", as defined in section 5 of the *Preclearance Act, 2016*, is guilty of an offence under this Act or the *Firearms Act* by reason only that the preclearance officer

(*a*) possesses a firearm, a prohibited weapon, a restricted weapon, a prohibited device or any prohibited ammunition in the course of or for the purpose of their duties or employment;

(*b*) transfers or offers to transfer a firearm, a prohibited weapon, a restricted weapon, a prohibited device, any ammunition or any prohibited ammunition in the course of their duties or employment;

(*c*) exports or imports a firearm, a prohibited weapon, a restricted weapon, a prohibited device or any prohibited ammunition in the course of their duties or employment; or

(*d*) fails to report the loss, theft or finding of any firearm, prohibited weapon, restricted weapon, prohibited device, ammunition, prohibited ammunition or explosive substance that occurs in the course of their duties or employment or the destruction of any such thing in the course of their duties or employment.

REGULATIONS PRESCRIBING PUBLIC OFFICERS

1. (1) A member of any of the following classes of persons, if employed in the public service of Canada or by the government of a province or municipality, is a public officer for the purposes of paragraph 117.07(2)(*g*) of the *Criminal Code*:

(*a*) employees who are responsible for the examination, inventory, storage, maintenance or transportation of court exhibits and evidence;

(*b*) employees of police forces or other public service agencies who are responsible for the acquisition, examination, inventory, storage, maintenance, issuance or transportation of firearms, prohibited weapons, restricted weapons, prohibited devices, prohibited ammunition or explosive substances;

(*c*) technicians, laboratory analysts and scientists who work at forensic or research laboratories;

(*d*) armourers and firearms instructors who work at police academies or similar institutions designated under subparagraph 117.07(2)(*e*)(ii) of the *Criminal Code*, or are employed by a federal or provincial department of natural resources, fisheries, wildlife, conservation or the environment, or by Revenue Canada;

(*e*) park wardens and other employees of a federal or provincial department who are responsible for the enforcement of laws and regulations dealing with natural resources, fisheries, wildlife, conservation or the environment;

(*f*) immigration officers;

(*g*) security personnel employed by the House of Commons or the Senate or by the Service, as defined in section 79.51 of the *Parliament of Canada Act*; and

(*h*) aircraft pilots employed by the Department of Transport or other public service agencies.

(2) For the purposes of subsection (1), the expression "public service agencies" has the same meaning as in section 1 of the Public Agents Firearms Regulations.

Coming into Force

2. These Regulations come into force on December 1, 1998. **SOR/98-466; SOR/98-472; SOR/2011-68; SOR/2015-166, s. 1.**

INDIVIDUALS ACTING FOR POLICE FORCE, CANADIAN FORCES AND VISITING FORCES.

117.08 Notwithstanding any other provision of this Act, but subject to section 117.1, no individual is guilty of an offence under this Act or the *Firearms Act* by reason only that the individual

(*a*) possesses a firearm, a prohibited weapon, a restricted weapon, a prohibited device, any prohibited ammunition or an explosive substance,

(*b*) manufactures or transfers, or offers to manufacture or transfer, a firearm, a prohibited weapon, a restricted weapon, a prohibited device, any ammunition or any prohibited ammunition,

(*c*) exports or imports a firearm, a prohibited weapon, a restricted weapon, a prohibited device or any prohibited ammunition,

(*d*) exports or imports a component or part designed exclusively for use in the manufacture of or assembly into an automatic firearm,

(*e*) alters a firearm so that it is capable of, or manufactures or assembles any firearm with intent to produce a firearm that is capable of, discharging projectiles in rapid succession during one pressure of the trigger,

(*f*) fails to report the loss, theft or finding of any firearm, prohibited weapon, restricted weapon, prohibited device, ammunition, prohibited ammunition or explosive substance or the destruction of any such thing, or

(*g*) alters a serial number on a firearm,

if the individual does so on behalf of, and under the authority of, a police force, the Canadian Forces, a visiting force, within the meaning of section 2 of the *Visiting Forces Act*, or a department of the Government of Canada or of a province. 1995, c. 39, s. 139.

CROSS-REFERENCES

"Peace officer", "Canadian forces", "firearm" and "weapon" are defined in s. 2. "Possession" is defined in s. 4(3). "Prohibited weapon", "restricted weapon", "prohibited device", "ammunition", "prohibited ammunition", "import", "export", "transfer", "automatic firearm", "chief firearms officer" and "firearms officer" are defined in s. 84(1).

Pursuant to s. 117.1, the exemption in this section does not apply where the person is subject to a prohibition order and the person acts contrary to the order or to an authorization or a licence issued under the authority of a sustenance or hunting order made under s. 113. Pursuant to s. 117.1, the exemption in this section does not apply where the person is subject to a prohibition order and the person acts contrary to the order or to an authorization or a licence issued under the authority of a sustenance or hunting order made under s. 113.

SYNOPSIS

This section, in effect, exempts persons from liability under this Act and the *Firearms Act* who supply or deal with the weapons and other regulated items on behalf of and under the authority of the police, Canadian forces and a visiting armed force. The person's acts must come within one of the activities covered by this section to take advantage of the exemption.

EMPLOYEES OF BUSINESS WITH LICENCE / Employees of business with licence / Employees of carriers / Employees of museums handling functioning imitation antique firearm / Employees of museums handling firearms generally / Public safety / Conditions.

117.09 (1) Notwithstanding any other provision of this Act, but subject to section 117.1, no individual who is the holder of a licence to possess and acquire restricted firearms and who is employed by a business as defined in subsection 2(1) of the *Firearms Act* that itself is the holder of a licence that authorizes the business to carry out specified activities in relation to prohibited firearms, prohibited weapons, prohibited devices or prohibited ammunition is guilty of an offence under this Act or the *Firearms Act* by reason only that the individual, in the course of the individual's duties or employment in relation to those specified activities,

(*a*) possesses a prohibited firearm, a prohibited weapon, a prohibited device or any prohibited ammunition;

(*b*) manufactures or transfers, or offers to manufacture or transfer, a prohibited weapon, a prohibited device or any prohibited ammunition;

(*c*) alters a firearm so that it is capable of, or manufactures or assembles any firearm with intent to produce a firearm that is capable of, discharging projectiles in rapid succession during one pressure of the trigger; or

(*d*) alters a serial number on a firearm.

(2) Notwithstanding any other provision of this Act, but subject to section 117.1, no individual who is employed by a business as defined in subsection 2(1) of the *Firearms Act* that itself is the holder of a licence is guilty of an offence under this Act or the *Firearms Act* by reason only that the individual, in the course of the individual's duties or employment, possesses, manufactures or transfers, or offers to manufacture or transfer, a partially manufactured barrelled weapon that, in its unfinished state, is not a

barrelled weapon from which any shot, bullet or other projectile can be discharged and that is capable of causing serious bodily injury or death to a person.

(3) Notwithstanding any other provision of this Act, but subject to section 117.1, no individual who is employed by a carrier, as defined in subsection 2(1) of the *Firearms Act*, is guilty of an offence under this Act or that Act by reason only that the individual, in the course of the individual's duties or employment, possesses any firearm, cross-bow, prohibited weapon, restricted weapon, prohibited device, ammunition or prohibited ammunition or transfers, or offers to transfer any such thing.

(4) Notwithstanding any other provision of this Act, but subject to section 117.1, no individual who is employed by a museum as defined in subsection 2(1) of the *Firearms Act* that itself is the holder of a licence is guilty of an offence under this Act or the *Firearms Act* by reason only that the individual, in the course of the individual's duties or employment, possesses or transfers a firearm that is designed or intended to exactly resemble, or to resemble with near precision, an antique firearm if the individual has been trained to handle and use such a firearm.

(5) Notwithstanding any other provision of this Act, but subject to section 117.1, no individual who is employed by a museum as defined in subsection 2(1) of the *Firearms Act* that itself is the holder of a licence is guilty of an offence under this Act or the *Firearms Act* by reason only that the individual possesses or transfers a firearm in the course of the individual's duties or employment if the individual is designated, by name, by a provincial minister within the meaning of subsection 2(1) of the *Firearms Act*.

(6) A provincial minister shall not designate an individual for the purpose of subsection (5) where it is not desirable, in the interests of the safety of any person, to designate the individual.

(7) A provincial minister may attach to a designation referred to in subsection (4) any reasonable condition that the provincial minister considers desirable in the particular circumstances and in the itnerests of the safety of any person. 1995, c. 39, s. 139.

CROSS-REFERENCES

"Firearm" and "weapon" are defined in s. 2. "Possession" is defined in s. 4(3). "Prohibited weapon", "prohibited firearm", "restricted weapon", "prohibited device", "ammunition", "prohibited ammunition", "import", "export", "transfer", "automatic firearm", "replica firearm", "licence", "chief firearms officer" and "firearms officer" are defined in s. 84(1). "Provincial Minister", although not defined in this part, probably bears the meaning assigned to that term in s. 2(1) of the *Firearms Act*.

Pursuant to s. 117.1, the exemption in this section does not apply where the person is subject to a prohibition order and the person acts contrary to the order or to an authorization or a licence issued under the authority of a sustenance or hunting order made under s. 113. The exemption in this section does not apply where the person is subject to a prohibition order and the person acts contrary to the order or to an authorization or a licence issued under the authority of a sustenance or hunting order made under s. 113.

SYNOPSIS

This section exempts from liability for offences under this Act and the *Firearms Act* certain classes of persons who perform the specified acts in the course of their duties in dealing with weapons and other regulated things. This section is important for persons engaged in the business of dealing in or manufacturing such things, common carriers and employees of museums designated by a provincial Minister. Subsection (5) provides that the Minister shall not designate a museum employee where it is not in the interests of the safety of any person that the individual be designated.

RESTRICTION.

117.1 Sections 117.07 to 117.09 do not apply if the public officer or the individual is subject to a prohibition order and acts contrary to that order or to an authorization or a licence issued under the authority of an order made under subsection 113(1). 1995, c. 39, s. 139.

CROSS-REFERENCES

"Prohibition order", "authorization" and licence" are defined in s. 84(1). The reference to "public officer" is a public officer as defined in s. 117.07(2). Section 113(1) gives the court the power to lift a prohibition order for sustenance hunting or trapping or for purposes of employment.

General

ONUS ON THE ACCUSED.

117.11 Where, in any proceedings for an offence under any of sections 89, 90, 91, 93, 97, 101, 104 and 105, any question arises as to whether a person is the holder of an authorization, a licence or a registration certificate, the onus is on the accused to prove that the person is the holder of the authorization, licence or registration certificate. 1995, c. 39, s. 139.

CROSS-REFERENCES

"Authorization", "licence" and "registration certificate" are defined in s. 84(1).

SYNOPSIS

This section places the onus on the accused to prove that the person is the holder of an authorization, licence or registration certificate where that is an issue on a prosecution for any of the offences listed in this section.

ANNOTATIONS

It was held that the predecessor to this section, at least as it applied to the offence of unlawful possession of restricted weapons, contrary to [former] s. 91(1) was not unconstitutional by reason of the guarantee to the presumption of innocence in s. 11(*d*) of the *Canadian Charter of Rights and Freedoms*: *R. v. Schwartz*, [1988] 2 S.C.R. 443, 45 C.C.C. (3d) 97.

AUTHORIZATIONS, ETC., AS EVIDENCE / Certified copies.

117.12 (1) In any proceedings under this Act or any other Act of Parliament, a document purporting to be an authorization, a licence or a registration certificate is evidence of the statements contained therein.

(2) In any proceedings under this Act or any other Act of Parliament, a copy of any authorization, licence or registration certificate is, if certified as a true copy by the Registrar or a chief firearms officer, admissible in evidence and, in the absence of evidence to the contrary, has the same probative force as the authorization, licence or registration certificate would have had if it had been proved in the ordinary way. 1995, c. 39, s. 139.

CROSS-REFERENCES

"Authorization", "licence", "registration certificate", "Registrar" and "chief firearms officer" are defined in s. 84(1).

SYNOPSIS

This section deals with the evidentiary value of an authorization, licence or registration certificate. Subsection (1) abrogates the hearsay rule by making the statements in the documents admissible for their truth. Subsection (2) gives a certified copy of any authorization, licence or registration certificate the same evidentiary value as the original, in the absence of evidence to the contrary.

CERTIFICATE OF ANALYST / Attendance of analyst / Notice of intention to produce certificate.

117.13 (1) A certificate purporting to be signed by an analyst stating that the analyst has analyzed any weapon, prohibited device, ammunition, prohibited ammunition or explosive substance, or any part or component of such a thing, and stating the results of the analysis is evidence in any proceedings in relation to any of those things under this Act or under section 19 of the *Export and Import Permits Act* in relation to subsection 15(2) of that Act without proof of the signature or official character of the person appearing to have signed the certificate.

(2) The party against whom a certificate of an analyst is produce may, with leave of the court, require the attendance of the analyst for the purposes of cross-examination.

(3) No certificate of an analyst may be admitted in evidence unless the party intending to produce it has, before the trial, given to the party against whom it is intended to be produced reasonable notice of that intention together with a copy of the certificate. 1995, c. 39, s. 139; 2008, c. 18, s. 2.

(4) and (5) [*Repealed*, 2008, c. 18, s. 2.]

CROSS-REFERENCES

"Weapon" and "explosive substance" are defined in s. 2. "Prohibited device", "ammunition", "prohibited ammunition", "authorization", "licence" and "registration certificate" are defined in s. 84(1).

SYNOPSIS

This section permits the evidence of an analyst to be presented by way of certificate. The results of an analysis of a weapon, prohibited device, ammunition, prohibited ammunition or explosive substance, or any part or component of such a thing as set out in the certificate is admissible as evidence, without proof of the signature, if the certificate purports to be signed by the analyst. The party intending to introduce the certificate must give the opposite party reasonable notice of such intention together with a copy of the certificate. Proof of service of the certificate may be made by way of affidavit. The party against whom the certificate is produced may apply for leave to have the analyst and the person who signed the affidavit attend for the purposes of cross-examination.

AMNESTY PERIOD / Purposes of amnesty period / Reliance on amnesty period / Proceedings are a nullity.

117.14 (1) The Governor in Council may, by order, declare for any purpose referred to in subsection (2) any period as an amnesty period with respect to any weapon, prohibited device, prohibited ammunition, explosive substance or component or part designed exclusively for use in the manufacture of or assembly into an automatic firearm.

(2) An order made under subsection (1) may declare an amnesty period for the purpose of

(*a*) permitting any person in possession of any thing to which the order relates to do anything provided in the order, including, without restricting the generality

of the foregoing, delivering the thing to a peace officer, a firearms officer or a chief firearms officer, registering it, destroying it or otherwise disposing of it; or

(*b*) permitting alterations to be made to any prohibited firearm, prohibited weapon, prohibited device or prohibited ammunition to which the order relates so that it no longer qualifies as a prohibited firearm, a prohibited weapon, a prohibited device or prohibited ammunition, as the case may be.

(3) No person who, during an amnesty period declared by an order made under subsection (1) and for a purpose described in the order, does anything provided for in the order, is, by reason only of the fact that the person did that thing, guilty of an offence under this Part.

(4) Any proceedings taken under this Part against any person for anything done by the person in reliance of this section are a nullity. 1995, c. 39, s. 139.

CROSS-REFERENCES

"Weapon", "peace officer" and "explosive substance" are defined in s. 2. "Prohibited device", "ammunition", "prohibited ammunition", "prohibited weapon", "prohibited firearm", "automatic firearm", "firearms officer", "chief firearms officer", "authorization", "licence" and "registration certificate" are defined in s. 84(1). "Possession" is defined in s. 4(3).

SYNOPSIS

This section permits the Governor in Council to declare amnesty periods to permit a person to deliver anything to which the order relates for destruction, or to permit alterations to be made to the thing so that it no longer qualifies as a prohibited firearm, prohibited weapon, prohibited device, or prohibited ammunition. See, for example, SOR/98-467 as amended by SOR/98-472.

ORDER DECLARING AN AMNESTY PERIOD (2018)

Definition of *firearm*

1. In this Order, *firearm* means any of the following prohibited firearms:
   (*a*) a SAN Swiss Arms Model Classic Green Sniper rifle;
   (*b*) a SAN Swiss Arms Model Ver rifle;
   (*c*) a SAN Swiss Arms Model Aestas rifle;
   (*d*) a SAN Swiss Arms Model Autumnus rifle; and
   (*e*) a SAN Swiss Arms Model Hiemis rifle.

Amnesty

2. (1) The amnesty period set out in subsection (3) is declared under section 117.14 of the *Criminal Code* for a person who
   (*a*) on the day before the day on which this Order is registered, possessed a firearm and held a licence that was issued under the *Firearms Act*; and
   (*b*) during the amnesty period, continues to hold a licence while in possession of the firearm.

Purpose

(2) The purpose of the amnesty period is to permit the person to do any of the following during that period:
   (*a*) possess the firearm;
   (*b*) deliver the firearm to a peace officer, firearms officer or chief firearms officer;
   (*c*) sell or give the firearm to a business — including a museum — authorized to acquire and possess prohibited firearms; and
   (*d*) transport the firearm for the purposes of paragraph (*b*) or (*c*).

Amnesty period

(3) The amnesty period begins on the day on which this Order is registered and ends on February 28, 2021.

Coming into force

3. This Order comes into force on the day on which it is registered. **SOR/2018-46.**

REGULATIONS / Restriction/ Non-restricted firearm / Restricted firearm.

117.15 (1) Subject to subsection (2), the Governor in Council may make regulations prescribing anything that by this Part is to be or may be prescribed.

(2) In making regulations, the Governor in Council may not prescribe any thing to be a prohibited firearm, a restricted firearm, a prohibited weapon, a restricted weapon, a prohibited device or prohibited ammunition if, in the opinion of the Governor in Council, the thing to be prescribed is reasonable for use in Canada for hunting or sporting purposes.

(3) Despite the definitions "prohibited firearm" and "restricted firearm" in subsection 84(1), a firearm that is prescribed to be a non-restricted firearm is deemed not to be a prohibited firearm or a restricted firearm.

(4) Despite the definition "prohibited firearm" in subsection 84(1), a firearm that is prescribed to be a restricted firearm is deemed not to be a prohibited firearm.1995, c. 39, s. 139; 2015, c. 27, s. 34.

CROSS-REFERENCES

"Prohibited firearm", "restricted firearm", "non-restricted firearm", "prohibited weapon", "restricted weapon", "prohibited device" and "prohibited ammunition" are defined in s. 84(1). Publication of regulations is governed by the *Statutory Instruments Act*, R.S.C. 1985, c. S-22. A much wider regulation power is included in s. 117 of the *Firearms Act*.

SYNOPSIS

This section gives the Governor in Council the power to make regulations prescribing anything that may be prescribed under this part, for example, prohibited ammunition, prohibited device, prohibited firearm, prohibited weapon, restricted firearm and restricted weapon. However, subsec. (2) prevents the Governor in Council from prescribing anything as prohibited ammunition, prohibited device, prohibited firearm, prohibited weapon, restricted firearm and restricted weapon if the thing to be prescribed is reasonable for use in Canada for hunting or sporting purposes. Subsections (3) and (4), respectively, entail that, notwithstanding the definitions given in s. 84(1), no firearm prescribed to be a non-restricted firearm can be considered to be a prohibited firearm or a restricted firearm, and that no firearm prescribed to be a restricted firearm can be considered to be a prohibited firearm.

Part IV / OFFENCES AGAINST THE ADMINISTRATION OF LAW AND JUSTICE

Interpretation

DEFINITIONS / "Evidence" or "statement" / "Government" / "Judicial proceeding" / "Office" / "Official" / "Witness".

118. In this Part

"evidence" or "statement" means an assertion of fact, opinion, belief or knowledge, whether material or not and whether admissible or not;

"government" means

(*a*) the Government of Canada,

(*b*) the government of a province, or

(*c*) Her Majesty in right of Canada or a province;

"judicial proceeding" means a proceeding

(*a*) in or under the authority of a court of justice,

(*b*) before the Senate or House of Commons or a committee of the Senate or House of Commons, or before a legislative council, legislative assembly or house of assembly or a committee thereof that is authorized by law to administer an oath,

(*c*) before a court, judge, justice, provincial court judge or coroner,

(*d*) before an arbitrator or umpire, or a person or body of persons authorized by law to make an inquiry and take evidence therein under oath, or

(*e*) before a tribunal by which a legal right or legal liability may be established,

whether or not the proceeding is invalid for want of jurisdiction or for any other reason;

"office" includes

(*a*) an office or appointment under the government,

(*b*) a civil or military commission, and

(*c*) a position or an employment in a public department;

"official" means a person who

(*a*) holds an office, or

(*b*) is appointed or elected to discharge a public duty;

"witness" means a person who gives evidence orally under oath or by affidavit in a judicial proceeding, whether or not he is competent to be a witness, and includes a child of tender years who gives evidence but does not give it under oath, because, in the opinion of the person presiding, the child does not understand the nature of an oath. R.S., c. C-34, s. 107; R.S.C. 1985, c. 27 (1st Supp.), s. 15; 2007, c. 13, s. 2.

CROSS-REFERENCES

In addition to the definitions set out in this section, applicable to offences created by this Part, reference should also be made to s. 2 and in particular the definitions of "justice", "provincial court judge", "peace officer", "public department", "public officer" and "Attorney General".

SYNOPSIS

This contains definitions which apply to this Part of the Code.

ANNOTATIONS

"evidence" – This definition, which has appeared in slightly different forms since the 1982 Code, was intended to avoid the difficulty at common law that, to prove perjury, it was necessary to show that the statement was material in the sense that, unless it related to the exact issue which was under consideration then the offence was not made out: *R. v. Drew* (1902), 6 C.C.C. 241 (Que. K.B., App. Side), affd 6 C.C.C. 424, 33 S.C.R. 228.

"judicial proceeding" – While it had been held in several earlier cases, notably *R. v. Kohel* (1926), 46 C.C.C. 279, [1926] 3 W.W.R. 478 (Sask. K.B.); *R. v. Rulofson* (1908), 14 C.C.C. 253 (B.C.S.C.), and *R. v. Allen* (1924), 43 C.C.C. 118, [1925] 1 D.L.R. 57 (Man. K.B.), that a civil examination for discovery is not a judicial proceeding where the official who administered the oath was not present during the examination, the Saskatchewan Court of Appeal has now held to the contrary in *R. v. Foster and Walton-Ball* (1982), 69 C.C.C. (2d) 484, and overruled *R. v. Kohel*. The absence of the official, in this case the deputy local registrar, was held not to invalidate the proceedings.

Properly interpreted, the relevant provision of the provincial *Securities Act* authorized the Registrar to require a person to submit to an examination under oath before him and, accordingly, such proceedings fell within para. (*d*) of this definition: *Re M.C. Shumiatcher*, [1962] S.C.R. 38, 131 C.C.C. 259 (Judson J. in chambers).

Although they were not entitled to make a final decision, persons, appointed under the provincial *Securities Act* to conduct an investigation and question witnesses under oath, were authorized by law to make an "inquiry" within the meaning of para. (*d*) and, accordingly, the proceeding was a judicial proceeding: *R. v. Thomson* (1974), 2 O.R. (2d) 644 (Co. Ct.).

"office" – This definition does not apply to an office under a municipal government so as to determine liability for the offence, contrary to s. 123, of offering a benefit to a municipal official [defined in s. 123(3), *inter alia*, as a person who holds an office under a municipal government]. The court, therefore, properly applied the dictionary definition of "office" as, *inter alia*, "A position to which certain duties are attached, esp. a place of trust, authority, or service under constituted authority.": *R. v. Belzberg*, [1962] S.C.R. 254, 131 C.C.C. 281 (5:0).

"Office" is not confined to provincial or federal governments and may include a position of duty, trust or authority, especially in the public service or in some corporation society or the like. Accordingly, a Health Director and Chief of the Siksika Nation held "office" and was an "official" within the meaning of this provision: *R. v. Yellow Old Woman (No. 2)* (2003), 181 C.C.C. (3d) 439, [2004] 10 W.W.R. 276 (Alta. C.A.), leave to appeal to S.C.C. refused [2004] 2 S.C.R. vii, 184 C.C.C. (3d) vi.

"official" – The expression "means" used in this definition is of an explanatory and restrictive nature and in contradistinction to the expression "includes", used in the definition of "office", *supra*, which is of an extensive nature. It follows that, the definition in this subsection being governed by the definition of "office", an official is a person who holds an office either within the meaning in para. (*a*), (*b*) or (*c*) of that definition, or within the usual meaning of the word office, which can be ascertained by reference to dictionaries, meaning in part, a "position of duty, trust, or authority, esp., in the public service, or in some corporation, society or the like" or a "position to which certain duties are attached, esp. a place of trust, authority, or service under constituted authority." An elected member of a municipal council was, therefore, an official holding an office within the meaning of para. (*a*) and was also within the definition in para. (*b*). As regards the latter, while the term "appointed" is often used in contrast to the word "elected", Parliament could not have intended any such distinction: *R. v. Sheets*, [1971] S.C.R. 614, 1 C.C.C. (2d) 508 (9:0). **Note**: It would appear that this meaning has now been codified by a 2007 amendment to include the term "elected".

A member of the Legislative Council of Quebec appointed by the Lieutenant Governor in the name of The Queen is an official within the meaning of subpara. (ii): *R. v. Martineau*, [1966] S.C.R. 103, [1966] 4 C.C.C. 327 (5:0).

A director of public security for a municipality is an official: *R. v. Boulanger*, [2006] 2 S.C.R. 49, 210 C.C.C. (3d) 1.

A paramedic is not an "official". Despite the public importance of a paramedic's job, he or she owes no duty to the public at large and holds no public "office": *R. v. Cosh* (2015), 327 C.C.C. (3d) 410 (N.S.C.A.).

"witness" – The reference to a "child of tender years" in this definition is apparently a reference to former s. 16 of the *Canada Evidence Act*, which provided for the taking of the unsworn evidence of such a child. Section 16 has now been amended to provide for the taking of unsworn evidence of a "person under fourteen years of age or a person whose mental capacity is challenged", who does not understand the nature of an oath or a solemn affirmation, but is able to communicate the evidence and who promises to tell the truth.

Section 14(2) of the *Canada Evidence Act* provides that evidence by a person, who makes a solemn affirmation in accordance with s. 14(1), has the same effect as if taken under oath and by s. 15(2), a person, who makes a solemn affirmation under s. 14(1), is liable to indictment and punishment for perjury in all respects as if he had been sworn. The form of the solemn affirmation is prescribed by s. 14(1).

While s. 13 of the *Canada Evidence Act* authorizes the administering of an oath, neither the *Criminal Code* nor the *Canada Evidence Act* prescribe a form of oath and no particular form was prescribed at common law. The essential element of an oath is that it be in a form which binds the conscience of the witness as a solemn appeal to the witness' deity: *R. v. Lee Tuck and Lung Tung* (1912), 19 C.C.C. 471, 5 D.L.R. 629 (Alta. S.C.).

A witness who takes a certain form of oath, without objection, in the form generally administered to persons of his faith, agreeing that it binds his conscience, cannot thereafter be heard to say that he was not sworn: *R. v. Shajoo Ram (No. 2)* (1915), 51 S.C.R. 392, 25 C.C.C. 69 (5:0).

Corruption and Disobedience

BRIBERY OF JUDICIAL OFFICERS, ETC. / Consent of Attorney General.

119. (1) Every one is guilty of an indictable offence and liable to imprisonment for a term not exceeding fourteen years who

(*a*) being the holder of a judicial office, or being a member of Parliament or of the legislature of a province, directly or in-directly, corruptly accepts, obtains, agrees to accept or attempts to obtain, for themselves or another person, any money, valuable consideration, office, place or employment in respect of anything done or omitted or to be done or omitted by them in their official capacity, or

(*b*) directly or indirectly, corruptly gives or offers to a person mentioned in paragraph (*a*), or to anyone for the benefit of that person, any money, valuable consideration, office, place or employment in respect of anything done or omitted or to be done or omitted by that person in their official capacity.

(2) No proceedings against a person who holds a judicial office shall be instituted under this section without the consent in writing of the Attorney General of Canada. R.S., c. C-34, s. 108; 2007, c. 13, s. 3.

CROSS-REFERENCES

The term "office" is defined in s. 118. The term "corruptly" is not defined in this Part but has been considered by the courts in relation to the secret commission offence in s. 426 where it was held not to mean wickedly or dishonestly but to refer to an act done *mala fides*, designed wholly or partially for the purpose of bringing about the effect forbidden by the section: *R. v. Brown* (1956), 116 C.C.C. 287 (Ont. C.A.).

This offence may be the basis for an application for an authorization to intercept private communications by reason of s. 183. Conviction for this offence may, in some circumstances, result in loss of the office by virtue of s. 748(1) and other disabilities as prescribed by s. 748(2).

Where the accused is the holder of a judicial office, the consent in writing of the Attorney General of Canada is required (subsec. (2)) and the offence may only be tried by a superior court of criminal jurisdiction (defined in s. 2) by virtue of ss. 468 and 469. [Note, attempt and conspiracy to commit the offence by the holder of a judicial office would not fall within the exclusive jurisdiction of the superior court.] It would also seem that, by virtue of s. 522, only a judge of a superior court can release on bail in such circumstances.

In all other cases, the accused has an election as to mode of trial under s. 536(2) and release pending trial is dealt with under s. 515.

SYNOPSIS

Sections 119 to 130 deal generally with corruption and disobedience of court orders. Section 119 creates *offences* which apply both to the person who directly or indirectly *accepts a bribe* and to the person who *offers a bribe*. The *offer,* the *acceptance,* the *agreement to accept* or the *attempt to obtain* make out the full offence. It is an element of both offences that the offer, acceptance or solicitation must be done *corruptly* and there must be an attempt to influence the office-holder *in his or her official capacity*.

The seriousness of this offence is recognized by the maximum sentence of 14 years imprisonment.

Subsection (2) requires the consent of the federal Attorney General before a prosecution can be launched against a judge.

ANNOTATIONS

The corrupt act of a Member of Parliament does not have to be in connection with his legislative duties, it may be in connection with his participation in an administrative act of government: *R. v. Bruneau*, [1964] 1 C.C.C. 97, 42 C.R. 93 (Ont. C.A.).

In *R. v. Arseneau*, [1979] 2 S.C.R. 136, 45 C.C.C. (2d) 321 (7:2), the majority of the court rejected the proposition that a member of the Legislature who is also a Minister of the Crown is to be taken not to be acting in his official capacity as a member in respect of acts and decisions which he makes in the administration of his ministry. In the absence of evidence to the contrary it must be accepted that it was as a member that he was appointed a Minister it being the generally accepted practice that a Minister participate in the process of obtaining legislative authority for implementing his policies and approving expenditures. Thus, his capacity as a member cannot be so severed from his functions as a Minister as to make it an offence under this section to bribe him as a member but no offence to bribe the same person in his capacity as Minister.

On a charge under this section the use to be made of the money received is irrelevant. Thus, it is no defence that the member used the money for non-reimbursable expenses he incurred as a Member of Parliament: *R. v. Yanakis* (1981), 64 C.C.C. (2d) 374 (Que. C.A.).

BRIBERY OF OFFICERS.

120. Every one is guilty of an indictable offence and liable to imprisonment for a term not exceeding fourteen years who

(*a*) being a justice, police commissioner, peace officer, public officer or officer of a juvenile court, or being employed in the administration of criminal law, directly or indirectly, corruptly accepts, obtains, agrees to accept or attempts to obtain, for themselves or another person, any money, valuable consideration, office, place or employment with intent

(i) to interfere with the administration of justice,

(ii) to procure or facilitate the commission of an offence, or

(iii) to protect from detection or punishment a person who has committed or who intends to commit an offence; or

(*b*) directly or indirectly, corruptly gives or offers to a person mentioned in paragraph (*a*), or to anyone for the benefit of that person, any money, valuable consideration, office, place or employment with intent that the person should do anything mentioned in subparagraph (*a*)(i), (ii) or (iii). R.S., c. C-34, s. 109; 2007, c. 13, s. 4.

CROSS-REFERENCES

The terms "justice", "peace officer" and "public officer" are defined in s. 2. The term "office" is defined in part in s. 118; see notes of that term under that section. The term "juvenile court" would appear to refer to an officer of the "juvenile court" as defined in s. 2 of the *Juvenile Delinquents Act*, R.S.C. 1970, c. J-3 (now repealed). The *Youth Criminal Justice Act* now only contains definitions of "youth justice court" and "youth worker". The term "corruptly" is not defined in this Part but has been considered by the courts in relation to the secret commission offence in s. 426 where it was held not to mean wickedly or dishonestly, but to refer to an act done *mala fides* designed wholly or partially for the purpose of bringing about the effect forbidden by the section: *R. v. Brown* (1956), 116 C.C.C. 287 (Ont. C.A.).

This offence may be the basis for an application for an authorization to intercept private communications by reason of s. 183 and falls within the definition of "enterprise crime offence" in s. 462.3 for the purposes of Part XII.2. Conviction for this offence may, in some circumstances, result in loss of the office by virtue of s. 748(1) and other disabilities as prescribed by s. 748(2).

The accused has an election as to mode of trial pursuant to s. 536(2). Release pending trial is governed by s. 515.

SYNOPSIS

This section parallels s. 119 in many ways, creating offences both relating to the *person offering* the bribe and the *person* who *accepts* or agrees to accept it. The group of public officers is different from those captured by s. 119, with this section targeting *police officers,* justices and others involved in the *administration of the criminal law*. Again, as with s. 119, the offer or acceptance must be done *corruptly* directly or indirectly. The maximum punishment for this offence is 14 years imprisonment.

The acts need not involve the officers in their public capacity. However, the *intent* must be to interfere with justice, making it easier for another person to commit an offence or to protect an offender from detection or punishment. There is no need to obtain the consent of the Attorney General to prosecute under this section.

ANNOTATIONS

"administration of justice" – It was held, considering the predecessor of this section, that the "administration of justice" is not limited to apprehended proceedings in respect of crimes in the strict sense but extends to proceedings in respect of provincial offences. Further it was immaterial whether the police officer actually intended to institute a prosecution; it sufficed if the accused was apprehensive of a prosecution and gave the bribe to prevent it: *R. v. Kalick* (1920), 61 S.C.R. 175, 35 C.C.C. 159 (5:1).

The term "the administration of justice" in this section refers to events leading up to the imposition of sentence and does not cover the administrative structure that governs convicts after they have been sentenced: *R. v. Smalbrugge* (1984), 19 C.C.C. (3d) 283 (B.C. Co. Ct.).

"an offence" – "Offence" in para. (*a*)(vi) includes the contravention of a valid provincial statute: *R. v. Sommerville*, [1963] 3 C.C.C. 240, 40 C.R. 384 (Sask. C.A.).

mens rea – The offence contrary to para. (*b*) is a specific intent offence for which drunkenness is a defence. Further, evidence of good character adduced by the accused may not only serve to support the accused's credibility but must be considered from the standpoint of whether the accused as a person of good character was likely to have committed this offence unless he was so drunk as to lack the capacity to form the requisite intent: *R. v. Dees* (1978), 40 C.C.C. (2d) 58 (Ont. C.A.).

FRAUDS ON THE GOVERNMENT / Contractor subscribing to election fund / Punishment.

121. (1) Every one commits an offence who

(*a*) directly or indirectly

(i) gives, offers or agrees to give or offer to an official or to any member of his family, or to any one for the benefit of an official, or

(ii) being an official, demands, accepts or offers or agrees to accept from any person for himself or another person,

a loan, reward, advantage or benefit of any kind as consideration for cooperation, assistance, exercise of influence or an act or omission in connection with

(iii) the transaction of business with or any matter of business relating to the government, or

(iv) a claim against Her Majesty or any benefit that Her Majesty is authorized or is entitled to bestow,

whether or not, in fact, the official is able to cooperate, render assistance, exercise influence or do or omit to do what is proposed, as the case may be;

(*b*) having dealings of any kind with the government, directly or indirectly pays a commission or reward to or confers an advantage or benefit of any kind on an employee or official of the government with which the dealings take place, or to any member of the employee's or official's family, or to anyone for the benefit of the employee or official, with respect to those dealings, unless the person has the consent in writing of the head of the branch of government with which the dealings take place;

(*c*) being an official or employee of the government, directly or indirectly demands, accepts or offers or agrees to accept from a person who has dealings with the government a commission, reward, advantage or benefit of any kind for themselves or another person, unless they have the consent in writing of the head of the branch of government that employs them or of which they are an official;

(*d*) having or pretending to have influence with the government or with a minister of the government or an official, directly or in-directly demands, accepts or offers or agrees to accept, for themselves or another person, a reward, advantage or benefit of any kind as consideration for cooperation, assistance, exercise of influence or an act or omission in connection with

(i) anything mentioned in subparagraph (*a*)(iii) or (iv), or

(ii) the appointment of any person, including themselves, to an office;

(*e*) directly or indirectly gives or offers, or agrees to give or offer, to a minister of the government or an official, or to anyone for the benefit of a minister or an official, a reward, advantage or benefit of any kind as consideration for cooperation, assistance, exercise of influence, or an act or omission, by that minister or official, in connection with

(i) anything mentioned in subparagraph (*a*)(iii) or (iv), or

(ii) the appointment of any person, including themselves, to an office; or

(*f*) having made a tender to obtain a contract with the government,

(i) directly or indirectly gives or offers, or agrees to give or offer, to another person who has made a tender, to a member of that person's family or to another person for the benefit of that person, a reward, advantage or benefit of any kind as consideration for the withdrawal of the tender of that person, or

(ii) directly or indirectly demands, accepts or offers or agrees to accept from another person who has made a tender a reward, advantage or benefit of any kind for themselves or another person as consideration for the withdrawal of their own tender.

(2) Every one commits an offence who, in order to obtain or retain a contract with the government, or as a term of any such contract, whether express or implied, directly or indirectly subscribes or gives, or agrees to subscribe or give, to any person any valuable consideration

(*a*) for the purpose of promoting the election of a candidate or a class or party of candidates to Parliament or the legislature of a province; or

(*b*) with intent to influence or affect in any way the result of an election conducted for the purpose of electing persons to serve in Parliament or the legislature of a province.

(3) Every one who commits an offence under this section is guilty of an indictable offence and liable to imprisonment for a term not exceeding five years. R.S., c. C-34, s. 110; 2007, c. 13, s. 5.

CROSS-REFERENCES

The terms "official" and "government" are defined in s. 118. The term "office" is defined, in part, in s. 118; see notes of that term under that section. The term "person" is defined in s. 2. With respect to the offences set out in subsec. (1)(*f*), also see "bid-rigging" offence in s. 47 of the *Competition Act*, R.S.C. 1985, c. C-34.

This offence may be the basis for an application for an authorization to intercept private communications by reason of s. 183 and falls within the definition of "enterprise crime offence" in s. 462.3 for the purposes of Part XII.2. Conviction for this offence bars the accused from contracting with Her Majesty or from receiving any benefit under a contract between Her Majesty and any other person or to hold office under Her Majesty, by virtue of s. 750(3), unless the capacity is restored by the Governor in Council under s. 750(4).

The accused has an election as to mode of trial pursuant to s. 536(2). Release pending trial is determined by s. 515, although the accused is eligible for release by the officer in charge under s. 498.

SYNOPSIS

Section 121 creates a number of offences relating to *frauds upon government* and is aimed, in part, at what is known as *influence peddling*. As with ss. 119 and 120, offences are created to catch both the government officials (or a family member of such officials) and the person offering the bribe. The offence is committed if the act is done directly or indirectly.

Section 121(1)(*a*), which deals specifically with influence peddling, catches a wide range of activities, including offers of *loans or benefits offered* for the *purpose* of *obtaining an advantage* in government business or benefits which the government may confer. There is no requirement that the official be actually able to be of assistance to bring about the result sought to be obtained. As with most offences created by this section, it is broad enough to encompass situations in which the intended recipient of the benefit is a *family member* of the government official.

Section 121(1)(*b*) creates an offence applicable to the *person who confers* an advantage or *benefit* upon an employee or an official of the government, by a *person who has any kind of dealings with the government*. The person offering the benefit must do so with *the intention* of conferring a benefit, however, no offence is committed where he has the *consent in writing* of the head of the branch of government, with which he deals, to do so. The accused must prove the existence of such consent.

Section 121(1)(*c*) creates a companion offence to the previous paragraph, and is aimed at the *employee* or official who *receives the reward* or benefit. The broad scope of this paragraph extends to benefits to *family members* of the accused official. As with the previous paragraph, the defence of consent by senior officials is provided and the onus is on the accused to demonstrate their consent.

Section 121(1)(*d*) and (*e*) create companion offences aimed at the *person demanding and the person accepting a reward* and the person offering the reward for the same *purposes* as in subsec. (1)(*a*) or to obtain the *appointment of any person to an office*. This offence requires the *intention* on the part of the person agreeing to accept the benefit of influencing, or pretending to do so, a minister or other employee of the government. The offence requires more than merely seeking access to governmental officials; the gravamen of the offence is attempting to *influence decisions*.

Section 121(1)(*f*) is aimed at the attempted *influencing* of *government tendering processes*. This paragraph creates offences for both sides of this type of corrupt deal-making. The key aspect of this offence is to offer or accept, the reward, advantage and so on, for the *purpose* of having *competing tenders withdrawn* from consideration.

Subsection (2) deals with attempts to curtail improper ties between those who have or seek to obtain government contracts and those who seek (or who wish to retain) elected office in the federal or provincial legislatures. The subsection is aimed at the intention to promote one or more candidate or to influence such elections to attain or retain government contracts. This offence prohibits *valuable consideration* being given, or promised, for such purpose directly or indirectly. The maximum punishment for the breach of this subsection is, by virtue of subsec. (3), five years' imprisonment.

ANNOTATIONS

Note: The cases noted below were decided before the amendment to this section adding the phrase "directly or indirectly".

Subsection (1) – In *R. v. Giguere*, [1983] 2 S.C.R. 448, 8 C.C.C. (3d) 1 (4:1), it was held by three of the five judges (including Wilson J., dissenting) that "influence" as used in this section refers to actually affecting a decision such as awarding a contract. However, co-operation and assistance are not so limited and would include opening doors or arranging meetings as the first step in an effort by another to secure a government contract. While the mere arranging of a meeting, for example, is not itself a crime it becomes so when a benefit is given, offered or demanded for the arranging of the meeting respecting the matters listed in this subsection and the person who receives or demands it is an official or one having or pretending to have influence in the relevant sense. A person having influence in the government in this sense is one who could affect, for example, a decision by the government to award a contract and similarly a person who pretends to have influence is a person who pretends he could affect such a government decision.

Subsection (1)(*a*) – The application of this subsection is not confined to a person who holds office or has responsibility for the administration of law or justice but is also aimed at a person who exercises legislative functions and thus the offence may be committed by an appointed member of the Legislative Council of Quebec. The gist of the offence is influence peddling and the section is aimed at the improper use, actual or pretended, of the real or pretended influence that the official enjoys. It is not necessary to prove that the prohibited conduct was committed by the person in his official capacity: *R. v. Martineau*, [1966] S.C.R. 103, [1966] 4 C.C.C. 327.

"Corruption" is not a required element of the *actus reus* or the *mens rea*. There is no requirement that the Crown prove that a benefit was conferred because of a person's position and, correspondingly, that the recipient knew that it was given because of his or her employment status. The Crown need only prove that the accused intentionally committed the prohibited act with a knowledge of the circumstances that are necessary elements of the offence. Accordingly, the accused must know that he is an official; he must intentionally demand or accept a loan, reward, advantage or benefit of any kind for himself or another person; and the accused must know that the reward is in consideration for co-operation, assistance or exercise of influence in connection with the transaction of business with or relating to the government: *R. v. Cogger*, [1997] 2 S.C.R. 842, 116 C.C.C. (3d) 322.

Subsection (1)(*b*) – It was held in *R. v. Cooper*, [1978] 1 S.C.R. 860, 34 C.C.C. (2d) 18, that the offence is not one of strict liability, but is one requiring proof of *mens rea* of the intention to confer a benefit with respect to dealings with the Government. It was also held (4:3) that the jury was not misdirected by the judge directing them that the offence was committed if the funds were conferred "directly or indirectly" in relation to the dealings. [**Note**: The use of that phrase has been codified by a 2007 amendment that added the words "directly or indirectly".]

In *R. v. Achtem* (1979), 52 C.C.C. (2d) 240, 13 C.R. (3d) 199 (Alta. C.A.), leave to appeal to S.C.C. refused C.C.C. *loc. cit.*, it was held that the accused had dealings with the "government" where his dealings were with the Alberta Housing Corporation, a corporation created by provincial statute whose board of directors was appointed by the Executive Council and consisted of Deputy Ministers and performed the functions designated by the Lieutenant Governor in Council. Where, as in this case, the statute does not specifically provide whether or not the corporation is a Crown corporation the test is the nature and degree of control exercised by the Crown over it.

The offence is made out if a gift is given for an ulterior purpose, even if no return is ultimately given and even if there is no acceptance by the official: *R. v. Pilarinos* (2002), 167 C.C.C. (3d) 97, 216 D.L.R. (4th) 680 (B.C.S.C.).

Subsection (1)(*c*) – This section is not limited to situations where the gift was motivated by the recipient's position in government. "Dealings", as used in this section, are limited to conduct whereby persons are in the process of having commercial dealings with the government at the time of the offence. The phrase "commission, reward, advantage or benefit of any kind" requires the beneficiary to have secured a material or tangible gain before falling into the parameters of the provision. It is important to consider the relationship between the parties as well as the scope of the benefit. The closer the relationship, the less likely the gift should be perceived as an advantage or benefit to the recipient. Whether a gift is a true "benefit" is a question of fact. To prove the requisite *mens rea*, it must be shown that the accused knew of the conduct and the circumstances in which it occurred. The crown is required to prove: (*a*) an employee's conscious decision to accept what in all of the circumstances is found to be a "commission, reward, advantage or benefit of any kind" and (*b*) knowledge (or wilful blindness) at the time of the receipt that the giver was having dealings with the government and that the employee's superior had not consented to his or her receipt of the "commission, reward, advantage or benefit of any kind": *R. v. Hinchey*, [1996] 3 S.C.R. 1128, 111 C.C.C. (3d) 353.

The offence under this subsection is committed even where the accused has received only the true value of services rendered outside his working hours where the compensation was received from a person who has dealings with the Government and the accused did not have the consent of his department head: *Dore v. Canada (Attorney General)*, [1975] 1 S.C.R. 756, 15 C.C.C. (2d) 542, reheard in part [1975] 1 S.C.R. at p. 784, 17 C.C.C. (2d) 359.

A government employee receives an "advantage" or "benefit" within the meaning of this paragraph when the employee receives something of value which, in all of the circumstances, the trier of fact concludes constitutes a profit to the employee (or a family member) derived, in part at least, because the employee is a government employee or because of the nature of the work done by the employee for the government. Thus, this would include not only arrangements involving a *quid pro quo* but also where the employee gets something because he is a government employee, even though the giver expects nothing in return and the employee has done nothing to earn the thing given. In making the determination of whether or not there has been an advantage or benefit, an objective assessment of all the relevant evidence must be made and not exclusively by reference to the employee's subjective state of mind. Once the prosecution has proved receipt of a benefit or advantage, there is no need for proof of any intent by the employee to exercise some undue influence in favour of the person giving the benefit. It is sufficient that there is proof that the employee decided to accept the thing offered with knowledge of the relevant circumstances: *R. v. Greenwood* (1991), 67 C.C.C. (3d) 435 (Ont. C.A.).

The fact that this paragraph does not set out the mental element required for proof of the offence or that the section is extremely broad does not render it so vague as to be unconstitutional and infringe the principles of fundamental justice as guaranteed by s. 7 of the Charter. However, the placing of the burden on the accused to prove the existence of written consent from the head of the department violates the guarantee to the presumption of innocence in s. 11(*d*) of the Charter. Accordingly, the words "the proof of which lies on him" must be deleted: *R. v. Fisher* (1994), 88 C.C.C. (3d) 103, 28 C.R. (4th) 63, 17 O.R. (3d) 295

(C.A.), leave to appeal to S.C.C. refused 94 C.C.C. (3d) vii, 119 D.L.R. (4th) vi, 25 C.R.R. (2d) 188*n*.

It is not a defence that the accused's family received a benefit but the accused did not. The words "for his benefit" modify the words "through anyone" and do not modify the words "through a member of his family". The phrase "through a member of his family" deems a benefit to a family member to be a benefit to the accused: *R. v. Mathur* (2010), 256 C.C.C. (3d) 97 (Ont. C.A.).

Subsection (1)(*d*) – This subsection is limited to persons who have, or pretend to have, a significant nexus with government. This means someone who could or pretends he could affect, for example, a decision by government to award a contract. It is not directed at persons who are merely able to arrange a meeting with government officials: *R. v. Giguere*, [1983] 2 S.C.R. 448, 8 C.C.C. (2d) 1, 37 C.R. (3d) 1.

In light of the wide definition of "person" in s. 2 an unincorporated political association such as the Nova Scotia Liberal Association may constitute a "person", within the meaning of this paragraph: *R. v. Barrow*, [1987] 2 S.C.R. 694, 38 C.C.C. (3d) 193.

As applied to subsec. (1)(*d*), a "matter of business" relates to the government if it depends on government action or could be facilitated by the government. These include publicly funded commercial transactions for which the government could impose or amend terms and conditions that would favour one vendor over others. The offence captures promises to exercise influence to change or expand government programs: *R. v. Carson*, 2018 SCC 12.

SELLING ETC., OF TOBACCO PRODUCTS AND RAW LEAF TOBACCO / Exceptions — subsections 30(2) and 32(2) and (3) of *Excise Act, 2001* / Exception — section 31 of *Excise Act, 2001* / Punishment / Subsequent offences.

121.1 (1) No person shall sell, offer for sale, transport, deliver, distribute or have in their possession for the purpose of sale a tobacco product, or raw leaf tobacco that is not packaged, unless it is stamped. The terms "tobacco product", "raw leaf tobacco", "packaged" and "stamped" have the same meanings as in section 2 of the *Excise Act, 2001*.

(2) Subsection (1) does not apply in any of the circumstances described in any of subsections 30(2) and 32(2) and (3) of the *Excise Act, 2001*.

(3) A tobacco grower does not contravene subsection (1) by reason only that they have in their possession raw leaf tobacco described in paragraph 31(*a*), (*b*) or (*c*) of the *Excise Act, 2001*.

(4) Every person who contravenes subsection (1)

- **(*a*) is guilty of an indictable offence and liable to imprisonment for a term of not more than five years and, if the amount of tobacco product is 10,000 cigarettes or more or 10 kg or more of any other tobacco product, or the amount of raw leaf tobacco is 10 kg or more,**
  - **(i) in the case of a second offence, to a minimum punishment of imprisonment for a term of 90 days,**
  - **(ii) in the case of a third offence, to a minimum punishment of imprisonment for a term of 180 days, and**
  - **(iii) in the case of a fourth or subsequent offence, to a minimum punishment of imprisonment for a term of two years less a day; or**
- **(*b*) is guilty of an offence punishable on summary conviction and liable to imprisonment for a term of not more than six months.**

(5) For the purpose of determining whether a convicted person has committed a second or subsequent offence, an offence under this section for which the person was previously convicted is considered to be an earlier offence whether it was prosecuted by indictment or by way of summary conviction proceedings. 2014, c. 23, s. 3.

CROSS-REFERENCES
Definitions and exceptions to liability relevant to this offence are found in the *Excise Act, 2001*, S.C. 2002, c. 22.

SYNOPSIS
Section 121.1 creates an offence in relation to the unauthorized sale of tobacco. The regulatory scheme enacted in the *Excise Act, 2001* is incorporated by reference in subsecs. (2) and (4), such that authorized selling, etc. is not caught by the provision. Subsection (4) distinguishes the indictable from the summary conviction offence based on the amount of tobacco involved, and provides for escalating penalties on subsequent offences.

BREACH OF TRUST BY PUBLIC OFFICER.

122. Every official who, in connection with the duties of his office, commits fraud or a breach of trust is guilty of an indictable offence and liable to imprisonment for a term not exceeding five years, whether or not the fraud or breach of trust would be an offence if it were committed in relation to a private person. R.S., c. C-34, s. 111.

CROSS-REFERENCES
The term "official" is defined in s. 118. The term "office" is defined, in part, in s. 118; see notes of that term under that section. Breach of trust by a trustee is an offence under s. 336. The secret commission offence is found in s. 426.

This offence may be the basis for an application for an authorization to intercept private communications by reason of s. 183 and falls within the definition of "enterprise crime offence" in s. 462.3 for the purposes of Part XII.2.

The accused has an election as to mode of trial pursuant to s. 536(2). Release pending trial is determined by s. 515, although the accused is eligible for release by the officer in charge under s. 498.

SYNOPSIS
Section 122 creates offences relating to *fraud* or *breach of trust* by a *public officer*. The offences are limited to activities in connection with the duties of the public office-holder. This section specifically imposes broader liability upon public officials than that which would apply to private persons who were involved in the same activities. This indictable offence is punishable by a maximum period of imprisonment of five years.

ANNOTATIONS
Breach of trust – In *R. v. Boulanger*, [2006] 2 S.C.R. 49, 210 C.C.C. (3d) 1, the Supreme Court of Canada held that the offence is made out where the Crown establishes the following elements beyond a reasonable doubt: (1) the accused is an official; (2) the accused was acting in connection with the duties of his or her office; (3) the accused breached the standard of responsibility and conduct demanded of him or her by the nature of the office; (4) the conduct of the accused represented a serious and marked departure from the standards expected of an individual in the accused's position of public trust; and (5) the accused acted with the intention to use his or her public office for a purpose other than the public good, for example, for a dishonest, partial, corrupt or oppressive purpose. Not every breach of the appropriate standard of conduct, however, will constitute an offence under this provision. The conduct must be sufficiently serious to move it from the realm of administrative fault to that of criminal behaviour. The *mens rea* turns on the intention to use one's public office for purposes other than the benefit of the public. An attempt to conceal his or her actions or the receipt of a significant personal benefit may provide evidence of the requisite *mens rea*. The receipt of a benefit, however, is not conclusive of a culpable *mens rea*. In this case, the accused, a director of public security for a municipality, did not commit a breach of trust

when he directed a police officer to produce a supplementary report regarding a motor vehicle accident involving his daughter. While the accused knew that he would benefit from a further police report, it is not misconduct to make a decision knowing it furthers one's personal interests if the decision is made honestly and in the belief that it is a proper exercise of the public power of the official. The accused's private purpose did not seek to undermine the public good, nor could the conduct be said to constitute a marked departure from the course of action that should have been taken.

The use of the phrase "breach of trust" does not render this provision unconstitutionally vague. Breach of trust can be interpreted by courts in part as a function of social norms of tolerance and community standards: *R. v. Lippé* (1996), 111 C.C.C. (3d) 187 (Que. C.A.).

The accused, the town's mayor, was properly convicted upon evidence that he misled a constituent as to the value of the constituent's land and endeavoured to procure it for himself for personal profit. The work of a public servant must be a real service in which no concealed pecuniary self-interest should bias the judgment of the officer and in which the substantial truth of every transaction should be made to appear: *R. v. McKitka* (1982), 66 C.C.C. (2d) 164 (B.C.C.A.), citing *R. v. Arnoldi* (1892), 23 O.R. 201 (H.C.J.).

"Official" / *Also see note under s. 118* – Despite s. 123 an elected municipal official is an official holding office under this section: *R. v. Sheets*, [1971] S.C.R. 614, 1 C.C.C. (2d) 508 (9:0).

MUNICIPAL CORRUPTION / Influencing municipal official / Definition of "municipal official".

123. (1) Every one is guilty of an indictable offence and liable to imprisonment for a term not exceeding five years who directly or indirectly gives, offers or agrees to give or offer to a municipal official or to anyone for the benefit of a municipal official — or, being a municipal official, directly or indirectly demands, accepts or offers or agrees to accept from any person for themselves or another person — a loan, reward, advantage or benefit of any kind as consideration for the official

(*a*) to abstain from voting at a meeting of the municipal council or a committee of the council;

(*b*) to vote in favour of or against a measure, motion or resolution;

(*c*) to aid in procuring or preventing the adoption of a measure, motion or resolution; or

(*d*) to perform or fail to perform an official act.

(2) Every one is guilty of an indictable offence and liable to imprisonment for a term not exceeding five years who influences or attempts to influence a municipal official to do anything mentioned in paragraphs (1)(*a*) to (*d*) by

(*a*) suppression of the truth, in the case of a person who is under a duty to disclose the truth;

(*b*) threats or deceit; or

(*c*) any unlawful means.

(3) In this section, "municipal official" means a member of a municipal council or a person who holds an office under a municipal government. R.S., c. C-34, s. 112; R.S.C. 1985, c. 27 (1st Supp.), s. 16; 2007, c. 13, s. 6.

CROSS-REFERENCES

A municipal official may also be convicted of the offence under s. 122. Bribery, etc., of other officials is dealt with in ss. 119 and 120.

This offence may be the basis for an application for an authorization to intercept private communications by reason of s. 183.

The accused has an election as to mode of trial pursuant to s. 536(2). Release pending trial is determined by s. 515, although the accused is eligible for release by the officer in charge under s. 498.

SYNOPSIS

This section is aimed at *municipal officials* who seek out or accept *benefits to be influenced* and those who offer such benefits. The section contains its own expanded definitions of the class of person included within the term "municipal official". The prohibited activities are limited to efforts at influencing such officials in the performance of *job related responsibilities,* including voting for a resolution, or doing (or not doing) an official act. Also, it is an offence to enlist the assistance of an official (or for the official to offer) to influence others to vote for or against any resolution.

Subsection (2) is aimed at the party seeking to influence officials in those actions outlined above (*i.e.*, voting for or against a resolution, or doing or not doing an official act) by a variety of means, including using threats, unlawful means or by the suppression of the truth by those who have a duty to tell the truth. This indictable offence has a maximum punishment of five years' imprisonment.

ANNOTATIONS

In *R. v. Belzberg*, [1962] S.C.R. 254, 131 C.C.C. 281, it was held that the chief building inspector in Calgary held office under a municipal government and that, if he had complied with the requests made to him, he would have failed to perform an official act. Note that the word "office" in subsec. (3) was interpreted by reference to dictionaries and that it was held that the definition in s. 118 does not apply to this section.

SELLING OR PURCHASING OFFICE.

124. Every one who

(*a*) purports to sell or agrees to sell an appointment to or a resignation from an office, or a consent to any such appointment or resignation, or receives or agrees to receive a reward or profit from the purported sale thereof, or

(*b*) purports to purchase or gives a reward or profit for the purported purchase of any such appointment, resignation or consent, or agrees or promises to do so,

is guilty of an indictable offence and liable to imprisonment for a term not exceeding five years. R.S., c. C-34, s. 113.

CROSS-REFERENCES

The term "office" is defined, in part, in s. 118; see notes with respect to that term under that section. Similar offences, relating to attempting to influence appointments to offices, are dealt with in s. 125.

Conviction for this offence bars the accused from contracting with Her Majesty or from receiving any benefit under a contract between Her Majesty and any other person or to hold office under Her Majesty, by virtue of s. 748(3), unless the capacity is restored by the Governor in Council under s. 748(4).

The accused has an election as to mode of trial pursuant to s. 536(2). Release pending trial is determined by s. 515, although the accused is eligible for release by the officer in charge under s. 498.

SYNOPSIS

This section creates the offence of *agreeing to sell or purchase a public office,* to arrange the resignation from such office or to arrange the appointment of a person to such office. No sale need take place; the agreement to carry out one side of transaction of the proposed buying, selling, purchasing, etc., establishes the criminal liability. This indictable offence carries a five-year maximum punishment.

INFLUENCING OR NEGOTIATING APPOINTMENTS OR DEALING IN OFFICES.

125. Every person is guilty of an indictable offence and liable to imprisonment for a term of not more than five years who

(*a*) receives, agrees to receive, gives or procures to be given, directly or indirectly, a reward, advantage or benefit of any kind as consideration for cooperation, assistance or exercise of influence to secure the appointment of any person to an office,

(*b*) solicits, recommends or negotiates in any manner with respect to an appointment to or resignation from an office, in expectation of a direct or indirect reward, advantage or benefit, or

(*c*) keeps without lawful authority a place for transacting or negotiating any business relating to

(i) the filling of vacancies in offices,

(ii) the sale or purchase of offices, or

(iii) appointments to or resignations from offices. R.S., c. C-34, s. 114; 2018, c. 29, s. 7.

CROSS-REFERENCES

The term "office" is defined, in part, in s. 118; see notes with respect to that term under that section. Similar offences, relating to purchasing or sale of offices, are dealt with in s. 125.

The accused has an election as to mode of trial pursuant to s. 536(2). Release pending trial is determined by s. 515, although the accused is eligible for release by the officer in charge under s. 498.

SYNOPSIS

Section 125 prohibits attempts to influence or negotiate appointments to, or resignations from, office. Paragraphs (*a*) and (*b*) create criminal liability for a person who agrees to receive any benefit and the person who offers such benefit, respectively. The expansive language includes *indirect benefits of any kind.*

Paragraph (*c*) prohibits keeping a place for the purpose of business relating to the resignation from or appointments to offices or sales or purchases of offices. This paragraph permits the *defence of lawful authority* but the accused has the burden of proof of establishing it. This indictable offence has a maximum punishment of five years' imprisonment.

ANNOTATIONS

Proof of corrupt intent is not an element of this offence: *R. v. Auger* (1942), 78 C.C.C. 136 (Que. Ct. Sess.). *Contra: R. v. Melnyk* (1938), 71 C.C.C. 362 (Alta. S.C.).

DISOBEYING A STATUTE / Attorney General of Canada may act.

126. (1) Every one who, without lawful excuse, contravenes an Act of Parliament by wilfully doing anything that it forbids or by wilfully omitting to do anything that it requires to be done is, unless a punishment is expressly provided by law, guilty of an indictable offence and liable to imprisonment for a term not exceeding two years.

(2) Any proceedings in respect of a contravention of or conspiracy to contravene an Act mentioned in subsection (1), other than this Act, may be instituted at the instance of the Government of Canada and conducted by or on behalf of that Government. R.S., c. C-34, s. 115; 1974-75-76, c. 93, s. 4.

CROSS-REFERENCES

Conspiracy is defined in s. 465.

The term "wilfully" does not have a fixed meaning and must take its meaning from the context. Generally speaking, however, it connotes an intention to bring about a proscribed consequence. See: *R. v. Buzzanga and Durocher* (1979), 49 C.C.C. (2d) 369 (Ont. C.A.).

The accused has an election as to mode of trial pursuant to s. 536(2). Release pending trial is determined by s. 515, although the accused is eligible for release by the officer in charge under s. 498.

SYNOPSIS

This section creates the offence of contravening any federal Act by *wilfully doing* any act prohibited thereby or *wilfully failing to do* any act required to be done by that Act. Such acts or omissions are punishable by a term of imprisonment not exceeding two years, *if the Act does not create its own punishment*. Up to two years is the minimum punishment created by the *Criminal Code* for indictable offences.

The section permits the defence of lawful excuse but, unlike many other sections in this Part of the Criminal Code, the onus of proving the lawful excuse is not shifted to the accused.

For offences covered by subsec. (1), other than those created by the *Criminal Code*, the *federal government may commence prosecution* for the offence, or conspiracy to commit the offence.

ANNOTATIONS

Subsection (1) – An accused's mistaken belief as to his legal obligations as imposed by the Act of Parliament does not constitute a lawful excuse within the meaning of this subsection: *R. v. Parrot* (1979), 51 C.C.C. (2d) 539 (Ont. C.A.), leave to appeal to S.C.C. refused *loc. cit*. C.C.C.

Subsection (2) – This subsection is *intra vires* Parliament: *R. v. Parrot, supra.* [Also see notes under definition of "Attorney General" in s. 2.]

DISOBEYING ORDER OF COURT / Attorney General of Canada may act.

127. (1) Every one who, without lawful excuse, disobeys a lawful order made by a court of justice or by a person or body of persons authorized by any Act to make or give the order, other than an order for the payment of money, is, unless a punishment or other mode of proceeding is expressly provided by law, guilty of

(*a*) an indictable offence and liable to imprisonment for a term not exceeding two years; or

(*b*) an offence punishable on summary conviction.

(2) Where the order referred to in subsection (1) was made in proceedings instituted at the instance of the Government of Canada and conducted by or on behalf of that Government, any proceedings in respect of a contravention of or conspiracy to contravene that order may be instituted and conducted in like manner. R.S., c. C-34, s. 116; 1974-75-76, c. 93, s. 5; 2005, c. 32, s. 1.

CROSS-REFERENCES

The term "Act" is defined in s. 2.

SYNOPSIS

The hybrid offence created by this section is disobeying an order of a court or other person or body established by legislation to give orders if there is no other penalty specified for such disobedience. Orders to pay money are specifically excluded from the operation of the section. The maximum punishment for this offence is two years' imprisonment where the

Crown proceeds by way of indictment and six months' imprisonment where the Crown proceeds by way of summary conviction.

As with s. 126, the federal government may prosecute if the order disobeyed was made by proceedings commenced by and prosecuted by (or on behalf of) the federal government.

ANNOTATIONS

The words "lawful order" apply to an order of a court either criminal or civil in nature, such as an order enjoining one party to a matrimonial dispute from molesting the other. Further, the inherent power of the court to punish for contempt is not a mode of proceeding expressly provided by law within the meaning of the exception so as to bar a conviction under subsec. (1): *R. v. Clement*, [1981] 2 S.C.R. 468, 61 C.C.C. (2d) 449 (7:0).

It was not open to an accused who had breached a non-publication order in respect of criminal proceedings to collaterally attack the validity of that order as a defence to a charge under this provision: *R. v. Domm* (1996), 111 C.C.C. (3d) 449 (Ont. C.A.), leave to appeal to S.C.C. refused 114 C.C.C. (3d) vi.

The "other mode of proceeding expressly provided by law" exception will be triggered where Parliament or a legislature has provided a legal foundation for the court's power to issue contempt orders, defined the circumstances in which a person will be found in contempt, and provided a specific punishment or mode of proceeding. The fact that rules of court address contempt proceedings is not sufficient to trigger the exception if the order was issued pursuant to the court's inherent common law power. Here, even though Ontario rules 60.11 and 60.12 set out in considerable detail the procedure to be followed on a motion for a contempt order, in light of the court's reasoning in *Clement*, *supra*, this alone is insufficient to trigger the exception: *R. v. Gibbons*, [2012] 2 S.C.R. 92, 283 C.C.C. (3d) 295.

Similarly, the provisions in the *Alberta Rules of Court* governing contempt of court flow from the court's inherent jurisdiction and do not trigger the "other mode of proceeding" exception: *R. v. Nielsen* (2015), 322 C.C.C. (3d) 457 (Alta. C.A.).

The weight of authority holds that breach of a common law peace bond may be prosecuted pursuant to this section: *R. v. Musoni* (2009), 243 C.C.C. (3d) 17 (Ont. S.C.J.), affirmed (2009), 248 C.C.C. (3d) 487 (Ont. C.A.), leave to appeal to S.C.C. refused (2010), 251 C.C.C. (3d) vii; *R. v. Petre* (2013), 299 C.C.C. (3d) 246 (Ont. S.C.J.); *R. v. Pope* (2013), 107 W.C.B. (2d) 750, 2013 YKTC 47; *R. v. Palosaari* (2012), 100 W.C.B. (2d) 827, [2012] B.C.J. No. 723 (Prov. Ct.). A minority view holds that breach of a common law peace bond results in monetary liability but not a criminal offence that can be prosecuted under this provision: *R. v. Mousseau* (2011), 273 C.C.C. (3d) 109 (Ont. C.J.).

MISCONDUCT OF OFFICERS EXECUTING PROCESS.

128. Every peace officer or coroner who, being entrusted with the execution of a process, wilfully

(*a*) misconducts himself in the execution of the process, or

(*b*) makes a false return to the process,

is guilty of an indictable offence and liable to imprisonment for a term not exceeding two years. R.S., c. C-34, s. 117.

CROSS-REFERENCES

The term "peace officer" is defined in s. 2. The term "wilfully" does not have a fixed meaning and must take its meaning from the context. Generally speaking, however, it connotes an intention to bring about a proscribed consequence. See: *R. v. Buzzanga and Durocher* (1979), 49 C.C.C. (2d) 369 (Ont. C.A.). Section 29 imposes certain duties on anyone executing a process. The use of force in enforcement of the law is principally dealt with under s. 25. Personating a peace officer is an offence under s. 130.

The accused has an election as to mode of trial pursuant to s. 536(2). Release pending trial is determined by s. 515, although the accused is eligible for release by the officer in charge under s. 498.

SYNOPSIS

Section 128 is limited in its application to offences committed by *peace officers* or *coroners* in connection with their duties to *execute process*. It is a criminal offence for such persons to *wilfully* engage in *misconduct* in the execution of this process or to make a *false return* to the process. Section 128 creates an indictable offence punishable by a maximum sentence of two years' imprisonment.

OFFENCES RELATING TO PUBLIC OR PEACE OFFICER.

129. Every one who

(*a*) resists or wilfully obstructs a public officer or peace officer in the execution of his duty or any person lawfully acting in aid of such an officer,

(*b*) omits, without reasonable excuse, to assist a public officer or peace officer in the execution of his duty in arresting a person or in preserving the peace, after having reasonable notice that he is required to do so, or

(*c*) resists or wilfully obstructs any person in the lawful execution of a process against lands or goods or in making a lawful distress or seizure,

is guilty of

(*d*) an indictable offence and is liable to imprisonment for a term not exceeding two years, or

(*e*) an offence punishable on summary conviction. R.S., c. C-34, s. 118; 1972, c. 13, s. 7.

CROSS-REFERENCES

The terms "peace officer" and "public officer" are defined in s. 2. The term "wilfully" does not have a fixed meaning and must take its meaning from the context. Generally speaking, however, it connotes an intention to bring about a proscribed consequence. See: *R. v. Buzzanga and Durocher* (1979), 49 C.C.C. (2d) 369 (Ont. C.A.) where, however, reference was made to *Rice v. Connolly*, [1966] 2 Q.B. 414 (C.A.), a case of wilfully obstructing a constable in the execution of his duty. In that case, "wilful" was held to mean not only intentional but "something which is done without lawful excuse".

Offence of assaulting a peace officer in execution of duty, see s. 270 and see also, notes under that section for further discussion of meaning of "execution of his duty". The offence of attempting to obstruct justice is in s. 139, of public mischief in s. 140 and escape offences in ss. 144 to 147. Misconduct by a peace officer in executing process is an offence under s. 128. Section 29 imposes certain duties on anyone executing a process. The use of force in enforcement of the law is principally dealt with under s. 25 and see notes under that section. Sections 494 and 495 deal specifically with warrantless arrest powers. Additional duties are imposed and powers given under other provisions of the Code, especially in Parts I and II, respecting breach of the peace and more serious disorders. Personating a peace officer is an offence under s. 130. As to power to enter dwelling house, see ss. 529-529.3.

Where the prosecution elects to proceed by way of summary conviction then the trial of this offence is conducted by a summary conviction court pursuant to Part XXVII. The punishment for the offence is then as set out in s. 787 and the limitation period is set out in s. 786(2). In either case, release pending trial is determined by s. 515, although the accused is eligible for release by a peace officer under ss. 496, 497 or by the officer in charge under s. 498.

A person found guilty of the offences in this section is, in certain circumstances, liable to the discretionary prohibition order prescribed by s. 110 for possession of firearms, ammunition and explosives.

SYNOPSIS

This section creates an offence of *wilfully obstructing* or resisting a peace or *public officer*, or a person assisting that officer in the execution of his duties.

As a precondition to conviction under para. (*a*), it must be shown that the *purpose* of the accused's actions was to *obstruct the officer and* that the officer was *engaged in the execution of his duties*.

Paragraphs (*a*) and (*c*) require proof that the accused either *resisted* or *wilfully obstructed* the carrying out of these duties. Section 129(*b*) dictates that the accused receive *reasonable notice* that the accused's *assistance* is required to arrest a person or to preserve the peace and the accused has *no reasonable excuse* for refusing to assist.

These offences are punishable by summary conviction proceedings or by way of indictment. In the latter case, the maximum punishment is two years' imprisonment.

ANNOTATIONS

Conduct amounting to obstruction of peace officer – The wilful obstruction of a police officer is a general intent offence. The conduct of an accused lawyer who instructed his client to leave the courtroom after a bench warrant for the client had been issued satisfied the *mens rea* requirement despite the accused's belief that the client's arrest was illegal: *R. v. Gunn* (1997), 113 C.C.C. (3d) 174 (Alta. C.A.), leave to appeal to S.C.C. refused 115 C.C.C. (3d) vi.

Paragraph (*a*) does not create two separate offences of "resisting" and "obstructing" an officer, but rather a single offence. The gravamen of the offence is interference with a peace officer engaged in the execution of his duty by resisting or by wilful obstruction. The concept of resisting has been subsumed in the larger concept of obstructing. It is a general intent offence: *R. v. Glowach* (2011), 277 C.C.C. (3d) 89 (B.C.S.C.).

Although the accused, a bicyclist, committed no provincial offence by refusing to identify himself to a police officer who had found him committing the summary conviction offence of going through a red light contrary to the *Motor Vehicle Act* (B.C.), since the officer had no power to arrest the accused under s. 495(2) (applicable to provincial offences by virtue of the *Summary Convictions Act* (B.C.) except if arrest was necessary to, *inter alia*, "establish the identity of the person", the officer by requesting the accused to identify himself was carrying out the duty of enforcing the law and when the accused refused to accede to the officer's request he was obstructing the officer in the performance of his duties: *R. v. Moore*, [1979] 1 S.C.R. 195, 43 C.C.C. (2d) 83 (5:2).

However, no charge lay under this section where the accused refused to identify herself in circumstances where the officer had no evidence that she had committed any offence: *R. v. Guthrie* (1982), 69 C.C.C. (2d) 216 (Alta. C.A.).

A person is not guilty of obstructing a peace officer merely by doing nothing, unless there is a legal duty to act arising at common law or by statute. The refusal of a motorist to hand over a radar detecting device could not constitute obstruction. The police officer had the right to arrest the accused if necessary to search him, but the refusal did not amount to obstruction. Willful obstruction of a police officer requires either some positive act, such as concealment of evidence, or an omission to do something which one is legally obliged to do: *R. v. Lavin* (1992), 76 C.C.C. (3d) 279 (Que. C.A.).

An accused could not be convicted of this offence for failing to comply with the order of a police officer to comply with a municipal by-law where the by-law was later held to be *ultra vires*. Moreover, even if the by-law were valid, since the applicable provincial legislation provided other means of enforcement such as ticketing the offender, and since the accused did not interfere with that procedure, the accused could not be charged with this offence merely for disobeying the officer's order: *R. v. Sharma*, [1993] 1 S.C.R. 650, 79 C.C.C. (3d) 142.

In *R. v. Long*, [1970] 1 C.C.C. 313 (B.C.C.A.), it was held that the exercise of the right of the prisoner or someone speaking for him to know the reason for arrest does not *per se* amount to obstruction.

Any privilege which a person placed under arrest may have to resist that arrest where he is not informed of the reason for the arrest does not extend to a friend of the person and will not constitute a defence to a charge of obstructing a police officer where the friend interferes with the arrest: *R. v. Saunders* (1977), 34 C.C.C. (2d) 243 (N.S.C.A.).

In *R. v. Westlie* (1971), 2 C.C.C. (2d) 315 (B.C.C.A.), the accused was convicted of wilfully obstructing a peace officer where on several occasions he stopped people in the "skid row" area of the city and pointed out to those people that the officer, who was in plain clothes for the purpose of detecting and arresting beggars, was a police officer. The members of the court in three separate opinions were of the view that the officer was in the execution of his duty at the time and that the accused's conduct constituted a wilful obstruction of that duty in that it completely frustrated him in the duty in which he was engaged.

It is the purpose of the wilful obstruction, not its result, that goes to the offence and accordingly the fact that the assault did not prevent the peace officer from executing his duty is not a defence: *R. v. Tortolano, Kelly and Cadwell* (1975), 28 C.C.C. (2d) 562 (Ont. C.A.), overruling *R. v. Bakin* (1973), 14 C.C.C. (2d) 541 (Ont. Co. Ct.).

Furthermore, the lawfulness of the accused's arrest is not dependent on whether the accused is convicted of the underlying offence of obstruction: *R. v. Anderson* (1996), 111 C.C.C. (3d) 540 (B.C.C.A.), leave to appeal to S.C.C. refused 114 C.C.C. (3d) vi.

Section 254(3) places a duty on a motorist to remain in the presence of the officer until he has completed the duties imposed on the officer by the section. Thus, an accused may be convicted of the offence contrary to this section where he flees the scene before the officer has had an opportunity to make a demand that he provide breath samples for analysis in the breathalyzer: *R. v. Quist* (1981), 61 C.C.C. (2d) 207, 11 Sask. R. 28 (C.A.).

However, in *R. v. Gall* (1984), 35 Sask. R. 138, 28 M.V.R. 91 (Q.B.), the accused was acquitted of the offence under this section where he took flight after he had registered a "fail" on the roadside screening device and *after* the officer had given him the breathalyzer demand. The accused's identity was known and the officer had completed his duties under the section. The accused should have been charged with failing or refusing to comply with the breathalyzer demand.

Conduct amounting to resisting – A charge of resisting an officer in the execution of his duty will lie under this section where the accused resists an officer to whom he has been delivered by other officers even when the accused is arrested for a summary conviction offence and is ultimately acquitted of that charge. Although s. 495(1)(*b*) of the Code limits the power of arrest to where an officer "finds [the accused] committing" the offence the validity of the arrest is to be determined in relation to the circumstances which were apparent to the officer at the time the arrest was made. In any event an officer who receives an accused into custody from other officers is in the execution of his duty pursuant to s. 31(2) of the Code: *R. v. Biron*, [1976] 2 S.C.R. 56, 23 C.C.C. (2d) 513 (5:3).

Resisting a peace officer requires more than being uncooperative — it requires active physical resistance: *R. v. Kennedy* (2016), 345 C.C.C. (3d) 530 (Ont. C.A.).

Execution of his duty / *Also see notes under s. 270* – An officer would be in the execution of his duty in forcibly entering private premises where he believes on reasonable and probable grounds that he is confronted with an emergency situation involving the preservation of life of a person in the dwelling-house, or the prevention of serious injury to that person, and if a proper announcement is made prior to entry: *R. v. Custer* (1984), 12 C.C.C. (3d) 372, [1984] 4 W.W.R. 133 (Sask. C.A.). Also see notes under s. 529.3.

There is an implied authority for a person to proceed from the gate to the front door of a house and police officers on premises by invitation may, as well, have a reasonable time to leave following revocation of an invitation to enter. Thereafter, however, in the absence of common law or statutory authority, the officer is no longer in the execution of his duty if he remains on the premises. A mere failure to keep the peace does not of itself empower the police to enter private premises: *R. v. Thomas* (1991), 67 C.C.C. (3d) 81, 91 Nfld. & P.E.I.R. 341 (Nfld. C.A.), affd [1993] 1 S.C.R. 835, 78 C.C.C. (3d) 575*n*; *R. v. Evans*, [1996] 1 S.C.R. 8, 104 C.C.C. (3d) 23.

An officer is not in the execution of his duty where he is seeking to enforce a law which has been repealed even though he honestly and reasonably believes that the law exists: *R. v. Houle* (1985), 24 C.C.C. (3d) 57, 48 C.R. (3d) 284 (Alta. C.A.).

A police officer who uses his powers associated with provincial highway safety legislation to detain an accused for an unrelated purpose is not acting in the execution of his duty: *R. v. Guénette* (1999), 136 C.C.C. (3d) 311, 2 M.V.R. (4th) 81 (Que. C.A.). In *R. v. Waugh* (2010), 251 C.C.C. (3d) 139, however, the Ontario Court of Appeal held that, by causing an uninsured vehicle to be impounded and towed to safety, the police were acting in the exercise of their common law duty to protect the life and property of the public (leave to appeal to S.C.C. refused [2010] 2 S.C.R. ix, 255 C.C.C. (3d) vi).

The police were not acting in lawful execution of their duty in unlawfully trespassing on private property at the time of the accused's arrest: *R. v. Lauda* (1999), 136 C.C.C. (3d) 358, 25 C.R. (5th) 320 (Ont. C.A.).

A peace officer need not be involved in the investigation of a specific crime, with an identifiable suspect, in order to be "in execution of his duty". The officer will be engaged "in execution of his duty" if, at any given time while on duty, a peace officer's activities fall within the duties and responsibilities of a peace officer described by statute or common law. However, something more than merely being "on duty" or "at work" is required before a peace officer will be "in the execution of his duty". Further, while the accused cannot be convicted unless he knew that the officer was engaged in the execution of a duty, the accused need not know the specifics of that duty in detail: *R. v. Noel* (1995), 101 C.C.C. (3d) 183 (B.C.C.A.).

Failing to assist officer / *para. (b)* – It is no defence to a charge under para. (*b*) that the person whom the officer sought to arrest was the accused's son. The assistance contemplated by para. (*b*) may be either verbal or physical depending on the circumstances but if the verbal assistance is obviously ineffectual then it is incumbent on the person to whom the request has been made to offer such physical assistance as may be required: *R. v. Foster* (1981), 65 C.C.C. (2d) 388, 27 C.R. (3d) 187 (Alta Q.B.).

The accused pawnbroker's conduct fell within the purview of para. (*b*) where he returned a pawned item to the holder of a pawnticket whom the accused knew or had reason to suspect was not the rightful owner. The accused's conduct could not be properly characterized as an omission because despite being advised by the police to retain possession of the item, the accused had deliberately committed an act intended to obstruct the police in the course of their investigation by rendering the item inaccessible to the police by returning it to the holder of the pawnticket. Furthermore, the existence of provincial legislation stating that the holder of a pawnticket is entitled to the item is not a defence to a charge under this provision as the provincial legislation cannot empower the return of a pledged item where to do so would constitute a criminal offence: *R. v. Akrofi* (1997), 113 C.C.C. (3d) 201, 96 O.A.C. 306 (C.A.).

Obstructing execution of process / *para. (c)* – It is no defence to a charge under this section arising out of the obstructing of a sheriff attempting to levy a distress pursuant to a warrant valid on its face, that the warrant may have been a nullity due to some procedural irregularity: *R. v. Fritz* (1979), 58 C.C.C. (2d) 285 (B.C.C.A.).

PERSONATING PEACE OFFICER / Punishment.

130. (1) Everyone commits an offence who

(*a*) falsely represents himself to be a peace officer or a public officer; or

(*b*) not being a peace officer or public officer, uses a badge or article of uniform or equipment in a manner that is likely to cause persons to believe that he is a peace officer or a public officer, as the case may be.

(2) Everyone who commits an offence under subsection (1)

(*a*) is guilty of an indictable offence and liable to imprisonment for a term of not more than five years; or

(*b*) is guilty of an offence punishable on summary conviction. R.S., c. C-34, s. 119; 2009, c. 28, s. 2.

CROSS-REFERENCES

The terms "peace officer" and "public officer" are defined in s. 2. The offence of obstructing a peace officer is in s. 129 and see notes under that section. Misconduct by a peace officer in executing process is an offence under s. 128. Other personation offences are dealt with in ss. 402.1 to 405.

SYNOPSIS

The final section in this group of offences creates the hybrid offence of *personating a peace officer*. The offence may be committed by a person either by actually *representing himself as a peace officer* or public officer, or by using a *badge or other equipment* which is likely to cause others to believe that he is such an officer.

ANNOTATIONS

Mens rea is an essential element of this offence and where a municipality-licensed bailiff mistakenly believes that he is a peace officer, he must be acquitted of impersonation: *R. v. Wallace, R. v. Hall, R. v. Leach* (1959), 125 C.C.C. 72 (Ont. Mag. Ct.).

The offence under para. (*a*) of this section requires proof of a misrepresentation as a peace officer or public officer as defined in s. 2, which implicitly means a person vested with powers within Canada. Thus, it would not be an offence under para. (*a*) for the accused to falsely represent that he was a United States Sheriff's officer: *R. v. Saleman* (1984), 19 C.C.C. (3d) 526 (Ont. Co. Ct.).

A peace officer as used in s. 2 of the *Criminal Code* does not include a person employed by a private bailiff company: *R. v. Burns* (2002), 170 C.C.C. (3d) 288, [2003] 2 W.W.R. 638 (Man. C.A.).

AGGRAVATING CIRCUMSTANCE.

130.1 If a person is convicted of an offence under section 130, the court imposing the sentence on the person shall consider as an aggravating circumstance the fact that the accused personated a peace officer or a public officer, as the case may be, for the purpose of facilitating the commission of another offence. 2014, c. 10, s. 1.

Misleading Justice

PERJURY / Video links, etc. / Idem / Application.

131. (1) Subject to subsection (3), every one commits perjury who, with intent to mislead, makes before a person who is authorized by law to permit it to be made before him a false statement under oath or solemn affirmation, by affidavit, solemn declaration or deposition or orally, knowing that the statement is false.

(1.1) Subject to subsection (3), every person who gives evidence under subsection 46(2) of the *Canada Evidence Act*, or gives evidence or a statement pursuant to an order made under section 22.2 of the *Mutual Legal Assistance in Criminal Matters Act*, commits perjury who, with intent to mislead, makes a false statement knowing that it is false, whether or not the false statement was made under oath or solemn affirmation in accordance with subsection (1), so long as the false statement was made in accordance with any formalities required by the law of the place outside Canada in which the person is virtually present or heard.

(2) Subsection (1) applies whether or not a statement referred to in that subsection is made in a judicial proceeding.

(3) Subsections (1) and (1.1) do not apply to a statement referred to in either of those subsections that is made by a person who is not specially permitted, authorized or required by law to make that statement. R.S., c. C-34, s. 120; R.S.C. 1985, c. 27 (1st Supp.), s. 17; 1999, c. 18, s. 92.

CROSS-REFERENCES

The terms "statement", and "judicial proceeding" are defined in s. 118. As to oath and solemn affirmation, see the notes concerning "witness" under s. 118 and ss. 13 to 16 of the *Canada Evidence Act*. Perjury is created an indictable offence by s. 132, which also prescribes the punishment. The requirement for corroboration is set out in s. 133. The related offence for cases excepted by the proviso in subsec. (3) is found in s. 134. The offence of giving contradictory evidence is in s. 136. The offence of fabricating evidence is in s. 137 and offences relating to affidavits in s. 138. The offence of attempting to obstruct justice is in s. 139. Note that s. 13 of the *Canadian Charter of Rights and Freedoms*, which otherwise protects against the use of prior testimony, does not apply to prosecutions for the offences of perjury and giving contradictory evidence. Section 5 of the *Canada Evidence Act*, which also protects against use of prior testimony, does not apply in a prosecution for perjury in the giving of that evidence.

Section 585 provides that no count charging perjury is insufficient by reason only that it does not state the nature of the authority of the tribunal before which the statement was made, or the subject of the inquiry, or the words used, or that it does not expressly negative the words used. However, s. 587(1)(*a*) provides for the furnishing of particulars in perjury cases.

The accused has an election as to mode of trial pursuant to s. 536(2). Release pending trial is determined by s. 515. This offence may be the basis for an application for an authorization to intercept private communications by reason of s. 183.

SYNOPSIS

This section spells out the parameters of the offence of *perjury*. It requires proof of several discrete elements, including that the *statement* made must be *false* and that the *accused knew that it was false*. There must also be an *intent to mislead*. The false statement may have been made *under oath or solemn affirmation,* orally, by affidavit or solemn declaration. Section 131 has been amended to encompass the contents of two earlier sections: one related to perjury committed in judicial proceedings, and the other to extra-judicial proceedings. Pursuant to subsec. (1.1), this provision applies to evidence given under s. 46(2) of the *Canada Evidence Act* and s. 22.2 of the *Mutual Legal Assistance in Criminal Matters Act*. Section 131(2) removes this distinction by stating that the offence may be committed regardless of whether the false statement was made in a judicial proceeding. Another element of the offence is that the person before whom the statement is sworn, affirmed or declared must be authorized to receive such statements, and includes persons such as a judge at trial, a commissioner for the taking of oaths and a notary public.

Subsection (3) excludes liability under this section if the person making the false statement was not specially authorized or required by law to make a statement.

ANNOTATIONS

Relationship to other offences – It would appear that the effect of the amendments to this section and former s. 122 are to create a single offence of perjury which may be committed either by making false statements in a judicial proceeding (former s. 120) or in extrajudicial proceedings (former s. 122). This would overcome the problems encountered in cases such as *R. v. Wilson* (1977), 33 C.C.C. (2d) 383, [1977] 2 W.W.R. 520 (Alta. C.A.), and *R. v. Hewson* (1977), 35 C.C.C. (2d) 407 (Ont. C.A.), where the accused who swore a false affidavit was held to have been improperly charged with the former s. 122 offence since the affidavit, being intended for use in judicial proceedings, civil or criminal, the offence, if any, was perjury as defined by the former s. 120.

Elements of offence generally – In *R. v. Calder*, [1960] S.C.R. 892, 129 C.C.C. 202 (9:0), Cartwright J. summarized the elements of this offence as requiring proof beyond a reasonable doubt that the evidence specified in the indictment was false in fact, that the accused when he gave it knew that it was false, and that he gave it with intent to mislead the court. Judson J. pointed out that where the most that can be found against the accused is that evidence he gave was in error then this affords no basis for the inference of the requisite knowledge and intent.

Mere carelessness or even recklessness in giving testimony on collateral matters, without any intent to mislead and give false evidence, does not amount to the offence of perjury: *R. v. Besner* (1975), 33 C.R.N.S. 122 (Que. C.A.).

Where the accused had given a complete statement to the police which he confirmed and then gave evidence at the preliminary inquiry that he knew to be false when he testified that he did not remember either being beaten or seeing at that time the two men who were charged with assaulting him, the argument that he could not be said to have had any intent to mislead the court when there was no other evidence before it against which his failure of recollection could be measured was rejected. It was held that those non-recollections were "evidence" as defined under this Part of the *Criminal Code*, and the fact that a court could or would not be misled does not alone preclude a finding that the accused intended to mislead it, for in the absence of other evidence as to the accused's intention the inference could properly be drawn that in so doing what he did he intended to mislead the court: *R. v. Wolf*, [1975] 2 S.C.R. 107, 17 C.C.C. (2d) 425 (9:0).

For there to be perjury, there has to be more than a deliberate false statement. The statement must also have been made with intent to mislead. In an exceptional case, an accused may be able to show that while he deliberately lied, he did not do so with intent to mislead: *R. v. Hebert*, [1989] 1 S.C.R. 233, 49 C.C.C. (3d) 59.

In assessing whether or not perjury has occurred, the trier of fact must have all of the evidence of the accused bearing on the impugned testimony. However, an outright confession to prior perjury in testimony given several weeks earlier in the same proceeding cannot qualify as an explanatory statement to show that there was no intent to mislead: *R. v. Zazulak* (1993), 84 C.C.C. (3d) 303 (Alta. C.A.), affd [1994] 25 S.C.R. 5*n*, 88 C.C.C. (3d) 415*n*.

Proof that testimony false – In *R. v. Farris*, [1965] 3 C.C.C. 245, [1965] 2 O.R. 396 (C.A.), it was held that it is no defence if the accused's statement is literally true if he well knew and intended that the statement should be taken in another sense.

It is no defence to say that the perjured evidence was so preposterous that it could not possibly be expected to mislead the court, and that the accused could therefore not have had an "intent to mislead". The accused's decision to withhold his evidence from the court was done with an intent to lead the court astray in the sense of not assisting the trier to arrive at a correct view of the facts: *R. v. Wilson* (2011), 272 C.C.C. (3d) 35 (Ont. S.C.J.).

In attempting to prove that the accused's sworn statement was knowingly false, the Crown may lead evidence that other people said similar things that were untrue in similar ways. The hearsay rule is not infringed because the probative value of multiple erroneous similarities arises from the unlikelihood of coincidence: *R. v. Bentley* (2013), 300 C.C.C. (3d) 273 (B.C.S.C.).

The Crown must prove the elements of perjury beyond a reasonable doubt, not the corroborative evidence mandated by s. 133 which is merely an evidentiary requirement: *R. v. O'Kane* (2012), 292 C.C.C. (3d) 222 (Man. C.A.); *R. v. Thind* (2018), 361 C.C.C. (3d) 117 (Ont. S.C.J.).

Proof of record – Proof of the record of proceedings in a civil action was made by exemplification, relying on s. 23 of the *Canada Evidence Act*. While s. 28 of the *Canada Evidence Act* requires at least 7 days notice where a "copy" of the record is produced, that requirement does not apply to exemplifications, being a "certified transcript under the great seal or under the seal of a particular court": *R. v. Kobold* (1927), 48 C.C.C. 290 (Man. C.A.). In *R. v. Tatomir* (1989), 51 C.C.C. (3d) 321 (Alta. C.A.), the court considered the admissibility of a certified copy of a driving prohibition to prove an offence under s. 259. The court held that, at common law, judicial documents could be proved by the production of the original record or an exemplification under the seal of the court to which the record belongs without notice.

Requirement of oath or solemn affirmation – A witness who takes a certain form of oath, without objection, in the form generally administered to persons of his faith, agreeing that it binds his conscience, cannot thereafter be heard to say that he was not sworn: *R. v. Shajoo Ram (No. 2)* (1915), 51 S.C.R. 392, 25 C.C.C. 69 (5:0).

There is no statutory requirement as to the method of proof of the fact of a witness being sworn and thus, evidence of the court reporter and the instructing police officer that they both heard the oath being administered to the accused was sufficient proof of the administration of the oath. That the proof might have been made by other or different means, such as by the official record of the court or the testimony of the official who administered the oath, did not render the evidence of these witnesses inadmissible: *R. v. Pfahler*, [1963] 2 C.C.C. 289 (Ont. C.A.).

There is no specific set of words required for an oath to be properly administered. Accordingly, even though the commissioner was unsure whether she employed the standard practice for swearing affidavit or whether she used a modified procedure, there was sufficient evidence to allow the judge to conclude that the accused appreciated that he had assumed a moral obligation to tell the truth: *R. v. Seath* (2000), 147 C.C.C. (3d) 133 (Alta. C.A.).

Effect of s. 5 of *Canada Evidence Act* – Where the accused had testified on a trial under the protection of s. 5 of the *Canada Evidence Act* that certain statements he had made at an earlier inquest and preliminary inquiry were false, his trial evidence could not later be used on prosecution for perjury in respect of his testimony at the inquest and preliminary inquiry. The provision in s. 5 applies only to perjury in the giving of "that evidence", *i.e.*, the evidence which it is alleged is false: *R. v. Kruchkovski* (1925), 43 C.C.C. 299, [1925] 2 D.L.R. 167 (Sask. C.A.).

Double jeopardy / *Also see notes under s. 613* – As long as it does not amount to a retrial of the original offence and particularly where the Crown is able to rely upon his subsequent contrary testimony an acquitted accused may be tried for his prior perjured denial of his commission of the original offence: *R. v. Gushue* (1976), 32 C.C.C. (2d) 189 (Ont. C.A.), affd [1980] 1 S.C.R. 798, 50 C.C.C. (2d) 417 (7:0), holding that this principle applies to a prosecution under s. 124 [now s. 136] as well. Also see *R. v. Grdic*, [1985] 1 S.C.R. 810, 19 C.C.C. (3d) 289, noted under s. 613, *infra*.

Permitted, authorized or required by law (subsec. (3)) / *Also see notes under s. 134* – An affidavit which the legislator has not permitted, authorized or required, in short, an affidavit which has no legal meaning or scope is exempted from the perjury offence: *R. v. Boisjoly*, [1972] S.C.R. 42, 5 C.C.C. (2d) 309 (5:0). [Considering former s. 122 of R.S.C. 1970, c. C-34 which made it an offence for a person being permitted, authorized or required by law to make a statement by affidavit, knowing it to be a false statement.]

Where the accused provided an affidavit merely as a witness for a party to matrimonial proceedings, the Crown had satisfied the criteria in subsec. (3). That statement was permitted, authorized or required by law. The affidavit in this case was never filed nor was the accused ever examined on it. However, the oath given in the context of matrimonial proceedings pursuant to the *Divorce Act* was required or authorized by the laws of Canada and Alberta and whether the affidavit was filed or not, it was intended to be relied upon: *R. v. Seath*, *supra*.

PUNISHMENT.

132. Every one who commits perjury is guilty of an indictable offence and liable to imprisonment for a term not exceeding fourteen years. R.S., c. C-34, s. 121; R.S.C. 1985, c. 27 (1st Supp.), s. 17; 1998, c. 35, s. 119.

CROSS-REFERENCES

The offence of perjury is defined in s. 131. The requirement for corroboration is set out in s. 133. As to related offences, see notes under s. 131. The accused has an election as to mode of trial pursuant to s. 536(2). Release pending trial is determined by s. 515. This offence may be the basis for an application for an authorization to intercept private communications by reason of s. 183.

SYNOPSIS

Section 132 states the punishment for the indictable offence of perjury. The maximum sentence is 14 years' imprisonment.

CORROBORATION.

133. No person shall be convicted of an offence under section 132 on the evidence of only one witness unless the evidence of that witness is corroborated in a material particular by evidence that implicates the accused. R.S., c. C-34, s. 122; R.S.C. 1985, c. 27 (1st Supp.), s. 17.

CROSS-REFERENCES

The offence of perjury is defined in s. 131 and punishment is set out in s. 132. For related offences, see notes under s. 131.

SYNOPSIS

This section deals with an evidentiary requirement in a perjury prosecution. Before an accused may be convicted of perjury, there must be *corroboration* of a *material particular* if there is only one witness to the offence giving evidence.

ANNOTATIONS

Application to party to offence – Although this section also applies to the offence of subornation of perjury as laid down under s. 21, where the charge is inciting [now counselling] to commit perjury that was not in fact committed this section does not apply to the proof of the lesser s. 464 offence: *R. v. Kyling*, [1970] S.C.R. 953, 2 C.C.C. (2d) 79 (5:0).

Evidence amounting to corroboration – While corroboration may be required on a charge of suborning perjury, it is only the perjury that requires corroboration not the accused's participation in the perjury and his knowledge of the falsity of the witness' evidence: *R. v. Doz* (1984), 12 C.C.C. (3d) 200 (Alta. C.A.).

There is a conflict in the authorities as to what element of the offence must be corroborated. Thus, it was held in *R. v. Nash* (1914), 23 C.C.C. 38 (Alta. C.A.), that it was sufficient to show corroboration of the element of the offence that the testimony was false. *R. v. Pattyson* (1973), 12 C.C.C. (2d) 174 (Sask. C.A.), seems to be to the same effect. However, in *R. v. Boisjoly* (1970), 11 C.R.N.S. 265 (Que. C.A.), it was held that there must be corroboration of the accused's knowledge of the falsity of the evidence.

While corroboration is required of a material particular it need not be with respect to a contested issue: *R. v. Van Straten* (1994), 89 C.C.C. (3d) 470 (Alta. C.A.). Also see *R. v. Kehler*, [2004] 1 S.C.R. 328, 181 C.C.C. (3d) 1.

In *R. v. B. (G.)*, [1990] 2 S.C.R. 3, 56 C.C.C. (3d) 161 (5:0), the court considered the effect of now repealed s. 586, which provided that no person shall be convicted on the unsworn evidence of a child "unless the evidence of the child is corroborated in a material particular by evidence that implicates the accused". The wording is thus almost identical to this section. It was there held that the requirement that the corroborating evidence implicate the accused requires only that the evidence confirm, in some material particular, the story of the witness giving the evidence which required corroboration. The confirming evidence need not also itself implicate the accused.

However, in *R. v. Thind* (1991), 64 C.C.C. (3d) 301 (B.C.C.A.), the court refused to apply *R. v. B. (G.), supra*, and held that, to be capable of corroboration under this section, the evidence from the other witness must be in contradiction to what has been sworn to by the accused in the previous proceeding. The requirement of more than one witness must be as to the falsity of the statement alleged to be perjured and it is not sufficient that the evidence simply confirms the reliability or trustworthiness of the other prosecution witness. Similarly, in *R. v. Neveu* (2004), 184 C.C.C. (3d) 18, the Quebec Court of Appeal held that where only one witness testifies, the corroboration must be more than evidence that strengthens the credibility of a witness whose credibility is not impugned. The corroboration must be of a material particular which implicates the accused. The corroboration requirement does not apply where the case against the accused is wholly circumstantial. See also *R. v. Evans* (1995), 101 C.C.C. (3d) 369 (Man. C.A.).

On the trial of two accused on a charge of perjury arising out of testimony given at a judicial inquiry a statement given by one accused to the police several months before the inquiry is capable of constituting corroboration against his co-accused if it was made in furtherance of a conspiracy to hide the truth with respect to a matter dealt with at the inquiry even if it was not made in furtherance of a conspiracy to testify falsely at the inquiry: *R. v. Zappia and Luppino* (1975), 27 C.C.C. (2d) 448 (Ont. C.A.).

Corroboration not required – As indicated above, corroboration is not required on a charge contrary to s. 464, counselling perjury which is not in fact committed: *R. v. Kyling, supra*. Nor is it required on a charge of conspiracy to commit perjury: *R. v. Fergusson and Petrie*, [1969] 1 C.C.C. 353 (B.C.C.A.).

In *R. v. Bouchard* (1982), 66 C.C.C. (2d) 338 (Man. C.A.), the court was divided as to whether corroboration was required where the perjury charge was proved by the accused's own confession to a police officer that he had lied at the original trial. O'Sullivan J.A. was of the view that this section nevertheless required corroboration. Matas J.A. allowed the accused's appeal on another ground and therefore did not consider the point. Monnin J.A., dissenting, was of the view that this section had no application in such circumstances. Also see *R. v. Evans, supra*.

The falsity of a statement by an accused as to his criminal record may be proved by production of a certificate of a fingerprint examiner as authorized by s. 667. Proof in such a manner must be considered an exception to the corroboration requirements of this section: *R. v. Predy* (1983), 17 C.C.C. (3d) 379 (Alta. C.A.).

Corroboration is not required where the case involves the contradictory statements of the accused: *R. v. Eriksen* (2006), 213 C.C.C. (3d) 374 (Y.T.C.A.). See also: *R. v. Wilson* (2011), 272 C.C.C. (3d) 35 (Ont. S.C.J.).

IDEM / Application.

134. (1) Subject to subsection (2), every one who, not being specially permitted, authorized or required by law to make a statement under oath or solemn affirmation, makes such a statement, by affidavit, solemn declaration or deposition or orally before a person who is authorized by law to permit it to be made before him, knowing that the statement is false, is guilty of an offence punishable on summary conviction.

(2) Subsection (1) does not apply to a statement referred to in that subsection that is made in the course of a criminal investigation. 1974-75-76, c. 93, s. 6; R.S.C. 1985, c. 27 (1st Supp.), s. 17.

CROSS-REFERENCES

The term "statement" is defined in s. 118. As to oath and solemn affirmation, see the notes concerning "witness" under s. 118 and ss. 13 to 16 of the *Canada Evidence Act*. This section covers most of the circumstances excepted from the perjury offence by s. 131(3). Other related offences are as follows: The offence of giving contradictory evidence is in s. 136. The offence of fabricating evidence is in s. 137 and other offences relating to affidavits in s. 138. The offence of attempting to obstruct justice is in s. 139. Note that subsec. (2), while exempting from liability statements made in the course of a criminal investigation, would not protect against conduct amounting to public mischief under s. 140. The trial of this offence is conducted by a summary conviction court pursuant to Part XXVII. The punishment for the offence is then as set out in s. 787 and the limitation period is set out in s. 786(2). Release pending trial is determined by s. 515, although the accused is eligible for release by a peace officer under ss. 496, 497 or by the officer in charge under s. 498.

Section 585 provides that no count charging the making of a false statement is insufficient by reason only that it does not state the nature of the authority of the tribunal before which the statement was made, or the subject of the inquiry, or the words used, or that it does not expressly negative the words used. However, s. 587(1)(*a*) provides for the furnishing of particulars in such cases.

SYNOPSIS

This section creates an offence covering the conduct excepted from the main offence of perjury by s. 131(3). This summary conviction offence prohibits the making of false statements before a person authorized to receive statements when the *accused was not specially required* or authorized to make the statement under oath or affirmation. Like s. 131, this section applies to false statements made under oath or solemn affirmation orally, by affidavit or solemn declaration. While there is a requirement that the accused know that the statement is false, there is no requirement of an intent to mislead.

This section also contains an exception which is found in subsec. (2) which removes from its ambit statements made during a criminal investigation.

ANNOTATIONS

Permitted, authorized or required by law – An affidavit which the legislator has not permitted, authorized or required, in short, an affidavit which has no legal meaning or scope is one which is not permitted, authorized or required by law: *R. v. Boisjoly*, [1972] S.C.R. 42, 5 C.C.C. (2d) 309 (5:0). [Considering former s. 122 of R.S.C. 1970, c. C-34, which made it an offence for a person being permitted, authorized or required by law to make a statement by affidavit, knowing it to be a false statement.]

There being no law which specifically required or authorized the use of an affidavit on a bail review hearing, until that affidavit was actually filed or used at the bail review, it had no legal significance and was thus not one permitted, authorized or required by law: *R. v. Hewson* (1977), 35 C.C.C. (2d) 407 (Ont. C.A.) (considering former s. 122).

Authorized by law to permit it to be made – Where the patent of the commissioner before whom the affidavits were sworn was limited to work in connection with a particular law firm and that firm had nothing whatever to do with the proceedings in which those affidavits were sworn then the commissioner had no authorization to take the oath of the accused and the offence is not made out: *R. v. Edwards* (1974), 20 C.C.C. (2d) 112 (Ont. C.A.) [considering former s. 122 of R.S.C. 1970, c. C-34 which contained a similar phrase].

135. [*Repealed*, R.S.C. 1985, c. 27 (1st Supp.), s. 17.]

WITNESS GIVING CONTRADICTORY EVIDENCE / Evidence in specific cases / Definition of "evidence" / Proof of former trial / Consent required.

136. (1) Every one who, being a witness in a judicial proceeding, gives evidence with respect to any matter of fact or knowledge and who subsequently, in a judicial proceeding, gives evidence that is contrary to his previous evidence is guilty of an indictable offence and liable to imprisonment for a term not exceeding fourteen years, whether or not the prior or later evidence or either is true, but no person shall be convicted under this section unless the court, judge or provincial court judge, as the case may be, is satisfied beyond a reasonable doubt that the accused, in giving evidence in either of the judicial proceedings, intended to mislead.

(1.1) Evidence given under section 714.1, 714.2, 714.3 or 714.4 or under subsection 46(2) of the *Canada Evidence Act* or evidence or a statement given pursuant to an order made under section 22.2 of the *Mutual Legal Assistance in Criminal Matters Act* is deemed to be evidence given by a witness in a judicial proceeding for the purposes of subsection (1).

(2) Notwithstanding the definition "evidence" in section 118, "evidence", for the purposes of this section, does not include evidence that is not material.

(2.1) Where a person is charged with an offence under this section, a certificate specifying with reasonable particularity the proceeding in which that person is alleged to have given the evidence in respect of which the offence is charged, is evidence that it was given in a judicial proceeding, without proof of the signature or official character of the person by whom the certificate purports to be signed if it purports to be signed by the clerk of the court or other official having the custody of the record of that proceeding or by his lawful deputy.

(3) No proceedings shall be instituted under this section without the consent of the Attorney General. R.S., c. C-34, s. 124; R.S.C. 1985, c. 27 (1st Supp.), s. 18; 1999, c. 18, s. 93.

CROSS-REFERENCES

The terms "witness", and "judicial proceeding" are defined in s. 118. "Attorney General" is defined in s. 2. Note that s. 13 of the *Canadian Charter of Rights*, which otherwise protects against the use of prior testimony, does not apply to prosecutions for the offences of perjury and giving contradictory evidence. Section 5 of the *Canada Evidence Act*, which also protects against use of prior testimony, does not apply in a prosecution for perjury in the giving of that evidence. Thus, statements made under the protection of s. 5 could not be used in a prosecution under this section. Related offences are found in: s. 131, perjury; s. 134, false statements under oath; s. 137, fabricating evidence; s. 138, offences relating to affidavits; s. 139, attempting to obstruct justice; s. 140, public mischief.

Section 585 provides that no count charging the making of a false statement is insufficient by reason only that it does not state the nature of the authority of the tribunal before which the statement was made, or the subject of the inquiry, or the words used, or that it does not expressly negative the words used. However, s. 587(1)(*a*) provides for the furnishing of particulars in such cases. These provisions may apply to the charging of the offence under this section. Section 583(*h*) provides that a count is not insufficient by reason only that it does not state that the consent has been obtained. As to proof of that consent, see notes under that section.

The accused has an election as to mode of trial pursuant to s. 536(2). Release pending trial is determined by s. 515.

SYNOPSIS

Section 136 is limited to *witnesses* who give *evidence* in a *judicial proceeding* and then give *contradictory evidence* in a judicial proceeding. Pursuant to subsec. (1.1), "judicial proceeding" includes evidence given under ss. 46(2), and 714.1 to 714.4 of the *Canada*

Evidence Act and pursuant to an order under s. 22.2 of the *Mutual Legal Assistance in Criminal Matters Act*. The issue on which the impugned evidence is given may be either about facts or knowledge. It is not necessary to prove which of the contradictory statements is false. However, it is an element of the offence that the accused *intended to mislead* by giving the evidence in either of the judicial proceedings. The seriousness of this indictable offence is reflected in its maximum penalty of 14 years.

Subsection (2) narrows the *definition* of *evidence* which would otherwise apply in this Part (see s. 118) by excluding *evidence* which is *not material.*

The proof of this offence is facilitated by subsec. (2.1) which permits the use of a certificate signed by a court clerk or other court official who has control of the record. The certificate can be used as proof that the evidence was given in a judicial proceeding, and the signature of the official character of the person signing need not be proved.

The availability of this section is further limited by a prerequisite under subsec. (3) that the Attorney General consent to all prosecutions under this section.

ANNOTATIONS

Elements of offence – Motive and intention are two separate matters and once the intention to mislead is established, even though it may have been for the highest motive, the offence, except for raising the successful defence of duress, is established: *R. v. Falkenberg* (1973), 13 C.C.C. (2d) 562 (Ont. Co. Ct.), revd on other grounds 16 C.C.C. (2d) 525 (C.A.), *infra.*

Double jeopardy / *Also see notes under ss. 131 and 613* – As long as it does not amount to a retrial of the original offence an acquitted accused may be tried under this section for his prior perjured denial of his commission of the original offence: *R. v. Gushue*, [1980] 1 S.C.R. 798, 50 C.C.C. (2d) 417 (7:0).

Consent of Attorney General / *Also see notes under s. 583(1)(h)* – A count for an offence for which the statutory consent of the Attorney-General to institute proceedings has been obtained cannot be amended if the amended count alleges another offence: *R. v. Falkenberg* (1974), 16 C.C.C. (2d) 525, 25 C.R.N.S. 374 (Ont. C.A.), quashing his conviction in 13 C.C.C. (2d) 562, *supra.*

FABRICATING EVIDENCE.

137. Every one who, with intent to mislead, fabricates anything with intent that it shall be used as evidence in a judicial proceeding, existing or proposed, by any means other than perjury or incitement to perjury is guilty of an indictable offence and liable to imprisonment for a term not exceeding fourteen years. R.S., c. C-34, s. 125.

CROSS-REFERENCES

The term "judicial proceeding" is defined in s. 118. Perjury is defined by s. 131. "Incite" is within the definition of "counsel" in s. 22(3). By s. 22(1), a person is party to the offence counselled.

Related offences are found in s. 131, perjury; s. 134, false statements under oath; s. 136, giving contradictory evidence; s. 138, offences relating to affidavits; s. 139, attempting to obstruct justice; s. 140, public mischief.

Section 585 provides that no count charging the fabricating of evidence is insufficient by reason only that it does not state the nature of the authority of the tribunal before which the statement was made, or the subject of the inquiry, or the evidence fabricated, or that it does not expressly negative the words used. However, s. 587(1)(*a*) provides for the furnishing of particulars in such cases.

Note that s. 25(1) of the *Interpretation Act*, R.S.C. 1985, c. I-21, provides, in effect, that a document, such as one produced under subsec. (2.1), is admissible in evidence and the fact is deemed to be established in the absence of evidence to the contrary.

The accused has an election as to mode of trial pursuant to s. 536(2). Release pending trial is determined by s. 515.

SYNOPSIS

Section 137 creates the indictable offence of *fabricating* anything which the accused *intends* to use in a *judicial proceeding*. This section is broadly worded to apply to circumstances in which such proceedings are either in existence or are proposed at the time that the fabrication occurs. It is an element of the offence that the accused did the act with the *intention to mislead*.

The maximum punishment under this section is 14 years' imprisonment.

ANNOTATIONS

An accused could not be convicted of this offence, by reason of her having signed notes alleging that she had been kidnapped by a certain person, since the notes would not be admissible in evidence at the trial of the person alleged to have committed the kidnapping: *R. v. Boyko* (1945), 83 C.C.C. 295 (Sask. C.A.).

OFFENCES RELATING TO AFFIDAVITS.

138. Every one who

(*a*) signs a writing that purports to be an affidavit or statutory declaration and to have been sworn or declared before him when the writing was not so sworn or declared or when he knows that he has no authority to administer the oath or declaration,

(*b*) uses or offers for use any writing purporting to be an affidavit or statutory declaration that he knows was not sworn or declared, as the case may be, by the affiant or declarant or before a person authorized in that behalf, or

(*c*) signs as affiant or declarant a writing that purports to be an affidavit or statutory declaration and to have been sworn or declared by him, as the case may be, when the writing was not so sworn or declared,

is guilty of an indictable offence and liable to imprisonment for a term not exceeding two years. R.S., c. C-34, s. 126.

CROSS-REFERENCES

Section 15 of the *Canada Evidence Act* provides for the form of solemn affirmation in the case of an affidavit or deposition. No particular form of oath is prescribed by law and see notes under "witness" in s. 118. A form of statutory declaration under the *Canada Evidence Act* is prescribed by s. 41 of that Act, but reference may also be made to the various provincial *Evidence Acts*.

Related offences are found in s. 131, perjury; s. 134, false statements under oath; s. 136, giving contradictory evidence; s. 137, fabricating evidence; s. 139, attempting to obstruct justice; s. 140, public mischief.

Section 585 provides that no count charging the making of a false oath is insufficient by reason only that it does not state the nature of the authority of the tribunal before which the oath was taken, or the subject of the inquiry. However, s. 587(1)(*a*) provides for the furnishing of particulars in such cases.

The accused has an election as to mode of trial pursuant to s. 536(2). Release pending trial is determined by s. 515, although the accused is eligible for release by the officer in charge under s. 498.

SYNOPSIS

This section creates offences relating to what may be referred to generally as "phoney affidavits" and it prohibits the use of such documents. It prohibits the accused, who may be either the affiant or the supposed witness, from signing a document saying that it is an affidavit or statutory declaration when the document was not so sworn or declared *or* if the accused *knows* that he is without authority to administer the oath or declaration. It also prohibits the use or offer for use of such documents if the person offering the document *knows* that the writing was not properly sworn or declared. It is not necessary to prove that the contents of such writings is false, only that it is not what it appears to be, namely a properly sworn or declared document.

The maximum punishment for this indictable offence is two years.

ANNOTATIONS

Paragraph (*a*) – The offence contrary to this paragraph requires proof of *mens rea* and the accused's mistaken belief as to the formalities requisite to constitute the ceremony of swearing and justify his completing the jurat is a defence to the charge: *R. v. Chow* (1978), 41 C.C.C. (2d) 143 (Sask. C.A.).

Paragraph (*b*) – The word "uses" in this paragraph simply means "employs for a purpose" and the offence contrary to this paragraph does not require proof that the use of the affidavit had as its purpose the misleading of justice. A use intended to bring about a result, which would adversely affect another's legal position was clearly within this paragraph. Finally, making use of a photocopy of the sham affidavit was using the original within the meaning of this paragraph: *R. v. Stevenson and McLean* (1980), 57 C.C.C. (2d) 526 (Ont. C.A.).

OBSTRUCTING JUSTICE / Idem / Idem.

139. (1) Every one who wilfully attempts in any manner to obstruct, pervert or defeat the course of justice in a judicial proceeding,

(*a*) by indemnifying or agreeing to indemnify a surety, in any way and either in whole or in part, or

(*b*) where he is a surety, by accepting or agreeing to accept a fee or any form of indemnity whether in whole or in part from or in respect of a person who is released or is to be released from custody,

is guilty of

(*c*) an indictable offence and is liable to imprisonment for a term not exceeding two years, or

(*d*) an offence punishable on summary conviction.

(2) Every one who wilfully attempts in any manner other than a manner described in subsection (1) to obstruct, pervert or defeat the course of justice is guilty of an indictable offence and liable to imprisonment for a term not exceeding ten years.

(3) Without restricting the generality of subsection (2), every one shall be deemed wilfully to attempt to obstruct, pervert or defeat the course of justice who in a judicial proceeding, existing or proposed,

(*a*) dissuades or attempts to dissuade a person by threats, bribes or other corrupt means from giving evidence;

(*b*) influences or attempts to influence by threats, bribes or other corrupt means a person in his conduct as a juror; or

(*c*) accepts or obtains, agrees to accept or attempts to obtain a bribe or other corrupt consideration to abstain from giving evidence, or to do or to refrain from doing anything as a juror. R.S., c. C-34, s. 127; R.S., c. 2 (2nd Supp.), s. 3; 1972, c. 13, s. 8.

CROSS-REFERENCES

The term "judicial proceeding" is defined in s. 118. Several provisions of the *Criminal Code* refer to sureties, see ss. 515, 679, 810, 816, 817. The responsibilities of sureties and procedure for rendering the accused into custody by his sureties are dealt with in ss. 762 to 773. The term "wilfully" does not have a fixed meaning and must take its meaning from the context. Generally speaking, however, it connotes an intention to bring about a proscribed consequence. See: *R. v. Buzzanga and Durocher* (1979), 49 C.C.C. (2d) 369 (Ont. C.A.). Section 649, which prohibits disclosure of jury proceedings, provides an exemption for the purposes of an investigation of an alleged offence under subsec. (2) of this section in relation to a juror, and for giving evidence in relation to such offence.

Related offences are as follows: s. 129, obstructing peace officer; s. 130, personation of peace officer; s. 131, perjury; s. 136, giving contradictory evidence; s. 137, fabricating evidence; s. 140, public mischief; s. 141, compounding indictable offence; s. 143, advertising reward and immunity. Also, see notes respecting contempt of court under ss. 9 and 10.

Where the prosecution elects to proceed by way of summary conviction on the charge contrary to subsec. (1) then the trial of this offence is conducted by a summary conviction court pursuant to Part XXVII. The punishment for the offence is then as set out in s. 787 and the limitation period is set out in s. 786(2). Where the Crown proceeds by way of indictment then the accused has an election as to mode of trial under s. 536(2). In either case, release pending trial is determined by s. 515, although the accused is eligible for release by a peace officer under s. 496, 497 or by the officer in charge under s. 498.

An accused charged with the offence under subsec. (2) has an election as to mode of trial under s. 536(2) and release pending trial is governed by s. 515.

This offence may be the basis for an application for an authorization to intercept private communications by reason of s. 183.

SYNOPSIS

Section 139 spells out the elements of the offence of *attempting to obstruct justice*.

The first group of offences relates to *sureties* and is found in subsec. (1). It prohibits anyone from indemnifying a surety (or agreeing to do so) for any loss arising from acting as surety ("signing bail") and also prohibits a surety from accepting or agreeing to accept an offer of a fee for so acting. The requisite *intention* is that the accused *wilfully* attempted to *obstruct, pervert or defeat the course of justice* in a judicial proceeding. This offence can be prosecuted by way of summary conviction or by way of indictment, and, in the latter case, is punishable by two years imprisonment.

Subsection (2) creates the offence of attempting to obstruct, pervert or defeat the course of justice in a manner apart from those described in s. 139(1). The actions of the accused must be proven to be *wilful*. The maximum sentence for this indictable offence is 10 years.

Section 139(3) provides a number of examples of how the offence created by subsec. (2) may be committed in the context of a *judicial proceeding*, either existing or proposed. This section is merely *illustrative not exhaustive*.

ANNOTATIONS

Course of justice – In *R. v. Hoggarth* (1957), 119 C.C.C. 234 (B.C.C.A.), a conviction for attempting to obstruct the course of justice was quashed. The court did not undertake to define "the course of justice" but held that, as no investigation of a possible crime was under way at the time nor had any charge been laid, there was nothing in the circumstances surrounding the making of the false statement in question that fell within that term.

The expression "the course of justice" in subsec. (2) includes judicial proceedings existing or proposed but is not limited to such proceedings. The offence under this subsection also includes attempts by a person to obstruct, prevent or defeat a prosecution which he contemplates may take place, notwithstanding that no decision to prosecute has been made: *R. v. Spezzano* (1977), 34 C.C.C. (2d) 87 (Ont. C.A.).

The term "the course of justice" includes the investigatory stage. The term is, as well, applicable to disciplinary proceedings of the law society. The course of justice includes all the judicial proceedings defined in s. 118. Any decision-making body would come within the phrase "the course of justice" if it was a body which judged; its authority to do so was derived from a statute; and the body, by the terms of its empowering statute, was required to act in a judicial manner: *R. v. Wijesinha*, [1995] 3 S.C.R. 422, 100 C.C.C. (3d) 410. Accordingly, a parole board hearing determining whether parole should be revoked is a judicial proceeding within the meaning of s. 118: *R. v. Heater* (1996), 111 C.C.C. (3d) 445 (Ont. C.A.).

***Mens rea* of offence** – In *R. v. Savinkoff*, [1963] 3 C.C.C. 163 (B.C.C.A.), the accused was charged under this section with attempting to persuade other persons to make statements connected with other offences. There was no proof that the accused knew the statements he was suggesting were false. It was held (2:1) that *mens rea* was a necessary element requiring proof of the knowledge of the falsity of the statement.

It is no defence that the accused believed that the evidence that he sought to suppress was false evidence: *R. v. Walker* (1972), 7 C.C.C. (2d) 270 (Ont. Prov. Ct.).

However, where the accused approached a witness who had testified against his friend and told the witness he should tell the truth, he was acquitted. The court found that his purpose was to protest an injustice, not to obstruct justice: *R. v. Belliveau* (1978), 42 C.C.C. (2d) 243 (N.B.S.C. App. Div.).

Attempts in any manner (subsec. (2)) – In *R. v. Balsdon*, [1968] 2 C.C.C. 164 (Ont. Co. Ct.), it was held, following the two doctrines *nemo tenetur seipsum accusare* — no man can be compelled to incriminate himself — and *nemo tenetur prodere seipsum* — no one is bound to betray himself, that, although attempts at service of warrants of committal following convictions for summary conviction offences is a part of the course of justice, deliberate misidentification of himself by the accused to police officers endeavouring to serve him is not obstruction of justice.

In *R. v. Spezzano, supra*, the court, without passing on the correctness of *R. v. Balsdon, supra*, distinguished it on the basis that whatever protection the common law right to remain silent confers on a person, it will not protect him when he not only denies his identity but gives the police a false name in order to protect himself. The court, however, pointed out that it is not every false statement to the police, such as a false denial of guilt, which will be capable of supporting a charge under this provision.

It would seem that subsec. (2) is wide enough to include a threat by an accused to cause bodily harm to the complainant who was present in court, notwithstanding at the time of the threat the accused had been convicted and sentenced for the offence which the complainant had initially reported: *R. v. Vermette* (1983), 6 C.C.C. (3d) 97 (Alta. C.A.), affd on other grounds [1987] 1 S.C.R. 577, 32 C.C.C. (3d) 519.

A charge under this subsection could be made out if the accused approached a police officer with a request that certain charges not be laid in exchange for a payment to the officer, even if the officer did not in fact attempt to obstruct justice: *R. v. Rousseau*, [1985] 2 S.C.R. 38, 21 C.C.C. (3d) 1 (7:0).

Any attempt to pay compensation in any form to a witness that has, as its purpose, a direct tendency to influence a witness not to give evidence in a judicial proceeding, irrespective of the motive for doing so, is a corrupt attempt to obstruct justice. Similarly, an attempt to pay compensation to the complainant in order to influence the proceeding by, for example, persuading the Crown to withdraw the charge is capable of amounting to an offence. The offence would not, however, cover a *bona fide* negotiation for the withholding, withdrawal or reduction of a given charge that is conducted with a law officer of the Crown. Nor would honestly approaching a witness who has made a false or mistaken statement and by reasoned arguments supported by material facts, trying to dissuade him from giving perjured or erroneous testimony constitute an offence: *R. v. Kotch* (1990), 61 C.C.C. (3d) 132 (Alta. C.A.). [Also, note s. 141(2).]

Subsection (2) of this section, although framed in the language of an attempt, in fact creates a substantive offence, the gist of which is the doing of an act which has a tendency to prevent or obstruct the course of justice and which is done for that purpose: *R. v. May* (1984), 13 C.C.C. (3d) 257 (Ont. C.A.), leave to appeal to S.C.C. refused [1984] 2 S.C.R. viii. It is not necessary to establish that the tendency materialized. Thus, an accused who sent a letter from jail requesting his brother to intimidate a witness could be convicted of this offence although the letter was intercepted by the jail authorities and never reached the brother. The acts of the accused went beyond an intention or even expression of an intention: *R. v. Graham* (1985), 20 C.C.C. (3d) 210 (Ont. C.A.), affd [1988] 1 S.C.R. 214, 38 C.C.C. (3d) 574 (5:0).

An attempt to dissuade someone from reporting an incident to the police may amount to an obstruction of justice: *R. v. Whalen* (1974), 17 C.C.C. (2d) 217 (Ont. Co. Ct.).

False courtroom testimony is a possible mode of committing this offence as s. 13 of the Charter provides no protection where the testimony is the *actus reus* of the offence: *R. v. Schertzer* (2015), 325 C.C.C. (3d) 202 (Ont. C.A.), leave to appeal to S.C.C. refused 2015 CarswellOnt 16494.

A lawyer is under a duty not to mislead the court and may be convicted of this offence where he participates in the client's deception by arranging for the client's friend to attend in court to answer a charge against the client, who had previously given the friend's name to the police as his own upon arrest: *R. v. Doz* (1984), 12 C.C.C. (3d) 200 (Alta. C.A.).

A police officer cannot be convicted of this offence solely because he improperly exercised his discretion not to charge someone, here a fellow officer, with a criminal offence. Rather, it must first be determined whether the conduct in issue can be regarded as a proper exercise of police discretion. If not, it must then be determined whether the offence of obstructing justice has been committed in the sense that the act tended to defeat or obstruct the course of justice. If the *actus reus* is established, the Crown must then prove that the accused did in fact intend to act in a way tending to obstruct, pervert or defeat the course of justice. A simple error in judgment will not be enough. An accused who acted in good faith has not committed the offence even if the conduct cannot be characterized as a legitimate exercise of discretion: *R. v. Beaudry*, [2007] 1 S.C.R. 190, 216 C.C.C. (3d) 353.

The offence of attempting to obstruct justice requires the specific intention to obstruct justice. Thus, in the case of a charge based on an attempt by the accused to obtain a false affidavit from a client, the accused's honest belief that the affidavit was true would constitute a defence: *R. v. Charbonneau* (1992), 74 C.C.C. (3d) 49 (Que. C.A.).

The gravamen of the offence under subsec. (2) is the wilful attempt to obstruct justice and it does not matter that the attempt was not only unsuccessful but could not have succeeded. Thus, it was no defence that the accused attempted to procure a witness to give false evidence on an issue which in law was irrelevant: *R. v. Hearn* (1989), 48 C.C.C. (3d) 376 (Nfld. C.A.), affd [1989] 2 S.C.R. 1180, 53 C.C.C. (3d) 352*n*.

"Other corrupt means" (subsec. (3)(*a*)) – Suggesting that a witness avoid testifying at the accused's preliminary inquiry by presenting a false doctor's certificate to the court amounted to "dissuading" the witness from testifying through "other corrupt means". Recommending a deceitful way of accomplishing the desired objective is just as much a part of the persuasion package as providing the incentive to carry out the desired objective in the first place: *R. v. Reynolds*, [2011] 1 S.C.R. 693, 268 C.C.C. (3d) 35.

Witness at preliminary inquiry – Where the procedure under s. 545 has been resorted to by the justice presiding at a preliminary inquiry then a charge will not lie under this section for the same conduct – the witness' refusal to be sworn and testify. However, if the justice did not act under s. 545 or if the conduct were repeated after an initial resort to s. 545, then a charge under this section or of contempt of court would lie: *R. v. Mercer* (1988), 43 C.C.C. (3d) 347 (Alta. C.A.); *R. v. Poulin* (1998), 127 C.C.C. (3d) 115 (Que. C.A.).

Procedure and evidence – Statements by the accused police officers, which were part of a plan to cover up the commission of a criminal offence by one of them, were part of the *actus reus* of the offence under this section and need not be proved voluntary on a *voir dire*: *R. v. Hanneson* (1989), 49 C.C.C. (3d) 467 (Ont. C.A.).

The words "attempts in any manner" in subsec. (2) include perjury as a means of committing this offence notwithstanding that by charging the accused with this offence rather than the offence under s. 131 the requirement of corroboration (s. 133) is avoided. Under this section, corroboration is not required either at law or as a matter of practice, although the conduct involves an allegation of perjury: *R. v. Simon* (1979), 45 C.C.C. (2d) 510 (Ont. C.A.); *R. v. Moore* (1980), 52 C.C.C. (2d) 202 (B.C.C.A.).

PUBLIC MISCHIEF / Punishment.

140. (1) Every one commits public mischief who, with intent to mislead, causes a peace officer to enter on or continue an investigation by

(*a*) making a false statement that accuses some other person of having committed an offence;

(*b*) doing anything intended to cause some other person to be suspected of having committed an offence that the other person has not committed, or to divert suspicion from himself;

(*c*) reporting that an offence has been committed when it has not been committed; or

(*d*) reporting or in any other way making it known or causing it to be made known that he or some other person has died when he or that other person has not died.

(2) Every one who commits public mischief

(*a*) is guilty of an indictable offence and liable to imprisonment for a term not exceeding five years; or

(*b*) is guilty of an offence punishable on summary conviction. R.S., c. C-34, s. 128; 1972, c. 13, s. 8; R.S.C. 1985, c. 27 (1st Supp.), s. 19.

CROSS-REFERENCES

The term "statement" is defined in s. 118. The term "peace officer" is defined in s. 2. Section 585 provides that no count charging the making of a false statement is insufficient by reason only that it does not state the nature of the authority of the tribunal before which the statement was made, or the subject of the inquiry, or the words used, or that it does not expressly negative the truth of the words used. However, s. 587(1)(*a*) provides for the furnishing of particulars in such cases.

Related offences are as follows: s. 129, obstructing peace officer; s. 130, personation of peace officer; s. 137, fabricating evidence; s. 139, attempting to obstruct justice; s. 141, compounding indictable offence; s. 143, advertising reward and immunity; s. 403, personation. This offence is to be contrasted to the property offences also referred to as mischief, in s. 430.

Where the prosecution elects to proceed by way of summary conviction then the trial of this offence is conducted by a summary conviction court pursuant to Part XXVII. The punishment for the offence is then as set out in s. 787 and the limitation period is set out in s. 786(2). Where the Crown proceeds by way of indictment then the accused has an election as to mode of trial under s. 536(2). In either case, release pending trial is determined by s. 515, although the accused is eligible for release by a peace officer under s. 496, 497 or by the officer in charge under s. 498.

SYNOPSIS

This section creates the offence of *public mischief* which involves causing peace officers to *begin,* or to *continue* an investigation with the *intention of misleading them.* The ways in which the offence may be committed are specified in subsec. (1). Among these are *falsely accusing another* of committing a criminal offence or *falsely reporting that an offence has occurred.* When public mischief is committed by either of these methods, the false report by the accused is the *actus reus* of the offence.

This offence is punishable by summary conviction or by way of indictment. If prosecuted by way of indictment, the maximum punishment is five years.

ANNOTATIONS

Meaning of "offence" – An "offence" referred to in this section is not restricted to only a *Criminal Code* offence but pertains to any breach of the law whether federal, provincial or otherwise that involves penal sanction: *R. v. Howard* (1972), 7 C.C.C. (2d) 211 (Ont. C.A.).

Meaning of "report" – "Reporting" need not be directly to the police and can include a report to an entity such as the CAS, who may in turn report to the police: *R. v. Delacruz* (2009), 249 C.C.C. (3d) 501 (Ont. S.C.J.).

Attempt to commit offence – On a charge of public mischief the accused may be convicted of an attempt to commit the offence where because the officer did not believe the accused he did not embark upon an investigation and was not misled: *R. v. Whalen* (1977), 34 C.C.C. (2d) 557 (B.C. Prov. Ct.).

Evidence – The statement by the accused to the police reporting the offence is the *actus reus* of the offence contrary to para. (*c*) and no *voir dire* is required to determine the voluntariness of such a statement: *R. v. Stapleton* (1982), 66 C.C.C. (2d) 231 (Ont. C.A.).

A similar result was reached in considering a statement taken from a young person, it being held that the special conditions for taking of statements as prescribed by [former] s. 56 of the *Young Offenders Act* were intended to apply only to young persons accused of committing crimes and not to a young person who provided a statement as a victim of the offence. Thus, on a charge under this section based on such a statement, the Crown need not prove compliance with s. 56. As in the case of an adult, the complaint is the *actus reus* of the offence and admissible without proof of voluntariness: *R. v. J.(J.)* (1988), 43 C.C.C. (3d) 257 (Ont. C.A.), leave to appeal to S.C.C. refused 101 N.R. 231*n*.

COMPOUNDING INDICTABLE OFFENCE / Exception for diversion agreements.

141. (1) Every one who asks for or obtains or agrees to receive or obtain any valuable consideration for himself or any other person by agreeing to compound or conceal an indictable offence is guilty of an indictable offence and liable to imprisonment for a term not exceeding two years.

(2) No offence is committed under subsection (1) where valuable consideration is received or obtained or is to be received or obtained under an agreement for compensation or restitution or personal services that is

(*a*) entered into with the consent of the Attorney General; or

(*b*) made as part of a program, approved by the Attorney General, to divert persons charged with indictable offences from criminal proceedings. R.S., c. C-34, s. 129; R.S.C. 1985, c. 27 (1st Supp.), s. 19.

CROSS-REFERENCES

The term "Attorney General" is defined in s. 2. An "indictable offence" would include a Crown option offence by virtue of s. 34 of the *Interpretation Act*, R.S.C. 1985, c. I-21. The term "compound" is not defined but may be taken to refer to the element of the common law offence of compounding a felony being an agreement not to prosecute or inform on a person who has committed an offence. See *R. v. Burgess* (1885), 15 Cox, C.C. 779 (C.A.). The reference to programmes in subsec. (2) presumably refers to restitution orders under s. 726 to 727.8, s. 737(2), a fine option programme under s. 718.1 and extrajudicial measures under ss. 4 to 10 of the *Youth Criminal Justice Act*.

Related offences are as follows: s. 23, accessory after the fact; s. 137, fabricating evidence; s. 139, attempting to obstruct justice; s. 140, public mischief; s. 142, corruptly taking reward; s. 143, advertising reward and immunity; s. 346, extortion. In addition it should be noted that courts will on occasion stay proceedings as an abuse of process where it is shown that the criminal proceedings were launched to collect a debt or realize on a civil claim, or following a threat to swear out an information to obtain payment of a debt. See *R. v. Leroux* (1928), 50 C.C.C. 52 (Ont. C.A.). Also see notes following s. 579.

The accused has an election as to mode of trial pursuant to s. 536(2). Release pending trial is determined by s. 515, although the accused is eligible for release by the officer in charge under s. 498.

SYNOPSIS

Section 141(1) creates an indictable offence applicable if a person asks for, obtains, or *agrees to accept* any form of *valuable consideration* in exchange for agreeing to compound or *conceal an indictable offence*. The maximum sentence for this offence is two years.

Subsection (2) provides two exceptions to the liability which would otherwise result from subsec. (1). Section 141(2)(*a*) excludes cases in which the valuable consideration is obtained (or will be so in the future) by virtue of an agreement made with the consent of the Attorney General. Section 141(2)(*b*) provides an exemption covering agreements made as part of a program for the diversion of persons from indictable criminal proceedings. To come within this paragraph, the diversion program must be approved by the Attorney General.

ANNOTATIONS

The Crown need not prove that an indictable offence was actually committed, it being sufficient to prove that the accused believed that an indictable offence had been committed: *R. v. H.L.* (1987), 57 C.R. (3d) 136 (Que. Ct. Sess.).

CORRUPTLY TAKING REWARD FOR RECOVERY OF GOODS.

142. Every one who corruptly accepts any valuable consideration, directly or indirectly, under pretence or on account of helping any person to recover anything obtained by the commission of an indictable offence is guilty of an indictable offence and liable to imprisonment for a term not exceeding five years. R.S., c. C-34, s. 130.

CROSS-REFERENCES

An "indictable offence" would include a Crown option offence by virtue of s. 34 of the *Interpretation Act*, R.S.C. 1985, c. I-21. The term "corruptly" is not defined in this Part but has been considered by the courts in relation to the secret commission offence in s. 426, where it was held not to mean wickedly or dishonestly, but to refer to an act done *mala fides*, designed wholly or partially for the purpose of bringing about the effect forbidden by the section: *R. v. Brown* (1956), 116 C.C.C. 287 (Ont. C.A.).

Related offences are as follows: s. 23, accessory after the fact; s. 137, fabricating evidence; s. 139, attempting to obstruct justice; s. 140, public mischief; s. 141, compounding indictable offence; s. 143, advertising reward and immunity; s. 346, extortion; ss. 354 and 355, possession of property obtained by crime; s. 462.31, laundering proceeds of crime.

The accused has an election as to mode of trial pursuant to s. 536(2). Release pending trial is determined by s. 515, although the accused is eligible for release by the officer in charge under s. 498.

SYNOPSIS

This section creates the indictable offence of *corruptly accepting valuable consideration* for the *recovery* of goods which were obtained by the commission of an indictable offence. It must be proven that the accused accepted the valuable consideration *corruptly* (directly or indirectly) and its receipt flowed from the pretence of helping or as the result of actually helping recover the goods. The maximum punishment for this offence is five years.

ANNOTATIONS

In *R. v. Butler* (1975), 26 C.C.C. (2d) 445 (Ont. Co. Ct.), the trial judge adopted the definition of the word "corruptly" given by Cussen J., in *R. v. Worthington*, [1921] V.L.R. 660, as "an act done by a man knowing that he is doing what is wrong, and doing it with an evil object" and found that in the factual circumstances the accused's acceptance of reward for obtaining the return of stolen goods was corrupt.

143. [*Repealed*, 2018, c. 29, s. 8.]

Escapes and Rescues

PRISON BREACH.

144. Every one who

(*a*) by force or violence breaks a prison with intent to set at liberty himself or any other person confined therein, or

(*b*) with intent to escape forcibly breaks out of, or makes any breach in, a cell or other place within a prison in which he is confined,

is guilty of an indictable offence and liable to imprisonment for a term not exceeding ten years. R.S., c. C-34, s. 132; 1976-77, c. 53, s. 5.

CROSS-REFERENCES

"Prison" is defined in s. 2. Section 149 provides an exception to the normal rule as set out in s. 743.1 that a sentence of less than two years is served in a reformatory. The court has the power to order that a sentence for escape may be served in a penitentiary. Escape is defined in s. 149 to include the offence under this section. Under s. 719(2), any time during which a convicted person is unlawfully at large does not count as part of any term of imprisonment. A finding of guilt in relation to the offence under para. (*a*) will require the court to impose an order prohibiting possession of firearms, ammunition or explosive substances under s. 109.

The related offence of escaping lawful custody and being unlawfully at large is in s. 145. Other related offences are as follows: s. 146, permitting or assisting escape; s. 147, rescue from lawful custody or officer permitting escape; s. 148, assisting prisoner of war to escape.

Murder of a warden, deputy warden, instructor, keeper, jailer, guard or other officer or permanent employee of a prison, acting in the course of his duties, is first degree murder by virtue of s. 231(4). This offence may be the basis for an application for an authorization to intercept private communications by reason of s. 183 or for a warrant to conduct video surveillance under s. 487.01(5).

The accused has an election as to mode of trial under s. 536(2). Release pending trial is determined by s. 515. However, by virtue of s. 519, the accused would not be released pursuant to any release order until the accused was not required to be detained in custody in respect of any other matter.

SYNOPSIS

This section sets out what constitutes prison breach and specifies that it is an indictable offence carrying a maximum sentence of 10 years.

The *actus reus* of the offence in s. 144(*a*) is the use of force or violence to break out of a prison. The mental element of this offence is the *intention* of the accused to set himself or another free.

The *actus reus* of the offence created in s. 144(*b*) is the action of *forcibly breaking* out or making a *breach* in a *cell* or any other part of a prison in which the *accused is incarcerated*. It must be shown that the accused did the act with the intention of *escaping*.

ESCAPE AND BEING AT LARGE WITHOUT EXCUSE / Failure to attend court / Failure to comply with condition of undertaking or recognizance / Failure to appear or to comply with summons / Failure to comply with appearance notice or promise to appear / Failure to comply with conditions of undertaking / Idem / Election of Crown under Contraventions Act / Proof of certain facts by certificate / Attendance and right to cross-examination / Notice of intention to produce.

145. (1) Every person is guilty of an indictable offence and liable to imprisonment for a term of not more than two years or is guilty of an offence punishable on summary conviction who

(*a*) escapes from lawful custody, or

(*b*) is, before the expiration of a term of imprisonment to which they were sentenced, at large in or out of Canada without lawful excuse.

(2) Every person is guilty of an indictable offence and liable to imprisonment for a term of not more than two years or is guilty of an offence punishable on summary conviction who,

(*a*) being at large on their undertaking or recognizance given to or entered into before a justice or judge, fails, without lawful excuse, to attend court in accordance with the undertaking or recognizance; or

(*b*) having appeared before a court, justice or judge, fails, without lawful excuse, to attend court as subsequently required by the court, justice or judge or to surrender themselves in accordance with an order of the court, justice or judge, as the case may be.

(3) Every person who is at large on an undertaking or recognizance given to or entered into before a justice or judge and is bound to comply with a condition of that undertaking or recognizance, and every person who is bound to comply with a direction under subsection 515(12) or 522(2.1) or an order under subsection 516(2), and who fails, without lawful excuse, to comply with the condition, direction or order is guilty of

(*a*) an indictable offence and is liable to imprisonment for a term not exceeding two years; or

(*b*) an offence punishable on summary conviction.

(4) Every person who is served with a summons and who fails, without lawful excuse, to appear at a time and place stated in it for the purposes of the *Identification of Criminals Act* or to attend court in accordance with it, is guilty of

(*a*) an indictable offence and liable to imprisonment for a term not exceeding two years; or

(*b*) an offence punishable on summary conviction.

(5) Every person who is named in an appearance notice or promise to appear, or in a recognizance entered into before an officer in charge or another peace officer, that has been confirmed by a justice under section 508 and who fails, without lawful excuse, to appear at the time and place stated in it, for the purposes of the *Identification of Criminals Act*, or to attend court in accordance with it, is guilty of

(*a*) an indictable offence and is liable to imprisonment for a term not exceeding two years; or

(*b*) an offence punishable on summary conviction.

(5.1) Every person who, without lawful excuse, fails to comply with any condition of an undertaking entered into under subsection 499(2) or 503(2.1)

(*a*) is guilty of an indictable offence and is liable to imprisonment for a term not exceeding two years; or

(*b*) is guilty of an offence punishable on summary conviction.

(6) For the purposes of subsection (5), it is not a lawful excuse that an appearance notice, promise to appear or recognizance states defectively the substance of the alleged offence.

(7) [*Repealed*, R.S.C. 1985, c. 27 (1st Supp.), s. 20(2).]

(8) For the purposes of subsections (3) to (5), it is a lawful excuse to fail to comply with a condition of an undertaking or recognizance or to fail to appear at a time and place stated in a summons, an appearance notice, a promise to appear or a recognizance for the purposes of the *Identification of Criminals Act* if before the failure the Attorney General, within the meaning of the *Contraventions Act*, makes an election under section 50 of that Act.

(9) In any proceedings under subsection (2), (4) or (5), a certificate of the clerk of the court or a judge of the court before which the accused is alleged to have failed to attend

or of the person in charge of the place at which it is alleged the accused failed to attend for the purposes of the *Identification of Criminals Act* stating that,

(*a*) in the case of proceedings under subsection (2), the accused gave or entered into an undertaking or recognizance before a justice or judge and failed to attend court in accordance therewith or, having attended court, failed to attend court thereafter as required by the court, justice or judge or to surrender in accordance with an order of the court, justice or judge, as the case may be,

(*b*) in the case of proceedings under subsection (4), a summons was issued to and served on the accused and the accused failed to attend court in accordance therewith or failed to appear at the time and place stated therein for the purposes of the *Identification of Criminals Act*, as the case may be, and

(*c*) in the case of proceedings under subsection (5), the accused was named in an appearance notice, a promise to appear or a recognizance entered into before an officer in charge or another peace officer, that was confirmed by a justice under section 508, and the accused failed to appear at the time and place stated therein for the purposes of the *Identification of Criminals Act*, failed to attend court in accordance therewith or, having attended court, failed to attend court thereafter as required by the court, justice or judge, as the case may be,

is evidence of the statements contained in the certificate without proof of the signature or the official character of the person appearing to have signed the certificate.

(10) An accused against whom a certificate described in subsection (9) is produced may, with leave of the court, require the attendance of the person making the certificate for the purposes of cross-examination.

(11) No certificate shall be received in evidence pursuant to subsection (9) unless the party intending to produce it has, before the trial, given to the accused reasonable notice of his intention together with a copy of the certificate. R.S., c. C-34, s. 133; R.S., c. 2 (2nd Supp.), s. 4; 1974-75-76, c. 93, s. 7; R.S.C. 1985, c. 27 (1st Supp.), s. 20; 1992, c. 47, s. 68; 1994, c. 44, s. 8; 1996, c. 7, s. 38; 1997, c. 18, s. 3; 2008, c. 18, s. 3; 2018, c. 29, s. 9(1)-(8), (10), (12).

CROSS-REFERENCES

The term "justice" is defined in s. 2. The terms "undertaking" and "recognizance" principally refer to forms of release authorized by Part XVI. In addition, pending appeal in indictable and summary conviction matters, an accused may be released on an undertaking or recognizance pursuant to ss. 679 and 816. The term "summons" refers to a form of process issued under Part XVI, while the terms "promise to appear" and "appearance notice" refer to process issued by a peace officer. Reference should also be made to the following provisions: ss. 494 and 495, warrantless arrest power; s. 510, issue of warrant for failing to comply with term of summons to appear for purposes of *Identification of Criminals Act*; s. 512, issuing of arrest warrant; s. 524, arrest of accused for misconduct while on a form of release; s. 475, accused absconding during trial; s. 544, accused absconding during preliminary inquiry; s. 598, accused failing to attend for jury trial; Part XXV, procedure for forfeiture of recognizances and for rendering of accused by sureties. Note that by virtue of s. 803(3), where the summary conviction court proceeds to try the accused *ex parte* then no proceedings may be taken under this section arising out of the failure of the accused to appear for trial except with the consent of the Attorney General.

Section 149 provides an exception to the normal rule as set out in s. 743.1 that a sentence of less than two years is served in a reformatory. The court has the power to order that a sentence for escape may be served in a penitentiary. "Escape" is defined in s. 149 to include the offence under subsec. (1) of this section. Under s. 719(2), any time during which a convicted person is unlawfully at large does not count as part of any term of imprisonment. A finding of guilt in relation to this offence may, in certain circumstances, give the court discretion to impose an order prohibiting possession of firearms, ammunition or explosive substances under s. 110.

The related offence of prison breach is in s. 145. Other related offences are as follows: s. 146, permitting or assisting escape; s. 147, rescue from lawful custody or officer permitting escape; s. 148, assisting prisoner of war to escape; s. 405, acknowledging bail in name of another person.

Murder of a peace officer, warden, deputy warden, instructor, keeper, jailer, guard or other officer or permanent employee of a prison, acting in the course of his duties, is first degree murder by virtue of s. 231(4). This offence in subsec. (1) may be the basis for an application for an authorization to intercept private communications by reason of s. 183 or a warrant to conduct video surveillance under s. 487.01(5).

The offences in this section are all Crown option offences. Where the prosecution elects to proceed by way of summary conviction then the trial of this offence is conducted by a summary conviction court pursuant to Part XXVII. The punishment for the offence is then as set out in s. 787 and the limitation period is set out in s. 786(2). Where the Crown proceeds by way of indictment then the accused has an election as to mode of trial under s. 536(2). In either case, release pending trial is determined by s. 515, although the accused is eligible for release by a peace officer under ss. 496 and 497 or by the officer in charge under s. 498. However, note s. 515(6) which puts the burden of proof on the accused to show why he should be released in certain circumstances, including the case where the accused is charged with an offence under subsecs. (2) to (5) of this section, or is charged with an indictable offence while at large after being released in respect of another indictable offence. Further, by virtue of s. 519, the accused would not be released pursuant to any release order until the accused was not required to be detained in custody in respect of any other matter.

SYNOPSIS

This section creates the offences of *escaping, being unlawfully at large,* and offences relating to *failing to comply* with various forms of process or judicial interim release. It also facilitates the prosecution of charges of failing to comply by authorizing the use of certificates to prove some aspects of these offences.

Subsection (1) deals with escapes and being unlawfully at large. Under s. 145(1)(*a*), it must be proven that the accused was in *lawful custody* at the time of the escape. Section 145(1)(*b*) states the elements of the offence of being unlawfully at large inside or outside of Canada before the expiration of the custodial portion of a sentence.

Section 145(2) creates offences pertaining to those who *fail to attend court* as required by the terms of an order of judicial interim release, or to appear subsequently as required by a court, judge or justice after initially appearing in court.

Subsection (3) creates the offence of failing to comply with a condition in a judicial interim release order and with directions or orders in detention orders or remand orders that the detainee not communicate with a victim, witness or other person identified in the order or direction.

Subsection (4) creates the offence of *failing to comply* with a requirement in a *summons* to attend court or at the specified place for fingerprinting as required by the *Identification of Criminals Act*.

Subsection (5) spells out the offence of *failing to comply* with a requirement in a *release order* entered into before the officer in charge of the station that the accused attend court or at the specified place for fingerprinting as required by the *Identification of Criminals Act*. This subsection only applies if the appearance notice, promise to appear or recognizance has been confirmed by a justice of the peace.

Subsections (2) to (5) permit the accused to rely upon a *lawful excuse,* but the onus is upon the accused to establish such excuse. As with other provisions placing a burden upon the accused, this aspect of the section is likely to be attacked as violating ss. 7 and 11(*d*) of the Charter. Subsection (6) specifically excludes from what might otherwise be a "lawful excuse" reliance upon a defect in the way in which the substance of the alleged offence is stated in the release documents described in subsec. (5).

The offences created in subsecs. (1) to (5.1) are punishable by way of summary conviction procedure or by indictment. In the latter event, the maximum punishment is two years.

Section 145(8) provides that for the sole purpose of the *Identification of Criminals Act*, an accused charged with or convicted of what is a summary conviction offence under this section, shall be deemed to have been charged with or convicted of an indictable offence.

Subsection (9) permits a *certificate* to be used to prove that an accused charged under s. 145(2), (4) or (5) *did fail* to attend court or for fingerprints as required. The certificate is to be provided by the clerk of the court or the person who is in charge of the place in which the accused was to have attended for fingerprints. It is proof of the statements contained in it without the need to prove the signature or the official character of the person who appears to have signed it.

Section 145(10) permits the cross-examination of the person who made the certificate in subsec. (9) but leave of the court is required. Subsection (11) provides that unless the accused is given notice of the intention to use a certificate along with a copy of it, a certificate made under subsec. (9) cannot be used as evidence.

ANNOTATIONS

Subsection (1) / Meaning of lawful custody – In *R. v. Piper*, [1965] 3 C.C.C. 135 (Man. C.A.), the accused was found guilty where he had escaped from the penitentiary confines but was still on penitentiary property.

In *R. v. Whitfield*, [1970] S.C.R. 46, [1970] 1 C.C.C. 129, it was held (5:2) that arrest is an undivided act that defies separation into "custodial" or "symbolic" arrest.

An arrest stated to be for one described offence cannot be validated by a later reliance upon another offence for which it might have been, but was not, made: *R. v. Huff* (1979), 50 C.C.C. (2d) 324 (Alta. C.A.).

Where an accused is informed at least of the general nature of the charge for which he was apprehended, his arrest is lawful: *R. v. Boughton* (1975), 23 C.C.C. (2d) 395, [1975] W.W.D. 79 (Alta. S.C. App. Div.).

Notwithstanding the applicable provincial legislation only permits the arrest of a person "found" to be intoxicated in a public place an accused may be convicted of escaping lawful custody provided he was apparently intoxicated when arrested even if the Judge finds as a fact he was not intoxicated: *R. v. Robertson* (1978), 42 C.C.C. 78 (B.C.C.A.).

A conviction under this section was imposed on an accused who was present in court when a sentence of incarceration was imposed but then left the court after a recess when the officer in charge briefly left the room. He was in custody within the meaning of the section as he was present when sentence was pronounced and submitted to arrest by asking permission of the officer to do various things, notwithstanding he was never placed in a prisoner's dock, handcuffed or otherwise physically placed under arrest: *R. v. Zajner* (1977), 36 C.C.C. (2d) 417 (Ont. C.A.).

An inmate of a transition house who leaves the house with permission of the management but fails to return to prison as required does not commit the offence under para. (*a*). A person cannot be convicted of escaping custody where his initial physical liberty was legally obtained. In such circumstances his offence, if any, is that created by para. (*b*): *R. v. Folchito* (1986), 26 C.C.C. (3d) 253 (Que. C.A.).

Unlawfully at large – An inmate, when released on a temporary pass, could be unlawfully at large immediately if at that moment he decided not to return to the institution when required: *R. v. MacCaud* (1975), 22 C.C.C. (2d) 445 (Ont. H.C.J.).

It is not every breach of a condition of a temporary absence permit which operates to deprive the inmate of a lawful excuse under this subsection, but rather only a wilful breach of a condition which shows an intention by the inmate to withdraw himself from the control, in the sense of the custody, of the correctional authorities even where the permit itself provided that apparent breach of the conditions rendered it null and void and deemed the inmate to be unlawfully at large: *R. v. Seymour* (1980), 52 C.C.C. (2d) 305 (Ont. C.A.).

Secure and open custody imposed pursuant to the [former] *Young Offenders Act* constitutes a form of imprisonment. Thus an offender who fails to return after expiry of a day pass may be convicted of the offence under para. (*b*): *R. v. McKay* (1985), 21 C.C.C. (3d) 191 (Man. C.A.); *R. v. B.D.* (1986), 24 C.C.C. (3d) 187 (Ont. C.A.). Similarly, *R. v. C.A.* (1986), 25 C.C.C. (3d) 133 (Sask. C.A.).

Proof of lawful custody – A calendar of sentence is sufficient proof that the accused is in lawful custody: *R. v. Ouellette* (1978), 39 C.C.C. (2d) 278 (B.C.C.A.).

In *R. v. Adams* (1978), 45 C.C.C. (2d) 459 (B.C.C.A.), two of the three members of the court held that it is not open to an accused to go behind a warrant of committal valid on its face.

Subsection (2) – An accused charged with a summary conviction offence and released on an undertaking to appear in court complies with that undertaking by appearing either personally or by counsel or agent, as permitted by s. 800(2), and where counsel appears on the court date the accused may not be charged with the offence under this section: *R. v. Okanee* (1981), 59 C.C.C. (2d) 149 (Sask. C.A.).

The *mens rea* requirement is largely objective. Lawful excuse requires the accused to establish due diligence, which includes an honest and reasonable belief in a state of facts that would excuse non-attendance. The defence was, however, made out where the accused did not attend because he was incorrectly advised by the complainant that the charge had been dropped: *R. v. Ludlow* (1999), 136 C.C.C. (3d) 460 (B.C.C.A.).

Failure to appear on a return date subsequent to the issuance of an arrest warrant marked "with discretion" cannot support a charge of failure to appear: *R. v. Bowen* (1999), 139 C.C.C. (3d) 131 (Ont. C.J.).

This provision creates one offence with subsections that describe three different methods of committing the offence: (1) being at large on an undertaking or recognizance and failing to attend court; (2) having appeared before a court and failing to attend thereafter as required by the court; and (3) having appeared before a court and failing to surrender in accordance with an order of the court. Accordingly, an information need not specify whether the offence was committed under para. (*a*) or (*b*): *R. v. Charles* (2006), 210 C.C.C. (3d) 289 (Alta. C.A.).

The offence under subsec. (2)(*b*) is committed where a person fails to appear in court after being required by the court to do so. It can be committed even where the underlying proceeding requiring the attendance is in respect of a non-criminal provincial offence: *R. v. Jerrett* (2017), 356 C.C.C. (3d) 285 (N.L.C.A.).

Subsection (3) – This is a true criminal offence and mere carelessness or failure to take the precautions that a reasonable person would take will not support a conviction. The Crown must prove that the accused had the requisite *mens rea* before any issue of lawful excuse arises: *R. v. Legere* (1995), 95 C.C.C. (3d) 555 (Ont. C.A.). Not folld: *R. v. Ludlow, supra.*

The *mens rea* of this offence requires proof that the accused knowingly or recklessly infringed the conditions of the undertaking. However, a mistake of law cannot negative *mens rea*. In this case, the accused was ordered to reside at a named apartment. When he could not obtain entry to the apartment, he decided to sleep in his car in the building's parking lot. The accused's mistaken belief that he was complying with the term of the undertaking was a mistake of law and no defence. The accused also failed to make out a lawful excuse by a showing of due diligence to satisfy the obligation: *R. v. Custance* (2005), 194 C.C.C. (3d) 225 (Man. C.A.), leave to appeal to S.C.C. refused 198 C.C.C. (3d) vi.

It is not a defence that the conviction which gave rise to the undertaking is subsequently set aside. Court orders must be obeyed until set aside or modified regardless of doubts or challenges as to their validity: *R. v. Gaudreault* (1996), 105 C.C.C. (3d) 270 (Que. C.A.), leave to appeal to S.C.C. refused 108 C.C.C. (3d) vi.

The Crown is required to prove beyond a reasonable doubt that the accused was bound by a recognizance condition on the date in question and it is only after this that the onus shifts to the accused to provide a lawful excuse: *R. v. Truong* (2008), 235 C.C.C. (3d) 547 (B.C.S.C.).

Subsection (5) – *Mens rea* is an element of the offence of failing to appear and accordingly the accused may raise the defence of honest mistake: *R. v. Bender* (1976), 30 C.C.C. (2d) 496 (B.C.S.C.).

Thus where an accused honestly forgot the date of his court appearance he has a defence to the charge even if he forgot due to his own negligence: *R. v. Stuart* (1981), 58 C.C.C. (2d) 203 (B.C.S.C.). Folld: *R. v. Neal* (1982), 67 C.C.C. (2d) 92 (Ont. Co. Ct.). See also: *R. v. Loutitt* (2011), 284 C.C.C. (3d) 518 (Alta. Q.B.).

Where the accused appeared pursuant to the first appearance notice but not for her trial date, the Crown had the option of proceeding under subsecs. (2) or (5). Subsection (5) applies not only to the "time and place stated" in the appearance notice, but also to attendance "in accordance therewith", which includes appearances "thereafter as required by the court": *R. v. Hubek* (2011), 277 C.C.C. (3d) 550 (Alta. C.A.).

Subsection (9) – A certificate under this subsection may be evidence not only that the accused failed to appear but that, for example, he was named in an appearance notice which was confirmed by a justice: *R. v. Dorigo* (1982), 69 C.C.C. (2d) 141 (B.C.S.C.).

PERMITTING OR ASSISTING ESCAPE.

146. Every one who

(*a*) permits a person whom he has in lawful custody to escape, by failing to perform a legal duty,

(*b*) conveys or causes to be conveyed into a prison anything, with intent to facilitate the escape of a person imprisoned therein, or

(*c*) directs or procures, under colour of pretended authority, the discharge of a prisoner who is not entitled to be discharged,

is guilty of an indictable offence and liable to imprisonment for a term not exceeding two years. R.S., c. C-34, s. 134.

CROSS-REFERENCES

The term "prison" is defined in s. 2.

The related offences of escaping lawful custody and being unlawfully at large are in s. 145. Other related offences are as follows: s. 144, prison breach; s. 147, rescue from lawful custody or officer permitting escape; s. 148, assisting prisoner of war to escape.

Murder of a peace officer, warden, deputy warden, instructor, keeper, jailer, guard or other officer or permanent employee of a prison, acting in the course of his duties, is first degree murder by virtue of s. 231(4).

The accused has an election as to mode of trial pursuant to s. 536(2). Release pending trial is determined by s. 515, although the accused is eligible for release by the officer in charge under s. 498.

SYNOPSIS

Section 146 creates an indictable offence of *permitting* or *assisting* a prisoner to *escape lawful custody* or *prison*.

Section 146(*a*) makes the *failure* to *perform* a *legal duty* which *permits* another to *escape* an offence. The principal in the offence must have *lawful custody* of the escapee.

Section 146(*b*) applies when a person takes anything into a prison or causes anything to be brought with the *intention* of *facilitating* an escape.

Section 146(*c*) spells out the offence of discharging a prisoner when the person who directs or procures such release does so under *pretended authority*. The accused must *know* that he or she does not have proper authority and that the *prisoner* is *not entitled* to be discharged.

The maximum punishment upon conviction is two years.

RESCUE OR PERMITTING ESCAPE.

147. Every one who

(*a*) rescues any person from lawful custody or assists any person in escaping or attempting to escape from lawful custody,

(*b*) being a peace officer, wilfully permits a person in his lawful custody to escape, or

(*c*) being an officer of or an employee in a prison, wilfully permits a person to escape from lawful custody therein,

is guilty of an indictable offence and liable to imprisonment for a term not exceeding five years. R.S., c. C-34, s. 135.

CROSS-REFERENCES

The terms "prison" and "peace officer" are defined in s. 2.

The related offence of escaping lawful custody and being unlawfully at large is in s. 145. Other related offences are as follows: s. 144, prison breach; s. 146, permitting or assisting escape; s. 148, assisting prisoner of war to escape.

Murder of a peace officer, warden, deputy warden, instructor, keeper, jailer, guard or other officer or permanent employee of a prison, acting in the course of his duties, is first degree murder by virtue of s. 231(4).

The accused has an election as to mode of trial pursuant to s. 536(2). Release pending trial is determined by s. 515, although the accused is eligible for release by the officer in charge under s. 498.

SYNOPSIS

Section 147 sets out three indictable offences of rescuing a person from lawful custody and prohibits actions of peace officers or prison employees which permit a person to escape.

Section 147(*a*) creates offences of assisting anyone to *escape* (or attempting to do so) or rescuing anyone from lawful custody.

Section 147(*b*) applies to peace officers and s. 147(*c*) to officers or employees of prisons who *wilfully permit* a person to escape from *lawful custody*.

The maximum sentence for these offences is five years.

ANNOTATIONS

A prisoner was still "escaping" within the meaning of this section although at the time the accused assisted him, he was in an area of the province which was landlocked and his flight from the authorities could only be transitory: *R. v. Stutt; R. v. Claussen* (1979), 52 C.C.C. (2d) 53 (B.C.C.A.).

In the absence of evidence to the contrary a police officer's testimony that he was transporting the prisoner in custody from police jail cells to court to set a trial date at the time he escaped was sufficient proof that the prisoner was in lawful custody and the Crown was not required to produce the actual warrant under which the prisoner was being held: *R. v. Stutt; R. v. Claussen, supra.*

Assistance is provided if the act of the accused joins in the enterprise of escape even if the act does not materially contribute to the escape: *R. v. Harrer* (1998), 124 C.C.C. (3d) 368, 172 W.A.C. 311 (B.C.C.A.).

ASSISTING PRISONER OF WAR TO ESCAPE.

148. Every one who knowingly and wilfully

(*a*) assists a prisoner of war in Canada to escape from a place where he is detained, or

(*b*) assists a prisoner of war, who is permitted to be at large on parole in Canada, to escape from the place where he is at large on parole,

is guilty of an indictable offence and liable to imprisonment for a term not exceeding five years. R.S., c. C-34, s. 136.

CROSS-REFERENCES

Related offences include the following: s. 50, assisting enemy alien; s. 54, assisting deserter; s. 55, assisting deserter from R.C.M.P.

Murder of a peace officer, warden, deputy warden, instructor, keeper, jailer, guard or other officer or permanent employee of a prison, acting in the course of his duties, is first degree murder by virtue of s. 231(4).

A finding of guilt in relation to this offence may, in certain circumstances, give the court a discretion to impose an order prohibiting possession of firearms, ammunition or explosive substances under s. 110.

The accused has an election as to mode of trial pursuant to s. 536(2). Release pending trial is determined by s. 515, although the accused is eligible for release by the officer in charge under s. 498.

SYNOPSIS

Section 148 creates the offence of assisting a *prisoner of war to escape*. Section 148(*a*) and (*b*) spell out the details of the prisoner of war's status at the time of the offence. Both offences require that the accused *know* of the status of the prisoner of war and *wilfully* assist in the escape. The maximum sentence for this indictable offence is five years' imprisonment.

SERVICE OF TERM FOR ESCAPE / Definition of "escape".

149. (1) Notwithstanding section 743.1, a court that convicts a person for an escape committed while undergoing imprisonment may order that the term of imprisonment be served in a penitentiary, even if the time to be served is less than two years.

(2) In this section, "escape" means breaking prison, escaping from lawful custody or, without lawful excuse, being at large before the expiration of a term of imprisonment to which a person has been sentenced. R.S., c. C-34, s. 137; 1972, c. 13, s. 9; 1976-77, c. 53, s. 6; 1992, c. 20, s. 199; 1995, c. 22, ss. 1 and 10.

CROSS-REFERENCES

"Penitentiary" is defined in s. 2 of the *Corrections and Conditional Release Act*, S.C. 1992, c. 20. Under s. 719(2), any time during which a convicted person is unlawfully at large does not count as part of any term of imprisonment.

SYNOPSIS

This section provides an exception to the normal rule as set out in s. 743.1 that a sentence of less than two years is served in a reformatory. The court has the power to order that a sentence for escape, as defined in subsec. (2), may be served in a penitentiary. Subsection (2) contains a broad definition of "escape" so that it includes prison breach (s. 144) and escaping or being unlawfully at large (s. 145(1)).

Part V / SEXUAL OFFENCES, PUBLIC MORALS AND DISORDERLY CONDUCT

Interpretation

DEFINITIONS / "Guardian" / "Public place" / "Theatre".

150. In this Part

"guardian" includes any person who has in law or in fact the custody or control of another person;

"public place" includes any place to which the public have access as of right or by invitation, express or implied;

"theatre" includes any place that is open to the public where entertainments are given, whether or not any charge is made for admission. R.S., c. C-34, s. 138.

CROSS-REFERENCES

In addition to the definitions in this section, see s. 2 and notes to that section. Despite the heading of this Part, in fact, many of the sexual offences are found in Part VIII and many of the offences dealing with public disorder are found in Part II.

SYNOPSIS

Section 150 provides definitions of the terms "guardian", "public place" and "theatre" which are used in a number of sections within Part V of the *Criminal Code*.

ANNOTATIONS

Public place – As the definitive words preceded by the word "includes" were not intended to be exhaustive and to exclude the ordinary dictionary meaning of those words, private property, frequented by members of the public with no objection by the owner, is a public place: *R. v. Lavoie*, [1968] 1 C.C.C. 265 (N.B.C.A.).

To constitute a public place it is not necessary that all segments of the public have a right of access thereto and accordingly a beverage room, from which a portion of the public may be excluded by law or by choice, is a public place under this section: *R. v. Tegstrom*, [1971] 1 W.W.R. 147 (Sask. D.C.).

"Public place" in this section was not meant to cover private places exposed to public view. The definition requires physical access to the place in which the impugned act was committed; visual access is not sufficient: *R. v. Clark*, [2005] 1 S.C.R. 6, 193 C.C.C. (3d) 289.

Sexual Offences

CONSENT NO DEFENCE / Exception — complainant aged 12 or 13 / Exception — complainant aged 14 or 15 / Exception for transitional purposes / Exception for transitional purposes / Exemption for accused aged twelve or thirteen / Mistake of age / Idem / Idem.

150.1 (1) Subject to subsections (2) to (2.2), when an accused is charged with an offence under section 151 or 152 or subsection 153(1), 160(3) or 173(2) or is charged with an offence under section 271, 272 or 273 in respect of a complainant under the age of 16 years, it is not a defence that the complainant consented to the activity that forms the subject-matter of the charge.

(2) When an accused is charged with an offence under section 151 or 152, subsection 173(2) or section 271 in respect of a complainant who is 12 years of age or more but under the age of 14 years, it is a defence that the complainant consented to the activity that forms the subject-matter of the charge if the accused

(*a*) is less than two years older than the complainant; and

(*b*) is not in a position of trust or authority towards the complainant, is not a person with whom the complainant is in a relationship of dependency and is not in a relationship with the complainant that is exploitative of the complainant.

(2.1) If an accused is charged with an offence under section 151 or 152, subsection 173(2) or section 271 in respect of a complainant who is 14 years of age or more but

under the age of 16 years, it is a defence that the complainant consented to the activity that forms the subject-matter of the charge if the accused

(*a*) is less than five years older than the complainant; and

(*b*) is not in a position of trust or authority towards the complainant, is not a person with whom the complainant is in a relationship of dependency and is not in a relationship with the complainant that is exploitative of the complainant.

(2.2) When the accused referred to in subsection (2.1) is five or more years older than the complainant, it is a defence that the complainant consented to the activity that forms the subject matter of the charge if, on the day on which this subsection comes into force,

(*a*) the accused is the common-law partner of the complainant, or has been cohabiting with the complainant in a conjugal relationship for a period of less than one year and they have had or are expecting to have a child as a result of the relationship; and

(*b*) the accused is not in a position of trust or authority towards the complainant, is not a person with whom the complainant is in a relationship of dependency and is not in a relationship with the complainant that is exploitative of the complainant.

(2.3) If, immediately before the day on which this subsection comes into force, the accused referred to in subsection (2.1) is married to the complainant, it is a defence that the complainant consented to the activity that forms the subject-matter of the charge.

(3) No person aged twelve or thirteen years shall be tried for an offence under section 151 or 152 or subsection 173(2) unless the person is in a position of trust or authority towards the complainant, is a person with whom the complainant is in a relationship of dependency or is in a relationship with the complainant that is exploitative of the complainant.

(4) It is not a defence to a charge under section 151 or 152, subsection 160(3) or 173(2), or section 271, 272 or 273 that the accused believed that the complainant was 16 years of age or more at the time the offence is alleged to have been committed unless the accused took all reasonable steps to ascertain the age of the complainant.

(5) It is not a defence to a charge under section 153, 159, 170, 171 or 172 or subsection 286.1(2), 286.2(2) or 286.3(2) that the accused believed that the complainant was eighteen years of age or more at the time the offence is alleged to have been committed unless the accused took all reasonable steps to ascertain the age of the complainant.

(6) An accused cannot raise a mistaken belief in the age of the complainant in order to invoke a defence under subsection (2) or (2.1) unless the accused took all reasonable steps to ascertain the age of the complainant. R.S.C. 1985, c. 19 (3rd Supp.), s. 1; 2005, c. 32, s. 2; 2008, c. 6, ss. 13, 54(*a*); 2014, c. 25, s. 4; 2015, c. 29, s. 6.

CROSS-REFERENCES

The term "complainant" is defined in s. 2. The terms "position of trust or authority" and "relationship of dependency" are not defined. Section 153(1.2) sets out circumstances from which a judge may infer that a person is in an exploitative relationship with a young person.

In effect, this section attempts to define the circumstances in which a child may legally consent to sexual activity and the parameters of the "defence" of mistake of fact where the mistake is as to the age of the complainant. As to other notes concerning the mistake defence generally, see notes following s. 19 and, with respect to consent in particular, the notes following s. 265.

Age is determined by s. 30 of the *Interpretation Act*, R.S.C. 1985, c. I-21. Section 658 provides means of proving the age of a child.

Special evidentiary and procedural provisions – Section 274 provides that no corroboration is required for a conviction for any of the offences in ss. 151 to 153.1, 155, 159, 160 and 170 to 173 and the judge shall not instruct the jury that it is unsafe to find the accused guilty in the absence of corroboration. That provision, in effect, reverses the common law rule of practice that required the trial judge to direct the jury as to the need for corroboration for most sexual offences, especially those involving children. Section 275 provides that the rule relating to evidence of recent complaint is abrogated respecting ss. 151 to 153.1, 155, 159, 160(2) and (3) and 170 to 173. Sections 276 to 276.4 enact special rules limiting the circumstances in which the complainant may be questioned with respect to his or her prior sexual conduct with persons other than the accused in proceedings under ss. 151 to 153.1, 155, 159, 160(2) and (3) and 170 to 173. Section 277 provides that evidence of sexual reputation is inadmissible in proceedings under ss. 151 to 153.1, 155, 159, 160(2) and (3) and 170 to 173. Production of records containing personal information for use by the accused at the trial of these offences is governed by ss. 278.1 to 278.9.

Section 486(1) and (2) provide that the judge may make an order excluding all or any members of the public where such order is in the interest of public morals, the maintenance of order or the proper administration of justice or is necessary to prevent injury to international relations or national defence or national security. The proper administration of justice includes safeguarding the interests of witnesses under the age of 18 years. Where the accused is charged with an offence in ss. 151 to 153.1, 155, 159, 160, 170 to 173 or 279.01 to 279.03 and the application by the accused or the prosecutor for the exclusion order is dismissed, the judge shall state the reason for not making the order. Section 486.1 sets out the circumstances in which the judge shall or may order a support person to be present and close to a witness while the witness testifies. Where the witness is under the age of 18 years or has a mental or physical disability, the order is to be made upon request, unless the judge is of the opinion that the order would interfere with the proper administration of justice. In the case of other witnesses, the order is to be made if necessary to obtain a full and candid account from the witness of the matters complained of. The application for this order may be made during the proceedings or before they begin to the judge who is to preside at the proceedings.

Similarly, s. 486.2 sets out the circumstances in which the judge shall or may order a witness to testify outside the courtroom or behind a screen or other device that would not allow the witness to see the accused. Where the witness is under the age of 18 years or may have difficulty communicating the evidence by reason of a mental or physical disability, the judge shall make the order unless the judge is of the opinion that the order would interfere with the proper administration of justice. In all other cases, the order may be made if the judge is of the opinion that the order is necessary to obtain a full and candid account from the witness of the acts complained of. Similarly, s. 486.3 provides that, on application by the prosecutor or a witness under the age of 18 years, the accused shall not personally cross-examine the witness unless the judge is of the opinion that the proper administration of justice requires the accused to personally conduct the cross-examination. In other cases, the judge may make an order that the accused not personally cross-examine the witness if the judge is of the opinion that the order is necessary to obtain a full and candid account from the witness of the acts complained of. The judge will appoint counsel to conduct the cross-examination.

Under s. 486.4, the judge may make an order directing that the identity of the complainant or a witness not be disclosed in any publication, broadcast or transmitted in any way. The order is mandatory where the complainant or a witness under the age of 18 years or the prosecutor applies for the order. Section 486.5 also gives the judge a discretion respecting non-publication orders in proceedings under these provisions in other circumstances.

Section 659 abrogates any rule requiring a warning about convicting the accused on the evidence of a child.

Where the accused is found guilty of the offences under ss. 151, 152, 155 or 159, 160(2) or (3), 163.1, 170, 171, 172.1, 173(2), 271, 272, 273 or 281 and the offence is in respect of a person who is under 16 years of age, then the court has the discretion to impose an order of prohibition under s. 161 prohibiting the accused from attending certain public areas and facilities or taking certain employment which will bring him into contact with persons under 16 years of age.

Section 715.1 provides that, in proceedings against the accused in which the victim (defined in s. 2) or other witness was under the age of 18 years at the time the offence is alleged to have been committed, a video recording made within a reasonable time after the alleged offence, in which the victim or witness describes the acts complained of, is admissible in evidence if the victim or witness, while testifying, adopts its contents, unless the judge is of the opinion that the admission of the video recoding would interfere with the proper administration of justice. Section 715.2 provides for a similar procedure where the victim or another witness may have difficulty communicating the evidence by reason of a mental or physical disability. Under s. 4(2) of the *Canada Evidence Act*, the spouse of an accused charged with an offence under ss. 151 to 153.1, 155, 159, 160(2), (3), 170 to 173, or 177 is a compellable witness at the instance of the prosecution. Sections 16 and 16.1 of the *Canada Evidence Act* deal with the competency of witnesses under the age of 14 years.

Section 718.01 provides that, in imposing a sentence for an offence involving the abuse of a person under the age of 18 years, the court shall give primary consideration to the objectives of denunciation and deterrence. Further, under s. 718.2, evidence that the offender, in committing the offence, abused a person under the age of 18 years is an aggravating circumstance.

SYNOPSIS

This section provides a series of rules that apply to enumerated sections to prevent an accused from relying on the consent of a complainant under a specified age. It also spells out when a mistake by the accused may be a defence.

Subsection (1) provides that the consent of the complainant, who is less than 16 years old, is no defence to the sexual assault offences (ss. 271 to 273) and no defence at all, no matter what the age of the complainant, to the other enumerated offences, such as sexual exploitation (s. 153(1)).

Subsection (2) provides an exception to subsec. (1) and permits the defence of consent to be raised to the offences of sexual interference (s. 151), invitation to sexual touching (s. 152), indecent exposure to a person under 16 (s. 173(2)), or sexual assault (s. 271) if the complainant is at least 12 but less than 14 years old and the additional requirements of the subsection are met. The further conditions which must be met for the exception to apply are as follows: (a) the accused is less than two years older than the complainant; (b) the accused is not in a position of trust or authority towards the complainant, the complainant is not in a relationship of dependency with the accused and the accused is not in a relationship with the complainant that is exploitative of the complainant.

Subsection (2.1) provides for a similar exception where the complainant is 14 years of age or more but under the age of 16 years. The conditions which must be met are as follow: (a) the accused is less than five years older than the complainant; and (b) the accused is not in a position of trust or authority towards the complainant, the complainant is not in a relationship of dependency with the accused and the accused is not in a relationship with the complainant that is exploitative of the complainant.

Importantly, subsec. (6) provides that mistake of fact cannot be invoked under subsecs. (2) or (2.1) unless the accused took all reasonable steps to ascertain the age of the complainant.

Subsection (2.2) provides a form of transitional provision for cases where the accused is five or more years older than the complainant when this section came into force (May 1, 2008) and (a) the accused and the complainant are either in a common-law relationship or cohabiting in a conjugal relationship and have or are expecting a child; and (b) the accused is not in a position of trust or authority towards the complainant, the complainant is not in a relationship of dependency with the accused and the accused is not in a relationship with the complainant that is exploitative of the complainant.

Subsection (2.3) provides a transitional provision that allows accused persons referred to in subsec. (2.1) who were married to the complainant when this subsection came into force to rely on the defence that the complainant consented to the activity that forms the subject-matter of the charge.

Subsection (3) prohibits the prosecution of a 12 or 13-year-old unless the accused comes within condition (b) noted above.

Under subsecs. (4) and (5), for the offences listed in this section, it is not an excuse that the accused believed the complainant was over 16 years or 18 years, as the case may be, unless the accused took all reasonable steps to ascertain the age of the complainant.

ANNOTATIONS

Note: Some of the cases noted below were decided when the age of consent was 14 years.

Application of Charter of Rights – This provision is not overbroad in contravention of s. 7 of the Charter. The close-in-age exceptions represent reasonable legislative line-drawing about when sexual contact becomes exploitative: *R. v. B. (A.)* (2015), 333 C.C.C. (3d) 382 (Ont. C.A.).

It has been held that former s. 246.1(2), which also limited the consent defence where the complainant was under fourteen years of age, did not constitute an unconstitutional violation of the equality rights guaranteed by s. 15 of the Charter: *R. v. Bearhead* (1986), 27 C.C.C. (3d) 546, 22 C.R.R. 211 (Alta. Q.B.); *R. v. Le Gallant* (1986), 29 C.C.C. (3d) 291, 54 C.R. (3d) 46 (B.C.C.A.); *R. v. Perkins* (1987), 59 C.R. (3d) 56, [1987] N.W.T.R. 308 (S.C.); *R. v. Halleran* (1989), 39 C.C.C. (3d) 177 (Nfld. C.A.). *Contra: R. v. Black* (1990), 11 W.C.B. (2d) 557 (B.C.S.C.), where it was held that former s. 246.1(2) infringed s. 7 of the Charter and was not a reasonable limit.

Elimination of the defence of consent by subsec. (1) where the complainant is under 14 years of age does not infringe s. 7 of the Charter: *R. v. M. (R.S.)* (1991), 69 C.C.C. (3d) 223, 10 C.R. (4th) 121 (P.E.I.C.A.).

The removal of the defence of consent to a charge contrary to s. 153 violates neither s. 7 nor s. 15 of the Charter: *R. v. Hann* (1992), 75 C.C.C. (3d) 355, 15 C.R. (4th) 355 (Nfld. C.A.).

Trial of child (Subsec. (3)) – It was held, considering a predecessor to subsec. (3) in relation to the former offence of rape, that the section merely enacted a rule of immunity not incapacity and therefore an accused who is over fourteen years of age may be convicted as a party although the principal being under fourteen years of age is immune from prosecution: *R. v. Cardinal* (1982), 3 C.C.C. (3d) 376, [1983] 1 W.W.R. 689 (Alta. C.A.), affd [1984] 2 S.C.R. 523, 18 C.C.C. (3d) 96 (7:0).

The fact that subsec. (3) does not extend immunity from prosecution to the offence of sexual assault under s. 271 does not violate an offender's rights under s. 7 of the Charter. Nevertheless, the discretion as to whether the accused should be charged with sexual assault must be exercised in a proper manner and for a proper motive and it would be for the Crown to ensure that a 12- or 13-year-old offender, who did not use force in circumstances which would only amount to an offence under s. 151 or s. 152, was not charged under s. 271 merely to avoid the immunity provisions of subsec. (3): *R. v. V. (K.S.)* (1994), 89 C.C.C. (3d) 477, 119 Nfld. & P.E.I.R. 290 (Nfld. C.A.), leave to appeal to S.C.C. refused 95 C.C.C. (3d) vi.

Mistake as to age – To convict an accused person who demonstrates an air of reality to the mistake of age defence, the Crown must prove, beyond a reasonable doubt, either that the accused person did not honestly believe the complainant was at least 16, or did not take all reasonable steps to ascertain the complainant's age. Determining what raises a reasonable doubt in respect of the objective element is a highly contextual, fact-specific exercise. In some cases, it may be reasonable to ask a partner's age. In some cases more may be required, given the obvious motivation for young people to misrepresent their age. One general rule may be recognized: the more reasonable an accused's perception of the complainant's age, the fewer steps will reasonably be required of them: *R. v. George*, [2017] 1 S.C.R. 1021, 349 C.C.C. (3d) 371.

The accused, in order to rely on the defence of mistake, need only raise a reasonable doubt. The accused must, however, have made an earnest inquiry or there should be some compelling factor that obviates the need for such an inquiry. Thus, the accused must show what steps he took and those steps were all that could be reasonably required of him in the circumstances: *R. v. Osborne* (1992), 17 C.R. (4th) 350, 102 Nfld. & P.E.I.R. 194 (Nfld. C.A.).

Where the accused raises the defence of honest but mistaken belief in the complainant's age, the Crown must prove beyond a reasonable doubt that the accused did not take all reasonable steps to ascertain the complainant's age or did not have an honest belief as to the complainant's age. The issue to be determined is what steps would have been reasonable for the accused to take in the circumstances. While in certain circumstances a visual observation may suffice, where it does not, further reasonable steps should be considered having regard to the complainant's physical appearance, her behaviour, the ages and appearance of those in whose company the complainant was found, the activities engaged in, the times, places and other circumstances in which the accused observes the complainant and her conduct. The accused's subjective belief is relevant but not conclusive of this determination: *R. v. P. (L.T.)* (1997), 113 C.C.C. (3d) 42, 142 W.A.C. 20 (B.C.C.A.).

Subsection (4) is not concerned with the accused's belief as to the complainant's age; it assumes that the accused believed the complainant to be old enough to give legal consent. This provision mandates an inquiry akin to a due diligence inquiry by the trier of fact, albeit with the onus of proof on the Crown. It was therefore an error of law for the trial judge to limit his analysis to the accused's own state of mind with no consideration of what steps were taken to confirm that belief: *R. v. Saliba* (2013), 304 C.C.C. (3d) 133 (Ont. C.A.). See also: *R. v. Dragos* (2012), 291 C.C.C. (3d) 350 (Ont. C.A.).

Where the circumstances in which the accused and the complainant met — including the complainant's appearance, her behaviour, and the apparent ages of the other partygoers — all indicated that she was at least 16 years old, subsec. (4) did not mandate any further inquiry: *R. v. Tannas* (2015), 324 C.C.C. (3d) 93 (Sask. C.A.).

Subsection (4) does not require the accused to have made every possible inquiry to ascertain the complainant's age in order to establish the mistake in age defence, nor does it necessarily require that the accused have expressly questioned the complainant on his or her age: *R. v. Chapman* (2016), 337 C.C.C. (3d) 269 (Ont. C.A.), leave to appeal to S.C.C. refused 2016 CarswellOnt 16186.

Subsection (5) does not create a reverse onus as the Crown must prove beyond a reasonable doubt that the accused did not take all reasonable steps or that he did not have an honest belief that the complainant was 18 years of age or more. However, where an accused does not lead any evidence other than through the Crown's case, his ability to obtain an acquittal on subsec. (5) may be compromised. Section 212(4) does not require the Crown to prove that a victim appeared to be less than 18 years of age in order to meet an argument that an accused who does not provide evidence has taken all reasonable steps to ascertain the victim's age merely on the basis of appearance: *R. v. Slater* (2005), 201 C.C.C. (3d) 85, 269 Sask. R. 42 (C.A.).

The accused must point to some evidence capable of giving rise to a reasonable doubt that the accused took all reasonable steps to ascertain the complainant's age. While the evidentiary burden on the accused is low, a mere assertion by the accused will be insufficient to give the defence an air of reality: *R. v. Moise* (2016), 343 C.C.C. (3d) 16 (Sask. C.A.).

Consent defence – The burden is on the accused to prove the consent defence provided by age proximity in subsec. (2)(*a*): *R. v. Thompson* (1992), 76 C.C.C. (3d) 142 (Alta. C.A.).

Whether the accused took "all reasonable steps" will depend on the circumstances. In order to rely on this provision, the accused need not necessarily directly ask the victim her age or ask collateral questions that would disclose her age. The age differential between the accused and the victim may be considered in determining whether the steps taken were reasonable and the greater the disparity in ages, the more inquiry will be required: *R. v. K. (R.A.)* (1996), 106 C.C.C. (3d) 93 (N.B.C.A.).

Whether the accused is in a position of trust for the purpose of subsec. (2)(*c*) must be considered with respect to the accused's position toward the complainant. While the position of the accused as viewed by other individuals, such as family members, may be relevant, it is not determinative. It will be an infrequent case in which the accused, who is a young person close in age to the complainant, will have been entrusted with sufficient responsibility to have been considered to have been in a position of trust toward the complainant, although such cases may arise where the accused was the complainant's baby-sitter, camp counsellor, lifeguard or tutor: *R. v. L. (D.B.)* (1995), 101 C.C.C. (3d) 406, 43 C.R. (4th) 252 (Ont. C.A.).

Expert evidence respecting child abuse – Evidence adduced solely for the purpose of bolstering the credibility of a witness is excluded by virtue of the rule against oath-helping: *R. v. Kyselka* (1962), 133 C.C.C. 103, 37 C.R. 391 (Ont. C.A.). Thus, the opinion of a child witness' teacher that she was a trustworthy witness is inadmissible: *R. v. Hill* (1986), 32 C.C.C. (3d) 314 (Ont. C.A.). Further the opinion of a psychologist that children rarely lie about sexual abuse is inadmissible: *R. v. Kostuck* (1986), 29 C.C.C. (3d) 190, 43 Man. R. (2d) 84 (C.A.). Expert evidence is admissible even if it relates directly to the ultimate question which the trier of fact must answer. In *R. v. R. (D.)*, [1996] 2 S.C.R. 291, 107 C.C.C. (3d) 289, therefore, the expert in child abuse who testified for the defence about the nature of the child complainant's memory was also entitled to also testify about conclusions on the reliability of the child's memory.

While expert evidence on the ultimate credibility of a witness is not admissible, expert evidence on human conduct and the psychological and physical factors which may lead to certain behaviour relevant to credibility is admissible, provided that the testimony goes beyond the ordinary experience of the trier of fact. Where such evidence is admitted, the jury must be carefully instructed as to its function and duty in making the final decision without being unduly influenced by the expert evidence: *R. v. Marquard*, [1993] 4 S.C.R. 223, 85 C.C.C. (3d) 193.

It did not violate the rule against "oath-helping" to ask an expert on child sexual abuse whether, as far as he was aware, the complainant had told him something that was untrue. The expert's evidence was directed to legitimate purposes having nothing to do with whether the complainant was truthful or not. The question and answer was admissible for the purpose of supporting the opinion of the expert expressed on other matters, such as his diagnosis of the complainant's condition and his explanation of her behaviour. His conclusions were based, in large part, on what the complainant had told him and those conclusions would be weakened if not invalidated if the expert did not believe what she had told him. It was therefore relevant to determine whether he believed her or not: *R. v. Burns*, [1994] 1 S.C.R. 656, 89 C.C.C. (3d) 193.

In *R. v. Beliveau* (1986), 30 C.C.C. (3d) 193 (B.C.C.A.), it was held that, while an expert could not be asked whether a child witness was truthful, the expert could give an opinion that certain observed behaviour, demeanour and other facts were consistent with the child having been sexually abused. Similarly *R. v. H. (E.L.)* (1990), 2 C.R. (4th) 187, 100 N.S.R. (2d) 1 (C.A.). In *R. v. J. (F.E.)* (1990), 53 C.C.C. (3d) 64, 74 C.R. (3d) 269 (Ont. C.A.), it was held that a psychologist and social worker could give expert evidence to the effect that a letter written by the child complainant, recanting the allegations of sexual abuse by her father, was typical of the recantations commonly seen among children who have been sexually abused when they realize the problems that their revelations have caused. However, the further opinion by the expert, that he had not found one case in which a child was being truthful when recanting, was inadmissible.

Expert evidence from a clinical psychologist, specializing in the treatment of young victims and perpetrators of sexual offences, that several behavioural characteristics noticed in the young victim were similar to those experienced by young victims of sexual offences is admissible on the trial of a charge of sexual assault and such evidence will often prove invaluable: *R. v. B. (G.)*, [1990] 2 S.C.R. 3, 56 C.C.C. (3d) 161 (5:0). However, expert evidence was not required to explain evidence from the complainant's mother regarding behavioural changes around the time of the offence. The trial judge was entitled to rely on common sense and experience in evaluating these behavioural changes: *R. v. N. (R.A.)* (2001), 152 C.C.C. (3d) 464, 277 A.R. 288 (C.A.).

On the trial of charges of sexual assault by the accused on his stepsons, expert evidence from a sexual abuse therapist was properly admitted to explain why the victims continued to associate with the accused, why the child did not immediately complain to the other parent, but did complain to outsiders, and why the memory of the events could improve as the self-protective mechanism of involuntary forgetting is overcome by the child being required to repeat the story on many occasions. This kind of evidence could be helpful to the jury on the issues of credibility by tending to show that the inferences which might well be drawn on the basis of common sense and common experience should not be drawn as a matter of course in cases of sexual abuse. The jury must, however, be warned as to the dangers in utilizing this kind of evidence, especially the danger of giving undue weight to the expert opinion: *R. v. C. (R.A.)* (1990), 57 C.C.C. (3d) 522, 78 C.R. (3d) 390 (B.C.C.A.).

In *R. v. D. (D.)*, [2000] 2 S.C.R. 275, 148 C.C.C. (3d) 41, the Supreme Court of Canada held that expert evidence regarding delayed disclosure was inadmissible as the expert's evidence was simply a statement of the law that the failure to make a timely complaint must not be the subject of a presumptive adverse inference against the complainant. Where there is an issue of delayed disclosure, the trial judge should instruct the jury that there is no inviolable rule relating to how people who are the victims of trauma like a sexual assault will behave. Some will make an immediate complaint, some will delay disclosure and some will not ever disclose the abuse. The reasons for delay are many and may include embarrassment, fear, guilt or a lack of understanding and knowledge. In assessing credibility, the timing of the complaint is simply one circumstance to consider the context of the case. Delayed disclosure, standing alone, will never give rise to an adverse inference against the credibility of the complainant.

In a case involving alleged physical abuse of a child, the opinion of an expert is admissible as to whether certain injuries were caused accidentally or intentionally; whether it is usual or rare to find injuries of a particular kind in a child of a particular age; the kind and degree of force required to cause the injuries; the age of the injuries; and the consistency or inconsistency of the injuries with explanations given for them. However, it is within the discretion of the trial judge to rule that the evidence be given in a less emotional but just as accurate form, for example, by use of the term "intentional force" rather than "child abuse". The judge may also require that a conclusory statement be excluded where opinion evidence can be given just as accurately in less conclusory terms, for example, in terms of the degree of likelihood of the injuries being caused in a particular manner, provided that this does not affect the honesty or accuracy of the opinion. Further, in a jury case, the trial judge must give a careful direction to the jury as to the manner in which this evidence must be analyzed and applied by the jury: *R. v. Millar* (1989), 49 C.C.C. (3d) 193, 71 C.R. (3d) 78 (Ont. C.A.).

Before an expert's opinion is admissible on behalf of the defence to show that the accused by reason of his disposition could not have been the perpetrator of the offence, the trial judge must be satisfied, as a matter of law, that either the perpetrator of the crime or the accused has a distinctive behavioural characteristic such that a comparison of one with the other will be of material assistance in determining innocence or guilt. The court must consider whether the scientific community has developed a standard profile for the offender who commits this type of crime: *R. v. Mohan*, [1994] 2 S.C.R. 9, 89 C.C.C. (3d) 402. See, however, *R. v. S. (J.T.)* (1996), 47 C.R. (4th) 240, 181 A.R. 181 *sub. nom R. v. Somers* (C.A.), in which expert evidence that there are three recognized psychological profiles of men who abuse young women and that the accused did not fit any of these profiles was admitted.

Where the Crown seeks to adduce expert evidence in respect of the accused, the condition for admission is that either the accused must be shown to be a member of a distinctive group capable of diagnosis by a psychiatrist or it must be shown that the perpetrator of the offence must have been a member of such a group. In this case, while expert evidence that the accused was a homosexual paedophile was relevant to determining the intent of the accused in touching the complainants, in the absence of a useful behavioural profile of the accused or homosexual paedophiles in general from which the jury could make its own judgment as to the accused's purpose at the time of the touching incidents, it was merely evidence of propensity or disposition: *R. v. Pascoe* (1997), 113 C.C.C. (3d) 126, 32 O.R. (3d) 37 (C.A.).

An expert may not testify that, based upon "statement validity analysis", the allegation by the complainant is credible. Evidence tendered for the specific purpose of bolstering the credibility of a witness is inadmissible and, in any event, this theory has not been shown to be scientifically valid: *R. v. Jmieff* (1994), 94 C.C.C. (3d) 157, 84 W.A.C. 213 (B.C.C.A.).

Similar fact evidence respecting child abuse – It was held in *R. v. D. (L.E.)*, [1989] 2 S.C.R. 111, 50 C.C.C. (3d) 142 (4:1), that testimony from the complainant, the accused's daughter, as to much more serious acts of sexual assault than those alleged in the charges, was inadmissible. This similar fact evidence bore nearly the entire burden of proving the Crown's case against the accused on the acts charged and its probative value was not sufficient to overcome its prejudicial effect. However, evidence from the complainant of other conduct, similar to the acts charged and more proximate in time, was properly admitted. Where similar fact evidence is admitted, the jury must be specifically warned that it is not to rely on the evidence as proof that the accused is the sort of person who would commit the offence charged and, on that basis, infer that the accused is in fact guilty of the offence charged.

In *R. v. B. (C.R.)*, [1990] 1 S.C.R. 717, 55 C.C.C. (3d) 1 (5:2), it was held that, on the trial of charges of sexual assault of the accused's natural daughter, evidence was admissible of sexual assaults by the accused upon the daughter of a woman with whom he had lived several years before. While there were differences between the conduct alleged by the complainant and by the similar fact witness it was open to the trial judge to conclude that the probative value of the similar fact evidence with respect to the credibility of the complainant outweighed its prejudicial effect.

On a charge of manslaughter involving the death of an infant, evidence was admissible of other injuries, suffered by the child in the weeks prior to his death, where there was evidence from which the jury could find that these other injuries were intentionally inflicted by the accused: *R. v. Millar* (1989), 49 C.C.C. (3d) 193, 71 C.R. (3d) 78 (Ont. C.A.).

As to similar fact evidence generally, see *R. v. Handy*, [2002] 2 S.C.R. 908, 164 C.C.C. (3d) 481.

Credibility of children – While the court must carefully assess the credibility of child witnesses the standard of a reasonable adult is not necessarily appropriate in assessing the credibility of young children. Young children may not be able to recount precise details and communicate the when and where of an event with exactitude, but this does not mean that they have misconceived what happened to them or who did it: *R. v. B. (G.), supra.*

There have been major changes in recent years with respect to the treatment of evidence of children. While, in a proper case, a child's evidence may be treated with caution, there is no assumption that children's evidence is always less reliable than the evidence of adults. Thus, if a court proceeds to discount a child's evidence automatically, without regard to the circumstances of the particular case, it will have fallen into error. It is also wrong to apply adult tests for credibility to the evidence of children. This does not mean that the evidence of children should not be subject to the same standard of proof as evidence of adult witnesses in criminal cases, but only that the evidence of children must not be approached from the perspective of rigid stereotypes but on the basis of common sense, taking into account the strengths and weaknesses which characterize the evidence offered in the particular case. The credibility of every witness of whatever age must be assessed by reference to criteria appropriate to her mental development, understanding and ability to communicate. In general, however, where an adult is testifying as to events which occurred when she was a child, her credibility should be assessed according to criteria applicable to her as an adult witness bearing in mind that the presence of inconsistencies, particularly as to peripheral matters such as time and location, should be considered in the context of the age of the witness at the time of the events to which she was testifying: *R. v. W. (R)*, [1992] 2 S.C.R. 122, 74 C.C.C. (3d) 134.

Hearsay exception – Reference should also be made to annotations found under s. 9 of the *Canada Evidence Act*.

It is open to the courts to create new hearsay exceptions where the circumstances meet the requirements for necessity, meaning "reasonably necessary", and reliability. In the case of out of court statements by children, necessity may be created where the child is found not to be competent to testify or where there is expert evidence that testimony in court might be traumatic for the child or harm the child. The requirement of necessity will probably mean that, in most cases, children will be called to give *viva voce* evidence. As regards the reliability requirement, the court would have to take into consideration many facts such as timing, demeanour, personality of the child, the intelligence and understanding of the child and the absence of any reason to expect fabrication. The trial judge might also attach conditions to the admission of the evidence in order to safeguard the interests of the accused. This might include the right to cross-examine the child, where the judge thinks it is possible and fair in all the circumstances: *R. v. Khan*, [1990] 2 S.C.R. 531, 59 C.C.C. (3d) 92 (5:0).

The necessity requirement includes a diverse number of circumstances ranging from total testimonial incompetence to traumatic consequences of the witness testifying. Necessity may be established on the basis of what has happened at trial or on the basis of extrinsic evidence. While expert evidence will often be required, evidence does not have to be called to establish necessity. Necessity may be established from the facts and circumstances of the case or from evidence called by the Crown. If the child cannot give evidence in a meaningful way, the trial judge may conclude that it is self-evident from the proceedings that out-of-court statements are necessary. In this case, it was open to the trial judge to find necessity had been established by the child's inability to respond in any way to questions about events: *R. v. F. (W.J.)*, [1999] 3 S.C.R. 569, 138 C.C.C. (3d) 1. See also *R. v. Rockey*, [1996] 3 S.C.R. 829, 110 C.C.C. (3d) 481; *R. v. Dubois* (1997), 118 C.C.C. (3d) 544 (Que. C.A.).

In a case where the child testifies, her hearsay statement will be admissible if reasonably necessary and if there are *indicia* of reliability present. Reasonable necessity in this context refers to the need to obtain an accurate and frank rendition of the child's version of events pertaining to the alleged assault: *Khan v. College of Physicians and Surgeons of Ontario* (1992), 76 C.C.C. (3d) 10 (Ont. C.A.).

In *R. v. Khelawon*, [2006] 2 S.C.R. 787, 215 C.C.C. (3d) 161, the Supreme Court of Canada considered the issue of threshold reliability. While at the threshold stage, the trial judge does not determine whether the statement will be relied upon as true, the truthfulness of the statement may be a concern in some cases at this initial stage. It might be appropriate to consider the presence of corroborating or conflicting evidence. In determining admissibility, courts should adopt a functional approach and focus on the particular danger raised by the hearsay evidence sought to be introduced, and on those attributes or circumstances relied upon by the proponent to overcome those dangers.

In *R. v. A. (S.)* (1992), 76 C.C.C. (3d) 522 (Ont. C.A.), the court set out guidelines to assist the trial judge in directing the jury as to the use to be made of a hearsay complaint. The court recommended that the jury be told they must determine whether the statement was made and, if it was, its contents; that the statement cannot be placed on the same footing as a statement made by a witness in the course of her testimony since out-of-court statements made by persons who do not testify, offered for the truth of their contents, are subject to frailties which warrant a cautious approach; and that the weight to be given to the statement will be affected by the other evidence which may support or undermine the reliability of the statement.

SEXUAL INTERFERENCE.

151. Every person who, for a sexual purpose, touches, directly or indirectly, with a part of the body or with an object, any part of the body of a person under the age of 16 years

(*a*) is guilty of an indictable offence and is liable to imprisonment for a term of not more than 14 years and to a minimum punishment of imprisonment for a term of one year; or

(*b*) is guilty of an offence punishable on summary conviction and is liable to imprisonment for a term of not more than two years less a day and to a minimum punishment of imprisonment for a term of 90 days. R.S.C. 1985, c. 19 (3rd Supp.), s. 1; 2005, c. 32, s. 3; 2008, c. 6, s. 54(b); 2012, c. 1, s. 11; 2015, c. 23, s. 2.

CROSS-REFERENCES

Age is determined by s. 30 of the *Interpretation Act*, R.S.C. 1985, c. I-21. Section 658 provides means of proving the age of a child. The term "sexual purpose" is not defined. The defences of consent and mistaken belief as to the age of the complainant are defined in s. 150.1. Under s. 150.1(3), a young offender aged 12 or 13 years may not be tried for an offence under subsec. (2) unless he is in a position of trust or authority. Section 170 creates an offence for a parent or guardian to procure a person under the age of 18 years for the purpose of engaging in any sexual activity prohibited by the Code. Section 171 creates an offence for a householder and other similarly situated persons to permit a person under the age of 18 years to resort to premises for the purpose of engaging in any sexual activity prohibited by the Code. Section 171.1 makes it an offence to transmit, make available, distribute or sell sexually explicit material to a person who is, or who the accused believes is under the age of 16 years for purpose of facilitating the commission of the offence created by this section. Section 172.1 makes it an offence to communicate by means of telecommunication with a person who is or who the accused believes is under the age of 16 years for the purpose of facilitating the commission of the offence under this section. Section 172.2 makes it an offence to agree with a person or make an arrangement with a person by means of telecommunication to commit an offence under this section with a person who is or who the accused believes is under the age of 16 years.

A person, found guilty of the offence in this section, may, depending on the circumstances, be liable to either the mandatory prohibition order in s. 109 or to the discretionary prohibition order prescribed by s. 110 for possession of weapons, ammunition and explosives. Where the accused is found guilty of this offence in respect of a person who is under 16 years of age, the court has the discretion to impose an order of prohibition under s. 161 prohibiting the accused from attending certain public areas and facilities or taking certain employment which will bring him into contact with persons under 16 years of age or using a computer system for the purpose of communicating with a person under the age of 16 years.

Special evidentiary and procedural provisions: see cross-references under s. 150.1.

As to cases concerning admissibility of evidence in child abuse cases, see notes under s. 150.1.

Section 718.01 provides that, in imposing a sentence for an offence involving the abuse of a person under the age of 18 years, the court shall give primary consideration to the objectives of denunciation and deterrence. Further, under s. 718.2, evidence that the offender, in committing the offence, abused a person under the age of 18 years is an aggravating circumstance.

The offence in this section is a primary designated offence for the purpose of making a forensic DNA data bank order. Under s. 490.012, on application by the prosecutor, where an offender is convicted of this offence, the judge shall make an order requiring the offender to comply with the *Sex Offender Information Registration Act*, S.C. 2004, c. 10.

SYNOPSIS

This section creates the offence of sexual interference with a person under 16 years and spells out the sentence for it. The offence may be committed by touching the complainant's body, directly or indirectly, with either a part of the accused's body or an object. It must be proven that the accused had a sexual purpose for the touching. This offence is punishable by way of summary conviction or by way of indictment. In the latter case, it is punishable by a maximum sentence of 14 years and to a minimum punishment of one year imprisonment. If the Crown proceeds by way of summary conviction, the offence is punishable by a maximum of two years less a day and a minimum of 90 days' imprisonment. Section 718.01 provides that, in imposing a sentence for an offence involving the abuse of a person under the age of 18 years, the court shall give primary consideration to the objectives of denunciation and deterrence. Further, under s. 718.2, evidence that the offender, in committing the offence, abused a person under the age of 18 years is an aggravating circumstance.

ANNOTATIONS

An accused who intends sexual interaction of any kind with a child and with that intent makes contact with the body of a child, "touches" the child within the meaning of this section, even where the sexual interaction is suggested by the child: *R. v. Sears* (1990), 58 C.C.C. (3d) 62 (Man. C.A.).

While the different minimum sentences applicable depending on Crown election violates s. 9 of the Charter, it is a reasonable limit pursuant to s. 1: *R. v. Lonegren* (2009), 250 C.C.C. (3d) 377 (B.C.S.C.), supp. reasons 260 C.C.C. (3d) 367 (B.C.S.C.).

The mandatory minimum sentence prescribed by para. (*a*) is contrary to s. 12 of the Charter and of no force or effect: *R. v. JED* (2018), 368 C.C.C. (3d) 212 (Man. C.A.).

The mandatory minimum sentence in para. (*b*) does not violate s. 15 of the Charter, as it does not perpetuate discrimination in the justice system against Aboriginal offenders: *R. v. B. (T.M.)* (2013), 299 C.C.C. (3d) 493 (Ont. S.C.J.).

INVITATION TO SEXUAL TOUCHING.

152. Every person who, for a sexual purpose, invites, counsels or incites a person under the age of 16 years to touch, directly or indirectly, with a part of the body or with an object, the body of any person, including the body of the person who so invites, counsels or incites and the body of the person under the age of 16 years,

(*a*) is guilty of an indictable offence and is liable to imprisonment for a term of not more than 14 years and to a minimum punishment of imprisonment for a term of one year; or

(*b*) is guilty of an offence punishable on summary conviction and is liable to imprisonment for a term of not more than two years less a day and to a minimum punishment of imprisonment for a term of 90 days. R.S.C. 1985, c. 19 (3rd Supp.), s. 1; 2005, c. 32, s. 3; 2008, c. 6, s. 54(*b*); 2012, c. 1, s. 12; 2015, c. 23, s. 3.

CROSS-REFERENCES

Age is determined by s. 30 of the *Interpretation Act*, R.S.C. 1985, c. I-21. Section 658 provides means of proving the age of a child. The term "counsels" is defined in s. 22 and in fact includes "incite". The term "sexual purpose" is not defined. The defences of consent and mistaken belief as to the age of the complainant are defined in s. 150.1. Under s. 150.1(3), a young offender aged 12 or 13 years may not be tried for an offence under subsec. (2) unless he is in a position of trust or authority. Section 170 creates an offence for a parent or guardian to procure a person under the age of 18 years for the purpose of engaging in any sexual activity prohibited by the Code. Section 171 creates an offence for a householder and other similarly situated persons to permit a person under the age of 18 years to resort to premises for the purpose of engaging in any sexual activity prohibited by the Code. Section 171.1 makes it an offence to transmit, make available, distribute or sell sexually explicit material to a person who is, or who the accused believes is under the age of 16 years for purpose of facilitating the commission of the offence created by this section. Section 172.1 makes it an offence to communicate by means of telecommunication with a person who is or who the accused believes is under the age of 16 years for the purpose of facilitating the commission of the offence under this section. Section 172.2 makes it an offence to agree with a person or make an arrangement with a person by means of telecommunication to commit an offence under this section with a person who is or who the accused believes is under the age of 16 years.

A person, found guilty of the offence in this section, may, depending on the circumstances, be liable to either the mandatory prohibition order in s. 109 or to the discretionary prohibition order prescribed by s. 110 for possession of weapons, ammunition and explosives. Where the accused is found guilty of this offence in respect of a person who is under 16 years of age, the court has the discretion to impose an order of prohibition under s. 161 prohibiting the accused from attending certain public areas and facilities or taking certain employment which will bring him into contact with persons under 16 years of age or using a computer system for the purpose of communicating with a person under the age of 16 years.

Special evidentiary and procedural provisions: see cross-references under s. 150.1.

As to cases concerning admissibility of evidence in child abuse cases, see notes under s. 150.1.

Section 718.01 provides that, in imposing a sentence for an offence involving the abuse of a person under the age of 18 years, the court shall give primary consideration to the objectives of denunciation and deterrence. Further, under s. 718.2, evidence that the offender, in committing the offence, abused a person under the age of 18 years is an aggravating circumstance.

The offence in this section is a primary designated offence for the purpose of making a forensic DNA data bank order. Under s. 490.012, on application by the prosecutor, where an offender is convicted of this offence, the judge shall make an order requiring the offender to comply with the *Sex Offender Information Registration Act*, S.C. 2004, c. 10.

SYNOPSIS

This section provides for the offence of inviting, counselling or inciting a person under 16 years of age to touch, directly or indirectly, any person's body. The touching may be with a part of the body or with an object. The person inviting the touching must do so for a sexual purpose. The section applies regardless of whether the accused invites the touching of his or herself or another person or incites the person under 16 to touch their own body. The offence is punishable by indictment or by way of summary conviction. In the former case, it is punishable by a maximum sentence of 14 years and to a minimum punishment of one year imprisonment. If the Crown proceeds by way of summary conviction, the offence is punishable by a maximum of two years less a day and a minimum of 90 days' imprisonment.

ANNOTATIONS

This offence does not require proof of actual physical contact between body parts or an invitation to engage in that level of contact. This section covers not only actual touching but "indirect" touching and thus includes an invitation by the accused to the complainant to hold a tissue onto which the accused ejaculated: *R. v. Fong* (1994), 92 C.C.C. (3d) 171 (Alta. C.A.), leave to appeal to S.C.C. refused 94 C.C.C. (3d) vii.

Incitement is more than mere passive acquiescence and requires some positive act by the accused to cause the complainant to engage in sexual touching. Failure to resist, therefore, is not inciting: *R. v. Rhynes* (2004), 186 C.C.C. (3d) 29 (P.E.I.S.C.), leave to appeal refused 2004 PESCAD 15 (P.E.I.C.A.).

SEXUAL EXPLOITATION / Punishment / Inference of sexual exploitation / Definition of "young person".

153. (1) Every person commits an offence who is in a position of trust or authority towards a young person, who is a person with whom the young person is in a relationship of dependency or who is in a relationship with a young person that is exploitative of the young person, and who

(*a*) for a sexual purpose, touches, directly or indirectly, with a part of the body or with an object, any part of the body of the young person; or

(*b*) for a sexual purpose, invites, counsels or incites a young person to touch, directly or indirectly, with a part of the body or with an object, the body of any person, including the body of the person who so invites, counsels or incites and the body of the young person.

(1.1) Every person who commits an offence under subsection (1)

(*a*) is guilty of an indictable offence and is liable to imprisonment for a term of not more than 14 years and to a minimum punishment of imprisonment for a term of one year; or

(*b*) is guilty of an offence punishable on summary conviction and is liable to imprisonment for a term of not more than two years less a day and to a minimum punishment of imprisonment for a term of 90 days.

(1.2) A judge may infer that a person is in a relationship with a young person that is exploitative of the young person from the nature and circumstances of the relationship, including

(a) the age of the young person;
(b) the age difference between the person and the young person;
(c) the evolution of the relationship; and
(d) the degree of control or influence by the person over the young person.

(2) In this section, "young person" means a person 16 years of age or more but under the age of eighteen years. R.S.C. 1985, c. 19 (3rd Supp.), s. 1; 2005, c. 32, s. 4; 2008, c. 6, s. 54(c); 2012, c. 1, s. 13; 2015, c. 23, s. 4.

CROSS-REFERENCES

Age is determined by s. 30 of the *Interpretation Act*, R.S.C. 1985, c. I-21. Section 658 provides means of proving the age of a child or young person. The term "counsels" is defined in s. 22 and in fact includes "incite". The term "sexual purpose" is not defined. The terms "position of trust or authority" and "relationship of dependency" are not defined. The Report of the Committee on Sexual Offences Against Children and Youths [The "Badgley" Report], released in 1984, contained many recommendations concerning the treatment of sexual offences against children and appears to have been the origin of many of the offences now found in this Part. That report, in its Recommendation 9, had suggested a definition of person in position of trust as including parent; step-parent; adoptive parent; foster parent; legal guardian; common-law partner of child's parent, step-parent, adoptive parent, foster parent, or legal guardian; grandparent; uncle, aunt; boarder in young person's home; teacher; baby-sitter, group home worker; youth group worker; and employer. The defences of consent and mistaken belief as to the age of the complainant are defined in s. 150.1. Section 170 creates an offence for a parent or guardian to procure a person under the age of 18 years for the purpose of engaging in any sexual activity prohibited by the Code. Section 171 creates an offence for a householder and other similarly situated persons to permit a person under the age of 18 years to resort to premises for the purpose of engaging in any sexual activity prohibited by the Code. Section 171.1 makes it an offence to transmit, make available, distribute or sell sexually explicit material to a person who is, or who the accused believes is under the age of 18 years for purpose of facilitating the commission of the offence created by this section. Section 172.1 makes it an offence to communicate by means of telecommunication with a person who is or who the accused believes is under the age of 18 years for the purpose of facilitating the commission of the offence under this section. Section 172.2 makes it an offence to agree with a person or make an arrangement with a person by means of telecommunication to commit an offence under this section with a person who is or who the accused believes is under the age of 18 years.

A person found guilty of the offence in this section, may, depending on the circumstances, be liable to the discretionary prohibition order prescribed by s. 110 for possession of weapons, ammunition and explosives.

Special evidentiary and procedural provisions: see cross-references under s. 150.1.

As to cases concerning admissibility of evidence in child abuse cases, see notes under s. 150.1.

Section 718.01 provides that, in imposing a sentence for an offence involving the abuse of a person under the age of 18 years, the court shall give primary consideration to the objectives of denunciation and deterrence. Further, under s. 718.2, evidence that the offender, in committing the offence, abused a person under the age of 18 years is an aggravating circumstance.

The offence in this section is a primary designated offence for the purpose of making a forensic DNA data bank order under s. 487.051. Under s. 490.012, on application by the prosecutor, where an offender is convicted of this offence, the judge shall make an order requiring the offender to comply with the *Sex Offender Information Registration Act*, S.C. 2004, c. 10.

SYNOPSIS

This section creates the hybrid offence of sexual exploitation of a young person. Subsection (2) provides a definition of "young person", namely a person between 16 and 17 years old inclusive. The offence is predicated upon either the accused being in a position of trust toward the young complainant, or the young person being in a relationship of dependency with the accused, or being in a relationship with a young person that is exploitative of the young person. If one of those relationships exist and the accused commits acts amounting to either sexual interference (s. 151) or invitation to sexual touching (s. 152), then the offence is committed. (Note that it must be shown that the accused had a sexual purpose.) The maximum sentence upon conviction for the indictable offence of sexual exploitation is 14 years and the minimum punishment is one year imprisonment. Where the Crown proceeds by way of summary conviction, the offence is punishable by a maximum of two years less a day imprisonment and not less than 90 days.

ANNOTATIONS

Note: Some of these cases were decided before the amendment to this section adding subsec. (1.2).

Sexual assault, as defined by s. 271, is not an included offence to the offence created by this section: *R. v. Nelson* (1989), 51 C.C.C. (3d) 150 (Ont. H.C.J.).

Unlike sexual assault, as defined by s. 271, the offence created by this section is a specific intent offence: *R. v. Nelson, supra.*

The Crown need not prove that the accused actually abused or exploited his position of trust or authority towards the young person: *R. v. Audet*, [1996] 2 S.C.R. 171, 106 C.C.C. (3d) 481.

The combined effect of this section and s. 150.1(1) does not result in violation of the equality provisions of s. 15 of the Charter, although some professions, such as teachers, are treated differently since the defence that the complainant consented is denied them. Nor does the denial of the consent defence violate s. 7 of the Charter: *R. v. Hann* (1992), 75 C.C.C. (3d) 355 (Nfld. C.A.).

"Authority" is not restricted to cases in which the relationship of authority stems from a role of the accused but extends to any relationship in which the accused actually exercises such a power. The word "trust" as used in this provision must be interpreted in accordance with its primary meaning of confidence or reliance. In considering whether the accused was in a "position of authority" or "position of trust", the age difference between the accused, the evolution of the relationship and the status of the accused in relation to the young person are relevant considerations. Teachers will usually be in a position of trust and authority towards their students: *R. v. Audet, supra.*

The Crown is required to prove a relationship that is exploitative of the young person independent of proof of the sexual conduct. Proof of consensual sexual relations between an accused and a young person is not by itself proof of a relationship that was exploitative of the young person. The scope of the meaning of an exploitative relationship should be determined to some extent by the scope of the other types of relationships set out in this section. There must be a power imbalance in favour of an accused person in circumstances other than where the accused is in a position of trust or authority, or circumstances where the young person has developed a reliance on the accused who has assumed a position of power over the young person. The evidence must demonstrate, or it must be possible for the court to draw, the inference from all of the circumstances that the young person is, as the result of this power imbalance, vulnerable to the actions and conduct of the accused who is taking advantage of the young person for his or her own benefit: *R. v. Anderson* (2009), 241 C.C.C. (3d) 432 (P.E.I.C.A.).

The accused's subjective belief that he was not in a position of trust or authority in relation to the complainant does not, in itself, provide a defence to a charge under subsec. (1): *R. v. R. (L.V.)* (2014), 316 C.C.C. (3d) 120 (B.C.C.A.), leave to appeal to S.C.C. refused 2015 CarswellBC 554.

A person who is relied upon by the young person's parent or guardian to exercise responsibility *vis-à-vis* the young person is generally in a position of trust for the purpose of this offence: *R. v. EJB* (2017), 352 C.C.C. (3d) 59 (Alta. C.A.).

The trial judge erred in relying on a school directive to conclude that a teaching assistant was presumptively in a position of trust. The determination of a relationship of trust or authority requires a factual consideration of the characteristics of the relationship in issue: *R. v. S. (J.S.)* (2010), 257 C.C.C. (3d) 403 (N.B.C.A.).

Although the accused was physically bigger than the complainant and ran the arcade where the complainant was employed, it was not shown that the accused was in a position of trust or authority or that the young person was in a relationship of dependency: *R. v. Caskenette* (1993), 80 C.C.C. (3d) 439 (B.C.C.A.).

It was a question of fact whether the accused was in a position of trust or authority towards the 17-year-old daughter of his common-law wife and whether she was in a relationship of dependency although they lived in the same house. The relationship of trust or authority on the part of the man or dependency on the part of the complainant could not be conclusively presumed to exist as a matter of law: *R. v. J. (R.H.)* (1993), 86 C.C.C. (3d) 354 (B.C.C.A.), leave to appeal to S.C.C. refused 87 C.C.C. (3d) vi.

The term "dependency" is to be read *ejusdem generis* with two other categories of trust or authority and contemplates a relationship in which there is a *de facto* reliance by a young person on a figure who has assumed a position of power, such as trust or authority over the young person along non-traditional lines. The disentitling condition of dependency must exist independently of a sexual relationship: *R. v. Galbraith* (1994), 90 C.C.C. (3d) 76 (Ont. C.A.), leave to appeal to S.C.C. refused 92 C.C.C. (3d) vi.

The Crown need only prove that the purpose of the touching was sexual in nature and need not prove that the accused touched the complainant for his own sexual gratification: *R. v. B. (G.)* (2009), 244 C.C.C. (3d) 185 (B.C.C.A.).

SEXUAL EXPLOITATION OF PERSON WITH DISABILITY / Definition of "consent" / Consent / Question of law / When no consent obtained / Subsection (3) not limiting / When belief in consent not a defence / Accused's belief as to consent.

153.1 (1) Every person who is in a position of trust or authority towards a person with a mental or physical disability or who is a person with whom a person with a mental or physical disability is in a relationship of dependency and who, for a sexual purpose, counsels or incites that person to touch, without that person's consent, his or her own body, the body of the person who so counsels or incites, directly or indirectly, with a part of the body or with an object, the body of any person, including the body of the person who so invites, counsels or incites and the body of the person with the disability, is guilty of

(*a*) an indictable offence and liable to imprisonment for a term not exceeding five years; or

(*b*) an offence punishable on summary conviction and liable to imprisonment for a term not exceeding eighteen months.

(2) Subject to subsection (3), "consent" means, for the purposes of this section, the voluntary agreement of the complainant to engage in the sexual activity in question.

(2.1) Consent must be present at the time the sexual activity in question takes place.

(2.2) The question of whether no consent is obtained under subsection (3) or (4) or 265(3) is a question of law.

(3) For the purposes of this section, no consent is obtained if

(*a*) the agreement is expressed by the words or conduct of a person other than the complainant;

(*a*.1) the complainant is unconscious;

(*b*) the complainant is incapable of consenting to the activity for any reason other than the one referred to in paragraph (*a*.1);

(*c*) the accused counsels or incites the complainant to engage in the activity by abusing a position of trust, power or authority;

(*d*) the complainant expresses, by words or conduct, a lack of agreement to engage in the activity; or

(*e*) the complainant, having consented to engage in sexual activity, expresses, by words or conduct, a lack of agreement to continue to engage in the activity.

(4) Nothing in subsection (3) shall be construed as limiting the circumstances in which no consent is obtained.

(5) It is not a defence to a charge under this section that the accused believed that the complainant consented to the activity that forms the subject-matter of the charge if

(*a*) the accused's belief arose from

(i) the accused's self-induced intoxication,

(ii) the accused's recklessness or wilful blindness, or

(iii) any circumstance referred to in subsection (3) or (4) or 265(3) in which no consent is obtained;

(*b*) the accused did not take reasonable steps, in the circumstances known to the accused at the time, to ascertain that the complainant was consenting.

(*c*) there is no evidence that the complainant's voluntary agreement to the activity was affirmatively expressed by words or actively expressed by conduct.

(6) If an accused alleges that he or she believed that the complainant consented to the conduct that is the subject-matter of the charge, a judge, if satisfied that there is sufficient evidence and that, if believed by the jury, the evidence would constitute a defence, shall instruct the jury, when reviewing all the evidence relating to the determination of the honesty of the accused's belief, to consider the presence or absence of reasonable grounds for that belief. 1998, c. 9, s. 2; 2018, c. 29, s. 10(1)-(2.1), (4)-(6).

CROSS-REFERENCES

Section 153 creates the related offence of sexual exploitation of a young person. Pursuant to s. 274, no corroboration is required for a conviction of the offence under this section and the judge shall not instruct the jury that it is unsafe to find the accused guilty in the absence of corroboration. Pursuant to s. 275, the rules relating to recent complaint are abrogated with respect to this offence. Sections 276 and 277, which limit cross-examination on prior sexual conduct of the complainant, apply to a prosecution for the offence under this section. Section 273.1 gives a similar definition of "consent" as in subsecs. (2) to (4) of this section, for the purposes of the sexual assault offences in ss. 271 to 273. Sections 278.1 to 278.9 govern the production of records containing personal information of the complainant or a witness. Section 273.2 gives a similar definition for the defence of belief in consent as in subsecs. (5) and (6) of this section, for the purposes of the sexual assault offences in ss. 271 to 273. Section 486(2.1) provides that, where an accused is charged with this offence and the complainant is, at the time of the trial or preliminary inquiry, under the age of 18 years or may have difficulty communicating the evidence by reason of a mental or physical disability, the judge may order that the complainant testify outside the courtroom or behind a screen where such procedure is necessary to obtain a full and candid account of the acts complained of. Section 627 provides that the judge may permit a juror with a physical disability who is otherwise qualified to serve as a juror to have technical, personal, interpretative or other support services. Sections 709 and 711 provide for the taking of commission evidence from a witness who is, by reason of physical disability arising out of illness not likely to be able to attend at the time the trial. Section 715.2 provides that, in proceedings under this section, a videotape, made within a reasonable time after the alleged offence, in which the complainant describes the acts complained of is admissible in evidence if the complainant adopts its contents and if the complainant may have difficulty communicating the evidence by reason of a mental or physical disability. Section 6 of the *Canada Evidence Act* provides that the court may order that a witness who has difficulty communicating, by reason of a physical or mental disability, be permitted to give evidence by any means that enables the evidence to be intelligible. Under s. 6.1 of the Act, a witness may give evidence as to the identity of an accused whom the witness is able to identify visually or in any other sensory manner.

The offence in this section is a primary designated offence for the purpose of making a forensic DNA data bank order under s. 487.051. Under s. 490.012, on application by the prosecutor, where an offender is convicted of this offence, the judge shall make an order requiring the offender to comply with the *Sex Offender Information Registration Act*, S.C. 2004, c. 10.

SYNOPSIS

This section creates the hybrid offence of sexual exploitation of a person with a mental or physical disability. The offence is predicated upon either the accused being in a position of trust toward the young complainant or the young person being in a relationship of dependency with the accused. If either relationship exists and the accused for a sexual purpose incites or counsels the complainant to touch any person's body directly or indirectly with an object or a part of the body, the offence is made out. Note that unlike the similar offences involving children it must be shown that the touching is without the complainant's consent. Consent is defined in subsecs. (2) to (4). Subsection (5) limits the availability of the defence of belief in consent and subsec. (6) sets out a mandatory jury instruction where such a defence is available. The maximum sentence upon conviction for the indictable offence of sexual exploitation is five years.

ANNOTATIONS

The definition of consent in this section and the limits of the defence of belief in consent are similar to the provisions of ss. 273.1 and 273.2 (respecting sexual assault) and therefore reference should be made to the notes under those sections. See in particular *R. v. Ewanchuk*, [1999] 1 S.C.R. 330, 131 C.C.C. (3d) 481, noted under both sections.

154. [*Repealed*, R.S.C. 1985, c. 19 (3rd Supp.), s. 1.]

INCEST / Punishment / Defence / Definition of "brother" and "sister".

155. (1) Every one commits incest who, knowing that another person is by blood relationship his or her parent, child, brother, sister, grandparent or grandchild, as the case may be, has sexual intercourse with that person.

(2) Everyone who commits incest is guilty of an indictable offence and is liable to imprisonment for a term of not more than 14 years and, if the other person is under the age of 16 years, to a minimum punishment of imprisonment for a term of five years.

(3) No accused shall be determined by a court to be guilty of an offence under this section if the accused was under restraint, duress or fear of the person with whom the accused had the sexual intercourse at the time the sexual intercourse occurred.

(4) In this section, "brother" and "sister", respectively, include half-brother and half-sister. R.S., c. C-34, s. 150; 1972, c. 13, s. 10; R.S.C. 1985, c. 27 (1st Supp.), s. 21; 2012, c. 1, s. 14.

CROSS-REFERENCES

Section 4(5) sets out a definition for sexual intercourse. Section 171.1 makes it an offence to transmit, make available, distribute or sell sexually explicit material to a person who is, or who the accused believes is under the age of 18 years for purpose of facilitating the commission of the offence created by this section. Section 172.1 makes it an offence to communicate by means of telecommunication with a person who is or who the accused believes is under the age of 18 years for the purpose of facilitating the commission of the offence under this section. Section 172.2 makes it an offence to agree with a person or make an arrangement with a person by means of telecommunication to commit an offence under this section with a person who is or who the accused believes is under the age of 18 years.

The accused may elect his mode of trial pursuant to s. 536(2) and release pending trial is determined by s. 515. Section 170 creates an offence for a parent or guardian to procure a person under the age of 18 years for the purpose of engaging in any sexual activity prohibited by the Code. Section 171 creates an offence for a householder and other similarly situated persons to permit a person under the age of 18 years to resort to premises for the purpose of engaging in any sexual activity prohibited by the Code.

A person, found guilty of the offence in this section, may, depending on the circumstances, be liable to the mandatory prohibition order prescribed by s. 109 for possession of certain weapons, ammunition and explosives. Where the accused is found guilty of this offence in respect of a person who is under 16 years of age, the court has the discretion to impose an order of prohibition under s. 161 prohibiting the accused from attending certain public areas and facilities or taking certain employment which will bring him into contact with persons under 16 years of age or using a computer system for the purpose of communicating with a person under the age of 16 years.

Special evidentiary and procedural provisions: see cross-references under s. 150.1.

As to cases concerning admissibility of evidence in child abuse cases, see notes under s. 150.1.

The offence in this section is a primary designated offence for the purpose of making a forensic DNA data bank order under s. 487.051. Under s. 490.012, on application by the prosecutor, where an offender is convicted of this offence, the judge shall make an order requiring the offender to comply with the *Sex Offender Information Registration Act*, S.C. 2004, c. 10.

SYNOPSIS

This section prohibits incest and provides for a maximum sentence for this indictable offence of 14 years' imprisonment and a minimum sentence of 5 years if the other person is under the age of 16 years.

The offence requires that *sexual intercourse* occur between the accused and another person whom the accused *knows* is one of the *blood relations* specified in subsec. (1). In addition, subsec. (4) expands the definitions of "brother" and "sister" to include half-siblings.

Section 155(3) prevents a finding of guilt in circumstances in which the *accused was in fear* of the relation involved, or under restraint or duress *when* intercourse took place.

ANNOTATIONS

This provision does not violate s. 7 of the Charter. In addition, the denial of the defence of consent does not violate s. 7: *R. v. F. (R.P.)* (1996), 105 C.C.C. (3d) 435 (N.S.C.A.). Nor does this provision violate ss. 2(*a*), 2(*d*) and 15 of the Charter: *R. v. S. (M.)* (1996), 111 C.C.C. (3d) 467 (B.C.C.A.), leave to appeal to S.C.C. refused 113 C.C.C. (3d) vii.

Incest is a general intent offence requiring no more than an intent to commit the *actus reus*: *R. v. B. (S.J.)* (2002), 166 C.C.C. (3d) 537 (Alta. C.A.).

Sexual assault and sexual interference are not included offences of this offence where the information simply charges that the accused committed incest with his daughter, even though the complainant was, to the accused's knowledge, under 14 years of age and thus incapable of consenting. Neither lack of consent, nor age of the complainant are elements of the offence under this section: *R. v. R. (G.)*, [2005] 2 S.C.R. 371, 198 C.C.C. (3d) 161.

156. [*Repealed*, R.S.C. 1985, c. 19 (3rd Supp.), s. 2.]

157. [*Repealed*, R.S.C. 1985, c. 19 (3rd Supp.), s. 2.]

158. [*Repealed*, R.S.C. 1985, c. 19 (3rd Supp.), s. 2.]

ANAL INTERCOURSE / Exception / Idem.

159. (1) Every person who engages in an act of anal intercourse is guilty of an indictable offence and liable to imprisonment for a term not exceeding ten years or is guilty of an offence punishable on summary conviction.

(2) Subsection (1) does not apply to any act engaged in, in private, between

(*a*) **husband and wife, or**

(*b*) **any two persons, each of whom is eighteen years of age or more, both of whom consent to the act.**

(3) For the purposes of subsection (2),

(*a*) **an act shall be deemed not to have been engaged in in private if it is engaged in in a public place or if more than two persons take part or are present; and**

(*b*) **a person shall be deemed not to consent to an act**

(i) if the consent is extorted by force, threats or fear of bodily harm or is obtained by false and fraudulent misrepresentations respecting the nature and quality of the act, or

(ii) if the court is satisfied beyond a reasonable doubt that that person could not have consented to the act by reason of mental disability. R.S.C. 1985, c. 19 (3rd Supp.), s. 3.

SYNOPSIS

Section 159 creates the offence of *anal intercourse* and also sets out a number of exemptions from its application. Section 159(1) sets out the prohibition against anal intercourse and provides for prosecution by way of summary conviction procedure or by indictment. In the latter case the maximum sentence is 10 years.

Section 159(2) provides an exemption from liability if the acts were done in *private,* with the *mutual consent* of those involved, by either *husband and wife* or by two persons both of whom are at least 18 years old.

Section 159(3) limits the scope of the exceptions in subsec. (2) in two ways. First, the meaning of "private" excludes acts done in a public place, or with more than two persons present. Second, s. 159(3)(*b*) limits what is meant by "consent". The accused cannot rely upon consent if it is proven beyond a reasonable doubt that the other person was unable to consent due to mental disability. In addition, consent is rendered invalid if it was obtained by force, threats, fear or fraud.

Two appellate courts have held this section to be unconstitutional.

ANNOTATIONS

Application of the Charter of Rights – It was held in *R. v. M. (C.)* (1995), 98 C.C.C. (3d) 481, 41 C.R. (4th) 134 (Ont. C.A.), that this section discriminates on the basis of age contrary to s. 15 of the Charter and is therefore of no force and effect.

Similarly, in *R. v. Roy* (1998), 125 C.C.C. (3d) 442, 161 D.L.R. (4th) 148 (Que. C.A.), it was held that this section infringes s. 15 of the Charter as it discriminates on the basis of age, sexual orientation and marital status and is therefore of no force and effect.

BESTIALITY / Compelling the commission of bestiality / Bestiality in presence of or by child.

160. (1) Every person who commits bestiality is guilty of an indictable offence and liable to imprisonment for a term not exceeding ten years or is guilty of an offence punishable on summary conviction.

(2) Every person who compels another to commit bestiality is guilty of an indictable offence and liable to imprisonment for a term not exceeding ten years or is guilty of an offence punishable on summary conviction.

(3) Despite subsection (1), every person who commits bestiality in the presence of a person under the age of 16 years, or who incites a person under the age of 16 years to commit bestiality,

(*a*) **is guilty of an indictable offence and is liable to imprisonment for a term of not more than 14 years and to a minimum punishment of imprisonment for a term of one year; or** (*b*) **is guilty of an offence punishable on summary conviction and is liable to imprisonment for a term of not more than two years less a day and to a minimum punishment of imprisonment for a term of six months. R.S.C. 1985, c. 19 (3rd Supp.), s. 3; 2008, c. 6, s. 54(*d*); 2012, c. 1, s. 15; 2015, c. 23, s. 5.**

CROSS-REFERENCES

Age is determined by s. 30 of the *Interpretation Act*, R.S.C. 1985, c. I-21. The term "incites" is within the definition of "counsels" in s. 22(3). A person convicted of the offence under subsec. (2) or (3), who is found to be loitering in or near a school ground, playground, public park or bathing area, is liable to be convicted of the vagrancy offence under s. 179. Section 170 creates an offence for a parent or guardian to procure a person under the age of 18 years for the purpose of engaging in any sexual activity prohibited by the Code. Section 171 creates an offence for a householder and other similarly situated persons to permit a person under the age of 18 years to resort to premises for the purpose of engaging in any sexual activity prohibited by the Code. Section 171.1 makes it an offence to transmit, make available, distribute or sell sexually explicit material to a person who is, or who the accused believes is under the age of 16 years for purpose of facilitating the commission of the offence created by subsec. (3). Section 172.1 makes it an offence to communicate by means of telecommunication with a person who is or who the accused believes is under the age of 16 years for the purpose of facilitating the commission of the offence under subsec. (3). Section 172.2 makes it an offence to agree with a person or make an arrangement with a person by means of telecommunication to commit an offence under subsec. (3) with a person who is or who the accused believes is under the age of 18 years.

Where the prosecution elects to proceed by indictment on this offence then the accused may elect his mode of trial pursuant to s. 536(2). Where the prosecution elects to proceed by way of summary conviction then the trial of this offence is conducted by a summary conviction court pursuant to Part XXVII. The punishment for the offence is then as set out in s. 787 and the limitation period is set out in s. 786(2). In either case, release pending trial is determined by s. 515, although the accused is eligible for release by a peace officer under s. 496, 497 or by the officer in charge under s. 498.

A person, found guilty of the offence in this section, may, depending on the circumstances, be liable to either the mandatory prohibition order under s. 109 or the discretionary prohibition order prescribed by s. 110 for possession of firearms, ammunition and explosives. Where the accused is found guilty of the offence under subsec. (2) or (3) in respect of a person who is under 16 years of age, the court has the discretion to impose an order of prohibition under s. 161 prohibiting the accused from attending certain public areas and facilities or taking certain employment which will bring him into contact with persons under 16 years of age or using a computer system for the purpose of communicating with a person under the age of 16 years.

Section 150.1(4) deals with the defence of mistake of age for the offence under subsec. (3).

Special evidentiary and procedural provisions: see cross-references under s. 150.1.

Section 486(1) and (2) provide that the judge may make an order excluding all or any members of the public where such order is in the interest of public morals, the maintenance of order or the proper administration of justice, or is necessary to prevent injury to international relations or national defence or national security. The proper administration of justice includes safeguarding the interests of witnesses under the age of 18 years. Section 486.1 sets out the circumstances in which the judge shall or may order a support person to be present and close to a witness while the witness testifies. Where the witness is under the age of 18 years or has a mental or physical disability, the order is to be made upon request unless the judge is of the opinion that the order would interfere with the proper administration of justice. In the case of other witnesses, the order is to be made if necessary to obtain a full and candid account from the witness of the matters complained of. The application for this order may be made during the proceedings or before they begin to the judge who is to preside at the proceedings.

Similarly, s. 486.2 sets out the circumstances in which the judge shall or may order a witness to testify outside the courtroom or behind a screen or other device that would not allow the witness to see the accused. Where the witness is under the age of 18 years or may have difficulty communicating the evidence by reason of a mental or physical disability, the judge shall make the order unless the judge is of the opinion that the order would interfere with the proper administration of justice. In all other cases, the order may be made if the judge is of the opinion that the order is necessary to obtain a full and candid account from the witness of the acts complained of. Similarly, s. 486.3 provides that, on application by the prosecutor or a witness under the age of 18 years, the accused shall not personally cross-examine the witness unless the judge is of the opinion that the proper administration of justice requires the accused to personally conduct the cross-examination. In other cases, the judge may make an order that the accused not personally cross-examine the witness if the judge is of the opinion that the order is necessary to obtain a full and candid account from the witness of the acts complained of. The judge will appoint counsel to conduct the cross-examination.

Under s. 486.4, the judge may make an order directing that the identity of a witness not be disclosed in any publication, broadcast or transmitted in any way. The order is mandatory where the complainant or a witness under the age of 18 years or the prosecutor applies for the order. Section 486.5 also gives the judge a discretion respecting non-publication orders in proceedings under these provisions in other circumstances.

Under s. 490.012, on application by the prosecutor, where an offender is convicted of the offence in subsec. (3), the judge shall make an order requiring the offender to comply with the *Sex Offender Information Registration Act*, S.C. 2004, c. 10.

SYNOPSIS

Section 160 prohibits *bestiality* and provides for its punishment.

Section 160(1) states the basic prohibition against the accused committing bestiality. Section 160(2) creates a parallel offence which applies if the accused *compels another* to commit bestiality. Section 160(3) creates criminal liability when the accused commits bestiality in the *presence* of another person who is *less than 16* years old or *incites* a person under 16 to commit the act.

All three offences created by this section may be prosecuted by way of summary conviction procedure or by indictment. The maximum sentence for the offences in subsecs. (1) and (2) where the Crown proceeds by way of indictment is 10 years. For the offence created by subsec. (3), the maximum sentence is 14 years and the minimum sentence is one year imprisonment, where the Crown proceeds by way of indictment. Where the Crown proceeds by way of summary conviction for the subsec. (3) offence, the maximum sentence is two years less one day and the minimum is six months' imprisonment.

ANNOTATIONS

This offence being one of "general intent" drunkenness is no defence to either the full offence or an attempt: *R. v. Triller* (1980), 55 C.C.C. (2d) 411 (B.C. Co. Ct.).

Penetration is an essential element of the offence of bestiality: *R. v. W. (D.L.)*, [2016] 1 S.C.R. 402, 335 C.C.C. (3d) 269.

---

161. (old provision) [*Repealed*, R.S.C. 1985, c. 19 (3rd Supp.), s. 4.]

ORDER OF PROHIBITION / Offences / Duration of prohibition / Court may vary order / Offence.

161. (1) When an offender is convicted, or is discharged on the conditions prescribed in a probation order under section 730, of an offence referred to in subsection (1.1) in respect of a person who is under the age of 16 years, the court that sentences the offender or directs that the accused be discharged, as the case may be, in addition to any other punishment that may be imposed for that offence or any other condition prescribed in the order of discharge, shall consider making and may make, subject to the conditions or exemptions that the court directs, an order prohibiting the offender from

(*a*) attending a public park or public swimming area where persons under the age of 16 years are present or can reasonably be expected to be present, or a daycare centre, schoolground, playground or community centre;

(*a*.1) being within two kilometres, or any other distance specified in the order, of any dwelling-house where the victim identified in the order ordinarily resides or of any other place specified in the order;

(*b*) seeking, obtaining or continuing any employment, whether or not the employment is remunerated, or becoming or being a volunteer in a capacity, that involves being in a position of trust or authority towards persons under the age of 16 years;

(*c*) having any contact — including communicating by any means — with a person who is under the age of 16 years, unless the offender does so under the supervision of a person whom the court considers appropriate; or

(*d*) using the Internet or other digital network, unless the offender does so in accordance with conditions set by the court.

(1.1) The offences for the purpose of subsection (1) are

(*a*) an offence under section 151, 152, 155 or 159, subsection 160(2) or (3), section 163.1, 170, 171, 171.1, 172.1 or 172.2, subsection 173(2), section 271, 272, 273 or 279.011, subsection 279.02(2) or 279.03(2), section 280 or 281 or subsection 286.1(2), 286.2(2) or 286.3(2);

(*b*) an offence under section 144 (rape), 145 (attempt to commit rape), 149 (indecent assault on female), 156 (indecent assault on male) or 245 (common assault) or subsection 246(1) (assault with intent) of the *Criminal Code*, chapter C-34 of the Revised Statutes of Canada, 1970, as it read immediately before January 4, 1983;

(*c*) an offence under subsection 146(1) (sexual intercourse with a female under 14) or section 153 (sexual intercourse with step-daughter), 155 (buggery or bestiality), 157 (gross indecency), 166 (parent or guardian procuring defilement) or 167 (householder permitting defilement) of the *Criminal Code*, chapter C-34 of the Revised Statutes of Canada, 1970, as it read immediately before January 1, 1988; or

(*d*) an offence under subsection 212(1) (procuring), 212(2) (living on the avails of prostitution of person under 18 years), 212(2.1) (aggravated offence in relation to living on the avails of prostitution of person under 18 years) or 212(4) (prostitution of person under 18 years) of this Act, as it read from time to time before the day on which this paragraph comes into force.

(2) The prohibition may be for life or for any shorter duration that the court considers desirable and, in the case of a prohibition that is not for life, the prohibition begins on the later of

(*a*) the date on which the order is made; and

(*b*) where the offender is sentenced to a term of imprisonment, the date on which the offender is released from imprisonment for the offence, including release on parole, mandatory supervision or statutory release.

(3) A court that makes an order of prohibition or, where the court is for any reason unable to act, another court of equivalent jurisdiction in the same province, may, on application of the offender or the prosecutor, require the offender to appear before it at any time and, after hearing the parties, that court may vary the conditions prescribed in the order if, in the opinion of the court, the variation is desirable because of changed circumstances after the conditions were prescribed.

(4) Every person who is bound by an order of prohibition and who does not comply with the order is guilty of

(*a*) an indictable offence and is liable to imprisonment for a term of not more than four years; or

(*b*) **an offence punishable on summary conviction and is liable to imprisonment for a term of not more than 18 months. 1993, c. 45, s. 1; 1995, c. 22, s. 18 (Sched. IV, item 26); 1997, c. 18, s. 4; 1999, c. 31, s. 67; 2002, c. 13, s. 4; 2005, c. 32, s. 5; 2008, c. 6, s. 54(*e*); 2012, c. 1, s. 16; 2014, c. 21, s. 1; 2014, c. 25, s. 5; 2015, c. 23, s. 6.**

CROSS-REFERENCES

Age is determined by s. 30 of the *Interpretation Act*, R.S.C. 1985, c. 1-21. Section 658 provides means of proving the age of a child.

By virtue of s. 42(2)(*j*) of the *Youth Criminal Justice Act*, an order cannot be made under this section with respect to a young person. Under s. 810.1, a person may apply to a provincial court judge for an order requiring the defendant to enter into a recognizance including conditions resembling the conditions which can be imposed as part of a prohibition order under this section.

SYNOPSIS

This provision permits the court to make an order prohibiting the offender from attending near certain public places and other facilities where persons under 16 years of age may be present, from obtaining employment which may involve the offender being in a position of trust or authority over persons under 16 years of age, having any contact with a person who is under the age of 16 years, unless the offender does so under the supervision of a person whom the court considers appropriate, and using the Internet or other digital network, unless the offender does so in accordance with conditions set by the court. The order may be made where the offender is found guilty of a specified sexual offence and the complainant was under 16 years of age. The order may be for life or some shorter period and its terms may be varied upon application of the offender or the prosecutor. Failure to comply with the prohibition order is a Crown option offence. It would seem that this section will now be resorted to rather than s. 179(1)(*b*) which has been held to be unconstitutional by the Supreme Court of Canada.

ANNOTATIONS

An order under subsec. (1) constitutes "punishment" for the purposes of s. 11(*i*) of the Charter. Therefore, an order under subsec. (1)(*c*) cannot be applied retrospectively to an offence committed prior to August 9, 2012 when the amended version of this provision came into force. However, with respect to subsec. (1)(*d*), retrospective application is demonstrably justified pursuant to s. 1 of the Charter and therefore permissible: *R. v. J. (K.R.)*, [2016] 1 S.C.R. 906, 337 C.C.C. (3d) 285.

"Public park" is a defined or discrete location that is accessible to the public for recreational use that involves or is reasonably likely to involve children under a specified age. In particular cases, other factors may be relevant, such as the presence of greenery or the public designation of the location as a park, but are not definitive: *R. v. Perron* (2009), 244 C.C.C. (3d) 369 (Ont. C.A.).

The term "community centre" in subsec. (1)(*a*) must be given an expansive meaning consistent with the objective of protecting children. A public library was held to fall within the definition: *R. v. Allaby* (2017), 353 C.C.C. (3d) 476 (Sask. C.A.).

"Public swimming area" includes a swimming pool open to members of a building complex: *R. v. D'Angelo* (2002), 8 C.R. (6th) 386 (Ont. C.A.).

"Playground" is an outdoor area the purpose of which is to accommodate play by children. A carnival was not a playground, but rather a commercial operation intended for the amusement of the public including children. Children's play was not its main object or purpose: *R. v. Lachapelle* (2009), 247 C.C.C. (3d) 59 (B.C.C.A.).

It was not an error to impose an order under subsec. (1) on an offender convicted of child pornography offences despite two risk assessments indicating that the accused was a "low risk" to re-offend. The circumstances of the offence itself were sufficient to justify the order: *R. v. Miller* (2017), 354 C.C.C. (3d) 58 (N.L.C.A.).

162. (old provision) [*Repealed*, R.S.C. 1985, c. 19 (3rd Supp.), s. 4.]

VOYEURISM / Definition of "visual recording" / Exemption / Printing, publication, etc., of voyeuristic recordings / Punishment / Defence / Question of law, motives

162. (1) Every one commits an offence who, surreptitiously, observes — including by mechanical or electronic means — or makes a visual recording of a person who is in circumstances that give rise to a reasonable expectation of privacy, if

(*a*) the person is in a place in which a person can reasonably be expected to be nude, to expose his or her genital organs or anal region or her breasts, or to be engaged in explicit sexual activity;

(*b*) the person is nude, is exposing his or her genital organs or anal region or her breasts, or is engaged in explicit sexual activity, and the observation or recording is done for the purpose of observing or recording a person in such a state or engaged in such an activity; or

(*c*) the observation or recording is done for a sexual purpose.

(2) In this section, "visual recording" includes a photographic, film or video recording made by any means.

(3) Paragraphs (1)(*a*) and (*b*) do not apply to a peace officer who, under the authority of a warrant issued under section 487.01, is carrying out any activity referred to in those paragraphs.

(4) Every one commits an offence who, knowing that a recording was obtained by the commission of an offence under subsection (1), prints, copies, publishes, distributes, circulates, sells, advertises or makes available the recording, or has the recording in his or her possession for the purpose of printing, copying, publishing, distributing, circulating, selling or advertising it or making it available.

(5) Every one who commits an offence under subsection (1) or (4)

(*a*) is guilty of an indictable offence and liable to imprisonment for a term not exceeding five years; or

(*b*) is guilty of an offence punishable on summary conviction.

(6) No person shall be convicted of an offence under this section if the acts that are alleged to constitute the offence serve the public good and do not extend beyond what serves the public good.

(7) For the purposes of subsection (6),

(*a*) it is a question of law whether an act serves the public good and whether there is evidence that the act alleged goes beyond what serves the public good, but it is a question of fact whether the act does or does not extend beyond what serves the public good; and

(*b*) the motives of an accused are irrelevant. 2005, c. 32, s. 6.

CROSS-REFERENCES

"Peace officer" is defined in s. 2. The offence of trespassing by night is defined in s. 177. Criminal harassment is defined in s. 264.

SYNOPSIS

This section creates the offence of voyeurism that is committed by surreptitiously observing a person in circumstances that give rise to a reasonable expectation of privacy if the person is in certain places defined in subsec. (1)(*a*), or the person is actually nude or exposing genital organs, anal region or a woman's breasts, or engaging in explicit sexual activity and the observation or recording is done for the purpose of observing or recording a person in such a state or engaged in the sexual activity (subsec. (1)(*b*)), or the observation or recording is done for a sexual purpose (subsec. (1)(*c*)). The offence is committed whether the observation is direct or done by mechanical or electronic means or through making a visual recording (defined in subsec. (2)). The offence is not committed by a peace officer acting under the authority of a general warrant issued under s. 487.01. This section also creates an offence in subsec. (4) of, in effect, trafficking or possessing for the purpose of trafficking recordings, if the accused knows that the recording was obtained by the commission of the offence under subsec. (1). The subsec. (4) offence is committed in any of the ways set out such as printing, copying, publishing or distributing. Subsection (6) provides for a defence where the alleged acts serve the public good. Subsection (7) provides that it is a question of law whether the act serves the public good and whether there is any evidence that the act alleged goes beyond what serves the public good. It is a question of fact whether or not the act does extend beyond what serves the public good. The accused's motives are irrelevant in determining the public good offence.

ANNOTATIONS

Circumstances that give rise to a reasonable expectation of privacy for this offence are circumstances in which a person would reasonably expect not to be the subject of the type of observation or recording that in fact occurred. The inquiry should take into account the entire context in which the impugned observation or recording took place. Relevant considerations may include: the location the person was in when she was observed or recorded; the nature of the impugned conduct (whether it consisted of observation or recording); awareness of or consent to potential observation or recording; the manner in which the observation or recording was done; the subject matter or content of the observation or recording; any rules, regulations or policies that governed the observation or recording in question; the relationship between the person who was observed or recorded and the person who did the observing or recording; the purpose for which the observation or recording was done; and the personal attributes of the person who was observed or recorded. The offence was made out where a teacher surreptitiously videotaped students in a public place for a sexual purpose: *R. v. Jarvis*, 2019 SCC 10.

PUBLICATION ETC., OF AN INTIMATE IMAGE WITHOUT CONSENT / Definition of "intimate image" / Defence / Question of fact and law, motives.

162.1 (1) Everyone who knowingly publishes, distributes, transmits, sells, makes available or advertises an intimate image of a person knowing that the person depicted in the image did not give their consent to that conduct, or being reckless as to whether or not that person gave their consent to that conduct, is guilty

(*a*) of an indictable offence and liable to imprisonment for a term of not more than five years; or

(*b*) of an offence punishable on summary conviction.

(2) In this section, "intimate image" means a visual recording of a person made by any means including a photographic, film or video recording,

(*a*) in which the person is nude, is exposing his or her genital organs or anal region or her breasts or is engaged in explicit sexual activity;

(*b*) in respect of which, at the time of the recording, there were circumstances that gave rise to a reasonable expectation of privacy; and

(*c*) in respect of which the person depicted retains a reasonable expectation of privacy at the time the offence is committed.

(3) No person shall be convicted of an offence under this section if the conduct that forms the subject-matter of the charge serves the public good and does not extend beyond what serves the public good.

(4) For the purposes of subsection (3),

CR. CODE

(*a*) it is a question of law whether the conduct serves the public good and whether there is evidence that the conduct alleged goes beyond what serves the public good, but it is a question of fact whether the conduct does or does not extend beyond what serves the public good; and

(*b*) the motives of an accused are irrelevant. 2014, c. 31, s. 3.

CROSS-REFERENCES

For notes on the "public good" defence provided by subsec. (3), see the notes under s. 163.

Section 164 enacts an alternative procedure, *in rem* proceedings, for the seizure, forfeiture and restoration of intimate images. Where an order has been made under s. 164, no proceedings may be taken under this section except with the consent of the Attorney General.

Section 164.1 sets out an *in rem* procedure for removal of intimate images from computer systems.

Section 164.2 provides that a court that convicts a person of an offence under this section may order that any thing, other than real property, be forfeited to the Crown if the court is satisfied that the thing was used in the commission of the offence and is the property of the offender, another person who was a party to the offence, or a person who acquired the thing from such a person in circumstances giving rise to a reasonable inference that it was transferred to avoid a forfeiture order.

This offence may be the basis for an application for an authorization to intercept private communications by reason of s. 183, or a video surveillance warrant under s. 487.01(5).

Where the victim of an offence under this section has incurred expenses to have the intimate image removed from the Internet, restitution of such expenses may be ordered pursuant to s. 738(1)(*e*) when sentence is imposed.

A "peace bond" is available under s. 810 where a person fears on reasonable grounds that another person will commit an offence under this section.

SYNOPSIS

This provision creates an offence in relation to the non-consensual distribution of intimate images. Under subsec. (1), the *actus reus* is satisfied if the person depicted did not consent to the image being distributed (or transmitted, etc.), and the *mens rea* is made out if the accused knows of or is reckless as to the person's non-consent. The subject matter of the offence ("intimate image") is defined in subsec. (2). The key concept is a "reasonable expectation of privacy" on the part of the person depicted, which must be present both at the time the recording was made and at the time the offence is committed. For guidance on "reasonable expectation of privacy", reference may be had to the annotations under s. 8 of the Charter.

Subsection (3) provides a "public good" defence, which is subject to subsec. (4). For guidance on this defence, see notes under s. 163.

PROHIBITION ORDER / Duration of prohibition / Court may vary order / Offence.

162.2 (1) When an offender is convicted, or is discharged on the conditions prescribed in a probation order under section 730, of an offence referred to in subsection 162.1(1), the court that sentences or discharges the offender, in addition to any other punishment that may be imposed for that offence or any other condition prescribed in the order of discharge, may make, subject to the conditions or exemptions that the court directs, an order prohibiting the offender from using the Internet or other digital network, unless the offender does so in accordance with conditions set by the court.

(2) The prohibition may be for any period that the court considers appropriate, including any period to which the offender is sentenced to imprisonment.

(3) A court that makes an order of prohibition or, if the court is for any reason unable to act, another court of equivalent jurisdiction in the same province may, on application of the offender or the prosecutor, require the offender to appear before it at any time and, after hearing the parties, that court may vary the conditions prescribed in the

order if, in the opinion of the court, the variation is desirable because of changed circumstances after the conditions were prescribed.

(4) Every person who is bound by an order of prohibition and who does not comply with the order is guilty of

(*a*) an indictable offence and is liable to imprisonment for a term of not more than four years; or

(*b*) an offence punishable on summary conviction and is liable to imprisonment for a term of not more than 18 months. 2014, c. 31, s. 3; 2015, c. 23, s. 33.

CROSS-REFERENCES

Section 161(1)(*d*) provides for a similar prohibition order available in respect of other sexual offences.

SYNOPSIS

This provision creates a new form of prohibition order that may be imposed on a person convicted or discharged of an offence in relation to intimate images under s. 162.1. It allows the court to prohibit the offender from using the Internet or other digital network except in accordance with conditions set by the court. The prohibition can be for any period deemed appropriate, and may be varied on application of the offender or the Crown. Subsection (4) creates a separate offence of failing to comply with such a prohibition.

Offences Tending to Corrupt Morals

OBSCENE MATERIALS / Idem / Defence of public good / Question of law and question of fact / Motives irrelevant / Ignorance of nature no defence / Obscene publication.

163. (1) Every person commits an offence who makes, prints, publishes, distributes, circulates or has in their possession for the purpose of publication, distribution or circulation any obscene written matter, picture, model, phonograph record or any other obscene thing.

(2) Every person commits an offence who knowingly, without lawful justification or excuse,

(*a*) sells, exposes to public view or has in their possession for that purpose any obscene written matter, picture, model, phonograph record or any other obscene thing; or

(*b*) publicly exhibits a disgusting object or an indecent show;

(*c*) [*Repealed*, 2018, c. 29, s. 11(3).]

(*d*) [*Repealed*, 2018, c. 29, s. 11(3).]

(3) No person shall be convicted of an offence under this section if the public good was served by the acts that are alleged to constitute the offence and if the acts alleged did not extend beyond what served the public good.

(4) For the purposes of this section, it is a question of law whether an act served the public good and whether there is evidence that the act alleged went beyond what served the public good, but it is a question of fact whether the acts did or did not extend beyond what served the public good.

(5) For the purposes of this section, the motives of an accused are irrelevant.

(6) [*Repealed*, 1993, c. 46, s. 1.]

(7) [*Repealed*, 2018, c. 29, s. 11(3).]

(8) For the purposes of this Act, any publication a dominant characteristic of which is the undue exploitation of sex, or of sex and any one or more of the following subjects,

namely, crime, horror, cruelty and violence, shall be deemed to be obscene. R.S., c. C-34, s. 159; 1993, c. 46, s. 1; 2018, c. 29, s. 11.

CROSS-REFERENCES

Possession is defined by s. 4(3). The punishment for this offence is set out in s. 169. Where the prosecution elects to proceed by indictment on this offence then the accused may elect his mode of trial pursuant to s. 536(2). Where the prosecution elects to proceed by way of summary conviction then the trial of this offence is conducted by a summary conviction court pursuant to Part XXVII. The punishment for the offence is then as set out in s. 787 [although note the maximum fine for a corporation is determined by s. 735(1)(*b*)] and the limitation period is set out in s. 786(2). In either case, release pending trial is determined by s. 515, although the accused is eligible for release by a peace officer under s. 496, 497 or by the officer in charge under s. 498. This offence is an enterprise crime offence for the purposes of Part XII.2 and the offence in subsec. (1)(*a*) may be the basis for an application for an authorization to intercept private communications by reason of s. 183 and a warrant for video surveillance by reason of s. 487.01(5). Section 584 deals with the sufficiency of an indictment in relation to obscene written material and s. 587(1)(*d*) provides for the ordering of particulars in such cases.

Section 164 enacts an alternative procedure, "*in rem*" proceedings, for determination of whether or not a publication is obscene or a crime comic. Where an order has been made under s. 164 then no proceedings may be taken under this section except with the consent of the Attorney General. Section 583(*h*) provides that a count in an indictment is not insufficient by reason only that it does not state that the required consent has been obtained. Section 165 makes it an offence to refuse to supply publications to a person because he refuses to purchase or acquire publications which he believes to be obscene or a crime comic. Section 166 makes it an offence to publish certain material calculated to injure public morals or in relation to marital and similar proceedings. Section 167 makes it an offence to take part in immoral theatrical performances. Section 168 makes it an offence to use the mail for the purpose of transmitting obscene material. Wilfully doing an indecent act is an offence under s. 173. Public nudity is an offence under s. 174. Exposing an indecent exhibition is an offence under s. 175(1)(*b*). Child pornography is dealt with in s. 163.1.

SYNOPSIS

Section 163 makes it an offence to produce, publish or distribute *obscene things or crime comics*.

Section 163(1)(*a*) is very broadly worded to prohibit all phases of the making, printing, publication, distribution and circulation, and the possession of *obscene things*, with the intention of doing any of the prohibited activities. The prohibited class of obscene things is expansive, covering written material, pictures, models, records or "any other thing whatsoever". Section 163(8) provides the sole definition of what is deemed to be obscene. It states that if a dominant characteristic of the publication is the *undue exploitation of sex*, or the combination of sex and at least one of crime, horror, cruelty or violence. The acts described within the section have received a broad interpretation, as reflected, for example, by a decision stating that the display of such objects in plain view within a store amounts to publication.

Section 163(1)(*b*), which deals with *crime comics*, prohibits many aspects of the publication process including the distribution and sale of crime comics, or their possession for such purposes. Section 163(7) defines what constitutes a crime comic.

Section 163(5) makes the accused's motives irrelevant. Subsection (6) purports to state that it is *no defence* that the accused was ignorant of the nature or presence of obscene content of the thing or of the crime comic. However, decisions made under the *Canadian Charter of Rights and Freedoms* have held that this subsection is unconstitutional and have established that it is a defence if the accused made an *honest* and *reasonable mistake of fact*. A mistake of law, which causes the accused to believe that the material he or she knows the nature or presence of is not obscene or a crime comic, is not a defence.

Section 163(2) makes it an offence to *knowingly* and *without lawful justification or excuse* engage in any of the acts listed in this subsection, which relate to obscenity, indecent objects, drugs and other things used to induce (or said to be useful to induce) abortions or miscarriages, and a number of other specified sex related materials.

Section 163(3) provides a defence if the accused *establishes* that the acts which make out the offence under this section *served the public good,* and extended no further than was required to achieve that objective. Subsection (4) states that whether an act served the public good, and whether there is any evidence that the act extended beyond what was required to achieve that end, are questions of law. That means that in a jury trial these issues would be determined by the trial judge. However, the subsection also provides that if it is determined that there is some evidence, the decision as to whether the act actually extended beyond what was needed to achieve the public good is a question of fact and will, therefore, be determined by the trier of fact.

ANNOTATIONS

Subsection (1) / Elements of offence generally / *Distinction between subsecs. (1) and (2)* – There is a difference between selling or having in possession for the purpose of selling contrary to subsec. (2) and distributing contrary to subsec. (1): *R. v. Fraser*, [1967] S.C.R. 38, [1967] 2 C.C.C. 43 (5:0).

In *R. v. Dorosz* (1971), 4 C.C.C. (2d) 203 (Ont. C.A.), the evidence upon conviction of possession of obscene matter for the purpose of distribution was simply the display for sale in a variety store of certain obscene publications. It was held (2:1) that Parliament had drawn a line in the chain from production to consumption of such material by virtue of mutually exclusive subsecs. (1) and (2), with the result that although the omission of proof of knowledge of obscenity is directed against the maker, circulator and distributor, that element must be proven against the person through whose hands the publication must finally pass before public consumption. Furthermore, it was the unanimous view of the Court that in any event the retail store clerk is not a distributor. Also see *R. v. Sudbury News Service Ltd.* (1978), 39 C.C.C. (2d) 1 (Ont. C.A.).

Meaning of "circulates" and "distributes" – A private showing of obscene films in the accused's home does not constitute circulation: *R. v. Rioux*, [1969] S.C.R. 599, [1970] 3 C.C.C. 149.

The rental of video movie cassettes comes within the meaning of distribution or circulation in this subsection: *R. v. Video Movieshop* (1982), 67 C.C.C. (2d) 87 (Nfld. S.C. T.D.). *Contra*: *R. v. Householders T.V. and Appliances Ltd.* (1984), 20 C.C.C. (3d) 561 (Ont. Co. Ct.), affd 20 C.C.C. (3d) 571 (C.A.).

While the mere renting of video movie cassettes may not constitute the offence under this paragraph, the offence was made out where the accused copied tapes for rental to other persons: *R. v. Harris and Lighthouse Video Centres Ltd.* (1987), 35 C.C.C. (3d) 1 (Ont. C.A.), leave to appeal to S.C.C. refused [1986] 2 S.C.R. vii, 38 C.C.C. (3d) vi.

***Mens rea* and mistake of fact** – While an intent to publish is not an element of all the offences created by this subsection, such as the offence of making, where the crown has framed its information to allege making an obscene publication, the allegation of publication cannot be said to be mere surplusage and the accused was entitled to be discharged where there was no evidence of publication or intent to publish: *R. v. Hawkshaw*, [1986] 1 S.C.R. 668, 26 C.C.C. (3d) 129 (7:0).

In *R. v. Metro News Ltd.* (1986), 29 C.C.C. (3d) 35 (Ont. C.A.), leave to appeal to S.C.C. refused C.C.C. *loc. cit.*, while the court held that subsec. (6) was unconstitutional as it had the effect of making the offences under this subsection absolute liability offences, nevertheless this holding did not have the effect of requiring the crown to prove *mens rea.* Rather, the act of distributing matter which is in fact obscene *prima facie* imports the offence, but it is open to an accused to avoid criminal liability by raising a reasonable doubt that he acted under an honest and reasonable belief in a state of facts which, if it had been as he believed them to be, would make his act innocent. However an accused's belief that the magazine did not exceed the community standards of tolerance and was not obscene did not constitute a reasonable mistake of fact nor give rise to a defence of due diligence. Whether a publication unduly exploits sex under subsec. (8) or whether the allegedly obscene matter exceeded the community's standard of tolerance constitutes a value judgment to which the doctrine of mistake of fact is inapplicable. An accused's belief that the publication was not legally obscene is not a defence.

Subsection (2) / Meaning of "knowingly" – The offence of "knowingly" selling obscene material requires proof of knowledge with respect to all aspects of the *actus reus*. It is not sufficient that the accused was aware that the dominant characteristic of the material was the exploitation of sex as the sale of such material is lawful. The Crown must show that the seller of the obscene material was aware of the relevant facts that made the material obscene. In the case of pornographic films and videos, it cannot easily be inferred that those selling the materials know their contents. While it may be inferred that the retailer is aware that the materials are erotic or pornographic and deal with the exploitation of sex, selling films dealing with the exploitation of sex is not illegal unless the material is obscene. Not only must the dominant characteristic of the material be the exploitation of sex, but the exploitation of sex must be undue. To prove knowledge, the Crown must prove beyond a reasonable doubt that the accused knew that the materials being sold have the qualities or contain the specific scenes which render such material obscene in law. This does not require proof that the retailer actually viewed the tapes. Knowledge can be proven by circumstantial evidence. In addition, in proper circumstances, the Crown can rely upon the principles of willful blindness. Where the accused knew of the presence of the ingredients of the subject-matter which rendered the exploitation of sex undue and thus obscene, the fact that the material had been approved by the provincial film review board does not constitute a lawful justification or excuse nor negative the necessary *mens rea*: *R. v. Jorgensen*, [1995] 4 S.C.R. 55, 102 C.C.C. (3d) 97.

Expose to public view – An obscene film was not exposed to public view within the meaning of this subsection where it was only shown to friends and relatives of the groom attending a private "stag party". The hall in which the film was shown was, at the time, not open to the public, but rather, was used for a private gathering. In this respect, the definition of "private" in the *Oxford English Dictionary* as "kept or removed from public view . . . not within the cognizance of people generally . . . not open to the public; intended only for the use of particular and privileged persons" accurately described the circumstances in which the film was shown: *R. v. Harrison* (1973), 12 C.C.C. (2d) 26 (Alta. Dist. Ct.).

On the other hand, where an obscene film was shown not only to invited guests but to others who merely paid an admission charge then there was an exposure to public view: *R. v. Vigue*, 13 C.C.C. (2d) 381 (B.C. Prov. Ct.).

Disgusting object, indecent show (para. (*b*)) – The offence created by para. (*b*) of exhibiting an indecent show is not so vague as to be an unconstitutional infringement of freedom of expression as guaranteed by s. 2(*b*) of the *Canadian Charter of Rights and Freedoms*. The test to be applied in determining indecency is that of the community standard of tolerance. A relevant consideration in applying that test is the nature of the audience, the issue being whether the show is inappropriate according to Canadian standards of tolerance because of the context in which it takes place: *R. v. Pelletier* (1985), 27 C.C.C. (3d) 77 (Que. C.A.).

The word "disgusting" was held to have a known dictionary as well as judicial meaning and, therefore, not to violate the due process guarantee under the *Canadian Bill of Rights*: *R. v. Isaacs' Gallery Ltd.* (1975), 19 C.C.C. (2d) 570 (Ont. C.A.), leave to appeal refused [1975] 1 S.C.R. ix.

The offence of exhibiting a disgusting object is unconstitutionally vague and violates ss. 2(*b*) and 7 of the *Canadian Charter of Rights and Freedoms* and is of no force and effect: *R. v. Glassman and Bogyo* (1986), 53 C.R. (3d) 164 (Ont. Prov. Ct.).

Note: Also see notes under ss. 174 and 175.

Subsection (3) (public good) – Where, although the book has certain literary merit particularly for the more sophisticated reader, it was available for the general public to whom the book was neither symbolism nor a psychological study the accused cannot rely on the defence of public good: *R. v. Delorme* (1973), 15 C.C.C. (2d) 350 (Que. C.A.) (2:1).

In *R. v. American News Co.* (1957), 118 C.C.C. 152 (Ont. C.A.), Laidlaw J.A. adopted as a definition of the words "public good" a formula used in Stephen's *Digest of Criminal Law*, namely, "necessary or advantageous to religion or morality to the administration of justice, the pursuit of science, literature or art, or other objects of general interest".

Subsection (6) – This subsection is of no force and effect by reason of its inconsistency with s. 7 of the *Canadian Charter of Rights and Freedoms*: *R. v. Metro News Ltd.* (1986), 29 C.C.C. (3d) 35 (Ont. C.A.), leave to appeal to S.C.C. refused C.C.C. *loc. cit.*; *R. v. Saint John News Co.* (1984), 17 C.C.C. (3d) 234 (N.B.Q.B.). *Contra*: *R. v. Red Hot Video Ltd.* (1984), 11 C.C.C. (3d) 389 (B.C. Co. Ct.), affd on other grounds 18 C.C.C. (3d) 1 (C.A.), leave to appeal to S.C.C. refused [1985] 2 S.C.R. x.

Subsection (8) [definition of obscenity] / Test for obscenity – In *R. v. Butler*, [1992] 1 S.C.R. 452, 70 C.C.C. (3d) 129, the court laid down a new comprehensive interpretation of subsec. (8). It would appear that this test is to be applied in two stages. The first stage involves a determination of whether the particular material involves the undue exploitation of sex. The second stage requires application of a test of "internal necessities". For the purposes of this definition, the court referred to three categories of pornography: (1) explicit sex with violence; (2) explicit sex without violence but which subjects people to treatment that is degrading or dehumanizing; and (3) explicit sex without violence that is neither degrading nor dehumanizing. Violence in this context includes both actual physical violence and threats of physical violence. In applying the definition to the three categories, the courts must determine what the community would tolerate others being exposed to on the basis of the degree of harm that may flow from such exposure. Harm in this context means that it predisposes persons to act in an anti-social manner as, for example, the physical or mental mistreatment of women by men or possibly the reverse. Anti-social conduct for this purpose is conduct which society formally recognizes as incompatible with its proper functioning. The stronger the inference of risk of harm, the lesser the likelihood of tolerance. Material falling in the first category will almost always constitute the undue exploitation of sex. Explicit sex which is degrading or dehumanizing may be undue if the risk of harm is substantial. Explicit sex that is not violent and neither degrading nor dehumanizing is generally tolerated and will not fall within the definition unless it employs children in its production. If material is not obscene under this framework, it does not become so by reason of the person to whom it is or may be shown or exposed nor by reason of the place or manner in which it is shown. Even if the work contains sexually explicit material that, by itself, would constitute the undue exploitation of sex, the portrayal of sex must then be viewed in context to determine whether that is the dominant theme of the work as a whole [the "internal necessities" test]. In other words, is undue exploitation of sex the main object of the work or is this portrayal of sex essential to a wider artistic, literary, or other similar purpose? Again, the community standards test applies at this stage, the court having to determine whether the sexually explicit material, when viewed in the context of the whole work, would be tolerated by the community as a whole. Since artistic expression rests at the heart of freedom of expression values, any doubt in this regard must be resolved in favour of freedom of expression.

Videotapes which merely display a large number of explicit sexual acts in a non-violent consensual manner, although devoid of any loving or affectionate relationship or any plot of meaningful value, are not necessarily degrading or dehumanizing. Further, even if the material could be found to be degrading or dehumanizing, it will not necessarily be found to be obscene. The material must also create a substantial risk of harm to society. Like any element of criminal allegation, it must be proved beyond a reasonable doubt and that proof must be found in the evidence adduced at trial. It does not follow from proof of portrayal of sexually explicit acts in a degrading or dehumanizing manner that the films are harmful and therefore obscene. It is open to the court to find that the harm component of the offence is not established. Where the participants appear as fully willing participants occupying substantially equal roles in a setting devoid of violence, bondage or bestiality or sex associated with crime, horror, cruelty, coercion or children, the risk of societal harm may not be evident. Further evidence may be required to prove that exposure to the impugned material will create a substantial risk of an identifiable harm that may cause persons to act in a manner inimical to the proper functioning of society. The question is essentially one of degree but the onus remains on the Crown to prove that the offence is made out: *R. v. Hawkins* (1993), 86 C.C.C. (3d) 246 (Ont. C.A.), leave to appeal to S.C.C. refused 87 C.C.C. (3d) vi.

In considering the requirement of proof of harm, reference may be made to *R. v. Labaye*, [2005] 3 S.C.R. 728, 203 C.C.C. (3d) 170; *R. v. Kouri*, [2005] 3 S.C.R. 798, 203 C.C.C. (3d) 217, noted under s. 197 and concerned with the related term of "indecency" in the definition of common bawdy house.

In determining whether the material depicts explicit sex, the trier of fact must consider the circumstances and context of the material. Even where no sexual act is depicted, material may still depict explicit sex. The trier of fact must consider whether a reasonable person viewing the material would consider whether the material was explicitly sexual in nature, taking into account the part of the body depicted; the nature of the depiction; the context; the accompanying dialogue, words, or gestures; and all other surrounding circumstances. However, so-called "sexualized nudity" would not itself be sufficient to constitute depiction of explicit sex. Explicit sex captures portrayals at the far end of the spectrum: *R. v. Smith* (2005), 198 C.C.C. (3d) 499 (Ont. C.A.), leave to appeal to S.C.C. refused 198 C.C.C. (3d) 499*n*.

Effect of audience to which publication directed – The audience viewing a publication is not relevant in determining whether the publication is obscene. Thus, the fact that articles were for sale in a store restricted to adults did not prevent a finding that the articles were obscene: *R. v. Germain*, [1985] 2 S.C.R. 241, 21 C.C.C. (3d) 289 (9:0); *R. v. Butler, supra.*

Application of subsection to articles other than publications – It was held in *R. v. Hawkshaw*, [1986] 1 S.C.R. 668, 26 C.C.C. (3d) 129 (7:0), that this subsection sets out the sole test for obscenity in charges under the *Criminal Code* whether based on publication or not, thus clearing up the issue left open in several earlier cases such as *R. v. Dechow*, [1978] 1 S.C.R. 951, 35 C.C.C. (2d) 22, and *Germain, supra.*

Application of Charter of Rights – The prohibition on obscene material as defined by subsec. (8) infringes freedom of expression but constitutes a reasonable limit prescribed by law within the meaning of s. 1: *R. v. Butler, supra.*

DEFINITION OF "CHILD PORNOGRAPHY" / Making child pornography / Distribution, etc. of child pornography / Possession of child pornography / Accessing child pornography / Interpretation / Aggravating factor / Defence / Defence / Question of law.

163.1 (1) In this section, "child pornography" means

(*a*) a photographic, film, video or other visual representation, whether or not it was made by electronic or mechanical means,

(i) that shows a person who is or is depicted as being under the age of eighteen years and is engaged in or is depicted as engaged in explicit sexual activity, or

(ii) the dominant characteristic of which is the depiction, for a sexual purpose, of a sexual organ or the anal region of a person under the age of eighteen years;

(*b*) any written material, visual representation or audio recording that advocates or counsels sexual activity with a person under the age of eighteen years that would be an offence under this Act;

(*c*) any written material whose dominant characteristic is the description, for a sexual purpose, of sexual activity with a person under the age of eighteen years that would be an offence under this Act; or

(*d*) any audio recording that has as its dominant characteristic the description, presentation or representation, for a sexual purpose, of sexual activity with a person under the age of eighteen years that would be an offence under this Act.

(2) Every person who makes, prints, publishes or possesses for the purpose of publication any child pornography is guilty of an indictable offence and liable to imprisonment for a term of not more than 14 years and to a minimum punishment of imprisonment for a term of one year.

(3) Every person who transmits, makes available, distributes, sells, advertises, imports, exports or possesses for the purpose of transmission, making available, distribution, sale, advertising or exportation any child pornography is guilty of an indictable offence and liable to imprisonment for a term of not more than 14 years and to a minimum punishment of imprisonment for a term of one year.

(4) Every person who possesses any child pornography is guilty of

(*a*) an indictable offence and is liable to imprisonment for a term of not more than 10 years and to a minimum punishment of imprisonment for a term of one year; or

(*b*) an offence punishable on summary conviction and is liable to imprisonment for a term of not more than two years less a day and to a minimum punishment of imprisonment for a term of six months.

(4.1) Every person who accesses any child pornography is guilty of

(*a*) an indictable offence and is liable to imprisonment for a term of not more than 10 years and to a minimum punishment of imprisonment for a term of one year; or

(*b*) an offence punishable on summary conviction and is liable to imprisonment for a term of not more than two years less a day and to a minimum punishment of imprisonment for a term of six months.

(4.2) For the purposes of subsection (4.1), a person accesses child pornography who knowingly causes child pornography to be viewed by, or transmitted to, himself or herself.

(4.3) If a person is convicted of an offence under this section, the court that imposes the sentence shall consider as an aggravating factor the fact that the person committed the offence with intent to make a profit.

(5) It is not a defence to a charge under subsection (2) in respect of a visual representation that the accused believed that a person shown in the representation that is alleged to constitute child pornography was or was depicted as being eighteen years of age or more unless the accused took all reasonable steps to ascertain the age of that person and took all reasonable steps to ensure that, where the person was eighteen years of age or more, the representation did not depict that person as being under the age of eighteen years.

(6) No person shall be convicted of an offence under this section if the act that is alleged to constitute the offence

(*a*) has a legitimate purpose related to the administration of justice or to science, medicine, education or art; and

(*b*) does not pose an undue risk of harm to persons under the age of eighteen years.

(7) For greater certainty, for the purposes of this section, it is a question of law whether any written material, visual representation or audio recording advocates or counsels

sexual activity with a person under the age of eighteen years that would be an offence under this Act. 1993, c. 46. s. 2; 2002, c. 13, s. 5; 2005, c. 32, s. 7; 201, c. 1, s. 17; 2015, c. 23, s. 7.

CROSS-REFERENCES

Possession is defined by s. 4(3). For notes on procedure on arrest and trial for this offence, see the notes under s. 163.

Section 164 enacts an alternative procedure, *in rem* proceedings, for determination of whether or not the representation or written material is child pornography. The offences in this section may be the basis for obtaining an authorization to intercept private communications or a warrant for video surveillance. Section 164.1 sets out an *in rem* procedure for removal of child pornography from a computer system. Section 164.2 provides that a court that convicts a person of an offence under this section may order that any thing, other than real property, be forfeited to the Crown if the court is satisfied that the thing was used in the commission of the offence and is the property of the offender, another person who was a party to the offence or a person who acquired the thing from such a person in circumstances giving rise to a reasonable inference that it was transferred to avoid a forfeiture order.

If the accused is found guilty of this offence in respect of a person who is under 16 years of age, the court may impose an order of prohibition under s. 161 prohibiting the accused from attending certain public areas and facilities or taking certain employment that will bring him into contact with persons under the age of 16 years. Section 171.1 makes it an offence to transmit, make available, distribute or sell sexually explicit material to a person who is, or who the accused believes is under the age of 18 years for purpose of facilitating the commission of the offence created by this section. Section 172.1 makes it an offence to communicate by means of telecommunication with a person who is or who the accused believes is under the age of 18 years for the purpose of facilitating the commission of the offence under this section. Section 172.2 makes it an offence to agree with a person or make an arrangement with a person by means of telecommunication to commit an offence under this section with a person who is or who the accused believes is under the age of 18 years.

Section 486(1) and (2) provide that the judge may make an order excluding all or any members of the public where such order is in the interest of public morals, the maintenance of order or the proper administration of justice, or is necessary to prevent injury to international relations or national defence or national security. The proper administration of justice includes safeguarding the interests of witnesses under the age of 18 years. Section 486.1 sets out the circumstances in which the judge shall or may order a support person to be present and close to a witness while the witness testifies. Where the witness is under the age of 18 years or has a mental or physical disability, the order is to be made upon request unless the judge is of the opinion that the order would interfere with the proper administration of justice. In the case of other witnesses, the order is to be made if necessary to obtain a full and candid account from the witness of the matters complained of. The application for this order may be made during the proceedings or before they begin to the judge who is to preside at the proceedings.

Similarly, s. 486.2 sets out the circumstances in which the judge shall or may order a witness to testify outside the courtroom or behind a screen or other device that would not allow the witness to see the accused. Where the witness is under the age of 18 years or may have difficulty communicating the evidence by reason of a mental or physical disability, the judge shall make the order unless the judge is of the opinion that the order would interfere with the proper administration of justice. In all other cases, the order may be made if the judge is of the opinion that the order is necessary to obtain a full and candid account from the witness of the acts complained of. Similarly, s. 486.3 provides that, on application by the prosecutor or a witness under the age of 18 years, the accused shall not personally cross-examine the witness unless the judge is of the opinion that the proper administration of justice requires the accused to personally conduct the cross-examination. In other cases, the judge may make an order that the accused not personally cross-examine the witness if the judge is of the opinion that the order is necessary to obtain a full and candid account from the witness of the acts complained of. The judge will appoint counsel to conduct the cross-examination.

Under s. 486.4, the judge may make an order directing that the identity of a witness not be disclosed in any publication, broadcast or transmitted in any way. The order is mandatory where the complainant or a witness under the age of 18 years or the prosecutor applies for the order. Under s. 486.4(3), the judge shall make an order directing that the identity of a witness who is under the age of 18 years and any person who is the subject of a representation, written material or recording that constitutes child pornography not be disclosed in any publication, broadcast or transmitted in any way. Section 486.5 also gives the judge a discretion respecting non-publication orders in proceedings under these provisions in other circumstances.

Section 718.01 provides that, in imposing a sentence for an offence involving the abuse of a person under the age of 18 years, the court shall give primary consideration to the objectives of denunciation and deterrence. Further, under s. 718.2, evidence that the offender, in committing the offence, abused a person under the age of 18 years is an aggravating circumstance.

The offence in this section is a primary designated offence for the purpose of making a forensic DNA data bank order under s. 487.051. Under s. 490.012, where an offender is convicted of this offence, the judge shall make an order requiring the offender to comply with the *Sex Offender Information Registration Act*, S.C. 2004, c. 10.

Bill C-22, *An Act respecting the mandatory reporting of Internet child pornography by persons who provide an Internet service*, in force as of December 8, 2011, requires Internet service providers to report tips they receive regarding Web sites where child pornography, as defined by this section, may be publicly available, to the Canadian Centre for Child Protection; and, to notify the police and safeguard evidence for 21 days (or longer pursuant to a court order) if they have reasonable grounds to believe that a child pornography offence has been or is being committed using an Internet service that they provide.

SYNOPSIS

This section creates various offences relating to child pornography, which is defined in subsec. (1). To determine whether the material offends para. (*b*) of the definition, resort will have to be made to the various sexual offences of the Code: ss. 151, 152, 153, 155, 159, 160, 170, 171, 172, and 271 to 273. Subsections (2) and (3) correspond to the similar offences under s. 163 and notes under that section should be referred to in determining whether the material has, for example, been published. Pursuant to subsec. (7), it is a question of law whether the written material, visual representation or audio recording advocates or counsels sexual activity with a person under the age of 18 years that would be an offence under the Code. The offences of making and distributing child pornography in subsecs. (2) and (3) are punishable by a maximum of 14 years and a minimum of one year imprisonment. Subsection (4) creates an offence of simple possession of child pornography. Where the Crown proceeds by way of indictment, the offence is punishable by a maximum of 10 years and a minimum of one year imprisonment. Where the Crown proceeds by way of summary conviction, the offence is punishable by two years less a day and a minimum of six months' imprisonment. Subsection (4.1) creates the offence of accessing any child pornography. Accessing is defined in subsec. (4.2). Where the Crown proceeds by way of indictment, the offence is punishable by a maximum of 10 years and a minimum of one year imprisonment. Where the Crown proceeds by way of summary conviction, the offence is punishable by two years less a day and a minimum of six months' imprisonment. In addition, the fact that the person committed the offence with intent to make a profit is a deemed aggravating factor under subsec. (4.3).

Subsections (5) to (7) set out certain defence. Subsection (5) allows for a limited defence of reasonable mistake of fact as to the age of the persons depicted. Subsection (6) recognizes a defence where the accused has a legitimate purpose related to the administration of justice or to science, medicine, education or art, provided the act does not pose an undue risk of harm to persons under the age of 18 years.

ANNOTATIONS

Note: Some of the cases noted under this section were decided prior to the revisions to this section that came into force on November 1, 2005 and should be read with that in mind and, in particular, in light of the expansion of the definition of child pornography in subsec. (1)(*c*) and (*d*) and the addition of subsec. (6)(*b*) that limits the legitimate purpose defence by providing that the act must not pose an undue risk of harm to persons under the age of 18 years.

Subsections (1)(*a*), (*b*) and (4) violate s. 2(*b*) of the Charter but are justified under s. 1: *R. v. Sharpe*, [2001] 1 S.C.R. 45, 150 C.C.C. (3d) 321.

Subsection (1) – "Person" includes both actual and imaginary human beings: *R. v. Sharpe, supra.*

"Advocates or counsels" concerns material that, viewed objectively, sends the message that sex with children could and should be pursued: *R. v. Sharpe, supra.*

Active inducement or encouragement may come from a message that is implicit in the stories themselves. Material that describes sex with children as enjoyable, normal, and beneficial, and the children as willing, may send the message that sex with children can and should be pursued and therefore falls within the definition in para. (*b*), even though the author does not expressly advocate the commission of criminal sexual acts with children: *R. v. Beattie* (2005), 201 C.C.C. (3d) 533 (Ont. C.A.), leave to appeal to S.C.C. refused 201 C.C.C. (3d) 533*n*.

Subsection (2) – This provision does not include private recordings of lawful sexual activity which includes any visual recording that did not depict unlawful sexual activity and was held by the accused exclusively for private use: *R. v. Sharpe, supra.*

The private use exception has three requirements: (1) the recording must depict lawful sexual activity; (2) the persons depicted must consent to the recording; and (3) the recording must be held for private use. There is no additional "exploitation" inquiry, as exploitation is already captured under lawfulness. Section 153 of the Code makes sexual exploitation of a young person a crime. Thus, where the Crown seeks to rely on s. 153 to negate the legality of the sexual activity depicted, the judge must consider whether it occurred in the context of an exploitative relationship. If so, the sexual activity is not lawful, and the private use exception does not apply: *R. v. Barabash*, [2015] 2 S.C.R. 522, 322 C.C.C. (3d) 287.

Constructive possession is complete where the accused: (i) has knowledge of the character of the object; (ii) knowingly puts or keeps the object in a particular place whether or not that place belongs to him; and (iii) intends to have the object in the particular place for his use or benefit, or that of another person. In dealing with virtual objects, such as computer images, the mere fact that an image has been accessed by or displayed in a Web browser does not, without more, constitute possession of that image. Previous access and the possibility of again accessing a website that contains digital images, located on a distant server over which the viewer has no control, do not constitute, either alone or together, constructive possession. Furthermore, the automatic caching of a file to the hard drive does not, without more, constitute possession. The cached file might be a place over which the computer user has control but in order to establish possession, it is necessary to satisfy the *mens rea* or fault requirement as well by showing that the file was knowingly stored and retained through the cache: *R. v. Morelli*, [2010] 1 S.C.R. 253, 252 C.C.C. (3d) 273.

Possession requires knowledge of the criminal character of the items in issue. Accordingly, the Crown must prove that the accused had knowledge of the contents of the videos in issue, although it is irrelevant whether the accused knew that the contents constituted child pornography. In addition, the Crown must also prove that an accused with the requisite knowledge had a measure of control over the item in issue, in that he had power or authority over the item whether it was exercised or not. There are circumstances of innocent possession where an individual has the requisite control and knowledge, but cannot be said to be in possession for the purpose of imposing criminal liability. Such circumstances include taking control of contraband exclusively for the purpose of immediately destroying it or otherwise placing it permanently beyond that person's ability to exercise any control over the contraband. In such cases, the intention is solely to divest oneself of control rather than to possess: *R. v. Chalk* (2007), 227 C.C.C. (3d) 141 (Ont. C.A.).

Wilful blindness was not present where the accused was merely "suspicious" that his partner had viewed child pornography on a computer owned by the accused and used by both men: *R. v. Farmer* (2014), 318 C.C.C. (3d) 322 (Ont. C.A.).

The accused had requested that clearly identified child pornography files be downloaded but aborted the downloading process. No images of child pornography were in fact found on the computer. The accused was in constructive possession of the files even though the images were not on the computer screen as he had knowledge of the nature of the materials, the intention or consent to have possession and the necessary control over the material by virtue of the ability to permit the files to be downloaded or to abort the process. It is the element of control, including deciding what will be done with the material, that is essential to possession. It is not necessary for the individual to have viewed the material. Once the downloading of the transmission commenced, the material was in a place over which the accused had control: *R. v. Daniels* (2004), 191 C.C.C. (3d) 393 (Nfld. & Lab. C.A.).

Subsection (3) – There is no requirement that the accused take a "positive step" to make child pornography available in order to be guilty of the offence. A possessor of child pornography who uses a file sharing program and passively acquiesces in the program making the material available (or is willfully blind to it) has committed the offence of making available: *R. v. Spencer*, [2014] 2 S.C.R. 212, 312 C.C.C. (3d) 215. See also: *R. v. Smith* (2011), 282 C.C.C. (3d) 494 (B.C.S.C.). *Contra*: *R. v. Pressacco* (2010), 352 Sask. R. 276 (Q.B.); *R. v. Lamb* (2010), 92 W.C.B. (2d) 408 (B.C.S.C.), requiring "actual intent" to make available.

Subsection (6) – The defences in this section should be liberally construed and based on an objective test. The accused can raise the defences by pointing to facts capable of supporting them and the Crown must disprove them beyond a reasonable doubt. The artistic merit defence includes any expression that might reasonably be viewed as art. Any objectively established artistic value, however small, can support the defence. The defences of medical, educational and scientific purpose should also be liberally construed and include possession by people in the justice system for purposes associated with prosecution, researchers studying the effects of child pornography and by those in possession of works for the purpose of addressing the political or philosophical aspects of child pornography: *R. v. Sharpe*, *supra*.

In order for a purpose to be "legitimate" under s. 163.1(6)(*a*), there must be: (1) an objective connection between the accused's actions and his or her purpose; and (2) an objective relationship between the accused's purpose and one or more of the protected activities (administration of justice, science, medicine, education, or art). However, this objective assessment does not involve the court in any assessment of the *value* of the particular scientific or artistic activity in question. "Undue risk of harm" under s. 163.1(6)(*b*) means a significant risk of objectively ascertainable harm as required by the law of obscenity, rather than the former "moral views of the community" approach: *R. v. Katigbak*, [2011] 3 S.C.R. 326, 276 C.C.C. (3d) 1.

This section provides no defence to a person who possesses or accesses child pornography for both a legitimate and an illegitimate purpose: *R. v. Kiefer* (2018), 368 C.C.C. (3d) 129 (Ont. C.A.).

Sentence – The minimum penalty in subsec. (3)(*a*) does not violate s. 12 of the Charter: *R. v. Schultz* (2008), 239 C.C.C. (3d) 535 (Alta. Q.B.).

The mandatory minimum sentence in subsec. (4)(*a*) violates s. 12 of the Charter and is of no force or effect: *R. v. John*, 2018 ONCA 702.

WARRANT OF SEIZURE / Summons to occupier / Owner and maker may appear / Order of forfeiture / Disposal of matter / Appeal / Consent / Definitions / "Advertisement of sexual services" / "Court" / "Crime comic" / "Judge" / "Voyeuristic recording".

164. (1) A judge may issue a warrant authorizing seizure of copies of a recording, a publication, a representation or any written material, if the judge is satisfied by information on oath that there are reasonable grounds to believe that

(*a*) the recording, copies of which are kept for sale or distribution in premises within the jurisdiction of the court, is a voyeuristic recording;

(*b*) the recording, copies of which are kept for sale or distribution in premises within the jurisdiction of the court, is an intimate image;

(*c*) the publication, copies of which are kept for sale or distribution in premises within the jurisdiction of the court, is *obscene*, within the meaning of subection 163(8);

(*d*) the representation, written material or recording, copies of which are kept in premises within the jurisdiction of the court, is child pornography as defined in section 163.1; or

(*e*) the representation, written material or recording, copies of which are kept in premises within the jurisdiction of the court, is an advertisement of sexual services.

(2) Within seven days of the issue of the warrant under subsection (1), the judge shall issue a summons to the occupier of the premises requiring him to appear before the court and show cause why the matter seized should not be forfeited to Her Majesty.

(3) The owner and the maker of the matter seized under subsection (1), and alleged to be obscene, child pornography, a voyeuristic recording, an intimate image or an advertisement of sexual services, may appear and be represented in the proceedings to oppose the making of an order for the forfeiture of the matter.

(4) If the court is satisfied, on a balance of probabilities, that the publication, representation, written material or recording referred to in subsection (1) is obscene, child pornography, a voyeuristic recording, an intimate image or an advertisement of sexual services, it may make an order declaring the matter forfeited to Her Majesty in right of the province in which the proceedings take place, for disposal as the Attorney General may direct.

(5) If the court is not satisfied that the publication, representation, written material or recording referred to in subsection (1) is obscene, child pornography, a voyeuristic recording, an intimate image or an advertisement of sexual services, it shall order that the matter be restored to the person from whom it was seized without delay after the time for final appeal has expired.

(6) An appeal lies from an order made under subsection (4) or (5) by any person who appeared in the proceedings

(*a*) on any ground of appeal that involves a question of law alone,

(*b*) on any ground of appeal that involves a question of fact alone, or

(*c*) on any ground of appeal that involves a question of mixed law and fact,

as if it were an appeal against conviction or against a judgment or verdict of acquittal, as the case may be, on a question of law alone under Part XXI and sections 673 to 696 apply with such modifications as the circumstances require.

(7) If an order is made under this section by a judge in a province with respect to one or more copies of a publication, a representation, written material or a recording, no proceedings shall be instituted or continued in that province under section 162, 162.1, 163, 163.1 or 286.4 with respect to those or other copies of the same publication, representation, written material or recording without the consent of the Attorney General.

(8) In this section,

"advertisement of sexual services" means any material — including a photographic, film, video, audio or other recording, made by any means, a visual representation or any written material — that is used to advertise sexual services contrary to section 286.4.

"court" means

(*a*) in the Province of Quebec, the Court of Quebec, the municipal court of Montreal and the municipal court of Quebec,

(*a*.1) in the Province of Ontario, the Superior Court of Justice,

(*b*) in the Provinces of New Brunswick, Manitoba, Saskatchewan and Alberta, the Court of Queen's Bench,

(*c*) in the Province of Newfoundland and Labrador, the Trial Division of the Supreme Court,

(*c*.1) [*Repealed.* 1992, c. 51, s. 34.]

(*d*) in the Provinces of Nova Scotia, British Columbia and Prince Edward Island, in Yukon and in the Northwest Territories, the Supreme Court, and

(*e*) in Nunavut, the Nunavut Court of Justice;

"crime comic" [*Repealed*, 2018, c. 29, s. 12(3).]

"intimate image" has the same meaning as in subsection 162.1(2).

"judge" means a judge of a court.

"voyeuristic recording" means a visual recording within the meaning of subsection 162(2) that is made as described in subsection 162(1). R.S., c. C-34, s. 160; 1974-75-76, c. 48, s. 25; 1978-79, c. 11, s. 10; R.S.C. 1985, c. 27 (2nd Supp.), s. 10; c. 40 (4th Supp.), s. 2; 1990, c. 16, s. 3; 1990, c. 17, s. 9; 1992, c. 1, s. 58; 1992, c. 51, s. 34; 1993, c. 28, Sch. III, s. 28 (repealed by 1999, c. 3, s. 12); 1993, c. 46, s. 3; 1997, c. 18, s. 5; 1998, c. 30, s. 14(*d*); 1999, c. 3, ss. 12, 27; 2002, c. 7, s. 139; c. 13, s. 6; 2005, c. 32, s. 8; 2014, c. 25, s. 6; 2014, c. 31, s. 4; 2015, c. 3, s. 46; 2018, c. 29, s. 12.

CROSS-REFERENCES

The definition of obscenity is in s. 163(8) and of child pornography in s. 163.1(1). The voyeurism offence is defined in s. 162. The offence of advertising sexual services is set out in s. 286.4. "Attorney General" is defined in s. 2. An ordinary search warrant to search for evidence of the obscenity, child pornography and voyeurism offences under other sections of the *Criminal Code* may be obtained under ss. 487 and 487.1. (See *R. v. Video Movies Ltd.* (1984), 16 C.C.C. (3d) 351, 59 N.B.R. (2d) 82 (Q.B.).) The procedure in this section relates only to the *in rem* proceedings.

SYNOPSIS

This provision authorizes special search and seizure powers in relation to obscene publications, crime comics, child pornography, voyeuristic recordings, intimate images and advertisements of sexual services, and for the restoration or forfeiture of seized items.

Section 164(1) permits a judge to issue a warrant to seize obscene publications, crime comics, child pornography, voyeuristic recordings, intimate images and advertisements of sexual services kept within the jurisdiction of the court.

The procedure is like that usually employed in the issuance of warrants. It requires that, after receiving information on oath, the judge is to be satisfied that there are reasonable grounds to believe there are copies of any publication kept for sale or distribution at the place to be searched or, in the case of child pornography and advertisements of sexual services, simply that the materials are kept in the premises to be searched. Subsection (8) provides definitions of "advertisements of sexual services", "court", "crime comic", "intimate image", "judge" and "voyeuristic recording" for the purposes of this section.

Section 164(2) commences the forfeiture proceedings, the details of which are set out in the rest of this section. The judge shall issue a summons within seven days of the issuance of the search warrant, to the occupier of the searched premises, requiring that person to show cause why the items should not be forfeited. Despite the wording of this subsection, it has been determined that the onus remains on the Crown.

Section 164(3) permits the owner and author of the seized items to be represented in the forfeiture proceedings and oppose the proposed forfeiture.

Section 164(4) provides that, if the court is satisfied on a balance of probabilities that the material is one of the listed items, it may make a forfeiture order. However, if the court is not satisfied that the items come within the prohibited categories, then the items shall be restored to the person from whom they were seized (subsec. (5)). An order under this subsection will not be made until the time for launching an appeal has passed. Subsection (6) provides for a right of appeal to any one who appeared in the proceedings as if it was an indictable appeal under Part XXI with such modifications as are required. The grounds of appeal are the broadest possible, ranging from questions of fact to questions of law, or a mixture of the two. The incorporation of the sections relating to indictable appeals specified in this subsection also incorporates an appeal to the Supreme Court of Canada, but only on the usual ground, *i.e.*, a question of law, and not the broader grounds permitted in the initial level of appeal.

Section 164(7) provides that if a judge has made an order of restoration or forfeiture under this section, no prosecution under s. 162 (voyeurism), s. 163 (which prohibits possessing obscene items or crime comics for certain purposes), s. 162.1 (publication of an intimate image without consent), s. 163.1 (child pornography) and s. 286.4 (advertising sexual services) may be brought in relation to the same publication, representation, written material or recording unless the Attorney General consents.

ANNOTATIONS

Sufficiency of warrant – The warrant under this subsection must specify the publications and the phrase "and others" following certain titles will be severed from the warrant as being too indefinite: *R. v. Laborde* (1972), 7 C.C.C. (2d) 86 (Sask. Q.B.).

For the purposes of this section a video tape is not a "publication": *R. v. Video Movies Ltd., supra. Contra: R. v. Nicols* (1984), 17 C.C.C. (3d) 555 (Ont. Co. Ct.).

Procedure on *in rem* proceedings – The summons must be returnable before the court and not a judge in chambers: *R. v. Belding* (1976), 37 C.R.N.S. 229, 16 N.B.R. (2d) 8 (C.A.).

Despite the wording of this subsection calling for the owner to "show cause" why the matter should not be forfeited, the burden of proof is on the Crown to show that the material is obscene and the ordinary rules of evidence apply: *R. v. Penthouse Magazine* (1977), 37 C.C.C. (2d) 376 (Ont. Co. Ct.). [An appeal by the owner to the Ont. C.A. was dismissed 46 C.C.C. (2d) 111 without reference to these issues.] Similarly, *R. v. H. H. Marshall Ltd.* (1982), 69 C.C.C. (2d) 197 (N.S.C.A.).

The burden on the Crown is to prove beyond a reasonable doubt that the publication is obscene: *R. v. Benjamin News (Montreal) Reg'd* (1978), 48 C.C.C. (2d) 399 (Que. C.A.).

The Superior Court has an inherent jurisdiction to quash a warrant issued under this section, where no show cause hearing has ever been held, even where the warrant is originally issued, as in Prince Edward Island, by another judge of the Superior Court: *R. v. Shama's Clover Farm* (1982), 1 C.C.C. (3d) 119 (P.E.I.S.C.).

Appeal procedure – This subsection only provides for an appeal to an appellate court and does not apply to a further appeal to the Supreme Court of Canada: *R. v. Provincial News Co.*, [1976] 1 S.C.R. 89, 20 C.C.C. (2d) 385 (3:2).

WARRANT OF SEIZURE / Notice to person who posted the material / Person who posted the material may appear / Non-appearance / Order / Destruction of copy / Return of material / Other provisions to apply / When order takes effect.

164.1 (1) If a judge is satisfied by information on oath that there are reasonable grounds to believe that there is material — namely, child pornography as defined in section 163.1, a voyeuristic recording, an intimate image or an advertisement of sexual services as defined in 164(8) or computer data as defined in subsection 342.1(2) that makes child pornography, a voyeuristic recording, an intimate image or an advertisement of sexual services available — that is stored on and made available through a computer system as defined in subsection 342.1(2) that is within the jurisdiction of the court, the judge may order the custodian of the computer system to

(*a*) give an electronic copy of the material to the court;

(*b*) ensure that the material is no longer stored on and made available through the computer system; and

(*c*) provide the information necessary to identify and locate the person who posted the material.

(2) Within a reasonable time after receiving the information referred to in paragraph (1)(*c*), the judge shall cause notice to be given to the person who posted the material, giving that person the opportunity to appear and be represented before the court, and show cause why the material should not be deleted. If the person cannot be identified or located or does not reside in Canada, the judge may order the custodian of the computer system to post the text of the notice at the location where the material was previously stored and made available, until the time set for the appearance.

(3) The person who posted the material may appear and be represented in the proceedings in order to oppose the making of an order under subsection (5).

(4) If the person who posted the material does not appear for the proceedings, the court may proceed *ex parte* to hear and determine the proceedings in the absence of the person as fully and effectually as if the person had appeared.

(5) If the court is satisfied, on a balance of probabilities, that the material is child pornography as defined in section 163.1, a voyeuristic recording, an intimate image or an advertisement of sexual services as defined in subsection 164(8) or computer data as defined in subsection 342.1(2) that makes child pornography, the voyeuristic recording, the intimate image or the advertisement of sexual services available, it may order the custodian of the computer system to delete the material.

(6) When the court makes the order for the deletion of the material, it may order the destruction of the electronic copy in the court's possession.

(7) If the court is not satisfied that the material is child pornography as defined in 163.1, a voyeuristic recording, an intimate image or an advertisement of sexual services as defined in subsection 164(8) or computer data as defined in subsection 342.1(2) that makes child pornography, the voyeuristic recording, the intimate image or the advertisement of sexual services available, the court shall order that the electronic copy be returned to the custodian of the computer system and terminate the order under paragraph (1)(*b*).

(8) Subsections 164(6) to (8) apply, with any modifications that the circumstances require, to this section.

(9) No order made under subsections (5) to (7) takes effect until the time for final appeal has expired. 2002, c. 13, s. 7; 2005, c. 32, s. 9; 2014, c. 25, s. 7; 2014, c. 31, s. 5.

CROSS-REFERENCES

"Judge" is defined in s. 164(8). Section 164 provides a procedure for the seizure of child pornography and voyeuristic recordings and *in rem* forfeiture proceedings. Section 164.2 provides for the forfeiture of any thing, other than real property, used in the commission of the offence under s. 163.1 (child pornography). Section 172.1 creates the offence of using a computer system to communicate with a child for the purpose of committing various sexual offences.

SYNOPSIS

This section provides a procedure for shutting down sites hosting child pornography, voyeuristic recordings, intimate images or advertisements of sexual services. The procedure begins with an order made under subsec. (1) directing the custodian of the computer system to provide a copy of the material to the court, ensure that the material is no longer stored on and made available through the computer system (para. (*b*)) and provide information necessary to identify and locate the person who posted the material. Under subsec. (2), the judge is then to cause notice to be given to the person who posted the material to show cause why the material should not be deleted. Following a hearing, if the judge is satisfied on a balance of probabilities that the material is one of the items in question, the court may order the custodian to delete the material. If not so satisfied, the judge shall order that the electronic copy be returned to the custodian and the order under subsec. (1)(*b*) is terminated. An appeal from an order made under this section lies to the court of appeal in accordance with s. 164(6).

FORFEITURE AFTER CONVICTION / Third party rights / Right of appeal — third party / Right of appeal — Attorney General / Application of Part XXI.

164.2 (1) On application of the Attorney General, a court that convicts a person of an offence under section 162.1, 163.1, 172.1 or 172.2, in addition to any other punishment that it may impose, may order that anything — other than real property — be forfeited to Her Majesty and disposed of as the Attorney General directs if it is satisfied, on a balance of probabilities, that the thing

(*a*) was used in the commission of the offence; and

(*b*) is the property of

(i) the convicted person or another person who was a party to the offence, or

(ii) a person who acquired the thing from a person referred to in subparagraph (i) under circumstances that give rise to a reasonable inference that it was transferred for the purpose of avoiding forfeiture.

(2) Before making an order under subsection (1), the court shall cause notice to be given to, and may hear, any person whom it considers to have an interest in the thing, and may declare the nature and extent of the person's interest in it.

(3) A person who was heard in response to a notice given under subsection (2) may appeal to the court of appeal against an order made under subsection (1).

(4) The Attorney General may appeal to the court of appeal against the refusal of a court to make an order under subsection (1).

(5) Part XXI applies, with any modifications that the circumstances require, with respect to the procedure for an appeal under subsections (3) and (4). 2002, c. 13, s. 7; 2008, c. 18, s. 4; 2012, c. 1, s. 18; 2014, c. 31, s. 6.

CROSS-REFERENCES

"Attorney General" is defined in s. 164.2. Section 164 provides for *in rem* forfeiture proceeding of *inter alia* child pornography. Section 164.1 provides for *in rem* proceedings for shutting down child pornography and other sites on a computer system. Section 164.3 provides a procedure for relief from a forfeiture order made under this section. An order made under this section falls within the definition of "sentence" for the purpose of appeal under Parts XXI and XXVII.

SYNOPSIS

This section sets out the procedure, following conviction of a child pornography offence under s. 163.1, the intimate image offence under s. 162.1, the child luring offence under s. 172.1 and the offence under s. 172.2 of making an arrangement to commit certain sexual offences by means of telecommuniction, for forfeiture of anything, other than real property, used in the commission of the offence. The court that convicts the person may make the forfeiture order if satisfied, on a balance of probabilities, that the thing was used in commission of the offence and is the property of the convicted person, or of a person to whom the property was transferred to avoid forfeiture. The court shall cause notice to be given to any person with an interest in the thing and may declare the nature and extent of the person's interest. A person to whom notice was given may appeal to the Court of Appeal, as may the Attorney General.

RELIEF FROM FORFEITURE / Hearing of application / Notice to Attorney General / Order / Appeal to court of appeal / Powers of Attorney General.

164.3 (1) Within thirty days after an order under subsection 164.2(1) is made, a person who claims an interest in the thing forfeited may apply in writing to a judge for an order under subsection (4).

(2) The judge shall fix a day — not less than thirty days after the application is made — for its hearing.

(3) At least fifteen days before the hearing, the applicant shall cause notice of the application and of the hearing day to be served on the Attorney General.

(4) The judge may make an order declaring that the applicant's interest in the thing is not affected by the forfeiture and declaring the nature and extent of the interest if the judge is satisfied that the applicant

(*a*) was not a party to the offence; and

(*b*) did not acquire the thing from a person who was a party to the offence under circumstances that give rise to a reasonable inference that it was transferred for the purpose of avoiding forfeiture.

(5) A person referred to in subsection (4) or the Attorney General may appeal to the court of appeal against an order made under that subsection. Part XXI applies, with any modifications that the circumstances require, with respect to the procedure for an appeal under this subsection.

(6) On application by a person who obtained an order under subsection (4), made after the expiration of the time allowed for an appeal against the order and, if an appeal is taken, after it has been finally disposed of, the Attorney General shall direct that

(*a*) the thing be returned to the person; or

(*b*) an amount equal to the value of the extent of the person's interest, as declared in the order, be paid to the person. 2002, c. 13, s. 7.

CROSS-REFERENCES

"Attorney General" is defined in s. 164.2. Section 164 provides for *in rem* forfeiture proceeding of *inter alia* child pornography. Section 164.1 provides for *in rem* proceedings for shutting down child pornography sites on a computer system.

SYNOPSIS

This section provides the procedure for a person claiming an interest in things forfeited under s. 164.2 to obtain an order declaring that the person's interest is not affected by the forfeiture order. Under subsec. (4) the order will be made if the judge is satisfied that the applicant was not a party to the offence under s. 163.1 and did not acquire the thing from a person who was a party to the offence under circumstances giving rise to a reasonable inference that it was transferred to the applicant for the purpose of avoiding forfeiture. Both the applicant and the Attorney General may appeal to the court of appeal in accordance with Part XXI.

165. [*Repealed*, 2018, c. 29, s. 13.]

166. [*Repealed*, 1994, c. 44, s. 9.]

IMMORAL THEATRICAL PERFORMANCE / Person taking part.

167. (1) Every one commits an offence who, being the lessee, manager, agent or person in charge of a theatre, presents or gives or allows to be presented or given therein an immoral, indecent or obscene performance, entertainment or representation.

(2) Every one commits an offence who takes part or appears as an actor, a performer or an assistant in any capacity, in an immoral, indecent or obscene performance, entertainment or representation in a theatre. R.S., c. C-34, s. 163.

CROSS-REFERENCES

The term "theatre" is defined in s. 150. The definition of obscenity is in s. 163(8). In addition to the obscenity offences in s. 163, related offences are: s. 173, wilfully doing an indecent act; s. 174, public nudity; s. 175(1)(*b*), exposing an indecent exhibition.

The punishment for this offence is set out in s. 169. Where the prosecution elects to proceed by indictment on this offence then the accused may elect his mode of trial pursuant to s. 536(2). Where the prosecution elects to proceed by way of summary conviction then the trial of this offence is conducted by a summary conviction court pursuant to Part XXVII. The punishment for the offence is then as set out in s. 787 [although, note the maximum fine for a corporation is determined by s. 735] and the limitation period is set out in s. 786(2). In either case, release pending trial is determined by s. 515, although the accused is eligible for release by a peace officer under s. 496, 497 or by the officer in charge under s. 498.

SYNOPSIS

Section 167 makes it an offence to either take part in an *immoral, indecent or obscene performance,* or to permit such a performance in a theatre.

Section 167(1) prohibits the lessee, manager, agent, or person in charge of the theatre, to give any of the forms of permission or acquiescence listed in the subsection for such a performance. Section 167(2) creates liability for those performing or assisting in such a performance. The determination of what is immoral, indecent or obscene is to be made with reference to Canadian contemporary community standards.

ANNOTATIONS

Relationship to public nudity offence – The fact that Parliament has made it an offence to be nude in a public place under s. 174 is irrelevant to a charge under this section. A performance is not rendered "immoral" solely because it is performed in the nude: *R. v. Johnson*, [1975] 2 S.C.R. 160, 13 C.C.C. (2d) 402 (6:3).

Application of obscenity definition – The definition of "obscenity" in s. 163(8) applies to a charge under this section of presenting an obscene entertainment where the entertainment is a movie and thus a "publication" within the meaning of s. 163(8): *R. v. Towne Cinema Theatres Ltd.*, [1985] 1 S.C.R. 494, 18 C.C.C. (3d) 193 (7:0).

So-called "lap dancing" constitutes an indecent performance within the meaning of this section. A performance is indecent if the social harm engendered by the performance, having reference to the circumstances in which it took place, is such that the community would not tolerate it taking place. While the tolerance basis of the community standards test is the same in indecency cases as in obscenity cases, indecency requires an assessment of the surrounding circumstances in applying the community standards test. What the community will tolerate will vary with the placed in which the acts take place and the composition of the audience. The social harm to be considered is the attitudinal harm on those watching the performance as perceived by the community as a whole. In this case, the conduct was harmful in many ways because it de-humanized women and publicly portrayed them n a servile and humiliating manner. Furthermore, it predisposes persons to act in an anti-social manner as if the treatment of women in this way was socially acceptable and normal conduct: *R. v. Mara*, [1997] 2 S.C.R. 630, 115 C.C.C. (3d) 539.

This is a full *mens rea* offence and thus to prove that the accused owner or manager allowed the indecent performance the Crown must prove either concerted acquiescence or wilful blindness. If the owner delegates responsibility in bad faith in an attempt to gain protection from the law rather than ensure compliance with the law, then in certain circumstances this would amount to wilful blindness: *R. v. Mara, supra.*

Charter Considerations – Sexual activity involving physical contact between performers and patrons and between performers is not a form of expression but rather physical activity not intended to convey meaning and consequently, s. 2(*b*) of the Charter is not engaged. Even if such activity could be characterized as a form of expression, the provision is saved by s. 1 of the Charter: *R. v. Ludacka* (1996), 105 C.C.C. (3d) 565 (Ont. C.A.).

MAILING OBSCENE MATTER / Exceptions.

168. (1) Every one commits an offence who makes use of the mails for the purpose of transmitting or delivering anything that is obscene, indecent, immoral or scurrilous.

(2) Subsection (1) does not apply to a person who

(*a*) prints or publishes any matter for use in connection with any judicial proceedings or communicates it to persons who are concerned in the proceedings;

(*b*) prints or publishes a notice or report under the direction of a court; or

(*c*) prints or publishes any matter

(i) in a volume or part of a genuine series of law reports that does not form part of any other publication and consists solely of reports of proceedings in courts of law, or

(ii) in a publication of a technical character that is intended, in good faith, for circulation among members of the legal or medical profession. R.S., c. C-34, s. 164; 1999, c. 5, s. 2.

CROSS-REFERENCES

The punishment for this offence is set out in s. 169. Where the prosecution elects to proceed by indictment on this offence then the accused may elect his mode of trial pursuant to s. 536(2). Where the prosecution elects to proceed by way of summary conviction then the trial of this offence is conducted by a summary conviction court pursuant to Part XXVII. The punishment for the offence is then as set out in s. 787 [although, note the maximum fine for a corporation is determined by s. 735(1)(*b*)] and the limitation period is set out in s. 786(2). In either case, release pending trial is determined by s. 515, although the accused is eligible for release by a peace officer under s. 496, 497 or by the officer in charge under s. 498. With respect to territorial jurisdiction of a mail in the course of the door-to-door delivery of the mail, see s. 476(*e*). As to definition of "mail", see s. 2 of the *Canada Post Corporation Act*, R.S.C. 1985, c. C-10.

SYNOPSIS

This section makes it an offence to *use the mails* to transmit, or deliver anything that is *obscene, scurrilous, immoral or indecent*. The accused must intend to use the mail for this purpose.

ANNOTATIONS

A private letter intended only for the recipient may fall under this section: *R. v. Lambert* (1965), 47 C.R. 12, 53 W.W.R. 186 (B.C.S.C.).

Where the matter involved is a magazine or newspaper, it is not necessary that the entire publication is found to be indecent, immoral or scurrilous. As with other offences under this Part the determination of what is immoral or indecent is judged by an objective standard, namely the community standard of tolerance of indecency or immorality. Evidence of such standards while sometimes helpful is not required: *R. v. Popert* (1981), 58 C.C.C. (2d) 505 (Ont. C.A.), affg 51 C.C.C. (2d) 485 *sub nom. R. v. Pink Triangle Press* (Ont. Co. Ct.).

PUNISHMENT.

169. Every one who commits an offence under section 163, 165, 167 or 168 is guilty of

(*a*) an indictable offence and liable to imprisonment for a term not exceeding two years; or

(*b*) an offence punishable on summary conviction. R.S., c. C-34, s. 165; 1999, c. 5, s. 3.

CROSS-REFERENCES

Where the prosecution elects to proceed by indictment on the offences set out in this section then the accused may elect his mode of trial pursuant to s. 536(2). Where the prosecution elects to proceed by way of summary conviction then the trial of the offence is conducted by a summary conviction court pursuant to Part XXVII. The punishment for the offence is then as set out in s. 787 [although, note the maximum fine for a corporation is determined by s. 735(1)(*b*)] and the limitation period is set out in s. 786(2). In either case, release pending trial is determined by s. 515, although the accused is eligible for release by a peace officer under s. 496, 497 or by the officer in charge under s. 498.

PARENT OR GUARDIAN PROCURING SEXUAL ACTIVITY.

170. Every parent or guardian of a person under the age of 18 years who procures the person for the purpose of engaging in any sexual activity prohibited by this Act with a person other than the parent or guardian is guilty of an indictable offence and liable to imprisonment for a term of not more than 14 years and to a minimum punishment of imprisonment for a term of one year. R.S.C. 1985, c. 19 (3rd Supp.), s. 5; 2005, c. 32, s. 9.1; 2008, c. 6, s. 54(*f*); 2012, c. 1, s. 19; 2015, c. 23, s. 8.

CROSS-REFERENCES

The term "guardian" is defined in s. 150. "Procures" is part of the definition of "counsels" in s. 22(3). Age is determined by reference to s. 30 of the *Interpretation Act*, R.S.C. 1985, c. I-21. The defence of mistake as to age is set out in s. 150.1(5). Section 658 provides means of proving the age of a child or young person. Sexual activity prohibited by this Act would refer to, *inter alia*, the offences in ss. 151 to 153, 155, 159, 160, the various forms of sexual assault in ss. 217 to 273 and may also refer to the prostitution offences in ss. 210 to 213. Where the accused is found guilty of this offence in respect of a person who is under 16 years of age, the court has the discretion to impose an order of prohibition under s. 161 prohibiting the accused from attending certain public areas and facilities or taking certain employment which will bring him into contact with persons under 16 years of age or using a computer system for the purpose of communicating with a person under the age of 16 years. Section 171.1 makes it an offence to transmit, make available, distribute or sell sexually explicit material to a person who is, or who the accused believes is under the age of 18 years for purpose of facilitating the commission of the offence created by this section. Section 172.1 makes it an offence to communicate by means of telecommunication with a person who is or who the accused believes is under the age of 18 years for the purpose of facilitating the commission of the offence under this section. Section 172.2 makes it an offence to agree with a person or make an arrangement with a person by means of telecommunication to commit an offence under this section with a person who is or who the accused believes is under the age of 18 years.

The accused has an election as to mode of trial pursuant to s. 536(2). Release pending trial is determined by s. 515, although the accused is eligible for release by the officer in charge under s. 498.

Special evidentiary and procedural provisions: see cross-references under s. 150.1.

As to cases concerning admissibility of evidence in child abuse cases, see notes under s. 150.1.

Section 718.01 provides that, in imposing a sentence for an offence involving the abuse of a person under the age of 18 years, the court shall give primary consideration to the objectives of denunciation and deterrence. Further, under s. 718.2, evidence that the offender, in committing the offence, abused a person under the age of 18 years is an aggravating circumstance.

The offence in this section is a primary designated offence for the purpose of making a forensic DNA data bank order under s. 487.051. Under s. 490.012, on application by the prosecutor, where an offender is convicted of this offence, the judge shall make an order requiring the offender to comply with the *Sex Offender Information Registration Act*, S.C. 2004, c. 10.

SYNOPSIS

This section creates an indictable offence for every parent or guardian of a person under the age of 18 to procure that person for the purpose of engaging in any sexual activity prohibited by the Code with a person other than the parent or guardian. The maximum sentence is 14 years and the minimum punishment is one year imprisonment. Thus, a conditional sentence is not available for this offence.

HOUSEHOLDER PERMITTING PROHIBITED SEXUAL ACTIVITY.

171. Every owner, occupier or manager of premises, or any other person who has control of premises or assists in the management or control of premises, who knowingly permits a person under the age of 18 years to resort to or to be in or on the premises for the purpose of engaging in any sexual activity prohibited by this Act is guilty of an indictable offence and liable to imprisonment for a term of not more than 14 years and to a minimum punishment of imprisonment for a term of one year. R.S.C. 1985, c. 19 (3rd Supp.), s. 5; 2005, c. 32, s. 9.1; 2008, c. 6, s. 54(*g*); 2012, c. 1, s. 20; 2015, c. 23, s. 9.

CROSS-REFERENCES

Age is determined by reference to s. 30 of the *Interpretation Act*, R.S.C. 1985, c. I-21. Section 658 provides means of proving the age of a child or young person. The defence of mistake as to age is set out in s. 150.1(5). Sexual activity prohibited by this Act would refer to, *inter alia*, the offences in ss. 151 to 153, 155, 159, 160, the various forms of sexual assault in ss. 217 to 273 and presumably the prostitution offences in ss. 210 to 213. Where the accused is found guilty of this offence in respect of a person who is under 16 years of age, the court has the discretion to impose an order of prohibition under s. 161 prohibiting the accused from attending certain public areas and facilities or taking certain employment which will bring him into contact with persons under 16 years of age or using a computer system for the purpose of communicating with a person under the age of 16 years. Section 171.1 makes it an offence to transmit, make available, distribute or sell sexually explicit material to a person who is, or who the accused believes is under the age of 18 years for purpose of facilitating the commission of the offence created by this section. Section 172.1 makes it an offence to communicate by means of telecommunication with a person who is or who the accused believes is under the age of 18 years for the purpose of facilitating the commission of the offence under this section. Section 172.2 makes it an offence to agree with a person or make an arrangement with a person by means of telecommunication to commit an offence under this section with a person who is or who the accused believes is under the age of 18 years.

The accused has an election as to mode of trial pursuant to s. 536(2). Release pending trial is determined by s. 515, although the accused is eligible for release by the officer in charge under s. 498.

Special evidentiary and procedural provisions: see cross-references under s. 150.1.

As to cases concerning admissibility of evidence in child abuse cases, see notes under s. 150.1.

Section 718.01 provides that, in imposing a sentence for an offence involving the abuse of a person under the age of 18 years, the court shall give primary consideration to the objectives of denunciation and deterrence. Further, under s. 718.2, evidence that the offender, in committing the offence, abused a person under the age of 18 years is an aggravating circumstance.

SYNOPSIS

This section is aimed at a householder who permits the premises to be used for sexual activities involving persons under the age of 18.

The class of accused is described as the owner, occupier, manager or other person with control over the premises, or a person who assists in its management and control. It is an indictable offence for an accused who comes within one of these categories of persons to knowingly permit a person under 18 to be in, or to resort to, the relevant premises for the purpose of engaging in any sexual act prohibited by the Act. The maximum sentence is 14 years and the minimum punishment is one year imprisonment.

MAKING SEXUALLY EXPLICIT MATERIAL AVAILABLE TO CHILD / Punishment / Presumption / No defence / Definition of "sexually explicit material".

171.1 (1) Every person commits an offence who transmits, makes available, distributes or sells sexually explicit material to

(*a*) a person who is, or who the accused believes is, under the age of 18 years, for the purpose of facilitating the commission of an offence with respect to that person under subsection 153(1), section 155, 163.1, 170, 171 or 279.011 or subsection 279.02(2), 279.03(2), 286.1(2), 286.2(2) or 286.3(2);

(*b*) a person who is, or who the accused believes is, under the age of 16 years, for the purpose of facilitating the commission of an offence under section 151 or 152, subsection 160(3) or 173(2) or section 271, 272, 273 or 280 with respect to that person; or

(*c*) a person who is, or who the accused believes is, under the age of 14 years, for the purpose of facilitating the commission of an offence under section 281 with respect to that person.

(2) Every person who commits an offence under subsection (1)

(*a*) is guilty of an indictable offence and is liable to imprisonment for a term of not more than 14 years and to a minimum punishment of imprisonment for a term of six months; or

(*b*) is guilty of an offence punishable on summary conviction and is liable to imprisonment for a term of not more than two years less a day and to a minimum punishment of imprisonment for a term of 90 days.

(3) Evidence that the person referred to in paragraph (1)(*a*), (*b*) or (*c*) was represented to the accused as being under the age of 18, 16 or 14 years, as the case may be, is, in the absence of evidence to the contrary, proof that the accused believed that the person was under that age.

(4) It is not a defence to a charge under paragraph (1)(*a*), (*b*) or (*c*) that the accused believed that the person referred to in that paragraph was at least 18, 16 or 14 years of age, as the case may be, unless the accused took reasonable steps to ascertain the age of the person.

(5) In subsection (1), "sexually explicit material" means material that is not child pornography, as defined in subsection 163.1(1), and that is

(*a*) a photographic, film, video or other visual representation, whether or not it was made by electronic or mechanical means,

(i) that shows a person who is engaged in or is depicted as engaged in explicit sexual activity, or

(ii) the dominant characteristic of which is the depiction, for a sexual purpose, of a person's genital organs or anal region or, if the person is female, her breasts;

(*b*) written material whose dominant characteristic is the description, for a sexual purpose, of explicit sexual activity with a person; or

(*c*) an audio recording whose dominant characteristic is the description, presentation or representation, for a sexual purpose, of explicit sexual activity with a person. 2012, c. 1, s. 21; 2014, c. 25, s. 8; 2015, c. 23, s. 10.

CROSS-REFERENCES

Related offences are offences in relation to child pornography, s. 163.1, child luring in s. 172.1 and making an arrangement by means of telecommunication to commit various child sexual offences. For further references, see Cross-References under s. 172.1.

SYNOPSIS

This section creates the hybrid offence of transmitting, making available, distributing or selling sexually explicit material for the purpose of facilitating the commission of the various sexual offences involving children. The offence is punishable by 14 years' imprisonment and a minimum punishment of six months where the Crown proceeds by indictment and by two years less a day imprisonment and a minimum punishment of 90 days where the Crown proceeds by way of summary conviction. Subsection (3) creates a rebuttable presumption that the accused believed that the person was under the age of 18, 16 or 14 years as the case may be if the person was represented to the accused as being under that age. By virtue of subsec. (4), it is no defence that the accused believed that the person was under the age of 18, 16 or 14 years as the case may be, unless the accused took reasonable steps to ascertain the age of the person. Subsection (5) defines "sexually explicit material".

CORRUPTING CHILDREN / Limitation / Definition of "child" / Who may institute prosecutions.

172. (1) Every one who, in the home of a child, participates in adultery or sexual immorality or indulges in habitual drunkenness or any other form of vice, and thereby endangers the morals of the child or renders the home an unfit place for the child to be in, is guilty of an indictable offence and liable to imprisonment for a term not exceeding two years.

(2) [*Repealed*, R.S.C. 1985, c. 19 (3rd Supp.), s. 6.]

(3) For the purposes of this section, "child" means a person who is or appears to be under the age of eighteen years.

(4) No proceedings shall be commenced under subsection (1) without the consent of the Attorney General, unless they are instituted by or at the instance of a recognized society for the protection of children or by an officer of a juvenile court. R.S., c. C-34, s. 168; R.S.C. 1985, c. 19 (3rd Supp.), s. 6.

CROSS-REFERENCES

Attorney General is defined in s. 2. The term "officer of a juvenile court" is not defined and presumably referred to an officer of the "juvenile court" as defined in s. 2(1) of the former *Juvenile Delinquents Act*, R.S.C. 1970, c. J-3. This section was not amended when that Act was repealed and the former *Young Offenders Act* proclaimed. Nor was it amended when the *Young Offenders Act* was repealed and the *Youth Criminal Justice Act* proclaimed. Section 583(*h*) provides that a count in an indictment is not insufficient by reason only that it does not state that the required consent has been obtained. Section 658 provides means of proving the age of a child. The defence of mistake as to age is set out in s. 150.1(5).

The accused has an election as to mode of trial of the offence described in subsec. (1) pursuant to s. 536(2). Release pending trial is determined by s. 515, although the accused is eligible for release by the officer in charge under s. 498.

Special evidentiary and procedural provisions: see cross-references under s. 150.1.

As to cases concerning admissibility of evidence in child abuse cases, see notes under s. 150.1.

SYNOPSIS

This section makes it an indictable offence to indulge in behaviour, in a *child's home,* which corrupts children. Children are defined in s. 172(3) as being *under or apparently under* the age of *18*. The prohibited activities listed in the section are expansively defined by adultery, sexual immorality, habitual drunkenness, or *any other form of vice*. However, it must be shown that the *result* of this behaviour is to *endanger the morals* of a child or to make the house unfit for a child to live in. It does not appear to be necessary that the accused intend that the conduct indulged in will have this result, only that the accused intended to behave in the proscribed way and certain results flowed from those actions. Conviction for this offence makes the accused liable to imprisonment for two years.

Prosecution under this section may only be undertaken with the Attorney General's consent, unless the prosecution is by a recognized society for the protection of children (such as a Children's Aid Society) or by an officer of a juvenile court.

ANNOTATIONS

Although the offence of engaging in sexual immorality in the home of a child violates s. 2(*b*) of the Charter, it is a reasonable limit within the meaning of s. 1 and is therefore valid: *R. v. E. (B.)* (1999), 139 C.C.C. (3d) 100 (Ont. C.A.).

The offence of engaging in sexual immorality in the home of a child requires proof that the accused intentionally engaged in the prohibited conduct including knowledge or at least wilful blindness that the children were aware of the sexually immoral conduct. "Sexual immorality" requires an objective consideration of conduct by reference to community standards of tolerance that are tied directly to the harm caused or threatened by the conduct. "Participation" requires proof of some form of conduct. "Morals" refers to those core values that are central to the maintenance of a free and democratic society. The morals of a child will be endangered by sexual immorality where: (1) the sexual conduct presents a real risk that the child will not develop an understanding that exploitive or non-consensual sexual activity is wrong; (2) the conduct degrades or dehumanizes women such that the child will not develop an understanding that all persons are equal and worthy of respect regardless of gender; (3) the conduct imperils the child's understanding of parents' responsibilities to protect and nurture their children; and (4) to the extent that the conduct actively involves the child, it may endanger the child's morals by leaving him or her without a proper sense of his or her own self-worth or autonomy: *R. v. E.(B.), supra.*

LURING A CHILD / Punishment / Presumption re age / No defence.

172.1 (1) Every person commits an offence who, by a means of telecommunication, communicates with

(*a*) a person who is, or who the accused believes is, under the age of 18 years, for the purpose of facilitating the commission of an offence with respect to that person under subsection 153(1), section 155, 163.1, 170, 171 or 279.011 or subsection 279.02(2), 279.03(2), 286.1(2), 286.2(2) or 286.3(2);

(*b*) a person who is, or who the accused believes is, under the age of 16 years, for the purpose of facilitating the commission of an offence under section 151 or

152, subsection 160(3) or 173(2) or section 271, 272, 273 or 280 with respect to that person; or

(*c*) a person who is, or who the accused believes is, under the age of 14 years, for the purpose of facilitating the commission of an offence under section 281 with respect to that person.

(2) Every person who commits an offence under subsection (1)

(*a*) is guilty of an indictable offence and is liable to imprisonment for a term of not more than 14 years and to a minimum punishment of imprisonment for a term of one year; or

(*b*) is guilty of an offence punishable on summary conviction and is liable to imprisonment for a term of not more than two years less a day and to a minimum punishment of imprisonment for a term of six months.

(3) Evidence that the person referred to in paragraph (1)(*a*), (*b*) or (*c*) was represented to the accused as being under the age of eighteen years, sixteen years or fourteen years, as the case may be, is, in the absence of evidence to the contrary, proof that the accused believed that the person was under that age.

(4) It is not a defence to a charge under paragraph (1)(*a*), (*b*) or (*c*) that the accused believed that the person referred to in that paragraph was at least eighteen years of age, sixteen years or fourteen years of age, as the case may be, unless the accused took reasonable steps to ascertain the age of the person. 2002, c. 13, s. 8; 2007, c. 20, s. 1; 2008, c. 6, s. 14; 2012, c. 1, s. 22; 2014, c. 25, s. 9; 2015, c. 23, s. 11.

CROSS-REFERENCES

Section 164.1 provides for *in rem* proceedings for shutting down child pornography sites on a computer system. If the accused is found guilty of this offence in respect of a person who is under 16 years of age, the court may impose an order of prohibition under s. 161 prohibiting the accused from attending certain public areas and facilities or taking certain employment that will bring him into contact with persons under the age of 16 years. Section 164.2 allows the Attorney General to apply to the court that convicts the accused of this offence for an order that any thing, other than real property, be forfeited to the Crown, if the thing was used in the commission of the offence and the property is the property of the offender, or another person who was a party to the offence, or from a third party who acquired the thing under circumstances giving rise to a reasonable inference that it was transferred for the purpose of avoiding forfeiture. The term "telecommunication" is defined in s. 35 of the *Interpretation Act*. Related offences are offences in relation to child pornography, s. 163.1, making sexually explicit material available to children for the purpose of committing various child sexual offences under s. 171.1 and making an arrangement by means of telecommunication to commit various child sexual offences under s. 172.2.

Section 486(1) and (2) provide that the judge may make an order excluding all or any members of the public where such order is in the interest of public morals, the maintenance of order or the proper administration of justice or is necessary to prevent injury to international relations or national defence or national security. The proper administration of justice includes safeguarding the interests of witnesses under the age of 18 years. Section 486.1 sets out the circumstances in which the judge shall or may order a support person to be present and close to a witness while the witness testifies. Where the witness is under the age of 18 years or has a mental or physical disability, the order is to be made upon request unless the judge is of the opinion that the order would interfere with the proper administration of justice. In the case of other witnesses, the order is to be made if necessary to obtain a full and candid account from the witness of the matters complained of. The application for this order may be made during the proceedings or before they begin to the judge who is to preside at the proceedings.

Similarly, s. 486.2 sets out the circumstances in which the judge shall or may order a witness to testify outside the courtroom or behind a screen or other device that would not allow the witness to see the accused. Where the witness is under the age of 18 years or may have difficulty communicating the evidence by reason of a mental or physical disability, the judge shall make the order unless the judge is of the opinion that the order would interfere with the proper administration of justice. In all other cases, the order may be made if the judge is of the opinion that the order is necessary to obtain a full and candid account from the witness of the acts complained of. Similarly, s. 486.3 provides that, on application by the prosecutor or a witness under the age of 18 years, the accused shall not personally cross-examine the witness unless the judge is of the opinion that the proper administration of justice requires the accused to personally conduct the cross-examination. In other cases, the judge may make an order that the accused not personally cross-examine the witness if the judge is of the opinion that the order is necessary to obtain a full and candid account from the witness of the acts complained of. The judge will appoint counsel to conduct the cross-examination.

Under s. 486.4, the judge may make an order directing that the identity of a witness not be disclosed in any publication, broadcast or transmitted in any way. The order is mandatory where the complainant or a witness under the age of 18 years or the prosecutor applies for the order. Section 486.5 also gives the judge a discretion respecting non-publication orders in proceedings under these provisions in other circumstances.

The offence in this section is a primary designated offence for the purpose of making a forensic DNA data bank order under s. 487.051. Under s. 490.012, on application by the prosecutor, where an offender is convicted of this offence, the judge shall make an order requiring the offender to comply with the *Sex Offender Information Registration Act*, S.C. 2004, c. 10.

SYNOPSIS

This section creates the offence of using means of telecommunication to communicate with children for the purpose of facilitating the commission of certain sexual offences. Paragraphs (1)(*a*), (*b*) and (*c*) set out the various sexual offences depending on the age of the child. The offence is committed if the person was under the particular age specified or if the accused believed the person to be under that age. Subsection (3) sets up a rebuttable presumption that the accused believed the person was under the relevant age if there is evidence that the person was represented to the accused as being under that age. Under subsec. (4), it is no defence that the accused believed that the person was over the relevant age unless the accused took reasonable steps to ascertain the age of the person. The offence is punishable by 14 years' imprisonment and a minimum punishment of one year imprisonment where the Crown proceeds by indictment and by two years less a day imprisonment and a minimum punishment of six months where the Crown proceeds by way of summary conviction.

ANNOTATIONS

Constitutional considerations – The presumption in subsec. (3) infringes s. 11(*d*) of the Charter, and cannot be saved under s. 1. However, the "reasonable steps" requirement in subsec. (4) does not infringe the Charter because it does not relieve the Crown of proving beyond a reasonable doubt that the accused actually believed the other person was underage: *R. v. Morrison*, 2019 SCC 15.

In *R. v. Morrison* (2017), 350 C.C.C. (3d) 161 (Ont. C.A.), the court struck down the mandatory minimum sentence in subsec. (2)(*a*) as contrary to s. 12 of the Charter. On further appeal, however, the court allowed the appeal on other grounds and set aside the declaration of invalidity without ruling on its correctness: *R. v. Morrison*, 2019 SCC 15.

Elements of the offence – Subsection (1)(*c*) creates an inchoate offence requiring proof of: (i) an intentional communication by computer; (ii) with a person who the accused knows or believes to be under 14 years of age; (iii) for the specific purpose of facilitating the commission of a specified secondary offence with respect to the underage person. Intention must be determined subjectively. Sexually explicit comments may be sufficient to establish the criminal purpose of the accused but the content of the communication is not necessarily determinative. "Facilitating" includes helping to bring about and making easier or more probable. It is not necessarily sufficient for the impugned acts of the accused to be objectively capable of facilitating the commission of the specified secondary offence. The court must be satisfied beyond a reasonable doubt that the accused communicated by computer with an underage person for the purpose of facilitating the commission of a specified secondary offence. Given the drafting of the section, it is not helpful to characterize the essential elements of the offence as either part of the *actus reus* or the *mens rea*: *R. v. Legare*, [2009] 3 S.C.R. 551, 249 C.C.C. (3d) 129.

The "reasonable steps" requirement in subsec. (4) bars accused persons from raising, as a defence, that they believed the other person was of legal age where they failed to take reasonable steps to ascertain the other person's age. However, this does not relieve the Crown of its ultimate burden of proving beyond a reasonable doubt that the accused believed the other person was underage. Thus, if the trier of fact can only conclude from the evidence that the accused was negligent or reckless with regard to the other person's age, the Crown has not met its burden, and the accused is entitled to an acquittal. However, willful blindness can substitute for belief: *R. v. Morrison*, 2019 SCC 15.

The offence in subsec. (1)(*c*) has three elements: (i) the accused must communicate by means of a computer; (ii) the communication must be with a person under 14 years of age or with a person who the accused believes is under the age of 14; and (iii) the accused's purpose in making the communication must be to facilitate the commission of one of the designated offences with the person with whom the communication is made. If the person to whom the communication is made is under 14, his or her age is a condition or circumstance that must be proven to complete the *actus reus*. If the person is over 14 but the accused believes that he or she is under the age of 14, the accused's belief is the circumstance or condition that the Crown must prove to establish the prohibited act. If the Crown proves the culpable *mens rea* existed, that is that the communication was for the purpose of the facilitation of the commission of a designated offence, the offence under this section is made out regardless of whether the designated crime is ever committed, attempted or is even factually possible. It is the belief that the person is under 14, not their actual age, that is relevant to the accused's purpose in engaging in the communication: *R. v. Alicandro* (2009), 246 C.C.C. (3d) 1 (Ont. C.A.), leave to appeal to S.C.C. refused [2010] 2 S.C.R. v, 255 C.C.C. (3d) vi.

Text messaging via cellular telephones satisfies the *actus reus* of communicating "by means of a computer system": *R. v. Woodward* (2011), 276 C.C.C. (3d) 86 (Ont. C.A.).

This provision is constitutionally valid. Properly interpreted, it does not violate ss. 7 or 11(*d*) of the Charter. Subsections (3) and (4) do not create reverse onuses or shift the burden to prove the accused's belief in the complainant's age away from the Crown, nor do they present a risk of convicting the morally innocent: *R. v. Ghotra* (2016), 334 C.C.C. (3d) 222 (Ont. S.C.J.).

AGREEMENT OR ARRANGEMENT — SEXUAL OFFENCE AGAINST CHILD / Punishment / Presumption / No defence / No defence.

172.2 (1) Every person commits an offence who, by a means of telecommunication, agrees with a person, or makes an arrangement with a person, to commit an offence

(*a*) under subsection 153(1), section 155, 163.1, 170, 171 or 279.011 or subsection 279.02(2), 279.03(2), 286.1(2), 286.2(2) or 286.3(2) with respect to another person who is, or who the accused believes is, under the age of 18 years;

(*b*) under section 151 or 152, subsection 160(3) or 173(2) or section 271, 272, 273 or 280 with respect to another person who is, or who the accused believes is, under the age of 16 years; or

(*c*) under section 281 with respect to another person who is, or who the accused believes is, under the age of 14 years.

(2) Every person who commits an offence under subsection (1)

(*a*) is guilty of an indictable offence and is liable to imprisonment for a term of not more than 14 years and to a minimum punishment of imprisonment for a term of one year; or

(*b*) is guilty of an offence punishable on summary conviction and is liable to imprisonment for a term of not more than two years less a day and to a minimum punishment of imprisonment for a term of six months.

(3) Evidence that the person referred to in paragraph (1)(*a*), (*b*) or (*c*) was represented to the accused as being under the age of 18, 16 or 14 years, as the case may be, is, in the absence of evidence to the contrary, proof that the accused believed that the person was under that age.

(4) It is not a defence to a charge under paragraph (1)(*a*), (*b*) or (*c*) that the accused believed that the person referred to in that paragraph was at least 18, 16 or 14 years of age, as the case may be, unless the accused took reasonable steps to ascertain the age of the person.

(5) It is not a defence to a charge under paragraph (1)(*a*), (*b*) or (*c*)

(*a*) that the person with whom the accused agreed or made an arrangement was a peace officer or a person acting under the direction of a peace officer; or

(*b*) that, if the person with whom the accused agreed or made an arrangement was a peace officer or a person acting under the direction of a peace officer, the person referred to in paragraph (1)(*a*), (*b*) or (*c*) did not exist. 2012, c. 1, s. 23; 2014, c. 25, s. 10; 2015, c. 23, s. 12.

CROSS-REFERENCES

Related offences are offences in relation to child pornography, s. 163.1, making sexually explicit material available to children for the purpose of facilitating sexual offences in relation to children under s. 171.1, and child luring in s. 172.1 Section 164.2 provides that a court that convicts a person of an offence under this section may order that any thing, other than real property, be forfeited to the Crown if the court is satisfied that the thing was used in the commission of the offence and is the property of the offender, another person who was a party to the offence or a person who acquired the thing from such a person in circumstances giving rise to a reasonable inference that it was transferred to avoid a forfeiture order. This offence is a designated offence for the purposes of s. 752. For further Cross-References, see notes under s. 172.1.

SYNOPSIS

This section creates an offence of agreeing with a person or making an arrangement with a person by means of telecommunications to commit various sexual offences. Paragraphs (1)(*a*), (*b*) and (*c*) set out the various sexual offences depending on the age of the child. The offence is committed if the person was under the particular age specified or if the accused believed the person to be under that age. Subsection (3) sets up a rebuttable presumption that the accused believed the person was under the relevant age if there is evidence that the person was represented to the accused as being under that age. Under subsec. (4), it is no defence that the accused believed that the person was over the relevant age unless the accused took reasonable steps to ascertain the age of the person. It is also no defence that the person with whom the accused agreed or made the arrangement was a peace officer or someone acting under the direction of a peace officer or that the "victim" did not exist, if the person with whom the accused agreed or made an arrangement was a peace officer or acting under the direction of a peace officer. The offence is punishable by 14 years' imprisonment and a minimum punishment of one year imprisonment where the Crown proceeds by indictment and by two years less a day imprisonment and a minimum punishment of six months where the Crown proceeds by way of summary conviction.

Disorderly Conduct

INDECENT ACTS / Exposure.

173. (1) Everyone who wilfully does an indecent act in a public place in the presence of one or more persons, or in any place with intent to insult or offend any person,

(*a*) is guilty of an indictable offence and is liable to imprisonment for a term of not more than two years; or

(*b*) is guilty of an offence punishable on summary conviction and is liable to imprisonment for a term of not more than six months.

(2) Every person who, in any place, for a sexual purpose, exposes his or her genital organs to a person who is under the age of 16 years

(*a*) is guilty of an indictable offence and is liable to imprisonment for a term of not more than two years and to a minimum punishment of imprisonment for a term of 90 days; or

(*b*) is guilty of an offence punishable on summary conviction and is liable to imprisonment for a term of not more than six months and to a minimum punishment of imprisonment for a term of 30 days. R.S., c. C-34, s. 169; R.S.C. 1985, c. 19 (3rd Supp.), s. 7; 2008, c. 6, s. 54(*h*); 2010, c. 17, s. 2; 2012, c. 1, s. 23.

CROSS-REFERENCES

The term "public place" is defined in s. 150. Age is determined by reference to s. 30 of the *Interpretation Act*, R.S.C. c. I-21. Section 658 provides means of proving the age of a child or young person. The defence of mistake as to the age of the victim is set out in s. 150.1(4). A limited defence of consent to the subsec. (2) offence is set out in s. 150.1(2). Under s. 150.1(3) a young offender aged 12 or 13 years may not be tried for an offence under subsec. (2) unless he is in a position of trust or authority. A person convicted of the offence under subsec. (2), who is found to be loitering in or near a school ground, playground, public park or bathing area, is liable to be convicted of the vagrancy offence under s. 179. Section 171.1 makes it an offence to transmit, make available, distribute or sell sexually explicit material to a person who is, or who the accused believes is under the age of 16 years for purpose of facilitating the commission of the offence created by subsec. (2). Section 172.1 makes it an offence to communicate by means of telecommunication with a person who is or who the accused believes is under the age of 16 years for the purpose of facilitating the commission of the offence under subsec. (2). Section 172.2 makes it an offence to agree with a person or make an arrangement with a person by means of telecommunication to commit an offence under subsec. (2) with a person who is or who the accused believes is under the age of 16 years.

The trial of these offences is conducted by a summary conviction court pursuant to Part XXVII. The punishment for the offence is then as set out in s. 787 and the limitation period is set out in s. 786(2). Release pending trial is determined by s. 515, although the accused is eligible for release by a peace officer under s. 496, 497 or by the officer in charge under s. 498.

Special evidentiary and procedural provisions: see cross-references under s. 150.1.

SYNOPSIS

This section creates offences for doing indecent acts or exposing oneself in certain circumstances.

Section 173(1) creates the offence of committing an indecent act in two ways. The first way requires that the indecent act be done in a public place in the presence of one or more other persons. It has been held that, if the place is one in which the public could witness the acts complained of, then it is public for the purposes of this section. Alternatively, the offence may be committed by doing an indecent act with the intention of insulting or offending another person. There must be proof that the accused acted wilfully. The hybrid offence is punishable by indictment or summary conviction. The maximum punishment by indictment is two years and the maximum punishment by way of summary conviction is six months.

Section 173(2) makes it an offence to expose one's genitals to a person under the age of 16, wherever the act occurs if the accused does so for a sexual purpose. Where the Crown proceeds by indictment, the maximum punishment is two years and the minimum punishment is 90 days. If the Crown proceeds by way of summary conviction, the maximum punishment is six months and the minimum punishment is 30 days.

ANNOTATIONS

Proof of intent – A presumption of intent to do the indecent act wilfully arises where it is seen by another person: *R. v. Parsons*, [1963] 3 C.C.C. 92 (B.C.S.C.). Folld *R. v. Dalen* (1978), 44 C.C.C. (2d) 228 (Sask. Dist. Ct.).

In *R. v. Sloan* (1994), 89 C.C.C. (3d) 97, 30 C.R. (4th) 156 (Ont. C.A.), leave to appeal to S.C.C. refused 91 C.C.C. (3d) vi, 77 O.A.C. 399*n*, the members of the court disagreed as to the elements of the offence. Galligan J.A. was of the view that the gravamen of the offence is the wilful commission of an indecent act in the presence of one or more persons and where there was no intention on the part of the accused to perform a sexual act in the presence of any person other than her "client" the surreptitious surveillance by police cannot turn what is essentially an act done in private into one which takes place in public. Goodman J.A. held that it was not necessary to determine whether the term "wilfully" applies both to the doing of the act and to the requirement that the act be done in the presence of one or more persons since the motor vehicle in the cirumstances of this case was not a public place. The mere fact that a vehicle is parked in a lot to which the public has access is not in itself sufficient to make that vehicle a public place, considering that the vehicle was parked late at night at the edge of the lot considerable distance from any other vehicle and where the activity could only be discerned by someone looking into the vehicle from a short distance. Since the place in which the act was done in this case was a private place, subsec. (1)(*a*) did not apply. Osborne J.A. dissenting held that the Crown need only prove that the indecent act was done wilfully and since the act was done in a car parked in a public place the offence was made out.

In *R. v. Mailhot* (1996), 108 C.C.C. (3d) 376 (Que. C.A.), the court held that conviction under subsec. (1)(*a*) of this provision required proof that the accused (1) wilfully committed an indecent act and (2) wilfully committed the act in a public place in the presence of one or more persons, excluding those who participated in the activity. In this case, the accused lacked the necessary intent where he mistakenly believed that an undercover police officer who observed him masturbate would participate in the act if only by looking at him and by getting emotional or sexual satisfaction from it.

An accused who walked down the streets with her breasts uncovered did not commit an indecent act. An indecent act need not have sexual context and may relate to other objectionable behaviour. The test of indecency is the community standard of tolerance. In applying this test, the court must consider what harm will accrue from exposure to the allegedly obscene act or material. The greater the harm, the less that the community will tolerate others being exposed to it: *R. v. Jacob* (1996), 112 C.C.C. (3d) 1, 142 D.L.R. (4th) 411 (Ont. C.A.).

Public place – In *R. v. McEwen*, [1980] 4 W.W.R. 85 (Sask. Prov. Ct.), the court, distinguishing *R. v. Hutt*, [1978] 2 S.C.R. 476, 38 C.C.C. (2d) 418, held that an accused did an indecent act in a "public place" where he exposed his private parts to pedestrians at a crosswalk although he was inside his own car at the time. Similarly, *R. v. Figliuzzi* (1981), 59 C.C.C. (2d) 144, 21 C.R. (3d) 326 (Alta. Q.B.); *R. v. Wise* (1982), 67 C.C.C. (2d) 231, [1982] 4 W.W.R. 658 (B.C. Co. Ct.). Also see note on *R. v. Sloan, supra*.

"Public place" within the meaning of subsec. (1)(*a*) and as defined in s. 150 means a place to which one is invited or where one has a right to be as in entering, visiting or using that place. It does not include simply access by way of looking or listening in from the outside.

Thus, the accused could not be convicted of the offence under subsec. (1)(*a*) where he performed the indecent act in the living room of his own private home, even if he could be observed by people outside the home: *R. v. Clark*, [2005] 1 S.C.R. 6, 193 C.C.C. (3d) 289.

Subsection (2) applies to images sent over the internet. The victim and the perpetrator need not be in the same physical place for an offence to be committed: *R. v. Alicandro* (2009), 246 C.C.C. (3d) 1 (Ont. C.A.), leave to appeal to S.C.C. refused [2010] 2 S.C.R. v, 255 C.C.C. (3d) vi.

The requirement in subsec. (1)(*a*) that the act be performed in the presence of one or more persons is not made out where the act is merely observed by an unmonitored video camera nor by the fact that there was another participant in the act: *R. v. Follett* (1994), 91 C.C.C. (3d) 435, 120 Nfld. & P.E.I.R. 230 (Nfld. S.C.), affd 98 C.C.C. (3d) 493 (Nfld. C.A.), leave to appeal to S.C.C. refused 101 C.C.C. (3d) vi, 42 C.R. (4th) 408*n*.

NUDITY / Nude / Consent of Attorney General.

174. (1) Every one who, without lawful excuse,

(*a*) is nude in a public place, or

(*b*) is nude and exposed to public view while on private property, whether or not the property is his own,

is guilty of an offence punishable on summary conviction.

(2) For the purposes of this section, a person is nude who is so clad as to offend against public decency or order.

(3) No proceedings shall be commenced under this section without the consent of the Attorney General. R.S., c. C-34, s. 170.

CROSS-REFERENCES

The term "public place" is defined in s. 150. Attorney General is defined in s. 2. Section 583(*h*) provides that a count in an indictment is not insufficient by reason only that it does not state that the required consent has been obtained. Related offences are: s. 163(2)(*b*), publicly exhibiting an indecent show; s. 167, immoral theatrical performance; s. 173, wilfully doing an indecent act; s. 175(1)(*b*), exposing an indecent exhibition.

The trial of this offence is conducted by a summary conviction court pursuant to Part XXVII. The punishment for the offence is then as set out in s. 787 and the limitation period is set out in s. 786(2). Release pending trial is determined by s. 515, although the accused is eligible for release by a peace officer under s. 496, 497 or by the officer in charge under s. 498.

SYNOPSIS

This section prohibits nudity in a public place, or a place which is exposed to the public, even if the accused is on private property. The accused may rely upon a lawful excuse for the behaviour.

Section 174(2) expands the usual definition of nudity to include being clothed so as to offend against public decency or order. In the absence of any greater specificity as to what offends public decency the courts have resorted to the standard used for obscenity, namely, contemporary Canadian standards of tolerance.

By virtue of subsec. (3), no one may be prosecuted for this summary conviction offence unless the Attorney General consents.

ANNOTATIONS

Application of provision – Where the accused is completely naked in a public place without lawful excuse the offence under this section is committed whether or not the nudity offends against public decency or order. Subsection (2) covers the situation where the accused is partially clothed, by creating the legal fiction that such a person is "nude" when clad as to offend public decency or order, but this subsection does not import the requirement of proof of offence against public decency or order where the accused is totally naked: *R. v. Verrette*, [1978] 2 S.C.R. 838, 40 C.C.C. (2d) 273, 85 D.L.R. (3d) 1 (9:0).

Notwithstanding the provision in s. 167 of the Code for the separate offence of appearing in an immoral or indecent performance in a theatre, an accused may be charged under this section since "public place" includes a theatre: *R. v. McCutcheon* (1977), 40 C.C.C. (2d) 555, 1 C.R. (3d) 39 (Que. C.A.).

This offence is not aimed at conduct such as swimming nude at an isolated beach, even where the accused misjudges the loneliness of the beach: *R. v. Benolkin* (1977), 36 C.C.C. (2d) 206 (Sask. Q.B.).

The mere fact that a female dancer is nude does not mean that her performance cannot be legitimate entertainment and therefore constitute a lawful excuse. The trial judge must, however, make this factual assessment in each case and a finding by the trial judge that the accused's dancing offended against public decency and order does not determine the issue of lawful excuse: *R. v. Zikman* (1990), 56 C.C.C. (3d) 430, 37 O.A.C. 277 (C.A.).

Offending against public decency or order (subsec. (2)) – The requirement of offence against public decency or order in subsec. (2) applies where the accused is partially, albeit lightly, dressed as where she wears only a transparent veil since such person is not "nude" in the dictionary sense of wearing no clothes: *R. v. McCutcheon* (1977), 40 C.C.C. (2d) 555, 1 C.R. (3d) 39 (Que. C.A.). [Note: this case was decided before *R. v. Verrette, supra*, and portions of it must therefore be read subject to that case.]

Although the accused is partially clad so that subsec. (2) applies, the Crown need not adduce evidence as to what offends public decency. Rather, the trial judge may make the finding that the manner of dress did offend public decency without such evidence: *R. v. Sidey* (1980), 52 C.C.C. (2d) 257 (Ont. C.A.).

The test of public decency in subsec. (2) is one of the community standard of tolerance to and for the actions of the accused in the circumstances in which they occur: *R. v. Giambalvo* (1982), 70 C.C.C. (2d) 324, 39 O.R. (2d) 588 (C.A.).

Attorney General's consent (subsec. 3) – In exercising the power under subsec. (3) the Attorney General is under no duty that can be enforced by the courts to act fairly and is not required to afford the accused a hearing before deciding whether or not to consent to the prosecution: *R. v. Warren* (1981), 61 C.C.C. (2d) 65, 22 C.R. (3d) 58 (Ont. H.C.J.).

The consent required by subsec. (3) may be endorsed on the face of the information and if done in that manner need not recite particulars of the charge: *R. v. Willard* (1984), 15 C.C.C. (3d) 350 (Ont. H.C.J.).

CAUSING DISTURBANCE, INDECENT EXHIBITION, LOITERING, ETC. / Evidence of peace officer.

175. (1) Every one who

(*a*) not being in a dwelling-house, causes a disturbance in or near a public place,

(i) by fighting, screaming, shouting, swearing, singing or using insulting or obscene language,

(ii) by being drunk, or

(iii) by impeding or molesting other persons,

(*b*) openly exposes or exhibits an indecent exhibition in a public place,

(*c*) loiters in a public place and in any way obstructs persons who are in that place, or

(*d*) disturbs the peace and quiet of the occupants of a dwelling-house by discharging firearms or by other disorderly conduct in a public place or who, not being an occupant of a dwelling-house comprised in a particular building or structure, disturbs the peace and quiet of the occupants of a dwelling-house comprised in the building or structure by discharging firearms or by other disorderly conduct in any part of a building or structure to which, at the time of such conduct, the occupants of two or more dwelling-houses

comprised in the building or structure have access as of right or by invitation, express or implied,

is guilty of an offence punishable on summary conviction.

(2) In the absence of other evidence, or by way of corroboration of other evidence, a summary conviction court may infer from the evidence of a peace officer relating to the conduct of a person or persons, whether ascertained or not, that a disturbance described in paragraph (1)(*a*) or (*d*) or an obstruction described in paragraph (1)(*c*) was caused or occurred. R.S., c. C-34, s. 171; 1972, c. 13, s. 11; 1974-75-76, c. 93, s. 9; 1997, c. 18, s. 6.

CROSS-REFERENCES

The terms "dwelling house" and "peace officer" are defined in s. 2, "public place" in s. 150. Section 84 contains a definition of "firearm" for Part III which, however, may be a useful reference for this section. Related offences are: ss. 63 to 69, offences in relation to unlawful and riotous assemblies; s. 163(2)(*b*), exhibiting an indecent show; s. 167, indecent theatrical performances; s. 173, wilfully doing indecent act; s. 174, public nudity; s. 179, vagrancy; s. 180, common nuisance. Sections 30 and 31 authorize the use of force to prevent a breach of the peace and arrest for breach of the peace. The offence of discharging a firearm with intent is in s. 244.

The trial of this offence is conducted by a summary conviction court pursuant to Part XXVII. The punishment for the offence is then as set out in s. 787 and the limitation period is set out in s. 786(2). Release pending trial is determined by s. 515, although the accused is eligible for release by a peace officer under s. 496, 497 or by the officer in charge under s. 498.

SYNOPSIS

This section creates summary conviction offences in relation to a variety of activities which cause a disturbance, including fighting, exposing an indecent exhibition, loitering and other public-nuisance activities.

Under s. 175(1)(*a*) it must be shown that the accused did one of the listed acts, that the accused was not in a dwelling-house and that the accused's acts resulted in a disturbance. The resulting disturbance must be at or near a public place. Paragraphs (*b*) and (*c*) contain straightforward prohibitions against certain types of actions in public. Paragraph (*d*) prohibits certain types of conduct which disrupt persons in a dwelling-house. First, liability may be shown by proving that the accused discharged a firearm, or engaged in other disorderly conduct in a public place which resulted in disturbing the peace and quiet of those occupying a dwelling-house. Second, liability may be shown by proving that the accused, who was not an occupant of the dwelling-house, disturbed the peace and quiet of those in the dwelling by discharging a firearm or engaging in other disorderly conduct within any part of the building or structure comprising the dwelling. An additional element for this second type of liability is the necessity to prove that the occupants of two or more units of the dwelling had a right or invitation to have access to that portion of the structure within which the accused created the disturbance. An example of the latter situation would be a disturbance created in the garage of an apartment building.

To facilitate the proof of these offences s. 175(2) permits the trial court to draw an inference, from the evidence of a peace officer who may testify as to the reactions of the members of the public who observed the accused's conduct, as proof that a disturbance did result from the accused's acts. Such evidence is permitted even if the peace officer did not know the identity of the members of the public whose reactions he observed.

ANNOTATIONS

Causing disturbance (subsec. (1)(*a*)) / Proof of disturbance – Subsection (1)(*a*)(i) requires proof of an externally manifested disturbance of the public peace, in the sense of interference with the ordinary or customary use of the premises by the public. There may be direct evidence of such an effect or interference, or it may be inferred by the evidence of a police officer as to the conduct of a person or persons under subsec. (2). The disturbance may consist of the impugned act itself, as in the case of a fight, interfering with the peaceful use of a barroom, or it may flow as a consequence of the impugned act, as where shouting and swearing produce a scuffle. An interference with the ordinary and customary conduct in or near the public place may consist of something as small as being distracted from one's work, but this interference must be present and must be externally manifested. The disturbance must be one which may reasonably have been foreseen in the particular circumstances of time and place: *R. v. Lohnes*, [1992] 1 S.C.R. 167, 69 C.C.C. (3d) 289.

Proof of disturbance requires that someone was affected or disturbed by the activity. Accordingly, where the accused engaged in a fight in a secluded laneway that was observed by his friends, there was no evidence of anyone being disturbed: *R. v. V.B. (J.G.)* (2002), 165 C.C.C. (3d) 494, 205 N.S.R. (2d) 391 *sub nom. R. v. B. (J.G.V.)* (C.A.).

One may be convicted of an attempt to cause a disturbance: *R. v. Kennedy* (1973), 11 C.C.C. (2d) 263, 21 C.R.N.S. 251 (Ont. C.A.).

"Swear" should be given its modern meaning of "to use bad or profane or obscene language" and is not limited to invoking the Deity or something sacred in condemnation of a person or object: *R. v. Clothier* (1975), 13 N.S.R. (2d) 141 (S.C. App. Div.) *Contra: R. v. Enns* (1968), 5 C.R.N.S. 115, 66 W.W.R. 318 (Sask. Dist. Ct.).

In *R. v. Berry* (1980), 56 C.C.C. (2d) 99 (Ont. C.A.), the court overruled *R. v. Goddard* (1971), 4 C.C.C. (2d) 396, [1971] 3 O.R. 517 (H.C.J.), and held that the offence under subsec. (1)(*a*)(iii) "by impeding" does not require proof of an affray, riot or unlawful assembly. The word "disturbance" is to be given its ordinary dictionary meaning.

It would seem that speaking normally into an electronic megaphone can constitute shouting within the meaning of para. (*a*)(i): *R. v. Reed* (1992), 76 C.C.C. (3d) 204 (B.C.C.A.).

A "public disturbance" requires more than a crowd observing — or even shouting anti-police sentiments at — police officers in the course of arrest. In order to satisfy the *actus reus* of causing a public disturbance by using obscene language, the offending language must *cause* an externally manifested disturbance: *R. v. Swinkels* (2010), 263 C.C.C. (3d) 49 (Ont. C.A.).

Exposing or exhibiting indecent exhibition (subsec. (1)(*b*)) – The words "openly" and "exhibits" in subsec. (1)(*b*) should be given meanings consistent with Parliament's intention in enacting the entire section, that is, to prevent acts which disturb the peace or interfere with the peaceful enjoyment of the street. Thus "openly" may be defined as "in an open manner without concealment so that all may see, hear or take cognizance in public" and "exhibit" may be defined as "to submit or to expose to view, to show, to display": *R. v. Bagu* (1981), 61 C.C.C. (2d) 355 (Ont. Prov. Ct.).

Loitering (subsec. (1)(*c*)) – The offence in subsec. (1)(*c*) is directed at a nuisance. To constitute the offence there must be evidence of obstruction in the sense of rendering impassable or difficult of passage. As well, the ordinary meaning of "loiter" is to hang idly about a place and does not embrace purposeful activity such as the conduct of a prostitute attempting to attract customers in circumstances falling short of soliciting as defined in s. 213: *R. v. Munroe* (1983), 5 C.C.C. (3d) 217 (Ont. C.A.). Similarly, *R. v. Gauvin* (1984), 11 C.C.C. (3d) 229 (Ont. C.A.), leave to appeal to S.C.C. refused November 13, 1984.

Meaning of "dwelling-house" – A beer parlour in a hotel is not part of a "dwelling-house" for the purposes of subsec. (1)(*a*). It is only those parts of the hotel kept or occupied as a residence which fall within the definition of dwelling-house in s. 2: *R. v. Garnot* (1979), 47 C.C.C. (2d) 355 (B.C.S.C.).

Although the patients' rooms in a hospital may constitute dwelling places, the television rooms and hallways to which the public have access are public places within the meaning of subsec. (1)(*a*): *R. v. Campbell* (1980), 22 C.R. (3d) 219 (Alta. Q.B.).

Constitutional considerations – The offence of causing a disturbance by swearing, although an infringement of freedom of expression under s. 2(*b*) of the Charter, is a reasonable limit on that freedom and the provision is therefore valid: *R. v. Lawrence* (1992), 74 C.C.C. (3d) 495, [1992] 5 W.W.R. 659 (Alta. Q.B.), affd without reference to the point 81 C.C.C. (3d) 159 (Alta. C.A.).

OBSTRUCTING OR VIOLENCE TO OR ARREST OF OFFICIATING CLERGYMAN / Disturbing religious worship or certain meetings / Idem.

176. (1) Every one who

(*a*) by threats or force, unlawfully obstructs or prevents or endeavours to obstruct or prevent an officiant from celebrating a religious or spiritual service or performing any other function in connection with their calling, or

(*b*) knowing that an officiant is about to perform, is on their way to perform or is returning from the performance of any of the duties or functions mentioned in paragraph (*a*)

(i) assaults or offers any violence to them, or

(ii) arrests them on a civil process, or under the pretence of executing a civil process,

is guilty of an indictable offence and liable to imprisonment for a term not exceeding two years.

(2) Every one who wilfully disturbs or interrupts an assemblage of persons met for religious worship or for a moral, social or benevolent purpose is guilty of an offence punishable on summary conviction.

(3) Every one who, at or near a meeting referred to in subsection (2), wilfully does anything that disturbs the order or solemnity of the meeting is guilty of an offence punishable on summary conviction. R.S., c. C-34, s. 172; 2018, c. 29, s. 13.1.

CROSS-REFERENCES

The accused has an election as to mode of trial of the offence described in subsec. (1) pursuant to s. 536(2). Release pending trial is determined by s. 515, although the accused is eligible for release by the officer in charge under s. 498. The trial of the offences in subsecs. (2) and (3) is conducted by a summary conviction court pursuant to Part XXVII. The punishment for the offence is then as set out in s. 787 and the limitation period is set out in s. 786(2). Release pending trial is determined by s. 515, although the accused is eligible for release by a peace officer under s. 496, 497 or by the officer in charge under s. 498.

SYNOPSIS

This section makes it an offence to interfere with religious services or worship and provides for punishment upon conviction for these offences.

Section 176(1) creates the indictable offence of obstructing or preventing *a clergyman* or minister from performing religious services or other religious functions. Subsection (1)(*a*) prohibits the use of *threats or force* to attempt to achieve this aim.

Section 176(1)(*b*) creates a similar offence. The elements consist of doing one of the acts listed in sub-para. (i) or (ii), together with proof that the accused intended to do the act alleged and that the accused *knew* that the clergyman or minister was on the way to or from, or was about to perform religious duties. The maximum sentence for this offence is two years' imprisonment.

Subsections (2) and (3) create summary conviction offences involving *intentional disruption of religious worship* or meetings assembled for one of the purposes stated in subsec. (2). To prove the offence, it must be shown that the accused *wilfully* did actions which were disruptive or which were productive of disorder or interruption, and not merely that the acts caused upset among the assembled.

ANNOTATIONS

Constitutional issues – This section does not violate the guarantee to freedom of speech and religion in s. 2 of the *Charter of Rights and Freedoms*: *R. v. Reed* (1983), 8 C.C.C. (3d) 153 (B.C. Co. Ct.), affd 10 C.C.C. (3d) 573 (C.A.), and *R. v. Reed* (1985), 19 C.C.C. (3d) 180 (B.C.C.A.). [It should be noted that while the question of the inconsistency of subsec. (3) with the guarantees to religious freedom in the *Bill of Rights* and the *Charter of Rights and Freedoms* was raised in *R. v. Skoke-Graham, infra*, the court having entered an acquittal on other grounds declined to deal with these issues.]

The offence created by subsec. (3) is *intra vires* Parliament being validly enacted under the criminal law power: *R. v. Skoke-Graham*, [1985] 1 S.C.R. 106, 17 C.C.C. (3d) 289 (6:0).

Subsection (2) – Where members of a congregation have assembled at the place of worship for Sunday service they have "met for religious worship" within the meaning of subsec. (2) although the service has not yet begun and an accused who at that time is using a loud hailer outside the place to condemn the beliefs of the worshippers may be convicted of the offence described in that subsection: *R. v. Reed, supra.*

Subsection (3) – The offence under subsec. (3) requires proof of some activity in the nature of a disorder. The conduct must either be disorderly in itself or productive of disorder. It is not sufficient that the accused's conduct produced annoyance, anxiety or emotional upset among the members of the assemblage meeting for religious worship, where the impugned acts, here kneeling to accept communion in violation of a diocesan directive, are brief, essentially passive and peaceful in nature and voluntarily desisted from upon request: *R. v. Skoke-Graham, supra.*

Two people are an assemblage of persons within the meaning of subsec. (2) and a meeting for the purpose of subsec. (3) occurs when people meet for religious worship and includes the period prior to the formal ceremony: *R. v. Reed* (1994), 91 C.C.C. (3d) 481, 24 C.R.R. (2d) 163 (B.C.C.A.), leave to appeal to S.C.C. refused 95 C.C.C. (3d) vi, 26 C.R.R. (2d) 188*n*.

While brief temporary annoyance would not be sufficient, the requisite element of "disturbs" is made out by deliberate continued annoyance constituting obstruction or partial obstruction of entrance to the place of worship: *R. v. Reed, supra.*

TRESPASSING AT NIGHT.

177. Every person who, without lawful excuse, loiters or prowls at night on the property of another person near a dwelling-house situated on that property is guilty of an offence punishable on summary conviction. R.S., c. C-34, s. 173; 2018, c. 29, s. 14.

CROSS-REFERENCES

The terms "dwelling-house" and "night" are defined in s. 2. While the term "property" is also defined in s. 2, the very broad definition in that provision appears unsuited to the context of this offence. Under s. 494(2), a property owner or person in lawful possession of property and anyone authorized by such person may arrest, without warrant, a person whom he finds committing a criminal offence on or in relation to that property. Reference should also be made to ss. 40 to 42 relating to use of force in defence of dwelling-house and other real property.

The trial of this offence is conducted by a summary conviction court pursuant to Part XXVII. The punishment for the offence is then as set out in s. 787 and the limitation period is set out in s. 786(2). Release pending trial is determined by s. 515, although the accused is eligible for release by a peace officer under s. 496, 497 or by the officer in charge under s. 498.

Section 162 creates the voyeurism offence.

SYNOPSIS

This section makes it a summary conviction offence to *loiter* or *prowl by night* near a dwelling house on another person's property. The accused may raise a lawful excuse but the burden of proving it is upon the accused. As with all sections which place a burden upon the accused, this aspect of the section is likely to attract scrutiny under the *Canadian Charter of Rights and Freedoms*.

ANNOTATIONS

This section creates two offences of prowling and loitering. The essence of loitering is the conduct of someone who is wandering about apparently without precise destination and is conduct which essentially has nothing reprehensible about it, if it does not take place on private property where the loiterer has no business. Prowling, on the other hand, involves some notion of evil. The prowler does not act without a purpose: *R. v. Cloutier* (1991), 66 C.C.C. (3d) 149 (Que. C.A.).

"Prowls" means to traverse stealthily in the sense of furtively, secretly, clandestinely or moving by imperceptible degrees. The Crown need not prove that the accused was looking for an opportunity to carry out an unlawful purpose. It is not a lawful excuse within the meaning of this section that the accused was trying to conceal himself following commission of a criminal offence: *R. v. Willis* (1987), 37 C.C.C. (3d) 184 (B.C. Co. Ct.).

The accused commits an offence under this section by intentionally loitering or prowling at night near a residence on another person's property unless the accused establishes a lawful excuse for his or her conduct. The Crown is not required to prove that the accused also had an intention to commit a specific evil act: *R. v. Priestap* (2006), 207 C.C.C. (3d) 490, 79 O.R. (3d) 561, 208 O.A.C. 351 (C.A.).

This section does not create an unconstitutional reverse onus provision inconsistent with the guarantee to the presumption of innocence in s. 11(*d*) of the *Canadian Charter of Rights and Freedoms*: *R. v. Tassou* (1984), 16 C.C.C. (3d) 567 (Alta. Prov. Ct.).

178. [*Repealed*, 2018, c. 29, s. 14.]

VAGRANCY / Punishment.

179. (1) Every one commits vagrancy who

(*a*) supports himself in whole or in part by gaming or crime and has no lawful profession or calling by which to maintain himself; or

(*b*) having at any time been convicted of an offence under section 151, 152 or 153, subsection 160(3) or 173(2) or section 271, 272 or 273, or of an offence under a provision referred to in paragraph (*b*) of the definition "serious personal injury offence" in section 687 of the *Criminal Code*, chapter C-34 of the Revised Statutes of Canada, 1970, as it read before January 4, 1983, is found loitering in or near a school ground, playground, public park or bathing area.

(2) Every one who commits vagrancy is guilty of an offence punishable on summary conviction. R.S., c. C-34, s. 175; 1972, c. 13, s. 12; 1984, c. 40, s. 20; R.S.C. 1985, c. 27 (1st Supp.), s. 22; c. 19 (3rd Supp.), s. 8.

CROSS-REFERENCES

"Gaming" is not defined in this section but presumably refers to the offences described by Part VII.

Section 687 of the *Criminal Code*, R.S.C. 1970, c. C-34, as it read prior to January 4, 1983 defined "serious personal injury offence" as follows:

> "(b) an offence mentioned in section 144 (rape) or 145 (attempted rape) or an offence or attempt to commit an offence mentioned in section 146 (sexual intercourse with a female under fourteen or between fourteen and sixteen), 149 (indecent assault on a female), 156 (indecent assault on a male) or 157 (gross indecency)"

Now also see s. 161 which makes it an offence to violate a prohibition order made against a sex offender.

The trial of this offence is conducted by a summary conviction court pursuant to Part XXVII. The punishment for the offence is then as set out in s. 787 and the limitation period is set out in s. 786(2). Release pending trial is determined by s. 515, although the accused is eligible for release by a peace officer under s. 496, 497 or by the officer in charge under s. 498.

Under s. 4(2) of the *Canada Evidence Act*, the spouse of an accused charged with this offence is a compellable witness at the instance of the prosecution. Section 16 of the Canada Evidence Act deals with the competency of witnesses under the age of 14 years.

SYNOPSIS

This section creates the summary conviction offence of *vagrancy*.

Section 179(1)(*a*) states that a person is guilty of vagrancy if that person has no visible, lawful means of support and the accused supports himself in part, or entirely, by gaming or crime.

Section 179(1)(*b*) states that a person is guilty of vagrancy if that person has been *convicted* of one of the offences specified in the paragraph and is found *loitering* in one of the listed *public places*. Loitering connotes hanging around for no valid purpose. It need not be shown that the accused had any particular intention beyond loitering in the prohibited location nor that the accused did any other act beyond being present.

ANNOTATIONS

Subsection (1)(*b*) of this section violates s. 7 of the Charter and is of no force and effect: *R. v. Heywood*, [1994] 3 S.C.R. 761, 94 C.C.C. (3d) 481, 34 C.R. (4th) 133.

Nuisances

COMMON NUISANCE / Definition.

180. (1) Every one who commits a common nuisance and thereby

(*a*) endangers the lives, safety or health of the public, or

(*b*) causes physical injury to any person,

is guilty of an indictable offence and liable to imprisonment for a term not exceeding two years.

(2) For the purposes of this section, every one commits a common nuisance who does an unlawful act or fails to discharge a legal duty and thereby

(*a*) endangers the lives, safety, health, property or comfort of the public; or

(*b*) obstructs the public in the exercise or enjoyment of any right that is common to all the subjects of Her Majesty in Canada. R.S., c. C-34, s. 176.

CROSS-REFERENCES

The accused has an election as to mode of trial pursuant to s. 536(2). Release pending trial is determined by s. 515, although the accused is eligible for release by the officer in charge under s. 498.

Related offences may be found in Part XI [wilful and forbidden act in relation to property]. Also note the intimidation offence in s. 423, explosive offences and duty in handling explosives in ss. 79 to 82, offences in relation to aircraft in ss. 76 to 78, sabotage in s. 52, careless handling of firearm in s. 86, duty to provide necessaries in s. 215 and duty of person undertaking dangerous acts in ss. 216, 217.

SYNOPSIS

The section creates the indictable offence of creating a *common nuisance*.

Subsection (2) sets out *what constitutes a common nuisance*. First, it must be proven that the accused either did an unlawful act or failed to discharge a legal duty. Secondly, it must be proven that the accused's act or omission resulted in one of the ill-effects described in s. 180(2)(*a*) or (*b*).

The offence created in subsec. (1) requires that, in addition to establishing proof that a *common nuisance* occurred, it must be shown that the nuisance *resulted in the harm* described in s. 180(1)(*a*) or (*b*). The maximum sentence for this offence is two years' imprisonment. As there is a substantial overlap between the two subsections, the "additional" elements set out in subsec. (1) may be satisfied by the same evidence that brought the accused within the definition of common nuisance under subsec. (2).

ANNOTATIONS

A common nuisance must be directed to the public generally and a conviction under this section cannot be supported where the acts were directed to three individuals: *R. v. Schula* (1956), 115 C.C.C. 382 (Alta. S.C. App. Div.).

Section 216 imposed a legal duty on the accused, who knew he was infected with the AIDS virus, to not donate blood to the Red Cross and breach of this duty may found a conviction under this section: *R. v. Thornton*, [1993] 2 S.C.R. 445, 82 C.C.C. (3d) 530 (9:0).

SPREADING FALSE NEWS.

181. Every one who wilfully publishes a statement, tale or news that he knows is false and that causes or is likely to cause injury or mischief to a public interest is guilty of an indictable offence and liable to imprisonment for a term not exceeding two years. R.S., c. C-34, s. 177.

ANNOTATIONS

This section violates the guarantee to freedom of expression under s. 2(*b*) of the Charter and is of no force and effect: *R. v. Zundel*, [1992] 2 S.C.R. 731, 75 C.C.C. (3d) 449.

DEAD BODY.

182. Every one who

(*a*) neglects, without lawful excuse, to perform any duty that is imposed on him by law or that he undertakes with reference to the burial of a dead human body or human remains, or

(*b*) improperly or indecently interferes with or offers any indignity to a dead human body or human remains, whether buried or not,

is guilty of an indictable offence and liable to imprisonment for a term not exceeding five years. R.S., c. C-34, s. 178.

CROSS-REFERENCES

The duty imposed by law, referred to in this section, presumably refers to provincial legislation which governs the burial of human remains.

The accused has an election as to mode of trial pursuant to s. 536(2). Release pending trial is determined by s. 515, although the accused is eligible for release by the officer in charge under s. 498.

A related offence is found in s. 243 which makes it an offence to dispose of the dead body of a child with intent to conceal the fact that its mother has been delivered of it.

SYNOPSIS

This rarely used section creates two indictable offences relating to the *neglect or improper interference with a dead body*. The first offence is *neglecting* to perform a *duty* imposed by law *or* which the accused agrees to undertake in connection with burying a dead person. The prosecution must prove that the accused did not have a *lawful excuse* for such neglect of the body.

The second offence is committed when an accused treats a dead body, buried or not, improperly, indecently or improperly interferes with it. Both offences under this section require proof that the accused knew that the body was dead. The maximum sentence is five years' imprisonment.

ANNOTATIONS

Paragraph (*b*) – Although it would be a defence to this charge if the accused did not know that the body was dead if on the facts as he believed them he was acting lawfully and innocently, such a defence is not open to an accused who believing the person is alive is attempting to have intercourse with the body because if, as he thought, the woman was alive he was raping her there being no suggestion he thought he had her consent to the act: *R. v. Ladue*, [1965] 4 C.C.C. 264 (Y.T.C.A.).

A physical interference with the human remains is not a necessary element of the offence under para. (*b*) and it applies to offering indignities to monuments that mark human remains because to offer indignities to such monuments is to offer indignities to the remains themselves: *R. v. Moyer*, [1994] 2 S.C.R. 899, 92 C.C.C. (3d) 1.

Part VI / INVASION OF PRIVACY

Definitions

DEFINITIONS / "authorization" / "electro-magnetic, acoustic, mechanical or other device" / "intercept" / "offence" / "police officer" / "private communication" / "public switched telephone network" / "radio-based telephone communication" / "sell" / "solicitor".

183. In this Part,

"authorization" means an authorization to intercept a private communication given under section 186 or subsection 184.2(3), 184.3(6) or 188(2);

"electro-magnetic, acoustic, mechanical or other device" means any device or apparatus that is used or is capable of being used to intercept a private communication, but does not include a hearing aid used to correct subnormal hearing of the user to not better than normal hearing;

"intercept" includes listen to, record or acquire a communication or acquire the substance, meaning or purport thereof;

"offence" means an offence contrary to, any conspiracy or attempt to commit or being an accessory after the fact in relation to an offence contrary to, or any counselling in relation to an offence contrary to

(*a*) any of the following provisions of this Act, namely,

(i) section 47 (high treason),

(ii) section 51 (intimidating Parliament or a legislature),

(iii) section 52 (sabotage),

(iii.1) section 56.1 (identity documents),

(iv) section 57 (forgery, etc.),

(v) section 61 (sedition),

(vi) section 76 (hijacking),

(vii) section 77 (endangering safety of aircraft or airport),

(viii) section 78 (offensive weapons, etc., on aircraft),

(ix) section 78.1 (offences against maritime navigation or fixed platforms),

(x) section 80 (breach of duty),

(xi) section 81 (using explosives),

(xii) section 82 (possessing explosives),

(xii.01) section 82.3 (possession, etc., of nuclear material, radioactive material or device),
(xii.02) section 82.4 (use or alteration of nuclear material, radioactive material or device),
(xii.03) section 82.5 (commission of indictable offence to obtain nuclear material, etc.),
(xii.04) section 82.6 (threats),
(xii.1) section 83.02 (providing or collecting property for certain activities),
(xii.2) section 83.03 (providing, making available, etc., property or services for terrorist purposes),
(xii.3) section 83.04 (using or possessing property for terrorist purposes),
(xii.4) section 83.18 (participation in activity of terrorist group),
(xii.41) section 83.181 (leaving Canada to participate in activity of terrorist group),
(xii.5) section 83.19 (facilitating terrorist activity),
(xii.51) section 83.191 (leaving Canada to facilitate terrorist activity),
(xii.6) section 83.2 (commission of offence for terrorist group),
(xii.61) section 83.201 (leaving Canada to commit offence for terrorist group),
(xii.62) section 83.202 (leaving Canada to commit offence that is terrorist activity),
(xii.7) section 83.21 (instructing to carry out activity for terrorist group),
(xii.8) section 83.22 (instructing to carry out terrorist activity),
(xii.81) subsection 83.221(1) (advocating or promoting commission of terrorism offences),
(xii.9) section 83.23 (harbouring or concealing),
(xii.91) section 83.231 (hoax — terrorist activity),
(xiii) section 96 (possession of weapon obtained by commission of offence),
(xiii.1) section 98 (breaking and entering to steal firearm),
(xiii.2) section 98.1 (robbery to steal firearm),
(xiv) section 99 (weapons trafficking),
(xv) section 100 (possession for purpose of weapons trafficking),
(xvi) section 102 (making automatic firearm),
(xvii) section 103 (importing or exporting knowing it is unauthorized),
(xviii) section 104 (unauthorized importing or exporting),
(xix) section 119 (bribery, etc.),
(xx) section 120 (bribery, etc.),
(xxi) section 121 (fraud on government),
(xxii) section 122 (breach of trust),
(xxiii) section 123 (municipal corruption),
(xxiv) section 132 (perjury),
(xxv) section 139 (obstructing justice),
(xxvi) section 144 (prison breach),
(xxvii) subsection 145(1) (escape, etc.),
(xxvii.1) section 162 (voyeurism),
(xxvii.2) section 162.1 (intimate image),
(xxviii) subsection 163(1) (obscene materials),
(xxix) section 163.1 (child pornography),
(xxix.1) section 170 (parent or guardian procuring sexual activity),
(xxix.2) section 171 (householder permitting sexual activity),
(xxix.3) section 171.1 (making sexually explicit material available to child),
(xxix.4) section 172.1 (luring a child),
(xxix.5) section 172.2 (agreement or arrangement — sexual offence against child),
(xxx) section 184 (unlawful interception),
(xxxi) section 191 (possession of intercepting device),
(xxxii) subsection 201(1) (keeping gaming or betting house),
(xxxiii) paragraph 202(1)(e) (pool-selling, etc.),

(xxxiv) subsection 210(1) (keeping common bawdy house),
(xxxv) [*Repealed*, 2014, c. 25, s. 11(1).]
(xxxvi) [*Repealed*, 2014, c. 25, s. 11(1).]
(xxxvii) [*Repealed*, 2014, c. 25, s. 11(1).]
(xxxviii) [*Repealed*, 2014, c. 25, s. 11(1).]
(xxxix) section 235 (murder),
(xxxix.1) section 244 (discharging firearm with intent),
(xxxix.2) section 244.2 (discharging firearm — recklessness),
(xl) section 264.1 (uttering threats),
(xli) section 267 (assault with a weapon or causing bodily harm),
(xlii) section 268 (aggravated assault),
(xliii) section 269 (unlawfully causing bodily harm),
(xliii.1) section 270.01 (assaulting peace officer with weapon or causing bodily harm),
(xliii.2) section 270.02 (aggravated assault of peace officer),
(xliv) section 271 (sexual assault),
(xlv) section 272 (sexual assault with a weapon, threats to a third party or causing bodily harm),
(xlvi) section 273 (aggravated sexual assault),
(xlvii) section 279 (kidnapping),
(xlvii.1) section 279.01 (trafficking in persons),
(xlvii.11) section 279.011 (trafficking of a person under the age of eighteen years),
(xlvii.2) section 279.02 (material benefit),
(xlvii.3) section 279.03 (withholding or destroying documents),
(xlviii) section 279.1 (hostage taking),
(xlix) section 280 (abduction of person under sixteen),
(l) section 281 (abduction of person under fourteen),
(li) section 282 (abduction in contravention of custody order),
(lii) section 283 (abduction),
(lii.1) 286.1 (obtaining sexual services for consideration),
(lii.2) 286.2 (material benefit from sexual services),
(lii.3) 286.3 (procuring),
(lii.4) 286.4 (advertising sexual services),
(liii) section 318 (advocating genocide),
(liv) section 327 (possession of device to obtain telecommunication facility or service),
(liv.1) section 333.1 (motor vehicle theft),
(lv) section 334 (theft),
(lvi) section 342 (theft, forgery, etc., of credit card),
(lvi.1) section 342.01 (instruments for copying credit card data or forging or falsifying credit cards),
(lvii) section 342.1 (unauthorized use of computer),
(lviii) section 342.2 (possession of device to obtain unauthorized use of computer system or to commit mischief),
(lix) section 344 (robbery),
(lx) section 346 (extortion),
(lxi) section 347 (criminal interest rate),
(lxii) section 348 (breaking and entering),
(lxii.1) section 353.1 (tampering with vehicle identification number),
(lxiii) section 354 (possession of property obtained by crime),
(lxiii.1) section 355.2 (trafficking in property obtained by crime),
(lxiii.2) section 355.4 (possession of property obtained by crime — trafficking),
(lxiv) section 356 (theft from mail),
(lxv) section 367 (forgery),

(lxvi) section 368 (use, trafficking or possession of forged document),
(lxvi.1) section 368.1 (forgery instruments),
(lxvii) section 372 (false information),
(lxviii) section 380 (fraud),
(lxix) section 381 (using mails to defraud),
(lxx) section 382 (fraudulent manipulation of stock exchange transactions),
(lxx.1) subsection 402.2(1) (identity theft),
(lxx.2) subsection 402.2(2) (trafficking in identity information),
(lxx.3) section 403 (identity fraud),
(lxxi) section 423.1 (intimidation of justice system participant or journalist),
(lxxii) section 424 (threat to commit offences against internationally protected person),
(lxxii.1) section 424.1 (threat against United Nations or associated personnel),
(lxxiii) section 426 (secret commissions),
(lxxiv) section 430 (mischief),
(lxxv) section 431 (attack on premises, residence or transport of internationally protected person),
(lxxv.1) section 431.1 (attack on premises, accommodation or transport of United Nations or associated personnel),
(lxxv.2) subsection 431.2(2) (explosive or other lethal device),
(lxxvi) section 433 (arson),
(lxxvii) section 434 (arson),
(lxxviii) section 434.1 (arson),
(lxxix) section 435 (arson for fraudulent purpose),
(lxxx) section 449 (making counterfeit money),
(lxxxi) section 450 (possession, etc., of counterfeit money),
(lxxxii) section 452 (uttering, etc., counterfeit money),
(lxxxiii) section 462.31 (laundering proceeds of crime),
(lxxxiv) subsection 462.33(11) (acting in contravention of restraint order),
(lxxxv) section 467.11 (participation in criminal organization),
(lxxxv.1) section 467.111 (recruitment of members — criminal organization),
(lxxxvi) section 467.12 (commission of offence for criminal organization), or
(lxxxvii) section 467.13 (instructing commission of offence for criminal organization),

(*b*) section 198 (fraudulent bankruptcy) of the *Bankruptcy and Insolvency Act*,

(*b*.1) any of the following provisions of the *Biological and Toxin Weapons Convention Implementation Act*, namely,
(i) section 6 (production, etc., of biological agents and means of delivery), or
(ii) section 7 (unauthorized production, etc., of biological agents),

(*b*.2) any of the following provisions of the *Cannabis Act*, namely,
(i) section 9 (distribution and possession for purpose of distributing),
(ii) section 10 (selling and possession for purpose of selling),
(iii) section 11 (importing and exporting and possession for purpose of exporting),
(iv) section 12 (production),
(v) section 13 (possession, etc., for use in production or distribution of illicit cannabis), or
(vi) section 14 (use of young person),

(*c*) any of the following provisions of the *Competition Act*, namely,
(i) section 45 (conspiracies, agreements or arrangements between competitors),
(ii) section 47 (bid-rigging), or
(iii) subsection 52.1(3) (deceptive telemarketing),

CR. CODE

(*d*) any of the following provisions of the *Controlled Drugs and Substances Act*, namely,
(i) section 5 (trafficking),
(ii) section 6 (importing and exporting);
(iii) section 7 (production); or
(iv) section 7.1 (possession, sale, etc., for use in production or trafficking),

(*d*.1) section 42 (offences related to infringement of copyright) of the *Copyright Act*,

(*e*) section 3 (bribing a foreign public official) of the *Corruption of Foreign Public Officials Act*,

(*e*.1) the *Crimes Against Humanity and War Crimes Act*,

(*f*) either of the following provisions of the *Customs Act*, namely,
(i) section 153 (false statements), or
(ii) section 159 (smuggling),

(*g*) any of the following provisions of the *Excise Act, 2001*, namely,
(i) section 214 (unlawful production, sale, etc., of tobacco, alcohol or cannabis),
(ii) section 216 (unlawful possession of tobacco product),
(iii) section 218 (unlawful possession, sale, etc., of alcohol),
(iii.1) section 218.1 (unlawful possession, sale, etc., of unstamped cannabis),
(iv) section 219 (falsifying or destroying records),
(v) section 230 (possession of property obtained by excise offences), or
(vi) section 231 (laundering proceeds of excise offences),

(*h*) any of the following provisions of the *Export and Import Permits Act*, namely,
(i) section 13 (export or attempt to export),
(ii) section 14 (import or attempt to import),
(iii) section 15 (diversion, etc.),
(iv) section 16 (no transfer of permits),
(v) section 17 (false information), or
(vi) section 18 (aiding and abetting),

Note: The preceding para. (*h*) of the definition "offence" is amended by 2018, c. 26, s. 23 (to come into force by order of the Governor in Council) by adding the following subpara. after subpara. (ii):
(ii.1) section 14.2 (broker or attempt to broker),

(*i*) any of the following provisions of the *Immigration and Refugee Protection Act*, namely,
(i) section 117 (organizing entry into Canada),
(ii) section 118 (trafficking in persons),
(iii) section 119 (disembarking persons at sea),
(iv) section 122 (offences related to documents),
(v) section 126 (counselling misrepresentation), or
(vi) section 129 (offences relating to officers),

(*j*) any offence under the *Security of Information Act*, or

(*k*) section 51.01 (offences related to goods, labels, packaging or services) of the *Trademarks Act*,

and includes any other offence that there are reasonable grounds to believe is a criminal organization offence or any other offence that there are reasonable grounds to believe is an offence described in paragraph (*b*) or (*c*) of the definition "terrorism offence" in section 2;

Note: Definition "offence" amended by 2001, c. 27, s. 245 (to come into force by order of the Governor in Council; however, repealed before coming into force, 2004, c. 15, s. 110).

"police officer" means any officer, constable or other person employed for the preservation and maintenance of the public peace;

"private communication" means any oral communication, or any telecommunication, that is made by an originator who is in Canada or is intended by the originator to be received by a person who is in Canada and that is made under circumstances in which it

is reasonable for the originator to expect that it will not be intercepted by any person other than the person intended by the originator to receive it, and includes any radio-based telephone communication that is treated electronically or otherwise for the purpose of preventing intelligible reception by any person other than the person intended by the originator to receive it;

"public switched telephone network" means a telecommunication facility the primary purpose of which is to provide a land line-based telephone service to the public for compensation;

"radio-based telephone communication" means any radiocommunication within the meaning of the *Radiocommunication Act* that is made over apparatus that is used primarily for connection to a public switched telephone network;

"sell" includes offer for sale, expose for sale, have in possession for sale or distribute or advertise for sale;

"solicitor" means, in the Province of Quebec, an advocate or notary and, in any other province, a barrister or solicitor. 1973-74, c. 50, s. 2; 1976-77, c. 53, s. 7; 1980-81-82-83, c. 125, s. 10; 1984, c. 21, s. 76; 1985, c. 27 (1st Supp.), ss. 7(2)(*a*), 23; R.S.C. 1985, c. 1 (2nd Supp.), s. 213; R.S.C. 1985, c. 1 (4th Supp.), s. 13; c. 29 (4th Supp.), s. 17; c. 42 (4th Supp.), s. 1; 1991, c. 28, s. 12; 1992, c. 27, s. 90; 1993, c. 7, s. 5; 1993, c. 25, s. 94; 1993, c. 40, s. 1; 1993, c. 46, s. 4; 1995, c. 39, s. 140; 1996, c. 19, s. 66; 1997, c. 18, s. 7; 1997, c. 23, s. 3; 1998, c. 34, s. 8; 1999, c. 2, s. 47; c. 5, s. 4; 2000, c. 24, s. 43; 2001, c. 32, s. 4; 2001, c. 41, ss. 5, 31, 133(2) and (5); 2002, c. 22, s. 409(2)(*b*); 2004, c. 15, s. 108; 2005, c. 32, s. 10; 2005, c. 43, s. 1; 2008, c. 6, s. 15; 2009, c. 22, s. 4; 2009, c. 28, s. 3; 2010, c. 3, s. 1; 2010, c. 17, s. 2; 2012, c. 1, s. 24; 2013, c. 8, s. 2; 2013, c. 9, s. 14; 2013, c. 13, s. 7; 2014, c. 17, s. 2; 2014, c. 25, s. 11; 2014, c. 31, s. 7; 2014, c. 32, s. 59; 2015, c. 20, s. 19; 2017, c. 7, s. 56; 2018, c. 12, s. 114; 2018, c. 16, s. 210; 2018, c. 29, s. 15.

CROSS-REFERENCES

In addition to the definitions in this section, see s. 2 and notes to that section. The term "telecommunication" is defined in s. 35 of the *Interpretation Act*, R.S.C. c. I-21, as "any transmission, emission or reception of signs, signals, writing, images or sounds or intelligence of any nature by wire, radio, visual or other electromagnetic system". "Radio" is also defined in s. 35. Note that s. 3 provides that a description in parenthesis after a section number is inserted for convenience of reference only and is no part of the provision.

Related offences may be found in s. 326, theft of telecommunication service and s. 327, unlawful possession of device to obtain telecommunication facility.

This Part is just one aspect of a more or less comprehensive scheme for regulating surreptitious use of electronic devices by agents of the state. Also see s. 487.01 which provides for a general warrant which would cover surreptitious electronic surveillance, s. 492.1 which regulates the use of tracking devices and s. 492.2 which regulates the use of telephone number recorders. In addition, provision is made in s. 487.02 for the making of an assistance order to require persons to co-operate in the carrying out of orders made under this Part.

The interception of private communications by the state constitutes a search or seizure for the purposes of s. 8 of the *Charter of Rights and Freedoms* and, therefore, in addition to the notes in this Part, see notes under s. 8 of the Charter.

At the time this Part was enacted, certain amendments to other federal statutes were made, in particular to the *Crown Liability and Proceedings Act*, R.S.C. 1985, c. C-50. Reference should also be made to the *Canadian Security Intelligence Service Act*, R.S.C. 1985, c. C-23, which provides authority for authorizations in national security matters.

SYNOPSIS

This section provides definitions which are used throughout Part VI of the *Criminal Code* dealing with intercepted private communications. The definition of "offence" contained in this section is pivotal because the offences contained in this list are the only offences which may form the basis of an application for an authorization to intercept private communications and a warrant for video surveillance under s. 487.01(5).

ANNOTATIONS

"Intercept" ***[Also see notes under s. 189(1), "Intercepted".]*** – Surreptitious electronic surveillance constitutes a search or seizure within the meaning of s. 8 of the *Charter of Rights and Freedoms*: *R. v. Duarte*, [1990] 1 S.C.R. 30, 53 C.C.C. (3d) 1.

The term "intercept", at least as used in s. 189, which deals with the admissibility of evidence, must be interpreted in context and in accordance with its primary dictionary meaning as an interference between the place of origination and the place of destination of the communication. Thus, there is no interception where the originator was simply mistaken as to the identity of the person to whom he was talking: *R. v. McQueen* (1975), 25 C.C.C. (2d) 262 (Alta. S.C.); *R. v. Singh* (1998), 127 C.C.C. (3d) 429 (B.C.C.A.).

This part has no application to a communication which is merely overheard by a third party without the use of any mechanical or other device: *R. v. Beckner* (1978), 43 C.C.C. (2d) 356 (Ont. C.A.). *Contra*: *R. v. Boutilier and Melnick* (1976), 35 C.C.C. (2d) 555 (N.S.S.C.).

The collection of text messages that have already been sent and received does not constitute an "intercept" and therefore does not require a Part VI authorization: *R. v. Jones* (2016), 338 C.C.C. (3d) 591 (Ont. C.A.), affd [2017] 2 S.C.R. 696; *R. v. Belcourt* (2015), 322 C.C.C. (3d) 93 (B.C.C.A.).

"Private communication" – For the purposes of this definition the "originator" of the private communication is the person who makes the remarks or series of remarks which the Crown seeks to adduce in evidence. Thus, if a person with a reasonable expectation of privacy, speaking in an electronically intercepted conversation, makes statements which the Crown seeks to use against him he has the protection of this Part: *R. v. Goldman*, [1980] 1 S.C.R. 976, 51 C.C.C. (2d) 1 (8:1).

An obscene or threatening phone call is a private communication even where it is that call which forms the substance of the charge: *R. v. Dunn* (1975), 28 C.C.C. (2d) 538 (N.S. Co. Ct.).

A telephone call to a police switchboard in which the accused threatened the life of a member of that force is not a private communication. It would not be reasonable to expect that such a communication would not be listened to or recorded by a person other than the switchboard operator: *R. v. Monachan* (1981), 60 C.C.C. (2d) 286 (Ont. C.A.), affd [1985] 1 S.C.R. 176, 16 C.C.C. (3d) 576 (7:0).

To a similar effect is *R. v. Lubovac* (1989), 52 C.C.C. (3d) 551 (Alta. C.A.), where it was held that pager messages were not private communications, since the pager simply broadcast a message to those who may happen to hear or overhear it. It was also held that retrieval, by the police, of messages left by the accused's accomplice at a computer message centre was not a violation of s. 8 of the Charter. The police had obtained a number from an informer which enabled them to retrieve any messages which had been left by the accomplice. The informer had, in turn, been given the number from the accomplice. The accomplice had no reasonable expectation that his messages would be sent out or received in confidence. Also see *R. v. Nin* (1985), 34 C.C.C. (3d) 89 (Que. Ct. Sess.).

However, it was held in *R. v. Solomon* (1996), 110 C.C.C. (3d) 354 (Que. C.A.), affd [1997] 3 S.C.R. 696, 118 C.C.C. (3d) 351, that even assuming that a conversation made from a cellular telephone is not a "private communication" within the meaning of this section, there is an expectation of privacy in the use of a cellular phone and therefore s. 8 of the Charter is violated unless the interceptions are authorized.

It was held in *R. v. Cheung* (1995), 100 C.C.C. (3d) 441 (B.C.S.C.), that, at least in 1990, conversations over a cellular telephone were private communications. While a person sending or receiving a call on a cellular telephone did face some risk of being overheard by someone who just happened to meet the combination of factors which matched a scanner to a call, the chance of someone, who set out to intercept the calls of a particular individual by scanner, to succeed in that venture was very small.

Use of a dial number recorder does not involve interception of a private communication. Communication in this section contemplates an exchange of information between persons: *R. v. Fegan* (1993), 80 C.C.C. (3d) 356 (Ont. C.A.). *Contra*: *R. v. Kutsak* (1993), 108 Sask. R. 241 (Q.B.). [Note that a warrant may now be obtained to install a dial number recorder pursuant to s. 492.2.]

A police officer's deception as to his identity with an online or text message interlocutor does not convert the interaction into an "interception" requiring authorization under this part: *R. v. Beairsto* (2018), 359 C.C.C. (3d) 376 (Alta. C.A.); *R. v. Mills* (2017), 136 W.C.B. (2d) 728, 2017 NLCA 12, leave to appeal to S.C.C. allowed 2017 CarswellNfld 483.

CONSENT TO INTERCEPTION.

183.1 Where a private communication is originated by more than one person or is intended by the originator thereof to be received by more than one person, a consent to the interception thereof by any one of those persons is sufficient consent for the purposes of any provision of this Part. 1993, c. 40, s. 2.

CROSS-REFERENCES

Consent to interception is relevant to s. 184 which creates the offence of interception of private communications and ss. 184.1 and 184.2 which authorize interception of private communications where one of the parties consents to the interception.

Interception of Communications

INTERCEPTION / Saving provision / Use or retention.

184. (1) Every one who, by means of any electro-magnetic, acoustic, mechanical or other device, wilfully intercepts a private communication is guilty of an indictable offence and liable to imprisonment for a term not exceeding five years.

(2) Subsection (1) does not apply to

(*a*) a person who has the consent to intercept, express or implied, of the originator of the private communication or of the person intended by the originator thereof to receive it;

(*b*) a person who intercepts a private communication in accordance with an authorization or pursuant to section 184.4 or any person who in good faith aids in any way another person who the aiding person believes on reasonable grounds is acting with an authorization or pursuant to section 184.4;

(*c*) a person engaged in providing a telephone, telegraph or other communication service to the public who intercepts a private communication,

(i) if the interception is necessary for the purpose of providing the service,

(ii) in the course of service observing or random monitoring necessary for the purpose of mechanical or service quality control checks, or

(iii) if the interception is necessary to protect the person's rights or property directly related to providing the service;

(*d*) an officer or servant of Her Majesty in right of Canada who engages in radio frequency spectrum management, in respect of a private communication intercepted by that officer or servant for the purpose of identifying, isolating or preventing an unauthorized or interfering use of a frequency or of a transmission; or

(*e*) a person, or any person acting on their behalf, in possession or control of a computer system, as defined in subsection 342.1(2), who intercepts a private

communication originating from, directed to or transmitting through that computer system, if the interception is reasonably necessary for

(i) managing the quality of service of the computer system as it relates to performance factors such as the responsiveness and capacity of the system as well as the integrity and availability of the system and data, or

(ii) protecting the computer system against any act that would be an offence under subsection 342.1(1) or 430(1.1).

(3) A private communication intercepted by a person referred to in paragraph (2)(*e*) can be used or retained only if

(*a*) it is essential to identify, isolate or prevent harm to the computer system; or

(*b*) it is to be disclosed in circumstances referred to in subsection 193(2). 1973-74, c. 50, s. 2; 1993, c. 40, s. 3; 2004, c. 12, s. 4.

CROSS-REFERENCES

The terms "electro-magnetic, acoustic, mechanical or other device", "intercept", "private communication" and "authorization" are defined in s. 183. The term "radio" is defined in s. 35 of the *Interpretation Act*, R.S.C. c. I-21. The term "wilfully" does not have a fixed meaning and must take its meaning from the context. Generally, however, it connotes an intention to bring about a proscribed consequence. See *R. v. Buzzanga and Durocher* (1979), 49 C.C.C. (2d) 369 (Ont. C.A.).

Consent to interception is given an expanded meaning in s. 183.1.

This provision is fundamental to the scheme enacted by this Part. It makes unlawful the interception of private communications by the devices defined in s. 183, subject to certain narrow exceptions in subsec. (2). Those exceptions are interceptions pursuant to a normal "60-day" authorization obtained under s. 186, interceptions under the emergency "36-hour" authorization obtained under s. 188, unauthorized interceptions in exceptional circumstances as set out in s. 184.4 and consent interceptions. The other exceptions listed essentially concern interceptions incidental to the providing of the telephone service. An important incentive to compliance with the law, in addition to the penalties under this section, is that if the interception is not lawfully made by agents of the state then it is probably a violation of s. 8 of the Charter and therefore subject to exclusion under s. 24(2) of the Charter.

Separate offences have been created for interception of cellular telephone communications under ss. 184.5 and 193.1.

It is an offence under s. 191 to unlawfully have possession of any device designed primarily for the surreptitious interception of private communications. Under s. 193, it is an offence to unlawfully disclose an intercepted private communication.

Pursuant to s. 192, any device, by means of which the offence under this section was committed, may be ordered forfeited. As well, pursuant to s. 194, the court that convicts the accused of the offence under this section may make an order for punitive damages. The offence in this section can itself be the basis for an authorization to intercept private communications, by virtue of the definition of "offence" in s. 183. Under s. 195(3), the annual reports of the Solicitor General and Attorneys General are to set out the number of prosecutions under this section of officers or servants of the Crown.

The accused has an election as to mode of trial pursuant to s. 536(2) and release pending trial is determined by s. 515, although the accused is eligible for release by the officer in charge under s. 498.

SYNOPSIS

This section makes it an *offence*, subject to a number of exceptions, *to intercept private communications by means of a specified device*, and provides for punishment upon conviction for this offence.

Subsection (1) creates the *indictable offence of unlawful interception*. The *device* used to intercept the private communication must be one listed in this section, as elaborated in the definition of such devices found in s. 183. The communication must be *private*, and this term is also defined in s. 183. The communication, must be *intercepted*, a defined term in s. 183. The act of the accused must be done *wilfully*, but no specific purpose beyond the interception need be shown. A person convicted under this subsection is liable to imprisonment for five years.

Subsection (2) provides a number of *exceptions to subsec. (1)*. Subsection (2)(*a*) states that subsec. (1) does not apply if one obtains the *consent* of either the *originator or the intended recipient* of the communication. The consent may be explicit or implied.

Section 184(2)(*b*) creates an exception to liability under subsec. (1) if the communication was intercepted *in accordance with an authorization* or pursuant to s. 184.4. It also exempts a person acting in good faith who assists another in the interception in any way, if that person believes, on reasonable grounds, that the person doing the interception is acting in accordance with an authorization.

Section 184(2)(*c*) and (*d*) permit certain types of interceptions required to provide or maintain the *service*, or quality control of a communication service or which are otherwise necessarily incidental to managing radio frequencies, if the interception is made by one of the specified categories of worker.

Subsection (2)(*e*) permits interceptions through a computer system by persons in control of a computer system if the interception is necessary to manage the quality of service of the system or to protect the system from unauthorized use as described in s. 342.1(1) or interfering with the use of the system as described in s. 430(1.1). However, subsec. (3) places limits on the use or retention of the intercepted communication.

ANNOTATIONS

Subsection (2)(*a*) – The consent contemplated by this section is one which is voluntary in the sense that it is free from coercion and made knowingly in that the consentor must be aware of what he is doing and aware of the significance of his act and the use which the police may be able to make of the consent. However, the test employed in determining the admissibility of a confession made by an accused to a person in authority has no application. If the consent which the person gives is the one he intended and given as a result of his own decision and not under external coercion the fact that his motives for so doing are selfish and even reprehensible will not vitiate it. Coercion in this context means the use of intimidating conduct or force or threats of force by the police, but coercion does not arise merely because the consent is given as a result of promised or expected leniency or immunity from prosecution: *R. v. Goldman*, [1980] 1 S.C.R. 976, 51 C.C.C. (2d) 1 (8:1).

A consent given by a police informer is valid and renders the interception lawful notwithstanding that the informer testifies at trial that he expected to be paid for his co-operation: *R. v. Playford* (1984), 17 C.C.C. (3d) 454 (Ont. H.C.J.), revd on other grounds 40 C.C.C. (3d) 142, 61 C.R. (3d) 101 (Ont. C.A.).

The Charter does not apply, where the interception was made by Bell Canada on its own in an attempt to identify the person who was using its services to make obscene and harassing telephone calls to its subscribers. Bell Canada was not an agent of the state: *R. v. Fegan* (1993), 80 C.C.C. (3d) 356, 21 C.R. (4th) 65 (Ont. C.A.).

An accused has standing to raise the violation of s. 8 of the *Charter of Rights and Freedoms* by reason of a consent interception between an alleged co-conspirator and an undercover police officer. The accused was entitled to have the evidence of this communication excluded pursuant to s. 24(2) of the Charter if to admit the evidence would bring the administration of justice into disrepute: *R. v. Montoute* (1991), 62 C.C.C. (3d) 481, 113 A.R. 95 (C.A.).

In using a dial number recorder, Bell Canada was not intercepting a "private communication". In any event, such conduct undertaken in an attempt to identify a person making obscene and harassing telephone calls, was lawful within the meaning of this paragraph, Bell Canada being the intended recipient of the signal caused by the originator in dialing a particular telephone number: *R. v. Fegan*, *supra*. *Contra*: *R. v. Kutsak* (1993), 108

Sask. R. 241 (Q.B.). [**Note:** An authorization to use a dial number recorder may now be obtained under s. 492.2.]

Subsection (2)(*c*) – In using a dial number recorder, Bell Canada was not intercepting a "private communication". In any event, such conduct, undertaken in an attempt to identify a person making obscene and harassing telephone calls, was lawful within the meaning of this paragraph, being necessary to protect the person's rights or property directly related to providing the telephone service within the meaning of subpara. (iii). The term "person" can refer to both the subscribers and Bell Canada: *R. v. Fegan, supra. Contra*: *R. v. Kutsak, supra.*

INTERCEPTION TO PREVENT BODILY HARM / Admissibility of intercepted communication / Destruction of recordings and transcripts / Definition of "agent of the state".

184.1 (1) An agent of the state may intercept, by means of any electro-magnetic, acoustic, mechanical or other device, a private communication if

- **(*a*) either the originator of the private communication or the person intended by the originator to receive it has consented to the interception;**
- **(*b*) the agent of the state believes on reasonable grounds that there is a risk of bodily harm to the person who consented to the interception; and**
- **(*c*) the purpose of the interception is to prevent the bodily harm.**

(2) The contents of a private communication that is obtained from an interception pursuant to subsection (1) are inadmissible as evidence except for the purpose of proceedings in which actual, attempted or threatened bodily harm is alleged, including proceedings in respect of an application for an authorization under this Part or in respect of a search warrant or a warrant for the arrest of any person.

(3) The agent of the state who intercepts a private communication pursuant to subsection (1) shall, as soon as is practicable in the circumstances, destroy any recording of the private communication that is obtained from an interception pursuant to subsection (1), any full or partial transcript of the recording and any notes made by that agent of the state of the private communication if nothing in that private communication suggests that bodily harm, attempted bodily harm or threatened bodily harm has occurred or is likely to occur.

(4) For the purposes of this section, "agent of the state" means

- **(*a*) a peace officer; and**
- **(*b*) a person acting under the authority of, or in cooperation with, a peace officer. 1993, c. 40, s. 4.**

CROSS-REFERENCES

Consent to interception is given an expanded meaning in s. 183.1. Although "bodily harm" is not defined in this Part, reference might be made to the definition in s. 267. The terms "electro-magnetic, acoustic, mechanical or other device", "intercept", "private communication" are defined in s. 183. The term "peace officer" is defined in s. 2.

Since the interception under this section is made with consent of one of the parties, no offence is committed under s. 184. The purpose of this section is to make lawful, interceptions by agents of the state even though the interception is made without court authorization. Since the exception is relatively narrowly drawn, the expectation would be that the evidence would not be rendered inadmissible by ss. 8 and 24(2) of the Charter. In normal circumstances, the police would be required to obtain an authorization under s. 184.2. In the limited circumstances where evidence which was obtained under this section is sought to be admitted at a trial, the Crown must comply with the provisions of s. 189. Section 188.2 provides protection against civil or criminal liability for a person acting under this section.

SYNOPSIS

This section permits interception of private communications by agents of the state [defined in subsec. (2)], although there is no court authorization. The section is narrowly focused and applies only where a party to the communication consents to the interception, the agent of the state believes on reasonable grounds that there is a risk of bodily harm to the person who consented, and the purpose of the interception is to prevent bodily harm. Thus, unlike the normal authorization provisions such as s. 186, the purpose of this section is not to obtain evidence. Thus, any evidence which is obtained is only admissible in certain limited circumstances set out in subsec. (2). Any recordings or notes which do not meet the requirements of subsec. (2) are to be destroyed.

INTERCEPTION WITH CONSENT / Application for authorization / Judge to be satisfied / Content and limitation of authorization / Related warrant or order.

184.2 (1) A person may intercept, by means of any electro-magnetic, acoustic, mechanical or other device, a private communication where either the originator of the private communication or the person intended by the originator to receive it has consented to the interception and an authorization has been obtained pursuant to subsection (3).

(2) An application for an authorization under this section shall be made by a peace officer, or a public officer who has been appointed or designated to administer or enforce any federal or provincial law and whose duties include the enforcement of this or any other Act of Parliament, *ex parte* and in writing to a provincial court judge, a judge of a superior court of criminal jurisdiction or a judge as defined in section 552, and shall be accompanied by an affidavit, which may be sworn on the information and belief of that peace officer or public officer or of any other peace officer or public officer, deposing to the following matters:

- **(*a*) that there are reasonable grounds to believe that an offence against this or any other Act of Parliament has been or will be committed;**
- **(*b*) the particulars of the offence;**
- **(*c*) the name of the person who has consented to the interception;**
- **(*d*) the period for which the authorization is requested; and**
- **(*e*) in the case of an application for an authorization where an authorization has previously been granted under this section or section 186, the particulars of the authorization.**

(3) An authorization may be given under this section if the judge to whom the application is made is satisfied that

- **(*a*) there are reasonable grounds to believe that an offence against this or any other Act of Parliament has been or will be committed;**
- **(*b*) either the originator of the private communication or the person intended by the originator to receive it has consented to the interception; and**
- **(*c*) there are reasonable grounds to believe that information concerning the offence referred to in paragraph (*a*) will be obtained through the interception sought.**

(4) An authorization given under this section shall

- **(*a*) state the offence in respect of which private communications may be intercepted;**
- **(*b*) state the type of private communication that may be intercepted;**
- **(*c*) state the identity of the persons, if known, whose private communications are to be intercepted, generally describe the place at which private communications may be intercepted, if a general description of that place can be given, and generally describe the manner of interception that may be used;**
- **(*d*) contain the terms and conditions that the judge considers advisable in the public interest; and**

(*e*) be valid for the period, not exceeding sixty days, set out therein.

(5) A judge who gives an authorization under this section may, at the same time, issue a warrant or make an order under any of sections 487, 487.01, 487.014 to 487.018, 487.02, 492.1 and 492.2 if the judge is of the opinion that the requested warrant or order is related to the execution of the authorization. 1993, c. 40, s. 4; 2014, c. 31, s. 8.

CROSS-REFERENCES

Consent to interception is given an expanded meaning in s. 183.1. The terms "electro-magnetic, acoustic, mechanical or other device", "intercept", "private communication" are defined in s. 183. The terms "peace officer" and "public officer" "provincial court judge" and "superior court judge" are defined in s. 2.

Since the interception under this section is made with consent of one of the parties and under an authorization, no offence is committed under s. 184. The purpose of this section is to deal with the implications of the decision of the Supreme Court of Canada in *R. v. Duarte*, [1990] 1 S.C.R. 30, 53 C.C.C. (3d) 1, 74 C.R. (3d) 281, which had held that a consent interception by agents of the state, although not unlawful under s. 184, was still a violation of s. 8 of the Charter, unless there was prior judicial authorization. Where evidence which was obtained through execution of the authorization is sought to be admitted at a trial, the Crown must comply with the provisions of s. 189.

Note that provision is made for obtaining the authorization through means of telecommunication under s. 184.3 in much the same way that a telewarrant may be obtained for seizure of things by search warrant. By virtue of s. 187, the material used on the application is to be kept secret and only disclosed in the circumstances set out in that section. The authorization may be executed anywhere in Canada in accordance with s. 188.1. Section 188.2 provides protection against civil or criminal liability for a person acting in accordance with an authorization. Provision is made in s. 487.02 for the making of an assistance order to require persons to co-operate in the carrying out of orders made under this section.

SYNOPSIS

This section permits the police to obtain a court authorization where one of the parties to the communication consents to the interception. Because one of the parties has consented, the requirements for obtaining the authorization are not as strict as for obtaining an authorization for surreptitious interceptions under ss. 185 and 186. The grounds for obtaining the authorization under this section more closely resemble the grounds for obtaining an ordinary search warrant under s. 487 and the authorization may be obtained for any federal offence, not just those specified in s. 183. Subsection (4) sets out the terms of the authorization and provides *inter alia* that the authorization be valid only for a period not exceeding 60 days. The time limit provided in subsec. (4)(*e*) does not apply in the case of criminal organizations, in which case the authorization may be valid for a period not exceeding one year.

ANNOTATIONS

Prior to the enactment of this section, the Supreme Court held that interception of private communications without a court authorization, even if with the consent of one of the parties to the communication, was an unreasonable search and seizure under s. 8 of the Charter: *R. v. Duarte*, [1990] 1 S.C.R. 30, 53 C.C.C. (3d) 1, 74 C.R. (3d) 281.

The absence of a requirement that other investigative means have been tried and failed does not violate s. 8 of the *Canadian Charter of Rights and Freedoms*: *R. v. Bordage* (2000), 146 C.C.C. (3d) 549 (Que. C.A.); *R. v. Largie* (2010), 258 C.C.C. (3d) 297 (Ont. C.A.), leave to appeal to S.C.C. refused 242 N.S.R. 400*n*.

This provision also applies to future crimes: *R. v. Bordage, supra.*

APPLICATION BY MEANS OF TELECOMMUNICATION / Application / Recording / Oath / Alternative to oath / Authorization / Giving authorization / Giving authorization where telecommunication produces writing.

184.3 (1) Notwithstanding section 184.2, an application for an authorization under subsection 184.2(2) may be made *ex parte* to a provincial court judge, a judge of a superior court of criminal jurisdiction or a judge as defined in section 552, by telephone or other means of telecommunication, if it would be impracticable in the circumstances for the applicant to appear personally before a judge.

(2) An application for an authorization made under this section shall be on oath and shall be accompanied by a statement that includes the matters referred to in paragraphs 184.2(2)(*a*) to (*e*) and that states the circumstances that make it inpracticable for the applicant to appear personally before a judge.

(3) The judge shall record, in writing or otherwise, the application for an authorization made under this section and, on determination of the application, shall cause the writing or recording to be placed in the packet referred to in subsection 187(1) and sealed in that packet, and a recording sealed in a packet shall be treated as if it were a document for the purposes of section 187.

(4) For the purposes of subsection (2), an oath may be administered by telephone or other means of telecommunication.

(5) An applicant who uses a means of telecommunication that produces a writing may, instead of swearing an oath for the purposes of subsection (2), make a statement in writing stating that all matters contained in the application are true to the knowledge or belief of the applicant and such a statement shall be deemed to be a statement made under oath.

(6) Where the judge to whom an application is made under this section is satisfied that the circumstances referred to in paragraphs 184.2(3)(*a*) to (*c*) exist and that the circumstances referred to in subsection (2) make it impracticable for the applicant to appear personally before a judge, the judge may, on such terms and conditions, if any, as are considered advisable, given an authorization by telephone or other means of telecommunication for a period of up to thirty-six hours.

(7) Where a judge gives an authorization by telephone or other means of telecommunication, other than a means of telecommunication that produces a writing,

(*a*) the judge shall complete and sign the authorization in writing, noting on its face the time, date and place at which it is given;

(*b*) the applicant shall, on the direction of the judge, complete a facsimile of the authorization in writing, noting on its face the name of the judge who gave it and the time, date and place at which it was given; and

(*c*) the judge shall, as soon as is practicable after the authorization has been given, cause the authorization to be placed in the packet referred to in subsection 187(1) and sealed in that packet.

(8) Where a judge gives an authorization by a means of telecommunication that produces a writing, the judge shall

(*a*) complete and sign the authorization in writing, noting on its face the time, date and place at which it is given;

(*b*) transmit the authorization by the means of telecommunication to the applicant, and the copy received by the applicant shall be deemed to be a facsimile referred to in paragraph (7)(*b*); and

(*c*) as soon as is practicable after the authorization has been given, cause the authorization to be placed in the packet referred to in subsection 187(1) and sealed in that packet. 1993, c. 40, s. 4.

CROSS-REFERENCES

This section supplements s. 184.2 and allows for the obtaining of an authorization to intercept private communications with the consent of one of the parties by means of telecommunications. The procedure is similar to the telewarrant procedure in s. 487.1 and thus see notes under that section. The material used in the application is to be kept secret in accordance with the provisions of s. 187. Provision is made in s. 487.02 for the making of an assistance order to require persons to co-operate in the carrying out of orders made under this section.

IMMEDIATE INTERCEPTION — IMMINENT HARM.

184.4 A police officer may intercept, by means of any electro-magnetic, acoustic, mechanical or other device, a private communication if the police officer has reasonable grounds to believe that

- **(*a*) the urgency of the situation is such that an authorization could not, with reasonable diligence, be obtained under any other provision of this Part;**
- **(*b*) the interception is immediately necessary to prevent an offence that would cause serious harm to any person or to property; and**
- **(*c*) either the originator of the private communication or the person intended by the originator to receive it is the person who would commit the offence that is likely to cause the harm or is the victim, or intended victim, of the harm. 1993, c. 40, s. 4; 2013, c. 8, s. 3**

CROSS-REFERENCES

The terms "electro-magnetic, acoustic, mechanical or other device", "intercept", "private communication" are defined in s. 183. An interception under this section is not unlawful by virtue of s. 184. The Crown must give notice of evidence obtained pursuant to this section in accordance with s. 189. Section 188.2 provides protection against civil or criminal liability for a person acting under this section. Section 195 makes the use of this provision reportable to Parliament. Section 196.1 requires written notice to be given to any person who was the object of the interception within 90 days after the day on which the interception occurred.

SYNOPSIS

This section authorizes warrantless interception of private communications in exigent circumstances where an authorization could not be obtained with reasonable diligence, there are reasonable grounds to believe that the interception is necessary to prevent an unlawful act that would cause serious harm and one of the parties to the communication is the person who would commit the unlawful act or is the intended victim.

The requirement that the authority to conduct a warrantless search in exigent circumstances be exercised only: (i) if there are reasonable grounds to believe that there is an urgent situation and (ii) that an authorization could not be obtained with reasonable diligence imports an objective standard of credibly based probability for each of the requirements. The provision incorporates strict temporal limitations and the onus rests on the Crown to show on balance that the conditions have been met. The provision does not violate s. 8 for this reason. [Note that the Supreme Court held that the provision did violate s. 8 as there was no mechanism for oversight through notice to persons. This constitutional defect was subsequently remedied by virtue of ss. 195 and 196.1 which require notice both to Parliament and the intercepted individual.]

INTERCEPTION OF RADIO-BASED TELEPHONE COMMUNICATIONS / Other provisions to apply.

184.5 (1) Every person who intercepts, by means of any electro-magnetic, acoustic, mechanical or other device, maliciously or for gain, a radio-based telephone communication, if the originator of the communication or the person intended by the

originator of the communication to receive it is in Canada, is guilty of an indictable offence and liable to imprisonment for a term not exceeding five years.

(2) Section 183.1, subsection 184(2) and sections 184.1 to 190 and 194 to 196 apply, with such modifications as the circumstances require, to interceptions of radio-based telephone communications referred to in subsection (1). 1993, c. 40, s. 4.

CROSS-REFERENCES

The terms "electro-magnetic, acoustic, mechanical or other device", "intercept", and "radio-based telephone communication" are defined in s. 183. Under s. 193.1 it is an offence to disclose the contents of radio-based telephone communications subject to certain exceptions.

SYNOPSIS

This section helps to fill the gap created by several cases which had held under the predecessor legislation that cellular telephone conversations were not private communications. This section now creates an offence to intercept such communications where the interception was made for gain or maliciously. Subsection (2) then integrates such communications with the rest of this Part of the Code, allowing for the obtaining of authorizations and warrantless interceptions in the same way as for private communications.

ONE APPLICATION FOR AUTHORIZATION SUFFICIENT.

184.6 For greater certainty, an application for an authorization under this Part may be made with respect to both private communications and radio-based telephone communications at the same time. 1993, c. 40, s. 4.

SYNOPSIS

This section makes clear that applications may be made at the same time for authorization to intercept private communications and radio-based telephone [i.e. cellular] communications. Such authorizations might be obtained under s. 184.2 where one of the parties consent or under s. 186 where there is no consent by any of the parties. It is unclear whether the authorization to intercept both types of communications can be contained in the same document, although there is no apparent reason why it could not. One limitation on the scope of this section is that the ordinary s. 186 authorization cannot be obtained through the telewarrant procedure in s. 184.3.

APPLICATION FOR AUTHORIZATION / Exception for criminal organizations and terrorist groups / Extension of period for notification / Where extension to be granted / Where extension not granted.

185. (1) An application for an authorization to be given under section 186 shall be made *ex parte* and in writing to a judge of a superior court of criminal jurisdiction or a judge as defined in section 552 and shall be signed by the Attorney General of the province in which the application is made or the Minister of Public Safety and Emergency Preparedness or an agent specially designated in writing for the purposes of this section by

(*a*) the Minister personally or the Deputy Minister of Public Safety and Emergency Preparedness personally, if the offence under investigation is one in respect of which proceedings, if any, may be instituted at the instance of the Government of Canada and conducted by or on behalf of the Attorney General of Canada, or

(*b*) the Attorney General of a province personally or the Deputy Attorney General of a province personally, in any other case,

and shall be accompanied by an affidavit, which may be sworn on the information and belief of a peace officer or public officer deposing to the following matters:

(*c*) the facts relied on to justify the belief that an authorization should be given together with particulars of the offence,

(*d*) the type of private communication proposed to be intercepted,

(*e*) the names, addresses and occupations, if known, of all persons, the interception of whose private communications there are reasonable grounds to believe may assist the investigation of the offence, a general description of the nature and location of the place, if known, at which private communications are proposed to be intercepted and a general description of the manner of interception proposed to be used,

(*f*) the number of instances, if any, on which an application has been made under this section in relation to the offence and a person named in the affidavit pursuant to paragraph (*e*) and on which the application was withdrawn or no authorization was given, the date on which each application was made and the name of the judge to whom each application was made,

(*g*) the period for which the authorization is requested, and

(*h*) whether other investigative procedures have been tried and have failed or why it appears they are unlikely to succeed or that the urgency of the matter is such that it would be impractical to carry out the investigation of the offence using only other investigative procedures.

(1.1) Notwithstanding paragraph (1)(*h*), that paragraph does not apply where the application for an authorization is in relation to

(*a*) an offence under section 467.11, 467.111, 467.12 or 467.13;

(*b*) an offence committed for the benefit of, at the direction of or in association with a criminal organization; or

(*c*) a terrorism offence.

(2) An application for an authorization may be accompanied by an application, personally signed by the Attorney General of the province in which the application for the authorization is made or the Minister of Public Safety and Emergency Preparedness if the application for the authorization is made by him or on his behalf, to substitute for the period mentioned in subsection 196(1) such longer period not exceeding three years as is set out in the application.

(3) Where an application for an authorization is accompanied by an application referred to in subsection (2), the judge to whom the applications are made shall first consider the application referred to in subsection (2) and where, on the basis of the affidavit in support of the application for the authorization and any other affidavit evidence submitted in support of the application referred to in subsection (2), the judge is of the opinion that the interests of justice warrant the granting of such application, he shall fix a period, not exceeding three years, in substitution for the period mentioned in subsection 196(1).

(4) Where the judge to whom an application for an authorization and an application referred to in subsection (2) are made refuses to fix a period in substitution for the period mentioned in subsection 196(1) or where the judge fixes a period in substitution therefor that is less than the period set out in the application referred to in subsection (2), the person appearing before the judge on the application for the authorization may withdraw the application for the authorization and thereupon the judge shall not proceed to consider the application for the authorization or to give the authorization and shall return to the person appearing before him on the application for the authorization both applications and all other material pertaining thereto. 1973-74, c. 50, s. 2; 1976-77, c. 53, s. 8; 1993, c. 40, s. 5; 1997, c. 18, s. 8; 1997, c. 23, s. 4; 2001, c. 32, s. 5; 2001, c. 41, s. 6 and 133(8); 2005, c. 10, ss. 22 and 34(1)(*f*)(v); 2014, c. 17, s. 3.

CROSS-REFERENCES

The terms "criminal organization", "superior court of criminal jurisdiction", "terrorism offences", "peace officer" and "public officer" are defined in s. 2. The terms "offence", and "private communication" are defined in s. 183. While the term "authorization" is defined in s. 183 to include an authorization under s. 186 and 188, it seems from the context that this section concerns an application for an authorization granted under s. 186. Prerequisites for applications for renewals of authorizations are set out in s. 186(6) and for emergency "36-hour" authorizations in s. 188. However, certain of the prerequisites in this section will be imported to the application under s. 188, in view of the lack of detail in the latter section. In addition, constitutional imperatives may require that some of the conditions in this section be imported into s. 188. By virtue of s. 187, the documents relating to an application under this section are confidential and placed in a sealed packet, which is kept in the custody of the court and not opened except pursuant to a judge's order or for the purpose of dealing with an application for a renewal. Other related provisions are as follows: s. 184, offence to unlawfully intercept private communications; s. 189, admissibility of evidence obtained through interceptions; s. 191, unlawful possession of devices for surreptitious interception; s. 193, unlawful disclosure of intercepted private communication; s. 194, provision for damages for unlawful interceptions; s. 195, report by Solicitor General of Canada and provincial Attorney General concerning applications for authorizations under this section.

Also see sections which provide for obtaining the following authorizations: s. 184.2 (consent interceptions); s. 487.01 (general warrant including video surveillance); s. 492.1 (tracking device); s. 492.2 (dial number recorder).

SYNOPSIS

This section sets out the *procedure and criteria for granting authorization* to intercept private communications, and *permits extensions* of the period within which *notice* must be given to the person whose communications are intercepted (see s. 196(1)).

The introductory words in 185(1) set out certain procedural matters which apply to an application for an authorization. It provides that the application shall be made *ex parte* and *in writing*. The only judges who may grant such authorizations are of the *superior court of criminal jurisdiction* or a *judge as defined in s. 552*. Only the Attorney General, the Solicitor General or their *agents specially designated in writing* for the purpose may sign such applications. Section 185(1)(*a*) and (*b*) set out the offences, in respect of which the Solicitor General, the Attorney General or their respective deputies may make such designations.

The written application must be accompanied by an *affidavit*, which may be *sworn* on *information and belief* by a peace officer or public officer. *Section 185(1)(c) to (h) specifies* the information the affidavit must contain.

Section 185(1)(*c*) dictates that the affidavit set out the *facts* which the application is based upon, including the *particulars of the offence*. Section 185(1)(*d*) requires that the affidavit state the *type of private communication* to be intercepted.

Section 185(1)(*e*) requires that the affidavit contain the following information: the identity of the *known persons* whose private communications are to be intercepted, a *general description* of the nature and location of the *place, if known*, where the private communications are to be intercepted and a *general description* of the *proposed manner of interception*. Note that, unlike the previous two requirements which must be satisfied only if known, the *description of the manner* of the interception *must* be given. The *person* whose private communications are to be intercepted is generally referred to as the *object of the interception*.

Section 185(1)(*f*) provides for the affidavit to give the *history of any prior applications*, including the details of any unsuccessful applications or applications which were withdrawn. Section 185(1)(*g*) states that the *period* for which the *authorization is sought* must be set out in the affidavit.

The final requirement is that the affidavit must state if *other investigative procedures have been tried and failed* or why they appear *unlikely to succeed* or why the matter is so *urgent* that it is *impractical* to pursue other means of investigation. However, this requirement does not apply in relation to an offence under ss. 467.11 to 467.13 or an offence committed for the benefit, etc., of a criminal organization, or a terrorism offence.

Pursuant to subsec. (1.1), the investigative necessity requirement is not a constitutional requirement. Accordingly, where the wiretap authorization relates to a criminal organization, the provision allowing the authorization without the need for investigative necessity does not violate s. 8 of the Charter. In addition, there is no constitutional requirement that an authorization be time-limited to 60 days. In this case, the extension of the wiretap authorization for a one-year period was not unreasonable or contrary to s. 8 of the Charter: *R. v. Doiron* (2007), 221 C.C.C. (3d) 97 (N.B.C.A.), leave to appeal to S.C.C. refused 223 C.C.C. (3d) vi.

Section 185(2) to (5) provides that the *notice period* within which the object of the interception is to be notified (s. 196(1)) may be *extended on application* of the Attorney General or Solicitor General. It permits a judge issuing an authorization to grant such an extension. Section 185(2) requires that either the Attorney General or Solicitor General must *personally sign* the application for this extension. The extension may be for up to *three years*. Subsection (3) requires that the judge considering the application for the authorization must first consider the application to extend notice under subsec. (2). The test to be applied by the judge, in granting the extension of notice, is that the *interests of justice* warrant the granting of it. However, subsec. (4) provides that, if the judge *declines to grant the application under subsection (2)*, the *applicant for the authorization* may *withdraw* it, in which event the judge shall not consider the application for an authorization and must return all *materials* relating to the application for the extension of the notice period under subsec. (2) and to the application for authorization to the applicant.

By virtue of s. 487.01(5), this section applies to general warrants to do video surveillance.

ANNOTATIONS

Jurisdiction of judge – As offences under the [former] *Narcotic Control Act* are ones in respect of which proceedings may be validly instituted at the instance of the Government of Canada and conducted by or on behalf of the Attorney General of Canada (in view of *R. v. Hauser*, [1979] 1 S.C.R. 984, 46 C.C.C. (2d) 481, 8 C.R. (3d) 89) an agent designated by the Solicitor General of Canada may apply for an authorization in respect of such offences: *R. v. Cordes*, [1979] 1 S.C.R. 1062, 47 C.C.C. (2d) 46 (7:0).

Since the definition of Attorney General of Canada in s. 2, *supra*, is in respect *inter alia* to both proceedings under other Federal Acts and a conspiracy under this Act to commit an offence under another Federal Act, only the provincial Attorney General has the power under para. (*b*) to designate an agent for applications in connection with the *Criminal Code* offences enumerated under this Part: *R. v. Hancock and Proulx* (1976), 30 C.C.C. (2d) 544 (B.C.C.A.).

The grounds for the application (subsec. (1)(*c*)) – An affidavit supporting an authorization must be full, frank, clear and concise. The use of boiler-plate language, which may be misleading, should be avoided. Although there is no legal requirement to do so, consideration should be given to obtaining affidavits directly from those with the best firsthand knowledge of the facts: *R. v. Araujo*, [2000] 2 S.C.R. 992, 149 C.C.C. (3d) 449. The prerequisite for the granting of the authorization, as set out in s. 186(1)(*a*), that the granting of the authorization be in the best interest of the administration of justice imports as a minimum requirement, consistent with s. 8 of the *Charter of Rights and Freedoms*, that the judge be satisfied that there are reasonable and probable grounds to believe that a particular offence or a conspiracy, attempt or incitement to commit it has been, or is being committed and that the authorization sought will afford evidence of that offence: *R. v. Duarte*, [1990] 1 S.C.R. 30, 53 C.C.C. (3d) 1.

The failure of the officer to swear that he had reasonable and probable grounds to support his belief was not a fatal defect. What is required is disclosure of the facts relied upon to justify the belief that an authorization should be granted: *R. v. Bicknell* (1988), 41 C.C.C. (3d) 545 (B.C.C.A.).

The failure of an explicit statement attesting to belief in the informer's reliability is not fatal to the authorization: *R. v. Al-Maliki* (2005), 201 C.C.C. (3d) 96 (B.C.C.A.).

Type of communication to be intercepted (subsec. (1)(*c*)) – The affidavit must comply frankly, fully and fairly with the provisions of this section and the authorities must not try to conceal their true intention from the authorizing judge. In *R. v. Gill* (1980), 56 C.C.C. (2d) 169 (B.C.C.A.), it was held that the affidavit by "obfuscation" concealed or failed to reveal the clear intention of the police to intercept the face-to-face oral communications between certain persons who were to be placed in the same gaol cell and as a consequence failed to comply with subsec. (1)(*c*) and (*e*).

Identification of "known" persons (subsec. (1)(*e*)) – A person is known within the meaning of subsec. (1)(*e*), if the police know of the existence of such person and have reasonable and probable grounds to believe that interception of her communications *may* assist. If the person meets both of those requirements then interception of her private communications cannot be lawfully made under a "basket clause" for unknown persons: *R. v. Chesson*, [1988] 2 S.C.R. 148, 43 C.C.C. (3d) 353 (4:0).

In the subsequent case of *R. v. Duarte, supra*, the court accepted that the prerequisite that the granting of the authorization be in the best interest of the administration of justice in s. 186(1)(*a*) imported as a minimum requirement, consistent with s. 8 of the *Charter of Rights and Freedoms*, that the judge be satisfied that there are reasonable and probable grounds to believe that an offence has been or is being committed and that the authorization sought *will* afford evidence of that offence. Care should therefore be taken in the drafting of the affidavit to ensure that, in simply following the wording of subsec. (1)(*e*), the authorities do not adopt too low a test in setting out the grounds required by subsec. (1)(*c*) upon which the authorization may be granted.

This provision does not distinguish between categories of "principal" known persons and "other" known persons: *R. v. Mahal* (2012), 292 C.C.C. (3d) 252 (Ont. C.A.), leave to appeal to S.C.C. refused 2013 CarswellOnt 4853.

The threshold for naming someone as a "known person" within the meaning of subsec. (1)(*e*) is not onerous: *R. v. Mahal, supra*; *R. v. Hafizi* (2016), 343 C.C.C. (3d) 380 (Ont. C.A.). However, a bare suspicion is not sufficient: *R. v. Ascencio-Chavez* (2016), 341 C.C.C. (3d) 147 (B.C.C.A.), leave to appeal to S.C.C. refused *R. v. Montgomery*, 2017 CarswellBC 637.

Necessity requirement (subsec. (1)(*h*)) – Investigative necessity requires that, practically speaking, there are no other reasonable means of investigation in the particular circumstances of the case: *R. v. Araujo*, [2000] 2 S.C.R. 992, 149 C.C.C. (3d) 449, 193 D.L.R. (4th) 440.

An authorization cannot be granted to prevent criminal activity in the future or to uncover evidence of unknown crimes. In this case, an authorization should not have been granted where the police were not investigating any specific crime known to them but were simply attempting to stop what they believed to be a continuing criminal activity by named individuals: *R. v. Grant* (1998), 130 C.C.C. (3d) 53 (Man. C.A.).

The fact that the police have enough information to lay a charge is not a bar to obtaining an authorization where there are grounds for permitting the investigation to continue by means of intercepted communications as where there is a reasonable expectation that evidence of a further offence might also be obtained: *R. v. Paulson* (1995), 97 C.C.C. (3d) 344 (B.C.C.A.).

Prior authorizations (subsec. (1)(*f*)) / *Also see cases noted under s. 186(6)* – On an application for a subsequent authorization in the same investigation there must be full and frank disclosure, but the requirements set out in s. 186(6) need not be complied with: *R. v.*

Moore; R. v. Bogdanich (1993), 81 C.C.C. (3d) 161 (B.C.C.A.), affd [1995] 1 S.C.R. 756, 95 C.C.C. (3d) 288.

JUDGE TO BE SATISFIED / Exception for criminal organizations and terrorism offences / Where authorization not to be given / Terms and conditions / Content and limitation of authorization / Persons designated / Installation and removal of device / Removal after expiry of authorization / Renewal of authorization / Renewal / Related warrant or order.

186. (1) An authorization under this section may be given if the judge to whom the application is made is satisfied

- **(*a*) that it would be in the best interests of the administration of justice to do so; and**
- **(*b*) that other investigative procedures have been tried and have failed, other investigative procedures are unlikely to succeed or the urgency of the matter is such that it would be impractical to carry out the investigation of the offence using only other investigative procedures.**

(1.1) Notwithstanding paragraph (1)(*b*), that paragraph does not apply where the judge is satisfied that the application for an authorization is in relation to

- **(*a*) an offence under section 467.11, 467.111, 467.12 or 467.13;**
- **(*b*) an offence committed for the benefit of, at the direction of or in association with a criminal organization; or**
- **(*c*) a terrorism offence.**

(2) No authorization may be given to intercept a private communication at the office or residence of a solicitor, or at any other place ordinarily used by a solicitor and by other solicitors for the purpose of consultation with clients, unless the judge to whom the application is made is satisfied that there are reasonable grounds to believe that the solicitor, any other solicitor practising with him, any person employed by him or any other such solicitor or a member of the solicitor's household has been or is about to become a party to an offence.

(3) Where an authorization is given in relation to the interception of private communications at a place described in subsection (2), the judge by whom the authorization is given shall include therein such terms and conditions as he considers advisable to protect privileged communications between solicitors and clients.

(4) An authorization shall

- **(*a*) state the offence in respect of which private communications may be intercepted;**
- **(*b*) state the type of private communication that may be intercepted;**
- **(*c*) state the identity of the persons, if known, whose private communications are to be intercepted, generally describe the place at which private communications may be intercepted, if a general description of that place can be given, and generally describe the manner of interception that may be used;**
- **(*d*) contain such terms and conditions as the judge considers advisable in the public interest; and**
- **(*e*) be valid for the period, not exceeding sixty days, set out therein.**

(5) The Minister of Public Safety and Emergency Preparedness or the Attorney General, as the case may be, may designate a person or persons who may intercept private communications under authorizations.

(5.1) For greater certainty, an authorization that permits interception by means of an electro-magnetic, acoustic, mechanical or other device includes the authority to install, maintain or remove the device covertly.

(5.2) On an *ex parte* application, in writing, supported by affidavit, the judge who gave an authorization referred to in subsection (5.1) or any other judge having jurisdiction to

give such an authorization may give a further authorization for the covert removal of the electro-magnetic, acoustic, mechanical or other device after the expiry of the original authorization

(*a*) under any terms or conditions that the judge considers advisable in the public interest; and

(*b*) during any specified period of not more than sixty days.

(6) Renewals of an authorization may be given by a judge of a superior court of criminal jurisdiction or a judge as defined in section 552 on receipt by him or her of an *ex parte* application in writing signed by the Attorney General of the province in which the application is made or the Minister of Public Safety and Emergency Preparedness — or an agent specially designated in writing for the purposes of section 185 by the Minister or the Attorney General, as the case may be — accompanied by an affidavit of a peace officer or public officer deposing to the following matters:

(*a*) the reason and period for which the renewal is required,

(*b*) full particulars, together with times and dates, when interceptions, if any, were made or attempted under the authorization, and any information that has been obtained by any interception, and

(*c*) the number of instances, if any, on which, to the knowledge and belief of the deponent, an application has been made under this subsection in relation to the same authorization and on which the application was withdrawn or no renewal was given, the date on which each application was made and the name of the judge to whom each such application was made,

and supported by such other information as the judge may require.

(7) A renewal of an authorization may be given if the judge to whom the application is made is satisfied that any of the circumstances described in subsection (1) still obtain, but no renewal shall be for a period exceeding sixty days.

(8) A judge who gives an authorization under this section may, at the same time, issue a warrant or make an order under any of sections 487, 487.01, 487.014 to 487.018, 487.02, 492.1 and 492.2 if the judge is of the opinion that the requested warrant or order is related to the execution of the authorization. 1973-74, c. 50, s. 2; 1976-77, c. 53, s. 9; 1993, c. 40, s. 6; 1997, c. 23, s. 5; 1999, c. 5, s. 5; 2001, c. 32, s. 6; 2001, c. 41, s. 6.1 and 133(8.1); 2005, c. 10, ss. 23 and 34(1)(*f*)(vi); 2014, c. 17, s. 4; 2014, c. 31, s. 9.

CROSS-REFERENCES

The reference to "judge" is a judge referred to in s. 185, being a judge of the superior court of criminal jurisdiction or a judge as defined in s. 552. The terms "solicitor", "intercept", "private communication" and "offence" are defined in s. 183. "Attorney General", "terrorism offence", and "criminal organization" are defined in s. 2. Procedure for obtaining an emergency "36-hour" authorization is set out in s. 188. The documents used on an application are confidential and must be dealt with in accordance with s. 187. Other related provisions are as follows: s. 184, offence to unlawfully intercept private communications [*i.e., inter alia*, not in accordance with an authorization]; s. 189, admissibility of evidence obtained through interceptions; s. 191, unlawful possession of devices for surreptitious interception; s. 193, unlawful disclosure of intercepted private communication; s. 194, provision for damages for unlawful interceptions; s. 195, reports by Solicitor General of Canada and provincial Attorney General concerning applications for authorizations under this section.

As to the impact of the Charter on the admissibility of evidence, also see notes under s. 189.

Provision is made in s. 487.02 for the making of an assistance order to require persons to co-operate in the carrying out of orders made under this section. The interception of "consent" interceptions may be authorized under s. 184.2. Also see s. 487.01 which makes this section applicable to obtaining a general warrant to conduct surreptitious video surveillance, s. 492.1 which regulates the use of tracking devices and s. 492.2 which regulates the use of telephone number recorders.

Authorizations may be executed anywhere in Canada in accordance with s. 188.1.

As to renewals of authorizations relating to "criminal organizations" see s. 186.1.

Section 188.2 provides protection against civil or criminal liability for a person acting in accordance with an authorization.

SYNOPSIS

This section sets out the *criteria which a judge is to apply* when considering whether to *grant a request for an authorization to intercept private communications.* It also sets out what must be *contained in an authorization,* and *who may intercept* private communications pursuant to an authorization. In addition, it provides for the *renewal of an authorization.*

Subsection (1) provides two conditions which must be met before a judge may issue an authorization. The first condition is that the interception must be in the *best interests of the administration of justice.* In addition, s. 186(1)(*b*) requires that the judge be satisfied of the *necessity of this means of investigation.* This requirement parallels the contents of the affidavit in support of the application as set out in s. 185(1)(*h*). As with s. 185, this requirement does not apply where the authorization is in relation to an offence under ss. 467.11 to 467.13 or an offence committed for the benefit, etc., of a criminal organization, or a terrorism offence.

Subsections (2) and (3) impose *strict limits* on when an authorization may be given in connection with the *home or office of a solicitor* or any *other place ordinarily used by solicitors for the purpose of consulting with their clients.* Before such an authorization may be issued, the judge must be satisfied that there are *reasonable grounds to believe* that the *solicitor*, or any of the other categories of people specified in subsec. (2) (generally those who have a close personal or business tie to the lawyer), *has been or is about to be a party to an offence.* As with all references to "offence" in this Part, it is limited to those offences listed in s. 183. Subsection (3) provides that, if such an authorization is granted, the judge *must impose terms and conditions to protect privileged conversations* between solicitors and clients. A typical condition which is imposed is that such authorizations be "live monitored", *i.e.*, listened to by an officer whenever communications are intercepted to ensure that no solicitor-client communications are unintentionally intercepted.

Subsection (4) sets out the *terms which must appear in all authorizations* and also provides a general power, in s. 186(4)(*d*), to impose *other terms and conditions* which the judge considers advisable *in the public interest.* Section 186(4)(*a*) requires that the *offence* in respect of which the authorization is given be stated. Section 186(4)(*b*) mandates that the *type of private communication that may be intercepted* be stated. Section 186(4)(*c*) parallels the requirements for the affidavit in support of the application set out in s. 185(1)(*e*) which deal with the *identity* of the *persons* whose communications are to be intercepted and a *description* of the *place and manner* of the interception. The final condition which must appear in the authorization is the *period for which it is valid, not exceeding 60 days.*

Section 186(5) permits the Solicitor General or the Attorney General to designate *who may make the authorized intercept.* Subsection (5.1) provides that an authorization includes the authority to install, maintain and remove the device covertly. Subsection (5.2) gives a judge authority to authorize covert removal of a device after the authorization has expired.

Subsection (6) deals with *renewal of authorizations.* The procedure set out for renewals parallels that in s. 185 dealing with initial applications, including that they be made *ex parte* and be supported by an *affidavit.* Section 186(6)(*c*) parallels s. 185(1)(*f*). The additional requirements relate to full disclosure of the reasons for the renewal and the interceptions made to date under the original authorization. In addition, the applicant must provide whatever other information the judge hearing the application may require. The *criteria* to be applied in deciding whether to *grant a renewal* are set out in subsec. (7). If the conditions set out in subsec. (1) still obtain, the judge *may* grant the *renewal* for *no more than 60 days.*

The time limit provided in subsecs. (4)(*e*) and (7) does not apply in the case of criminal organizations, in which case the authorization or renewal may be valid for a period not exceeding one year.

ANNOTATIONS

Unlawful interception – Evidence of private communications, intercepted by the police with the consent of one of the parties to the communication but without an authorization, violates s. 8 of the *Canadian Charter of Rights and Freedoms* and the evidence will be inadmissible if its admission would bring the administration of justice into disrepute within the meaning of s. 24(2) of the Charter. Where, however, the police acted in good faith, in reasonable reliance on what they understood the law to be as set out in s. 184(2)(*a*), then the evidence should be admitted: *R. v. Duarte*, [1990] 1 S.C.R. 30, 53 C.C.C. (3d) 1.

Where the evidence of the intercepted communication was inadmissible against the co-conspirator by reason of a violation of the Charter then it was not admissible against the accused. Where the Crown seeks to rely on the co-conspirators exception to the hearsay rule, there is a threshold condition that the tendered evidence be admissible against the person who actually made the statements in question: *R. v. Montoute* (1991), 62 C.C.C. (3d) 481 (Alta. C.A.).

Conversations between the accused and the co-accused were admissible only against the co-accused because the accused's rights under s. 8 of the Charter were violated. The authorization named the co-accused but did not name the accused and did not include a basket clause: *R. v. Mooring* (1999), 137 C.C.C. (3d) 324 (B.C.C.A.).

Where there is a clear dividing line between the good and bad parts of an authorization so that they are not so interwoven that they cannot be separated but are actually separate authorizations given in the same order, the court can divide the order, preserve the valid portion which then forms the authorization: *R. v. Grabowski*, [1985] 2 S.C.R. 434, 22 C.C.C. (3d) 449 (7:0).

Subsection (1)(*a*) – Surreptitious electronic surveillance constitutes a search or seizure within the meaning of s. 8 of the Charter: *R. v. Duarte, supra.*

In *R. v. Duarte, supra*, the court accepted that the prerequisite that the granting of the authorization be in the best interest of the administration of justice imported as a minimum requirement, consistent with s. 8 of the Charter, that the judge be satisfied that there are reasonable and probable grounds to believe that an offence has been, or is being, committed and that the authorization sought will afford evidence of that offence.

Hearsay statements of an informer may provide reasonable and probable grounds to justify the granting of an authorization to intercept private communications. A tip from an informer by itself, however, is insufficient to establish reasonable and probable grounds. The reliability of the tip is to be assessed by recourse to the totality of the circumstances. The court will look to a variety of factors including the degree of detail of the tip, the informer's source of knowledge, and any *indicia* of the informer's reliability such as past performance or confirmation from other investigative sources. The results of the interception cannot, however, *ex post facto* provide evidence of the reliability of the information: *R. v. Garofoli*, [1990] 2 S.C.R. 1421, 60 C.C.C. (3d) 161 (5:2).

Subsection (1)(*b*) – See notes under heading **Necessity requirement (subsec. (1)(*h*))** in s. 185.

Subsection (1.1) – The investigative necessity requirement is not a constitutional requirement. Accordingly, where the wiretap authorization relates to a criminal organization, the provision allowing the authorization without the need for investigative necessity does not violate s. 8 of the Charter. In addition, there is no constitutional requirement that an authorization be time-limited to 60 days. In this case, the extension of the wiretap authorization for a one-year period was not unreasonable or contrary to s. 8 of the Charter: *R. v. Doiron* (2007), 221 C.C.C. (3d) 97 (N.B.C.A.), leave to appeal to S.C.C. refused 223 C.C.C. (3d) vi (S.C.C.). See also: *R. v. Lucas* (2014), 313 C.C.C. (3d) 159 (Ont. C.A.), leave to appeal to S.C.C. refused 2015 CarswellOnt 639.

Subsections (2), (3) / *Interception of solicitor-client communications* – In seeking to admit private communications intercepted pursuant to an authorization there is no burden on the

Crown to prove this subsection has not been breached: *R. v. Lyons* (1979), 52 C.C.C. (2d) 113 (B.C. Co. Ct.).

A police cell block where lawyers were permitted to consult with their clients was nevertheless held not to be a place ordinarily used by a solicitor for the purpose of consultation with clients. Use of the cells in this manner constituted an unusual or extraordinary use: *R. v. Johnny and Billy* (1981), 62 C.C.C. (2d) 33 (B.C.S.C.), affd 5 C.C.C. (3d) 538 (C.A.).

A jail telephone is not a "place" where a solicitor ordinarily consults with clients. Accordingly, the imposition of a live monitoring condition requiring the recording to be stopped when the accused was speaking to a solicitor struck the appropriate balance: *R. v. Blais* (2003), 182 C.C.C. (3d) 39 (Ont. C.A.).

In *R. v. Taylor* (1997), 121 C.C.C. (3d) at p. 353 (B.C.C.A.), affd [1998] 1 S.C.R. 26, 121 C.C.C. (3d) 353, the court held that a term in an authorization prohibiting interceptions "at" the office of a solicitor was not violated where the interception was of the communication by a named target while using his cellular phone, even though the recipient was at a law office. The place of interception was not at the office but at the distribution centre for cellular calls.

A practicing solicitor can be named in an authorization as a known person in limited circumstances even though the provisions of this section had not been established — for instance, where there is a credibly based probability that a non-privileged communication of potential investigative assistance would occur between a practicing solicitor and another at a location other than a solicitor's home or office: *R. v. Mastop* (2012), 296 C.C.C. (3d) 205 (B.C.S.C.).

Subsection (3) – This subsection does not require that the judge impose conditions if he does not consider them advisable: *R. v. Chambers* (1983), 9 C.C.C. (3d) 132 (B.C.C.A.), affd [1986] 2 S.C.R. 29, 26 C.C.C. (3d) 353.

Subsection (4) / Contents of authorization / The offence (para. (*a*)) – The purpose of this requirement is to demonstrate, on the face of the authorization, that the judge has exercised his jurisdiction within the limits described in s. 183 and thus a simple generic statement of the offence, in this case "murder" and "conspiracy to commit murder", is sufficient: *R. v. Mathurin* (1978), 41 C.C.C. (2d) 263 (Que. C.A.).

Basket clause (para. (*c*)) – In a case involving consideration of the former s. 178.13(2)(*c*) it was held that an authorization providing for the interception of the private communications of a certain named person and that "such interceptions" may be made at certain addresses does not authorize the interception of the communications of other unnamed persons at those addresses. It was clear from the wording of the clause that it was not intended to operate as a "basket clause" so as to authorize the interception of conversations of unknown persons at those addresses: *R. v. Douglas* (1977), 33 C.C.C. (2d) 395 (Ont. C.A.).

An authorization simply authorizing the interception of conversations of certain named persons and "other persons as yet unknown who may become identified within the time limit of this authorization" did not sufficiently comply with the former s. 178.13(2) in so far as it purported to authorize the interception of private communications of unknown persons. Nor was this defect cured by inclusion in the authorization of the standard clause authorizing the installation of electromagnetic and other devices. This clause was not a description of the manner of interception within the meaning of that subsection: *R. v. Badovinac* (1977), 34 C.C.C. (2d) 65 (Ont. C.A.).

A "basket clause" must identify the class of persons who are to be intercepted and may not simply delegate that function to the police by identifying the unknown persons who may be intercepted as persons of whom there are reasonable and probable grounds to believe that the interception of their private communications may assist the investigation of any of the offences named in the order. This wording, virtually identical to s. 185(1)(*e*) simply vests a discretion in the police to determine who may be intercepted: *R. v. Paterson* (1985), 18 C.C.C. (3d) 137 (Ont. C.A.), affd [1987] 2 S.C.R. 291, 39 C.C.C. (3d) 575 (7:0).

To be named in the authorization as a known person, the existence of that person must be known to the police and must be one the interception of whose private communications there are reasonable grounds to believe may assist the investigation of the offence. If at the time the police apply for an authorization a person meets these criteria she will be a known person and therefore if her communications are to be admitted, she must be named in the authorization as a target for interception: *R. v. Chesson*, [1988] 2 S.C.R. 148, 43 C.C.C. (3d) 353 (4:0).

This provision does not distinguish between categories of "principal" known persons and "other" known persons: *R. v. Mahal* (2012), 292 C.C.C. (3d) 252 (Ont. C.A.), application for judicial review refused 2013 CarswellOnt 4853 (S.C.C.), leave to appeal to S.C.C. refused 2013 CarswellOnt 4853.

A new authorization does not have to be obtained for each unknown person as soon as he becomes known during the duration of an authorization: *R. v. Gray* (1998), 132 C.C.C. (3d) 565 (N.B.C.A.).

Place of interception (para. (*c*)) – A clause in an authorization purporting to authorize the interception of a named person's communications without any limitation as to place is invalid: *R. v. Ritch* (1982), 69 C.C.C. (2d) 289 (Alta. C.A.) affd [1984] 2 S.C.R. 333 *sub nom. R. v. Brese* 16 C.C.C. (3d) 191*n* (7:0). Similarly, *R. v. Grabowski*, [1985] 2 S.C.R. 434, 22 C.C.C. (3d) 449 (7:0), where it was held that a clause was invalid which authorized interception of the private communications of named persons and unknown persons provided for by the "basket clause" at any place where such persons could be found. As it stood, the authorization contained no limitations as to persons or place or interception. However, the authorization was severable and the offending clause relating to interception at unspecified locations could be excluded.

A clause in an authorization may validly provide for interception of private communications at places resorted to by the named targets. Inclusion of such a clause does not, *per se,* infringe s. 8 of the Charter. The judge can properly find that there are reasonable and probable grounds for believing that evidence will be obtained as to the commission of the offence with respect to certain classes of places. Further, there is no requirement that the authorization include the most specific description possible, and thus a general resort to a clause was sufficient to include pay telephones resorted to by the targets. However, in some circumstances interceptions at pay telephones may violate s. 8. Thus, in this case, although prior to seeking the first of several authorizations, it was known to the police that the named targets resorted to public telephones, there was nothing in the authorizations to indicate that such telephones were to be wire-tapped nor that the slightest consideration was given to protection of the public interest by imposing conditions as contemplated by para. (*d*). At a minimum, where it is intended to intercept pay telephones pursuant to a resort to a clause, the authorization should provide that conversations at a public telephone not be intercepted unless there are reasonable and probable grounds for believing that the target was using the telephone at the time that the device was activated: *R. v. Thompson*, [1990] 2 S.C.R. 1111, 59 C.C.C. (3d) 225 (4:2).

An automobile is a "place" within the meaning of this subsection: *R. v. Papalia*, [1988] 2 S.C.R. 137, 43 C.C.C. (3d) 129 (4:0).

An authorization to intercept private communications of the accused and his parents at any place resorted to or used by the named persons did not extend to the interception of a communication where the accused was detained and the police provided a room for the accused and his parents to talk. *R. v. Mojtahedpour* (2003), 171 C.C.C. (3d) 428 (B.C.C.A.).

Where the authorization fails to describe the place at which the private communication of named persons may be intercepted, where such a description must be given as required by s. 186(4)(*c*), then interceptions made pursuant to such an authorization are not lawfully made: *R. v. Blacquiere* (1980), 57 C.C.C. (2d) 330, 28 Nfld. & P.E.I.R. 336 (P.E.I.S.C.).

Interceptions of private communications pursuant to an authorization which permits installation of a device in a motor vehicle is not rendered unlawful by reason of the fact that the device used is attached to the vehicle's battery: *R. v. Chesson*, [1988] 2 S.C.R. 148, 43 C.C.C. (3d) 353.

Description of manner of interception (para. (*c*)) – It was held in *R. v. Glesby* (1982), 66 C.C.C. (2d) 332, 135 D.L.R. (3d) 524 (Man. Q.B.), affd 70 C.C.C. (2d) 148, [1982] 5 W.W.R. 351, *sub nom. R. v. Diamond* (C.A.), that an authorization complied with the present subsec. (2)(*c*) as to generally describing the manner of interception where it authorized the police to "intercept or cause to be intercepted private communications as hereunder specified and for such purposes to take all steps as are reasonably necessary to install, make use of, monitor and remove any electro-magnetic, acoustic, mechanical and other device as may be required to implement this authorization".

An authorization complies with the requirement in para. (*c*) as to description of the manner of interception although that description authorizes the use of any electromagnetic, accoustic, mechanical or other device which in the opinion of the police is required to investigate the offence: *R. v. Lawrence*, [1988] 1 S.C.R. 619, 40 C.C.C. (3d) 192*n*.

Surreptitious entry – It is implied in the authorization that the police officer may make a surreptitious entry into private premises to install a device such as a radio transmitter where such entry is necessary to implement the authorization and the authorizing judge has not included in the authorization any limitations on or prohibition of such entry. However, the judge in the exercise of his supervisory jurisdiction should designate the procedures, devices and conditions which are necessary in the public interest: *R. v. Lyons*, [1984] 2 S.C.R. 633, 15 C.C.C. (3d) 417 (4:2); *Reference re an Application for an Authorization*, [1984] 2 S.C.R. 697, 15 C.C.C. (3d) 466 (4:2). [Also, now see subsecs. (5.1) and (5.2).]

However, the guarantee to protection against unreasonable search and seizure in s. 8 of the Charter requires that, with respect to private residences, the authorizing judge should consider what conditions, if any, are required in the public interest. In order to ensure that the authorizing judge has at least considered these matters, the authorization should, at minimum, refer specifically to each place that is a private residence and designate the type of devices that may be employed. In the absence of express mention of a private residence in the authorization, and hence this minimal protection, the safeguards provided by the judicial role are illusory. Surreptitious entry of a private dwelling which has not been specifically mentioned in the authorization is unreasonable and contrary to s. 8 of the Charter. Evidence obtained pursuant to such an entry may be excluded under s. 24(2) of the Charter: *R. v. Thompson, supra*. [However, now see subsec. (5.1).]

Constitutional considerations – "Public interest" as used in subsec. (4)(*d*) is not so vague so as to violate s. 7 of the *Canadian Charter of Rights and Freedoms*: *R. v. Shalala* (2000), 224 N.B.R. (2d) 118 (C.A.), leave to appeal to S.C.C. refused 262 N.R. 400*n*.

Other terms and conditions (para. (*d*)) – Failure to include a clause in an authorization imposing a duty on police to minimize interception of irrelevant conversations is not a violation of the guarantee to protection against unreasonable search or seizure in s. 8 of the Charter: *R. v. Garofoli*, [1990] 2 S.C.R. 1421, 60 C.C.C. (3d) 161 (5:2).

Period of time (para. (*e*)) – The authorization to comply with para. (*e*) may state merely that it is valid for a period not exceeding a certain number of days commencing on a specified date. It need not set out a specific number of identifiable days to be valid: *R. v. Murphy and Holme* (1982), 69 C.C.C. (2d) 152 (B.C.C.A.), leave to appeal to S.C.C. refused 43 N.R. 450*n*.

A statement in the preamble of the authorization to the effect that interception was to be by "electronic" means was an adequate description of the manner of interception: *R. v. Rowbotham* (1988), 41 C.C.C. (3d) 1, 63 C.R. (3d) 113 (Ont. C.A.); *Williams v. R.* (2018), 367 C.C.C. (3d) 263 (N.B.C.A.).

Severance – An authorization is severable and an offending clause relating to interception at unspecified locations, a clause which was never resorted to, may be severed and the balance of the authorization upheld: *R. v. Grabowski, supra.*

Where, however, the good and bad parts of the authorization are so interwoven that they cannot be separated, then it is not possible to sever the valid portions of the authorization from the invalid portion and the trial court has no power to amend the authorization so as to place a limit on the places where the interception of communications of unknown persons could have been made: *R. v. Braithwaite* (1986), 30 C.C.C. (3d) 348, 72 A.R. 227 (C.A.).

Review of validity of authorization – Since a wiretap constitutes a search or seizure within the meaning of s. 8 of the Charter, statutory provisions authorizing interception of private communications must conform to the minimum constitutional requirements demanded by s. 8 of the Charter. Thus, before granting an authorization, a judge must be satisfied that the granting of the authorization is in the best interests of the administration of justice. This requires that the judge be satisfied by affidavit that there are reasonable and probable grounds to believe that a specified crime has been or is being committed and that the interception of the private communications in question will afford evidence of the crime. In addition, the applicant must meet the requirements of subsec. (1)(*b*) with respect to the unavailability of other investigative procedures. The statutory requirements of subsec. (1)(*a*) are identical to the constitutional requirements. The review to determine compliance with the statutory minimum requirements and hence the minimum constitutional requirements is to be conducted by the trial judge rather than a judge of the court which granted the authorization. The judge conducting the review must hear evidence and submissions as to whether the interception constitutes an unreasonable search and seizure. Since this is an issue as to the admissibility of evidence, it is an issue which may be raised at trial. Applications for review should be made to the trial judge. If the judge concludes that the minimum statutory conditions set out in subsec. (1)(*a*) have not been complied with then the search is not authorized by law and is unlawful. The judge should not, however, review the authorization *de novo* and should not substitute his view for that of the authorizing judge. If based on the record which was before the authorizing judge as amplified on the review, the trial judge concludes that the authorizing judge could have granted the authorization then he should not interfere. In this process, the existence of fraud, non-disclosure, misleading evidence and new evidence are not prerequisites to a review but merely relevant factors, their sole impact being to determine whether there continues to be any basis for the decision of the authorizing judge: *R. v. Garofoli, supra.*

In *R. v. Garofoli, supra*, the court set out a procedure to be followed when editing the materials in the sealed packet containing the affidavits on which the authorization was granted. If the Crown can support the authorization on the basis of the edited material, the authorization is confirmed. If the editing renders the authorization unsupportable, the Crown may apply to have the trial judge consider so much of the excised material as is necessary to support the authorization. If the judge accedes to this request, the defence must be provided with a summary of the excised material that is sufficient to allow it to challenge the authorization, while not identifying a confidential informer. In *R. v. Crevier* (2015), 330 C.C.C. (3d) 305 (Ont. C.A.), the court provided detailed guidance in respect of this so-called "step six" *Garofoli* procedure, holding that the judicial summary must enable the accused to mount a facial or sub-facial challenge to the authorization. The adequacy of the summary plays a key role in the court's assessment of whether the accused is sufficiently aware of the redacted material so that "step six" can be employed.

Even though the accused may not have been directly incriminated by conversations recorded pursuant to an authorization, where incriminating remarks made by other individuals during the conversations would be admissible as evidence against the accused under the co-conspirators exception to the rule against hearsay, then it would seem that the accused has standing to challenge the validity of the authorization: *R. v. Durette*, [1994] 1 S.C.R. 469, 88 C.C.C. (3d) 1, 28 C.R. (4th) 1.

While an accused has standing to challenge the validity of an authorization to intercept the private communications of a third party if the accused's communications were also intercepted, he has no standing to challenge the legality of the interception of conversations of co-conspirators where he was not a party to those conversations: *R. v. Rendon* (1999), 140 C.C.C. (3d) 12, 33 C.R. (5th) 311 (Que. C.A.), affd [2001] 1 S.C.R. 997, 156 C.C.C. (3d) 222 *sub nom. R. v. Peters.*

Errors in the information presented to the authorizing judge, whether advertent or even fraudulent, are only factors to be considered in deciding whether or not to set aside the authorization. The trial judge should examine the information in the affidavit which was independent of the evidence found to be misleading to determine whether there was sufficient reliable information to support an authorization: *R. v. Bisson*, [1994] 3 S.C.R. 1097, 94 C.C.C. (3d) 94, 65 Q.A.C. 241.

Where the information filed in support of the authorization included a reference to a Crime Stoppers tip which was subject to the police informer privilege, the Crown should have been entitled to withdraw the reference to the tip from the information and to defend the authorization without reference to this information: *R. v. Leipert*, [1997] 1 S.C.R. 281, 112 C.C.C. (3d) 385, 4 C.R. (5th) 259.

An affidavit supporting an authorization must be full, frank, clear and concise. The use of boiler-plate language, which may be misleading, should be avoided. Although there is no legal requirement to do so, consideration should be given to obtaining affidavits directly from those with the best firsthand knowledge of the facts. Where the reliability of the content of the affidavit is challenged, the question is whether there was at least some evidence that might reasonably be believed on the basis of which the authorization could have been granted. The question is not whether in the opinion of the reviewing judge, the application should have been granted at all by the authorizing judge. In engaging in this analysis, the reviewing judge must exclude erroneous information. If the police acted in good faith, then the reviewing judge may consider the amplification of the record on the review. Amplification, however, must not become a means of circumventing the prior authorization requirement. Amplification is permissible where the police had the requisite reasonable and probable grounds and demonstrated investigative necessity but have, in good faith, made some minor, technical error in the drafting of their affidavit material: *R. v. Araujo*, [2000] 2 S.C.R. 992, 149 C.C.C. (3d) 449, 193 D.L.R. (4th) 440.

In *R. v. Araujo, supra*, the court referred with apparent approval to the decision in *R. v. Morris* (1998), 134 C.C.C. (3d) 539, 23 C.R. (5th) 354 (N.S.C.A.), where it was held that while even fraudulent errors do not automatically invalidate the warrant, this does not mean that errors, particularly deliberate ones, are irrelevant in the review process. While not leading to automatic vitiation of the warrant, there remains the need to protect the prior authorization process. In appropriate circumstances the reviewing judge may conclude on the totality of the circumstances that the conduct of the police in seeking prior authorization was so subversive of that process that the resulting warrant must be set aside to protect the process and the preventive function it serves.

Where the wiretap authorization has been granted but evidence has not yet been obtained pursuant to it, an application to review the granting of the authorization may be brought before the authorizing judge. In any other case, there will necessarily be an issue to the admissibility of the evidence obtained, which should be determined by the trial judge: *R. v. Santos*, [2000] W.W.R. 103 (Man. Q.B.).

The absence of a complete jurat on the affidavit for the authorization did not render it invalid. The jurat is a certificate; it is not the oath itself: *Williams v. R.* (2018), 367 C.C.C. (3d) 263 (N.B.C.A.).

Cross-examination of deponent of affidavit – While the accused has no right to cross-examine the deponent of the affidavit, the trial judge should grant leave to cross-examine where satisfied that cross-examination is necessary to enable the accused to make full answer and defence. A basis must be shown by the accused for the view that the cross-examination will elicit testimony tending to discredit the existence of one of the preconditions to the authorization, as, for example, the existence of reasonable and probable grounds. The test previously applied by most of the lower courts, refusing to permit counsel for the accused to cross-examine the deponent of the affidavit unless there was *prima facie* proof of a deliberate falsehood or reckless disregard for the truth in respect of statements in the affidavit and that this false statement is necessary to the finding that there were grounds for granting the authorization, was too strict. Cross-examination will be limited by the trial judge to questions that are directed to establish that there was no basis upon which the authorization could have been granted. With respect to confidential informers, there is no right to cross-examine. The informer is not a witness and cannot be identified, unless the accused brings himself within the exception which permits disclosure of the informer's identity where the accused's innocence is at stake: *R. v. Garofoli, supra.*

In *R. v. Pires; R. v. Lising*, [2005] 3 S.C.R. 343, 201 C.C.C. (3d) 449, 33 C.R. (6th) 241, the Supreme Court of Canada held that subsequent Charter jurisprudence did not result in the abolition or relaxation of the *Garofoli, supra*, leave requirement. The *Garofoli* threshold was consistent with Charter principles. The review hearing was not intended to test the merits of the Crown's allegations in respect of the offence charged, but only the sufficiency of the information supporting the wiretap authorization. Accordingly, cross-examination could not be permitted where there was no reasonable likelihood that it would impact on the admissibility of the evidence, particularly having regard to the concern over the prolixity of proceedings and the need to protect informants.

Where the actual deponent of the affidavit had only a limited role in the investigation, the accused should be permitted to cross-examine the sub-affiant police officers who were actively involved in the investigation and provided the deponent with the information used for the affidavit: *R. v. Pasaluko* (1992), 77 C.C.C. (3d) 190 (B.C.S.C.).

A judge presiding at a preliminary inquiry has jurisdiction to grant leave to the accused to cross-examine police witnesses on affidavits used to obtain an authorization: *R. v. Dawson* (1998), 123 C.C.C. (3d) 385, 15 C.R. (5th) 201 (Ont. C.A.).

Subsection (5) / *[Designation of persons who may intercept]* – A designation by the provincial Attorney General is valid notwithstanding it is not expressly limited to offences within provincial jurisdiction (*i.e.*, Code offences). A designation in general terms will be construed as being so limited: *R. v. Miller and Thomas (No. 2)* (1975), 28 C.C.C. (2d) 115 (B.C. Co. Ct.). Furthermore, this subsection does not mean that interceptions may only be made by designated interceptors: *R. v. Miller and Thomas (No. 3)* (1975), 28 C.C.C. (2d) 118 (B.C. Co. Ct.).

If an interceptor is named in the authorization and described as a person designated by the Attorney General, the presumption of regularity applies and the Crown is not required to prove the designation in the absence of evidence to indicate some irregularity: *R. v. Shaw* (1983), 4 C.C.C. (3d) 348, 45 N.B.R. (2d) 21 (C.A.).

Where authority to intercept was given to a particular commanding officer or persons acting under his authority then the right to intercept would include a person acting within the scope or ambit of the general authority conferred upon him by his commanding officer. Such person need not be specifically and personally authorized by the commanding officer: *R. v. Vrany, Zikan and Dvorak* (1979), 46 C.C.C. (2d) 14 (Ont. C.A.).

Where the authorization names a certain interceptor and "any person acting under his authority" it is incumbent on the Crown to establish that the persons participating in the interceptions were in fact acting under his authority. On the other hand, interceptions recorded automatically at times when the equipment was not being monitored are admissible: *R. v. Shaw, supra.*

Subsections (6), (7) / *[Renewals]* – A renewal may only extend the time of the original authorization. It may not extend or modify the terms of the original authorization by including, for example, a person not provided for in the original authorization: *R. v. Badovinac, supra.* Nor may the renewal change the address of the place of interception: *R. v.*

Dass (1979), 47 C.C.C. (2d) 194, 8 C.R. (3d) 224 (Man. C.A.), leave to appeal to S.C.C. refused 4 Man. R. (2d) 86*n*, 30 N.R. 609*n*.

Where, however, it is apparent that the second order was intended to be both a renewal of the original authorization and a new authorization it may properly include persons not included in the original authorization: *R. v. Vrany* (1979), 46 C.C.C. (2d) 14 (Ont. C.A.), application for leave to appeal to S.C.C. dismissed May 6, 1980.

Where the authorities seek to intercept the private communications of more targets then they may apply for a fresh authorization with respect to all of the proposed targets. There is no requirement that a renewal be obtained with respect to the persons named in the original authorization: *R. v. Thompson, supra*.

Further, where the authorities do obtain a second authorization, which includes additional persons and places, they do not have to comply with the provisions of subsec. (6) and thus do not have to disclose all of the details of each and every piece of incriminating evidence known to the authorities. The material in support of the fresh authorization should, however, include a full, fair and frank disclosure of relevant intercepted private communications obtained up to the time of the second authorization: *R. v. Moore: R. v. Bogdanich* (1993), 81 C.C.C. (3d) 161, 21 C.R. (4th) 387 (B.C.C.A.), affd [1995] 1 S.C.R. 756, 95 C.C.C. (3d) 288, 38 C.R. (4th) 44.

TIME LIMITATION IN RELATION TO CRIMINAL ORGANIZATIONS AND TERRORISM OFFENCES.

186.1 Notwithstanding paragraphs 184.2(4)(*e*) and 186(4)(*e*) and subsection 186(7), an authorization or any renewal of an authorization may be valid for one or more periods specified in the authorization exceeding sixty days, each not exceeding one year, where the authorization is in relation to

(*a*) an offence under section 467.11, 467.111, 467.12 or 467.13;

(*b*) an offence committed for the benefit of, at the direction of or in association with a criminal organization; or

(*c*) a terrorism offence. 1997, c. 23, s. 6; 2001, c. 32, s. 7; 2001, c. 41, s. 7 and 133(9); 2014, c. 17, s. 5.

CROSS-REFERENCES

The terms "criminal organization" and "terrorism offence" are defined in s. 2. Sections 467.11 to 467.13 create offences with respect to criminal organizations. Section 184.2 provides for an authorization to intercept communications with the consent of one of the participants. Section 186 provides for the granting of an authorization to surreptitiously intercept private communications. Section 196(5) also gives a judge power to extend the notification required under that section in case of criminal organization investigations.

MANNER IN WHICH APPLICATION TO BE KEPT SECRET / Exception / Opening for further application / Opening on order of judge / Opening on order of trial judge / Order for destruction of documents / Order of judge / Idem / Editing of copies / Accused to be provided with copies / Original documents to be returned / Deleted parts / Documents to be kept secret — related warrant or order.

187. (1) All documents relating to an application made pursuant to any provision of this Part are confidential and, subject to subsection (1.1), shall be placed in a packet and sealed by the judge to whom the application is made immediately on determination of the application, and that packet shall be kept in the custody of the court in a place to which the public has no access or in such other place as the judge may authorize and shall not be dealt with except in accordance with subsections (1.2) to (1.5).

(1.1) An authorization given under this Part need not be placed in the packet except where, pursuant to subsection 184.3(7) or (8), the original authorization is in the hands

of the judge, in which case that judge must place it in the packet and the facsimile remains with the applicant.

(1.2) The sealed packet may be opened and its contents removed for the purpose of dealing with an application for a further authorization or with an application for renewal of an authorization.

(1.3) A provincial court judge, a judge of a superior court of criminal jurisdiction or a judge as defined in section 552 may order that the sealed packet be opened and its contents removed for the purpose of copying and examining the documents contained in the packet.

(1.4) A judge or provincial court judge before whom a trial is to be held and who has jurisdiction in the province in which an authorization was given may order that the sealed packet be opened and its contents removed for the purpose of copying and examining the documents contained in the packet if

- **(*a*) any matter relevant to the authorization or any evidence obtained pursuant to the authorization is in issue in the trial; and**
- **(*b*) the accused applies for such an order for the purpose of consulting the documents to prepare for trial.**

(1.5) Where a sealed packet is opened, its contents shall not be destroyed except pursuant to an order of a judge of the same court as the judge who gave the authorization.

(2) An order under subsection (1.2), (1.3), (1.4) or (1.5) made with respect to documents relating to an application made pursuant to section 185 or subsection 186(6) or 196(2) may only be made after the Attorney General or the Minister of Public Safety and Emergency Preparedness by whom or on whose authority the application for the authorization to which the order relates was made has been given an opportunity to be heard.

(3) An order under subsection (1.2), (1.3), (1.4) or (1.5) made with respect to documents relating to an application made pursuant to subsection 184.2(2) or section 184.3 may only be made after the Attorney General has been given an opportunity to be heard.

(4) Where a prosecution has been commenced and an accused applies for an order for the copying and examination of documents pursuant to subsection (1.3) or (1.4), the judge shall not, notwithstanding those subsections, provide any copy of any document to the accused until the prosecutor has deleted any part of the copy of the document that the prosecutor believes would be prejudicial to the public interest, including any part that the prosecutor believes could

- **(*a*) compromise the identity of any confidential informant;**
- **(*b*) compromise the nature and extent of ongoing investigations;**
- **(*c*) endanger persons engaged in particular intelligence-gathering techniques and thereby prejudice future investigations in which similar techniques would be used; or**
- **(*d*) prejudice the interests of innocent persons.**

(5) After the prosecutor has deleted the parts of the copy of the document to be given to the accused under subsection (4), the accused shall be provided with an edited copy of the document.

(6) After the accused has received an edited copy of a document, the prosecutor shall keep a copy of the original document, and an edited copy of the document and the original document shall be returned to the packet and the packet resealed.

(7) An accused to whom an edited copy of a document has been provided pursuant to subsection (5) may request that the judge before whom the trial is to be held order that any part of the document deleted by the prosecutor be made available to the accused, and the judge shall order that a copy of any part that, in the opinion of the judge, is

required in order for the accused to make full answer and defence and for which the provision of a judicial summary would not be sufficient, be made available to the accused.

(8) The rules provided for in this section apply to all documents relating to a request for a related warrant or order referred to in subsection 184.2(5), 186(8) or 188(6) with any necessary modifications. 1973-74, c. 50, s. 2, R.S.C. 1985, c. 27 (1st Supp.), s. 24; 1993, c. 40, s. 7; 2005, c. 10, s. 24; 2014, c. 31, s. 10.

CROSS-REFERENCES

Note that s. 24 of the *Access to Information Act*, R.S.C. 1985, c. A-1, provides that the head of a government institution shall refuse to disclose any record requested under that Act that contains information, the disclosure of which is restricted by or pursuant to this section.

SYNOPSIS

This section sets out the manner in which certain documents relating to applications under this Part are to be kept confidential. Subject to subsec. (1.1), all documents are to be placed in a sealed packet and kept in the custody of the court. By virtue of subsec. (1.1), the authorization itself is not placed in the packet except in the case of the telecommunication procedure under s. 184.3 in which case the authorization is placed in the sealed packet and the facsimile remains with the applicant.

The other provisions of this section deal with the circumstances in which the sealed packet can be opened and the material used on the application disclosed. Under subsec. (1.2), the packet may be opened for the purpose of a renewal or further authorization. Under subsec. (1.3), a judge may permit the packet to be opened and the contents copied and examined. Similarly, the trial judge, under subsec. (1.4), may permit the packet to be opened and the contents copied and examined where application is made by the accused for the purpose of preparing for trial and any matter relevant to the authorization or any evidence obtained pursuant to the authorization is "in issue" in the trial. These applications must be made upon notice to the Attorney General.

Subsections (4) to (7) then set out the editing procedure. In summary Crown counsel will first edit the material to remove information, the disclosure of which would be prejudicial to the public interest. The accused is then provided with the edited copy. The accused, however, may apply to the trial judge for an order that portions which were deleted be disclosed to the accused. The further disclosure order will be made where the judge is of the opinion that the additional material is necessary in order for the accused to make full answer and defence and where provision of a "judicial summary" of the deleted material would not be sufficient. This process roughly tracks the decisions of the Supreme Court of Canada in *Dersch v. Canada (Attorney General)*, [1990] 2 S.C.R. 1505, 60 C.C.C. (3d) 132, 80 C.R. (3d) 299, and *R. v. Garofoli*, [1990] 2 S.C.R. 1421, 60 C.C.C. (3d) 161, 80 C.R. (3d) 317. The former decision had held under the predecessor legislation that, as a result of the enactment of the *Charter of Rights and Freedoms*, the accused had the right to access to the sealed packet in order to make full answer and defence. The latter decision had laid out a procedure for editing the affidavit and is noted below and noted under s. 186 in reference to the right to cross-examine the deponent of the affidavit.

ANNOTATIONS

Note: The cases noted under this section were decided under the predecessor legislation but were considered to be of assistance in applying this legislation.

Access to sealed packet – An application for access to the sealed packet may be made to a superior court judge prior to the preliminary inquiry. That judge may also edit the affidavit. Where, however, the accused claims that he needs access to the identity of a secret informer then that issue will probably have to be determined by the trial judge: *R. v. Giannakopoulos* (1991), 66 C.C.C. (3d) 541, 82 Alta. L.R. (2d) 243 (Q.B.).

The right to full disclosure requires that an accused, against whom wiretap evidence is to be adduced, have access to an edited copy of the affidavit in the sealed packet prior to electing his mode of trial. At this initial stage, the affidavit is to be edited by Crown counsel since only the trial judge has the power to make the final determination as to what material should be edited from the affidavit: *R. v. Aranda* (1992), 69 C.C.C. (3d) 420 (Ont. Ct. (Gen. Div.)).

Where there is likely no affidavit in the sealed packet because the application was brought on an emergency basis pursuant to s. 188 the accused is entitled to cross-examine the person upon whose submissions the order was granted: *R. v. Graves* (1987), 31 C.C.C. (3d) 552 (N.S.S.C.).

A non-accused target may apply pursuant to subsec. (1.3) to examine the contents of the packet. Different considerations, however, apply to a non-accused target who does not face the threat of imprisonment. The non-accused target's substantive constitutional rights do not compel absolute access to confidential information held by the state where the applicant does not face the jeopardy of the criminal process. In the balancing process, the state's pressing interests in the confidentiality of the package is the dominant consideration in the exercise of this discretion. A judge should normally only exercise discretion in favour of granting access to the packet to a non-accused target on the presentation of some evidence that law enforcement officials engaged in fraud or wilful non-disclosure in obtaining the authorization although such a judicial order may be justified in other cases. If the target is successful in securing access to the packet, he may only then seek access to the recording materials upon a new motion in a subsequent proceeding: *Michaud v. Quebec (Attorney General)*, [1996] 3 S.C.R. 3, 109 C.C.C. (3d) 289, 1 C.R. (5th) 1.

Editing of affidavit – If the Crown can support the authorization on the basis of the material as edited then the authorization is confirmed. If, however, the editing renders the authorization insupportable then the Crown may apply to have the trial judge consider as much of the excised material as is necessary to support the authorization. The trial judge should accede to such a request only if satisfied that the accused is sufficiently aware of the nature of the excised material to challenge it in argument or by evidence. In this respect, a judicial summary of the excised material should be provided if it will fulfil that function: *R. v. Garofoli*, [1990] 2 S.C.R. 1421, 60 C.C.C. (3d) 161, 80 C.R. (3d) 317 (5:2).

When determining whether the contents of a wiretap affidavit should be disclosed to an accused, full disclosure should be the rule, subject to certain exceptions based upon overriding public interests which may justify non-disclosure. It was improper to edit out material which had already been disclosed in earlier proceedings arising out of the same investigation. Since it is only confidential information that should be edited, the affidavits as edited at the earlier trial should have been the starting point in this case. It was also an error to excise not only information which might tend to identify informers but information obtained from informers and others and material characterized merely as commentary, summary or opinion. The discretion to determine what editing is required to ensure that the public interest is protected does not include the power to edit material whose continued confidentiality clearly is not justified by any of the public interest concerns: *R. v. Durette*, [1994] 1 S.C.R. 469, 88 C.C.C. (3d) 1, 28 C.R. (4th) 1.

Cross-examination of deponent of affidavit – See notes under s. 186 above.

Appeal or review of decision refusing or granting access – No appeal lies to the Court of Appeal from the decision of the authorizing judge refusing an application to open the sealed packet so as to prepare to review and set aside the authorization: *R. v. Meltzer* (1986), 29 C.C.C. (3d) 266 (B.C.C.A.), affd on other grounds [1989] 1 S.C.R. 1764, 49 C.C.C. (3d) 453, 70 C.R. (3d) 383; *R. v. Kumar* (1987), 35 C.C.C. (3d) 477 (Sask. C.A.), leave to appeal to S.C.C. refused [1987] 1 S.C.R. ix, 79 N.R. 395, 58 Sask. R. 80*n*.

Similarly, where the Director of Civil Forfeiture brought a civil action seeking forfeiture of property and a judge made an order unsealing wiretap affidavits under subsec. (1.3), the Director's appeal of that order to the Court of Appeal was quashed. The court held (2:1) that the unsealing order was criminal in nature, despite having taken place in the context of a civil proceeding: *British Columbia (Director of Civil Forfeiture) v. Hells Angels Motorcycle Corp.* (2014), 314 C.C.C. (3d) 229 (B.C.C.A.).

APPLICATIONS TO SPECIALLY APPOINTED JUDGES / Authorizations in emergency / Certain interceptions deemed not lawful / Definition of "Chief Justice" / Inadmissibility of evidence / Related warrant or order.

188. (1) Notwithstanding section 185, an application made under that section for an authorization may be made *ex parte* to a judge of a superior court of criminal jurisdiction, or a judge as defined in section 552, designated from time to time by the Chief Justice, by a peace officer specially designated in writing, by name or otherwise, for the purposes of this section by

(*a*) the Minister of Public Safety and Emergency Preparedness, if the offence is one in respect of which proceedings, if any, may be instituted by the Government of Canada and conducted by or on behalf of the Attorney General of Canada, or

(*b*) the Attorney General of a province, in respect of any other offence in the province,

if the urgency of the situation requires interception of private communications to commence before an authorization could, with reasonable diligence, be obtained under section 186.

(2) Where the judge to whom an application is made pursuant to subsection (1) is satisfied that the urgency of the situation requires that interception of private communications commence before an authorization could, with reasonable diligence, be obtained under section 186, he may, on such terms and conditions, if any, as he considers advisable, give an authorization in writing for a period of up to thirty-six hours.

(3) [*Repealed*, 1993, c. 40, s. 8.]

(4) In this section, "Chief Justice" means

(*a*) in the Province of Ontario, the Chief Justice of the Ontario Court;

(*b*) in the Province of Quebec, the Chief Justice of the Superior Court;

(*c*) in the Provinces of Nova Scotia, British Columbia and Prince Edward Island, and in the Yukon and the Northwest Territories, the Chief Justice of the Supreme Court;

(*d*) in the Provinces of New Brunswick, Manitoba, Saskatchewan and Alberta, the Chief Justice of the Court of Queen's Bench;

(*e*) in the Province of Newfoundland and Labrador, the Chief Justice of the Supreme Court, Trial Division; and

(*f*) in Nunavut, the Chief Justice of the Nunavut Court of Justice.

(5) The trial judge may deem inadmissible the evidence obtained by means of an interception of a private communication pursuant to a subsequent authorization given under this section, where he finds that the application for the subsequent authorization was based on the same facts, and involved the interception of the private communications of the same person or persons, or related to the same offence, on which the application for the original authorization was based.

(6) A judge who gives an authorization under this section may, at the same time, issue a warrant or make an order under any of sections 487, 487.01, 487.014 to 487.018, 487.02, 492.1 and 492.2 if the judge is of the opinion that the requested warrant or order is related to the execution of the authorization, that the urgency of the situation requires the warrant or the order and that it can be reasonably executed or complied with within

36 hours. 1973-74, c. 50, s. 2; 1974-75-76, c. 19, s. 1; 1978-79, c. 11, s. 10; R.S.C. 1985, c. 27 (1st Supp.), s. 25; c. 27 (2nd Supp.), s. 10; 1990, c. 17, s. 10; 1992, c. 1, s. 58; 1992, c. 51, s. 35; 1993, c. 28, Sch. III, s. 29 (repealed by 1999, c. 3, s. 12); 1993, c. 40, s. 8; 1999, c. 3, ss. 12, 28; 2002, c. 7, s. 140; 2005, c. 10, s. 34(1)(*f*)(vii); 2014, c. 31, s. 11; 2015, c. 3, s. 47; 2017, c. 33, s. 255.

CROSS-REFERENCES

The terms "intercept", "offence" and "private communication" are defined in s. 183. "Peace officer" and "superior court of criminal jurisdiction" are defined in s. 2.

The procedure for applying for and granting of a normal "60-day" authorization is dealt with in ss. 185 and 186. Admissibility of evidence obtained as a result of execution of the authorization is dealt with in s. 189. The unlawful interception offence in s. 184 would not apply to a person acting under an authorization granted under this section by virtue of s. 184(2)(*b*).

Authorizations may be executed anywhere in Canada in accordance with s. 188.1. Provision is made in s. 487.02 for the making of an assistance order to require persons to co-operate in the carrying out of orders made under this section. Section 188.2 provides protection against civil or criminal liability for a person acting in accordance with an authorization.

SYNOPSIS

This section authorizes *emergency applications* for *authorizations to be issued to a designated judge* and sets out an *evidentiary rule* regarding the *admission of such evidence* at trial.

Section 188(1) permits such applications to be made *ex parte* by a peace officer to a judge designated by the Chief Justice of a province, if the *urgency of the situation* requires that an *interception be made before* one could, *with reasonable diligence*, bring an application in accordance with s. 186. "Chief Justice" is defined in s. 188(4). The *peace officer* bringing the application must be *designated in writing* by either the Attorney General or the Solicitor General (depending on whose behalf the application is made) *for the purpose of this section*. Subsection (2) provides that, if the *judge is satisfied* that the *urgency* of the situation requires that the interception should begin before a conventional application could, with reasonable diligence, be made, he *may* issue a written authorization. This type of authorization can *last for a maximum of 36 hours* and may contain whatever *terms and conditions* the judge deems advisable.

Subsection (5) gives a *trial judge* the *discretion to exclude* evidence of private communications intercepted under a *subsequent emergency authorization* under certain circumstances. The circumstances triggering the discretion are that the *judge finds* that the *subsequent authorization* was based on the *same facts*, and involved the *same targeted persons or the same offence*, as the *first application* for an authorization was based upon.

ANNOTATIONS

To comply with the requirements of s. 8 of the Charter, the information which forms the basis for the application under this section must be made on oath or affirmation, or *semble*, the informant must undertake to confirm the information under oath. It may also be that s. 8 requires that the process relating to the obtaining of the authorization includes some form of memorializing or recording the gist of the sworn allegations: *R. v. Galbraith* (1989), 49 C.C.C. (3d) 178, 70 C.R. (3d) 392 (Alta. C.A.). Folld: *R. v. Laudicina* (1990), 53 C.C.C. (3d) 281, 41 C.R.R. 142 (Ont. H.C.J.).

The certificate referred to in subsec. (3) may be given at the same time as the authorization is granted and based on the same material: *R. v. Laudicina, supra.*

EXECUTION OF AUTHORIZATIONS / Execution in another province.

188.1 (1) Subject to subsection (2), the interception of a private communication authorized pursuant to section 184.2, 184.3, 186 or 188 may be carried out anywhere in Canada.

(2) Where an authorization is given under section 184.2, 184.3, 186 or 188 in one province but it may reasonably be expected that it is to be executed in another province and the execution of the authorization would require entry into or upon the property of any person in the other province or would require that an order under section 487.02 be made with respect to any person in that other province, a judge in the other province may, on application, confirm the authorization and when the authorization is so confirmed, it shall have full force and effect in that other province as though it had originally been given in that other province. 1993, c. 40, s. 9.

CROSS-REFERENCES

The various orders referred to in this section are the authorizations to intercept with consent of one of the parties [ss. 184.2 and 184.3]; the normal 60-day order for surreptitious interception [s. 186] and the emergency 36-hour authorization [s. 188]. This section also applies to general warrants to conduct video surveillance under s. 487.01(5).

SYNOPSIS

This section reverses case law under the predecessor legislation which had held that a judge in one province could not grant an authorization to intercept private communications in another province. By virtue of subsec. (1), the authorization may be carried out anywhere in Canada. The only caveat is that, pursuant to subsec. (2), if it will be necessary to enter private property in the other province or to obtain an assistance order under s. 487.02, then the authorization must be confirmed in the other province. It is unclear what material, other than the authorization, needs to be placed before the judge in the other province.

ANNOTATIONS

A confirmation order was not required to effect an interception obtained in one province where the telephone company employees in the other province voluntarily assisted the police by re-routing calls to equipment in the police interception room. Neither of the two circumstances set out in this section that require a confirmation order existed: *R. v. Pham* (1997), 122 C.C.C. (3d) 90, 164 W.A.C. 55 (B.C.C.A.), leave to appeal to S.C.C. refused 128 C.C.C. (3d) vi.

This provision is permissive rather than mandatory. Accordingly, there is no requirement for an authorization made in one province but executed in another province to be confirmed by a judge in the province of execution: *R. v. Doiron* (2007), 221 C.C.C. (3d) 97 (N.B.C.A.), leave to appeal to S.C.C. refused 223 C.C.C. (3d) vi (S.C.C.).

NO CIVIL OR CRIMINAL LIABILITY.

188.2 No person who acts in accordance with an authorization or under section 184.1 or 184.4 or who aids, in good faith, a person who he or she believes on reasonable grounds is acting in accordance with an authorization or under one of those sections incurs any criminal or civil liability for anything reasonably done further to the authorization or to that section. 1993, c. 40, s. 9.

CROSS-REFERENCES

"Authorization" is defined in s. 183. This section would therefore apply to persons executing authorizations granted under ss. 184.2, 184.3, 186 and 188, in addition to persons acting under ss. 184.1 [interception without authorization but with consent of party to communication where risk of bodily harm] and s. 184.4 [interception without authorization in exigent circumstances].

NOTICE OF INTENTION TO PRODUCE EVIDENCE / Privileged evidence.

189. (1) to (4) [*Repealed*, 1993, c. 40, s. 10.]

(5) The contents of a private communication that is obtained from an interception of the private communication pursuant to any provision of, or pursuant to an authorization given under, this Part shall not be received in evidence unless the party intending to adduce it has given to the accused reasonable notice of the intention together with

(*a*) a transcript of the private communication, where it will be adduced in the form of a recording, or a statement setting out full particulars of the private communication, where evidence of the private communication will be given *viva voce*; and

(*b*) a statement respecting the time, place and date of the private communication and the parties thereto, if known.

(6) Any information obtained by an interception that, but for the interception, would have been privileged remains privileged and inadmissible as evidence without the consent of the person enjoying the privilege. 1973-74, c. 50, s. 2; 1976-77, c. 53, s. 10; 1993, c. 40, s. 10.

CROSS-REFERENCES

The terms "intercept" and "private communication" are defined in s. 183. Section 190 makes provision for the giving of further particulars of the private communication that is intended to be adduced in evidence. The notice requirement in subsec. (5) of this section is distinct from the requirements of s. 196 which requires the Attorney General or Solicitor General to give notice to a person who has been the target of an interception pursuant to an authorization.

SYNOPSIS

This section imposes *notice and disclosure requirements* which must be complied *with before evidence* of lawfully intercepted private communications *may be received* in evidence. The accused must receive *reasonable notice of the intention to introduce* such evidence along with either a *transcript* of the intercepted private communications or a statement setting out the full particulars of the communication (depending on how it is intended that the evidence be adduced) *and* details of the place, date, time of, and parties to, the communication (if known).

Subsection (6) *protects the character* of intercepted otherwise *privileged communications* by providing that such evidence is inadmissible without the consent of the person who enjoys the privilege.

ANNOTATIONS

Many of the annotations under this section have been removed, consequent upon the amendment of this section to remove the automatic exclusionary rule for unlawfully intercepted private communications. Nevertheless, where private communications have been unlawfully intercepted then there will likely be a violation of s. 8 of the Charter. It has previously been held that a search will be reasonable if it is authorized by law, if the law itself is reasonable and if the manner in which the search was carried out is reasonable: *R. v. Collins*, [1987] 1 S.C.R. 265, 33 C.C.C. (3d) 1, 56 C.R. (3d) 193. In considering whether the particular interception was lawful, reference should be made to the notes under ss. 184 to 186 which authorize interceptions and to the notes under this section which deal with circumstances in which the interception has been lawfully made. If the search or seizure of the evidence is unlawful and unreasonable then the evidence is subject to exclusion if the conditions in s. 24(2) of the Charter have been fulfilled. Reference should also be made to the notes under ss. 8 and 24(2) of the Charter, *infra*.

The amendment to this section removing the automatic rule of exclusion where the interception was not lawfully made applies retrospectively. Thus, admission of the evidence at the accused's trial is to be determined under s. 24(2) of the *Canadian Charter of Rights and Freedoms*, and not under the provisions of this section as they stood at the time the accused was charged: *R. v. Rendon* (1999), 140 C.C.C. (3d) 12, 33 C.R. (5th) 311 (Que. C.A.), leave to appeal to S.C.C. granted 143 C.C.C. (3d) vi.

Intercepted private communications are not "conscriptive" evidence for the purpose of analysis under s. 24(2) of the Charter as explained in *R. v. Stillman*, [1997] 1 S.C.R. 607, 113 C.C.C. (3d) 321, 5 C.R. (5th) 1 [noted under s. 24 of the Charter, *infra*]: *R. v. Fliss*, [2002] 1 S.C.R. 535, 161 C.C.C. (3d) 225, 49 C.R. (5th) 395.

Meaning of "intercepted" – "Intercepted" means an interference by a third party between the place of origin and the place of destination of the communication and does not include the situation where there are only two people involved although the originator is mistaken as to the identity of the party receiving the communication: *R. v. McQueen* (1975), 25 C.C.C. (2d) 262, [1975] 6 W.W.R. 604 (Alta. S.C. App. Div.); *R. v. Singh* (1998), 127 C.C.C. (3d) 429, 178 W.A.C. 198 (B.C.C.A.).

Eavesdropping by a police officer as to the private conversation between two accused in a prison cell constitutes the interception of a private communication within the meaning of this section: *R. v. Boutilier and Melnick* (1976), 35 C.C.C. (2d) 555, 76 D.L.R. (3d) 291 (N.S. T.D.). *Contra: R. v. Beckner* (1978), 43 C.C.C. (2d) 356 (Ont. C.A.), where it was held that Part VI has no application where the conversation is merely overheard by a third party without the use of any mechanical or other device. Similarly, where the recipient of the conversation testifies as to its contents, the provisions of this Part have no application: *R. v. Gamble and Nichols* (1978), 40 C.C.C. (2d) 415 (Alta. S.C. App. Div.).

The collection of text messages that have already been sent and received does not constitute an "intercept" and therefore does not require a Part VI authorization: *R. v. Jones* (2016), 338 C.C.C. (3d) 591 (Ont. C.A.), affd [2017] 2 S.C.R. 696; *R. v. Belcourt* (2015), 322 C.C.C. (3d) 93 (B.C.C.A.).

Subsection (5) [Notice] / Persons entitled to notice – On a joint trial all the accused must be served with the notice prescribed by this subsection not merely those accused who were the subject of the interception: *R. v. Viscount* (1977), 37 C.C.C. (2d) 533 (Ont. Co. Ct.).

A co-accused has the right to notice of another accused's intention to adduce the contents of intercepted communications during the course of their joint trial: *R. v. Proudfoot* (1995), 102 C.C.C. (3d) 260, 102 W.A.C. 241 *sub nom. R. v. Steel*, 34 Alta. L.R. (3d) 426 (C.A.).

It was held in *R. v. Nygaard*, [1989] 2 S.C.R. 1074, 51 C.C.C. (3d) 417, 72 C.R. (3d) 257 (8:1), that this section applies where Crown counsel sought to cross-examine a defence witness on intercepted private communications which she had with the accused. The effect of the cross-examination substantially undermined the alibi evidence given by this witness and in reality the private communications were used as evidence against the accused. Accordingly it was necessary for the Crown to prove that subsec. (5) has been complied with.

Notice given at preliminary inquiry – A notice given prior to the preliminary inquiry remains valid for all subsequent proceedings including a trial on a preferred indictment where the accused is discharged at the preliminary hearing: *R. v. Welsh and Iannuzzi (No. 6), supra.*

The fact that the intercepted private communication was introduced at the accused's preliminary hearing does not satisfy the specific notice provisions of this subsection: *R. v. Dunn* (1975), 28 C.C.C. (2d) 538 (N.S. Co. Ct.).

Transcript (para. (*a*)) – A "transcript" within the meaning of this subsection need not be absolutely word perfect nor need it be certified by a court stenographer: *R. v. Dunn* (1977), 36 C.C.C. (2d) 495 (Sask. C.A.), affd 52 C.C.C. (2d) 127*n*, [1979] 2 S.C.R. 1012 *sub nom. R. v. Yee.*

This subsection is complied with where the transcript is in one of the official languages even where the conversation was in another language: *R. v. Ma, Ho and Lai* (1975), 28 C.C.C. (2d) 16 (B.C. Co. Ct.); *R. v. Johnny and Billy* (1981), 62 C.C.C. (2d) 33 (B.C.S.C.), affd 5 C.C.C. (3d) 538 (C.A.).

The requirement of a "transcript" is satisfied by giving the accused a copy of the actual tape recording: *R. v. Dass* (1977), 39 C.C.C. (2d) 465 (Man. Q.B.).

While it is the tapes themselves which constitute the evidence which should be and must be considered by the jury, it is nonetheless appropriate, in many instances, that transcripts not only be read while the tapes are being played but also be retained by the jury during their deliberations. Examples of cases where the trial judge might properly exercise his discretion are where the tape is in a foreign language or where the communications are lengthy or numerous. Where, however, the jury is permitted to retain the transcripts, there must be instructions by the trial judge that it is the tapes which constitute the evidence and the necessary equipment must be made available so that the jury may listen to the tapes during their deliberations. A police officer who has listened to the tapes may give evidence as to the identification of the voices reproduced and may, as well, tender a transcript which he has prepared and which he testifies accurately represents the conversations heard on the tape. The officer can, of course, be cross-examined both on voice identification and accuracy of the transcripts and it would be open to the defence to tender a witness who also has listened to the tapes and prepared a transcript setting out an alternate interpretation. The two transcripts could then go to the jury: *R. v. Rowbotham* (1988), 41 C.C.C. (3d) 1 (Ont. C.A.).

Whether the tapes of communications in a foreign language will be played for the jury during the course of the trial and whether the tapes should be left with the jury during its deliberations are matters within the trial judge's discretion. Where the communications are in a foreign language, secondary opinion evidence in the form of a translation will be essential to the trier of fact. If the translation is in the form of a transcript, the transcript should be filed but the extent to which the transcripts are read during the course of the trial and left with the jury during deliberations falls within the discretion of the trial judge: *R. v. Shayesteh* (1996), 111 C.C.C. (3d) 225 (Ont. C.A.).

While a police officer who has prepared a transcript of the conversations may not be an "expert" on voice identification, it was open to the trial judge to point out to the jury the greater opportunities the officer had for identification, provided the jury was clearly told that they were not bound to accept the officer's opinion: *R. v. Rowbotham* (1988), 41 C.C.C. (3d) 1 (Ont. C.A.).

Contents of notice (para. (*b*)) – This subsection was complied with where the accused was served with copies of the transcripts showing time, date, telephone number and parties to the conversation and told that the transcripts could be used at trial, and where his solicitor was given written notice of intention which also contained details of the date, place and parties to the conversations: *R. v. Schmitke and Mudry* (1981), 60 C.C.C. (2d) 180 (B.C.C.A.).

The words "if known" in subpara. (*b*) modify the entire phrase "time, place and date of the private communication and the parties thereto" and therefore only if the time, place and date are known need those particulars be given. Where, however, the evidence establishes that the police did have this information but did not supply it to the accused, the taped conversation is inadmissible: *R. v. Allen (No. 4)* (1979), 47 C.C.C. (2d) 55 (Ont. H.C.J.).

Identification of the place of the interception requires the prosecution to inform the accused of the location of the two telephones at the opposite ends of the communication, where they are known. Thus, where the police knew the location of the pay telephone from which a call was made it should have been identified in the notice: *R. v. Morello* (1987), 40 C.C.C. (3d) 278 (Alta. C.A.).

Subsection (6) / *Privilege* – This subsection renders inadmissible intercepted private communications between the accused husband and his wife where the wife could not be a competent or compellable witness at the instance of the Crown. The privilege attaching to husband and wife communications is not destroyed where the communication is obtained by an interception within the meaning of this Part: *R. v. Jean and Piesinger* (1979), 46 C.C.C. (2d) 176, 7 C.R. (3d) 338 (Alta. S.C. App. Div.), affd [1980] 1 S.C.R. 400, 51 C.C.C. (2d) 192*n*, 20 A.R. 360; *R. v. Lloyd and Lloyd*, [1981] 2 S.C.R. 645, 64 C.C.C. (2d) 169, 31 C.R. (3d) 157 (6:3).

While this subsection preserves privileges which are recognized at law, although the conversations have been intercepted pursuant to an authorization, the police informer privilege had no application so as to exclude conversations between the accused, a former police informer, and his co-accused a police officer. To be protected by the privilege, the actions of the informer must relate to his function as a police informer. On the evidence accepted by the trial judge in this case, the conduct and communications between the accused and other parties had nothing to do with the accused's function as an informer. The evidence showed that the accused was acting in his own interests and that of his co-accused. The fact that the accused was a police informer did not give him licence to commit criminal offences solely in his own interests: *R. v. Hiscock; R. v. Sauvé* (1992), 46 Q.A.C. 263 (C.A.)

There is no class privilege for communications between parent and child that would render intercepted communications inadmissible at the trial of the child (a young offender): *R. v. E. (T.K.)* (2005), 194 C.C.C. (3d) 496, 28 C.R. (6th) 366, 281 N.B.R. (2d) 360 (C.A.), leave to appeal to S.C.C. refused 198 C.C.C. (3d) vi. [Also see note of this case under s. 146 of the *Youth Criminal Justice Act*.]

FURTHER PARTICULARS.

190. Where an accused has been given notice pursuant to subsection 189(5), any judge of the court in which the trial of the accused is being or is to be held may at any time order that further particulars be given of the private communication that is intended to be adduced in evidence. 1973-74, c. 50, s. 2.

CROSS-REFERENCES

The term "private communication" is defined in s. 183.

The particulars referred to in this section should not be confused with particulars ordered by a court under s. 587 to supplement an information or indictment.

SYNOPSIS

This section permits a *judge of the trial court* to order that *additional particulars pertaining to private communications* be provided to an *accused who has received a notice* under s. 189(5) that the actual private communications (*i.e.*, primary evidence) will be introduced as evidence against him.

POSSESSION, ETC. / Exemptions / Terms and conditions of licence.

191. (1) Every one who possesses, sells or purchases any electromagnetic, acoustic, mechanical or other device or any component thereof knowing that the design thereof renders it primarily useful for surreptitious interception of private communications is guilty of an indictable offence and liable to imprisonment for a term not exceeding two years.

(2) Subsection (1) does not apply to

(*a*) a police officer in possession of a device or component described in subsection (1) in the course of his employment;

(*b*) a person in possession of such a device or component for the purpose of using it in an interception made or to be made in accordance with an authorization;

(*b*.1) a person in possession of such a device or component under the direction of a police officer in order to assist that officer in the course of his duties as a police officer;

(*c*) an officer or a servant of Her Majesty in right of Canada or a member of the Canadian Forces in possession of such a device or component in the course of his duties as such an officer, servant or member, as the case may be; and

(*d*) any other person in possession of such a device or component under the authority of a licence issued by the Minister of Public Safety and Emergency Preparedness.

(3) A licence issued for the purpose of paragraph (2)(*d*) may contain such terms and conditions relating to the possession, sale or purchase of a device or component described in subsection (1) as the Minister of Public Safety and Emergency Preparedness may prescribe. 1973-74, c. 50, s. 2; R.S.C. 1985, c. 27 (1st Supp.), s. 26; 2005, c. 10, s. 34(1)(*f*)(viii); 2013, c. 8, s. 4.

CROSS-REFERENCES

The terms "authorization", "electro-magnetic, acoustic, mechanical or other device", "intercept", "private communication" and "sell" are defined in s. 183. Possession is defined in s. 4(3). "Canadian Forces" is defined in s. 2 and police officer and police constable are within the definition of "peace officer" in s. 2. Under s. 193 it is an offence to unlawfully disclose an intercepted private communication.

Pursuant to s. 192, any device by means of which the offence under this section was committed may be ordered forfeited. The offence in this section can itself be the basis for an authorization to intercept private communications, by virtue of the definition of "offence" in s. 183. Related offences are the interception offence in s. 184 and the disclosure offence in s. 193.

The accused has an election as to mode of trial of the offence described in subsec. (1) pursuant to s. 536(2). Release pending trial is determined by s. 515, although the accused is eligible for release by the officer in charge under s. 498.

Note: By virtue of s. 487.01(5) the offence and exceptions in this section also apply to video surveillance in circumstances where persons have a reasonable expectation of privacy.

SYNOPSIS

Section 191 makes it an *indictable offence* to do any of the specified things in relation to *any of the devices* listed (which may be used to *surreptitiously intercept private communications*). The prohibited devices include not only any electromagnetic, acoustic, mechanical device, but extend also to *any other device or component* thereof, if *its design makes it useful primarily* for the *surreptitious interception of private communications.* It must be shown that the accused *knew* of the *nature or abilities* of the device or component. The wide-ranging description of the prohibited activities with such devices is *possessing, selling, or purchasing*. The penalty upon conviction is a maximum of two years' imprisonment.

Subsection (2) provides a series of *exceptions to liability under subsec. (1)*. Subsection (2)(*a*) to (*c*) exclude the operation of subsec. (1) to certain *classes of persons*, generally police officers, those carrying out lawful interceptions, those working under the direction of the police, or members of the Canadian forces. Such possession by the police or Canadian forces members must generally be in the course of their employment. Section 191(2)(*d*) exempts those who *hold licences to possess such devices* from criminal liability under subsec. (1). These licences are *issued by the federal Solicitor General* and may contain, pursuant to subsec. (3), terms and conditions.

ANNOTATIONS

A radio receiver tuned to a police band is not a device prohibited by this section where the evidence shows that the police are aware that members of the public have receivers capable of intercepting their communications. In such circumstances it could not be said that the device was intercepting "private communications" as those words are defined by s. 183: *R. v. Pitts* (1975), 29 C.C.C. (2d) 150 (Ont. Co. Ct.).

Similarly, *R. v. Comeau* (1984), 11 C.C.C. (3d) 61, 37 C.R. (3d) 286 (N.B.C.A.), where it was held that the use of codes by the police to disguise the broadcasts while showing an intention that they only be understood by the police was insufficient to produce any reasonable expectation that the broadcasts would not be intercepted. The originators would still expect many persons to continue to "listen" to the broadcasts.

FORFEITURE / Limitation.

192. (1) Where a person is convicted of an offence under section 184 or 191, any electro-magnetic, acoustic, mechanical or other device by means of which the offence was committed or the possession of which constituted the offence, on the conviction, in addition to any punishment that is imposed, may be ordered forfeited to Her Majesty whereupon it may be disposed of as the Attorney General directs.

(2) No order for forfeiture shall be made under subsection (1) in respect of telephone, telegraph or other communication facilities or equipment owned by a person engaged in providing telephone, telegraph or other communication service to the public or forming part of the telephone, telegraph or other communication service or system of that person by means of which an offence under section 184 has been committed if that person was not a party to the offence. 1973-74, c. 50, s. 2.

CROSS-REFERENCES

The terms "electro-magnetic, acoustic, mechanical or other device", are defined in s. 183. "Attorney-General" is defined in s. 2. A party to an offence is defined by ss. 21 and 22.

In addition to the penalties set out in ss. 184 and 191 and the order under this section, a court that convicts an accused of the s. 184 offence or an offence under s. 193 may make an award of punitive damages under s. 194.

SYNOPSIS

This section authorizes the *forfeiture of any device* which was the *means of committing an offence* for which the accused has been convicted under s. 184 (unlawful interception of private communications) or s. 191 (unlawful possession, etc., of such devices). Such an order may be made *upon sentencing, in addition* to any other punishment. The section provides that the device is to be turned over to Her Majesty, and the Attorney General may then direct how it will be disposed of.

Subsection (2) *exempts* from such order, the *listed equipment owned by a person who is involved in providing telephone* services (and other specified lawful activities) to the public. However, the exception only applies if the owner was *not a party to the offence.*

DISCLOSURE OF INFORMATION / Exemptions / Publishing of prior lawful disclosure.

193. (1) Where a private communication has been intercepted by means of an electro-magnetic, acoustic, mechanical or other device without the consent, express or implied, of the originator thereof or of the person intended by the originator thereof to receive it, every one who, without the express consent of the originator thereof or of the person intended by the originator thereof to receive it, wilfully

(*a*) uses or discloses the private communication or any part thereof or the substance, meaning or purport thereof or of any part thereof, or

(*b*) discloses the existence thereof,

is guilty of an indictable offence and liable to imprisonment for a term not exceeding two years.

(2) Subsection (1) does not apply to a person who discloses a private communication or any part thereof or the substance, meaning or purport thereof or of any part thereof or who discloses the existence of a private communication

(*a*) in the course of or for the purpose of giving evidence in any civil or criminal proceedings or in any other proceedings in which the person may be required to give evidence on oath;

(*b*) in the course of or for the purpose of any criminal investigation if the private communication was lawfully intercepted;

(*c*) in giving notice under section 189 or furnishing further particulars pursuant to an order under section 190;

(*d*) in the course of the operation of

(i) a telephone, telegraph or other communication service to the public,

(ii) a department or an agency of the Government of Canada, or

(iii) services relating to the management or protection of a computer system, as defined in subsection 342.1(2),

if the disclosure is necessarily incidental to an interception described in paragraph 184(2)(*c*), (*d*) or (*e*);

(*e*) where disclosure is made to a peace officer or prosecutor in Canada or to a person or authority with responsibility in a foreign state for the investigation or prosecution of offences and is intended to be in the interests of the administration of justice in Canada or elsewhere; or

(*f*) where the disclosure is made to the Director of the Canadian Security Intelligence Service or to an employee of the Service for the purpose of enabling the Service to perform its duties and functions under section 12 of the *Canadian Security Intelligence Service Act*.

(3) Subsection (1) does not apply to a person who discloses a private communication or any part thereof or the substance, meaning or purport thereof or of any part thereof or who discloses the existence of a private communication where that which is disclosed by him was, prior to the disclosure, lawfully disclosed in the course of or for the purpose of giving evidence in proceedings referred to in paragraph (2)(*a*). 1973-74, c. 50, s. 2; 1976-77, c. 53, s. 11; 1984, c. 21, s. 77; R.S.C. 1985, c. 30 (4th Supp.), s. 45; 1993, c. 40, s. 11; 2004, c. 12, s. 5.

CROSS-REFERENCES

The terms "authorization", "electro-magnetic, acoustic, mechanical or other device", "intercept", "private communication" and "sell" are defined in s. 183. "Peace officer" is defined in s. 2. As to cases on the meaning of consent, see notes under s. 184. As to the meaning of "lawfully intercepted", reference should be made to the exception in s. 184(2) to the unlawful interception offence. The term "wilfully" does not have a fixed meaning and must take its meaning from the context. Generally, however, it connotes an intention to bring about a proscribed consequence. See *R. v. Buzzanga and Durocher* (1979), 49 C.C.C. (2d) 369 (Ont. C.A.).

Pursuant to s. 194, the court that convicts the accused of the offence under this section may make an order for punitive damages. Under s. 195(3), the annual report of the Solicitor General and Attorneys General are to set out the number of prosecutions under this section of officers or servants of the Crown.

The accused has an election as to mode of trial pursuant to s. 536(2) and release pending trial is determined by s. 515, although the accused is eligible for release by the officer in charge pursuant to s. 498.

Note that s. 24 of the *Access to Information Act*, R.S.C. 1985, c. A-1, provides that the head of a government institution shall refuse to disclose any record requested under that Act that contains information, the disclosure of which is restricted by or pursuant to this section.

SYNOPSIS

This section makes it an indictable offence to *disclose* certain information *pertaining to intercepted private communications*, subject to certain exceptions.

The offence created by subsec. (1) contains three elements. First, the interception must have been *made by one of the devices* listed, and it must have been done *without the consent* of either the originator or the person intended to receive it. (Thus, only interceptions made lawful pursuant to s. 183.1 are excluded by this aspect of s. 193.) Second, there must be *no express consent* of such persons to use information or disclose its contents or meaning as set out in s. 193(1)(*a*) or to disclose its existence. Third, the *actions of the accused* must be proven to be *wilful*. The maximum punishment for this offence is two years.

Section 193(2)(*a*) and (*c*) and subsec. (3) are *exceptions* to subsec. (1) and apply generally to the use of such information in relation to *evidence being given in proceedings or procedural matters* in relation to such proceedings. Section 193(2)(*c*) complements ss. 189 and 190, which require certain information to be disclosed in order to provide additional information to the accused. Section 193(2)(*b*) and (*e*) relate to *law enforcement and prosecutorial needs* and permit *disclosure of lawfully intercepted private communications* to assist in the investigation or prosecution of offences. In the case of the exception under s. 193(2)(*e*), there is the additional requirement that the disclosure be intended to be *in the interests of the administration of justice*. As this paragraph also authorizes disclosure to foreign police and prosecutors, the reference to the administration of justice may refer to its benefit in Canada or elsewhere. Section 193(2)(*d*) complements s. 184(2)(*c*) and (*d*) and exempts disclosure which is necessarily incidental to interceptions described in those paragraphs which basically relate to running and servicing public telephone or other communications services or monitoring them. Disclosure to *employees of the Canadian Security Intelligence Service (CSIS)* for the purpose of carrying out its duties as specified is also exempted from liability under subsection (1). Subsection (3) exempts persons who disclose information which has already been lawfully disclosed in court proceedings.

ANNOTATIONS

Subsection (1) – The essence of this offence is the making known to another person the existence of an unlawfully intercepted private communication. It is irrelevant that the tape recordings given to the other person were of such poor quality that the voices on it were not discernible, so long as the existence of the unlawful interception was revealed: *R. v. Simm* (1976), 31 C.C.C. (2d) 322 (Alta. S.C.T.D.).

In one of the few successful prosecutions under this section the court held that the system which the accused had installed in his office and adjoining boardroom fell under the prohibition in subsec. (1). The system allowed for the surreptitious interception of private conversations in both rooms through use of hidden microphones and interception of private conversations of anyone using the accused's telephone. The accused's own testimony that he wished to use the devices to ascertain if unauthorized persons were making use of his office or boardroom constituted an admission that they would be used for surreptitious interceptions: *R. v. McLelland* (1986), 30 C.C.C. (3d) 134 (Ont. C.A.).

Subsection (2) – A witness required to testify at a public inquiry established by the provincial Government and to disclose the contents of an intercepted private communication comes within the exception in this subsection: *Re Royal Commission of Inquiry into Activities of Royal American Shows Inc.* (1977), 39 C.C.C. (2d) 22 (Laycraft J. Com'r).

A party to a civil proceeding can request the disclosure of recordings of private communications intercepted by the state in the course of a criminal investigation. Nothing in the words of para. (2)(*a*) limits its application to the time when evidence is being given at trial. The documents requested at the discovery stage of any civil proceeding may be requested "for the purpose" of testifying at the hearing. However, this section creates neither an actual disclosure mechanism nor a right of access. Recourse must be had to the applicable rules of civil procedure: *Imperial Oil v. Jacques*, [2014] 3 S.C.R. 287, 316 C.C.C. (3d) 1.

The protection afforded by this subsection also extends to civil proceedings over which the province has jurisdiction and the words "for the purpose of giving evidence" would protect the production of the tape recording prior to trial: *Tide Shore Logging Ltd. v. Commonwealth Ins. Co.* (1979), 47 C.C.C. (2d) 215 (B.C.S.C.).

Either para. (*a*) or (*b*) of this subsection permits defence counsel to cross-examine a Crown witness on intercepted private communications even if the lawfulness of the interception has not been established. In particular, as regards para. (*b*), the phrase "any criminal investigation" is not limited to a police investigation but would include the investigation carried out by counsel in the course of cross-examination at a trial: *R. v. Lessard (No. 3)* (1986), 33 C.C.C. (3d) 569 (Que. S.C.).

Paragraph (2)(*e*) does not offend s. 8 of the Charter. It reasonably limits the scope of disclosure of the products of wiretap authorizations, requiring that the disclosing party must subjectively believe that disclosure will further the interests of justice in Canada or the foreign state. A disclosing party who knows little or nothing about the justice system in the foreign state or for what purpose the state intends to use the information will have a hard time satisfying a court that this burden has been met. The same holds true for a disclosing party who has reason to believe that the information will be used in relation to torture or other human rights violations. The section incentivizes disclosing parties to proceed cautiously: *United States of America v. Wakeling*, [2014] 3 S.C.R. 549, 318 C.C.C. (3d) 134.

DISCLOSURE OF INFORMATION RECEIVED FROM INTERCEPTION OF RADIO-BASED TELEPHONE COMMUNICATIONS / Other provisions to apply.

193.1 (1) Every person who wilfully uses or discloses a radio-based telephone communication or who wilfully discloses the existence of such a communication is guilty of an indictable offence and liable to imprisonment for a term not exceeding two years, if

(*a*) the originator of the communication or the person intended by the originator of the communication to receive it was in Canada when the communication was made;

(*b*) the communciation was intercepted by means of an electromagnetic, acoustic, mechanical or other device without the consent, express or implied, of the originator of the communication or of the person intended by the originator to receive the communication; and

(*c*) the person does not have the express or implied consent of the originator of the communication or of the person intended by the originator to receive the communication.

(2) Subsections 193(2) and (3) apply, with such modifications as the circumstances require, to disclosures of radio-based telephone communications. 1993, c. 40, s. 12.

CROSS-REFERENCES

The terms "electro-magnetic, acoustic, mechanical or other device", "intercept", and "radio-based telephone communication" are defined in s. 183. The interception of radio-based telephone communications is itself an offence under s. 184.5 if the interception was done maliciously or for gain. No such limitation applies to the offence created by this section. Disclosure is permitted, however, with the consent of one of the parties or if any of the exemptions in s. 193(2) or (3) apply. Thus, see the synopsis and notes under s. 193.

SYNOPSIS

This section makes it an indictable offence to disclose certain information pertaining to intercepted radio-based telephone communications [*e.g.*, cellular phones] if one of the parties to the communication was in Canada, the communication was intercepted by means of an electro-magnetic, acoustic, mechanical or other device without the consent of one of the parties and the disclosure was not consented to. Disclosure is permitted where any of the conditions set out in s. 193(2) or (3) apply.

DAMAGES / No damages where civil proceedings commenced / Judgment may be registered / Moneys in possession of accused may be taken.

194. (1) Subject to subsection (2), a court that convicts an accused of an offence under section 184, 184.5, 193 or 193.1 may, on the application of a person aggrieved, at the time sentence is imposed, order the accused to pay to that person an amount not exceeding five thousand dollars as punitive damages.

(2) No amount shall be ordered to be paid under subsection (1) to a person who has commenced an action under Part II of the *Crown Liability Act*.

(3) Where an amount that is ordered to be paid under subsection (1) is not paid forthwith, the applicant may, by filing the order, enter as a judgment, in the superior court of the province in which the trial was held, the amount ordered to be paid, and that judgment is enforceable against the accused in the same manner as if it were a judgment rendered against the accused in that court in civil proceedings.

(4) All or any part of an amount that is ordered to be paid under subsection (1) may be taken out of moneys found in the possession of the accused at the time of his arrest, except where there is a dispute respecting ownership of or right of possession to those moneys by claimants other than the accused. 1973-74, c. 50, s. 2; 1993, c. 40, s. 13.

CROSS-REFERENCES

In addition to an order under this section, where a person is convicted of an offence under s. 184 or 191, any electro-magnetic, acoustic, mechanical or other device, by means of which the offence was committed or the possession of which constituted the offence, may be ordered forfeited to the Crown.

An order under this section may be appealed under Part XXI as a sentence appeal.

SYNOPSIS

This section permits a *court, which convicts a person* of an offence under s. 184 (unlawful interception) or s. 193 (unlawful possession, etc., of devices), to order *punitive damages* be awarded to a person aggrieved by the offence. The order is only to be made *on application by the aggrieved person* and must be made at the *time of sentencing*. The *maximum amount* of such an order is *$5000*. If there is no dispute about the ownership or right of possession (by persons other than the accused), funds located in the possession of the accused at the time of his arrest may be used to satisfy an order made under subsec. (1). If the amount of damages awarded is not paid forthwith, subsec. (3) permits the order to be *treated as if it were a civil judgment* for enforcement purposes.

Subsection (2) prohibits money being paid under this section to a person who has begun an action under Part II of the *Crown Liability Act*.

ANNUAL REPORT / Information respecting authorizations — sections 185 and 188 / Information respecting interceptions — section 184.4 / Other information / Report to be laid before Parliament / Report by Attorneys General.

195. (1) The Minister of Public Safety and Emergency Preparedness shall, as soon as possible after the end of each year, prepare a report relating to

- **(*a*) authorizations for which that Minister and agents specially designated in writing by that Minister for the purposes of section 185 applied and the interceptions made under those authorizations in the immediately preceding year;**
- **(*b*) authorizations given under section 188 for which peace officers specially designated by that Minister for the purposes of that section applied and the interceptions made under those authorizations in the immediately preceding year; and**

(*c*) **interceptions made under section 184.4 in the immediately preceding year if the interceptions relate to an offence for which proceedings may be commenced by the Attorney General of Canada.**

(2) The report shall, in relation to the authorizations and interceptions referred to in paragraphs (1)(*a*) and (*b*), set out

(*a*) **the number of applications made for authorizations;**

(*b*) **the number of applications made for renewal of authorizations;**

(*c*) **the number of applications referred to in paragraphs (*a*) and (*b*) that were granted, the number of those applications that were refused and the number of applications referred to in paragraph (*a*) that were granted subject to terms and conditions;**

(*d*) **the number of persons identified in an authorization against whom proceedings were commenced at the instance of the Attorney General of Canada in respect of**

(i) **an offence specified in the authorization,**

(ii) **an offence other than an offence specified in the authorization but in respect of which an authorization may be given, and**

(iii) **an offence in respect of which an authorization may not be given;**

(*e*) **the number of persons not identified in an authorization against whom proceedings were commenced at the instance of the Attorney General of Canada in respect of**

(i) **an offence specified in such an authorization,**

(ii) **an offence other than an offence specified in such an authorization but in respect of which an authorization may be given, and**

(iii) **an offence other than an offence specified in such an authorization and for which no such authorization may be given,**

and whose commission or alleged commission of the offence became known to a peace officer as a result of an interception of a private communication under an authorization;

(*f*) **the average period for which authorizations were given and for which renewals thereof were granted;**

(*g*) **the number of authorizations that, by virtue of one or more renewals thereof, were valid for more than sixty days, for more than one hundred and twenty days, for more than one hundred and eighty days and for more than two hundred and forty days;**

(*h*) **the number of notifications given pursuant to section 196;**

(*i*) **the offences in respect of which authorizations were given, specifying the number of authorizations given in respect of each of those offences;**

(*j*) **a description of all classes of places specified in authorizations and the number of authorizations in which each of those classes of places was specified;**

(*k*) **a general description of the methods of interception involved in each interception under an authorization;**

(*l*) **the number of persons arrested whose identity became known to a peace officer as a result of an interception under an authorization;**

(*m*) **the number of criminal proceedings commenced at the instance of the Attorney General of Canada in which private communications obtained by interception under an authorization were adduced in evidence and the number of those proceedings that resulted in a conviction; and**

(*n*) **the number of criminal investigations in which information obtained as a result of the interception of a private communication under an authorization was used although the private communication was not adduced in evidence in criminal proceedings commenced at the instance of the Attorney General of Canada as a result of the investigations.**

(2.1) The report shall, in relation to the interceptions referred to in paragraph (1)(*c*), set out

(*a*) the number of interceptions made;

(*b*) the number of parties to each intercepted private communication against whom proceedings were commenced in respect of the offence that the police officer sought to prevent in intercepting the private communication or in respect of any other offence that was detected as a result of the interception;

(*c*) the number of persons who were not parties to an intercepted private communication but whose commission or alleged commission of an offence became known to a police officer as a result of the interception of a private communication, and against whom proceedings were commenced in respect of the offence that the police officer sought to prevent in intercepting the private communication or in respect of any other offence that was detected as a result of the interception;

(*d*) the number of notifications given under section 196.1;

(*e*) the offences in respect of which interceptions were made and any other offences for which proceedings were commenced as a result of an interception, as well as the number of interceptions made with respect to each offence;

(*f*) a general description of the methods of interception used for each interception;

(*g*) the number of persons arrested whose identity became known to a police officer as a result of an interception;

(*h*) the number of criminal proceedings commenced in which private communications obtained by interception were adduced in evidence and the number of those proceedings that resulted in a conviction;

(*i*) the number of criminal investigations in which information obtained as a result of the interception of a private communication was used even though the private communication was not adduced in evidence in criminal proceedings commenced as a result of the investigations; and

(*j*) the duration of each interception and the aggregate duration of all the interceptions related to the investigation of the offence that the police officer sought to prevent in intercepting the private communication.

(3) The report shall, in addition to the information referred to in subsections (2) and (2.1), set out

(*a*) the number of prosecutions commenced against officers or servants of Her Majesty in right of Canada or members of the Canadian Forces for offences under section 184 or 193; and

(*b*) a general assessment of the importance of interception of private communications for the investigation, detection, prevention and prosecution of offences in Canada.

(4) The Minister of Public Safety and Emergency Preparedness shall cause a copy of each report prepared by him under subsection (1) to be laid before Parliament forthwith on completion thereof, or if Parliament is not then sitting, on any of the first fifteen days next thereafter that Parliament is sitting.

(5) The Attorney General of each province shall, as soon as possible after the end of each year, prepare and publish or otherwise make available to the public a report relating to

(*a*) authorizations for which the Attorney General and agents specially designated in writing by the Attorney General for the purposes of section 185 applied and to the interceptions made under those authorizations in the immediately preceding year;

(*b*) authorizations given under section 188 for which peace officers specially designated by the Attorney General for the purposes of that section applied and to the interceptions made under those authorizations in the immediately preceding year; and

(*c*) interceptions made under section 184.4 in the immediately preceding year, if the interceptions relate to an offence not referred to in paragraph (1)(*c*).

The report must set out, with any modifications that the circumstances require, the information described in subsections (2) to (3). 1973-74, c. 50, s. 2; 1976-77, c. 53, s. 11.1; R.S.C. 1985, c. 27 (1st Supp.), s. 27; 2005, c. 10, s. 34(1)(*f*)(ix) and (x); 2013, c. 8, s. 5; 2015, c. 20, s. 20.

CROSS-REFERENCES

The term "authorization" is defined in s. 183. "Peace officer", "Canadian Forces", and "Attorney General" are defined in s. 2.

SYNOPSIS

This section imposes a number of *annual reporting requirements upon the Solicitor General of Canada and the Attorneys General of the provinces*, relating to *activity under this Part* of the *Criminal Code*. Subsections (1) to (4), require the Solicitor General to cause a report to be prepared annually and *presented to Parliament*. The details of what must be in the report are set out in subsecs. (2) and (3). In broad terms, the report must provide detailed information relating to applications for authorization (whether successful or not), and the contents of authorizations which were given under the normal powers in s. 185 or emergency orders made under ss. 184.4 and 188. In addition, the results of the authorizations (for example, the number of cases in which such evidence was used and if the prosecution resulted in a conviction) must be set out. Attorneys General have similar duties imposed upon them under subsec. (5).

WRITTEN NOTIFICATION TO BE GIVEN / Extension of period for notification / Where extension to be granted / Application to be accompanied by affidavit / Exception for criminal organization and terrorist groups.

196. (1) The Attorney General of the province in which an application under subsection 185(1) was made or the Minister of Public Safety and Emergency Preparedness if the application was made by or on behalf of that Minister shall, within 90 days after the period for which the authorization was given or renewed or within such other period as is fixed pursuant to subsection 185(3) or subsection (3) of this section, notify in writing the person who was the object of the interception pursuant to the authorization and shall, in a manner prescribed by regulations made by the Governor in Council, certify to the court that gave the authorization that the person has been so notified.

(2) The running of the 90 days referred to in subsection (1), or of any other period fixed pursuant to subsection 185(3) or subsection (3) of this section, is suspended until any application made by the Attorney General or the Minister to a judge of a superior court of criminal jurisdiction or a judge as defined in section 552 for an extension or a subsequent extension of the period for which the authorization was given or renewed has been heard and disposed of.

(3) Where the judge to whom an application referred to in subsection (2) is made, on the basis of an affidavit submitted in support of the application, is satisfied that

(*a*) the investigation of the offence to which the authorization relates, or

(*b*) a subsequent investigation of an offence listed in section 183 commenced as a result of information obtained from the investigation referred to in paragraph (*a*),

is continuing and is of the opinion that the interests of justice warrant the granting of the application, the judge shall grant an extension, or a subsequent extension, of the period, each extension not to exceed three years.

(4) An application pursuant to subsection (2) shall be accompanied by an affidavit deposing to

(*a*) the facts known or believed by the deponent and relied on to justify the belief that an extension should be granted; and

(*b*) the number of instances, if any, on which an application has, to the knowledge or belief of the deponent, been made under that subsection in relation to the particular authorization and on which the application was withdrawn or the application was not granted, the date on which each application was made and the judge to whom each application was made.

(5) Notwithstanding subsections (3) and 185(3), where the judge to whom an application referred to in subsection (2) or 185(2) is made, on the basis of an affidavit submitted in support of the application, is satisfied that the investigation is in relation to

(*a*) an offence under section 467.11, 467.111, 467.12 or 467.13,

(*b*) an offence committed for the benefit of, at the direction of, or in association with, a criminal organization, or

(*c*) a terrorism offence.

and is of the opinion that the interests of justice warrant the granting of the application, the judge shall grant an extension, or a subsequent extension, of the period, but no extension may exceed three years. 1973-74, c. 50, s. 2; 1976-77, c. 53, s. 12; R.S.C. 1985, c. 27 (1st Supp.), s. 28; 1993, c. 40, s. 14; 1997, c. 23, s. 7; 2001, c. 32, s. 8; 2001, c. 41, s. 8 and 133(10); 2005, c. 10, s. 25; 2014, c. 17, s. 6.

REGULATIONS: PROTECTION OF PRIVACY REGULATIONS

2. For the purposes of subsection [196(1)] of the *Criminal Code*, the Attorney General of a province who gave a notice required to be given by that subsection, or the Solicitor General of Canada where the notice was given by him, shall certify to the court that issued the authorization that such notice was given by filing with a judge of the court a certificate signed by the person who gave the notice specifying

(*a*) the name and address of the person who was the object of the interception;

(*b*) the date on which the authorization and any renewal thereof expired;

(*c*) if any delay for the giving of notice was granted under section [196] or subsection [185(3)] of the *Criminal Code*, the period of such delay; and

(*d*) the date, place and method of the giving of the notice.

3. [*Revoked.* SOR/81-859, s. 2.]

4. A certificate filed pursuant to section 2 shall be treated as a confidential document, shall be placed in a packet, sealed by the judge with whom it is filed and kept with the packet sealed pursuant to section [187] of the *Criminal Code* that relates to the authorization to which the certificate relates. **C.R.C. 1978, c. 440; SOR/81-859, *Can. Gaz., Part II*, 26/10/81, p. 3153.**

CROSS-REFERENCES

The terms "Attorney General", "criminal organization", "peace officer", "public officer" and "superior court of criminal jurisdiction" are defined in s. 2. The documents relating to an application under subsec. (2) are to be kept confidential in accordance with s. 187.

SYNOPSIS

Section 196 provides that those persons, whose private communications have been intercepted pursuant to an authorization, be *notified that they have been the object of such an interception.*

Subsection (1) requires the Attorney General or the Solicitor General (depending on who made the application for the authorization) to provide the notification *within 90 days* after the period for which the authorization was given or renewed, unless an order was made varying such period; (the period of time for giving notice may be altered by an order under s. 185(3) or 196(3). The notice must be *in writing* but it need not tell the person the contents or the details of the authorization. After notice is given, the person who gave the notice must *certify to the court issuing the authorization* that the *notice has been given*. The Governor in Council may pass regulations providing for the contents of such certification.

Subsections (2) to (4) permit an *application to be made to a judge, before the period for the giving of notice has run, to extend the period for up to three years*. A subsequent application for the extension of such period may be made. The application may be brought by either the Attorney General or the Solicitor General, depending on whose behalf the application for the authorization is made. The same types of judges, who are authorized by this Part to grant authorizations under s. 185, may extend the notice. An application to extend the time for notice must be accompanied by an *affidavit sworn on the basis of information and belief of a peace or public officer*. The running of the 90 days or any other period is suspended once the application for an extension is made, until the application can be heard and disposed of. Subsection (4) sets out the required contents of such an affidavit which include (in addition to information regarding prior applications for authorization — whether successful, withdrawn or refused) the *facts which the deponent relies upon* for support that the notice period should be extended. Subsection (3) spells out the *criteria to be applied by the judge* hearing such an application. The affidavit must first satisfy the judge that either: (a) the *investigation of an offence* to which the authorization relates; or (b) subsequent investigation for an offence listed in s. 183, obtained as a result of the investigation noted in (a), *is continuing*. Finally, the judge must be of the opinion that the *interests of justice warrant* the granting of the application. If these conditions are met, the judge *must* fix an extended period, of *less than three years*, for the notice to be given.

Subsection (5) sets out special provisions relating to "criminal organizations".

ANNOTATIONS

Subsection (1) is complied with merely by notifying the person that he was the object of an interception. The person has no right to any wider notification such as receipt of a copy of the authorization: *R. v. Zaduk* (1978), 38 C.C.C. (2d) 349 (Ont. H.C.J.), affd (1979), 46 C.C.C. (2d) 327, 98 D.L.R. (3d) 133 (Ont. C.A.).

The Crown, having informed the accused that they were not the targets of any wiretap investigation in relation to the charges for which they were then being tried, had no obligation to disclose whether or not the accused were named as targets in any other authorizations. Before the Crown would be required to disclose this information, the defence must meet a threshold test of showing some basis which would enable the presiding judge to conclude that there is in existence material which is potentially relevant: *R. v. Chaplin*, [1995] 1 S.C.R. 727, 96 C.C.C. (3d) 225, 36 C.R. (4th) 201.

WRITTEN NOTICE — INTERCEPTION IN ACCORDANCE WITH SECTION 184.4 / Extension of period for notification / Where extension to be granted / Application to be accompanied by affidavit / Exception — criminal organization or terrorism offence.

196.1 (1) Subject to subsections (3) and (5), the Attorney General of the province in which a police officer intercepts a private communication under section 184.4 or, if the interception relates to an offence for which proceedings may be commenced by the Attorney General of Canada, the Minister of Public Safety and Emergency Preparedness shall give notice in writing of the interception to any person who was the object of the interception within 90 days after the day on which it occurred.

(2) The running of the 90-day period or of any extension granted under subsection (3) or (5) is suspended until any application made by the Attorney General of the province or the Minister to a judge of a superior court of criminal jurisdiction or a judge as defined in section 552 for an extension or a subsequent extension of the period has been heard and disposed of.

(3) The judge to whom an application under subsection (2) is made shall grant an extension or a subsequent extension of the 90-day period — each extension not to exceed

three years — if the judge is of the opinion that the interests of justice warrant granting the application and is satisfied, on the basis of an affidavit submitted in support of the application, that one of the following investigations is continuing:

(*a*) the investigation of the offence to which the interception relates; or

(*b*) a subsequent investigation of an offence commenced as a result of information obtained from the investigation referred to in paragraph (*a*).

(4) An application shall be accompanied by an affidavit deposing to

(*a*) the facts known or believed by the deponent and relied on to justify the belief that an extension should be granted; and

(*b*) the number of instances, if any, on which an application has, to the knowledge or belief of the deponent, been made under subsection (2) in relation to the particular interception and on which the application was withdrawn or the application was not granted, the date on which each application was made and the judge to whom each application was made.

(5) Despite subsection (3), the judge to whom an application under subsection (2) is made shall grant an extension or a subsequent extension of the 90-day period — each extension not to exceed three years — if the judge is of the opinion that the interests of justice warrant granting the application and is satisfied, on the basis of an affidavit submitted in support of the application, that the interception of the communication relates to an investigation of

(*a*) an offence under section 467.11, 467.12 or 467.13;

(*b*) an offence committed for the benefit of, at the direction of or in association with a criminal organization; or

(*c*) a terrorism offence. 2013, c. 8, s. 6.

Part VII / DISORDERLY HOUSES, GAMING AND BETTING

Interpretation

DEFINITIONS / "bet" / "common bawdy-house" / "common betting house" / "common gaming house" / "disorderly house" / "game" / "gaming equipment" / "keeper" / "place" / "public place" / Exception / Onus / Effect when game partly played on premises.

197. (1) In this Part

"bet" means a bet that is placed on any contingency or event that is to take place in or out of Canada, and without restricting the generality of the foregoing, includes a bet that is placed on any contingency relating to a horse-race, fight, match or sporting event that is to take place in or out of Canada;

"common bawdy-house" means for the practice of acts of indecency, a place that is kept or occupied or resorted to by one or more persons;

"common betting house" means a place that is opened, kept or used for the purpose of

(*a*) enabling, encouraging or assisting persons who resort thereto to bet between themselves or with the keeper, or

(*b*) enabling any person to receive, record, register, transmit or pay bets or to announce the results of betting;

"common gaming house" means a place that is

(*a*) kept for gain to which persons resort for the purpose of playing games, or

(*b*) kept or used for the purpose of playing games

(i) in which a bank is kept by one or more but not all of the players,

(ii) in which all or any portion of the bets on or proceeds from a game is paid, directly or indirectly, to the keeper of the place,

(iii) in which, directly or indirectly, a fee is charged to or paid by the players for the privilege of playing or participating in a game or using gaming equipment, or

(iv) in which the chances of winning are not equally favourable to all persons who play the game, including the person, if any, who conducts the game;

"disorderly house" means a common bawdy-house, a common betting house or a common gaming house;

"game" means a game of chance or mixed chance and skill;

"gaming equipment" means anything that is or may be used for the purpose of playing games or for betting;

"keeper" includes a person who

(*a*) is an owner or occupier of a place,

(*b*) assists or acts on behalf of an owner or occupier of a place,

(*c*) appears to be, or to assist or act on behalf of an owner or occupier of a place,

(*d*) has the care or management of a place, or

(*e*) uses a place permanently or temporarily, with or without the consent of the owner or occupier thereof;

"place" includes any place, whether or not

(*a*) it is covered or enclosed,

(*b*) it is used permanently or temporarily, or

(*c*) any person has an exclusive right of user with respect to it;

"prostitute" [*Repealed*, 2014, c. 25, s. 12(1).]

"public place" includes any place to which the public have access as of right or by invitation, express or implied.

(2) A place is not a common gaming house within the meaning of paragraph (*a*) or subparagraph (*b*)(ii) or (iii) of the definition "common gaming house" in subsection (1) while it is occupied and used by an incorporated genuine social club or branch thereof, if

(*a*) the whole or any portion of the bets on or proceeds from games played therein is not directly or indirectly paid to the keeper thereof; and

(*b*) no fee is charged to persons for the right or privilege of participating in the games played therein other than under the authority of and in accordance with the terms of a licence issued by the Attorney General of the province in which the place is situated or by such other person or authority in the province as may be specified by the Attorney General thereof.

(3) The onus of proving that, by virtue of subsection (2), a place is not a common gaming house is on the accused.

(4) A place may be a common gaming house notwithstanding that

(*a*) it is used for the purpose of playing part of a game and another part of the game is played elsewhere;

(*b*) the stake that is played for is in some other place; or

(*c*) it is used on only one occasion in the manner described in paragraph (*b*) of the definition "common gaming house" in subsection (1), if the keeper or any person acting on behalf of or in concert with the keeper has used another place on another occasion in the manner described in that paragraph. R.S., c. C-34, s. 179; 1972, c. 13, s. 13; 1980-81-82-83, c. 125, s. 11; R.S.C. 1985, c. 27 (1st Supp.), s. 29; 2014, c. 25, s. 12.

CROSS-REFERENCES

In addition to the definitions in this section, see s. 2 and notes to that section. The gaming, betting and lottery offences are found in ss. 201 to 209; bawdy house and prostitution offences in ss. 210 to 213.

SYNOPSIS

Section 197(1) provides exhaustive definitions for a number of terms which are used in several sections throughout Part VII of the *Criminal Code*. The definition of "common gaming house" in subsec. (1) must be read together with subsec. (2) which provides a number of exceptions to the definition.

Section 197(3) provides that the onus of proving that the house comes within one of the exclusions within s. 197(2) is upon the accused.

Section 197(4) clarifies and extends the meaning of *common gaming house*. It is aimed at foreclosing methods of avoiding conviction by the use of techniques such as using a number of different locations for a "floating crap game".

ANNOTATIONS

"bet" – "Bets" or "betting" under the *Criminal Code* do not have the same connotation as found in civil law of contract, and there are other considerations in determining illegal betting: *R. v. Benwell* (1972), 9 C.C.C. (2d) 158, [1972] 3 O.R. 906 (C.A.) (2:1), affd [1973] S.C.R. v, 10 C.C.C. (2d) 503.

"common bawdy-house" / *[Also see notes under s. 210]* – **Note**: the following cases were decided under a previous version of this section in which "prostitution" was part of the definition of "common bawdy house" and should be read with caution in light of the amended language which focuses solely on "indecency".

The words "kept or occupied" or "resorted to" connote a frequent or habitual use of the premises for the purpose of prostitution: *R. v. Patterson*, [1968] S.C.R. 157, [1968] 2 C.C.C. 247 (5:0). In that case Spence J., summarized the type of evidence from which the court has found that the prohibited nature of the premises was established, as follows:

first, there has been actual evidence of the continued and habitual use of the premises for prostitution . . .

secondly, there has been evidence of the reputation in the neighbourhood of the premises as a common bawdy-house, or,

thirdly, there has been evidence of such circumstances as to make the inference that the premises were resorted to habitually as a place of prostitution, a proper inference for the Court to draw from such evidence.

"Acts of indecency" and "prostitution" are not vague so as to violate s. 7 of the Charter: *R. v. DiGiuseppe* (2002), 161 C.C.C. (3d) 424, 155 O.A.C. 62 (C.A.), leave to appeal to S.C.C. refused [2002] 3 S.C.R. vii, 167 C.C.C. 93d) vi.

Indecency requires proof beyond a reasonable doubt of two elements: (1) that, by its nature, the conduct at issue causes harm or presents a significant risk of harm to individuals or society in a way that undermines or threatens to undermine a value reflected in, and thus formally endorsed through, the Constitution or similar fundamental laws by, for example: (a) confronting members of the public with conduct that significantly interferes with their autonomy and liberty; (b) predisposing others to anti-social behaviour; or (c) physically or psychologically harming persons involved in the conduct; and (2) that the harm or risk of harm is of a degree that is incompatible with the proper functioning of society.

The first requirement is not based on individual notions of harm, nor on the teachings of a particular ideology, but on what society, through its fundamental laws, has recognized as essential. Views about the harm that the sexual conduct at issue may produce, however widely held, do not suffice to ground a conviction. Unlike the community standard of tolerance test, the requirement of formal recognition inspires confidence that the values upheld by judges and jurors are truly those of Canadian society. Autonomy, liberty, equality and human dignity are among these values. The list of harms is not closed. Bad taste does not suffice and moral views, even if strongly held, do not suffice. Similarly, the fact that most members of the community might disapprove of the conduct does not suffice. The second requirement requires proof that the conduct, not only by its nature but also in degree, rises to the level of threatening the proper functioning of our society. If the harm is based on the threat to autonomy and liberty arising from unwanted confrontation by a particular kind of sexual conduct, the Crown must establish a real risk that the way people live will be significantly and adversely affected by the conduct. If the only people involved in or observing the conduct were willing participants, indecency on the basis of this harm will not be made out. If the harm is based on predisposing others to antisocial behaviour, a real risk that the conduct will have this effect must be proved. Vague generalizations that the sexual conduct at issue will lead to attitudinal changes and hence antisocial behaviour will not suffice. The causal link between images of sexuality and antisocial behaviour cannot be assumed. Attitudes in themselves are not crimes, however deviant they may be or disgusting they may appear. What is required is proof of links, first between the sexual conduct at issue and the formation of negative attitudes, and second between those attitudes and real risk of antisocial behaviour. Finally, if the harm is based on physical or psychological injury to participants, it must be shown that the harm has occurred or that there is a real risk that this will occur. Witnesses may testify as to actual harm. Expert witnesses may give evidence on the risks of potential harm. In considering psychological harm, care must be taken to avoid substituting disgust for the conduct involved, for proof of harm to the participants. In the case of vulnerable participants, it may be easier to infer psychological harm than in cases where participants operate on an equal and autonomous basis. As a general rule, these are matters that can and should be established by evidence. In most cases, expert evidence will be required to establish that the nature and degree of the harm makes it incompatible with the proper functioning of society: *R. v. Labaye*, [2005] 3 S.C.R. 728, 203 C.C.C. (3d) 170; *R. v. Kouri*, [2005] 3 S.C.R. 789, 203 C.C.C. (3d) 217.

"common betting house" / ***[Also see notes under s. 201]*** – Use of a hotel room on only one occasion will not come within this definition which requires proof that the activity is frequent or habitual in nature. While the word "opened" may have a very wide meaning it must take its meaning from the context, in this case the words "kept or used" which have been held to require proof of a frequent or habitual use: *R. v. Grainger* (1978), 42 C.C.C. (2d) 119 (Ont. C.A.).

"common gaming house" / ***[Also see notes under s. 201]*** – In *R. v. Rockert*, [1978] 2 S.C.R. 704, 38 C.C.C. (2d) 438 (7:2), it was held that premises which are used on only one occasion do not fall within either para. (*a*) or (*b*) of this definition. The words "kept" and "resort" in para. (*a*) connote frequent or habitual activity, as does "kept" in para. (*b*). The word "used" in para. (*b*) means "that is made use of" and requires a practice of employing the premises in the prohibited manner or at least a practice consisting of more than one use or occasion. Following this decision, subsec. (4) was amended to add para. (*c*) to that subsection with the result that, in some cases, in the circumstances therein described, a single use of premises may nevertheless suffice to constitute the premises a common gaming house.

A place to which persons who have paid a membership fee resort nightly to play rummy and at which the accused sells refreshments comes within para. (*a*) of the definition notwithstanding the membership fee is devoted to a *bona fide* soccer club (which however was not incorporated under subsec. (2)) where the accused kept the proceeds from the refreshment sales and was clearly carrying on a business for gain: *R. v. Karavasilis* (1980), 54 C.C.C. (2d) 530 (Ont. C.A.).

In addition to proof of the elements in the definition in para. (*a*) the Crown must prove as an element of the offence of gaming that the participants had the chance of both winning and losing money or money's worth. Thus, possible outcomes must be a result, direct or indirect, of wagering or hazarding a stake prior to or during the game. Where no money changed hands between the players, this element of gaming is not made out merely because it is customary for the loser of the card game to pay for the refreshments. The players in such circumstances were not putting up a stake on the outcome of the game but had merely found a convenient way for taking turns at who would purchase drinks which would normally be consumed: *R. v. Di Pietro and Di Pietro*, [1986] 1 S.C.R. 250, 25 C.C.C. (3d) 100 (7:0), approving *R. v. Irwin* (1982), 1 C.C.C. (3d) 212, 39 O.R. (2d) 314 (C.A.).

In this case, a scheme devised by the accused, in which persons purchased memberships in a club which purchased provincial government lottery tickets, constituted keeping a common gaming house. A portion of the fee was used to pay the accused's expenses and the other portion was used to purchase the tickets. The accused guaranteed that each group would have a certain number of winning combinations or he would give a refund. This was more than a group of persons getting together to purchase tickets and play a lottery. Rather, it was a new game of chance. It was a game played for a consideration and in accordance with rules developed by the accused. Under the accused's scheme, he and each of the members stood the chance of both winning and losing money or money's worth. The requisite element of wagering was therefore made out: *R. v. Herger* (1991), 4 O.R. (3d) 359 (C.A.).

"gain" – As used in para. (*a*), "gain" can include direct winnings. Consequently, where the accused was an exceptionally skilled professional gambler who supported the commercial gambling establishment and paid employees out of his large winnings, the premises fell within the meaning of "common gaming house": *R. v. Turmel* (1996), 109 C.C.C. (3d) 162 (Ont. C.A.).

"game" – In *R. v. Ross, Banks and Dyson*, [1968] S.C.R. 786, [1969] 1 C.C.C. 1, it was held (by four judges to one) following the rule of literal interpretation in the absence of ambiguity that the word "mixed" in this definition implies no indication of the proportions of chance and skill and therefore bridge is a game within this subsection.

A carnival operation where the patrons toss coins at glasses and other vessels, winning the glass or vessel on which the coin lands, is a game within the meaning of this definition: *R. v. Touzin and Touzin* (1979), 49 C.C.C. (2d) 183 (Que. C.A.).

In *R. v. Riesberry*, [2015] 3 S.C.R. 1167, 331 C.C.C. (3d) 23, the trial judge erred in entering an acquittal on a charge under s. 209 without considering evidence that a horse race is a game with a systematic resort to chance to determine outcomes. There was evidence that post position is determined at random and that certain post positions are more advantageous than others, leading to a possible conclusion that a horse race qualifies as a "game" under this definition.

"keeper" – It was held in *R. v. Kerim*, [1963] S.C.R. 124, [1963] 1 C.C.C. 233 (3:2), that not every person who falls within this definition as a "keeper" keeps a common gaming house. Rather, there must be some act of participation in the wrongful use of the place. Presumably, this reasoning would apply to the other keeping offences, keeping a common betting house and keeping a common bawdy house. [Note: While this decision would seem to render this definition redundant, it is suggested that, in any of the keeping offences, it must be proved as a minimum that the person fell within the definition of keeper in this section and also committed some act as indicated by the court in *Kerim*. Some of the difficulty in interpretation of this section appears to be as a result of its derivation from s. 229(3) of the 1927 Code, which enacted a presumption that a person was a keeper of a disorderly house if he or she "appears, acts or behaves" as, *inter alia*, the person having the care, government, or management of the premises.]

While it has been held that, for premises to be considered a common gaming house, there must be evidence of frequent or habitual use: *R. v. Rockert, supra*, it is not necessary to prove that the person charged with keeping the common gaming house acted as such frequently or habitually, particularly in light of para. (*e*) of this definition which refers to a permanent or temporary use of the place: *R. v. Lamolinara* (1989), 53 C.C.C. (3d) 250 (Que. C.A.).

Social club exemption [subsec. (2)] – It was held in *R. v. MacDonald*, [1966] S.C.R. 3, [1966] 2 C.C.C. 307 (5:0), that a branch of the Royal Canadian Legion was not entitled to the social club exemption where bingo was carried out on a large scale and on a daily basis. The court held that this was not an "occupation and use by a *bona fide* social club". However, following that decision, this subsection was substantially amended so that the activities carried on in that case might fall within this exemption, provided that the requisite licence was obtained and complied with.

A gaming house, which falls within the definition of "common gaming house" in para. (*b*)(i), being a place kept or used for the purpose of playing games in which a bank is kept by one or more but not all of the players, is not entitled to the exemption in this subsection: *R. v. Pon Chung and Mow Chong Social Club*, [1965] 2 C.C.C. 331 (Ont. C.A.).

The social club's "*bona fides*" is not lost merely because some of the avowed objects of the club were not carried out: *R. v. Pon Chung and Mow Chong Social Club, supra.*

Presumptions

198. [*Repealed*, 2018, c. 29, s. 16.]

Search

WARRANT TO SEARCH / Search without warrant, seizure and arrest / Disposal of property seized / When declaration or direction may be made / Conversion into money / Telephones exempt from seizure / Exception.

199. (1) A justice who is satisfied by information on oath that there are reasonable grounds to believe that an offence under section 201, 202, 203, 206, 207 or 210 is being committed at any place within the jurisdiction of the justice may issue a warrant authorizing a peace officer to enter and search the place by day or night and seize anything found therein that may be evidence that an offence under section 201, 202, 203, 206, 207 or 210, as the case may be, is being committed at that place, and to take into custody all persons who are found in or at that place and requiring those persons and things to be brought before that justice or before another justice having jurisdiction, to be dealt with according to law.

(2) A peace officer may, whether or not he is acting under a warrant issued pursuant to this section, take into custody any person whom he finds keeping a common gaming house and any person whom he finds therein, and may seize anything that may be evidence that such an offence is being committed and shall bring those persons and things before a justice having jurisdiction, to be dealt with according to law.

(3) Except where otherwise expressly provided by law, a court, judge, justice or provincial court judge before whom anything that is seized under this section is brought may declare that the thing is forfeited, in which case it shall be disposed of or dealt with as the Attorney General may direct if no person shows sufficient cause why it should not be forfeited.

(4) No declaration or direction shall be made pursuant to subsection (3) in respect of anything seized under this section until

(*a*) it is no longer required as evidence in any proceedings that are instituted pursuant to the seizure; or

(*b*) the expiration of thirty days from the time of seizure where it is not required as evidence in any proceedings.

(5) The Attorney General may, for the purpose of converting anything forfeited under this section into money, deal with it in all respects as if he were the owner thereof.

(6) Nothing in this section or in section 489 authorizes the seizure, forfeiture or destruction of telephone, telegraph or other communication facilities or equipment that may be evidence of or that may have been used in the commission of an offence under section 201, 202, 203, 206, 207 or 210 and that is owned by a person engaged in providing telephone, telegraph or other communication service to the public or forming

part of the telephone, telegraph or other communication service or system of that person.

(7) Subsection (6) does not apply to prohibit the seizure, for use as evidence, of any facility or equipment described in that subsection that is designed or adapted to record a communication. R.S., c. C-34, s. 181; 1994, c. 44, s. 10.

CROSS-REFERENCES

The terms "justice", "peace officer", "day", "night" and "Attorney General" are defined in s. 2.

Section 29 sets out duties of persons executing a warrant and, *inter alia*, the officer must have it with him, where it is feasible to do so, and produce it when requested to do so.

As to the use of force generally in enforcement of the law, see ss. 25, 26, 27 and 31.

Warrants in relation to the offences described in this section could also be obtained pursuant to ss. 487 and 487.1. The declaration of forfeiture under subsec. (3) may be appealed as a sentence appeal under Part XXI or Part XXVII, as the case may be.

SYNOPSIS

Section 199 creates search, seizure and forfeiture provisions relating to the offences within Part VII listed in s. 199(1). In addition it authorizes taking into custody persons found within the places searched.

Section 199(1) permits a justice who is satisfied by information on oath that there are reasonable grounds to believe that one of the offences listed in the subsection (all "vice"-type offences) is being committed at a place, to issue a warrant authorizing the search of the place. It allows the search to take place day or night and gives the police authority to detain any person or thing found on the premises and then to bring them before a justice.

Section 199(2) permits a police officer who enters a *common gaming house* to detain the *keeper* of the house and all those who are *found in* the house, and to seize all things within the house. There is no requirement that the police have a warrant to enter or seize property from the *common gaming house* at the time the seizures are made under this subsection.

It should be noted that s. 199(6) adds certain restrictions to what may be seized by warrant under this section or s. 489. These restrictions deal basically with communication facilities and equipment.

Section 199(7) permits the seizure of items otherwise included within subsec. (6) if the item is designed or adapted to record conversations and it is seized for evidentiary purposes.

Section 199(3) creates a broad discretion in judicial officers to direct that whatever is seized be forfeited. It appears that the onus is upon the person who seeks to avoid forfeiture to "show sufficient cause" why it *should not be forfeited*. The Attorney General controls how items ordered seized are to be dealt with, including requiring that they be disposed of as directed. Section 199(5) gives the Attorney General the same powers as the owner to convert a forfeited item into money. Section 199(4) provides certain time-limits within which an item seized is not to be the subject of a declaration or direction.

ANNOTATIONS

Constitutional considerations – This provision meets the constitutional requirement of prior judicial authorization: *R. v. Huynh* (2009), 249 C.C.C. (3d) 569 (Alta. Q.B.).

Forfeiture – For forfeiture of seized funds it is not necessary that the Crown prove their identity with the specific proven offence: *R. v. Owens* (1971), 5 C.C.C. (2d) 125 (Ont. C.A.).

A declaration for forfeiture may be made only after a hearing in conformity with the provisions of this section, notice of which has been given to all interested parties: *R. v. Tobin* (1982), 69 C.C.C. (2d) 137 (Nfld. S.C.T.D.).

A forfeiture order may be made under this section at the conclusion of the trial of an accused for an offence under s. 201. Subsection (4) does not require that the court await the outcome of any appeal proceedings before making the declaration: *R. v. Anderson and Blackie* (1983), 10 C.C.C. (3d) 183 (B.C.C.A.).

Items, such as money, which may be evidence of the gaming-house offence may be seized from the keeper under subsec. (2) and declared forfeited under subsec. (3) although he is not on the premises at the time of the execution of the warrant: *R. v. Anderson and Blackie*, *supra*.

A forfeiture order may be made under subsec. (3), where the gaming equipment was seized pursuant to a search warrant issued under s. 487: *R. v. Harb* (1994), 88 C.C.C. (3d) 204 (N.S.C.A.).

200. [*Repealed*, R.S.C. 1985, c. 27 (1st Supp.), s. 30.]

Gaming and Betting

KEEPING GAMING OR BETTING HOUSE / Person found in or owner permitting use.

201. (1) Every one who keeps a common gaming house or common betting house is guilty of an indictable offence and liable to imprisonment for a term not exceeding two years.

(2) Every one who

(*a*) is found, without lawful excuse, in a common gaming house or common betting house, or

(*b*) as owner, landlord, lessor, tenant, occupier or agent, knowingly permits a place to be let or used for the purposes of a common gaming house or common betting house,

is guilty of an offence punishable on summary conviction. R.S., c. C-34, s. 185.

CROSS-REFERENCES

The terms "keeper", "common gaming house" and "common betting house" are defined in s. 197(1) and (4). The exemptions for genuine social clubs is set out in s. 197(2). Section 198 sets out certain presumptions which aid in proof that premises are a common gaming house or common betting house. In particular, note s. 198(2) and (3) respecting slot machines. Sections 204 and 207 enact certain exemptions respecting gaming and betting. While s. 206 enacts exemptions for certain kinds of gaming and lotteries, those sections do not in specific terms exempt an accused from liability under this section. Accordingly, the reach of those exemptions is uncertain, see cases below in particular respecting the Agricultural fair exemption. Related offences are found in s. 203, placing bets on behalf of others; s. 206, lotteries and games of chance; s. 209, cheating at play.

The offence in subsec. (1) may be the basis for an application for an authorization to intercept private communications by reason of s. 183 or a warrant for video surveillance under s. 487.01(5) and falls within the definition of "enterprise crime offence" in s. 462.3 for the purposes of Part XII.2. As regards special search and seizure powers in relation to gaming houses and betting houses, see s. 199.

The offence in subsec. (1) is a pure indictable offence, but, by virtue of s. 553, it is an offence over which a provincial court judge has absolute jurisdiction and does not depend on the consent of the accused. That is, the accused does not have an election as to mode of trial, although the provincial court judge may, by virtue of s. 555(1), elect to continue the proceedings as a preliminary inquiry, in which case the accused is deemed to have elected trial by judge and jury pursuant to s. 565(1)(*a*). The trial of the offences in subsec. (2) are conducted by a summary conviction court pursuant to Part XXVII. The punishment for the offences in subsec. (2) are as set out in s. 787 and the limitation period is set out in s. 786(2). For all offences under this section, release pending trial is determined by s. 515, although the accused is eligible for release by a peace officer under s. 496, 497 or by the officer in charge under s. 498.

SYNOPSIS

This section creates offences in relation to *keeping a common gaming or betting house.*

Section 201(1) makes it an indictable offence to *keep* such a premises. The maximum punishment upon conviction is two years' imprisonment.

Section 201(2) creates two summary conviction offences. Paragraph (2)(*a*) makes it an offence for an accused to be a *found in* at a *common gaming house* or *common betting house*. It must be shown that the accused had *no lawful excuse* for being present in such a premises.

Section 201(2)(*b*) prohibits *permitting* a place to be used as a *common gaming house* or a *common betting house* if the accused is in the capacity of an owner, landlord, tenant, occupier or agent. It must be shown that the accused *knew* the use being made of the place and permitted it to occur.

ANNOTATIONS

Meaning of "keeps" / *Also see notes under heading "Keeper" in s. 197* – Not every person who falls within the definition of "keeper" within s. 197 "keeps" a common gaming house. To constitute that offence there must be some act of participation in the wrongful use of the place. Thus the accused who was the owner of the premises and rented them out to various charitable organizations but who in no way participated in the promotion, organization or operation of the games was acquitted of this charge. The fact that he operated a refreshment stand for the patrons of the games which was entirely independent of the activities of the organization renting the premises is immaterial. The accused in such circumstances may, however, come within the offence in subsec. (2)(*b*): *R. v. Kerim*, [1963] S.C.R. 124, [1963] 1 C.C.C. 233 (3:2).

R. v. Kerim, supra, was distinguished and the accused's conviction upheld where the accused leased the premises, provided cards and score pads and sold refreshments, notwithstanding there was no "rake-off". The accused had involved himself in the use of the premises to such an extent that he was participating in the illegal use. His own activities in providing the accommodation and facilities and selling the refreshments made the premises a common gaming house: *R. v. Karavasilis* (1980), 54 C.C.C. (2d) 530 (Ont. C.A.).

Where the game's rules do not preclude some or all of its players from having equal opportunity to becoming its banker and that position does not confer some advantage over the players then the banker cannot be said to be the keeper of a common gaming house: *R. v. Monroe* (1970), 1 C.C.C. (2d) 68 (B.C.C.A.).

Mere participation in an illegal gaming activity, for example through employment at a bingo hall, does not render an individual a party to the offence of keeping a common gaming house: *R. v. Bragdon* (1996), 112 C.C.C. (3d) 91 (N.B.C.A.).

Common gaming house / *Also see notes under s. 197* – In *R. v. Rockert*, [1978] 2 S.C.R. 704, 38 C.C.C. (2d) 438 (7:2), it was held that premises which are used on only one occasion do not fall within either para. (*a*) or para. (*b*) of the definition of common gaming house in s. 197(1). However, following this decision, subsec. (4) of s. 197 was amended to add para. (*c*) to that subsection with the result that in some cases, in the circumstances therein described, a single use of premises may nevertheless suffice to constitute the premises a common gaming house.

Common betting house / *Also see notes under s. 197* – Use of premises on one occasion will not constitute such premises a common betting house as defined in s. 197: *R. v. Grainger* (1978), 42 C.C.C. (2d) 119 (Ont. C.A.).

The recording of bets, let alone proof of the method of recording, is not an ingredient of keeping a common betting house and there need not even be direct evidence of the accused having received a bet. It is enough that premises were kept by the accused for the purpose of enabling any person to receive bets: *R. v. Silvestro*, [1965] S.C.R. 155, [1965] 2 C.C.C. 253 (3:2).

First Nations gambling – The accused members of the Shawanaga First Nations failed to adduce evidence to demonstrate that gambling, or the regulation of gambling, was an integral part of their distinctive cultures. They therefore failed to demonstrate that the high stakes bingo and other gambling activities in which they were engaged, and their Band's regulation of those activities, took place pursuant to an aboriginal right recognized and affirmed by s. 35(1) of the *Constitution Act, 1982*. The accused were properly convicted of offences under this section: *R. v. Gardner; R. v. Jones*, [1996] 2 S.C.R. 821, 109 C.C.C. (3d) 275, *sub nom. R. v. Pamajewon.*

Agricultural fair exemptions – Notwithstanding there is no exemption clause for offences charged under this section, if the charge could have been laid under s. 206(1)(*f*) or (*g*) and the accused can bring himself within the exemption clause in s. 206(3) (games operated at an exhibition or fair) the accused is entitled to the protection of any exemption set out in that subsection: *R. v. Andrews and five others* (1975), 28 C.C.C. (2d) 450 (Sask. C.A.). Also see *R. v. Beasley* (1936), 65 C.C.C. 337 (Ont. C.A.). But see: *R. v. Cross* (1978), 40 C.C.C. (2d) 505 (Alta. S.C. App. Div.) where slot machines are involved; noted under s. 198(2), *supra.*

BETTING, POOL-SELLING, BOOK-MAKING, ETC. / Punishment.

202. (1) Every one commits an offence who

(*a*) uses or knowingly allows a place under his control to be used for the purpose of recording or registering bets or selling a pool;

(*b*) imports, makes, buys, sells, rents, leases, hires or keeps, exhibits, employs or knowingly allows to be kept, exhibited or employed in any place under his control any device or apparatus for the purpose of recording or registering bets or selling a pool, or any machine or device for gambling or betting;

(*c*) has under his control any money or other property relating to a transaction that is an offence under this section;

(*d*) records or registers bets or sells a pool;

(*e*) engages in book-making or pool-selling, or in the business or occupation of betting, or makes any agreement for the purchase or sale of betting or gaming privileges, or for the purchase or sale of information that is intended to assist in book-making, pool-selling or betting;

(*f*) prints, provides or offers to print or provide information intended for use in connection with book-making, pool-selling or betting on any horse-race, fight, game or sport, whether or not it takes place in or outside of Canada or has or has not taken place;

(*g*) imports or brings into Canada any information or writing that is intended or is likely to promote or be of use in gambling, book-making, pool-selling or betting on a horse-race, fight, game or sport, and where this paragraph applies it is immaterial

(i) whether the information is published before, during or after the race, fight, game or sport, or

(ii) whether the race, fight, game or sport takes place in Canada or elsewhere,

but this paragraph does not apply to a newspaper, magazine or other periodical published in good faith primarily for a purpose other than the publication of such information;

(*h*) advertises, prints, publishes, exhibits, posts up, or otherwise gives notice of any offer, invitation or inducement to bet on, to guess or to foretell the result of a contest, or a result of or contingency relating to any contest;

(*i*) wilfully and knowingly sends, transmits, delivers or receives any message that conveys any information relating to book-making, pool-selling, betting or wagering, or that is intended to assist in book-making, poolselling, betting or wagering; or

(*j*) aids or assists in any manner in anything that is an offence under this section.

(2) Every one who commits an offence under this section is guilty of an indictable offence and liable

(*a*) for a first offence, to imprisonment for not more than two years;

(*b*) for a second offence, to imprisonment for a term not more than two years and not less than fourteen days; and

(*c*) for each subsequent offence, to imprisonment for not more than two years and not less than three months. R.S., c. C-34, s. 186; 1974-75-76, c. 93, s. 11; 2008, c. 18, s. 5.

CROSS-REFERENCES

The terms "bet", "gaming equipment", and "place" are defined in s. 197.

The offence in para. (1)(*e*) may be the basis for an application for an authorization to intercept private communications by reason of s. 183 or a warrant for video surveillance by reason of s. 487.01(5), and the offences in this section fall within the definition of "enterprise crime offence" in s. 462.3 for the purposes of Part XII.2. As regards special search and seizure powers in relation to gaming houses and betting houses, see s. 199. Sections 204 and 207 enact certain exemptions respecting gaming and betting. While s. 206 enacts exemptions for certain kinds of gaming and lotteries, that section does not, in specific terms, exempt an accused from liability under this section. Accordingly, the reach of those exemptions is uncertain, see cases noted under heading **Agricultural fair exemption**, under s. 201.

The offence in subsec. (2) is a pure indictable offence, but by virtue of s. 553 it is an offence over which a provincial court judge has absolute jurisdiction and does not depend on the consent of the accused. That is, the accused does not have an election as to mode of trial, although the provincial court judge may, by virtue of s. 555(1), elect to continue the proceedings as a preliminary inquiry, in which case, the accused is deemed to have elected trial by judge and jury pursuant to s. 565(1)(*a*). Release pending trial is determined by s. 515, although the accused is eligible for release by a peace officer under s. 496, 497 or by the officer in charge under s. 498.

Where the prosecution seeks the higher penalty prescribed by subsec. (2)(*b*) or (*c*), it must comply with the provisions of s. 665. Section 667 provides one method of proof of the prior conviction. Note that no reference to the prior conviction may be made in the information by virtue of s. 664.

Related offences are: s. 201, keeping common gaming or betting house; s. 203, placing bets on behalf of others; s. 206, offences in relation to lotteries and games of chance; s. 209, cheating at play.

SYNOPSIS

This section creates indictable offences prohibiting betting, pool selling, bookmaking, importing equipment to engage in any of these activities, and other similar illicit gambling activities. It also provides for punishment upon conviction for such offences. To determine the scope of liability under this section it is necessary to read it together with s. 204 which provides for a number of exemptions.

Section 202(1) creates a number of specific prohibitions set out in paras. (*a*), (*b*), (*d*) to (*i*), which spell out the prohibited acts and in the case of certain paragraphs also spell out the mental element. One such paragraph is para. (*i*) which specifies certain actions such as sending, transmitting, delivering or receiving any message by one of the means specified in the paragraph which is related to bookmaking, pool-selling, or wagering, or that is intended to *assist* in such activity. It must be shown that the accused's actions were both wilful and done knowingly.

Section 202(1)(*c*) and (*j*) create broad offences which extend the liability created by the more specific paragraphs. Section 202(1)(*c*) makes it an offence for the accused to have *control* over any *money* or property relating to a transaction prohibited by this subsection. Similarly subsec. (1)(*j*) makes it an offence to *aid or assist in any manner* anything which is otherwise an offence under subsec. (1). It must be shown that the accused *knew* that the acts assisted in the commission of the other offence created by the subsection but it does not appear that it must be shown that the accused's *purpose was to assist*.

Section 202(2) creates an escalating punishment scale based on the number of prior offences for which the accused has been convicted.

ANNOTATIONS

Constitutional Considerations: This offence is a valid exercise of Parliament's criminal law power: *R. v. J.B.L. Amusements Ltd.* (1998), 123 C.C.C. (3d) 419 (Nfld. C.A.).

Subsection (1)(*b*) – The accused's honest but mistaken belief that the devices were legal even where such belief is the result of reasonable inquiries made of Customs officials is no defence to this charge, by virtue of s. 19: *R. v. Potter* (1978), 39 C.C.C. (2d) 538 (P.E.I.S.C.).

To obtain a conviction for the offence under subsec. (1)(*b*), the Crown was required to prove that the accused kept devices in a place under her control, that the devices were gambling devices, and that the accused knew that the devices were gambling devices and knowingly kept them. Gambling or gaming must, as well, involve a chance of gain and a risk of loss. The Crown, however, was not required to show that the machines were actually used for the purpose of gambling: *R. v. Kent*, [1994] 3 S.C.R. 133, 92 C.C.C. (3d) 344.

The offence of keeping a device for gambling or betting constitutes a valid exercise of Parliament's criminal law power: *R. v. J.B.L. Amusements Ltd.* (1998), 123 C.C.C. (3d) 419 (Nfld. C.A.).

Subsection (1)(*d*) – The registering or recording must be of the bookmaker's, not the bettor's, record of bets: *R. v. Michael* (1974), 18 C.C.C. (2d) 282 (Alta. S.C. App. Div.).

Subsection (1)(*e*) – The keeper of a common betting house is one who does something for the purpose of aiding and abetting other persons to engage in the business or occupation of betting and thus he may be convicted of the offence under this section: *R. v. Silvestro*, [1965] S.C.R. 155, [1965] 2 C.C.C. 253 (3:2).

The term "bookmaking" is not limited to horse races. A bookmaker is one who engages in the occupation of taking bets or negotiating bets and the keeping of accounts, regardless of whether the bet is on a horse-race or is more general in scope. Thus, bookmaking describes an enterprise, the business of taking bets and of keeping accounts: *R. v. Decome* (1991), 63 C.C.C. (3d) 460 (Que. C.A.).

The accused's scheme in which persons purchased memberships in a club which purchased provincial government lottery tickets did not amount to pool-selling or selling a pool. The scheme was not one in which the participants or members bet with one another and one or more of the members or participants won, as is usually the case in pool-betting or pool-selling. Rather the members shared equally in the winnings:*R. v. Herger* (1991), 4 O.R. (3d) 359 (C.A.).

Subsection (1)(*f*) – The Crown was not required to prove that the British football pools, which were the source of the information provided or conveyed by the accused, were illegal pools in England: *R. v. Ede* (1993), 84 C.C.C. (3d) 447*n*, 63 O.A.C. 319 (C.A.).

Lotteries constitute a form of gaming and betting: *R. v. World Media Brokers Inc.* (1998), 132 C.C.C. (3d) 180 (Ont. Ct. (Prov. Div.)), affd 174 C.C.C. (3d) 385 (Ont. C.A.).

PLACING BETS ON BEHALF OF OTHERS.

203. Every one who

(*a*) places or offers or agrees to place a bet on behalf of another person for a consideration paid or to be paid by or on behalf of that other person,

(*b*) engages in the business or practice of placing or agreeing to place bets on behalf of other persons, whether for a consideration or otherwise, or

(*c*) holds himself out or allows himself to be held out as engaging in the business or practice of placing or agreeing to place bets on behalf of other persons, whether for a consideration or otherwise,

is guilty of an indictable offence and liable

(*d*) for a first offence, to imprisonment for not more than two years,

(*e*) for a second offence, to imprisonment for not more than two years and not less than fourteen days, and

(*f*) for each subsequent offence, to imprisonment for not more than two years and not less than three months. R.S., c. C-34, s. 187; 1974-75-76, c. 93, s. 11.

CROSS-REFERENCES

The term "bet" is defined in s. 197.

Section 204 enacts certain exemptions respecting betting, for offences under ss. 201 and 202, but not this section. Section 206 enacts exemptions for certain kinds of gaming but does not, in specific terms, exempt an accused from liability under this section. Accordingly, the reach of those exemptions is uncertain, see cases noted under heading **Agricultural fair exemption**, under s. 201. The exemption in s. 207 would, however, apply to conduct otherwise within this section.

The offences under this section are pure indictable offences, but, by virtue of s. 553, are offences over which a provincial court judge has absolute jurisdiction and does not depend on the consent of the accused. That is, the accused does not have an election as to mode of trial, although the provincial court judge may, by virtue of s. 555(1), elect to continue the proceedings as a preliminary inquiry, in which case, the accused is deemed to have elected trial by judge and jury pursuant to s. 565(1)(*a*). Release pending trial is determined by s. 515, although the accused is eligible for release by a peace officer under s. 496, 497 or by the officer in charge under s. 498.

Where the prosecution seeks the higher penalty prescribed by para. (*e*) or (*f*), it must comply with the provisions of s. 665. Section 667 provides one method of proof of the prior conviction. Note that no reference to the prior conviction may be made in the information by virtue of s. 664.

SYNOPSIS

Section 203 prohibits the activities of the actions of "bookies" and other off-track betting schemes and sets out a schedule of available sentences based on whether the accused is a repeat offender.

Section 203(*a*) makes it an indictable offence to *place* a *bet* for another in exchange for *consideration*. The offence is also stated to encompass *offers* or *agreements* to place the bet. The consideration may be received either at the time of the act described or it may be agreed that the consideration may be received at a later time.

Section 203(*b*) makes it an indictable offence to engage in the business or practice of either placing or agreeing to place bets, whether or not for consideration.

Section 203(*c*) makes it an indictable offence to hold oneself out to be a "bookie", or allow oneself to be so held out.

ANNOTATIONS

This section, which was first introduced following the decision of the Ontario Court of Appeal in *R. v. Gruhl and Brennan*, [1970] 1 C.C.C. 104, has been amended from time to time and liability extended as various off-track betting schemes have come before the courts. Thus, cases such as *R. v. Williams and Adams* (1970), 2 C.C.C. (2d) 476 (Alta. S.C. App. Div.), affd [1971] S.C.R. vi, 3 C.C.C. (2d) 91*n* (5:0), and *R. v. Benwell* (1972), 9 C.C.C. (2d) 158 (Ont. C.A.) (2:1), affd [1973] S.C.R. vi, 10 C.C.C. (2d) 503 (9:0), decided before the enactment of subsecs. (*b*) and (*c*) must be read with care.

EXEMPTION / Exception / Presumption / Operation of pari-mutuel system / Supervision of pari-mutuel system / Percentage that may be deducted and retained / Percentage that may be deducted and retained / Stopping of betting / Regulations / Approvals / Idem / 900 metre zone / Contravention / Definition of "association".

204. (1) Sections 201 and 202 do not apply to

(*a*) any person or association by reason of his or their becoming the custodian or depository of any money, property or valuable thing staked, to be paid to

(i) the winner of a lawful race, sport, game or exercise,

(ii) the owner of a horse engaged in a lawful race, or

(iii) the winner of any bets between not more than ten individuals;

(*b*) a private bet between individuals not engaged in any way in the business of betting;

(*c*) bets made or records of bets made through the agency of a pari-mutuel system on running, trotting or pacing horse-races if

(i) the bets or records of bets are made on the race-course of an association in respect of races conducted at that race-course or another race-course in or out of Canada, and, in the case of a race conducted on a race-course situated outside Canada, the governing body that regulates the race has been certified as acceptable by the Minister of Agriculture and Agri-Food or a person designated by that Minister pursuant to subsection (8.1) and that Minister or person has permitted pari-mutuel betting in Canada on the race pursuant to that subsection, and

(ii) the provisions of this section and the regulations are complied with.

(1.1) For greater certainty, a person may, in accordance with the regulations, do anything described in section 201 or 202, if that person does it for the purposes of legal pari-mutuel betting.

(2) For the purposes of paragraph (1)(*c*), bets made, in accordance with the regulations, in a betting theatre referred to in paragraph (8)(*e*), or by any means of telecommunication to the racecourse of an association or to such a betting theatre, are deemed to be made on the racecourse of the association.

(3) No person or association shall use a pari-mutuel system of betting in respect of a horse-race unless the system has been approved by and its operation is carried on under the supervision of an officer appointed by the Minister of Agriculture and Agri-Food.

(4) Every person or association operating a pari-mutuel system of betting in accordance with this section in respect of a horse-race, whether or not the person or association is conducting the race-meeting at which the race is run, shall pay to the Receiver General in respect of each individual pool of the race and each individual feature pool one-half of one per cent, or such greater fraction not exceeding one per cent as may be fixed by the Governor in Council, of the total amount of money that is bet through the agency of the pari-mutuel system of betting.

(5) Where any person or association becomes a custodian or depository of any money, bet or stakes under a pari-mutuel system in respect of a horse-race, that person or association shall not deduct or retain any amount from the total amount of money, bets or stakes unless it does so pursuant to subsection (6).

(6) An association operating a pari-mutuel system of betting in accordance with this section in respect of a horse-race, or any other association or person acting on its behalf, may deduct and retain from the total amount of money that is bet through the agency of the pari-mutuel system, in respect of each individual pool of each race or each individual feature pool, a percentage not exceeding the percentage prescribed by the regulations plus any odd cents over any multiple of five cents in the amount calculated in accordance with the regulations to be payable in respect of each dollar bet.

(7) Where an officer appointed by the Minister of Agriculture and Agri-Food is not satisfied that the provisions of this section and the regulations are being carried out in good faith by any person or association in relation to a race-meeting, he may, at any time, order any betting in relation to the race-meeting to be stopped for any period that he considers proper.

(8) The Minister of Agriculture and Agri-Food may make regulations

(*a*) prescribing the maximum number of races for each race-course on which a race meeting is conducted, in respect of which a pari-mutuel system of betting may be used for the race meeting or on any one calendar day during the race meeting, and the circumstances in which the Minister of Agriculture and Agri-Food or a person designated by him for that purpose may approve of the use of that system in respect of additional races on any race-course for a particular race meeting or on a particular day during the race meeting;

(*b*) prohibiting any person or association from using a pari-mutuel system of betting for any race-course on which a race meeting is conducted in respect of more than the maximum number of races prescribed pursuant to paragraph (*a*) and the additional races, if any, in respect of which the use of a pari-mutuel system of betting has been approved pursuant to that paragraph;

(*c*) prescribing the maximum percentage that may be deducted and retained pursuant to subsection (6) by or on behalf of a person or association operating a pari-mutuel system of betting in respect of a horse-race in accordance with this section and providing for the determination of the percentage that each such person or association may deduct and retain;

(*d*) respecting pari-mutuel betting in Canada on horse-races conducted on a race-course situated outside Canada; and

(*e*) authorizing pari-mutuel betting and governing the conditions for pari-mutuel betting, including the granting of licences therefor, that is conducted by an association in a betting theatre owned or leased by the association in a province in which the Lieutenant Governor in Council, or such other person or authority in the province as may be specified by the Lieutenant Governor in Council thereof, has issued a licence to that association for the betting theatre.

(8.1) The Minister of Agriculture and Agri-Food or a person designated by that Minister may, with respect to a horse-race conducted on a race-course situated outside Canada,

(*a*) certify as acceptable, for the purposes of this section, the governing body that regulates the race; and

(*b*) permit pari-mutuel betting in Canada on the race.

(9) The Minister of Agriculture and Agri-Food may make regulations respecting

(*a*) the supervision and operation of pari-mutuel systems related to race meetings, and the fixing of the dates on which and the places at which an association may conduct such meetings;

(*b*) the method of calculating the amount payable in respect of each dollar bet;

(*c*) the conduct of race-meetings in relation to the supervision and operation of pari-mutuel systems, including photo-finishes, video patrol and the testing of bodily substances taken from horses entered in a race at such meetings, including, in the case of a horse that dies while engaged in racing or immediately before or after the race, the testing of any tissue taken from its body;

(*d*) the prohibition, restriction or regulation of

(i) the possession of drugs or medicaments or of equipment used in the administering of drugs or medicaments at or near race-courses, or

(ii) the administering of drugs or medicaments to horses participating in races run at a race meeting during which a pari-mutuel system of betting is used; and

(*e*) the provision, equipment and maintenance of accommodation, services or other facilities for the proper supervision and operation of pari-mutuel systems related to race meetings, by associations conducting those meetings or by other associations.

(9.1) For the purposes of this section, the Minister of Agriculture and Agri-Food may designate, with respect to any race-course, a zone that shall be deemed to be part of the race-course, if

(*a*) the zone is immediately adjacent to the race-course;

(*b*) the farthest point of that zone is not more than 900 metres from the nearest point on the race track of the race-course; and

(*c*) all real property situated in that zone is owned or leased by the person or association who owns or leases the race-course.

(10) Every person who contravenes or fails to comply with any of the provisions of this section or of any regulations made under this section is guilty of

(*a*) an indictable offence and liable to imprisonment for a term not exceeding two years; or

(*b*) an offence punishable on summary conviction.

(11) For the purposes of this section, "association" means an association incorporated by or pursuant to an Act of Parliament or of the legislature of a province that owns or leases a race-course and conducts horse-races in the ordinary course of its business and, to the extent that the applicable legislation requires that the purposes of the association be expressly stated in its constating instrument, having as one of its purposes the conduct of horse-races. R.S., c. C-34, s. 188; 1980-81-82-83, c. 99, s. 1; R.S.C. 1985, c. 47 (1st Supp.), s. 1; 1989, c. 2, s. 1; 1994, c. 38, ss. 14, 25; 2008, c. 18, s. 6.

CROSS-REFERENCES

Where the prosecution elects to proceed by indictment on the offence under subsec. (10) then the accused may elect his mode of trial pursuant to s. 536(2). Where the prosecution elects to proceed by way of summary conviction then the trial of this offence is conducted by a summary conviction court pursuant to Part XXVII. The punishment for the offence is then as set out in s. 787 and the limitation period is set out in s. 786(2). In either case, release pending trial is determined by s. 515, although the accused is eligible for release by a peace officer under s. 496, 497 or by the officer in charge under s. 498.

SYNOPSIS

Section 204 creates *exemptions* from liability which would otherwise arise under s. 201 or 202, and it also creates a system of legalized *pari-mutuel betting*.

Section 204(1) creates *three types* of exemptions. Section 204(1)(*a*) exempts the *custodian* or the *stakeholder of moneys* when such person pays out the stakes or money to one of the class of persons described in subparas. (i) to (iii).

Section 204(1)(*c*) excludes bets made or records of bets made through the *pari-mutuel system* if the conditions in subparas. (i) and (ii) are satisfied. Subsection (2) deems bets made in accordance with the regulations in a betting theatre, or by means of telecommunication to the race-course or betting theatre, to have been made at the race-course.

Section 204(3) to (9.1) permit the setting of and functioning of a pari-mutuel betting operation for *horse races*. It provides for regulations to be made dealing with many aspects of system described in subsec. (8). Subsection (1.1) states that if the person does an act described in ss. 201 to 202 for the *purpose of legal pari-mutuel* betting it is exempt from liability if the acts are done in accordance with the regulations.

Section 204(11) provides an exhaustive *definition* of the word *association* for the purposes of the section.

Section 204(10) creates the *offence* of contravening the section or the regulations made under it. In addition it provides for punishment by way of summary conviction procedure or by way of indictment. In the latter case the maximum sentence is two years.

205. [*Repealed*, R.S.C. 1985, c. 52 (1st Supp.), s. 1.]

OFFENCE IN RELATION TO LOTTERIES AND GAMES OF CHANCE / Definition of "three-card monte" / Exemption for fairs / Definition of "fair or exhibition" / Offence / Lottery sale void / *Bona fide* exception / Foreign lottery included / Saving.

206. (1) Every one is guilty of an indictable offence and liable to imprisonment for a term not exceeding two years who

(*a*) makes, prints, advertises or publishes, or causes or procures to be made, printed, advertised or published, any proposal, scheme or plan for advancing, lending, giving, selling or in any way disposing of any property by lots, cards, tickets or any mode of chance whatever;

(*b*) sells, barters, exchanges or otherwise disposes of, or causes or procures, or aids or assists in, the sale, barter, exchange or other disposal of, or offers for sale, barter or exchange, any lot, card, ticket or other means or device for advancing, lending, giving, selling or otherwise disposing of any property by lots, tickets or any mode of chance whatever;

(*c*) knowingly sends, transmits, mails, ships, delivers or allows to be sent, transmitted, mailed, shipped or delivered, or knowingly accepts for carriage or transport or conveys any article that is used or intended for use in carrying out any device, proposal, scheme or plan for advancing, lending, giving, selling or otherwise disposing of any property by any mode of chance whatever;

(*d*) conducts or manages any scheme, contrivance or operation of any kind for the purpose of determining who, or the holders of what lots, tickets, numbers or chances, are the winners of any property so proposed to be advanced, lent, given, sold or disposed of;

(*e*) conducts, manages or is a party to any scheme, contrivance or operation of any kind by which any person, on payment of any sum of money, or the giving of any valuable security, or by obligating himself to pay any sum of money or give any valuable security, shall become entitled under the scheme, contrivance or operation to receive from the person conducting or managing the scheme, contrivance or operation, or any other person, a larger sum of money or amount of valuable security than the sum or amount paid or given, or to be paid or given, by reason of the fact that other persons have paid or given, or obligated themselves to pay or give any sum of money or valuable security under the scheme, contrivance or operation;

(*f*) disposes of any goods, wares or merchandise by any game of chance or any game of mixed chance and skill in which the contestant or competitor pays money or other valuable consideration;

(*g*) induces any person to stake or hazard any money or other valuable property or thing on the result of any dice game, three-card monte, punch board, coin table or on the operation of a wheel of fortune;

(*h*) for valuable consideration carries on or plays or offers to carry on or to play, or employs any person to carry on or play in a public place or a place to which the public have access, the game of three-card monte;

(*i*) receives bets of any kind on the outcome of a game of three-card monte; or

(*j*) being the owner of a place, permits any person to play the game of three-card monte therein.

(2) In this section "three-card monte" means the game commonly known as three-card monte and includes any other game that is similar to it, whether or not the game is

played with cards and notwithstanding the number of cards or other things that are used for the purpose of playing.

(3) Paragraphs (1)(*f*) and (*g*), in so far as they do not relate to a dice game, three-card monte, punch board or coin table, do not apply to the board of an annual fair or exhibition, or to any operator of a concession leased by that board within its own grounds and operated during the fair or exhibition on those grounds.

(3.1) For the purposes of this section, "fair or exhibition" means an event where agricultural or fishing products are presented or where activities relating to agriculture or fishing take place.

(4) Every one who buys, takes or receives a lot, ticket or other device mentioned in subsection (1) is guilty of an offence punishable on summary conviction.

(5) Every sale, loan, gift, barter or exchange of any property, by any lottery, ticket, card or other mode of chance depending on or to be determined by chance or lot, is void, and all property so sold, lent, given, bartered or exchanged is forfeited to Her Majesty.

(6) Subsection (5) does not affect any right or title to property acquired by any *bona fide* purchaser for valuable consideration without notice.

(7) This section applies to the printing or publishing, or causing to be printed or published, of any advertisement, scheme, proposal or plan of any foreign lottery, and the sale or offer for sale of any ticket, chance or share, in any such lottery, or the advertisement for sale of such ticket, chance or share, and the conducting or managing of any such scheme, contrivance or operation for determining the winners in any such lottery.

(8) This section does not apply to

(*a*) the division by lot or chance of any property by joint tenants or tenants in common, or persons having joint interests in any such property; or

(*b*) [*Repealed*, 1999, c. 28, s. 156.]

(*c*) bonds, debentures, debenture stock or other securities recallable by drawing of lots and redeemable with interest and providing for payment of premiums on redemption or otherwise. R.S., c. C-34, s. 189; R.S.C. 1985, c. 52 (1st Supp.), s. 2; 1999, c. 28, s. 156.

CROSS-REFERENCES

The term "bet" is defined in s. 197 and "property" and "valuable security" in s. 2. The game of "three-card monte", referred to in subsec. (2), was described in *Re Rosen* (1920), 37 C.C.C. 381 (Que. C.A.), as "a game played with three cards, say, two black ones and a red one, shuffled or manipulated by the dealer and placed face down and the opponent backs his ability to spot the position of a particular card. By sleight of hand or quickness of movement, the dealer endeavours to induce the person backing his opinion to put his hand on the wrong card."

The offences under subsec. (1) are pure indictable offences, but by virtue of s. 553 are offences over which a provincial court judge has absolute jurisdiction and does not depend on the consent of the accused. That is, the accused does not have an election as to mode of trial, although the provincial court judge may by virtue of s. 555(1) elect to continue the proceedings as a preliminary inquiry, in which case, the accused is deemed to have elected trial by judge and jury pursuant to s. 565(1)(*a*). The trial of the offence in subsec. (4) is conducted by a summary conviction court pursuant to Part XXVII. The punishment for the offence in subsec. (4) is as set out in s. 787 and the limitation period is set out in s. 787(2). For all offences under this section, release pending trial is determined by s. 515, although the accused is eligible for release by a peace officer under s. 496, 497 or by the officer in charge under s. 498. As regards special search and seizure powers in relation to offences under this section, see s. 199.

Section 207 provides for certain types of permitted lotteries. As regards pyramid selling and similar schemes, reference should be made to ss. 55 and 56 of the *Competition Act*, R.S.C. 1985,

c. C-34, and respecting the conduct of promotional contests involving a lottery or other game, see s. 59 of the same Act. Section 207.1 authorizes lotteries on international cruise ships.

Related offences are: s. 201, keeping common gaming or betting house; s. 203, placing bets on behalf of others; s. 209, cheating at play.

The offence in s. 206(1)(*e*) is an enterprise crime offence pursuant to s. 462.3.

SYNOPSIS

Sections 206, 207 and 207.1, when read together, create liability for acts in relation to *lotteries and games of chance* and create *exceptions* to such liability.

Section 206(1) creates the indictable offence of doing the acts specified on paras. (*a*) to (*j*). No purpose beyond the doing of the acts described need be proven. The maximum sentence upon imprisonment is two years.

Section 206(2) defines "three-card monte" for the purposes of this section.

Section 204(3) creates an exception from s. 206(1)(*f*) to (*g*) for the use of a board located at an *annual fair or exhibition* or the operator of such a board. However, the exemption does not include dice games, three-card monte, punch board or coin tables. Subsection (3.1) sets out an exhaustive definition of the phrase "fair or exhibition" – see where it is used in subsec. (3).

Section 206(4) creates a summary conviction offence applicable to any one who takes or receives a lot, ticket or other item mentioned in subsec. (1).

Section 206(5) provides that any right of property involved in the specified acts relating to lotteries and games of chance is void and is forfeited to the Crown. However, s. 206(6) is a saving provision which states that if a person acquires the property as a *bona fide purchaser for valuable consideration* without notice their rights are protected.

Section 206(7) sets out that application of this section to a foreign lottery.

Section 206(8) sets out additional general exemptions to the operation of this section.

ANNOTATIONS

Subsection (1)(*a*) – A conviction was upheld where the scheme was that 20 ticket holders would be chosen by chance and then those 20 would compete in a potato-peeling contest to see who would win the 10 cars which were offered as prizes. The court held that the whole scheme was one of chance determining the result, as "the twenty drawn to enter the contest might well be without any real skill in paring a potato, and the cars would go to the ten least unskilful or inefficient . . . or what is also important, if any of the twenty should prove skilful, they were chosen as contestants by chance": *R. v. Wallace* (1954), 109 C.C.C. 351 (Alta. S.C. App. Div.). This case was distinguished in *R. v. Young* (1957), 119 C.C.C. 389 (B.C.C.A.), where it was held that the selection by chance of the persons entitled to participate in the contest of skill did not render the whole scheme a lottery.

The burden is on the Crown to prove that the proposed disposition of property was by mode of chance alone, involving the absence of any genuine skill and if the "skill testing question" constitutes an exercise of skill then the scheme is not a prohibited lottery. Where the police halt the lottery before the draw is held there is no burden on the accused to prove that the intended question would be a genuine test of skill: *R. v. Young* (1978), 45 C.C.C. (2d) 565 (Alta. S.C. App. Div.).

This provision prohibits the sale of a share of lottery tickets: *R. v. Stromberg* (1999), 131 C.C.C. (3d) 546 (B.C.C.A.), leave to appeal to S.C.C. refused 140 C.C.C. (3d) vi.

Furthermore, a new element of risk or chance in addition to that already implicit in the lottery itself need not be established in relation to a scheme for the sale of shares in a lottery: *R. v. World Media Brokers Inc.* (1998), 132 C.C.C. (3d) 180 (Ont. Ct. (Prov. Div.)), affd 174 C.C.C. (3d) 385 (Ont. C.A.).

Subsection (1)(*d*) – Where the lucky draw and skill-testing scheme was found to simply be a device to attempt to avoid prosecution, a conviction for operating a lottery was affirmed: *R. v. Robert Simpson (Regina) Limited* (1958), 121 C.C.C. 39 (Sask. C.A.).

A scheme which is one of skill or mixed skill and chance does not contravene this subsection: *R. v. Roe*, [1949] S.C.R. 652, 94 C.C.C. 273.

The Montreal voluntary tax plan was reviewed under appeal in *Montreal (City) v. Quebec (Attorney General)*, [1970] 2 C.C.C. 1 (S.C.C.). The court, agreeing that the prize offering of silver ingots was a cash prize and that the scheme was based essentially on chance, held (7:0) that the plan was a lottery.

The accused's belief that the *Criminal Code* lottery provisions did not apply to bingo games held on an Indian Reserve was a mistake of law and, thus, no defence to the charge under this paragraph: *R. v. Jones*, [1991] 3 S.C.R. 110, 66 C.C.C. (3d) 512 (7:0).

The accused members of the Eagle Lake First Nations failed to adduce evidence to demonstrate that gambling, or the regulation of gambling, was an integral part of their distinctive cultures. They therefore failed to demonstrate that the bingo operation in which they were engaged, and their Band's regulation of that activity, took place pursuant to an aboriginal right recognized and affirmed by s. 35(1) of the *Constitution Act, 1982*. The accused were therefore properly convicted of offences under this section: *R. v. Gardner; R. v. Jones*, [1996] 2 S.C.R. 821, 109 C.C.C. (3d) 275, *sub nom. R. v. Pamajewon*.

Any aboriginal rights the First Nations may have in relation to economic activity on the reserves did not include the right to regulate high-stakes gambling on the reserve. By the valid exercise of the criminal law power, Parliament has made such activities a criminal offence: *R. v. Gardner; R. v. Jones* (1994), 95 C.C.C. (3d) 97 (Ont. C.A.).

Subsection (1)(*e*) – Chance and skill are not factors in the offence of conducting a lottery as the offence is committed if a purchaser stands to receive back a larger amount than he contributed because other persons have contributed. Further, the offence was committed even where the accused deposited with the trust company running the contest sufficient funds to pay for the prize even if only one ticket was sold. The deposit of the funds with the trust company was only made by the accused by reason of the fact that it was part of a scheme by which contestants would pay money to enter the contest and such contest clearly contemplated, at its inception and throughout, that the prize would be awarded at the conclusion of the contest by reason of the payments for tickets of all the non-successful contestants: *R. v. Dream Home Contests (Edmonton) Ltd.; R. v. Hodges*, [1960] S.C.R. 414, 126 C.C.C. 241 (5:0). Folld: *R. v. Canus Of North America Ltd.*, [1965] 1 C.C.C. 91 (Sask. C.A.).

The legitimacy of a business is not a factor to be considered if a part of its operation is a lottery scheme. Furthermore, the key to this offence is that a participant shall become entitled to receive from others under the scheme an amount larger than his investment, and accordingly it does not matter whether that larger amount was in existence in the scheme before or after he joined it: *R. v. Golden Canada Products* (1973), 15 C.C.C. (2d) 1 (Alta. C.A.).

The essential element of this offence is the scheme and it is not necessary that money has been paid by the new recruits so long as it is contemplated that it will be payable and that a participant will receive a larger sum than he paid in as a result of the participation of others. It is not a requisite of the scheme that there be a banker: *R. v. Mackenzie, Ennis and Meilleur* (1982), 66 C.C.C. (2d) 528 (Ont. C.A.); *R. v. Fehr* (1983), 4 C.C.C. (3d) 382 (B.C.C.A.).

The value of the product in relation to the price for which it is sold is one of many relevant factors in determining whether a multi-marketing scheme violates this provision. The entire scheme must be examined to determine whether it is a recruitment scheme which will inevitably lead to loss by some who have paid into it by way of contribution in the expectation of receiving a larger amount from amounts paid in by subsequent recruits: *R. v. Friskie* (2003), 177 C.C.C. (3d) 72 (Sask. C.A.).

The Crown is not required to prove that at the time of the alleged offence other people had already paid money so that one of the persons in the scheme had already been paid a sum greater than what he had earlier paid. It is sufficient that the Crown establishes that the scheme whereby that result could obtain was in existence: *R. v. Stead* (1981), 60 C.C.C. (2d) 397 (Sask. Prov. Ct.).

Where a significant part of the scheme operated in the province it is no defence that part of the scheme, such as the actual payment of the money, also operated in the United States: *R. v. Stead, supra.*

Subsection 1(*f*) – Simply because there is an increased level of difficulty or because some elements of the game are out of the player's control does not necessarily render the game one of mixed chance and skill. In this case, however, a "crane machine" in which the player operates a joystick to move the crane to a location and uses the claw to obtain toys and novelties was a game of mixed chance and skill as virtually all of the elements of the game were out of the control of the player: *R. v. Balance Group International Trading Inc.* (2002), 162 C.C.C. (3d) 126 (Ont. C.A.).

Subsection (1)(*g*) – A wheel of fortune is a gambling device bearing some resemblance to a revolving wheel with sections indicating chances taken or bets placed: *R. v. Andrews and five others* (1975), 28 C.C.C. (2d) 450 (Sask. C.A.).

Subsection (3) – An accused who can bring himself within this subsection is entitled to its protection even on a charge of keeping a common gaming house under s. 201: *R. v. Andrews and five others, supra.*

However, this principle does not apply where the games involved are slot machines: *R. v. Cross* (1978), 40 C.C.C. (2d) 505 (Alta. S.C. App. Div.).

Subsection (7) – This section is not unconstitutionally vague: *R. v. Stromberg, infra.*

Subsection (8) – The exemption in para. (*a*) does not apply to a bingo game where, although all participants must be members of the sponsoring association, the prize money is derived from the sale of the bingo cards: *R. v. Gladue and Kirby* (1986), 30 C.C.C. (3d) 308 (Alta. Prov. Ct.).

PERMITTED LOTTERIES / Terms and conditions of licence / Offence / Definition of "lottery scheme" / Exception — charitable or religious organization / Definition of "slot machine" / Exception re: pari-mutuel betting.

207. (1) Notwithstanding any of the provisions of this Part relating to gaming and betting, it is lawful

(*a*) for the government of a province, either alone or in conjunction with the government of another province, to conduct and manage a lottery scheme in that province, or in that and the other province, in accordance with any law enacted by the legislature of that province;

(*b*) for a charitable or religious organization, pursuant to a licence issued by the Lieutenant Governor in Council of a province or by such other person or authority in the province as may be specified by the Lieutenant Governor in Council thereof, to conduct and manage a lottery scheme in that province if the proceeds from the lottery scheme are used for a charitable or religious object or purpose;

(*c*) for the board of a fair or of an exhibition or an operator of a concession leased by that board, to conduct and manage a lottery scheme in a province where the Lieutenant Governor in Council of the province or such other person or authority in the province as may be specified by the Lieutenant Governor in Council thereof has

(i) designated that fair or exhibition as a fair or exhibition where a lottery scheme may be conducted and managed, and

(ii) issued a licence for the conduct and management of a lottery scheme to that board or operator;

(*d*) for any person, pursuant to a licence issued by the Lieutenant Governor in Council of a province or by such other person or authority in the province as may be specified by the Lieutenant Governor in Council thereof, to conduct and manage a lottery scheme at a public place of amusement in that province if

(i) the amount or value of each prize awarded does not exceed five hundred dollars, and

(ii) the money or other valuable consideration paid to secure a chance to win a prize does not exceed two dollars;

(*e*) for the government of a province to agree with the government of another province that lots, cards or tickets in relation to a lottery scheme that is by any of paragraphs (*a*) to (*d*) authorized to be conducted and managed in that other province may be sold in the province;

(*f*) for any person, pursuant to a licence issued by the Lieutenant Governor in Council of a province or such other person or authority in the province as may be designated by the Lieutenant Governor in Council thereof, to conduct and manage in the province a lottery scheme that is authorized to be conducted and managed in one or more other provinces where the authority by which the lottery scheme was first authorized to be conducted and managed consents thereto;

(*g*) for any person, for the purpose of a lottery scheme that is lawful in a province under any of paragraphs (*a*) to (*f*), to do anything in the province, in accordance with the applicable law or licence, that is required for the conduct, management or operation of the lottery scheme or for the person to participate in the scheme; and

(*h*) for any person to make or print anywhere in Canada or to cause to be made or printed anywhere in Canada anything relating to gaming and betting that is to be used in a place where it is or would, if certain conditions provided by law are met, be lawful to use such a thing, or to send, transmit, mail, ship, deliver or allow to be sent, transmitted, mailed, shipped or delivered or to accept for carriage or transport or convey any such thing where the destination thereof is such a place.

(2) Subject to this Act, a licence issued by or under the authority of the Lieutenant Governor in Council of a province as described in paragraph (1)(*b*), (*c*), (*d*) or (*f*) may contain such terms and conditions relating to the conduct, management and operation of or participation in the lottery scheme to which the licence relates as the Lieutenant Governor in Council of that province, the person or authority in the province designated by the Lieutenant Governor in Council thereof or any law enacted by the legislature of that province may prescribe.

(3) Every one who, for the purposes of a lottery scheme, does anything that is not authorized by or pursuant to a provision of this section

(*a*) in the case of the conduct, management or operation of that lottery scheme,

(i) is guilty of an indictable offence and liable to imprisonment for a term not exceeding two years, or

(ii) is guilty of an offence punishable on summary conviction; or

(*b*) in the case of participating in that lottery scheme, is guilty of an offence punishable on summary conviction.

(4) In this section, "lottery scheme" means a game or any proposal, scheme, plan, means, device, contrivance or operation described in any of paragraphs 206(1)(*a*) to (*g*), whether or not it involves betting, pool selling or a pool system of betting other than

(*a*) three-card monte, punch board or coin table;

(*b*) bookmaking, pool selling or the making or recording of bets, including bets made through the agency of a pool or pari-mutuel system, on any race or fight, or on a single sport event or athletic contest; or

(*c*) for the purposes of paragraphs (1)(*b*) to (*f*), a game or proposal, scheme, plan, means, device, contrivance or operation described in any of paragraphs 206(1)(*a*) to (*g*) that is operated on or through a computer, video device, slot machine or a dice game.

(4.01) In paragraph 4(*c*), "slot machine" means any automatic machine or slot machine, other than any automatic machine or slot machine that dispenses as prizes only one or more free games on that machine, that

(*a*) is used or intended to be used for any purpose other than selling merchandise or services; or

(*b*) is used or intended to be used for the purpose of selling merchandise or services if

(i) the result of one of any number of operations of the machine is a matter of chance or uncertainty to the operator,

(ii) as a result of a given number of successive operations by the operator, the machine produces different results, or

(iii) on any operation of the machine, it discharges or emits a slug or token.

(4.1) The use of a computer for the sale of a ticket, selection of a winner or the distribution of a prize in a raffle, including a 50/50 draw, is excluded from paragraph (4)(*c*) in so far as the raffle is authorized under paragraph (1)(*b*) and the proceeds are used for a charitable or religious object or purpose.

(5) For greater certainty, nothing in this section shall be construed as authorizing the making or recording of bets on horse-races through the agency of a pari-mutuel system other than in accordance with section 204. R.S., c. C-34, s. 190; 1974-75-76, c. 93, s. 12; R.S.C. 1985, c. 27 (1st Supp.), s. 31, c. 52 (1st Supp.), s. 3; 1999, c. 5, s. 6; 2014, c. 39, s. 171; 2018, c. 29, s. 17.

CROSS-REFERENCES

The terms "bet" and "game" are defined in s. 197. Pari-mutuel systems are dealt with in s. 204. The game of "three-card monte", referred to in subsec. (4), was described in *Re Rosen* (1920), 37 C.C.C. 381 (Que. C.A.), as a "a game played with three cards, say, two black ones and a red one, shuffled or manipulated by the dealer and placed face down and the opponent backs his ability to spot the position of a particular card. By sleight of hand or quickness of movement, the dealer endeavours to induce the person backing his opinion to put his hand on the wrong card".

Where the Crown elects to proceed by indictment on the offence described in subsec. (3)(*a*) then the accused has an election as to mode of trial under s. 536(2). Where the Crown elects to proceed by way of summary conviction for the offence under subsec. (3)(*a*) and for any case under subsec. (3)(*b*), the trial is conducted by a summary conviction court pursuant to Part XXVII. The punishment for these summary conviction offences is as set out in s. 787 and the limitation period is set out in s. 786(2). For all offences under this section, release pending trial is determined by s. 515, although the accused is eligible for release by a peace officer under ss. 496, 497 or by the officer in charge under s. 498. As regards special search and seizure powers in relation to offences under this section, see s. 199.

As regards pyramid selling and similar schemes, reference should be made to ss. 55 and 56 of the *Competition Act*, R.S.C. 1985, c. C-34, and respecting the conduct of promotional contests involving a lottery or other game, see s. 59 of the same Act. Section 207.1 authorizes lotteries on international cruise ships.

Related offences are: s. 201, keeping common gaming or betting house; s. 203, placing bets on behalf of others; s. 209, cheating at play.

SYNOPSIS

Section 207 legalizes the *creation* and *operation* of *lotteries* run by any of the bodies specified in s. 207(1)(*a*) to (*d*). In addition it provides for the *regulation* of such schemes and creates an offence of operating or participating in a lottery not created or run in accordance with s. 207.

Section 207(1) permits lotteries to be created by a *province*, or *under licence* by charitable or religious organizations, by a board of a fair or exhibition or by any other person to whom a licence has been issued. The last-mentioned category only applies to lotteries in which the ticket cost no more than two dollars and the prize does not exceed $500.

Section 207(1)(*e*) to (*h*) permits persons to do specified activities required to carry out the operation of lawful lotteries under this section.

Section 207(4) *exhaustively defines* the term *lottery scheme* for the purposes of this section and also specifically excludes the activities noted in s. 207(4)(*a*) to (*c*) which are dealt with (either by way of prohibition or regulation) in ss. 202 to 206.

Section 207(4.1) clarifies that the use of a computer in a raffle or 50/50 draw does not place it within the exemption in subsec. (4)(*c*).

Section 207(5) clarifies the scope of the exclusion in s. 207(4)(*b*) in relation to pari-mutuel schemes.

Section 207(2) permits *terms and conditions* to be imposed in a *licence* under this section to regulate the conduct, management, and operation or participation in a lottery scheme.

Section 207(3) makes it an offence to do anything not authorized by this section if the act is done for the purpose of a lottery scheme. It is a summary conviction offence or an indictable offence punishable by up to two years imprisonment if the act is done in relation to the conduct, management or operation of such scheme. It is a summary conviction offence to participate in an unlawful scheme.

ANNOTATIONS

Since a "pull-ticket" vending machine falls within the definition of a slot machine in s. 198(3) the provincial gaming commission acts properly in refusing to issue licenses to charities or religious organizations seeking to use such machines: *Charity Vending Ltd. v. Alberta (Gaming Commission)* (1988), 45 C.C.C. (3d) 455 (Alta. C.A.).

The statutory scheme established by this section and s. 206 which, in effect, decriminalizes certain forms of gambling and creates a regulated industry does not constitute an unconstitutional delegation to the province, although the power to impose terms and conditions on licenses is delegated to the Lieutenant Governor: *R. v. Furtney*, [1991] 3 S.C.R. 89, 66 C.C.C. (3d) 498, 8 C.R. (4th) 121 (7:0).

EXEMPTION — LOTTERY SCHEME ON AN INTERNATIONAL CRUISE SHIP / Paragraph 207(1)(*h*) and subsection 207(5) apply / Offence / Definitions.

207.1 (1) Despite any of the provisions of this Part relating to gaming and betting, it is lawful for the owner or operator of an international cruise ship, or their agent, to conduct, manage or operate and for any person to participate in a lottery scheme during a voyage on an international cruise ship when all of the following conditions are satisfied:

(*a*) all the people participating in the lottery scheme are located on the ship;

(*b*) the lottery scheme is not linked, by any means of communication, with any lottery scheme, betting, pool selling or pool system of betting located off the ship;

(*c*) the lottery scheme is not operated within five nautical miles of a Canadian port at which the ship calls or is scheduled to call; and

(*d*) the ship is registered

(i) in Canada and its entire voyage is scheduled to be outside Canada, or

(ii) anywhere, including Canada, and its voyage includes some scheduled voyaging within Canada and the voyage

(A) is of at least forty-eight hours duration and includes some voyaging in international waters and at least one non-Canadian port of call including the port at which the voyage begins or ends, and

(B) is not scheduled to disembark any passengers at a Canadian port who have embarked at another Canadian port, without calling on at least one non-Canadian port between the two Canadian ports.

(2) For greater certainty, paragraph 207(1)(*h*) and subsection 207(5) apply for the purposes of this section.

(3) Every one who, for the purpose of a lottery scheme, does anything that is not authorized by this section

(*a*) in the case of the conduct, management or operation of the lottery scheme,

(i) is guilty of an indictable offence and liable to imprisonment for a term of not more than two years, or

(ii) is guilty of an offence punishable on summary conviction; and

(*b*) in the case of participating in the lottery scheme, is guilty of an offence punishable on summary conviction.

(4) The definitions in this subsection apply in this section.

"international cruise ship" means a passenger ship that is suitable for continuous ocean voyages of at least forty-eight hours duration, but does not include such a ship that is used or fitted for the primary purpose of transporting cargo or vehicles.

"lottery scheme" means a game or any proposal, scheme, plan, means, device, contrivance or operation described in any of paragraphs 206(1)(*a*) to (*g*), whether or not it involves betting, pool selling or a pool system of betting. It does not include

(*a*) three-card monte, punch board or coin table; or

(*b*) bookmaking, pool selling or the making or recording of bets, including bets made through the agency of a pool or pari-mutuel system, on any race or fight, or on a single sporting event or athletic contest. 1999, c. 5, s. 7.

CROSS-REFERENCES

For other exemptions from liability for lottery schemes, see ss. 206(3), (7) and 207.

SYNOPSIS

This section creates an exemption from liability for the gaming and betting offences created by this Part for lottery schemes conducted on international cruise ships. To take advantage of the exemption the operator must comply with all of the conditions set out in subsec. (1). Subsection (4) defines "international cruise ship" and "lottery scheme". Subsection (2) makes it clear that it is lawful to make or print items for use in a scheme authorized by this section and that this section does not authorize the making or recording of bets on horse-races through the agency of a pari-mutuel system other than in accordance with s. 204. Subsection (3) creates two offences: para. (*a*) for a person conducting, managing or operating the lottery scheme not authorized by this section and para. (*b*) participating in an unauthorized lottery scheme. The former is a hybrid offence. The latter is a summary conviction offence.

ANNOTATIONS

Paragraph (*b*) prohibits either extra-provincial or international sales of lottery tickets and accordingly, charitable lottery tickets marketed via the Internet were not lawful: *Reference re: Earth Future Lottery and Criminal Code s. 207* (2002), 166 C.C.C. (3d) 373, 215 D.L.R. (4th) 656, 211 Nfld. & P.E.I.R. 311 (P.E.I.C.A.), affd [2003] 1 S.C.R. 123, 171 C.C.C. (3d) 225, 222 D.L.R. (4th) 383.

---

208. [*Repealed*, R.S.C. 1985, c. 27 (1st Supp.), s. 32.]

CHEATING AT PLAY.

209. Every one who, with intent to defraud any person, cheats while playing a game or in holding the stakes for a game or in betting is guilty of an indictable offence and liable to imprisonment for a term not exceeding two years. R.S., c. C-34, s. 192.

CROSS-REFERENCES

The terms "game" and "bet" are defined in s. 197.

This offence is a pure indictable offence, but, by virtue of s. 553, it is an offence over which a provincial court judge has absolute jurisdiction and does not depend on the consent of the accused. That is, the accused does not have an election as to mode of trial, although the provincial court judge may, by virtue of s. 555(1), elect to continue the proceedings as a preliminary inquiry, in which case, the accused is deemed to have elected trial by judge and jury pursuant to s. 565(1)(*a*). Release pending trial is determined by s. 515, although the accused is eligible for release by a peace officer under s. 496, 497 or by the officer in charge under s. 498.

Related offences are: s. 201, keeping common gaming or betting house; s. 202, offences in relation to betting, pool-selling and book-making, etc.; s. 203, placing bets on behalf of others; s. 380, fraud.

SYNOPSIS

This section makes it an indictable offence to *cheat at play*. The *actus reus* of the offence is to cheat while doing any of the following: playing a game; holding the stakes; or betting. The requisite mental element is the *intention of defrauding* any person. The maximum sentence upon conviction is two years.

ANNOTATIONS

In *R. v. McGarey*, [1974] S.C.R. 278, 6 C.C.C. (2d) 525, 26 D.L.R. (3d) 231, the booth operator was convicted in the operation of a midway milk bottle toss game where the unsuspecting patron was unaware that the bottom bottles of each pyramid were heavily weighted. It was held (5:0) that in this game of mixed chance and skill the booth operator was a player and the surreptitious weighting of the bottom bottles constituted his intent to defraud the patron player by creating a false visual impression of the game, which false impression in itself was the ill-practice of cheating.

However, simple measures taken to increase the degree of skill required for success are not improper: *R. v. Reilly* (1979), 48 C.C.C. (2d) 286 (Ont. C.A.).

Bawdy-houses

KEEPING COMMON BAWDY-HOUSE / Landlord, inmate, etc. / Notice of conviction to be served on owner / Duty of landlord on notice.

210. (1) Every one who keeps a common bawdy-house is guilty of an indictable offence and liable to imprisonment for a term not exceeding two years.

(2) Every one who

(*a*) is an inmate of a common bawdy-house,

(*b*) is found, without lawful excuse, in a common bawdy-house, or

(*c*) as owner, landlord, lessor, tenant, occupier, agent or otherwise having charge or control of any place, knowingly permits the place or any part thereof to be let or used for the purposes of a common bawdy-house,

is guilty of an offence punishable on summary conviction.

(3) Where a person is convicted of an offence under subsection (1), the court shall cause a notice of the conviction to be served on the owner, landlord or lessor of the place in

respect of which the person is convicted or his agent, and the notice shall contain a statement to the effect that it is being served pursuant to this section.

(4) Where a person on whom a notice is served under subsection (3) fails forthwith to exercise any right he may have to determine the tenancy or right of occupation of the person so convicted, and thereafter any person is convicted of an offence under subsection (1) in respect of the same premises, the person on whom the notice was served shall be deemed to have committed an offence under subsection (1) unless he proves that he has taken all reasonable steps to prevent the recurrence of the offence. R.S., c. C-34, s. 193.

CROSS-REFERENCES

The terms "keeper", "common bawdy-house" and "place" are defined in s. 197. Section 198(1)(*a*) and (*d*) set out certain presumptions which aid in proof that premises are a common bawdy-house.

As regards special search and seizure powers in relation to bawdy-houses, see s. 199.

The offence in subsec. (1) is a pure indictable offence, but, by virtue of s. 553, it is an offence over which a provincial court judge has absolute jurisdiction and does not depend on the consent of the accused. That is, the accused does not have an election as to mode of trial, although the provincial court judge may, by virtue of s. 555(1), elect to continue the proceedings as a preliminary inquiry, in which case, the accused is deemed to have elected trial by judge and jury pursuant to s. 565(1)(*a*). The trial of the offences in subsec. (2) are conducted by a summary conviction court pursuant to Part XXVII. The punishment for the offences in subsec. (2) are as set out in s. 787 and the limitation period is set out in s. 786(2). For all offences under this section, release pending trial is determined by s. 515, although the accused is eligible for release by a peace officer under s. 496, 497 or by the officer in charge under s. 498.

This offence falls within the definition of "enterprise crime offence" in s. 462.3 for the purposes of Part XII.2.

Other offences related to prostitution may be found in ss. 211 to 213.

As to production of records containing personal information of the complainant or a witness, see ss. 278.1 to 278.9.

Section 486(1) and (2) provide that the judge may make an order excluding all or any members of the public where such order is in the interest of public morals, the maintenance of order or the proper administration of justice, or is necessary to prevent injury to international relations or national defence or national security. The proper administration of justice includes safeguarding the interests of witnesses under the age of 18 years. Section 486.1 sets out the circumstances in which the judge shall or may order a support person to be present and close to a witness while the witness testifies. Where the witness is under the age of 18 years or has a mental or physical disability, the order is to be made upon request unless the judge is of the opinion that the order would interfere with the proper administration of justice. In the case of other witnesses, the order is to be made if necessary to obtain a full and candid account from the witness of the matters complained of. The application for this order may be made during the proceedings or before they begin to the judge who is to preside at the proceedings.

Similarly, s. 486.2 sets out the circumstances in which the judge shall or may order a witness to testify outside the courtroom or behind a screen or other device that would not allow the witness to see the accused. Where the witness is under the age of 18 years or may have difficulty communicating the evidence by reason of a mental or physical disability, the judge shall make the order unless the judge is of the opinion that the order would interfere with the proper administration of justice. In all other cases, the order may be made if the judge is of the opinion that the order is necessary to obtain a full and candid account from the witness of the acts complained of. Similarly, s. 486.3 provides that, on application by the prosecutor or a witness under the age of 18 years, the accused shall not personally cross-examine the witness unless the judge is of the opinion that the proper administration of justice requires the accused to personally conduct the cross-examination. In other cases, the judge may make an order that the accused not personally cross-examine the witness if the judge is of the opinion that the order is necessary to obtain a full and candid account from the witness of the acts complained of. The judge will appoint counsel to conduct the cross-examination.

Under s. 486.4, the judge may make an order directing that the identity of the complainant or a witness not be disclosed in any publication, broadcast or transmitted in any way. The order is mandatory where the complainant or a witness under the age of 18 years or the prosecutor applies for the order. Section 486.5 also gives the judge a discretion respecting non-publication orders in proceedings under these provisions in other circumstances.

SYNOPSIS

This section creates a number of offences in relation to a common bawdy-house.

Section 210(1) makes it an indictable offence to *keep a common bawdy-house*. The maximum sentence upon conviction is two years.

Section 210(2) creates three summary conviction offences. Section 210(2)(*a*) makes it an offence to be an *inmate* in a common bawdy-house. "Inmate" is not defined in the *Criminal Code* but would include a resident or regular occupant of the premises. Section 210(2)(*b*) makes it an offence to be *found in* a common bawdy-house. It must be shown that there was no lawful excuse for the accused's presence. The term "found in" is not defined. Section 210(2)(*c*) makes it an offence for any of the named persons to *knowingly permit* any part of a premises to be used or let for the *purposes* of a common bawdy-house. The category of persons who are caught by this paragraph are those who have actual control or charge over the premises. To demonstrate that the conduct satisfies the necessary mental element of having *knowingly permitted* the use, it must be shown that the accused was aware of the use of the premises and either acquiesced or encouraged its continued use for the illicit purposes.

Subsections (3) and (4) must be read together and create a duty upon the owner, landlord or lessor of the premises which was the subject of a conviction under subsec. (1) (keeping a common bawdy-house). Subsection (3) provides for a notice to be served upon such person or his agent advising of the conviction, and upon receipt of the notice the landlord, owner or lessor must either *forthwith* attempt to terminate the tenancy or other arrangement permitting the keeper to be on the premises or face possible later prosecution. If there is a conviction under subsec. (1) in relation to the same premises after the notice has served upon the owner (or other person mentioned in the subsection) the person who had received the notice *shall be deemed* to also be a keeper pursuant to subsec. (1). To accord with fundamental fairness, at the least it must be shown that the later conviction involving the same premises related to activity which occurred after the notice has been served. The effect of the deeming provision may be ousted if the accused establishes that all reasonable steps were taken to prevent the reoccurrence of the offence under subsec. (1).

ANNOTATIONS

Note: The following cases were decided with reference to a former version of s. 197 in which "prostitution" was part of the definition of "common bawdy house". The amendment was in response to the Supreme Court's decision in *Canada (Attorney General) v. Bedford*, [2013] 3 S.C.R. 1101, 303 C.C.C. (3d) 146, which struck the word "prostitution" from the former definition. The following cases should be read with caution in light of the amended definition which focuses solely on "indecency".

Common bawdy-house / *Also see notes under s. 197* – Any defined space is capable of being a common bawdy-house, even a parking lot, if there is localization of a number of acts of prostitution within its specified boundaries. However, mere presence by prostitutes in the parking lot on a number of occasions, where they did not exercise any control or management over the lot and had no right or interest in the lot as owners, tenants or licensees, is not sufficient to establish them as keeping a common bawdy-house: *R. v. Pierce* (1982), 66 C.C.C. (2d) 388 (Ont. C.A.).

That the premises are a common bawdy-house may be proved by evidence of the general reputation of the house in the community: *R. v. Theirlynck*, [1931] S.C.R. 478, 56 C.C.C. 156.

As well, where there is evidence that the place has the reputation as a common bawdy-house, evidence was admissible as to the accused's reputation as a prostitute. Such evidence is not admitted to show that the accused was the keeper but that the place is occupied by a person whose reputation is consistent with the reputation which it is said the place bears: *R. v. West* (1950), 96 C.C.C. 349 (Ont. C.A.).

"Acts of indecency" and "prostitution" are not vague so as to violate s. 7 of the Charter: *R. v. DiGiuseppe* (2002), 161 C.C.C. (3d) 424 (Ont. C.A.), leave to appeal to S.C.C. refused [2002] 3 S.C.R. vii, 167 C.C.C. (3d) vi.

As to the meaning of acts of indecency, see *R. v. Labaye*, [2005] 3 S.C.R. 728, 203 C.C.C. (3d) 170; *R. v. Kouri*, [2005] 3 S.C.R. 789, 203 C.C.C. (3d) 217, noted under s. 197.

Keeps (subsec. (1)) – As not every "keeper" as defined in s. 197 "keeps" a common bawdy-house, an information charging that the accused "were the keepers of a common bawdy-house" does not charge an offence known to law: *R. v. Catalano* (1977), 37 C.C.C. (2d) 255 (Ont. C.A.).

Thus the offence requires proof of provision of accommodation by the accused. A prostitute who on several occasions over a two-week period resorted to the same hotel must be acquitted of this offence where there is no evidence she was given any particular room, or had rented a particular room or even that she had paid the rent on the room: *R. v. McLellan* (1980), 55 C.C.C. (2d) 543 (B.C.C.A.).

To establish the offence of keeping there must be proof that the accused had some degree of control over the care and management of the premises, and that the accused participated to some extent in the illicit activities of the common bawdy-house. This element of participation does not, however, require personal participation in the sexual acts which occur in the house. It is sufficient that the accused participated in the use of the house as a common bawdy-house. Thus, a person who satisfies the definition of "keeper" in s. 197(1) does not necessarily commit the offence under subsec. (1): *R. v. Corbeil*, [1991] 2 S.C.R. 830, 64 C.C.C. (3d) 272 (4:1).

It is unnecessary to show that the accused participated in the day-to-day running of the premises where he is shown to be the directing mind of the corporation which owned the premises, participated in the management, received the proceeds and was aware of the activities being carried on: *R. v. Woszczyna; R. v. Soucy* (1983), 6 C.C.C. (3d) 221 (Ont. C.A.).

Even where the accused uses her own residence by herself for the purposes of prostitution she may be convicted under this section: *R. v. Worthington* (1972), 10 C.C.C. (2d) 311 (Ont. C.A.).

The Crown must establish an element of control over the care and regular management of the place which harboured the acts of indecency. Willful blindness on the part of the owner or delegation of responsibility are insufficient: *R. v. Kouri, supra*.

Prostitution is not limited to conventional sexual activities and includes lewd acts for payment for the sexual gratification of customers. In this case, sado-masochistic acts were lewd activities in that although they involved pain and humiliation, this did not detract from their sexuality nor the sexual gratification obtained by the clients: *R. v. Bedford* (2000), 143 C.C.C. (3d) 311 (Ont. C.A.), leave to appeal to S.C.C. refused 147 C.C.C. (3d) vi.

Indecency is not inherent in the offence of prostitution. In this case, even though there was no physical contact, the fact that dancers stimulated the customer by engaging in various sexual acts while the customers masturbated was sufficient to constitute prostitution: *R. v. St-Onge* (2001), 155 C.C.C. (3d) 517 (Que. C.A.), leave to appeal to S.C.C. refused [2002] 1 S.C.R. x, 160 C.C.C. (3d) vi.

And, in *R. v. Ni* (2002), 158 O.A.C. 230 (C.A.), the court held that the charge under this section could be made out on the basis of acts of prostitution consisting of acts of masturbation by employees of a massage parlour upon customers. It was unnecessary for the Crown to prove that the conduct also amounted to acts of indecency.

Found in (subsec. (2)(*b*)) – The offence of being found in a common bawdy-house is not a lesser offence included in the charge of keeping a common bawdy-house: *R. v. Labelle*, [1957] Que. Q.B. 81 (C.A.).

The offence under subsec. (2)(*b*) requires that the accused was found in the common bawdy house and it was not sufficient that the accused "was present". Mere proof of presence on the premises in question at some earlier time is not sufficient, the accused must have been perceived there or seen by someone. On the other hand, evidence that the accused was seen entering and leaving was sufficient to prove the offence, his presence in the bawdy house not being the object of subsequent admission but being discovered by the contemporaneous observation or inspection by the police: *R. v. Lemieux* (1991), 70 C.C.C. (3d) 434 (Que. C.A.).

Permitting (subsec. (2)(*c*)) – Where the accused knowingly allowed the premises to be used as a place to which men and women resorted for the purpose of illicit sexual intercourse then a conviction will be sustained even though there was no evidence that the women were charging money for their services or that the couples resorting to the premises were unmarried: *R. v. Turkiewich* (1962), 133 C.C.C. 301 (Man. C.A.).

A charge of being an occupier unlawfully permitting premises to be used as a common bawdy-house was held to be a lesser offence included in the charge of keeping a common bawdy-house: *R. v. Lafreniere*, [1965] 1 C.C.C. 31 (Ont. H.C.J.).

The words "or otherwise having charge or control" qualify the earlier words in the subsection and make it clear that the section is not directed at an owner or landlord, *per se*, but rather at such persons as being the ones having charge or control of the premises. Even where the landlord has power to acquire the charge or control of the premises by immediate termination of the lease, still, once he leased the premises, it was the tenant who had charge or control. The section is directed at a landlord who has actual charge or control in the sense that he has the right to intervene forthwith and whose failure to do so can be considered the granting of permission: *R. v. Wong* (1977), 33 C.C.C. (2d) 6 (Alta. S.C. App. Div.).

TRANSPORTING PERSON TO BAWDY-HOUSE.

211. Every one who knowingly takes, transports, directs, or offers to take, transport or direct, any other person to a common bawdy-house is guilty of an offence punishable on summary conviction. R.S., c. C-34, s. 194.

CROSS-REFERENCES

The term "common bawdy-house" is defined in s. 197.

The trial of this offence is conducted by a summary conviction court pursuant to Part XXVII. The punishment for the offence is as set out in s. 787 and the limitation period is set out in s. 786(2). Release pending trial is determined by s. 515, although the accused is eligible for release by a peace officer under s. 496, 497 or by the officer in charge under s. 498. Other offences in relation to bawdy-houses are found in s. 210. Offences in relation to prostitution are found in ss. 212 and 213.

As to production of records containing personal information of the complainant or a witness, see ss. 278.1 to 278.9.

Section 486(1) and (2) provide that the judge may make an order excluding all or any members of the public where such order is in the interest of public morals, the maintenance of order or the proper administration of justice, or is necessary to prevent injury to international relations or national defence or national security. The proper administration of justice includes safeguarding the interests of witnesses under the age of 18 years. Section 486.1 sets out the circumstances in which the judge shall or may order a support person to be present and close to a witness while the witness testifies. Where the witness is under the age of 18 years or has a mental or physical disability, the order is to be made upon request unless the judge is of the opinion that the order would interfere with the proper administration of justice. In the case of other witnesses, the order is to be made if necessary to obtain a full and candid account from the witness of the matters complained of. The application for this order may be made during the proceedings or before they begin to the judge who is to preside at the proceedings.

Similarly, s. 486.2 sets out the circumstances in which the judge shall or may order a witness to testify outside the courtroom or behind a screen or other device that would not allow the witness to see the accused. Where the witness is under the age of 18 years or may have difficulty communicating the evidence by reason of a mental or physical disability, the judge shall make the order unless the judge is of the opinion that the order would interfere with the proper administration of justice. In all other cases, the order may be made if the judge is of the opinion that the order is necessary to obtain a full and candid account from the witness of the acts complained of. Similarly, s. 486.3 provides that, on application by the prosecutor or a witness under the age of 18 years, the accused shall not personally cross-examine the witness unless the judge is of the opinion that the proper administration of justice requires the accused to personally conduct the cross-examination. In other cases, the judge may make an order that the accused not personally cross-examine the witness if the judge is of the opinion that the order is necessary to obtain a full and candid account from the witness of the acts complained of. The judge will appoint counsel to conduct the cross-examination.

Under s. 486.4, the judge may make an order directing that the identity of the complainant or a witness not be disclosed in any publication, broadcast or transmitted in any way. The order is mandatory where the complainant or a witness under the age of 18 years or the prosecutor applies for the order. Section 486.5 also gives the judge a discretion respecting non-publication orders in proceedings under these provisions in other circumstances.

SYNOPSIS

This section makes it a summary conviction offence to *transport a person to a common bawdy-house*. The actions encompassed by the section are broadly defined as including taking, transporting, directing or offering to do any of these things. The *mens rea* for the offence is that the action be done *knowingly*, namely, that the accused knew that the place was a common bawdy-house.

[*Heading repealed*, 2014, c. 25, s. 13.]

212. [*Repealed*, 2014, c. 25, s. 13.]

Offences in Relation to Offering, Providing or Obtaining Sexual Services for Consideration

2014, c. 25, s. 14.

STOPPING OR IMPEDING TRAFFIC / Communicating to provide sexual services for consideration / Definition of "public place".

213. (1) Everyone is guilty of an offence punishable on summary conviction who, in a public place or in any place open to public view, for the purpose of offering, providing or obtaining sexual services for consideration,

(*a*) stops or attempts to stop any motor vehicle, or

(*b*) impedes the free flow of pedestrian or vehicular traffic or ingress to or egress from premises adjacent to that place.

(*c*) [*Repealed*, 2014, c. 25, s. 15(2).]

(1.1) Everyone is guilty of an offence punishable on summary conviction who communicates with any person — for the purpose of offering or providing sexual services for consideration — in a public place, or in any place open to public view, that is or is next to a school ground, playground or daycare centre.

(2) In this section, "public place" includes any place to which the public have access as of right or by invitation, express or implied, and any motor vehicle located in a public place or in any place open to public view. 1972, c. 13, s. 15; R.S.C. 1985, c. 50 (1st Supp.), s. 1; 2014, c. 25, s. 15.

CROSS-REFERENCES

"Place" is defined in s. 197. "Motor vehicle" is defined in s. 2.

Other offences relating to sexual services are found in ss. 286.1, 286.2, 286.3 and 286.4.

The trial of this offence is conducted by a summary conviction court pursuant to Part XXVII. The punishment for the offence is as set out in s. 787 and the limitation period is set out in s. 786(2). Release pending trial is determined by s. 515, although the accused is eligible for release by a peace officer under s. 496, 497 or by the officer in charge under s. 498. Other offences in relation to prostitution are found in ss. 211 and 212. Offences in relation to bawdy-houses are found in ss. 210 and 211.

As to production of records containing personal information of the complainant or a witness, see ss. 278.1 to 278.9.

Section 486(2.1) provides that, where an accused is charged with this offence and the complainant is, at the time of the trial or preliminary inquiry, under the age of 18 years or may have difficulty communicating the evidence by reason of a mental or physical disability, the judge may order that the complainant testify outside the courtroom or behind a screen where such procedure is necessary to obtain a full and candid account of the acts complained of. Section 715.1 provides that, in proceedings under subsec. (2) or (3), a videotape, made within a reasonable time after the alleged offence, in which the complainant describes the acts complained of, is admissible in evidence if the complainant adopts its contents. Similarly, s. 715.2 provides that, in proceedings under this section in which the complainant or another witness may have difficulty communicating the evidence by reason of a mental or physical disability, a videotape made within a reasonable time after the alleged offence, in which the complainant or witness describes the acts complained of, is admissible in evidence if the complainant or witness adopts its contents.

SYNOPSIS

This section makes it an offence to do any of the prohibited acts (described in subsec. (1)(*a*) to (*c*)) if accompanied by the intention of offering, providing or obtaining sexual services for consideration. This summary conviction offence applies to the acts described below only if they are done in a *public place* (as defined by s. 213(2)) or a place open to public view.

Section 213(1)(*a*) applies to the act of either stopping a motor vehicle or attempting to do so for the prohibited purpose.

Section 213(1)(*b*) prohibits impeding either pedestrian or motor vehicle traffic, or impeding others from going in or out of any premises adjacent to a public place, or one open to the public for the purposes described above.

Section 213(1.1) creates an offence of communicating near schools, etc. for the purpose of offering or providing sexual services. Section 213(2) clarifies what counts as a public place for purposes of this section.

Part VIII / OFFENCES AGAINST THE PERSON AND REPUTATION

Interpretation

DEFINITIONS / "abandon" or "expose" / "aircraft" / "child" / "form of marriage" / "guardian" / "operate" / "vessel".

214. In this Part

"abandon" or "expose" includes

(*a*) a wilful omission to take charge of a child by a person who is under a legal duty to do so, and

(*b*) dealing with a child in a manner that is likely to leave that child exposed to risk without protection;

"aircraft" [*Repealed*, 2018, c. 21, s. 13.]

"child" [*Repealed*, 2002, c. 13, s. 9.]

"form of marriage" includes a ceremony of marriage that is recognized as valid

(*a*) by the law of the place where it was celebrated, or

(*b*) by the law of the place where an accused is tried, notwithstanding that it is not recognized as valid by the law of the place where it was celebrated;

"guardian" includes a person who has in law or in fact the custody or control of a child. R.S., c. C-34, s. 196; R.S.C. 1985, c. 27 (1st Supp.), s. 33; c. 32 (4th Supp.), s. 56; 2018, c. 21, s. 13.

"operate" [*Repealed*, 2018, c. 21, s. 13.]

"vessel" [*Repealed*, 2018, c. 21, s. 13.]

CROSS-REFERENCES

In addition to the definitions in this section, see s. 2 and notes to that section. The terms "motor vehicle" and "railway equipment" are defined in s. 2. The term "wilfully" does not have a fixed meaning and must take its meaning from the context. Generally speaking, however, it connotes an intention to bring about a proscribed consequence. See: *R. v. Buzzanga and Durocher* (1979), 49 C.C.C. (2d) 369 (Ont. C.A.). Most of the legal duties referred to in the definition of "abandon" or "expose" may be found in ss. 215 to 217. Age is determined by reference to s. 30 of the *Interpretation Act*, R.S.C. 1985, c. I-21.

ANNOTATIONS

"abandon or expose" – A relative who undertakes to babysit young children is under a legal duty to take the same care of the children as their parents are at law required to do: *R. v. Reedy (No. 2)* (1981), 60 C.C.C. (2d) 104 (Ont. Dist. Ct.).

"vessel" – A canoe is a "vessel" for the purpose of Part VIII of the *Code*: *R. v. Sillars* (2018), 368 C.C.C. (3d) 452 (Ont. C.J.).

Duties Tending to Preservation of Life

DUTY OF PERSONS TO PROVIDE NECESSARIES / Offence / Punishment / Presumptions.

215. (1) Every one is under a legal duty

(*a*) as a parent, foster parent, guardian or head of a family, to provide necessaries of life for a child under the age of sixteen years;

(*b*) to provide necessaries of life to their spouse or common-law partner; and

(*c*) to provide necessaries of life to a person under his charge if that person

(i) is unable, by reason of detention, age, illness, mental disorder or other cause, to withdraw himself from that charge, and

(ii) is unable to provide himself with necessaries of life.

(2) Every person commits an offence who, being under a legal duty within the meaning of subsection (1), fails without lawful excuse to perform that duty, if

(*a*) with respect to a duty imposed by paragraph (1)(*a*) or (*b*),

(i) the person to whom the duty is owed is in destitute or necessitous circumstances, or

(ii) the failure to perform the duty endangers the life of the person to whom the duty is owed, or causes or is likely to cause the health of that person to be endangered permanently; or

(*b*) with respect to a duty imposed by paragraph (1)(*c*), the failure to perform the duty endangers the life of the person to whom the duty is owed or causes or is likely to cause the health of that person to be injured permanently.

(3) Every one who commits an offence under subsection (2)

(*a*) is guilty of an indictable offence and liable to imprisonment for a term not exceeding five years; or

(*b*) is guilty of an offence punishable on summary conviction and liable to imprisonment for a term not exceeding eighteen months.

(4) For the purpose of proceedings under this section,

(*a*) [*Repealed*, 2000, c. 12, s. 93(2).];

(*b*) evidence that a person has in any way recognized a child as being his child is, in the absence of any evidence to the contrary, proof that the child is his child;

(*c*) evidence that a person has failed for a period of one month to make provision for the maintenance of any child of theirs under the age of sixteen years is, in the absence of any evidence to the contrary, proof that the person has failed without lawful excuse to provide necessaries of life for the child; and

(*d*) the fact that a spouse or common-law partner or child is receiving or has received necessaries of life from another person who is not under a legal duty to provide them is not a defence. R.S., c. C-34, s. 197; 1974-75-76, c. 66, s. 8; 1991, c. 43, s. 9; 2000, c. 12, ss. 93, 95(*a*); 2005, c. 32, s. 11; 2018, c. 29, s. 18.

CROSS-REFERENCES

The terms "child" and "guardian" are defined in s. 214. The terms "mental disorder" and "common-law partner" are defined in s. 2. Omission to perform the duty imposed by subsec. (1) may, in some circumstances, amount to criminal negligence as defined in s. 219 and, if conduct results in death or bodily harm, will amount to an offence under ss. 220 and 221 respectively. Criminal negligence causing death is also a form of culpable homicide for the purposes of ss. 222 to 237. The related offence of abandoning a child is in s. 218. Neglecting to obtain assistance in child birth is an offence under s. 242. The accused's spouse is a competent and compellable witness at the instance of the Crown by virtue of s. 4(2).

Where the prosecution elects to proceed by indictment on this offence then the accused may elect his mode of trial pursuant to s. 536(2). Where the prosecution elects to proceed by way of summary conviction then the trial of this offence is conducted by a summary conviction court pursuant to Part XXVII. The punishment for the offence is then as set out in s. 787 and the limitation period is set out in s. 786(2). In either case, release pending trial is determined by s. 515, although the accused is eligible for release by a peace officer under s. 496, 497 or by the officer in charge under s. 498.

Section 718.01 provides that, in imposing a sentence for an offence involving the abuse of a person under the age of 18 years, the court shall give primary consideration to the objectives of denunciation and deterrence. Further, under s. 718.2, evidence that the offender, in committing the offence, abused a person under the age of 18 years is an aggravating circumstance.

SYNOPSIS

This section creates an offence for *failing to provide the necessaries of life* and contains a number of *rebuttable presumptions which facilitate proof of certain elements of the offence.*

Section 215(1) establishes three classes of relationships in which one party has a legal duty to provide the necessaries of life to the other party: (a) a parent, foster parent, guardian or head of a family must provide the necessaries of life to a child under the age of 16; (b) a married person must provide for his spouse; and (c) a person who has charge of another must provide the necessaries of life to that person if for one of the specified reasons that person is unable to withdraw from the charge and is unable to provide himself with the necessaries of life.

Section 215(2) states that failure to carry out the legal duty specified in subsec. (1) constitutes an offence. The first element of this offence is that the accused failed, without lawful excuse, to fulfil a duty imposed by subsec. (1) if the additional conditions in either s. 215(2)(*a*) or (*b*) are established. The onus of establishing a lawful excuse is on the accused and, as with all such burdens placed on the accused, it has been attacked as an alleged violation of ss. 7 and 11(*d*) of the Charter.

Section 215(2)(*a*) applies to cases in which the legal duty owed by the accused arises as a result of s. 215(1)(*a*) or (*b*) (basically parents and spouses). Under s. 215(2)(*a*), the offence will be made out if the person to whom the duty is owed is either *destitute or in necessitous circumstances* or if the result of the failure to fulfil the duty *endangers the life* of the person to whom the duty is owed or *causes or is likely to cause* permanent endangerment to the health of that person. Section 215(2)(*b*) applies if the duty upon the accused arose from s. 215(1)(*c*) (a person under the charge of the accused if certain circumstances pertain). The failure to fulfil that duty makes out the offence, if the result is that the *life* of the person to whom the duty is owed is *endangered* or it is *likely to cause the health* of that person to be *injured permanently*.

Subsection (3) provides that the offence created may be prosecuted by way of summary conviction procedure or by indictment. Where the Crown proceeds by way of indictment, the maximum sentence is five years and where the Crown proceeds by summary conviction, the maximum sentence is 18 months.

Section 215(4)(*b*) to (*c*) set out *rebuttable evidentiary presumptions* that evidence of the things specified is *proof* of certain elements of the offence *unless* there is *any evidence to the contrary*. Section 215(4)(*d*) limits what constitutes a defence to the charge of failing to provide the necessaries of life. It provides that it is not a defence that some one else, who is not under a legal duty to do so, provided a spouse or child the necessaries of life.

ANNOTATIONS

"Necessaries of life" – The words "necessaries of life" mean such necessaries as tend to preserve life, and not necessaries in their ordinary legal sense and may include medical aid: *R. v. Brooks* (1902), 5 C.C.C. 372 (B.C.S.C.).

Failure to provide medical treatment can amount to "necessitous circumstances" and can therefore lead to liability under either of subparas. (2)(*a*)(i) or (ii): *R. v. J. (S.)* (2015), 320 C.C.C. (3d) 524 (Ont. C.A.), leave to appeal to S.C.C. refused 2015 CarswellOnt 10364.

Lawful excuse – The accused's inability to support his wife may constitute a lawful excuse: *R. v. Yuman* (1910), 17 C.C.C. 474 (Ont. C.A.).

It is not a lawful excuse for a parent who, knowing that a child is in need of medical assistance, refused to obtain such assistance because to do so would be contrary to a tenet of his own particular faith. The guarantee to freedom of conscience and religion in s. 2(*a*) of the *Charter of Rights and Freedoms* does not affect that issue: *R. v. Tutton and Tutton* (1985), 18 C.C.C. (3d) 328 (Ont. C.A.), affd [1989] 1 S.C.R. 1392, 48 C.C.C. (3d) 129 (6:0).

Where an accused is charged with manslaughter in an indictment so worded as to make the offence under this subsection an included offence, it must be made clear to the jury that the issue of lawful excuse and the onus on the accused on that issue is not applicable on the manslaughter charge: *R. v. Tutton and Tutton, supra*.

Placing the persuasive burden of establishing lawful excuse upon the accused violates s. 11(*d*) of the Charter and does not constitute a reasonable limit pursuant to s. 1 of the Charter. Accordingly, the words "the proof of which lies on him" are of no force and effect: *R. v. Curtis* (1998), 123 C.C.C. (3d) 178 (Ont. C.A.). See also *R. v. Scott* (1996), 110 C.C.C. (3d) 473 (Sask. Q.B.).

Mens rea – This offence imposes liability on an objective basis. On a charge contrary to subsec. (2)(*a*)(ii), the Crown must prove a marked departure from the conduct of a reasonably prudent parent in circumstances where it was objectively foreseeable that the failure to provide the necessaries of life would lead to a risk of danger to the life, or a risk of permanent endangerment to the health, of the child: *R. v. Naglik*, [1993] 3 S.C.R. 122, 83 C.C.C. (3d) 526.

In a series of cases, the Supreme Court of Canada had occasion to explore the fault element in cases of so-called "penal negligence" apparently as distinguished from criminal negligence. Failure to provide necessaries would be one of these offences. In *R. v. Creighton*, [1993] 3 S.C.R. 3, 83 C.C.C. (3d) 346, McLachlin J., writing for a majority of the court, suggested the following approach to proof of such offences. The first question is whether the *actus reus* is established. This requires that the negligence constitute a marked departure from the standards of a reasonable person in all the circumstances of the case. The next question is whether the *mens rea* is established. Normally the *mens rea* for objective foresight of risk of harm is inferred from the facts. The standard is that of the reasonable person in the circumstances of the accused. The normal inference that a person who committed a manifestly dangerous act failed to direct their mind to the risk and the need to take care may be negated by evidence raising a reasonable doubt as to lack of capacity to appreciate the risk. Short of incapacity, personal factors are not relevant whether those factors might indicate, for example, either a lack of experience or a special experience. Also see: *R. v. Naglik*, *supra*.

Under subsec. (2)(*a*)(ii), the Crown must prove that the failure to obtain medical attention would likely put the child at risk of permanent harm: *R. v. Barry* (2004), 187 C.C.C. (3d) 176 (Nfld. & Lab. C.A.).

There are differences between criminal negligence and failing to provide the necessaries of life. Criminal negligence requires conduct that constitutes a marked and substantial departure from what a reasonably prudent person would do under the circumstances. Failing to provide the necessaries of life requires proof only that the conduct constitutes a marked departure from the standard of care expected of a reasonably prudent person in the circumstances. Criminal negligence requires proof that the accused showed a wanton or reckless disregard for the life or safety of another, whereas failure to provide the necessaries of life requires proof that the accused's failure endangered the life of the person to whom he or she owed a duty, or that the accused caused, or was likely to cause, the health of that person to be endangered permanently. Finally, criminal negligence is the more serious of the two offences: *R. v. F. (J.)*, [2008] 3 S.C.R. 215, 236 C.C.C. (3d) 421.

"Under his charge" – This phrase imposed a duty where one person was under the other's charge, was unable to withdraw from that charge and was unable to provide himself or herself with the necessaries of life which include food, shelter, care, medical attention necessary to sustain life and protection from harm. "Charge" connoted the duty or responsibility of taking care of a person or thing and included the exercise of an element of control by one person and a dependency on the part of the other. Factors to be considered are the relative positions of the parties and their ability to understand and appreciate their circumstances and whether the accused had explicitly assumed responsibility for the other such as by obtaining a power of attorney for personal care. The offence is made out where there is a marked departure from the conduct of a reasonably prudent person having the charge of another in circumstances where it was reasonably foreseeable that failure to provide necessaries of life would risk danger to life or permanent endangerment of the health of the person under the charge of the accused. In this case, the accused's elderly and ill father was properly found to be under his charge having regard to the fact that the victim was dependent, had a familial relationship with the accused, the accused was fully aware of his father's need of the necessaries of life, the accused controlled the victim's living conditions and kept him in an unsafe environment, the accused had control over the victim's personal care, the accused chose not to make decisions such as contacting community services and the fact that the victim was incapable of withdrawing from the accused's charge having regard to his age and mental illness: *R. v. Peterson* (2005), 201 C.C.C. (3d) 220 (Ont. C.A.), leave to appeal to S.C.C. refused 204 C.C.C. (3d) vi.

DUTY OF PERSONS UNDERTAKING ACTS DANGEROUS TO LIFE.

216. Every one who undertakes to administer surgical or medical treatment to another person or to do any other lawful act that may endanger the life of another person is, except in cases of necessity, under a legal duty to have and to use reasonable knowledge, skill and care in so doing. R.S., c. C-34, s. 198.

CROSS-REFERENCES

Omission to perform the duty imposed by this section may, in some circumstances, amount to criminal negligence as defined in s. 219 and, if conduct results in death or bodily harm, will amount to an offence under ss. 220 and 221 respectively. Criminal negligence causing death is also a form of culpable homicide for the purposes of ss. 222 to 237. Also note s. 217 respecting the duty of persons undertaking acts. Section 45 protects a person from criminal responsibility for performing surgical operations in certain circumstances.

SYNOPSIS

This section creates a *legal duty* upon those who undertake *lawful* acts that may endanger the life of another to have and to *use reasonable knowledge, skill and care* in so doing. Section 216 specifically addresses those administering surgical or medical treatment, but also extends to anyone who does any other *lawful* act *that may endanger the life of another person*. This section explicitly *excludes* those cases in which the act was performed out of *necessity*.

ANNOTATIONS

Whether or not the accused, who were acting as midwives at a home birth, were administering medical treatment within the meaning of this section their conduct did constitute "any other lawful act that may endanger the life of another person" and they were therefore under a legal duty to have and use reasonable knowledge, skill and care and were to be held to the standard of a competent childbirth attendant notwithstanding their lack of formal training as midwives: *R. v. Sullivan* (1986), 31 C.C.C. (3d) 62, 55 C.R. (3d) 48 (B.C. Co. Ct.). [Appeal to Court of Appeal dismissed on other grounds (1988), 43 C.C.C. (3d) 65, 65 C.R. (3d) 256, 31 B.C.L.R. (2d) 145, further appeal to S.C.C. allowed on other grounds [1991] 1 S.C.R. 489, 63 C.C.C. (3d) 97, 3 C.R. (4th) 277.]

This section imposed a legal duty on the accused, who knew he was infected with the AIDS virus, to not donate blood to the Red Cross and breach of this duty may found a conviction for common nuisance under s. 180: *R. v. Thornton*, [1993] 2 S.C.R. 445, 82 C.C.C. (3d) 530, 21 C.R. (4th) 215 (9:0).

DUTY OF PERSONS UNDERTAKING ACTS.

217. Every one who undertakes to do an act is under a legal duty to do it if an omission to do the act is or may be dangerous to life. R.S., c. C-34, s. 199.

CROSS-REFERENCES

Omission to perform the duty imposed by this section may, in some circumstances, amount to criminal negligence as defined in s. 219 and, if conduct results in death or bodily harm, will amount to an offence under ss. 220 and 221 respectively. Criminal negligence causing death is also a form of culpable homicide for the purposes of ss. 222 to 237.

SYNOPSIS

Section 217 imposes a *legal duty* upon any one who undertakes to do an act if omitting to do it *is or may be dangerous to life*.

ANNOTATIONS

An "undertaking" must generally be something in the nature of a commitment upon which reliance is reasonably placed. The mere expression of words indicating a willingness to do an act cannot trigger a legal duty: *R. v. Browne* (1997), 116 C.C.C. (3d) 183, 33 O.R. (3d) 775, 100 O.A.C. 152 (C.A.), leave to appeal to S.C.C. refused 118 C.C.C. (3d) vi, 110 O.A.C. 200*n*, 225 N.R. 396*n*.

DUTY OF PERSONS DIRECTING WORK.

217.1 Every one who undertakes, or has the authority, to direct how another person does work or performs a task is under a legal duty to take reasonable steps to prevent bodily harm to that person, or any other person, arising from that work or task. 2003, c. 21, s. 3.

CROSS-REFERENCES

"Bodily harm", "every one" and "person" are defined in s. 2. Omission to perform the duty imposed by this section may, in some circumstances, amount to criminal negligence as defined in s. 219 and, if conduct results in death or bodily harm, will amount to an offence under ss. 220 and 221 respectively. Criminal negligence causing death is also a form of culpable homicide for the purposes of ss. 222 to 237. The liability of an organization for offences of negligence is set out in s. 22.1 and for offences requiring proof of fault, other than negligence, is set out in s. 22.2. Also note s. 217 respecting the duty of persons undertaking acts. Section 45 protects a person from criminal responsibility for performing surgical operations in certain circumstances.

SYNOPSIS

This section codifies a legal duty on everyone who undertakes or has authority to direct how others work or perform a task, to take reasonable steps to prevent bodily harm to the person performing the work or task, and to any other person.

ABANDONING CHILD.

218. Every one who unlawfully abandons or exposes a child who is under the age of ten years, so that its life is or is likely to be endangered or its health is or is likely to be permanently injured,

(*a*) is guilty of an indictable offence and liable to imprisonment for a term not exceeding five years; or

(*b*) is guilty of an offence punishable on summary conviction and liable to imprisonment for a term not exceeding eighteen months. R.S., c. C-34, s. 200; 2005, c. 32, s. 12.

CROSS-REFERENCES

The terms "child", "abandon" and "expose" are defined in s. 214. Age is determined by reference to s. 30 of the *Interpretation Act*, R.S.C. 1985, c. I-21. The related offence of failing to provide necessaries is found in s. 215. Neglecting to obtain assistance in child birth is an offence under s. 242.

The accused's spouse is a competent and compellable witness at the instance of the Crown by virtue of s. 4(2).

The accused has an election as to mode of trial pursuant to s. 536(2). Release pending trial is determined by s. 515, although the accused is eligible for release by the officer in charge under s. 498.

Section 718.01 provides that, in imposing a sentence for an offence involving the abuse of a person under the age of 18 years, the court shall give primary consideration to the objectives of denunciation and deterrence. Further, under s. 718.2, evidence that the offender, in committing the offence, abused a person under the age of 18 years is an aggravating circumstance.

SYNOPSIS

This section creates the hybrid offence of abandoning or exposing a child under 10 years of age so that the child's life is or is likely to be endangered or the health of the child is or is likely to be permanently injured. Since the abandonment or exposure must be unlawful, it would seem that the accused must intend to expose or abandon the child.

ANNOTATIONS

This provision requires proof of subjective *mens rea*: *R. v. H. (A.D.)*, [2013] 2 S.C.R. 269, 295 C.C.C. (3d) 376.

While the Crown, to prove this offence, must prove not only that the child was abandoned but that, *inter alia*, its life was likely to be endangered, the offence was made out where the accused abandoned her child in a motor vehicle for an indefinite period of time in an environment which posed a threat to its life due to the cold temperatures and risk of abduction. It was no excuse that the accused intended to return several hours later at a time, when according to expert evidence, the child would still be alive. It is the act of endangering that constitutes the offence: *R. v. Holzer* (1988), 63 C.R. (3d) 301 (Alta. Q.B.).

Criminal Negligence

CRIMINAL NEGLIGENCE / Definition of "duty".

219. (1) Every one is criminally negligent who

(*a*) in doing anything, or

(*b*) in omitting to do anything that it is his duty to do,

shows wanton or reckless disregard for the lives or safety of other persons.

(2) For the purposes of this section, "duty" means a duty imposed by law. R.S., c. C-34, s. 202.

CROSS-REFERENCES

The offences of criminal negligence causing death and causing bodily harm are set out in ss. 220 and 221 respectively. Criminal negligence is also a form of culpable homicide for the purposes of s. 222. Duties imposed under sections of the *Criminal Code* include the following: s. 33, duty to disperse rioters; s. 79, duty of care re explosives; s. 86, duty of care re firearms; s. 215, duty to provide necessaries; s. 216, duty of person undertaking acts dangerous to life; s. 217, duty of persons undertaking acts; s. 217.1, duty of persons directing work; s. 263(1) and (2), duty to safeguard opening in ice and excavations.

Related offences where the conduct results only in damage to property or animals are found in Part XI. Liability of an organization for an offence requiring proof of negligence is set out in s. 22.1.

SYNOPSIS

Section 219 defines the term *criminal negligence*.

Criminal negligence can arise from either acts or omissions, if the accused was under a *legal duty* to do the omitted act. If the act or omission shows a *wanton or reckless disregard for the lives or safety of other persons*, this makes out criminal negligence. Despite the reference to "other persons" the offence *need only* result in potential harm to *one* other person.

ANNOTATIONS

Meaning of criminal negligence – The mere breach of a duty imposed by a provincial statute does not *per se* constitute criminal negligence: *R. v. Titchner* (1961), 131 C.C.C. 64, 29 D.L.R. (2d) 1 (Ont. C.A.), but it is proper for the judge to refer the jury to the legislation which governs the particular activity in which the accused is engaged: *R. v. Leblanc*, [1977] 1 S.C.R. 339, 29 C.C.C. (2d) 97, 68 D.L.R. (3d) 243 (6:3).

Criminal negligence does not require proof of intention or deliberation, indifference being sufficient. Thus, the accused may be convicted on proof of driving amounting to a marked and substantial departure from the standard of a reasonable driver in circumstances where the accused either recognized and ran an obvious and serious risk to the lives and safety of others or, alternatively, gave no thought to that risk: *R. v. Sharp* (1984), 12 C.C.C. (3d) 428, 39 C.R. (3d) 367, 26 M.V.R. 279 (Ont. C.A.).

In two cases *R. v. Waite*, [1989] 1 S.C.R. 1436, 48 C.C.C. (3d) 1, 69 C.R. (3d) 323, and *R. v. Tutton*, [1989] 1 S.C.R. 1392, 48 C.C.C. (3d) 129, 69 C.R. (3d) 289, the Supreme Court considered the *mens rea* of the criminal negligence offence as it applied to acts of commission [*Waite*, operation of a motor vehicle] and omission [*Tutton*, failure of parents to provide medical treatment to a child]. In each case there were three judgments and no clear consensus emerged as to the requisite *mens rea*. On two points, there was agreement as follows: (1) There is no distinction between acts of commission or omission in determining the requisite *mens rea*; (2) It is an error to direct the jury that the Crown must prove elements of deliberateness and wilfulness. The court divided equally however on whether the *mens rea* required was subjective or objective. Three members of the court (McIntyre, Lamer and L'Heureux-Dubé JJ.) were of the view that an objective standard was to be applied. Thus, proof of conduct which reveals a marked and significant departure from the standard which could be expected of a reasonably prudent person in the circumstances will justify a conviction. The decision must be made, however, on a consideration of the facts existing at the time and in relation to the accused's perception of those facts. Thus, an honest and reasonably held belief in the existence of certain facts may be a relevant consideration in assessing the reasonableness of the accused's conduct. Further, McIntyre J., writing for himself and L'Heureux-Dubé J., adopted the reasons for judgment of Cory J.A. in the Ontario Court of Appeal in *R. v. Waite* (1986), 28 C.C.C. (3d) 326, 52 C.R. (3d) 355, 41 M.V.R. 119. This would appear to represent approval of that court's principle of fault as it applies to this offence, especially in the driving context. The clearest explanation of this principle may be found in *R. v. Sharp, supra*, where the Court of Appeal held that, while the jury may find the required fault in the nature of the accused's driving which amounts to a marked and substantial departure from the standard of a reasonable driver in the circumstances, the accused may be acquitted if there is an explanation which arises from the evidence that would account for the deviant conduct in a manner which would negative the element of fault, such as a cause resulting from circumstances beyond the accused's control, for example, a sudden mechanical malfunction. Lamer J. in his concurring reasons in both cases, while accepting the objective standard, was of the view that, in applying this, a generous allowance must be made for factors which are particular to the accused, such as youth, mental development, education. [*Quaere* whether such a generous allowance applies in the case of licensed activity such as driving.]

Wilson J. writing for herself, Dickson C.J.C. and Le Dain J., while explicitly adopting the fault notion as explained in *R. v. Sharp, supra*, in the motor vehicle context, would also require proof of some minimal blameworthy state of mind described as advertence to the risk or wilful blindness to the risk. In the driving context, however, where risks to lives and safety of others is constant and obvious, the accused's claim that he or she gave no thought to the risk or has simply a negative state of mind would, in most cases, amount to the culpable positive mental state of wilful blindness to the prohibited risk. More generally it was explained [*Tutton, supra*, at p. 154 C.C.C.]:

> "Conduct which shows a wanton or reckless disregard for the lives and safety of others will by its nature constitute *prima facie* evidence of the mental element, and in the absence of some evidence that casts doubt on the normal degree of mental awareness, proof of the act and reference to what a reasonable person in the circumstances must have realized will lead to a conclusion that the accused was aware of the risk or wilfully blind to the risk."

In the subsequent cases of *R. v. Nelson* (1990), 54 C.C.C. (3d) 285, 75 C.R. (3d) 70 , 21 M.V.R. (2d) 245 (Ont. C.A.), and *R. v. Cabral* (1990), 54 C.C.C. (3d) 317 , 21 M.V.R. (2d) 252 (Ont. C.A.), held that, until the Supreme Court of Canada holds otherwise, it is still open to that court to follow its decisions in *R. v. Sharp, supra*, and in *R. v. Waite* (1986), 28 C.C.C. (3d) 326, and apply the objective test as enunciated in those decisions. Further, the court noted that in the context of a charge of criminal negligence involving the operation of a motor vehicle, in most cases, as a practical matter, there will be very little difference between the limited subjective approach of Wilson J. and the objective approach in *R. v. Sharp, supra*, and in *R. v. Waite* (1986), 28 C.C.C. (3d) 326.

In *R. v. Anderson*, [1990] 1 S.C.R. 265, 53 C.C.C. (3d) 481, 75 C.R. (3d) 50 (7:0), the court returned to the question of criminal negligence in the context of a driving case. Sopinka J. for the court, while not attempting to resolve the objective/subjective issue, pointed out that fundamental to either approach is a finding that the conduct of the accused constituted a marked departure from the norm. He also pointed out that, as the risk created increases, the objective and subjective approaches begin to converge, since the easier it is to conclude that both a reasonably prudent person would have foreseen the consequences [the objective approach] and that the particular accused must have foreseen the consequences [the subjective approach]. In this case, it was unnecessary to resolve the issue because the trial judge had a reasonable doubt whether the conduct of the accused in driving in an impaired condition and failing to stop at a red light was a marked departure from the norm. That being the case, a conclusion that the accused had a wanton or reckless disregard for the lives and safety of others could not be drawn on either a subjective or objective basis.

The *mens rea* for a party to this offence requires the aider to do something with intent to assist conduct that is criminally negligent and to know sufficient details of the assisted conduct to render that conduct criminally negligent. Thus, the conduct that the aider knows he is assisting must constitute a marked and substantial departure from what is reasonable in the circumstances. It is not necessary that the aider know the law, nor that he appreciate the legal consequences of the conduct being assisted. The aider will have aided the commission of the offence if he or she intentionally assists conduct which constitutes the offence and knows the principal intends to commit it. In those circumstances, the aider did something "for the purpose of" assisting the commission of the offence. In addition, it is not necessary that the aider have subjective foresight of the consequence of the criminally negligent act he or she is assisting. It is sufficient to show that a reasonable person, in all the circumstances, would have appreciated a consequence — bodily harm that is not trivial or transient — would result. An individual who was the "flagman" in a street race could be held liable as a party as it was open to conclude that the race, as the accused anticipated it, was a marked and substantial departure from what was reasonable in the circumstances, and the bodily harm was a foreseeable consequence of the street race: *R. v. R. (M.)* (2011), 275 C.C.C. (3d) 45 (Ont. C.A.).

Death caused by dangerous driving and death caused by criminal negligence involve different degrees of moral blameworthiness. Further, proof of the offence under this section requires establishing a reckless disregard, rather than a marked departure from the standard of reasonable conduct, which is all that is required for dangerous driving: *R. v. Fortier* (1998), 127 C.C.C. (3d) 217 (Que. C.A.).

Fault is determined by considering whether the conduct constitutes a marked departure from that expected of a reasonable person in the circumstances. While the fault requirement applies uniformly to both acts and omissions, there may be situations in which a failure to act where there is a duty to do so will not fall below the standard, whereas actions which actually create a risk will fall below the standard: *R. v. Canhoto* (1999), 140 C.C.C. (3d) 321, 29 C.R. (5th) 170 (Ont. C.A.).

Reasonable foreseeability of harm is relevant in the analysis of legal causation in negligence based offences. Where conduct is inherently dangerous and carries with it a reasonable foreseeable risk of immediate and substantial harm, the test for legal causation will have been met. Independent voluntary human intervention in the events started by an accused may break the chain of causation: *R. v. Shilon* (2006), 240 C.C.C. (3d) 401 (Ont. C.A.), leave to appeal to S.C.C. refused [2007] 2 S.C.R. vi.

A finding of criminal negligence first requires the trial judge to find that there was a marked and substantial departure from the standard of care of a reasonable person in both the physical and mental elements of the offence. In this case, the trial judge erred in concluding that, because the accused realized there was a risk of injury to the deceased, he was wanton or reckless without making specific consideration of whether the accused's physical act was a marked departure from the norm: *R. v. L. (J.)* (2006), 204 C.C.C. (3d) 324, 206 O.A.C. 205 (C.A.).

In determining whether the conduct of the accused, a 16-year-old boy, constituted criminal negligence the standard to be used is that of a sane and sober 16-year-old. The question then was whether or not the conduct amounted to a marked and substantial departure from that standard. In this case the accused lightly pushed his friend at the top of a staircase who then fell to his death. While such conduct constituted negligence it involved only minimal force and momentary inadvertence and was not sufficient to amount to a marked and substantial departure from the standard of a reasonable person: *R. v. Barron* (1985), 23 C.C.C. (3d) 544, 48 C.R. (2d) 334 (Ont. C.A.).

Evidence that the accused suffered from mental retardation was relevant to determining whether he possessed the capacity to understand and appreciate the risks entailed by his conduct and could therefore be held to be criminally negligent: *R. v. Ubhi* (1994), 27 C.R. (4th) 332, 1 M.V.R. (3d) 161 (B.C.C.A.), leave to appeal to S.C.C. refused 31 C.R. (4th) 405, 5 M.V.R. (3d) 249*n*.

A "duty imposed by law" may be a duty arising by virtue of either statute or common law: *R. v. Coyne* (1958), 124 C.C.C. 176, 31 C.R. 335 (N.B.C.A.).

A parent is under a legal duty at common law to take reasonable steps to protect his child from illegal violence used by the other parent towards the child which the parent foresees or ought to foresee. Such a parent is criminally liable for failing to discharge that duty in circumstances which show a wanton or reckless disregard for the child's safety, where the failure to discharge the legal duty has contributed to the death of the child or resulted in bodily harm to the child: *R. v. Popen* (1981), 60 C.C.C. (2d) 232 (Ont. C.A.).

Criminal negligence requires conduct that constitutes a marked and substantial departure from what a reasonably prudent person would do under the circumstances. Failing to provide the necessaries of life requires proof only that the conduct constitutes a marked departure from the standard of care expected of a reasonably prudent person in the circumstances. Criminal negligence requires proof that the accused showed a wanton or reckless disregard for the life or safety of another, whereas failure to provide the necessaries of life requires proof that the accused's failure endangered the life of the person to whom he or she owed a duty, or that the accused caused, or was likely to cause, the health of that person to be endangered permanently. Finally, criminal negligence is the more serious of the two offences. Where criminal negligence and a failure to provide the necessaries of life are both alleged, the jury should first determine whether the accused had a duty to protect the victim and failed in that duty. If the offence of failing to provide the necessaries of life is established, the jury should then determine whether this constituted a wanton or reckless disregard for the life or safety of the victim so as to constitute criminal negligence: *R. v. F. (J.)*, [2008] 3 S.C.R. 215, 236 C.C.C. (3d) 421.

Constitutional considerations – Section 7 of the *Charter of Rights and Freedoms* does not require proof of subjective foresight for a conviction for criminal negligence: *R. v. Nelson, supra*.

CAUSING DEATH BY CRIMINAL NEGLIGENCE.

220. Every person who by criminal negligence causes death to another person is guilty of an indictable offence and liable

(*a*) where a firearm is used in the commission of the offence, to imprisonment for life and to a minimum punishment of imprisonment for a term of four years; and

(*b*) in any other case, to imprisonment for life. R.S., c. C-34, s. 203; 1995, c. 39, s. 141.

CROSS-REFERENCES

Criminal negligence is defined in s. 219. "Firearm" and "person" are defined in s. 2. Pursuant to s. 255.1, where the offence was committed by means of a motor vehicle, vessel or aircraft, evidence that the accused's blood alcohol level exceeded .160 at the time when the offence was committed is deemed to be an aggravating factor on sentencing. See s. 259 re driving prohibition orders. Note s. 732.1(3)(*g*.1) and (*g*.2), which allow for terms of probation that the offender attend for curative treatment in relation to the consumption of alcohol and drugs and participate in an alcohol ignition interlock device program. For liability of an organization for an offence requiring proof of negligence, see s. 22.1.

Section 249.2 creates the offence of causing death by criminal negligence while street racing (defined in s. 2). The penalty for that offence, as in this section, is a maximum of life imprisonment.

ANNOTATIONS

The word "person" should be interpreted in the same manner as "human being" as defined for the homicide provisions by s. 223. Thus for this section to apply the child must have been completely extruded from its mother's body and be born alive. Where the child dies while it is in the birth canal it is not at that time a "person" and the offence under this section could not be committed: *R. v. Sullivan*, [1991] 1 S.C.R. 489, 63 C.C.C. (3d) 97.

Evidence of the type of driving by the accused immediately after the accident is admissible as part of the *res gestae* and also for consideration on the issue of his wanton and reckless disregard prior to and at the time of the accident: *R. v. Balcerczyk*, [1957] 3 S.C.R. 20, 117 C.C.C. 71 (4:1).

For conviction the Crown must prove the breaching of an obligation imposed by law with a wanton or reckless disregard for the lives or safety of others and, to assist in the proof of *mens rea*, may lead evidence of previous similar conduct: *R. v. Leblanc*, [1977] 1 S.C.R. 339, 29 C.C.C. (2d) 97 (6:3).

A trial judge is not obliged to use the phrase "obvious and serious risk to others" in charging the jury. The phrase "a wanton or reckless disregard for the lives or safety of others", drawn from the language of s. 219, was adequate: *R. v. Kerr* (2013), 305 C.C.C. (3d) 127 (B.C.C.A.).

The test for causation for homicide is whether the acts of the accused were a significant contributing cause to the death: *R. v. Nette*, [2001] 3 S.C.R. 488, 158 C.C.C. (3d) 486.

Foreseeability of the risk of death is not a factor which the jury should consider on the question of whether the accused's conduct amounts to criminal negligence: *R. v. Pinske* (1988), 6 M.V.R. (2d) 19, 30 B.C.L.R. (2d) 114 (C.A.), affd [1989] 2 S.C.R. 979, 100 N.R. 399 (7:0).

The minimum sentence does not violate s. 12 of the Charter. The minimum sentence may, however, be reduced by considering the time spent in pre-trial custody: *R. v. Morrisey*, [2000] 2 S.C.R. 90, 148 C.C.C. (3d) 1.

CAUSING BODILY HARM BY CRIMINAL NEGLIGENCE.

221. Every one who by criminal negligence causes bodily harm to another person is guilty of an indictable offence and liable to imprisonment for a term not exceeding ten years. R.S., c. C-34, s. 204.

CROSS-REFERENCES

Criminal negligence is defined in s. 219. "Bodily harm" and "every one" are defined in s. 2. For liability of an organization for an offence requiring proof of negligence, see s. 22.1.

As to included offences, see s. 662(5).

The accused's spouse is a competent and compellable witness at the instance of the Crown by virtue of s. 4(4) where the victim is under the age of 14 years. Age is determined by reference to s. 30 of the *Interpretation Act*, R.S.C. 1985, c. I-21.

The accused has an election as to mode of trial pursuant to s. 536(2). Release pending trial is determined by s. 515. An accused convicted of this offence may, pursuant to s. 259, be ordered prohibited from operating a motor vehicle, vessel, aircraft or railway equipment for any period not exceeding ten years where the offence under this section was committed by means of a motor vehicle, vessel, aircraft or railway equipment. The procedure respecting the making of that order of prohibition is found in s. 260. It may be that, in some circumstances, the accused will also be liable to the mandatory prohibition order respecting firearms, ammunition and explosives by virtue of s. 109. With respect to causation see notes under ss. 220, 249 and 255.

Pursuant to s. 255.1, where the offence was committed by means of a motor vehicle, vessel or aircraft, evidence that the accused's blood alcohol level exceeded .160 at the time when the offence was committed is deemed to be an aggravating factor on sentencing. See s. 259 re driving prohibition orders. Note s. 732.1(3)(*g*.1) and (*g*.2), which allow for terms of probation that the offender attend for curative treatment in relation to the consumption of alcohol and drugs and participate in an alcohol ignition interlock device program.

Section 249.3 creates the offence of causing bodily harm by criminal negligence while street racing (defined in s. 2). The penalty for that offence is a maximum of 14 years.

Homicide

HOMICIDE / Kinds of homicide / Non culpable homicide / Culpable homicide / Idem / Exception.

222. (1) A person commits homicide when, directly or indirectly, by any means, he causes the death of a human being.

(2) Homicide is culpable or not culpable.

(3) Homicide that is not culpable is not an offence.

(4) Culpable homicide is murder or manslaughter or infanticide.

(5) A person commits culpable homicide when he causes the death of a human being,

(*a*) by means of an unlawful act,

(*b*) by criminal negligence,

(*c*) by causing that human being, by threats or fear of violence or by deception, to do anything that causes his death, or

(*d*) by wilfully frightening that human being, in the case of a child or sick person.

(6) Notwithstanding anything in this section, a person does not commit homicide within the meaning of this Act by reason only that he causes the death of a human being by procuring, by false evidence, the conviction and death of that human being by sentence of the law. R.S., c. C-34, s. 205.

CROSS-REFERENCES

The scheme of the homicide provisions is that this section defines culpable homicide and then other provisions determine whether culpable homicide is murder, manslaughter or infanticide. The distinction is largely, although not exclusively, dependent on the intent accompanying the conduct which resulted in death. Murder is defined in ss. 229 and 230. The punishment for murder is set out in s. 235. Infanticide is defined in s. 233. The punishment for infanticide is set out in s. 237.

Manslaughter is defined in ss. 232, 234 and 263. The punishment for manslaughter is set out in s. 236.

As to causation, see ss. 223(2) and 224 to 227. As to definition of "human being" see s. 233.

Criminal negligence is defined in s. 219 and criminal negligence causing death is also a separate offence under s. 220. For liability of an organization for an offence requiring proof of negligence, see s. 22.1.

SYNOPSIS

This section spells out *what constitutes homicide* and sets out the *distinction between culpable and non-culpable homicide*.

Section 222(1) states that *homicide* is committed when a person *causes the death*, directly or indirectly, of another person. Homicide may be either culpable or not, and non-culpable homicide is not an offence. Subsection (6) provides a clarification by excluding from the ambit of homicide procuring the death of another by false evidence which leads to that person's conviction and the imposition of the death penalty.

Subsection (4) exhaustively *defines culpable homicide as being murder, manslaughter or infanticide*. Subsection (5) deals with the ways in which culpable homicide may be committed such as by an unlawful act (s. 222(5)(*a*)) or by criminal negligence (s. 222(5)(*b*)).

ANNOTATIONS

Causation – Where an issue of causation arises the jury in deciding the question is not limited to considering the testimony of expert witnesses but may also consider the evidence of lay witnesses who witnessed the assault alleged by the Crown to have been the cause of death. Causation as a question of fact is for the jury not the experts. Further, where it is established that the assault by the accused was at least a contributing cause of death, outside the *de minimis* range, then causation as a matter of law has been established. The accused must take his victim as he finds him and it is no defence to a charge of manslaughter that death was unexpected and the physical reactions of the victim to the assault unforseen or that death ordinarily would not result from the unlawful act: *R. v. Smithers*, [1978] 1 S.C.R. 506, 34 C.C.C. (2d) 427 (9:0).

Causation has both a factual and legal component. Factual causation is concerned with an inquiry about how the victim died in a medical, mechanical or physical sense. Legal causation is concerned with whether the person should be held responsible in law for the death. While causation is distinct from *mens rea*, the proper standard of causation expresses an element of fault that is sufficient to base responsibility. When an unlawful act is combined with the requisite mental element for the offence charged, causation is generally not an issue. The applicable standard for causation in relation to manslaughter is a contributing cause outside the *de minimis* range. For first degree murder during the commission of another offense, the causation must be a substantial and integral part of the killing. This causation requirement refers to the increased degree of moral culpability that is required before an accused can be found guilty of first degree murder. In charging the jury, there is a need to distinguish between the terms used to describe the relevant standard of causation and the terminology used to express it. Latin expressions and formulations that are negative should not be used. It is preferable to explain the standard of causation in terms of phrases such as "significant contributing cause" rather than "not a trivial cause" or "not insignificant": *R. v. Nette*, [2001] 3 S.C.R. 488, 158 C.C.C. (3d) 486.

The test for the time of death is whether any of the victim's vital organs including the heart continue to operate. The criminal law does not recognize brain death or cessation of brain function as the legal standard of determining when death occurs: *R. v. Green* (1988), 43 C.C.C. (3d) 413 (B.C.S.C.).

Intervening cause cases constitute a unique category of case such that the trial judge is obliged to give the jury a clear and specific instruction with respect to the intervening events. The jury must understand their obligation to consider whether or not any independent, intervening and therefore exculpatory factors occurred after the accused's act, thereby severing the link in the chain of events leading to the victim's death: *R. v. Reid* (2003), 180 C.C.C. (3d) 151, 18 C.R. (6th) 282 (N.S.C.A.).

Even in cases where it is alleged that an intervening act has interrupted the chain of legal causation, the causation test remains whether the dangerous and unlawful acts of the accused are a significant contributing cause of the victim's death. An intervening act that is reasonably foreseeable will usually not break or rupture the chain of causation so as to relieve the offender of legal responsibility for the unintended result. The time to assess reasonable foreseeability is at the time of the initial unlawful act, rather than at the time of the intervening act. It is the general nature of the intervening acts and the accompanying risk of harm, not the precise details, that need to be reasonably foreseeable. If they are, then the accused's actions may remain a significant contributing cause of death: *R. v. Maybin*, [2012] 2 S.C.R. 30, 283 C.C.C. (3d) 275.

Where the entire episode involving a series of unlawful acts is one continuing transaction then it is not open to the accused to rely upon the defence of honest but mistaken belief on the basis that at the time of the final act which actually resulted in the death of the victim the accused believed the victim to be already dead: *R. v. Frizzell* (1993), 81 C.C.C. (3d) 463, 22 C.R. (4th) 400 (B.C.C.A.).

The common law definition of causation requiring proof that the unlawful act was at least a contributing cause of death outside the *de minimis* range complies with the principles of fundamental justice as guaranteed by s. 7 of the Charter. When combined with the requisite fault element for manslaughter by an unlawful act, being commission of an unlawful dangerous act, in circumstances where a reasonable person would have foreseen the risk of bodily harm which is neither trivial nor transitory, there is no risk that a person who is morally innocent will be convicted for consequences that should not be attributed to him: *R. v. Cribbin* (1994), 89 C.C.C. (3d) 67, 28 C.R. (4th) 137 (Ont. C.A.).

Homicide by "unlawful act" – The *mens rea* of unlawful act manslaughter under subsec. (5)(*a*) is, in addition to the *mens rea* of the underlying offence, objective foreseeability of the risk of bodily harm which is neither trivial nor transitory: *R. v. Creighton*, [1993] 3 S.C.R. 3, 83 C.C.C. (3d) 346.

The unlawful act must also be objectively dangerous, that is, likely to injure another person: *R. v. DeSousa*, [1992] 2 S.C.R. 944, 76 C.C.C. (3d) 124; *R. v. Creighton, supra.*

Where the Crown relies on subsec. (5)(*a*), the unlawful act must be identified and the trial judge must determine whether the *actus reus* and *mens rea* of that offence have been proven beyond a reasonable doubt, and whether objective foreseeability of bodily harm was neither transitory nor trivial. It is insufficient to simply conclude that that the accused's conduct was dangerous without identifying the underlying unlawful act: *R. v. T. (K.)* (2005), 199 C.C.C. (3d) 551, 31 C.R. (6th) 187 (Man. C.A.), leave to appeal to S.C.C. quashed (improperly brought pursuant to s. 40 of the *Supreme Court Act*) [2006] 1 S.C.R. xiii, 205 C.C.C. (3d) vi, leave to appeal to S.C.C. refused [2006] 1 S.C.R. xiii, 208 C.C.C. (3d) vi.

Where the defence of self-defence is made out then the act done in self-defence is not unlawful, the homicide is not culpable and the accused must be acquitted: *R. v. Baker* (1988), 45 C.C.C. (3d) 368 (B.C.C.A.).

The unlawful act can be a breach of a federal or provincial statute as long as it is not an offence or absolute liability (or otherwise constitutionally deficient) and provided it is objectively dangerous. Here, the accused bar owners may have breached the provincial *Liquor Licence Act* by allowing someone to become intoxicated on their premises, but the act was not objectively dangerous. Therefore, the fact that the impaired person later caused a fatal car crash could not make the accused guilty of unlawful act manslaughter: *R. v. Sztejnmiler* (2013), 299 C.C.C. (3d) 456 (Ont. C.J.).

Homicide by criminal negligence – See notes under ss. 219 and 220.

Homicide by causing person to do something that causes own death – The purpose of subsec. (5)(*c*) is to deter dangerous conduct that, while not illegal in itself, causes the death of a human being. The *actus reus* is a threat conveyed to the victim and a fear of violence thereby created in the victim; or deception that leads the victim to personally commit the fatal act. The *mens rea* is object foresight of bodily harm that is neither trivial nor transient. Properly interpreted, the provision is neither unconstitutionally vague nor overbroad: *R. c. Charbonneau* (2016), 343 C.C.C. (3d) 204 (C.A. Que.).

WHEN CHILD BECOMES HUMAN BEING / Killing child.

223. (1) A child becomes a human being within the meaning of this Act when it has completely proceeded, in a living state, from the body of its mother whether or not

(*a*) it has breathed,

(*b*) it has an independent circulation, or

(*c*) the navel string is severed.

(2) A person commits homicide when he causes injury to a child before or during its birth as a result of which the child dies after becoming a human being. R.S., c. C-34, s. 206.

CROSS-REFERENCES

Culpable homicide is defined in s. 222 and see cross-references under that section respecting murder, manslaughter and infanticide. The effect of this section is that killing of a child who has become a human being can amount to homicide or also found the offence of criminal negligence causing death under s. 220. Where the child's death is caused in the act of birth before it becomes a human being then the accused commits the offence under s. 238. Neglecting to obtain assistance in child-birth is an offence under s. 242 and concealing the body of a child an offence under s. 243. Other causation provisions are found in ss. 224 to 226 and 228.

SYNOPSIS

This section establishes the point at which a *child becomes a human being* for the purpose of determining if a homicide has been committed.

Section 223(1) defines that a child is a human being if it has completely proceeded from its mother in a *living state*, even if it has not done one of the things listed in s. 223(1)(*a*) to (*c*). Subsection (2) provides that homicide is committed if a child dies after meeting the definition of human being, in subsec. (1) even if the cause of death was injuries sustained by the child before or during its birth.

ANNOTATIONS

A person who attacks an obviously pregnant woman with intent to harm her is guilty of at least manslaughter if the foetus being subsequently born alive dies from injury or disease caused by the attack: *R. v. Prince* (1988), 44 C.C.C. (3d) 510, [1989] 1 W.W.R. 80 (Man. C.A.).

The exclusion of fetuses from the definition of "human being" is constitutional and there was no basis for revisiting the settled authority to that effect: *R. v. Mary Wagner* (2016), 352 C.C.C. (3d) 112 (Ont. S.C.J.).

DEATH THAT MIGHT HAVE BEEN PREVENTED.

224. Where a person, by an act or omission, does any thing that results in the death of a human being, he causes the death of that human being notwithstanding that death from that cause might have been prevented by resorting to proper means. R.S., c. C-34, s. 207.

CROSS-REFERENCES

Culpable homicide is defined in s. 222 and see cross-references under that section respecting murder, manslaughter and infanticide. Other causation provisions are found in ss. 223(2) and 225 to 228. "Human being" is defined in s. 223(1). This provision would also apply to the offences of criminal negligence causing death under s. 220, dangerous driving causing death under s. 249(4) and impaired operation causing death under s. 255(3).

SYNOPSIS

Section 224 deals with the issue of a *death which might have been prevented*, which arises as a question of causation in relation to homicide cases.

This section provides that a person commits homicide if that person does anything which results in the death of another person, even if proper treatment could have prevented death from that cause. The person may have caused the death by act or omission. This satisfies the first requirement of all homicides: proof that the person caused the death of another person (see s. 222(1)).

DEATH FROM TREATMENT OF INJURY.

225. Where a person causes to a human being a bodily injury that is of itself of a dangerous nature and from which death results, he causes the death of that human being notwithstanding that the immediate cause of death is proper or improper treatment that is applied in good faith. R.S., c. C-34, s. 208.

CROSS-REFERENCES

Culpable homicide is defined in s. 222 and see cross-references under that section respecting murder, manslaughter and infanticide. Other causation provisions are found in ss. 223(2), 224, 226 and 228. "Human being" is defined in s. 223(1). This provision would also apply to the offences of criminal negligence causing death under s. 220, dangerous driving causing death under s. 249(4) and impaired operation causing death under s. 255(3). The term "bodily injury" is not defined in this section. Some assistance may, however, be obtained from the definition of "bodily harm" in s. 2.

SYNOPSIS

Section 225 deals with one aspect of the issue of causation in homicide cases, namely, the effect of the *immediate cause of death being treatment* applied after the accused *caused a dangerous injury* to the deceased. The section provides that, if the *treatment was given in good faith*, it is irrelevant whether it was proper or not. The key is whether the *injury, caused by the accused* to the deceased, was of a *dangerous nature and that death resulted from it*. Thus, causation will be supplied by this section so long as the act of the accused causing injury was an operative factor, even if it was only one of the causes of the death.

ANNOTATIONS

In *R. v. Kitching and Adams* (1976), 32 C.C.C. (2d) 159, [1976] 6 W.W.R. 697 (Man. C.A.), the defence raised was that the cause of death was the act of doctors who, having detected no sign of brain activity, removed the deceased's kidneys and then disconnected the deceased from the mechanical devices which were used to keep his heart and other organs functioning. Matas J.A., for four of the judges, held that the jury had been adequately instructed on the effects of ss. 207 to 209 [now ss. 224 to 226]. O'Sullivan J.A., in a concurring opinion pointed out that those sections extend liability in certain cases and do not affect the principle that it is not necessary to prove that a criminal is the sole cause of his crime and that even if it could be shown that the actions of the doctors constituted an operative cause of death, still, that would not exonerate the accused unless the evidence left a reasonable doubt that the accused's actions also constituted an operative cause of the deceased's death.

A similar result was reached in *R. v. Malcherek; R. v. Steel* (1981), 73 Cr. App. R. 173 (C.A.).

In *R. v. Torbiak and Gillis* (1978), 40 C.C.C. (2d) 193 (Ont. C.A.), the court held that there could be no doubt that the cause of death in law was a gunshot wound to the groin inflicted by one of the accused although the doctors, because of the elderly victim's age decided to follow a conservative course of non-interventional treatment following the shooting until three weeks later the victim's condition deteriorated and he died on the operating table.

ACCELERATION OF DEATH.

226. Where a person causes to a human being a bodily injury that results in death, he causes the death of that human being notwithstanding that the effect of the bodily injury is only to accelerate his death from a disease or disorder arising from some other cause. R.S., c. C-34, s. 209.

CROSS-REFERENCES

Culpable homicide is defined in s. 222 and see cross-references under that section respecting murder, manslaughter and infanticide. Other causation provisions are found in ss. 223(2), 224, 225 and 228. "Human being" is defined in s. 223(1). This provision would also apply to the offences of criminal negligence causing death under s. 220, dangerous driving causing death under s. 249(4) and impaired operation causing death under s. 255(3). The term "bodily injury" is not defined in this section. Some assistance may, however, be obtained from the definition of "bodily harm" in s. 2.

SYNOPSIS

Section 226 deals with the legal effect of actions which *accelerate the death* of another person.

This section states that when a person causes bodily injury to another person which results in death, that person causes the death of the deceased, even if the only effect of the injury was to hasten the unavoidable death of that person.

EXEMPTION FOR MEDICAL ASSISTANCE IN DYING / Exemption for person aiding practitioner / Reasonable but mistaken belief / Non-application of section 14 / Definitions.

227. (1) No medical practitioner or nurse practitioner commits culpable homicide if they provide a person with medical assistance in dying in accordance with section 241.2.

(2) No person is a party to culpable homicide if they do anything for the purpose of aiding a medical practitioner or nurse practitioner to provide a person with medical assistance in dying in accordance with section 241.2.

(3) For greater certainty, the exemption set out in subsection (1) or (2) applies even if the person invoking it has a reasonable but mistaken belief about any fact that is an element of the exemption.

(4) Section 14 does not apply with respect to a person who consents to have death inflicted on them by means of medical assistance in dying provided in accordance with section 241.2.

(5) In this section, *medical assistance in dying*, *medical practitioner* and *nurse practitioner* have the same meanings as in section 241.1. 2016, c. 3, s. 2.

CROSS-REFERENCES

Culpable homicide is defined in s. 122. The prohibition against counseling or aiding suicide (with an exception for medically assisted dying) is contained in s. 241. The medically assisted dying regime is set out in ss. 241.1 through 241.4.

SYNOPSIS

This exemption was enacted in tandem with the assisted dying regime created in response to the Supreme Court's decision in *Carter v. Canada (Attorney General)*, [2015] 1 S.C.R. 331, 320 C.C.C. (3d) 1. It provides an exemption from liability for culpable homicide to a health professional who complies with the requirements of the regime.

KILLING BY INFLUENCE ON THE MIND.

228. No person commits culpable homicide where he causes the death of a human being

(*a*) by any influence on the mind alone, or

(*b*) by any disorder or disease resulting from influence on the mind alone,

but this section does not apply where a person causes the death of a child or sick person by wilfully frightening him. R.S., c. C-34, s. 211.

CROSS-REFERENCES

Culpable homicide is defined in s. 222 and see cross-references under that section respecting murder, manslaughter and infanticide. Other causation provisions are found in ss. 223(2), 224, 225, 226 and 228. "Human being" is defined in s. 223(1). The proviso in this section respecting death caused to a child or sick person relates back to s. 222(5)(*d*). Similarly, it would seem that, if the conduct fell within s. 222(5)(*c*) it would not likely come within the term "by any influence on the *mind alone*" in para. (*a*).

SYNOPSIS

This section excludes certain acts, which can be referred to as *killing by influence of the mind,* from what would otherwise constitute culpable homicide.

The acts excluded are causing the death of a human being as means of influence of the mind or as a consequence of any disorder or disease resulting from such influence. However, it does not exclude such acts if the person *wilfully frightens* a sick person or child and thereby causes the death. This exception is a corollary of s. 222(5)(*d*) which makes such conduct culpable homicide.

ANNOTATIONS

This section was applied and the accused's conviction for manslaughter quashed where the evidence indicated that the deceased died from acute heart failure precipitated by the fear and emotional stress of a break-in by the accused and an ensuing struggle. There was no evidence that either the physical exertion of the struggle or an assault during the struggle was a contributing factor to the victim's death. The victim did have a pre-existing heart condition: *R. v. Powder* (1981), 29 C.R. (3d) 183 (Alta. C.A.), leave to appeal to S.C.C. refused *loc. cit.*

Murder, Manslaughter and Infanticide

MURDER.

229. Culpable homicide is murder

(*a*) where the person who causes the death of a human being

(i) means to cause his death, or

(ii) means to cause him bodily harm that he knows is likely to cause his death, and is reckless whether death ensues or not;

(*b*) where a person, meaning to cause death to a human being or meaning to cause him bodily harm that he knows is likely to cause his death, and being reckless whether death ensues or not, by accident or mistake causes death to another human being, notwithstanding that he does not mean to cause death or bodily harm to that human being; or

(c) where a person, for an unlawful object, does anything that he knows or ought to know is likely to cause death, and thereby causes death to a human being, notwithstanding that he desires to effect his object without causing death or bodily harm to any human being. R.S., c. C-34, s. 212.

CROSS-REFERENCES

Culpable homicide is defined in s. 222. Culpable homicide is also defined as murder in the circumstances set out in s. 230. Murder is classified as first or second degree murder under s. 231. The punishment for murder is, pursuant to s. 235, a minimum of life imprisonment. Eligibility for parole for a person convicted of murder is determined by ss. 742 to 747. [Respecting parole eligibility, see further cross-references under s. 235.] A person convicted of murder will also be liable to the mandatory prohibition order respecting certain weapons, ammunition and explosives by virtue of s. 109. As to included offences, see s. 662. For special provision respecting the plea of *autrefois*, see s. 610(2) to (4).

Pursuant to s. 582, no person may be convicted of first degree murder unless he is specifically charged with that offence in the indictment. Under s. 589, no count that charges an offence other than murder shall be joined in an indictment to a count that charges murder.

The offence of attempted murder is set out in s. 239, accessory after the fact to murder in s. 240 and conspiracy to commit murder in s. 465(1)(*a*).

This offence may be the basis for an application for an authorization to intercept private communications by reason of s. 183 or a warrant to conduct video surveillance under s. 487.01(5), and falls within the definition of "enterprise crime offence" in s. 462.3 for the purposes of Part XII.2.

Section 7(3) enacts special jurisdictional rules for commission of this offence outside Canada when the offence is in relation to an internationally protected person or property referred to in s. 431 [official premises, etc.].

The accused's spouse is a competent and compellable witness at the instance of the Crown by virtue of s. 4(4) where the victim is under the age of 14 years. Age is determined by reference to s. 30 of the *Interpretation Act*, R.S.C. 1985, c. I-21.

Section 17 limits the availability of the statutory defence of compulsion by threats. As to other defences see: s. 16, insanity; s. 25, use of force in enforcement of law; s. 27, use of force to prevent commission of certain offences; ss. 34 to 37, self defence and defence of person under accused's protection; ss. 38 to 41, defence of property; s. 44, use of force by master of vessel; s. 232, provocation. As to notes respecting the necessity defence, see s. 8.

Trial of murder is by the superior court of criminal jurisdiction (defined in s. 2) by virtue of ss. 468 and 469. By virtue of s. 522, only a judge of the superior court of criminal jurisdiction may release an accused charged with this offence.

SYNOPSIS

This section defines *culpable homicide* as murder in three circumstances.

Section 229(*a*)(i) provides the simplest definition, namely intentionally causing the death of a human being by s. 229(*a*)(ii), death caused by a person, who *means to cause bodily harm* that he *knows is likely to cause death* and is reckless whether death ensues or not, is also culpable homicide. The key elements of the mental element in this offence is the intention to cause the requisite degree of bodily harm, coupled with the necessary recklessness as to its effect.

Section 229(*b*) deals with the situation in which an *unintended victim is killed* as a result of accused's acts. The requisite *mental element described in s. 229(a)* must be proven in this paragraph, except that it is satisfied by proof *in relation to the intended victim.* If the mental element as well as the fact that the accused caused the death of the unintended victim are proven, then the fact that the death of that person is caused by accident or mistake is irrelevant and the acts will still render the accused guilty of culpable homicide. The paragraph specifically states that it is culpable homicide, even if the accused did not intend to cause death or inflict any bodily harm upon the person who was killed.

Section 229(*c*) deals with homicides which occur while a person commits another unlawful object. If a person does anything for an *unlawful object* that he *knows or ought to know* is *likely to cause death* and death results from this act, it is culpable homicide. The fact that the accused wanted to carry out the purpose without any death or bodily injury to anyone is legally irrelevant for the purposes of this paragraph. The unlawful object desired by the accused must be some additional object beyond the very act which resulted in the death.

ANNOTATIONS

Proof of intent – Notwithstanding that the accused's primary defence is self-defence where there is also evidence of alcohol consumption and provocation the jury should be directed to consider the cumulative effect of that evidence in determining whether the requisite intent is made out: *R. v. Desveaux* (1986), 26 C.C.C. (3d) 88 (Ont. C.A.); *R. v. Clow* (1985), 44 C.R. (3d) 228 (Ont. C.A.). Similarly, *R. v. Nealy* (1986), 30 C.C.C. (3d) 460 (Ont. C.A.), where there was evidence of alcohol consumption, provocation, anger and fear. However, intense anger alone is insufficient to reduce murder to manslaughter: *R. v. Parent*, [2001] 1 S.C.R. 761, 154 C.C.C. (3d) 1. See also *R. v. Walle* (2007), 230 C.C.C. (3d) 181 (Alta. C.A.).

The purpose of a "rolled-up" instruction on intent is to ensure that the jurors do not compartmentalize evidence that may be relevant to more than one of these issues. It brings together the evidence relevant to stand-alone defences such as intoxication and provocation with evidence related to proof of the basic fault requirement for murder, and invites the jury to consider the cumulative impact of several items of evidence in its decision about the accused's state of mind: *R. v. Flores* (2011), 269 C.C.C. (3d) 194 (Ont. C.A.).

The trial judge erroneously distinguished between intoxication and intention in instructing the jury on intent separately from the defence of intoxication. Furthermore, the trial judge made no reference to the evidence of intoxication in instructing the jury on the common sense inference: *R. v. Carriere* (2001), 159 C.C.C. (3d) 51 (Ont. C.A.).

Where the trial judge has clearly directed the jury as to the requirement of proof of intent there is no requirement for a "residual direction" as to the effect of self-defence and provocation. The judge could, however, give such a direction having regard to the equities and needs of a particular case: *R. v. Ferber* (1987), 36 C.C.C. (3d) 157 (Alta. C.A.), leave to appeal to S.C.C. refused *loc. cit.* To a similar effect, see *R. v. Smith* (1990), 53 C.C.C. (3d) 97 (N.S.C.A.).

Willful blindness can substitute for actual knowledge whenever knowledge is a component of *mens rea*. The doctrine of willful blindness imputes knowledge to an accused whose suspicion is aroused to the point where he or she sees the need for further inquiries but deliberately chooses not to make those inquiries. This is distinct from recklessness and involves no departure from the subjective inquiry into the accused's state of mind. Willful blindness is not simply a failure to inquire but deliberate ignorance: *R. v. Briscoe*, [2010] 1 S.C.R. 411, 253 C.C.C. (3d) 140.

Paragraph *(a)*(ii) represents only a slight relaxation of the *mens rea* for murder and requires proof of a subjective intent to cause bodily harm and subjective knowledge that the bodily harm is of such a nature that it is likely to result in death. Further, this *mens rea* must be concurrent with the impugned act. However, it is not always necessary for the guilty act and the intent to be completely concurrent or that the requisite *mens rea* persist throughout the entire commission of the wrongful act. If death results from a series of wrongful acts that are part of a single transaction, then it must be established that the requisite intent coincided at some point with the wrongful acts: *R. v. Cooper*, [1993] 1 S.C.R. 146, 78 C.C.C. (3d) 289.

The variation in the degree of culpability as between the fault elements in subparas. (*a*)(i) and (*a*)(ii) is too slight to warrant distinction. The requirement in subpara. (*a*)(ii) that the fatal assault be carried out in a reckless way by heedlessly proceeding with the deadly assault, knowing the obvious risks, adds nothing to the vital element of the intent to cause bodily harm that the killer knows is likely to cause death and yet persists in the assault. Anyone who causes bodily harm that knows is likely to cause death must, in those circumstances, have a deliberate disregard for the fatal consequences that he knows are likely to happen and accordingly, be reckless: *R. v. Cooper*, [1993] 1 S.C.R. 146, 78 C.C.C. (3d) 289; *R. v. Moo* (2009), 247 C.C.C. (3d) 34 (Ont. C.A.), leave to appeal to S.C.C. refused [2010] 2 S.C.R. viii, 255 C.C.C. (3d) vi.

The trial judge erred in charging the jury that the mental element was satisfied if they found that the accused had an "attitude of recklessness": *R. v. Dempsey* (2002), 165 C.C.C. (3d) 440 (B.C.C.A.).

In the case of a genuine suicide pact, the surviving party should have a defence to murder. This defence will only be available when the parties are in such a mental state that they have formed a common and irrevocable intent to commit suicide together simultaneously and by the same act where the risk of death is identical and equal for both: *R. v. Gagnon* (1993), 84 C.C.C. (3d) 143 (Que. C.A.).

Where the accused claimed that the firearm discharged accidentally, the trial judge erred by instructing the jury solely on intent as it related to the required *mens rea*, but not on how the claim of accident related to the voluntary act component of the *actus reus*: *Primeau v. R.* (2017), 356 C.C.C. (3d) 329 (C.A. Que.).

Intoxication defence ***[Also see notes under s. 33.1]*** – The rules in *D.P.P. v. Beard* (1920), 14 Cr. App. R. 159 (H.L.), violate ss. 7 and 11(*d*) of the Charter because they limit the defence of intoxication to the capacity of an accused to form the specific intent. Before a trial judge charges a jury on the issue of intoxication, the judge must be satisfied that the effect of the intoxication was such that its effect might have impaired the accused's foresight of consequences sufficient to raise a reasonable doubt. Once this threshold test is met, the judge must make clear to the jury that the issue is whether the Crown has satisfied them beyond a reasonable doubt that the accused had the requisite intent. In most circumstances, a one-step charge which omits any reference to "capacity" or "capability" and focuses the jury on the question of "intent in fact" is appropriate. Consequently, the jury must consider whether the accused possessed the requisite specific intent having regard to the evidence of intoxication, along with all of the other evidence in the case. In certain cases, however, in light of the facts of the case and/or the admission of expert evidence, a two-step charge may be appropriate. In this case, the jury is charged both with regard to the capacity to form the requisite intent and with regard to the need to determine in all of the circumstances whether the requisite intent was in fact formed by the accused. In these circumstances, the jury might be instructed that their overall duty is to determine whether or not the accused possessed the requisite intent for the crime. If, on the basis of the expert evidence, the jury is left with a reasonable doubt as to whether, as a result of the consumption of the alcohol, the accused had the capacity to form the requisite intent then that ends the inquiry and the accused must be acquitted of the offence and consideration must then be given to any included lesser offences. If the jury is not left with a reasonable doubt as a result of the expert evidence as to the capacity to form the intent then they must consider and take into account all the surrounding circumstances and the evidence pertaining to those circumstances in determining whether or not the accused possessed the requisite intent for the offence. Furthermore, the presumption that a person intends the natural consequences of their act refers only to a common-sense and logical inference that the jury can but is not compelled to make. Where there is some evidence of intoxication, the trial judge must link the instructions on intoxication with the instruction on the common-sense inference so that the jury is specifically instructed that evidence of intoxication can rebut the inference: *R. v. Robinson*, [1996] 1 S.C.R. 683, 105 C.C.C. (3d) 97. See also *R. v. McMaster*, [1996] 1 S.C.R. 740, 105 C.C.C. (3d) 193; *R. v. Lemky*, [1996] 1 S.C.R. 757, 105 C.C.C. (3d) 137; *R. v. Seymour*, [1996] 2 S.C.R. 252, 106 C.C.C. (3d) 520.

The trial judge need not explicitly link the effect of intoxication to the ability to foresee the consequences. A functional approach should be taken to the issue of linking of foreseeability and intoxication: *R. v. Daley*, [2007] 3 S.C.R. 523, 226 C.C.C. (3d) 1.

The distinction between conduct of a deceased relevant to an accused's state of mind and conduct that may qualify as provocation under s. 232 is especially important where there is evidence of intoxication. To qualify as provocation under s. 232, the jury must be satisfied that the conduct was sufficient to deprive an ordinary person of self-control. In making that assessment, the jury does not take into consideration the alcohol consumption of the particular accused. However, potentially provocative conduct that fails the ordinary person test and, therefore, cannot qualify as provocation under s. 232, must still be considered by a jury in assessing whether an accused lacked the necessary intent due to intoxication: *R. v. Bouchard* (2013), 305 C.C.C. (3d) 240 (Ont. C.A.), affd [2014] 3 S.C.R. 283, 316 C.C.C. (3d) 85.

It is essential in a case where the Crown relies upon the intent described in para. (*a*)(ii) that the jury receive an explanation of the essential difference between that intent and the intent in para. (*a*)(i), namely, that the former requires foresight of the likely consequences of the acts which cause bodily harm combined with recklessness as to that consequence: *R. v. Korzepa* (1991), 64 C.C.C. (3d) 489 (B.C.C.A.).

It was held in *R. v. Young*, [1981] 2 S.C.R. 39, 59 C.C.C. (2d) 305 (5:4), that where the only defence relied upon was drunkenness and the accused's acts were such as, in the normal course of events, to give rise to a probability of serious injury that would likely cause death, then in the absence of any indication that the accused lacked the normal intent which accompanies such acts the inference to be drawn from the facts, absent drunkenness, was that the accused intended to cause bodily harm which he knew was likely to cause death and was reckless as to whether death ensued or not. It did not constitute fatal non-direction for the trial judge not to direct the jury that manslaughter was an available verdict if apart from drunkenness the jury had a reasonable doubt as to the accused's intent.

A psychiatrist may give opinion evidence that an accused lacked capacity to form the intent required for murder, provided that there is a proper basis for such opinion. Thus, the psychiatrist may not express an opinion that the accused as a normal person did not have the capacity to form the required intent, based on his conclusion that the personality of the accused is such that he could not have had the intent requisite for murder in committing a crime of such brutality as was involved in the particular case. Such an opinion does not involve the application of knowledge within the expertise of the psychiatrist. On the other hand, an opinion that, for example, the accused had an organic amnesia as the result of the consumption of alcohol is within the expertise of a psychiatrist: *R. v. Gowland* (1978), 45 C.C.C. (2d) 303 (Ont. C.A.).

Included offences – Attempted murder is an included offence to murder: *R. v. Sarrazin*, [2011] 3 S.C.R. 505, 276 C.C.C. (3d) 210.

Liability of party – The accused's liability as a party to a killing cannot be determined simply by application of a principle that the accused was party to some single ongoing transaction. In the case of an accused who aids or abets in the killing of another, the requisite intent that the aider or abettor must have to warrant conviction for murder must be the same as that of the principal offender. The aider or abettor must intend that he or the perpetrator cause bodily harm of a kind likely to result in death and be reckless whether death ensues or not. If the intent of the aiding party is insufficient to support a conviction for murder, then the party may still be convicted of manslaughter if the unlawful act which was aided or abetted is one he knows is likely to cause some harm short of death: *R. v. Kirkness*, [1990] 3 S.C.R. 74, 60 C.C.C. (3d) 9 (5:2).

Where the accused was charged with first degree murder and the jury was instructed on liability for aiding and abetting, it was essential that the jury be clearly and correctly instructed as to the principal's constitutionally required *mens rea* for murder under para. (*a*)(i) and (ii): *R. v. Zoldi* (2018), 360 C.C.C. (3d) 476 (Ont. C.A.).

It was reversible error to instruct the jury that the aider simply needed to foresee that the principal would cause someone's death. Rather, it needed to be made clear that the aider must have foreseen that the principal would cause someone's death while possessing one of the culpable mental states in para. (*a*)(i) and (ii): *R. v. McLellan* (2018), 362 C.C.C. (3d) 183 (Ont. C.A.).

On a charge of conspiracy to commit murder, the jury should be instructed on the culpable states of mind in both subparas. (*a*)(i) and (ii): *R. v. Correia* (2016), 339 C.C.C. (3d) 321 (B.C.C.A.).

Transferred intent [para. (*b*)] – Even where the provisions of this paragraph apply the Crown must prove a concurrence of *mens rea* and *actus reus*; that at the time of the act, which killed the deceased, the accused had the specified intent with respect to the proposed victim: *R. v. Droste* (1979), 49 C.C.C. (2d) 52, 18 C.R. (3d) 64 (Ont. C.A.).

The doctrine of transferred intent has no application where an accused mistakenly kills someone else while attempting to kill himself. The harm caused and the harm intended must be of the same legal kind and accordingly, the *mens rea* for suicide and murder cannot be equated: *R. v. Fontaine* (2002), 168 C.C.C. (3d) 263, 7 C.R. (6th) 139 (Man. C.A.), affd 199 C.C.C. (3d) 349, 31 C.R. (6th) 273 (Man. C.A.). *Contra*: *R. v. Brown* (1983), 4 C.C.C. (3d) 571 (Ont. H.C.J.).

Homicide in course of effecting unlawful purpose [para. (*c*)] – Liability for murder cannot be based on any *mens rea* less than subjective foresight of death and, accordingly, that part of para. (*c*) allowing for a conviction upon proof that the accused ought to have known that death was likely to result is unconstitutional: *R. v. Martineau*, [1990] 2 S.C.R. 633, 58 C.C.C. (3d) 353 (5:2). See also *R. v. Haché* (2007), 227 C.C.C. (3d) 162 (N.B.C.A.).

Under para. (*c*), the unlawful object must be different from the assault that gives rise to the charge of murder. The act that causes death need not be unlawful, although it will almost invariably be a dangerous act and unlawful. The test for causation is the same as under s. 222(5) as described in *R. v. Smithers*, [1978] 1 S.C.R. 506, 34 C.C.C. (2d) 427, noted under that section. While the unlawful object does not have to include an intent or object to assault or kill the deceased, it must be an object or conduct that would constitute a serious crime which is an indictable offence requiring *mens rea*. The second *mens rea* requirement is proof of subjective foresight of death. In the context of an unintentional death, the subjective foresight element does not require that an accused foresee the precise situation or all of the events that resulted in death. It is sufficient if the accused has the subjective foresight that the acts done for the unlawful object are likely to cause death and those acts are sufficiently linked to the death to have caused the death within the meaning of the section: *R. v. Meiler* (1999), 136 C.C.C. (3d) 11 (Ont. C.A.).

This provision does not violate s. 7 of the Charter. Subsection (*c*) requires the subjective foresight of death together with the intent to pursue an unlawful object which is itself an indictable offence requiring full *mens rea*. The elements of the offence are as follows: (a) the accused must pursue an unlawful object other than to cause the death of the victim or bodily harm to the victim knowing that death is likely; (b) the unlawful object must itself be an indictable offence requiring *mens rea*; (c) in furtherance of the unlawful object, the accused must intentionally commit a dangerous act; (d) the dangerous act must be distinct from the unlawful object only in the sense that the unlawful object must be something other than the likelihood of death, which is the harm that is foreseen as a consequence of the dangerous act; (e) the dangerous act must be a specific act or series of acts that, in fact, result in death, although the dangerous act need not itself constitute an offence; and (f) when the dangerous act is committed, the accused must have subjective knowledge that death is likely to result. It is insufficient to prove the intention to carry out the unlawful object. The Crown must also establish an additional component of *mens rea* — the intent to commit the dangerous act knowing that it is likely to cause death. Vague realization that death is possible will not be sufficient. Similarly, if the dangerous act was done as a reaction and out of panic, this may suggest that the required subjective foresight of death was not present. "Likely" requires more than an awareness of risk or a possibility or chance of death. What is necessary is subjective knowledge that death is likely, which must be present at some point during the acts committed by the accused that caused the death: *R. v. Shand* (2011), 266 C.C.C. (3d) 137 (Ont. C.A.), leave to appeal to S.C.C. refused (2012), 295 O.A.C. 398*n*.

Inferring actual knowledge from the "common sense inference" risks substituting a constitutionally impermissible mental or fault element for subjective foresight. In the absence of any direct evidence on the foresight or knowledge issue, it can only be proven beyond a reasonable doubt if the only rational inference available on the evidence is that the accused knew the dangerous act was likely to cause someone's death: *R. v. Roks* (2011), 274 C.C.C. (3d) 1 (Ont. C.A.), additional reasons (2011), 284 C.C.C. (3d) 510 (Ont. C.A.).

MURDER IN COMMISSION OF OFFENCES.

230. Culpable homicide is murder where a person causes the death of a human being while committing or attempting to commit high treason or treason or an offence mentioned in section 52 (sabotage), 75 (piratical acts), 76 (hijacking an aircraft), 144 or subsection 145(1) or sections 146 to 148 (escape or rescue from prison or lawful custody), section 270 (assaulting a peace officer), section 271 (sexual assault), 272 (sexual assault with a weapon, threats to a third party or causing bodily harm), 273 (aggravated sexual assault), 279 (kidnapping and forcible confinement), 279.1 (hostage taking), 343 (robbery), 348 (breaking and entering) or 433 or 434 (arson), whether or not the person means to cause death to any human being and whether or not he knows that death is likely to be caused to any human being, if

(*a*) he means to cause bodily harm for the purpose of

(i) facilitating the commission of the offence, or

(ii) facilitating his flight after committing or attempting to commit the offence,

and the death ensues from the bodily harm;

(*b*) he administers a stupefying or overpowering thing for a purpose mentioned in paragraph (*a*), and the death ensues therefrom; or

(*c*) he wilfully stops, by any means, the breath of a human being for a purpose mentioned in paragraph (*a*), and the death ensues therefrom. R.S., c. C-34, s. 213; 1974-75-76, c. 93, s. 13, c. 105, s. 29; 1980-81-82-83, c. 125, s. 15; R.S.C. 1985, c. 27 (1st Supp.), s. 40(2); 1991, c. 4, s. 1.

(*d*) [*Repealed*, 1991, c. 4, s. 1.]

CROSS-REFERENCES

Note that s. 3 provides that the descriptions in parenthesis after the section number are inserted for convenience of reference only and are no part of the provision.

Culpable homicide is defined in s. 222. Culpable homicide is also defined as murder in the circumstances set out in s. 229. Murder is classified as first or second degree murder under s. 231. The punishment for murder is, pursuant to s. 235, a minimum of life imprisonment.

ANNOTATIONS

Constitutional considerations – In two cases, *R. v. Vaillancourt*, [1987] 2 S.C.R. 636, 39 C.C.C. (3d) 118, and *R. v. Martineau*, [1990] 2 S.C.R. 633, 58 C.C.C. (3d) 353, the Supreme Court has considered the constitutionality of the provisions of this section. In the latter case, a majority of the court held that liability for murder cannot be based on any *mens rea* less than subjective foresight of death and that, accordingly, all of this section is unconstitutional.

In the subsequent case of *R. v. Sit*, [1991] 3 S.C.R. 124, 66 C.C.C. (3d) 449, the court confirmed the scope of its earlier decisions and, in particular, held that para. (*c*) is of no force and effect.

CLASSIFICATION OF MURDER / Planned and deliberate murder / Contracted murder / Murder of peace officer, etc. / Hijacking, sexual assault or kidnapping / Criminal harassment / Murder — terrorist activity / Murder — criminal organization / Intimidation / Second degree murder.

231. (1) Murder is first degree murder or second degree murder.

(2) Murder is first degree murder when it is planned and deliberate.

(3) Without limiting the generality of subsection (2), murder is planned and deliberate when it is committed pursuant to an arrangement under which money or anything of value passes or is intended to pass from one person to another, or is promised by one person to another, as consideration for that other's causing or assisting in causing the death of anyone or counselling another person to do any act causing or assisting in causing that death.

(4) Irrespective of whether a murder is planned and deliberate on the part of any person, murder is first degree murder when the victim is

(*a*) a police officer, police constable, constable, sheriff, deputy sheriff, sheriff's officer or other person employed for the preservation and maintenance of the public peace, acting in the course of his duties;

(*b*) a warden, deputy warden, instructor, keeper, jailer, guard or other officer or a permanent employee of a prison, acting in the course of his duties; or

(*c*) a person working in a prison with the permission of the prison authorities and acting in the course of his work therein.

(5) Irrespective of whether a murder is planned and deliberate on the part of any person, murder is first degree murder in respect of a person when the death is caused by that person while committing or attempting to commit an offence under one of the following sections:

(*a*) section 76 (hijacking an aircraft);

(*b*) section 271 (sexual assault);

(*c*) section 272 (sexual assault with a weapon, threats to a third party or causing bodily harm);

(*d*) section 273 (aggravated sexual assault);

(*e*) section 279 (kidnapping and forcible confinement); or

(*f*) section 279.1 (hostage taking).

(6) [*Repealed*, R.S.C. 1985, c. 27 (1st Supp.), s. 35.]

(6) Irrespective of whether a murder is planned and deliberate on the part of any person, murder is first degree murder when the death is caused by that person while committing or attempting to commit an offence under section 264 and the person committing that offence intended to cause the person murdered to fear for the safety of the person murdered or the safety of anyone known to the person murdered.

(6.01) Irrespective of whether a murder is planned and deliberate on the part of a person, murder is first degree murder when the death is caused by that person while committing or attempting to commit an indictable offence under this or any other Act of Parliament if the act or omission constituting the offence also constitutes a terrorist activity.

(6.1) Irrespective of whether a murder is planned and deliberate on the part of a person, murder is first degree murder when

(*a*) the death is caused by that person for the benefit of, at the direction of or in association with a criminal organization; or

(*b*) the death is caused by that person while committing or attempting to commit an indictable offence under this or any other Act of Parliament for the benefit of, at the direction of or in association with a criminal organization.

(6.2) Irrespective of whether a murder is planned and deliberate on the part of a person, murder is first degree murder when the death is caused by that person while committing or attempting to commit an offence under section 423.1.

(7) All murder that is not first degree murder is second degree murder. R.S., c. C-34, s. 214; R.S. c. C-35, s. 4; 1973-74, c. 38, s. 2; 1974-75-76, c. 105, s. 4; 1980-81-82-83, c. 125, s. 16; R.S.C. 1985, c. 27 (1st Supp.), ss. 7(2)(*b*), 35, 40(2); 1997, c. 16, s. 3; 1997, c. 23, s. 8; 2001, c. 32, s. 9(2); 2001, c. 41, s. 9; 2009, c. 22, s. 5.

CROSS-REFERENCES

Note that s. 3 provides that the descriptions in parenthesis after the section number are inserted for convenience of reference only and are no part of the provision.

Murder is defined in ss. 229 and 230. The terms "prison", "criminal organization" and "terrorist activity" are defined in s. 2. The punishment for murder is, pursuant to s. 235, a minimum of life imprisonment. Eligibility for parole for a person convicted of murder is determined by ss. 745 to 746.1. [Respecting parole eligibility, see further cross-references under s. 235.] However, note that under s. 745, a person convicted of second degree murder must be sentenced to life imprisonment without eligibility for parole for 25 years where he has previously been convicted of murder, however described. A person convicted of murder will also be liable to the mandatory prohibition order respecting firearms, ammunition and explosives by virtue of s. 100(1). As to included offences, see s. 662. With respect to other notes concerning procedure and evidence, see CROSS-REFERENCES under ss. 229 and 230.

SYNOPSIS

This section *classifies* convictions for *murder* into first and second degree murder for the purpose of setting a parole eligibility date.

The effect of subsecs. (1) and (7) is that a murder which does not come within subsections (2) to (6.2) is second degree murder.

Subsection (2) states that murder is *first degree* murder when it is *planned and deliberate*. Subsection (3) deems conduct described in the subsection, which may be generally referred to as *contract killings*, to be planned and deliberate, and therefore, by definition, first degree murder.

The following subsections deem murders of specified victims (subsec. (4)) or while committing or attempting to commit specified offences (subsecs. (5) to (6.2)) to be first degree murder. The phrase "while committing" only requires proof that the underlying offence and the death were part of the same transaction, not that they occurred at the same moment. However, the death must have been caused "by that person". As to the meaning of that phrase, see the annotations in this section under the heading "**Liability of party**".

ANNOTATIONS

Subsection (2) [Planning and Deliberation] / ***Meaning of planning and deliberation*** – This subsection brings back the concept of "planned and deliberate" which was formerly part of the definition of capital murder. Some of the following cases were decided under the former capital murder sections.

The word "deliberate" means "considered, not impulsive" and as used in the subsection cannot have simply the meaning "intentional" because it is only if the accused's act was intentional that he can be guilty of murder. The subsection is creating an additional element. Psychiatric evidence that at the critical moment the accused was suffering from a depressive psychosis resulting in impairment of his ability to decide even inconsequential things would have a direct bearing on the issue of whether the act was deliberate and the trial judge's failure to adequately deal with this evidence in his charge to the jury necessitated a new trial: *R. v. More*, [1963] S.C.R. 522, [1963] 3 C.C.C. 289 (5:2).

In *R. v. Mitchell*, [1964] S.C.R. 471, [1965] 1 C.C.C. 155, the court was unanimous (7:0) on the manner in which a trial judge should instruct a jury to determine whether a murder, which they have found to have been committed by the accused, was "planned and deliberate". After referring to *R. v. More, supra,* and *R. v. McMartin*, [1964] S.C.R. 484, [1965] 1 C.C.C. 142, Spence J., wrote at p. 162 C.C.C.:

> I am of the opinion that the judgments in these two cases have as their *ratio decidendi* the principle that in determining whether the accused committed the crime of capital murder in that it was "planned and deliberate on the part of such person" the jury should have available and should be directed to consider all the circumstances including not only the evidence of the accused's actions but of his condition, his state of mind as affected by either real or imagined insults and provoking actions of the victim and by the accused's consumption of alcohol.

In *R. v. Widdifield* (1961), 6 Crim. L.Q. 152 (Ont. H.C.J.), Gale J. charged the jury in part as follows:

> I think that in the Code "planned" is to be assigned, I think, its natural meaning of a calculated scheme or design which has been carefully thought out, and the nature and consequences of which have been considered and weighed. But that does not mean, of course, to say that the plan need be a complicated one. It may be a very simple one, and the simpler it is perhaps the easier it is to formulate.
>
> The important element, it seems to me, so far as time is concerned, is the time involved in developing the plan, not the time between the development of the plan and the doing of the act. One can carefully prepare a plan and immediately it is prepared set out to do the planned act, or, alternatively, you can wait an appreciable time to do it once it has been formed.
>
> As far as the word "deliberate" is concerned, I think that the Code means that it should also carry its natural meaning of "considered," "not impulsive," "slow in deciding," "cautious," implying that the accused must take time to weigh the advantages and disadvantages of his intended action. That is what, as it seems to me, "deliberate" means.

The direction in *R. v. Widdifield, supra*, as to the definition of "planned" was approved in *R. v. Reynolds* (1978), 44 C.C.C. (2d) 129, 22 O.R. (2d) 353 (C.A.).

Planning in this context requires evidence that the killing was the result of a scheme or design previously formulated. A murder committed on a sudden impulse and without prior consideration would not meet this test: *R. v. Smith* (1979), 51 C.C.C. (2d) 381, 1 Sask. R. 213 (C.A.).

The deliberation required under this subsection must occur before the act of murder commences: *R. v. Ruptash* (1982), 68 C.C.C. (2d) 182 (Alta. C.A.).

Intoxication – In *R. v. Reynolds* (1978), 44 C.C.C. (2d) 129, 22 O.R. (2d) 353 (C.A.), it was held that evidence of intoxication was not limited to the question of the accused's ability to plan and deliberate and that it would be open to the jury to find that the accused acted impulsively without deliberation due to the consumption of alcohol and other circumstances even though he was *able* to plan and deliberate.

In *R. v. Wallen*, [1990] 1 S.C.R. 827, 54 C.C.C. (3d) 383 (3:2), all members of the court agreed that the trial judge must direct the jury to consider the issue of intoxication as it applies to planning and deliberation separately from the issue of intoxication as a defence to murder. However, the court divided on whether it is mandatory in all cases for the trial judge to make it clear that a lesser degree of intoxication may suffice to negative planning and deliberation than to negative the intent to kill. In any event, all members of the court agreed that such a direction will be helpful to the jury.

Mental disorder – The existence of a mental disorder is not incompatible with the commission of a planned and deliberate murder. In particular, the word "deliberate" has not imported a requirement that the accused's previous determination to kill the victim must have been the result of normal thinking or must have been rationally motived: *R. v. Kirkby* (1985), 21 C.C.C. (3d) 31, 47 C.R. (3d) 97 (Ont. C.A.).

Liability of party – An accused sought to be made liable for first degree murder as an aider or abettor must be shown to have intended to aid a planned and deliberate murder: *R. v. Peters and Eldridge* (1985), 23 C.C.C. (3d) 171 (B.C.C.A.).

Application to murder defined in ss. 229 and 230 – This section does not create a separate substantive offence of first degree murder, but rather constitutes a characterization, for sentencing purposes, of the substantive offence of murder in ss. 229 and 230. A murder is first degree murder within the meaning of this subsection if there is planning and deliberation in relation to the specific *mens rea* of the applicable section, which in the case of a murder described by s. 229(*b*) is the intent to cause the death to one person although by accident or mistake, another is killed. While there may be certain mental states specified in ss. 229 and 230 which are incompatible with planning and deliberation, the *mens rea* of s. 229(*b*) is not one of them: *R. v. Droste*, [1984] 1 S.C.R. 208, 10 C.C.C. (3d) 404 (7:0).

However, the mental state described in s. 229(*a*)(ii) is not incompatible with planning and deliberation. There can be no doubt that a person can plan and deliberate to cause terrible bodily harm that he knows is likely to result in death. Nothing is added to the aspect of planning and deliberation by the requirement under s. 229(*a*)(ii) that the fatal assault be carried out in a reckless manner: *R. v. Nygaard*, [1989] 2 S.C.R. 1074, 51 C.C.C. (3d) 417.

Subsection (4) [Murder of police officer, etc.] / *Mens rea* – In a case decided under the former s. 202A(2) it was held that knowledge by the accused that the person killed was a police officer or other person employed for the preservation and maintenance of public peace is requisite for a conviction under that section: *R. v. Shand* (1971), 3 C.C.C. (2d) 8 (Man. C.A.).

It was held in *R. v. Collins* (1989), 48 C.C.C. (3d) 343 (Ont. C.A.), that for the offence to constitute first degree murder pursuant to this subsection, the Crown must prove that the deceased was a person who falls within the designation of the occupations set forth in that subsection acting in the course of his duties to the knowledge of the accused or with recklessness on his part as to whether or not the deceased was such a person so acting.

"Acting in the course of his duties" – Evidence that the victim was a member of a police detachment and performing regular police duties, was assigned to a police cruiser and was in uniform when his body was discovered and that he made a radio transmission shortly before his death was, in the absence of evidence to the contrary, sufficient to discharge the evidentiary burden on the Crown to prove that the deceased was acting in the course of his duties, notwithstanding the lack of any evidence as to exactly what the officer was doing at the time of his death: *R. v. Fitzgerald and Schoenberger* (1982), 70 C.C.C. (2d) 87 (Ont. C.A.).

The term "acting in the course of his duty" while wider than the phrase "engaged in the execution of his duty" will generally encompass the whole time-span of a police officer's tour of duty and would include any activity related to the performance of a duty or to the ability of the officer to perform his duty, including for example having lunch or receiving medical attention during a tour of duty: *R. v. Prevost* (1988), 42 C.C.C. (3d) 314 (Ont. C.A.), leave to appeal to S.C.C. refused [1989] 1 S.C.R. xii.

Constitutional considerations – The classification of murder of a police officer as first degree murder thus mandating a life sentence without eligibility for parole for 25 years does not offend the *Charter of Rights and Freedoms*, ss. 7, 9, 12 and 15: *R. v. Bowen* (1990), 59 C.C.C. (3d) 515 (Alta. C.A.); *R. v. Lefebvre* (1989), 71 C.R. (3d) 213 (Que. C.A.).

Subsection (5) / *Unlawful confinement* – In *R. v. Pritchard*, [2008] 3 S.C.R. 195, 236 C.C.C. (3d) 301, the Supreme Court of Canada reconciled conflicting appellate case law in respect of the requisite temporal and causal connection between the enumerated offence and any ancillary offence. While proof of robbery does not by itself trigger subsec. (5), proof of robbery does not bar or alter its application either. The phrase "while committing or attempting to commit" requires the killing to be closely connected, temporally and causally, with an enumerated offence. Although every robbery involves an element of violence or threatened violence, the level of violence does not always occasion confinement of the significant duration required to satisfy s. 279(2). Not all robberies involve domination of the victim and accordingly, not all robbery-murders will satisfy subsec. (5)(*e*). Even a confinement which satisfies s. 279(2) will not trigger this provision if it is consumed in the very act of killing. As set out in *R. v. Kimberley* (2001), 157 C.C.C. (3d) 129 (Ont. C.A.), in order to trigger this provision, the confinement and the murder must constitute distinct criminal acts. Where the jury is satisfied that there was confinement not limited to what was "integral to" the particular act of killing disclosed by the evidence, the Crown has established a distinct criminal act under s. 279(2). If the jury is satisfied that the murder was committed in the course of that confinement, such that the series of events may be characterized as a "single transaction", then the requirements of subsec. (5)(*e*) are met. The fact that the accused confined the victim for the purpose of committing a non-enumerated offence does not alter the operation of subsec. (5)(*e*). Second degree murder will be elevated to first degree murder whether the murder and the predicate offence, such as unlawful confinement, are linked together both causally and temporally in circumstances that make the entire course of conduct a single transaction. The temporal-causal connection is established where the unlawful confinement creates a "continuing illegal domination of the victim" that provides the accused with a position of power which he or she chooses to exploit to murder the victim. If these factors are established, the fact that, along the way other offences, such as robbery, are committed, is not a bar to the application of subsec. (5).

The predicate offence under subsec. (5) need not precede the mortal wound so long as the act of killing and the predicate offence, while distinct offences, remain part of the same transaction: *R. v. Mullings* (2014), 319 C.C.C. (3d) 1 (Ont. C.A.), leave to appeal to S.C.C. refused 2015 CarswellOnt 18931.

There is no basis for directing the jury that the unlawful confinement had ceased and thus that this subsection did not apply where the accused, having held the deceased and her relatives at gunpoint for a substantial period of time, shot his wife a short time after she indicated that she intended to leave: *R. v. Francella*, [1990] 2 S.C.R. 1420, 60 C.C.C. (3d) 96*n* (5:0), affg 46 C.C.C. (3d) 93 (Ont. C.A.).

This provision applies even if the victim of the murder and the victim of the enumerated offence are not the same. The purpose of the provision is to punish murders committed in connection with crimes of domination more severely. The provision is restricted to its appropriate context by the requirement that there must be a close temporal and causal connection between the murder and the enumerated offence: *R. v. Russell*, [2001] 2 S.C.R. 804, 157 C.C.C. (3d) 1.

Murder is treated as an exceptionally serious crime and elevated to first degree under this provision because the murder is committed by someone already abusing his or her power by illegally dominating another person, or because it is committed by someone who chooses to exploit his or her position of dominance and power to the point of murder. In this case, the accused did not illegally dominate the deceased where the victim had consented to having the accused pull a belt around the victim's neck while engaged in sexual activity. While consent to the tightening of the belt could not exclude the accused's responsibility for the victim's death, that fact could not retroactively make the confinement forcible: *R. v. McIlwaine* (1996), 111 C.C.C. (3d) 426 (Que. C.A.).

It was not an error for the jury to find that the victim was unlawfully confined within the meaning of this section where she had locked herself in the bathroom and the accused had broken the door down in order to attack her: *R. v. Johnstone* (2014), 313 C.C.C. (3d) 34 (Ont. C.A.).

Not every killing in a moving motor vehicle invokes this provision. A person who initially voluntarily enters a vehicle is not unlawfully confined because a person who consents to *de facto* confinement is not unlawfully confined: *R. v. Millard* (2016), 340 C.C.C. (3d) 388 (Ont. S.C.J.).

This section is subservient to s. 229; it classifies for sentencing purposes the offences in that section as either first or second degree murder. Thus, an accused charged with second degree murder may be convicted of that offence even though the facts would support a conviction of first degree murder, as where death ensues as a result of the use of a weapon in the course of an unlawful confinement: *R. v. Farrant*, [1983] 1 S.C.R. 124, 4 C.C.C. (3d) 354 (5:2).

Subsection (6) / Murder in the course of criminal harassment – Just as a single act can amount to criminal harassment under s. 264, so too can the added mental element in subsec. (6) be inferred from a single act: *R. v. Smith* (2014), 308 C.C.C. (3d) 254 (Ont. C.A.).

Liability of party – The words "when the death is caused by that person" limit the application of this subsection and a person could not be convicted of first degree murder under this subsection when his liability for murder depended solely on the combined operation of ss. 21(2) and 230. The court noted that those words had been omitted from the

French version of the *Criminal Code* but adopted the approach that the provision being a penal one the accused was entitled to rely on the interpretation which was most favourable to him, in this case the English version of s. 231(5): *R. v. Woods and Gruener* (1980), 57 C.C.C. (2d) 220 (Ont. C.A.).

The phrase, "when death is caused by that person" is broad enough to include a person who assists in the murder where that person is a substantial cause of the death. The Crown must establish that the accused has committed an act or series of acts which are of such a nature that they must be regarded as a substantial and integral cause of the death. The accused must play a very active, usually physical, role in the killing. In addition, the Crown must show that there was no intervening act of another which resulted in the accused no longer being substantially connected to the death of the victim and that the underlying offence and the murder were a part of the same transaction: *R. v. Harbottle*, [1993] 3 S.C.R. 306, 84 C.C.C. (3d) 1.

Thus, s. 21(2) cannot be a source of criminal liability for first-degree murder under this subsection: *R. v. Michaud* (2000), 144 C.C.C. (3d) 62 (N.B.C.A.).

"While committing" – There need not be an exact coincidence between the act causing death and the acts constituting the underlying offence. It is sufficient if they form part of one continuous sequence of events forming a single transaction: *R. v. Paré*, [1987] 2 S.C.R. 618, 38 C.C.C. (3d) 97 (7:0).

It was not necessary for the Crown to prove the exact time of death and that the sexual assault occurred prior to death provided it was shown that the sexual assault and the death were part of a continuous sequence of events: *R. v. Ganton* (1992), 77 C.C.C. (3d) 259 (Sask. C.A.).

In determining whether the sexual assault and murder are inextricably linked, it must be determined whether the temporal and causal connections between the murder and the sexual assault are so close together so as to form a continuous single transaction: *R. v. Muchikekwanape* (2002), 166 C.C.C. (3d) 144 (Man. C.A.).

As long as the murder and sexual assault are part of the same transaction, it makes no difference that the death preceded the sexualized conduct: *R. v. Niemi* (2017), 355 C.C.C. (3d) 344 (Ont. C.A.).

This subsection does not apply where the murder was committed after the completion of the underlying offence even if to facilitate flight after commission of that offence: *R. v. Sargent* (1983), 5 C.C.C. (3d) 429 (Sask. C.A.).

Constitutional considerations – The combined effect of subsec. (5) and s. 745(*a*), requiring that a person, convicted of first degree murder where the murder is committed while comitting one of the offences specified in subsec. (5), must be sentenced to life imprisonment without eligibility for parole for 25 years, does not infringe ss. 7, 9 and 12 of the Charter: *R. v. Luxton*, [1990] 2 S.C.R. 711, 58 C.C.C. (3d) 449 (7:0); *R. v. Arkell*, [1990] 2 S.C.R. 695, 59 C.C.C. (3d) 65 (7:0).

MURDER REDUCED TO MANSLAUGHTER / What is provocation / Questions of fact / Death during illegal arrest.

232. (1) Culpable homicide that otherwise would be murder may be reduced to manslaughter if the person who committed it did so in the heat of passion caused by sudden provocation.

(2) Conduct of the victim that would constitute an indictable offence under this Act that is punishable by five or more years of imprisonment and that is of such a nature as to be sufficient to deprive an ordinary person of the power of self-control is provocation for the purposes of this section, if the accused acted on it on the sudden and before there was time for their passion to cool.

(3) For the purposes of this section, the questions

(*a*) whether the conduct of the victim amounted to provocation under subsection (2), and

(*b*) whether the accused was deprived of the power of self-control by the provocation that he alleges he received,

are questions of fact, but no one shall be deemed to have given provocation to another by doing anything that he had a legal right to do, or by doing anything that the accused incited him to do in order to provide the accused with an excuse for causing death or bodily harm to any human being.

(4) Culpable homicide that otherwise would be murder is not necessarily manslaughter by reason only that it was committed by a person who was being arrested illegally, but the fact that the illegality of the arrest was known to the accused may be evidence of provocation for the purpose of this section. R.S., c. C-34, s. 215; 2015, c. 29, s. 7.

CROSS-REFERENCES

Culpable homicide is defined in s. 222. Murder is defined by ss. 229 and 230. The punishment for manslaughter is set out in s. 236. It is not unusual for the excuse of provocation to be raised in circumstances where the accused also relies on the defence of intoxication [thus see notes under ss. 33.1 and 229]; use of force to prevent commission of certain offences [thus see s. 27]; self defence and defence of property [thus see ss. 34 to 42].

A person convicted of manslaughter may be subject to a dangerous offender application under Part XXIV.

SYNOPSIS

Section 232 sets out some of the circumstances under which *murder will be reduced to manslaughter*.

The first three subsections spell out the defence of *provocation*. Before subsec. (1) becomes relevant, it must be shown that the culpable homicide would *otherwise have been murder*. Despite the use of the word "may" in the section, murder will be reduced to manslaughter if the murder was committed as a result of provocation. Provocation occurs if the person who committed the act did so in the *heat of passion caused by sudden provocation*.

Pursuant to subsec. (2), the act which provokes the accused must be conduct that would constitute an indictable offence that is punishable by five or more years' imprisonment. It further requires a mix of subjective and objective factors in determining if that conduct constituted provocation. The *objective aspect* of the test is whether the wrongful act or insult is of such a nature as to be sufficient to deprive an ordinary man of self-control. Even in this aspect of the test, there appears to be some element of subjectivity as the ordinary person may include some of the general characteristics of the accused such as sex, race or age. The *subjective aspect* of the test is that the accused *did act on the provocation* and did so *before* there was *time for his passion to cool*. In this second part of the test, the background, temperament, idiosyncrasies or drunkenness of the accused may be considered. The requirement of suddenness must apply both to the provocation and to the accused's reaction to it.

Subsection (3) states that the issues of whether a particular wrongful act or insult amounted to provocation and whether the accused was deprived of his self-control as a result of the provocation are *questions of fact*. This means that the jury will ultimately determine these issues, although the judge will first consider, as a question of law, whether there is *any evidence* which could amount to provocation. The subsection makes it clear that if a person does anything which he has a legal right to do or which he does as a result of incitement by the accused to do for the purpose of providing the accused with an excuse to cause the person death or bodily harm, this does not amount to provocation. One example of a person who has a legal right to do something which might otherwise constitute provocation is a person who is justified in using force against the accused in self-defence.

Subsection (4) deals with the effect of an illegal arrest as it relates to provocation in this section. The fact that a person was arrested illegally does not necessarily reduce what would otherwise be murder to manslaughter. It also provides that an unlawful arrest of a person may constitute provocation if that person was aware of the illegality of the arrest.

ANNOTATIONS

Note: The cases annotated below should be relied upon with caution. They were decided before amendments in 2015 which specified that the defence of provocation only applies where the conduct of the victim constitutes an indictable offence punishable by five or more years in prison. Previously, subsec. (2) stated that the conduct of the victim need merely be a "wrongful act or insult".

Sufficiency of evidence to raise defence – In *R. v. Squire*, [1977] 2 S.C.R. 13, 29 C.C.C. (2d) 497, the accused's counsel at trial for non-capital murder relied only on the defence of drunkenness. On appeal against the conviction the defence of provocation was successfully raised. On further appeal by the Crown it was held (9:0) that a trial judge is under no duty to invite a jury to consider defences of which there is no evidence or which cannot reasonably be inferred from the evidence and where, as here, it can be said that no jury acting judicially on the evidence at trial could find a wrongful act or insult sufficient to deprive an ordinary person of self-control, the trial judge was not in error in not charging the jury on the defence of provocation.

An accused, who at the time of the offence had and kept the initiative in a situation where the acts of the deceased, whether they were insults or physical acts, were predictable, cannot avail himself of the defence of "sudden" provocation within the meaning of this section: *R. v. Louison* (1975), 26 C.C.C. (2d) 266, [1975] 6 W.W.R. 289 (Sask. C.A.), affd [1979] 1 S.C.R. 100, 51 C.C.C. (2d) 479*n* (9:0).

The words of the victim terminating her relationship with the accused cannot amount to a wrongful act or insult within this section: *R. v. Young* (1993), 78 C.C.C. (3d) 538, 117 N.S.R. (2d) 166 (C.A.), leave to appeal to S.C.C. refused 81 C.C.C. (3d) vi.

Nature of objective test of "ordinary person" – Provocation under this section is subject to a dual test. One must first consider the effect on an ordinary person of the particular wrongful act or insult relied on. This constitutes an objective test. If this first test is satisfied then the subjective test is to determine whether the accused acted actually upon the provocation, on the sudden and before there was time for his passion to cool. While the character, background, temperament, idiosyncracies, or the drunkenness of the accused are matters to be considered in the second test they are excluded from consideration in the first test: *R. v. Wright*, [1969] S.C.R. 335, [1969] 3 C.C.C. 258 (5:0); *R. v. Taylor*, [1947] S.C.R. 462, 89 C.C.C. 209; *R. v. Olbey*, [1980] 1 S.C.R. 1008, 50 C.C.C. (2d) 257 (6:1).

In relation to the objective element of the test, it is proper to consider the background of the relationship between the deceased and accused, including earlier insults which culminated in the final provocative actions or words. The "ordinary person" must be of the same age and sex, and share with the accused such other factors as would give the act or insult in question a special significance, and must have experienced the same series of acts or insults as those experienced by the accused. The defence may be available even if the insults might induce a desire for revenge so long as immediately before the last insult, the accused did not intend to kill: *R. v. Thibert*, [1996] 1 S.C.R. 37, 104 C.C.C. (3d) 1 (3:2).

The "ordinary person" standard is informed by contemporary norms of behaviour, including fundamental values such as the commitment to equality provided for in the Charter. The accused must have a justifiable sense of being wronged. The proper approach is one that takes into account some, but not all, of the individual characteristics of the accused. Personal circumstances may be relevant to determining whether the accused was in fact provoked (the subjective element), but they do not shift the ordinary person standard to suit the individual accused. There is an important distinction between contextualizing the objective standard, which is necessary and proper, and individualizing it, which would only serve to defeat its purpose: *R. v. Tran*, [2010] 3 S.C.R. 350, 261 C.C.C. (3d) 435. Thus, the trial judge did not err in directing the jury not to consider the accused's intellectual capacity and psychological makeup in applying the "ordinary person" test: *R. v. Berry* (2017), 345 C.C.C. (3d) 32 (Ont. C.A.), leave to appeal to S.C.C. refused 2017 CarswellOnt 13984.

A trier of fact is not required to consider the defences of provocation and intoxication together, or to take into account the accused's degree of intoxication when deciding whether an ordinary person would have lost self-control in response to the deceased's insult: *R. v. Sheehan* (2010), 264 C.C.C. (3d) 520 (N.B.C.A.).

The "ordinary person" test merely requires consideration of whether the ordinary person would have lost the power of self-control not whether the ordinary person would have done what the accused did: *R. v. Carpenter* (1993), 83 C.C.C. (3d) 193, 14 O.R. (3d) 641 (C.A.).

It was held in *R. v. Hill*, [1986] 1 S.C.R. 313, 25 C.C.C. (3d) 322 (6:3), that the ordinary or reasonable person under the objective test has a normal temperament and level of self-control and is not exceptionally excitable, pugnacious or in a state of drunkenness. Further, particular characteristics that are not peculiar or idiosyncratic can be ascribed to an ordinary person without subverting the logic of the objective test. However, the jury need not be instructed that the ordinary person is, for example, someone of the same age, sex or race as the accused, since the jury will naturally as a matter of good sense ascribe to the ordinary person any general characteristics relevant to the provocation in question. For example, if the provocation is a racial slur, the jury will think of an ordinary person with the racial background that forms the substance of the insult. Features such as sex, age or race do not detract from a person's characterization as ordinary.

The accused advanced provocation on the basis that his deceased wife's behaviour was contrary to the Sikh community values and brought shame to the accused. The trial judge was entitled to conclude that, although there was a reasonable doubt on the subjective element of provocation, the Crown had proven the objective requirement beyond a reasonable doubt. The trial judge could conclude that, even taking into account the accused's cultural background, an ordinary person would not have lost his power of self-control: *R. v. Nahar* (2004), 181 C.C.C. (3d) 449, 20 C.R. (6th) 30 (B.C.C.A.).

It was held that there is no air of reality to the proposition that an ordinary person in the accused's circumstances would be deprived of self-control when scolded about her level of education by her sister-in-law: *R. v. Mayuran*, [2012] 2 S.C.R. 162, 284 C.C.C. (3d) 1.

The application of the air of reality test assumes that the version of events in an accused's confession is true. However, an air of reality cannot spring from bare, unsupported assertions by the accused not reasonably borne out by the evidence. Here, there was no air of reality to the accused's assertion that he "snapped" after the victim, who had been extorting him for some time, threatened to continue the extortion. The subjective element of provocation was therefore lacking: *R. v. Pappas*, [2013] 3 S.C.R. 452, 302 C.C.C. (3d) 295.

Charge to jury / *Also see notes on "nature of objective test" above* – It had been held in a series of cases, *R. v. Daniels* (1983), 7 C.C.C. (3d) 542, 47 A.R. 149 (C.A.); *R. v. Conway* (1985), 17 C.C.C. (3d) 481 (Ont. C.A.); *R. v. Desveaux* (1986), 26 C.C.C. (3d) 88, 51 C.R. (3d) 173 (Ont. C.A.), that the jury must consider in relation to the objective test the same external pressures of insult by acts or words as were on the accused. Thus, the application of the objective test is not limited to the events which immediately triggered the attack by the accused, but also includes all of the events which put pressure on the accused and may have coloured and given meaning to the final triggering act or insult. These cases were decided prior to *R. v. Hill*, *supra*, but were not explicitly overruled. However, to the extent that these decisions like *R. v. Hill*, in the Ontario Court of Appeal (1982), 2 C.C.C. (3d) 394, 32 C.R. (3d) 88, reflect a mandatory requirement as to the component of the trial judge's charge, they should be read with care bearing in mind the admonishment from the Supreme Court majority in *R. v. Hill* that although a direction as to the particular relevant attributes of the "ordinary person" may be helpful in clarifying the application of the ordinary person standard it is neither wise nor necessary to make this a mandatory component of all jury charges on provocation and that whenever possible the court "should retain simplicity in charges to the jury and have confidence that the words of the *Criminal Code* will provide sufficient guidance to the jury". Again, it must be pointed out that the court was there only specifically considering the necessity of a mandatory direction concerning the age and sex of the "ordinary person".

The word "wrongful" only modifies "act" and not insult since an insult is always wrongful. However a reference to a "wrongful insult" while an error in English usage is not an error of law: *R. v. Murdock* (1978), 40 C.C.C. (2d) 97, [1978] 3 W.W.R. 313 (Man. C.A.).

It is misdirection to tell the jury that provocation operates to negate the intent for murder. Provocation may reduce murder to manslaughter even if the accused had the intention to kill: *R. v. Oickle* (1984), 11 C.C.C. (3d) 180, 61 N.S.R. (2d) 239 (S.C. App. Div.).

It was an error for the trial judge to refer to the accused's size and athletic ability and the difference in size between the accused and the victim when instructing the jury on the "ordinary person" component of the defence. Having been invited to draw these comparisons, the jury may have thought that the reasonableness or even justifiability of the accused's response to the provocative acts was a relevant consideration in the application of the ordinary person test. However, unlike some defences, provocation does not measure the conduct of the accused against standards of reasonableness or proportionality: *R. v. Hill* (2015), 330 C.C.C. (3d) 1 (Ont. C.A.).

Intense anger alone is insufficient to reduce murder to manslaughter. While anger can play a role in reducing murder to manslaughter in connection with the defence under this section, anger is not a stand-alone defence. Thus, the trial judge erred in directing the jury to the effect that they could find the accused guilty of manslaughter, on the basis of the anger felt by the accused, even if they concluded that the conditions set out in this section were not met: *R. v. Parent*, [2001] 1 S.C.R. 761, 154 C.C.C. (3d) 1.

Although subsec. (1) uses the word "may" the jury does not have a discretion to return a verdict of manslaughter where provocation is made out. Accordingly, it should be made clear to the jury that if they find there is provocation or if they have a reasonable doubt in that regard then the only verdict for what otherwise might be murder is manslaughter: *R. v. Leblanc* (1985), 22 C.C.C. (3d) 126 (Ont. C.A.).

Mistake of fact and transferred intent – If an accused, acting under such provocation as would reduce murder to manslaughter, shoots at one person with the intention of killing him, but accidentally kills a third person, the intention extenuated by provocation is transferred from the intended victim to the actual victim and the accused is guilty of manslaughter: *R. v. Droste (No. 2)* (1981), 63 C.C.C. (2d) 418, 34 O.R. (2d) 588 (C.A.), affd on other grounds [1984] 1 S.C.R. 208, 10 C.C.C. (3d) 404 (7:0).

Similarly, mistake of fact is relevant to the objective test, if any ordinary person would also have misinterpreted the facts which confronted the accused: *R. v. Hansford* (1987), 33 C.C.C. (3d) 74, 55 C.R. (3d) 347 (Alta. C.A.), leave to appeal to S.C.C. refused 79 A.R. 239.

Application to attempted murder – Provocation is not a defence to a charge of attempted murder so as to reduce the offence to one of attempted manslaughter. However, there may be cases where the conduct of the victim amounting to provocation produced in the accused a state of excitement, anger or disturbance as a result of which he might not contemplate the consequences of his acts and might not, in fact, intend to bring about those consequences: *R. v. Campbell* (1977), 38 C.C.C. (2d) 6, 17 O.R. (2d) 673 (C.A.).

Self-induced provocation [subsec. (3)] – The phrase "legal right" in subsec. (3) means a right which is sanctioned by law as distinct from something which a person may do without incurring legal liability. The defence of provocation is open to someone who is "insulted", and the words or act put forward as provocation need not be words or acts which are specifically prohibited by the law: *R. v. Thibert*, [1996] 1 S.C.R. 37, 104 C.C.C. (3d) 1 (3:2).

In considering whether a deceased was within his legal rights his action cannot be considered in isolation and in cases of "self-induced" provocation it is only where the actions by the deceased go to extreme lengths in the circumstances that such actions can form the basis of the defence of provocation. Where the only possible interpretation of the events was that the provocative act was self-induced in circumstances in which the deceased had the legal right to use as much force as necessary to attempt to effect his escape or protect his life, then subsec. (3)(*b*) applied: *R. v. Louison* (1975), 26 C.C.C. (2d) 266 (Sask. C.A.), affd [1979] 1 S.C.R. 100, 51 C.C.C. (2d) 479*n* (9:0).

Self-induced provocation is not a special category of the defence attracting special principles, but rather describes a particular application of the general principles that govern the defence of provocation. There is no absolute rule that a person who instigates a confrontation cannot rely on the defence of provocation. However, the fact that the victim's response to the accused's confrontational conduct fell within a range of reasonably predictable reactions may suggest that an ordinary person would not have lost self-control: *R. v. Cairney*, [2013] 3 S.C.R. 420, 302 C.C.C. (3d) 1.

Constitutional considerations – The fact that provocation operates as a defence only where the act or insult relied upon as provocation meets a threshold test that an ordinary person would have been deprived of self-control does not infringe the principles of fundamental justice as guaranteed by s. 7 of the Charter. This section does not impose liability where subjective fault does not exist but reduces the liability even when that fault does exist: *R. v. Cameron* (1992), 71 C.C.C. (3d) 272 (Ont. C.A.).

INFANTICIDE.

233. A female person commits infanticide when by a wilful act or omission she causes the death of her newly-born child, if at the time of the act or omission she is not fully recovered from the effects of giving birth to the child and by reason thereof or of the effect of lactation consequent on the birth of the child her mind is then disturbed. R.S., c. C-34, s. 216.

CROSS-REFERENCES

The term "newly-born child" is defined in s. 2. When a child becomes a human being is defined by s. 223(1). The punishment for infanticide is set out in s. 237. Related offences are as follows: s. 238, killing unborn child in act of birth; s. 242, neglect to obtain assistance in child-birth; s. 243, concealing body of child; s. 215, failing to provide necessaries; s. 218, abandoning child. Under s. 223(2) a person commits homicide when she causes injury to a child before or during its birth as a result of which the child dies after becoming a human being. As to other provisions respecting causation, see ss. 224 to 226.

As to included offences, see s. 662(4) which makes the offence under s. 243 an included offence. Reference should also be made to s. 663 which provides for conviction of infanticide although some of the elements of this offence are not made out.

For special provision respecting the plea of *autrefois*, see s. 610(2) and (4).

The accused's spouse is a competent and compellable witness at the instance of the Crown by virtue of s. 4(4).

SYNOPSIS

Section 233 defines what constitutes *infanticide*. It is one of four offences in Part VIII of the *Criminal Code* which deal with infants as victims of offences (also see ss. 238, 242 and 243).

The principal in this offence is the *mother* of a newly-born child. The *actus reus* occurs when the new mother, by *wilful act or omission*, causes the death of the newly-born child. The offence must occur at a time when the woman has *not fully recovered* from the effects of *giving birth and*, as a result of either those effects or lactation following the birth, her *mind* is *disturbed*. The child must have been born alive for this section to apply. Unlike murder and manslaughter (the other forms of culpable homicide), infanticide does not have either a minimum or maximum sentence of life imprisonment.

ANNOTATIONS

In *R. v. Borowiec*, [2016] 1 S.C.R. 80, 333 C.C.C. (3d) 435, the Supreme Court held that infanticide applies where (1) a mother, by a wilful act or omission, kills her newborn child and, (2) at the time of the act or omission, the mother's mind is "disturbed" either because she is not fully recovered from the effects of giving birth or by reason of the effect of lactation. The word "disturbed" is not a legal or medical term of art but should be applied in its grammatical and ordinary sense. The disturbance need not constitute a defined mental or psychological condition or a mental illness, and there is no requirement to prove that the act or omission was caused by the disturbance. However, the disturbance must be present at the time of the act or omission that caused the child's death, and it must occur at a time when the accused is not fully recovered from the effects of giving birth or of lactation. The disturbance is part of the *actus reus* of infanticide; the *mens rea* is the same as for manslaughter.

There is no reverse onus on the accused to prove the applicability of the defence of infanticide on the balance of probabilities: *R. v. Effert* (2009), 244 C.C.C. (3d) 510 (Alta. Q.B.).

Infanticide is both a discrete indictable offence and a partial defence to murder. To prove infanticide, the Crown must establish the *mens rea* associated with the unlawful act that caused the child's death and objective foreseeability of the risk of bodily harm to the child from that assault. It is the unique *actus reus* of infanticide that distinguishes it from murder and manslaughter. The presence of the *mens rea* for murder, while not negating the partial defence of infanticide, is not a condition precedent to the existence of that partial defence: *R. v. B. (L.)* (2011), 270 C.C.C. (3d) 208 (Ont. C.A.), leave to appeal to S.C.C. refused (2011), 291 O.A.C. 398*n*.

If there is an air of reality to the defence of infanticide and the Crown proves that the accused committed a culpable homicide, the jury should be told to consider infanticide first. If the Crown fails to negate at least one of the elements of infanticide beyond a reasonable doubt, the jury should be instructed to return a verdict of not guilty of murder, but guilty of infanticide: *R. v. B. (L.)*, *supra*.

MANSLAUGHTER.

234. Culpable homicide that is not murder or infanticide is manslaughter. R.S., c. C-34, s. 217.

CROSS-REFERENCES

Murder is defined in ss. 229 and 230. Infanticide is defined in s. 233. As to included offences, see s. 662. As to special provisions respecting the plea of *autrefois*, see s. 610(2) to (4). The punishment for manslaughter is set out in s. 236. As to limits on intoxification defence, see s. 33.1.

SYNOPSIS

This section provides that all culpable homicide which is not murder (s. 229 or 230) or infanticide (s. 233) is manslaughter. Thus, manslaughter is defined both by specific provisions which reduce murder to manslaughter (see s. 232) and by declaring the residual category of acts amounting to culpable homicide to be manslaughter. Drunkenness, which is defined by common law principles and is not dealt with in the *Criminal Code*, also reduces murder to manslaughter. The mental element varies depending on what principle operates to reduce a culpable homicide to manslaughter. Thus, the intention ranges from the intention to do an unlawful act (s. 222(5)(*a*)) to the intention to kill which is mitigated by the presence of provocation (s. 232).

ANNOTATIONS

Intent – Once the jury has found that the homicide was culpable it must decide the accused's intent, and if at that stage there is a reasonable doubt that he intended to commit murder they should then consider the offence of manslaughter: *R. v. Kuzmack*, [1955] S.C.R. 292, 111 C.C.C. 1 (8:1).

Unlike the crime of murder which requires proof of a special intent to commit that offence, manslaughter only requires a general intent: *R. v. Mack* (1975), 22 C.C.C. (2d) 257, 29 C.R.N.S. 270 (Alta. S.C. App. Div.) (5:0).

Where there is evidence of mental illness or disorder at the time of the murder it would be prudent for the judge to instruct the jury that it would be open for them to find that although the accused was not at the time insane, he did not have the mental capacity to form the specific intent to commit murder, but had the general intent to warrant a conviction for manslaughter: *R. v. Baltzer* (1974), 27 C.C.C. (2d) 118 (N.S.S.C. App. Div.); *R. v. Hilton* (1977), 34 C.C.C. (2d) 206 (Ont. C.A.); *R. v. Browning* (1976) 34 C.C.C. (2d) 200 (Ont. C.A.); *R. v. Lechasseur* (1977), 38 C.C.C. (2d) 319 (Que. C.A.).

Unlawful act manslaughter – The *mens rea* of unlawful act manslaughter under subsec. (5)(*a*) is, in addition to the *mens rea* of the underlying offence, objective foreseeability of the risk of bodily harm which is neither trivial nor transitory. In applying this objective test personal characteristics not directly relevant to an element of the offence such as experience, education and psychological defences serve as a defence only when there is an incapacity to appreciate the risk involved in the conduct. Likewise, the standard is not raised because the particular accused may have special experience or training. On the other hand, the particular activity may impose a higher *de facto* standard than others: *R. v. Creighton*, [1993] 3 S.C.R. 3, 83 C.C.C. (3d) 346.

The unlawful act must also be objectively dangerous, that is, likely to injure another person: *R. v. DeSousa*, [1992] 2 S.C.R. 944, 76 C.C.C. (3d) 124; *R. v. Creighton, supra*.

Party to manslaughter – An accused who lacks the necessary *mens rea* for murder may be convicted of manslaughter by aiding or abetting another in the offence of murder pursuant to s. 21(1), where a reasonable person in all the circumstances would have appreciated that bodily harm was the foreseeable consequence of the dangerous act which was being undertaken. Further, if the accused party did not foresee the probability of murder by the principal offender but a reasonable person in all the circumstances would have foreseen at least a risk of harm to another as a result of carrying out the common intention, the party could be found guilty of manslaughter pursuant to s. 21(2). Liability for manslaughter under s. 21(2) does not depend upon proof that a reasonable person would have foreseen the risk of death: *R. v. Jackson*, [1993] 4 S.C.R. 573, 86 C.C.C. (3d) 385.

Manslaughter by criminal negligence / *Also see notes under ss. 219 and 220* – On a trial for murder the verdicts left to the jury were murder, manslaughter due to intoxication and not guilty due to accident. On the accused's appeal from conviction for murder it was argued that the trial judge should have left with the jury the verdict of manslaughter as a result of criminal negligence. The court held however that such a theory was based on speculation, that there was no evidence to support criminal negligence as distinct from accident and, accordingly, the defence was not entitled to have this theory placed before the jury: *R. v. Charbonneau*, [1977] 2 S.C.R. 805, 33 C.C.C. (2d) 469 (8:1).

Constitutional considerations – Manslaughter is not one of those offences which because of its gravity or the stigma attached to it requires proof of a minimum *mens rea* of foreseeability of death to comply with s. 7 of the Charter. Thus, the offence of unlawful act manslaughter as interpreted by the courts and requiring only objective foreseeability of the risk of bodily harm does not violate s. 7. Thus, the so-called "thin skull" rule which renders offenders liable for the unforeseen consequences of their dangerous acts as well does not violate s. 7: *R. v. Creighton, supra*.

PUNISHMENT FOR MURDER / Minimum punishment.

235. (1) Every one who commits first degree murder or second degree murder is guilty of an indictable offence and shall be sentenced to imprisonment for life.

(2) For the purposes of Part XXIII, the sentence of imprisonment for life prescribed by this section is a minimum punishment. R.S., c. C-34, s. 218; 1973-74, c. 38, s. 3; 1974-75-76, c. 105, s. 5.

CROSS-REFERENCES

Murder is defined in ss. 229 and 230 and classified as first or second degree murder by s. 231. The determination of parole ineligibility is made in accordance with ss. 745 to 746.1. That scheme as applied to adults may, however, be briefly summarized as follows. A person convicted of first degree murder is liable to imprisonment for life without eligibility for parole for 25 years [s. 745], but may apply for judicial review of the period of ineligibility after 15 years [s. 745.6]. A person convicted of second degree murder is liable to imprisonment for life without eligibility for parole for a period between 10 and 25 years [s. 745]. This period is set by the trial judge under s. 745.4 after taking the recommendation, if any, from the jury [where the case has been tried by a jury] pursuant to s. 745.2. Note, however, that where an accused is convicted of second degree murder, the period of parole ineligibility must be set at 25 years where the accused was previously convicted of murder however described under the *Criminal Code* [s. 745] [Note s. 664 which prohibits reference in the indictment to the previous conviction. However, s. 665 which requires service of notice of intention to seek greater punishment does not apply.] Again, the accused may apply for judicial review of the period of ineligibility after 15 years where the period set under s. 745.4 exceeds 15 years [s. 745.6]. A person convicted of murder will also be liable to the mandatory prohibition order respecting firearms, ammunition and explosives by virtue of s. 109. Pursuant to s. 745.5, where the accused was under 18 years of age at the time of the offence but has been transferred to the ordinary courts then the period of parole ineligibility may be between five and ten years whether the accused is convicted of first or second degree murder.

Section 17 limits the availability of the statutory defence of compulsion by threats. As to other notes respecting defences to murder, see ss. 229 and 230. As to included offences, see s. 662.

This offence may be the basis for an application for an authorization to intercept private communications by reason of s. 183 or a warrant to conduct video surveillance by reason of s. 487.01(5), and falls within the definition of "enterprise crime offence" in s. 462.3 for the purposes of Part XII.2.

Section 7(3) enacts special jurisdictional rules for commission of this offence outside Canada when the offence is in relation to an internationally protected person or property referred to in s. 431 [official premises, etc.]. A threat to commit an offence under this section against an internationally protected person (defined in s. 2) is an offence under s. 424.

Special provision respecting the plea of *autrefois* see s. 610(2) to (4).

Pursuant to s. 582, no person may be convicted of first degree murder unless he is specifically charged with that offence in the indictment. Under s. 589, no count that charges an offence other than murder shall be joined in an indictment to a count that charges murder.

Trial of murder is by the superior court of criminal jurisdiction (defined in s. 2) by virtue of ss. 468 and 469. By virtue of s. 522, only a judge of the superior court of criminal jurisdiction may release an accused charged with this offence.

The accused's spouse is a competent and compellable witness at the instance of the Crown by virtue of s. 4(4) where the victim is under the age of 14 years. Age is determined by reference to s. 30 of the *Interpretation Act*, R.S.C. 1985, c. I-21.

MANSLAUGHTER.

236. Every person who commits manslaughter is guilty of an indictable offence and liable

(*a*) where a firearm is used in the commission of the offence, to imprisonment for life and to a minimum punishment of imprisonment for a term of four years; and

(*b*) in any other case, to imprisonment for life. R.S., c. C-34, s. 219; 1995, c. 39, s. 142.

CROSS-REFERENCES

Manslaughter is defined by ss. 232, 234 and 263(3).

Section 7(3) enacts special jurisdictional rules for commission of this offence outside Canada when the offence is in relation to an internationally protected person or property referred to in s. 432 [official premises, etc.]. Firearm is defined in s. 2.

As to included offences see s. 662(5). For special provision respecting the plea of *autrefois*, see s. 610(2) to (4).

The accused's spouse is a competent and compellable witness at the instance of the Crown by virtue of s. 4(4) where the victim is under the age of 14 years. Age is determined by reference to s. 30 of the *Interpretation Act*, R.S.C. 1985, c. I-21.

The accused has an election as to mode of trial pursuant to s. 536(2). Release pending trial is determined by s. 515. An accused convicted of this offence may, pursuant to s. 259, be ordered prohibited from operating a motor vehicle, vessel, aircraft or railway equipment for during any period that the court considers proper, where the offence under this section was committed by means of a motor vehicle, vessel, aircraft or railway equipment. The procedure respecting the making of that order of prohibition is found in s. 260. In some circumstances, the accused will also be liable to the mandatory prohibition order respecting weapons, ammunition and explosives by virtue of s. 109. Where the offence was committed by means of a motor vehicle, vessel, aircraft or railway equipment, evidence that the accused's blood alcohol level exceeded .16 at the time of the offence is deemed an aggravating factor, for purposes of sentencing, under s. 255.1.

SYNOPSIS

Section 236 provides that the *maximum sentence* upon conviction for *manslaughter* is *life imprisonment*. This is to be contrasted to the punishment for murder for which the minimum sentence is life, and for which there are restrictions in the *Criminal Code* regarding eligibility for parole. There is no minimum sentence for manslaughter except where a firearm is used in the commission of the offence. In such a case, the minimum punishment is four years' imprisonment.

ANNOTATIONS

This provision does not violate s. 12 of the Charter: *R. v. Ferguson*, [2008] 1 S.C.R. 96, 228 C.C.C. (3d) 385.

PUNISHMENT FOR INFANTICIDE.

237. Every female person who commits infanticide is guilty of an indictable offence and liable to imprisonment for a term not exceeding five years. R.S., c. C-34, s. 220.

CROSS-REFERENCES

Infanticide is defined in ss. 233 and 663.

The accused has an election as to mode of trial pursuant to s. 536(2). Release pending trial is determined by s. 515. In some circumstances, the accused will also be liable to the discretionary prohibition order respecting firearms, ammunition and explosives by virtue of s. 110.

The accused's spouse is a competent and compellable witness at the instance of the Crown by virtue of s. 4(4). For other notes concerning the offence of infanticide, see s. 233.

SYNOPSIS

Section 237 sets out the *punishment for infanticide* (see s. 233). There is *no minimum* sentence for this offence. The maximum sentence upon conviction is five years.

ANNOTATIONS

Where the expert evidence indicated that the accused was seriously mentally ill at the time of the offence (even raising doubts as to her liability for this offence) the court on appeal against a prison sentence allowed the appeal and substituted a conditional discharge. The principle of deterrence simply had no application in the circumstances, the only real consideration being rehabilitation: *R. v. Szola* (1977), 33 C.C.C. (2d) 572 (Ont. C.A.).

KILLING UNBORN CHILD IN ACT OF BIRTH / Saving.

238. (1) Every one who causes the death, in the act of birth, of any child that has not become a human being, in such a manner that, if the child were a human being, he would be guilty of murder, is guilty of an indictable offence and liable to imprisonment for life.

(2) This section does not apply to a person who, by means that, in good faith, he considers necessary to preserve the life of the mother of a child, causes the death of that child. R.S., c. C-34, s. 221.

CROSS-REFERENCES

As to when a child becomes a human being, see s. 223(1). The accused has an election as to mode of trial pursuant to s. 536(2). Release pending trial is determined by s. 515. Murder is defined in ss. 229 and 230. The offence of infanticide is defined in s. 233. Related offences are as follows: s. 243, neglect to obtain assistance in child-birth; s. 243, concealing body of child; s. 215, failing to provide necessaries; s. 218, abandoning child.

SYNOPSIS

This section creates the indictable offence of *killing an unborn child in the act of birth*. This offence applies in circumstances where the death was caused in such a way that, had the child become a human being (see s. 223), the crime would have been murder. The maximum sentence upon conviction is imprisonment for life.

Section 238(2) provides an exception to liability for such acts dealing with cases in which the act, resulting in the death of the unborn child, was done to save the life of the mother. The person doing the act must consider *in good faith* that such act was necessary for that purpose.

ATTEMPT TO COMMIT MURDER / Subsequent offences / Sequence of convictions only.

239. (1) Every person who attempts by any means to commit murder is guilty of an indictable offence and liable

- **(*a*) if a restricted firearm or prohibited firearm is used in the commission of the offence or if any firearm is used in the commission of the offence and the offence is committed for the benefit of, at the direction of, or in association with, a criminal organization, to imprisonment for life and to a minimum punishment of imprisonment for a term of**
  - **(i) in the case of a first offence, five years, and**
  - **(ii) in the case of a second or subsequent offence, seven years;**
- **(*a*.1) in any other case where a firearm is used in the commission of the offence, to imprisonment for life and to a minimum punishment of imprisonment for a term of four years; and**
- **(*b*) in any other case, to imprisonment for life.**

(2) In determining, for the purpose of paragraph (1)(*a*), whether a convicted person has committed a second or subsequent offence, if the person was earlier convicted of any of the following offences, that offence is to be considered as an earlier offence:

- **(*a*) an offence under this section;**
- **(*b*) an offence under subsection 85(1) or (2) or section 244 or 244.2; or**
- **(*c*) an offence under section 220, 236, 272 or 273, subsection 279(1) or section 279.1, 344 or 346 if a firearm was used in the commission of the offence.**

However, an earlier offence shall not be taken into account if 10 years have elapsed between the day on which the person was convicted of the earlier offence and the day on which the person was convicted of the offence for which sentence is being imposed, not taking into account any time in custody.

(3) For the purposes of subsection (2), the only question to be considered is the sequence of convictions and no consideration shall be given to the sequence of commission of offences or whether any offence occurred before or after any conviction. R.S., c. C-34, s. 222; 1995, c. 39, s. 143; 2008, c. 6, s. 16; 2009, c. 22, s. 6.

CROSS-REFERENCES

Attempt is defined in s. 24. "Firearm" is defined in s. 2. "Criminal organization" is defined in ss. 2 and 467.1(1). "Restricted firearm" and "prohibited firearm" are defined in s. 84.

Section 17 limits the availability of the statutory defence of compulsion by threats. Under s. 662(2), an accused may be convicted of "attempted second degree murder" on an indictment charging first degree murder. Presumably, where the indictment charges second degree murder then the accused can be convicted of attempted second degree murder by virtue of s. 662(1)(*b*). Under s. 661, where an attempt is charged but the evidence proves commission of the full offence, the accused may be convicted of the attempt.

The accused's spouse is a competent and compellable witness at the instance of the Crown by virtue of s. 4(4) where the victim is under the age of 14 years. Age is determined by reference to s. 30 of the *Interpretation Act*, R.S.C. 1985, c. I-21.

The accused has an election as to mode of trial pursuant to s. 536(2). Release pending trial is determined by s. 515. A person convicted of attempted murder will be liable to the mandatory prohibition order respecting weapons, ammunition and explosives by virtue of s. 109. While s. 239 is not listed in s. 183 as an "offence" for the purposes of obtaining an authorization to intercept private communications, an authorization may be obtained in respect of an attempt to commit any of the offences listed in s. 183 and "235 (murder)" is listed in s. 183. Similarly, while s. 239 is not listed in s. 462.3 as an "enterprise crime offence" for the purposes of Part XII.1, "section 235 (punishment for murder)" is listed in s. 462.3 and para. (*c*) of the definition of enterprise crime offence provides that an attempt to commit any of the listed offences is as well an enterprise crime offence. A person convicted of attempted murder may be subject to a dangerous offender application under Part XXIV.

SYNOPSIS

This section makes it an indictable offence to attempt to commit murder. This part of the section is redundant as s. 24(1) would create such an offence. The key aspect of this section provides the maximum and minimum punishments. This is a departure from the general rule expressed in s. 463(*a*) that a person is liable to a sentence of 14 years upon conviction for attempting to commit an offence which would be punishable by life imprisonment upon completion of the full offence. The mental element for this offence is the intention to kill.

The sentencing regime operates as follows. In all cases, the maximum punishment is life imprisonment. Under subsec. (1)(*a*), where a restricted firearm or prohibited firearm is used or if any firearm is used where the offence is committed for the benefit of, at the direction of, or in association with a criminal organization, the minimum punishment for a first offence is five years, and seven years for a second or subsequent offence. The rules for determining second and subsequent offences are set out in subsecs. (2) and (3). Thus, certain earlier convictions for related offences, such as certain firearm offences or other offences involving use of a firearm, are deemed to be earlier offences. However, an earlier offence is not to be taken into account if 10 years have elapsed (not counting time spent in custody). Subsection (3) reverses the common law rule and provides that, in determining whether an offence is an earlier offence, the only question is whether the conviction was registered earlier; the sequence of commission of the offences is not relevant. Under subsec. (1)(*a*.1), in any other case in which a firearm is used, the minimum punishment is four years. Where no firearm is used there is no minimum, pursuant to subsec. (1)(*b*).

ANNOTATIONS

Intent – A conviction for attempted murder requires proof of the specific intent to kill. No lesser *mens rea* will suffice, and in particular a conviction under this section may not be based on the lesser intents described in s. 229(*a*)(ii) or s. 230: *R. v. Ancio*, [1984] 1 S.C.R. 225, 10 C.C.C. (3d) 385 (7:1).

The common law doctrine of transferred intent does not apply to attempted murder although it clearly applies to murder. Inchoate crimes such as attempted murder do not require a result of harm as part of the *actus reus*. The *actus reus* is complete upon the first act beyond preparation. Section 229(*b*) makes the accused liable for murder if innocent bystanders died from their injuries, but it does not speak to the application of transferred intent principles to attempted murder. Where both the *mens rea* and *actus reus* of an attempted are established, an accused is liable for an inchoate crime in relation to the intended victim, and might also be subject to punishment in connection with an unintended victim in accordance with his moral culpability and the injury caused: *R. v. Gordon* (2009), 241 C.C.C. (3d) 388 (Ont. C.A.), leave to appeal to S.C.C. refused 243 C.C.C. (3d) vi.

Neither excessive force in self-defence nor provocation are defences to this charge so as to reduce the offence to one of attempted manslaughter. However, the conduct of the victim may be a relevant piece of evidence on the question of whether the accused had the requisite intent to kill if the provocation by the victim produced in the accused a state of anger, excitement or disturbance to the extent that he did not contemplate the consequences of his act and did not intend those consequences: *R. v. Campbell* (1977), 38 C.C.C. (2d) 6, 17 O.R. (2d) 673 (C.A.).

To make out the offence under this section the Crown must prove that the accused, having the specific intent to cause the death of a human being, did anything for the purpose of carrying out that intent, by any means. The Crown need not prove that the accused had the specific intent to murder each of the victims, specified in the indictment, by name in a case where the accused intending to kill an occupant of a tavern returned to the tavern and opened fire on the area in which a number of patrons were standing: *R. v. Marshall* (1986), 25 C.C.C. (3d) 151 (N.S.C.A.).

Liability of party – A party cannot be convicted of this offence based on the objective foreseeability under s. 21(2). Accordingly, the words "ought to have known" in s. 21(2) are inoperative where liability is sought to be imposed on a party for the offence in this section: *R. v. Logan*, [1990] 2 S.C.R. 731, 58 C.C.C. (3d) 391.

Included offences – An indictment charging attempted murder *simpliciter* only includes the offence of attempting to unlawfully cause bodily harm: *R. v. Simpson (No. 2)* (1981), 58 C.C.C. (2d) 122, 20 C.R. (3d) 36 (Ont. C.A.); *R. v. Colburne* (1991), 66 C.C.C. (3d) 235 (Que. C.A.).

ACCESSORY AFTER FACT TO MURDER.

240. Every one who is an accessory after the fact to murder is guilty of an indictable offence and liable to imprisonment for life. R.S., c. C-34, s. 223.

CROSS-REFERENCES

The definition of accessory after the fact is in s. 23. Sections 23.1 and 592 deal with the trial of and charging of the accessory although the principal has not or cannot be convicted. Murder is defined in ss. 229 and 230.

Trial of accessory after the fact to murder is by the superior court of criminal jurisdiction (defined in s. 2) by virtue of ss. 468 and 469. By virtue of s. 522, only a judge of the superior court of criminal jurisdiction may release an accused charged with this offence. A person convicted of this offence may be liable to the mandatory prohibition order respecting firearms, ammunition and explosives by virtue of s. 109.

While s. 240 is not listed in s. 183 as an "offence" for the purposes of obtaining an authorization to intercept private communications, an authorization may be obtained for being an accessory after the fact in relation to any of the offences listed in s. 183 and "235 (murder)" is listed in s. 183. Similarly, while s. 240 is not listed in s. 462.3 as an "enterprise crime offence" for the purposes of Part XII.1, "section 235 (punishment for murder)" is listed in s. 462.3 and s. 462.3(*c*) provides that being an accessory after the fact in relation to any of the offences listed in the section is as well an enterprise crime offence.

The accused's spouse is a competent and compellable witness at the instance of the Crown by virtue of s. 4(4) where the victim is under the age of 14 years. Age is determined by reference to s. 30 of the *Interpretation Act*, R.S.C. 1985, c. I-21.

SYNOPSIS

This section provides that it is an indictable offence to be an *accessory after the fact* to the commission of a *murder*. This aspect of the section is redundant in light of s. 23 of the *Criminal Code*. The important aspect of the section is one which places the *maximum sentence*, upon conviction, at *life imprisonment*. This is an exception to the general rule as stated in s. 463(*a*) that the punishment for being an accessory after the fact is punishable by 14 years, if the sentence, to which the principal accused is subject, is life imprisonment. For a description of what constitutes being an accessory after the fact, see s. 23.

ANNOTATIONS

The offence of being an accessory after the fact to manslaughter under s. 463(*a*) is a lesser and included offence to that of being an accessory after the fact to murder: *R. v. Webber* (1995), 102 C.C.C. (3d) 248, 106 W.A.C. 161 (B.C.C.A.).

Suicide

COUNSELLING OR AIDING SUICIDE / Exemption for medical assistance in dying / Exemption for person aiding practitioner / Exemption for pharmacist / Exemption for person aiding patient / Clarification / Reasonable but mistaken belief / Definitions.

241 (1) Everyone is guilty of an indictable offence and liable to imprisonment for a term of not more than 14 years who, whether suicide ensues or not,

(*a*) counsels a person to die by suicide or abets a person in dying by suicide; or

(*b*) aids a person to die by suicide.

(2) No medical practitioner or nurse practitioner commits an offence under paragraph (1)(*b*) if they provide a person with medical assistance in dying in accordance with section 241.2.

(3) No person is a party to an offence under paragraph (1)(*b*) if they do anything for the purpose of aiding a medical practitioner or nurse practitioner to provide a person with medical assistance in dying in accordance with section 241.2.

(4) No pharmacist who dispenses a substance to a person other than a medical practitioner or nurse practitioner commits an offence under paragraph (1)(*b*) if the pharmacist dispenses the substance further to a prescription that is written by such a practitioner in providing medical assistance in dying in accordance with section 241.2.

(5) No person commits an offence under paragraph (1)(*b*) if they do anything, at another person's explicit request, for the purpose of aiding that other person to self-administer a substance that has been prescribed for that other person as part of the provision of medical assistance in dying in accordance with section 241.2.

(5.1) For greater certainty, no social worker, psychologist, psychiatrist, therapist, medical practitioner, nurse practitioner or other health care professional commits an offence if they provide information to a person on the lawful provision of medical assistance in dying.

(6) For greater certainty, the exemption set out in any of subsections (2) to (5) applies even if the person invoking the exemption has a reasonable but mistaken belief about any fact that is an element of the exemption.

(7) In this section, *medical assistance in dying*, *medical practitioner*, *nurse practitioner* and *pharmacist* have the same meanings as in section 241.1. R.S., c. C-34, s. 224; R.S.C. 1985, c. 27 (1st Supp.), s. 7(3); 2016, c. 3, s. 3.

CROSS-REFERENCES

Culpable homicide is defined in s. 222. Section 227 provides an exemption to liability for culpable homicide applicable to persons participating in a medically assisted death in compliance with the *Criminal Code* regime. The medically assisted dying regime is set out in ss. 241.1 through 241.4.

SYNOPSIS

This section makes it an indictable offence to counsel the act of suicide or to assist in such an act. At one time, attempting suicide was an offence, but that section has been repealed so that the person who attempts to commit suicide does not commit an offence: only the person who counsels or assists is guilty of a crime. The offence is made out regardless of whether a suicide ensues. A person convicted of this offence is liable to imprisonment for a period of not more than 14 years. Enacted in response to *Carter v. Canada (Attorney General)*, [2015] 1 S.C.R. 331, 320 C.C.C. (3d) 1, subsecs. (2) through (7) now create exemptions for persons who participate in a medically assisted death in compliance with the *Criminal Code* regime, or persons with a reasonable but mistaken belief that they are in compliance with that regime.

ANNOTATIONS

In *Carter v. Canada (Attorney General)*, [2015] 1 S.C.R. 331, 320 C.C.C. (3d) 1, the court revisited its earlier 5:4 holding in *Rodriguez v. British Columbia (Attorney General)*, [1993] 3 S.C.R. 519, 85 C.C.C. (3d) 15, and struck down the prohibition on physician-assisted suicide. The court held that, insofar as the law prohibits physician-assisted dying for competent adults who seek such assistance as a result of a grievous and irremediable medical condition that causes enduring and intolerable suffering, it is unconstitutionally overbroad in violation of s. 7. The exemptions in this provision and the medically assisted dying regime in ss. 241.1 through 241.4 were enacted in response to the court's decision.

In the case of a genuine suicide pact, the surviving party should have a defence to murder. This defence will only be available when the parties are in such a mental state that they have formed a common and irrevocable intent to commit suicide together simultaneously and by the same act where the risk of death is identical and equal for both. The survivor may, however, be liable to be convicted of the offence under this section: *R. v. Gagnon* (1993), 84 C.C.C. (3d) 143 (Que. C.A.).

Medical Assistance in Dying 2016, c. 3, s. 3.

DEFINITIONS.

241.1 The following definitions apply in this section and in sections 241.2 to 241.4.

***medical assistance in dying* means**

(*a*) the administering by a medical practitioner or nurse practitioner of a substance to a person, at their request, that causes their death; or

(*b*) the prescribing or providing by a medical practitioner or nurse practitioner of a substance to a person, at their request, so that they may self-administer the substance and in doing so cause their own death.

medical practitioner **means a person who is entitled to practise medicine under the laws of a province.**

nurse practitioner **means a registered nurse who, under the laws of a province, is entitled to practise as a nurse practitioner — or under an equivalent designation — and to autonomously make diagnoses, order and interpret diagnostic tests, prescribe substances and treat patients.**

pharmacist **means a person who is entitled to practice pharmacy under the laws of a province. 2016, c. 3, s. 3.**

CROSS-REFERENCES

Culpable homicide is defined in s. 222. Section 227 provides an exemption to liability for culpable homicide applicable to persons participating in a medically assisted death in compliance with the *Criminal Code* regime. Section 241 likewise provides exemptions to the offence of counseling or assisting a suicide.

SYNOPSIS

Sections 241.1 to 241.4, enacted in response to the Supreme Court's decision in *Carter v. Canada (Attorney General)*, [2015] 1 S.C.R. 331, 320 C.C.C. (3d) 1, are intended to create a comprehensive regime for legally permissible, medically assisted dying.

ELIGIBILITY FOR MEDICAL ASSISTANCE IN DYING / Grievous and irremediable medical condition / Safeguards / Unable to sign / Independent witness / Independence — medical practitioners and nurse practitioners / Reasonable knowledge, care and skill / Informing pharmacist / Clarification.

241.2 (1) A person may receive medical assistance in dying only if they meet all of the following criteria:

(*a*) they are eligible — or, but for any applicable minimum period of residence or waiting period, would be eligible — for health services funded by a government in Canada;

(*b*) they are at least 18 years of age and capable of making decisions with respect to their health;

(*c*) they have a grievous and irremediable medical condition;

(*d*) they have made a voluntary request for medical assistance in dying that, in particular, was not made as a result of external pressure; and

(*e*) they give informed consent to receive medical assistance in dying after having been informed of the means that are available to relieve their suffering, including palliative care.

(2) A person has a grievous and irremediable medical condition only if they meet all of the following criteria:

(*a*) they have a serious and incurable illness, disease or disability;

(*b*) they are in an advanced state of irreversible decline in capability;

(*c*) that illness, disease or disability or that state of decline causes them enduring physical or psychological suffering that is intolerable to them and that cannot be relieved under conditions that they consider acceptable; and

(*d*) their natural death has become reasonably foreseeable, taking into account all of their medical circumstances, without a prognosis necessarily having been made as to the specific length of time that they have remaining.

(3) Before a medical practitioner or nurse practitioner provides a person with medical assistance in dying, the medical practitioner or nurse practitioner must

(*a*) be of the opinion that the person meets all of the criteria set out in subsection (1);

(*b*) ensure that the person's request for medical assistance in dying was

(i) made in writing and signed and dated by the person or by another person under subsection (4), and

(ii) signed and dated after the person was informed by a medical practitioner or nurse practitioner that the person has a grievous and irremediable medical condition;

(*c*) be satisfied that the request was signed and dated by the person — or by another person under subsection (4) — before two independent witnesses who then also signed and dated the request;

(*d*) ensure that the person has been informed that they may, at any time and in any manner, withdraw their request;

(*e*) ensure that another medical practitioner or nurse practitioner has provided a written opinion confirming that the person meets all of the criteria set out in subsection (1);

(*f*) be satisfied that they and the other medical practitioner or nurse practitioner referred to in paragraph (*e*) are independent;

(*g*) ensure that there are at least 10 clear days between the day on which the request was signed by or on behalf of the person and the day on which the medical assistance in dying is provided or — if they and the other medical practitioner or nurse practitioner referred to in paragraph (*e*) are both of the opinion that the person's death, or the loss of their capacity to provide informed consent, is imminent — any shorter period that the first medical practitioner or nurse practitioner considers appropriate in the circumstances;

(*h*) immediately before providing the medical assistance in dying, give the person an opportunity to withdraw their request and ensure that the person gives express consent to receive medical assistance in dying; and

(*i*) if the person has difficulty communicating, take all necessary measures to provide a reliable means by which the person may understand the information that is provided to them and communicate their decision.

(4) If the person requesting medical assistance in dying is unable to sign and date the request, another person — who is at least 18 years of age, who understands the nature of the request for medical assistance in dying and who does not know or believe that they are a beneficiary under the will of the person making the request, or a recipient, in any other way, of a financial or other material benefit resulting from that person's death — may do so in the person's presence, on the person's behalf and under the person's express direction.

(5) Any person who is at least 18 years of age and who understands the nature of the request for medical assistance in dying may act as an independent witness, except if they

(*a*) know or believe that they are a beneficiary under the will of the person making the request, or a recipient, in any other way, of a financial or other material benefit resulting from that person's death;

(*b*) are an owner or operator of any health care facility at which the person making the request is being treated or any facility in which that person resides;

(*c*) are directly involved in providing health care services to the person making the request; or

(*d*) directly provide personal care to the person making the request.

(6) The medical practitioner or nurse practitioner providing medical assistance in dying and the medical practitioner or nurse practitioner who provides the opinion referred to in paragraph (3)(*e*) are independent if they

(*a*) are not a mentor to the other practitioner or responsible for supervising their work;

(*b*) do not know or believe that they are a beneficiary under the will of the person making the request, or a recipient, in any other way, of a financial or other material benefit resulting from that person's death, other than standard compensation for their services relating to the request; or

(*c*) do not know or believe that they are connected to the other practitioner or to the person making the request in any other way that would affect their objectivity.

(7) Medical assistance in dying must be provided with reasonable knowledge, care and skill and in accordance with any applicable provincial laws, rules or standards.

(8) The medical practitioner or nurse practitioner who, in providing medical assistance in dying, prescribes or obtains a substance for that purpose must, before any pharmacist dispenses the substance, inform the pharmacist that the substance is intended for that purpose.

(9) For greater certainty, nothing in this section compels an individual to provide or assist in providing medical assistance in dying. 2016, c. 3, s. 3.

FAILURE TO COMPLY WITH SAFEGUARDS / Forgery / Destruction of documents / Punishment / Definition of *document*.

241.3 A medical practitioner or nurse practitioner who, in providing medical assistance in dying, knowingly fails to comply with all of the requirements set out in paragraphs 241.2(3)(*b*) to (*i*) and subsection 241.2(8) is guilty of an offence and is liable

(*a*) on conviction on indictment, to a term of imprisonment of not more than five years; or

(*b*) on summary conviction, to a term of imprisonment of not more than 18 months. 2016, c. 3, s. 3.

FILING INFORMATION — MEDICAL PRACTITIONER OR NURSE PRACTITIONER / Filing information — pharmacist / Regulations / Guidelines — information on death certificates / Offence and punishment / Offence and punishment.

241.31 (1) Unless they are exempted under regulations made under subsection (3), a medical practitioner or nurse practitioner who receives a written request for medical assistance in dying must, in accordance with those regulations, provide the information required by those regulations to the recipient designated in those regulations.

(2) Unless they are exempted under regulations made under subsection (3), a pharmacist who dispenses a substance in connection with the provision of medical assistance in dying must, in accordance with those regulations, provide the information required by those regulations to the recipient designated in those regulations.

(3) The Minister of Health must make regulations that he or she considers necessary

(*a*) respecting the provision and collection, for the purpose of monitoring medical assistance in dying, of information relating to requests for, and the provision of, medical assistance in dying, including

(i) the information to be provided, at various stages, by medical practitioners or nurse practitioners and by pharmacists, or by a class of any of them,

(ii) the form, manner and time in which the information must be provided,

(iii) the designation of a person as the recipient of the information, and

(iv) the collection of information from coroners and medical examiners;

(*b*) respecting the use of that information, including its analysis and interpretation, its protection and its publication and other disclosure;

(*c*) respecting the disposal of that information; and

(*d*) exempting, on any terms that may be specified, a class of persons from the requirement set out in subsection or (2).

(3.1) The Minister of Health, after consultation with representatives of the provincial governments responsible for health, must establish guidelines on the information to be included on death certificates in cases where medical assistance in dying has been provided, which may include the way in which to clearly identify medical assistance in dying as the manner of death, as well as the illness, disease or disability that prompted the request for medical assistance in dying.

(4) A medical practitioner or nurse practitioner who knowingly fails to comply with subsection (1), or a pharmacist who knowingly fails to comply with subsection (2),

(*a*) is guilty of an indictable offence and liable to a term of imprisonment of not more than two years; or

(*b*) is guilty of an offence punishable on summary conviction.

(5) Everyone who knowingly contravenes the regulations made under subsection (3)

(*a*) is guilty of an indictable offence and liable to a term of imprisonment of not more than two years; or

(*b*) is guilty of an offence punishable on summary conviction. 2016, c. 3, s. 4.

FORGERY / Destruction of documents / Punishment / Definition of "document".

241.4 (1) Everyone commits an offence who commits forgery in relation to a request for medical assistance in dying.

(2) Everyone commits an offence who destroys a document that relates to a request for medical assistance in dying with intent to interfere with

(*a*) another person's access to medical assistance in dying;

(*b*) the lawful assessment of a request for medical assistance in dying; or

(*c*) another person invoking an exemption under any of subsections 227(1) or (2), 241(2) to (5) or 245(2); or

(*d*) the provision by a person of information under section 241.31.

(3) Everyone who commits an offence under subsection (1) or (2) is liable

(*a*) on conviction on indictment, to a term of imprisonment of not more than five years; or

(*b*) on summary conviction, to a term of imprisonment of not more than 18 months.

(4) In subsection (2), *document* has the same meaning as in section 321. 2016, c. 3, ss. 3, 5.

Neglect in Child-birth and Concealing Dead Body

NEGLECT TO OBTAIN ASSISTANCE IN CHILD-BIRTH.

242. A female person who, being pregnant and about to be delivered, with intent that the child shall not live or with intent to conceal the birth of the child, fails to make provision for reasonable assistance in respect of her delivery is, if the child is permanently injured as a result thereof or dies immediately before, during or in a short time after birth, as a result thereof, guilty of an indictable offence and liable to imprisonment for a term not exceeding five years. R.S., c. C-34, s. 226.

CROSS-REFERENCES

Related offences are infanticide, defined in s. 237, killing unborn child in act of birth in s. 238 and concealing body of child in s. 243. See s. 223(2) as to when causing death to child during or before birth amounts to homicide.

The accused has an election as to mode of trial pursuant to s. 536(2). Release pending trial is determined by s. 515, although the accused is eligible for release by the officer in charge under s. 498.

A person convicted of this offence may be liable to the mandatory prohibition order respecting firearms, ammunition and explosives by virtue of s. 109.

SYNOPSIS

Section 242 makes it an indictable offence to *neglect to obtain help in child-birth* if the act or omission is done with the requisite intent, and the consequences to the child are as specified in the section. The *pregnant woman is liable as a principal* if she is about to give birth and fails to make provision for reasonable assistance for the delivery. This liability only attaches if the woman fails to get assistance *with the intention that the child should not live or to conceal the birth* and certain results follow. The *consequences* which must be proven are that the *child dies* immediately before, during or in a short time after the birth or is permanently injured *as result of the woman's failure to obtain assistance*. The maximum sentence on conviction for this offence is five years' imprisonment.

ANNOTATIONS

The death or injury must be a direct result of deliberate failure to obtain reasonable assistance at birth: *R. v. Bryan* (1959), 123 C.C.C. 160, [1959] O.W.N. 103 (C.A.) (2:1).

CONCEALING BODY OF CHILD.

243. Every one who in any manner disposes of the dead body of a child, with intent to conceal the fact that its mother has been delivered of it, whether the child died before, during or after birth, is guilty of an indictable offence and liable to imprisonment for a term not exceeding two years. R.S., c. C-34, s. 227.

CROSS-REFERENCES

By virtue of s. 662(4), this offence is an included offence where a count charges murder of a child or charges infanticide.

The accused has an election as to mode of trial pursuant to s. 536(2). Release pending trial is determined by s. 515, although the accused is eligible for release by the officer in charge under s. 498.

Related offences are infanticide, defined in s. 237, killing unborn child in act of birth in s. 238 and neglecting to obtain assistance in child birth in s. 243.

ANNOTATIONS

For the purposes of this section, a fetus becomes a child when it has reached a stage in its development when, but for some external event or other circumstances, it would likely have been born alive. This standard provides sufficient precision to comply with the s. 7 principle of fundamental justice that criminal laws must not be vague: *R. v. Levkovic*, [2013] 2 S.C.R. 204, 296 C.C.C. (3d) 457.

Bodily Harm and Acts and Omissions Causing Danger to the Person

DISCHARGING FIREARM WITH INTENT / Punishment / Subsequent offences / Sequence of convictions only.

244. (1) Every person commits an offence who discharges a firearm at a person with intent to wound, maim or disfigure, to endanger the life of or to prevent the arrest or

detention of any person — whether or not that person is the one at whom the firearm is discharged.

(2) Every person who commits an offence under subsection (1) is guilty of an indictable offence and liable

(*a*) if a restricted firearm or prohibited firearm is used in the commission of the offence or if the offence is committed for the benefit of, at the direction of, or in association with, a criminal organization, to imprisonment for a term not exceeding 14 years and to a minimum punishment of imprisonment for a term of

(i) in the case of a first offence, five years, and

(ii) in the case of a second or subsequent offence, seven years; and

(*b*) in any other case, to imprisonment for a term not exceeding 14 years and to a minimum punishment of imprisonment for a term of four years.

(3) In determining, for the purpose of paragraph (2)(*a*), whether a convicted person has committed a second or subsequent offence, if the person was earlier convicted of any of the following offences, that offence is to be considered as an earlier offence:

(*a*) an offence under this section;

(*b*) an offence under subsection 85(1) or (2) or section 244.2; or

(*c*) an offence under section 220, 236, 239, 272 or 273, subsection 279(1) or section 279.1, 344 or 346 if a firearm was used in the commission of the offence.

However, an earlier offence shall not be taken into account if 10 years have elapsed between the day on which the person was convicted of the earlier offence and the day on which the person was convicted of the offence for which sentence is being imposed, not taking into account any time in custody.

(4) For the purposes of subsection (3), the only question to be considered is the sequence of convictions and no consideration shall be given to the sequence of commission of offences or whether any offence occurred before or after any conviction. R.S., c. C-34, s. 228; 1980-81-82-83, c. 125, s. 17; 1995, c. 39, s. 144; 2008, c. 6, s. 17; 2009, c. 22, s. 7.

CROSS-REFERENCES

"Firearm" is defined in s. 2. "Criminal organization" is defined in ss. 2 and 467.1(1). "Restricted firearm" and "prohibited firearm" are defined in s. 84. Related offences are as follows: s. 239, attempted murder; s. 129, resisting arrest; s. 270(1)(*b*) assault with intent to resist arrest; s. 267, assault causing bodily harm and assault with a weapon; s. 268, aggravated assault; s. 269, unlawfully causing bodily harm; s. 272, sexual assault with a weapon and sexual assault causing bodily harm; s. 273, aggravated sexual assault; and s. 244.2, discharging firearm into a place. An authorization to intercept private communications may be obtained in relation to this offence.

The accused has an election as to mode of trial pursuant to s. 536(2). Release pending trial is determined by s. 515.

A person convicted of this offence may be liable to the mandatory prohibition order respecting weapons, ammunition and explosives by virtue of s. 109. A person convicted of this offence may be subject to a dangerous offender application under Part XXIV. This offence is also a primary designated offence under s. 487.04.

SYNOPSIS

This section makes it an indictable offence to discharge a firearm with one of the intentions specified in the section. The doing of any of the aforementioned acts with any of the intentions set out in paras. (*a*) to (*c*), namely, wounding, maiming or disfiguring any person, endangering the life of anyone or preventing the arrest of a person, makes out the offence. The offence is made out even if the person referred to in paras. (*a*) or (*b*) is not the person who was, in fact, fired at.

The sentencing regime operates as follows. In all cases, the maximum punishment is 14 years. Under subsec. (2)(*a*), where a restricted firearm or prohibited firearm is used or if any firearm is used where the offence is committed for the benefit of, at the direction of, or in association with a criminal organization, the minimum punishment for a first offence is five years, and seven years for a second or subsequent offence. The rules for determining second and subsequent offences are set out in subsecs. (3) and (4). Thus, certain earlier convictions for related offences, such as certain firearm offences or other offences involving use of a firearm, are deemed to be earlier offences. However, an earlier offence is not to be taken into account if 10 years have elapsed (not counting time spent in custody). Subsection (4) reverses the common law rule and provides that, in determining whether an offence is an earlier offence, the only question is whether the conviction was registered earlier; the sequence of commission of the offences is not relevant. Under subsec. (2)(*b*), in any other case, the minimum punishment is four years.

ANNOTATIONS

In *R. v. Schultz* (1962), 133 C.C.C. 174, 38 C.R. 76 (Alta. S.C. App. Div.), the court considered various definitions of the word "maim" all to the effect that the person is maimed when he is rendered less able to fight. In that case it was held that the breaking of a man's leg is a sufficiently serious injury to amount to a maiming.

In *R. v. Innes and Brotchie* (1972), 7 C.C.C. (2d) 544 (B.C.C.A.), Robertson J.A. considered various definitions of the words "wound, maim or disfigure" including that "maim" means to render the victim less able to defend himself and "disfigure" denotes more than a temporary marring of the figure or appearance of a person.

An acquittal on a charge of attempted murder and a conviction on a charge of discharging a firearm with intent to endanger life are not inconsistent verdicts as the intent to endanger life is different from the intent to murder: *R. v. Boomhower* (1974), 20 C.C.C. (2d) 89, 27 C.R.N.S. 188 (Ont. C.A.).

Assault as defined by s. 265(1)(*b*) is an included offence of this offence: *R. v. Colburne* (1991), 66 C.C.C. (3d) 235, [1991] R.J.Q. 1199 (C.A.).

Proof of an actual arrest pursuant to subsec. (*c*), whether in progress or intended, is not part of the *actus reus* of the offence: *R. v. Jackson* (2002), 163 C.C.C. (3d) 451, 58 O.R. (3d) 593 (C.A.).

The four-year minimum sentence prescribed for the offence under para. (*b*) does not infringe the guarantee to protection against cruel and unusual punishment under s. 12 of the *Canadian Charter of Rights and Freedoms*: *R. v. Roberts* (1998), 125 C.C.C. (3d) 471, 199 N.B.R. (2d) 387 (C.A.).

CAUSING BODILY HARM WITH INTENT — AIR GUN OR PISTOL.

244.1 Every person who, with intent

(*a*) to wound, maim or disfigure any person,

(*b*) to endanger the life of any person, or

(*c*) to prevent the arrest or detention of any person,

discharges an air or compressed gas gun or pistol at any person, whether or not that person is the person mentioned in paragraph (*a*), (*b*) or (*c*), is guilty of an indictable offence and liable to imprisonment for a term not exceeding fourteen years. 1995, c. 39, s. 144.

CROSS-REFERENCES

The comparable offence where a firearm is used is found in s. 244. The accused has an election as to mode of trial pursuant to s. 536(2). Release pending trial is determined by s. 515. A person convicted of this offence may be liable to the weapons prohibition under s. 109.

SYNOPSIS

This section makes it an indictable offence to discharge an air gun or pistol at any person with one of the intentions specified in the section. The offence is made out even if the person referred to in paras. (*a*) or (*b*) is not the person who was in fact fired at. The maximum punishment to which the offender is liable upon conviction is 14 years.

DISCHARGING FIREARM — RECKLESSNESS / Definition of "place" / Punishment / Subsequent offences / Sequence of convictions only.

244.2 (1) Every person commits an offence

(*a*) who intentionally discharges a firearm into or at a place, knowing that or being reckless as to whether another person is present in the place; or

(*b*) who intentionally discharges a firearm while being reckless as to the life or safety of another person.

(2) For the purpose of paragraph (1)(*a*), "place" means any building or structure — or part of one — or any motor vehicle, vessel, aircraft, railway vehicle, container or trailer.

(3) Every person who commits an offence under subsection (1) is guilty of an indictable offence and

(*a*) if a restricted firearm or prohibited firearm is used in the commission of the offence or if the offence is committed for the benefit of, at the direction of or in association with a criminal organization, is liable to imprisonment for a term of not more than 14 years and to a minimum punishment of imprisonment for a term of

(i) five years, in the case of a first offence, and

(ii) seven years, in the case of a second or subsequent offence; and

(*b*) in any other case, is liable to imprisonment for a term of not more than 14 years and to a minimum punishment of imprisonment for a term of four years.

(4) In determining, for the purpose of paragraph (3)(*a*), whether a convicted person has committed a second or subsequent offence, if the person was earlier convicted of any of the following offences, that offence is to be considered as an earlier offence:

(*a*) an offence under this section;

(*b*) an offence under subsection 85(1) or (2) or section 244; or

(*c*) an offence under section 220, 236, 239, 272 or 273, subsection 279(1) or section 279.1, 344 or 346 if a firearm was used in the commission of the offence.

However, an earlier offence shall not be taken into account if 10 years have elapsed between the day on which the person was convicted of the earlier offence and the day on which the person was convicted of the offence for which sentence is being imposed, not taking into account any time in custody.

(5) For the purpose of subsection (4), the only question to be considered is the sequence of convictions and no consideration shall be given to the sequence of commission of offences or whether any offence occurred before or after any conviction. 2009; c. 22, s. 8.

CROSS-REFERENCES

"Firearm" and "criminal organization" are defined in s. 2. Pursuant to s. 2.1, "restricted firearm" and "prohibited firearm" have the same meaning as in s. 84. For related offences, see the note under s. 244. An authorization to intercept private communications may be obtained in relation to this offence. This offence is a primary designated offence for the purposes of the DNA Forensic Analysis provisions.

SYNOPSIS

This section creates an offence similar to the offence under s. 244. Under s. 244, the accused must discharge the firearm at a person. This offence merely requires that the accused discharged a firearm intentionally into or at a place knowing that, or being reckless whether, another person was present (subsec. (1)(*a*)), or intentionally discharging a firearm while being reckless as to the life or safety of another person. "Place" is defined in subsec. (2).

The sentencing regime operates as follows. In all cases, the maximum punishment is 14 years. However, where the accused used a restricted or prohibited firearm or the offence was committed for the benefit of, at the direction of, or in association with, a criminal organization there is a minimum punishment of five years for a first offence and seven years for second and subsequent offences. Subsections (4) and (5) set out the rules for whether a person has committed a second or subsequent offence. Note in particular that, if the accused has been out of custody for 10 years since the earlier offence, that offence will not be taken into account. Note also that subsec. (5) reverses the common law rule and it is simply the order of convictions that is considered, not the sequence in which the underlying offences were committed.

ANNOTATIONS

Constitutional considerations – The mandatory minimum sentence of four years' imprisonment provided by subsec. (3)(*b*) is not contrary to s. 12 of the Charter: *R. v. Oud* (2016), 339 C.C.C. (3d) 379 (B.C.C.A.).

ADMINISTERING NOXIOUS THING / Exemption / Definitions.

245. (1) Every one who administers or causes to be administered to any person or causes any person to take poison or any other destructive or noxious thing is guilty of an indictable offence and liable

(*a*) to imprisonment for a term not exceeding fourteen years, if he intends thereby to endanger the life of or to cause bodily harm to that person; or

(*b*) to imprisonment for a term not exceeding two years, if he intends thereby to aggrieve or annoy that person.

(2) Subsection (1) does not apply to

(*a*) a medical practitioner or nurse practitioner who provides medical assistance in dying in accordance with section 241.2; and

(*b*) a person who does anything for the purpose of aiding a medical practitioner or nurse practitioner to provide medical assistance in dying in accordance with section 241.2.

(3) In subsection (2), *medical assistance in dying*, *medical practitioner* and *nurse practitioner* have the same meanings as in section 241.1. R.S., c. C-34, s. 229; 2016, c. 3, s. 6.

CROSS-REFERENCES

The term "bodily harm" is defined in s. 2.

The offence of supplying a noxious thing intended to procure a miscarriage is found in s. 288.

The accused has an election as to mode of trial pursuant to s. 536(2). Release pending trial is determined by s. 515, although the accused is eligible for release by the officer in charge under s. 498 where charged with the offence under para. (*b*).

A person convicted of the offence under para. (*a*) may be liable to the mandatory prohibition order respecting weapons, ammunition and explosives by virtue of s. 109 and a person found guilty of the offence under para. (*b*) liable to the discretionary prohibition order under s. 110. A person convicted of the offence under para. (*a*) may be subject to a dangerous offender application under Part XXIV.

SYNOPSIS

Section 245 makes it an indictable *offence to administer a noxious thing*. The *actus reus* of the offence consists of administering, causing to be administered or causing to be taken a noxious thing, poison or destructive thing. To be guilty of an offence under this section, it must be proven that the accused intended to do the physical acts described. However, for sentencing purposes, a distinction is made between different intentions. If the accused intended that, by doing any of the acts described, he would endanger the life of another or cause that person bodily harm, the maximum sentence is 14 years. If the accused does any of the acts to aggrieve or annoy that person, the maximum sentence is two years.

ANNOTATIONS

The *mens rea* required by this section is proof that the accused intended a consequence defined in the section. A "noxious thing" is any substance which in the light of all the circumstances attendant upon its administration is capable of effecting or, in the normal course of events, will effect one of the defined consequences. Even an innocuous substance may in some circumstances come within the section. The Crown need not prove that the accused knew the substance was noxious, although this would be relevant in establishing intent, but only that the substance was in fact noxious: *R. v. Burkholder* (1977), 34 C.C.C. (2d) 214, [1977] 1 W.W.R. 627 (Alta. S.C. App. Div.).

Administration does not require that the accused intend that the noxious substance be taken internally: *R. v. Clark* (2008), 234 C.C.C. (3d) 12 (Alta. C.A.).

OVERCOMING RESISTANCE TO COMMISSION OF OFFENCE.

246. Every one who, with intent to enable or assist himself or another person to commit an indictable offence,

(*a*) attempts, by any means, to choke, suffocate or strangle another person, or by any means calculated to choke, suffocate or strangle, attempts to render another person insensible, unconscious or incapable of resistance, or

(*b*) administers or causes to be administered to any person, or attempts to administer to any person, or causes or attempts to cause any person to take a stupefying or overpowering drug, matter or thing,

is guilty of an indictable offence and liable to imprisonment for life. R.S., c. C-34, s. 230; 1972, c. 13, s. 70.

CROSS-REFERENCES

An "indictable offence" will include a hybrid offence, punishable on indictment or on summary conviction: *Interpretation Act*, R.S.C. 1985, c. I-21, s. 34(1)(*a*).

Note that where death is caused in the commission of certain offences by means similar to those referred to in this section then the accused will be liable to be convicted of murder under s. 230(*b*) or (*c*) [constructive murder]. The related offence of administering a noxious thing is found in s. 245.

The accused has an election as to mode of trial pursuant to s. 536(2). Release pending trial is determined by s. 515. A person convicted of this offence will be liable to the mandatory prohibition order respecting firearms, ammunition and explosives by virtue of s. 109. A person convicted of this offence may be subject to a dangerous offender application under Part XXIV.

SYNOPSIS

This section makes it an indictable offence for any person to *overcome resistance for the purpose of committing an indictable offence* or to do so to assist another person. The offence is made out by proving that the accused did any of the acts described in paras. (*a*) or (*b*) for this purpose. The maximum sentence upon conviction is life imprisonment.

TRAPS LIKELY TO CAUSE BODILY HARM / Bodily harm / Offence-related place / Offence-related place — bodily harm / Death.

247. (1) Every one is guilty of an indictable offence and is liable to imprisonment for a term not exceeding five years, who with intent to cause death or bodily harm to a person, whether ascertained or not,

(*a*) sets or places a trap, device or other thing that is likely to cause death or bodily harm to a person; or

(*b*) being in occupation or possession of a place, knowingly permits such a trap, device or other thing to remain in that place.

(2) Every one who commits an offence under subsection (1) and thereby causes bodily harm to any other person is guilty of an indictable offence and liable to imprisonment for a term not exceeding ten years.

(3) Every one who commits an offence under subsection (1), in a place kept or used for the purpose of committing another indictable offence, is guilty of an indictable offence and is liable to a term of imprisonment not exceeding ten years.

(4) Every one who commits an offence under subsection (1), in a place kept or used for the purpose of committing another indictable offence, and thereby causes bodily harm to a person is guilty of an indictable offence and liable to a term of imprisonment not exceeding fourteen years.

(5) Every one who commits an offence under subsection (1) and thereby causes the death of any other person is guilty of an indictable offence and liable to imprisonment for life. R.S., c. C-34, s. 231; 2004, c. 12, s. 6.

CROSS-REFERENCES

The term "property" is defined in s. 2. The term "bodily harm" is not defined in this section. Some assistance may, however, be obtained from the definition of "bodily harm" in s. 2.

The accused has an election as to mode of trial pursuant to s. 536(2). Release pending trial is determined by s. 515, although the accused is eligible for release by the officer in charge under s. 498. A person found guilty of this offence may be liable to the discretionary prohibition order respecting weapons, ammunition and explosives by virtue of s. 109, depending on the circumstances in which the offence was committed.

The related offences of criminal negligence causing death and causing bodily harm are found in ss. 220 and 221, respectively. The offences of failing to guard an opening in the ice and failing to guard excavations are found in s. 263.

SYNOPSIS

This section makes it an indictable offence to set or permit traps and other similar devices which are likely to cause death or bodily harm to any person.

The physical acts that make up the offence under subsec. (1) are setting, placing a trap, device or other thing that is likely to cause death or bodily harm to any person or being in occupation or possession of the place where such traps have been set or placed. The requisite intent is to cause death or bodily harm. Where the accused is merely in occupation or possession of the place, the prosecution must also proved that he or she knowingly permitted the trap to remain in the place. The simple offence carries a five-year maximum term of imprisonment.

Where the commission of the offence causes bodily harm, the maximum penalty is ten years and life if death is caused. Where the place is also kept or used for the purpose of committing another indictable offence such as producing marihuana, the maximum penalty is ten years and fourteen years if as a result of commission of the offence under subsec. (1) bodily harm is caused to a person.

INTERFERING WITH TRANSPORTATION FACILITIES.

248. Every one who, with intent to endanger the safety of any person, places anything on or does anything to any property that is used for or in connection with the transportation of persons or goods by land, water or air that is likely to cause death or bodily harm to persons is guilty of an indictable offence and liable to imprisonment for life. R.S., c. C-34, s. 232.

CROSS-REFERENCES

The term "bodily harm" is not defined in this section. Some assistance may, however, be obtained from the definition of "bodily harm" in s. 2. Related offences are as follows: ss. 76 to 78, offences involving aircraft; ss. 80 to 82, offences involving explosives; ss. 220 to 222, criminal negligence; s. 247, setting trap with intent; ss. 430 to 436, damage to property.

The accused has an election as to mode of trial pursuant to s. 536(2). Release pending trial is determined by s. 515. A person convicted of this offence may be liable to the mandatory prohibition order respecting firearms, ammunition and explosives by virtue of s. 109, depending on the circumstances in which the offence was committed.

SYNOPSIS

Section 248 creates the indictable offence of *interfering with transportation facilities* with the *intention of endangering the safety* of any *person*. The physical acts outlined in the section are placing anything on, or doing anything to property used in connection with transporting people or goods by land, water or air. In addition to proof of the physical act and the intention, it must be established that the act is likely to cause death or bodily harm. The maximum sentence for this offence is life imprisonment.

EDITOR'S NOTE: The former offences under the heading "Motor Vehicles, Vessels and Aircraft" have been repealed and replaced with Part VIII.1, "Offences Relating to Conveyances" (ss. 320.11 through 320.4). The cross-references, synopses, and annotations under the former offences have been retained to the extent that they may be helpful in applying the equivalent offences in the new Part VIII.1.

[*Heading repealed*, 2018, c. 21, s. 14.]

---

249. [*Repealed*, 2018, c. 21, s. 14.]

Editor's Note: The offence of dangerous operation of a conveyance is now found in s. 320.13. The annotations below should be approached with caution in relation to the new offence.

CROSS-REFERENCES

The terms "motor vehicle" and "railway equipment" are defined in s. 2. The terms "aircraft", "vessel" and "operates" are defined in s. 214. The term "bodily harm" is defined in s. 2.

With respect to the offence in subsec. (4) and the issue of causation, see ss. 224 to 226. For special jurisdictional rules relating to offences committed on the water or on aircraft in the course of a flight see s. 476. Also see s. 477 respecting offences committed on the territorial sea or on internal waters [defined in s. 3 of the *Territorial Sea and Fishing Zones Act*, R.S.C. 1985, c. T-8]. Section 662(5) makes the offences under this section included offences where the count charges an offence of criminal negligence causing death [s. 220], criminal negligence causing bodily harm [s. 221] or manslaughter [s. 236] arising out of the operation of a vehicle or navigation of a vessel or aircraft. The related offences of impaired driving causing death and bodily harm are found in s. 255. The offence of failing to stop at the scene of an accident is found in s. 252. Where the accused not only commits the offence under subsec. (3) or (4), but at the time was being pursued by a peace officer operating a motor vehicle and in order to evade the officer fails without reasonable excuse to stop the vehicle as soon as possible, the accused commits an offence under s. 249.1(3) and is liable to the penalties set out in s. 249.1(4).

Where the prosecution elects to proceed by indictment on the offence in subsec. (2), dangerous operation, *simpliciter*, then the accused may elect his mode of trial pursuant to s. 536(2). Where the prosecution elects to proceed by way of summary conviction then the trial of this offence is conducted by a summary conviction court pursuant to Part XXVII. The punishment for the offence is then as set out in s. 787 and the limitation period is set out in s. 786(2). In either case, release pending trial is determined by s. 515, although the accused is eligible for release by a peace officer under s. 496, 497 or by the officer in charge under s. 498. The accused has an election as to mode of trial of the offences in subsecs. (3) and (4) pursuant to s. 536(2). Release pending trial is determined by s. 515.

An accused found guilty of these offences may, pursuant to s. 259, be ordered prohibited from operating a motor vehicle, vessel, aircraft or railway equipment, as the case may be, where the offence under this section was committed by means of a motor vehicle, vessel, aircraft or railway equipment. The length of the prohibition order is as follows: offence under subsec. (2), during any period not exceeding 3 years plus any period to which the offender is sentenced to imprisonment; offence under either subsec. (3) or (4), during any period not exceeding 10 years. The procedure respecting the making of the order of prohibition is found in s. 260. Evidence that the accused's blood alcohol level exceeded .16 at the time of the offence is deemed an aggravating factor, for purposes of sentencing, under s. 255.1.

Section 249.4 creates the offence of dangerous operation of a motor vehicle while street racing (defined in s. 2). That section provides for greater penalties where bodily harm or death is caused while street racing.

SYNOPSIS

Section 249 makes it an offence to operate motor vehicles, vessels or aircraft in a dangerous manner and provides for punishment upon conviction for these offences.

Section 249(1)(*a*) makes it an offence to *operate a motor vehicle* in a manner that is *dangerous*. To determine if the driving is dangerous, the paragraph indicates that one must *consider all of the circumstances* such as the nature, condition and the use of the place as well as the amount of traffic that is or might reasonably be expected to be present. In addition, it is essential that there be *danger to the public* who either were *present or who might have been expected to be present*. A passenger in the car is part of the public. The mental element for the offence requires proof of an intention to operate the vehicle in a way which, objectively viewed, constitutes a departure from the standard of care expected of a prudent driver in the circumstances.

Section 249(1)(*b*) creates a parallel offence in relation to the *dangerous operation of a vessel* or water skis, surf board, water sled or other towed object. The offence may be committed in the internal waters of Canada or on its territorial seas. Section 249(1)(*c*) creates a parallel offence in relation to the dangerous operation of an aircraft. Finally, s. 249(1)(*d*) sets out the similar offence of dangerous operation of railway equipment.

Subsection (2) provides that the aforementioned offences may be tried by way of summary conviction procedure or by way of indictment. In the latter case, the maximum sentence is five years' imprisonment.

Subsections (3) and (4) create more *aggravated* indictable offences which occur when a *particular consequence* flows from the commission of any of the offences described in subsec. (1). Subsection (3) applies if the acts described in subsec. (1) *result in bodily harm* to another person and it provides for a maximum sentence not exceeding 10 years. Subsection (4) creates the offence of doing one of the acts described in subsec. (1), when this *causes the death* of another person. A person convicted pursuant to subsec. (4) is liable to up to 14 years' imprisonment. In both subsecs. (3) and (4), there must be a *link proven between the accused's acts and the result*. Though it is not yet clearly defined how strong a link need be proven, the accused's act must at least be a cause of the consequences.

ANNOTATIONS

Elements of offence of dangerous operation – In *R. v. Peda*, [1969] S.C.R. 905, [1969] 4 C.C.C. 245, Judson J. (Fauteaux, Abbott, Martland and Ritchie JJ., concurring), held that subsec. (1)(*a*) contains its own definition of dangerous driving, and a court is not required to charge the jury other than in terms of the subsection itself.

In considering whether the manner of driving endangered the public, it was an error for the trial judge to simply consider the absence of other traffic in the course of a high speed police chase. The passenger in the accused's car and the officer in the police cruiser were included in the public contemplated by this section: *R. v. Edlund* (1990), 23 M.V.R. (2d) 37, 104 A.R. 354 (C.A.).

It is unnecessary for the Crown to prove that the lives or safety of others were actually endangered. The offence is proved where the Crown establishes that the driving complained of was dangerous to the public, that is, either the public actually present at the time of the offence or the public which might reasonably have been expected to be in the particular vicinity at the time: *R. v. Mueller* (1975), 29 C.C.C. (2d) 243, 32 C.R.N.S. 188 (Ont. C.A.).

The appropriate *mens rea* for this offence is based on a modified objective test. As a general rule, personal factors need not be taken into account and the accused may be convicted if it is proven that, viewed objectively, the accused was driving in a manner that was dangerous to the public, having regard to all of the circumstances. In making this assessment, the court should be satisfied that the conduct amounted to a marked departure from the standard of care that a reasonable person would observe in the accused's situation. An explanation, such as the sudden onset of an unexpected illness would negative liability if a reasonable person in the position of the accused would not have been aware of the risk: *R. v. Hundal*, [1993] 1 S.C.R. 867, 79 C.C.C. (3d) 97.

In *R. v. Beatty*, [2008] 1 S.C.R. 49, 228 C.C.C. (3d) 225, the Supreme Court of Canada fully considered the requisite *mens rea* and *actus reus*. The modified objective test requires a marked departure from the civil norm in the circumstances of the case. A mere departure from the standard expected of a reasonably prudent person will meet the threshold for civil negligence but will not be sufficient for penal negligence. The distinction between a mere departure and a marked departure is a question of degree. The *actus reus* requires proof beyond a reasonable doubt that, viewed objectively, the accused was driving in a manner that was dangerous to the public, having regard to all of the circumstances, including the nature, condition and use of the place at which the motor vehicle is being operated and the amount of traffic that, at the time, is or might reasonably be expected to be at that place. It is the manner in which the vehicle was operated that is at issue, not the consequence of the driving. While the consequence may assist in assessing the risk involved, it does not answer the question of whether or not the vehicle was operated in a manner dangerous to the public.

The *mens rea* requires the trier of fact to be satisfied on the basis of all of the evidence, including evidence, if any, about the accused's actual state of mind, that the conduct amounted to a marked departure from the standard of care that a reasonable person would observe in the accused's circumstances. If the trier of fact is convinced beyond a reasonable doubt that the objectively dangerous conduct constitutes a marked departure from the norm, the trier of fact must consider evidence, if any, about the actual state of mind of the accused to determine whether it raises a reasonable doubt about whether a reasonable person in the accused's position would have been aware of the risk created by this conduct. Subjective *mens rea* of intentionally creating a danger for other users of the highway will always constitute a marked departure from the standard expected of a reasonably prudent driver. Subjective *mens rea*, however, is not necessary. A lack of care must be serious enough to merit punishment. If an explanation is offered by the accused, then, in order to convict, the trier of fact must be satisfied that a reasonable person in similar circumstances ought to have been aware of the risk and of the danger involved in the conduct manifested by the accused. The objective *mens rea* is based on the premise that a reasonable person in the accused's position would have been aware of the risks arising from the conduct. The objective test must be modified to give the accused the benefit of any reasonable doubt about whether the reasonable person would have appreciated the risk or could and would have done something to avoid creating the danger. In addition, a reasonably held mistake of fact may provide a complete defence if, based on the accused's reasonable perception of the facts, the conduct measured up to the requisite standard of care. The modified objective test must be applied in the context of the events surrounding the incident. Personal attributes such as age, experience and education are not relevant. The reasonable person, however, must be put in the circumstances that the accused found himself in when the events occurred in order to assess the reasonableness of the conduct. See also *R. v. Roy* (2012), 281 C.C.C. (3d) 433 (S.C.C.), where in snowy and foggy conditions the accused had pulled onto a highway into the path of an oncoming tractor trailer, resulting in the death of his passenger. The accused had no memory of the collision. The accused's decision to pull onto the highway was consistent with a simple misjudgment and could not reasonably support an inference of a marked departure.

Under certain circumstances, excessive speed alone may be sufficient to constitute dangerous driving: *R. v. Richards* (2003), 174 C.C.C. (3d) 154, 169 O.A.C. 339 (C.A.).

A sleeping driver is not driving of their own volition and acts committed while in an automatic state of mind cannot form the *actus reus* of this offence. The elements of the offence are made out, however, where the driver embarked on driving in circumstances in which he knew or ought to have known that there was a real risk that he would fall asleep at the wheel: *R. v. Jiang* (2007), 220 C.C.C. (3d) 55, 48 C.R. (6th) 49 (B.C.C.A.).

A trier of fact is not precluded by issue estoppel from taking into consideration the consumption of alcohol by an accused in determining guilty on dangerous driving causing bodily harm, where the accused is acquitted of impaired driving in circumstances that arise from the same incident: *R. v. Settle* (2010), 261 C.C.C. (3d) 45 (B.C.C.A.).

Constitutional considerations – The offence created by subsec. (1)(*a*) is not unconstitutionally vague in violation of s. 7 of the *Charter of Rights and Freedoms*: *R. v. Demeyer* (1986), 27 C.C.C. (3d) 575, 40 M.V.R. 231 (Alta. C.A.).

Imposing liability for this offence on the basis of a modified objective test for fault does not infringe s. 7 of the Charter: *R. v. Hundal, supra.*

Causation (subsecs. (3) and (4)) – It was held in relation to the offence of criminal negligence causing death that the element of causation is satisfied if the evidence shows that the criminally negligent conduct of the accused meets the test in *R. v. Smithers*, [1978] 1 S.C.R. 506, 34 C.C.C. (2d) 427, being at least a contributing cause of death outside the *de minimis* range. It is misdirection to instruct the jury that the conduct must be shown to be a substantial cause: *R. v. Pinske* (1988), 30 B.C.L.R. (2d) 114, 6 M.V.R. (2d) 19 (B.C.C.A.), affd [1989] 2 S.C.R. 979, 100 N.R. 399. The *Smithers* test has been adopted for prosecutions under this section and the similar offences of impaired driving causing bodily harm or death under s. 255(2) and (3): *R. v. Larocque* (1988), 5 M.V.R. (2d) 221 (Ont. C.A.); *R. v. Halkett* (1988), 73 Sask. R. 241, 11 M.V.R. (2d) 109 (C.A.); *R. v. Singhal* (1988), 5 M.V.R. (2d) 173 (B.C.C.A.); *R. v. Arsenault* (1992), 16 C.R. (4th) 301, 104 Nfld. & P.E.I.R. 29 (P.E.I.C.A.); *R. v. Colby* (1989), 52 C.C.C. (3d) 321, 100 A.R. 142 (C.A.), and *R. v. Ewart* (1989), 53 C.C.C. (3d) 153, 100 A.R. 118 (C.A.), leave to appeal to S.C.C. refused 109 A.R. 320*n*. The court seems to have adopted a somewhat stricter test for causation in *R. v. F. (D.)* (1989), 52 C.C.C. (3d) 357, 73 C.R. (3d) 391 (C.A.).

In considering whether the *Smithers* test has been made out, reference should also now be made to *R. v. Nette*, [2001] 3 S.C.R. 488, 158 C.C.C. (3d) 486, where a majority of the court explained that causing death outside the *de minimis* range means that the acts of the accused were a significant contributing cause to the death.

249.1 [*Repealed*, 2018, c. 21, s. 14.]

Editor's Note: The offence of flight from a peace officer is now found in s. 320.17. The annotations below should be approached with caution in relation to the new offence.

CROSS-REFERENCES

The terms "motor vehicle", "peace officer" and "bodily harm" are defined in s. 2. The term "operates" is defined in s. 214.

With respect to causation and death, see ss. 224 to 226. Section 662(5) makes the offences under this section included offences where the count charges an offence of criminal negligence causing death [s. 220], criminal negligence causing bodily harm [s. 221] or manslaughter [s. 236] arising out of the operation of a vehicle or navigation of a vessel or aircraft. The related offences of impaired driving causing death and bodily harm are found in s. 255. The offence of failing to stop at the scene of an accident is found in s. 252. The offence of dangerous operation is found in s. 249. The related offence of obstructing a peace office is found in s. 129.

Where the prosecution elects to proceed by indictment on the offence in subsec. (1), dangerous operation, the accused may elect his mode of trial pursuant to s. 536(2). Where the prosecution elects to proceed by way of summary conviction then the trial of this offence is conducted by a summary conviction court pursuant to Part XXVII. The punishment for the offence is then as set out in s. 787 and the limitation period is set out in s. 786(2). In either case, release pending trial is determined by s. 515, although the accused is eligible for release by a peace officer under ss. 496, 497 or by the officer in charge under s. 498. The accused has an election as to mode of trial of the offences in subsecs. (3). Release pending trial is determined by s. 515.

An accused found guilty of these offences may, pursuant to s. 259, be ordered prohibited from operating a motor vehicle. The length of the prohibition order is as follows: offence under subsec. (1), during any period not exceeding 3 years; offence under subsec. (4)(*a*), during any period not exceeding 10 years; offence under subsec. (4)(*b*), during any period that the court considers proper. The procedure respecting the making of the order of prohibition is found in s. 260. Evidence that the accused's blood alcohol level exceeded .16 at the time of the offence is deemed an aggravating factor, for purposes of sentencing, under s. 255.1.

SYNOPSIS

This section creates three offences of increasing gravity for motorists attempting to evade the police. The gravamen of each offence is failing without reasonable excuse to stop the motor vehicle as soon as is reasonable in the circumstances while being pursued by a peace officer. The offence requires proof of an intention (in order to) to evade the police officer. The flight offence *simpliciter* is a hybrid offence under subsec. (1).

Subsection (3) in effect creates an aggravated form of dangerous operation. Where the motorist not only engages in the conduct prohibited by subsec. (1), but operates the vehicle in a dangerous manner as described in s. 249 and causes death or bodily harm to another person, the motorist is liable to imprisonment for 14 years (where bodily harm caused) and life (where death caused).

ANNOTATIONS

A pursuit within the meaning of this provision includes an effort to catch up with, and does not require that the peace officer intended to overtake or pass the other vehicle: *R. v. Briltz* (2016), 331 C.C.C. (3d) 338 (Sask. C.A.).

249.2 [*Repealed*, 2018, c. 21, s. 14.]

249.3 [*Repealed*, 2018, c. 21, s. 14.]

249.4 [*Repealed*, 2018, c. 21, s. 14.]

---

250. [*Repealed*, 2018, c. 21, s. 14.]

251. [*Repealed*, 2018, c. 21, s. 14.]

CROSS-REFERENCES

The terms "aircraft", "vessel" and "operates" are defined in s. 214. The term "railway equipment" is defined in s. 2. Section 583(*h*) provides that a count in an indictment is not insufficient by reason only that it does not state that the required consent has been obtained. [For notes on consent see s. 583.] The accused has an election as to mode of trial pursuant to s. 536(2). Release pending trial is determined by s. 515, although the accused is eligible for release by the officer in charge under s. 498.

An accused convicted of this offence may, pursuant to s. 259, be ordered prohibited from operating a motor vehicle, vessel, aircraft or railway equipment, as the case may be, during any period not exceeding 3 years. The procedure respecting the making of that order of prohibition is found in s. 260.

SYNOPSIS

This section makes it an indictable offence to endanger the life of any person by knowingly sending or taking a licensed or registered vessel that is unseaworthy on a voyage from a place in Canada to another place in or out of Canada or from a place on the inland waters of the United States to a place in Canada. Similarly, it is an indictable offence to endanger the life of any person by sending or operating an unfit or unsafe aircraft on a flight or by sending or operating railway equipment that is not fit and safe for operation. The maximum penalty for this offence is a term of imprisonment of five years. Subsection (2) provides that no criminal liability will attach to an accused person who establishes that he/she used all reasonable means to ensure that the vessel was seaworthy or that the aircraft or railway equipment was fit and safe. Furthermore, if an accused can establish that the operation of the unseaworthy vessel, or the unfit or unsafe aircraft or railway equipment was, under the circumstances, reasonable and justifiable, he/she cannot be convicted of this offence. The written consent of the Attorney General of Canada is necessary before any proceedings are instituted under this section.

---

252. [*Repealed*, 2018, c. 21, s. 14.]

Editor's Note: The offence of failure to stop after an accident is now found in s. 320.16. The annotations below should be approached with caution in relation to the new offence.

CROSS-REFERENCES

The term "vehicle" is not defined, although "motor vehicle" is defined in s. 2. The terms "aircraft" and "vessel" are defined in s. 214.

Where the prosecution elects to proceed by indictment on the offence in subsec. (1) then the accused may elect his mode of trial pursuant to s. 536(2). Where the prosecution elects to proceed by way of summary conviction on the offence contrary to subsec. (1.1) then the trial of this offence is conducted by a summary conviction court pursuant to Part XXVII. The punishment for the offence is then as set out in s. 787 and the limitation period is set out in s. 786(2). In either case, release pending trial is determined by s. 515, although the accused is eligible for release by a peace officer under s. 496, 497 or by the officer in charge under s. 498. Where the offence involved the operation of a motor vehicle, vessel, aircraft or railway equipment then an accused found guilty of this offence may, pursuant to s. 259, be ordered prohibited from operating a motor vehicle, vessel, aircraft or railway equipment, as the case may be, during any period not exceeding 3 years. The procedure respecting the making of that order of prohibition is found in s. 260. Related offences: s. 249, dangerous operation; ss. 253 and 255, impaired operation and "over 80"; s. 254, failing to comply with screening device or breathalyzer demand; ss. 220 and 221, criminal negligence causing death or bodily harm.

The penalties for this offence were increased by S.C. 1999, c. 32. The transitional provisions of that Act provide that the lesser penalty or punishment applies in respect of any offence that was committed before the coming into force of the Act. Pursuant to s. 255.1, evidence that the accused's blood alcohol level exceeded .160 at the time when the offence was committed is deemed to be an aggravating factor on sentencing. Note s. 732.1(3)(*g*.1) and (*g*.2), which allow for terms of probation that the offender attend for curative treatment in relation to the consumption of alcohol and drugs and participate in an alcohol ignition interlock device program.

SYNOPSIS

This section makes it an offence, for any person who has the care, charge or control of a vehicle, vessel or aircraft that is involved in an accident with another person, vehicle, vessel or aircraft, to fail to stop at the scene of the accident in order to avoid civil or criminal liability. The person who is involved in the accident must give his name and address and, if there are injuries, offer assistance. By subsec. (2), uncontroverted evidence of his failure to do so is proof of an intent to escape civil or criminal liability. The offence contrary to subsec. (1.1) is hybrid and punishable on indictment by a maximum term of imprisonment of five years. Where the accused fails to stop knowing that bodily harm has been caused to another person, the offence is indictable and punishable by 10 years' imprisonment. Where the accused knows that another person is dead or knows that bodily harm has been caused and is reckless as to whether the death of the other person resulted from the bodily harm, the maximum punishment is life imprisonment.

ANNOTATIONS

Elements of offence generally – The offence is made out when it is established that the defendant failed to perform any one of the three statutory duties set out in the information. Furthermore, naming the defendant as the driver in the charge is within the designation of one who has care and control of the vehicle: *R. v. Steere* (1972), 6 C.C.C. (2d) 403, 19 C.R.N.S. 115 (B.C.C.A.).

Contemporaneous knowledge of the accident by the accused is an element of this offence which the Crown must prove. It is not sufficient that the accused "should have known" of the accident: *R. v. Slessor*, [1970] 2 C.C.C. 247, 7 C.R.N.S. 379 (Ont. C.A.); *R. v. Faulkner (No. 2)* (1977), 37 C.C.C. (2d) 217 (N.S. Co. Ct.).

In *R. v. Slessor, supra,* the majority divided on the liability of a passenger under this subsection. Gale C.J.O., held that a passenger in the vehicle, including the owner, who is asleep or otherwise unconscious at the time of an accident cannot be convicted of this offence unless, after the automobile has in fact been stopped in compliance with the section, the owner, upon regaining consciousness causes it to be driven off before the other requisites of the section are met. Further, *per* Gale C.J.O., apart from joint ventures, only one person in the car would have care, charge or control and if that person is the passenger he must have a degree of exercisable or exercised control over the actual driver. His Lordship would leave open the question whether the subsection is directed solely to the person who has care, charge or control at the moment of impact. Laskin J.A., held that the subsection could not apply to a person who did not have care, charge or control at the time the car was involved in the accident. Schroeder J.A., dissenting, held that if both the driver and the owner/passenger had care and control at the relevant time both could be liable for failing to comply with the subsection.

The court in *R. v. Shea* (1982), 17 M.V.R. 40, 37 Nfld. & P.E.I.R. 457 (Nfld. C.A.), considered that the law was correctly stated by Gale C.J.O. in *R. v. Slessor, supra,* and affirmed the acquittal of the owner of the vehicle because of the trial judge's finding that he only took over driving of the car some distance, albeit a short distance, from the accident scene.

Civil or criminal liability – The "civil or criminal liability" contemplated by this section includes any liability, civil or criminal, which might properly arise from the operation of the motor vehicle by the accused at the time the accident takes place. The liability a driver seeks to evade does not need to arise solely from the consequences of the accident itself, but may also encompass offences connected to the driving, such as impaired driving, driving while suspended, criminal negligence, and dangerous driving. Being the driver of a stolen car when involved in an accident, and fleeing to avoid detection as the driver, is sufficiently related to the event to be captured by this provision: *R. v. Seipp* (2017), 344 C.C.C. (3d) 401 (B.C.C.A.), affd [2018] 1 S.C.R. 3.

"Accident" – A deliberate act of mischief by the accused in relation to property, here lining up his car behind the car of another and then deliberately pushing it into a wall is not an "accident" within the meaning of this section: *R. v. O'Brien* (1987), 39 C.C.C. (3d) 528, 67 Nfld. & P.E.I.R. 68 (Nfld. S.C.T.D.).

The obligation to stop at the scene of an accident does not depend on the existence of damage or injury: *R. v. Chase* (2006), 209 C.C.C. (3d) 43 (B.C.C.A.).

This section does not apply where the accident involves the accused's car and a pole. The reference in subsec. (1)(*b*) is to another vehicle: *R. v. Vellow* (1990), 27 M.V.R. (2d) 59 (Ont. Ct. (Prov. Div.)).

Subsection (1)(*a*) – "Another person" includes a passenger in a single vehicle accident: *R. v. McColl* (2008), 235 C.C.C. (3d) 319, 60 C.R. (6th) 78 (Alta. C.A.).

Admissibility of statement – The existence of the statutory duty under this subsection does not dispense with the onus upon the Crown to establish that any statement made was not otherwise involuntary: *R. v. Fex* (1973), 14 C.C.C. (2d) 188, 23 C.R.N.S. 368 (Ont. C.A.), and *R. v. Cleavely* (1966), 49 C.R. 326, 57 W.W.R. 301 (Sask. Q.B.). *Contra: R. v. Smith* (1973), 15 C.C.C. (2d) 113, 25 C.R.N.S. 246 (Alta. C.A.). Also see *R. v. White*, [1999] 2 S.C.R. 417, 135 C.C.C. (3d) 257, noted under s. 7 of the *Canadian Charter of Rights and Freedoms.*

Presumption of intent [subsec. (2)] – This subsection is to be read disjunctively and thus the presumption applies where the accused fails to perform any of the three duties imposed on him: *R. v. Roche*, [1983] 1 S.C.R. 491, 3 C.C.C. (3d) 193 (7:0).

As to the meaning of the phrase "in the absence of any evidence to the contrary", see *R. v. Proudlock*, [1979] 1 S.C.R. 525, 43 C.C.C. (2d) 321, noted under s. 348, *infra.*

Evidence which is not rejected by the trier of fact and which tends to show that the accused may not have had the requisite intent is evidence to the contrary. Evidence of drunkenness may constitute evidence to the contrary: *R. v. Nolet (Charette)* (1980), 4 M.V.R. 265 (Ont. C.A.).

Evidence that the accused, prior to walking away from the scene of the accident, was under the influence of alcohol and unresponsive to questions was capable of being evidence to the contrary and thus rebut the presumption: *R. v. Adler* (1981), 59 C.C.C. (2d) 517, [1981] 4 W.W.R. 379 (Sask. C.A.).

Constitutional considerations – This subsection is not an unconstitutional infringement on the guarantee to the presumption of innocence in s. 11(*d*) of the *Canadian Charter of Rights and Freedoms*: *R. v. T.* (1985), 18 C.C.C. (3d) 125, 43 C.R. (3d) 307 (N.S. S.C. App. Div.); *R. v. Gosselin* (1988), 45 C.C.C. (3d) 568, 9 M.V.R. (2d) 290 (Ont. C.A.).

---

253. [*Repealed*, 2018, c. 21, s. 14.]

Editor's Note: The offences of impaired operation of a conveyance and operating a conveyance with a drug or alcohol level over the prescribed limit are now found in s. 320.14. The annotations below should be approached with caution in relation to the new offence.

CROSS-REFERENCES

The terms "motor vehicle" and "railway equipment" are defined in s. 2. The terms "aircraft", "vessel" and "operate" are defined in s. 214. The presumption respecting "care or control" is found in s. 258(1)(*a*). Procedure for making a breathalyzer or approved screening device [A.L.E.R.T.]

demand is found in s. 254 and for obtaining a warrant to obtain blood samples in s. 256. The adverse inference respecting the impaired offence for failing to comply with a demand under s. 254 is found in s. 258(3). The presumptions respecting the accused's blood alcohol level arising from analysis of a breath sample or blood sample are found in s. 258(1)(*c*), (*d*), (*d*.01) and (*d*.1). Procedure for admission of certificates of an analyst, qualified technician and medical practitioner is in s. 258(1)(*e*) to (*i*) and (6) and (7).

The punishment for these offences is set out in s. 255. Evidence that the accused's blood alcohol level exceeded .16 at the time of the offence is deemed to be an aggravating factor, for purposes of sentencing, under s. 255.1. Where the prosecution elects to proceed by indictment on this offence then the accused may elect his mode of trial pursuant to s. 536(2). Where the prosecution elects to proceed by way of summary conviction then the trial of this offence is conducted by a summary conviction court pursuant to Part XXVII. In either case, release pending trial is determined by s. 515, although the accused is eligible for release by a peace officer under s. 496, 497 or by the officer in charge under s. 498. Where the accused is charged with impaired operation causing death or causing bodily harm under s. 255(2) or (3) then he has an election as to mode of trial pursuant to s. 536(2) and release pending trial is determined by s. 515. An accused found guilty of this offence is subject to an order prohibiting him from operating a motor vehicle, vessel, aircraft or railway equipment, as the case may be. The length of the order is as follows: for a first offence, during a period of not more than three years and not less than one year; for a second offence, during a period of not more than five years and not less than two years; for each subsequent offence, during a period of not less than three years plus any period to which the offender is sentenced to imprisonment. For prohibition order where the accused is convicted of the offence of impaired causing bodily harm or causing death, see notes under s. 255. The procedure respecting the making of that order of prohibition is found in s. 260.

SYNOPSIS

This section makes it an offence for a person to operate a motor vehicle or vessel, operate or assist in the operation of an aircraft or railway equipment or have the care or control of a motor vehicle, vessel, aircraft or railway equipment, if that peron's ability to do so is impaired by alcohol or a drug or if that person has a concentration of alcohol in the blood exceeding eighty milligrams of alcohol in one hundred millilitres of blood. The fact that the motor vehicle, vessel, aircraft or railway equipment is not in motion is not a defence. Subsection (2) makes it clear that impairment can arise from a combination of alcohol and a drug.

ANNOTATIONS

Proof of care or control / *Also see notes under s. 258(1)(a)* – An intention to drive is not an element of the care or control offence. Care or control may be exercised without such intent where the accused performs some act or series of acts involving the use of the car, its fittings or equipment, whereby the vehicle may unintentionally be set in motion creating the danger this section is designed to prevent: *R. v. Ford*, [1982] 1 S.C.R. 231, 65 C.C.C. (2d) 392 (7:2).

"Care or control" signifies: (1) an intentional course of conduct associated with a motor vehicle; (2) by a person whose ability to drive is impaired, or whose blood alcohol level exceeds the legal limit; (3) in circumstances that create a realistic risk of danger to persons or property. The risk of danger must be realistic and not just theoretically possible. Parliament's objective in enacting this provision was to prevent the risk of danger to public safety that normally arises from the mere combination of alcohol and automobile. Conduct that presents no such risk falls outside the intended reach of the offence. Here, the judge did not err in acquitting an accused who fell asleep in his truck with the engine running while waiting for a taxi: *R. v. Boudreault*, [2012] 3 S.C.R. 157, 290 C.C.C. (3d) 222.

To convict the accused of the care or control offence, it is not necessary to establish some overt action on the part of the accused to indicate that he was involved with the vehicle in a way as to cause danger to the public. Where the accused had the immediate capacity and means of operating the vehicle, there existed the risk that he would put it in motion and become a danger to the public, even though at the time he was found by the police he was asleep in the front seat of the vehicle: *R. v. Diotte* (1991), 64 C.C.C. (3d) 209 (N.B.C.A.). See also *R. v. Rousseau* (1997), 121 C.C.C. (3d) 571 (Que. C.A.).

The intent to drive or the presence of danger is an essential element of the offence. If the person's interaction with the vehicle did not pose an immediate or potential risk of harm or risk to public safety, a conviction cannot be made out: *R. v. Mallery* (2008), 231 C.C.C. (3d) 203, 59 C.R. (6th) 209 (N.B.C.A.).

A course of conduct associated with the vehicle that would involve the risk of putting the vehicle in motion can constitute care and control. Accordingly, care and control was established where the accused was asleep in the driver's seat with the keys on the floor of the vehicle: *R. v. Pilon* (1998), 131 C.C.C. (3d) 236, 115 O.A.C. 324 (C.A.).

The mere fact that an individual is a custodian of a vehicle does not alone constitute care and control. There must be a risk of danger that the car might be put in motion or of other danger. Where there is no risk that the vehicle will unintentionally be set in motion or any other risk, care and control is not established: *R. v. Decker* (2002), 162 C.C.C. (3d) 503, 2 C.R. (6th) 352 (Nfld. C.A.), leave to appeal to S.C.C. refused [2004] 4 S.C.R. vi, 231 Nfld. & P.E.I.R. 355*n*.

Motor vehicle – The decision of the Supreme Court of Canada in *R. v. Saunders*, [1967] 3 C.C.C. 278, 1 C.R.N.S. 249, that the definition of a motor vehicle in s. 2 contemplates a kind of vehicle, not whether a vehicle is actually operable or effectively functionable, now renders irrelevant all the previous decisions on when a motor vehicle is a motor vehicle in spite of internal or external conditions causing malfunctioning or immobilization of the vehicle.

An automobile which is out of gas is still a motor vehicle for the purposes of this section: *R. v. Lloyd*, [1988] 4 W.W.R. 423, 6 M.V.R. (2d) 240 (Sask. C.A.).

On this issue, also see the note by J. Watson, "Proving the Actus Reus of Motor Vehicle Crimes: What is a Motor Vehicle?", 21 M.V.R. (2d) 93.

Operation of vessel – In *R. v. Wade* (1975), 23 C.C.C. (2d) 572 (N.S. Co. Ct.), it was considered that a dragger immobilized by its fishing nets being entangled around other vessels' mooring cables was not then navigated or operated by its captain.

However, a person "operates" a vessel which is merely drifting with its engine turned off: *R. v. Ernst* (1979), 50 C.C.C. (2d) 320, 34 N.S.R. (2d) 318 (C.A.).

Proof of impairment (para. (*a*)) – The *Criminal Code* does not prescribe any special test for determining impairment such as a "marked departure" from normal behaviour. If the evidence of impairment establishes any degree of impairment ranging from slight to great, the offence is made out: *R. v. Stellato* (1993), 78 C.C.C. (3d) 380, 18 C.R. (4th) 127 (Ont. C.A.), affd [1994] 2 S.C.R. 478*n*, 90 C.C.C. (3d) 160*n*.

It cannot be assumed, however, that, where a person's functional ability is affected in some respects by the consumption of alcohol, his ability to drive is also automatically impaired. Where the proof of impairment consists of observations of conduct, in most cases, if the conduct is a slight departure from normal conduct, it would be unsafe to conclude beyond a reasonable doubt that the ability to drive was impaired by alcohol: *R. v. Andrews* (1996), 104 C.C.C. (3d) 392, 110 W.A.C. 182 (Alta. C.A.), leave to appeal to S.C.C. refused 106 C.C.C. (3d) vi, 135 W.A.C. 79*n*.

An accused may be convicted of this offence although his impaired condition is due partly to fatigue and partly to the consumption of alcohol: *R. v. Pelletier* (1989), 51 C.C.C. (3d) 161 (Sask. Q.B.).

On a charge of impaired driving the trial judge was entitled to take the certificate of analysis into account as part of the whole case and as evidence that prior to being stopped the accused most likely had consumed alcohol. In so doing the judge was not drawing on any technical or special knowledge: *R. v. Dinelle* (1986), 44 M.V.R. 109 (N.S.C.A.).

The word "drug" includes not only drugs in the medicinal sense, but any substance consumed which will bring about the impairment contemplated by this section. In particular the word includes the ingredient in glue which produces a "high" from glue sniffing and which may impair a person's ability to drive: *R. v. Marionchuk* (1978), 42 C.C.C. (2d) 573, 4 C.R. (3d) 178 (Sask. C.A.).

Admissibility of opinion evidence of impairment – A qualified breathalyzer technician is not, without further credentials, capable of relating the defendant's reading to his ability to operate a motor vehicle: *R. v. Edson* (1976), 30 C.C.C. (2d) 470, [1976] 3 W.W.R. 695 (B.C. Co. Ct.).

A layman or police officer may give his opinion based on his own observations as to whether or not the accused's ability to drive was impaired. However, a police officer's opinion is entitled to no special regard: *R. v. Graat*, [1982] 2 S.C.R. 819, 2 C.C.C. (3d) 365 (7:0).

R. v. Graat, supra, was applied in *R. v. Polturak* (1988), 9 M.V.R. (2d) 89, 90 A.R. 158 (C.A.), upholding the admission of the opinion of police officers with experience in narcotics control that the accused's ability to drive was impaired by drugs or drugs and alcohol.

***Mens rea* of impairment offence** – In *R. v. King*, [1962] S.C.R. 746, 133 C.C.C. 1, an appeal by the Crown, affirming 129 C.C.C. 391, 34 C.R. 264, the question before the court was whether *mens rea* relating to both the act of driving and to the state of being impaired by alcohol or a drug is an essential ingredient of the offence of impaired driving. Ritchie J. (Martland J., concurring), decided that neither necessary implication nor express language disclosed any intention of Parliament to rule out *mens rea* as an essential ingredient of this offence but was of the opinion that (at p. 19 C.C.C.):

> . . . that element need not necessarily be present in relation both to the act of driving and to the state of being impaired in order to make the offence complete. That is to say, that a man who becomes impaired as the result of taking a drug on medical advice without knowing its effect cannot escape liability if he became aware of his impaired condition before he started to drive his car just as a man who did not appreciate his impaired condition when he started to drive cannot escape liability on the ground that his lack of appreciation was brought about by voluntary consumption of liquor or drug.

The *mens rea* for the care or control offence is the intent to assume care or control after the voluntary consumption of alcohol or a drug and the *actus reus* is the act of assumption of care or control when the voluntary consumption of alcohol or a drug has impaired the ability to drive: *R. v. Toews*, [1985] 2 S.C.R. 119, 21 C.C.C. (3d) 24 (7:0).

Thus, the necessary *mens rea* was established where the accused voluntarily consumed a sedative drug which he knew might impair his ability to drive even if the accused as a result of previous experience believed the drug would not take effect until he completed driving: *R. v. Murray* (1985), 22 C.C.C. (3d) 502, 36 M.V.R. 12 (Ont. C.A.). In addition, the intent to become voluntarily intoxicated includes recklessness where the accused was aware that impairment could result, but persisted despite the risk: *R. v. Mavin* (1997), 119 C.C.C. (3d) 38, 154 Nfld. & P.E.I.R. 242 (Nfld. C.A.).

Drunkenness is no defence to the charge of impaired care or control under para. (*a*). The only mental element involved in the offence is voluntary intoxication: *R. v. Penno*, [1990] 2 S.C.R. 865, 59 C.C.C. (3d) 344 (7:0).

Even where the accused is in a state of automatism or "near automatism" brought about by the consumption of intoxicants, it would seem that this is no defence to the charge: *R. v. Honish* (1991), 68 C.C.C. (3d) 329 (Alta. C.A.).

***Mens rea* of "over 80" offence [para. (*b*)]** – The requirement and the actual proof of *mens rea* are two different matters. This offence requires *mens rea,* but once there is established driving with an excessive amount of alcohol in his system the defendant then faces the rebuttable presumption of *mens rea* which may be negated by defence evidence. A mistaken belief by the accused, based on an inaccurate chart as to the progressive absorption of alcohol into the blood, that his blood-alcohol would not exceed .08 was held not to be a defence to this charge: *R. v. Penner* (1974), 16 C.C.C. (2d) 334, [1974] 3 W.W.R. 176 (Man. C.A.).

The requisite *mens rea* or fault for this offence is supplied by proof of the accused's voluntary consumption of alcohol. It is not necessary to prove that the accused either knew or was reckless to the fact that his blood-alcohol exceeded the legal limit: *R. v. MacCannell* (1980), 54 C.C.C. (2d) 188, 6 M.V.R. 19 (Ont. C.A.). Folld: *R. v. Lynch* (1982), 69 C.C.C. (2d) 88, 38 Nfld. & P.E.I.R. 267 (Nfld. C.A.): *R. v. Patterson* (1982), 69 C.C.C. (2d) 274, 15 M.V.R. 283 (N.S.C.A.).

Proof of "over 80" offence – Where the Crown is unable to rely on the presumption in s. 258(1)(*c*) the court cannot take judicial notice of the progressive absorption of alcohol into the blood to prove that a blood-alcohol reading which exceeded .08 at the time of the test exceeded .08 at the time of the offence: *R. v. Stevenson* (1972), 14 C.C.C. (2d) 412 (B.C.C.A.); *R. v. McBurney* (1974), 21 C.C.C. (2d) 207, [1975] 2 W.W.R. 448 (Man. C.A.); *R. v. Chandok* (1973), 12 C.C.C. (2d) 500 (N.S. Co. Ct.); *R. v. Wolff* (1976), 31 C.C.C. (2d) 337 (Ont. H.C.J.). In the latter case it was also held that the evidence that the accused displayed obvious signs of impairment likewise did not prove the offence under this section, following *R. v. Coach* (1971), 4 C.C.C. (2d) 333, [1971] 3 O.R. 466 (H.C.J.). Similarly, *R. v. Robertson* (1979), 47 C.C.C. (2d) 159 (B.C.C.A.).

Where the *viva voce* evidence of the intoxilyzer technician was adduced instead of, or in addition to, the filing of the certificate, there was no need to rely on the presumption of accuracy. Accordingly, the trial judge did not err in considering the breathalyzer results when assessing the credibility of the defence: *R. v. Chow* (2010), 260 C.C.C. (3d) 289 (Ont. C.A.).

In *R. v. Perossa* (1974), 19 C.C.C. (2d) 553 (B.C.S.C.), a conviction for this offence was upheld despite the lack of expert evidence relating the results of analysis of a blood sample back to the time of the offence where there was evidence of erratic driving and a high degree of intoxication. In view of this other evidence the court distinguished *R. v. Stevenson, supra.*

When the toxicologist's opinion that the accused's blood-alcohol level exceeded 80 mg of alcohol at the time of driving was dependent on the assumption that the accused had not been drinking large quantities of alcohol immediately before being stopped, the Crown was required to prove the lack of such drinking by the accused. There was no burden on the accused to show that he had not been drinking immediately before being stopped nor was there a basis to create a presumption that in absence of evidence to the contrary, the accused is deemed not to have consumed large quantities of alcohol immediately before providing a breath sample. The trial judge was entitled, however, to consider the circumstantial evidence in determining whether the Crown had met the burden and could take into account the accused's failure to testify about what would be an unusual drinking pattern: *R. v. Grosse* (1996), 107 C.C.C. (3d) 97, 91 O.A.C. 40 (C.A.), leave to appeal to S.C.C. refused 112 C.C.C. (3d) vi, 99 O.A.C. 239*n*.

In *R. v. Paszczenko*; *R. v. Lima* (2010), 81 C.R. (6th) 97 (Ont. C.A.), the Court of Appeal reiterated that the trier of fact is entitled to make a "common sense" inference of no "bolus drinking" where the accused has not pointed to anything in the evidence to suggest such an unusual drinking pattern. The court was also "inclined to the view" that courts are entitled to take judicial notice of the fact that (a) the majority of human beings eliminate alcohol in a range of 10-20 milligrams of alcohol per 100 millilitres of blood per hour, and (b) after rising relatively quickly during the first 30 minutes or so after the last drink, a person's BAC generally hits a plateau for a period of up to two hours, during which time the absorption rate and the elimination rate remain about equal and the BAC neither rises nor falls. See also: *R. v. Saul* (2015), 322 C.C.C. (3d) 356 (B.C.C.A.).

Pursuant to this section, breathalzyer results must be determined on the basis of milligrams of alcohol per 100 ml of blood and cannot be expressed as "grams percent": *R. v. Nyman* (1998), 131 C.C.C. (3d) 124, 113 O.A.C. 356 (C.A.).

In *R. v. Doell* (2007), 221 C.C.C. (3d) 336, the Saskatchewan Court of Appeal held that *R. v. Boucher* (2005), 202 C.C.C. (3d) 34 (S.C.C.), stood for the proposition that breath test results cannot be used to assess the credibility of a witness in the context of the inquiry into whether the accused has presented evidence to the contrary. It did not address, however, the question of whether those test results may be considered in determining if a .08 offence has been established. If evidence to the contrary is adduced and the presumption set aside, both breathalyzer and roadside test results may nonetheless be considered in determining whether an offence has been made out.

Included offences – The care or control offence is included in the offence of driving and thus an accused charged with the driving offence may be convicted of the care and control offence: *R. v. Drolet* (1988), 20 Q.A.C. 94, [1989] R.J.Q. 295 (C.A.), affd [1990] 2 S.C.R. 1107*n*. Where the charge is care or control evidence that the accused was in fact driving may be sufficient to sustain the conviction on the charge as laid: *R. v. Coultis* (1982), 66 C.C.C. (2d) 385, 29 C.R. (3d) 189 (Ont. C.A.); *R. v. Pielle* (1982), 18 M.V.R. 46 (B.C.S.C.).

There is generally nothing unfair about the Crown changing its theory of the case during trial and seeking a conviction on the included offence of care and control where the driving offence was originally charged: *R. v. Pawluk* (2017), 357 C.C.C. (3d) 86 (Ont. C.A.).

However, where the Crown's case on a charge of care or control is based on evidence of the finding of the accused in the driver's seat, a conviction may not be entered on an admission by the accused that at some time prior to his arrest he had been driving the vehicle. The Crown is bound by the case it presents to the court and when it fails to prove that case, the accused having successfully rebutted the presumption in s. 258(1)(*a*), it cannot ask for a conviction of another offence disclosed by the accused's own evidence: *R. v. Pendleton* (1982), 1 C.C.C. (3d) 228 (Ont. C.A.). This holding has been attenuated, however, *R. v. Khawaja* (2010), 273 C.C.C. (3d) 415 (Ont. C.A.), affd [2012] 3 S.C.R. 555, 290 C.C.C. (3d) 361.

Where the trial judge finds that although the accused has consumed alcohol he has a reasonable doubt as to her impairment and thus acquits on the charge contrary to para. (*a*), he may still convict on the charge under para. (*b*). In such circumstances the doctrine of issue estoppel has no application so as to bar a conviction on the latter offence: *R. v. Casson* (1976), 30 C.C.C. (2d) 506 (Alta. C.A.).

Multiple convictions – A motorist cannot be convicted of both offences under this section occurring at one time: *R. v. Houchen* (1976), 31 C.C.C. (2d) 274 (B.C.C.A.) (2:1); *R. v. Boivin* (1976), 34 C.C.C. (2d) 203 (Que. C.A.).

A motorist may not choose which of the over-80 or ability-impaired charges he will plead guilty to; the court will first dispose of the charge on which the Crown seeks a conviction: *R. v. Butler* (1975), 27 C.C.C. (2d) 26 (B.C. Prov. Ct.).

A 24-hour driving suspension imposed under provincial legislation does not bar a conviction under this section although the suspension and the charge under this section arose out of the same incident: *R. v. Art* (1987), 39 C.C.C. (3d) 563 (B.C.C.A.).

Charging offence – In *R. v. Hawryluk,* [1967] 3 C.C.C. 356 (Sask. C.A.), an information that followed the wording of the statute, "while his ability to drive a motor vehicle was impaired by alcohol or a drug, did unlawfully drive a motor vehicle", was held to be valid as it only charged one of the two alternative offences of driving while impaired or having the care or control of a motor vehicle while impaired, and as each offence may be committed in more than one way it is proper to set out both factors, "by alcohol or drug", in the charge.

253.1 [*Repealed*, 2018, c. 21, s. 14.]

254. [*Repealed*, 2018, c. 21, s. 14.]

Editor's Note: The authority of the police to demand breath samples, blood samples and bodily substances (and to require an individual to perform physical coordination tests or submit to drug evaluation) in the investigation of drug- and alcohol-related driving offences is now set out in ss. 320.27 and 320.28. The annotations below should be approached with caution in relation to the new provisions, especially in light of s. 320.27(2) which now allows for an approved screening device breath sample demand to be made even in absence of a reasonable suspicion of the presence of alcohol.

REGULATIONS: ORDER APPROVING BLOOD SAMPLE CONTAINERS

Approved Containers

1. The following containers, being containers of a kind that is designed to receive a sample of blood of a person for analysis, are hereby approved as suitable, in respect of blood samples, for the purposes of section 258 of the *Criminal Code*:

(a) Vacutainer® XF947;
(b) BD Vacutainer TM 367001;
(c) Vacutainer® 367001;
(d) Tri-Tech Inc. TUG10;
(e) BD Vacutainer® REF 367001; and
(f) TRITECHFORENSICS TUG10.

Repeal

2. The Approved Blood Sample Container Order is repealed.

Coming into force

3. This Order comes into force on the day on which it is registered. **SOR/2005-37; SOR/2010-64, s. 1; SOR/2012-60, s. 1.**

REGULATIONS: APPROVED BREATH ANALYSIS INSTRUMENTS ORDER

Approved Instruments

2. The following instruments, each being an instrument of a kind that is designed to receive and make an analysis of a sample of the breath of a person in order to measure the concentration of alcohol in the blood of that person, are hereby approved as suitable for the purposes of section 258 of the *Criminal Code*:

(a) [*Repealed*, SOR/2012-237, s. 1(1).]
(b) [*Repealed*, SOR/2012-237, s. 1(1).]
(c) [*Repealed*, SOR/2012-237, s. 1(1).]
(d) [*Repealed*, SOR/2013-107, s. 1(1).]
(e) [*Repealed*, SOR/2013-107, s. 1(1).]
(f) [*Repealed*, SOR/2013-107, s. 1(1).]
(g) [*Repealed*, SOR/2013-107, s. 1(1).]
(h) Intoxilyzer® 5000C;
(i) [*Repealed*, SOR/2012-237, s. 1(2).]
(j) [*Repealed*, SOR/2013-107, s. 1(2).]
(k) BAC Datamaster C;
(l) Alco-Sensor IV-RBT IV;
(m) [*Repealed*, SOR/2013-107, s. 1(3).]
(n) Alco-Sensor IV/RBT IV-K;
(o) Alcotest 7110 MKIII Dual C;
(p) Intoxilyzer® 8000 C;
(q) DataMaster DMT-C; and
(r) Intox EC/IR II.

SI/85-201, *Can. Gaz. Part II*, 27/11/85, p. 4692; SI/92-105, *Can. Gaz. Part II*, 17/6/92, p. 2577; SI/92-167, *Can. Gaz. Part II*, 23/9/92, p. 3807; SI/93-61, *Can. Gaz., Part II*, 5/5/93, p. 2198; SI/93-175, *Can. Gaz., Part II*, 8/9/93, p. 3714; SOR/94-422, *Can. Gaz., Part II*, 15/6/94, p. 2451; SOR/94-572, *Can. Gaz., Part II*, 7/9/94, p. 3132; SOR/95-312, *Can. Gaz., Part II*, 12/7/95, p. 1885; SOR/2000-200, *Can. Gaz., Part II*, s. 1; SOR/2002-99, *Can. Gaz., Part II*, s. 1; SOR/2007-197, s. 1; SOR/2008-106, s. 1; SOR/2009-205, s. 1; SOR/2012-237, s. 1; SOR/2013-107, s. 1.

REGULATIONS: APPROVED SCREENING DEVICES ORDER

Approved Screening Devices

2. The following devices, each being a device of a kind that is designed to ascertain the presence of alcohol in the blood of a person, are hereby approved for the purposes of section 254 of the *Criminal Code*:

(*a*) Alcolmeter S-L2;

(*b*) Alco-Sûr;

(*c*) Alcotest® 7410 PA3;

(*d*) Alcotest® 7410 GLC;

(*e*) Alco-Sensor IV DWF;

(*f*) Alco-Sensor IV PWF;

(*g*) Intoxilyzer 400D;

(*h*) Alco-Sensor FST; and

(*i*) Dräger Alcotest 6810.

SI/85-200, *Can. Gaz. Part II*, 27/11/85, p. 4691; SI/88-136, *Can. Gaz. Part II*, 28/9/88, p. 4074; SOR/93-263, *Can. Gaz., Part II*, 2/6/93, p. 2403; SOR/94-193, *Can. Gaz., Part II*, 9/3/94, p. 1232; SOR/94-423, *Can. Gaz., Part II*, 15/6/94, p. 2453; SOR/96-81, *Can. Gaz., Part II*, 24/1/96, p. 609; SOR/97-116, *Can. Gaz., Part II*, 53/97, p. 649; SOR/2009-239, s. 1; SOR/2011-313, s. 1; SOR/2012-61, s. 1.

CROSS-REFERENCES

The terms "peace officer", "motor vehicle" and "railway equipment" are defined in s. 2. The terms "aircraft", "vessel" and "operates" are defined in s. 214. The procedure for obtaining a warrant to obtain blood samples is set out in s. 256. The adverse inference respecting the impaired offence for failing to comply with a demand under this section is found in s. 258(3). The presumptions respecting the accused's blood alcohol level arising from analysis of a breath sample or blood sample are found in s. 258(1)(*c*), (*d*) and (*d*.1). Procedure for admission of certificates of an analyst, qualified technician and medical practitioner is set out in s. 258(1)(*e*) to (*i*) and (6) and (7). Note s. 258(4) which provides for summary application to a judge within 3 months of the date the blood sample was taken for an order releasing one of the samples for the purpose of testing by the defence.

The punishment for this offence is set out in s. 255. Under s. 255(2.2) and (3.2), an accused who is convicted of the offence under s. 254(5) and knew or ought to have known that operation of the vehicle caused an accident resulting in bodily harm or death, as the case may be, is liable to the same penalty as if the offender were convicted of impaired operation causing bodily harm or death, *i.e.* 10 years of life imprisonment, as the case may be. Where the prosecution elects to proceed by indictment on this offence then the accused may elect his mode of trial pursuant to s. 536(2). Where the prosecution elects to proceed by way of summary conviction then the trial of this offence is conducted by a summary conviction court pursuant to Part XXVII. In either case, release pending trial is determined by s. 515, although the accused is eligible for release by a peace officer under s. 496, 497 or by the officer in charge under s. 498. An accused found guilty of this offence is subject to an order prohibiting him from operating a motor vehicle, vessel, aircraft or railway equipment, as the case may be, where the accused was operating or had the care or control of a motor vehicle, vessel, aircraft or railway equipment or was assisting in the operation of an aircraft or of railway equipment at the time the offence was committed or within the two hours preceding that time. The length of the order is as follows: for a first offence, during a period of not more than three years and not less than three months; for a second offence, during a period of not more than three years and not less than six months; for each subsequent offence, during a period of not more than three years and not less than one year. The procedure respecting the making of that order of prohibition is found in s. 260. Pursuant to s. 255.1, evidence that the accused's blood alcohol level exceeded .160 at the time when the offence was committed is deemed to be an aggravating factor on sentencing. Note s. 732.1(3)(*g*.1) and (*g*.2), which allow for imposition of terms of probation that the offender attend for curative treatment in relation to the consumption of alcohol and drugs and participate in an alcohol ignition interlock device program.

Related offences: s. 249, dangerous operation; s. 252, failing to stop at scene of accident; ss. 253 and 255, impaired operation and "over 80"; ss. 220 and 221, criminal negligence causing death or bodily harm.

Section 257 protects the medical practitioner and qualified technician from criminal and civil liability when proceeding under this section. Section 258.1 enacts provisions to protect the privacy of the accused by prohibiting unauthorized use of bodily samples taken under this section and unauthorized disclosure of the results of physical coordination tests.

SYNOPSIS

Subsection (1) defines certain terms relating to demands for breath and blood and samples of other bodily substances. Subsection 254(2) provides that a peace officer may make a demand requiring a person to take part in certain investigatory tests if the officer has reasonable grounds to suspect that the person has alcohol or a drug in their body and that the person operated or had care or control of a motor vehicle, vessel, aircraft or railway equipment within the preceding three hours. If the suspicion relates to a drug, the officer may demand that the person perform physical coordination tests prescribed by regulations made under s. 254.1. If the suspicion relates to alcohol, the officer may demand that the person perform the coordination tests and/or supply a breath sample in an approved screening device. A peace officer may make a video recording of the physical coordination tests.

Under subsec. (3), if the peace officer has reasonable grounds to believe that a person is or has, during the preceding three hours, committed an offence under s. 253 by reason of the consumption of alcohol, the peace officer may make a demand of that person for breath samples (the breathalyzer or intoxilyzer demand). When the peace officer has reasonable grounds to believe that the physical condition of the person is such that he or she may not be capable of providing the breath sample or that it would be impractical to do so, a demand may be made that blood samples be taken by or under the supervision of a qualified physician as long as the physician is satisfied that this procedure would not endanger the life of the person (blood demand).

Subsection (3.1) sets up a system for detecting impairment by drugs or a combination of drugs and alcohol. If the peace officer has reasonable grounds to believe that a person is or has, during the preceding three hours, committed an offence under s. 253(1)(*a*) (impaired operation or care or control) by reason of the consumption of drugs or drugs and alcohol, the peace officer may make a demand that the person submit to an evaluation by an evaluating officer. If the evaluating officer has reasonable grounds to suspect that the person has alcohol in their body, the officer may make a demand for breath samples (subsec. (3.3)). If the evaluating officer has reasonable grounds to believe that the person's ability to operate is impaired by drugs or a combination of drugs and alcohol, the evaluating officer may make a demand that the person provide (a) oral fluid or urine, or (b) samples of blood.

Samples of blood may only be taken by or under the direction of a qualified medical practitioner who is satisfied that taking the samples would not endanger the person's life or health (subsec. (4)).

It is an offence to refuse to comply with a peace officer's demand under this section, pursuant to subsec. (5). Pursuant to subsec. (6), an accused can only be convicted of one offence under this section arising out of the same transaction.

ANNOTATIONS

Subsection (1) / Validity of designation of technician – Designation as a qualified technician by the Deputy Attorney General is valid: *R. v. Bourassa* (1972), 6 C.C.C. (2d) 414 (B.C.S.C.).

The designation in Ontario of a person as a qualified technician by the provincial Solicitor General is valid by virtue of the combined operation of this subsection and s. 2 which defines "Attorney General" in part as the Attorney General or Solicitor General of the province: *R. v.*

Wilkes; R. v. Foshay (1979), 48 C.C.C. (2d) 362 (Ont. C.A.), leave to appeal to S.C.C. refused March 17, 1980.

A police officer designated as a qualified technician under the former s. 237 but who was not redesignated under this section, when many other technicians were, was not a qualified technician within the meaning of this section. Section 44(*a*) of the *Interpretation Act*, R.S.C. 1985, c. I-21, providing that a person acting under a former enactment shall continue to act, as if appointed under the new enactment, until another is appointed in his stead, could not apply in view of the designation under this section of other technicians: *R. v. Schemenauer* (1987), 34 C.C.C. (3d) 573 (Sask. C.A.).

In *R. v. Novis* (1987), 36 C.C.C. (3d) 275 (Ont. C.A.), s. 44 of the *Interpretation Act* was applied to find that the officer's original designation under former s. 237 was valid until his new designation became effective. There was, however, no evidence that another officer had been appointed in his stead.

By virtue of s. 7 of the *Interpretation Act*, R.S.C. 1985, c. I-21, a designation is valid although made prior to proclamation of this section. The effect of s. 7 is that the designation takes effect when the new provision is proclaimed in force: *R. v. Janes* (1987), 40 C.C.C. (3d) 209 (N.S.C.A.).

The flaw in the designation of an officer which referred to him as a "qualified technician" when in fact he was qualified to take only breath samples and not blood samples did not affect the admissibility of his certificate in relation to analysis of breath samples: *R. v. MacDonald* (1986), 65 Nfld. & P.E.I.R. 72, 46 M.V.R. 76 (P.E.I.S.C.), affd 39 C.C.C. (3d) 189, 7 M.V.R. (2d) 128 (P.E.I.C.A.). Similarly: *R. v. Janes, supra.*

Proof of designation of technician – If the designation by the Attorney General of a breathalyzer officer as a "qualified technician" is sought to be proved by Gazette the publication must be before the court; otherwise the officer's own evidence of his appointment being made and gazetted is, in the absence of evidence to the contrary, sufficient: *R. v. Leavitt* (1971), 5 C.C.C. (2d) 141 (Alta. S.C.).

Judicial notice must be taken of a designation made by the Attorney General and duly gazetted: *R. v. Betts* (1977), 34 C.C.C. (2d) 562 (N.B.S.C.).

The qualified technician's *viva voce* evidence that he had been so qualified by the Attorney General and his appointment had been gazetted establishes a rebuttable presumption of his position. In addition judicial notice may be taken that the Borkenstein breathalyzer is an approved instrument: *R. v. Leblanc* (1972), 7 C.C.C. (2d) 525 (N.S.C.A.).

Production of an original letter of appointment purportedly signed by the Attorney General is proof in the absence of any evidence to the contrary that the breathalyzer operator was a qualified technician: *R. v. Baskier* (1971), 4 C.C.C. (2d) 552 (Sask. C.A.).

Testimony by the breathalyzer operator that he was a qualified technician and production by him of a letter from the Attorney General to that effect is sufficient proof in the absence of evidence to the contrary that he is a qualified technician. The designation need not be proved by production of the provincial Gazette containing the designation: *R. v. Gettle* (1977), 34 C.C.C. (2d) 569 (B.C.C.A.).

The accused does not satisfy the evidential burden upon him to adduce evidence tending to negative the presumption of due appointment of the technician, which is raised by the Crown showing that the officer had acted in the requisite capacity, merely by cross-examination of the officer directed to show that the officer was unsure who had signed the letter notifying him of his appointment: *R. v. Adams* (1986), 30 C.C.C. (3d) 469 (Sask. C.A.).

The statement in the technician's signed certificate as to his designation as a qualified technician by the Attorney General is evidence of his official character: *R. v. Evanson* (1973), 11 C.C.C. (2d) 275 (Man. C.A.); *R. v. Novis* (1987), 36 C.C.C. (3d) 275 (Ont. C.A.).

Approved instrument – It was held considering a technician's certificate issued pursuant to the former s. 237 that a statement in the technician's certificate that the breath sample was received into a "Borkenstein Breathalyzer, an approved instrument pursuant to section

237(6)" is sufficient proof that the instrument was approved even though the particular model number of the Borkenstein Breathalyzer was not specified in the certificate: *R. v. Gorman* (1976), 32 C.C.C. (2d) 222 (N.B.C.A.); *R. v. Gilbert* (1976), 31 C.C.C. (2d) 251 (Ont. C.A.); *R. v. Pedrotti* (1976), 30 C.C.C. (2d) 575*n* (B.C.S.C.); *R. v. Gregorwich* (1975), 27 C.C.C. (2d) 267 (Alta. C.A.). *Contra: R. v. Foley* (1975), 25 C.C.C. (2d) 514 (Sask. Q.B.).

A breathalyzer Model 900A is an approved instrument notwithstanding that the instrument has been modified to eliminate the instrument's susceptibility to radio frequency interference. Minor alterations to improve an instrument's efficiency do not alter the kind of instrument approved. It is only evidence of a modification to the instrument which goes to the issue of the kind, nature or character of the breathalyzer that should create a reasonable doubt as to whether the particular breathalyzer remains in a class of approved instruments: *R. v. Bebbington* (1988), 43 C.C.C. (3d) 456 (Ont. C.A.).

There is no requirement to adduce expert evidence regarding the reliability of or the manner in which the "Beckman CX-7" analyzes blood. It is sufficient if the expert operating the machine testified that it was capable of making the required measurements or producing the required data and that the machine was in good working order and was properly used: *R. v. Delorey* (2004), 188 C.C.C. (3d) 372 (N.S.C.A.).

Subsection (2) [Physical coordination test demand] – An officer who carries out field sobriety tests pursuant to subsec. (2)(*a*) does not need to be qualified as an expert to testify about how he or she developed reasonable grounds through administering the tests. Neither a "*Mohan*" *voir dire* nor notice under s. 657.3 is required: *R. v. Parada* (2016), 341 C.C.C. (3d) 337 (Sask. C.A.).

Subsection (2) [Approved screening device demand] / Proof of reasonable suspicion – There is no requirement that the officer apprehending the motorist administer the test. A second officer attending the scene subsequently, who forms the requisite belief, may make the demand and administer the test: *R. v. Telford* (1979), 50 C.C.C. (2d) 322 (Alta. C.A.). See also *R. v. Padavattan* (2007), 223 C.C.C. (3d) 221 (Ont. S.C.J.).

However, the officer who makes the demand must also formulate the opinion as to the adequacy of the sample provided by the motorist: *R. v. Shea* (1979), 49 C.C.C. (2d) 497, 3 M.V.R. 134 (P.E.I.S.C.).

Reasonable suspicion can be achieved either by the officer's personal knowledge and observation or the communicated observations of others or a combination of both. It is not necessary for an officer to independently investigate and verify the grounds for reasonable suspicion conveyed to him as long as he subjectively believes them: *R. v. Nahorniak* (2010), 256 C.C.C. (3d) 147 (Sask. C.A.).

The test for making the demand is consumption of alcohol alone, and not its amount or behavioural consequence: *R. v. Gilroy* (1987), 3 M.V.R. (2d) 123 (Alta. C.A.), leave to appeal to S.C.C. refused 87 N.R. 236*n*. Furthermore, the police officer only needs reasonable suspicion that the person operating the vehicle has alcohol in their body and need not believe that the accused has committed any offence: *R. v. Lindsay* (1999), 134 C.C.C. (3d) 159 (Ont. C.A.), or was operating or had care and control of the motor vehicle: *R. v. MacPherson* (2000), 150 C.C.C. (3d) 540 (Ont. C.A.). Similarly, *R. v. Butchko* (2004), 192 C.C.C. (3d) 552 (Sask. C.A.).

There is no requirement for the Crown to prove that the screening device was an approved device before relying on the results of the test to show that the police had reasonable grounds to make a breathalyzer demand: *R. v. Jacob* (2013), 296 C.C.C. (3d) 1 (Man. C.A.).

Breath sample to be provided "forthwith" – The term "forthwith" suggests that the breath sample is to be provided immediately. Thus, a demand made by a police officer, who is without the device and requires half an hour for the device to arrive, does not satisfy the conditions of this subsection. Since the demand was invalid, the accused was under no obligation to comply with it and his failure to comply could not constitute an offence: *R. v. Grant*, [1991] 3 S.C.R. 139, 67 C.C.C. (3d) 268.

In *R. v. Wilson* (1999), 41 M.V.R. (3d) 1 (B.C.C.A.), the court held that the Crown need not prove in every case that an approved screening device is in the possession of the police or immediately available. The mere absence of evidence that an approved screening device was immediately available is not enough to raise any doubt about the validity of the demand where it was made and immediately refused.

The demand did not comply with this subsection where the officer did not have the screening device with him and had to take the accused to the detachment. A total of 14 minutes elapsed between the making of the demand and the time when the device was ready. For the sample to be provided "forthwith" it must be provided immediately, meaning very shortly after the accused has been requested to accompany the officer for the purpose of providing the sample, usually at the side of the road or in the immediate vicinity: *R. v. Cote* (1992), 70 C.C.C. (3d) 280 (Ont. C.A.).

"Forthwith" means immediately or without delay. This provision requires that both the demand and the provision of the sample be made forthwith. In this case, the accused had refused to provide a roadside breath sample but, approximately one hour later at the police station, after speaking to counsel, he decided to do so. The second demand made more than one hour later at the police station was not lawful as it was not made forthwith. As the legitimacy of the breathalyzer demand was based on the legitimacy of the ASD demand, the breathalyzer demand was similarly unlawful: *R. v. Woods*, [2005] 2 S.C.R. 205, 197 C.C.C. (3d) 353.

In unusual circumstances, "forthwith" may be given a more flexible interpretation than its ordinary meaning strictly suggests. However, "forthwith" is not limited to circumstances in which there is sufficient delay such that a realistic opportunity to consult counsel was available but not provided. In considering the immediacy requirement, the court should consider the following: (i) the analysis must be contextual; (ii) the demand must be made by the police officer promptly once he or she forms the reasonable suspicion that the driver has alcohol in his or her body. The immediate requirement commences at the stage of reasonable suspicion; (iii) "forthwith" connotes a prompt demand and an immediate response, although in unusual circumstances a more flexible interpretation may be given. In the end, the time from the formation of reasonable suspicion to the making of the demand to the detainee's response to the demand by refusing or providing a sample must be no more than is reasonably necessary to enable the officer to discharge his or her duty as contemplated by subsec. (2); (iv) the immediacy requirement must take into account all the circumstances including a reasonably necessary delay where breath tests cannot immediately be performed because an ASD is not immediately available, or where a short delay is needed to ensure an accurate result of an immediate ASD test or where a short delay is required due to articulated and legitimate safety concerns. These are delays that are no more than are reasonably necessary to enable the officer to properly discharge his or her duty. Any delay not so justified exceeds the immediacy requirement; (v) one of the circumstances for consideration is whether the police could realistically have fulfilled their obligation to implement the detainee's s. 10(*b*) rights before requiring the sample. If so, the "forthwith" criterion is not met: *R. v. Quansah* (2012), 286 C.C.C. (3d) 307 (Ont. C.A.).

Where there is evidence that the officer knew that the suspect had recently consumed alcohol and expert evidence shows that the subsequent screening test would be unreliable due to the presence of alcohol in the mouth, and the officer knows that the resultant test will provide inaccurate results, the fact that the suspect failed the test could not itself provide the requisite reasonable and probable grounds to make a demand under subsec. (3). However, the officer is not required to wait 15 minutes on each occasion that the officer makes the demand. It is only where the officer had reason to believe that, without waiting, the test may be inaccurate, that the officer needs to delay the administration of the test. Where the particular screening device used has been approved under the statutory scheme, the officer is entitled to rely on its accuracy unless there is credible evidence to the contrary: *R. v. Bernshaw*, [1995] 1 S.C.R. 254, 95 C.C.C. (3d) 193.

The officer is entitled to delay taking the sample where there are grounds to believe that the delay is necessary to obtain accurate results, as where the suspect has recently consumed alcohol: *R. v. Dewald; R. v. Pierman* (1994), 92 C.C.C. (3d) 160 (Ont. C.A.), affd (*R. v. Dewald*) [1996] 1 S.C.R. 68, 103 C.C.C. (3d) 382.

The mere possibility that alcohol has been consumed within the 15 or 20-minute period prior to the administration of the tests does not preclude an officer from relying on the screening device. Where an officer honestly and reasonably concludes that he cannot form an opinion as to whether alcohol has been consumed within the preceding 15 or 20 minutes, he is entitled to rely on the screening device and administer the test without delay: *R. v. Einarson* (2004), 183 C.C.C. (3d) 19 (Ont. C.A.).

The approved screening device does not have to be warmed up and tested as operational before a demand is made: *R. v. Danychuk* (2004), 183 C.C.C. (3d) 337 (Ont. C.A.).

There is a relationship between the practicability of providing samples and the test for impracticability of obtaining a breath sample. The decision in respect of these issues must be made at about the same time and in light of the circumstances that exist at that time. In considering impracticability, the police officer must also consider the time period that might be required to pass before it would be practical to obtain a breath sample rather than a blood sample: *R. v. Salmon* (1999), 141 C.C.C. (3d) 207 (B.C.C.A.), leave to appeal to S.C.C. refused 150 C.C.C. (3d) vi.

Although the officer did not have the device when he stopped the accused, it was brought to him in less than five minutes at which time the demand was made. This was a valid demand and therefore there was no need to inform the accused of his rights under s. 10(*b*) of the Charter: *R. v. Misasi* (1993), 79 C.C.C. (3d) 339 (Ont. C.A.). Similarly: *R. v. Higgins* (1994), 88 C.C.C. (3d) 232, [1994] 3 W.W.R. 305 (Man. C.A.).

The fact that the device was not on the person of the police officer or in his police vehicle when the demand was made or that he did not know the time frame for the arrival of the device does not necessarily take the demand outside subsec. (2). The determination of whether the test has been administered forthwith is not a question of the number of seconds which have elapsed from the time the demand was made to the time the test was administered but rather is a question of the circumstances of the case. It would seem that if the time between the demand and the administering of the test is more than 30 minutes then in most situations the demand would be invalid, but if there are no more than 30 minutes between the demand and administering of the test the court must examine the circumstances: *R. v. Payne* (1994), 91 C.C.C. (3d) 144 (Nfld. C.A.).

In *R. v. Megahy* (2008), 233 C.C.C. (3d) 142, however, the Alberta Court of Appeal held that a delayed demand due to the failure of the officer to have a roadside device available when he was specifically tasked to conduct roadside stops was not forthwith. In particular, the demand was not made until the accused had walked four minutes to the location of the device.

There is no statutory requirement that the word "forthwith" be used when making the demand and its omission does not render the demand invalid. The demand need not be in any particular form provided that it is made clear to the driver that a sample must be provided forthwith. This can be accomplished through words or conduct, including the tenor of the officer's discussion with the accused: *R. v. Torsney* (2007), 217 C.C.C. (3d) 571 (Ont. C.A.), leave to appeal to S.C.C. refused [2007] 2 S.C.R. viii, 218 C.C.C. (3d) vi.

Similarly, in *R. v. Neitsch* (2007), 224 C.C.C. (3d) 91, the Alberta Court of Appeal concluded that there is no need for the officer to use the word "forthwith" in order for the demand to be valid. In determining whether the demand was made "forthwith", all of the contextual circumstances must be considered, not solely the initial conversation between the officer and the accused. In this case, the accused had been stopped, a demand was made, he was immediately taken to a nearby machine, and he did comply, all of which occurred within five minutes. All of the evidence was relevant to conclude that immediacy had been conveyed to the accused.

Validity of stop / random stops, R.I.D.E., etc. – The random stopping of a motor vehicle as part of a well-publicized program to reduce impaired driving such as the R.I.D.E. program is authorized at common law and therefore does not affect the validity of a demand made under this subsection once the officer forms the requisite suspicions: *R. v. Dedman*, [1985] 2 S.C.R. 2, 20 C.C.C. (3d) 97 (4:3).

The random stopping of a motorist for the purposes of a spot check procedure, even if of relatively brief duration, results in a detention within the meaning of s. 9 of the *Charter of Rights and Freedoms* and such detention is arbitrary in violation of s. 9 where, although the stop is done pursuant to statutory [provincial] authority and for lawful purposes there are no criteria for the selection of the drivers to be stopped and subjected to the spot check procedure. However, the authorization of such stops by the provincial legislation is a reasonable limit within the meaning of s. 1 of the Charter, having regard to the importance of highway safety and the role to be played in relation to it by a random stop authority for the purpose of increasing both the detection and the perceived risk of detection of motor vehicle offences, many of which cannot be detected by mere observation of driving. Finally, the demand by the police officer that the motorist surrender his driver's licence and proof of insurance for inspection as required by the provincial legislation does not infringe the motorist's right to be secure against unreasonable search and seizure as guaranteed by s. 8 of the Charter: *R. v. Hufsky*, [1988] 1 S.C.R. 621, 40 C.C.C. (3d) 398 (7:0).

It was held that, although there was no comparable legislation in Saskatchewan to the Ontario legislation considered in *R. v. Hufsky*, *supra*, the common law power to stop vehicles in the course of a checkpoint programme also constituted a reasonable limit on the right guaranteed by s. 9 of the Charter. Thus, evidence obtained as to the accused's blood-alcohol level following such a stop is admissible: *R. v. Burke* (1988), 45 C.C.C. (3d) 434 (Sask. C.A.).

Further, even purely random stops, not part of an organized programme such as the R.I.D.E. program, but permitted by provincial legislation and *semble* common law, are a reasonable limit on the s. 9 Charter rights where the stop is for a legal reason, such as to check the driver's licence and insurance, the driver's sobriety or the mechanical fitness of the vehicle: *R. v. Ladouceur*, [1990] 1 S.C.R. 1257, 56 C.C.C. (3d) 22; *R. v. Wilson*, [1990] 1 S.C.R. 1291, 56 C.C.C. (3d) 142. However, in *R. v. Griffin* (1996), 111 C.C.C. (3d) 490 (Nfld. C.A.), leave to appeal to S.C.C. refused 113 C.C.C. (3d) vi, the Court of Appeal concluded that a roving random stop amounted to an arbitrary detention as it was neither authorized by the *Criminal Code* nor by provincial legislation. The provincial legislation which requires a driver to produce a vehicle license on request by a police officer does not expressly confer a power on the police to stop vehicles and, accordingly, such a random stop power could not be inferred merely as a result of the existence of a statutory duty on a motorist to carry and produce documents and maintain the vehicle properly. Furthermore, the statutory power to direct traffic could not be relied upon to conduct a random stop program.

Right to counsel under s. 10(*b*) of Charter – It was held that a motorist required to supply a breath sample under the predecessor to this subsection is detained within the meaning of s. 10(*b*) of the Charter, but it is a reasonable limitation on the right to retain and instruct counsel as guaranteed by that provision that the motorist supply the breath sample without being entitled to consult counsel: *R. v. Thomsen*, [1988] 1 S.C.R. 640, 40 C.C.C. (3d) 411.

Even where there is a delay to ensure that the officer can obtain a proper sample, as where the officer knows that the suspect has just recently consumed alcohol, the suspect is not entitled to his or her rights under s. 10(*b*) of the Charter: *R. v. Bernshaw*, [1995] 1 S.C.R. 254, 95 C.C.C. (3d) 193.

Where the demand is invalid, it could not constitute a reasonable limit. Accordingly, since the accused was detained, he should have been informed of his rights under s. 10(*b*): *R. v. Grant*, [1991] 3 S.C.R. 139, 67 C.C.C. (3d) 268.

Where the demand was made but the police officer had to wait for the device to arrive some 16 minutes later, the demand was not made forthwith. Accordingly, the police were required to provide the accused with a realistic opportunity to consult with counsel during the time between the issuance of the demand and the arrival of the screening device. The officer had to take reasonable steps to facilitate the accused's access to counsel having regard to the availability of a cell phone or pay phones in the vicinity: *R. v. George* (2004), 187 C.C.C. (3d) 289 (Ont. C.A.).

A "realistic opportunity to consult with counsel" cannot be equated with the mere chance to place a call to a lawyer. The central question was whether, in all of the circumstances, there was a realistic opportunity to the accused, in the space of six or seven minutes, to contact, seek and receive advice from counsel. In this case, denying the accused the opportunity to use a cell phone to call counsel in the early morning hours did not infringe any rights, as there was no realistic possibility that the accused would have been able to locate his counsel at this time: *R. v. Torsney* (2007), 217 C.C.C. (3d) 571 (Ont. C.A.), leave to appeal to S.C.C. refused [2007] 2 S.C.R. viii, 218 C.C.C. (3d) vi.

Note: Some of the cases noted below were decided before the enactment of subsec. (2)(*a*).

Right to counsel / *Sobriety tests other than screening device demand* – A motorist detained and requested to perform physical sobriety tests and answer questions about prior alcohol consumption does not have the right to consult counsel or be informed of that right under s. 10(*b*) of the *Canadian Charter of Rights and Freedoms*. Although there is no express statutory limit on the right to counsel, these measures fall within the scope of reasonable police authority conferred by necessary implication from the operational requirements of the governing provincial and federal legislative provisions — namely the right to stop vehicles under provincial highway traffic legislation and in the police duty to enforce this section and constitute a reasonable limit on the s. 10(*b*) rights: *R. v. Elias; R. v. Orbanski*, [2005] 2 S.C.R. 3, 196 C.C.C. (3d) 481. [Now see s. 254(2)(*a*).]

In *R. v. Milne* (1996), 107 C.C.C. (3d) 118 (Ont. C.A.), leave to appeal to S.C.C. refused 110 C.C.C. (3d) vi, the court concluded that the use of evidence obtained through roadside co-ordination tests is limited to determining whether to make a demand under this section. The right to counsel is not impaired as little as possible if the compelled and self-created incriminatory evidence gathered at the roadside, and before the accused has been informed of the right to counsel, could be used for trial purposes. Admission at trial of the co-ordination test results to prove impairment on a charge of impaired driving would render the trial unfair. See also *R. v. Oldham* (1996), 109 C.C.C. (3d) 392 (N.B.C.A.); and *R. v. Roy* (1997), 117 C.C.C. (3d) 243 (Que. C.A.). Similarly, see *R. v. Sundquist* (2000), 145 C.C.C. (3d) 145 (Sask. C.A.).

As noted above, in *R. v. Elias; R. v. Orbanski*, *supra*, the court held that a motorist requested to perform physical sobriety tests and answer questions about prior alcohol consumption does not have the right to consult counsel or be informed of that right under s. 10(*b*) of the *Canadian Charter of Rights and Freedoms*. In holding that this was a reasonable limit on the s. 10(*b*) rights, the court noted that the Crown conceded that evidence obtained as a result of the motorist's participation without the right to counsel can only be used as an investigative tool and cannot be used as direct evidence to incriminate the driver. The court thus appears to have approved this line of cases.

Similarly, statements given at the roadside are generally inadmissible on a charge of refusing to provide a breath sample under s. 254(5). The admission of any roadside utterances as part of the Crown's case is forbidden, other than on the basis of establishing grounds for the demand or the *actus reus* of the offence: *R. v. Rivera* (2011), 270 C.C.C. (3d) 469 (Ont. C.A.), leave to appeal to S.C.C. refused (2011), 291 O.A.C. 398*n*.

Where an accused is directed to exit the vehicle and answer questions about his alcohol consumption, the officer's observations about how the accused behaves after exiting the car are admissible only to establish grounds for the breathalyzer demand and not to incriminate the accused on an impaired driving charge: *R. v. Visser* (2013), 300 C.C.C. (3d) 388 (B.C.C.A.).

A request by an officer to "blow in his face" was a permissible sobriety test: *R. v. Weintz* (2008), 233 C.C.C. (3d) 365 (B.C.C.A.), leave to appeal to S.C.C. refused 235 C.C.C. (3d) vi.

Provincial legislation which authorizes the police to require a driver to stop for the purpose of determining whether there is sufficient evidence to justify making either an approved screening device demand or a breathalyzer demand constitutes a reasonable limit on the right to counsel. In addition, the right to silence was not infringed as a result of brief police questioning. In the absence of the right to counsel, the right to make an informed choice as to whether to speak to the police requires only that the police not engage in conduct that effectively and unfairly deprives the detainee of the right to choose whether to speak to the police: *R. v. Smith, supra*; *R. v. Housley* (1996), 105 C.C.C. (3d) 83 (Ont. C.A.), leave to appeal to S.C.C. refused 108 C.C.C. (3d) vi.

Effect of other Charter of Rights guarantees – Failure to show the accused the results of the test with the roadside screening device does not constitute a violation of the *Canadian Charter of Rights and Freedoms*: *R. v. Tanner* (1986), 41 M.V.R. 92 (N.S.C.A.).

Section 8 of the Charter does not impose an obligation on the police in all cases to inform a person of the right to refuse to provide a blood or saliva sample: *R. v. Blackstock* (1997), 10 C.R. (5th) 385 (Ont. C.A.).

This subsection does not violate the guarantee to fundamental justice under s. 7 of the Charter despite the lack of criteria in the legislation for determining when the peace officer might reasonably suspect there is alcohol in the person's body. Nor does it authorize an unreasonable search and seizure in violation of s. 8 of the Charter: *R. v. Broadhurst* (1985), 24 C.C.C. (3d) 27, 38 M.V.R. 35 (Ont. H.C.J.); *R. v. Dawson* (1986), 28 C.C.C. (3d) 46 (Alta. Q.B.). *Contra*: *R. v. Ward* (1989), 50 C.C.C. (3d) 376 (P.E.I.S.C.).

Subsection (3)(*a*)(i) [Breath demand] / *Grounds for demand* – Where the accused challenges the admissibility of the breath tet results on the basis of a violation of s. 8 of the Charter, the onus is on the Crown to prove that the officer had reasonable and probable grounds to make the demand because the Crown seeks to rely on breath samples obtained as a result of a warrantless search. There is both a subjective and objective component to establishing reasonable and probable grounds. In this case, the officer's subjective believe was supported objectively by the accused's erratic driving pattern and the various indicia of impairment upon arrest: *R. v. Shepherd* (2009), 245 C.C.C. (3d) 137 (S.C.C.).

The reasonable and probable grounds do not have to be based upon the actual operation of a vehicle as the officer's observations of the motorist's condition may disclose the grounds to give him the necessary belief: *R. v. Conway* (1974), 16 C.C.C. (2d) 233 (P.E.I.S.C.). Further, such grounds may be based on information supplied by third parties, not necessarily fellow police officers, and the officer may testify as to the contents of the conversations which caused him to make the demand: *R. v. Strongquill* (1978), 43 C.C.C. (2d) 232 (Sask. C.A.).

The motorist's failure to pass the test with the roadside screening device pursuant to subsec. (2), itself constitutes grounds for the demand under this section. There is no requirement that the device be proved to have been operating properly: *R. v. Arthurs* (1981), 63 C.C.C. (2d) 572 (Sask. C.A.); *R. v. Beaudette* (1981), 61 C.C.C. (2d) 61 (Man. Co. Ct.); *R. v. Hurley* (1980), 29 Nfld. & P.E.I.R. 263, 9 M.V.R. 46 (Nfld. C.A.); *R. v. Yurechuk*, [1983] 1 W.W.R. 460 (Alta. C.A.); *R. v. Denney* (1985), 34 M.V.R. 111 (N.S.S.C. App. Div.); or even that it is an approved instrument: *R. v. Seymour* (1986), 75 N.S.R. (2d) 174, 45 M.V.R. 132 (S.C. App. Div.).

If the accused does not challenge the admissibility of the results of the Intoxilizer/Breathalyzer analysis on the basis that Charter rights were violated, the Crown is not required to establish that the officer had reasonable and probable grounds to make the demand. Reasonable and probable grounds involve an objective and subjective test. Where the grounds depend upon a "fail" from an approved screening device, the Crown must prove that the officer reasonably believed that he or she was using an approved device. In the absence of credible evidence to the contrary, the officer's testimony that he or she made a demand with an approved screening device is sufficient evidence that the officer had the requisite belief and it is not necessary for the officer to provide the particular model number or otherwise identify the device: *R. v. Gundy* (2008), 231 C.C.C. (3d) 26 (Ont. C.A.).

The fact that the screening device was one day past its scheduled recalibration date did not automatically make it unreasonable for the officer to rely on the device's "fail" reading to make a breath demand: *R. v. Biccum* (2012), 286 C.C.C. (3d) 536 (Alta. C.A.).

Validity of demand – A peace officer is only vested with the authority to make a demand in the territorial jurisdiction in which his appointment is effective: *R. v. Soucy* (1975), 23 C.C.C. (2d) 561 (N.B.S.C. App. Div.); *R. v. Arsenault* (1980), 55 C.C.C. (2d) 38 (N.B.C.A.).

Even though a demand for blood samples has been made and complied with, if thereafter it became practicable to make a demand under this paragraph for breath samples, then such demand may properly be made and the results of analysis of the breath samples is admissible: *R. v. Hiltz* (1988), 82 N.S.R. (2d) 387 (C.A.).

Form of demand – It is unnecessary that the demand be in any particular form provided it is made clear to the accused that he has to give a sample of his breath: *R. v. Nicholson* (1970), 8 C.C.C. (2d) 170 (N.S.S.C. App. Div.); *R. v. Flegel* (1972), 7 C.C.C. (2d) 55 (Sask. C.A.).

The demand under this subsection must be unequivocal and should not leave the accused with any doubt that he must comply, and that it is not a mere request or invitation: *R. v. Boucher* (1986), 73 N.B.R. (2d) 113 (Q.B.).

A demand that the accused supply "a sample" of his breath is a sufficient demand under this subsection despite the fact that the subsection refers to "such samples": *R. v. Rentoul* (1977), 37 C.C.C. (2d) 78 (Alta. S.C.T.D.).

Offence committed within preceding two hours [Note: This section now provides that the officer must form the belief that within the preceeding three hours the accused committed the offence.] – For a demand to be valid, the officer making the demand must form a belief within two hours of the time that he believes that an offence under s. 253 was committed. It is not necessary, however, that the demand be made within the two hour period or that the tests be performed within two hours: *R. v. Deruelle*, [1992] 2 S.C.R. 663, 75 C.C.C. (3d) 118.

Demand to be made "as soon as practicable" – "As soon as practicable" means within a reasonably prompt time, not "as soon as possible". In this case, a 59-minute delay while the officer satisfied himself that the accused had received medical treatment was appropriate: *R. v. Squires* (2002), 166 C.C.C. (3d) 65 (Ont. C.A.).

The failure to make a demand as soon as practicable does not render the evidence inadmissible, although it may afford the accused an argument pursuant to the Charter: *R. v. Forsythe* (2009), 250 C.C.C. (3d) 90 (Man. C.A.), leave to appeal to S.C.C. refused 254 C.C.C. (3d) vi.

Although the general practice is that the demand for a breath sample is made at the scene of the stop, a demand made by the breathalyzer technician at the station may also comply with subsec. (3) provided that he formed reasonable grounds within the three-hour limit and made the demand as soon as practicable thereafter: *R. v. Guenter* (2016), 340 C.C.C. (3d) 351 (Ont. C.A.), leave to appeal to S.C.C. refused 2017 CarswellOnt 705.

Constitutionality of provision – In a lengthy judgment which considered many of the provisions of the *Canadian Bill of Rights* it was held that the compulsory breath test did not offend the Bill and in particular did not offend the provisions with respect to self-crimination, due process and protection of the law: *R. v. Curr*, [1972] S.C.R. 889, 7 C.C.C. (2d) 181 (9:0).

Similarly, these provisions do not offend the *Charter of Rights and Freedoms*: *R. v. Altseimer* (1982), 1 C.C.C. (3d) 7 (Ont. C.A.); *R. v. Gaff* (1984), 15 C.C.C. (3d) 126 (Sask. C.A.), leave to appeal to S.C.C. refused C.C.C. *loc. cit.*

Although this section gives the officer the right to detain the motorist for the purpose of complying with the demand, it is open to the officer to arrest the motorist pursuant to s. 495 and such arrest will not violate the accused's rights against arbitrary detention or imprisonment under s. 9 of the *Charter of Rights and Freedoms* where it was not unreasonable to prevent a repetition or continuation of the offence: *R. v. Cayer* (1988), 66 C.R. (3d) 30, 6 M.V.R. (2d) 1 (Ont. C.A.), or for the accused's own safety: *R. v. Faulkner* (1988), 9 M.V.R. (2d) 137 (B.C.C.A.). Similarly: *R. v. Baker* (1988), 9 M.V.R. (2d) 165 (N.S.C.A.).

As to other cases respecting the effect of a police officer or police department policy to arrest all impaired drivers prior to having them comply with the demand under this subsection and whether an arrest in such circumstances violates s. 9 of the *Charter of Rights and Freedoms*, see notes under s. 495, *infra*.

Right to counsel under s. 10(*b*) of Charter / generally – In *R. v. Therens*, [1985] 1 S.C.R. 613, 18 C.C.C. (3d) 481 (6:2), the court considered whether a motorist to whom a demand under this subsection is made is under detention within the meaning of s. 10(*b*) of the *Canadian Charter of Rights and Freedoms*. Estey J. (Beetz, Chouinard and Wilson JJ. concurring) held that, when the police officers administered the breathalyzer test, the motorist, who was not under arrest, was detained and accordingly prior to his complying with the demand, the police were required to inform him of his right to counsel. Le Dain J. (Dickson C.J.C., McIntyre and Lamer JJ. concurring on this issue) held that the motorist was under detention when the demand was made under this section to accompany the police officer and submit to a breathalyzer test. He was, accordingly, entitled at the time of his detention to be informed of his right to instruct counsel without delay.

The scope of available legal advice in this context is necessarily limited, but it is improper to speculate about the nature of the advice that a detainee would have received and whether the evidence would have been obtained had the right not been infringed. The burden is on the Crown to show that the accused would not have acted any differently had his s. 10(*b*) rights been fully respected and that, accordingly, the evidence would have been obtained irrespective of the breach. One of the purposes of s. 10(*b*) is to provide detainees with an opportunity to make informed choices about their legal rights and obligations. This opportunity is no less significant when breathalyzer charges are involved: *R. v. Bartle*, [1994] 3 S.C.R. 173, 92 C.C.C. (3d) 289; *R. v. Pozniak*, [1994] 3 S.C.R. 310, 92 C.C.C. (3d) 472.

Once it was proved that the accused had been informed of his right to counsel and indicated he understood his rights, there was no obligation on the Crown to establish that he waived the right to consult counsel merely because he had not sought legal advice: *R. v. Shannon* (1987), 34 C.C.C. (3d) 525 (N.W.T.C.A.). Also see: *R. v. Elgie* (1987), 35 C.C.C. (3d) 332 (B.C.C.A.), leave to appeal to S.C.C. refused 82 N.R. 185*n*. Similarly, see *R. v. Baig*, [1987] 2 S.C.R. 537, 37 C.C.C. (3d) 181 (7:0).

In *R. v. Stein* (1989), 14 M.V.R. (2d) 229 (B.C.C.A.), the court adopted the test approved by the Supreme Court of Canada in *R. v. Baig*, [1987] 2 S.C.R. 537, 37 C.C.C. (3d) 181, that absent proof of circumstances indicating that the accused did not understand his right to counsel when he was informed of it, the onus was on the accused to prove that he asked for the right but it was denied or he was denied any opportunity to even ask for it.

There is no burden on the Crown to establish that the accused was advised of his rights under s. 10 of the Charter, rather it is for the accused to put any alleged infringement in issue: *R. v. Roach* (1985), 23 C.C.C. (3d) 262 (Alta. C.A.).

At least where the relevant information can be obtained from the accused motorist, s. 10(*b*) of the Charter does not require that the officer answer counsel's questions before counsel speaks to the accused: *R. v. Fitzsimmons* (2006), 216 C.C.C. (3d) 141 (Ont. C.A.), leave to appeal to S.C.C. refused [2007] 1 S.C.R. ix, 217 C.C.C. (3d) vi.

Right to counsel / duty to inform – The duty imposed upon the police under s. 10(*b*) of the *Canadian Charter of Rights and Freedoms* is to inform the accused of his rights at a time when he was capable of understanding them and not to require the accused to provide potentially incriminating evidence prior to affording the accused a reasonable opportunity to make a reasoned choice to retain legal counsel. Thus the accused's rights under s. 10(*b*) were infringed where the police proceeded with the test under this paragraph at a time that the accused was so drunk that he could not understand what had been said to him: *R. v. Mohl* (1987), 34 C.C.C. (3d) 435 (Sask. C.A.), reversed on other grounds [see note below]; *R. v. D. (P.A.)*, [1987] 6 W.W.R. 175, 58 Sask. R. 48 (C.A.), or where as a result of a concussion he was incapable of understanding his right to counsel: *R. v. McAvena* (1987), 34 C.C.C. (3d) 461 (Sask. C.A.). **Note:** an appeal by the Crown was allowed in the case of *R. v. Mohl*, [1989] 1 S.C.R. 1389, 47 C.C.C. (3d) 575 (9:0), the court holding that, assuming there had been a violation of s. 10(*b*), to admit the evidence of the results of the breathalyzer test would not bring the administration of justice into disrepute within the meaning of s. 24(2) of the Charter. The court adopted the reasons of Sirois J. in the summary conviction appeal court.

The accused's right to be informed of his right to counsel under s. 10(*b*) was infringed where the information was given in English but the accused, to the knowledge of the officer, was French-speaking. The accused testified that he did not understand his right to counsel. Special circumstances existed requiring the officer to reasonably ascertain that the accused's rights were understood by him: *R. v. Vanstaceghem* (1987), 36 C.C.C. (3d) 142 (Ont. C.A.).

The accused's right to counsel is infringed where police inform him that he has the right to retain and instruct counsel without delay and then instruct him that he has the right to make only one telephone call, a statement with the detainee believes to be correct, and he thereupon makes one call which proves to be abortive and which he believes exhausts his right to further endeavour to contact counsel: *R. v. Pavel, supra*.

The accused, having been informed of his right to counsel in relation to the offence of dangerous driving for which he was arrested, need not again be informed of his rights under s. 10(*b*) of the *Charter of Rights and Freedoms* 10 minutes later, prior to the making of a breathalyzer demand under this paragraph: *R. v. MacDonald* (1986), 25 C.C.C. (3d) 572 (N.S.C.A.).

The officer, having advised the accused of his rights under s. 10(*b*) of the *Canadian Charter of Rights and Freedoms* before requiring that he comply with the demand to provide samples for analysis in the screening device, need not repeat the rights prior to requiring compliance with the breathalyzer demand: *R. v. Schechtel* (1985), 32 M.V.R. 316 (Sask. Q.B.).

The two preceding cases should now be read in light of the decision of the Supreme Court of Canada in *R. v. Black*, [1989] 2 S.C.R. 138, 50 C.C.C. (3d) 1 (5:0), where the court held that s. 10(*b*) of the Charter must be considered in light of s. 10(*a*) which requires the police to inform the detainee of the reason for the detention. A detainee can exercise her s. 10(*b*) rights in a meaningful way only if she knows the extent of her jeopardy and thus, the accused's rights under s. 10(*b*) were violated where she was initially arrested on a charge of attempted murder and not reinformed of her rights when the victim died and she was charged with first degree murder. The two charges were "significantly different".

However, in *R. v. Schmautz*, [1990] 1 S.C.R. 398, 53 C.C.C. (3d) 556, it was held that the accused's rights under s. 10(*b*) were not infringed in the following circumstances. The police informed the accused of his right to retain and instruct counsel and gave him the usual police caution after informing him that they were investigating an accident. The accused was not detained at that time. After several questions, the officers made a breathalyzer demand and the accused refused. While the accused was detained when the demand was made there was no requirement that he again be informed of his rights under s. 10(*b*). While there must be a close factual connection or linkage relating the warning to the detention and the reason therefor, here, by giving the accused both the police and Charter warnings at the outset of the short interview, the police alerted the accused that he was suspected and was being investigated in relation to a serious offence. The situation that arose with the breathalyzer demand was directly connected to the investigation. This was not a case where another more serious offence was suddenly being investigated because of changed circumstances external to the encounter. In this case, the demand arose directly and immediately out of the inquiry; it was part of a single incident at which the accused was fully made aware of his rights.

The accused having been informed of his rights under s. 10(*b*) of the Charter at the scene of an accident, following the making of a blood demand, he need not again be informed of his rights at the hospital, although the demand itself was repeated at that time: *R. v. Scott* (1991), 30 M.V.R. (2d) 42, 104 N.S.R. (2d) 112 (C.A.).

In *R. v. Brydges*, [1990] 1 S.C.R. 190, 53 C.C.C. (3d) 330 (7:0), a majority of the court, for the first time, laid down the rule that the police, as a matter of routine, must, as part of the duty to inform the accused of his right to counsel under s. 10(*b*), inform him of the availability of legal aid and duty counsel. The court left open the further question as to the effect this new caution will have on what constitutes due diligence, on the part of the accused, in the exercise of the right to counsel. The court noted, however, that the right to consult counsel of choice upon arrest or detention may now have to be considered, having regard to the immediate availability of duty counsel in most jurisdictions.

The detainee is entitled under the information component of s. 10(*b*) of the Charter to be advised of whatever system for free and immediate, preliminary legal advice exists in the jurisdiction at the time of detention and how such advice can be accessed: *R. v. Pozniak*, [1994] 3 S.C.R. 310, 92 C.C.C. (3d) 472.

The police officer complied with the informational component of the right to counsel when he indicated that the detainee could speak to a lawyer "now" during a roadside stop. The use of this phrase was not misleading and the officer was not required to advise the detainee that this contact would occur at the police station: *R. v. Devries* (2009), 244 C.C.C. (3d) 354 (Ont. C.A.).

Right to consult counsel in private – The right to privacy is inherent in the right to counsel as guaranteed by s. 10(*b*). The accused does not waive that right merely by acquiescing to conditions imposed by the police officer: *R. v. Lepage* (1986), 32 C.C.C. (3d) 171 (N.S.C.A.); *R. v. Rudolph* (1986), 32 C.C.C. (3d) 179 (Alta. Q.B.); *R. v. Young* (1987), 38 C.C.C. (3d) 452 (N.B.C.A.); *R. v. McKane* (1987), 35 C.C.C. (3d) 481 (Ont. C.A.).

The test to determine whether the right to privacy has been violated is whether it was more probable than not that the police did or could overhear the accused's conversation with counsel. The test is objective and requires a determination as to whether there was a real or substantial possibility that the police could have overheard the accused's conversation with counsel: *R. v. O'Donnell* (2004), 185 C.C.C. (3d) 367 (N.B.C.A.).

The right to privacy inherent in s. 10(*b*) of the Charter is the right to consult counsel and does not necessarily start with the attempt to reach a lawyer: *R. v. Standish* (1988), 41 C.C.C. (3d) 340, 5 M.V.R. (2d) 239 (B.C.C.A.).

The private communication to which the detainee is entitled is not restricted to a communication with his lawyer and includes communication with any person to whom the detainee wishes to speak in the process of exercising his rights under s. 10(*b*) of the Charter: *R. v. McNeilly* (1988), 10 M.V.R. (2d) 142 (Y.T.S.C.).

Where the circumstances surrounding the giving of information to an accused with respect to his rights under s. 10(*b*) of the Charter are such as to lead the accused to reasonably believe that he does not have the right to retain and instruct counsel in private or will not be given such right, and where such circumstances are known or ought to be known to the officer and the officer knows or ought to know the effect that such circumstances may reasonably have on the accused, there is a duty on the officer to explain to the accused that he has such right to privacy and that it will be given to him. Again, the failure to give such explanation constitutes a violation of s. 10(*b*): *R. v. Jackson* (1993), 86 C.C.C. (3d) 233 (Ont. C.A.).

Opportunity to consult counsel – Section 10(*b*) does not create a constitutional obligation on governments to ensure that free and immediate, preliminary legal advice is available to all detainees: *R. v. Matheson*, [1994] 3 S.C.R. 328, 92 C.C.C. (3d) 434. Nevertheless, where a detainee has indicated a desire to exercise his right to counsel, the state is required to provide him with a reasonable opportunity to do so. During this period, state agents must refrain from eliciting incriminating evidence from the detainee until he has had a reasonable opportunity to reach counsel. The police are obliged to "hold off" from attempting to elicit criminatory evidence from the detainee until he has had a reasonable opportunity to reach counsel. While there may be compelling and urgent circumstances in which despite a detainee's being unable to contact a lawyer due to the unavailability of duty counsel, police will not be required to hold off in requiring the detainee to comply with a breathalyzer demand, as the existence of the two-hour evidentiary presumption available to the Crown under s. 258(1)(*c*)(ii) does not by itself constitute such a compelling or urgent circumstance. Urgency is not created by a mere investigatory and evidentiary expediency in circumstances where duty counsel is unavailable to detainees who have asserted their desire to contact a lawyer and have been duly diligent in exercising their rights: *R. v. Prosper*, [1994] 3 S.C.R. 236, 92 C.C.C. (3d) 353.

Police officers making an arrest in a potentially volatile situation may be justified in denying the detainee the right then and there to call counsel in order to prevent any new factors from entering the situation. Once the police are clearly in control of the situation, however, they must afford the accused an opportunity to contact counsel in private: *R. v. Taylor* (1990), 54 C.C.C. (3d) 152 (N.S.C.A.).

Where the accused has been properly informed and provided with a reasonable opportunity to consult with counsel, there is no positive duty on police officers to inquire of the detainee whether he was successful in making contact with counsel before continuing the investigation. The accused's impairment does not relieve him of the duty to be reasonably diligent in exercising the right to counsel: *R. v. Maloney* (1995), 147 N.S.R. (2d) 139 (C.A.).

The refusal of the police to permit the accused's lawyer into the breathalyzer room to observe the administering of the test does not constitute a denial of the right to counsel as guaranteed by s. 10(*b*) of the Charter: *R. v. Atchison* (1991), 68 C.C.C. (3d) 241 (B.C.S.C.).

The right to consult in privacy, while requiring that the consultation be out of hearing of other persons, need not be out of sight of other persons: *R. v. Walkington* (1974), 17 C.C.C. (2d) 553 (Sask. C.A.); *R. v. Doherty* (1974), 16 C.C.C. (2d) 494 (N.S.C.A.); *R. v. Holmes* (1982), 2 C.C.C. (3d) 471 (Ont. C.A.).

That an enclosed glass booth in the police station may not be absolutely soundproof does not establish that a conversation carried on within it between the accused and his lawyer can be overheard. The test to be applied in determining whether the accused's right to consult in private has been complied with is whether the accused was afforded such privacy as would permit a discussion without fear of being overheard: *R. v. Miller* (1990), 87 Nfld. & P.E.I.R. 55 (Nfld. C.A.).

Subsection (3)(*a*)(ii) [blood demand] [Note: The period is now three hours.] – For a demand to be valid under this paragraph, the officer making the demand must have formed a belief within two hours of the time that he believes that an offence under s. 253 was committed. It is not necessary, however, that the demand be made within the two hour period or that the tests be performed within two hours: *R. v. Deruelle*, [1992] 2 S.C.R. 663, 75 C.C.C. (3d) 118. Nor is it necessary that the officer have formed a belief before the expiration of the two hour period that one of the preconditions within subpara. (i) or (ii) existed. Thus, a demand will be valid under this paragraph where, having formed the belief that the accused committed an offence under s. 253 within the preceding two hours, the officer first makes a demand for breath samples but later finds it to be impossible or impracticable to obtain a breath sample and therefore then makes a demand for blood samples, even if this latter demand is made after expiration of the two hour period: *R. v. Pavel, supra*; *R. v. Gale* (1991), 13 W.C.B. (2d) 408 (Nfld. C.A.).

It is the officer making the demand who must have formed the belief as to the commission of the offence within the two hour period. Where, initially, a breath demand was made which could not be complied with, a subsequent blood demand by another officer was invalid where this latter officer had no belief that the offence under s. 253 had been committed within the preceding two hours: *R. v. Pavel, supra.*

A demand for a blood sample was properly made where the motorist, although willing to take a breathalyzer test, had sustained a head injury, was receiving treatment in a hospital and the officer was concerned that the two hour limit would expire before the treatment was completed. The words "any physical condition of the person" give the officer a wide discretion to determine the practicability or capability of the motorist to provide a breath sample: *R. v. Wytiuk* (1989), 17 M.V.R. (2d) 18 (Man. Q.B.).

A demand made under this paragraph must make reference to the conditions set out in subsec. (4), namely that the samples of blood may only be taken by demand if the samples are taken by or under the direction of a qualified medical practitioner and the practitioner is satisfied that the taking of those samples will not endanger the life or health of the person: *R. v. Green*, [1992] 1 S.C.R. 614, 70 C.C.C. (3d) 285. On the other hand, the officer need not obtain the prior approval of the medical practitioner before making the demand: *R. v. Green* (1990), 60 C.C.C. (3d) 362 (N.S.C.A.).

Where the police have failed to comply with the requirements of *R. v. Green, supra*, the taking of the sample contravenes ss. 7 and 8 even if the accused would have complied with the demand in the absence of medical assurances. Where, however, the accused complies despite the lack of medical assurances, the admission of the blood samples will rarely bring the "administration of justice into disrepute": *R. v. Knox*, [1996] 3 S.C.R. 199, 109 C.C.C. (3d) 481.

An accused, who has been involved in a motor vehicle accident and taken to the hospital because of his serious injuries, is detained within the meaning of s. 10(*b*) of the Charter when a demand is made by a police officer under this paragraph that he consent to the taking of blood samples. While any actual physical restraint arose from his injuries, there was a detention from the psychological compulsion of the demand: *R. v. Harder* (1989), 49 C.C.C. (3d) 565 (B.C.C.A.).

A motorist, confined to hospital as a result of injuries received in the motor vehicle accident under investigation, is not detained when the officer merely asks some questions at the beginning of the investigation. He is only detained when the demand for a blood sample was made and it was only then that he was entitled to be informed of his rights under s. 10(*b*) of the Charter: *R. v. Kay* (1990), 53 C.C.C. (3d) 500 (B.C.C.A.).

The nature of the charge is irrelevant to the validity of the demand. The accused need not be advised of the specific offence for which he is being detained and is only entitled to be told that he was being detained for the purpose of effecting compliance with this section: *R. v. Nagy* (1997), 115 C.C.C. (3d) 473 (Ont. C.A.).

The demand under this paragraph need not be made in the presence of the qualified medical practitioner. Further, the word "impracticable" in subpara. (ii) does not mean impossible and connotes a degree of reason and involves some regard for practice: *R. v. Pearce* (1988), 56 Man. R. (2d) 77, 13 M.V.R. (2d) 116 (Q.B.).

The Crown is not required to prove the consent of the accused to the giving of a blood sample: *R. v. Knox, supra.*

Subsection (3.1) [drug evaluation demand] – Subsection (3.1) does not provide for the automatic admissibility at trial of drug recognition expert ("DRE") opinion evidence; accordingly, the common law rules set out in *R. v. Mohan*, [1994] 2 S.C.R. 9, 89 C.C.C. (3d) 402, apply. The *Mohan* requirement for special expertise, which is normally addressed on a *voir dire*, is conclusively answered by subsec. (3.1). A DRE's expertise has been conclusively and irrebuttably established by Parliament: *R. v. Bingley*, [2017] 1 S.C.R. 170, 345 C.C.C. (3d) 306.

Subsection (5) [Failure to comply with A.L.E.R.T. demand under subsec. (2)] – The Crown is not required to prove that the device which would have been used, had there been no refusal, was an approved device: *R. v. Reimer* (1980), 54 C.C.C. (2d) 127 (Sask. Q.B.). *R. v. Lemieux* (1990), 24 M.V.R. (2d) 157, 41 O.A.C. 326 (C.A.); *R. v. McCauley* (1997), 161 N.S.R. (2d) 154, 28 M.V.R. (3d) 257 (C.A.).

The criminalization of the refusal to comply with the demand under subsec. (2) does not infringe s. 7 of the *Canadian Charter of Rights and Freedoms* and is a reasonable limit on the rights under s. 10(*b*): *R. v. Thompson* (2001), 151 C.C.C. (3d) 339 (Ont. C.A.).

Subsection (5) [Failure to comply with breath demand] / Elements of offence – This subsection creates the single offence of non-compliance which may be committed either by failure or refusal, and it is immaterial whether or not a breathalyzer machine was available at the time of the demand: *R. v. Kitchemonia* (1973), 12 C.C.C. (2d) 225 (Sask. C.A.). See also: *R. v. Gesner* (1979), 46 C.C.C. (2d) 252 (N.B.C.A.).

Where the accused refused to blow into an approved screening device, it is not a defence to the offence under this subsection that the accused offered to provide a breath sample at a machine at the police station: *R. v. Wilson* (1996), 125 W.A.C. 223, 18 M.V.R. (3d) 298 (B.C.C.A.).

Similarly, the offence may be committed by either refusing to accompany the officer or refusing to supply breath samples and the Crown need only show the offence of refusing to comply with the demand was committed in either one of these modes even though both modes are set out in the information. The additional averment in the information is mere surplusage: *R. v. MacNeil* (1978), 41 C.C.C. (2d) 46 (Ont. C.A.); *B.C. (Attorney General) (Re)*, [1980] 3 W.W.R. 193 (B.C.S.C.).

The word "refuses" is fully comprised within the word "fails" and thus a verbal refusal to take the test will support a conviction on an information charging that the accused failed to comply: *R. v. Gesner* (1979), 46 C.C.C. (2d) 252 (N.B.C.A.).

As the combined effect of this section and s. 258(1) has been held to require that at least two samples be taken, an accused who refuses to give more than one sample may be convicted of the offence under this subsection and it is no defence to such a charge that the technician considered the first sample satisfactory: *R. v. Faulkner (No. 2)* (1977), 37 C.C.C. (2d) 217 (N.S. Co. Ct.); *R. v. Hatt* (1978), 41 C.C.C. (2d) 442 (N.B.C.A.); *R. v. Quiring* (1979), 46 C.C.C. (2d) 51 (B.C.C.A.); *R. v. Boswell* (1978), 44 C.C.C. (2d) 356 (P.E.I.S.C.); *R. v. Hazzard* (1978), 51 C.C.C. (2d) 344 (N.W.T.C.A.); *R. v. Giroux, supra.*

Statements made to a police officer at the roadside subsequent to an accident pursuant to a statutory requirement are compelled statements. Following *R. v. Powers* (2006), 213 C.C.C. (3d) 351 (B.C.C.A.), the court held that statutorily compelled statements were not admissible for any purpose, including establishing grounds for making either the approved screening device demand, or the breath demand: *R. v. Soules* (2011), 273 C.C.C. (3d) 496 (Ont. C.A.), leave to appeal to S.C.C. refused (2011), 294 O.A.C. 399*n*.

As to the *mens rea* of the refusal offence, the case law is divided. One view is that the Crown must prove that the accused intentionally refused or failed to provide a suitable sample: *R. v. Lewko* (2002), 169 C.C.C. (3d) 359 (Sask. C.A.); *R. v. Sullivan*, [2001] O.J. No. 2799 (C.J.); *R. v. Soucy* (2014), 316 C.C.C. (3d) 153 (Ont. C.J.); *R. v. Greenshields* (2014), 111 W.C.B. (2d) 674, [2014] O.J. No. 475 (C.J.). The other view is that the accused need only have knowledge or awareness of the prohibited act; the accused's intention to produce the prohibited consequence is relevant only to whether there was a "reasonable excuse": *R. v. Porter* (2012), 103 W.C.B. (2d) 246, [2012] O.J. No. 2841 (S.C.J.); *R. v. Pletsas* (2014), 112 W.C.B. (2d) 111, [2014] O.J. No. 1136 (S.C.J.); *R. v. Singh* (2013), 55 M.V.R. (6th) 39 (Ont. S.C.J.).

Charging offence – An information which, although it omits the words "without reasonable excuse", is otherwise in the words of the section and sets out the proper section number of the offence, is not defective: *R. v. Cote*, [1978] 1 S.C.R. 8, 33 C.C.C. (2d) 353 (8:0).

Change of mind – An offer by an accused to provide a breath sample after consulting his counsel is not a defence to this charge where the accused made two clear and unconditional refusals without giving any reason for refusing: *R. v. McGauley* (1974), 16 C.C.C. (2d) 419 (B.C.C.A.). Similarly, in *R. v. McKeen* (2001), 151 C.C.C. (3d) 449 (N.S.C.A.), leave to appeal to S.C.C. refused 154 C.C.C. (3d) vi, the court held that despite the accused's change of mind at the detachment, the offence of refusal to provide a breath sample was complete where the accused repeatedly refused to invoke the right to counsel at the roadside. Once the right to consult with counsel had been waived, there was no duty on the police to provide an opportunity for the accused to consult with counsel and not to elicit a response to the breathalyzer demand. The fact that the police subsequently asked the accused at the detachment if he wished to consult with counsel did not revive a right which the accused had previously refused to exercise.

But compare *R. v. Jumaga*, [1977] 1 S.C.R. 486, 29 C.C.C. (2d) 269, where it was held on the facts that a first refusal really constituted a request to consult counsel and it was so treated by the police and was therefore itself not sufficient to sustain the charge.

A definitive refusal can only be established once the accused, who is seeking access to counsel's advice, has received it at the police station and has then refused, or confirmed an earlier refusal, to provide a sample. Here, the accused had failed a roadside screening test, been arrested, and indicated that he wanted to speak to counsel. Subsequently, he said that he did not want to accompany the police to provide a breath sample and was arrested for refusal, then released from the scene. The trial judge erred in convicting him, because in the circumstances there was no final or definitive refusal: *R. v. Mandryk* (2012), 291 C.C.C. (3d) 182 (Ont. S.C.J.).

The requirement that the accused "comply" with the demand must be read as requiring compliance within a reasonable time, not necessarily forthwith. Where the accused initially refused to accompany the technician but later, within the two-hour period, offered to comply after consultation with a lawyer, the charge was not made out: *R. v. Brotton* (1983), 24 M.V.R. 76, 28 Sask. R. 78 (C.A.).

In determining whether an accused, who initially refused and later changed his mind, is guilty of this offence, the court ought not to minutely dissect a single conversation or take a single sentence out of context. It would seem that whether there has been a refusal depends on consideration of all the circumstances of each individual case, including the time elapsed and whether it can be said that the accused's offer to take the test was severable from his earlier words to the contrary: *R. v. Cunningham* (1989), 49 C.C.C. (3d) 521 (Alta. C.A.).

Where the original refusal was not unequivocal and was closely followed by an offer to provide a sample then the offence is not made out: *R. v. Sagh* (1981), 62 C.C.C. (2d) 299 (Alta. Q.B.).

Where, however, the accused unequivocally refuses and only changes his mind 15 minutes later, at which time the technician advised him that it was too late, the charge was made out. The two events were sufficiently separate as to constitute different transactions: *R. v. Butt* (1983), 23 M.V.R. 273, 44 Nfld. & P.E.I.R. 297 (Nfld. C.A.).

Proof of offence – The words of refusal need not be proved voluntary and therefore there is no necessity to hold a *voir dire* to determine the voluntariness of such utterance: *R. v. Gallaher* (1977), 37 C.C.C. (2d) 191 (B.C. Co. Ct.); *R. v. Stapleton* (1982), 66 C.C.C. (2d) 231 (Ont. C.A.); *R. v. Zerebeski* (1982), 66 C.C.C. (2d) 284 (Sask. Q.B.).

It is a question of fact whether or not the accused blew adequately or whether there is some other explanation for the accused's failure to provide adequate sample, namely, that the breathalyzer was not operating properly. The Crown is not as a matter of law required to prove that the breathalyzer was in working order: *R. v. Leveque* (1985), 22 C.C.C. (3d) 559, 37 M.V.R. 166 (B.C.C.A.).

Similarly, in *R. v. Fillier* (1995), 15 M.V.R. (3d) 272, 132 Nfld. & P.E.I.R. 339 (Nfld. S.C.), the court held that there is no requirement that the Crown adduce evidence as to the training and/or experience of the peace officer in the operation of the screening device for the officer's opinion to be received in respect of the failure to provide a suitable sample.

On a charge of refusal, there is no requirement that the police officer have a reasonable belief that he or she could administer the demand at the time it is made. Neither is there a requirement for the Crown to prove that an ASD would have been available within the "forthwith" period. Because the offence is complete upon the refusal, the police officer's ability to actually take the sample in accordance with the demand is not relevant to culpability: *R. v. Degiorgio* (2011), 275 C.C.C. (3d) 1 (Ont. C.A.).

Violation of right to counsel generally – Where the accused immediately refuses after the demand was made and before he was given his rights under s. 10(*b*) of the Charter, he should be informed of his right to counsel, that he was not bound by his earlier answers and that it was open to the accused to change his mind and consult counsel if he so wished: *R. v. MacIsaac* (1988), 72 Nfld. & P.E.I.R. 220, 9 M.V.R. (2d) 239 (P.E.I.S.C.).

However, compare *R. v. Cote* (1988), 8 M.V.R. (2d) 256, 87 N.B.R. (2d) 190 (C.A.), where it was held that while the accused's refusal was not irrevocable in such circumstances, evidence of the refusal was properly admitted where the accused was advised of her right to counsel, subsequently was given an opportunity to speak to a lawyer and never made a request to take the test. The court was divided on whether, since the original refusal is not irrevocable, the accused should be given another demand.

Where the act of refusal occurred after the time when the accused should have been informed of his right to counsel under s. 10(*b*) of the *Canadian Charter of Rights and Freedoms*, that is, immediately upon the making of the demand, the accused's rights under s. 10(*b*) have been infringed and the evidence of the refusal must be excluded under s. 24(2). It must be assumed that had the accused consulted counsel he would have complied with the demand: *R. v. Phillips; R. v. Reid* (1986), 26 C.C.C. (3d) 60 (Alta. C.A.).

R. v. Brownridge, [1972] S.C.R. 926, 7 C.C.C. (2d) 417 (6:3), decided the issue whether or not the fact that the police would not allow a suspected impaired motorist to contact his lawyer for advice after their demand for his breath sample was a "reasonable excuse" for his refusal to comply. In the first majority judgment, *per* Ritchie J. (Fauteux C.J.C., Martland and Spence JJ., concurring), it was held that as there was a genuine reason for the motorist to seek legal advice it would run contrary to s. 2(*c*)(ii) (the right of a detained person to instruct counsel without delay) of the Bill of Rights to hold that the withholding of that right from him was incapable of constituting a reasonable excuse for him to provide a breath sample. In the second majority judgment Laskin J. (Hall J., concurring), held that s. 2 of the Bill of Rights enjoins a construction upon former s. 235 that would infringe any right recognized under the Bill of Rights and if efforts to reach counsel expend the time beyond the two-hour-limitation period primacy must be given the protection accorded by the Bill of Rights over the statutory rule of evidence under s. 258(1)(*c*)(ii). Moreover, denial of right to counsel does not constitute a "reasonable excuse" rather this right exists independently of those words and its denial vitiates a conviction for this offence. Pigeon J. (Abbott and Judson JJ., concurring) dissenting, was of the opinion that regardless of whether or not the suspected motorist was under arrest the denial of his request for counsel was not to be a reasonable excuse for him to refuse to provide his breath sample.

Although replacing the criminal offence of refusal with the presumption that failure or refusal to provide a roadside breath sample would constitute grounds for a breathalyzer demand would be less intrusive, it would undermine the effectiveness of roadside screening programs. Any infringement of ss. 7 or 10(*b*) of the Charter constitute a reasonable limit under s. 1: *R. v. Thompson* (2001), 151 C.C.C. (3d) 339 (Ont. C.A.).

Where a demand is made under subsec. (3) and the accused is not advised of his rights under s. 10(*b*) of the *Canadian Charter of Rights and Freedoms* then he has a reasonable excuse for refusing to comply with the demand: *R. v. Mackinnon* (1985), 21 C.C.C. (3d) 264 (P.E.I.C.A.).

Denial of the right to counsel is not a reasonable excuse for refusing to comply with the demand. Where, however, the accused proves that his right to counsel was violated then he would be entitled to an exclusion of evidence of the refusal if the accused can prove that to admit evidence would bring the administration of justice into disrepute within the meaning of s. 24(2) of the Charter. Since the onus is on the accused to establish the violation on a balance of probabilities, merely raising a reasonable doubt as to whether his right to counsel had been violated would not be sufficient: *R. v. Williams* (1992), 78 C.C.C. (3d) 72 (Ont. C.A.).

The accused's rights were violated when he was charged with refusal despite repeated unsuccessful attempts to reach a lawyer. The accused refused to comply with the demand until he spoke to a lawyer. He had been diligent in asserting his right and there was no urgency, the demand having been made only 45 minutes after he was arrested: *R. v. Dunnett* (1990), 62 C.C.C. (3d) 14 (N.B.C.A.), leave to appeal to S.C.C. refused 62 C.C.C. (3d) vi.

The refusal of the police to first await the motorist's lawyer's attendance before administering the breathalyzer test following a consultation on the telephone is not a reasonable excuse for the motorist to refuse to take the test: *R. v. Bond* (1973), 14 C.C.C. (2d) 497 (N.S.C.A.); *R. v. Kavanagh* (1981), 62 C.C.C. (2d) 518 (B.C.S.C.); *R. v. Giroux* (1981), 63 C.C.C. (2d) 555 (Que. C.A.), leave to appeal to S.C.C. refused C.C.C. *loc. cit.*

Where the accused was informed of his right to counsel and given a reasonable opportunity to consult, his inability to speak to his lawyer, which he did not communicate to the police, did not constitute a reasonable excuse for refusing to comply with the demand. Without any request on the part of the accused for more time to consult counsel, the police were entitled to conclude that the accused had refused without reasonable excuse: *R. v. Ferron* (1989), 49 C.C.C. (3d) 432 (B.C.C.A.).

Where the accused unsuccessfully attempted to contact two lawyers and then indicated that he no longer wished to consult with counsel and would not provide a breath sample, the officer was required to inform the accused again of the right to a reasonable opportunity to contact counsel as well as the fact that the police officer would not renew the demand for a breath sample during that time: *R. v. Russell* (2000), 150 C.C.C. (3d) 243 (N.B.C.A.).

Inability to consult in private – As indicated in the cases noted under s. 254(3), *supra*, it has been held that under s. 10(*b*) of the Charter, the right to consult with counsel in private is inherent in the right and there need not be any request for privacy. Nevertheless, it was held in *R. v. Young* (1987), 38 C.C.C. (3d) 452 (N.B.C.A.), that having regard to all the circumstances the trial judge did not err in refusing to exclude under s. 24(2) of the Charter the evidence of the accused's refusal notwithstanding the violation of s. 10(*b*) by reason of the failure of the police officer to move out of earshot. The court did not consider whether the breach of s. 10(*b*) provided the accused with a reasonable excuse. Also see: *R. v. Dempsey* (1987), 77 N.S.R. (2d) 284, 46 M.V.R. 179 (C.A.).

The right to consult with counsel includes the right to do so in privacy. The failure of the police to comply with a request for privacy constitutes a denial of the right to counsel and therefore a reasonable excuse to refuse to comply with the demand: *R. v. Penner* (1973), 12 C.C.C. (2d) 468 (Man. C.A.).

Reasonable excuse / burden of proof – By virtue of s. 794(2), an accused who asserts a "reasonable excuse" for failing or refusing to comply with a breathalyzer demand bears the burden of proving the factual foundation for that excuse on a balance of probabilities: *R. v. Goleski* (2014), 307 C.C.C. (3d) 1 (B.C.C.A.), affd [2015] 1 S.C.R. 399, 320 C.C.C. (3d) 433.

Reasonable excuse / legal advice – An accused's statement that "My lawyer advised me not to take the test" in response to the making of a breathalyzer demand was a refusal within this subsection: *R. v. Hurley* (1980), 29 Nfld. & P.E.I.R. 263, 9 M.V.R. 46 (Nfld. C.A.).

The police officer's refusal to permit the accused's lawyer to verify the results of the first breathalyzer test does not constitute a reasonable excuse, nor does the accused's mistaken belief, based on the advice of the lawyer, that it would constitute a reasonable excuse: *R. v. Giroux* (1981), 63 C.C.C. (2d) 555 (Que. C.A.), leave to appeal to S.C.C. refused C.C.C. *loc. cit.*

A motorist's mistaken belief, based on an erroneous judgment of a provincial court judge, that a police officer had no right to make the demand is not a reasonable excuse: *R. v. MacIntyre* (1983), 24 M.V.R. 67 (Ont. C.A.).

Reasonable excuse / grounds for demand – It is not a "reasonable excuse" for refusing to provide a breath sample that the accused is subsequently acquitted of the charge under former s. 234 [now s. 253], where the demand for the breath sample was lawfully made and the offence under this subsection is otherwise established. "Reasonable excuse" refers to matters which stand outside of the requirements which must be met (*i.e.*, those under subsec. (3)(*a*)) before a charge can be supported under this subsection: *R. v. Taraschuk*, [1977] 1

S.C.R. 385, 25 C.C.C. (2d) 108 (9:0). Note, this case overrules: *R. v. Canstone* (1971), 3 C.C.C. (2d) 539 (B.C.S.C.), and *R. v. Mitchell* (1973), 11 C.C.C. (2d) 12 (B.C.S.C.).

While it is a defence to a charge under this subsection that the officer did not have reasonable and probable grounds to believe that the accused had committed an offence under former s. 234 [now s. 253]: *R. v. MacDonald* (1974), 22 C.C.C. (2d) 350 (N.S.C.A.), to sustain the charge there need not be direct evidence from the officer that he had such a belief. Rather, the existence of the necessary belief can be inferred by the court: *R. v. Fraelic* (1977), 36 C.C.C. (2d) 473 (N.S. Co. Ct.); *R. v. Blanchette* (1978), 41 C.C.C. (2d) 205 (Alta. Dist. Ct.).

Reasonable excuse / offer of blood sample – An offer to provide a blood sample in lieu of a breath sample is not a reasonable excuse for refusing to comply with the demand under subsec. (3)(*a*): *R. v. Wall* (1974), 19 C.C.C. (2d) 146 (Sask. C.A.); *R. v. Weir* (1993), 79 C.C.C. (3d) 538 (N.S.C.A.); *R. v. Richardson* (1993), 80 C.C.C. (3d) 287 (Ont. C.A.); *R. v. Taylor* (1993), 39 W.A.C. 201, 43 M.V.R. (2d) 240 (B.C.C.A.).

Where, however, the accused's offer to supply a blood sample is taken up and it is not made clear to him that this is not a suitable alternative to complying with the demand the accused had a reasonable excuse to refuse: *Saskatchewan (Attorney General) v. Chrun*, [1973] 5 W.W.R. 611 (Sask. Dist. Ct.); *R. v. Larkin* (1979), 27 Nfld. & P.E.I.R. 284, 4 M.V.R. 149 (P.E.I.S.C.).

While evidence of sobriety cannot provide the basis for a "reasonable excuse", it can be relevant evidence of *mens rea.* In this case, the accused claimed that he tried to produce a breath sample but was unable; he offered to provide a blood sample instead. He then went on his own accord and had a blood test which demonstrated that he was, in fact, sober. The trial judge erred in refusing to consider this evidence because it properly bolstered the credibility of the accused's claim that, knowing himself to be sober, he genuinely tried to provide a breath sample: *R. v. Sceviour* (2010), 258 C.C.C. (3d) 196 (Nfld. & Lab. C.A.)).

Reasonable excuse / impairment – Establishing that the defendant's mind was so affected by alcohol or a drug that he could not grasp the demand at all would constitute a reasonable excuse for non-compliance: *R. v. Laybolt* (1974), 17 C.C.C. (2d) 16 (P.E.I.S.C.). *Contra: R. v. Warnica* (1980), 56 C.C.C. (2d) 100 (N.S.C.A.), where it was held that once it was shown that the accused appeared to understand the demand a rebuttable presumption arose that he intended the natural consequences of his own conduct which however may *not* be rebutted by testimony from the accused that he was too drunk to understand the demand. Further, lack of understanding is not a reasonable excuse.

Reasonable excuse / physical disability – In *R. v. Nadeau* (1974), 19 C.C.C. (2d) 199 (N.B.C.A.), Hughes C.J.N.B. expressed the view that "the "reasonable excuse' envisaged must be some circumstance which renders compliance with the demand either extremely difficult or likely to involve a substantial risk to the health of the person on whom the demand has been made".

The physical inability of the accused to take the test is a reasonable excuse within this subsection notwithstanding the inability is the result of the voluntary consumption of alcohol: *R. v. Henderson* (1976), 34 C.C.C. (2d) 40 (Ont. Co. Ct.).

The defence of reasonable excuse should not be confined to matters in the mind of the accused, to the exclusion of dangerous conditions not fully known or recognized by the accused. The defence should include rare situations where there is a reason at the time not to make the demand or to require compliance under threat of prosecution, but that reason is not fully known, either to the investigating officer or to the suspect. There is a reasonable excuse where both police and the accused have been seriously misled by mistaken medical diagnosis on a matter so fundamental to the interests of both. In this case, even though the accused was unaware of the exact nature of his injury, he did know that he was injured, perhaps seriously, and consequently, on the advice of counsel, he refused to comply with the police request until he was examined by a physician whom he knew and trusted. The accused had been examined briefly by a physician who advised the police that the accused was fit to comply with the demand. In fact, the accused had a very serious spinal injury and had he complied with the demand, he might well have become paralyzed. The fact that the accused was unaware of the specific danger to which he was exposed was no basis for a conclusion that he was not fearful for his safety and not justified in accepting the advice of his lawyer: *R. v. Moser* (1992), 71 C.C.C. (3d) 165 (Ont. C.A.).

Reasonable excuse / generally – The accused's belief that the results of the breathalyzer test would be inaccurate is not a reasonable excuse to refuse to comply with the demand. The accused must rely on the safeguard in s. 258(1)(*c*) which permits "evidence to the contrary" to rebut the presumption, which arises from the results of the breathalyzer test, taken pursuant to a demand under subsec. (3) that the blood alcohol reading from the breathalyzer is the same as at the time of the offence: *R. v. Campbell* (1978), 40 C.C.C. (2d) 570 (Alta. C.A.) (2:1). Similarily, *R. v. Roy* (1979), 11 C.R. (3d) 178 (Que. C.A.); *R. v. Dunn* (1980), 8 M.V.R. 198 (B.C.C.A.).

Thus the accused's fear that, because he was on medication, the results would be inaccurate is not a reasonable excuse for refusing to comply with the demand: *R. v. Frohwerk* (1979), 48 C.C.C. (2d) 214 (Man. C.A.).

Anxiety caused by accurate information supplied at the accused's request by the police officer as to the penalty for a second conviction for a drinking and driving offence (including information that a jail term would also result for a conviction under this subsection) is not a reasonable excuse: *R. v. Broda* (1983), 21 M.V.R. 85, 22 Sask. R. 239 (C.A.).

An extremely helpful review of the various factors which could constitute a "reasonable excuse" is found in the decision of the court in *R. v. Phinney* (1979), 49 C.C.C. (2d) 81 (N.S.C.A.), where the majority of the court concluded that the accused's honest belief based on reasonable grounds that the particular breathalyzer machine might not be functioning properly was a reasonable excuse to refuse to comply with the demand. The court emphasized, however, that this fear must be based on objective evidence.

Where the accused was to be taken 100 miles away for the breathalyzer test where he would be effectively stranded with no way to get home and no place to stay it was held that he had a reasonable excuse as contemplated by this subsection: *R. v. Iron* (1977), 35 C.C.C. (2d) 279 (Sask. Q.B.).

A possible financial loss for the accused if he were required to leave his vehicle and accompany the officer is not a reasonable excuse. In this case the accused claimed that he needed to remain with his truck to clean up the spilled cargo of fish otherwise there was risk that the cargo would be condemned resulting in a substantial financial loss: *R. v. Gidney* (1987), 7 M.V.R. (2d) 90, 81 N.S.R. (2d) 404 (C.A.).

Grounds of compassion, in this case the accused's desire to go to the hospital when he learned that his nephew who was at the hospital was in serious condition, do not constitute grounds for refusing to comply with the demand: *R. v. Heim* (1989), 98 N.S.R. (2d) 447, 13 M.V.R. (2d) 301 (C.A.).

A genuine religious belief is not an excuse for refusal to provide a breath sample: *R. v. Chomokowski* (1973), 11 C.C.C. (2d) 562 (Man. C.A.).

The accused had a reasonable excuse for refusing to comply with the demand because of her concern about sanitation when the officer gave her an unwrapped mouthpiece: *R. v. Pittendreigh* (1994), 83 W.A.C. 169, 162 A.R. 169 (C.A.).

A reasonably held belief of a threat of unfairness or illegality by the police would support a reasonable excuse: *R. v. Dawson* (1996), 140 Nfld. & P.E.I.R. 176, 21 M.V.R. (3d) 299 (Nfld. C.A.).

Right to production – Failure to provide the accused with the mouthpiece he used in his attempt to blow into the breathalyzer did not violate the accused's rights under s. 7. It was highly improbable that a broken mouthpiece would not have been detected by even a brief inspection: *R. v. Mayer* (1989), 16 M.V.R. (2d) 174 (B.C. Co. Ct.).

Records concerning the history and performance of the device used to measure the accused's blood alcohol concentration were third party records not subject to automatic

Stinchcombe disclosure. Because there was nothing to indicate any problem with the operation of the instrument, the accused failed to meet the "likely relevant" threshold for production: *R. v. Jackson* (2015), 332 C.C.C. (3d) 466 (Ont. C.A.), leave to appeal to S.C.C. refused 2016 CarswellOnt 10528.

Only those maintenance records that are contemporaneous with the criminal charge are "fruits of the investigation" which must be included in the information provided by the police to the Crown. These are primarily time-of-test results. Maintenance records that are temporally remote from the charge or relate only to the historical background of the instrument are not subject to *Stinchcombe* disclosure: *R. v. Vallentgoed* (2016), 344 C.C.C. (3d) 85 (Alta. C.A.), affd 2018 SCC 44.

Multiple convictions – The offences under this section and under s. 253(*a*) constitute separate and distinct acts or delicts and therefore the accused may be convicted of both offences though they arise out of one incident: *R. v. Schilbe* (1976), 30 C.C.C. (2d) 113 (Ont. C.A.).

254.01 [*Repealed*, 2018, c. 21, s. 14.]

254.1 [*Repealed*, 2018, c. 21, s. 14.]

255. [*Repealed*, 2018, c. 21, s. 14.]

Editor's Note: The punishment for drug- and alcohol-related driving offences is now set out in ss. 320.19, 320.2 (bodily harm), and 320.21 (death). Statutory aggravating factors are now enumerated in s. 320.22. The annotations below should be approached with caution in relation to the new sentencing regime, which includes increased maximum penalties.

CROSS-REFERENCES

Mode of trial – Where the prosecution elects to proceed by indictment on the offences in subsec. (1) then the accused may elect his mode of trial pursuant to s. 536(2). Where the prosecution elects to proceed by way of summary conviction then the trial of the offence is conducted by a summary conviction court pursuant to Part XXVII. In either case, release pending trial is determined by s. 515, although the accused is eligible for release by a peace officer under s. 496, 497 or by the officer in charge under s. 498. Where the accused is charged with an offence under subsec. (2) or (3) then he has an election as to mode of trial pursuant to s. 536(2) and release pending trial is determined by s. 515.

Causation – With respect to the offence in subsec. (3) and the issue of causation, see ss. 224 to 226. As to case law, in addition to the notes under this section, see the notes under s. 249. The term "bodily harm" is defined s. 2.

Punishment – The maximum fine for the offences in subsec. (1), where the prosecution proceeds by way of summary conviction, is $2000 as set out in s. 787 and the limitation period is set out in s. 786(2). There is no limit on the fine where the prosecution proceeds by way of indictment. Where the prosecution seeks the higher penalty prescribed by para. (*a*)(ii) or (iii), it must comply with the provisions of s. 727. Section 667 provides one method of proof of the prior conviction. No reference to the prior conviction may be made in the information by virtue of s. 664. Note the extended definition of the meaning of previous convictions in subsec. (4). The wording of para. (4)(*c*) is somewhat confusing because the numbers refer to the section numbers of R.S.C. 1985 immediately prior to the *Criminal Law Amendment Act*, 1985, c. 19, proclaimed in force on December 4, 1985. For convenience, the following sets out a description of the offence referred to and in square brackets, the R.S.C. 1985 number as used in this subsection followed by the R.S.C. 1970 section number: impaired driving and care or control of motor vehicle [250/234]; refusing to comply with roadside screening device demand [251/234.1]; refusing to comply with breathalyzer demand [252/235]; "over 80" re motor vehicles [253/236]; refusal to comply with breath demand re operation of vessel [259/240.1]; "over 80" re vessels [260/240.2]; and impaired operation of vessel [258(4)/240(4)]. By reason of the change in the minimum term from 3 months to 90 days, a person sentenced to the minimum term of 90 days under para. (*a*)(iii) may be ordered to serve the sentence on an intermittent basis pursuant to s. 732. By reason of s. 730, since subsec. (1) prescribes a minimum punishment, a discharge is not available in relation to the offence under s. 254 nor for the offence under s. 253 in provinces where subsec. (5) has not been proclaimed in force.

An accused convicted of the offence under subsec. (2) or (3) may, pursuant to s. 259, be ordered prohibited from operating a motor vehicle, vessel, aircraft or railway equipment, as the case may be, for life if convicted of the offence under subsec. (3) and during any period not exceeding 10 years for the offence under subsec. (2). The prohibition order for the offence under subsec. (1) is mandatory by virtue of s. 259(1). The length of the order is as follows: for a first offence, during a period of not more than three years and not less than one year; for a second offence, during a period of not more than five years and not less than two years; for each subsequent offence, during a period of not less than three years plus any period to which the offender is sentenced to imprisonment. The procedure respecting the making of that order of prohibition is found in s. 260.

Pursuant to s. 255.1, evidence that the accused's blood alcohol level exceeded .160 at the time when the offence was committed is deemed to be an aggravating factor on sentencing. Note s. 732.1(3)(*g*.1) and (*g*.2), which allow for imposition of terms of probation that the offender attend for curative treatment in relation to the consumption of alcohol and drugs and participate in an alcohol ignition interlock device program.

SYNOPSIS

When a person is convicted of the basic offence under ss. 253 or 254, that person is liable to a maximum term of imprisonment of five years if prosecuted by indictment, and 18 months if prosecuted summarily. The minimum punishment upon a conviction for a first offence under ss. 253 or 254 is a fine of $1000; for a second offence, imprisonment for not less than 30 days; and for each subsequent offence, imprisonment for not less than 120 days, whether or not the offence is prosecuted summarily or by indictment. A person convicted of an offence under s. 253(1)(*a*) (impaired) who has caused either bodily harm or death to another person, is guilty of an indictable offence and is subject to a maximum term of imprisonment — in the case of bodily harm, for 10 years: and in the case of death, for life. A person who is convicted of an offence under s. 253(1)(*b*) (over "80") and causes an accident resulting in bodily harm to another or death is guilty of an indictable offence and is subject to a maximum term of imprisonment — in the case of bodily harm, for 10 years, and in the case of death, for life. Note that it does not appear that there needs to be a causal connection between the blood-alcohol level and the causing of the accident.

Subsections (2.2) and (3.2) enact the same penalties (*i.e.* 10 years or life) where the person is convicted of a refusal offence under s. 254(5) and knew or ought to have known that the operation of the vehicle, vessel, aircraft or railway equipment caused an accident resulting in bodily harm or death as the case may be.

Subsection (3.1) clarifies that the minimum punishments set out in subsec. (1)(*a*) also apply to the offences described in subsecs. (2) and (3). Thus, for example, a conditional sentence would not be available for second or subsequent offences.

A conviction under ss. 253 or 254(5) will be considered a second or subsequent offence, if a person has previously been convicted of an offence under any of these provisions, subsecs. (2) or (3) of this section, or ss. 250, 251, 252, 253, 259, or 260, or the former s. 258(4). Where it is proclaimed in force, subsec. (5) gives discretion to discharge the person, charged with a s. 253 offence, on the conditions set out in a probation order (which must include a requirement that the person seek treatment), provided there is evidence that a person has an alcohol or drug problem and a finding that it would not be contrary to the public interest to discharge him, notwithstanding that the person would otherwise not be eligible for discharge under s. 736(1) because the offence carries a minimum penalty.

ANNOTATIONS

Sentencing under subsec. (1) generally – It was open to the trial court to adopt a series of detailed guidelines for the imposition of penalties in drinking and driving offences, provided that the guidelines are used in conjunction with the appropriate principles and factors as they apply to the situation before the judge in the particular case: *R. v. Stephens* (1989), 51 C.C.C. (3d) 557 (P.E.I.C.A.).

In *R. v. Bradshaw*, [1976] 1 S.C.R. 162, 21 C.C.C. (2d) 69 (8:0), decided prior to the enactment of subsec. (5), it was held that a minimum fine is a minimum punishment within the meaning of s. 662.1 [now s. 736] and therefore a discharge is not available.

Second or subsequent offence [subsec. (1)(*a*)(ii) and (iii)] – The increased penalty for a "second" or "subsequent" offence does not apply where the offence is committed prior to the conviction for the offence relied upon as a prior offence even if committed after this prior offence: *R. v. Negridge* (1980), 54 C.C.C. (2d) 304 (Ont. C.A.); *R. v. Rahko* (1983), 29 M.V.R. 37 (B.C.C.A.). Similarly where the accused is convicted on the same day of impaired driving and refusing to comply with a breathalyzer demand arising out of the same transaction he has only one prior conviction for the purposes of penalty and is to be sentenced on the basis of para. (*a*)(ii) rather than para. (*a*)(iii): *R. v. Skolnick* (1981), 59 C.C.C. (2d) 286 (Ont. C.A.), affd [1982] 2 S.C.R. 47, 68 C.C.C. (2d) 385 (9:0).

Two prior convictions which are entered at the same time but arise out of separate incidents are properly considered a single prior conviction: *R. v. Robertson* (1998), 124 C.C.C. (3d) 558 (Nfld. C.A.), leave to appeal to S.C.C. refused 129 C.C.C. (3d) vi.

A curative discharge is not a conviction for the purpose of subsec. (1): *R. v. Conn* (2004), 190 C.C.C. (3d) 313 (Man. C.A.).

In deciding whether to seek an increased penalty, the Crown must exercise its discretion in a way that is consistent with the principles of fundamental justice. While a trial judge can review the prosecutor's exercise of discretion to determine whether it offends s. 7 of the Charter, this does not involve an assessment of the reasonableness of the prosecutor's decision but rather a consideration of whether the Crown's decision is arbitrary; undermines the integrity of the administration of justice; renders the sentencing proceedings fundamentally unfair; or if it results in a limit on the accused's liberty that is grossly disproportionate to the state interest in proving the notice: *R. v. Gill*, 2012 ONCA 607.

Consistent with *Gladue* and *Ipeelee*, the Crown must consider the accused's aboriginal status in determining whether to request a mandatory minimum sentence of imprisonment: *R. v. Anderson* (2013), 295 C.C.C. (3d) 262 (N.L.C.A.), leave to appeal to S.C.C. allowed [2013] S.C.C.A. No. 85.

Note: These cases were decided before the minimum punishment was increased to 120 days.

Constitutionality of minimum punishment – The mandatory jail term prescribed by para. (*a*) does not offend the fundamental justice guarantee in s. 7 of the *Charter of Rights and Freedoms*: *R. v. Tardif* (1983), 9 C.C.C. (3d) 223 (Sask. C.A.), nor s. 15 of the Charter: *R. v. Aucoin* (1987), 79 N.S.R. (2d) 32, 48 M.V.R. 154 (S.C. App. Div.).

The minimum punishment of 90 days prescribed by subsec. (1)(*a*)(iii) does not violate the guarantee to protection against imposition of cruel and unusual punishment under s. 12 of the Charter: *R. v. Parsons* (1988), 40 C.C.C. (3d) 128 (Nfld. S.C.T.D.).

The minimum jail sentence for repeat offenders will not ordinarily violate ss. 7 and 12 of the Charter and thus subsec. (1)(*a*)(ii) is not unconstitutional. However, in a particular case, as where there is a very significant time gap between the first and second offences, the minimum punishment may be grossly disproportionate in which case the accused may be entitled to a constitutional exemption under s. 24(1) of the Charter: *R. v. Kumar* (1993), 85 C.C.C. (3d) 417 (B.C.C.A.). However, now see *R. v. Ferguson*, [2008] 1 S.C.R. 96, 228 C.C.C. (3d) 385.

Causation — impairment (subsecs. (2) and (3)) – It was held in relation to the offence of criminal negligence causing death that the element of causation is satisfied if the evidence shows that the criminally negligent conduct of the accused meets the test in *R. v. Smithers*, [1978] 1 S.C.R. 506, 34 C.C.C. (2d) 427 (a manslaughter case noted under s. 222) being at least a contributing cause of death outside the *de minimis* range. It is misdirection to instruct the jury that the conduct must be shown to be a substantial cause: *R. v. Pinske* (1988), 30 B.C.L.R. (2d) 114, 6 M.V.R. (2d) 19 (B.C.C.A.), affd [1989] 2 S.C.R. 979. The *Smithers* test has been adopted for prosecutions under this section and the similar offences of dangerous driving causing bodily harm or death under s. 249(3) and (4): *R. v. Larocque* (1988), 5 M.V.R. (2d) 221 (Ont. C.A.); *R. v. Halkett* (1988), 73 Sask. R. 241, 11 M.V.R. (2d) 109 (C.A.); *R. v. Singhal* (1988), 5 M.V.R. (2d) 173 (B.C.C.A.); *R. v. Arsenault* (1992), 16 C.R. (4th) 301, 104 Nfld. & P.E.I.R. 29 (P.E.I.C.A.); *R. v. Colby* (1989), 52 C.C.C. (3d) 321 (Alta. C.A.), and *R. v. Ewart* (1989), 53 C.C.C. (3d) 153 (Alta. C.A.), leave to appeal to S.C.C. refused 109 A.R. 320*n*. The court seems to have adopted a somewhat stricter test for causation in *R. v. F. (D.)* (1989), 52 C.C.C. (3d) 357 (Alta. C.A.).

In considering whether the *Smithers* test has been made out, reference should also now be made to *R. v. Nette*, [2001] 3 S.C.R. 488, 158 C.C.C. (3d) 486, where a majority of the court explained that causing death outside the *de minimis* range means that the acts of the accused were a significant contributing cause to the death.

Evidence of impairment *per se* is not sufficient to satisfy the test of causation even when coupled with expert opinion evidence as to the physiology of alcohol, an opinion, however, which was expressed in terms of averages and statistical probabilities and couched in qualifying language: *R. v. Fisher* (1992), 13 C.R. (4th) 222, 36 M.V.R. (2d) 6 (B.C.C.A.).

While it is sufficient to prove that the accused's impairment contributed in the smallest degree to the death, mere evidence that the accused's ability to drive was impaired is insufficient to establish causation. The Crown must prove unusual conduct on the part of the accused or that the accused's state of intoxication could have contributed in more than a minor way to the victim's death. The absence of an explanation from the accused can also lead to an adverse inference that his intoxication contributed to the victim's death: *R. v. Laprise* (1996), 113 C.C.C. (3d) 87 (Que. C.A.).

Where there is evidence to support a conviction beyond the fact of the accident, and no evidence to suggest a reason for the accident other than impairment, it is not an error for the trial judge to take account of the circumstances of the accident to establish both impairment and causation: *R. v. Rhyason* (2006), 214 C.C.C. (3d) 337 (Alta. C.A.), affd [2007] 3 S.C.R. 108, 221 C.C.C. (3d) 1.

Causation — "over 80" (subsecs. (2.1) and (3.1)) – One line of authority holds that the offences of driving "over 80" causing death and bodily harm do *not* require a causal link between the accused's blood alcohol level and the accident to be proven: *R. c. Gaulin* (2017), 353 C.C.C. (3d) 330 (C.A. Que.); *R. v. Koma* (2015), 329 C.C.C. (3d) 29 (Sask. C.A.). Other authorities hold that the "over 80 driving" must be a real factor in causing the accident: *R. v. Jagoe* (2012), 302 C.C.C. (3d) 454 (N.B.C.A.).

Definition of "accident" (subsec. (3.1)) – A purposive rather than literalist reading must be given. Thus, there was no "accident" within the meaning of subsec. (3.1) where the deceased had jumped on the hood of the car and struck the windshield with a baseball bat, then fallen to the ground and struck his head when the accused applied the brakes to try to get him off the hood. The deceased's conduct was deliberate and criminal, so any "accident" was not caused by the accused's driving: *R. v. Jagoe* (2012), 302 C.C.C. (3d) 454 (N.B.C.A.).

Rule precluding multiple convictions [*Kienapple rule*] – Where the act of the accused, which amounts to dangerous driving, is operating her motor vehicle while her ability to do so was substantially impaired by alcohol, the rule precluding multiple convictions enunciated in *R. v. Kienapple*, [1975] 1 S.C.R. 725, 15 C.C.C. (2d) 524, applies and the accused cannot be convicted of this offence and the offence under s. 249(4). Since a conviction for the offence under this subsection more accurately describes the *delict*, the conviction should be entered on that charge and the charge under s. 249(4) stayed: *R. v. Colby* (1989), 52 C.C.C. (3d) 321 (Alta. C.A.).

The rule precluding multiple convictions does not prevent the conviction of the accused for the offence under subsec. (2) and the offence of criminal negligence causing bodily harm, although the injuries underlying both offences were to the same victim. The evidence disclosed facts concerning both the accused's manner of driving and, as well, her capacity to drive. The act of impaired operation did not encompass the manner of driving which, in this case, formed a part of the sequence of actions which constituted criminal negligence: *R. v. Andrew* (1990), 57 C.C.C. (3d) 301 (B.C.C.A.).

Discharge for curative treatment [subsec. (5)] / Constitutional considerations – While the validity of the selective proclamation of this subsection has been attacked as a violation of the equality rights in s. 15 of the *Canadian Charter of Rights and Freedoms*, most courts have held either that there is no violation or that the courts have no power to, in effect, proclaim this provision in force: *R. v. Killen* (1985), 24 C.C.C. (3d) 40 (N.S.C.A.); *R. v. Ellsworth* (1988), 46 C.C.C. (3d) 442 (Que. C.A.); *R. v. Van Vliet* (1988), 45 C.C.C. (3d) 481 (B.C.C.A.). Moreover, in *R. v. Turpin*, [1989] 1 S.C.R. 1296, 48 C.C.C. (3d) 8 (6:0), the court doubted the correctness of the decision of the Ontario Court of Appeal in *R. v. Hamilton; R. v. Asselin; R. v. McCullagh* (1986), 30 C.C.C. (3d) 257, where that court had found a violation of s. 15 and in effect proclaimed this subsection to be in effect. Thus in *R. v. Alton* (1989), 53 C.C.C. (3d) 252 (Ont. C.A.), the court reversed the decision in *R. v. Hamilton, supra*, and held that this subsection is not available to an accused in Ontario.

However, in *R. v. Daybutch* (2015), 325 C.C.C. (3d) 568 (Ont. C.J.), the court held that the unavailability of a curative discharge for Aboriginal offenders in Ontario as a result of the province's policy not to proclaim it in force was discriminatory and violated the offender's s. 15 Charter right.

Circumstances where discharge should be granted – Where this subsection has been proclaimed in force, the court is entitled to assume that adequate facilities will be provided for curative treatment. Before invoking this subsection the court must be satisfied on a balance of probabilities that the accused is in need of curative treatment and that a discharge would not be contrary to the public interest. However, notwithstanding the accused has a lengthy record for *Criminal Code* driving offences this subsection may be resorted to where evidence adduced shows that the appropriate treatment for the accused's addiction is available and that the accused is now well-motivated and has a good chance of overcoming his alcoholism: *R. v. Beaulieu* (1980), 53 C.C.C. 342 (N.W.T.S.C.).

In considering whether a curative discharge would be contrary to the public interest, the court should consider, among other things, the circumstances of the offence and whether the accused was involved in an accident causing death, bodily harm or significant property damage; the *bona fides* of the accused; the accused's criminal record as it relates to alcohol-related driving offences; whether the accused was subject to a driving prohibition at the time of the offence; whether the accused had received the benefit of a prior curative discharge and what, if anything, the accused had done to facilitate his rehabilitation under the prior discharge: *R. v. Storr* (1995), 102 W.A.C. 65, 174 A.R. 65 (C.A.).

It will not always be contrary to the public interest to grant a discharge under this subsection to a recidivist. In some cases public protection may well be best served by effective measures to reduce the risk of repetition of the offence through rehabilitation of the offender. On the other hand it would be contrary to the public interest to grant a discharge if there was a real risk of repetition of the offence: *R. v. Wallner* (1988), 44 C.C.C. (3d) 358 (Alta. C.A.).

It was improper for the trial judge to adjourn the sentencing of the accused for a lengthy period of time presumably to determine whether he was an appropriate candidate for a discharge for curative treatment by seeing whether he would stop drinking. If the evidence was not sufficient at the time of the application for the discharge, then the judge should have invited the accused to call medical or other evidence: *R. v. Kidder* (1992), 127 A.R. 136, 38 M.V.R. (2d) 98 (C.A.).

In determining whether to grant a discharge, regard must be had to the circumstances and gravity of the offence, the motive of the offender to rehabilitate, the alcohol-related criminal record, whether there was a driving prohibition at the time and whether a previous curative discharge had been granted: *R. v. Soosay* (2001), 160 C.C.C. (3d) 437 (Alta. C.A.).

"Other evidence" must be evidence which is similar in quality and kind to medical evidence including evidence from other professionals who are able to provide information on treatment and rehabilitation. Accordingly, evidence of the accused and a youth justice committee worker was insufficient to support a discharge: *R. v. Soosay*, *supra*.

255.1 [*Repealed*, 2018, c. 21, s. 14.]

CROSS-REFERENCES

"Motor vehicle" is defined in s. 2. "Aircraft" and "vessel" are defined in s. 214. Section 258(1)(*c*) and (*d*) assist the prosecution in establishing the accused's blood alcohol level at the time of the offence. Those provisions, however, only apply to proceedings for offences under s. 255. There are a number of other offences to which this section might have application. See in particular ss. 220 and 221 [criminal negligence], s. 252 [failing to stop], and s. 259 [operating a motor vehicle, vessel or aircraft while disqualified]. For notes on sentencing for driving offences, see s. 718.2.

SYNOPSIS

The effect of this section is that if the offence was committed by means of a motor vehicle, vessel or aircraft, evidence that the accused's blood alcohol level exceeded .160 at the time when the offence was committed is deemed to be an aggravating factor on sentencing. This section must be read with s. 718.2, which sets out other statutory aggravating factors.

256. [*Repealed*, 2018, c. 21, s. 14.]

Editor's Note: The power to issue a warrant authorizing a peace officer to acquire a blood sample from a person incapable of providing consent is now provided in s. 320.29. The annotations below should be approached with caution in relation to the new provision.

CROSS-REFERENCES

The terms "peace officer" and "justice" are defined in s. 2 and the terms "qualified medical practitioner" and "qualified technician" in s. 254. The reference to s. 487.1 is to the telewarrant procedure set out in that section. The term "bodily harm" is defined in s. 2.

The normal procedure for obtaining blood samples by demand is set out in s. 254. Section 257 protects the medical practitioner and qualified technician from criminal and civil liability when proceeding under this section. Section 258.1 enacts provisions to protect the privacy of the accused by prohibiting unauthorized use of bodily samples taken under this section.

The presumption respecting the accused's blood alcohol level arising from analysis of a blood sample is found in s. 258(1)(*d*). Procedure for admission of certificates of an analyst, qualified technician and medical practitioner is set out in s. 258(1)(*e*) to (*i*) and (6) and (7). Note s. 258(4) which provides for summary application to a judge, within 3 months of the date the blood sample was taken, for an order releasing one of the samples for the purpose of testing by the defence.

Section 489.1 [which incorrectly refers to s. 258 rather than this section] requires that the peace officer make a report to a justice as soon as practicable following execution of the warrant.

SYNOPSIS

This section authorizes a justice who has reasonable grounds to believe: (a) that a person has committed an offence under s. 253 within the preceding four hours; (b) that the person has been involved in an accident resulting in bodily harm to himself or anyone else or death to another person; (c) that a physician is of the opinion that the person is physically or mentally unable to consent to the taking of blood samples; and (d) that the physician is also of the opinion that the taking of the blood samples would not endanger the life or health of the person, to issue a warrant authorizing a peace officer to require a physician to take or to supervise the taking of sufficient blood from the person to allow analysis for the concentration of alcohol or drugs. The information to obtain the warrant must be in Form 1 or, if obtained by telephone or other means of telecommunication, pursuant to s. 487.1, modified to contain a statement setting out the alleged offence and the identity of the person from whom blood samples are to be taken. The warrant may be in Form 5 or 5.1, varied to suit the case. The warrant may only be executed if the physician continues to be satisfied that the condition of the person precludes consent and that the person's health will not be endangered. If blood is taken pursuant to the warrant, the peace officer must give a copy or a facsimile of the warrant (as soon as practicable) to the person from whom the samples are obtained.

ANNOTATIONS

Constitutional considerations – The non-consensual taking of a blood sample from an unconscious motorist without a warrant and without any statutory authority is a serious intrusion into the person's privacy and this violation of s. 8 of the Charter warrants exclusion of the evidence obtained: *R. v. Pohoretsky*, [1987] 1 S.C.R. 945, 33 C.C.C. (3d) 398 (7:0). [**Note:** This case arose prior to the statutory amendments providing for the taking of blood samples in certain cases.] Similarly: *R. v. Tomaso* (1989), 70 C.R. (3d) 152, 33 O.A.C. 106 (C.A.).

To a similar effect, see *R. v. Dyment*, [1988] 2 S.C.R. 417, 45 C.C.C. (3d) 244 (5:0), where a blood sample originally taken from the accused for medical reasons was turned over to a police officer. The physician held the blood sample subject to a duty to respect the patient's privacy and this was sufficient to qualify the police officer's taking of the sample as a seizure. The officer had no warrant to seize the sample and the Crown adduced no evidence to justify a warrantless seizure. The seizure was unlawful and unreasonable under s. 8 of the Charter and the results of the analysis of the sample were inadmissible pursuant to s. 24(2) of the Charter.

Similarly, *R. v. Dersch*, [1993] 3 S.C.R. 768, 85 C.C.C. (3d) 1, where it was held that the accused's rights were violated when the police, without consent or a warrant, obtained confidential information from the physician as to the results of a blood alcohol test. The accused had repeatedly refused to provide a blood sample and the sample was only obtained, for medical purposes, when the accused was unconscious. Also, *R. v. Colarusso*, [1994] 1 S.C.R. 20, 87 C.C.C. (3d) 193, where it was held that the accused's rights under s. 8 of the Charter were violated when the results of analysis of blood samples originally obtained by the coroner for his purposes were appropriated for use in a criminal prosecution.

There was no violation of the Charter where the officer merely asked hospital personnel to not destroy a blood sample taken for medical purposes until the officer could obtain a warrant. The hospital staff were not agents of the state and the subsequent seizure pursuant to the warrant was valid: *R. v. Lunn* (1990), 61 C.C.C. (3d) 193 (B.C.C.A.).

It was proper for the police officer to take control of one of several blood samples taken by hospital personnel for medical purposes to preserve its continuity until a search warrant could be obtained. Such action did not violate s. 8 of the Charter where the officer had reasonable and probable grounds to protect the blood sample: *R. v. Katsigiorgis* (1987), 39 C.C.C. (3d) 256 (Ont. C.A.).

Procedural requirements – The failure of the officer to file the written report as required by s. 487.1(9) did not invalidate the warrant nor render inadmissible the results of analysis of a blood sample taken pursuant to the warrant: *R. v. Skin* (1988), 13 M.V.R. (2d) 130 (B.C. Co. Ct.).

257. [*Repealed*, 2018, c. 21, s. 14.]

258. [*Repealed*, 2018, c. 21, s. 14.]

Editor's Note: The evidentiary shortcuts and presumptions governing drug- and alcohol-related driving offences are now set out in ss. 320.31 through 320.35. The annotations below should be approached with caution in relation to the new provisions.

CROSS-REFERENCES

The terms "peace officer", "motor vehicle", "railway equipment", "superior court of criminal jurisdiction" and "court of criminal jurisdiction" are defined in s. 2. The terms "aircraft", "vessel" and "operates" are defined in s. 214. The terms "analyst", "approved container", "approved instrument", "qualified medical practitioner" and "qualified technician" are defined in s. 254. The offence of impaired operation is defined in ss. 253 and 255, of "over 80" in s. 253 and refusing to comply with a breath or blood demand in s. 254.

Section 25(1) of the *Interpretation Act*, R.S.C. 1985, c. I-21 provides that "Where an enactment provides that a document is evidence of a fact without anything in the context to indicate that the document is conclusive evidence, then, in any judicial proceedings, the document is admissible in evidence and the fact is deemed to be established in the absence of any evidence to the contrary."

As to proof of service by affidavit, see s. 4(6).

Section 258.1 enacts provisions to protect the privacy of the accused by prohibiting unauthorized use of bodily samples taken under ss. 254 or 256 and unauthorized disclosure of the results of physical coordination tests.

SYNOPSIS

This section provides that, where the prosecution establishes in proceedings under s. 255(1) with respect to an offence under ss. 253, 254(5) or 255(2) to (3.2) that the accused was sitting in the operator's seat of the vehicle, the accused is deemed to have care or control of that vehicle. This presumption can be overturned if the accused is able to establish that the purpose of occupying that seat was not for setting the vehicle in motion.

In addition, the result of an analysis of a breath or blood sample along with samples of urine or other bodily substances, may be admitted in evidence even if there was no warning prior to the taking of the sample that the accused need not consent to the procedure, nor that the result might be used in evidence. No person is required, however, to give a sample of urine or other bodily substance except as required under s. 254 and evidence of a failure or refusal to give such a sample is not admissible at trial, nor may it be made the subject of comment. When the technical requirements described in s. 258(1)(*c*), (*d*) and (*d*.1) are met, the evidence of the results of analysis is, in the absence of evidence to the contrary, proof of the concentration of alcohol in the accused's blood at the time of the offence and proof, where applicable, that the concentration of alcohol in blood exceeded 80 mg alcohol in 100 ml of blood. If more than one sample is analyzed and the results are different, the evidence of the lowest of the concentrations will be used in the proceedings.

To rebut the presumption in para. (*c*) (the presumption of identity for breath samples), the accused must show that the approved instrument was malfunctioning or was operated improperly, that the malfunction or improper operation resulted in the determination that the concentration of alcohol in the accused's blood exceeded 80 mg of alcohol in 100 mL of blood, and that the concentration of alcohol in the accused's blood would not, in fact, have exceeded 80 mg of alcohol in 100 mL of blood at the time when the offence was alleged to have been committed. Under para. (*d*.01), the presumption cannot be defeated by evidence of the amount of alcohol consumed, the rate of absorption or elimination of alcohol or a calculation based on what the concentration of alcohol in the accused's blood would have been at the time when the offence was alleged to have been committed. Further, under para. (*d*.1), where the analysis shows a concentration exceeding .08, the presumption of identity applies in the absence of evidence tending to show that the accused's consumption of alcohol was consistent with both (i) a concentration of alcohol in the accused's blood that did not exceed 80 mg of alcohol in 100 mL of blood at the time when the offence was alleged to have been committed, and (ii) the concentration of alcohol in the accused's blood as determined under para. (*c*) or (*d*), as the case may be, at the time when the sample or samples were taken.

The conditions for rebutting the presumption in para. (*d*) (the presumption of identity for blood samples) are almost identical except that the accused must show, not that the instrument was malfunctioning or operated improperly, but that the analysis was performed improperly, that the improper performance resulted in the determination that the concentration of alcohol in the accused's blood exceeded 80 mg of alcohol in 100 mL of blood, and that the concentration of alcohol in the accused's blood would not, in fact, have exceeded 80 mg of alcohol in 100 mL of blood at the time when the offence was alleged to have been committed. Paragraph (*d*.1) also applies to an attempt to rebut the para. (*d*) presumption.

It would seem that these provisions, which came into force on May 1, 2008, attempt to reverse a long line of cases that allowed the accused to rebut the presumption of identity by adducing expert evidence that, based on the defence testimony as to the amount of alcohol consumed, the blood-alcohol would not have exceeded .08. That kind of evidence would not seem to be sufficient since *inter alia* the evidence would not show that the machine was malfunctioning or that the analysis was performed improperly. It should be pointed out that, even before these provisions came into force on May 1, 2008, the value of this kind of evidence was placed in doubt by the decision of the Supreme Court of Canada in *R. v. Gibson*, 2008 SCC 16. In view of these amendments, the notes of decisions concerning this kind of expert evidence have been removed. If readers require information on these decisions they should refer to the 2008 edition of *Martin's Annual Criminal Code*.

Subsection (1)(*e*), (*f*), (*g*), (*h*) and (*i*) provide that the certificates of analysts, medical practitioners and qualified technicians are themselves evidence of the facts set out therein without the need to prove the signature or the official character of the person signing the certificate. The presumptions of accuracy enacted by these provisions can be rebutted by evidence to the contrary as provided for in s. 25(1) of the *Interpretation Act*, R.S.C. 1985, c. I-21. The party intending to produce the certificate as evidence must, prior to trial, give the other party reasonable notice of his intention, along with a copy of the certificate. An accused person may, with leave of the court, require the attendance for cross-examination of the medical practitioner, analyst or technician who signed the certificate.

Under subsec. (4), if an additional sample of blood was taken, the accused may apply to a judge of a superior court or court of criminal jurisdiction within six months of the date upon which the blood samples were taken for an order for the release of one of the samples for analysis. In proceedings under s. 255(1) in respect of an offence committed under s. 253(1)(*a*), or in proceedings under s. 255(2) or (3), evidence of failure by the accused to comply with a demand made under s. 254 is admissible. The court may draw an inference adverse to the accused from such evidence. Under subsec. (5), a blood sample taken for analysis of alcohol concentration may also be tested for the presence of drugs.

ANNOTATIONS

General – The amendments to subsec. (1) do not apply retrospectively to offences committed before July 2, 2009: *R. v. Dineley*, [2012] 3 S.C.R. 272, 290 C.C.C. (3d) 190.

Presumption of care or control [subsec. (1)(*a*)] – Proof of indecision on the part of the accused is not sufficient to rebut the presumption in subsec. (1)(*a*). While it may be that the accused need not establish on a balance of probabilities that he had a settled purpose at the time of initially occupying the driver's seat other than that of setting the vehicle in motion, he must nevertheless prove on a balance of probabilities that he did not occupy that seat for the purpose of putting the vehicle in motion: *R. v. George* (1994), 90 C.C.C. (3d) 502 (Nfld. C.A.).

The fact that the accused is able to rebut the presumption in this paragraph does not entitle him to an acquittal where the Crown is able to establish that he had care or control without reliance on the presumption. This paragraph does not import into the care or control offence an intent to drive and the accused may be convicted of that offence where although he does not have an intent to drive he performs some act or series of acts involving the use of a car, its fittings or equipment, whereby the vehicle may unintentionally be set in motion: *R. v. Ford*, [1982] 1 S.C.R. 231, 65 C.C.C. (2d) 392 (7:2).

The Crown does not have to make a formal election before it can rely on the presumption in this paragraph: *R. v. Journeaux* (1992), 38 M.V.R. (2d) 323 (Ont. C.A.).

The Crown was not entitled to rely on the presumption in this paragraph where the accused was lying across the seat with his head on the passenger side and his legs were encased in a sleeping-bag under the steering wheel. It could not be said that he was occupying the seat ordinarily occupied by the driver. It was further held that the Crown had not otherwise made out care or control. Acts of care or control, short of driving, are acts which involve some use of the vehicle or its fittings, or some course of conduct associated with the vehicle which would involve the risk of putting the vehicle in motion so that it could become dangerous, and in this case the accused was asleep in the sleeping-bag: *R. v. Toews*, [1985] 2 S.C.R. 119, 21 C.C.C. (3d) 24 (7:0).

Constitutionality of care or control presumption – It has been held that the predecessor to this paragraph, although it required the accused to prove on a balance of probabilities that he did not enter the vehicle with the intention of setting it in motion, is a reasonable limit on the guarantee to the presumption of innocence in s. 11(*d*) of the *Canadian Charter of Rights and Freedoms* and is therefore valid: *R. v. Whyte*, [1988] 2 S.C.R. 3, 42 C.C.C. (3d) 97 (6:0).

Applicability of presumption (para. (1)(*c*)) – To rebut the presumptions in subsec. (1)(*c*), an accused must adduce evidence tending to show that the malfunctioning or improper operation of the approved instrument casts doubt on the reliability of the results. The burden is discharged if: (1) the accused adduces evidence relating directly to the malfunctioning or improper operation of the instrument; and (2) the accused establishes that this defect tends to cast doubt on the reliability of the results. In the case of improper operation of an instrument, while abstract evidence alone may sometimes meet the requirement of raising a reasonable doubt about the reliability of the results, it is more likely that evidence that relates more concretely to the facts in issue will be required. What is essential is that the possibility that the defect affected the reliability of the results is serious enough to raise a reasonable doubt: *R. c. Cyr-Langlois* (2018), 368 C.C.C. (3d) 415 (S.C.C.).

The Crown may rely on the presumption in this paragraph not only where it proceeds by way of certificate under subsec. (1)(*g*) but where the technician gives *viva voce* evidence: *R. v. Lightfoot*, [1981] 1 S.C.R. 566, 59 C.C.C. (2d) 414 (9:0).

When the Crown proceeds by way of *viva voce* evidence of the qualified technician and seeks to rely on the presumption in this paragraph, it need only meet the requirements of this subsection and therefore, *inter alia*, the provisions of subsec. (1)(*f*) have no application: *R. v. Walters* (1975), 26 C.C.C. (2d) 56, 11 N.S.R. (2d) 443 (App. Div.).

Where the Crown is unable to rely on the presumption in this paragraph it may still prove the offence by adducing expert evidence as to the progressive absorption of alcohol into the bloodstream in order to relate the readings in the certificate back to the time of the offence: *R. v. Bozek* (1977), 34 C.C.C. (2d) 457 (Sask. Dist. Ct.); *R. v. Burnison* (1979), 70 C.C.C. (2d) 38 (Ont. C.A.).

When proceeding by way of *viva voce* evidence from the breathalyzer technician rather than by certificate there is no requirement of proof as to the suitability of the substance or solution before the Crown may rely on the presumption in this subsection: *R. v. Lightfoot*, *supra*.

The presumption applies equally to the included offence of care and control "over 80" where the offence charged was driving "over 80": *R. v. Pawluk* (2017), 357 C.C.C. (3d) 86 (Ont. C.A.).

Requirement of two samples – The words "each sample" must be interpreted in conjunction with s. 254(3) meaning each sample which in the opinion of the qualified technician is necessary to enable a proper analysis to be made. It would not include for example, a breath sample a portion of which escapes due to a malfunction in the machine and which in the opinion of the technician will not give a proper analysis: *R. v. Perrier* (1984), 15 C.C.C. (3d) 506, 29 M.V.R. 92 (Ont. C.A.).

Despite the use of the superlative "lowest" the Crown may still rely on the presumption where only two samples were taken. It is not necessary that three or more samples be taken: *R. v. Schultz* (1977), 38 C.C.C. (2d) 39 (Ont. H.C.J.).

It was held in *R. v. Norman* (1978), 40 C.C.C. (2d) 27, [1978] 3 W.W.R. 542 (Alta. C.A.), that considering the certificate as a whole the fact that the certificate referred to the results of analysis of "one of the said samples" and "another of the said samples" did not leave open as a reasonable conclusion that a third sample was taken the results of which were not given in the certificate. In the absence of anything to suggest to the contrary "another" is to be read in the sense of "the other". Folld: *R. v. Grace* (1979), 47 C.C.C. (2d) 301 (N.S.C.A.).

Similarly, the fact that the printed form of the certificate has spaces for the results of three breath tests, only two of which were filled out does not give rise to an inference that a third sample was taken but that the results were not recorded: *R. v. Dempsey* (1979), 45 C.C.C. (2d) 267 (N.B.C.A.).

Similarly, the mere fact that the accused blew into the breathalyzer three times is not evidence that more than two "samples" were taken: *R. v. Mangialaio* (1984), 15 C.C.C. (3d) 331, 29 M.V.R. 244 (B.C.C.A.).

Where only one breath sample was obtained, although the Crown may not rely on the technician's certificate or the presumption in this section, it may still secure a conviction under s. 253(*b*) by proceeding by *viva voce* expert evidence where the technician is able to testify that the one sample was suitable: *R. v. Jones* (1976), 33 C.C.C. (2d) 50, 16 N.B.R. (2d) 32 (C.A.).

Requirement samples received directly into approved instrument [para. (*c*)(iii)] – Evidence from the technician, merely that samples were received into a "breathalyzer instrument" is not proof that the samples were received directly into an approved instrument as required by subpara. (iii): *R. v. Alatyppo* (1983), 4 C.C.C. (3d) 514, 20 M.V.R. 39 (Ont. C.A.).

The court may take judicial notice of the workings of the Borkenstein Breathalyzer, or at least refer to standard textbooks on the subject, and so take note of the fact that the only way to introduce the breath sample is by blowing directly into a tube attached to the machine. Thus, evidence that the breath sample was "introduced" is proof that it was received "directly" into the breathalyzer: *R. v. Walters* (1975), 26 C.C.C. (2d) 56 (C.A.).

Time element / interval of 15 minutes between samples – It was held by Seaton J.A., in *R. v. Perry* (1978), 41 C.C.C. (2d) 182 (B.C.C.A.), that there was no basis for extending the provisions of s. 25(2) of the *Interpretation Act*, R.S.C. 1970, c. I-23, to minutes and thus breath tests taken at 3:00 a.m. and 3:15 a.m. complied with the requirement that the breath samples be taken "at least 15 minutes" apart. This holding, which was contrary to the conclusion reached by several other provincial appellate courts, was apparently upheld by the Supreme Court of Canada which dismissed the appeal by the accused on June 11, 1980, [1980] 1 S.C.R. 1104, 51 C.C.C. (2d) 576*n*, N.R. *loc. cit.* p. 106, in brief reasons to the effect that the court was in agreement with the reasons of Taggart J.A. Taggart J.A. concurred in the reasons of Seaton J.A., but in addition relied on a finding of fact by the trial judge that the actual time between the tests was 15 complete minutes.

In *R. v. Taylor* (1983), 7 C.C.C. (3d) 293 (Ont. C.A.), leave to appeal to S.C.C. refused C.C.C. *loc. cit.*, the court considered the judgments in *R. v. Perry, supra,* and the majority of the court concluded that while a bare 15 minutes is sufficient for compliance, that interval is the interval of time from the point when everything necessary to complete the taking of the first sample has been done and the point when the first act is done to commence the taking of the second sample. The requirement will not be met by a certificate which merely states that the samples were taken at, for example, 3:00 a.m. and 3:17 a.m. since such a certificate is open to the conclusion that the taking of the samples commenced at those two times and without additional information as to the length of time needed to finish taking the first sample, the trial judge would not be able to determine the interval between them. Folld: *R. v. Dawson* (1984), 12 C.C.C. (3d) 152 (P.E.I.S.C. *in banco*); not followed: *R. v. Kornak* (1984), 12 C.C.C. (3d) 182 (Alta. C.A.); *R. v. Moore* (1984), 13 C.C.C. (3d) 281 (B.C.C.A.); *R. v. Scott* (1984), 36 Sask. R. 216 (C.A.); *R. v. DeCoste* (1984), 15 C.C.C. (3d) 289 (N.S.S.C. App. Div.); *R. v. Hepditch* (1989), 47 C.C.C. (3d) 286, 13 M.V.R. (2d) 101, 75 Nfld. & P.E.I.R. 201 (Nfld. C.A.).

In a subsequent case, *R. v. Hayes* (1985), 19 C.C.C. (3d) 569 (Ont. C.A.), the court held that for the purpose of this paragraph the sample is taken once the accused's breath sample is inside the breathalyzer and in computing the time interval it is not necessary to take into account the period of time for the machine to analyze and indicate the results of each sample. Similarly, *R. v. Daly* (1985), 32 M.V.R. 213 (Ont. C.A.); *R. v. Atkinson* (1986), 42 M.V.R. 78 (N.S.C.A.); *R. v. Arsenault* (1986), 43 M.V.R. 287 (P.E.I.S.C.).

The requirement that the samples were taken at least 15 minutes apart applies to samples of which in the opinion of the technician a proper analysis can be made. Thus, where a "sample" is taken but not analyzed because the machine was not properly hooked up, the technician need not wait 15 minutes to take a proper sample: *R. v. Weselowski* (1984), 11 C.C.C. (3d) 574 (B.C.C.A.); *R. v. Denton* (1985), 32 M.V.R. 250 (Sask. Q.B.).

Time element / as soon as practicable and within two hours – A breath sample was taken "as soon as practicable" where it was taken one hour after the accused's arrival at the police station where the delay was due to the necessity of repairing the breathalyzer: *R. v. Finlayson* (1974), 21 C.C.C. (2d) 511 (Sask. C.A.).

The test for determining whether or not breath samples were taken as soon as practicable is whether they were taken within a reasonably prompt time under the circumstances. The court must take into account both subjective and objective factors, including whether the police officer involved acted reasonably: *R. v. Van Der Veen* (1988), 44 C.C.C. (3d) 38 (Alta. C.A.); *R. v. Vanderbruggen* (2006), 206 C.C.C. (3d) 489 (Ont. C.A.).

The phrase "as soon as practicable" must be applied with reason having regard to the whole chain of events and bearing in mind that the *Criminal Code* permits an outside limit of two hours from the time of the offence to the taking of the first test. There is no requirement that the Crown provide a detailed explanation of what occurred during every minute that the accused is in custody: *R. v. Vanderbruggen, supra.*

The approach articulated in *Vanderbruggen, supra*, also applies to delay *between* the taking of the first and second samples: *R. v. Singh* (2014), 310 C.C.C. (3d) 285 (Ont. C.A.).

The phrase "as soon as practicable" does not require that the tests be taken at the very earliest moment. In the circumstances a 20-minute delay while the accused was kept under observation was permissible: *R. v. Mudry; R. v. Coverly* (1979), 50 C.C.C. (2d) 518 (Alta. C.A.). Folld: *R. v. Carter* (1980), 55 C.C.C. (2d) 405 (B.C.C.A.); *R. v. Ashby* (1980), 57 C.C.C. (2d) 348 (Ont. C.A.); *R. v. Cander* (1981), 59 C.C.C. (2d) 490 (B.C.C.A.), leave to appeal to S.C.C. refused 38 N.R. 450*n*. Similarly: *R. v. Phillips* (1988), 42 C.C.C. (3d) 150 (Ont. C.A.).

Similarly, a 21-minute delay between the time of the arrival at the police station and the time of the first test is not evidence that the tests were not taken as soon as practicable. The requirement that the tests be taken as soon as practicable must be applied with reason. There is no need to explain every incident which occurred from the time of the offence to the time the samples were taken unless the trial judge is not satisfied on the evidence before him that the samples were taken as soon as practicable: *R. v. Carter* (1981), 59 C.C.C. (2d) 450 (Sask. C.A.). Folld: *R. v. Cambrin* (1982), 1 C.C.C. (3d) 59 (B.C.C.A.).

The critical issue in each case, where it is alleged that the tests were not taken as soon as practicable, is whether the conduct of the police was reasonable, having regard to all the circumstances. The act of the arresting officer in commencing the preparation of the alcohol influence report for a period of nine minutes before turning the accused over to the breathalyzer technician, was not an unreasonable procedure: *R. v. Payne* (1990), 56 C.C.C. (3d) 548 (Ont. C.A.).

Although the officer has grounds to make an immediate demand under s. 254(3), the fact that he first makes a demand under s. 254(2) does not prevent the samples subsequently obtained pursuant to the s. 254(3) demand from being obtained as soon as practicable: *R. v. Jensen* (1982), 2 C.C.C. (3d) 11 (N.S.C.A.).

Judicial notice – It was held in *R. v. Dickson* (1973), 5 N.S.R. (2d) 240 (C.A.), that the trial Judge erred in taking judicial notice of the tolerance for error in the Borkenstein Breathalyzer.

And, it was held to be an error for the judge to base his decision in part on a breathalyzer manual which he obtained from the police and which was not properly introduced into evidence: *R. v. Robertson* (1979), 47 C.C.C. (2d) 159 (B.C.C.A.).

Note: Some of the cases noted below were decided prior to the significant amendments to this section in subsec. (1)(*c*), (*d*), (*d*.01) and (*d*.1).

Evidence to the contrary / generally – As to the meaning generally of the words "any evidence to the contrary" see *R. v. Proudlock*, [1979] 1 S.C.R. 525, 43 C.C.C. (2d) 321, noted under s. 348, *infra.*

"Evidence to the contrary" must be evidence which tends to establish that the proportion of alcohol in the accused's blood at the time of the offence was not the same as indicated by the approved instrument. No evidence is "evidence to the contrary" when its only effect is to demonstrate in general terms the possible uncertainty of the elements of the legislative scheme established by these provisions or the inherent fallibility of the instruments which are approved under statutory authority. Thus, for example, evidence that the particular type of Borkenstein Breathalyzer is subject to a possible margin of error is not evidence to the contrary: *R. v. Moreau*, [1979] 1 S.C.R. 261, 42 C.C.C. (2d) 525 (5:4).

Evidence that is disbelieved, such as testimony from the accused as to the amount he had to drink, cannot form the basis for an expert's opinion so as to constitute evidence to the contrary. Further, the absence of symptoms other than the smell of alcohol, while relevant to a charge of impaired driving, is a neutral factor and is not evidence to the contrary: *R. v. Boucher* (2005), 202 C.C.C. (3d) 34, 33 C.R. (6th) 32 (S.C.C.).

The prohibition against using breathalyzer readings in assessing credibility applies only to cases in which the accused challenges the presumption of accuracy because, in such circumstances, it would be circular to use readings as proof of their own accuracy. However, where defence counsel only challenges the presumption of identity, the consideration of breathalyzer readings does not raise the spectre of circular reasoning. They are part of the body of evidence which the trial judge has to consider in deciding whether there was a reasonable doubt: *R. v. Kernighan* (2010), 257 C.C.C. (3d) 12 (Ont. C.A.).

In *R. v. Kozun* (1981), 64 C.C.C. (2d) 62 (Sask. C.A.), it was held that the fact that a third test was taken, the results of which were not disclosed in the certificate did not constitute evidence to the contrary.

Rounding down or truncating the breathalyzer reading to the second digit does not produce a false result nor constitute evidence to the contrary: *R. v. Hanson* (1989), 75 C.R. (3d) 110, 18 M.V.R. (2d) 172 (Ont. C.A.); *R. v. Goosen* (1985), 34 Man. R. (2d) 242, 35 M.V.R. 145 (Q.B.).

Evidence that the accused failed a roadside screening test may not be used to discredit evidence capable of constituting "evidence to the contrary" as to do so would render the trial unfair: *R. v. Coutts* (1999), 136 C.C.C. (3d) 225 (Ont. C.A.). Also see *R. v. Milne* (1996), 107 C.C.C. (3d) 118 (Ont. C.A.), leave to appeal to S.C.C. refused 110 C.C.C. (3d) vi, noted under s. 254, *supra.*

Contra: *R. v. Fox* (2003), 178 C.C.C. (3d) 223 (Sask. C.A.), and *R. v. Beston* (2006), 214 C.C.C. (3d) 509 (Sask. C.A.), where it was held that the results of the approved screening device test cannot be used to incriminate the accused but can be used to test the credibility of the accused giving evidence to the contrary in order to rebut the presumption of accuracy of a certificate of a breath test.

Results of a breathalyzer test without reliance on the statutory presumptions may be considered as part of the totality of evidence to discredit evidence to the contrary: *R. v. Bernard* (1999), 140 C.C.C. (3d) 412 (Que. C.A.).

Similarly, *R. v. Suttie* (2004), 188 C.C.C. (3d) 167 (Ont. C.A.), held that where the accused challenges the accuracy of the blood alcohol readings in the certificate by calling evidence tending to show that his or her blood alcohol level at the time of testing must have been below .08, subsec. (1)(*g*) permits the court to consider the certificate as some evidence of the facts contained in it in determining whether to accept or reject the accused's "evidence to the contrary".

The proper interpretation of subsec. (1)(*c*)(iii) is that the breath sample from the accused must be received into an approved instrument either from an approved container if one is used or, if not, directly into the approved instrument itself: *R. v. Mulroney* (2009), 248 C.C.C. (3d) 311 (Ont. C.A.).

Evidence to the contrary/constitutional considerations – In *R. c. St-Onge Lamoureux*, [2012] 3 S.C.R. 187, 294 C.C.C. (3d) 42, the court considered a constitutional challenge to the new restrictions on "evidence to the contrary". It held (5:2) that, while ss. 258(1)(*c*), 258(1)(*d*.01) and 258(1)(*d*.1) do not infringe ss. 7 and 11(*c*) of Charter, they do infringe s. 11(*d*). Sections 258(1)(*d*.01) and 258(1)(*d*.1) are justified under s. 1, but s. 258(1)(*c*) is only justified once two restrictions on the defence are severed. Section 258(1)(*c*)(iv) contains three separate and cumulative new requirements that the accused must satisfy to rebut the presumptions of accuracy and identity: (1) there must be evidence that the instrument was malfunctioning or was operated improperly; (2) there must be evidence tending to show that the malfunction or improper operation of the instrument resulted in a reading according to which the blood alcohol level of the accused exceeded .08; and (3) there must be evidence that the accused's blood alcohol level would not, in fact, have exceeded .08 at the time of the alleged offence. While (1) is demonstrably justified under s. 1, both (2) and (3) constitute serious infringements of the right to be presumed innocent that cannot be justified in a democratic society. The court therefore read down s. 258(1)(*c*)(iv) to exclude these two requirements.

Subsection (1)(*d*) [Special considerations re blood samples] Subparagraph (i) requires that the accused have notice within the three-month period [now six-month] that he is charged with an impaired driving offence, that the Crown has had a sample of the accused's blood analysed and that a second sample was taken and is available to permit an analysis of it by him or on his behalf. If the accused is given notice within this three-month [now six-month] period and then does not exercise his right to request production then, absent special circumstances, this would foreclose any complaints that the prosecution was later unable to produce the sample by reason of its destruction following the expiry of the three-month period. The most appropriate and convenient way to notify the accused of the existence of the second sample is by service of the certificate of the qualified technician or certificate of the qualified medical practitioner as the case may be. This does not mean that notice by other means cannot be given so long as it is to the same effect and it is proved in accordance with the criminal standard that the accused was made aware in a timely fashion. The accused must receive the information with enough time to apply for an order releasing the sample for analysis under subsec. (4). However, where the accused has been given proper notice of the availability of the second sample then the fact that he did not apply for its release for testing would not effect the availability of the presumption: *R. v. Egger*, [1993] 2 S.C.R. 451, 82 C.C.C. (3d) 193. However, the failure to give notice of the existence of the second sample merely precludes the Crown from relying on the presumption. The Crown is entitled to present *viva voce* evidence from an analyst and physician as to the blood-alcohol content: *R. v. Ross* (1996), 108 C.C.C. (3d) 168 (N.S.C.A.).

The "offence" referred to in para. (*d*)(ii) means not only the offence specified in the information but also any other offence properly included therein: *R. v. Cyr* (1983), 25 M.V.R. 62, 60 N.S.R. (2d) 159 (C.A.).

Where the Crown does not rely on the provisions of the *Criminal Code* respecting the obtaining of blood samples and proof of the blood alcohol level pursuant to this section, but rather relies on an analysis made at the hospital, the evidence of the hospital technologists as to the results of the analysis performed by the hospital equipment is admissible, notwithstanding that the technologists were unable to give evidence as to the capability or reliability of the equipment nor as to the accuracy of the results of the analyses. It is not necessary for evidence to be given to explain precisely how the machine operates, it being sufficient that the expert operating the machine establishes that the machine is capable of making the required measurements or producing the required data, that the machine was in good working order at the relevant times, and that it was properly used: *R. v. Redmond* (1990), 54 C.C.C. (3d) 273 (Ont. C.A.). *Contra*: *R. v. Bird* (1989), 71 C.R. (3d) 52, 76 Sask. R. 275 (C.A.).

The fact that the blood samples, taken from the accused for hospital purposes, were destroyed before the accused could apply for release of a sample for independent testing did not result in violation of the accused's rights under s. 7, although the Crown relied upon the analysis performed at the hospital to prove the accused's blood alcohol level. The Crown was not seeking to rely on the presumption in this paragraph and thus there was no reason for requiring that a blood sample should have been preserved for analysis: *R. v. Redmond*, *supra*.

Subsection (1)(*d*.1) ("straddle" evidence) – In *R. v. Gibson*, [2008] 1 S.C.R. 397, 230 C.C.C. (3d) 97, the Supreme Court held that expert evidence of alcohol elimination rates in the general population and "straddle" evidence can be relevant and are therefore not inherently inadmissible for the purpose of rebutting the presumption in subsec. (1)(*d*.1). However, because of variation between individuals, the probative value of evidence based on rates in the general population will often be so low that it will fail to raise a reasonable doubt that the accused had a blood alcohol content exceeding 80 mg. Expert evidence of the elimination rate of the accused as established by a test is potentially more probative of the blood alcohol content he or she had while driving than evidence based on elimination rates in the general population. However, because an individual's elimination rate varies over time based on a number of factors, the probative value of evidence based on the elimination rate of the accused will logically depend on the number of variables controlled for in the elimination rate test. Evidence of the elimination rate of the accused at the time of the offence would be more likely to rebut the presumption in subsec. (1)(*d*.1) than mere evidence of the elimination rate of the accused under testing conditions. In *R. v. Ibanescu*, [2013] 2 S.C.R. 400, 303 C.C.C. (3d) 1, the court confirmed that the reasons of LeBel J. in *Gibson*, summarized above, reflect the governing law.

Subsection (1)(*e*) [certificate of analyst] – It is not necessary for the certificate to name the defendant but it must identify the bodily substance in such a way so that that substance may be linked to the defendant by other evidence: *R. v. Larson* (1971), 3 C.C.C. (2d) 537 (Alta. C.A.).

Subsection (1)(*f*) [certificate of analyst re alcohol standard] – A rubber stamp facsimile of the analyst's signature is not the equivalent of his signature: *R. v. Faber* (1972), 9 C.C.C. (2d) 353 (B.C.S.C.).

This subsection is merely evidentiary providing the Crown with the means by which to rebut any evidence that the substance or solution was unsuitable: *R. v. Ware* (1975), 30 C.R.N.S. 308 (Ont. C.A.).

Subsection (1)(*g*) [qualified technician's certificate] / Identification of suitable alcohol standard – There is no requirement of proof by means of a separate certificate from an analyst under subsec. (1)(*f*) that the testing standard was suitable. Absent evidence to the contrary, the technician is the judge of the suitability of the standard and the technician's statement as to the suitability of the alcohol standard is sufficient. Further, unless there is some evidence that the certificate under s. 258(1)(*g*) is not reliable, there is no duty on the

Crown to produce at or before trial a certificate under subsec. (1)(*f*) or to disclose that the standard used was suitable: *R. v. Squires* (1994), 87 C.C.C. (3d) 430 (Nfld. C.A.). Similarly, the technician's testimony that he had ascertained that the breathalyzer was in proper working order by means of alcohol standard was sufficient even though the operator testified that he did not personally examine the analyst's certificate accompanying ampoules of the standard alcohol solution: *R. v. Harding* (1994), 88 C.C.C. (3d) 97 (Ont. C.A.).

Other prerequisites to admissibility – The "place" is adequately identified for the purposes of para. (*g*)(iii)(B) where the municipality in which the tests were administered is set out in the certificate: *R. v. Padula* (1981), 59 C.C.C. (2d) 572 (Ont. C.A.).

The certificate is inadmissible when only one breath sample was taken nor *semble* may the Crown rely on the presumption in subsec. (1)(*c*) when only one sample was taken: *R. v. Noble*, [1978] 1 S.C.R. 632, 37 C.C.C. (2d) 193 (9:0).

The necessary nexus between the certificate and the charge may be inferred from circumstantial evidence based on the arresting officer's testimony as to the times of the tests and the identity of the technician and the contents of the notice of intention with the certificate of analysis attached thereto. In any event, it would seem that in determining the evidentiary link and the certificate's admissibility, the judge may refer to the contents of the certificate itself: *R. v. Andraishek* (1988), 9 M.V.R. (2d) 121 (Alta. C.A.). Similarly, *R. v. Walsh* (1980), 53 C.C.C. (2d) 568 (Ont. C.A.).

The only conditions precedent to the admissibility of the technician's certificate are that samples of breath be taken and that they be taken pursuant to a demand under s. 254. There is no further requirement that there be *viva voce* evidence from the technician that suitable samples had been taken by him: *R. v. Hall* (1981), 57 C.C.C. (2d) 305 (Alta. C.A.).

It is not necessary for the Crown to prove by extrinsic evidence that two or more samples were taken. While the Crown, to have the benefit of this paragraph, must establish a link between the breathalyzer demand and the test which resulted in the analysis, that link is established by proof that the test dealt with in the certificate was made pursuant to the demand: *R. v. Schlegel* (1985), 22 C.C.C. (3d) 436 (B.C.C.A.), leave to appeal to S.C.C. refused 66 N.R. 79*n*.

Paragraph (*g*)(iii)(B) does not require that the certificate record the time when the taking of the first sample commenced, where the certificate did set out the time when the taking of the first sample was complete and when the taking of the second sample commenced: *R. v. Eggen* (1988), 42 C.C.C. (3d) 94 (Sask. C.A.); *R. v. Hogg* (1990), 25 M.V.R. (2d) 1 (Ont. C.A.).

Forms vary from province to province and the issue is not compliance with a prescribed form but rather whether the requirements of subsec. (1)(*c*)(ii) are met given the particular certificate at issue. The requirements of this provision are satisfied without the necessity of stating the start and end times of when the accused began and finished providing a breath sample: *R. v. Gunn* (2010), 253 C.C.C. (3d) 1 (Sask. C.A.).

There is no requirement that the exact offences be stated in the notice: *R. v. Gazica* (2002), 168 C.C.C. (3d) 446 (Alta. C.A.).

Errors in certificate – Even though it seems obvious that there is only a minor typographical error an inaccurate certificate must be rejected: *R. v. Gosby* (1974), 26 C.R.N.S. 161, 8 N.S.R. (2d) 183 (C.A.). See also: *R. v. Michel* (2011), 276 C.C.C. (3d) 526 (Sask. Q.B.).

It was held, however, in *R. v. Bykowski* (1980), 54 C.C.C. (2d) 398 (Alta. C.A.) (2:1), that what was obviously a typographical error in the certificate the dates of the two samples being given as March "1978" and March "1979" could be "corrected" by evidence of a person other than a qualified technician, such as evidence from the arresting officer that all events occurred in March, 1979.

Effect of absence of grounds for making demand – While absence of reasonable and probable grounds for belief of impairment [or *semble* as result of the recent amendments, belief that the offence under s. 253(*b*) was committed] may afford a defence to a charge under s. 254(5) it does not render inadmissible certificate evidence of a qualified technician on a charge under s. 255: *R. v. Rilling*, [1976] 2 S.C.R. 183, 24 C.C.C. (2d) 81 (5:3).

In *R. v. Alex*, [2017] 1 S.C.R. 967, 349 C.C.C. (3d) 383, the court rejected a challenge to the decision in *Rilling, supra*. The Crown does not have to prove the existence of a lawful demand to avail itself of the evidentiary shortcuts in subsec. (1)(*c*) and (*g*). The court found it unnecessary to decide whether *Rilling* was correct when decided. The scientific reliability of the results of properly administered breath tests is now firmly established. Section 8 of the Charter, in combination with s. 24(2), provides a comprehensive and direct protection against unreasonable searches and seizures, including those of breath samples.

In *R. v. Charette* (2009), 243 C.C.C. (3d) 480, the Ontario Court of Appeal held that *R. v. Rilling, supra*, applies with equal force to s. 258(1)(*g*). For the purposes of s. 258(1)(*g*), where an accused is charged with driving "over 80", the Crown need not concern itself with proving the existence of reasonable and probable grounds under s. 254(3) unless the accused brings a Charter application challenging the admissibility of the test results.

Evidentiary effect of certificate – Section 25(1) of the *Interpretation Act*, R.S.C. 1985, c. I-21, applies to this paragraph and has the effect that the facts set out in the certificate are deemed to be established "in the absence of any evidence to the contrary". Evidence to the contrary would include evidence raising a reasonable doubt that the results of the analyses set out in the certificate correctly state the blood alcohol level at the time of those analyses: *R. v. Stewart* (1983), 8 C.C.C. (3d) 368 (B.C.C.A.).

Where the accused has adduced evidence to the contrary challenging the accuracy of the blood-alcohol readings, the trial judge may consider the certificate as some evidence of the facts contained in it in determining whether to accept or reject the evidence to the contrary. It will be in the rarest of cases, however, that the certificate alone is a sufficient basis to reject otherwise credible defence evidence to the contrary: *R. v. Suttie* (2004), 188 C.C.C. (3d) 167 (Ont. C.A.).

Subsection (1)(*h*) [certificate re blood samples] – The results of analysis of blood samples, taken for medical purposes and performed on hospital equipment, were inadmissible without some evidence from a qualified person that the machines used were capable of performing the function in question and that, if operated properly, would produce an accurate and reliable result. In the absence of such evidence, the results of the analyses produced by the machines lack any evidentiary value. It was precisely to avoid these problems of proof that this provision and s. 254 were enacted. Where the Crown is unable to rely on these provisions then it must prove its case in the usual way: *R. v. Bird* (1989), 71 C.R. (3d) 52, 76 Sask. R. 275 (C.A.).

The certificate of the qualified technician (a registered nurse) was not inadmissible although the technician failed to indicate what class of persons she fell into by marking one of the alternatives on the certificate. The omission was not substantially prejudicial to the accused since the technician signed the certificate and included the initials "R.N." In addition, the certificate of the qualified medical practitioner referred to the samples having been taken by a "qualified technician": *R. v. Fedun* (1993), 50 M.V.R. (2d) 286, 114 Sask. R. 127 (Q.B.).

Subsection (2) [No legal compulsion to provide samples] – Since this subsection is for the protection of the defence it is not improper for defence counsel to cross-examine to show that the accused's refusal to take a breathalyzer test reflected an attitude which would make it unlikely that her inculpatory statement was given voluntarily: *R. v. Lapinsky*, [1966] 3 C.C.C. 97 (B.C.S.C.).

In *R. v. Brager*, [1965] 4 C.C.C. 251 (B.C.C.A.), the court held that if defence counsel had elicited the fact that no physical sobriety tests were made then Crown counsel would be entitled to re-examine to disclose the reasons for that omission, not to prove guilt, but to alleviate any inference that such tests were not made because they would not support the charge.

Subsection (3) [Adverse inference from refusal to comply with demand] – Where the accused was acquitted of the charge under s. 254(5) and no appeal was taken the Crown is bound to accept the correctness of the verdict and may not rely on the adverse inference in this subsection on the accused's appeal from his conviction of the offence under s. 253: *R. v. Zink* (1977), 38 C.C.C. (2d) 97 (Alta. C.A.).

On the other hand the fact that the Crown by reliance on this subsection secures a conviction for the offence under s. 253(*a*) is not a bar to a conviction for the offence contrary to s. 254(5): *R. v. Mazurek* (1978), 41 C.C.C. (2d) 353 (Alta. Dist. Ct.).

Where the acquittal on the s. 254 charge is not the result of a finding that the accused did not comply with the demand but rather due to the "technicality" that the Crown failed to prove that the demand was made by the officer named in the information then this subsection may be invoked: *R. v. Fredrek* (1979), 17 A.R. 613 (C.A.); *R. v. Ranger* (1983), 26 M.V.R. 83 (B.C.C.A.).

The adverse inference arises merely upon proof that the accused refused without reasonable excuse to comply with the demand. There need not be proof also that the refusal was due to the accused's fear that the results would show that he was impaired: *R. v. Garneau* (1982), 66 C.C.C. (2d) 90 (Alta. Q.B.).

The adverse inference provided for by this subsection does not offend the guarantee to the presumption of innocence in s. 11(*d*) of the Charter: *R. v. Mackenzie* (1983), 6 C.C.C. (3d) 86 (Alta. Q.B.); *R. v. Van Den Elzen* (1983), 10 C.C.C. (3d) 532 (B.C.C.A.).

Subsection (4) [Application for order releasing sample] – See notes under heading: "Special considerations re blood samples" under subsec. (1)(*c*), (*d*) above.

Subsection (6) [Attendance of technician, etc.] – The analyst or qualified technician testifying under this subsection is a witness for the Crown and his evidence in chief would be the statements in his certificate: *R. v. Latter* (1971) 2 C.C.C. (2d) 453 (N.S.C.A.).

This subsection is neither pre-emptive nor exclusive and it is open to the accused to apply to a justice of the peace for a subpoena pursuant to s. 698 to compel the attendance of the analyst although the analyst would then be the accused's witness. In determining whether or not to issue the subpoena however, the same test should be applied by the justice of the peace as must be met under this subsection: *R. v. Forsythe* (1980), 54 C.C.C. (2d) 44 (Alta. Q.B.).

Leave to call the technician should not be given unless there is an indication in the evidence, or an affidavit or in the submissions or undertakings by counsel, of a material irregularity in the testing procedure followed by the technician which, if substantiated, could provide a legal basis for doubting the accuracy of the certificate. Further, it should be apparent that the evidence sought is within the peculiar knowledge of the technician *qua* technician and not evidence which, for example, could be given by any other officer present at the relevant time: *R. v. Davis* (1983), 4 C.C.C. (3d) 53 (Alta. C.A.).

Subsection (7) [Notice of intention to introduce certificate] / Reasonable notice / form and content of notice – The notice does not have to be in writing, but it must be exact for the specific offence proceeded upon. Accordingly notice given for use of a certificate for a s. 253(*a*) offence is of no avail upon the withdrawal of that charge and the proceeding upon a s. 253(*b*) offence: *R. v. Hannan* (1970), 1 C.C.C. (2d) 447 (Sask. Q.B.).

Written notice which is clear and unambiguous is not nullified by the fact that at the time the police officer serves it, he tells the accused the certificate would be used "if necessary": *R. v. Good, Schmidt and Winnipeg; R. v. Neubert* (1983), 6 C.C.C. (3d) 105 (Alta. C.A.).

It is not enough for an accused to point to an error in a notice and then allege that, by reason of the error alone, there is ambiguity or confusion which results in the notice not being reasonable. The bald generalization of ambiguity or confusion must be brought down to concrete terms, based on the facts of the case, to show a particular ambiguity or confusion which relates to the reasonableness of the notice. Thus, an accused charged with the offence under s. 253(*b*) was given reasonable notice, although the notice he was given referred to that charge as well as a charge under s. 253(*a*). The accused at all times knew he was facing a charge under s. 253(*b*) and that he had been given a notice which said that the Crown intended to tender the certificate in evidence at the trial on that charge. There was nothing confusing or ambiguous in this information and the superfluous reference to s. 253(*a*) could in no way have altered the impact of what was undoubtedly a straightforward statement: *R. v. McCullagh* (1990), 53 C.C.C. (3d) 130 (Ont. C.A.).

The Crown is required to prove compliance with the requirements of subsec. (7) on a balance of probabilities, not beyond a reasonable doubt: *R. v. Redford* (2014), 319 C.C.C. (3d) 170 (Alta. C.A.).

Section 4(6)(*a*) and (*b*) of the *Criminal Code* provides an alternative way of proving service and notice for the purpose of this section: *R. v. Veinot* (2010), 265 C.C.C. (3d) 193 (N.S.S.C.).

A printed notice of intention in which, through an apparent typographical error, the wrong section number was checked off, was not invalid and it was open to the trial judge to find that the accused was given reasonable notice: *R. v. Brebner* (1989), 49 C.C.C. (3d) 97 (Ont. C.A.).

This provision has no application where the Crown proceeds by way of *viva voce* evidence of the qualified technician rather than relying on his certificate: *R. v. Walters* (1975), 26 C.C.C. (2d) 56 (N.S.S.C. App. Div.).

Reasonable notice / time of service – For the purposes of this subsection the trial commences with the taking of the evidence and accordingly service of a notice after plea was taken about one month earlier was held to be sufficient: *R. v. Vereschagin* (1972), 10 C.C.C. (2d) 529 (B.C.S.C.).

A certificate of intention to use the resulting certificate of analysis was served upon the defendant a few minutes after he completed his breathalyzer test even though the information against him was not laid until two days later. It was held that since the primary purpose of service was to notify him of the use at trial of the certificate, there would not be any prejudice to him not knowing at the time of service whether he would be charged under the ability impaired or in excess of 80 mg. of alcohol section of the Code: *R. v. Goerz* (1971), 5 C.C.C. (2d) 92 (Alta. C.A.). Folld: *R. v. MacIsaac* (1972), 9 C.C.C. (2d) 46 (N.B.C.A.); *R. v. Ratto; R. v. Gillis; R. v. McMullin* (1972), 9 C.C.C. (2d) 63 (N.S.C.A.); *R. v. Faber* (1972), 8 C.C.C. (2d) 10 (B.C.C.A.); *R. v. Ledoux* (1972), 7 C.C.C. (2d) 18 (Sask. C.A.); and *R. v. Evanson* (1973), 11 C.C.C. (2d) 275 (Man. C.A.).

The notice of intention and the certificate may be served on the accused prior to the laying of an information and the certificate may be used on the trial of even a third information, where the first and second informations were quashed prior to plea, without service of a new notice, at least where the Crown has proceeded promptly in laying the new information: *R. v. Nykiforuk* (1981), 60 C.C.C. (2d) 128 (Alta. C.A.), leave to appeal to S.C.C. refused 33 A.R. 467*n*.

Similarly, *R. v. Koback* (1986), 43 M.V.R. 272 (Sask. C.A.), where the Crown withdrew one information charging the care or control offence and promptly relaid another information charging the driving offence.

Similarly, on a re-trial ordered after a successful appeal, the Crown may rely on the original notice of intention: *R. v. Nickerson* (1984), 27 M.V.R. 124, 64 N.S.R. (2d) 164 (S.C. App. Div.).

In the absence of evidence of the date of service, even though defence counsel did not object, the court is not entitled to infer that the defendant had been given both reasonable notice of the Crown's intention and a copy of the certificate: *R. v. Tunke* (1975), 25 C.C.C. (2d) 518 (Alta. S.C.).

Reasonable notice / capacity to understand – In *R. v. Hamm*, [1977] 2 S.C.R. 85, 28 C.C.C. (2d) 257 (6:3), the court held that the presumption that a person understood what was going on when he was served with the notice under this section was not rebutted merely by the high blood-alcohol reading set out in the certificate of the results of a breathalyzer test performed at the time since the effect of the consumption of alcohol varies among individuals. The trial judge therefore erred in finding that because of the high reading the accused was so intoxicated at the time of service as to be incapable of being served with reasonable notice. The majority accordingly did not consider the propriety of effecting service on a person in an even more intoxicated state. Spence J., dissenting, took a different view of the facts and would have upheld the trial judge's finding of fact of lack of reasonable notice. His Lordship also held that notice under this subsection could not validly be given until an information was laid for it is only then that there is an "accused".

The presumption that the accused understood the notice and certificate which were in English was not rebutted merely by evidence that the demand and other conversation between the accused and the police was in French: *R. v. Saulnier (No. 2)* (1980), 53 C.C.C. (2d) 237, 38 NS.R. (2d) 538 (C.A.).

The rebuttable presumption that the accused understood the notice was applied where the accused was hard of hearing: *R. v. Bender* (1980), 3 Sask. R. 277, 6 M.V.R. 44 (C.A.).

Service on persons other than accused – Service of the certificate and the notice of intention on a law student appearing to fix a date is sufficient compliance with this subsection just as service on the accused's counsel would constitute sufficient compliance: *R. v. Meyer* (1973), 29 C.C.C. (2d) 165 (B.C.C.A.).

Similarly, service on a lawyer who acknowledges that he acts for the accused is compliance with this subsection: *R. v. Monty* (1981), 65 C.C.C. (2d) 54, [1982] 1 W.W.R. 283 (Alta. Q.B.).

Proof of service – A certificate of an analysis is a document within the meaning of s. 4(6) and therefore proof of service may be by way of affidavit: *R. v. Spreen* (1987), 40 C.C.C. (3d) 190, 82 A.R. 318, 8 M.V.R. (2d) 148 (C.A.).

Copy of certificate – The copy of the certificate, served along with the notice of intention to produce the original at trial, does not have to be signed as a duplicate original, but is sufficient if it is a true copy in all essential particulars and conveys to the defendant all of the required information: *R. v. Glass* (1973), 12 C.C.C. (2d) 450 (Sask. C.A.).

Evidence that the copy of the certificate was prepared using a preassembled form containing carbon paper is *prima facie* proof that the copy given to the accused was a copy of the certificate and there is no requirement that the copy and the certificate have been specifically compared: *R. v. Bergstrom* (1982), 65 C.C.C. (2d) 351 (Man. C.A.). Also see: *R. v. Pederson* (1973), 15 C.C.C. (2d) 323 (B.C.S.C.); *R. v. Morgan* (1995), 104 C.C.C. (3d) 342 (Nfld. C.A.).

Proof that a copy has been served is *prima facie* evidence of its accuracy unless there is an issue raised that the copy is not a true counterpart of the original. It is not a requirement that the police officer serving the copy observe the certificate being typed or compare the copy with the original: *R. v. Mavin* (1997), 119 C.C.C. (3d) 38 (Nfld. C.A.).

The service on the accused of the top of three copies of the certificate, the lower two of which are carbon copies, complies with the requirement in this subsection that the accused be served with a "copy" of the certificate: *R. v. Walsh* (1980), 53 C.C.C. (2d) 568, 6 M.V.R. 125 (Ont. C.A.).

258.1 [*Repealed*, 2018, c. 21, s. 14.]

Editor's Note: The unauthorized use or disclosure of samples and test results obtained under the regime governing drug- and alcohol-related driving offences is now addressed in s. 320.36.

CROSS-REFERENCES

"Peace officer" is defined in s. 2.

SYNOPSIS

This section enacts safeguards to prevent the unauthorized use of bodily substances that have been seized as part of the drinking and driving regime set out in ss. 254 and 256. Subsection (1) makes it an offence to use these substances other than for authorized purposes, namely for the analysis referred to in the provision authorizing the seizure, or pursuant to an order by a court under s. 258(4), to test for drugs under s. 258(5) or for medical purposes in accordance with subsec. (3) of this section. Subsection (3) creates a similar offence for unauthorized disclosure of the results of physical coordination tests, the results of analysis of bodily substances and medical samples seized under warrant. Under subsec. (4), the results of tests and analysis may be disclosed to the person to whom they relate. The offences in subsecs. (2) and (3) are summary conviction offences.

259. [*Repealed*, 2018, c. 21, s. 14.]

Editor's Note: **Driving prohibition orders are now governed by s. 320.24. The annotations below should be approached with caution in relation to the new provisions.**

CROSS-REFERENCES

The terms "highway", "motor vehicle" and "railway equipment" are defined in s. 2. The terms "aircraft", "vessel" and "operate" are defined in s. 214. Where the prosecution seeks the longer prohibition order prescribed by para. (1)(*b*) or (*c*), it probably must comply with the provisions of s. 665. Section 667 provides one method of proof of the prior conviction. No reference to the prior conviction may be made in the information by virtue of s. 664. Procedure for making the prohibition order is set out in s. 260(1) to (3). Provision respecting a means of proof of notice of the disqualification and proof of the disqualification is set out in s. 260(4) to (7). Section 261 provides for an order staying the prohibition order pending appeal against a conviction or discharge. An order under this section is within the definition of "sentence" in ss. 673 and 785 for the purposes of appeals in proceedings by indictment and summary conviction respectively.

Where the Crown elects to proceed by indictment on the offence described in subsec. (4), the accused has an election as to mode of trial. Where the Crown elects to proceed by way of summary conviction for the offence under subsec. (4) then the trial is conducted by a summary conviction court pursuant to Part XXVII. The punishment for the summary conviction offence is as set out in s. 787 and the limitation period is set out in s. 786(2). The accused is also liable to imposition of a prohibition order under this section for a period not exceeding three years. For all offences under this section, release pending trial is determined by s. 515, although the accused is eligible for release by a peace officer under ss. 496 and 497, or by the officer in charge under s. 498.

Pursuant to s. 255.1, evidence that the accused's blood alcohol level exceeded .160 at the time when the offence was committed is deemed to be an aggravating factor on sentencing.

The maximum punishment for this offence and the length of the prohibition periods were increased by S.C. 1999, c. 32. The transitional provisions of that Act provide that the lesser penalty or punishment applies in respect of any offence that was committed before the coming into force of the Act.

Note s. 732.1(3)(*g*.1) and (*g*.2), which allow for terms of probation that the offender attend for curative treatment in relation to the consumption of alcohol and drugs and participate in an alcohol ignition interlock device program.

SYNOPSIS

This section describes the circumstances under which a judge is required to impose an order prohibiting an offender from operating a motor vehicle, vessel, aircraft or railway equipment. If an offender is convicted of an offence under ss. 253, 254 or this section, discharged of an offence under s. 253, and had at the time of the offence, or in the case of an offence under s. 254, three hours preceding that time, care or control of or was operating a motor vehicle, a vessel, an aircraft or railway equipment, the judge must impose a prohibition order. Such an order will last for a period of not more than three years and not less than one year for a first

offence, not more than five years and not less than two years for a second offence, and not less than three years for each subsequent offence, plus any period to which the offender is sentenced to imprisonment. An exception is made in subsecs. (1.1) to (1.2) where the province in which the offender resides has established an alcohol ignition interlock device program, in which case the offender may operate a vehicle equipped with the device while registered in and complying with the conditions of the program, unless the court orders otherwise. The authorization has no effect until expiry of at least three months for a first offence, at least six months for a second offence, at least 12 months for a subsequent offence, or any period that may be fixed by order of the court that is greater than these minimums. If an offender is convicted or discharged of an offence under ss. 220, 221, 236, 249, 250, 251, 252 and 255(2) to (3.2), the judge may make an order prohibiting the offender from operating the motor vehicle, vessel, aircraft or railway equipment for any period that the court considers appropriate if the offender is liable to a maximum sentence of life imprisonment. If the offender is liable to a sentence greater than five years but less than life imprisonment, the prohibition order may last for a period of up to ten years plus any period to which the offender is sentenced to imprisonment. In any other case, the maximum length of the order is three years plus any period to which the offender is sentenced to imprisonment. Subsection (2.1) permits the court to make a prohibition order imposed under this section consecutive to other prohibition orders made under this section. Subsections (3.1) to (3.4) create enhanced prohibitions where the accused has been convicted or discharged of one of the street racing offences created by ss. 249.2 to 249.4. The principal difference is the creation of minimum prohibitions for the various street racing offences. The minimum and maximum penalties vary depending upon the number of prior convictions for the offence and whether the offender was convicted of an aggravated form of the offence because bodily harm or death was caused. This section also holds that no order under subsec. (1) or (2) shall prevent a person from acting as master, mate or engineer or a vessel required to carry such qualified individuals. Any person who is convicted of operating a motor vehicle, vessel, aircraft or railway equipment in Canada while disqualified is guilty of a hybrid offence punishable upon indictment to a maximum term of imprisonment of five years. If is an offence under the *Criminal Code* to drive while disqualified, even if the disqualification was made pursuant to a provincial statute or federal legislation other than the *Criminal Code*, provided that the disqualification arose from a conviction for an offence referred to in subsec. (1) or (2).

ANNOTATIONS

Principles in making prohibition order – The order made under subsec. (1) is an aspect of the sentence and the duty on the judge is to determine what is a fit period of prohibition applying proper sentencing principles. It is not proper to simply impose a one-year prohibition because the accused, an out-of-province resident, would not otherwise be suspended from driving for the one year prescribed by provincial legislation: *R. v. Goulding* (1987), 40 C.C.C. (3d) 244 (N.S.C.A.).

Where an order is made under subsec. (2)(*a*.1), the period of driving prohibition is the aggregate of two components: (i) the period of imprisonment, and (ii) the period of driving prohibition specified by the court. Sentencing judges should articulate the two components of the prohibition, both in the sentence pronounced and in the documents issued to give effect to the prohibition: *R. v. Bansal* (2017), 352 C.C.C. (3d) 374 (B.C.C.A.).

There is no power to provide for exceptions from the prohibition order to, for example, permit the accused to drive for the purposes of employment: *R. v. Girard* (1993), 79 C.C.C. (3d) 174 (N.B.C.A.).

Elements of offence – The offence under former s. 238(3) was held to be a true criminal offence requiring proof of *mens rea*. Further, the existence of a provincial licence suspension was a question of fact and ignorance of that fact is a defence to this charge, notwithstanding the suspension arises automatically by operation of a provincial law as a consequence of a conviction for a *Criminal Code* motor vehicle offence: *R. v. Prue; R. v. Baril*, [1979] 2 S.C.R. 547, 46 C.C.C. (2d) 257 (4:3).

An accused whose licence is suspended by virtue of provincial legislation should be convicted of the criminal offence only where he is driving in circumstances in which a licence is required by provincial legislation: *R. v. Mansour*, [1979] 2 S.C.R. 916, 47 C.C.C. (3d) 129 (9:0).

Both under the provincial legislation and the *Criminal Code*, upon conviction for the offences specified in the Registrar's certificate, the accused is to be informed by the court that he is disqualified from driving and under the provincial legislation where the accused is a resident of the province, the convicting judge is to secure the driver's licence, if any, from the accused. As well, under the provincial legislation, the accused would not be entitled to reinstatement of his licence so long as he was disqualified from driving. In the circumstances, the doctrine of regularity applies with the result that the only reasonable presumption was that the accused was notified of his disqualification. Accordingly, the Registrar's certificate together with the application of the doctrine of regularity was sufficient to constitute *prima facie* proof of the *mens rea* for the offence of driving while disqualified, that is proof that the accused knew he was disqualified from driving: *R. v. Larsen* (1992), 71 C.C.C. (3d) 335 (Sask. C.A.). [Also see notes under s. 260.] In certain circumstances, however, the presumption of regularity, together with the certificate of disqualification, is insufficient to establish *mens rea* where by the combined operation of s. 259(2) and the provincial statute it was possible that the offender was subject to a disqualification from driving without notification: *R. v. Miskiman*, [1997] 8 W.W.R. 280, 140 W.A.C. 256 (Sask. C.A.).

A prohibition order indicating that everyone who operated a motor vehicle while disqualified is "upon conviction, guilty of an offence and is liable to a term of custody and supervision" failed to comply with s. 260(1)(*c*) of the *Criminal Code*, in that it did not bring home to the individual the specifics of this provision. In particular, it must be clear that the individual could be found guilty of an indictable offence and imprisoned for up to five years or found guilty of an offence punishable on summary conviction: *R. v. Molina* (2008), 231 C.C.C. (3d) 193 (Ont. C.A.).

Knowledge of the prohibition order is an essential element. In this case, knowledge was not proven having regard to the fact that although the accused was subject to a three-year driving prohibition, he believed that the prohibition was over after one year subsequent to taking a driving test and receiving an apprentice driving license: *R. v. Lariviere* (2000), 38 C.R. (5th) 130, 15 M.V.R. (4th) 304 (Que. C.A.), quashed [2001] 3 S.C.R. 1013, 160 C.C.C. (3d) 129.

The onus of proving registration in and compliance with an ignition interlock program is on the accused, pursuant to s. 794(2) of the Code: *R. v. Whatmore* (2011), 281 C.C.C. (3d) 95 (Alta. Prov. Ct.).

Procedure – In order to obtain the greater driving prohibition mandated by subsec. (1)(*c*) the prosecution must give notice as required by s. 665: *R. v. Keldsen* (1987), 1 W.C.B. (2d) 75 (B.C.S.C.).

Constitutional considerations – It was held in *R. v. Boggs*, [1981] 1 S.C.R. 49, 58 C.C.C. (2d) 7 (7:0), that the predecessor to this subsection (s. 238(3)) was unconstitutional because it had the effect of attaching penal consequences to a breach of an order made under a provincial statute although the provincial order of disqualification did not arise out of a conviction for a criminal offence. This particular problem would seem to have been remedied by the limited definition of "disqualification" in subsec. (5).

This section does not violate the equality rights guaranteed by s. 15 of the Charter even though a person may be disqualified by reason of subsec. (5)(*b*) pursuant to a suspension imposed by provincial legislation and the length of suspension varies from province to province: *R. v. Buchanan* (1989), 46 C.C.C. (3d) 468 (N.S.C.A.).

260. [*Repealed*, 2018, c. 21, s. 14.]

Editor's Note: The procedure governing driving prohibition orders is now set out in s. 320.24. The annotations below should be approached with caution in relation to the new provisions.

CROSS-REFERENCES

The term "offender" is defined in s. 2. The term "motor vehicle" is defined in s. 2. The terms "aircraft", "vessel" and "operate" are defined in s. 214. Procedure for stay of the prohibition order pending appeal is set out in s. 261.

With respect to the notice prescribed by subsec. (6), note s. 27(1) of the *Interpretation Act*, R.S.C. 1985, c. I-21, which provides that, where there is reference to "at least" a number of days between two events, in calculating that number of days, the days on which the events happened are excluded.

Section 25(1) of the *Interpretation Act* provides that "Where an enactment provides that a document is evidence of a fact without anything in the context to indicate that the document is conclusive evidence, then, in any judicial proceedings, the document is admissible in evidence and the fact is deemed to be established in the absence of any evidence to the contrary."

SYNOPSIS

This section sets out the steps that a court must take in imposing a prohibition order under s. 259(1) and (2). The court must ensure that the order is read by or to the offender, that a copy is given to the offender, and that the offender is informed of the criminal consequences of disobeying the order. After these steps are taken, the offender must endorse the order and acknowledge both receipt of it and the fact that the order has been explained. The order will be valid even if the offender fails to endorse it.

Where it is proved that a notice of disqualification as defined in s. 259 has been mailed by registered or certified mail to an offender, in the absence of evidence to the contrary, after five days of the mailing of the notice, the offender is deemed to have received it and to have knowledge of the disqualification, the date of its commencement and its duration. A certificate describing in reasonably particular terms that a person has been disqualified from driving a motor vehicle or operating a vessel or aircraft is evidence of the facts without further proof. The accused must be given at least seven days' notice in writing that the certificate will be used in evidence.

ANNOTATIONS

Note: Some of the decisions noted below, although decided under the predecessor legislation, were felt to be relevant to these provisions.

Procedure in making order [subsec. (1)] – While the judge may delegate to an appropriate official of the court compliance with this subsection, the duties cannot be delegated to the agent of the accused who appeared on his behalf and entered the plea of guilty: *R. v. Materi* (1987), 35 C.C.C. (3d) 273 (Sask. C.A.).

An accused cannot be convicted of the offence contrary to s. 259(4) in the absence of proof of compliance with this subsection, even where there is proof that the accused was aware of the prohibition order: *R. v. Kean* (1989), 22 M.V.R. (2d) 279, 80 Nfld. & P.E.I.R. 159 (Nfld. Prov. Ct.).

A prohibition order indicating that everyone who operated a motor vehicle while disqualified is "upon conviction, guilty of an offence and is liable to a term of custody and supervision" failed to comply with subsec. (1)(*c*) of the *Criminal Code*, in that it did not bring home the specifics of this provision and in particular, that they could be found guilty of an indictable offence and imprisoned for up to five years or found guilty of an offence punishable on summary conviction: *R. v. Molina* (2008), 231 C.C.C. (3d) 193 (Ont. C.A.).

Proof of knowledge of disqualification [subsec. (4)] – It was held in relation to former s. 238, which did not contain a provision respecting proof of knowledge, that nevertheless with the establishment of the accused's licence suspension the Crown is entitled to rely on the presumption that a man intends the natural consequences of his act in order to prove the necessary *mens rea* and if, in order to make his suspension order effective, the registrar was required to give notice of his suspension to the accused there is no obligation on the Crown to prove that such notice had been served on the accused prior to his driving as, in the absence of evidence to the contrary, the presumption that all acts required by law have been taken will apply: *R. v. Heisler*, [1967] 1 C.C.C. 97 (N.S.S.C.).

Similarly, it was held that once the Crown proves that the accused drove while disqualified it makes out a *prima facie* case notwithstanding there is no direct evidence that the accused knew of the suspension. The accused then runs the risk of being convicted unless he discharges the evidential burden of introducing evidence of lack of knowledge although if at the end of the case there is a reasonable doubt with respect to any element of the offence, including such knowledge, he is entitled to be acquitted: *R. v. Lock* (1974), 18 C.C.C. (2d) 477 (Ont. C.A.).

This provision is simply one method through which the Crown may prove *mens rea*: *R. v. Gale* (1995), 168 A.R. 212, 16 M.V.R. (3d) 33 (Q.B.).

The presumption of regularity applies to this provision but can be rebutted by evidence to the contrary arising from the Crown's case or led by the defence. Accordingly, where a record relied upon by the Crown to prove *mens rea* is defective on its face, evidence to the contrary arises from the Crown's case and the Crown is required to lead evidence to prove compliance with this provision beyond a reasonable doubt. Where no evidence to the contrary arises, the accused must rebut the *prima facie* case of knowledge: *R. v. Guilbault* (2010), 251 C.C.C. (3d) 563 (N.S.S.C.), affd 268 C.C.C. (3d) 48 (N.S.C.A.).

Sufficiency of certificate under subsec. (5) – It was held in relation to former s. 238(4), which was worded similarly to this subsection, that the certificate is not admissible to prove additionally that notice of suspension had been given to the accused: *R. v. Lock* (1974), 18 C.C.C. (2d) 477 (Ont. C.A.). *Quaere*, whether the same result would be reached now, in light of subsec. (4).

A notice which complied with the provisions of this subsection but went on to name the wrong date of the offence was held to be valid. This latter piece of information was not essential to the giving of notice and did not vitiate the effectiveness of the notice given: *R. v. Spezzano* (1976), 32 C.C.C. (2d) 303 (Ont. C.A.).

A typographical error will not render the certificate inadmissible provided that the identity of the accused, the period of suspension and the fact of prohibition are clear: *R. v. Alexis* (1999), 181 D.L.R. (4th) 719, 48 M.V.R. (3d) 1 (B.C.C.A.).

A stamped impression of the registrar's signature on the certificate is sufficient: *R. v. Layton* (1978), 40 C.C.C. (2d) 457 (B.C.S.C.).

However, a form which is pre-printed with the registrar's signature on it and then filled out later and which is never seen by the registrar does not comply: *R. v. Zwicker* (1979), 49 C.C.C. (2d) 340 (N.S. Mag. Ct.), affd (1980), 53 C.C.C. (2d) 239 (N.S.C.A.).

Sufficiency of notice under subsec. (6) – Service of the notice of intention in the period between the accused's first appearance and his trial is permissible, provided the notice is given to the accused seven days before the trial date: *R. v. Heisler*, [1967] 1 C.C.C. 97 (N.S.S.C.).

The Crown may not resort to provincial legislation which permits the admissibility of documents in the possession of the Registrar without notice: *R. v. Delyon* (1979), 47 C.C.C. (2d) 173 (Ont. Prov. Ct.), aprvd *R. v. Morrison* (1980), 53 C.C.C. (2d) 478 (Ont. H.C.J.). See also: *R. v. Albright*, [1987] 2 S.C.R. 383, 37 C.C.C. (3d) 105, noted under s. 645.

Other means of proof of disqualification – A certified copy of an order of driving prohibition, signed by a justice of the peace for the clerk of the court and bearing the seal of the provincial court, although not admissible under subsec. (5) because the notice required by this subsection was not given, is admissible at common law. At common law, judicial documents could be proved by production of the original record or an exemplification under the seal of the court, without notice: *R. v. Tatomir* (1989), 51 C.C.C. (3d) 321 (Alta. C.A.).

It was held in *R. v. Gramik* (1988), 9 M.V.R. (2d) 141 (Alta. Q.B.), that an order of a driving prohibition made by a court is admissible under the common law public documents exception to the hearsay rule.

However, it was held in *R. v. Kuzma* (1988), 5 M.V.R. (2d) 232, 66 Sask. R. 153 (C.A.), that a certified copy of the order of driving prohibition was not properly tendered under s. 667 since on its face it was a copy of an order by a clerk of the court and not a certified copy of an order made pursuant to s. 259. The court left open whether if there were a certified copy of a court order of prohibition this would be a certificate within the meaning of s. 667.

261. [*Repealed*, 2018, c. 21, s. 14.]

Editor's Note: Stays of driving prohibition orders pending appeal are now governed by s. 320.25. The annotations below should be approached with caution in relation to the new provisions.

CROSS-REFERENCES

An order under this section is itself within the definition of "sentence" in ss. 673 and 785 for the purposes of appeals in proceedings by indictment and summary conviction respectively.

SYNOPSIS

This section empowers a judge of the court to which an appeal is taken against conviction or discharge under s. 730 for an offence committed under ss. 220, 221, 236, 249 to 255 or 259, to direct a stay of any prohibition order until the appeal is disposed of, or the court orders otherwise. In staying the order, the judge may impose conditions, but the inclusion of such conditions does not decrease the period of the prohibition. An application to stay a prohibition order pending an appeal to the Supreme Court of Canada is also made to a judge of the court of appeal, not a judge of the Supreme Court of Canada.

ANNOTATIONS

The burden is on the appellant to show that a stay of the order should be granted. The appellant must show that the appeal is not frivolous, that continuation of the driving prohibition pending appeal is not necessary in the public interest, and that to grant the stay would not detrimentally affect the confidence of the public in the effective enforcement and administration of criminal law: *R. v. Jay and MacLean* (1987), 66 Nfld. & P.E.I.R. 84, 50 M.V.R. 137 (P.E.I.S.C.).

The standard of frivolousness has two different aspects: (1) whether the appeal is brought for a motivation different than having success in the appeal, and (2) the appeal has little chance of success. In addition, the court must consider the hardship on the appellant and the protection of the public: *R. v. McPherson* (1999), 140 C.C.C. (3d) 316 (B.C.C.A.).

The Court of Appeal does not have jurisdiction to stay a driving prohibition pending an appeal to the Supreme Court of Canada: *R. v. Reed* (1997), 120 C.C.C. (3d) 556 (B.C.C.A.).

IMPEDING ATTEMPT TO SAVE LIFE.

262. Every one who

(*a*) prevents or impedes or attempts to prevent or impede any person who is attempting to save his own life, or

(*b*) without reasonable cause prevents or impedes or attempts to prevent or impede any person who is attempting to save the life of another person,

is guilty of an indictable offence and liable to imprisonment for a term not exceeding ten years. R.S., c. C-34, s. 241.

CROSS-REFERENCES

The accused has an election as to mode of trial pursuant to s. 536(2). Release pending trial is determined by s. 515.

SYNOPSIS

This section sets out the criminal consequences for preventing or impeding, or attempting to prevent or impede, any person who is attempting to save his own life or that of another person. Where the circumstances involve a person attempting to save the life of another person, an accused under this section has the defence of reasonable excuse. The offence is indictable and punishable upon conviction to a maximum term of imprisonment of ten years.

DUTY TO SAFEGUARD OPENING IN ICE / Excavation on land / Offences.

263. (1) Every one who makes or causes to be made an opening in ice that is open to or frequented by the public is under a legal duty to guard it in a manner that is adequate to prevent persons from falling in by accident and is adequate to warn them that the opening exists.

(2) Every one who leaves an excavation on land that he owns or of which he has charge or supervision is under a legal duty to guard it in a manner that is adequate to prevent persons from falling in by accident and is adequate to warn them that the excavation exists.

(3) Every one who fails to perform a duty imposed by subsection (1) or (2) is guilty of

(*a*) manslaughter, if the death of any person results therefrom;

(*b*) an offence under section 269, if bodily harm to any person results therefrom; or

(*c*) an offence punishable on summary conviction. R.S., c. C-34, s. 242; 1980-81-82-83, c. 125, s. 18.

CROSS-REFERENCES

The offence of manslaughter is punishable pursuant to s. 236. An accused charged with manslaughter has an election as to mode of trial pursuant to s. 536(2) and release pending trial is determined under s. 515.

The offence under s. 269, referred to in subsec. (3)(*b*), is the offence of unlawfully causing bodily harm. "Bodily harm" is defined in s. 2. An accused, charged with the offence under s. 269, has an election as to mode of trial pursuant to s. 536(2) and release pending trial is determined under s. 515.

For the offence under subsec. (3)(*c*), the trial is conducted by a summary conviction court pursuant to Part XXVII. The punishment for the summary conviction offence is as set out in s. 787 [although, note that the maximum fine for a corporation is determined by s. 735(1)(*b*)] and the limitation period is set out in s. 786(2).

Related offences: ss. 219 to 221, criminal negligence; s. 247, setting traps with intent.

SYNOPSIS

This section sets out the legal requirements incumbent upon anyone who makes a hole in ice that is, or could be used by the public, or who leaves an excavation on land that he owns or supervises. A person who fails to guard such openings in the land or the ice in such manner as to prevent other persons from falling in, and to adequately warn them of the opening, is guilty of a criminal offence punishable on summary conviction.

If a person dies as a result of the failure to comply with this section, the offender will be guilty, upon conviction, of manslaughter. If a person suffers bodily harm, the offender, upon conviction, will be subject to the terms of s. 269.

ANNOTATIONS

This section sets up a statutory duty which if breached will lead to a conviction for manslaughter even in circumstances which would not amount to criminal negligence as defined by s. 219: *R. v. Aldergrove Competition Motorcycle Association and Levy* (1982), 69 C.C.C. (2d) 183 (B.C. Co. Ct.), affd 5 C.C.C. (3d) 114 (B.C.C.A.).

264. [*Repealed* (old provision), R.S.C. 1985, c. 27 (1st Supp.), s. 37.]

CRIMINAL HARASSMENT / Prohibited conduct / Punishment / Factors to be considered / Reasons.

264. (1) No person shall, without lawful authority and knowing that another person is harassed or recklessly as to whether the other person is harassed, engage in conduct referred to in subsection (2) that causes that other person reasonably, in all the circumstances, to fear for their safety or the safety of anyone known to them.

(2) The conduct mentioned in subsection (1) consists of

(*a*) repeatedly following from place to place the other person or anyone known to them;

(*b*) repeatedly communicating with, either directly or indirectly, the other person or anyone known to them;

(*c*) besetting or watching the dwelling-house, or place where the other person, or anyone known to them, resides, works, carries on business or happens to be; or

(*d*) engaging in threatening conduct directed at the other person or any member of their family.

(3) Every person who contravenes this section is guilty of

(*a*) an indictable offence and is liable to imprisonment for a term not exceeding ten years; or

(*b*) an offence punishable on summary conviction.

(4) Where a person is convicted of an offence under this section, the court imposing the sentence on the person shall consider as an aggravating factor that, at the time the offence was committed, the person contravened

(*a*) the terms or conditions of an order made pursuant to section 161 or a recognizance entered into pursuant to section 810, 810.1 or 810.2; or

(*b*) the terms or conditions of any other order or recognizance made or entered into under the common law or a provision of this or any other Act of Parliament or of a province that is similar in effect to an order or recognizance referred to in paragraph (*a*).

(5) Where the court is satisfied of the existence of an aggravating factor referred to in subsection (4), but decides not to give effect to it for sentencing purposes, the court shall give reasons for its decision. 1993, c. 45, s. 2; 1997, c. 16. s. 4; 1997, c. 17, s. 9; 2002, c. 13, s. 10.

CROSS-REFERENCES

Other related offences are: s. 177, trespassing by night; s. 264.1, uttering threats; s. 372, indecent and harassing telephone calls; s. 423, intimidation; s. 430, mischief. In addition, ss. 810 and 810.1 authorize a provincial court judge to require the defendant to enter into a recognizance and comply with conditions. A person convicted of this offence must have imposed a weapon, ammunition and explosives prohibition under s. 109. Other statutory aggravating factors for the purposes of sentencing are set out in s. 718.2(*a*). While this section requires the court to give reasons in certain circumstances, s. 726.2 requires the court to give reasons for sentence in every case.

Section 486(1) and (2) provide that the judge may make an order excluding all or any members of the public where such order is in the interest of public morals, the maintenance of order or the proper administration of justice, or is necessary to prevent injury to international relations or national defence or national security. The proper administration of justice includes safeguarding the interests of witnesses under the age of 18 years. Section 486.1 sets out the circumstances in which the judge shall or may order a support person to be present and close to a witness while the witness testifies. Where the witness is under the age of 18 years or has a mental or physical disability, the order is to be made upon request unless the judge is of the opinion that the order would interfere with the proper administration of justice. In the case of other witnesses, the order is to be made if necessary to obtain a full and candid account from the witness of the matters complained of. The application for this order may be made during the proceedings or before they begin to the judge who is to preside at the proceedings.

Similarly, s. 486.2 sets out the circumstances in which the judge shall or may order a witness to testify outside the courtroom or behind a screen or other device that would not allow the witness to see the accused. Where the witness is under the age of 18 years or may have difficulty communicating the evidence by reason of a mental or physical disability, the judge shall make the order unless the judge is of the opinion that the order would interfere with the proper administration of justice. In all other cases, the order may be made if the judge is of the opinion that the order is necessary to obtain a full and candid account from the witness of the acts complained of. Similarly, s. 486.3(4) provides that, on application by the prosecutor or the victim (defined in s. 2), the accused shall not personally cross-examine the witness unless the judge is of the opinion that the proper administration of justice requires the accused to personally conduct the cross-examination. The judge will appoint counsel to conduct the cross-examination.

Under s. 486.5, the judge may make an order directing that the identity of the victim or a witness not be disclosed in any publication, broadcast or transmitted in any way if the judge is satisfied that the order is necessary for the proper administration of justice.

Section 715.1 provides that, in proceedings against the accused in which the victim or other witness was under the age of 18 years at the time the offence is alleged to have been committed, a video recording made within a reasonable time after the alleged offence, in which the victim or witness describes the acts complained of, is admissible in evidence if the victim or witness, while testifying, adopts its contents, unless the judge is of the opinion that the admission of the video recoding would interfere with the proper administration of justice. Section 715.2 provides for a similar procedure where the victim or another witness may have difficulty communicating the evidence by reason of a mental or physical disability.

SYNOPSIS

This section creates the Crown option offence of criminal harassment. It is an offence to engage in harassing conduct as defined in subsec. (2). Knowing that the person is harassed [or being reckless in that respect] causes the other person to reasonably fear for their safety or the safety of anyone known to them. Subsection (4) deems the contravention of certain types of court orders in the commission of the offence to be aggravating factors for the purpose of sentencing. Where the court is satisfied that one of these factors exist, but decides not to give effect to it, the court must give reasons for its decisions.

ANNOTATIONS

The *mens rea* required for this offence is that the accused knew that his conduct caused the complainant to be harassed or that he was aware of such a risk and was reckless or willfully blind as to whether or not the person was harassed. Accordingly, honest mistake is a defence to this offence. Furthermore, this provision does not violate s. 7 of the Charter as foresight of the prohibited consequence of causing actual fear is not required in order to hold the accused responsible for the results of the unlawful activity. It must be established that: (1) the accused has engaged in conduct set out in s. 264(2)(*a*), (*b*), (*c*) or (*d*); (2) the complainant was harassed; (3) the accused who engaged in such conduct knew that the complainant was harassed or was reckless or willfully blind as to whether the complainant was harassed; (4) the conduct caused the complainant to fear for his or her safety or the safety of anyone known to the person; and (5) the complainants fear in all of the circumstances was reasonable: *R. v. Sillipp* (1997), 120 C.C.C. (3d) 384 (Alta. C.A.), leave to appeal to S.C.C.

refused 123 C.C.C. (3d) vi. Folld: *R. v. Krushel* (2000), 142 C.C.C. (3d) 1 (Ont. C.A.), leave to appeal to S.C.C. refused [2004] 4 S.C.R. vi *sub nom. R. v. Grey*, 169 C.C.C. (3d) vi.

Nor does this section constitute an unconstitutional violation of s. 2(*b*) of the *Canadian Charter of Rights and Freedoms*: *R. v. Krushel, supra*. See also *R. v. Davis* (2000), 224 W.A.C. 99, 148 Man. R. (2d) 99 (C.A.).

A single incident can constitute threatening conduct: *R. v. Kosikar* (1999), 138 C.C.C. (3d) 217 (Ont. C.A.), leave to appeal to S.C.C. refused 142 C.C.C. (3d) vi; *R. v. Hawkins* (2006), 215 C.C.C. (3d) 419 (B.C.C.A.).

Harassment is proven if as a consequence of the prohibited act, the complainant was in a state of being harassed or felt harassed in the sense of feeling tormented, troubled, worried continually or chronically plagued, bedeviled and badgered. *R. v. Kosikar, supra.*

Even though conduct occurred over a relatively short period of time and there was no prior contact, the requisite elements of the offence were met where it was highly threatening and persistent. In this case, the accused had jumped out from the bushes and blocked the path of a stranger jogging in a residential neighbourhood at night. He then chased the complainant to a house and stared at her while she waited for someone to answer the door: *R. v. K. (K.)* (2009), 241 C.C.C. (3d) 284 (Ont. C.A.), supp. reasons 244 C.C.C. (3d) 124 (Ont. C.A.), leave to appeal to S.C.C. refused 243 C.C.C. (3d) vi. See also *R. v. O'Connor* (2008), 234 O.A.C. 135 (C.A.), leave to appeal to S.C.C. refused [2008] 3 S.C.R. ix.

The words "tormented, troubled, worried continually or chronically, plagued, bedeviled and badgered" are not cumulative and are individually synonymous with the word "harrassed". Accordingly, establishing any of these factors can constitute harrassment: *R. v. Kordrostami* (2000), 143 C.C.C. (3d) 488 (Ont. C.A.).

Harassment should not be given a restrictive definition and includes "requests, solicitations, incitements" that have the effect of bothering someone because of their continuity or repetition: *R. v. Lamontagne* (1998), 129 C.C.C. (3d) 181 (Que. C.A.).

In considering whether repeated communications constitute criminal harassment, regard must be had to both the content and the repetitious nature of the calls, together with the context in which the calls were made: *R. v. Scuby* (2004), 181 C.C.C. (3d) 97 (B.C.C.A.).

"Watching" in para. (*c*) requires continuous observation for a particular purpose. Merely looking and smiling at someone, standing alone, is not sufficient to constitute "watching". The term must be construed with reference to the relationship between "watching" and "besetting": *R. v. Eltom* (2010), 258 C.C.C. (3d) 224 (Ont. S.C.J.).

Conduct can be repeated only if it occurs on two occasions. The trier of fact must consider the conduct that was the subject matter of the charge against the background of the relationship and the history between the complainant and the accused. In this case, where the accused had been previously convicted of threatening the complainant, two letters sent 18 months apart could constitute "repeated" communication: *R. v. Ohenhen* (2005), 200 C.C.C. (3d) 309 (Ont. C.A.).

An objective standard must apply in determining whether threatening conduct in subsec. (2)(*d*) amounts to intimidation designed to instill a sense of fear in the recipient: *R. v. George* (2002), 162 C.C.C. (3d) 337 (Y.T.C.A.).

Evidence of prior incidents of discreditable conduct may be admissible to provide context to assess the effect of the incident on the complainant and whether the accused knew that the conduct would cause the complainant to be fearful or that the accused was reckless as to whether the complainant would be fearful: *R. v. D. (D.)* (2005), 203 C.C.C. (3d) 6 (Ont. C.A.).

Assaults

UTTERING THREATS / Punishment / Idem.

264.1 (1) Every one commits an offence who, in any manner, knowingly utters, conveys or causes any person to receive a threat

(*a*) to cause death or bodily harm to any person;
(*b*) to burn, destroy or damage real or personal property; or
(*c*) to kill, poison or injure an animal or bird that is the property of any person.

(2) Every one who commits an offence under paragraph (1)(*a*) is guilty of
(*a*) an indictable offence and liable to imprisonment for a term not exceeding five years; or
(*b*) an offence punishable on summary conviction and liable to imprisonment for a term not exceeding eighteen months.

(3) Every one who commits an offence under paragraph (1)(*b*) or (*c*)
(*a*) is guilty of an indictable offence and liable to imprisonment for a term not exceeding two years; or
(*b*) is guilty of an offence punishable on summary conviction. R.S.C. 1985, c. 27 (1st Supp.), s. 38; 1994, c. 44, s. 16.

CROSS-REFERENCES

The terms "bodily harm" and "property" are defined in s. 2. The term "person" is defined in s. 35 of the *Interpretation Act*, R.S.C. 1985, c. I-21.

This offence may be the basis for an application for an authorization to intercept private communications by reason of s. 183.

Where the threat is in relation to the use of nuclear material see s. 7(3.4).

An alternative to this offence is the procedure for requiring the offender to enter into a recognizance to keep the peace, either at common law or pursuant to s. 810. Related offences: s. 346, extortion; s. 423, intimidation; s. 423.1 intimidation of a justice system participant; s. 424, threat to commit offence against internationally protected person; ss. 430 to 432, damage to property; ss. 433 to 436, arson and other fires; ss. 444 to 447, offences in relation to animals.

SYNOPSIS

This section describes the kinds of threats that will attract criminal consequences. Any person who utters, conveys or causes another person to receive a threat of death, or serious bodily harm, is guilty of an indictable offence and liable to imprisonment for a maximum term of five years, or a summary conviction offence. If a person threatens to burn, damage or destroy another person's real or personal property or to kill, poison or injure an animal or bird belonging to another person, he is guilty of an indictable offence, with a maximum term of imprisonment of two years, or of a summary conviction offence.

ANNOTATIONS

Meaning of threat – A "conditional" threat, that if the police officer did not leave he would be shot, comes within the ordinary meaning of "threat" and can constitute an offence under this section. In this case the court adopted a dictionary definition of threat as "a denunciation to a person of ill to befall him; esp. a declaration of hostile determination or of loss, pain, punishment, or damage to be inflicted in retribution for or conditionally upon some course; a menace": *R. v. Ross* (1986), 26 C.C.C. (3d) 413 (Ont. C.A.).

Serious bodily harm in subsec. (1)(*a*) means any hurt or injury, whether physical or psychological, that interferes in a substantial way with the physical or psychological integrity, health or well-being of the complainant. The issue to be determined is whether looked at objectively in the context of all the words written and having regard to the person to whom they were directed, would the questioned words convey a threat of serious bodily harm to a reasonable person? A threat to rape is capable of constituting a threat to cause serious bodily harm: *R. v. McCraw*, [1991] 3 S.C.R. 72, 66 C.C.C. (3d) 517 (7:0).

Elements of offence generally – Aside from cases where the words might have a secondary, innocent meaning as between the parties it is immaterial whether the "victim" appreciated he was being threatened. The Crown is only required to prove the accused uttered the threat by one of the means specified: *R. v. Carons* (1978), 42 C.C.C. (2d) 19 (Alta. C.A.).

The *actus reus* will be made out if a reasonable person aware of the circumstances in which the words were uttered would have perceived them to be a threat of death or bodily harm. The Crown need not prove that the intended recipient of the threat was made aware of it, or if aware of it, that he or she was intimidated by it or took it seriously. Nor must the words be directed toward a specific person; a threat against an ascertained group of people is sufficient. The *mens rea* is made out if the accused intended the words uttered or conveyed to intimidate or to be taken seriously. It is not necessary to prove an intent that the words be conveyed to the subject of the threat or that the accused intended to carry out the threat: *R. v. McRae*, [2013] 3 S.C.R. 931, 307 C.C.C. (3d) 291.

In determining whether or not the accused's statements were a threat, the words are to be viewed objectively in the context or circumstances in which they were spoken, the issue being whether they would convey a threat of serious bodily harm to a reasonable person. The *mens rea* of the offence is that the words to be spoken or written as a threat to cause death or serious bodily harm; that is, they were meant to intimidate or to be taken seriously. Words spoken in jest or in such a manner that they could not be taken seriously could not lead a reasonable person to conclude that the words conveyed a threat. There is no requirement that the intended victim of the threat be aware of the threat: *R. v. Clemente*, [1994] 2 S.C.R. 758, 91 C.C.C. (3d) 1.

In considering whether a poem constituted a threat, regard must be had to a reasonable person's consideration of all of the relevant circumstances: *R. v. Batista* (2008), 238 C.C.C. (3d) 97 (Ont. C.A.).

In *R. v. Leblanc*, [1989] 1 S.C.R. 1583, 50 C.C.C. (3d) 192*n* (7:0), the court overturned the decision of the New Brunswick Court of Appeal, 44 C.C.C. (3d) 18, and restored the accused's conviction for the offence under this section, holding that the jury had been properly directed. The issue in the case was the *mens rea* of the offence and the trial judge, in directing the jury, had distinguished between a threat innocently made which was no offence and a threat which was an actual menace.

The fact that the victim of the offence was unknown at the time the threat was made did not preclude a conviction for the offence under this section. A threat to cause the death of a member of an ascertained group of persons contravenes this section: *R. v. Rémy* (1993), 82 C.C.C. (3d) 176 (Que. C.A.).

"Repeatedly" means conduct that is repeated on more than one occasion: *R. v. Ryback* (1996), 105 C.C.C. (3d) 240 (B.C.C.A.), leave to appeal to S.C.C. refused 107 C.C.C. (3d) vi.

Pre-charge conduct of the accused is relevant to whether the complainant's fear of the accused was reasonable, as well as to the accused's intent in knowing or being reckless as to whether conduct harassed the complainant: *R. v. Ryback, supra.*

ASSAULT / Application / Consent / Accused's belief as to consent.

265. (1) A person commits an assault when

(*a*) without the consent of another person, he applies force intentionally to that other person, directly or indirectly;

(*b*) he attempts or threatens, by an act or a gesture, to apply force to another person, if he has, or causes that other person to believe upon reasonable grounds that he has, present ability to effect his purpose; or

(*c*) while openly wearing or carrying a weapon or an imitation thereof, he accosts or impedes another person or begs.

(2) This section applies to all forms of assault, including sexual assault, sexual assault with a weapon, threats to a third party or causing bodily harm and aggravated sexual assault.

(3) For the purposes of this section, no consent is obtained where the complainant submits or does not resist by reason of

(*a*) the application of force to the complainant or to a person other than the complainant;

(*b*) threats or fear of the application of force to the complainant or to a person other than the complainant;

(*c*) fraud; or

(*d*) the exercise of authority.

(4) Where an accused alleges that he believed that the complainant consented to the conduct that is the subject-matter of the charge, a judge, if satisfied that there is sufficient evidence and that, if believed by the jury, the evidence would constitute a defence, shall instruct the jury, when reviewing all the evidence relating to the determination of the honesty of the accused's belief, to consider the presence or absence of reasonable grounds for that belief. R.S., c. C-34, s. 244; 1974-75-76, c. 93, s. 21; 1980-81-82-83, c. 125, s. 19.

CROSS-REFERENCES

The terms "complainant" and "weapon" are defined in s. 2. The offences described in subsec. (2) may be found as follows: s. 266, punishment for assault *simpliciter* [formerly common assault]; s. 267, assault with weapon and assault causing bodily harm; s. 268, aggravated assault; s. 270, assault police; s. 271, sexual assault; s. 272, sexual assault with weapon, threats to a third party and causing bodily harm; s. 273, aggravated sexual assault.

As to defences see: s. 16, insanity; s. 17, compulsion by threats; s. 25, use of force in enforcement of law; s. 27, use of force to prevent commission of certain offences; s. 33.1 intoxication; ss. 34 to 37, self defence and defence of person under accused's protection; ss. 38 to 41, defence of property; s. 43, use of force by way of correction; s. 44, use of force by master of vessel.

As to notes respecting the intoxication and necessity defences see s. 8. These latter defences, especially intoxication are of limited application since most of the assault offences are general intent offences.

Section 273.1 defines consent for the sexual offences in ss. 271, 272 and 273 and, in particular, defines circumstances additional to those set out in s. 265(3) in which no consent is obtained. For the same group of offences, s. 273.2 sets out circumstances where belief in consent is not a defence. For additional notes concerning the defence of honest belief in consent, see the notes following s. 273.2.

As to mode of trial and punishment, see the cross-references under particular assault offence.

SYNOPSIS

This section describes what an assault is, when an assault is aggravated, and the extent to which *consent* can be used as a defence to a charge of assault. A person who directly or indirectly applies force *intentionally* to another person, or who attempts or threatens to do so, has committed an assault. If a person stops another person while openly wearing a weapon or an imitation weapon, he is also guilty of assault. All forms of assault, including sexual assault are covered by this section, but now see also s. 273.1. Consent may constitute a defence to a charge of assault but it cannot be invoked if the victim submits because force has been applied to, or is threatened to be applied to, the victim or another person. Furthermore, the defence of consent will not apply if a person has submitted as a result of fraud or the exercise of authority by the accused.

Section 265(4) requires that the jury in a case in which the defence of consent is raised, and which would be effective if accepted, be instructed by the judge to consider whether the accused had reasonable grounds for an honest belief that there was consent.

ANNOTATIONS

Elements of offence other than consent – Where the application of force is the result of carelessness, as in *R. v. Starratt* (1971), 5 C.C.C. (2d) 32 (Ont. C.A.), or through a reflex action as in *R. v. Wolfe* (1974), 20 C.C.C. (2d) 382 (Ont. C.A.), the essential element of intent is lacking and the accused must be acquitted.

An accused may commit an assault although he exerts no degree of strength or power when touching the victim: *R. v. Burden* (1981), 64 C.C.C. (2d) 68 (B.C.C.A.).

In *R. v. Byrne*, [1968] 3 C.C.C. 179 (B.C.C.A.), it was held that words alone unaccompanied by any gesture do not constitute the act of assault.

Whether or not there has been an assault as defined by subsec. (1)(*b*) depends on the facts of a particular case. Thus, where the accused school teacher, by acts and gestures, directed his pupils to perform various sexual acts upon him, the trier of fact could find that there were not mere invitations but threats to apply force, coupled with a present ability to effect that purpose and thus an assault, or, as here, a sexual assault: *R. v. Cadden* (1989), 48 C.C.C. (3d) 122 (B.C.C.A.).

An assault is committed when a person threatens to apply force and has the ability to do so: *R. v. Horncastle* (1972), 8 C.C.C. (2d) 253 (N.B.C.A.).

An assault is committed within the meaning of subsec. (1)(*b*) where the accused fires a gun at someone who was within range, even if the shot missed and the victim had no idea that he was being shot at: *R. v. Melaragni* (1992), 75 C.C.C. (3d) 546 (Ont. Ct. (Gen. Div.)).

Meaning of consent – To be effective the consent to the assault must be freely given with appreciation of all the risks and not merely submission to an apparently inevitable situation: *R. v. Stanley* (1977), 36 C.C.C. (2d) 216 (B.C.C.A.).

In *R. v. Cey* (1989), 48 C.C.C. (3d) 480 (Sask. C.A.), the court had to consider the scope of consent as a result of a charge of assault causing bodily harm, arising out of events in the course of an amateur hockey game. By agreeing to play the game, a hockey player consents to some forms of intentional bodily contact and to the risk of injury therefrom. Those forms of bodily contact sanctioned by the rules are the clearest examples but, as well, even those forms denounced by the rules, but falling within the accepted standards by which the game is played, may also come within the scope of the implied consent. While ordinarily, consent, being a state of mind, is a wholly subjective matter to be determined accordingly, when it comes to implied consent in the context of a team sport such as hockey, the scope of the implied consent must be determined by reference to objective criteria, at least in respect of those forms of conduct covered by the initial general consent. In determining the scope of the implied consent, the court will have regard to the conditions under which the game is played and the risk and degree of injury. Some forms of bodily contact carry with them such a high risk of injury and such a distinct probability of serious harm as to go beyond what, in fact, the players commonly consent to or what, in law, they are capable of consenting to.

In determining the scope of implied consent, the court must employ objective criteria and have regard to a number of factors, including the setting of the game, the extent of the force employed, the degree of risk of injury, the probabilities of serious harm and whether or not the rules of the game contemplate contact. Contact which evinces a deliberate purpose to inflict injury will generally be held to be outside of the immunity provided by implied consent in sporting events, but this does not mean that the prosecution must in all cases prove such deliberate purpose. Conversely, the fact that the rules do not allow for bodily contact is not itself determinative, especially where the ideal of non-contact is frequently breached in a spirited hockey game: *R. v. Leclerc* (1991), 67 C.C.C. (3d) 563 (Ont. C.A.).

In *R. v. M. (M.L.)*, [1994] 2 S.C.R. 3*n*, 89 C.C.C. (3d) 96*n*, it was held that the court of appeal erred in holding that the 16-year-old complainant, who was the accused's step-daughter, had to have offered some minimal word or gesture of objection in order for there to be proof that she did not consent and erred in holding that lack of resistance could be equated with consent.

Consensual fights – The common law limits on consent imposed for policy reasons apply to assaults as defined by this section and, thus, consent is vitiated where adults intentionally apply force causing serious hurt or non-trivial bodily harm to each other in the course of a fist fight or brawl. These limits do not, however, affect the validity or effectiveness of freely given consent to participate in rough sporting activities, so long as the intentional application of force to which one consents is within the customary norms and rules of the game. This limitation on consent would also not apply to medical treatment or appropriate surgical intervention nor would it necessarily nullify consent between stuntmen engaged in the creation of a socially valuable cultural product. Finally, these limits do not apply to ordinary school yard scuffles between children who immaturely seek to resolve differences through fighting: *R. v. Jobidon*, [1991] 2 S.C.R. 714, 66 C.C.C. (3d) 454 (7:0).

Serious bodily harm must be both intended and caused for consent to be vitiated: *R. v. Paice*, [2005] 1 S.C.R. 339, 195 C.C.C. (3d) 97.

Where the accused did not intend to cause bodily harm, consent is available as a defence if bodily harm is inadvertently caused: *R. v. Zhao* (2013), 297 C.C.C. (3d) 533 (Ont. C.A.).

Valid consent to a fight does not require a consent to each and every blow but rather what might reasonably occur during the fight: *R. v. Gardiner* (2018), 366 C.C.C. (3d) 119 (Alta. C.A.).

In view of the 16-year-old offender's intention to cause serious harm to the complainant who was of the same age, the nature of the force applied, and the serious consequences of those actions, the complainant's consent could not nullify the offender's culpability on a charge of assault causing bodily harm notwithstanding the young age of both the accused and the complainant. The offender's actions were more than socially useless, they were dangerous and intended to be dangerous. It was unnecessary to decide in this case whether the consent could operate as a defence where a young person engages in a consensual fight, not intending to cause serious harm: *R. v. W. (G.)* (1994), 90 C.C.C. (3d) 139 (Ont. C.A.).

However, where the 15-year-old offender did not intend to cause the victim more than trivial bodily harm, the consent was not vitiated notwithstanding that more serious harm may have been caused: *R. v. B. (T.B.)* (1994), 93 C.C.C. (3d) 191, 34 C.R. (4th) 241 (P.E.I.C.A.).

Similarly, where the 16-year-old offender did not intend to cause the victim harm and only minor bodily harm resulted, the offender's honest belief that the victim consented to the fight was a defence: *R. v. M. (S.)* (1995), 97 C.C.C. (3d) 281, 39 C.R. (4th) 60 (Ont. C.A.).

Mistaken belief in consent [subsec. (4)] – This subsection which is consistent with the common law applicable to all defences does not infringe either s. 11(*d*) or (*f*) of the Charter. The accused who seeks to rely upon the defence of mistaken belief only bears a tactical evidentiary burden: *R. v. Osolin*, [1993] 4 S.C.R. 595, 86 C.C.C. (3d) 481. [Also see s. 273.2.]

As to when there is an air of reality of a defence, see note of *R. v. Cinous*, [2002] 2 S.C.R. 3, 162 C.C.C. (3d) 129, under s. 273.2.

Consent obtained by threats or fear of use of force [subsec. (3)(*b*)] – The threats referred to in this paragraph are threats of the application of force. A threat made by the accused to expose certain pictures of the complainant was not the type of threat contemplated. As the conduct did not otherwise fall within this subsection, which is exhaustive of the circumstances vitiating consent, then no assault was committed: *R. v. Guerrero* (1988), 64 C.R. (3d) 65 (Ont. C.A.).

Consent obtained by fraud [subsec. (3)(*c*)] – An accused who knows that he is HIV-positive and fails to disclose that fact has obtained consent by a type of fraud that may vitiate consent to sexual intercourse within the meaning of subsec. (3)(*c*). In addition to fraud that relates to the nature and quality of the act, fraud is made out by dishonest action or behaviour including non-disclosure that results in deprivation. Deprivation in this context means that the dishonest act (either falsehoods or failure to disclose) had the effect of exposing the complainant to a significant risk of serious bodily harm. In addition, the Crown must prove that the complainant would have refused to engage in unprotected sex with the accused if she had been advised that he was HIV-positive: *R. v. Cuerrier*, [1998] 2 S.C.R. 371, 127 C.C.C. (3d) 1. See also *R. v. Williams*, [2003] 2 S.C.R. 134, 176 C.C.C. (3d) 449.

The *Cuerrier* requirement of "significant risk of serious bodily harm" should be read as requiring disclosure of HIV status if there is a realistic possibility of transmission of HIV. If there is no realistic possibility of transmission of HIV, failure to disclose that one has HIV will not constitute fraud vitiating consent to sexual relations under subsec. (3)(*c*). A realistic possibility of transmission is negated if: (i) the accused's viral load at the time of sexual relations was low and (ii) condom protection was used. This general proposition does not preclude the common law from adapting to future advances in treatment and to circumstances where risk factors other than those considered in this case are at play: *R. v. Mabior*, [2012] 2 S.C.R. 584, 290 C.C.C. (3d) 32.

Where a complainant has chosen not to become pregnant, deceptions that expose her to an increased risk of becoming pregnant may constitute a sufficiently serious deprivation to vitiate consent under subsec. (3)(*c*). This application of "fraud" is consistent with Charter values of equality and autonomy, while recognizing that not every deception that induces consent should be criminalized. Here, where the accused had surreptitiously poked holes in the condom, there was no consent by reason of fraud: *R. v. Hutchinson*, [2014] S.C.J. No. 19.

Consent obtained by exercise of authority [subsec. (3)(*d*)] – Exercise of authority in this paragraph is not limited to relationships where there is a right to issue orders and to enforce obedience. Consent in the context of sexual relationships implies a reasonably informed choice, freely exercised. No such choice has been exercised where a person engages in sexual activity if, because of her mental state, she is incapable of understanding the sexual nature of the act or of realizing that she may choose to decline participation. Where there is a significant power imbalance between the accused and the complainant, this can have an effect on the apparent consent. It would be open to the court to find that there was no consent by reason of the overwhelming imbalance of power in the relationship between the accused psychiatrist and the particular patients: *R. v. Saint-Laurent* (1994), 90 C.C.C. (3d) 291 (Que. C.A.), leave to appeal to S.C.C. refused 66 Q.A.C. 160*n*, 175 N.R. 240*n*.

An accused stands in a position of authority over a complainant if the accused can coerce the complainant into consent by virtue of their relationship. The existence of a position of authority does not mean that any sexual activity between the accused and the complainant is non-consensual. The Crown must also prove beyond a reasonable doubt that the accused secured the complainant's apparent consent to the sexual activity which is the subject matter of the charge by the exercise of that coercive authority over the complainant: *R. v. Geddes* (2015), 322 C.C.C. (3d) 414 (Ont. C.A.). See also *R. v. Matheson* (1999), 134 C.C.C. (3d) 289 (Ont. C.A.).

ASSAULT.

266. Every one who commits an assault is guilty of

(*a*) an indictable offence and liable to imprisonment for a term not exceeding five years; or

(*b*) an offence punishable on summary conviction. R.S., c. C-34, s. 245; 1972, c. 13, s. 21; 1974-75-76, c. 93, s. 22; 1980-81-82-83, c. 125, s. 19.

CROSS-REFERENCES

Assault is defined in s. 265. For cases respecting consent, especially assaults in course of a "consensual fight", see notes under s. 265. Where the prosecution elects to proceed by indictment on this offence, then the accused may elect his mode of trial pursuant to s. 536(2). Where the prosecution elects to proceed by way of summary conviction, then the trial of this offence is conducted by a summary conviction court pursuant to Part XXVII. The punishment for the offence is then as set out in s. 787 and the limitation period is set out in s. 786(2). In either case, release pending trial is determined by s. 515, although the accused is eligible for release by a peace officer under ss. 496, 497 or by the officer in charge under s. 498.

A person, found guilty of the offence in this section, will be liable to the discretionary prohibition order prescribed by s. 110, for possession of weapons, ammunition and explosives.

Section 7(3) enacts special jurisdictional rules for commission of this offence outside Canada when the offence is in relation to an internationally protected person or property referred to in s. 431 (official premises, etc.). A threat to commit an offence under this section against an internationally protected person (defined in s. 2) is an offence under s. 424. Section 33.1 limits the availability of the drunkenness defence.

The accused's spouse is a competent and compellable witness at the instance of the Crown by virtue of s. 4(4) of the *Canada Evidence Act*, R.S.C. 1985, c. C-5, where the complainant is under the age of 14 years. Age is determined by reference to s. 30 of the *Interpretation Act*, R.S.C. 1985, c. I-21.

Section 486(1) and (2) provide that the judge may make an order excluding all or any members of the public where such order is in the interest of public morals, the maintenance of order or the proper administration of justice, or is necessary to prevent injury to international relations or national defence or national security. The proper administration of justice includes safeguarding the interests of witnesses under the age of 18 years. Section 486.1 sets out the circumstances in which the judge shall or may order a support person to be present and close to a witness while the witness testifies. Where the witness is under the age of 18 years or has a mental or physical disability, the order is to be made upon request unless the judge is of the opinion that the order would interfere with the proper administration of justice. In the case of other witnesses, the order is to be made if necessary to obtain a full and candid account from the witness of the matters complained of. The application for this order may be made during the proceedings or before they begin to the judge who is to preside at the proceedings.

Similarly, s. 486.2 sets out the circumstances in which the judge shall or may order a witness to testify outside the courtroom or behind a screen or other device that would not allow the witness to see the accused. Where the witness is under the age of 18 years or may have difficulty communicating the evidence by reason of a mental or physical disability, the judge shall make the order unless the judge is of the opinion that the order would interfere with the proper administration of justice. In all other cases, the order may be made if the judge is of the opinion that the order is necessary to obtain a full and candid account from the witness of the acts complained of. Similarly, s. 486.3 provides that, on application by the prosecutor or a witness under the age of 18 years, the accused shall not personally cross-examine the witness unless the judge is of the opinion that the proper administration of justice requires the accused to personally conduct the cross-examination. In other cases, the judge may make an order that the accused not personally cross-examine the witness if the judge is of the opinion that the order is necessary to obtain a full and candid account from the witness of the acts complained of. The judge will appoint counsel to conduct the cross-examination.

Under s. 486.4, the judge may make an order directing that the identity of the complainant or a witness not be disclosed in any publication, broadcast or transmitted in any way. The order is mandatory where the complainant or a witness under the age of 18 years or the prosecutor applies for the order. Section 486.5 also gives the judge a discretion respecting non-publication orders in proceedings under these provisions in other circumstances.

Section 659 abrogates any rule requiring a warning about convicting the accused on the evidence of a child.

Section 715.1 provides that, in proceedings against the accused in which the victim (defined in s. 2) or other witness was under the age of 18 years at the time the offence is alleged to have been committed, a video recording made within a reasonable time after the alleged offence, in which the victim or witness describes the acts complained of, is admissible in evidence if the victim or witness, while testifying, adopts its contents, unless the judge is of the opinion that the admission of the video recoding would interfere with the proper administration of justice. Section 715.2 provides for a similar procedure where the victim or another witness may have difficulty communicating the evidence by reason of a mental or physical disability. Under s. 4(2) of the *Canada Evidence Act*, the spouse of an accused charged with this offence is a compellable witness at the instance of the prosecution. Sections 16 and 16.1 of the *Canada Evidence Act* deal with the competency of witnesses under the age of 14 years.

The offence in this section is a secondary designated offence for the purpose of making a forensic DNA data bank order under s. 487.051.

ANNOTATIONS

The conduct of the accused in pushing the complainant aside in order to leave his office, even if it amounted to an assault, was of such a trifling nature that the maxim *de minimis non curat lex* applied, and the accused was acquitted: *R. v. Lepage* (1989), 74 C.R. (3d) 368 (Sask. Q.B.).

The double jeopardy guarantee in s. 11(*h*) of the Charter is not a bar to the trial of an officer for an offence under this section notwithstanding his previous conviction for a major service offence under the *Royal Canadian Mounted Police Act*, R.S.C. 1970, c. R-9, as a result of that assault: *R. v. Wigglesworth*, [1987] 2 S.C.R. 541, 37 C.C.C. (3d) 385, 60 C.R. (3d) 193 (6:1). Also see *R. v. Shubley*, [1990] 1 S.C.R. 3, 52 C.C.C. (3d) 481, 65 D.L.R. (4th) 193 (3:2), noted under s. 267.

ASSAULT WITH A WEAPON OR CAUSING BODILY HARM.

267. Every one who, in committing an assault,

(*a*) carries, uses or threatens to use a weapon or an imitation thereof, or

(*b*) causes bodily harm to the complainant,

is guilty of an indictable offence and liable to imprisonment for a term not exceeding ten years or an offence punishable on summary conviction and liable to imprisonment for a term not exceeding eighteen months. 1980-81-82-83, c. 125, s. 19; 1994, c. 44, s. 17.

CROSS-REFERENCES

The terms "bodily harm", "complainant" and "weapon" are defined in s. 2. Assault is defined in s. 265. Limits on availability of drunkenness defence, see s. 33.1.

For cases respecting consent, especially assaults in the course of a "consensual fight", see notes under s. 265.

This offence may be the basis for an application for an authorization to intercept private communications by reason of s. 183.

Section 7(3) enacts special jurisdictional rules for commission of this offence outside Canada when the offence is in relation to an internationally protected person or property referred to in s. 431 (official premises, etc.).

The accused's spouse is a competent and compellable witness at the instance of the Crown by virtue of s. 4(4) of the *Canada Evidence Act*, where the complainant is under the age of 14 years. Age is determined by reference to s. 30 of the *Interpretation Act*, R.S.C. 1985, c. I-21.

Where the Crown elects to proceed by indictment, the accused may elect the mode of trial pursuant to s. 536(2). Release pending trial is determined by s. 515. A person, found guilty of the offence in this section, will be liable to the mandatory prohibition order in s. 109 for possession of certain weapons, ammunition and explosives where the Crown proceeds by indictment. Otherwise, the accused may be subject to an order under s. 110. A person found guilty of this offence may be subject to a dangerous offender application under Part XXIV.

Where the acts described in this section also involve a sexual assault, see s. 272. Using a firearm in commission of an indictable offence is an offence under s. 85. Unlawfully causing bodily harm is an offence under s. 269.

Section 486(1) and (2) provide that the judge may make an order excluding all or any members of the public where such order is in the interest of public morals, the maintenance of order or the proper administration of justice, or is necessary to prevent injury to international relations or national defence or national security. The proper administration of justice includes safeguarding the interests of witnesses under the age of 18 years. Section 486.1 sets out the circumstances in which the judge shall or may order a support person to be present and close to a witness while the witness testifies. Where the witness is under the age of 18 years or has a mental or physical disability, the order is to be made upon request unless the judge is of the opinion that the order would interfere with the proper administration of justice. In the case of other witnesses, the order is to be made if necessary to obtain a full and candid account from the witness of the matters complained of. The application for this order may be made during the proceedings or before they begin to the judge who is to preside at the proceedings.

Similarly, s. 486.2 sets out the circumstances in which the judge shall or may order a witness to testify outside the courtroom or behind a screen or other device that would not allow the witness to see the accused. Where the witness is under the age of 18 years or may have difficulty communicating the evidence by reason of a mental or physical disability, the judge shall make the order unless the judge is of the opinion that the order would interfere with the proper administration of justice. In all other cases, the order may be made if the judge is of the opinion that the order is necessary to obtain a full and candid account from the witness of the acts complained of. Similarly, s. 486.3 provides that, on application by the prosecutor or a witness under the age of 18 years, the accused shall not personally cross-examine the witness unless the judge is of the opinion that the proper administration of justice requires the accused to personally conduct the cross-examination. In other cases, the judge may make an order that the accused not personally cross-examine the witness if the judge is of the opinion that the order is necessary to obtain a full and candid account from the witness of the acts complained of. The judge will appoint counsel to conduct the cross-examination.

Under s. 486.4, the judge may make an order directing that the identity of the complainant or a witness not be disclosed in any publication, broadcast or transmitted in any way. The order is mandatory where the complainant or a witness under the age of 18 years or the prosecutor applies for the order. Section 486.5 also gives the judge a discretion respecting non-publication orders in proceedings under these provisions in other circumstances.

Section 659 abrogates any rule requiring a warning about convicting the accused on the evidence of a child.

Section 715.1 provides that, in proceedings against the accused in which the victim (defined in s. 2) or other witness was under the age of 18 years at the time the offence is alleged to have been committed, a video recording made within a reasonable time after the alleged offence, in which the victim or witness describes the acts complained of, is admissible in evidence if the victim or witness, while testifying, adopts its contents, unless the judge is of the opinion that the admission of the video recoding would interfere with the proper administration of justice. Section 715.2 provides for a similar procedure where the victim or another witness may have difficulty communicating the evidence by reason of a mental or physical disability. Under s. 4(2) of the *Canada Evidence Act*, the spouse of an accused charged with this offence is a compellable witness at the instance of the prosecution. Sections 16 and 16.1 of the *Canada Evidence Act* deal with the competency of witnesses under the age of 14 years.

The offence in this section is a primary designated offence for the purpose of making a forensic DNA data bank order under s. 487.051.

SYNOPSIS

This section specifies that a person who commits an assault while using or carrying a weapon or an imitation weapon, or who causes any hurt or injury that is not transient or trifling in nature and interferes with the complainant's health or comfort, is guilty of an indictable offence and liable to imprisonment for a maximum term of 10 years.

ANNOTATIONS

Assault with weapon [para. (*a*)] – The offence under subsec. (1)(*a*) of this section or s. 272(*a*) [now s. 272(1)(*a*)] may be committed although the accused did not in fact have possession of the weapon at the time of the threat: *R. v. Kelly* (1983), 37 C.R. (3d) 190 (B.C. Co. Ct.).

Provided the instrument used by the accused in the course of the assault falls within the definition of weapon, then this offence is made out. It is not necessary to show that the weapon also caused injuries to the complainant: *R. v. Richard* (1992), 72 C.C.C. (3d) 349, 110 N.S.R. (2d) 345 (C.A.).

The term "weapon" is not limited to inanimate objects and can include a dog which the accused ordered to attack the complainant: *R. v. McLeod* (1993), 84 C.C.C. (3d) 336 (Y.T.C.A.).

A blade used by a father in a misguided attempt to circumcise his four-year-old son was a "weapon" notwithstanding that the accused did not attempt to harm the child. What prevents a normal surgical operation from constituting an offence in s. 45 is reasonable care and skill: *R. v. W. (D.J.)* (2011), 282 C.C.C. (3d) 352 (B.C.C.A.), affd (2012), 294 C.C.C. (3d) 480 (S.C.C.).

Assault causing bodily harm – Reasonable foreseeability that harm will occur as a result of the assault is not a necessary element of this offence: *R. v. Brooks*, *infra*. Similarly, *R. v. Swenson* (1994), 91 C.C.C. (3d) 541, [1994] 9 W.W.R. 124, 74 W.A.C. 106 (Sask. C.A.).

Where the evidence fails to show whether the bruising caused by the accused's acts was more than merely transient or trifling in nature the element of "bodily harm" as defined in subsec. (2) is not made out: *R. v. Dupperon* (1984), 16 C.C.C. (3d) 453, 43 C.R. (3d) 70, [1985] 2 W.W.R. 369 (Sask. C.A.).

In *R. v. Dixon* (1988), 42 C.C.C. (3d) 318, 64 C.R. (3d) 372, [1988] 5 W.W.R. 577 (Yukon Terr. C.A.), only Esson J.A. discussed at length the definition of bodily harm in subsec. (2) and considered that the words "transient or trifling in nature" import a very short period of time and an injury of a very minor degree which results in a very minor degree of distress.

Bodily harm need not meet a standard of interfering in a grave or substantial way with the physical integrity or well-being of the complainant. A functional impairment is not necessary. Interference with comfort is sufficient to constitute bodily harm if it is more than trifling and transient: *R. v. Moquin* (2010), 253 C.C.C. (3d) 96, 73 C.R. (6th) 310 (Man. C.A.).

As to the consent defence, also see cases noted under s. 265(1), *supra*.

Constitutional considerations – The offence created by subsec. (1)(*b*) does not violate the principles of fundamental justice as guaranteed by s. 7 of the Charter although there is no requirement of objective foreseeability that the consequences of the assault would be bodily harm: *R. v. Brooks* (1988), 41 C.C.C. (3d) 157, 64 C.R. (3d) 322 (B.C.C.A.).

Section 11(*h*) of the *Charter of Rights and Freedoms* (the double jeopardy provision) does not prevent the trial of an accused for an offence of assault causing bodily harm arising out of an assault by the accused, an inmate of a provincial correctional institution, on a fellow inmate, notwithstanding that the accused had previously been punished for the same conduct by the authorities within the institution. These prison disciplinary proceedings did not result in the accused being punished for an "offence" within the meaning of s. 11(*h*): *R. v. Shubley*, [1990] 1 S.C.R. 3, 52 C.C.C. (3d) 481, 65 D.L.R. (4th) 193 (3:2).

AGGRAVATED ASSAULT / Punishment / Excision / Consent.

268. (1) Every one commits an aggravated assault who wounds, maims, disfigures or endangers the life of the complainant.

(2) Every one who commits an aggravated assault is guilty of an indictable offence and liable to imprisonment for a term not exceeding fourteen years.

(3) For greater certainty, in this section, "wounds" or "maims" includes to excise, infibulate or mutilate, in whole or in part, the labia majora, labia minora or clitoris of a person, except where

- **(*a*) a surgical procedure is performed, by a person duly qualified by provincial law to practise medicine, for the benefit of the physical health of the person or for the purpose of that person having normal reproductive functions or normal sexual appearance or function; or**
- **(*b*) the person is at least eighteen years of age and there is no resulting bodily harm.**

(4) For the purposes of this section and section 265, no consent to the excision, infibulation or mutilation, in whole or in part, of the labia majora, labia minora or clitoris of a person is valid, except in the cases described in paragraphs (3)(*a*) and (*b*). 1980-81-82-83, c. 125, s. 19; 1997, c. 16, s. 5.

CROSS-REFERENCES

The term "complainant" is defined in s. 2. Assault is defined in s. 265.

This offence may be the basis for an application for an authorization to intercept private communications by reason of s. 183.

Section 7(3) enacts special jurisdictional rules for commission of this offence outside Canada when the offence is in relation to an internationally protected person or property referred to in s. 431 (official premises, etc.).

The accused's spouse is a competent and compellable witness at the instance of the Crown by virtue of s. 4(4) of the *Canada Evidence Act*, R.S.C. 1985, c. C-5, where the complainant is under the age of 14 years. Age is determined by reference to s. 30 of the *Interpretation Act*, R.S.C. 1985, c. I-21.

The accused may elect his mode of trial pursuant to s. 536(2). Release pending trial is determined by s. 515. A person, found guilty of the offence in this section, will be liable to the mandatory prohibition order in s. 109 for possession of certain weapons, ammunition and explosives. A person found guilty of this offence may be subject to a dangerous offender application under Part XXIV.

Where the acts described in this section also involve a sexual assault, see s. 273.

Limits on the availability of drunkenness defence, see s. 33.1.

Section 486(1) and (2) provide that the judge may make an order excluding all or any members of the public where such order is in the interest of public morals, the maintenance of order or the proper administration of justice, or is necessary to prevent injury to international relations or national defence or national security. The proper administration of justice includes safeguarding the interests of witnesses under the age of 18 years. Section 486.1 sets out the circumstances in which the judge shall or may order a support person to be present and close to a witness while the witness testifies. Where the witness is under the age of 18 years or has a mental or physical disability, the order is to be made upon request unless the judge is of the opinion that the order would interfere with the proper administration of justice. In the case of other witnesses, the order is to be made if necessary to obtain a full and candid account from the witness of the matters complained of. The application for this order may be made during the proceedings or before they begin to the judge who is to preside at the proceedings.

Similarly, s. 486.2 sets out the circumstances in which the judge shall or may order a witness to testify outside the courtroom or behind a screen or other device that would not allow the witness to see the accused. Where the witness is under the age of 18 years or may have difficulty communicating the evidence by reason of a mental or physical disability, the judge shall make the order unless the judge is of the opinion that the order would interfere with the proper administration of justice. In all other cases, the order may be made if the judge is of the opinion that the order is necessary to obtain a full and candid account from the witness of the acts complained of. Similarly, s. 486.3 provides that, on application by the prosecutor or a witness under the age of 18 years, the accused shall not personally cross-examine the witness unless the judge is of the opinion that the proper administration of justice requires the accused to personally conduct the cross-examination. In other cases, the judge may make an order that the accused not personally cross-examine the witness if the judge is of the opinion that the order is necessary to obtain a full and candid account from the witness of the acts complained of. The judge will appoint counsel to conduct the cross-examination.

Under s. 486.4, the judge may make an order directing that the identity of the complainant or a witness not be disclosed in any publication, broadcast or transmitted in any way. The order is mandatory where the complainant or a witness under the age of 18 years or the prosecutor applies for the order. Section 486.5 also gives the judge a discretion respecting non-publication orders in proceedings under these provisions in other circumstances.

Section 659 abrogates any rule requiring a warning about convicting the accused on the evidence of a child.

Section 715.1 provides that, in proceedings against the accused in which the victim (defined in s. 2) or other witness was under the age of 18 years at the time the offence is alleged to have been committed, a video recording made within a reasonable time after the alleged offence, in which the victim or witness describes the acts complained of, is admissible in evidence if the victim or witness, while testifying, adopts its contents, unless the judge is of the opinion that the admission of the video recording would interfere with the proper administration of justice. Section 715.2 provides for a similar procedure where the victim or another witness may have difficulty communicating the evidence by reason of a mental or physical disability. Under s. 4(2) of the *Canada Evidence Act*, the spouse of an accused charged with this offence is a compellable witness at the instance of the prosecution. Sections 16 and 16.1 of the *Canada Evidence Act* deal with the competency of witnesses under the age of 14 years.

The offence in this section is a primary designated offence for the purpose of making a forensic DNA data bank order under s. 487.051.

SYNOPSIS

This section describes what constitutes an aggravated assault and sets out the punishment for such an assault. When a person wounds, maims, disfigures or endangers the life of a complainant that person is guilty of aggravated assault and is liable to a maximum term of imprisonment of 14 years.

ANNOTATIONS

The element of wounding requires a breaking of the skin but is satisfied by proof that the blows of the accused led to a perforation of the victim's ear-drum: *R. v. Littletent* (1985), 17 C.C.C. (3d) 520 (Alta. C.A.).

While endangerment of life does not require proof of bodily harm, the conduct must endanger the complainant's life and not merely have the potential to endanger life. Accordingly, where the accused made stabbing motions towards the victim's chest but did not injure the victim, the requisite endangerment of life was not proven: *R. v. De Freitas* (1999), 132 C.C.C. (3d) 333 (Man. C.A.).

Consent is no defence to this offence where the injuries were caused by use of a weapon such as a knife: *R. v. Carriere* (1987), 35 C.C.C. (3d) 276 (Alta. C.A.).

This section creates a form of assault offence and the offence of assault causing bodily harm in s. 267(*b*) is an included offence: *R. v. Lucas* (1987), 34 C.C.C. (3d) 28 (Que. C.A.). See also *R. v. Soluk* (2001), 157 C.C.C. (3d) 473 (B.C.C.A.).

The *mens rea* of this offence is objective foresight of bodily harm and does not require proof of an intent to maim, wound or disfigure: *R. v. Godin*, [1994] 2 S.C.R. 484, 89 C.C.C. (3d) 574*n*.

The Crown need not show that an accused alleged to be a party to the offence pursuant to s. 21(1)(*b*) had any greater *mens rea* than the actual perpetrator and, in particular, need not show an objective foresight of the specific wounds resulting from the assault: *R. v. Cuadra* (1998), 125 C.C.C. (3d) 289 (B.C.C.A.). Similarly, where the accused is alleged to be a party under s. 21(2): *R. v. Vang* (1999), 132 C.C.C. (3d) 32 (Ont. C.A.), leave to appeal to S.C.C. refused 137 C.C.C. (3d) vi.

The offence under this section is made out where the accused endangered the life of the complainant and intentionally applied force without the complainant's consent. The first element is made out where the accused, who was HIV-positive, had unprotected sexual intercourse with the complainant. It was unnecessary to establish that the complainant was in fact infected with the virus. The lack of consent is made out where the accused failed to disclose that he was HIV-positive thus vitiating consent by fraud: *R. v. Cuerrier*, [1998] 2 S.C.R. 371, 127 C.C.C. (3d) 1.

The *mens rea* for aggravated assault is the *mens rea* for assault plus objective foresight of the risk of bodily harm. Part of the *actus reus* is the endangerment of the victim's life. The *mens rea* and the *actus reus* must coincide. Where during his relationship with the victim, the accused had learned that he was HIV positive and continued to have unprotected intercourse without disclosing it to the victim, the offence of aggravated assault was not made out. It could not be shown that sexual activity after learning of his infected status harmed the victim or even exposed her to a significant risk of harm because, at that point, she was possibly already infected with HIV. While prior to the test, there was endangerment but no criminal intent, after the test, there was criminal intent but no proof of endangerment. In the circumstances, the accused was properly convicted of attempted aggravated assault: *R. v. Williams* (2003), 176 C.C.C. (3d) 449 (S.C.C.).

The *Cuerrier* requirement of "significant risk of serious bodily harm" should be read as requiring disclosure of HIV status if there is a realistic possibility of transmission of HIV. If there is no realistic possibility of transmission of HIV, failure to disclose that one has HIV will not constitute fraud vitiating consent to sexual relations. A realistic possibility of transmission is negated if: (i) the accused's viral load at the time of sexual relations was low and (ii) condom protection was used. This general proposition does not preclude the common law from adapting to future advances in treatment and to circumstances where risk factors other than those considered in this case are at play: *R. v. Mabior*, [2012] 2 S.C.R. 584, 290 C.C.C. (3d) 32.

Following an arrest for an unrelated offence, the accused proclaimed that he was HIV positive and proceeded to spit in the face of an officer. Though there was no evidence of a realistic possibility of transmission, the proper verdict on the evidence was guilty of attempted aggravated assault given the accused's clear intent to transmit HIV by spitting: *R. v. Bear* (2013), 304 C.C.C. (3d) 185 (Man. C.A.).

UNLAWFULLY CAUSING BODILY HARM.

269. Every one who unlawfully causes bodily harm to any person is guilty of

(*a*) an indictable offence and liable to imprisonment for a term not exceeding ten years; or

(*b*) an offence punishable on summary conviction and liable to imprisonment for a term not exceeding eighteen months. 1980-81-82-83, c. 125, s. 19; 1994, c. 44, s. 18.

CROSS-REFERENCES

"Bodily harm" is defined in s. 2.

This offence may be the basis for an application for an authorization to intercept private communications by reason of s. 183.

Section 7(3) enacts special jurisdictional rules for commission of this offence outside Canada when the offence is in relation to an internationally protected person or property referred to in s. 431 (official premises, etc.).

The accused's spouse is a competent and compellable witness at the instance of the Crown by virtue of s. 4(4) of the *Canada Evidence Act*, R.S.C. 1985, c. C-5, where the complainant is under the age of 14 years. Age is determined by reference to s. 30 of the *Interpretation Act*, R.S.C. 1985, c. I-21.

The accused may elect the mode of trial pursuant to s. 536(2) where the Crown proceeds by indictment. Release pending trial is determined by s. 515. A person found guilty of the offence in para. (*a*) will be liable to the mandatory prohibition order in s. 109 for possession of certain weapons, ammunition and explosives in such a case. Otherwise, the accused may be subject to an order under s. 110. A person found guilty of this offence may be subject to a dangerous offender application under Part XXIV.

The offence of assault causing bodily harm is found in s. 267(*b*). Limits on the availability of drunkenness defence, see s. 33.1.

ANNOTATIONS

The term "unlawfully" in this section refers only to provincial or federal offences and would not include any underlying offence of absolute liability. As well, the unlawful act must be at least objectively dangerous, an act that a reasonable person would inevitably realize would subject another person to the risk of bodily harm. This bodily harm must be more than merely trivial or transitory in nature and will, in most cases, involve an act of violence done deliberately to another person. So interpreted, this section does not violate s. 7 of the Charter, even though neither an intention to cause bodily harm nor subjective foresight of bodily harm is an element of the offence: *R. v. DeSousa*, [1992] 2 S.C.R. 944, 76 C.C.C. (3d) 124 (5:0).

An accused may be convicted of the offence under this section although the bodily harm was caused by an assault and a charge under s. 267(*b*) could have been laid: *R. v. Glowacki* (1984), 16 C.C.C. (3d) 574 (B.C.C.A.).

Consent is no defence to the charge under this section. However the accused's good faith belief as to the effectiveness of the treatment that he as a "healer" was providing the victim was evidence which could negative the *mens rea* of the offence. The fact that the treatment was not authorized by provincial legislation regulating treatment of illness did not fully determine the accused's guilt for this offence even though the treatment caused bodily harm: *R. v. Daigle* (1987), 39 C.C.C. (3d) 542, [1987] R.J.Q. 2374 (C.A.).

Although this offence is one of general intent and thus voluntary intoxication is no defence, an attempt to unlawfully cause bodily harm is an offence of specific intent and intoxication is a defence: *R. v. Colburne* (1991), 66 C.C.C. (3d) 235, [1991] R.J.Q. 1199 (C.A.).

Some appellate courts have held that objective foreseeability of bodily harm is an essential element of this offence: *R. v. Dewey* (1998), 132 C.C.C. (3d) 348 (Alta. C.A.); *R. v. Nurse* (1993), 83 C.C.C. (3d) 546 (Ont. C.A). Others have held that the Crown only need prove that bodily harm was caused, not that it was foreseeable: *R. v. Brooks* (1988), 41 C.C.C. (3d) 157 (B.C.C.A.); *R. v. Swenson* (1994), 91 C.C.C. (3d) 541 (Sask. C.A.).

AGGRAVATING CIRCUMSTANCE — ASSAULT AGAINST A PUBLIC TRANSIT OPERATOR / Definitions.

269.01 (1) When a court imposes a sentence for an offence referred to in paragraph 264.1(1)(*a*) or any of sections 266 to 269, it shall consider as an aggravating circumstance the fact that the victim of the offence was, at the time of the commission of the offence, a public transit operator engaged in the performance of his or her duty.

(2) The following definitions apply in this section.

"public transit operator" means an individual who operates a vehicle used in the provision of passenger transportation services to the public, and includes an individual who operates a school bus.

"vehicle" includes a bus, paratransit vehicle, licensed taxi cab, train, subway, tram and ferry. 2015, c. 1, s. 1.

CROSS-REFERENCES

For other deemed aggravating factors on sentencing, see s. 718.2.

SYNOPSIS

This section provides that, when a person is convicted of an assault or threatening offence, it is deemed to be an aggravating factor that the victim was a public transit operator engaged in the performance of his or her duties. It must be read with s. 718.2, which sets out other statutory aggravating factors.

TORTURE / definitions / "official" / "torture" / no defence / evidence.

269.1 (1) Every official, or every person acting at the instigation of or with the consent or acquiescence of an official, who inflicts torture on any other person is guilty of an indictable offence and liable to imprisonment for a term not exceeding fourteen years.

(2) For the purposes of this section,
"official" means

(*a*) a peace officer,
(*b*) a public officer,
(*c*) a member of the Canadian Forces, or
(*d*) any person who may exercise powers, pursuant to a law in force in a foreign state, that would, in Canada, be exercised by a person referred to in paragraph (*a*), (*b*), or (*c*),

whether the person exercises powers in Canada or outside Canada;
"torture" means any act or omission by which severe pain or suffering, whether physical or mental, is intentionally inflicted on a person

(*a*) for a purpose including
(i) obtaining from the person or from a third person information or a statement,
(ii) punishing the person for an act that the person or a third person has committed or is suspected of having committed, and
(iii) intimidating or coercing the person or a third person, or
(*b*) for any reason based on discrimination of any kind,

but does not include any act or omission arising only from, inherent in or incidental to lawful sanctions.

(3) It is no defence to a charge under this section that the accused was ordered by a superior or a public authority to perform the act or omission that forms the subject-matter of the charge or that the act or omission is alleged to have been justified by exceptional circumstances, including a state of war, a threat of war, internal political instability or any other public emergency.

(4) In any proceedings over which Parliament has jurisdiction, any statement obtained as a result of the commission of an offence under this section is inadmissible in evidence, except as evidence that the statement was so obtained. R.S.C. 1985, c. 10 (3rd Supp.), s. 2.

CROSS-REFERENCES

The terms "peace officer", "public officer", "Canadian Forces" are defined in s. 2.

Section 7(3.7) enacts special jurisdictional rules where commission of this offence was outside Canada.

The accused may elect his mode of trial pursuant to s. 536(2). Release pending trial is determined by s. 515. A person, found guilty of the offence in this section, will be liable to the mandatory prohibition order in s. 109 for possession of certain weapons, ammunition and explosives. A person found guilty of this offence may be subject to a dangerous offender application under Part XXIV.

In light of subsec. (3), the scope of the defence of obedience to *de facto* law in s. 15 is uncertain.

SYNOPSIS

This section makes it an offence for any person, either acting in an official capacity or acting at the instigation or acquiescence of an official, to inflict torture on another person. This is an indictable offence punishable by a maximum term of imprisonment of 14 years. The section contains complete definitions of the terms "official" and "torture". A person accused of an offence under this section may not escape criminal liability as a result of the fact that he was following the orders of a superior or a public authority, or that exceptional circumstances justified the action.

The contents of any statement obtained as a result of the commission of an offence under this section is inadmissible in evidence in any proceedings over which Parliament has jurisdiction.

ASSAULTING A PEACE OFFICER / Punishment.

270. (1) Every one commits an offence who

(*a*) assaults a public officer or peace officer engaged in the execution of his duty or a person acting in aid of such an officer;

(*b*) assaults a person with intent to resist or prevent the lawful arrest or detention of himself or another person; or

(*c*) assaults a person

(i) who is engaged in the lawful execution of a process against lands or goods or in making a lawful distress or seizure, or

(ii) with intent to rescue anything taken under lawful process, distress or seizure.

(2) Every one who commits an offence under subsection (1) is guilty of

(*a*) an indictable offence and liable to imprisonment for a term not exceeding five years; or

(*b*) an offence punishable on summary conviction. R.S., c. C-34, s. 246; 1972, c. 13, s. 22; 1980-81-82-83, c. 125, s. 19.

CROSS-REFERENCES

The terms "peace officer" and "public officer" are defined in s. 2. It is an offence to disarm a peace officer under s. 270.1. Assault is defined in s. 265. Where the accused in committing this offence carries, uses or threatens to use a weapon or an imitation of one, or causes bodily harm to the complainant, they commit the separate offence under s. 270.01 and are subject to the more severe penalties set out in that section. Where the accused in committing this offence wounds, maims, disfigures or endangers the life of the complainant, they commit the offence under s. 270.02 and are liable to a term of imprisonment of 14 years. Section 718.02 provides that, in imposing sentence for this offence, the court is to give primary consideration to the objectives of denunciation and deterrence.

This offence may be the basis for a conviction for constructive murder under s. 230 and murder of a peace officer, acting in the course of his duties, is first degree murder under s. 231(4).

Where the prosecution elects to proceed by indictment on this offence, then the accused may elect his mode of trial pursuant to s. 536(2). Where the prosecution elects to proceed by way of summary conviction, then the trial of this offence is conducted by a summary conviction court pursuant to Part XXVII.

The punishment for the offence is then as set out in s. 787 and the limitation period is set out in s. 786(2). In either case, release pending trial is determined by s. 515, although the accused is eligible for release by a peace officer under s. 496, 497 or by the officer in charge under s. 498.

A person, found guilty of the offence in this section, will be liable to the discretionary prohibition order prescribed by s. 110 for possession of certain weapons, ammunition and explosives.

The related offence of obstructing a peace officer in the execution of his duty is set out in s. 129. Misconduct by a peace officer in executing process is an offence under s. 128. Section 29 imposes certain duties on anyone executing a process. The use of force in enforcement of the law is principally dealt with under s. 25 and see notes under that section. Sections 494 and 495 deal specifically with warrantless arrest powers. Additional duties are imposed under other provisions of the Code, especially in Parts I and II respecting breach of the peace and more serious disorders. Personating a peace officer is an offence under s. 130.

SYNOPSIS

This section describes the offence of assaulting a peace officer. Any person who assaults a public officer or peace officer engaged in the execution of his duty, or a person assisting such an officer, or who assaults a person with intent to resist or prevent a lawful arrest, or who assaults a person engaged in the lawful execution of a process against lands or goods is guilty of an offence under this section. An offence under this section is punishable on summary conviction, or, on indictment, to a term of imprisonment not exceeding five years.

ANNOTATIONS

"Engaged in the execution of his duty" [subsec. (1)(*a*)] – Taking the facts as found by the trial Judge, regardless as to whether or not the police officer was a trespasser on private property when he was engaged in investigating a possible unlawful entry into the building, he was at the time in the execution of his duty and since he was not unlawfully interfering with either the liberty or the property of the respondent, who assaulted him while being questioned, an offence was proven under this subsection: *R. v. Stenning*, [1970] S.C.R. 631, [1970] 3 C.C.C. 145.

In *R. v. Bushman,* [1968] 4 C.C.C. 17 (B.C.C.A.), it was held (2:1) that where the accused failed to give police officers investigating a hit and run offence reasonable opportunity to depart from his residence's vestibule, it cannot be said that he properly revoked the implied leave and licence to attend at a convenient outer door to converse with him, and accordingly his striking an officer amounted to assaulting a policeman.

The police officer was not in the execution of her duty when she entered the accused's trailer for the purpose of investigating an allegation of assault as there was no common law or statutory foundation which would justify the entry without consent: *R. v. Plamondon* (1997), 121 C.C.C. (3d) 314 (B.C.C.A.).

Validity of arrest – An officer is in execution of his duty where he is empowered to make a warrantless arrest by s. 495(1)(*a*), although the arrest is effected by entry on to private premises without the consent of the occupier, provided the officer has reasonable and probable grounds for the belief that the person sought is within the premises and proper announcement was made before entry: *R. v. Landry*, [1986] 1 S.C.R. 145, 25 C.C.C. (3d) 1 (8:1).

In *R. v. Cottam and Cottam*, [1970] 1 C.C.C. 117 (B.C.C.A.), it was held that to determine whether the officers in apprehending the accused were engaged in the execution of their duty a jury should be instructed (a) as to circumstances in which the arrest would be lawful and (b), if the arrest was unlawful, whether the officers had thereby so far exceeded their duty and authority as to be no longer in the execution of their duty.

An arrest is a submission to restraint on one's freedom and physical force is not an essential ingredient of that act. Where on the facts it was found that the accused was not told by the officer that he was under arrest or the reason for his arrest, when it was feasible to do so, he cannot be convicted of assaulting the officer under this section: *R. v. Acker,* [1970] 4 C.C.C. 269 (N.S.S.C. App. Div.).

A police officer arresting an accused pursuant to an outstanding warrant, but without possession of the warrant, fully discharges his duty under s. 29 by telling the person that the reason for the arrest is the existence of the warrant, he need not obtain the warrant, or ascertain its contents in order to tell the accused. An arrest in such circumstances is therefore lawful and a conviction under this subsection will lie where the accused assaults the officer: *R. v. Gamracy*, [1974] S.C.R. 640, 12 C.C.C. (2d) 209 (3:2).

Note: Also see notes under s. 129 and s. 495.

ASSAULTING PEACE OFFICER WITH WEAPON OR CAUSING BODILY HARM / Punishment.

270.01 (1) Everyone commits an offence who, in committing an assault referred to in section 270,

(*a*) carries, uses or threatens to use a weapon or an imitation of one; or
(*b*) causes bodily harm to the complainant.

(2) Everyone who commits an offence under subsection (1) is guilty of

(*a*) an indictable offence and liable to imprisonment for a term of not more than 10 years; or
(*b*) an offence punishable on summary conviction and liable to imprisonment for a term of not more than 18 months. 2009, c. 22, s. 9.

CROSS-REFERENCES
"Weapon", "bodily harm" and "complainant" are defined in s. 2. This offence is a primary designated offence for the purposes of the DNA Forensic Analysis provisions. For additional CROSS-REFERENCES, see s. 270. Section 718.02 provides that, in imposing sentence for this offence, the court is to give primary consideration to the objectives of denunciation and deterrence.

AGGRAVATED ASSAULT OF PEACE OFFICER.

270.02 Everyone who, in committing an assault referred to in section 270, wounds, maims, disfigures or endangers the life of the complainant is guilty of an indictable offence and liable to imprisonment for a term of not more than 14 years. 2009, c. 22, s. 9.

CROSS-REFERENCES
"Complainant" is defined in s. 2. This offence is a primary designated offence for the purposes of the DNA Forensic Analysis provisions. For additional CROSS-REFERENCES, see s. 270. For the meaning of the terms "wounds", "maims", "disfigures" or "endangers the life", see the notes under s. 268, which creates the related offence of aggravated assault. Section 718.02 provides that, in imposing sentence for this offence, the court is to give primary consideration to the objectives of denunciation and deterrence.

SENTENCES TO BE SERVED CONSECUTIVELY.

270.03 A sentence imposed on a person for an offence under subsection 270(1) or 270.01(1) or section 270.02 committed against a law enforcement officer, as defined in subsection 445.01(4), shall be served consecutively to any other punishment imposed on the person for an offence arising out of the same event or series of events. 2015, c. 34, s. 2.

DISARMING A PEACE OFFICER / Definition of "weapon" / Punishment.

270.1 (1) Every one commits an offence who, without the consent of a peace officer, takes or attempts to take a weapon that is in the possession of the peace officer when the peace officer is engaged in the execution of his or her duty.

(2) For the purpose of subsection (1), "weapon" means any thing that is designed to be used to cause injury or death to, or to temporarily incapacitate, a person.

(3) Every one who commits an offence under subsection (1) is guilty of

(*a*) an indictable offence and liable to imprisonment for a term of not more than five years; or
(*b*) an offence punishable on summary conviction and liable to imprisonment for a term of not more than eighteen months. 2002, c. 13, s. 11.

CROSS-REFERENCES
"Peace officer" is defined in s. 2. Section 270 creates the offence of assaulting a peace officer in the execution of his duty. See notes under that section for the meaning of the phrase "engaged in the execution of his or her duty". Obstructing a peace officer in the execution of his duty is an offence under s. 129.

SYNOPSIS

This section creates the hybrid offence of disarming a peace officer. It is an offence to take or attempt to take a weapon from the officer's possession when the officer is engaged in the execution of his or her duty. "Weapon" is defined in subsec. (2).

SEXUAL ASSAULT.

271. Everyone who commits a sexual assault is guilty of

(*a*) an indictable offence and is liable to imprisonment for a term of not more than 10 years or, if the complainant is under the age of 16 years, to imprisonment for a term of not more than 14 years and to a minimum punishment of imprisonment for a term of one year; or

(*b*) an offence punishable on summary conviction and is liable to imprisonment for a term of not more than 18 months or, if the complainant is under the age of 16 years, to imprisonment for a term of not more than two years less a day and to a minimum punishment of imprisonment for a term of six months. 1980-81-82-83, c. 125, c. 19; R.S.C. 1985, c. 19 (3rd Supp.), s. 10; 1994, c. 44, s. 19; 2012, c. 1, s. 25; 2015, c. 23, s. 14.

CROSS-REFERENCES
While assault is defined in s. 265 as, in effect, a touching without the consent of the complainant, s. 273.1 gives a specific definition of consent for the purpose of the offence in this section. Section 265(4) deals with the defence of mistaken belief in consent generally but again, s. 273.2 deals specifically with that defence in the context of this offence. A spouse may be charged with this offence (s. 278). Section 17 limits the availability of the statutory defence of compulsion by threats. Section 33.1 limits the availability of the intoxication defence.

Section 150.1(1) and (2) set out the circumstances in which consent is a defence where the complainant is under 14 years of age. Age is determined by s. 30 of the *Interpretation Act*, R.S.C. 1985, c. I-21. Section 658 provides a means of proving the age of a child. Section 150.1(4) provides a limited defence of mistake as to the age of the complainant.

A person found guilty of the offence in this section, may, depending on the circumstances, be liable to either the mandatory prohibition order in s. 109 or to the discretionary prohibition order prescribed by s. 110 for possession of certain weapons, ammunition and explosives. Where the accused is found guilty of this offence in respect of a person who is under 16 years of age, the court has the discretion to impose an order of prohibition under s. 161 prohibiting the accused from attending certain public areas and facilities or taking certain employment which will bring him into contact with persons under 16 years of age or using a computer system for the purpose of communicating with a person under the age of 16 years. This offence may be the basis for an application for an authorization to intercept private communications by reason of s. 183, or a video surveillance warrant under s. 487.01. This offence may be the basis for a conviction for first degree murder under s. 231(5) and also for a finding that the accused is a dangerous offender under Part XXIV. Section 7(3) enacts special jurisdictional rules for commission of this offence outside Canada, when the offence is in relation to an internationally protected person or property referred to in s. 431 (official premises, etc.).

The offences in this section and ss. 272 and 273 are primary designated offences for the purpose of making a forensic DNA data bank order under s. 487.051. Under s. 490.012, on application by the prosecutor, where an offender is convicted of these offences, the judge shall make an order requiring the offender to comply with the *Sex Offender Information Registration Act*, S.C. 2004, c. 10.

Other sexual offences are found in ss. 151 to 160 and 170 to 174. Section 171.1 makes it an offence to transmit, make available, distribute or sell sexually explicit material to a person who is, or who the accused believes is under the age of 16 years for the purpose of facilitating the commission of the offence created by this section or ss. 272 and 273. Section 172.1 makes it an offence to communicate by means of telecommunication with a person who is or who the accused believes is under the age of 16 years for the purpose of facilitating the commission of the offence under this section or ss. 272 and 273. Section 172.2 makes it an offence to agree with a person or make an arrangement with a person by means of telecommunication to commit an offence under this section or ss. 272 and 273 with a person who is or who the accused believes is under the age of 16 years.

Special evidentiary and procedural provisions – Section 274 specifically provides that no corroboration is required for a conviction for this offence and the offences in ss. 272 and 273 and the judge shall not instruct the jury that it is unsafe to find the accused guilty in the absence of corroboration. Section 275 provides that the rule relating to evidence of recent complaint is abrogated respecting this section. While assault is defined in s. 265 as, in effect, a touching without the consent of the complainant, s. 273.1 gives a specific definition of consent for the purpose of the offence in this section. Section 265(4) deals with the defence of mistaken belief in consent generally but again, s. 273.2 deals specifically with that defence in the context of this offence. Section 277 provides that evidence of sexual reputation is inadmissible in proceedings under this section. Production of records containing personal information of the complainant or a witness for use by the accused at the trial is governed by ss. 278.1 to 278.9. Section 486(1) and (2) provide that the judge may make an order excluding all or any members of the public where such order is in the interest of public morals, the maintenance of order or the proper administration of justice, or is necessary to prevent injury to international relations or national defence or national security. The proper administration of justice includes safeguarding the interests of witnesses under the age of 18 years. Where the accused is charged with an offence under this section and the application by the accused or the prosecutor for the exclusion order is dismissed, the judge shall state the reason for not making the order. Section 486.1 sets out the circumstances in which the judge shall or may order a support person to be present and close to a witness while the witness testifies. Where the witness is under the age of 18 years or has a mental or physical disability, the order is to be made upon request unless the judge is of the opinion that the order would interfere with the proper administration of justice. In the case of other witnesses, the order is to be made if necessary to obtain a full and candid account from the witness of the matters complained of. The application for this order may be made during the proceedings or before they begin to the judge who is to preside at the proceedings.

Similarly, s. 486.2 sets out the circumstances in which the judge shall or may order a witness to testify outside the courtroom or behind a screen or other device that would not allow the witness to see the accused. Where the witness is under the age of 18 years or may have difficulty communicating the evidence by reason of a mental or physical disability, the judge shall make the order unless the judge is of the opinion that the order would interfere with the proper administration of justice. In all other cases, the order may be made if the judge is of the opinion that the order is necessary to obtain a full and candid account from the witness of the acts complained of. Similarly, s. 486.3 provides that, on application by the prosecutor or a witness under the age of 18 years, the accused shall not personally cross-examine the witness unless the judge is of the opinion that the proper administration of justice requires the accused to personally conduct the cross-examination. In other cases, the judge may make an order that the accused not personally cross-examine the witness if the judge is of the opinion that the order is necessary to obtain a full and candid account from the witness of the acts complained of. The judge will appoint counsel to conduct the cross-examination.

Under s. 486.4, the judge may make an order directing that the identity of the complainant or a witness not be disclosed in any publication, broadcast or transmitted in any way. The order is mandatory where the complainant or a witness under the age of 18 years or the prosecutor applies for the order. Section 486.5 also gives the judge a discretion respecting non-publication orders in proceedings under these provisions in other circumstances.

Section 659 abrogates any rule requiring a warning about convicting the accused on the evidence of a child.

Section 715.1 provides that, in proceedings against the accused in which the victim (defined in s. 2) or other witness was under the age of 18 years at the time the offence is alleged to have been committed, a video recording made within a reasonable time after the alleged offence, in which the victim or witness describes the acts complained of, is admissible in evidence if the victim or witness, while testifying, adopts its contents, unless the judge is of the opinion that the admission of the video recoding would interfere with the proper administration of justice. Section 715.2 provides for a similar procedure where the victim or another witness may have difficulty communicating the evidence by reason of a mental or physical disability. Under s. 4(2) of the *Canada Evidence Act*, the spouse of an accused charged with this offence is a compellable witness at the instance of the prosecution. Sections 16 and 16.1 of the *Canada Evidence Act* deal with the competency of witnesses under the age of 14 years.

ANNOTATIONS

Meaning of "sexual assault" – Sexual assault is an assault, within any one of the definitions of that concept in s. 265(1), which is committed in circumstances of a sexual nature such that the sexual integrity of the victim is violated. The test to be applied in determining whether the impugned conduct has the requisite sexual nature is an objective one: whether viewed in the light of all the circumstances the sexual or carnal context of the assault is visible to a reasonable observer. The part of the body touched, the nature of the contact, the situation in which it occurred, the words and gestures accompanying the act, and all other circumstances surrounding the conduct, including threats, which may or may not be accompanied by force, will be relevant. The intent or purpose of the person committing the act, to the extent that this may appear from the evidence, may also be a factor in considering whether the conduct is sexual. If the motive of the accused is sexual gratification, to the extent that this may appear from the evidence it may be a factor in determining whether the conduct is sexual. The existence of such a motive is, however, merely one of many factors to be considered: *R. v. Chase*, [1987] 2 S.C.R. 293, 37 C.C.C. (3d) 97 (6:0).

The offence of sexual assault is one of general intent so that the issue is whether, notwithstanding the absence of a proven sexual intent, the touching was committed in circumstances of a sexual nature: *R. v. S. (P.L.)*, [1991] 1 S.C.R. 909, 64 C.C.C. (3d) 193.

The importance of the accused's purpose as a factor in determining whether or not there has been a sexual assault will vary depending on the circumstances. In this case, where the conduct involved "skylarking" which had been part of the regular life of the family for many years without any sexual connotations, the jury, in order to convict, would have to find that the impugned conduct had changed, from being incidental to the romping or "skylarking" but without sexual connotation, to acts with sexual intent. In such a case, the accused's purpose or motivation would be very relevant: *R. v. J. (C.)* (1990), 58 C.C.C. (3d) 167 (Nfld. C.A.).

Sexual assault does not require proof of sexuality or sexual gratification which are merely factors. The conduct of the accused in grabbing his young child's genitals as a form of "discipline" was an aggressive act of domination which violated the sexual integrity of the child which could be found to be a sexual assault: *R. v. V. (K.B.)* (1992), 71 C.C.C. (3d) 65 (Ont. C.A.), affd [1993] 2 S.C.R. 857, 82 C.C.C. (3d) 382. Therefore, the requisite *mens rea* was established where the accused had touched the complainants's breasts and testicles without hostility in the context of joking as a reasonable person would perceive the sexual context of the touchings: *R. v. Bernier* (1997), 119 C.C.C. (3d) 467 (Que. C.A.), affd [1998] 1 S.C.R. 975, 124 C.C.C. (3d) 383.

A fraudulent gynecological exam constituted a sexual assault even though the accused, posing as a medical doctor, was in a consensual sexual relationship with the victim at the time: *R. v. Mastronardi* (2014), 313 C.C.C. (3d) 295 (B.C.C.A.).

Abuse of process – The burden is on the accused to establish the facts which he alleges amount to an abuse of process. Even lengthy delay in the laying of charges alleging sexual assault by a person in *loco parentis* will not of itself amount to an abuse of process nor necessarily lead to an unfair trial. An allegation by the accused that his right to make full answer and defence has been prejudiced by delay, as a result of the death of potential defence witnesses, is to be determined at trial and not by way of a pre-trial motion to stay proceedings: *R. v. D. (E.)* (1990), 57 C.C.C. (3d) 151 (Ont. C.A.). To a similar effect, see: *R. v. G. (W.G.)* (1990), 58 C.C.C. (3d) 263 (Nfld. C.A.).

For further notes on abuse of process, see the annotations following s. 579.

SEXUAL ASSAULT WITH A WEAPON, THREATS TO A THIRD PARTY OR CAUSING BODILY HARM / Punishment / Subsequent offences / Sequence of convictions only.

272. (1) Every person commits an offence who, in committing a sexual assault,

(*a*) carries, uses or threatens to use a weapon or an imitation of a weapon;

(*b*) threatens to cause bodily harm to a person other than the complainant;

(*c*) causes bodily harm to the complainant; or

(*d*) is a party to the offence with any other person.

(2) Every person who commits an offence under subsection (1) is guilty of an indictable offence and liable

(*a*) if a restricted firearm or prohibited firearm is used in the commission of the offence or if any firearm is used in the commission of the offence and the offence is committed for the benefit of, at the direction of, or in association with, a criminal organization, to imprisonment for a term not exceeding 14 years and to a minimum punishment of imprisonment for a term of

(i) in the case of a first offence, five years, and

(ii) in the case of a second or subsequent offence, seven years;

(*a*.1) in any other case where a firearm is used in the commission of the offence, to imprisonment for a term not exceeding 14 years and to a minimum punishment of imprisonment for a term of four years;

(*a*.2) if the complainant is under the age of 16 years, to imprisonment for life and to a minimum punishment of imprisonment for a term of five years; and

(*b*) in any other case, to imprisonment for a term not exceeding fourteen years.

(3) In determining, for the purpose of paragraph (2)(*a*), whether a convicted person has committed a second or subsequent offence, if the person was earlier convicted of any of the following offences, that offence is to be considered as an earlier offence:

(*a*) an offence under this section;

(*b*) an offence under subsection 85(1) or (2) or section 244 or 244.2; or

(*c*) an offence under section 220, 236, 239 or 273, subsection 279(1) or section 279.1, 344 or 346 if a firearm was used in the commission of the offence.

However, an earlier offence shall not be taken into account if 10 years have elapsed between the day on which the person was convicted of the earlier offence and the day on which the person was convicted of the offence for which sentence is being imposed, not taking into account any time in custody.

(4) For the purposes of subsection (3), the only question to be considered is the sequence of convictions and no consideration shall be given to the sequence of commission of offences or whether any offence occurred before or after any conviction. 1980-81-82-83, c. 125, s. 19; 1995, c. 39, s. 145; 2008, c. 6, s. 28; 2009, c. 22, s. 10; 2012, c. 1, s. 26; 2015, c. 23, s. 15.

CROSS-REFERENCES

"Criminal organization" is defined in ss. 2 and 476.1. Pursuant to s. 2.1, "restricted firearm" and "prohibited firearm" are defined in s. 84. A person found guilty of the offence in this section will be liable to the mandatory prohibition order in s. 109 for possession of certain weapons, ammunition and explosives. For other cross-references, see CROSS-REFERENCES under s. 271.

SYNOPSIS

This section provides that any person who, in committing a sexual assault, carries, uses or threatens to use a weapon or imitation, who threatens to cause bodily harm to a person other than the complainant, who causes bodily harm to the complainant, or who is party to the offence, is guilty of an indictable offence. The maximum punishment for the offence is life imprisonment if the complainant is under the age of 16 years, or 14 years' imprisonment if the complainant is 16 or older. Where a restricted or prohibited firearm is used or the offence was committed for the benefit of, at the direction of, or in association with, a criminal organization, the offender is liable to a minimum punishment of at least five years' imprisonment for a first offence and seven years for a second or subsequent offence. The rules for determining whether the offender has committed a second or subsequent offence are set out in subsecs. (3) and (4) and, for example, provide that a prior offence includes not only convictions under this section, but other specified offences involving use of a firearm. However, an earlier offence is not to be taken into account if 10 years have elapsed from the conviction of the earlier offence, not counting time in custody. Subsection (4) reverses the common law rule and provides that the court only takes into account the sequence of convictions, not the order in which the offences were committed. In any other case where a firearm is used, the offender is liable to a minimum term of imprisonment of four years. Where no firearm is used, there is no minimum punishment, unless the complainant is under the age of 14 years, in which case the offender is liable to a minimum punishment of five years.

ANNOTATIONS

If an object is used in inflicting injury, be it physical or psychological, in the commission of a sexual assault, it is not necessary that the injury amount to bodily harm to trigger the application of para. (1)(*a*): *R. v. Lamy* (1993), 80 C.C.C. (3d) 558 (Man. C.A.).

The offence under [now] para. (*a*) does not require proof that the accused was actually in possession of a weapon. The offence is complete if the complainant believes, on reasonable grounds, that the accused had the present ability to affect his purpose: *R. v. Worobec* (1991), 63 C.C.C. (3d) 412 (B.C.C.A.).

The offence described by para. (*c*) is a general intent offence for which drunkenness due to voluntary consumption of alcohol is no defence: *R. v. Bernard* (1985), 18 C.C.C. (3d) 574 (Ont. C.A.). [Also see s. 33.1.]

Bodily harm as used in para. (*c*) can include psychological harm: *R. v. Mathieu* (1996), 111 C.C.C. (3d) 291 (Alta. C.A.), leave to appeal to S.C.C. refused 114 C.C.C. (3d) vi.

An object constitutes a "weapon" where it contributed to the harm caused to the victim. The object does not have to be designed or intended to injure in order to qualify as a weapon. Injury is not synonymous with "bodily harm" and includes any object used in inflicting psychological or physical injury: *R. v. Lamy*, [2002] 1 S.C.R. 860, 162 C.C.C. (3d) 353.

Consent is not vitiated in all circumstances of sexual assault causing bodily harm, but only where bodily harm was intended and in fact caused. Where the accused did not intend to cause bodily harm, consent is available as a defence if bodily harm is inadvertently caused: *R. v. Zhao* (2013), 297 C.C.C. (3d) 533 (Ont. C.A.).

AGGRAVATED SEXUAL ASSAULT / Punishment / Subsequent offences / Sequence of convictions only.

273. (1) Every one commits an aggravated sexual assault who, in committing a sexual assault, wounds, maims, disfigures or endangers the life of the complainant.

(2) Every person who commits an aggravated sexual assault is guilty of an indictable offence and liable

(*a*) if a restricted firearm or prohibited firearm is used in the commission of the offence or if any firearm is used in the commission of the offence and the offence is committed for the benefit of, at the direction of, or in association with, a criminal organization, to imprisonment for life and to a minimum punishment of imprisonment for a term of

(i) in the case of a first offence, five years, and

(ii) in the case of a second or subsequent offence, seven years;

(*a*.1) in any other case where a firearm is used in the commission of the offence, to imprisonment for life and to a minimum punishment of imprisonment for a term of four years;

(*a*.2) if the complainant is under the age of 16 years, to imprisonment for life and to a minimum punishment of imprisonment for a term of five years; and

(*b*) in any other case, to imprisonment for life.

(3) In determining, for the purpose of paragraph (2)(*a*), whether a convicted person has committed a second or subsequent offence, if the person was earlier convicted of any of the following offences, that offence is to be considered as an earlier offence:

(*a*) an offence under this section;

(*b*) an offence under subsection 85(1) or (2) or section 244 or 244.2; or

(*c*) an offence under section 220, 236, 239 or 272, subsection 279(1) or section 279.1, 344 or 346 if a firearm was used in the commission of the offence.

However, an earlier offence shall not be taken into account if 10 years have elapsed between the day on which the person was convicted of the earlier offence and the day on which the person was convicted of the offence for which sentence is being imposed, not taking into account any time in custody.

(4) For the purposes of subsection (3), the only question to be considered is the sequence of convictions and no consideration shall be given to the sequence of commission of offences or whether any offence occurred before or after any conviction. 1980-81-82-83, c. 125, s. 19; 1995, c. 39, s. 146; 2008, c. 6, s. 29; 2009, c. 22, s. 11; 2012, c. 1, s. 27.

CROSS-REFERENCES

"Criminal organization" is defined in ss. 2 and 476.1. Pursuant to s. 2.1, "restricted firearm" and "prohibited firearm" are defined in s. 84. A person found guilty of the offence in this section will be liable to the mandatory prohibition order in s. 109 for possession of certain weapons, ammunition and explosives. For other cross-references, see CROSS-REFERENCES under s. 271.

SYNOPSIS

If a person wounds, maims, disfigures or endangers the life of a complainant during the commission of a sexual assault, that person is guilty of the indictable offence of aggravated sexual assault and liable to imprisonment for life. The section also enacts minimum punishments. Where a restricted or prohibited firearm is used or the offence was committed for the benefit of, at the direction of, or in association with, a criminal organization, the offender is liable to a minimum punishment of at least five years' imprisonment for a first offence and seven years for a second or subsequent offence. The rules for determining whether the offender has committed a second or subsequent offence are set out in subsecs. (3) and (4) and, for example, provide that a prior offence includes not only convictions under this section but other specified offences involving firearms. However, an earlier offence is not to be taken into account if 10 years have elapsed from the conviction of the earlier offence, not counting time in custody. Subsection (4) reverses the common law rule and provides that the court only takes into account the sequence of convictions, not the order in which the offences were committed. In any other case where a firearm is used, the offender is liable to a minimum term of imprisonment of four years. Where no firearm is used, there is no minimum punishment, unless the victim was under the age 16 years, in which case the minimum punishment is five years.

MEANING OF "CONSENT" / Consent / Question of law / No consent obtained / Subsection (2) not limiting.

273.1 (1) Subject to subsection (2) and subsection 265(3), "consent" means, for the purposes of sections 271, 272 and 273, the voluntary agreement of the complainant to engage in the sexual activity in question.

(1.1) Consent must be present at the time the sexual activity in question takes place.

(1.2) The question of whether no consent is obtained under subsection 265(3) or subsection (2) or (3) is a question of law.

(2) For the purpose of subsection (1), no consent is obtained if

- **(*a*) the agreement is expressed by the words or conduct of a person other than the complainant;**
- **(*a*.1) the complainant is unconscious;**
- **(*b*) the complainant is incapable of consenting to the activity for any reason other than the one referred to in paragraph (*a*.1);**
- **(*c*) the accused induces the complainant to engage in the activity by abusing a position of trust, power or authority;**
- **(*d*) the complainant expresses, by words or conduct, a lack of agreement to engage in the activity; or**
- **(*e*) the complainant, having consented to engage in sexual activity, expresses, by words or conduct, a lack of agreement to continue to engage in the activity.**

(3) Nothing in subsection (2) shall be construed as limiting the circumstance in which no consent is obtained. 1992, c. 38, s. 1; 2018, c. 29, s. 19(1)-(2.1).

CROSS-REFERENCES

The term "complainant" is defined in s. 2. Section 265(3) sets out additional circumstances in which no valid consent is given as where, for example, the consent is obtained by fraud or the exercise of authority. As to mistaken belief in consent as a defence, see s. 265(4) which sets out the minimum evidentiary requirement and the mandatory jury direction. Section 273.2 sets out circumstances where belief in consent is no defence.

SYNOPSIS

This section supplements the definition of consent in s. 265 which defines assault for all of the assault offences including sexual assault. The definition in this section applies only to the sexual assault offences. Subsection (1) provides a general definition which focuses on the voluntary agreement by the complainant. Subsection (2) then sets out a number of circumstances where the apparent agreement by the complainant cannot amount to consent. Subsection (2) makes a number of points: agreement cannot be based on the words or conduct of someone other than the complainant and there is no agreement where the complainant is incapable of giving consent [although incapacity is not defined], agreement is the result of abuse of a position of trust, power or authority, the complainant expresses lack of consent or the complainant, having initially consented, expresses a change of mind. This subsection is in addition to the circumstances set out in s. 265(3) where there is no consent to an assault generally.

ANNOTATIONS

There is no defence of implied consent to sexual assault. The absence of consent is subjective and must be determined by reference to the complainant's subjective internal state of mind towards the touching at the time it occurred. The complainant's statement that she did not consent is a matter of credibility to be weighed in light of all of the evidence including any ambiguous conduct. If the trier of fact accepts the complainant's testimony that she did not consent, no matter how strongly conduct may contradict her claim, the absence of consent is established. The trier of fact need only consider s. 265(3) if the complainant has chosen to participate in sexual activity or her ambiguous conduct or submission has given rise to doubt regarding the absence of consent. There is no consent where the complainant consents because she honestly believes that she will otherwise suffer physical violence. While the plausibility of the alleged fear and any overt expressions of it are relevant in assessing the complainant's credibility that she consented out of fear, the approach is subjective: *R. v. Ewanchuk*, [1999] 1 S.C.R. 330, 131 C.C.C. (3d) 481.

Capacity is a factual issue to be decided by the jury and there is no mandatory requirement for expert testimony in assessing a special needs complainant's capacity to consent: *R. v. A. (A.)* (2001), 155 C.C.C. (3d) 279 (Ont. C.A.).

Subsection (2)(*d*) is not void for vagueness so as to constitute a breach of s. 7 of the *Canadian Charter of Rights and Freedoms*: *R. v. Darrach* (1998), 122 C.C.C. (3d) 225 (Ont. C.A.), leave to appeal to S.C.C. granted 124 C.C.C. (3d) vi.

A person cannot consent in advance to sexual activity expected to occur while unconscious. The definition of consent requires ongoing, conscious consent throughout the sexual activity in question: *R. v. A. (J.)*, [2011] 2 S.C.R. 440, 271 C.C.C. (3d) 1 (5:4).

The 15-year-old complainant could not be said to have given a valid consent where she consented under the influence of a drug given to her by the accused. The complainant was at first unaware that the drug had been put in her drink and testified that thereafter she felt "out of control": *R. v. Daigle* (1998), 127 C.C.C. (3d) 130 (Que. C.A.), affd [1998] 1 S.C.R. 1220*n*, 127 C.C.C. (3d) 129. [Note: This case was decided before the age of consent was raised to 16 years; see s. 150.1.] Also see *R. v. Bernier* (1997), 119 C.C.C. (3d) 467 (Que. C.A.), affd [1998] 1 S.C.R. 975, 124 C.C.C. (3d) 383, a case involving acts, committed prior to this section coming into force, by a nurse's aid against patients who were mentally handicapped persons.

Where the complainant denied having freely consented to the sexual activity and the accused admitted to extorting her to have sex by threatening to expose her nude photos, the complainant cannot be said to have freely consented within the meaning of subsec. (1): *R. v. Stender* (2004), 188 C.C.C. (3d) 514 (Ont. C.A.), affd [2005] 1 S.C.R. 914, 201 C.C.C. (3d) 319.

Inducing consent by abusing the relationships set out in subsec. (2)(*c*) does not imply the same degree of coercion contemplated by s. 265(3)(*d*), which speaks to consent obtained where the complainant submits or does not resist by reason of the "exercise of authority". It includes circumstances in which a person in a position of trust over another uses the personal feelings and confidence engendered by that relationship to secure an apparent consent to sexual activity: *R. v. Snelgrove*, 2019 SCC 16; *R. v. Lutoslawski* (2010), 258 C.C.C. (3d) 1 (Ont. C.A.), affd [2010] 3 S.C.R. 60, 262 C.C.C. (3d) 1.

A drug dealer may be in a position of power pursuant to subsec. (2)(*c*) in relation to an addicted client if the supplying of drugs created a relationship of dependency that could be exploited by the accused: *R. v. Hogg* (2000), 148 C.C.C. (3d) 86 (Ont. C.A.), revd (unreported, May 1, 2002, Court File No. C38095, Ont. C.A.).

The misrepresentation of an undercover police officer's occupation did not constitute fraud so as to vitiate the accused's consent in circumstances in which the accused invited the police officer to touch him to prove that he was not a police officer: *R. v. P. (N.M.)* (2000), 146 C.C.C. (3d) 167 (N.S.C.A.), motion for leave to intervene adjourned 149 C.C.C. (3d) 446 (S.C.C.), leave to appeal to S.C.C. refused 193 D.L.R. (4th) vi.

Voluntary agreement to the "sexual activity in question" in subsec. (1) means that the complainant must subjectively agree to the specific physical act itself, its sexual nature and the specific identity of the partner. The "sexual activity in question" does not include conditions or qualities of the physical act, such as birth control measures or the presence of sexually transmitted diseases. Here, the "sexual activity in question" was sexual intercourse and the complainant voluntarily agreed to it, notwithstanding the fact that her partner had furtively poked holes in the condom. However, where the complainant has chosen not to become pregnant, deceptions that expose her to an increased risk of becoming pregnant may constitute a sufficiently serious deprivation to vitiate consent via fraud under s. 265(3)(*c*): *R. v. Hutchinson*, [2014] 1 S.C.R. 346, 308 C.C.C. (3d) 413.

WHERE BELIEF IN CONSENT NOT A DEFENCE.

273.2 It is not a defence to a charge under section 271, 272 or 273 that the accused believed that the complainant consented to the activity that forms the subject-matter of the charge, where

(*a*) the accused's belief arose from

(i) the accused's self-induced intoxication,

(ii) the accused's recklessness or wilful blindness, or

(iii) any circumstance referred to in subsection 265(3) or 273.1(2) or (3) in which no consent is obtained;

(*b*) the accused did not take reasonable steps, in the circumstances known to the accused at the time, to ascertain that the complainant was consenting.

(*c*) there is no evidence that the complainant's voluntary agreement to the activity was affirmatively expressed by words or actively expressed by conduct. 1992, c. 38, s. 1; 2018, c. 29, s. 20.

CROSS-REFERENCES

The term "complainant" is defined in s. 2. Sections 265 and 273.1 set out circumstances in which no valid consent in fact is given. As to mistaken belief in consent as a defence see s. 265(4) which sets out the minimum evidentiary requirement and the mandatory jury direction. Also see s. 150.1 re mistake as to age.

SYNOPSIS

This section attempts to clarify the circumstances in which the common law defence of mistaken belief in consent is a defence to a charge of sexual assault. Paragraph (*a*)(i) is consistent with the common law rule that self-induced intoxication is no defence to sexual assault and para. (*a*)(ii) reflects the decision of the Supreme Court of Canada in *R. v. Sansregret*, *infra*. Paragraph (*b*) is something of a departure from the common law in that it introduces a partly objective standard in determining whether the accused's belief was honestly held. Note, however, that it is reasonable steps in the circumstances known to the accused. In this respect, the defence is not unlike other sections of the Code, such as self-defence under s. 34, which impose an objective and subjective standard.

ANNOTATIONS

The defence of honest but mistaken belief does not impose any burden of proof on the accused and may arise on any evidence including the Crown's case-in-chief. Honest but mistaken belief can be raised if it is established that the accused believed that the complainant affirmatively communicated consent through her words or actions. A belief that silence, passivity or ambiguous conduct constitutes consent provides no defence. An accused also cannot rely upon his purported belief that the complainant's expressed lack of agreement to sexual touching constituted an invitation to more persistent or aggressive contact. Once the complainant has expressed an unwillingness to engage in sexual contact, the accused must make certain that she has truly changed her mind before proceeding with any further intimacies. The accused cannot rely on the mere lapse of time, the complainant's silence or equivocal conduct to indicate that there has been a change of heart and that the consent now exists nor can he engage in further sexual touching to "test the waters". In this case, the complainant had clearly said no to any further contact. There was no evidence of anything that occurred between the communication of non-consent and the subsequent sexual touching which would lead the accused to honestly have believed that there was consent: *R. v. Ewanchuk*, [1999] 1 S.C.R. 330, 131 C.C.C. (3d) 481.

In *R. v. Cinous*, [2002] 2 S.C.R. 3, 162 C.C.C. (3d) 129, the court considered at length the test for when there is an air of reality requiring that a defence be left to the jury. While the court did not consider this section or s. 265(4), since the issue arose in the context of self-defence to a murder charge, the comments may be of assistance. While a trial judge has a duty to put to the jury any defence for which there is an air of reality, the judge also has a duty not to put defences for which there is no air of reality. A defence possesses an air of reality if a properly instructed jury acting reasonably could acquit the accused on the basis of the defence. In applying the air of reality test, a trial judge considers the totality of the evidence, and assumes the evidence relied upon by the accused to be true. The evidential foundation can be indicated by evidence emanating from the examination-in-chief or cross-examination of the accused, of defence witnesses, or of Crown witnesses. It can also rest upon the factual circumstances of the case or from any other evidential source on the record. There is no requirement that the evidence be adduced by the accused or that the accused's evidence be corroborated by other evidence. The trial judge does not make determinations about the credibility of witnesses, weigh the evidence, make findings of fact, or draw determinate factual inferences. Nor is the air of reality test intended to assess whether the defence is likely, unlikely, somewhat likely, or very likely to succeed at the end of the day. The question for the trial judge is whether the evidence discloses a real issue to be decided by the jury, and not how the jury should ultimately decide the issue. A single air of reality test applies to all defences. The question remains whether there is (1) evidence (2) upon which a properly instructed jury acting reasonably could acquit if it believed the evidence to be true. The second part of this question can be rendered by asking whether the evidence put forth is reasonably capable of supporting the inferences required to acquit the accused. This is the current state of the law, uniformly applicable to all defences. There is no special test for sexual offences.

The air of reality test applies to affirmative defences such as self-defence, but it is never the function of the trial judge in a jury trial to assess the evidence and make a determination that the Crown has proven one or more of the essential elements of the offence and direct the jury accordingly. It does not matter how obvious the judge may believe the answer to be or that the judge may be of the view that any other conclusion would be perverse. The trial judge may give an opinion on the matter but never a direction: *R. v. Gunning*, [2005] 1 S.C.R. 627, 196 C.C.C. (3d) 123.

While this section does not require in all cases that the accused first determine "unequivocally" that the complainant was consenting, there may be circumstances where nothing short of an unequivocal indication of consent from the complainant, at the time of the alleged offence, will suffice to meet the threshold test. In general, para. (*b*) creates a proportionate relationship between what will be required in the way of reasonable steps by the accused and the circumstances known to the accused at the time: *R. v. G. (R.)* (1994), 38 C.R. (4th) 123, 87 W.A.C. 254 (B.C.C.A.).

Assuming that sexual assault is an offence requiring proof of subjective *mens rea* to meet minimum constitutional standards, this section meets that requirement. The accused is not under an obligation to determine all relevant circumstances — the issue is what the accused actually knew, not what he or she ought to have known. Further, the accused is not required to have taken all reasonable steps. Finally, while this section and s. 265(4) may have the effect of placing a tactical or evidential burden on an accused to adduce some evidence capable of raising a reasonable doubt, this does not infringe the accused's right not to be compelled to be a witness. Accordingly, this section does not infringe ss. 7 and 11(*c*) of the *Canadian Charter of Rights and Freedoms*: *R. v. Darrach* (1998), 122 C.C.C. (3d) 225 (Ont. C.A.), affd on other grounds [2000] 2 S.C.R. 443, 148 C.C.C. (3d) 97.

Where the defences of consent and honest but mistaken belief in consent are raised, it must be determined whether it is proven beyond a reasonable doubt that sexual activity took place which, if there was no consent, constituted a sexual assault, whether it occurred without the consent of the victim and, if it occurred without the victim's consent, whether the defendant did not have an honest but mistaken belief in consent. It is only when the trial judge has reached the third step that this section is considered: *R. v. Butler* (1998), 13 C.R. (5th) 372 (Ont. C.A.).

This provision applies to offences of sexual assault only and did not apply to a charge of forcible confinement: *R. v. Niedermier* (2005), 193 C.C.C. (3d) 199 (B.C.C.A.), leave to appeal to S.C.C. refused 196 C.C.C. (3d) vi.

This provision applies to all sexual assaults, regardless of the age of the complainant. Accordingly, where a defence of mistake of fact as to the age of the complainant is raised, the court must consider if recklessness, willful blindness, or self-induced intoxication affected the honesty of the accused's belief: *R. v. Nguyen* (2017), 348 C.C.C. (3d) 238 (Sask. C.A.).

The following case arose prior to the enactment of this section.

The fact that the stories of the accused and the complainant are diametrically opposed is but one factor in determining whether or not there is an air of reality to the defence. If it is not realistically possible for a properly instructed jury, acting judiciously, to splice together some of each person's evidence with respect to the encounter, and settle upon a reasonably coherent set of facts, supported by the evidence, that is capable of sustaining a defence of mistaken belief in consent then the issue really is purely one of credibility, of consent or no consent, and the defence of mistaken belief in consent should not be put to the jury. When the complainant and the accused give similar versions of the facts, and the only material contradiction is in their interpretation of what happened, the defence of honest but mistaken belief in consent should generally be put to the jury, except in cases where the accused's conduct demonstrates recklessness or wilful blindness to the absence of consent. There is no requirement that the accused explicitly testify that he mistakenly believed that the complainant was consenting. Consent is a mental state experienced only by the complainant and thus an assertion by the accused that the complainant consented must mean that he in fact believed that she was consenting. The real question will be whether that belief was on honest one: *R. v. Park*, [1995] 2 S.C.R. 836, 99 C.C.C. (3d) 1. Also see: *R. v. Livermore*, [1995] 4 S.C.R. 123, 102 C.C.C. (3d) 212; *R. v. Esau*, [1997] 2 S.C.R. 777, 116 C.C.C. (3d) 289.

REMOVAL OF CHILD FROM CANADA / Punishment.

273.3 (1) No person shall do anything for the purpose of removing from Canada a person who is ordinarily resident in Canada and who is

- **(*a*) under the age of 16 years, with the intention that an act be committed outside Canada that if it were committed in Canada would be an offence against section 151 or 152 or subsection 160(3) or 173(2) in respect of that person;**
- **(*b*) 16 years of age or more but under the age of eighteen years, with the intention that an act be committed outside Canada that if it were committed in Canada would be an offence against section 153 in respect of that person; or**
- **(*c*) under the age of eighteen years, with the intention that an act be committed outside Canada that if it were committed in Canada would be an offence against section 155 or 159, subsection 160(2) or section 170, 171, 267, 268, 269, 271, 272 or 273 in respect of that person; or**
- **(*d*) under the age of 18 years, with the intention that an act be committed outside Canada that, if it were committed in Canada, would be an offence against section 293.1 in respect of that person or under the age of 16 years, with the intention that an act be committed outside Canada that, if it were committed in Canada, would be an offence against section 293.2 in respect of that person.**

(2) Every person who contravenes this section is guilty of

- **(*a*) an indictable offence and is liable to imprisonment for a term not exceeding five years; or**
- **(*b*) an offence punishable on summary conviction. 1993, c. 45, s. 3; 1997, c. 18, s. 13; 2008, c. 6, s. 54(*i*); 2015, c. 29, s. 8.**

SYNOPSIS

This section makes it an offence to do anything for the purpose of removing certain classes of persons from Canada who are ordinarily resident in Canada. It must be shown that the person to be removed from Canada is under a specified age and that the accused's intention was that an act be committed which would constitute one of the specified sexual offences if committed in Canada.

ANNOTATIONS

This section rebuts the general presumption against the extraterritorial application of criminal law. While the accused need not be present in Canada while committing the relevant act, the victim must be present in Canada in order to be removed from it: *R. v. Oler* (2018), 364 C.C.C. (3d) 380 (B.C.C.A.).

CORROBORATION NOT REQUIRED.

274. If an accused is charged with an offence under section 151, 152, 153, 153.1, 155, 159, 160, 170, 171, 172, 173, 271, 272, 273, 286.1, 286.2 or 286.3, no corroboration is required for a conviction and the judge shall not instruct the jury that it is unsafe to find the accused guilty in the absence of corroboration. 1980-81-82-83, c. 125, s. 19; R.S.C. 1985, c. 19 (3rd Supp.), s. 11; 2002, c. 13, s. 12; 2014, c. 25, s. 16.

CROSS-REFERENCES

As to other evidentiary and procedural provisions respecting the offences listed in this section, see the cross-references in relation to those provisions and the notes under s. 150.1.

SYNOPSIS

This section states that in the trial of an offence under ss. 151, 152, 153, 155, 159,160, 170, 171, 172, 173, 271, 272, 273, 286.1, 286.2 or 286.3, *corroboration* is not required for a conviction and the judge shall not instruct the jury that it is unsafe to find the accused guilty in the absence of corroboration. The section is designed to ensure that, with the repeal of the statutory corroboration requirement, the courts do not revert to the common law position requiring corroboration of a sexual complainant's evidence. [See *R. v. Camp* (1977), 36 C.C.C. (2d) 511 (Ont. C.A.).] Also see s. 659 abrogating any mandatory rule as to the danger of acting on the evidence of children.

ANNOTATIONS

Notwithstanding this section, the trial judge still has a discretion when reviewing the facts with a jury to discuss with them the weight they might see fit to attach to the unsupported evidence of the complainant: *R. v. Saulnier* (1989), 48 C.C.C. (3d) 301 (N.S.C.A.).

There is no common law rule of practice which requires a judge to charge the jury as to the danger of acting on the uncorroborated evidence of the complainant on a charge of gross indecency under former s. 157 of the *Criminal Code*, R.S.C. 1970, c. C-34. The trial judge does, however, have a discretion to give the jury an instruction with respect to the weight of the unsupported testimony of the complainant: *R. v. Stymiest* (1993), 79 C.C.C. (3d) 408 (B.C.C.A.).

No corroboration is required in respect of the offence of incest (s. 155) for a charge laid in 2002, although the offence allegedly occurred in 1982, at a time when corroboration was required: *R. v. D. (A.)* (2005), 193 C.C.C. (3d) 314 (Sask. C.A.).

RULES RESPECTING RECENT COMPLAINT ABROGATED.

275. The rules relating to evidence of recent complaint are hereby abrogated with respect to offences under sections 151, 152, 153, 153.1, 155 and 159, subsections 160(2)

and (3) and sections 170, 171, 172, 173, 271, 272 and 273. 1980-81-82-83, c. 125, s. 19; R.S.C. 1985, c. 19 (3rd Supp.), s. 11; 2002, c. 13, s. 12.

CROSS-REFERENCES

The "recent complaint" rule abrogated by this section was the rule, developed at common law, which permitted the prosecution to elicit from the complainant or other person a complaint of a sexual assault made at the first reasonable opportunity. The complaint was admitted, not for its truth, but, to show consistency and rebut the adverse inference, which the trier of fact would otherwise be invited to draw, that the victim's allegation was untrue. The rule was an exception to the rule at common law, that a witness's testimony in chief may not be buttressed by the party calling the witness by proving that she has made a prior consistent statement. The recent complaint rule was often criticized because of the anachronistic assumptions underlying it (see *R. v. Timm*, [1981] 2 S.C.R. 315, 59 C.C.C. (2d) 396) and was finally abolished by this provision. However, a form of this rule has now been revived in the case of youthful complainants by the provisions of s. 715.1 which permits the admission of a videotape of a complaint in some circumstances.

As to other evidentiary and procedural provisions respecting the offences listed in this section, see the cross-references in relation to those provisions and the notes under s. 150.1.

ANNOTATIONS

The effect of this section is that the Crown during its case in chief may not adduce evidence of recent complaints. However, since there was never a prohibition against the accused attempting to exploit the lack of a recent complaint, and since only the right of the Crown to lead the evidence in chief has been negated by this section, the defence can elect to cross-examine on this issue. In addition, prior consistent statements may be admissible as part of the Crown's case in chief if they fall within one of the other existing exceptions to the rule against prior consistent statements such as to rebut an allegation of recent fabrication, as part of the *res gestae*, or as narrative. If the Crown is relying upon recent fabrication as the basis for admissibility of prior consistent statements, it must wait until the defence has clearly opened the door by making an opening statement, or through cross-examination of the complainant or other Crown witnesses or by the allegtion of fabrication becoming implicit from the defence conduct of the case. The *res gestae* exception is limited to cases where the words spoken are so interrelated to the fact in issue that they become part of the fact itself. The statements by children who have allegedly been sexually assaulted may properly be admitted as part of the narrative in the sense that the statement advances the story from offence to prosecution or explains why so little was done to terminate the abuse or bring the perpetrator to justice. It is part of the narrative of a complainant's testimony when she recounts the assaults, how they came to be terminated, and how the matter came to the attention of the police. This part of the narrative provides chronological cohesion and eliminates gaps which would divert the mind of the listener from the central issue. It may be supportive of the central allegation in the sense of creating a logical framework for its presentation but it cannot be used and the jury must be warned of this as confirmation of the truthfulness of the sworn allegations: *R. v. F. (J.E.)* (1993), 85 C.C.C. (3d) 457 (Ont. C.A.).

In determining whether there has been an allegation of recent fabrication so as to permit evidence of a complaint to be given as an exception to this provision, it is not sufficient to merely look at defence counsel's statements expressly disclaiming any such allegation. If having regard to the manner in which the complainant has been cross-examined, with defence counsel having elicited some but not all of the complainant's statements after the offence, so that the jury would wrongly infer that the complainant made no complaint on an earlier occasion, then the Crown must be permitted to correct the erroneous impression by re-examination and the adducing of other evidence. The accused cannot have an automatic unlimited power to choose among the complainant's various statements: *R. v. N. (L.)* (1989), 52 C.C.C. (3d) 1 (N.W.T.C.A.).

This section does not prevent evidence being given as to the fact of a complaint where such evidence is a necessary part of the narrative to understand an admission made by the accused when confronted with the complaint: *R. v. George* (1985), 23 C.C.C. (3d) 42 (B.C.C.A.).

If the full purpose underlying Parliament's abrogation of this rule is to be achieved, evidence of when a complaint was first made, why it was not made at the first available opportunity if that was the case, and what it was that precipitated the complaint eventually made, must be receivable as part of the narrative, in order to ensure that the jury has all of the evidence of the complainant's conduct necessary to enable the jury to draw the right inference with respect to her credibility. The prior complaint, admissible under the narrative exception to the rule against prior consistent statements, is not, however, admissible to gauge the consistency and thus the credibility of the complainant's evidence at trial. Accordingly, unless it is necessary to provide the context for some other circumstance relevant to the jury's consideration, the actual content of the prior complaint has no relevance and is inadmissible: *R. v. Ay* (1994), 93 C.C.C. (3d) 456 (B.C.C.A.).

For other cases approving the narrative exception see *R. v. Foster* (1995), 128 Sask. R. 292, 85 W.A.C. 292 (C.A.), leave to appeal to S.C.C. refused 152 Sask. R. 316*n* and *R. v. B. (O.)* (1995), 103 C.C.C. (3d) 531 (N.S.C.A.).

Where the Crown adduces prior complaint evidence that is part of the narrative, the trial judge will be required to provide a limiting instruction to the jury to the effect that such evidence is to be used only to assess the complainant's credibility and not for the truth of its contents. The defence should also be able to explore the issue of the timing of a complaint because it relates to the issue of the complainant's credibility. The trier of fact may, but need not, draw an adverse inference against the complainant's credibility by the reason of the lack of recent complaint: *R. v. Henrich* (1996), 108 C.C.C. (3d) 97 (Ont. C.A.).

In *R. v. D. (D.)*, [2000] 2 S.C.R. 275, 148 C.C.C. (3d) 41, the Supreme Court of Canada held that expert evidence regarding delayed disclosure was inadmissible as the expert's evidence was simply a statement of the law that the failure to make a timely complaint must not be the subject of a presumptive adverse inference against the complainant. Where there is an issue of delayed disclosure, the trial judge should instruct the jury that there is no inviolable rule relating to how people who are the victims of trauma like a sexual assault will behave. Some will make an immediate complaint, some will delay disclosure and some will not ever disclose the abuse. The reasons for delay are many and may include embarrassment, fear, guilt or a lack of understanding and knowledge. In assessing credibility, the timing of the complaint is simply one circumstance to consider the context of the case. Delayed disclosure, standing alone, will never give rise to an adverse inference against the credibility of the complainant.

Where evidence of failure to complain is adduced, the jury should be warned against the stereotype that a wronged woman will always complain. The jury must decide whether the complainant's conduct after the incident is consistent with her story by considering the complainant's state of mind at the time, the age and level of maturity of the complainant, the complainant's sense of confidence and composure and the relationship between the accused and the complainant: *R. v. M. (T.E.)* (1996), 110 C.C.C. (3d) 179 (Alta. C.A.), leave to appeal to S.C.C. refused 114 C.C.C. (3d) vi.

The child victims' complaints to their parents were admissible where the defence contended that the children's sworn testimony was inconsistent in vital respects with their prior statements and was the result of their parents' coaching or the product of suggestions made to them by their parents, and was not based on the children's antecedent memory of the event. The prior complaints became admissible under the common law exception to admission of prior consistent statements: *R. v. Owens* (1986), 33 C.C.C. (3d) 275 (Ont. C.A.).

In *R. v. B. (D.C.)* (1994), 91 C.C.C. (3d) 357 (Man. C.A.), the court held that the judge-made rule against prior consistent statements should no longer apply to the evidence of a child's complaint of sexual abuse.

EVIDENCE OF COMPLAINANT'S SEXUAL ACTIVITY / Conditions for admissibility / Factors that judge must consider / Interpretation.

276. (1) In proceedings in respect of an offence under section 151, 152, 153, 153.1, 155 or 159, subsection 160(2) or (3) or section 170, 171, 172, 173, 271, 272 or 273, evidence that the complainant has engaged in sexual activity, whether with the accused or with any other person, is not admissible to support an inference that, by reason of the sexual nature of that activity, the complainant

(*a*) is more likely to have consented to the sexual activity that forms the subject-matter of the charge; or

(*b*) is less worthy of belief.

(2) In proceedings in respect of an offence referred to in subsection (1), evidence shall not be adduced by or on behalf of the accused that the complainant has engaged in sexual activity other than the sexual activity that forms the subject-matter of the charge, whether with the accused or with any other person, unless the judge, provincial court judge or justice determines, in accordance with the procedures set out in sections 278.93 and 278.94, that the evidence

(*a*) is not being adduced for the purpose of supporting an inference described in subsection (1);

(*b*) is relevant to an issue at trial; and

(*c*) is of specific instances of sexual activity; and

(*d*) has significant probative value that is not substantially outweighed by the danger of prejudice to the proper administration of justice.

(3) In determining whether evidence is admissible under subsection (2), the judge, provincial court judge or justice shall take into account

(*a*) the interests of justice, including the right of the accused to make a full answer and defence;

(*b*) society's interest in encouraging the reporting of sexual assault offences;

(*c*) whether there is a reasonable prospect that the evidence will assist in arriving at a just determination in the case;

(*d*) the need to remove from the fact-finding process any discriminatory belief or bias;

(*e*) the risk that the evidence may unduly arouse sentiments of prejudice, sympathy or hostility in the jury;

(*f*) the potential prejudice to the complainant's personal dignity and right of privacy;

(*g*) the right of the complainant and of every individual to personal security and to the full protection and benefit of the law; and

(*h*) any other factor that the judge, provincial court judge or justice considers relevant.

(4) For the purpose of this section, "sexual activity" includes any communication made for a sexual purpose or whose content is of a sexual nature. 1980-81-82-83, c. 125, s. 19; R.S.C. 1985, c. 19 (3rd Supp.), s. 12; c. 27 (1st Supp.), s. 203; 1992, c. 38, s. 2; 2002, c. 13, s. 13; 2018, c. 29, s. 21.

CROSS-REFERENCES

The terms "complainant", "justice" and "provincal court judge" are defined in s. 2.

As to other evidentiary and procedural provisions respecting the offences listed in this section, see the cross-references in relation to those provisions and the notes under s. 150.1 However, note in particular the companion provision in s. 277 respecting evidence of sexual reputation.

As to the procedure for determining the admissibility of sexual conduct evidence, see ss. 276.1 and 276.2. Section 276.3 limits the publications of the proceedings. Section 276.4 requires the judge to instruct the jury as to the proper use of sexual conduct evidence and s. 276.5 makes the determination of admissibility a question of law, thus giving the Attorney General a right of appeal.

SYNOPSIS

This section was enacted following the decision of the Supreme Court of Canada in *R. v. Seaboyer*, *infra*. Unlike the predecessor provision which was found to violate s. 7 of the Charter, this section does not attempt to delineate all the circumstances in which sexual conduct activity would be admissible. Rather, subsec. (1) sets out the *purpose* for which the evidence is not admissible, *i.e.*, the evidence is not admissible for the now discredited purposes of merely showing the complainant is more likely to have consented or is less worthly of belief. In this sense, the section is structured in a way similar to s. 277 which was found in the same case to be constitutional. Subsection (2) codifies the test enunciated in *Seaboyer* that defence evidence which is probative of an issue in the case can only be excluded if the prejudicial effect of that evidence substantially outweighs the probative value. The requirement that the evidence relate to specific instances of sexual activity excludes the use of more general character evidence. It is unclear as to the extent that this section could apply to expert psychiatric or psychological evidence of disposition. Subsection (3) attempts to identify a non-exhaustive list of factors to assist the judge in determining the prejudicial effect of the evidence as weighed against its probative value. Of the various factors, perhaps those in paras. (*c*) to (*e*) will prove to be most significant as they relate directly to the probative value and prejudicial effect of evidence as traditionally understood, *i.e.* whether the evidence will be misused by the trier of fact. In making this determination, the judge will bear in mind the mandatory requirement in s. 276.4 that the jury be instructed as to the proper use of the evidence. The other factors listed in subsec. (3) reflect the decision by Parliament that certain evidence may be excluded despite its apparent probative value because of policy considerations not strictly related to the potential improper use of the evidence by the trier of fact. The weight to be attached to these broader policy issues will be somewhat more difficult to quantify in the particular case.

ANNOTATIONS

Constitutional considerations – This provision, including the procedural requirements, does not violate ss. 7 or 11(*d*) of the Charter: *R. v. Darrach*, [2000] 2 S.C.R. 443, 148 C.C.C. (3d) 97.

Application – This provision applies to all sexual activity whether with the accused or with someone else and also applies to non-consensual as well as consensual sexual activity: *R. v. Darrach*, *supra*.

Where this provision is used to substantiate a claim of honest but mistaken belief in consent, the accused must provide some evidence of what he believed at the time of the alleged assault in the context of the *voir dire* pursuant to s. 276.1: *R. v. Darrach*, *supra*.

Evidence of a sexual relationship between the accused and the complainant proximate in time to the alleged offences might well support a defence of honest but mistaken belief in consent in some circumstances. However, such evidence should not have been admitted where the accused's defence to one count was consent, not mistaken belief in consent, and with respect to the other three counts a denial that the incidents ever occurred: *R. v. Dickson* (1993), 81 C.C.C. (3d) 224 (Y.T.C.A.), affd [1994] 1 S.C.R. 153, 86 C.C.C. (3d) 576*n*.

Where evidence of prior sexual activity between the parties is offered in support of the defence of honest but mistaken belief in consent, it must be tested on a case-by-case basis having regard to all circumstances, including, but not limited to: the viability of the defence itself; the nature and extent of the prior sexual activity as compared to the sexual activity forming the subject-matter of the charge; the time frame separating the incidents; and the nature of the relationship between the parties: *R. v. Harris* (1997), 118 C.C.C. (3d) 498 (Ont. C.A.).

"Sexual activity" includes a prior conviction for communicating for the purposes of prostitution: *R. v. Drakes* (1998), 122 C.C.C. (3d) 498 (B.C.C.A.).

This section applies to evidence of a sexual relationship between the accused and complainant, even where the proposed evidence does not relate to specific instances of sexual activity but merely the general fact of a sexual relationship: *R. v. L.S.* (2017), 354 C.C.C. (3d) 71 (Ont. C.A.).

While the admissibility of evidence that the complainant was a virgin prior to the alleged assault by the accused is not covered either by this section or s. 277, the jury must be warned against the improper use of such evidence and in particular that the fact the complainant was a virgin does not mean that she was of better character and therefore more truthful: *R. v. Brothers* (1995), 99 C.C.C. (3d) 64 (Alta. C.A.).

Where the Crown adduced evidence from the complainant that she terminated her relationship with the accused prior to the alleged assault because she had a sexual preference for women with the apparent intention of asking the jury to draw the inference that the complainant was not the type of person to consent to intercourse with the male accused, then the defence should have been permitted to adduce evidence that the complainant, two days before the alleged assault, had sexual intercourse with a man. Such evidence would have been admissible according to the guidelines set out in *R. v. Seaboyer*, *supra*; *R. v. Morden* (1991), 69 C.C.C. (3d) 123 (B.C.C.A.).

The trial judge did not err in refusing to permit defence counsel to cross-examine the complainant (his step-daughter) as to whether she had lied in telling a police-officer that she had been sexually assaulted by persons other than the accused. There was no indication that the complainant's evidence on this collateral matter might be false. The evidence was of tenuous relevancy but had a significant potential to mislead the jury: *R. v. W.(B.A.)*, [1992] 3 S.C.R. 811.

The trial judge did not err in curtailing cross-examination of the complainant concerning an allegation she made about another man, nor did he err in refusing the defence permission to call this man who would deny the allegation and testify that he had been charged with sexually assaulting the victim and had been acquitted. The only legal basis which would justify this cross-examination would be to lay the foundation for a pattern of fabrication by the complainant of similar allegations of sexual assault against other men. This should not be encouraged unless the defence is in a position to establish that the complainant has recanted her earlier accusations or that they are demonstrably false. The cross-examination was on a collateral matter being in the nature of an attack on the general character of the complainant: *R. v. Riley* (1992), 11 O.R. (3d) 151 (C.A.).

The trial judge did not err in refusing to permit cross-examination of the complainant about allegations of sexual abuse by her biological father made at the same time she claimed abuse by the accused, her uncle. The complainant made it clear in her evidence at the preliminary inquiry that the sexual activity with her father ceased before the accused began abusing her. The accused did not intend to call the biological father to confirm or refute her allegations against him. The proposed evidence was not relevant to the accused's denial that the sexual activity took place or to the identity of the perpetrators: *R. v. T. (M.)* (2012), 289 C.C.C. (3d) 115 (Ont. C.A.).

This section and the procedure set out in ss. 276.1 and 276.2 have no application to evidence tending to show that the complainant has fabricated stories of sexual activity in which she has admittedly never engaged. However, the trial judge must nevertheless determine whether the proposed evidence is sufficiently probative to warrant its admission: *R. v. Gauthier* (1995), 100 C.C.C. (3d) 563 (B.C.C.A.).

Where evidence of sexual conduct between the accused and the complainant after the alleged offence became relevant because of testimony given by the complainant in examination-in-chief, the trial judge should have permitted defence counsel to cross-examine the complainant on that conduct, notwithstanding an earlier pre-trial ruling to exclude the evidence: *R. v. Potvin* (1998), 124 C.C.C. (3d) 568 (Que. C.A.).

The trial judge erred in precluding cross-examination of the complainant on her statement to the police, wherein she admitted to having engaged in consensual sexual intercourse with the accused three days before the alleged assault and stated that was the reason for visiting the accused on the date of the alleged assault. At trial, the complainant denied visiting the accused on the date of the alleged assault with the intention of having sex with him. Ordinarily, nothing would prevent defence counsel from cross-examining the complainant on such a material inconsistency. The fact that the material inconsistency was inextricably linked in the police questioning to the earlier consensual sexual contact between the complainant and the accused should not prevent the cross-examination. Where the defence of honest but mistaken belief is not realistically advanced by the accused at trial, then evidence of prior, unrelated sexual activity between the complainant and the accused will seldom be relevant to an issue at trial. However, the circumstances of this case were exceptional, as the only reason the unrelated prior sexual activity was at all implicated was because it was directly referred to by the police while posing a question which did bear on the sexual activity forming the subject matter of the charge. It would be unfair for an accused to be denied access to evidence which is otherwise admissible and relevant to his defence if the prejudice related to admitting that evidence is uniquely attributable to the authorities' conduct: *R. v. Crosby*, [1995] 2 S.C.R. 912, 98 C.C.C. (3d) 225.

The trial judge erred in precluding the accused from cross-examining the complainant in relation to prior complaints of sexual assault regarding other persons. The questions were relevant to credibility in that they established the improbability of assaults involving virtually identical comments and actions by a number of alleged assailants in different circumstances over the years: *R. v. Anstey* (2002), 162 C.C.C. (3d) 567 (Nfld. C.A.).

This section applies to evidence of specific sexual activity, not sexual inactivity. Therefore, the defence was permitted to cross-examine the complainant on her purported prior statement to the accused that she had not had sex in six months: *R. v. Antonelli* (2011), 280 C.C.C. (3d) 96 (Ont. S.C.J.).

Where the Crown led the complainant's pregnancy as evidence of the accused's guilt, the accused had the right to cross-examine the complainant that sexual activity with someone else could have explained the pregnancy. The trial judge therefore erred in denying the accused's application under this section: *R. v. R.V.* (2018), 362 C.C.C. (3d) 434 (Ont. C.A.), leave to appeal to S.C.C. allowed 2018 CarswellOnt 21618.

Subsection (2) – In considering the inadmissibility of the evidence under this subsection, the trial judge must consider the factors set out in subsec. (3). "Significant probative value" requires that the evidence not be so trifling as to be incapable, in the context of all the evidence, of raising a reasonable doubt. It is not necessary for the accused to demonstrate strong and compelling reasons for the admission of the evidence. Furthermore, the use of the word "substantially" raises the standard for exclusion once the accused has shown it to have significant probative value: *R. v. Darrach, supra.*

The exception in subsec. (2) has no application at a preliminary inquiry: *R. v. S. (M.P.)* (2014), 338 C.C.C. (3d) 200 (B.C.C.A.). *Contra*: *R. v. Alibhai* (1998), 123 C.C.C. (3d) 556 (Ont. Gen. Div.).

EDITOR'S NOTE: The former provisions under ss. 276.1 through 276.5 have been repealed and replaced with ss. 278.93 through 278.97. The annotations under the former provisions have been retained to the extent that they may be helpful in applying the new equivalent provisions.

276.1 [*Repealed*, 2018, c. 29, s. 22.]

Editor's Note: Section 276.1 was repealed and replaced with s. 278.93. The annotations below should be approached with caution in relation to the new provision.

ANNOTATIONS

Constitutional considerations – The requirement in subsec. (2)(*a*) that the accused supply detailed particulars does not infringe the rights guaranteed by ss. 7 and 11(*c*) of the *Canadian Charter of Rights and Freedoms*: *R. v. Darrach*, [2000] 2 S.C.R. 443, 148 C.C.C. (3d) 97.

Evidentiary requirements – While the trial judge may allow an information and belief affidavit at the first stage of presenting detailed particulars of the evidence, it must be a personal affidavit of a person who has relevant information and who can personally testify as to its truth. The Crown's cross-examination must be limited to what is necessary to determine whether the proposed evidence is admissible. Furthermore, the accused's testimony on the *voir dire* is protected pursuant to s. 13 of the *Canadian Charter of Rights and Freedoms* and can only be used at trial to impugn his credibility and not establish his culpability: *R. v. Darrach, supra.*

The inquiry under this section entails only a facial consideration of the matter and a tentative decision as to whether the evidence appears capable of being admissible. Any doubts that might exist at this stage are better left to be resolved at the evidentiary hearing under s. 276.2. The courts must be cautious in applying limits on the right of an accused to cross-examine and adduce evidence and so, unless the evidence clearly appears to be incapable of being admissible, having regard for the criteria set out in s. 276(2) and the *indicia* in s. 276(3), the judge should proceed to the evidentiary hearing stage: *R. v. Ecker* (1995), 96 C.C.C. (3d) 161 (Sask. C.A.).

Having excluded the accused's statements due to a Charter violation, the trial judge did not err under this section in refusing to admit the accused's statements during the course of a *voir dire*, although in the result, the accused was required to testify on the *voir dire*: *R. v. Mathieu* (1996), 111 C.C.C. (3d) 291 (Alta. C.A.), leave to appeal to S.C.C. refused 114 C.C.C. (3d) vi.

A preliminary inquiry judge has jurisdiction to hear and decide an application under this section: *R. v. Alibhai* (1998), 123 C.C.C. (3d) 556 (Ont. Ct. (Gen. Div.)). *Contra: R. v. T. (W.S.)* (1997), 33 W.C.B. (2d) 212 (B.C.S.C.).

276.2 [*Repealed*, 2018, c. 29, s. 22.]

Editor's Note: Section 276.2 was repealed and replaced with s. 278.94. The annotation below should be approached with caution in relation to the new provision.

ANNOTATIONS

The non-compellability of the complainant does not violate the accused's right to make full answer and defence pursuant to ss. 7 and 11(*d*) of the *Canadian Charter of Rights and Freedoms*: *R. v. Darrach*, [2000] 2 S.C.R. 443, 148 C.C.C. (3d) 97.

276.3 [*Repealed*, 2018, c. 29, s. 22.]

Editor's Note: Section 276.3 was repealed and replaced with s. 278.95.

276.4 [*Repealed*, 2018, c. 29, s. 22.]

Editor's Note: Section 276.4 was repealed and replaced with s. 278.96. The annotations below should be approached with caution in relation to the new provision.

ANNOTATIONS

Cross-examination of the complainant on allegedly deviant and aberrant sexual behaviour, to support a defence by the accused psychologist that his acts were legitimate therapy, had a great potential for undue prejudice and the trial judge erred in failing to direct the jury as to the limited use of that evidence: *R. v. Fiqia* (1993), 87 C.C.C. (3d) 377 (Alta. C.A.). [**Note:** this case was tried prior to the enactment of this section.]

Where evidence of a prior sexual act has been admitted, even if it was not admitted under s. 276 on the basis that the act was non-consensual, it is incumbent on the trial judge to instruct the jury as to the proper and limited use of the evidence and, where necessary, that the evidence was not to be used for some other, improper, purpose that was suggested in the course of defence counsel's jury address: *R. v. Bell* (1998), 126 C.C.C. (3d) 94 (N.W.T.C.A.).

276.5 [*Repealed*, 2018, c. 29, s. 22.]

Editor's Note: Section 276.5 was repealed and replaced with s. 278.97.

REPUTATION EVIDENCE.

277. In proceedings in respect of an offence under section 151, 152, 153, 153.1, 155 or 159, subsection 160(2) or (3) or section 170, 171, 172, 173, 271, 272 or 273, evidence of sexual reputation, whether general or specific, is not admissible for the purpose of challenging or supporting the credibility of the complainant. 1980-81-82-83, c. 125, s. 19; R.S.C. 1985, c. 19 (3rd Supp.), s. 13; 2002, c. 13, s. 14.

CROSS-REFERENCES

The term "complainant" is defined in s. 2. As to other evidentiary and procedural provisions respecting the offences listed in this section, see the cross-references in relation to those provisions and the notes under s. 150.1. However, note in particular the companion provisions in s. 276 respecting evidence of sexual conduct with persons other than the accused.

SYNOPSIS

This section states that evidence of sexual reputation is not admissible to challenge or support the credibility of the complainant in proceedings under ss. 151, 152, 153, 155, 159, 170, 171, 172, 173, 271, 272, 273, or s. 160(2) or (3). It, in effect, reverses the common law rule that evidence of a reputation for sexual promiscuity was relevant to the complainant's credibility.

ANNOTATIONS

This section is not unconstitutional by reason of ss. 7 and 11(*d*) of the Charter: *R. v. Seaboyer*, [1991] 2 S.C.R. 577, 66 C.C.C. (3d) 321 (7:2).

SPOUSE MAY BE CHARGED.

278. A husband or wife may be charged with an offence under section 271, 272 or 273 in respect of his or her spouse, whether or not the spouses were living together at the time the activity that forms the subject-matter of the charge occurred. 1980-81-82-83, c. 125, s. 19.

CROSS-REFERENCES

As to other evidentiary and procedural provisions respecting the offences listed in this section, see the cross-references in relation to those provisions and the notes under s. 150.1.

SYNOPSIS

This section specifies that a person may be charged with the offences of sexual assault, sexual assault with a weapon or causing bodily harm, or aggravated sexual assault against his or her spouse, whether or not they were living together at the time of the alleged offence. This reverses the common law rule that a husband could not be guilty of rape committed, by himself, upon his lawful wife, on the basis that, by virtue of the marriage contract, she was deemed to have irrevocably consented to intercourse.

CR. CODE

Editor's Note: PERSONAL INFORMATION RECORDS
The following ss. 278.1 to 278.91 were enacted in response to the decision of the Supreme Court of Canada in *R. v. O'Connor*, [1995] 4 S.C.R. 411, 103 C.C.C. (3d) 1, 44 C.R. (4th) 1, which mandated the disclosure of therapeutic records in the possession of the Crown and set out a common law procedure for production and disclosure of records in the possession of third parties. *O'Connor* and related cases are noted under s. 650.

These provisions are triggered by an application by the accused charged with any of the sexual offences, enumerated in s. 278.2, for disclosure or production of records as defined in s. 278.1. That section contains a wide definition to include any record that contains personal information for which there is a reasonable expectation of privacy. Certain types of documents are listed and, as well, the definition includes documents protected under provincial or other federal legislation. Hospital records would be an obvious example of such documents. The only exception is a record created by a person responsible for the investigation or prosecution of the offence. Further, the procedure set out in these sections applies even to records in the possession of the Crown, thus expressly overruling a part of the holding in *O'Connor*, unless the complainant or the person to whom the records relate expressly waives the application of these sections. The Crown's disclosure obligation with respect to such records is limited to notifying the accused that they are in the possession of the prosecution, but without disclosing the their contents.

Sections 278.3 to 278.7 envisage a careful multi-staged procedure. Under s. 278.3, the accused first makes a written application for production to the trial judge identifying the record, the person in control of the record and the grounds for seeking production. Section 278.3(3) identifies the two purposes for which a record may be produced, *i.e.*, that it is relevant to an issue at trial or to the competence of a witness. A key provision is subsec. (4), which deems certain assertions that, on their own, are not to be sufficient to provide grounds for production of the record. The application must be served on the prosecutor, the person in control of the record and the complainant or witness to whom the records relate. At the same time, the accused must serve a subpoena in Form 16.1 on the person having control of the record. This form of subpoena notifies the person that the record need not be disclosed to any other party nor brought to court until a judge has made an order for their production. A judge presiding at a preliminary inquiry has no jurisdiction to order production of records under these sections.

The next stage in the process requires the judge to conduct an in camera hearing in accordance with s. 278.4 to determine whether to require production of the records to the judge for review. The person in control of the records and the complainant or witness, as the case may be, have standing to make submissions at this hearing. No order for costs may be made against any such person in respect of their participation in the hearing. The basis upon which the judge may decide to require production of the records is set out in s. 278.5. It would seem clear that the judge is to make this determination without necessarily reviewing the documents, on the basis of submissions. It may be that the parties are entitled to call evidence on this hearing, but the person in control of the records, the complainant or the witness to whom the records relate, are not compellable witnesses. Before ordering that the records be produced, the judge must be satisfied that the application is in accordance with s. 278.3, that the accused has established that the record is likely to be relevant to an issue at trial or to the competence of a witness and that production is necessary in the interests of justice. Section 278.5(2) sets out the test the judge must apply. In general terms, the judge is required to consider the accused's right to make full answer and defence as well as the privacy and equality rights of the person to whom the records relate. The judge is also directed in mandatory terms to consider a number of listed factors that focus not only on the probative value of the evidence and the privacy interests of any person, but broader societal concerns such as the interest in encouraging complainants to obtain treatment. Section 278.8 requires the judge to give reason for the decision.

The third stage in the procedure is set out in s. 278.6. If the judge decides that the record should be produced to the judge, the judge must then decide whether to disclose the record to the accused. This determination will ordinarily be made by the judge in private in the absence of the parties. However, the judge may hold an in camera hearing if it will assist in making the determination. The person to whom the records relate or the person in control of the records is not a compellable witness at this hearing. This may pose a difficulty for the judge if, for example, the need for the hearing is the difficulty in deciphering or understanding the documents. The test for determining whether to order disclosure is set out in s. 278.7(1) and (2) and involves application of the same factors that the judge applied under s. 278.5. Section 278.8 requires the judge to give reason for the decision.

The final stage in the procedure is set out in s. 278.7(3) to (6), which applies where the judge decides that a record or part of a record should be produced to the accused. Subsection (3) permits the judge to impose conditions on the disclosure. For example, the judge may require that the record be edited, that copies of the record not be made and that it be examined only at the court offices. The judge will also order a copy of the record be disclosed to the prosecutor unless the judge determines that it is not in the interests of justice to do so. Production of the record is made subject to the condition that it not be used in any other proceeding. If the judge decides not to order production of the record, a copy is to be kept in a sealed packet pending any appeal proceedings.

A decision whether or not to order production of the record to the judge under s. 278.5 or to the accused under s. 278.7 is deemed to be a question of law for the purposes of appeal by the accused or the Crown under s. 675 or s. 676.

It is a summary conviction offence under s. 278.9 to publish, broadcast or transmit in any way the contents of the application or any of the proceedings at the in camera hearings. Moreover, it is also an offence to publish, broadcast or transmit in any way the judge's reasons unless the judge orders that the determination may be published taking into account the interests of justice and privacy interests. The penalty for this offence is as prescribed in s. 787. The limitation period for instituting proceedings for this offence is six months pursuant to s. 786(2).

DEFINITION OF "RECORD".

278.1 For the purposes of sections 278.2 to 278.92, "record" means any form of record that contains personal information for which there is a reasonable expectation of privacy and includes medical, psychiatric, therapeutic, counselling, education, employment, child welfare, adoption and social services records, personal journals and diaries, and records containing personal information the production or disclosure of which is protected by any other Act of Parliament or a provincial legislature, but does not include records made by persons responsible for the investigation or prosecution of the offence. 1997, c. 30, s. 1; 2018, c. 29, s. 23.

ANNOTATIONS

The definition of "record" is not overly broad and applies only to documents that truly raise a legally recognized privacy interest: *R. v. Mills*, [1999] 3 S.C.R. 668, 139 C.C.C. (3d) 321.

The definition only applies to records in which the complainant or witness has a reasonable expectation of privacy. However, absent evidence from the accused to the contrary, a trial judge is entitled to assume that a reasonable expectation of privacy attaches to any of the records falling within the enumerated categories and that, accordingly, the accused must comply with the provisions in order to gain access to the records. The fact that the accused was present for some of the complainant's counselling sessions and may have been privy to some of the disclosures by the complainant and the advice from the counsellor did not undermine her reasonable expectation of privacy: *R. v. Clifford* (2001), 163 C.C.C. (3d) 3 (Ont. C.A.).

Police occurrence reports prepared in the investigation of previous incidents involving a complainant or witness other than the offence being prosecuted count as "records" and are subject to the *Mills* regime. Given the sensitive nature of the information frequently contained in such police occurrence reports, and the impact that their disclosure can have on the privacy interests of complainants and witnesses, there will generally be a reasonable expectation of privacy in such reports. Further, the exemption for investigatory and prosecutorial records does not exempt such reports from the *Mills* regime: *R. v. Quesnelle*, [2014] 2 S.C.R. 390, 312 C.C.C. (3d) 187.

This provision had no application where the defence sought to call a witness, who worked in the complainant's home with the child protection agency, to testify about the complainant's reputation for truthfulness: *R. v. P-P. (S.H.)* (2003), 176 C.C.C. (3d) 281 (N.S.C.A.).

The court file number of another prosecution involving the same complainant was not a "record" within the meaning of this section and should be disclosed. This information would allow the accused to obtain publicly available information associated with the court file and potentially pursue an application for further material under the statutory regime: *R. v. Shaugnessy* (2012), 288 C.C.C. (3d) 195 (Alta. Q.B.).

PRODUCTION OF RECORD TO ACCUSED / Application of provisions / Duty of prosecutor to give notice.

278.2 (1) Except in accordance with sections 278.3 to 278.91, no record relating to a complainant or a witness shall be produced to an accused in any proceedings in respect of any of the following offences or in any proceedings in respect of two or more offences at least one of which is any of the following offences:

(*a*) an offence under section 151, 152, 153, 153.1, 155, 159, 160, 170, 171, 172, 173, 210, 211, 213, 271, 272, 273, 279.01, 279.011, 279.02, 279.03, 286.1, 286.2 or 286.3, or

(*b*) any offence under this Act, as it read from time to time before the day on which this paragraph comes into force, if the conduct alleged would be an offence referred to in paragraph (*a*) if it occurred on or after that day.

(*c*) [*Repealed*, 2014, c. 25, s. 17(3).]

(2) Section 278.1, this section and sections 278.3 to 278.91 apply where a record is in the possession or control of any person, including the prosecutor in the proceedings, unless, in the case of a record in the possession or control of the prosecutor, the complainant or witness to whom the record relates has expressly waived the application of those sections.

(3) In the case of a record in respect of which this section applies that is in the possession or control of the prosecutor, the prosecutor shall notify the accused that the record is in the prosecutor's possession but, in doing so, the prosecutor shall not disclose the record's contents. 1997, c. 30, s. 1; 1998, c. 9, s. 3; 2014, c. 25, ss. 17, 48(5); 2015, c. 13, s. 5(2).

ANNOTATIONS

Constitutional considerations – Sections 278.1 to 278.91 do not violate ss. 7, 8, 11(*d*) or 15 of the Charter: *R. v. Mills*, [1999] 3 S.C.R. 668, 139 C.C.C. (3d) 321.

General – Neither these provisions nor the principles set out in *R. v. O'Connor*, [1995] 4 S.C.R. 411, 103 C.C.C. (3d) 1, 44 C.R. (4th) 1, have any application to the use of the complainant's diary which was in the defence's possession and had not been wrongfully taken. The balancing tests set out with respect to third party records have no application with respect to the scope of cross-examination. The issue was whether the complainant's privacy interest substantially outweighed the accused's right to test the complainant's memory by cross-examination on the absence of entries in the diary recording abuse: *R. v. Shearing*, [2002] 3 S.C.R. 33, 165 C.C.C. (3d) 225.

Where the accused was charged with historical sexual assaults under the former s. 246.1 (now s. 271), the third-party records regime under ss. 278.1 to 278.9, and not the common law regime, applied. As the enactment was purely procedural, the presumption of retroactive application was engaged: *R. v. Gibson* (2010), 264 C.C.C. (3d) 121 (Ont. S.C.J.).

APPLICATION FOR PRODUCTION / No application in other proceedings / Form and content of application / Insufficient grounds / Service of application and subpoena / Service on other persons.

278.3 (1) An accused who seeks production of a record referred to in subsection 278.2(1) must make an application to the judge before whom the accused is to be, or is being, tried.

(2) For greater certainty, an application under subsection (1) may not be made to a judge or justice presiding at any other proceedings, including a preliminary inquiry.

(3) An application must be made in writing and set out

(*a*) particulars identifying the record that the accused seeks to have produced and the name of the person who has possession or control of the record; and

(*b*) the grounds on which the accused relies to establish that the record is likely relevant to an issue at trial or to the competence of a witness to testify.

(4) Any one or more of the following assertions by the accused are not sufficient on their own to establish that the record is likely relevant to an issue at trial or to the competence of a witness to testify:

(*a*) that the record exists;

(*b*) that the record relates to medical or psychiatric treatment, therapy or counselling that the complainant or witness has received or is receiving;

(*c*) that the record relates to the incident that is the subject-matter of the proceedings;

(*d*) that the record may disclose a prior inconsistent statement of the complainant or witness;

(*e*) that the record may relate to the credibility of the complainant or witness;

(*f*) that the record may relate to the reliability of the testimony of the complainant or witness merely because the complainant or witness has received or is receiving psychiatric treatment, therapy or counselling;

(*g*) that the record may reveal allegations of sexual abuse of the complainant by a person other than the accused;

(*h*) that the record relates to the sexual activity of the complainant with any person, including the accused;

(*i*) that the record relates to the presence or absence of a recent complaint;

(*j*) that the record relates to the complainant's sexual reputation; or

(*k*) that the record was made close in time to a complaint or to the activity that forms the subject-matter of the charge against the accused.

(5) The accused shall serve the application on the prosecutor, on the person who has possession or control of the record, on the complainant or witness, as the case may be, and on any other person to whom, to the knowledge of the accused, the record relates, at least 60 days before the hearing referred to in subsection 278.4(1) or any shorter interval that the judge may allow in the interests of justice. The accused shall also serve a subpoena issued under Part XXII in Form 16.1 on the person who has possession or control of the record at the same time as the application is served.

(6) The judge may at any time order that the application be served on any person to whom the judge considers the record may relate. 1997, c. 30, s. 1; 2015, c. 13, s. 6; 2018, c. 29, s. 24.

ANNOTATIONS

Subsection (4) – This provision does not prevent an accused from relying on the enumerated factors but rather prevents reliance on bare assertions of the listed matters where there is no other evidence and the bare assertion stands on its own. With the exception of "recent complaint", the accused may rely on the listed assertions where there is an evidentiary or informational foundation to suggest that they may be related to likely relevance. The evidentiary threshold the accused must meet is to point to case-specific evidence or information to show that the record in issue is likely relevant to an issue at trial or the competence of a witness to testify. The issue of likely relevance, however, is a matter for the trial judge's discretion: *R. v. Mills*, [1999] 3 S.C.R. 668, 139 C.C.C. (3d) 321.

Where the records contain statements made by a complainant on matters potentially relevant to credibility, the likely relevance threshold will be met if there is some basis for concluding that the statements have some potential to provide some added information not already available to the defence or have some potential impeachment value. For example, material differences between the initial statement and preliminary inquiry testimony coupled with the fact that the complainant spoke to a therapist about the matters between these two events is sufficient to satisfy likely relevance: *R. v. Batte* (2000), 145 C.C.C. (3d) 449.

The mere assertion that the complainant had written about the accused in her diary was insufficient to meet the likely relevance test: *R. v. L. (D.W.)* (2001), 156 C.C.C. (3d) 152 (N.S.C.A.).

HEARING *IN CAMERA* / Persons who may appear at hearing / Right to counsel / Costs.

278.4 (1) The judge shall hold a hearing *in camera* to determine whether to order the person who has possession or control of the record to produce it to the court for review by the judge.

(2) The person who has possession or control of the record, the complainant or witness, as the case may be, and any other person to whom the record relates may appear and make submissions at the hearing, but they are not compellable as witnesses at the hearing.

(2.1) The judge shall, as soon as feasible, inform any person referred to in subsection (2) who participates in the hearing of their right to be represented by counsel.

(3) No order for costs may be made against a person referred to in subsection (2) in respect of their participation in the hearing. 1997, c. 30, s. 1; 2015, c. 13, s. 7.

JUDGE MAY ORDER PRODUCTION OF RECORD FOR REVIEW / Factors to be considered.

278.5 (1) The judge may order the person who has possession or control of the record to produce the record or part of the record to the court for review by the judge if, after the hearing referred to in subsection 278.4(1), the judge is satisfied that

(*a*) the application was made in accordance with subsections 278.3(2) to (6);

(*b*) the accused has established that the record is likely relevant to an issue at trial or to the competence of a witness to testify; and

(*c*) the production of the record is necessary in the interests of justice.

(2) In determining whether to order the production of the record or part of the record for review pursuant to subsection (1), the judge shall consider the salutary and deleterious effects of the determination on the accused's right to make a full answer and defence and on the right to privacy, personal security and equality of the complainant or witness, as the case may be, and of any other person to whom the record relates. In particular, the judge shall take the following factors into account:

(*a*) the extent to which the record is necessary for the accused to make a full answer and defence;

(*b*) the probative value of the record;

(*c*) the nature and extent of the reasonable expectation of privacy with respect to the record;

(*d*) whether production of the record is based on a discriminatory belief or bias;
(*e*) the potential prejudice to the personal dignity and right to privacy of any person to whom the record relates;
(*f*) society's interest in encouraging the reporting of sexual offences;
(*g*) society's interest in encouraging the obtaining of treatment by complainants of sexual offences; and
(*h*) the effect of the determination on the integrity of the trial process. 1997, c. 30, s. 1; 2015, c. 13, s. 8.

ANNOTATIONS

The requirement that production be "necessary in the interests of justice" at this stage refers to whether production to the judge is necessary in the interests of justice. The first factor in subsec. (2) requires the judge to consider the accused's right to make full answer and defence. If the judge concludes that it is necessary to examine the documents in order to determine whether they should be produced to enable the accused to make full answer and defence, then production to the judge is "necessary in the interests of justice". If the record is "likely relevant" and after considering the factors set out in subsec. (2), the judge is uncertain about whether production is necessary to make full answer and defence, the judge should also rule in favour of inspecting the documents. This provision does not require that the judge engage in a conclusive evaluation of each of the factors, but rather requires the judge to take these factors into account to the extent possible at this early stage of the proceedings in deciding whether to order the production of documents for inspection by the court. While the enumerated factors are relevant, the trial judge is free to make whatever order is necessary in the interests of justice. A sufficient evidentiary basis to support production to the court can be established through Crown disclosure, defence witnesses, the cross-examination of Crown witnesses at the preliminary inquiry and the trial, expert evidence, as well as the nature of the records in question: *R. v. Mills*, [1999] 3 S.C.R. 668, 139 C.C.C. (3d) 321.

In considering the application of the test under this section, the trial judge might well find that there is a somewhat reduced expectation of privacy in respect of records relating to counselling sessions where the accused was present. On the other hand, because the accused was present at the session, he should be in a position to provide specific details of the information sought: *R. v. Clifford* (2001), 163 C.C.C. (3d) 3 (Ont. C.A.).

REVIEW OF RECORD BY JUDGE / Hearing *in camera* / Provision re hearing.

278.6 (1) Where the judge has ordered the production of the record or part of the record for review, the judge shall review it in the absence of the parties in order to determine whether the record or part of the record should be produced to the accused.

(2) The judge may hold a hearing *in camera* if the judge considers that it will assist in making the determination.

(3) Subsections 278.4(2) to (3) apply in the case of a hearing under subsection (2). 1997, c. 30, s. 1; 2015, c. 13, s. 9.

JUDGE MAY ORDER PRODUCTION OF RECORD TO ACCUSED / Factors to be considered / Conditions on production / Copy to prosecutor / Record not to be used in other proceedings / Retention of record by court.

278.7 (1) Where the judge is satisfied that the record or part of the record is likely relevant to an issue at trial or to the competence of a witness to testify and its production is necessary in the interests of justice, the judge may order that the record or part of the record that is likely relevant be produced to the accused, subject to any conditions that may be imposed pursuant to subsection (3).

(2) In determining whether to order the production of the record or part of the record to the accused, the judge shall consider the salutary and deleterious effects of the

determination on the accused's right to make a full answer and defence and on the right to privacy, personal security and equality of the complainant or witness, as the case may be, and of any other person to whom the record relates and, in particular, shall take the factors specified in paragraphs 278.5(2)(*a*) to (*h*) into account.

(3) If the judge orders the production of the record or part of the record to the accused, the judge may impose conditions on the production to protect the interests of justice and, to the greatest extent possible, the privacy, personal security and equality interests of the complainant or witness, as the case may be, and of any other person to whom the record relates, including, for example, the following conditions:

(*a*) that the record be edited as directed by the judge;

(*b*) that a copy of the record, rather than the original, be produced;

(*c*) that the accused and counsel for the accused not disclose the contents of the record to any other person, except with the approval of the court;

(*d*) that the record be viewed only at the offices of the court;

(*e*) that no copies of the record be made or that restrictions be imposed on the number of copies of the record that may be made; and

(*f*) that information regarding any person named in the record, such as their address, telephone number and place of employ ment, be severed from the record.

(4) Where the judge orders the production of the record or part of the record to the accused, the judge shall direct that a copy of the record or part of the record be provided to the prosecutor, unless the judge determines that it is not in the interests of justice to do so.

(5) The record or part of the record that is produced to the accused pursuant to an order under subsection (1) shall not be used in any other proceedings.

(6) Where the judge refuses to order the production of the record or part of the record to the accused, the record or part of the record shall, unless a court orders otherwise, be kept in a sealed package by the court until the later of the expiration of the time for any appeal and the completion of any appeal in the proceedings against the accused, whereupon the record or part of the record shall be returned to the person lawfully entitled to possession or control of it. 1997, c. 30, s. 1; 2015, c. 13, s. 10.

ANNOTATIONS

In considering whether to order production to the accused, the trial judge must again consider the factors set out in s. 278.5(2). The trial judge is not required to rule conclusively on each of the enumerated factors, nor are they required to determine whether factors relating to the privacy and equality of the complainant or witness outweigh factors relating to the accused's right to make full answer and defence. The societal interest factors in s. 278.5(2)(*f*) and (*g*) are not given controlling weight in the determination regarding production. In considering s. 278.5(2)(*h*), the trial judge is required to consider, along with the other enumerated factors, whether the search for truth would be advanced by the production of the records in question or whether the material would introduce discriminatory biases and beliefs into the fact-finding process: *R. v. Mills*, [1999] 3 S.C.R. 668, 139 C.C.C. (3d) 321.

Having granted production of the complainant's psychiatric records, the trial judge erred in relying on the *R. v. O'Connor*, [1995] 4 S.C.R. 411, 103 C.C.C. (3d) 1, procedure in determining the scope of cross-examination. Once production is granted, the propriety of cross-examination is to be determined based on the application of fundamental rules of evidence: *R. v. Pontbriand* (2004), 189 C.C.C. (3d) 30 (Que. C.A.), leave to appeal to S.C.C. refused [2005] 1 S.C.R. xiv. Similarly, in *R. v. C. (T.)* (2004), 189 C.C.C. (3d) 473 (Ont. C.A.), leave to appeal to S.C.C. refused [2005] 2 S.C.R. xi, 198 C.C.C. (3d) vi, the Ontario Court of Appeal held that the third party record provisions govern production, not admissibility or use, and therefore were not applicable to a social worker's report that was lawfully in the possession of the accused. Nonetheless, the trial judge was entitled to exclude the report on the basis that the prejudicial effect of the report substantially outweighed its probative value having regard to the distortion of the fact-finding process and the therapeutic relationship.

REASONS FOR DECISION / Record of reasons.

278.8 (1) The judge shall provide reasons for ordering or refusing to order the production of the record or part of the record pursuant to subsection 278.5(1) or 278.7(1).

(2) The reasons referred to in subsection (1) shall be entered in the record of the proceedings or, where the proceedings are not recorded, shall be provided in writing. 1997, c. 30, s. 1.

PUBLICATION PROHIBITED / Offence.

278.9 (1) No person shall publish in any document, or broadcast or transmit in any way, any of the following:

(*a*) the contents of an application made under section 278.3;

(*b*) any evidence taken, information given or submissions made at a hearing under subsection 278.4(1) or 278.6(2); or

(*c*) the determination of the judge pursuant to subsection 278.5(1) or 278.7(1) and the reasons provided pursuant to section 278.8, unless the judge, after taking into account the interests of justice and the right to privacy of the person to whom the record relates, orders that the determination may be published.

(2) Every person who contravenes subsection (1) is guilty of an offence punishable on summary conviction. 1997, c. 30, s. 1; 2005, c. 32, s. 14.

APPEAL.

278.91 For the purposes of sections 675 and 676, a determination to make or refuse to make an order pursuant to subsection 278.5(1) or 278.7(1) is deemed to be a question of law. 1997, c. 30, s. 1.

ADMISSIBILITY — ACCUSED IN POSSESSION OF RECORDS RELATING TO COMPLAINANT / Requirements for admissibility / Factors that judge shall consider.

278.92 (1) Except in accordance with this section, no record relating to a complainant that is in the possession or control of the accused — and which the accused intends to adduce — shall be admitted in evidence in any proceedings in respect of any of the following offences or in any proceedings in respect of two or more offences at least one of which is any of the following offences:

(*a*) an offence under section 151, 152, 153, 153.1, 155, 160, 170, 171, 172, 173, 210, 211, 213, 271, 272, 273, 279.01, 279.011, 279.02, 279.03, 286.1, 286.2 or 286.3; or

(*b*) any offence under this Act, as it read from time to time before the day on which this paragraph comes into force, if the conduct alleged would be an offence referred to in paragraph (*a*) if it occurred on or after that day.

(2) The evidence is inadmissible unless the judge, provincial court judge or justice determines, in accordance with the procedures set out in sections 278.93 and 278.94,

(*a*) if the admissibility of the evidence is subject to section 276, that the evidence meets the conditions set out in subsection 276(2) while taking into account the factors set out in subsection (3); or

(*b*) in any other case, that the evidence is relevant to an issue at trial and has significant probative value that is not substantially outweighed by the danger of prejudice to the proper administration of justice.

(3) In determining whether evidence is admissible under subsection (2), the judge, provincial court judge or justice shall take into account

(*a*) the interests of justice, including the right of the accused to make a full answer and defence;

(*b*) society's interest in encouraging the reporting of sexual assault offences;

(*c*) society's interest in encouraging the obtaining of treatment by complainants of sexual offences;

(*d*) whether there is a reasonable prospect that the evidence will assist in arriving at a just determination in the case;

(*e*) the need to remove from the fact-finding process any discriminatory belief or bias;

(*f*) the risk that the evidence may unduly arouse sentiments of prejudice, sympathy or hostility in the jury;

(*g*) the potential prejudice to the complainant's personal dignity and right of privacy;

(*h*) the right of the complainant and of every individual to personal security and to the full protection and benefit of the law; and

(*i*) any other factor that the judge, provincial court judge or justice considers relevant. 2018, c. 29, s. 25.

CROSS-REFERENCES

The terms "complainant", "justice", and "provincial court judge" are defined in s. 2. The term "record" is defined in s. 278.1. The procedure for admitting records relating to the complainant that are in the possession or control of the accused is established in ss. 278.93 and 278.94. Section 278.95 limits the publication of the proceedings. Section 278.96 requires the judge to instruct the jury as to the proper use of the records. Section 278.97 makes the determination of admissibility a question of law, thus giving the Attorney General a right of appeal.

SYNOPSIS

This section makes any record relating to a complainant that is in the possession or control of the accused (and which the accused intends to adduce) presumptively inadmissible in proceedings involving sexual offences. If the admissibility of the evidence is also subject to s. 276 (*i.e.* evidence of the complainant's sexual activity), the evidence is inadmissible unless the court determines that the evidence meets the conditions set out in s. 276(2) while also taking the factors in s. 278.92(3) into account. In any other case, the evidence is inadmissible unless the court determines that the evidence is relevant to an issue at trial and has significant probative value that is not substantially outweighed by the danger of prejudice to the proper administration of justice. Section 278.92(3) requires the court to take a number of factors into account when determining whether the evidence is admissible under s. 278.92(2).

ANNOTATIONS

An order under s. 278.92 is required before defence counsel may put the contents of a record in the possession of the accused in which the complainant has a reasonable expectation of privacy to a witness in the trial of a sexual offence (even if the record itself is not admitted into evidence as an exhibit): *R. v. Boyle*, 2019 ONCJ 226.

The requirement that the evidence have "significant probative value" means that the evidence must have more than "trifling relevance" and is capable of leaving the trier of fact with a reasonable doubt (in the context of all of the evidence). The requirement that the significant probative value is not "substantially" outweighed by the danger of prejudice to the proper administration of justice serves to protect the accused by raising the standard for the judge to exclude evidence once the accused has shown it to have significant probative value. Evidence of a prior inconsistent statement by a complainant in a case where the most significant evidence is the testimony of the complainant is of more than trifling relevance, because inconsistent statements by witnesses are among the more important methods to determine the credibility and reliability of witnesses. Conversely, the relevance requirement under s. 278.92(2) was not met where the evidentiary record did not establish a rational basis for the inference that the failure to document an instance of abuse in a therapeutic record was circumstantial evidence that the alleged abuse never happened: *R. v. Boyle*, 2019 ONCJ 232, citing *R. v. L.S.* (2017), 354 C.C.C. (3d) 71 (Ont. C.A.), and *R. v. Darrach*, [2000] 2 S.C.R. 443, 148 C.C.C. (3d) 97.

Records "in the possession or control" of the accused include records provided to the accused in disclosure. In a case where the records included information that was at odds with the information that the complainant gave to the police, factors (*a*) and (*d*) in s. 278.92(3) weighed heavily in favour of permitting the records to be used for the limited purpose of impeaching the anticipated testimony of the complainant. The court considered the accused's right to make full answer and defence and ruled that the records could be used by the accused during the trial for the purpose of cross-examination, even though there was an obvious concern in relation to factors (*c*), (*g*) and (*h*), because "it would be unjust not to permit the accused the use of these records to prove prior inconsistent statements": see *R. v. Brown*, 2019 ONSC 1335 (S.C.J.).

APPLICATION FOR HEARING — SECTIONS 276 AND 278.92 / Form and content of application / Jury and public excluded / Judge may decide to hold hearing.

278.93 (1) Application may be made to the judge, provincial court judge or justice by or on behalf of the accused for a hearing under section 278.94 to determine whether evidence is admissible under subsection 276(2) or 278.92(2).

(2) An application referred to in subsection (1) must be made in writing, setting out detailed particulars of the evidence that the accused seeks to adduce and the relevance of that evidence to an issue at trial, and a copy of the application must be given to the prosecutor and to the clerk of the court.

(3) The judge, provincial court judge or justice shall consider the application with the jury and the public excluded.

(4) If the judge, provincial court judge or justice is satisfied that the application was made in accordance with subsection (2), that a copy of the application was given to the prosecutor and to the clerk of the court at least seven days previously, or any shorter interval that the judge, provincial court judge or justice may allow in the interests of justice and that the evidence sought to be adduced is capable of being admissible under subsection 276(2), the judge, provincial court judge or justice shall grant the application and hold a hearing under section 278.94 to determine whether the evidence is admissible under subsection 276(2) or 278.92(2). 2018, c. 29, s. 25.

Editor's Note: This provision was formerly found in s. 276.1. Reference should be made, with appropriate caution, to the annotations summarizing the case law under that provision.

CROSS-REFERENCES

The terms "complainant", "justice", "provincial court judge", and "clerk of the court" are defined in s. 2. The term "prosecutor" is defined in ss. 2 and 785. As to the procedure for determining the admissibility of sexual conduct evidence or records relating to a complainant that are in the possession or control of the accused, see s. 278.94. Section 278.95 limits the publication of the proceedings. Section 278.96 requires the judge to instruct the jury as to the proper use of the evidence admitted under s. 278.94, and s. 278.97 makes the determination under s. 278.94 a question of law, thus giving the Attorney General a right of appeal.

SYNOPSIS

This section sets out the first step for making an application to admit evidence of the sexual conduct of the complainant (other than the sexual activity which forms the subject matter of the charge) or to admit records relating to a complainant that are in the possession or control of the accused. This section requires a written application setting out the particulars of the evidence sought to be adduced by the accused and the relevance of that evidence. The application to admit the evidence is actually a two-stage proceeding. Under this section, the judge determines whether the formal requirements have been met such as the written application and notice (seven days unless otherwise ordered) and whether the evidence is capable of being admissible. If these requirements are met, then the accused is entitled to an evidentiary hearing, conducted in accordance with s. 278.94, to determine whether the evidence should be admitted. The test for the admissibility of evidence of the sexual conduct of the complainant is set out in s. 276(2), while the test for the admissibility of records relating to a complainant that are in the possession or control of the accused is set out in s. 278.92(2).

HEARING — JURY AND PUBLIC EXCLUDED / Complainant not compellable / Right to counsel / Judge's determination and reasons / Record of reasons.

278.94 (1) The jury and the public shall be excluded from a hearing to determine whether evidence is admissible under subsection 276(2) or 278.92(2).

(2) The complainant is not a compellable witness at the hearing but may appear and make submissions.

(3) The judge shall, as soon as feasible, inform the complainant who participates in the hearing of their right to be represented by counsel.

(4) At the conclusion of the hearing, the judge, provincial court judge or justice shall determine whether the evidence, or any part of it, is admissible under subsection 276(2) or 278.92(2) and shall provide reasons for that determination, and

- **(*a*) if not all of the evidence is to be admitted, the reasons must state the part of the evidence that is to be admitted;**
- **(*b*) the reasons must state the factors referred to in subsection 276(3) or 278.92(3) that affected the determination; and**
- **(*c*) if all or any part of the evidence is to be admitted, the reasons must state the manner in which that evidence is expected to be relevant to an issue at trial.**

(5) The reasons provided under subsection (4) shall be entered in the record of the proceedings or, if the proceedings are not recorded, shall be provided in writing. 2018, c. 29, s. 25.

Editor's Note: This provision was formerly found in s. 276.2. Reference should be made, with appropriate caution, to the annotation summarizing the case law under that provision.

CROSS-REFERENCES
The terms "complainant", "justice", and "provincial court judge" are defined in s. 2. As to the procedure for determining whether the accused is entitled to an evidentiary hearing prescribed by this section, see s. 278.93. Section 278.95 limits the publication of the proceedings. Section 278.96 requires the judge to instruct the jury as to the proper use of the evidence admitted under s. 278.94, and s. 278.97 makes the determination of admissibility a question of law, thus giving the Attorney General a right of appeal.

SYNOPSIS
This section sets out the final step in the procedure for making an application to admit evidence of the sexual conduct of the complainant (other than the sexual activity which forms the subject matter of the charge) or to admit records relating to a complainant that are in the possession or control of the accused. If the prerequisites set out in s. 278.93 have been met, then the accused becomes entitled to an evidentiary hearing, conducted in accordance with this section, to attempt to show that the evidence sought to be adduced meets the test for

admissibility as set out in ss. 276(2) or 278.92(2). The hearing under this section is held *in camera* and in the absence of the jury. Moreover, the complainant is not a compellable witness at the hearing. Rather, the complainant is granted standing to make submissions at the hearing and must be informed by the judge of his or her right to be represented by counsel for this purpose. This section also requires the court to provide reasons for the decision and to specify what parts of the evidence are to be admitted, the factors in ss. 276(3) or 278.92(3) that affected the determination, and the manner in which the evidence that is to be admitted is expected to be relevant to an issue at trial.

ANNOTATIONS

The jurisprudence under s. 276 is applicable to applications under s. 278.94(2): *R. v. Boyle*, 2019 ONCJ 232.

PUBLICATION PROHIBITED / Offence.

278.95 (1) A person shall not publish in any document, or broadcast or transmit in any way, any of the following:

(*a*) the contents of an application made under subsection 278.93;

(*b*) any evidence taken, the information given and the representations made at an application under section 278.93 or at a hearing under section 278.94;

(*c*) the decision of a judge or justice under subsection 278.93(4), unless the judge or justice, after taking into account the complainant's right of privacy and the interests of justice, orders that the decision may be published, broadcast or transmitted; and

(*d*) the determination made and the reasons provided under subsection 278.94(4), unless

(i) that determination is that evidence is admissible, or

(ii) the judge or justice, after taking into account the complainant's right of privacy and the interests of justice, orders that the determination and reasons may be published, broadcast or transmitted.

(2) Every person who contravenes subsection (1) is guilty of an offence punishable on summary conviction. 2018, c. 29, s. 25.

Editor's Note: This provision was formerly found in s. 276.3.

CROSS-REFERENCES

The terms "complainant", "justice" and "provincial court judge" are defined in s. 2. Procedure for summary conviction offences is found in Part XXVII, which sets out the maximum penalties and the time limitation. Whether or not proceedings may be published under this section, publishers should bear in mind the provisions of s. 648 restricting publication of proceedings in the absence of the jury.

SYNOPSIS

This section makes it an offence to publish in any document or broadcast or transmit in any way certain aspects of the hearing held under ss. 278.93 and 278.94, which are held *in camera* and in the absence of the jury, to determine the admissibility of sexual activity evidence as permitted by s. 276 or of records relating to a complainant that are in the possession or control of the accused as permitted by s. 278.92. This section prohibits publication, broadcast or transmission of the application and the proceedings under ss. 278.93 and 278.94 and of the court's decision under s. 278.93, unless otherwise ordered by the judge. As well, the decision under s. 278.94 cannot be published, broadcasted or transmitted unless it is determined that the evidence is admissible or the court orders otherwise.

JUDGE TO INSTRUCT JURY — RE USE OF EVIDENCE.

278.96 If evidence is admitted at trial on the basis of a determination made under subsection 278.94(4), the judge shall instruct the jury as to the uses that the jury may and may not make of that evidence. 2018, c. 29, s. 25.

Editor's Note: This provision was formerly found in s. 276.4. Reference should be made, with appropriate caution, to the annotations summarizing the case law under that provision.

CROSS-REFERENCES

The procedure for determining whether evidence is admissible under ss. 276 and 278.92 is set out in ss. 278.93 and 278.94.

APPEAL.

278.97 For the purposes of sections 675 and 676, a determination made under subsection 278.94(4) shall be deemed to be a question of law. 2018, c. 29, s. 25.

Editor's Note: This provision was formerly found in s. 276.5.

CROSS-REFERENCES

Sections 675 and 676 govern rights of appeal by the accused and the Attorney General respectively. The main importance of this section lies in the fact that decisions to admit sexual activity evidence or records related to the complainant that are in the possession of the accused are questions of law and are, therefore, appealable by the Crown should the accused be acquitted.

Kidnapping, Trafficking in Persons, Hostage Taking and Abduction

2005, c. 43, s. 2.

KIDNAPPING / Punishment / Subsequent offences / Factors to consider / Sequence of convictions only / Forcible confinement.

279. (1) Every person commits an offence who kidnaps a person with intent

(*a*) to cause the person to be confined or imprisoned against the person's will;

(*b*) to cause the person to be unlawfully sent or transported out of Canada against the person's will; or

(*c*) to hold the person for ransom or to service against the person's will.

(1.1) Every person who commits an offence under subsection (1) is guilty of an indictable offence and liable

(*a*) if a restricted firearm or prohibited firearm is used in the commission of the offence or if any firearm is used in the commission of the offence and the offence is committed for the benefit of, at the direction of, or in association with, a criminal organization, to imprisonment for life and to a minimum punishment of imprisonment for a term of

(i) in the case of a first offence, five years, and

(ii) in the case of a second or subsequent offence, seven years;

(*a*.1) in any other case where a firearm is used in the commission of the offence, to imprisonment for life and to a minimum punishment of imprisonment for a term of four years;

(*a*.2) if the person referred to in paragraph (1)(*a*), (*b*) or (*c*) is under 16 years of age, to imprisonment for life and, unless the person who commits the offence is a parent, guardian or person having the lawful care or charge of the person referred to in that paragraph, to a minimum punishment of imprisonment for a term of five years; and

(*b*) in any other case, to imprisonment for life.

(1.2) In determining, for the purpose of paragraph (1.1)(*a*), whether a convicted person has committed a second or subsequent offence, if the person was earlier convicted of any of the following offences, that offence is to be considered as an earlier offence:

(*a*) an offence under subsection (1);

(*b*) an offence under subsection 85(1) or (2) or section 244 or 244.2; or

(*c*) an offence under section 220, 236, 239, 272, 273, 279.1, 344 or 346 if a firearm was used in the commission of the offence.

However, an earlier offence shall not be taken into account if 10 years have elapsed between the day on which the person was convicted of the earlier offence and the day on which the person was convicted of the offence for which sentence is being imposed, not taking into account any time in custody.

(1.21) In imposing a sentence under paragraph (1.1)(*a*.2), the court shall take into account the age and vulnerability of the victim.

(1.3) For the purposes of subsection (1.2), the only question to be considered is the sequence of convictions and no consideration shall be given to the sequence of commission of offences or whether any offence occurred before or after any conviction.

(2) Every one who, without lawful authority, confines, imprisons or forcibly seizes another person is guilty of

(*a*) an indictable offence and liable to imprisonment for a term not exceeding ten years; or

(*b*) an offence punishable on summary conviction and liable to imprisonment for a term not exceeding eighteen months. R.S., c. C-34, s. 247; R.S.C. 1985, c. 27 (1st Supp.), s. 39; 1995, c. 39, s. 147; 1997, c. 18, s. 14; 2008, c. 6, s. 30; 2009, c. 22, s. 12; 2013, c. 32, s. 1; 2018, c. 29, s. 26.

(3) [*Repealed*, 2018, c. 29, s. 26.]

CROSS-REFERENCES

"Victim" is defined in s. 2. Section 279.04 defines when a person exploits another person for the purpose of this section. Section 279.02 makes it an offence to receive a financial or other material benefit from the commission of the offence under this section. Under s. 279.03, it is an offence to withhold or destroy travel or identity documents for the purpose of committing the offence under this section.

The related offence of trafficking in persons under the age of 18 years is set out in s. 279.011. The two offences are virtually identical except that the s. 279.011 offence includes minimum punishments. The offences, referred to in this section, of kidnapping, aggravated assault and aggravated sexual assault are found in ss. 279, 268 and 273 respectively. Also see s. 212, which creates various offences relating to procuring persons for the purpose of prostitution, whether in or out of Canada.

Section 17 limits the availability of the statutory defence of compulsion by threats to the offence of "forcible abduction". However, forcible abduction has been held not to include kidnapping: *R. v. Robins* (1982), 66 C.C.C. (2d) 550 (Que. C.A.). This offence may be the basis for an application for an authorization to intercept private communications by reason of s. 183.

Section 486 provides that the judge may exclude members of the public from the courtroom where it is in the interests of the proper administration of justice, which includes ensuring that witnesses under the age of 18 years are safeguarded in all proceedings. If the prosecutor or the accused applies for an order excluding the public at proceedings for an offence under this section and the judge fails to make the order, the judge is required to give reasons for that decision. Under s. 486.4, where an accused is charged with the offence under this section, the judge may make an order directing that any information that could identify the complainant or a witness not be published, broadcast or transmitted in any way. The judge is to inform the complainant or any witness under the age of 18 years of the right to make an application under s. 486.4.

This offence is a primary designated offence for the DNA provisions and a designated offence for the sex offender information provisions of Part XV and is a designated offence for the dangerous offender and long-term offender provisions in Part XXIV.

SYNOPSIS

This section describes the offences of kidnapping and forcible confinement, the punishment for these offences, and the defence of non-resistance. Any person who kidnaps another person against his will, with intent to confine him, to cause him to be sent out of Canada, or to hold him for ransom or to service, is guilty of an indictable offence and liable to life imprisonment. The section also enacts minimum punishments for the kidnapping offence. Under para. (1.1)(*a*.2), if the victim was under 16 years of age, the accused is subject to a minimum punishment of five years' imprisonment, unless the accused is a parent, guardian or person having the lawful care or charge of the victim. In any event, in imposing sentence under this paragraph, the court shall take into consideration the age and vulnerability of the victim. Where a restricted or prohibited firearm is used or the offence was committed for the benefit of, at the direction of, or in association with, a criminal organization, the offender is liable to a minimum punishment of at least five years' imprisonment for a first offence and seven years for a second or subsequent offence. The rules for determining whether the offender has committed a second or subsequent offence are set out in subsecs. (2.1) and (2.2) and, for example, provide that a prior offence includes not only convictions under this subsection, but other specified offences involving firearms. However, an earlier offence is not to be taken into account if 10 years have elapsed from the conviction of the earlier offence, not counting time in custody. Subsection (2.2) reverses the common law rule and provides that the court only takes into account the sequence of convictions, not the order in which the offences were committed. In any other case where a firearm is used, the offender is liable to a minimum term of imprisonment of four years. Where no firearm is used, there is no minimum punishment. Anyone who confines, imprisons or forcibly seizes another person without lawful authority is guilty of an indictable offence punishable by a maximum term of imprisonment of 10 years where the Crown proceeds by indictment, and 18 months where the Crown proceeds by summary conviction. Evidence of the fact that the victim did not resist does not constitute a defence unless the accused proves that such failure to resist was not caused by threats, duress or force.

ANNOTATIONS

Kidnapping [subsec. (1)] – To constitute kidnapping there must be a movement or taking of the person from one place to another and not simply the placing of the person in the area of confinement. Where an accused binds the victim who originally voluntarily entered his truck, places her in the back of the truck and continues on his trip until he can find a suitable place to sexually assault her the offence is made out: *R. v. Oakley* (1977), 36 C.C.C. (2d) 436 (Alta. C.A.).

In *R. v. Elder* (1978), 40 C.C.C. (2d) 122 (Sask. Dist. Ct.), the accused was acquitted of the offences under both subsecs. (1) and (2) where during a hostage-taking incident at a prison while he assisted in moving the hostage from one area to another his only purpose was to remove him from danger. The accused's purpose negatived the element of *mens rea* for both offences.

False statements by the accused which induced his victim to willingly enter into his custody constitutes kidnapping: *R. v. Brown* (1972), 8 C.C.C. (2d) 13 (Ont. C.A.).

Similarly, *R. v. Metcalfe* (1983), 10 C.C.C. (3d) 114 (B.C.C.A.), where it was held that "kidnap" includes to take and carry away a person against his will by unlawful force or by fraud. Leave to appeal to S.C.C. was refused April 2, 1984.

The *mens rea* of the offence under subsec. (1)(*b*) does not require proof that the accused knew that transportation of the victim out of Canada was unlawful: *R. v. Kear* (1989), 51 C.C.C. (3d) 574 (Ont. C.A.).

The powers which the accused, who were acting for an American bail bondsman, had to arrest a fugitive did not extend outside the United States and could not give them authority to violate Canadian sovereignty. Accordingly, the accused, in seizing the fugitive in Canada, were acting unlawfully and were properly convicted of the offence under subsec. (1)(*b*): *R. v. Kear*, *supra*.

Kidnapping is a "continuing" offence, which begins with the taking of the victim and ends only when the victim is released or consents to the detention. Therefore, the accused was guilty as a party to kidnapping where he did not participate in the initial taking, but aided and abetted the victim's subsequent confinement and forced movements between locations: *R. v. Hernandez* (2011), 270 C.C.C. (3d) 546, *sub nom. R. v. Vu* (B.C.C.A.).

Kidnapping is a "continuing" offence which begins with the taking of the victim and ends only when the victim is released or consents to the detention. It is an aggravated form of unlawful confinement — aggravated by the additional element of movement, which increases the risk of harm to the victim by isolating him or her from a place where detection and rescue are more likely. Because kidnapping is a continuing offence, a person who chooses to participate in the victim's confinement — after having learned that the victim has been kidnapped — may be held responsible for the offence of kidnapping under s. 21(1): *R. v. Vu*, [2012] 2 S.C.R. 411, affg 270 C.C.C. (3d) 546 *sub nom. R. v. Hernandez* (B.C.C.A.).

Minimum sentence [subsec. (1.1)] – Credit for time spent in pre-trial custody may reduce the sentence to be imposed below the minimum prescribed by this subsection: *R. v. Mills* (1999), 133 C.C.C. (3d) 451 (B.C.C.A.).

Unlawful confinement [subsec. (2)] – The offence under this subsection does not require proof of total physical restraint of the victim: *R. v. Gratton* (1985), 18 C.C.C. (3d) 462 (Ont. C.A.), leave to appeal to S.C.C. refused [1985] 1 S.C.R. viii.

Forcible confinement deprives the individual of liberty to move from point to point while kidnapping consists of taking control of a person and carrying them away from one point to another. While kidnapping entails forcible confinement, forcible confinement can occur without kidnapping: *R. v. Tremblay* (1997), 117 C.C.C. (3d) 86 (Que. C.A.).

Constitutional considerations [subsec. (3)] – The reverse onus provision created by this subsection is of no force and effect being inconsistent with the guarantee to the presumption of innocence in s. 11(*d*) of the Charter: *R. v. Gough* (1985), 18 C.C.C. (3d) 453 (Ont. C.A.); *R. v. Grift* (1986), 28 C.C.C. (3d) 120 (Alta. Q.B.); *R. v. Pete* (1998), 131 C.C.C. (3d) 233 (B.C.C.A.).

TRAFFICKING IN PERSONS / Consent.

279.01 (1) Every person who recruits, transports, transfers, receives, holds, conceals or harbours a person, or exercises control, direction or influence over the movements of a person, for the purpose of exploiting them or facilitating their exploitation is guilty of an indictable offence and liable

(*a*) to imprisonment for life and to a minimum punishment of imprisonment for a term of five years if they kidnap, commit an aggravated assault or aggravated sexual assault against, or cause death to, the victim during the commission of the offence; or

(*b*) to imprisonment for a term of not more than 14 years and to a minimum punishment of imprisonment for a term of four years in any other case.

(2) No consent to the activity that forms the subject-matter of a charge under subsection (1) is valid. 2005, c. 43, s. 3; 2014, c. 25, s. 18; 2014, c. 25, s. 18.

Note: Section 279.01 amended by enacting subsec. (3), 2015, c. 16, s. 1 (to come into force by order of the Governor in Council):

Presumption

(3) For the purposes of subsections (1) and 279.011(1), evidence that a person who is not exploited lives with or is habitually in the company of a person who is exploited is, in the absence of evidence to the contrary, proof that the person exercises control, direction or influence over the movements of that person for the purpose of exploiting them or facilitating their exploitation.

CROSS-REFERENCES

"Victim" is defined in s. 2. Section 279.04 defines when a person exploits another person for the purpose of this section. Section 279.02 makes it an offence to receive a financial or other material benefit from the commission of the offence under this section. Under s. 279.03, it is an offence to withhold or destroy travel or identity documents for the purpose of committing the offence under this section.

The related offence of kidnapping is set out in s. 279. The offences of aggravated assault and aggravated sexual assault are found in ss. 268 and 273 respectively. The offence of trafficking of a person when the victim is under the age of 18 years is set out at s. 279.011.

Section 17 limits the availability of the statutory defence of compulsion by threats to the offence of "forcible abduction". However, forcible abduction has been held not to include kidnapping: *R. v. Robins* (1982), 66 C.C.C. (2d) 550 (Que. C.A.). This offence may be the basis for an application for an authorization to intercept private communications by reason of s. 183.

Section 486 provides that the judge may exclude members of the public from the courtroom where it is in the interests of the proper administration of justice, which includes ensuring that witnesses under the age of 18 years are safeguarded in all proceedings. If the prosecutor or the accused applies for an order excluding the public at proceedings for an offence under this section and the judge fails to make the order, the judge is required to give reasons for that decision. Under s. 486.4, where an accused is charged with the offence under this section, the judge may make an order directing that any information that could identify the complainant or a witness not be published, broadcast or transmitted in any way. The judge is to inform the complainant or any witness under the age of 18 years of the right to make any application under s. 486.4.

SYNOPSIS

This section creates the offence of trafficking in persons. It is an offence to recruit, transport or deal with persons in any other methods specified in the section for the purpose of exploiting them or facilitating their exploitation. Exploitation is defined in s. 279.04 and, broadly speaking, envisages two circumstances. One circumstance is where the victim is forced to provide services or labour because they fear for their safety or the safety of someone they know. The other form of exploitation is using deception or coercion to have an organ or tissue removed. The exploited person's consent is no defence to the charge by virtue of subsec. (2). Subsection (3) creates a presumption that subsec. (1) is met if, in the absence of evidence to the contrary, the accused, who is not exploited, lives or is habitually in the company of a person who is exploited. The penalty depends upon whether the accused commits other offences while committing this offence. If the accused kidnaps or commits an aggravated assault or aggravated sexual assault or causes death to the victim during the commission of the offence, the accused is liable to imprisonment for life. Otherwise the accused is liable to imprisonment for 14 years.

ANNOTATIONS

This provision is not unconstitutionally overbroad or void for vagueness: *R. v. D'Souza* (2016), 339 C.C.C. (3d) 494 (Ont. S.C.J.).

TRAFFICKING OF A PERSON UNDER THE AGE OF EIGHTEEN YEARS / Consent.

279.011 (1) Every person who recruits, transports, transfers, receives, holds, conceals or harbours a person under the age of eighteen years, or exercises control, direction or influence over the movements of a person under the age of eighteen years, for the purpose of exploiting them or facilitating their exploitation is guilty of an indictable offence and liable

(*a*) to imprisonment for life and to a minimum punishment of imprisonment for a term of six years if they kidnap, commit an aggravated assault or aggravated sexual assault against, or cause death to, the victim during the commission of the offence; or

(*b*) to imprisonment for a term of not more than fourteen years and to a minimum punishment of imprisonment for a term of five years, in any other case.

(2) No consent to the activity that forms the subject-matter of a charge under subsection (1) is valid. 2010, c. 3, s. 2.

CROSS-REFERENCES

"Victim" is defined in s. 2. Section 279.04 defines when a person exploits another person for the purpose of this section. Section 279.02 makes it an offence to receive a financial or other material benefit from the commission of the offence under this section. Under s. 279.03, it is an offence to withhold or destroy travel or identity documents for the purpose of committing the offence under this section.

The related offence of trafficking in persons is set out in s. 279.01, kidnapping is set out in s. 279. The presumption created by s. 279.01(3) applies to s. 279.011(1). The offences of aggravated assault and aggravated sexual assault are found in ss. 268 and 273 respectively. Also see s. 212, which creates various offences relating to procuring persons for the purpose of prostitution, including persons under the age of 18 years, whether in or out of Canada.

Section 17 limits the availability of the statutory defence of compulsion by threats to the offence of "forcible abduction". However, forcible abduction has been held not to include kidnapping: *R. v. Robins* (1982), 66 C.C.C. (2d) 550 (Que. C.A.). This offence may be the basis for an application for an authorization to intercept private communications by reason of s. 183.

Section 486 provides that the judge may exclude members of the public from the courtroom where it is in the interests of the proper administration of justice, which includes ensuring that witnesses under the age of 18 years are safeguarded in all proceedings. If the prosecutor or the accused applies for an order excluding the public at proceedings for an offence under this section and the judge fails to make the order, the judge is required to give reasons for that decision. Under s. 486.4, where an accused is charged with the offence under this section, the judge may make an order directing that any information that could identify the complainant or a witness not be published, broadcast or transmitted in any way. The judge is to inform the complainant or any witness under the age of 18 years of the right to make an application under s. 486.4.

This offence is a primary designated offence for the DNA provisions and a designated offence for the sex offender information provisions of Part XV and is a designated offence for the dangerous offender and long-term offender provisions in Part XXIV.

SYNOPSIS

This section creates the offence of trafficking in persons under the age of 18 years. It is an offence to recruit, transport or deal with persons under the age of 18 years in any other methods specified in the section for the purpose of exploiting them or facilitating their exploitation. Exploitation is defined in s. 279.04 and, broadly speaking, envisages two circumstances. One circumstance is where the victim is forced to provide services or labour because they fear for their safety or the safety of someone they know. The other form of exploitation is using deception or coercion to have an organ or tissue removed. The exploited person's consent is no defence to the charge by virtue of subsec. (2). Section 279.01(3) creates a presumption that s. 279.011(1) is met if, in the absence of evidence to the contrary, the accused, who is not exploited, lives or is habitually in the company of a person who is exploited. The penalty depends upon whether the accused commits other offences while committing this offence. If the accused kidnaps or commits an aggravated assault or aggravated sexual assault or causes death to the victim during the commission of the offence, the accused is liable to imprisonment for life and to a minimum term of imprisonment of six years. Otherwise the accused is liable to imprisonment for 14 years and to a minimum punishment of five years.

ANNOTATIONS

The fault element of this offence focuses on an accused's purpose in exercising control, direction or influence over the movements of a person in the proscribed age group. No exploitation need actually occur or be facilitated by the accused's conduct for an accused to be convicted of human trafficking: *R. v. A. (A.)* (2015), 327 C.C.C. (3d) 377 (Ont. C.A.); *R. c. Urizar* (2013), 99 C.R. (6th) 370 (C.A. Que.).

This provision is not unconstitutionally overbroad or void for vagueness: *R. v. D'Souza* (2016), 339 C.C.C. (3d) 494 (Ont. S.C.J.).

MATERIAL BENEFIT — TRAFFICKING / Material benefit — trafficking of person under 18 years.

279.02 (1) Everyone who receives a financial or other material benefit, knowing that it is obtained by or derived directly or indirectly from the commission of an offence under subsection 279.01(1), is guilty of an indictable offence and liable to imprisonment for a term of not more than 10 years.

(2) Everyone who receives a financial or other material benefit, knowing that it is obtained by or derived directly or indirectly from the commission of an offence under subsection 279.011(1), is guilty of an indictable offence and liable to imprisonment for a term of not more than 14 years and to a minimum punishment of imprisonment for a term of two years. 2005, c. 43, s. 3; 2010, c. 3, s. 3; 2014, c. 25, s. 19.

CROSS-REFERENCES

Sections 279.01 and 279.011, referred to in this section, create the offences of trafficking in persons and trafficking in persons under the age of 18 years respectively. Section 279.03 makes it an offence to withhold or destroy documents for the purpose of committing the s. 279.01 offence. Under s. 486.4, where an accused is charged with the offence under this section, the judge may make an order directing that any information that could identify the complainant or a witness not be published, broadcast or transmitted in any way. The judge is to inform the complainant or any witness under the age of 18 years of the right to make any application under s. 486.4.

SYNOPSIS

This section complements the offences in ss. 279.01 and 279.011 by making it an offence to receive a financial or other material benefit, knowing that it results from the commission of the offences under those sections.

ANNOTATIONS

This provision is not unconstitutionally overbroad or void for vagueness: *R. v. D'Souza* (2016), 339 C.C.C. (3d) 494 (Ont. S.C.J.).

WITHHOLDING OR DESTROYING DOCUMENTS — TRAFFICKING / Withholding or destroying documents — trafficking of person under 18 years.

279.03 (1) Everyone who, for the purpose of committing or facilitating an offence under subsection 279.01(1), conceals, removes, withholds or destroys any travel document that

belongs to another person or any document that establishes or purports to establish another person's identity or immigration status — whether or not the document is of Canadian origin or is authentic — is guilty of an indictable offence and liable to imprisonment for a term of not more than five years.

(2) Everyone who, for the purpose of committing or facilitating an offence under subsection 279.011(1), conceals, removes, withholds or destroys any travel document that belongs to another person or any document that establishes or purports to establish another person's identity or immigration status — whether or not the document is of Canadian origin or is authentic — is guilty of an indictable offence and liable to imprisonment for a term of not more than 10 years and to a minimum punishment of imprisonment for a term of one year. 2005, c. 43, s. 3; 2010, c. 3, s. 3; 2014, c. 25, s. 19.

CROSS-REFERENCES

Sections 279.01 and 279.011 create the offences of trafficking in persons and trafficking in persons under the age of 18 years respectively.

Section 486 provides that the judge may exclude members of the public from the courtroom where it is in the interests of the proper administration of justice, which includes ensuring that witnesses under the age of 18 years are safeguarded in all proceedings. If the prosecutor or the accused applies for an order excluding the public at proceedings for an offence under this section and the judge fails to make the order, the judge is required to give reasons for that decision. Under s. 486.4, the judge may make an order protecting the identity of the complainant or witness in proceedings for an offence under this section.

SYNOPSIS

This section complements the trafficking in persons offences in ss. 279.01 and 279.011 by making it an offence to conceal or otherwise deal with travel or identity documents of another person for the purpose of committing those offences. The offence is committed whether or not the documents are of Canadian origin or authentic.

EXPLOITATION / Factors / Organ or tissue removal.

279.04 (1) For the purposes of sections 279.01 to 279.03, a person exploits another person if they cause them to provide, or offer to provide, labour or a service by engaging in conduct that, in all the circumstances, could reasonably be expected to cause the other person to believe that their safety or the safety of a person known to them would be threatened if they failed to provide, or offer to provide, the labour or service.

(2) In determining whether an accused exploits another person under subsection (1), the Court may consider, among other factors, whether the accused

(*a*) used or threatened to use force or another form of coercion;
(*b*) used deception; or
(*c*) abused a position of trust, power or authority.

(3) For the purposes of sections 279.01 to 279.03, a person exploits another person if they cause them, by means of deception or the use or threat of force or of any other form of coercion, to have an organ or tissue removed. 2005, c. 43, s. 3; 2012, c. 15, s. 2.

CROSS-REFERENCES

Section 279.01 creates the offence of trafficking in persons. Section 279.04 defines when a person exploits another person for the purpose of this section. Section 279.02 makes it an offence to receive a financial or other material benefit from the commission of the offence under this section. Section 279.03 makes it an offence to withhold or destroy documents for the purpose of committing the s. 279.01 offence. Under s. 486.4, where an accused is charged with the offence under this section, the judge may make an order directing that any information that could identify the complainant or a witness not be published, broadcast or transmitted in any way. The judge is to inform the complainant or any witness under the age of 18 years of the right to make any application under s. 486.4.

SYNOPSIS

This section defines when a person exploits another for the purposes of the offences in ss. 279.01 to 279.03. The section is of greatest importance for applying s. 279.01, which makes it an offence to deal with persons in the ways set out in the section for the purpose of exploiting them or facilitating their exploitation. Exploitation is made out where, in effect, the accused causes the victim to provide labour or services by making the victim fear for their safety (or the safety of a person known to them). Subsection (2) provides factors to consider in determining whether exploitation has been proved. Subsection (3) specifies that exploitation has occurred where organ or tissue removal is brought about by threats or deception.

ANNOTATIONS

One person exploits another if they cause that other person to provide labour by doing something that, in all the circumstances, could reasonably be expected to cause the other person to believe that their safety or the safety of a person known to them would be threatened if they failed to provide the labour. The expectation of the specific belief engendered by the accused's conduct must be reasonable, thus introducing an objective element. The person's safety need not actually be threatened. In addition, the term "safety" is not limited to the state of being protected from physical harm, but also extends to psychological harm: *R. v. A. (A.)* (2015), 327 C.C.C. (3d) 377 (Ont. C.A.).

Note: Section 279.05 enacted, to come after s. 279.04, 2015, c. 16, s. 3 (to come into force by order of the Governor in Council):

Sentences to be served consecutively

279.05 A sentence imposed on a person for an offence under sections 279.01 to 279.03 shall be served consecutively to any other punishment imposed on the person for an offence arising out of the same event or series of events and to any other sentence to which the person is subject at the time the sentence is imposed on the person for an offence under any of those sections.

HOSTAGE TAKING / Punishment / Subsequent offences / Sequence of convictions only.

279.1 (1) Everyone takes a person hostage who — with intent to induce any person, other than the hostage, or any group of persons or any state or international or intergovernmental organization to commit or cause to be committed any act or omission as a condition, whether express or implied, of the release of the hostage —

(*a*) confines, imprisons, forcibly seizes or detains that person; and

(*b*) in any manner utters, conveys or causes any person to receive a threat that the death of, or bodily harm to, the hostage will be caused or that the confinement, imprisonment or detention of the hostage will be continued.

(2) Every person who takes a person hostage is guilty of an indictable offence and liable

(*a*) if a restricted firearm or prohibited firearm is used in the commission of the offence or if any firearm is used in the commission of the offence and the offence is committed for the benefit of, at the direction of, or in association with, a criminal organization, to imprisonment for life and to a minimum punishment of imprisonment for a term of

(i) in the case of a first offence, five years, and

(ii) in the case of a second or subsequent offence, seven years;

(*a*.1) in any other case where a firearm is used in the commission of the offence, to imprisonment for life and to a minimum punishment of imprisonment for a term of four years; and

(*b*) in any other case, to imprisonment for life.

(2.1) In determining, for the purpose of paragraph (2)(*a*), whether a convicted person has committed a second or subsequent offence, if the person was earlier convicted of any of the following offences, that offence is to be considered as an earlier offence:

(*a*) an offence under this section;

(*b*) an offence under subsection 85(1) or (2) or section 244 or 244.2; or

(*c*) an offence under section 220, 236, 239, 272 or 273, subsection 279(1) or section 344 or 346 if a firearm was used in the commission of the offence.

However, an earlier offence shall not be taken into account if 10 years have elapsed between the day on which the person was convicted of the earlier offence and the day on which the person was convicted of the offence for which sentence is being imposed, not taking into account any time in custody.

(2.2) For the purposes of subsection (2.1), the only question to be considered is the sequence of convictions and no consideration shall be given to the sequence of commission of offences or whether any offence occurred before or after any conviction. R.S.C. 1985, c. 27 (1st Supp.), s. 40(1); 1995, c. 39, s. 148; 2008, c. 6, s. 31; 2009, c. 22, s. 13; 2018, c. 29, s. 27.

(3) [*Repealed*, 2018, c. 29, s. 27.]

CROSS-REFERENCES

Section 17 limits the availability of the statutory defence of compulsion by threats to the offence of hostage taking. Firearm is defined in s. 2. Pursuant to s. 2.1, "restricted firearm" and "prohibited firearm" are defined in s. 84.

This offence may be the basis for an application for an authorization to intercept private communications by reason of s. 183 and for warrant to conduct video surveillance by reason of s. 487.01(5). This offence may be the basis for a conviction for constructive murder under s. 230 and first degree murder under s. 231(5). Section 7(3) and (3.1) enacts special jurisdictional rules where this offence is committed outside Canada. A threat to commit an offence under this section against an internationally protected person (defined in s. 2) is an offence under s. 424.

The accused may elect his mode of trial pursuant to s. 536(2). Release pending trial is determined by s. 515. A person found guilty of the offence in this section will be liable to the mandatory prohibition order in s. 109 for possession of certain weapons, ammunition and explosives. A person found guilty of this offence may be subject to a dangerous offender application under Part XXIV.

Uttering threats is an offence under s. 264.1. The related offences of kidnapping and unlawful confinement are found in s. 279.

SYNOPSIS

This section describes the offence of hostage-taking. Any one commits this offence when he unlawfully confines a person and threatens that the safety of that person will be compromised or that his detention will continue if another person or group of persons, including states or international governments, does not comply with the offender's demands. Anyone convicted of an offence under this section is guilty of an indictable offence and liable to a maximum term of life imprisonment and to a minimum punishment of four years if a firearm is used in the commission of the offence. The *defence* of non-resistance applies in the same circumstances as are set out in s. 279(3).

ABDUCTION OF PERSON UNDER SIXTEEN / Definition of "guardian".

280. (1) Every one who, without lawful authority, takes or causes to be taken an unmarried person under the age of sixteen years out of the possession of and against the will of the parent or guardian of that person or of any other person who has the lawful care or charge of that person is guilty of an indictable offence and liable to imprisonment for a term not exceeding five years.

(2) In this section and sections 281 to 283, "guardian" includes any person who has in law or in fact the custody or control of another person. R.S., c. C-34, s. 249; 1980-81-82-83, c. 125, s. 20.

CROSS-REFERENCES

Section 17 limits the availability of the statutory defence of compulsion by threats.

Section 7(3) enacts special jurisdictional rules for commission of this offence outside Canada when the offence is in relation to an internationally protected person. This offence may be the basis for an application to intercept private communications by reason of s. 183 and for a warrant to conduct video surveillance by reason of s. 487.01(5).

The accused may elect his mode of trial pursuant to s. 536(2). Release pending trial is determined by s. 515, although the accused is eligible for release by the officer in charge under s. 498.

The accused's spouse is a competent and compellable witness at the instance of the Crown by virtue of s. 4(2). Age is determined by s. 30 of the *Interpretation Act*, R.S.C. 1985, c. I-21. Section 658 provides a means of proving the age of a child.

Related offences: s. 279, kidnapping and unlawful confinement; s. 279.1, hostage taking; s. 281, abduction of child under 14 years of age; s. 282, abduction of child under 14 years of age in contravention of custody order; s. 283, abduction of child under 14 years of age where no custody order with intent to deprive parent, etc., of possession of child. Section 171.1 makes it an offence to transmit, make available, distribute or sell sexually explicit material to a person who is, or who the accused believes is under the age of 16 years for purpose of facilitating the commission of the offence created by this section. Section 172.1 makes it an offence to communicate by means of telecommunication with a person who is or who the accused believes is under the age of 16 years for the purpose of facilitating the commission of the offence under this section. Section 172.2 makes it an offence to agree with a person or make an arrangement with a person by means of telecommunication to commit an offence under this section with a person who is or who the accused believes is under the age of 16 years.

Defences: s. 285, where court satisfied that taking, etc., was necessary to protect young person from imminent harm; s. 286, *no* defence that young person consented to or suggested any conduct of the accused. As to mistake defence generally, see notes under ss. 19 and 150.1.

SYNOPSIS

This section makes it an offence for anyone to cause to be taken, without lawful authority, any unmarried person under the age of 16 from the possession of the parent, the guardian, or any other person who has the lawful care or charge of that person. This taking must occur without the consent of the parent, guardian or other responsible person. A person convicted under this section is guilty of an indictable offence and liable to a maximum term of imprisonment of five years.

ANNOTATIONS

The phrase "takes or causes to be taken" requires some participation by the accused in the removal of the girl either through physical involvement or inducement or enticement. The mere fact that the girl is aware she can find refuge with the accused does not constitute any inducement on his part: *R. v. Johnson* (1977), 37 C.C.C. (2d) 352 (Sask. Dist. Ct.).

Proof of the taking away does not require any element of persuasion and even if the girls involved took a very active, if not leading part, in what occurred a conviction will follow if it is proved that the taking was against the will of the parent: *R. v. Langevin and LaPensee* (1962), 133 C.C.C. 257, 38 C.R. 421 (Ont. C.A.). In this case the dicta by Lebel J.A., in *R. v. Bebee* (1958), 120 C.C.C. 310 (Ont. C.A.), that persuasion by the accused was a necessary element of the offence, was disapproved.

Possession includes physical possession as well as the right of a parent to exercise his or her right of control over the child. The Crown need not demonstrate some element of coercion or control over the child. Furthermore, consent is no defence pursuant to s. 286 of the *Criminal Code* such that a runaway child cannot extinguish the right of a parent or guardian to exercise parental control: *R. v. Vokey* (2005), 202 C.C.C. (3d) 236 (B.C.C.A.). See also *R. v. Flick* (2005), 202 C.C.C. (3d) 244, 34 C.R. (6th) 174 (B.C.C.A.).

ABDUCTION OF PERSON UNDER FOURTEEN.

281. Every one who, not being the parent, guardian or person having the lawful care or charge of a person under the age of fourteen years, unlawfully takes, entices away, conceals, detains, receives or harbours that person with intent to deprive a parent or guardian, or any other person who has the lawful care or charge of that person, of the possession of that person is guilty of an indictable offence and liable to imprisonment for a term not exceeding ten years. R.S., c. C-34, s. 250; 1980-81-82-83, c. 125, s. 20.

CROSS-REFERENCES

The term "guardian" is defined in s. 280(2).

Section 17 limits the availability of the statutory defence of compulsion by threats. Section 7(3) enacts special jurisdictional rules for commission of this offence outside Canada when the offence is in relation to an internationally protected person. This offence may be the basis for a warrant to intercept private communications by reason of s. 183 and for a warrant to conduct video surveillance by reason of s. 487.01(5).

The accused may elect his mode of trial pursuant to s. 536(2). Release pending trial is determined by s. 515.

The accused's spouse is a competent and compellable witness at the instance of the Crown by virtue of s. 4(2). Age is determined by s. 30 of the *Interpretation Act*, R.S.C. 1985, c. I-21. Section 658 provides a means of proving the age of a child.

Related offences: s. 279, kidnapping and unlawful confinement; s. 279.1, hostage taking; s. 280, abduction of person under 16 years of age against will of parent; s. 282, abduction of child under 14 years of age in contravention of custody order; s. 283, abduction of child under 14 years of age where no custody order with intent to deprive parent, etc., of possession of child.

Defences: s. 284, where the accused establishes that the taking away, etc., was with the consent of the parent, guardian or other person having the lawful possession, care or charge of the young person; s. 285, where court satisfied that taking, etc., was necessary to protect young person from imminent harm; s. 286 *no* defence that young person consented to or suggested any conduct of the accused. As to mistake defence generally, see notes under ss. 19 and 150.1.

Where the accused is found guilty of this offence in respect of a person who is under 14 years of age, the court has the discretion to impose an order of prohibition under s. 161 prohibiting the accused from attending certain public areas and facilities or taking certain employment which will bring him into contact with persons under 14 years of age or using a computer system for the purpose of communicating with a person under the age of 14 years.

SYNOPSIS

This section describes the offence of abduction of a person under the age of 14 years. Anyone other than the parent, guardian or person lawfully in charge of a person under 14, who takes, entices away, conceals, detains, receives or harbours such a person, with the intention of depriving a parent, guardian or person in charge of possession of the person under 14, commits this offence. The offence is indictable, and punishable by imprisonment not exceeding 10 years.

ANNOTATIONS

It was held under the predecessor to this section that the word "detains" was to be given its dictionary meaning of "withhold". Thus the gravamen of the offence was not merely the keeping or confinement of the child but the intentional withholding of the child from the accused's wife, who had lawful custody of the child, which had the effect of depriving her of her custodial rights. Thus, in Ontario, where the child had lived with its mother, the courts had jurisdiction to try an offence of detaining, although the child was taken and held by the accused in another province: *R. v. Bigelow* (1982), 69 C.C.C. (2d) 204, 37 O.R. (2d) 304 (C.A.), leave to appeal to S.C.C. refused C.C.C. *loc. cit.*

The word "unlawfully" in the English version of this section is surplusage and does not require proof of commission of some additional unlawful act in the taking of the child. The term "possession" is not limited to circumstances in which the parent or guardian is actually in physical control of the child at the time of the taking. The concept of deprivation of possession relates to the ability of a parent to exercise his right of control over the child. Although proof of the intent required by this section can be met by the intentional and purposeful deprivation of the parent's control over the child, the *mens rea* of the offence can also be proven by the mere fact of the deprivation of possession of the child through a taking as long as the trier of fact can infer that the accused knew or foresaw that his actions would be certain or substantially certain to result in the parents being deprived of the ability to exercise control over the child: *R. v. Chartrand*, [1994] 2 S.C.R. 864, 91 C.C.C. (3d) 396, 31 C.R. (4th) 1.

ABDUCTION IN CONTRAVENTION OF CUSTODY ORDER / Where no belief in validity of custody order.

282. (1) Every one who, being the parent, guardian or person having the lawful care or charge of a person under the age of fourteen years, takes, entices away, conceals, detains, receives or harbours that person, in contravention of the custody provisions of a custody order in relation to that person made by a court anywhere in Canada, with intent to deprive a parent or guardian, or any other person who has the lawful care or charge of that person, of the possession of that person is guilty of

(*a*) an indictable offence and liable to imprisonment for a term not exceeding ten years; or

(*b*) an offence punishable on summary conviction.

(2) Where a count charges an offence under subsection (1) and the offence is not proven only because the accused did not believe that there was a valid custody order but the evidence does prove an offence under section 283, the accused may be convicted of an offence under section 283. 1980-81-82-83, c. 125, s. 20; 1993, c. 45, s. 4.

CROSS-REFERENCES

The term "guardian" is defined in s. 280(2).

Section 17 limits the availability of the statutory defence of compulsion by threats. Section 7(3) enacts special jurisdictional rules for commission of this offence outside Canada when the offence is in relation to an internationally protected person. This offence may be the basis for an authorization to intercept private communications by reason of s. 183 and for a warrant to conduct video surveillance by reason of s. 487.01(5).

The accused's spouse is a competent and compellable witness at the instance of the Crown by virtue of s. 4(2). Age is determined by s. 30 of the *Interpretation Act*, R.S.C. 1985, c. I-21. Section 658 provides a means of proving the age of a child.

Where the prosecution elects to proceed by indictment on this offence then the accused may elect his mode of trial pursuant to s. 536(2). Where the prosecution elects to proceed by way of summary conviction then the trial of this offence is conducted by a summary conviction court pursuant to Part XXVII. The punishment for the offence is then as set out in s. 787 and the limitation period is set out in s. 786(2). In either case, release pending trial is determined by s. 515, although the accused is eligible for release by a peace officer under s. 496, 497 or by the officer in charge under s. 498.

Related offences: s. 279, kidnapping and unlawful confinement; s. 279.1, hostage taking; s. 280, abduction of person under 16 years of age against will of parent; s. 281, abduction of child under 14 years of age by person other than parent, guardian or person having lawful care of child; s. 283, abduction of child under 14 years of age where no custody order with intent to deprive parent, etc., of possession of child.

Defences: s. 284, where the accused establishes that the taking away, etc., was with the consent of the parent, guardian or other person having the lawful possession, care or charge of the young person; s. 285, where court satisfied that taking, etc., was necessary to protect young person from imminent harm; s. 286, *no* defence that young person consented to or suggested any conduct of the accused. As to mistake defence generally, see notes under ss. 19 and 150.1.

SYNOPSIS

Subsection (1) describes the offence of abduction of a person under the age of 14 years in contravention of a custody order. Anyone who is the parent, guardian or person lawfully in charge of a person under 14 who takes, entices away, conceals, detains, receives or harbours that person in violation of a custody order of a Canadian court, with the intention of depriving another parent, guardian or person in charge of possession of the person under 14, commits this offence. The offence may be prosecuted by indictment or summarily, and is punishable on indictment by imprisonment not exceeding 10 years.

Where the accused would otherwise be found not guilty only because he or she did not believe there was a valid custody order in existence then by virtue of subsec. (2) the accused may be convicted of the offence under s. 283, if that offence is made out.

ANNOTATIONS

The words "lawful care or charge" do not modify the word "parent" and the parent may therefore be convicted of the offence under this section although at the time of the taking he did not have lawful care or charge of the child: *R. v. Van Herk* (1984), 12 C.C.C. (3d) 359, 40 C.R. (3d) 264 (Alta. C.A.).

The *mens rea* of the offence under this section is proof that the accused intended to deprive the person with lawful care of the child, of the possession of the child, and with an intent to do so in contravention of a valid and subsisting court order. A mistaken belief as to the legal effect of a custody order is a defence to this charge. Such a mistake although a mistake of law is an error as to the legal effect of civil law and therefore a defence. However, the fact that the accused knew the terms of the custody order and acted in contravention of its terms would, in most cases, be sufficient to persuade the trier of fact that she intended to do so. *Quaere*, whether the mistaken belief as to the legal effect of the order must be based on reasonable grounds: *R. v. Ilczyszyn* (1988), 45 C.C.C. (3d) 91 (Ont. C.A.).

In the subsequent case of *R. v. Hammerbeck* (1991), 68 C.C.C. (3d) 161 (B.C.C.A.), that court held that an honest belief by the accused that he was not bound by the terms of the custody order was a defence and that the mistake need not be based on reasonable grounds.

The term "detain" in this section means "withhold" and thus the mere fact that a parent keeps a child longer than the prescribed access period would not necessarily constitute a withholding and thus a detention of the child. Further, to prove the requisite intent for the offence, there must be proof that the act was done for the express purpose of depriving the other parent of possession of the child. Mere recklessness would not suffice. There must be an intention to somehow put the child beyond the reach of the other parent's custody or control. An intention not to assist or co-operate in the regaining of physical control of the child by the other parent cannot be equated with the intention to deprive that parent of possession of the child: *R. v. McDougall* (1990), 62 C.C.C. (3d) 174, 3 C.R. (4th) 112 (Ont. C.A.).

A clause in a custody order, providing that neither parent may remove any of the children without consent of the other party or a court order, was a "custody provision" of the custody order within the meaning of this section. Further, although, by virtue of the order, the accused's wife did not have a right to custody of the child, the right of access given to her by the court order involved transfer of the lawful care or charge of the child to the mother for the duration of the access. While the order was not one contemplating joint custody, what is granted by such an "access" order is more than merely a right to visit while the child is in the possession, care or charge of the other parent. It involves transfer of the child from the possession, care or charge of the custodial parent, here the accused, to that of the non-custodial parent. If prevented from the exercise of the right to lawful care or charge of the child during these access periods, then the person entitled to such access is denied possession of the child for that period within the meaning of this section: *R. v. Petropoulos* (1990), 59 C.C.C. (3d) 393, 29 R.F.L. (3d) 289 (B.C.C.A.).

Where the order made under the *Divorce Act*, R.S.C. 1985, c. 3 (2nd Supp.), while providing for rights of access for the accused spouse, made no provision for custody of the child then the Territorial legislation making the spouses joint guardians applied and the accused could not be convicted of the offence under this section. While the order was a custody order, it did not contain "custody provisions": *R. v. Gustaw* (1991), 65 C.C.C. (3d) 296 (N.W.T.S.C.).

Every custody order is subject to variation and particularly where the order is only an interim custody order, police officers before attempting to arrest a parent for abduction in contravention of such an order should take reasonable steps and make such inquiries as are appropriate and possible to ensure that the order accurately reflects the true legal relationship between the parties: *R. v. McCoy* (1984), 17 C.C.C. (3d) 114 (Ont. Prov. Ct.).

Breach of an access order is insufficient to establish the requisite intent. An essential element of the offence was whether the accused had the intent to deprive the mother of possession of the child. In this case, the accused's uncontradicted evidence was that he kept the child in the United States only temporarily because he had been requested to keep the child available pending a child protective services investigation: *R. v. Muirhead* (2008), 230 C.C.C. (3d) 236 (P.E.I.C.A.).

ABDUCTION / Consent required.

283. (1) Every one who, being the parent, guardian or person having the lawful care or charge of a person under the age of fourteen years, takes, entices away, conceals, detains, receives or harbours that person, whether or not there is a custody order in relation to that person made by a court anywhere in Canada, with intent to deprive a parent or guardian, or any other person who has the lawful care or charge of that person, of the possession of that person, is guilty of

(*a*) an indictable offence and is liable to imprisonment for a term not exceeding ten years; or

(*b*) an offence punishable on summary conviction.

(2) No proceedings may be commenced under subsection (1) without the consent of the Attorney General or counsel instructed by him for that purpose. 1980-81-82-83, c. 125, s. 20; 1993, c. 45, s. 5.

CROSS-REFERENCES

The term "guardian" is defined in s. 280(2). "Attorney General" is defined in s. 2. Section 583(*h*) provides that a count in an indictment is not insufficient by reason only that it does not state that the required consent has been obtained (as to notes concerning sufficiency of consent, see s. 583).

Section 17 limits the availability of the statutory defence of compulsion by threats. Section 7(3) enacts special jurisdictional rules for commission of this offence outside Canada when the offence is in relation to an internationally protected person. This offence may be the basis of an application for an authorization to intercept private communications by reason of s. 183 and for a warrant to conduct video surveillance by reason of s. 487.01(5).

The accused's spouse is a competent and compellable witness at the instance of the Crown by virtue of s. 4(2). Age is determined by s. 30 of the *Interpretation Act*, R.S.C. 1985, c. I-21. Section 658 provides a means of proving the age of a child.

Where the prosecution elects to proceed by indictment on this offence then the accused may elect his mode of trial pursuant to s. 536(2). Where the prosecution elects to proceed by way of summary conviction then the trial of this offence is conducted by a summary conviction court pursuant to Part XXVII. The punishment for the offence is then as set out in s. 787 and the limitation period is set out in s. 786(2). In either case, release pending trial is determined by s. 515, although the accused is eligible for release by a peace officer under s. 496, 497 or by the officer in charge under s. 498.

Related offences: s. 279, kidnapping and unlawful confinement; s. 279.1, hostage taking; s. 280, abduction of person under 16 years of age against will of parent; s. 281, abduction of child under 14 years of age by person other than parent, guardian or person having lawful care of child; s. 282, abduction of child under 14 years of age in contravention of custody order with intent to deprive parent, etc., of possession of child.

Defences: s. 284, where the accused establishes that the taking away, etc., was with the consent of the parent, guardian or other person having the lawful possession, care or charge of the young person; s. 285, where court satisfied that taking, etc., was necessary to protect young person from imminent harm; s. 286, *no* defence that young person consented to or suggested any conduct of the accused. As to mistake defence generally, see notes under ss. 19 and 150.1.

SYNOPSIS

This section describes the offence of abduction by a parent, guardian or person lawfully in charge of a person under 14 years of age whether or not there is a custody order of a Canadian court in existence. In such circumstances, the offence is committed if the person under 14 is taken, enticed away, concealed, detained, received or harboured with the intention of depriving another parent, guardian or person lawfully in charge, of possession of the person under 14. The offence may be prosecuted by indictment or summarily, but only with the consent of an Attorney General, or counsel instructed by him. The offence is punishable, on indictment, by imprisonment not exceeding 10 years.

ANNOTATIONS

"Taking" occurs where the accused causes the child to come or go with him and in the process, excludes the authority of another person who has lawful care or charge of the child. Nothing in this provision requires the deprived parent, guardian or other person to actually have had possession of the child at the moment of the offence. To "deprive" a person of something means, among other things, to keep that person from that which he or she would otherwise have. "Possession" is not limited to circumstances in which the deprived parent is actually in physical control of the child at the time of the taking but extends to the ability to exercise control over the child. The intent to deprive of possession will exist whenever the taker knows or foresees that his or her actions would be certain or substantially certain to result in the parent being deprived of the ability to exercise control over the child. The *actus reus* of the offence requires nothing more than preventing a parent, guardian or other person having lawful care of charge of the child from exercising control over that child. Status as the custodial parent or the other parent's status as an access parent does not constitute a defence to this provision: *R. v. Dawson*, [1996] 3 S.C.R. 783, 111 C.C.C. (3d) 1.

While provincial legislation may define "parent" it is not clear whether such definition could apply or whether the common law definition applies. At common law "parent" is *prima facie* confined to the lawful mother and father and exceptionally includes the father of a child born out of wedlock: *R. v. Levesque* (1984), 15 C.C.C. (3d) 413 (N.S. Co. Ct.).

DEFENCE.

284. No one shall be found guilty of an offence under sections 281 to 283 if he establishes that the taking, enticing away, concealing, detaining, receiving or harbouring of any young person was done with the consent of the parent, guardian or other person having the lawful possession, care or charge of that young person. 1980-81-82-83, c. 125, s. 20.

CROSS-REFERENCES

The term "guardian" is defined in s. 280(2). The term "young person" is not defined but presumably was intended to refer to the child under the age of fourteen years referred to in ss. 281 to 283.

SYNOPSIS

This section provides a defence of consent to the abduction offences found in ss. 281 to 283. The consent must be given by the parent, guardian or other person in charge of a person under 14 who has lawful possession, care, or charge of that person. Consent of a young person provides no defence, by virtue of s. 286.

The consent must come from the person whom the accused intended to deprive of possesion of the child not from the accused himself. Therefore, the accused who was the parent who had lawful possession of the child at the time of the alleged offence could not rely on his own consent as a defence to the offence under s. 283: *R. v. Dawson*, [1996] 3 S.C.R. 783, 111 C.C.C. (3d) 1.

DEFENCE.

285. No one shall be found guilty of an offence under sections 280 to 283 if the court is satisfied that the taking, enticing away, concealing, detaining, receiving or harbouring of any young person was necessary to protect the young person from danger of imminent harm or if the person charged with the offence was escaping from danger of imminent harm. 1980-81-82-83, c. 125, s. 20; 1993, c. 45, s. 6.

CROSS-REFERENCES

The term "young person" is not defined but presumably was intended to refer to the child under the age of fourteen years or sixteen years, as the case may be, referred to in ss. 280 to 283.

SYNOPSIS

This section provides a defence of necessity to the abduction offences found in ss. 280 to 283. For the defence to succeed, the court must be satisfied that the taking or other conduct in relation to a young person prohibited by ss. 280 to 283 was necessary to protect the young person from danger of imminent harm or if the accused was escaping from danger or imminent harm.

ANNOTATIONS

In considering whether there is an air of reality to the defence of necessity, there must be some evidence that: (1) from the accused's point of view, using the modified objective standard, there was a danger of imminent harm to the children; (2) from the accused's point of view, using the modified objective standard, there were no reasonable legal alternatives to taking the children in breach of the custody order, and (3) viewed objectively, the harm to the children by taking them in contravention of the custody order was proportional to the potential harm to the children that was being avoided. The accused's honest belief that the trial judge in a family law matter would deprive her of all access to her children thereby causing them harm did not constitute imminent harm. There was no emergent situation and the accused had other legal avenues in which to address the issue: *R. v. VandenElsen* (2003), 177 C.C.C. (3d) 332, 230 D.L.R. (4th) 640, 175 O.A.C. 71 (C.A.).

An honest but mistaken belief that the child is in danger of imminent harm is a defence, provided that the taking of the child was necessary, in an objective sense, based on the circumstances as the accused honestly believed them to be. In considering the defence, the jury should be instructed to consider other remedial steps which might have been taken and to consider the reasonableness of the accused's mistaken belief: *R. v. Adams* (1993), 79 C.C.C. (3d) 193, 19 C.R. (4th) 277, 12 O.R. (3d) 248 (C.A.).

Where the accused invokes this provision on the basis that they were "escaping from the danger of imminent harm", there must be a connection between the taking of the child and the non-custodial parent's escape from the danger of imminent harm. In this case, even if the accused thought that he was in danger, he did not have to take his child in order to escape the harm: *R. v. Mendez* (1997), 113 C.C.C. (3d) 304, 320 O.R. (3d) 67 (C.A.), leave to appeal to S.C.C. refused 121 C.C.C. (3d) vi.

NO DEFENCE.

286. In proceedings in respect of an offence under sections 280 to 283, it is not a defence to any charge that a young person consented to or suggested any conduct of the accused. 1980-81-82-83, c. 125, s. 20.

CROSS-REFERENCES

The term "young person" is not defined but presumably was intended to refer to the child under the age of fourteen years or sixteen years, as the case may be, referred to in ss. 280 to 283.

SYNOPSIS

This section clarifies the fact that although a defence of consent by a person in charge of a young person exists with respect to ss. 281 to 283 (see s. 284), the consent or suggestion of *a young person* cannot provide a defence to abduction under any of ss. 280 to 283. They might, however, be relevant to establish necessity under s. 285.

Commodification of Sexual Activity 2014, c. 25, s. 20.

OBTAINING SEXUAL SERVICES FOR CONSIDERATION / Obtaining sexual services for consideration from person under 18 years / Subsequent offences / Sequence of convictions only / Definitions of "place" and "public place"

286.1 (1) Everyone who, in any place, obtains for consideration, or communicates with anyone for the purpose of obtaining for consideration, the sexual services of a person is guilty of

(*a*) an indictable offence and liable to imprisonment for a term of not more than five years and a minimum punishment of,

(i) in the case where the offence is committed in a public place, or in any place open to public view, that is or is next to a park or the grounds of a school or religious institution or that is or is next to any other place where persons under the age of 18 can reasonably be expected to be present,

(A) for a first offence, a fine of $2,000, and

(B) for each subsequent offence, a fine of $4,000, or

(ii) in any other case,

(A) for a first offence, a fine of $1,000, and

(B) for each subsequent offence, a fine of $2,000; or

(*b*) an offence punishable on summary conviction and liable to imprisonment for a term of not more than 18 months and a minimum punishment of,

(i) in the case referred to in subparagraph (*a*)(i),

(A) for a first offence, a fine of $1,000, and

(B) for each subsequent offence, a fine of $2,000, or

(ii) in any other case,

(A) for a first offence, a fine of $500, and

(B) for each subsequent offence, a fine of $1,000.

(2) Everyone who, in any place, obtains for consideration, or communicates with anyone for the purpose of obtaining for consideration, the sexual services of a person under the age of 18 years is guilty of an indictable offence and liable to imprisonment for a term of not more than 10 years and to a minimum punishment of imprisonment for a term of

(*a*) for a first offence, six months; and

(*b*) for each subsequent offence, one year.

(3) In determining, for the purpose of subsection (2), whether a convicted person has committed a subsequent offence, if the person was earlier convicted of any of the following offences, that offence is to be considered as an earlier offence:

(*a*) an offence under that subsection; or

(*b*) an offence under subsection 212(4) of this Act, as it read from time to time before the day on which this subsection comes into force.

(4) In determining, for the purposes of this section, whether a convicted person has committed a subsequent offence, the only question to be considered is the sequence of convictions and no consideration shall be given to the sequence of commission of offences, whether any offence occurred before or after any conviction or whether offences were prosecuted by indictment or by way of summary conviction proceedings.

(5) For the purposes of this section, "place" and "public place" have the same meaning as in subsection 197(1). 2014, c. 25, s. 20.

CROSS-REFERENCES

"Place" and "public place" are defined in s. 197.

Other offences relating to sexual services are found in ss. 213, 286.2, 286.3 and 286.4.

Certain immunities to a charge on this provision are provided by s. 286.5.

Where the prosecution elects to proceed by indictment on this offence, then the accused may elect his mode of trial pursuant to s. 536(2). Where the prosecution elects to proceed by way of summary conviction, then the trial of this offence is conducted by a summary conviction court pursuant to Part XXVII. The punishment for the offence is then set out in s. 787 and the limitation period is set out in s. 786(2). In either case, release pending trial is determined by s. 515, although the accused is eligible for release by a peace officer under ss. 496 or 497, or by the officer in charge under s. 498.

This offence may be the basis for an application for an authorization to intercept private communications by reason of s. 183, or a video surveillance warrant under s. 487.01(5).

As to production of records containing personal information of the complainant or a witness, see ss. 278.1 to 278.9.

Section 486(1) and (2) provide that the judge may make an order excluding all or any members of the public where such order is in the interest of public morals, the maintenance of order or the proper administration of justice, or is necessary to prevent injury to international relations or national defence or national security. The proper administration of justice includes safeguarding the interests of witnesses under the age of 18 years.

Section 486.1 sets out the circumstances in which the judge shall or may order a support person to be present and close to a witness while the witness testifies. Where the witness is under the age of 18 years or had a mental or physical disability, the order is to be made upon request unless the judge is of the opinion that the order would interfere with the proper administration of justice. In the case of other witnesses, the order is to be made if necessary to obtain a full and candid account from the witness of the matters complained of. The application for this order may be made during the proceedings or before they begin to the judge who is to preside at the proceedings.

Similarly, s. 486.2 sets out the circumstances in which the judge shall or may order a witness to testify outside the courtroom or behind a screen or other device that would not allow the witness to see the accused. Where the witness is under the age of 18 years or may have difficulty communicating the evidence by reason of mental or physical disability, the judge shall make the order unless the judge is of the opinion that the order would interfere with the proper administration of justice. In all other cases, the order may be made if the judge is of the opinion that the order is necessary to obtain a full and candid account from the witness of the acts complained of.

Section 486.3 provides that, on application by the prosecutor or a witness under the age of 18 years, the accused shall not personally cross-examine the witness unless the judge is of the opinion that the proper administration of justice requires the accused to personally conduct the cross-examination. In other cases, the judge may make an order that the accused not personally cross-examine the witness if the judge is of the opinion that the order is necessary to obtain a full and candid account from the witness of the acts complained of. The judge will appoint counsel to conduct the cross-examination.

Under s. 486.4, the judge may make an order directing that the identity of a witness not be disclosed in any publication, broadcast or transmitted in any way. The order is mandatory where the complainant or a witness is under the age of 18 years or the prosecutor applies for the order. Section 486.5 also gives the judge a discretion respecting non-publication orders.

Section 718.01 provides that, in imposing a sentence for an offence involving the abuse of a person under the age of 18 years, the court shall give primary consideration to the objectives of denunciation and deterrence. Further, under s. 718.2, evidence that the offender, in committing the offence, abused a person under the age of 18 years is an aggravating circumstance.

The offence in subsec. (1) is a secondary designated offence for the purpose of making a forensic DNA data bank order under s. 487.051. The offence in subsec. (2) is a primary designated offence.

Pursuant to s. 490.012, where an offender is convicted of the offence under subsec. (2), the judge shall make an order requiring the offender to comply with the *Sex Offender Information Registration Act*, S.C. 2004, c. 10. Where an offender is convicted under subsec. (1), such an order shall be made on application of the prosecutor if certain circumstances are present.

If a person is found guilty of the offence in subsec. (2) in respect of a person who is under 16 years of age, the court may impose an order of prohibition under s. 161 prohibiting the accused from attending certain public areas and facilities or taking certain employment that will bring him into contact with persons under the age of 16 years.

Section 171.1 makes it an offence to transmit, make available, distribute or sell sexually explicit material to a person who is, or who the accused believes is under the age of 18 years for the purpose of facilitating the commission of an offence under subsec. (2).

Section 172.2 makes it an offence to agree with a person or make an arrangement with a person by means of telecommunication to commit an offence under subsec. (2) with a person who is or who the accused believes is under the age of 18 years.

SYNOPSIS

Sections 286.1 to 286.5 represent Parliament's response to the Supreme Court's decision in *Canada (Attorney General) v. Bedford*, [2013] 3 S.C.R. 1101, 303 C.C.C. (3d) 146, which struck down a number of prostitution-related prohibitions. In general, with certain exceptions, they enact an "asymmetrical" model which criminalizes the purchasing of sexual services but not the selling.

Section 286.1 creates offences related to obtaining sexual services for consideration, or communicating with anyone for that purpose.

Subsection (1) creates the basic offences, which may be prosecuted summarily or by indictment, and which stipulate escalating minimum penalties for subsequent offences.

Subsection (2) creates an aggravated form of the same offence with a minimum sentence of imprisonment, which is committed where the person providing the sexual services is under the age of 18.

Subsection (3) provides that a previous conviction for the equivalent offence under the former s. 212(4) counts as a prior conviction for the purposes of subsec. (2).

Subsection (4) places strictures on how the court determines whether a conviction counts as a "subsequent offence". Only the sequence of convictions is to be considered.

In relation to the former s. 212(4) — now s. 286.1(2) — it was held that the six-month mandatory minimum sentence was contrary to s. 12 of the Charter and of no force or effect: *R. v. J.L.M.* (2017), 353 C.C.C. (3d) 40 (B.C.C.A.), leave to appeal to S.C.C. refused 2018 CarswellBC 680.

MATERIAL BENEFIT FROM SEXUAL SERVICES / Material benefit from sexual services provided by person under 18 years / Presumption / Exception / No exception / Aggravating factor

286.2 (1) Everyone who receives a financial or other material benefit, knowing that it is obtained by or derived directly or indirectly from the commission of an offence under subsection 286.1(1), is guilty of an indictable offence and liable to imprisonment for a term of not more than 10 years.

(2) Everyone who receives a financial or other material benefit, knowing that it is obtained by or derived directly or indirectly from the commission of an offence under subsection 286.1(2), is guilty of an indictable offence and liable to imprisonment for a term of not more than 14 years and to a minimum punishment of imprisonment for a term of two years.

(3) For the purposes of subsections (1) and (2), evidence that a person lives with or is habitually in the company of a person who offers or provides sexual services for consideration is, in the absence of evidence to the contrary, proof that the person received a financial or other material benefit from those services.

(4) Subject to subsection (5), subsections (1) and (2) do not apply to a person who receives the benefit

(*a*) in the context of a legitimate living arrangement with the person from whose sexual services the benefit is derived;

(*b*) as a result of a legal or moral obligation of the person from whose sexual services the benefit is derived;

(*c*) in consideration for a service or good that they offer, on the same terms and conditions, to the general public; or

(*d*) in consideration for a service or good that they do not offer to the general public but that they offered or provided to the person from whose sexual services the benefit is derived, if they did not counsel or encourage that person to provide sexual services and the benefit is proportionate to the value of the service or good.

(5) Subsection (4) does not apply to a person who commits an offence under subsection (1) or (2) if that person

(*a*) used, threatened to use or attempted to use violence, intimidation or coercion in relation to the person from whose sexual services the benefit is derived;

(*b*) abused a position of trust, power or authority in relation to the person from whose sexual services the benefit is derived;

(*c*) provided a drug, alcohol or any other intoxicating substance to the person from whose sexual services the benefit is derived for the purpose of aiding or abetting that person to offer or provide sexual services for consideration;

(*d*) engaged in conduct, in relation to any person, that would constitute an offence under section 286.3; or

(*e*) received the benefit in the context of a commercial enterprise that offers sexual services for consideration.

(6) If a person is convicted of an offence under this section, the court that imposes the sentence shall consider as an aggravating factor the fact that that person received the

benefit in the context of a commercial enterprise that offers sexual services for consideration. 2014, c. 25, s. 20.

CROSS-REFERENCES

Other offences relating to sexual services are found in ss. 213, 286.1, 286.3 and 286.4.

Certain immunities to a charge on this provision are provided by s. 286.5.

This offence may be the basis for an application for an authorization to intercept private communications by reason of s. 183, or a video surveillance warrant under s. 487.01(5).

The accused may elect his mode of trial pursuant to s. 536(2).

For special procedures in respect of vulnerable witnesses, see cross-references under s. 286.1.

Section 718.01 provides that, in imposing a sentence for an offence involving the abuse of a person under the age of 18 years, the court shall give primary consideration to the objectives of denunciation and deterrence. Further, under s. 718.2, evidence that the offender, in committing the offence, abused a person under the age of 18 years is an aggravating circumstance.

This offence is a primary designated offence for the purpose of making a forensic DNA data bank order under s. 487.051.

Pursuant to s. 490.012, where an offender is convicted of the offence under subsec. (2), the judge shall make an order requiring the offender to comply with the *Sex Offender Information Registration Act*, S.C. 2004, c. 10. Where an offender is convicted under subsec. (1), such an order shall be made on application of the prosecutor if certain circumstances are present.

If a person is found guilty of the offence in subsec. (2) in respect of a person who is under 16 years of age, the court may impose an order of prohibition under s. 161 prohibiting the accused from attending certain public areas and facilities or taking certain employment that will bring him into contact with persons under the age of 16 years.

Section 171.1 makes it an offence to transmit, make available, distribute or sell sexually explicit material to a person who is, or who the accused believes is under the age of 18 years for the purpose of facilitating the commission of an offence under subsec. (2).

Section 172.2 makes it an offence to agree with a person or make an arrangement with a person by means of telecommunication to commit an offence under subsec. (2) with a person who is or who the accused believes is under the age of 18 years.

SYNOPSIS

This provision creates the indictable offence of receiving a material benefit from sexual services. In essence, it replaces the former s. 212(1)(*j*) — living on the avails of prostitution — which the Supreme Court struck down in *Canada (Attorney General) v. Bedford* , [2013] 3 S.C.R. 1101, 303 C.C.C. (3d) 146. The court held that the former law captured a number of non-exploitative relationships which were not connected to the law's purpose, and also that its negative effect on the security and safety of prostitutes was grossly disproportionate to its objective of protecting prostitutes from harm. This provision attempts to remedy those problems by way of a number of exceptions to liability in subsec. (4).

Subsection (1) sets out the basic offence, while subsec. (2) creates an aggravated form of the offence with a minimum sentence of imprisonment where the sexual services in question are provided by someone under the age of 18.

Subsection (3) creates an evidentiary presumption that a person who lives with (or is habitually in the company of) someone who provides sexual services is committing the offence.

Subsection (4) creates exceptions to liability, apparently targeting the kind of non-exploitative relationships that concerned the court in *Bedford*, *supra*.

Subsection (5) in turn creates a number of exceptions to the exceptions in subsec. (4).

Finally, subsec. (6) stipulates that committing this offence in the context of a commercial enterprise is to be considered an aggravating factor on sentence.

PROCURING / Procuring — person under 18 years

286.3 (1) Everyone who procures a person to offer or provide sexual services for consideration or, for the purpose of facilitating an offence under subsection 286.1(1), recruits, holds, conceals or harbours a person who offers or provides sexual services for consideration, or exercises control, direction or influence over the movements of that person, is guilty of an indictable offence and liable to imprisonment for a term of not more than 14 years.

(2) Everyone who procures a person under the age of 18 years to offer or provide sexual services for consideration or, for the purpose of facilitating an offence under subsection 286.1(2), recruits, holds, conceals or harbours a person under the age of 18 who offers or provides sexual services for consideration, or exercises control, direction or influence over the movements of that person, is guilty of an indictable offence and liable to imprisonment for a term of not more than 14 years and to a minimum punishment of imprisonment for a term of five years. 2014, c. 25, s. 20.

CROSS-REFERENCES

Other offences relating to sexual services are found in ss. 213, 286.1, 286.2 and 286.4.

Certain immunities to a charge on this provision are provided by s. 286.5.

This offence may be the basis for an application for an authorization to intercept private communications by reason of s. 183, or a video surveillance warrant under s. 487.01(5).

The accused may elect his mode of trial pursuant to s. 536(2).

For special procedures in respect of vulnerable witnesses, see cross-references under s. 286.1.

Section 718.01 provides that, in imposing a sentence for an offence involving the abuse of a person under the age of 18 years, the court shall give primary consideration to the objectives of denunciation and deterrence. Further, under s. 718.2, evidence that the offender, in committing the offence, abused a person under the age of 18 years is an aggravating circumstance.

This offence is a primary designated offence for the purpose of making a forensic DNA data bank order under s. 487.051.

Pursuant to s. 490.012, where an offender is convicted of the offence under subsec. (2), the judge shall make an order requiring the offender to comply with the *Sex Offender Information Registration Act*, S.C. 2004, c. 10. Where an offender is convicted under subsec. (1), such an order shall be made on application of the prosecutor if certain circumstances are present.

If a person is found guilty of the offence in subsec. (2) in respect of a person who is under 16 years of age, the court may impose an order of prohibition under s. 161 prohibiting the accused from attending certain public areas and facilities or taking certain employment that will bring him into contact with persons under the age of 16 years.

Section 171.1 makes it an offence to transmit, make available, distribute or sell sexually explicit material to a person who is, or who the accused believes is under the age of 18 years for the purpose of facilitating the commission of an offence under subsec. (2).

Section 172.2 makes it an offence to agree with a person or make an arrangement with a person by means of telecommunication to commit an offence under subsec. (2) with a person who is or who the accused believes is under the age of 18 years.

SYNOPSIS

This provision creates the indictable offence of procuring a person to provide sexual services. It is similar in many respects to the "receiving material benefits" offence under s. 286.2, but requires a more active degree of involvement.

Subsection (1) sets out the basic offence, while subsec. (2) creates an aggravated form of the offence with a minimum sentence of imprisonment where the sexual services in question are provided by someone under the age of 18.

ADVERTISING SEXUAL SERVICES.

286.4 Everyone who knowingly advertises an offer to provide sexual services for consideration is guilty of

(*a*) an indictable offence and liable to imprisonment for a term of not more than five years; or

(*b*) an offence punishable on summary conviction and liable to imprisonment for a term of not more than 18 months. 2014, c. 25, s. 20.

CROSS-REFERENCES

"Advertisement of sexual services" is defined in s. 164(8) for the purposes of that section.

Other offences relating to sexual services are found in ss. 213, 286.1, 286.2 and 286.3.

Certain immunities to a charge on this provision are provided by s. 286.5.

This offence may be the basis for an application for an authorization to intercept private communications by reason of s. 183, or a video surveillance warrant under s. 487.01(5).

Section 164 enacts an alternative procedure, *in rem* proceedings, for the seizure, forfeiture and restoration of advertisements for sexual services. Where an order has been made under s. 164, no proceedings may be taken under this section except with the consent of the Attorney General.

Section 164.1 sets out an *in rem* procedure for removal of advertisements for sexual services from computer systems.

Section 164.2 provides that a court that convicts a person of an offence under this section may order that any thing, other than real property, be forfeited to the Crown if the court is satisfied that the thing was used in the commission of the offence and is the property of the offender, another person who was a party to the offence, or a person who acquired the thing from such a person in circumstances giving rise to a reasonable inference that it was transferred to avoid a forfeiture order.

Where the prosecution elects to proceed by indictment on this offence then the accused may elect his mode of trial pursuant to s. 536(2). Where the prosecution elects to proceed by way of summary conviction then the trial of this offence is conducted by a summary conviction court pursuant to Part XXVII. In either case, release pending trial is determined by s. 515, although the accused is eligible for release by a peace officer under ss. 496 or 497, or by the officer in charge under s. 498.

For special procedures in respect of vulnerable witnesses, see cross-references under s. 286.1.

SYNOPSIS

This provision creates the offence of advertising sexual services.

In s. 164(8), "advertisement of sexual services" is defined to mean "any material — including a photographic, film, video, audio or other recording, made by any means, a visual representation or any written material — that is used to advertise sexual services contrary to section 286.4".

IMMUNITY — MATERIAL BENEFIT AND ADVERTISING / Immunity — aiding, abetting, etc.

286.5 (1) No person shall be prosecuted for

(*a*) an offence under section 286.2 if the benefit is derived from the provision of their own sexual services; or

(*b*) an offence under section 286.4 in relation to the advertisement of their own sexual services.

(2) No person shall be prosecuted for aiding, abetting, conspiring or attempting to commit an offence under any of sections 286.1 to 286.4 or being an accessory after the fact or counselling a person to be a party to such an offence, if the offence relates to the offering or provision of their own sexual services. 2014, c. 25, s. 20.

CROSS-REFERENCES
Sections 286.1 to 286.4 set out the offences to which this immunity-granting provision relates.

SYNOPSIS
This provision creates certain immunities to the offences in ss. 286.1 to 286.4, apparently meant to address some of the constitutional defects in the previous prostitution-related provisions identified by the court in *Canada (Attorney General) v. Bedford*, [2013] 3 S.C.R. 1101, 303 C.C.C. (3d) 146. Because the new regime is meant primarily to criminalize the buyers rather than the sellers of sexual services, this provision closes off avenues of principal and accessorial liability under which sex workers could otherwise face conviction. In particular, it provides that a person cannot be criminally liable for advertising or obtaining a material benefit from the person's own sexual services, nor can a person be guilty as a party to any of the offences where the sexual services in question are the person's own.

Abortion

PROCURING MISCARRIAGE / Woman procuring her own miscarriage / Definition of "means" / Exceptions / Information requirement / Definitions / "accredited hospital" / "approved hospital" / "board" / "Minister of Health" / "qualified medical practitioner" / "therapeutic abortion committee" / Requirement of consent not affected.

287. (1) Every one who, with intent to procure the miscarriage of a female person, whether or not she is pregnant, uses any means for the purpose of carrying out his intention is guilty of an indictable offence and liable to imprisonment for life.

(2) Every female person who, being pregnant, with intent to procure her own miscarriage, uses any means or permits any means to be used for the purpose of carrying out her intention is guilty of an indictable offence and liable to imprisonment for a term not exceeding two years.

(3) In this section, "means" includes
(*a*) the administration of a drug or other noxious thing;
(*b*) the use of an instrument; and
(*c*) manipulation of any kind.

(4) Subsections (1) and (2) do not apply to
(*a*) a qualified medical practitioner, other than a member of a therapeutic abortion committee for any hospital, who in good faith uses in an accredited or approved hospital any means for the purpose of carrying out his intention to procure the miscarriage of a female person, or
(*b*) a female person who, being pregnant, permits a qualified medical practitioner to use in an accredited or approved hospital any means for the purpose of carrying out her intention to procure her own miscarriage,

if, before the use of those means, the therapeutic abortion committee for that accredited or approved hospital, by a majority of the members of the committee and at a meeting of the committee at which the case of the female person has been reviewed,
(*c*) has by certificate in writing stated that in its opinion the continuation of the pregnancy of the female person would or would be likely to endanger her life or health, and
(*d*) has caused a copy of such certificate to be given to the qualified medical practitioner.

(5) The Minister of Health of a province may by order
(*a*) require a therapeutic abortion committee for any hospital in that province, or any member thereof, to furnish him with a copy of any certificate described in

paragraph (4)(*c*) issued by that committee, together with such other information relating to the circumstances surrounding the issue of that certificate as he may require, or

(*b*) require a medical practitioner who, in that province, has procured the miscarriage of any female person named in a certificate described in paragraph (4)(*c*), to furnish him with a copy of that certificate, together with such other information relating to the procuring of the miscarriage as he may require.

(6) For the purposes of subsections (4) and (5) and this subsection,

"accredited hospital" means a hospital accredited by the Canadian Council on Hospital Accreditation in which diagnostic services and medical, surgical and obstetrical treatment are provided;

"approved hospital" means a hospital in a province approved for the purposes of this section by the Minister of Health of that province;

"board" means the board of governors, management or directors, or the trustees, commission or other person or group of persons having the control and management of an accredited or approved hospital;

"Minister of Health" means

(*a*) in the Provinces of Ontario, Quebec, New Brunswick, Manitoba, Prince Edward Island and Newfoundland and Labrador, the Minister of Health,

(*b*) in the Provinces of Nova Scotia and Saskatchewan, the Minister of Public Health, and

(*c*) in the Province of British Columbia, the Minister of Health Services and Hospital Insurance,

(*d*) in the Province of Alberta, the Minister of Hospitals and Medical Care,

(*e*) in Yukon, the Northwest Territories and Nunavut, the Minister of Health;

"qualified medical practitioner" means a person entitled to engage in the practice of medicine under the laws of the province in which the hospital referred to in subsection (4) is situated;

"therapeutic abortion committee" for any hospital means a committee, comprised of not less than three members each of whom is a qualified medical practitioner, appointed by the board of that hospital for the purpose of considering and determining questions relating to terminations of pregnancy within that hospital.

(7) Nothing in subsection (4) shall be construed as making unnecessary the obtaining of any authorization or consent that is or may be required, otherwise than under this Act, before any means are used for the purpose of carrying out an intention to procure the miscarriage of a female person. R.S., c. C-34, s. 251; 1974-75-76, c. 93, s. 22.1; 1993, Sch. III, s. 30; 1996, c. 8, s. 32(1)(*d*); 2002, c. 7, s. 141; 2015, c. 3, s. 48.

CROSS-REFERENCES

The related offence of supplying noxious things, etc., for purpose of procuring a miscarriage is found in s. 288.

ANNOTATIONS

This section is of no force and effect by reason of its violation of s. 7 of the Charter: *R. v. Morgentaler, Smoling and Scott*, [1988] 1 S.C.R. 30, 37 C.C.C. (3d) 449, 62 C.R. (3d) 1 (5:2).

Provincial legislation, whose central purpose and dominant characteristic was the restriction of abortion as a socially undesirable practice which should be suppressed or punished, is *ultra vires* the province. The prohibition of the performance of abortions in certain circumstances with penal consequences is traditionally regarded as a part of the criminal law. The legislation in this case was designed to prevent the defendant from opening free-standing abortion clinics within the province: *R. v. Morgentaler*, [1993] 3 S.C.R. 463, 85 C.C.C. (3d) 118, 25 C.R. (4th) 179.

There are no substantive rights under the Quebec *Charter of Human Rights and Freedoms*, R.S.Q. 1977, c. C-12, nor the *Civil Code of Lower Canada*, upon which an injunction could be founded to restrain a woman from having an abortion. Similarly, the common law did not recognize any right in the foetus until born alive. Additionally, a father's interest in a foetus cannot support a right to veto a woman's decision in respect of that foetus, including the decision to have an abortion. Accordingly, the courts of Quebec were not entitled to grant an injunction to the father to restrain the mother from having an abortion: *Tremblay v. Daigle*, [1989] 2 S.C.R. 530, 62 D.L.R. (4th) 634, 102 N.R. 81 (9:0).

288. [*Repealed*, 2018, c. 29, s. 28.]

Venereal Diseases

289. [*Repealed*, R.S.C. 1985, c. 27 (1st Supp.), s. 41.]

Offences Against Conjugal Rights

BIGAMY / Matters of defence / Incompetency no defence / Validity presumed / Act or omission by accused.

290. (1) Every one commits bigamy who

(*a*) in Canada,

(i) being married, goes through a form of marriage with another person,

(ii) knowing that another person is married, goes through a form of marriage with that person, or

(iii) on the same day or simultaneously, goes through a form of marriage with more than one person; or

(*b*) being a Canadian citizen resident in Canada leaves Canada with intent to do anything mentioned in subparagraphs (*a*)(i) to (iii) and, pursuant thereto, does outside Canada anything mentioned in those subparagraphs in circumstances mentioned therein.

(2) No person commits bigamy by going through a form of marriage if

(*a*) that person in good faith and on reasonable grounds believes that his spouse is dead,

(*b*) the spouse of that person has been continuously absent from him for seven years immediately preceding the time when he goes through the form of marriage, unless he knew that his spouse was alive at any time during those seven years,

(*c*) that person has been divorced from the bond of the first marriage, or

(*d*) the former marriage has been declared void by a court of competent jurisdiction.

(3) Where a person is alleged to have committed bigamy, it is not a defence that the parties would, if unmarried, have been incompetent to contract marriage under the law of the place where the offence is alleged to have been committed.

(4) Every marriage or form of marriage shall, for the purpose of this section, be deemed to be valid unless the accused establishes that it was invalid.

(5) No act or omission on the part of an accused who is charged with bigamy invalidates a marriage or form of marriage that is otherwise valid. R.S., c. C-34, s. 254.

CROSS-REFERENCES

"Form of marriage" is defined in s. 214.

The punishment for bigamy is found in s. 291(1). The accused may elect his mode of trial pursuant to s. 536(2). Release pending trial is determined by s. 515, although the accused is eligible for release by the officer in charge under s. 498.

The accused's spouse is a competent and compellable witness at the instance of the Crown by virtue of s. 4(2). Section 291(2) provides for a means of proof of the marriage by way of certificate. Section 25(1) of the *Interpretation Act*, R.S.C. 1985, c. I-21, provides that "Where an enactment provides that a document is evidence of a fact without anything in the context to indicate that the document is conclusive evidence, then, in any judicial proceedings, the document is admissible in evidence and the fact is deemed to be established in the absence of any evidence to the contrary".

The related offence of polygamy is found in s. 293 and of solemnizing a marriage in contravention of the laws of the province in s. 295.

SYNOPSIS

This section describes the offence of bigamy. Every one commits this offence who, in Canada goes through a form of marriage with a person while already married to another person, who goes through a form of marriage with another person knowing that person to be married to someone else, or who goes through a form of marriage with more than one other person simultaneously. If a resident Canadian citizen leaves Canada to do any of the things described above, that person also commits the offence of bigamy. These general prohibitions do not apply if the person in *good faith* and on *reasonable grounds* believes that his spouse is dead, if the person has been divorced from the spouse, if the spouse of the person has been absent for seven years without interruption and nothing has been heard of the spouse during that time, or if the former marriage has been declared void by a court of competent jurisdiction. A person charged under this section cannot use as a defence the fact that there would be a legal impediment to the original marriage in the place where the offence is alleged to have been committed. Unless the accused establishes otherwise, there is a presumption in this section that all forms of marriage are valid and no act or omission of the accused may be set up as invalidating the marriage.

ANNOTATIONS

All that is necessary is to prove that the ceremony was one known to and recognized by the law as capable of producing a valid marriage, and accordingly independent circumstances, such as the lack of a marriage licence, which might otherwise create a legal disability, are irrelevant: *R. v. Howard,* [1966] 3 C.C.C. 91, 54 W.W.R. 484 (B.C. Co. Ct.).

It has been held in a number of cases that a *bona fide* but mistaken belief that the first marriage had been dissolved through divorce was no defence to a charge under this section: *R. v. Bleiler* (1912), 19 C.C.C. 249, 1 D.L.R. 787 (Alta. S.C.); *R. v. Morgan* (1942), 78 C.C.C. 129, [1942] 4 D.L.R. 321 (N.S.S.C.); *R. v. Brinkley* (1907), 12 C.C.C. 454, 14 O.L.R. 434 (C.A.); *R. v. Queneau* (1949), 95 C.C.C. 187, 8 C.R. 235 (Que. C.A.). These cases are in accord with what was the leading English case of *R. v. Wheat and Stocks* (1921), 15 Cr. App. R. 134. In the later case of *R. v. King* (1963), 48 Cr. App. R. 17, *R. v. Wheat and Stocks* was distinguished and explained as being limited to the case where the accused's belief is that the first marriage was dissolved as a result of a divorce. In *R. v. King*, the court held that a belief that the first marriage was invalid would be a defence although the defence was rejected on the facts of the case. Interestingly, the accused's belief that the first marriage was invalid was due to his mistaken belief that he had not been validly divorced from an even earlier marriage. *R. v. Wheat and Stocks* was finally overruled by the Court of Appeal in *R. v. Gould* (1968), 52 Cr. App. R. 152, where it was held that a belief that the former marriage had been dissolved is a defence to the charge. It was held in *Gould* that the belief must be an honest one based on reasonable grounds.

The defence was accepted in *R. v. Woolridge* (1979), 49 C.C.C. (2d) 300 (Sask. Prov. Ct.), where the trial judge held that an honest *and* reasonable belief that the previous marriage had been dissolved by divorce was a defence to the charge under this section applying *R. v. Haugen* (1923), 41 C.C.C. 132, [1923] 2 W.W.R. 709 (Sask. C.A.), where it was held that an honest and reasonable belief that the accused's first marriage was a nullity because his first wife was still validly married was a defence.

It is submitted that such a defence is properly recognized and that a mistaken belief that the previous marriage had been dissolved by divorce should be a defence if the belief is honestly held. While some cases have foundered on the issue of whether the accused's mistake is one of fact or law, it is submitted that applying the decision of the Supreme Court of Canada in *R. v. Prue; R. v. Baril*, [1979] 2 S.C.R. 547, 46 C.C.C. (2d) 257, 8 C.R. (3d) 68 (a case under former s. 238(3)) this kind of mistake should be recognized as a mistake of fact. Finally, it is submitted that it is sufficient if the belief is honestly held and need not be based on reasonable grounds, applying *R. v. Rees*, [1956] S.C.R. 640, 115 C.C.C. 1, 24 C.R. 1; *D.P.P. v. Morgan* (1975), 61 Cr. App. R. 136 (H.L.); and *R. v. Pappajohn*, [1980] 2 S.C.R. 120, 52 C.C.C. (2d) 481, 111 D.L.R. (3d) 1.

PUNISHMENT / Certificate of marriage.

291. (1) Every one who commits bigamy is guilty of an indictable offence and liable to imprisonment for a term not exceeding five years.

(2) For the purposes of this section a certificate of marriage issued under the authority of law is evidence of the marriage or form of marriage to which it relates without proof of the signature or official character of the person by whom it purports to be signed. R.S., c. C-34, s. 255.

CROSS-REFERENCES

"Form of marriage" is defined in s. 214.

The offence of bigamy is defined in s. 290. The accused may elect his mode of trial pursuant to s. 536(2). Release pending trial is determined by s. 515, although the accused is eligible for release by the officer in charge under s. 498.

The accused's spouse is a competent and compellable witness at the instance of the Crown by virtue of s. 4(2).

With respect to subsec. (2), note than s. 25(1) of the *Interpretation Act*, R.S.C. 1985, c. I-21, provides that "Where an enactment provides that a document is evidence of a fact without anything in the context to indicate that the document is conclusive evidence, then, in any judicial proceedings, the document is admissible in evidence and the fact is deemed to be established in the absence of any evidence to the contrary".

For notes respecting mistake generally, see notes under s. 19.

The related offence of polygamy is found in s. 293 and of solemnizing a marriage in contravention of the laws of the province in s. 295.

SYNOPSIS

This section sets out the punishment for bigamy and facilitates the proof of a prior marriage. A person convicted of bigamy is guilty of an indictable offence and liable to a maximum term of imprisonment of five years. It is not necessary to prove the signature or official character of a person signing a marriage certificate for it to be admissible as evidence of a lawful prior marriage.

PROCURING FEIGNED MARRIAGE / Corroboration.

292. (1) Every person who procures or knowingly aids in procuring a feigned marriage between himself and another person is guilty of an indictable offence and liable to imprisonment for a term not exceeding five years.

(2) No person shall be convicted of an offence under this section on the evidence of only one witness unless the evidence of that witness is corroborated in a material particular by evidence that implicates the accused. R.S., c. C-34, s. 256; 1980-81-82-83, c. 125, s. 21.

CROSS-REFERENCES
"Form of marriage" is defined in s. 214.

The accused's spouse is a competent and compellable witness at the instance of the Crown by virtue of s. 4(2).

The accused may elect his mode of trial pursuant to s. 536(2). Release pending trial is determined by s. 515, although the accused is eligible for release by the officer in charge under s. 498.

The related offence of pretending to solemnize a marriage is found in s. 294 and of solemnizing a marriage in contravention of the laws of the province in s. 295.

SYNOPSIS

This section imposes criminal liability upon any person, *male* or *female*, who procures or *knowingly* aids in procuring a feigned marriage between that person and another person. The offence is indictable and the maximum sentence is a term of five years of imprisonment. No person can be convicted of an offence under this section on the *uncorroborated evidence* of one witness.

ANNOTATIONS

In *R. v. B. (G.)*, [1990] 2 S.C.R. 3, 56 C.C.C. (3d) 161 (5:0), the court considered the effect of, now repealed, s. 586 which provided that no person shall be convicted on the unsworn evidence of a child, "unless the evidence of the child is corroborated in a material particular by evidence that implicates the accused". The wording is thus almost identical to subsec. (2) of this section. It was there held that the requirement that the corroborating evidence implicate the accused requires only that the evidence confirm in some material particular the story of the witness giving the evidence which required corroboration. The confirming evidence need not also itself implicate the accused.

POLYGAMY / Evidence in case of polygamy.

293. (1) Every one who

(*a*) practises or enters into or in any manner agrees or consents to practise or enter into

(i) any form of polygamy, or

(ii) any kind of conjugal union with more than one person at the same time,

whether or not it is by law recognized as a binding form of marriage; or

(*b*) celebrates, assists or is a party to a rite, ceremony, contract or consent that purports to sanction a relationship mentioned in subparagraph (*a*)(i) or (ii),

is guilty of an indictable offence and liable to imprisonment for a term not exceeding five years.

(2) Where an accused is charged with an offence under this section, no averment or proof of the method by which the alleged relationship was entered into, agreed to or consented to is necessary in the indictment or upon the trial of the accused, nor is it necessary on the trial to prove that the persons who are alleged to have entered into the relationship had or intended to have sexual intercourse. R.S., c. C-34, s. 257.

CROSS-REFERENCES
"Form of marriage" is defined in s. 214.

The accused's spouse is a competent and compellable witness at the instance of the Crown by virtue of s. 4(2).

The accused may elect his mode of trial pursuant to s. 536(2). Release pending trial is determined by s. 515, although the accused is eligible for release by the officer in charge under s. 498.

The related offence of bigamy is found in s. 291 and of solemnizing a marriage in contravention of the laws of the province in s. 295.

SYNOPSIS

This section makes it a criminal offence to agree, consent to or practise any form of polygamy or conjugal union with more than one person at the same time. It also imposes criminal liability on anyone who celebrates, assists or is party to a rite, ceremony, contract or consent that sanctions a relationship described above. The offence is indictable with a maximum term of imprisonment of five years. Subsection (2) states that it is not necessary to include in the indictment or to prove at trial the method by which the relationship was entered into, agreed to or consented to, nor is it necessary to establish at trial that the parties had, or intended to have, sexual intercourse.

ANNOTATIONS

In *Reference re: Criminal Code (Can), s. 293* (2011), 279 C.C.C. (3d) 1, the British Columbia Supreme Court held that this provision is constitutionally valid, but should be read down to exclude the criminalization of persons under 18 who enter into a prohibited marriage. Though the offence triggers a breach of s. 2(*a*) in respect of religious minorities who avow a commitment to plural marriage, it is demonstrably justified under s. 1 because of the social and individual harms associated with polygamy.

The words "any kind of conjugal union" in subsec. (1)(*a*)(ii) predicate some form of union under the guise of marriage and were not intended to apply to adultery even where one or both of the persons are married at the time they are living together: *R. v. Tolhurst, R. v. Wright* (1937), 68 C.C.C. 319 (Ont. C.A.).

There is no requirement for the Crown to prove harm, compulsion, or lack of consent as an essential element of the polygamy offence. The offence embraces both a marriage and a conjugal union but does not require proof of both: *R. v. Blackmore* (2017), 350 C.C.C. (3d) 429 (B.C.S.C.).

FORCED MARRIAGE.

293.1 Everyone who celebrates, aids or participates in a marriage rite or ceremony knowing that one of the persons being married is marrying against their will is guilty of an indictable offence and liable to imprisonment for a term not exceeding five years. 2015, c. 29, s. 9.

CROSS-REFERENCES

The terms "marriage rite" and "marriage ceremony" are not defined.

SYNOPSIS

This section makes it an offence to celebrate, aid or participate in a marriage rite or ceremony where one of the persons being married is being forced to do so. The offence is indictable and punishable by up to five years' imprisonment.

MARRIAGE UNDER AGE OF 16 YEARS.

293.2 Everyone who celebrates, aids or participates in a marriage rite or ceremony knowing that one of the persons being married is under the age of 16 years is guilty of an indictable offence and liable to imprisonment for a term not exceeding five years. 2015, c. 29, s. 9.

CROSS-REFERENCES

The terms "marriage rite" and "marriage ceremony" are not defined.

SYNOPSIS

This section makes it an offence to celebrate, aid or participate in a marriage rite or ceremony where one of the persons being married is under the age of 16, regardless of whether that person is doing so voluntarily. The offence is indictable and punishable by up to five years' imprisonment.

Unlawful Solemnization of Marriage

PRETENDING TO SOLEMNIZE MARRIAGE.

294. Every person is guilty of an indictable offence and liable to imprisonment for a term of not more than two years who

(*a*) solemnizes or pretends to solemnize a marriage without lawful authority; or

(*b*) procures a person to solemnize a marriage knowing that he is not lawfully authorized to solemnize the marriage. R.S., c. C-34, s. 258; 2018, c. 29, s. 29.

CROSS-REFERENCES

"Form of marriage" is defined in s. 214.

The accused's spouse is a competent and compellable witness at the instance of the Crown by virtue of s. 4(2).

The accused may elect his mode of trial pursuant to s. 536(2). Release pending trial is determined by s. 515, although the accused is eligible for release by the officer in charge under s. 498.

The related offence of procuring a feigned marriage is found in s. 292.

SYNOPSIS

This section prohibits any person who does not have the lawful authority to do so from solemnizing or pretending to solemnize a marriage. It also prohibits any person from knowingly procuring an unqualified person to solemnize a marriage. A person charged with an offence under this section must prove that he is, in fact, lawfully entitled to solemnize a marriage — a requirement that has potential Charter implications.

A person convicted under this section is guilty of an indictable offence and liable to a maximum term of imprisonment of two years.

MARRIAGE CONTRARY TO LAW.

295. Everyone who, being lawfully authorized to solemnize marriage, knowingly solemnizes a marriage in contravention of federal law or the laws of the province in which the marriage is solemnized is guilty of an indictable offence and liable to imprisonment for a term not exceeding two years. R.S., c. C-34, s. 259; 2015, c. 29, s. 10.

CROSS-REFERENCES

"Form of marriage" is defined in s. 214.

The accused may elect his mode of trial pursuant to s. 536(2). Release pending trial is determined by s. 515, although the accused is eligible for release by the officer in charge under s. 498.

The related offence of bigamy is found in s. 291, of polygamy in s. 293, of forced marriage in s. 293.1, and of marriage under the age of 16 years in s. 293.2.

SYNOPSIS

This section imposes criminal liability on any person who is lawfully authorized to solemnize a marriage, but who *knowingly* solemnizes a marriage which contravenes either federal law or the law of the province where the marriage takes place. The offence is indictable and the maximum term of imprisonment is two years.

[*Heading repealed*, 2018, c. 29, s. 30.]

296. [*Repealed*, 2018, c. 29, s. 30.]

Defamatory Libel

DEFINITION OF "NEWSPAPER".

297. In sections 303, 304 and 308, "newspaper" means any paper, magazine or periodical containing public news, intelligence or reports of events, or any remarks or observations thereon, printed for sale and published periodically or in parts or numbers, at intervals not exceeding thirty-one days between the publication of any two such papers, parts or numbers, and any paper, magazine or periodical printed in order to be dispersed and made public, weekly or more often, or at intervals not exceeding thirty-one days, that contains advertisements, exclusively or principally. R.S., c. C-34, s. 261.

CROSS-REFERENCES

The calculation of days is dealt with in s. 27 of the *Interpretation Act*, R.S.C. 1985, c. I-21.

SYNOPSIS

This section defines the term "newspaper" for the purpose of ss. 303, 304 and 308. Whether a publication is a newspaper depends on the frequency of publication and subject matter.

DEFINITION / Mode of expression.

298. (1) A defamatory libel is matter published, without lawful justification or excuse, that is likely to injure the reputation of any person by exposing him to hatred, contempt or ridicule, or that is designed to insult the person of or concerning whom it is published.

(2) A defamatory libel may be expressed directly or by insinuation or irony

(*a*) in words legibly marked on any substance; or

(*b*) by any object signifying a defamatory libel otherwise than by words. R.S., c. C-34, s. 262.

CROSS-REFERENCES

Publishing a libel is defined in s. 299.

The punishment for publishing a defamatory libel known to be false is a maximum of five years under s. 300. The punishment for publishing a defamatory libel is a maximum of two years under s. 301. The punishment for extortion by libel is a maximum of five years under s. 302. For all these offences, the accused may elect his mode of trial pursuant to s. 536(2). Release pending trial is determined by s. 515, although the accused is eligible for release by the officer in charge under s. 498.

Liability of the proprietor of a newspaper is dealt with in s. 303. Various defences or excuses for publishing a defamatory libel are set out in ss. 304 to 316. Section 317 provides for a special verdict in the case of defamatory libel. Section 584(1) provides that no count for publishing a defamatory libel is insufficient by reason only that it does not set out the words that are alleged to be libellous. However, under s. 587(1)(*e*), particulars may be ordered further describing any writing or words that are the subject of the charge. Under s. 584(2), a count for publishing a libel may charge that the published matter was written in a sense that, by innuendo, made the publication thereof criminal and may specify that sense without any introductory assertion to show how the matter was written in that sense. Under s. 584(3), it is sufficient to prove that the matter was libellous, with or without innuendo. The plea of justification in cases of defamatory libel is dealt with in ss. 607(2), 611 and 612. Under s. 612(3), where the accused is convicted, the court may consider, in pronouncing sentence, whether the offence was aggravated or mitigated by the plea. Under s. 637, a private prosecutor has no right to stand jurors aside. Sections 728 and 729 make special provision for costs in cases of defamatory libel.

Seditious libel is dealt with in ss. 59 to 61, blasphemous libel in s. 296 and hate propaganda in ss. 318 to 320. Publishing false news is an offence under s. 181.

SYNOPSIS

This section defines defamatory libel and specifies that it may be expressed directly or by insinuation or irony in words legibly marked or through an object otherwise than by words. A defamatory libel is a matter published that is likely to injure the reputation of any person by exposing that person to hatred, contempt, ridicule or insult. Furthermore, a defamatory libel must be published *without lawful justification.*

ANNOTATIONS

This section is not so vague as to infringe s. 7 of the *Canadian Charter of Rights and Freedoms.* While this section infringes the guarantee to freedom of expression in s. 2(*b*) of the Charter, properly interpreted it is valid as a reasonable limit under s. 1 of the Charter. In particular, when regard is had to the French version of this section, it is apparent that the phrase "designed to insult" in subsec. (1) requires proof of a grave insult: *R. v. Lucas*, [1998] 1 S.C.R. 439, 123 C.C.C. (3d) 97.

PUBLISHING.

299. A person publishes a libel when he
- **(*a*) exhibits it in public;**
- **(*b*) causes it to be read or seen; or**
- **(*c*) shows or delivers it, or causes it to be shown or delivered, with intent that it should be read or seen by any person other than the person whom it defames. R.S., c. C-34, s. 263; 2018, c. 29, s. 31.**

CROSS-REFERENCES

Defamatory libel is defined in s. 298.

SYNOPSIS

This section defines the term "publishing" as it relates to libel. The section holds that a person publishes a libel when that person exhibits it in public, causes it to be read or viewed, or causes it to be shown or delivered *with the intent* that it should be read or seen by any other person.

ANNOTATIONS

This section is not so vague as to infringe s. 7 of *Canadian Charter of Rights and Freedoms.* While this section infringes the guarantee to freedom of expression in s. 2(*b*) of the Charter, it is valid as a reasonable limit under s. 1 of the Charter, except for that part of para. (*c*) that makes it an offence, although the intent is only to show it to the person defamed. Accordingly, the words "by the person whom it defames or" should be severed from para. (*c*). The phrase "any other person" will not pertain to the situation where only the person defamed is shown the defamatory libel: *R. v. Lucas*, [1998] 1 S.C.R. 439, 123 C.C.C. (3d) 97.

PUNISHMENT OF LIBEL KNOWN TO BE FALSE.

300. Every one who publishes a defamatory libel that he knows is false is guilty of an indictable offence and liable to imprisonment for a term not exceeding five years. R.S., c. C-34, s. 264.

CROSS-REFERENCES

Defamatory libel is defined in s. 298 and see cross-references under that section concerning related offences, special procedural provisions and defences or excuses. Publishing is defined in s. 299. As to vicarious liability of a newspaper proprietor, see s. 303.

The accused may elect his mode of trial pursuant to s. 536(2). Release pending trial is determined by s. 515, although the accused is eligible for release by the officer in charge under s. 498.

SYNOPSIS

This section imposes criminal liability upon any person who publishes, as defined in s. 299, a defamatory libel, as defined in s. 298. The Crown must prove that the accused intended to defame the victim. Any person convicted under this section is guilty of an indictable offence with a maximum term of imprisonment of five years.

ANNOTATIONS

This section is not so vague as to infringe s. 7 of the *Canadian Charter of Rights and Freedoms*. While this section infringes the guarantee to freedom of expression in s. 2(*b*) of the Charter, properly interpreted, it is valid as a reasonable limit under s. 1 of the Charter. It would be contrary to constitutional principles to interpret this section as requiring anything less than a subjective intent to defame. Accordingly, the Crown can only make out the offence if it proves beyond a reasonable doubt that the accused intended to defame the victim: *R. v. Lucas*, [1998] 1 S.C.R. 439, 123 C.C.C. (3d) 97.

PUNISHMENT FOR DEFAMATORY LIBEL.

301. Every one who publishes a defamatory libel is guilty of an indictable offence and liable to imprisonment for a term not exceeding two years. R.S., c. C-34, s. 265.

CROSS-REFERENCES

Defamatory libel is defined in s. 298 and see cross-references under that section concerning related offences, special procedural provisions and defences or excuses. Publishing is defined in s. 299. As to vicarious liability of a newspaper proprietor, see s. 303.

The accused may elect his mode of trial pursuant to s. 536(2). Release pending trial is determined by s. 515, although the accused is eligible for release by the officer in charge under s. 498.

SYNOPSIS

This section provides that a person who is convicted of publishing a defamatory libel is guilty of an indictable offence, with a maximum term of imprisonment of two years. The difference between this section and s. 300 is that there is no requirement in this section that the libel be false.

ANNOTATIONS

This section was held to be of no force and effect as violating s. 2 of the *Canadian Charter of Rights and Freedoms* and not constituting a reasonable limit under s. 1: *R. v. Prior* (2008), 231 C.C.C. (3d) 12 (Nfld. & Lab. S.C.T.D.); *R. v. Gill* (1996), 29 O.R. (3d) 250 (Gen. Div.); and *R. v. Lucas* (1995), 129 Sask. R. 53 (Q.B.). [**Note:** There was no appeal from the finding in *R. v. Lucas* that this section is unconstitutional. The decision of the Supreme Court of Canada with respect to the constitutionality of s. 300 in *Lucas* is noted above, under that section.]

EXTORTION BY LIBEL / Idem / Punishment.

302. (1) Every one commits an offence who, with intent

(*a*) to extort money from any person, or

(*b*) to induce a person to confer on or procure for another person an appointment or office of profit or trust,

publishes or threatens to publish or offers to abstain from publishing or to prevent the publication of a defamatory libel.

(2) Every one commits an offence who, as the result of the refusal of any person to permit money to be extorted or to confer or procure an appointment or office of profit or trust, publishes or threatens to publish a defamatory libel.

(3) Every one who commits an offence under this section is guilty of an indictable offence and liable to imprisonment for a term not exceeding five years. R.S., c. C-34, s. 266.

CROSS-REFERENCES

Defamatory libel is defined in s. 298 and see cross-references under that section concerning related offences, special procedural provisions and defences or excuses. Publishing is defined in s. 299. The accused may elect his mode of trial pursuant to s. 536(2). Release pending trial is determined by s. 515, although the accused is eligible for release by the officer in charge under s. 498.

The general extortion offence is found in s. 346.

SYNOPSIS

This section describes the offence of extortion by libel. It states that anyone who, *with intent*, publishes, threatens to publish, or offers to refrain from or prevent the publication of a defamatory libel in order to extort money from a person or to induce that person to confer an appointment or office of profit or trust upon another person, commits an offence. An offence under this section is also committed if, as a result of a person's refusal to do any of the things described in subsec. (1), anyone threatens to publish, or in fact publishes a defamatory libel. The offences set out in this section are indictable and carry a maximum term of imprisonment of five years.

PROPRIETOR OF NEWSPAPER PRESUMED RESPONSIBLE / General authority to manager when negligence / Selling newspapers.

303. (1) The proprietor of a newspaper shall be deemed to publish defamatory matter that is inserted and published therein, unless he proves that the defamatory matter was inserted in the newspaper without his knowledge and without negligence on his part.

(2) Where the proprietor of a newspaper gives to a person general authority to manage or conduct the newspaper as editor or otherwise, the insertion by that person of defamatory matter in the newspaper shall, for the purposes of subsection (1), be deemed not to be negligence on the part of the proprietor unless it is proved that

(*a*) he intended the general authority to include authority to insert defamatory matter in the newspaper; or

(*b*) he continued to confer general authority after he knew that it had been exercised by the insertion of defamatory matter in the newspaper.

(3) No person shall be deemed to publish a defamatory libel by reason only that he sells a number or part of a newspaper that contains a defamatory libel, unless he knows that

the number or part contains defamatory matter or that defamatory matter is habitually contained in the newspaper. R.S., c. C-34, s. 267.

CROSS-REFERENCES

The term "newspaper" is defined in s. 303. Defamatory libel is defined in s. 298 and see cross-references under that section concerning related offences, special procedural provisions and defences or excuses. Publishing is defined in s. 299. The liability of a party generally is set out in ss. 21 and 22.

SYNOPSIS

This section sets out the conditions under which a proprietor or vendor of a newspaper, as that term is defined in s. 297, is *deemed to publish defamatory matter*. The proprietor of a newspaper must prove that any *defamatory matter* in his newspaper was inserted *without* his *knowledge* and *without negligence* on his part or else he is deemed to have published it. If the proprietor has given authority to another person as manager or editor of the newspaper and that person has inserted *defamatory matter* in the newspaper, no negligence will be ascribed to the proprietor unless the prosecution proves that he intended to give the manager or editor the authority to insert *defamatory matter* in the newspaper, or allowed the manager or editor to continue to exercise general authority after the *defamatory matter* had been inserted in the newspaper. Subsection (3) states that a vendor of newspapers containing a *defamatory libel* will not be deemed to have published that *defamatory libel* unless the vendor *knows* that such material is, in fact, contained in the newspaper or that the newspaper habitually carries it.

SELLING BOOK CONTAINING DEFAMATORY LIBEL / Sale by servant.

304. (1) No person shall be deemed to publish a defamatory libel by reason only that he sells a book, magazine, pamphlet or other thing, other than a newspaper that contains a defamatory matter if, at the time of the sale, he does not know that it contains the defamatory matter.

(2) Where a servant, in the course of his employment, sells a book, magazine, pamphlet or other thing, other than a newspaper, the employer shall be deemed not to publish any defamatory matter contained therein unless it is proved that the employer authorized the sale knowing that

(*a*) defamatory matter was contained therein; or

(*b*) defamatory matter was habitually contained therein, in the case of a periodical. R.S., c. C-34, s. 268.

CROSS-REFERENCES

The term "newspaper" is defined in s. 303. Defamatory libel is defined in s. 298 and see cross-references under that section concerning related offences, special procedural provisions and other defences or excuses. Publishing is defined in s. 299. As to vicarious liability of a newspaper proprietor, see s. 303.

SYNOPSIS

This section sets out the circumstances in which a person who sells a book, pamphlet or publication other than a newspaper that contains *defamatory matter* is not deemed to have published a *defamatory libel*. The seller of the item mentioned in subsec. (1) is not deemed to have published a *defamatory libel* if, at the time of sale, he did not know that the item contained *defamatory matter*. Similarly, where an employee sells an item containing *defamatory matter*, the employer will not be deemed to have published that *defamatory matter* unless the prosecution proves that the employer knew the matter was contained in the item or, in the case of a periodical, that the item habitually contained such *defamatory matter*.

PUBLISHING PROCEEDINGS OF COURTS OF JUSTICE.

305. No person shall be deemed to publish a defamatory libel by reason only that he publishes defamatory matter

- **(*a*) in a proceeding held before or under the authority of a court exercising judicial authority; or**
- **(*b*) in an inquiry made under the authority of an Act or by order of Her Majesty, or under the authority of a public department or a department of the government of a province. R.S., c. C-34, s. 269.**

CROSS-REFERENCES

The term "newspaper" is defined in s. 303. Defamatory libel is defined in s. 298 and see cross-references under that section concerning related offences, special procedural provisions and other defences or excuses. Publishing is defined in s. 299. As to vicarious liability of a newspaper proprietor, see s. 303.

Note s. 166 which makes it an offence to publish certain judicial proceedings calculated to injure public morals or respecting marriage, judicial separation or restitution of conjugal rights.

SYNOPSIS

This section describes a general exemption from the provisions that apply to publishing *defamatory libel* for those persons who publish *defamatory matter* in a court proceeding or an authorized inquiry.

PARLIAMENTARY PAPERS.

306. No person shall be deemed to publish a defamatory libel by reason only that he

- **(*a*) publishes to the Senate or House of Commons or to a legislature of a province, defamatory matter contained in a petition to the Senate or House of Commons or to the legislature of a province, as the case may be;**
- **(*b*) publishes by order or under the authority of the Senate or House of Commons or of a legislature of a province, a paper containing defamatory matter; or**
- **(*c*) publishes, in good faith and without ill-will to the person defamed, an extract from or abstract of a petition or paper mentioned in paragraph (*a*) or (*b*). R.S., c. C-34, s. 270.**

CROSS-REFERENCES

Defamatory libel is defined in s. 298 and see cross-references under that section concerning related offences, special procedural provisions and other defences or excuses. Publishing is defined in s. 299. As to vicarious liability of a newspaper proprietor, see s. 303. Section 307 creates the related defence of publication of fair reports of parliamentary, legislative or judicial proceedings. Section 316 contains provision for proof that the matter alleged to be defamatory was published by order or under the authority of Parliament or of the legislature.

SYNOPSIS

This section, like s. 305, describes a general exemption from the provisions that apply to publishing a *defamatory libel* for those persons who publish *defamatory matter* contained in a petition to the Senate, House of Commons, or legislature of a province, who publish under the authority of these bodies a paper containing *defamatory matter*, or who publish, *in good faith* and without *ill-will* to the person defamed, an extract from or abstract of the documents referred to above.

FAIR REPORTS OF PARLIAMENTARY OR JUDICIAL PROCEEDINGS / Divorce proceedings an exception.

307. (1) No person shall be deemed to publish a defamatory libel by reason only that he publishes in good faith, for the information of the public, a fair report of the proceedings of the Senate or House of Commons or the legislature of a province, or a committee thereof, or of the public proceedings before a court exercising judicial authority, or publishes, in good faith, any fair comment on any such proceedings.

(2) This section does not apply to a person who publishes a report of evidence taken or offered in any proceeding before the Senate or House of Commons or any committee thereof, on a petition or bill relating to any matter of marriage or divorce, if the report is published without authority from or leave of the House in which the proceeding is held or is contrary to any rule, order or practice of that House. R.S., c. C-34, s. 271.

CROSS-REFERENCES

Defamatory libel is defined in s. 298 and see cross-references under that section concerning related offences, special procedural provisions and other defences or excuses. Publishing is defined in s. 299. As to vicarious liability of a newspaper proprietor, see s. 303. Section 306 creates the related defence of publication of parliamentary or legislative papers. Section 316 contains provision for proof that the matter alleged to be defamatory was published by order or under the authority of Parliament or of the legislature.

With reference to subsec. (2) of this section, note that s. 166 makes it an offence to publish certain judicial proceedings calculated to injure public morals or respecting marriage, judicial separation or restitution of conjugal rights.

SYNOPSIS

This section, like ss. 305 and 306, establishes an exemption from the provisions that apply to publishing a *defamatory libel* to a person who publishes *in good faith* or *for public information*, a fair report of, or fair comment on the proceedings of the Senate, House of Commons, provincial legislature, a committee of any of these bodies, or court matters that are open to the public. This exemption does not apply in relation to publication of evidence or a petition or bill relating to a matter of marriage or divorce in proceedings before the Senate, the House of Commons, or any committee thereof if the person who publishes the material does so without the authority of the appropriate House or the publication is contrary to any rule, order or practice of that House.

FAIR REPORT OF PUBLIC MEETING.

308. No person shall be deemed to publish a defamatory libel by reason only that he publishes in good faith, in a newspaper, a fair report of the proceedings of any public meeting if

(*a*) the meeting is lawfully convened for a lawful purpose and is open to the public;

(*b*) the report is fair and accurate;

(*c*) the publication of the matter complained of is for the public benefit; and

(*d*) he does not refuse to publish in a conspicuous place in the newspaper a reasonable explanation or contradiction by the person defamed in respect of the defamatory matter. R.S., c. C-34, s. 272.

CROSS-REFERENCES

The term "newspaper" is defined in s. 303. Defamatory libel is defined in s. 298 and see cross-references under that section concerning related offences, special procedural provisions and other defences or excuses. Publishing is defined in s. 299. As to vicarious liability of a newspaper proprietor, see s. 303. The general defence of publication for the public benefit is set out in s. 309.

SYNOPSIS

This section provides an exemption for any person who publishes defamatory libel when that person publishes in a newspaper, in *good faith*, a *fair report* of what occurred at a public meeting. The person who publishes the report may only resort to this exemption if the meeting is *lawfully convened* for a *lawful purpose* and is open to the public, the report is *fair* and *accurate*, the publication of the material complained of is for the *benefit of the public*, and the person agrees to publish, in a conspicuous place in the newspaper, any explanation or contradiction of the offending material by the person defamed. This section applies to publication of defamatory matter in newspapers only.

PUBLIC BENEFIT.

309. No person shall be deemed to publish a defamatory libel by reason only that he publishes defamatory matter that, on reasonable grounds, he believes is true, and that is relevant to any subject of public interest, the public discussion of which is for the public benefit. R.S., c. C-34, s. 273.

CROSS-REFERENCES

Defamatory libel is defined in s. 298 and see cross-references under that section concerning related offences, special procedural provisions and other defences or excuses. Note however, in particular, that the plea of justification in cases of defamatory libel is dealt with in ss. 607(2), 611 and 612. Under s. 612(3), where the accused is convicted, the court may consider, in pronouncing sentence, whether the offence was aggravated or mitigated by the plea. Publishing is defined in s. 299. As to vicarious liability of a newspaper proprietor, see s. 303. The special defence of publication for the public benefit in a newspaper is set out in s. 308.

SYNOPSIS

This section provides a more general exemption than the one found in s. 308 in that it applies to any publication, not just newspapers. So long as the person who publishes the defamatory matter believes, on *reasonable grounds*, that the material is true, relevant to a subject of public interest and that it is in the public interest to discuss it, the exemption in this section applies.

FAIR COMMENT ON PUBLIC PERSON OR WORK OF ART.

310. No person shall be deemed to publish a defamatory libel by reason only that he publishes fair comments

(*a*) on the public conduct of a person who takes part in public affairs; or

(*b*) on a published book or other literary production, or on any composition or work of art or performance publicly exhibited, or on any other communication made to the public on any subject, if the comments are confined to criticism thereof. R.S., c. C-34, s. 274.

CROSS-REFERENCES

Defamatory libel is defined in s. 298 and see cross-references under that section concerning related offences, special procedural provisions and other defences or excuses. Publishing is defined in s. 299. As to vicarious liability of a newspaper proprietor, see s. 303.

SYNOPSIS

This section provides that a person will not be deemed to have published a defamatory libel by reason of the fact that he makes *fair comment* about the *public* conduct of a person who participates in *public* affairs. Similarly, a person who makes *fair comment* in the form of criticism of any published book, literary production, publicly exhibited composition, work of art, performance or other communication, may avail himself of this section. This section allows for fair comment on public matters only.

WHEN TRUTH A DEFENCE.

311. No person shall be deemed to publish a defamatory libel where he proves that the publication of the defamatory matter in the manner in which it was published was for the public benefit at the time when it was published and that the matter itself was true. R.S., c. C-34, s. 275.

CROSS-REFERENCES

Defamatory libel is defined in s. 298 and see cross-references under that section concerning related offences, special procedural provisions and other defences or excuses. Note however, in particular, that the plea of justification in cases of defamatory libel is dealt with in ss. 607(2), 611 and 612. Under s. 612(3), where the accused is convicted, the court may consider, in pronouncing sentence, whether the offence was aggravated or mitigated by the plea. Publishing is defined in s. 299. As to vicarious liability of a newspaper proprietor, see s. 303. The related defence of publication for the public benefit is set out in ss. 308 and 309.

SYNOPSIS

This section, like s. 309, provides an exemption from criminal liability under s. 300 for any person who publishes defamatory matter that was true and the publication of which, both in manner and time, was for the public benefit. This section, unlike s. 309, however, requires the person charged under s. 300 to prove both of these elements.

PUBLICATION INVITED OR NECESSARY.

312. No person shall be deemed to publish a defamatory libel by reason only that he publishes defamatory matter

(*a*) on the invitation or challenge of the person in respect of whom it is published, or

(*b*) that it is necessary to publish in order to refute defamatory matter published in respect of him by another person,

if he believes that the defamatory matter is true and it is relevant to the invitation, challenge or necessary refutation, as the case may be, and does not in any respect exceed what is reasonably sufficient in the circumstances. R.S., c. C-34, s. 276.

CROSS-REFERENCES

Defamatory libel is defined in s. 298 and see cross-references under that section concerning related offences, special procedural provisions and other defences or excuses. Note however, in particular, that the plea of justification in cases of defamatory libel is dealt with in ss. 311, 607(2), 611 and 612. Under s. 612(3), where the accused is convicted, the court may consider, in pronouncing sentence, whether the offence was aggravated or mitigated by the plea. Publishing is defined in s. 299. As to vicarious liability of a newspaper proprietor, see s. 303. The related defence of publication for the public benefit is set out in ss. 308 and 309.

SYNOPSIS

This section provides an exemption to an offence under s. 300 for any person who publishes defamatory matter upon the invitation or challenge of the person to whom the matter is relevant, or which is necessary to refute defamatory matter published by another person in respect of himself. In order to qualify for this exemption, the person using it must believe that the defamatory matter is true, relevant to the invitation, challenge or refutation, and does not go beyond what could be considered to be reasonably sufficient in the circumstances.

ANSWERS TO INQUIRIES.

313. No person shall be deemed to publish a defamatory libel by reason only that he publishes, in answer to inquiries made to him, defamatory matter relating to a subject-matter in respect of which the person by whom or on whose behalf the inquiries are made has an interest in knowing the truth or who, on reasonable grounds, the person who publishes the defamatory matter believes has such an interest, if

(*a*) the matter is published, in good faith, for the purpose of giving information in answer to the inquiries;

(*b*) the person who publishes the defamatory matter believes that it is true;

(*c*) the defamatory matter is relevant to the inquiries; and

(*d*) the defamatory matter does not in any respect exceed what is reasonably sufficient in the circumstances. R.S., c. C-34, s. 277.

CROSS-REFERENCES

Defamatory libel is defined in s. 298 and see cross-references under that section concerning related offences, special procedural provisions and other defences or excuses. Note however, in particular, that the plea of justification in cases of defamatory libel is dealt with in ss. 311, 607(2), 611 and 612. Under s. 612(3), where the accused is convicted, the court may consider, in pronouncing sentence, whether the offence was aggravated or mitigated by the plea. Publishing is defined in s. 299. As to vicarious liability of a newspaper proprietor, see s. 303.

SYNOPSIS

If a person publishes defamatory matter in response to inquiries made by another person who has, or is believed to have, an interest in knowing the truth, that person, subject to certain restrictions, will not be guilty of an offence under s. 300. This excuse applies if the person who publishes the defamatory matter believes that it is true, if the defamatory matter is relevant to the inquiries and does not exceed what is *reasonably sufficient* in the circumstances, and if the defamatory matter is published in *good faith* for the purpose of responding to the inquiries.

GIVING INFORMATION TO PERSON INTERESTED.

314. No person shall be deemed to publish a defamatory libel by reason only that he publishes to another person defamatory matter for the purpose of giving information to that person with respect to a subject-matter in which the person to whom the information is given has, or is believed on reasonable grounds by the person who gives it to have, an interest in knowing the truth with respect to that subject-matter if

(*a*) the conduct of the person who gives the information is reasonable in the circumstances;

(*b*) the defamatory matter is relevant to the subject-matter; and

(*c*) the defamatory matter is true, or if it is not true, is made without ill-will toward the person who is defamed and is made in the belief, on reasonable grounds, that it is true. R.S., c. C-34, s. 278.

CROSS-REFERENCES

Defamatory libel is defined in s. 298 and see cross-references under that section concerning related offences, special procedural provisions and other defences or excuses. Note however, in particular, that the plea of justification in cases of defamatory libel is dealt with in ss. 311, 607(2), 611 and 612. Under s. 612(3), where the accused is convicted, the court may consider, in pronouncing sentence, whether the offence was aggravated or mitigated by the plea. Publishing is defined in s. 299. As to vicarious liability of a newspaper proprietor, see s. 303.

SYNOPSIS

This section, like s. 313, provides an exemption from criminal liability under s. 300 to a person who publishes defamatory matter to another person whom the person *believes*, on *reasonable grounds*, has an interest in knowing the truth. This section applies only if the conduct of the person who gives out this matter is *reasonable*, if the defamatory matter is relevant to the subject, and if the defamatory matter is true or, if not true, if the person who gives the defamatory matter does so *without ill-will* and *believes*, on *reasonable grounds*, that the matter is true.

PUBLICATION IN GOOD FAITH FOR REDRESS OF WRONG.

315. No person shall be deemed to publish a defamatory libel by reason only that he publishes defamatory matter in good faith for the purpose of seeking remedy or redress for a private or public wrong or grievance from a person who has, or who on reasonable grounds he believes has, the right or is under an obligation to remedy or redress the wrong or grievance, if

(*a*) he believes that the defamatory matter is true;

(*b*) the defamatory matter is relevant to the remedy or redress that is sought; and

(*c*) the defamatory matter does not in any respect exceed what is reasonably sufficient in the circumstances. R.S., c. C-34, s. 279.

CROSS-REFERENCES

Defamatory libel is defined in s. 298 and see cross-references under that section concerning related offences, special procedural provisions and other defences or excuses. Note however, in particular, that the plea of justification in cases of defamatory libel is dealt with in ss. 311, 607(2), 611 and 612. Under s. 612(3), where the accused is convicted, the court may consider, in pronouncing sentence, whether the offence was aggravated or mitigated by the plea. Publishing is defined in s. 299. As to vicarious liability of a newspaper proprietor, see s. 303.

SYNOPSIS

A person will not be criminally liable under s. 300 only by reason of the fact that he publishes defamatory matter in *good faith* for the purpose of seeking a redress for a private or public wrong from another person whom he *believes*, on *reasonable grounds*, to be obliged to remedy that wrong or grievance. This section requires that the person who publishes the defamatory matter believes that this material is true, that it is relevant to the remedy being sought, and that it does not exceed what is reasonably sufficient in the circumstances.

PROVING PUBLICATION BY ORDER OF LEGISLATURE / Directing verdict / Certificate of order.

316. (1) An accused who is alleged to have published a defamatory libel may, at any stage of the proceedings, adduce evidence to prove that the matter that is alleged to be defamatory was contained in a paper published by order or under the authority of the Senate or House of Commons or a legislature of a province.

(2) Where at any stage in proceedings referred to in subsection (1) the court, judge, justice or provincial court judge is satisfied that the matter alleged to be defamatory was contained in a paper published by order or under the authority of the Senate or House of Commons or a legislature of a province, he shall direct a verdict of not guilty to be entered and shall discharge the accused.

(3) For the purposes of this section, a certificate under the hand of the Speaker or clerk of the Senate or House of Commons or a legislature of a province to the effect that the matter that is alleged to be defamatory was contained in a paper published by order or under the authority of the Senate, House of Commons or legislature of a province, as the case may be, is conclusive evidence thereof. R.S., c. C-34, s. 280.

CROSS-REFERENCES

Defamatory libel is defined in s. 298 and see cross-references under that section concerning related offences, special procedural provisions and other defences or excuses. This section relates back to the defence set out in s. 307.

SYNOPSIS

This section provides a means by which a person, charged under s. 300, may prove that the matter alleged to be defamatory, was contained in a paper published by order or under the authority of the Senate or House of Commons or provincial legislature. (See s. 306(*b*).) The accused may raise s. 306(*b*) at any stage of the proceedings and, if the court is satisfied that the section applies, he shall direct a verdict of not guilty and discharge the accused. A certificate of the Speaker or clerk of the Senate, House of Commons or provincial legislature, to the effect that the matter alleged to be defamatory was contained in a paper published by order or under the authority of any of the bodies specified in s. 306(*b*), is conclusive evidence of facts contained in that certificate.

Verdicts

VERDICTS IN CASES OF DEFAMATORY LIBEL.

317. Where, on the trial of an indictment for publishing a defamatory libel, a plea of not guilty is pleaded, the jury that is sworn to try the issue may give a general verdict of guilty or not guilty on the whole matter put in issue on the indictment, and shall not be required or directed by the judge to find the defendant guilty merely on proof of publication by the defendant of the alleged defamatory libel, and of the sense ascribed thereto in the indictment, but the judge may, in his discretion, give a direction or opinion to the jury on the matter in issue as in other criminal proceedings, and the jury may, on the issue, find a special verdict. R.S., c. C-34, s. 281.

CROSS-REFERENCES

Defamatory libel is defined in s. 298 and see cross-references under that section concerning related offences, special procedural provisions and other defences or excuses. Note however, in particular, that the plea of justification in cases of defamatory libel is dealt with in ss. 311, 607(2), 611 and 612. Under s. 612(3), where the accused is convicted, the court may consider, in pronouncing sentence, whether the offence was aggravated or mitigated by the plea. Section 584(1) provides that no count for publishing a defamatory libel is insufficient by reason only that it does not set out the words that are alleged to be libellous. However, under s. 587(1)(*e*), particulars may be ordered further describing any writing or words that are the subject of the charge. Under s. 584(2), a count for publishing a libel may charge that the published matter was written in a sense that, by innuendo, made the publication thereof criminal and may specify that sense without any introductory assertion to show how the matter was written in that sense. Under s. 584(3), it is sufficient to prove that the matter was libellous, with or without innuendo.

SYNOPSIS

This section describes the kinds of verdicts that may flow from the trial on an indictment for publishing a defamatory libel. When the accused pleads not guilty to such an indictment, the jury may give a general verdict of guilty or not guilty on the whole matter. The judge is not empowered to direct the jury to find the accused guilty merely on the basis of proof of publication of the defamatory libel. The jury may, if the judge has exercised his discretion to give an opinion or direction to the jury on the matter in issue, find a special verdict.

Hate Propaganda

ADVOCATING GENOCIDE / Definition of "genocide" / Consent / Definition of "identifiable group".

318. (1) Every one who advocates or promotes genocide is guilty of an indictable offence and liable to imprisonment for a term not exceeding five years.

(2) In this section, "genocide" means any of the following acts committed with intent to destroy in whole or in part any identifiable group, namely,

(*a*) killing members of the group; or

(*b*) deliberately inflicting on the group conditions of life calculated to bring about its physical destruction.

(3) No proceeding for an offence under this section shall be instituted without the consent of the Attorney General.

(4) In this section, "identifiable group" means any section of the public distinguished by colour, race, religion, national or ethnic origin, age, sex, sexual orientation, gender identity or expression, or mental or physical disability. R.S., c. 11 (1st Supp.), s. 1; 2004, c. 14, s. 1; 2014, c. 31, s. 12; 2017, c. 13, s. 3.

CROSS-REFERENCES

"Attorney General" is defined in s. 2. Section 583(*h*) provides that a count in an indictment is not insufficient by reason only that it does not state that the required consent has been obtained. [As to notes concerning sufficiency of consent, see s. 583.]

The accused may elect his mode of trial pursuant to s. 536(2). Release pending trial is determined by s. 515, although the accused is eligible for release by the officer in charge under s. 498.

This offence may be the basis for an application for an authorization to intercept private communications by reason of s.183.

Procedure for an *in rem* proceeding against hate propaganda, which includes material advocating genocide, is set out in s. 320. The offences in relation to inciting hatred and hate propaganda are set out in s. 319. The offence of publishing false news is in s. 181. The offence of defamatory libel is dealt with in ss. 297 to 317.

SYNOPSIS

This section describes the offence of advocating or promoting genocide. Genocide is defined as the act of killing members of an identifiable group or of deliberately inflicting conditions on an identifiable group calculated to bring about the destruction of that group, in whole or in part. An identifiable group is defined as any section of the public distinguished by colour, race, religion, national or ethnic origin, age, sex, sexual orientation, or mental or physical disability. The offence is indictable, and may be prosecuted only with the consent of an Attorney General and is punishable by imprisonment not exceeding five years.

ANNOTATIONS

In *Mugesera v. Canada (Minister of Citizenship and Immigration)*, [2005] 2 S.C.R. 100, 197 C.C.C. (3d) 233, 30 C.R. (6th) 39, the Supreme Court of Canada held that this provision does not require proof that genocide had in fact occurred. The act of incitement has to be direct and public. The guilty mind required is an intent to directly prompt or provoke another to commit genocide. In this case, the applicant's public speech contained a deliberate call for the murder of Tutsis, which was sufficient to make a finding that he had attempted to incite citizens to act against one another. This finding and the fact that the applicant was aware of ethnic massacres that were taking place was sufficient to make out the necessary *mens rea*.

PUBLIC INCITEMENT OF HATRED / Wilful promotion of hatred / Defences / Forfeiture / Exemption from seizure of communication facilities / Consent / Definitions / "communicating" / "identifiable group" / "public place" / "statements".

319. (1) Every one who, by communicating statements in any public place, incites hatred against any identifiable group where such incitement is likely to lead to a breach of the peace is guilty of

(*a*) an indictable offence and is liable to imprisonment for a term not exceeding two years; or

(*b*) an offence punishable on summary conviction.

(2) Every one who, by communicating statements, other than in private conversation, wilfully promotes hatred against any identifiable group is guilty of

(*a*) an indictable offence and is liable to imprisonment for a term not exceeding two years; or

(*b*) an offence punishable on summary conviction.

(3) No person shall be convicted of an offence under subsection (2)

(*a*) if he establishes that the statements communicated were true;

(*b*) if, in good faith, the person expressed or attempted to establish by an argument an opinion on a religious subject or an opinion based on a belief in a religious text;

(*c*) if the statements were relevant to any subject of public interest, the discussion of which was for the public benefit, and if on reasonable grounds he believed them to be true; or

(*d*) if, in good faith, he intended to point out, for the purpose of removal, matters producing or tending to produce feelings of hatred toward an identifiable group in Canada.

(4) Where a person is convicted of an offence under section 318 or subsection (1) or (2) of this section, anything by means of or in relation to which the offence was committed, on such conviction, may, in addition to any other punishment imposed, be ordered by the presiding provincial court judge or judge to be forfeited to Her Majesty in right of the province in which that person is convicted, for disposal as the Attorney General may direct.

(5) Subsections 199(6) and (7) apply with such modifications as the circumstances require to section 318 or subsection (1) or (2) of this section.

(6) No proceeding for an offence under subsection (2) shall be instituted without the consent of the Attorney General.

(7) In this section,

"communicating" includes communicating by telephone, broadcasting or other audible or visible means;

"identifiable group" has the same meaning as in section 318;

"public place" includes any place to which the public have access as of right or by invitation, express or implied;

"statements" includes words spoken or written or recorded electronically or electro-magnetically or otherwise, and gestures, signs or other visible representations. R.S., c. 11 (1st Supp.), s. 1; 2004, c. 14, s. 2.

CROSS-REFERENCES

"Attorney General" is defined in s. 2. Section 583(*h*) provides that a count in an indictment is not insufficient by reason only that it does not state that the required consent has been obtained. [As to notes concerning sufficiency of consent, see s. 583.]

Where the prosecution elects to proceed by indictment on either of these offences then the accused may elect his mode of trial pursuant to s. 536(2). Where the prosecution elects to proceed by way of summary conviction then the trial of this offence is conducted by a summary conviction court pursuant to Part XXVII. The punishment for the offence is then as set out in s. 787 and the limitation period is set out in s. 786(2). In either case, release pending trial is determined by s. 515, although the accused is eligible for release by a peace officer under s. 496, 497 or by the officer in charge under s. 498.

Procedure for an *in rem* proceeding against hate propaganda is set out in s. 320. The offence of advocating genocide is in s. 318. The offence of publishing false news is in s. 181. The offence of defamatory libel is dealt with in ss. 297 to 317.

SYNOPSIS

This section creates two offences involving the inciting or promoting of hatred against an identifiable group.

In subsec. (1), the offence is committed if such hatred is incited by the communication, in a public place, of words likely to lead to a breach of the peace.

In subsec. (2) the offence is committed only by the *wilful* promotion of hatred against an identifiable group through the communication of statements other than in private conversation.

Subsection (3) creates defences to the offence where it is established that the statements are true, that they amount to the good faith expression of an opinion on a religious subject or an opinion based on a belief in a religious text, that they are reasonably believed to be true and are published with respect to a matter of public interest and to the public good, or that they are published in a good faith effort to identify hate engendering matters in order to have them removed. The wording seems to place the onus of establishing only the first of these four defences on the accused.

Both offences created in this section may be prosecuted by indictment or summarily, and are punishable, on indictment, to a term of imprisonment not exceeding two years. The offence in subsec. (2) may only be prosecuted with the consent of an Attorney General.

Subsections (4) and (5) specify that where a person is convicted of offences under this section or s. 318, the means of communication by which the offence is committed may be forfeited to the Crown, with the exception of communication facilities and equipment as described in s. 199(6) and (7).

Subsection (7) defines "communicating" to include audible or visible means, defines "identifiable group" as in s. 318, defines "public place" to include places in which the public has access by right or by express or implied invitation, and defines "statement" to include spoken, written or recorded words, and gestures, signs, or other visible representation.

ANNOTATIONS

Subsections (1) and (2) – "Wilful" in this subsection means with the intention of promoting hatred and does not include recklessness. The offence would therefore be made out only if the accused had as their conscious purpose the promotion of hatred against the identifiable group or if they foresaw that the promotion of hatred against that group was certain or morally certain to result and communicated the statements as a means of achieving some other purpose: *R. v. Buzzanga and Durocher* (1979), 49 C.C.C. (2d) 369 (Ont. C.A.).

This definition of the term "wilful" was approved by the Supreme Court of Canada in *R. v. Keegstra*, [1990] 3 S.C.R. 397, 61 C.C.C. (3d) 1. In that case, the court also considered the meaning to be attached to the other elements of the offence. The term "promotes" indicates active support or instigation. The term "hatred" connotes emotion of an intense and extreme nature that is clearly associated with vilification and detestation. It is an emotion that, if exercised against members of an identifiable group, implies that those individuals are to be despised, scorned, denied respect and made subject to ill-treatment on the basis of group affiliation.

"Promotes" means actively supports or instigates and requires more than mere encouragement. "Hatred" connotes emotions of an intense and extreme nature that is clearly associated with vilification and detestation. Only the most intense forms of dislike fall within the ambit of this offence. This offence does not require proof that the communication caused actual hatred. In determining whether the communication expressed hatred, the court must look at the understanding of a reasonable person in context. Although this requires the trier of fact to engage in a subjective interpretation of the communicated message to determine whether "hatred" was what the speaker intended to promote, it is insufficient that the message be offensive or that the trier of fact dislike the statements. The analysis must focus on the speech's audience and on its social and historical context. The speech is to be considered objectively having regard to the circumstances in which the speech was given, the manner and tone used and the persons to whom the message was addressed. In considering the *mens rea*, subsec. (1) requires something less than the intentional promotion of hatred while subsec. (2) requires the accused to have had, as a conscious purpose, the promotion of hatred against the identifiable group, or foresight that the promotion of hatred against that group was certain to result and nevertheless communicated the statements. In many instances, the *mens rea* will flow from the establishment of the elements of the criminal act of the offence: *Mugesera v. Canada (Minister of Citizenship and Immigration)*, [2005] 2 S.C.R. 100, 197 C.C.C. (3d) 233.

It constitutes misdirection to instruct the jury that if they found that the accused in his actions was aware that there was a danger that his conduct would cause the promotion of hatred against an identifiable group and knowing this he chose to persist in his conduct then the jury could make a finding of wilfullness. At most, the jury should be instructed that they may consider the risks known to the accused: *R. v. Keegstra* (1991), 63 C.C.C. (3d) 110 (Alta. C.A.).

"Willfully" includes willful blindness: *R. v. Harding* (2001), 40 C.R. (5th) 119 (Ont. S.C.J.), affd 160 C.C.C. (3d) 225 (Ont. C.A.), leave to appeal to S.C.C. refused [2003] 3 S.C.R. viii, 167 C.C.C. (3d) vi.

Although this subsection infringes freedom of expression, as guaranteed by s. 2(*b*) of the Charter, it constitutes a reasonable limit on that right and is therefore valid legislation: *R. v. Keegstra, supra.*

New forms of Internet-based communication do not amount to changed circumstances justifying reconsideration of *Keegstra, supra.* This provision remains constitutional: *R. v. Topham* (2017), 345 C.C.C. (3d) 542 (B.C.S.C.).

In *R. v. Krymowski*, [2005] 1 S.C.R. 101, 193 C.C.C. (3d) 129, the Crown particularized the identifiable group as being "Roma". The evidence showed that the accused referred to "gypsies" as the object of their hatred. To make out the offence, however, there was no need to prove any interchangeability between the specific hateful terms employed and the name by which the target group was identified in the information. The relevant questions to be asked were whether the Crown had proved beyond a reasonable doubt that the accused made some or all of the statements alleged in the information and whether the statements made, as a matter of fact, promoted hatred of the Roma. Moreover, dictionary definitions presented to the trial judge showed that "gypsy" can refer to an ethnic group properly known as "Roma", "Rom", or "Romany". The trial judge could therefore have taken judicial notice of that fact and then considered it, together with the rest of the evidence, to determine whether there was proof beyond a reasonable doubt that the accused did in fact intend to target Roma.

Subsection (3)(*a*) – Reversing the burden of proof to the defence that the statements were true as provided for in this paragraph while infringing the guarantee to the presumption of innocence in s. 11(*d*) of the Charter is a reasonable limit and therefore valid: *R. v. Keegstra, supra.* See also *R. v. Keegstra*, [1996] 1 S.C.R. 458, 105 C.C.C. (3d) 19.

Subsection (3)(*d*) – It would seem that this defence was simply provided out of an abundance of caution since it would be rare that a person could successfully invoke this exemption where it was shown that he *wilfully* promoted hatred: *R. v. Buzzanga and Durocher, supra.*

WARRANT OF SEIZURE / Summons to occupier / Owner and author may appear / Order of forfeiture / Disposal of matter / Appeal / Consent / Definitions / "court" / "genocide" / "hate propaganda" / "judge".

320. (1) A judge who is satisfied by information on oath that there are reasonable grounds for believing that any publication, copies of which are kept for sale or distribution in premises within the jurisdiction of the court, is hate propaganda, shall issue a warrant under his hand authorizing seizure of the copies.

(2) Within seven days of the issue of the warrant under subsection (1), the judge shall issue a summons to the occupier of the premises requiring him to appear before the court and show cause why the matter seized should not be forfeited to Her Majesty.

(3) The owner and the author of the matter seized under subsection (1) and alleged to be hate propaganda may appear and be represented in the proceedings in order to oppose the making of an order for the forfeiture of the matter.

(4) If the court is satisfied that the publication referred to in subsection (1) is hate propaganda, it shall make an order declaring the matter forfeited to Her Majesty in right of the province in which the proceedings take place, for disposal as the Attorney General may direct.

(5) If the court is not satisfied that the publication referred to in subsection (1) is hate propaganda, it shall order that the matter be restored to the person from whom it was seized forthwith after the time for final appeal has expired.

(6) An appeal lies from an order made under subsection (4) or (5) by any person who appeared in the proceedings

(*a*) on any ground of appeal that involves a question of law alone,

(*b*) on any ground of appeal that involves a question of fact alone, or

(*c*) on any ground of appeal that involves a question of mixed law and fact,

as if it were an appeal against conviction or against a judgment or verdict of acquittal, as the case may be, on a question of law alone under Part XXI, and sections 673 to 696 apply with such modifications as the circumstances require.

(7) No proceeding under this section shall be instituted without the consent of the Attorney General.

(8) In this section,

"court" means

(*a*) in the Province of Quebec, the Court of Quebec,

(*a*.1) in the Province of Ontario, the Superior Court of Justice,

(*b*) in the Provinces of New Brunswick, Manitoba, Saskatchewan and Alberta, the Court of Queen's Bench,

(*c*) in the Province of Newfoundland and Labrador, the Supreme Court, Trial Division,

(*c*.1) [*Repealed.* 1992, c. 51, s. 36.]

(*d*) in the Provinces of Nova Scotia, British Columbia and Prince Edward Island, in Yukon and in the Northwest Territories, the Supreme Court, and

(*e*) in Nunavut, the Nunavut Court of Justice;

"genocide" has the same meaning as in section 318;

"hate propaganda" means any writing, sign or visible representation that advocates or promotes genocide or the communication of which by any person would constitute an offence under section 319;

"judge" means a judge of a court. R.S., c. 11 (1st Supp.), s. 1; 1974-75, c. 48, s. 25; 1978-79, c. 11, s. 10; R.S.C. 1985, c. 27 (2nd Supp.), s. 10; c. 40 (4th Supp.), s. 2; 1990, c. 16, s. 4; 1990, c. 17, s. 11; 1992, c. 1, s. 58; 1993, c. 28, Sch. III, s. 31 (repealed 1999, c. 3, s. 12); 1998, c. 30, s. 14(*d*); 1999, c. 3, ss. 12, 29; 2002, c. 7, s. 142; 2015, c. 3, s. 49.

CROSS-REFERENCES

The procedure in this section resembles the *in rem* procedure for obscene publications in s. 164 and thus see notes under that section respecting procedure. The procedure for obtaining a normal search warrant to obtain evidence of commission of an offence is set out in ss. 487 and 487.1. The procedure for shutting down a hate-propaganda site on the internet is set out in s. 320.1.

SYNOPSIS

This section authorizes a judge of a court as defined in subsec. (8), with the consent of an Attorney General, to issue a warrant to seize copies of any publication where *reasonable grounds* exist *for believing* that the subject publication is hate propaganda and that copies are kept for sale or distribution in premises located within the court's jurisdiction. Hate propaganda means writings, signs or representations that advocate or promote genocide or which would constitute the incitement or promotion of hatred against an identifiable group contrary to s. 319. Subsection (2) requires the judge to issue a summons to the occupier of the premises that have been searched within seven days of the issuance of the warrant, requiring him to show cause why the seized copies should not be forfeited. The owner and author of the publication may appear and oppose forfeiture. Subsections (4) to (6) describe the procedure for forfeiture, restoration and appeal.

ANNOTATIONS

A warrant may be issued under the general search warrant provision, s. 487, although the investigation relates to hate literature offences: *R. v. Keegstra* (1984), 19 C.C.C. (3d) 254 (Alta. Q.B.), revd on other grounds 43 C.C.C. (3d) 150 (C.A.).

WARRANT OF SEIZURE / Notice to person who posted the material / Person who posted the material may appear / Non-appearance / Order / Destruction of copy / Return of material / Other provisions to apply / When order takes effect.

320.1 (1) If a judge is satisfied by information on oath that there are reasonable grounds to believe that there is material that is hate propaganda within the meaning of subsection 320(8) or computer data within the meaning of subsection 342.1(2) that makes hate propaganda available, that is stored on and made available to the public through a computer system within the meaning of subsection 342.1(2) that is within the jurisdiction of the court, the judge may order the custodian of the computer system to

(*a*) give an electronic copy of the material to the court;

(*b*) ensure that the material is no longer stored on and made available through the computer system; and

(*c*) provide the information necessary to identify and locate the person who posted the material.

(2) Within a reasonable time after receiving the information referred to in paragraph (1)(*c*), the judge shall cause notice to be given to the person who posted the material, giving that person the opportunity to appear and be represented before the court and show cause why the material should not be deleted. If the person cannot be identified or located or does not reside in Canada, the judge may order the custodian of the computer system to post the text of the notice at the location where the material was previously stored and made available, until the time set for the appearance.

(3) The person who posted the material may appear and be represented in the proceedings in order to oppose the making of an order under subsection (5).

(4) If the person who posted the material does not appear for the proceedings, the court may proceed *ex parte* to hear and determine the proceedings in the absence of the person as fully and effectually as if the person had appeared.

(5) If the court is satisfied, on a balance of probabilities, that the material is available to the public and is hate propaganda within the meaning of subsection 320(8) or computer data within the meaning of subsection 342.1(2) that makes hate propaganda available, it may order the custodian of the computer system to delete the material.

(6) When the court makes the order for the deletion of the material, it may order the destruction of the electronic copy in the court's possession.

(7) If the court is not satisfied that the material is available to the public and is hate propaganda within the meaning of subsection 320(8) or computer data within the meaning of subsection 342.1(2) that makes hate propaganda available, the court shall order that the electronic copy be returned to the custodian and terminate the order under paragraph (1)(*b*).

(8) Subsections 320(6) to (8) apply, with any modifications that the circumstances require, to this section.

(9) No order made under subsections (5) to (7) takes effect until the time for final appeal has expired. 2001, c. 41, s. 10; 2014, c. 31, s. 13.

CROSS-REFERENCES

"Judge" and "court" are defined in s. 320(8). No proceedings under this section shall be instituted without consent of the Attorney General in view of the combined operation of subsec. (8) and s. 320(7). Appeal rights are governed by s. 320(6).

SYNOPSIS

This section provides a procedure for shutting down sites on the Internet that contain material falling within the definition of hate propaganda. The procedure commences with an order made by a judge (defined in s. 320(8)) upon the judge being satisfied by information on oath of the matters set out in subsec. (1). Proceedings under this section cannot be instituted, however, without the consent of the Attorney General, in view of the combined operation of subsec. (8) and s. 320(7). Under the order, the custodian of the computer system must give an electronic copy to the court, ensure that the material is no longer stored on and made available through the computer system and provide information to identify and locate the person who posted the material. The judge must then cause notice to be given to the person who posted the material in accordance with subsec. (2). The person is then given an opportunity to show cause why the material should not be deleted from the computer system. If the person does not appear, the court may proceed *ex parte*. If the court is satisfied that the material is available to the public and is hate propaganda or data that makes hate propaganda available, the court may order the custodian of the computer system to delete the material (subsec. (5)) and destroy the electronic copy (subsec. (6)). If the court is not so satisfied, the electronic copy of the material is returned to the custodian and the order under subsec. (1) is terminated (subsec. (7)). Appeal rights are as provided for in s. 320. No order made under subsec. (5) to (7) takes effect until the time for final appeal has expired.

ANNOTATIONS

See *Citron v. Zundel* (2002), 41 C.H.R.R. D/274, a case concerning the Internet decided under s. 13 of the *Canadian Human Rights Act,* which proscribes telephonic communication of hate messages as a discriminatory practice if there is repeated communication of "any matter that is likely to expose a person or persons to hatred or contempt by reason of the fact that that person or those persons are identifiable on the basis of a prohibited ground of discrimination."

PART VIII.1 / OFFENCES RELATING TO CONVEYANCES

EDITOR'S NOTE: This Part, enacted in 2018, replaces the provisions in the former ss. 249 through 261. According to the government, the new regime was intended to: repeal and replace all transportation offences with a modern, simplified and coherent structure; authorize mandatory alcohol screening at the roadside where police have already made a lawful stop under provincial law or at common law; increase certain minimum fines and certain maximum penalties; facilitate investigation and proof of blood alcohol concentration; eliminate and restrict defences that encourage risk-taking behaviour and make it harder to enforce laws against drinking and driving; clarify Crown disclosure requirements; and permit an earlier enrolment in a provincial ignition interlock program. The voluminous case law under the previous regime will continue to provide guidance as courts and practitioners begin to apply the new provisions. We have therefore retained the annotations under the former ss. 249 through 261. Caution will need to be taken, however, in adapting the existing case law to the new regime given some significant differences. Among these are: the creation of a police power in s. 320.27 to demand an approved screening device breath sample without any suspicion of the presence of alcohol; the intended elimination of the "bolus" and "post-offence" drinking defences by way of the provisions of s. 320.14 making it an offence to be over the legal limit within two hours of driving; the stipulation of defence disclosure entitlements in relation to breath sample machinery in s. 320.34; and the increase of the maximum penalties for *simpliciter* offences to 10 years (indictable) and two years less a day (summary conviction) and for bodily harm offences to 14 years (indictable).

Interpretation

DEFINITIONS.

320.11 The following definitions apply in this Part.

"analyst" means a person who is, or a person who is a member of a class of persons that is, designated by the Attorney General under subparagraph 320.4(*b*)(ii) or paragraph 320.4(*c*).

"approved container" means a container that is designed to receive a sample of a person's blood for analysis and that is approved by the Attorney General of Canada under paragraph 320.39(*d*).

"approved drug screening equipment" means equipment that is designed to ascertain the presence of a drug in a person's body and that is approved by the Attorney General of Canada under paragraph 320.39(*b*).

"approved instrument" means an instrument that is designed to receive and make an analysis of a sample of a person's breath to determine their blood alcohol concentration and that is approved by the Attorney General of Canada under paragraph 320.39(*c*).

"approved screening device" means a device that is designed to ascertain the presence of alcohol in a person's blood and that is approved by the Attorney General of Canada under paragraph 320.39(*a*).

"conveyance" means a motor vehicle, a vessel, an aircraft or railway equipment.

"evaluating officer" means a peace officer who has the qualifications prescribed by regulation that are required in order to act as an evaluating officer.

"operate" means

(*a*) in respect of a motor vehicle, to drive it or to have care or control of it;

(*b*) in respect of a vessel or aircraft, to navigate it, to assist in its navigation or to have care or control of it; and

(*c*) in respect of railway equipment, to participate in the direct control of its motion, or to have care or control of it as a member of the equipment's crew, as

a person who acts in lieu of a member of the equipment's crew by remote control, or otherwise.

"qualified medical practitioner" means a person who is qualified under provincial law to practise medicine.

"qualified technician" means

(*a*) in respect of breath samples, a person who is designated by the Attorney General under paragraph 320.4(*a*); and

(*b*) in respect of blood samples, a person who is, or a person who is a member of a class of persons that is, designated by the Attorney General under subparagraph 320.4(*b*)(i).

"vessel" includes a hovercraft. 2018, c. 21, s. 15.

Recognition and Declaration

RECOGNITION AND DECLARATION.

320.12 It is recognized and declared that

(*a*) operating a conveyance is a privilege that is subject to certain limits in the interests of public safety that include licensing, the observance of rules and sobriety;

(*b*) the protection of society is well served by deterring persons from operating conveyances dangerously or while their ability to operate them is impaired by alcohol or a drug, because that conduct poses a threat to the life, health and safety of Canadians;

(*c*) the analysis of a sample of a person's breath by means of an approved instrument produces reliable and accurate readings of blood alcohol concentration; and

(*d*) an evaluation conducted by an evaluating officer is a reliable method of determining whether a person's ability to operate a conveyance is impaired by a drug or by a combination of alcohol and a drug. 2018, c. 21, s. 15.

Offences and Punishment

DANGEROUS OPERATION / Operation causing bodily harm / Operation causing death.

320.13 (1) Everyone commits an offence who operates a conveyance in a manner that, having regard to all of the circumstances, is dangerous to the public.

(2) Everyone commits an offence who operates a conveyance in a manner that, having regard to all of the circumstances, is dangerous to the public and, as a result, causes bodily harm to another person.

(3) Everyone commits an offence who operates a conveyance in a manner that, having regard to all of the circumstances, is dangerous to the public and, as a result, causes the death of another person. 2018, c. 21, s. 15.

CROSS-REFERENCES

The term "conveyance" is defined in s. 320.11. That definition includes the terms "motor vehicle" and "railway equipment", which are defined in s. 2. With respect to the offences in subsecs. (2) and (3) and the issue of causation, see ss. 224 to 226. For special jurisdictional rules relating to offences committed on the water or on aircraft in the course of a flight, see s. 476. Section 662(5) makes the offences under this section included offences where the count charges an offence of criminal negligence causing death (s. 220), criminal negligence causing bodily harm (s. 221), or manslaughter (s. 236) arising out of the operation of a conveyance. The related offences of impaired operation, refusal to comply with a demand, failure to stop after an accident, flight from a peace officer, and operation while prohibited are found in ss. 320.14, 320.15, 320.16, 320.17, and 320.18, respectively. The punishment provisions for this and the other related offences are found in ss. 320.19, 320.2, and 320.21. Other provisions relevant to sentencing are found in ss. 320.22 through 320.26, including driving prohibition orders in s. 320.24.

OPERATION WHILE IMPAIRED / Operation causing bodily harm / Operation causing death / Operation — low blood drug concentration / Exception — alcohol / Exception — drugs / Exception — combination of alcohol and drug.

320.14 (1) Everyone commits an offence who

(*a*) operates a conveyance while the person's ability to operate it is impaired to any degree by alcohol or a drug or by a combination of alcohol and a drug;

(*b*) subject to subsection (5), has, within two hours after ceasing to operate a conveyance, a blood alcohol concentration that is equal to or exceeds 80 mg of alcohol in 100 mL of blood;

(*c*) subject to subsection (6), has, within two hours after ceasing to operate a conveyance, a blood drug concentration that is equal to or exceeds the blood drug concentration for the drug that is prescribed by regulation; or

(*d*) subject to subsection (7), has, within two hours after ceasing to operate a conveyance, a blood alcohol concentration and a blood drug concentration that is equal to or exceeds the blood alcohol concentration and the blood drug concentration for the drug that are prescribed by regulation for instances where alcohol and that drug are combined.

(2) Everyone commits an offence who commits an offence under subsection (1) and who, while operating the conveyance, causes bodily harm to another person.

(3) Everyone commits an offence who commits an offence under subsection (1) and who, while operating the conveyance, causes the death of another person.

(4) Subject to subsection (6), everyone commits an offence who has, within two hours after ceasing to operate a conveyance, a blood drug concentration that is equal to or exceeds the blood drug concentration for the drug that is prescribed by regulation and that is less than the concentration prescribed for the purposes of paragraph (1)(*c*).

(5) No person commits an offence under paragraph (1)(*b*) if

(*a*) they consumed alcohol after ceasing to operate the conveyance;

(*b*) after ceasing to operate the conveyance, they had no reasonable expectation that they would be required to provide a sample of breath or blood; and

(*c*) their alcohol consumption is consistent with their blood alcohol concentration as determined in accordance with subsection 320.31(1) or (2) and with their having had, at the time when they were operating the conveyance, a blood alcohol concentration that was less than 80 mg of alcohol in 100 mL of blood.

(6) No person commits an offence under paragraph (1)(*c*) or subsection (4) if

(*a*) they consumed the drug after ceasing to operate the conveyance; and

(*b*) after ceasing to operate the conveyance, they had no reasonable expectation that they would be required to provide a sample of a bodily substance.

(7) No person commits an offence under paragraph (1)(*d*) if

(*a*) they consumed the drug or the alcohol or both after ceasing to operate the conveyance;

(*b*) after ceasing to operate the conveyance, they had no reasonable expectation that they would be required to provide a sample of a bodily substance; and

(*c*) their alcohol consumption is consistent with their blood alcohol concentration as determined in accordance with subsection 320.31(1) or (2) and with their having had, at the time when they were operating the conveyance, a blood

alcohol concentration less than the blood alcohol concentration established under paragraph 320.38(*c*). 2018, c. 21, s. 15.

Editor's Note: Reference should be made to the case law summarized in the annotations under the former s. 253, which (with appropriate modifications) will no doubt inform the courts' interpretation of the new offence.

CROSS-REFERENCES

The term "conveyance" is defined in s. 320.11. That definition includes the terms "motor vehicle" and "railway equipment", which are defined in s. 2. With respect to the offences in subsecs. (2) and (3) and the issue of causation, see ss. 224 to 226. For special jurisdictional rules relating to offences committed on the water or on aircraft in the course of a flight, see s. 476. The related offences of dangerous operation, refusal to comply with a demand, failure to stop after an accident, flight from a peace officer, and operation while prohibited are found in ss. 320.13, 320.15, 320.16, 320.17, and 320.18, respectively. The punishment provisions for this and the other related offences are found in ss. 320.19, 320.2, and 320.21. Other provisions relevant to sentencing are found in ss. 320.22 through 320.26, including mandatory prohibition orders in s. 320.24. Provisions governing the collection of evidence of the conveyance-related offences are found in ss. 320.27 through 320.3. Evidentiary rules pertaining to bodily samples are set out in ss. 320.31 through 320.35.

SYNOPSIS

This section creates the offence of operating a conveyance while impaired by alcohol and/or drug or while having a blood alcohol level or blood drug concentration in excess of the prescribed limit. Notably, paras. (1)(*b*), (*c*), and (*d*) also prohibit being over the legal limit within two hours of driving. This novel extension of the law is subject to exceptions for innocent intervening consumption in subsecs. (5), (6), and (7), which carve out consumption that occurred after driving, where the individual had no reason to expect a demand, and where the quantity consumed was consistent with a level that was under the limit at the time of driving. This has the effect of criminalizing consumption prior to driving in quantities sufficient to result in a reading over the limit, even where the level or concentration at the time of driving may have not yet risen above the limit. It also criminalizes consumption after driving, in situations where the individual had a reasonable expectation that he or she may be required to provide a sample (for example, after an accident), and that may serve to obstruct investigation of the offence. These provisions are designed to defeat the "bolus drinking" and "post-offence drinking defences".

FAILURE OR REFUSAL TO COMPLY WITH DEMAND / Accident resulting in bodily harm / Accident resulting in death / Only one conviction.

320.15 (1) Everyone commits an offence who, knowing that a demand has been made, fails or refuses to comply, without reasonable excuse, with a demand made under section 320.27 or 320.28.

(2) Everyone commits an offence who commits an offence under subsection (1) and who, at the time of the failure or refusal, knows that, or is reckless as to whether, they were involved in an accident that resulted in bodily harm to another person.

(3) Everyone commits an offence who commits an offence under subsection (1) and who, at the time of the failure or refusal, knows that, or is reckless as to whether, they were involved in an accident that resulted in the death of another person or in bodily harm to another person whose death ensues.

(4) A person who is convicted of an offence under this section is not to be convicted of another offence under this section with respect to the same transaction. 2018, c. 21, s. 15.

Editor's Note: The offence of failure or refusal to comply with a lawful breath demand was formerly found in s. 254(5). Reference should be made, with appropriate caution, to the annotations summarizing the case law under that provision.

CROSS-REFERENCES

The related offences of dangerous operation, impaired operation, failure to stop after an accident, flight from a peace officer, and operation while prohibited are found in ss. 320.13, 320.14, 320.16, 320.17, and 320.18, respectively. The punishment provisions for this and the other related offences are found in ss. 320.19, 320.2, and 320.21. Other provisions relevant to sentencing are found in ss. 320.22 through 320.26, including mandatory prohibition orders in s. 320.24. Provisions governing the collection of evidence of the conveyance-related offences are found in ss. 320.27 through 320.3. Evidentiary rules pertaining to bodily samples are set out in ss. 320.31 through 320.35.

FAILURE TO STOP AFTER ACCIDENT / Accident resulting in bodily harm / Accident resulting in death.

320.16 (1) Everyone commits an offence who operates a conveyance and who at the time of operating the conveyance knows that, or is reckless as to whether, the conveyance has been involved in an accident with a person or another conveyance and who fails, without reasonable excuse, to stop the conveyance, give their name and address and, if any person has been injured or appears to require assistance, offer assistance.

(2) Everyone commits an offence who commits an offence under subsection (1) and who at the time of committing the offence knows that, or is reckless as to whether, the accident resulted in bodily harm to another person.

(3) Everyone commits an offence who commits an offence under subsection (1) and who, at the time of committing the offence, knows that, or is reckless as to whether, the accident resulted in the death of another person or in bodily harm to another person whose death ensues. 2018, c. 21, s. 15.

Editor's Note: The offence of failing to stop at the scene of an accident was formerly found in s. 252. Reference should be made, with appropriate caution, to the annotations summarizing the case law under that provision.

CROSS-REFERENCES

The related offences of dangerous operation, impaired operation, failure to comply with a breath demand, flight from a peace officer, and operation while prohibited are found in ss. 320.13, 320.14, 320.15, 320.17, and 320.18, respectively. The punishment provisions for this and the other related offences are found in ss. 320.19, 320.2, and 320.21. Other provisions relevant to sentencing are found in ss. 320.22 through 320.26, including mandatory prohibition orders in s. 320.24.

FLIGHT FROM PEACE OFFICER.

320.17 Everyone commits an offence who operates a motor vehicle or vessel while being pursued by a peace officer and who fails, without reasonable excuse, to stop the motor vehicle or vessel as soon as is reasonable in the circumstances. 2018, c. 21, s. 15.

Editor's Note: The offence of flight from a peace officer was formerly found in s. 249.1. Reference should be made, with appropriate caution, to the annotations summarizing the case law under that provision.

CROSS-REFERENCES

The related offences of dangerous operation, impaired operation, failure to comply with a breath demand, failure to stop after an accident, and operation while prohibited are found in ss. 320.13, 320.14, 320.15, 320.16, and 320.18, respectively. The punishment provisions for this and the other related offences are found in ss. 320.19, 320.2, and 320.21. Other provisions relevant to sentencing are found in ss. 320.22 through 320.26, including mandatory prohibition orders in s. 320.24.

OPERATION WHILE PROHIBITED / Exception.

320.18 (1) Everyone commits an offence who operates a conveyance while prohibited from doing so

(*a*) by an order made under this Act; or

(*b*) by any other form of legal restriction imposed under any other Act of Parliament or under provincial law in respect of a conviction under this Act or a discharge under section 730.

(2) No person commits an offence under subsection (1) arising out of the operation of a motor vehicle if they are registered in an alcohol ignition interlock device program established under the law of the province in which they reside and they comply with the conditions of the program. 2018, c. 21, s. 15.

Editor's Note: The offence of driving while prohibited was formerly found in s. 259(4). Reference should be made, with appropriate caution, to the annotations summarizing the case law under that provision.

PUNISHMENT / Summary conviction / Minimum fines for high blood alcohol concentrations / Minimum fine — subsection 320.15(1) / Punishment — dangerous operation and other offences.

320.19 (1) Everyone who commits an offence under subsection 320.14(1) or 320.15(1) is liable on conviction on indictment or on summary conviction

(*a*) to the following minimum punishment, namely,

(i) for a first offence, a fine of $1,000,

(ii) for a second offence, imprisonment for a term of 30 days, and

(iii) for each subsequent offence, imprisonment for a term of 120 days;

(*b*) if the offence is prosecuted by indictment, to imprisonment for a term of not more than 10 years; and

(*c*) if the offence is punishable on summary conviction, to imprisonment for a term of not more than two years less a day.

(2) Everyone who commits an offence under subsection 320.14(4) is liable on summary conviction to a fine of not more than $1,000.

(3) Despite subparagraph (1)(*a*)(i), everyone who commits an offence under paragraph 320.14(1)(*b*) is liable, for a first offence, to

(*a*) a fine of not less than $1,500, if the person's blood alcohol concentration is equal to or exceeds 120 mg of alcohol in 100 mL of blood but is less than 160 mg of alcohol in 100 mL of blood; and

(*b*) a fine of not less than $2,000, if the person's blood alcohol concentration is equal to or exceeds 160 mg of alcohol in 100 mL of blood.

(4) Despite subparagraph (1)(*a*)(i), everyone who commits an offence under subsection 320.15(1) is liable, for a first offence, to a fine of not less than $2,000.

(5) Everyone who commits an offence under subsection 320.13(1) or 320.16(1), section 320.17 or subsection 320.18(1) is liable

(*a*) on conviction on indictment, to imprisonment for a term of not more than 10 years; or

(*b*) on summary conviction, to imprisonment for a term of not more than two years less a day. 2018, c. 21, s. 15.

Editor's Note: The punishment provisions for the drug- and alcohol-related driving offences were previously located in s. 255. Reference should be made, with appropriate caution, to the annotations summarizing the case law under that provision.

PUNISHMENT IN CASE OF BODILY HARM.

320.2 Everyone who commits an offence under subsection 320.13(2), 320.14(2), 320.15(2) or 320.16(2) is liable on conviction on indictment or on summary conviction

(*a*) to the following minimum punishment, namely,

(i) for a first offence, a fine of $1,000,

(ii) for a second offence, imprisonment for a term of 30 days, and

(iii) for each subsequent offence, imprisonment for a term of 120 days;

(*b*) if the offence is prosecuted by indictment, to imprisonment for a term of not more than 14 years; and

(*c*) if the offence is punishable on summary conviction, to imprisonment for a term of not more than two years less a day. 2018, c. 21, s. 15.

Editor's Note: The punishment provisions for the drug- and alcohol-related driving offences were previously located in s. 255. Reference should be made, with appropriate caution, to the annotations summarizing the case law under that provision.

PUNISHMENT IN CASE OF DEATH.

320.21 Everyone who commits an offence under subsection 320.13(3), 320.14(3), 320.15(3) or 320.16(3) is liable on conviction on indictment to imprisonment for life and to a minimum punishment of,

(*a*) for a first offence, a fine of $1,000;

(*b*) for a second offence, imprisonment for a term of 30 days; and

(*c*) for each subsequent offence, imprisonment for a term of 120 days. 2018, c. 21, s. 15.

Editor's Note: The punishment provisions for the drug- and alcohol-related driving offences were previously located in s. 255. Reference should be made, with appropriate caution, to the annotations summarizing the case law under that provision.

AGGRAVATING CIRCUMSTANCES FOR SENTENCING PURPOSES.

320.22 A court imposing a sentence for an offence under any of sections 320.13 to 320.18 shall consider, in addition to any other aggravating circumstances, the following:

(*a*) the commission of the offence resulted in bodily harm to, or the death of, more than one person;

(*b*) the offender was operating a motor vehicle in a race with at least one other motor vehicle or in a contest of speed, on a street, road or highway or in another public place;

(*c*) a person under the age of 16 years was a passenger in the conveyance operated by the offender;

(*d*) the offender was being remunerated for operating the conveyance;

(*e*) the offender's blood alcohol concentration at the time of committing the offence was equal to or exceeded 120 mg of alcohol in 100 mL of blood;

(*f*) the offender was operating a large motor vehicle; and

(*g*) the offender was not permitted, under a federal or provincial Act, to operate the conveyance. 2018, c. 21, s. 15.

DELAY OF SENTENCING / Exception to minimum punishment.

320.23 (1) The court may, with the consent of the prosecutor and the offender, and after considering the interests of justice, delay sentencing of an offender who has been found guilty of an offence under subsection 320.14(1) or 320.15(1) to allow the offender to attend a treatment program approved by the province in which the offender resides. If the court delays sentencing, it shall make an order prohibiting the offender from

operating, before sentencing, the type of conveyance in question, in which case subsections 320.24(6) to (9) apply.

(2) If the offender successfully completes the treatment program, the court is not required to impose the minimum punishment under section 320.19 or to make a prohibition order under section 320.24, but it shall not direct a discharge under section 730. 2018, c. 21, s. 15.

MANDATORY PROHIBITION ORDER / Prohibition period / Discretionary order of prohibition — low blood drug concentration / Discretionary order of prohibition — other offences / Prohibition period / Effect of order / Obligation of court / Validity of prohibition order not affected / Application — public place / Consecutive prohibition periods / Minimum absolute prohibition period.

320.24 (1) If an offender is found guilty of an offence under subsection 320.14(1) or 320.15(1), the court that sentences the offender shall, in addition to any other punishment that may be imposed for that offence, make an order prohibiting the offender from operating the type of conveyance in question during a period to be determined in accordance with subsection (2).

(2) The prohibition period is

(*a*) for a first offence, not less than one year and not more than three years, plus the entire period to which the offender is sentenced to imprisonment;

(*b*) for a second offence, not less than two years and not more than 10 years, plus the entire period to which the offender is sentenced to imprisonment; and

(*c*) for each subsequent offence, not less than three years, plus the entire period to which the offender is sentenced to imprisonment.

(3) If an offender is found guilty of an offence under subsection 320.14(4), the court that sentences the offender may, in addition to any other punishment that may be imposed for that offence, make an order prohibiting the offender from operating the type of conveyance in question during a period of not more than one year.

(4) If an offender is found guilty of an offence under section 320.13, subsection 320.14(2) or (3), 320.15(2) or (3) or under any of sections 320.16 to 320.18, the court that sentences the offender may, in addition to any other punishment that may be imposed for that offence, make an order prohibiting the offender from operating the type of conveyance in question during a period to be determined in accordance with subsection (5).

(5) The prohibition period is

(*a*) if the offender is liable to imprisonment for life in respect of that offence, of any duration that the court considers appropriate, plus the entire period to which the offender is sentenced to imprisonment;

(*b*) if the offender is liable to imprisonment for more than five years but less than life in respect of that offence, not more than 10 years, plus the entire period to which the offender is sentenced to imprisonment; and

(*c*) in any other case, not more than three years, plus the entire period to which the offender is sentenced to imprisonment.

(5.1) Subject to subsection (9), a prohibition order takes effect on the day that it is made.

(6) A court that makes a prohibition order under this section shall cause the order to be read by or to the offender or a copy of the order to be given to the offender.

(7) A failure to comply with subsection (6) does not affect the validity of the prohibition order.

(8) A prohibition order in respect of a motor vehicle applies only to its operation on a street, road or highway or in any other public place.

(9) If the offender is, at the time of the commission of the offence, subject to an order made under this Act prohibiting the offender from operating a conveyance, a court that makes a prohibition order under this section that prohibits the offender from operating the same type of conveyance may order that the prohibition order be served consecutively to that order.

(10) A person may not be registered in an alcohol ignition interlock device program referred to in subsection 320.18(2) until the expiry of

(*a*) in the case of a first offence, a period, if any, that may be fixed by order of the court;

(*b*) in the case of a second offence, a period of three months after the day on which the sentence is imposed or any longer period that may be fixed by order of the court; and

(*c*) in the case of a subsequent offence, a period of six months after the day on which the sentence is imposed or any longer period that may be fixed by order of the court. 2018, c. 21, s. 15.

Editor's Note: Driving prohibition orders were previously governed by s. 259. Reference should be made, with appropriate caution, to the annotations summarizing the case law under that provision.

STAY OF ORDER PENDING APPEAL / **Appeals to Supreme Court of Canada / Effect of conditions.**

320.25 (1) Subject to subsection (2), if an appeal is taken against a conviction or sentence for an offence under any of sections 320.13 to 320.18, a judge of the court to which the appeal is taken may direct that the prohibition order under section 320.24 arising out of the conviction shall, on any conditions that the judge imposes, be stayed pending the final disposition of the appeal or until otherwise ordered by that court.

(2) In the case of an appeal to the Supreme Court of Canada, a direction may be made only by a judge of the court from which the appeal was taken.

(3) The imposition of conditions on a stay of a prohibition order does not operate to decrease the prohibition period provided in the prohibition order. 2018, c. 21, s. 15.

Editor's Note: Stays of driving prohibition orders pending appeal were previously governed by s. 259. Reference should be made, with appropriate caution, to the annotations summarizing the case law under that provision.

EARLIER AND SUBSEQUENT OFFENCES.

320.26 In determining, for the purpose of imposing a sentence for an offence under subsection 320.14(1) or 320.15(1), whether the offence is a second, third or subsequent offence, any of the following offences for which the offender was previously convicted is considered to be an earlier offence:

(*a*) an offence under any of subsections 320.14(1) to (3) or section 320.15; or

(*b*) an offence under any of sections 253, 254 and 255, as those sections read from time to time before the day on which this section comes into force. 2018, c. 21, s. 15.

Investigative Matters

TESTING FOR PRESENCE OF ALCOHOL OR DRUG / **Mandatory alcohol screening.**

320.27 (1) If a peace officer has reasonable grounds to suspect that a person has alcohol or a drug in their body and that the person has, within the preceding three hours, operated a conveyance, the peace officer may, by demand, require the person to comply

with the requirements of either or both of paragraphs (*a*) and (*b*) in the case of alcohol or with the requirements of either or both of paragraphs (*a*) and (*c*) in the case of a drug:

(*a*) to immediately perform the physical coordination tests prescribed by regulation and to accompany the peace officer for that purpose;

(*b*) to immediately provide the samples of breath that, in the peace officer's opinion, are necessary to enable a proper analysis to be made by means of an approved screening device and to accompany the peace officer for that purpose;

(*c*) to immediately provide the samples of a bodily substance that, in the peace officer's opinion, are necessary to enable a proper analysis to be made by means of approved drug screening equipment and to accompany the peace officer for that purpose.

(2) If a peace officer has in his or her possession an approved screening device, the peace officer may, in the course of the lawful exercise of powers under an Act of Parliament or an Act of a provincial legislature or arising at common law, by demand, require the person who is operating a motor vehicle to immediately provide the samples of breath that, in the peace officer's opinion, are necessary to enable a proper analysis to be made by means of that device and to accompany the peace officer for that purpose. 2018, c. 21, s. 15.

Editor's Note: Screening demands for breath samples, bodily substances, and physical coordination tests were previously governed by s. 254. Reference should be made, with appropriate caution, to the annotations summarizing the case law under that provision. It should be noted that s. 320.27(2) now authorizes an approved screening device breath sample demand to be made even where the peace officer lacks a reasonable suspicion that there is alcohol in the driver's body.

SAMPLES OF BREATH OR BLOOD — ALCOHOL / Evaluation and samples of blood — drugs / Samples of breath — alcohol / Samples of bodily substances / Types of drugs / Condition / Approved containers / Retained sample / Validity of analysis not affected / Release of retained sample.

320.28 (1) If a peace officer has reasonable grounds to believe that a person has operated a conveyance while the person's ability to operate it was impaired to any degree by alcohol or has committed an offence under paragraph 320.14(1)(*b*), the peace officer may, by demand made as soon as practicable,

(*a*) require the person to provide, as soon as practicable,

(i) the samples of breath that, in a qualified technician's opinion, are necessary to enable a proper analysis to be made by means of an approved instrument, or

(ii) if the peace officer has reasonable grounds to believe that, because of their physical condition, the person may be incapable of providing a sample of breath or it would be impracticable to take one, the samples of blood that, in the opinion of the qualified medical practitioner or qualified technician taking the samples, are necessary to enable a proper analysis to be made to determine the person's blood alcohol concentration; and

(*b*) require the person to accompany the peace officer for the purpose of taking samples of that person's breath or blood.

(2) If a peace officer has reasonable grounds to believe that a person has operated a conveyance while the person's ability to operate it was impaired to any degree by a drug or by a combination of alcohol and a drug, or has committed an offence under paragraph 320.14(1)(*c*) or (*d*) or subsection 320.14(4), the peace officer may, by demand, made as soon as practicable, require the person to comply with the requirements of either or both of paragraphs (*a*) and (*b*):

(*a*) to submit, as soon as practicable, to an evaluation conducted by an evaluating officer to determine whether the person's ability to operate a conveyance is impaired by a drug or by a combination of alcohol and a drug, and to accompany the peace officer for that purpose; or

(*b*) to provide, as soon as practicable, the samples of blood that, in the opinion of the qualified medical practitioner or qualified technician taking the samples, are necessary to enable a proper analysis to be made to determine the person's blood drug concentration, or the person's blood drug concentration and blood alcohol concentration, as the case may be, and to accompany the peace officer for that purpose.

(3) An evaluating officer who has reasonable grounds to suspect that a person has alcohol in their body may, if a demand was not made under subsection (1), by demand made as soon as practicable, require the person to provide, as soon as practicable, the samples of breath that, in a qualified technician's opinion, are necessary to enable a proper analysis to be made by means of an approved instrument.

(4) If, on completion of the evaluation, the evaluating officer has reasonable grounds to believe that one or more of the types of drugs set out in subsection (5) — or that a combination of alcohol and one or more of those types of drugs — is impairing the person's ability to operate a conveyance, the evaluating officer shall identify the type or types of drugs in question and may, by demand made as soon as practicable, require the person to provide, as soon as practicable,

(*a*) a sample of oral fluid or urine that, in the evaluating officer's opinion, is necessary to enable a proper analysis to be made to ascertain the presence in the person's body of one or more of the types of drugs set out in subsection (5); or

(*b*) the samples of blood that, in the opinion of the qualified medical practitioner or qualified technician taking the samples, are necessary to enable a proper analysis to be made to ascertain the presence in the person's body of one or more of the types of drugs set out in subsection (5) or to determine the person's blood drug concentration for one or more of those types of drugs.

(5) For the purpose of subsection (4), the types of drugs are the following:

(*a*) a depressant;
(*b*) an inhalant;
(*c*) a dissociative anaesthetic;
(*d*) cannabis;
(*e*) a stimulant;
(*f*) a hallucinogen; or
(*g*) a narcotic analgesic.

(6) A sample of blood may be taken from a person under this section only by a qualified medical practitioner or a qualified technician, and only if they are satisfied that taking the sample would not endanger the person's health.

(7) A sample of blood shall be received into an approved container that shall be subsequently sealed.

(8) A person who takes samples of blood under this section shall cause one of the samples to be retained for the purpose of analysis by or on behalf of the person from whom the blood samples were taken.

(9) A failure to comply with subsection (7) or (8) does not by itself affect the validity of the taking of the sample or of an analysis made of the sample.

(10) A judge of a superior court of criminal jurisdiction or a court of criminal jurisdiction shall, on the summary application of the person from whom samples of blood were taken under this section, made within six months after the day on which the samples were taken, order the release of any sample that was retained to the person for

the purpose of examination or analysis, subject to any terms that the judge considers appropriate to ensure that the sample is safeguarded and preserved for use in any proceedings in respect of which it was taken. 2018, c. 21, s. 15.

Editor's Note: Demands for breath samples, blood samples, and bodily substances were previously governed by s. 254. Reference should be made, with appropriate caution, to the annotations summarizing the case law under that provision.

WARRANTS TO OBTAIN BLOOD SAMPLES / Form / Procedure — telephone or other means of telecommunication / Duration of warrant / Copy or facsimile to person / Taking of samples.

320.29 (1) A justice may issue a warrant authorizing a peace officer to require a qualified medical practitioner or a qualified technician to take the samples of a person's blood that, in the opinion of the practitioner or technician taking the samples, are necessary to enable a proper analysis to be made to determine the person's blood alcohol concentration or blood drug concentration, or both, if the justice is satisfied, on an information on oath in Form 1 or on an information on oath submitted to the justice by telephone or other means of telecommunication, that

(*a*) there are reasonable grounds to believe that the person has, within the preceding eight hours, operated a conveyance that was involved in an accident that resulted in bodily harm to themselves or another person or in the death of another person;

(*b*) there are reasonable grounds to suspect that the person has alcohol or a drug in their body; and

(*c*) a qualified medical practitioner is of the opinion that

(i) by reason of any physical or mental condition of the person, the person is unable to consent to the taking of samples of their blood, and

(ii) the taking of samples of the person's blood will not endanger their health.

(2) A warrant issued under subsection (1) may be in Form 5 or 5.1, varied to suit the case.

(3) Section 487.1 applies, with any modifications that the circumstances require, in respect of an application for a warrant that is submitted by telephone or other means of telecommunication.

(4) Samples of blood may be taken from a person under a warrant issued under subsection (1) only during the time that a qualified medical practitioner is satisfied that the conditions referred to in subparagraphs (1)(*c*)(i) and (ii) continue to exist.

(5) If a warrant issued under subsection (1) is executed, the peace officer shall, as soon as practicable, give a copy of it — or, in the case of a warrant issued by telephone or other means of telecommunication, a facsimile — to the person from whom the samples of blood are taken.

(6) Subsections 320.28(7) to (10) apply with respect to the taking of samples of blood under this section. 2018, c. 21, s. 15.

Editor's Note: Warrant to obtain blood samples from individuals incapable of giving consent to the taking were previously governed by s. 256. Reference should be made, with appropriate caution, to the annotations summarizing the case law under that provision.

TESTING BLOOD — DRUG OR ALCOHOL.

320.3 Samples of a person's blood that are taken for the purposes of this Part may be analyzed to determine the person's blood alcohol concentration or blood drug concentration, or both. 2018, c. 21, s. 15.

Evidentiary Matters

BREATH SAMPLES / Blood samples — concentration when sample taken / Evidence not included / Presumption — blood alcohol concentration / Admissibility of evaluating officer's opinion / Presumption — drug / Admissibility of result of analysis / Evidence of failure to provide sample / Admissibility of statement / Evidence of failure to comply with demand.

320.31 (1) If samples of a person's breath have been received into an approved instrument operated by a qualified technician, the results of the analyses of the samples are conclusive proof of the person's blood alcohol concentration at the time when the analyses were made if the results of the analyses are the same — or, if the results of the analyses are different, the lowest of the results is conclusive proof of the person's blood alcohol concentration at the time when the analyses were made — if

(*a*) before each sample was taken, the qualified technician conducted a system blank test the result of which is not more than 10 mg of alcohol in 100 mL of blood and a system calibration check the result of which is within 10% of the target value of an alcohol standard that is certified by an analyst;

(*b*) there was an interval of at least 15 minutes between the times when the samples were taken; and

(*c*) the results of the analyses, rounded down to the nearest multiple of 10 mg, did not differ by more than 20 mg of alcohol in 100 mL of blood.

(2) The result of an analysis made by an analyst of a sample of a person's blood is proof of their blood alcohol concentration or their blood drug concentration, as the case may be, at the time when the sample was taken in the absence of evidence tending to show that the analysis was performed improperly.

(3) Evidence of the following does not constitute evidence tending to show that an analysis of a sample of a person's blood was performed improperly:

(*a*) the amount of alcohol or a drug that they consumed;

(*b*) the rate at which the alcohol or the drug would have been absorbed or eliminated by their body; or

(*c*) a calculation based on the evidence referred to in paragraphs (*a*) and (*b*) of what their blood alcohol concentration or blood drug concentration would have been at the time the sample was taken.

(4) For the purpose of paragraphs 320.14(1)(*b*) and (*d*), if the first of the samples of breath was taken, or the sample of blood was taken, more than two hours after the person ceased to operate the conveyance and the person's blood alcohol concentration was equal to or exceeded 20 mg of alcohol in 100 mL of blood, the person's blood alcohol concentration within those two hours is conclusively presumed to be the concentration established in accordance with subsection (1) or (2), as the case may be, plus an additional 5 mg of alcohol in 100 mL of blood for every interval of 30 minutes in excess of those two hours.

(5) An evaluating officer's opinion relating to the impairment, by a type of drug that they identified, or by a combination of alcohol and that type of drug, of a person's ability to operate a conveyance is admissible in evidence without qualifying the evaluating officer as an expert.

(6) If the analysis of a sample provided under subsection 320.28(4) demonstrates that the person has a drug in their body that is of a type that the evaluating officer has identified as impairing the person's ability to operate a conveyance, that drug — or, if the person has also consumed alcohol, the combination of alcohol and that drug — is presumed, in the absence of evidence to the contrary, to be the drug, or the combination of alcohol and that drug, that was present in the person's body at the time when the

person operated the conveyance and, on proof of the person's impairment, to have been the cause of that impairment.

(7) The result of an analysis of a sample of a person's breath, blood, urine, sweat or other bodily substance that they were not required to provide under this Part may be admitted in evidence even if the person was not warned before they provided the sample that they were not required to do so or that the result of the analysis of the sample might be used in evidence.

(8) Unless a person is required to provide a sample of a bodily substance under this Part, evidence that they failed or refused to provide a sample for analysis or that a sample was not taken is not admissible and the failure, refusal or fact that a sample was not taken shall not be the subject of comment by any person in any proceedings under this Part.

(9) A statement made by a person to a peace officer, including a statement compelled under a provincial Act, is admissible in evidence for the purpose of justifying a demand made under section 320.27 or 320.28.

(10) In any proceedings in respect of an offence under section 320.14, evidence that the accused, without reasonable excuse, failed or refused to comply with a demand made under section 320.27 or 320.28 is admissible and the court may draw an inference adverse to the accused from that evidence. 2018, c. 21, s. 15.

Editor's Note: The evidentiary shortcuts and presumptions facilitating proof of drug- and alcohol-related driving offences were previously contained in s. 258. Reference should be made, with appropriate caution, to the annotations summarizing the case law under that provision.

CERTIFICATES / Notice of intention to produce certificate / Attendance and cross-examination / Form and content of application / Time of hearing / Certificate admissible in evidence / Onus.

320.32 (1) A certificate of an analyst, qualified medical practitioner or qualified technician made under this Part is evidence of the facts alleged in the certificate without proof of the signature or the official character of the person who signed the certificate.

(2) No certificate shall be received in evidence unless the party intending to produce it has, before the trial, given to the other party reasonable notice of their intention to produce it and a copy of the certificate.

(3) A party against whom the certificate is produced may apply to the court for an order requiring the attendance of the person who signed the certificate for the purposes of cross-examination.

(4) The application shall be made in writing and set out the likely relevance of the proposed cross-examination with respect to the facts alleged in the certificate. A copy of the application shall be given to the prosecutor at least 30 days before the day on which the application is to be heard.

(5) The hearing of the application shall be held at least 30 days before the day on which the trial is to be held.

(6) In proceedings in respect of an offence under subsection 320.18(1), the following certificates are evidence of the facts alleged in them without proof of the signature or official character of the person who signed them:

- **(*a*) a certificate setting out with reasonable particularity that the person named in it is prohibited from operating a motor vehicle in the province specified in the certificate, signed by the person who is responsible for the registration of motor vehicles in that province or any person authorized by the responsible person to sign it; and** (*b*) **a certificate setting out with reasonable particularity that the person named in it is prohibited from operating a conveyance other than a motor vehicle, signed by the Minister of Transport or any person authorized by him or her to sign it.**

(7) If it is proved that a prohibition under paragraph 320.18(1)(*b*) has been imposed on a person and that notice of the prohibition has been mailed to them at their last known address, that person is, beginning on the tenth day after the day on which the notice is mailed, in the absence of evidence to the contrary, presumed to have received the notice and to have knowledge of the prohibition, of the date of its commencement and of its duration. 2018, c. 21, s. 15.

PRINTOUT FROM APPROVED INSTRUMENT.

320.33 A document that is printed out from an approved instrument and signed by a qualified technician who certifies it to be the printout produced by the approved instrument when it made an analysis of a sample of a person's breath is evidence of the facts alleged in the document without proof of the signature or official character of the person who signed it. 2018, c. 21, s. 15.

DISCLOSURE OF INFORMATION / Application for further disclosure / Form and content of application / Time of hearing / For greater certainty.

320.34 (1) In proceedings in respect of an offence under section 320.14, the prosecutor shall disclose to the accused, with respect to any samples of breath that the accused provided under section 320.28, information sufficient to determine whether the conditions set out in paragraphs 320.31(1)(*a*) to (*c*) have been met, namely:

(*a*) **the results of the system blank tests;**

(*b*) **the results of the system calibration checks;**

(*c*) **any error or exception messages produced by the approved instrument at the time the samples were taken;**

(*d*) **the results of the analysis of the accused's breath samples; and**

(*e*) **a certificate of an analyst stating that the sample of an alcohol standard that is identified in the certificate is suitable for use with an approved instrument.**

(2) The accused may apply to the court for a hearing to determine whether further information should be disclosed.

(3) The application shall be in writing and set out detailed particulars of the information that the accused seeks to have disclosed and the likely relevance of that information to determining whether the approved instrument was in proper working order. A copy of the application shall be given to the prosecutor at least 30 days before the day on which the application is to be heard.

(4) The hearing of the application shall be held at least 30 days before the day on which the trial is to be held.

(5) For greater certainty, nothing in this section limits the disclosure to which the accused may otherwise be entitled. 2018, c. 21, s. 15.

PRESUMPTION OF OPERATION.

320.35 In proceedings in respect of an offence under section 320.14 or 320.15, if it is proved that the accused occupied the seat or position ordinarily occupied by a person who operates a conveyance, the accused is presumed to have been operating the conveyance unless they establish that they did not occupy that seat or position for the purpose of setting the conveyance in motion. 2018, c. 21, s. 15.

Editor's Note: The presumption established here was provided for in the former s. 258(1)(*a*). Reference should be made, with appropriate caution, to the annotations summarizing the case law under that provision.

General Provisions

UNAUTHORIZED USE OF BODILY SUBSTANCE / Unauthorized use or disclosure of results / Exception / Offence.

320.36 (1) No person shall use a bodily substance obtained under this Part for any purpose other than for an analysis under this Part.

(2) No person shall use, disclose or allow the disclosure of the results obtained under this Part of any evaluation, physical coordination test or analysis of a bodily substance, except for the purpose of the administration or enforcement of a federal or provincial Act related to drugs and/or alcohol and/or to the operation of a motor vehicle, vessel, aircraft or railway equipment.

(3) The results of an evaluation, test or analysis referred to in subsection (2) may be disclosed to the person to whom they relate, and may be disclosed to any other person if the results are made anonymous and the disclosure is made for statistical or research purposes.

(4) Everyone who contravenes subsection (1) or (2) commits an offence punishable on summary conviction. 2018, c. 21, s. 15.

REFUSAL TO TAKE SAMPLE / No liability.

320.37 (1) No qualified medical practitioner or qualified technician shall be found guilty of an offence by reason only of their refusal to take a sample of blood from a person for the purposes of this Part if they have a reasonable excuse for refusing to do so.

(2) No qualified medical practitioner, and no qualified technician, who takes a sample of blood from a person under this Part incurs any liability for doing anything necessary to take the sample that was done with reasonable care and skill. 2018, c. 21, s. 15.

REGULATIONS.

320.38 The Governor in Council may make regulations

(*a*) prescribing the qualifications required for a peace officer to act as an evaluating officer and respecting the training of evaluating officers;

(*b*) prescribing the blood drug concentration for a drug for the purpose of paragraph 320.14(1)(*c*);

(*c*) prescribing a blood alcohol concentration and a blood drug concentration for a drug for the purposes of paragraph 320.14(1)(*d*);

(*d*) prescribing the blood drug concentration for a drug for the purpose of subsection 320.14(4);

(*e*) prescribing the physical coordination tests to be conducted under paragraph 320.27(1)(*a*); and

(*f*) prescribing the tests to be conducted and procedures to be followed during an evaluation under paragraph 320.28(2)(*a*) and the forms to be used in recording the results of the evaluation. 2018, c. 21, s. 15.

APPROVAL — ATTORNEY GENERAL OF CANADA.

320.39 The Attorney General of Canada may, by order, approve

(*a*) a device that is designed to ascertain the presence of alcohol in a person's blood;

(*b*) equipment that is designed to ascertain the presence of a drug in a person's body;

(*c*) an instrument that is designed to receive and make an analysis of a sample of a person's breath to determine their blood alcohol concentration; and

(*d*) a container that is designed to receive a sample of a person's blood for analysis. 2018, c. 21, s. 15.

DESIGNATION — ATTORNEY GENERAL.

320.4 The Attorney General may designate

(*a*) a person as qualified, for the purposes of this Part, to operate an approved instrument;

(*b*) a person or class of persons as qualified, for the purposes of this Part,

(i) to take samples of blood, or

(ii) to analyze samples of bodily substances; and

(*c*) a person or class of persons as qualified, for the purposes of this Part, to certify that an alcohol standard is suitable for use with an approved instrument. 2018, c. 21, s. 15.

Part IX / OFFENCES AGAINST RIGHTS OF PROPERTY

Interpretation

DEFINITIONS / "break" / "credit card" / "document" / "exchequer bill" / "exchequer bill paper" / "false document" / "revenue paper".

321. In this Part

"break" means

(*a*) to break any part, internal or external, or

(*b*) to open any thing that is used or intended to be used to close or to cover an internal or external opening;

"Credit card" means any card, plate, coupon book or other device issued or otherwise distributed for the purpose of being used

(*a*) on presentation to obtain, on credit, money, goods, services or any other thing of value, or

(*b*) in an automated teller machine, a remote service unit or a similar automated banking device to obtain any of the services offered through the machine, unit or device;

"document" means any paper, parchment or other material on which is recorded or marked anything that is capable of being read or understood by a person, computer system or other device, and includes a credit card, but does not include trademarks on articles of commerce or inscriptions on stone or metal or other like material;

"exchequer bill" means a bank-note, bond, note, debenture or security that is issued or guaranteed by Her Majesty under the authority of Parliament or the legislature of a province;

"exchequer bill paper" means paper that is used to manufacture exchequer bills;

"false document" means a document

(*a*) the whole or a material part of which purports to be made by or on behalf of a person

(i) who did not make it or authorize it to be made, or

(ii) who did not in fact exist,

(*b*) that is made by or on behalf of the person who purports to make it but is false in some material particular,

(*c*) that is made in the name of an existing person, by him or under his authority, with a fraudulent intention that it should pass as being made by a person, real or fictitious, other than the person who makes it or under whose authority it is made;

"revenue paper" means paper that is used to make stamps, licences or permits or for any purpose connected with the public revenue. R.S., c. C-34, s. 282; R.S.C. 1985, c. 27 (1st Supp.), s. 42; 2014, c. 20, s. 366(1).

CROSS-REFERENCES

In addition to the definitions in this section, see s. 2 and notes to that section.

SYNOPSIS

This section contains definitions for a number of key terms that are employed throughout Part IX of the *Criminal Code* entitled "Offences Against Rights of Property".

ANNOTATIONS

False document – It is sufficient that the accused knows that the document purports to be a genuine document issued by an entity such as the government or other official authority that did not make the document or is non-existent. There is no requirement that there be an existing authentic document and a false document that so closely resembled the original as to raise a inference that it purported to be a copy of the authentic document: *R. v. Sommani* (2007), 218 C.C.C. (3d) 168 (B.C.C.A.), leave to appeal to S.C.C. refused 379 N.R. 394*n*.

Theft

THEFT / Time when theft completed / Secrecy / Purpose of taking / Wild living creature.

322. (1) Every one commits theft who fraudulently and without colour of right takes, or fraudulently and without colour of right converts to his use or to the use of another person, anything whether animate or inanimate, with intent,

- **(*a*) to deprive, temporarily or absolutely, the owner of it, or a person who has a special property or interest in it, of the thing or of his property or interest in it;**
- **(*b*) to pledge it or deposit it as security;**
- **(*c*) to part with it under a condition with respect to its return that the person who parts with it may be unable to perform; or**
- **(*d*) to deal with it in such a manner that it cannot be restored in the condition in which it was at the time it was taken or converted.**

(2) A person commits theft when, with intent to steal anything, he moves it or causes it to move or to be moved, or begins to cause it to become movable.

(3) A taking or conversion of anything may be fraudulent notwithstanding that it is effected without secrecy or attempt at concealment.

(4) For the purposes of this Act, the question whether anything that is converted is taken for the purpose of conversion, or whether it is, at the time it is converted, in the lawful possession of the person who converts it is not material.

(5) For the purposes of this section, a person who has a wild living creature in captivity shall be deemed to have a special property or interest in it while it is in captivity and after it has escaped from captivity. R.S., c. C-34, s. 283.

CROSS-REFERENCES

The punishment for theft is set out in s. 334 and therefore see that section for cross-references respecting mode of trial and release pending trial as well as special procedural provisions. For notes on the defence of mistake generally, see notes under s. 19. Section 323 deals with special property or interest in the case of oyster beds. Also, note s. 588 which deems certain persons to have a property interest in property of which they have the management, control or custody.

Section 583(*b*) deals with sufficiency of an indictment which fails to name the person who owns or has a special property or interest in property mentioned in the count. Sections 324 to 333 define other means by which theft may be committed. Offences resembling theft are set out in ss. 335 to 342. The related offence of false pretences is dealt with in ss. 361 to 363. Fraudulently obtaining food and lodging is an offence under s. 364. The general offence of fraud is contained in s. 380. The offence of secret commissions is set out in s. 426. The offence of possession of goods obtained by commission of an indictable offence is set out in ss. 354 and 355. The break and enter offences are dealt with in ss. 348 to 352. Robbery is dealt with in ss. 343 and 344. For notes on doctrine of recent possession, see s. 354.

SYNOPSIS

This section describes the offence of theft.

Subsection (1) states that a person commits theft when the person takes or converts anything with the intent to deprive the owner or person who has special property in it, to deposit it as security, to part with it under conditions that make its return dubious, or to deal with it in a manner that makes it impossible to return it in the condition it was in when it was taken. The person who commits theft as defined above must deal *fraudulently* and *without colour of right* with the subject matter of the charge. Subsection (3) states that a taking or conversion of a thing may be fraudulent even if it is done without secrecy or attempt at concealment. The section further sets out that a person who moves or causes a thing to be moved, or begins to make the thing moveable, with the *intent to steal* that thing, commits the offence of theft. Under subsection (4), the question of whether a converted item was taken for the purpose of conversion, or whether it is lawfully in the possession of the person who converted it is not material to an offence under this section. Finally, subsection (4) establishes that a person who has kept a wild living creature in captivity is deemed to have a special property or interest in the creature when it is in captivity and after it has escaped.

ANNOTATIONS

Special property or interest [also see s. 328] – The special property or interest must be in the very thing alleged to have been stolen. The interest a person may have in protecting himself against loss or damage resulting from the use of a forged document by and in the possession of another is neither property nor special property nor interest in the forged document. Further, the property or the special property or interest must exist at the time at which the theft, either by taking or conversion, is committed: *R. v. Smith*, [1962] S.C.R. 215, 131 C.C.C. 403.

In *R. v. Ben Smith; R. v. Harry Smith*, [1963] 1 C.C.C. 68 (Ont. C.A.), convictions for theft were upheld where the accused, who were directors of a company, without the knowledge of the other directors and without any authority from the company used the company's money to purchase certain shares which they then pledged with a bank to cover a personal overdraft. It was immaterial that the accused honestly intended, with reasonable prospects, to redeem the shares and pay back the company or that they in fact did so to the eventual profit of the company or that the accused were trustees for the company. On the facts the accused had temporarily deprived the company of a special property or interest in the shares, which includes the equitable interest of a *cestui que trust*.

A holder of a conditional sale agreement has an interest in his goods which are in the possession of the conditional buyer: *R. v. Maroney*, [1975] 2 S.C.R. 306, 18 C.C.C. (2d) 257 (5:0).

Notwithstanding that it is being illegally held, a narcotic may be the subject of a theft as defined in this section, the person with *de facto* ownership of the narcotic having a special property or interest in it: *R. v. Grasser* (1981), 64 C.C.C. (2d) 520 (N.S.S.C. App. Div.).

"Anything" – In *R. v. Scallen* (1974), 15 C.C.C. (2d) 441 (B.C.C.A.), it was held that the word "anything" in this section was wide enough to include a bank credit and that "anything" need not be something tangible or material.

Similarly, in *R. v. Hardy* (1980), 57 C.C.C. (2d) 73 (B.C.C.A.), a conviction for theft of "money" from his employer was upheld where the accused caused cheques to be made out to himself as additional salary, caused other cheques to be issued to cover repairs to his own cars and home, and instructed the company bookkeeper to offset a supplier's invoice for supplies or services delivered to the accused against the supplier's indebtedness of the company. The majority of the court were of the view that these various money credits with the employer's banker and with its customers which the accused diverted to himself or to his benefit were "anything" within the meaning of this section. Lambert J.A. although concurring in the result was of the view that dealings whereby the employer's accounts receivable were set-off were not within the indictment, a trade account receivable not properly being described as "money".

To come within the term "anything" in this section, the thing which is taken, whether tangible or intangible, must be of a nature such that it can be the subject of a proprietary right and the property must be capable of being taken or converted in a manner that results in the deprivation of the victim. Confidential information per se, rather than a list or other tangible object containing confidential information does not fall within this definition. Confidential information does not qualify as property for the purposes of this section and except in very unusual circumstances is not of a nature such that it can be taken or converted: *R. v. Stewart*, [1988] 1 S.C.R. 963, 41 C.C.C. (3d) 481 (6:0).

A promissory note falls within the definition of property in s. 2 and is thus "anything" capable of being stolen within the meaning of this section: *R. v. Cinq-Mars* (1989), 51 C.C.C. (3d) 248 (Que. C.A.).

Proof of ownership – In *R. v. Little and Wolski*, [1976] 1 S.C.R. 20, 19 C.C.C. (2d) 385 (5:0), an appeal from conviction for theft was dismissed where although the owner of the goods allegedly stolen was named in the indictment as "Westwood Jewellers Limited" the only evidence was that the goods were stolen from "Westwood Jewellers" which was owned and managed by one of the witnesses. The court divided on the effect of this apparent failure to prove ownership in the entity named in the indictment. de Grandpré J., for the majority held that if the owner of the object allegedly stolen is mentioned in the indictment and if his ownership is not proven and there are no other circumstances to indicate to the accused the true nature of the charge, an acquittal should be entered. However, when, as in the present case there cannot be any possibility for the accused to fail to identify the transaction about which they are charged, there is no reason to discharge the accused for the sole reason that the owner mentioned in the indictment has not been mentioned in the evidence. Dickson J., for himself and Beetz J., while agreeing that the conviction was proper, held that except in exceptional circumstances as where the theft can be inferred from the suspicious circumstances of the accused's possession, an allegation of ownership is not mere surplusage. However, the identity of the owner is sufficiently established in instances in which the owner is named in the indictment when, (i) the evidence adduced by the Crown reasonably identifies the owner with the person named in the indictment as owner, and (ii) it is clear that failure to prove the identity of the owner with greater precision has not misled or prejudiced the accused in preparation or presentation of his defence. In this case both (i) and (ii) were met and therefore the conviction was proper.

Conversion – In *R. v. Konken* (1971), 3 C.C.C. (2d) 348 (B.C.C.A.), the accused was acquitted of theft through conversion of a water pump. The majority held that the accused's explanation for retaining the pump, after overhearing conversation which might have led him to believe the pump was not abandoned as he thought, was reasonable and therefore the Crown had failed to prove that the accused had fraudulently and without colour of right converted the pump. Nemetz J.A., agreed that the accused should be acquitted and went on to hold that where a person retains goods innocently taken the essential element to support a conversion is that the knowledge subsequently acquired by the person must be of an unequivocal and unambiguous nature. In this case no knowledge of ownership was brought home to the accused.

Intent to deprive owner – In *R. v. O'Mahoney,* [1966] 2 C.C.C. 264 (B.C.C.A.), the accused was personally responsible for any shortages in accounts. Some shortages he made up by switching funds from one account to the other, but the ultimate deficiency he always made up from his own pocket. It was held that he did not have an intent to steal as set out in s. 322(1).

"Fraudulently" including "prank" defence – In *R. v. Ben Smith; R. v. Harry Smith, supra,* with respect to the issue of fraudulent intent the Court stated as follows (at p. 83 C.C.C.): "In *Stephen's History of the Criminal Law,* 1883, vol. II, pp. 121-2 two essential elements of fraudulent intent are stated to be "deceit or an intention to deceive or in some cases mere secrecy; and, secondly, either actual injury or possible injury or an intent to expose some person either to actual injury or to a risk of possible injury by means of that deceit or secrecy'. In vol. III of the same work the learned author adds to these two essential elements a possible third element, really implicit in the first one, which is that the conduct must not only be wrongful but intentionally and knowingly wrongful."

In *R. v. Kerr,* [1965] 4 C.C.C. 37 (Man. C.A.), the accused openly took a large ashtray "as a prank", intending to return it. It was held that there was no *animus furandi* as is required by the Code. The "prank" defence was rejected in *R. v. Heminger and Hornigold,* [1969] 3 C.C.C. 201 (Man. C.A.), the court distinguishing *Kerr* on the facts. In this case the accused had taken a chair from a beer parlour.

In *R. v. Bogner* (1975), 33 C.R.N.S. 349 (2:1) (Que. C.A.), the court appears to have rejected the concept of a "prank" defence. The majority held that a general dishonest state of mind in addition to the intent to do the acts constituting the *actus reus* was not required.

In *R. v. Théroux*, [1993] 2 S.C.R. 5, 79 C.C.C. (3d) 449, the court considered the *mens rea* of fraud under s. 380 of the *Criminal Code*. In that context, the court held that "an act of deceit which is made carelessly without any expectation of consequences, as for example, an innocent prank or a statement made in debate which is not intended to be acted upon, would not amount to fraud because the accused would have no knowledge that the prank would put the property of those who heard it at risk." It is unclear whether this would have any application to the question of prank under this section.

The element of fraud cannot be inferred merely from the accused's failure to return goods which were given to him by the owner, although the time set for the return of the goods has expired: *Washington (State) v. Johnson,* [1988] 1 S.C.R. 327, 40 C.C.C. (3d) 546 (4:3).

Colour of right – The term "colour of right" denotes an honest belief in a state of facts that, if true, would at law justify or excuse the act done. An accused bears the onus of showing that there is an "air of reality" to the asserted defence — *i.e.*, whether there is some evidence upon which a trier of fact, properly instructed and acting reasonably, could be left in a state of reasonable doubt about colour of right: *R. v. Simpson,* [2015] 2 S.C.R. 827, 327 C.C.C. (3d) 360.

In *R. v. DeMarco* (1973), 13 C.C.C. (2d) 369 (Ont. C.A.), it was held that an honestly asserted proprietary or possessory claim constitutes a colour of right notwithstanding it is unfounded in law or fact. Further, an absence of fraudulent intent may exist apart from a colour of right as conduct to be fraudulent must be dishonest and morally wrong. Also see *R. v. Howson,* [1966] 3 C.C.C. 348 (Ont. C.A.).

It was held in *R. v. Pace,* [1965] 3 C.C.C. 55 (N.S.C.A.), that theft may still be committed though the object is of no use or value to the owner. The court considered that a belief that the owner would consent to the taking if asked might constitute a colour of right defence but such a defence is not made out where the accused's belief is merely that no one would object to the taking.

The accused did not act under a colour of right where he obtained and then destroyed a promissory note evidencing his indebtedness to the complainant, because he believed that he was the victim of a fraud and feared losing his money. It was apparent that the accused was acting merely on the basis of a moral right in order to avoid having to exercise his legal rights through the court. A moral right cannot of itself found a colour of right: *R. v. Cinq-Mars* (1989), 51 C.C.C. (3d) 248 (Que. C.A.).

On a charge of theft involving alleged misappropriation by a real estate broker, of money held in his trust account, the issue on the availability of the defence of colour of right was not what the jury thought the accused's rights were in relation to the account but whether the accused had an honest belief he had a right to the money: *R. v. Lilly*, [1983] 1 S.C.R. 794, 5 C.C.C. (3d) 1 (7:0).

An honest belief in a moral as opposed to a legal right cannot constitute a colour of right defence. However, a belief in a moral right may negative a fraudulent intent: *R. v. Hemmerly* (1976), 30 C.C.C. (2d) 141 (Ont. C.A.).

Colour of right refers to a situation where there is an assertion of a proprietary or possessory right to the thing that is the subject of the alleged theft. Colour of right can either be a mistake concerning the facts or an honest mistaken belief in a civil claim to the thing. In the latter case, the issue is not whether the civil claim was well founded but rather whether the accused honestly believed he had such a claim: *R. v. Dorosh* (2004), 183 C.C.C. (3d) 224 (Sask. C.A.).

Passing of property – In determining whether property passed so that the offence, if any, could not constitute theft, the focus should be on the knowledge of the accused rather than the knowledge of the victim. Where a transferor mistakenly transfers property to a recipient, and the recipient knows of the mistake, property does not pass for the purpose of the criminal law if the law of property creates a right of recovery, no matter whether the original transfer is said to be void or voidable. If the recipient then converts the property to his own use, fraudulently and without colour of right, and with intent to deprive the transferor of the property, then he is guilty of theft: *R. v. Milne*, [1992] 1 S.C.R. 697, 70 C.C.C. (3d) 481 (5:0).

Where the accused received goods because the victim was induced to deliver them through the accused's fraud in providing a cheque which the accused knew would be dishonoured, then no title in the goods passed to the accused and he could be convicted of conversion. The civil law, such as the provincial *Sale of Goods Act*, had no application, provided that, as here, the victim had a right to recover the goods. It would be open to find an act of conversion when the accused took delivery and asserted ownership and control or later when he effected sales to third parties: *R. v. Smith* (1992), 77 C.C.C. (3d) 182 (Ont. C.A.), affd [1993] 3 S.C.R. 635, 84 C.C.C. (3d) 160*n* (5:0).

Included offence – On a charge of theft, possession of property obtained by crime is a lesser included offence pursuant to s. 662(1): *R. v. Francis* (2011), 279 C.C.C. (3d) 541 (Ont. S.C.J.).

OYSTERS / Oyster bed.

323. (1) Where oysters and oyster brood are in oyster beds, layings or fisheries that are the property of any person and are sufficiently marked out or known as the property of that person, that person shall be deemed to have a special property or interest in them.

(2) An indictment is sufficient if it describes an oyster bed, laying or fishery by name or in any other way, without stating that it is situated in a particular territorial division.

R.S., c. C-34, s. 284.

CROSS-REFERENCES

The general offence of theft is set out in s. 322 and see cross-references under that section respecting related offences. The punishment for theft is set out in s. 334 and therefore see that section for cross-references respecting mode of trial and release pending trial as well as special procedural provisions. Also, note s. 588 which deems certain persons to have a property interest in property of which they have the management, control or custody. Section 583(*b*) deals with sufficiency of an indictment which fails to name the person who owns or has a special property or interest in property mentioned in the count. Sections 324 to 333 define other means by which theft may be committed. Offences resembling theft are set out in ss. 335 to 342.

SYNOPSIS

This section bestows a special property interest in oysters and oyster brood contained in an oyster bed upon a person who owns the oysters and who has marked out or let it be known that they belong to him. An indictment charging on offence under this section does not require that the oyster bed be described as being situated in a particular territorial division so long as it is described by name or in some other way.

THEFT BY BAILEE OF THINGS UNDER SEIZURE.

324. Every one who is a bailee of anything that is under lawful seizure by a peace officer or public officer in the execution of the duties of his office, and who is obliged by law or agreement to produce and deliver it to that officer or to another person entitled thereto at a certain time and place, or on demand, steals it if he does not produce and deliver it in accordance with his obligation, but he does not steal it if his failure to produce and deliver it is not the result of a wilful act or omission by him. R.S., c. C-34, s. 285.

CROSS-REFERENCES

The term "steal" is defined in s. 2 as committing theft. The general offence of theft is defined in s. 322. The terms "peace officer" and "public officer" are defined in s. 2. The punishment for theft is set out in s. 334 and therefore see that section for cross-references respecting mode of trial and release pending trial as well as special procedural provisions. Also, note s. 588 which deems certain persons to have a property interest in property of which they have the management, control or custody. Section 583(*b*) deals with sufficiency of an indictment which fails to name the person who owns or has a special property or interest in property mentioned in the count. Sections 325 to 333 define other means by which theft may be committed. Offences resembling theft are set out in ss. 335 to 342. See, in particular, criminal breach of trust under s. 336 and public servant refusing to deliver property under s. 337. The offence of secret commission by an agent is set out in s. 426. See cross-references under s. 322 respecting other related offences.

SYNOPSIS

This section describes the offence of theft by a bailee of things under seizure. When a person is the bailee of any item that has been lawfully seized by a peace officer or a public officer and is obliged by law or agreement to produce that item to a specific person at a certain time and place, or on demand, he is deemed by this section to have stolen the item if he does not deliver it in accordance with his obligation. This section only applies if his failure to deliver the item is the result of a wilful act or omission on his part.

ANNOTATIONS

It is a necessary element of the offence under this section that the goods were lawfully seized. Where there is no evidence that the bailiff had ascertained that the goods which he purported to seize were on the premises at the time there was no valid seizure. An undertaking signed by the accused acknowledging the seizure and agreeing to hold the goods as a bailee could not be taken as an admission that the goods were on the premises if in fact they were not. Moreover whatever the civil consequences of signing the undertaking, in the absence of evidence that the accused read the undertaking it could not be taken as an admission in criminal proceedings: *R. v. Vroom* (1975), 23 C.C.C. (2d) 345, 58 D.L.R. (3d) 565 (Alta. S.C. App. Div.) (2:1).

AGENT PLEDGING GOODS, WHEN NOT THEFT.

325. A factor or an agent does not commit theft by pledging or giving a lien on goods or documents of title to goods that are entrusted to him for the purpose of sale or for any other purpose, if the pledge or lien is for an amount that does not exceed the sum of

(*a*) the amount due to him from his principal at the time the goods or documents are pledged or the lien is given; and

(*b*) the amount of any bill of exchange that he has accepted for or on account of his principal. R.S., c. C-34, s. 286.

CROSS-REFERENCES

The general offence of theft is defined in s. 322. The punishment for theft is set out in s. 334 and therefore see that section for cross-references respecting mode of trial and release pending trial as well as special procedural provisions. As to meaning of "bill of exchange", see *Bills of Exchange Act*, R.S.C. 1985, c. B-4. Sections 324, 326 and 328 to 333 define other means by which theft may be committed. Offences resembling theft are set out in ss. 335 to 342. See cross-references under s. 322 respecting other related offences.

SYNOPSIS

This section sets out the circumstances in which an agent *does not* commit the offence of theft when dealing with goods entrusted to him for the purpose of sale or otherwise. An agent who pledges or gives a lien on goods is not guilty of theft if the pledge or lien is for an amount that does not exceed the sum of the amount due to him from his principal or the amount of any bill of exchange that he has accepted for or on account of his principal.

THEFT OF TELECOMMUNICATION SERVICE / Definition of "telecommunication".

326. (1) Every one commits theft who fraudulently, maliciously, or without colour of right,

(*a*) abstracts, consumes or uses electricity or gas or causes it to be wasted or diverted; or

(*b*) uses any telecommunication facility or obtains any telecommunication service. R.S., c. C-34, s. 287; 1974-75-76, c. 93, s. 23; 2014, c. 31, s. 14(2).

(2) [*Repealed.* 2014, c. 31, s. 14(2).]

CROSS-REFERENCES

The term "radio" is defined in s. 35 of the *Interpretation Act*, R.S.C. 1985, c. I-21. The general offence of theft is defined in s. 322. The punishment for theft is set out in s. 334 and therefore see that section for cross-references respecting mode of trial and release pending trial as well as special procedural provisions. Section 327(2) provides for an order of forfeiture of an instrument or device in relation to which an offence under para. (1)(*b*) was committed. Sections 328 to 333 define other means by which theft may be committed. Offences resembling theft are set out in ss. 335 to 342. The related offence of possession of a device for unlawfully obtaining a telecommunication facility or service is in s. 327 and unauthorized use of a computer service in s. 342.1. See cross-references under s. 322 respecting other related offences. Part VI deals with interception of private communications and note, in particular, the offence in s. 191 of possession of a device designed for surreptitious interception of private communications.

SYNOPSIS

This section describes the offence of theft of electricity or gas, and also theft of a telecommunication service. Any person who *fraudulently, maliciously*, or *without colour of right*, abstracts, consumes, uses, diverts or wastes electricity or gas, or who uses any telecommunication facility or obtains any telecommunication services is guilty of theft.

ANNOTATIONS

The word "fraudulently" does not mean that the Crown must prove that the accused deceived the utility company into willingly providing the service; the expression only connotes an intentional and deliberate taking of service that was not his to obtain: *R. v. Brais* (1972), 7 C.C.C. (2d) 301 (B.C.C.A.).

A charge of fraudulently using a telecommunication wire requires that the accused acted intentionally and deliberately with knowledge that the service was not the accused's to obtain. Where the accused added several extension phones to the one properly installed by the telephone company the evidence failed to prove the element of knowledge that the incoming wire was not made available to him for use as he did and he was acquitted: *R. v. Renz* (1974), 18 C.C.C. (2d) 492 (B.C.C.A.).

The unauthorized use of the programmes and other information stored in a university computer did not involve use of a telecommunication facility within the meaning of this section notwithstanding access was gained to the computer through a remote terminal. This section is aimed at theft of information from a facility through which it is channelled; and a computer system is not a facility constructed to serve a telecommunication function as defined in subsec. (2) but is rather a data processing facility: *R. v. McLaughlin*, [1980] 2 S.C.R. 331, 53 C.C.C. (2d) 417 (5:0). [**Note:** now see s. 342.1, *infra*.]

The offence under para. (*b*) is not made out where the accused having innocently obtained the pay-TV signal continued to watch the signal without paying the cable company: *R. v. Miller and Miller* (1984), 12 C.C.C. (3d) 466 (Alta. C.A.).

POSSESSION OF DEVICE TO OBTAIN USE OF TELECOMMUNICATION FACILITY OR SERVICE / Forfeiture / Limitation / Definition of "device".

327. (1) Every person who, without lawful excuse, makes, possesses, sells, offers for sale, imports, obtains for use, distributes or makes available a device that is designed or adapted primarily to use a telecommunication facility or obtain a telecommunication service without payment of a lawful charge, knowing that the device has been used or is intended to be used for that purpose, is

(*a*) guilty of an indictable offence and liable to imprisonment for a term of not more than two years; or

(*b*) guilty of an offence punishable on summary conviction.

(2) If a person is convicted of an offence under subsection (1) or paragraph 326(1)(*b*), in addition to any punishment that is imposed, any device in relation to which the offence was committed or the possession of which constituted the offence may be ordered forfeited to Her Majesty and may be disposed of as the Attorney General directs.

(3) No order for forfeiture is to be made in respect of telecommunication facilities or equipment by means of which an offence under subsection (1) is committed if they are owned by a person engaged in providing a telecommunication service to the public or form part of such a person's telecommunication service or system and that person is not a party to the offence.

(4) In this section, "device" includes

(*a*) a component of a device; and

(*b*) a computer program within the meaning of subsection 342.1(2). 1974-75-76, c. 93, s. 24; 2014, c. 31, s. 15; 2018, c. 29, s. 32.

CROSS-REFERENCES

Possession is defined in s. 4(3). A party to an offence is defined in ss. 21 and 22. The related offence of theft of a telecommunication service is in s. 326. See cross-references under s. 322 respecting other related offences. See similar offences in relation to instruments for forging or falsifying credit cards (s. 342.01) and for unlawfully obtaining computer services (s. 342.2). Part VI deals with interception of private communications and note, in particular, the offence in s. 191 of possession of a device designed for surreptitious interception of private communications.

Where the Crown proceeds by indictment, the accused may elect the mode of trial pursuant to s. 536(2). Release pending trial is determined by s. 515, although the accused is eligible for release by the officer in charge under s. 498. This offence may be the basis of an application for an authorization to intercept private communications by reason of s. 183 and for a warrant to conduct video surveillance by reason of s. 487.01(5).

SYNOPSIS

This section makes it an offence for a person to manufacture, possess, sell or offer for sale, or distribute any device or component which is primarily useful in the activity described in s. 326(1)(*b*), *i.e.*, theft of a telecommunication service. The section specifies that no criminal liability will be found where the accused has a lawful excuse for possession of the described device. The section puts the onus of establishing the lawful excuse upon the accused and may thereby give rise to a challenge under s. 11(*d*) of the Charter. Subsections (2) and (3) deal with the issue of forfeiture of the device described above upon conviction, but such forfeiture will not be imposed in respect of a telephone, telegraph or other communications equipment which is owned by a person in the business of providing a telecommunications service to the public who was not a party to the offence.

ANNOTATIONS

A device used to descramble pay-TV signals is a device the design of which renders it primarily useful for obtaining the use of a telecommunication service within the meaning of this section although the pay-TV service is carried on the same cable as the regular television service which the accused legitimately receives: *R. v. Lefave* (1984), 15 C.C.C. (3d) 287 (Ont. Gen. Sess. Peace).

The possession offence under this section does not require proof that the accused intended to use the device himself and would cover circumstances where the accused is in possession for storage purposes under circumstances which give rise to a reasonable inference that he knows that the intended use of the device is to be by other persons who will eventually receive them for the purposes of obtaining the telecommunications service without payment of lawful charges: *R. v. Fulop* (1988), 46 C.C.C. (3d) 427 (Ont. C.A.), affd 63 C.C.C. (3d) 288*n* (S.C.C.).

A computer program on a computer disc by which the accused could make long-distance telephone calls without charge constitutes an instrument or device within the meaning of this section: *R. v. Duck* (1985), 21 C.C.C. (3d) 529 (Ont. Dist. Ct.).

THEFT BY OR FROM PERSON HAVING SPECIAL PROPERTY OR INTEREST.

328. A person may be convicted of theft notwithstanding that anything that is alleged to have been stolen was stolen

- **(*a*) by the owner of it from a person who has a special property or interest in it;**
- **(*b*) by a person who has a special property or interest in it from the owner of it;**
- **(*c*) by a lessee of it from his reversioner;**
- **(*d*) by one of several joint owners, tenants in common or partners of or in it from the other persons who have an interest in it; or**
- **(*e*) by the representatives of an organization from the organization. R.S., c. C-34, s. 288; 2003, c. 21, s. 4.**

CROSS-REFERENCES

The terms "organization", "representative" and "steal" are defined in s. 2 as committing theft. The general offence of theft is defined in s. 322. The punishment for theft is set out in s. 334 and therefore see that section for cross-references respecting mode of trial and release pending trial as well as special procedural provisions. Also, note s. 588 which deems certain persons to have a property interest in property of which they have the management, control or custody. Section 583(*b*) deals with sufficiency of an indictment which fails to name the person who owns or has a special property or interest in property mentioned in the count. Sections 324, 326 and 330 to 333 define other means by which theft may be committed. Offences resembling theft are set out in ss. 335 to 342. See cross-references under s. 322 respecting other related offences.

SYNOPSIS

This section describes the circumstances in which the offence of theft may be committed by the owner of an item or a person who has a special property or interest in it. The following are situations in which the offence will have been committed: (a) when an item is taken by the owner from a person who has a special property or interest in it; (b) when a person who has a special property or interest in an item steals it from the owner; (c) when an item is stolen by a lessee from the person to whom it reverts; (d) when one of several joint owners, tenants in common or partners of or in an item, takes it from the others; and (e) when the representatives of an organization steal from that organization.

ANNOTATIONS

In *R. v. Ben Smith; R. v. Harry Smith,* [1963] 1 C.C.C. 68 (Ont. C.A.), it was held that a special property or interest included the equitable interest of a *cestui que trust*. In this case the accused had converted the shares of a company for their own personal use. See s. 322.

A neighbour taking care of a dwelling-house in the absence of the owner, at the owner's request, has a special property or interest in the house and the moveable property in it: *R. v. Rodrigue* (1987), 61 C.R. (3d) 381 (Que. C.A.).

---

329. [*Repealed*, 2000, c. 12, s. 94.]

THEFT BY PERSON REQUIRED TO ACCOUNT / Effect of entry in account.

330. (1) Every one commits theft who, having received anything from any person on terms that require him to account for or pay it or the proceeds of it or a part of the proceeds to that person or another person, fraudulently fails to account for or pay it or the proceeds of it or the part of the proceeds of it accordingly.

(2) Where subsection (1) otherwise applies, but one of the terms is that the thing received or the proceeds or part of the proceeds of it shall be an item in a debtor and creditor account between the person who receives the thing and the person to whom he is to account for or to pay it, and that the latter shall rely only on the liability of the other as his debtor in respect thereof, a proper entry in that account of the thing received or the proceeds or part of the proceeds of it, as the case may be, is a sufficient accounting therefor, and no fraudulent conversion of the thing or the proceeds or part of the proceeds of it thereby accounted for shall be deemed to have taken place. R.S., c. C-34, s. 290.

CROSS-REFERENCES

As to limitation on restitution of property see s. 491.1(3). The general offence of theft is defined in s. 322. The punishment for theft is set out in s. 334 and therefore see that section for cross-references respecting mode of trial and release pending trial as well as special procedural provisions. Sections 324, 326, 328 and 331 to 333 define other means by which theft may be committed. Offences resembling theft are set out in ss. 335 to 342. See, in particular, criminal breach of trust under s. 336. The offence of secret commission by an agent is set out in s. 426. See cross-references under s. 322 respecting other related offences.

SYNOPSIS

This section describes a kind of theft which can be committed by a person who is required to account for, pay for or account for the proceeds of anything received from another person and *fraudulently* fails to do so. Subsection (2) creates an exception to this offence where a debtor-creditor account has been set up between two parties and a proper entry of the transaction is entered into that account.

ANNOTATIONS

Fraudulently – The element of fraud cannot be inferred merely from the accused's failure to return the goods within a reasonable time: *Washington (State) v. Johnson*, [1988] 1 S.C.R. 327, 40 C.C.C. (3d) 546 (4:3).

Terms requiring accused to account – In *R. v. Preston* (1958), 28 C.R. 51 (N.S.S.C., *in banco*), it was held (4:1) that the conviction failed upon lack of proof of the terms of accounting and fraudulent failure to account.

This section does not apply where the accused is required to return the specific article entrusted to him: *R. v. Kimbrough* (1918), 30 C.C.C. 56 (Alta. S.C. App. Div.).

An accused may be convicted of the offence described by this section where he failed to account for the proceeds of a cheque which he had been given while employed by a corporation, even if the improper dealings with the cheque may have arisen after the accused was fired by the corporation. The accused's obligation to account did not necessarily cease with his termination from the company: *R. v. Fischer* (1987), 31 C.C.C. (3d) 303 (Sask. C.A.).

Debtor and creditor account (subsec. (2)) – The saving provision of subsec. (2) does not apply where although the accused has a debtor and creditor relationship with persons to whom he is to pay the funds, it is no part of the terms on which the accused received the funds from a third party that the funds would be an item in a debtor and creditor account between the accused and the person to whom the funds were to be paid: *R. v. Lowden* (1981), 59 C.C.C. (2d) 1 (Alta. C.A.), affd on other grounds [1982] 2 S.C.R. 60, 68 C.C.C. (2d) 531 (9:0).

Charging offence – In *R. v. McKenzie*, [1972] S.C.R. 409, 4 C.C.C. (2d) 296, the accused was convicted on a charge that "unlawfully did commit theft of the sum of approximately sixteen dollars and fifty cents, the property of Dominic Louis Christian contrary to the form of the statute in such case made and provided", where as a taxi driver he failed to remit to the taxi's owner all the money due to him. On appeal by the Crown it was held (5:0), that the information was by virtue of s. 492(2)(*b*) [now s. 581(2)(*b*)] framed to declare the matter charged to be an indictable offence in the words of s. 280 [now s. 334] and was therefore sufficient and that the accused's failure to account to his employer was theft within this section.

THEFT BY PERSON HOLDING POWER OF ATTORNEY.

331. Every one commits theft who, being entrusted, whether solely or jointly with another person, with a power of attorney for the sale, mortgage, pledge or other disposition of real or personal property, fraudulently sells, mortgages, pledges or otherwise disposes of the property or any part of it, or fraudulently converts the proceeds of a sale, mortgage, pledge or other disposition of the property, or any part of the proceeds, to a purpose other than that for which he was entrusted by the power of attorney. R.S., c. C-34, s. 291.

CROSS-REFERENCES

The general offence of theft is defined in s. 322. The punishment for theft is set out in s. 334 and therefore see that section for cross-references respecting mode of trial and release pending trial as well as special procedural provisions. Sections 324, 326, 328, 330, 332 and 333 define other means by which theft may be committed. Offences resembling theft are set out in ss. 335 to 342. See, in particular, criminal breach of trust under s. 336. The offence of secret commission by an agent is set out in s. 426. See cross-references under s. 322 respecting other related offences.

As to limitation on restitution of property see, s. 491.1(3).

SYNOPSIS

This section sets out the offence of theft committed by a person who holds power of attorney. Any person entrusted solely or jointly with a power of attorney for the sale, mortgage, or other disposition of real or personal property, who *fraudulently* disposes of all or part of that property or *fraudulently* converts the proceeds of such disposition to a purpose other than that which the power of attorney specifies, commits the offence of theft.

MISAPPROPRIATION OF MONEY HELD UNDER DIRECTION / Effect of entry in account.

332. (1) Every one commits theft who, having received, either solely or jointly with another person, money or valuable security or a power of attorney for the sale of real or personal property, with a direction that the money or a part of it, or the proceeds or a part of the proceeds of the security or the property shall be applied to a purpose or paid to a person specified in the direction, fraudulently and contrary to the direction applies to any other purpose or pays to any other person the money or proceeds or any part of it.

(2) This section does not apply where a person who receives anything mentioned in subsection (1) and the person from whom he receives it deal with each other on such terms that all money paid to the former would, in the absence of any such direction, be properly treated as an item in a debtor and creditor account between them, unless the direction is in writing. R.S., c. C-34, s. 292.

CROSS-REFERENCES

The term "valuable security" is defined in s. 2 and its value determined by reference to s. 4(2). The general offence of theft is defined in s. 322. The punishment for theft is set out in s. 334 and therefore see that section for cross-references respecting mode of trial and release pending trial as well as special procedural provisions. Sections 324, 326, 328, 329 to 331 and 333 define other means by which theft may be committed. Offences resembling theft are set out in ss. 335 to 342. See, in particular, criminal breach of trust under s. 336. The offence of secret commission by an agent is set out in s. 426. See cross-references under s. 322 respecting other related offences.

As to limitation on restitution of property see, s. 491.1(3).

SYNOPSIS

This section describes the offence of theft of money held under direction. Any person who, *fraudulently* and *contrary to a direction* that money or valuable security be applied or paid to a specific person, applies to another purpose or pays to another person, part or all of the money or proceeds, commits the offence of theft. Subsection (1) does not apply if a debtor-creditor account exists, unless the direction referred to in subsec. (1) is in writing.

ANNOTATIONS

Fraudulent requires an intentional misappropriation, without mistake. The dishonesty inherent in the offence lies in the intentional and unmistaken application of funds to an improper purpose. In this case, it was established that the accused was aware of receiving the money with a direction and applied it intentionally to another purpose contrary to that direction: *R. v. Skalbania*, [1997] 3 S.C.R. 1235, 120 C.C.C. (3d) 217.

A conviction under this section was upheld where the accused, president of a brokerage house, received money for the purchase of a portion of a bond issue and on the date that the bonds were to be delivered was unable to effect delivery as the bonds were held by a bank and the accused lacked the funds to obtain delivery. The accused in the meantime had applied the money received for the purchase of the bonds to cover debts of his company. The offence under this section does not depend on the existence of a mandate. All that is required is a direction which in this case was the confirmation given by the accused confirming the sale and the date of delivery. The defence under subsec. (2) did not apply as by the terms of the agreement the accused was not to apply the funds to the credit of the victim's account generally but was to use the funds for a particular purpose, namely to pay for the bonds on the day they were issued. Finally, it was no defence to the charge that the accused was not required to keep the money *in specie*: *R. v. Legare*, [1978] 1 S.C.R. 275, 36 C.C.C. (2d) 463 (4:3).

The existence of a debtor and creditor relationship in the absence of a direction is a question of fact to be decided by the jury: *R. v. Finlay*, [1968] 2 C.C.C. 157 (Y.T.C.A.).

Where the only evidence of a direction is the expectation on the part of the person who gave the money to the accused then the offence under this section is not made out. However, expectations known to the accused as a result of express instructions are directions and there need not also be instructions as to what not to do with the money. Thus, an accused travel agent was properly convicted where money was paid to him by his clients for the express purpose of purchasing airline tickets for a particular trip on a regular carrier and the accused accepted the money for the purpose of satisfying those expectations and then dealt with the money so as to defeat that purpose: *R. v. Lowden*, [1982] 2 S.C.R. 60, 68 C.C.C. (2d) 531 (9:0).

TAKING ORE FOR SCIENTIFIC PURPOSE.

333. No person commits theft by reason only that he takes, for the purpose of exploration or scientific investigation, a specimen of ore or mineral from land that is not enclosed and is not occupied or worked as a mine, quarry or digging. R.S., c. C-34, s. 293.

CROSS-REFERENCES

The general offence of theft is defined in s. 322. The punishment for theft is set out in s. 334. For offences in relation to minerals and mines, see ss. 394 to 396.

SYNOPSIS

This section creates an exception to the offence of theft where a person takes, for the purpose of exploration or scientific investigation, a specimen of ore or mineral from land that is neither enclosed nor is being worked as a mine or quarry.

MOTOR VEHICLE THEFT / Subsequent offences.

333.1 (1) Everyone who commits theft is, if the property stolen is a motor vehicle, guilty of an offence and liable

- **(*a*) on proceedings by way of indictment, to imprisonment for a term of not more than 10 years, and to a minimum punishment of imprisonment for a term of six months in the case of a third or subsequent offence under this subsection; or**
- **(*b*) on summary conviction, to imprisonment for a term of not more than 18 months.**

(2) For the purpose of determining whether a convicted person has committed a third or subsequent offence, an offence for which the person was previously convicted is considered to be an earlier offence whether it was prosecuted by indictment or by way of summary conviction proceedings. 2010, c. 14, s. 3.

CROSS-REFERENCES

"Motor vehicle" is defined in s. 2. The offence of theft is defined in s. 322 and the punishment for the general offence of theft is set out in s. 334. The summary conviction offence of "joy-riding" is set out in s. 335. Also see s. 353 for offences with respect to automobile master keys, s. 353.1, offence of tampering with vehicle identification numbers, and s. 354(2), the presumption of knowing possession of stolen goods from possession of a vehicle or part with an obliterated vehicle identification number.

SYNOPSIS

This section simply creates elevated penalties for theft of automobiles. While the general theft offence in s. 334 would also apply to theft of motor vehicles, this section creates a different penalty structure which, *inter alia*, does not depend upon the value of the vehicle as would be the case under s. 334. In addition, this section creates a minimum penalty of six months' imprisonment for a third or subsequent offence under this section.

PUNISHMENT FOR THEFT.

334. Except where otherwise provided by law, every one who commits theft

(*a*) is guilty of an indictable offence and liable to imprisonment for a term not exceeding ten years, where the property stolen is a testamentary instrument or the value of what is stolen exceeds five thousand dollars; or

(*b*) is guilty

(i) of an indictable offence and is liable to imprisonment for a term not exceeding two years, or

(ii) of an offence punishable on summary conviction,

where the value of what is stolen does not exceed five thousand dollars. R.S., c. C-34, s. 294; 1972, c. 13, s. 23; 1974-75-76, c. 93, s. 25; R.S.C. 1985, c. 27 (1st Supp.), s. 43; 1994, c. 44, s. 20.

CROSS-REFERENCES

This section applies to theft as defined in ss. 322, 324, 326, 328 and 330 to 332. The terms "property" and "testamentary instrument" are defined in s. 2.

This offence may be the basis for an application for an authorization to intercept private communications by reason of s. 183 or for a warrant to conduct video surveillance by reason of s. 487.01(5). Theft is an enterprise crime offence for the purposes of Part XII.2.

As to admission of photographic evidence of property, see s. 491.2. For proof by way of affidavit of ownership, lawful possession, value, and that the person was deprived of property by fraud or otherwise without the person's lawful consent, see s. 657.1.

Where the offence, although committed outside Canada, is in relation to the use of nuclear material, see s. 7(3.4).

The offence in para. (*a*) is an indictable offence for which the accused may elect his mode of trial under s. 536(2). Where the prosecution elects to proceed by indictment for the offence under para. (*b*) then, by virtue of s. 553, it is an offence over which a provincial court judge has absolute jurisdiction and does not depend on the consent of the accused. That is, the accused does not have an election as to mode of trial, although the provincial court judge may, by virtue of s. 555(1), elect to continue the proceedings as a preliminary inquiry, in which case, the accused is deemed to have elected trial by judge and jury pursuant to s. 565(1)(*a*). As well, under s. 555(2), where, in the course of the trial, evidence establishes that the subject-matter of the offence is a testamentary instrument or that its value exceeds $5,000 then the provincial court judge shall put the accused to his election under s. 536(2). Where the prosecution elects to proceed by way of summary conviction then the proceedings are conducted by a summary conviction court pursuant to Part XXVII. The punishment is then as set out in s. 787 and the limitation period is set out in s. 786(2). For the offence under para. (*b*), release pending trial is determined by s. 515, although the accused is eligible for release by a peace officer under s. 496, 497 or by the officer in charge under s. 498. The value of a valuable security is determined in accordance with s. 4(2) and of a postal card or stamp in accordance with s. 4(1).

Section 588 deems certain persons to have a property interest in property of which they have the management, control or custody. By virtue of s. 583(*b*), an indictment which otherwise complies with s. 581 is not insufficient by reason that it fails to name the person who owns or has a special property or interest in property mentioned in the count. Offences resembling theft are set out in ss. 335 to 342. The related offence of false pretences is dealt with in ss. 361 to 363. Fraudulently obtaining food and lodging is an offence under s. 364. The general offence of fraud is contained in s. 380. The offence of secret commission is set out in s. 426. The offence of possession of goods obtained by commission of an indictable offence is set out in ss. 354 and 355. The break and enter offences are dealt with in ss. 348 to 352. Robbery is dealt with in ss. 343 and 344. Under s. 357, it is an offence to bring into or have in Canada anything that the accused has obtained outside Canada by an act that, if it had been committed in Canada, would have been the offence of theft.

SYNOPSIS

This section sets out the punishment for the offence of theft as described in the preceding sections. Where the value of the property stolen is greater than $5,000 or it is a testamentary instrument, the offence of theft is indictable and a person convicted of the offence faces a maximum term of 10 years' imprisonment. In other cases, the offence is either indictable, with a maximum of two years of imprisonment, or summary. This section only applies if there is no other specific provision for punishment in law [for example, theft of a credit card under s. 342 which contains its own punishment section].

Offences Resembling Theft

TAKING MOTOR VEHICLE OR VESSEL OR FOUND THEREIN WITHOUT CONSENT / Exception / Definition of "vessel".

335. (1) Subject to subsection (1.1), every one who, without the consent of the owner, takes a motor vehicle or vessel with intent to drive, use, navigate or operate it or cause it to be driven, used, navigated or operated, or is an occupant of a motor vehicle or vessel knowing that it was taken without the consent of the owner, is guilty of an offence punishable on summary conviction.

(1.1) Subsection (1) does not apply to an occupant of a motor vehicle or vessel who, on becoming aware that it was taken without the consent of the owner, attempted to leave the motor vehicle or vessel, to the extent that it was feasible to do so, or actually left the motor vehicle or vessel.

(2) For the purposes of subsection (1), "vessel" has the same meaning as in section 320.11. R.S., c. C-34, s. 296; 1972, c. 13, s. 23; R.S.C. 1985, c. 1 (4th Supp.), s. 15; 1997, c. 18, s. 15; 2018, c. 21, s. 16.

CROSS-REFERENCES

The term "motor vehicle" is defined in s. 2.

Trial of this offence is conducted by a summary conviction court pursuant to Part XXVII. The punishment is set out in s. 787 and the limitation period is set out in s. 786(2). Release pending trial is determined by s. 515, although the accused is eligible for release by a peace officer under ss. 496, 497 or by the officer in charge under s. 498.

The related offence of theft is defined in s. 322 and punished in accordance with s. 334. While the offence under this section is not specifically made an included offence of theft under s. 334, under s. 606(4), the accused may be permitted to plead guilty to this offence with the consent of the prosecutor.

SYNOPSIS

This section describes the offence of taking a motor vehicle or vessel, as defined in s. 214, with the intent to drive, operate, use or navigate it, or cause it to be driven, operated, used or navigated. The taking of the motor vehicle or vessel must be accomplished *without the owner's consent*. It is also an offence to be an occupant knowing it was taken without the consent of the owner. The offence is punishable on summary conviction. No offence is committed by the occupant if the occupant attempted to leave, to the extent feasible, upon becoming aware of the unlawful taking.

ANNOTATIONS

The offence under this section is not an included offence of theft under s. 334. The two offences are separate and in certain fact situations the accused may be prosecuted under either section at the option of the Crown. In particular an intent by the accused to return the vehicle does not preclude his conviction for theft: *R. v. LaFrance*, [1975] 2 S.C.R. 201, 13 C.C.C. (2d) 289 (6:3).

The offence of "occupant joyriding" created by this section does not violate ss. 7 or 11(*d*) of the *Canadian Charter of Rights and Freedoms*: *R. v. H. (P.)* (2000), 143 C.C.C. (3d) 223 (Ont. C.A.).

Section 794(2), which places the burden on the defendant to prove an exception, exemption, proviso, excuse or qualification prescribed by law, does not apply to the defence set out in subsec. (1.1): *R. v. H. (P.), supra.*

CRIMINAL BREACH OF TRUST.

336. Every one who, being a trustee of anything for the use or benefit, whether in whole or in part, of another person, or for a public or charitable purpose, converts, with intent to defraud and in contravention of his trust, that thing or any part of it to a use that is not authorized by the trust is guilty of an indictable offence and liable to imprisonment for a term not exceeding fourteen years. R.S., c. C-34, s. 296.

CROSS-REFERENCES

The term "trustee" is defined in s. 2.

Related offences: s. 122, breach of trust by official (defined in s. 118); s. 426, secret commission; s. 331, theft by person holding power of attorney; s. 322, conversion; s. 332, theft by person holding money, etc., under direction; s. 380, fraud.

Pursuant to s. 583, an indictment, which otherwise complies with s. 581, is not insufficient by reason (*b*), that it does not name the person who owns the property or (*c*), that it charges an intent to defraud without naming the person whom it was intended to defraud.

The accused may elect his mode of trial pursuant to s. 536(2). Release pending trial is determined by s. 515.

SYNOPSIS

This section describes the offence of criminal breach of trust. Any person who acts as a trustee and who, *with intent to defraud* and *in contravention of his trust*, converts the object of the trust, or any part of it, to a use not authorized by the trust, commits an indictable offence and is liable to a maximum term of imprisonment of 14 years.

ANNOTATIONS

The intent to defraud in this section is a limited intent directed to the trust duties: *R. v. Petricia* (1974), 17 C.C.C. (2d) 27 (B.C.C.A.).

Having charged the individual accused with the offence under this section in that "being a trustee of funds" he converted those funds to an unauthorized use, the Crown was required to prove that the accused was a trustee and it was not sufficient to prove he was party to an offence committed by the actual trustee, a corporate entity: *R. v. Rosen*, [1985] 1 S.C.R. 83, 16 C.C.C. (3d) 481 (7:0).

337. [*Repealed*, 2018, c. 29, s. 33.]

FRAUDULENTLY TAKING CATTLE OR DEFACING BRAND / Punishment for theft of cattle / Evidence of property in cattle / Presumption from possession.

338. (1) Every one who, without the consent of the owner,

(*a*) fraudulently takes, holds, keeps in his possession, conceals, receives, appropriates, purchases or sells cattle that are found astray, or

(*b*) fraudulently, in whole or in part,

(i) obliterates, alters or defaces a brand or mark on cattle, or

(ii) makes a false or counterfeit brand or mark on cattle,

is guilty of an indictable offence and liable to imprisonment for a term not exceeding five years.

(2) Every one who commits theft of cattle is guilty of an indictable offence and liable to imprisonment for a term not exceeding ten years.

(3) In any proceedings under this Act, evidence that cattle are marked with a brand or mark that is recorded or registered in accordance with any Act is, in the absence of any evidence to the contrary, proof that the cattle are owned by the registered owner of that brand or mark.

(4) Where an accused is charged with an offence under subsection (1) or (2), the burden of proving that the cattle came lawfully into the possession of the accused or his employee or into the possession of another person on behalf of the accused is on the accused, if the accused is not the registered owner of the brand or mark with which the cattle are marked, unless it appears that possession of the cattle by an employee of the accused or by another person on behalf of the accused was without the knowledge and authority, sanction or approval of the accused. R.S., c. C-34, s. 298; 1974-75-76, c. 93, s. 26.

CROSS-REFERENCES

The term "cattle" is defined in s. 2. Possession is defined by s. 4(3). The general theft offence is defined in s. 322 and the general offence of possession of goods obtained by crime in s. 354. Other offences in relation to cattle are in s. 444. Under s. 357, it is an offence to bring into or have in Canada anything that the accused has obtained outside Canada by an act that, if it had been committed in Canada, would have been the offence of theft.

Pursuant to s. 583(*b*), an indictment, which otherwise complies with s. 581, is not insufficient by reason that it does not name the person who owns the property.

The accused may elect his mode of trial pursuant to s. 536(2). Release pending trial is determined by s. 515, although the accused is eligible for release by the officer in charge pursuant to s. 498 for the offence under subsec. (1).

SYNOPSIS

This section sets up a code to govern the offence of stealing cattle, the punishment for this offence and some evidence and procedural provisions. Subsection (1) states that any person who, without the consent of the owner, *fraudulently* takes, keeps in his possession, holds, conceals, receives, appropriates, purchases or sells stray cattle is guilty of an indictable offence and liable to a maximum term of imprisonment of five years. Subsection (1) applies the same punishment to any person who *fraudulently* obliterates, alters or defaces a brand or mark, in whole or in part, on cattle, or who makes a false or counterfeit brand or mark on cattle. Subsection (2) describes the punishment for the more serious offence of cattle theft. This offence is also indictable but carries a maximum term of imprisonment of 10 years. Subsection (3) states that, in any proceedings under the *Criminal Code*, evidence that cattle are marked with a brand or mark registered in accordance with any Act is proof, in the absence of evidence to the contrary, that the cattle are owned by the registered owner of that brand. Subsection (4) puts the burden upon a person charged under subsec. (1) or (2) of proving that the cattle came lawfully into his possession or constructive possession, if that person is not the registered owner of the brand with which the cattle are marked. The accused will not bear the burden of proof under subsec. (4), if it appears that the possession of the cattle by an employee or other person on his behalf, was without the knowledge and authority, sanction or approval of the accused.

ANNOTATIONS

A charge under this section was dismissed where, although the circumstances were suspicious and established negligence on the part of the accused in that he failed to make any attempt to verify the identity of the cattle and make those inspections which a reasonably prudent rancher would make, still the Crown had not established the requisite *mens rea.* This case was interesting in that expert evidence was adduced as to the behaviour of cows in "mothering up" to their own calves in order to establish that certain calves were not the offspring of the accused's own cattle: *R. v. Galpin* (1977), 34 C.C.C. (2d) 545 (B.C. Prov. Ct.).

TAKING POSSESSION ETC., OF DRIFT TIMBER / Dealer in second-hand goods / Search for timber unlawfully detained / Evidence of property in timber / Presumption from possession / Definitions / "coastal waters of Canada" / "lumber" / "lumbering equipment".

339. (1) Every one is guilty of an indictable offence and liable to imprisonment for a term not exceeding five years who, without the consent of the owner,

- **(*a*) fraudulently takes, holds, keeps in his possession, conceals, receives, appropriates, purchases or sells,**
- **(*b*) removes, alters, obliterates or defaces a mark or number on, or**
- **(*c*) refuses to deliver up to the owner or to the person in charge thereof on behalf of the owner or to a person authorized by the owner to receive it,**

any lumber or lumbering equipment that is found adrift, cast ashore or lying on or embedded in the bed or bottom, or on the bank or beach, of a river, stream or lake in Canada, or in the harbours or any of the coastal waters of Canada.

(2) Every one who, being a dealer in second-hand goods of any kind, trades or traffics in or has in his possession for sale or traffic any lumbering equipment that is marked with the mark, brand, registered timber mark, name or initials of a person, without the written consent of that person, is guilty of an offence punishable on summary conviction.

(3) A peace officer who suspects, on reasonable grounds, that any lumber owned by any person and bearing the registered timber mark of that person is kept or detained in or on any place without the knowledge or consent of that person, may enter into or on that place to ascertain whether or not it is detained there without the knowledge or consent of that person.

(4) Where any lumber or lumbering equipment is marked with a timber mark or a boom chain brand registered under any Act, the mark or brand is, in proceedings under subsection (1), and, in the absence of any evidence to the contrary, proof that it is the property of the registered owner of the mark or brand.

(5) Where an accused or his servants or agents are in possession of lumber or lumbering equipment marked with the mark, brand, registered timber mark, name or initials of another person, the burden of proving that it came lawfully into his possession or into possession of his servants or agents is, in proceedings under subsection (1), on the accused.

(6) In this section,

"coastal waters of Canada" includes all of Queen Charlotte Sound, all of the Strait of Georgia and the Canadian waters of the Strait of Juan de Fuca;

"lumber" means timber, mast, spar, shingle bolt, sawlog or lumber of any description;

"lumbering equipment" includes a boom chain, chain, line and shackle. R.S., c. C-34, s. 299.

CROSS-REFERENCES

Possession is defined by s. 4(3). The term "peace officer" is defined in s. 2. The power given a peace officer under subsec. (3) would seem to be a search within the meaning of s. 8 of the Charter of Rights and Freedoms and therefore see notes under that section.

Pursuant to s. 583(*b*), an indictment, which otherwise complies with s. 581, is not insufficient by reason that it does not name the person who owns the property.

The accused may elect his mode of trial pursuant to s. 536(2) for the offence under subsec. (1) and release pending trial is determined by s. 515, although the accused is eligible for release by the officer in charge pursuant to s. 498. Trial of the offence described by subsec. (2) is conducted by a summary conviction court pursuant to Part XXVII. The punishment is as set out in s. 787 [although note the maximum fine for a corporation is as set out in s. 735] and the limitation period is set out in s. 786(2). Release pending trial is determined by s. 515, although the accused is eligible for release by a peace officer under s. 496, 497 or by the officer in charge under s. 498.

SYNOPSIS

This section sets out a number of provisions that deal with offences in relation to certain specified kinds of lumber and lumbering equipment. Subsection (1)(*a*) states that any person who, *without the consent of the owner, fraudulently* takes, holds, keeps in his possession, appropriates, purchases or sells any lumber or lumbering equipment found adrift or embedded in the shore, bottom or bed of any river, stream or lake in Canada, or in the harbours of coastal waters of Canada commits an indictable offence with a maximum term of imprisonment of five years. Subsection (1)(*b*) and (*c*) apply the same punishment to any person who, *without the consent of the owner*, removes, alters, obliterates or defaces a mark or number, or who refuses to deliver to the owner or person authorized to receive it, any lumber found in the places described above. It is to be noted that subsec. (1)(*a*) specifies that the acts described therein be committed *fraudulently* whereas subsec. (1)(*b*) and (*c*) do not have the same requirement. Subsection (2) makes it a summary conviction offence for a second-hand dealer to trade, or have in his possession to sell, lumbering equipment that is marked with the name or initials of a person or with a name, brand or registered timber mark, unless the dealer has the *written consent* of that person. Subsection (3) empowers a peace officer, who has *reasonable grounds to suspect* that lumber owned by another person is being kept or detained in any place without the owner's knowledge or consent, to enter that place to ascertain whether or not his suspicions are founded. This section, which permits entry into a place without a warrant, may be found to offend s. 8 of the Charter. Any lumber or lumbering equipment marked with a registered timber mark or boom chain brand is presumed to be the property of the registered owner of the mark or brand in proceedings under subsec. (1), unless there is evidence to the contrary. Subsection (5) places on a person charged under subsec. (1) the burden of proving that lumber or lumbering equipment marked with a brand mark, registered timber mark, name or initials of another person, that is in the possession of the accused came to be so possessed lawfully.

DESTROYING DOCUMENTS OF TITLE.

340. Every one who, for a fraudulent purpose, destroys, cancels, conceals or obliterates

(*a*) a document of title to goods or lands,

(*b*) a valuable security or testamentary instrument, or

(*c*) a judicial or official document,

is guilty of an indictable offence and liable to imprisonment for a term not exceeding ten years. R.S., c. C-34, s. 300.

CROSS-REFERENCES

The terms "document of title to goods", "document of title to lands", "valuable security" and "testamentary instrument" are defined in s. 2. The value of a valuable security is determined in accordance with s. 4(2).

The accused may elect his mode of trial pursuant to s. 536(2). Release pending trial is determined by s. 515.

SYNOPSIS

This section describes the offence of destroying, cancelling, concealing or obliterating a document of title to lands or goods, a valuable security or testamentary instrument, or a judicial or official document. The action must be done with a *fraudulent purpose*. The offence is indictable and carries a maximum term of imprisonment of 10 years.

FRAUDULENT CONCEALMENT.

341. Every one who, for a fraudulent purpose, takes, obtains, removes or conceals anything is guilty of an indictable offence and liable to imprisonment for a term not exceeding two years. R.S., c. C-34, s. 301.

CROSS-REFERENCES

The accused may elect his mode of trial pursuant to s. 536(2). Release pending trial is determined by s. 515, although the accused is eligible for release by the officer in charge pursuant to s. 498. The related offences of fraudulent concealment of title documents are in ss. 340 and 385.

Where the offence, although committed outside Canada, is in relation to the use of nuclear material, see s. 7(3.4).

SYNOPSIS

This section describes the offence of fraudulent concealment. Any person who, *for a fraudulent purpose*, takes, removes or conceals *anything* commits the offence. The offence is indictable and carries a maximum term of two years' imprisonment.

THEFT, FORGERY, ETC., OF CREDIT CARD / Jurisdiction / Unauthorized use of credit card data / Definitions.

342. (1) Every person who

(*a*) steals a credit card,

(*b*) forges or falsifies a credit card,

(*c*) possesses, uses or traffics in a credit card or a forged or falsified credit card, knowing that it was obtained, made or altered

(i) by the commission in Canada of an offence, or

(ii) by an act or omission anywhere that, if it had occurred in Canada, would have constituted an offence, or

(*d*) uses a credit card knowing that it has been revoked or cancelled,

is guilty of

(*e*) an indictable offence and is liable to imprisonment for a term not exceeding ten years, or

(*f*) an offence punishable on summary conviction.

(2) An accused who is charged with an offence under subsection (1) may be tried and punished by any court having jurisdiction to try that offence in the place where the offence is alleged to have been committed or in the place where the accused is found, is arrested or is in custody, but where the place where the accused is found, is arrested or is in custody is outside the province in which the offence is alleged to have been committed, no proceedings in respect of that offence shall be commenced in that place without the consent of the Attorney General of that province.

(3) [*Repealed* (old provision), R.S.C. 1985, c. 27 (1st Supp.), s. 44.]

(3) Every person who, fraudulently and without colour of right, possesses, uses, traffics in or permits another person to use credit card data, including personal authentication information, whether or not the data is authentic, that would enable a person to use a credit card or to obtain the services that are provided by the issuer of a credit card to credit card holders is guilty of

(*a*) an indictable offence and is liable to imprisonment for a term not exceeding ten years; or

(*b*) an offence punishable on summary conviction.

(4) In this section,

"personal authentication information" means a personal identification number or any other password or information that a credit card holder creates or adopts to be used to authenticate his or her identity in relation to the credit card;

"traffic" means, in relation to a credit card or credit card data, to sell, export from or import into Canada, distribute or deal with in any other way. 1974-75-76, c. 93, s. 27; R.S.C. 1985, c. 27 (1st Supp.), s. 44; 1997, c. 18, s. 16; 2009, c. 28, s. 4.

CROSS-REFERENCES

The term "credit card" is defined in s. 321. The term "steal" is defined in s. 2 as theft. Possession is defined by s. 4(3), however, s. 358 defines circumstances in which possession is complete. "Attorney General" is defined in s. 2. Section 583(*h*) provides that a count in an indictment is not insufficient by reason only that it does not state that the required consent has been obtained. [As to notes concerning sufficiency of consent, see s. 583.] Section 359 enacts a special evidentiary rule. Under s. 359, evidence that stolen property was found in the accused's possession in the previous 12 months is admissible to prove knowledge that the property that forms the subject-matter of the proceedings was stolen property. For the section to be invoked, notice must be given to the accused. Under s. 657.2 evidence that anyone was found guilty of theft of the property is proof that the property was stolen.

The general theft offence is defined by s. 322; the general offence of possession of goods obtained by crime by s. 354; the general forgery and uttering offences by ss. 366 to 368. Obtaining credit by fraud or by false pretences is an offence under s. 362. Bringing into Canada anything obtained outside Canada by an act that, if committed in Canada, would have been an offence under this section if committed in Canada, is an offence under s. 357. Section 342.01 creates offences respecting instruments adapted or intended for use in forging or falsifying credit cards. Section 56.1 creates offences in relation to the unlawful possession, sale and transfer of identity documents.

It would seem that where the prosecution elects to proceed by indictment then the accused may elect his mode of trial pursuant to s. 536(2). However, s. 553(*a*) provides that a provincial court judge has absolute jurisdiction to try an accused charged with "theft" where the value of the subject-matter of the offence does not exceed $5000 and, therefore, query whether the offence described by para. (1)(*a*) is governed by s. 553(*a*). Where the prosecution elects to proceed by way of summary conviction then the trial of the offence is conducted by a summary conviction court pursuant to Part XXVII. The punishment is as set out in s. 787 and the limitation period is set out in s. 786(2). Release pending trial in any case is determined by s. 515, although the accused is eligible for release by a peace officer under s. 496, 497 or by the officer in charge under s. 498. This offence may be the basis of an application for authorization to intercept private communications by reason of s. 183 and for a warrant to conduct video surveillance by reason of s. 487.01(5).

SYNOPSIS

This section deals with offences in relation to a credit card. Subsection (1) makes it a hybrid offence, with a maximum term of imprisonment of ten years upon conviction for the indictable offence, to steal, forge or falsify a credit card, or to use a credit card which the accused knows has been revoked or cancelled. Subsection (1) further states that any person who has in his possession, uses or traffics in any way with a credit card which that person *knows* was obtained anywhere by an action which, in Canada, is or would be an offence, commits an offence. Subsection (2) provides that the trial of an offence under subsec. (1) may be held either where the offence is alleged to have been committed or anywhere the accused is found, arrested or in custody. If the accused is found, arrested or in custody outside the province where the offence under subsec. (1) is alleged to have been committed, *the consent of the Attorney General* of that province is required before a trial may be commenced. Subsection (3) creates offences in relation to fraudulent possession, use, trafficking in (defined in subsec. (4)), or permitting another person to use credit card data, including personal authentication information (defined in subsec. (4)).

ANNOTATIONS

Where the information is drafted to come within subsec. (1)(*c*)(ii) but specifies that the credit card was obtained by an "offence" that if it had occurred in Canada would have constituted an offence then the Crown having particularized the act or omission as an "offence" must prove that it was an offence known to the law of the place where it allegedly took place. This would require proof of the foreign law: *R. v. Ingram* (1978), 43 C.C.C. (2d) 211 (Ont. Prov. Ct.).

It was held in *R. v. Colman,* [1981] 3 W.W.R. 572, 29 A.R. 170 (Q.B.), that inasmuch as subsec. (1)(*c*) in the French version creates only one offence an accused charged with possession of the credit card may successfully plead *autrefois acquit* based on a prior acquittal on an information charging that she unlawfully did "use or deal" with the credit card. Since the French version was more favourable to the accused it was that version which must be adopted. Cavanagh J. noted that the Yukon Territory Court of Appeal came to a contrary conclusion in *R. v. McKay* (1978), 39 C.C.C. (2d) 101, 3 C.R. (3d) 1, but without any reference to the French version of this subsection.

A credit card was "obtained by" commission of an indictable offence where it was originally simply found by the accused but he subsequently formed the intention to convert the card to his own use: *R. v. Costello* (1982), 1 C.C.C. (3d) 403, [1983] 1 W.W.R. 666 (B.C.C.A.). Folld: *R. v. Zurowski* (1983), 5 C.C.C. (3d) 285, 33 C.R. (3d) 93 (Alta. C.A.); *R. v. Elias* (1986), 33 C.C.C. (3d) 476 (Que. C.A.), affd [1989] 1 S.C.R. 423, 46 C.C.C. (3d) 447 (5:0).

The offence under subsec. (3) is committed even where the credit card in question has been blocked and could not have been used successfully: *R. v. Tuduce* (2014), 314 C.C.C. (3d) 429 (Ont. C.A.), leave to appeal to S.C.C. refused 2015 CarswellOnt 18924. *Contra*: *R. v. Jahanrakhshan* (2011), 96 W.C.B. (2d) 158, [2011] B.C.J. No. 1657 (S.C.), affirmed (2013), 296 C.C.C. (3d) 553 (B.C.C.A.), additional reasons (2013), 301 C.C.C. (3d) 334 (B.C.C.A.), affirmed (2013), 582 W.A.C. 69 (B.C.C.A.).

INSTRUMENTS FOR COPYING CREDIT CARD DATA OR FORGING OR FALSIFYING CREDIT CARDS / Forfeiture / Limitation.

342.01 (1) Every person is guilty of an indictable offence and liable to imprisonment for a term of not more than 10 years, or is guilty of an offence punishable on summary conviction, who, without lawful justification or excuse, makes, repairs, buys, sells, exports from Canada, imports into Canada or possesses any instrument, device, apparatus, material or thing that they know has been used or know is adapted or intended for use

(*a*) in the copying of credit card data for use in the commission of an offence under subsection 342(3); or

(*b*) in the forging or falsifying of credit cards.

(2) Where a person is convicted of an offence under subsection (1), any instrument, device, apparatus, material or thing in relation to which the offence was committed or the possession of which constituted the offence may, in addition to any other punishment that may be imposed, be ordered forfeited to Her Majesty, whereupon it may be disposed of as the Attorney General directs.

(3) No order of forfeiture may be made under subsection (2) in respect of any thing that is the property of a person who was not a party to the offence under subsection (1). 1997, c. 18, s. 17; 2009, c. 28, s. 5.

CROSS-REFERENCES

"Attorney General" is defined in s. 2. Section 327 creates a similar offence in relation to instruments used for unlawfully obtaining telecommunication facilities. Section 342.2 creates a similar offence in relation to instruments used for obtaining unauthorized use of computers. As to the meaning of "reasonable inference", reference might be made to cases noted under s. 351.

SYNOPSIS

This section creates a Crown-option offence to complement the offence under s. 342 by making it an offence to make, possess, repair, buy, sell, export or import any instrument, device, material, apparatus or thing, that the person knows has been used or is adapted or intended for use in copying of credit card data for use in committing the offence under s. 342(3), or forging or falsifying credit cards. Upon conviction, the device, instrument etc. may be forfeited to the Crown, except if the matter was not the property of a person party to the offence.

UNAUTHORIZED USE OF COMPUTER / Definitions / "computer password" / "computer program" / "computer service" / "computer system" / "data" / "electro-magnetic, acoustic, mechanical or other device" / "function" / "intercept" / "traffic".

342.1 (1) Everyone is guilty of an indictable offence and liable to imprisonment for a term of not more than 10 years, or is guilty of an offence punishable on summary conviction who, fraudulently and without colour of right,

(*a*) obtains, directly or indirectly, any computer service;

(*b*) by means of an electro-magnetic, acoustic, mechanical or other device, intercepts or causes to be intercepted, directly or indirectly, any function of a computer system;

(*c*) uses or causes to be used, directly or indirectly, a computer system with intent to commit an offence under paragraph (*a*) or (*b*) or under section 430 in relation to computer data or a computer system; or

(*d*) uses, possesses, traffics in or permits another person to have access to a computer password that would enable a person to commit an offence under paragraph (*a*), (*b*) or (*c*).

(2) In this section,

"computer data" means representations, including signs, signals or symbols, that are in a form suitable for processing in a computer system;

"computer password" means any computer data by which a computer service or computer system is capable of being obtained or used;

"computer program" means computer data representing instructions or statements that, when executed in a computer system, causes the computer system to perform a function;

"computer service" includes data processing and the storage or retrieval of computer data;

"computer system" means a device that, or a group of interconnected or related devices one or more of which,

(*a*) contains computer programs or other computer data, and

(*b*) by means of computer programs,

(i) performs logic and control, and

(ii) may perform any other function;

"data" [*Repealed.* 2014, c. 31, s. 16(2).]

"electro-magnetic, acoustic, mechanical or other device" means any device or apparatus that is used or is capable of being used to intercept any function of a computer system, but does not include a hearing aid used to correct subnormal hearing of the user to not better than normal hearing;

"function" includes logic, control, arithmetic, deletion, storage and retrieval and communication or telecommunication to, from or within a computer system;

"intercept" includes listen to or record a function of a computer system, or acquire the substance, meaning or purport thereof.

"traffic" means, in respect of a computer password, to sell, export from or import into Canada, distribute or deal with in any other way. R.S.C. 1985, c. 27 (1st Supp.), s. 45; 1997, c. 18, s. 18; 2014, c. 31, s. 16.

CROSS-REFERENCES

The term "telecommunication" is defined in s. 35 of the *Interpretation Act*, R.S.C. 1985, c. I-21. As to notes respecting the term "colour of right", see notes under s. 322. This offence may be the basis of an application to intercept private communications by reason of s. 183 or for a warrant to conduct video surveillance by reason of s. 487.01(5).

Related offences: s. 184, unlawful interception of private communications; s. 326, theft of telecommunication service; s. 327, possession of device to unlawfully obtain telecommunication facility or service; s. 342.2, possession or sale of instruments for committing an offence under this section; s. 430(1.1), mischief in relation to data.

The accused may elect the mode of trial pursuant to s. 536(2) where the prosecution elects to proceed by way of indictment. Where the prosecution elects to proceed by way of summary conviction then the trial is conducted by a summary conviction court pursuant to Part XXVII. The punishment is as set out in s. 787 [although note the maximum fine for a corporation is as set out in s. 735] and the limitation period is set out in s. 786(2). Release pending trial is determined by s. 515, although the accused is eligible for release by a peace officer under s. 496, 497 or by the officer in charge under s. 498.

SYNOPSIS

This section makes it a hybrid offence for a person *fraudulently* and *without colour of right* to obtain, directly or indirectly, any computer service, or to intercept or cause to be intercepted, directly or indirectly, any function of a computer service by means of any device. It further states that it is an offence to use or cause to be used, directly or indirectly, a computer system *with intent* to commit either of the offences described above or an offence under s. 430, or to use, possess, traffic in or permit access to a computer password enabling a person to commit the offence in this section. Subsection (2) contains an extensive set of definitions of terms relevant to this offence. The maximum term of imprisonment upon conviction for the indictable offence described in this section is ten years.

ANNOTATIONS

"Computer system" includes text messaging via cellular telephones: *R. v. Woodward* (2011), 276 C.C.C. (3d) 86 (Ont. C.A.).

However, in *R. v. Cockell* (2013), 299 C.C.C. (3d) 221 (Alta. C.A.), leave to appeal to S.C.C. refused [2013] 3 S.C.R. x, the court held that the trial judge had erred by deeming the accused's Blackberry to be a "computer system" within the meaning of subsec. (2) in the absence of any expert evidence on this point.

POSSESSION OF DEVICE TO OBTAIN UNAUTHORIZED USE OF COMPUTER SYSTEM OR TO COMMIT MISCHIEF / Forfeiture / Limitation / Definition of "device".

342.2 (1) Every person who, without lawful excuse, makes, possesses, sells, offers for sale, imports, obtains for use, distributes or makes available a device that is designed or adapted primarily to commit an offence under section 342.1 or 430, knowing that the device has been or is intended to be used to commit such an offence, is

(*a*) guilty of an indictable offence and liable to imprisonment for a term of not more than two years; or

(*b*) guilty of an offence punishable on summary conviction.

(2) If a person is convicted of an offence under subsection (1), in addition to any punishment that is imposed, any device in relation to which the offence was committed or the possession of which constituted the offence may be ordered forfeited to Her Majesty and may be disposed of as the Attorney General directs.

(3) No order of forfeiture may be made under subsection (2) in respect of any thing that is the property of a person who was not a party to the offence under subsection (1).

(4) In this section, "device" includes

(*a*) a component of a device; and

(*b*) a computer program within the meaning of subsection 342.1(2). 1997, c. 18, s. 19; 2014, c. 31, s. 17; 2018, c. 29, s. 34.

CROSS-REFERENCES

"Attorney General" is defined in s. 2. Section 327 creates a similar offence in relation to instruments used for unlawfully obtaining telecommunication facilities. Section 342.01 creates a similar offence in relation to instruments used for forging or falsifying credit cards. As to the meaning of "reasonable inference", reference might be made to cases noted under s. 351. This offence may be the basis of an application to intercept private communications by reason of s. 183 or for a warrant to conduct video surveillance by reason of s. 487.01(5).

SYNOPSIS

This section creates a Crown-option offence to complement the offence under s. 342.1 by making it an offence to make, possess, sell, offer for sale or distribute any instrument, device or component thereof, the design of which renders it primarily useful for committing the offence under that section or under s. 430. The Crown must also prove that the person had the device under circumstances giving rise to a reasonable inference that the device, instrument or component was used or intended for use to commit the s. 342.1 or s. 430 offence. Upon conviction the device, instrument or component may be forfeited to the Crown, except if the matter was not the property of a person party to the offence.

Robbery and Extortion

ROBBERY.

343. Every one commits robbery who

(*a*) steals, and for the purpose of extorting whatever is stolen or to prevent or overcome resistance to the stealing, uses violence or threats of violence to a person or property;

(*b*) steals from any person and, at the time he steals or immediately before or immediately thereafter, wounds, beats, strikes or uses any personal violence to that person;

(*c*) assaults any person with intent to steal from him; or

(*d*) steals from any person while armed with an offensive weapon or imitation thereof. R.S., c. C-34, s. 302.

CROSS-REFERENCES

The terms "offensive weapon" and "property" are defined in s. 2. The term "steal" is defined in s. 2 as committing theft. Theft is defined in ss. 322 to 333, but principally in s. 322. Assault is defined in s. 265. The punishment for robbery is set out in s. 344.

Section 17 limits the availability of the statutory defence of compulsion by threats to the offence of "robbery". As to admission of photographic evidence of property, see s. 491.2. Under s. 583, an indictment, which otherwise complies with s. 581, is not insufficient by reason only that (*a*), it does not name the person injured or intended to be injured; (*b*), it does not name the person who owns or has a special property or interest in the property mentioned in the count, however, see s. 587 as to when particulars may be ordered. Also note s. 588 which deems certain persons to have a property interest in property of which they have the management, control or custody. This offence has often posed problems respecting included offences. Thus, see notes under s. 662.

This offence may be the basis for an application for an authorization to intercept private communications by reason of s. 183 or a warrant to conduct video surveillance by reason of s. 487.01(5). Robbery is an enterprise crime offence for the purposes of Part XII.2.

Where the offence, although committed outside Canada, is in relation to the use of nuclear material, see s. 7(3.4).

The accused may elect his mode of trial pursuant to s. 536(2). Release pending trial is determined by s. 515. A person convicted of the offence in this section will be liable to the mandatory prohibition order in s. 109 for possession of certain weapons, ammunition and explosives.

Related offences: s. 85, using firearm during commission or attempted commission of indictable offence; s. 244, discharging firearm with intent to wound; s. 264.1, uttering threats; s. 266, assault; s. 267, assault with a weapon or causing bodily harm; s. 268, aggravated assault; s. 272, sexual assault with a weapon; s. 273, aggravated sexual assault; s. 279, kidnapping and unlawful confinement; s. 345, stopping mail with intent to rob; s. 346, extortion; s. 348, break and enter; s. 351(2), disguised with intent. Section 98.1 creates a robbery offence where the object of the theft is a firearm.

Pursuant to s. 348.1, if a person is convicted of this offence in relation to a dwelling-house, it is an aggravating factor in sentencing that the dwelling-house was occupied at the time and the offender knew or was reckless as to whether the dwelling-house was occupied and used violence or threats of violence to a person or property.

SYNOPSIS

This section describes the offence of robbery. Every person who *steals* and uses violence or threats of violence to another person or property in order to overcome resistance to the stealing or to extort whatever is stolen, commits the form of robbery set out in para. (*a*). Everyone who *steals* from any person and, during the course of the stealing, or *immediately* before or after, wounds, beats or uses any personal violence to that person commits the form of robbery set out in para. (*b*). A person who assaults another person *with the intent to steal* from him commits the offence of robbery described in para. (*c*). Finally, everyone who *steals* from any person while armed, with an offensive weapon or an imitation thereof, commits the offence of robbery described in para. (*d*). It is to be noted that paras. (*a*), (*b*) and (*d*) require proof of the act of stealing as one of the elements of the offence. Paragraph (*c*) requires proof only of an intent to steal as an essential element.

ANNOTATIONS

Use of violence or threats of violence (para. (*a*)) – Assault, for which only a general intent is required, may be a lesser and included offence in the charge of unlawfully and by violence stealing, which also requires proof of the specific intent to carry out that purpose: *R. v. George*, [1960] S.C.R. 871, 128 C.C.C. 289 (4:1).

The offence under this paragraph is not made out in a "purse snatching" case where the accused simply snatches the purse before the victim could offer any resistance and he uses no other violence to the victim: *R. v. Picard* (1976), 39 C.C.C. (2d) 57 (Que. Sess. Ct.).

However, where the victim's arms are held to prevent resistance while the money is taken, then the offence is made out: *R. v. Trudel* (1984), 12 C.C.C. (3d) 342 (Que. C.A.).

Paragraph (*a*) requires the violence to be before or contemporaneous with the theft. In this case, the accused got into an altercation with a security guard in the parking lot after committing the theft in the store. As the theft was complete once the accused had left the store, a conviction for robbery could not be made out: *R. v. Newell* (2007), 217 C.C.C. (3d) 483 (Nfld. & Lab. C.A.). See also *R. v. Jean* (2012), 293 C.C.C. (3d) 66 (B.C.C.A.), leave to appeal to S.C.C. refused 2013 CarswellBC 1314 (S.C.C.); *R. v. McKay* (2014), 305 C.C.C. (3d) 409 (Sask. C.A.).

In *R. v. Katrensky* (1975), 24 C.C.C. (2d) 350 (B.C. Prov. Ct.), the accused was convicted of robbery as defined in this section where he merely handed the bank teller a note stating "empty your till". It was held that to constitute a threat of violence the Crown must prove that the victim felt threatened and that she had reasonable and probable grounds for her fear. In this case while there may not have been any immediate fear of violence, the implied threat of violence if the request was not carried out was sufficient to constitute the act of the accused robbery.

Threats of violence within the meaning of this paragraph would include any demonstration from which physical injury to the victim may be reasonably apprehended: *R. v. Sayers and McCoy* (1983), 8 C.C.C. (3d) 572 (Ont. C.A.).

A threat of violence is characterized by conduct which reflects an intent to have recourse to violence in order to carry out the theft or to prevent resistance to the theft. A threat may be expressed or implicit and made by means of words, writings or actions. There is no requirement that the accused be armed or utter words such as "This is a hold up". The question is whether the actions and words of the accused, in light of the context and circumstances in which they took place, could reasonably create a feeling of apprehension on the part of the victims: *R. v. Pelletier* (1992), 71 C.C.C. (3d) 438 (Que. C.A.).

Once a threat is established, there is no additional requirement of some minimum level of violence: *R. v. Lecky* (2001), 157 C.C.C. (3d) 351 (Ont. C.A.).

Stealing and using violence (para. (*b*)) – In order to avoid an interpretation repetitious to para. (a), this paragraph should be regarded as setting out what one might call constructive robbery occurring with theft and a proximate application of violence *R. v. Lieberman*, [1970] 5 C.C.C. 300, 11 C.R.N.S. 168 (Ont. C.A.) (2:1). It is not necessary that the violence be used to accomplish or further the theft. The purpose for which the personal violence is used is immaterial provided it accompanies the act of stealing or immediately precedes it or follows it: *R. v. Downer* (1978), 40 C.C.C. (2d) 532 (Ont. C.A.).

The "violence" contemplated by this paragraph requires proof of more than a mere assault. Thus the mere nudging of the victim to steal her purse is not sufficient: *R. v. Lew* (1978), 40 C.C.C. (2d) 140 (Ont. C.A.). Similarly: *R. v. Oakley* (1986), 24 C.C.C. (3d) 351 (Ont. C.A.).

In determining whether the conduct amounted to the use of threats or violence, a trier of fact may apply a partly subjective and partly objective test. In this case, the accused had given a note to the teller and indicated through gestures and grunts that he wanted money. Given the teller's evidence that the accused's hand was in his pocket throughout and that she assumed that he had a weapon in his pocket, the offence was made out: *R. v. Bourassa* (2004), 189 C.C.C. (3d) 438 (N.S.C.A.).

Assault with intent to steal (para. (*c*)) – A charge that the accused "did commit robbery [of the victim] of approximately $15" particularizes a completed stealing and where the Crown fails to prove that any money was stolen the Crown cannot rely on the definition of robbery in this paragraph to make out the offence. The accused may, however, be convicted of attempted robbery: *R. v. Bob* (1980), 54 C.C.C. (2d) 169 (B.C.C.A.).

Stealing while armed (para. (*d*)) – To be "armed" means to be equipped with or possessed of an instrument: *R. v. Sloan* (1974), 19 C.C.C. (2d) 190 (B.C.C.A.).

A charge of robbery was dismissed where the accused was charged that he "simulated with his fist that he was armed". It was held that this paragraph requires that the accused be armed with a weapon or an imitation thereof and no part of the body can resemble an offensive weapon: *R. v. Gouchie* (1976), 33 C.C.C. (2d) 120 (Que. Sess. Peace).

The offence under this paragraph does not require that the accused intended to use the weapon or that the victim be frightened or intimidated by its presence: *Tremblay v. Quebec (Attorney General)* (1984), 43 C.R. (3d) 92 (Que. C.A.).

***Mens rea* generally** – An honest belief that a debt was due from the victim to himself will vitiate the element of theft in a robbery charge against the accused: *R. v. Carroll* (1975), 27 C.C.C. (2d) 276 (Ont. C.A.).

Included offences – This section creates only one offence, namely robbery, which may be committed in any of the different ways described. On a charge of stealing while armed, under para. (*d*) while theft is an included offence, assault is not as the mere fact of being armed does not necessarily involve an assault. Where the Crown alleges in the indictment the particular means by which the robbery was committed, as here, "did steal . . . while armed with an imitation of an offensive weapon" it is required to prove every essential averment of the charge and could not require the trial judge instruct the jury to consider whether robbery was committed in one of the other ways described in the section: *R. v. Johnson* (1977), 35 C.C.C. (2d) 439 (B.C.C.A.).

It is an error for the trial judge to instruct the jury that "simple robbery" is an included offence to "armed robbery". Notwithstanding that the trial judge erroneously left robbery with the jury and the indictment included the words "use a firearm, to wit: a sawed-off shotgun", the accused was still properly convicted. The words "sawed-off shotgun" did not particularize an element of the offence but rather put the accused on notice that he faced the minimum sentence for robbery where a firearm is used: *R. v. Manley* (2011), 269 C.C.C. (3d) 40 (Ont. C.A.).

The fact that robbery may be committed in ways which do not include an assault does not alter the fact that robbery as described in this section does include the offence of assault. It is sufficient that an offence such as assault is included in the enactment creating the principal offence, it need not be necessarily included. Thus common assault was an included offence although the indictment merely alleged that the accused "unlawfully did commit robbery of [the victim] of a quantity of cigarettes and approximately $4.00 in cash": *R. v. Luckett*, [1980] 1 S.C.R. 1140, 50 C.C.C. (2d) 489 (7:0).

The accused may be convicted of assault causing bodily harm on an indictment charging robbery *simpliciter*. The inclusion of the word "wounds" in the definition of robbery in para. (*b*) makes assault causing bodily harm an included offence: *R. v. Horsefall* (1990), 61 C.C.C. (3d) 245 (B.C.C.A.).

An indictment which charges robbery under para. (*c*) includes attempted theft so that the accused may be convicted of that offence where the evidence establishes a theft but no assault: *R. v. Boisvert* (1991), 68 C.C.C. (3d) 478 (Que. C.A.).

Property which may be subject-matter of offence – A narcotic may be the subject of a robbery notwithstanding it constitutes an offence for the victim to be in possession of it: *R. v. Janzic* (1982), 1 C.C.C. (3d) 246 (Ont. C.A.), leave to appeal to S.C.C. refused 46 N.R. 90*n*.

ROBBERY / Subsequent offences / Sequence of convictions only.

344. (1) Every person who commits robbery is guilty of an indictable offence and liable

(*a*) if a restricted firearm or prohibited firearm is used in the commission of the offence or if any firearm is used in the commission of the offence and the

offence is committed for the benefit of, at the direction of, or in association with, a criminal organization, to imprisonment for life and to a minimum punishment of imprisonment for a term of

(i) in the case of a first offence, five years, and

(ii) in the case of a second or subsequent offence, seven years;

(*a*.1) in any other case where a firearm is used in the commission of the offence, to imprisonment for life and to a minimum punishment of imprisonment for a term of four years; and

(*b*) in any other case, to imprisonment for life.

(2) In determining, for the purpose of paragraph (1)(*a*), whether a convicted person has committed a second or subsequent offence, if the person was earlier convicted of any of the following offences, that offence is to be considered as an earlier offence:

(*a*) an offence under this section;

(*b*) an offence under subsection 85(1) or (2) or section 244 or 244.2; or

(*c*) an offence under section 220, 236, 239, 272 or 273, subsection 279(1) or section 279.1 or 346 if a firearm was used in the commission of the offence.

However, an earlier offence shall not be taken into account if 10 years have elapsed between the day on which the person was convicted of the earlier offence and the day on which the person was convicted of the offence for which sentence is being imposed, not taking into account any time in custody.

(3) For the purposes of subsection (2), the only question to be considered is the sequence of convictions and no consideration shall be given to the sequence of commission of offences or whether any offence occurred before or after any conviction. R.S., c. C-34, s. 303; 1972, c. 13, s. 70; 1995, c. 39, s. 149; 2008, c. 6, s. 32; 2009, c. 22, s. 14.

CROSS-REFERENCES

Robbery is defined in s. 343. "Firearm" is defined in s. 2. "Criminal organization" is defined in ss. 2 and 476.1. Pursuant to s. 2.1, "restricted firearm" and "prohibited firearm" are defined in s. 84.

As to admission of photographic evidence of property see, s. 491.2.

Section 17 limits the availability of the statutory defence of compulsion by threats to the offence of "robbery". Under s. 583, an indictment, which otherwise complies with s. 581, is not insufficient by reason only that (*a*), it does not name the person injured or intended to be injured; (*b*), it does not name the person who owns or has a special property or interest in the property mentioned in the count, however, see s. 587 as to when particulars may be ordered. Also note s. 588 which deems certain persons to have a property interest in property of which they have the management, control or custody. This offence has often posed problems respecting included offences. Thus, see notes under s. 662.

This offence may be the basis for an application for an authorization to intercept private communications by reason of s. 183 or a warrant to conduct video surveillance by reason of s. 487.01(5). Robbery is an enterprise crime offence for the purposes of Part XII.2.

The accused may elect his mode of trial pursuant to s. 536(2). Release pending trial is determined by s. 515. A person convicted of the offence in this section will be liable to the mandatory prohibition order in s. 109 for possession of certain weapons, ammunition and explosives.

Related offences: s. 85, using firearm during commission or attempted commission of indictable offence; s. 244, discharging firearm with intent to wound; s. 264.1, uttering threats; s. 266, assault; s. 267, assault with a weapon or causing bodily harm; s. 268, aggravated assault; s. 272, sexual assault with a weapon; s. 273, aggravated sexual assault; s. 279, kidnapping and unlawful confinement; s. 345, stopping mail with intent to rob; s. 346, extortion; s. 348, break and enter; s. 351(2), disguised with intent. Section 98.1 creates a robbery offence where the object of the theft is a firearm.

SYNOPSIS

This section sets out the penalties for the robbery offences described in s. 343. The maximum punishment is life imprisonment. The section also enacts minimum punishments. Where a restricted or prohibited firearm is used or the offence was committed for the benefit of, at the direction of, or in association with, a criminal organization, the offender is liable to a minimum punishment of at least five years' imprisonment for a first offence and seven years for a second or subsequent offence. The rules for determining whether the offender has committed a second or subsequent offence are set out in subsecs. (2) and (3) and, for example, provide that a prior offence includes not only convictions under this section, but other specified offences involving firearms. However, an earlier offence is not to be taken into account if 10 years have elapsed from the conviction of the earlier offence, not counting time in custody. Subsection (4) reverses the common law rule and provides that the court only takes into account the sequence of convictions, not the order in which the offences were committed. In any other case where a firearm is used, the offender is liable to a minimum term of imprisonment of four years. Where no firearm is used, there is no minimum punishment.

ANNOTATIONS

Note: These cases were decided before the increase in the minimum punishment as now set out in subsec. (1)(*a*).

Prior to the enactment of para. (*a*) it was held where the underlying offence is robbery, the minimum penalty prescribed for the offence contrary to s. 85 [using a firearm in the commission of an indictable offence] did not infringe s. 12 of the Charter although it could result in the imposition of a number of consecutive sentences for offences arising out of the same series of events: *R. v. Brown*, [1994] 3 S.C.R. 749, 93 C.C.C. (3d) 97.

The minimum punishment of four years set out in former para. (*a*) does not violate s. 12 of the Charter: *R. v. Lapierre* (1998), 123 C.C.C. (3d) 332, 15 C.R. (5th) 283 (Que. C.A.); *R. v. Wust* (1998), 125 C.C.C. (3d) 43, 17 C.R. (5th) 45 *sub nom. R. v. W. (L.W.)* (B.C.C.A.), revd on other grounds [2000] 1 S.C.R. 455, 143 C.C.C. (3d) 129; *R. v. McDonald* (1998), 127 C.C.C. (3d) 57, 17 C.R. (5th) 1 (Ont. C.A.).

The court may deduct the time spent in pre-sentence custody pursuant to s. 719(3) even if the resulting sentence is less than the four-year minimum. There is no mechanical formula for crediting pre-sentencing custody. While approximately two months' credit for each month spent in pre-sentence custody is entirely appropriate to reflect the harshness of pre-trial custody, a different rationale could also be applied depending on the circumstances of the detention. Accordingly, the amount of credit given for pre-trial custody should be left to the discretion of the sentencing judge: *R. v. Wust*, [2000] 1 S.C.R. 455, 143 C.C.C. (3d) 129. See also *R. v. Arrance*, [2000] 1 S.C.R. 488, 143 C.C.C. (3d) 154, and *R. v. Arthurs*, [2000] 1 S.C.R. 481, 143 C.C.C. (3d) 149.

It was held that former s. 85 could be resorted to only where there is a conviction for the underlying offence and the use of the firearm was in the actual commission or attempted commission of the underlying offence. Thus, the accused could not be convicted of using a firearm while a party to a robbery where, although a firearm was used to compel a third person to commit the robbery, this third person did not actually use the firearm to commit the robbery: *R. v. Ingraham* (1991), 66 C.C.C. (3d) 27, 46 O.A.C. 216 (C.A.).

STOPPING MAIL WITH INTENT.

345. Every one who stops a mail conveyance with intent to rob or search it is guilty of an indictable offence and liable to imprisonment for life. R.S., c. C-34, s. 304.

CROSS-REFERENCES

Robbery is defined in s. 343. The term "mail conveyance" is defined in s. 2 of the *Canada Post Corporation Act*, R.S.C. 1985, c. C-10, as meaning "any physical, electronic, optical or other means used to transmit the mail". That section also contains the definition of "mail".

Section 476(*e*) contains a special provision for territorial jurisdiction where an offence is committed in respect of a mail in the course of door-to-door delivery.

The related offence of theft from the mail is in s. 356. Using a firearm during commission or attempted commission of an indictable offence is an offence under s. 85. Disguised with intent is an offence under s. 351(2).

The accused may elect his mode of trial pursuant to s. 536(2). Release pending trial is determined by s. 515. A person convicted of the offence in this section may be liable to the mandatory prohibition order in s. 109 for possession of certain weapons, ammunition and explosives.

SYNOPSIS

This section describes the offence of stopping a mail conveyance with *the intent to rob or search* it. The offence is punishable by way of indictment and carries a maximum term of life imprisonment and a minimum punishment of four years where a firearm is used in the commission of the offence.

EXTORTION / Punishment / Subsequent offences / Sequence of convictions only / Saving.

346. (1) Every one commits extortion who, without reasonable justification or excuse and with intent to obtain anything, by threats, accusations, menaces or violence induces or attempts to induce any person, whether or not he is the person threatened, accused or menaced or to whom violence is shown, to do anything or cause anything to be done.

(1.1) Every person who commits extortion is guilty of an indictable offence and liable

(*a*) if a restricted firearm or prohibited firearm is used in the commission of the offence or if any firearm is used in the commission of the offence and the offence is committed for the benefit of, at the direction of, or in association with, a criminal organization, to imprisonment for life and to a minimum punishment of imprisonment for a term of

(i) in the case of a first offence, five years, and

(ii) in the case of a second or subsequent offence, seven years;

(*a*.1) in any other case where a firearm is used in the commission of the offence, to imprisonment for life and to a minimum punishment of imprisonment for a term of four years; and

(*b*) in any other case, to imprisonment for life.

(1.2) In determining, for the purpose of paragraph (1.1)(*a*), whether a convicted person has committed a second or subsequent offence, if the person was earlier convicted of any of the following offences, that offence is to be considered as an earlier offence:

(*a*) an offence under this section;

(*b*) an offence under subsection 85(1) or (2) or section 244 or 244.2; or

(*c*) an offence under section 220, 236, 239, 272 or 273, subsection 279(1) or section 279.1 or 344 if a firearm was used in the commission of the offence.

However, an earlier offence shall not be taken into account if 10 years have elapsed between the day on which the person was convicted of the earlier offence and the day on which the person was convicted of the offence for which sentence is being imposed, not taking into account any time in custody.

(1.3) For the purposes of subsection (1.2), the only question to be considered is the sequence of convictions and no consideration shall be given to the sequence of commission of offences or whether any offence occurred before or after any conviction.

(2) A threat to institute civil proceedings is not a threat for the purposes of this section. R.S., c. C-34, s. 305; R.S.C. 1985, c. 27 (1st Supp.), s. 46; 1995, c. 39, s. 150; 2008, c. 6, s. 33; 2009, c. 22, s. 15.

CROSS-REFERENCES

This offence may be the basis for an application for an authorization to intercept private communications by reason of s. 183 or a warrant to conduct video surveillance by reason of s. 487.01(5). Extortion is an enterprise crime offence for the purposes of Part XII.2.

Where the offence, although committed outside Canada, is in relation to the use of nuclear material, see s. 7(3.4). Firearm is defined in s. 2. "Criminal organization" is defined in ss. 2 and 476.1. Pursuant to s. 2.1, "restricted firearm" and "prohibited firearm" are defined in s. 84.

Related offences: s. 85, using firearm during commission or attempted commission of indictable offence; s. 244, discharging firearm with intent to wound; s. 264.1, uttering threats; s. 266, assault; s. 267, assault with a weapon or causing bodily harm; s. 268, aggravated assault; s. 279, kidnapping and unlawful confinement; s. 343, robbery; s. 347, criminal interest rate; s. 302, extortion by libel.

The accused may elect his mode of trial pursuant to s. 536(2). Release pending trial is determined by s. 515. A person convicted of the offence in this section may be liable to the mandatory prohibition order in s. 109 for possession of certain weapons, ammunition and explosives. Pursuant to s. 486(3), the judge or justice may make an order banning publication of the identity of the complainant or witness and any information that could disclose the identity of the complainant or witness.

Pursuant to s. 348.1, if a person is convicted of the offence under this section in relation to a dwelling-house, it is an aggravating factor in sentencing that the dwelling-house was occupied at the time and the offender knew or was reckless as to whether the dwelling-house was occupied and used violence or threats of violence to a person or property.

Under s. 486.4, where an accused is charged with the offence under this section, the judge may make an order directing that any information that could identify the complainant or a witness not be published, broadcast or transmitted in any way. The judge is to inform the complainant or any witness under the age of 18 years of the right to make any application under s. 486.4. Under s. 486.6, it is an offence to violate the order made.

SYNOPSIS

This section describes the offence of extortion. Any person who, *without reasonable justification* or excuse and *with intent to obtain anything*, induces or attempts to induce another person by means of threats, accusations, menaces or violence, to do anything or cause anything to be done, commits the offence of extortion. The person threatened or menaced does not necessarily have to be the person from whom the accused is expecting action. This is an indictable offence with a maximum term of life imprisonment. The section also enacts minimum punishments. Where a restricted or prohibited firearm is used or the offence was committed for the benefit of, at the direction of, or in association with, a criminal organization, the offender is liable to a minimum punishment of at least five years' imprisonment for a first offence and seven years for a second or subsequent offence. The rules for determining whether the offender has committed a second or subsequent offence are set out in subsecs. (1.2) and (1.3) and, for example, provide that a prior offence includes not only convictions under this section, but other specified offences involving use of a firearm. However, an earlier offence is not to be taken into account if 10 years have elapsed from the conviction of the earlier offence, not counting time in custody. Subsection (1.3) reverses the common law rule and provides that the court only takes into account the sequence of convictions, not the order in which the offences were committed. In any other case where a firearm is used, the offender is liable to a minimum term of imprisonment of four years. Where no firearm is used, there is no minimum punishment.

Subsection (2) clarifies that a threat to institute civil proceedings is not a threat for the purposes of this section.

ANNOTATIONS

"Anything" – The purpose of the provision is to protect against interference with freedom of choice. The word "anything" should be given a wide, unrestricted application and can include extorting sexual favours: *R. v. Davis*, [1999] 3 S.C.R. 759, 139 C.C.C. (3d) 193.

Threats or menaces – A "threat" to come within this section does not necessarily connote a menace of ill to be personally inflicted by the threatener. Thus a false statement by the accused that if the victim does not do a certain thing he will be dealt with by a third person of known violent propensities or associations will constitute this offence: *R. v. Swartz* (1977), 37 C.C.C. (2d) 409 (Ont. C.A.), affd without reference to the point [1979] 2 S.C.R. 256, 45 C.C.C. (2d) 1, *sub nom. R. v. Cotroni; R. v. Papalia.*

A veiled reference may constitute a threat if it is sufficient, in light of all the circumstances, to convey to the complainant the consequences which he or she fears or would prefer to avoid. Whether such words amount to a threat must be considered contextually, including in light of the shared knowledge of the complainant and accused: *R. v. Barros*, [2011] 3 S.C.R. 368, 273 C.C.C. (3d) 129.

There is no requirement that the threats or menaces be shown to be of such a nature as to deprive the victim of the free and voluntary exercise of his will: *R. v. Syrmalis; R. v. Laurie* (1981), 63 C.C.C. (2d) 452 (Que. C.A.).

The offence is made out even if the victim does not capitulate to the accused's wishes: *R. v. Noel* (2001), 156 C.C.C. (3d) 169, 46 C.R. (5th) 189 (N.B.C.A.).

An approach by a lawyer to a lawyer acting for another party to have certain criminal charges dropped in exchange for a sum of money, if made without threats, accusations, menaces or violence does not constitute an offence under this section: *R. v. Rousseau*, [1985] 2 S.C.R. 38, 21 C.C.C. (3d) 1.

Subsection (1) is broadly worded to criminalize threats of any kind made with an attempt to induce any person to do anything, if those threats are made with the intention of obtaining anything. A legal justification must be reasonable and the burden is on the Crown to demonstrate beyond a reasonable doubt the absence of any reasonable excuse or justification. In this case, a threat to have the complainant fired if she did not repay money owed to the accused's wife constituted a threat within this provision as the threat to have the complainant fired was unlawful: *R. v. Alexander* (2005), 206 C.C.C. (3d) 233, 32 C.R. (6th) 159 (Ont. C.A.), leave to appeal to S.C.C. refused 352 N.R. 197*n*.

Reasonable justification of excuse – In *R. v. Natarelli and Volpe*, [1967] S.C.R. 539, [1968] 1 C.C.C. 154, 1 C.R.N.S. 302, it was held that in determining whether there could be reasonable justification or excuse for making the demand or using threats, the accused's entire course of conduct, and not one isolated item thereof, must be considered; and once it is proved that the accused made threats to cause death or bodily injury with intent to obtain consideration, then they are guilty regardless of whether they honestly believed that they did have or whether they actually had a right to the consideration demanded.

On a charge contrary to this section, arising out of seizure of certain property, evidence was admissible as to what the accused had been told by a bailiff to whom he had spoken. This information was not admissible for its truth, but was admissible to show the accused's state of mind and the honesty of his belief and whether he had reasonable justification or excuse for his actions: *R. v. Toth* (1989), 8 W.C.B. (2d) 255 (Ont. C.A.).

Criminal Interest Rate

CRIMINAL INTEREST RATE / Definitions / "credit advanced" / "criminal rate" / "insurance charge" / "interest" / "official fee" / "overdraft charge" / "required deposit balance" / Presumption / Proof of effective annual rate / Notice / Cross-examination with leave / Consent required for proceedings / Application.

347. (1) Despite any other Act of Parliament, every one who enters into an agreement or arrangement to receive interest at a criminal rate, or receives a payment or partial payment of interest at a criminal rate, is

(*a*) guilty of an indictable offence and liable to imprisonment for a term not exceeding five years; or

(*b*) guilty of an offence punishable on summary conviction and liable to a fine not exceeding $25,000 or to imprisonment for a term not exceeding six months or to both.

(2) In this section,

"credit advanced" means the aggregate of the money and the monetary value of any goods, services or benefits actually advanced or to be advanced under an agreement or arrangement minus the aggregate of any required deposit balance and any fee, fine, penalty, commission and other similar charge or expense directly or indirectly incurred under the original or any collateral agreement or arrangement;

"criminal rate" means an effective annual rate of interest calculated in accordance with generally accepted actuarial practices and principles that exceeds sixty per cent on the credit advanced under an agreement or arrangement;

"insurance charge" means the cost of insuring the risk assumed by the person who advances or is to advance credit under an agreement or arrangement, where the face amount of the insurance does not exceed the credit advanced;

"interest" means the aggregate of all charges and expenses, whether in the form of a fee, fine, penalty, commission or other similar charge or expense or in any other form, paid or payable for the advancing of credit under an agreement or arrangement, by or on behalf of the person to whom the credit is or is to be advanced, irrespective of the person to whom any such charges and expenses are or are to be paid or payable, but does not include any repayment of credit advanced or any insurance charge, official fee, overdraft charge, required deposit balance or, in the case of a mortgage transaction, any amount required to be paid on account of property taxes;

"official fee" means a fee required by law to be paid to any governmental authority in connection with perfecting any security under an agreement or arrangement for the advancing of credit;

"overdraft charge" means a charge not exceeding five dollars for the creation of or increase in an overdraft, imposed by a credit union or caisse populaire the membership of which is wholly or substantially comprised of natural persons or a deposit taking institution the deposits in which are insured, in whole or in part, by the Canada Deposit Insurance Corporation or guaranteed, in whole or in part, by the Quebec Deposit Insurance Board;

"required deposit balance" means a fixed or an ascertainable amount of the money actually advanced or to be advanced under an agreement or arrangement that is required, as a condition of the agreement or arrangement, to be deposited or invested by or on behalf of the person to whom the advance is or is to be made and that may be available, in the event of his defaulting in any payment, to or for the benefit of the person who advances or is to advance the money.

(3) Where a person receives a payment or partial payment of interest at a criminal rate, he shall, in the absence of evidence to the contrary, be deemed to have knowledge of the nature of the payment and that it was received at a criminal rate.

(4) In any proceedings under this section, a certificate of a Fellow of the Canadian Institute of Actuaries stating that he has calculated the effective annual rate of interest on any credit advanced under an agreement or arrangement and setting out the calculations and the information on which they are based is, in the absence of evidence to the contrary, proof of the effective annual rate without proof of the signature or official character of the person appearing to have signed the certificate.

(5) A certificate referred to in subsection (4) shall not be received in evidence unless the party intending to produce it has given to the accused or defendant reasonable notice of that intention together with a copy of the certificate.

(6) An accused or a defendant against whom a certificate referred to in subsection (4) is produced may, with leave of the court, require the attendance of the actuary for the purposes of cross-examination.

(7) No proceedings shall be commenced under this section without the consent of the Attorney General.

(8) This section does not apply to any transaction to which the *Tax Rebate Discounting Act* applies. 1980-81-82-83, c. 43, s. 9; 2007, c. 9, s. 1.

CROSS-REFERENCES

"Attorney General" is defined in s. 2. Section 583(*h*) provides that a count in an indictment is not insufficient by reason only that it does not state that the required consent has been obtained. [As to notes concerning sufficiency of consent, see s. 583.] This offence may be the basis for an application for an authorization to intercept private communications by reason of s. 183 and an enterprise crime offence within the meaning of s. 462.3.

Where the prosecution elects to proceed by indictment on this offence then the accused may elect his mode of trial pursuant to s. 536(2). Where the prosecution elects to proceed by way of summary conviction then the trial of this offence is conducted by a summary conviction court pursuant to Part XXVII.

The limitation period is set out in s. 786(2). In either case, release pending trial is determined by s. 515, although the accused is eligible for release by a peace officer under s. 496, 497 or by the officer in charge under s. 498.

The related offence of extortion is found in s. 346. Under s. 486.4, where an accused is charged with the offence under this section, the judge may make an order directing that any information that could identify the complainant or a witness not be published, broadcast or transmitted in any way. The judge is to inform the complainant or any witness under the age of 18 years of the right to make any application under s. 486.4. Under s. 486.6, it is an offence to violate the order made.

Pursuant to s. 347.1, this section does not apply to certain payday loans by persons other than financial institutions where the loan is for $1500 or less, for a term of 62 days or less, and the lender is in a designated province and is licensed or authorized by the laws of the province. Payday loan is defined in s. 347.1 as "an advancement of money in exchange for a post-dated cheque, a pre-authorized debit or a future payment of a similar nature but not for any guarantee, suretyship, overdraft protection or security on property and not through a margin loan, pawnbroking, a line of credit or a credit card".

SYNOPSIS

This section describes the offence of charging a criminal interest rate. The offence is committed by anyone who enters into an agreement or arrangement to receive interest at a criminal rate, or who actually receives a payment or partial payment of interest at a criminal rate. The term "criminal rate" means an effective annual rate that exceeds 60 per cent on the credit advanced, calculated according to accepted actuarial principles and practices. The term "interest" means the aggregate of all charges and expenses, in any form, but with certain listed and defined exceptions, paid or payable for the advancing of credit. The offence may be tried by indictment, with a maximum penalty of five years, or by summary conviction, with a maximum penalty of a fine of $25,000 and imprisonment for six months, but only with the consent of an Attorney General. Subsection (3) creates a presumption, in the absence of evidence to the contrary, that a person receiving payment or partial payment of interest at a criminal rate does so *knowingly*. Subsections (4) and (5) permit, for the purposes of this section, proof of a rate of interest by a certificate of a fellow of the Canadian Institute of Actuaries, provided that the accused is given reasonable notice and a copy of the certificate. Subsection (6) permits the court to require the attendance of the actuary for cross-examination. The section applies, notwithstanding any other federal enactment, but does not apply to transactions governed by the *Tax Rebate Discounting Act*.

ANNOTATIONS

"Interest" – The term "interest" in this section is broadly defined and included in a "facility fee" which the borrower agreed to pay to obtain the loan: *William E. Thomson Associates Inc. v. Carpenter* (1989), 61 D.L.R. (4th) 1, 69 O.R. (2d) 545 (C.A.), leave to appeal to S.C.C. refused 65 D.L.R. (4th) viii, 71 O.R. (2d) x.

The stipulation that the borrower was to pay a share of the anticipated profit from a real estate deal was a condition of the borrower receiving the loan and fell within the all-inclusive definition of "interest": *677950 Ontario Ltd. v. Artell Developments Ltd.* (1992), 75 C.C.C. (3d) 343, 93 D.L.R. (4th) 334 (Ont. C.A.), affd [1993] 2 S.C.R. 443, 82 C.C.C. (3d) 192*n*, *sub nom. Horvat v. Artell Developments Ltd.*

A late payment penalty on a utility bill is capable of constituting interest within the meaning of this section: *Garland v. Consumers' Gas Co.*, [1998] 3 S.C.R. 112, 129 C.C.C. (3d) 97.

"Credit advanced" – In *Garland v. Consumers' Gas Co., supra*, the court had to consider a late payment penalty that the utility company imposed on accounts not paid by the due date. Merely because a particular charge constitutes a penalty, does not bring it within the meaning of "interest". The issue is whether that penalty constitutes, in substance, a cost incurred by customers to receive credit, which in turn depended on whether the relationship between the customer and the company involved any advancement of credit within this section. The definition of "credit advanced" includes a deferral of payment for goods, services or benefits. There must be a specified amount owing, and that amount must actually be due in the absence of an arrangement permitting later payment. In this case, the company provides goods and services to its customers for which a specified amount of money is payable each month on a certain date. The deferral of that payment past the due date constitutes credit advanced under an agreement or arrangement which in effect permits the two payment options: paying by the due date, which costs nothing, and a longer-term option, which involves an additional charge. Also see *Garland v. Consumers' Gas Co.*, [2004] 1 S.C.R. 629, 237 D.L.R. (4th) 385, as to customers' remedy for violation of this section.

Elements of the offence – The *mens rea* of this offence is proof that the accused voluntarily entered into a loan agreement providing for receipt by him of a criminal rate of interest. The Crown is not also required to prove that the accused knew that charging a rate above 60% was unlawful: *William E. Thomson Associates Inc. v. Carpenter* (1989), 61 D.L.R. (4th) 1, 69 O.R. (2d) 545 (C.A.), leave to appeal to S.C.C. refused 65 D.L.R. (4th) viii, 71 O.R. (2d) x.

The Crown must prove that the accused knew (or was willfully blind to the fact) that the terms of the agreement charged an effective annual rate of interest in excess of 60 percent: *R. v. Saikaley* (2017), 348 C.C.C. (3d) 290 (Ont. C.A.), leave to appeal to S.C.C. refused 2017 CarswellOnt 19047.

In considering whether a fee or charge constituted interest within the meaning of this provision, the court must determine whether it was for the advancing of credit and whether the credit was being advanced pursuant to an agreement or arrangement. Charging a satellite subscriber for the cost of collecting an overdue account was a recovery of a disbursement rather than a cost for advancing credit and, accordingly, did not constitute interest: *De Wolf v. Bell ExpressVu Inc.* (2009), 247 C.C.C. (3d) 258, 311 D.L.R. (4th) 68 (Ont. C.A.), leave to appeal to S.C.C. refused 251 C.C.C. (3d) vii.

The offence under subsec. (1)(*a*) is to be narrowly construed. Whether an agreement or arrangement for credit violates this paragraph is determined as of the time the transaction is entered into. If the agreement permits but does not require the payment of interest at a criminal rate then there is no violation of subsec. (1)(*a*). However, subsec. (1)(*b*) is to be broadly construed and whether an interest payment violates this paragraph is determined as of the time the payment is received. The effective annual rate for the purposes of subsec. (1)(*b*) is calculated over the period during which credit is actually outstanding. There is no violation of that paragraph where the payment of interest at a criminal rate arises from a voluntary act of the debtor and not compelled by the lender or the occurrence of a determining event set out in the agreement: *Degelder Construction Co. v. Dancorp Developments Ltd.*, [1998] 3 S.C.R. 90, 129 C.C.C. (3d) 129.

Defences – It is no defence that the borrowers were willing to participate in the agreement and that the accused was not engaged in swindling or other trickery. It would, however, be a defence if in certain circumstances the accused had made an honest mistake as to the terms of the agreement: *R. v. McRobb* (1984), 20 C.C.C. (3d) 493 (Ont. Co. Ct.), vard 32 C.C.C. (3d) 479*n* (Ont. C.A.).

Admissibility of evidence – Although the Crown has proceeded by way of summary conviction, so that the six-month limitation period applies, evidence of payments made by the victims of the offence prior to this period is relevant and admissible to establish the effective annual rate of interest: *R. v. Duzan* (1993), 79 C.C.C. (3d) 552, 32 W.A.C. 295 (Sask. C.A.).

Effect on validity of contract – It was held in *William E. Thomson Associates Inc. v. Carpenter* (1989), 61 D.L.R. (4th) 1, 69 O.R. (2d) 545 (C.A.), leave to appeal to S.C.C. refused 65 D.L.R. (4th) viii, 71 O.R. (2d) x, a civil action, that the unlawfulness of the transaction did not render the entire loan agreement void. The illegal part of the agreement could be severed and the borrower required to repay the principal.

Constitutional considerations – This section is *intra vires* Parliament: *677950 Ontario Ltd. v. Artell Developments Ltd., supra.*

DEFINITIONS / "interest" / "payday loan" / Non-application / Designation of province / Revocation.

347.1 (1) The following definitions apply in subsection (2).

"interest" has the same meaning as in subsection 347(2).

"payday loan" means an advancement of money in exchange for a post-dated cheque, a pre-authorized debit or a future payment of a similar nature but not for any guarantee, suretyship, overdraft protection or security on property and not through a margin loan, pawnbroking, a line of credit or a credit card.

(2) Section 347 and section 2 of the *Interest Act* do not apply to a person, other than a financial institution within the meaning of paragraphs (*a*) to (*d*) of the definition "financial institution" in section 2 of the *Bank Act*, in respect of a payday loan agreement entered into by the person to receive interest, or in respect of interest received by that person under the agreement, if

- **(*a*) the amount of money advanced under the agreement is $1,500 or less and the term of the agreement is 62 days or less;**
- **(*b*) the person is licensed or otherwise specifically authorized under the laws of a province to enter into the agreement; and**

(c) the province is designated under subsection (3).

(3) The Governor in Council shall, by order and at the request of the lieutenant governor in council of a province, designate the province for the purposes of this section if the province has legislative measures that protect recipients of payday loans and that provide for limits on the total cost of borrowing under the agreements.

(4) The Governor in Council shall, by order, revoke the designation made under subsection (3) if requested to do so by the lieutenant governor in council of the province or if the legislative measures described in that subsection are no longer in force in that province. 2007, c. 9, s. 2.

CROSS-REFERENCES

The criminal interest rate offence is defined in s. 347.

SYNOPSIS

This section exempts certain types of so-called payday loans from the criminal interest rate offence in s. 347 and the similar offence in s. 2 of the *Interest Act*, R.S.C. 1985, c. I-15. Payday loans are defined in subsec. (1) and are, in effect, short-term loans made by persons other than financial institutions as defined in the *Bank Act*, S.C. 1991, c. 46. The exemption applies only if the conditions in subsec. (2) are met, that the loan is for $1500 or less, for a term of 62 days or less, and made by a lender that is licensed or specifically authorized by the laws of the province, and the province is designated by the Governor in Council in accordance with subsec. (3). Subsection (4) provides for the revocation of the designation.

Breaking and Entering

BREAKING AND ENTERING WITH INTENT, COMMITTING OFFENCE OR BREAKING OUT / Presumptions / Definition of "place".

348. (1) Every one who

(*a*) breaks and enters a place with intent to commit an indictable offence therein,

(*b*) breaks and enters a place and commits an indictable offence therein, or

(*c*) breaks out of a place after

(i) committing an indictable offence therein, or

(ii) entering the place with intent to commit an indictable offence therein,

is guilty

(*d*) if the offence is committed in relation to a dwelling-house, of an indictable offence and liable to imprisonment for life, and

(*e*) if the offence is committed in relation to a place other than a dwelling-house, of an indictable offence and liable to imprisonment for a term not exceeding ten years or of an offence punishable on summary conviction.

(2) For the purposes of proceedings under this section, evidence that an accused

(*a*) broke and entered a place or attempted to break and enter a place is, in the absence of evidence to the contrary, proof that he broke and entered the place or attempted to do so, as the case may be, with intent to commit an indictable offence therein; or

(*b*) broke out of a place is, in the absence of any evidence to the contrary, proof that he broke out after

(i) committing an indictable offence therein, or

(ii) entering with intent to commit an indictable offence therein.

(3) For the purposes of this section and section 351, "place" means

(*a*) a dwelling-house;

(*b*) a building or structure or any part thereof, other than a dwelling-house;

(*c*) a railway vehicle, a vessel, an aircraft or a trailer; or

(*d*) a pen or an enclosure in which fur-bearing animals are kept in captivity for breeding or commercial purposes. R.S., c. C-34, s. 306; 1972, c. 13, s. 24; R.S.C. 1985, c. 27 (1st Supp.), s. 47; 1997, c. 18, s. 20.

CROSS-REFERENCES

The term "dwelling house" is defined in s. 2. The term "break" is defined in s. 321. "Enter" is defined in s. 350(*a*) and s. 350(*b*) deems a person to have broken and entered in circumstances defined therein. An indictable offence includes a Crown-option offence, which may be prosecuted by indictment, by virtue of s. 34(1) of the *Interpretation Act*, R.S.C. 1985, c. I-21.

As to admission of photographic evidence of property, see s. 491.2. For proof by way of affidavit of ownership, lawful possession, value, and that the person was deprived of property by fraud or otherwise without the person's lawful consent, see s. 657.1.

Section 662(6) provides that a person, charged with the offence under subsec. (1)(*b*), may be convicted of the offence under subsec. (1)(*a*) where the evidence does not prove the former offence but does prove the latter. Under s. 583, an indictment, which otherwise complies with s. 581, is not insufficient by reason only that (*a*) it does not name the person injured or intended to be injured; (*b*) it does not name the person who owns or has a special property or interest in the property mentioned in the count, however, see s. 587 as to when particulars may be ordered. Also note s. 588 which deems certain persons to have a property interest in property of which they have the management, control or custody.

This offence may be the basis for an application for an authorization to intercept private communications by reason of s. 183 or a warrant to conduct video surveillance under s. 487.01(5).

The accused may elect the mode of trial pursuant to s. 536(2) unless the Crown proceeds by way of summary conviction where the offence does not relate to a dwelling-house. Release pending trial is determined by s. 515. A person convicted of the offence in this section may be liable to the mandatory prohibition order in s. 109 for possession of certain weapons, ammunition and explosives.

The offence of forcible entry is in s. 72 and trespassing by night in s. 177. Being unlawfully in a dwelling house is an offence under s. 349. Possession of break-in instruments is an offence under s. 351(1). Defence of property is dealt with in ss. 38 to 42. Section 494 gives the owner of property or person in possession and persons authorized by them a power to arrest, without warrant, a person found committing a criminal offence on or in relation to that property. The offence which is most often alleged to be the indictable offence intended to be committed is theft under s. 334. Section 98 creates offences similar to the offences in this section where the object of the break and enter is a firearm. The only important distinction between the two provisions is that the s. 98 offence carries a maximum punishment of life imprisonment whether or not the place is a dwelling-house.

Pursuant to s. 348.1, if a person is convicted of the offence under this section in relation to a dwelling-house, it is an aggravating factor in sentencing that the dwelling-house was occupied at the time and the offender knew or was reckless as to whether the dwelling-house was occupied and used violence or threats of violence to a person or property.

SYNOPSIS

This section describes the offence of breaking and entering. The offence is committed by anyone: (a) who breaks and enters a place *with intent to commit an indictable offence* therein; (b) who breaks and enters a place and actually commits an indictable offence; or (c) breaks out of a place after committing an indictable offence, or after having entered intending to commit an indictable offence. The offence is indictable, with a maximum punishment of life imprisonment if the place is a dwelling house. For a non-dwelling-house the offence is a hybrid, the maximum punishment being 10 years by indictment and 6 months if the Crown elects to proceed summarily. The meaning of "place", for the purpose of this section, is defined by subsec. (3). Subsection (2) creates two presumptions. Where a person breaks and enters a place or attempts to do so, those acts are proof, in the absence of evidence to the contrary, that the person had the intent to commit an indictable offence therein. Similarly, where a person breaks out of a place, that act is proof that he committed, or entered with intent to commit, an indictable offence therein.

ANNOTATIONS

Intoxication defence – In *R. v. Gawel*, [1984] 6 W.W.R. 672*n* (Sask. C.A.), varg [1984] 5 W.W.R. 608, 40 C.R. (3d) 93 (Q.B.), on a charge of break and enter and committing assault, the accused was convicted of assault only, the evidence showing that the accused, who was in a highly intoxicated state, mistakenly believed he was in his own house when he assaulted the occupant.

Presumption of intent [subsec. (2)] – Once a *prima facie* case is made out using this presumption the accused need only raise a reasonable doubt, which he may do by adducing evidence of an explanation that may reasonably be true. However, an explanation that is disbelieved does not constitute "any evidence to the contrary" as it is no evidence. The evidence upon which the accused relies must at least raise a reasonable doubt as to his guilt, and if it does not meet this test then the *prima facie* case remains: *R. v. Proudlock*, [1979] 1 S.C.R. 525, 43 C.C.C. (2d) 321. [**Note:** Since this decision the *Criminal Code* has been amended to delete the word "any" from the phrase "in the absence of any evidence to the contrary". However, the majority judgment in *R. v. Proudlock* indicates that there is no basis for a distinction depending on the presence of the word "any"; the phrases "evidence to the contrary" and "any evidence to the contrary" both being the converse of "no evidence to the contrary".]

When there is any evidence to the contrary, in the sense of evidence tending to negative the existence of the necessary intent, the onus is then upon the Crown to prove the existence of the necessary intent beyond a reasonable doubt. Evidence of the accused's condition due to the consumption of alcohol and drugs which caused him to act in an irrational manner was evidence to the contrary in that it tended to negative an intent to commit an indictable offence: *R. v. Campbell* (1974), 17 C.C.C. (2d) 320 (Ont. C.A.).

Evidence that the accused is of good character is not of itself "evidence to the contrary": *R. v. Khan* (1982), 66 C.C.C. (2d) 32 (Ont. C.A.).

The presumption in this subsection is not available where the indictment specifies the particular indictable offence such as theft or mischief: *R. v. Khan, supra*.

Doctrine of recent possession / *Also see notes under s. 354* – Upon proof of unexplained possession of recently stolen goods the trier of fact may, but not must, draw an inference of guilt of not only the possession offence but an offence such as break and enter committed in obtaining the goods: *R. v. Kowlyk*, [1988] 2 S.C.R. 59, 43 C.C.C. (3d) 1 (4:1).

"Place" – The definition of "place" in subsec. (4)(*b*) contemplates a type of structure within which human beings function and not, for example, a glass show-case on the exterior wall of a building which gives no access to any part of the building: *R. v. Desjatnik* (1981), 64 C.C.C. (2d) 408 (Que. Ct. Sess. of Peace).

On the other hand a small boutique in a shopping mall which is a permanent structure closed in on all sides at night is a "place" notwithstanding it has no roof: *R. v. McKerness* (1983), 4 C.C.C. (3d) 233 (Que. Ct. Sess. Peace).

An oil bulk plant compound enclosed by a permanent fence in which are situated fuel storage tanks, an office and warehouse is a structure and hence a "place" within the meaning of this section: *R. v. Thibault* (1982), 66 C.C.C. (2d) 422 (N.S.C.A.).

Similarly, an area containing an office building surrounded by a 10 foot high fence is a place: *R. v. Fajtl* (1986), 53 C.R. (3d) 396 (B.C.C.A.).

A yard does not constitute a "place". "Structure" can include empty spaces that are enclosed but does not apply to open, unenclosed spaces: *R. v. Ausland* (2010), 251 C.C.C. (3d) 207 (Alta. C.A.).

Included offences – Possession of stolen goods contrary to s. 322 is included in a charge of break, enter and theft: *R. v. L'Hirondelle* (1992), 72 C.C.C. (3d) 254 (Alta. C.A.). *Contra: R. v. Rivet* (1975), 29 C.R.N.S. 301 (Ont. C.A.).

Being unlawfully in a dwelling house pursuant to s. 349 is an included offence under s. 349(1)(*a*). In addition, s. 348(1)(*a*) is an included offence under s. 348(1)(*b*): *R. v. Liang* (2008), 240 C.C.C. (3d) 197 (Alta. C.A.).

Constitutional considerations – While subsec. (2)(*b*) infringes the presumption of innocence in s. 11(*d*) of the Charter, it constitutes a reasonable limit within the meaning of s. 1 of the Charter and is therefore valid: *R. v. Slavens* (1991), 64 C.C.C. (3d) 29 (B.C.C.A.).

AGGRAVATING CIRCUMSTANCE — HOME INVASION.

348.1 If a person is convicted of an offence under section 98 or 98.1, subsection 279(2) or section 343, 346 or 348 in relation to a dwelling-house, the court imposing the sentence on the person shall consider as an aggravating circumstance the fact that the dwelling-house was occupied at the time of the commission of the offence and that the person, in committing the offence,

(*a*) knew that or was reckless as to whether the dwelling-house was occupied; and

(*b*) used violence or threats of violence to a person or property. 2002, c. 13, s. 15; 2008, c. 6, s. 34.

CROSS-REFERENCES

The terms "dwelling-house" and "property" are defined in s. 2. For other deemed aggravating circumstances on sentencing, see s. 718.2.

ANNOTATIONS

"Home invasion" in this section is not synonymous with "home invasion robbery". The essential elements of a home invasion are: (i) occupancy of a dwelling-house at the time one of the listed crimes was committed; (ii) knowledge or recklessness on the part of the offender as to whether the dwelling-house was occupied; and (iii) actual or threatened use of violence to persons or property: *R. v. C. (D.J.)* (2009), 245 C.C.C. (3d) 258 (Sask. C.A.).

Where the assailants showed up at the victim's house, pulled him outside the front door and assaulted him there, this aggravating circumstance still applied even though the assault was not strictly speaking in the "home": *R. v. Ginnish* (2014), 306 C.C.C. (3d) 118 (N.B.C.A.).

BEING UNLAWFULLY IN DWELLING-HOUSE / Presumption.

349. (1) Every person who, without lawful excuse, enters or is in a dwelling-house with intent to commit an indictable offence in it is guilty of an indictable offence and liable to imprisonment for a term of not more than 10 years or of an offence punishable on summary conviction.

(2) For the purposes of proceedings under this section, evidence that an accused, without lawful excuse, entered or was in a dwelling-house is, in the absence of any evidence to the contrary, proof that he entered or was in the dwelling-house with intent to commit an indictable offence therein. R.S., c. C-34, s. 307; 1997, c. 18, s. 21; 2018, c. 29, s. 35.

CROSS-REFERENCES

The term "dwelling house" is defined in s. 2. "Enter" is defined in s. 350(*a*). The offence which is most often alleged to be the indictable offence intended to be committed is theft under s. 334.

The accused may elect his mode of trial pursuant to s. 536(2) unless the Crown elects to proceed by way of summary conviction. Release pending trial is determined by s. 515. A person convicted of the offence in this section may, depending on the circumstances, be liable to the mandatory prohibition order in s. 109 for possession of certain weapons, ammunition and explosives or the discretionary order in s. 110 where the Crown proceeds summarily.

The offence of forcible entry is in s. 72 and trespassing by night in s. 177. Being unlawfully in a dwelling house is an offence under s. 349. Possession of break-in instruments is an offence under s. 351(1). Defence of property is dealt with in ss. 38 to 42. Section 494 gives the owner of property or person in possession and persons authorized by them a power to arrest, without warrant, a person found committing a criminal offence on or in relation to that property.

SYNOPSIS

This section describes the offence of being unlawfully in a dwelling house. Anyone who enters or is in a dwelling house, with intent to commit an indictable offence therein, commits the offence. A person is not guilty if he has a lawful excuse for entering or being present in the dwelling house, but the onus is on that person to so establish, on a balance of probabilities. It is important to note that the accused need not have entered with the requisite intent, provided that he formulates that intent while present in the dwelling house. Subsection (2) provides that evidence of entry or presence in a dwelling house without lawful excuse, in the absence of evidence to the contrary, is proof of the existence of the requisite intent.

ANNOTATIONS

"dwelling house" – A motel unit is a dwelling house: *R. v. Henderson,* [1975] 1 W.W.R. 360 (B.C. Prov. Ct.).

Presumption of intent (subsec. (2)) – Prior to the amendment of this subsection which replaced the words "*prima facie* evidence" with the words "in the absence of any evidence to the contrary, proof" it was held that even where the Crown could rely on the presumption because of proof of an unlawful entry there was no onus on the accused to provide a reasonable and logical explanation for his presence in the premises since the evidence, while not establishing a lawful excuse for the accused's presence, might well create a reasonable doubt as to his intent to commit an indictable offence therein which is a vital element in the commission of the offence: *R. v. Austin*, [1969] 1 C.C.C. 97 (S.C.C.) (3:2). In *R. v. Proudlock*, [1979] 1 S.C.R. 525, 43 C.C.C. (2d) 321, Pigeon J., whose judgment was concurred in by five members of the court, was of the view that the change in the wording had not affected the meaning which should be attributed to the presumption. In particular an explanation which is not believed does not constitute "any evidence to the contrary".

Evidence of drunkenness which discloses that the accused did not have the necessary specific intent is evidence to the contrary neutralizing the statutory presumption: *R. v. Johnnie* (1975), 23 C.C.C. (2d) 68 (B.C.C.A.).

Evidence to the contrary is evidence in either the prosecution or the defence case which is not disbelieved by the trier of fact and which gives rise to a reasonable doubt with respect to the existence of the intent to commit an indictable offence on the part of the accused: *R. v. Nagy* (1988), 45 C.C.C. (3d) 350 (Ont. C.A.).

Included offences – The offence of mischief as described in s. 430(1)(*d*) is an included offence: *R. v. E. (S.)* (1993), 80 C.C.C. (3d) 502 (N.W.T.C.A.). *Contra*: *R. v. Drake* (1974), 16 C.C.C. (2d) 505 (N.S.C.A.); *R. v. Beyo* (2000), 144 C.C.C. (3d) 15 (Ont. C.A.), leave to appeal to S.C.C. refused 147 C.C.C. (3d) vi.

Constitutional considerations – It was held in *R. v. Nagy* (1988), 45 C.C.C. (3d) 350 (Ont. C.A.), that this subsection creates a mandatory presumption so that if the prosecution proves entry or presence in a dwelling-house without lawful excuse the trier of fact must, not may, convict in the absence of any evidence to the contrary and therefore this subsection offends the presumption of innocence guarantee in s. 11(*d*) of the Charter. However, it constitutes a reasonable limit within the meaning of s. 1 of the Charter and therefore the subsection is valid.

ENTRANCE.

350. For the purposes of sections 348 and 349,

(*a*) a person enters as soon as any part of his body or any part of an instrument that he uses is within any thing that is being entered; and

(*b*) a person shall be deemed to have broken and entered if

(i) he obtained entrance by a threat or artifice or by collusion with a person within, or

(ii) he entered without lawful justification or excuse by a permanent or temporary opening. R.S., c. C-34, s. 308; 2018, c. 29, s. 36.

CROSS-REFERENCES

The term "break" is defined in s. 321.

SYNOPSIS

For the purposes of s. 348 and 349, entry occurs as soon as any part of the body of, or an instrument used by, a person is within anything being entered. A person is deemed to have broken and entered if entry is obtained, by threat, artifice or collusion with a person inside, or through a permanent or temporary opening, without lawful justification. The onus is on the accused to establish that justification.

ANNOTATIONS

Entry by artifice, etc. (para. (*b*)(i)) – By artifice is by a manoeuvre or stratagem such as sneaking into premises behind someone making a lawful entry: *R. v. Leger* (1976), 31 C.C.C. (2d) 413 (Ont. C.A.).

Entry without lawful justification or excuse (para. (*b*)(ii)) – The words "by a permanent or temporary opening" are clear and should be given their ordinary meaning and embrace an entry not only through the further opening of a temporary opening, but any entry through any temporary opening. Thus entry by the accused through a doorway in a partly constructed house which was open, as the door had not yet been installed, comes within this provision: *R. v. Johnson*, [1977] 2 S.C.R. 646, 34 C.C.C. (2d) 12 (9:0).

In determining whether there was lawful justification or excuse, the time to be considered is the time of the entry. Thus, this paragraph did not apply to an accused who was licenced to enter a store as were other members of the public during normal business hours, notwithstanding he harboured an intent to remain in the store until after closing and then steal a quantity of goods: *R. v. Farbridge* (1984), 15 C.C.C. (3d) 521 (Alta. C.A.).

Constitutional considerations – The phrase "the proof of which lies upon him" in para. (*b*)(ii) is unconstitutional as violating s. 11(*d*) of the Charter. However, with that phrase eliminated this paragraph is valid: *R. v. Singh* (1987), 41 C.C.C. (3d) 278 (Alta. C.A.).

While para. (*b*)(ii) infringes the presumption of innocence as guaranteed by s. 11(*d*) of the *Canadian Charter of Rights and Freedoms*, it constitutes a reasonable limit and is therefore valid: *R. v. K. (T.B.)* (1998), 49 C.R.R. (2d) 328 (Ont. C.A.), leave to appeal to S.C.C. refused 55 C.R.R. (2d) 374*n*.

POSSESSION OF BREAK-IN INSTRUMENT / Disguise with intent.

351. (1) Every person who, without lawful excuse, has in their possession any instrument suitable for the purpose of breaking into any place, motor vehicle, vault or safe knowing that the instrument has been used or is intended to be used for that purpose,

(*a*) is guilty of an indictable offence and liable to imprisonment for a term not exceeding ten years; or

(*b*) is guilty of an offence punishable on summary conviction.

(2) Every one who, with intent to commit an indictable offence, has his face masked or coloured or is otherwise disguised is guilty of an indictable offence and liable to imprisonment for a term not exceeding ten years. R.S., c. C-34, s. 309; 1972, c. 13, s. 25; R.S.C. 1985, c. 27 (1st Supp.), s. 48; 2008, c. 18, s. 9; 2018, c. 29, s. 37.

CROSS-REFERENCES

The term "motor vehicle" is defined in s. 2. The term "place" is defined in s. 351. Possession is defined in s. 4(3). An indictable offence include a Crown-option offence, which may be prosecuted by indictment, by virtue of s. 34(1) of the *Interpretation Act*, R.S.C. 1985, c. I-21.

The accused may elect his mode of trial pursuant to s. 536(2). Release pending trial is determined by s. 515.

Related offences: s. 85, using firearm during commission or attempted commission of indictable offence; s. 343, robbery; s. 348, break and enter; s. 349, unlawfully in dwelling house; s. 352, breaking into coin-operated device; s. 353, selling, etc., automobile master key.

SYNOPSIS

This section describes two offences — that of being in possession of a break-in instrument and that of being disguised with intent to commit an indictable offence. Subsection (1) makes it clear that the person accused of this offence may escape criminal liability, if he can establish a *lawful excuse* for possessing the instrument described above. Subsection (2) makes it an indictable offence, with a maximum term of imprisonment of 10 years, for a person to mask, colour or otherwise disguise his face with intent to commit an indictable offence.

ANNOTATIONS

Meaning of instrument (subsec. (1)) – Nitric acid, sulphuric acid, bicarbonate of soda and various implements, being proved sufficient to make nitroglycerine, were held to be an "instrument" within this section: *R. v. Benischek*, [1963] 3 C.C.C. 286 (Ont. C.A.).

Liability of party – In *R. v. Zanini*, [1967 S.C.R. 715, [1968] 2 C.C.C. 1 (5:0), the accused and his companions were charged with breaking and entering and committing theft in a dwelling-house and possession of house-breaking instruments. The two companions pleaded guilty to the former charge and the latter charge was withdrawn as against them. The accused was acquitted of the former charge as the stolen money could not be identified by the owner, but by application of s. 21(2) of the Code was convicted of the latter charge. The accused's appeal was dismissed, it being held that the fact that the possession charge was withdrawn against the two active principals did not affect the right of the Crown to proceed against the accused, as there is no requirement in s. 21(2) that the active participants must be convicted of possession; and it was open to the jury to find, as it did, that the accused knew or ought to have known that one of his confederates, for the purpose of effecting their common design of breaking and entering the dwelling-house at least would, of necessity, be in possession of house-breaking instruments.

Reasonable inference of intended use of instrument (subsec. (1)) – The phrase "a reasonable inference", in a criminal statute, requires proof beyond a reasonable doubt. Accordingly, the burden on the Crown to prove every element of the offence beyond a reasonable doubt requires proof beyond a reasonable doubt of (*a*) possession by the accused of the instruments specified in the indictment; (*b*) the suitability of the instruments for the prohibited purpose; and (*c*) and intention to use the instruments for the prohibited purpose. In the result, the phrase "without lawful excuse, the proof of which lies on him" added to a predecessor to this subsection to make available to the accused the defence of innocent purpose is now superfluous and was presumably kept in the provision, with subsequent amendments, out of an abundance of caution. The phrase does not encompass excuses or justifications that would exist if those words were omitted from the section and thus general common law excuses such as duress or authorization by law need not be proved by the accused on a balance of probabilities. In the result, this provision does not offend the guarantee to the presumption of innocence in s. 11(*d*) of the *Charter of Rights and Freedoms*: *R. v. Holmes*, [1988] 1 S.C.R. 914, 41 C.C.C. (3d) 497 (5:0).

It was not necessary for the Crown to establish a nexus between the accused's possession of instruments and a "target" vehicle where it was alleged that the tools were used for breaking into and theft of automobiles. The absence of a nexus in time and place between the possession of instruments and a particular automobile is, however, a significant factor in determining whether it is appropriate to draw an inference of intent to use instruments for the prohibited purpose: *R. v. K. (S.)* (1995), 103 C.C.C. (3d) 572, 108 W.A.C. 311 (B.C.C.A.).

Where an exculpatory explanation is given by an accused contemporaneously with his arrest, it is admissible at the instance of the accused without a determination as to whether there was an opportunity for concoction: *R. v. Crossley* (1997), 117 C.C.C. (3d) 533, 154 W.A.C. 61 (B.C.C.A.).

Masked with intent (subsec. (2)) – The Crown must prove the intention to commit one or more specific indictable offences: *R. v. Shay* (1976), 32 C.C.C. (2d) 13 (Ont. C.A.).

POSSESSION OF INSTRUMENTS FOR BREAKING INTO COIN-OPERATED OR CURRENCY EXCHANGE DEVICES.

352. Every person who, without lawful excuse, has in their possession any instrument suitable for the purpose of breaking into a coin-operated device or a currency exchange device, knowing that the instrument has been used or is intended to be used for that purpose, is guilty of an indictable offence and liable to imprisonment for a term of not more than two years. R.S., c. C-34, s. 310; 1972, c. 13, s. 26; 1974-75-76, c. 93, s. 28; 2018, c. 29, s. 38.

CROSS-REFERENCES

Possession is defined in s. 4(3).

The accused may elect his mode of trial pursuant to s. 536(2). Release pending trial is determined by s. 515, although the accused is eligible for release by the officer in charge pursuant to s. 498.

The related offence of possession of break-in instruments is in s. 351 and of selling, etc., automobile master key in s. 353.

SYNOPSIS

This section describes the offence of possession of any instrument for breaking into coin-operated or currency exchange devices in circumstances which give rise to a *reasonable inference* that the instrument has been used, or is or was intended to be used for such a purpose. This section, like s. 351, puts the onus of proof on the accused to establish that such possession was *with lawful excuse*. This is an indictable offence with a maximum term of two years' imprisonment.

ANNOTATIONS

An instrument is "suitable" within the meaning of this section provided any reasonable person would assume or believe that it was capable, adequate or suitable for the purpose notwithstanding there is evidence that in fact the instruments could not break into the device: *R. v. Garland* (1978), 41 C.C.C. (2d) 346, 3 C.R. (3d) 206 (Nfld. Dist. Ct.).

Expert evidence merely to the effect that the instrument was suitable for picking locks is not evidence that it was within the specific category of instruments suitable for breaking into a coin-operated device: *R. v. Mackie* (1978), 43 C.C.C. (2d) 269, 4 C.R. (3d) 263 (Ont. H.C.J.).

k. A conviction for theft of the coins from a coin-operated device is a bar to a conviction under this section arising out of the same circumstances in view of the rule in *R. v. Kienapple*, [1975] 1 S.C.R. 729, 15 C.C.C. (2d) 524, where there is no evidence that the key had been used prior to the theft and the accused was arrested immediately after the theft so that there was no evidence from which an inference could be drawn of any intended future use of it: *R. v. Stanziale* (1979), 47 C.C.C. (2d) 348, 9 C.R. (3d) 281 (Ont. C.A.).

SELLING, ETC., AUTOMOBILE MASTER KEY / Exception / Terms and conditions of licence / Fees / Record to be kept / Failure to comply with subsection (3) / Definitions / "automobile master key" / "licence".

353. (1) Every one who

(*a*) sells, offers for sale or advertises in a province an automobile master key otherwise than under the authority of a licence issued by the Attorney General of that province, or

(*b*) purchases or has in his possession in a province an automobile master key otherwise than under the authority of a licence issued by the Attorney General of that province,

is guilty of an indictable offence and liable to imprisonment for a term not exceeding two years.

(1.1) A police officer specially authorized by the chief of the police force to possess an automobile master key is not guilty of an offence under subsection (1) by reason only that the police officer possesses an automobile master key for the purposes of the execution of the police officer's duties.

(2) A licence issued by the Attorney General of a province as described in paragraph (1)(*a*) or (*b*) may contain such terms and conditions relating to the sale, offering for sale, advertising, purchasing, having in possession or use of an automobile master key as the Attorney General of that province may prescribe.

(2.1) The Attorney General of a province may prescribe fees for the issue or renewal of licences as described in paragraph (1)(*a*) or (*b*).

(3) Every one who sells an automobile master key

(*a*) shall keep a record of the transaction showing the name and address of the purchaser and particulars of the licence issued to the purchaser as described in paragraph (1)(*b*); and

(*b*) shall produce the record for inspection at the request of a peace officer.

(4) Every one who fails to comply with subsection (3) is guilty of an offence punishable on summary conviction.

(5) The definitions in this subsection apply in this section.

"automobile master key" includes a key, pick, rocker key or other instrument designed or adapted to operate the ignition or other switches or locks of a series of motor vehicles.

"licence" includes any authorization.R.S., c. C-34, s. 311; 1997, c. 18, s. 22.

CROSS-REFERENCES

The terms "Attorney General" and "motor vehicle" are defined in s. 2. Possession is defined in s. 4(3). The accused may elect his mode of trial for the offence in subsec. (1), pursuant to s. 536(2). Release pending trial is determined by s. 515, although the accused is eligible for release by the officer in charge pursuant to s. 498. The offence under subsec. (4) is tried by a summary conviction court under Part XXVII. The punishment is as set out in s. 787 [although see s. 735(1)(*b*) respecting maximum fine for corporation] and the limitation period is set out in s. 786(2). Release pending trial is determined by s. 515, although the accused is eligible for release by a peace officer under s. 496, 497 or by the officer in charge under s. 498.

Related offences: s. 351, possession of break-in instruments; s. 352, possession of instruments for breaking into coin-operated devices; s. 334, theft; s. 335, joy-riding; s. 96, possession of weapons obtained by crime.

SYNOPSIS

This section creates several offences in relation to "automobile master key" (defined in subsec. (5)).

Subsection (1) describes the offence of selling, offering for sale, advertising in a province, purchasing, or possessing in a province an automobile master key *otherwise than under the authority* of *a licence* issued by the Attorney General of the province. That offence is indictable and carries a maximum term of two years' imprisonment. Subsection (2) states that a licence issued by the Attorney General of a province may contain such terms and conditions relating to the sale, offering for sale, advertising, purchasing or possession of an automobile master key as the Attorney General of that province may prescribe. Subsection (3) requires that any person who sells an automobile master key keep a record of the transaction, showing the name, address and particulars of the licence referred to in subsec. (1) of the purchaser. Subsection (3) further requires the vendor of the master key to produce the record at the request of a peace officer. A failure to comply with either of the requirements described in subsection (3) gives rise to a summary conviction offence. Subsection (1.1) creates an exemption for a police officer authorized by the chief of police to be in possession of an automobile master key for the purpose of the execution of the officer's duties.

ANNOTATIONS

This section contemplates a device which may be the subject of commerce, the sale and possession of which is lawful only under licence. A coat hanger although so fashioned as to be capable of lifting the latch on locked vehicles does not fall within the meaning of "automobile master key": *R. v. Young* (1983), 3 C.C.C. (3d) 395 (Ont. C.A.).

TAMPERING WITH VEHICLE IDENTIFICATION NUMBER / Definition of "vehicle identification number" / Exception / Punishment.

353.1 (1) Every person commits an offence who, without lawful excuse, wholly or partially alters, removes or obliterates a vehicle identification number on a motor vehicle.

(2) For the purpose of this section, "vehicle identification number" means any number or other mark placed on a motor vehicle for the purpose of distinguishing it from other similar motor vehicles.

(3) Despite subsection (1), it is not an offence to wholly or partially alter, remove or obliterate a vehicle identification number on a motor vehicle during regular maintenance or any repair or other work done on the vehicle for a legitimate purpose, including a modification of the vehicle.

(4) Every person who commits an offence under subsection (1)

(*a*) is guilty of an indictable offence and liable to imprisonment for a term of not more than five years; or

(*b*) is guilty of an offence punishable on summary conviction. 2010, c. 14, s. 4.

CROSS-REFERENCES

"Motor vehicle" is defined in s. 2. Section 354(2) creates a presumption of knowing possession of stolen goods from possession of a vehicle or part with an obliterated vehicle identification number. Section 333.1 creates an offence of theft of an automobile.

SYNOPSIS
This section creates the Crown-option offence of tampering, in any of the ways set out in subsec. (2), with vehicle identification numbers on a motor vehicle. There is a saving provision in subsec. (3) for alteration of the number during regular maintenance.

Possession and Trafficking

2010, c. 14, s. 5.

POSSESSION OF PROPERTY OBTAINED BY CRIME / Obliterated vehicle identification number / Definition of "vehicle identification number" / Exception.

354. (1) Every one commits an offence who has in his possession any property or thing or any proceeds of any property or thing knowing that all or part of the property or thing or of the proceeds was obtained by or derived directly or indirectly from

(*a*) the commission in Canada of an offence punishable by indictment; or

(*b*) an act or omission anywhere that, if it had occurred in Canada, would have constituted an offence punishable by indictment.

(2) In proceedings in respect of an offence under subsection (1), evidence that a person has in their possession a motor vehicle the vehicle identification number of which has been wholly or partially removed or obliterated or a part of a motor vehicle being a part bearing a vehicle identification number that has been wholly or partially removed or obliterated is, in the absence of any evidence to the contrary, proof that the motor vehicle or part, as the case may be, was obtained,

(*a*) by the commission in Canada of an offence punishable by indictment; or

(*b*) by an act or omission anywhere that, if it had occurred in Canada, would have constituted an offence punishable by indictment.

(3) For the purposes of subsection (2), "vehicle identification number" means any number or other mark placed on a motor vehicle for the purpose of distinguishing the motor vehicle from other similar motor vehicles.

(4) A peace officer or a person acting under the direction of a peace officer is not guilty of an offence under this section by reason only that the peace officer or person possesses property or a thing or the proceeds of property or a thing mentioned in subsection (1) for the purposes of an investigation or otherwise in the execution of the peace officer's duties. R.S., c. C-34, s. 312; 1972, c. 13, s. 27; 1974-75-76, c. 93, s. 29; 1997, c. 18, s. 23; 2018, c. 29, s. 39.

CROSS-REFERENCES
The terms "motor vehicle", "peace officer" and "property" are defined in s. 2. Possession is defined in s. 4(3), however, s. 358 defines circumstances in which possession is complete. An indictable offence includes Crown-option offences which may be prosecuted by indictment, by virtue of s. 34(1) of the *Interpretation Act*, R.S.C. 1985, c. I-21.

The punishment for this offence is set out in s. 355 and see notes under that section respecting mode of trial and release pending trial. The offence which is most often alleged to be the indictable offence by which the goods were obtained is theft under s. 334. Other related offences are: s. 333.1, theft of automobile; s. 342, theft, etc., of credit card; s. 343, robbery; s. 346, extortion; s. 348, break and enter; s. 349, unlawfully in dwelling house; s. 351, possession of break-in instruments; s. 352, possession of instruments for breaking into coin-operated devices; s. 353.1, tampering with vehicle identification number; s. 362, obtaining by false pretences; s. 380, fraud; s. 355.2, trafficking in property obtained by crime; s. 355.3, prohibition on importing or exporting stolen property; s. 355.4, possession of property obtained by crime for the purpose of trafficking.

By virtue of s. 583(*b*), an indictment which otherwise complies with s. 581 is not insufficient by reason that it fails to name the person who owns or has a special property or interest in property mentioned in the count. Also note s. 588 which deems certain persons to have a property interest in property of which they have the management, control or custody. Sections 359 and 360 enact special evidentiary rules. Under s. 359, evidence that stolen property was found in the accused's possession in the previous 12 months is admissible to prove knowledge that the property which forms the subject-matter of the proceedings was stolen property. Under s. 360, evidence may be given that the accused was convicted in the previous 5 years of theft or an offence under this section, to prove that knowledge that the property which forms the subject-matter of the proceedings was unlawfully obtained. Note that, for both sections, notice must be given to the accused.

As to admission of photographic evidence of property, see s. 491.2. For proof by way of affidavit of ownership, lawful possession, value, and that the person was deprived of property by fraud or otherwise without the person's lawful consent, see s. 657.1. Under s. 657.2, evidence that any person was convicted or discharged for the theft of the property is proof that the property was stolen.

This offence may be the basis for an application for an authorization to intercept private communications by reason of s. 183 or a warrant to conduct video surveillance pursuant to s. 487.01(5). In some circumstances, the offence under this section will constitute an enterprise crime offence for the purposes of Part XII.2 [see s. 462.3, definition of enterprise crime offence para. (*b*)].

Bringing into Canada anything obtained outside Canada by an act that, if committed in Canada, would have been an offence under this section if committed in Canada is an offence under s. 357. Possession of mail, etc., obtained by theft is an offence under s. 356(1)(*b*).

The equivalent offence in the *Controlled Drugs and Substances Act* is s. 8.

SYNOPSIS

This section describes the offence of possession of property obtained by crime. Subsection (1) states that if a person has in his possession any property or the proceeds of any property, knowing that such property or proceeds were obtained or derived directly or indirectly from the commission in Canada of an indictable offence or an act or omission in any location which would in Canada constitute an indictable offence, that person is guilty of an offence. Subsection (2) states that evidence that the vehicle identification number of a motor vehicle, or a part of a motor vehicle, has been wholly or partially obliterated or removed is, absent evidence to the contrary, proof that *the item was obtained* and that the person in possession of it *knew that it was obtained* by the commission of an indictable offence. No offence is committed if a peace officer or a person acting under the direction of a peace officer has possession for the purpose of an investigation or in the execution of the officer's duties.

ANNOTATIONS

Doctrine of recent possession – A review of the elements of the "doctrine" of recent possession is found in *R. v. Kowlyk*, [1988] 2 S.C.R. 59, 43 C.C.C. (3d) 1 (4:1). Those elements, as set out in that case and distilled from the various decisions as approved in *Kowlyk*, may be summarized as follows:

1. No adverse inference may be drawn against an accused from the fact of possession alone unless it were recent: *R. v. Graham*, [1974] S.C.R. 59, 7 C.C.C. (2d) 93 (7:0);
2. If a pre-trial explanation of such possession were given by the accused, and if it possessed that degree of contemporaneity with the possession making evidence of it admissible, no adverse inference could be drawn on the basis of recent possession alone if the explanation were one which could reasonably be true: *R. v. Graham, supra*;
3. In the absence of such explanation, recent possession alone is quite sufficient to raise a factual inference of theft;
4. Where the accused does not testify, a jury instruction as to the inference arising from unexplained possession does not constitute a "comment" within the meaning of s. 4(6): *R. v. Newton*, [1977] 1 S.C.R. 399, 28 C.C.C. (2d) 286 (9:0);
5. Where an explanation which could reasonably be true is given for the possession, then no inference of guilt on the basis of recent possession alone may be drawn, even if the

trier of fact is not satisfied as to the truth of the explanation and thus, to obtain a conviction in the face of such an explanation, it must establish by other evidence the guilt of the accused beyond a reasonable doubt;
6. The unexplained possession of stolen goods, standing alone, will also warrant an inference of guilt of breaking and entering and theft of those goods;
7. Upon proof of the unexplained possession of recently stolen goods, the trier of fact may – but not must – draw an inference of guilt of theft or of offences incidental thereto;
8. Where the circumstances are such that a question could arise as to whether the accused was a thief or merely a possessor, it will be for the trier of fact, upon a consideration of all the circumstances, to decide which, if either, inference should be drawn.

In the subsequent case of *R. v. Wiseman* (1989), 52 C.C.C. (3d) 160 (N.S.C.A.), the court interpreted *Kowlyk* as also standing for the proposition that, in charging the jury, the trial judge should avoid the use of the phrase "doctrine of recent possession". The court stated that what is really involved is an inference from unexplained possession of recently stolen goods. The court seems to have been concerned that use of a term such as "doctrine" implies some mandatory rule of law, rather than application of a common sense inference.

Although the doctrine is stated in terms of the inference applying in the absence of any reasonable explanation, there is no burden on the Crown to prove that no explanation was given prior to trial or that such explanation, if given, could not reasonably be true: *R. v. Graham, supra*. It would seem, however, that where an explanation was given to the police, then defence counsel can adduce it through the police: *R. v. Newton, supra*, per Dickson J. The exact basis for its admissibility is unclear, although the suggestion from *R. v. Graham, supra*, is that if made contemporaneously with the finding in possession, it is admissible as part of the *res gestae*. In that case, it was held that a statement made a few hours later was not admissible at the instance of the defence. In *R. v. Graham* and other cases such as *R. v. Ungaro*, [1950] S.C.R. 430, 96 C.C.C. 245, it was pointed out that where the accused gives a statement to the police, but also testifies, it is the explanation under oath which, if reasonably true, negatives the inference of guilty knowledge.

The trier of fact need not *believe* the explanation, it is enough that it raises a reasonable doubt: *R. v. L'Heureux*, [1985] 2 S.C.R. 159, 21 C.C.C. (3d) 574 (7:0). However, an explanation which is disbelieved cannot constitute a reasonable explanation: *R. v. Proudlock*, [1979] 1 S.C.R. 525, 43 C.C.C. (2d) 321.

Since no adverse inference may be drawn from the accused's failure to give an explanation for his possession of stolen goods upon his arrest and after he has been informed of his right to remain silent, then it would seem that evidence of silence at that time is irrelevant and should not be admitted. Where evidence has been admitted of silence at the time of arrest and following the caution, it is clearly misdirection to tell the jury that, in assessing the accused's explanation given on the witness stand, they may consider that an explanation given at once is more convincing than one given at some later time. Rather, the jury should be told that, while an explanation given before arrest or not too long after the arrest is more convincing than one given at some later time, they must not take into account that the accused, upon being arrested and warned, said nothing and they should be directed that he had the right to say nothing and to consult a lawyer: *R. v. Machado* (1989), 50 C.C.C. (3d) 133 (B.C.C.A.).

Where it was the theory of the Crown that the accused was the actual thief and the Crown did not rely on the doctrine of recent possession the trial Judge is not in error in failing to direct the jury on the doctrine: *R. v. Hewson*, [1978] 2 S.C.R. 111, 42 C.C.C. (2d) 507 (5:4).

In *R. v. Saieva*, [1982] 1 S.C.R. 897, 68 C.C.C. (2d) 97 (7:0), the court in considering whether possession was sufficiently "recent" to entitle reliance on the doctrine of recent possession approved the statement in *R. v. Killam* (1973), 12 C.C.C. (2d) 114 (B.C.C.A.), that the criteria to be used are the nature of the object "its rareness, the readiness in which it can, and is likely to, pass from hand to hand, the ease of its identification and the likelihood of transferability".

Proof of offence – This offence is an offence of dishonesty and requires proof of blameworthy conduct. The accused, having only become aware that the goods were stolen, panicked and drove them away from his premises. He was not guilty of this offence although he failed to inform the police. His conduct was inconsistent with any intention to retain or deal with the goods: *R. v. York* (2005), 193 C.C.C. (3d) 331 (B.C.C.A.).

Wilful blindness – To engage the doctrine of willful blindness, there must be a real suspicion in the mind of the accused that is ignored. Where an accused makes a single inquiry, willful blindness can still be found if the accused has real suspicions after the inquiry but did not make any further inquiry: *R. v. Lagace* (2003), 181 C.C.C. (3d) 12 (Ont. C.A.).

Proof that goods obtained by crime – An admission by the accused is admissible for its truth, even if the admission itself contains hearsay, provided that the accused indicates a belief in the acceptance of the truth of the hearsay statement. If, however, the accused merely reports a hearsay statement without either adopting it or indicating a belief in its truth then the statement is not admissible for the truth of its contents. Thus, out of court statements by an accused, charged with the offence under this section, that he did not know the origin of the goods but his friend had stolen the goods and he knew they were "hot", made in circumstances indicating he believed the statements were true, were admissible not only to prove guilty knowledge but that, in fact, the goods were stolen: *R. v. Streu*, [1989] 1 S.C.R. 1521, 48 C.C.C. (3d) 321 (5:0).

While the *mens rea* requirement is satisfied by actual knowledge or willful blindness, mere recklessness is insufficient: *R. v. Vinokurov* (2001), 156 C.C.C. (3d) 300 (Alta. C.A.).

Where the indictable offence is specified in the indictment as "theft" it is misdirection to instruct the jury that the offence is proven if the goods were obtained by fraud: *R. v. Beaudet* (1977), 34 C.C.C. (2d) 150 (Ont. C.A.).

Although it is alleged that the goods were obtained by the commission "in Canada" of an indictable offence the Crown is not required to prove whether the crime was committed in Canada as long as it is, or would have been if committed in Canada, an indictable offence: *R. v. Elliott* (1984), 15 C.C.C. (3d) 195 (Alta. C.A.).

Meaning of "obtained by" – The words "obtained by", apply only where the indictable offence was committed in respect of the thing obtained. Thus where the owner willingly parts with the goods as part of a scheme to defraud his own insurance company by falsely reporting that the goods were stolen the goods have not been obtained by the commission of an indictable offence. They have however been "indirectly derived" from the commission of a crime within the meaning of this subsection: *R. v. Geauvreau* (1979), 51 C.C.C. (2d) 75 (Ont. C.A.), affd [1982] 1 S.C.R. 485, 66 C.C.C. (2d) 375 (9:0).

Goods were not, however, obtained by or derived directly or indirectly from commission of the offence of fraud where the goods were sold to the accused by the owner even if, to the knowledge of the accused, the owner had attempted to defraud his insurance company by arranging for a fake break and enter in which these goods were "stolen". In those circumstances the goods were not the proceeds of crime: *R. v. Epp* (1988), 42 C.C.C. (3d) 572 (Sask. C.A.).

Goods which the accused originally found were "obtained by" the commission of an indictable offence where she subsequently fraudulently converted them to her own use and then retained them in her possession: *R. v. Hayes* (1985), 20 C.C.C. (3d) 385 (Ont. C.A.).

Charging offence – Where a count named the property's owner with some imprecision, but still furnished the accused with reasonable information to identify the alleged owner, there was no error fatal to conviction: *R. v. Emmons* (1970), 1 C.C.C. (2d) 468 (Alta. S.C. App. Div.).

A charge of possession of stolen clothes the property of a person or persons unknown was held to be valid on the ground that for either theft or possession the Crown need only prove ownership in some person or persons other than the accused: *R. v. McDowell,* [1970] 5 C.C.C. 374 (Ont. C.A.), affd [1971] S.C.R. vi.

A count alleging possession of property without alleging the owner or without even in the alternative alleging ownership in a person or persons unknown is valid: *R. v. Halliday* (1975), 25 C.C.C. (2d) 131 (N.S.S.C. App. Div.).

Where the indictment spells out the particulars of the actual commission of the offence punishable by indictment, from which the property originated, it is not necessary for the Crown to prove knowledge of those particulars on the part of the accused: *R. v. Gowing and Johnson* (1970), 2 C.C.C. (2d) 105 (Alta. C.A.).

Rule precluding multiple convictions – The majority theory (6:1) in *R. v. Cote*, [1975] 1 S.C.R. 303, 18 C.C.C. (2d) 321 (6:1), that in law there is no bar to a convicted thief, who is subsequently found with the very stolen articles, being convicted of unlawful possession should be carefully considered in view of the difficulty of establishing when the thief had consummated his theft and when the offence of his unlawful possession of the same property commenced. Although there is a division of opinion the weight of the previous authorities seems to be in favour of the proposition that where possession and theft are proximate the thief cannot also be convicted of illegal possession of the same articles: *R. v. Fergusson*, [1962] S.C.R. 229, 132 C.C.C. 112; *R. v. Siggins* (1960), 127 C.C.C. 409 (Ont. C.A.); *R. v. Varkonyi*, [1964] 1 C.C.C. 311 (Man. C.A.); *R. v. Pryce*, [1967] 3 C.C.C. 13 (B.C.C.A.); and *R. v. Hunt*, [1968] 4 C.C.C. 366 (N.S. Co. Ct.). *Contra, R. v. MacQuarrie*, [1964] 3 C.C.C. 261, 43 C.R. 97 (P.E.I.S.C.), *per* MacGuigan J., dissenting, and *R. v. McKay*, [1968] 4 C.C.C. 355 (N.W.T.T.C.).

Presumption for removal of V.I.N. number [subsec. (2)] – The presumption does not operate to provide proof of the type of indictable offence specified in the indictment by which the vehicle left the hands of its rightful possessor: *R. v. Leslie* (1975), 23 C.C.C. (2d) 343 (Ont. C.A.).

The presumption in this subsection may be rebutted by evidence that merely raises a reasonable doubt and is not rejected by the trier of fact: *R. v. Boyle, infra; R. v. Hill* (1983), 4 C.C.C. (3d) 519 (Ont. C.A.).

The term "obliterate" in this subsection includes the destruction of the integrity of the original vehicle identification number by altering some of the numbers and letters comprising it to produce a new and spurious vehicle identification number: *R. v. Hodgkins* (1985), 19 C.C.C. (3d) 109 (Ont. C.A.).

"Motor vehicle" includes agricultural implements: *R. v. Petrisor*, [1998] 3 W.W.R. 516, 160 Sask. R. 126 (Q.B.).

Constitutional considerations – Application of the doctrine of recent possession does not offend the guarantees in s. 11(*c*) and (*d*) of the *Charter of Rights and Freedoms*: *R. v. Russell* (1983), 4 C.C.C. (3d) 460 (N.S.C.A.).

Subsection (2) creates two presumptions: that the vehicle was obtained by commission of an indictable offence and that the accused had guilty knowledge. However, only the first is constitutionally valid. The presumption of guilty knowledge is arbitrary and contravenes the guarantee to the presumption of innocence in s. 11(*d*) of the *Charter of Rights and Freedoms*. Accordingly, while the Crown may rely on this subsection to prove that the vehicle was unlawfully obtained, guilty knowledge must be proved by inferences from other circumstances such as the unexplained possession of recently stolen goods: *R. v. Boyle* (1983), 5 C.C.C. (3d) 193 (Ont. C.A.).

PUNISHMENT.

355. Every one who commits an offence under section 354

(*a*) is guilty of an indictable offence and liable to imprisonment for a term not exceeding ten years, where the subject-matter of the offence is a testamentary instrument or the value of the subject-matter of the offence exceeds five thousand dollars; or

(*b*) is guilty

(i) of an indictable offence and liable to imprisonment for a term not exceeding two years, or

(ii) of an offence punishable on summary conviction,

where the value of the subject-matter of the offence does not exceed five thousand dollars. R.S., c. C-34, s. 313; 1972, c. 13, s. 28; 1974-75-76, c. 93, s. 30; R.S.C. 1985, c. 27 (1st Supp.), s. 49; 1994, c. 44, s. 21.

CROSS-REFERENCES

The offence in para. (*a*) is an indictable offence for which the accused may elect his mode of trial under s. 536(2). Release pending trial is determined under s. 515. Where the prosecution elects to proceed by indictment for the offence under para. (*b*) then, by virtue of s. 553, it is an offence over which a provincial court judge has absolute jurisdiction and does not depend on the consent of the accused. That is, the accused does not have an election as to mode of trial, although the provincial court judge may, by virtue of s. 555(1), elect to continue the proceedings as a preliminary inquiry, in which case, the accused is deemed to have elected trial by judge and jury pursuant to s. 565(1)(*a*). As well, under s. 555(2), where, in the course of the trial, evidence establishes that the subject-matter of the offence is a testamentary instrument or that its value exceeds $5,000 then the provincial court judge shall put the accused to his election under s. 536(2). Where the prosecution elects to proceed by way of summary conviction then the proceedings are conducted by a summary conviction court pursuant to Part XXVII. The punishment is then as set out in s. 787 and the limitation period is set out in s. 786(2). For the offence under para. (*b*), release pending trial is determined by s. 515, although the accused is eligible for release by a peace officer under s. 496, 497 or by the officer in charge under s. 498. The value of a valuable security (defined in s. 2) is determined in accordance with s. 4(2) and of a postal card or stamp in accordance with s. 4(1). The term "testamentary instrument" is defined in s. 2.

SYNOPSIS

This section sets out the punishment for an offence under s. 354. Paragraph (*a*) states that when the subject-matter of the offence is a testamentary instrument or when the value of the subject-matter of the offence exceeds $5,000, the offence is indictable with a maximum term of 10 years' imprisonment. Paragraph (*b*) states that when the value of the subject-matter of the offence does not exceed $5,000, it is a Crown election offence with a maximum term of imprisonment of two years on indictment.

ANNOTATIONS

An item's retail value *prima facie* establishes its value: *R. v. Belanger* (1972), 6 C.C.C. (2d) 210 (B.C.C.A.).

On a charge of possession of stolen property the value is not an essential ingredient of the offence but rather goes only to jurisdiction and sentence. Where the charge alleged the offence under para. (*a*) but there was no evidence to show that the value was in excess of that amount the court would be justified in entering a conviction under para. (*b*) provided there was evidence that the property was of some value: *R. v. Gillis* (1977), 35 C.C.C. (2d) 418 (N.S.C.A.).

DEFINITION OF "TRAFFIC".

355.1 For the purposes of sections 355.2 and 355.4, "traffic" means to sell, give, transfer, transport, export from Canada, import into Canada, send, deliver or deal with in any other way, or to offer to do any of those acts. 2010, c. 14, s. 6.

CROSS-REFERENCES

The offence of possession of property obtained by crime is set out in s. 354. The penalty for that offence is in s. 355. Section 357 makes it an offence to have possession of property obtained by crime outside of Canada. Section 355.2 creates the offence of trafficking in property obtained by crime or in the proceeds of such property. Section 355.3 prohibits the importing or exporting of property or proceeds obtained by an offence. Section 355.4 creates the offence of possession for the purpose of trafficking. The penalties for the offences in ss. 355.2 and 355.4 are set out in s. 355.5. The related offence of bringing stolen goods into Canada is found in s. 357. The offence which is most often alleged to be the indictable offence by which the goods were obtained is theft under s. 334. The specific offence of theft of a motor vehicle is set out in s. 333.1. Other related offences are: s. 342, theft, etc., of credit card; s. 343, robbery; s. 346, extortion; s. 348, break and enter; s. 349, unlawfully in dwelling house; s. 351, possession of break-in instruments; s. 352, possession of instruments for breaking into coin-operated devices; s. 362, obtaining by false pretences; s. 380, fraud.

Section 491.2 provides for use of photographic evidence to prove the offences under ss. 355.2 and 355.4. The offences under ss. 355.2 and 355.4 are offences for which the Attorney General may apply for a disclosure order under s. 462.48 of information from the Commissioner of Revenue.

TRAFFICKING IN PROPERTY OBTAINED BY CRIME.

355.2 Everyone commits an offence who traffics in any property or thing or any proceeds of any property or thing knowing that all or part of the property, thing or proceeds was obtained by or derived directly or indirectly from

(*a*) the commission in Canada of an offence punishable by indictment; or

(*b*) an act or omission anywhere that, if it had occurred in Canada, would have constituted an offence punishable by indictment. 2010, c. 14, s. 6.

CROSS-REFERENCES

"Traffic" is defined in s. 355.1. The punishment for this offence is set out in s. 355.5. Possession of property obtained by crime for the purpose of trafficking is an offence under s. 355.4. Section 355.3 prohibits the importing or exporting of property or proceeds obtained by an offence. As to admission of photographic evidence of property, see s. 491.2. For proof by way of affidavit of ownership, lawful possession, value, and that the person was deprived of property by fraud or otherwise without the person's lawful consent, see s. 657.1. For other Cross-References as to related offences, see s. 355.1.

IN REM PROHIBITION.

355.3 The importation into Canada or exportation from Canada of any property or thing or any proceeds of any property or thing is prohibited if all or part of the property, thing or proceeds was obtained by or derived directly or indirectly from

(*a*) the commission in Canada of an offence punishable by indictment; or

(*b*) an act or omission anywhere that, if it had occurred in Canada, would have constituted an offence punishable by indictment. 2010, c. 14, s. 6.

CROSS-REFERENCES

Section 355.2 creates the offence of trafficking in property obtained by crime or in the proceeds of such property. Section 355.4 creates the offence of possession for the purpose of trafficking. The penalties for the offences in ss. 355.2 and 355.4 are set out in s. 355.5. The offence of bringing stolen goods into Canada is found in s. 357. For other Cross-References as to related offences, see s. 355.1.

SYNOPSIS

This section does not itself create an offence, but rather prohibits importation into Canada or exportation from Canada of any property or thing or any proceeds of any property or thing if all or part of the property, thing or proceeds was obtained by or derived from the commission in Canada of an offence punishable by indictment, which would include Crown-option offences, or an act or omission that, if it had occurred in Canada, would have constituted an offence punishable by indictment. It would appear that this section was enacted to assist officers of the Canada Border Services Agency in investigating the illegal export or import of property obtained by crime.

POSSESSION OF PROPERTY OBTAINED BY CRIME — TRAFFICKING.

355.4 Everyone commits an offence who has in their possession, for the purpose of trafficking, any property or thing or any proceeds of any property or thing knowing that all or part of the property, thing or proceeds was obtained by or derived directly or indirectly from

(*a*) the commission in Canada of an offence punishable by indictment; or

(*b*) an act or omission anywhere that, if it had occurred in Canada, would have constituted an offence punishable by indictment. 2010, c. 14, s. 6.

CROSS-REFERENCES

"Property" is defined in s. 2. Possession is defined in s. 4(3); however, s. 358 defines circumstances in which possession is complete. "Traffic" is defined in s. 355.1. The punishment for this offence is set out in s. 355.5. Trafficking in property obtained by crime is an offence under s. 355.2. Section 355.3 prohibits the importing or exporting of property or proceeds obtained by an offence. By virtue of s. 583(*b*), an indictment which otherwise complies with s. 581 is not insufficient by reason that it fails to name the person who owns or has a special property or interest in property mentioned in the count. Also note s. 588 which deems certain persons to have a property interest in property of which they have the management, control or custody. Under s. 593, any number of persons may be charged in the same indictment with an offence under this section, notwithstanding that the property was in possession at different times or the person by whom the property was obtained is not indicted or is not in custody or is not amendable to justice. As to admission of photographic evidence of property, see s. 491.2. For proof by way of affidavit of ownership, lawful possession, value, and that the person was deprived of property by fraud or otherwise without the person's lawful consent, see s. 657.1. For other Cross-References as to related offences, see s. 355.1.

PUNISHMENT.

355.5 Everyone who commits an offence under section 355.2 or 355.4

(*a*) is, if the value of the subject matter of the offence is more than $5,000, guilty of an indictable offence and liable to imprisonment for a term of not more than 14 years; or

(*b*) is, if the value of the subject matter of the offence is not more than $5,000,

(i) guilty of an indictable offence and liable to imprisonment for a term of not more than five years, or

(ii) guilty of an offence punishable on summary conviction. 2010, c. 14, s. 6.

CROSS-REFERENCES

See Cross-References under s. 355.1.

THEFT FROM MAIL / Allegation of value not necessary / Punishment.

356. (1) Everyone commits an offence who

(*a*) steals

(i) anything sent by post, after it is deposited at a post office and before it is delivered, or after it is delivered but before it is in the possession of the addressee or of a person who may reasonably be considered to be authorized by the addressee to receive mail,

(ii) a bag, sack or other container or covering in which mail is conveyed, whether or not it contains mail, or

(iii) a key suited to a lock adopted for use by the Canada Post Corporation;

(*a*.1) with intent to commit an offence under paragraph (*a*), makes, possesses or uses a copy of a key suited to a lock adopted for use by the Canada Post Corporation, or a key suited to obtaining access to a receptacle or device provided for the receipt of mail;

(*b*) has in their possession anything that they know has been used to commit an offence under paragraph (*a*) or (*a*.1) or anything in respect of which they know that such an offence has been committed; or

(*c*) fraudulently redirects, or causes to be redirected, anything sent by post.

(2) In proceedings for an offence under this section it is not necessary to allege in the indictment or to prove on the trial that anything in respect of which the offence was committed had any value.

(3) Everyone who commits an offence under subsection (1)

(*a*) is guilty of an indictable offence and liable to imprisonment for a term of not more than 10 years; or

(*b*) is guilty of an offence punishable on summary conviction. R.S., c. C-34, s. 314; 1980-81-82-83, c. 54, s. 56; 2009, c. 28, s. 6.

CROSS-REFERENCES

Possession is defined by s. 4(3), however, s. 358 defines circumstances in which possession is complete. The terms "mail", "post" and "post office" are defined in s. 2(1) of the *Canada Post Corporation Act*, R.S.C. 1985, c. C-10 and "delivery" in s. 2(2) of that Act.

This offence may be the basis for an application for an authorization to intercept private communications by reason of s. 183 or a warrant to conduct video surveillance under s. 487.01(5).

The accused may elect his mode of trial pursuant to s. 536(2). Release pending trial is determined by s. 515.

Section 476(*e*) contains a special provision for territorial jurisdiction where an offence is committed, in respect of a mail, in the course of door-to-door delivery.

The related offence of stopping mail with intent to rob or search is in s. 345.

For the offence under subsec. (1)(*b*), ss. 359 and 360 enact special evidentiary rules.

Under s. 359, evidence that stolen property was found in the accused's possession in the previous 12 months is admissible to prove knowledge that the property that forms the subject-matter of the proceedings was stolen property. Under s. 360, evidence may be given that the accused was convicted in the previous 5 years, of theft or an offence under s. 354, that to prove that knowledge that the property which forms the subject-matter of the proceedings was unlawfully obtained. Note that, for both sections, notice must be given to the accused.

SYNOPSIS

This section creates various offences in relation to theft from the mail. Paragraph (1)(*a*) describes the offence of stealing mail and covers anything sent by post until it is in the possession of the addressee or of the person who may reasonably be considered to be authorized by the addresses to receive mail; stealing a container or covering in which mail is conveyed; and stealing a key suited to a lock adopted for use by the Canada Post Corporation. It is an offence under para. (1)(*a*.1), with intent to create an offence under para. (1)(*a*), to make, possess or use a copy of a key suited to a lock adopted by Canada Post, or a key suited to obtaining access to a receptacle or device for receiving mail. The complementary offence of possession of anything known to have been used to commit an offence under paras. (1)(*a*) and (*a*.1) is found in para. (1)(*b*). And, fraudulently redirected mail is an offence under para. (1)(*c*). By virtue of subsec. (2), it is not necessary to prove that anything in respect of which the offence was committed was of any value.

ANNOTATIONS

By virtue of s. 588 a letter once it is deposited at the post office becomes the property of the Postmaster General: *R. v. Wendland* (1970), 1 C.C.C. (2d) 382 (Sask. C.A.).

By virtue of the definition of "delivery" in the *Post Office Act*, R.S.C. 1970, c. P-14 [now s. 2(2) of the *Canada Post Corporation Act*, R.S.C. 1985, c. C-10], mail in a lock box is already delivered: *R. v. Burgess* (1976), 33 C.C.C. (2d) 126 (B.C.C.A.).

Mail is not "delivered" until it is in a receptacle to which the addressee has access and may remove the mail: *R. v. Weaver, Warwick and Smurthwaite* (1980), 55 C.C.C. (2d) 564 (Ont. C.A.).

BRINGING INTO CANADA PROPERTY OBTAINED BY CRIME.

357. Every one who brings into or has in Canada anything that he has obtained outside Canada by an act that, if it had been committed in Canada, would have been the offence of theft or an offence under section 342 or 354, is guilty of an indictable offence and liable to a term of imprisonment not exceeding ten years. R.S., c. C-34, s. 315; R.S.C. 1985, c. 27 (1st Supp.), s. 50.

CROSS-REFERENCES

The offence of theft is described in ss. 322 to 334 and 338. The accused may elect his mode of trial pursuant to s. 536(2). Release pending trial is determined by s. 515.

SYNOPSIS

This section makes it an offence to import into Canada or to have possession of anything so imported that the accused obtained by an act that would have been the offence of theft or an offence under s. 342 (credit card offences) or 354 (possession of goods obtained by crime) if it had been committed in Canada. The offence is indictable and carries a maximum term of imprisonment of 10 years.

HAVING IN POSSESSION WHEN COMPLETE.

358. For the purposes of sections 342 and 354 and paragraph 356(1)(*b*), the offence of having in possession is complete when a person has, alone or jointly with another person, possession of or control over anything mentioned in those sections or when he aids in concealing or disposing of it, as the case may be. R.S., c. C-34, s. 316; R.S.C. 1985, c. 27 (1st Supp.), s. 50.

CROSS-REFERENCES

For the definition of possession generally, see s. 4(3).

SYNOPSIS

This section states that the offence of possession, for the purposes of ss. 342, 354 and 356(1)(*b*), is complete when a person has, alone or jointly with another person, possession of or control over anything mentioned in those sections. Similarly, the offence of possession is complete when the accused aids in concealing or disposing of anything referred to in those sections.

ANNOTATIONS

It was held in *R. v. MacPherson; R. v. Resnick*, [1964] 3 C.C.C. 170, 43 C.R. 272 (Ont. C.A.), that a person aiding in concealing or disposing of stolen goods is held to be in possession of these goods.

It was found in *R. v. Hanson; R. v. Klepeck*, [1966] 4 C.C.C. 86 (B.C.C.A.), that the intention of the accused to possess only a part of the whole is inconsistent with an intention to possess the whole.

359. [*Repealed*, 2018, c. 29, s. 40.]

360. [*Repealed*, 2018, c. 29, s. 40.]

False Pretences

FALSE PRETENCE / Exaggeration / Question of fact.

361. (1) A false pretence is a representation of a matter of fact either present or past, made by words or otherwise, that is known by the person who makes it to be false and that is made with a fraudulent intent to induce the person to whom it is made to act on it.

(2) Exaggerated commendation or depreciation of the quality of anything is not a false pretence unless it is carried to such an extent that it amounts to a fraudulent misrepresentation of fact.

(3) For the purposes of subsection (2) it is a question of fact whether commendation or depreciation amounts to a fraudulent misrepresentation of fact. R.S., c. C-34, s. 319.

CROSS-REFERENCES

The offences relating to false pretences are found in ss. 362 and 363. See the cross-references under those sections for mode of trial, release pending trial and special evidentiary provisions. The related offence of theft is defined in ss. 322 to 334, theft, etc., of credit card in s. 342 and fraud in s. 380.

SYNOPSIS

This section defines a false pretence as a representation of a matter of fact made in any fashion that is *known by the person who makes it* to be false *and* that is made with a *fraudulent intent* to induce the person to whom it is made to act on it. Both of the mental elements described above must be present in order to fall within the definition of a false pretence. Subsection (2) states that an exaggeration or depreciation of the quality of anything does not amount to a false pretence unless it amounts to a *fraudulent misrepresentation of fact*. Whether or not the exaggeration or depreciation described in subsec. (2) is a fraudulent misrepresentation is a question of fact.

ANNOTATIONS

A false representation amounting to a mere promise or profession of intention is not a false pretence within this section unless such promise or profession of intention necessarily and irresistibly involves a representation of an existing fact. Thus a false promise to pay for goods in the future is not within this section: *R. v. Reid* (1940), 74 C.C.C. 156 (B.C.C.A.). [Note however that where the means of payment is a cheque, Parliament has enacted a special rule set out in s. 362(4).]

FALSE PRETENCE OR FALSE STATEMENT / Punishment / Idem / Presumption from cheque issued without funds / Definition of "cheque".

362. (1) Every one commits an offence who

(*a*) by a false pretence, whether directly or through the medium of a contract obtained by a false pretence, obtains anything in respect of which the offence of theft may be committed or causes it to be delivered to another person;

(*b*) obtains credit by a false pretence or by fraud;

(*c*) knowingly makes or causes to be made, directly or indirectly, a false statement in writing with intent that it should be relied on, with respect to the financial condition or means or ability to pay of himself or herself or any person or organization that he or she is interested in or that he or she acts for, for the purpose of procuring, in any form whatever, whether for his or her benefit or the benefit of that person or organization,

(i) the delivery of personal property,

(ii) the payment of money,

(iii) the making of a loan,

(iv) the grant or extension of credit,

(v) the discount of an account receivable, or

(vi) the making, accepting, discounting or endorsing of a bill of exchange, cheque, draft, or promissory note; or

(*d*) knowing that a false statement in writing has been made with respect to the financial condition or means or ability to pay of himself or herself or another person or organization that he or she is interested in or that he or she acts for, procures on the faith of that statement, whether for his or her benefit or for the benefit of that person or organization, anything mentioned in subparagraphs (*c*)(i) to (vi).

(2) Every one who commits an offence under paragraph (1)(*a*)

(*a*) is guilty of an indictable offence and liable to a term of imprisonment not exceeding ten years, where the property obtained is a testamentary instrument or the value of what is obtained exceeds five thousand dollars; or

(*b*) is guilty

(i) of an indictable offence and liable to imprisonment for a term not exceeding two years, or

(ii) of an offence punishable on summary conviction,

where the value of what is obtained does not exceed five thousand dollars.

(3) Every one who commits an offence under paragraph (1)(*b*), (*c*) or (*d*) is guilty of an indictable offence and liable to imprisonment for a term not exceeding ten years.

(4) Where, in proceedings under paragraph (1)(*a*), it is shown that anything was obtained by the accused by means of a cheque that, when presented for payment within a reasonable time, was dishonoured on the ground that no funds or insufficient funds were on deposit to the credit of the accused in the bank or other institution on which the cheque was drawn, it shall be presumed to have been obtained by a false pretence, unless the court is satisfied by evidence that when the accused issued the cheque he believed on reasonable grounds that it would be honoured if presented for payment within a reasonable time after it was issued.

(5) In this section, "cheque" includes, in addition to its ordinary meaning, a bill of exchange drawn on any institution that makes it a business practice to honour bills of exchange or any particular kind thereof drawn on it by depositors. R.S., c. C-34, s. 320; 1972, c. 13, s. 29; 1974-75-76, c. 93, s. 31; R.S.C. 1985, c. 27 (1st Supp.), s. 52; 1994, c. 44, s. 22; 2003, c. 21, s. 5.

CROSS-REFERENCES

A false pretence is defined in s. 361. "Organization" and "person" are defined in s. 2.

As to admission of photographic evidence of property, see s. 491.2. For proof by way of affidavit of ownership, lawful possession, value, and that the person was deprived of property by fraud or otherwise without the person's lawful consent, see s. 657.1. By virtue of s. 583(*b*), an indictment which otherwise complies with s. 581 is not insufficient by reason only that (*b*), it fails to name the person who owns or has a special property or interest in property mentioned in the count or (*c*), it charges an intent to defraud without naming or describing the person whom it was intended to defraud. Also note s. 588 which deems certain persons to have a property interest in property of which they have the management, control or custody. Under s. 586, no count alleging false pretences or fraud is insufficient by reason only that it does not set out in detail the nature of the false pretences or fraud. However, under s. 587(1)(*b*), the court may order particulars of any false pretence or fraud that is alleged.

For the meaning of "bill of exchange", see *Bills of Exchange Act*, R.S.C. 1985, c. B-4.

Where the offence under subsec. (1)(*a*), although committed outside Canada, is in relation to the use of nuclear material, see s. 7(3.4).

The offence in para. (2)(*a*) is a pure indictable offence for which the accused may elect his mode of trial under s. 536(2). Where the prosecution elects to proceed by indictment for the offence under para. 2(*b*) then, by virtue of s. 553, it is an offence over which a provincial court judge has absolute jurisdiction and does not depend on the consent of the accused. That is, the accused does not have an election as to mode of trial, although the provincial court judge may, by virtue of s. 555(1), elect to continue the proceedings as a preliminary inquiry, in which case, the accused is deemed to have elected trial by judge and jury pursuant to s. 565(1)(*a*). As well, under s. 555(2), where, in the course of the trial, evidence establishes that the subject-matter of the offence is a testamentary instrument or that its value exceeds $5,000 then the provincial court judge shall put the accused to his election under s. 536(2). Where the prosecution elects to proceed by way of summary conviction then the proceedings are conducted by a summary conviction court pursuant to Part XXVII. The punishment is then as set out in s. 787 and the limitation period is set out in s. 786(2). For the offences under subsec. (2), release pending trial is determined by s. 515, although in case of the offence under subsec. (2)(*b*) the accused is eligible for release by a peace officer under s. 496, 497 or by the officer in charge under s. 498. The value of a valuable security (defined in s. 2) is determined in accordance with s. 4(2) and of a postal card or stamp in accordance with s. 4(1). The term "testamentary instrument" is defined in s. 2.

For the offences punished under subsec. (3), the accused may elect his mode of trial under s. 536(2) and release pending trial is governed by s. 515.

SYNOPSIS

This section describes the offence of false pretences and the punishment for the offence. Subsection (1) states that any person who, by a false pretence or fraud, obtains credit, or who *knowingly makes a false statement in writing*, intending it to be relied upon, with respect to his own financial state, or that of any entity in which he has an interest, in order to procure any of the benefits listed in subsec. (1)(*c*), is guilty of an offence. Subsection (1) further states that every one commits an offence who *knows that a false written statement* about his own financial state or that of any entity in which he has an interest has been made and, on the basis of that statement, procures anything mentioned in subsec. (1)(*c*). Finally, an offence under this section is committed when a person, by false pretence, directly or indirectly as described in subsec. (1)(*a*), obtains anything for himself or another person in respect of which the offence of theft may be committed. The form of the offence described in subsec. (1)(*a*) is indictable, with a maximum term of 10 years' imprisonment when the property obtained is a testamentary instrument, or its value exceeds $5,000. Where the value does not exceed $5,000, the offence is hybrid with a maximum term of imprisonment of two years on indictment. The forms of the offence described in subsec. (1)(*b*), (*c*) and (*d*) are all punishable by indictment only, with a maximum term of 10 years' imprisonment. Subsection (4) enacts a presumption that in proceedings under subsec. (1)(*a*) where the goods have been obtained by an N.S.F. cheque, it shall be presumed that those goods have been obtained by false pretences unless the court is satisfied that the accused *believed on reasonable grounds* that the cheque would be honoured when he wrote it. Subsection (5) gives a wide definition to the term "cheque" for the purposes of this section.

ANNOTATIONS

Whether property must pass – The word "obtains" does not mean that the goods must wholly or entirely pass to the accused; the passing of their possession and a property interest, *e.g.,* an insurable interest, in them is sufficient for conviction: *R. v. Hemingway,* [1955] S.C.R. 712, 112 C.C.C. 321.

Subsequently the view was expressed (2:1) that the acquiring of mere possession would satisfy the requirements of the offence of obtaining anything by a false pretence: *R. v. Campbell,* [1968] 1 C.C.C. 104 (B.C.C.A.).

A very useful review of the conflicting authorities on the issue whether or not, for the establishment of this offence, in addition to bare possession some aspect of ownership must also pass is found in *R. v. Vallillee* (1974), 15 C.C.C. (2d) 409 (Ont. C.A.).

Proof of offence of obtaining by false pretences [subsec. (1)(*a*)] – Where on appeal the court finds that a lesser amount than that set out in the indictment was proved to have been obtained it may amend the conviction accordingly and dismiss the appeal: *R. v. Lake,* [1969] S.C.R. 49, [1969] 2 C.C.C. 224 (5:0).

Where the victim made his own thorough investigation, not relying on the representations by the accused, a conviction under this section cannot be sustained: *R. v. Thornton* (1926), 46 C.C.C. 249 (B.C.C.A.).

Obtaining credit by fraud or false pretences [subsec. (1)(*b*)] – The credit obtained does not have to be that of the accused; it is sufficient for conviction if he obtained goods by falsely charging them to his employer's account. Furthermore, it is no defence for the accused to argue successfully that he could have been convicted under subsec. (1)(*a*) of obtaining by a false pretence: *R. v. Dvornek* (1962), 132 C.C.C. 231 (B.C.C.A.).

A loan of money secured by a property mortgage amounts to the obtaining of credit. Furthermore, there is a presumption that where money was obtained by a false pretence, *prima facie,* there is an intent to defraud. Even where the victim makes its own investigation, if the false representation by the accused is the operative inducement in the obtaining of the credit the offence is made out: *R. v. Dyke and Dyke* (1976), 33 C.C.C. (2d) 556 (Nfld. Dist. Ct.).

False statement respecting financial condition [subsec. (1)(*c*)] – It was held prior to the recent amendment to subpara. (iv), which added the word "grant", that the phrase "extension of credit" means granting or according credit and therefore does not include conduct by the accused which merely serves to keep open an existing line of credit: *R. v. Cohen* (1984), 15 C.C.C. (3d) 231 (Que. C.A.).

Presumption from N.S.F. cheque [subsec. (4)] – Where the case against the accused was that he obtained goods by a cheque drawn against a non-existent bank account it is not necessary, once the Crown has satisfactorily proven the non-existence of the account, to prove the presentment and dishonouring of the cheque: *R. v. Morphett* (1970), 1 C.C.C. (2d) 98 (B.C.C.A.).

More than a reasonable doubt is required to rebut the presumption which may be satisfied by evidence whether or not it flows from the accused: *R. v. Druckman* (1974), 31 C.R.N.S. 177 (Ont. Co. Ct.).

The accused's explanation is to be judged using a subjective test and a real belief that funds would be available even though considered objectively the belief was unreasonable will lead to an acquittal: *R. v. Lane* (1978), 42 C.C.C. (2d) 375 (Ont. Prov. Ct.).

This subsection is of no force and effect by reason of its violation of the guarantee to the presumption of innocence in s. 11(*d*) of the *Charter of Rights and Freedoms*: *R. v. Driscoll* (1987), 38 C.C.C. (3d) 28 (Alta. C.A.); *R. v. Ferguson* (1992), 70 C.C.C. (3d) 330 (P.E.I.S.C.). *Contra: R. v. Bunka* (1984), 12 C.C.C. (3d) 437 (Sask. Q.B.).

OBTAINING EXECUTION OF VALUABLE SECURITY BY FRAUD.

363. Every one who, with intent to defraud or injure another person, by a false pretence causes or induces any person

(*a*) to execute, make, accept, endorse or destroy the whole or any part of a valuable security, or

(*b*) to write, impress or affix a name or seal on any paper or parchment in order that it may afterwards be made or converted into or used or dealt with as a valuable security,

is guilty of an indictable offence and liable to imprisonment for a term not exceeding five years. R.S., c. C-34, s. 321.

CROSS-REFERENCES

The term "valuable security" is defined in s. 2 and its value determined in accordance with s. 4(2).

By virtue of s. 583, an indictment which otherwise complies with s. 581 is not insufficient by reason only that (*b*), it fails to name the person who owns or has a special property or interest in property mentioned in the count or (*c*), it charges an intent to defraud without naming or describing the person whom it was intended to defraud. Also note s. 588 which deems certain persons to have a property interest in property of which they have the management, control or custody. Under s. 586, no count alleging false pretences or fraud is insufficient by reason only that it does not set out in detail the nature of the false pretences or fraud. However, under s. 587(1)(*b*), the court may order particulars of any false pretence or fraud that is alleged.

The accused may elect his mode of trial pursuant to s. 536(2). Release pending trial is determined by s. 515, although the accused is eligible for release by the officer in charge pursuant to s. 498.

SYNOPSIS

This section describes the indictable offence of obtaining the execution of a valuable security by means of a false pretence. The accused must have *the intent to defraud or injure* another person. The maximum term of imprisonment upon conviction for this offence is five years.

FRAUDULENTLY OBTAINING FOOD, BEVERAGE OR ACCOMMODATION / Presumption / Definition of "cheque".

364. (1) Every one who fraudulently obtains food, a beverage or accommodation at any place that is in the business of providing those things is guilty of an offence punishable on summary conviction

(2) In proceedings under this section, evidence that the accused obtained food, a beverage or accommodation at a place that is in the business of providing those things and did not pay for it and

(*a*) made a false or fictitious show or pretence of having baggage,

(*b*) had any false or pretended baggage,

(*c*) surreptitiously removed or attempted to remove his baggage or any material part of it,

(*d*) absconded or surreptitiously left the premises,

(*e*) knowingly made a false statement to obtain credit or time for payment, or

(*f*) offered a worthless cheque, draft or security in payment for the food, beverage or accommodation,

is, in the absence of any evidence to the contrary, proof of fraud.

(3) In this section, "cheque" includes, in addition to its ordinary meaning, a bill of exchange drawn on any institution that makes it a business practice to honour bills of exchange or any particular kind thereof drawn on it by depositors. R.S., c. C-34, s. 322; 1994, c. 44, s. 23.

CROSS-REFERENCES
The terms "food", "beverage" and "accommodation" are not defined in this section. However, reference might be made to the definition of "food" in the *Food and Drugs Act*, s. 2. While there is no definition of "fraudulently" which is universally applicable, generally speaking, it refers to conduct which is dishonest and morally wrong: *R. v. DeMarco* (1973), 13 C.C.C. (2d) 369 (Ont. C.A.).

This offence resembles the offence of obtaining by false pretences and thus, see notes under s. 361 respecting related offences. Trial of this offence is conducted by a summary conviction court pursuant to Part XXVII. The punishment is as set out in s. 787 and the limitation period is set out in s. 786(2). Release pending trial is determined by s. 515, although the accused is eligible for release by a peace officer under s. 496, 497 or by the officer if charge under s. 498.

SYNOPSIS
This section describes the summary conviction offence of fraudulently obtaining food, beverage or accommodation at a place that is in the business of providing those things. Subsection (2) sets out a number of fact situations which, in conjunction with evidence that an accused obtained any of the accommodations described in subsec. (1) without paying, will constitute proof of the fraud, in the absence of evidence to the contrary.

---

365. [*Repealed*, 2018, c. 29, s. 41.]

Forgery and Offences Resembling Forgery

FORGERY / Making false document / When forgery complete / Forgery complete though document incomplete / Exception.

366. (1) Every one commits forgery who makes a false document, knowing it to be false, with intent

(*a*) that it should in any way be used or acted on as genuine, to the prejudice of any one whether within Canada or not; or

(*b*) that a person should be induced, by the belief that it is genuine, to do or to refrain from doing anything, whether within Canada or not.

(2) Making a false document includes

(*a*) altering a genuine document in any material part;

(*b*) making a material addition to a genuine document or adding to it a false date, attestation, seal or other thing that is material; or

(*c*) making a material alteration in a genuine document by erasure, obliteration, removal or in any other way.

(3) Forgery is complete as soon as a document is made with the knowledge and intent referred to in subsection (1), notwithstanding that the person who makes it does not intend that any particular person should use or act on it as genuine or be induced, by the belief that it is genuine, to do or refrain from doing anything.

(4) Forgery is complete notwithstanding that the false document is incomplete or does not purport to be a document that is binding in law, if it is such as to indicate that it was intended to be acted on as genuine.

(5) No person commits forgery by reason only that the person, in good faith, makes a false document at the request of a police force, the Canadian Forces or a department or agency of the federal government or of a provincial government. R.S., c. C-34, s. 324; 2009, c. 28, s. 7.

CROSS-REFERENCES
The terms "document" and "false document" are defined in s. 321.

The punishment for forgery is set out in s. 367 and for uttering a forged document in s. 368. For either offence, the accused may elect the mode of trial pursuant to s. 536(2) unless the Crown proceeds by way of summary conviction. Release pending trial is determined by s. 515.

Forgery and uttering offences may be the basis for an application for an authorization to intercept private communications by reason of s. 183 and a warrant to conduct video surveillance under s. 487.01(5), and are enterprise crime offences for the purposes of Part XII.2. Offences resembling forgery and uttering, but referring to specific types of documents, are in the following sections: s. 369, exchequer bill paper, public seals, etc.; s. 370, counterfeit government proclamation; ss. 371, 372, false telegram, etc.; s. 374, drawing document without authority; s. 375, obtaining by forged document; s. 376, counterfeiting stamp, mark, etc.; s. 377, defacing official documents; s. 378, offences in relation to registers; ss. 397 to 402, falsification of books and documents in relation to contracts and trade; ss. 406 to 414, forgery of trade-marks and trade descriptions; ss. 416 to 421, offences in relation to public stores; Part XII, offences in relation to currency, counterfeiting, etc. For forgery of credit card, see ss. 342, 342.01.

Also see s. 56.1, offences in relation to identity documents; s. 368.1, offences in relation to instruments for use in committing forgery; and s. 402.1, identity theft.

By virtue of s. 368.2, a public officer does not commit this offence where the acts were for the sole purpose of establishing or maintaining a covert identity for use in the course of the public officer's duties or employment.

SYNOPSIS

This section describes the offence of forgery. Every person who makes a false document, *knowing it to be false, with the intent* that it should be used as genuine to the prejudice of another person, or that another person should be induced, believing the document to be genuine, to do or refrain from doing anything, commits the offence of forgery. The action contemplated or the person to be induced may be inside or outside Canada. Subsection (2) defines the term "making a false document" in the context of altering a genuine document. Subsection (3) states that a forgery is complete as soon as the document is made with the intent and knowledge referred to in subsection (1), whether or not the accused intends a specific person to act on it. Subsection (4) further states that the offence of forgery is complete even if the false document is incomplete or of no binding legal effect so long as it can be demonstrated that it was intended to be acted upon as genuine.

ANNOTATIONS

Meaning of false document – The provisions of this subsection do not exclude the definition of "false document" in s. 321. Thus an accused may be convicted of forgery where he makes a "false document" as that phrase is defined in s. 321. Specifically, the accused makes a "false document" where he prepares a document which is false in some material particular. A document which is false in reference to the very purpose for which it was created is clearly one which is false in a material particular. Thus the act of the accused in preparing inventory sheets which contained false information as to the very matter which they purported to certify and so were false in a number of material particulars comes within this section: *R. v. Gaysek*, [1971] S.C.R. 888, 2 C.C.C. (2d) 545 (3:2).

It is not necessarily the case that a document which merely contains a lie falls within the definition of a false document. However, a document which is false in reference to the very purpose for which it was created is one that is false in a material particular within the meaning of s. 321 and therefore capable of founding a conviction under this section: *R. v. Ogilvie* (1993), 81 C.C.C. (3d) 125 (Que. C.A.).

It is open to the trier of fact to find a document to be a false document where it is a photocopy which purports to be a true copy of the state of a particular instrument at the time of its reproduction. In this case the accused photocopied parts of two documents so that it appeared that what had been copied was a certified cheque: *R. v. Sebo* (1988), 42 C.C.C. (3d) 536 (Alta. C.A.), leave to appeal to S.C.C. refused 93 A.R. 240*n*. Similarly: *R. v. Nuosci*

(1991), 69 C.C.C. (3d) 64 (C.A.), leave to appeal to S.C.C. refused 71 C.C.C. (3d) vii, 56 O.A.C. 159*n*.

In *R. v. Paquette*, [1975] 2 S.C.R. 168, 45 C.C.C. (2d) 575 (7:0), the court in reversing the accused notary's acquittal on a charge of uttering approved the dissenting reasons of Montgomery J.A., in the Quebec Court of Appeal, 42 C.C.C. (2d) 57, who had held that in adding a false attestation to an affidavit the accused made a false document within the meaning of this subsection notwithstanding he was unaware that the entire document was a forgery. The accused had attested to the signature of one of the purported witnesses although he had not seen the "witness" sign the document.

Authorized signings are excluded from the ambit of this offence, even where the document fails on its face to specifically indicate that the actual signatory is acting as a proxy of another. Such documents may be misleading as a result, but they do not have the property of falsity inherent in forgery: *R. v. Foley* (1994), 90 C.C.C. (3d) 390 (Nfld. C.A.).

The Crown must establish that the document is false and that it was false in relation to the very purpose for which it was created: *R. v. Benson* (2012), 294 C.C.C. (3d) 109 (Man. C.A.).

Offences involving cheques – The accused was convicted of forgery where he endorsed the signature of the payee of a cheque. As the cheque was made out to the payee the payee could be the only endorser. When the accused signed the payee's name as endorser he did it to the prejudice of the payee and the offence was made out. Moreover, it was no defence that the payor had authorized the accused to deal with the cheque in that manner since such authorization could not come from the payor: *R. v. Cowan*, [1962] S.C.R. 476, 132 C.C.C. 352 (3:2).

A forged endorsement on an otherwise valid cheque converts the cheque into a false document: *R. v. Elkin* (1978), 42 C.C.C. (2d) 185 (B.C.C.A.); *R. v. Jones,* [1970] 4 C.C.C. 284 (Ont. C.A.); *R. v. Keshane* (1974), 20 C.C.C. (2d) 542 (Sask. C.A.).

The figures on a cheque are a material part: *R. v. O'Hearn,* [1964] 3 C.C.C. 296 (B.C.C.A.).

PUNISHMENT FOR FORGERY.

367. Every one who commits forgery

(*a*) is guilty of an indictable offence and liable to imprisonment for a term not exceeding ten years; or

(*b*) is guilty of an offence punishable on summary conviction. R.S.C., c. C-34, s. 325; 1994, c. 44, s. 24; 1997, c. 18, s. 24.

CROSS-REFERENCES

Forgery is defined in s. 366. This offence may be the basis for an application for an authorization to intercept private communications by reason of s. 183. Forgery is an enterprise crime offence for the purposes of Part XII.2.

The accused may elect the mode of trial pursuant to s. 536(2) unless the Crown proceeds by way of summary conviction. Release pending trial is determined by s. 515. For related offences, see cross-references under s. 366. The offence of uttering is defined in s. 368.

By virtue of s. 368.2, a public officer does not commit this offence where the acts were for the sole purpose of establishing or maintaining a covert identity for use in the course of the public officer's duties or employment.

SYNOPSIS

This section states that forgery is a hybrid offence with a maximum term of imprisonment of 10 years, where the Crown proceeds by indictment, and six months if the Crown proceeds by summary conviction pursuant to s. 787.

USE, TRAFFICKING OR POSSESSION OF FORGED DOCUMENT / Punishment / Wherever forged.

368. (1) Everyone commits an offence who, knowing or believing that a document is forged,

(*a*) uses, deals with or acts on it as if it were genuine;

(*b*) causes or attempts to cause any person to use, deal with or act on it as if it were genuine;

(*c*) transfers, sells or offers to sell it or makes it available, to any person, knowing that or being reckless as to whether an offence will be committed under paragraph (*a*) or (*b*); or

(*d*) possesses it with intent to commit an offence under any of paragraphs (*a*) to (*c*).

(1.1) Everyone who commits an offence under subsection (1)

(*a*) is guilty of an indictable offence and liable to imprisonment for a term of not more than 10 years; or

(*b*) is guilty of an offence punishable on summary conviction.

(2) For the purposes of proceedings under this section, the place where a document was forged is not material. R.S., c. C-34, s. 326; 1997, c. 18, s. 25; 2009, c. 28, s. 8.

CROSS-REFERENCES

The term "document" is defined in s. 321. The offence of forgery is defined in s. 366 and punished under s. 367.

This offence may be the basis for an application for an authorization to intercept private communications by reason of s. 183. Uttering a forged document is an enterprise crime offence for the purposes of Part XII.2. The accused may elect the mode of trial pursuant to s. 536(2) unless the Crown proceeds by way of summary conviction. Release pending trial is determined by s. 515.

Offences resembling forgery and uttering but referring to specific types of documents are in the following sections: s. 369, exchequer bill paper, public seals, etc.; s. 370, counterfeit government proclamation; ss. 371, 372, false telegram, etc.; s. 374, drawing document without authority; s. 375, obtaining by forged document; s. 376, counterfeiting stamp, mark, etc.; s. 377, defacing official documents; s. 378, offences in relation to registers; ss. 397 to 402, falsification of books and documents in relation to contracts and trade; ss. 406 to 414, forgery of trade-marks and trade descriptions; ss. 416 to 421, offences in relation to public stores; Part XII, offences in relation to currency, counterfeiting, etc.

Also see s. 56.1, offences in relation to identity documents; s. 368.1, offences in relation to instruments for use in committing forgery; and s. 402.1, identity theft.

By virtue of s. 368.2, a public officer does not commit this offence where the acts were for the sole purpose of establishing or maintaining a covert identity for use in the course of the public officer's duties or employment.

SYNOPSIS

This section replaces the offence of uttering forged documents. Paragraphs (1)(*a*) and (*b*) correspond to the old uttering offence in that they make it an offence to use, deal with, or act upon a document known or believed to be forged, or cause or attempt to cause any person to deal with or act on a document as if it were genuine. The new offences are found in paras. (1)(*c*) and (*d*) and make it an offence to transfer, sell, offer to sell or to make available a document to any person knowing that or being reckless as to whether an offence under para. (1)(*a*) or (*b*) was committed, and possession of a document within intent to commit an offence under any of paras. (1)(*a*), (*b*) or (*c*). The place where the document was forged is not material for the purposes of the offences under this section.

ANNOTATIONS

The requirement of corroboration only applies to the offence of forgery, not to the offence of uttering: *R. v. Susimaki,* [1968] 3 C.C.C. 381 (B.C.C.A.).

A forgery within the meaning of s. 366 must exist before an offence under this section can be committed. It is not sufficient that the document was a "false document" as defined by s. 321 if the document was not made with one of the intents specified in s. 366(1): *R. v. Hawrish* (1986), 32 C.C.C. (3d) 446 (Sask. C.A.). *Contra: R. v. Lapointe* (1984), 12 C.C.C. (3d) 238 (Que. C.A.), where it was held, relying in part on *R. v. Keshane* (1974), 20 C.C.C. (2d) 542 (Sask. C.A.), leave to appeal to S.C.C. refused C.C.C. *loc. cit.*, [1974] S.C.R. ix, now overruled on this point, that while on a charge under subsec. (1)(*b*) the Crown must establish that the accused intended that the other person use the document as genuine or that he was reckless in that respect, what need not be shown is the intent described in s. 366 with which the document was forged. And it was held in *R. v. Sebo* (1988), 42 C.C.C. (3d) 536 (Alta. C.A.), that an intention to defraud is not an element of the offence under this section. Rather, the intent required is the intent to deceive, such an interpretation is consistent with the forgery offence defined by s. 366(1)(*b*) which as well does not require proof of an intent to defraud.

The fact that the accused ought to have known that certain facts existed does not by itself form a basis for the application of the doctrine of wilful blindness: *R. v. Currie* (1975), 24 C.C.C. (2d) 292 (Ont. C.A.) (2:1).

Acts of the accused in preparing fictitious bills for fees which were to be used if necessary to cover the payment of a benefit to a bank manager, did not constitute uttering where the bills were never used and never seen either by the bank or the revenue authorities: *R. v. Valois*, [1986] 1 S.C.R. 278, 25 C.C.C. (3d) 97 (7:0).

FORGERY.

368.1 Everyone is guilty of an indictable offence and liable to imprisonment for a term of not more than 14 years, or is guilty of an offence punishable on summary conviction, who, without lawful authority or excuse, makes, repairs, buys, sells, exports from Canada, imports into Canada or possesses any instrument, device, apparatus, material or thing that they know has been used or know is adapted or intended for use by any person to commit forgery. 2009, c. 28, s. 9.

CROSS-REFERENCES

The related offences of forgery are found in ss. 366 and 367; trafficking or possession of forged documents in s. 368; and unlawful possession of exchequer bill paper, revenue paper or paper to make bank notes in s. 369. For further related offences, see the CROSS-REFERENCES under s. 366. By virtue of s. 368.2, a public officer does not commit this offence where the acts were for the sole purpose of establishing or maintaining a covert identity for use in the course of the public officer's duties or employment.

PUBLIC OFFICERS ACTING IN THE COURSE OF THEIR DUTIES OR EMPLOYMENT.

368.2 No public officer, as defined in subsection 25.1(1), is guilty of an offence under any of sections 366 to 368.1 if the acts alleged to constitute the offence were committed by the public officer for the sole purpose of establishing or maintaining a covert identity for use in the course of the public officer's duties or employment. 2009, c. 28, s. 9.

CROSS-REFERENCES

The similar defence providing immunity for public officers from what might otherwise be considered criminal conduct is set out in great detail in ss. 25.1 to 25.4.

EXCHEQUER BILL PAPER, PUBLIC SEALS, ETC.

369. Everyone is guilty of an indictable offence and liable to imprisonment for a term of not more than 14 years who, without lawful authority or excuse,

(*a*) makes, uses or possesses

(i) any exchequer bill paper, revenue paper or paper that is used to make bank-notes, or

(ii) any paper that is intended to resemble paper mentioned in subparagraph (i); or

(*b*) makes, reproduces or uses a public seal of Canada or of a province, or the seal of a public body or authority in Canada or of a court of law. R.S., c. C-34, s. 327; 2009, c. 28, s. 9.

CROSS-REFERENCES

The terms "exchequer bill", "exchequer bill paper", and "revenue paper" are defined in s. 321. The terms "bank-note" and "writing" are defined in s. 2. "Writing" is also defined in s. 35 of the *Interpretation Act*, R.S.C. 1985, c. I-21.

This offence resembles the offences of forgery and using, trafficking and possession of forged documents under ss. 366 to 368. Other related offences are as follows: s. 56.1, offences in relation to identity documents; s. 368.1, offences in relation to instruments for use in committing forgery; s. 370, counterfeit government proclamation; ss. 371, 372, false telegram, etc.; s. 374, drawing document without authority; s. 375, obtaining by forged document; s. 376, counterfeiting stamp, mark, etc.; s. 377, defacing official documents; s. 378, offences in relation to registers; ss. 397 to 402, falsification of books and documents in relation to contracts and trade; ss. 402.1 to 403, identity theft and fraud; ss. 406 to 414, forgery of trade-marks and trade descriptions; ss. 416 to 421, offences in relation to public stores; Part XII, offences in relation to currency, counterfeiting, etc.

SYNOPSIS

Paragraph (*a*) of this section describes the indictable offence of making use of or possessing exchequer bill paper, revenue bill paper, paper used to make bank notes, or any paper that is intended to look like those papers, without lawful authority or excuse. It further describes the offence of making, disposing of, or knowingly possessing any item that is intended to be used to commit forgery, and the offence of making or using a public seal of Canada, a province, a public body or a court of law. The maximum term of imprisonment for this offence is 14 years.

ANNOTATIONS

The word "other" in para. (*b*) relates back only to the word "instrument", which is used as meaning a written document. Thus there is no common category into which "plate, die, machinery and instrument" fall to warrant the *ejusdem generis* interpretation rule, so cheques and an unemployment insurance card found on the accused were held to be unlawful items: *R. v. Evans* (1962), 132 C.C.C. 271, 37 C.R. 341 (B.C.C.A.).

In *R. v. Griffiths* (1969), 7 C.R.N.S. 196 (Que. Q.B., App. Side), it was held that proof of mere possession of an unendorsed forged cheque, in the absence of proof that the cheque was intended to be used to commit forgery, is not an offence. Furthermore Rivard J., refused to follow *R. v. Evans, supra.*

Having regard to the definition of revenue paper in s. 321 as paper used to make stamps, licences or permits, the offence is not made out where the accused is in possession of a false birth certificate. The definition contemplates present possession of paper for the future purpose of making or manufacturing certain government documents. It was not intended to apply to completed documents: *R. v. Hagerman* (1988), 46 C.C.C. (3d) 432 (B.C. Co. Ct.).

The term "adapted" in para. (*b*) means "suitable for": *R. v. Mac*, [2002] 1 S.C.R. 856, 163 C.C.C. (3d) 1.

370. [*Repealed*, 2018, c. 29, s. 42.]

371. [*Repealed*, 2018, c. 29, s. 42.]

FALSE INFORMATION / Indecent communications / Harassing communications / Punishment.

372. (1) Everyone commits an offence who, with intent to injure or alarm a person, conveys information that they know is false, or causes such information to be conveyed by letter or any means of telecommunication.

(2) Everyone commits an offence who, with intent to alarm or annoy a person, makes an indecent communication to that person or to any other person by a means of telecommunication.

(3) Everyone commits an offence who, without lawful excuse and with intent to harass a person, repeatedly communicates, or causes repeated communications to be made, with them by a means of telecommunication.

(4) Everyone who commits an offence under this section is

(*a*) guilty of an indictable offence and liable to imprisonment for a term of not more than two years; or

(*b*) guilty of an offence punishable on summary conviction. R.S., c. C-34, s. 330; 2014, c. 31, s. 18.

CROSS-REFERENCES

Section 4(8) provides that, if an offence contains an element of communication, it is deemed to include telecommunication.

On the definition of "indecent", see the notes under s. 163.

The accused may elect his mode of trial pursuant to s. 536(2) for the offence described in subsec. (1) and release pending trial is determined by s. 515, although the accused is eligible for release by the officer in charge under s. 498. It may be that, in some circumstances, the accused found guilty of this offence would be liable to the discretionary order prohibiting possession of firearms, ammunition or explosives.

Trial of the offences described by subsecs. (2) and (3) is conducted by a summary conviction court pursuant to Part XXVII. The punishment is as set out in s. 787 and the limitation period is set out in s. 786(2). Release pending trial is determined by s. 515, although the accused is eligible for release by a peace officer under s. 496, 497 or by the officer in charge under s. 498.

An alternative to this offence is the procedure for requiring the offender to enter into a recognizance to keep the peace either at common law or pursuant to s. 810. Other related offences: s. 175, causing disturbance; s. 264, criminal harassment; s. 264.1, uttering threats; s. 346, extortion; s. 423, intimidation and watching and besetting; s. 424, threat to commit offence against internationally protected person; s. 371, sending false telegram, etc., with intent to defraud.

SYNOPSIS

This section creates hybrid offences of conveying false information, and making indecent or harassing communications. Subsection (1) provides that anyone who *knowingly* conveys false information with intent to injure or alarm creates an offence. Subsection (2) creates an offence of making an indecent communication with intent to alarm or annoy. Subsection (3) prohibits harassing communications, provided they are made repeatedly and with intent to harass.

ANNOTATIONS

Subsection (2) – This subsection applies, although the calls were made to an answering machine. The accused was aware that the calls were being recorded and would be heard by the victim at a later time: *R. v. Manicke* (1993), 81 C.C.C. (3d) 255, 109 Sask. R. 126 (C.A.).

Subsection (3) – The victim of an offence under this subsection must be the recipient of the harassing telephone calls. Thus, the accused was acquitted where he made repeated calls intending to harass his wife, but the calls were intercepted by a friend: *R. v. Wood* (1983), 8 C.C.C. (3d) 217 (Ont. Prov. Ct.).

The term "harass" in this subsection is synonymous with annoy and could include conduct of the accused in repeatedly telephoning a person and simply hanging up when the call was answered: *R. v. Sabine* (1990), 57 C.C.C. (3d) 209, 78 C.R. (3d) 34 (N.B.Q.B.).

373. [*Repealed*, R.S.C. 1985, c. 27 (1st Supp.), s. 53.]

DRAWING DOCUMENT WITHOUT AUTHORITY, ETC.

374. Every one who

(*a*) with intent to defraud and without lawful authority makes, executes, draws, signs, accepts or endorses a document in the name or on the account of another person by procuration or otherwise, or

(*b*) makes use of or utters a document knowing that it has been made, executed, signed, accepted or endorsed with intent to defraud and without lawful authority, in the name or on the account of another person, by procuration or otherwise,

is guilty of an indictable offence and liable to imprisonment for a term not exceeding fourteen years. R.S., c. C-34, s. 332.

CROSS-REFERENCES

The term "document" is defined in s. 321.

The accused may elect his mode of trial pursuant to s. 536(2). Release pending trial is determined by s. 515.

This offence resembles the offences of forgery and uttering under ss. 367 and 368. Other related offences are as follows: s. 369, exchequer bill paper, public seals, etc.; s. 370, counterfeit government proclamation; ss. 371, 372, false telegram, etc.; s. 375, obtaining by forged document; s. 376, counterfeiting stamp, mark, etc.; s. 377, defacing official documents; s. 378, offences in relation to registers; ss. 397 to 402, falsification of books and documents in relation to contracts and trade; ss. 406 to 414, forgery of trade-marks and trade descriptions; ss. 416 to 421, offences in relation to public stores; Part XII, offences in relation to currency, counterfeiting, etc.

SYNOPSIS

This section describes the offence of drawing or using a document without authority. Anyone who makes, executes, draws, signs, accepts or endorses a document in the name of or on behalf of another person without lawful authority, and with an intention to defraud, or who knowingly makes use of, or utters such a document, commits an indictable offence. The maximum term of punishment is 14 years' imprisonment.

OBTAINING, ETC., BY INSTRUMENT BASED ON FORGED DOCUMENT.

375. Every one who demands, receives or obtains anything, or causes or procures anything to be delivered or paid to any person under, on, or by virtue of any instrument issued under the authority of law, knowing that it is based on a forged document, is guilty of an indictable offence and liable to imprisonment for a term not exceeding fourteen years. R.S., c. C-34, s. 333.

CROSS-REFERENCES

The term "document" is defined in s. 321.

The accused may elect his mode of trial pursuant to s. 536(2). Release pending trial is determined by s. 515.

This offence resembles the offences of forgery and uttering under ss. 367 and 368. Other related offences are as follows: s. 369, exchequer bill paper, public seals, etc.; s. 370, counterfeit government proclamation; ss. 371, 372, false telegram, etc.; s. 374, drawing document without authority; s. 376, counterfeiting stamp, mark, etc.; s. 377, defacing official documents; s. 378, offences in relation to registers; ss. 397 to 402, falsification of books and documents in relation to contracts and trade; ss. 406 to 414, forgery of trade-marks and trade descriptions; ss. 416 to 421, offences in relation to public stores; Part XII, offences in relation to currency, counterfeiting, etc.

SYNOPSIS

This section creates the offence of using an instrument based on a forged document. Anyone who demands, receives or obtains anything, or causes anything to be delivered or paid, by virtue of an instrument issued under legal authority, but knowing that it is based on a forged document, commits an indictable offence. The maximum term or punishment is 14 years.

COUNTERFEITING STAMP, ETC. / Counterfeiting mark / Definitions / "mark" / "stamp".

376. (1) Every person is guilty of an indictable offence and liable to imprisonment for a term of not more thatn 14 years who

(*a*) fraudulently uses, mutilates, affixes, removes or counterfeits a stamp or part thereof,

(*b*) knowingly and without lawful excuse has in their possession

(i) a counterfeit stamp or a stamp that has been fraudulently mutilated, or

(ii) anything bearing a stamp of which a part has been fraudulently erased, removed or concealed, or

(*c*) without lawful excuse makes or knowingly has in their possession a die or instrument that is capable of making the impression of a stamp or part of a stamp.

(2) Every one who, without lawful authority,

(*a*) makes a mark,

(*b*) sells, or exposes for sale, or has in his possession a counterfeit mark,

(*c*) affixes a mark to anything that is required by law to be marked, branded, sealed or wrapped other than the thing to which the mark was originally affixed or was intended to be affixed, or

(*d*) affixes a counterfeit mark to anything that is required by law to be marked, branded, sealed or wrapped,

is guilty of an indictable offence and liable to imprisonment for a term not exceeding fourteen years.

(3) In this section

"mark" means a mark, brand, seal, wrapper or design used by or on behalf of

(*a*) the government of Canada or of a province,

(*b*) the government of a state other than Canada, or

(*c*) a department, board, commission or agent established by a government mentioned in paragraph (*a*) or (*b*) in connection with the service or business of that government;

"stamp" means an impressed or adhesive stamp used for the purpose of revenue by the government of Canada or a province or by the government of a state other than Canada. R.S., c. C-34, s. 334; 2018, c. 29, s. 43.

CROSS-REFERENCES

Possession is defined in s. 4(3). While there is no definition of "fraudulently" which is universally applicable, generally speaking, it refers to conduct which is dishonest and morally wrong: *R. v. DeMarco* (1973), 13 C.C.C. (2d) 369 (Ont. C.A.).

The accused may elect his mode of trial pursuant to s. 536(2). Release pending trial is determined by s. 515.

This offence resembles the offences of forgery and uttering under ss. 367 and 368. Other related offences are as follows: s. 369, exchequer bill paper, public seals, etc.; s. 370, counterfeit government proclamation; s. 374, drawing document without authority; ss. 397 to 402, falsification of books and documents in relation to contracts and trade; ss. 406 to 414, forgery of trade-marks and trade descriptions; ss. 416 to 421, offences in relation to public stores; Part XII, offences in relation to currency, counterfeiting, etc.

SYNOPSIS

This section describes the offences of counterfeiting a stamp or a mark. *Stamp* and *mark* are both defined in subsec. (3), and are limited to government uses. Subsection (1) provides that an indictable offence is committed where anyone counterfeits a stamp or part of a stamp, fraudulently deals with a stamp or part of a stamp in a variety of ways, possesses a counterfeit or fraudulently mutilated stamp, or something bearing a stamp of which part has been fraudulently erased, removed or concealed, or makes or knowingly possesses a die or instrument capable of making the impression of a stamp or part thereof. In the case of the possession offences and the offence of making a die or instrument, the accused will not be convicted if he can establish that the act in question was done with a lawful excuse. Subsection (2) provides that an indictable offence is committed where anyone, without lawful authority, makes a mark, sells or exposes for sale a counterfeit mark, affixes a mark originally affixed, or intended to be affixed, to one thing to something else legally requiring a mark, or affixes a counterfeit mark to something requiring a mark. The maximum term of punishment for both offences is 14 years' imprisonment.

ANNOTATIONS

The *actus reus* of subsec. (1)(*a*) is established by proof that the use of the stamp is objectively impressed with a fraudulent element: *R. v. Lemay* (1999), 144 C.C.C. (3d) 74 (Que. C.A.).

DAMAGING DOCUMENTS / Definition of "election document".

377. (1) Every one who unlawfully

(*a*) destroys, defaces or injures a register, or any part of a register, of births, baptisms, marriages, deaths or burials that is required or authorized by law to be kept in Canada, or a copy or any part of a copy of such a register that is required by law to be transmitted to a registrar or other officer,

(*b*) inserts or causes to be inserted in a register or copy referred to in paragraph (*a*) an entry, that he knows is false, of any matter relating to a birth, baptism, marriage, death or burial, or erases any material part from that register or copy,

(*c*) destroys, damages or obliterates an election document or causes an election document to be destroyed, damaged or obliterated, or

(*d*) makes or causes to be made an erasure, alteration or interlineation in or on an election document,

is guilty of an indictable offence and liable to imprisonment for a term not exceeding five years.

(2) In this section, "election document" means any document or writing issued under the authority of an Act of Parliament or the legislature of a province with respect to an election held pursuant to the authority of that Act. R.S., c. C-34, s. 335.

CROSS-REFERENCES

The term "document" is defined in s. 321.

The accused may elect his mode of trial pursuant to s. 536(2). Release pending trial is determined by s. 515, although the accused is eligible for release by the officer in charge under s. 498.

This offence resembles the offences of forgery and uttering under ss. 367 and 368. Other related offences are as follows: s. 369, exchequer bill paper, public seals, etc.; s. 370, counterfeit government proclamation; s. 374, drawing document without authority; s. 375, obtaining by instrument issued under authority of law knowing it is based on a forged document; s. 376, counterfeiting stamp, mark, etc.; s. 377, defacing official documents.

SYNOPSIS

This section describes the offence of damaging or interfering with certain registers and election documents. Paragraph (1)(*a*) prohibits a person from destroying, defacing or injuring a register or part of a register of births, baptisms, marriages, deaths or burials lawfully required or authorized to be kept, or a copy or partial copy lawfully required to be transmitted. Subsection (1)(*b*) prohibits false insertions or erasures in such a register or copy. Subsection (1)(*c*) prohibits a person from damaging or obliterating an election document, or causing such an act to be done. Subsection (1)(*d*) proscribes erasures, alterations or interlineations in election documents. An election document is defined in subsec. (2), and relates only to elections authorized by federal or provincial enactments. This offence is indictable and carries a maximum term of five years' imprisonment.

OFFENCES IN RELATION TO REGISTERS.

378. Every one who

(*a*) being authorized or required by law to make or issue a certified copy of, extract from or certificate in respect of a register, record or document, knowingly makes or issues a false certified copy, extract or certificate,

(*b*) not being authorized or required by law to make or issue a certified copy of, extract from or certificate in respect of a register, record or document, fraudulently makes or issues a copy, extract or certificate that purports to be certified as authorized or required by law, or

(*c*) being authorized or required by law to make a certificate or declaration concerning any particular required for the purpose of making entries in a register, record or document, knowingly and falsely makes the certificate or declaration,

is guilty of an indictable offence and liable to imprisonment for a term not exceeding five years. R.S., c. C-34, s. 336.

CROSS-REFERENCES

The term "document" is defined in s. 321. The term "register" is not defined but probably refers to the registers described in s. 377.

The accused may elect his mode of trial pursuant to s. 536(2). Release pending trial is determined by s. 515, although the accused is eligible for release by the officer in charge under s. 498.

This offence resembles the offences of forgery and uttering under ss. 367 and 368. Other related offences are as follows: s. 369, exchequer bill paper, public seals, etc.; s. 370, counterfeit government proclamation; s. 374, drawing document without authority; s. 375, obtaining by instrument issued under authority of law knowing it is based on a forged document; s. 376, counterfeiting stamp, mark, etc.; s. 377, defacing official documents.

SYNOPSIS

This section describes the offence of issuing false or unauthorized certifications. Paragraph (*a*) prohibits persons legally required or authorized to issue certified copies of, extracts from, or certificates in respect of a register, record or document, from knowingly doing so falsely. Paragraph (*b*) prohibits other persons from *fraudulently issuing* such documents if they purport to be certified as legally required or authorized. Paragraph (*c*) prohibits persons legally authorized or required to make certificates or declarations concerning any particular required for making entries in such register, record or document from *knowingly* doing so falsely. In each case, the offence is indictable, with a maximum term of punishment of five years' imprisonment.

Part X / FRAUDULENT TRANSACTIONS RELATING TO CONTRACTS AND TRADE

Interpretation

DEFINITIONS OF GOODS.

379. In this Part, "goods" means anything that is the subject of trade or commerce. R.S., c. C-34, s. 337; 2018, c. 29, s. 43.1.

CROSS-REFERENCES

In addition to the definitions in this section, see s. 2 and notes to that section.

SYNOPSIS

This section provides a definition of the term *goods* and *trading stamps* for the purpose of Part X, which concerns fraudulent transactions relating to contracts and trade.

ANNOTATIONS

"Trading stamps" – The definition of "trading stamps" in this section is exhaustive notwithstanding the use of the word "includes": *R. v. Loblaw Groceterias Co. (Man.) Ltd.; R. v. Thomson (Niagara IGA Grocery)*, [1961] S.C.R. 138, 129 C.C.C. 223 (5:0).

Fraud

FRAUD / Minimum punishment / Affecting public market.

380. (1) Every one who, by deceit, falsehood or other fraudulent means, whether or not it is a false pretence within the meaning of this Act, defrauds the public or any person, whether ascertained or not, of any property, money or valuable security or any service,

(*a*) is guilty of an indictable offence and liable to a term of imprisonment not exceeding fourteen years, where the subject-matter of the offence is a testamentary instrument or the value of the subject-matter of the offence exceeds five thousand dollars; or

(*b*) is guilty

(i) of an indictable offence and liable to imprisonment for a term not exceeding two years, or

(ii) of an offence punishable on summary conviction,

where the value of the subject-matter of the offence does not exceed five thousand dollars.

(1.1) When a person is prosecuted on indictment and convicted of one or more offences referred to in subsection (1), the court that imposes the sentence shall impose a

minimum punishment of imprisonment for a term of two years if the total value of the subject-matter of the offences exceeds one million dollars.

(2) Every one who, by deceit, falsehood or other fraudulent means, whether or not it is a false pretence within the meaning of this Act, with intent to defraud, affects the public market price of stocks, shares, merchandise or anything that is offered for sale to the public is guilty of an indictable offence and liable to imprisonment for a term not exceeding fourteen years. R.S., c. C-34, s. 338; 1974-75-76, c. 93, s. 32; R.S.C. 1985, c. 27 (1st Supp.), s. 54; 1994, c. 44, s. 25; 1997, c. 18, s. 26; 2004, c. 3, s. 2; 2011, c. 6, s. 2.

CROSS-REFERENCES

The terms "every one", "person", "property" and "valuable security" are defined in s. 2.

As to admission of photographic evidence of property, see s. 491.2. For proof by way of affidavit of ownership, lawful possession, value, and that the person was deprived of property by fraud or otherwise without the person's lawful consent, see s. 657.1.

By virtue of s. 583, an indictment which otherwise complies with s. 581 is not insufficient by reason only that: para. (*b*), it fails to name the person who owns or has a special property or interest in property mentioned in the count or para. (*c*), it charges an intent to defraud without naming or describing the person whom it was intended to defraud. Also note s. 588 which deems certain persons to have a property interest in property of which they have the management, control or custody. Under s. 586, no count alleging fraud is insufficient by reason only that it does not set out in detail the nature of the fraud. However, under s. 587(1)(*b*) the court may order particulars of any fraud that is alleged.

This offence may be the basis for an application for an authorization to intercept private communications by reason of s. 183 and a warrant to conduct video surveillance under s. 487.01(5). Fraud is an enterprise crime offence for the purposes of Part XII.2.

Where the offence, although committed outside Canada, is in relation to the use of nuclear material, see s. 7(3.4).

The offence in para. (1)(*a*) is an indictable offence for which the accused may elect the mode of trial under s. 536(2) and release pending trial is determined in accordance with s. 515. Where the prosecution elects to proceed by indictment for the offence under subsec. (1)(*b*) then, by virtue of s. 553, it is an offence over which a provincial court judge has absolute jurisdiction and does not depend on the consent of the accused. That is, the accused does not have an election as to mode of trial, although the provincial court judge may, by virtue of s. 555(1), elect to continue the proceedings as a preliminary inquiry, in which case the accused is deemed to have elected trial by judge and jury pursuant to s. 565(1)(*a*). As well, under s. 555(2), where, in the course of the trial, evidence establishes that the subject-matter of the offence is a testamentary instrument or that its value exceeds $5,000 then the provincial court judge shall put the accused to his election under s. 536(2). Where the prosecution elects to proceed by way of summary conviction then the proceedings are conducted by a summary conviction court pursuant to Part XXVII. The punishment is then as set out in s. 787 and the limitation period is set out in s. 786(2). For the offence under para. (*b*), release pending trial is determined by s. 515, although the accused is eligible for release by a peace officer under s. 496, 497 or by the officer in charge under s. 498. The value of a valuable security is determined in accordance with s. 4(2) and of a postal card or stamp in accordance with s. 4(1). The term "testamentary instrument" is defined in s. 2.

For the offence under subsec. (2), the accused may elect his mode of trial under s. 536(2) and release pending trial is determined in accordance with s. 515.

The related offence of theft is generally described in s. 322 and false pretences in s. 362. Other offences relating to trading in securities, etc., are in ss. 382 to 384 and include "wash trading" (s. 382) and insider trading (s. 382.1) and in s. 400 (false prospectus). Section 380.1 provides that, in sentencing an offender for this offence, the court shall consider as aggravating circumstances the magnitude, complexity, duration or degree of planning of the fraud; that the offence adversely affected or had the potential to adversely affect the stability of the Canadian economy or financial system or any financial market in Canada or investor confidence in such markets; the offence involved a large number of victims; the offence had a significant impact on the victims given their personal circumstances such as age, health and financial situation; in committing the offence, the offender took advantage of the high regard in which the offender was held in the community; the offender did not comply with a licensing requirement or professional standard; and that the offender concealed or destroyed records. As well, the offender's employment, employment skills, or status or reputation in the community are not to be considered as mitigating factors if those circumstances were relevant to, contributed to, or were used in the commission of the offence. Section 380.1(3) requires the sentencing court to state the aggravating and mitigating circumstances that it took into account. Section 380.2 provides for the making of a prohibition order, prohibiting the offender from being involved in any capacity that involves authority over the property of another person. Section 380.3 directs the court to consider making a restitution order under ss. 738 or 739. Section 380.4 allows the court to consider a community impact statement.

Sections 487.012 to 487.017 provide procedures for the making of production orders that would require persons to produce documents, data or information to police officers or public officers designated in the order.

SYNOPSIS

This section describes the offences of defrauding the public, or any person, of property, money, valuable security or any service, and of affecting the public market price of stocks, shares, merchandise or anything offered for sale to the public. The activities described above must be accomplished by deceit, falsehood or other fraudulent means, whether or not they constitute false pretences within the meaning of the *Criminal Code*. The accused must have the intent to defraud to attract criminal liability for affecting the market price of stocks, shares, or publicly offered merchandise and this form of the offence is punishable on indictment by a maximum term of 14 years' imprisonment. The more general offence of defrauding the public is indictable, with a maximum punishment of 14 years, when the subject-matter of the offence is a testamentary instrument or has a value greater than $5,000. In other circumstances, this form of the offence is hybrid, with a maximum punishment on indictment of two years. Where the Crown proceeds by indictment and the value of the subject matter of the offences exceeds one million dollars, the offender is subject to a minimum sentence of two years' imprisonment.

ANNOTATIONS

Meaning of defrauds generally – The classic definition of fraud is found in the judgment of Buckley J., in *London & Globe Finance Corp. Ltd. (Re)*, [1903] 1 Ch. 728 at pp. 732-3: "To defraud is to deprive by deceit: it is by deceit to induce a man to act to his injury. More tersely it may be put, that to deceive is by falsehood to induce a state of mind; to defraud is by deceit to induce a course of action."

It was held, however, in *Scott v. Metropolitan Police Commissioner* (1974), 60 Cr. App. R. 124 (H.L.), that this definition is not exhaustive and that to "defraud" ordinarily means: "to deprive a person dishonestly of something which is his or of something to which he is or would or might but for the perpetration of the fraud, be entitled."

In *R. v. Renard* (1974), 17 C.C.C. (2d) 355 (Ont. C.A.), the court held that, a victim may be defrauded by being deprived of something and he may be deprived of something either by being fraudulently induced to part with it or by having that to which he is entitled fraudulently diverted or withheld from him.

An accused's acts in procuring a third person to put him in a position to take money to which the complainant would be otherwise entitled constitutes fraud: *R. v. Kribbs,* [1968] 1 C.C.C. 345, [1967] 2 O.R. 539 (C.A.).

A charge of fraud is valid against the principle shareholder who fraudulently depletes the assets of his *alter ego,* a limited company: *R. v. Marquardt* (1972), 6 C.C.C. (2d) 372, 18 C.R.N.S. 162 (B.C.C.A.).

Meaning of falsehood – It is a falsehood for a person to promise to pay cash for the purchase of an item without any intention of honouring the promise: *R. v. Stanley* (1957), 119 C.C.C. 220, 26 C.R. 180 (B.C.C.A.).

Meaning of "other fraudulent means" generally – In *R. v. Cox and Paton,* [1963] S.C.R. 500, [1963] 2 C.C.C. 148 (5:0), although no exhaustive definition of "other fraudulent means" was given it was held that if all the directors of a company were to join together to purchase a worthless asset with company funds in order to enrich themselves then even "supposing it could be said that the directors being the "mind of the company' and well knowing the true facts, the company was not deceived . . . it is clear that . . . the directors would have defrauded the company, if not by deceit or falsehood, by "other fraudulent means' ".

In *R. v. Olan, Hudson and Hartnett*, [1978] 2 S.C.R. 1175, 41 C.C.C. (2d) 145 (9:0), the court considered the application of *R. v. Cox and Paton, supra,* in a situation where the accused had caused a company over which they had control to divest its holdings in "blue chip" securities and to purchase shares in a company whose major asset was a debt owed to it by a company controlled by two of the accused. It was held that where it is alleged a corporation was defrauded by its directors' deception of the corporation is not an essential element of the offence, the words "other fraudulent means" include not only means which are in the nature of a falsehood or deceit but also all other means which can properly be stigmatized as dishonest. Further, while no exhaustive definition of "defraud" was attempted the Crown at least must prove dishonesty and deprivation. The element of deprivation is satisfied on proof of detriment, prejudice, or risk of prejudice to the economic interest of the victims. The issue in this case was whether the use of the victim's assets in this manner was in furtherance of a *bona fide* business interest of the victim or was it expended in advancing the personal interests of the accused and whether the victim suffered deprivation as a result. The court disagreed with the Ontario Court of Appeal view that there was no evidence of fraud and ordered a new trial. It was not necessary for the Crown to prove the new investment was worthless or negligible.

At least where the Crown relies on "other fraudulent means" rather than deceit or falsehood there need not be some form of relationship or nexus between the accused and the victim. Thus, the infringement of copyright by "counterfeiting" of video tapes may constitute fraud, whether or not it would also amount to theft, notwithstanding there is no relationship between the accused and the victim, the holder of the copyright or distribution rights to the tapes: *R. v. Kirkwood* (1983), 5 C.C.C. (3d) 393, 35 C.R. (3d) 97 (Ont. C.A.), relying on *Scott v. Metropolitan Police Commissioner, supra.* Folld: *R. v. Fitzpatrick* (1984), 11 C.C.C. (3d) 46 (B.C.C.A.).

Other fraudulent means includes mere omission where, through silence, an individual hides from the other person a fundamental and essential information. The silence or omission must be such that it would mislead a reasonable person: *R. v. Emond* (1997), 117 C.C.C. (3d) 275 (Que. C.A.), leave to appeal to S.C.C. refused 117 C.C.C. (3d) vi.

In considering whether the acts of the accused can properly be stigmatized as dishonest, the standard to be applied is that of a reasonable person. It connotes an underhanded design which has the effect, or which engenders the risk, of depriving others of what is theirs. The dishonesty lies in the wrongful use of something in which another person has an interest, in such a manner that this other's interest is extinguished or put at risk. The use is wrongful in this sense if it constitutes conduct which reasonable decent persons would consider dishonest and unscrupulous: *R. v. Zlatic*, [1993] 2 S.C.R. 29, 79 C.C.C. (3d) 466.

The requisite *mens rea* cannot be inferred from a finding that an accused's conduct was objectively dishonest when the *actus reus* is based on "other fraudulent means". Dishonesty with respect to the *actus reus* is to be measured against the objective standard of what a reasonable person would consider to be dishonest without regard for what the accused actually knew: *R. v. Wolsey* (2008), 233 C.C.C. (3d) 205 (B.C.C.A.).

Risk of deprivation – Where the "owner" of certain confidential information had no intention of dealing with it in a commercial way it could not be said that a person who obtains that information has committed fraud, since there was no risk of economic loss amounting to deprivation: *R. v. Stewart*, [1988] 1 S.C.R. 963, 41 C.C.C. (3d) 481 (6:0).

While there need not be actual economic loss there must be an actual risk of prejudice and where the victim named in the indictment merely acted as a conduit in the transactions so that there was no actual risk of prejudice to her economic interests the charge was not made out: *R. v. Campbell and Kotler*, [1986] 2 S.C.R. 376, 29 C.C.C. (3d) 97 (5:0).

In *R. v. Knowles* (1979), 51 C.C.C. (2d) 237 (Ont. C.A.), the court found the requisite dishonest deprivation where the victim was induced to make a loan which it would not have made had it known the true state of affairs, namely that the true borrower was an officer of a company which was a subsidiary of the victim. The deceit practised by the accused placed the accused in a conflict of interest and thus imperilled the victim's economic interests notwithstanding the loan was secured and used for the purpose for which it was advanced.

Economic loss does not have to be proven by the Crown and fraud is complete when money is paid for corporate shares to which the accused falsely ascribed certain attributes: *R. v. Knelson and Baran* (1962), 133 C.C.C. 210, 38 C.R. 181 (B.C.C.A.).

Mens rea – The *mens rea* of fraud is established by proof of subjective knowledge of the prohibited act, and subjective knowledge that the act could have as a consequence deprivation, in the sense of causing another to lose their pecuniary interest in certain property or in placing that interest at risk. There is no requirement that the accused subjectively appreciate the dishonesty of his acts: *R. v. Théroux*, [1993] 2 S.C.R. 5, 79 C.C.C. (3d) 449; *R. v. Zlatic*, *supra*.

An accused's honest belief that he was entitled to the property in question is a mistake of law and does not negate the *mens rea* of fraud. While lack of "colour of right" is an element of theft and therefore provides a defence, it does not provide a defence to a charge of fraud: *R. v. Kingsbury* (2012), 297 C.C.C. (3d) 255 (B.C.C.A.).

Expectation of subsequent validation – Where pursuant to the suggestion of his superior, who approved but would not authorize a salary increase, the accused submitted fictitious expense accounts to the Quebec government, it was held (4:3) that such a direction was not a valid defence to a charge of defrauding the public in general and the Government of the Province of Quebec in particular, and that the accused's expectation that such a practice would ultimately be validated was also not a proper defence in law: *R. v. Lemire*, [1965] S.C.R. 174, [1965] 4 C.C.C. 11.

Proof of charge as particularized – Proprietorships are not in and of themselves persons capable of being defrauded but are merely the registered names under which persons capable of being defrauded do business. Where the prosecution alleges in an indictment that the victim is a proprietorship then it in effect has particularized as the victim the person who used the propriertorship to carry on business and that it was in the operation of that proprietorship that he was defrauded and not otherwise: *R. v. Campbell and Kotler*, [1986] 2 S.C.R. 376, 29 C.C.C. (3d) 97 (5:0). [However, now see definition of "person" in s. 2, which includes an organization, which in turn includes a partnership.]

On a charge under this section it is not necessary for the Crown to prove the accused actually obtained the property which was the subject of the charge, only that the victim was deprived of the property as a result of the accused's dishonest acts: *R. v. Huggett* (1978), 42 C.C.C. (2d) 198 (Ont. C.A.).

A charge of conspiracy or attempt to commit fraud may be made out although the victim is unascertained. Further, the victim need not be particularized in the indictment: *R. v. Vezina; R. v. Cote*, [1986] 1 S.C.R. 2, 23 C.C.C. (3d) 481 (7:0).

An indictment alleging that certain individuals were defrauded of "$2,500", rather than a sum of money, is sufficient to support a conviction although the evidence showed the individuals were induced by deceit, falsehood or other fraudulent means merely to part with a cheque in that amount drawn, moreover, on the bank accounts of corporations of which they were principal owners or co-owners: *R. v. Scheel* (1978), 42 C.C.C. (2d) 31, 3 C.R. (3d) 359 (Ont. C.A.).

Meaning of "property" [Also see "Risk of deprivation", *supra*] – The word "property" does not mean ownership, but is only descriptive of the thing of which one is defrauded and the offence is completed once there is a passing over of possession under deceitful circumstances: *R. v. Vallillee* (1974), 15 C.C.C. (2d) 409, 24 C.R.N.S. 319 (Ont. C.A.).

Other notes – Although the acts of the accused may also constitute a breach of provincial welfare legislation it is open to the Crown to proceed under this section: *R. v. Gladu* (1986), 29 C.C.C. (3d) 186 (Ont. C.A.); *R. v. Gallant* (1987), 34 C.C.C. (3d) 190, 64 Nfld. & P.E.I.R. 89 (P.E.I.C.A.). *R. v. Rouse* (1988), 39 C.C.C. (3d) 115, 85 A.R. 60 (C.A.).

Affecting public market [subsec. (2)] – In one of the few cases decided under this subsection a conviction was upheld where the accused was one of several persons involved in operating a "box". While ostensibly set up to maintain orderly marketing in shares the two companies involved in the "box" were in fact used to give the illusion of arms length transactions in the trading of the shares and gave the impression that the shares were continually rising in value: *R. v. McNaughton* (1976), 43 C.C.C. (2d) 293, 33 C.R.N.S. 279 (Que. C.A.).

Constitutional considerations – The mandatory minimum sentence imposed by subsec. (1.1) for frauds exceeding $1 million violates s. 12 of the Charter and is not justified under s. 1: *R. v. Plange* (2018), 359 C.C.C. (3d) 273 (Ont. S.C.J.).

SENTENCING — AGGRAVATING CIRCUMSTANCES / Aggravating circumstance — value of the fraud / Non-mitigating factors / Record of proceedings.

380.1 (1) Without limiting the generality of section 718.2, where a court imposes a sentence for an offence referred to in section 380, 382, 382.1 or 400, it shall consider the following as aggravating circumstances:

(*a*) the magnitude, complexity, duration or degree of planning of the fraud committed was significant;

(*b*) the offence adversely affected, or had the potential to adversely affect, the stability of the Canadian economy or financial system or any financial market in Canada or investor confidence in such a financial market;

(*c*) the offence involved a large number of victims;

(*c*.1) the offence had a significant impact on the victims given their personal circumstances including their age, health and financial situation;

(*d*) in committing the offence, the offender took advantage of the high regard in which the offender was held in the community;

(*e*) the offender did not comply with a licensing requirement, or professional standard, that is normally applicable to the activity or conduct that forms the subject-matter of the offence; and

(*f*) the offender concealed or destroyed records related to the fraud or to the disbursement of the proceeds of the fraud.

(1.1) Without limiting the generality of section 718.2, when a court imposes a sentence for an offence referred to in section 382, 382.1 or 400, it shall also consider as an aggravating circumstance the fact that the value of the fraud committed exceeded one million dollars.

(2) When a court imposes a sentence for an offence referred to in section 380, 382, 382.1 or 400, it shall not consider as mitigating circumstances the offender's employment, employment skills or status or reputation in the community if those circumstances were relevant to, contributed to, or were used in the commission of the offence.

(3) The court shall cause to be stated in the record the aggravating and mitigating circumstances it took into account when determining the sentence. 2004, c. 3, s. 2; 2011, c. 6, s. 3.

CROSS-REFERENCES

Section 380 describes the general offence of defrauding the public or any person and stock fraud. Section 382 creates the offence of fraudulent manipulation of stock exchange transactions. Section 382.1 creates offences of insider trading. Section 400 creates offences in relation to making a false prospectus.

Section 718.2 sets out other principles of sentencing including other deemed aggravating circumstances, such as para. (*a*)(iii), that the offender abused a position of trust or authority in relation to the victim. Section 380.2 provides for the making of a prohibition order, prohibiting the offender from being involved in any capacity that involves authority over the property of another person. Section 380.3 directs the court to consider making a restitution order under ss. 738 or 739. Section 380.4 allows the court to consider a community impact statement.

SYNOPSIS

This section deals with principles of sentencing specific to the various fraud offences created by ss. 380, 382, 382.1 and 400. Subsection (1) sets out various aggravating circumstances that the court is to take into account. Subsection (1.1) sets out the additional aggravating circumstances that the value of the fraud exceeded one million dollars for the offences in ss. 382, 382.1 and 400. Section 380(1.1) already takes that circumstance into account for the offence committed under s. 380 by creating a minimum punishment of two years' imprisonment where the value of the fraud exceeds one million dollars. Subsection (3) requires the sentencing court to set out the aggravating and mitigating circumstances that were taken into account.

PROHIBITION ORDER / Duration / Court may vary order / Offence.

380.2 (1) When an offender is convicted, or is discharged on the conditions prescribed in a probation order under section 730, of an offence referred to in subsection 380(1), the court that sentences or discharges the offender, in addition to any other punishment that may be imposed for that offence or any other condition prescribed in the order of discharge, may make, subject to the conditions or exemptions that the court directs, an order prohibiting the offender from seeking, obtaining or continuing any employment, or becoming or being a volunteer in any capacity, that involves having authority over the real property, money or valuable security of another person.

(2) The prohibition may be for any period that the court considers appropriate, including any period to which the offender is sentenced to imprisonment.

(3) A court that makes an order of prohibition or, if the court is for any reason unable to act, another court of equivalent jurisdiction in the same province, may, on application of the offender or the prosecutor, require the offender to appear before it at any time and, after hearing the parties, that court may vary the conditions prescribed in the order if, in the opinion of the court, the variation is desirable because of changed circumstances.

(4) Every person who is bound by an order of prohibition and who does not comply with the order is guilty of

(*a*) an indictable offence and is liable to imprisonment for a term not exceeding two years; or

(*b*) an offence punishable on summary conviction. 2011, c. 6, s. 4.

CROSS-REFERENCES

Section 380(1) describes the general offence of defrauding the public or any person. Section 380.1 provides that, in sentencing an offender for the offence under s. 380, the court shall consider as aggravating circumstances the magnitude, complexity, duration or degree of planning of the fraud; that the offence adversely affected or had the potential to adversely affect the stability of the Canadian economy or financial system or any financial market in Canada or investor confidence in such markets; the offence involved a large number of victims; the offence had a significant impact on the victims given their personal circumstances such as age, health and financial situation; in committing the offence, the offender took advantage of the high regard in which the offender was held in the community; the offender did not comply with a licensing requirement or professional standard; and that the offender concealed or destroyed records. As well, the offender's employment, employment skills, or status or reputation in the community are not to be considered as mitigating factors if those circumstances were relevant to, contributed to, or were used in the commission of the offence. Section 380.1(3) requires the sentencing court to state the aggravating and mitigating circumstances that it took into account. Section 380.3 directs the court to consider making a restitution order under ss. 738 or 739. Section 380.4 allows the court to consider a community impact statement.

SYNOPSIS

This section gives the court the power to impose a prohibition order where the offender is convicted of the general fraud offence described in s. 380(1). The order prohibits the offender from any involvement (employment or volunteering) in authority over the property of another. The court can impose conditions or exemptions as part of the prohibition order and can be for any period the court considers appropriate. Failure to comply with the order is a Crown-option offence.

ANNOTATIONS

The sanction authorized by subsec. (1) imposes significant restrictions on an offender's liberty and security of the person and the presumption against retrospectivity therefore applies. It can only be applied to frauds committed after this provision came into force in November, 2011: *R. v. Hooyer* (2016), 332 C.C.C. (3d) 97 (Ont. C.A.).

380.3 [*Repealed*, 2015, c. 13, s. 11.]

380.4 [*Repealed*, 2015, c. 13, s. 11.]

USING MAILS TO DEFRAUD.

381. Every one who makes use of the mails for the purpose of transmitting or delivering letters or circulars concerning schemes devised or intended to deceive or defraud the public, or for the purpose of obtaining money under false pretences, is guilty of an indictable offence and liable to imprisonment for a term not exceeding two years. R.S., c. C-34, s. 339.

CROSS-REFERENCES

The term "mail" is defined in s. 2 of the *Canada Post Corporation Act*, R.S.C. 1985, c. C-10. By virtue of s. 583, an indictment, which otherwise complies with s. 581, is not insufficient by reason only that: para. (*c*), it charges an intent to defraud without naming or describing the person whom it was intended to defraud. Under s. 586, no count alleging false pretences or fraud is insufficient by reason only that it does not set out in detail the nature of the false pretences or fraud. However, under s. 587(1)(*b*), the court may order particulars of any false pretence or fraud that is alleged.

This offence may be the basis for an application for an authorization to intercept private communications by reason of s. 183 and a warrant to conduct video surveillance under s. 487.01(5).

The accused may elect his mode of trial pursuant to s. 536(2). Release pending trial is determined by s. 515, although the accused is eligible for release by the officer in charge pursuant to s. 498.

The related offence of fraud is described in s. 380 and of circulating a false prospectus in s. 400.

SYNOPSIS

This section makes it an offence to use the mails to deliver letters or circulars that either describe schemes intended to deceive the public, or that are to be used for the purpose of obtaining money under false pretences. This is an indictable offence with a maximum term of two years' imprisonment.

FRAUDULENT MANIPULATION OF STOCK EXCHANGE TRANSACTIONS.

382. Every one who, through the facility of a stock exchange, curb market or other market, with intent to create a false or misleading appearance of active public trading in a security or with intent to create a false or misleading appearance with respect to the market price of a security,

(*a*) effects a transaction in the security that involves no change in the beneficial ownership thereof,

(*b*) enters an order for the purchase of the security, knowing that an order of substantially the same size at substantially the same time and at substantially the same price for the sale of the security has been or will be entered by or for the same or different persons, or

(*c*) enters an order for the sale of the security, knowing that an order of substantially the same size at substantially the same time and at substantially the same price for the purchase of the security has been or will be entered by or for the same or different persons,

is guilty of an indictable offence and liable to imprisonment for a term not exceeding ten years. R.S., c. C-34, s. 340; 2004, c. 3, s. 4.

CROSS-REFERENCES

This offence may be the basis for an application for an authorization to intercept private communications by reason of s. 183 and is an enterprise crime offence for the purposes of Part XII.2. The accused may elect his mode of trial pursuant to s. 536(2). Release pending trial is determined by s. 515, although the accused is eligible for release by the officer in charge pursuant to s. 498.

The related offence of fraud is described in s. 380, of insider trading and tipping in s. 382.1 and of circulating a false prospectus in s. 400.

Section 380.1 provides that, in sentencing an offender for the offence under this section, the court shall consider as aggravating circumstances the magnitude, complexity, duration or degree of planning of the fraud; that the offence adversely affected or had the potential to adversely affect the stability of the Canadian economy or financial system or any financial market in Canada or investor confidence in such markets; the offence involved a large number of victims; the offence had a significant impact on the victims given their personal circumstances such as age, health and financial situation; in committing the offence, the offender took advantage of the high regard in which the offender was held in the community; the offender did not comply with a licensing requirement or professional standard; and that the offender concealed or destroyed records. As well, the offender's employment, employment skills, or status or reputation in the community are not to be considered as mitigating factors if those circumstances were relevant to, contributed to, or were used in the commission of the offence. Section 380.1(2) requires the court to consider as an aggravating circumstance that the value of the fraud committed exceeded one million dollars. Section 380.1(3) requires the sentencing court to state the aggravating and mitigating circumstances that it took into account.

Sections 487.012 to 487.017 provide procedures for the making of production orders that would require persons to produce documents, data or information to police officers or public officers designated in the order.

SYNOPSIS

This section sets out the offence of manipulation of transactions on a stock exchange, curb market or other market and is colloquially known as "wash-trading". Every person who uses one of these institutions with *intent to create a false or misleading appearance* with respect to the market price, or activity of a security, and who engages in any of the activities specified in paras. (*a*), (*b*) or (*c*), commits an indictable offence and is liable to a maximum term of 10 years' imprisonment. Paragraph (*a*) describes a transaction in a security that involves no change in the *beneficial ownership*. Paragraphs (*b*) and (*c*) describe the entering of an order for the sale or purchase of a security, *knowing* that a substantially matching or counter balancing purchase or sale order has been, or will be entered on behalf of the same or different persons.

ANNOTATIONS

The section requires an "intent to create a false or misleading appearance of active public interest", and if the purpose is merely to stabilize the market price in the accused's own interest, an offence has not been committed: *R. v. Jay,* [1966] 1 C.C.C. 70 (Ont. C.A.).

For the offence of knowingly entering a cross-order the Crown need not prove that the cross-trade involved either fictitious persons or persons involved with the accused in a fraudulent conspiracy, since the purpose of this section is to prevent fraudulent misuse of the facilities of a market for profit: *R. v. MacMillan,* [1969] 2 C.C.C. 289, 66 D.L.R. (2d) 680 (Ont. C.A.).

The words "or other market" in this section include an "over-the-counter" market: *R. v. Bluestein* (1982), 70 C.C.C. (2d) 336, 36 C.R. (3d) 46, 142 D.L.R. (3d) 71 (Que. C.A.).

PROHIBITED INSIDER TRADING / Tipping / Saving / Definition of "inside information".

382.1 (1) A person is guilty of an indictable offence and liable to imprisonment for a term not exceeding ten years who, directly or indirectly, buys or sells a security, knowingly using inside information that they

(*a*) possess by virtue of being a shareholder of the issuer of that security;

(*b*) possess by virtue of, or obtained in the course of, their business or professional relationship with that issuer;

(*c*) possess by virtue of, or obtained in the course of, a proposed takeover or reorganization of, or amalgamation, merger or similar business combination with, that issuer;

(*d*) possess by virtue of, or obtained in the course of, their employment, office, duties or occupation with that issuer or with a person referred to in paragraphs (*a*) to (*c*); or

(*e*) obtained from a person who possesses or obtained the information in a manner referred to in paragraphs (*a*) to (*d*).

(2) Except when necessary in the course of business, a person who knowingly conveys inside information that they possess or obtained in a manner referred to in subsection (1) to another person, knowing that there is a risk that the person will use the information to buy or sell, directly or indirectly, a security to which the information relates, or that they may convey the information to another person who may buy or sell such a security, is guilty of

(*a*) an indictable offence and liable to imprisonment for a term not exceeding five years; or

(*b*) an offence punishable on summary conviction.

(3) For greater certainty, an act is not an offence under this section if it is authorized or required, or is not prohibited, by any federal or provincial Act or regulation applicable to it.

(4) In this section, "inside information" means information relating to or affecting the issuer of a security or a security that they have issued, or are about to issue, that

(*a*) has not been generally disclosed; and

(*b*) could reasonably be expected to significantly affect the market price or value of a security of the issuer. 2004, c. 3, s. 5.

CROSS-REFERENCES

Other offences relating to trading in securities, etc., include fraud (s. 380), "wash trading" (s. 382) and false prospectus (s. 400).

Section 380.1 provides that, in sentencing an offender for the offence under this section, the court shall consider as aggravating circumstances the magnitude, complexity, duration or degree of planning of the fraud; that the offence adversely affected or had the potential to adversely affect the stability of the Canadian economy or financial system or any financial market in Canada or investor confidence in such markets; the offence involved a large number of victims; the offence had a significant impact on the victims given their personal circumstances such as age, health and financial situation; in committing the offence, the offender took advantage of the high regard in which the offender was held in the community; the offender did not comply with a licensing requirement or professional standard; and that the offender concealed or destroyed records. As well, the offender's employment, employment skills, or status or reputation in the community are not to be considered as mitigating factors if those circumstances were relevant to, contributed to, or were used in the commission of the offence. Section 380.1(2) requires the court to consider as an aggravating circumstance that the value of the fraud committed exceeded one million dollars. Section 380.1(3) requires the sentencing court to state the aggravating and mitigating circumstances that it took into account.

Sections 487.012 to 487.017 provide procedures for the making of production orders that would require persons to produce documents, data or information to police officers or public officers designated in the order.

SYNOPSIS

This section creates the offence of insider trading. Provincial statutes create offences or provide a civil remedy for some forms of insider trading. This section recognizes the provincial interest by providing in subsec. (3) that an act is not an offence under this section if it is authorized or required, or is not prohibited, by any other federal or provincial Act or regulation. The section creates two types of offences: insider trading where the insider uses the information for his or her own benefit by buying or selling securities, and tipping where the insider provides the information to another person to use for their benefit. Subsection (1) defines the insider trading offence and provides that the offender is liable to a maximum term of imprisonment of 10 years. The essence of that offence is directly or indirectly buying or selling a security knowingly using inside information that the person has acquired in any of the ways set out in paras. (*a*) to (*e*), for example by virtue of being a shareholder or because of a professional relationship with the security issuer. Subsection (2) defines the tipping offence where the person knowingly conveys to another inside information that they possess or obtained in a manner referred to in subsec. (1), knowing that there is a risk that the other person will use the information themselves to buy or sell, directly or indirectly, a security to which the information relates or convey the information to another person who will buy or sell such security. The tipping offence is a hybrid offence and on indictment is punishable by a maximum of five years' imprisonment.

Subsection (4) defines inside information as information that has not generally been disclosed and could reasonably be expected to "significantly" affect the market price or value of a security.

GAMING IN STOCKS OR MERCHANDISE / Onus.

383. (1) Every one is guilty of an indictable offence and liable to imprisonment for a term not exceeding five years who, with intent to make gain or profit by the rise or fall in price of the stock of an incorporated or unincorporated company or undertaking, whether in or outside Canada, or of any goods, wares or merchandise,

(*a*) makes or signs, or authorizes to be made or signed, any contract or agreement, oral or written, purporting to be for the purchase or sale of shares of stock or goods, wares or merchandise, without the *bona fide* intention of acquiring the shares, goods, wares or merchandise or of selling them, as the case may be, or

(*b*) makes or signs, or authorizes to be made or signed, any contract or agreement, oral or written, purporting to be for the sale or purchase of shares of stock or goods, wares or merchandise in respect of which no delivery of the thing sold or purchased is made or received, and without the *bona fide* intention of making or receiving delivery thereof, as the case may be,

but this section does not apply where a broker, on behalf of a purchaser, receives delivery, notwithstanding that the broker retains or pledges what is delivered as security for the advance of the purchase money or any part thereof.

(2) Where, in proceedings under this section, it is established that the accused made or signed a contract or agreement for the sale or purchase of shares of stock or goods, wares or merchandise, or acted, aided or abetted in the making or signing thereof, the burden of proof of a *bona fide* intention to acquire or to sell the shares, goods, wares or merchandise or to deliver or to receive delivery thereof, as the case may be, lies on the accused. R.S., C. C-34, s. 341.

CROSS-REFERENCES

The term "goods" is defined in s. 379.

The accused may elect his mode of trial pursuant to s. 536(2). Release pending trial is determined by s. 515, although the accused is eligible for release by the officer in charge pursuant to s. 498.

The related offence of fraud is described in s. 380, of wash-trading in s. 382, of a broker reducing stock by selling for his own account in s. 384 and of circulating a false prospectus in s. 400.

SYNOPSIS

This section describes the indictable offence of dealing in stocks or merchandise *with the intention of profiting* by the variation in the price of those goods but *without* the *bona fide intention of acquiring, selling*, or *making* or *receiving delivery* of the goods. Subsection (1) exempts brokers from this offence in certain circumstances. Subsection (2) states that when it has been established that the accused has made or signed an agreement for the sale or purchase of stocks or merchandise, or acted, aided and abetted in such a transaction, the burden of proof to establish the *bona fide* intention described in subsec. (1), lies on the accused. The maximum term of imprisonment upon conviction is five years.

BROKER REDUCING STOCK BY SELLING FOR HIS OWN ACCOUNT.

384. Every one is guilty of an indictable offence and liable to imprisonment for a term not exceeding five years who, being an individual, or a member or an employee of a partnership, or a director, an officer or an employee of a corporation, where he or the partnership or corporation is employed as a broker by any customer to buy and carry on margin any shares of an incorporated or unincorporated company or undertaking, whether in or out of Canada, thereafter sells or causes to be sold shares of the company or undertaking for any account in which

(*a*) he or his firm or a partner thereof, or

(*b*) the corporation or a director thereof,

has a direct or indirect interest, if the effect of the sale is, otherwise than unintentionally, to reduce the amount of those shares in the hands of the broker or under his control in the ordinary course of business below the amount of those shares that the broker should be carrying for all customers. R.S., c. C-34, s. 342.

CROSS-REFERENCES

The accused may elect his mode of trial pursuant to s. 536(2). Release pending trial is determined by s. 515, although the accused is eligible for release by the officer in charge pursuant to s. 498.

The related offence of fraud is described in s. 380, of wash-trading in s. 382, of gaming in stocks or merchandise in s. 383 and of circulating a false prospectus in s. 400.

SYNOPSIS

This section describes an indictable offence in which a broker sells shares that have been bought and carried on margin for any account in which the broker, his firm, partner, corporation or corporate director has direct or indirect interest. The effect of the sale must be to reduce *intentionally* the amount of those shares in the hands or under the control of the broker below the amount of those shares that the broker should be carrying for all customers. The maximum term of imprisonment for this offence is five years.

FRAUDULENT CONCEALMENT OF TITLE DOCUMENTS / Consent required.

385. (1) Every one who, being a vendor or mortgagor of property or of a chose in action or being a solicitor for or agent of a vendor or mortgagor of property or a chose in action, is served with a written demand for an abstract of title by or on behalf of the purchaser or mortgagee before the completion of the purchase or mortgage, and who

(*a*) with intent to defraud and for the purpose of inducing the purchaser or mortgagee to accept the title offered or produced to him, conceals from him any settlement, deed, will or other instrument material to the title, or any encumbrance on the title, or

(*b*) falsifies any pedigree on which the title depends,

is guilty of an indictable offence and liable to imprisonment for a term not exceeding two years.

(2) No proceedings shall be instituted under this section without the consent of the Attorney General. R.S., c. C-34, s. 343.

CROSS-REFERENCES

"Property" and "Attorney General" are defined in s. 2. Section 583(*h*) provides that a count in an indictment is not insufficient by reason only that it does not state that the required consent has been obtained. [As to notes concerning sufficiency of consent, see s. 583.]

Other offences relating to registers are found ss. 377 and 378 and the offence of fraudulent registration of title is in s. 386 and of fraudulent sale of real property in s. 387. By virtue of s. 583, an indictment which otherwise complies with s. 581 is not insufficient by reason only that: para. (*b*), it fails to name the person who owns or has a special property or interest in property mentioned in the count or para. (*c*), it charges an intent to defraud without naming or describing the person whom it was intended to defraud. Also note s. 588 which deems certain persons to have a property interest in property of which they have the management, control or custody. Under s. 586, no count alleging fraud is insufficient by reason only that it does not set out in detail the nature of the fraud. However, under s. 587(1)(*b*), the court may order particulars of any fraud that is alleged.

The accused may elect his mode of trial pursuant to s. 536(2). Release pending trial is determined by s. 515, although the accused is eligible for release by the officer in charge pursuant to s. 498.

CR. CODE

SYNOPSIS

This section describes the indictable offence of concealing any settlement, deed, will or other instrument material to title, concealing any encumbrance on the title (subsec. (1)(*a*)), or falsifying any pedigree on which the title depends (subsec. (1)(*b*)). The accused must be a vendor or mortgagor of property or a chose in action or a solicitor or agent for the vendor or mortgagor, and must have been served with a written demand for an abstract of title by or on behalf of the purchaser or mortgagee prior to the completion of the purchase or mortgage. In proceedings under subsec. (1)(*a*), the accused must both intend to defraud and to induce the purchaser or mortgagee to accept the title offered. Subsection (2) requires the consent of the Attorney General for the institution of proceedings under this section. The maximum term of imprisonment for this offence is two years.

FRAUDULENT REGISTRATION OF TITLE.

386. Every one who, as principal or agent, in a proceeding to register title to real property, or in a transaction relating to real property that is or is proposed to be registered, knowingly and with intent to deceive,

(*a*) makes a material false statement or representation,

(*b*) suppresses or conceals from a judge or registrar, or any person employed by or assisting the registrar, any material document, fact, matter or information, or

(*c*) is privy to anything mentioned in paragraph (*a*) or (*b*),

is guilty of an indictable offence and liable to imprisonment for a term not exceeding five years. R.S., c. C-34, s. 344.

CROSS-REFERENCES

The accused may elect his mode of trial pursuant to s. 536(2). Release pending trial is determined by s. 515, although the accused is eligible for release by the officer in charge pursuant to s. 498.

Related offences: s. 380, fraud; s. 385, fraudulent concealment of title document; s. 387, fraudulent sale of real property.

SYNOPSIS

This section describes the indictable offence of knowingly, and with intent to deceive, making a *material false* statement or representation, of suppressing or concealing from a judge, a registrar, or any person assisting the registrar, any *material* document, fact, matter or information, or of being privy to any of these activities, in a proceeding to register title to real property. The accused must be either the principal or agent in the real estate transaction. The maximum term of imprisonment upon conviction is five years.

FRAUDULENT SALE OF REAL PROPERTY.

387. Every one who, knowing of an unregistered prior sale or of an existing unregistered grant, mortgage, hypothec, privilege or encumbrance of or on real property, fraudulently sells the property or any part thereof is guilty of an indictable offence and liable to imprisonment for a term not exceeding two years. R.S., c. C-34, s. 345.

CROSS-REFERENCES

While there is no definition of "fraudulently" which is universally applicable, generally speaking, it refers to conduct which is dishonest and morally wrong: *R. v. DeMarco* (1973), 13 C.C.C. (2d) 369 (Ont. C.A.).

The accused may elect his mode of trial pursuant to s. 536(2). Release pending trial is determined by s. 515, although the accused is eligible for release by the officer in charge pursuant to s. 498.

Related offences: s. 380, fraud; s. 385, fraudulent concealment of title documents; s. 386, fraudulent registration of title.

SYNOPSIS

This section describes the fraudulent sale of real estate. Any person who fraudulently sells property, either in whole or in part, knowing of the existence of an unregistered prior sale or an existing unregistered grant, mortgage or other encumbrance on real property, is guilty of an indictable offence and liable to a maximum term of two years' imprisonment.

MISLEADING RECEIPT.

388. Every one who wilfully

(*a*) with intent to mislead, injure or defraud any person, whether or not that person is known to him, gives to a person anything in writing that purports to be a receipt for or an acknowledgment of property that has been delivered to or received by him, before the property referred to in the purported receipt or acknowledgment has been delivered to or received by him, or

(*b*) accepts, transmits or uses a purported receipt or acknowledgment to which paragraph (*a*) applies,

is guilty of an indictable offence and liable to imprisonment for a term not exceeding two years. R.S., c. C-34, s. 346.

CROSS-REFERENCES

The terms "person" and "property" are defined in s. 2.

Note that s. 391 provides that where an offence is committed under this section by a person who acts in the name of a corporation, firm or partnership, no person other than the person who does the act by means of which the offence is committed or who is secretly privy to it is guilty of the offence.

The accused may elect his mode of trial pursuant to s. 536(2). Release pending trial is determined by s. 515, although the accused is eligible for release by the officer in charge pursuant to s. 498.

SYNOPSIS

This section describes the offence of dealing with a misleading receipt. Every person who *wilfully*, with *intent to mislead, injure*, or *defraud* another person, gives to any person anything in writing that purports to be a receipt for property prior to the delivery of that property is guilty of an offence. Any person who *wilfully* accepts, transmits or uses a receipt as described above is also guilty of an offence. The offence is indictable and carries a maximum term of two years' imprisonment.

FRAUDULENT DISPOSAL OF GOODS ON WHICH MONEY ADVANCED / Saving.

389. (1) Every one who

(*a*) having shipped or delivered to the keeper of a warehouse or to a factor, an agent or a carrier, anything on which the consignee thereof has advanced money or has given valuable security, thereafter, with intent to deceive, defraud or injure the consignee, disposes of it in a manner that is different from and inconsistent with any agreement that has been made in that behalf between him and the consignee, or

(*b*) knowingly and wilfully aids or assists any person to make a disposition of anything to which paragraph (*a*) applies for the purpose of deceiving, defrauding or injuring the consignee,

is guilty of an indictable offence and liable to imprisonment for a term not exceeding two years.

(2) No person is guilty of an offence under this section where, before disposing of anything in a manner that is different from and inconsistent with any agreement that has been made in that behalf between him and the consignee, he pays or tenders to the consignee the full amount of money or valuable security that the consignee has advanced. R.S., c. C-34, s. 347.

CROSS-REFERENCES

The term "valuable security" is defined in s. 2.

By virtue of s. 583, an indictment which otherwise complies with s. 581 is not insufficient by reason only that: para. (*b*), it fails to name the person who owns or has a special property or interest in property mentioned in the count or para. (*c*), it charges an intent to defraud without naming or describing the person whom it was intended to defraud. Also note s. 588 which deems certain persons to have a property interest in property of which they have the management, control or custody. Under s. 586, no count alleging fraud is insufficient by reason only that it does not set out in detail the nature of the fraud. However, under s. 587(1)(*b*), the court may order particulars of any fraud that is alleged.

Note that s. 391 provides that where an offence is committed under this section by a person who acts in the name of a corporation, firm or partnership, no person other than the person who does the act by means of which the offence is committed or who is secretly privy to it is guilty of the offence.

The accused may elect his mode of trial pursuant to s. 536(2). Release pending trial is determined by s. 515, although the accused is eligible for release by the officer in charge pursuant to s. 498.

SYNOPSIS

This section describes the offence of fraudulently disposing of goods that have been shipped or delivered to the keeper of a warehouse or to a factor, an agent or a carrier. Every person who has shipped to one of the above-named individuals goods upon which the consignee has advanced money, and who, *with intent to defraud* or *injure* the consignee, disposes of the goods in a fashion that is inconsistent with any agreement made between himself and the consignee, is guilty of an indictable offence and liable to a maximum term of two years' imprisonment. A person who *knowingly* and *wilfully* aids or assists another person to commit the offence described above *for the purpose of deceiving, defrauding or injuring* the consignee, is also guilty of the offence and subject to the same punishment. Subsection (2) provides a defence to the charge where a person pays back the full amount of money advanced by the consignee *prior* to disposing of anything in a fashion that contravenes their agreement.

FRAUDULENT RECEIPTS UNDER *BANK ACT*.

390. Every one is guilty of an indictable offence and liable to imprisonment for a term not exceeding two years who

(*a*) wilfully makes a false statement in any receipt, certificate or acknowledgment for anything that may be used for a purpose mentioned in the *Bank Act*; or

(*b*) wilfully,

(i) after giving to another person,

(ii) after a person employed by him has, to his knowledge, given to another person, or

(iii) after obtaining and endorsing or assigning to another person,

any receipt, certificate or acknowledgment for anything that may be used for a purpose mentioned in the *Bank Act*, without the consent in writing of the holder or endorsee or the production and delivery of the receipt, certificate or acknowledgment, alienates or parts with, or does not deliver

to the holder or owner the property mentioned in the receipt, certificate or acknowledgment. R.S., c. C-34, s. 348.

CROSS-REFERENCES

The terms "every one", "person" and "property" are defined in s. 2.

Note that s. 391 provides that where an offence is committed under this section by a person who acts in the name of a corporation, firm or partnership, no person other than the person who does the act by means of which the offence is committed or who is secretly privy to it is guilty of the offence.

The accused may elect his mode of trial pursuant to s. 536(2). Release pending trial is determined by s. 515, although the accused is eligible for release by the officer in charge pursuant to s. 498.

SYNOPSIS

This section describes the offence of *fraudulently* dealing in receipts made for a purpose mentioned in the *Bank Act*. Paragraph (*a*) states that any person who *wilfully* makes a false statement in a receipt or other similar document that may be used for a purpose mentioned in the *Bank Act* commits an indictable offence and is liable to a maximum term of imprisonment of two years. Paragraph (*b*) also makes it an offence punishable on the same terms for a person to *wilfully* dispose of or fail to deliver the relevant property to a person to whom the accused has given or endorsed over a *Bank Act* receipt mentioning that property. The accused can raise the defence of written consent by the holder or endorsee of the receipt, or produce and deliver the receipt.

ANNOTATIONS

The words "receipt, certificate or acknowledgment for anything that may be used for a purpose mentioned in the *Bank Act*" have the same meaning in both paras. (*a*) and (*b*) and refer to documents which are evidence of title to property and which may be transferred by endorsement or delivery: *R. v. Dubois* (1979), 45 C.C.C. (2d) 531 (Ont. C.A.).

391. [*Repealed*, 2003, c. 21, s. 6.]

DISPOSAL OF PROPERTY TO DEFRAUD CREDITORS.

392. Every one who,

(*a*) with intent to defraud his creditors,

(i) makes or causes to be made a gift, conveyance, assignment, sale, transfer or delivery of his property, or

(ii) removes, conceals or disposes of any of his property, or

(*b*) with intent that any one should defraud his creditors, receives any property by means of or in relation to which an offence has been committed under paragraph (*a*),

is guilty of an indictable offence and liable to imprisonment for a term not exceeding two years. R.S., c. C-34, s. 350.

CROSS-REFERENCES

The term "property" is defined in s. 2.

By virtue of s. 583, an indictment which otherwise complies with s. 581 is not insufficient by reason only that: para. (*b*), it fails to name the person who owns or has a special property or interest in property mentioned in the count or para. (*c*), it charges an intent to defraud without naming or describing the person whom it was intended to defraud. Also note s. 588 which deems certain persons to have a property interest in property of which they have the management, control or custody.

Reference should also be made to the offences created by the *Bankruptcy Act* [now *Bankruptcy and Insolvency Act*], R.S.C. 1985, c. B-2.

The accused may elect his mode of trial pursuant to s. 536(2). Release pending trial is determined by s. 515, although the accused is eligible for release by the officer in charge pursuant to s. 498.

SYNOPSIS

This section describes the offence of disposing of property in order to defraud creditors. Every person who makes a gift, assignment or transfer of his property, or who conceals or disposes of it *with the intent to defraud his creditors* commits an indictable offence under para. (*a*). Similarly, a person who receives any property that has been dealt with in a fashion described in para. (*a*) *with the intent that anyone should defraud his creditors* is guilty of an indictable offence and liable to the same punishment of a maximum term of two years' imprisonment.

ANNOTATIONS

The giving of a third mortgage comes within the meaning of the words "makes an assignment" in this section: *R. v. Ehresman* (1980), 58 C.C.C. (2d) 574, 121 D.L.R. (3d) 505 (B.C.C.A.).

The word "conceals" in para. (*a*)(ii) is used in its primary sense of a positive act of secreting. Thus, the mere failure of a bankrupt to disclose the existence of property to the trustee and Official Receiver, as required by the *Bankruptcy Act*, R.S.C. 1970, c. B-3, does not constitute an offence under para. (*a*)(ii): *R. v. Goulis* (1981), 60 C.C.C. (2d) 347, 20 C.R. (3d) 360 (Ont. C.A.).

FRAUD IN RELATION TO FARES, ETC. / Idem / Fraudulently obtaining transportation.

393. (1) Every one whose duty it is to collect a fare, toll, ticket or admission who wilfully

(*a*) fails to collect it,

(*b*) collects less than the proper amount payable in respect thereof, or

(*c*) accepts any valuable consideration for failing to collect it or for collecting less than the proper amount payable in respect thereof,

is guilty of an indictable offence and liable to imprisonment for a term not exceeding two years.

(2) Every one who gives or offers to a person whose duty it is to collect a fare, toll, ticket or admission fee any valuable consideration

(*a*) for failing to collect it, or

(*b*) for collecting an amount less than the amount payable in respect thereof,

is guilty of an indictable offence and liable to imprisonment for a term not exceeding two years.

(3) Every one who, by any false pretence or fraud, unlawfully obtains transportation by land, water or air is guilty of an offence punishable on summary conviction. R.S., c. C-34, s. 351.

CROSS-REFERENCES

By virtue of s. 583, an indictment which otherwise complies with s. 581 is not sufficient by reason only that: para. (*b*), it fails to name the person who owns or has a special property or interest in property mentioned in the count or para. (*c*), it charges an intent to defraud without naming or describing the person whom it was intended to defraud. Under s. 586, no count alleging false pretences or fraud is insufficient by reason only that it does not set out in detail the nature of the false pretences or fraud. However, under s. 587(1)(*b*), the court may order particulars of any false pretence or fraud that is alleged.

The offences in subsecs. (1) and (2) are indictable offences, but, by virtue of s. 553(*c*)(viii), are offences over which a provincial court judge has absolute jurisdiction and does not depend on the consent of the accused. That is, the accused does not have an election as to mode of trial, although the provincial court judge may, by virtue of s. 555(1), elect to continue the proceedings as a preliminary inquiry, in which case, the accused is deemed to have elected trial by judge and jury pursuant to s. 565(1)(*a*). The trial of the offence in subsec. (3) is conducted by a summary conviction court pursuant to Part XXVII. The punishment for the offence in subsec. (3) is as set out in s. 787 and the limitation period is set out in s. 786(2). For all offences under this section, release pending trial is determined by s. 515, although the accused is eligible for release by a peace officer under s. 496, 497 or by the officer in charge under s. 498.

Also see s. 454 which creates the offence of producing, etc., or possession of slugs to be fraudulently used in substitution for coins or tokens of value.

SYNOPSIS

This section describes the offence of fraud in relation to fares. Subsection (1) states that any person who *has a duty to collect* a fare, toll, ticket or admission and who *wilfully* fails to collect it, collects less than the full amount, or accepts valuable consideration for failing to collect, or collecting less than the proper amount, is guilty of an indictable offence and liable to a term of imprisonment not exceeding two years. Subsection (2) makes it an offence to give or offer to a person whose duty it is to collect a fare, toll, ticket or admission any valuable consideration for failing to collect the amount payable. This offence is indictable and carries a maximum term of imprisonment of two years. Subsection (3) describes the summary conviction offence of unlawfully obtaining transportation by any false pretence or fraud.

FRAUD IN RELATION TO VALUABLE MINERALS / Sale of valuable minerals / Purchase of valuable minerals / Presumption / Offence / Forfeiture / Exception.

394. (1) No person who is the holder of a lease or licence issued under an Act relating to the mining of valuable minerals, or by the owner of land that is supposed to contain valuable minerals, shall

(*a*) by a fraudulent device or contrivance, defraud or attempt to defraud any person of

(i) any valuable minerals obtained under or reserved by the lease or licence, or

(ii) any money or valuable interest or thing payable in respect of valuable minerals obtained or rights reserved by the lease or licence; or

(*b*) fraudulently conceal or make a false statement with respect to the amount of valuable minerals obtained under the lease or licence.

(2) No person, other than the owner or the owner's agent or someone otherwise acting under lawful authority, shall sell any valuable mineral that is unrefined, partly refined, uncut or otherwise unprocessed.

(3) No person shall buy any valuable mineral that is unrefined, partly refined, uncut or otherwise unprocessed from anyone who the person has reason to believe is not the owner or the owner's agent or someone otherwise acting under lawful authority.

(4) In any proceeding in relation to subsection (2) or (3), in the absence of evidence raising a reasonable doubt to the contrary, it is presumed that

(*a*) in the case of a sale, the seller is not the owner of the valuable mineral or the owner's agent or someone otherwise acting under lawful authority; and

(*b*) in the case of a purchase, the purchaser, when buying the valuable mineral, had reason to believe that the seller was not the owner of the mineral or the owner's agent or someone otherwise acting under lawful authority.

(5) A person who contravenes subsection (1), (2) or (3) is guilty of an indictable offence and liable to imprisonment for a term of not more than five years.

(6) If a person is convicted of an offence under this section, the court may order anything by means of or in relation to which the offence was committed, on such conviction, to be forfeited to Her Majesty.

(7) Subsection (6) does not apply to real property other than real property built or significantly modified for the purpose of facilitating the commission of an offence under this section. R.S., c. C-34, s. 352; R.S.C. 1985, c. 27 (1st Supp.), s. 186; 1999, c. 5, s. 10.

CROSS-REFERENCES

"Valuable mineral" is defined in s. 2. Section 394.1 makes it an offence to possess any unprocessed mineral that has been stolen or dealt with contrary to this section. A justice may issue a search warrant to search for any valuable mineral that is deposited contrary to this Act or any other Act of Parliament, under s. 395. Offences in relation to mines are set out in s. 396. Section 656 creates a presumption of theft or unlawful possession in any proceeding in relation to theft or possession of a valuable mineral that is unrefined, partly refined, uncut or otherwise unprocessed by any person actively engaged in or on a mine.

SYNOPSIS

This section creates a number of offences that in general deal with fraud in relation to valuable minerals (as defined in s. 2). Subsection (1) creates fraud offences for persons holding a lease or licence relating to mining of valuable minerals or persons owning land purporting to contain valuable minerals. Subsection (2) prohibits the sale of unrefined, partly refined, uncut or otherwise unprocessed valuable minerals except by the owner, the owner's agent or a person acting under lawful authority. Under subsec. (4)(*a*), the seller is presumed not to be the owner, the owner's agent or a person acting under lawful authority in the absence of evidence raising a reasonable doubt. Subsection (3) makes it an offence to buy such material from anyone other than a person the accused has reason to believe is not the owner, the owner's agent or a person acting under lawful authority. Subsection (4)(*b*) creates a presumption that the purchaser knew the seller was not the owner, the owner's agent or a person acting under lawful authority, in the absence of evidence raising a reasonable doubt. The offences under this section are indictable and punishable by not more than five years' imprisonment. Under subsec. (6), anything by means of or in relation to which the offence was committed may be forfeited to the Crown. That subsection, however, does not apply to real property, unless the real property has been built or significantly modified for the purpose of facilitating commission of an offence under this section.

POSSESSION OF STOLEN OR FRAUDULENTLY OBTAINED VALUABLE MINERALS / Evidence / Offence / Forfeiture / Exception.

394.1 (1) No person shall possess any valuable mineral that is unrefined, partly refined, uncut or otherwise unprocessed that has been stolen or dealt with contrary to section 394.

(2) Reasonable grounds to believe that the valuable mineral has been stolen or dealt with contrary to section 394 are, in the absence of evidence raising a reasonable doubt to the contrary, proof that the valuable mineral has been stolen or dealt with contrary to section 394.

(3) A person who contravenes subsection (1) is guilty of an indictable offence and liable to imprisonment for a term of not more than five years.

(4) If a person is convicted of an offence under this section, the court may, on that conviction, order that anything by means of or in relation to which the offence was committed be forfeited to Her Majesty.

(5) Subsection (4) does not apply to real property, other than real property built or significantly modified for the purpose of facilitating the commission of an offence under subsection (3). 1999, c. 5, s. 10.

CROSS-REFERENCES

"Valuable mineral" is defined in s. 2. Section 394 creates fraud offences for persons holding a lease or licence relating to mining of valuable minerals or persons owning land purporting to contain valuable minerals and prohibits the unauthorized sale or purchase of unrefined, partly refined, uncut or otherwise unprocessed valuable minerals. A justice may issue a search warrant to search for any valuable mineral that is deposited contrary to this Act or any other Act of Parliament, under s. 395. Offences in relation to mines are set out in s. 396. Section 656 creates a presumption of theft or unlawful possession in any proceeding in relation to theft or possession of a valuable mineral that is unrefined, partly refined, uncut or otherwise unprocessed by any person actively engaged in or on a mine.

SYNOPSIS

This section creates offences that complement the offences under s. 394 by making it an offence to possess unrefined, partly refined, uncut or otherwise unprocessed valuable minerals that have been dealt with contrary to s. 394 or have been stolen. Subsection (2) creates a presumption that the valuable mineral was stolen or dealt with contrary to s. 394, in the absence of evidence raising a reasonable doubt, if there are reasonable grounds to believe that the valuable mineral has been stolen or dealt with contrary to s. 394. The offences under this section are indictable and punishable by not more than five years' imprisonment. Under subsec. (4), anything by means of or in relation to which the offence was committed may be forfeited to the Crown. That subsection, however, does not apply to real property, unless the real property has been built or significantly modified for the purpose of facilitating commission of an offence under this section.

SEARCH FOR VALUABLE MINERALS / Power to seize / Appeal.

395. (1) If an information in writing is laid under oath before a justice by a peace officer or by a public officer who has been appointed or designated to administer or enforce a federal or provincial law and whose duties include the enforcement of this Act or any other Act of Parliament and the justice is satisfied that there are reasonable grounds to believe that, contrary to this Act or any other Act of Parliament, any valuable mineral is deposited in a place or held by a person, the justice may issue a warrant authorizing a peace officer or a public officer, if the public officer is named in it, to search any of the places or persons mentioned in the information.

(2) Where, on search, anything mentioned in subsection (1) is found, it shall be seized and carried before the justice who shall order

(*a*) that it be detained for the purposes of an inquiry or a trial; or

(*b*) if it is not detained for the purposes of an inquiry or a trial,

(i) that it be restored to the owner, or

(ii) that it be forfeited to Her Majesty in right of the province in which the proceedings take place if the owner cannot be ascertained.

(3) An appeal lies from an order made under paragraph (2)(*b*) in the manner in which an appeal lies in summary conviction proceedings under Part XXVII and the provisions of that Part relating to appeals apply to appeals under this subsection. R.S., c. C-34, s. 353; 1999, c. 5, s. 11.

CROSS-REFERENCES

The term "justice", "peace officer", "public officer" and "valuable mineral" are defined in s. 2.

SYNOPSIS

This section sets out a scheme for obtaining a warrant to search for valuable minerals. Subsection (1) requires that an information in writing and under oath be laid before a justice by a peace officer or public officer. The information must state that the valuable mineral is unlawfully held by a person or deposited in a place. The justice may issue a warrant to search any of the places or persons in the information. Subsection (2) provides that anything found as a result of a search conducted under subsec. (1) must be seized and carried before the justice who shall order that it be detained for inquiry or trial, or that it be restored to the owner, or forfeited to Her Majesty in right of the province in which the proceedings took place if the owner cannot be ascertained. Subsection (3) provides a right of appeal from any order that the items seized be given to the owner or Her Majesty.

OFFENCES IN RELATION TO MINES / Presumption.

396. (1) Every one who

(*a*) adds anything to or removes anything from any existing or prospective mine, mining claim or oil well with a fraudulent intent to affect the result of an assay, a test or a valuation that has been made or is to be made with respect to the mine, mining claim or oil well, or

(*b*) adds anything to, removes anything from or tampers with a sample or material that has been taken or is being or is about to be taken from any existing or prospective mine, mining claim or oil well for the purpose of being assayed, tested or otherwise valued, with a fraudulent intent to affect the result of the assay, test or valuation,

is guilty of an indictable offence and liable to imprisonment for a term not exceeding ten years.

(2) For the purposes of proceedings under subsection (1), evidence that

(*a*) something has been added to or removed from anything to which subsection (1) applies, or

(*b*) anything to which subsection (1) applies has been tampered with,

is, in the absence of any evidence to the contrary, proof of a fraudulent intent to affect the result of an assay, a test or a valuation. R.S., c. C-34, s. 354.

CROSS-REFERENCES

The accused may elect his mode of trial pursuant to s. 536(2). Release pending trial is determined by s. 515.

Other offences relating to mines are found in ss. 394 and 394.1.

Section 395 provides for the issuance of a search warrant to search for valuable minerals alleged to be unlawfully deposited or held contrary to law.

See s. 333 for defence on charge of theft where ore is taken for exploration or scientific investigation.

SYNOPSIS

This section describes two offences in relation to mines. Both offences relate to specified activities that would affect the result of a test or valuation of a mine, a mining claim or an oil well. Both offences also require that the accused have the *fraudulent intent* to affect the results of the test. These offences are indictable and carry a maximum term of 10 years' imprisonment. Subsection (2) creates a presumption that the prosecution may rely on to prove, in the absence of evidence to the contrary, the fraudulent intent required under subsec. (1). Evidence of the addition to, the removal from, or the tampering with anything to which subsec. (1) applies proves the criminal intent required for conviction under this section.

Falsification of Books and Documents

BOOKS AND DOCUMENTS / Privy.

397. (1) Every one who, with intent to defraud,

(*a*) destroys, mutilates, alters, falsifies, or makes a false entry in, or

(*b*) omits a material particular from, or alters a material particular in, a book, paper, writing, valuable security or document is guilty of an indictable offence and liable to imprisonment for a term not exceeding five years.

(2) Every one who, with intent to defraud his creditors, is privy to the commission of an offence under subsection (1) is guilty of an indictable offence and liable to imprisonment for a term not exceeding five years. R.S., c. C-34, s. 355.

CROSS-REFERENCES

The terms "valuable security" and "writing" are defined in s. 2. The term "document" is not defined for this Part but reference might be made to the definition in s. 321 for Part IX. By virtue of s. 583, an indictment which otherwise complies with s. 581 is not insufficient by reason only that: para. (*c*), it charges an intent to defraud without naming or describing the person whom it was intended to defraud. Under s. 586, no count alleging fraud is insufficient by reason only that it does not set out in detail the nature of the fraud. However, under s. 587(1)(*b*), the court may order particulars of any fraud that is alleged.

The accused may elect his mode of trial pursuant to s. 536(2). Release pending trial is determined by s. 515, although the accused is eligible for release by the officer in charge pursuant to s. 498.

This offence resembles the forgery and uttering offences and therefore see cross-references under ss. 366 to 368. Also see s. 392, disposal of property with intent to defraud creditors.

SYNOPSIS

This section describes the offence of destroying, mutilating, altering, falsifying, or omitting or altering a material particular in a book, paper, writing, valuable security or document. The accused must engage in the above-described activity with the *intent to defraud*. This is an indictable offence with a maximum term of five years' imprisonment. Subsection (2) states that every person who, *with the intent to defraud* his creditors, is privy to the offence described above is also guilty of an indictable offence which carries a maximum term of five years' imprisonment.

FALSIFYING EMPLOYMENT RECORD.

398. Every one who, with intent to deceive, falsifies an employment record by any means, including the punching of a time clock, is guilty of an offence punishable on summary conviction. R.S., c. C-34, s. 356.

CROSS-REFERENCES

Trial of this offence is conducted by a summary conviction court pursuant to Part XXVII.

The punishment is as set out in s. 787 and the limitation period is set out in s. 786(2).

Release pending trial is determined by s. 515, although the accused is eligible for release by a peace officer under s. 496, 497 or by the officer in charge under s. 498.

SYNOPSIS

This section describes the offence of falsifying an employment record. It states that every person who, *with the intent to deceive*, falsifies an employment record *by any means*, including the punching of a time clock, is guilty of a summary conviction offence.

FALSE RETURN BY PUBLIC OFFICER.

399. Every one who, being entrusted with the receipt, custody or management of any part of the public revenues, knowingly furnishes a false statement or return of

(*a*) any sum of money collected by him or entrusted to his care, or

(*b*) any balance of money in his hands or under his control,

is guilty of an indictable offence and liable to imprisonment for a term not exceeding five years. R.S., c. C-34, s. 357.

CROSS-REFERENCES

The accused may elect his mode of trial pursuant to s. 536(2). Release pending trial is determined by s. 515, although the accused is eligible for release by the officer in charge pursuant to s. 498.

Related offences: s. 122, breach of trust by public officer; s. 336, criminal breach of trust; s. 337, public servant refusing to deliver property.

SYNOPSIS

This section describes the offence of making a false return by a public officer. The offence is committed where a person entrusted with public revenues *knowingly* furnishes a false statement of any sum or balance of money entrusted to or controlled by him. The offence is indictable, with a maximum punishment of five years' imprisonment.

FALSE PROSPECTUS, ETC. / Definition of "company".

400. (1) Every one who makes, circulates or publishes a prospectus, a statement or an account, whether written or oral, that he knows is false in a material particular, with intent

- **(*a*) to induce persons, whether ascertained or not, to become shareholders or partners in a company,**
- **(*b*) to deceive or defraud the members, shareholders or creditors, whether ascertained or not, of a company, or**
- **(*c*) to induce any person to**
  - **(i) entrust or advance anything to a company, or**
  - **(ii) enter into any security for the benefit of a company,**

is guilty of an indictable offence and liable to imprisonment for a term not exceeding ten years.

(2) In this section, "company" means a syndicate, body corporate or company, whether existing or proposed to be created. R.S., c. C-34, s. 358; 1994, c. 44, s. 26.

CROSS-REFERENCES

The term "person" is defined in s. 2.

By virtue of s. 583, an indictment which otherwise complies with s. 581 is not insufficient by reason only that: para. (*c*), it charges an intent to defraud without naming or describing the person whom it was intended to defraud. Under s. 586, no count alleging fraud is insufficient by reason only that it does not set out in detail the nature of the fraud. However, under s. 587(1)(*b*), the court may order particulars of any fraud that is alleged.

Other offences relating to trading in securities, etc., are in ss. 380(2) and 382 to 384.

The accused may elect his mode of trial pursuant to s. 536(2). Release pending trial is determined by s. 515.

Section 380.1 provides that, in sentencing an offender for the offence under this section, the court shall consider as aggravating circumstances the magnitude, complexity, duration or degree of planning of the fraud; that the offence adversely affected or had the potential to adversely affect the stability of the Canadian economy or financial system or any financial market in Canada or investor confidence in such markets; the offence involved a large number of victims; the offence had a significant impact on the victims given their personal circumstances such as age, health and financial situation; in committing the offence, the offender took advantage of the high regard in which the offender was held in the community; the offender did not comply with a licensing requirement or professional standard; and that the offender concealed or destroyed records. As well, the offender's employment, employment skills, or status or reputation in the community are not to be considered as mitigating factors if those circumstances were relevant to, contributed to, or were used in the commission of the offence. Section 380.1(2) requires the court to consider as an aggravating circumstance that the value of the fraud committed exceeded one million dollars. Section 380.1(3) requires the sentencing court to state the aggravating and mitigating circumstances that it took into account.

Sections 487.012 to 487.017 provide procedures for the making of production orders that would require persons to provide documents or data.

SYNOPSIS

This section describes offences in relation to a false prospectus. Anyone who makes, circulates or publishes a prospectus, statement or account, whether written or oral, which he knows is false in a material particular, commits an indictable offence, if his purpose in so doing is one of those listed in subsec. (1)(*a*) to (*d*). Those purposes are: to induce anyone to become a shareholder or partner in a company; to deceive or defraud members, shareholders or creditors of a company; to induce anyone to entrust or advance anything to a company; or to enter into any security for the benefit of a company. The maximum punishment for this offence is imprisonment for 10 years.

ANNOTATIONS

The falsity, which need not amount to a false pretence, may be found in a statement of purposes, which the author never had any intention of carrying out. Furthermore, for a para. (*c*) offence, a count is not duplicitious merely because it expresses the alternative modes of carrying out the offence by making, circulating or publishing a false prospectus, and the phrase "any person" includes all unascertained persons of the class of people to whom it was intended to give the prospectus at the time of its preparation: *R. v. Cox and Paton,* [1963] S.C.R. 500, [1963] 2 C.C.C. 148, 40 C.R. 52 (5:0).

A material omission may render a statement false: *R. v. Colucci,* [1965] 4 C.C.C. 56, 46 C.R. 256 (Ont. C.A.).

Where the defence is that the false material particular was a mistaken belief as to the correctness of that particular the jury must determine whether the belief was an honest one which negatived the guilty knowledge required to be proven by the Crown: *R. v. Davidson* (1971), 3 C.C.C. (2d) 509, [1971] 4 W.W.R. 731 (B.C.C.A.) (2:1).

The intent to defraud is not an element of the para. (*a*) offence which only requires falsity in a material particular, the accused's knowledge of it, and an overt act with the intent to induce members of the public to become shareholders: *R. v. Scallen* (1974), 15 C.C.C. (2d) 441 (B.C.C.A.).

OBTAINING CARRIAGE BY FALSE BILLING / Forfeiture.

401. (1) Every one who, by means of a false or misleading representation, knowingly obtains or attempts to obtain the carriage of anything by any person into a country, province, district or other place, whether or not within Canada, where the importation or transportation of it is, in the circumstances of the case, unlawful is guilty of an offence punishable on summary conviction.

(2) Where a person is convicted of an offence under subsection (1), anything by means of or in relation to which the offence was committed, on such conviction, in addition to any punishment that is imposed, is forfeited to Her Majesty and shall be disposed of as the court may direct. R.S., c. C-34, s. 359.

CROSS-REFERENCES

Trial of this offence is conducted by a summary conviction court pursuant to Part XXVII.

The punishment is as set out in s. 787 and the limitation period is set out in s. 786(2).

Release pending trial is determined by s. 515, although the accused is eligible for release by a peace officer under s. 496, 497 or by the officer in charge under s. 498.

Section 414 provides for a presumption as to the port of shipment where an offence relates to imported goods.

The similar offence of fraudulently obtaining food and lodging is in s. 364 and fraud in relation to fares, etc., is in s. 393.

SYNOPSIS

This section describes the offence of obtaining carriage by false billing. Anyone *knowingly* obtaining or attempting to obtain the unlawful carriage or importation of anything to any place within or outside Canada by means of a false or misleading representation, commits a summary conviction offence. Upon conviction, anything by means of, or in relation to which the offence is committed is forfeited to the Crown, to be disposed of as the court directs.

402. [*Repealed*, 2018, c. 29, s. 44.]

Identity Theft and Identity Fraud

DEFINITION OF "IDENTITY INFORMATION".

402.1 For the purposes of sections 402.2 and 403, "identity information" means any information — including biological or physiological information — of a type that is commonly used alone or in combination with other information to identify or purport to identify an individual, including a fingerprint, voice print, retina image, iris image, DNA profile, name, address, date of birth, written signature, electronic signature, digital signature, user name, credit card number, debit card number, financial institution account number, passport number, Social Insurance Number, health insurance number, driver's licence number or password. 2009, c. 28, s. 10.

IDENTITY THEFT / Trafficking in identity information / Clarification / Jurisdiction / Punishment.

402.2 (1) Every person commits an offence who obtains or possesses another person's identity information with intent to use it to commit an indictable offence that includes fraud, deceit or falsehood as an element of the offence.

(2) Everyone commits an offence who transmits, makes available, distributes, sells or offers for sale another person's identity information, or has it in their possession for any of those purposes, knowing that or being reckless as to whether the information will be used to commit an indictable offence that includes fraud, deceit or falsehood as an element of the offence.

(3) For the purposes of subsections (1) and (2), an indictable offence referred to in either of those subsections includes an offence under any of the following sections:

(*a*) section 57 (forgery of or uttering forged passport);
(*b*) section 58 (fraudulent use of certificate of citizenship);
(*c*) section 130 (personating peace officer);
(*d*) section 131 (perjury);
(*e*) section 342 (theft, forgery, etc., of credit card);
(*f*) section 362 (false pretence or false statement);
(*g*) section 366 (forgery);
(*h*) section 368 (use, trafficking or possession of forged document);
(*i*) section 380 (fraud); and
(*j*) section 403 (identity fraud).

(4) An accused who is charged with an offence under subsection (1) or (2) may be tried and punished by any court having jurisdiction to try that offence in the place where the offence is alleged to have been committed or in the place where the accused is found, is

arrested or is in custody. However, no proceeding in respect of the offence shall be commenced in a province without the consent of the Attorney General of that province if the offence is alleged to have been committed outside that province.

(5) Everyone who commits an offence under subsection (1) or (2)

- **(*a*) is guilty of an indictable offence and liable to imprisonment for a term of not more than five years; or**
- **(*b*) is guilty of an offence punishable on summary conviction. 2009, c. 28, s. 10; 2018, c. 29, s. 45.**

CROSS-REFERENCES

"Attorney General" is defined in s. 2. "Identity information" is defined in s. 402.1. Section 403 creates the related offence of identity fraud. Section 56.1 creates the offence of procuring, making, possessing or transferring identity documents. Other related offences are: s. 57, offences in relation to passports; s. 130, personating a peace officer; s. 340, destroying identity documents; s. 342, unauthorized use of credit cards; s. 342.01, possession of instrument for copying credit cards; s. 362, obtaining by false pretences; s. 367, forgery; s. 368, use and trafficking in a forged document; s. 368.1, possession of instruments for purpose of committing forgery; s. 374, drawing a false document; s. 380, fraud; s. 403, identity fraud; s. 404, personation at an examination.

SYNOPSIS

This section, part of Bill S-4, a comprehensive scheme for dealing with identity theft and related offences, defines various forms of identity theft. Subsection (1) makes it an offence to knowingly obtain or possess another person's identity information under circumstances giving rise to a reasonable inference that the information is intended to be used to commit an indictable offence that includes fraud, deceit, or falsehood as an element of the offence. Subsection (2) in effect creates an offence of trafficking in identity information. Subsection (3) includes a non-exhaustive list of offences for the purposes of subsecs. (1) and (2). Subsection (4) creates a special rule for the place of trial of the offences in this section. The offence may be tried in the place where the offence is alleged to be committed or the place where the accused is found, arrested, or is in custody. However, where the offence was committed in another province, the consent of the Attorney General of the province where the offence is to be tried is required.

IDENTITY FRAUD / Clarification / Punishment.

403. (1) Everyone commits an offence who fraudulently personates another person, living or dead,

- **(*a*) with intent to gain advantage for themselves or another person;**
- **(*b*) with intent to obtain any property or an interest in any property;**
- **(*c*) with intent to cause disadvantage to the person being personated or another person; or**
- **(*d*) with intent to avoid arrest or prosecution or to obstruct, pervert or defeat the course of justice.**

(2) For the purposes of subsection (1), personating a person includes pretending to be the person or using the person's identity information — whether by itself or in combination with identity information pertaining to any person — as if it pertains to the person using it.

(3) Everyone who commits an offence under subsection (1)

- **(*a*) is guilty of an indictable offence and liable to imprisonment for a term of not more than 10 years; or**
- **(*b*) is guilty of an offence punishable on summary conviction. R.S., c. C-34, s. 361; 1994, c. 44, s. 27; 2009, c. 28, s. 10.**

CROSS-REFERENCES

"Identity information" is defined in s. 402.1. The related offence of identity theft is found in s. 402.2. Attempting to obstruct justice is also an offence under s. 139 and the general offence of fraud is found in s. 380. For other related offences, see notes under s. 402.1.

SYNOPSIS

This section, part of Bill S-4, a comprehensive scheme for dealing with identity theft and related offences, defines various forms of identity fraud, in general the fraudulent personation of another person, living or dead, to gain an advantage (paras. (1)(*a*) and (*b*)); to cause a disadvantage to another (para. (1)(*c*)); or with the intent to avoid arrest or prosecution or obstruct the course of justice (para. (1)(*d*)). Subsection (2) clarifies that personating a person includes pretending to be the person or using the person's identity information (a term defined in s. 402.1) as if it pertained to the person using it.

ANNOTATIONS

The word "advantage" in para. (*a*) is to be given its ordinary meaning and includes that which advances or serves or which gives profit and is thus not restricted to a pecuniary or economic advantage. Thus a personation to avoid arrest comes within this section: *R. v. Rozon* (1974), 28 C.R.N.S. 232 (Que. C.A.).

An impersonation in Canada to United States immigration authorities in order to obtain clearance to board an aircraft bound for the United States comes within this section. The offence is completely committed in Canada. Further, "advantage" is not confined to an economic or proprietary advantage and would include such a clearance. It does not matter that the ultimate effect of commission of the offence would be breach of the laws of a friendly country: *R. v. Hetsberger* (1980), 51 C.C.C. (2d) 257 (Ont. C.A.).

The word "person" in this section refers to a human being and does not include a fictitious person: *R. v. Northrup* (1982), 1 C.C.C. (3d) 210, 41 N.B.R. (2d) 610 (C.A.).

404. [*Repealed*, 2018, c. 29, s. 46.]

ACKNOWLEDGING INSTRUMENT IN FALSE NAME.

405. Every person who, without lawful authority or excuse, acknowledges, in the name of another person before a court or a judge or other person authorized to receive the acknowledgment, a recognizance of bail, a confession of judgment, a consent to judgment or a judgment, deed or other instrument, is guilty of an indictable offence and liable to imprisonment for a term of not more than five years. R.S., c. C-34, s. 363; 2018, c. 29, s. 46.

CROSS-REFERENCES

The accused may elect his mode of trial pursuant to s. 536(2). Release pending trial is determined by s. 515, although the accused is eligible for release by the officer in charge pursuant to s. 498.

Related offences: s. 130, personating a peace officer; s. 403, personation with intent; s. 404, personation at examination.

SYNOPSIS

This section describes the offence of acknowledging an instrument in a false name. The offence is committed where a person acknowledges before a court or other authorized person any of a variety of legal documents in the name of another person. A defence is available where the accused can establish that he committed the act with lawful authority or excuse. The offence is indictable, and punishable by a maximum term of five years' imprisonment.

ANNOTATIONS

To make out the offence under this section where the recognizance purports to be issued by an officer in charge pursuant to s. 503(2), other than the officer for the time being in command of the police force responsible for the lock-up or other place where the accused is taken after arrest, the Crown must prove that the accused acknowledged the recognizance in a name other than his own, that he acknowledged it before a person who is an officer in charge of the lock-up or place at the time the accused was taken to that place to be detained in custody and that the officer in charge is a peace officer who has been designated for the purpose of Part XVI by the officer for the time being in command of the police force responsible for the lock-up or other place to which the accused was taken after arrest: *R. v. Gendron* (1985), 22 C.C.C. (3d) 312 (Ont. C.A.).

Forgery of Trademarks and Trade Descriptions 2014, c. 20, s. 366(1).

FORGING TRADEMARK.

406. For the purposes of this Part, every one forges a trademark who

(*a*) without the consent of the proprietor of the trademark, makes or reproduces in any manner that trademark or a mark so nearly resembling it as to be calculated to deceive; or

(*b*) falsifies, in any manner, a genuine trademark. R.S., c. C-34, s. 364; 2014, c. 20, s. 366(1).

CROSS-REFERENCES

The term trade-mark is defined in s. 2 of the *Trade-marks Act*, R.S.C. 1985, c. T-13. The offences created in this Part relating to trade-marks and trade-names are found in ss. 407 to 411 and punished pursuant to s. 412. Some of those offences resemble the general fraud offence which is defined in s. 380 and forgery as defined in ss. 366 to 368.

SYNOPSIS

This section defines the offence of forgery of a trade-mark for the purposes of Part X of the Code, respecting fraudulent transactions. A person forges a trade-mark where he makes or reproduces the mark, or a mark so nearly resembling it as to be calculated to deceive, without the consent of the proprietor, or where he falsifies a genuine mark in any manner.

OFFENCE.

407. Every one commits an offence who, with intent to deceive or defraud the public or any person, whether ascertained or not, forges a trademark. R.S., c. C-34, s. 365; 2014, c. 20, s. 366(1).

CROSS-REFERENCES

The term "person" is defined in s. 2. The term trade-mark is defined in s. 2 of the *Trade-marks Act*, R.S.C. 1985, c. T-13.

Forging a trade-mark is defined in s. 406. By virtue of s. 583, an indictment which otherwise complies with s. 581 is not insufficient by reason only that: para. (*c*), it charges an intent to defraud without naming or describing the person whom it was intended to defraud. Under s. 586, no count alleging fraud is insufficient by reason only that it does not set out in detail the nature of the fraud. However, under s. 587(1)(*b*), the court may order particulars of any fraud that is alleged.

The punishment for this offence is set out in s. 412 and therefore see notes under that section with respect to mode of trial and release pending trial. Section 412(2) also provides for forfeiture of anything by means of or in relation to which a person commits an offence under this section.

This offence resembles the general forgery offence and therefore see ss. 366 to 368.

SYNOPSIS

This section creates the offence of forging a trade-mark. The offence is committed where the acts described in s. 406 are done with the intention to deceive or defraud any person or the public.

PASSING OFF.

408. Every one commits an offence who, with intent to deceive or defraud the public or any person, whether ascertained or not,

(*a*) passes off other wares or services as and for those ordered or required; or

(*b*) makes use, in association with wares or services, of any description that is false in a material respect regarding

(i) the kind, quality, quantity or composition,

(ii) the geographical origin, or

(iii) the mode of the manufacture, production or performance

of those wares or services. R.S., c. C-34, s. 366.

CROSS-REFERENCES

The term "person" is defined in s. 2.

By virtue of s. 583, an indictment which otherwise complies with s. 581 is not insufficient by reason only that: para. (*c*), it charges an intent to defraud without naming or describing the person whom it was intended to defraud. Under s. 586, no count alleging fraud is insufficient by reason only that it does not set out in detail the nature of the fraud. However, under s. 587(1)(*b*), the court may order particulars of any fraud that is alleged.

The punishment for this offence is set out in s. 412 and therefore see notes under that section with respect to mode of trial and release pending trial. Section 412(2) also provides for forfeiture of anything by means of or in relation to which a person commits an offence under this section.

Reference should also be made to the *Trade-marks Act*, R.S.C. 1985, c. T-13.

SYNOPSIS

This section describes the offence of "passing off". This offence is committed where a person, with the intention of deceiving any person or the public, passes off wares or services as being those actually ordered or required, or uses a description which is false in any of the material particulars enumerated in para. (*b*) in association with those wares or services.

INSTRUMENTS FOR FORGING TRADEMARK / Saving.

409. (1) Every one commits an offence who makes, has in his possession or disposes of a die, block, machine or other instrument, designed or intended to be used in forging a trademark.

(2) No person shall be convicted of an offence under this section where he proves that he acted in good faith in the ordinary course of his business or employment. R.S., c. C-34, s. 367; 2014, c. 20, s. 366(1).

CROSS-REFERENCES

The term trade-mark is defined in the *Trade-marks Act*, R.S.C. 1985, c. T-13. Forging a trade-mark is defined in s. 406. Possession is defined in s. 4(3). The punishment for this offence is set out in s. 412 and therefore see notes under that section with respect to mode of trial and release pending trial. Section 412(2) also provides for forfeiture of anything by means of or in relation to which a person commits an offence under this section.

SYNOPSIS

This section creates the offence of dealing with instruments for forging a trade-mark. The offence is committed where any person makes, possesses or disposes of an instrument designed or intended to be used in forging a trade-mark. A defence exists where the accused establishes that he acted in *good faith* in the ordinary course of his business or employment.

ANNOTATIONS

While the Crown need not show that the trade-mark was or is registered it must prove it to be a trade-mark as defined by the *Trade-marks Act*: *R. v. Strong Cobb Arner of Canada Ltd.* (1973), 15 C.C.C. (2d) 288, 2 O.R. (2d) 220 (H.C.J.), affd 16 C.C.C. (2d) 150, 2 O.R. (2d) 692 (C.A.).

OTHER OFFENCES IN RELATION TO TRADEMARKS.

410. Every one commits an offence who, with intent to deceive or defraud,

(*a*) defaces, conceals or removes a trademark or the name of another person from anything without the consent of that other person; or

(*b*) being a manufacturer, dealer, trader or bottler, fills any bottle or siphon that bears the trademark or name of another person, without the consent of that other person, with a beverage, milk, by-product of milk or other liquid commodity for the purpose of sale or traffic. R.S., c. C-34, s. 368; 2014, c. 20, s. 366(1).

CROSS-REFERENCES

The term trade-mark is defined in s. 2 of the *Trade-marks Act*, R.S.C. 1985, c. T-13. The term "person" is defined in s. 2. By virtue of s. 583, an indictment which otherwise complies with s. 581 is not insufficient by reason only that: para. (*c*), it charges an intent to defraud without naming or describing the person whom it was intended to defraud. Under s. 586, no count alleging fraud is insufficient by reason only that it does not set out in detail the nature of the fraud. However, under s. 587(1)(*b*), the court may order particulars of any fraud that is alleged.

The punishment for this offence is set out in s. 412 and therefore see notes under that section with respect to mode of trial and release pending trial. Section 412(2) also provides for forfeiture of anything by means of or in relation to which a person commits an offence under this section.

SYNOPSIS

This section creates additional offences in relation to trade-marks. Paragraph (*a*) provides that an offence is committed where any person defaces, conceals or removes a trade-mark or the name of another person from anything without consent, and with the intention to deceive or defraud. Paragraph (*b*) provides that an offence is committed where a manufacturer, dealer, trader or bottler for the purpose of sale or traffic, fills a bottle or siphon bearing a trade-mark, or the name of a person, with any liquid commodity without consent, and with the intention to deceive or defraud.

USED GOODS SOLD WITHOUT DISCLOSURE.

411. Every one commits an offence who sells, exposes or has in his possession for sale, or advertises for sale, goods that have been used, reconditioned or remade and that bear the trademark or the trade-name of another person, without making full disclosure that the goods have been reconditioned, rebuilt or remade for sale and that they are not then in the condition in which they were originally made or produced. R.S., c. C-34, s. 369; 2014, c. 20, s. 366(1).

CROSS-REFERENCES

The terms "trade-mark" and "trade-name" are defined in s. 2 of the *Trade-marks Act*, R.S.C. 1985, c. T-13. The term "goods" is defined in s. 379. Possession is defined in s. 4(3). The term "person" is defined in s. 2.

The punishment for this offence is set out in s. 412 and therefore see notes under that section with respect to mode of trial and release pending trial. Section 412(2) also provides for forfeiture of anything by means of or in relation to which a person commits an offence under this section.

SYNOPSIS

This section describes the offence of selling used goods without appropriate disclosure. The offence is committed where a person sells, exposes for sale, possesses for sale or advertises goods bearing a trade-mark or trade name of another person without disclosing that the goods were used, reconditioned or remade for sale.

PUNISHMENT / Forfeiture.

412. (1) Every one who commits an offence under section 407, 408, 409, 410 or 411 is guilty of

- **(*a*) an indictable offence and liable to imprisonment for a term not exceeding two years; or**
- **(*b*) an offence punishable on summary conviction.**

(2) Anything by means of or in relation to which a person commits an offence under section 407, 408, 409, 410 or 411 is, unless the court otherwise orders, forfeited on the conviction of that person for that offence. R.S., c. C-34, s. 370.

CROSS-REFERENCES

Where the prosecution elects to proceed by indictment for these offences then the accused may elect his mode of trial under s. 536(2). Where the prosecution elects to proceed by way of summary conviction then the proceedings are conducted by a summary conviction court pursuant to Part XXVII. The punishment is then as set out in s. 787 [although see s. 735(1)(*b*) where the accused is a corporation] and the limitation period is set out in s. 786(2).

Release pending trial for the offences is determined under s. 515, although the accused is eligible for release by a peace officer under s. 496, 497 or by the officer in charge under s. 498.

SYNOPSIS

This section provides that the offences described in ss. 407 to 411 may be prosecuted by indictment, with a maximum punishment of imprisonment for two years, or by summary conviction. Anything by means of or in relation to which any of these offences is committed is forfeited upon conviction, unless the court orders otherwise.

413. [*Repealed*, 2018, c. 29, s. 47.]

PRESUMPTION FROM PORT OF SHIPMENT.

414. Where, in proceedings under this Part, the alleged offence relates to imported goods, evidence that the goods were shipped to Canada from a place outside Canada is, in the absence of any evidence to the contrary, proof that the goods were made or produced in the country from which they were shipped. R.S., c. C-34, s. 372.

CROSS-REFERENCES

The term "goods" is defined in s. 379.

SYNOPSIS

This section creates a presumption concerning the origin of goods in proceedings under Part X. Evidence that goods were shipped into Canada from another country is proof that the goods were produced in that country, in the absence of evidence to the contrary.

Wreck

OFFENCES IN RELATION TO WRECK.

415. Every one who

(*a*) secretes wreck, defaces or obliterates the marks on wreck or uses any means to disguise or conceal the fact that anything is wreck, or in any manner conceals the character of wreck, from a person who is entitled to inquire into the wreck,

(*b*) receives wreck, knowing that it is wreck, from a person other than the owner thereof or a receiver of wreck, and does not within forty-eight hours thereafter inform the receiver of wreck thereof,

(*c*) offers wreck for sale or otherwise deals with it, knowing that it is wreck, and not having a lawful authority to sell or deal with it,

(*d*) keeps wreck in his possession knowing that it is wreck, without lawful authority to keep it, for any time longer than the time reasonably necessary to deliver it to the receiver of wreck, or

(*e*) boards, against the will of the master, a vessel that is wrecked, stranded or in distress unless he is a receiver of wreck or a person acting under orders of a receiver of wreck,

is guilty of

(*f*) an indictable offence and liable to imprisonment for a term not exceeding two years, or

(*g*) an offence punishable on summary conviction. R.S., c. C-34, s. 373.

CROSS-REFERENCES

The term "wreck" is defined in s. 2. The term "master" is defined in s. 2 of the *Canada Shipping Act*, R.S.C. 1985, c. S-9. The term "receiver of wreck" refers to a person appointed under s. 423 of the *Canada Shipping Act*, R.S.C. 1985, c. S-9 or a person acting under s. 424 of that Act. The *Canada Shipping Act* contains additional offences respecting wreck. In addition, s. 439(2) of that Act enacts a presumption applicable in "any indictment or prosecution of an accused for receiving, secreting or disguising any wreck, for having the possession thereof, for selling or dealing therewith or for defacing or obliterating marks thereon" and s. 439(3) permits evidence to be adduced of a prior conviction "on any indictment or prosecution of an accused for receiving, secreting, defacing, possessing, selling, dealing with or concealing the character of any wreck." The wide terms in which these provisions are cast would appear to make them applicable (assuming their constitutionality) to a prosecution under this section.

Where the prosecution elects to proceed by indictment then the accused may elect his mode of trial under s. 536(2). Where the prosecution elects to proceed by way of summary conviction then the proceedings are conducted by a summary conviction court pursuant to Part XXVII. The punishment is then as set out in s. 787 [although see s. 735(1)(*b*) where the accused is a corporation] and the limitation period is set out in s. 786(2). Release pending trial is determined under s. 515, although the accused is eligible for release by a peace officer under s. 496, 497 or by the officer in charge under s. 498.

Also see s. 438 which makes it an offence to interfere with the saving of a wrecked vessel.

SYNOPSIS

This section describes a series of offences in relation to wreck. "Wreck" is defined in s. 2 and includes the cargo, stores and parts of a vessel which are separated from it, and the property of persons who belong to, are on board or have left a wrecked vessel. An offence is committed where anyone secretes, disguises or conceals the character of wreck, *knowingly* receives wreck from a person other than the owner or a receiver of wreck without informing the receiver within 48 hours, *knowingly* deals with wreck without lawful authority, *knowingly* keeps wreck in possession without lawful authority longer than the time reasonably necessary to deliver it to the receiver; or, not being a receiver of wreck or a person acting under a receiver's orders, boards a wrecked, stranded or distressed vessel against the will of the master. The offence may be prosecuted by indictment or summarily. The maximum term of punishment on indictment is two years.

Public Stores

DISTINGUISHING MARK ON PUBLIC STORES.

416. The Governor in Council may, by notice to be published in the *Canada Gazette*, prescribe distinguishing marks that are appropriated for use on public stores to denote the property of Her Majesty therein, whether the stores belong to Her Majesty in right of Canada or to Her Majesty in any other right. R.S., c. C-34, s. 374.

CROSS-REFERENCES

The term "Her Majesty" is defined in s. 35 of the *Interpretation Act*, R.S.C. 1985, c. I-21. The terms "property" and "public stores" are defined in s. 2.

SYNOPSIS

This section authorizes the Governor in Council to prescribe distinguishing marks for use on public stores to denote that the stores belong to Her Majesty.

APPLYING OR REMOVING MARKS WITHOUT AUTHORITY / Unlawful transactions in public stores / Definition of "distinguishing mark".

417. (1) Every person is guilty of an indictable offence and liable to imprisonment for a term of not more than two years who,

(*a*) without lawful authority applies a distinguishing mark to anything, or

(*b*) with intent to conceal the property of Her Majesty in public stores, removes, destroys or obliterates, in whole or in part, a distinguishing mark.

(2) Every person who, without lawful authority, receives, possesses, keeps, sells or delivers public stores that they know bear a distinguishing mark is guilty of

(*a*) an indictable offence and liable to imprisonment for a term not exceeding two years; or

(*b*) an offence punishable on summary conviction.

(3) For the purposes of this section, "distinguishing mark" means a distinguishing mark that is appropriated for use on public stores pursuant to section 416. R.S., c. C-34, s. 375; 2018, c. 29, s. 48.

CROSS-REFERENCES

The term "Her Majesty" is defined in s. 35 of the *Interpretation Act*, R.S.C. 1985, c. I-21. The terms "property" and "public stores" are defined in s. 2. Possession is defined in s. 4(3). Under s. 421(1), evidence that a person was at any time performing duties in the Canadian Forces [defined in s. 2] is, in the absence of evidence to the contrary, proof that his enrolment in the Canadian Forces prior to that time was regular. Under s. 421(2), an accused charged with the offence under subsec. (2) is presumed to have known that the stores bore a distinguishing mark if he was at the time of the offence in the service or employment of Her Majesty or was a dealer in marine stores or in old metals.

The accused may elect his mode of trial for the offence under subsec. (1) pursuant to s. 536(2). Release pending trial is determined by s. 515, although the accused is eligible for release by the officer in charge pursuant to s. 498. Where the prosecution elects to proceed by indictment for the offence under subsec. (2) then the accused may elect his mode of trial under s. 536(2). Where the prosecution elects to proceed by way of summary conviction then the proceedings are conducted by a summary conviction court pursuant to Part XXVII. The punishment is then as set out in s. 787 [although see s. 735(1)(*b*) where the accused is a corporation] and the limitation period is set out in s. 786(2). Release pending trial for the offence under subsec. (2) is determined under s. 515, although the accused is eligible for release by a peace officer under s. 496, 497 or by the officer in charge under s. 498.

Related offences concerning public stores are in ss. 418 and 420.

SYNOPSIS

This section describes offences with respect to distinguishing marks prescribed pursuant to s. 416. An offence is committed contrary to subsec. (1) where anyone applies a distinguishing mark *without lawful authority*, the onus of proof of which lies on him, or removes, destroys or obliterates a distinguishing mark in whole or in part, with intent to conceal Her Majesty's ownership. The offence is indictable, with a maximum term of imprisonment of two years. An offence is committed contrary to subsec. (2) where anyone knowingly receives, possesses, keeps, sells, or delivers public stores bearing a distinguishing mark *without lawful authority*, the proof of which lies on the accused. This offence may be prosecuted by indictment, with a maximum term of two years' imprisonment, or by summary conviction.

SELLING DEFECTIVE STORES TO HER MAJESTY / Offences by representatives.

418. (1) Every one who knowingly sells or delivers defective stores to Her Majesty or commits fraud in connection with the sale, lease or delivery of stores to Her Majesty or the manufacture of stores for Her Majesty is guilty of an indictable offence and liable to imprisonment for a term not exceeding fourteen years.

(2) Every one who, being a representative of an organization that commits, by fraud, an offence under subsection (1),

- **(*a*) knowingly takes part in the fraud, or**
- **(*b*) knows or has reason to suspect that the fraud is being committed or has been or is about it be committed and does not inform the responsible government, or a department thereof, of Her Majesty,**

is guilty of an indictable offence and liable to imprisonment for a term not exceeding fourteen years. R.S., c. C-34, s. 376; 2003, c. 21, s. 6.1.

CROSS-REFERENCES

The terms "organization", "every one" and "representative" are defined in s. 2. The term "Her Majesty" is defined in s. 35 of the *Interpretation Act*, R.S.C. 1985, c. I-21.

Under s. 421(1), evidence that a person was at any time performing duties in the Canadian Forces (defined in s. 2) is, in the absence of evidence to the contrary, proof that his enrolment in the Canadian Forces prior to that time was regular.

The accused may elect his mode of trial for the offence under subsec. (1) pursuant to s. 536(2). Release pending trial is determined by s. 515.

Related offences concerning public stores are in ss. 417 and 420.

SYNOPSIS

This section describes the offence of selling defective stores to Her Majesty. An indictable offence is committed where a person *knowingly* sells or delivers defective stores to Her Majesty, or commits fraud in connection with the sale, lease, or delivery of stores to, or manufacture of stores for Her Majesty. The maximum term of imprisonment is 14 years.

Subsection (2) provides that an officer, director, employee or agent of a corporation committing this offence by fraud is also guilty of an indictable offence with a maximum term of imprisonment of 14 years if he *knowingly* participates in the fraud, or *knows* or *has reason to suspect* that the fraud has been, is being or is about to be committed and fails to inform the responsible government department.

UNLAWFUL USE OF MILITARY UNIFORMS OR CERTIFICATES.

419. Every person is guilty of an offence punishable on summary conviction who, without lawful authority,

(*a*) wears a uniform of the Canadian Forces or any other naval, army or air force or a uniform that is so similar to the uniform of any of those forces that it is likely to be mistaken therefor,

(*b*) wears a distinctive mark relating to wounds received or service performed in war, or a military medal, ribbon, badge, chevron or any decoration or order that is awarded for war services, or any imitation thereof, or any mark or device or thing that is likely to be mistaken for any such mark, medal, ribbon, badge, chevron, decoration or order,

(*c*) has in his possession a certificate of discharge, certificate of release, statement of service or identity card from the Canadian Forces or any other naval, army or air force that has not been issued to and does not belong to him, or

(*d*) has in his possession a commission or warrant or a certificate of discharge, certificate of release, statement of service or identity card, issued to an officer or person in or who has been in the Canadian Forces or any other naval, army or air force, that contains any alteration that is not verified by the initials of the officer who issued it, or by the initials of some officer thereto lawfully authorized. R.S., c. C-34, s. 377; 2018, c. 29, s. 49.

CROSS-REFERENCES

Under s. 421(1), evidence that a person was at any time performing duties in the Canadian Forces (defined in s. 2) is, in the absence of evidence to the contrary, proof that his enrolment in the Canadian Forces prior to that time was regular.

Trial of this offence is conducted by a summary conviction court pursuant to Part XXVII. The punishment is as set out in s. 787 and the limitation period is set out in s. 786(2). Release pending trial is determined by s. 515, although the accused is eligible for release by a peace officer under s. 496, 497 or by the officer in charge under s. 498.

The offence of personation with intent is found in s. 403 and of personating a police officer in s. 130.

SYNOPSIS

This section describes the offence of unlawful use of military uniforms or certificates or imitations thereof. The wearing or, in certain cases, possession of a wide variety of military apparel, marks, certificates, commissions and warrants without lawful authority, the proof of which lies on the accused, is a summary conviction offence.

MILITARY STORES / Exception.

420. (1) Every one who buys, receives or detains from a member of the Canadian Forces or a deserter or an absentee without leave therefrom any military stores that are owned by Her Majesty or for which the member, deserter or absentee without leave is accountable to Her Majesty is guilty of

(*a*) an indictable offence and liable to imprisonment for a term not exceeding five years; or

(*b*) an offence punishable on summary conviction.

(2) No person shall be convicted of an offence under this section where he establishes that he did not know and had no reason to suspect that the military stores in respect of which the offence was committed were owned by Her Majesty or were military stores for which the member, deserter or absentee without leave was accountable to Her Majesty. R.S., c. C-34, s. 378.

CROSS-REFERENCES

The term "military" is defined in s. 2.

Under s. 421(1), evidence that a person was at any time performing duties in the Canadian Forces (defined in s. 2) is, in the absence of evidence to the contrary, proof that his enrolment in the Canadian Forces prior to that time was regular.

Where the prosecution elects to proceed by indictment then the accused may elect his mode of trial under s. 536(2). Where the prosecution elects to proceed by way of summary conviction then the proceedings are conducted by a summary conviction court pursuant to Part XXVII. The punishment is then as set out in s. 787 [although see s. 735(1)(*b*) where the accused is a corporation] and the limitation period is set out in s. 786(2). Release pending trial is determined under s. 515, although the accused is eligible for release by a peace officer under ss. 496, 497 or by the officer in charge under s. 498.

Related offences concerning public stores are in ss. 417 and 418.

Other offences relating to deserters are in ss. 54 and 62.

SYNOPSIS

This section describes the offence of unauthorized use of military stores. An offence is committed where a person buys, receives or detains military stores of Her Majesty from a member of the Canadian Forces, a deserter or an absentee without leave of the forces. The offence may be prosecuted by indictment, with a maximum term of imprisonment of five years, or by summary conviction. Subsection (2) creates a defence where the accused establishes that he did not know and had no reason to suspect that the stores were owned by Her Majesty.

EVIDENCE OF ENLISTMENT / Presumption when accused a dealer in stores.

421. (1) In proceedings under sections 417 to 420, evidence that a person was at any time performing duties in the Canadian Forces is, in the absence of any evidence to the contrary, proof that his enrolment in the Canadian Forces prior to that time was regular.

(2) An accused who is charged with an offence under subsection 417(2) shall be presumed to have known that the stores in respect of which the offence is alleged to have been committed bore a distinguishing mark within the meaning of that subsection at the time the offence is alleged to have been committed if he was, at that time, in the service or employment of Her Majesty or was a dealer in marine stores or in old metals. R.S., c. C-34, s. 379.

CROSS-REFERENCES

The term "Canadian Forces" is defined in s. 2. The term "Her Majesty" is defined in s. 35 of the *Interpretation Act*, R.S.C. 1985, c. I-21.

SYNOPSIS

This section creates certain presumptions relating to ss. 417 to 420. By virtue of subsec. (1), in proceedings under ss. 417 to 420, evidence that a person performed duties in the armed forces is proof of his earlier regular enrolment in the absence of evidence to the contrary. By virtue of subsec. (2), if the accused was in the service or employment of Her Majesty, or was a dealer in marine stores or old metals at the time he is alleged to have committed an offence contrary to s. 417(2), he is presumed to know that the stores in question bore a distinguishing mark at the time.

Breach of Contract, Intimidation and Discrimination Against Trade Unionists

CRIMINAL BREACH OF CONTRACT / Saving / Consent required.

422. (1) Every one who wilfully breaks a contract, knowing or having reasonable cause to believe that the probable consequences of doing so, whether alone or in combination with others, will be

(*a*) to endanger human life,

(*b*) to cause serious bodily injury,

(*c*) to expose valuable property, real or personal, to destruction or serious injury,

(*d*) to deprive the inhabitants of a city or place, or part thereof, wholly or to a great extent, of their supply of light, power, gas or water, or

(*e*) to delay or prevent the running of any locomotive engine, tender, freight or passenger train or car, on a railway that is a common carrier,

is guilty of

(*f*) an indictable offence and liable to imprisonment for a term not exceeding five years, or

(*g*) an offence punishable on summary conviction.

(2) No person wilfully breaks a contract within the meaning of subsection (1) by reason only that

(*a*) being the employee of an employer, he stops work as a result of the failure of his employer and himself to agree on any matter relating to his employment, or,

(*b*) being a member of an organization of employees formed for the purpose of regulating relations between employers and employees, he stops work as a result of the failure of the employer and a bargaining agent acting on behalf of the organization to agree on any matter relating to the employment of members of the organization,

if, before the stoppage of work occurs, all steps provided by law with respect to the settlement of industrial disputes are taken and any provision for the final settlement of differences, without stoppage of work, contained in or by law deemed to be contained in a collective agreement is complied with and effect given thereto.

(3) No proceedings shall be instituted under this section without the consent of the Attorney General. R.S., c. C-34, s. 380.

CROSS-REFERENCES

"Attorney General" is defined in s. 2. Section 583(*h*) provides that a count in an indictment is not insufficient by reason only that it does not state that the required consent has been obtained. [As to notes concerning sufficiency of consent, see s. 583.]

Where the prosecution elects to proceed by indictment then the accused may elect his mode of trial under s. 536(2). Where the prosecution elects to proceed by way of summary conviction then the proceedings are conducted by a summary conviction court pursuant to Part XXVII. The punishment is then as set out in s. 787 [although see s. 719(*b*) where the accused is a corporation] and the limitation period is set out in s. 786(2). Release pending trial is determined under s. 515, although the accused is eligible for release by a peace officer under ss. 496, 497 or by the officer in charge under s. 498.

Also see s. 466 which creates the offence of conspiracy in restraint of trade.

SYNOPSIS

This section describes the offence of criminal breach of contract. The offence is committed where a person *wilfully* breaches a contract, *knowing* or *having reasonable cause to believe* that the consequences will endanger life, cause serious bodily injury, expose valuable property to destruction or serious injury, deprive people wholly or substantially of light, power, gas, or water, or delay or prevent the running of a common carrier railway. These consequences may flow from a breach by the accused or by the accused in combination with others. The offence may be prosecuted by indictment, with a maximum term of punishment of five years' imprisonment, or by summary conviction. Subsection (2) provides that a contract is not broken within the meaning of this section where an employee lawfully stops work because matters relating to his employment are not agreed upon, or where he stops work as part of a lawful work stoppage by a union. Proceedings under this section may only be instituted with the consent of an Attorney General.

INTIMIDATION / Exception.

423. (1) Every one is guilty of an indictable offence and liable to imprisonment for a term of not more than five years or is guilty of an offence punishable on summary conviction who, wrongfully and without lawful authority, for the purpose of compelling another person to abstain from doing anything that he or she has a lawful right to do, or to do anything that he or she has a lawful right to abstain from doing,

(*a*) uses violence or threats of violence to that person or his or her spouse or common-law partner or children, or injures his or her property;

(*b*) intimidates or attempts to intimidate that person or a relative of that person by threats that, in Canada or elsewhere, violence or other injury will be done to or punishment inflicted on him or her or a relative of his or hers, or that the property of any of them will be damaged;

(*c*) persistently follows that person;

(*d*) hides any tools, clothes or other property owned or used by that person, or deprives him or her of them or hinders him or her in the use of them;

(*e*) with one or more other persons, follows that person, in a disorderly manner, on a highway;

(*f*) besets or watches the place where that person resides, works, carries on business or happens to be; or

(*g*) blocks or obstructs a highway.

(2) A person who attends at or near or approaches a dwelling-house or place, for the purpose only of obtaining or communicating information, does not watch or beset within the meaning of this section. R.S., c. C-34, s. 381; 1980-81-82-83, c. 125, s. 22; 2000, c. 12, s. 95(*b*); 2001, c. 32, s. 10.

CROSS-REFERENCES

Where the offence, although committed outside Canada, is in relation to a demand for nuclear material, see s. 7(3.4). "Common-law partner" and "dwelling-house" are defined in s. 2.

Trial of this offence is conducted by a summary conviction court pursuant to Part XXVII. The punishment is as set out in s. 787 and the limitation period is set out in s. 786(2). Release pending trial is determined by s. 515, although the accused is eligible for release by a peace officer under ss. 496, 497 or by the officer in charge under s. 498. In some circumstances, the accused found guilty of this offence would be liable to the discretionary order prohibiting possession of firearms, ammunition or explosives.

An alternative to this offence is the procedure for requiring the offender to enter into a recognizance to keep the peace either at common law or pursuant to s. 810. Other related offences: s. 175, causing disturbance; s. 264, criminal harassment; s. 264.1, uttering threats; s. 346, extortion; s. 424, threat to commit offence against internationally protected person; s. 371, sending false telegram, etc., with intent to defraud; s. 372, conveying false messages, harassing or indecent telephone calls.

SYNOPSIS

This section describes the offence of intimidation. The offence is committed where a person intending to compel someone to abstain from doing something he has a right to do, or to do something that he has the right to abstain from doing, *wrongfully* and *without authority*: uses violence or threats of violence against the person or his spouse or children; injures his property; intimidates or attempts to intimidate the person or a relative by threats of violence or injury to property; persistently follows the person; hides or deprives the person of the use of his property; with another or others follows the person in a disorderly manner on a highway; watches or besets the residence, work place or other place where the person happens to be; or blocks a highway. The offence may be prosecuted by summary conviction or indictment. By virtue of s. (2), where a person approaches a place for the sole purpose of obtaining or communicating information, he does not watch or beset within the meaning of this section.

ANNOTATIONS

A picket line, staffed by non-employees, advocating a collective bargaining agreement was held to be just as effective an interference with contractual relations as any other restraint might be and on the facts was held to involve the proposition that the defendants were in breach of subsec. (1)(*f*): *Smith Bros. Construction Co. v. Jones* (1955), 113 C.C.C. 16 (Ont. H.C.J.).

This section is not confined to industrial disputes and trade-union activity: *R. v. Basaraba* (1975), 24 C.C.C. (2d) 296 (Man. C.A.).

A road in a company town owned by the company but which the public have a *de facto* right to use constitutes a "highway" for the purposes of subsec. (1)(*g*): *R. v. Stockley* (1977), 36 C.C.C. (2d) 387 (Nfld. C.A.).

INTIMIDATION OF A JUSTICE SYSTEM PARTICIPANT OR A JOURNALIST / Prohibited conduct / Punishment.

423.1 (1) No person shall, without lawful authority, engage in any conduct with the intent to provoke a state of fear in

(*a*) a group of persons or the general public in order to impede the administration of criminal justice;

(*b*) a justice system participant in order to impede him or her in the performance of his or her duties; or

(*c*) a journalist in order to impede him or her in the transmission to the public of information in relation to a criminal organization.

(2) [*Repealed*, 2015, c. 13, s. 12(2).]

(3) Every person who contravenes this section is guilty of an indictable offence and is liable to imprisonment for a term of not more than fourteen years. 2001, c. 32, s. 11; 2015, c. 13, s. 12.

CROSS-REFERENCES

"Justice system participant" is defined in s. 2. "Criminal organization" is defined in ss. 2 and 467.1(1). An alternative to this offence is the procedure for requiring the offender to enter into a recognizance to keep the peace either at common law or pursuant to s. 810. Other related offences: s. 175, causing disturbance; s. 264, criminal harassment; s. 346, extortion; s. 371, sending false telegram etc. with intent to defraud; s. 372, conveying false messages, harassing or indecent telephone calls; s. 423 intimidation and watching and besetting; s. 424, threat to commit offence against internationally protected person.

Section 486.5 sets out a procedure that allows a victim, witness, the prosecutor or a justice system participant to apply for an order prohibiting publication, broadcast or transmission in any way of information that would identify the person.

Section 718.02 provides that, in imposing sentence for the offence created by para. (1)(*b*), the court is to give primary consideration to the objectives of denunciation and deterrence.

SYNOPSIS

This section describes a form of intimidation directed to interference with the administration of justice and at journalists investigating criminal organizations. It is an offence to engage in the conduct set out in subsec. (2) without lawful excuse with intent to provoke a state of fear in (a) a group of persons or the public to impede the administration of justice; (b) justice system participants to impede them in their performance of their duties; or (c) journalists to impede them in transmission to the public of information in relation to a criminal organization. Subsection (2) sets out the kinds of prohibited conduct. This is an indictable offence with a maximum penalty of 14 years.

This section requires the Crown to prove a specific intent to impede a justice system participant in the exercise of his or her duties: *R. v. Armstrong* (2012), 288 C.C.C. (3d) 282 (B.C.C.A.), leave to appeal to S.C.C. refused 2013 CarswellBC 761.

THREAT AGAINST INTERNATIONALLY PROTECTED PERSON.

424. Every one who threatens to commit an offence under section 235, 236, 266, 267, 268, 269, 269.1, 271, 272, 273, 279 or 279.1 against an internationally protected person or who threatens to commit an offence under section 431 is guilty of an indictable offence and liable to imprisonment for a term of not more than five years. 1974-75-76, c. 93, s. 33; R.S.C. 1985, c. 27 (1st Supp.), s. 55; 2001, c. 41, s. 11.

CROSS-REFERENCES

The term "internationally protected person" is defined in s. 2. Section 7(10) provides for admissibility of a certificate from the Minister of Foreign Affairs stating any fact relevant to the question of whether any person is a person who is entitled, pursuant to international law, to special protection from any attack on his person, freedom or dignity.

This offence may be the basis for an application for an authorization to intercept private communications by reason of s. 183 and a warrant to conduct video surveillance under s. 487.01(5).

Section 7(3) enacts special jurisdictional rules for commission of this offence outside Canada when the offence is in relation to an internationally protected person or property referred to in s. 431 [official premises, etc.]. The related offence for United Nations personnel or associated personnel is in s. 424.1.

The accused may elect his mode of trial pursuant to s. 536(2). Release pending trial is determined by s. 515, although the accused is eligible for release by the officer in charge pursuant to s. 498. In some circumstances, the accused found guilty of this offence would be liable to the discretionary order prohibiting possession of firearms, ammunition or explosives.

SYNOPSIS

This section describes the offence of threatening to commit an offence against an internationally protected person. A person charged under this section must have threatened to commit one of the listed offences and the threats must be directed against an internationally protected person. A person who threatens to commit the offence under s. 431 of attacking the premises, residence or transport of an internationally protected person is also guilty of an offence under this section. This offence is indictable and carries a maximum term of five years' imprisonment.

THREAT AGAINST UNITED NATIONS OR ASSOCIATED PERSONNEL.

424.1 Every one who, with intent to compel any person, group of persons, state or any international or intergovernmental organization to do or refrain from doing any act, threatens to commit an offence under section 235, 236, 266, 267, 268, 269, 269.1, 271, 272, 273, 279 or 279.1 against a member of United Nations personnel or associated personnel or threatens to commit an offence under section 431.1 is guilty of an indictable offence and liable to imprisonment for a term of not more than ten years. 2001, c. 41, s. 11.

CROSS-REFERENCES

The terms "associated personnel" and "United Nations personnel" are defined in s. 2. This offence may be the basis for an application for an authorization to intercept private communications by reason of s. 183 and a warrant to conduct video surveillance under s. 487.01(5). Section 7(3.71) enacts special jurisdictional rules for commission of this offence outside Canada when the offence is in relation to United Nations personnel or associated personnel or property referred to in s. 431.1 [official premises, etc.]. The certificate of the Minister of Foreign Affairs is proof of facts relevant to the question of whether any person is a member of United Nations personnel or a member of associated personnel under s. 7(10).

SYNOPSIS

This section describes the offence of threatening to commit an offence against United Nations personnel or personnel associated with the United Nations. A person charged under this section must have threatened to commit one of the listed offences, and the threats must be directed against United Nations personnel or associated personnel with the intent to compel any person, group, state or international or intergovernmental organization to do or refrain from doing any act. A person who threatens to commit the offence under s. 431.1 of attacking the premises, residence or transport of a member of United Nations personnel or associated personnel is also guilty of an offence under this section. This offence is indictable and carries a maximum term of 10 years' imprisonment.

OFFENCES BY EMPLOYERS.

425. Every one who, being an employer or the agent of an employer, wrongfully and without lawful authority

- **(*a*) refuses to employ or dismisses from his employment any person for the reason only that the person is a member of a lawful trade union or of a lawful association or combination of workmen or employees formed for the purpose of advancing, in a lawful manner, their interests and organized for their protection in the regulation of wages and conditions of work,**
- **(*b*) seeks by intimidation, threat of loss of position or employment, or by causing actual loss of position or employment, or by threatening or imposing any pecuniary penalty, to compel workmen or employees to abstain from belonging to a trade union, association or combination to which they have a lawful right to belong, or**
- **(*c*) conspires, combines, agrees or arranges with any other employer or his agent to do anything mentioned in paragraph (*a*) or (*b*),**

is guilty of an offence punishable on summary conviction. R.S., c. C-34, s. 382.

CROSS-REFERENCES

Trial of this offence is conducted by a summary conviction court pursuant to Part XXVII. The punishment is as set out in s. 787 and the limitation period is set out in s. 786(2). Release pending trial is determined by s. 515, although the accused is eligible for release by a peace officer under s. 496, 497 or by the officer in charge under s. 498.

The related offence of intimidation is found in s. 423. With respect to the offence in para. (*c*), see the saving provisions with respect to refusing to work and trade combinations in s. 467.

SYNOPSIS

This section describes several offences relating to labour disputes with which an employer can be charged. Any person who is either an employer or an agent of an employer and who *wrongfully and without lawful authority* refuses to hire or continue the employment of another person because he is a member of a *lawful* trade union or association, or who, employing the methods described in para. (*b*), attempts to keep his employees from joining a union or association to which they have a lawful right to belong is guilty of a summary conviction offence. Paragraph (*c*) imposes liability to summary conviction upon any person who *conspires, combines, agrees* or *arranges* with the employer or his agent to do any of the things described above.

ANNOTATIONS

Paragraph (*a*) – The "reason only" means the primary reason, the *causa causans,* the reason behind the act in question, and may be inferred from the attitudes or decisions not expressly outlined in detail: *R. ex rel. Perreault v. Alex Pelletier And Sons Ltd.* (1960), 33 C.R. 84 (Que. Mag. Ct.).

A charge under this subsection was dismissed where police officers, called by the employer, removed employees from the employer's premises but without instructions to do so from the employer. There was held to be no dismissal either directly or indirectly by the employer: *R. v. J. Alepin Freres Ltee*, [1965] S.C.R. 359, [1965] 3 C.C.C. 1.

Paragraph (*b*) – The offence of seeking to compel workmen or employees to abstain from belonging to a trade union is the prohibited activity expressed in two methods which may both be incorporated into one charge: *R. v. Hickey, ex p. Hebb Motors Ltd.*, [1965] 2 C.C.C. 170 (N.S.S.C.).

THREATS AND RETALIATION AGAINST EMPLOYEES / Punishment.

425.1 (1) No employer or person acting on behalf of an employer or in a position of authority in respect of an employee of the employer shall take a disciplinary measure against, demote, terminate or otherwise adversely affect the employment of such an employee, or threaten to do so,

(*a*) with the intent to compel the employee to abstain from providing information to a person whose duties include the enforcement of federal or provincial law, respecting an offence that the employee believes has been or is being committed contrary to this or any other federal or provincial Act or regulation by the employer or an officer or employee of the employer or, if the employer is a corporation, by one or more of its directors; or

(*b*) with the intent to retaliate against the employee because the employee has provided information referred to in paragraph (*a*) to a person whose duties include the enforcement of federal or provincial law.

(2) Any one who contravenes subsection (1) is guilty of

(*a*) an indictable offence and liable to imprisonment for a term not exceeding five years; or

(*b*) an offence punishable on summary conviction. 2004, c. 3, s. 6.

CROSS-REFERENCES

Sections 487.012 to 487.017 provide procedures for the making of production orders that would require persons to provide documents or data.

SYNOPSIS

This section creates a form of whistle-blower protection. The section makes it an offence for an employer or anyone acting on behalf of an employer to take or threaten to take disciplinary or other measures such as termination against an employee with the intent to compel the employee not to provide information to persons whose duties include enforcement of federal or provincial law respecting an offence that the employee believes has been or is being committed by the employer, an officer or employee of the employer or directors of a corporation. The section also makes it an offence for such persons to retaliate against the employee for having taken any of these steps. The offence created is a hybrid offence and the maximum penalty is five years if the Crown proceeds by indictment.

Secret Commissions

SECRET COMMISSIONS / Privity to offence / Punishment / Definition of "agent" and "principal".

426. (1) Every one commits an offence who

(*a*) directly or indirectly, corruptly gives, offers or agrees to give or offer to an agent or to anyone for the benefit of the agent — or, being an agent, directly or indirectly, corruptly demands, accepts or offers or agrees to accept from any person, for themselves or another person — any reward, advantage or benefit of any kind as consideration for doing or not doing, or for having done or not done, any act relating to the affairs or business of the agent's principal, or for showing or not showing favour or disfavour to any person with relation to the affairs or business of the agent's principal; or

(*b*) with intent to deceive a principal, gives to an agent of that principal, or, being an agent, uses with intent to deceive his principal, a receipt, an account, or other writing

(i) in which the principal has an interest,

(ii) that contains any statement that is false or erroneous or defective in any material particular, and

(iii) that is intended to mislead the principal.

(2) Every one commits an offence who is knowingly privy to the commission of an offence under subsection (1).

(3) A person who commits an offence under this section is guilty of an indictable offence and liable to imprisonment for a term not exceeding five years.

(4) In this section "agent" includes an employee, and "principal" includes an employer.
R.S., c. C-34, s. 383; R.S.C. 1985, c. 27 (1st Supp.), s. 56; 2007, c. 13, s. 7.

CROSS-REFERENCES

This offence may be the basis for an application for an authorization to intercept private communications by reason of s. 183 and is an enterprise crime offence for the purposes of Part XII.2.

The accused may elect his mode of trial pursuant to s. 536(2). Release pending trial is determined by s. 515, although the accused is eligible for release by a peace officer under s. 496, 497 or by the officer in charge under s. 498.

This offence is often charged with the offence of fraud defined in s. 380. Other forms of breach of trust are as follows: s. 122, breach of trust by public officer; s. 330, theft by person required to account; s. 331, theft by person holding power of attorney; s. 332, theft of money held under direction; s. 336, criminal breach of trust; s. 384, broker selling for his own account.

SYNOPSIS

This section describes the offence of giving secret commissions. Subsection (1)(*a*) states that a person who directly or indirectly *corruptly* gives, offers or agrees to give or offer to an agent, or who, being an agent, *corruptly* demands, accepts or offers or agrees to accept any reward, advantage or benefit of any kind in return for doing or not doing an act, or for showing favour or disfavour to another person, in relation to the business of his principal, commits this indictable offence. Subsection (1)(*b*) describes another form of this offence which involves the giving to an agent or the using by an agent of a *receipt*, *account*, or *other writing* in which the principal has an interest and in which a false, erroneous or defective statement, intended to mislead the principal, is contained. In order to be convicted of an offence under subsec. (1)(*b*), the accused must have *the intent to deceive* a principal. Subsection (2) makes it an offence for a person to be *knowingly privy* to an offence under subsec. (1). The maximum term of imprisonment for offences under this section is five years.

ANNOTATIONS

Elements of offence – Where the person charged with the offence under subsec. (1)(*a*)(ii) is the agent, then the Crown must establish as elements of the *actus reus* the existence of an agency relationship; the accepting by an agent of a benefit as consideration for doing or forbearing to do any act in relation to the affairs of the agent's principals; and the failure by the agent to make adequate and timely disclosure of the source, amount and nature of the benefit. The requisite *mens rea* is proof that the agent was aware of the agency relationship; that the agent knowingly accepted the benefit as consideration for an act to be undertaken in relation to the affairs of the principal; and that the agent was aware of the extent of the disclosure to the principal or lack thereof. If the accused was aware that some disclosure was made, then it will be for the court to determine whether in all the circumstances of the particular case it was in fact adequate and timely. The term "corruptly" means secretly or without requisite disclosure. There is no requirement of any corrupt bargain. Thus, it is possible to convict the agent who has accepted or taken a reward despite the innocence of the giver of the reward or benefit. The non-disclosure will be established if the Crown demonstrates that adequate and timely disclosure of the source, amount and nature of the benefit has not been made by the agent to the principal. A general and vague disclosure that the agent is receiving commissions will not meet the objective of the section. The agent must disclose the nature of the benefit which is being received, the amount of that benefit calculated to the best of the agent's ability and the source of the benefit. It may not be possible for the agent to be exact as to the amount of commission which will be received and it will, therefore, be sufficient if a reasonable effort is made to alert the principal as to the approximate amount and source of commission to be received. The disclosure must be timely in the sense that the principal must be aware of the benefit as soon as possible. The disclosure must be made at the point when the reward may influence the agent in relation to the principal's affairs and it is essential then that the agent clearly disclose to the principal as promptly as possible the source and amount or approximate amount of the benefit: *R. v. Kelly*, [1992] 2 S.C.R. 170, 73 C.C.C. (3d) 385, 14 C.R. (4th) 181; *R. v. Arnold*, [1992] 2 S.C.R. 208, 73 C.C.C. (3d) 31, 113 N.S.R. (2d) 271.

The evil to which this section is directed is secret transactions with an agent concerning the affairs of his principal, and it is no defence that the accused believed that he had a right to have a certain thing done by the agent's principal: *R. v. Brown* (1956), 116 C.C.C. 287, 24 C.R. 404 (Ont. C.A.) (2:1).

Meaning of "agent" – While the offence, contrary to subsec. (1)(*a*)(i), requires proof that the person who was offered the secret commission was in fact an agent, the agent need not have a specific principal at the time of the prohibited offer, nor need the agent intend to carry out the purpose for which the offer was made: *R. v. Wile* (1990), 58 C.C.C. (3d) 85, 79 C.R. (3d) 32, 74 O.R. (2d) 289 (C.A.).

The mere giving of advice with respect to investments does not establish an agency relationship: *R. v. Arnold* (1994), 88 C.C.C. (3d) 92, 129 N.S.R. (2d) 356 (C.A.).

[*Heading repealed*, 2018, c. 29, s. 50.]

427. [*Repealed*, 2018, c. 29, s. 50.]

Part XI / WILFUL AND FORBIDDEN ACTS IN RESPECT OF CERTAIN PROPERTY

Interpretation

DEFINITION OF "PROPERTY"

428. In this Part, "property" means real or personal corporeal property. R.S., c. C-34, s. 385.

CROSS-REFERENCES

In addition to the definition of this section, see s. 2 and notes to that section. For definition of "wilfully", see s. 429.

SYNOPSIS

This section defines the term "property" for the purposes of Part XI of the Code. The definition is more restricted than the one found in s. 2 of the Code and encompasses real or personal corporeal property.

WILFULLY CAUSING EVENT TO OCCUR / Colour of right / Interest.

429. (1) Every one who causes the occurrence of an event by doing an act or by omitting to do an act that it is his duty to do, knowing that the act or omission will probably cause the occurrence of the event and being reckless whether the event occurs or not, shall be deemed, for the purposes of this Part, wilfully to have caused the occurrence of the event.

(2) A person shall not be convicted of an offence under sections 430 to 446 if they act with legal justification or excuse or colour of right.

(3) Where it is an offence to destroy or to damage anything,

(*a*) the fact that a person has a partial interest in what is destroyed or damaged does not prevent him from being guilty of the offence if he caused the destruction or damage; and

(*b*) the fact that a person has a total interest in what is destroyed or damaged does not prevent him from being guilty of the offence if he caused the destruction or damage with intent to defraud. R.S., c. C-34, s. 386; 2018, c. 29, s. 51.

CROSS-REFERENCES

For other notes on the meaning of "colour of right", see s. 322 and with respect to mistake generally, see s. 19. With respect to subsec. (3)(*b*), note that where the accused is charged with an offence under s. 433 or 434, then s. 435 enacts a presumption of intent to defraud where the accused is the holder of or is named as the beneficiary under a policy of fire insurance relating to the property, and where intent to defraud is material.

SYNOPSIS

This section contains three provisions relevant to Part XI of the Code. Subsection (1) states that any person who does something (or fails to do something which it is his or her duty to do) knowing that this action or inaction will *probably cause* the occurrence of an event and who is *reckless* as to the outcome of his action, is deemed, for the purposes of this Part of the Code, to have wilfully caused the occurrence of the event. Subsection (2) makes it clear that no person who proves that he acted with *legal justification or excuse* and *with colour of right* shall be convicted of an offence under ss. 430 to 446. Subsection (3)(*a*) provides that where it is an offence to destroy or damage anything, a person who causes damage or destruction can be found guilty, notwithstanding the fact that he has a partial interest in that thing. Subsection (3)(*a*) states that a person who has a total interest in the damaged property can be found guilty of an offence if he caused the damage or destruction *with the intent to defraud.*

ANNOTATIONS

Application of definition of "wilfully" [subsec. (1)] – In view of this extended definition of "wilfully" an information containing an allegation of unlawfully damaging property is valid: *R. v. Rese,* [1968] 1 C.C.C. 363 (Ont. C.A.).

Legal justification or excuse and colour of right [subsec. (2)] – To come within this exception the accused must show that he believed in a state of facts which, if it actually existed, would constitute a legal justification or excuse: *R. v. Ninos and Walker,* [1964] 1 C.C.C. 326 (N.S.S.C. *in Banco*).

Where the accused shot and killed a dog which he had accidentally wounded in an attempt to frighten it off his land which he had turned into a wildlife refuge it was held that the first shot was justified as it was not done with the intent to wound or kill the dog and that the second shot, which was done for humanitarian reasons to put the dog out of its misery, was also justified. The accused's honest belief (proved to be wrong at trial) that the dog could not be saved provided him with a colour of right. The court left open the question whether the intentional shooting of dogs to protect wildlife would itself constitute a lawful justification or excuse: *R. v. Comber* (1975), 28 C.C.C. (2d) 444 (Ont. Co. Ct.).

The defence of colour of right is based on the accused's subjective, honest belief that at the time of the offence, he had a color of right. The color of right defence is an honest belief in a state of facts or civil law that, if it existed, would negate the *mens rea* of the offence. While the belief does not have to be reasonable, the reasonableness of the belief is a factor in determining if there is an honest belief. It is not sufficient, however, that the accused have a moral belief in a colour of right. Colour of right includes errors of fact and law and is not limited to areas of law respecting proprietary or possessory rights. In this case, however, the defence of color of right did not apply where it was based on the accused's ignorance of the jurisdiction of the *Criminal Code*: *R. v. Watson* (1999), 137 C.C.C. (3d) 422 (Nfld. C.A.).

The word "and" in this subsection should be read as "or" so it is sufficient if the accused establishes that he acted either with legal justification or excuse, or with a colour of right. Colour of right means an honest belief in a state of fact which, if it existed, would be a legal justification or excuse: *R. v. Creaghan* (1982), 1 C.C.C. (3d) 449 (Ont. C.A.).

It would seem that placing the onus on the accused to prove the legal justification or excuse is unconstitutional as violating s. 11(*d*) of the Charter: *R. v. Gamey* (1993), 80 C.C.C. (3d) 117 (Man. C.A.).

Destruction or damage to person's own property [subsec. (3)] – Where a trustee's interest is only a bare legal title the trustee does not have any sufficient interest in the property to remove the application of this paragraph: *R. v. Griffith,* [1987] 2 W.W.R. 564 (Man. Q.B.).

Mischief

MISCHIEF / Mischief in relation to computer data / Punishment / Punishment / Idem / Mischief relating to religious property, educational institutions, etc. / Definition of "property" / Mischief relating to war memorials / Mischief in relation to cultural property / Mischief in relation to computer data / Offence / Saving / Idem / Definition of "computer data".

430. (1) Every one commits mischief who wilfully

(*a*) destroys or damages property;

(*b*) renders property dangerous, useless, inoperative or ineffective;

(*c*) obstructs, interrupts or interferes with the lawful use, enjoyment or operation of property; or

(*d*) obstructs, interrupts or interferes with any person in the lawful use, enjoyment or operation of property.

(1.1) Everyone commits mischief who wilfully

(*a*) destroys or alters computer data;

(*b*) renders computer data meaningless, useless or ineffective;

(*c*) obstructs, interrupts or interferes with the lawful use of computer data; or

(*d*) obstructs, interrupts or interferes with a person in the lawful use of computer data or denies access to computer data to a person who is entitled to access to it.

(2) Every one who commits mischief that causes actual danger to life is guilty of an indictable offence and liable to imprisonment for life.

(3) Every one who commits mischief in relation to property that is a testamentary instrument or the value of which exceeds five thousand dollars

(*a*) is guilty of an indictable offence and liable to imprisonment for a term not exceeding ten years; or

(*b*) is guilty of an offence punishable on summary conviction.

(4) Every one who commits mischief in relation to property, other than property described in subsection (3),

(*a*) is guilty of an indictable offence and liable to imprisonment for a term not exceeding two years; or

(*b*) is guilty of an offence punishable on summary conviction.

(4.1) Everyone who commits mischief in relation to property described in any of paragraphs (4.101)(*a*) to (*d*), if the commission of the mischief is motivated by bias, prejudice or hate based on colour, race, religion, national or ethnic origin, age, sex, sexual orientation, gender identity or expression or mental or physical disability,

(*a*) is guilty of an indictable offence and liable to imprisonment for a term not exceeding ten years; or

(*b*) is guilty of an offence punishable on summary conviction and liable to imprisonment for a term not exceeding eighteen months.

(4.101) For the purposes of subsection (4.1), "property" means

(*a*) a building or structure, or part of a building or structure, that is primarily used for religious worship — including a church, mosque, synagogue or temple — , an object associated with religious worship located in or on the grounds of such a building or structure, or a cemetery;

(*b*) a building or structure, or part of a building or structure, that is primarily used by an "identifiable group" as defined in subsection 318(4) as an educational institution — including a school, daycare centre, college or university — , or an object associated with that institution located in or on the grounds of such a building or structure;

(*c*) a building or structure, or part of a building or structure, that is primarily used by an "identifiable group" as defined in subsection 318(4) for administrative,

social, cultural or sports activities or events — including a town hall, community centre, playground or arena — , or an object associated with such an activity or event located in or on the grounds of such a building or structure; or

(*d*) a building or structure, or part of a building or structure, that is primarily used by an "identifiable group" as defined in subsection 318(4) as a residence for seniors or an object associated with that residence located in or on the grounds of such a building or structure.

(4.11) Everyone who commits mischief in relation to property that is a building, structure or part thereof that primarily serves as a monument to honour persons who were killed or died as a consequence of a war, including a war memorial or cenotaph, or an object associated with honouring or remembering those persons that is located in or on the grounds of such a building or structure, or a cemetery is guilty of an indictable offence or an offence punishable on summary conviction and is liable,

(*a*) whether the offence is prosecuted by indictment or punishable on summary conviction, to the following minimum punishment, namely,

(i) for a first offence, to a fine of not less than $1,000,

(ii) for a second offence, to imprisonment for not less than 14 days, and

(iii) for each subsequent offence, to imprisonment for not less than 30 days;

(*b*) if the offence is prosecuted by indictment, to imprisonment for a term not exceeding 10 years; and

(*c*) if the offence is punishable on summary conviction, to imprisonment for a term not exceeding 18 months.

(4.2) Every one who commits mischief in relation to cultural property as defined in Article 1 of the Convention for the Protection of Cultural Property in the Event of Armed Conflict, done at The Hague on May 14, 1954, as set out in the schedule to the *Cultural Property Export and Import Act*,

(*a*) is guilty of an indictable offence and liable to imprisonment for a term not exceeding ten years; or

(*b*) is guilty of an offence punishable on summary conviction.

(5) Everyone who commits mischief in relation to computer data

(*a*) is guilty of an indictable offence and liable to imprisonment for a term not exceeding ten years; or

(*b*) is guilty of an offence punishable on summary conviction.

(5.1) Everyone who wilfully does an act or wilfully omits to do an act that it is their duty to do, if that act or omission is likely to constitute mischief causing actual danger to life, or to constitute mischief in relation to property or computer data,

(*a*) is guilty of an indictable offence and liable to imprisonment for a term not exceeding five years; or

(*b*) is guilty of an offence punishable on summary conviction.

(6) No person commits mischief within the meaning of this section by reason only that

(*a*) he stops work as a result of the failure of his employer and himself to agree on any matter relating to his employment; or

(*b*) he stops work as a result of the failure of his employer and a bargaining agent acting on his behalf to agree on any matter relating to his employment; or

(*c*) he stops work as a result of his taking part in a combination of workmen or employees for their own reasonable protection as workmen or employees.

(7) No person commits mischief within the meaning of this section by reason only that he attends at or near or approaches a dwelling-house or place for the purpose only of obtaining or communicating information.

(8) In this section, "computer data" has the same meaning as in subsection 342.1(2). R.S., c. C-34, s. 387; 1972, c. 13, s. 30; R.S.C. 1985, c. 27 (1st Supp.), s. 57; 1994, c. 44, s. 28; 2001, c. 41, s. 12; 2005, c. 40, s. 3; 2014, c. 9, s. 1; 2014, c. 31, s. 19; 2017, c. 23, ss. 1, 2.

CROSS-REFERENCES

The term "property" is defined in s. 428. The term "wilfully" is defined in s. 429(1). The defence of legal justification or excuse and colour of right is set out in s. 429(2). Where the accused has an interest in the thing destroyed, see s. 429(3). This offence may be the basis of an application for an authorization to intercept private communications pursuant to s. 183 or for a warrant to conduct video surveillance by reason of s. 487.01(5).

The definition of "cultural property" referred to in subsec. (4.2) is as follows:

For the purposes of the present Convention, the term "cultural property" shall cover, irrespective of origin or ownership:

(*a*) movable or immovable property of great importance to the cultural heritage of every people, such as monuments of architecture, art or history, whether religious or secular; archaeological sites; groups of buildings which, as a whole, are of historical or artistic interest; works of art; manuscripts, books and other objects of artistic, historical or archaeological interest; as well as scientific collections and important collections of books or archives or of reproductions of the property defined above;

(*b*) buildings whose main and effective purpose is to preserve or exhibit the movable cultural property defined in subparagraph (*a*) such as museums, large libraries and depositories of archives, and refuges intended to shelter, in the event of armed conflict, the movable cultural property defined in subparagraph (*a*);

(*c*) centres containing a large amount of cultural property as defined in subparagraphs (*a*) and (*b*), to be known as "centres containing monuments".

The offence in subsec. (2) is an indictable offence for which the accused may elect his mode of trial under s. 536(2). Release pending trial is determined under s. 515. Where the prosecution elects to proceed by indictment for the offence under subsecs. (3) to (5.1) the accused may elect the mode of trial under s. 536(2). Release pending trial is determined under s. 515, although the accused is eligible for release by a peace officer under s. 496, 497 or by the officer in charge under s. 498. Where the prosecution elects to proceed by way of summary conviction then the proceedings are conducted by a summary conviction court pursuant to Part XXVII. The punishment is then as set out in s. 787 and the limitation period is set out in s. 786(2). Where the prosecution elects to proceed by indictment for the offence under subsec. (4) then, by virtue of s. 553(*a*)(v), it is an offence over which a provincial court judge has absolute jurisdiction and does not depend on the consent of the accused. That is, the accused does not have an election as to mode of trial, although the provincial court judge may, by virtue of s. 555(1), elect to continue the proceedings as a preliminary inquiry, in which case, the accused is deemed to have elected trial by judge and jury pursuant to s. 565(1)(*a*). As well, under s. 555(2), where, in the course of the trial, evidence establishes that the subject-matter of the offence is a testamentary instrument or that its value exceeds $5,000 then the provincial court judge shall put the accused to his election under s. 536(2). Where the prosecution elects to proceed by way of summary conviction then the proceedings are conducted by a summary conviction court pursuant to Part XXVII. The punishment is then as set out in s. 787 and the limitation period is set out in s. 786(2). Release pending trial is determined by s. 515, although the accused is eligible for release by a peace officer under s. 496, 497 or by the officer in charge under s. 498. The value of a valuable security is determined in accordance with s. 4(2) and of a postal card or stamp in accordance with s. 4(1). The term "testamentary instrument" is defined in s. 2. Where the prosecution elects to proceed by indictment for the offence under subsec. (5) or (5.1) then the accused may elect his mode of trial under s. 536(2). Where the prosecution elects to proceed by way of summary conviction then the proceedings are conducted by a summary conviction court pursuant to Part XXVII. The punishment is then as set out in s. 787 and the limitation period is set out in s. 786(2). Release pending trial for the offences in subsec. (5) or (5.1) is determined under s. 515, although the accused is eligible for release by a peace officer under s. 496, 497 or by the officer in charge under s. 498.

Using a computer facility with intent to commit an offence under this section is an offence under s. 342.1(1)(*c*). The offence of public mischief [*i.e.*, misleading a peace officer] is in s. 140. Under s. 718.2(*a*)(i) evidence that the offence was motivated by bias, prejudice or hate based on certain grounds such as religion is an aggravating factor on sentencing.

SYNOPSIS

This section describes the offence of mischief in its various forms. It also sets out the punishment that will be applied after a finding of guilt under this section. Every person who *wilfully* does any of the things listed in subsec. (1) or (1.1) commits the offence of mischief. The punishment for this offence, depending on the circumstances of the case, can be life imprisonment. The penalty depends on the nature of the conduct or the property involved, such as religious property under subsec. (4.1), or cultural property under subsec. (4.2). Subsections (6) and (7) provide exemptions from the offence of mischief for the specific actions described therein. Subsection (6) would appear to apply to a situation involving a labour dispute.

ANNOTATIONS

Mischief to property [subsec. (1)] – The gravamen of this offence is the commission of mischief and an information that sets out the alternative modes in para. (*c*) is not duplicitous: *R. v. Hibbs* (1973), 10 C.C.C. (2d) 513 (Alta. S.C.).

This subsection defines one offence of mischief which has been classified for sentencing purposes by application of subsecs. (2), (3) or (4): *R. v. Lebrun* (1988), 65 C.R. (3d) 280 (Que. C.A.).

The offence under para. (*a*) of this subsection is a general intent offence for which intoxication as a result of voluntary consumption of alcohol or drugs is not a defence: *R. v. Schmidtke* (1985), 19 C.C.C. (3d) 390 (Ont. C.A.).

The offence in para. (*a*) requires proof that the property was rendered less suited for its intended purpose or that at least temporarily the usefulness or the value of the property was impaired. Putting a poster on a lamp-post did not impair the use or value of the property and could not amount to the offence: *R. v. Quickfall* (1993), 78 C.C.C. (3d) 563 (Que. C.A.), leave to appeal to S.C.C. refused 83 C.C.C. (3d) vi. To similar effect, see *R. v. Jeffers* (2012), 280 C.C.C. (3d) 54 (Ont. C.A.).

A person who as part of a labour dispute forms part of a human barricade so as to block access to the premises, in violation of an injunction limiting the number of picketers, may be found guilty of the offence under para. (*c*) either as a principal or a party though he neither says nor does anything other than stand shoulder to shoulder with other persons: *R. v. Mammolita* (1983), 9 C.C.C. (3d) 85 (Ont. C.A.).

However, members of a trade union lawfully on strike may picket an employer's place of business with the purpose of bringing economic pressure to bear on that employer and subsec. (1)(*c*) should not be interpreted so as to make this lawful activity an offence. The offence requires proof of some physical act on the part of the accused which operates as, or has the effect of causing, some sort of obstruction, interruption, or interference with the use or enjoyment or potential use or enjoyment of the property that goes beyond the mere communication of information through picketing. The fact that persons may be persuaded voluntarily not to do business with the owner or that the employer's attention is diverted from his business to deal with the actions of the accused is simply the inevitable consequence of the give and take of the economic pressures that are necessarily incidental to any labour dispute: *R. v. Dooling* (1994), 94 C.C.C. (3d) 525 (Nfld. S.C.).

Enjoyment of property as used in subsec. (1)(*c*) refers to "use" or "pleasure". Conduct of the accused in having a loud party, thus interfering with his neighbour's ability to sleep, can constitute interference with possessory rights so as to amount to an offence under subsec. (1)(*c*): *R. v. W. (T.)* (1993), 21 W.C.B. (2d) 194 (B.C.S.C.). Similarly, in *R. v. Maddeaux*

(1997), 115 C.C.C. (3d) 122 (Ont. C.A.), leave to appeal to S.C.C. refused 118 C.C.C. (3d) vi, the court held that "use, enjoyment or operation" are to be read *ejusdem generis*. "Use" and "enjoyment" include presence for purposes of cooking, eating, cleaning, resting, sleeping, listening to the radio or watching television. "Operation" would normally apply to a commercial, institutional or industrial enterprise.

In *R. v. Nicol* (2002), 170 C.C.C. (3d) 59 (Man. C.A.), the court held that "enjoyment" is not limited to proprietary rights and includes taking pleasure from the use of the property.

The term "any person" in para. (*d*) includes employees or invitees and is not limited to the owner or leaseholder: *R. v. Biggin* (1980), 55 C.C.C. (2d) 408 (Ont. C.A.).

In *R. v. Drapeau* (1995), 96 C.C.C. (3d) 554 (Que. C.A.), a majority of the court held that the accused could not be convicted of the offence under subsec. (1)(*d*) based on his conduct in watching or staring at his neighbours and by making objectionable noises. Beauregard J.A. held that there was a doubt that the accused intended to interfere with the complainants' enjoyment of their land. Fish J.A. held that the term "enjoyment" must be restricted to the entitlement or exercise of a right in relation to property. It could not apply to conduct which merely diminishes the pleasure derived from a property by its owner. Chamberland J.A. dissenting would have upheld the accused's conviction on the basis that "enjoyment" should include the satisfaction which the property can provide to the owner.

Actual danger to life [subsec. (2)] – The actual danger to life must be the direct result of a deliberate act of mischief and not just merely incidental thereto: *R. v. Nairn* (1955), 112 C.C.C. 272 (Nfld. S.C.).

There is no requirement that the actual danger to life be caused by the damage as opposed to the act which caused the damage: *R. v. Humphrey* (1986), 21 O.A.C. 36 (C.A.).

Punishment [subsecs. (3) and (4)] – Other than a testamentary instrument it is the value of the property damaged not the amount of the damage which determines whether the charge lies under this subsection or subsec. (4). Accordingly the information should allege either the value of the property or make reference to subsec. (3) or (4): *R. v. Sargent and Hinds* (1986), 55 C.R. (3d) 78 (Ont. Prov. Ct.).

An information which merely fails to allege the value of the property still discloses an offence known to law and is capable of amendment to allege the value of the property: *R. v. Fediash* (1988), 44 C.C.C. (3d) 233 (Sask. Q.B.).

Subsection (5.1) – The *mens rea* for this offence is objective. Accordingly, the *mens rea* was made out where the accused lit a bag of chips on fire, a reasonable person would perceive that the resultant damage to property was a likely consequence: *R. v. D. (S.D.)* (2002), 164 C.C.C. (3d) 1 (Nfld. & Lab. C.A.).

Saving [subsec. (7)] – This subsection does not provide a defence to a person who trespasses on private property in order to communicate his message: *R. v. Waters* (1990), 54 C.C.C. (3d) 40 (Sask. Q.B.).

The accused's conduct in parking his truck near his property line and placing a sign on his truck directed at his neighbours fell within subsec. (7). The acts constituted no more than communication of a message and posed no danger to anyone or to the complainant's property, notwithstanding the fact that the message negatively affected the complainant's ability to sell their property: *R. v. Tremblay* (2010), 256 C.C.C. (3d) 389 (Ont. C.A.).

ATTACK ON PREMISES, RESIDENCE OR TRANSPORT OF INTERNATIONALLY PROTECTED PERSON.

431. Every one who commits a violent attack on the official premises, private accommodation or means of transport of an internationally protected person that is likely to endanger the life or liberty of such a person is guilty of an indictable offence and liable to imprisonment for a term of not more than fourteen years. 1974-75-76, c. 93, s. 34; R.S.C. 1985, c. 27 (1st Supp.), s. 58; 2001, c. 41, s. 13.

CROSS-REFERENCES

The term "internationally protected person" is defined in s. 2. Section 7(10) provides for admissibility of a certificate from the Secretary of State for External Affairs stating any fact relevant to the question of whether any person is a person who is entitled, pursuant to international law, to special protection from any attack on his person, freedom or dignity.

This offence may be the basis for an application for an authorization to intercept private communications by reason of s. 183 and for a warrant to conduct video surveillance by reason of s. 487.01(5).

Section 7(3) enacts special jurisdictional rules for commission of this offence outside Canada when the offence is in relation to an internationally protected person or property referred to in this section. A threat to commit an offence under this section is an offence under s. 424.

The accused may elect the mode of trial pursuant to s. 536(2). Release pending trial is determined by s. 515. A person convicted of the offence in this section may be liable to the mandatory prohibition order in s. 109 for possession of weapons, ammunition and explosives.

SYNOPSIS

This section describes the offence of attacking the official premises, private accommodation or means of transport of an internationally protected person. The attack must be likely to endanger the life or liberty of such a protected person. The offence is indictable and carries a maximum term of 14 years. This offence is related to s. 424.

ATTACK ON PREMISES, ACCOMMODATION OR TRANSPORT OF UNITED NATIONS OR ASSOCIATED PERSONNEL.

431.1 Every one who commits a violent attack on the official premises, private accommodation or means of transport of a member of United Nations personnel or associated personnel that is likely to endanger the life or liberty of such a person is guilty of an indictable offence and liable to imprisonment for a term of not more than fourteen years. 2001, c. 41, s. 13.

CROSS-REFERENCES

The terms "associated personnel" and "United Nations personnel" are defined in s. 2. This offence may be the basis for an application for an authorization to intercept private communications by reason of s. 183 and a warrant to conduct video surveillance under s. 487.01(5). Section 7(3) enacts special jurisdictional rules for commission of this offence outside Canada. A threat to commit an offence under this section is an offence under s. 424.1. The certificate of the Minister of Foreign Affairs is proof of facts relevant to the question of whether any person is a member of United Nations personnel or a member of associated personnel under s. 7(10).

SYNOPSIS

This section describes the offence of violently attacking the official premises, private accommodation or means of transport of a member of United Nations personnel or personnel associated with the United Nations. The attack must be likely to endanger the life or liberty of such a person. The offence is indictable and carries a maximum term of 14 years. This offence is related to s. 424.1.

DEFINITIONS / Explosive or other lethal device / Armed forces.

431.2 (1) The following definitions apply in this section.

"explosive or other lethal device" means

(*a*) an explosive or incendiary weapon or device that is designed to cause, or is capable of causing, death, serious bodily injury or substantial material damage; or

(*b*) a weapon or device that is designed to cause, or is capable of causing, death, serious bodily injury or substantial material damage through the release, dissemination or impact of toxic chemicals, biological agents or toxins or similar substances, or radiation or radioactive material.

"infrastructure facility" means a publicly or privately owned facility that provides or distributes services for the benefit of the public, including services relating to water, sewage, energy, fuel and communications.

"military forces of a state" means the armed forces that a state organizes, trains and equips in accordance with the law of the state for the primary purpose of national defence or national security, and every person acting in support of those armed forces who is under their formal command, control and responsibility.

"place of public use" means those parts of land, a building, street, waterway or other location that are accessible or open to members of the public, whether on a continuous, periodic or occasional basis, and includes any commercial, business, cultural, historical, educational, religious, governmental, entertainment, recreational or other place that is accessible or open to the public on such a basis.

"public transportation system" means a publicly or privately owned facility, conveyance or other thing that is used in connection with publicly available services for the transportation of persons or cargo.

(2) Every one who delivers, places, discharges or detonates an explosive or other lethal device to, into, in or against a place of public use, a government or public facility, a public transportation system or an infrastructure facility, either with intent to cause death or serious bodily injury or with intent to cause extensive destruction of such a place, system or facility that results in or is likely to result in major economic loss, is guilty of an indictable offence and liable to imprisonment for life.

(3) For greater certainty, subsection (2) does not apply to an act or omission that is committed during an armed conflict and that, at the time and in the place of its commission, is in accordance with customary international law or conventional international law applicable to the conflict, or to activities undertaken by military forces of a state in the exercise of their official duties, to the extent that those activities are governed by other rules of international law. 2001, c. 41, s. 13.

CROSS-REFERENCES

The other offences concerning explosives are found in ss. 79 to 82. Section 7(3.72) enacts special jurisdictional rules for commission of this offence outside Canada. This offence may be the basis for an application for an authorization to intercept private communications by reason of s. 183 and a warrant to conduct video surveillance under s. 487.01(5). "Government or public facility" is defined in s. 2.

SYNOPSIS

Although many of the acts covered by this section would also be covered by the general explosive offences especially under s. 81, this creates a specific offence for delivering, placing, discharging or detonating explosives or other lethal devices in public places, or government or public facilities, or public transportation systems or infrastructure facilities. The acts must be done with the intent to cause death, serious bodily harm or extensive destruction of such place or facility resulting in or likely to result in major economic loss. The maximum penalty for the offence is life imprisonment. There is a saving provision in subsec. (3) for acts carried out in times of war or by military forces of a state.

---

432. [*Repealed*, R.S.C. 1985, c. 27 (1st Supp.), s. 58 (old provision).]

UNAUTHORIZED RECORDING OF A MOVIE / Unauthorized recording for purpose of sale, etc. / Forfeiture / Forfeiture — limitation.

432. (1) A person who, without the consent of the theatre manager, records in a movie theatre a performance of a cinematographic work within the meaning of section 2 of the *Copyright Act* or its soundtrack

(*a*) is guilty of an indictable offence and liable to imprisonment for a term of not more than two years; or

(*b*) is guilty of an offence punishable on summary conviction.

(2) A person who, without the consent of the theatre manager, records in a movie theatre a performance of a cinematographic work within the meaning of section 2 of the *Copyright Act* or its soundtrack for the purpose of the sale, rental or other commercial distribution of a copy of the cinematographic work

(*a*) is guilty of an indictable offence and liable to imprisonment for a term of not more than five years; or

(*b*) is guilty of an offence punishable on summary conviction.

(3) In addition to any punishment that is imposed on a person who is convicted of an offence under this section, the court may order that anything that is used in the commission of the offence be forfeited to Her Majesty in right of the province in which the proceedings are taken. Anything that is forfeited may be disposed of as the Attorney General directs.

(4) No order may be made under subsection (3) in respect of anything that is the property of a person who is not a party to the offence. 2007, c. 28, s. 1.

CROSS-REFERENCES

"Attorney General" is defined in s. 2. Parties to offences are defined in ss. 21 to 22.2. This offence complements the offence under s. 42 of the *Copyright Act*, R.S.C. 1985, c. C-42, which makes it an offence to record for commercial purposes *e.g.* for sale or rental or distribution of copyright works. This section relies on the definitions in the *Copyright Act* for "cinematographic work" and "performance", which are as follows:

"cinematographic work" includes any work expressed by any process analogous to cinematography, whether or not accompanied by a soundtrack;

"performance" means any acoustic or visual representation of a work, performer's performance, sound recording or communication signal, including a representation made by means of any mechanical instrument, radio receiving set or television receiving set;

SYNOPSIS

This section creates two offences. Subsection (1) simply makes it an offence to record a performance in a movie theatre without the manager's consent. The Crown need not prove that the person had a commercial purpose. Subsection (2) overlaps with the offence under the *Copyright Act* and similarly makes it an offence to record without the consent of the theatre manager for purposes of sale, rental or other commercial distribution. Subsection (3) permits the sentencing court to order forfeiture of the equipment used in the commission of the offence. However, by virtue of subsec. (4), no order for forfeiture may be made in respect of anything that is the property of a person who is not a party to the offence.

Arson and Other Fires

ARSON / Disregard for human life.

433. Every person who intentionally or recklessly causes damage by fire or explosion to property, whether or not that person owns the property, is guilty of an indictable offence and liable to imprisonment for life where

(*a*) the person knows that or is reckless with respect to whether the property is inhabited or occupied; or

(*b*) the fire or explosion causes bodily harm to another person. R.S., c. C-34, s. 389; 1990, c. 15, s. 1.

CROSS-REFERENCES

The term "bodily harm" is defined in s. 2. The term "property" is defined in s. 428. The term "recklessly" is not defined, but reference might be made to *R. v. Sansregret*, [1985] 1 S.C.R. 570, 18 C.C.C. (3d) 223, where recklessness was defined as being found "in the attitude of one who, aware that there is danger that his conduct could bring about the result prohibited by the criminal law, nevertheless persists, despite the risk. It is, in other words, the conduct of one who sees the risk and who takes the chance." The defence of legal justification or excuse and colour of right is set out in s. 429(2).

This offence may be the basis for an application for an authorization to intercept private communications by reason of s. 183 and a warrant to conduct video surveillance under s. 487.01. Arson is an enterprise crime offence for the purposes of Part XII.2.

Section 17 limits the availability of the statutory defence of compulsion by threats to the offence of "arson".

The accused may elect this mode of trial pursuant to s. 536(2). Release pending trial is determined by s. 515.

Related offences: s. 81, using explosives; s. 434, intentionally or recklessly causing damage by fire or explosion to property not wholly owned by accused; s. 434.1, intentionally or recklessly causing damage by fire or explosion to property wholly owned by accused; s. 435, causing damage by fire or explosion with intent to defraud; s. 436, causing fire or explosion through negligence; s. 436.1, possession of incendiary material.

SYNOPSIS

The section creates the offence of *intentionally* or *recklessly* causing *damage to property* by fire or explosion. It must be shown either that: (1) the accused knew, or was reckless as to whether or not the property was inhabited or occupied; or (2) bodily harm to another person resulted from the fire or explosion. It is irrelevent whether or not the accused owns the property. This is an indictable offence carrying a maximum sentence of life imprisonment.

ANNOTATIONS

The offence contrary to s. 434 is not included in the offence of arson as described in this section. The offence of mischief under s. 430 is, however, an included offence: *R. v. Pascal* (1994), 90 C.C.C. (3d) 575 (Man. C.A.).

Recklessness requires proof that the accused actually knew that damage by fire to the property specified was the probable consequence of the proposed action and the accused proceeded with the conduct in the face of the risk. In this case, proof of the intentional burning of a bag of chips, without knowledge of the probable consequence that the building would burn, was insufficient to establish the requisite *mens rea*: *R. v. D. (S.D.)* (2002), 164 C.C.C. (3d) 1 (Nfld. & Lab. C.A.).

The inhabitation or occupation required by para. (*a*) means inhabitation or occupation by someone other than the accused himself: *R. v. Ludwig* (2018), 367 C.C.C. (3d) 341 (Ont. C.A.).

ARSON / Damage to property.

434. Every person who intentionally or recklessly causes damage by fire or explosion to property that is not wholly owned by that person is guilty of an indictable offence and liable to imprisonment for a term not exceeding fourteen years. R.S., c. C-34, s. 390; 1990, c. 15, s. 1.

CROSS-REFERENCES

The term "property" is defined in s. 428. The term "recklessly" is not defined but reference might be made to *R. v. Sansregret*, [1985] 1 S.C.R. 570, 18 C.C.C. (3d) 223, where recklessness was defined as being found "in the attitude of one who, aware that there is danger that his conduct could bring about the result prohibited by the criminal law, nevertheless persists, despite the risk. It is, in other words, the conduct of one who sees the risk and who takes the chance." The defence of legal justification or excuse and colour of right is set out in s. 429(2).

This offence may be the basis for a conviction for constructive murder under s. 230.

Section 17 limits the availability of the statutory defence of compulsion by threats to the offence of "arson".

The accused may elect his mode of trial under s. 536(2). Release pending trial is determined under s. 515.

Related offences: s. 81, using explosives; s. 433, intentionally or recklessly causing damage by fire or explosion to property where bodily harm is caused or where person knows property is occupied; s. 434.1, intentionally or recklessly causing damage by fire or explosion to property wholly owned by accused; s. 435, causing damage by fire or explosion with intent to defraud; s. 436, causing fire or explosion through negligence; s. 436.1, possession of incendiary material.

SYNOPSIS

The section creates the offence of willfully or recklessly causing damage by fire or explosion to property that the accused does not wholly own. This is an indictable offence carrying a maximum sentence of 14 years.

ANNOTATIONS

This is a general intent offence for which intoxication falling short of automatism is not available as a defence. The *actus reus* is the damaging of property by fire. The mental element is the intentional or reckless performance of the illegal act. No additional knowledge or purpose is needed. In assessing the issue of intent, the trier of fact must consider all of the surrounding circumstances. The manner in which the fire started is likely to be an important consideration. Ultimately, the question is whether it can be inferred that the accused intended to damage someone else's property or was reckless whether damage ensued or not: *R. v. Tatton*, [2015] 2 S.C.R. 574, 323 C.C.C. (3d) 166.

The term "damage" does not require proof that the property was diminished in value by the fire. Damage may include physical harm to the property: *R. v. V. (M.)* (1998), 123 C.C.C. (3d) 138 (Ont. C.A.).

Recklessness requires proof that the accused actually knew that damage by fire to the property specified was the probable consequence of the proposed action and the accused proceeded with the conduct in the face of the risk. In this case, proof of intentional burning of a bag of chips, without knowledge of the probable consequence that the building would burn, was insufficient to establish the requisite *mens rea*: *R. v. D. (S.D.)* (2002), 164 C.C.C. (3d) 1 (Nfld. & Lab. C.A.).

ARSON / Own property.

434.1 Every person who intentionally or recklessly causes damage by fire or explosion to property that is owned, in whole or in part, by that person is guilty of an indictable offence and liable to imprisonment for a term not exceeding fourteen years, where the

fire or explosion seriously threatens the health, safety or property of another person. 1990, c. 15, s. 1.

CROSS-REFERENCES

The term "property" is defined in s. 428. The term "recklessly" is not defined but reference might be made to *R. v. Sansregret*, [1985] 1 S.C.R. 570, 18 C.C.C. (3d) 223, where recklessness was defined as being found "in the attitude of one who, aware that there is danger that his conduct could bring about the result prohibited by the criminal law, nevertheless persists, despite the risk. It is, in other words, the conduct of one who sees the risk and who takes the chance." The defence of legal justification or excuse and colour of right is set out in s. 429(2).

Section 17 limits the availability of the statutory defence of compulsion by threats to the offence of "arson".

The accused may elect his mode of trial under s. 536(2). Release pending trial is determined under s. 515.

Related offences: s. 81, using explosives; s. 433, intentionally or recklessly causing damage by fire or explosion to property where bodily harm is caused or where person knows property is occupied; s. 434, intentionally or recklessly causing damage by fire or explosion to property not wholly owned by accused; s. 435, causing damage by fire or explosion with intent to defraud; s. 436, causing fire or explosion through negligence; s. 436.1, possession of incendiary material.

SYNOPSIS

The section creates the offence of willfully or recklessly causing damage by fire or explosion to property owned, in whole or in part, by the accused, where the fire or explosion *seriously threatens* the health, safety or property of *another person*. This is an indictable offence carrying a maximum sentence of 14 years.

ANNOTATIONS

The Crown is not required to prove that the accused knew that the fire threatened the health, safety, or property of others: *R. v. Bastien* (2017), 349 C.C.C. (3d) 149 (B.C.C.A.).

ARSON FOR FRAUDULENT PURPOSE / Holder or beneficiary of fire insurance policy.

435. (1) Every person who, with intent to defraud any other person, causes damage by fire or explosion to property, whether or not that person owns, in whole or in part, the property, is guilty of an indictable offence and liable to imprisonment for a term not exceeding ten years.

(2) Where a person is charged with an offence under subsection (1), the fact that the person was the holder of or was named as a beneficiary under a policy of fire insurance relating to the property in respect of which the offence is alleged to have been committed is a fact from which intent to defraud may be inferred by the court. R.S., c. C-34, s. 391; 1990, c. 15, s. 1.

CROSS-REFERENCES

The term "property" is defined in s. 428. Section 17 limits the availability of the statutory defence of compulsion by threats to the offence of "arson". The accused may elect his mode of trial under s. 536(2). Release pending trial is determined under s. 515.

Related offences: s. 81, using explosives; s. 433, intentionally or recklessly causing damage by fire or explosion to property where bodily harm is caused or where person knows property is occupied; s. 434, intentionally or recklessly causing damage by fire or explosion to property not wholly owned by accused; s. 434.1, intentionally or recklessly causing damage by fire or explosion to property wholly owned by accused; s. 436, causing fire or explosion through negligence; s. 436.1, possession of incendiary material.

SYNOPSIS

The section creates the offence of causing damage to property by fire or explosion with the *intent to defraud* another person. It is irrelevent whether or not the accused owns the property, in whole or in part. By subsec. (2), a court may *infer intention* to defraud from the fact that the accused is the holder of, or named beneficiary under, a policy of fire insurance in respect of damaged property. This is an indictable offence carrying a maximum sentence of 10 years.

ANNOTATIONS

Application of inference – It was held in relation to former s. 435 that the presumption did not apply where the accused were insured only in respect to loss of personal property within the burned premises: *R. v. Drouin and Drouin*, [1973] S.C.R. 747, 10 C.C.C. (2d) 381.

ARSON BY NEGLIGENCE / Non-compliance with prevention laws.

436. (1) Every person who owns, in whole or in part, or controls property is guilty of an indictable offence and liable to imprisonment for a term not exceeding five years where, as a result of a marked departure from the standard of care that a reasonably prudent person would use to prevent or control the spread of fires or to prevent explosions, that person is a cause of a fire or explosion in that property that causes bodily harm to another person or damage to property.

(2) Where a person is charged with an offence under subsection (1), the fact that the person has failed to comply with any law respecting the prevention or control of fires or explosions in the property is a fact from which a marked departure from the standard of care referred to in that subsection may be inferred by the court. R.S., c. C-34, s. 392; 1990, c. 15, s. 1.

CROSS-REFERENCES

The term "bodily harm" is defined in s. 2. The term "property" is defined in s. 428. The defence of legal justification or excuse and colour of right is set out in s. 429(2). The standard of liability in this section resembles the test adopted for the criminal negligence offences in ss. 220 and 221. Thus, see notes under those sections and s. 219.

Section 17 limits the availability of the statutory defence of compulsion by threats to the offence of "arson".

The accused may elect his mode of trial pursuant to s. 536(2). Release pending trial is determined by s. 515.

Related offences; s. 81, using explosives; s. 434, intentionally or recklessly causing damage by fire or explosion to property not wholly owned by accused; s. 434.1, intentionally or recklessly causing damage by fire or explosion to property wholly owned by accused; s. 435, causing damage by fire or explosion with intent to defraud; s. 436.1, possession of incendiary material.

SYNOPSIS

The section creates the offence of being a cause of any fire or explosion in a *property owned, in whole or in part, or controlled* by the accused where: (1) a marked departure from the standard of care that a reasonably prudent person would use, to prevent or control the spread of fires or to prevent explosions, is shown to be the cause of the fire or explosion; and (2) the fire or explosion resulted in bodily harm to another person, or damage to property. By subsec. (2), a court may *infer marked departure* from the subsec. (1) standard of care, from the fact that the accused has *failed to comply* with any law respecting the prevention or control of fires or explosions in the property. This is an indictable offence carrying a maximum sentence of five years.

ANNOTATIONS

This provision imposes a duty to prevent or control the spread of fires and thus an accused may be convicted under this section even if the fire may have originally been caused by an agency other than that of the accused. The section does, however, require proof of a causal connection between the accused's breach of duty, the resulting spread of the fire, and the injury or damage: *R. v. Harricharan* (1995), 98 C.C.C. (3d) 145, 23 O.R. (3d) 233 (C.A.).

POSSESSION OF INCENDIARY MATERIAL.

436.1 Every person who possesses any incendiary material, incendiary device or explosive substance for the purpose of committing an offence under any of sections 433 to 436 is guilty of an indictable offence and liable to imprisonment for a term not exceeding five years. 1990, c. 15, s. 1.

CROSS-REFERENCES

Possession is defined in s. 4(3). For definition of "explosive substance", see s. 2. The accused may elect his mode of trial pursuant to s. 536(2). Release pending trial is determined by s. 515.

Related offences: s. 81, using explosives; s. 82, possession of explosive substance without lawful excuse; s. 434, intentionally or recklessly causing damage by fire or explosion to property not wholly owned by accused; s. 434.1, intentionally or recklessly causing damage by fire or explosion to property wholly owned by accused; s. 435, causing damage by fire or explosion with intent to defraud; s. 436, causing fire or explosion through negligence.

SYNOPSIS

The section creates the offence of *possessing* any incendiary material or device, or explosive substance for the purpose of committing a ss. 433 to 436 offence. This is an indictable offence carrying a maximum term of five years.

Other Interference with Property

FALSE ALARM OF FIRE.

437. Every one who wilfully, without reasonable cause, by outcry, ringing bells, using a fire alarm, telephone or telegraph, or in any other manner, makes or circulates or causes to be made or circulated an alarm of fire is guilty of

(*a*) an indictable offence and liable to imprisonment for a term not exceeding two years; or

(*b*) an offence punishable on summary conviction. R.S., c. C-34, s. 393; 1972, c. 13, s. 31.

CROSS-REFERENCES

The term "wilfully" is defined in s. 429(1). The defence of legal justification or excuse and colour of right is set out in s. 429(2).

Where the prosecution elects to proceed by indictment on this offence then the accused may elect his mode of trial pursuant to s. 536(2). Where the prosecution elects to proceed by way of summary conviction then the trial of this offence is conducted by a summary conviction court pursuant to Part XXVII. The limitation period is set out in s. 786(2). In either case, release pending trial is determined by s. 515, although the accused is eligible for release by a peace officer under ss. 496, 497 or by the officer in charge under s. 498.

SYNOPSIS

This section describes the offence of raising a false alarm of fire. Every person who *wilfully* and *without reasonable cause* makes or circulates, or causes to be made or circulated, an alarm of fire is guilty of an offence punishable on summary conviction or by indictment. A person convicted of the indictable offence is liable to a maximum term of two years' imprisonment.

INTERFERING WITH SAVING OF WRECKED VESSEL / Interfering with saving of wreck.

438. (1) Every one who wilfully prevents or impedes, or who wilfully endeavours to prevent or impede,

(*a*) the saving of a vessel that is wrecked, stranded, abandoned or in distress, or

(*b*) a person who attempts to save a vessel that is wrecked, stranded, abandoned or in distress,

is guilty of an indictable offence and liable to imprisonment for a term not exceeding five years.

(2) Every one who wilfully prevents or impedes or wilfully endeavours to prevent or impede the saving of wreck is guilty of an offence punishable on summary conviction. R.S., c. C-34, s. 394.

CROSS-REFERENCES

The term "wreck" is defined in s. 2. The term "wilfully" is defined in s. 429(1). The defence of legal justification or excuse and colour of right is set out in s. 429(2).

For the offence under subsec. (1), the accused may elect his mode of trial under s. 536(2). Release pending trial is determined under s. 515, although the accused is eligible for release by the officer in charge under s. 498.

Trial of the offence under subsec. (2) is conducted by a summary conviction court pursuant to Part XXVII. The punishment is as set out in s. 787 and the limitation period is set out in s. 786(2). Release pending trial is determined by s. 515, although the accused is eligible for release by a peace officer under s. 496, 497 or by the officer in charge under s. 498. Other offences in relation to wreck are in s. 415 and see cross-references under that section.

SYNOPSIS

This section describes the offence of interfering with the saving of a wrecked vessel. Any person who *wilfully* prevents or impedes, or who *wilfully* endeavours to prevent or impede the saving of a vessel that is wrecked, stranded, abandoned or in distress is guilty of an indictable offence and liable to a maximum term of five years. Subsection (2) makes it a summary conviction offence to *wilfully* prevent or impede the saving of wreck.

INTERFERING WITH MARINE SIGNAL, ETC. / Idem.

439. (1) Every one who makes fast a vessel or boat to a signal, buoy or other sea-mark that is used for purposes of navigation is guilty of an offence punishable on summary conviction.

(2) Every one who wilfully alters, removes or conceals a signal, buoy or other sea-mark that is used for purposes of navigation is guilty of an indictable offence and liable to imprisonment for a term not exceeding ten years. R.S., c. C-34, s. 395.

CROSS-REFERENCES

The term "wilfully" is defined in s. 429(1). The defence of legal justification or excuse and colour of right is set out in s. 429(2).

Trial of the offence under subsec. (1) is conducted by a summary conviction court pursuant to Part XXVII. The punishment is as set out in s. 787 and the limitation period is set out in s. 786(2). Release pending trial is determined by s. 515, although the accused is eligible for release by a peace officer under s. 496, 497 or by the officer in charge under s. 498.

For the offence under subsec. (2), the accused may elect his mode of trial under s. 536(2). Release pending trial is determined under s. 515.

The more serious offence of destroying or causing serious damage to or interfering with the operation of any maritime navigational facility where the act is likely to endanger the safe navigation of a ship or the safety of a fixed platform is found in s. 78.1(2)(*c*).

SYNOPSIS

This section describes the offence of interfering with a marine signal. The summary conviction offence is committed by fastening a boat or vessel to a sea-mark used for navigation. A person who *wilfully* alters, removes or conceals a sea-mark that is used for navigation is guilty of the indictable form of the offence and is liable upon conviction to a maximum term of 10 years' imprisonment.

REMOVING NATURAL BAR WITHOUT PERMISSION.

440. Every one who wilfully and without the written permission of the Minister of Transport, the burden of proof of which lies on the accused, removes any stone, wood, earth or other material that forms a natural bar necessary to the existence of a public harbour, or that forms a natural protection to such a bar, is guilty of an indictable offence and liable to imprisonment for a term not exceeding two years. R.S., c. C-34, s. 396.

CROSS-REFERENCES

The term "wilfully" is defined in s. 429(1). The defence of legal justification or excuse and colour of right is set out in s. 429(2).

The accused may elect his mode of trial under s. 536(2). Release pending trial is determined under s. 515 although the accused is eligible for release by the officer in charge under s. 498.

SYNOPSIS

This section describes the indictable offence of removing any material that forms, or is protection to a natural bar necessary to the existence of a public harbour. The accused must act *wilfully* and *without the written permission* of the Minister of Transport, the proof of which lies upon him.

OCCUPANT INJURING BUILDING.

441. Every one who, wilfully and to the prejudice of a mortgagee or owner, pulls down, demolishes or removes, all or any part of a dwelling-house or other building of which he is in possession or occupation, or severs from the freehold any fixture fixed therein or thereto, is guilty of an indictable offence and liable to imprisonment for a term not exceeding five years. R.S., c. C-34, s. 397.

CROSS-REFERENCES

The term "wilfully" is defined in s. 429(1). The term "dwelling-house" is defined in s. 2. The defence of legal justification or excuse and colour of right is set out in s. 429(2). Where the accused has an interest in the thing destroyed see s. 429(3). The accused may elect his mode of trial under s. 536(2). Release pending trial is determined under s. 515 although the accused is eligible for release by the officer in charge under s. 498.

SYNOPSIS

In this section, an occupant of a dwelling-house or other building commits an indictable offence if he *wilfully* and *to the prejudice* of a mortgagee or owner demolishes or removes any part of the building or severs from the freehold any fixture. The maximum term of imprisonment upon conviction is five years.

ANNOTATIONS

The offence under this section is complete when any of the specified acts, done with the requisite intent, negatively affect the security interest of the mortgagee. The interest of the mortgagee may still be inchoate before any steps have been taken by the mortgagee to realize on its security: *R. v. Lundgard* (1991), 63 C.C.C. (3d) 368, [1991] 4 W.W.R. 259 (Alta. C.A.).

INTERFERING WITH BOUNDARY LINES.

442. Every one who wilfully pulls down, defaces, alters or removes anything planted or set up as the boundary line or part of the boundary line of land is guilty of an offence punishable on summary conviction. R.S., c. C-34, s. 398.

CROSS-REFERENCES

The term "wilfully" is defined in s. 429(1). The defence of legal justification or excuse and colour of right is set out in s. 429(2).

The related offence of interfering with boundary marks is in s. 443.

Trial of this offence is conducted by a summary conviction court pursuant to Part XXVII. The punishment is as set out in s. 787 and the limitation period is set out in s. 786(2). Release pending trial is determined by s. 515 although the accused is eligible for release by a peace officer under ss. 496, 497, or by the officer in charge under s. 498.

SYNOPSIS

This section describes the summary conviction offence of interfering with a boundary line. A person who *wilfully* defaces, alters or removes anything that forms a part of a boundary line is guilty of an offence under this section.

INTERFERING WITH INTERNATIONAL BOUNDARY MARKS, ETC. / Saving provision.

443. (1) Every one who wilfully pulls down, defaces, alters or removes

(*a*) a boundary mark lawfully placed to mark any international, provincial, county or municipal boundary, or

(*b*) a boundary mark lawfully placed by a land surveyor to mark a limit, boundary or angle of a concession, range, lot or parcel of land,

is guilty of an indictable offence and liable to imprisonment for a term not exceeding five years.

(2) A land surveyor does not commit an offence under subsection (1) where, in his operations as a land surveyor,

(*a*) he takes up, when necessary, a boundary mark mentioned in paragraph (1)(*b*) and carefully replaces it as it was before he took it up; or

(*b*) he takes up a boundary mark mentioned in paragraph (1)(*b*) in the course of surveying for a highway or other work that, when completed, will make it impossible or impracticable for that boundary mark to occupy its original position, and he establishes a permanent record of the original position sufficient to permit such position to be ascertained. R.S., c. C-34, s. 399.

CROSS-REFERENCES

The term "wilfully" is defined in s. 429(1). The terms "county" and "province" are defined in s. 35 of the *Interpretation Act*, R.S.C. 1985, c. I-21. The defence of legal justification or excuse and colour of right is set out in s. 429(2). Section 476 enacts special rules of territorial jurisdiction where an offence is committed on the boundary between territorial divisions.

The accused may elect his mode of trial under s. 536(2). Release pending trial is determined under s. 515 although the accused is eligible for release by the officer in charge under s. 498.

The related summary conviction offence of interfering with boundary lines is in s. 442.

SYNOPSIS

This section describes the offence of interfering with international and other boundary marks. Any person who *wilfully* defaces, alters or removes a boundary mark lawfully placed to mark an international, provincial, county or municipal boundary, or a boundary mark lawfully placed by a land surveyor, is guilty of an indictable offence and subject to a maximum term of five years' imprisonment. Subsection (2) describes specific circumstances in which a land surveyor who takes up boundary marks is not criminally liable under this section.

Animals **2018, c. 29, s. 52.**

444. [*Repealed*, 2018, c. 29, s. 52.]

INJURING OR ENDANGERING OTHER ANIMALS / Punishment.

445. (1) Every one commits an offence who, wilfully and without lawful excuse,

(*a*) kills, maims, wounds, poisons or injures dogs, birds or animals that are kept for a lawful purpose; or

(*b*) places poison in such a position that it may easily be consumed by dogs, birds or animals that are kept for a lawful purpose.

(2) Every one who commits an offence under subsection (1) is guilty of

(*a*) an indictable offence and liable to imprisonment for a term of not more than five years; or

(*b*) an offence punishable on summary conviction and liable to a fine not exceeding ten thousand dollars or to imprisonment for a term of not more than eighteen months or to both. R.S., c. C-34, s. 401, 2008, c. 12, s. 1; 2018, c. 29, s. 53.

CROSS-REFERENCES

The term "wilfully" is defined in s. 429(1). The defence of legal justification or excuse and colour of right is set out in s. 429(2). Other offences in relation to animals are set out in ss. 445.1 and 447.

In addition to any other sentence, the court may make an order under s. 447.1(1)(*a*) prohibiting the accused from owning, having the custody or control of or residing in the same premises as an animal or a bird during any period that the court considers appropriate but, in the case of a second or subsequent offence, for a minimum of five years. Further, under s. 447.1(1)(*b*), the court may order that the accused pay reasonable costs to a person or an organization that has taken care of an animal or a bird as a result of the commission of the offence, provided the costs are readily ascertainable.

SYNOPSIS

This section describes the offence of injuring or endangering animals. Any person who *wilfully and without lawful excuse* kills, maims, wounds, injures or poisons dogs, birds or animals that are kept for a lawful purpose or who places poison in a position that it might be easily consumed by those creatures, is guilty of a summary conviction offence.

ANNOTATIONS

These provisions are designed to protect domesticated or domestic animals and do not apply to stray animals, the words "kept for a lawful purpose" contemplating a keeper of the animal and a measure of control exercised by that person: *R. v. Deschamps* (1978), 43 C.C.C. (2d) 45 (Ont. Prov. Ct.).

Once the dog that the defendant believed had been worrying his sheep had left the scene and was no longer a danger, he had no justification for wounding it: *R. v. Etherington*, [1963] 2 C.C.C. 230 (Ont. Mag. Ct.).

An accused would have a defence to a charge under this section involving the injury to a police service dog where the use of the dog in the circumstances constituted excessive use of force: *R. v. Barr* (1982), 1 C.C.C. (3d) 47 (Alta. Prov. Ct.).

KILLING OR INJURING CERTAIN ANIMALS / Punishment / Sentences to be served consecutively / Definitions.

445.01 (1) Every one commits an offence who, wilfully and without lawful excuse, kills, maims, wounds, poisons or injures a law enforcement animal while it is aiding a law enforcement officer in carrying out that officer's duties, a military animal while it is aiding a member of the Canadian Forces in carrying out that member's duties or a service animal.

(2) Every one who commits an offence under subsection (1) is guilty of

(*a*) an indictable offence and liable to imprisonment for a term of not more than five years and, if a law enforcement animal is killed in the commission of the offence, to a minimum punishment of imprisonment for a term of six months; or

(*b*) an offence punishable on summary conviction and liable to a fine of not more than $10,000 or to imprisonment for a term of not more than 18 months or to both.

(3) A sentence imposed on a person for an offence under subsection (1) committed against a law enforcement animal shall be served consecutively to any other punishment imposed on the person for an offence arising out of the same event or series of events.

(4) The following definitions apply in this section.

"law enforcement animal" means a dog or horse that is trained to aid a law enforcement officer in carrying out that officer's duties.

"law enforcement officer" means a police officer, a police constable or any person referred to in paragraph (*b*), (*c*.1), (*d*), (*d*.1), (*e*) or (*g*) of the definition "peace officer" in section 2.

"military animal" means an animal that is trained to aid a member of the Canadian Forces in carrying out that member's duties.

"service animal" means an animal that is required by a person with a disability for assistance and is certified, in writing, as having been trained by a professional service animal institution to assist a person with a disability. 2015, c. 34, s. 3.

CROSS-REFERENCES

The term "wilfully" is defined in s. 429(1). The defence of legal justification or excuse and colour of right is set out in s. 429(2). Section 718.03 provides that, when imposing a sentence for an offence under s. 445.01(1), the primary considerations are denunciation and deterrence.

SYNOPSIS

This section creates the hybrid offence of injuring or endangering law enforcement or military animals that are assisting officers or members in their duties, or service animals.

Cruelty to Animals

CAUSING UNNECESSARY SUFFERING / Punishment / Failure to exercise reasonable care as evidence / Presence at baiting as evidence.

445.1 (1) Every one commits an offence who

(*a*) wilfully causes or, being the owner, wilfully permits to be caused unnecessary pain, suffering or injury to an animal or a bird;

(*b*) in any manner encourages, aids or assists at the fighting or baiting of animals or birds;

(*c*) wilfully, without reasonable excuse, administers a poisonous or an injurious drug or substance to a domestic animal or bird or an animal or a bird wild by nature that is kept in captivity or, being the owner of such an animal or a bird, wilfully permits a poisonous or an injurious drug or substance to be administered to it;

(*d*) promotes, arranges, conducts, assists in, receives money for or takes part in any meeting, competition, exhibition, pastime, practice, display or event at or in the course of which captive birds are liberated by hand, trap, contrivance or any other means for the purpose of being shot when they are liberated; or

(*e*) being the owner, occupier or person in charge of any premises, permits the premises or any part thereof to be used for a purpose mentioned in paragraph (*d*).

(2) Every one who commits an offence under subsection (1) is guilty of

(*a*) an indictable offence and liable to imprisonment for a term of not more than five years; or

(*b*) an offence punishable on summary conviction and liable to a fine not exceeding ten thousand dollars or to imprisonment for a term of not more than eighteen months or to both.

(3) For the purposes of proceedings under paragraph (1)(*a*), evidence that a person failed to exercise reasonable care or supervision of an animal or a bird thereby causing it pain, suffering or injury is, in the absence of any evidence to the contrary, proof that the pain, suffering or injury was caused or was permitted to be caused wilfully, as the case may be.

(4) For the purpose of proceedings under paragraph (1)(*b*), evidence that an accused was present at the fighting or baiting of animals or birds is, in the absence of any evidence to the contrary, proof that he or she encouraged, aided or assisted at the fighting or baiting. 2008, c. 12, s. 1.

CROSS-REFERENCES

"Wilfully" is defined in s. 429(1). Sections 444 and 445 create offences dealing with killing or endangering animals. Section 446 creates offences relating to the damaging or injuring of animals and birds while they are being driven or conveyed, or abandoning animals and birds. In addition to any other sentence, the court may make an order under s. 447.1(1)(*a*) prohibiting the accused from owning, having the custody or control of or residing in the same premises as an animal or a bird during any period that the court considers appropriate but, in the case of a second or subsequent offence, for a minimum of five years. Further, under s. 447.1(1)(*b*), the court may order that the accused pay reasonable costs to a person or an organization that has taken care of an animal or a bird as a result of the commission of the offence, provided the costs are readily ascertainable.

SYNOPSIS

This section is one of three dealing with cruelty to animals. Subsection (1) sets out a number of ways in which the offence is committed, including causing unnecessary cruelty, encouraging fighting or baiting animals or birds, administering poison or injurious drugs without reasonable excuse, and promoting meetings and similar pastimes where captive birds are liberated for the purpose of being shot. Subsections (3) and (4) create presumptions to aid in the prosecution of the offences.

ANNOTATIONS

Note: Some of the cases noted below were decided before the recent amendments but were thought to still be of assistance.

Subsection (1)(*a*) – "Unnecessary" in this context means that man in the pursuit of his legitimate purposes is obliged not to inflict pain, suffering or injury which is not inevitable taking into account the purpose sought and the circumstances of the particular case. Thus while euthanasia of stray animals is itself justified, where the method used by the accused causes pain and suffering which was not inevitable in view of alternative economically feasible methods available, the accused should be convicted: *R. v. Menard* (1978), 43 C.C.C. (2d) 458 (Que. C.A.).

Determining whether there is an absence of reasonable care or supervision is an objective exercise. In the absence of any evidence to the contrary, evidence that a person failed to exercise reasonable care is proof of wilfulness for the purposes of subsec. (1)(*a*). Where there is evidence to the contrary, the Crown must prove willful conduct and s. 429(1), which engages the subjective element of recklessness, applies: *R. v. Gerling*, [2016] B.C.J. No. 264 (C.A.).

Subsection (1)(*b*) – In *Pitts v. Miller* (1874), L.R. 9, Q.B. 380 (Q.B.), Cockburn C.J. considered baiting in terms of an animal either tied to a stake or unable to escape, and Quain J. relied upon dictionary definitions of attacking with violence or harassing with the help of others.

Subsection (1)(*d*) – The mischief sought to be prevented in this paragraph is cruelty to birds by their sudden release for the purpose of being shot at: *R. v. Prefontaine* (1973), 26 C.R.N.S. 367 (Que. C.A.).

CAUSING DAMAGE OR INJURY / Punishment / Failure to exercise reasonable care as evidence.

446. (1) Every one commits an offence who

(*a*) by wilful neglect causes damage or injury to animals or birds while they are being driven or conveyed; or

(*b*) being the owner or the person having the custody or control of a domestic animal or a bird or an animal or a bird wild by nature that is in captivity, abandons it in distress or wilfully neglects or fails to provide suitable and adequate food, water, shelter and care for it.

(2) Every one who commits an offence under subsection (1) is guilty of

(*a*) an indictable offence and liable to imprisonment for a term of not more than two years; or

(*b*) an offence punishable on summary conviction and liable to a fine not exceeding five thousand dollars or to imprisonment for a term of not more than six months or to both.

(3) For the purposes of proceedings under paragraph (1)(*a*), evidence that a person failed to exercise reasonable care or supervision of an animal or a bird thereby causing it damage or injury is, in the absence of any evidence to the contrary, proof that the damage or injury was caused by willful neglect. R.S., c. C-34, s. 402; 1974-75-76, c. 93, s. 35; 2008, c. 12, s. 1.

CROSS-REFERENCES
"Wilfully" is defined in s. 429(1). Sections 444 and 445 create offences dealing with killing or endangering animals. Section 445 creates offences relating to the causing of unnecessary suffering to animals or birds. In addition to any other sentence, the court may make an order under s. 447.1(1)(*a*) prohibiting the accused from owning, having the custody or control of or residing in the same premises as an animal or a bird during any period that the court considers appropriate but, in the case of a second or subsequent offence, for a minimum of five years. Further, under s. 447.1(1)(*b*), the court may order that the accused pay reasonable costs to a person or an organization that has taken care of an animal or a bird as a result of the commission of the offence, provided the costs are readily ascertainable.

SYNOPSIS
This section creates offences in the nature of wilful neglect of animals and birds in (a) the conveying of them, and (b) the abandoning of them. Subsection (3) creates a presumption to assist in the prosecution of the offence under subsec. (1)(*a*) arising out of the failure to exercise reasonable care or supervision.

KEEPING COCKPIT / Punishment / Confiscation.

447. (1) Every one commits an offence who builds, makes, maintains or keeps a cockpit on premises that he or she owns or occupies, or allows a cockpit to be built, made, maintained or kept on such premises.

(2) Every one who commits an offence under subsection (1) is guilty of

- **(*a*) an indictable offence and liable to imprisonment for a term of not more than five years; or**
- **(*b*) an offence punishable on summary conviction and liable to a fine not exceeding ten thousand dollars or to imprisonment for a term of not more than eighteen months or to both.**

(3) A peace officer who finds cocks in a cockpit or on premises where a cockpit is located shall seize them and take them before a justice who shall order them to be destroyed. R.S., c. C-34, s. 403; 2008, c. 12, s. 1.

CROSS-REFERENCES
The term "peace officer" is defined in s. 2. This offence applies to a person who may be described as the keeper of the cockpit. The offence, if any, committed by another person is described in s. 445.1(1)(*d*).

In addition to any other sentence, the court may make an order under s. 447.1(1)(*a*) prohibiting the accused from owning, having the custody or control of or residing in the same premises as an animal or a bird during any period that the court considers appropriate but, in the case of a second or subsequent offence, for a minimum of five years. Further, under s. 447.1(1)(*b*), the court may order that the accused pay reasonable costs to a person or an organization that has taken care of an animal or a bird as a result of the commission of the offence, provided the costs are readily ascertainable.

SYNOPSIS
This section makes it an offence for a person to build or maintain, or to allow to be built or maintained, a cockpit on premises which that person owns or occupies. Subsection (3) empowers a peace officer who finds cocks in a cockpit, or on premises where there is a cockpit, to seize the birds and take them before a justice, who must order them destroyed.

ORDER OF PROHIBITION OR RESTITUTION / Breach of order / Application.

447.1 (1) The court may, in addition to any other sentence that it may impose under subsection 445(2), 445.1(2), 446(2) or 447(2),

(*a*) make an order prohibiting the accused from owning, having the custody or control of or residing in the same premises as an animal or a bird during any period that the court considers appropriate but, in the case of a second or subsequent offence, for a minimum of five years; and

(*b*) on application of the Attorney General or on its own motion, order that the accused pay to a person or an organization that has taken care of an animal or a bird as a result of the commission of the offence the reasonable costs that the person or organization incurred in respect of the animal or bird, if the costs are readily ascertainable.

(2) Every one who contravenes an order made under paragraph (1)(*a*) is guilty of an offence punishable on summary conviction.

(3) Sections 740 to 741.2 apply, with any modifications that the circumstances require, to orders made under paragraph (1)(*b*). 2008, c. 12, s. 1; 2018, c. 29, s. 54.

CROSS-REFERENCES

"Attorney General" is defined in s. 2.

SYNOPSIS

This section provides for making a prohibition order for persons convicted of the offences relating to mistreatment of animals and birds. In addition, under subsec. (2), the sentencing court may require the offender to pay the reasonable costs of the person or organization that has had to care for the animals or birds as a result of the commission of the offence by the offender, provided the costs are readily ascertainable.

Part XII / OFFENCES RELATING TO CURRENCY

Interpretation

DEFINITIONS / "counterfeit money" / "counterfeit token of value" / "current" / "utter".

448. In this Part,

"counterfeit money" includes

(*a*) a false coin or false paper money that resembles or is apparently intended to resemble or pass for a current coin or current paper money,

(*b*) a forged bank-note or forged blank bank-note, whether complete or incomplete,

(*c*) a genuine coin or genuine paper money that is prepared or altered to resemble or pass for a current coin or current paper money of a higher denomination,

(*d*) a current coin from which the milling is removed by filing or cutting the edges and on which new milling is made to restore its appearance,

(*e*) a coin cased with gold, silver, or nickel, as the case may be, that is intended to resemble or pass for a current gold, silver or nickel coin, and

(*f*) a coin or a piece of metal or mixed metals that is washed or coloured by any means with a wash or material capable of producing the appearance of gold, silver or nickel and that is intended to resemble or pass for a current gold, silver or nickel coin;

"counterfeit token of value" means a counterfeit excise stamp, postage stamp or other evidence of value, by whatever technical, trivial or deceptive designation it may be described, and includes genuine coin or paper money that has no value as money;

"current" means lawfully current in Canada or elsewhere by virtue of a law, proclamation or regulation in force in Canada or elsewhere as the case may be;

"utter" includes sell, pay, tender and put off. R.S., c. C-34, s. 406.

CROSS-REFERENCES

In addition to the definitions in this section, see s. 2 and notes to that section. The term "bank-note" is defined in s. 2. Section 461(2) provides for admission of a certificate of an examiner of counterfeit money as proof that any money, coin or bank-note is counterfeit or genuine, as the case may be, and is or is not, as the case may be, current in Canada or elsewhere. Section 462 provides that counterfeit money, counterfeit tokens of value and anything used or intended to be used to make counterfeit money or tokens of value belong to Her Majesty. Section 462(2) gives a peace officer power to seize and detain these items.

SYNOPSIS

This section contains definitions of the terms "counterfeit money", "counterfeit token of value", "current" and "utter" for the purpose of Part XII of the *Criminal Code*.

ANNOTATIONS

A forged Government of Canada cheque does not constitute "counterfeit money" as defined in this provision: *R. v. Kirkness* (2004), 191 C.C.C. (3d) 17 (Man. C.A.).

Making

MAKING.

449. Every one who makes or begins to make counterfeit money is guilty of an indictable offence and liable to imprisonment for a term not exceeding fourteen years. R.S., c. C-34, s. 407.

CROSS-REFERENCES

The term "counterfeit money" is defined in s. 448. Section 461(1) enacts a conclusive presumption as to when the offence is complete. Section 461(2) provides for admission of a certificate of an examiner of counterfeit money as proof that any money, coin or bank-note is counterfeit or genuine and is or is not, as the case may be, current in Canada or elsewhere.

This offence may be the basis for an application for an authorization to intercept private communications by reason of s. 183 and is an enterprise crime offence for the purposes of Part XII.2.

The accused may elect his mode of trial under s. 536(2). Release pending trial is determined under s. 515. Section 462 provides that counterfeit money and anything used or intended to be used to make counterfeit money belong to Her Majesty. Section 462(2) gives a peace officer power to seize and detain these items.

Possession

POSSESSION, ETC., OF COUNTERFEIT MONEY.

450. Every person is guilty of an indictable offence and liable to imprisonment for a term of not more than 14 years who, without lawful justification or excuse,

(*a*) buys, receives or offers to buy or receive counterfeit money;

(*b*) has in their custody or possession counterfeit money; or

(*c*) introduces counterfeit money into Canada. R.S., c. C-34, s. 408; 2018, c. 29, s. 55.

CROSS-REFERENCES

Possession is defined in s. 4(3). The term "counterfeit money" is defined in s. 448. Section 461(1) enacts a conclusive presumption as to when the offence is complete. Section 461(2) provides for admission of a certificate of an examiner of counterfeit money as proof that any money, coin or bank-note is counterfeit or genuine and is or is not, as the case may be, current in Canada or elsewhere.

This offence may be the basis for an application for an authorization to intercept private communications by reason of s. 183 and is an enterprise crime offence for the purposes of Part XII.2.

The accused may elect his mode of trial under s. 536(2). Release pending trial is determined under s. 515. Section 462 provides that counterfeit money and anything used or intended to be used to make counterfeit money belong to Her Majesty. Section 462(2) gives a peace officer power to seize and detain these items.

SYNOPSIS

This section describes the indictable offence of buying, receiving, offering to buy or receive, possessing or bringing into Canada counterfeit money. A person who is charged under this section and who has dealt with counterfeit money in a fashion described above, bears the onus of proving that he had *lawful justification or excuse* for his actions. The maximum term of imprisonment upon conviction is 14 years.

ANNOTATIONS

In *R. v. Robinson*, [1974] S.C.R. 573, 10 C.C.C. (2d) 505, it was held *per* Ritchie J. (Abbott, Judson, Spence and Laskin JJ., concurring), that it was no defence that the accused was in possession of counterfeit U.S. 1941/42 dimes (the genuine coins, because of some imperfections upon minting, having a numismatic value of between $100 and $800 each) for the purpose of sale as a numismatic curiosity and not for circulation as legal tender. The coins' primary characteristic was that they were intended to resemble a current coin within the definition of s. 448 of the Code. On the question of lawful justification or excuse upon the accused Laskin J., agreed with Ritchie J., on the merits that there was no evidence to support such a finding, but held that if evidence of a want of intention by the accused to use the counterfeit coins as currency had been led then the accused could be said to have discharged the shifting burden cast upon him by the section.

The offence under para. (*b*) does not require proof of an intention to use the money as currency: *R. v. Duane* (1984), 12 C.C.C. (3d) 368, 57 A.R. 227 (C.A.), affd [1985] 2 S.C.R. 612, 22 C.C.C. (3d) 448*n* (7:0).

It is not necessary as a foundation to the opinion of the Crown's expert witness as to the bank-note being counterfeit that he first prove the authenticity of the bank-note copied: *R. v. Gagnon* (1975), 31 C.R.N.S. 332 (Ont. Co. Ct.).

Proof that the accused knew of the counterfeit nature of the bills is an essential element of the "possession" required for the offence and the burden of proof is on the Crown to prove such knowledge beyond a reasonable doubt; lack of such knowledge is not a matter of "lawful excuse" which the accused has to prove. It is only after the Crown has proved possession, including knowledge of the counterfeit nature of the money, that the issue of lawful justification or excuse, arises: *R. v. Santeramo* (1976), 32 C.C.C. (2d) 35, 36 C.R.N.S. 1 (Ont. C.A.). Folld: *R. v. Freng* (1993), 86 C.C.C. (3d) 91 (B.C.C.A.).

The accused's knowledge may be inferred from the quality of the counterfeit bill: *R. v. Mak* (2000), 46 W.C.B. (2d) 581 (B.C.C.A.).

HAVING CLIPPINGS, ETC.

451. Every person is guilty of an indictable offence and liable to imprisonment for a term of not more than five years who, without lawful justification or excuse, has in their

custody or possession, knowing that it has been produced or obtained by impairing, diminishing or lightening a current gold or silver coin,

(*a*) gold or silver filings or clippings,

(*b*) gold or silver bullion, or

(*c*) gold or silver in dust, solution or otherwise. R.S., c. C-34, s. 409; 2018, c. 29, s. 56.

CROSS-REFERENCES

Possession is defined in s. 4(3). The term "current" is defined in s. 448. Section 461(2) provides for admission of a certificate of an examiner of counterfeit money as proof that any coin is or is not, as the case may be, current in Canada or elsewhere.

The accused may elect his mode of trial under s. 536(2). Release pending trial is determined under s. 515, although the accused is eligible for release by the officer in charge under s. 498.

The related offence of clipping or uttering clipped coin is in s. 455.

SYNOPSIS

This section describes the offence of possessing gold or silver filings, clippings, bullion or dust in any form, which has been produced by diminishing a *current* gold or silver coin. The prosecution must prove that the accused *knew* that the gold or silver was produced or obtained in the fashion described above. As in s. 450, the accused must prove *lawful justification or excuse* for the knowing possession of the items set out in this section. This is an indictable offence with a maximum term of five years' imprisonment.

Uttering

UTTERING, ETC., COUNTERFEIT MONEY

452. Every person is guilty of an indictable offence and liable to imprisonment for a term of not more than 14 years who, without lawful justification or excuse,

(*a*) utters or offers to utter counterfeit money or uses counterfeit money as if it were genuine, or

(*b*) exports, sends or takes counterfeit money out of Canada. R.S., c. C-34, s. 410; 2018, c. 29, s. 57.

CROSS-REFERENCES

The terms "counterfeit money" and "utter" are defined in s. 448. Section 461(1) enacts a conclusive presumption as to when the offence is complete. Section 461(2) provides for admission of a certificate of an examiner of counterfeit money as proof that any money, coin or bank-note is counterfeit or genuine and is or is not, as the case may be, current in Canada or elsewhere.

This offence may be the basis for an application for an authorization to intercept private communications by reason of s. 183 and is an enterprise crime offence for the purposes of Part XII.2.

The accused may elect his mode of trial under s. 536(2). Release pending trial is determined under s. 515. Section 462 provides that counterfeit money and anything used or intended to be used to make counterfeit money belong to Her Majesty. Section 462(2) gives a peace officer power to seize and detain these items.

The related offence of uttering coin that is not current is in s. 453.

SYNOPSIS

This section describes the offences of uttering or offering to utter counterfeit money, or using it as though it were genuine, and of exporting counterfeit money out of Canada. This is an indictable offence with a maximum term of 14 years' imprisonment.

ANNOTATIONS

Uttering counterfeit money includes the sale of counterfeit money as counterfeit to be put into circulation as currency notwithstanding the immediate purchaser is not deceived as to the genuineness of the money: *R. v. Kelly and Lauzon* (1979), 48 C.C.C. (2d) 560 (Ont. C.A.).

UTTERING COIN.

453. Every one who, with intent to defraud, knowingly utters

(*a*) a coin that is not current, or

(*b*) a piece of metal or mixed metals that resembles in size, figure or colour a current coin for which it is uttered,

is guilty of an indictable offence and liable to imprisonment for a term not exceeding two years. R.S., c. C-34, s. 411.

CROSS-REFERENCES

Possession is defined in s. 4(3). The terms "current" and "utter" are defined in s. 448. Section 461(2) provides for admission of a certificate of an examiner of counterfeit money as proof that any coin is or is not, as the case may be, current in Canada or elsewhere. By virtue of s. 583, an indictment which otherwise complies with s. 581 is not insufficient by reason only that: para. (*c*), it charges an intent to defraud without naming or describing the person whom it was intended to defraud.

The accused may elect his mode of trial under s. 536(2). Release pending trial is determined under s. 515, although the accused is eligible for release by the officer in charge under s. 498.

SYNOPSIS

This section describes the offence of *knowingly* uttering a coin that is not current, or a piece of metal that resembles a current coin in size, figure or colour. A person charged under this section must have an *intent to defraud* to be convicted. The offence is indictable and carries a maximum term of two years' imprisonment.

SLUGS AND TOKENS.

454. Every person is guilty of an offence punishable on summary conviction who, without lawful excuse, manufactures, produces, sells or has in their possession anyting that is intended to be fraudulently used in substitution for a coin or token of value that any coin or token-operated device is designed to receive,

(*a*) manufactures, produces or sells, or

(*b*) has in his possession. R.S., c. C-34, s. 412; 1972, c. 13, s. 32; 2018, c. 29, s. 58.

CROSS-REFERENCES

Possession is defined in s. 4(3). While there is no definition of "fraudulently" which is universally applicable, generally speaking, it refers to conduct which is dishonest and morally wrong: *R. v. DeMarco* (1973), 13 C.C.C. (2d) 369 (Ont. C.A.). This offence supplements the offence of fraudulently obtaining transportation in s. 393(3). Note also the offence of possession of instruments for breaking into coin-operated devices in s. 352. Trial of this offence is conducted by a summary conviction court pursuant to Part XXVII. The punishment is as set out in s. 787 and the limitation period is set out in s. 786(2). Release pending trial is determined by s. 515, although the accused is eligible for release by a peace officer under s. 496, 497 or by the officer in charge under s. 498.

SYNOPSIS

This section describes the summary conviction offence of manufacturing, producing, selling or possessing slugs or tokens. A person charged under this section must have the *intent* that these items be fraudulently used in substitution for a coin or a valuable token in a coin or token-operated device. Like ss. 450 and 451, the accused bears the onus of proving that the possession of these slugs and tokens for the purposes described in the section was with *lawful excuse*.

ANNOTATIONS

For the offence of possession the accused must be aware of the article's potential fraudulent use: *R. v. Kolot* (1975), 27 C.C.C. (2d) 79 (B.C. Co. Ct.).

Subway fare boxes monitored by operators who may scrutinize tickets and refuse entry do not constitute "token-operated devices". Furthermore, a subway ticket is not a token of value that a "token-operated device is designed to receive": *R. v. Aeso* (1996), 105 C.C.C. (3d) 283 (Ont. Ct. (Prov. Div.)).

Defacing or Impairing

CLIPPING AND UTTERING CLIPPED COIN.

455. Every one who

(*a*) impairs, diminishes or lightens a current gold or silver coin with intent that it should pass for a current gold or silver coin, or

(*b*) utters a coin knowing that it has been impaired, diminished or lightened contrary to paragraph (*a*),

is guilty of an indictable offence and liable to imprisonment for a term not exceeding fourteen years. R.S., c. C-34, s. 413.

CROSS-REFERENCES

The terms "current" and "utter" are defined in s. 448. Section 461(2) provides for admission of a certificate of an examiner of counterfeit money as proof that any coin is or is not, as the case may be, current in Canada or elsewhere.

The accused may elect his mode of trial under s. 536(2). Release pending trial is determined under s. 515.

The related offence of possession of clippings or filings is in s. 451.

SYNOPSIS

This section describes the offences of diminishing, impairing or lightening a current gold or silver coin *with intent* that it should pass for a current gold or silver coin, and of uttering a coin, knowing that it has been so diminished, impaired or lightened. These are indictable offences with a maximum of 14 years' imprisonment.

DEFACING CURRENT COINS.

456. Every one who

(*a*) defaces a current coin, or

(*b*) utters a current coin that has been defaced,

is guilty of an offence punishable on summary conviction. R.S., c. C-34, s. 414.

CROSS-REFERENCES

The terms "current" and "utter" are defined in s. 448. Section 461(2) provides for admission of a certificate of an examiner of counterfeit money as proof that any coin is or is not, as the case may be, current in Canada or elsewhere.

Trial of this offence is conducted by a summary conviction court pursuant to Part XXVII. The punishment is as set out in s. 787 and the limitation period is set out in s. 786(2). Release pending trial is determined by s. 515, although the accused is eligible for release by a peace officer under ss. 496, 497 or by the officer in charge under s. 498.

LIKENESS OF BANK-NOTES / Exception / Offence / Defence.

457. (1) No person shall make, publish, print, execute, issue, distribute or circulate, including by electronic or computer-assisted means, anything in the likeness of

(*a*) a current bank-note; or

(*b*) an obligation or a security of a government or bank.

(2) Subsection (1) does not apply to

(*a*) the Bank of Canada or its employees when they are carrying out their duties;

(*b*) the Royal Canadian Mounted Police or its members or employees when they are carrying out their duties; or

(*c*) any person acting under a contract or licence from the Bank of Canada or Royal Canadian Mounted Police.

(3) A person who contravenes subsection (1) is guilty of an offence punishable on summary conviction.

(4) No person shall be convicted of an offence under subsection (3) in relation to the printed likeness of a Canadian bank-note if it is established that the length or width of the likeness is less than three-fourths or greater than one-and-one-half times the length or width, as the case may be, of the bank-note and

(*a*) the likeness is in black-and-white only; or

(*b*) the likeness of the bank-note appears on only one side of the likeness. R.S., c. C-34, s. 415; 1999, c. 5, s. 12.

CROSS-REFERENCES

The term "current" is defined in s. 448. "Bank-note" is defined in s. 2. "Bank" is defined in s. 35 of the *Interpretation Act*, R.S.C. 1985, c. I-21. Section 461(2) provides for admission of a certificate of an examiner of counterfeit money as proof that any money or bank-note is or is not, as the case may be, current in Canada or elsewhere.

Trial of these offences is conducted by a summary conviction court pursuant to Part XXVII. The punishment is as set out in s. 787 [although see s. 719(*b*) where the accused is a corporation] and the limitation period is set out in s. 786(2). Release pending trial is determined by s. 515, although the accused is eligible for release by a peace officer under s. 496, 497 or by the officer in charge under s. 498.

SYNOPSIS

This section describes the offence of making, issuing, publishing, printing, distributing, executing or circulating anything that has a *likeness* to or the *appearance* of a current banknote or any obligation or security of a government or a bank. The offence is punishable by summary conviction. The section stipulates that no person shall be convicted of an offence in relation to a printed likeness if the provisions set out in subsec. (4) are met. There is also exemption for employees of the Bank of Canada and the Royal Canadian Mounted Police or any person acting under contract or licence to the Bank or the R.C.M.P. when carrying out their duties.

ANNOTATIONS

It was held under the predecessor legislation that the act of importing and distributing goods, with the likeness or appearance of current bank-notes, to wholesalers and retailers comes within the prohibition against publishing: *R. v. Giftcraft Ltd.* (1984), 13 C.C.C. (3d) 192 (Ont. H.C.J.).

Instruments or Materials

MAKING, HAVING OR DEALING IN INSTRUMENTS FOR COUNTERFEITING.

458. Every person who, without lawful justification or excuse, makes, repairs, buys, sells or has in their custody or possession any machine, engine, tool, instrument, material or other thing that they know has been used or is adapted and intended for use in making counterfeit money or counterfeit tokens of value, is guilty of an indictable offence and liable to imprisonment for a term of not more than 14 years. R.S., c. C-34, s. 416; 2018, c. 29, s. 59.

CROSS-REFERENCES

The terms "counterfeit money" and "counterfeit tokens of value" are defined in s. 448. Possession is defined in s. 4(3). Section 461(2) provides for admission of a certificate of an examiner of counterfeit money as proof that any money, coin or bank-note is counterfeit or genuine, as the case may be, and is or is not, as the case may be, current in Canada or elsewhere. Section 461(1) enacts a conclusive presumption as to when the offence is complete. Section 462 provides that counterfeit money, counterfeit tokens of value and anything used or intended to be used to make counterfeit money or tokens of value belong to Her Majesty. Section 462(2) gives a peace officer power to seize and detain these items. The accused may elect his mode of trial under s. 536(2). Release pending trial is determined under s. 515.

SYNOPSIS

This section describes the offence of possessing, making or repairing, beginning to make or repair, or buying or selling any instrument, material or thing that has been used or is intended to be used to make counterfeit money or valuable tokens. The prosecution must establish that the accused *knows* the use to which these items have been or are intended to be put. The section requires the accused to establish lawful justification or excuse for the acts described in paras. (*a*) to (*d*) and may thus be challenged under s. 11(*d*) of the Charter. The offence is indictable and carries a maximum term of 14 years' imprisonment.

CONVEYING INSTRUMENTS FOR COINING OUT OF MINT.

459. Every person is guilty of an indictable offence and liable to imprisonment for a term of not more than 14 years who, without lawful justification or excuse, knowingly conveys out of any of Her Majesty's mints in Canada,

(*a*) any machine, engine, tool, instrument, material or thing used or employed in connection with the manufacture of coins,

(*b*) a useful part of anything mentioned in paragraph (*a*), or

(*c*) coin, bullion, metal or a mixture of metals. R.S., c. C-34, s. 417; 2018, c. 29, s. 60.

CROSS-REFERENCES

The accused may elect his mode of trial under s. 536(2). Release pending trial is determined under s. 515.

SYNOPSIS

This section describes the offence of conveying certain items out of any of Her Majesty's mints in Canada. The accused person must establish lawful justification or excuse for any of the actions described in the section — a provision which could be challenged under the Charter. Any person who *knowingly* conveys out of the mint any machine, engine, tool, instrument, material or thing used in connection with the manufacture of coins, a useful part of any of these items, or coin, bullion, metal, or a mixture of metals, commits this indictable offence and is liable to a maximum term of 14 years' imprisonment.

Advertising and Trafficking in Counterfeit Money or Counterfeit Tokens of Value

ADVERTISING AND DEALING IN COUNTERFEIT MONEY, ETC. / Fraudulent use of money genuine but valueless.

460. (1) Every one who

- **(*a*) by an advertisement or any other writing, offers to sell, procure or dispose of counterfeit money or counterfeit tokens of value or to give information with respect to the manner in which or the means by which counterfeit money or counterfeit tokens of value may be sold, procured or disposed of, or**
- **(*b*) purchases, obtains, negotiates or otherwise deals with counterfeit tokens of value, or offers to negotiate with a view to purchasing or obtaining them,**

is guilty of an indictable offence and liable to imprisonment for a term not exceeding five years.

(2) No person shall be convicted of an offence under subsection (1) in respect of genuine coin or genuine paper money that has no value as money unless, at the time when the offence is alleged to have been committed, he knew that the coin or paper money had no value as money and he had a fraudulent intent in his dealings with or with respect to the coin or paper money. R.S., c. C-34, s. 418.

CROSS-REFERENCES

The terms "counterfeit money" and "counterfeit tokens of value" are defined in s. 448. The term "writing" is defined in s. 2. Section 461(2) provides for admission of a certificate of an examiner of counterfeit money as proof that any money, coin or bank-note is counterfeit or genuine, as the case may be, and is or is not, as the case may be, current in Canada or elsewhere. Section 461(1) enacts a conclusive presumption as to when the offence is complete. Section 462 provides that counterfeit money, counterfeit tokens of value and anything used or intended to be used to make counterfeit money or tokens of value belong to Her Majesty. Section 462(2) gives a peace officer power to seize and detain these items. The accused may elect his mode of trial under s. 536(2). Release pending trial is determined under s. 515, although the accused is eligible for release by the officer in charge under s. 498.

SYNOPSIS

This section describes the offence of dealing in counterfeit money or counterfeit tokens.

Subsection (1)(*a*) provides that any person who, by advertisement or other writing offers to sell, obtain or dispose of counterfeit items, or to give information on how to sell, obtain or dispose of such things is guilty of an offence.

Subsection (1)(*b*) similarly makes it an offence to purchase, obtain, negotiate or offer to negotiate the purchase of such counterfeit items.

Subsection (2) provides that a person who deals in genuine coin or paper money that has no value is not guilty of an offence under subsec. (1), unless he *knew* that the items had no value and he had a *fraudulent* intent in his dealings. The offence is indictable and carries a maximum term of five years' imprisonment.

CR. CODE

Special Provisions as to Proof

WHEN COUNTERFEIT COMPLETE / Certificate of examiner of counterfeit / Notice of intention to produce certificate / Attendance and cross-examination.

461. (1) Every offence relating to counterfeit money or counterfeit tokens of value shall be deemed to be complete notwithstanding that the money or tokens of value in respect of which the proceedings are taken are not finished or perfected or do not copy exactly the money or tokens of value that they are apparently intended to resemble or for which they are apparently intended to pass.

(2) In any proceedings under this Part, a certificate signed by a person designated as an examiner of counterfeit by the Minister of Public Safety and Emergency Preparedness, stating that any coin, paper money or bank-note described therein is counterfeit money or that any coin, paper money or bank-note described therein is genuine and is or is not, as the case may be, current in Canada or elsewhere, is evidence of the statements contained in the certificate without proof of the signature or official character of the person appearing to have signed the certificate.

(3) No certificate shall be received in evidence unless the party intending to produce it has, before the trial, given to the other party reasonable notice of their intention and a copy of the certificate.

(4) A party against whom the certificate is produced may, with leave of the court, require the attendance of the person who signed the certificate for the purposes of cross-examination. R.S., c. C-34, s. 419; 1992, c. 1, s. 58; 2005, c. 10, s. 34(1)(*f*)(xi); 2018, c. 21, s. 17.

CROSS-REFERENCES

The terms "counterfeit money", "counterfeit tokens of value" and "current" are defined in s. 448. The term "bank-note" is defined in s. 2.

With respect to subsec. (2), note that s. 25(1) of the *Interpretation Act*, R.S.C. 1985, c. I-21, provides that "where an enactment provides that a document is evidence of a fact without anything in the context to indicate that the document is conclusive evidence, then, in any judicial proceedings, the document is admissible in evidence and the fact is deemed to be established in the absence of any evidence to the contrary".

With respect to subsec. (3), s. 258(6) and (7) require that the party intending to introduce the certificate give reasonable notice of his intention and a copy of the certificate and give the judge power to order that the examiner be produced for the purposes of cross-examination.

SYNOPSIS

This section sets out certain special provisions in relation to proving offences relating to counterfeiting.

Subsection (1) provides that counterfeiting offences are complete, even if the counterfeit money or tokens are not finished, perfected or are not exact copies of the genuine articles.

Subsection (2) provides that any certificate signed by a person designated by the Solicitor General of Canada as an examiner of counterfeit is evidence of the statements relating to the genuineness or currency of the money without proof of the signature or official character of the person appearing to have signed the certificate.

ANNOTATIONS

On a charge contrary to s. 450(*b*) the Crown may establish a *prima facie* case by having a police officer testify that he has been employed as an examiner of counterfeit bills and that having compared the bills with genuine bills he was of the opinion that they were counterfeit and that if they had been genuine, they would be lawfully current. It is not necessary that the Crown produce a certificate signed by a person designated as an examiner of counterfeit by the Solicitor General of Canada nor that it lead some documentary evidence or call some official from the Bank of Canada who was in a position to make reference to the proper law or proper proclamation or regulation pursuant to this section: *R. v. MacIntosh* (1971), 5 C.C.C. (2d) 239 (Ont. C.A.).

Similarly a member of the R.C.M.P. designated as an examiner of counterfeit by the Solicitor-General of Canada may give a *viva voce* opinion based on his training and experience that certain bills are not genuine and were intended to resemble paper money which was current legal tender in the United States: *R. v. Serratore* (1980), 53 C.C.C. (2d) 106 (Ont. C.A.).

Forfeiture

OWNERSHIP / Seizure.

462. (1) Counterfeit money, counterfeit tokens of value and anything that is used or is intended to be used to make counterfeit money or counterfeit tokens of value belong to Her Majesty.

(2) A peace officer may seize and detain

(*a*) counterfeit money,

(*b*) counterfeit tokens of value, and

(*c*) machines, engines, tools, instruments, materials or things that have been used or that have been adapted and are intended for use in making counterfeit money or counterfeit tokens of value,

and anything seized shall be sent to the Minister of Finance to be disposed of or dealt with as he may direct, but anything that is required as evidence in any proceedings shall not be sent to the Minister until it is no longer required in those proceedings. R.S., c. C-34, s. 420.

CROSS-REFERENCES

The terms "counterfeit money" and "counterfeit tokens of value" are defined in s. 448. "Her Majesty" is defined in s. 35 of the *Interpretation Act*, R.S.C. 1985, c. I-21. The normal search warrant provisions are found in ss. 487 and 487.1.

SYNOPSIS

This section describes a procedure for seizing counterfeit money, tokens of value and instruments designed or adapted for use in counterfeiting.

Subsection (2) states that a peace officer may seize and detain any of these items and shall send them to the Minister of Finance for disposal unless they are needed as evidence in any proceedings.

Subsection (1) makes it clear that any of the items described in this section belong to Her Majesty.

This section creates a power to seize, without warrant, which might attract scrutiny under s. 8 of the Charter.

Part XII.1

[*Heading repealed*, 2018, c. 16, s. 211.]

[*Heading repealed*, 2018, c. 16, s. 211.]

462.1 [*Repealed*, 2018, c. 16, s. 211.]

CROSS-REFERENCES

In addition to the definitions of this section, see s. 2 and notes to that section.

SYNOPSIS

This section provides definitions of the terms relevant to the offence described in Part XII.1 of the Code.

ANNOTATIONS

The prohibition in this Part in relation to "literature for illicit drug use" violates s. 2(*b*) of the Charter and is of no force and effect. Accordingly, the definition of "literature for illicit drug use" must be severed from the section: *Iorfida v. MacIntyre* (1994), 93 C.C.C. (3d) 395 (Ont. Ct. (Gen. Div.)).

[*Heading repealed*, 2018, c. 16, s. 211.]

462.2 [*Repealed*, 2018, c. 16, s. 211.]

CROSS-REFERENCES

The terms "illicit drug use", "sell", "literature for illicit drug use", and "instrument for illicit drug use" are defined in s. 462.1.

The trial of this offence is conducted by a summary conviction court pursuant to Part XXVII. The limitation period is set out in s. 786(2). Release pending trial is determined by s. 515, although the accused is eligible for release by a peace officer under s. 496, 497 or by the officer in charge under s. 498.

Where the prosecution seeks the higher penalty prescribed by para. (*b*), it must comply with the provisions of s. 665. Section 667 provides one method of proof of the prior conviction. No reference to the prior conviction may be made in the information by virtue of s. 664.

SYNOPSIS

This section describes the offence of *knowingly* importing into Canada, exporting from Canada, manufacturing, promoting, or selling instruments or literature for *illicit* drug use. The offence is a summary one, punishable on a first conviction by a maximum fine of $100,000 and/or a term of imprisonment not exceeding six months. For every offence following a first conviction, the punishment increases to a maximum fine of $300,000 and/or a term of imprisonment not exceeding one year.

ANNOTATIONS

The prohibition in this section in relation to literature for illicit drug use violates s. 2(*b*) of the Charter and is of no force and effect. Accordingly, the words "or literature" must be severed from the section: *Iorfida v. MacIntyre* (1994), 93 C.C.C. (3d) 395, 21 O.R. (3d) 186 (Gen. Div.).

This provision is neither vague nor overbroad contrary to s. 7 of the Charter: *R. v. Spindloe* (2001), 154 C.C.C. (3d) 8, 42 C.R. (5th) 58 (Sask. C.A.).

Part XII.2 / PROCEEDS OF CRIME

Interpretation

DEFINITIONS / "designated drug offence" / "designated offence" / "enterprise crime offence" / "judge" / "proceeds of crime" / Regulations / Powers of Attorney General of Canada / Powers of Attorney General of a province.

462.3 (1) In this Part,

"designated drug offence" [*Repealed*, 1996, c. 19, s. 68(1).]

"designated offence" means

(*a*) any offence that may be prosecuted as an indictable offence under this or any other Act of Parliament, other than an indictable offence prescribed by regulation, or

(*b*) a conspiracy or an attempt to commit, being an accessory after the fact in relation to, or any counselling in relation to, an offence referred to in paragraph (*a*);

"designated substance offence" [*Repealed*, 2001, c. 32, s. 12(3).]

"enterprise crime offence" [*Repealed*, 2001, c. 32, s. 12(2).]

Note: Definition "enterprise crime offence" amended 2001, c. 27, s. 246; however definition repealed by 2001, c. 32, s. 12(2).

"judge" means a judge as defined in section 552 or a judge of a superior court of criminal jurisdiction;

"proceeds of crime" means any property, benefit or advantage, within or outside Canada, obtained or derived directly or indirectly as a result of

(*a*) the commission in Canada of a designated offence, or

(*b*) an act or omission anywhere that, if it had occurred in Canada, would have constituted a designated offence.

(2) The Governor in Council may make regulations prescribing indictable offences that are excluded from the definition "designated offence" in subsection (1).

(3) Despite the definition "Attorney General" in section 2, the Attorney General of Canada may

(*a*) exercise all the powers and perform all the duties and functions assigned to the Attorney General by or under this Act in respect of a designated offence if the alleged offence arises out of conduct that in whole or in part is in relation to an alleged contravention of an Act of Parliament or a regulation made under such an Act, other than this Act or a regulation made under this Act; and

(*b*) conduct proceedings and exercise all the powers and perform all the duties and functions assigned to the Attorney General by or under this Act in respect of

(i) an offence referred to in section 354, 355.2, 355.4 or 462.31, if the alleged offence arises out of conduct that in whole or in part is in relation to an alleged contravention of an Act of Parliament, other than this Act, or a regulation made under such an Act, and

(ii) an offence under subsection 462.33(11) if the restraint order was made on application of the Attorney General of Canada.

(4) Subsection (3) does not affect the authority of the Attorney General of a province to conduct proceedings in respect of a designated offence or to exercise any of the powers or perform any of the duties and functions assigned to the Attorney General by or under this Act. R.S.C. 1985, c. 42 (4th Supp.), s. 2; 1993, c. 25, s. 95; 1993, c. 37, s. 32; 1993, c. 46, s. 5; 1994, c. 44, s. 29; 1995, c. 39, s. 151; 1996, c. 19, ss. 68, 70(*a*); 1997, c. 18, s. 27; 1997, c. 23, s. 9; 1998, c. 34, ss. 9, 11; 1999, c. 5, s. 52; 2001, c. 32, s. 12; 2001, c. 41, ss. 14, 33; 2005, c. 44, s. 1; 2010, c. 14, s. 7.

CROSS-REFERENCES

The scope of what is considered an attempt is set out in s. 24 of the *Criminal Code*. The meaning of being an accessory after the offence is found in s. 23. Section 22 determines the meaning of counselling. The effect of the recent amendment to this section is that all indictable offences under the *Criminal Code* or other federal statutes are designated offences for the purpose of this Part, unless they are prescribed by regulations. Comparable provisions relating to drugs are found in ss. 14 to 27 of the *Controlled Drugs and Substances Act*.

SYNOPSIS

This section provides definitions for the proceeds of crime provisions of the *Criminal Code*.

The term "proceeds of crime" is also defined, and encompasses any property, benefit or advantage within or outside Canada, obtained or derived directly or indirectly as a result of an enterprise crime or designated drug offence or conduct that would have constituted such an offence if it had occurred in Canada.

ANNOTATIONS

The ability to impose a fine in lieu of forfeiture pursuant to subsec. (3) is discretionary and, unlike the sentencing provisions in s. 734(2), the judge may, but need not, consider the means of the accused to pay. The amount of the fine must be equal to the value of the property and not a lesser amount: *R. v. Neves* (2005), 202 C.C.C. (3d) 375 (Man. C.A.).

Offence

LAUNDERING PROCEEDS OF CRIME / Punishment / Exception.

462.31 (1) Every one commits an offence who uses, transfers the possession of, sends or delivers to any person or place, transports, transmits, alters, disposes of or otherwise deals with, in any manner and by any means, any property or any proceeds of any property with intent to conceal or convert that property or those proceeds, knowing or believing that all or a part of that property or of those proceeds was obtained or derived directly or indirectly as a result of

(*a*) the commission in Canada of a designated offence; or

(*b*) an act or omission anywhere that, if it had occurred in Canada, would have constituted a designated offence.

(2) Every one who commits an offence under subsection (1)

(*a*) is guilty of an indictable offence and is liable to imprisonment for a term not exceeding ten years; or

(*b*) is guilty of an offence punishable on summary conviction.

(3) A peace officer or a person acting under the direction of a peace officer is not guilty of an offence under subsection (1) if the peace officer or person does any of the things mentioned in that subsection for the purposes of an investigation or otherwise in the execution of the peace officer's duties. R.S.C. 1985, c. 42 (4th Supp.), s. 2; 1996, c. 19, s. 70; 1997, c. 18, s. 28; 2001, c. 32, s. 13.

CROSS-REFERENCES

The meaning of "property" and "person" are contained in s. 2.

The term "designated offence" is defined in s. 462.3. Section 4(3) sets out what being in "possession" means in this Act.

This offence has been added to the list of offences in relation to which, according to s. 183, an authorization for interception of private communications may be obtained or a warrant to conduct video surveillance may be obtained by reason of s. 487.01(5).

If the accused is prosecuted by indictment under s. 462.31(2)(*a*), the accused has a right to make an election under s. 536(2). If tried by summary conviction, Part XXVII will govern the procedure and s. 787(1) sets out the maximum punishment upon conviction as six months imprisonment or a $2,000 fine, or both [except in the case of a corporation, see s. 719(*b*)].

SYNOPSIS

This section describes the offence of laundering the proceeds of crime. The offence is committed when a person deals with any property, or any proceeds of property, in any manner and by any means, with the intent to conceal or convert it, knowing or believing that the property or proceeds were, in whole or in part, obtained or derived directly or indirectly as a result of the conduct described in the definition of the term "proceeds of crime".

The offence may be prosecuted by indictment, with a maximum punishment of imprisonment for 10 years, or by summary conviction.

By virtue of subsec. (3), no offence is committed by a peace officer or a person acting under the direction of a peace officer if the acts are done for the purpose of an investigation or otherwise in the execution of the officer's duties.

ANNOTATIONS

"Transfer of possession" is the act of a person who has control or possession of the object and then tries to pass it on to another. This provision applies only to the party originally having control of the property, not the recipient of the property. The act of purchasing the merchandise is not the equivalent of transferring its possession. A recipient of the property would be guilty of possession of property obtained by crime pursuant to s. 354 of the *Criminal Code*: *R. v. Daoust*, [2004] 1 S.C.R. 217, 180 C.C.C. (3d) 449.

The *mens rea* requires proof of an intent to conceal or convert property or proceeds of property and knowledge or belief that the property or proceeds were derived from a designated offence. "Convert" must be given its ordinary meaning and does not include an intent to disguise or conceal: *R. v. Daoust*, *supra*.

Search, Seizure and Detention of Proceeds of Crime

SPECIAL SEARCH WARRANT / Procedure / Execution of warrant / Execution in another province / Detention and record of property seized / Return of proceeds / Notice / Undertaking by Attorney General.

462.32 (1) Subject to subsection (3), if a judge, on application of the Attorney General, is satisfied by information on oath in Form 1 that there are reasonable grounds to believe that there is in any building, receptacle or place, within the province in which the judge has jurisdiction or any other province, any property in respect of which an order of forfeiture may be made under subsection 462.37(1) or (2.01) or 462.38(2), in respect of a designated offence alleged to have been committed within the province in which the judge has jurisdiction, the judge may issue a warrant authorizing a person named in the warrant or a peace officer to search the building, receptacle or place for that property and to seize that property and any other property in respect of which that person or peace officer believes, on reasonable grounds, that an order of forfeiture may be made under that subsection.

(2) An application for a warrant under subsection (1) may be made *ex parte*, shall be made in writing and shall include a statement as to whether any previous applications have been made under subsection (1) with respect to the property that is the subject of the application.

(2.1) Subject to subsection (2.2), a warrant issued pursuant to subsection (1) may be executed anywhere in Canada.

(2.2) Where a warrant is issued under subsection (1) in one province but it may be reasonably expected that it is to be executed in another province and the execution of the warrant would require entry into or on the property of any person in the other province, a judge in the other province may, on *ex parte* application, confirm the warrant, and when the warrant is so confirmed it shall have full force and effect in that other province as though it had originally been issued in that province.

(3) Subsections 487(2) to (4) and section 488 apply, with such modifications as the circumstances require, to a warrant issued under this section.

(4) Every person who executes a warrant issued by a judge under this section shall

(*a*) detain or cause to be detained the property seized, taking reasonable care to ensure that the property is preserved so that it may be dealt with in accordance with the law;

(*b*) as soon as practicable after the execution of the warrant but within a period not exceeding seven days thereafter, prepare a report in Form 5.3, identifying the property seized and the location where the property is being detained and cause the report to be filed with the clerk of the court; and

(*c*) cause a copy of the report to be provided, on request, to the person from whom the property was seized and to any other person who, in the opinion of the judge, appears to have a valid interest in the property.

(4.1) Subject to this or any other Act of Parliament, a peace officer who has seized anything under a warrant issued by a judge under this section may, with the written consent of the Attorney General, on being issued a receipt for it, return the thing seized to the person lawfully entitled to its possession, if

(*a*) the peace officer is satisfied that there is no dispute as to who is lawfully entitled to possession of the thing seized;

(*b*) the peace officer is satisfied that the continued detention of the thing seized is not required for the purpose of forfeiture; and

(*c*) the thing seized is returned before a report is filed with the clerk of the court under paragraph (4)(*b*).

(5) Before issuing a warrant under this section in relation to any property, a judge may require notice to be given to and may hear any person who, in the opinion of the judge, appears to have a valid interest in the property unless the judge is of the opinion that giving such notice before the issuance of the warrant would result in the disappearance, dissipation or reduction in value of the property or otherwise affect the property so that all or a part thereof could not be seized pursuant to the warrant.

(6) Before issuing a warrant under this section, a judge shall require the Attorney General to give such undertakings as the judge considers appropriate with respect to the payment of damages or costs, or both, in relation to the issuance and execution of the warrant. R.S.C. 1985, c. 42 (4th Supp.), s. 2; 1997, c. 18, s. 29; 2001, c. 32, s. 14; 2005, c. 44, s. 3.

CROSS-REFERENCES

The terms "property", "peace officer", "clerk of the court" and "person" are defined in s. 2. "Judge" and "Attorney General" are defined in ss. 2 and 462.3(3), (4).

Sections 487 to 489 deal with search warrants generally, and telewarrants are dealt with in s. 487.1. Form 5.3 has been created to report of what property is seized under a search warrant authorized by this section. Section 462.35 provides that the order detaining property seized under such warrants automatically expires after six months unless the Attorney General brings an application to extend the order within that time. In addition, any person with an interest in the property seized under this type of warrant may apply under s. 462.34 to examine the property or to have the property returned.

Section 462.34 provides that if a warrant is issued under this section and the accused is later committed to trial for a designated offence (as defined in s. 462.3) a copy of the report of what was seized shall be forwarded to the clerk of the court in which the accused is ordered to stand trial.

Property seized pursuant to a warrant issued under section may be managed in accordance with an order made under s. 462.331.

SYNOPSIS

This section provides for special search warrants with respect to property which falls into the category of proceeds of crime and which is subject to forfeiture under this Part.

An application for such a search warrant must be brought in writing, by an Attorney General, to a judge as defined in s. 462.3. It may be made *ex parte* and must include a statement as to whether any previous applications have been made in respect of the same property.

Where information on oath in Form 1 satisfies the judge that such property is in a building, receptacle or place, the judge may issue a warrant authorizing a named person or a peace officer to search for that property in that place, and to seize it and any other property which the person believes, on reasonable grounds, falls within this provision.

The warrant may be executed anywhere in Canada but if it is to be executed in another province and execution would require entry into or on the property of any person, it must first be confirmed by a judge in the other province.

The backing and time of execution provisions in ss. 487 and 488 apply to these special warrants.

Subsection (4) requires that a person executing a warrant under this section must detain and preserve the property seized and prepare a report within seven days of seizure which shall be given to the court, the person from whom the seizure was made and any other person whom the issuing judge decides has an apparent valid interest in the property. Subsection (4.1) sets out the circumstances in which the peace officer may, with the consent of the Attorney General, return the items seized before the report is filed.

Subsection (5) provides that, prior to issuing a warrant, a judge may require that notice be given to and may hear any person who, in the judge's opinion, appears to have a valid interest in the property, unless he believes that notice would result in disappearance, dissipation or reduction in value of the property, or otherwise affect the property so that all or part of it could not be seized.

Subsection (6) compels a judge, before issuing a warrant, to require the Attorney General to give such undertaking as the judge considers appropriate with respect to the payment of damages or costs in relation to the warrant.

ANNOTATIONS

The court may set aside an *ex parte* order made under this section where the court that made the order was misled because of the failure of the Crown to disclose material evidence: *R. v. Derksen* (1998), 126 C.C.C. (3d) 554 (Sask. Q.B.), affd 140 C.C.C. (3d) 184 (Sask. C.A.), leave to appeal to S.C.C. refused 142 C.C.C. (3d) vi.

APPLICATION FOR RESTRAINT ORDER / Procedure / Restraint order / Appointment of Minister of Public Works and Government Services / Property outside Canada / Notice / Order in writing / Undertakings by Attorney General / Service of order / Registration of order / Continues in force / Offence.

462.33 (1) The Attorney General may make an application in accordance with subsection (2) for a restraint order under subsection (3) in respect of any property.

(2) An application made under subsection (1) for a restraint order under subsection (3) in respect of any property may be made *ex parte* and shall be made in writing to a judge and be accompanied by an affidavit sworn on the information and belief of the Attorney General or any other person deposing to the following matters, namely,

(*a*) the offence or matter under investigation;

(*b*) the person who is believed to be in possession of the property;

(*c*) the grounds for the belief that an order of forfeiture may be made under subsection 462.37(1) or (2.01) or 462.38(2) in respect of the property;

(*d*) a description of the property; and

(*e*) whether any previous applications have been made under this section with respect to the property.

(3) A judge who hears an application for a restraint order made under subsection (1) may — if the judge is satisfied that there are reasonable grounds to believe that there exists, within the province in which the judge has jurisdiction or any other province, any property in respect of which an order of forfeiture may be made under subsection

462.37(1) or (2.01) or 462.38(2), in respect of a designated offence alleged to have been committed within the province in which the judge has jurisdiction — make an order prohibiting any person from disposing of, or otherwise dealing with any interest in, the property specified in the order otherwise than in the manner that may be specified in the order.

(3.01) Subsections 462.32(2.1) and (2.2) apply, with such modifications as the circumstances require, in respect of a restraint order.

(3.1) A restraint order may be issued under this section in respect of property situated outside Canada, with any modifications that the circumstances require.

(4) An order made by a judge under subsection (3) may be subject to such reasonable conditions as the judge thinks fit.

(5) Before making an order under subsection (3) in relation to any property, a judge may require notice to be given to and may hear any person who, in the opinion of the judge, appears to have a valid interest in the property unless the judge is of the opinion that giving such notice before making the order would result in the disappearance, dissipation or reduction in value of the property or otherwise affect the property so that all or a part thereof could not be subject to an order of forfeiture under subsection 462.37(1) or (2.01) or 462.38(2).

(6) An order made under subsection (3) shall be made in writing.

(7) Before making an order under subsection (3), a judge shall require the Attorney General to give such undertakings as the judge considers appropriate with respect to the payment of damages or costs, or both, in relation to

- **(*a*) the making of an order in respect of property situated within or outside Canada; and**
- **(*b*) the execution of an order in respect of property situated within Canada.**

(8) A copy of an order made by a judge under subsection (3) shall be served on the person to whom the order is addressed in such manner as the judge directs or as may be prescribed by rules of court.

(9) A copy of an order made under subsection (3), shall be registered against any property in accordance with the laws of the province in which the property is situated.

(10) An order made under subsection (3) remains in effect until

- **(*a*) it is revoked or varied under subsection 462.34(4) or revoked under paragraph 462.43(*a*);**
- **(*b*) it ceases to be in force under section 462.35; or**
- **(*c*) an order of forfeiture or restoration of the property is made under subsection 462.37(1) or (2.01), 462.38(2) or 462.41(3) or any other provision of this or any other Act of Parliament.**

(11) Any person on whom an order made under subsection (3) is served in accordance with this section and who, while the order is in force, acts in contravention of or fails to comply with the order is guilty of an indictable offence or an offence punishable on summary conviction. R.S.C. 1985, c. 42 (4th Supp.), s. 2; 1993, c. 37, s. 21; 1996, c. 16, s. 60(1)(d); 1997, c. 18, s. 30; 2001, c. 32, s. 15; 2005, c. 44, s. 4.

CROSS-REFERENCES

The terms "property" and "person" are defined in s. 2. "Judge" and "designated offence" are defined in s. 462.3. "Attorney General" is defined in ss. 2 and 462.3(3), (4). Section 4(3) sets out when a person is in possession. Section 482 gives courts the power to make their own rules of court.

The offence created by 462.33(11) is one for which an application to intercept private communications may be made under s. 183. As there is no specified punishment if the prosecution is by way of indictment, s. 730 provides that the maximum period of imprisonment upon conviction is five years. In addition, an accused prosecuted by indictment would have a right to make an election under s. 536(2). If tried by summary conviction, Part XXVII will govern the procedure, and s. 787(1) sets out the maximum punishment upon conviction as six months imprisonment or a $2,000 fine, or both.

Section 462.35 provides for the automatic expiry of a restraint order made under this section after six months unless the Attorney General has, within that time, successfully applied for an extension of the order.

Section 462.36 provides that if the court makes a restraint order and the accused is later committed to trial for a designated offence (as defined in s. 462.3) a copy of the restraint order shall be forwarded to the clerk of the court in which the accused is ordered to stand trial.

If notice is given under subsec. (8), the court may use s. 462.4(*b*) to set aside any conveyance or transfer of property relating to the property subject to the restraint order unless the transaction was made for valuable consideration to a purchaser acting in good faith and without notice of the order.

Section 462.43 provides for the residual disposal of property seized under a restraint order.

As to restraint orders in relation to "offence-related property" under the *Controlled Drugs and Substances Act*, see s. 14 of that Act.

Property restrained pursuant to a restraint order made under this section on application of the Attorney General may be managed in accordance with an order made under s. 462.331.

SYNOPSIS

This section provides for the issuance of restraint orders with respect to property which falls into the definition of "proceeds of crime" and is subject to forfeiture under this part.

An application for such an order must be made in writing by an Attorney General to a judge as defined in s. 462.3. It may be made *ex parte* and shall be accompanied by an affidavit sworn on information or belief. The affidavit must identify the offence in question; the person believed to be in possession of the property; the grounds for the belief that the property is subject to forfeiture, and its description and a statement whether any previous application had been made with respect to the property.

If the judge is satisfied that reasonable grounds exist to believe that the property is subject to forfeiture, the judge may make an order in writing prohibiting any dealing with or disposing of any interest in the property. The judge may also impose such reasonable conditions as the judge thinks fit. Before making a restraint order, the judge may require notice be given to and may hear any person who in the judge's opinion appears to have a valid interest in the property unless he believes that giving such notice would result in the disappearance, dissipation or reduction in value of the property, or otherwise affect the property so that all or part of it could not be subject to an order of forfeiture. An order is valid throughout Canada, but if it is to be executed in another province and execution would require entry into or on the property of any person, it must first be confirmed by a judge in the other province.

Subsection (7) requires the judge, before making an order, to require the Attorney General to give such undertakings as the judge considers appropriate with respect to the payment of damages or costs in relation to the warrant.

A copy of an order must be served on the person to whom it is addressed, and a copy shall be registered in accordance with provincial law.

An order remains in effect until its revocation, variation or automatic expiry, or until an order of forfeiture or restoration is made.

Subsection (11) creates an offence triable by indictment or on summary conviction for contravening or failing to comply with a restraint order which has been served as required. As no punishment is specially provided for this offence, the indictable offence is punishable by imprisonment for a term not exceeding five years [s. 743], and the summary conviction offence is punishable by up to six months and a $2000 fine [s. 787].

ANNOTATIONS

An order made under this section is a seizure within the meaning of s. 8 of the *Canadian Charter of Rights and Freedoms*. However, the owner's rights under s. 8 were not violated because an agent of a provincial regulatory authority conducting an audit of the owner's business for compliance with provincial statutes passed on to the police information later used in a criminal investigation. The owner was required to keep the information under the provincial legislation and must have known that the legislation was not private in relation to the government. Transmitting information to the police, to initiate an investigation into the irregularities that had been observed, was connected with performance of the agent's duties and that information could be used by the police to support an application for an order under this section: *Quebec (Attorney General) v. Laroche*, [2002] 3 S.C.R. 708, 169 C.C.C. (3d) 97. [Also see note of this case under s. 462.34, *infra*.]

Offence-related property extends the proceeds of sale of offence-related property: *Scotia Mortgage Corp. v. Leung* (2007), 221 C.C.C. (3d) 505 (B.C.C.A.), leave to appeal to S.C.C. refused 223 C.C.C. (3d) vi.

While subsec. (3) refers to a forfeiture order under, *inter alia* s. 462.37(1), that necessarily includes an order that could be made on the basis of s. 462.37(2) because, although the evidence does not establish that the designated offence was committed in relation to property, the sentencing court is nevertheless satisfied beyond a reasonable doubt that the property is proceeds of crime: *Quebec (Attorney General) v. Laroche, supra.*

MANAGEMENT ORDER / Appointment of Minister of Public Works and Government Services / Power to manage / Application for destruction order / Notice / Manner of giving notice / Destruction order / Forfeiture order / When management order ceases to have effect / For greater certainty / Application to vary conditions.

462.331 (1) With respect to property seized under section 462.32 or restrained under section 462.33, other than a "controlled substance", within the meaning of the *Controlled Drugs and Substances Act*, or "cannabis", as defined in subsection 2(1) of the *Cannabis Act*, on application of the Attorney General or of any other person with the written consent of the Attorney General, if a judge is of the opinion that the circumstances so require, the judge may

(*a*) appoint a person to take control of and to manage or otherwise deal with all or part of the property in accordance with the directions of the judge; and

(*b*) require any person having possession of that property to give possession of the property to the person appointed under paragraph (*a*).

(2) When the Attorney General of Canada so requests, a judge appointing a person under subsection (1) shall appoint the Minister of Public Works and Government Services.

(3) The power to manage or otherwise deal with property under subsection (1) includes

(*a*) the power to make an interlocutory sale of perishable or rapidly depreciating property;

(*b*) the power to destroy, in accordance with subsections (4) to (7), property that has little or no value; and

(*c*) the power to have property, other than real property or a conveyance, forfeited to Her Majesty in accordance with subsection (7.1).

(4) Before a person who is appointed to manage property destroys property that has little or no value, they shall apply to a court for a destruction order.

(5) Before making a destruction order, a court shall require notice in accordance with subsection (6) to be given to and may hear any person who, in the court's opinion, appears to have a valid interest in the property.

(6) A notice shall

(*a*) be given in the manner that the court directs or that may be specified in the rules of the court; and

(*b*) specify the effective period of the notice that the court considers reasonable or that may be set out in the rules of the court.

(7) A court shall order that the property be destroyed if it is satisfied that the property has little or no financial or other value.

(7.1) On application by a person who is appointed to manage the property, a court shall order that the property, other than real property or a conveyance, be forfeited to Her Majesty to be disposed of or otherwise dealt with in accordance with the law if

(*a*) a notice is given or published in the manner that the court directs or that may be specified in the rules of the court;

(*b*) the notice specifies a period of 60 days during which a person may make an application to the court asserting their interest in the property; and

(*c*) during that period, no one makes such an application.

(8) A management order ceases to have effect when the property that is the subject of the management order is returned in accordance with the law, destroyed or forfeited to Her Majesty.

(8.1) For greater certainty, if property that is the subject of a management order is sold, the management order applies to the net proceeds of the sale.

(9) The Attorney General may at any time apply to the judge to cancel or vary any condition to which a management order is subject but may not apply to vary an appointment made under subsection (2). 2001, c. 32, s. 16; 2017, c. 7, s. 58; 2018, c. 16, s. 212.

CROSS-REFERENCES

"Property" is defined in s. 2. "Judge" is defined in s. 462.3. "Attorney General" is defined in ss. 2 and 462.3(3), (4).

SYNOPSIS

This section allows the Attorney General or a person with the written consent of the Attorney General to apply to a judge for a management order in relation to property seized in accordance with a warrant issued under s. 462.32 or restrained under an order made under s. 462.33. The power to make the order includes the power to sell perishable or rapidly depreciating property and, if authorized by a destruction order, to destroy property of little or no value. Notice is to be given to persons with a valid interest in the property before a destruction order is made. A management order expires when it is returned or ordered forfeited. The Attorney General may apply to cancel or vary any conditions of the management order.

APPLICATION FOR REVIEW OF SPECIAL WARRANTS AND RESTRAINT ORDERS / Notice to Attorney General / Terms of examination order / Order of restoration of property or revocation or variation of order / Hearing / Expenses / Taxing legal fees / Conditions to be satisfied / Saving provision / Form of recognizance.

462.34 (1) Any person who has an interest in property that was seized under a warrant issued pursuant to section 462.32 or in respect of which a restraint order was made under subsection 462.33(3) may, at any time, apply to a judge

(*a*) for an order under subsection (4); or

(*b*) for permission to examine the property.

(2) Where an application is made under paragraph (1)(*a*),

(*a*) the application shall not, without the consent of the Attorney General, be heard by a judge unless the applicant has given to the Attorney General at least two clear days notice in writing of the application; and

(*b*) the judge may require notice of the application to be given to and may hear any person who, in the opinion of the judge, appears to have a valid interest in the property.

(3) A judge may, on an application made to the judge under paragraph (1)(*b*), order that the applicant be permitted to examine property subject to such terms as appear to the judge to be necessary or desirable to ensure that the property is safeguarded and preserved for any purpose for which it may subsequently be required.

(4) On an application made to a judge under paragraph (1)(*a*) in respect of any property and after hearing the applicant and the Attorney General and any other person to whom notice was given pursuant to paragraph (2)(*b*), the judge may order that the property or a part thereof be returned to the applicant or, in the case of a restraint order made under subsection 462.33(3), revoke the order, vary the order to exclude the property or any interest in the property or part thereof from the application of the order or make the order subject to such reasonable conditions as the judge thinks fit,

(*a*) if the applicant enters into a recognizance before the judge, with or without sureties, in such amount and with such conditions, if any, as the judge directs and, where the judge considers it appropriate, deposits with the judge such sum of money or other valuable security as the judge directs;

(*b*) if the conditions referred to in subsection (6) are satisfied; or

(*c*) for the purpose of

(i) meeting the reasonable living expenses of the person who was in possession of the property at the time the warrant was executed or the order was made or any person who, in the opinion of the judge, has a valid interest in the property and of the dependants of that person,

(ii) meeting the reasonable business and legal expenses of a person referred to in subparagraph (i), or

(iii) permitting the use of the property in order to enter into a recognizance under Part XVI,

if the judge is satisfied that the applicant has no other assets or means available for the purposes set out in this paragraph and that no other person appears to be the lawful owner of or lawfully entitled to possession of the property.

(5) For the purpose of determining the reasonableness of legal expenses referred to in subparagraph (4)(*c*)(ii), a judge shall hold an in camera hearing, without the presence of the Attorney General, and shall take into account the legal aid tariff of the province.

(5.1) For the purpose of determining the reasonableness of expenses referred to in paragraph (4)(*c*), the Attorney General may

(*a*) at the hearing of the application, make representations as to what would constitute the reasonableness of the expenses, other than legal expenses; and

(*b*) before or after the hearing of the application held in camera pursuant to subsection (5), make representations as to what would constitute reasonable legal expenses referred to in subparagraph (4)(*c*)(ii).

(5.2) The judge who made an order under paragraph (4)(*c*) may, and on the application of the Attorney General shall, tax the legal fees forming part of the legal expenses referred to in subparagraph (4)(*c*)(ii) and, in so doing, shall take into account

(*a*) the value of property in respect of which an order of forfeiture may be made;

(*b*) the complexity of the proceedings giving rise to those legal expenses;

(*c*) the importance of the issues involved in those proceedings;

(*d*) the duration of any hearings held in respect of those proceedings;

(*e*) whether any stage of those proceedings was improper or vexatious;

(*f*) any representations made by the Attorney General; and

(*g*) any other relevant matter.

(6) An order under paragraph (4)(*b*) in respect of property may be made by a judge if the judge is satisfied

(*a*) where the application is made by

(i) a person charged with a designated offence, or

(ii) any person who acquired title to or a right of possession of that property from a person referred to in subparagraph (i) under circumstances that give rise to a reasonable inference that the title or right was transferred from that person for the purpose of avoiding the forfeiture of the property,

that a warrant should not have been issued pursuant to section 462.32 or a restraint order under subsection 462.33(3) should not have been made in respect of that property, or

(*b*) in any other case, that the applicant is the lawful owner of or lawfully entitled to possession of the property and appears innocent of any complicity in a designated offence or of any collusion in relation to such an offence, and that no other person appears to be the lawful owner of or lawfully entitled to possession of the property,

and that the property will no longer be required for the purpose of any investigation or as evidence in any proceeding.

(7) Sections 354, 355.2 and 355.4 do not apply to a person who comes into possession of any property that, by virtue of an order made under paragraph (4)(*c*), was returned to any person after having been seized or was excluded from the application of a restraint order made under subsection 462.33(3).

(8) A recognizance entered into pursuant to paragraph (4)(*a*) may be in Form 32. R.S.C. 1985, c. 42 (4th Supp.), s. 2; 1996, c. 19, ss. 69 and 70; 1997, c. 18, ss. 31, 140; 2001, c. 32, s. 17; 2010, c. 14, s. 8.

CROSS-REFERENCES

The terms "property" and "person" are defined in s. 2. "Judge" and "designated offence" are defined in s. 462.3. "Attorney General" is defined in ss. 2 and 462.3(3), (4). Pursuant to s. 462.341, certain parts of this section may apply to moneys seized under this Act or the *Controlled Drugs and Substances Act*.

If the Attorney General is required to return documents as part of a successful application under this section, copies can be made, pursuant to s. 462.46, of such documents before they are returned, and may be used as evidence as if they were the originals. Section 462.45 provides that an order returning property pursuant to s. 462.34(4) is suspended if an appeal from such an order or an application for restoration is made.

SYNOPSIS

This section provides for an application to a judge, as defined in s. 462.3, for an order returning property seized under s. 462.32, revoking a restraint order made under s. 462.34, or permitting the examination of seized or restrained property on such terms as the judge may require. Two clear days' notice must be given the Attorney General, unless the judge requires notice to be given to and hearing accorded to other interested parties.

The judge may also exclude property from the warrant or order if: the warrant or order should not have been issued with respect to that property; the property belongs to an innocent third party and the property is not required for evidence; the property is required for reasonable living, business or legal expenses (if the applicant has no other assets or means); or the applicant enters into a recognizance. The judge who made the order respecting release of funds to meet reasonable legal expenses shall tax those fees on application by the Attorney General.

Possession of property returned or excluded pursuant to this section is not an offence.

ANNOTATIONS

Standard of review – The review of a special warrant or restraint order which is designed to prevent the depletion of illegal property requires a different approach than that used in reviewing wiretap authorizations. The reviewing judge must determine whether the same decision would have been made, not merely whether there was a sufficient basis for the decision. In so doing, the judge must consider any evidence presented by the applicant to rebut or undermine the justifications for the authorization. Even if the judge concludes that the authorization should not have been granted, the Crown may request that the property remain under restraint if it is still required for a criminal investigation or as evidence in other cases. In addition, the rule against collateral attack is also relaxed to accommodate challenges to the underlying general search warrant while reviewing a special warrant or restraint order. *Quebec (Attorney General) v. Laroche*, [2002] 3 S.C.R. 708, 169 C.C.C. (3d) 97.

This provision does not violate ss. 7, 10(*b*), 11(*c*) or 11(*d*) of the Charter: *R. v. Trang* (2001), 161 C.C.C. (3d) 210 (Alta. Q.B.).

Legal expenses – The application to vary the order must be made by the client, not the lawyer. On the hearing of the application, the client, who is still facing charges, cannot be examined as to the source of his assets. Further, the client should not be required to answer any questions which may assist the Crown to prosecute him on further charges in other proceedings. Once the accused has established that the variation is required to meet legal expenses, the judge will hold an *in camera* hearing in the absence of Crown counsel to determine the amount which should be released from the restraint order: *R. v. Morra* (1992), 77 C.C.C. (3d) 380 (Ont. Ct. (Gen. Div.)).

Before succeeding on an application to access funds under this section, the accused must first attempt to avail himself of legal aid funding: *R. v. Cheng* (2011), 284 C.C.C. (3d) 240 (Ont. S.C.J.). *Contra*: *R. v. Bedi*, [2003] O.J. No. 5825 (S.C.J.).

There is no right of appeal to the Court of Appeal from the dismissal of an application under subsec. (4)(*c*)(ii). The only avenue of appeal is pursuant to s. 40 of the *Supreme Court Act*, R.S.C. 1985, c. S-26: *R. v. Martin* (2011), 266 C.C.C. (3d) 262 (Nfld. & Lab. C.A.).

Monies released for legal expenses pursuant to this provision are still subject to a fine in lieu of forfeiture under s. 462.37(3): *R. v. Rafilovich* (2017), 353 C.C.C. (3d) 293 (Ont. C.A.), additional reasons (2017), 142 W.C.B. (2d) 289, 2017 ONCA 824, leave to appeal to S.C.C. allowed 2018 CarswellOnt 11223.

[Now also see subsecs. (5.1)(*b*) and (5.2).]

APPLICATION OF PROPERTY RESTITUTION PROVISIONS.

462.341 Subsection 462.34(2), paragraph 462.34(4)(*c*) and subsections 462.34(5), (5.1) and (5.2) apply, with any modifications that the circumstances require, to a person who has an interest in money or bank-notes that are seized under this Act, the *Controlled Drugs and Substances Act* or the *Cannabis Act* and in respect of which proceedings may be taken under subsection 462.37(1) or (2.01) or 462.38(2). 1997, c. 18, ss. 32, 140; 1999, c. 5, s. 14; 2005, c. 44, s. 5; 2018, c. 16, s. 213.

EXPIRATION OF SPECIAL WARRANTS AND RESTRAINT ORDERS/Where proceedings instituted/Where application made.

462.35 (1) Subject to this section, where property has been seized under a warrant issued pursuant to section 462.32 or a restraint order has been made under section 462.33 in relation to property, the property may be detained or the order may continue in force, as the case may be, for a period not exceeding six months from the seizure or the making of the order, as the case may be.

(2) The property may continue to be detained, or the order may continue in force, for a period that exceeds six months if proceedings are instituted in respect of which the thing detained may be forfeited.

(3) The property may continue to be detained or the order may continue in force for a period or periods that exceed six months if the continuation is, on application made by the Attorney General, ordered by a judge, where the judge is satisfied that the property is required, after the expiration of the period or periods, for the purpose of section 462.37 or 462.38 or any other provision of this or any other Act of Parliament respecting forfeiture or for the purpose of any investigation or as evidence in any proceeding. R.S.C. 1985, c. 42 (4th Supp.), s. 2; 1997, c. 18, s. 33.

CROSS-REFERENCES

The term "property" is defined in s. 2. "Judge" is defined in s. 462.3. "Attorney General" is defined in ss. 2 and 462.3(3), (4).

If a successful application is not made by the Attorney General to extend the length of a restraint order or a search warrant issued under s. 462.32, the property seized will be disposed of under s. 462.32 or 462.43. If the Attorney General is required to return documents under this section, copies can be made, pursuant to s. 462.46, of such documents before they are returned, and may be used as evidence as if they were the originals.

Unlike most of the provisions in this Part, there is no right of appeal from a decision under this section.

SYNOPSIS

This section provides for the automatic expiry of warrants and restraint orders after six months, unless forfeiture proceedings are instituted; or a judge is satisfied by the Attorney General that the property may be required after the expiration of that period for the purpose of ss. 462.37, 462.38, any other provision of the Code, or any other federal Act respecting forfeiture, or for the purpose of any investigation or as evidence in any proceeding, extends the time. This section also pertains to property seized or restrained under ss. 462.32 and 462.33.

ANNOTATIONS

Even where the Crown complies with the provisions of this section, a judge has a discretion to refuse to order the continuing detention of the goods. The order was refused where the Crown had misled the judge who granted the initial *ex parte* order under s. 462.32 by failing to disclose that prior to the seizure of the goods an agreement had been reached between Crown counsel and counsel for the owner that would allow the owner to remain in possession of the goods: *R. v. Derksen* (1998), 126 C.C.C. (3d) 554 (Sask. Q.B.), affd 140 C.C.C. (3d) 184 (Sask. C.A.), leave to appeal to S.C.C. refused 142 C.C.C. (3d) vi.

FORWARDING TO CLERK WHERE ACCUSED TO STAND TRIAL.

462.36 Where a judge issues a warrant under section 462.32 or makes a restraint order under section 462.33 in respect of any property, the clerk of the court shall, when an accused is ordered to stand trial for a designated offence, cause to be forwarded to the clerk of the court to which the accused has been ordered to stand trial a copy of the report filed pursuant to paragraph 462.32(4)(*b*) or of the restraint order in respect of the property. R.S.C. 1985, c. 42 (4th Supp.), s. 2; 2001, c. 32, s. 18.

CROSS-REFERENCES

The terms "property" and "clerk of the court" are defined in s. 2. "Judge" and "designated offence" are defined in s. 462.3.

SYNOPSIS

This section provides for the transmission to the clerk of the court, to which an accused has been ordered to stand trial for a designated offence, of a copy of the report filed under s. 462.32(4)(*b*), or the restraint order under s. 462.33, with respect to the seized or restrained property.

Forfeiture of Proceeds of Crime

ORDER OF FORFEITURE OF PROPERTY / Proceeds of crime — other offences / Order of forfeiture — particular circumstances / Offences / Offender may establish that property is not proceeds of crime / Pattern of criminal activity / Conditions — pattern of criminal activity / Application under subsection (1) not prevented / Exception / Property outside Canada / Fine instead of forfeiture / Imprisonment in default of payment of fine / Fine option program not available to offender.

462.37 (1) Subject to this section and sections 462.39 to 462.41, if an offender is convicted, or discharged under section 730, of a designated offence and the court imposing sentence on or discharging the offender, on application of the Attorney General, is satisfied, on a balance of probabilities, that any property is proceeds of crime obtained through the commission of the designated offence, the court shall order that the property be forfeited to Her Majesty to be disposed of as the Attorney General directs or otherwise dealt with in accordance with the law.

(2) If the evidence does not establish to the satisfaction of the court that property in respect of which an order of forfeiture would otherwise be made under subsection (1) was obtained through the commission of the designated offence of which the offender is convicted or discharged, but the court is satisfied, beyond a reasonable doubt, that the property is proceeds of crime, the court may make an order of forfeiture under subsection (1) in relation to that property.

(2.01) A court imposing sentence on an offender convicted of an offence described in subsection (2.02) shall, on application of the Attorney General and subject to this section and sections 462.4 and 462.41, order that any property of the offender that is identified by the Attorney General in the application be forfeited to Her Majesty to be disposed of as the Attorney General directs or otherwise dealt with in accordance with the law if the court is satisfied, on a balance of probabilities, that

(*a*) within 10 years before the proceedings were commenced in respect of the offence for which the offender is being sentenced, the offender engaged in a pattern of criminal activity for the purpose of directly or indirectly receiving a material benefit, including a financial benefit; or

(*b*) the income of the offender from sources unrelated to designated offences cannot reasonably account for the value of all the property of the offender.

(2.02) The offences are the following:

(*a*) a criminal organization offence punishable by five or more years of imprisonment;

(*b*) an offence under section 5, 6 or 7 of the *Controlled Drugs and Substances Act* — or a conspiracy or an attempt to commit, being an accessory after the fact in relation to, or any counselling in relation to an offence under those sections — prosecuted by indictment; and

(*c*) an offence under subsection 9(1) or (2), 10(1) or (2), 11(1) or (2), 12(1), (4), (5), (6) or (7), 13(1) or 14(1) of the *Cannabis Act* — or a conspiracy or an attempt to commit, being an accessory after the fact in relation to, or any counselling in relation to an offence under any of those subsections — prosecuted by indictment.

Note: Subsection 462.37(2.02) amended by striking out "and" at the end of para. (*a*), by adding "and" at the end of para. (*b*), and by enacting para. (*c*), 2015, c. 16, s. 4 (to come into force by order of the Governor in Council):

(*c*) an offence under any of sections 279.01 to 279.03.

Note: Subsection 462.37(2.02) is replaced, 2018, c. 16, s. 225, on the first day on which both of *An Act to amend the Criminal Code (exploitation and trafficking in persons)*, 2015, c. 16, s. 4 and 2018, c. 16, s. 214 are in force:

Offences

(2.02) The offences are the following:

(*a*) a criminal organization offence punishable by five or more years of imprisonment;

(*b*) an offence under section 5, 6 or 7 of the *Controlled Drugs and Substances Act* — or a conspiracy or an attempt to commit, being an accessory after the fact in relation to, or any counselling in relation to an offence under any of those sections — prosecuted by indictment;

(*c*) an offence under subsection 9(1) or (2), 10(1) or (2), 11(1) or (2), 12(1), (4), (5), (6) or (7), 13(1) or 14(1) of the *Cannabis Act* — or a conspiracy or an attempt to commit, being an accessory after the fact in relation to, or any counselling in relation to an offence under any of those subsections — prosecuted by indictment; and

(*d*) an offence under any of sections 279.01 to 279.03.

(2.03) A court shall not make an order of forfeiture under subsection (2.01) in respect of any property that the offender establishes, on a balance of probabilities, is not proceeds of crime.

(2.04) In determining whether the offender has engaged in a pattern of criminal activity described in paragraph (2.01)(*a*), the court shall consider

(*a*) the circumstances of the offence for which the offender is being sentenced;

(*b*) any act or omission — other than an act or omission that constitutes the offence for which the offender is being sentenced — that the court is satisfied, on a balance of probabilities, was committed by the offender and constitutes an offence punishable by indictment under any Act of Parliament;

(*c*) any act or omission that the court is satisfied, on a balance of probabilities, was committed by the offender and is an offence in the place where it was committed and, if committed in Canada, would constitute an offence punishable by indictment under any Act of Parliament; and

(*d*) any other factor that the court considers relevant.

(2.05) A court shall not determine that an offender has engaged in a pattern of criminal activity unless the court is satisfied, on a balance of probabilities, that the offender committed, within the period referred to in paragraph (2.01)(*a*),

(*a*) acts or omissions — other than an act or omission that constitutes the offence for which the offender is being sentenced — that constitute at least two serious offences or one criminal organization offence;

(*b*) acts or omissions that are offences in the place where they were committed and, if committed in Canada, would constitute at least two serious offences or one criminal organization offence; or

(*c*) an act or omission described in paragraph (*a*) that constitutes a serious offence and an act or omission described in paragraph (*b*) that, if committed in Canada, would constitute a serious offence.

(2.06) Nothing in subsection (2.01) shall be interpreted as preventing the Attorney General from making an application under subsection (1) in respect of any property.

(2.07) A court may, if it considers it in the interests of justice, decline to make an order of forfeiture against any property that would otherwise be subject to forfeiture under subsection (2.01). The court shall give reasons for its decision.

(2.1) An order may be issued under this section in respect of property situated outside Canada, with any modifications that the circumstances require.

(3) If a court is satisfied that an order of forfeiture under subsection (1) or (2.01) should be made in respect of any property of an offender but that the property or any part of or interest in the property cannot be made subject to an order, the court may, instead of ordering the property or any part of or interest in the property to be forfeited, order the offender to pay a fine in an amount equal to the value of the property or the part of or interest in the property. In particular, a court may order the offender to pay a fine if the property or any part of or interest in the property

(*a*) cannot, on the exercise of due diligence, be located;

(*b*) has been transferred to a third party;

(*c*) is located outside Canada;

(*d*) has been substantially diminished in value or rendered worthless; or

(*e*) has been commingled with other property that cannot be divided without difficulty.

(4) Where a court orders an offender to pay a fine pursuant to subsection (3), the court shall

(*a*) impose, in default of payment of that fine, a term of imprisonment

(i) not exceeding six months, where the amount of the fine does not exceed ten thousand dollars,

(ii) of not less than six months and not exceeding twelve months, where the amount of the fine exceeds ten thousand dollars but does not exceed twenty thousand dollars,

(iii) of not less than twelve months and not exceeding eighteen months, where the amount of the fine exceeds twenty thousand dollars but does not exceed fifty thousand dollars,

(iv) of not less than eighteen months and not exceeding two years, where the amount of the fine exceeds fifty thousand dollars but does not exceed one hundred thousand dollars,

(v) of not less than two years and not exceeding three years, where the amount of the fine exceeds one hundred thousand dollars but does not exceed two hundred and fifty thousand dollars,

(vi) of not less than three years and not exceeding five years, where the amount of the fine exceeds two hundred and fifty thousand dollars but does not exceed one million dollars, or

(vii) of not less than five years and not exceeding ten years, where the amount of the fine exceeds one million dollars; and

(*b*) direct that the term of imprisonment imposed pursuant to paragraph (*a*) be served consecutively to any other term of imprisonment imposed on the offender or that the offender is then serving.

(5) Section 736 does not apply to an offender against whom a fine is imposed pursuant to subsection (3). R.S.C. 1985, c. 42 (4th Supp.), s. 2; 1995, c. 22, s. 10; 2001, c. 32, s. 19; 2005, c. 44, s. 6; 2017, c. 7, s. 59(1); 2018, c. 16, s. 214.

CROSS-REFERENCES

The terms "criminal organization offence", "serious offence", and "property" are defined in s. 2. The terms "designated offence" and "proceeds of crime" are defined in s. 462.3. "Attorney General" is defined in ss. 2 and 462.3(3), (4). The order may be executed in another province in accordance with s. 462.371.

Section 462.39 provides for an inference to be drawn that the property was obtained as a result of an "enterprise crime offence" if the conditions of that section are satisfied. Section 462.41 requires that notice be given to any person who may have a valid interest in the property before an order is made for the forfeiture of the property. In addition, before any property is forfeited under this section, the court may set aside any improper conveyances, using its powers under s. 462.4. Section 462.42 allows persons with a valid interest in the property which is to be forfeited to apply to have their interest declared not affected by any forfeiture, and to either retrieve the portion of the property in which they have an interest or an equivalent sum of money. Section 462.43 provides for the disposal of any residual property remaining after all persons with a valid interest have had their claims determined. If documents are returned under s. 462.37, the Attorney General has the right to make copies before returning the documents and to use them as evidence as if they were originals, pursuant to s. 462.46.

Section 673, which defines "sentence" for the purpose of indictable offences, includes an order under this section so that s. 683 permits an appeal to the appropriate appellate court. Section 462.45 provides that a forfeiture order is not to be carried out for 30 days and is stayed if it is under appeal, an application is made for restoration of the property or there are any proceedings in which the right to seize the property is questioned.

As to forfeiture of proceeds from a designated substance offence, see s. 23 of the *Controlled Drugs and Substances Act*.

Reference should also be made to the *Seized Property Management Act*, S.C. 1993, c. 37 [found in *Martin's Related Criminal Statutes*], where property is forfeited to Her Majesty and disposed of, or where a fine is imposed pursuant to this section.

SYNOPSIS

This section deals with the forfeiture of proceeds of crime after an accused person has been convicted of a designated offence.

Subsection (1) provides for an order, for the forfeiture of property, by the judge imposing sentence when a person is found guilty of the designated offence. If the Attorney General satisfies the judge, on a balance of probabilities, that any property is the proceeds of crime, and that the designated offence that was the subject of the trial was committed in relation to such property, the judge shall order its forfeiture.

Subsection (2) provides that, where in the proceedings described in subsec. (1), the connection between the offence and the property is not established, but the judge is satisfied beyond a reasonable doubt that the property is proceeds of crime, the judge may order its forfeiture.

Subsection (2.1) gives the judge extraterritorial jurisdiction in the sense that an order may be made under this section even where the property is outside Canada.

Subsections (2.01) to (2.07) provide an expanded jurisdiction to order forfeiture of property that is not directly connected to the crime for which the accused has been convicted, where the accused has been convicted of a criminal organization offence or an offence or a conspiracy, attempt or accessory after the fact to an offence under ss. 5 to 7 of the *Controlled Drugs and Substances Act*. Under subsec. (2.01), the forfeiture order may be made in relation to any property identified in an application by the Attorney General, where the court is satisfied on a balance of probabilities that, within the 10 years before the proceedings were commenced, the offender was engaged in a pattern of criminal activity for the purpose of directly or indirectly receiving a material benefit, or the offender's income from non-designated offences cannot reasonably account for the offender's wealth. However, under subsec. (2.03), the court shall not make a forfeiture order if the offender establishes on a balance of probabilities that the property identified in the application is not proceeds of crime. Subsection (2.04) sets out the circumstances the judge is to consider in determining whether the offender engaged in a pattern of criminal activity. Among other things, this subsection allows the judge to take into account other offences that have been shown to have likely been committed by the offender. However, under subsec. (2.05), the court shall not find that the offender engaged in a pattern of criminal activity unless the court is satisfied that, within the 10-year period referred to in subsec. (2.01), the offender probably committed certain offences; namely one criminal organization offence or two serious offences (terms defined in s. 2), or similar offences committed outside of Canada as specified in paras. (*b*) and (*c*). Further, under subsec. (2.07), the judge may decline to make the order but must give reasons for not doing so.

Where an order should be made under subsec. (1) or (2.01), but the property cannot be found after the exercise of due diligence, it has been transferred, it is outside Canada, or it has been diminished or commingled, the court may, instead of ordering forfeiture, impose a fine of equal value to such property on the offender.

Subsection (4) provides a sliding scale for consecutive imprisonment in lieu of payment of the fine.

ANNOTATIONS

The trial judge at the time of sentencing erred in refusing to make an order under subsec. (1) with respect to certain monies seized from the accused at the time of his arrest, in part because the judge believed that the monies had been given the accused by his mother. The entitlement claims of other persons to the proceeds are not to be dealt with in conjunction with a sentence hearing but rather pursuant to s. 462.42 after the order of forfeiture has been made: *R. v. Pawlyk* (1991), 65 C.C.C. (3d) 63 (Man. C.A.).

The forfeiture order is part of the sentence and, once the order has been made, the trial judge is *functus*. Thus, the judge had no jurisdiction to subsequently vacate a portion of the order on the application of the mortgagee: *R. v. Sterling* (1992), 71 C.C.C. (3d) 222 (B.C.S.C.). *Contra*: *Wilson v. Canada* (1993), 86 C.C.C. (3d) 464 (Ont. C.A.), where it was held that third party claims can be considered at the sentence hearing in view of s. 462.41.

The burden on the applicant seeking the return of property is less onerous at the forfeiture stage as opposed to the restraint order stage, in that the applicant need only show that he or she appears innocent of any complicity or collusion with respect to the offences regarding which the forfeiture order is sought: *Antillas Communication inc. v. La Reine* (2007), 232 C.C.C. (3d) 553 (Que. C.A.).

A valid security interest can attach to funds subsequently found to constitute proceeds of crime. In such circumstances, a corporation's interest is voidable but not void *ab initio*. Accordingly, in this case, although the bank had a valid security interest in moneys in an account pursuant to a security agreement, it was not appropriate in the circumstances to exercise the court's discretion in favour of the bank in respect of funds which were identifiable proceeds of crime that should be returned to the victims. The portion of the funds in the account which were not identifiable proceeds of crime were not properly the subject of a forfeiture order and should be returned to the bank: *R. v. Canadian Imperial Bank of Commerce* (2000), 151 C.C.C. (3d) 439 (Ont. C.A.).

It was not appropriate to impose a fine under subsec. (3) where the proceeds had been used by the accused to enter into a recognizance and then for lawyer fees. If the Crown had moved to seize the funds, they would have been available for these purposes in any event by an application under s. 462.34: *R. v. Gagnon* (1993), 80 C.C.C. (3d) 508 (Alta. Q.B.).

A provincial court judge acting as a trial judge has the jurisdiction to order the forfeiture of property under this section: *R. v. Rosenblum* (1998), 130 C.C.C. (3d) 481 (B.C.C.A.).

The fact that property is registered in the name of a third party does not create a discretion to impose a fine in lieu of forfeiture where the criteria of subsec. (1) have been met: *R. v. Rosenblum, infra*.

In view of the provisions of subsecs. (3) and (4) a lawyer, representing the accused, who has taken an assignment of seized funds is in a potential conflict of interest. If the court makes an order in favour of the lawyer then the accused is liable to have a fine (and jail in default) imposed in the equivalent amount. On the other hand, it would be inappropriate for the lawyer to wait until after sentencing and then make a claim under s. 462.42 in an effort to circumvent the scheme of the legislation: *R. v. Wilson, supra*.

While the judge has a discretion whether or not to impose a fine and as to the determination of the value of the property, the fine must equal the value of the property. The offender's ability to pay is not a factor reducing the amount of the fine and is not a factor to be considered in whether to impose a fine. However, the ability to pay may be taken into consideration in determining the time limit for payment of the fine: *R. v. Lavigne*, [2006] 1 S.C.R. 392, 206 C.C.C. (3d) 449.

An order for a fine in lieu of forfeiture can be made only where the offender has possession or control of the property in question or at least had possession of the property at some point. This conclusion flows from the use of the phrase "any property of an offender" in subsec. (3) and the definition of "property" in s. 2: *R. v. Dwyer* (2013), 296 C.C.C. (3d) 193 (Ont. C.A.), additional reasons 2013 ONCA 306.

It is an error to decline to order a fine in lieu of forfeiture out of concern for the accused's rehabilitative prospects and his ability to satisfy restitution orders made against him: *R. v. Angelis* (2016), 340 C.C.C. (3d) 477 (Ont. C.A.), leave to appeal to S.C.C. refused (2017), [2016] S.C.C.A. No. 484.

It is an error to decline to order a fine in lieu of forfeiture in respect of certain proceeds simply because those proceeds were released by the court pursuant to s. 462.34(4) to pay legal expenses: *R. v. Rafilovich* (2017), 353 C.C.C. (3d) 293 (Ont. C.A.), additional reasons 2017 ONCA 824, leave to appeal to S.C.C. allowed 2018 CarswellOnt 11223.

DEFINITION OF "ORDER" / Execution / Filing of order from another province / Attorney General of Canada / Effect of registered order / Notice / Application of section 462.42 / Application under section 462.42 to be made in one province / Finding in one court binding

462.371 (1) In this section, "order" means an order made under section 462.37 or 462.38.

(2) An order may be executed anywhere in Canada.

(3) Where the Attorney General of a province in which property that is the subject of an order made in another province is situated receives a certified copy of the order and files it with the superior court of criminal jurisdiction of the province in which the property is situated, the order shall be entered as a judgment of that court.

(4) Where the Attorney General of Canada receives a certified copy of an order made in a province in respect of property situated in another province and files the order with the superior court of criminal jurisdiction of the province in which the property is situated, the order shall be entered as a judgment of that court.

(5) An order has, from the date it is filed in a court of a province under subsection (3) or (4), the same effect as if it had been an order originally made by that court.

(6) Where an order has been filed in a court under subsection (3) or (4), it shall not be executed before notice in accordance with subsection 462.41(2) is given to every person who, in the opinion of the court, appears to have a valid interest in the property.

(7) Section 462.42 applies, with such modifications as the circumstances require, in respect of a person who claims an interest in property that is the subject of an order filed under subsection (3) or (4).

(8) No person may make an application under section section 462.42 in relation to property that is the subject of an order filed under subsection (3) or (4) if that person has previously made an application in respect of the same property in another province.

(9) The finding by a court of a province in relation to property that is the subject of an order filed under subsection (3) or (4) as to whether or not an applicant referred to in subsection 462.42(4) is affected by the forfeiture referred to in that subsection or declaring the nature and extent of the interest of the applicant under that subsection is binding on the superior court of criminal jurisdiction of the province where the order is entered as a judgment. 1997, c. 18, s. 34.

CROSS-REFERENCES
"Property" and "superior court of criminal jurisdiction" are defined in s. 2. "Attorney General" is defined in ss. 2 and 462.3(3), (4).

SYNOPSIS

This section sets out the procedure for executing forfeiture orders made under ss. 462.37 and 462.38 where the property is situated in another province. Upon receiving the order the Attorney General causes the order to be filed in the superior court of criminal jurisdiction and the order is then entered as a judgment of that court. However, the order cannot be executed until notice has been given in accordance with s. 462.41(2). A person affected by the order may then apply to the superior court in accordance with s. 462.42, provided that the person has not made an application in respect of the same property in another province. An order under s. 462.42 as to whether an applicant is affected by the forfeiture or declaring the nature and extent of the interest is binding on the superior court.

APPLICATION FOR FORFEITURE / Order of forfeiture of property / Property outside Canada / Person deemed absconded.

462.38 (1) Where an information has been laid in respect of a designated offence, the Attorney General may make an application to a judge for an order of forfeiture under subsection (2) in respect of any property.

(2) Subject to sections 462.39 to 462.41, where an application is made to a judge under subsection (1), the judge shall, if the judge is satisfied that

(*a*) any property is, beyond a reasonable doubt, proceeds of crime,

(*b*) that property was obtained through the commission of a designated offence in respect of which proceedings were commenced, and

(*c*) the accused charged with the offence referred to in paragraph (*b*) has died or absconded,

order that the property be forfeited to Her Majesty to be disposed of as the Attorney General directs or otherwise dealt with in accordance with the law.

(2.1) An order may be issued under this section in respect of property situated outside Canada, with any modifications that the circumstances require.

(3) For the purposes of this section, a person shall be deemed to have absconded in connection with a designated offence if

(*a*) an information has been laid alleging the commission of the offence by the person,

(*b*) a warrant for the arrest of the person or a summons in respect of an organization has been issued in relation to that information, and

(*c*) reasonable attempts to arrest the person pursuant to the warrant or to serve the summons have been unsuccessful during the period of six months commencing on the day the warrant or summons was issued, or, in the case of a person who is not or never was in Canada, the person cannot be brought within that period to the jurisdiction in which the warrant or summons was issued,

and the person shall be deemed to have so absconded on the last day of that period of six months. R.S.C. 1985, c. 42 (4th Supp.), s. 2; 1997, c. 18, s. 35(2); 2001, c. 32, s. 20; 2003, c. 21, s. 7; 2017, c. 7, s. 60(1).

CROSS-REFERENCES
The terms "organization", "property" and "person" are defined in s. 2. The terms "judge", "proceeds of crime" and "designated offence" are defined in s. 462.3. "Attorney General" is defined in ss. 2 and 462.3(3), (4). The order is executed in accordance with s. 462.371.

Section 462.39 provides for an inference to be drawn that the property was obtained as a result of a "designated offence" if the conditions of that section are satisfied. Section 462.41 requires that notice be given to any person who may have a valid interest in the property before an order is made for the forfeiture of the property. In addition, before any property is forfeited under this section, the court may set aside any improper conveyances using its powers under s. 462.4. Section 462.42 allows persons with a valid interest in the property which is to be forfeited to apply to have their interest declared not affected by any forfeiture, and to either retrieve the portion of the property in which they have an interest or an equivalent sum of money. Section 462.43 provides for the disposal of any residual property remaining after all persons with a valid interest have had their claims determined. If documents are returned under s. 462.37, the Attorney General has the right to make copies before returning the documents and to use them as evidence as if they were originals, pursuant to s. 462.46.

Section 462.44 provides for a right of appeal from a forfeiture order. Section 462.45 provides that a forfeiture order is not to be carried out for 30 days and is stayed if it is under appeal, an application is made for restoration of the property or there are any proceedings in which the right to seize the property is questioned.

Similar provisions relating to a designated substance offence are found in s. 17 of the *Controlled Drugs and Substances Act*.

Reference should also be made to the *Seized Property Management Act*, S.C. 1993, c. 37, where property is forfeited to Her Majesty under this section.

SYNOPSIS

This section provides for an *in rem* forfeiture hearing for proceeds of crime in certain circumstances. The Attorney General may apply for such a hearing if an information has been laid in respect of a designated offence. On such an application, the judge shall order forfeiture if the Attorney General establishes that the property is, *beyond reasonable doubt*, proceeds of crime, that related enterprise crime proceedings were commenced, and that the accused has died or absconded.

Subsection (3) deems a person to have absconded if an information has been laid, a warrant issued, and reasonable attempts to arrest have been unsuccessful during the six-month period after the issuance of the warrant.

ANNOTATIONS

In establishing that any seized property is beyond a reasonable doubt the "proceeds of crime", there is no burden on the Crown to prove that the funds seized were the proceeds of any specific illegal transaction such as sale of naroctics. Thus, the fact that the funds or other property are proceeds of crime may be established by circumstantial evidence. The hearing under s. 462.38 is in its nature between a criminal trial proper where the strict rules of evidence apply and a sentence hearing. Thus, while it must be proved beyond a reasonable doubt that the property was the proceeds of crime, the fact that proceedings in respect of an enterprise crime offence had been commenced and that the accused absconded need only be proved on a balance of probabilities. Similarly, bearing in mind the standard of proof beyond a reasonable doubt as to the source of the funds sought to be forefeited, the general rule that all relevant evidence is admissible applies and the effect of exclusionary rules of evidence is to be left to the judge hearing the application. This includes the weight, if any, to be accorded to hearsay evidence, bearing in mind its reliability and the explanation for not making better evidence available: *R. v. Clymore* (1992), 74 C.C.C. (3d) 217 (B.C.S.C.).

Where the prerequisites set out in subsec. (3) have been met so that the accused is deemed to have absconded, the requirement in subsec. (1)(*c*) has been made out even if, in the course of the proceedings, the accused's whereabouts become known. Thus, in this case, the accused had still absconded for the purpose of the Crown's application, even if during the course of the proceedings his whereabouts were discovered as a result of his arrest by American authorities while apparently attempting to import drugs into that country. There was no requirement that the Crown attempt to extradite the accused before the end of the proceedings under this section. His status as an absconding accused continues for the purpose of this section: *R. v. Clymore, supra.* [Now see also subsec. (3)(*c*).]

Although the proceedings under this section lead only to the forfeiture of property, it would be open to the accused to rely on s. 8 of the Charter and to argue for exclusion of the funds seized, on the basis that his right to protection against unreasonable search and seizure was violated: *R. v. Clymore, supra.*

Property is not limited to physical property and can apply to an interest in property. The property does not have to be in existence at the time that the charges are laid providing that the property is proceeds of crime from the charge period. Property can appreciate or be converted to substitute property after the charge period but still constitute proceeds of crime: *R. v. Stone Estate* (2001), 155 C.C.C. (3d) 168, 42 C.R. (5th) 339 (N.S.C.A.).

INFERENCE.

462.39 For the purpose of subsection 462.37(1) or 462.38(2), the court may infer that property was obtained or derived as a result of the commission of a designated offence where evidence establishes that the value, after the commission of that offence, of all the property of the person alleged to have committed the offence exceeds the value of all the property of that person before the commission of that offence and the court is satisfied that the income of that person from sources unrelated to designated offences committed by that person cannot reasonably account for such an increase in value. R.S.C. 1985, c. 42 (4th Supp.), s. 2; 1996, c. 19, s. 70; 2001, c. 32, s. 21.

CROSS-REFERENCES

The terms "property" and "person" are defined in s. 2. The term "designated offence" is defined in s. 462.3. This section is incorporated into the *Controlled Drugs and Substances Act.* See s. 23 of that Act.

SYNOPSIS

This section provides that the court may infer in forfeiture hearings under this Part that property was obtained or derived from an enterprise crime offence where it is established that the value of all of a person's property after the commission of such an offence exceeds the previous value, and that unrelated legitimate income cannot reasonably account for the increase.

VOIDABLE TRANSFERS.

462.4 A court may,

(*a*) prior to ordering property to be forfeited under subsection 462.37(1) or (2.01) or 462.38(2), and

(*b*) in the case of property in respect of which a restraint order was made under section 462.33, where the order was served in accordance with subsection 462.33(8),

set aside any conveyance or transfer of the property that occurred after the seizure of the property or the service of the order under section 462.33, unless the conveyance or transfer was for valuable consideration to a person acting in good faith. R.S. 1985, c. 42 (4th Supp.) s. 2; 1997, c. 18, s. 36; 2005, c. 44, s. 7.

CROSS-REFERENCES

The term "property" is defined in s. 2. This property could have been seized by a warrant issued under s. 462.32.

This section is incorporated into the *Controlled Drugs and Substances Act* by s. 23 of that Act.

SYNOPSIS

This section provides that, prior to ordering forfeiture, a court may void any transfers of seized or restrained property. The court is authorized to so order in the case of restrained property if the order was served and unless the transfer was made for valuable consideration to a person acting in good faith.

NOTICE / Manner of giving notice / Order of restoration of property.

462.41 (1) Before making an order under subsection 462.37(1) or (2.01) or 462.38(2) in relation to any property, a court shall require notice in accordance with subsection (2) to be given to and may hear any person who, in the opinion of the court, appears to have a valid interest in the property.

(2) A notice shall

(*a*) be given in the manner that the court directs or that may be specified in the rules of the court;

(*b*) specify the period that the court considers reasonable or that may be set out in the rules of the court during which a person may make an application to the court asserting their interest in the property; and

(*c*) set out the designated offence charged and a description of the property.

(3) Where a court is satisfied that any person, other than

(*a*) a person who is charged with, or was convicted of, a designated offence, or

(*b*) a person who acquired title to or a right of possession of that property from a person referred to in paragraph (*a*) under circumstances that give rise to a reasonable inference that the title or right was transferred for the purpose of avoiding the forfeiture of the property,

is the lawful owner or is lawfully entitled to possession of any property or any part thereof that would otherwise be forfeited pursuant to subsection 462.37(1) or (2.01) or 462.38(2) and that the person appears innocent of any complicity in an offence referred to in paragraph (*a*) or of any collusion in relation to such an offence, the court may order that the property or part thereof be returned to that person. R.S.C. 1985, c. 42 (4th Supp.), s. 2; 1996, c. 19, s. 70; 1997, c. 18, ss. 37, 140; 2001, c. 32, s. 22; 2005, c. 44, s. 8; 2017, c. 7, s. 61.

CROSS-REFERENCES

The terms "property" and "person" are defined in s. 2. The term "designated offence" is defined in s. 462.3. The powers of a court to make rules is stated in s. 482.

Persons who receive notice under this section and seek to prevent their property from being forfeited can apply under s. 462.42 for relief from forfeiture.

A right of appeal from an order under subsec. (3) is provided by s. 462.44 and the order is stayed pursuant to s. 462.45. If a proceeding is brought, under which the restoration of the property under s. 462.41(3) is challenged, s. 462.45 will stay the restoration pending the completion of the further proceedings to determine the validity of the restoration order.

If documents are ordered returned under s. 462.41(3), the Attorney General has the right to make copies before returning the documents and to use them as evidence as if they were originals, pursuant to s. 462.46.

This section is incorporated into the *Controlled Drugs and Substances Act* by s. 23 of that Act.

SYNOPSIS

This section provides for notice to and the hearing of interested parties before forfeiture is ordered, and for the return of property to such persons if they are innocent of complicity.

Before making a forfeiture order, whether after a conviction or in an *in rem* proceeding, a court must require notice to be given in accordance with subsec. (2) to any person whom the court believes has a valid interest in the property in question, and may hear such person.

Where the court is satisfied that a person is the lawful owner of, or is entitled to possession of, all or part of the property in question, and appears innocent of complicity of collusion in a designated offence, the court may order it returned to that person, unless that person was charged with or convicted of a designated offence, or derived his or her interest in the property from such persons, in circumstances giving rise to a reasonable inference that the transfer was made to avoid forfeiture.

ANNOTATIONS

This section provides for both notice to interested third parties and an opportunity for them to be heard on the application. They need not apply under s. 462.42 after forfeiture has been made for an order that their property is not forfeited: *R. v. Sankar* (2010), 270 C.C.C. (3d) 410 (Ont. S.C.J.).

Where the process under this section makes otherwise forfeitable property not subject to forfeiture, the judge may impose a fine equivalent pursuant to s. 462.37: *Wilson v. Canada* (1993), 86 C.C.C. (3d) 464, 25 C.R. (4th) 239 (Ont. C.A.).

Forfeited funds can be released for the purpose of paying legal fees to counsel and the Legal Aid Plan: *R. v. Thomas* (2001), 153 C.C.C. (3d) 94 (Ont. C.A.).

A deceased's estate can have a valid interest in seized properties even if the interest did not exist at the time of the seizure. In this case, the judge had the jurisdiction to order a partial return of seized monies in order to pay for the estate's reasonable legal costs in responding to the Crown's forfeiture application: *Beaulieu Estate v. Canada* (2001), 165 C.C.C. (3d) 563, 214 D.L.R. (4th) 663, 243 N.B.R. (2d) 338 *sub nom. R. v. Beaulieu Estate* (C.A.).

APPLICATION BY PERSON CLAIMING INTEREST FOR RELIEF FROM FORFEITURE / Fixing day for hearing / Notice / Order declaring interest not subject to forfeiture / Appeal from order under subsection (4) / Return of property.

462.42 (1) Any person who claims an interest in property that is forfeited to Her Majesty under subsection 462.37(1) or (2.01) or 462.38(2) may, within thirty days after the forfeiture, apply by notice in writing to a judge for an order under subsection (4) unless the person is

- **(*a*) a person who is charged with, or was convicted of, a designated offence that resulted in the forfeiture; or**
- **(*b*) a person who acquired title to or a right of possession of the property from a person referred to in paragraph (*a*) under circumstances that give rise to a reasonable inference that the title or right was transferred from that person for the purpose of avoiding the forfeiture of the property.**

(2) The judge to whom an application is made under subsection (1) shall fix a day not less than thirty days after the date of filing of the application for the hearing thereof.

(3) An applicant shall serve a notice of the application made under subsection (1) and of the hearing thereof on the Attorney General at least fifteen days before the day fixed for the hearing.

(4) Where, on the hearing of an application made under subsection (1), the judge is satisfied that the applicant is not a person referred to in paragraph (1)(*a*) or (*b*) and appears innocent of any complicity in any designated offence that resulted in the forfeiture or of any collusion in relation to any such offence, the judge may make an order declaring that the interest of the applicant is not affected by the forfeiture and declaring the nature and extent of the interest.

(5) An applicant or the Attorney General may appeal to the court of appeal from an order under subsection (4) and the provisions of Part XXI with respect to procedure on appeals apply, with such modifications as the circumstances require, to appeals under this subsection.

(6) The Attorney General shall, on application made to the Attorney General by any person who has obtained an order under subsection (4) and where the periods with respect to the taking of appeals from that order have expired and any appeal from that order taken under subsection (5) has been determined,

(*a*) direct that the property or the part thereof to which the interest of the applicant relates be returned to the applicant; or

(*b*) direct that an amount equal to the value of the interest of the applicant, as declared in the order, be paid to the applicant. R.S.C. 1985, c. 42 (4th Supp.), s. 2; 1996, c. 19, s. 70; 1997, c. 18, ss. 38, 140; 2001, c. 32, s. 23; 2005, c. 44, s. 9.

CROSS-REFERENCES

The terms "property" and "person" are defined in s. 2. The terms "judge" and "designated offence" are defined in s. 462.3. "Attorney General" is defined in ss. 2 and 462.3(3), (4).

This section is incorporated into the *Controlled Drugs and Substances Act* by s. 23 of that Act.

SYNOPSIS

This section provides for written applications by innocent third parties for relief from forfeiture under this part within 30 days after such forfeiture is ordered.

Such application may be brought by any person who claims an interest in forfeited property, other than a person described in subsec. (1)(*a*) or (*b*), that is, a person who was charged with or convicted of a designated offence in relation to the property, or a person who acquired his interest from such person, in circumstances giving rise to a reasonable inference that the transfer was made to avoid forfeiture.

A judge to whom such application is made shall fix a hearing date not less than 30 days after the application is filed. The Attorney General is entitled to at least 15 days notice of the hearing.

The judge hearing the application may make an order declaring the nature and extent of the applicant's interest, and also declaring that it is not affected by the forfeiture, if he is satisfied that the applicant was not a person described in subsec. (1)(*a*) or (*b*) and that he appears innocent of complicity or collusion in the offence that resulted in the forfeiture.

Appeals are available from orders under this section to the Court of Appeal.

Upon the application of a person who has obtained an order under this section, if the appeal period has expired and any appeal has been determined, the Attorney General is required to direct the return of the property or the repayment of its value as declared in the order to the applicant.

ANNOTATIONS

An application under this provision is more properly made to a superior court judge since that judge is not subject to the jurisdictional limitations of a kind that might hamper the inquiry of a provincial court judge: *R. v. Rosenblum* (1998), 130 C.C.C. (3d) 481, 167 D.L.R. (4th) 639 (B.C.C.A.).

Even where the applicant has met the conditions in this section, the judge has a discretion to refuse to make a declaration in favour of the applicant. In exercising the discretion, the judge must consider whether the innocent third party should suffer so that the goal of divesting the accused of his proceeds of crime can be achieved: *R. v. Wilson* (1993), 86 C.C.C. (3d) 464, 25 C.R. (4th) 239 (Ont. C.A.).

In *R. v. Wilson*, *supra*, the accused and his wife had assigned their interest in seized funds to their lawyers for the payment of legal fees. At the time of sentencing, an order was made forfeiting those funds pursuant to s. 462.37. Once that order was made, any interest that the accused and his wife had in the funds was extinguished as was the interest that the lawyers had. Accordingly, they had no assertable interest in the funds within the meaning of this section.

The victim of an offence who had served a garnishee summons upon a company holding funds owed to the accused, before the Attorney General applied for forfeiture of those funds, was entitled to an order declaring an interest in those funds: *R. v. Tatarchuk*, [1993] 1 W.W.R. 349, 4 Alta. L.R. (3d) 300 (Q.B.).

An ordinary creditor does not have an enforceable interest in any particular asset of the debtor and in principle does not enjoy a right of recourse in relation to the asset. Accordingly, ordinary creditors do not have a valid interest in the proceeds of an enterprise crime offence committed by the debtor as contemplated by subsec. (4) of this provision: *Lumen Inc. v. Canada (Attorney General)* (1997), 119 C.C.C. (3d) 91, 10 C.R. (5th) 246 (Que. C.A.), leave to appeal to S.C.C. refused 119 C.C.C. (3d) vi, 152 D.L.R. (4th) vi. However, where the interest in the property goes beyond that of an unsecured creditor, a claim may be brought. In *R. v. 1431633 Ontario Inc.* (2010), 250 C.C.C. (3d) 354 (Ont. S.C.J.), the court recognized the right of a creditor that had erroneously failed to perfect a construction lien as a result of counsel's error.

An interest in a property may be acquired where a third party creditor registered a mortgage after a restraint order had been made but before the order of forfeiture. The applicant must establish an absence of complicity or collusion in the enterprise crime offence on a balance of probabilities in order to obtain an interest in the property: *Villeneuve v. Canada* (1999), 140 C.C.C. (3d) 564 (Que. C.A.).

This section provides a mechanism by which third parties who claim an interest in property forfeited under s. 462.37 may apply to a judge for relief from the forfeiture order made at the sentencing stage of the trial. Where the applicant under this section establishes a valid claim, the forfeiture order is not rescinded. Rather, the Attorney General is required, pursuant to subsec. (6), to either return the property to the applicant or remit to the applicant an amount equal to the value of the applicant's interest: *R. v. 170888 Canada Ltee* (1999), 135 C.C.C. (3d) 367, 174 D.L.R. (4th) 340 (Que. C.A.).

In an unusual case, it was held that a corporation could bring an application under this section for an order under subsec. (4) in respect of a shareholder's loan, which had been declared forfeited under s. 462.37 as proceeds of crime at the shareholder's sentence hearing, although the corporation denied having received the loan. Even though it claimed that the loan was never received, the corporation had a sufficient interest in that forfeited property to seek relief under this section: *R. v. 170888 Canada Ltee., supra.*

RESIDUAL DISPOSAL OF PROPERTY SEIZED OR DEALT WITH PURSUANT TO SPECIAL WARRANTS OR RESTRAINT ORDERS / Property outside Canada.

462.43 (1) Where property has been seized under a warrant issued pursuant to section 462.32, a restraint order has been made under section 462.33 in relation to any property or a recognizance has been entered into pursuant to paragraph 462.34(4)(*a*) in relation to any property and a judge, on application made to the judge by the Attorney General or any person having an interest in the property or on the judge's own motion, after notice given to the Attorney General and any other person having an interest in the property, is satisfied that the property will no longer be required for the purpose of section 462.37, 462.38 or any other provision of this or any other Act of Parliament respecting forfeiture or for the purpose of any investigation or as evidence in any proceeding, the judge

(*a*) in the case of a restraint order, shall revoke the order;

(*b*) in the case of a recognizance, shall cancel the recognizance; and

(*c*) in the case of property seized under a warrant issued pursuant to section 462.32 or property under the control of a person appointed pursuant to paragraph 462.331(1)(*a*),

(i) if possession of it by the person from whom it was taken is lawful, shall order that it be returned to that person,

(ii) if possession of it by the person from whom it was taken is unlawful and the lawful owner or person who is lawfully entitled to its possession is known,

shall order that it be returned to the lawful owner or the person who is lawfully entitled to its possession, or

(iii) if possession of it by the person from whom it was taken is unlawful and the lawful owner or person who is lawfully entitled to its possession is not known, may order that it be forfeited to Her Majesty, to be disposed of as the Attorney General directs, or otherwise dealt with in accordance with the law.

(2) An order may be issued under this section in respect of property situated outside Canada, with any modifications that the circumstances require. R.S.C. 1985, c. 42 (4th Supp.), s. 2; 2001, c. 32, s. 24; 2004, c. 12, s. 7.

CROSS-REFERENCES

The terms "property" and "person" are defined in s. 2. "Attorney General" is defined in ss. 2 and 462.3(3), (4). "Judge" is defined in s. 462.3.

If documents are returned under s. 462.43, the Attorney General has the right to make copies before returning the documents and to use them as evidence as if they were originals, pursuant to s. 462.46.

Section 462.44 provides a right of appeal from a decision made under this section. Section 462.45 provides that a forfeiture order is not to be carried out for 30 days and is stayed if it is under appeal, an application is made for restoration of the property or there are any proceedings in which the right to seize the property is questioned.

Reference should also be made to the *Seized Property Management Act*, S.C. 1993, c. 37 [found in *Martin's Related Criminal Statutes*], where property is forfeited to Her Majesty under this section.

SYNOPSIS

This section provides for the revocation of restraint orders, the cancellation of any recognizances, and the return of seized property (or its forfeiture where the owner is not known), on application by the Attorney General or an interested party, where the property is no longer required for the purposes of this Part, or of any Act of Parliament, or for any investigation or as evidence.

ANNOTATIONS

Standard of review – The review of a special warrant or restraint order, which is designed to prevent the depletion of illegal property, requires a different approach than that used in reviewing wiretap authorizations. The reviewing judge must determine whether the same decision would have been made, not merely whether there was a sufficient basis for the decision. In so doing, the judge must consider any evidence presented by the applicant to rebut or undermine the justifications for the authorization. Even if the judge concludes that the authorization should not have been granted, the Crown may request that the property remain under restraint if it is still required for a criminal investigation or as evidence in other cases. In addition, the rule against collateral attack is also relaxed to accommodate challenges to the underlying general search warrant while reviewing a special warrant or restraint order. *Quebec (Attorney General) v. Laroche*, [2002] 3 S.C.R. 708, 169 C.C.C. (3d) 97.

APPEALS FROM CERTAIN ORDERS

462.44 Any person who considers that they are aggrieved by an order made under subsection 462.38(2) or 462.41(3) or section 462.43 may appeal from the order as if the order were an appeal against conviction or against a judgment or verdict of acquittal, as the case may be, under Part XXI, and that Part applies, with such modifications as

the circumstances require, to such an appeal. R.S.C. 1985, c. 42 (4th Supp.), s. 2; 1997, c. 18, s. 39.

CROSS-REFERENCES

The term "person" is defined in s. 2.

Section 462.45 provides that any order for forfeiture or restoration is stayed if an appeal is brought.

Section 462.44 does not refer to orders made pursuant to s. 462.37 as they come within the definition of "sentence" under s. 673 (applicable to indictable offences), and s. 689(1) provides for the stay of such orders pending the appeal.

Section 462.42 provides an avenue for those not implicated in the "designated offence" to seek relief from a forfeiture order.

This section is incorporated into the *Controlled Drugs and Substances Act* by s. 23 of that Act.

SYNOPSIS

This section provides for appeals from *in rem* forfeiture decisions, and decisions under s. 462.43, as if they were appeals from convictions or acquittal in proceedings by indictment.

SUSPENSION OF FORFEITURE PENDING APPEAL.

462.45 Despite anything in this Part, the operation of an order of forfeiture or restoration of property under subsection 462.34(4), 462.37(1) or (2.01), 462.38(2) or 462.41(3) or section 462.43 is suspended pending

(*a*) any application made in respect of the property under any of those provisions or any other provision of this or any other Act of Parliament that provides for the restoration or forfeiture of such property,

(*b*) any appeal taken from an order of forfeiture or restoration in respect of the property, or

(*c*) any other proceeding in which the right of seizure of the property is questioned,

and property shall not be disposed of within thirty days after an order of forfeiture is made under any of those provisions. R.S.C. 1985, c. 42 (4th Supp.), s. 2; 2005, c. 44, s. 10.

CROSS-REFERENCES

The term "property" is defined in s. 2. Section 490(12), which also deals with the return, forfeiture and disposition of seized property, contains a similar provision requiring a 30 day stay of all such orders, in addition to stays pending any appeals or similar challenges to the order made under that section. If the order appealed from is made under s. 462.37(1), s. 689(1) stays the operation of the order if it was made in relation to an indictable offence and an appeal is launched against the order. This section is incorporated into the *Controlled Drugs and Substances Act* by s. 23 of that Act.

SYNOPSIS

This section provides for the automatic suspension of forfeiture or restoration orders pending applications or appeals under this Part, or other proceedings in which the right of seizure is questioned. In addition, it also stipulates that property may not be disposed of 30 days after being ordered forfeit.

COPIES OF DOCUMENTS RETURNED OR FORFEITED / Probative force.

462.46 (1) If any document is returned or ordered to be returned, forfeited or otherwise dealt with under subsection 462.34(3) or (4), 462.37(1) or (2.01), 462.38(2) or 462.41(3) or section 462.43, the Attorney General may, before returning the document or complying with the order, cause a copy of the document to be made and retained.

(2) Every copy made under subsection (1) shall, if certified as a true copy by the Attorney General, be admissible in evidence and, in the absence of evidence to the contrary, shall have the same probative force as the original document would have had if it had been proved in the ordinary way. R.S.C. 1985, c. 42 (4th Supp.), s. 2; 2005, c. 44, s. 11.

CROSS-REFERENCES

The term "Attorney General" is defined in s. 2.

This provision is quite similar to the power given under s. 490(13) and (14) to use photocopies of documents returned to their owner although those provisions require the Attorney General to certify that the copies are true before they may be admitted as if they were original documents.

This section is incorporated into the *Controlled Drugs and Substances Act* by s. 23 of that Act.

SYNOPSIS

This section permits the Attorney General to make and retain copies of documents returned or ordered to be returned, forfeited or otherwise dealt with under this Part. Such copies, if certified by the Attorney General, are admissible in evidence, and have the same probative force as the original, in the absence of evidence to the contrary.

Disclosure Provisions

NO CIVIL OR CRIMINAL LIABILITY INCURRED BY INFORMANTS.

462.47 For greater certainty but subject to section 241 of the *Income Tax Act*, a person is justified in disclosing to a peace officer or the Attorney General any facts on the basis of which that person reasonably suspects that any property is proceeds of crime or that any person has committed or is about to commit a designated offence. R.S.C. 1985, c. 42 (4th Supp.), s. 2; 1996, c. 19, s. 70; 2001, c. 32, s. 25.

CROSS-REFERENCES

The terms "property", "peace officer" and "person" are defined in s. 2. The terms "proceeds of crime" and "designated offence" are defined in s. 462.3. "Attorney General" is defined in ss. 2 and 462.3(3), (4). For protection of "whistle blowers", see s. 425.1.

SYNOPSIS

This section clarifies that, subject to s. 241 of the *Income Tax Act*, a person may disclose to a peace officer or the Attorney General information resulting in a reasonable suspicion that property is proceeds of crime, or that a person has committed or is about to commit an enterprise crime or designated drug offence.

DEFINITION OF "DESIGNATED SUBSTANCE OFFENCE" / Disclosure of income tax information / Application / Order for disclosure of information / Service of order / Extension of period for compliance with order / Objection to disclosure of information / Determination of objection / Judge may examine information / Limitation period / Appeal to Federal Court of Appeal / Limitation period for appeal / Special rules for hearings / *Ex parte* representations / Copies / Further disclosure / Form / Definitions of "police officer".

462.48 (1) In this section, "designated substance offence" means

(*a*) an offence under Part I of the *Controlled Drugs and Substances Act*, except subsection 4(1) of that Act;

(*a*.1) an offence under Division 1 of Part 1 of the *Cannabis Act*, except subsection 8(1) of that Act; or

(*b*) a conspiracy or an attempt to commit, being an accessory after the fact in relation to, or any counselling in relation to, an offence referred to in paragraph (*a*) or (*a*.1).

(1.1) The Attorney General may make an application in accordance with subsection (2) for an order for disclosure of information under subsection (3), for the purposes of an investigation in relation to

(*a*) a designated substance offence;

(*b*) an offence against section 354, 355.2, 355.4 or 462.31 if the offence is alleged to have been committed in relation to any property, thing or proceeds obtained or derived directly or indirectly as a result of

(i) the commission in Canada of a designated substance offence, or

(ii) an act or omission anywhere that, if it had occurred in Canada, would have constituted a designated substance offence;

(*c*) an offence against section 467.11, 467.111, 467.12 or 467.13 or a conspiracy or an attempt to commit, or being an accessory after the fact in relation to, such an offence; or

(*d*) a terrorism offence.

(2) An application under subsection (1.1) shall be made *ex parte* in writing to a judge and be accompanied by an affidavit sworn on the information and belief of the Attorney General or a person specially designated by the Attorney General for that purpose deposing to the following matters, namely,

(*a*) the offence or matter under investigation;

(*b*) the person in relation to whom the information or documents referred to in paragraph (*c*) are required;

(*c*) the type of information or book, record, writing, return or other document obtained by or on behalf of the Minister of National Revenue for the purposes of the *Income Tax Act*, Part IX of the *Excise Tax Act* or the *Excise Act, 2001* to which access is sought or that is proposed to be examined or communicated; and

(*d*) the facts relied on to justify the belief, on reasonable grounds, that the person referred to in paragraph (*b*) has committed or benefited from the commission of any of the offences referred to in subsection (1.1) and that the information or documents referred to in paragraph (*c*) are likely to be of substantial value, whether alone or together with other material, to the investigation for the purposes of which the application is made.

(3) Where the judge to whom an application under subsection (1.1) is made is satisfied

(*a*) of the matters referred to in paragraph (2)(*d*), and

(*b*) that there are reasonable grounds for believing that it is in the public interest to allow access to the information or documents to which the application relates, having regard to the benefit likely to accrue to the investigation if the access is obtained,

the judge may, subject to any conditions that the judge considers advisable in the public interest, order the Commissioner of Revenue or any person specially designated in writing by the Commissioner for the purposes of this section

(*c*) to allow a police officer named in the order access to all such information and documents and to examine them, or

(*d*) where the judge considers it necessary in the circumstances, to produce all such information and documents to the police officer and allow the police officer to remove the information and documents from the possession of that person,

within such period as the judge may specify after the expiration of seven clear days following the service of the order pursuant to subsection (4).

(4) A copy of an order made by a judge under subsection (3) shall be served on the person to whom the order is addressed in such manner as the judge directs or as may be prescribed by rules of court.

(5) A judge who makes an order under subsection (3) may, on application of the Minister of National Revenue, extend the period within which the order is to be complied with.

(6) The Minister of National Revenue or any person specially designated in writing by that Minister for the purposes of this section may object to the disclosure of any information or document in respect of which an order under subsection (3) has been made by certifying orally or in writing that the information or document should not be disclosed on the ground that

- **(*a*) the Minister of National Revenue is prohibited from disclosing the information or document by any bilateral or international treaty, convention or other agreement respecting taxation to which the Government of Canada is a signatory;**
- **(*b*) a privilege is attached by law to the information or document;**
- **(*c*) the information or document has been placed in a sealed package pursuant to law or an order of a court of competent jurisdiction; or**
- **(*d*) disclosure of the information or document would not, for any other reason, be in the public interest.**

(7) Where an objection to the disclosure of information or a document is made under subsection (6), the objection may be determined, on application, in accordance with subsection (8), by the Chief Justice of the Federal Court, or by such other judge of that court as the Chief Justice may designate to hear such applications.

(8) A judge who is to determine an objection pursuant to subsection (7) may, if the judge considers it necessary to determine the objection, examine the information or document in relation to which the objection is made and shall grant the objection and order that disclosure of the information or document be refused where the judge is satisfied of any of the grounds mentioned in subsection (6).

(9) An application under subsection (7) shall be made within ten days after the objection is made or within such greater or lesser period as the Chief Justice of the Federal Court, or such other judge of that court as the Chief Justice may designate to hear such applications, considers appropriate.

(10) An appeal lies from a determination under subsection (7) to the Federal Court of Appeal.

(11) An appeal under subsection (10) shall be brought within ten days from the date of the determination appealed from or within such further time as the Federal Court of Appeal considers appropriate in the circumstances.

(12) An application under subsection (7) or an appeal brought in respect of that application shall

- **(*a*) be heard in camera; and**
- **(*b*) on the request of the person objecting to the disclosure of information, be heard and determined in the National Capital Region described in the schedule to the *National Capital Act*.**

(13) During the hearing of an application under subsection (7) or an appeal brought in respect of that application, the person who made the objection in respect of which the application was made or the appeal was brought shall, on the request of that person, be given the opportunity to make representations *ex parte*.

(14) When any information or document is examined or provided under subsection (3), the person by whom it is examined or to whom it is provided or any officer of the Canada Revenue Agency may make, or cause to be made, one or more copies of it, and

any copy purporting to be certified by the Minister of National Revenue or an authorized person to be a copy made under this subsection is evidence of the nature and content of the original information or document and has the same probative force as the original information or document would have had if it had been proved in the ordinary way.

(15) No person to whom information or documents have been disclosed or provided pursuant to this subsection or pursuant to an order made under subsection (3) shall further disclose the information or documents except for the purposes of the investigation in relation to which the order was made.

(16) An order made under subsection (3) may be in Form 47.

(17) In this section, "police officer" means any officer, constable or other person employed for the preservation and maintenance of the public peace. R.S.C. 1985, c. 42 (4th Supp.), s. 2; 1994, c. 13, s. 7; 1996, c. 19, s. 70; 1997, c. 23, s. 10; 1999, c. 17, s. 120; 2001, c. 32, s. 26; 2001, c. 41, s. 133(11); 2005, c. 38, ss. 138(*e*), 140(*b*); 2010, c. 14, s. 9; 2013, c. 9, s. 15; 2014, c. 17, s. 7; 2018, c. 16, s. 215; 2018, c. 27, s. 28.

CROSS-REFERENCES

The term "property" is defined in s. 2. The term "judge" is defined in s. 462.3. "Attorney General" is defined in ss. 2 and 462.3(3), (4). Section 46 of the *Federal Courts Act* gives that court the power to make rules of court. The meaning of "clear days" (see s. 462.3) is to be determined by referring to s. 27(1) of the *Interpretation Act*.

This section is incorporated into the *Controlled Drugs and Substances Act* by s. 23 of that Act.

SYNOPSIS

This section authorizes *ex parte* applications in writing by an Attorney General to a judge for an order that the Commissioner of Customs and Revenue, or designate, allow access to a peace officer, or produce information and documents.

The Attorney General must depose by affidavit sworn on his information and belief, or that of his designate, that the information is sought for the purpose of an investigation in relation to a designated substance offence (or certain related offences) or an offence under ss. 467.11 to 467.13 (and related offences). The Attorney General must also identify the person in relation to whom the information or documents are required, as well as the type of information sought, and set out the facts relied upon to justify the *belief on reasonable grounds* that the person has committed or benefited from the offence. Finally, the Attorney General must state that the information or documents are likely to be of substantial value.

In determining whether to grant the order the judge shall consider the facts attested to in the affidavit, the public interest and the likely benefit to the investigation.

Where an order is issued, it may be subject to such terms as the judge considers advisable in the public interest. The order shall also set out the period of its validity (commencing seven days after service), and shall provide for service in some manner on the person to whom it is addressed.

The section further provides for objection by the Minister of National Revenue or his/her designate to the disclosure of information and for extension of time to comply, and for certain appeals.

Where information or documents are examined or provided, they may be copied. Copies certified by the Minister of National Revenue may be used in evidence. No person to whom information or documents have been disclosed or provided can make further disclosure except for the purpose of the particular investigation.

Specific Rules of Forfeiture

SPECIFIC FORFEITURE PROVISIONS UNAFFECTED BY THIS PART / Priority for restitution to victims of crime.

462.49 (1) This Part does not affect the operation of any other provision of this or any other Act of Parliament respecting the forfeiture of property.

(2) The property of an offender may be used to satisfy the operation of a provision of this or any other Act of Parliament respecting the forfeiture of property only to the extent that is is not required to satisfy the operation of any other provision of this or any other Act of Parliament respecting the restitution or compensation of persons affected by the commission of offences. R.S.C. 1985, c. 42 (4th Supp.), s. 2.

CROSS-REFERENCES

The term "property" is defined in s. 2. Provisions regarding restitution of property are to be found in s. 491.1 and those regarding compensation to victims of crime are in ss. 737.1 to 741.2.

This section is incorporated into the *Controlled Drugs and Substances Act* by s. 23 of that Act.

SYNOPSIS

This section clarifies that this Part does not affect the operation of other forfeiture provisions in the Code or in any other Act of Parliament. It also provides that the property of an offender may be used to satisfy such other forfeiture provisions only to the extent not required to satisfy orders for restitution or compensation of victims of crime made pursuant to federal enactment.

Regulations

REGULATIONS.

462.5 The Attorney General may make regulations governing the manner of disposing of or otherwise dealing with, in accordance with the law, property forfeited under this Part. R.S.C. 1985, c. 42 (4th Supp.), s. 2.

CROSS-REFERENCES

The term "property" is defined in s. 2. "Attorney General" is defined in ss. 2 and 462.3(3), (4).

This section is incorporated into the *Controlled Drugs and Substances Act*.

SYNOPSIS

This section provides for the making of regulations governing the disposition of forfeited property.

Part XIII / ATTEMPTS – CONSPIRACIES – ACCESSORIES

ATTEMPTS, ACCESSORIES.

463. Except where otherwise expressly provided by law, the following provisions apply in respect of persons who attempt to commit or are accessories after the fact to the commission of offences:

(*a*) every one who attempts to commit or is an accessory after the fact to the commission of an indictable offence for which, on conviction, an accused is liable to be sentenced to imprisonment for life is guilty of an indictable offence and liable to imprisonment for a term not exceeding fourteen years;

(*b*) every one who attempts to commit or is an accessory after the fact to the commission of an indictable offence for which, on conviction, an accused is liable to imprisonment for fourteen years or less is guilty of an indictable offence and liable to imprisonment for a term that is one-half of the longest term to which a person who is guilty of that offence is liable;

(*c*) every one who attempts to commit or is an accessory after the fact to the commission of an offence punishable on summary conviction is guilty of an offence punishable on summary conviction; and

(*d*) every one who attempts to commit or is an accessory after the fact to the commission of an offence for which the offender may be prosecuted by indictment or for which he is punishable on summary conviction

(i) is guilty of an indictable offence and liable to imprisonment for a term not exceeding a term that is one-half of the longest term to which a person who is guilty of that offence is liable, or

(ii) is guilty of an offence punishable on summary conviction. R.S., c. C-34, s. 421; R.S.C. 1985, c. 27 (1st Supp.), s. 59; 1998, c. 35, s. 120.

CROSS-REFERENCES

Attempt is defined in s. 24. Accessory after the fact is defined in s. 23. Also see s. 23.1.

The offence of attempted murder is punishable under s. 239, of accessory after the fact to murder under s. 240. As to mode of trial for these offences, see the cross-references under those sections. Note that where the substantive offence, for example theft of goods of a value not exceeding $1,000, is within the absolute jurisdiction of a provincial court judge by virtue of s. 553, then an attempt to commit or being an accessory after the fact to the commission of the offence is, by virtue of s. 553(*b*), also within the absolute jurisdiction of the provincial court judge. For notes concerning the operation of that section as it applies to the particular offence, see the cross-references under the section creating the substantive offence.

Similarly, for other offences, the rights of election and mode of trial generally follow the substantive offence and therefore see notes under the section creating the substantive offence. Note however that attempted murder, unlike murder, is not within the exclusive jurisdiction of the superior court under s. 469.

See s. 7 enacting territorial jurisdictional rules respecting offences committed on aircraft, offences in relation to nuclear material, attempt to commit or being an accessory after the fact to the offence in s. 269.1 (torture), war crimes and crimes against humanity.

Under s. 586, no count that alleges an attempt by fraudulent means is insufficient by reason only that it does not set out in detail the nature of the fraudulent means. Section 587(1) however gives the court power to order that further particulars be provided of the alleged attempt by fraudulent means.

SYNOPSIS

This section sets out a general scheme of punishment for attempting to commit, or being an accessory after the fact, to the commission of all offences which are not otherwise expressly dealt with by law.

Paragraph (*a*) provides that a person who attempts to commit or is an accessory after the fact to the commission of an indictable offence which carries a maximum punishment of life imprisonment, is guilty of an indictable offence and liable to a term of imprisonment not exceeding 14 years.

Paragraph (*b*) provides that a person who attempts to commit, or is an accessory after the fact to the commission of an indictable offence which carries a maximum term of 14 years' imprisonment or less, is guilty of an indictable offence and liable to imprisonment for a term not exceeding one-half the maximum punishment set out for the actual commission of that offence.

Paragraph (*c*) provides that any person who attempts to commit, or is an accessory after the fact to the commission of a summary conviction offence is also guilty of a summary conviction offence.

Paragraph (*d*) states that any person who attempts to commit, or is an accessory after the fact to the commission of a hybrid offence is guilty of an indictable offence and liable to a term of imprisonment that is half the maximum provided for the actual commission of the offence, or is guilty of a summary conviction offence.

COUNSELLING OFFENCE THAT IS NOT COMMITTED.

464. Except where otherwise expressly provided by law, the following provisions apply in respect of persons who counsel other persons to commit offences, namely,

(*a*) every one who counsels another person to commit an indictable offence is, if the offence is not committed, guilty of an indictable offence and liable to the same punishment to which a person who attempts to commit that offence is liable; and

(*b*) every one who counsels another person to commit an offence punishable on summary conviction is, if the offence is not committed, guilty of an offence punishable on summary conviction. R.S., c. C-34, s. 422; R.S.C. 1985, c. 27 (1st Supp.), s. 60.

CROSS-REFERENCES

"Counsel" is defined in s. 22(3). The liability of a person who counsels commission of an offence and an offence is committed is defined in s. 22(1) and (2). Punishment for attempt to commit an offence is set out in s. 463 with the exception of attempted murder (s. 239) and thus see cross-references under s. 463. Note that where the substantive offence, for example theft of goods of a value not exceeding $1000, is within the absolute jurisdiction of a provincial court judge by virtue of s. 553, then counselling the offence is by virtue of s. 553(*b*) also within the absolute jurisdiction of the provincial court judge. Presumably, that provision would also apply to counselling an offence listed in s. 553 which is not committed. For counselling all other indictable offences which are not committed, the accused would have an election as to mode of trial under s. 536(2). For the offence in para. (*b*), the trial of the offence is conducted by a summary conviction court pursuant to Part XXVII. The limitation period is set out in s. 786(2).

See s. 7 enacting special territorial jurisdictional rules respecting offences committed on aircraft, offences in relation to nuclear material, counselling the offence in s. 269.1 (torture), war crimes and crimes against humanity.

SYNOPSIS

This section makes it an offence to counsel another person to commit an offence, where that offence is not committed.

Paragraph (*a*) states that every one who counsels another person to commit an indictable offence, provided that the offence is not committed, is him/herself guilty of an indictable offence and liable to the same punishment as would be imposed for an attempt to commit that offence.

Paragraph (*b*) likewise makes it a summary conviction offence to counsel another person to commit an offence punishable on summary conviction, given that the offence is not committed.

ANNOTATIONS

The accused was properly convicted of procuring the death of his wife where he accepted the offer of an undercover police officer posing as a contract killer and agreed to pay the officer for the killing. Further, although the officer had no intention of carrying out the plan and the accused's acts had no influence on the officer's conduct or state of mind, the accused was properly convicted of the full offence under this section rather than merely an attempt: *R. v.*

Glubisz (1979), 47 C.C.C. (2d) 232, 9 C.R. (3d) 300 (B.C.C.A.). Similarly, *R. v. Walia (No. 1)* (1975), 9 C.R. (3d) 293 (B.C.C.A.).

A person may be convicted of this offence although the person counselled would only be a party to the offence if it were committed: *R. v. Meikle* (1983), 9 C.C.C. (3d) 91 (Ont. H.C.J.).

"Procure" means to instigate, persuade or solicit. The offence is complete when the solicitation or incitement occurs even though it is immediately rejected by the person solicited and it is no defence to the charge that the accused subsequently renounces the criminal purpose: *R. v. Gonzague* (1983), 4 C.C.C. (3d) 505, 34 C.R. (3d) 169 (Ont. C.A.).

In *R. v. Hamilton*, [2005] 2 S.C.R. 432, 198 C.C.C. (3d) 1, the court considered the application of this section in the context of e-mails advertising software that would enable purchasers to generate credit card numbers that could be used to illegally obtain funds. The *actus reus* for counselling requires proof that the materials or statements made or transmitted actively induce or advocate, and do not merely describe, the commission of an offence. The *mens rea* requires proof, either of an intention that the offence counselled be committed, or knowingly counselling the commission of the offence while aware of the unjustified risk that the offence counselled was in fact likely to be committed as a result of the accused's conduct. The fact that the accused's motive was mercenary did not negative the *mens rea*.

Where the accused was charged with counseling murder for distributing a poster appearing to invite the killing of a local politician, the Crown had to prove that a reasonable person viewing the poster objectively would take it as an invitation to kill, and that the accused knowingly counseled the murder while aware of the unjustified risk that murder was likely to be committed: *R. v. Jeffers* (2012), 280 C.C.C. (3d) 54 (Ont. C.A.).

CONSPIRACY / Conspiracy to commit offences / Idem / Jurisdiction / Appearance of accused at trial / If previously tried outside Canada.

465. (1) Except where otherwise expressly provided by law, the following provisions apply in respect of conspiracy:

(*a*) every one who conspires with any one to commit murder or to cause another person to be murdered, whether in Canada or not, is guilty of an indictable offence and liable to a maximum term of imprisonment for life;

(*b*) every one who conspires with any one to prosecute a person for an alleged offence, knowing that he did not commit that offence, is guilty of an indictable offence and liable

(i) to imprisonment for a term not exceeding ten years, if the alleged offence is one for which, on conviction, that person would be liable to be sentenced to imprisonment for life or for a term not exceeding fourteen years, or

(ii) to imprisonment for a term not exceeding five years, if the alleged offence is one for which, on conviction, that person would be liable to imprisonment for less than fourteen years; and

(*c*) every one who conspires with any one to commit an indictable offence not provided for in paragraph (*a*) or (*b*) is guilty of an indictable offence and liable to the same punishment as that to which an accused who is guilty of that offence would, on conviction, be liable; and

(*d*) every one who conspires with any one to commit an offence punishable on summary conviction is guilty of an offence punishable on summary conviction.

(2) [*Repealed*, R.S.C. 1985, c. 27 (1st Supp.), s. 61(3).]

(3) Every one who, while in Canada, conspires with any one to do anything referred to in subsection (1) in a place outside Canada that is an offence under the laws of that place shall be deemed to have conspired to do that thing in Canada.

(4) Every one who, while in a place outside Canada, conspires with any one to do anything referred to in subsection (1) in Canada shall be deemed to have conspired in Canada to do that thing.

(5) Where a person is alleged to have conspired to do anything that is an offence by virtue of subsection (3) or (4), proceedings in respect of that offence may, whether or not that person is in Canada, be commenced in any territorial division in Canada, and the accused may be tried and punished in respect of that offence in the same manner as if the offence had been committed in that territorial division.

(6) For greater certainty, the provisions of this Act relating to

(*a*) requirements that an accused appear at and be present during proceedings, and

(*b*) the exceptions to those requirements,

apply to proceedings commenced in any territorial division pursuant to subsection (5).

(7) If a person is alleged to have conspired to do anything that is an offence by virtue of subsection (3) or (4) and that person has been tried and dealt with outside Canada in respect of the offence in such a manner that, if the person had been tried and dealt with in Canada, they would be able to plead *autrefois acquit, autrefois convict*, pardon or an expungement order under the *Expungement of Historically Unjust Convictions Act*, the person shall be deemed to have been so tried and dealt with in Canada. R.S., c. C-34, s. 423; 1974-75-76, c. 93, s. 36; 1980-81-82-83, c. 125, s. 23; R.S.C. 1985, c. 27 (1st Supp.), s. 61; 1998, c. 35, s. 121; 2018, c. 11, s. 28.

CROSS-REFERENCES

Trial of the offence of conspiracy to commit the offences listed in s. 469(*a*), namely: s. 47, treason; s. 49, alarming Her Majesty; s. 51, intimidating Parliament or a legislature; s. 53, inciting to mutiny; s. 61, seditious offences; s. 74, piracy; s. 75, piratical acts; s. 235, murder, is by the superior court of criminal jurisdiction (defined in s. 2) by virtue of ss. 468 and 469. By virtue of s. 522, only a judge of the superior court of criminal jurisdiction may release an accused charged with any of those offences. For the offence described in subsec. (1)(*b*), the accused has his election as to mode of trial pursuant to s. 536(2) and release is determined by s. 515, although the accused is eligible for release by the officer in charge pursuant to s. 498 for the offence described in para. (*b*)(ii). For conspiracy to commit all other indictable offences, including the indictable offences within the absolute jurisdiction of a provincial court judge under s. 553, the accused has his election as to mode of trial under s. 536(2). Release pending trial is determined by s. 515, although the accused is eligible for release by the officer in charge pursuant to s. 498 where the substantive offence is punishable by five years imprisonment or less.

For conspiracy to commit a summary conviction offence (para. (*d*)) then the proceedings are conducted by a summary conviction court pursuant to Part XXVII. The punishment is then as set out in s. 787 [although see s. 719(*b*) where the accused is a corporation] and the limitation period is set out in s. 786(2). Release pending trial is determined under s. 515, although the accused is eligible for release by a peace officer under s. 496, 497 or by the officer in charge under s. 498.

In addition to the special jurisdictional rules in subsecs. (3) to (6), see s. 7 respecting offences committed on aircraft, offences in relation to nuclear material, conspiracy to commit the offence in s. 269.1 (torture), war crimes and crimes against humanity.

The procedure respecting the pleas of *autrefois* is found in ss. 607 to 610.

Under s. 586, no count that alleges a conspiracy by fraudulent means is insufficient by reason only that it does not set out in detail the nature of the fraudulent means. Section 587(1), however, gives the court power to order that further particulars be provided of the alleged conspiracy by fraudulent means.

See s. 467, a saving provision in respect of refusing to work and trade combinations.

As to offences relating to the activities of "criminal organizations" see ss. 467.1 and 467.2.

SYNOPSIS

This section sets out various offences of conspiracy and provides for punishment upon conviction for each of these offences.

Subsection (1) states that the provisions contained therein apply except where otherwise expressly provided by law.

Subsection (1)(*a*) provides that any person who conspires with another person to commit murder anywhere is guilty of an indictable offence and liable to a maximum term of life imprisonment.

Subsection (1)(*b*) sets out the punishments applied to a person who is guilty of conspiring to prosecute another person for an alleged offence, *knowing* that that person did not commit the offence.

Subsection (1)(*c*) and (*d*) described the offences of conspiracy to commit either an indictable or a summary conviction offence and the punishment upon conviction for these offences.

Subsection (3) states that any person who, while in Canada, conspires to do anything described in subsec. (1) in a place outside Canada that is against the law in that place is deemed to have committed the conspiracy in Canada.

Subsection (4) provides that a person who conspires to do anything referred to in subsec. (1) in Canada while outside Canada is deemed to have committed the offence of conspiracy in Canada.

Subsection (5) states that proceedings against any person under subsecs. (3) or (4) may be commenced anywhere in Canada and that the accused may be tried and punished in the same manner as if the offence had been committed in that location.

Subsection (6) clarifies that, subject to certain exceptions the accused must appear and be present during proceedings commenced under subsec. (5).

Subsection (7) states that if a person has been tried and dealt with outside Canada in relation to offences under subsecs. (3) and (4), in such a manner that would, in Canada, give rise to the pleas of *autrefois acquit, autrefois convict*, or pardon, the person shall be deemed to have been so tried and dealt with in Canada.

ANNOTATIONS

Meaning of conspiracy – The essential elements of a conspiracy are an agreement by two or more persons to commit a criminal offence, or to achieve a lawful object by commission of a criminal offence; an intention by two or more persons to agree, and an intention to put this common design into effect. It is not necessary that there be proof of any overt act in furtherance of the conspiracy, to complete the crime. Where there are alleged to be only two conspirators and one of them had no intention of carrying out the common design, then there is no proof of a conspiracy: *R. v. O'Brien*, [1954] S.C.R. 666, 110 C.C.C. 1 (3:2).

Impossibility is not a defence to a charge of conspiracy, except that conspiracy to commit an imaginary crime cannot give rise to criminal liability: *United States of America v. Dynar*, [1997] 2 S.C.R. 462, 115 C.C.C. (3d) 481, 8 C.R. (5th) 79.

On the trial of a charge contrary to subsec. (1)(*c*) of conspiracy to commit a specified indictable offence the Crown must establish an intention by the accused to enter into an agreement to commit that offence. Mere recklessness with respect to the subject of the agreement is not sufficient where the evidence indicates that a number of courses of actions were being considered only some of which were illegal: *R. v. Lessard* (1982), 10 C.C.C. (3d) 61 (Que. C.A.).

Aiding and abetting pursuant to a common intent and design in the commission of a substantive offence is not necessarily the same thing as conspiring to commit the same offence, and accordingly an acquittal of the conspiracy is not inconsistent with a conviction on the substantive count: *R. v. Koury*, [1964] S.C.R. 212, [1964] 2 C.C.C. 97 (6:3).

It was held in *R. v. Cotroni; R. v. Papalia*, [1979] 2 S.C.R. 256, 45 C.C.C. (2d) 1 (7:0), that to have a conspiracy it was essential that there be an agreement between the co-conspirators, and that there must be a common purpose of a single enterprise. In this case although there was in the most general terms an adventure with a common object, namely to possess certain extorted funds, there was no general agreement, rather, two competing and mutually exclusive objects: the agreement of one group of conspirators being to relieve the others of the extorted funds. There were therefore two separate conspiracies revealed by the evidence and since only one took place in Ontario, the venue of the trial, it was to be assumed that it was this conspiracy which was embraced by the indictment.

The *actus reus* is proven where there is a formation of an agreement, tacit or express, between two or more individuals, to act together in pursuit of a mutual criminal objective. There must be a common goal borne out of a meeting of the minds whereby each agrees to act together with the other to achieve a common goal. A conspiracy is not established merely by proof of knowledge of the existence of a scheme to commit a crime or by the doing of acts in furtherance of that scheme. Neither knowledge nor participation in a criminal scheme can be equated with the *actus reus* necessary to prove conspiracy. Absent a true consensus to achieve a mutual criminal objective, conspiracy does not criminalize joint conduct that falls short of an attempt to commit the substantive crime: *R. v. Alexander* (2005), 206 C.C.C. (3d) 233 (Ont. C.A.), leave to appeal to S.C.C. refused 352 N.R. 197*n*. See also *R. v. Cebulak* (1988), 46 C.C.C. (3d) 437 (Ont. H.C.J.).

Where one member of an alleged two-person conspiracy is only pretending to agree, there is no conspiracy and both accused must be acquitted: *R. v. Nicholson* (2018), 365 C.C.C. (3d) 268 (Sask. C.A.).

Liability as a party to a conspiracy is limited to cases where the accused aids or abets the initial formation of the agreement, or aids or abets a new member to join a pre-existing agreement. Aiding or abetting the furtherance of the unlawful object does not establish aiding or abetting the principal with any element of the offence of conspiracy, and thus cannot ground party liability for conspiracy. However, where a person, with knowledge of a conspiracy, does or omits to do something for the purpose of furthering the unlawful object, with the knowledge and consent of one or more of the existing conspirators, this provides powerful circumstantial evidence from which membership in the conspiracy can be inferred: *R. v. F. (J.)*, [2013] 1 S.C.R. 565, 293 C.C.C. (3d) 377. See also: *R. v. Trieu* (2008), 429 A.R. 200 (C.A.). The broader approach to party liability proposed in *R. v. McNamara (No. 1)* (1981), 56 C.C.C. (2d) 193 (Ont. C.A.), affd [1985] 1 S.C.R. 662, *sub nom. Canadian Dredge & Dock Co. v. R.*, 19 C.C.C. (3d) 1, must now be read in light of *R. v. F. (J.), supra*.

Where the accused is alleged to have joined a pre-existing conspiracy, it is insufficient to merely prove that the accused had knowledge of an unlawful plan. It must be established that the accused adopted the plan as his own and consented to participate in achieving it. Mere recklessness as to the object of the agreement cannot establish conspiracy: *R. v. Lamontagne* (1999), 142 C.C.C. (3d) 561 (Que. C.A.).

Conspiracy between spouses – A husband and wife cannot be found guilty of conspiring together: *R. v. Kowbel*, [1954] S.C.R. 498, 110 C.C.C. 47 (4:1).

Effect of acquittal of co-conspirator or where co-conspirator cannot be convicted – Where two alleged co-conspirators are tried separately the acquittal of one does not necessarily invalidate the conviction of the other. Moreover, where the evidence against one of two conspirators is substantially stronger the better course is to direct separate trials, particularly when a damaging statement admissible only against the one is to be tendered by the Crown. Of course when substantially the same evidence is admissible against jointly-tried conspirators as a matter of logic (although not any imperative rule of law) both should be either convicted or acquitted: *R. v. Guimond*, [1979] 1 S.C.R. 960, 44 C.C.C. (2d) 481 (7:2).

Moreover, even where one of the two parties to the agreement cannot, as a matter of law, be convicted of the conspiracy, such as the prostitute on a charge of conspiracy to live on the avails of her prostitution, the other person may be convicted of conspiracy: *R. v. Murphy and Bieneck* (1981), 60 C.C.C. (2d) 1 (Alta. C.A.).

Proof of conspiracy alleged – Although the gravamen of the offence of conspiracy to import narcotics is the agreement to import narcotics rather than a particular narcotic, where the Crown has chosen to particularize the narcotic, in this case heroin, the Crown was required to prove that offence and not some other conspiracy. To allow the Crown to prove some other offence characterized by different particulars would be to undermine the purpose of providing particulars: that purpose is to permit the accused to be reasonably informed of the transaction alleged against him, thus giving him the possibility of a full defence and a fair trial. In this case, it was not appropriate to amend the indictment on appeal to remove reference to the term "heroin". No such amendment was sought at trial and the trial had proceeded originally on the basis that the Crown must prove a conspiracy relating to heroin and, on this basis, one of the accused took the stand and testified that he was only involved in a conspiracy relating to cocaine. It would be unfair and prejudicial to the accused after that course of events to permit an amendment fundamentally and retroactively changing the nature of what the Crown must prove: *R. v. Saunders*, [1990] 1 S.C.R. 1020, 56 C.C.C. (3d) 220.

Conspiracy having more than one object – A single conspiracy may have more than one illegal object, and it is proper to allege in one count a conspiracy to commit several crimes. If the Crown proves a conspiracy to do any of the prohibited acts alleged in the indictment as the objects of the conspiracy then that is sufficient to support a conviction. In fact, where there is but one agreement and not separate agreements as to the different unlawful objects there can be only one conviction. On the other hand, where the prosecution proves only that some of those accused had conspired with one of their number for their own purposes no common purpose such as that alleged has been established. However, where the evidence establishes the conspiracy alleged against two or more accused or against one accused and an unknown person, where the indictment alleges that the accused conspired together with persons unknown, it is immaterial that the evidence also discloses another wider conspiracy to which the accused or some of them were also parties: *R. v. Paterson, Ackworth and Kovach* (1985), 18 C.C.C. (3d) 137 (Ont. C.A.), affd [1987] 2 S.C.R. 291, 39 C.C.C. (3d) 575 (7:0).

Indictments charging conspiracy may raise problems as to whether a conspiracy count has charged the accused with two or more conspiracies, which raises an issue of duplicity. In the alternative, the count may charge only one conspiracy but the proof at trial may demonstrate that there was more than one conspiracy. In the latter case, the issue is whether the Crown has proved the conspiracy charged despite the evidence of a second conspiracy. In determining this issue, the court will have regard to the wording of the indictment and may also look to the opening of the Crown. In order to find that a specific conspiracy lies within the scope of the indictment, it is sufficient if the evidence adduced demonstrates that the conspiracy proven included some of the accused; established that it occurred at some time within the time frame alleged in the indictment; and had as its object the type of crime alleged: *R. v. Douglas*, [1991] 1 S.C.R. 301, 63 C.C.C. (3d) 29 (5:0).

Multiple convictions ["Kienapple rule"] – The doctrine in *R. v. Kienapple*, [1975] 1 S.C.R. 729, 15 C.C.C. (2d) 524, 26 C.R.N.S. 1, which precludes multiple convictions for the same delict does not prevent a conviction for conspiracy and for a substantive offence which also formed some of the evidence relied upon by the Crown in proof of the conspiracy: *R. v. Sheppe*, [1980] 2 S.C.R. 22, 51 C.C.C. (2d) 481 (7:0).

Conspiracy and attempt – Attempting to conspire to commit a substantive offence is not a crime in Canadian law: *R. v. Déry*, [2006] 2 S.C.R. 669, 213 C.C.C. (3d) 289.

Conspiracy to commit the offence contrary to s. 139(2) of attempting to obstruct justice is an offence known to law: *R. v. May* (1984), 13 C.C.C. (3d) 257 (Ont. C.A.), leave to appeal to S.C.C. refused [1984] 2 S.C.R. vii.

Effect of withdrawal from conspiracy – It is no defence that an accused having agreed to carry out the unlawful act with the intention to carry out the common design later withdraws from the conspiracy, since the offence is already complete: *R. v. O'Brien, supra.*

Co-conspirator's exception to hearsay rule – The case of *R. v. Baron and Wertman* (1976), 31 C.C.C. (2d) 525 (Ont. C.A.), contains a detailed review of the law of evidence which permits evidence of the acts and declarations of one conspirator done in furtherance of the conspiracy to be admitted against other co-conspirators. Martin J.A., for the court, suggests that the following procedure be followed:

1. At the end of the whole case the trial judge must decide as a matter of law, whether there is any admissible evidence against an accused from his own acts and declarations, that he is a participant in the conspiracy charged.
2. If there is no evidence directly admissible against an accused connecting him with the conspiracy the trial judge must direct the jury to acquit that accused.
3. If the trial judge concludes that there is some evidence admissible directly against an accused that he was a party to the conspiracy, he will instruct the jury that they must first find from evidence admissible directly against an accused (that is by evidence other than the acts and declarations of alleged co-conspirators) that he was a party to the conspiracy charged. The trial judge will then instruct the jury that if they find from such evidence that the accused was a party to the conspiracy the acts and declarations of alleged co-conspirators in furtherance of the conspiracy may be used as evidence against him . . .
4. As a general rule, it would be desirable for the trial judge to *then* refer the jury to the principal evidence admissible *directly* against each accused from which they may find that such accused was a party to the conspiracy but the jury should be instructed that it is for them to say if the evidence has this effect.
5. Finally, he must instruct the jury that on the whole of the evidence they must be satisfied beyond a reasonable doubt that the accused was a member of the conspiracy.

In *R. v. Filiault and Kane* (1981), 63 C.C.C. (2d) 321 (Ont. C.A.), affd [1984] 1 S.C.R. 389, 15 C.C.C. (3d) 352*n* (7:0), it was held that in determining whether the condition in rule (1), *supra,* was met the trial judge is entitled to view the accused's own acts and declarations against the picture provided by the acts of the alleged co-conspirators. The judge is not required to view the accused's acts and declarations in isolation, divorced from the context in which they occurred.

Hearsay evidence is inadmissible on the initial determination whether the alleged conspiracy or alleged common design existed: *R. v. Jamieson* (1989), 48 C.C.C. (3d) 287, 90 N.S.R. (2d) 164 (C.A.).

In *R. v. Sutton* (1999), 140 C.C.C. (3d) 336, 222 N.B.R. (2d) 78 (C.A.), affd [2000] 2 S.C.R. 595, 148 C.C.C. (3d) 513, 38 C.R. (5th) 39, the court held that all hearsay evidence that meets the necessity and reliability criteria may be considered at the first step of determining whether the existence of a conspiracy has been proven.

The co-conspirators exception to the hearsay rule as applied in *R. v. Carter*, *infra*, meets the requirements of necessity and reliability and remains a valid exception to the hearsay rule. Such evidence is therefore admissible in all but the most exceptional cases: *R. v. Mapara*, [2005] 1 S.C.R. 358, 195 C.C.C. (3d) 225, 28 C.R. (6th) 1.

In charging the jury on the applicability of the co-conspirator's exception to the hearsay rule the trial judge should instruct them to consider whether on all the evidence they are satisfied beyond a reasonable doubt that the conspiracy charged in the indictment existed. If they conclude that a conspiracy as alleged did exist, they must then review the evidence and decide whether, on the basis of the evidence directly received against the accused, a probability is raised that he was a member of the conspiracy. If this conclusion is reached, they then become entitled to apply the hearsay exception and consider evidence of the acts and declarations performed and made by the co-conspirators in furtherance of the objects of the conspiracy as evidence against the accused on the issue of his guilt. They should be told, however, that the ultimate determination of guilt is for them alone and that the mere fact that they have found sufficient evidence directly admissible against the accused to enable them to consider his participation in the conspiracy probable, and to apply the hearsay exception, does not make a conviction automatic: *R. v. Carter*, [1982] 1 S.C.R. 938, 67 C.C.C. (2d) 568, 31 C.R. (3d) 97 (5:0).

On the difficult issue of applying the co-conspirator's exception to a two-person conspiracy, see *R. v. Bogiatzis* (2010), 285 C.C.C. (3d) 437 (Ont. C.A.).

In *R. v. Puddicombe* (2013), 299 C.C.C. (3d) 534 (Ont. C.A.), leave to appeal to S.C.C. refused 2014 CarswellOnt 2577, a five-judge panel re-affirmed the position in *Bogiatzis, supra*, that the *Carter* approach applies to a two-person conspiracy.

Conspiracy to commit offence outside Canada (subsec. (3)) – In *R. v. Gunn*, [1982] 1 S.C.R. 522, 66 C.C.C. (2d) 294, 27 C.R. (3d) 120, the Supreme Court of Canada, having allowed the accused's appeal from the decision of the Manitoba Court of Appeal (1980), 54 C.C.C. (2d) 163, 4 Man. R. (2d) 269 *sub nom. R. v. Apaya and Gunn* on other grounds, did not find it necessary to give any direction in detail as to how the charge of conspiracy involving breach of foreign criminal law as envisaged by this subsection should be framed. However, it was held that the statutory fiction of a conspiracy in Canada in violation of foreign law can only become operative if a breach of the foreign law is charged.

And in *R. v. Baldini and Gullekson* (1984), 39 C.R. (3d) 43, 31 Alta. L.R. (2d) 69 (C.A.), the court considered that the charge should also make specific reference to subsec. (3).

Although the accused had agreed to supply narcotics to an undercover police officer in the United States, there was a substantial link between the offence alleged and Canada. Thus, *inter alia*, the accused were in Canada for the negotiations with the officer and when the agreement was finally made. Accordingly, there was no need for the Crown to charge the accused under subsec. (3), but could rely on the general conspiracy provisions in subsec. (1)(*c*): *R. v. Douglas* (1989), 51 C.C.C. (3d) 129, 72 C.R. (3d) 309 (Ont. C.A.).

The accused could properly be convicted of conspiracy to traffic in narcotics without reference to subsec. (3) where the evidence showed that they agreed in Canada to sell or offered to sell narcotics to a third person, even if the deal was to be completed in the United States. Under the *Narcotic Control Act*, a simple offer to sell can constitute trafficking and the absence of delivery of the drug or receipt of the proceeds in Canada is not relevant: *R. v. Rowbotham; R. v. Roblin* (1992), 76 C.C.C. (3d) 542, 60 O.A.C. 75 (C.A.), affd [1993] 4 S.C.R. 834, 85 C.C.C. (3d) 575*n*, 69 O.A.C. 267, supplementary reasons [1994] 2 S.C.R. 463, 90 C.C.C. (3d) 449, 30 C.R. (4th) 141.

Conspiracy outside Canada to commit offence in Canada (subsec. (4)) – Where the indictment alleges that the conspiracy actually took place in Canada it is not open to the Crown to rely on the provisions of subsec. (4) to prove all the components of the charge. If the agreement took place wholly outside Canada the indictment must so allege: *R. v. Dass* (1979), 47 C.C.C. (2d) 194, 8 C.R. (3d) 224 (Man. C.A.), leave to appeal to S.C.C. refused 30 N.R. 609*n*, 4 Man. R. (2d) 86*n*.

Territorial jurisdiction (subsec. (5)) – An offence is "an offence by virtue of subsection . . . (4)" although it could also be tried in Canada, albeit in another province, at common law. Subsection (4) is not restricted to cases which would not have been offences against Canadian law before the passage of that provision: *R. v. Lai and Lau* (1985), 24 C.C.C. (3d) 237 (B.C.C.A.).

CONSPIRACY IN RESTRAINT OF TRADE / Trade union, exception.

466. (1) A conspiracy in restraint of trade is an agreement between two or more persons to do or to procure to be done any unlawful act in restraint of trade.

(2) The purposes of a trade union are not, by reason only that they are in restraint of trade, unlawful within the meaning of subsection (1). R.S., c. C-34, s. 424.

CROSS-REFERENCES

Conspiracy in restraint of trade is a common law offence. As this section does not create an offence and with the repeal of s. 465(2) (common law conspiracy), it is entirely possible that the offence of conspiracy in restraint of trade can no longer be charged nor punished and that resort must be had to the substantive offences in other parts of the Code such as ss. 422 to 425 or to the offences under Part VI of the *Competition Act*, R.S.C. 1985, c. C-34.

SYNOPSIS

This section provides a definition of conspiracy in restraint of trade.

Subsection (1) states that such a conspiracy is an agreement between two or more persons to do, or arrange to have done, any *unlawful act* in restraint of trade.

Subsection (2) specifically provides that a trade union does not commit an offence under this section only by reason of the fact that its purposes are in restraint of trade.

SAVING / Definition of "trade combination".

467. (1) No person shall be convicted of the offence of conspiracy by reason only that he

(*a*) refuses to work with a workman or for an employer; or

(*b*) does any act or causes any act to be done for the purpose of a trade combination, unless that act is an offence expressly punishable by law.

(2) In this section, "trade combination" means any combination between masters or workmen or other persons for the purpose of regulating or altering the relations between masters or workmen, or the conduct of a master or workman in or in respect of his business, employment or contract of employment or service. R.S., c. C-34, s. 425.

CROSS-REFERENCES

These provisions would appear to apply to any conspiracy offence, not just those punishable under s. 465. Thus see, for example, s. 425(*c*).

SYNOPSIS

This section provides an exception to the general offence of conspiracy.

Subsection (1) states that no person shall be convicted of conspiracy *by reason only* that he refuses to work with a workman or for an employer, or that he does any *lawful act* for the purpose of trade combination.

Subsection (2) defines the term "trade combination" for the purposes of subsec. (1).

DEFINITIONS / "Criminal organization" / "Serious offence" / Facilitation / Commission of offence / Regulations.

467.1 (1) The following definitions apply in this Act.

"criminal organization" means a group, however organized, that

(*a*) is composed of three or more persons in or outside Canada; and

(*b*) has as one of its main purposes or main activities the facilitation or commission of one or more serious offences that, if committed, would likely result in the direct or indirect receipt of a material benefit, including a financial benefit, by the group or by any of the persons who constitute the group.

It does not include a group of persons that forms randomly for the immediate commission of a single offence.

"serious offence" means an indictable offence under this or any other Act of Parliament for which the maximum punishment is imprisonment for five years or more, or another offence that is prescribed by regulation.

(2) For the purposes of this section, section 467.11 and 467.111, facilitation of an offence does not require knowledge of a particular offence the commission of which is facilitated, or that an offence actually be committed.

(3) In this section and in sections 467.11 to 467.13, committing an offence means being a party to it or counselling any person to be a party to it.

(4) The Governor in Council may make regulations prescribing offences that are included in the definition "serious offence" in subsection (1). 1997, c. 23, s. 11; 2001, c. 32, s. 27; 2014, c. 17, s. 8.

ANNOTATIONS

The definition of "criminal organization" does not violate ss. 2(*d*) or 7 of the Charter: *R. v. Terezakis* (2007), 223 C.C.C. (3d) 344, 51 C.R. (6th) 165 (B.C.C.A.), leave to appeal to S.C.C. refused 226 C.C.C. (3d) vi.

"Criminal organization" was neither vague nor overbroad and, accordingly, did not violate s. 7 of the Charter: *R. v. Lindsay* (2009), 245 C.C.C. (3d) 301 (Ont. C.A.).

By insisting that criminal groups be "organized", Parliament has made plain that some form of structure and degree of continuity are required to engage the organized crime provisions. However, courts must not limit the scope of the provisions to the stereotypical model of organized crime: *R. v. Venneri*, [2012] 2 S.C.R. 211, 286 C.C.C. (3d) 1.

In order to prove that commission of serious offences is one of the "main purposes or main activities", the Crown is not required to lead evidence comparing the legal and illegal components of the business on a quantitative basis: *R. v. Beauchamp* (2015), 326 C.C.C. (3d) 280 (Ont. C.A.).

PARTICIPATION IN ACTIVITIES OF CRIMINAL ORGANIZATION / Prosecution / Factors.

467.11 (1) Every person who, for the purpose of enhancing the ability of a criminal organization to facilitate or commit an indictable offence under this or any other Act of Parliament, knowingly, by act or omission, participates in or contributes to any activity of the criminal organization is guilty of an indictable offence and liable to imprisonment for a term not exceeding five years.

(2) In a prosecution for an offence under subsection (1), it is not necessary for the prosecutor to prove that

(*a*) the criminal organization actually facilitated or committed an indictable offence;

(*b*) the participation or contribution of the accused actually enhanced the ability of the criminal organization to facilitate or commit an indictable offence;

(*c*) the accused knew the specific nature of any indictable offence that may have been facilitated or committed by the criminal organization; or

(*d*) the accused knew the identity of any of the persons who constitute the criminal organization.

(3) In determining whether an accused participates in or contributes to any activity of a criminal organization, the Court may consider, among other factors, whether the accused

(*a*) uses a name, word, symbol or other representation that identifies, or is associated with, the criminal organization;

(*b*) frequently associates with any of the persons who constitute the criminal organization;

(*c*) receives any benefit from the criminal organization; or

(*d*) repeatedly engages in activities at the instruction of any of the persons who constitute the criminal organization. 2001, c. 32, s. 27.

CROSS-REFERENCES

"Criminal organization" is defined in s. 467.1. Under s. 467.1(2) "facilitation of an offence" does not require knowledge of a particular offence, the commission of which is facilitated, or that an offence actually be committed. Further "committing an offence" means being a party to it or counselling any person to be a party to it. Related offences include: possession of explosives for the benefit of a criminal organization [s. 82(2)] and first degree murder where death is caused while committing the using explosive offence in s. 81 for the benefit of a criminal organization [s. 231(6.1)]. A wiretap authorization may be obtained in relation to this offence. It is also an enterprise crime offence for the purpose of Part XII.2. Evidence that an offence was committed for the benefit of a criminal organization is a deemed aggravating factor for the purposes of sentencing pursuant to s. 718.2. A person who fears that another person will commit a criminal organization offence may lay an information seeking to have the person enter into a recognizance pursuant to s. 810.01. The authority of the Attorney General of Canada to conduct proceedings in respect of this offence is set out in s. 467.2. The sentence for this offence is to be served consecutively to any other punishment imposed on the person for an offence arising out of the same event or series of events and to any other sentence that the person is subject. As to parole ineligibility, see s. 743.6. Sections 490.1 to 490.81 set out a scheme for the forfeiture of "offence-related property" (defined in s. 2). Special protections for victims or witnesses in proceedings against an accused for this offence are set out in s. 486.

SYNOPSIS

This section creates the least serious of the criminal organization offences, making it an offence to participate in or contribute to any activity of the criminal organization for the purpose of enhancing the ability of a criminal organization to facilitate or commit an indictable offence. Subsection (2) sets out a series of things the prosecution need not prove in order to make out the offence. Subsection (3) sets out certain types of evidence that the court may consider in determining whether the offence has been made out.

ANNOTATIONS

This provision does not violate s. 7 of the Charter: *R. v. Lindsay* (2009), 245 C.C.C. (3d) 301 (Ont. C.A.), leave to appeal to S.C.C. refused March 4, 2010. See also *R. v. Pereira* (2008), 247 C.C.C. (3d) 311 (B.C.S.C.), holding that these provisions also did not violate s. 2(*d*) of the Charter.

RECRUITMENT OF MEMBERS BY A CRIMINAL ORGANIZATION.

467.111 Every person who, for the purpose of enhancing the ability of a criminal organization to facilitate or commit an indictable offence under this Act or any other Act of Parliament, recruits, solicits, encourages, coerces or invites a person to join the criminal organization, is guilty of an indictable offence and liable,

(*a*) in the case where the person recruited, solicited, encouraged or invited is under 18 years of age, to imprisonment for a term not exceeding five years, and to a minimum punishment of imprisonment for a term of six months; and

(*b*) in any other case, to imprisonment for a term not exceeding five years. 2014, c. 17, s. 9.

COMMISSION OF OFFENCE FOR CRIMINAL ORGANIZATION / Prosecution.

467.12 (1) Every person who commits an indictable offence under this or any other Act of Parliament for the benefit of, at the direction of, or in association with, a criminal organization is guilty of an indictable offence and liable to imprisonment for a term not exceeding fourteen years.

(2) In a prosecution for an offence under subsection (1), it is not necessary for the prosecutor to prove that the accused knew the identity of any of the persons who constitute the criminal organization. 2001, c. 32, s. 27.

CROSS-REFERENCES

"Criminal organization" is defined in s. 467.1. Related offences include: possession of explosives for the benefit of a criminal organization [s. 82(2)] and first degree murder where death is caused while committing the using explosive offence in s. 81 for the benefit of a criminal organization [s. 231(6.1)]. A wiretap authorization may be obtained in relation to this offence. It is also an enterprise crime offence for the purpose of Part XII.2. A person who fears that another person will commit a criminal organization offence may lay an information seeking to have the person enter into a recognizance pursuant to s. 810.01. The authority of the Attorney General of Canada to conduct proceedings in respect of a criminal organization offence is set out in s. 467.2. Pursuant to s. 467.14, the sentence for this offence is to be served consecutively to any other punishment imposed on the person for an offence arising out of the same event or series of events and to any other sentence that the person is subject. Evidence that an offence was committed for the benefit of a criminal organization is a deemed aggravating factor for the purposes of sentencing pursuant to s. 718.2. As to parole ineligibility, see s. 743.6. Sections 490.1 to 490.81 set out a scheme for the forfeiture of "offence-related property" (defined in s. 2).

Special protections for victims or witnesses in proceedings against an accused for this offence are set out in s. 486.

SYNOPSIS

This section creates one of the three special criminal organization offences, making it an offence to commit an indictable offence for the benefit of, at the direction of, or in association with a criminal organization. Under subsec. (2) it is not necessary to prove that the accused knew the identity of any of the persons constituting the criminal organization.

ANNOTATIONS

This provision was neither vague nor overbroad contrary to s. 7 of the Charter: *R. v. Lindsay* (2009), 245 C.C.C. (3d) 301 (Ont. C.A.), leave to appeal to S.C.C. refused March 4, 2010. See also *R. v. Pereira* (2008), 247 C.C.C. (3d) 311 (B.C.S.C.), holding that these provisions also did not violate s. 2(*d*) of the Charter.

The phrase "in association with" captures offences that advance, at least to some degree, the interests of a criminal organization. It requires a connection between the predicate offence and the organization, as opposed to simply an association between the accused and the organization. The Crown must also demonstrate that an accused knowingly dealt with a criminal organization. The fact that the accused was not a member of the organization did not preclude a finding that he operated "in association with" the organization when he acted as its client and its supplier contrary: *R. v. Venneri*, [2012] 2 S.C.R. 211, 286 C.C.C. (3d) 1.

INSTRUCTING COMMISSION OF OFFENCE FOR CRIMINAL ORGANIZATION / Prosecution.

467.13 (1) Every person who is one of the persons who constitute a criminal organization and who knowingly instructs, directly or indirectly, any person to commit an offence under this or any other Act of Parliament for the benefit of, at the direction of, or in association with, the criminal organization is guilty of an indictable offence and liable to imprisonment for life.

(2) In a prosecution for an offence under subsection (1), it is not necessary for the prosecutor to prove that

(*a*) an offence other than the offence under subsection (1) was actually committed;
(*b*) the accused instructed a particular person to commit an offence; or
(*c*) the accused knew the identity of all of the persons who constitute the criminal organization. 2001, c. 32, s. 27.

CROSS-REFERENCES

"Criminal organization" is defined in s. 467.1. Related offences include: possession of explosives for the benefit of a criminal organization [s. 82(2)] and first degree murder where death is caused while committing the using explosive offence in s. 81 for the benefit of a criminal organization [s. 231(6.1)]. A wiretap authorization may be obtained in relation to this offence. It is also an enterprise crime offence for the purpose of Part XII.2. A person who fears that another person will commit a criminal organization offence may lay an information seeking to have the person enter into a recognizance pursuant to s. 810.01. The authority of the Attorney General of Canada to conduct proceedings in respect of a criminal organization offence is set out in s. 467.2. Pursuant to

s. 467.14, the sentence for this offence is to be served consecutively to any other punishment imposed on the person for an offence arising out of the same event or series of events and to any other sentence that the person is subject. Evidence that an offence was committed for the benefit of a criminal organization is a deemed aggravating factor for the purposes of sentencing pursuant to s. 718.2. As to parole ineligibility, see s. 743.6. Sections 490.1 to 490.81 set out a scheme for the forfeiture of "offence-related property" (defined in s. 2).

Special protections for victims or witnesses in proceedings against an accused for this offence are set out in s. 486.

SYNOPSIS

This section creates the most serious offence apparently aimed at the leaders of the criminal organization, making it an offence for a member of the organization to knowingly instruct any person to commit an offence for the benefit of, at the direction of, or in association with a criminal organization. Under subsec. (2), it is not necessary to prove that the offence was actually committed, that the accused instructed a particular person or that the accused knew the identity of all of the persons constituting the criminal organization.

ANNOTATIONS

This provision does not violate ss. 2(*d*) or 7 of the Charter: *R. v. Terezakis* (2007), 223 C.C.C. (3d) 344, 51 C.R. (6th) 165 (B.C.C.A.), leave to appeal to S.C.C. refused 226 C.C.C. (3d) vi.

"Knowingly" applies to all elements of the *actus reus*, which requires proof of being a member of a criminal organization and instructing the commission of an offence linked to a criminal organization. The *mens rea* requires proof of membership in a group, however organized; knowledge that a main purpose or activity of the group is the facilitation or commission of serious crime; knowledge that the crime likely would result in a direct or indirect benefit to the group or any person in the group; and, as a member of the group, knowingly instructing another to commit a crime for the benefit of the group, at its direction or in association with the group. An accused's assertion that he did not share the main criminal purpose or subscribe to the main criminal activity of the group has relevance to the conviction to be determined on a case by case basis. There is no doubt, however, that the citizen knows the zone of risk and the implications of being part of such a group and instructing others to commit crimes for the benefit of, at the direction of, or in association with the group. In addition, the Crown is not required to prove that the accused had authority in, or was the leader of, the criminal organization: *R. v. Terezakis, supra.*

SENTENCES TO BE SERVED CONSECUTIVELY.

467.14 A sentence imposed on a person for an offence under section 467.11, 467.111, 467.12 or 467.13 shall be served consecutively to any other punishment imposed on the person for an offence arising out of the same event or series of events and to any other sentence to which the person is subject at the time the sentence is imposed on the person for an offence under any of those sections. 2001, c. 32, s. 27; 2014, c. 17, s. 10.

POWERS OF ATTORNEY GENERAL OF CANADA / Powers of the Attorney General of a province.

467.2 (1) Notwithstanding the definition of "Attorney General" in section 2, the Attorney General of Canada may conduct proceedings in respect of

(*a*) an offence under section 467.11 or 467.111; or

(*b*) another criminal organization offence where the alleged offence arises out of conduct that in whole or in part is in relation to an alleged contravention of an Act of Parliament or a regulation made under such an Act, other than this Act or a regulation made under this Act.

For those purposes, the Attorney General of Canada may exercise all the powers and perform all the duties and functions assigned to the Attorney General by or under this Act.

(2) Subsection (1) does not affect the authority of the Attorney General of a province to conduct proceedings in respect of an offence referred to in section 467.11, 467.111, 467.12 or 467.13 or to exercise any of the powers or perform any of the duties and functions assigned to the Attorney General by or under this Act. 1997, c. 23, s. 11; 2001, c. 32, s. 28; 2014, c. 17, s. 11.

CROSS-REFERENCES
"Criminal organization offence" is defined in s. 2.

Part XIV / JURISDICTION

General

SUPERIOR COURT OF CRIMINAL JURISDICTION.

468. Every superior court of criminal jurisdiction has jurisdiction to try any indictable offence. R.S., c. C-34, s. 426.

CROSS-REFERENCES
The term "superior court of criminal jurisdiction" is defined in s. 2.

Note on mode of trial – The scheme of the *Criminal Code* is to classify offences as purely indictable (*e.g.*, robbery, s. 344), purely summary (*e.g.*, soliciting, s. 213) or hybrid, *i.e.*, the prosecution may elect whether to proceed by way of summary conviction or by indictment (*e.g.*, assault, s. 266). The effect of s. 468 is that the superior court of criminal jurisdiction may try any purely indictable offence or any hybrid offence where the prosecution elects to proceed by way of indictment. Other courts of criminal jurisdiction (defined in s. 2) may, however, try indictable offences except those offences listed in s. 469 (*e.g.*, murder, s. 235). The offences listed in s. 469 may only be tried by the superior court of criminal jurisdiction with a jury subject to a re-election in conformity with s. 473. Indictable offences not listed in s. 469 fall into two categories. For the majority of the indictable offences not listed in s. 469, the accused may elect the mode of trial as set out in s. 536(2) and, within limits, may change that election (see, *e.g.*, s. 561). While the Attorney General is given a narrow discretion to override this election and require a jury trial under s. 568 in the circumstances defined therein and, in addition, a provincial court judge has a discretion to override or not record an accused's election for trial by provincial court judge and hold a preliminary inquiry (see, for example, ss. 555 and 567), the thrust of the provisions is to give the accused the right to determine the manner of trial. The other group of offences are those offences listed in s. 553 (*e.g.*, keeping common bawdy house, s. 210(1)) that fall within the absolute jurisdiction of a provincial court judge, meaning that the accused does not have a normal election as to the mode of trial under s. 536(2). Nevertheless, the other courts with jurisdiction to try indictable offences have jurisdiction to try the offences listed in s. 553, if the provincial court judge elects not to try the offence and requires that the case proceed by way of preliminary inquiry pursuant to s. 555(1), or in the course of the trial it is disclosed that, in fact, the offence is not one over which the provincial court judge has absolute jurisdiction, in which case, the accused must then be put to his election under s. 536(2). [For example, a charge of theft of goods of a value not exceeding $5,000 where the evidence discloses that the value of the goods exceeds $5,000.]

For all summary conviction offences, meaning purely summary conviction or hybrid offences, where the prosecution elects to proceed by way of summary conviction, only the summary conviction court (defined in s. 785) may try the accused. The procedure for trial of summary conviction offences generally resembles trial of an indictable offence by a provincial court judge but that procedure, including special rights of appeal, is set out in Part XXVII.

ANNOTATIONS

A superior court of criminal jurisdiction has the right to try those offences within the absolute jurisdiction of a provincial court judge: *R. v. Holliday* (1973), 12 C.C.C. (2d) 56, [1973] 5 W.W.R. 363 (Alta. S.C. App. Div.).

COURT OF CRIMINAL JURISDICTION / Accessories / Corrupting justice / Attempts / Conspiracy.

469. Every court of criminal jurisdiction has jurisdiction to try an indictable offence other than

(*a*) an offence under any of the following sections:

(i) section 47 (treason),

(ii) [*Repealed*, 2018, c. 29, s. 61.]

(iii) section 51 (intimidating Parliament or a legislature),

(iv) section 53 (inciting to mutiny),

(v) section 61 (seditious offences),

(vi) section 74 (piracy),

(vii) section 75 (piratical acts), or

(viii) section 235 (murder);

(*b*) the offence of being an accessory after the fact to high treason or treason or murder;

(*c*) an offence under section 119 (bribery) by the holder of a judicial office;

(*c*.1) an offence under any of sections 4 to 7 of the *Crimes Against Humanity and War Crimes Act*;

(*d*) the offence of attempting to commit any offence mentioned in subparagraphs (*a*)(i) to (vii); or

(*e*) the offence of conspiring to commit any offence mentioned in paragraph (*a*).

R.S., c. C-34, s. 427; 1972, c. 13, s. 33; 1974-75-76, c. 93, s. 37, c. 105, s. 29; R.S.C. 1985, c. 27 (1st Supp.), s. 62; 2000, c. 24, s. 44; 2018, c. 29, s. 61.

CROSS-REFERENCES

Note that s. 3 provides that the descriptions in parenthesis after the section number are inserted for convenience of reference only and are no part of the provision.

The term "court of criminal jurisdiction" is defined in s. 2. Only the superior court of criminal jurisdiction has jurisdiction to try the offences listed in this section. As well, only a judge of the superior court of criminal jurisdiction may release an accused pending trial for these offences, by virtue of s. 522. The ordinary mode of trial for these offences is by virtue of the combined effect of ss. 468 and 471, by way of jury. However, provision is made for re-election for trial by judge alone under s. 473.

As to mode of trial generally, see the note under s. 468.

ANNOTATIONS

Neither the superior court of criminal jurisdiction nor the court of criminal jurisdiction have jurisdiction to try a summary conviction offence *ab initio*: *R. v. Rahim* (1977), 36 C.C.C. (2d) 533 (Ont. Co. Ct.).

JURISDICTION OVER PERSON.

470. Subject to this Act, every superior court of criminal jurisdiction and every court of criminal jurisdiction that has power to try an indictable offence is competent to try an accused for that offence

(*a*) if the accused is found, is arrested or is in custody within the territorial jurisdiction of the court; or

(*b*) if the accused has been ordered to be tried by

(i) that court, or

(ii) any other court, the jurisdiction of which has by lawful authority been transferred to that court. R.S., c. C-34, s. 428; R.S.C. 1985, c. 27 (1st Supp.), s. 101(3).

CROSS-REFERENCES

The terms "superior court of criminal jurisdiction" and "court of criminal jurisdiction" are defined in s. 2. The effect of this section is to overcome the common law rule that a criminal court's jurisdiction to try the accused was strictly local and subject to a statutory exception, *e.g.*, for offences committed at sea, the court had no jurisdiction to try an accused for an offence committed in some other country. In the circumstances set out in this section, the court can try the accused, although the offence was not committed within the territorial division (defined in s. 2), provided that the accused is found, arrested or is in custody within the territorial jurisdiction (defined by provincial legislation) of the court or has been ordered to be tried by that court, *e.g.*, by an order for change of venue under s. 599. [Note that this section deals only with territorial jurisdiction over the person of the accused, some other section must be resorted to to ensure that the information or indictment is also before the court, *e.g.*, as in s. 599(4) where an order for a change of venue is made. An alternative is by laying the information under s. 504.]

In addition to this section, a court may also acquire territorial jurisdiction over an accused by reason of special statutory provisions such as those found in s. 7, s. 465(5), or ss. 477 to 481. Sections 478 and 479 are especially useful in providing that offences committed in a number of different divisions or provinces may, with consent of the Crown, be transferred to the jurisdiction where the accused is for guilty pleas. Further, s. 476 attempts to resolve difficult issues of territorial jurisdiction where an offence is committed near the border of a territorial division, such as on a bridge between two divisions.

As to mode of trial, see the note under s. 468.

SYNOPSIS

This section provides that every superior court of criminal jurisdiction and every court of criminal jurisdiction that has power to try an indictable offence is also *competent to try* a person for that offence: (a) if the person is physically found within the territorial jurisdiction of the court; or (b) if the person has been ordered to be tried by that court, or any other court, the jurisdiction of which has been *lawfully* transferred to that court.

ANNOTATIONS

Where proceedings were properly commenced under permissible territorial jurisdiction of a justice and the accused was committed for trial to a particular court of criminal jurisdiction that court has jurisdiction to hear and determine the charges even though the offence was committed in another territorial division within the same province: *R. v. McMorris and Francis* (1971), 4 C.C.C. (2d) 268, [1971] 3 O.R. 748 (Co. Ct.).

Where an accused appears and enters a plea the court before which he appears has jurisdiction by virtue of para. (*a*) in that the accused is "in custody within the territorial jurisdiction of the Court" notwithstanding the offence was not committed in that territorial division. Alternatively, if an objection is taken to the court's jurisdiction and the objection is overruled then the accused has been "ordered to be tried by that Court" within the meaning of para. (*b*)(i) and the court by virtue of that section has jurisdiction: *R. v. Rice, ex p. Katz and Lavitch*, [1968] 3 C.C.C. 85, 63 W.W.R. 64 (Man. C.A.).

At common law the accused has a *prima facie* right to be tried in the county in which the offence was committed and this rule, in the absence of a court-ordered change of venue, continues except as modified by this section. However, the words "is in custody within the territorial jurisdiction of the court" do not give the court of one county jurisdiction where the accused, arrested in another county where the offence was committed, is merely brought to the former county in custody and then released on bail. If this section were to apply in such circumstances then it would be open to the Crown to select the venue of the trial by simply arranging to have an accused held in custody in the jurisdiction of its choice: *R. v. Sarazin and Sarazin* (1978), 39 C.C.C. (2d) 131, 3 C.R. (3d) 97 (P.E.I.S.C.).

Where an indictment had been preferred and the accused had appeared in Superior Court and waived arraignment, the court had jurisdiction over the application from release for custody pursuant to this provision. Neither s. 485(2) or (3) operated to deprive the Superior Court of jurisdiction over the accused: *R. v. Holowaychuk* (2009), 244 C.C.C. (3d) 352 (Ont. C.A.).

TRIAL BY JURY COMPULSORY.

471. Except where otherwise expressly provided by law, every accused who is charged with an indictable offence shall be tried by a court composed of a judge and jury. R.S., c. C-34, s. 429.

CROSS-REFERENCES

The Code has, of course, enacted a number of exceptions to the rule set out in this section, generally, but not always conditional on the accused's consent to some other form of trial. As to mode of trial generally, see the note under s. 468. Also see notes under s. 11(*f*) of the Charter concerning the constitutional right to a jury trial.

472. [*Repealed*, R.S.C. 1985, c. 27 (1st Supp.), s. 63.]

TRIAL WITHOUT JURY / Joinder of other offences / Withdrawal of consent.

473. (1) Notwithstanding anything in this Act, an accused charged with an offence listed in section 469 may, with the consent of the accused and the Attorney General, be tried without a jury by a judge of a superior court of criminal jurisdiction.

(1.1) Where the consent of the accused and the Attorney General is given in accordance with subsection (1), the judge of the superior court of criminal jurisdiction may order that any offence be tried by that judge in conjunction with the offence listed in section 469.

(2) Notwithstanding anything in this Act, where the consent of an accused and the Attorney General is given in accordance with subsection (1), that consent shall not be withdrawn unless both the accused and the Attorney General agree to the withdrawal. R.S., c. C-34, s. 430; R.S.C. 1985, c. 27 (1st Supp.), s. 63; 1994, c. 44, s. 30.

CROSS-REFERENCES

The terms "Attorney General" and "superior court of criminal jurisdiction" are defined in s. 2. Also see the note as to mode of trial under s. 468.

SYNOPSIS

This section describes the circumstances in which a person charged with an offence listed in s. 469 may have a trial without a jury. If the accused and the Attorney General consent, a s. 469 offence may be tried by judge of a superior court of criminal jurisdiction without a jury. Consent given under this section cannot be withdrawn unless both the accused and the Attorney General agree to the withdrawal.

ANNOTATIONS

Where an accused who is represented by counsel consents under this section to be tried on a charge of murder by a judge alone there is no duty on the judge to inquire into the accused's understanding of his choice. Specifically no such duty arises merely because the accused is only 16 years of age: *R. v. Davis (No. 2)* (1977), 35 C.C.C. (2d) 464, [1977] 4 W.W.R. 47 (Alta. S.C. App. Div.).

A Crown Attorney, as agent of the Attorney General, may consent to the re-election under this section. On the other hand, no re-election is required where the jury has not been empanelled and the accused merely intends to plead guilty to the offence charged or an included offence: *R. v. Luis* (1989), 50 C.C.C. (3d) 398 (Ont. H.C.J.).

It was held in *R. v. Turpin*, [1989] 1 S.C.R. 1296, 48 C.C.C. (3d) 8 (6:0), that s. 11(*f*) of the Charter confers no constitutional right to be tried by a judge without a jury. The purpose of s. 11(*f*) is to give an accused the right to a jury trial and to ensure that if a jury trial is not of benefit to the accused, the accused may waive the constitutional right to a jury trial. However, where the *Criminal Code* requires a jury trial then s. 11(*f*) gives the accused no right to elect another mode of trial.

The prosecutor's refusal to consent must be motivated by a desire to achieve fundamental fairness and not by the desire to obtain a tactical or strategic advantage. In this case, the refusal of the Crown to consent was improper and was motivated in part by a consideration of the identity of the assigned trial judge. Accordingly, the consent of the Crown was dispensed with: *R. v. Bird* (1996), 107 C.C.C. (3d) 186, 39 Alta. L.R. (3d) 128 (Q.B.). See also *R. v. McGregor* (1999), 134 C.C.C. (3d) 570, 22 C.R. (5th) 233 (Ont. C.A.).

The accused relied on the defence of intoxication and led evidence from a psychologist of the difficulty juries experience in applying the intoxication instructions. However, this evidence was of limited weight since it was unrelated to the particular circumstances of this case. The accused was not entitled to a constitutional remedy dispensing with the Crown's consent to trial by judge alone: *R. v. Jensen* (2005), 195 C.C.C. (3d) 14, 27 C.R. (6th) 240 (Ont. C.A.).

There is no requirement that the Crown provide reasons for refusing to consent and the failure to provide reasons for such a refusal is not a basis for judicial intervention. The exercise of prosecutorial discretion must be arbitrary, capricious or motivated by improper considerations to constitute an abuse of process: *R. v. Ng* (2003), 173 C.C.C. (3d) 349, 12 C.R. (6th) 1 (Alta. C.A.), leave to appeal to S.C.C. refused 183 C.C.C. (3d) vi.

ADJOURNMENT WHEN NO JURY SUMMONED / Adjournment on instruction of judge.

474. (1) Where the competent authority has determined that a panel of jurors is not to be summoned for a term or sittings of the court for the trial of criminal cases in any territorial division, the clerk of the court may, on the day of the opening of the term or sittings, if a judge is not present to preside over the court, adjourn the court and the business of the court to a subsequent day. R.S., c. C-34, s. 431.

(2) A clerk of the court for the trial of criminal cases in any territorial division may, at any time, on the instructions of the presiding judge or another judge of the court, adjourn the court and the business of the court to a subsequent day. R.S., c. C-34, s. 431; 1994, c. 44, s. 31.

CROSS-REFERENCES

The terms "territorial division" and "clerk of the court" are defined in s. 2. See s. 763 respecting the accused's recognizance remaining in force.

SYNOPSIS

This section empowers the clerk of the court, where no judge is present at the opening of the term, to adjourn court proceedings to a subsequent day if the competent authority has determined that a panel of jurors is not to be summoned for a term or sittings of the court. It also provides in subsec. (2) that, on instructions of a judge, the clerk may, at any time, adjourn the court.

ACCUSED ABSCONDING DURING TRIAL / Adverse inference / Accused not entitled to re-opening / Counsel for accused may continue to act.

475. (1) Notwithstanding any other provision of this Act, where an accused, whether or not he is charged jointly with another, absconds during the course of his trial,

(*a*) he shall be deemed to have waived his right to be present at his trial, and

(*b*) the court may

(i) continue the trial and proceed to a judgment or verdict and, if it finds the accused guilty, impose a sentence on him in his absence, or

(ii) if a warrant in Form 7 is issued for the arrest of the accused, adjourn the trial to await his appearance,

but where the trial is adjourned pursuant to subparagraph (*b*)(ii), the court may, at any time, continue the trial if it is satisfied that it is no longer in the interests of justice to await the appearance of the accused.

(2) Where a court continues a trial pursuant to subsection (1), it may draw an inference adverse to the accused from the fact that he has absconded.

(3) Where an accused reappears at his trial that is continuing pursuant to subsection (1), he is not entitled to have any part of the proceedings that was conducted in his absence re-opened unless the court is satisfied that because of exceptional circumstances it is in the interests of justice to re-open the proceedings.

(4) Where an accused has absconded during the course of his trial and the court continues the trial, counsel for the accused is not thereby deprived of any authority he may have to continue to act for the accused in the proceedings. 1974-75-76, c. 93, s. 39.

CROSS-REFERENCES

The term "counsel" is defined in s. 2. A similar provision respecting an accused who absconds in the course of his preliminary inquiry is found in s. 544 and in the course of his summary conviction trial in s. 803(2). As well, an accused who fails to appear for his trial or remain at his trial may lose his right to trial by jury by virtue of s. 598.

Section 650 provides for other circumstances in which an accused may be absent from the trial.

SYNOPSIS

This section deals with the situation where an accused person absconds *during the course* of a trial.

Subsection (1) provides that an absconding accused, whether or not he is charged jointly with another, is deemed to have waived his right to be present at his trial. Subsection (1)(*b*) also provides that the court may continue the trial to its conclusion and impose a sentence on the absconding accused, or issue an arrest warrant and adjourn the trial until the accused appears. If the court adjourns the trial under subsec. (1)(*b*), that court may at any time continue the trial if it is satisfied that it is no longer in the interests of justice to await the appearance of the accused.

Subsection (2) allows the court to draw an adverse inference from the fact that the accused has absconded.

Subsection (3) provides that when an accused reappears at a trial that has continued in his absence, he is not entitled to have any portion of the proceedings conducted when he was not present reopened unless he establishes that because of exceptional circumstances, it is in the best interests of justice to re-open such proceedings.

Subsection (4) states that counsel for an absconding accused has the authority to continue to act for the accused during the proceedings.

ANNOTATIONS

Meaning of absconds – The word "absconds" in this section means more than mere failure to appear and imports a requirement that the accused has voluntarily absented himself from his trial for the purpose of impeding or frustrating the trial, or with the intention of avoiding its consequences. The necessary intent can however be inferred from proof that the accused deliberately absented himself. Upon proof that the accused absconded, the trial may proceed although defence counsel has been permitted to withdraw: *R. v. Garofoli* (1988), 41 C.C.C. (3d) 97, 64 C.R. (3d) 193 (Ont. C.A.), affd on this point [1990] 2 S.C.R. 1421, 60 C.C.C. (3d) 161. See also *R. v. Taylor* (2010), 252 C.C.C. (3d) 197 (B.C.C.A.).

Procedure – Once the accused absconds, he has waived his right to be present as required by s. 650 and even after he has been apprehended the trial may continue in his absence until it was reasonably practicable to return him to court: *R. v. Tzimopoulos* (1986), 29 C.C.C. (3d) 304, 54 C.R. (3d) 1 (Ont. C.A.), leave to appeal to S.C.C. refused [1987] 1 S.C.R. xv, 54 C.R. (3d) xxviii.

It is for the trial judge to determine whether or not the accused has absconded and in directing the jury as to the adverse inference as permitted by subsec. (2) the judge need not leave it to the jury to first determine whether the accused absconded: *R. v. Tzimopoulos, supra.*

Notwithstanding subsec. (4) in most cases it would be unfair to require defence counsel to continue to represent an accused who has absconded. This subsection does not confer any authority on counsel to continue to act, nor does it interfere with or restrict counsel's right, in accordance with professional standards, to cease to act for the accused: *R. v. Garofoli* (1988), 41 C.C.C. (3d) 97, 64 C.R. (3d) 193 (Ont. C.A.), revd on other grounds [1990] 2 S.C.R. 1421, 60 C.C.C. (3d) 161, 80 C.R. (3d) 317.

Constitutional considerations – This provision does not offend the guarantee to fundamental justice in s. 7 of the *Canadian Charter of Rights and Freedoms*: *R. v. Czuczman* (1986), 26 C.C.C. (3d) 43, 49 C.R. (3d) 385, 27 D.L.R. (4th) 694 (Ont. C.A.), nor the right to a fair trial under s. 11(*d*): *R. v. Tzimopoulos* (1986), 29 C.C.C. (3d) 304, 54 C.R. (3d) 1 (Ont. C.A.).

Special Jurisdiction

SPECIAL JURISDICTIONS.

476. For the purposes of this Act,

(*a*) where an offence is committed in or on any water or on a bridge between two or more territorial divisions, the offence shall be deemed to have been committed in any of the territorial divisions;

(*b*) where an offence is committed on the boundary of two or more territorial divisions or within five hundred metres of any such boundary, or the offence was commenced within one territorial division and completed within another, the offence shall be deemed to have been committed in any of the territorial divisions;

(*c*) where an offence is committed in or on a vehicle employed in a journey, or on board a vessel employed on a navigable river, canal or inland water, the offence shall be deemed to have been committed in any territorial division through which the vehicle or vessel passed in the course of the journey or voyage on which the offence was committed, and where the center or other part of the road, or navigable river, canal or inland water on which the vehicle or vessel passed in the course of the journey or voyage is the boundary of two or more territorial divisions, the offence shall be deemed to have been committed in any of the territorial divisions;

(*d*) where an offence is committed in an aircraft in the course of a flight of that aircraft, it shall be deemed to have been committed

(i) **in the territorial division in which the flight commenced,**
(ii) **in any territorial division over which the aircraft passed in the course of the flight, or**
(iii) **in the territorial division in which the flight ended; and**

(*e*) **where an offence is committed in respect of the mail in the course of its door-to-door delivery, the offence shall be deemed to have been committed in any territorial division through which the mail was carried on that delivery. R.S., c. C-34, s. 432; R.S.C. 1985, c. 27 (1st Supp.), s. 186; 1992, c. 1, s. 58.**

CROSS-REFERENCES

The term "territorial division" is defined in s. 2. The term "mail" is defined in s. 2 of the *Canada Post Corporation Act*, R.S.C. 1985, c. C-10. For other notes respecting territorial jurisdiction, see cross-references under ss. 6, 7 and 470.

SYNOPSIS

This section clarifies territorial jurisdiction in a number of unusual or special sets of circumstances.

ANNOTATIONS

Offences committed in more than one division [para. (*b*)] – Jurisdiction in inferior courts must be established like any essential ingredient of an offence and is not presumed, as in the case of superior courts, so where the Crown in a questionable boundary case failed strictly to prove jurisdiction over the accused by a county magistrate an acquittal was ordered: *R. v. O'Blenis,* [1965] 2 C.C.C. 165, (N.B.S.C. App. Div.).

In *R. v. Bigelow* (1982), 69 C.C.C. (2d) 204, 37 O.R. (2d) 304 (C.A.), the court in holding that the effect of this paragraph was to establish a broad basis for jurisdiction over interprovincial offences reviewed the case law as to its application and drew the following conclusions: (i) this paragraph conferred jurisdiction over crimes involving continuity of operation extending over more than one province in any province where a component of the offence took place; (ii) the courts in one province have assumed jurisdiction where an overt act referrable to or in furtherance of a criminal plan extending beyond that province was committed in the province; and (iii) where the act of the accused in one province generates effects in another this paragraph confers jurisdiction on the courts of the second province.

A province may try an offence which is completed partly in that province and partly in another province or territory. Consequently, sexual assaults which occurred for several years in several provinces could be prosecuted in any of the provinces in which an assault was committed: *R. v. L. (D.A.)* (1996), 107 C.C.C. (3d) 178, 125 W.A.C. 65 (B.C.C.A.).

Offences committed on vehicle or vessel [para. (*c*)] – The word "deemed" in this paragraph means "deemed conclusively". Thus even where evidence is led that the offence actually took place in a particular territorial division, not the division named in the indictment, as long as the vehicle passed through the territorial division named in the indictment in the course of the journey in which the offence was committed, the offence is proved: *R. v. Moore and Grazier* (1970), 1 C.C.C. (2d) 521, [1971] 1 W.W.R. 656 (B.C.C.A.).

This provision does not have application where none of the constituent elements of the offence occurred in Canada. In this case, although the offence involved Canadians in a Canadian vehicle in the United States, there was no significant link between Canada and the formulation, initiation or commission of the offence: *R. v. B. (O.)* (1997), 116 C.C.C. (3d) 189, 99 O.A.C. 313 (C.A.).

CR. CODE

WORDS AND EXPRESSIONS / Saving.

477. (1) In sections 477.1 to 477.4, "ship" includes any description of vessel, boat or craft designed, used or capable of being used solely or partly for marine navigation, without regard to method or lack of propulsion.

(2) Nothing in sections 477.1 to 477.4 limits the operation of any other Act of Parliament or the jurisdiction that a court may exercise apart from those sections. 1990, c. 44, s. 15; 1996, c. 31, s. 67.

OFFENCES IN, ABOVE OR BEYOND CONTINENTAL SHELF.

477.1 Every person who commits an act or omission that, if it occurred in Canada, would be an offence under a federal law, within the meaning of section 2 of the *Oceans Act*, is deemed to have committed that act or omission in Canada if it is an act or omission

(*a*) in the exclusive economic zone of Canada that

(i) is committed by a person who is in the exclusive economic zone of Canada in connection with exploring or exploiting, conserving or managing the natural resources, whether living or non-living, of the exclusive economic zone of Canada, and

(ii) is committed by or in relation to a person who is a Canadian citizen or a permanent resident within the meaning of subsection 2(1) of the *Immigration and Refugee Protection Act*.

(*b*) that is committed in a place in or above the continental shelf of Canada and that is an offence in that place by virtue of section 20 of the *Oceans Act*;

(*c*) that is committed outside Canada on board or by means of a ship registered or licensed, or for which an identification number has been issued, pursuant to any Act of Parliament:

(*d*) that is committed outside Canada in the course of hot pursuit; or

(*e*) that is committed outside the territory of any state by a Canadian citizen. 1990, c. 44, s. 15; 1996, c. 31, s. 68; 2001, c. 27, s. 247.

CROSS-REFERENCES

The term "ship" is defined in s. 477. Section 2 of the *Oceans Act*, S.C. 1996, c. 31, defines "federal law" as follows:

> "federal laws" includes Acts of Parliament, regulations as defined in section 2 of the *Interpretation Act* and any other rules of law within the jurisdiction of Parliament, but does not include ordinances within the meaning of the *Northwest Territories Act* or the *Yukon Act* or, after section 3 of the *Nunavut Act* comes into force, laws made by the Legislature for Nunavut or continued by section 29 of that Act;

Section 20 of the *Oceans Act* provides:

> 20(1) Subject to any regulations made pursuant to paragraph 26(1)(*j*) or (*k*), federal laws apply
>
> (*a*) on or under any marine installation or structure from the time it is attached or anchored to the continental shelf of Canada in connection with the exploration of that shelf or the exploitation of its mineral or other non-living resources until the marine installation or structure is removed from the waters above the continental shelf of Canada;
>
> (*b*) on or under any artificial island constructed, erected or placed on the continental shelf of Canada; and
>
> (*c*) within such safety zone surrounding any marine installation or structure or artificial island referred to in paragraph (*a*) or (*b*) as is determined by or pursuant to the regulations.
>
> (2) For the purposes of subsection (1), federal laws shall be applied
>
> (*a*) as if the places referred to in that subsection formed part of the territory of Canada;
>
> (*b*) notwithstanding that by their terms their application is limited to Canada; and

(*c*) in a manner that is consistent with the rights and freedoms of other states under international law and, in particular, with the rights and freedoms of other states in relation to navigation and overflight.

Pursuant to s. 477.2, the consent of the Attorney General of Canada is required to continue indictable proceedings if the accused is not a Canadian citizen and the offence is alleged to have been committed on board any ship registered outside Canada. The consent of the Attorney General of Canada is also required to continue proceedings where the courts only have jurisdiction by virtue of para. (*a*) or (*b*) if the accused is not a Canadian citizen and the offence is alleged to have been committed on board any ship registered outside Canada. Finally, the consent of the Attorney General of Canada is also required if the courts have jurisdiction by virtue of para. (*d*) or (*e*). The consent must be obtained not later than eight days after the proceedings are commenced. Section 477.3 gives the same powers of arrest, entry, search or seizure as may be exercise d in Canada in respect of an act or omission referred to in this section in the circumstances set out in that section. However, where the offence is alleged to have been committed on board a ship registered outside Canada, the powers shall not be exercised outside Canada without the consent of the Attorney General of Canada. A judge or justice also has the same powers to authorize an arrest, search or other investigative measure in the circumstances set out in s. 477.3(2). Section 477.4 provides for proof of certain matters by certificate issued under s. 23(1) of the *Oceans Act*.

Reference should also be made to s. 7 which sets out other circumstances in which Canadian courts have jurisdiction over offences not actually committed on Canadian territory.

SYNOPSIS

This section gives Canadian courts jurisdiction over offenders by deeming certain acts or omissions to have been committed in Canada although they were committed outside the territory of Canada.

ANNOTATIONS

In *R. v. Macooh*, [1993] 2 S.C.R. 802, 82 C.C.C. (3d) 481, 22 C.R. (4th) 70, the court adopted the definition of "hot pursuit" suggested by R.E. Salhany in *Canadian Criminal Procedure*, 5th ed. (Aurora, Ontario: Canada Law Book Inc., 1989), p. 44: "Generally, the essence of fresh pursuit is that it must be continuous pursuit conducted with reasonable diligence, so that pursuit and capture along with the commission of the offence may be considered as forming part of a single transaction."

CONSENT OF ATTORNEY GENERAL / Exception / Consent of Attorney General / Idem / Consent to be filed.

477.2 (1) No proceedings in respect of an offence committed in or on the territorial sea of Canada shall be continued unless the consent of the Attorney General of Canada is obtained not later than eight days after the proceedings are commenced, if the accused is not a Canadian citizen and the offence is alleged to have been committed on board any ship registered outside Canada.

(1.1) Subsection (1) does not apply to proceedings by way of summary conviction.

(2) No proceedings in respect of which courts have jurisdiction by virtue only of paragraph 477.1(*a*) or (*b*) shall be continued unless the consent of the Attorney General of Canada is obtained not later than eight days after the proceedings are commenced, if the accused is not a Canadian citizen and the offence is alleged to have been committed on board any ship registered outside Canada.

(3) No proceedings in respect of which courts have jurisdiction by virtue only of paragraph 477.1(*d*) or (*e*) shall be continued unless the consent of the Attorney General of Canada is obtained not later than eight days after the proceedings are commenced.

(4) The consent of the Attorney General required by subsection (1), (2) or (3) must be filed with the clerk of the court in which the proceedings have been instituted. 1990, c. 44, s. 15; 1994, c. 44, s. 32; 1996, c. 31, s. 69.

ANNOTATIONS

Note: Some of the following cases were decided prior to the re-enactment of this section but were considered of assistance in interpreting this section.

Where consent required – Consent is required where the offence is a hybrid offence for such offence is deemed to be indictable by s. 34(1) of the *Interpretation Act*, R.S.C. 1985, c. I-21: *R. v. Gallagher* (1981), 62 C.C.C. (2d) 3 (B.C. Co. Ct.).

There must at least be some evidence in the case to indicate that the accused is not a Canadian citizen before the Crown must prove that the accused was a Canadian citizen and that the consent of the Attorney General was not required: *R. v. Erickson* (1989), 49 C.C.C. (3d) 33, 14 M.V.R. (2d) 122 (B.C.C.A.), leave to appeal to S.C.C. refused 50 C.C.C. (3d) vi, 104 N.R. 109*n*.

Proof of consent – Failure to obtain the necessary consent will result in a conviction being quashed: *R. v. Ford; R. v. Gilkey* (1956), 115 C.C.C. 113, 18 W.W.R. 563 (B.C.C.A.).

The decision to consent under this section is not an administrative decision which can be delegated to an official such as the Assistant Deputy Attorney General: *R. v. Sunila* (1987), 35 C.C.C. (3d) 289, 78 N.S.R. (2d) 24 (S.C. App. Div.).

A consent given by the Deputy Attorney General is valid in view of the provision of s. 24(2)(*c*) of the *Interpretation Act*, R.S.C. 1985, c. I-21. Further, a consent referring to a charge of "murder" was sufficient to permit trial of the accused on a charge of first degree murder, there being nothing to indicate that the consent was restricted to a charge of second degree murder: *R. v. Frisbee* (1989), 48 C.C.C. (3d) 386 (B.C.C.A.) , leave to appeal to S.C.C. refused 50 C.C.C. (3d) vi.

An objection to the validity of the form of consent cannot be raised for the first time near the conclusion of the trial just prior to the charge to the jury: *R. v. Sunila* (1987), 35 C.C.C. (3d) 289, 78 N.S.R. (2d) 24 (S.C. App. Div.).

EXERCISING POWERS OF ARREST, ENTRY, ETC. / Arrest, search, seizure, etc. / Limitation.

477.3 (1) Every power of arrest, entry, search or seizure or other power that could be exercised in Canada in respect of an act or omission referred to in section 477.1 may be exercised, in the circumstances referred to in that section.

- **(*a*) at the place or on board the ship or marine installation or structure, within the meaning of section 2 of the *Oceans Act*, where the act or omission occurred; or**
- **(*b*) where hot pursuit has been commenced, at any place on the seas, other than a place that is part of the territorial sea of any other state.**

(2) A justice or judge in any territorial division in Canada has jurisdiction to authorize an arrest, entry, search or seizure or an investigation or other ancillary matter related to an offence

- **(*a*) committed in or on the territorial sea of Canada or any area of the sea that forms part of the internal waters of Canada, or**
- **(*b*) referred to in section 477.1 in the same manner as if the offence had been committed in that territorial division.**

(3) Where an act or omission that is an offence by virtue only of section 477.1 is alleged to have been committed on board any ship registered outside Canada, the powers referred to in subsection (1) shall not be exercised outside Canada with respect to that act or omission without the consent of the Attorney General of Canada. 1990, c. 44, s. 15; 1996, c. 31, s. 70.

CROSS-REFERENCES

"Justice" is defined in s. 2. For other cross-references respecting jurisdiction for offences committed outside Canada, see the notes following s. 477.1. For references to powers of search, entry and arrest generally see notes following ss. 487, 529 and 495, respectively.

SYNOPSIS

This section sets out the powers of arrest, search, seizure and entry that may be exercised in relation to offences mentioned in s. 477.1. Note that pursuant to subsec. (3), where the offence is alleged to have been committed on board any ship registered outside Canada, the powers of arrest, search, seizure and entry shall not be exercised outside Canada without the consent of the Attorney General of Canada.

ANNOTATIONS

In *R. v. Macooh*, [1993] 2 S.C.R. 802, 82 C.C.C. (3d) 481, 22 C.R. (4th) 70, the court adopted the definition of "hot pursuit" suggested by R.E. Salhany in *Canadian Criminal Procedure*, 5th ed. (Aurora, Ontario: Canada Law Book Inc., 1989), p. 44: "Generally, the essence of fresh pursuit is that it must be continuous pursuit conducted with reasonable diligence, so that pursuit and capture along with the commission of the offence may be considered as forming part of a single transaction."

TERRITORIAL DIVISION FOR PROSECUTION / Evidence / Certificate cannot be compelled.

477.4 (1) [*Repealed*, 1996, c. 31, s. 71.]

(2) [*Repealed*, 1996, c. 31, s. 71.]

(3) In proceedings in respect of an offence,

(*a*) a certificate referred to in subsection 23(1) of the *Oceans Act*, or

(*b*) a certificate issued by or under the authority of the Minister of Foreign Affairs containing a statement that any geographical location specified in the certificate was, at any time material to the proceedings, in an area of a fishing zone of Canada that is not within the internal waters of Canada or the territorial sea of Canada or outside the territory of any state,

is conclusive proof of the truth of the statement without proof of the signature or official character of the person appearing to have issued the certificate.

(4) A certificate referred to in subsection (3) is admissible in evidence in proceedings referred to in that subsection but its production cannot be compelled. 1990, c. 44, s. 15; 1995, c. 5, s. 25; 1996, c. 31, s. 71.

CROSS-REFERENCES

Section 23(1) of the *Oceans Act*, S.C. 1996, c. 31, provides as follows:

> 23(1) In any legal or other proceedings, a certificate issued by or under the authority of the Minister of Foreign Affairs containing a statement that any geographic location specified in the certificate was, at any time material to the proceedings,
>
> (*a*) in the internal waters of Canada,
>
> (*b*) in the territorial sea of Canada,
>
> (*c*) in the contiguous zone of Canada,
>
> (*d*) in the exclusive economic zone of Canada, or
>
> (*e*) or above the continental shelf of Canada
>
> is conclusive proof of the truth of the statement without proof of the signature or official character of the person appearing to have issued the certificate.

For other cross-references respecting jurisdiction over offences committed outside Canada, see the notes following s. 477.1.

OFFENCE COMMITTED ENTIRELY IN ONE PROVINCE / Exception / Idem / Where accused committed to stand trial / Definition of "newspaper".

478. (1) Subject to this Act, a court in a province shall not try an offence committed entirely in another province.

(2) Every proprietor, publisher, editor or other person charged with the publication of a defamatory libel in a newspaper or with conspiracy to publish a defamatory libel in a newspaper shall be dealt with, indicted, tried and punished in the province where he resides or in which the newspaper is printed.

(3) An accused who is charged with an offence that is alleged to have been committed in Canada outside the province in which the accused is, may, if the offence is not an offence mentioned in section 469 and

(*a*) in the case of proceedings instituted at the instance of the Government of Canada and conducted by or on behalf of that Government, if the Attorney General of Canada consents, or

(*b*) in any other case, if the Attorney General of the province where the offence is alleged to have been committed consents,

appear before a court or judge that would have had jurisdiction to try that offence if it had been committed in the province where the accused is, and where the accused consents to plead guilty and pleads guilty to that offence, the court or judge shall determine the accused to be guilty of the offence and impose the punishment warranted by law, but where the accused does not consent to plead guilty and does not plead guilty, the accused shall, if the accused was in custody prior to appearance, be returned to custody and shall be dealt with according to law.

(4) Notwithstanding that an accused described in subsection (3) has been ordered to stand trial or that an indictment has been preferred against the accused in respect of the offence to which he desires to plead guilty, the accused shall be deemed simply to stand charged of that offence without a preliminary inquiry having been conducted or an indictment having been preferred with respect thereto.

(5) In this section, "newspaper" has the same meaning as in section 297. R.S., c. C-34, s. 434; 1974-75-76, c. 93, s. 40; R.S.C. 1985, c. 27 (1st Supp.), ss. 64, 101(3); 1994, c. 44, s. 33.

CROSS-REFERENCES

The term "province" is defined in s. 35 of the *Interpretation Act*, R.S.C. 1985, c. I-21. "Attorney General" is defined in s. 2. Section 583(*h*) provides that a count in an indictment is not insufficient by reason only that it does not state that the required consent has been obtained. [As to notes concerning sufficiency of consent, see s. 583.] Defamatory libel is dealt with under ss. 297 to 317. A related provision for transfer of charges between territorial divisions within the same province is in s. 479. Respecting transfer of probation orders between provinces, see s. 739. For other notes respecting territorial jurisdiction, see cross-references under ss. 6, 7 and 470.

SYNOPSIS

This section deals with offences committed within the jurisdiction of one province.

Subsection (1) provides that subject to exceptions found within the Code, a court in one province shall not try an offence entirely committed in another province.

Subsection (2) states that any person charged with the offence of publishing, or conspiring to publish, a defamatory libel in a newspaper must deal with in the province where he resides or where the newspaper is printed.

Subsection (3) provides that any person charged with an offence, other than an offence listed in s. 469, that is alleged to have been committed outside the province in which that person is, may plead guilty before a court having jurisdiction over the offence in that province and be sentenced in that location. The appropriate Attorney General must consent to this procedure.

Subsection (4) makes it clear that an accused person pleading guilty under subsec. (3), whether or not he has been ordered to stand trial, or an indictment has been preferred against him in the province where the offence was committed, shall be deemed to stand charged of that offence in the province in which the plea is entered without a preliminary inquiry having been held or an indictment preferred.

Subsection (5) gives the term "newspaper" the same meaning as is found in s. 297.

ANNOTATIONS

Subsection (1) – In determining jurisdiction it is questionable whether civil law should be employed to locate the *actus reus,* particularly where the offence is of a continuing character that might occur in more than one jurisdiction: *R. v. Trudel, ex p. Horbas and Myhaluk,* [1969] 3 C.C.C. 95, 5 C.R.N.S. 342 *sub nom. R. v. Horbas and Myhaluk* (Man. C.A.).

Subsection (3) – The authorities of one province did not notify the accused of an indictable offence warrant that they held for him while he was being tried, convicted and then serving his sentence in another province for other offences committed there. Upon appeal against the sentence finally imposed upon him when he was brought back for trial some years later the appellate court indicated its disapproval of this procedure by substantially reducing the sentence: *R. v. Parisien* (1971), 3 C.C.C. (2d) 433, [1971] 4 W.W.R. 81 (B.C.C.A.).

If the accused can show that the exercise of the discretion by the Attorney General to refuse to consent to the transfer is arbitrary, then the accused would be entitled to a remedy under s. 24 of the Charter on the basis that there has been an infringement of s. 7 of the Charter. However, if reasonable grounds exist for the exercise of the discretion one way or another and there has been a fair consideration as to whether, or in what way, the discretion should be exercised, the ultimate decision cannot be said to be arbitrary. In this case, Crown counsel provided the accused with a letter setting out several valid reasons for refusing to consent to the transfer including that, as a general rule, the accused should be sentenced in the community where the offence occurred in order for the deterrent affect of that sentence; disposition of the offence in the jurisdiction where it arose will most likely ensure the application of local provincial sentencing standards for like defences; and the more serious the offence the more appropriate it is to dispose of the case where the offence occurred: *R. v. Fleming* (1992), 72 C.C.C. (3d) 133 (Man. Q.B.).

OFFENCE OUTSTANDING IN SAME PROVINCE.

479. Where an accused is charged with an offence that is alleged to have been committed in the province in which he is, he may, if the offence is not an offence mentioned in section 469, and

- **(*a*) in the case of proceedings instituted at the instance of the Government of Canada and conducted by or on behalf of that Government, the Attorney General of Canada consents, or**
- **(*b*) in any other case, the Attorney General of the province where the offence is alleged to have been committed consents,**

appear before a court or judge that would have had jurisdiction to try that offence if it had been committed in the place where the accused is, and where the accused consents to plead guilty and pleads guilty to that offence, the court or judge shall determine the accused to be guilty of the offence and impose the punishment warranted by law, but where the accused does not consent to plead guilty and does not plead guilty, the accused shall, if the accused was in custody prior to his appearance, be returned to custody and shall be dealt with according to law. R.S., c. C-34, s. 435; 1974-75-76, c. 93, s. 41; R.S.C. 1985, c. 27 (1st Supp.), s. 65; 1994, c. 44, s. 34.

CROSS-REFERENCES

"Attorney General" is defined in s. 2. Section 583(*h*) provides that a count in an indictment is not insufficient by reason only that it does not state that the required consent has been obtained. [As to notes concerning sufficiency of consent, see s. 583.] For a related provision for transfer of charges between provinces, see s. 478. For other notes respecting territorial jurisdiction, see cross-references under ss. 6, 7 and 470. Change of venue for trial within the province but in another territorial division is governed by s. 599.

SYNOPSIS

This section allows an accused person to plead guilty to an offence, other than the one listed in s. 469, before a court or a judge within the province where the offence was committed but not within the territorial division of that province having jurisdiction over the offender. The appropriate Attorney General must consent to this procedure and the accused must, in fact, plead guilty to the offence.

OFFENCE IN UNORGANIZED TERRITORY / New territorial division.

480. (1) Where an offence is committed in an unorganized tract of country in any province or on a lake, river or other water therein, not included in a territorial division or in a provisional judicial district, proceedings in respect thereof may be commenced and an accused may be charged, tried and punished in respect thereof within any territorial division or provisional judicial district of the province in the same manner as if the offence had been committed within that territorial division or provisional judicial district.

(2) Where a provisional judicial district or a new territorial division is constituted in an unorganized tract referred to in subsection (1), the jurisdiction conferred by that subsection continues until appropriate provision is made by law for the administration of criminal justice within the provisional judicial district or new territorial division. R.S., c. C-34, s. 436.

CROSS-REFERENCES

The term "territorial division" is defined in s. 2. The term "province" is defined in s. 35 of the *Interpretation Act*, R.S.C. 1985, c. I-21. Also see s. 481 and for other notes respecting territorial jurisdiction, see cross-references under ss. 6, 7 and 470.

SYNOPSIS

This section clarifies jurisdiction in situations where an offence is committed in an unorganized tract in any province that is not included in a territorial division or provisional judicial district.

Subsection (1) states that the trial of an offence committed in such a location may take place in any territorial division or provisional judicial district in that province.

Subsection (2) provides that when a provincial judicial district or new territorial division is constituted in an unorganized tract, subsec. (1) will continue to apply until provision for the administration of justice within that division or district is made.

OFFENCE NOT IN A PROVINCE.

481. Where an offence is committed in a part of Canada not in a province, proceedings in respect thereof may be commenced and the accused may be charged, tried and punished within any territorial division in any province in the same manner as if that offence had been committed in that territorial division. R.S., c. C-34, s. 437.

CROSS-REFERENCES

The term "territorial division" is defined in s. 2. The term "province" is defined in s. 35 of the *Interpretation Act*, R.S.C. 1985, c. I-21. Also see s. 480 and for other notes respecting territorial jurisdiction, see cross-references under ss. 6, 7 and 470.

SYNOPSIS

This section provides that an accused who commits an offence in a part of Canada which is not a province may be tried and punished within any territorial division in any province of Canada.

OFFENCE IN CANADIAN WATERS.

481.1 Where an offence is committed in or on the territorial sea of Canada or any area of the sea that forms part of the internal waters of Canada, proceedings in respect thereof may, whether or not the accused is in Canada, be commenced and an accused may be charged, tried and punished within any territorial division in Canada in the same manner as if the offence had been committed in that territorial division. 1996, c. 31, s. 72.

CROSS-REFERENCES

The definition of territorial sea is in the *Territorial Sea and Fishing Zones Act*, R.S.C. 1985, T-8. "Attorney General" is defined in s. 2. See s. 477.2 as to when the consent of the Attorney General is required. Section 583(*h*) provides that a count in an indictment is not insufficient by reason only that it does not state that the required consent has been obtained. [As to other notes concerning sufficiency of consent, see s. 583.] The term "Canadian ship" is defined in s. 2 of the *Canada Shipping Act*, R.S.C. 1985, c. S-9. For definition of Canadian citizen, see *Citizenship Act*, R.S.C. 1985, c. C-29. For other notes respecting territorial jurisdiction, see cross-references under ss. 6, 7 and 470.

SYNOPSIS

This section states that where an offence is committed by any person on Canadian seas or waters off the Canadian coast, whether or not such offence was committed on a Canadian ship, the offence is within the jurisdiction of Canadian law. The offence will be tried in the same manner as it had been committed in that territorial jurisdiction.

ANNOTATIONS

This section gives Canadian courts jurisdiction to try offences committed on the territorial sea of Canada, although neither the accused nor the victim are Canadian citizens and the offence was committed on a foreign ship. This section is not limited to offences having extraterritorial effect such as piracy: *R. v. Frisbee* (1989), 48 C.C.C. (3d) 386 (B.C.C.A.), leave to appeal to S.C.C. refused 50 C.C.C. (3d) vi.

OFFENCE OUTSIDE CANADA.

481.2 Subject to this or any other Act of Parliament, where an act or omission is committed outside Canada and the act or omission is an offence when committed outside Canada under this or any other Act of Parliament, proceedings in respect of the offence may, whether or not the accused is in Canada, be commenced, and an accused may be charged, tried and punished within any territorial division in Canada in the same manner as if the offence had been committed in that territorial division. 1996, c. 31, s. 72; 2008, c. 18, s. 10.

CROSS-REFERENCES

A number of provisions of this Act and other federal legislation provide that an act or omission committed outside Canada is an offence in Canada. Many of the provisions are found in s. 7, which contains a provision similar to this in s. 7(5). Similarly, see s. 481.1 for offences committed on the territorial sea or the internal waters of Canada. Where this section applies, the provisions of the *Criminal Code* for the requirement of the appearance of the accused at proceedings apply, pursuant to s. 481.3.

APPEARANCE OF ACCUSED AT TRIAL.

481.3 For greater certainty, the provisions of this Act relating to

(*a*) the requirement of the appearance of an accused at proceedings, and

(*b*) the exceptions to that requirement

apply to proceedings commenced in any territorial division pursuant to section 481, 481.1 or 481.2. 1996, c. 31, s. 72.

Rules of Court

POWER TO MAKE RULES / Idem / Purpose of rules / Publication / Regulations to secure uniformity.

482. (1) Every superior court of criminal jurisdiction and every court of appeal may make rules of court not inconsistent with this or any other Act of Parliament, and any rules so made apply to any prosecution, proceeding, action or appeal, as the case may be, within the jurisdiction of that court, instituted in relation to any matter of a criminal nature or arising from or incidental to any such prosecution, proceeding, action or appeal.

(2) The following courts may, subject to the approval of the lieutenant governor in council of the relevant province, make rules of court not inconsistent with this Act or any other Act of Parliament that are applicable to any prosecution, proceeding, including a preliminary inquiry or proceedings within the meaning of Part XXVII, action or appeal, as the case may be, within the jurisdiction of that court, instituted in relation to any matter of a criminal nature or arising from or incidental to the prosecution, proceeding, action or appeal:

(*a*) every court of criminal jurisdiction for a province;

(*b*) every appeal court within the meaning of section 812 that is not a court referred to in subsection (1);

(*c*) the Ontario Court of Justice;

(*d*) the Court of Quebec and every municipal court in the Province of Quebec;

(*e*) the Provincial Court of Nova Scotia;

(*f*) the Provincial Court of New Brunswick;

(*g*) the Provincial Court of Manitoba;

(*h*) the Provincial Court of British Columbia;

(*i*) the Provincial Court of Prince Edward Island;

(*j*) the Provincial Court of Saskatchewan;

(*k*) the Provincial Court of Alberta;

(*l*) the Provincial Court of Newfoundland and Labrador;

(*m*) the Territorial Court of Yukon;

(*n*) the Territorial Court of the Northwest Territories; and

(*o*) the Nunavut Court of Justice.

(3) Rules under subsection (1) or (2) may be made

(*a*) generally to regulate the duties of the officers of the court and any other matter considered expedient to attain the ends of justice and carry into effect the provisions of the law;

(*b*) to regulate the sittings of the court or any division thereof, or of any judge of the court sitting in chambers, except in so far as they are regulated by law;

(*c*) to regulate the pleading, practice and procedure in criminal matters, including pre-hearing conferences held under section 625.1, proceedings with respect to judicial interim release and preliminary inquiries and, in the case of rules under subsection (1), proceedings with respect to mandamus, certiorari, habeas corpus, prohibition and procedendo and proceedings on an appeal under section 830; and

(*d*) to carry out the provisions of this Act relating to appeals from conviction, acquittal or sentence and, without restricting the generality of this paragraph,

(i) for furnishing necessary forms and instructions in relation to notices of appeal or applications for leave to appeal to officials or other persons requiring or demanding them,

(ii) for ensuring the accuracy of notes taken at a trial and the verification of any copy or transcript,

(iii) for keeping writings, exhibits or other things connected with the proceedings on the trial,

(iv) for securing the safe custody of property during the period in which the operation of an order with respect to that property is suspended under subsection 689(1), and

(v) for providing that the Attorney General and counsel who acted for the Attorney General at the trial be supplied with certified copies of writings, exhibits and things connected with the proceedings that are required for the purposes of their duties.

(4) Rules of court that are made under the authority of this section shall be published in the *Canada Gazette*.

(5) Notwithstanding anything in this section, the Governor in Council may make such provision as he considers proper to secure uniformity in the rules of court in criminal matters, and all uniform rules made under the authority of this subsection prevail and have effect as if enacted by this Act. R.S., c. C-34, s. 438; 1974-75-76, c. 93, s. 42; R.S.C. 1985, c. 27 (1st Supp.), s. 66; 1994, c. 44, s. 35; 2002, c. 13, s. 17; 2015, c. 3, s. 50.

CROSS-REFERENCES

The terms "Attorney General", "superior court of criminal jurisdiction", "court of appeal", "court of criminal jurisdiction" and "writing" are defined in s. 2. Section 745.5 makes separate provision for making of rules of procedure on applications for review of parole ineligibility of a person convicted of murder.

Where rules made under this section provide that the accused need not appear personally, by virtue of s. 485, jurisdiction over the person is not lost. Section 482.1 gives the courts mentioned in this section the power to make case management rules.

SYNOPSIS

Subsection (1) provides that every superior court of criminal jurisdiction and every court of appeal may make rules of court in relation to any criminal proceedings or matters incidental to a prosecution arising before it.

Subsection (2) states that every court of criminal jurisdiction for a province, every appeal court within the meaning of s. 812 that is not a court referred to in subsec. (1) and the trial courts that are not the superior court of justice, such as the provincial court, may, with the approval of the Lieutenant Governor in Council of the province, make similar rules that are applicable to any prosecution, proceeding, including a preliminary inquiry or summary conviction proceedings, action or appeal, as the case may be, within the jurisdiction of that court, instituted in relation to any matter of a criminal nature or arising from or incidental to the prosecution, proceeding, action or appeal. The rules made under both subsecs. (1) and (2) may not be inconsistent with the Code or any other Act of Parliament.

Subsection (3) sets out the matters which such rules may regulate and subsec. (4) requires publication of the rules in the Canada Gazette. Subsection (5) empowers the Governor in Council to ensure uniformity of the rules of court in criminal matters and any uniform rules made under this subsection prevail.

ANNOTATIONS

In *R. v. Jacobs*, [1971] S.C.R. 92, 2 C.C.C. (2d) 26, the Que. C.A. had, on March 24, 1969, dismissed the accused's appeal when his counsel failed to appear to argue the appeal. Subsequently, on April 18, 1969, the court rescinded its order, and from that order the Crown appealed. It was held (5:0) that both of the Appeal Court orders, neither of which dealt with the merits of the accused's appeal, were made in the exercise of its discretionary power relating to practice concerning the proper administration of justice in criminal matters.

While subsec. (3)(*c*) does not authorize the making of rules which would permit the court to award costs on an application for *habeas corpus,* in a criminal matter the Superior Court has the power to award costs by virtue of its inherent jurisdiction to control proceedings, to penalize abuses and to maintain its authority. However, the power to award costs arises only in circumstances similar to a contempt of court, such as misconduct or dishonesty by a party, or a serious interference with the administration of justice: *Quebec (Attorney General) v. Cronier* (1981), 63 C.C.C. (2d) 437 (Que. C.A.).

Similarly, while the Superior Court has an inherent jurisdiction to award costs against the inferior court, the power is to be used sparingly and only where the circumstances were akin to a contempt of court or reveal malice or bad faith thereby creating a flagrant injustice. Moreover, before the order is made the judge of the inferior court is entitled to notice and an opportunity to be heard on the question of costs: *Mayrand v. Cronier* (1981), 63 C.C.C. (2d) 561 (Que. C.A.).

POWER TO MAKE RULES RESPECTING CASE MANAGEMENT / Compliance with directions / Summons or warrant / Provisions to apply / Approval of lieutenant governor in council / Subsections 482(4) and (5) to apply.

482.1 (1) A court referred to in subsection 482(1) or (2) may make rules for case management, including rules

- **(*a*) for the determination of any matter that would assist the court in effective and efficient case management;**
- **(*b*) permitting personnel of the court to deal with administrative matters relating to proceedings out of court if the accused is represented by counsel; and**
- **(*c*) establishing case management schedules.**

(2) The parties to a case shall comply with any direction made in accordance with a rule made under subsection (1).

(3) If rules are made under subsection (1), a court, justice or judge may issue a summons or warrant to compel the presence of the accused at case management proceedings.

(4) Section 512 and subsection 524(1) apply, with any modifications that the circumstances require, to the issuance of a summons or a warrant under subsection (3).

(5) Rules made under this section by a court referred to in subsection 482(2) must be approved by the lieutenant governor in council of the relevant province in order to come into force.

(6) Subsections 482(4) and (5) apply, with any modifications that the circumstances require, to rules made under subsection (1). 2002, c. 13, s. 18.

CROSS-REFERENCES

The general power to make rules is set out in s. 482. By virtue of s. 485, where rules made under this section provide that the accused need not appear personally, jurisdiction over the person is not lost.

SYNOPSIS

This section gives all trial and appellate courts the powers to make case management rules in respect of proceedings in those courts. Importantly, the court is given the power to make rules delegating certain administrative tasks to court personnel, provided the accused is represented by counsel. The parties are required to comply with any directions made in accordance with the rules and the court may issue a summons or warrant to ensure the attendance of the accused at a case management conference. Where the rules are not made by the Court of Appeal or a superior court of criminal jurisdiction, they must be approved by the lieutenant governor in council in order to come into force. The rules must be published in the Canada Gazette and the Governor in Council must make such provisions as considered necessary to ensure uniformity of the rules of court in criminal matters and any uniform rules prevail.

Part XV / SPECIAL PROCEDURE AND POWERS

General Powers of Certain Officials

OFFICIALS WITH POWERS OF TWO JUSTICES.

483. Every judge or provincial court judge authorized by the law of the province in which he is appointed to do anything that is required to be done by two or more justices may do alone anything that this Act or any other Act of Parliament authorizes two or more justices to do. R.S., c. C-34, s. 439.

CROSS-REFERENCES

The terms "provincial court judge" and "justice" are defined in s. 2.

SYNOPSIS

This section authorizes every judge or provincial court judge who is authorized by the law of a province to do anything required to be done by two or more justices to also act in the place of two or more justices when such a provision is found in the Code or any other Act of Parliament.

PRESERVING ORDER IN COURT.

484. Every judge or provincial court judge has the same power and authority to preserve order in a court over which he presides as may be exercised by the superior court of criminal jurisdiction of the province during the sittings thereof. R.S., c. C-34, s. 440.

CROSS-REFERENCES

The terms "provincial court judge", "justice" and "superior court of criminal jurisdiction" are defined in s. 2.

For notes on the common law power over contempt of court, see notes following ss. 9 and 10.

SYNOPSIS

This section gives to every judge or provincial court judge the same power as may be exercised by the superior court of criminal jurisdiction to preserve order during the sittings of courts over which they preside.

ANNOTATIONS

A provincial court judge has the power to punish for contempt on preliminary inquiry a person who refused to rise when the Court was called to order: *R. v. Hume, ex p. Hawkins*, [1966] 3 C.C.C. 43, 53 D.L.R. (2d) 453, 53 W.W.R. 406 *sub nom. Hawkins Habeas Corpus Application (Re)* (B.C.S.C.).

This section gives a provincial court judge presiding at a preliminary hearing power to convict for contempt in the face of the court where required to preserve order in the court. Thus, a counsel's refusal despite the judge's order to remove a tape recorder from the court room during a preliminary hearing could in certain circumstances amount to contempt: *R. v. Barker* (1980), 53 C.C.C. (2d) 322, [1980] 4 W.W.R. 202 (Alta. C.A.).

This section gives a provincial court judge power to cite for contempt an accused who appears for his trial in such an intoxicated condition that the trial is unable to proceed: *R. v. Heer* (1982), 68 C.C.C. (2d) 333, 38 B.C.L.R. 176 (S.C.).

Under this section one judge of the Alberta Provincial Court has no jurisdiction to try a contempt of court charge initiated by another judge as a result of conduct by the accused committed in the face of the court: *R. v. Doz*, [1987] 2 S.C.R. 463, 38 C.C.C. (3d) 479, 55 Alta. L.R. (2d) 289 (7:0).

The words "order in a court" do not embrace a refusal by a witness to testify and thus this section cannot be invoked to authorize a provincial court judge presiding at a preliminary hearing to punish such refusal as a contempt of court. The judge's only power in such circumstances is to use the procedure in s. 545: *R. v. Bubley* (1976), 32 C.C.C. (2d) 79, [1976] 6 W.W.R. 179 (Alta. S.C. App. Div.).

PROCEDURAL IRREGULARITIES / Where accused not present / Summons or warrant / Dismissal for want of prosecution / Adjournment and order / Part XVI to apply.

485. (1) Jurisdiction over an offence is not lost by reason of the failure of any court, judge, provincial court judge or justice to act in the exercise of that jurisdiction at any particular time, or by reason of a failure to comply with any of the provisions of this Act respecting adjournments or remands.

(1.1) Jurisdiction over an accused is not lost by reason of the failure of the accused to appear personally, so long as subsection 515(2.2), paragraph 537(1)(*j*), (*j*.1) or (*k*), subsection 650(1.1) or (1.2), paragraph 650(2)(*b*) or 650.01(3)(*a*), subsection 683(2.1) or 688(2.1) or a rule of court made under section 482 or 482.1 applies.

(2) Where jurisdiction over an accused or a defendant is lost and has not been regained, a court, judge, provincial court judge or justice may, within three months after the loss of jurisdiction, issue a summons, or if it or he considers it necessary in the public interest, a warrant for the arrest of the accused or defendant.

(3) Where no summons or warrant is issued under subsection (2) within the period provided therein, the proceedings shall be deemed to be dismissed for want of prosecution and shall not be recommenced except in accordance with section 485.1.

(4) Where, in the opinion of the court, judge, provincial court judge or justice, an accused or a defendant who appears at a proceeding has been misled or prejudiced by reason of any matter referred to in subsection (1), the court, judge, provincial court judge or justice may adjourn the proceeding and may make such order as it or he considers appropriate.

(5) The provisions of Part XVI apply with such modifications as the circumstances require where a summons or warrant is issued under subsection (2). 1974-75-76, c. 93, s. 43; R.S.C. 1985, c. 27 (1st Supp.), s. 67; 1997, c. 18, s. 40; 2002, c. 13, s. 19.

CROSS-REFERENCES

The terms "provincial court judge" and "justice" are defined in s. 2.

Calculation of a period of months is determined in accordance with s. 28 of the *Interpretation Act*, R.S.C. 1985, c. I-21.

SYNOPSIS

This section deals with specific examples of procedural irregularities as they relate to jurisdiction over the offender and the offence.

Subsection (1) states that jurisdiction over an offence is not lost when the court fails to exercise jurisdiction at any particular time, or when it fails to comply with any of the provisions in the Code with respect to adjournments or remands.

Subsection (1.1) provides that jurisdiction over the person is not lost at the preliminary inquiry or the trial where the person was to appear by counsel or appear by video or similar system as permitted in the sections listed in the subsection or by a rule of court made under ss. 482 or 482.1.

Subsection (2) empowers a court to issue a summons or, if necessary in the public interest, a warrant for the arrest of an accused person within three months after jurisdiction over that person has been lost and has not been regained.

Subsection (3) states that if no summons or warrant is issued within the three-month period stipulated in subsec. (2), the proceedings shall be deemed dismissed for want of prosecution. Such proceedings cannot be reinstituted except in accordance with s. 485.1.

Subsection (4) empowers a court to adjourn a proceeding and make such order as is considered appropriate when it appears that an accused person has been misled or prejudiced by reason of any matter referred to in subsec. (1).

Subsection (5) provides that the provisions of Part XVI, which deal with compelling the appearance of an accused before a justice and interim release, apply with the necessary modifications when a summons or warrant is issued under subsec. (2).

ANNOTATIONS

This section was applied to cure a failure to comply with [former] s. 537(1)(a), the preliminary hearing having been adjourned for longer than eight days without the accused's consent. The court noted that *R. v. Doyle*, [1977] 1 S.C.R. 597, 29 C.C.C. (2d) 177, 68 D.L.R. (3d) 270, which held that adjourning a case for longer than eight days without the accused's consent resulted in a loss of jurisdiction over the person of the accused, was decided at a time when this section did not apply: *R. v. Ulrich* (1977), 38 C.C.C. (2d) 1, [1978] 1 W.W.R. 422 (Alta. S.C.T.D.).

It was held in *R. v. Krannenburg*, [1980] 1 S.C.R. 1053, 51 C.C.C. (2d) 205, 17 C.R. (3d) 357 (7:0), that the predecessor to this section could not cure a loss of jurisdiction which resulted when there was a proper adjournment to a fixed day but upon that day nothing happened. The court distinguished between a loss of jurisdiction "over the person" such as a remand in excess of eight days without consent, and a loss of jurisdiction "over the offence" when nothing is done on the return date of a proper adjournment. However, the recent amendment to this section with the addition of the reference to the failure to exercise jurisdiction at any particular time, may well cover the loss of jurisdiction dealt with in *R. v. Krannenburg*.

Where an accused did not appear, and nothing was done on the return date of an adjournment because the accused, on being remanded to a hospital for observation had been found unfit and not returned to court, the court regained jurisdiction over him on a subsequent appearance one month later. *R. v. Fogarty* (1988), 46 C.C.C. (3d) 289 (N.S.C.A.).

RECOMMENCEMENT WHERE DISMISSAL FOR WANT OF PROSECUTION.

485.1 Where an indictment in respect of a transaction is dismissed or deemed by any provision of this Act to be dismissed for want of prosecution, a new information shall not be laid and a new indictment shall not be preferred before any court in respect of the same transaction without

(*a*) the personal consent in writing of the Attorney General or Deputy Attorney General, in any prosecution conducted by the Attorney General or in which the Attorney General intervenes; or

(*b*) the written order of a judge of that court, in any prosecution conducted by a prosecutor other than the Attorney General and in which the Attorney General does not intervene. R.S.C. 1985, c. 27 (1st Supp.), s. 67.

CROSS-REFERENCES

The terms "indictment" and "prosecutor" are defined in s. 2. The latter term is also defined in s. 785 for summary conviction proceedings.

SYNOPSIS

This section sets out the circumstances under which a proceeding may be recommenced after it has been dismissed for want of prosecution. No new information can be laid, or indictment preferred, in this situation unless the personal written consent of the Attorney General or the Deputy Attorney General is obtained, or, in the case of a matter that is not prosecuted by the Attorney General and in which the Attorney General has not intervened, a judge of the relevant court issues a written order.

ANNOTATIONS

This section does not apply where the indictment is quashed by the trial judge for failing to comply with the sufficiency requirements of s. 581. Thus the Attorney General's consent is not required to lay a new information: *R. v. Richardson* (1987), 39 C.C.C. (3d) 262 (N.S.C.A.).

Although the charges which were initially dismissed for want of prosecution were laid by a private prosecutor, the Attorney General may consent to the laying of a new information by agents of the Crown: *R. v. Proctor & Gamble Inc.* (1993), 82 C.C.C. (3d) 477 (Alta. C.A.).

EXCLUSION OF PUBLIC / Application / Factors to be considered / Reasons to be stated / No adverse inference.

486. (1) Any proceedings against an accused shall be held in open court, but the presiding judge or justice may, on application of the prosecutor or a witness or on his or her own motion, order the exclusion of all or any members of the public from the court room for all or part of the proceedings, or order that the witness testify behind a screen or other device that would allow the witness not to be seen by members of the public, if the judge or justice is of the opinion that such an order is in the interest of public morals, the maintenance of order or the proper administration of justice or is necessary to prevent injury to international relations or national defence or national security.

(1.1) The application may be made, during the proceedings, to the presiding judge or justice or, before the proceedings begin, to the judge or justice who will preside at the proceedings or, if that judge or justice has not been determined, to any judge or justice having jurisdiction in the judicial district where the proceedings will take place.

(2) In determining whether the order is in the interest of the proper administration of justice, the judge or justice shall consider

(*a*) society's interest in encouraging the reporting of offences and the participation of victims and witnesses in the criminal justice process;

(*b*) the safeguarding of the interests of witnesses under the age of 18 years in all proceedings;

(*c*) the ability of the witness to give a full and candid account of the acts complained of if the order were not made;

(*d*) whether the witness needs the order for their security or to protect them from intimidation or retaliation;

(*e*) the protection of justice system participants who are involved in the proceedings;

(*f*) whether effective alternatives to the making of the proposed order are available in the circumstances;

(*g*) the salutary and deleterious effects of the proposed order; and

(*h*) any other factor that the judge or justice considers relevant.

(3) If an accused is charged with an offence under section 151, 152, 153, 153.1, 155 or 159, subsection 160(2) or (3) or section 163.1, 170, 171, 171.1, 172, 172.1, 172.2, 173, 271, 272, 273, 279.01, 279.011, 279.02, 279.03, 286.1, 286.2, 286.3 and the prosecutor or the accused applies for an order under subsection (1), the judge or justice shall, if no such order is made, state, by reference to the circumstances of the case, the reason for not making an order.

(4) No adverse inference may be drawn from the fact that an order is, or is not, made under this section. R.S., c. C-34, s. 442; 1974-75-76, c. 93, s. 44; 1980-81-82-83, c. 110, s. 74, c. 125, s. 25; R.S.C. 1985, c. 19 (3rd Supp.), s. 14; c. 23 (4th Supp.), s. 1; 1992, c. 21, s. 9; 1993, c. 45, s. 7; 1997, c. 16, s. 6; 1999, c. 25, s. 2; 2001, c. 32, s. 29; 2001, c. 41, s. 16, 34 and 133(13), (14); 2002, c. 13, s. 20; 2005, c. 32, s. 15; 2005, c. 43, ss. 4 and 8(3)(*a*); 2010, c. 3, s. 4; 2012, c. 1, s. 28; 2014, c. 25, s. 21; 2015, c. 13, s. 13; c. 20, s. 21.

CROSS-REFERENCES

The terms "justice" and "justice system participant" are defined in s. 2. Age is determined by reference to s. 30 of the *Interpretation Act*, R.S.C. 1985, c. I-21.

Section 486.1 provides for the making of an order to allow for a support person to be present and to be close to a witness while the witness testifies. Section 486.2 provides for taking testimony outside the courtroom or behind a screen so that the witness cannot see the accused. Section 486.3 provides for making of orders that the accused not personally cross-examine witnesses. Sections 486.4 and 486.5 provide for the making of non-publication orders.

SYNOPSIS

This section sets out the circumstances in which a judge may exclude the public from the courtroom.

Subsection (1) enacts the presumption that proceedings will be held in open court. If the judge or justice is of the opinion that, for any of the reasons set out therein, the public should be excluded from the courtroom, the judge or justice may make such an order. Subsection (1.1) governs when and to whom such an application may be made. One reason for exclusion is the proper administration of justice, which is defined in part in subsec. (2). Under subsec. (3), where the accused is charged with certain offences set out therein and the judge refuses to make the exclusion order, the judge shall state reasons for the refusal. Generally speaking, the offences referred to are the various sexual offences and the human trafficking offences. Finally, subsec. (4) prohibits any adverse inference being drawn from the making of (or refusal to make) such an order.

ANNOTATIONS

Note: The cases noted below were decided under the predecessor section.

Grounds for exclusion of public generally – The trial judge must exercise his or her discretion under subsec. (1) in conformity with the Charter. The trial judge must consider the following factors: (a) available options and whether there are any other reasonable and effective alternatives available; (b) whether the order is limited as much as possible, and (c) balance the objectives of the particular order and its probable effects against the importance of openness and the particular expression that will be limited in order to ensure that the positive and negative effects of the order are proportionate. The party making the application bears the burden of establishing that the rule of openness should be displaced by showing that the order is necessary to the proper administration of justice, that the order is as limited as possible and that the salutary effects of the order are proportionate to its deleterious effects. If the order sought is to protect a constitutional right, this factor must be considered in respect of proportionality. Where the facts are not in dispute, the statement of counsel is sufficient. However, if the facts are in dispute or there is insufficient evidence placed before the trial judge, the applicant should adduce evidence at the hearing held *in camera*: *Canadian Broadcasting Corp. v. New Brunswick (Attorney General)*, [1996] 3 S.C.R. 480, 110 C.C.C. (3d) 193.

On the trial of a drug charge, an application was made under the predecessor to this section to exclude the public while the accused testified, as she would be revealing the fact that she was a police informer. The application was refused and, on appeal, it was held there was no error in the refusal of the judge to exercise his power in this section. The reason put forward was not sufficient reason to exclude the public since it had already been revealed in open court that she was an informer and it could not be said that the disclosure that she intended to do it again added in any substantial way to whatever danger was alleged to attend her testifying in open court. It would, however, have been preferable for the trial judge to at least have listened *in camera* to defence counsel's reasons for seeking exclusion: *R. v. Douglas* (1977), 33 C.C.C. (2d) 395 (Ont. C.A.).

An order excluding the public may properly be made where the complainant in a sexual offence would otherwise be too nervous to give evidence. In such circumstances, the order is necessary for the proper administration of justice: *R. v. Lefebvre* (1984), 17 C.C.C. (3d) 277 (Que. C.A.).

A provincial court judge has no power under this section to order a newspaper reporter to be excluded from court so as to prevent the reporter from publishing the names of witnesses (in this case, the inmates of a bawdy-house). Such an order is a misuse of the section in attempting to prevent conduct that is not unlawful, interfering with freedom of the press, and it could not be justified on the basis of the proper administration of justice: *R. v. F.P. Publications (Western) Ltd.* (1979), 51 C.C.C. (2d) 110 (Man. C.A.) (4:1).

It was held in *R. v. Musitano* (1985), 24 C.C.C. (3d) 65 (Ont. C.A.), leave to appeal to S.C.C. refused 79 N.R. 79*n*, that the trial judge properly exercised his discretion in excluding the public in the interest of the proper administration of justice when conducting an inquiry in the course of the trial to determine the impartiality of several jurors.

Requirement of reasons in sexual offence cases [subsec. (3)] – The fact that the judge is required to give reasons does not enlarge the grounds, set out in subsec. (1), for excluding the public: *R. v. Brint* (1979), 45 C.C.C. (2d) 560 (Alta. S.C.).

Constitutional considerations – It was held that the predecessor to this section was a reasonable limit on the freedoms guaranteed by s. 2(*b*) of the Charter: *Canadian Broadcasting Corp. v. New Brunswick (Attorney General)*, [1996] 3 S.C.R. 480, 110 C.C.C. (3d) 193.

It has also been held that the section does not violate the rights of victims and their families as guaranteed by s. 7 of the *Canadian Charter of Rights and Freedoms*. In particular, the "public morals" exception to the open court rule is not vague or overly broad, nor is the provision procedurally defective, although the victim is not granted automatic standing. The fact that public access to child or coerced pornography will result in undue harm or violate the privacy interests of the victims or their families are matters properly coming within the ambit of the administration of justice branch of this subsection: *French Estate v. Ontario (Attorney General)* (1998), 122 C.C.C. (3d) 475 (Ont. C.A.), leave to appeal to S.C.C. refused 132 C.C.C. (3d) vi.

SUPPORT PERSON — WITNESSES UNDER 18 OR WHO HAVE A DISABILITY / Other witnesses / Application / Factors to be considered / Witness not to be a support person / No communication while testifying / No adverse inference.

486.1 (1) In any proceedings against an accused, the judge or justice shall, on application of the prosecutor in respect of a witness who is under the age of 18 years or who has a mental or physical disability, or on application of such a witness, order that a support person of the witness' choice be permitted to be present and to be close to the witness while the witness testifies, unless the judge or justice is of the opinion that the order would interfere with the proper administration of justice.

(2) In any proceedings against an accused, the judge or justice may, on application of the prosecutor in respect of a witness, or on application of a witness, order that a support person of the witness' choice be permitted to be present and to be close to the witness while the witness testifies if the judge or justice is of the opinion that the order would facilitate the giving of a full and candid account by the witness of the acts complained of or would otherwise be in the interest of the proper administration of justice.

(2.1) An application referred to in subsection (1) or (2) may be made, during the proceedings, to the presiding judge or justice or, before the proceedings begin, to the judge or justice who will preside at the proceedings or, if that judge or justice has not been determined, to any judge or justice having jurisdiction in the judicial district where the proceedings will take place.

(3) In determining whether to make an order under subsection (2), the judge or justice shall consider

(*a*) the age of the witness;
(*b*) the witness' mental or physical disabilities,if any;
(*c*) the nature of the offence;
(*d*) the nature of any relationship between the witness and the accused;
(*e*) whether the witness needs the order for their security or to protect them from intimidation or retaliation;
(*f*) society's interest in encouraging the reporting of offences and the participation of victims and witnesses in the criminal justice process; and
(*g*) any other factor that the judge or justice considers relevant.

(4) The judge or justice shall not permit a witness to be a support person unless the judge or justice is of the opinion that doing so is necessary for the proper administration of justice.

(5) The judge or justice may order that the support person and the witness not communicate with each other while the witness testifies.

(6) No adverse inference may be drawn from the fact that an order is, or is not, made under this section. 2005, c. 32, s. 15; 2015, c. 13, s. 14.

CROSS-REFERENCES

"Justice" and "prosecutor" are defined in s. 2. Age is determined by reference to s. 30 of the *Interpretation Act*, R.S.C. 1985, c. I-21.

Section 486 provides for the making of an order to exclude the public. Section 486.2 provides for taking testimony outside the courtroom or behind a screen so that the witness cannot see the accused. Section 486.3 provides for making of orders that the accused not personally cross-examine witnesses. Sections 486.4 and 486.5 provide for the making of non-publication orders.

SYNOPSIS

This section sets out the circumstances in which the judge or justice may make an order to permit a support person to be present and close to a witness while the witness testifies. The section envisages two sets of circumstances. Under subsec. (1), where the witness is under the age of 18 years or has a mental or physical disability, the order will be made where the prosecutor or the witness applies for it, unless the judge or justice is of the opinion that the order would interfere with the proper administration of justice. Under subsec. (2), in the case of all other witnesses, the order will only be made where the judge or justice is of the opinion that the order is necessary to obtain a full and candid account from the witness of the acts complained of. The application may be made during the proceedings or before they begin to the judge or justice who will preside at the proceedings (subsec. (2.1)). The factors to be considered in making the order under subsec. (2) are set out in subsec. (3). Ordinarily, another witness cannot be the support person except where it is necessary for the proper administration of justice (subsec. (4)). The judge or justice may order the witness and the support person not to communicate while the witness testifies (subsec. (5)). Under subsec. (6), no adverse inference may be drawn from the fact that an order is or is not made.

ANNOTATIONS

The complainant's mother was an appropriate support person, notwithstanding that she was a witness in the matter, given that, at the time that she acted as a support person, the mother had already testified and been fully cross-examined: *R. v. C. (D.)* (2008), 238 C.C.C. (3d) 16 (N.S.C.A.).

TESTIMONY OUTSIDE COURT ROOM — WITNESSES UNDER 18 OR WHO HAVE A DISABILITY / Other witnesses / Application / Factors to be considered / Same procedure for determination / Conditions of exclusion / No adverse inference.

486.2 (1) Despite section 650, in any proceedings against an accused, the judge or justice shall, on application of the prosecutor in respect of a witness who is under the age of 18 years or who is able to communicate evidence but may have difficulty doing so by reason of a mental or physical disability, or on application of such a witness, order that the witness testify outside the court room or behind a screen or other device that would allow the witness not to see the accused, unless the judge or justice is of the opinion that the order would interfere with the proper administration of justice.

(2) Despite section 650, in any proceedings against an accused, the judge or justice may, on application of the prosecutor in respect of a witness, or on application of a witness, order that the witness testify outside the court room or behind a screen or other device that would allow the witness not to see the accused if the judge or justice is of the opinion that the order would facilitate the giving of a full and candid account by the witness of the acts complained of or would otherwise be in the interest of the proper administration of justice.

(2.1) An application referred to in subsection (1) or (2) may be made, during the proceedings, to the presiding judge or justice or, before the proceedings begin, to the judge or justice who will preside at the proceedings or, if that judge or justice has not been determined, to any judge or justice having jurisdiction in the judicial district where the proceedings will take place.

(3) In determining whether to make an order under subsection (2), the judge or justice shall consider

- **(*a*) the age of the witness;**
- **(*b*) the witness' mental or physical disabilities, if any;**
- **(*c*) the nature of the offence;**
- **(*d*) the nature of any relationship between the witness and the accused;**
- **(*e*) whether the witness needs the order for their security or to protect them from intimidation or retaliation;**

(*f*) whether the order is needed to protect the identity of a peace officer who has acted, is acting or will be acting in an undercover capacity, or of a person who has acted, is acting or will be acting covertly under the direction of a peace officer;

(*f*.1) whether the order is needed to protect the witness's identity if they have had, have or will have responsibilities relating to national security or intelligence;

(*g*) society's interest in encouraging the reporting of offences and the participation of victims and witnesses in the criminal justice process; and

(*h*) any other factor that the judge or justice considers relevant.

(4) If the judge or justice is of the opinion that it is necessary for a witness to testify in order to determine whether an order under subsection (2) should be made in respect of that witness, the judge or justice shall order that the witness testify in accordance with that subsection.

(5) A witness shall not testify outside the court room in accordance with an order made under subsection (1) or (2) unless arrangements are made for the accused, the judge or justice and the jury to watch the testimony of the witness by means of closed-circuit television or otherwise and the accused is permitted to communicate with counsel while watching the testimony.

(6) No adverse inference may be drawn from the fact that an order is, or is not, made under subsection (1) or (2). 2005, c. 32, s. 15; 2014, c. 17, s. 12; 2015, c. 13, s. 15; 2015, c. 20, s. 38(2).

(7) [*Repealed*, 2015, c. 13, s. 15.]

(8) [*Repealed*, 2015, c. 13, s. 15.]

CROSS-REFERENCES

"Criminal organization", "justice", "prosecutor" and "terrorism offence" are defined in s. 2. Age is determined by reference to s. 30 of the *Interpretation Act*, R.S.C. 1985, c. I-21.

Section 486 provides for the making of an order to exclude the public. Section 486.1 provides for permitting a support person to be present while a witness testifies. Section 486.3 provides for making of orders that the accused not personally cross-examine witnesses. Sections 486.4 and 486.5 provide for the making of non-publication orders.

SYNOPSIS

This section sets out circumstances in which a witness may be permitted to testify outside the courtroom or behind a screen or device that would not allow the witness to see the accused. The section envisages three different situations. The first concerns witnesses who are under age of 18 years or may have difficulty communicating testimony because of a mental or physical disability. Where the witness or the prosecutor applies for the order, the judge is to make the order unless of the opinion that the order would interfere with the proper administration of justice.

The second situation is set out in subsec. (2) and concerns other witnesses. In that case, the order will be made only if the judge is of the opinion that it is necessary to obtain a full and candid account from the witness of the acts complained of. In making this determination, the judge takes into account the factors set out in s. 486.1(3) such as the nature of the offence and the relationship between the witness and the accused.

The third situation relates to a certain class of offences. These offences are listed in subsec. (5) and include various criminal organization offences, terrorism offences and national security offences listed in the *Security of Information Act*, R.S.C. 1985, c. O-5, such as communicating secret information to terrorist groups or foreign entities. The order is to be made under subsec. (4) permitting the witness to testify outside the courtroom if necessary to protect the safety of the witness, or outside the courtroom or behind a screen if the judge is of the opinion that the order is necessary to obtain a full and candid account from the witness.

If it is necessary to hear from the witness to decide whether an order should be made under subsec. (2) or (4), subsec. (6) provides that the witness may testify on that inquiry outside the courtroom or behind the screen as the case may be. A witness shall not testify outside the courtroom unless facilities are available to allow the accused, the judge and the jury to watch the testimony, and the accused has a means of communicating with counsel while watching the testimony. No adverse inference may be drawn from the fact that an order is or is not made.

ANNOTATIONS

Note: Some of these cases noted below were decided under the predecessor section and may be of greatest assistance in applying subsecs. (2) and (4).

When order should be made – It was held that the circumstances under which a judge may make an order under the predecessor to this section did not require that exceptional and inordinate stress be caused to the child. The trial judge has substantial latitude in deciding whether the use of the screen should be permitted and the evidence in support of the application need not take any particular form. In exercising the discretion under the section, the trial judge may consider evidence of the capabilities and demeanour of the child, the nature of the allegations and the circumstances of the case. It may well be that the trial judge may also consider the fact that the accused is unrepresented in determining whether or not to permit the use of the screen: *R. v. Levogiannis*, [1993] 4 S.C.R. 475, 85 C.C.C. (3d) 327 (9:0).

Before permitting the witness to testify outside of court, the trial judge may hold a *voir dire* to determine whether such an order is necessary to obtain a full and candid account. On that *voir dire*, however, the Crown may not ask witnesses who are not qualified as experts to give their opinion on that issue: *R. v. H. (B.C.)* (1990), 58 C.C.C. (3d) 16 (Man. C.A.). [Now see subsec. (6).]

It was held under the predecessor to this section that the trial judge is not empowered to form the requisite opinion that a screen is necessary unless there is an evidential base relating to the standard of necessity set out in this subsection. The necessary evidential base was lacking, where there was merely testimony from the complainant that she did not feel comfortable talking in front of a lot of people and the accused and that she would find it easier if people were excluded from the courtroom: *R. v. M. (P.)* (1990), 1 O.R. (3d) 341 (C.A.).

The court has the jurisdiction to make an order requiring the Attorney General to assume responsibility for the payment of the appointed lawyer's fees: *R. v. S. (B.)* (2007), 240 C.C.C. (3d) 375 (Que. C.A.).

Constitutional considerations – This provision does not violate ss. 7 or 11(*d*) of the Charter: *R. v. S. (J.)* (2008), 238 C.C.C. (3d) 522 (B.C.C.A.), affd 251 C.C.C. (3d) 1 (S.C.C.).

Procedure – Ordinarily, the trial judge should instruct the jury to the effect that the use of the screen is a procedure that is allowed in cases of this kind by reason of the youth of the witness and that, since it has nothing to do with the guilt or innocence of the accused, the jury must not draw any inference of any kind from its use, and, in particular, that no adverse inference should be drawn against the accused because of the screen: *R. v. Levogiannis*, *supra*. [Now see subsec. (8).]

The trial judge does not have independent discretion to determine which testimonial accommodation would be better in the circumstances, unless the requested testimonial accommodation would interfere with the proper administration of justice: *R. v. T. (S.B.)* (2008), 232 C.C.C. (3d) 115 (B.C.S.C.).

ACCUSED NOT TO CROSS-EXAMINE WITNESSES UNDER 18 / Accused not to cross-examine complainant — certain offences / Other witnesses / Factors to be considered / Application / No adverse inference.

486.3 (1) In any proceedings against an accused, the judge or justice shall, on application of the prosecutor in respect of a witness who is under the age of 18 years, or on application of such a witness, order that the accused not personally cross-examine the witness, unless the judge or justice is of the opinion that the proper administration of justice requires the accused to personally conduct the cross-examination. If such an order is made, the judge or justice shall appoint counsel to conduct the cross-examination.

(2) In any proceedings against an accused in respect of an offence under any of sections 264, 271, 272 and 273, the judge or justice shall, on application of the prosecutor in respect of a witness who is a victim, or on application of such a witness, order that the accused not personally cross-examine the witness, unless the judge or justice is of the opinion that the proper administration of justice requires the accused to personally conduct the cross-examination. If such an order is made, the judge or justice shall appoint counsel to conduct the cross-examination.

(3) In any proceedings against an accused, the judge or justice may, on application of the prosecutor in respect of a witness who is not entitled to make an application under subsection (1) or (2), or on application of such a witness, order that the accused not personally cross-examine the witness if the judge or justice is of the opinion that the order would allow the giving of a full and candid account from the witness of the acts complained of or would otherwise be in the interest of the proper administration of justice. If the order is made, the judge or justice shall appoint counsel to conduct the cross-examination.

(4) In determining whether to make an order under subsection (3), the judge or justice shall consider

- **(*a*) the age of the witness;**
- **(*b*) the witness' mental or physical disabilities, if any;**
- **(*c*) the nature of the offence;**
- **(*d*) whether the witness needs the order for their security or to protect them from intimidation or retaliation;**
- **(*e*) the nature of any relationship between the witness and the accused;**
- **(*f*) society's interest in encouraging the reporting of offences and the participation of victims and witnesses in the criminal justice process; and**
- **(*g*) any other factor that the judge or justice considers relevant.**

(4.1) An application referred to in any of subsections (1) to (3) may be made during the proceedings to the presiding judge or justice or, before the proceedings begin, to the judge or justice who will preside at the proceedings or, if that judge or justice has not been determined, to any judge or justice having jurisdiction in the judicial district where the proceedings will take place.

(5) No adverse inference may be drawn from the fact that counsel is, or is not, appointed under this section. 2005, c. 32, s. 15; 2015, c. 13, s. 16.

CROSS-REFERENCES

"Justice", "prosecutor" and "victim" are defined in s. 2. Age is determined by reference to s. 30 of the *Interpretation Act*, R.S.C. 1985, c. I-21.

Section 486 provides for the making of an order to exclude the public. Section 486.1 provides for permitting a support person to be present while a witness testifies. Section 486.2 provides for taking testimony outside the courtroom or behind a screen so that the witness cannot see the accused. Sections 486.4 and 486.5 provide for the making of non-publication orders.

SYNOPSIS

This section sets out circumstances in which the judge may order that the accused not personally cross-examine prosecution witnesses. Where the order is made, the judge appoints counsel to conduct the cross-examination. The section envisages three different situations. The first concerns witnesses who are under the age of 18 years. Where the witness or the prosecutor applies for the order, the judge is to make the order unless the judge is of the opinion that the proper administration of justice requires the accused to personally conduct the cross-examination.

The second situation is set out in subsec. (2) and concerns other witnesses. In that case, the order will be made only if the judge is of the opinion that it is necessary to obtain a full and candid account from the witness of the acts complained of. In making this determination, the judge takes into account the factors set out in s. 486.1(3), such as the nature of the offence and the relationship between the witness and the accused.

The third situation relates to an accused charged with the criminal harassment offence in s. 264. On application by the victim or the prosecutor, the accused shall not personally cross-examine the victim unless the judge is of the opinion that the proper administration of justice requires the accused to personally conduct the cross-examination.

Under subsec. (4.1), the application for an order under this section may be made during the proceedings or before they begin to the judge who will preside at the proceedings. No adverse inference may be drawn from the fact that an order is, or is not, made.

ANNOTATIONS

An evidentiary foundation must be laid before an order under this provision is made. At a minimum, there must be reliable, trustworthy evidence from sources with intimate knowledge of the individual witnesses so that the court could be satisfied, on the balance of probabilities, that a full and candid account could not have been achieved if the witnesses were cross-examined by the accused: *R. v. Tehrankari* (2008), 246 C.C.C. (3d) 70 (Ont. S.C.J.).

Where the accused's testimony made allegations against the complainants that had not been put to them in cross-examination by counsel appointed pursuant to subsec. (2), the trial judge erred by relying on the rule in *Browne v. Dunn* (1893), 6 R. 67 (U.K.H.L.), as a reason to reject the accused's evidence and convict him. It was not clear that the accused understood what he was required to do in relation to briefing appointed counsel about his anticipated testimony: *R. v. Wapass* (2014), 314 C.C.C. (3d) 561 (Sask. C.A.).

Subsection (1) contains a presumption that an accused cannot cross-examine a young witness personally unless a judge decides it is necessary for the proper administration of justice. It would defeat the purpose of this provision if the accused were allowed to question the young witness personally on the *voir dire* of this issue: *R. v. M. (C.G.)* (2015), 334 C.C.C. (3d) 88 (Alta. C.A.), leave to appeal to S.C.C. refused 2016 CarswellAlta 1751.

NON-DISCLOSURE OF WITNESS' IDENTITY / Hearing may be held / Factors to be considered / No adverse inference.

486.31 (1) In any proceedings against an accused, the judge or justice may, on application of the prosecutor in respect of a witness, or on application of a witness, make an order directing that any information that could identify the witness not be disclosed in the course of the proceedings if the judge or justice is of the opinion that the order is in the interest of the proper administration of justice.

(2) The judge or justice may hold a hearing to determine whether the order should be made, and the hearing may be in private.

(3) In determining whether to make the order, the judge or justice shall consider

(*a*) the right to a fair and public hearing;

(*b*) the nature of the offence;

(*c*) whether the witness needs the order for their security or to protect them from intimidation or retaliation;

(*d*) whether the order is needed to protect the security of anyone known to the witness;

(*e*) whether the order is needed to protect the identity of a peace officer who has acted, is acting or will be acting in an undercover capacity, or of a person who has acted, is acting or will be acting covertly under the direction of a peace officer;

(*e*.1) whether the order is needed to protect the witness's identity if they have had, have or will have responsibilities relating to national security or intelligence;

(*f*) society's interest in encouraging the reporting of offences and the participation of victims and witnesses in the criminal justice process;

(*g*) the importance of the witness' testimony to the case;

(*h*) whether effective alternatives to the making of the proposed order are available in the circumstances;

(*i*) the salutary and deleterious effects of the proposed order; and

(*j*) any other factor that the judge or justice considers relevant.

(4) No adverse inference may be drawn from the fact that an order is, or is not, made under this section. 2015, c. 13, s. 17; c. 20, s. 38(3).

CROSS-REFERENCES

"Justice" and "prosecutor" are defined in s. 2.

SYNOPSIS

This section allows the court, on application of the prosecutor or a witness, to make an order directing that any information that could identify the witness not be disclosed in the course of the proceedings when such an order is in the interest of the proper administration of justice. Subsection (2) provides that the hearing of such an application may be in private. Subsection (3) provides a list of mandatory considerations for the court to weigh in deciding whether to make an order. Subsection (4) prohibits any adverse inference being drawn from the making of (or refusal to make) such an order.

ORDER RESTRICTING PUBLICATION — SEXUAL OFFENCES / Mandatory order on application / Victim under 18 — other offences / Mandatory order on application / Child pornography / Limitation.

486.4 (1) Subject to subsection (2), the presiding judge or justice may make an order directing that any information that could identify the victim or a witness shall not be published in any document or broadcast or transmitted in any way, in proceedings in respect of

(*a*) any of the following offences:

(i) an offence under section 151, 152, 153, 153.1, 155, 159, 160, 162, 163.1, 170, 171, 171.1, 172, 172.1, 172.2, 173, 210, 211, 213, 271, 272, 273, 279.01, 279.011, 279.02, 279.03, 280, 281, 286.1, 286.2, 286.3, 346 or 347, or

(ii) any offence under this Act, as it read from time to time before the day on which this subparagraph comes into force, if the conduct alleged would be an offence referred to in subparagraph (i) if it occurred on or after that day; or

(iii) [*Repealed*, 2014, c. 25, s. 22(2).]

(*b*) two or more offences being dealt with in the same proceeding, at least one of which is an offence referred to in paragraph (*a*).

(2) In proceedings in respect of the offences referred to in paragraph (1)(*a*) or (*b*), the presiding judge or justice shall

(*a*) at the first reasonable opportunity, inform any witness under the age of eighteen years and the victim of the right to make an application for the order; and

(*b*) on application made by the victim, the prosecutor or any such witness, make the order.

(2.1) Subject to subsection (2.2), in proceedings in respect of an offence other than an offence referred to in subsection (1), if the victim is under the age of 18 years, the presiding judge or justice may make an order directing that any information that could identify the victim shall not be published in any document or broadcast or transmitted in any way.

(2.2) In proceedings in respect of an offence other than an offence referred to in subsection (1), if the victim is under the age of 18 years, the presiding judge or justice shall

(*a*) as soon as feasible, inform the victim of their right to make an application for the order; and

(*b*) on application of the victim or the prosecutor, make the order.

(3) In proceedings in respect of an offence under section 163.1, a judge or justice shall make an order directing that any information that could identify a witness who is under the age of eighteen years, or any person who is the subject of a representation, written material or a recording that constitutes child pornography within the meaning of that section, shall not be published in any document or broadcast or transmitted in any way.

(4) An order made under this section does not apply in respect of the disclosure of information in the course of the administration of justice when it is not the purpose of the disclosure to make the information known in the community. 2005, c. 32, s. 15; c. 43, s. 8(3)(*b*); 2010, c. 3, s. 5; 2012, c. 1, s. 29; 2014, c. 25, ss. 22, 48(6); 2015, c. 13, s. 18(1), (2), (4).

CROSS-REFERENCES

"Justice" and "prosecutor" are defined in s. 2. Age is determined by reference to s. 30 of the *Interpretation Act*, R.S.C. 1985, c. I-21.

Section 486 provides for the making of an order to exclude the public. Section 486.1 provides for permitting a support person to be present while a witness testifies. Section 486.2 provides for taking testimony outside the courtroom or behind a screen so that the witness cannot see the accused. Section 486.3 provides for making of orders that the accused not personally cross-examine witnesses. Section 486.5 provides for the making of non-publication orders not covered by this section. Failure to comply with an order made under this section is a summary conviction offence under s. 486.6.

SYNOPSIS

This section provides that when an accused is charged under any of the specified sections, the court may make an order directing that the identity of, or any information that would identify, the victim or another witness not be published, broadcasted or transmitted in any way. Generally speaking, the offences listed in subsec. (1) are sexual offences, but also included are the human trafficking offences (ss. 279.01 to 279.03) and offences such as extortion (s. 346) and charging a criminal interest rate (s. 347). Subsection (2) requires the presiding judge or justice to inform any witness under the age of 18 and the victim, at the first reasonable opportunity, of the right to make an application under subsec. (1). If such an application is made by the victim, the prosecutor, or a witness under the age of 18, the judge or justice must make the order.

Subsection (3) sets out a special rule in relation to the child pornography offence. The order is to be made for any witness who is under the age of 18 and any person who is the subject of a representation, written material or recording that constitutes child pornography.

Subsection (4) provides an exception for disclosure in the course of the administration of justice, where disclosure is not for the purpose of making the information known to the community.

ANNOTATIONS

Note: Some of the cases noted below were decided under the predecessor section.

Meaning of publication – The accused media organization did not violate a publication ban by refusing to take down a news article on its website identifying the 14-year-old victim of a homicide. The article was posted before the ban was issued. Refusal to remove a lawfully published story does not amount to publishing within the meaning of this provision: *R. v. Canadian Broadcasting Corporation* (2018), 368 C.C.C. (3d) 396 (Alta. C.A.).

Procedure – It was held under a predecessor to this section that the order (which was mandatory upon application by the prosecutor) must be made, at the latest, at the time the complainant begins her testimony: *R. v. Calabrese* (1981), 64 C.C.C. (2d) 71 (Que. S.C.).

It was held considering the predecessor to this section that, where the complainant or the prosecutor wishes to obtain a more specific order prohibiting the naming of the accused or other persons or places on the ground that such information would disclose the identity of the complainant, evidence must be provided to support the application. The order cannot properly be made merely with the consent of the prosecutor and the complainant and without any supporting evidence. However, such evidence can be supplied either by *viva voce* evidence, affidavit or submissions of counsel, and the discretion of a judge to make a non-publication order beyond an order as to the name of the complainant is not restricted to a limited category of cases such as those of incest and other familial crimes. On the other hand, great weight should always be given by judges in the exercise of their discretion to the tradition of openness of the courts to the public and the constitutional guarantee of freedom of the media in s. 2(*b*) of the Charter: *R. v. Southam Inc.* (1989), 47 C.C.C. (3d) 21 (Ont. C.A.).

It was held that a court may not unilaterally revoke an order under this section. If, however, both the Crown and the complainant consent to a revocation of the order, then the circumstances which make the publication ban mandatory are no longer present, and, subject to any rights that the accused may have under subsec. (3), the trial judge can revoke the order: *R. v. Adams*, [1995] 4 S.C.R. 707, 103 C.C.C. (3d) 262.

A publication ban continues in effect during appellate proceedings: *R. v. K. (V.)* (1991), 68 C.C.C. (3d) 18 (B.C.C.A.).

Where a judge is *functus officio*, a judge of the superior court has inherent jurisdiction to vary or lift the ban on publication of the complainant's identity: *R. v. Ireland* (2005), 203 C.C.C. (3d) 443 (Ont. S.C.J.).

Constitutional considerations – While the predecessor to this section was held to infringe freedom of expression as guaranteed under s. 2(*b*) of the Charter it was also held to constitute a reasonable limit on that freedom and was valid: *Canadian Newspapers Co. v. Canada (Attorney General)*, [1988] 2 S.C.R. 122, 43 C.C.C. (3d) 24 (6:0). [Note: The court left open the question whether, in a proper case, the accused's right to a fair trial as guaranteed by s. 11(*d*) of the Charter would require that the complainant's name be published.]

Note: The following cases were decided prior to the amendment to these provisions and the inclusion of s. 486.5, which expand the statutory bases for non-publication orders.

Publication bans other than pursuant to statute – A trial judge has jurisdiction to prohibit the publication of the names of certain witnesses where the circumstances are sufficiently compelling, as where the witnesses are prison inmates who justifiably fear for their safety should their identity be disclosed: *R. v. McArthur* (1984), 13 C.C.C. (3d) 152 (Ont. H.C.J.). [These circumstances would likely now be covered by this section and s. 486.5.]

The superior court has an inherent jurisdiction to make an order prohibiting publication of the identity of the accused where such an order is necessary to protect a trial that is then being conducted before it. As well, the superior court has power under its inherent jurisdiction to render assistance to inferior courts to enable them to administer justice fully and effectively: *R. v. Unnamed Person* (1985), 22 C.C.C. (3d) 284 (Ont. C.A.).

To seek or challenge a ban on appeal, the Crown and the accused must follow the regular avenues of appeal available to them through the *Criminal Code*. For a third party, such as the media, who has been affected by the publication ban, where the ban has been imposed by a provincial court judge, then the third party may apply to the superior court by way of *certiorari* and may then follow the appellate routes prescribed in the *Criminal Code*. When the order has been made by a superior court judge, then the third party may apply for leave to appeal to the Supreme Court of Canada under s. 40 of the *Supreme Court Act*, R.S.C. 1985, c. S-26. The judge hearing the application for a ban has the discretion to direct that third parties, such as the media, be given notice in accordance with the provincial rules of criminal procedure and has the discretion to grant standing to interested third parties and determine what rights the third parties should have on the hearing of the application. A judge has the discretion at common law to impose a ban on publication to protect the fairness of the trial only where: (a) such a ban is necessary in order to prevent a real and substantial risk to the fairness of the trial, because reasonably available alternative measures will not prevent the risk; and (b) the salutary effects of the publication ban outweigh the deleterious: *Dagenais v. Canadian Broadcasting Corp.*, [1994] 3 S.C.R. 835, 94 C.C.C. (3d) 289.

The rights of an adult accused to equality as protected by s. 15 of the Charter are not infringed, notwithstanding that the judge may make an order prohibiting publication of the identity of the complainant or an accused young offender. Further, s. 7 of the Charter does not give the accused a right to privacy which may be enforced by a ban on publication of his identity: *R. v. D. (G.)* (1991), 63 C.C.C. (3d) 134 (Ont. C.A.), leave to appeal to S.C.C. refused 64 C.C.C. (3d) vi.

A trial judge, presiding at a retrial following the accused's successful appeal, has an inherent power to make an order prohibiting publication of aspects of the previous proceedings which could prejudice the jury hearing the retrial. Such an order does not violate the right to freedom of the press in s. 2(*b*) of the *Canadian Charter of Rights and Freedoms*: *R. v. Barrow* (1989), 48 C.C.C. (3d) 308, 91 N.S.R. (2d) 176 (S.C.T.D.).

ORDER RESTRICTING PUBLICATION — VICTIMS AND WITNESSES / Justice system participants / Offences / Limitation / Application and notice / Grounds / Hearing may be held / Factors to be considered / Conditions / Publication prohibited.

486.5 (1) Unless an order is made under section 486.4, on application of the prosecutor in respect of a victim or a witness, or on application of a victim or a witness, a judge or justice may make an order directing that any information that could identify the victim or witness shall not be published in any document or broadcast or transmitted in any way if the judge or justice is of the opinion that the order is in the interest of the proper administration of justice.

(2) On application of the prosecutor in respect of a justice system participant who is involved in proceedings in respect of an offence referred to in subsection (2.1), or on application of such a justice system participant, a judge or justice may make an order directing that any information that could identify the justice system participant shall not be published in any document or broadcast or transmitted in any way if the judge or justice is of the opinion that the order is in the interest of the proper administration of justice.

(2.1) The offences for the purposes of subsection (2) are

(*a*) an offence under section 423.1, 467.11, 467.111, 467.12 or 467.13, or a serious offence committed for the benefit of, at the direction of, or in association with, a criminal organization;

(*b*) a terrorism offence;

(*c*) an offence under subsection 16(1) or (2), 17(1), 19(1), 20(1) or 22(1) of the *Security of Information Act*; or

(*d*) an offence under subsection 21(1) or section 23 of the *Security of Information Act* that is committed in relation to an offence referred to in paragraph (*c*).

(3) An order made under this section does not apply in respect of the disclosure of information in the course of the administration of justice if it is not the purpose of the disclosure to make the information known in the community.

(4) An applicant for an order shall

(*a*) apply in writing to the presiding judge or justice or, if the judge or justice has not been determined, to a judge of a superior court of criminal jurisdiction in the judicial district where the proceedings will take place; and

(*b*) provide notice of the application to the prosecutor, the accused and any other person affected by the order that the judge or justice specifies.

(5) An applicant for an order shall set out the grounds on which the applicant relies to establish that the order is necessary for the proper administration of justice.

(6) The judge or justice may hold a hearing to determine whether an order should be made, and the hearing may be in private.

(7) In determining whether to make an order, the judge or justice shall consider

(*a*) the right to a fair and public hearing;

(*b*) whether there is a real and substantial risk that the victim, witness or justice system participant would suffer harm if their identity were disclosed;

(*c*) whether the victim, witness or justice system participant needs the order for their security or to protect them from intimidation or retaliation;

(*d*) society's interest in encouraging the reporting of offences and the participation of victims, witnesses and justice system participants in the criminal justice process;

(*e*) whether effective alternatives are available to protect the identity of the victim, witness or justice system participant;

(*f*) the salutary and deleterious effects of the proposed order;

(*g*) the impact of the proposed order on the freedom of expression of those affected by it; and

(*h*) any other factor that the judge or justice considers relevant.

(8) An order may be subject to any conditions that the judge or justice thinks fit.

(9) Unless the judge or justice refuses to make an order, no person shall publish in any document or broadcast or transmit in any way

(*a*) the contents of an application;

(*b*) any evidence taken, information given or submissions made at a hearing under subsection (6); or

(*c*) any other information that could identify the person to whom the application relates as a victim, witness or justice system participant in the proceedings. 2005, c. 32, s. 15; 2015, c. 13, s. 19.

CROSS-REFERENCES

"Justice", "justice system participant", "prosecutor", "superior court of criminal jurisdiction" and "victim" are defined in s. 2.

Section 486 provides for the making of an order to exclude the public. Section 486.1 provides for permitting a support person to be present while a witness testifies. Section 486.2 provides for taking testimony outside the courtroom or behind a screen so that the witness cannot see the accused. Section 486.3 provides for making of orders that the accused not personally cross-examine witnesses. Section 486.4 provides for the making of non-publication orders in relation to various enumerated offences such as the various sexual offences, child pornography, extortion and charging a criminal interest rate. Failure to comply with an order made under this section is a summary conviction offence under s. 486.6.

SYNOPSIS

This section creates a code of procedure for the prosecutor, a victim or a witness (subsec. (1)), or a justice system participant (subsec. (2)) to apply for a non-publication order. The basis for making the order is whether the judge is satisfied that the order is necessary for the proper administration of justice. Where the order is made, it applies to prohibit publication, broadcast or transmission in any way of any information that could identify the person. Subsection (3) provides an exception for disclosure in the course of the administration of justice, where disclosure is not for the purpose of making the information known to the community.

Subsection (4) requires that the applicant apply in writing either to the presiding judge or, if a judge has not been determined, to a judge of the superior court of justice. The application must be on notice to the accused, prosecutor and any other person affected by the order as required by the judge and, pursuant to subsec. (5), must set out the grounds for the making of the order. The judge may hold a hearing, which may be *in camera*, to determine whether the order should be made The factors the judge must consider are set out in subsec. (7). The judge may include conditions in the order. Unless the judge refuses to make the order, the contents of the application, the proceedings at the hearing and any other information that would identify the person shall also not be published, broadcasted or transmitted in any way.

OFFENCE / Application of order.

486.6 (1) Every person who fails to comply with an order made under subsection 486.4(1), (2) or (3) or 486.5(1) or (2) is guilty of an offence punishable on summary conviction.

(2) For greater certainty, an order referred to in subsection (1) applies to prohibit, in relation to proceedings taken against any person who fails to comply with the order, the publication in any document or the broadcasting or transmission in any way of information that could identify a victim, witness or justice system participant whose identity is protected by the order. 2005, c. 32, s. 15.

CROSS-REFERENCES

"Victim" and "justice system participant" are defined in s. 2. Sections 486.4 and 486.5 provide for the making of orders prohibiting the publication, broadcasting or transmitting in any way of information that could identify the person named in the order.

SYNOPSIS

This section is complementary to ss. 486.4 and 486.5 and makes it a summary conviction offence to violate the orders made under those sections. The orders made under those sections also apply to protect the identity of the persons named in the orders in proceedings under this section.

ANNOTATIONS

It was held that a person could be cited for contempt of court in the superior court for violation of an order made under the predecessor to s. 486.4, notwithstanding the availability of the punishment under what is now this section: *Quebec (Procureur Général) v. Publications Photo-Police Inc.*, [1990] 1 S.C.R. 851 (7:0).

The accused journalist's conduct in writing and filing an article that identified the victim was sufficient to make out the *actus reus* of party liability under s. 21(1)(*b*) and (*c*) for the offence committed by the newspaper's publisher. However, whatever the fault element for the principal offender, party liability depended upon proof of intention to aid or abet the principal: *R. v. Helsdon* (2007), 216 C.C.C. (3d) 1 (Ont. C.A.).

SECURITY OF WITNESSES / Application / Factors to be considered / No adverse inference.

486.7 (1) In any proceedings against an accused, the presiding judge or justice may, on application of the prosecutor or a witness or on his or her own motion, make any order, other than one that may be made under any of sections 486 to 486.5, if the judge or justice is of the opinion that the order is necessary to protect the security of any witness and is otherwise in the interest of the proper administration of justice.

(2) The application may be made, during the proceedings, to the presiding judge or justice or, before the proceedings begin, to the judge or justice who will preside at the proceedings or, if that judge or justice has not been determined, to any judge or justice having jurisdiction in the judicial district where the proceedings will take place.

(3) In determining whether to make the order, the judge or justice shall consider

(*a*) the age of the witness;

(*b*) the witness's mental or physical disabilities, if any;

(*c*) the right to a fair and public hearing;

(*d*) the nature of the offence;

(*e*) whether the witness needs the order to protect them from intimidation or retaliation;

(*f*) whether the order is needed to protect the security of anyone known to the witness;

(*g*) society's interest in encouraging the reporting of offences and the participation of victims and witnesses in the criminal justice process;

(*h*) the importance of the witness's testimony to the case;

(*i*) whether effective alternatives to the making of the proposed order are available in the circumstances;

(*j*) the salutary and deleterious effects of the proposed order; and

(*k*) any other factor that the judge or justice considers relevant.

(4) No adverse inference may be drawn from the fact that an order is, or is not, made under this section. 2015, c. 20, s. 22.

CROSS-REFERENCES

"Justice" and "prosecutor" are defined in s. 2.

SYNOPSIS

This section allows the court to make "any order" — other than those available under ss. 486 to 486.5 — to protect the security of a witness. For example, this may allow for the use of testimonial aids not contemplated by any of the foregoing sections. Subsection (2) governs the timing and venue of such an application, while subsec. (3) sets out a list of mandatory considerations for the court to weigh in deciding whether to make an order. Subsection (4) prohibits any adverse inference being drawn from the making of (or refusal to make) such an order.

INFORMATION FOR SEARCH WARRANT / Endorsement of search warrant / Operation of computer system and copying equipment / Duty of person in possession or control / Form / Effect of endorsement.

487. (1) A justice who is satisfied by information on oath in Form 1 that there are reasonable grounds to believe that there is in a building, receptacle or place

(*a*) anything on or in respect of which any offence against this Act or any other Act of Parliament has been or is suspected to have been committed,

(*b*) anything that there are reasonable grounds to believe will afford evidence with respect to the commission of an offence, or will reveal the whereabouts of a person who is believed to have committed an offence, against this Act or any other Act of Parliament,

(*c*) anything that there are reasonable grounds to believe is intended to be used for the purpose of committing any offence against the person for which a person may be arrested without warrant, or

(*c*.1) any offence-related property,

may at any time issue a warrant authorizing a peace officer or a public officer who has been appointed or designated to administer or enforce a federal or provincial law and whose duties include the enforcement of this Act or any other Act of Parliament and who is named in the warrant

(*d*) to search the building, receptacle or place for any such thing and to seize it, and

(*e*) subject to any other Act of Parliament, to, as soon as practicable, bring the thing seized before, or make a report in respect thereof to, the justice or some other justice for the same territorial division in accordance with section 489.1.

(2) If the building, receptacle or place is in another territorial division, the justice may issue the warrant with any modifications that the circumstances require, and it may be executed in the other territorial division after it has been endorsed, in Form 28, by a justice who has jurisdiction in that territorial division. The endorsement may be made on the original of the warrant or on a copy of the warrant transmitted by any means of telecommunication.

(2.1) A person authorized under this section to search a computer system in a building or place for data may

(*a*) use or cause to be used any computer system at the building or place to search any data contained in or available to the computer system;

(*b*) reproduce or cause to be reproduced any data in the form of a print-out or other intelligible output;

(*c*) seize the print-out or other output for examination or copying; and

(*d*) use or cause to be used any copying equipment at the place to make copies of the data.

(2.2) Every person who is in possession or control of any building or place in respect of which a search is carried out under this section shall, on presentation of the warrant, permit the person carrying out the search

(*a*) to use or cause to be used any computer system at the building or place in order to search any data contained in or available to the computer system for data that the person is authorized by this section to search for;

(*b*) to obtain a hard copy of the data and to seize it; and

(*c*) to use or cause to be used any copying equipment at the place to make copies of the data.

(3) A search warrant issued under this section may be in the form set out as Form 5 in Part XXVIII, varied to suit the case.

(4) An endorsement that is made in accordance with subsection (2) is sufficient authority to the peace officers or public officers to whom the warrant was originally directed, and to all peace officers within the jurisdiction of the justice by whom it is endorsed, to execute the warrant and to deal with the things seized in accordance with section 489.1 or as otherwise provided by law. R.S., c. C-34, s. 443; R.S.C. 1985, c. 27 (1st Supp.), s. 68; 1994, c. 44, s. 36; 1997, c. 18, s. 41; 1997, c. 23, s. 12; 1999, c. 5, s. 16; 2008, c. 18, s. 11.

CROSS-REFERENCES

The terms "justice", "offence-related property", "peace officer", "public officer" and "territorial division" are defined in s. 2. A definition of "data", albeit for that section, is provided in s. 342.1.

Provision for granting of a telewarrant is made in s. 487.1. Section 487.11 allows a peace officer to search without a warrant in exigent circumstances. Restriction on publicity, see s. 487.2. A search warrant is executed in accordance with s. 488. If it is desired to execute the warrant at night, the grounds for doing so must be set out in the information. Execution of a warrant to search a lawyer's office is governed by s. 488.1. Section 489 provides for seizure of things not named in the warrant but which the person executing the warrant believes on reasonable grounds have been obtained by or have been used in the commission of an offence or may afford evidence. Section 489.1 sets out the procedure for restitution of goods to the lawful owner and s. 490 the procedure for detention of things which have been seized but not returned under s. 489.1. As to forfeiture of weapons and contraband, see ss. 491 and 491.1. Section 491.2 makes provision for use of photographic evidence in lieu of the actual property so that the property itself may be returned to the lawful owner. Other search or seizure powers: ss. 117.02 to 117.06, search and seizure re weapons; s. 164, *in rem* proceedings re obscene publications and crime comics; ss. 185 to 188, authorization to intercept private communications; ss. 254, 256 and 257, demand for breath and blood samples, warrant for blood sample; s. 199, disorderly house search warrant; s. 320, *in rem* proceedings re hate propaganda; s. 395, precious metals etc.; s. 462, seizure of counterfeit money, tokens and instruments for use in making counterfeit; s. 462.32, proceeds of crimes; s. 492, seizure of explosives. Also see s. 487.01 which allows for the obtaining of a "general" warrant in circumstances where a warrantless search or seizure would violate s. 8 of the Charter; s. 492.1, warrant to use tracking device; and s. 492.2, warrant to use telephone number recorder or obtain records of telephone calls.

Section 487.05 allows a provincial court judge to issue a warrant to seize bodily substances for forensic DNA analysis. For other cross-references respecting DNA analysis, see the summary immediately preceding s. 487.04. Section 487.091 provides that a justice may issue a warrant to obtain handprint, fingerprint, footprint, foot impression, teeth impression or other print or impression of the body or any part of the body.

Also see s. 487.11, which gives a peace officer or public officer appointed or designated to administer or enforce any federal or provincial law and whose duties also include the enforcement of the *Criminal Code* or any other Act of Parliament, a broad warrantless power of search and seizure in exigent circumstances. The officer may exercise the power to search and seizure in subsec. (1) without a warrant, provided that the conditions for granting a warrant exist but by reason of exigent circumstances it would be impracticable to obtain a warrant.

Note s. 31(1) of the *Interpretation Act*, R.S.C. 1985, c. I-21, which provides that where anything is required or authorized to be done by or before, *inter alia*, a justice of the peace it shall be done by or before one whose jurisdiction or powers extend to the place where the thing is to be done.

With respect to protection of persons executing warrants, see ss. 25 to 27. Also note s. 29(1) which imposes a duty on a person executing a warrant to have it with him, where it is feasible to do so, and produce it when requested.

Sections 487.012 and 487.013 provide alternatives to the search warrant procedure in this section by providing for an application for production orders.

Also see notes under s. 8 of the Charter.

SYNOPSIS

This section sets out the procedure that must be followed to obtain a search warrant.

Subsection (1) makes it clear that the justice must be *satisfied that there are reasonable grounds to believe* that the prescribed items will be found in a building, receptacle or place. The items being searched for may include anything in respect of which an offence against an Act of Parliament *has been*, or is *suspected* of *having been committed*, anything that there is *reasonable ground to believe* will afford evidence of an offence against an Act of Parliament, anything that will reveal the whereabouts of a person believed to have committed an offence, or anything that there are *reasonable grounds to believe* is intended to be used for the purpose of committing an offence against the person, for which a person may be arrested without a warrant. The justice may only be satisfied of the preceding if the information that comes before him is on oath and in Form 1.

The justice may issue a warrant authorizing a person named in that warrant, or a peace officer to search the building, receptacle or place for the specified items and to seize such items. The warrant will also require that the items seized be brought before a justice or that a report be made as soon as practicable.

Subsection (2) makes it clear that, if the building, receptacle or place in which the items sought are believed to be located is in another territorial division, the justice may issue the warrant in a form modified to fit the circumstances. This warrant must then be endorsed in Form 28, by a justice having jurisdiction, before it can be executed. This endorsement, which may be made on the original warrant or on a copy of the warrant transmitted by telecommunication, is sufficient authority to the person to whom the warrant was originally directed and to all peace officers within the new territorial division to execute the warrant. Once the warrant is endorsed, subsec. (4) provides that the warrant is authority for the officers to whom it was originally directed and officers in the jurisdiction of the justice to execute the warrant.

Subsections (2.1) and (2.2) provide for execution of the warrant in relation to data by using the computer system at the place to be searched.

ANNOTATIONS

Constitutional requirements generally – Where it is feasible to obtain prior authorization, such authorization, usually in the form of a warrant issued by a person able to act judicially and to assess the evidence as to whether the appropriate standard has been met in an entirely neutral and impartial manner, is a precondition for a valid search and seizure in conformity with s. 8 of the *Canadian Charter of Rights and Freedoms*. The person seeking to justify a warrantless search must rebut the presumption that such search is unreasonable in violation of s. 8: *Hunter v. Southam Inc.*, [1984] 2 S.C.R. 145, 14 C.C.C. (3d) 97 (8:0).

This section complies with s. 8 of the Charter: *R. v. Times Square Book Store* (1985), 21 C.C.C. (3d) 503, 48 C.R. (3d) 132 (Ont. C.A.).

Generally speaking, conformity to law is an essential component of reasonableness, although mere minor or technical defects in the warrant would not necessarily make an ensuing search or seizure unreasonable in violation of s. 8 of the Charter. However, a search or seizure conducted under a search warrant that is invalid in substance because it was issued upon information that did not set out facts upon which a justice acting judicially could be satisfied that there were grounds for issuing the warrant under subsec. (1)(*b*), or did not meet the minimum requirements of particularity respecting the things to be searched for, is unreasonable under s. 8: *R. v. Harris and Lighthouse Video Centres Ltd.* (1987), 35 C.C.C. (3d) 1, 57 C.R. (3d) 356 (Ont. C.A.), leave to appeal to S.C.C. refused [1986] 2 S.C.R. vii, 38 C.C.C. (3d) vi.

In considering the validity of a search warrant, facts obtained as a result of an unreasonable search must be excised. The court must then determine whether the warrant would have been issued without the improperly obtained facts: *R. v. Grant*, [1993] 3 S.C.R. 223, 84 C.C.C. (3d) 173 (9:0).

In *R. v. Tessling*, [2004] 3 S.C.R. 432, 189 C.C.C. (3d) 129, the Supreme Court of Canada held that the use of an infrared camera to obtain information about the patterns of heat distribution on the external surfaces of a house did not constitute a search within the meaning of s. 8 of the Charter. Information obtained via this technology cannot, by itself, constitute sufficient grounds to obtain a search warrant. The technology, at its current stage of development, was non-intrusive, did not "see" through the wall of a building and did not disclose a biographical core of information or reveal intimate details about the accused's lifestyle. Accordingly, there was no reasonable expectation of privacy in respect of this information.

Grounds for issuing warrant – Information supplied by a reliable informer, even though it is hearsay, may in some circumstances provide the necessary ground to justify granting of a search warrant. However, the mere statement by the informant that he was told by a reliable informer that a certain person is carrying on criminal activity or that contraband would be found at a certain place would be insufficient basis for granting a warrant. The underlying circumstances disclosed by the informer for his conclusion must be set out thus enabling the justice to satisfy himself that the requisite reasonable grounds exist: *R. v. Debot* (1986), 30 C.C.C. (3d) 207, 54 C.R. (3d) 120 (Ont. C.A.). A further appeal by the accused to the Supreme Court of Canada was dismissed [1989] 2 S.C.R. 1140, 52 C.C.C. (3d) 193 (5:0). The court agreed that the appropriate standard to establish reasonable grounds for a search is one of "reasonable probability" and, in making this determination, the court must have regard to the totality of the circumstances. The court also held that the suspect's criminal record and reputation could be taken into account provided that, *inter alia*, the reputation is related to the ostensible reasons for the search. Where the police rely on information from an informer, it is not necessary for the police to confirm each detail in the informer's tip, so long as the sequence of events actually observed conforms sufficiently to the anticipated pattern to remove the possibility of innocent coincidence. On the other hand, the level of verification required may be higher where the police rely on an informant whose credibility cannot be assessed or where fewer details are provided and the risk of innocent coincidence is greater.

Information from unnamed confidential sources was not a sufficient basis for issuing the warrant where there was no evidence to substantiate the veracity of the informers, no information as to how the informers acquired this knowledge and no independent evidence to support the story of the informers: *R. v. Berger* (1989), 48 C.C.C. (3d) 185, 74 Sask. R. 198 (C.A.).

Before granting the warrant the justice must be satisfied, *inter alia*, that the grounds stated for obtaining the warrant are current and that there is a nexus between the grounds for believing an offence has been committed and that evidence of the commission of the offence will be found on the premises to be searched: *R. v. Turcotte* (1987), 39 C.C.C. (3d) 193, [1982] 2 W.W.R. 97 (Sask. C.A.).

"Peace officer" includes a person appointed as a Special Provincial Constable under the *Police Act*, R.S.B.C. 1996, c. 367, with appointment restricted to "the performance of duties in respect to the mandate of the Ministry of Finance": *R. v. Semeniuk* (2007), 224 C.C.C. (3d) 71 (B.C.C.A.).

Things for which warrant may be obtained – A search warrant may authorize the removal and seizure of fixtures such as doors and windows: *R. v. Spitzer* (1984), 15 C.C.C. (3d) 98 (Sask. Q.B.). *Contra: R. v. Munn (No. 1)* (1938), 71 C.C.C. 139, [1938] 3 D.L.R. 772 (P.E.I.S.C.).

A search warrant is not available under this section to seize funds deposited in a savings account at a bank. A credit balance in a bank account is an intangible, merely proof that the bank has certain sums on deposit, and such funds are not segregated from the bank's other assets: *R. v. Banque Royale du Canada* (1985), 18 C.C.C. (3d) 98, 44 C.R. (3d) 387 (Que. C.A.), leave to appeal to S.C.C. refused C.C.C. *loc. cit*. [However, now see s. 462.33.]

The purpose of subsec. (1) is to allow the investigators to unearth and preserve as much relevant evidence as possible. They should therefore be able to locate, examine and preserve all the evidence relevant to events that may have given rise to criminal liability. Thus, this section is not limited to authorizing a search for evidence of the elements of the offence and may authorize a search for and seizure of evidence of negligence in the investigation of a strict liability offence going to a possible due diligence defence: *CanadianOxy Chemicals Ltd. v. Canada (Attorney General)*, [1999] 1 S.C.R. 743, 133 C.C.C. (3d) 426.

Seizure of hospital records – It was held in *R. v. French* (1977), 37 C.C.C. (2d) 201 (Ont. C.A.), affd on other grounds [1980] 1 S.C.R. 158, 47 C.C.C. (2d) 411, that in order to obtain hospital records the provincial legislation which brought those records into existence and safeguards their use must be complied with, even where the records are sought in criminal proceedings. Thus, see *R. v. Lyons* (1981), 64 C.C.C. (2d) 73 (Ont. H.C.J.), where an order was made within the terms of the provincial legislation. Also see *R. v. Coon* (1992), 74 C.C.C. (3d) 146 (Ont. Ct. (Gen. Div.)), noted under s. 698.

In *R. v. Waterford Hospital* (1983), 6 C.C.C. (3d) 481, 35 C.R. (3d) 348 (Nfld. C.A.), a search warrant to obtain hospital records made during a remand of the accused under s. 537(1)(*c*) was quashed, *inter alia*, because the Department of Justice could have applied under the provincial legislation to examine the records.

Where the applicable provincial legislation contained no code of procedure for obtaining medical records, a search warrant issued under this section was available to obtain the relevant records. The duty of confidentiality, which the hospital and staff owed to the accused, was not breached as the records were required to be released by law pursuant to the order of the justice: *R. v. Worth* (1989), 54 C.C.C. (3d) 215 (Ont. H.C.J.), affd 54 C.C.C. (3d) 223*n* (C.A.).

In *R. v. Serendip Physiotherapy Clinic* (2004), 189 C.C.C. (3d) 417, 25 C.R. (6th) 30, leave to appeal to S.C.C. refused [2005] 1 S.C.R. xv, 248 D.L.R. (4th) vii, the Ontario Court of Appeal held that there was no requirement that a search warrant for the seizure of physiotherapy records contain conditions protecting the patients' privacy. The search of a physiotherapy clinic did not risk the breach of an established class privilege and, accordingly, records seized from such a clinic were *prima facie* admissible.

Jurisdiction of justice – A justice of the peace appointed in and for the province has jurisdiction to issue a search warrant to be executed in one county although at the time the justice is sitting in another county, and such a warrant need not be endorsed pursuant to subsec. (2): *R. v. Haley* (1986), 27 C.C.C. (3d) 454, 51 C.R. (3d) 363 (Ont. C.A.). *Contra: R. v. Ciment Independant Inc., R. v. Ciment St-Laurent Inc.* (1985), 21 C.C.C. (3d) 429, 47 C.R. (3d) 83 (Que. C.A.).

A justice of the peace had jurisdiction to issue a search warrant to seize documents from a federal government department containing confidential information acquired under the *Old Age Security Act* (Can.) which was sought as evidence in relation to a fraud on provincial welfare authorities. The Act itself and the *Privacy Act* (Can.) created an exemption to the privilege and duty of non-disclosure in such circumstances. It was still open to the federal Minister to object to disclosure but this must be done under s. 37 of the *Canada Evidence Act*. On the other hand, in view of the confidential nature of the material sought, it would have been prudent for the justice of the peace to impose conditions and restrictions on the manner in which the warrant was executed: *Canada (Procureur General) v. Belanger* (1987), 42 C.C.C. (3d) 82, 61 C.R. (3d) 388 (Que. C.A.).

A provincial court judge has jurisdiction to issue the warrant on the same material where a justice of the peace refused to issue a warrant on the same material. A justice of the peace and provincial court judge have the same jurisdiction and the application before the provincial court judge is a *de novo* hearing. Furthermore, successive applications are not prohibited and do not constitute an abuse of process particularly where, as in this case, the officer had added paragraphs explaining that an application had been sought and rejected by the justice of the peace: *R. v. Duchcherer* (2006), 208 C.C.C. (3d) 201 (B.C.C.A.).

Search of persons / *Search incident of arrest* – Police officers have the power to search an accused as an incident to a lawful arrest and to seize anything in his possession or immediate surroundings to guarantee the safety of the police and the accused, prevent the accused's escape or provide evidence against him. The existence of reasonable and probable grounds to believe that the accused is in possession of weapons or evidence is not a prerequisite to the existence of the power to search, provided, however, that the search is for a valid objective and not unrelated to the objectives of the proper administration of justice. Proper objectives are to prevent the accused evading arrest and to collect evidence. Accordingly, a search done for weapons or other dangerous articles is necessary as an elementary precaution to preclude the possibility of their use against the police, the nearby public or the accused himself. A search is also proper to collect evidence that can be used in establishing the guilt of the accused. Further, the search must not be conducted in an abusive fashion and the use of physical or psychological constraint should be proportionate to the objectives sought and the other circumstances of the situation. A "frisk" or pat down search is a relatively non-intrusive procedure and, if done for valid reasons, is not a disproportionate interference with the freedom of persons lawfully arrested: *Cloutier c. Langlois*, [1990] 1 S.C.R. 158, 53 C.C.C. (3d) 257 (7:0). Also see *R. v. Caslake*, [1998] 1 S.C.R. 51, 121 C.C.C. (3d) 97.

Police have a limited power to detain for investigation where there are reasonable grounds to detain. The detention must be viewed as reasonably necessary on an objective view of the totality of the circumstances, informing the officer's suspicion that there is a clear nexus between the person to be detained and a recent or on-going criminal offence. The officer must have a reasonable suspicion that the particular individual is implicated in the criminal activity under investigation. The overall reasonableness of the decision to detain must further be assessed against all of the circumstances, most importantly the extent to which the interference with individual liberty is necessary to perform the officer's duty, the liberty interfered with, and the nature and extent of that interference. The power to detain cannot be exercised on the basis of a hunch, nor can it become a *de facto* arrest. Where the officer has lawfully detained the person for investigation, the officer may undertake a protective pat-down search where the officer believes on reasonable grounds that his or her safety or the safety of others is at risk. The search must be confined in scope to an intrusion reasonably designed to locate weapons. The detention and the pat-down search must be conducted in a reasonable manner: *R. v. Mann*, [2004] 3 S.C.R. 59, 185 C.C.C. (3d) 308.

Search and right to counsel – As a general rule, police proceeding to search are not obligated to suspend the search and give a person the opportunity to retain and instruct counsel, as, for example, when the search is of a home pursuant to a search warrant. Where a person is detained for a search, as in the case of a body search incident to arrest, then, immediately upon detention, the detainee has the right to be informed of the right to counsel under s. 10(*b*) of the *Charter of Rights and Freedoms*. However, the police are not obligated to suspend the search incident to arrest until the detainee has the opportunity to retain counsel. The police are, however, required to suspend the search where the lawfulness of the search is dependent on the detainee's consent or where the statute gives a person a right to seek review of the decision to search: *R. v. Debot*, [1989] 2 S.C.R. 1140, 52 C.C.C. (3d) 193.

Once the police have the situation clearly under control in the course of execution of a search warrant then they are required to afford an occupant of the premises, who has been arrested, an opportunity to exercise his rights under s. 10(*b*) of the Charter: *R. v. Strachan*, [1988] 2 S.C.R. 980, 46 C.C.C. (3d) 479 (7:0).

Execution of warrant [Also see notes under s. 488] – A police officer may have the assistance of persons, who are neither named in the warrant nor peace officers, provided that the police officer remains in control of and accountable for the search: *R. v. B. (J.E.)* (1989), 52 C.C.C. (3d) 224 (N.S.C.A.).

An officer executing a search warrant is required to have the warrant with her [see s. 29]. However, where the officer forgot to bring the warrant through inadvertence and the accused consented to the search commencing while the warrant was being brought to his home, then it was not shown that the search was unlawful: *R. v. B. (J.E.), supra*.

Where the police depart from the knock and announce principle, there is an onus on them to explain why they thought it was necessary to do so. The Crown must be able to lay an evidentiary framework to support the conclusion that the police had reasonable grounds to be concerned about the possibility of harm to themselves or occupants, or about the destruction of evidence. The greater the departure from the principle of announced entry, the heavier the onus. The evidence to justify such a departure must be judged by what was or should have reasonably been known to the police at the time. In addition, police must be allowed a certain amount of latitude in the manner in which they decide to enter premises and cannot be expected to measure in advance with nuanced precision the amount of force the situation will require. In this case, an unannounced, forced entry while masked was reasonable in all of the circumstances: *R. v. Cornell*, [2010] 2 S.C.R. 142, 258 C.C.C. (3d) 429.

A search is not presumptively unreasonable because the tactical team first entering did not have the warrant. The purpose of the provision is to allow the occupant to know why the search is being carried out, to allow an assessment of his or her legal position, and to know that there is a color of authority for the search making forcible resistance improper. This requirement is met if the warrant is in the possession of at least one member of the team executing the warrant: *R. v. Cornell, supra.*

Contents of warrant – The person whose premises are being searched is entitled to know from examination of the search warrant for what reason the search is taking place and the seizing officer must know in relation to what offence or circumstances the articles are to be seized. The failure, therefore, to describe the offence sufficiently in the search warrant is fatal to the validity of the warrant. A warrant merely setting out a conspiracy to defraud certain named companies "and other financial institutions" and not alleging the means of fraud nor what the victims were defrauded of was held to be defective and was quashed and the items seized ordered to be returned: *R. v. Alder* (1977), 37 C.C.C. (2d) 234, [1977] 5 W.W.R. 132 (Alta. S.C.T.D.).

In determining the degree of specificity required of things to be searched for, regard must be had to the nature of the offence alleged in the information to obtain the search warrant. In this case the court was required to consider the size and sophisticated nature of the target of the search as well as the continuing nature of the alleged offences and the lengthy period of time during which they were alleged to have been committed. Thus a warrant authorizing search and seizure of broad classes of documents was justified. Even where the informant did not allege the precise nexus between a thing to be searched for and an alleged offence, the justice of the peace who issued the warrant was entitled to draw reasonable inferences of such nexus from the allegations in the information. Where, by the very nature of the things to be searched for, it is not possible to describe them with precision or great particularity, it is inevitable that the executing officers will have to exercise some discretion in determining whether things found on the premises fall within the description of the things or classes of things described in the warrant: *R. v. Church of Scientology (No. 6)*; *R. v. Walsh* (1987), 31 C.C.C. (3d) 449 (C.A.).

The offence for which the items are sought need not be set out in the warrant with the same precision as would be required for an indictment, provided that the person in charge of the premises is reasonably informed from the warrant as to the nature of the offence and the object of the search: *R. v. PSI Mind Development Institute Ltd* (1977), 37 C.C.C. (2d) 263 (Ont. H.C.J.).

Religious privilege / freedom of religion – While it is not the function of the court to pass on the validity of religious beliefs sincerely held by any organization, the mere fact that an organization claims to be a religion does not bar the Crown or any other litigant from seeking the assistance of the courts in the determination of either criminal or civil wrong, including resort to the investigative tool of a search warrant: *R. v. Church of Scientology (No. 6); R. v. Walsh, supra.*

There is no recognized class privilege accorded to the priest penitent relationship and so while s. 2(*a*) of the *Charter of Rights and Freedoms* may have enhanced the claim that communications made in the course of that relationship may have to be afforded privilege, its applicability must be determined on a case by case basis. The justice would have jurisdiction to issue a warrant to seize files which allegedly contained priest penitent communications where the information to obtain the warrant discloses a *prima facie* case of criminality and that no reasonable alternative source of obtaining the information was available: *R. v. Church of Scientology (No. 6); R. v. Walsh, supra.*

The *Canadian Charter of Rights and Freedoms* does not require the application of a strict test such as the test of scrupulous exactitude in the assessment of the particularity of the search warrant, notwithstanding that the search allegedly involved intrusion into areas of protected freedoms such as freedom of religion: *R. v. Church of Scientology (No. 6)*; *R. v. Walsh, supra*.

Freedom of expression (media) – Even where the minimum requirements set out in this section have been met, the justice has a discretion whether or not to issue the warrant and, if so, whether to attach conditions to its execution. In the case of the media and in light of the guarantee to freedom of expression in s. 2(*b*) of the Charter, there must be a careful consideration as to whether the warrant should issue and also the conditions which might be imposed. Ordinarily, the information to obtain the warrant should disclose whether there are alternative sources from which the information may reasonably be obtained and if there is an alternative source, that it has been investigated and all reasonable efforts to obtain the information have been exhausted. If a search will impede the media from fulfilling its functions of news gatherer and disseminator, then a warrant should only be issued where a compelling state interest is demonstrated. The fact that the information sought has already been disseminated in whole or in part, to the public by the media will ordinarily favour the granting of the warrant: *Canadian Broadcasting Corp. v. New Brunswick (Attorney General)*, [1991] 3 S.C.R. 459, 67 C.C.C. (3d) 544 (6:1); *Canadian Broadcasting Corp. v. Lessard*, [1991] 3 S.C.R. 421, 67 C.C.C. (3d) 517 (6:1).

Obscene material [Also see notes under s. 164] – Where a search warrant is sought in relation to allegedly obscene magazines, it is not sufficient that the justice of the peace is satisfied that the items sought could be of assistance in establishing the commission of an offence. Rather, the justice must be satisfied on reasonable and probable grounds that the magazines to be seized are obscene and can be found at the specified premises. Further, the warrant should be reasonably specific when dealing with books and magazines since sexually explicit material, however distasteful it may be, so long as it is not obscene, is entitled to the same protection as other forms of expression. On the other hand, neither the material presented in support of the application for a warrant nor the warrant itself need specify the title of each magazine or book sought to be seized: *R. v. Times Square Book Store* (1985), 21 C.C.C. (3d) 503, 48 C.R. (3d) 132 (Ont. C.A.); *R. v. Comic Legends* (1987), 40 C.C.C. (3d) 203, 56 Alta. L.R. (2d) 170 (Q.B.).

Disclosure of identity of confidential informers – Where an accused seeks to attack the lawfulness and reasonableness of a search of his home on the basis that there were not sufficient grounds, in the information, for the issuance of the warrant then there should be reasonable disclosure made of the information which was used to obtain the search warrant, if it is needed and requested, despite the fact that it may disclose the identity of an informer. However, upon receipt of such a request, the trial judge should review the information with the object of deleting all references to the identity of the informer. The information so edited should then be made available to the accused. If, at the conclusion of the editing procedure, the Crown still believes that the informer would become known to the accused upon production of the information, then a decision would have to be made by the Crown. The informer might by this time be willing to consent to being identified. Alternatively, the informer's identity might have become so notorious in the community or become so well known to the accused that his identification would no longer be a significant issue. If the Crown is of the view that to produce the informer would be prejudicial to the administration of justice the Crown may elect not to proceed with the evidence or to proceed on the basis of a warrantless search. In those circumstances, the trial judge will have to consider the application of s. 24(2) of the Charter: *R. v. Hunter* (1987), 34 C.C.C. (3d) 14, 57 C.R. (3d) 1 (Ont. C.A.).

In *R. v. Collins* (1989), 48 C.C.C. (3d) 343, 69 C.R. (3d) 235 (Ont. C.A.), the court considered the related problem of disclosure of the identity of a confidential informer who is not named in the information to obtain the search warrant but whose information was the basis, at least in part, for obtaining the search warrant. It was held that the common law rules of evidence, which prohibit judicial disclosure of a police informer's identity by police officers who have learned the informer's identity in the course of their duties, were applicable. There is only one exception to this principle and that is where disclosure of the identity of the informer is necessary to demonstrate the innocence of the accused.

In *R. v. Leipert*, [1997] 1 S.C.R. 281, 112 C.C.C. (3d) 385, the court considered the problem of an information based upon a tip from an anonymous informer under a Crime Stoppers programme. Absent a basis for concluding that disclosure of the information that may reveal the identity of the informer is necessary to establish the innocence of the accused, the information remains privileged and cannot be produced, whether on a hearing into the reasonableness of the search or on the trial proper. Therefore anonymous tip sheets should not be edited with a view to disclosing them to the defence unless the accused's case falls within the innocence at stake exception. To do so runs the risk that the court will deprive the informer of the privilege that belongs to him or her absolutely, subject only to the innocence at stake exception. It also undermines the efficacy of programs such as Crime Stoppers that depend on guarantees of anonymity to those who volunteer information on crimes. When an accused seeks disclosure of privileged informer information on the basis of the exception, the accused must first show some basis to conclude that without the disclosure sought, his or her innocence is at stake. If such a basis is shown, the court may then review the information to determine whether, in fact, the information is necessary to prove the accused's innocence. If the court concludes that disclosure is necessary, the court should only reveal as much information as is essential to allow proof of innocence. Before disclosing the information to the accused, the Crown should be given the option of staying the proceedings. If the Crown chooses to proceed, disclosure of the information essential to establish innocence may be provided to the accused. If the accused cannot bring the case within the exception, the trial judge should permit the Crown to defend the warrant on the material in the information with the reference to the anonymous tip deleted.

Review of sufficiency of warrant / When review application should be brought – Where the sole purpose for attacking the validity of the search warrant issued by a justice of the peace is to lay a foundation for exclusion of evidence, obtained as a result of its execution, pursuant to ss. 8 and 24(2) of the *Charter of Rights and Freedoms*, then the issue should be determined at trial and not by way of an application to the superior court prior to trial. The rule against collateral attack of orders of a superior court does not extend to the orders of an inferior court: *R. v. Zevallos* (1987), 37 C.C.C. (3d) 79, 59 C.R. (3d) 153 (Ont. C.A.); *R. v. Williams* (1987), 38 C.C.C. (3d) 319, 17 B.C.L.R. (2d) 223 (Y.T.C.A.); *R. v. Jamieson* (1989), 48 C.C.C. (3d) 287, 90 N.S.R. (2d) 164 (C.A.); *R. v. Bailey* (1988), 87 N.S.R. (2d) 245, 39 C.R.R. 378 (C.A.). *Contra: R. v. Komadowski* (1986), 27 C.C.C. (3d) 319, [1986] 3 W.W.R. 657 (Man. C.A.), leave to appeal to S.C.C. refused C.C.C. *loc. cit.*, 44 Man. R. (2d) 79.

Scope of review – On an application to quash a search warrant the superior court judge may not substitute his opinion as to the sufficiency of the evidence. Rather he is limited to determining whether or not there is evidence upon which the justice acting judicially could determine that a warrant should be issued and whether the warrant contained sufficient particulars of the items to be seized so that it could not be said that the discretion of the officer was substituted for that of the justice as to the items to be seized: *R. v. Times Square Book Store, supra; Quebec (Attorney General) v. Mathieu* (1986), 50 C.R. (3d) 156 (Que. C.A.); *R. v. Turcotte*, [1988] 2 W.W.R. 97 (Sask. C.A.). The enactment of the *Canadian Charter of Rights and Freedoms* has not altered the scope of review which is limited to jurisdictional error: *R. v. Church of Scientology (No. 6); R. v. Walsh, supra.*

In determining the validity of an information or search warrant the court is not entitled to look at the results of the search: *Liberal Party of Quebec v. Mierzwinski* (1978), 46 C.C.C. (2d) 118 (Que. S.C.).

Procedure on review – Most of the recent cases on the procedure to review prior judicial authorization, including the threshold for permitting cross-examination of the affiant have taken place in the wiretap context. Accordingly, reference should be made to the cases noted under s. 186 and especially those noted under the headings "**Review of validity of authorization**" and "**Cross-examination of deponent of affidavit**". See in particular the notes of *R. v. Garofoli*, [1990] 2 S.C.R. 1421, 60 C.C.C. (3d) 161 and *R. v. Araujo*, [2000] 2 S.C.R. 992, 149 C.C.C. (3d) 449.

While in the result the court did not find it necessary to decide the point, some doubt was expressed as to whether a justice of the peace was a compellable witness to testify with respect to his mental processes in exercising the judicial function whether or not to grant a search warrant: *R. v. Moran* (1987), 36 C.C.C. (3d) 225, 21 O.A.C. 257 (C.A.), leave to appeal to S.C.C. refused [1988] 1 S.C.R. xi. [And now see: *MacKeigan v. Hickman*, [1989] 2 S.C.R. 796, 50 C.C.C. (3d) 449.]

Standing – In the absence of showing some possessory or proprietary interest either in the things seized or the premises, a third person has no standing to attempt to quash the search warrant even where the items seized relate to transactions by the applicant: *R. v. Model Power* (1980), 21 C.R. (3d) 195 (Ont. C.A.), leave to appeal to S.C.C. refused C.R. *loc. cit.*.

The accused had standing to challenge a search warrant executed at a property that he owned but did not reside in. The accused had the authority to regulate access to the property. While a non-resident might not have the same expectation of privacy as a resident, there was no evidence that the accused had given up possession or control to any other occupant: *R. v. Vi* (2008), 239 C.C.C. (3d) 57 (B.C.C.A.).

Severance of warrant – Where a search warrant is defective in part that part only may be severed: *R. v. Johnson & Franklin Wholesale Distributors Ltd.* (1971), 3 C.C.C. (2d) 484, 16 C.R.N.S. 107 (B.C.C.A.).

Although on an application to quash a search warrant the superior court has power to sever off bad parts of a warrant there is no authority to permit the court on a *certiorari* application to amend the warrant by, for example, narrowing the time period of the alleged offence to conform with the evidence disclosed in the information to obtain the warrant: *R. v. Dobney Holdings* (1985), 18 C.C.C. (3d) 238 (B.C.C.A.).

Return of items seized – Where the search warrant had a fatal defect it was wrong for the judge on *certiorari* to allow the Crown to decide which documents should be retained, and an order will be made directing that all documents and copies be returned to the applicant: *Bergeron v. Deschamps*, [1978] 1 S.C.R. 243, 33 C.C.C. (2d) 461 (9:0). The court without passing on the correctness of *R. v. Black* (1973), 13 C.C.C. (2d) 446, 24 C.R.N.S. 203 (B.C.S.C.), where it had been held that an order should go returning the seized goods provided they were not required as evidence, distinguished the case on the basis that in *R. v. Black* there was not the same fatal frailties as existed in this case. In *R. v. Black* the warrant was quashed because of failure of the person signing it to indicate he was a justice of the peace.

Even where charges have been laid and the items seized under the invalid warrant are required as evidence, the court, in quashing the warrant, has a discretion to order the items returned. This power existed prior to the *Charter of Rights and Freedoms* and exists as a remedy under s. 24(1): *R. v. Chapman* (1984), 12 C.C.C. (3d) 1, 9 D.L.R. (4th) 244 (Ont. C.A.).

In determining whether or not to make an order returning items seized after the warrant has been quashed the court will have regard to the conduct of the prosecuting authorities in relation to the search and seizure, the seriousness of the offence, the degree of potential cogency of the things seized in proving the charge, the nature of the defect in the warrant and the potential prejudice to the owner in being kept out of possession. In proper circumstances the court may give the authorities an opportunity to obtain a new warrant before ordering the return of the items seized: *R. v. Dobney Foundry Ltd. (No. 2)* (1985), 19 C.C.C. (3d) 465, [1985] 3 W.W.R. 626 (B.C.C.A.).

The court, having quashed the warrant, may in appropriate circumstances provide that the items are to be returned within a specified number of days unless the Crown obtains a fresh search warrant within that time: *R. v. Dobney Foundry Ltd. (No. 3)* (1986), 29 C.C.C. (3d) 285, [1987] 1 W.W.R. 281 (B.C.C.A.).

The Superior Court's inherent jurisdiction to order the return of items wrongfully seized under an invalid search warrant and which are not required as evidence also extends to items seized without a search warrant and which are wrongfully held by the police: *Butler and Butler v. Canada (Solicitor General)* (1981), 61 C.C.C. (2d) 512 (B.C.S.C.).

Application to other statutes – Although the former *Bankruptcy Act*, R.S.C. 1970, c. B-3, contained its own search and seizure provisions, the authorities could resort to this section to obtain evidence in relation to an offence under that Act. The addition of the words "or any other Act of Parliament" unambiguously show that every Act of Parliament could fall within the ambit of subsec. (1)(*a*) and (*b*): *R. v. Multiform Manufacturing Co.*, [1990] 2 S.C.R. 624, 58 C.C.C. (3d) 257 (7:0).

A search warrant may be obtained under this section to search for narcotics. In such a case, however, the authorities were not entitled to rely upon the broad powers in s. 12 of the [former] *Narcotic Control Act* for execution of the warrant: *R. v. Grant*, [1993] 3 S.C.R. 223, 84 C.C.C. (3d) 173.

INFORMATION FOR GENERAL WARRANT / Limitation / Search or seizure to be reasonable / Video surveillance / Other provisions to apply / Other provisions to apply / Telewarrant provisions to apply.

487.01 (1) A provincial court judge, a judge of a superior court of criminal jurisdiction or a judge as defined in section 552 may issue a warrant in writing authorizing a peace officer to, subject to this section, use any device or investigative technique or procedure or do any thing described in the warrant that would, if not authorized, constitute an unreasonable search or seizure in respect of a person or a person's property if

(*a*) the judge is satisfied by information on oath in writing that there are reasonable grounds to believe that an offence against this or any other Act of Parliament has been or will be committed and that information concerning the offence will be obtained through the use of the technique, procedure or device or the doing of the thing;

(*b*) the judge is satisfied that it is in the best interests of the administration of justice to issue the warrant; and

(*c*) there is no other provision in this or any other Act of Parliament that would provide for a warrant, authorization or order permitting the technique, procedure or device to be used or the thing to be done.

(2) Nothing in subsection (1) shall be construed as to permit interference with the bodily integrity of any person.

(3) A warrant issued under subsection (1) shall contain such terms and conditions as the judge considers advisable to ensure that any search or seizure authorized by the warrant is reasonable in the circumstances.

(4) A warrant issued under subsection (1) that authorizes a peace officer to observe, by means of a television camera or other similar electronic device, any person who is engaged in activity in circumstances in which the person has a reasonable expectation of privacy shall contain such terms and conditions as the judge considers advisable to ensure that the privacy of the person or of any other person is respected as much as possible.

(5) The definition "offence" in section 183 and sections 183.1, 184.2, 184.3 and 185 to 188.2, subsection 189(5), and sections 190, 193 and 194 to 196 apply, with such modifications as the circumstances require, to a warrant referred to in subsection (4) as though references in those provisions to interceptions of private communications were read as references to observations by peace officers by means of television cameras or similar electronic devices of activities in circumstances in which persons had reasonable expectations of privacy.

(5.1) A warrant issued under subsection (1) that authorizes a peace officer to enter and search a place covertly shall require, as part of the terms and conditions referred to in subsection (3), that notice of the entry and search be given within any time after the execution of the warrant that the judge considers reasonable in the circumstances.

(5.2) Where the judge who issues a warrant under subsection (1) or any other judge having jurisdiction to issue such a warrant is, on the basis of an affidavit submitted in support of an application to vary the period within which the notice referred to in subsection (5.1) is to be given, is satisfied that the interests of justice warrant the granting of the application, the judge may grant an extension, or a subsequent extension, of the period, but no extension may exceed three years.

(6) Subsections 487(2) and (4) apply, with such modifications as the circumstances require, to a warrant issued under subsection (1).

(7) Where a peace officer believes that it would be impracticable to appear personally before a judge to make an application for a warrant under this section, a warrant may be issued under this section on an information submitted by telephone or other means of telecommunication and, for that purpose, section 487.1 applies, with such modifications as the circumstances require, to the warrant. 1993, c. 40, s. 15; 1997, c. 18, s. 42; 1997, c. 23, s. 13.

CROSS-REFERENCES

This section is part of a more or less comprehensive scheme relating to search and seizure. Interception of private communications are dealt with in Part VI. Use of telephone number recorders is regulated under s. 492.2 and use of tracking devices is regulated under s. 492.1. Section 487 deals with the granting of ordinary search warrants to seize tangible things. Provision is made in s. 487.02 for the making of an assistance order to require persons to co-operate in the carrying out of orders made under this section. As to warrants to obtain bodily substances for DNA analysis, see ss. 487.04 to 487.09, and for impression warrant, see s. 487.091.

The terms "peace officer", "provincial court judge" and "superior court judge" are defined in s. 2.

SYNOPSIS

This section allows for the obtaining of a warrant in circumstances where a warrantless search or seizure would violate s. 8 of the Charter. In effect, it fills a gap noted by various courts. For example, the Supreme Court had held in *R. v. Wong*, [1990] 3 S.C.R. 36, 60 C.C.C. (3d) 460, that warrantless surreptitious video surveillance by agents of the state in circumstances where the target has a reasonable expectation of privacy is a violation of s. 8 and yet no provision was made for obtaining a warrant or court authorization. A warrant for such surveillance could now be obtained under this section.

The warrant may be issued for any device or investigative technique or procedure or "any thing" except, pursuant to subsec. (2), anything which would interfere with the bodily integrity of any person. Subsection (3) permits the judge to impose appropriate conditions.

Subsection (5) makes special provision for video surveillance in circumstances where persons have a reasonable expectation of privacy. The effect of this subsection is that the authorization procedure under Part VI applies with the necessary modifications. In other words, a general warrant for this type of surveillance can only be obtained in the same circumstances as where an authorization to intercept private communications may be obtained. Thus, while a general warrant under subsec. (1) may be obtained in relation to any federal offence, a warrant in relation to video surveillance in circumstances where persons have a reasonable expectation of privacy can only be obtained for the offences listed in s. 183. To obtain the warrant, the police must meet the tests set out in Part VI rather than the test in subsec. (1) of this section. As well, the prohibition on disclosure of information from such surveillance in s. 193 is incorporated, as is notice of intention to introduce into evidence in s. 189(5), and the notice to targets provision in s. 196.

Subsection (4) requires the judge to impose conditions to protect the privacy of the targeted person and others in a case where the warrant is issued to authorize video surveillance in circumstances where persons have a reasonable expectation of privacy.

Subsection (5.1) and (5.2) deal with notice following a covert entry and search by a peace officer.

Subsection (6) makes applicable the provisions of s. 487 for "backing" the warrant if it is to be executed in another territorial division. Note that if the warrant is to be executed in another province and the investigative technique requires entry into private property or an assistance order under s. 487.02 then the warrant must be confirmed by a judge of the other province.

The warrant may be obtained by telephone etc. in accordance with subsec. (7).

ANNOTATIONS

Properly interpreted, this provision does not violate s. 8 of the Charter: *R. v. Lucas* (2014), 313 C.C.C. (3d) 159 (Ont. C.A.), leave to appeal to S.C.C. refused 2015 CarswellOnt 639.

A peace officer is not precluded from obtaining a general warrant solely because he has sufficient information to obtain a search warrant. A general warrant may be used with a view to gathering additional and possibly better evidence than that which could be seized immediately through the execution of a search warrant. Accordingly, the police were permitted to utilize the general warrant to covertly enter the premises where they detected evidence of a drug operation, and to subsequently use these observations as a basis to obtain a search warrant under s. 11 of the *Controlled Drugs and Substances Act*: *R. v. Brand* (2008), 229 C.C.C. (3d) 443 (B.C.C.A.).

A general warrant was validly issued under this section requiring employees of the Canada Post Corporation to photocopy the outside of envelopes and packages of mailable material after it was delivered to certain post office boxes. Compliance with the warrant would not require the employees to contravene the *Canada Post Corporation Act*: *Canada Post Corp. v. Canada (Attorney General)* (1995), 95 C.C.C. (3d) 568 (Ont. Ct. (Gen. Div.)).

An "anticipatory" search warrant for the re-seizure of items returned to the owner later the same day is authorized by this section: *R. v. Noseworthy* (1997), 116 C.C.C. (3d) 376, 33 O.R. (3d) 641 (C.A.).

In *R. v. Brooks* (2003), 178 C.C.C. (3d) 361, 15 C.R. (6th) 319 (Ont. C.A.), the court held that there should be explicit, clear and narrowly drawn pre-conditions to the issuance of a general warrant.

In *R. v. Brand* (2008), 229 C.C.C. (3d) 443, 56 C.R. (6th) 39, the British Columbia Court of Appeal held that a general warrant was properly utilized to allow for a covert entry to obtain information with a view to gathering additional and possibly better evidence than that which could be seized immediately through the execution of a search warrant.

This provision can authorize repeated covert entries and searches of private property. Covert entries constitute an "investigative technique or procedure". This provision is not limited to electronic devices to record and intercept communications. The focus of para. (*c*) was not on whether there were other investigative techniques that might accomplish the purported investigative purposes or goals of the police, but on the particular investigative technique or procedure that the police sought to utilize and whether it could be properly authorized by another provision. In this case, there was no other provision that could authorize repeated, covert entries and searches on private property over a two-month period. Further, the fact that some of the purposes of the investigation could have been obtained through the issuance of a traditional search warrant did not preclude reliance on this section: *R. v. Ha* (2009), 245 C.C.C. (3d) 546 (Ont. C.A.), leave to appeal to S.C.C. refused 247 C.C.C. (3d) vi.

Section 487.01(1)(*c*) should be broadly construed to ensure that the general warrant is not used to circumvent the more specific or rigorous pre-authorization requirements for warrants, such as those found in Part VI. A general warrant is not available to obtain an intercept of private communications, which includes text messages: *R. v. Telus Communication Co.*, [2013] 2 S.C.R. 3, 294 C.C.C. (3d) 498.

The validity of the warrant was not affected by the fact that the search warrant was signed before the information to obtain was sworn: *R. v. Ho* (2012), 293 C.C.C. (3d) 185 (Alta. C.A.).

A general warrant is not the proper form of authorization for the search of a computer. A regular search warrant under s. 487 is available: *R. v. Z. (K.)* (2014), 312 C.C.C. (3d) 346 (Alta. Q.B.).

A general warrant cannot authorize the breach of a person's s. 10(*a*) right to be informed of the reasons for one's detention. Therefore, where a general warrant authorized police to execute a "ruse" traffic stop on a suspect in a drug investigation, it was not permissible to include a term authorizing police not to inform the suspect of the actual reason for the traffic stop: *R. v. Croft* (2014), 332 C.C.C. (3d) 241 (Alta. Q.B.).

This provision can in principle authorize a "bedpan vigil" in respect of an accused who has secreted contraband in his rectum. However, a general warrant cannot override the terms of s. 503, which require an arrested person to be brought before a justice without unreasonable delay and in any event within 24 hours of arrest: *R. v. Poirier* (2016), 342 C.C.C. (3d) 407 (Ont. C.A.).

DEFINITIONS.

487.011 The following definitions apply in this section and in sections 487.012 to 487.0199.

"computer data" has the same meaning as in subsection 342.1(2).

"data" means representations, including signs, signals or symbols, that are capable of being understood by an individual or processed by a computer system or other device.

"document" means a medium on which data is registered or marked.

"judge" means a judge of a superior court of criminal jurisdiction or a judge of the Court of Quebec.

"public officer" means a public officer who is appointed or designated to administer or enforce a federal or provincial law and whose duties include the enforcement of this Act or any other Act of Parliament.

"tracking data" means data that relates to the location of a transaction, individual or thing.

"transmission data" means data that

(*a*) relates to the telecommunication functions of dialling, routing, addressing or signalling;

(*b*) is transmitted to identify, activate or configure a device, including a computer program as defined in subsection 342.1(2), in order to establish or maintain access to a telecommunication service for the purpose of enabling a communication, or is generated during the creation, transmission or reception of a communication and identifies or purports to identify the type, direction, date, time, duration, size, origin, destination or termination of the communication; and

(*c*) does not reveal the substance, meaning or purpose of the communication. 2004, c. 3, s. 7; 2014, c. 31, s. 20.

PRESERVATION DEMAND / Conditions for making demand / Limitation / Expiry and revocation of demand / Conditions in demand / No further demand.

487.012 (1) A peace officer or public officer may make a demand to a person in Form 5.001 requiring them to preserve computer data that is in their possession or control when the demand is made.

(2) The peace officer or public officer may make the demand only if they have reasonable grounds to suspect that

(*a*) an offence has been or will be committed under this or any other Act of Parliament or has been committed under a law of a foreign state;

(*b*) in the case of an offence committed under a law of a foreign state, an investigation is being conducted by a person or authority with responsibility in that state for the investigation of such offences; and

(*c*) the computer data is in the person's possession or control and will assist in the investigation of the offence.

(3) A demand may not be made to a person who is under investigation for the offence referred to in paragraph (2)(*a*).

(4) A peace officer or public officer may revoke the demand by notice given to the person at any time. Unless the demand is revoked earlier, the demand expires

(*a*) in the case of an offence that has been or will be committed under this or any other Act of Parliament, 21 days after the day on which it is made; and

(*b*) in the case of an offence committed under a law of a foreign state, 90 days after the day on which it is made.

(5) The peace officer or public officer who makes the demand may impose any conditions in the demand that they consider appropriate — including conditions prohibiting the disclosure of its existence or some or all of its contents — and may revoke a condition at any time by notice given to the person.

(6) A peace officer or public officer may not make another demand requiring the person to preserve the same computer data in connection with the investigation. 2004, c. 3, s. 7; 2014, c. 31, s. 20.

(7) [*Repealed*, 2014, c. 31, s. 20.]

(8) [*Repealed*, 2014, c. 31, s. 20.]

CROSS-REFERENCES

"Computer data" is defined in ss. 487.011 and 342.1.

"Peace officer" is defined in s. 2, and "public officer" is defined in s. 487.011.

Section 487.013 provides for a preservation order in relation to computer data.

Section 487.014 provides for general production orders.

Sections 487.015 to 487.018 provide for other forms of production orders in relation to specified types of data.

Sections 487.019, 487.0191 and 487.0192 set out certain procedural requirements and options applicable to all preservation or production orders made under the foregoing provisions.

Section 487.0193 provides a procedure by which the target of a production order can seek to have the order varied or revoked.

Section 487.0194 governs the destruction of data following the expiration of a preservation demand or order.

Section 487.0195 clarifies that none of the foregoing provisions prevent a request for the voluntary preservation or production of data or documents.

Section 487.0196 provides that self-incrimination concerns do not excuse compliance with orders made under the foregoing provisions; however, immunity against subsequent incriminating use is provided.

Sections 487.0197 to 487.0199 create summary conviction offences for contravening preservation demands, preservation orders and production orders.

SYNOPSIS

This provision allows a peace officer or public officer to demand that a person preserve computer data in their possession. A demand may be made on the basis of a reasonable belief that an offence has been or will be committed under the *Criminal Code* or other Act of

Parliament, or that an offence has been committed under a law of a foreign state provided an investigation is being carried out in the foreign state by someone with appropriate authority to do so. The demand must also be made on reasonable belief that the data in question will assist the investigation of the offence.

Subsection (3) provides that a demand cannot be made to the subject of the investigation.

Subsection (4) provides time periods for the expiry of the demand.

Subsection (5) allows the officer making the demand to stipulate appropriate conditions.

Subsection (6) prohibits subsequent demands for preservation of the same data.

PRESERVATION ORDER — COMPUTER DATA / Conditions for making order / Offence against law of foreign state / Form / Limitation / Expiry of order.

487.013 (1) On *ex parte* application made by a peace officer or public officer, a justice or judge may order a person to preserve computer data that is in their possession or control when they receive the order.

(2) Before making the order, the justice or judge must be satisfied by information on oath in Form 5.002

- **(*a*) that there are reasonable grounds to suspect that an offence has been or will be committed under this or any other Act of Parliament or has been committed under a law of a foreign state, that the computer data is in the person's possession or control and that it will assist in the investigation of the offence; and**
- **(*b*) that a peace officer or public officer intends to apply or has applied for a warrant or an order in connection with the investigation to obtain a document that contains the computer data.**

(3) If an offence has been committed under a law of a foreign state, the justice or judge must also be satisfied that a person or authority with responsibility in that state for the investigation of such offences is conducting the investigation.

(4) The order is to be in Form 5.003.

(5) A person who is under investigation for an offence referred to in paragraph (2)(*a*) may not be made subject to an order.

(6) Unless the order is revoked earlier, it expires 90 days after the day on which it is made. 2004, c. 3. s. 7; 2014, c. 31, s. 20.

CROSS-REFERENCES

"Computer data" is defined in ss. 487.011 and 342.1.

"Peace officer" is defined in s. 2, and "public officer" is defined in s. 487.011.

"Justice" is defined in s. 2 and "judge" is defined in s. 487.011.

For references to the other production and preservation order-related sections, see the cross-references under s. 487.012.

SYNOPSIS

This section provides for the making of a preservation order by a justice or judge in respect of computer data.

Pursuant to subsec. (2), the order may be made only where the justice or judge is satisfied on an *ex parte* application containing information on oath in writing that there are reasonable grounds to believe that an offence has been or will be committed under the *Criminal Code* or other Act of Parliament, or that an offence has been committed under a law of a foreign state; that the computer data is in the person's possession or control and that it will assist in the investigation of the offence; and that the officer intends to apply (or has applied) for a warrant or order to obtain the data.

Under subsec. (3), if a foreign offence is alleged to have been committed, the justice or judge must also be satisfied that it is being investigated by someone with appropriate authority in that jurisdiction.

Subsection (5) prohibits such an order from being made against a person under investigation for an offence.

GENERAL PRODUCTION ORDER / Conditions for making order / Form / Limitation.

487.014 (1) Subject to sections 487.015 to 487.018, on *ex parte* application made by a peace officer or public officer, a justice or judge may order a person to produce a document that is a copy of a document that is in their possession or control when they receive the order, or to prepare and produce a document containing data that is in their possession or control at that time.

(2) Before making the order, the justice or judge must be satisfied by information on oath in Form 5.004 that there are reasonable grounds to believe that

(*a*) an offence has been or will be committed under this or any other Act of Parliament; and

(*b*) the document or data is in the person's possession or control and will afford evidence respecting the commission of the offence.

(3) The order is to be in Form 5.005.

(4) A person who is under investigation for the offence referred to in subsection (2) may not be made subject to an order. 2004, c. 3, s. 7; 2014, c. 31, s. 20.

CROSS-REFERENCES

"Data" and "document" are defined in s. 487.011.

"Peace officer" is defined in s. 2, and "public officer" is defined in s. 487.011.

"Justice" is defined in s. 2 and "judge" is defined in s. 487.011.

For references to the other production and preservation order-related sections, see the cross-references under s. 487.012.

SYNOPSIS

This section provides for the making of a production order by a justice or judge against a person other than a person under investigation for an offence under the *Criminal Code* or other Act of Parliament. The order may require the person to produce a copy of a document in their possession or to prepare and produce a document containing data in their possession. The order may be made only where the justice or judge is satisfied on an *ex parte* application containing information on oath in writing that there are reasonable grounds to believe that an offence has been or will be committed, that the document or data will afford evidence of the offence, and that the document or data is in the person's possession or control.

ANNOTATIONS

A judge does not have power to make it a term or condition of a production order that the police compensate a third party for expenses incurred in complying with the order. Where the financial costs of compliance are unreasonable, the remedy lies in a full or partial exemption from the production order. In order to meet the threshold, the financial consequences must be so burdensome that it would be unreasonable in the circumstances to expect compliance. What is reasonable will be informed by a variety of factors including the breadth of the order being sought, the size and economic viability of the object of the order, and the extent of the order's financial impact on the party. Where the party is a repeated target of production orders, the cumulative impact of multiple orders may also be relevant: *Ontario v. Tele-Mobile Co.*, [2008] 1 S.C.R. 305, 229 C.C.C. (3d) 417.

The law regarding search warrants should also apply to production orders. Accordingly, the test for review of a production order is the same as the *Garofoli* test. Where the target of the production order is a media outlet, the reviewing judge must apply a somewhat modified *Garofoli* test. The media are entitled to particularly careful consideration because of the importance of their role in a democratic society. While this does not import any new or additional requirements for the issuance of a production order, the authorizing judge must consider all of the circumstances and conduct a balancing test in exercising his or her discretion having regard to the constitutional protection afforded by s. 2(*b*) of the Charter: *Canadian Broadcasting Corp. v. Manitoba (Attorney General)* (2009), 250 C.C.C. (3d) 61, [2010] 1 W.W.R. 389 (Man. C.A.).

A production order continues to compel the third party to release the information sought even if the period for compliance set out on the face of the order has expired: *R. v. Goulbourne* (2011), 267 C.C.C. (3d) 568 (Ont. S.C.J.).

The police were not entitled to use a production order to search the accused's safety deposit boxes and should have obtained a search warrant instead: *R. v. Huynh* (2012), 283 C.C.C. (3d) 189 (Alta. C.A.).

Police can obtain a production order for past text messages. An authorization under Part VI is only needed for the prospective interception of future text messages: *R. v. Jones* (2016), 338 C.C.C. (3d) 591 (Ont. C.A.), affd [2017] 2 S.C.R. 696.

While a production order may only issue against a person in Canada, a virtual presence may be sufficient. Therefore, a production order could issue against an internet business whose virtual presence constituted a real and substantial connection to the jurisdiction. Nothing in this provision requires the targeted records to be physically present in the jurisdiction: *British Columbia (Attorney General) v. Brecknell* (2018), 358 C.C.C. (3d) 179 (B.C.C.A.).

PRODUCTION ORDER TO TRACE SPECIFIED COMMUNICATION / Conditions for making order / Form / Service / Limitation / Report.

487.015 (1) On *ex parte* application made by a peace officer or public officer for the purpose of identifying a device or person involved in the transmission of a communication, a justice or judge may order a person to prepare and produce a document containing transmission data that is related to that purpose and that is, when they are served with the order, in their possession or control.

(2) Before making the order, the justice or judge must be satisfied by information on oath in Form 5.004 that there are reasonable grounds to suspect that

- **(*a*) an offence has been or will be committed under this or any other Act of Parliament;**
- **(*b*) the identification of a device or person involved in the transmission of a communication will assist in the investigation of the offence; and**
- **(*c*) transmission data that is in the possession or control of one or more persons whose identity is unknown when the application is made will enable that identification.**

(3) The order is to be in Form 5.006.

(4) A peace officer or public officer may serve the order on any person who was involved in the transmission of the communication and whose identity was unknown when the application was made

- **(*a*) within 60 days after the day on which the order is made; or**
- **(*b*) within one year after the day on which the order is made, in the case of an offence under section 467.11, 467.12 or 467.13, an offence committed for the benefit of, at the direction of or in association with a criminal organization, or a terrorism offence.**

(5) A person who is under investigation for the offence referred to in subsection (2) may not be made subject to an order.

(6) A peace officer or public officer named in the order must provide a written report to the justice or judge who made the order as soon as feasible after the person from whom the communication originated is identified or after the expiry of the period referred to in subsection (4), whichever occurs first. The report must state the name and address of each person on whom the order was served, and the date of service. 2004, c. 3, s. 7; 2014, c. 31, s. 20.

CROSS-REFERENCES

"Transmission data" and "document" are defined in s. 487.011.

"Peace officer" is defined in s. 2, and "public officer" is defined in s. 487.011.

"Justice" is defined in s. 2 and "judge" is defined in s. 487.011.

For references to the other production and preservation order-related sections, see the cross-references under s. 487.012.

SYNOPSIS

This section provides for the making of a production order to trace specified communications by a justice or judge against a person whose identity is unknown other than a person under investigation for an offence under the *Criminal Code* or other Act of Parliament. The order may require the person to produce a document containing transmission data that is related to that purpose and that is in their possession or control when they are served with the order. The order may be made only where the justice or judge is satisfied on an *ex parte* application containing information on oath in writing that there are reasonable grounds to suspect that an offence has been or will be committed, that the identification of a device or person involved in the transmission of a communication will assist in the investigation of the offence, and that transmission data that is in the possession or control of one or more unknown persons will enable the identification of the device or person involved in the offence.

Subsection (4) permits an officer to serve the order on any person involved in the transmission of the communication and whose identity was previously unknown at the time of the application. Service must be made within 60 days of the order, though it can be made up to one year after the order in the case of terrorism offences and offences in relation criminal organizations.

Subsection (6) sets out timelines for the making of a report to the justice or judge who made the order, with details of service.

PRODUCTION ORDER — TRANSMISSION DATA / Conditions for making order / Form / Limitation.

487.016 (1) On *ex parte* application made by a peace officer or public officer, a justice or judge may order a person to prepare and produce a document containing transmission data that is in their possession or control when they receive the order.

(2) Before making the order, the justice or judge must be satisfied by information on oath in Form 5.004 that there are reasonable grounds to suspect that

(*a*) an offence has been or will be committed under this or any other Act of Parliament; and

(*b*) the transmission data is in the person's possession or control and will assist in the investigation of the offence.

(3) The order is to be in Form 5.007.

(4) A person who is under investigation for the offence referred to in subsection (2) may not be made subject to an order. 2004, c. 3, s. 7; 2014, c. 31, s. 20.

CROSS-REFERENCES

"Transmission data" and "document" are defined in s. 487.011.

"Peace officer" is defined in s. 2, and "public officer" is defined in s. 487.011.

"Justice" is defined in s. 2 and "judge" is defined in s. 487.011.

For references to the other production and preservation order-related sections, see the cross-references under s. 487.012.

SYNOPSIS

This section provides for the making of a more specific production order than the order under s. 487.014. Under this section, a justice or judge may require a person, other than a person under investigation for an offence under the *Criminal Code* or other Act of Parliament, to produce a document containing transmission data that is in their possession or control when they receive the order. The order may be made only where the justice or judge is satisfied on an *ex parte* application containing information on oath in writing that there are reasonable grounds to suspect that an offence has been or will be committed, that the transmission data will assist in the investigation of the offence, and that the transmission data is in the person's possession or control.

PRODUCTION ORDER — TRACKING DATA / Conditions for making order / Form / Limitation.

487.017 (1) On *ex parte* application made by a peace officer or public officer, a justice or judge may order a person to prepare and produce a document containing tracking data that is in their possession or control when they receive the order.

(2) Before making the order, the justice or judge must be satisfied by information on oath in Form 5.004 that there are reasonable grounds to suspect that

(*a*) an offence has been or will be committed under this or any other Act of Parliament; and

(*b*) the tracking data is in the person's possession or control and will assist in the investigation of the offence.

(3) The order is to be in Form 5.007.

(4) A person who is under investigation for the offence referred to in subsection (2) may not be made subject to an order. 2004, c. 7, s. 7; 2014, c. 31, s. 20.

CROSS-REFERENCES

"Tracking data" and "document" are defined in s. 487.011.

"Peace officer" is defined in s. 2, and "public officer" is defined in s. 487.011.

"Justice" is defined in s. 2 and "judge" is defined in s. 487.011.

For references to the other production and preservation order-related sections, see the cross-references under s. 487.012.

SYNOPSIS

This section provides for the making of a more specific production order than the order under s. 487.014. Under this section, a justice or judge may require a person, other than a person under investigation for an offence under the *Criminal Code* or other Act of Parliament, to produce a document containing tracking data that is in their possession or control when they receive the order. The order may be made only where the justice or judge is satisfied on an *ex parte* application containing information on oath in writing that there are reasonable grounds to suspect that an offence has been or will be committed, that the tracking data will assist in the investigation of the offence, and that the tracking data is in the person's possession or control.

PRODUCTION ORDER — FINANCIAL DATA / Identification of person / Conditions for making order / Form / Limitation.

487.018 (1) On *ex parte* application made by a peace officer or public officer, a justice or judge may order a financial institution, as defined in section 2 of the *Bank Act*, or a person or entity referred to in section 5 of the *Proceeds of Crime (Money Laundering) and Terrorist Financing Act*, to prepare and produce a document setting out the following data that is in their possession or control when they receive the order:

(*a*) either the account number of a person named in the order or the name of a person whose account number is specified in the order;

(*b*) the type of account;

(*c*) the status of the account; and

(*d*) the date on which it was opened or closed.

(2) For the purpose of confirming the identity of a person who is named or whose account number is specified in the order, the order may also require the institution, person or entity to prepare and produce a document setting out the following data that is in their possession or control:

(*a*) the date of birth of a person who is named or whose account number is specified in the order;

(*b*) that person's current address; and

(*c*) any previous addresses of that person.

(3) Before making the order, the justice or judge must be satisfied by information on oath in Form 5.004 that there are reasonable grounds to suspect that

(*a*) an offence has been or will be committed under this or any other Act of Parliament; and

(*b*) the data is in the possession or control of the institution, person or entity and will assist in the investigation of the offence.

(4) The order is to be in Form 5.008.

(5) A financial institution, person or entity that is under investigation for the offence referred to in subsection (3) may not be made subject to an order. 2014, c. 31, s. 20.

CROSS-REFERENCES

"Data" and "document" are defined in s. 487.011.

"Peace officer" is defined in s. 2, and "public officer" is defined in s. 487.011.

"Justice" is defined in s. 2 and "judge" is defined in s. 487.011.

For references to the other production and preservation order-related sections, see the cross-references under s. 487.012.

SYNOPSIS

This section provides for the making of a more specific production order than the order under s. 487.014. Under this section, a justice or judge may require a financial institution or person or entity referred to in s. 5 of the *Proceeds of Crime (Money Laundering) and Terrorist Financing Act*, to produce account information about a person named in the order unless the institution, person or entity is under investigation for the offence that is under investigation. The order may also require the institution, person or entity to produce the person's date of birth, current address or previous address to confirm the identity of the person named in the order. The order may be made only where the justice or judge is satisfied on an *ex parte* application containing information on oath in writing that there are reasonable grounds to suspect that an offence against the *Criminal Code* or other federal legislation has been or is suspected to have been committed, that the information will assist in investigating the offence, and that the institution, person or entity has possession or control of the information.

CONDITIONS IN PRESERVATION AND PRODUCTION ORDERS / Effect of order / Power to revoke or vary order.

487.019 (1) An order made under any of sections 487.013 to 487.018 may contain any conditions that the justice or judge considers appropriate including, in the case of an order made under section 487.014, conditions to protect a privileged communication between a person who is qualified to give legal advice and their client.

(2) The order has effect throughout Canada and, for greater certainty, no endorsement is needed for the order to be effective in a territorial division that is not the one in which the order is made.

(3) On *ex parte* application made by a peace officer or public officer, the justice or judge who made the order — or a judge in the judicial district where the order was made — may, on the basis of an information on oath in Form 5.0081, revoke or vary the order. The peace officer or public officer must give notice of the revocation or variation to the person who is subject to the order as soon as feasible. 2014, c. 31, s. 20.

CROSS-REFERENCES

"Peace officer" is defined in s. 2, and "public officer" is defined in s. 487.011.

"Justice" is defined in s. 2 and "judge" is defined in s. 487.011.

For references to the other production and preservation order-related sections, see the cross-references under s. 487.012.

SYNOPSIS

This section provides certain procedural powers in relation to preservation and production orders under ss. 487.013 to 487.018. Subsection (2) provides that such orders have effect throughout Canada. Subsection (1) provides that the order may contain terms or conditions including terms and conditions to protect solicitor-client communications. Subsection (3) provides that, on an *ex parte* application made by a peace officer or public officer, the judge or justice who made the order, or a judge from the same judicial district, has the power to revoke or vary the order. Notice of the revocation or variation must be given to the person subject to the order as soon as feasible.

ORDER PROHIBITING DISCLOSURE / Conditions for making order / Form / Application to revoke or vary order.

487.0191 (1) On *ex parte* application made by a peace officer or public officer, a justice or judge may make an order prohibiting a person from disclosing the existence or some or all of the contents of a preservation demand made under section 487.012 or a preservation or production order made under any of sections 487.013 to 487.018 during the period set out in the order.

(2) Before making the order, the justice or judge must be satisfied by information on oath in Form 5.009 that there are reasonable grounds to believe that the disclosure during that period would jeopardize the conduct of the investigation of the offence to which the preservation demand or the preservation or production order relates.

(3) The order is to be in Form 5.0091.

(4) A peace officer or a public officer or a person, financial institution or entity that is subject to an order made under subsection (1) may apply in writing to the justice or judge who made the order — or to a judge in the judicial district where the order was made — to revoke or vary the order. 2014, c. 31, s. 20.

CROSS-REFERENCES

"Peace officer" is defined in s. 2, and "public officer" is defined in s. 487.011.

"Justice" is defined in s. 2 and "judge" is defined in s. 487.011.

For references to the other production and preservation order-related sections, see the cross-references under s. 487.012.

SYNOPSIS

Under this section, a judge or justice may make an order prohibiting the disclosure of the contents of a preservation demand under s. 487.012 or a preservation or production order under ss. 487.013 to 487.018 during the period of the order. The order may be made an *ex parte* application by a peace officer or public officer, containing information on oath in writing that there are reasonable grounds to believe that disclosure during the period would jeopardize the conduct of the investigation to which the demand or order under ss. 487.012 to 487.018 relates. Subsection (4) provides that a peace officer or public officer or a person, financial institution or entity that is subject to the non-disclosure order may apply in writing to have the order revoked or varied.

PARTICULARS — PRODUCTION ORDERS / Particulars — production order to trace specified communication / Form of production / Non-application / Probative force of copies / *Canada Evidence Act*.

487.0192 (1) An order made under any of sections 487.014 and 487.016 to 487.018 must require a person, financial institution or entity to produce the document to a peace officer or public officer named in the order within the time, at the place and in the form specified in the order.

(2) An order made under section 487.015 must require a person to produce the document to a peace officer or public officer named in the order as soon as feasible after they are served with the order at the place and in the form specified in the order.

(3) For greater certainty, an order under any of sections 487.014 to 487.018 may specify that a document may be produced on or through an electro-magnetic medium.

(4) For greater certainty, sections 489.1 and 490 do not apply to a document that is produced under an order under any of sections 487.014 to 487.018.

(5) Every copy of a document produced under section 487.014 is admissible in evidence in proceedings under this or any other Act of Parliament on proof by affidavit that it is a true copy and has the same probative force as the document would have if it were proved in the ordinary way.

(6) A document that is prepared for the purpose of production is considered to be original for the purposes of the *Canada Evidence Act*. 2014, c. 31, s. 20.

CROSS-REFERENCES

"Document" is defined in s. 487.011.

"Peace officer" is defined in s. 2, and "public officer" is defined in s. 487.011.

"Justice" is defined in s. 2 and "judge" is defined in s. 487.011.

For references to the other production and preservation order-related sections, see the cross-references under s. 487.012.

SYNOPSIS

This section provides for particulars regarding production orders under ss. 487.014 to 487.018. Subsections (1) and (2) require that the order provide specifics as to the time, place and form of the required production. Such orders may specify that the document may be produced on or through an electro-magnetic medium. Subsection (4) provides that the procedural requirements under ss. 489.1 and 490 regarding the restitution of property, reports by a peace officer and the detention of things seized, do not apply to documents produced under production orders.

The evidentiary provisions in subsecs. (5) and (6) provide that a document prepared for the purpose of production is considered to be an original under the *Canada Evidence Act*, and that copies of a document produced under the general production order provision in s. 487.014 are admissible in proceedings under the *Criminal Code* or other federal legislation on proof by affidavit that it is a true copy.

APPLICATION FOR REVIEW OF PRODUCTION ORDER / Notice required / No obligation to produce / Revocation or variation of order.

487.0193 (1) Before they are required by an order made under any of sections 487.014 to 487.018 to produce a document, a person, financial institution or entity may apply in writing to the justice or judge who made the order — or to a judge in the judicial district where the order was made — to revoke or vary the order.

(2) The person, institution or entity may make the application only if they give notice of their intention to do so to a peace officer or public officer named in the order within 30 days after the day on which the order is made.

(3) The person, institution or entity is not required to prepare or produce the document until a final decision is made with respect to the application.

(4) The justice or judge may revoke or vary the order if satisfied that

(*a*) it is unreasonable in the circumstances to require the applicant to prepare or produce the document; or

(*b*) production of the document would disclose information that is privileged or otherwise protected from disclosure by law. 2014, c. 31, s. 20.

CROSS-REFERENCES

"Document" is defined in s. 487.011.

"Peace officer" is defined in s. 2, and "public officer" is defined in s. 487.011.

"Justice" is defined in s. 2 and "judge" is defined in s. 487.011.

For references to the other production and preservation order-related sections, see the cross-references under s. 487.012.

SYNOPSIS

This section sets out the procedure by which the target of a production order under ss. 487.014 to 487.018 can, before producing a document, seek to have the order varied or revoked. An application in writing may be made to the justice or judge who made the order, or to a judge in the same judicial district. Notice of the application must be given to the peace officer or public officer named within the order within 30 days of the production order. The order may be revoked or varied if the justice or judge is satisfied that production is unreasonable in the circumstances or production would disclose information that is privileged or otherwise protected from disclosure by law.

Where a media organization challenges a production order, the same standard of review applies as when a non-media target challenges an order: *R. v. Vice Media Canada Inc.* (2017), 352 C.C.C. (3d) 355 (Ont. C.A.), affd 2018 SCC 53.

Where an affected party sought to revoke or vary a production order under this section, and also sought prerogative relief in the nature of *certiorari*, an appeal to the Court of Appeal lay under s. 784: *R. v. Vice Media Canada Inc.*, *supra*.

DESTRUCTION OF PRESERVED COMPUTER DATA AND DOCUMENTS — PRESERVATION DEMAND / Destruction of preserved computer data and documents — preservation order / Destruction of preserved computer data and documents — production order / Destruction of preserved computer data and documents — warrant.

487.0194 (1) A person to whom a preservation demand is made under section 487.012 shall destroy the computer data that would not be retained in the ordinary course of business and any document that is prepared for the purpose of preserving computer data under that section as soon as feasible after the demand expires or is revoked, unless they are subject to an order made under any of sections 487.013 to 487.017 with respect to the computer data.

(2) A person who is subject to a preservation order made under section 487.013 shall destroy the computer data that would not be retained in the ordinary course of business and any document that is prepared for the purpose of preserving computer data under that section as soon as feasible after the order expires or is revoked, unless they are subject to a new preservation order or to a production order made under any of sections 487.014 to 487.017 with respect to the computer data.

(3) A person who is subject to a production order made under any of sections 487.014 to 487.017 with respect to computer data that they preserved under a preservation demand or order made under section 487.012 or 487.013 shall destroy the computer data that would not be retained in the ordinary course of business and any document that is prepared for the purpose of preserving computer data under that section as soon as feasible after the earlier of

(*a*) the day on which the production order is revoked, and

(*b*) the day on which a document that contains the computer data is produced under the production order.

(4) Despite subsections (1) to (3), a person who preserved computer data under a preservation demand or order made under section 487.012 or 487.013 shall destroy the computer data that would not be retained in the ordinary course of business and any document that is prepared for the purpose of preserving computer data under that section when a document that contains the computer data is obtained under a warrant. 2014, c. 31, s. 20.

CROSS-REFERENCES

"Computer data" is defined in ss. 487.011 and 342.1(2).

"Document" is defined in s. 487.011.

For references to the other production and preservation order-related sections, see the cross-references under s. 487.012.

Under s. 487.0199, it is a summary conviction offence to contravene this section without lawful excuse.

SYNOPSIS

This section governs the destruction of data following the expiration of a preservation demand or order under ss. 487.012 or 487.013. A person who receives a preservation demand or order is required, after the demand or order expires, or after the data has been given to the law enforcement agency under a production order or search warrant, to destroy the computer data that would not be retained in the ordinary course of business as soon as feasible.

FOR GREATER CERTAINTY / No civil or criminal liability.

487.0195 (1) For greater certainty, no preservation demand, preservation order or production order is necessary for a peace officer or public officer to ask a person to voluntarily preserve data that the person is not prohibited by law from preserving or to

voluntarily provide a document to the officer that the person is not prohibited by law from disclosing.

(2) A person who preserves data or provides a document in those circumstances does not incur any criminal or civil liability for doing so. 2014, c. 31, s. 20.

CROSS-REFERENCES

"Data" and "document" are defined in s. 487.011.

"Peace officer" is defined in s. 2, and "public officer" is defined in s. 487.011.

"Justice" is defined in s. 2 and "judge" is defined in s. 487.011.

For references to the other production and preservation order-related sections, see the cross-references under s. 487.012.

SYNOPSIS

This section clarifies that none of the foregoing provisions on production demands, production orders or preservation orders prevent a request for the voluntary preservation or production of data or documents that a person is not prohibited by law from disclosing. No civil or criminal liability will be incurred for production or preservation of data in such circumstances.

SELF-INCRIMINATION.

487.0196 No one is excused from complying with an order made under any of sections 487.014 to 487.018 on the ground that the document that they are required to produce may tend to incriminate them or subject them to a proceeding or penalty. However, no document that an individual is required to prepare may be used or received in evidence against them in a criminal proceeding that is subsequently instituted against them, other than a prosecution for an offence under section 132, 136 or 137. 2014, c. 31, s. 20.

CROSS-REFERENCES

"Data" and "document" are defined in s. 487.011.

For references to the other production and preservation order-related sections, see the cross-references under s. 487.012.

Note that, under s. 487.0193, a person may apply for an variation or revocation of a production order on the basis that the order would require production of privileged information, documents or data or material that is otherwise protected by law.

Under s. 487.0198, it is an offence not to comply with a production order.

SYNOPSIS

A person is not excused from complying with a production order on the grounds of self-incrimination. However, where an individual is required to prepare a document under ss. 487.014 to 487.018, that document cannot be used or received in evidence against the individual in any criminal proceedings subsequently instituted against the individual except for proceedings under s. 132 (perjury), s. 136 (giving contradictory evidence) or s. 137 (fabricating evidence).

OFFENCE — PRESERVATION DEMAND.

487.0197 A person who contravenes a preservation demand made under section 487.012 without lawful excuse is guilty of an offence punishable on summary conviction and is liable to a fine of not more than $5,000. 2014, c. 31, s. 20.

CROSS-REFERENCES
For references to the other production and preservation order-related sections, see the cross-references under s. 487.012.

OFFENCE — PRESERVATION OR PRODUCTION ORDER.

487.0198 A person, financial institution or entity that contravenes an order made under any of sections 487.013 to 487.018 without lawful excuse is guilty of an offence punishable on summary conviction and is liable to a fine of not more than $250,000 or to imprisonment for a term of not more than six months, or to both. 2014, c. 31, s. 20.

CROSS-REFERENCES
For references to the other production and preservation order-related sections, see the cross-references under s. 487.012.

Note that, under s. 487.0193, a person may apply for a variation or revocation of a production order on the basis that the order would require production of privileged information, documents or data, or material that is otherwise protected by law.

OFFENCE — DESTRUCTION OF PRESERVED DATA.

487.0199 A person who contravenes section 487.0194 without lawful excuse is guilty of an offence punishable on summary conviction. 2014, c. 31, s. 20.

CROSS-REFERENCES
For references to the other production and preservation order-related sections, see the cross-references under s. 487.012.

ASSISTANCE ORDER.

487.02 If an authorization is given under section 184.2, 184.3, 186 or 188 or a warrant is issued under this Act, the judge or justice who gives the authorization or issues the warrant may order a person to provide assistance, if the person's assistance may reasonably be considered to be required to give effect to the authorization or warrant. 1993, c. 40, s. 15; 1997, c. 18, s. 43; 2014, c. 31, s. 20.

CROSS-REFERENCES
Although violation of an order under this section is not specifically made an offence, presumably the failure to comply could be punished under s. 127.

SYNOPSIS

This section provides for the making of an order requiring persons to assist in the execution of various authorizations and warrants. For example, the assistance of the telephone company may be required to implement an authorization under s. 186 to intercept private communications.

ANNOTATIONS

An assistance order could be validly made under this section requiring employees of the Canada Post Corporation to photocopy the outside of envelopes and packages of mailable material after it was delivered to certain post office boxes and requiring the employees not to divulge the existence of the warrant and the order. *Canada Post Corp. v. Canada (Attorney General)* (1995), 95 C.C.C. (3d) 568 (Ont. Ct. (Gen. Div.)).

An assistance order was not required to effect an interception obtained in one province where the telephone company employees in the other province were prepared to assist the police by re-routing calls to equipment in the police interception room: *R. v. Pham* (1997), 122 C.C.C. (3d) 90 (B.C.C.A.), leave to appeal to S.C.C. refused 128 C.C.C. (3d) vi.

REVIEW / Report.

487.021 (1) Within seven years after the coming into force of this section, a comprehensive review of the provisions and operation of sections 487.011 to 487.02 shall be undertaken by such committee of the House of Commons as may be designated or established by the House for that purpose.

(2) The committee referred to in subsection (1) shall, within a year after a review is undertaken pursuant to that subsection or within such further time as the House may authorize, submit a report on the review to the Speaker of the House, including a statement of any changes the committee recommends. 2014, c. 31, s. 20.

CROSS-REFERENCES

Section 487.012 provides for a demand to preserve computer data.

Section 487.013 provides for a preservation order in relation to computer data.

Section 487.014 provides for general production orders.

Sections 487.015 to 487.018 provide for other forms of production orders in relation to specified types of data.

Sections 487.019, 487.0191 and 487.0192 set out certain procedural requirements and options applicable to all preservation or production orders made under the foregoing provisions.

Section 487.0193 provides a procedure by which the target of a production order can seek to have the order varied or revoked.

Section 487.0194 governs the destruction of data following the expiration of a preservation demand or order.

Section 487.0195 clarifies that none of the foregoing provisions prevent a request for the voluntary preservation or production of data or documents.

Section 487.0196 provides that self-incrimination concerns do not excuse compliance with orders made under the foregoing provisions; however, immunity against subsequent incriminating use is provided.

Sections 487.0197 to 487.0199 create summary conviction offences for contravening preservation demands, preservation orders and production orders.

Section 487.02 provides for an assistance order.

SYNOPSIS

This provision requires that a committee of the House of Commons undertake a comprehensive review of the provisions and operation of ss. 487.011 to 487.02 within seven years of the coming into force of this section, and the production of a report within a year after the review is undertaken.

EXECUTION IN ANOTHER PROVINCE / Endorsement.

487.03 (1) If a warrant is issued under section 487.01, 487.05 or 492.1 or subsection 492.2(1) in one province, a judge or justice, as the case may be, in another province may, on application, endorse the warrant if it may reasonably be expected that it is to be executed in the other province and that its execution would require entry into or on the property of any person, or would require that an order be made under section 487.02 with respect to any person, in that province.

(1.1) The endorsement may be made on the original of the warrant or on a copy of the warrant that is transmitted by any means of telecommunication and, once endorsed, the warrant has the same force in the other province as though it had originally been issued there. 1993, c. 40, s. 15; 1995, c. 27, s. 1; 2000, c. 10, s. 13; 2007, c. 22, s. 7; 2008, c. 18, s. 12.

(2) [*Repealed*, 2007, c. 22, s. 7.]

SYNOPSIS

Subsection (1) provides that a warrant may be confirmed where it is to be executed in another province. Such confirmation is in addition to the backing procedure set out in s. 487(2) [applicable to a general warrant issued under s. 487.01] and is required where it will be necessary to enter private premises or where an assistance order is made under s. 487.02.

Subsection (1.1) provides that the endorsement may be made on the original warrant or a copy of the warrant that is transmitted by any means of telecommunication.

Forensic DNA Analysis

DEFINITIONS / "Adult" / "Designated offence" / "DNA" / "Forensic DNA analysis" / "Primary designated offence" / "Provincial court judge" / "Secondary designated offence" / "Young Offenders Act" / "Young person".

487.04 In this section and in sections 487.05 to 487.0911,

"adult" has the meaning assigned by subsection 2(1) of the *Youth Criminal Justice Act*;

"designated offence" means a primary designated offence or a secondary designated offence;

"DNA" means deoxyribonucleic acid;

"forensic DNA analysis"

(*a*) in relation to a bodily substance that is taken from a person in execution of a warrant under section 487.05, means forensic DNA analysis of the bodily substance and the comparison of the results of that analysis with the results of the analysis of the DNA in the bodily substance referred to in paragraph 487.05(1)(*b*), and includes any incidental tests associated with that analysis, and

(*b*) in relation to a bodily substance that is provided voluntarily in the course of an investigation of a designated offence or is taken from a person under an order made under section 487.051 or an authorization granted under section 487.055 or 487.091, or to a bodily substance referred to in paragraph 487.05(1)(*b*), means forensic DNA analysis of the bodily substance;

"primary designated offence" means

(*a*) an offence under any of the following provisions, namely,

(i) subsection 7(4.1) (offence in relation to sexual offences against children),

(i.1) section 151 (sexual interference),

(i.2) section 152 (invitation to sexual touching),

(i.3) section 153 (sexual exploitation),

(i.4) section 153.1 (sexual exploitation of person with disability),

(i.5) section 155 (incest),

(i.6) subsection 160(2) (compelling the commission of bestiality),

(i.7) subsection 160(3) (bestiality in presence of or by a child),

(i.8) section 163.1 (child pornography),

(i.9) section 170 (parent or guardian procuring sexual activity),

(i.901) section 171.1 (making sexually explicit material available to child),

(i.91) section 172.1 (luring a child),

(i.911) section 172.2 (agreement or arrangement — sexual offence against child),

(i.92) subsection 173(2) (exposure),

(i.93) [*Repealed*, 2014, c. 25, s. 23(1).]

(i.94) [*Repealed*, 2014, c. 25, s. 23(1).]

(i.95) [*Repealed*, 2014, c. 25, s. 23(1).]

(i.96) [*Repealed*, 2014, c. 25, s. 23(1).]

(ii) section 235 (murder),
(iii) section 236 (manslaughter),
(iv) section 239 (attempt to commit murder),
(v) section 244 (discharging firearm with intent),
(vi) section 244.1 (causing bodily harm with intent — air gun or pistol),
(vi.1) section 244.2 (discharging firearm — recklessness),
(vii) paragraph 245(a) (administering noxious thing with intent to endanger life or cause bodily harm),
(viii) section 246 (overcoming resistance to commission of offence),
(ix) section 267 (assault with a weapon or causing bodily harm),
(x) section 268 (aggravated assault),
(xi) section 269 (unlawfully causing bodily harm),
(xi.1) section 270.01 (assaulting peace officer with weapon or causing bodily harm),
(xi.2) section 270.02 (aggravated assault of peace officer),
(xi.3) section 271 (sexual assault),
(xii) section 272 (sexual assault with a weapon, threats to a third party or causing bodily harm),
(xiii) section 273 (aggravated sexual assault),
(xiii.1) subsection 273.3(2) (removal of a child from Canada),
(xiv) section 279 (kidnapping),
(xiv.1) section 279.011 (trafficking — person under 18 years),
(xiv.2) subsection 279.02(2) (material benefit — trafficking of person under 18 years),
(xiv.3) subsection 279.03(2) (withholding or destroying documents — trafficking of person under 18 years),
(xiv.4) subsection 286.1(2) (obtaining sexual services for consideration from person under 18 years),
(xiv.5) subsection 286.2(2) (material benefit from sexual services provided by person under 18 years),
(xiv.6) subsection 286.3(2) (procuring — person under 18 years),
(xv) section 344 (robbery), and
(xvi) section 346 (extortion),

(*a*.1) an offence under any of the following provisions, namely,
(i) section 75 (piratical acts),
(i.01) section 76 (hijacking),
(i.02) section 77 (endangering safety of aircraft or airport),
(i.03) section 78.1 (seizing control of ship or fixed platform),
(i.04) subsection 81(1) (using explosives),
(i.041) section 82.3 (possession, etc., of nuclear material, radioactive material or device),
(i.042) section 82.4 (use or alteration of nuclear material, radioactive material or device),
(i.043) section 82.5 (commission of indictable offence to obtain nuclear material, etc.),
(i.044) section 82.6 (threats),
(i.05) section 83.18 (participation in activity of terrorist group),
(i.051) section 83.181 (leaving Canada to participate in activity of terrorist group),
(i.06) section 83.19 (facilitating terrorist activity),
(i.061) section 83.191 (leaving Canada to facilitate terrorist activity),
(i.07) section 83.2 (commission of offence for terrorist group),
(i.071) section 83.201 (leaving Canada to commit offence for terrorist group),
(i.072) section 83.202 (leaving Canada to commit offence that is terrorist activity),
(i.08) section 83.21 (instructing to carry out activity for terrorist group),

(i.09) section 83.22 (instructing to carry out terrorist activity),
(i.091) subsection 83.221(1) (advocating or promoting commission of terrorism offences),
(i.1) section 83.23 (harbouring or concealing),
(i.11) [*Repealed*, 2010, c. 17, s. 3(4).]
(ii) [*Repealed*, 2010, c. 17, s. 3(4).]
(iii) [*Repealed*, 2010, c. 17, s. 3(4).]
(iii.1) [*Repealed*, 2010, c. 17, s. 3(4).]
(iv) [*Repealed*, 2014, c. 25, s. 23(3).]
(iv.1) [*Repealed*, 2010, c. 17, s. 3(4).]
(iv.2) [*Repealed*, 2010, c. 17, s. 3(4).]
(iv.3) [*Repealed*, 2010, c. 17, s. 3(4).]
(iv.4) [*Repealed*, 2010, c. 17, s. 3(4).]
(iv.5) [*Repealed*, 2010, c. 17, s. 3(4).]
(v) [*Repealed*, 2014, c. 25, s. 23(3).]
(v.1) [*Repealed*, 2010, c. 17, s. 3(4).]
(v.2) [*Repealed*, 2010, c. 17, s. 3(4).]
(vi) section 233 (infanticide),
(vii) [*Repealed*, 2010, c. 17, s. 3(5).]
(vii.1) section 279.01 (trafficking in persons),
(vii.11) subsection 279.02(1) (material benefit — trafficking),
(vii.12) subsection 279.03(1) (withholding or destroying documents — trafficking),
(viii) section 279.1 (hostage taking),
(viii.1) subsection 286.2(1) (material benefit from sexual services),
(viii.2) subsection 286.3(1) (procuring),
(ix) paragraph 348(1)(*d*) (breaking and entering a dwelling-house),
(x) section 423.1 (intimidation of a justice system participant or journalist),
(xi) section 431 (attack on premises, residence or transport of internationally protected person),
(xii) section 431.1 (attack on premises, accommodation or transport of United Nations or associated personnel),
(xiii) subsection 431.2(2) (explosive or other lethal device),
(xiv) section 467.11 (participation in activities of criminal organization),
(xiv.1) section 467.111 (recruitment of members — criminal organization),
(xv) section 467.12 (commission of offence for criminal organization), and
(xvi) section 467.13 (instructing commission of offence for criminal organization),
(xvi.1) [*Repealed*, 2005, c. 25, s. 1(4).]
(xvii) [*Repealed*, 2005, c. 25, s. 1(4).]
(xviii) [*Repealed*, 2005, c. 25, s. 1(4).]
(xix) [*Repealed*, 2005, c. 25, s. 1(4).]
(xx) [*Repealed*, 2005, c. 25, s. 1(4).]

(*b*) an offence under any of the following provisions of the *Criminal Code*, chapter C-34 of the Revised Statutes of Canada, 1970, as they read from time to time before January 4, 1983, namely,
(i) section 144 (rape),
(i.1) section 145 (attempt to commit rape),
(ii) section 146 (sexual intercourse with female under fourteen and between fourteen and sixteen),
(iii) section 148 (sexual intercourse with feeble-minded, etc.),
(iv) section 149 (indecent assault on female),
(v) section 156 (indecent assault on male),
(vi) section 157 (acts of gross indecency), and

(vii) subsection 246(1) (assault with intent) if the intent is to commit an offence referred to in subparagraphs (i) to (vi),

(*c*) an offence under any of the following provisions of the *Criminal Code*, chapter C-34 of the Revised Statutes of Canada, 1970, as they read from time to time before January 1, 1988:

(i) subsection 146(1) (sexual intercourse with a female under age of 14),

(ii) subsection 146(2) (sexual intercourse with a female between ages of 14 and 16),

(iii) section 153 (sexual intercourse with step-daughter),

(iv) section 157 (gross indecency),

(v) section 166 (parent or guardian procuring defilement), and

(vi) section 167 (householder permitting defilement),

(*c*.01) an offence under any of the following provisions of the *Criminal Code*, chapter C-34 of the Revised Statutes of Canada, 1970, as enacted by section 19 of *An Act to amend the Criminal Code in relation to sexual offences and other offences against the person and to amend certain other Acts in relation thereto or in consequence thereof*, chapter 125 of the Statutes of Canada, 1980-81-82-83:

(i) section 246.1 (sexual assault),

(ii) section 246.2 (sexual assault with a weapon, threats to a third party or causing bodily harm), and

(iii) section 246.3 (aggravated sexual assault),

(*c*.02) an offence under any of the following provisions of this Act, as they read from time to time before the day on which this paragraph comes into force:

(i) paragraph 212(1)(i) (stupefying or overpowering for the purpose of sexual intercourse),

(ii) subsection 212(2) (living on the avails of prostitution of person under 18 years),

(iii) subsection 212(2.1) (aggravated offence in relation to living on the avails of prostitution of person under 18 years), and

(iv) subsection 212(4) (prostitution of person under 18 years),

(*c*.03) an offence under any of paragraphs 212(1)(*a*) to (*h*) (procuring) of this Act, as they read from time to time before the day on which this paragraph comes into force,

(*c*.1) an offence under any of the following provisions of the *Security of Information Act*, namely,

(i) section 6 (approaching, entering, etc., a prohibited place),

(ii) subsection 20(1) (threats or violence), and

(iii) subsection 21(1) (harbouring or concealing), and

(*d*) an attempt to commit or, other than for the purposes of subsection 487.05(1), a conspiracy to commit an offence referred to in any of paragraphs (*a*) to (*c*.03);

"provincial court judge", in relation to a young person, includes a youth court judge within the meaning of subsection 2(1) of the *Youth Criminal Justice Act*;

"secondary designated offence" means an offence, other than a primary designated offence, that is

(*a*) an offence under this Act that may be prosecuted by indictment — or, for section 487.051 to apply, is prosecuted by indictment — for which the maximum punishment is imprisonment for five years or more,

(*a*.1) an offence under any of the following provisions of the *Cannabis Act* that may be prosecuted by indictment — or, for section 487.051 to apply, is prosecuted by indictment — for which the maximum punishment is imprisonment for five years or more:

(i) section 9 (distribution and possession for purpose of distributing)

(ii) section 10 (selling and possession for purpose of selling),

(iii) section 11 (importing and exporting and possession for purpose of exporting),
(iv) section 12 (production),
(v) section 13 (possession, etc., for use in production or distribution of illicit cannabis), and
(vi) section 14 (use of young person),

(*b*) an offence under any of the following provisions of the *Controlled Drugs and Substances Act* that may be prosecuted by indictment — or, for section 487.051 to apply, is prosecuted by indictment — for which the maximum punishment is imprisonment for five years or more
(i) section 5 (trafficking in substance and possession for purpose of trafficking),
(ii) section 6 (importing and exporting), and
(iii) section 7 (production of substance),

(*c*) an offence under any of the following provisions of this Act:
(i) section 145 (escape and being at large without excuse),
(i.1) section 146 (permitting or assisting escape),
(i.2) section 147 (rescue or permitting escape),
(i.3) section 148 (assisting prisoner of war to escape),
(i.4) and (ii) [*Repealed*, 2010, c. 17, s. 3(10).]
(iii) subsection 173(1) (indecent acts),
(iv) [*Repealed*, 2018, c. 21, s. 18(1).]
(v) section 264 (criminal harassment),
(vi) section 264.1 (uttering threats),
(vii) section 266 (assault),
(viii) section 270 (assaulting a peace officer),
(viii.1) subsection 286.1(1) (obtaining sexual services for consideration),
(viii.2) subsection 320.16(1) (failure to stop after accident),
(ix) paragraph 348(1)(*e*) (breaking and entering a place other than a dwelling-house),
(x) section 349 (being unlawfully in dwelling-house), and
(xi) section 423 (intimidation),

(*d*) an offence under any of the following provisions of the *Criminal Code*, as they read from time to time before July 1, 1990:
(i) section 433 (arson), and
(ii) section 434 (setting fire to other substance),

(*d*.1) an offence under section 252, as it read from time to time before the day on which section 14 of *An Act to amend the Criminal Code (offences relating to conveyances) and to make consequential amendments to other Acts* comes into force;

(*d*.2) an offence under any of sections 249, 249.1, 249.2, 249.3, 249.4, 253, 254 and 255, as they read from time to time before the day on which section 14 of *An Act to amend the Criminal Code (offences relating to conveyances) and to make consequential amendments to other Acts* comes into force, that may be prosecuted by indictment or, for section 487.051 to apply, is prosecuted by indictment; and

(*e*) an attempt to commit or, other than for the purposes of subsection 487.05(1), a conspiracy to commit
(i) an offence referred to in paragraph (*a*) or (*b*) — which, for section 487.051 to apply, is prosecuted by indictment, or
(ii) an offence referred to in any of paragraphs (*c*) to (*d*.2);

"Young Offenders Act" means chapter Y-1 of the Revised Statutes of Canada, 1985.

"young person" has the meaning assigned by subsection 2(1) of the *Youth Criminal Justice Act* or subsection 2(1) of the *Young Offenders Act*, as the case may be. 1995, c.

27, s. 1; 1998, c. 37, s. 15; 2001, c. 41, s. 17; 2002, c. 1, s. 175; 2005, c. 25, s. 1; 2005, c. 43, ss. 5, 9(2); 2007, c. 22, ss. 2, 8; 2008, c. 6, s. 35, 63(2); 2009, c. 22, s. 16; 2010, c. 3, s. 6; 2010, c. 17, s. 3; 2012, c. 1, s. 30; 2013, c. 9, s. 16; 2013, c. 13, s. 8; 2014, c. 17, s. 13; 2014, c. 25, s. 23; 2015, c. 20, s. 23; 2018, c. 16, s. 216; 2018, c. 21, s. 18.

ANNOTATIONS

Although only kidnapping is specifically referenced in brackets in this provision, forcible confinement by reference to s. 279 is also a primary designated offence: *R. v. R. (J.J.)* (2004), 181 C.C.C. (3d) 7 (Ont. C.A.).

INFORMATION FOR WARRANT TO TAKE BODILY SUBSTANCES FOR DNA ANALYSIS / Criteria / Telewarrant.

487.05 (1) A provincial court judge who on *ex parte* application made in Form 5.01 is satisfied by information on oath that there are reasonable grounds to believe

- **(*a*) that a designated offence has been committed,**
- **(*b*) that a bodily substance has been found or obtained**
  - **(i) at the place where the offence was committed,**
  - **(ii) on or within the body of the victim of the offence,**
  - **(iii) on anything worn or carried by the victim at the time when the offence was committed, or**
  - **(iv) on or within the body of any person or thing or at any place associated with the commission of the offence,**
- **(*c*) that a person was a party to the offence, and**
- **(*d*) that forensic DNA analysis of a bodily substance from the person will provide evidence about whether the bodily substance referred to in paragraph (*b*) was from that person**

and who is satisfied that it is in the best interests of the administration of justice to do so may issue a warrant in Form 5.02 authorizing the taking, from that person, for the purpose of forensic DNA analysis, of any number of samples of one or more bodily substances that is reasonably required for that purpose, by means of the investigative procedures described in subsection 487.06(1).

(2) In considering whether to issue the warrant, the provincial court judge shall have regard to all relevant matters, including

- **(*a*) the nature of the designated offence and the circumstances of its commission; and**
- **(*b*) whether there is**
  - **(i) a peace officer who is able, by virtue of training or experience, to take samples of bodily substances from the person, by means of the investigative procedures described in subsection 487.06(1), or**
  - **(ii) another person who is able, by virtue of training or experience, to take, under the direction of a peace officer, samples of bodily substances from the person, by means of those investigative procedures.**

(3) Where a peace officer believes that it would be impracticable to appear personally before a judge to make an application for a warrant under this section, a warrant may be issued under this section on an information submitted by telephone or other means of telecommunication and, for that purpose, section 487.1 applies, with such modifications as the circumstances require, to the warrant. 1995, c. 27, s. 1; 1997, c. 18, s. 44; 1998, c. 37, s. 16.

CROSS-REFERENCES

The terms "provincial court judge", "designated offence", "DNA", and "forensic DNA analysis" are defined in s. 487.04. "Peace officer" is defined in s. 2. Under s. 487.057, the peace officer who is authorized to take or cause to be taken the samples of bodily substances is to make a report to the provincial court judge after the samples have been taken. Section 487.058 protects the peace officer or person acting under the direction of a peace officer from civil liability. Section 487.06(1) sets out those "bodily substances" that may be seized pursuant to a warrant issued under this section. Section 487.06(2) requires the judge to include appropriate terms and conditions. Section 487.07 sets out the special requirements with respect to execution of a warrant obtained under this section. Section 487.08 limits the use of evidence obtained as a result of the execution of a warrant obtained under this section. Section 487.09 contains special directions respecting destruction of bodily substances obtained under the warrant. Section 487.092 provides that a justice may issue a warrant to obtain handprint, fingerprint, footprint, foot impression, teeth impression or other print or impression of the body or any part of the body. Other provisions respecting search warrants include s. 487 [warrant to search for evidence and contraband] and s. 487.01 ["general warrant"]. Under s. 487.3, the judge may make a sealing order.

SYNOPSIS

This section permits a provincial court judge to issue a warrant for the taking of bodily samples for forensic DNA analysis. The judge may issue the warrant where there are reasonable grounds to believe that a designated offence (defined in s. 487.04) has been committed; that a bodily substance has been found or obtained at the scene, on or in the victim or on anything worn or carried by the victim or on or within the body of any person or thing or at any place associated with the commission of the designated offence; the person was a party to the offence; and that forensic DNA analysis of the suspect's bodily substance will provide evidence, in effect, by a comparison of the suspect's DNA with the analysis of the substance associated with the crime. In considering whether to grant the warrant, the judge must consider the nature of the designated offence and the circumstances of its commission and whether there is a peace officer or other person with the necessary training who is able to take the bodily samples from the suspect. The warrant may be obtained through the telewarrant procedure in s. 487.1.

ANNOTATIONS

The DNA warrant provisions under this section and the companion provisions in ss. 487.04 and 487.06 to 487.09 do not violate s. 8 of the *Canadian Charter of Rights and Freedoms*. In particular, there is no need to import a "last resort" requirement. The sections already strike the appropriate balance between the public interest in effective law enforcement and the rights of individuals to control the release of personal information about themselves. Further, the principles of fundamental justice, like the principle against self-incrimination said to be implicated by this section, are more appropriately considered under s. 8. There is no need for a separate s. 7 analysis: *R. v. B. (S.A.)*, [2003] 2 S.C.R. 678, 178 C.C.C. (3d) 193.

Reference to *ex parte* proceedings in this section is not mandatory. Subsection (1) does not deprive a judge of the option of requiring a contested hearing in a suitable case. An issuing judge may find it advisable to require notice to ensure reasonableness and fairness in the circumstances. However, such a hearing is not constitutionally mandated because of the risk that the suspect would take steps to frustrate the proper execution of the warrant: *R. v. B. (S.A.)*, *supra*.

Although this section authorizes an *ex parte* hearing, the judge is not bound to proceed in that manner and could in a proper case require that the accused be served with the application, as where the accused is already in custody: *R. v. F. (S.)* (2000), 141 C.C.C. (3d) 225 (Ont. C.A.). See also *R. v. Feeney* (2001), 152 C.C.C. (3d) 390 (B.C.C.A.).

It was held, in a case where the evidence was seized prior to the enactment of this section, that the taking of hair samples and buccal swabs without prior judicial authorization could not be justified as a search incident to arrest and violated the accused's rights under ss. 7 and 8 of the Charter: *R. v. Stillman*, [1997] 1 S.C.R. 607, 113 C.C.C. (3d) 321.

Where the Crown seeks to adduce novel scientific evidence, the trial judge's function is limited to an overview of the evidence to be satisfied that it reflects a scientific theory or technique that has either gained acceptance in the scientific community or, if not accepted, is considered otherwise reliable in accordance with the methodology validating it. The trial judge is required to hear sufficient evidence to determine reliability as a preliminary matter. The trial judge must not pass judgment on the particular application of the methodology by the expert. That is a question of weight for the jury. In charging the jury as to the weight to be attached to DNA evidence, in addition to the usual instructions concerning expert evidence, the trial judge would be well advised to instruct the jury not to be overwhelmed by the aura of scientific infallibility associated with scientific evidence. The judge should tell the jurors to use their common sense in their assessment of all of the evidence on the DNA issue and determine if it is reliable and valid as a piece of circumstantial evidence: *R. v. Terceira* (1998), 123 C.C.C. (3d) 1 (Ont. C.A.), affd [1999] 3 S.C.R. 866, 142 C.C.C. (3d) 95.

ORDER — PRIMARY DESIGNATED OFFENCES / Order — primary designated offences / Order — persons found not criminally responsible and secondary designated offences / Order to offender

487.051 (1) The court shall make an order in Form 5.03 authorizing the taking of the number of samples of bodily substances that is reasonably required for the purpose of forensic DNA analysis from a person who is convicted, discharged under section 730 or found guilty under the *Youth Criminal Justice Act* or the *Young Offenders Act*, of an offence committed at any time, including before June 30, 2000, if that offence is a primary designated offence within the meaning of paragraphs (*a*) and (*c*.02) of the definition "primary designated offence" in section 487.04 when the person is sentenced or discharged.

(2) The court shall make such an order in Form 5.03 in relation to a person who is convicted, discharged under section 730 or found guilty under the *Youth Criminal Justice Act* or the *Young Offenders Act*, of an offence committed at any time, including before June 30, 2000, if that offence is a primary designated offence within the meaning of any of paragraphs (*a*.1) to (*c*.01) and (*c*.03) to (*d*) of the definition "primary designated offence" in section 487.04 when the person is sentenced or discharged. However, the court is not required to make the order if it is satisfied that the person has established that the impact of such an order on their privacy and security of the person would be grossly disproportionate to the public interest in the protection of society and the proper administration of justice, to be achieved through the early detection, arrest and conviction of offenders.

(3) The court may, on application by the prosecutor and if it is satisfied that it is in the best interests of the administration of justice to do so, make such an order in Form 5.04 in relation to

(*a*) a person who is found not criminally responsible on account of mental disorder for an offence committed at any time, including before June 30, 2000, if that offence is a designated offence when the finding is made; or

(*b*) a person who is convicted, discharged under section 730 or found guilty under the *Youth Criminal Justice Act* or the *Young Offenders Act*, of an offence committed at any time, including before June 30, 2000, if that offence is a secondary designated offence when the person is sentenced or discharged.

In deciding whether to make the order, the court shall consider the person's criminal record, whether they were previously found not criminally responsible on account of mental disorder for a designated offence, the nature of the offence, the circumstances surrounding its commission and the impact such an order would have on the person's privacy and security of the person and shall give reasons for its decision.

(4) When the court makes an order authorizing the taking of samples of bodily substances, it may make an order in Form 5.041 to require the person to report at the place, day and time set out in the order and submit to the taking of the samples. 1998, c. 37, s. 17; 2002, c. 1, s. 176; 2005, c. 25, s. 3; 2007, c. 22, s. 9; 2014, c. 25, s. 24.

CROSS-REFERENCES

The terms "designated offence", "primary designated offence", "secondary designated offence", "DNA", "forensic DNA analysis", and "young person" are defined in s. 487.04. Section 487.05 allows for the issuance of a warrant to obtain bodily samples for forensic DNA analysis in the course of an investigation.

SYNOPSIS

This section and ss. 487.052 to 487.091 create the scheme for collecting bodily substances from offenders for forensic DNA analysis and storage of the results in the national DNA data bank established under the *DNA Identification Act*, S.C. 1998, c. 37. The foundation provisions are: this section, which gives the court that finds the adult or young offender guilty or not criminally responsible of certain offences the power to authorize the taking of the bodily substances, including the power in respect of offenders convicted of certain offences committed before June 30, 2000 when s. 5(1) of the *DNA Identification Act* came into force, and which directs the Solicitor General of Canada, for criminal identification purposes, to establish a national DNA data bank, consisting of a crime scene index and a convicted offenders index, to be maintained by the Commissioner of the R.C.M.P.; and s. 487.055, which gives a provincial court judge, on *ex parte* application, the power to authorize the taking of bodily substances for forensic DNA analysis from certain offenders who had previously been convicted of certain serious offences and are still serving sentence. These sections and the related provisions for implementing the scheme are summarized below.

Under this section, the nature of the power to order the taking of bodily substances for forensic DNA analysis depends on the offence of which the person was found guilty.

The order shall be made if the person was convicted of a primary designated offence as defined in paras. (*a*) and (*c*.02) of the definition of primary designated offence in s. 487.04, such as aggravated sexual assault whether or not the offence was committed before June 30, 2000. For primary designated offences defined in paras. (*a*.1) to (*d*) of the definition of primary designated offences, such as sexual assault, the order is also to be made, whether or not the offence was committed before June 30, 2000, but subject to the discretion described in subsec. (2), where the impact on a person's privacy and security of the person is grossly disproportionate to the public interest in the protection of society and the proper administration of justice, to be achieved through the early detection, arrest and conviction of offenders.

The order may be made if the person was found not criminally responsible on account of mental disorder for a primary or secondary designated offence committed at any time or convicted or found guilty of a secondary designated offence (also defined in s. 487.04), whether or not committed before June 30, 2000, and the court is satisfied that it is in the best interests of justice. In deciding whether to make the order, the court is directed under subsec. (3) to consider the offender's record, whether the person was previously found not criminally responsible on account of mental disorder, the nature of the offence, the circumstances surrounding its commission and the impact on the offender's privacy and security of the person. The court is required to give reasons for the decision.

The order is to be made at the time of disposition or, if the court did not consider the matter at that time, it shall within 90 days set a date for a hearing to do so, pursuant to s. 487.053.

Pursuant to s. 487.054, the decision of the court under s. 487.051 may be appealed by the offender or the prosecutor as the case may be. Section 487.056 sets out when the order is to be executed and allows for the issuing of a warrant if the person fails to appear as required.

Section 487.055 deals with persons who were convicted prior to these provisions coming into force. It allows for an *ex parte* application to a provincial court judge for authorization to take bodily substances for the purpose of forensic DNA analysis from persons (a) declared to be dangerous offenders; (b) dangerous offenders or dangerous sexual offenders under the former legislation; (c) convicted of murder; (c.1) convicted of attempted murder, or conspiracy to commit murder or to cause another person to be murdered and, on the date of the application, is serving a sentence of imprisonment for that offence; (d) convicted of a sexual offence and, on the date of the application, is serving a sentence of imprisonment for that offence; or (e) convicted of manslaughter and, on the date of the application, is serving a sentence of imprisonment for that offence. "Sexual offence" for this purpose is defined in s. 487.055(3). The application must be accompanied by a certificate under s. 667(1)(*a*) as proof of the finding or conviction as the case may be. In deciding whether to grant the authorization, the judge is to consider, under s. 487.055(3.1), the offender's criminal record, the nature of the offence and the circumstances surrounding its commission, and the impact on the offender's privacy and security of the person and is to give reasons for the decision. Although the application under subsec. (1) may be made *ex parte*, the section contemplates that the offender may be given notice. If so, and the person wishes to attend, subsec. (3.01) provides for attendance by closed-circuit television or similar means. If the offender is on conditional release, a summons may issue directing the offender to attend at the specified time and place for the purpose of submitting to the taking of the samples (subsecs. (3.11) and (4)). The summons is to be accompanied by a copy of the authorization and is to be served by a peace officer in the manner directed by subsec. (5). If the offender does not report as required, a justice of the peace may issue a warrant for the person's arrest pursuant to subsec. (8). Section 487.0551 allows for the issuing of a warrant to a person who fails to appear in accordance with an order or warrant made under these provisions. And, s. 487.0552 makes it an offence to fail, without reasonable excuse, to comply with an order or summons as the case may be.

Section 487.091 provides that, if a DNA profile could not be derived from the bodily substances obtained in execution of an order made under s. 487.051 or an authorization under s. 487.055, an *ex parte* application may be made to a provincial court judge for authorization to take further samples. The application must state the reasons why the DNA profile could not be derived. Section 487.055(5) and (6) apply, with the necessary modifications, so as to obtain the samples from a person who is not in custody. Thus, a summons may be issued to require the offender to attend for the taking of the samples and, if necessary, a justice of the peace may issue a warrant for that purpose.

Section 487.056 sets out when and where the sample is to be taken, depending upon the provision under which the order was made. Under s. 487.056(6), the samples of bodily substances are to be taken by a peace officer, or another person acting under the direction of a peace officer who is able by virtue of training or experience to take the samples. The peace officer is then required under s. 487.057 to make a written report as soon as is feasible after the samples have been taken. The report is to be filed with the court that made the order, or the provincial court judge who granted the authorization, as the case may be, and include the time and date that the samples were taken and a description of the bodily substances that were taken. The peace officer and the person acting under the officer's direction are protected from civil and criminal liability under s. 487.058 for anything necessarily done with reasonable care and skill in the taking of the samples in execution of the order or authorization. Section 487.06(1) sets out the means by which the bodily substances may be taken, namely, plucking of hairs, taking of buccal swabs or the taking of blood by a shallow pricking of the skin. Section 487.06(2) directs the court or provincial court judge to include terms or conditions that the judge or court considers advisable to ensure that the taking of the samples is reasonable in the circumstances. Under s. 487.06(3) the peace officer may also take fingerprints from the persons for the purpose of the *DNA Identification Act*. (Section 5(5)(*b*) of that Act provides that the profile in the convicted offenders index of the DNA data bank shall contain information as to the identity of the person from whose bodily substance the profile was derived.) Before taking the samples, the peace officer is, pursuant to s. 487.071, to verify that the DNA data bank does not already contain the person's DNA profile and, if it is already in the convicted offenders' index, the bodily sample is not to be taken. Before taking the sample the officer is to inform the offender of the matters set forth in s. 487.07(1), such as the means by which the samples will be taken, the purpose of taking the samples, and the contents of the authorization or order. Under subsec. (2), the offender may be detained for the purpose of taking the substances for a reasonable period and may be required to accompany the peace officer for that purpose. The peace officer is also to take reasonable steps to ensure the person's privacy while the samples are being taken. There are special provisions in s. 487.07(4) and (5) in the case of young persons.

The bodily samples and a copy of the order or authorization are to be transmitted to the Commissioner of the R.C.M.P. for entry into the convicted offenders index of the national DNA data bank (s. 487.071(3)). (Under s. 10(1) of the *DNA Identification Act*, the Commissioner shall safely and securely store, for the purpose of forensic DNA analysis, the portions of the samples of the bodily substances that the Commissioner considers appropriate and, without delay, destroy any remaining portions. Under subsec. (2), forensic DNA analysis of stored bodily substances may be performed if the Commissioner is of the opinion that the analysis is justified because significant technological advances have been made since the time when a DNA profile of the person who provided the bodily substances, or from whom they were taken, was last derived.) Section 487.08(1.1) limits the use of bodily substances taken pursuant to an order or authorization to use for forensic DNA analysis or to transmit any unused portions to the Commissioner. Contravention of these provisions is a Crown-option offence pursuant to s. 487.08(4).

Section 487.09 provides for the destruction of bodily substances or removal of electronic records in certain circumstances, as where the person has been finally acquitted of the designated offence. However, subsec. (2) provides that a provincial court judge may order that the bodily substances or results of the analyses not be destroyed if they might reasonably be required in an investigation or prosecution. Under subsec. (3), bodily substances that were provided voluntarily are to be destroyed and the results of the analysis destroyed where it is determined that the profile did not match the substance found at the place referred to in s. 487.05(1)(*b*), for example the scene of the offence. Section 487.091 allows a provincial court judge to make an *ex parte* order authorizing the taking of additional samples where, among other things, it was not possible to obtain a DNA profile from the original samples.

ANNOTATIONS

Note: Some of the cases cited below were decided prior to the amendments to this section.

The risk of re-offence is not a prerequisite to the making of an order: *R. v. Durham* (2007), 221 C.C.C. (3d) 304 (B.C.C.A.).

Strictly speaking there is no burden on either Crown or defence under [now] subsec. (3)(*b*). However, as the party seeking the order, the Crown bears an evidential burden to produce sufficient information to raise the issue. The trial judge must then be satisfied after weighing and balancing all the relevant considerations that the order should be made: *R. v. Hendry* (2001), 161 C.C.C. (3d) 275, 48 C.R. (5th) 310 (Ont. C.A.).

In cases falling under [now] subsec. (3)(*b*), the trial judge is to make the order sought if satisfied that it is in the best interests of the administration of justice to do so. The court is instructed to consider the offender's criminal record, the nature of the offence and the circumstances surrounding its commission, and the impact on the person's privacy and security of the person. Given an adult offender's diminished expectation of privacy following conviction, the minimal intrusion into the security of the person in the ordinary case and the important interests served by the DNA data bank, it will usually be in the best interests of the administration of justice for the judge to make the order: *R. v. Hendry supra*.

An order may be grossly disproportionate if the circumstances of the particular offender or the offence or risk of breach of privacy or security of the person varied markedly from the usual cases contemplated by the scheme. The order should be refused only if the imposition of terms and conditions of the authorizing order would not adequately restore the appropriate balance. In balancing law enforcement objectives with the person's privacy interests, regard should be had to the offender's criminal record, the nature of the offence and the specific risk of misuse or of particular dangers to the health of the offender: *R. v. Jordan* (2002), 162 C.C.C. (3d) 385, 1 C.R. (6th) 141 (N.S.C.A.).

For the purposes of [now] subsec. (2)(*b*), criminal record includes a youth court record: *R. v. S. (O.S.)* (2002), 168 C.C.C. (3d) 360, 317 A.R. 163 (C.A.).

Although the public interest is presumed to outweigh privacy interests in the case of primary designated offences, in [now] subsec. (2), that subsection recognizes that this is a rebuttable presumption. In balancing the privacy interest against the public interest, regard should be had to the criminal record of the offender, the nature of the offence, the circumstances surrounding its commission and the impact on the offender's privacy and security of the person. The offender must establish that the public interest is clearly and substantially outweighed by the individual's privacy and security interests. The purposes and principles set out in the *Youth Criminal Justice Act*, S.C. 2002, c. 1, should be considering in determining whether an order should be granted: *R. v. C. (R.W.)* (2005), 201 C.C.C. (3d) 321, 32 C.R. (6th) 201 (S.C.C.).

The words "best interests of the administration of justice" do not import a requirement that the order can only be made where there are reasonable and probable grounds to believe that a further offence will be committed where the offender's DNA will be of assistance in proving the case. The application of the provision requires a balancing between the competing rights of society and the interests of the accused. The state's interest is not simply detection of crime, but includes deterrence of potential repeat offenders, promotion of safety of the community, detecting the work of a serial offender, assistance in solving "cold crimes", streamlining investigations and assisting the innocent by early exclusion from investigative suspicion: *R. v. Briggs* (2001), 157 C.C.C. (3d) 38, 45 C.R. (5th) 99 (Ont. C.A.), leave to appeal to S.C.C. refused [2002] 2 S.C.R. v, 162 C.C.C. (3d) vi.

The judge may consider offences committed by the offender both before and after the commission of the designated offence. The existence of DNA at the scene of the offence is not necessarily a relevant consideration: *R. v. Briggs, supra.*

It was held, considering the predecessor to this section, that the Court of Appeal is not "the court" within the meaning of this section. Although the Court of Appeal had substituted a conviction for second degree murder, it did not become the "convicting" court for the purpose of this section: *R. v. Bellegarde* (2003), 181 C.C.C. (3d) 69, [2004] 5 W.W.R. 459 (Sask. C.A.).

It was held that the predecessor to this section allowing for taking of samples from a person convicted before June 30, 2000 did not offend ss. 7, 9 or 11(*i*) of the Charter: *R. v. Murrins* (2002), 162 C.C.C. (3d) 412, 1 C.R. (6th) 166 (N.S.C.A.). See also *R. v. Ku* (2002), 169 C.C.C. (3d) 535, 7 C.R. (6th) 241 (B.C.C.A.), leave to appeal to S.C.C. refused [2003] 3 S.C.R. vii, 178 C.C.C. (3d) vi.

This section does not offend ss. 7 or 8 of the Charter in its application to young offenders: *R. v. S. (C.)* (2011), 269 C.C.C. (3d) 431 (Ont. C.A.).

487.052 [*Repealed*, 2005, c. 25, s. 4; 2007, c. 22, s. 3.]

TIMING OF ORDER / Hearing.

487.053 (1) The court may make an order under section 487.051 authorizing the taking of samples of bodily substances when it imposes a sentence on a person, finds the person not criminally responsible on account of mental disorder or directs that they be discharged under section 730.

(2) If the court does not consider the matter at that time, it

(*a*) shall, within 90 days after the day on which it imposes the sentence, makes the finding or directs that the person be discharged, set a date for a hearing to do so;

(*b*) retains jurisdiction over the matter; and

(*c*) may require the person to appear by closed-circuit television or any other means that allows the court and the person to engage in simultaneous visual and oral communication, as long as the person is given the opportunity to communicate privately with counsel if they are represented by counsel. 1998, c. 37, s. 17; 2000, c. 10, s. 14; 2005, c. 25, s. 4; 2007, c. 22, s. 3.

SYNOPSIS

For a synopsis of this and the related sections, see the synopsis under s. 487.051.

APPEAL.

487.054 The offender or the prosecutor may appeal from a decision of the court under any of subsections 487.051(1) to (3). 1998, c. 37, s. 17; 2007, c. 22, s. 10.

CROSS-REFERENCES

See cross-references under s. 487.051.

SYNOPSIS

For a synopsis of this and the related sections, see the synopsis under s. 487.051. For a synopsis of the provisions for DNA warrants, see the editor's note preceding s. 487.04.

ANNOTATIONS

The appeal route follows the scheme in the *Criminal Code* generally. That is, in indictable proceedings the appeal from the making or refusal to make the order lies to the Court of Appeal and in summary conviction proceedings the appeal is taken in accordance with Part XXVII of the *Criminal Code*. The appeal court has the power to make the order that should have been made by the trial court: *R. v. Hendry* (2001), 161 C.C.C. (3d) 275, 48 C.R. (5th) 310 (Ont. C.A.). See also *R. v. R. (B.)* (2011), 274 C.C.C. (3d) 490 (Nfld. & Lab. C.A.).

There is no jurisdiction to stay a DNA order pending an appeal from conviction: *R. v. Zurowski* (2003), 175 C.C.C. (3d) 494, [2003] 9 W.W.R. 400 (Alta. C.A.), motion to quash dismissed 183 C.C.C. (3d) 448 (S.C.C.). *Contra R. v. Briggs* (2001), 53 O.R. (3d) 124 (C.A.), leave to appeal to S.C.C. refused 154 O.A.C. 198*n*.

A DNA order is a discretionary decision that is entitled to deference on appeal: *R. v. Briggs* (2001), 157 C.C.C. (3d) 38, 45 C.R. (5th) 99 (Ont. C.A.), leave to appeal to S.C.C. refused 162 C.C.C. (3d) vi, 91 C.R.R. (2d) 187*n*.

In cases under [now] s. 487.051(2) and (3), absent an error in principle, failure to consider a relevant factor, or an overemphasis of the appropriate factors, a court of appeal should only intervene to vary a decision to either make or refuse to make a DNA data bank order if the decision was clearly unreasonable: *R. v. Hendry, supra*.

OFFENDERS SERVING SENTENCES / Certificate / Definition of "sexual offence" / Manner of appearance / Criteria / Order / Summons / Service on individual.

487.055 (1) A provincial court judge may, on *ex parte* application made in Form 5.05, authorize in Form 5.06 the taking, for the purpose of forensic DNA analysis, of any number of samples of bodily substances that is reasonably required for that purpose, by means of the investigative procedures described in subsection 487.06(1), from a person who, before June 30, 2000,

(*a*) had been declared a dangerous offender under Part XXIV;

(*b*) had been declared a dangerous offender or a dangerous sexual offender under Part XXI of the *Criminal Code*, being chapter C-34 of the Revised Statutes of Canada, 1970, as it read from time to time before January 1, 1988;

(*c*) had been convicted of murder;

(*c*.1) had been convicted of attempted murder or conspiracy to commit murder or to cause another person to be murdered and, on the date of the application, is serving a sentence of imprisonment for that offence;

(*d*) had been convicted of a sexual offence within the meaning of subsection (3) and, on the date of the application, is serving a sentence of imprisonment for that offence; or

(*e*) had been convicted of manslaughter and, on the date of the application, is serving a sentence of imprisonment for that offence.

(2) The application shall be accompanied by a certificate referred to in paragraph 667(1)(*a*) that establishes that the person is a person referred to in subsection (1). The certificate may be received in evidence without giving the notice referred to in subsection 667(4).

(3) For the purposes of subsection (1), "sexual offence" means

(*a*) an offence under any of the following provisions, namely,

(i) section 151 (sexual interference),

(ii) section 152 (invitation to sexual touching),

(iii) section 153 (sexual exploitation),

(iv) section 155 (incest),

(v) subsection 212(4) (offence in relation to juvenile prostitution),

(vi) section 271 (sexual assault),

(vii) section 272 (sexual assault with a weapon, threats to a third party or causing bodily harm), and

(viii) section 273 (aggravated sexual assault);

(*a*.1) an offence under subsection 348(1) if the indictable offence referred to in that subsection is a sexual offence within the meaning of paragraph (*a*), (*b*), (*c*) or (*d*);

(*b*) an offence under any of the following provisions of the *Criminal Code*, chapter C-34 of the Revised Statutes of Canada, 1970, as they read from time to time before January 4, 1983, namely,

(i) section 144 (rape),

(ii) section 146 (sexual intercourse with female under fourteen or between fourteen and sixteen),

(iii) section 148 (sexual intercourse with feeble-minded, etc.),

(iv) section 149 (indecent assault on female),

(v) section 156 (indecent assault on male), or

(vi) section 157 (acts of gross indecency);

(*c*) an offence under paragraph 153(1)(*a*) (sexual intercourse with step-daughter, etc.) of the *Criminal Code*, chapter C-34 of the Revised Statutes of Canada, 1970, as it read from time to time before January 1, 1988; and

(*d*) an attempt to commit an offence referred to in any of paragraphs (*a*) to (*c*).

(3.01) The court may require a person who is given notice of an application under subsection (1) and who wishes to appear at the hearing to appear by closed-circuit television or any other means that allows the court and the person to engage in simultaneous visual and oral communication, as long as the person is given the opportunity to communicate privately with counsel if they are represented by counsel.

(3.1) In deciding whether to grant an authorization under subsection (1), the court shall consider the person's criminal record, the nature of the offence and the circumstances surrounding its commission and the impact such an authorization would have on the privacy and security of the person and shall give reasons for its decision.

(3.11) If the court authorizes the taking of samples of bodily substances from a person who is on conditional release and who has appeared at the hearing, it shall make an order in Form 5.041 to require the person to report at the place, day and time set out in the order and submit to the taking of the samples.

(4) However, if a person who is on conditional release has not appeared at the hearing, a summons in Form 5.061 setting out the information referred to in paragraphs 487.07(1)(*b*) to (*d*) shall be directed to them requiring them to report at the place, day and time set out in the summons and submit to the taking of the samples.

(5) The summons shall be accompanied by a copy of the authorization referred to in subsection (1) and be served by a peace officer who shall either deliver it personally to the person to whom it is directed or, if that person cannot conveniently be found, leave it for the person at their latest or usual place of residence with any person found there who appears to be at least sixteen years of age. 1998, c. 37, s. 17; 2000, c. 10, s. 15; 2005, c. 25, s. 5; 2007, c. 22, s. 11; 2008, c. 18, s. 13.

(6) [*Repealed*, 2008, c. 18, s. 13.]

(7) to (10) [*Repealed*, 2007, c. 22, s. 11(4).]

CROSS-REFERENCES

"Prosecutor" and "peace officer" are defined in s. 2. "Forensic DNA analysis" and "provincial court judge" are defined in s. 487.04. Also, see cross-references under s. 487.051.

SYNOPSIS

For a synopsis of this and the related sections, see the synopsis under s. 487.051.

ANNOTATIONS

It was held that the predecessor to this section, which also permitted an *ex parte* application, is clear and unambiguous and there is no requirement that the judge consider giving notice to the offender. Further, the section does not infringe either ss. 7 or 8 of the *Charter of Rights and Freedoms* and, since the taking of DNA samples is not a punishment, the retroactive application of the provision does not infringe ss. 11(*h*) or 11(*i*) of the Charter: *R. v. Rodgers* (2006), 207 C.C.C. (3d) 225, 37 C.R. (6th) 1 (S.C.C.).

Although there is no appeal from an order under this section, the decision of the judge is reviewable on *certiorari*: *R. v. Rodgers, supra.*

FAILURE TO APPEAR / Execution of warrant.

487.0551 (1) If a person fails to appear at the place, day and time set out in an order made under subsection 487.051(4) or 487.055(3.11) or in a summons referred to in subsection 487.055(4) or 487.091(3), a justice of the peace may issue a warrant for their arrest in Form 5.062 to allow samples of bodily substances to be taken.

(2) The warrant may be executed anywhere in Canada by a peace officer who has jurisdiction in that place or over the person. The warrant remains in force until it is executed. 2007, c. 22, s. 12.

CROSS-REFERENCES

"Peace officer" is defined in s. 2.

SYNOPSIS

For a synopsis of this and the related sections, see the synopsis under s. 487.051.

FAILURE TO COMPLY WITH ORDER OR SUMMONS / For greater certainty

487.0552 (1) Every person who, without reasonable excuse, fails to comply with an order made under subsection 487.051(4) or 487.055(3.11) of this Act or under subsection 196.14(4) or 196.24(4) of the *National Defence Act*, or with a summons referred to in subsection 487.055(4) or 487.091(3) of this Act, is guilty of

(*a*) an indictable offence and liable to imprisonment for a term of not more than two years; or

(*b*) an offence punishable on summary conviction.

(2) For greater certainty, a lawful command that prevents a person from complying with an order or summons is a reasonable excuse if, at the time, the person is subject to the Code of Service Discipline within the meaning of subsection 2(1) of the *National Defence Act*. 2007, c. 22, s. 12.

SYNOPSIS

For a synopsis of this and the related sections, see the synopsis under s. 487.051.

WHEN COLLECTION TO TAKE PLACE / When collection to take place / When collection to take place / Appeal / Collection of samples / Who collects samples.

487.056 (1) Samples of bodily substances shall be taken as authorized under section 487.051

(*a*) at the place, day and time set out in an order made under subsection 487.051(4) or as soon as feasible afterwards; or

(*b*) in any other case, on the day on which the order authorizing the taking of the samples is made or as soon as feasible afterwards.

(2) Samples of bodily substances shall be taken as authorized under section 487.055 or 487.091

(*a*) at the place, day and time set out in an order made under subsection 487.055(3.11) or a summons referred to in subsection 487.055(4) or 487.091(3) or as soon as feasible afterwards; or

(*b*) in any other case, as soon as feasible after the authorization is granted.

(3) If a person fails to appear as required by an order made under subsection 487.051(4) or 487.055(3.11) or a summons referred to in subsection 487.055(4) or 487.091(3), samples of bodily substances shall be taken

(*a*) when the person is arrested under a warrant issued under subsection 487.0551(1) or as soon as feasible afterwards; or

(*b*) as soon as feasible after the person appears at the place set out in the order or summons if no warrant is issued.

(4) Subsections (1) to (3) apply even if the order or authorization to take the samples of bodily substances is appealed.

(5) A peace officer who is authorized under section 487.051, 487.055 or 487.091 to take samples of bodily substances may cause the samples to be taken in any place in Canada in which the person who is subject to the order or authorization is located.

(6) The samples shall be taken by a peace officer who has jurisdiction over the person or in the place in which the samples are taken — or a person acting under their direction — who is able, by virtue of training or experience, to take them. 1998, c. 37, s. 17; 2000, c. 10, s. 16; 2002, c. 1, s. 179; 2005, c. 25, s. 6; 2007, c. 22, s. 13.

CROSS-REFERENCES

"Peace officer" is defined in s. 2. Under s. 487.057, after taking the samples, the peace officer is to make a written report. Section 487.058 protects the peace officer and the person acting under the officer's direction from civil and criminal liability. Also, see cross-references under s. 487.051.

SYNOPSIS

For a synopsis of this and the related sections, see the synopsis under s. 487.051.

ANNOTATIONS

There is no jurisdiction to stay a DNA order pending an appeal from conviction: *R. v. Zurowski* (2003), 175 C.C.C. (3d) 494, [2003] 9 W.W.R. 400 (Alta. C.A.), motion to quash dismissed February 9, 2004, Court File No. 30074, S.C.C. *Contra R. v. Briggs* (2001), 53 O.R. (3d) 124, 142 O.A.C. 41 (C.A.), leave to appeal to S.C.C. refused 154 O.A.C. 198*n*. See also *R. v. Gibson* (2011), 277 C.C.C. (3d) 247 (B.C.S.C.), holding that subsec. (4) does not remove a superior court's inherent jurisdiction to grant a stay of a DNA order pending a conviction appeal.

REPORT OF PEACE OFFICER / Contents of report / Copy of report.

487.057 (1) A peace officer who takes samples of bodily substances from a person or who causes a person who is not a peace officer to take samples under their direction shall, as soon as feasible after the samples are taken, make a written report in Form 5.07 and cause the report to be filed with

(*a*) the provincial court judge who issued the warrant under section 487.05 or granted the authorization under section 487.055 or 487.091 or another judge of that provincial court; or

(*b*) the court that made the order under section 487.051.

(2) The report shall include

(*a*) a statement of the time and date the samples were taken; and

(*b*) a description of the bodily substances that were taken.

(3) A peace officer who takes the samples or causes the samples to be taken under their direction at the request of another peace officer shall send a copy of the report to the other peace officer unless that other peace officer had jurisdiction to take the samples. 1998, c. 37, s. 17; 2000, c. 10, s. 17; 2007, c. 22, s. 14.

CROSS-REFERENCES

"Peace officer" is defined in s. 2. Also, see cross-references under s. 487.051.

SYNOPSIS

For a synopsis of this and the related sections with respect to taking of samples from persons found guilty of certain offences, see the synopsis under s. 487.051.

NO CRIMINAL OR CIVIL LIABILITY.

487.058 No peace officer, and no person acting under a peace officer's direction, incurs any criminal or civil liability for anything necessarily done with reasonable care and skill in the taking of samples of bodily substances from a person under a warrant issued under section 487.05, an order made under section 487.051 or an authorization granted under section 487.055 or 487.091. 1998, c. 37, s. 17; 2000; c. 10, s. 18; 2007, c. 22, s. 15.

CROSS-REFERENCES

"Peace officer" is defined in s. 2. For other cross-references see ss. 487.05 and 487.051.

SYNOPSIS

For a synopsis of this and the related sections with respect to taking of samples for forensic DNA analysis from persons found guilty of certain offences, see the synopsis under s. 487.051.

INVESTIGATIVE PROCEDURES / Terms and conditions / Fingerprints.

487.06 (1) A peace officer or a person acting under a peace officer's direction is authorized by a warrant issued under section 487.05, an order made under section

487.051 or an authorization granted under section 487.055 or 487.091 to take samples of bodily substances by any of the following means:

- **(*a*) the plucking of individual hairs from the person, including the root sheath;**
- **(*b*) the taking of buccal swabs by swabbing the lips, tongue and inside cheeks of the mouth to collect epithelial cells; or**
- **(*c*) the taking of blood by pricking the skin surface with a sterile lancet.**

(2) The warrant, order or authorization shall include any terms and conditions that the provincial court judge or court, as the case may be, considers advisable to ensure that the taking of the samples authorized by the warrant, order or authorization is reasonable in the circumstances.

(3) A peace officer who is authorized to take samples of bodily substances from a person by an order made under section 487.051 or an authorization granted under section 487.055 or 487.091, or a person acting under their direction, may take fingerprints from the person for the purpose of the *DNA Identification Act*. 1995, c. 27, s. 1; 1998, c. 37, s. 18; 2000, c. 10, s. 19; 2007, c. 22, s. 16.

CROSS-REFERENCES

The term "provincial court judge" is defined in s. 487.04. "Peace officer" is defined in s. 2. Section 487.05 sets out the circumstances in which a provincial court judge may issue a warrant to seize the bodily substances referred to in this section for forensic DNA analysis. Section 487.07 sets out the special requirements with respect to execution of a warrant obtained under this section. Section 487.08 limits the use of evidence obtained as a result of the execution of a warrant obtained under this section. Section 487.09 contains special directions respecting destruction of bodily substances obtained under the warrant. Section 487.091 provides that a justice may issue a warrant to obtain handprint, fingerprint, footprint, foot impression, teeth impression or other print or impression of the body or any part of the body. Other provisions respecting search warrants include s. 487 [warrant to search for evidence and contraband] and s. 487.01 ["general warrant"]. For other cross-references respecting search warrants, see notes following s. 487. For other cross-references with respect to taking of samples from persons found guilty of certain offences, see the cross-references under s. 487.051.

SYNOPSIS

For a synopsis of this and the related sections with respect to taking of samples for forensic DNA analysis from persons found guilty of certain offences, see the synopsis under s. 487.051.

ANNOTATIONS

This provision does not violate s. 7 of the Charter: *R. v. Ku* (2002), 169 C.C.C. (3d) 535, 7 C.R. (6th) 241 (B.C.C.A.), leave to appeal to S.C.C. refused 178 C.C.C. (3d) vi. See also *R. v. F. (S.)* (2000), 141 C.C.C. (3d) 225, 32 C.R. (5th) 79 (Ont. C.A.), which upheld the constitutional validity of the predecessor to this section.

DUTY TO INFORM / Detention of person / Respect of privacy / Execution of warrant against young person / Waiver of rights of young person.

487.07 (1) Before taking samples of bodily substances from a person, or causing samples to be taken under their direction, in execution of a warrant issued under section 487.05 or an order made under section 487.051 or under an authorization granted under section 487.055 or 487.091, a peace officer shall inform the person of

- **(*a*) the contents of the warrant, order or authorization;**
- **(*b*) the nature of the investigative procedures by means of which the samples are to be taken;**
- **(*c*) the purpose of taking the samples;**

(*d*) the authority of the peace officer and any other person under the direction of the peace officer to use as much force as is necessary for the purpose of taking the samples; and

(*d*.1) [*Repealed*, 2000, c. 10, s. 20(2).]

(*e*) in the case of samples of bodily substances taken in execution of a warrant,

(i) the possibility that the results of forensic DNA analysis may be used in evidence, and

(ii) if the sample is taken from a young person, the rights of the young person under subsection (4).

(2) A person from whom samples of bodily substances are to be taken may

(*a*) be detained for that purpose for a period that is reasonable in the circumstances; and

(*b*) be required to accompany a peace officer for that purpose.

(3) A peace officer who takes samples of bodily substances from a person, or a person who takes such samples under the direction of a peace officer, shall ensure that the person's privacy is respected in a manner that is reasonable in the circumstances.

(4) A young person against whom a warrant is executed has, in addition to any other rights arising from his or her detention under the warrant,

(*a*) the right to a reasonable opportunity to consult with, and

(*b*) the right to have the warrant executed in the presence of

counsel and a parent or, in the absence of a parent, an adult relative or, in the absence of a parent and an adult relative, any other appropriate adult chosen by the young person.

(5) A young person may waive his or her rights under subsection (4) but any such waiver

(*a*) must be recorded on audio tape or video tape or otherwise; or

(*b*) must be made in writing and contain a statement signed by the young person that he or she has been informed of the right being waived. 1995, c. 27, ss. 1 and 3; 1998, c. 37, s. 19; 2000, c. 10, s. 20; 2007, c. 22, s. 17.

CROSS-REFERENCES

The terms "young person", "adult", "DNA" and "forensic DNA analysis" are defined in s. 487.04. "Peace officer" is defined in s. 2. Section 487.05 sets out the circumstances in which a provincial court judge may issue a warrant to seize bodily substances for forensic DNA analysis. Section 487.06(1) sets out those "bodily substances" that may be seized pursuant to a warrant issued under s. 487.05. Section 487.06(2) requires the judge to include appropriate terms and conditions. Section 487.08 limits the use of evidence obtained as a result of the execution of a warrant obtained under this section. Section 487.09 contains special directions respecting destruction of bodily substances obtained under the warrant. Section 487.091 provides that a justice may issue a warrant to obtain handprint, fingerprint, footprint, foot impression, teeth impression o r other print or impression of the body or any part of the body. A warrant is executed in accordance with s. 29. Where a person is detained, the peace officer must comply with the provisions of s. 10 of the Charter, subject to reasonable limitations as permitted by s. 1 of the Charter. For protection of persons executing warrants, see ss. 25 to 28.

Other provisions respecting search warrants include s. 487 [warrant to search for evidence and contraband] and s. 487.01 ["general warrant"]. For other cross-references respecting search warrants, see notes following s. 487. Also, see cross-references under s. 487.051.

SYNOPSIS

For a synopsis of this and the related sections with respect to taking of samples for forensic DNA analysis from persons found guilty of certain offences, see the synopsis under s. 487.051.

VERIFICATION / DNA profile in data bank / DNA profile not in data bank.

487.071 (1) Before taking samples of bodily substances from a person under an order made under section 487.051 or an authorization granted under section 487.055 or 487.091, a peace officer, or a person acting under their direction, shall verify whether the convicted offenders index of the national DNA data bank, established under the *DNA Identification Act*, contains the person's DNA profile.

(2) If the person's DNA profile is in the convicted offenders index of the national DNA data bank, the peace officer or person acting under their direction shall not take any bodily substances from the person but shall

(*a*) confirm in writing on the order or authorization that he or she has been advised that the person's DNA profile is in the DNA data bank; and

(*b*) transmit a copy of the order or authorization containing that confirmation and any other information prescribed by regulations made under the *DNA Identification Act* to the Commissioner of the Royal Canadian Mounted Police.

(3) If the person's DNA profile is not in the convicted offenders index of the national DNA data bank, the peace officer or person acting under their direction shall execute the order or authorization and transmit to the Commissioner of the Royal Canadian Mounted Police

(*a*) any bodily substances taken; and

(*b*) a copy of the order or authorization and any other information prescribed by regulations made under the *DNA Identification Act*. 1998, c. 37, s. 20; 2000, c. 10, s. 21; 2005, c. 25, s. 8; 2007, c. 22, s. 18.

CROSS-REFERENCES

"Forensic DNA analysis" is defined in s. 487.04. Section 5(1) of the *DNA Identification Act* directs the Solicitor General of Canada, for criminal identification purposes, to establish a national DNA data bank, consisting of a crime scene index and a convicted offenders index, to be maintained by the Commissioner of the R.C.M.P.

SYNOPSIS

For a synopsis of this and the related sections with respect to taking of samples from persons found guilty of certain offences, see the synopsis under s. 487.051.

USE OF BODILY SUBSTANCES — WARRANT / Use of bodily substances — order, authorization / Use of results — warrant / Offence / Offence.

487.08 (1) No person shall use bodily substances that are taken in execution of a warrant under section 487.05 or under section 196.12 of the *National Defence Act* except to use them for the purpose of forensic DNA analysis in the course of an investigation of a designated offence.

(1.1) No person shall use bodily substances that are taken in execution of an order made under section 487.051 of this Act or section 196.14 of the *National Defence Act*, or under an authorization granted under section 487.055 or 487.091 of this Act or section 196.24 of the *National Defence Act*, except to transmit them to the Commissioner of the Royal Canadian Mounted Police for the purpose of forensic DNA analysis in accordance with the *DNA Identification Act*.

(2) No person shall use the results of forensic DNA analysis of bodily substances that are taken in execution of a warrant under section 487.05 or under section 196.12 of the *National Defence Act* except

(*a*) in the course of an investigation of the designated offence or any other designated offence in respect of which a warrant was issued or a bodily substance was found in the circumstances described in paragraph 487.05(1)(*b*) or in paragraph 196.12(1)(*b*) of the *National Defence Act*; or

(*b*) in any proceeding for such an offence.

(2.1) [*Repealed*, 2005, c. 25, s. 9(2).]

(3) Every person who contravenes subsection (1) or (2) is guilty of an offence punishable on summary conviction.

(4) Every person who contravenes subsection (1.1)

(*a*) is guilty of an indictable offence and liable to imprisonment for a term not exceeding two years; or

(*b*) is guilty of an offence punishable on summary conviction and liable to a fine not exceeding $2,000 or to imprisonment for a term not exceeding six months, or to both. 1995, c. 27, s. 1; 1998, c. 37, s. 21; 2000, c. 10, s. 22; 2005, c. 25, s. 9; 2007, c. 22, s. 19.

CROSS-REFERENCES

The terms "designated offence", "DNA", and "forensic DNA analysis" are defined in s. 487.04. Section 487.05 sets out the circumstances in which a provincial court judge may issue a warrant to seize bodily substances for forensic DNA analysis. Section 487.06(1) sets out those "bodily substances" that may be seized pursuant to a warrant issued under this section. Section 487.06(2) requires the judge to include appropriate terms and conditions. Section 487.07 sets out the special requirements with respect to execution of a warrant obtained under that section. Section 487.09 contains special directions respecting destruction of bodily substances obtained under the warrant. Section 487.091 provides that a justice may issue a warrant to obtain handprint, fingerprint, footprint, foot impression, teeth impression or other print or impression of the body or any part of the body. Other provisions respecting search warrants include s. 487 [warrant to search for evidence and contraband] and s. 487.01 ["general warrant"]. For other cross-references respecting search warrants, see notes following s. 487. For other cross-references with respect to taking of samples from persons found guilty of certain offences, see the cross-references under s. 487.051.

The limitation period for a summary conviction offence is six months as specified in s. 786(2). The maximum penalty for a summary conviction offence is set out in s. 687.

SYNOPSIS

For a synopsis of this and the related sections with respect to taking of samples for forensic DNA analysis from persons found guilty of certain offences, see the synopsis under s. 487.051.

DESTRUCTION OF BODILY SUBSTANCES, etc. — WARRANT / Exception / Destruction of bodily substances, etc., voluntarily given.

487.09 (1) Subject to subsection (2), bodily substances that are taken from a person in execution of a warrant under section 487.05 and the results of forensic DNA analysis shall be destroyed or, in the case of results in electronic form, access to those results shall be permanently removed, without delay after

(*a*) the results of that analysis establish that the bodily substance referred to in paragraph 487.05(1)(*b*) was not from that person;

(*b*) the person is finally acquitted of the designated offence and any other offence in respect of the same transaction; or

(*c*) the expiration of one year after

(i) the person is discharged after a preliminary inquiry into the designated offence or any other offence in respect of the same transaction,

(ii) the dismissal, for any reason other than acquittal, or the withdrawal of any information charging the person with the designated offence or any other offence in respect of the same transaction, or

(iii) any proceeding against the person for the offence or any other offence in respect of the same transaction is stayed under section 579 or under that section as applied by section 572 or 795,

unless during that year a new information is laid or an indictment is preferred charging the person with the designated offence or any other offence in respect of the same transaction or the proceeding is recommenced.

(2) A provincial court judge may order that the bodily substances that are taken from a person and the results of forensic DNA analysis not be destroyed during any period that the provincial court judge considers appropriate if the provincial court judge is satisfied that the bodily substances or results might reasonably be required in an investigation or prosecution of the person for another designated offence or of another person for the designated offence or any other offence in respect of the same transaction.

(3) Bodily substances that are provided voluntarily by a person and the results of forensic DNA analysis shall be destroyed or, in the case of results in electronic form, access to those results shall be permanently removed, without delay after the results of that analysis establish that the bodily substance referred to in paragraph 487.05(1)(*b*) was not from that person. 1995, c. 27, s. 1; 1998, c. 37, s. 22.

CROSS-REFERENCES

The terms "provincial court judge", "designated offence", "DNA" and "forensic DNA analysis" are defined in s. 487.04. The term "indictment" which includes an "information" is defined in s. 2. Section 487.05 sets out the circumstances in which a provincial court judge may issue a warrant to seize bodily substances for forensic DNA analysis. Section 487.06(1) sets out those "bodily substances" that may be seized pursuant to a warrant issued under that section. Section 487.06(2) requires the judge to include appropriate terms and conditions. Section 487.07 sets out the special requirements with respect to execution of a warrant obtained under this section. Section 487.08 limits the use of evidence obtained as a result of the execution of a warrant obtained under this section. Section 487.091 provides that a justice may issue a warrant to obtain hand print, fingerprint, footprint, foot impression, teeth impression or other print or impression of the body or any part of the body. Other provisions respecting search warrants include s. 487 [warrant to search for evidence and contraband] and s. 487.01 ["general warrant"]. For other cross-references respecting search warrants, see notes following s. 487. Section 579, referred to in subsec. (1), gives the Attorney General or counsel instructed by the Attorney General for that purpose the power to direct a stay of proceedings. Those proceedings may be recommenced, without laying a new information or preferring a new indictment, within one year of the entering of the stay.

COLLECTION OF ADDITIONAL BODILY SUBSTANCES / Reasons / Persons not in custody.

487.091 (1) A provincial court judge may, on *ex parte* application made in Form 5.08, authorize in Form 5.09 the taking from a person, for the purpose of forensic DNA analysis, of any number of additional samples of bodily substances that is reasonably required for that purpose, by means of the investigative procedures described in subsection 487.06(1), if

(*a*) a DNA profile cannot be derived from the bodily substances that were taken from that person under an order made under section 487.051 or an authorization granted under section 487.055; or

(*b*) the information or bodily substances required by regulations made under the *DNA Identification Act* were not transmitted in accordance with the requirements of the regulations or were lost.

(2) The application shall state the reasons why a DNA profile cannot be derived from the bodily substances or why the information or bodily substances were not transmitted in accordance with the regulations or were lost.

(3) If the court authorizes the taking of samples of bodily substances from a person who is not in custody, a summons in Form 5.061 setting out the information referred to in paragraphs 487.07(1)(*b*) to (*d*) shall be directed to the person requiring them to report at the place, day and time set out in the summons and submit to the taking of the samples. Subsections 487.055(5) and (6) apply, with any modifications that the circumstances require. 1998, c. 37, s. 23; 2000, c. 10, s. 23; 2005, c. 25, s. 10; 2007, c. 22, s. 20.

CROSS-REFERENCES

"Provincial court judge" is defined in ss. 2 and 487.04. "Forensic DNA analysis" is defined in s. 487.04. "DNA profile" is defined in s. 2 of the *DNA Identification Act* as "the results of forensic DNA analysis of a bodily substance". Also, see cross-references under s. 487.051.

SYNOPSIS

For a synopsis of this and the related sections with respect to taking of samples for forensic DNA analysis from persons found guilty of certain offences, see the synopsis under s. 487.051.

REVIEW BY ATTORNEY GENERAL / Clerical error / Substantive defect / No defect.

487.0911 (1) On receipt of a notice from the Commissioner of the Royal Canadian Mounted Police under subsection 5.2(1) of the *DNA Identification Act* that an order made under section 487.051 or an authorization granted under section 487.091 appears to be defective, the Attorney General shall review the order or authorization and the court record.

(2) If the Attorney General is of the opinion that the defect is due to a clerical error, the Attorney General shall

(*a*) apply, *ex parte*, to the judge who made the order or authorization, or to a judge of the same court, to have it corrected; and

(*b*) transmit a copy of the corrected order or authorization, if any, to the Commissioner.

(3) If the Attorney General is of the opinion that the offence referred to in the order or authorization is not a designated offence, the Attorney General shall inform the Commissioner of that opinion.

(4) If the Attorney General is of the opinion that the offence referred to in the order or authorization is a designated offence, the Attorney General shall transmit that opinion, with written reasons, to the Commissioner. 2005, c. 25, s. 11; 2007, c. 22, s. 21.

INFORMATION FOR IMPRESSION WARRANT / Search or seizure to be reasonable / Provisions to apply / Telewarrant

487.092 (1) A justice may issue a warrant in writing authorizing a peace officer to do any thing, or cause any thing to be done under the direction of the peace officer, described in the warrant in order to obtain any handprint, fingerprint, footprint, foot impression, teeth impression or other print or impression of the body or any part of the body in respect of a person if the justice is satisfied

(*a*) by information on oath in writing that there are reasonable grounds to believe that an offence against this or any other Act of Parliament has been committed and that information concerning the offence will be obtained by the print or impression; and

(*b*) that it is in the best interests of the administration of justice to issue the warrant.

(2) A warrant issued under subsection (1) shall contain such terms and conditions as the justice considers advisable to ensure that any search or seizure authorized by the warrant is reasonable in the circumstances.

(3) Subsections 487(2) and (4) apply, with such modifications as the circumstances require, to a warrant issued under subsection (1).

(4) Where a peace officer believes that it would be impracticable to appear personally before a justice to make an application for a warrant under this section, a warrant may be issued under this section on an information submitted by telephone or other means of telecommunication and, for that purpose, section 487.1 applies, with such modifications as the circumstances require, to the warrant. 1997, c. 18, s. 45; 1998, c. 37, s. 23.

CROSS-REFERENCES

The terms "justice" and "peace officer" are defined in s. 2. Section 487.05 sets out the circumstances in which a provincial court judge may issue a warrant to seize bodily substances for forensic DNA analysis. Other provisions respecting search warrants include s. 487 [warrant to search for evidence and contraband] and s. 487.01 ["general warrant"]. For other cross-references respecting search warrants, see notes following s. 487. A warrant is executed in accordance with s. 29. Where a person is detained, the peace officer must comply with the provisions of s. 10 of the Charter, subject to reasonable limitations as permitted by s. 1 of the Charter. For protection of persons executing warrants, see ss. 25 to 28.

SYNOPSIS

This section provides that a justice may issue a warrant authorizing the taking of impressions of the body or any part of the body, including teeth impressions, handprints, footprints and foot impressions. The justice must be satisfied that there are reasonable grounds to believe that an offence under the *Criminal Code* or another Act of Parliament has been committed, that information concerning the offence will be obtained and that it is in the best interests of the administration of justice to issue the warrant. The justice shall include such terms and conditions as considered advisable. Where it is not practicable for the peace officer to appear in person before the justice, the officer may apply for a telewarrant in accordance with the procedures set out in s. 487.1. Section 487(2) to (4) allows the justice to issue a warrant to be executed in another territorial division. A justice having jurisdiction in that territorial division must, however, endorse the warrant.

ANNOTATIONS

It was held, prior to the enactment of this section, that the taking of dental impressions without prior judicial authorization could not be justified as a search incident to arrest and violated the accused's rights under ss. 7 and 8 of the *Canadian Charter of Rights and Freedoms*: *R. v. Stillman*, [1997] 1 S.C.R. 607, 113 C.C.C. (3d) 321.

Other Provisions Respecting Search Warrants, Preservation Orders and Production Orders

2014, c. 31, s. 21.

TELEWARRANTS / Information submitted by telephone / Information submitted by other means of telecommunication / Administration of oath / Alternative to oath / Contents of information / Issuing warrant / Formalities respecting warrant and facsimiles / Issuance of warrant where telecommunication produces writing / Providing facsimile / Affixing fascimile / Report of peace officer / Bringing before justice / Proof of authorization / Duplicates and facsimiles acceptable.

487.1 (1) If a peace officer believes that an indictable offence has been committed and that it would be impracticable to appear personally before a justice to make an application for a warrant in accordance with section 487, the peace officer may submit an information on oath by telephone or other means of telecommunication to a justice designated for the purpose by the chief judge of the provincial court having jurisdiction in the matter.

(2) An information submitted by telephone or other means of telecommunication, other than a means of telecommunication that produces a writing, shall be on oath and shall be recorded verbatim by the justice, who shall, as soon as practicable, cause to be filed, with the clerk of the court for the territorial division in which the warrant is intended for execution, the record or a transcription of it, certified by the justice as to time, date and contents.

(2.1) The justice who receives an information submitted by a means of telecommunication that produces a writing shall, as soon as practicable, cause to be filed, with the clerk of the court for the territorial division in which the warrant is intended for execution, the information certified by the justice as to time and date of receipt.

(3) For the purposes of subsection (2), an oath may be administered by telephone or other means of telecommunication.

(3.1) A peace officer who uses a means of telecommunication referred to in subsection (2.1) may, instead of swearing an oath, make a statement in writing stating that all matters contained in the information are true to his or her knowledge and belief and such a statement is deemed to be a statement made under oath.

(4) An information submitted by telephone or other means of telecommunication shall include

- **(*a*) a statement of the circumstances that make it impracticable for the peace officer to appear personally before a justice;**
- **(*b*) a statement of the indictable offence alleged, the place or premises to be searched and the items alleged to be liable to seizure;**
- **(*c*) a statement of the peace officer's grounds for believing that items liable to seizure in respect of the offence alleged will be found in the place of premises to be searched; and**
- **(*d*) a statement as to any prior application for a warrant under this section or any other search warrant, in respect of the same matter, of which the peace officer has knowledge.**

(5) A justice referred to in subsection (1) may issue a warrant to a peace officer conferring the same authority respecting search and seizure as may be conferred by a warrant issued under subsection 487(1) if the justice is satisfied that an information submitted by telephone or other means of telecommunication

- **(*a*) is in respect of an indictable offence and conforms to the requirements of subsection (4);**
- **(*b*) discloses reasonable grounds for dispensing with an information presented personally and in writing; and**

(*c*) discloses reasonable grounds in accordance with paragraph 487(1)(*a*), (*b*) or (*c*), as the case may be, for the issuance of a warrant in respect of an indictable offence.

The justice may require that the warrant be executed within the period that he or she may order.

(6) Where a justice issues a warrant by telephone or other means of telecommunication, other than a means of telecommunication that produces a writing,

(*a*) the justice shall complete and sign the warrant in Form 5.1, noting on its face the time, date and place of issuance;

(*b*) the peace officer, on the direction of the justice, shall complete, in duplicate, a facsimile of the warrant in Form 5.1, noting on its face the name of the issuing justice and the time, date and place of issuance; and

(*c*) the justice shall, as soon as practicable after the warrant has been issued, cause the warrant to be filed with the clerk of the court for the territorial division in which the warrant is intended for execution.

(6.1) Where a justice issues a warrant by a means of telecommunication that produces a writing,

(*a*) the justice shall complete and sign the warrant in Form 5.1, noting on its face the time, date and place of issuance;

(*b*) the justice shall transmit the warrant by the means of telecommunication to the peace officer who submitted the information and the copy of the warrant received by the peace officer is deemed to be a facsimile within the meaning of paragraph (6)(*b*);

(*c*) the peace officer shall procure another facsimile of the warrant; and

(*d*) the justice shall, as soon as practicable after the warrant has been issued, cause the warrant to be filed with the clerk of the court for the territorial division in which the warrant is intended for execution.

(7) A peace officer who executes a warrant issued by telephone or other means of telecommunication shall, before or as soon as practicable after entering the place or premises to be searched, give a facsimile of the warrant to any person who is present and ostensibly in control of the place or premises.

(8) A peace officer who, in any unoccupied place or premises, executes a warrant issued by telephone or other means of telecommunication shall, on entering or as soon as practicable after entering the place or premises, cause a facsimile of the warrant to be suitably affixed in a prominent place within the place or premises.

(9) A peace officer to whom a warrant is issued by telephone or other means of telecommunication shall file a written report with the clerk of the court for the territorial division in which the warrant was intended for execution as soon as practicable but within a period not exceeding seven days after the warrant has been executed, which report shall include

(*a*) a statement of the time and date the warrant was executed or, if the warrant was not executed, a statement of the reasons why it was not executed;

(*b*) a statement of the things, if any, that were seized pursuant to the warrant and the location where they are being held; and

(*c*) a statement of the things, if any, that were seized in addition to the things mentioned in the warrant and the location where they are being held, together with a statement of the peace officer's grounds for believing that those additional things had been obtained by, or used in, the commission of an offence.

(10) The clerk of the court shall, as soon as practicable, cause the report, together with the information and the warrant to which it pertains, to be brought before a justice to be dealt with, in respect of the things seized referred to in the report, in the same manner as if the things were seized pursuant to a warrant issued, on an information

presented personally by a peace officer, by that justice or another justice for the same territorial division.

(11) In any proceeding in which it is material for a court to be satisfied that a search or seizure was authorized by a warrant issued by telephone or other means of telecommunication, the absence of the information or warrant, signed by the justice and carrying on its face a notation of the time, date and place of issuance, is, in the absence of evidence to the contrary, proof that the search or seizure was not authorized by a warrant issued by telephone or other means of telecommunication.

(12) A duplicate or a facsimile of an information or a warrant has the same probative force as the original for the purposes of subsection (11). R.S.C. 1985, c. 27 (1st Supp.), s. 69; 1992, c. 1, ss. 58, 59; 1994, c. 44, s. 37; 2018, c. 21, s. 19.

CROSS-REFERENCES

The terms "clerk of the court", "justice", "peace officer" and "territorial division" are defined in s. 2. The term "telecommunication" is defined in s. 35(1) of the *Interpretation Act*, R.S.C. 1985, c. I-21. The usual provision for granting of a warrant is in s. 487 and note that, unlike s. 487, this section is restricted to cases involving allegations of commission of an indictable offence, which would, however, include a hybrid offence by virtue of s. 34(1)(*a*) of the *Interpretation Act*, R.S.C. 1985, c. I-21. Restriction on publicity, see s. 487.2. A search warrant is executed in accordance with s. 488. Execution of a warrant to search a lawyer's office is governed by s. 488.1. Section 489 provides for seizure of things not named in the warrant but which the person executing the warrant believes on reasonable grounds have been obtained by or have been used in the commission of an offence. Section 489.1 sets out the procedure for restitution of goods to the lawful owner and s. 490 sets out the procedure for detention of things which have been seized but not returned under s. 489.1. As to forfeiture of weapons and contraband, see ss. 491 and 491.1. Section 491.2 makes provision for use of photographic evidence in lieu of the actual property so that the property itself may be returned to the lawful owner. For notes on other search or seizure powers, see s. 487. Power to obtain a telewarrant to enter a dwelling-house to effect an arrest is found in s. 529.5, and to obtain a telewarrant to obtain bodily impressions is found in s. 487.092(4).

Note s. 31(1) of the *Interpretation Act*, R.S.C. 1985, c. I-21 which provides that where anything is required or authorized to be done by or before, *inter alia*, a justice of the peace, it shall be done by or before one whose jurisdiction or powers extend to the place where the thing is to be done.

Also see notes under s. 8 of the Charter.

SYNOPSIS

This section sets out the requirements that must be met when a peace officer wishes to obtain a telewarrant.

Subsection (1) requires that the peace officer believe that an indictable offence has been committed and it is impracticable to appear personally before the justice to apply for the warrant. Under such circumstances, the peace officer may submit his sworn information by telephone or other means of telecommunication to a justice. This justice must have been designated for this purpose by the chief judge of the provincial court.

Subsection (2) states that the information referred to in subsec. (1) must be on oath, recorded verbatim by the justice, and filed with the clerk of the court having territorial jurisdiction as soon as practicable. The justice must certify the record of this information as to time, date and contents.

Subsections (2.1), (3.1) and (6.1) allow for receiving the information by use of a "fax" machine.

Subsection (4) sets out the requirements for an information or oath submitted by telephone or other means of telecommunication. Where the justice is satisfied that the requirements described in subsec. (5) have been met, that justice may issue a warrant to the peace officer authorizing the same powers as were found in ss. 256(1) or 487(1). The justice may also require that the warrant be executed within a specific time period.

Subsection (6) sets out specific obligations upon the justice and the peace officer who are involved in the application for telewarrants.

Subsection (7) requires that a peace officer who executes a telewarrant (other than a warrant under subsec. 256(1)) must give a facsimile of the warrant to any person present and apparently in control of the premises before entering. If the premises are unoccupied and the telewarrant does not relate to subsec. 256(1), the peace officer must affix the facsimile in a prominent place upon entering the premises or as soon as practicable thereafter.

Subsection (9) requires a peace officer who has executed a telewarrant to file a written report with the clerk of the court for the territorial jurisdiction in which the warrant was executed within seven days of the execution of the warrant. The report must include the things set out in paras. (*a*) to (*c*) in subsec. (9).

Subsection (10) makes it clear that the clerk of the court must place before a justice the report referred to in subsec. (9) along with the information and the warrant. There is no difference in the treatment of these items and that of similar documents produced upon personal applications for warrants.

Subsection (11) states that in any proceeding challenging a search authorized by telewarrant, the absence of a transcribed and certified information on oath or warrant is, unless there is evidence to the contrary, proof that the search and seizure was not authorized by a warrant.

ANNOTATIONS

The term "facsimile" in subsec. (6)(*b*) means a reasonable copy, being one without significant and misleading errors. Since the two documents are prepared in two different locations by two different persons, there will inevitably be differences, but if they are not significant nor misleading and could not have prejudiced the accused, then the statutory requirement has been fulfilled. Further, the failure of the officer to file the written report as required by subsec. (9) did not invalidate the warrant nor render inadmissible the results of analysis of a blood sample taken pursuant to the warrant: *R. v. Skin* (1988), 13 M.V.R. (2d) 130 (B.C. Co. Ct.).

WHERE WARRANT NOT NECESSARY.

487.11 A peace officer, or a public officer who has been appointed or designated to administer or enforce any federal or provincial law and whose duties include the enforcement of this or any other Act of Parliament, may, in the course of his or her duties, exercise any of the powers described in subsection 487(1) or 492.1(1) without a warrant if the conditions for obtaining a warrant exist but by reason of exigent circumstances it would be impracticable to obtain a warrant. 1997, c. 18, s. 46.

CROSS-REFERENCES

The terms "peace officer" and "public officer" are defined s. 2. Several other sections of the Code give a peace officer a warrantless search or seizure power, usually in exigent circumstances, including s. 101, weapons, and s. 529.3, entry of dwelling-house to effect arrest. Also see s. 11(7) of *Controlled Drugs and Substances Act* which gives a warrantless search and seizure power in exigent circumstances in relation to offences under that Act. The term "exigent circumstances" is not defined, but some assistance may be obtained from the definition of that phrase as contained in s. 529.3(2).

SYNOPSIS

This provision gives a peace officer or public officer appointed or designated to administer or enforce any federal or provincial law and whose duties also include the enforcement of the *Criminal Code* or any other Act of Parliament, a broad warrantless power of search and seizure in exigent circumstances. The officer may exercise the power to search and seizure granted by the two sections referred to without a warrant, provided that the conditions for granting a warrant exist, but by reason of exigent circumstances it would be impracticable to obtain a warrant. Section 487 is the normal search warrant power and allows a justice to issue a warrant to search for and seize in any "building receptacle or place" contraband [subsec. (1)(*a*)], evidence [subsec. (1)(*b*)], anything that is reasonably believed is intended for use for the purpose of committing an offence against the person for which a person may be arrested without warrant [subsec. (1)(*c*)], and offence-related property [subsec. (1)(*d*)]. Section 492.1 allows a justice to issue a warrant to install and monitor a tracking device. Reference must be made to ss. 487 and 492.1 to determine the grounds that the officer must have to obtain the warrant and hence to exercise the same powers without a warrant under this section in exigent circumstances. Section 489(2) gives the officer power to seize without warrant anything that the officer believes on reasonable grounds has been obtained by the commission of an offence, has been used in the commission of an offence or will afford evidence in respect of any offence under the *Criminal Code* or other federal statute, provided that the officer is lawfully present in the place pursuant to a warrant or in the execution of duties.

ANNOTATIONS

It would appear that this section was enacted partly in response to the decision of the Supreme Court of Canada in *R. v. Silveira*, [1995] 2 S.C.R. 297, 97 C.C.C. (3d) 450. The majority judgment in that case cast considerable doubt on the existence of a common law power to search and seize, especially a dwelling-house, in exigent circumstances as where the entry was required to prevent the destruction of evidence. In determining the meaning of "exigent circumstances", some assistance may be obtained by reference to the concurring opinion of L'Heureux-Dubé J. who would have recognized a common law power of warrantless search and seizure in exigent circumstances.

In the course of executing a warrant at the residence, the police conducted a safety check in the outbuildings where a grow operation was located. When a warrant has been issued to search one place or premises, the police, in the course of the execution of the warrant, have the authority at common law to inspect and enter other places or premises on that property to the extent reasonably necessary to protect themselves and others. Such action cannot be taken as a matter of course or on the basis of generalized, non-specific concerns. Before acting, they must have a reasonable basis for believing that there is a possibility that their immediate safety or the safety of others is at risk. While safety concerns can trigger a statutory exigent circumstances exception to a warrant requirement, such concerns will not always satisfy those exceptions. Those concerns must make obtaining a warrant impracticable: *R. v. Chuhaniuk* (2010), 261 C.C.C. (3d) 486 (B.C.C.A.).

RESTRICTION ON PUBLICATION.

487.2 If a search warrant is issued under section 487 or 487.1 or a search is made under such a warrant, every one who publishes in any document, or broadcasts or transmits in any way, any information with respect to

(*a*) the location of the place searched or to be searched, or

(*b*) the identity of any person who is or appears to occupy or be in possession or control of that place or who is suspected of being involved in any offence in relation to which the warrant was issued,

without the consent of every person referred to in paragraph (*b*) is, unless a charge has been laid in respect of any offence in relation to which the warrant was issued, guilty of an offence punishable on summary conviction. R.S.C. 1985, c. 27 (1st Supp.), s. 69; 2005, c. 32, s. 16.

(2) [*Repealed*, 2005, c. 32, s. 16(2).]

SYNOPSIS

This section applies certain restrictions on publication, broadcast or transmission in any way of certain information in relation to search warrants. It is a summary conviction offence to publish the location of the place searched or to be searched, or the identity of any person who appears to occupy, possess or control that place, or who is suspected of being involved in any offence relating to the warrant. Such information may be published if the consent of all of the persons described above has been obtained or if a charge in respect of any offence in relation to which the warrant was issued has been laid.

ANNOTATIONS

It has now been held that this section is of no force and effect in view of the unreasonable restrictions it places on freedom of expression as guaranteed by s. 2(*b*) of the *Charter of Rights and Freedoms*: *Canadian Newspapers Co. v. Canada (Attorney General)* (1986), 28 C.C.C. (3d) 379 (Man. Q.B.); *Canadian Newspapers Co. v. Canada (Attorney General)* (1986), 29 C.C.C. (3d) 109 (Ont. H.C.J.); *Girard (informant) v. Ouellet* (2001), 153 C.C.C. (3d) 217, 43 C.R. (5th) 161 *sub nom. Thibault v. Demers* (Que. C.A.), leave to appeal to S.C.C. refused 157 C.C.C. (3d) vi.

ORDER DENYING ACCESS TO INFORMATION / Reasons / Procedure / Application for variance of order.

487.3 (1) **On application made at the time an application is made for a warrant under this or any other Act of Parliament, an order under any of sections 487.013 to 487.018 or an authorization under section 529 or 529.4, or at a later time, a justice, a judge of a superior court of criminal jurisdiction or a judge of the Court of Quebec may make an order prohibiting access to, and the disclosure of, any information relating to the warrant, order or authorization on the ground that**

(*a*) the ends of justice would be subverted by the disclosure for one of the reasons referred to in subsection (2) or the information might be used for an improper purpose; and

(*b*) the reason referred to in paragraph (*a*) outweighs in importance the access to the information.

(2) For the purposes of paragraph (1)(*a*), an order may be made under subsection (1) on the ground that the ends of justice would be subverted by the disclosure

(*a*) if disclosure of the information would

(i) compromise the identity of a confidential informant,

(ii) compromise the nature and extent of an ongoing investigation

(iii) endanger a person engaged in particular intelligence-gathering techniques and thereby prejudice future investigations in which similar techniques would be used, or

(iv) prejudice the interests of an innocent person; and

(*b*) for any other sufficient reason

(3) Where an order is made under subsection (1), all documents relating to the application shall, subject to any terms and conditions that the justice or judge considers desirable in the circumstances, including, without limiting the generality of the foregoing, any term or condition concerning the duration of the prohibition, partial disclosure of a document, deletion of any information or the occurrence of a condition, be placed in a packet and sealed by the justice or judge immediately on determination of the application, and that packet shall be kept in the custody of the court in a place to which the public has no access or in any other place that the justice or judge may authorize and shall not be dealt with except in accordance with the terms and conditions specified in the order or as varied under subsection (4).

(4) An application to terminate the order or vary any of its terms and conditions may be made to the justice or judge who made the order or a judge of the court before which

any proceedings arising out of the investigation in relation to which the warrant or production order was obtained may be held. 1997, c. 23, s. 14; 1997, c. 39, s. 1; 2004, c. 3, s. 8; 2014, c. 31, s. 22.

CROSS-REFERENCES

The term "justice" is defined in s. 2. For other cross-references with respect to search warrants, see s. 487.

SYNOPSIS

This section gives a judge or justice the power to make an order denying access to and the disclosure of any information relating to a warrant, a preservation or production order, or an authorization to enter a dwelling house under ss. 529 or 529.4. The application for such an order is to be made at the time of the issuing of the warrant or authorization. The order may be made only where the ends of justice would be subverted by disclosure or the information might be used for an improper purpose and the justice or judge is satisfied that these grounds outweigh the importance of access to the information. While the phrase "ends of justice would be subverted" is defined in subsec. (2), and refers to matter such as disclosure compromising the identity of a confidential informer, the phrase also includes "for any other sufficient reason". Where the order is made, all documents relating to the application are to be sealed, subject to any terms and conditions that the justice or judge considers desirable in the circumstances pursuant to subsec. (3). The wording of this subsection contemplates that the justice or judge may order the sealing of parts of the information or may allow access to some of the information on certain terms. For example, it would seem to be open to the judge to allow access to the material but prohibit publication for some period of time. Under subsec. (4), an application may be made to the justice or judge who made the order or to a judge of the court before which any proceedings arising out of the investigation may be held to terminate the order or vary any of its terms and conditions.

ANNOTATIONS

Note: Some of the following cases were decided prior to the enactment of this section but may be useful in interpreting its provisions.

Where a search warrant is executed and nothing is found then the public has no right to see either the warrant or the information. Where, however, the search warrant has been executed, and objects found as a result of the search are brought before a justice pursuant to s. 490, then any member of the public is entitled to inspect the warrant and the information upon which it has been issued pursuant to this section, unless it is established that the ends of justice would be subverted by disclosure or that the judicial documents might be used for an improper purpose. Finally, the public has no right to attend the hearing at which application is made for the issuance of a search warrant. That hearing may be held *in camera: Nova Scotia (Attorney General)*, [1982] 1 S.C.R. 175, 65 C.C.C. (2d) 129, 26 C.R. (3d) 193 (5:4).

This discretion must be judicially exercised with regard for the right of the accused to a fair trial and the guarantee of freedom of the press. The phrase "for any other sufficient reason" includes a serious threat to the fairness of the accused's trial. In this case, the publication of allegations including information from an accomplice prior to trial would have undermined the accused's right to a fair trial. Where an order of a provincial court judge imposing or refusing a publication ban would imperil the right to a fair trial, the accused who has elected to be tried by a judge and jury is entitled to challenge the order by way of *certiorari*: *R. v. Flahiff* (1998), 123 C.C.C. (3d) 79, 17 C.R. (5th) 94 (Que. C.A.).

In *Toronto Star Newspapers Ltd. v. Ontario*, [2005] 2 S.C.R. 188, 197 C.C.C. (3d) 1, 29 C.R. (6th) 251, the Supreme Court of Canada held that a sealing order should be made only when necessary to prevent serious risk to the proper administration of justice because reasonably alternative measures would not prevent the risk and the salutary effects of a publication ban outweighed the deleterious effects. This test is applied to all discretionary court orders that limit freedom of expression and freedom of the press in relation to legal proceedings. The test should not be applied mechanistically but with regard to the circumstances in which a sealing order was sought. It is not enough to rely on the general proposition that pre-trial publication of the details of a police investigation risks the tainting of statements taken from potential witnesses. See also *Ottawa Citizen Group Inc. v. Canada (Attorney General)* (2005), 197 C.C.C. (3d) 514, 31 C.R. (6th) 144, 255 D.L.R. (4th) 149 (Ont. C.A.), supp. reasons 197 C.C.C. (3d) 514 at p. 532, 255 D.L.R. (4th) 149 at p. 167, 75 O.R. (3d) 607 (C.A.).

This provision applies to the *Extradition Act: United States of America v. M. (D.J.)* (2001), 156 C.C.C. (3d) 276 (Ont. S.C.J.), leave to appeal to S.C.C. refused 158 C.C.C. (3d) vi.

Although nothing is seized during the search the accused who was the object of the investigation, as an interested party, is entitled to inspect the information, the warrant and the related documentation: *R. v. Jany* (1983), 9 C.C.C. (3d) 349 (B.C.S.C.).

The media were not entitled to access to portions of the information to obtain a search warrant which included references to intercepted communications: *National Post Co. v. Ontario* (2003), 176 C.C.C. (3d) 432 (Ont. S.C.J.), leave to appeal to S.C.C. refused 197 O.A.C. 200*n*.

An application to the Superior Court to gain access to documents relating to execution of a search warrant is premature while an application is pending in the provincial court to have the documents sealed: *Henderson v. Jolicouer* (1983), 9 C.C.C. (3d) 79 (Ont. H.C.J.).

When charges are not laid, the judge making the sealing order is not the only judge capable of varying the order: *Phillips v. Vancouver Sun* (2004), 182 C.C.C. (3d) 483, 19 C.R. (6th) 55, 238 D.L.R. (4th) 167 (B.C.C.A.).

EXECUTION OF SEARCH WARRANT.

488. A warrant issued under section 487 or 487.1 shall be executed by day, unless

(*a*) the justice is satisfied that there are reasonable grounds for it to be executed by night;

(*b*) the reasonable grounds are included in the information; and

(*c*) the warrant authorizes that it be executed by night. R.S., c. C-34, s. 444; R.S.C. 1985, c. 27, (1st. Supp.), s. 70; 1997, c. 18, s. 47.

CROSS-REFERENCES

The terms "justice", "day" and "night" are defined in s. 2. With respect to protection of persons executing warrants, see ss. 25 to 27. Also note s. 29(1) which imposes a duty on a person executing a warrant to have it with him, where it is feasible to do so, and produce it when requested.

SYNOPSIS

This section states that a warrant issued pursuant to ss. 487 or 487.1 must be executed by day unless the justice, by the warrant, authorizes its execution by night. The grounds for execution at night must be set out in the authorization.

ANNOTATIONS

The execution of a search warrant at night is justified only in exceptional circumstances. A search warrant executed at night without justification constitutes a serious Charter violation: *R. v. Sutherland* (2000), 150 C.C.C. (3d) 231, 39 C.R. (5th) 310 (C.A.).

The fact that the affiant knew no one would be home when the warrant was executed was highly relevant and the reviewing judge was correct to hold that this reduced the degree to which privacy interests would be affected by a night search: *R. v. R. (L.V.)* (2014), 316 C.C.C. (3d) 120 (B.C.C.A.), leave to appeal to S.C.C. refused 2015 CarswellBC 554.

Once the warrant has expired with the completion of the search the officers' right to be on the premises is terminated and they become trespassers if they remain on, or return to the premises: *R. v. Moran* (1987), 36 C.C.C. (3d) 225 (Ont. C.A.).

In appropriate circumstances a search warrant may be issued for an extended period of time and its execution delayed for the purpose of apprehending a suspect who is at the premises only at certain times: *R. v. Coull and Dawe* (1986), 33 C.C.C. (3d) 186 (B.C.C.A.).

Where there is a risk of loss or destruction of evidence so that rapid action is required or where there is a real threat of violent behaviour whether directed at the police or third parties then the police may be justified in using special procedures in executing the warrant. However, the consideration of the possibility of violence must be carefully limited and should not amount to a *carte blanche* for the police to ignore completely all restrictions on police behaviour. The greater the departure from the standards of behaviour required by the commnon law and the *Charter of Rights and Freedoms*, then the heavier the onus on the police to show why they thought it necessary to use force in the execution of the warrant: *R. v. Genest*, [1989] 1 S.C.R. 59, 45 C.C.C. (3d) 385, 67 C.R. (3d) 224 (7:0).

This provision does not apply to a telewarrant issued under s. 11(2) of the *Controlled Drugs and Substances Act*: *R. v. Dueck* (2005), 200 C.C.C. (3d) 378 (B.C.C.A.).

DEFINITIONS / "data" / "document" / "journalist" / "journalistic source" / "officer" / Warrant, Authorization and Order / Warrant, Authorization and Order / Special Advocate / Offence by Journalist — Exception / Offence by Journalist — Order / Conditions / Powers / Discovery of Relation to Journalist / Powers of Judge.

488.01 (1) The following definitions apply in this section and in section 488.02.

"data" has the same meaning as in section 487.011.

"document" has the same meaning as in section 487.011.

"journalist" has the same meaning as in subsection 39.1(1) of the *Canada Evidence Act*.

"journalistic source" has the same meaning as in subsection 39.1(1) of the *Canada Evidence Act*.

"officer" means a peace officer or public officer.

(2) Despite any other provision of this Act, if an applicant for a warrant under section 487.01, 487.1, 492.1 or 492.2, a search warrant under this Act, notably under section 487, an authorization under section 184.2, 184.3, 186 or 188, or an order under any of sections 487.014 to 487.017 knows that the application relates to a journalist's communications or an object, document or data relating to or in the possession of a journalist, they shall make an application to a judge of a superior court of criminal jurisdiction or to a judge as defined in section 552. That judge has exclusive jurisdiction to dispose of the application.

(3) A judge may issue a warrant, authorization or order under subsection (2) only if, in addition to the conditions required for the issue of the warrant, authorization or order, he or she is satisfied that

(*a*) there is no other way by which the information can reasonably be obtained; and

(*b*) the public interest in the investigation and prosecution of a criminal offence outweighs the journalist's right to privacy in gathering and disseminating information.

(4) The judge to whom the application for the warrant, authorization or order is made may, in his or her discretion, request that a special advocate present observations in the interests of freedom of the press concerning the conditions set out in subsection (3).

(5) Subsections (3) and (4) do not apply in respect of an application for a warrant, authorization or order that is made in relation to the commission of an offence by a journalist.

(6) If a warrant, authorization or order referred to in subsection (2) is sought in relation to the commission of an offence by a journalist and the judge considers it necessary to protect the confidentiality of journalistic sources, the judge may order that some or all documents obtained pursuant to the warrant, authorization or order are to be dealt with in accordance with section 488.02.

(7) The warrant, authorization or order referred to in subsection (2) may contain any conditions that the judge considers appropriate to protect the confidentiality of journalistic sources and to limit the disruption of journalistic activities.

(8) The judge who rules on the application for the warrant, authorization or order referred to in subsection (2) has the same powers, with the necessary adaptations, as the authority who may issue the warrant, authorization or order.

(9) If an officer, acting under a warrant, authorization or order referred to in subsection (2) for which an application was not made in accordance with that subsection, becomes aware that the warrant, authorization or order relates to a journalist's communications or an object, document or data relating to or in the possession of a journalist, the officer shall, as soon as possible, make an *ex parte* application to a judge of a superior court of criminal jurisdiction or a judge as defined in section 552 and, until the judge disposes of the application,

- **(*a*) refrain from examining or reproducing, in whole or in part, any document obtained pursuant to the warrant, authorization or order; and**
- **(*b*) place any document obtained pursuant to the warrant, authorization or order in a sealed packet and keep it in a place to which the public has no access.**

(10) On an application under subsection (9), the judge may

- **(*a*) confirm the warrant, authorization or order if the judge is of the opinion that no additional conditions to protect the confidentiality of journalistic sources and to limit the disruption of journalistic activities should be imposed;**
- **(*b*) vary the warrant, authorization or order to impose any conditions that the judge considers appropriate to protect the confidentiality of journalistic sources and to limit the disruption of journalistic activities;**
- **(*c*) if the judge considers it necessary to protect the confidentiality of journalistic sources, order that some or all documents that were or will be obtained pursuant to the warrant, authorization or order are to be dealt with in accordance with section 488.02; or**
- **(*d*) revoke the warrant, authorization or order if the judge is of the opinion that the applicant knew or ought reasonably to have known that the application for the warrant, authorization or order related to a journalist's communications or an object, document or data relating to or in the possession of a journalist. 2017, c. 22, s. 3.**

DOCUMENTS / Notice / Application / Disclosure: Prohibition / Disclosure Order / Examination / Order.

488.02 (1) Any document obtained pursuant to a warrant, authorization or order issued in accordance with subsection 488.01(3), or that is the subject of an order made under subsection 488.01(6) or paragraph 488.01(10)(*c*), is to be placed in a packet and sealed by the court that issued the warrant, authorization or order and is to be kept in the custody of the court in a place to which the public has no access or in such other place as the judge may authorize and is not to be dealt with except in accordance with this section.

(2) No officer is to examine or reproduce, in whole or in part, a document referred to in subsection (1) without giving the journalist and relevant media outlet notice of his or her intention to examine or reproduce the document.

(3) The journalist or relevant media outlet may, within 10 days of receiving the notice referred to in subsection (2), apply to a judge of the court that issued the warrant, authorization or order to issue an order that the document is not to be disclosed to an officer on the grounds that the document identifies or is likely to identity a journalistic source.

(4) A document that is subject to an application under subsection (3) is to be disclosed to an officer only following a disclosure order in accordance with paragraph (7)(*b*).

(5) The judge may order the disclosure of a document only if he or she is satisfied that

- **(*a*) there is no other way by which the information can reasonably be obtained; and**
- **(*b*) the public interest in the investigation and prosecution of a criminal offence outweighs the journalist's right to privacy in gathering and disseminating information.**

(6) The judge may, if he or she considers it necessary, examine a document to determine whether it should be disclosed.

(7) The judge must,

- **(*a*) if he or she is of the opinion that the document should not be disclosed, order that it be returned to the journalist or the media outlet, as the case may be; or**
- **(*b*) if he or she is of the opinion that the document should be disclosed, order that it be delivered to the officer who gave the notice under subsection (2), subject to such restrictions and conditions as the judge deems appropriate. 2017, c. 22, s. 3.**

DEFINITIONS / "custodian" / "document" / "judge" / "lawyer" / "officer" / Examination or seizure of certain documents where privilege claimed / Application to judge / Disposition of application / Privilege continues / Order to custodian to deliver / Application to another judge / Prohibition / Authority to make copies / Hearing in private / Exception.

488.1 (1) In this section,

"custodian" means a person in whose custody a package is placed pursuant to subsection (2);

"document", for the purposes of this section, has the same meaning as in section 321;

"judge" means a judge of a superior court of criminal jurisdiction of the province where the seizure was made;

"lawyer" means, in the Province of Quebec, an advocate, lawyer or notary and, in any other province, a barrister or solicitor;

"officer" means a peace officer or public officer.

(2) Where an officer acting under the authority of this or any other Act of Parliament is about to examine, copy or seize a document in the possession of a lawyer who claims that a named client of his has a solicitor-client privilege in respect of that document, the officer shall, without examining or making copies of the document,

- **(*a*) seize the document and place it in a package and suitably seal and identify the package; and**
- **(*b*) place the package in the custody of the sheriff of the district or county in which the seizure was made or, if there is agreement in writing that a specified person act as custodian, in the custody of that person.**

(3) Where a document has been seized and placed in custody under subsection (2), the Attorney General or the client or the lawyer on behalf of the client, may

- **(*a*) within fourteen days from the day the document was so placed in custody, apply, on two days notice of motion to all other persons entitled to make application, to a judge for an order**

(i) appointing a place and a day, not later than twenty-one days after the date of the order, for the determination of the question whether the document should be disclosed, and

(ii) requiring the custodian to produce the document to the judge at that time and place;

(*b*) serve a copy of the order on all other persons entitled to make application and on the custodian within six days of the date on which it was made; and

(*c*) if he has proceeded as authorized by paragraph (*b*), apply, at the appointed time and place, for an order determining the question.

(4) On an application under paragraph (3)(*c*), the judge

(*a*) may, if the judge considers it necessary to determine the question whether the document should be disclosed, inspect the document;

(*b*) where the judge is of the opinion that it would materially assist him in deciding whether or not the document is privileged, may allow the Attorney General to inspect the document;

(*c*) shall allow the Attorney General and the person who objects to the disclosure of the document to make representations; and

(*d*) shall determine the question summarily and,

(i) if the judge is of the opinion that the document should not be disclosed, ensure that it is repackaged and resealed and order the custodian to deliver the document to the lawyer who claimed the solicitor-client privilege or to the client, or

(ii) if the judge is of the opinion that the document should be disclosed, order the custodian to deliver the document to the officer who seized the document or some other person designated by the Attorney General, subject to such restrictions or conditions as the judge deems appropriate,

and shall, at the same time, deliver concise reasons for the determination in which the nature of the document is described without divulging the details thereof.

(5) Where the judge determines pursuant to paragraph (4)(*d*) that a solicitor-client privilege exists in respect of a document, whether or not the judge has, pursuant to paragraph (4)(*b*), allowed the Attorney General to inspect the document, the document remains privileged and inadmissible as evidence unless the client consents to its admission in evidence or the privilege is otherwise lost.

(6) Where a document has been seized and placed in custody under subsection (2) and a judge, on the application of the Attorney General, is satisfied that no application has been made under paragraph (3)(*a*) or that following such an application no further application has been made under paragraph (3)(*c*), the judge shall order the custodian to deliver the document to the officer who seized the document or to some other person designated by the Attorney General.

(7) Where the judge to whom an application has been made under paragraph (3)(*c*) cannot act or continue to act under this section for any reason, subsequent applications under that paragraph may be made to another judge.

(8) No officer shall examine, make copies of or seize any document without affording a reasonable opportunity for a claim of solicitor-client privilege to be made under subsection (2).

(9) At any time while a document is in the custody of a custodian under this section, a judge may, on an *ex parte* application of a person claiming a solicitor-client privilege under this section, authorize that person to examine the document or make a copy of it in the presence of the custodian or the judge, but any such authorization shall contain provisions to ensure that the document is repackaged and that the package is resealed without alteration or damage.

(10) An application under paragraph (3)(*c*) shall be heard in private.

(11) This section does not apply in circumstances where a claim of solicitor-client privilege may be made under the *Income Tax Act* or under the *Proceeds of Crime (Money Laundering) and Terrorist Financing Act*. R.S.C. 1985, c. 27 (1st Supp.), s. 71; 2000, c. 17, s. 89; 2001, c. 41, s. 80.

CROSS-REFERENCES

The terms "peace officer", "public officer", "superior court of criminal jurisdiction" and "Attorney General" are defined in s. 2. With respect to protection of persons executing warrants, see ss. 25 to 27. Also note s. 29(1) which imposes a duty on a person executing a warrant to have it with him, where it is feasible to do so, and produce it when requested.

For notes on other search powers see s. 487.

SYNOPSIS

This section sets out a procedure for determining a claim of solicitor-client privilege in relation to documents in the possession of a lawyer.

Subsection (2) states that where a peace officer or public officer is about to examine, copy or seize a document in the possession of a lawyer who makes a claim of solicitor-client privilege, that officer must place the document in a sealed and identified package and place the package in the custody of the sheriff of the relevant district or county or another person who, by written agreement, is empowered to act as custodian.

When documents have been dealt with in accordance with subsec. (1), the Attorney General, the client or the lawyer on behalf of the client may apply within 14 days and upon two days' notice to all other parties, to a judge for an order that would deal with the documents. The judge may make an order that a date and place for the determination of the issue of privilege be set within not more than 21 days. The judge may also order that the custodian produce the documents to the judge on the date and at the location fixed for determining the issue. Paragraph (*b*) provides for service of the order on all parties while para. (*c*) authorizes the application for an order determining the issue.

Subsection (4) describes the procedure on an application for an order determining the issue.

Subsection (5) provides that when the judge decides that a document is privileged, it will remain inadmissible as evidence unless the client consents to its admission, or the privilege is otherwise lost. This is so even if the document has been inspected by the Attorney General.

Subsection (6) states that upon determination that no claim of privilege is being pursued the custodian must deliver it to the Attorney General, a designate or the seizing officer.

Subsection (7) authorizes another judge to hear applications under subsec. (3)(*c*) where the original judge cannot act or continue to act.

Subsection (8) makes it clear that the authorized officer must give a reasonable opportunity for a claim of solicitor-client privilege to be made before seizing or copying documents. A person claiming privilege may make an *ex parte* application to a judge to examine or make copies of documents that are in the custody of a custodian. Any such order must contain provisions to ensure that no damage or alteration to the documents occurs during an examination of this sort. Furthermore, the documents may only be examined under this subsection in the presence of the custodian or judge.

Subsection (10) provides that an application under subsec. (3)(*c*) shall be heard in private.

Subsection (11) specifically exempts any claim of solicitor-client privilege in relation to proceedings under the *Income Tax Act* or the *Proceeds of Crime (Money Laundering) Act* from this section.

ANNOTATIONS

Constitutional Considerations: This provision violates s. 8 of the Charter and accordingly, is of no force and effect: *Lavallee, Rackel & Heintz v. Canada (Attorney General); White,*

Ottenheimer & Baker v. Canada (Attorney General); R. v. Fink, [2002], 3 S.C.R. 209, 167 C.C.C. (3d) 1, 3 C.R. (6th) 209.

Search of Law Offices: In *Lavallee, Rackel & Heintz v. Canada (Attorney General), supra*, the Supreme Court of Canada struck down this section and set out the following procedure for the search of law offices in the absence of new legislation. No search warrant can issue for documents that are known to be protected by solicitor-client privilege. A search warrant for a law office can only issue if there is no reasonable alternative to the search. Documents must be sealed unless the warrant specifically authorizes the immediate examination, copying and seizure of an identified document. Counsel and the client should be contacted at the time that the warrant is executed. Failing that, a representative of the Bar should supervise the sealing and seizure of documents. The police officer must advise the justice of the efforts made to contact privilege holders and they must be given a reasonable opportunity to assert privilege. If notification of privilege holders is not possible, then a lawyer appointed by the Law Society or court should examine the documents and determine whether a claim of privilege should be made. At such a hearing, the Attorney General is not entitled to inspect the documents beforehand.

The principle of minimization must be reflected in the wording of the authorization and affidavits in support of the authorization: *Maranda v. Richer*, [2003] 3 S.C.R. 193, 178 C.C.C. (3d) 321, 15 C.R. (6th) 1 *sub nom. Maranda v. Quebec (Juge de la Cour du Quebec)*.

"Law office" should be broadly interpreted to include "any place where privileged documents may reasonably be expected to be located" including a lawyer's home, a lawyer's office in multi-disciplinary business premises, the offices of in-house counsel for a business, and storage facilities where lawyers store their files. The word "document" should also be interpreted expansively as set out in s. 321 of the *Criminal Code*: *Festing v. Canada (Attorney General)* (2003), 172 C.C.C. (3d) 321, 223 D.L.R. (4th) 448, [2003] 5 W.W.R. 53 (B.C.C.A.).

Similarly, privilege was found to be engaged where the order was directed, not at a law office, but at the use of cellular and landline phone equipment belonging to the lawyer that was suspected of being used by the client. The process from *Lavallee, supra*, should have been followed: *R. v. B. (A.)* (2014), 307 C.C.C. (3d) 514 (N.L.C.A.).

Solicitor-client Privilege: Prior to the enactment of this section, the Supreme Court of Canada in *Descoteaux v. Mierzwinski*, [1982] 1 S.C.R. 860, 70 C.C.C. (2d) 385, 28 C.R. (3d) 289 (7:0), considered at length the relationship between solicitor-client privilege and the execution of a search warrant at a solicitor's office. The holding by the court may be summarized as follows: Although solicitor-client privilege was originally a rule of evidence, it is not necessary to wait for the trial or preliminary inquiry at which the communication is to be adduced in evidence before raising its confidentiality. The confidentiality of communications between solicitor and client may be raised in any circumstance where such communications are likely to be disclosed without the client's consent. A justice of the peace must be more demanding before authorizing the search of a lawyer's office or one of his files and, where necessary, should set out special procedures for the execution of the warrant in order to limit to what is absolutely inevitable the breach of confidentiality. Further, where the documents sought would in fact be inadmissible in evidence by reason of the solicitor-client privilege then the justice of the peace would have no jurisdiction to authorize the search pursuant to s. 443(1)(*b*) [now s. 487(1)(*b*)] of this section. In any case where the justice of the peace has the necessary jurisdiction to authorize the search because, for example, the documents, while originally subject to solicitor-client privilege, have lost that privilege as they would fall within an exception to the rule, nevertheless, the search should be limited to what is absolutely necessary in order to seize the things for which the search was authorized. Moreover, a justice of the peace has a discretion to refuse a warrant even where the conditions set out in this section have been met. Thus, where the search would interfere with rights as fundamental as freedom of the press or a solicitor's client's right to confidentiality, a justice of the peace may and should refuse to issue the warrant unless there is material to show (*a*) whether a reasonable alternative source of obtaining the information is or is not available, and (*b*) if available, that reasonable steps have been taken to obtain it from that alternative source. Where what is sought is evidence, then even where the justice of the peace is satisfied that there is such evidence on the premises of the lawyer, he should only allow a lawyer's office to be searched if, in addition, he is satisfied that there is no reasonable alternative to a search.

Billing information, including fees and disbursements, fall within the purview of solicitor-client privilege: *Maranda v. Richer, supra.*

Legal correspondence, including reporting letters, have a rebuttable presumption that it is subject to solicitor-client privilege. It was therefore improper for a search warrant to authorize the seizure of legal correspondence: *R. v. Douglas* (2017), 351 C.C.C. (3d) 58 (Man. C.A.), leave to appeal to S.C.C. refused 2017 CarswellMan 584.

No appeal lies from the determination under this section by the superior court judge as to whether the documents should be disclosed despite the claim of solicitor client privilege: *R. v. King* (1992), 74 C.C.C. (3d) 191 (P.E.I.C.A.). See also *R. v. Wilder* (1996), 110 C.C.C. (3d) 186, 130 W.A.C. 17 (B.C.C.A.).

SEIZURE OF THINGS NOT SPECIFIED / Seizure without warrant

489. (1) Every person who executes a warrant may seize, in addition to the things mentioned in the warrant, any thing that the person believes on reasonable grounds

(*a*) has been obtained by the commission of an offence against this or any other Act of Parliament;

(*b*) has been used in the commission of an offence against this or any other Act of Parliament; or

(*c*) will afford evidence in respect of an offence against this or any other Act of Parliament.

(2) Every peace officer, and every public officer who has been appointed or designated to administer or enforce any federal or provincial law and whose duties include the enforcement of this or any other Act of Parliament, who is lawfully present in a place pursuant to a warrant or otherwise in the execution of duties may, without a warrant, seize any thing that the officer believes on reasonable grounds

(*a*) has been obtained by the commission of an offence against this or any other Act of Parliament;

(*b*) has been used in the commission of an offence against this or any other Act of Parliament; or

(*c*) will afford evidence in respect of an offence against this or any other Act of Parliament. R.S. c. C-34, s. 445; R.S.C 1985, c. 27 (1st. Supp.), s. 72; c. 42 (4th Supp.), s. 3; 1993, 40, s. 16; 1997, c. 18, s. 48.

CROSS-REFERENCES

For other notes on search powers, see s. 487. With respect to protection of persons executing warrants, see ss. 25 to 27. Also note s. 29(1) which imposes a duty on a person executing a warrant to have it with him, where it is feasible to do so, and produce it when requested.

SYNOPSIS

Subsection (1) authorizes the seizure of items not specified in a warrant. Where a person executing such a warrant *believes on reasonable grounds* that a thing, not mentioned in the warrant, has been obtained by, or has been used in the commission of an offence or will afford evidence, the officer may seize that thing.

Subsection (2) allows seizure of such items where the officer is lawfully present pursuant to a warrant or otherwise in the execution of duties.

ANNOTATIONS

This is a self-contained provision, separate from the plain view doctrine. Thus, it does not require the police to meet all of the requirements of that common law doctrine: *R. v. B. (E.)* (2011), 269 C.C.C. (3d) 227 (Ont. C.A.), leave to appeal to S.C.C. refused (2012), 295 O.A.C. 398*n*; *R. v. Frieburg* (2013), 299 C.C.C. (3d) 254 (Man. C.A.), leave to appeal to S.C.C. refused 2013 CarswellMan 603; *R. v. T. (R.M.J.)* (2014), 311 C.C.C. (3d) 185 (Man. C.A.).

RESTITUTION OF PROPERTY OR REPORT BY PEACE OFFICER / Idem / Form.

489.1 (1) Subject to this or any other Act of Parliament, where a peace officer has seized anything under a warrant issued under this Act or under section 487.11 or 489 or otherwise in the execution of duties under this or any other Act of Parliament, the peace officer shall, as soon as is practicable,

(*a*) where the peace officer is satisfied,

(i) that there is no dispute as to who is lawfully entitled to possession of the thing seized, and

(ii) that the continued detention of the thing seized is not required for the purposes of any investigation or a preliminary inquiry, trial or other proceeding,

return the thing seized, on being issued a receipt therefor, to the person lawfully entitled to its possession and report to the justice who issued the warrant or some other justice for the same territorial division or, if no warrant was issued, a justice having jurisdiction in respect of the matter, that he has done so; or

(*b*) where the peace officer is not satisfied as described in subparagraphs (*a*)(i) and (ii),

(i) bring the thing seized before the justice referred to in paragraph (*a*), or

(ii) report to the justice that he has seized the thing and is detaining it or causing it to be detained

to be dealt with by the justice in accordance with subsection 490(1).

(2) Subject to this or any other Act of Parliament, where a person, other than a peace officer, has seized anything under a warrant issued under this Act or under section 487.11 or 489 or otherwise in the execution of duties under this or any other Act of Parliament, that person shall, as soon as is practicable,

(*a*) bring the thing seized before the justice who issued the warrant or some other justice for the same territorial division or, if no warrant was issued, before a justice having jurisdiction in respect of the matter, or

(*a*) report to the justice referred to in paragraph (*a*) that he has seized the thing and is detaining it or causing it to be detained,

to be dealt with by the justice in accordance with subsection 490(1).

(3) A report to a justice under this section shall be in the form set out as Form 5.2 in Part XXVIII, varied to suit the case and shall include, in the case of a report in respect of a warrant issued by telephone or other means of telecommunication, the statements referred to in subsection 487.1(9). R.S.C. 1985, c. 27 (1st Supp.), s. 72; 1993, c. 40, s. 17; 1997, c. 18, s. 49.

CROSS-REFERENCES

The terms "justice", "peace officer" and "territorial division" are defined in s. 2.

In the case of property which is not returned to the person lawfully entitled to its possession, then the provisions of s. 490 must be complied with respecting continued detention. Under s. 491.2, before any property that would otherwise be required to be used in evidence under proceedings for offences under ss. 334, 344, 348, 354, 362 or 380 is returned or otherwise dealt with under this section, a peace officer or other person under the direction of a peace officer may take and retain a photograph for use in evidence. With respect to restitution or forfeiture of contraband, see ss. 491, 491.1 and 492.

Note that the reference in this section to "section 258" is obviously in error. The reference should be to s. 256.

This section also applies to material produced to a peace officer or public officer in accordance with a production order under s. 487.012.

SYNOPSIS

This section deals with the disposition of property that has been seized by a peace officer either under a warrant issued pursuant to ss. 258, 487, 487.01 or 487.1, or without warrant under ss. 487.11 or 489, or otherwise as a result of the execution of the peace officer's duties under any Act of Parliament.

Subsection (1)(*a*) provides that where the peace officer is satisfied that lawful possession is not in issue and the continued detention of the thing seized is not required for the purposes of any investigation or court proceedings, the peace officer shall, as soon as practicable, return the item seized to the person lawfully entitled to it. The peace officer must obtain a receipt for the returned item and make a report to a justice having jurisdiction.

Subsection (1)(*b*) states that where the peace officer is not satisfied as required in para. (*a*), he must bring the item seized to a justice having jurisdiction *or* report to the justice that the thing has been seized and is detained. The justice must then deal with the item in accordance with s. 490(1).

Subsection (2) provides a scheme for the disposition of items seized by a person other than a peace officer either under a warrant or without warrant under ss. 487.11 or 489 or otherwise in the execution of that person's duties under any Act of Parliament. That person is required, as soon as practicable, to bring the items seized before a justice having jurisdiction or make a report to such a justice indicating that the item has been seized and is detained.

Any report made under this section must be in accordance with Form 5.2 in Part XXVIII, varied to suit the case. When a report is made in respect of a telewarrant, it must include the statements referred to in s. 487.1(9).

ANNOTATIONS

This section applies to a warrantless search and seizure as an incident to a lawful arrest for an offence under the *Criminal Code*: *R. v. Backhouse* (2005), 194 C.C.C. (3d) 1 (Ont. C.A.).

An officer's failure to comply with subsec. (1) violated s. 8 of the Charter, because an individual retains a residual, post-taking reasonable expectation of privacy in items lawfully seized: *R. v. Garcia-Machado* (2015), 327 C.C.C. (3d) 215 (Ont. C.A.); *R. v. Craig* (2016), 335 C.C.C. (3d) 28 (B.C.C.A.); *R. v. Villaroman* (2018), 363 C.C.C. (3d) 141 (Alta. C.A.).

DETENTION OF THINGS SEIZED / Further detention / Idem / Detention without application where consent / When accused ordered to stand trial / Where continued detention no longer required / Idem / Application for order of return / Exception / Disposal of things seized / Exception / Application by lawful owner / Order / Detention pending appeal, etc. / Copies of documents returned / Probative force / Access to things seized / Conditions / Appeal / Waiver of notice.

490. (1) Subject to this or any other Act of Parliament, where, pursuant to paragraph 489.1(1)(*b*) or subsection 489.1(2), anything that has been seized is brought before a justice or a report in respect of anything seized is made to a justice, the justice shall,

(*a*) where the lawful owner or person who is lawfully entitled to possession of the thing seized is known, order it to be returned to that owner or person, unless the prosecutor, or the peace officer or other person having custody of the thing seized, satisfies the justice that the detention of the thing seized is required for the purposes of any investigation or a preliminary inquiry, trial or other proceeding; or

(*b*) where the prosecutor, or the peace officer or other person having custody of the thing seized, satisfies the justice that the thing seized should be detained for a reason set out in paragraph (*a*), detain the thing seized or order that it be detained, taking reasonable care to ensure that it is preserved until the conclusion of any investigation or until it is required to be produced for the purposes of a preliminary inquiry, trial or other proceeding.

(2) Nothing shall be detained under the authority of paragraph (1)(*b*) for a period of more than three months after the day of the seizure, or any longer period that ends when an application made under paragraph (*a*) is decided, unless

(*a*) a justice, on the making of a summary application to him after three clear days' notice thereof to the person from whom the thing detained was seized, is satisfied that, having regard to the nature of the investigation, its further detention for a specified period is warranted and the justice so orders; or

(*b*) proceedings are instituted in which the thing detained may be required.

(3) More than one order for further detention may be made under paragraph (2)(*a*) but the cumulative period of detention shall not exceed one year from the day of the seizure, or any longer period that ends when an application made under paragraph (*a*) is decided, unless

(*a*) a judge of a superior court of criminal jurisdiction or a judge as defined in section 552, on the making of a summary application to him after three clear days notice thereof to the person from whom the thing detained was seized, is satisfied, having regard to the complex nature of the investigation, that the further detention of the thing seized is warranted for a specified period and subject to such other conditions as the judge considers just, and he so orders; or

(*b*) proceedings are instituted in which the thing detained may be required.

(3.1) A thing may be detained under paragraph (1)(*b*) for any period, whether or not an application for an order under subsection (2) or (3) is made, if the lawful owner or person who is lawfully entitled to possession of the thing seized consents in writing to its detention for that period.

(4) When an accused has been ordered to stand trial, the justice shall forward anything detained pursuant to subsections (1) to (3) to the clerk of the court to which the accused has been ordered to stand trial to be detained by the clerk of the court and disposed of as the court directs.

(5) Where at any time before the expiration of the periods of detention provided for or ordered under subsections (1) to (3) in respect of anything seized, the prosecutor, or the peace officer or other person having custody of the thing seized, determines that the continued detention of the thing seized is no longer required for any purpose mentioned in subsection (1) or (4), the prosecutor, peace officer or other person shall apply to

(*a*) a judge of a superior court of criminal jurisdiction or a judge as defined in section 552, where a judge ordered its detention under subsection (3), or

(*b*) a justice, in any other case,

who shall, after affording the person from whom the thing was seized or the person who claims to be the lawful owner thereof or person entitled to its possession, if known, an opportunity to establish that he is lawfully entitled to the possession thereof, make an order in respect of the property under subsection (9).

(6) Where the periods of detention provided for or ordered under subsections (1) to (3) in respect of anything seized have expired and proceedings have not been instituted in which the thing detained may be required, the prosecutor, peace officer or other person shall apply to a judge or justice referred to in paragraph 5(*a*) or (*b*) in the circumstances set out in that paragraph, for an order in respect of the property under subsection (9) or (9.1).

(7) A person from whom anything has been seized may, after the expiration of the periods of detention provided for or ordered under subsections (1) to (3) and on three clear days notice to the Attorney General, apply summarily to

(*a*) a judge of a superior court of criminal jurisdiction or a judge as defined in section 552, where a judge ordered the detention of the thing seized under subsection (3), or

(*b*) a justice, in any other case,

for an order under paragraph (9)(*c*) that the thing seized be returned to the applicant.

(8) A judge of a superior court of criminal jurisdiction or a judge as defined in section 552, where a judge ordered the detention of the thing seized under subsection (3), or a justice, in any other case, may allow an application to be made under subsection (7) prior to the expiration of the periods referred to therein where he is satisfied that hardship will result unless the application is so allowed.

(9) Subject to this or any other Act of Parliament, if

(*a*) a judge referred to in subsection (7), where a judge ordered the detention of anything seized under subsection (3), or

(*b*) a justice, in any other case,

is satisfied that the periods of detention provided for or ordered under subsections (1) to (3) in respect of anything seized have expired and proceedings have not been instituted in which the thing detained may be required or, where those periods have not expired, that the continued detention of the thing seized will not be required for any purpose mentioned in subsection (1) or (4), he shall

(*c*) if possession of it by the person from whom it was seized is lawful, order it to be returned to that person; or

(*d*) if possession of it by the person from whom it was seized is unlawful and the lawful owner or person who is lawfully entitled to its possession is known, order it to be returned to the lawful owner or to the person who is lawfully entitled to its possession,

and may, if possession of it by the person from whom it was seized is unlawful, or if it was seized when it was not in the possession of any person, and the lawful owner or person who is lawfully entitled to its possession is not known, order it to be forfeited to Her Majesty, to be disposed of as the Attorney General directs, or otherwise dealt with in accordance with the law.

(9.1) Notwithstanding subsection (9), a judge or justice referred to in paragraph (9)(*a*) or (*b*) may, if the periods of detention provided for or ordered under subsections (1) to (3) in respect of a thing seized have expired but proceedings have not been instituted in which the thing may be required, order that the thing continue to be detained for such period as the judge or justice considers necessary if the judge or justice is satisfied

(*a*) that the continued detention of the thing might reasonably be required for a purpose mentioned in subsection (1) or (4); and

(*b*) that it is in the interests of justice to do so.

(10) Subject to this or any other Act of Parliament, a person, other than a person who may make an application under subsection (7), who claims to be the lawful owner or person lawfully entitled to possession of anything seized and brought before or reported to a justice under section 489.1 may, at any time, on three clear days notice to the Attorney General and the person from whom the thing was seized, apply summarily to

(*a*) a judge referred to in subsection (7), where a judge ordered the detention of the thing seized under subsection (3), or

(*b*) a justice, in any other case,

for an order that the thing detained be returned to the applicant.

(11) Subject to this or any other Act of Parliament, on an application under subsection (10), where a judge or justice is satisfied that

(*a*) the applicant is the lawful owner or lawfully entitled to possession of the thing seized, and

(*b*) the periods of detention provided for or ordered under subsections (1) to (3) in respect of the thing seized have expired and proceedings have not been instituted in which the thing detained may be required or, where such periods have not expired, that the continued detention of the thing seized will not be required for any purpose mentioned in subsection (1) or (4),

the judge or justice shall order that

(*c*) the thing seized be returned to the applicant; or

(*d*) except as otherwise provided by law, where, pursuant to subsection (9), the thing seized was forfeited, sold or otherwise dealt with in such a manner that it cannot be returned to the applicant, the applicant be paid the proceeds of sale or the value of the thing seized.

(12) Notwithstanding anything in this section, nothing shall be returned, forfeited or disposed of under this section pending any application made, or appeal taken, thereunder in respect of the thing or proceeding in which the right of seizure thereof is questioned or within thirty days after an order in respect of the thing is made under this section.

(13) The Attorney General, the prosecutor or the peace officer or other person having custody of a document seized may, before bringing it before a justice or complying with an order that the document be returned, forfeited or otherwise dealt with under subsection (1), (9) or (11), make or cause to be made, and may retain, a copy of the document.

(14) Every copy made under subsection (13) that is certified as a true copy by the Attorney General, the person who made the copy or the person in whose presence the copy was made is admissible in evidence and, in the absence of evidence to the contrary, has the same probative force as the original document would have if it had been proved in the ordinary way.

(15) Where anything is detained pursuant to subsections (1) to (3.1), a judge of a superior court of criminal jurisdiction, a judge as defined in section 552 or a provincial court judge may, on summary application on behalf of a person who has an interest in what is detained, after three clear days notice to the Attorney General, order that the person by or on whose behalf the application is made be permitted to examine anything so detained.

(16) An order that is made under subsection (15) shall be made on such terms as appear to the judge to be necessary or desirable to ensure that anything in respect of which the order is made is safeguarded and preserved for any purpose for which it may subsequently be required.

(17) A person who feels aggrieved by an order made under subsection (8), (9), (9.1) or (11) may appeal from the order

(*a*) to the court of appeal as defined in section 673 if the order was made by a judge of a superior court of criminal jurisdiction, in which case sections 678 to 689 apply with any modifications that the circumstances require; or

(*b*) to the appeal court as defined in section 812 in any other case, in which case sections 813 to 828 apply with any modifications that the circumstances require.

(18) Any person to whom three days notice must be given under paragraph (2)(*a*) or (3)(*a*) or subsection (7), (10) or (15) may agree that the application for which the notice is given be made before the expiration of the three days. R.S., c. C-34, s. 446; R.S.C. 1985, c. 27 (1st Supp.), s. 73; 1994, c. 44, s. 38; 1997, c. 18, s. 50; 2008, c. 18, s. 14.

CROSS-REFERENCES

The terms "Attorney General", "superior court of criminal jurisdiction", "justice", "peace officer" and "prosecutor" are defined in s. 2. Calculation of a period of months is determined in accordance with s. 28 of the *Interpretation Act*, R.S.C. 1985, c. I-21. As to calculation of "clear days" notice, see s. 27(1) of the *Interpretation Act*.

Under s. 491.2, before any property that would otherwise be required to be used in evidence under proceedings for offences under ss. 334, 344, 348, 354, 362 or 380 is forfeited or otherwise dealt with under this section, a peace officer or other person under the direction of a peace officer may take and retain a photograph for use in evidence. With respect to restitution or forfeiture of contraband, see ss. 491, 491.1 and 492. Section 490.1 (as enacted by 1997, c. 18, s. 51; see **note** before s. 490.1) provides a procedure for dealing with perishable goods. Sections 490.2 to 490.9 deal with forfeiture of "offence-related property".

An application for a management order under the *Seized Property Management Act*, S.C. 1993, c. 37, may be made at the same time as an application under this section. Where property that was subject to a management order has been forfeited under subsec. (9), the proceeds may be shared in accordance with the *Seized Property Management Act*.

This section also applies to material produced to a peace officer or public officer in accordance with a production order under s. 487.012.

SYNOPSIS

This section provides a comprehensive scheme that governs procedure when seized items are brought before a justice or a report is made and further detention of these items is requested.

Subsection (1) stipulates that the justice must return the goods to the lawfully entitled owner, if such information is available, unless the prosecutor satisfies the justice that their detention is required for the purposes of any investigation or proceedings. When the prosecutor satisfies this burden, the justice must order the detention of the seized items, taking care to ensure their preservation until the conclusion of the investigation or until they are required for further proceedings.

Subsection (2) makes it clear that any order under subsec. (1) must have a maximum life of three months from the day of the seizure unless the justice is satisfied upon a summary application that further detention for a specified period is required or that proceedings have been initiated which may require the detained items. Three clear days' notice to the person from whom the items were seized is necessary before such an application may be made.

However, subsec. (9.1) now allows a judge or justice to make an order for the further detention of the property even if the detention orders previously made have expired.

Subsection (3) states that more than one order under subsec. (2) may be made but that the cumulative period of detention cannot exceed one year from the date of seizure except in two circumstances. If an application on three days' notice is brought before a judge of a superior court of criminal jurisdiction or a judge as defined in s. 552, and that judge is satisfied that further detention is required due to the complex nature of the investigation, an order may be made detaining the seized items for a specified period, subject to such conditions as the judge may impose. If proceedings have been instituted in which the thing detained may be required, the cumulative period of detention may exceed one year. No order is required where the owner consents in writing to the detention under subsec. (3.1).

Subsection (4) provides that when an accused person has been ordered to stand trial, the justice shall forward the detained items to the clerk of the court having jurisdiction. The clerk will then detain the items and dispose of them as the court directs.

Subsection (5) states that when a prosecutor determines that the detained items are no longer required for the purposes described in subsec. (1) or (4), an application to the appropriate judge or justice shall be made. The judge or justice must give any person claiming to be the lawful owner of the items an opportunity to establish this claim. An order with respect to the items will be made in accordance with subsec. (9).

Subsection (6) provides for an application by the prosecutor for an order under subsec. (9) where the period of detention has expired and proceedings have not been instituted.

Subsection (7) likewise allows a person from whom anything has been seized to make an application, on three days' notice to the Attorney General, for the return of those items after the expiration of the period of detention. A judge or a justice may allow an application under subsec. (7) to be made prior to the expiration of the ordered period of detention where he has been satisfied that hardship will result if such an application is not allowed.

Subsection (9) states that if a judge or a justice is satisfied that the detention period has expired or that the continued detention of seized goods will not be required for any of the purposes referred to in the section, he shall order those goods returned to their lawful owner. If the lawful owner cannot be determined, the judge or justice may order the seized goods to be forfeited to Her Majesty, to be disposed of as directed by the Attorney General or in accordance with law. An order under subsec. (9) is subject to the other provisions in the Code or any other Act of Parliament. Pursuant to s. 490.9(2), where an order is made under s. 490(9)(*c*), and the property involved is offence-related property, the judge may require the applicant to enter into a recognizance.

Subsection (10) sets out the requirements for an application for the return of detained goods by a person, other than the person from whom these items were seized, who claims to be the lawful owner. The judge or justice who hears this application shall, if the requirements of subsec. (1) are met, order the return of the seized items to the applicant, or where those items have been sold and cannot be returned to the applicant, order the proceeds of such sale to be paid to the applicant.

Subsection (12) states that nothing shall be returned, forfeited or disposed of under this section pending any application or appeal of the seizure or within 30 days after an order is made.

Subsections (13) and (14) grant to the Attorney General, the prosecutor, peace officer or custodian of the documents the right to make copies of documents ordered to be returned or forfeited and if such copies are certified as true copies by the Attorney General, they are admissible in evidence with the same probative force, absent evidence to the contrary, as the original document.

Subsection (15) makes provision for an application by a person who has interest in seized property to examine the detained items. Such an examination must be regulated according to subsec. (16) in such a way as to safeguard and preserve the detained items.

Subsection (17) sets out the rights of appeal for any person who is not content with an order made under subsecs. (8), (9), (9.1) or (11).

Subsection (18) allows for an expedited hearing on consent.

ANNOTATIONS

Subsection (1) – The initial detention order made under this subsection is not an extension of the initial judicial process authorizing a search warrant and ss. 7 and 8 of the Charter of Rights and Freedoms are not applicable. Accordingly, the hearing may be held *ex parte* without notice to the owner of the goods. This is the case under the former legislation: *R. v. Church of Scientology (No. 6); R. v. Walsh* (1987), 31 C.C.C. (3d) 449 (Ont. C.A.), and the present legislation: *R. v. Barnable P.C.J.* (1986), 27 C.C.C. (3d) 565 (Nfld. S.C.T.D.).

Where articles have been brought before the justice pursuant to s. 489.1 having been seized in the execution of a warrant, the justice must determine whether or not the article falls within the description contained in the warrant of things which may be searched for and seized and whether it is protentially relevant to the offence set out in the warrant. On the other hand, there is no requirement in the provisions that the justice give reasons for making the detention order under this subsection and until the contrary is shown, a superior court is not entitled to infer that the justice did not decide the issues that were confided to him for determination: *Famous Players Ltd. v. Director of Investigation and Research* (1986), 29 C.C.C. (3d) 251, 11 C.P.R. (3d) 161 (Ont. H.C.J.); *Radok v. Joubert* (1988), 44 C.C.C. (3d) 317 (B.C.S.C.).

Whether the court is proceeding under this subsection or subsec. (9), the person from whom the money was seized need only show that he was in lawful possession of the money.

Upon such proof, the applicant's right to possession is presumed and the onus is then on the Crown to prove beyond a reasonable doubt that applicant is not lawfully entitled to the money by, for example, proof that the possession is tainted: *R. v. Mac* (1995), 97 C.C.C. (3d) 115, 80 O.A.C. 26 (C.A.).

Subsection (2) – The amendment to this subsection would appear to give statutory recognition to the holding in *R. v. Papalia* (1987), 38 C.C.C. (3d) 37 (B.C.S.C.), that it is sufficient that the application for further detention is made within three months and that there is no requirement that the detention order itself be made within three months. As well, Parliament has now added subsec. (9.1) to allow for an order of continued detention even though the detention order has expired.

A justice has no jurisdiction to make an order requiring the police to make photocopies of the detained documents. Jurisdiction to deal with the items seized after their further detention has been authorized is given to a judge, as under subsec. (15): *Filion v. Savard* (1988), 42 C.C.C. (3d) 182 (Que. C.A.).

Where the items seized have been held by the police, but under seal pending the determination of an application in the superior court to quash the warrant, then the owner is not entitled to the return of the items although no extension was obtained after expiration of the original three-month detention order. In the circumstances, the owner must be taken to have acquiesced to the continued detention, and the terms of subsec. (2) would not appear to contemplate a case where the reason for the delay is an application by the owner testing the validity of the seizure: *Société Radio-Canada v. Québec (Procureur-Général)* (1992), 78 C.C.C. (3d) 175, [1993] R.J.Q. 15 (C.A.), leave to appeal to S.C.C. refused 89 C.C.C. (3d) vi, 57 Q.A.C. 29*n*.

This subsection deals only with extending the time of detention beyond three months and does not give the judge jurisdiction to order the return of items allegedly improperly seized. The legal vehicle for the return of goods unlawfully taken or held is the civil action of replevin or an application under the *Charter of Rights and Freedoms* in the superior court: *R. v. Raponi*, [2004] 3 S.C.R. 35, 185 C.C.C. (3d) 338, 21 C.R. (6th) 197.

No appeal lies from an order made under subsec. (2): *R. v. Raponi, supra.*

Subsection (3) – An investigation is not "complex" within the meaning of this subsection merely because a large volume of documents were seized and a larger number of suspects have been identified than was initially thought to be the case. Had the authorities dedicated greater resources to the case, the investigation could have been completed within one year: *Moyer (Re)* (1994), 95 C.C.C. (3d) 174 (Ont. Ct. (Gen. Div.)).

The onus is on the Crown to establish the complexity of the investigation and the need for further detention of the items seized. In assessing the complexity of the investigation, the court may consider what work is yet to be done, the estimated time for completion, and whether the work should reasonably have been done earlier. In absence of evidence that a full year is required, it should not be granted automatically: *Canada Revenue Agency v. Okoroafor* (2010), 259 C.C.C. (3d) 87 (Ont. S.C.J.).

Subsection (7) – Where, prior to an application for return of moneys seized from the accused, the police have returned the moneys to the insurers of the victims of a robbbery which the accused were suspected of having committed (although the charge was stayed), then the judge should decline to make an order either under this section or pursuant to the superior court's inherent jurisdiction. In such circumstances the conflicting claims are most appropriately resolved by the civil courts: *R. v. Taylor* (1986), 31 C.C.C. (3d) 21 (B.C.S.C.).

A longer detention can only be permitted having regard to the complexity of the investigation but not the complexity of the potential charges or the number of hours required to review the material seized. The onus is on the applicant to establish the complexity of the investigation and the need for further detention. A non-complex investigation that investigators have had insufficient time to complete does not warrant a further detention order. A complex investigation is one that has many varied interrelated parts, patterns, or elements and consequently is hard to understand fully. Some factors that may be considered in determining whether the investigation is complex are: the number of police services and/or government departments involved; the involvement of foreign government; the investigation requires the assistance of lawyers, accountants, computer technicians and/or other professionals to decipher the documents or for other purposes; the investigation requires the cooperation of police services other than the applicant in Canada or elsewhere; the investigation requires witnesses to be interviewed outside Canada; the investigation covers an extensive timeframe or geographical area; there is a confusing paper trail; the offences were committed in more than one jurisdiction by more than one person or with nominees; complicated and time-consuming net worth calculations are required; it is a paper case; the investigative agency has no control over the timely responses of third parties; or documents require translation or transcripts of intercepted private communications must be prepared: *Canada Revenue Agency v. Okoroafor* (2010), 259 C.C.C. (3d) 87 (Ont. S.C.J.).

Applicants under subsec. (7) are under a duty to make full and frank disclosure so that the court can make an informed decision about, among other things, whether other interested parties must be given notice of the proceeding: *R. v. Floward Enterprises Ltd. (H. Williams and Co.)* (2017), 348 C.C.C. (3d) 409 (Ont. C.A.), additional reasons 2017 ONCA 643.

Subsection (9) – The Crown may seek an order of forfeiture under this subsection of moneys alleged to be the proceeds of crime. It is not restricted to the procedure set out in Part XII.2. Further, a conviction is not a condition precedent to an order under this subsection: *British Columbia (Attorney General) v. Forseth* (1995), 99 C.C.C. (3d) 296 (B.C.C.A.), leave to appeal to S.C.C. refused 104 C.C.C. (3d) vi.

Given that the Crown bears the burden of proof beyond a reasonable doubt, this provision requires adherence to the strict rules of evidence such as the exclusion of hearsay: *R. v. West* (2005), 199 C.C.C. (3d) 449 (Ont. C.A.). See also *Canada (Attorney General) v. Acero* (2006), 210 C.C.C. (3d) 549 (B.C.S.C.).

This subsection does not permit the judge to return items seized on the basis that the seizure was unlawful. The legal vehicle for the return of goods unlawfully taken or held is the civil action of replevin or an application under the *Charter of Rights and Freedoms* in the superior court: *R. v. Raponi*, [2004] 3 S.C.R. 35, 185 C.C.C. (3d) 338.

While s. 8 of the Charter has application to a forfeiture hearing, the same considerations did not apply with the same force as when an individual's liberty is at stake: *R. v. Daley* (2001), 156 C.C.C. (3d) 225 (Alta. C.A.).

An order under subsec. (9) cannot defeat a civil claim against the very property ordered returned: *Lin v. Ontario (Attorney General)* (2008), 240 C.C.C. (3d) 541 (Ont. S.C.J.).

Where the provincial court had made an order pursuant to subsec. (9)(*c*) for the return of property and the Crown had not appealed, the Crown's application for a preservation order in respect of that property under the Ontario *Civil Remedies Act* was held to be an impermissible collateral attack: *Ontario (Attorney General) v. $787,940 in Canadian Currency (In Rem)* (2014), 312 C.C.C. (3d) 150 (Ont. S.C.J.), additional reasons (2014), 243 A.C.W.S. (3d) 299, [2014] O.J. No. 2989 (S.C.J.).

Subsection (15) – It was held in relation to the predecessor to this subsection that there is no appeal from a decision made under this subsection: *R. v. Stewart,* [1970] 3 C.C.C. 428 (Sask. C.A.).

It was held that the word "examine" in the predecessor to this subsection includes making copies. Accordingly, a judge may order that the applicant be permitted to visually examine and make copies of documents under seizure: *R. v. Sutherland* (1977), 38 C.C.C. (2d) 252 (Ont. Co. Ct.). *Contra: R. v. Labrador Tool Supply Ltd.* (1982), 3 C.C.C. (3d) 269 (Nfld. S.C.T.D.).

Subsection (17) – An appeal lies to the court of appeal with leave pursuant to s. 839(1) from a decision under this subsection: *R. v. Church of Scientology of Toronto* (1991), 63 C.C.C. (3d) 328 (Ont. C.A.).

No appeal lies against an initial decision returning a thing seized to its owner pursuant to subsec. (1)(*a*): *SPCA Montérégie v. Langelier* (2017), 354 C.C.C. (3d) 513 (C.A. Que.).

If the accused had the right to make an application under subsecs. (8) or (9), then he has the right to appeal the dismissal of the motion pursuant to subsec. (17) whether or not the order is interlocutory in nature: *R. v. Scott* (2015), 322 C.C.C. (3d) 448 (Man. C.A.).

Where a third party with a claim to seized property was not given notice of an application under subsec. (7) because the applicant failed to make full and frank disclosure to the court, the third party has a right of appeal under subsec. (17): *R. v. Floward Enterprises Ltd. (H. Williams and Co.)* (2017), 348 C.C.C. (3d) 409 (Ont. C.A.), additional reasons 2017 ONCA 643.

PERISHABLE THINGS.

490.01 Where any thing seized pursuant to this Act is perishable or likely to depreciate rapidly, the person who seized the thing or any other person having custody of the thing

- **(*a*) may return it to its lawful owner or the person who is lawfully entitled to possession of it; or**
- **(*b*) where, on *ex parte* application to a justice, the justice so authorizes, may**
  - **(i) dispose of it and give the proceeds of disposition to the lawful owner of the thing seized, if the lawful owner was not a party to an offence in relation to the thing or, if the identity of that lawful owner cannot be reasonably ascertained, the proceeds of disposition are forfeited to Her Majesty, or**
  - **(ii) destroy it. 1997, c. 18, s. 51; 1999, c. 5, s. 17.**

SYNOPSIS

This section operates as an exception to the rules set out in s. 490 respecting the detention of things seized under the *Criminal Code*. Goods that are perishable or likely to rapidly depreciate may immediately be returned to their lawful owner or the person lawfully entitled to possession. Alternatively, an application may be made without notice to a justice for authorization to dispose of the goods, with the proceeds to be given to the lawful owner, or the justice may authorize destruction of the goods.

SEX OFFENDER INFORMATION

Interpretation

DEFINITIONS / Interpretation.

490.011 (1) The following definitions apply in this section and in sections 490.012 to 490.032.

"crime of a sexual nature" means a crime referred to in subsection 3(2) of the *Sex Offender Information Registration Act*.

"database" has the same meaning as in subsection 3(1) of the *Sex Offender Information Registration Act*.

"designated offence" means

- **(*a*) an offence under any of the following provisions:**
  - **(i) subsection 7(4.1) (offence in relation to sexual offences against children),**
  - **(ii) section 151 (sexual interference),**
  - **(iii) section 152 (invitation to sexual touching),**
  - **(iv) section 153 (sexual exploitation),**
  - **(v) section 153.1 (sexual exploitation of person with disability),**
  - **(vi) section 155 (incest),**
  - **(vi.1) subsection 160(2) (compelling the commission of bestiality),**
  - **(vii) subsection 160(3) (bestiality in presence of or by a child),**
  - **(viii) section 163.1 (child pornography),**

(ix) section 170 (parent or guardian procuring sexual activity),
(ix.1) section 171.1 (making sexually explicit material available to child),
(x) section 172.1 (luring a child),
(x.1) section 172.2 (agreement or arrangement — sexual offence against child),
(xi) subsection 173(2) (exposure),
(xii) [*Repealed*, 2014, c. 25, s. 25(1).]
(xiii) [*Repealed*, 2014, c. 25, s. 25(1).]
(xiv) [*Repealed*, 2014, c. 25, s. 25(1).]
(xv) [*Repealed*, 2014, c. 25, s. 25(1).]
(xvi) section 271 (sexual assault),
(xvii) section 272 (sexual assault with a weapon, threats to a third party or causing bodily harm),
(xviii) paragraph 273(2)(*a*) (aggravated sexual assault — use of a restricted firearm or prohibited firearm or any firearm in connection with criminal organization),
(xviii.1) paragraph 273(2)(*a*.1) (aggravated sexual assault — use of a firearm),
(xix) paragraph 273(2)(*b*) (aggravated sexual assault),
(xx) subsection 273.3(2) (removal of a child from Canada),
(xxi) section 279.011 (trafficking — person under 18 years),
(xxii) subsection 279.02(2) (material benefit — trafficking of person under 18 years),
(xxiii) subsection 279.03(2) (withholding or destroying documents — trafficking of person under 18 years),
(xxiv) subsection 286.1(2) (obtaining sexual services for consideration from person under 18 years),
(xxv) subsection 286.2(2) (material benefit from sexual services provided by person under 18 years), and
(xxvi) subsection 286.3(2) (procuring — person under 18 years);

(*b*) an offence under any of the following provisions:
(i) section 162 (voyeurism),
(i.1) subsection 173(1) (indecent acts),
(ii) section 177 (trespassing at night),
(iii) section 230 (murder in commission of offences),
(iii.1) section 231 (murder),
(iv) section 234 (manslaughter),
(v) paragraph 246(*b*) (overcoming resistance to commission of offence),
(vi) section 264 (criminal harassment),
(vii) section 279 (kidnapping),
(vii.1) section 279.01 (trafficking in persons),
(vii.11) subsection 279.02(1) (material benefit — trafficking),
(vii.12) subsection 279.03(1) (withholding or destroying documents — trafficking),
(viii) section 280 (abduction of a person under age of sixteen),
(ix) section 281 (abduction of a person under age of fourteen),
(ix.1) subsection 286.1(1) (obtaining sexual services for consideration),
(ix.2) subsection 286.2(1) (material benefit from sexual services),
(ix.3) subsection 286.3(1) (procuring),
(x) paragraph 348(1)(*d*) (breaking and entering a dwelling house with intent to commit an indictable offence),
(xi) paragraph 348(1)(*d*) (breaking and entering a dwelling house and committing an indictable offence),
(xii) paragraph 348(1)(*e*) (breaking and entering a place other than a dwelling house with intent to commit an indictable offence), and
(xiii) paragraph 348(1)(*e*) (breaking and entering a place other than a dwelling house and committing an indictable offence);

(*c*) an offence under any of the following provisions of the *Criminal Code*, chapter C-34 of the Revised Statutes of Canada, 1970, as they read from time to time before January 4, 1983:

(i) section 144 (rape),

(ii) section 145 (attempt to commit rape),

(iii) section 149 (indecent assault on female),

(iv) section 156 (indecent assault on male), and

(v) subsection 246(1) (assault with intent) if the intent is to commit an offence referred to in any of subparagraphs (i) to (iv);

(*c*.1) an offence under any of the following provisions of the *Criminal Code*, chapter C-34 of the Revised Statutes of Canada, 1970, as enacted by section 19 of *An Act to amend the Criminal Code in relation to sexual offences and other offences against the person and to amend certain other Acts in relation thereto or in consequence thereof*, chapter 125 of the Statutes of Canada, 1980-81-82-83:

(i) section 246.1 (sexual assault),

(ii) section 246.2 (sexual assault with a weapon, threats to a third party or causing bodily harm), and

(iii) section 246.3 (aggravated sexual assault);

(*d*) an offence under any of the following provisions of the *Criminal Code*, chapter C-34 of the Revised Statutes of Canada, 1970, as they read from time to time before January 1, 1988:

(i) subsection 146(1) (sexual intercourse with a female under age of fourteen),

(ii) subsection 146(2) (sexual intercourse with a female between ages of fourteen and sixteen),

(iii) section 153 (sexual intercourse with step-daughter),

(iv) section 157 (gross indecency),

(v) section 166 (parent or guardian procuring defilement), and

(vi) section 167 (householder permitting defilement);

(*d*.1) an offence under any of the following provisions of this Act, as they read from time to time before the day on which this paragraph comes into force:

(i) paragraph 212(1)(i) (stupefying or overpowering for the purpose of sexual intercourse),

(ii) subsection 212(2) (living on the avails of prostitution of person under 18 years),

(iii) subsection 212(2.1) (aggravated offence in relation to living on the avails of prostitution of person under 18 years), and

(iv) subsection 212(4) (prostitution of person under 18 years);

(*e*) an attempt or conspiracy to commit an offence referred to in any of paragraphs (*a*), (*c*), (*c*.1), (*d*) and (*d*.1); or

(*f*) an attempt or conspiracy to commit an offence referred to in paragraph (*b*).

"Ontario Act" means *Christopher's Law (Sex Offender Registry), 2000*, S.O. 2000, c. 1.

"pardon" means a conditional pardon granted under Her Majesty's royal prerogative of mercy or under section 748 that has not been revoked.

"record suspension" means a record suspension, as defined in subsection 2(1) of the *Criminal Records Act*, that has not been revoked or ceased to have effect.

"registration centre" has the same meaning as in subsection 3(1) of the *Sex Offender Information Registration Act*.

"Review Board" means the Review Board established or designated for a province under subsection 672.38(1).

"verdict of not criminally responsible on account of mental disorder" means a verdict of not criminally responsible on account of mental disorder within the meaning of subsection 672.1(1) or a finding of not responsible on account of mental disorder within the meaning of subsection 2(1) of the *National Defence Act*, as the case may be.

(2) For the purpose of this section and sections 490.012 to 490.032, a person who is convicted of, or found not criminally responsible on account of mental disorder for, a designated offence does not include a young person

(*a*) within the meaning of subsection 2(1) of the *Youth Criminal Justice Act* unless they are given an adult sentence within the meaning of that subsection for the offence; or

(*b*) within the meaning of subsection 2(1) of the *Young Offenders Act*, chapter Y-1 of the Revised Statutes of Canada, 1985, unless they are convicted of the offence in ordinary court within the meaning of that subsection. 2004, c. 10, s. 20; 2005, c. 43, s. 6; 2007, c. 5, s. 11; 2008, c. 6, s. 36; 2010, c. 3, s. 7; 2010, c. 17, s. 4; 2012, c. 1, s. 141(2) and (3); 2012, c. 1, s. 31; 2014, c. 25, s. 25.

CROSS-REFERENCES

Sections 490.011 to 490.032 were enacted by the *Sex Offender Information Registration Act*, S.C. 2004, c. 10. Section 3(2) of that Act (referred to in the definition of "crime of a sexual nature") provides as follows:

> (2) For the purposes of this Act, a crime is of a sexual nature if it consists of one or more acts that
> (*a*) are either sexual in nature or committed with the intent to commit an act or acts that are sexual in nature; and
> (*b*) constitute an offence.

Section 18 of that Act provides that the lieutenant governor in council of a province may designate places or classes of places in the province as registration centres, and the area of the province served by each registration centre.

Section 5(*b*) of the *Criminal Records Act*, R.S.C. 1985, c. C-47, provides that the legal restrictions imposed by ss. 490.012 and 490.019 continue, notwithstanding that the individual has been granted a pardon under that Act.

ANNOTATIONS

The provisions of the *Sex Offender Information Registration Act*, S.C. 2004, c. 10, and these provisions were intended to be retrospective in application and to apply to any convicted offender sentenced after the coming into force of the legislation for an offence that is a designated offence. Further, registration is not a "punishment" so as to trigger the offender's right under s. 11(*i*) of the *Charter of Rights and Freedoms* to the benefit of lesser punishment where the punishment has varied between the time of the commission and the time of sentencing: *R. v. Cross* (2006), 205 C.C.C. (3d) 289 (N.S.C.A.), leave to appeal to S.C.C. refused [2006] 2 S.C.R. vi, 210 C.C.C. (3d) vi; *R. v. Rouschop*, [2005] O.J. No. 1336 (C.J.); *R. v. G. (M.)* (2005), 132 C.R.R. (2d) 289 (B.C.S.C.). Similarly, see *R. v. Dyck* (2005), 203 C.C.C. (3d) 365 (Ont. S.C.J.), holding that registration under *Christopher's Law (Sex Offender Registry), 2000*, S.O. 2000, c. 1, is not punishment for the purpose of s. 11(*i*). [Note: also now see *R. v. Rodgers* (2006), 207 C.C.C. (3d) 225 (S.C.C.), considering the retroactive application of the DNA data bank provision, s. 487.055.]

Christopher's Law (Sex Offender Registry), 2000, S.O. 2000, c. 1 (the "Ontario Act"), is valid legislation. It is *intra vires* the province, does not violate ss. 7 and 12 of the *Canadian Charter of Rights and Freedoms* and has not been rendered inoperative by enactment of the *Criminal Code* provisions and the *Sex Offender Information Registration Act*: *R. v. Dyck*, *supra*.

Order to Comply with the *Sex Offender Information Registration Act*

2007, c. 5, s. 12.

ORDER / Order — if intent established / Order — if previous offence established / Failure to make order.

490.012 (1) When a court imposes a sentence on a person for an offence referred to in paragraph *(a)*, *(c)*, *(c*.1), *(d)*, *(d*.1) or *(e)* of the definition "designated offence" in subsection 490.011(1) or renders a verdict of not criminally responsible on account of mental disorder for such an offence, it shall make an order in Form 52 requiring the person to comply with the *Sex Offender Information Registration Act* for the applicable period specified in section 490.013.

(2) When a court imposes a sentence on a person for an offence referred to in paragraph *(b)* or *(f)* of the definition "designated offence" in subsection 490.011(1), it shall, on application of the prosecutor, make an order in Form 52 requiring the person to comply with the *Sex Offender Information Registration Act* for the applicable period specified in section 490.013 if the prosecutor establishes beyond a reasonable doubt that the person committed the offence with the intent to commit an offence referred to in paragraph *(a)*, *(c)*, *(c*.1), *(d)*, *(d*.1) or *(e)* of that definition.

(3) When a court imposes a sentence on a person for a designated offence in connection with which an order may be made under subsection (1) or (2) or renders a verdict of not criminally responsible on account of mental disorder for such an offence, it shall, on application of the prosecutor, make an order in Form 52 requiring the person to comply with the *Sex Offender Information Registration Act* for the applicable period specified in section 490.013 if the prosecutor establishes that

- **(*a*) the person was, before or after the coming into force of this paragraph, previously convicted of, or found not criminally responsible on account of mental disorder for, an offence referred to in paragraph *(a)*, *(c)*, *(c*.1), *(d)*, *(d*.1) or *(e)* of the definition "designated offence" in subsection 490.011(1) or in paragraph *(a)* or *(c)* of the definition "designated offence" in section 227 of the *National Defence Act*;**
- **(*b*) the person was not served with a notice under section 490.021 or 490.02903 or under section 227.08 of the *National Defence Act* in connection with that offence; and**
- **(*c*) no order was made under subsection (1) or under subsection 227.01(1) of the *National Defence Act* in connection with that offence.**

(4) If the court does not consider the matter under subsection (1) or (3) at that time, the court

- **(*a*) shall, within 90 days after the day on which it imposes the sentence or renders the verdict, set a date for a hearing to do so;**
- **(*b*) retains jurisdiction over the matter; and**
- **(*c*) may require the person to appear by closed-circuit television or any other means that allows the court and the person to engage in simultaneous visual and oral communication, as long as the person is given the opportunity to communicate privately with counsel if they are represented by counsel. 2004, c. 10, s. 20; 2007, c. 5, s. 13; 2010, c. 17, s. 5; 2014, c. 25, s. 26.**

CROSS-REFERENCES

This section must be read with the *Sex Offender Information Registration Act*, S.C. 2004, c. 10. That Act sets out the reporting requirements of a person subject to an order under this section. That Act may be found in *Martin's Related Criminal Statutes*.

The duration of the order made under this section is determined by s. 490.013. If the order was made under subsec. (1) or (2) of this section, it ends 10 years after it was made if the offence was a summary conviction offence or punishable by two or five years. If the maximum penalty for the offence is 10 or 14 years, the order ends 20 years after it was made. However, if the order was made under s. 490.012(1) and the person was convicted of, or found not criminally responsible on account of mental disorder for more than one offence referred to in paras. (*a*), (*c*), (*c*.1), (*d*) or (*e*) of the definition of designated offence in s. 490.011(1) then the order applies for life. The order is also a lifetime order if the maximum penalty for the offence was life imprisonment or the person was already under an obligation under ss. 490.019 or 490.02901 or s. 227.06 of the *National Defence Act*, R.S.C. 1985, c. N-5, or s. 36.1 of the *International Transfer of Offenders Act*, S.C. 2004, c. 21. The Attorney General or minister of justice, as the case may be, may serve notice to comply with the registration requirements in accordance with s. 490.02 where on the day this Act came into force (December 15, 2004) the person was still serving sentence for or had not received an absolute discharge under Part XX.1 from an offence listed in paras. (*a*), (*c*), (*d*) or (*e*) of the definition of designated offence in s. 490.011(1), or the person was already listed in the sex offender registry established under the Ontario Act for such an offence and the person was a resident of Ontario at any time between April 23, 2001 and December 15, 2004.

The prosecutor or a person who is subject to an order under subsec. (2) of this section may appeal on any ground of law or mixed law and fact under s. 490.014. Under s. 490.015, the person may apply for a termination order. That section sets out the dates when an application may first be made for a termination order. The circumstances in which the termination may be made are set out in s. 490.016. Section 490.017 sets out the appeal provisions in relation to a termination order application. Section 490.018 sets out the requirements placed on a court that makes an order under this section. Section 490.03 sets out the circumstances in which information in the sex offender database may be disclosed. Section 490.031 creates the offence for failing to comply with an order under this section.

Sections 490.02901 to 490.02911 establish a similar scheme for registration under the *Sex Offender Information Registration Act* for persons who arrive in Canada and have been convicted or found not criminally responsible for offences outside of Canada that are equivalent to the definition of designated offence as defined in s. 490.011(1). Sections 490.02912 to 490.02915 deal with applications for termination of registration orders made under s. 36.1 of the *International Transfer of Offenders Act*.

Section 5(*b*) of the *Criminal Records Act*, R.S.C. 1985, c. C-47, provides that the legal restriction imposed by this section continues, notwithstanding that the individual has been granted a pardon under that Act. The person may, however, apply for a termination order at that point.

Sections 227 to 227.21 of the *National Defence Act* contain the analogous provisions in relation to court martial proceedings.

Under s. 487.051, persons convicted or found not criminally responsible of primary designated offences as defined in s. 487.04 are subject to orders for taking of bodily samples to allow for forensic DNA analysis. The court has a discretion to make such an order for persons convicted of secondary designated offences.

SYNOPSIS

This section provides that a court may make an order requiring the offender to comply with the requirements of the *Sex Offender Information Registration Act*, S.C. 2004, c. 10. The order is mandatory for the offences listed in subsec. (1) and is mandatory upon application of the prosecutor in the circumstances set out in subsecs. (2) and (3). The order is to be made when the offender is sentenced or the court renders a verdict of not criminally responsible on account of mental disorder. However, under subsec. (4), the court retains jurisdiction to make an order and is to do so by setting a date within 90 days of the sentence or the verdict. The court may require the person to appear by close-circuit television or other means. The court must give reasons for its decision.

This section contemplates three different circumstances in which the order will be made. Where the offence is listed in paras. (*a*), (*c*), (*c*.1), (*d*), (*d*.1) or (*e*) of the definition of designated offence in s. 490.011(1), no further finding is required. Those offences are the various sexual offences under the present Code or predecessor provisions (subsec. (1)).

Where the offence is one listed in paras. (*b*) or (*f*), the court must make a further finding that the offence, such as trespassing by night (s. 177), was committed with the intent to commit one of the offences referred in paras. (*a*), (*c*), (*c*.1), (*d*), (*d*.1) or (*e*). The burden is on the prosecution to establish this intent beyond a reasonable doubt (subsec. (2)). Finally, where the offence falls within the definition of a designated offence under any of paras. (*a*) to (*f*), the order will be made where the offender was previously convicted of or found criminally responsible on account of mental disorder for an offence listed in paras. (*a*), (*c*), (*c*.1), (*d*), (*d*.1) or (*e*) of the definition of designated offence (subsec. (3)).

ANNOTATIONS

There is no right to appeal an order pursuant to subsec. (1) as it is not a sentence within the meaning of s. 673 of the Code: *R. v. Chisholm* (2012), 292 C.C.C. (3d) 132 (N.B.C.A.). See also *R. v. W. (J.J.)* (2012), 292 C.C.C. (3d) 292 (N.S.C.A.).

It was held under the predecessor to this section that, in a case where the application for registration must be initiated by the prosecutor and the issue was first raised by the sentencing judge and not pursued by the prosecutor, the judge did not err in failing to make the order: *R. v. R. (B.E.)* (2005), 32 C.R. (6th) 151 (B.C.C.A.).

The sentencing judge has no discretion to make the reporting period less than required by the applicable *Criminal Code* provisions: *R. v. R. (R.J.)* (2005), 252 Nfld. & P.E.I.R. 166 (Nfld. & Lab. C.A.).

As applied to persons who have been found not criminally responsible by reason of mental disorder and who have received an absolute discharge, the sex offender registration provisions are contrary to s. 15 of the Charter and of no force or effect: *G. v. Ontario (Attorney General)*, 2019 ONCA 264.

This provision has no application where the accused receives an absolute or conditional discharge: *R. v. Jayswal* (2011), 266 C.C.C. (3d) 388 (Ont. C.J.).

Where the court imposed a 20-year SOIRA order in circumstances in which a lifetime order was mandatory, the court did not fail to "consider the matter" within the meaning of subsec. (4). As a result, the court was *functus officio* and dismissed the Crown's application to correct the defective order: *R. v. B. (C.D.)* (2013), 306 C.C.C. (3d) 369 (B.C.S.C.). *Contra*: *R. v. Merrick* (2013), 108 W.C.B. (2d) 821, [2013] O.J. No. 3965 (C.J.).

DATE ORDER BEGINS / Duration of order / Duration of order / Duration of order / Duration of order / Duration of order.

490.013 (1) An order made under section 490.012 begins on the day on which it is made.

(2) An order made under subsection 490.012(1) or (2)

- **(*a*) ends 10 years after it was made if the offence in connection with which it was made was prosecuted summarily or if the maximum term of imprisonment for the offence is two or five years;**
- **(*b*) ends 20 years after it was made if the maximum term of imprisonment for the offence is 10 or 14 years; and**
- **(*c*) applies for life if the maximum term of imprisonment for the offence is life.**

(2.1) An order made under subsection 490.012(1) applies for life if the person is convicted of, or found not criminally responsible on account of mental disorder for, more than one offence referred to in paragraph (*a*), (*c*), (*c*.1), (*d*), (*d*.1) or (*e*) of the definition "designated offence" in subsection 490.011(1).

(3) An order made under subsection 490.012(1) or (2) applies for life if the person is, or was at any time, subject to an obligation under section 490.019 or 490.02901, under section 227.06 of the *National Defence Act* or under section 36.1 of the *International Transfer of Offenders Act*.

(4) An order made under subsection 490.012(1) or (2) applies for life if the person is, or was at any time, subject to an order made previously under section 490.012 of this Act or section 227.01 of the *National Defence Act*.

(5) An order made under subsection 490.012(3) applies for life. 2004, c. 10, s. 20; 2007, c. 5, s. 14; 2010, c. 17, s. 6; 2014, c. 25, s. 27.

CROSS-REFERENCES

"Prosecutor" is defined in s. 2. For other cross-references, see s. 490.012.

SYNOPSIS

This section sets out the duration of the order to comply with registration requirements that is made under s. 490.012. If the order was made under subsec. (1) or (2) of s. 490.012, it ends 10 years after it was made if the offence was a summary conviction offence or punishable by two or five years. If the maximum penalty for the offence is 10 or 14 years, the order ends 20 years after it was made. If the maximum punishment was life or the order was made under s. 490.012(3), the order applies for life. The order is also a lifetime order if the person was convicted or found not criminally responsible for more than one offence referred to in paras. (*a*), (*c*), (*c*.1), (*d*), (*d*.1) or (*e*) of the definition of designated offence, or the offender was under an obligation under ss. 490.019 or 490.02901. The Attorney General or minister of justice, as the case may be, may serve notice to comply with the registration requirements in accordance with s. 490.02 where on the day this Act came into force (December 15, 2004) the person was still serving sentence for or had not received an absolute discharge under Part XX.1 from an offence listed in paras. (*a*), (*c*), (*d*), (*d*.1) or (*e*) of the definition of designated offence in s. 490.011, or the person was already listed in the sex offender registry established under the Ontario Act for such an offence and the person was a resident of Ontario at any time between April 23, 2001 and December 15, 2004. Finally, the order is for life if the person is or at any time was subject to an order made previously under either s. 490.012(1) or (2).

ANNOTATIONS

Under subsec. (2.1), an offender will be subject to a lifetime SOIRA order if convicted of multiple designated offences, even if he is sentenced for those offences simultaneously: *R. v. Burns* (2012), 285 C.C.C. (3d) 328 (Sask. C.A.).

The triggering of a mandatory lifetime order by more than one offence is not unconstitutionally overbroad or grossly disproportionate. The commission of multiple offences is not an unreasonable proxy for an increased risk of re-offending: *R. v. Long*, 2018 ONCA 282.

APPEAL.

490.014 The prosecutor, or a person who is subject to an order under subsection 490.012(2), may appeal from a decision of the court under that subsection on any ground of appeal that raises a question of law or of mixed law and fact. The appeal court may dismiss the appeal, or allow it and order a new hearing, quash the order or make an order that may be made under that subsection. 2004, c. 10, s. 20; 2010, c. 17, s. 7.

CROSS-REFERENCES

"Prosecutor" is defined in s. 2. Section 490.018 imposes on the appeal court the same obligations as a trial court where the appeal court makes an order under s. 490.012. For other cross-references, see s. 490.012.

SYNOPSIS

This section gives the prosecutor or the person against whom an order was made under s. 490.012(2) a right of appeal on a question of law or mixed law and fact. The appeal court may dismiss the appeal, or allow the appeal and order a new hearing, quash the order or make an order that may be made under s. 490.012(2).

ANNOTATIONS

Section 487.054 provides for appeals in relation to making of DNA orders. Like this section, it does not specify the appeal court. In *R. v. Hendry* (2001), 161 C.C.C. (3d) 275, 48 C.R. (5th) 310 (Ont. C.A.), the court held that the appeal route follows the scheme in the *Criminal Code* generally. That is, in indictable proceedings, the appeal from the making or refusal to make the order lies to the Court of Appeal and, in summary conviction proceedings, the appeal is taken in accordance with Part XXVII of the *Criminal Code*.

There is no right of appeal from an order made under s. 490.012(1): *R. v. Chisholm* (2012), 292 C.C.C. (3d) 132 (N.B.C.A.); *R. v. W. (J.J.)* (2012), 292 C.C.C. (3d) 292 (N.S.C.A.); *R. v. Whiting* (2013), 304 C.C.C. (3d) 342 (Sask. C.A.); *R. v. R. (L.V.)* (2016), 334 C.C.C. (3d) 464 (B.C.C.A.), leave to appeal to S.C.C. refused 2016 CarswellBC 2581.

APPLICATION FOR TERMINATION ORDER / Multiple orders / Pardon or record suspension / Scope of application / Re-application / Jurisdiction.

490.015 (1) A person who is subject to an order may apply for a termination order

(*a*) if five years have elapsed since the order was made, in the case of an order referred to in paragraph 490.013(2)(*a*);

(*b*) if 10 years have elapsed since the order was made, in the case of an order referred to in paragraph 490.013(2)(*b*); or

(*c*) if 20 years have elapsed since the order was made, in the case of an order referred to in paragraph 490.013(2)(*c*) or subsection 490.013(2.1), (3) or (5).

(2) A person who is subject to more than one order made under section 490.012 of this Act, or under that section and section 227.01 of the *National Defence Act*, may apply for a termination order if 20 years have elapsed since the most recent order was made.

(3) Despite subsections (1) and (2), a person may apply for a termination order once they receive a pardon or once a record suspension is ordered.

(4) The application shall be in relation to every order that is in effect. If a person is subject to an obligation under section 490.019 or 490.02901, under section 227.06 of the *National Defence Act* or under section 36.1 of the *International Transfer of Offenders Act*, the application shall also be in relation to that obligation.

(5) A person whose application is refused may re-apply if five years have elapsed since they made the previous application. They may also re-apply once they receive a pardon or once a record suspension is ordered. However, they may not re-apply under this subsection if an order is made with respect to them under section 490.012 of this Act or section 227.01 of the *National Defence Act* after the previous application was made.

(6) The application shall be made to

(*a*) a superior court of criminal jurisdiction if

(i) one or more of the orders to which it relates were made by such a court under section 490.012, or

(ii) one or more of the orders to which it relates were made under section 227.01 of the *National Defence Act* and the Chief Military Judge does not have jurisdiction to receive the application under subsection 227.03(6) of that Act; or

(*b*) a court of criminal jurisdiction, in any other case in which the application relates to one or more orders made under section 490.012. 2004, c. 10, s. 20; 2007, c. 5, s. 15; 2010, c. 17, s. 8; 2012, c. 1, s. 142.

CROSS-REFERENCES

"Superior court of criminal jurisdiction" and "court of criminal jurisdiction" are defined in s. 2. "Pardon" and "record suspension" are defined in s. 490.011. For other cross-references, see s. 490.012. Section 490.026 provides for an application to terminate an order made under s. 490.019. Section 490.02908 provides for an application to terminate an obligation to comply with the *Sex Offender Information Registration Act*, S.C. 2004, c. 10, in relation to convictions or findings made outside Canada. It would appear that, in light of subsec. (3) of this section, a person subject to an order under s. 490.012 and an obligation under ss. 490.019 or 490.02901 makes an application under this section to terminate both.

SYNOPSIS

This section provides for the person who is subject to an order to comply with registration requirements made under s. 490.012 to apply for a termination order. The time for making the application depends on the duration of the order. If it was a 10-year order, the person may apply after five years. If the order was for 20 years, the person may apply after 10 years. If the order was for life, the person may apply after 20 years. Or, the person may apply on or after the day on which they receive a pardon or record suspension. If the person is subject to multiple orders, the order must be in relation to all of the orders and the application can only be made after 20 years or on or after the day on which the person receives a pardon or record suspension. Pursuant to subsec. (3), a person who is subject to an obligation under ss. 490.019 or 490.02901 must include an application to terminate that obligation as well. Where the person's application was unsuccessful, they may not reapply for five years, but if, in the meantime, a new s. 490.012 order was made, they may not reapply. The application is made to a court of criminal jurisdiction unless the original order was made by a superior court of criminal jurisdiction, in which case the application must be made to that court.

TERMINATION ORDER / Reasons for decision / Requirements relating to notice.

490.016 (1) The court shall make a termination order if it is satisfied that the person has established that the impact on them of continuing an order or an obligation, including on their privacy or liberty, would be grossly disproportionate to the public interest in protecting society through the effective prevention or investigation of crimes of a sexual nature, to be achieved by the registration of information relating to sex offenders under the *Sex Offender Information Registration Act*.

(2) The court shall give reasons for its decision.

(3) If the court makes a termination order, it shall cause the Commissioner of the Royal Canadian Mounted Police and the Attorney General of the province, or the minister of justice of the territory, to be notified of the decision. 2004, c. 10, s. 20; 2007, c. 15, s. 16; 2010, c. 17, s. 9.

CROSS-REFERENCES

The time for making an application for a termination order is set out in s. 490.015. Section 490.017 provides for an appeal from a decision under this section. For other cross-references, see s. 490.012.

SYNOPSIS

This section sets out the circumstances when a court may terminate an order. The test is similar to the test set out in s. 490.012(4) for when the court may refuse to initially make the order. The applicant must establish that the impact of continuing the order or orders, and any obligation, to which the application relates, including on their privacy or liberty, would be grossly disproportionate to the public interest in the protection of society through the effective prevention or investigation of crimes of a sexual nature, to be achieved by the registration of information relating to sex offenders. The court must give reasons for the decision.

ANNOTATIONS

Note: the following cases were decided under s. 490.012(4) which, at that time, gave a judge a discretion to refuse to initially make an order requiring compliance with the *Sex Offender Information Registration Act*, S.C. 2004, c. 10. That discretion has now been removed. Notes of the following decisions have been included because s. 490.012(4) was worded similarly to the present s. 490.016(1), although the latter now specifically refers to the importance of protecting society through prevention of crimes of a sexual nature, whereas former s. 490.012(4) only referred to investigation of such crimes.

The standard of "grossly disproportionate" is very high. While registration will have some impact on the offender's privacy, this must be balanced against the purpose of the legislation and its confidentiality requirements. The purpose of registration is not to identify sex offenders to the community but, in accordance with this section, to help police services investigate crimes of a sexual nature by requiring the registration of certain information relating to sex offenders. The provisions of the *Sex Offender Information Registration Act* indicate an intention to keep information collected confidential and for use only by those with a legitimate reason in keeping with the purposes of investigation of crime and protection of society: *R. v. Casaway* (2005), 64 W.C.B. (2d) 610 (N.W.T.S.C.). Similarly, *R. v. Clarke* (2005), 197 C.C.C. (3d) 443 (N.S.S.C.), affd 208 C.C.C. (3d) 243 (N.S.C.A.), and *R. v. S. (L.)* (2005), 78 W.C.B. (2d) 378 (B.C. Prov. Ct.).

The impact to be assessed is the impact of the registration requirements on the offender's current and prospective circumstances. This includes a consideration of the impact of registration on the offender's privacy and liberty interests. The evidence upon which the convicted offender may rely to invoke and satisfy the exception may emerge from the trial or sentencing proceedings. Relevant factors include the nature of the offence, the risk to re-offend, the offender's criminal record and other matters personal to the offender's circumstances. The registration is not limited, however, to likely recidivism and the diminished risk of recidivism is not a basis to enhance the impact on the offender or dilute the public interest in registration: *R. v. Debidin* (2008), 241 C.C.C. (3d) 152 (Ont. C.A.).

The focus on the inquiry must be on the offender's present and possible future circumstances and not on the offence itself. In considering whether the order would be grossly disproportionate, the court must assess the impact of the order on the offender, including the impact on his privacy and liberty interests, and determine whether that impact is grossly disproportionate to the public interest. Factors that may be considered include unique individual circumstances such as a personal handicap, which would require the offender to obtain assistance to report, intangible effects such as stigma, undermining rehabilitation and reintegration in the community, and whether the order might result in police harassment. Absent disproportional impact, the length of the reporting obligation alone does not constitute gross disproportionality: *R. v. Redhead* (2006), 206 C.C.C. (3d) 315 (Alta. C.A.), leave to appeal to S.C.C. refused [2006] 2 S.C.R. x, 210 C.C.C. (3d) vi.

APPEAL / Requirements relating to notice.

490.017 (1) The prosecutor or the person who applied for a termination order may appeal from a decision made under subsection 490.016(1) on any ground of appeal that raises a question of law or of mixed law and fact. The appeal court may dismiss the appeal, or allow it and order a new hearing, quash the termination order or make an order that may be made under that subsection.

(2) If the appeal court makes an order that may be made under subsection 490.016(1), it shall cause the Commissioner of the Royal Canadian Mounted Police and the Attorney General of the province, or the minister of justice of the territory, in which the

application for the order was made to be notified of the decision. 2004, c. 10, s. 20; 2007, c. 5, s. 17; 2010, c. 17, s. 10.

CROSS-REFERENCES

"Prosecutor" is defined in s. 2. For other cross-references, see s. 490.012.

SYNOPSIS

This section gives the prosecutor or the person who applied for a termination order a right of appeal on a question of law or mixed law and fact. The appeal court may dismiss the appeal, or allow the appeal and order a new hearing, quash the termination order or make an order that may be made under s. 490.016(1).

ANNOTATIONS

Section 487.054 provides for appeals in relation to making of DNA orders. Like this section, it does not specify the appeal court. In *R. v. Hendry* (2001), 161 C.C.C. (3d) 275, 48 C.R. (5th) 310 (Ont. C.A.), the court held that the appeal route follows the scheme in the *Criminal Code* generally. That is, in indictable proceedings, the appeal from the making or refusal to make the order lies to the Court of Appeal and, in summary conviction proceedings, the appeal is taken in accordance with Part XXVII of the *Criminal Code*.

REQUIREMENTS RELATING TO NOTICE / Endorsement / Notice on disposition by Review Board / Notice before release.

490.018 (1) When a court or appeal court makes an order under section 490.012, it shall cause

(*a*) the order to be read by or to the person who is subject to it;

(*b*) a copy of the order to be given to that person;

(*c*) that person to be informed of sections 4 to 7.1 of the *Sex Offender Information Registration Act*, sections 490.031 and 490.0311 of this Act and section 119.1 of the *National Defence Act*; and

(*d*) a copy of the order to be sent to

(i) the Review Board that is responsible for making a disposition with respect to that person, if applicable,

(ii) the person in charge of the place in which that person is to serve the custodial portion of a sentence or is to be detained in custody as part of a disposition under Part XX.1, if applicable,

(iii) the police service whose member charged that person with the offence in connection with which the order is made, and

(iv) the Commissioner of the Royal Canadian Mounted Police.

(2) After paragraphs (1)(*a*) to (*c*) have been complied with, the person who is subject to the order shall endorse the order.

(3) A Review Board shall cause a copy of the order to be given to the person who is subject to it when it directs

(*a*) under paragraph 672.54(*a*), that the person be discharged absolutely; or

(*b*) under paragraph 672.54(*b*), that the person be discharged subject to conditions, unless the conditions restrict the person's liberty in a manner and to an extent that prevent them from complying with sections 4, 4.1, 4.3 and 6 of the *Sex Offender Information Registration Act*.

(4) The person in charge of the place in which the person is serving the custodial portion of a sentence, or is detained in custody, before their release or discharge shall give the person a copy of the order not earlier than 10 days before their release or discharge. 2004, c. 10, s. 20; 2007, c. 5, s. 18; 2010, c. 17, s. 11.

CROSS-REFERENCES

"Review Board" is defined in s. 490.011. For other cross-references, see s. 490.012.

Section 119.1 of the *National Defence Act* provides as follows:

> 119.1 Every person who, without reasonable excuse, fails to comply with an order made under section 227.01 of this Act or section 490.012 of the *Criminal Code*, or with an obligation under section 227.06 of this Act or section 490.019 of the *Criminal Code*, is guilty of an offence and on conviction is liable to imprisonment for less than two years or to less punishment.

SYNOPSIS

This section sets out the notice requirements where a court makes an order to comply with registration requirements under the *Sex Offender Information Registration Act*, S.C. 2004, c. 10. Sections 4 to 7 of that Act set out the obligations of the person for reporting to a registration centre and providing information. A copy of the order is to be sent to the place where the person is detained, the Review Board, if applicable, and the police service that charged the offender. The offender is required to endorse the order. This section also places notice obligations on the Review Board. The person in charge of the place where the offender is serving sentence or is detained is required to give the person a copy of the order not earlier than 10 days before the offender's release or discharge.

Notice and Obligation to Comply with the *Sex Offender Information Registration Act* — Convictions Before December 15, 2004

2010, c. 17, s. 12.

OBLIGATION TO COMPLY.

490.019 A person who is served with a notice in Form 53 shall comply with the *Sex Offender Information Registration Act* for the applicable period specified in section 490.022 unless a court makes an exemption order under subsection 490.023(2). 2004, c. 10, s. 20.

CROSS-REFERENCES

Section 4(2) of the *Sex Offender Information Registration Act*, S.C. 2004, c. 10, provides as follows:

> (2) A person who is subject to an obligation under section 490.019 or 490.02901 of the *Criminal Code*, section 227.06 of the *National Defence Act* or section 36.1 of the *International Transfer of Offenders Act* shall report to a registration centre referred to in section 7.1
>
> (*a*) if they are not in custody on the day on which they become subject to the obligation, within seven days — or, if they are required to report to a registration centre designated under the *National Defence Act*, within 15 days — after that day; and
>
> (*b*) in any other case, within seven days — or, if they are required to report to a registration centre designated under the *National Defence Act*, within 15 days — after
>
> (i) they receive an absolute or conditional discharge under Part XX.1 of the *Criminal Code*,
>
> (i.1) they receive an absolute or conditional discharge or are released from custody under Division 7 of Part III of the *National Defence Act*,
>
> (i.2) an imprisonment or a detention to which they are sentenced is suspended under section 215 or 216 of the *National Defence Act*,
>
> (ii) they are released from custody pending the determination of an appeal, or
>
> (iii) they are released from custody after serving the custodial portion of a sentence.

Section 5(*b*) of the *Criminal Records Act*, R.S.C. 1985, c. C-47, provides that the legal restriction imposed by this section continues, notwithstanding that the individual has been granted a pardon under that Act.

Section 490.02 sets out the persons who may be served with a notice. Under s. 490.021, the notice must be served within one year after the day on which the *Sex Offender Information Registration Act* came into force (December 15, 2004). That section sets out the manner of service. Section 490.022 sets out the date that the obligation to comply begins and ends. Section 490.023 allows the person to apply to a court for an exemption order. Section 490.024 provides for an appeal from the refusal to make an exemption order or by the Attorney General from the making of the exemption order. Section 490.025 provides for notice to the person that they have not been granted an exemption order. Under s. 490.026, the person may apply for a termination order under s. 490.027. Section 490.028 deals with the case where the offender is eligible to apply for an exemption order and a termination order. Section 490.029 allows for appeals in relation to termination orders. Section 490.03 deals with disclosure of the material in the database. Section 490.031 creates an offence for failing to comply with an obligation as required by this section. The similar scheme for offenders who have been convicted or found not criminally responsible in relation to offences committed outside Canada is set out in ss. 490.02901 to 490.02911.

SYNOPSIS

This section creates the obligation to comply with the *Sex Offender Information Registration Act*, S.C. 2004, c. 10, for persons who fall within s. 490.02 and have been served with a notice, and the court has not made an exemption order.

ANNOTATIONS

These provisions do not violate ss. 7 or 11 of the Charter: *C. (P.S.) v. British Columbia (Attorney General)* (2007), 222 C.C.C. (3d) 230 (B.C.S.C.); *R. v. B. (C.L.)* (2007), 225 C.C.C. (3d) 237, [2007] 12 W.W.R. 120 (Alta. Q.B.).

The retrospective application of the SOIRA provisions does not offend s. 7 of the Charter: *R. v. Warren* (2010), 254 C.C.C. (3d) 264 (Alta. C.A.).

PERSONS WHO MAY BE SERVED / Exception.

490.02 (1) The Attorney General of a province or minister of justice of a territory may serve a person with a notice only if the person was convicted of, or found not criminally responsible on account of mental disorder for, an offence referred to in paragraph *(a)*, *(c)*, *(c.1)*, *(d)* or *(e)* of the definition "designated offence" in subsection 490.011(1) and

(*a*) on the day on which the *Sex Offender Information Registration Act* comes into force, they are subject to a sentence for, or have not received an absolute discharge under Part XX.1 from, the offence; or

(*b*) in any other case,

(i) their name appears in connection with the offence, immediately before the *Sex Offender Information Registration Act* comes into force, in the sex offender registry established under the Ontario Act, and

(ii) they either were a resident of Ontario at any time between April 23, 2001 and the day on which the *Sex Offender Information Registration Act* comes into force or committed the offence in Ontario.

(2) A notice shall not be served on a person

(*a*) if they have been finally acquitted of, or have received a free pardon granted under Her Majesty's royal prerogative of mercy or under section 748 for, every offence in connection with which a notice may be served on them under section 490.021 of this Act or section 227.08 of the *National Defence Act*;

(*b*) if an application has been made for an order under subsection 490.012(3) of this Act or subsection 227.01(3) of the *National Defence Act* in relation to any offence in connection with which a notice may be served on them under section 490.021 of this Act or section 227.08 of the *National Defence Act*; or

(*c*) who is referred to in paragraph (1)(*b*) if they have provided proof of a pardon in accordance with subsection 9(1) of the Ontario Act. 2004, c. 10, s. 20; 2007, c. 5, s. 20.

CROSS-REFERENCES

"Attorney General" is defined in s. 2. Section 490.021 provides that the notice must be served within one year of the day the *Sex Offender Information Registration Act*, S.C. 2004, c. 10, came into force (December 15, 2004) and sets out the manner of service. Section 490.022 sets out the date that the obligation to comply begins and its duration. Section 490.023 allows the person to apply to a court for an exemption order. Section 490.024 provides for an appeal from the refusal to make an exemption order or by the Attorney General from the making of the exemption order. Section 490.025 provides for notice to the person that they have not been granted an exemption order. Under s. 490.026, the person may apply for a termination order under s. 490.027. Section 490.028 deals with the case where the offender is eligible to apply for an exemption order and a termination order. Section 490.029 allows for appeals in relation to termination orders. Section 490.03 deals with disclosure of the material in the database. Section 490.031 creates an offence for failing to comply with an obligation as required by s. 490.019.

SYNOPSIS

This section deals with cases where the offender is not before a court and therefore not liable to an order made under s. 490.012. Presumably, it was intended to deal with offenders who were dealt with before the *Sex Offender Information Registration Act*, S.C. 2004, c. 10, came into force on December 15, 2004. It sets out two circumstances where a person may be served with a notice to comply with the *Sex Offender Information Registration Act*. The first is where the person was convicted or found not criminally responsible for one of the sexual offences listed in the definition of designated offences in s. 490.011(1)(*a*), (*c*), (*d*) or (*e*) and was still under sentence or had not received an absolute discharge on the day the Act came into force. The second circumstance is where the person's name appears in connection with the offence on the sex offender registry created by the Ontario Act and the person was a resident of Ontario between April 23, 2001 and December 15, 2004. However, the notice shall not be served if the person has received a free pardon, has already been served with a notice under s. 490.012 or, in the case of a person in the Ontario registry, they have provided proof of a pardon in accordance with the Ontario Act. Section 490.012(5) and (6) set out the manner of proof of service.

ANNOTATIONS

The provisions of the *Sex Offender Information Registration Act*, S.C. 2004, c. 10, and these provisions were intended to be retrospective in application and to apply to any convicted offender sentenced after the coming into force of the legislation for an offence that is a designated offence. Further, registration is not a "punishment" so as to trigger the offender's right under s. 11(*i*) of the *Charter of Rights and Freedoms* to the benefit of lesser punishment where the punishment has varied between the time of the commission and the time of sentencing: *R. v. Cross* (2006), 205 C.C.C. (3d) 289, 37 C.R. (6th) 81 (N.S.C.A.), leave to appeal to S.C.C. refused [2006] 2 S.C.R. (3d) vi, 210 C.C.C. (3d) vi; *R. v. C. (S.S.)* (2008), 234 C.C.C. (3d) 365, 59 C.R. (6th) 237 (B.C.C.A.). See also *R. v. B. (C.L.)* (2010), 253 C.C.C. (3d) 486, 477 A.R. 365 (C.A.). Similarly, see *R. v. Dyck* (2005), 203 C.C.C. (3d) 365, 35 C.R. (6th) 56 (Ont. S.C.J.), holding that registration under *Christopher's Law (Sex Offender Registry), 2000*, S.O. 2000, c. 1, is not punishment for the purpose of s. 11(*i*). [Note: also now see *R. v. Rodgers* (2006), 207 C.C.C. (3d) 225, 37 C.R. (6th) 1 (S.C.C.), considering the retroactive application of the DNA data bank provision, s. 487.055.]

Christopher's Law (Sex Offender Registry), 2000, S.O. 2000, c. 1 (the "Ontario Act"), is valid legislation. It is *intra vires* the province, does not violate ss. 7 and 12 of the *Canadian*

Charter of Rights and Freedoms and has not been rendered inoperative by enactment of this Act and the related *Criminal Code* provisions: *R. v. Dyck, supra.*

Someone who is subject to a firearms prohibition under s. 109 is "subject to a sentence" within the meaning of subsec. (1)(*a*): *T. (R.A.) v. British Columbia (Attorney General)* (2011), 277 C.C.C. (3d) 334 (B.C.C.A.).

PERIOD FOR AND METHOD OF SERVICE / Exception / Exception / Exception / Proof of Service / Requirements relating to notice.

490.021 (1) The notice shall be personally served within one year after the day on which the *Sex Offender Information Registration Act* comes into force.

(2) If a person referred to in paragraph 490.02(1)(*a*) is unlawfully at large or is in breach of any terms of their sentence or discharge, or of any conditions set under this Act or under Part III of the *National Defence Act*, that relate to residence, the notice may be served by registered mail at their last known address.

(3) If a person referred to in paragraph 490.02(1)(*b*) is not in compliance with section 3 of the Ontario Act on the day on which the *Sex Offender Information Registration Act* comes into force, the notice may be served by registered mail at their last known address.

(4) If a person referred to in paragraph 490.02(1)(*b*) is in compliance with section 3 and subsection 7(2) of the Ontario Act on the day on which the *Sex Offender Information Registration Act* comes into force but fails to comply with subsection 3(1) or 7(2) of the Ontario Act within one year after that day, the notice shall be served within one year after the day on which they failed to comply and may be served by registered mail at their last known address.

(5) An affidavit of the person who served the notice, sworn before a commissioner or other person authorized to take affidavits, is evidence of the service and the notice if it sets out that

(*a*) the person who served the notice has charge of the appropriate records and has knowledge of the facts in the particular case;

(*b*) the notice was personally served on, or mailed to, the person to whom it was directed on a named day; and

(*c*) the person who served the notice identifies a true copy of the notice as an exhibit attached to the affidavit.

(6) The person who served the notice shall, without delay, send a copy of the affidavit and the notice to the Attorney General of the province, or the minister of justice of the territory, in which the person was served. 2004, c. 10, s. 20; 2007, c. 5, s. 21(2).

CROSS-REFERENCES

"Attorney General" is defined in s. 2. "Pardon" is defined in s. 490.011. Section 490.02 sets out the persons who may be served with a notice to comply with the obligations under s. 490.019. Section 490.022 sets out the date that the obligation to comply begins and its duration. Section 490.023 allows the person to apply to a court for an exemption order. Section 490.024 provides for an appeal from the refusal to make an exemption order or by the Attorney General from the making of the exemption order. Section 490.025 provides for notice to the person that they have not been granted an exemption order. Under s. 490.026, the person may apply for a termination order under s. 490.027. Section 490.028 deals with the case where the offender is eligible to apply for an exemption order and a termination order. Section 490.029 allows for appeals in relation to termination orders. Section 490.03 deals with disclosure of the material in the database. Section 490.031 creates an offence for failing to comply with an obligation as required by s. 490.019.

SYNOPSIS

The notice to comply with the *Sex Offender Information Registration Act*, S.C. 2004, c. 10, must be served within one year after the day on which the Act came into force (December 15, 2004). The notice must be served personally unless the person is unlawfully at large or in breach of the terms of the sentence or discharge or in breach of s. 3 of the Ontario Act, which sets out the times for the offender to report to the police force, in which case service may be effected by registered mail at the last known address. Subsections (5) and (6) provide for proof of service.

DATE OBLIGATION BEGINS / Date obligation ends / Duration of obligation.

490.022 (1) The obligation under section 490.019 begins

(*a*) either one year after the day on which the person is served with the notice or when an exemption order is refused under subsection 490.023(2), whichever is later; or

(*b*) when an exemption order is quashed.

(2) The obligation ends on the earliest of

(*a*) the day on which an exemption order is made on an appeal from a decision made under subsection 490.023(2),

(*b*) the day on which the obligation of a person referred to in paragraph 490.02(1)(*b*) to comply with section 3 of the Ontario Act ends under paragraph 7(1)(*a*) of that Act, or

(*c*) the day on which a person referred to in paragraph 490.02(1)(*b*) provides satisfactory proof of a pardon or record suspension to a person who collects information, as defined in subsection 3(1) of the *Sex Offender Information Registration Act*, at a registration centre.

(3) If none of paragraphs (2)(*a*) to (*c*) applies earlier, the obligation

(*a*) ends 10 years after the person was sentenced, or found not criminally responsible on account of mental disorder, for the offence listed in the notice if the offence was prosecuted summarily or if the maximum term of imprisonment for the offence is two or five years;

(*b*) ends 20 years after the person was sentenced, or found not criminally responsible on account of mental disorder, for the offence listed in the notice if the maximum term of imprisonment for the offence is 10 or 14 years;

(*c*) applies for life if the maximum term of imprisonment for the offence listed in the notice is life; or

(*d*) applies for life if, at any time, the person was convicted of, or found not criminally responsible on account of mental disorder for, more than one offence that is referred to in paragraph (*a*), (*c*), (*c*.1), (*d*) or (*e*) of the definition "designated offence" in subsection 490.011(1) of this Act or in paragraph (*a*) or (*c*) of the definition "designated offence" in section 227 of the *National Defence Act* and if more than one of those offences is listed in the notice. 2004, c. 10, s. 20; 2007, c. 5, s. 22; 2012, c. 1, s. 143.

CROSS-REFERENCES

"Ontario Act", "pardon" and "record suspension" are defined in s. 490.011. Section 490.02 sets out the persons who may be served with a notice to comply with the obligations under s. 490.019. Section 490.023 allows the person to apply to a court for an exemption order. Section 490.024 provides for an appeal from the refusal to make an exemption order or by the Attorney General from the making of the exemption order. Section 490.025 provides for notice to the person that they have not been granted an exemption order. Under s. 490.026, the person may apply for a termination order under s. 490.027. Section 490.028 deals with the case where the offender is eligible to apply for an exemption order and a termination order. Section 490.029 allows for appeals in relation to termination orders. Section 490.03 deals with disclosure of the material in the database. Section 490.031 creates an offence for failing to comply with an obligation as required by s. 490.019.

SYNOPSIS

This section sets out the length of the obligation to comply with the relevant provisions of the *Sex Offender Information Registration Act*, S.C. 2004, c. 10, in accordance with s. 490.019. The obligation begins one year after the date of service with the notice of the obligation or when a court decides not to make an exemption order, whichever is later, or when an exemption order is quashed. The obligation ends when an exemption order is made, when the obligation of a person who is registered under the Ontario Act ends, or the person provides proof of a pardon or record suspension. Subsection (3) sets out the duration of the obligation to comply.

APPLICATION FOR EXEMPTION ORDER / Jurisdiction / Exemption order / Reasons for decision / Removal of information from database.

490.023 (1) A person who is not subject to an order under section 490.012 of this Act or section 227.01 of the *National Defence Act* may apply for an order exempting them from the obligation within one year after they are served with a notice under section 490.021 of this Act or section 227.08 of the *National Defence Act*.

(1.1) The application shall be made to a court of criminal jurisdiction if

(*a*) it relates to an obligation under section 490.019 of this Act; or

(*b*) it relates to an obligation under section 227.06 of the *National Defence Act* and the Chief Military Judge does not have jurisdiction to receive the application under subsection 227.1(2) of that Act.

(2) The court shall make an exemption order if it is satisfied that the person has established that the impact of the obligation on them, including on their privacy or liberty, would be grossly disproportionate to the public interest in protecting society through the effective prevention or investigation of crimes of a sexual nature, to be achieved by the registration of information relating to sex offenders under the *Sex Offender Information Registration Act*.

(3) The court shall give reasons for its decision.

(4) If the court makes an exemption order, it shall also make an order requiring the Royal Canadian Mounted Police to permanently remove from the database all information that relates to the person that was registered in the database on receipt of the copy of the notice. 2004, c. 10, s. 20; 2007, c. 5, s. 23; 2010, c. 17, s. 13.

CROSS-REFERENCES

"Court of criminal jurisdiction" is defined in s. 2. "Database" is defined in s. 490.011. Section 490.02 sets out the persons who may be served with a notice to comply with the obligations under s. 490.019. Section 490.022 sets out the date that the obligation to comply begins and its duration. Section 490.024 provides for an appeal from the refusal to make an exemption order or by the Attorney General from the making of the exemption order. Section 490.025 provides for notice to the person that they have not been granted an exemption order. Under s. 490.026, the person may apply for a termination order under s. 490.027. Section 490.028 deals with the case where the offender is eligible to apply for an exemption order and a termination order. Section 490.029 allows for appeals in relation to termination orders. Section 490.03 deals with disclosure of the material in the database. Section 490.031 creates an offence for failing to comply with an obligation as required by s. 490.019.

SYNOPSIS

This section provides that a person may apply for an order exempting them from complying with an obligation under s. 490.019. The application must be brought within one year from the date they were served with the notice of the obligation. Subsection (2) sets out the test the court is to apply in deciding whether to make the order. The court is required to give reasons for the decision. If the court makes the exemption order, they are also required to remove all information from the database relating to the person.

ANNOTATIONS

The court has no power to make a partial exemption order, such as an order relieving the offender from complying with the temporarily absent reporting conditions in s. 6 of the *Sex Offender Information Registration Act*. The fact that there is no such power may be taken into account in considering the impact the order would have on the applicant's ability to seek more remunerative employment in the long distance trucking industry. In considering whether to make an exemption order, it is open to the court to consider the broader public interest including the public interest in rehabilitation, which might be impaired by the reporting requirements: *R. v. W. (G.E.)* (2006), 396 A.R. 149 (Q.B.).

There is no jurisdiction to alter the duration of the order: *R. v. R. (M.J.)* (2007), 224 C.C.C. (3d) 80, 257 N.S.R. (2d) 120 (C.A.).

APPEAL / Removal of information from database.

490.024 (1) The Attorney General or the person who applied for an exemption order may appeal from a decision of the court under subsection 490.023(2) on any ground of appeal that raises a question of law or of mixed law and fact. The appeal court may dismiss the appeal, or allow it and order a new hearing, quash the exemption order or make an order that may be made under that subsection.

(2) If the appeal court makes an exemption order, it shall also make an order requiring the Royal Canadian Mounted Police to permanently remove from the database all information that relates to the person that was registered in the database on receipt of the copy of the notice. 2004, c. 10, s. 20; 2010, c. 17, s. 14.

CROSS-REFERENCES

"Attorney General" is defined in s. 2. Section 490.02 sets out the persons who may be served with a notice to comply with the obligations under s. 490.019. Section 490.022 sets out the date that the obligation to comply begins and its duration. Section 490.023 allows the person to apply to a court for an exemption order. Section 490.025 provides for notice to the person that they have not been granted an exemption order. Under s. 490.026, the person may apply for a termination order under s. 490.027. Section 490.028 deals with the case where the offender is eligible to apply for an exemption order and a termination order. Section 490.029 allows for appeals in relation to termination orders. Section 490.03 deals with disclosure of the material in the database. Section 490.031 creates an offence for failing to comply with an obligation as required by s. 490.019.

SYNOPSIS

This section creates a right of appeal in the Attorney General or the person who applied for the exemption. The appeal is limited to questions of law or mixed law and fact.

ANNOTATIONS

Section 487.054 provides for appeals in relation to making of DNA orders. Like this section, it does not specify the appeal court. In *R. v. Hendry* (2001), 161 C.C.C. (3d) 275, 48 C.R. (5th) 310 (Ont. C.A.), the court held that the appeal route follows the scheme in the *Criminal Code* generally. That is, in indictable proceedings, the appeal from the making or refusal to make the order lies to the Court of Appeal and, in summary conviction proceedings, the appeal is taken in accordance with Part XXVII of the *Criminal Code*.

REQUIREMENTS RELATING TO NOTICE.

490.025 If a court refuses to make an exemption order or an appeal court dismisses an appeal from such a decision or quashes an exemption order, it shall cause the Commissioner of the Royal Canadian Mounted Police and the Attorney General of the province, or the minister of justice of the territory, in which the application for the order was made to be notified of the decision and shall cause the person who applied for the order to be informed of sections 4 to 7.1 of the *Sex Offender Information Registration Act*, sections 490.031 and 490.0311 of this Act and section 119.1 of the *National Defence Act*. 2004, c. 10, s. 20; 2007, c. 5, s. 24; 2010, c. 17, s. 15.

CROSS-REFERENCES

Section 490.02 sets out the persons who may be served with a notice to comply with the obligations under s. 490.019. Section 490.022 sets out the date that the obligation to comply begins and its duration. Section 490.023 allows the person to apply to a court for an exemption order. Section 490.024 provides for an appeal from the refusal to make an exemption order or by the Attorney General from the making of the exemption order. Under s. 490.026, the person may apply for a termination order under s. 490.027. Section 490.028 deals with the case where the offender is eligible to apply for an exemption order and a termination order. Section 490.029 allows for appeals in relation to termination orders. Section 490.03 deals with disclosure of the material in the database. Section 490.031 creates an offence for failing to comply with an obligation as required by s. 490.019.

SYNOPSIS

This section provides the mechanism to ensure that the person who has been unsuccessful either at first instance or on appeal in an application for an exemption order is notified of the result and of their obligation to therefore comply with the relevant provisions of the *Sex Offender Information Registration Act*, S.C. 2004, c. 10, and that it is an offence under s. 490.031 not to comply.

APPLICATION FOR TERMINATION ORDER / Time for application / More than one offence / Pardon or record suspension / Re-application / Jurisdiction.

490.026 (1) A person who is subject to an obligation under section 490.019 may apply for a termination order unless they are also subject to an obligation under section 490.02901, under section 227.06 of the *National Defence Act* or under section 36.1 of the *International Transfer of Offenders Act* — or an order under section 490.012 or under section 227.01 of the *National Defence Act* — that began later.

(2) A person may apply for a termination order if the following period has elapsed since they were sentenced, or found not criminally responsible on account of mental disorder, for an offence referred to in paragraph (*a*), (*c*), (*c*.1), (*d*) or (*e*) of the definition "designated offence" in subsection 490.011(1) of this Act or in paragraph (*a*) or (*c*) of the definition "designated offence" in section 227 of the *National Defence Act*:

- **(*a*) five years if the offence was prosecuted summarily or if the maximum term of imprisonment for the offence is two or five years;**
- **(*b*) 10 years if the maximum term of imprisonment for the offence is 10 or 14 years; or**
- **(*c*) 20 years if the maximum term of imprisonment for the offence is life.**

(3) If more than one offence is listed in the notice served under section 490.021, the person may apply for a termination order if 20 years have elapsed since they were sentenced, or found not criminally responsible on account of mental disorder, for the most recent offence referred to in paragraph (*a*), (*c*), (*c*.1), (*d*) or (*e*) of the definition "designated offence" in subsection 490.011(1) of this Act or in paragraph (*a*) or (*c*) of the definition "designated offence" in section 227 of the *National Defence Act*.

(4) Despite subsections (2) and (3), a person may apply for a termination order once they receive a pardon or once a record suspension is ordered.

(5) A person whose application is refused may apply again if five years have elapsed since they made the previous application. They may also apply again once they receive a pardon or once a record suspension is ordered. However, they may not apply again if, after the previous application was made, they become subject to an obligation under section 490.02901, under section 227.06 of the *National Defence Act* or under section 36.1 of the *International Transfer of Offenders Act* or to an order under section 490.012 or under section 227.01 of the *National Defence Act*.

(6) The application shall be made to a court of criminal jurisdiction if

(*a*) it relates to an obligation under section 490.019 of this Act; or

(*b*) it relates to an obligation under section 227.06 of the *National Defence Act* and the Chief Military Judge does not have jurisdiction to receive the application under subsection 227.12(6) of that Act. 2004, c. 10, s. 20; 2007, c. 5, s. 24; 2010, c. 17, s. 16; 2012, c. 1, s. 144.

CROSS-REFERENCES

"Court of criminal jurisdiction" is defined in s. 2. "Pardon" and "record suspension" are defined in s. 490.011. Section 490.02 sets out the persons who may be served with a notice to comply with the obligations under s. 490.019. Section 490.022 sets out the date that the obligation to comply begins and its duration. Section 490.023 allows the person to apply to a court for an exemption order. Section 490.024 provides for an appeal from the refusal to make an exemption order or by the Attorney General from the making of the exemption order. Section 490.025 provides for notice to the person that they have not been granted an exemption order. The termination order is made under s. 490.027. Section 490.028 deals with the case where the offender is eligible to apply for an exemption order and a termination order. Section 490.029 allows for appeals in relation to termination orders. Section 490.03 deals with disclosure of the material in the database. Section 490.031 creates an offence for failing to comply with an obligation as required by s. 490.019. Pursuant to s. 490.015(3), a person who is subject to an obligation under s. 490.019 and has applied for a termination order under s. 490.015 must include an application to terminate the obligation as well.

SYNOPSIS

This section sets out the circumstances in which the person may apply for an order terminating the obligation under s. 490.019. The person cannot be subject to an order under s. 490.012. (If they are, they must apply under s. 490.015 to terminate the order and the obligation.) Subsection (2) sets out the times when the application may be made. Where the person has committed more than one offence, they can only apply to terminate the obligation after 20 years from the date when they were sentenced or found not criminally responsible, pursuant to subsec. (3). The person may reapply after five years from the date of the application or if they have received a pardon or record suspension, unless in the interim they became subject to an obligation under s. 490.02901 for offences committed outside Canada or obligations or orders made under certain provisions of the *National Defence Act*, R.S.C. 1985, c. N-5, or the *International Transfer of Offenders Act*, S.C. 2004, c. 21.

TERMINATION ORDER / Reasons for decision / Requirements relating to notice.

490.027 (1) The court shall make an order terminating the obligation if it is satisfied that the person has established that the impact on them of continuing the obligation, including on their privacy or liberty, would be grossly disproportionate to the public interest in protecting society through the effective prevention or investigation of crimes of a sexual nature, to be achieved by the registration of information relating to sex offenders under the *Sex Offender Information Registration Act*.

(2) The court shall give reasons for its decision.

(3) If the court makes a termination order, it shall cause the Commissioner of the Royal Canadian Mounted Police and the Attorney General of the province, or the minister of justice of the territory, to be notified of the decision. 2004, c. 10, s. 20; 2007, c. 5, s. 25; 2010, c. 17, s. 17.

CROSS-REFERENCES

"Crime of a sexual nature" is defined in s. 490.011. Section 490.02 sets out the persons who may be served with a notice to comply with the obligations under s. 490.019. Section 490.022 sets out the date that the obligation to comply begins and its duration. Section 490.023 allows the person to apply to a court for an exemption order. Section 490.024 provides for an appeal from the refusal to make an exemption order or by the Attorney General from the making of the exemption order. Section 490.025 provides for notice to the person that they have not been granted an exemption order. Under s. 490.026, the person may apply for a termination order under this section. Section 490.028 deals with the case where the offender is eligible to apply for an exemption order and a termination order. Section 490.029 allows for appeals in relation to termination orders. Section 490.03 deals with disclosure of the material in the database. Section 490.031 creates an offence for failing to comply with an obligation as required by s. 490.019.

SYNOPSIS

This section sets out the circumstances in which the court may make an order terminating the obligation. The test is whether the impact of continuing the obligation would be grossly disproportionate to the public interest in the protection of society through the effective prevention or investigation of crimes of a sexual nature to be achieved through registration.

ANNOTATIONS

Note: The following cases were decided under s. 490.012(4) which, at that time, gave a judge a discretion to refuse to initially make an order requiring compliance with the *Sex Offender Information Registration Act*, S.C. 2004, c. 10. That discretion has now been removed. Notes of the following decisions have been included because s. 490.012(4) was worded similarly to the present s. 490.027(1), although the latter now specifically refers to the importance of protecting society through prevention of crimes of a sexual nature, whereas former s. 490.012(4) only referred to investigation of such crimes.

The standard of "grossly disproportionate" is very high. While registration will have some impact on the offender's privacy, this must be balanced against the purpose of the legislation and its confidentiality requirements. The purpose of registration is not to identify sex offenders to the community but, in accordance with this section, to help police services investigate crimes of a sexual nature by requiring the registration of certain information relating to sex offenders. The provisions of the *Sex Offender Information Registration Act* indicate an intention to keep information collected confidential and for use only by those with a legitimate reason in keeping with the purposes of investigation of crime and protection of society: *R. v. Casaway* (2005), 64 W.C.B. (2d) 610 (N.W.T.S.C.). Similarly, *R. v. Clarke* (2005), 197 C.C.C. (3d) 443 (N.S.S.C.), affd 208 C.C.C. (3d) 243 (N.S.C.A.), and *R. v. S. (L.)* (2005), 78 W.C.B. (2d) 378 (B.C. Prov. Ct.).

The impact to be assessed is the impact of the registration requirements on the offender's current and prospective circumstances. This includes a consideration of the impact of registration on the offender's privacy and liberty interests. The evidence upon which the convicted offender may rely to invoke and satisfy the exception may emerge from the trial or sentencing proceedings. Relevant factors include the nature of the offence, the risk to re-offend, the offender's criminal record and other matters personal to the offender's circumstances. The registration is not limited, however, to likely recidivism and the diminished risk of recidivism is not a basis to enhance the impact on the offender or dilute the public interest in registration: *R. v. Debidin* (2008), 241 C.C.C. (3d) 152 (Ont. C.A.).

The focus on the inquiry must be on the offender's present and possible future circumstances and not on the offence itself. In considering whether the order would be grossly disproportionate, the court must assess the impact of the order on the offender, including the impact on his privacy and liberty interests, and determine whether that impact is grossly disproportionate to the public interest. Factors that may be considered include unique individual circumstances such as a personal handicap, which would require the offender to obtain assistance to report, intangible effects such as stigma, undermining rehabilitation and reintegration in the community, and whether the order might result in police harassment. Absent disproportional impact, the length of the reporting obligation alone does not constitute gross disproportionality: *R. v. Redhead* (2006), 206 C.C.C. (3d) 315 (Alta. C.A.), leave to appeal to S.C.C. refused [2006] 2 S.C.R. x, 210 C.C.C. (3d) vi.

DEEMED APPLICATION.

490.028 If a person is eligible to apply for both an exemption order under section 490.023 and a termination order under section 490.026 within one year after they are served with a notice under section 490.021 of this Act or section 227.08 of the *National Defence Act*, an application within that period for one order is deemed to be an application for both. 2004, c. 10, s. 20; 2007, c. 5, s. 26.

CROSS-REFERENCES

Section 490.02 sets out the persons who may be served with a notice to comply with the obligations under s. 490.019. Section 490.022 sets out the date that the obligation to comply begins and its duration. Section 490.023 allows the person to apply to a court for an exemption order. Section 490.024 provides for an appeal from the refusal to make an exemption order or by the Attorney General from the making of the exemption order. Section 490.025 provides for notice to the person that they have not been granted an exemption order. Under s. 490.026, the person may apply for a termination order under s. 490.027. Section 490.029 allows for appeals in relation to termination orders. Section 490.03 deals with disclosure of the material in the database. Section 490.031 creates an offence for failing to comply with an obligation as required by s. 490.019.

SYNOPSIS

It would seem that this section is designed to avoid duplication of applications. Thus, a person who is eligible for an exemption order and a termination order within one year after they were served with a notice of an obligation to comply with the provisions of the *Sex Offender Registration Act*, S.C. 2004, c. 10, is deemed to have applied for both orders.

APPEAL / Requirements relating to notice.

490.029 (1) The Attorney General or the person who applied for a termination order may appeal from a decision of the court made under subsection 490.027(1) on any ground of appeal that raises a question of law or of mixed law and fact. The appeal court may dismiss the appeal, or allow it and order a new hearing, quash the termination order or make an order that may be made under that subsection.

(2) If the appeal court makes an order that may be made under subsection 490.027(1), it shall cause the Commissioner of the Royal Canadian Mounted Police and the Attorney General of the province, or the minister of justice of the territory, in which the application for the order was made to be notified of the decision. 2004, c. 10, s. 20; 2007, c. 5, s. 26; 2010, c. 17, s. 18.

CROSS-REFERENCES

Section 490.02 sets out the persons who may be served with a notice to comply with the obligations under s. 490.019. Section 490.022 sets out the date that the obligation to comply begins and its duration. Section 490.023 allows the person to apply to a court for an exemption order. Section 490.024 provides for an appeal from the refusal to make an exemption order or by the Attorney General from the making of the exemption order. Section 490.025 provides for notice to the person that they have not been granted an exemption order. Under s. 490.026, the person may apply for a termination order under s. 490.027. Section 490.028 deals with the case where the offender is eligible to apply for an exemption order and a termination order. Section 490.03 deals with disclosure of the material in the database. Section 490.031 creates an offence for failing to comply with an obligation as required by s. 490.019.

SYNOPSIS

This section creates a right of appeal in the Attorney General or the person who applied for a termination order. The appeal is limited to questions of law or mixed law and fact.

ANNOTATIONS

Section 487.054 provides for appeals in relation to making of DNA orders. Like this section, it does not specify the appeal court. In *R. v. Hendry* (2001), 161 C.C.C. (3d) 275, 48 C.R. (5th) 310 (Ont. C.A.), the court held that the appeal route follows the scheme in the *Criminal Code* generally. That is, in indictable proceedings, the appeal from the making or refusal to make the order lies to the Court of Appeal and, in summary conviction proceedings, the appeal is taken in accordance with Part XXVII of the *Criminal Code*.

Notice and Obligation to Comply with the *Sex Offender Information Registration Act* — Convictions Outside Canada

OBLIGATION.

490.02901 A person who is served with a notice in Form 54 shall comply with the *Sex Offender Information Registration Act* for the applicable period specified in section 490.02904 unless a court makes an exemption order under subsection 490.02905(2). 2010, c. 17, s. 19.

CROSS-REFERENCES

Sections 490.02901 to 490.02911 establish a scheme requiring registration under the *Sex Offender Information Registration Act*, S.C. 2004, c. 10, for offences committed outside Canada. The scheme is, in many ways, similar to the scheme obliging persons who were convicted of offences before the Act came into force to register. Thus, see Cross-References under s. 490.019. The basic scheme for making an order against a person convicted or found not criminally responsible of a designated offence in Canada is set out in ss. 490.012 to 490.018.

This section sets out the basic obligation to comply with the Act for a person convicted or found not criminal responsible on account of mental disorder of an offence outside Canada that is, in the opinion of the Attorney General or minister of justice, equivalent to an offence referred to in para. (*a*) of the definition of designated offence in s. 490.011(1). Section 4(2) of the *Sex Offender Information Registration Act*, provides as follows:

(2) A person who is subject to an obligation under section 490.019 or 490.02901 of the *Criminal Code*, section 227.06 of the *National Defence Act* or section 36.1 of the *International Transfer of Offenders Act* shall report to a registration centre referred to in section 7.1

(*a*) if they are not in custody on the day on which they become subject to the obligation, within seven days — or, if they are required to report to a registration centre designated under the *National Defence Act*, within 15 days — after that day; and

(*b*) in any other case, within seven days — or, if they are required to report to a registration centre designated under the *National Defence Act*, within 15 days — after

(i) they receive an absolute or conditional discharge under Part XX.1 of the *Criminal Code*,

(i.1) they receive an absolute or conditional discharge or are released from custody under Division 7 of Part III of the *National Defence Act*,

(i.2) an imprisonment or a detention to which they are sentenced is suspended under section 215 or 216 of the *National Defence Act*,
(ii) they are released from custody pending the determination of an appeal, or
(iii) they are released from custody after serving the custodial portion of a sentence.

Failure to comply with the obligation is an offence under s. 490.031. Section 490.02902 sets out the persons who may be served with the obligation. In short, it is persons convicted of or found not criminally responsible on account of mental disorder for an offence outside Canada that is, in the opinion of the Attorney General or minister of justice, equivalent to an offence referred to in para. (*a*) of the definition of designated offence in s. 490.011(1). Section 490.02903 sets out the notice requirements for complying with the obligation. Section 490.02904 sets out the time frame for the length of the reporting obligations. The person may apply for an order exempting them from an obligation to register under the Act within one year after they are served. Section 490.02905 sets out the circumstances under which a court is to make an exemption order. Section 490.02906(1) provides a right of appeal by the Attorney General or the person who applied for the exemption. Sections 490.02906(2) and 490.02907 set out the consequences of an appeal. Section 490.02908 gives a person subject to an obligation the right to apply for a termination order. That section sets out when the person may apply for the termination order. Section 490.02909 sets out the test the court is to apply in deciding whether to make the order. An appeal from the decision under s. 490.02909 is taken in accordance with s. 490.0291. Section 490.02911 places an obligation on a person who was convicted or found not criminally responsible of an equivalent offence to advise the police within seven days after they arrive in Canada of their name and other identifying information. The failure to comply with the obligation under that section is an offence under s. 490.0312.

SYNOPSIS

This section sets out the obligation of a person, who has been convicted or found not criminally responsible of the equivalent of designated offence, and is served with a notice to comply with the *Sex Offender Information Registration Act*. The person must comply unless a court makes an exemption order under s. 490.02905(2).

PERSONS WHO MAY BE SERVED / Exception.

490.02902 (1) The Attorney General of a province, or the minister of justice of a territory, may serve a person with a notice in Form 54 only if the person arrived in Canada after the coming into force of this subsection and they were convicted of or found not criminally responsible on account of mental disorder for an offence outside Canada — other than a service offence as defined in subsection 2(1) of the *National Defence Act* — that is, in the opinion of the Attorney General or minister of justice, equivalent to an offence referred to in paragraph (*a*) of the definition "designated offence" in subsection 490.011(1).

(2) The notice shall not be served on a person who has been acquitted of every offence in connection with which a notice may be served on them under section 490.02903. 2010, c. 17, s. 19.

CROSS-REFERENCES

"Attorney General" is defined in s. 2. For other Cross-References, see s. 490.02901.

SYNOPSIS

This section sets out which persons, convicted or found not criminal responsible of offences outside Canada, may be served with an obligation to comply with the *Sex Offender Information Registration Act*, S.C. 2004, c. 10. A person may be served with the notice only if they entered Canada after this section came into force on April 15, 2011 and the person has been convicted or found not criminally responsible of the equivalent of a designated offence, in the opinion of the Attorney General of the province or the minister of justice of the territory.

PERIOD FOR AND METHOD OF SERVICE / Proof of service / Requirements relating to notice.

490.02903 (1) A notice in Form 54 shall be personally served.

(2) An affidavit of the person who served the notice, sworn before a commissioner or other person authorized to take affidavits, is evidence of the service and the notice if it sets out that

- **(*a*) the person who served the notice has charge of the appropriate records and has knowledge of the facts in the particular case;**
- **(*b*) the notice was personally served on the person to whom it was directed on a named day; and**
- **(*c*) the person who served the notice identifies a true copy of the notice as an exhibit attached to the affidavit.**

(3) The person who served the notice shall, without delay, send a copy of the affidavit and the notice to the Attorney General of the province, or the minister of justice of the territory, in which the person was served. 2010, c. 17, s. 19.

CROSS-REFERENCES

"Attorney General" is defined in s. 2. For other Cross-References, see s. 490.02901.

SYNOPSIS

This section sets out the notice requirements for compliance with the *Sex Offender Information Registration Act*, S.C. 2004, c. 10, for persons, convicted or found not criminally responsible, of offences outside Canada of the equivalent of a designated offence. There must be personal service in accordance with subsec. (1). Subsection (2) provides for an affidavit of service, which is to be sent to the Attorney General of the province or minister of justice pursuant to subsec. (3).

WHEN OBLIGATION BEGINS / When obligation ends / Duration of obligation.

490.02904 (1) The obligation under section 490.02901 begins on the day on which the person is served with the notice.

(2) The obligation ends on the day on which an exemption order is made.

(3) If subsection (2) does not apply, the obligation

- **(*a*) ends 10 years after the person was sentenced or found not criminally responsible on account of mental disorder if the maximum term of imprisonment provided for in Canadian law for the equivalent offence is two or five years;**
- **(*b*) ends 20 years after the person was sentenced or found not criminally responsible on account of mental disorder if the maximum term of imprisonment provided for in Canadian law for the equivalent offence is 10 or 14 years;**
- **(*c*) applies for life if the maximum term of imprisonment provided for in Canadian law for the equivalent offence is life; or**
- **(*d*) applies for life if, before or after the coming into force of this paragraph, the person was convicted of, or found not criminally responsible on account of mental disorder for, more than one offence referred to in paragraph (*a*), (*c*), (*c*.1), (*d*), (*d*.1) or (*e*) of the definition "designated offence" in subsection 490.011(1) or referred to in paragraph (*a*) or (*c*) of the definition "designated**

offence" in section 227 of the *National Defence Act* and if more than one of those offences is listed in the notice. 2010, c. 17, s. 19; 2014, c. 25, s. 28.

CROSS-REFERENCES

For Cross-References, see s. 490.02901.

SYNOPSIS

This section sets out the length of the obligation for compliance with the *Sex Offender Information Registration Act*, S.C. 2004, c. 10, for persons convicted or found not criminally responsible of offences outside Canada of the equivalent of a designated offence. The obligation to comply begins on the day the person is served with the notice and ends when an exemption order is made, or if no exemption order is made, after expiration of the times set out in subsec. (3): 10 years after the person was sentenced or found not criminally responsible if the maximum penalty for the equivalent Canadian offence is imprisonment for two or five years; 20 years after the person was sentenced or found not criminally responsible if the maximum penalty for the equivalent Canadian offence is imprisonment for 10 or 14 years; life if the maximum term for the equivalent Canadian offence is life imprisonment; and life if the person was convicted or found not criminally responsible for more than one offence referred to in paras. (*a*), (*c*), (*d*), (*d*.1) or (*e*) of the definition of designated offence in s. 490.011(1) or similar offences in the *National Defence Act*, R.S.C. 1985, c. N-5.

APPLICATION FOR EXEMPTION ORDER / Exemption order / Reasons for decision / Removal of information from database / Notification.

490.02905 (1) A person who is served with a notice in Form 54 under section 490.02903 may apply to a court of criminal jurisdiction for an order exempting them from the obligation within one year after they are served.

(2) The court

(*a*) shall make an exemption order if it is satisfied that the person has established that

(i) they were not convicted of or found not criminally responsible on account of mental disorder for or were acquitted of the offence in question, or

(ii) the offence in question is not equivalent to an offence referred to in paragraph (*a*) of the definition "designated offence" in subsection 490.011(1); and

(*b*) shall order that the notice be corrected if it is satisfied that the offence in question is not equivalent to the offence referred to in the notice but is equivalent to another offence referred to in paragraph (*a*) of the definition "designated offence" in subsection 490.011(1).

(3) The court shall give reasons for its decision.

(4) If the court makes an exemption order, it shall also make an order requiring the Royal Canadian Mounted Police to permanently remove from the database all information that relates to the person that was registered in the database on receipt of the copy of the notice.

(5) If the court makes an order referred to in paragraph (2)(*b*), it shall cause the Commissioner of the Royal Canadian Mounted Police and the Attorney General of the province, or the minister of justice of the territory, in which the application for the order was made to be notified of the decision. 2010, c. 17, s. 19.

CROSS-REFERENCES

An appeal from a decision under this section is provided for in s. 490.02906. For other Cross-References, see s. 490.02901.

SYNOPSIS

This section sets out the process for an offender, who has been served with a s. 490.02903 notice, to apply for an exemption from the registration requirements under the *Sex Offender Information Registration Act*, S.C. 2004, c. 10, in relation to offences committed outside Canada. The application must be made within one year after the person was served with the notice. Subsection (2) sets out two grounds for the exemption order, namely: the person was not convicted or not found criminally responsible or acquitted of the offence, or the offence is not an equivalent of a designated offence as defined in s. 490.011(1). Alternatively, the court may correct the notice if the person was convicted of an equivalent offence, although not the one named in the notice. The court is required to give reasons for its decision. Subsections (3) and (4) set out the process for either removing the person's information from the database or correcting the record.

APPEAL / Removal of information from database.

490.02906 (1) The Attorney General or the person who applied for an exemption order may appeal from a decision under subsection 490.02905(2) on any ground of appeal that raises a question of law or of mixed law and fact. The appeal court may

(*a*) dismiss the appeal;

(*b*) allow the appeal and order a new hearing;

(*c*) quash the exemption order; or

(*d*) make an order that may be made under that subsection.

(2) If an appeal court makes an exemption order, it shall also make an order requiring the Royal Canadian Mounted Police to permanently remove from the database all information that relates to the person that was registered in the database on receipt of the copy of the notice. 2010, c. 17, s. 19.

CROSS-REFERENCES

"Attorney General" is defined in s. 2. For other Cross-References, see s. 490.02901.

SYNOPSIS

This section provides for an appeal from an order granting or refusing an exemption order in relation to an obligation to comply with the *Sex Offender Information Registration Act*, S.C. 2004, c. 10, in relation to offences committed outside Canada. The person or the Attorney General may appeal on any ground of law or mixed law and fact. The appellate court may dismiss the appeal, allow the appeal and order a new hearing, quash the exemption order or make any order, such as an exemption order or an order correcting the notice, that the court at first instance could have made. If the court makes an exemption order it must also make an order requiring the R.C.M.P. to permanently remove all information from the database. Section 490.02907 sets out the requirements for notifying the police and the Attorney General or minister of justice, if the appeal court quashes the exemption order.

REQUIREMENTS RELATING TO NOTICE.

490.02907 If an appeal court quashes an exemption order, it shall cause the Commissioner of the Royal Canadian Mounted Police and the Attorney General of the province, or the minister of justice of the territory, in which the application for the order was made to be notified of the decision and shall cause the person who applied for the order to be informed of sections 4 to 7.1 of the *Sex Offender Information Registration Act*, sections 490.031 and 490.0311 of this Act and section 119.1 of the *National Defence Act*. 2010, c. 17, s. 19.

CROSS-REFERENCES
"Attorney General" is defined in s. 2. If the court makes an exemption order, the process for notifying the R.C.M.P. is set out in s. 490.02906(2). For other Cross-References, see s. 490.02901.

APPLICATION FOR TERMINATION ORDER / Time for application — one offence / Time for application — more than one offence / Re-application.

490.02908 (1) A person who is subject to an obligation under section 490.02901 may apply to a court of criminal jurisdiction for a termination order unless they are also subject to another obligation under that section — or to an obligation under section 490.019, under section 227.06 of the *National Defence Act* or under section 36.1 of the *International Transfer of Offenders Act* or an order under section 490.012 or under section 227.01 of the *National Defence Act* — that began later.

(2) The person may apply for a termination order if the following period has elapsed since the sentence was imposed or the verdict of not criminally responsible on account of mental disorder was rendered:

- **(*a*) five years if the maximum term of imprisonment provided for in Canadian law for the equivalent offence is two or five years;**
- **(*b*) 10 years if the maximum term of imprisonment provided for in Canadian law for the equivalent offence is 10 or 14 years; or**
- **(*c*) 20 years if the maximum term of imprisonment provided for in Canadian law for the equivalent offence is life.**

(3) If more than one offence is listed in the notice served under section 490.02903, the person may apply for a termination order if 20 years have elapsed since the sentence was imposed, or the verdict of not criminally responsible on account of mental disorder was rendered, for the most recent offence.

(4) A person whose application is refused may apply again if five years have elapsed since the application was made. 2010, c. 17, s. 19.

CROSS-REFERENCES
If the person is subject to other obligations or orders to comply with the *Sex Offender Information Registration Act*, S.C. 2004, c. 10, in addition to an obligation for offences committed outside Canada, the application for a termination order must be made under s. 490.015. "Court of criminal jurisdiction" is defined in s. 2. The test for making a termination order is set out in s. 490.02909. An appeal from an order made under s. 490.02909 is provided for in s. 490.0291. For other Cross-References, see s. 490.02901.

SYNOPSIS

This section allows a person, subject only to an obligation under s. 490.02901 to comply with the provisions of the *Sex Offender Information Registration Act* for offences committed outside Canada, to terminate the obligation. When the person may apply depends upon the nature of the equivalent Canadian offence. The person may apply five years after the person was sentenced or found not criminally responsible if the maximum penalty for the equivalent Canadian offence is imprisonment for two or five years; 10 years after the person was sentenced or found not criminally responsible if the maximum penalty for the equivalent Canadian offence is imprisonment for 10 or 14 years; 20 years if the maximum term for the equivalent Canadian offence is life imprisonment or if more than one offence is listed in the notice. A person whose application is refused may apply again in five years.

TERMINATION ORDER / Reasons for decision / Requirements relating to notice.

490.02909 (1) The court shall make an order terminating the obligation if it is satisfied that the person has established that the impact on them of continuing the obligation, including on their privacy or liberty, would be grossly disproportionate to the public

interest in protecting society through the effective prevention or investigation of crimes of a sexual nature to be achieved by the registration of information relating to sex offenders under the *Sex Offender Information Registration Act*.

(2) The court shall give reasons for its decision.

(3) If the court makes a termination order, it shall cause the Commissioner of the Royal Canadian Mounted Police and the Attorney General of the province, or the minister of justice of the territory, to be notified of the decision. 2010, c. 17, s. 19.

CROSS-REFERENCES

If the person is subject to other obligations or orders to comply with the *Sex Offender Information Registration Act*, S.C. 2004, c. 10, in addition to an obligation for offences committed outside Canada, the application for a termination order must be made under s. 490.015. An appeal from an order made under this section is provided for in s. 490.0291. The test for making a termination order under this section is similar to the test for making similar orders under s. 490.015. Accordingly, see Cross-References and Annotations under that section. For other Cross-References, see s. 490.02901.

SYNOPSIS

This section sets out the test for making an order terminating obligations under the *Sex Offender Information Registration Act* in relation to offences committed outside Canada. The test is set out in subsec. (1). The court is required to give reasons for the decision. If the termination order is made, the court is required to notify the Commissioner of the R.C.M.P. accordingly.

APPEAL / Requirements relating to notice.

490.0291 (1) The Attorney General or the person who applied for a termination order may appeal from a decision under subsection 490.02909(1) on any ground of appeal that raises a question of law or of mixed law and fact. The appeal court may dismiss the appeal, allow the appeal and order a new hearing, quash the termination order or make an order that may be made under that subsection.

(2) If the appeal court makes an order that may be made under subsection 490.02909(1), it shall cause the Commissioner of the Royal Canadian Mounted Police and the Attorney General of the province, or the minister of justice of the territory, in which the application for the order was made to be notified of the decision. 2010, c. 17, s. 19.

CROSS-REFERENCES

"Attorney General" is defined in s. 2. The basis for an appeal under this section is similar to the appeal from similar orders made under s. 490.017. Accordingly, see Cross-References and Annotations under that section. For other Cross-References, see s. 490.02901.

SYNOPSIS

This section sets out the grounds of appeal for a decision made on an application for an order terminating obligations to comply with the *Sex Offender Information Registration Act*, S.C. 2004, c. 10, in relation to offences committed outside Canada. The applicant and the Attorney General may appeal on any ground of law or mixed law and fact. The appeal court may dismiss the appeal, allow the appeal and order a new hearing, quash the termination order or make a termination order. If the termination order is made, the court is required to notify the Commissioner of the R.C.M.P. accordingly.

OBLIGATION TO ADVISE POLICE SERVICE / Change in address / Information to be provided to Attorney General / Obligation ends.

490.02911 (1) A person who was convicted of or found not criminally responsible on account of mental disorder for an offence outside Canada shall, if the offence is equivalent to one referred to in paragraph (*a*) of the definition "designated offence" in subsection 490.011(1), advise a police service within seven days after the day on which they arrive in Canada of that fact and of their name, date of birth, gender and address. They are not required to so advise the police service again unless they are later convicted of or found not criminally responsible on account of mental disorder for another such offence.

(2) The person shall, if they are in Canada, advise a police service of a change in address within seven days after the day on which the change is made.

(3) The police service shall cause the Attorney General of the province, or the minister of justice of the territory, in which it is located to be provided with the information.

(4) A person's obligation under subsection (2) ends when they are served under section 490.02902 or, if it is earlier, one year after the day on which they advise the police service under subsection (1). 2010, c. 17, s. 19.

CROSS-REFERENCES

"Attorney General" is defined in s. 2. The failure to comply with the obligation under this section is an offence under s. 490.0312. For other Cross-References, see s. 490.02901.

SYNOPSIS

This section places an obligation on persons, who were convicted of or found not criminally responsible on account of mental disorder for offences committed outside Canada that are the equivalent to offences referred to in para. (*a*) of the definition "designated offence" in s. 490.011(1), to advise the police service within seven days after the day on which they arrive in Canada of that fact and of their name, date of birth, gender and address. The police will then notify the Attorney General of the province or the minister of justice of the territory, presumably so that they can consider whether to serve a notice under s. 490.02901. The person must also notify the police service of any change of address within seven days of the change. The obligation to notify the police of change of address ends once they are served with the notice to comply with provisions of the *Sex Offender Information Registration Act*, S.C. 2004, c. 10, or one year after they originally advised the police service.

International Transfer of Offenders Act

APPLICATION FOR TERMINATION ORDER / Time for application — one offence / More than one offence / Re-application.

490.02912 (1) A person who is subject to an obligation under section 36.1 of the *International Transfer of Offenders Act* may apply to a court of criminal jurisdiction for a termination order unless they are also subject to an obligation under section 490.019 or 490.02901 or under section 227.06 of the *National Defence Act* — or to an order under section 490.012 or under section 227.01 of the *National Defence Act* — that began later.

(2) The person may apply for a termination order if the following period has elapsed since the sentence was imposed or the verdict of not criminally responsible on account of mental disorder was rendered:

- **(*a*) five years if the maximum term of imprisonment provided for in Canadian law for the equivalent offence is two or five years;**

(b) 10 years if the maximum term of imprisonment provided for in Canadian law for the equivalent offence is 10 or 14 years; or

(c) 20 years if the maximum term of imprisonment provided for in Canadian law for the equivalent offence is life.

(3) If more than one offence is listed in the copy of the Form 1 that was delivered under subparagraph 8(4)(*a*)(ii) of the *International Transfer of Offenders Act*, the person may apply for a termination order if 20 years have elapsed since the sentence was imposed, or the verdict of not criminally responsible on account of mental disorder was rendered, for the most recent offence.

(4) A person whose application is refused may apply again if five years have elapsed since the application was made. 2010, c. 17, s. 19.

CROSS-REFERENCES

This section and ss. 490.02913 to 490.02914 establish a procedure for an offender subject to an obligation to comply with the *Sex Offender Information Registration Act*, S.C. 2004, c. 10, under s. 36.1 of the *International Transfer of Offenders Act*, S.C. 2004, c. 21, to terminate that obligation. The obligation to comply begins on the day of the person's transfer. Section 4(2) of the *Sex Offender Information Registration Act*, provides as follows:

> (2) A person who is subject to an obligation under section 490.019 or 490.02901 of the *Criminal Code*, section 227.06 of the *National Defence Act* or section 36.1 of the *International Transfer of Offenders Act* shall report to a registration centre referred to in section 7.1
>
> (*a*) if they are not in custody on the day on which they become subject to the obligation, within seven days — or, if they are required to report to a registration centre designated under the *National Defence Act*, within 15 days — after that day; and
>
> (*b*) in any other case, within seven days — or, if they are required to report to a registration centre designated under the *National Defence Act*, within 15 days — after
>
> (i) they receive an absolute or conditional discharge under Part XX.1 of the *Criminal Code*,
>
> (i.1) they receive an absolute or conditional discharge or are released from custody under Division 7 of Part III of the *National Defence Act*,
>
> (i.2) an imprisonment or a detention to which they are sentenced is suspended under section 215 or 216 of the *National Defence Act*,
>
> (ii) they are released from custody pending the determination of an appeal, or
>
> (iii) they are released from custody after serving the custodial portion of a sentence.

Section 8(4) of the *International Transfer of Offenders Act* provides as follows:

> (4) The Minister
>
> (*a*) shall inform a Canadian offender, in writing, as to how their foreign sentence is to be served in Canada and, in the case of an offender who is required to comply with the *Sex Offender Information Registration Act*,
>
> (i) inform them, in writing, of that obligation and of sections 4 to 7.1 of that Act and sections 490.031 and 490.0311 of the *Criminal Code*, and
>
> (ii) on the day of the transfer at the earliest, deliver a copy of Form 1 of the schedule to
>
> (A) the offender,
>
> (B) the Attorney General of the province, or the minister of justice of the territory, in which the person is to be detained in custody, and
>
> (C) the person in charge of the place in which the person is to be detained in custody; and

Section 36.2 of the *International Transfer of Offenders Act* provides for the point at which the obligation terminates and the duration of the obligation to comply. The process for terminating the obligation is similar to that established under ss. 490.015 to 490.017; thus, see Cross-References under those sections. If the person is subject to other obligations or orders to comply with the *Sex Offender Information Registration Act*, the application for a termination order must be made under s. 490.015. The test for making the termination order is set out in s. 490.02913. An appeal from an order made under this section is provided for in s. 490.02904. Failure to comply with the s. 36.1 obligation is an offence under s. 490.031.

SYNOPSIS

This section allows a person, subject only to an obligation under s. 36.1 of the *International Transfer of Offenders Act* to comply with the provisions of the *Sex Offender Information Registration Act*, to terminate the obligation. When the person may apply depends upon the nature of the equivalent Canadian offence. The person may apply five years after the person was sentenced or found not criminally responsible if the maximum penalty for the equivalent Canadian offence is imprisonment for two or five years; 10 years after the person was sentenced or found not criminally responsible if the maximum penalty for the equivalent Canadian offence is imprisonment for 10 or 14 years; 20 years if the maximum term for the equivalent Canadian offence is life imprisonment or if more than one offence is listed in the Form 1 that was delivered to the person under s. 8(4) of the *International Transfer of Offenders Act*. A person whose application is refused may apply again in five years.

TERMINATION ORDER / Reasons for decision / Requirements relating to notice.

490.02913 (1) The court shall make an order terminating the obligation if it is satisfied that the person has established that the impact on them of continuing the obligation, including on their privacy or liberty, would be grossly disproportionate to the public interest in protecting society through the effective prevention or investigation of crimes of a sexual nature to be achieved by the registration of information relating to sex offenders under the *Sex Offender Information Registration Act*.

(2) The court shall give reasons for its decision.

(3) If the court makes a termination order, it shall cause the Commissioner of the Royal Canadian Mounted Police and the Attorney General of the province, or the minister of justice of the territory, to be notified of the decision. 2010, c. 17, s. 19.

CROSS-REFERENCES

If the person is subject to other obligations or orders to comply with the *Sex Offender Information Registration Act*, S.C. 2004, c. 10, in addition to an obligation under s. 36.1 of the *International Transfer of Offenders Act*, S.C. 2004, c. 21, the application for a termination order must be made under s. 490.015. An appeal from an order made under this section is provided for in s. 490.02914. The test for making a termination order under this section is similar to the test for making similar orders under s. 490.015. Accordingly, see Cross-References and Annotations under that section. For other Cross-References, see s. 490.02912.

SYNOPSIS

This section sets out the test for making an order terminating obligations under the *Sex Offender Information Registration Act* as a result of s. 36.1 of the *International Transfer of Offenders Act*. The test is set out in subsec. (1). The court is required to give reasons for the decision. If the termination order is made, the court is required to notify the Commissioner of the R.C.M.P. accordingly.

APPEAL / Requirements relating to notice.

490.02914 (1) The Attorney General or the person who applied for a termination order may appeal from a decision under subsection 490.02913(1) on any ground of appeal that raises a question of law or of mixed law and fact. The appeal court may dismiss the appeal, allow the appeal and order a new hearing, quash the termination order or make an order that may be made under that subsection.

(2) If the appeal court makes an order that may be made under subsection 490.02913(1), it shall cause the Commissioner of the Royal Canadian Mounted Police and the Attorney General of the province, or the minister of justice of the territory, in which the application for the order was made to be notified of the decision. 2010, c. 17, s. 19.

CROSS-REFERENCES

"Attorney General" is defined in s. 2. The basis for an appeal under this section is similar to the appeal for similar orders made under s. 490.017. Accordingly, see Cross-References and Annotations under that section. For other Cross-References, see s. 490.02912.

SYNOPSIS

This section sets out the grounds of appeal for a decision made on an application for an order terminating obligations to comply with the *Sex Offender Information Registration Act*, S.C. 2004, c. 10, in relation to s. 36.1 of the *International Transfer of Offenders Act*, S.C. 2004, c. 21. The applicant and the Attorney General may appeal on any ground of law or mixed law and fact. The appeal court may dismiss the appeal, allow the appeal and order a new hearing, quash the termination order or make a termination order. If the termination order is made, the court is required to notify the Commissioner of the R.C.M.P. accordingly.

NOTICE BEFORE RELEASE / Notice on disposition by Review Board.

490.02915 (1) The person in charge of the place in which a person who is subject to an obligation under section 36.1 of the *International Transfer of Offenders Act* is serving the custodial portion of a sentence, or is detained in custody before their release or discharge, shall give the person a copy of the Form 1 referred to in subsection 490.02912(3) not earlier than 10 days before their release or discharge.

(2) A Review Board shall cause a copy of the Form 1 to be given to the person when it directs

- **(*a*) under paragraph 672.54(*a*), that the person be discharged absolutely; or**
- **(*b*) under paragraph 672.54(*b*), that the person be discharged subject to conditions unless the conditions restrict the person's liberty in a manner and to an extent that prevent them from complying with sections 4, 4.1, 4.3 and 6 of the *Sex Offender Information Registration Act*. 2010, c. 17, s. 19.**

CROSS-REFERENCES

See Cross-References under s. 490.02912.

SYNOPSIS

This section sets out an administrative procedure to ensure that, when persons transferred to Canada under the *International Transfer of Offenders Act*, S.C. 2004, c. 21, are released from custody, they are aware of their obligations to report in accordance with s. 36.1 of that Act and the *Sex Offender Information Registration Act*, S.C. 2004, c. 10.

Disclosure of Information

DISCLOSURE BY COMMISSIONER / Disclosure in connection with proceedings / Disclosure in proceedings.

490.03 (1) The Commissioner of the Royal Canadian Mounted Police or a person authorized by the Commissioner shall, on request, disclose information that is registered in the database or the fact that such information is registered in the database

- **(*a*) to the prosecutor if the disclosure is necessary for the purpose of a proceeding under section 490.012; or**
- **(*b*) to the Attorney General if the disclosure is necessary for the purpose of a proceeding under subsection 490.016(1), 490.023(2), 490.027(1), 490.02905(2), 490.02909(1) or 490.02913(1) or for the purpose of an appeal from a decision made in any of those proceedings or in a proceeding under subsection 490.012(2).**

(2) The Commissioner or that person shall, on request, disclose to the prosecutor or Attorney General the information that is registered in the database relating to a person if the person discloses, in connection with a proceeding or appeal other than one referred to in subsection (1), the fact that information relating to them is registered in the database.

(3) The prosecutor or the Attorney General may, if the information is relevant to the proceeding, appeal or any subsequent appeal, disclose it to the presiding court. 2004, c. 10, s. 20; 2007, c. 5, s. 27; 2010, c. 17, s. 20.

CROSS-REFERENCES

"Attorney General" and "prosecutor" are defined in s. 2. "Database" and "crime of a sexual nature" are defined in s. 490.011. Section 490.02 sets out the persons who may be served with a notice to comply with the obligations under s. 490.019. Section 490.022 sets out the date that the obligation to comply begins and its duration. Section 490.023 allows the person to apply to a court for an exemption order. Section 490.024 provides for an appeal from the refusal to make an exemption order or by the Attorney General from the making of the exemption order. Section 490.025 provides for notice to the person that they have not been granted an exemption order. Under s. 490.026, the person may apply for a termination order under s. 490.027. Section 490.028 deals with the case where the offender is eligible to apply for an exemption order and a termination order. Section 490.029 allows for appeals in relation to termination orders. Section 490.031 creates an offence for failing to comply with an obligation as required by s. 490.019.

SYNOPSIS

This section sets out the circumstances in which information in the sex offender database may be disclosed. There are, in effect, four circumstances in which information may be disclosed. At the request of the Attorney General or the prosecutor, information may be disclosed under subsec. (1) for proceedings in relation to the making or terminating an order or obligation or granting an exemption or appeals in such proceeding, or under subsec. (2) where the person him or herself disclose information. Under subsec. (3), the Attorney General or the prosecutor may disclose information to a court in connection with such proceedings. Finally, under subsec. (4), information may be disclosed to a judge or justice on an application for a search warrant in connection with an investigation of a crime that there are reasonable grounds to suspect is of a sexual nature.

Offences

OFFENCE / Reasonable excuse / Proof of certain facts by certificate / Attendance and cross-examination / Notice of intention to produce.

490.031 (1) Every person who, without reasonable excuse, fails to comply with an order made under section 490.012 or under section 227.01 of the *National Defence Act* or with an obligation under section 490.019 or 490.02901, under section 227.06 of the *National Defence Act* or under section 36.1 of the *International Transfer of Offenders Act* is guilty of an offence and liable

- **(*a*) on conviction on indictment, to a fine of not more than $10,000 or to imprisonment for a term of not more than two years, or to both; or**
- **(*b*) on summary conviction, to a fine of not more than $10,000 or to imprisonment for a term of not more than six months, or to both.**

(2) For greater certainty, a lawful command that prevents a person from complying with an order or obligation is a reasonable excuse if, at the time, the person is subject to the Code of Service Discipline within the meaning of subsection 2(1) of the *National Defence Act*.

(3) In proceedings under subsection (1), a certificate of a person referred to in paragraph 16(2)(*b*) of the *Sex Offender Information Registration Act* stating that the sex offender failed to report under section 4, 4.1, 4.2 or 4.3 — or provide information under section 5 or notify a person under subsection 6(1) — of that Act is evidence of the statements contained in it without proof of the signature or official character of the person appearing to have signed it.

Note: Subsection 490.031(3) replaced, 2015, c. 23, s. 30 (to come into force by order of the Governor in Council):

Proof of certain facts by certificate

(3) In proceedings under subsection (1), a certificate of a person referred to in paragraph 16(2)(*b*) of the *Sex Offender Information Registration Act* stating that the sex offender failed to report under section 4, 4.1, 4.2 or 4.3 — or provide information under section 5 or notify a person under subsection 6(1) or (1.01) — of that Act is evidence of the statements contained in it without proof of the signature or official character of the person appearing to have signed it.

(4) The sex offender named in the certificate may, with the leave of the court, require the attendance of the person who signed it for the purpose of cross-examination.

(5) A certificate is not to be received in evidence unless, before the commencement of the trial, the party who intends to produce it gives the sex offender a copy of it and reasonable notice of their intention to produce it. 2004, c. 10, s. 20; 2007, c. 5, s. 28; 2010, c. 17, s. 21.

CROSS-REFERENCES

Section 490.02 sets out the persons who may be served with a notice to comply with the obligations under s. 490.019. Section 490.022 sets out the date that the obligation to comply begins and its duration. Section 490.023 allows the person to apply to a court for an exemption order. Section 490.024 provides for an appeal from the refusal to make an exemption order or by the Attorney General from the making of the exemption order. Section 490.025 provides for notice to the person that they have not been granted an exemption order. Under s. 490.026, the person may apply for a termination order under s. 490.027. Section 490.028 deals with the case where the offender is eligible to apply for an exemption order and a termination order. Section 490.029 allows for appeals in relation to termination orders. Section 490.03 deals with disclosure of the material in the database. For Cross-References in relation to obligations imposed in relation to offences committed outside Canada or where the person has been transferred to Canada under the *International Transfer of Offenders Act*, S.C. 2004, c. 21, see ss. 490.02901 and 490.02912 respectively.

SYNOPSIS

This section creates the offence for failing to comply with an order made by a court under s. 490.012 or an obligation under s. 490.019 or s. 490.02901. Subsection (3) provides for proof, by way of certificate, of the person's failure to comply with the *Sex Offender Information Registration Act*, S.C. 2004, c. 10. The prosecutor must give notice of the intention to produce the certificate and, under subsec. (4), the offender may seek leave of the court to require the attendance of the person who signed the certificate for purposes of cross-examination.

OFFENCE.

490.0311 Every person who knowingly provides false or misleading information under subsection 5(1) or 6(1) of the *Sex Offender Information Registration Act* is guilty of an offence and liable

Note: The portion of section 490.0311 before para. (*a*) replaced, 2015, c. 23, s. 31 (to come into force by order of the Governor in Council):

Offence

490.0311 Every person who knowingly provides false or misleading information under subsection 5(1) or 6(1) or (1.01) of the *Sex Offender Information Registration Act* is guilty of an offence and liable

(*a*) on conviction on indictment, to a fine of not more than $10,000 or to imprisonment for a term of not more than two years, or to both; or

(*b*) on summary conviction, to a fine of not more than $10,000 or to imprisonment for a term of not more than six months, or to both. 2007, c. 5, s. 29; 2010, c. 17, s. 22.

OFFENCE.

490.0312 Every person who, without reasonable excuse, fails to comply with an obligation under subsection 490.02911(1) or (2) is guilty of an offence punishable on summary conviction. 2010, c. 17, s. 23.

Regulations

REGULATIONS.

490.032 The Governor in Council may make regulations

(*a*) requiring that additional information be contained in a notice under Form 53 or Form 54; and

(*b*) prescribing, for one or more provinces, the form and content of that information. 2004, c. 10, s. 20; 2010, c. 17, s. 24.

Forfeiture of Offence-related Property

ORDER OF FORFEITURE OF PROPERTY ON CONVICTION / Property related to other offences / Property outside Canada / Appeal.

490.1 (1) Subject to sections 490.3 to 490.41, if a person is convicted, or discharged under section 730, of an indictable offence under this Act or the *Corruption of Foreign Public Officials Act* and, on application of the Attorney General, the court is satisfied, on a balance of probabilities, that offence-related property is related to the commission of the offence, the court shall

(*a*) if the prosecution of the offence was commenced at the instance of the government of a province and conducted by or on behalf of that government, order that the property be forfeited to Her Majesty in right of that province to be disposed of or otherwise dealt with in accordance with the law by the Attorney General or Solicitor General of that province; and

(*b*) in any other case, order that the property be forfeited to Her Majesty in right of Canada to be disposed of or otherwise dealt with in accordance with the law by the member of the Queen's Privy Council for Canada that is designated by the Governor in Council for the purpose of this paragraph.

(1.1) [*Repealed*, 2001, c. 41, s. 130(7.1).]

(2) Subject to sections 490.3 to 490.41, if the evidence does not establish to the satisfaction of the court that property in respect of which an order of forfeiture would otherwise be made under subsection (1) is related to the commission of the indictable offence under this Act or the *Corruption of Foreign Public Officials Act* of which a person is convicted or discharged, but the court is satisfied, beyond a reasonable doubt, that the property is offence-related property, the court may make an order of forfeiture under subsection (1) in relation to that property.

(2.1) An order may be issued under this section in respect of property situated outside Canada, with any modifications that the circumstances require.

(3) A person who has been convicted of an indictable offence under this Act or the *Corruption of Foreign Public Officials Act*, or the Attorney General, may appeal to the court of appeal from an order or a failure to make an order under subsection (1) as if the appeal were an appeal against the sentence imposed on the person in respect of the offence. 1997, c. 23, s. 15; 2001, c. 32, s. 30(2); 2001, c. 41, s. 18, 130(7.1); 2007, c. 13, s. 8; 2017, c. 7, s. 64.

CROSS-REFERENCES

"Attorney General", "offence-related property" and "property" are defined in s. 2. A related scheme for forfeiture of proceeds of crime is set out in Part XII.2. An order made under subsec. (1) is, pursuant to s. 490.7, stayed pending appeal.

SYNOPSIS

Sections 490.1 to 490.9 set up a legislative scheme for dealing with property believed to be "offence-related property". The scheme is similar to the parallel scheme enacted in Part XII.2 for Proceeds of Crime. These provisions were enacted as part of a package of legislative measures to deal with criminal organizations but that connection has been removed in view of the broad definition of "offence-related property" in s. 2 being any property, within or outside Canada, by means of or in respect of which any indictable offence under the Code is committed, that is used in any manner in connection with the commission of any indictable offence or that is intended for use for the purpose of committing an indictable offence.

This property may have been seized under one of the seizure powers in this Act or some other federal statute such as the *Controlled Drugs and Substances Act*. Alternatively, it may be under the control of the state as a result of an application for a restraint order under s. 490.8. The restraint order may be granted if the judge is satisfied that there are reasonable grounds to believe that the property is offence-related property and may be made in relation to property in or outside Canada. Failure to comply with a restraint order is a hybrid offence. As no punishment is specially provided for this offence, the indictable offence is punishable by imprisonment for a term not exceeding five years [s. 743] and the summary conviction offence is punishable by up to six months and a $2000 fine [s. 787]. Unlike the proceeds of crime restraint order obtained under s. 462.33, s. 490.8 does not expressly give the judge power to require that notice be given to persons having an interest in the property. Further, s. 490.8 does not mandate that the judge require the Attorney General to give undertakings with respect to the payment of damages or costs [compare s. 462.33(7)]. As well, no express provision is made for exempting from the restraint order, property required for living expenses or payment of legal fees [compare s. 462.34]. A judge may make an order for management of offence-related property subject to a restraint order or seized pursuant to a search warrant under s. 487, in accordance with s. 490.81. The judge may also make a destruction order where the property is of little or no value after notice to persons with a valid interest.

These sections envisage essentially two different procedures by which offence-related property will be forfeited to the Crown. Under s. 490.1, forfeiture is triggered upon the conviction of the person for an indictable offence. If the court is satisfied on a balance of probabilities that the offence was committed in relation to the offence-related property, it is ordered forfeited. If the court is not so satisfied but is satisfied beyond a reasonable doubt that the property was nevertheless offence-related property, the property may also be forfeited. An order made under s. 490.1 or the failure to make the order may be appealed as if it were a sentence appeal. Section 490.2 sets out an alternative *in rem* procedure because the accused who was charged with the criminal organization offence has died or absconded. The forfeiture order may only be made where the judge is satisfied beyond a reasonable doubt that the property is offence-related property. Any person aggrieved by an order made under s.

490.2 may appeal that order pursuant to s. 490.6 to the Court of Appeal as if the order were a conviction or acquittal as the case may be.

Section 490.3 gives the court an additional power, prior to making the forfeiture order, to set aside transactions that occurred after the seizure of the property or the making of a restraint order. The transaction will not be set aside if the person acquiring the property gave valuable consideration and was acting in good faith. Pursuant to s. 490.4, the judge shall require notice to be given to any person who appears to have a valid interest in the property and such a person has standing to oppose the forfeiture order. The judge may order the property returned to the lawful owner provided that person is not charged with a criminal organization offence and has not acquired property from a person charged with a criminal organization offence in circumstances giving rise to a reasonable inference that the transfer was made to avoid a forfeiture order. Special provision is made in s. 490.41, where the property is a dwelling-house, for notice to persons residing in the house.

Even where the property has been forfeited, s. 490.5 allows an application by innocent persons for an order that their interest in the property is not affected by the forfeiture. Where the application has been successful, the applicant applies to the Attorney General under s. 490.5(6) for the return of the property or an amount equal in value to the value of the interest of the applicant, as declared by the court. The applicant and the Attorney General may appeal an order made under s. 490.5 to the Court of Appeal.

Any of the orders made under ss. 490.1(1), 490.2(2) and 490.5(4) are stayed pending any appeal or any other proceedings relating to restoration or forfeiture of the property.

Section 490.9 makes ss. 489.1 and 490 applicable to any offence-related property subject to ss. 490.1 to 490.7. References should be made to the notes under those sections. Section 489.1 requires the seizing officer to return the property or take it before a justice to be dealt with under s. 490. Section 490 deals with the detention and restoration of goods that have been seized. The reference in s. 490.9(2) to an order under s. 490(9)(*c*) refers to an order returning goods to their lawful owner because the order detaining the goods has expired and proceedings have not been instituted in which the thing detained may be required. Where the property involved is offence-related property, the judge may require the applicant to enter into a recognizance.

Forfeiture does not form part of the sentencing proceedings. Accordingly, the normal rules of evidence apply and hearsay is inadmissible: *R. v. Faulkner* (2007), 222 C.C.C. (3d) 359 (N.B.C.A.).

APPLICATION FOR *IN REM* FORFEITURE / Order of forfeiture of property / Accused deemed absconded / Who may dispose of property / Property outside Canada / Definition of "judge".

490.2 (1) If an information has been laid in respect of an indictable offence under this Act or the *Corruption of Foreign Public Officials Act*, the Attorney General may make an application to a judge for an order of forfeiture under subsection (2).

(2) Subject to sections 490.3 to 490.41, the judge to whom an application is made under subsection (1) shall order that the property that is subject to the application be forfeited and disposed of in accordance with subsection (4) if the judge is satisfied

(*a*) beyond a reasonable doubt that the property is offence-related property;

(*b*) that proceedings in respect of an indictable offence under this Act or the *Corruption of Foreign Public Officials Act* in relation to the property were commenced; and

(*c*) that the accused charged with the offence has died or absconded.

(3) For the purpose of subsection (2), an accused is deemed to have absconded in connection with the indictable offence if

(*a*) an information has been laid alleging the commission of the offence by the accused,

(b) a warrant for the arrest of the accused has been issued in relation to that information, and

(c) reasonable attempts to arrest the accused under the warrant have been unsuccessful during a period of six months beginning on the day on which the warrant was issued,

and the accused is deemed to have so absconded on the last day of that six month period.

(4) For the purpose of subsection (2), the judge shall

(a) if the prosecution of the offence was commenced at the instance of the government of a province and conducted by or on behalf of that government, order that the property be forfeited to Her Majesty in right of that province to be disposed of or otherwise dealt with in accordance with the law by the Attorney General or Solicitor General of that province; and

(b) in any other case, order that the property be forfeited to Her Majesty in right of Canada to be disposed of or otherwise dealt with in accordance with the law by the member of the Queen's Privy Council for Canada that is designated by the Governor in Council for the purpose of this paragraph.

(4.1) An order may be issued under this section in respect of property situated outside Canada, with any modifications that the circumstances require.

(5) In this section and sections 490.5 and 490.8, "judge" means a judge as defined in section 552 or a judge of a superior court of criminal jurisdiction. 1997, c. 23, s. 15; 2001, c. 32, s. 31; 2007, c. 13, s. 9; 2017, c. 7, s. 65.

CROSS-REFERENCES

"Attorney General", "offence-related property" and "property" are defined in s. 2. A related scheme for forfeiture of proceeds of crime is set out in Part XII.2. Any person aggrieved by an order made under subsec. (2) may appeal to the court of appeal pursuant to s. 490.6. The order is stayed pending the appeal, pursuant to s. 490.7.

SYNOPSIS

See synopsis under s. 490.1.

VOIDABLE TRANSFERS.

490.3 A court may, before ordering that offence-related property be forfeited under subsection 490.1(1) or 490.2(2), set aside any conveyance or transfer of the property that occurred after the seizure of the property, or the making of a restraint order in respect of the property, unless the conveyance or transfer was for valuable consideration to a person acting in good faith. 1997, c. 23, s. 15.

CROSS-REFERENCES

"Offence-related property" is defined in s. 2.

SYNOPSIS

See synopsis under s. 490.1.

NOTICE / Manner of giving notice / Order of restoration of property.

490.4 (1) Before making an order under subsection 490.1(1) or 490.2(2) in relation to any property, a court shall require notice in accordance with subsection (2) to be given to, and may hear, any person who, in the opinion of the court, appears to have a valid interest in the property.

(2) A notice shall

(*a*) be given in the manner that the court directs or that may be specified in the rules of the court;

(*b*) specify the period that the court considers reasonable or that may be set out in the rules of the court during which a person may make an application to the court asserting their interest in the property; and

(*c*) set out the offence charged and a description of the property.

(3) A court may order that all or part of the property that would otherwise be forfeited under subsection 490.1(1) or 490.2(2) be returned to a person — other than a person who was charged with an indictable offence under this Act or the *Corruption of Foreign Public Officials Act* or a person who acquired title to or a right of possession of the property from such a person under circumstances that give rise to a reasonable inference that the title or right was transferred for the purpose of avoiding the forfeiture of the property — if the court is satisfied that the person is the lawful owner or is lawfully entitled to possession of all or part of that property, and that the person appears innocent of any complicity in, or collusion in relation to, the offence. 1997, c. 23, s. 15; 2001, c. 32, s. 32; 2007, c. 13, s. 10; 2017, c. 7, s. 66.

CROSS-REFERENCES

"Property" is defined in s. 2.

SYNOPSIS

See synopsis under s. 490.1.

NOTICE / Manner of giving notice / Non-forfeiture of property / Factors in relation to dwelling-house.

490.41 (1) If all or part of offence-related property that would otherwise be forfeited under subsection 490.1(1) or 490.2(2) is a dwelling-house, before making an order of forfeiture, a court shall require that notice in accordance with subsection (2) be given to, and may hear, any person who resides in the dwelling-house and is a member of the immediate family of the person charged with or convicted of the indictable offence under this Act or the *Corruption of Foreign Public Officials Act* in relation to which the property would be forfeited.

(2) A notice shall

(*a*) be given in the manner that the court directs or that may be specified in the rules of the court;

(*b*) specify the period that the court considers reasonable or that may be set out in the rules of the court during which a member of the immediate family who resides in the dwelling-house may make themselves known to the court; and

(*c*) set out the offence charged and a description of the property.

(3) Subject to an order made under subsection 490.4(3), if a court is satisfied that the impact of an order of forfeiture made under subsection 490.1(1) or 490.2(2) would be disproportionate to the nature and gravity of the offence, the circumstances surrounding the commission of the offence and the criminal record, if any, of the person charged with or convicted of the offence, as the case may be, it may decide not to order the forfeiture of the property or part of the property and may revoke any restraint order made in respect of that property or part.

(4) Where all or part of the property that would otherwise be forfeited under subsection 490.1(1) or 490.2(2) is a dwelling-house, when making a decision under subsection (3), the court shall also consider

(*a*) the impact of an order of forfeiture on any member of the immediate family of the person charged with or convicted of the offence, if the dwelling-house was

the member's principal residence at the time the charge was laid and continues to be the member's principal residence; and

(*b*) whether the member referred to in paragraph (*a*) appears innocent of any complicity in the offence or of any collusion in relation to the offence. 2001, c. 32, s. 33; 2007, c. 13, s. 11; 2017, c. 7, s. 67.

CROSS-REFERENCES

"Property" and "dwelling-house" are defined in s. 2.

SYNOPSIS

See synopsis under s. 490.1.

APPLICATION / Fixing day for hearing / Notice / Order declaring interest not affected by forfeiture / Appeal from order made under subsection (4) / Return of property.

490.5 (1) Where any offence-related property is forfeited to Her Majesty pursuant to an order made under subsection 490.1(1) or 490.2(2), any person who claims an interest in the property, other than

(*a*) in the case of property forfeited pursuant to an order made under subsection 490.1(1), a person who was convicted of the indictable offence in relation to which the property was forfeited,

(*b*) in the case of property forfeited pursuant to an order made under subsection 490.2(2), a person who was charged with the indictable offence in relation to which the property was forfeited, or

(*c*) a person who acquired title to or a right of possession of the property from a person referred to in paragraph (*a*) or (*b*) under circumstances that give rise to a reasonable inference that the title or right was transferred from that person for the purpose of avoiding the forfeiture of the property,

may, within thirty days after the forfeiture, apply by notice in writing to a judge for an order under subsection (4).

(2) The judge to whom an application is made under subsection (1) shall fix a day not less than thirty days after the date of the filing of the application for the hearing of the application.

(3) An applicant shall serve a notice of the application made under subsection (1) and of the hearing of it on the Attorney General at least fifteen days before the day fixed for the hearing.

(4) Where, on the hearing of an application made under subsection (1), the judge is satisfied that the applicant

(*a*) is not a person referred to in paragraph (1)(*a*), (*b*) or (*c*) and appears innocent of any complicity in any indictable offence that resulted in the forfeiture of the property or of any collusion in relation to such an offence, and

(*b*) exercised all reasonable care to be satisfied that the property was not likely to have been used in connection with the commission of an unlawful act by the person who was permitted by the applicant to obtain possession of the property or from whom the applicant obtained possession or, where the applicant is a mortgagee or lienholder, by the mortgagor or lien-giver,

the judge may make an order declaring that the interest of the applicant is not affected by the forfeiture and declaring the nature and the extent or value of the interest.

(5) An applicant or the Attorney General may appeal to the court of appeal from an order made under subsection (4), and the provisions of Part XXI with respect to procedure on appeals apply, with any modifications that the circumstances require, in respect of appeals under this subsection.

(6) The Attorney General shall, on application made to the Attorney General by any person in respect of whom a judge has made an order under subsection (4), and where the periods with respect to the taking of appeals from that order have expired and any appeal from that order taken under subsection (5) has been determined, direct that

(*a*) the property, or the part of it to which the interest of the applicant relates, be returned to the applicant; or

(*b*) an amount equal to the value of the interest of the applicant, as declared in the order, be paid to the applicant. 1997, c. 23, s. 15; 2001, c. 32, s. 34.

CROSS-REFERENCES

"Attorney General", "offence-related property" and "property" are defined in s. 2. "Judge" is defined in s. 490.2(5). An order made under subsec. (4) is, pursuant to s. 490.7, stayed pending appeal.

SYNOPSIS

See synopsis under s. 490.1.

APPEALS FROM ORDERS UNDER SUBSECTION 490.2(2).

490.6 Any person who, in their opinion, is aggrieved by an order made under subsection 490.2(2) may appeal from the order as if the order were an appeal against conviction or against a judgment or verdict of acquittal, as the case may be, under Part XXI, and that Part applies, with any modifications that the circumstances require, in respect of such an appeal. 1997, c. 23, s. 15.

CROSS-REFERENCES

The order is stayed pending appeal, pursuant to s. 490.7.

SYNOPSIS

See synopsis under s. 490.1.

SUSPENSION OF ORDER PENDING APPEAL.

490.7 Notwithstanding anything in this Act, the operation of an order made in respect of property under subsection 490.1(1), 490.2(2) or 490.5(4) is suspended pending

(*a*) any application made in respect of the property under any of those provisions or any other provision of this or any other Act of Parliament that provides for restoration or forfeiture of the property, or

(*b*) any appeal taken from an order of forfeiture or restoration in respect of the property,

and the property shall not be disposed of or otherwise dealt with until thirty days have expired after an order is made under any of those provisions. 1997, c. 23, s. 15.

SYNOPSIS

See synopsis under s. 490.1.

APPLICATION FOR RESTRAINT ORDER / Procedure / Restraint order / Property outside Canada / Conditions / Order in writing / Service of order / Registration of order / Order continues in force / Offence.

490.8 (1) The Attorney General may make an application in accordance with this section for a restraint order under this section in respect of any offence-related property.

(2) An application made under subsection (1) for a restraint order in respect of any offence-related property may be made *ex parte* and shall be made in writing to a judge and be accompanied by an affidavit sworn on the information and belief of the Attorney General or any other person deposing to the following matters:

(*a*) the indictable offence to which the offence-related property relates;

(*b*) the person who is believed to be in possession of the offence-related property; and

(*c*) a description of the offence-related property.

(3) Where an application for a restraint order is made to a judge under subsection (1), the judge may, if satisfied that there are reasonable grounds to believe that the property is offence-related property, make a restraint order prohibiting any person from disposing of, or otherwise dealing with any interest in, the offence-related property specified in the order otherwise than in the manner that may be specified in the order.

(3.1) A restraint order may be issued under this section in respect of property situated outside Canada, with any modifications that the circumstances require.

(4) A restraint order made by a judge under this section may be subject to any reasonable conditions that the judge thinks fit.

(5) A restraint order made under this section shall be made in writing.

(6) A copy of a restraint order made under this section shall be served on the person to whom the order is addressed in any manner that the judge making the order directs or in accordance with the rules of the court.

(7) A copy of a restraint order made under this section shall be registered against any property in accordance with the laws of the province in which the property is situated.

(8) A restraint order made under this section remains in effect until

(*a*) an order is made under subsection 490(9) or (11), 490.4(3) or 490.41(3) in relation to the property; or

(*b*) an order of forfeiture of the property is made under section 490 or subsection 490.1(1) or 490.2(2).

(9) Any person on whom a restraint order made under this section is served in accordance with this section and who, while the order is in force, acts in contravention of or fails to comply with the order is guilty of an indictable offence or an offence punishable on summary conviction. 1997, c. 23, s. 15; 2001, c. 32, s. 35.

CROSS-REFERENCES

"Attorney General", "offence-related property" and "property" are defined in s. 2. A related scheme for restraining disposition of proceeds of crime is set out in Part XII.2. "Judge" is defined in s. 490.2(5).

SYNOPSIS

See synopsis under s. 490.1.

MANAGEMENT ORDER / Appointment of Minister of Public Works and Government Services / Power to manage / Application for destruction order / Notice / Manner of giving notice / Destruction order / Forfeiture order / When management order ceases to have effect / For greater certainty / Application to vary conditions.

490.81 (1) With respect to offence-related property other than a "controlled substance" within the meaning of the *Controlled Drugs and Substances Act* or cannabis as defined in subsection 2(1) of the *Cannabis Act*, on application of the Attorney General or of any other person with the written consent of the Attorney General, a judge or justice in the case of offence-related property seized under section 487, or a judge in the case of

offence-related property restrained under section 490.8, may, if he or she is of the opinion that the circumstances so require,

(*a*) appoint a person to take control of and to manage or otherwise deal with all or part of the property in accordance with the directions of the judge or justice; and

(*b*) require any person having possession of that property to give possession of the property to the person appointed under paragraph (*a*).

(2) When the Attorney General of Canada so requests, a judge or justice appointing a person under subsection (1) shall appoint the Minister of Public Works and Government Services.

(3) The power to manage or otherwise deal with property under subsection (1) includes

(*a*) the power to make an interlocutory sale of perishable or rapidly depreciating property;

(*b*) the power to destroy, in accordance with subsections (4) to (7), property that has little or no value; and

(*c*) the power to have property, other than real property or a conveyance, forfeited to Her Majesty in accordance with subsection (7.1).

(4) Before a person who is appointed to manage property destroys property that has little or no value, they shall apply to a court for a destruction order.

(5) Before making a destruction order, a court shall require notice in accordance with subsection (6) to be given to and may hear any person who, in the court's opinion, appears to have a valid interest in the property.

(6) A notice shall

(*a*) be given in the manner that the court directs or that may be specified in the rules of the court; and

(*b*) specify the effective period of the notice that the court considers reasonable or that may be set out in the rules of the court.

(7) A court shall order that the property be destroyed if it is satisfied that the property has little or no financial or other value.

(7.1) On application by a person who is appointed to manage the property, a court shall order that the property, other than real property or a conveyance, be forfeited to Her Majesty to be disposed of or otherwise dealt with in accordance with the law if

(*a*) a notice is given or published in the manner that the court directs or that may be specified in the rules of the court;

(*b*) the notice specifies a period of 60 days during which a person may make an application to the court asserting their interest in the property; and

(*c*) during that period, no one makes such an application.

(8) A management order ceases to have effect when the property that is the subject of the management order is returned in accordance with the law, destroyed or forfeited to Her Majesty.

(8.1) For greater certainty, if property that is the subject of a management order is sold, the management order applies to the net proceeds of the sale.

(9) The Attorney General may at any time apply to the judge or justice to cancel or vary any condition to which a management order is subject, but may not apply to vary an appointment made under subsection (2). 2001, c. 32, s. 36; 2017, c. 7, s. 68; 2018, c. 16, s. 217.

CROSS-REFERENCES

"Attorney General", "offence-related property" and "property" are defined in s. 2. A related scheme for management of proceeds of crime is set out in Part XII.2.

SYNOPSIS

See synopsis under s. 490.1.

SECTIONS 489.1 AND 490 APPLICABLE / Recognizance.

490.9 (1) Subject to sections 490.1 to 490.7, sections 489.1 and 490 apply, with any modifications that the circumstances require, to any offence-related property that is the subject of a restraint order made under section 490.8.

(2) Where, pursuant to subsection (1), an order is made under paragraph 490(9)(*c*) for the return of any offence-related property that is the subject of a restraint order under section 490.8, the judge or justice making the order may require the applicant for the order to enter into a recognizance before the judge or justice, with or without sureties, in any amount and with any conditions that the judge or justice directs and, where the judge or justice considers it appropriate, require the applicant to deposit with the judge or justice any sum of money or other valuable security that the judge or justice directs. 1997, c. 23, s. 15.

CROSS-REFERENCES

"Offence-related property" and "property" are defined in s. 2.

SYNOPSIS

See synopsis under s. 490.1.

FORFEITURE OF WEAPONS AND AMMUNITION / Return to lawful owner / Application of proceeds.

491. (1) Subject to subsection (2), where it is determined by a court that

- **(*a*) a weapon, an imitation firearm, a prohibited device, any ammunition, any prohibited ammunition or an explosive substance was used in the commission of an offence and that thing has been seized and detained, or**
- **(*b*) that a person has committed an offence that involves, or the subject-matter of which is, a firearm, a cross-bow, a prohibited weapon, a restricted weapon, a prohibited device, ammunition, prohibited ammunition or an explosive substance and any such thing has been seized and detained,**

the thing so seized and detained is forfeited to Her Majesty and shall be disposed of as the Attorney General directs.

(2) If the court by which a determination referred to in subsection (1) is made is satisfied that the lawful owner of any thing that is or may be forfeited to Her Majesty under subsection (1) was not a party to the offence and had no reasonable grounds to believe that the thing would or might be used in the commission of an offence, the court shall order that the thing be returned to that lawful owner, that the proceeds of any sale of the thing be paid to that lawful owner or, if the thing was destroyed, that an amount equal to the value of the thing be paid to the owner.

(3) Where any thing in respect of which this section applies is sold, the proceeds of the sale shall be paid to the Attorney General or, where an order is made under subsection (2), to the person who was, immediately prior to the sale, the lawful owner of the thing. 1972, c. 13, s. 37; 1991, c. 40, s. 30; 1995, c. 39, s. 152.

CROSS-REFERENCES

The terms "weapon", "firearm" and "Attorney General" are defined in s. 2. Liability of a person as a party to an offence is defined in ss. 21 and 22. For other provisions respecting forfeiture of contraband, see ss. 491.1 and 492. For special provision for search and seizure of weapons, see ss. 117.02 to 117.06.

Pursuant to s. 2.1, the terms "cross-bow", "prohibited weapon", "restricted weapon", "prohibited device", "ammunition", and "prohibited ammunition" have the same meaning as in s. 84(1).

SYNOPSIS

This section sets out a special code for dealing with forfeiture of weapons and ammunition and their subsequent disposal.

Subsection (1) provides that, where a court determines (a) that a weapon was used in the commission of an offence and it has been seized and detained, or (b) that a person has committed an offence involving, or the subject matter of which is, a firearm or other listed weapon or ammunition, that weapon or ammunition is forfeited and will be dealt with as the Attorney General directs. This determination is subject to the provisions of subsec. (2).

Subsection (2) provides that where the court determines that the lawful owner of the weapon or ammunition referred to in subsec. (1) was not a party to the offence and had no reason to believe that the weapon or ammunition would be so used, the court shall order the weapon returned to that person. Where the weapon or ammunition has been sold, the proceeds will be paid, either to the Attorney General, or the lawful owner described in subsec. (2). Subsection (3) deals with the proceeds of sale.

ANNOTATIONS

Due to the amendment to this provision, however, forfeiture is mandatory pursuant to subsec. (1)(*b*) where the item has not been used but is merely involved in the offence. Accordingly, where the accused was stopped and two loaded firearms were found in his vehicle, the items were properly forfeited under this provision: *R. v. Roberts* (2005), 199 C.C.C. (3d) 442 (Sask. Prov. Ct.).

A firearms forfeiture order made under this section is one of the consequences that forms part of the punishment, and is therefore appealable with leave under s. 675(1)(*b*): *R. v. Montague* (2014), 312 C.C.C. (3d) 1 (Ont. C.A.), leave to appeal to S.C.C. refused 2014 CarswellOnt 16354.

Forfeiture of a large firearms collection pursuant to this section does not constitute cruel and unusual punishment within the meaning of s. 12 of the Charter: *R. v. Montague*, *supra*.

The wording of subsec. (2) contemplates that lawful owners can apply for return of their seized property either before or after forfeiture is ordered: *R. v. Saunders* (2014), 317 C.C.C. (3d) 246 (N.L.C.A.).

ORDER FOR RESTITUTION OR FORFEITURE OF PROPERTY OBTAINED BY CRIME / Idem / When certain orders not to be made / By whom order executed.

491.1 (1) Where an accused or defendant is tried for an offence and the court determines that an offence has been committed, whether or not the accused has been convicted or discharged under section 730 of the offence, and at the time of the trial any property obtained by the commission of the offence

(*a*) is before the court or has been detained so that it can be immediately dealt with, and

(*b*) will not be required as evidence in any other proceedings,

section 490 does not apply in respect of the property and the court shall make an order under subsection (2) in respect of the property.

(2) In the circumstances referred to in subsection (1), the court shall order, in respect of any property,

(*a*) if the lawful owner or person lawfully entitled to possession of the property is known, that it be returned to that person; and

(*b*) if the lawful owner or person lawfully entitled to possession of the property is not known, that it be forfeited to Her Majesty, to be disposed of as the Attorney General directs or otherwise dealt with in accordance with the law.

(3) An order shall not be made under subsection (2)

(*a*) in the case of proceedings against a trustee, banker, merchant, attorney, factor, broker or other agent entrusted with the possession of goods or documents of title to goods, for an offence under section 330, 331, 332 or 336; or

(*b*) in respect of

(i) property to which a person acting in good faith and without notice has acquired lawful title for valuable consideration,

(ii) a valuable security that has been paid or discharged in good faith by a person who was liable to pay or discharge it,

(iii) a negotiable instrument that has, in good faith, been taken or received by transfer or delivery for valuable consideration by a person who had no notice and no reasonable cause to suspect that an offence had been committed, or

(iv) property in respect of which there is a dispute as to ownership or right of possession by claimants other than the accused or defendant.

(4) An order made under this section shall, on the direction of the court, be executed by the peace officers by whom the process of the court is ordinarily executed. R.S.C. 1985, c. 27 (1st Supp.), s. 74.

CROSS-REFERENCES

The terms "Attorney General", "valuable security", "document of title", "peace officer" and "property" are defined in s. 2.

Forfeiture of the proceeds of crime seized or subject to a restraint order pursuant to Part XII.2 is dealt with under the provisions of that Part. Forfeiture of "offence-related property" is dealt with in ss. 490.1 to 490.9.

SYNOPSIS

This section deals with the disposition of property which has been obtained by crime.

Subsection (1) describes the situation where, during the trial of an accused or defendant, the court determines that an offence has been committed and any property obtained by the commission of the offence is before the court or detained and will not be required as evidence in any other proceedings. Under such circumstances, s. 490 will not apply in respect of this property, but the court will make an order under subsec. (2) to dispose of it.

Subsection (2) states that the court shall order that the property be returned to the lawful owner, if such person is known. If the identity of the lawful owner is not known, the property will be ordered forfeit to Her Majesty, to be dealt with as the Attorney General directs or otherwise in accordance with the law.

Subsection (3) sets out the circumstances in which an order under subsec. (2) will not be made.

Subsection (4) provides that an order made under this section shall be executed, on the direction of the court, by such peace officers as normally execute process of the court.

ANNOTATIONS

It was held in *R. v. Kolstad* (1959), 123 C.C.C. 170, 30 C.R. 176 (Alta. C.A.), affd [1960] S.C.R. 110, 125 C.C.C. 254, that money paid by the accused for the purpose of bribery and filed as an exhibit at his trial should not be paid out to the accused, but rather held in court until further order.

This provision does not apply where the accused has been found not guilty. In such circumstances, the court has the jurisdiction to deal with an application for the return of seized funds as part of its inherent jurisdiction or under s. 24(1) of the Charter: *R. v. Perello* (2005), 207 C.C.C. (3d) 209 (Sask. Q.B.), affd 216 C.C.C. (3d) 327, 289 Sask. R. 214 (C.A.).

PHOTOGRAPHIC EVIDENCE / Certified photograph admissible in evidence / Statements made in certificate / Secondary evidence of peace officer / Notice of intention to produce certified photograph / Attendance for examination / Production of property in court / Definition of "photograph".

491.2 (1) Before any property that would otherwise be required to be produced for the purposes of a preliminary inquiry, trial or other proceeding in respect of an offence under section 334, 344, 348, 354, 355.2, 355.4, 362 or 380 is returned or ordered to be returned, forfeited or otherwise dealt with under section 489.1 or 490 or is otherwise returned, a peace officer or any person under the direction of a peace officer may take and retain a photograph of the property.

(2) Every photograph of property taken under subsection (1), accompanied by a certificate of a person containing the statements referred to in subsection (3), shall be admissible in evidence and, in the absence of evidence to the contrary, shall have the same probative force as the property would have had if it had been proved in the ordinary way.

(3) For the purposes of subsection (2), a certificate of a person stating that

- **(*a*) the person took the photograph under the authority of subsection (1),**
- **(*b*) the person is a peace officer or took the photograph under the direction of a peace officer, and**
- **(*c*) the photograph is a true photograph**

shall be admissible in evidence and, in the absence of evidence to the contrary, is evidence of the statements contained in the certificate without proof of the signature of the person appearing to have signed the certificate.

(4) An affidavit or solemn declaration of a peace officer or other person stating that the person has seized property and detained it or caused it to be detained from the time that person took possession of the property until a photograph of the property was taken under subsection (1) and that the property was not altered in any manner before the photograph was taken shall be admissible in evidence and, in the absence of evidence to the contrary, is evidence of the statements contained in the affidavit or solemn declaration without proof of the signature or official character of the person appearing to have signed the affidavit or solemn declaration.

(5) Unless the court orders otherwise, no photograph, certificate, affidavit or solemn declaration shall be received in evidence at a trial or other proceeding pursuant to subsection (2), (3) or (4) unless the prosecutor has, before the trial or other proceeding, given to the accused a copy thereof and reasonable notice of intention to produce it in evidence.

(6) Notwithstanding subsection (3) or (4), the court may require the person who appears to have signed a certificate, an affidavit or a solemn declaration referred to in that subsection to appear before it for examination or cross-examination in respect of the issue of proof of any of the facts contained in the certificate, affidavit or solemn declaration.

(7) A court may order any property seized and returned pursuant to section 489.1 or 490 to be produced in court or made available for examination by all parties to a proceeding at a reasonable time and place, notwithstanding that a photograph of the property has been received in evidence pursuant to subsection (2), where the court is satisfied that the interests of justice so require and that it is possible and practicable to do so in the circumstances.

(8) In this section, "photograph" includes a still photograph, a photographic film or plate, a microphotographic film, a photostatic negative, an X-ray film, a motion picture and a videotape. R.S.C. 1985, c. 23 (4th Supp.), s. 2; 1992, c. 1, s. 58; 2010, c. 14, s. 10.

CROSS-REFERENCES

The terms "prosecutor", "peace officer" and "property" are defined in s. 2. "Prosecutor" is also defined in s. 785 for the purpose of summary conviction proceedings. Section 4(6) provides that service of any document may be proved by oral evidence or by way of affidavit.

SEIZURE OF EXPLOSIVES / Forfeiture / Application of proceeds.

492. (1) Every person who executes a warrant issued under section 487 or 487.1 may seize any explosive substance that he suspects is intended to be used for an unlawful purpose, and shall, as soon as possible, remove to a place of safety anything that he seizes by virtue of this section and detain it until he is ordered by a judge of a superior court to deliver it to some other person or an order is made pursuant to subsection (2).

(2) Where an accused is convicted of an offence in respect of anything seized by virtue of subsection (1), it is forfeited and shall be dealt with as the court that makes the conviction may direct.

(3) Where anything to which this section applies is sold, the proceeds of the sale shall be paid to the Attorney General. R.S., c. C-34, s. 447; R.S.C. 1985, c. 27 (1st Supp.), s. 70.

CROSS-REFERENCES

The terms "explosive substance" and "Attorney General" are defined in s. 2. For other provisions respecting forfeiture of contraband, see ss. 491 and 491.1.

SYNOPSIS

This section sets out special provisions for seizing and disposing of explosives.

Subsection (1) provides that a person who executes a warrant under s. 487 may seize any explosives which are suspected to be held for an unlawful purpose. Such person must, as soon as possible, put these explosives in a safe place and hold them there until ordered by a judge of a superior court to deliver them to another person, or in accordance with subsec. (2).

Subsection (2) states that where a person is convicted of an offence in relation to the seized explosives, such explosives are forfeited and will be dealt with in accordance with the direction of the court that imposed the conviction.

Subsection (3) ensures that the proceeds from the sale of any explosives seized under this section will be paid to the Attorney General.

WARRANT FOR TRACKING DEVICE — TRANSACTIONS AND THINGS / Warrant for tracking device — individuals / Scope of warrant / Conditions / Period of validity / Period of validity — organized crime and terrorism offence / Removal after expiry of warrant / Definitions.

492.1 (1) A justice or judge who is satisfied by information on oath that there are reasonable grounds to suspect that an offence has been or will be committed under this or any other Act of Parliament and that tracking the location of one or more transactions or the location or movement of a thing, including a vehicle, will assist in the investigation of the offence may issue a warrant authorizing a peace officer or a public officer to obtain that tracking data by means of a tracking device.

(2) A justice or judge who is satisfied by information on oath that there are reasonable grounds to believe that an offence has been or will be committed under this or any other Act of Parliament and that tracking an individual's movement by identifying the location of a thing that is usually carried or worn by the individual will assist in the investigation of the offence may issue a warrant authorizing a peace officer or a public officer to obtain that tracking data by means of a tracking device.

(3) The warrant authorizes the peace officer or public officer, or a person acting under their direction, to install, activate, use, maintain, monitor and remove the tracking device, including covertly.

(4) A warrant may contain any conditions that the justice or judge considers appropriate, including conditions to protect a person's interests.

(5) Subject to subsection (6), a warrant is valid for the period specified in it as long as that period ends no more than 60 days after the day on which the warrant is issued.

(6) A warrant is valid for the period specified in it as long as that period ends no more than one year after the day on which the warrant is issued, if the warrant relates to

- **(*a*) an offence under any of sections 467.11 to 467.13;**
- **(*b*) an offence committed for the benefit of, at the direction of, or in association with a criminal organization; or**
- **(*c*) a terrorism offence.**

(7) On *ex parte* application supported by an affidavit, the justice or judge who issued a warrant or another justice or judge who has jurisdiction to issue such warrants may authorize the covert removal of the tracking device after the expiry of the warrant under any conditions that the justice or judge considers advisable in the public interest. The authorization is valid for the period specified in it as long as that period is not more than 90 days.

(8) The following definitions apply in this section.

"data" means representations, including signs, signals or symbols, that are capable of being understood by an individual or processed by a computer system or other device.

"judge" means a judge of a superior court of criminal jurisdiction or a judge of the Court of Quebec.

"public officer" means a public officer who is appointed or designated to administer or enforce a federal or provincial law and whose duties include the enforcement of this or any other Act of Parliament.

"tracking data" means data that relates to the location of a transaction, individual or thing.

"tracking device" means a device, including a computer program within the meaning of subsection 342.1(2), that may be used to obtain or record tracking data or to transmit it by a means of telecommunication. 1993, c. 40, s. 18; 1999, c. 5, s. 18; 2014, c. 31, s. 23.

CROSS-REFERENCES

"Peace officer" and "justice" are defined in s. 2.

This section is part of a more or less comprehensive scheme relating to surreptitious electronic surveillance. Interception of private communications are dealt with in Part VI. Use of transmission data recorders under ss. 492.2 and 487.01 would cover the use of other electronic devices, authorizing the collection of telephonic data and internet communications. Provision is made in s. 487.02 for the making of an assistance order to require persons to co-operate in the carrying out of orders made under this section.

SYNOPSIS

This section provides for the granting of a warrant to authorize the use of "tracking devices", as defined in subsec. (8). Subsection (1) permits a justice or a judge to authorize the tracking of the movement of a *thing*, including a vehicle, if he or she is satisfied by information on oath, that there are reasonable grounds to suspect that an offence has been committed or will be committed, and that tracking the location of the thing will assist in the investigation of the offence. Subsection (2) relates to the authorization to track the movements of a *thing usually carried or worn by an individual*, and requires reasonable grounds to believe that an offence has been committed or will be committed, and that tracking the location of the thing will assist in the investigation of the offence.

Warrants issued under this section may contain any conditions that the justice or judge considers appropriate. They are valid for a specified period, which can be no longer than one year in relation to specific terrorism and criminal organization offences, and can be no longer than 60 days for all other offences. Under subsec. (7), the justice or judge may authorize the covert removal of the device after the expiration of the warrant.

WARRANT FOR TRANSMISSION DATA RECORDER / Scope of warrant / Limitation / Period of validity / Period of validity — organized crime or terrorism offence / Definitions.

492.2 (1) A justice or judge who is satisfied by information on oath that there are reasonable grounds to suspect that an offence has been or will be committed against this or any other Act of Parliament and that transmission data will assist in the investigation of the offence may issue a warrant authorizing a peace officer or a public officer to obtain the transmission data by means of a transmission data recorder.

(2) The warrant authorizes the peace officer or public officer, or a person acting under their direction, to install, activate, use, maintain, monitor and remove the transmission data recorder, including covertly.

(3) No warrant shall be issued under this section for the purpose of obtaining tracking data.

(4) Subject to subsection (5), a warrant is valid for the period specified in it as long as that period ends no more than 60 days after the day on which the warrant is issued.

(5) The warrant is valid for the period specified in it as long as that period ends no more than one year after the day on which the warrant is issued, if the warrant relates to

- **(*a*) an offence under any of sections 467.11 to 467.13;**
- **(*b*) an offence committed for the benefit of, at the direction of, or in association with a criminal organization; or**
- **(*c*) a terrorism offence.**

(6) The following definitions apply in this section.

"data" means representations, including signs, signals or symbols, that are capable of being understood by an individual or processed by a computer system or other device.

"judge" means a judge of a superior court of criminal jurisdiction or a judge of the Court of Quebec.

"public officer" means a public officer who is appointed or designated to administer or enforce a federal or provincial law and whose duties include the enforcement of this or any other Act of Parliament.

"transmission data" means data that

- **(*a*) relates to the telecommunication functions of dialling, routing, addressing or signalling;**
- **(*b*) is transmitted to identify, activate or configure a device, including a computer program as defined in subsection 342.1(2), in order to establish or maintain access to a telecommunication service for the purpose of enabling a communication, or is generated during the creation, transmission or reception of a communication and identifies or purports to identify the type, direction, date, time, duration, size, origin, destination or termination of the communication; and**
- **(*c*) does not reveal the substance, meaning or purpose of the communication.**

"transmission data recorder" means a device, including a computer program within the meaning of subsection 342.1(2), that may be used to obtain or record transmission data

or to transmit it by a means of telecommunication. 1993, c. 40, s. 18; 1999, c. 5, s. 19; 2014, c. 31, s. 23.

CROSS-REFERENCES

The terms "justice" and "peace officer" are defined in s. 2. This section is part of a more or less comprehensive scheme relating to surreptitious electronic surveillance. Interception of private communications are dealt with in Part VI. Use of tracking devices as regulated under s. 492.1 and s. 487.01 would cover the use of other electronic devices such as video cameras. Provision is made in s. 487.02 for the making of an assistance order to require persons to co-operate in the carrying out of orders made under this section.

SYNOPSIS

This section provides for the granting of a warrant to authorize the covert use of a "transmission data recorder" to obtain "transmission data", as defined in subsec. (6). The justice or judge must be satisfied by information on oath that there are reasonable grounds to suspect that an offence has been or will be committed and that transmission data will assist in the investigation of the offence. Warrants issued under this section are valid for a specified period, which can be no longer than one year in relation to specific terrorism and criminal organization offences, and can be no longer than 60 days for all other offences.

Part XVI / COMPELLING APPEARANCE OF ACCUSED BEFORE A JUSTICE AND INTERIM RELEASE

Interpretation

DEFINITIONS / "accused" / "appearance notice" / "judge" / "officer in charge" / "promise to appear" / "recognizance" / "summons" / "undertaking" / "warrant".

493. In this Part,

"accused" includes

(*a*) a person to whom a peace officer has issued an appearance notice under section 496, and

(*b*) a person arrested for a criminal offence;

"appearance notice" means a notice in Form 9 issued by a peace officer;

"judge" means

(*a*) in the Province of Ontario, a judge of the superior court of criminal jurisdiction of the Province,

(*b*) in the Province of Quebec, a judge of the superior court of criminal jurisdiction of the province or three judges of the Court of Quebec,

(*c*) [*Repealed*, 1992, c. 51, s. 37.]

(*d*) in the Provinces of Nova Scotia, New Brunswick, Manitoba, British Columbia, Prince Edward Island, Saskatchewan, Alberta and Newfoundland and Labrador, a judge of the superior court of criminal jurisdiction of the Province,

(*e*) in Yukon and the Northwest Territories, a judge of the Supreme Court, and

(*f*) in Nunavut, a judge of the Nunavut Court of Justice;

"officer in charge" means the officer for the time being in command of the police force responsible for the lock-up or other place to which an accused is taken after arrest or a peace officer designated by him for the purposes of this Part who is in charge of that place at the time an accused is taken to that place to be detained in custody;

"promise to appear" means a promise in Form 10;

"recognizance", when used in relation to a recognizance entered into before an officer in charge, or other peace officer, means a recognizance in Form 11, and when used in relation to a recognizance entered into before a justice or judge, means a recognizance in Form 32;

"summons" means a summons in Form 6 issued by a justice or a judge;

"undertaking" means an undertaking in Form 11.1 or 12;

"warrant", when used in relation to a warrant for the arrest of a person, means a warrant in Form 7 and, when used in relation to a warrant for the committal of a person, means a warrant in Form 8. R.S., c. C-34, s. 448; R.S., c. 2 (2nd Supp.), s. 5; 1972, c. 17, s. 3; 1974-75-76, c. 48, s. 25(1); 1978-79, c. 11, s. 10; R.S.C. 1985, c. 11 (1st Supp.), s. 2; c. 27 (2nd Supp.), s. 10; c. 40 (4th Supp.), s. 2; 1990, c. 16, s. 5; 1990, c. 17, s. 12; 1992, c. 51, s. 37; 1993, c. 28, Sch. III, s. 32 (repealed 1999, c. 3, s. 12); 1994, c. 44, s. 39; 1999, c. 3, ss. 12, 30; 2002, c. 7, s. 143; 2015, c. 3, s. 51.

CROSS-REFERENCES

The terms "peace officer", "property", "justice", "superior court of criminal jurisdiction" and "Attorney General" are defined in s. 2. In addition to the definition in this section see s. 2 and notes to that section. Section 841 provides that forms varied to suit the case and forms to the like effect shall be deemed to be good, valid and sufficient in the circumstances for which, respectively, they are provided. Also note s. 849(3) requiring preprinted portions of forms to be printed in both official languages.

SYNOPSIS

This section contains definitions of key terms found in Part XVI of the *Criminal Code*. Part XVI provides a legislative scheme for compelling the appearance of an accused person before a justice and for judicial interim release.

ANNOTATIONS

"Officer in charge" – This definition contemplates a delegation of authority by the officer for the time being in command of the police force to a police officer who is at the time in charge of the place of detention. The officer in charge of such place does not have the powers conferred and imposed under this Part unless and until he has been designated for such purposes: *R. v. Gendron* (1985), 22 C.C.C. (3d) 312 (Ont. C.A.).

Arrest Without Warrant and Release from Custody

ARREST WITHOUT WARRANT BY ANY PERSON / Arrest by owner, etc. of property / Delivery to peace officer / For greater certainty.

494. (1) Any one may arrest without warrant

(*a*) a person whom he finds committing an indictable offence; or

(*b*) a person who, on reasonable grounds, he believes

(i) has committed a criminal offence, and

(ii) is escaping from and freshly pursued by persons who have lawful authority to arrest that person.

(2) The owner or a person in lawful possession of property, or a person authorized by the owner or by a person in lawful possession of property, may arrest a person without a warrant if they find them committing a criminal offence on or in relation to that property and

(*a*) they make the arrest at that time; or

(*b*) they make the arrest within a reasonable time after the offence is committed and they believe on reasonable grounds that it is not feasible in the circumstances for a peace officer to make the arrest.

(3) Any one other than a peace officer who arrests a person without warrant shall forthwith deliver the person to a peace officer.

(4) For greater certainty, a person who is authorized to make an arrest under this section is a person who is authorized by law to do so for the purposes of section 25. R.S., c. C-34, s. 449; R.S., c. 2 (2nd Supp.), s. 5; 2012, c. 9, s. 3.

CROSS-REFERENCES

The term "peace officer" is defined in s. 2. Indictable offence includes a hybrid offence by virtue of s. 34(1)(*a*) of the *Interpretation Act*, R.S.C. 1985, c. I-21. See *R. v. Huff* (1979), 50 C.C.C. (2d) 324 (Alta. C.A.). With respect to protection of persons acting in the administration or enforcement of the law see ss. 25 to 27. Also note s. 29(2) which imposes a duty on a person making an arrest to give notice of the reason for the arrest. An additional power of arrest is given under s. 30 with respect to breach of the peace. The additional powers of arrest by peace officers are dealt with in ss. 31 and 495.

Section 529.3 gives a peace officer power to enter a dwelling-house to effect the arrest without a warrant in exigent circumstances. The officer may enter the dwelling-house without prior announcement in the circumstances set out in s. 529.4(3). Power to issue a warrant to arrest a person in a dwelling-house is set out in ss. 529 and 529.1.

SYNOPSIS

This section describes the power of any person, whether or not they are a peace officer, to arrest another person without a warrant.

Subsection (1) grants to every person the authority to arrest without warrant another person in two sets of circumstances. If a person is found committing an indictable offence, he may be arrested without a warrant by any other person. A person who is not a peace officer may also arrest without a warrant another person whom the individual making the arrest has reasonable grounds to believe has committed a criminal offence and has escaped from, and is being freshly pursued by persons with the lawful authority to make the arrest.

Subsection (2) states that anyone who is either the owner of, in lawful possession of, or has been authorized by the owner of the person in lawful possession of property, may arrest without a warrant a person whom they find committing a criminal offence in relation to or on that property provided they make the arrest at the time they find them committing the offence or within a reasonable time after the offence is committed, and they believe on reasonable grounds that it is not feasible in the circumstances for a peace officer to make the arrest.

Subsection (3) requires that any person, other than a peace officer, who arrests another person without a warrant, must deliver the arrested person forthwith to a peace officer.

Under subsec. (4), a person who makes a lawful arrest under this section is a person authorized by law to do so for purposes of s. 25. Section 25 authorizes the use of force to *inter alia* carry out an arrest.

ANNOTATIONS

Constitutional considerations – The arrest of a citizen by another private citizen is a governmental function to which the Charter applies and thus a search incident to that arrest must comply with s. 8 of the Charter: *R. v. Lerke* (1986), 24 C.C.C. (3d) 129, 49 C.R. (3d) 324, 25 D.L.R. (4th) 403 (Alta. C.A.). *Contra*: See *R. v. J. (A.M.)* (1999), 137 C.C.C. (3d) 213, 204 W.A.C. 238 (B.C.C.A.), in which the court held that a person other than a peace officer making a citizen's arrest is not required to give the accused the requisite Charter warnings.

Grounds for arrest (subsec. (1)) – A citizen must have reasonable grounds to believe that a person was apparently in the process of committing an indictable offence in his or her presence: *R. v. Abel* (2008), 229 C.C.C. (3d) 465 (B.C.C.A.).

Meaning of "forthwith" (subsec. (3)) – "Forthwith" does not mean instantly but merely as soon as is reasonably practicable under all the circumstances: *R. v. Cunningham* (1979), 49 C.C.C. (2d) 390 (Man. Co. Ct.).

ARREST WITHOUT WARRANT BY PEACE OFFICER / Limitation / Consequences of arrest without warrant.

495. (1) A peace officer may arrest without warrant

(*a*) a person who has committed an indictable offence or who, on reasonable grounds, he believes has committed or is about to commit an indictable offence;

(*b*) a person whom he finds committing a criminal offence; or

(*c*) a person in respect of whom he has reasonable grounds to believe that a warrant of arrest or committal, in any form set out in Part XXVIII in relation thereto, is in force within the territorial jurisdiction in which the person is found.

(2) A peace officer shall not arrest a person without warrant for

(*a*) an indictable offence mentioned in section 553,

(*b*) an offence for which the person may be prosecuted by indictment or for which he is punishable on summary conviction, or

(*c*) an offence punishable on summary conviction,

in any case where

(*d*) he believes on reasonable grounds that the public interest, having regard to all the circumstances including the need to

(i) establish the identity of the person,

(ii) secure or preserve evidence of or relating to the offence, or

(iii) prevent the continuation or repetition of the offence or the commission of another offence,

may be satisfied without so arresting the person, and

(*e*) he has no reasonable grounds to believe that, if he does not so arrest the person, the person will fail to attend court in order to be dealt with according to law.

(3) Notwithstanding subsection (2), a peace officer acting under subsection (1) is deemed to be acting lawfully and in the execution of his duty for the purposes of

(*a*) any proceedings under this or any other Act of Parliament; and

(*b*) any other proceedings, unless in any such proceedings it is alleged and established by the person making the allegation that the peace officer did not comply with the requirements of subsection (2). R.S., c. C-34, s. 450; R.S., c. 2 (2nd Supp.), s. 5; R.S.C. 1985, c. 27 (1st Supp.), s. 75.

CROSS-REFERENCES

The term "peace officer" is defined in s. 2. Indictable offence includes a hybrid offence by virtue of s. 34(1)(*a*) of the *Interpretation Act*, R.S.C. 1985, c. I-21. See *R. v. Huff* (1979), 50 C.C.C. (2d) 324 (Alta. C.A.). With respect to protection of persons acting in the administration or enforcement of the law see ss. 25 to 27. Section 28 protects the peace officer in case of arrest of the wrong person when executing a warrant. Also note s. 29(1), which requires the person executing the warrant to have it with him where feasible and produce it upon request, and s. 29(2) which imposes a duty on a person making an arrest to give notice of the warrant under which he makes the arrest and the reason for the arrest. An additional power of arrest is given under s. 31 with respect to breach of the peace. Section 10 of the Charter, as well, imposes duties with respect to reason for arrest and right to counsel and see notes under that section. A peace officer of course also may exercise the powers of arrest given to a private citizen under ss. 30 and 494.

Section 529.3 gives a peace officer power to enter a dwelling-house to effect the arrest without a warrant in exigent circumstances. The officer may enter the dwelling-house without prior announcement in the circumstances set out in s. 529.4(3). Power to issue a warrant to arrest a person in a dwelling-house is set out in ss. 529 and 529.1.

Note the special procedure set out in s. 507.1 where a private prosecutor lays an information under s. 504 and seeks to have a summons or warrant issued.

Note on the scheme for pre-trial release – Where an officer does not arrest the person by virtue of s. 495(2) because the accused is alleged to have committed a hybrid offence, a summary conviction offence or an offence listed in s. 553 and there is not cause for arrest to, for example, establish identity, preserve evidence, prevent commission of an offence, or ensure attendance in court, then he shall issue an appearance notice under s. 496. Where the officer arrests the person but the person falls within the categories set out in s. 497(1) then he shall release him pursuant to s. 497 on an appearance notice (defined in s. 493), or with the intention of compelling his appearance by way of summons (defined in s. 493), once there is no cause for further detention. If the person is arrested and not released under s. 497 then he shall be released by the officer in charge (defined in s. 493) or another officer pursuant to s. 498 on a promise to appear or recognizance (defined in s. 493) once there is no cause for further detention. The officer may release not only for the offences described in s. 495(2) but for any offence punishable by imprisonment for five years or less. While the provisions of ss. 495(2), 497 and 498 are stated in mandatory terms, in effect requiring the accused's release unless there is cause to further detain him where he is charged with one of the specified offences, s. 503(2) gives the peace officer and officer in charge a discretion to release an accused charged with other offences (except an offence listed in s. 469) on a promise to appear or recognizance, if the officer is satisfied that the accused "should be released from custody conditionally". The contents of the appearance notice, promise to appear and recognizance are described in s. 501 and may also require that the accused attend at a time and place stated therein for the purposes of the *Identification of Criminals Act*, R.S.C. 1985, c. I-1. The officer may also require the accused to enter into an undertaking including terms in s. 503(2.1). The accused and the prosecutor can apply to replace this undertaking. Where the accused does not attend as required then a justice may issue a warrant for the accused's arrest pursuant to s. 502. In all cases where the accused is given process by the peace officer or officer in charge an information is to be laid before a justice as soon as practicable and, in any event, before the return date set out in the process pursuant to s. 505. The justice then will either confirm the process or cancel it pursuant to s. 508. Where the accused is not released by the peace officer or officer in charge then he must be taken before a justice pursuant to s. 503, usually within 24 hours. The justice will then deal with release pursuant to s. 515 unless the accused is charged with an offence listed in s. 469 such as murder. In the latter case the justice will order that the accused be detained in custody and the onus is upon the accused to bring an application under s. 522 to a judge of the superior court of criminal jurisdiction (defined in s. 2) for release pending trial. Section 503 also makes special provision for an accused who is arrested for an offence alleged to have been committed in another province.

Where the accused is not released on a form of process by a peace officer or officer in charge then an information will be laid before the justice pursuant to s. 504. Where the accused has not yet been arrested then the justice may issue a summons or warrant [both defined in s. 493] pursuant to s. 507. The contents of the summons is described in s. 509 and served in accordance with s. 509(2) and may also require that the accused attend at a time and place stated therein for the purposes of the *Identification of Criminals Act*. Where the accused does not attend as required then a justice may issue a warrant for the accused's arrest pursuant to s. 510. Once the person is arrested on a warrant then again he will be taken before a justice pursuant to s. 503, unless the warrant has been endorsed permitting the officer in charge to release under s. 499. The contents of the warrant are described in ss. 511 and 513. The warrant is executed pursuant to s. 513. The duties of a peace officer executing an arrest warrant are described in ss. 29 and 10 of the Charter. Further, under s. 512, notwithstanding that an accused has been released on a form of process by a peace officer or officer in charge, or a summons has been issued, a justice may issue a summons or warrant where he believes on reasonable and probable grounds that this action is necessary in the public interest. The information laid under s. 504 or s. 505 may be in Form 2 pursuant to s. 506.

Failure to attend court as required, comply with conditions in a recognizance or undertaking or attend for the purposes of the *Identification of Criminals Act* is an offence under s. 145. A warrant may issue under s. 512 where the accused fails to appear for court as required.

A warrant, summons, appearance notice, promise to appear, undertaking or recognizance may be issued, executed, given or entered into on a holiday by virtue of s. 20.

SYNOPSIS

This section specifies the powers of a peace officer to arrest without a warrant, and the limitations thereon.

Subsection (1) states that a peace officer may arrest without warrant any person whom he finds committing a criminal offence, any person whom he believes on reasonable grounds has committed or is about to commit an indictable offence, or any person whom he reasonably believes is the subject of a warrant of arrest or committal.

Subsection (2) limits the powers of arrest without warrant available to a peace officer. A peace officer shall not arrest a person without warrant for an indictable offence within the absolute jurisdiction of a provincial court judge, for a Crown election offence, or for a summary conviction offence, in any of the circumstances set out in subsec. (2)(*d*) and (*e*). In other words, the peace officer should arrest without warrant persons committing the offences listed in paras. (*a*), (*b*) or (*c*) only where it is necessary to establish the identity of the person, to preserve evidence of the offence, to prevent the continuation of or repetition of the offence, or to secure the attendance of the accused in court.

Subsection (3) makes it clear that a peace officer, acting under subsec. (1), is deemed to be acting lawfully and in the execution of his duty for the purposes of any Act of Parliament, notwithstanding subsec. (2). This deeming provision also extends to any other proceedings, unless it is established that the peace officer did not comply with subsec. (2).

ANNOTATIONS

Meaning of "reasonable grounds" (subsec. (1)(*a*)) – For an arrest to be valid on the basis of reasonable and probable grounds, it is not sufficient for the police officer to subjectively believe that he has reasonable and probable grounds to make an arrest. Rather, it must also be shown that a reasonable person, standing in the shoes of the officer, would have believed that reasonable and probable grounds existed to make the arrest. However, the police need not go further and establish a *prima facie* case. An arrest which is lawfully made does not become unlawful simply because the police intend to continue their investigation after the arrest, nor does the arrest thereby constitute a violation of s. 9 of the Charter: *R. v. Storrey*, [1990] 1 S.C.R. 241, 53 C.C.C. (3d) 316 (7:0).

For a peace officer to have reasonable and probable grounds his belief in the person's guilt must take into account all the information available to him. He is entitled to disregard only what he has good reason for believing is not reliable: *Chartier v. Quebec (Attorney General)*, [1979] 2 S.C.R. 474, 48 C.C.C. (2d) 34.

Although the accused's arrest was based on the information of a third party civilian who was unknown to the police, the police were not required to obtain confirmation of the civilian's information in order to have reasonable and probable grounds to arrest the accused. The officer must conduct the inquiry which the circumstances reasonably permit to determine whether there are reasonable and probable grounds. In so doing, the officer must take into account all information available to him and is entitled to disregard only information which he has good reason to believe is unreliable. In this case, the third party witnessed the events, provided a specific and detailed complaint and made no claim to anonymity. Accordingly, the police were able to assess the third party's reliability and had no reason to discount his information: *R. v. Golub* (1997), 117 C.C.C. (3d) 193, 9 C.R. (5th) 98 (Ont. C.A.), leave to appeal to S.C.C. refused 128 C.C.C. (3d) vi.

Finds committing criminal offence (subsec. (1)(*b*)) – Where a peace officer makes an arrest under para. *(b)*, the validity of the arrest does not depend upon a subsequent conviction for the commission of that offence, but rather upon the circumstances which were apparent to the officer at the time: *R. v. Biron*, [1976] 2 S.C.R. 56, 23 C.C.C. (2d) 513 (5:3), and *R. v. Fuhr*, [1975] 4 W.W.R. 403 (Alta. S.C. App. Div.).

In *R. v. Stevens* (1976), 33 C.C.C. (2d) 429, 18 N.S.R. (2d) 96 (S.C. App. Div.), the court, considering *R. v. Biron, supra,* held that in order to arrest a person without a warrant for a summary conviction offence it is not sufficient for the arresting officer to show that he had reasonable and probable grounds to believe such offence had been, or was about to be, committed, rather he must go further and show that he found a situation in which a person was apparently committing an offence. Where the accused is acquitted on a charge of causing a disturbance on the basis that the accused was in a dwelling home at the time a charge of resisting an officer in the execution of his duty in attempting to arrest for that offence must also fail, the arrest being unlawful.

The police officer did not find the accused committing an offence where the police officer stopped the accused in his vehicle and smelled burning marihuana emanating from the vehicle. The officer did not see, hear or smell the accused committing the offence of possession of marihuana. Observation of recently smoked marihuana is not an observation of current possession of additional unsmoked marihuana, nor is it objectively reasonable to conclude that more, unsmoked marihuana is present: *R. v. Janvier* (2007), 227 C.C.C. (3d) 294 (Sask. C.A.).

However, the smell of raw (as opposed to burnt) marihuana detected by an experienced officer as emanating from a vehicle did amount to the observation that a crime (possession of marihuana) was being committed at that time. The possession of marihuana was not a past event and the officer did not need to infer that he could find more marihuana by conducting a search. Because the smell alone was sufficient to conclude that the subject was contemporaneously in possession of marihuana, the arrest was lawful under s. 495(1)(*b*): *R. v. Harding* (2010), 256 C.C.C. (3d) 284 (Alta. C.A.). See also *R. v. Loewen* (2010), 260 C.C.C. (3d) 296 (Alta. C.A.), affd on other grounds [2011] 2 S.C.R. 167, 273 C.C.C. (3d) 1, in which the court held that the smell of burned marihuana did not preclude the possibility of continuing possession of a controlled substance. The amount of cash seized during a valid pat-down search and the odour of burnt drugs constituted objective reasonable grounds.

Similarly, in *R. v. MacCannell* (2014), 314 C.C.C. (3d) 514 (B.C.C.A.), the court held that "odour alone" — whether burnt or fresh — *may* be sufficient to support an arrest under para. (1)(*b*), depending on the facts of the case.

Person for whom arrest warrant outstanding (subsec. (1)(*c*)) – It is not necessary that the peace officer ascertain the nature of the offence for which the warrant is outstanding: *R. v. Gamracy*, [1974] S.C.R. 640, 12 C.C.C. (2d) 209 (3:2).

Where it was clearly feasible for a police officer to possess the warrant his failure to do so vitiated any lawful arrest: *R. v. Richard* (1974), 27 C.R.N.S. 337 (Que. S.C.).

Right to enter premises to effect arrest – See notes following s. 529.3.

Search incident to arrest – Police officers have the power to search an accused as an incident to a lawful arrest and to seize anything in his possession or immediate surroundings to guarantee the safety of the police and the accused, prevent the accused's escape or provide evidence against him. The existence of reasonable and probable grounds to believe that the accused is in possession of weapons or evidence is not a prerequisite to the existence of the power to search, provided, however, that the search is for a valid objective and not unrelated to the objectives of the proper administration of justice. Accordingly, a search done for weapons or other dangerous articles is necessary as an elementary precaution to preclude the possibility of their use against the police, the nearby public or the accused himself. A search is also proper to collect evidence that can be used in establishing the guilt of the accused. Further, the search must not be conducted in an abusive fashion and the use of physical or psychological constraint should be proportionate to the objectives sought and the other circumstances of the situation. A "frisk" or pat down search is a relatively non-intrusive procedure and, if done for valid reasons, is not a disproportionate interference with the freedom of persons lawfully arrested: *Cloutier c. Langlois*, [1990] 1 S.C.R. 158, 53 C.C.C. (3d) 257 (7:0).

A strip search is the removal or rearrangement of some or all of the clothing of a person to permit a visual inspect of a person's private areas or undergarments. This is distinguishable from the less intrusive "frisk" or "pat down" searches, which do not involve the removal of clothing, and the more intrusive body cavity searches. Before a strip search may be justified as an incident to arrest, the arrest itself must be lawful and the search must be truly incident to the arrest in the sense that it must be related to the reasons for the arrest. The reasonableness of the search for evidence is governed by the need to preserve the evidence and to prevent its disposal by the detainee. Where only a strip search will expose the evidence, the risk of disposal must be realistically assessed. A search incident to arrest may also be focused on weapons. Usually, a pat down or frisk search will suffice for determining whether a person has a weapon on his person. Only if the frisk search reveals a possible weapon or if the particular circumstances of the case raise the risk that a weapon is concealed will a strip search be justified. The mere possibility that evidence or weapons are concealed on the body of the accused is not sufficient to justify a strip search. Strip searches cannot be carried out as a matter of routine policy. A strip search will always be unreasonable if carried out abusively. Merely because the police have reasonable and probable grounds to carry out an arrest does not confer authority on them to automatically carry out a strip search. Additional grounds pertaining to the purpose of the strip search are required. To meet the constitutional standard of reasonableness, the police must establish that they have reasonable and probable grounds for concluding that a strip search is necessary to discover weapons or evidence related to the reason for the arrest. Beyond this, the search must still be carried out in a reasonable manner.

Several factors should be considered in determining whether and, if so, how to conduct a strip search, such as, whether the search can be conducted at the police station, whether it can be done in a manner that ensures the health and safety of all involved, whether the search will be authorized by a police officer acting in a supervisory capacity, whether the search will be carried out by officers of the same gender as the accused and whether the search is carried out with minimum force. Strip searches should only be conducted in police stations unless exigent circumstances exist. Strip searches conducted in the field can only be justified where there is a demonstrated necessity and urgency to search for weapons and objects that could be used to threaten the safety of the accused, arresting officers or other individuals: *R. v. Golden*, [2001] 3 S.C.R. 679, 159 C.C.C. (3d) 449.

The warrantless search of a home incident to arrest is generally prohibited subject to exceptional circumstances where the law enforcement interest is so compelling that it overrides the individual's right to privacy within the home. The state interest upon arrest is the effective administration of justice, the various components of which include the need to secure the arrested person, protect those at the scene of the arrest and preserve evidence. The frustration of the effective enforcement of justice is the hallmark of exceptional circumstances. The risk of physical harm to those at the scene of the arrest constitutes exceptional circumstances justifying the warrantless entry and search of a residence. If the circumstances of an arrest give rise to a legitimate cause for concern with respect to the safety of those at the scene, reasonable steps to allay that concern may be taken. The nature of the apprehended risk, the potential consequences of not taking protective measures, the availability of alternative measures and the likelihood of the contemplated danger actually existing, must all be considered. The officers making this assessment must do so on the spot with no time for careful reflection: *R. v. Golub*, *supra*.

The common law power to search incident to arrest permits the search of cell phones and similar devices found on the suspect. Because the search of a cell phone has the potential to be a much more significant invasion of privacy than the typical search incident to arrest, four conditions must be met in order for the search to comply with s. 8. First, the arrest must be lawful. Second, the search must be truly incidental to the arrest. This requirement should be strictly applied to permit searches that must be done promptly upon arrest in order to effectively serve the law enforcement purposes. In this context, those purposes are protecting the police, the accused or the public; preserving evidence; and, if the investigation will be stymied or significantly hampered absent the ability to promptly conduct the search, discovering evidence. Third, the nature and the extent of the search must be tailored to its purpose. In practice, this will mean that only recently sent or drafted emails, texts, photos and the call log will, generally, be available, although other searches may, in some circumstances, be justified. Finally, the police must take detailed notes of what they have examined on the device and how they examined it. The notes should generally include the applications searched, the extent of the search, the time of the search, its purpose and its duration: *R. v. Fearon*, [2014] 3 S.C.R. 621, 318 C.C.C. (3d) 182 (4:3).

Right to counsel on arrest – Where a person is detained for a search, as in the case of a body search incident to arrest, then, immediately upon detention, the detainee has the right to be informed of the right to counsel under s. 10(*b*) of the Charter. However, the police are not obligated to suspend the search incident to arrest until the detainee has the opportunity to retain counsel. The police are, however, required to suspend the search where the lawfulness of the search is dependent on the detainee's consent or where the statute gives a person a right to seek review of the decision to search: *R. v. Debot*, [1989] 2 S.C.R. 1140, 52 C.C.C. (3d) 193.

Arrest to establish identity – It was held in *R. v. Moore*, [1979] 1 S.C.R. 195, 43 C.C.C. (2d) 83 (5:2), which arose out of an arrest for a summary conviction provincial traffic offence for which these provisions are applicable by virtue of the provincial *Summary Convictions Act*, that as a constable has no power to arrest an accused for a summary conviction offence by virtue of this subsection unless, *inter alia,* the arrest was necessary to establish the person's identity, a constable in requesting that the person whom he finds committing such an offence identify himself is in the execution of his duty and the accused's refusal to accede to the request constitutes the offence of obstructing police under s. 129.

Arrest and arbitrary detention under s. 9 of Charter [Also see meaning of "reasonable grounds", *supra*] – In *R. v. Grant*, [2009] 2 S.C.R. 353, 245 C.C.C. (3d) 1, the Supreme Court of Canada held that an unlawful detention will necessarily be arbitrary within the meaning of s. 9 of the Charter. Earlier suggestions that an unlawful detention was not necessarily arbitrary (see *R. v. Duguay* (1985), 18 C.C.C. (3d) 289 (Ont. C.A.)) should not be followed. Mirroring the framework developed for assessing unreasonable searches and seizures under s. 8 of the Charter, it should now be understood that, for a detention to be non-arbitrary, it must be authorized by a law which is itself non-arbitrary. As with other rights, the s. 9 prohibition of arbitrary detention may be limited under s. 1 by such measures "prescribed by law as can be demonstrably justified in a free and democratic society": see *R. v. Hufsky*, [1988] 1 S.C.R. 621, 40 C.C.C. (3d) 398, and *R. v. Ladouceur*, [1990] 1 S.C.R. 1257, 56 C.C.C. (3d) 22.

The police advised the accused that he was being detained in relation to an investigation into the death of his daughter but he was formally arrested only subsequent to questioning at the police station. The initial detention of the accused was not arbitrary. The police officer put the accused under *de facto* arrest through the use of words that conveyed clearly to the accused that he was under arrest, the conduct of the officers and the accused's submission to police authority and this arrest was lawful as it was based on reasonable and probable grounds: *R. v. Latimer*, [1997] 1 S.C.R. 217, 112 C.C.C. (3d) 193.

Also see *R. v. Keeling* (1988), 10 M.V.R. (2d) 57 (B.C.C.A.), where the accused was arrested only after he had been detained as a consequence of the breathalyzer demand. In those circumstances, the imposition of the arrest, even if pursuant to the police officer's policy that he arrests all impaired drivers, was inconsequential. At all times, the accused was lawfully detained for a legitimate reason. To a similar effect is: *R. v. Sieben* (1989), 51 C.C.C. (3d) 343, 73 C.R. (3d) 33 (Alta. C.A.).

It was held in *R. v. Fosseneuve* (1995), 101 C.C.C. (3d) 61, 43 C.R. (4th) 260 (Man. Q.B.), that subsec. (2)(*d*) of this section is invalid to the extent that it permits an arrest without warrant for the offences mentioned therein, solely on the ground of the "public interest". However, it is valid to the extent that it permits the arrest in a public interest, limited to the needs to establish identity, secure evidence, and prevent the continuation or repetition of the offence or the commission of another offence.

Subsection (3) – Subsection (3) must be construed to mean that no reliance can be placed on a peace officer's failure to comply with subsec. (2) to support the argument that he was not acting in the execution of his duty in making an arrest: *R. v. Adams* (1972), 21 C.R.N.S. 257, [1973] 1 W.W.R. 371 (Sask.C.A.). Folld: *R. v. McKibbon* (1973), 12 C.C.C. (2d) 66 (B.C.C.A.); *R. v. Bunn* (1986), 29 C.C.C. (3d) 133 (Man. Q.B.).

This subsection had no application to charges of assault of police under s. 270 where there was no allegation of a failure to comply with subsec. (2) but, rather, it was alleged that the officers were not in execution of their duty because, when they attempted to arrest the accused at his home, they were trespassers and the arrest was illegal: *R. v. Delong* (1989), 47 C.C.C. (3d) 402, 69 C.R. (3d) 147 (Ont. C.A.).

ISSUE OF APPEARANCE NOTICE BY PEACE OFFICER.

496. Where, by virtue of subsection 495(2), a peace officer does not arrest a person, he may issue an appearance notice to the person if the offence is

(*a*) an indictable offence mentioned in section 553;

(*b*) an offence for which the person may be prosecuted by indictment or for which he is punishable on summary conviction; or

(*c*) an offence punishable on summary conviction. R.S., c. C-34, s. 451; R.S., c. 2 (2nd Supp.), s. 5.

CROSS-REFERENCES

The term "peace officer" is defined in s. 2. The term "appearance notice" is defined in s. 493. An appearance notice may be issued or entered into on a holiday by virtue of s. 20. A warrant may issue under s. 512 where the accused fails to appear for court as required. For discussion of the pre-trial release provisions see the *Note on the scheme for pre-trial release* under s. 495.

SYNOPSIS

This section authorizes a peace officer to issue an appearance notice where the officer decides not to arrest a person on the basis of subsec. 495(2).

RELEASE FROM CUSTODY BY PEACE OFFICER / Exception / Where subsection (1) does not apply / Consequences of non-release.

497. (1) Subject to subsection (1.1), if a peace officer arrests a person without warrant for an offence described in paragraph 496(*a*), (*b*) or (*c*), the peace officer shall, as soon as practicable,

(*a*) release the person from custody with the intention of compelling their appearance by way of summons; or

(*b*) issue an appearance notice to the person and then release them.

(1.1) A peace officer shall not release a person under subsection (1) if the peace officer believes, on reasonable grounds,

(*a*) that it is necessary in the public interest that the person be detained in custody or that the matter of their release from custody be dealt with under another provision of this Part, having regard to all the circumstances including the need to

(i) establish the identity of the person,

(ii) secure or preserve evidence of or relating to the offence,

(iii) prevent the continuation or repetition of the offence or the commission of another offence, or

(iv) ensure the safety and security of any victim of or witness to the offence; or

(*b*) that if the person is released from custody, the person will fail to attend court in order to be dealt with according to law.

(2) Subsection (1) does not apply in respect of a person who has been arrested without warrant by a peace officer for an offence described in subsection 503(3).

(3) A peace officer who has arrested a person without warrant for an offence described in subsection (1) and who does not release the person from custody as soon as practicable in the manner described in that subsection shall be deemed to be acting lawfully and in the execution of the peace officer's duty for the purposes of

(*a*) any proceedings under this or any other Act of Parliament; and

(*b*) any other proceedings, unless in any such proceedings it is alleged and established by the person making the allegation that the peace officer did not comply with the requirements of subsection (1). R.S., c. C-34, s. 452; R.S., c. 2 (2nd Supp.), s. 5; 1999, c. 25, s. 3.

CROSS-REFERENCES

The terms "peace officer" and "victim" are defined in s. 2. The terms "appearance notice" and "summons" are defined in s. 493. The contents of the appearance notice are set out in s. 501. An appearance notice may be issued or entered into on a holiday by virtue of s. 20. A warrant may issue under s. 512 where the accused fails to appear for court as required. For discussion of the pre-trial release provisions see the *Note on the scheme for pre-trial release* under s. 495.

SYNOPSIS

This section sets out the powers of a peace officer to release a person who has been arrested without a warrant.

Subsection (1) provides that where a peace officer arrests a person without a warrant for an offence set out in s. 496(*a*), the officer must, as soon as practicable, release the person from custody with the intention of issuing a summons. The peace officer may also decide to issue an appearance notice to the person and then release him. However, the officer shall not release the accused if the officer believes on reasonable grounds that the accused's detention is necessary in the public interest as defined in subsec. (1.1)(*a*) or because the accused will fail to attend court.

Subsection (2) makes it clear that the requirements of subsec. (1) do not apply where a person has been arrested without warrant by a peace officer for an indictable offence alleged to have been committed in Canada but in a different province.

Subsection (3) provides that a peace officer is deemed to be acting lawfully and in the execution of his or her duties even if he or she does not comply with subsec. (1) for the purposes set out in paras. (*a*) and (*b*), unless it is established that the provisions of subsec. (1) were not complied with.

ANNOTATIONS

The continued detention of a motorist, arrested for impaired driving, until he has sobered up is authorized by subsec. (1)(*f*) of this section and does not violate the guarantee against arbitrary detention in s. 9 of the *Charter of Rights and Freedoms*: *R. v. Williamson* (1986), 25 C.C.C. (3d) 139, 40 M.V.R. 15 (Alta. Q.B.). Similarly: *R. v. Pashovitz* (1987), 59 C.R. (3d) 396, 59 Sask. R. 165 (C.A.).

Where the alleged breach of the Charter does not give rise to a defence, did not lead to the obtaining of evidence and could not have had a bearing on the sentence, then it ought not to be the subject of inquiry at trial, as in this case where the alleged breach of s. 9 resulted from the continued detention of the motorist several hours after it was safe for him to go: *R. v. Cutforth*, (1987), 40 C.C.C. (3d) 253, 61 C.R. (3d) 187 (Alta. C.A.). However, compare *R. v. Davidson* (1988), 46 C.C.C. (3d) 403, 88 N.S.R. (2d) 271 (C.A.).

There was a sufficient temporal nexus to warrant the application of s. 24(2) of the *Charter of Rights and Freedoms* to permit exclusion of a notice of intention to produce a certificate of analysis in a drinking and driving case, where the notice was served following the period of arbitrary detention: *R. v. Weaver* (2005), 194 C.C.C. (3d) 350, 27 C.R. (6th) 397 (Alta. C.A.).

RELEASE FROM CUSTODY BY OFFICER IN CHARGE / Exception / Where subsection (1) does not apply / Consequences of non-release.

498. (1) Subject to subsection (1.1), if a person who has been arrested without warrant by a peace officer is taken into custody, or if a person who has been arrested without warrant and delivered to a peace officer under subsection 494(3) or placed in the custody of a peace officer under subsection 163.5(3) of the *Customs Act* is detained in custody under subsection 503(1) for an offence described in paragraph 496(*a*), (*b*) or (*c*), or any other offence that is punishable by imprisonment for five years or less, and has not been taken before a justice or released from custody under any other provision of this Part, the officer in charge or another peace officer shall, as soon as practicable,

(*a*) release the person with the intention of compelling their appearance by way of summons;

(*b*) release the person on their giving a promise to appear;

(*c*) release the person on the person's entering into a recognizance before the officer in charge or another peace officer without sureties in an amount not exceeding $500 that the officer directs, but without deposit of money or other valuable security; or

(*d*) if the person is not ordinarily resident in the province in which the person is in custody or does not ordinarily reside within 200 kilometres of the place in which the person is in custody, release the person on the person's entering into a recognizance before the officer in charge or another peace officer without sureties in an amount not exceeding $500 that the officer directs and, if the officer so directs, on depositing with the officer a sum of money or other valuable security not exceeding in amount or value $500, that the officer directs.

(1.1) The officer in charge or the peace officer shall not release a person under subsection (1) if the officer in charge or peace officer believes, on reasonable grounds,

(*a*) that it is necessary in the public interest that the person be detained in custody or that the matter of their release from custody be dealt with under another provision of this Part, having regard to all the circumstances including the need to

(i) establish the identity of the person,

(ii) secure or preserve evidence of or relating to the offence,

(iii) prevent the continuation or repetition of the offence or the commission of another offence, or

(iv) ensure the safety and security of any victim of or witness to the offence; or

(*b*) that, if the person is released from custody, the person will fail to attend court in order to be dealt with according to law.

(2) Subsection (1) does not apply in respect of a person who has been arrested without warrant by a peace officer for an offence described in subsection 503(3).

(3) An officer in charge or another peace officer who has the custody of a person taken into or detained in custody for an offence described in subsection (1) and who does not release the person from custody as soon as practicable in the manner described in that subsection shall be deemed to be acting lawfully and in the execution of the officer's duty for the purposes of

(*a*) any proceedings under this or any other Act of Parliament; or

(*b*) any other proceedings, unless in any such proceedings it is alleged and established by the person making the allegation that the officer in charge or other peace officer did not comply with the requirements of subsection (1). R.S., c. C-34, s. 453; R.S., c. 2 (2nd Supp.), s. 5; R.S.C. 1985, c. 27 (1st Supp.), s. 186; 1997, c. 18, s. 52; 1998, c. 7, s. 2; 1999, c. 25, ss. 4, 30.

CROSS-REFERENCES

The terms "officer in charge", "recognizance", "summons" and "promise to appear" are defined in s. 493. The terms "peace officer", "valuable security", "justice" and "victim" are defined in s. 2. Money or other valuable security deposited with the officer in charge is to be delivered to a justice under s. 500. The contents of the promise to appear and recognizance are set out in s. 501. A promise to appear or recognizance may be issued, given or entered into on a holiday by virtue of s. 20. A warrant may issue under s. 512 where the accused fails to appear for court as required. For discussion of the pre-trial release provisions see the *Note on the scheme for pre-trial release* under s. 495.

SYNOPSIS

This section describes the powers of an officer in charge or another peace officer to effect the release of a person who has been arrested without warrant by a peace officer and who has been taken into custody or detained in custody under s. 503(1), for an offence described in s. 496(*a*), (*b*) or (*c*).

Subsection (1) provides that if the person has not been taken before a justice, or released from custody under any other provision in Part XVI, the officer must, subject to certain specified exceptions, release that person as soon as practicable with the intention of compelling their appearance by way of summons. If the officer does not release in that manner, the officer may release if the accused enters into some form of release as specified in para. (*b*), (*c*) or (*d*). Subsection (1.1) describes the circumstances in which the officer may decide not to release the person.

In accordance with subsec. (2), subsec. (1) does not apply where a person has been arrested without a warrant by a peace officer for an indictable offence alleged to have been committed in a different province.

Subsection (3) provides that an officer is deemed to be acting lawfully and in the execution of duty even if the officer does not release the person as soon as practicable and in accordance with subsec. (1) for the purposes described in subsec. (3)(*a*) or (*b*), unless it is established that the officer did not comply with the requirements of subsec. (1).

RELEASE FROM CUSTODY BY OFFICER IN CHARGE WHERE ARREST MADE WITH WARRANT / Additional conditions / Application to justice / Application by prosecutor.

499. (1) Where a person who has been arrested with a warrant by a peace officer is taken into custody for an offence other than one mentioned in section 522, the officer in charge may, if the warrant has been endorsed by a justice under subsection 507(6),

(*a*) release the person on the person's giving a promise to appear;

(*b*) release the person on the person's entering into a recognizance before the officer in charge without sureties in the amount not exceeding five hundred dollars that the officer in charge directs, but without deposit of money or other valuable security; or

(*c*) if the person is not ordinarily resident in the province in which the person is in custody or does not ordinarily reside within two hundred kilometres of the place in which the person is in custody, release the person on the person's entering into a recognizance before the officer in charge without sureties in the amount not exceeding five hundred dollars that the officer in charge directs and, if the officer in charge so directs, on depositing with the officer in charge

such sum of money or other valuable security not exceeding in amount or value five hundred dollars, as the officer in charge directs.

(2) In addition to the conditions for release set out in paragraphs (1)(*a*), (*b*) and (*c*), the officer in charge may also require the person to enter into an undertaking in Form 11.1 in which the person, in order to be released, undertakes to do one or more of the following things:

(*a*) to remain within a territorial jurisdiction specified in the undertaking;

(*b*) to notify a peace officer or another person mentioned in the undertaking of any change in his or her address, employment or occupation;

(*c*) to abstain from communicating, directly or indirectly, with any victim, witness or other person identified in the undertaking, or from going to a place specified in the undertaking, except in accordance with the conditions specified in the undertaking;

(*d*) to deposit the person's passport with the peace officer or other person mentioned in the undertaking,

(*e*) to abstain from possessing a firearm and to surrender any firearm in the possession of the person and any authorization, licence or registration certificate or other document enabling that person to acquire or possess a firearm;

(*f*) to report at the times specified in the undertaking to a peace officer or other person designated in the undertaking;

(*g*) to abstain from

(i) the consumption of alcohol or other intoxicating substances, or

(ii) the consumption of drugs except in accordance with a medical prescription; and

(*h*) to comply with any other condition specified in the undertaking that the officer in charge considers necessary to ensure the safety and security of any victim of or witness to the offence.

(3) A person who has entered into an undertaking under subsection (2) may, at any time before or at his or her appearance pursuant to a promise to appear or recognizance, apply to a justice for an order under subsection 515(1) to replace his or her undertaking, and section 515 applies, with such modifications as the circumstances require, to such a person.

(4) Where a person has entered into an undertaking under subsection (2), the prosecutor may

(*a*) at any time before the appearance of the person pursuant to a promise to appear or recognizance, after three days notice has been given to that person, or

(*b*) at the appearance,

apply to a justice for an order under subsection 515(2) to replace the undertaking, and section 515 applies, with such modifications as the circumstances require, to such a person. R.S., c. 2 (2nd Supp.), s. 5; R.S.C. 1985, c. 27 (1st Supp.), s. 186; 1994, c. 44, s. 40, 1997, c. 18, s. 53; 1999, c. 25, s. 5.

CROSS-REFERENCES

The terms "officer in charge", "recognizance" and "promise to appear" are defined in s. 493. The terms "peace officer", "valuable security", "justice" and "victim" are defined in s. 2. Money or other valuable security deposited with the officer in charge is to be delivered to a justice under s. 500. The contents of the promise to appear and recognizance are set out in s. 501. A warrant, summons, appearance notice, promise to appear, undertaking or recognizance may be issued, executed, given or entered into on a holiday by virtue of s. 20. A warrant may issue under s. 512 where the accused fails to appear for court as required. For discussion of the pre-trial release provisions see the *Note on the scheme for pre-trial release* under s. 495.

SYNOPSIS

This section describes the powers of an officer in charge to release a person from custody when that person has been arrested with a warrant.

The provisions of this section apply only if the warrant has been endorsed by a justice under s. 507(6) and the arrest for a non- s. 522 offence.

The officer in charge may order the release of such a person on a promise to appear or a recognizance in accordance with the terms set out in subsec. (1) and may also require the accused to enter into an undertaking including terms set out in subsec. (2). Either the accused or the prosecutor may apply to replace the undertaking.

MONEY OR OTHER VALUABLE SECURITY TO BE DEPOSITED WITH JUSTICE.

500. If a person has, under paragraph 498(1)(*d*) or 499(1)(*c*), deposited any sum of money or other valuable security with the officer in charge, the officer in charge shall, without delay after the deposit, cause the money or valuable security to be delivered to a justice for deposit with the justice. R.S., c. 2 (2nd Supp.), s. 5; 1999, c. 5, s. 20; c. 25, s. 6.

CROSS-REFERENCES

The term "officer in charge" is defined in s. 493. The terms "valuable security", "peace officer" and "justice" are defined in s. 2.

SYNOPSIS

This section requires the officer in charge who has received a deposit of money or valuable security from a person pursuant to s. 498(1)(*d*) or s. 499(1)(*c*) to ensure that such money or security is delivered forthwith to a justice for deposit.

CONTENTS OF APPEARANCE NOTICE, PROMISE TO APPEAR AND RECOGNIZANCE / Idem / Attendance for purposes of *Identification of Criminals Act* / Signature of accused.

501. (1) An appearance notice issued by a peace officer or a promise to appear given to, or a recognizance entered into before, an officer in charge or another peace officer shall

(*a*) set out the name of the accused;

(*b*) set out the substance of the offence that the accused is alleged to have committed; and

(*c*) require the accused to attend court at a time and place to be stated therein and to attend thereafter as required by the court in order to be dealt with according to law.

(2) An appearance notice issued by a peace officer or a promise to appear given to, or a recognizance entered into before, an officer in charge or another peace officer shall set out the text of subsections 145(5) and (6) and section 502.

(3) An appearance notice issued by a peace officer or a promise to appear given to, or a recognizance entered into before, an officer in charge or another peace officer may require the accused to appear at a time and place stated in it for the purposes of the *Identification of Criminals Act*, where the accused is alleged to have committed an indictable offence and, in the case of an offence designated as a contravention under the *Contraventions Act*, within the meaning of the Act, has not made an election under section 50 of that Act.

(4) An accused shall be requested to sign in duplicate his appearance notice, promise to appear or recognizance and, whether or not he complies with that request, one of the duplicates shall be given to the accused, but if the accused fails or refuses to sign, the lack of his signature does not invalidate the appearance notice, promise to appear or recognizance, as the case may be. R.S., c. 2 (2nd Supp.), s. 5; R.S.C. 1985, c. 27 (1st Supp.), s. 76; 1992, c. 47, s. 69; 1994, c. 44, s. 41; 1996, c. 7, s. 38; 2008, c. 18, s. 15.

(5) [*Repealed*, 2008, c. 18, s. 15.]

CROSS-REFERENCES

The terms "officer in charge", "appearance notice", "recognizance" and "promise to appear" are defined in s. 493. The terms "valuable security", "peace officer" and "justice" are defined in s. 2. Where the accused does not attend as required for the purpose of the *Identification of Criminals Act*, R.S.C. 1985, c. I-1, then a justice may issue a warrant for the accused's arrest pursuant to s. 502. A warrant may issue under s. 512 where the accused fails to appear for court as required. For discussion of the pre-trial release provisions see the *Note on the scheme for pre-trial release* under s. 495.

SYNOPSIS

This section describes the required contents of an appearance notice, a promise to appear and a recognizance and deals with several related issues.

Subsection (1) states that an appearance notice, a promise to appear or a recognizance must set out the name of the accused, describe the substance of the offence alleged to have been committed, and require that the accused attend court at a time and place stated therein and attend thereafter as required by the court. These documents must also set out the text of ss. 145(5) and (6) and 502.

Subsection (3) provides that a promise to appear, and appearance notice or a recognizance may also require that the accused appear at the stated time and place for the purposes of the *Identification of Criminals Act*. This further requirement can be imposed only where the accused is alleged to have committed an indictable offence.

Subsection (4) requires that the accused be requested to sign in duplicate the appearance notice, the promise to appear or the recognizance. Even if the accused does not comply with this request, one of the duplicate copies must be given to him. If the accused fails, or refuses to sign, the lack of a signature does not invalidate the appearance notice, the promise to appear or the recognizance.

ANNOTATIONS

Subsection (1)(*b*) – An appearance notice that merely sets out for the substance of the offence a section and paragraph number without even identifying the statute does not meet the test of sufficiency: *R. v. Powers* (1973), 10 C.C.C. (2d) 395, 21 C.R.N.S. 116 (N.B.Q.B.).

Subsection (1)(*c*) – The officer in charge has no jurisdiction to designate another territorial jurisdiction other than the county in which the accused was arrested as the place he is to appear before a justice to answer to the charge: *R. v. Simons* (1976), 30 C.C.C. (2d) 162, 34 C.R.N.S. 273 (Ont. C.A.).

To attend court within the meaning of this paragraph involves making one's presence known to the presiding justice, and not simply being physically present in the courtroom: *R. v. Anderson* (1983), 9 C.C.C. (3d) 539, 37 C.R. (3d) 67 (Alta. C.A.).

Subsection (2) – The omission in a promise to appear to set out the complete text of s. 145(5) does not affect the court's jurisdiction to proceed with the trial where the accused appears, whether under protest or not: *R. v. Gougeon; R. v. Haesler; R. v. Gray* (1980), 55 C.C.C. (2d) 218 (Ont. C.A.), leave to appeal to S.C.C. refused 35 N.R. 83*n*.

Subsection (3) – The discretionary power to require an accused to attend for fingerprinting does not violate the principles of fundamental justice as guaranteed by s. 7 of the *Charter of Rights and Freedoms*: *R. v. Beare; R. v. Higgins*, [1988] 2 S.C.R. 387, 45 C.C.C. (3d) 57.

A Crown option offence is deemed to be indictable until Crown counsel elects otherwise and thus an accused can be compelled to attend for fingerprinting in relation to such offence as provided for in the *Identification of Criminals Act*, R.S.C. 1985, c. I-1. Moreover, it was open to the Crown to delay electing the mode of proceeding on a Crown option offence until the accused had complied with a condition in the appearance notice or promise to appear to attend for fingerprinting: *R. v. Abarca* (1980), 57 C.C.C. (2d) 410 (Ont. C.A.); *R. v. Lavoie* (1990), 58 C.C.C. (3d) 246 (Que. S.C.).

FAILURE TO APPEAR.

502. Where an accused who is required by an appearance notice or promise to appear or by a recognizance entered into before an officer in charge or another peace officer to appear at a time and place stated therein for the purposes of the *Identification of Criminals Act* does not appear at that time and place, a justice may, where the appearance notice, promise to appear or recognizance has been confirmed by a justice under section 508, issue a warrant for the arrest of the accused for the offence with which the accused is charged. R.S., c. 2 (2nd Supp.), s. 5; 1992, c. 47, s. 70; 1996, c. 7, s. 38; 1997, c. 18, s. 54.

CROSS-REFERENCES

The terms "officer in charge", "appearance notice", "recognizance" and "promise to appear" are defined in s. 493. The terms "justice" and "peace officer" are defined in s. 2. A warrant may issue under s. 512 where the accused fails to appear for court as required.

SYNOPSIS

This section describes the consequences of failing to appear for the purposes of the *Identification of Criminals Act* as required by a promise to appear, an appearance notice or a recognizance. Should the accused not appear at the time and place stipulated, a justice may issue a warrant for the arrest of the accused for the charged offence. The justice may only issue a warrant if the appearance notice, the promise to appear or the recognizance has been confirmed by a justice under s. 508.

ANNOTATIONS

Once the court has become *functus* with respect to the original charge because it has been disposed of completely, the justice has no power to issue a warrant under this section for failure of the accused to attend for fingerprinting as required by the appearance notice: *R. v. McHardy* (1980), 53 C.C.C. (2d) 91, [1980] 5 W.W.R. 1 (Sask. Q.B.).

Appearance of Accused Before Justice

TAKING BEFORE JUSTICE / Conditional release / Undertaking / Application by prosecutor / Application to justice / Remand to custody for return to jurisdiction where offence alleged to have been committed / Interim release / Release of person about to commit indictable offence / Consequences of non-release.

503. (1) A peace officer who arrests a person with or without warrant or to whom a person is delivered under subsection 494(3) or into whose custody a person is placed under subsection 163.5(3) of the *Customs Act* shall cause the person to be detained in custody and, in accordance with the following provisions, to be taken before a justice to be dealt with according to law:

- **(*a*) where a justice is available within a period of twenty-four hours after the person has been arrested by or delivered to the peace officer, the person shall be taken before a justice without unreasonable delay and in any event within that period, and**
- **(*b*) where a justice is not available within a period of twenty-four hours after the person has been arrested by or delivered to the peace officer, the person shall be taken before a justice as soon as possible,**

unless, at any time before the expiration of the time prescribed in paragraph (*a*) or (*b*) for taking the person before a justice,

(*c*) the peace officer or officer in charge releases the person under any other provision of this Part, or

(*d*) the peace officer or officer in charge is satisfied that the person should be released from custody, whether unconditionally under subsection (4) or otherwise conditionally or unconditionally, and so releases him.

(2) If a peace officer or an officer in charge is satisfied that a person described in subsection (1) should be released from custody conditionally, the officer may, unless the person is detained in custody for an offence mentioned in section 522, release that person on the person's giving a promise to appear or entering into a recognizance in accordance with paragraphs 498(1)(*b*) to (*d*) and subsection (2.1).

(2.1) In addition to the conditions referred to in subsection (2), the peace officer or officer in charge may, in order to release the person, require the person to enter into an undertaking in Form 11.1 in which the person undertakes to do one or more of the following things:

(*a*) to remain within a territorial jurisdiction specified in the undertaking;

(*b*) to notify the peace officer or another person mentioned in the undertaking of any change in his or her address, employment or occupation;

(*c*) to abstain from communicating, directly or indirectly, with any victim, witness or other person identified in the undertaking, or from going to a place specified in the undertaking, except in accordance with the conditions specified in the undertaking;

(*d*) to deposit the person's passport with the peace officer or other person mentioned in the undertaking,

(*e*) to abstain from possessing a firearm and to surrender any firearm in the possession of the person and any authorization, licence or registration certificate or other document enabling that person to acquire or possess a firearm;

(*f*) to report at the times specified in the undertaking to a peace officer or other person designated in the undertaking;

(*g*) to abstain from

(i) the consumption of alcohol or other intoxicating substances, or

(ii) the consumption of drugs except in accordance with a medical prescription; or

(*h*) to comply with any other condition specified in the undertaking that the peace officer or officer in charge considers necessary to ensure the safety and security of any victim of or witness to the offence.

(2.2) A person who has entered into an undertaking under subsection (2.1) may, at any time before or at his or her appearance pursuant to a promise to appear or recognizance, apply to a justice for an order under subsection 515(1) to replace his or her undertaking, and section 515 applies, with such modifications as the circumstances require, to such a person.

(2.3) Where a person has entered into an undertaking under subsection (2.1), the prosecutor may

(*a*) at any time before the appearance of the person pursuant to a promise to appear or recognizance, after three days notice has been given to that person, or

(*b*) at the appearance,

apply to a justice for an order under subsection 515(2) to replace the undertaking, and section 515 applies, with such modifications as the circumstances require, to such a person.

(3) Where a person has been arrested without warrant for an indictable offence alleged to have been committed in Canada outside the territorial division to where the arrest took place, the person shall, within the time prescribed in paragraph (1)(*a*) or (*b*), be taken before a justice within whose jurisdiction the person was arrested unless, where the offence was alleged to have been committed within the province in which the person was arrested, the person was taken before a justice within whose jurisdiction the offence was alleged to have been committed, and the justice within whose jurisdiction the person was arrested

(*a*) if the justice is not satisfied that there are reasonable grounds to believe that the person arrested is the person alleged to have committed the offence, shall release that person; or

(*b*) if the justice is satisfied that there are reasonable grounds to believe that the person arrested is the person alleged to have committed the offence, may

(i) remand the person to the custody of a peace officer to await execution of a warrant for his or her arrest in accordance with section 528, but if no warrant is so executed within a period of six days after the time he or she is remanded to such custody, the person in whose custody he or she then is shall release him or her, or

(ii) where the offence was alleged to have been committed within the province in which the person was arrested, order the person to be taken before a justice having jurisdiction with respect to the offence.

(3.1) Notwithstanding paragraph (3)(*b*), a justice may, with the consent of the prosecutor, order that the person referred to in subsection (3), pending the execution of a warrant for the arrest of that person, be released

(*a*) unconditionally; or

(*b*) on any of the following terms to which the prosecutor consents, namely,

(i) giving an undertaking, including an undertaking to appear at a specified time before the court that has jurisdiction with respect to the indictable offence that the person is alleged to have committed, or

(ii) entering into a recognizance described in any of paragraphs 515(2)(*a*) to (*e*) with such conditions described in subsection 515(4) as the justice considers desirable and to which the prosecutor consents.

(4) A peace officer or an officer in charge having the custody of a person who has been arrested without warrant as a person about to commit an indictable offence shall release that person unconditionally as soon as practicable after he is satisfied that the continued detention of that person in custody is no longer necessary in order to prevent the commission by him of an indictable offence.

(5) Notwithstanding subsection (4), a peace officer or an officer in charge having the custody of a person referred to in that subsection who does not release the person before the expiration of the time prescribed in paragraph (1)(*a*) or (*b*) for taking the person before the justice shall be deemed to be acting lawfully and in the execution of his duty for the purposes of

(*a*) any proceedings under this or any other Act of Parliament; or

(*b*) any other proceedings, unless in such proceedings it is alleged and established by the person making the allegation that the peace officer or officer in charge did not comply with the requirements of subsection (4). R.S., c. C-34, s. 454; R.S., c. 2 (2nd Supp.), s. 5; 1974-75-76, c. 93, s. 46; R.S.C. 1985, c. 27 (1st Supp.), s. 77; 1994, c. 44, s. 42; 1997, c. 18, s. 55; 1998, c. 7, s. 3; 1999, c. 25, s. 7.

CROSS-REFERENCES

The terms "officer in charge", "undertaking" and "recognizance" are defined in s. 493. The terms "peace officer", "prosecutor", "justice" and "victim" are defined in s. 2. For discussion of the pre-trial release provisions see the *Note on the scheme for pre-trial release* under s. 495.

SYNOPSIS

This section describes the requirements placed on a peace officer to ensure that a person arrested with or without a warrant be brought before a justice to be dealt with according to law.

Subsection (1) provides that where a justice is available within 24 hours of a person's arrest or delivery to a peace officer, that person shall be taken before the justice without unreasonable delay and, in any event, within that period. If a justice is not available within a period of 24 hours, the person shall be taken before a justice as soon as possible. These requirements apply unless, prior to the expiration of time periods described above, the peace officer or officer in charge releases the person under any other provision in Part XVI, under s. 503(4), or otherwise, conditionally or unconditionally.

Subsection (2) provides that where a peace officer or officer in charge is satisfied that a person described in subsec. (1) should be released upon conditions, that officer may make such a release in accordance with s. 498(1)(*b*) to (*d*). In addition, the officer can require the accused to enter into an undertaking containing the conditions set out in subsec. (2.1). Note in particular that the officer may impose conditions necessary to ensure the safety and security of any victm or witness. Both the accused and the prosecutor may apply to a justice to replace the undertaking. Subsection (2) may not be resorted to if the person is being held in custody pursuant to s. 522.

Subsection (3) deals with the situation in which a person has been arrested, without a warrant, for an indictable offence alleged to have been committed outside the territorial division in which he has been apprehended. Such a person must be brought before a justice within the time periods described in subsec. (1)(*a*) or (*b*) above and the justice shall release that person if there are no reasonable grounds to believe that the person committed the offence. If the justice is satisfied that there are reasonable grounds to believe that the arrested person is the person alleged to have committed the offence, the justice may remand the person in the custody of the peace officer to await the execution of an arrest warrant pursuant to s. 528. If no warrant is executed within six days of this remand, the accused person must be released. If the offence was committed in the same province, the justice may order that the accused be taken before a justice having jurisdiction over the offence.

Subsection (3.1) provides that a justice may order the release of a person referred to in subsec. (3), with the consent of the prosecutor, pending the execution of the arrest warrant. Such a release may be unconditional or according to the terms set out in subsec. (3.1).

Subsection (4) provides that a peace officer or officer in charge having custody of a person who has been arrested without a warrant as a person about to commit an indictable offence shall release that person unconditionally as soon as practicable after the officer is satisfied that the continued detention of that person is no longer necessary to prevent the commission of an indictable offence.

Subsection (5) makes it clear that a peace officer having custody of a person referred to in subsec. (4) and who does not release that person within the time limits prescribed by subsec. (1)(*a*) and (*b*), is deemed to be acting lawfully and in the execution of his or her duty for the purposes specified in subsec. (5)(*a*) and (*b*), unless it is established that the officer did not comply with the requirements of subsec. (4).

ANNOTATIONS

An 18-hour delay, following the arrest of the accused before he was taken before a justice, so that a line-up could be arranged, did not infringe this section nor constitute a violation of s. 9 of the Charter: *R. v. Storrey*, [1990] 1 S.C.R. 241, 53 C.C.C. (3d) 316 (7:0).

The breach of this section resulting in the accused's detention for 36 hours before being brought before a justice constituted a violation of s. 9 of the Charter: *R. v. Charles* (1987), 36 C.C.C. (3d) 286, 59 C.R. (3d) 94 (Sask. C.A.). See, however, *R. v. Tam* (1995), 100 C.C.C. (3d) 196, 100 W.A.C. 40 (B.C.C.A.), in which a delay of over 24 hours rendered the detention "unlawful" contrary to this section but not "arbitrary" within the meaning of s. 9 of the Charter.

In *R. v. W. (E.)* (2002), 168 C.C.C. (3d) 38, 7 C.R. (6th) 343, the Manitoba Court of Appeal held that 24 hours merely establishes the outer limit of permissible detention. A detention of more than 6 hours was, in the circumstances, unlawful and constituted a violation of s. 9 of the Charter.

The actions of the police in purposely keeping the accused in custody beyond the statutory limit so that they could obtain an inculpatory statement constituted a breach of s. 9 of the *Canadian Charter of Rights and Freedoms*: *R. v. Mangat* (2006), 209 C.C.C. (3d) 225 (Ont. C.A.).

An accused arrested on the strength of Telex information of a warrant outstanding elsewhere in the province must be brought before a justice within 24 hours. The court which issued the warrant does not have exclusive jurisdiction to deal with the matter of the accused's release. If the Crown because of a lack of information is unable to proceed with the show cause hearing at that time the proper course is to apply for an adjournment for three days under s. 515 during which time the Crown can either transport the accused to the locale where the warrant was issued or obtain the necessary information: *R. v. Ragan* (1974), 21 C.C.C. (2d) 115, [1975] 2 W.W.R. 284 (B.C. Prov. Ct.).

The provisions of subsec. (3) are mandatory and require that the person arrested be personally brought before the justice for the identity hearing. On the hearing the onus is on the Crown. In calculating the six-day period in para. (*b*) neither the remand date nor the release date should be excluded. The remand order under para. (*b*) should provide for the accused's release unless a warrant is executed within that six-day period: *R. v. Marshall* (1984), 13 C.C.C. (3d) 73 (Ont. H.C.J.).

Information, Summons and Warrant

IN WHAT CASES JUSTICE MAY RECEIVE INFORMATION.

504. Any one who, on reasonable grounds, believes that a person has committed an indictable offence may lay an information in writing and under oath before a justice, and the justice shall receive the information, where it is alleged

(*a*) that the person has committed, anywhere, an indictable offence that may be tried in the province in which the justice resides, and that the person

(i) is or is believed to be, or

(ii) resides or is believed to reside,

within the territorial jurisdiction of the justice;

(*b*) that the person, wherever he may be, has committed an indictable offence within the territorial jurisdiction of the justice;

(*c*) that the person has, anywhere, unlawfully received property that was unlawfully obtained within the territorial jurisdiction of the justice; or

(*d*) that the person has in his possession stolen property within the territorial jurisdiction of the justice. R.S., c. C-34, s. 455; R.S., c. 2 (2nd Supp.), s. 5.

CROSS-REFERENCES

The terms "justice", "property" and "steal" are defined in s. 2. Indictable offence includes a hybrid offence by virtue of s. 34(1)(*a*) of the *Interpretation Act*, R.S.C. 1985, c. I-21. The determination as to whether process should issue is made in accordance with s. 507. Under s. 506 an information may be laid in Form 2. For discussion of the pre-trial release provisions see the *Note on the scheme for pre-trial release* under s. 495. The information may be laid by means of telecommunication in accordance with s. 508.1.

SYNOPSIS

This section describes the process by which any person may lay an information before a justice that another person has committed an indictable offence.

The information must be in writing and under oath. The justice must receive the information if it contains any of the allegations set out in paras. (*a*) to (*d*).

ANNOTATIONS

Constitutional considerations – This provision is *intra vires* Parliament, and provincial provisions such as those contained in the *Youth Protection Act, 1977* (Que.), c. 20, which attempt to prevent anyone from laying an information unless the person has consent of a government official are inoperative: *Quebec (Attorney General) v. Lechasseur*, [1981] 2 S.C.R. 253, 63 C.C.C. (2d) 301 (9:0).

In *Ellis v. Ontario* (2009), 244 C.C.C. (3d) 438, 67 C.R. (6th) 313 (Ont. C.A.), the court held that "territorial jurisdiction" refers to the entire province of Ontario and not to administrative regions created by the *Courts of Justice Act*, R.S.O. 1990, c. C.43. Territorial jurisdiction requires the justice of the peace to receive information. provided that there is a connection between the alleged offender and the justice's territorial jurisdiction.

Duty of justice – The act of receiving an information is ministerial rather than judicial: *R. v. Jean Talon Fashion Center Inc.* (1975), 22 C.C.C. (2d) 223, 56 D.L.R. (3d) 296 (Que. Q.B.).

When information laid – In *R. v. Southwick, ex p. Gilbert Steel Ltd.*, [1968] 1 C.C.C. 356, 2 C.R.N.S. 46 (Ont. C.A.), it was held that on the swearing of the written complaint the information is "laid" and becomes the commencement of criminal proceedings.

Separate informations outstanding – It does not affect the validity of either information to have two separate informations charging the same offence outstanding at the same time: *R. v. Policha, ex p. Hrischuk,* [1970] 5 C.C.C. 165, 11 C.R.N.S. 99 *sub nom. Hrischuk v. Clark and Policha.* (Sask. Q.B.).

Defects in jurat [Also see notes under s. 789] – The cases are divided as to the effect of the failure to indicate the date in the jurat upon which the information may be sworn. In *R. v. Bobcaygeon (Village)* (1974), 17 C.C.C. (2d) 236 (Ont. C.A.), the court left open whether such an omission was fatal to the validity of the information, but doubted whether the trial court's power to amend an information could extend to inserting the date in the jurat. The court upheld the refusal to issue *mandamus* in that case to require the judge to continue with the trial since by reason of the absence of the date when the information was sworn it did not disclose that it was sworn within the applicable limitation period. The defendant and the trial judge were entitled to know by perusing the information the components of the offence, the time and place of its commission and that the informant had laid the information within the prescribed time. The information, which failed to convey to them this information, was a nullity.

However, in *R. v. Government of Saskatchewan* (1982), 20 Sask. R. 213 (C.A.), the court refused to follow *R. v. Bobcaygeon (Village), supra*, and held that an information was not a nullity even though, by reason of the failure to complete the jurat, it was not clear whether the information was laid within the limitation period. The court held that whether or not the prosecution was commenced within the limitation period was a matter to be decided by the trial judge upon hearing evidence.

To a similar effect is *R. v. Dean* (1985), 17 C.C.C. (3d) 410 (Alta. Q.B.), where the validity of the information was upheld although the year that the information was sworn was missing from the jurat. In view of the five-year limitation period, there was no possibility that the information was laid outside the limitation period. *Contra: R. v. Platt; R. v. Cowan*, [1981] 4 W.W.R. 601, 9 Man. R. (2d) 75 (Q.B.).

And in *R. v. Akey* (1990), 11 W.C.B. (2d) 594 (Ont. Ct. (Gen. Div.)), it was held that the absence from the jurat, of the month in which the information was sworn, did not render the information invalid when it was apparent that the information, charging Crown option offences upon which the Crown elected to proceed by way of summary conviction, must have been sworn within six months of the offence.

Illegibility of justice's signature – The illegibility in the jurat of the signature of the justice of the peace who took the information does not render the information invalid where the identity of the person signing the information appears on the face of the information. Thus, in this case, below the illegible signature were the words "A justice of the peace in and for the Province of Ontario": *R. v. Kapoor* (1989), 52 C.C.C. (3d) 41 (Ont. H.C.J.).

Other defects – In *R. v. Zastawny* (1970), 10 C.R.N.S. 155, 72 W.W.R. 537 (Sask. Q.B.), an information that failed to state on its face the site of the offence was quashed as not disclosing an offence within the territorial jurisdiction of the Magistrate.

Omission of the informant's name and occupation from the place indicated in Form 2 does not invalidate the information: *R. v. Eddy* (1982), 69 C.C.C. (2d) 568 (B.C.S.C.).

TIME WITHIN WHICH INFORMATION TO BE LAID IN CERTAIN CASES.

505. Where

(*a*) an appearance notice has been issued to an accused under section 496, or

(*b*) an accused has been released from custody under section 497 or 498,

an information relating to the offence alleged to have been committed by the accused or relating to an included or other offence alleged to have been committed by him shall be laid before a justice as soon as practicable thereafter and in any event before the time stated in the appearance notice, promise to appear or recognizance issued to or given or entered into by the accused for his attendance in court. R.S., c. 2 (2nd Supp.), s. 5.

CROSS-REFERENCES

The term "justice" is defined in s. 2. The terms "appearance notice", "recognizance" and "promise to appear" are defined in s. 493. The determination as to whether process issued by the officer should be confirmed or cancelled is made in accordance with s. 508. Under s. 506 an information may be laid in Form 2. For discussion of the pre-trial release provisions see the *Note on the scheme for pre-trial release* under s. 495.

SYNOPSIS

This section sets out the time periods within which informations must be laid in specified cases.

The section requires that where an appearance notice has been issued under s. 496 or an accused has been released from custody under ss. 497 or 498, an information shall be laid before a justice as soon as practicable thereafter. The information must be laid, in any event, prior to the first appearance of the accused in court.

ANNOTATIONS

It was held in *R. v. Naylor* (1978), 42 C.C.C. (2d) 12 (Ont. C.A.), that this section sets out two time-limits both of which are mandatory, (1) that the information be laid as soon as practicable and (2) that it be laid before the time (meaning time of day) of the appearance in court. However, where there is a failure to comply with these time-limits while no charge of fail to appear under s. 145(5) will lie and the court has no power to issue a warrant under s. 512(2), if the accused does appear this is sufficient to give the court jurisdiction. The failure to follow the procedure in this section does not invalidate the information nor result in a loss of jurisdiction over the offence and the accused's appearance in court gives the court jurisdiction over the person. Folld: *R. v. Hrankowski* (1980), 54 C.C.C. (2d) 174, [1980] 5 W.W.R. 684 (Alta. C.A.), leave to appeal to S.C.C. refused C.C.C. *loc. cit.*, 26 A.R. 268*n*.

The court has jurisdiction even if the accused appears under protest to the court's jurisdiction: *R. v. Gougeon; R. v. Haesler; R. v. Gray* (1980), 55 C.C.C. (2d) 218 (Ont. C.A.), leave to appeal to S.C.C. refused 35 N.R. 83*n*.

Similarly, in *Alberta v. Sinopec Shanghai Engineering Co.* (2011), 286 C.C.C. (3d) 406 (Alta. C.A.), leave to appeal to S.C.C. refused (2012), 438 N.R. 391*n*, the court held that any attempt to appear conditionally to challenge the efficacy of service will be ineffective and result in attornment to the court's jurisdiction. This is to be distinguished from a challenge to the court's jurisdiction to try to the offence, in which case a conditional appearance is possible.

The manner in which the accused is brought before the court does not affect jurisdiction over the offence of the accused. Failure to comply with the time limitation in this section does not cause the provincial court to lose jurisdiction: *R. v. Black* (2010), 255 C.C.C. (3d) 62 (N.B.C.A.), leave to appeal to S.C.C. refused [2011] 1 S.C.R. vi, 261 C.C.C. (3d) iv.

The failure to follow the time requirements in para. (*b*) does not invalidate the information or result in a loss of jurisdiction over the offence. Where there has been a failure to comply, the court must determine whether the accused was prejudiced in the circumstances: *R. v. Markovic* (2005), 200 C.C.C. (3d) 449, 77 O.R. (3d) 752 (C.A.), leave to appeal to S.C.C. refused 204 C.C.C. (3d) vi.

Similarly a "conditional appearance" by counsel on the required date gives the court jurisdiction. The criminal law does not recognize "conditional" appearances: *R. v. Harnish* (1979), 49 C.C.C. (2d) 190 (N.S.S.C. App. Div.).

The laying of an information after the time stated in the appearance notice is only an administrative failure and while that information does not qualify as an information under this section it will qualify as an information under s. 507 so that the accused's appearance in court brings him within the court's jurisdiction: *R. v. Powers* (1973), 10 C.C.C. (2d) 395, 21 C.R.N.S. 116 (N.S.Q.B.). *Contra: R. v. Fleming* (1979), 47 C.C.C. (2d) 406 (B.C.S.C.).

The fact that an appearance notice has been given to the accused does not preclude the officer, because the return date on the notice is wrong, from subsequently invoking the procedure under s. 507 by going before a justice and laying an information and serving the accused with a summons: *R. v. Benteau* (1975), 24 C.C.C. (2d) 96 (Ont. H.C.J.).

FORM

506. An information laid under section 504 or 505 may be in Form 2. R.S., c. 2 (2nd Supp.), s. 5.

CROSS-REFERENCES

Note that s. 788(1) requires that Form 2 be used to initiate summary conviction proceedings. Section 841 provides that forms varied to suit the case and forms to the like effect shall be deemed to be good, valid and sufficient in the circumstances for which, respectively, they are provided. Also note s. 841(3) requiring preprinted portions of forms to be printed in both official languages.

ANNOTATIONS

The information may be laid in the name of the complainant alone: *R. v. Ostler, ex p. A.-G. B.C.*, [1966] 1 C.C.C. 249, 52 W.W.R. 483, *sub nom. R. v. Harvey*, and *R. v. Gyles, ex p. Mandelbaum*, [1969] 3 C.C.C. 119, 5 C.R.N.S. 307 *sub nom. Mandelbaum v. Denstedt* (Man. C.A.).

JUSTICE TO HEAR INFORMANT AND WITNESSES — PUBLIC PROSECUTIONS / Process compulsory / Procedure when witnesses attend / Summons to be issued except in certain cases / No process in blank / Endorsement of warrant by justice / Promise to appear or recognizance deemed to have been confirmed / Issue of summons or warrant.

507. (1) Subject to subsection 523(1.1), a justice who receives an information laid under section 504 by a peace officer, a public officer, the Attorney General or the Attorney General's agent, other than an information laid before the justice under section 505, shall, except if an accused has already been arrested with or without a warrant,

(*a*) hear and consider, *ex parte*,

(i) the allegations of the informant, and

(ii) the evidence of witnesses, where he considers it desirable or necessary to do so; and

(*b*) where he considers that a case for so doing is made out, issue, in accordance with this section, either a summons or a warrant for the arrest of the accused to compel the accused to attend before him or some other justice for the same territorial division to answer to a charge of an offence.

(2) No justice shall refuse to issue a summons or warrant by reason only that the alleged offence is one for which a person may be arrested without warrant.

(3) A justice who hears the evidence of a witness pursuant to subsection (1) shall

(*a*) take the evidence on oath; and

(*b*) cause the evidence to be taken in accordance with section 540 in so far as that section is capable of being applied.

(4) Where a justice considers that a case is made out for compelling an accused to attend before him to answer to a charge of an offence, he shall issue a summons to the accused unless the allegations of the informant or the evidence of any witness or witnesses taken in accordance with subsection (3) discloses reasonable grounds to believe that it is necessary in the public interest to issue a warrant for the arrest of the accused.

(5) A justice shall not sign a summons or warrant in blank.

(6) A justice who issues a warrant under this section or section 508 or 512 may, unless the offence is one mentioned in section 522, authorize the release of the accused pursant to section 499 by making an endorsement on the warrant in Form 29.

(7) Where, pursuant to subsection (6), a justice authorizes the release of an accused pursuant to section 499, a promise to appear given by the accused or a recognizance entered into by the accused pursuant to that section shall be deemed, for the purposes of subsection 145(5), to have been confirmed by a justice under section 508.

(8) Where, on an appeal from or review of any decision or matter of jurisdiction, a new trial or hearing or a continuance or renewal of a trial or hearing is ordered, a justice may issue either a summons or a warrant for the arrest of the accused in order to compel the accused to attend at the new or continued or renewed trial or hearing. R.S., c. 2 (2nd Supp.), s. 5; 1972, c. 13, s. 35; R.S.C. 1985, c. 27 (1st Supp.), s. 78; 1994, c. 44, s. 43; 2002, c. 13, s. 21.

CROSS-REFERENCES

The terms "Attorney General", "justice", "peace officer" and "public officer" are defined in s. 2. With respect to oaths and solemn affirmations, see ss. 13 to 15 of the *Canada Evidence Act*, R.S.C. 1985, c. C-5. The terms "summons" and "warrant" are defined in s. 493. The contents of a summons and the means of service are set out in s. 509. The contents of a warrant are set out in ss. 511 and 513. It is executed in accordance with s. 514. A warrant or summons may be issued, executed, given or entered into on a holiday by virtue of s. 20. Where the information is laid under s. 505, then the process issued by the peace officer or officer in charge is confirmed or cancelled in accordance with s. 508. This section sets out the procedure where the information is laid in a public prosecution. Where the information is laid by a private prosecutor, the procedure set out in s. 507.1 is to be followed. For discussion of the pre-trial release provisions see the Note on the scheme for pre-trial release under s. 495.

Note s. 31(1) of the *Interpretation Act*, R.S.C. 1985, c. I-21, which provides that where anything is required or authorized to be done by or before, *inter alia*, a justice of the peace it shall be done by or before one whose jurisdiction or powers extend to the place where the thing is to be done.

Failure to attend court as required or attend for the purposes of the *Identification of Criminals Act* is an offence under s. 145. As well a warrant may issue under s. 510 for failure to attend for the purposes of the *Identification of Criminals Act*, R.S.C. 1985, c. I-1, as required in a summons.

A warrant may issue under s. 512 where the accused fails to appear for court as required or where a summons cannot be served because the accused is evading service.

Probative value of electronically transmitted copy of summons or warrant, see s. 708.1.

SYNOPSIS

This section sets out the procedure to be followed for issuing process where an information is laid under s. 504 in a public prosecution. Section 507.1 sets out the procedure to be followed for private prosecutions. Section 508 governs the procedure where process has been issued under s. 505, before the information has been laid.

Subsection (1) states that except where an accused has already been arrested, the justice shall hear and consider, *ex parte*, the allegations of the informant. Where the justice considers it desirable or necessary, he shall also hear the evidence of witnesses. Where the justice considers that a case for so doing has been established, he shall issue a summons or a warrant for the arrest of the accused. A justice may not refuse to issue a summons or a warrant only for the reason that the offence is one which permits arrest without a warrant.

Subsection (3) requires that any evidence heard pursuant to subsec. (1) must be taken on oath and in accordance with s. 540 to the extent that this is possible.

Subsection (4) provides that the justice may issue a summons to compel the attendance of the accused to answer a charge of an offence if a case for doing so is made out. The justice may issue a warrant for the arrest of the accused if there are reasonable grounds to believe that this is necessary in the public interest. The justice may not sign a warrant or a summons in blank.

Subsection (6) empowers the justice who issues a warrant under this section, s. 508 or 512, where the offence is one described in paras. (*a*) to (*d*), to authorize the release of the accused pursuant to s. 499 by endorsing the warrant. Where an accused is released under subsec. (6), the promise to appear or recognizance shall be deemed to have been confirmed under s. 508 for the purposes of s. 145(5).

Subsection (8) states that a justice may issue a summons or a warrant to compel the attendance of the accused where a new trial or hearing is ordered on appeal or review or a continuance of a trial is ordered.

ANNOTATIONS

Minimum requirements of information – Although the information may not comply with the requirements as to sufficiency in s. 581(3) such a defect does not render the information null and void *ab initio* and incapable of founding jurisdiction to compel the appearance of the accused before the court to answer the allegation that he committed an indictable offence: *R. v. Bahinipaty* (1983), 5 C.C.C. (3d) 439, 23 Sask. R. 36 (C.A.).

To be valid, an information cannot be laid against an unknown person but must be sworn against a named person or against a person who can be sufficiently described so as to be identifiable. As a precondition to the exercise of the power to hear and consider the evidence of witnesses under this section, the information must comply with ss. 504 and 581 and the name or sufficient description of the accused is an essential part of an information. The justice of the peace has no power to embark on an inquiry on an information which does not conform with the provisions of s. 581 in order to obtain sufficient information to take a proper information: *R. v. Buchbinder* (1985), 20 C.C.C. (3d) 481, 47 C.R. (3d) 135 (Ont. C.A.).

Duty to hold inquiry [subsec. (1)(*a*)] – The justice's failure to hold an inquiry as required by this section prior to issuing the summons does not affect the jurisdiction of the provincial court judge: *R. v. Pottle* (1979), 49 C.C.C. (2d) 113 (Nfld. C.A.); *R. v. Bachman*, [1979] 6 W.W.R. 468 (B.C.C.A.). It would seem that the law in Ontario is to the contrary: *R. v. Gougeon; R. v. Haesler; R. v. Gray* (1980), 55 C.C.C. (2d) 218 (Ont. C.A.), leave to appeal to S.C.C. refused 35 N.R. 83*n*.

Procedure in holding inquiry [subsec. (3)] – The inquiry under this section is to be held *in camera* and the accused has no right to attend and no right to notice. On the hearing Crown counsel may attend as counsel for the informant: *R. v. Whitmore* (1987), 41 C.C.C. (3d) 555 (Ont. H.C.J.), affd 51 C.C.C. (3d) 294 (Ont. C.A.), as to propriety of holding an *ex parte* hearing, and the attendance of Crown counsel.

While the requirement that the hearing be held *in camera* is an infringement on the guarantee to freedom of expression under s. 2(*b*) of the Charter, it represents a reasonable limit: *Southam Inc. v. Coulter* (1990), 60 C.C.C. (3d) 267, 75 O.R. (3d) 1, 40 O.A.C. 341 (C.A.).

A justice of the peace, although appointed by the Attorney General and as court administrator required to maintain a good working relationship with other components of the justice system, had the necessary independence and impartiality to carry out her duties under this section. Of importance in this respect is the oath that she must take to truly and faithfully execute her duties as a justice of the peace: *R. v. Isaac* (1989), 47 C.C.C. (3d) 353 (B.C.S.C.).

Nature of decision to issue process – In determining whether to issue a summons or a warrant a provincial court judge exercises his discretion and accordingly *mandamus* cannot lie against him: *R. v. Coughlan, ex p. Evans,* [1970] 3 C.C.C. 61, 8 C.R.N.S. 201 (Alta. S.C.). In any event the supervisory court may only order the inferior court to hear the matter again: *R. v. Jones, ex p. Cohen,* [1970] 2 C.C.C. 374 (B.C.S.C.).

A justice has jurisdiction to withdraw and annul his warrant where he issued it under a misconception of the facts: *R. v. Eckersley* (1972), 7 C.C.C. (2d) 314 (Que. Mun. Ct.).

If the justice's refusal to issue process was based on extraneous considerations, or if his discretion was not exercised judicially following a proper hearing, *mandamus* will lie: *R. v. Blythe* (1973), 13 C.C.C. (2d) 192 (B.C.S.C.); *R. v. Swan* (1979), 48 C.C.C. (2d) 501 (Ont. H.C.J.).

A justice acts judicially in determining whether or not he will issue a process requiring attendance in court. A refusal does not invalidate an information; the informant is entitled to re-apply before the same or another justice for process to be issued: *R. v. Allen* (1974), 20 C.C.C. (2d) 447 (Ont. C.A.).

Access to evidence taken on hearing – Although the justice presiding at a preliminary hearing has no power to order production of any statements given before a justice under this section, as a matter of fairness such statements should be made available to the accused notwithstanding the proceedings under this section are conducted *ex parte* and *in camera*. If the defence has these statements he may cross-examine the witness on them in the same manner as any other prior statement: *R. v. Cohen* (1976), 32 C.C.C. (2d) 446, 34 C.R.N.S. 362 *sub nom. Quebec (Attorney General) v. Cohen* (Que. C.A.). An appeal by the Crown to the S.C.C. was allowed 46 C.C.C. (2d) 473, 13 C.R. (3d) 36, the court holding that the decision of the justice refusing such cross-examination was not reviewable on *certiorari*. In the result the court did not consider the correctness of the justice's ruling.

The Crown is entitled to documentation and information relating to the *in camera* hearing: *R. v. Billingham* (1995), 26 O.R. (3d) 226 (Gen. Div.).

Right to proceed under this section where s. 501 or 505 not complied with – Where there has been non-compliance with the mandatory provisions of s. 505, it is open to the Crown to proceed by way of an information laid under s. 504 and the justice may issue either a summons or a warrant under this section in order to compel the accused's attendance unless it can be said that the subsequent proceedings constitute an abuse of process: *R. v. Riley* (1981), 60 C.C.C. (2d) 193 (Ont. C.A.).

Where the provisions of s. 505 have not been complied with, the information having been sworn after the return date in the appearance notice, a warrant or summons may issue under this section: *R. v. Gagné* (1989), 53 C.C.C. (3d) 89 (Que. C.A.). There is no necessity to cancel the appearance notice and in fact no jurisdiction to do so: *R. v. Tremblay* (1982), 68 C.C.C. (2d) 273, 28 C.R. (3d) 262 (B.C.C.A.).

A summons may also issue under this section although the appearance notice was invalid for failure to comply with s. 501(4) and the information laid under s. 505 was neither cancelled nor confirmed by the justice: *R. v. Thomson* (1984), 11 C.C.C. (3d) 435, 51 A.R. 273 (C.A.).

Until such time as the accused comes before a judge capable of taking his election and plea, the court has not assumed any jurisdiction in the matter and should any error be made in the method of summoning the accused to court then it may be corrected by the issuance of a new summons or warrant. It is only when the accused has appeared in court and made his election or plea that the court has become seized with jurisdiction which can be lost if nothing is done on a court date: *R. v. Macaskill* (1981), 58 C.C.C. (2d) 361, 45 N.S.R. (2d) 181 (S.C. App. Div.). Similarly, *R. v. Kennedy* (1983), 8 C.C.C. (3d) 322, [1983] 6 W.W.R. 673 (B.C.C.A.).

Other notes – The issuance of a summons by a justice of the peace other than the justice before whom the complaint was sworn is legal: *R. v. Southwick, ex p. Gilbert Steel Ltd.*, [1968] 1 C.C.C. 356, 2 C.R.N.S. 46 (Ont. C.A.).

REFERRAL WHEN PRIVATE PROSECUTION / Summons or warrant / Conditions for issuance / Appearance of Attorney General / Information deemed not to have been laid / Information deemed not to have been laid — proceedings commenced / New evidence required for new hearing / Subsections 507(2) to (8) to apply / Non-application — informations laid under sections 810 and 810.1 / Definition of "designated justice" / Meaning of "Attorney General".

507.1 (1) A justice who receives an information laid under section 504, other than an information referred to in subsection 507(1), shall refer it to a provincial court judge or, in Quebec, a judge of the Court of Quebec, or to a designated justice, to consider whether to compel the appearance of the accused on the information.

(2) A judge or designated justice to whom an information is referred under subsection (1) and who considers that a case for doing so is made out shall issue either a summons or warrant for the arrest of the accused to compel him or her to attend before a justice to answer to a charge of the offence charged in the information.

(3) The judge or designated justice may issue a summons or warrant only if he or she

(*a*) has heard and considered the allegations of the informant and the evidence of witnesses;

(*b*) is satisfied that the Attorney General has received a copy of the information;

(*c*) is satisfied that the Attorney General has received reasonable notice of the hearing under paragraph (*a*); and

(*d*) has given the Attorney General an opportunity to attend the hearing under paragraph (*a*) and to cross-examine and call witnesses and to present any relevant evidence at the hearing.

(4) The Attorney General may appear at the hearing held under paragraph (3)(*a*) without being deemed to intervene in the proceeding.

(5) If the judge or designated justice does not issue a summons or warrant under subsection (2), he or she shall endorse the information with a statement to that effect. Unless the informant, not later than six months after the endorsement, commences proceedings to compel the judge or designated justice to issue a summons or warrant, the information is deemed never to have been laid.

(6) If proceedings are commenced under subsection (5) and a summons or warrant is not issued as a result of those proceedings, the information is deemed never to have been laid.

(7) If a hearing in respect of an offence has been held under paragraph (3)(*a*) and the judge or designated justice has not issued a summons or a warrant, no other hearings may be held under that paragraph with respect to the offence or an included offence

unless there is new evidence in support of the allegation in respect of which the hearing is sought to be held.

(8) Subsections 507(2) to (8) apply to proceedings under this section.

(9) Subsections (1) to (8) do not apply in respect of an information laid under section 810 or 810.1.

(10) In this section, "designated justice" means a justice designated for the purpose by the chief judge of the provincial court having jurisdiction in the matter or, in Quebec, a justice designated by the chief judge of the Court of Quebec.

(11) In this section, "Attorney General" includes the Attorney General of Canada and his or her lawful deputy in respect of proceedings that could have been commenced at the instance of the Government of Canada and conducted by or on behalf of that Government. 2002, c. 13, s. 22; 2008, c. 18, s. 16.

CROSS-REFERENCES

The terms "Attorney General", "justice" and "provincial court judge" are defined in s. 2. The procedure for issuing process in public prosecutions is set out in s. 507. Section 579.01 permits the Attorney General to intervene in private prosecutions by calling witnesses and examining and cross-examining witnesses without actually taking over the prosecution.

The terms "summons" and "warrant" are defined in s. 493. The contents of a summons and the means of service are set out in s. 509. The contents of a warrant are set out in ss. 511 and 513. It is executed in accordance with s. 514. A warrant or summons may be issued, executed, given or entered into on a holiday by virtue of s. 20. Where the information is laid under s. 505 then the process issued by the peace officer or officer in charge is confirmed or cancelled in accordance with s. 508. For discussion of the pre-trial release provisions see the Note on the scheme for pre-trial release under s. 495.

Failure to attend court as required or attend for the purposes of the *Identification of Criminals Act* is an offence under s. 145. As well a warrant may issue under s. 510 for failure to attend for the purposes of the *Identification of Criminals Act*, R.S.C. 1985, c. I-1, as required in a summons. A warrant may issue under s. 512 where the accused fails to appear for court as required or where a summons cannot be served because the accused is evading service.

Probative value of electronically transmitted copy of summons or warrant, see s. 708.1.

SYNOPSIS

This section sets out the procedure to be followed before process is issued in a private prosecution, *i.e.* where the information is not laid by a police officer, public officer, the Attorney General or the Attorney General's agent, under s. 504. The section contains additional protections not found in the companion provision for public prosecutions under s. 507. (In accordance with subsec. (9) this section does not apply to the "peace bond" provisions in ss. 810 and 810.1.) The justice must refer the information to a provincial court judge or a judge of the Court of Quebec, as the case may be, or a designated justice of the peace. Before issuing process, whether a summons or a warrant, the judge or designated justice must hear the allegations of the informant and evidence, be satisfied that the Attorney General has received a copy of the information and reasonable notice of the hearing and given the Attorney General an opportunity to attend the hearing, cross-examine witnesses and present evidence. The Attorney General may participate in the proceedings without being deemed to have intervened in the prosecution, thus allowing the private prosecutor to continue the prosecution, should process be issued.

If the judge or designated judge does not issue process, no further hearings may be held unless there is new evidence to support the allegations. If a summons or warrant is not issued and no proceedings are instituted, e.g. through *mandamus*, to compel the judge or designated justice to issue process within six months or the proceedings are instituted but process is not issued as a result, the information is deemed never to have been laid.

The procedure for conducting the hearing under this section is set out in s. 507(2) to (8). Subsection (10) provides for the appointment of designated justices. Subsection (11) gives the Attorney General of Canada the same rights as the Attorney General of the province in respect of proceedings that could have been commenced at the instance of the Government of Canada and conducted by or on behalf of that government.

ANNOTATIONS

A Crown does not have the jurisdiction to withdraw an information before the pre-enquete hearing: *R. v. McHale* (2009), 251 C.C.C. (3d) 283 (Ont. S.C.J.), affd 256 C.C.C. (3d) 26 (Ont. C.A.), leave to appeal to S.C.C. refused 259 C.C.C. (3d) iv.

If the justice's refusal to issue process was based on extraneous considerations, or if his discretion was not exercised judicially following a proper hearing, *mandamus* will lie: *R. v. Blythe* (1973), 13 C.C.C. (2d) 192 (B.C.S.C.); *Swan (Re)* (1979), 48 C.C.C. (2d) 501 (Ont. H.C.J.).

Unlike s. 507(1)(*a*)(ii), s. 507.1(3)(*a*) appears to make the introduction of "evidence of witnesses" mandatory. Such a requirement serves as an important control over invocation of the criminal process by private informants: *R. v. Vasarhelyi* (2011), 272 C.C.C. (3d) 193 (Ont. C.A.), leave to appeal to S.C.C. refused (2012), 295 O.A.C. 400*n*.

For other annotations, see notes under s. 507.

JUSTICE TO HEAR INFORMANT AND WITNESSES / Procedure when witnesses attend.

508. (1) A justice who receives an information laid before him under section 505 shall

(*a*) hear and consider, *ex parte*,

(i) the allegations of the informant, and

(ii) the evidence of witnesses, where he considers it desirable or necessary to do so;

(*b*) where he considers that a case for so doing is made out, whether the information relates to the offence alleged in the appearance notice, promise to appear or recognizance or to an included or other offence,

(i) confirm the appearance notice, promise to appear or recognizance, as the case may be, and endorse the information accordingly, or

(ii) cancel the appearance notice, promise to appear or recognizance, as the case may be, and issue, in accordance with section 507, either a summons or a warrant for the arrest of the accused to compel the accused to attend before him or some other justice for the same territorial division to answer to a charge of an offence and endorse on the summons or warrant that the appearance notice, promise to appear or recognizance, as the case may be, has been cancelled; and

(*c*) where he considers that a case is not made out for the purposes of paragraph (*b*), cancel the appearance notice, promise to appear or recognizance, as the case may be, and cause the accused to be notified forthwith of such cancellation.

(2) A justice who hears the evidence of a witness pursuant to subsection (1) shall

(*a*) take the evidence on oath; and

(*b*) cause the evidence to be taken in accordance with section 540 in so far as that section is capable of being applied. R.S., c. 2 (2nd Supp.), s. 5; R.S.C. 1985, c. 27 (1st Supp.), s. 79.

CROSS-REFERENCES

The term "justice" is defined in s. 2. With respect to oaths and solemn affirmations see ss. 13 to 15 of the *Canada Evidence Act*, R.S.C. 1985, c. C-5. The terms "appearance notice", "promise to appear" and "recognizance" are defined in s. 493. The contents of these forms of release are set out in s. 501. Under s. 512 even though the accused has been released on one of these forms of release the justice may issue a summons or warrant. Where the information is laid under s. 504 then the process is issued by the justice in accordance with s. 507. The information may be laid by a peace officer by telecommunication in accordance with s. 508.1. For discussion of the pre-trial release provisions see the *Note on the scheme for pre-trial release* under s. 495.

Note s. 31(1) of the *Interpretation Act*, R.S.C. 1985, c. I-21, which provides that where anything is required or authorized to be done by or before, *inter alia*, a justice of the peace it shall be done by or before one whose jurisdiction or powers extend to the place where the thing is to be done.

Failure to attend court as required or attend for the purposes of the *Identification of Criminals Act*, R.S.C. 1985, c. I-1, is an offence under s. 145.

SYNOPSIS

This section sets out the procedure that must be followed when a justice receives an information laid before him under s. 505.

Subsection (1) requires a justice in this situation to hear and consider, *ex parte*, the allegations of the informant and, where it is considered desirable or necessary, the evidence of witnesses. Where a case is made out, the justice shall confirm the appearance notice, the promise to appear or the recognizance and endorse the information accordingly. The justice may also cancel the appearance notice, the promise to appear, or the recognizance and compel the accused, by summons or warrant, to appear in order to answer to a charge of an offence. If the justice considers that a case is not made out for the purposes of para. (*b*), the justice may cancel the appearance notice, promise to appear or recognizance and order that the accused be notified of this cancellation.

Subsection (2) requires that a justice, who hears the evidence of a witness pursuant to subsec. (1), must take the evidence on oath and, in so far as is possible, in accordance with s. 540.

ANNOTATIONS

Failure to confirm the appearance notice has relevance only to any proceedings taken against the accused should he fail to attend court as required therein. Such failure does not void the information and once the accused appears there is no necessity that the appearance notice be confirmed: *R. v. Wetmore* (1976), 32 C.C.C. (2d) 347 (N.S. S.C. App. Div.); *R. v. Maximick* (1979), 48 C.C.C. (2d) 417 (B.C.C.A.); *R. v. McGinnis* (1979), 51 C.C.C. (2d) 301 (Alta. C.A.); *R. v. Romanchuk* (2011), 278 C.C.C. (3d) 92 (Sask. C.A.); *R. v. Duran* (2011), 285 C.C.C. (3d) 46 (Ont. S.C.J.); *R. v. Millar* (2012), 285 C.C.C. (3d) 208 (Ont. S.C.J.). *Contra: R. v. Harris* (1978), 39 C.C.C. (2d) 256 (Ont. Prov. Ct.), and *semble, R. v. Gougeon; R. v. Haesler; R. v. Gray* (1980), 55 C.C.C. (2d) 218 (Ont. C.A.), at least where timely objection is made.

Prior to confirming the appearance notice, the justice must be satisfied that the notice complies with provisions of the *Criminal Code* including the requirement that the accused was served with copy of the notice. Where the accused fails to appear as required, a judge may issue a summons or warrant without proof of service of the appearance notice: *R. v. DeMelo* (1994), 92 C.C.C. (3d) 52, 73 O.A.C. 371 (C.A.).

Where an accused challenges the sufficiency of the *ex parte* hearing required by subsec. (1), the presumption of regularity applies and the burden is on the accused to show on a balance of probabilities that the requisite hearing had not taken place. For there to be compliance with this subsection, there need not be a "formal" hearing, although it would be preferable for the justice of the peace to ask the informant to briefly divulge the factual basis of the charge: *R. v. Morton* (1992), 70 C.C.C. (3d) 244, 7 O.R. (3d) 625 (Gen. Div.), affd 83 C.C.C. (3d) 95*n* (C.A.).

A charge of failing to comply with a requirement that the accused attend for fingerprinting must be dismissed if the promise to appear is only confirmed after the date set out for attendance for fingerprinting: *R. v. Tulloch* (1987), 40 C.C.C. (3d) 90 (Ont. Prov. Ct.).

INFORMATION LAID OTHERWISE THAN IN PERSON / Alternative to oath.

508.1 (1) For the purposes of sections 504 to 508, a peace officer may lay an information by any means of telecommunication that produces a writing.

(2) A peace officer who uses a means of telecommunication referred to in subsection (1) shall, instead of swearing an oath, make a statement in writing stating that all matters contained in the information are true to the officer's knowledge and belief, and such a statement is deemed to be a statement made under oath. 1997, c. 18, s. 56.

ANNOTATIONS

An officer is entitled to use a fax machine to lay an information. Section 507(1)(*a*) does not require that another person read the faxed material out loud to the justice so that she could "hear" it: *R. v. Lupyrypa* (2011), 270 C.C.C. (3d) 571 (Alta. C.A.).

SUMMONS / Service on individual / Content of summons / Attendance for purposes of *Identification of Criminals Act*.

509. (1) A summons issued under this Part shall

(*a*) be directed to the accused;

(*b*) set out briefly the offence in respect of which the accused is charged; and

(*c*) require the accused to attend court at a time and place to be stated therein and to attend thereafter as required by the court in order to be dealt with according to law.

(2) A summons shall be served by a peace officer who shall deliver it personally to the person to whom it is directed or, if that person cannot conveniently be found, shall leave it for him at his last or usual place of abode with some inmate thereof who appears to be at least sixteen years of age.

(3) [*Repealed*, 2008, c. 18, s. 17.]

(4) There shall be set out in every summons the text of subsection 145(4) and section 510.

(5) A summons may require the accused to appear at a time and place stated in it for the purposes of the *Identification of Criminals Act*, where the accused is alleged to have committed an indictable offence and, in the case of an offence designated as a contravention under the *Contraventions Act*, the Attorney General, within the meaning of that Act, has not made an election under section 50 of that Act. R.S., c. 2 (2nd Supp.), s. 5; R.S.C. 1985, c. 27 (1st Supp.), s. 80; 1992, c. 47, s. 71; 1996, c. 7, s. 38; 2008, c. 18, s. 17.

CROSS-REFERENCES

The term "peace officer" is defined in s. 2. Summons is defined in s. 493 as a summons in Form 6. Section 841 provides that forms varied to suit the case and forms to the like effect shall be deemed to be good, valid and sufficient in the circumstances for which, respectively, they are provided. A summons may be issued or given on a holiday by virtue of s. 20. For protection of person executing process see ss. 25 to 28. Service of a summons on a corporation, see s. 703.2.

Failure to attend court as required or attend for the purposes of the *Identification of Criminals Act*, R.S.C. 1985, c. I-1, is an offence under s. 145. As well a warrant may issue under s. 510 for failure to attend for the purposes of the *Identification of Criminals Act*. A warrant may issue under s. 512 where the accused fails to appear for court as required or where a summons cannot be served because the accused is evading service. A summons is effective throughout Canada (s. 703.1). Probative value of electronically transmitted copy, see s. 708.1.

SYNOPSIS

This section deals with the summons.

Subsection (1) requires that a summons issued under Part XVI be directed to the accused, set out the offence with which the accused is charged, and require the accused to attend in court at a time and place to be stated and thereafter as required by the court.

Subsection (2) states that a summons must be served by a peace officer for personal delivery upon the person to whom it is directed. If that person cannot be *conveniently* found, the peace officer must leave the summons at the person's latest or usual residence with a person who lives in the premises and who appears to be at least 16 years old.

Subsection (4) requires that the text of ss. 145(4) and 510 be set out in every summons.

Subsection (5) states that a summons may require the accused to appear at a stated time and place for the purposes of the *Identification of Criminals Act*, if the offence the accused is alleged to have committed is an indictable one.

ANNOTATIONS

There is no jurisdiction in a court to proceed *ex parte* against a defendant served with a summons outside Canada: *R. v. Shulman* (1975), 23 C.C.C. (2d) 242, 58 D.L.R. (3d) 586 (B.C.C.A.).

A justice has no power to issue a summons to an accused solely for the purpose of the *Identification of Criminals Act* and not in conjunction with procuring his attendance at court: *R. v. Michelsen* (1983), 4 C.C.C. (3d) 371, 33 C.R. (3d) 285 (Man. Q.B.).

Subsection (5) – The discretionary power to require an accused to attend for fingerprinting does not violate the principles of fundamental justice as guaranteed by s. 7 of the *Charter of Rights and Freedoms*: *R. v. Beare; R. v. Higgins*, [1988] 2 S.C.R. 387, 45 C.C.C. (3d) 57 (7:0).

FAILURE TO APPEAR.

510. Where an accused who is required by a summons to appear at a time and place stated in it for the purposes of the *Identification of Criminals Act* does not appear at that time and place and, in the case of an offence designated as a contravention under the *Contraventions Act*, the Attorney General, within the meaning of the Act, has not made an election under section 50 of that Act, a justice may issue a warrant for the arrest of the accused for the offence with which the accused is charged. R.S., c. 2 (2nd Supp.), s. 5; 1992, c. 47, s. 72; 1996, c. 7, s. 38.

CROSS-REFERENCES

The term "justice" is defined in s. 2. The terms "summons" and "warrant" are defined in s. 493. Failure to attend for the purposes of the *Identification of Criminals Act*, R.S.C. 1985, c. I-1, is an offence under s. 145. A warrant may also issue for failure to attend for the purposes of the *Identification of Criminals Act* as required in a promise-to-appear appearance notice or recognizance pursuant to s. 502. A warrant may issue under s. 512 where the accused fails to appear for court as required or where a summons cannot be served because the accused is evading service.

SYNOPSIS

This section deals with the failure to appear by an accused, who is required by summons to appear at a stated time and place for the *Identification of Criminals Act*. If the accused does not appear as required, the justice may issue a warrant for the arrest of the accused for the offence with which he is charged.

CONTENTS OF WARRANT TO ARREST / No return day / Discretion to postpone execution / Deemed execution of warrant.

511. (1) A warrant issued under this Part shall

(*a*) name or describe the accused;

(*b*) set out briefly the offence in respect of which the accused is charged; and

(*c*) order that the accused be forthwith arrested and brought before the judge or justice who issued the warrant or before some other judge or justice having jurisdiction in the same territorial division, to be dealt with according to law.

(2) A warrant issued under this Part remains in force until it is executed and need not be made returnable at any particular time.

(3) Notwithstanding paragraph (1)(*c*), a judge or justice who issues a warrant may specify in the warrant the period before which the warrant shall not be executed, to allow the accused to appear voluntarily before a judge or justice having jurisdiction in the territorial division in which the warrant was issued.

(4) Where the accused appears voluntarily for the offence in respect of which the accused is charged, the warrant is deemed to be executed. R.S., c. C-34, s. 456; R.S., c. 2 (2nd Supp.), s. 5; R.S.C. 1985, c. 27 (1st. Supp.), s. 81; 1997, c. 18, s. 57.

CROSS-REFERENCES

The term "justice" is defined in s. 2. Section 31(1) of the *Interpretation Act*, R.S.C. 1985, c. I-21, provides that where anything is required or authorized to be done by or before, *inter alia*, a justice of the peace it shall be done by or before one whose jurisdiction or powers extend to the place where the thing is to be done. The terms "accused" and "warrant" are defined in s. 493.

Formalities in a warrant are set out in s. 513. Under s. 20 a warrant may be executed on a holiday. A warrant is executed in accordance with ss. 29 and 514, and s. 10 of the Charter. For protection of person executing warrants and other process see ss. 25 to 28.

SYNOPSIS

This section sets out the necessary contents of a warrant to arrest issued under Part XVI.

Subsection (1) states that a warrant issued under Part XVI shall name or describe the accused, set out briefly the charge, and order the immediate arrest of the accused, who must then be brought before a judge or justice having jurisdiction, in order to be dealt with according to law.

Subsection (2) states that a warrant issued under Part XVI remains in force until it is executed. It is not necessary that it be made returnable at any specific time.

Subsection (3) allows the justice to require that the warrant be held for a specified time to allow the accused to appear voluntarily.

ANNOTATIONS

There is no jurisdiction for the Provincial Court Judges to seize themselves of release hearings by requiring that the accused be brought before the issuer of the warrant: *R. v. Davidson* (2004), 193 C.C.C. (3d) 63, 26 C.R. (6th) 264, 357 A.R. 353 (C.A.).

CERTAIN ACTIONS NOT TO PRECLUDE ISSUE OF WARRANT / Warrant in default of appearance.

512. (1) A justice may, where the justice has reasonable and probable grounds to believe that it is necessary in the public interest to issue a summons or a warrant for the arrest of the accused, issue a summons or warrant notwithstanding that

(*a*) an appearance notice or a promise to appear or a recognizance entered into before an officer in charge or another peace officer has been confirmed or cancelled under subsection 508(1);

(*b*) a summons has previously been issued under subsection 507(4); or

(*c*) the accused has been released unconditionally or with the intention of compelling his appearance by way of summons.

(2) Where

(*a*) service of a summons is proved and the accused fails to attend court in accordance with the summons,

(*b*) an appearance notice or a promise to appear or a recognizance entered into before an officer in charge or another peace officer has been confirmed under subsection 508(1) and the accused fails to attend court in accordance therewith in order to be dealt with according to law, or

(*c*) it appears that a summons cannot be served because the accused is evading service,

a justice may issue a warrant for the arrest of the accused. R.S., c. 2 (2nd Supp.), s. 5; R.S.C. 1985, c. 27 (1st Supp.), s. 82; 1997, c. 18, s. 58.

CROSS-REFERENCES

The terms "justice" and "peace officer" are defined in s. 2. The terms "accused", "appearance notice", "officer in charge", "promise to appear", "summons", "warrant" and "recognizance" are defined in s. 493. As to contents of warrant see ss. 511 and 513. A warrant is executed in accordance with ss. 29 and 514, and s. 10 of the Charter. For protection of person executing warrants and other process see ss. 25 to 28.

SYNOPSIS

This section empowers a justice to issue a warrant in certain specific situations.

Subsection (1) states that a justice may issue a summons or a warrant for the arrest of an accused notwithstanding that an appearance notice, a promise to appear or a recognizance has been confirmed or cancelled under s. 508(1). A summons or warrant may also be issued by a justice under this subsection even if another summons has been issued under s. 507(4) or the accused has been released unconditionally or with the intention of compelling his appearance by way of summons. However, in all of these instances the justice must believe that it is in the public interest to issue the summons or warrant.

Subsection (2) provides that a justice may issue a warrant for the arrest of the accused where service of summons is proved and the accused fails to appear in court. The justice may also issue a warrant when an appearance notice, a promise to appear or a recognizance has been confirmed under s. 508(1) and the accused fails to appear in court, or when a summons cannot be served because the accused appears to be evading service.

ANNOTATIONS

Subsection (1) – An accused's release from custody because of non-compliance with s. 525 does not preclude a justice from issuing a warrant for his arrest again for the same offence: *Ex p. Chung* (1975), 26 C.C.C. (2d) 497, [1976] 1 W.W.R. 453 (B.C.C.A.).

This subsection gives a judge a residual power to issue a warrant where the accused after an initial appearance in court fails to appear, even if the initial appearance was pursuant to defective process such as a failure to comply with s. 505: *R. v. Gougeon; R. v. Haesler; R. v. Gray* (1980), 55 C.C.C. (2d) 218 (Ont. C.A.), leave to appeal to S.C.C. refused 35 N.R. 83*n*. Folld: *R. v. Siller* (1980), 59 C.C.C. (2d) 169 (B.C.C.A.).

Subsection (2) – There is no jurisdiction to issue a warrant simply to preserve jurisdiction where the accused is already in custody but has not been brought before the court: *R. v. Inverarity* (1984), 18 C.C.C. (3d) 74 (Sask. Q.B.). [**Note:** as to whether jurisdiction would be lost in such circumstances regard must be had to s. 485.]

However, to the contrary is *R. v. Hartmann* (1986), 30 C.C.C. (3d) 286 (Ont. H.C.J.), where it was held that a warrant could issue under this subsection, and possibly under subsec. (1), to preserve jurisdiction where the accused was not brought to court on a remand date. It is not a condition precedent to the issuance of a warrant under this subsection that its issuance be necessary in the public interest and resort to this subsection does not depend on the fact that the accused did not have a lawful excuse for failing to attend in court.

FORMALITIES OF WARRANT.

513. A warrant in accordance with this Part shall be directed to the peace officers within the territorial jurisdiction of the justice, judge or court by whom or by which it is issued. R.S., c. 2 (2nd Supp.), s. 5.

CROSS-REFERENCES

"Warrant" is defined in s. 493. The contents of the warrant are described in s. 511. Under s. 20 a warrant may be executed on a holiday. A warrant is executed in accordance with ss. 29 and 514, and s. 10 of the Charter. For protection of person executing warrants and other process see ss. 25 to 28.

SYNOPSIS

This section requires that a warrant issued under Part XVI be directed to the peace officers within the territorial jurisdiction of the issuing justice, judge or court.

EXECUTION OF WARRANT / By whom warrant may be executed.

514. (1) A warrant in accordance with this Part may be executed by arresting the accused

(*a*) wherever he is found within the territorial jurisdiction of the justice, judge or court by whom or by which the warrant was issued; or

(*b*) wherever he is found in Canada, in the case of fresh pursuit.

(2) A warrant in accordance with this Part may be executed by a person who is one of the peace officers to whom it is directed, whether or not the place in which the warrant is to be executed is within the territory for which the person is a peace officer. R.S., c. 2 (2nd Supp.), s. 5.

CROSS-REFERENCES

"Justice" and "peace officer" are defined in s. 2. "Warrant" is defined in s. 493. The contents of the warrant are described in ss. 511 and 513. Under s. 20 a warrant may be executed on a holiday. A warrant is executed in accordance with ss. 29 and 513, and s. 10 of the Charter. For protection of person executing warrants see ss. 25 to 28. Where the warrant cannot be executed in accordance with this section then an application may be made under s. 528 to a justice, in whose jurisdiction the accused is believed to be, who may endorse the warrant authorizing the arrest within his jurisdiction. As to effect of warrant from superior court in another province, see s. 703.

As to execution of a warrant where the accused is believed to be in a dwelling-house, see ss. 529 to 529.5.

SYNOPSIS

This section describes the execution of a warrant issued under Part XVI on the accused.

Subsection (1) states that a warrant may be executed by arresting the accused wherever he is found within the territorial jurisdiction of the issuing court. In the case of fresh pursuit, the warrant may be executed wherever the accused is found in Canada.

Subsection (2) provides that the warrant may be executed by one of the peace officers to whom it is directed, even if the place where the warrant is to be executed is not part of that peace officer's territory.

Judicial Interim Release

ORDER OF RELEASE / Release on undertaking with conditions, etc. / Power of justice to name sureties in order / Alternative to physical presence / Where consent required / Release on undertaking with conditions, etc. / Conditions authorized / Condition prohibiting possession of firearms, etc. / Surrender, etc. / Reasons / Additional conditions / Offences / Detention in custody / Order of detention / Reasons / Order of release / Idem / Sufficiency of record / Written reasons / Justification for detention in custody / Detention in custody for offence mentioned in s. 469 / Order re no communication / Consideration of victim's safety and security / Copy to victim.

515. (1) Subject to this section, where an accused who is charged with an offence other than an offence listed in section 469 is taken before a justice, the justice shall, unless a plea of guilty by the accused is accepted, order, in respect of that offence, that the accused be released on his giving an undertaking without conditions, unless the prosecutor, having been given a reasonable opportunity to do so, shows cause, in respect of that offence, why the detention of the accused in custody is justified or why an order under any other provision of this section should be made and where the justice makes an order under any other provision of this section, the order shall refer only to the particular offence for which the accused was taken before the justice.

(2) Where the justice does not make an order under subsection (1), he shall, unless the prosecutor shows cause why the detention of the accused is justified, order that the accused be released

(*a*) on his giving an undertaking with such conditions as the justice directs;

(*b*) on his entering into a recognizance before the justice, without sureties, in such amount and with such conditions, if any, as the justice directs but without deposit of money or other valuable security;

(*c*) on his entering into a recognizance before the justice with sureties in such amount and with such conditions, if any, as the justice directs but without deposit of money or other valuable security;

(*d*) with the consent of the prosecutor, on his entering into a recognizance before the justice, without sureties, in such amount and with such conditions, if any, as the justice directs and on his depositing with the justice such sum of money or other valuable security as the justice directs; or

(*e*) if the accused is not ordinarily resident in the province in which the accused is in custody or does not ordinarily reside within two hundred kilometres of the place in which he is in custody, on his entering into a recognizance before the justice with or without sureties in such amount and with such conditions, if any, as the justice directs, and upon his depositing with the justice such sum of money or other valuable security as the justice directs.

(2.1) Where, pursuant to subsection (2) or any other provision of this Act, a justice, judge or court orders that an accused be released on his entering into a recognizance with sureties, the justice, judge or court may, in the order, name particular persons as sureties.

(2.2) Where, by this Act, the appearance of an accused is required for the purposes of judicial interim release, the appearance shall be by actual physical attendance of the accused but the justice may, subject to subsection (2.3), allow the accused to appear by means of any suitable telecommunication device, including telephone, that is satisfactory to the justice.

(2.3) The consent of the prosecutor and the accused is required for the purposes of an appearance if the evidence of a witness is to be taken at the appearance and the accused cannot appear by closed-circuit television or any other means that allow the court and the accused to engage in simultaneous visual and oral communication.

(3) The justice shall not make an order under any of paragraphs (2)(*b*) to (*e*) unless the prosecution shows cause why an order under the immediately preceding paragraph should not be made.

(4) The justice may direct as conditions under subsection (2) that the accused shall do any one or more of the following things as specified in the order:

- **(*a*) report at times to be stated in the order to a peace officer or other person designated in the order;**
- **(*b*) remain within a territorial jurisdiction specified in the order;**
- **(*c*) notify the peace officer or other person designated under paragraph (*a*) of any change in his address or his employment or occupation;**
- **(*d*) abstain from communicating, directly or indirectly, with any victim, witness or other person identified in the order, or refrain from going to any place specified in the order, except in accordance with the conditions specified in the order that the justice considers necessary;**
- **(*e*) where the accused is the holder of a passport, deposit his passport as specified in the order;**
- **(*e*.1) comply with any other condition specified in the order that the justice considers necessary to ensure the safety and security of any victim of or witness to the offence; and**
- **(*f*) comply with such other reasonable conditions specified in the order as the justice considers desirable.**

(4.1) When making an order under subsection (2), in the case of an accused who is charged with

- **(*a*) an offence in the commission of which violence against a person was used, threatened or attempted,**
- **(*a*.1) a terrorism offence,**
- **(*b*) an offence under section 264 (criminal harassment),**
- **(*b*.1) an offence under section 423.1 (intimidation of a justice system participant),**
- **(*b*.2) an offence relating to the contravention of any of sections 9 to 14 of the *Cannabis Act*,**
- **(*c*) an offence relating to the contravention of any of sections 5 to 7 of the *Controlled Drugs and Substances Act*,**
- **(*d*) an offence that involves, or the subject-matter of which is, a firearm, a cross-bow, a prohibited weapon, a restricted weapon, a prohibited device, ammunition, prohibited ammunition or an explosive substance, or**
- **(*e*) an offence under subsection 20(1) of the *Security of Information Act*, or an offence under subsection 21(1) or 22(1) or section 23 of that Act that is committed in relation to an offence under subsection 20(1) of that Act,**

the justice shall add to the order a condition prohibiting the accused from possessing a firearm, cross-bow, prohibited weapon, restricted weapon, prohibited device, ammunition, prohibited ammunition or explosive substance, or all those things, until the accused is dealt with according to law unless the justice considers that such a condition is not required in the interests of the safety of the accused or the safety and security of a victim of the offence or of any other person.

(4.11) Where the justice adds a condition described in subsection (4.1) to an order made under subsection (2), the justice shall specify in the order the manner and method by which

- **(*a*) the things referred to in subsection (4.1) that are in the possession of the accused shall be surrendered, disposed of, detained, stored or dealt with; and**
- **(*b*) the authorizations, licences and registration certificates held by the person shall be surrendered.**

(4.12) Where the justice does not add a condition described in subsection (4.1) to an order made under subsection (2), the justice shall include in the record a statement of the reasons for not adding the condition.

(4.2) Before making an order under subsection (2), in the case of an accused who is charged with an offence referred to in subsection (4.3), the justice shall consider whether it is desirable, in the interests of the safety and security of any person, particularly a victim of or witness to the offence or a justice system participant, to include as a condition of the order

(*a*) that the accused abstain from communicating, directly or indirectly, with any victim, witness or other person identified in the order, or refrain from going to any place specified in the order; or

(*b*) that the accused comply with any other condition specified in the order that the justice considers necessary to ensure the safety and security of those persons.

(4.3) The offences for the purposes of subsection (4.2) are

(*a*) a terrorism offence;

(*b*) an offence described in section 264 or 423.1

(*c*) an offence in the commission of which violence against a person was used, threatened or attempted; and

(*d*) an offence under subsection 20(1) of the *Security of Information Act*, or an offence under subsection 21(1) or 22(1) or section 23 of that Act that is committed in relation to an offence under subsection 20(1) of that Act.

(5) Where the prosecutor shows cause why the detention of the accused in custody is justified, the justice shall order that the accused be detained in custody until he is dealt with according to law and shall include in the record a statement of his reasons for making the order.

(6) Unless the accused, having been given a reasonable opportunity to do so, shows cause why the accused's detention in custody is not justified, the justice shall order, despite any provision of this section, that the accused be detained in custody until the accused is dealt with according to law, if the accused is charged

(*a*) with an indictable offence, other than an offence listed in section 469,

(i) that is alleged to have been committed while at large after being released in respect of another indictable offence pursuant to the provisions of this Part or section 679 or 680,

(ii) that is an offence under section 467.11, 467.111, 467.12 or 467.13, or a serious offence alleged to have been committed for the benefit of, at the direction of, or in association with, a criminal organization,

(iii) that is an offence under any of sections 83.02 to 83.04 and 83.18 to 83.23 or otherwise is alleged to be a terrorism offence,

(iv) an offence under subsection 16(1) or (2), 17(1), 19(1), 20(1) or 22(1) of the *Security of Information Act*,

(v) an offence under subsection 21(1) or 22(1) or section 23 of the *Security of Information Act* that is committed in relation to on offence referred to in subparagraph (iv),

(vi) that is an offence under section 99, 100 or 103,

(vii) that is an offence under section 244 or 244.2, or an offence under section 239, 272 or 273, subsection 279(1) or section 279.1, 344 or 346 that is alleged to have been committed with a firearm, or

(viii) that is alleged to involve, or whose subject-matter is alleged to be, a firearm, a cross-bow, a prohibited weapon, a restricted weapon, a prohibited device, any ammunition or prohibited ammunition or an explosive substance, and that is alleged to have been committed while the accused was under a prohibition order within the meaning of subsection 84(1);

(b) with an indictable offence, other than an offence listed in section 469 and is not ordinarily resident in Canada,

(c) with an offence under any of subsections 145(2) to (5) that is alleged to have been committed while he was at large after being released in respect of another offence pursuant to the provisions of this Part or section 679, 680 or 816, or

(d) with having committed an offence punishable by imprisonment for life under any of sections 5 to 7 of the *Controlled Drugs and Substances Act* or the offence of conspiring to commit such an offence.

(6.1) If the justice orders that an accused to whom subsection (6) applies be released, the justice shall include in the record a statement of the justice's reasons for making the order.

(7) Where an accused to whom paragraph 6(*a*), (*c*) or (*d*) applies shows cause why the accused's detention in custody is not justified, the justice shall order that the accused be released on giving an undertaking or entering into a recognizance described in any of paragraphs (2)(*a*) to (*e*) with the conditions described in subsections (4) to (4.2) or, where the accused was at large on an undertaking or recognizance with conditions, the additional conditions described in subsections (4) to (4.2), that the justice considers desirable, unless the accused, having been given a reasonable opportunity to do so, shows cause why the conditions or additional conditions should not be imposed.

(8) Where an accused to whom paragraph (6)(*b*) applies shows cause why the accused's detention in custody is not justified, the justice shall order that the accused be released on giving an undertaking or entering into a recognizance described in any of paragraphs (2)(*a*) to (*e*) with the conditions, described in subsections (4) to (4.2), that the justice considers desirable.

(9) For the purposes of subsections (5) and (6), it is sufficient if a record is made of the reasons in accordance with the provisions of Part XVIII relating to the taking of evidence at preliminary inquiries.

(9.1) Despite subsection (9), if the justice orders that the accused be detained in custody primarily because of a previous conviction of the accused, the justice shall state that reason, in writing, in the record.

(10) For the purposes of this section, the detention of an accused in custody is justified only on one or more of the following grounds:

(a) where the detention is necessary to ensure his or her attendance in court in order to be dealt with according to law;

(b) where the detention is necessary for the protection or safety of the public, including any victim of or witness to the offence, or any person under the age of 18 years, having regard to all the circumstances including any substantial likelihood that the accused will, if released from custody, commit a criminal offence or interfere with the administration of justice; and

(c) if the detention is necessary to maintain confidence in the administration of justice, having regard to all the circumstances, including

(i) the apparent strength of the prosecution's case,

(ii) the gravity of the offence,

(iii) the circumstances surrounding the commission of the offence, including whether a firearm was used, and

(iv) the fact that the accused is liable, on conviction, for a potentially lengthy term of imprisonment or, in the case of an offence that involves, or whose subject-matter is, a firearm, a minimum punishment of imprisonment for a term of three years or more.

(11) Where an accused who is charged with an offence mentioned in section 469 is taken before a justice, the justice shall order that the accused be detained in custody until he is

dealt with according to law and shall issue a warrant in Form 8 for the committal of the accused.

(12) A justice who orders that an accused be detained in custody under this section may include in the order a direction that the accused abstain from communicating, directly or indirectly, with any victim, witness or other person identified in the order, except in accordance with such conditions specified in the order as the justice considers necessary.

(13) A justice who makes an order under this section shall include in the record of the proceedings a statement that he or she considered the safety and security of every victim of the offence when making the order.

(14) If an order is made under this section, the justice shall, on request by a victim of the offence, cause a copy of the order to be given to the victim. R.S., c. C-34, s. 457; R.S., c. 2 (2nd Supp.), s. 5; 1974-75-76, c. 93, s. 47; R.S.C. 1985, c. 27 (1st Supp.), ss. 83, 186 (Sched. IV, item 7); 1991, c. 40, s. 31; 1993, c. 45, s. 8; 1994, c. 44, s. 44; 1995, c. 39, ss. 153, 188(*b*); 1996, c. 19, ss. 71, 93.3; 1997, c. 18, s. 59; c. 23, s. 16; 1999, c. 5, s. 21; c. 25, s. 8; 2001, c. 32, s. 37; c. 41, ss. 19, 133(15)-(17); 2008, c. 6, s. 37; 2009, c. 22, s. 17; c. 29, s. 2; 2010, c. 20, s. 1; 2012, c. 1, s. 32; 2014, c. 17, s. 14; 2015, c. 13, s. 20; 2018, c. 16, s. 218.

CROSS-REFERENCES

The terms "justice", "criminal organization", "terrorism offence", "justice system participant" and "victim" are defined in s. 2. The terms "recognizance" and "undertaking" are defined in s. 493. "Sureties" is defined in s. 35 of the *Interpretation Act*, R.S.C. 1985, c. I-21, as sufficient sureties and when those words are used one person is sufficient therefor, unless otherwise expressly required.

Pursuant to s. 2.1, the terms "cross-bow", "prohibited weapon", "restricted weapon", "prohibited device", "ammunition", and "prohibited ammunition" have the same meaning as in s. 84(1).

Where the justice stated in writing on the record, in accordance with subsec. (9.1) of this section, that the reason for detention was primarily because of a previous conviction, the sentencing judge may not give more than 1 for 1 credit for pre-sentence custody, pursuant to s. 719(3.1). The term "conviction" is not defined in this section, but presumably has the same meaning as "convicted of a criminal offence" in s. 518(1)(*c*).

Note on judicial interim release – Where the accused is not released by the arresting officer or the officer in charge (defined in s. 493) then s. 503 requires that he be taken before a justice (defined in s. 2) without unreasonable delay and within 24 hours where a justice is available. Upon being taken before a justice the accused is entitled to a bail hearing under s. 515 unless he is charged with an offence listed in s. 469, such as murder, or he pleads guilty. Following is a brief discussion of the procedure and the relationship between the various provisions as they apply to an accused charged with an offence other than an offence listed in s. 469. For the s. 469 offences see the note under s. 522.

The hearing under s. 515 is variously described in the case law as a judicial interim release hearing or "show cause" hearing because in most cases the onus is on the prosecution to show cause why the accused should not be released on an undertaking (defined in s. 493) without conditions. There are certain exceptions, listed in s. 515(6), where the onus is reversed and it is the accused who must show cause why he should not be detained. The justice must provide reasons in accordance with s. 515(6.1) if the justice nevertheless releases the accused. In either case cause for detention is set out in s. 515(10). Where the prosecutor shows cause why the accused should not be released on an unconditional undertaking then the onus is on the prosecutor to show why the accused should not be released on a form of release representing the least interference with the accused's liberty, from an undertaking with conditions to a recognizance (defined in s. 493), with or without sureties (defined in s. 35 of the *Interpretation Act*), and finally a detention order. These forms of release are described in s. 515(2) and the conditions which may be imposed are set out in s. 515(4), (4.1) and (4.3). Note that where a prohibition order is made under subsec. (4.1), pursuant to s. 113, the justice or judge may make an order authorizing a chief firearms officer or the

Registrar to issue, in accordance with such terms and conditions as is considered appropriate, an authorization, a licence or a registration certificate, as the case may be, to the accused for sustenance or employment purposes. Under s. 114, the prohibition order may require the accused to surrender anything the possession of which is prohibited by the order and every authorization, licence and registration certificate relating to any such thing. Unless the prohibition order provides otherwise, everything the possession of which is prohibited by the order is forfeited to the Crown pursuant to s. 115, subject to the true owner making an application under s. 117. Under s. 116, every authorization, licence and registration certificate relating to anything the possession of which is prohibited by a prohibition order and issued to the accused is, on the commencement of the prohibition order, revoked, or amended, as the case may be, to the extent of the prohibitions in the order. In certain cases, described in s. 515(2)(*d*), and (*e*), the justice may also make an order requiring a cash deposit with or without sureties. Where the onus is on the prosecutor to show cause s. 515(5) requires the justice to give reasons for making a detention order. Where the onus is on the accused then s. 515(6) requires that the justice give reasons for making a release order. Even where the accused is detained for some other reason, *e.g.*, because he is serving sentence, he is entitled to a hearing under s. 515, however, if the justice makes a release order then by virtue of s. 519 the accused will still remain in custody until he is no longer required to be detained for some other reason. If the justice detains the accused "primarily" because of a previous conviction, subsec. (9.1) requires the justice to record that fact in writing (presumably on the information). The purpose of this record is that it limits the amount of credit that can be awarded for pre-sentence custody in accordance with s. 719(3.1).

Sections 516 to 518 set out the procedure to be followed on the bail hearing. Section 516 deals with adjournments and permits the justice to order the accused to abstain from communicating with witnesses or other named persons. Section 517 provides for a non-publication order. Section 518 sets out the kind of evidence which may be tendered on the hearing. The effect of s. 518 is to give a relatively wide latitude to the justice permitting him to receive and base his decision on evidence "considered credible or trustworthy". Thus the rules of evidence which would apply at a trial would not apply on the bail hearing. One limit on the receipt of evidence is the proviso in s. 518(1)(*b*), which prohibits questioning of the accused respecting the offence with which he is charged. The scope of this subsection is uncertain, there being some case law noted under s. 518 holding that, while the accused cannot be asked by the justice or the prosecutor about the offence, he is entitled to volunteer his testimony concerning the offence. Where a release order is made then s. 519 sets out the procedure for putting the order into effect and the circumstances in which the accused will be released.

The Code also sets out an elaborate system of review. Under s. 515.1 the undertaking or recognizance may be "varied" with consent of the prosecutor. Under s. 520 the accused may apply to a judge (defined in s. 493) to review a detention order or to review the terms upon which he was released. Section 521 gives a similar right of review to the prosecutor to review any release order made by a justice. It would also seem that orders made under ss. 520 or 521 can in turn be reviewed under those sections. The application is on notice to the prosecutor or accused as the case may be (ss. 520(2) and 521(2)). The procedure on the review hearing resembles the procedure on the original s. 515 hearing, except that the onus is on the applicant to show cause why the original order should be vacated (ss. 520(7) and 521(8)). The presence of the accused would not appear to be mandatory but the judge may make an order requiring the accused's presence which order may be enforced through issuance of a warrant (ss. 520(3), (5) and 521(3), (5)). Ordinarily, the judge will consider the transcript of proceedings sought to be reviewed but has power to consider other additional evidence or exhibits (ss. 520(7) and 521(8)). Adjournment of the proceeding is provided for in ss. 520(4) and 521(4).

Section 523(2) also provides for a more informal review process at various stages of the proceedings by a justice, a preliminary inquiry judge, a judge of the trial court, or the trial judge. Note, however, that the release or detention order can only be vacated under this subsection upon cause being shown and, in some circumstances, the review can only be undertaken where both the accused and the prosecutor consent. Section 524 enacts a procedure for dealing with cases where it is alleged that the accused has violated or is about to violate any form of release either issued by a peace officer or by a justice or has committed an indictable offence while on a form of release.

That section gives a power to arrest with (subsec. (1)) or without warrant (subsec. (2)). Upon arrest under this section the accused will be taken before a justice and where it is shown that his arrest was justified (subsec. (8)) then the release order is cancelled and the accused ordered detained unless he can show cause why he should not be detained in custody. If the accused shows cause then s. 524(9) provides for the types of release order which may be made. Any order made under s. 524 may be reviewed under ss. 520 and 521 by the accused or the prosecutor as the case may be. The procedure on the s. 524 hearing is similar to the original show cause hearing (subsec. (12)). Finally, s. 525 sets out a procedure for an automatic review, by a judge, of the detention of any accused who is ordered detained either under s. 515, 521 or 524. The time when the review occurs depends on whether the accused is charged with an indictable offence (90 days) or a summary conviction offence (30 days). The scope of s. 525 remains subject to some uncertainty. In particular it is not clear whether the accused is entitled to a review where he has been ordered released but is unable to comply with the terms of the recognizance and it is unclear whether the section applies where the accused has previously unsuccessfully applied to a judge under s. 520. The procedure under the s. 525 hearing resembles the procedure under s. 515, except that notwithstanding where the onus originally lay the judge must be satisfied that the accused's continued detention is justified within the meaning of s. 515(10) (subsec. (4)). Subsections (5) to (7) describe a procedure for cancelling any release order made under s. 525, a procedure which resembles the s. 524 procedure. Aside from those subsections there would not appear to be any mechanism for reviewing a release order made under s. 525. Subsection (9) also requires the judge in any event to give directions for expediting the trial. A similar discretionary power is given to any justice or judge conducting a hearing under any of the other sections, pursuant to s. 526.

Barring a review under these provisions the effect of s. 523(1) is that the release or detention order remains in effect until verdict. Where the accused is found guilty then the release order remains in effect unless the judge orders that he be taken into custody pending sentence. Section 523(1.1) provides a procedure for the release order in respect of one information to apply to a new information charging the same offence, or an included offence.

Where the accused pleads guilty either prior to the show cause hearing under s. 515 or in the course of the hearing then, pursuant to s. 518(2), the justice may make an order provided for in s. 515 for his release pending sentence.

The procedure for enforcement of a recognizance is set out in Part XXV. That Part sets out the responsibilities of sureties (s. 764); procedure for rendering of accused by his sureties (ss. 766, 767 and 769); substitution of a new surety (s. 767.1), and the new release hearing where the accused is rendered into custody by his sureties (s. 769). That Part also sets out the procedure in case of default by the accused, including endorsing the fact of the default (s. 770); the hearing for estreat of the bail (s. 771); levying execution to enforce a writ of *fieri facias* where the recognizance is ordered forfeited (ss. 772 and 773).

There are special limitations on the making of interim release and detention orders where the court makes an assessment order under Part XX.1. See in particular ss. 672.16, 672.17 and 672.18.

ANNOTATIONS

Jurisdiction – A justice has continuing jurisdiction to hear an application for release under subsec. (1) regardless of the point in the proceedings. Jurisdiction is not lost merely because the accused has been committed for trial in the superior court and the charging document is no longer before the provincial court. However, where an accused is being tried in the superior court and no order in respect of bail or detention has been made, the superior court judge may exercise his or her inherent jurisdiction to entertain an initial bail application: *R. v. Mayen* (2014), 311 C.C.C. (3d) 225 (Man. Q.B.).

A person appearing pursuant to a summons is not "taken before a justice" within the meaning of subsec. (1) and cannot be made subject to a release order: *R. v. Nowazek* (2018), 366 C.C.C. (3d) 389 (Y.T.C.A.).

Burden of proof – The evidentiary burden upon the Crown at this early stage is upon the minimum standard, the balance of probability: *R. v. Julian* (1972), 20 C.R.N.S. 227 (N.S.S.C).

Forms of release (subsec. (2)) – A central part of the law of bail consists of the ladder principle and the authorized forms of release, which are found in subsecs. (1) to (3). Save for exceptions, an unconditional release on an undertaking is the default position when granting release. Alternative forms of release are to be imposed in accordance with the ladder principle, which must be adhered to strictly: release is favoured at the earliest reasonable opportunity and on the least onerous grounds. If the Crown proposes an alternate form of release, it must show why this form is necessary for a more restrictive form of release to be imposed. Each rung of the ladder must be considered individually and must be rejected before moving to a more restrictive form of release. Where the parties disagree on the form of release, it is an error of law for a judge to order a more restrictive form without justifying the decision to reject the less onerous forms. A recognizance with sureties is one of the most onerous forms of release, and should not be imposed unless all the less onerous forms have been considered and rejected as inappropriate: *R. v. Antic*, [2017] 1 S.C.R. 509, 347 C.C.C. (3d) 231.

Cash bail – It is not necessary to impose cash bail on accused persons if they or their sureties have reasonably recoverable assets and are able to pledge those assets to the satisfaction of the court. A recognizance is functionally equivalent to cash bail and has the same coercive effect. Cash bail should be relied on only in exceptional circumstances in which release on a recognizance with sureties is unavailable. When cash bail is ordered, the amount must not be set so high that it effectively amounts to a detention order, which means that the amount should be no higher than necessary to satisfy the concern that would otherwise warrant detention and proportionate to the means of the accused and the circumstances of the case. The judge is under a positive obligation to inquire into the ability of the accused to pay: *R. v. Antic*, *supra*.

It was held in *R. v. Garrington* (1972), 9 C.C.C. (2d) 472 (Ont. H.C.J.), that it was wrong to fix the amount of the cash deposit as some portion of the amount still unrecovered (the accused were charged with a robbery of a large amount of money) or to fix the amount so high that it was effectively a detention order.

Fixing amount of surety – Where the amount fixed for sureties is so high that in effect it amounts to a detention order it will be reduced accordingly: *R. v. Cichanski* (1976), 25 C.C.C. (2d) 84 (Ont. H.C.J.).

Naming sureties – The inclusion of subsec. (2.1) confers a permissive authority. The court is not required to name sureties and, because a prospective surety is not in court or is as yet unidentified, the court is often not in a position to in effect pre-approve a surety to be named in the order. It then falls to the justice exercising the compliance jurisdiction in s. 519 to approve, or not, the sureties before release can occur. There is no legal requirement that a surety be present in court and testify in order for judicial interim release to be considered. While there may be circumstances where the judge may wish to see a surety, a blanket requirement that all prospective sureties in every case must appear before the court at the show cause hearing amounts to an abuse of discretion: *R. v. Brooks* (2001), 153 C.C.C. (3d) 533 (Ont. S.C.J.); *R. v. Villota* (2002), 163 C.C.C. (3d) 507 (Ont. S.C.J.).

Reasonable conditions (subsec. (4)) – Conditions of release under s. 515(4) should only be imposed to the extent that they are necessary to address concerns related to the statutory criteria for detention and to ensure that the accused is released. They must not be imposed to change an accused person's behaviour or to punish an accused person: *R. v. Antic*, *supra*.

To come within the meaning of the term "reasonable conditions", the particular term must be related to a purpose which would otherwise justify the accused's detention pending trial: *R. v. Keenan* (1979), 57 C.C.C. (2d) 267 (Que. C.A.).

The justice may validly impose a condition that the accused remain out of a certain part of the city where the term is designed to prevent the commission of further offences while the accused is on judicial interim release: *R. v. Bielefeld* (1981), 64 C.C.C. (2d) 216 (B.C.S.C.).

Effect of order to stand trial on lesser offence – Where an accused who has been ordered detained on a charge of robbery is committed for trial on the lesser offence of attempted robbery the original order remains in effect: *Ex p. Walker* (1974), 20 C.C.C. (2d) 539 (Ont. H.C.J.); *cf. R. v. Lafontaine* (1973), 13 C.C.C. (2d) 316 (Ont. H.C.J.), noted under s. 522.

Requirement of reasons – The requirement of reasons is directory only and the failure to give reasons does not affect the validity of the detention order: *R. v. Baker* (1973), 13 C.C.C. (2d) 340 (B.C.S.C.).

Adjournment – There is no need for a full hearing before a justice exercises discretion concerning the length of the remand: *R. v. F. (C.G.)* (2003), 181 C.C.C. (3d) 422 (N.S.C.A.).

Right to counsel – An unrepresented accused charged with an indictable offence may have the right to counsel at a bail hearing or bail review. The presiding judge has a duty to inquire whether the accused wishes to be represented by counsel. The determination must be made on a case-by-case basis having regard to the complexity of the proceedings and the seriousness of the charge: *R. v. Chan* (2000), 146 C.C.C. (3d) 494 (Alta. C.A.).

Police officer acting as prosecutor – The differing definitions of "prosecutor" under s. 2 (applicable generally) and s. 785 (applicable only to summary conviction matters) make clear that Parliament intended prosecutors at bail hearing on indictable offences to be legally trained. It is not permissible for a police officer to act as the prosecutor at a bail hearing where an indictable offence is charged: *Alberta (Attorney General) v. Edmonton Police Service* (2017), 344 C.C.C. (3d) 357 (Alta. Q.B.).

Reverse onus (subsec. (6)) – Notwithstanding an accused may fall within this subsection the basic philosophy of the interim release provisions is that prior to conviction all those persons who do not constitute a danger to public and who will show up for trial ought not to be detained in custody. Where as a result of this subsection the onus is on the accused the justice must still consider the two grounds set out in subsec. (10) in determining whether or not to release the accused. The justice does not have a residual discretion to refuse bail: *R. v. Quinn* (1977), 34 C.C.C. (2d) 473 (N.S. Co. Ct.); *Batson (Re)* (1977), 21 N.B.R. (2d) 275 (C.A.).

The reverse onus prescribed by subsec. (2)(*d*) does not violate ss. 7, 9 or 11(*e*) of the Charter. The onus which subsec. (2)(*d*) imposes is reasonable in the sense that it requires the accused to provide information which he is most capable of providing. The special rules combat the pre-trial recidivism and absconding problems which are characteristic of systematic drug trafficking which usually occurs in a highly sophisticated and lucrative commercial setting. While the provision also applies to the small or casual drug dealers, they will normally have no difficulty in justifying their release and obtaining bail: *R. v. Pearson*, [1992] 3 S.C.R. 665, 77 C.C.C. (3d) 124.

Similarly, the scopt of subsec. (6)(*a*) is sufficiently narrow to constitute just cause under s. 11(*e*) and is constitutional: *R. v. Morales*, [1992] 3 S.C.R. 711, 77 C.C.C. (3d) 91.

It was an error in principle for the bail judge to simply "decide the application on its substantive merits" without deciding the question of onus. The grounds for detention cannot be read in isolation from the question of who bears the onus of justifying continued detention: *R. v. Reyat* (2008), 340 C.C.C. (3d) 252 (B.C.C.A., In Chambers).

The determination of whether a person is ordinarily resident in Canada is a question of fact and status as a refugee claimant is but one factor bearing on this determination. Undue weight should not be given to refugee status as compared to landed immigrant or citizenship status. Absent special factors, such as an imminent appeal hearing where the individual has been advised success will be unlikely or the complete lack of any surrounding indicia of stability, a refugee claimant ought not to be automatically saddled with the reverse onus: *R. v. Oladipo* (2004), 191 C.C.C. (3d) 237 (Ont. S.C.J.).

Grounds for detention (subsec. (10)) – The public safety component or para. (*b*), namely where there is a substantial likelihood that the accused if released will interfere with the administration of justice or commit further crimes, constitutes just cause for the denial of bail within the meanings of s. 11(*e*) of the Charter: *R. v. Morales, supra.* In this case the court struck down the "public interest" ground under former subsec. (10)(*b*) as a basis for pre-trial detention because it authorized detention in terms which were vague and imprecise and thus authorizes a denial of bail without just cause. This component is thus unconstitutional and the words "in the public interest or" should be struck down: *R. v. Morales, supra.* This subsection has since been amended to delete "public interest" and add para. (*c*).

The constitutionality of the predecessor to para. (*c*) was considered in *R. v. Hall*, [2002] 3 S.C.R. 309, 167 C.C.C. (3d) 449. The court held that the words "on any other just cause being shown and, without restricting the generality of the foregoing", which have now been removed, violated ss. 7 and 11(*e*) of the Charter and were accordingly inoperative. The remainder of the former provision, however, was not unconstitutional. To allow an accused to be released in the face of a heinous crime and overwhelming evidence may erode the public's confidence in the administration of justice. In considering whether detention is necessary to maintain confidence in the administration of justice, the inquiry must focus on the reasonable community perception of the necessity of denying bail to maintain confidence in the administration of justice, judicially determined through the objective lens having regard to all the circumstances including the strength of the case, the gravity of the nature of the offence, the circumstances surrounding the offence and the potential for a lengthy term of imprisonment.

Even where there is very strong evidence against the accused this is merely one factor to be taken into account by the judge: *R. v. Perron* (1989), 51 C.C.C. (3d) 518 (Que. C.A.).

In *R. v. St-Cloud*, [2015] 2 S.C.R. 328, 321 C.C.C. (3d) 307, the court clarified that para. (*c*) is a distinct ground for detention, not a residual ground that applies only where the first two grounds in paras. (*a*) and (*b*) are not satisfied. It should not be interpreted narrowly or applied sparingly. Its application is not limited to exceptional circumstances, to unexplainable crimes, to the most heinous of crimes or to certain classes of offence. In applying this ground, the justice must first consider the four circumstances that are expressly referred to in para. (*c*), then consider any other relevant circumstances. At the end of this balancing exercise, the ultimate question is whether detention is necessary to maintain confidence in the administration of justice. The court must not order detention automatically even where the four listed circumstances support such a result. Some other circumstances that might be relevant are the personal circumstances of the accused (age, criminal record, physical or mental condition, and membership in a criminal organization), the status of the victim and the impact on society of a crime committed against that person, and the fact that the trial of the accused will be held at a much later date.

Cases dictating that para. (*c*) should be invoked rarely and in a narrow set of circumstances should now be read cautiously in light of *St-Cloud, supra.* See, *e.g.*: *R. v. B. (A.)* (2006), 204 C.C.C. (3d) 490 (Ont. S.C.J.); *R. v. LaFramboise* (2005), 203 C.C.C. (3d) 492 (Ont. C.A. [In Chambers]).

No one factor in para. (*c*) is determinative. The factors should be analyzed together having regard to their combined effect. Where each of the four factors is assessed as having maximum force, a determination that refusal of bail is necessary to maintain public confidence in the administration of justice is expected: *R. v. Mordue* (2006), 223 C.C.C. (3d) 407 (Ont. C.A.).

No communication (subsec. 12) – A no-contact order only remains in effect while the accused is detained under s. 515. Accordingly, after the accused was found guilty and remanded into custody pending sentence, his detention was no longer pursuant to this provision and the original remand order containing the no-contact provision was no longer in effect: *R. v. Brown* (2000), 151 C.C.C. (3d) 85 (N.S.C.A.).

CR. CODE

VARIATION OF UNDERTAKING OR RECOGNIZANCE.

515.1 An undertaking or recognizance pursuant to which the accused was released that has been entered into under section 499, 503 or 515 may, with the written consent of the prosecutor, be varied, and where so varied, is deemed to have been entered into pursuant to section 515. 1997, c. 18, s. 60.

ANNOTATIONS

The surety is released from his obligations if the conditions of release in the recognizance have been altered without the knowledge of the surety: *R. v. Millward* (1998), 128 C.C.C. (3d) 67 (Alta. Q.B.).

This provision allows for the amendment or variation of an existing release order without the necessity of vacating or cancelling the prior release order. Accordingly, the accused does not have to surrender into custody, the sureties do not need to reattend and a new order does not have to be signed. Where the original release was made by a judge, however, the variation must nonetheless be approved by the court. It is necessary that the surety have notice of the application and that evidence, such as an affidavit, be put before the court proving notice and confirming that the surety agrees to be bound by the new recognizance. It is also necessary to establish that the accused has knowledge that the variation has been allowed and that he is bound by the new order. This may be accomplished by requiring the applicant to sign a witnessed acknowledgment that he had read and received a copy of the order and agreed to be bound by its terms on a certified copy of the variation order: *R. v. Ford* (1998), 129 C.C.C. (3d) 189 (Ont. Ct. (Gen. Div.)).

REMAND IN CUSTODY.

516. (1) A justice may, before or at any time during the course of any proceedings under section 515, on application by the prosecutor or the accused, adjourn the proceedings and remand the accused to custody in prison by warrant in Form 19, but no adjournment shall be for more than three clear days except with the consent of the accused.

(2) A justice who remands an accused to custody under subsection (1) or subsection 515(11) may order that the accused abstain from communicating directly or indirectly, with any victim, witness or other person identified in the order, except in accordance with any conditions specified in the order that the justice considers necessary. R.S., c. 2 (2nd Supp.), s. 5; 1999, c. 5, s. 22; c. 25, s. 31(3).

CROSS-REFERENCES

The term "justice" is defined in s. 2. As to calculation of "clear days" see s. 27(1) of the *Interpretation Act*, R.S.C. 1985, c. I-21. For an overview of the application of this Part and the procedure respecting release pending trial see *Note on judicial interim release* under s. 515, or the *Note on judicial interim release* under s. 522 where the accused is charged with an offence listed in s. 469.

SYNOPSIS

This section authorizes a justice at any time, either before or during a hearing under s. 515, to adjourn proceedings and remand the accused to custody in prison. Such a remand will be made in Form 19 and shall not be for a longer period than three clear days, unless the accused person consents. The remand may be made upon application by either the prosecutor or the accused. The justice may order the accused to abstain from communicating with witnesses or other persons named in the order.

ANNOTATIONS

Failure to comply with this section, *i.e.*, by failing to issue a warrant of committal, though it may render unlawful his detention during the period does not affect the court's jurisdiction over the accused or the offence: *R. v. Morrison* (1975), 29 C.C.C. (2d) 323 (B.C.S.C.).

The proceedings must be continued within the three clear days. Thus an adjournment on the 22nd day of the month to the 26th day of the month without the accused's consent does not comply with this section: *R. v. Khabra* (1978), 39 C.C.C. (2d) 475 (B.C.S.C.).

On a court-ordered remand in custody if gaol facilities are available the accused must be held there separate from police investigation holding-cells: *R. v. Precourt* (1976), 39 C.C.C. (2d) 311 (Ont. C.A.).

ORDER DIRECTING MATTERS NOT TO BE PUBLISHED FOR SPECIFIED PERIOD / Failure to comply / Definition of "newspaper".

517. (1) If the prosecutor or the accused intends to show cause under section 515, he or she shall so state to the justice and the justice may, and shall on application by the accused, before or at any time during the course of the proceedings under that section, make an order directing that the evidence taken, the information given or the representations made and the reasons, if any, given or to be given by the justice shall not be published in any document, or broadcast or transmitted in any way before such time as

(*a*) if a preliminary inquiry is held, the accused in respect of whom the proceedings are held is discharged; or

(*b*) if the accused in respect of whom the proceedings are held is tried or ordered to stand trial, the trial is ended.

(2) Every person who fails, without lawful excuse, to comply with an order made under subsection (1) is guilty of an offence punishable on summary conviction. R.S., c. 2 (2nd Supp.), s. 5; 1974-75-76, c. 93, s. 48; R.S.C. 1985, c. 27 (1st Supp.), s. 101(2)(*a*); 2005, c. 32, s. 17; 2018, c. 29, s. 62.

(3) [*Repealed*, 2005, c. 32, s. 17(2).]

CROSS-REFERENCES

The terms "prosecutor" and "justice" are defined in s. 2. For an overview of the application of this Part and the procedure respecting release pending trial see *Note on judicial interim release* under s. 515, or the *Note on judicial interim release* under s. 522 where the accused is charged with an offence listed in s. 469.

Trial of the offence under subsec. (2) is conducted by a summary conviction court pursuant to Part XXVII. The punishment is as set out in s. 787 [except note the maximum fine provided for in s. 719 in the case of a corporation] and the limitation period is set out in s. 786(2).

SYNOPSIS

This section authorizes a justice dealing with a hearing under s. 515 to make an order directing that matters not be published for a specified period.

Subsection (1) provides that the justice shall, upon application by the accused during proceedings under s. 515, make an order that evidence, information, representations and reasons given, not be published, broadcast or transmitted in any way. Such an order may be made to last, if a preliminary hearing is held, until such time, if applicable, as the accused is discharged or, if the accused is committed for trial, until the trial ends. The justice may also make such an order on his or her own initiative.

Subsection (2) makes failure to comply with an order under this section a summary conviction offence. The accused must prove that such a failure to comply was with lawful excuse.

ANNOTATIONS

While this provision violates s. 2(*b*) of the Charter, it is saved under s. 1: *Toronto Star Newspapers Ltd. v. Canada*, [2010] 1 S.C.R. 721, 255 C.C.C. (3d) 473.

A judge has no power to prohibit publication of his decision granting or refusing release. He may only prohibit publication of his reasons for the decision: *R. v. Forget* (1982), 65 C.C.C. (2d) 373 (Ont. C.A.).

A judge has no power under this section to also order a ban on publication of the identity of the accused or on information which journalists have obtained from the police: *Southam Inc. v. Brassard* (1987), 38 C.C.C. (3d) 74 (Que. S.C.), where however it was pointed out that publication of material which would interfere in some manner with the course of justice would amount to contempt of court.

Subsection (1) is to be broadly interpreted to include even non-prejudicial information: *R. v. Daly* (2003), 178 C.C.C. (3d) 31 (B.C.S.C.), affd on other grounds 198 C.C.C. (3d) 185 (B.C.C.A.).

It was no defence that the reporter had obtained legal advice prior to the publication: *R. v. Daly, supra.*

This provision is applicable to proceedings under the *Extradition Act*: *United States of America v. Amhaz* (2001), 159 C.C.C. (3d) 570 (B.C.S.C.).

INQUIRIES TO BE MADE BY JUSTICE AND EVIDENCE / Release pending sentence.

518. (1) In any proceedings under section 515,

(*a*) the justice may, subject to paragraph (*b*), make such inquiries, on oath or otherwise, of and concerning the accused as he considers desirable;

(*b*) the accused shall not be examined by the justice or any other person except counsel for the accused respecting the offence with which the accused is charged, and no inquiry shall be made of the accused respecting that offence by way of cross-examination unless the accused has testified respecting the offence;

(*c*) the prosecutor may, in addition to any other relevant evidence, lead evidence

(i) to prove that the accused has previously been convicted of a criminal offence,

(ii) to prove that the accused has been charged with and is awaiting trial for another criminal offence,

(iii) to prove that the accused has previously committed an offence under section 145, or

(iv) to show the circumstances of the alleged offence, particularly as they relate to the probability of conviction of the accused;

(*d*) the justice may take into consideration any relevant matters agreed on by the prosecutor and the accused or his counsel;

(*d*.1) the justice may receive evidence obtained as a result of an interception of a private communication under and within the meaning of Part VI, in writing, orally or in the form of a recording and, for the purposes of this section, subsection 189(5) does not apply to that evidence;

(*d*.2) the justice shall take into consideration any evidence submitted regarding the need to ensure the safety or security of any victim of or witness to an offence; and

(*e*) the justice may receive and base his decision on evidence considered credible or trustworthy by him in the circumstances of each case.

(2) Where, before or at any time during the course of any proceedings under section 515, the accused pleads guilty and that plea is accepted, the justice may make any order provided for in this Part for the release of the accused until the accused is sentenced. R.S., c. 2 (2nd Supp.), s. 5; 1974-75-76, c. 93, s. 49; R.S.C. 1985, c. 27 (1st Supp.), s. 84; 1994, c. 44, s. 45; 1999, c. 25, s. 9.

CROSS-REFERENCES

The terms "prosecutor", "justice" and "victim" are defined in s. 2. For an overview of the application of this Part and the procedure respecting release pending trial see *Note on judicial interim release* under s. 515, or the *Note on judicial interim release* under s. 522 where the accused is charged with an offence listed in s. 469.

SYNOPSIS

This section describes the kinds of inquiries that may be made and evidence that may be led in proceedings under s. 515.

While the justice is empowered to make such inquiries as he considers desirable, para. (*b*) makes it clear that the accused may not be cross-examined respecting the offence with which he has been charged unless the accused has testified in chief respecting the offence. The prosecutor may lead evidence on issues that are enumerated in para. (*c*) as well as on other relevant matters. The justice may consider any relevant information agreed to by the prosecutor and the accused or counsel for the accused.

Paragraph (*d*.1) states that the justice may receive evidence obtained as a result of an interception of private communications. Section 189(5), which deals with admission into evidence of intercepted communications, does not apply. Paragraph (*d*.2) requires the justice to take into consideration evidence concerning the need to ensure the safety or security of any victim or witness.

Subsection (2) allows a justice to make any order of release found in Part XVI when the accused pleads guilty and is remanded for sentence.

ANNOTATIONS

Examination of accused (subsec. (1)(*b*)) – This subsection does not preclude the Crown from tendering evidence as to the accused's extra-judicial statements and such statements to persons in authority are admissible without a *voir dire* to determine voluntariness: *R. v. Bouffard* (1979), 16 C.R. (3d) 373 (Que. S.C.).

A statement obtained from the accused during the hearing in violation of this paragraph is not admissible in subsequent court proceedings against the accused: *R. v. Deom* (1981), 64 C.C.C. (2d) 222 (B.C.S.C.). This is so even where the violation is initiated by the accused's own counsel in examination of the accused: *R. v. Paonessa and Paquette* (1982), 66 C.C.C. (2d) 300 (Ont. C.A.), affd on other grounds [1983] 1 S.C.R. 660, 3 C.C.C. (3d) 384 (5:0).

Matters agreed upon (subsec. (1)(*d*)) – The bail hearing may proceed on the basis of counsel's submissions including submissions challenging the accuracy and weight of factors asserted by the opposing party: *R. v. Courchene* (1999), 141 C.C.C. (3d) 431 (Man. Q.B.).

Meaning of "credible or trustworthy" (subsec. (1)(*e*)) – Credible and trustworthy evidence includes evidence ordinarily inadmissible at trial as long as the other party has fair opportunity to correct or contradict it: *R. v. Powers* (1972), 9 C.C.C. (2d) 533 (Ont. H.C.J.). Similarly *R. v. Woo* (1994), 90 C.C.C. (3d) 404 (B.C.S.C.).

While this paragraph entitles the justice to act on hearsay evidence considered trustworthy as well as direct evidence considered credible, it is not authority for Crown counsel simply reading a statement of the circumstances of the offence, a procedure which deprives the accused of his right to cross-examine: *R. v. Hajdu* (1984), 14 C.C.C. (3d) 563 (Ont. H.C.J.). Similarly, *R. v. Woo, supra*; *R. v. Courchene, supra*.

However, consider *R. v. Dhindsa* (1986), 30 C.C.C. (3d) 368 (B.C.S.C.), holding that both Crown and defence counsel may make statements as to the anticipated evidence. Where there is a controversy or contradiction, then affidavits may be tendered and relied upon and if affidavits will not suffice to resolve the conflict, then *viva voce* evidence could be called and cross-examination take place.

The attendance of sureties is not always required to effect the release of an accused ordered to be released on a recognizance with sureties. Counsel was permitted to file surety questionnaires completed by prospective sureties unable to attend court on the basis that the questionnaires were credible and trustworthy: *R. v. Brooks* (2001), 153 C.C.C. (3d) 533 (Ont. S.C.J.).

Right to make submissions – A show cause hearing is an adversarial proceeding and both sides including the prosecutor have a right to be heard. The court is not entitled to frustrate this right by predicting the Crown's submissions: *R. v. Villota* (2002), 163 C.C.C. (3d) 507, 3 C.R. (6th) 342 (Ont. S.C.J.).

RELEASE OF ACCUSED / Discharge from custody / Warrant for committal.

519. (1) Where a justice makes an order under subsection 515(1), (2), (7) or (8),

(*a*) if the accused thereupon complies with the order, the justice shall direct that the accused be released

(i) forthwith, if the accused is not required to be detained in custody in respect of any other matter, or

(ii) as soon thereafter as the accused is no longer required to be detained in custody in respect of any other matter; and

(*b*) if the accused does not thereupon comply with the order, the justice who made the order or another justice having jurisdiction shall issue a warrant for the committal of the accused and may endorse thereon an authorization to the person having the custody of the accused to release the accused when the accused complies with the order

(i) forthwith after the compliance, if the accused is not required to be detained in custody in respect of any other matter, or

(ii) as soon thereafter as the accused is no longer required to be detained in custody in respect of any other matter

and if the justice so endorses the warrant, he shall attach to it a copy of the order.

(2) Where the accused complies with an order referred to in paragraph (1)(*b*) and is not required to be detained in custody in respect of any other matter, the justice who made the order or another justice having jurisdiction shall, unless the accused has been or will be released pursuant to an authorization referred to in that paragraph, issue an order for discharge in Form 39.

(3) Where the justice makes an order under subsection 515(5) or (6) for the detention of the accused, he shall issue a warrant for the committal of the accused. R.S., c. 2 (2nd Supp.), s. 5; 1974-75-76, c. 93, s. 50; R.S.C. 1985, c. 27 (1st Supp.), s. 85.

CROSS-REFERENCES

The term "justice" is defined in s. 2. "Warrant of committal" is defined in s. 493. Section 841 provides that forms varied to suit the case and forms to the like effect shall be deemed to be good, valid and sufficient in the circumstances for which, respectively, they are provided. For an overview of the application of this Part and the procedure respecting release pending trial see *Note on judicial interim release* under s. 515, or the *Note on judicial interim release* under s. 522 where the accused is charged with an offence listed in s. 469.

SYNOPSIS

This section deals with the release of the accused after a justice has made an order under s. 515(1), (2), (7) or (8).

Subsection (1) provides that where a justice makes a release order under s. 515, the accused shall be released if he complies with the order. Such release will be immediate if the accused is not required to be held in custody on another matter, or as soon as the accused is not required to be detained on another matter. If the accused does not comply with the order under s. 515, a justice having jurisdiction must issue a warrant for the accused's committal.

In such a case, the justice may endorse on the warrant an authorization to release the accused when he complies with the order. The timing of this release will depend on the matters set out in para. (*b*)(i) and (ii).

Subsection (2) states that when the accused complies with an order referred to in subsec. (1)(*b*) and is not required to be detained in custody on another matter, the accused may also be released by way of an order for discharge in Form 39.

Subsection (3) states that a justice who has ordered the detention of the accused must issue a warrant of committal.

ANNOTATIONS

A judge has no power to make a "release" order permitting an accused serving a penitentiary sentence to be released on condition that he reside at the penitentiary except where entitled to be absent pursuant to passes granted by the Parole Board: *R. v. Arviv* (1987), 38 C.C.C. (3d) 283 (Ont. Dist. Ct.).

It is the duty of the justice or judge to determine the sufficiency of a proposed surety not the Crown Attorney: *R. v. Dewsbury* (1989), 50 C.C.C. (3d) 163 (Ont. H.C.J.).

REVIEW OF ORDER / Notice to prosecutor / Accused to be present / Adjournment of proceedings / Failure of accused to attend / Execution / Evidence and powers of judge on review / Limitation of further applications / Application of ss. 517, 518 and 519.

520. (1) If a justice, or a judge of the Nunavut Court of Justice, makes an order under subsection 515(2), (5), (6), (7), (8) or (12) or makes or vacates any order under paragraph 523(2)(*b*), the accused may, at any time before the trial of the charge, apply to a judge for a review of the order.

(2) An application under this section shall not, unless the prosecutor otherwise consents, be heard by a judge unless the accused has given to the prosecutor at least two clear days notice in writing of the application.

(3) If the judge so orders or the prosecutor or the accused or his counsel so requests, the accused shall be present at the hearing of an application under this section and, where the accused is in custody, the judge may order, in writing, the person having the custody of the accused to bring him before the court.

(4) A judge may, before or at any time during the hearing of an application under this section, on application by the prosecutor or the accused, adjourn the proceedings, but if the accused is in custody no adjournment shall be for more than three clear days except with the consent of the accused.

(5) Where an accused, other than an accused who is in custody, has been ordered by a judge to be present at the hearing of an application under this section and does not attend the hearing, the judge may issue a warrant for the arrest of the accused.

(6) A warrant issued under subsection (5) may be executed anywhere in Canada.

(7) On the hearing of an application under this section, the judge may consider

(*a*) the transcript, if any, of the proceedings heard by the justice and by any judge who previously reviewed the order made by the justice,

(*b*) the exhibits, if any, filed in the proceedings before the justice, and

(*c*) such additional evidence or exhibits as may be tendered by the accused or the prosecutor,

and shall either

(*d*) dismiss the application, or

(*e*) if the accused shows cause, allow the application, vacate the order previously made by the justice and make any other order provided for in section 515 that he considers is warranted.

(8) Where an application under this section or section 521 has been heard, a further or other application under this section or section 521 shall not be made with respect to that same accused, except with leave of a judge, prior to the expiration of thirty days from the date of the decision of the judge who heard the previous application.

(9) The provisions of section 517, 518 and 519 apply with such modifications as the circumstances require in respect of an application under this section. R.S., c. 2 (2nd Supp.), s. 5; 1974-75-76, c. 93, s. 51; R.S.C. 1985, c. 27 (1st Supp.), s. 86; 1994, c. 44, s. 46; 1999, c. 3, s. 31.

CROSS-REFERENCES

The terms "prosecutor" and "justice" are defined in s. 2 and "judge" in s. 493. As to calculation of "at least two clear days" see s. 27 of the *Interpretation Act*, R.S.C. 1985, c. I-21. For an overview of the application of this Part and the procedure respecting release pending trial see *Note on judicial interim release* under s. 515, or the *Note on judicial interim release* under s. 522 where the accused is charged with an offence listed in s. 469. As to the Nunavut Courtof Justice, see the note under s. 536.1.

SYNOPSIS

This section sets out the procedure by which an accused may obtain a review of the order made by a justice under s. 515(2), (5), (6), (7), (8) or (12). The decision of a justice to vacate an order under s. 523(2)(*b*) may also be reviewed by the accused under this section.

Subsection (1) allows the accused to apply to a judge for a review of the order at any time prior to trial.

Unless the prosecutor consents, subsec. (2) requires that a review under this section be heard only if the accused has given to the prosecutor two clear days' notice.

If the prosecutor, the accused or his counsel requests, or the judge so orders, the accused shall be present at the hearing of an application under this section.

Subsection (3) provides that where the accused is in custody, the judge may order in writing the person having custody of the accused to bring him to court.

Subsection (4) authorizes a judge to adjourn the hearing of the application at the request of the prosecutor or the accused. Such application may be brought prior to or during the hearing. If the accused is in custody, no adjournment for more than three clear days will be granted unless the accused consents.

If an accused who is not in custody is ordered by a judge to be present at the hearing and does not attend, the judge is authorized by subsec. (5) to issue an arrest warrant. This warrant may be executed anywhere in Canada.

Subsection (7) lists in paras. (*a*), (*b*) and (*c*) the items that the judge hearing the application may consider. Subsection (7)(*d*) and (*e*) empower the judge to either dismiss the application or, if the accused shows cause, allow the application, vacate the earlier order and make any other order under s. 515 that is appropriate.

Subsection (8) makes it clear that the accused may make further applications under this section or s. 521 only after 30 days have expired since the previous application, unless the judge gives leave.

Subsection (9) states that the provisions of ss. 517, 518 and 519 will apply with necessary modifications in an application under this section.

ANNOTATIONS

Jurisdiction – While subsec. (1) only refers to review of an order by a "justice", the wording of this subsection indicates that the accused may apply for review of an order of a judge made either under this section or s. 521: *R. v. Gouveia* (1982), 1 C.C.C. (3d) 143 (Ont. H.C.J.); *R. v. Saracino* (1989), 47 C.C.C. (3d) 185 (Ont. H.C.J.). *Contra: R. v. Lahooti* (1978), 38 C.C.C. (2d) 481 (Ont. H.C.J.).

While a judge of the Manitoba Court of Appeal has jurisdiction to review a refusal to make an order for judicial interim release, in the absence of special circumstances the further application for review should be made to a judge of the Court of Queen's Bench: *R. v. Petrie*, [1985] 2 W.W.R. 128, 30 Man. R. (2d) 145 (C.A. in chambers); *R. v. Semenick*, [1985] 2 W.W.R. 132, 30 Man. R. (2d) 147 (C.A. in chambers). See also: *R. v. Durrani* (2008), 242 C.C.C. (3d) 103 (Ont. C.A.); *R. v. Parsons* (2010), 259 C.C.C. (3d) 347 (Nfld. & Lab. C.A.).

Where a superior court judge allows an application for review and vacates the bail order, the parties have no further right to apply to a superior court judge for a further review: *R. v. Smith* (2003), 171 C.C.C. (3d) 383 (Sask. C.A.).

Nature of review – In *R. v. St-Cloud*, [2015] 2 S.C.R. 328, 321 C.C.C. (3d) 307, the court comprehensively explained the review process set out in ss. 520 and 521. It held that these provisions do not confer an open-ended discretion on the reviewing judge to vary the initial decision concerning the detention or release of the accused. They establish not a *de novo* proceeding, but a hybrid remedy. The judge must determine whether it is appropriate to exercise his or her power of review. Exercising this power will be appropriate in only three situations: (1) where there is admissible new evidence if that evidence shows a material and relevant change in the circumstances of the case; (2) where the impugned decision contains an error of law; or (3) where the decision is clearly inappropriate. A decision may be clearly inappropriate if the justice gave excessive weight to one relevant factor or insufficient weight to another. However, the reviewing judge does not have the power to interfere with the initial decision simply because he or she would have weighed the relevant factors differently.

Procedure on review – Upon review the onus is upon the applicant to demonstrate an error in law or principle by the justice of the peace who made the order under review: *R. v. Horvat* (1972), 9 C.C.C. (2d) 1 (B.C.S.C.).

The order of a justice of the peace vacated in para. (*e*) is not rendered *void ab initio* so as to negative any charge laid for breaching it, but instead is terminated in favour of the substituted order: *R. v. Goldrick* (1974), 17 C.C.C. (2d) 74 (Ont. H.C.J.).

While the judge may hear additional evidence, the transcript of the proceedings before the justice should be filed with the court, otherwise it would be impossible to determine whether or not the justice was in error: *R. v. Hunter* (1973), 24 C.R.N.S. 197 (Ont. Co. Ct.).

However, a transcript is not always required, particularly where no *viva voce* evidence was heard before the justice, merely counsel's submissions, and to require the transcript might defeat the intent of this legislation which was to encourage expeditious disposition of bail matters: *R. v. Carrier, supra*.

It has been held, considering the predecessor to para. (*e*), that even where the accused demonstrates some error by the justice in the making of the initial detention order or the conduct of the hearing, the judge is not required to vacate the detention order and make a release order unless the accused shows why the detention order was not justified on the primary or secondary ground. On the review the Crown may rely on the evidence at the original hearing and may adduce additional evidence to justify the accused's continued detention: *R. v. English* (1983), 8 C.C.C. (3d) 487 (Ont. Co. Ct.); *R. v. Saswirsky* (1984), 17 C.C.C. (3d) 341 (Ont. H.C.J.).

Right to counsel – An unrepresented accused charged with an indictable offence may have the right to counsel at a bail hearing or bail review. The presiding judge has a duty to inquire whether the accused wishes to be represented by counsel. The determination must be made on a case-by-case basis having regard to the complexity of the proceedings and the seriousness of the charge: *R. v. Chan* (2000), 146 C.C.C. (3d) 494 (Alta. C.A.).

Subsection (7) [new evidence] – The four criteria from *R. v. Palmer* (1979), [1980] 1 S.C.R. 759, 50 C.C.C. (2d) 193, for the admission of fresh evidence on appeal are relevant to the determination of what constitutes admissible new evidence for the purposes of the review provided for in ss. 520 and 521. Given the generally expeditious nature of the interim release process and the risks of violating the rights of the accused, and since the release hearing takes place at the very start of criminal proceedings, a reviewing judge must be flexible in applying these four criteria: *R. v. St-Cloud*, [2015] 2 S.C.R. 328, 321 C.C.C. (3d) 307.

Subsection (8) – Leave should not be granted unless the decision of the reviewing judge was clearly wrong in law or there have been intervening events which require granting of leave in the interests of justice: *R. v. McCue*, *infra*. See also *R. v. MacIver* (1998), 157 W.A.C. 84, 131 Man. R. (2d) 84 (C.A.).

REVIEW OF ORDER / Notice to accused / Accused to be present / Adjournment of proceedings / Failure of accused to attend / Warrant for detention / Execution / Evidence and powers of judge on review / Limitation of further applications / Application of ss. 517, 518 and 519.

521. (1) If a justice, or a judge of the Nunavut Court of Justice, makes an order under subsection 515(1), (2), (7), (8) or (12) or makes or vacates any order under paragraph 523(2)(*b*), the prosecutor may, at any time before the trial of the charge, apply to a judge for a review of the order.

(2) An application under this section shall not be heard by a judge unless the prosecutor has given to the accused at least two clear days notice in writing of the application.

(3) If the judge so orders or the prosecutor or the accused or his counsel so requests, the accused shall be present at the hearing of an application under this section and, where the accused is in custody, the judge may order, in writing, the person having the custody of the accused to bring him before the court.

(4) A judge may, before or at any time during the hearing of an application under this section, on application of the prosecutor or the accused, adjourn the proceedings, but if the accused is in custody no adjournment shall be for more than three clear days except with the consent of the accused.

(5) Where an accused, other than an accused who is in custody, has been ordered by a judge to be present at the hearing of an application under this section and does not attend the hearing, the judge may issue a warrant for the arrest of the accused.

(6) Where, pursuant to paragraph (8)(*e*), the judge makes an order that the accused be detained in custody until he is dealt with according to law, he shall, if the accused is not in custody, issue a warrant for the committal of the accused.

(7) A warrant issued under subsection (5) or (6) may be executed anywhere in Canada.

(8) On the hearing of an application under this section, the judge may consider

- **(*a*) the transcript, if any, of the proceedings heard by the justice and by any judge who previously reviewed the order made by the justice,**
- **(*b*) the exhibits, if any, filed in the proceedings before the justice, and**
- **(*c*) such additional evidence or exhibits as may be tendered by the prosecutor or the accused,**

and shall either

- **(*d*) dismiss the application, or**
- **(*e*) if the prosecutor shows cause, allow the application, vacate the order previously made by the justice and make any other order provided for in section 515 that he considers to be warranted.**

(9) Where an application under this section or section 520 has been heard, a further or other application under this section or section 520 shall not be made with respect to the same accused, except with leave of a judge, prior to the expiration of thirty days from the date of the decision of the judge who heard the previous application.

(10) The provisions of sections 517, 518 and 519 apply with such modifications as the circumstances require in respect of an application under this section. R.S., c. 2 (2nd

Supp.), s. 5; 1974-75-76, c. 93, s. 52; R.S.C. 1985, c. 27 (1st Supp.), s. 87; 1994, c. 44, s. 47; 1999, c. 3, s. 32.

CROSS-REFERENCES

The terms "prosecutor" and "justice" are defined in s. 2 and "judge" in s. 493. As to calculation of "at least two clear days" see s. 27 of the *Interpretation Act*, R.S.C. 1985, c. I-21. For an overview of the application of this Part and the procedure respecting release pending trial see *Note on judicial interim release* under s. 515, or the *Note on judicial interim release* under s. 522 where the accused is charged with an offence listed in s. 469.

SYNOPSIS

This section is the companion to s. 520. It describes the procedure that the prosecutor must follow to review an order made by a justice under s. 515(1), (2), (7), (8) or (12) or vacated by a justice under s. 523(2)(*b*).

Subsection (2) requires that the prosecutor give the accused at least two clear days' notice in writing of the application.

Subsection (3) provides for the presence of the accused if the judge so orders or the prosecutor or the accused so requests. Where the accused is in custody, the judge may order in writing the person having custody of the accused to bring him to court.

Subsection (4) authorizes the judge to adjourn the proceedings at any time prior to or during the hearing upon application by the prosecutor or the accused. If the accused is in custody, no adjournment shall be longer than three days unless the accused consents.

Subsection (5) states that when an accused who is not in custody and who has been ordered by the judge to be present at the hearing of an application under this section, fails to attend, the judge may issue an arrest warrant.

If the judge makes an order under this section that the accused be detained in custody, he must issue a warrant of committal if the accused is not in custody. A warrant issued under this subsection or subsec. (5) may be executed anywhere in Canada.

Subsection (8) sets out items that a judge may consider in a hearing under this section. It also describes the dispositions available to the judge at the conclusion of the hearing.

Subsection (9), like s. 520(8), requires a waiting period of 30 days between applications under this section or s. 520, unless a judge gives leave.

Subsection (10) makes the provision of ss. 517, 518 and 519 applicable to a proceeding under this section with such modifications as circumstances require.

ANNOTATIONS

Note: see also the notes under s. 520, in particular concerning the Supreme Court's explanation of the bail review regime in *R. v. St-Cloud*, [2015] 2 S.C.R. 328, 321 C.C.C. (3d) 307.

In the absence of evidence of excess of jurisdiction or error in principle, a judge on review, even though he would not have come to the same decision as did the justice, should not alter it unless the prosecutor can show cause by additional evidence or by pointing to a demonstrable error: *R. v. La Chapelle and La Chapelle* (1974), 19 C.C.C. (2d) 70 (N.S.S.C.).

An application may be made under this section although the order sought to be reviewed is that of a judge under s. 520 rather than an order of a justice. However, except where there has been a substantial change in circumstances, the judge conducting the second review should not interfere with the existing order unless it is established that the judge conducting the first review made an error in principle in application of the relevant provisions which materially affected the outcome of the initial application: *R. v. Saracino* (1989), 47 C.C.C. (3d) 185 (Ont. H.C.J.).

The refusal to hear submissions by the Crown is a breach of natural justice and constitutes jurisdictional error: *R. v. Villota* (2002), 163 C.C.C. (3d) 507 (Ont. S.C.J.).

Where a superior court judge allows an application for review and vacates the bail order, the parties have no further right to apply to a superior court judge for a further review: *R. v. Smith* (2003), 171 C.C.C. (3d) 383 (Sask. C.A.).

INTERIM RELEASE BY JUDGE ONLY / Idem / Order re no communication / Release of accused / Order not reviewable except under s. 680 / Application of sections 517, 518 and 519 / Other offences.

522. (1) Where an accused is charged with an offence listed in section 469, no court, judge or justice, other than a judge of or a judge presiding in a superior court of criminal jurisdiction for the province in which the accused is so charged, may release the accused before or after the accused has been ordered to stand trial.

(2) Where an accused is charged with an offence listed in section 469, a judge of or a judge presiding in a superior court of criminal jurisdiction for the province in which the accused is charged shall order that the accused be detained in custody unless the accused, having been given a reasonable opportunity to do so, shows cause why his detention in custody is not justified within the meaning of subsection 515(10).

(2.1) A judge referred to in subsection (2) who orders that an accused be detained in custody under this section may include in the order a direction that the accused abstain from communicating, directly or indirectly, with any victim, witness or other person identified in the order except in accordance with such conditions specified in the order as the judge considers necessary.

(3) If the judge does not order that the accused be detained in custody under subsection (2), the judge may order that the accused be released on giving an undertaking or entering into a recognizance described in any of paragraphs 515(2)(*a*) to (*e*) with such conditions described in subsections 515(4), (4.1) and (4.2) as the judge considers desirable.

(4) An order made under this section is not subject to review, except as provided in section 680.

(5) The provisions of sections 517, 518 except subsection (2) thereof, and 519 apply with such modifications as the circumstances require in respect of an application for an order under subsection (2).

(6) Where an accused is charged with an offence mentioned in section 469 and with any other offence, a judge acting under this section may apply the provisions of this Part respecting judicial interim release to that other offence. R.S., c. 2 (2nd Supp.), s. 5; 1972, c. 13, s. 36; 1974-75-76, c. 93, s. 53; R.S.C. 1985, c. 27 (1st Supp.), s. 88; 1991, c. 40, s. 32; 1994, c. 44, s. 48; 1999, c. 25, s. 10.

CROSS-REFERENCES

The terms "superior court of criminal jurisdiction" and "victim" are defined in s. 2. The terms "accused", "recognizance" and "undertaking" are defined in s. 493.

Note on judicial interim release – Where the accused is charged with an offence listed in s. 469 such as murder then he may not be released by a peace officer, officer in charge or justice. Section 503 requires that he be taken before a justice (defined in s. 2) without unreasonable delay and, in any event, within 24 hours, where a justice is available. The justice will then make a detention order (s. 515(11)). The onus is then on the accused to apply for a show cause hearing by making an application under s. 522 to a judge of the superior court of criminal jurisdiction (defined in s. 2). The procedure on the s. 522 hearing is similar to the show cause hearing under s. 515 except that the onus is on the accused in all cases to show why his detention is not justified for the reasons set out in s. 515(10). Where the accused shows cause then the judge may order the accused's release on an undertaking or recognizance on the same terms as may a justice acting under s. 515(2), (4) and (4.1) and thus see the discussion under s. 515.

Sections 517 and 518 set out the procedure to be followed on the bail hearing. Section 517 provides for a non-publication order. Section 518 sets out the kind of evidence which may be tendered on the hearing. The effect of s. 518 is to give a relatively wide latitude to the judge permitting him to receive and base his decision on evidence "considered credible or trustworthy". Thus the rules of evidence which would apply at a trial would not apply on the bail hearing. One limit on the receipt of evidence is the proviso in s. 518(1)(*b*) which prohibits questioning of the accused respecting the offence with which he is charged. The scope of this subsection is uncertain, there being some case law noted under s. 518 holding that while the accused cannot be asked by the judge or the prosecutor about the offence he is entitled to volunteer his testimony concerning it. The presence of the accused would not appear to be mandatory. Where a release order is made then s. 519 sets out the procedure for putting the order into effect and the circumstances in which the accused will be released.

The system for review of either a release or detention order is more restricted than is the case of an accused charged with a non-s. 469 offence. There is no *right* to a review. The only formal review mechanism is set out in s. 680 and requires an application to the Chief Justice or acting Chief Justice of the Court of Appeal for directions referring the case to the Court of Appeal (defined in ss. 2 and 673). Where the Chief Justice gives such directions then the Court of Appeal will hear the review application and may confirm the decision, vary the decision or substitute such other decision as, in its opinion, should have been made. Under s. 680(2) with the consent of the parties the review directed by the Chief Justice may be heard by a single judge rather than by three judges of the Court of Appeal.

Section 523(2) also provides for a more informal review process at various stages of the proceedings but only by a judge of the superior court of criminal jurisdiction. Note, however, that the release or detention order can only be vacated under this subsection upon cause being shown and in some circumstances the review can only be undertaken where both the accused and the prosecutor consent. Section 524 enacts a procedure for dealing with cases where it is alleged that the accused has violated or is about to violate the release order or has committed an indictable offence while on a form of release. That section gives a power to arrest with (subsec. (1)) or without warrant (subsec. (2)). Upon arrest under this section the accused will be taken before a justice who is required to remand the accused to appear before a judge of the superior court of criminal jurisdiction. Where it is shown that his arrest was justified (subsec. (4)) then the release order is cancelled by the judge. The accused is then ordered detained unless he can show cause why he should not be detained in custody. If the accused shows cause then s. 524(5) provides for the types of release order which may be made. Any order made under s. 524 may only be reviewed pursuant to s. 680. The procedure on the s. 524 hearing is similar to the original show cause hearing (subsec. (12)). There is some uncertainty as to the scope of s. 524 where the accused is arrested for an indictable offence while on a s. 522 release order. It would seem that the procedure to be followed is that unless the prosecutor elects to proceed under s. 524 the justice will have jurisdiction to proceed with a bail hearing in relation to the new non-s. 469 charge under s. 515. See *R. v. Yarema* (1989), 52 C.C.C. (3d) 242 (Ont. H.C.J.), noted under s. 524.

The automatic review procedure set out in s. 525 does not apply to an accused charged with a s. 469 offence. Section 526 however provides that the judge conducting a hearing under this Part may give directions for expediting the trial.

Barring a review under ss. 680, 523(2) or 524 then the effect of s. 523(1) is that the release order remains in effect until the trial is completed. Section 523(1.1) provides a procedure for the release order in respect of one information to apply to a new information charging the same offence or an included offence.

Under s. 522(6) where the accused is also charged with an offence not listed in s. 469 the judge to whom an application is made under s. 522 may also make an order for release or detention in respect of this other offence. Invoking subsec. (6) will avoid the necessity of multiple hearings in the case of an accused charged with an offence listed in s. 469 and some other offence.

The procedure for enforcement of a recognizance is set out in Part XXV. That Part sets out the responsibilities of sureties (s. 764); procedure for rendering of the accused by his sureties (ss. 766, 767, 769); substitution of a new surety (s. 767.1), and the new release hearing where the accused is rendered into custody by his sureties (s. 769). That Part also sets out the procedure in case of default by the accused, including endorsing the fact of the default (s. 770); the hearing for estreat of bail (s. 771), and levying execution to enforce a writ of *fieri facias* where the recognizance is ordered forfeited (ss. 772, 773).

There are special limitations on the making of interim release and detention orders where the court makes an assessment order under Part XX.1. See in particular ss. 672.16, 672.17 and 672.18.

ANNOTATIONS

Prior to the recent amendments to this section there was some uncertainty as to whether a detention or release order made under this section in relation to a murder charge lapsed when the accused was committed for trial on a charge of manslaughter (an offence not specified in s. 469). The following cases hold that in such circumstances there should be a new bail hearing before a justice or provincial court judge: *R. v. LaFontaine* (1973), 13 C.C.C. (2d) 316 (Ont. H.C.J.); *R. v. Manuel* (1981), 60 C.C.C. (2d) 97 (Ont. H.C.J.); *R. v. Favel* (1985), 19 C.C.C. (3d) 335 (Sask. Q.B.). To the contrary is *R. v. Degerness* (1980), 57 C.C.C. (2d) 534 (B.C.S.C.).

The Superior Court has the jurisdiction, notwithstanding s. 680 of the *Criminal Code*, to entertain successive applications for bail in respect of a murder charge where the correctness of the earlier decision is conceded, but it is alleged that there has been a material change in circumstances. The matter requires a *de novo* consideration of the request for release: *R. v. Saleh* (2007), 252 C.C.C. (3d) 521 (Ont. S.C.J.).

A detention order made on a charge of first degree murder does not lapse when the accused is committed for trial on a charge of second degree murder and is reviewable only pursuant to s. 680: *R. v. Archer* (1981), 59 C.C.C. (2d) 384 (Ont. C.A.). *Contra, R. v. Turner* (1999), 133 C.C.C. (3d) 180 (Nfld. C.A.), holding that the proper procedure is to reapply under this section in view of the change in circumstances.

The reverse onus in subsec. (2) does not offend the guarantee to reasonable bail pursuant to s. 11(*e*) of the Charter. The provision is only applicable in a narrow set of circumstances in that bail is denied only to those who cannot show cause why their detention is not justified: *R. v. Sanchez* (1999), 136 C.C.C. (3d) 31 (N.S.C.A.). See also *R. v. Bray* (1983), 2 C.C.C. (3d) 325 (Ont. C.A.), and *R. v. Dubois (No. 2)* (1983), 8 C.C.C. (3d) 344 (Que. S.C.), which upheld the constitutionality of the predecessor to this section.

The reverse onus requires the accused to establish that on a balance of probabilities his detention is not justified on either the primary or secondary ground. However, there is no burden on the accused to disprove the offence or his implication in it; the onus is on the Crown to adduce evidence of the accused's implication in the offence: *R. v. Bray, supra.*

Where the "substantial likelihood" of committing an offence or interfering with the administration of justice involves an assessment of the likelihood of dangerousness, the court must consider the following:

(1) the nature of the offence;

(2) the relevant circumstances of the offence which may put into issue events prior to and subsequent to the offence;

(3) the likelihood of conviction, the degree of participation of the accused;

(4) the relationship between the accused and the victim;

(5) the profile of the accused which includes occupation, lifestyle, criminal record, family situation and mental state;

(6) his conduct prior to the commission of the alleged offence, and

(7) the danger which the interim release of the accused represents for the community specifically affected by the matter: *R. v. Rondeau* (1996), 108 C.C.C. (3d) 474, [1996] R.J.Q. 1155 (C.A.).

The overwhelming nature of the evidence of guilt and the probability of conviction are merely factors to be considered and are the determining factors in deciding whether the accused should be released pending trial. The accused is entitled to the benefit of the presumption of innocence and the judge should not decide the result of the trial: *R. v. Braun* (1994), 91 C.C.C. (3d) 237 (Sask. C.A.).

Subsection (4) of this section must be read with s. 523(2) which gives a judge of the trial court power to vacate any order previously made upon cause being shown. While resort must be had to the procedure under s. 680 where the allegation is that the original judge made an error, where it is submitted that there has been a change in circumstances the parties should resort to s. 523(2). Where the Crown's consent is required for the review powers to be exercised by a superior court judge, it would be expected that in cases of new circumstances the Crown would not unreasonably withhold its consent: *R. v. Patterson* (1985), 19 C.C.C. (3d) 149 (Alta. C.A.).

A superior court judge has the jurisdiction to vary an order made by the Court of Appeal, where the variation was based on a change in circumstances and the correctness of the original order was not in issue: *R. v. Klymchuk* (2007), 220 C.C.C. (3d) 439 (Ont. S.C.J.).

PERIOD FOR WHICH APPEARANCE NOTICE, ETC., CONTINUES IN FORCE / Where new information charging same offence / When direct indictment is preferred charging same offence / Order vacating previous order for release or detention / Provisions applicable to proceedings under subsection (2).

523. (1) **Where an accused, in respect of an offence with which he is charged, has not been taken into custody or has been released from custody under or by virtue of any provision of this Part, the appearance notice, promise to appear, summons, undertaking or recognizance issued to, given or entered into by the accused continues in force, subject to its terms, and applies in respect of any new information charging the same offence or an included offence that was received after the appearance notice, promise to appear, summons, undertaking or recognizance was issued, given or entered into,**

(*a*) where the accused was released from custody pursuant to an order of a judge made under subsection 522(3), until his trial is completed; or

(*b*) in any other case,

(i) until his trial is completed, and

(ii) where the accused is, at his trial, determined to be guilty of the offence, until a sentence within the meaning of section 673 is imposed on the accused unless, at the time the accused is determined to be guilty, the court, judge or justice orders that the accused be taken into custody pending such sentence.

(1.1) Where an accused, in respect of an offence with which he is charged, has not been taken into custody or is being detained or has been released from custody under or by virtue of any provision of this Part and after the order for interim release or detention has been made, or the appearance notice, promise to appear, summons, undertaking or recognizance has been issued, given or entered into, a new information, charging the same offence or an included offence, is received, section 507 or 508, as the case may be, does not apply in respect of the new information and the order for interim release or detention of the accused and the appearance notice, promise to appear, summons, undertaking or recognizance, if any, applies in respect of the new information.

(1.2) When an accused, in respect of an offence with which the accused is charged, has not been taken into custody or is being detained or has been released from custody under or by virtue of any provision of this Part and after the order for interim release or detention has been made, or the appearance notice, promise to appear, summons, undertaking or recognizance has been issued, given or entered into, and an indictment is preferred under section 577 charging the same offence or an included offence, the order for interim release or detention of the accused and the appearance notice, promise to appear, summons, undertaking or recognizance, if any, applies in respect of the indictment.

(2) Despite subsections (1) to (1.2),

(*a*) the court, judge or justice before whom an accused is being tried, at any time,
(*b*) the justice, on completion of the preliminary inquiry in relation to an offence for which an accused is ordered to stand trial, other than an offence listed in section 469, or
(*c*) with the consent of the prosecutor and the accused or, where the accused or the prosecutor applies to vacate an order that would otherwise apply pursuant to subsection (1.1), without such consent, at any time
(i) where the accused is charged with an offence other than an offence listed in section 469, the justice by whom an order was made under this Part or any other justice,
(ii) where the accused is charged with an offence listed in section 469, a judge of or a judge presiding in a superior court of criminal jurisdiction for the province, or
(iii) the court, judge or justice before which or whom an accused is to be tried,

may, on cause being shown, vacate any order previously made under this Part for the interim release or detention of the accused and make any other order provided for in this Part for the detention or release of the accused until his trial is completed that the court, judge or justice considers to be warranted.

(3) The provisions of sections 517, 518 and 519 apply, with such modifications as the circumstances require, in respect of any proceedings under subsection (2), except that subsection 518(2) does not apply in respect of an accused who is charged with an offence listed in section 469. R.S., c. 2 (2nd Supp.), s. 5; 1974-75-76, c. 93, s. 54; R.S.C. 1985, c. 27 (1st Supp.), s. 89; 2011, c. 16, s. 2.

CROSS-REFERENCES

The term "justice" is defined in s. 2 and "accused", "appearance notice", "promise to appear", "undertaking", "recognizance" and "summons" in s. 493. An order under subsec. (2)(*b*) is reviewable pursuant to s. 520 or s. 521 by the accused or the prosecutor as the case may be. For an overview of the application of this Part and the procedure respecting release pending trial see *Note on judicial interim release* under s. 515, or the *Note on judicial interim release* under s. 522 where the accused is charged with an offence listed in s. 469.

SYNOPSIS

This section describes the periods of time for which various specified forms of release continue to be in force.

Subsection (1) provides that an appearance notice, promise to appear, summons, undertaking or recognizance remains in force until the completion of the accused's trial and, unless the judge orders the accused to be detained prior to the imposition of sentence, until the sentencing has been completed. For an accused charged with an offence listed under s. 469, the form of release remains valid until the completion of the trial. Subsection (1.1) provides that, when an accused is at liberty on a form of release and a new information charging the same or an included offence is received, the original form of release continues to apply. Under subsec. (1.2), a similar procedure applies where a direct indictment is preferred under s. 577.

Subsection (2) applies notwithstanding subsecs. (1) to (1.2), and authorizes any order previously made under Part XVI to be vacated and replaced with any other order provided for by this Part.

Subsection (3) states that ss. 517, 518 and 519 apply with such modifications as are necessary in respect of any proceedings under subsec. (2).

ANNOTATIONS

Subsection (1.1) – The Crown cannot proceed on a revised information in reliance upon process issued under s. 507 by a justice of the peace on a prior information. A provincial court judge has jurisdiction over the accused by virtue of the accused's appearance before him. It is not necessary for process to issue with respect to the relaid information in order for the provincial court judge to have jurisdiction over the offences: *R. v. McCarthy* (1998), 131 C.C.C. (3d) 102 (B.C.S.C.).

Subsection (2) – The mere fact that the accused has been ordered to stand trial is not sufficient cause to warrant the revocation of the accused's release order under para. (*a*) and the making of a detention order: *R. v. Braithwaite* (1980), 57 C.C.C. (2d) 351 (N.S.S.C. App. Div.).

Unless the accused was being tried by a superior court judge, there was no jurisdiction to vary a release order in the absence of the consent of the Crown, where the accused had been released on conditions by a superior court judge acting under s. 522. The appropriate venue to vary bail conditions in the absence of Crown consent was the Court of Appeal pursuant to s. 680: *R. v. Hardiman* (2003), 172 C.C.C. (3d) 211, 211 N.S.R. (2d) 358 (C.A.).

Subsection (2)(*a*) may only be invoked once the trial has actually commenced. This provision, therefore, did not authorize the judge seized of the trial to conduct a bail review one month prior to the scheduled trial date: *R. v. McCreery* (1996), 110 C.C.C. (3d) 561 (B.C.S.C.).

The superior court lacks jurisdiction to review a detention order made by the provincial court under subsec. (2)(*a*), either by way of inherent jurisdiction or *habeas corpus*: *R. v. Passera* (2017), 352 C.C.C. (3d) 478 (Ont. C.A.).

The justice may exercise his jurisdiction under para. (*b*) even where the release order was made by a judge on a review: *R. v. Wedow* (1981), 62 C.C.C. (2d) 381 (Alta. Q.B.).

A judge has the jurisdiction to issue an arrest warrant where the accused, previously appearing by counsel, did not subsequently attend court in person on a plea date. There is no requirement that the judge specifically order the accused to appear in person. Warrants should not be issued on arbitrary or capricious grounds or for any indirect motive not directed to compelling the accused's attendance where his presence is necessary: *R. v. Sidorov* (2001), 160 C.C.C. (3d) 122, 281 A.R. 357 (C.A.), leave to appeal to S.C.C. refused *loc. cit.* C.C.C. at p. vi.

A provincial court judge before whom an application is made to have an accused found to be a dangerous offender has jurisdiction under subsec. (2)(*a*) to release the accused pending the hearing: *R. v. Davidson* (1999), 140 C.C.C. (3d) 166 (B.C.S.C.).

No appeal lies to the Court of Appeal from an order made by a superior court of criminal jurisdiction pursuant to this section. Such an order can be reviewed only by the Supreme Court of Canada under s. 40(1) of the *Supreme Court Act*, R.S.C. 1985, c. S-26: *R. v. Bukmeier* (1996), 107 C.C.C. (3d) 272, 123 W.A.C. 312 (B.C.C.A.).

Arrest of Accused on Interim Release

ISSUE OF WARRANT FOR ARREST OF ACCUSED / Arrest of accused without warrant / Hearing / Retention of accused / Release of accused / Order not reviewable / Release of accused / Powers of justice after hearing / Release of accused / Reasons / Where justice to order that accused be released / Provisions applicable to proceedings under this section / Certain provisions applicable to order under this section.

524. (1) Where a justice is satisfied that there are reasonable and probable grounds to believe that an accused

- **(*a*) has contravened or is about to contravene any summons, appearance notice, promise to appear, undertaking or recognizance that was issued or given to him or entered into by him, or**
- **(*b*) has committed an indictable offence after any summons, appearance notice, promise to appear, undertaking or recognizance was issued or given to him or entered into by him,**

he may issue a warrant for the arrest of the accused.

(2) Notwithstanding anything in this Act, a peace officer who believes on reasonable grounds that an accused

(*a*) has contravened or is about to contravene any summons, appearance notice, promise to appear, undertaking or recognizance that was issued or given to him or entered into by him, or

(*b*) has committed an indictable offence after any summons, appearance notice, promise to appear, undertaking or recognizance was issued or given to him or entered into by him,

may arrest the accused without warrant.

(3) Where an accused who has been arrested with a warrant issued under subsection (1), or who has been arrested under subsection (2), is taken before a justice, the justice shall

(*a*) where the accused was released from custody pursuant to an order made under subsection 522(3) by a judge of the superior court of criminal jurisdiction of any province, order that the accused be taken before a judge of that court; or

(*b*) in any other case, hear the prosecutor and his witnesses, if any, and the accused and his witnesses, if any.

(4) Where an accused described in paragraph (3)(*a*) is taken before a judge and the judge finds

(*a*) that the accused has contravened or had been about to contravene his summons, appearance notice, promise to appear, undertaking or recognizance, or

(*b*) that there are reasonable grounds to believe that the accused has committed an indictable offence after any summons, appearance notice, promise to appear, undertaking or recognizance was issued or given to him or entered into by him,

he shall cancel the summons, appearance notice, promise to appear, undertaking or recognizance and order that the accused be detained in custody unless the accused, having been given a reasonable opportunity to do so, shows cause why his detention in custody is not justified within the meaning of subsection 515(10).

(5) Where the judge does not order that the accused be detained in custody pursuant to subsection (4), he may order that the accused be released on his giving an undertaking or entering into a recognizance described in any of paragraphs 515(2)(*a*) to (*e*) with such conditions described in subsection 515(4) or, where the accused was at large on an undertaking or a recognizance with conditions, such additional conditions, described in subsection 515(4), as the judge considers desirable.

(6) Any order made under subsection (4) or (5) is not subject to review, except as provided in section 680.

(7) Where the judge does not make a finding under paragraph (4)(*a*) or (*b*), he shall order that the accused be released from custody.

(8) Where an accused described in subsection (3), other than an accused to whom paragraph (*a*) of that subsection applies, is taken before the justice and the justice finds

(*a*) that the accused has contravened or had been about to contravene his summons, appearance notice, promise to appear, undertaking or recognizance, or

(*b*) that there are reasonable grounds to believe that the accused has committed an indictable offence after any summons, appearance notice, promise to appear, undertaking or recognizance was issued or given to him or entered into by him,

he shall cancel the summons, appearance notice, promise to appear, undertaking or recognizance and order that the accused be detained in custody unless the accused, having been given a reasonable opportunity to do so, shows cause why his detention in custody is not justified within the meaning of subsection 515(10).

(9) Where the accused shows cause why his detention in custody is not justified within the meaning of subsection 515(10), the justice shall order that the accused be released on his giving an undertaking or entering into a recognizance described in any of paragraphs 515(2)(*a*) to (*e*) with such conditions, described in subsection 515(4), as the justice considers desirable.

(10) Where the justice makes an order under subsection (9), he shall include in the record a statement of his reasons for making the order, and subsection 515(9) is applicable with such modifications as the circumstances require in respect thereof.

(11) Where the justice does not make a finding under paragraph (8)(*a*) or (*b*), he shall order that the accused be released from custody.

(12) The provisions of sections 517, 518 and 519 apply with such modifications as the circumstances require in respect of any proceedings under this section, except that subsection 518(2) does not apply in respect of an accused who is charged with an offence mentioned in section 522.

(13) Section 520 applies in respect of any order made under subsection (8) or (9) as though the order were an order made by a justice or a judge of the Nunavut Court of Justice under subsection 515(2) or (5), and section 521 applies in respect of any order made under subsection (9) as though the order were an order made by a justice or a judge of the Nunavut Court of Justice under subsection 515(2). R.S., c. C-34, s. 458; R.S., c. 2 (2nd Supp.), s. 5; 1974-75-76, c. 93, s. 55; 1999, c. 3, s. 33.

CROSS-REFERENCES

The term "justice" is defined in s. 2 and "accused", "appearance notice", "promise to appear", "undertaking", "recognizance" and "summons" in s. 493. Breach of the terms of a release order issued by a peace officer, officer in charge, justice or judge is an offence under s. 145. The procedure for enforcement of a recognizance is set out in Part XXV. That Part sets out the responsibilities of sureties (s. 764); procedure for rendering of the accused by his sureties (ss. 766, 767, 769); substitution of a new surety (s. 767.1); and the new release hearing where the accused is rendered into custody by his sureties (s. 769). That Part also sets out the procedure in case of default by the accused, including endorsing the fact of the default (s. 770); the hearing for estreat of the bail (s. 771); levying execution to enforce a writ of *fieri facias* where the recognizance is ordered forfeited (ss. 772, 773). For an overview of the application of this Part and the procedure respecting release pending trial see *Note on judicial interim release* under s. 515, or the *Note on judicial interim release* under s. 522 where the accused is charged with an offence listed in s. 469. As to the Nunavut Court of Justice, see the note under s. 536.1.

Where the accused was detaining prior to sentencing under subsec. (4) or (8), the sentencing judge may not give more than 1 for 1 credit for pre-sentence custody, pursuant to s. 719(3.1).

SYNOPSIS

This section sets out the procedure to be followed when a warrant for the arrest of an accused who is on interim release is sought.

Subsection (1) provides that where a justice is satisfied that there are reasonable grounds to believe that an accused person has contravened or is about to contravene his form of release or has committed an indictable offence after entering into a form of release, that justice may issue a warrant for the arrest of the accused.

Subsection (2) states that when a peace officer has reasonable grounds to believe that the accused has done any of the things listed above, the officer may arrest the accused without a warrant.

Subsection (3) requires the justice before whom an accused, apprehended under subsec. (1) or (2), is brought, to hear the prosecutor, the accused and any witness. If the accused was released in relation to an offence under s. 469, the justice must order that the accused be taken before a judge of the superior court of criminal jurisdiction.

Subsection (4) requires a judge of the superior court of criminal jurisdiction before whom an accused, charged with an offence under s. 469, appears pursuant to subsec. (3), to cancel the accused's form of release if that judge finds that the accused has done any of the things listed in subsec. (4)(*a*) and (*b*). The judge must order that the accused be detained in custody unless the accused, after being given a reasonable opportunity to do so, shows cause why such detention is not justified.

Subsection (5) allows the judge to release the accused, on conditions, if the judge considers this to be desirable. Any order made under subsec. (4) or (5) above can be reviewed only as provided for in s. 680. If the judge does not find that the accused has done the things described in subsec. (4)(*a*) and (*b*), he shall order the release of the accused.

Subsections (8), (9), (10) and (11) provide for a similar scheme to deal with an accused who has been taken into custody after release on charges relating to offences other than those listed in s. 469. In this situation, a justice is empowered to deal with the accused when that person is apprehended.

Subsection (12) provides that ss. 517, 518 and 519 apply, with any necessary modifications, to proceedings under this section except that s. 518(2) does not apply in respect of an accused charged with an offence under s. 469.

Subsection (13) provides that the review procedures described in ss. 520 and 521 apply to a judge under this section.

ANNOTATIONS

Subsection (1) – A justice may without the necessity of a specific charge in writing being laid before him issue a warrant for arrest pursuant to this section: *R. v. Fulton* (1972), 10 C.C.C. (2d) 120 (Sask. Q.B.).

In acting under this subsection the justice must act judicially. A provincial court judge who has himself been witness to the reasonable and probable grounds has no jurisdiction to issue the warrant or conduct the subsequent hearing under subsec. (3). Such a judge does not have the requisite measure of neutrality and detachment: *R. v. Kot* (1983), 10 C.C.C. (3d) 297 (Ont. H.C.J.). [**Note:** an appeal to the Ontario Court of Appeal was quashed the issue being moot: 11 C.C.C. (3d) 96*n* (Ont. C.A.).]

A judge has the jurisdiction to issue an arrest warrant where the accused, previously appearing by counsel, did not subsequently attend court in person on a plea date. There is no requirement that the judge specifically order the accused to appear in person. Warrants should not be issued on arbitrary or capricious grounds or for any indirect motive not directed to compelling the accused's attendance where his presence is necessary: *R. v. Sidorov* (2001), 160 C.C.C. (3d) 122 (Alta. C.A.), leave to appeal to S.C.C. refused *loc. cit.* C.C.C. at p. vi.

As it is not a term of an appearance notice that the accused keep the peace and be of good behaviour, a justice has no power to issue a warrant under this subsection based merely upon the fact that the accused is charged with subsequently committing a similar offence: *R. v. S.* (1986), 33 C.C.C. (3d) 383 (Sask. Q.B.).

Where the accused is released pursuant to an order of the Court of Appeal pending a new trial, a single judge of the court of appeal has jurisdiction to hear an application to revoke a release order: *R. v. Parsons* (1997), 124 C.C.C. (3d) 92 (Nfld. C.A.).

Subsection (3) – An application under this subsection to cancel the accused's recognizance is properly brought before a justice notwithstanding the release order was made by a judge on a review under s. 520: *R. v. Kinger* (1982), 65 C.C.C. (2d) 483 (Alta. C.A.).

Where an accused appears before a justice for alleged misconduct, either under subsec. (1) or (2), as a result of misconduct alleged to have occurred after release by a superior court judge pursuant to s. 522, the justice should first ascertain the basis of the accused's appearance. Where the only reason for the appearance is that the accused has been arrested for alleged misconduct then the justice must order that the accused appear before a superior court judge pursuant to subsec. (3)(*a*). If, however, in addition, charges have been laid under

s. 145 for failing to comply with the release order or for commission of some other criminal offence then the prosecutor should indicate whether or not he proposes to proceed under this section. If the prosecutor elects to proceed under this section then again the justice should order that the accused appear before a superior court judge pursuant to subsec. (3)(*a*) before dealing with release on the new charges. Where, however, the prosecutor does not so elect then the justice has jurisdiction to deal with release of the accused on the new charges pursuant to s. 515: *R. v. Yarema* (1989), 52 C.C.C. (3d) 242 (Ont. H.C.J.), affd 64 C.C.C. (3d) 260 (Ont. C.A.).

This section and s. 515 are not mutually exclusive. Thus, even where a hearing has been held before a justice under s. 515 for offences committed while the accused was at large on a release order made by a superior court judge under s. 522, the Crown is not precluded from subsequently applying to the superior court under this section to review the original release order: *R. v. Yarema, supra.*

Where an accused has not only failed to comply with the conditions of the recognizance but has been charged with new offences then the justice has jurisdiction to hear an application for bail on the new charges as well as to cancel the previous release order: *R. v. Gabrielson* (1991), 62 C.C.C. (3d) 571 (Ont. Ct. (Gen. Div.)).

Subsection (8) – It was held in *R. v. Lafond* (1975), 25 C.C.C. (2d) 568 (Que. Sess. Peace), that where an accused who has previously been released is brought before the justice for a show cause hearing for an offence committed while released then even though the accused does not technically come within subsec. (3) the justice may exercise the jurisdiction under this subsection and cancel the previous form of release. Such a situation would arise where the accused was arrested under s. 495 and not as the result of a warrant issued under subsec. (1) or as a result of a police officer's belief under subsec. (2).

In determining whether the conditions of release have been violated any issue as to whether the conditions allegedly violated were ambiguous must be determined on the basis of where the original burden lay for interim release. Thus where the offence was one for which the original burden was on the accused to show cause why he should be released, for example, on a charge of conspiracy to traffic in narcotics, then any ambiguity in the terms must be resolved in favour of the Crown: *Ex p. Clarke (No. 2)* (1978), 42 C.C.C. (2d) 23 (Nfld. S.C.T.D.).

The court had jurisdiction to proceed under subsec. (8) notwithstanding that the accused had not formally been arrested pursuant to subsecs. (1) or (2). Because the accused had been lawfully arrested, was lawfully detained, and had repeatedly been given notice of the Crown's intention to seek revocation of her existing bail, an arrest specifically pursuant to subsecs. (1) or (2) was unnecessary: *R. v. Ramage* (2011), 273 C.C.C. (3d) 331 (Ont. S.C.J.).

Where the Crown has elected to proceed summarily in respect of the new offence(s) alleged to have been committed by the accused, there is no "indictable offence" within the meaning of subsec. (8)(*b*) and the court has no jurisdiction to proceed with a hearing under this section: *R. v. Webley* (2015), 325 C.C.C. (3d) 239 (Ont. S.C.J.).

Review of Detention Where Trial Delayed

TIME FOR APPLICATION TO JUDGE / Notice of hearing / Matters to be considered on hearing / Order / Warrant of judge for arrest / Arrest without warrant by peace officer / Hearing and order / Provisions applicable to proceedings / Directions for expediting trial.

525. (1) Where an accused who has been charged with an offence other than an offence listed in section 469 and who is not required to be detained in custody in respect of any other matter is being detained in custody pending his trial for that offence and the trial has not commenced

(*a*) in the case of an indictable offence, within ninety days from

(i) the day on which the accused was taken before a justice under section 503, or

(ii) where an order that the accused be detained in custody has been made under section 521 or 524, or a decision has been made with respect to a review under section 520, the later of the day on which the accused was taken into custody under that order and the day of the decision, or

(*b*) in the case of an offence for which the accused is being prosecuted in proceedings by way of summary conviction, within thirty days from

(i) the day on which the accused was taken before a justice under subsection 503(1), or

(ii) where an order that the accused be detained in custody has been made under section 521 or 524, or a decision has been made with respect to a review under section 520, the later of the day on which the accused was taken into custody under that order and the day of the decision,

the person having the custody of the accused shall, forthwith on the expiration of those ninety or thirty days, as the case may be, apply to a judge having jurisdiction in the place in which the accused is in custody to fix a date for a hearing to determine whether or not the accused should be released from custody.

(2) On receiving an application under subsection (1), the judge shall

(*a*) fix a date for the hearing described in subsection (1) to be held in the jurisdiction

(i) where the accused is in custody, or

(ii) where the trial is to take place; and

(*b*) direct that notice of the hearing be given to such persons, including the prosecutor and the accused, and in such manner, as the judge may specify.

(3) On the hearing described in subsection (1), the judge may, in deciding whether or not the accused should be released from custody, take into consideration whether the prosecutor or the accused has been responsible for any unreasonable delay in the trial of the charge.

(4) If, following the hearing described in subsection (1), the judge is not satisfied that the continued detention of the accused in custody is justified within the meaning of subsection 515(10), the judge shall order that the accused be released from custody pending the trial of the charge on his giving an undertaking or entering into a recognizance described in any of paragraphs 515(2)(*a*) to (*e*) with such conditions described in subsection 515(4) as the judge considers desirable.

(5) Where a judge having jurisdiction in the province where an order under subsection (4) for the release of an accused has been made is satisfied that there are reasonable grounds to believe that the accused

(*a*) has contravened or is about to contravene the undertaking or recognizance on which he has been released, or

(*b*) has, after his release from custody on his undertaking or recognizance, committed an indictable offence,

he may issue a warrant for the arrest of the accused.

(6) Notwithstanding anything in this Act, a peace officer who believes on reasonable grounds that an accused who has been released from custody under subsection (4)

(*a*) has contravened or is about to contravene the undertaking or recognizance on which he has been released, or

(*b*) has, after his release from custody on his undertaking or recognizance, committed an indictable offence,

may arrest the accused without warrant and take him or cause him to be taken before a judge having jurisdiction in the province where the order for his release was made.

(7) A judge before whom an accused is taken pursuant to a warrant issued under subsection (5) or pursuant to subsection (6) may, where the accused shows cause why

his detention in custody is not justified within the meaning of subsection 515(10), order that the accused be released on his giving an undertaking or entering into a recognizance described in any of paragraphs 515(2)(*a*) to (*e*) with such conditions, described in subsection 515(4), as the judge considers desirable.

(8) The provisions of sections 517, 518 and 519 apply with such modifications as the circumstances require in respect of any proceedings under this section.

(9) Where an accused is before a judge under any of the provisions of this section, the judge may give directions for expediting the trial of the accused. R.S., c. C-34, s. 459; R.S., c. 2 (2nd Supp.), s. 5; 1974-75-76, c. 93, s. 56; R.S.C. 1985, c. 27 (1st Supp.), s. 90; 1994, c. 44, s. 49; 1997, c. 18, s. 61.

CROSS-REFERENCES

The term "justice" is defined in s. 2 and "judge", "recognizance" and "undertaking" in s. 493. As to calculation of "within" a certain number of days see s. 27(5) of the *Interpretation Act*, R.S.C. 1985, c. I-21. For an overview of the application of this Part and the procedure respecting release pending trial see *Note on judicial interim release* under s. 515, or the *Note on judicial interim release* under s. 522 where the accused is charged with an offence listed in s. 469.

The accused of course has a constitutional right to trial within a reasonable time and thus see notes under s. 11(*b*) of the Charter.

SYNOPSIS

This section provides for a review of the detention of an accused person when that person's trial has been delayed. This review applies only to persons charged with offences other than those listed in s. 469.

Subsection (1) places an obligation on the person having custody of the accused to apply to the judge having jurisdiction to fix a date for a hearing to determine whether an accused should be released after the applicable time period has expired. The time periods vary according to the type of offence alleged to have been committed and the section under which the accused has been detained.

Subsection (2) requires a judge, upon receipt of the application under subsec. (1), to fix a date for the hearing, and to direct that notice be given to the prosecutor and the accused.

Subsection (3) authorizes the judge to consider whether the prosecutor or the accused has been responsible for any unreasonable delay in the trial of the charge.

Under subsec. (4), the judge must consider, following the hearing, whether the continued detention of the accused is justified on the primary or secondary grounds as outlined in s. 515(10). The judge may decide to release the accused under this section using any of the forms of release described in s. 515(2)(*a*) to (*e*) with such conditions described in s. 515(4) as are appropriate.

Subsections (5) and (6) authorize the arrest of an accused person who has been released under subsec. (4) with or without a warrant where there are grounds to believe that he has violated or is about to violate his undertaking or recognizance, or that he has committed an indictable offence subsequent to release.

Subsection (7) states that the onus is on the accused brought before a justice under subsec. (5) or (6) to show cause why detention is not justified. Section 515(10), (2) and (4) are applicable, depending on the circumstances. Sections 517, 518 and 519 are applicable with such modifications as circumstances require.

Subsection (9) gives the judge dealing with an accused under this section a discretion to give directions for expediting the trial.

ANNOTATIONS

General – In *R. v. Myers*, 2019 SCC 18, the court undertook a comprehensive analysis of this provision, holding that its purpose is to prevent accused persons from languishing in pre-trial custody and to ensure a prompt trial. The provision imposes an independent responsibility on the reviewing judge to consider whether the continued detention of the accused is justified, and establishes a discretionary mechanism designed to prevent unreasonable delay and to expedite the trials of individuals in remand. The jailer has an obligation to apply for the detention review hearing immediately upon the expiration of 90 days following the day on which the accused was initially taken before a justice under s. 503. Where there is an intervening detention order under ss. 520, 521 or 524, the 90-day period begins again. Accused persons who have not had a full bail hearing are also entitled to a review under s. 525. Upon receiving the application from the jailer, the judge must fix a date and hold a hearing at the earliest opportunity. At the hearing, the reviewing judge may refer to the transcript, exhibits and reasons from any initial judicial interim release hearing and from any subsequent review hearings, and should show respect for any findings of fact made by the first-level decision-maker if there is no cause to interfere with them. Both parties are also entitled to make submissions on the basis of any additional credible or trustworthy information which is relevant or material to the judge's analysis, and pre-existing material is subject to the criteria of due diligence and relevance. Unreasonable delay is not a threshold that must be met before the detention of the accused is reviewed. The overarching question is whether the continued detention of the accused in custody is justified within the meaning of s. 515(10). In determining whether the detention of the accused is still justified, the reviewing judge may consider any new evidence or change in the circumstances of the accused, the impact of the passage of time and any unreasonable delay on the proportionality of the detention, and the rationale offered for the original detention order, if one was made. If there was no initial bail hearing, the s. 525 judge is responsible for conducting one, taking into account the time the accused has already spent in pre-trial custody. The judge must provide the accused with reasons why their continued detention is or is not justified. Where appropriate, the judge should make use of the discretion under ss. 525(9) and 526 to give directions for expediting the trial and related proceedings.

Procedure – An application brought on a week later and then set for hearing is reasonable compliance with this section: *R. v. Kozak and Lewis* (1975), 32 C.R.N.S. 245, [1976] 1 W.W.R. 356 (B.C.S.C.).

Jurisdiction over the offence is not affected by the fact that due to inadvertence nothing was done on the date to which a review under this section was adjourned: *R. v. Gagliardi* (1981), 60 C.C.C. (2d) 267 (B.C.C.A.), leave to appeal to S.C.C. refused C.C.C. *loc. cit.*.

A youth court judge has jurisdiction to conduct the 90-day review pursuant to the *Youth Criminal Justice Act*: *R. v. O. (A.J.)* (2004), 185 C.C.C. (3d) 120 (Ont. S.C.J.).

Effect of failure to comply with section – It was held by the court in *Ex. p. Cordes* (1976), 31 C.C.C. (2d) 279 (Alta. S.C. App. Div.), that failure to comply with this section does not *ipso facto* vacate the previous detention order and render the accused's detention illegal entitling him to release on *habeas corpus*. On a *habeas corpus* application brought because of unreasonable delay the judge would have regard to the same considerations set out in this section. Where the section has not been complied with the appropriate remedy is *mandamus* to require compliance therewith.

To a similar effect is *R. v. Pomfret* (1990), 53 C.C.C. (3d) 56 (Man. C.A.), where the court also held that the failure to hold the review as required by this section did not, in the circumstances, result in arbitrary detention in violation of s. 9 of the Charter. The lapse of time was not of such an extent that the court could infer deliberateness or design on the part of the gaoler. Finally, refusing to release the accused on his application for *habeas corpus* did not violate s. 10(*c*) of the Charter. The *habeas corpus* application brought to the court's attention that the accused was entitled to a review under this section and resulted in him receiving that to which he was entitled under the law, namely a bail review hearing.

The reverse onus contained in s. 515(6) of the *Criminal Code* applies to a review under this provision and cannot be eliminated merely through a delay: *R. v. Thorsteinson* (2006), 238 C.C.C. (3d) 83 (Man. Q.B.).

The accused's detention does not become unlawful merely upon the expiration of the 90 days. The custodian is under a statutory obligation to seek the hearing required under this section as soon as practicable after the expiration of the 90-day period. Where an application for a hearing has been made by the custodian, the appropriate disposition of a claim to release on *habeas corpus* is to refer that claim to the judge conducting the hearing under this section. Where no application has been made, *habeas corpus* may lie to determine whether the lapse of time has tainted the legality of the detention. Alternatively, an accused may apply by way of *mandamus* to compel the director to comply: *Vukelich v. Vancouver Pre-Trial Centre, Director* (1993), 87 C.C.C. (3d) 32, 27 C.R. (4th) 15 (B.C.C.A.).

DIRECTIONS FOR EXPEDITING PROCEEDINGS.

526. Subject to subsection 525(9), a court, judge or justice before which or whom an accused appears pursuant to this Part may give directions for expediting any proceedings in respect of the accused. R.S., c. 2 (2nd Supp.), s. 5; R.S.C. 1985, c. 27 (1st Supp.), s. 91.

CROSS-REFERENCES

The term "justice" is defined in s. 2 and "accused" and "judge" in s. 493. The accused of course has a constitutional right to trial within a reasonable time and thus see notes under s. 11(*b*) of the Charter. For an overview of the application of this Part and the procedure respecting release pending trial see *Note on judicial interim release* under s. 515, or the *Note on judicial interim release* under s. 522 where the accused is charged with an offence listed in s. 469.

SYNOPSIS

This section authorizes a court, judge, or justice dealing with an accused under Part XVI of the Code to give directions for expediting any proceedings relating to the accused.

Procedure to Procure Attendance of a Prisoner

PROCURING ATTENDANCE / Provincial court judge's order / Conveyance of prisoner / Detention of prisoner required as witness / Detention in other cases / Application of sections respecting sentence / Transfer of prisoner / Conveyance of prisoner / Return.

527. (1) A judge of a superior court of criminal jurisdiction may order in writing that a person who is confined in a prison be brought before the court, judge, justice or provincial court judge before whom the prisoner is required to attend, from day to day as may be necessary, if

(*a*) the applicant for the order sets out the facts of the case in an affidavit and produces the warrant, if any; and

(*b*) the judge is satisfied that the ends of justice require that an order be made.

(2) A provincial court judge has the same powers for the purposes of subsection (1) or (7) as a judge has under that subsection where the person whose attendance is required is within the province in which the provincial court judge has jurisdiction.

(3) An order that is made under subsection (1) or (2) shall be addressed to the person who has custody of the prisoner, and on receipt thereof that person shall

(*a*) deliver the prisoner to any person who is named in the order to receive him; or

(*b*) bring the prisoner before the court, judge, justice or provincial court judge, as the case may be, on payment of his reasonable charges in respect thereof.

(4) Where a prisoner is required as a witness, the judge or provincial court judge shall direct, in the order, the manner in which the prisoner shall be kept in custody and returned to the prison from which he is brought.

(5) Where the appearance of a prisoner is required for the purposes of paragraph (1)(*a*) or (*b*), the judge or provincial court judge shall give appropriate directions in the order with respect to the manner in which the prisoner is

(*a*) to be kept in custody, if he is ordered to stand trial; or

(*b*) to be returned, if he is discharged on a preliminary inquiry or if he is acquitted of the charge against him.

(6) Sections 718.3 and 743.1 apply where a prisoner to whom this section applies is convicted and sentenced to imprisonment by the court, judge, justice or provincial court judge.

(7) On application by the prosecutor, a judge of a superior court of criminal jurisdiction may, if a prisoner or a person in the custody of a peace officer consents in writing, order the transfer of the prisoner or other person to the custody of a peace officer named in the order for a period specified in the order, where the judge is satisfied that the transfer is required for the purpose of assisting a peace officer acting in the execution of his or her duties.

(8) An order under subsection (7) shall be addressed to the person who has custody of the prisoner and on receipt thereof that person shall deliver the prisoner to the peace officer who is named in the order to receive him.

(9) When the purposes of any order made under this section have been carried out, the prisoner shall be returned to the place where he was confined at the time the order was made. R.S., c. C-34, s. 460; R.S.C. 1985, c. 27 (1st Supp.), ss. 92, 101(2)(*b*); 1994, c. 44, s. 50; 1995, c. 22, s. 10; 1997, c. 18, s. 62.

CROSS-REFERENCES

"Provincial court judge", "superior court of criminal jurisdiction", "prosecutor", "justice", "prison", and "peace officer" are defined in s. 2. Section 672.85 gives the chairperson of the Criminal Code Review Board the power to order the attendance of the accused for a review hearing under s. 672.81.

SYNOPSIS

This section sets out the procedure to procure the attendance of a prisoner at his preliminary hearing, the trial of his charge, or to give evidence in criminal proceedings.

Subsection (1) states that when a prisoner's attendance is required, an application must be made to a judge of a superior court of criminal jurisdiction. The applicant must set out the facts of the case in an affidavit and produce any warrant to the judge. The judge may, if satisfied that the ends of justice require it, make a written order to bring the prisoner before the court.

Subsection (2) provides that a provincial court judge has the same powers as the judges described in subsecs. (1) and (7) except that the provincial court judge may only order the appearance of a prisoner being held in that province.

Subsection (3) describes the requirements of an order made under subsecs. (1) and (2).

Subsection (4) states that the judge or provincial court judge must direct the manner in which a prisoner, required to testify as a witness, shall be kept in custody and returned to prison.

Subsection (5) sets out the kinds of directions a judge or provincial court judge must include in an order compelling the attendance of a prisoner at his preliminary hearing or trial.

Subsection (7) authorizes a superior court judge (or a provincial court judge if the prisoner is in the judge's province) to order the transfer of a prisoner to a named peace officer for a specified period where such a transfer would assist the peace officer in the execution of his duties. The prisoner must consent in writing to this procedure. An order under subsec. (7) must be addressed to the person having custody of the prisoner and, upon receipt, that person must deliver the prisoner to the named peace officer.

Subsection (9) requires that the prisoner be returned to the place of confinement when the purposes of any order made under this section have been accomplished.

ANNOTATIONS

A witness brought to court pursuant to an order under this section may be compelled to testify notwithstanding he has not been served with a subpoena and there is no warrant issued under s. 698 outstanding: *R. v. Ayres* (1984), 15 C.C.C. (3d) 208 (Ont. C.A.).

The judge in making an order under this section in relation to an accused who is detained in another district has power under subsec. (5) to order that the accused be brought to the local gaol several days prior to the actual trial date to afford him a reasonable opportunity to properly prepare his defence: *Auclair v. Dube J.S.P. and R.* (1984), 39 C.R. (3d) 398 (Que. S.C.).

Although this section provides a convenient procedure for securing the attendance at court of persons confined in custody on other matters, it was open to a justice of the peace to resort to the provisions of s. 512 and issue a bench warrant for the arrest of an accused where the accused, detained on another matter, was not brought to court to set a date for his trial: *R. v. Hartmann* (1986), 30 C.C.C. (3d) 286 (Ont. H.C.J.).

Endorsement of Warrant

ENDORSING WARRANT / Copy of affidavit or warrant / Effect of endorsement.

528. (1) Where a warrant for the arrest or committal of an accused, in any form set out in Part XXVIII in relation thereto, cannot be executed in accordance with section 514 or 703, a justice within whose jurisdiction the accused is or is believed to be shall, on application and proof on oath or by affidavit of the signature of the justice who issued the warrant, authorize the arrest of the accused within his jurisdiction by making an endorsement, which may be in Form 28, on the warrant.

(1.1) A copy of an affidavit or warrant submitted by a means of telecommunication that produces a writing has the same probative force as the original for the purposes of subsection (1).

(2) An endorsement that is made on a warrant pursuant to subsection (1) is sufficient authority to the peace officers to whom it was originally directed, and to all peace officers within the territorial jurisdiction of the justice by whom it is endorsed, to execute the warrant and to take the accused before the justice who issued the warrant or before any other justice for the same territorial division. R.S., c. C-34, s. 461; 1974-75-76, c. 93, s. 57; R.S.C. 1985, c. 27 (1st Supp.), s. 93; 1994, c. 44, s. 51.

CROSS-REFERENCES

"Justice" and "peace officer" are defined in s. 2. "Warrant" is defined in s. 493. Under s. 20, a warrant may be executed on a holiday. A warrant is executed in accordance with this section and s. 29 and s. 10 of the Charter. For protection of persons executing warrants see ss. 25 to 28.

SYNOPSIS

This section empowers a justice to authorize the arrest of an accused person who is believed to be in that justice's jurisdiction, when a warrant for arrest or committal cannot be executed in accordance with ss. 514 or 703. The justice being asked to authorize the arrest of the accused will endorse the warrant only upon proof on oath or by affidavit of the signature of the justice who issued the warrant. Under subsec. (1.1), a faxed copy has the same probative value as the original.

Subsection (2) states that an endorsement on the warrant pursuant to subsec. (1) is sufficient authority to the peace officers to whom it was originally directed, along with all peace officers within the territorial jurisdiction of the endorsing justice, to execute the warrant.

ANNOTATIONS

The trial judge correctly found that a warrant issued by a justice of the peace in Ontario was ineffective in Saskatchewan because it had never been endorsed by a justice in Saskatchewan in accordance with this section. However, the judge erred in finding the arrest illegal without considering whether it was a valid warrantless arrest for an indictable offence pursuant to s. 495(1): *R. v. Charles* (2012), 289 C.C.C. (3d) 170 (Sask. C.A.).

529. [*Repealed* (old provision, with heading), 1994, c. 44, s. 52.]

Powers to Enter Dwelling-houses to Carry out Arrests

INCLUDING AUTHORIZATION TO ENTER IN WARRANT OF ARREST / Execution

529. (1) A warrant to arrest or apprehend a person issued by a judge or justice under this or any other Act of Parliament may authorize a peace officer, subject to subsection (2), to enter a dwelling-house described in the warrant for the purpose of arresting or apprehending the person if the judge or justice is satisfied by information on oath in writing that there are reasonable grounds to believe that the person is or will be present in the dwelling-house.

(2) An authorization to enter a dwelling-house granted under subsection (1) is subject to the condition that the peace officer may not enter the dwelling-house unless the peace officer has, immediately before entering the dwelling-house, reasonable grounds to believe that the person to be arrested or apprehended is present in the dwelling-house. 1994, c. 44, s. 52; 1997, c. 39, s. 2.

CROSS-REFERENCES

"Justice", "dwelling-house" and "peace officer" are defined in s. 2. A warrant to arrest may be issued under various provisions of this Act. The most important provision is s. 507. Sections 511 and 512 set out the contents of the arrest warrant. Section 514 contains other provisions concerning execution of an arrest warrant. Under s. 20, a warrant may be executed on a holiday. A warrant is executed in accordance with ss. 29 and 10 of the Charter. For protection of persons executing warrants, see ss. 25 to 28. Section 528 deals with endorsing the warrant where it cannot be executed in accordance with s. 514. Section 529.1 permits a justice or judge to issue a warrant authorizing a peace officer to enter a dwelling-house for the purpose of arresting or apprehending a person, where a warrant is already in force anywhere in Canada or where grounds exist for a warrantless arrest. Section 529.2 requires the justice or judge to include terms and conditions in the warrant to ensure that the entry is reasonable in the circumstances. Section 529.3 allows for warrantless entry to effect an arrest in exigent circumstances. Section 529.4 sets out the circumstances in which a peace officer may enter without prior announcement. Section 529.5 permits application for a telewarrant where it is impracticable to appear personally before a judge or justice to obtain a warrant to enter a dwelling-house or the authorization to enter or enter without announcement under ss. 529 or 529.4. The provisions respecting issuance of a telewarrant are set out in s. 487.1.

Section 34.1 of the *Interpretation Act*, R.S.C. 1985, c. I-21, provides that any person who may issue a warrant to arrest or apprehend a person under any other Act of Parliament may also authorize entry into a dwelling-house to effect the arrest and without prior announcement.

For notes on warrantless search of the home, see annotations following s. 529.3. For notes with respect to prior announcement, see annotations following s. 529.4.

Section 489(2) gives the officer power to seize without warrant anything that the officer believes on reasonable grounds has been obtained by the commission of an offence, has been used in the commission of an offence or will afford evidence in respect of any offence under the *Criminal Code* or other federal statute, provided that the officer is lawfully present in the place pursuant to a warrant or in the execution of duties.

SYNOPSIS

This section allows a justice or judge to include in a warrant to arrest or apprehend, the power to authorize the peace officer to enter a dwelling-house for the purpose of effect the arrest or apprehension. This authorization is dependent upon the judge or justice being satisfied by information on oath in writing that there are reasonable grounds to believe that the person is or will be present. Nevertheless, the warrant mus t include a condition that the officer only enter the dwelling-house if the officer has, immediately before entering, reasonable grounds to believe the person is in the dwelling-house. This provision and the companion provisions in ss. 529.1 to 529.5 were apparently enacted in response to the decision of the Supreme Court of Canada in *R. v. Feeney*, noted below.

ANNOTATIONS

It was held in *R. v. Feeney*, [1997] 2 S.C.R. 13, 115 C.C.C. (3d) 129, that the common law right to make a warrantless arrest on private premises must now be adjusted to comport with Charter values. In general, the privacy interest in a dwelling-house now outweighs the interests of the police and warrantless arrests in dwelling-houses are prohibited. An arrest warrant alone is insufficient protection of a suspect's privacy rights. [**Note:** This case was decided prior to the enactment of this section and the companion provisions of ss. 529.1 to 529.5. This section and s. 529.1 now provide for judicial authorization of entry into a dwelling-house to effect an arrest. In addition, s. 529.2 now gives statutory authority for a warrantless entry in exigent circumstances.]

The warrant requirement to effect an arrest of the accused is not restricted to an accused's dwelling house. Accordingly, a warrant to enter a dwelling house was required where the accused was arrested in a laundry room of a rooming house shared with others: *R. v. Adams* (2001), 157 C.C.C. (3d) 220, 203 D.L.R. (4th) 290, 148 O.A.C. 253 (C.A.).

WARRANT TO ENTER DWELLING-HOUSE

529.1 A judge or justice may issue a warrant in Form 7.1 authorizing a peace officer to enter a dwelling-house described in the warrant for the purpose of arresting or apprehending a person identified or identifiable by the warrant if the judge or justice is satisfied by information on oath that there are reasonable grounds to believe that the person is or will be present in the dwelling-house and that

(*a*) a warrant referred to in this or any other Act of Parliament to arrest or apprehend the person is in force anywhere in Canada;

(*b*) grounds exist to arrest the person without warrant under paragraph 495(1)(*a*) or (*b*) or section 672.91; or

(*c*) grounds exist to arrest or apprehend without warrant the person under an Act of Parliament, other than this Act. 1997, c. 39, s. 2; 2002, c. 13, s. 23.

CROSS-REFERENCES

"Justice", "dwelling-house" and "peace officer" are defined in s. 2. Section 495 sets out the circumstances in which a peace officer may make an arrest without warrant. A warrant to arrest may be issued under various provisions of this Act. The most important provision is s. 507. Sections 511 and 512 set out the contents of the arrest warrant. Section 514 contains other provisions concerning execution of an arrest warrant. Under s. 20, a warrant may be executed on a holiday. A warrant is executed in accordance with ss. 29 and 10 of the Charter. For protection of persons executing warrants, see ss. 25 to 28. Section 528 deals with endorsing the warrant where it cannot be executed in accordance with s. 514. Section 529 permits a justice or judge to include a term in an arrest warrant authorizing a peace officer to enter a dwelling-house for the purpose of arresting or apprehending a person. Section 529.2 requires the justice or judge to include terms and conditions in the warrant to ensure that the entry is reasonable in the circumstances. Section 529.3 allows for warrantless entry to effect an arrest in exigent circumstances. Section 529.4 sets out the circumstances in which a peace officer may enter without prior announcement. Section 529.5 permits application for a telewarrant where it is impracticable to appear personally before a judge or justice to obtain a warrant to enter a dwelling-house or the authorization to enter or enter without announcement under s. 529 or s. 529.4. The provisions respecting issuance of a telewarrant are set out in s. 487.1.

Section 34.1 of the *Interpretation Act*, R.S.C. 1985, c. I-21, provides that any person who may issue a warrant to arrest or apprehend a person under any other Act of Parliament may also authorize entry into a dwelling-house to effect the arrest and without prior announcement.

For notes on warrantless search of the home, see annotations following s. 529.3. For notes with respect to prior announcement, see annotations following s. 529.4.

Section 489(2) gives the officer power to seize without warrant anything that the officer believes on reasonable grounds has been obtained by the commission of an offence, has been used in the commission of an offence or will afford evidence in respect of any offence under the *Criminal Code* or other federal statute, provided that the officer is lawfully present in the place pursuant to a warrant or in the execution of duties.

SYNOPSIS

This section allows a justice or judge to issue a warrant to authorize the peace officer to enter a dwelling-house for the purpose of effecting the arrest or apprehension. This authorization is dependent upon the judge or justice being satisfied by information on oath in writing that there are reasonable grounds to believe that the person is or will be present and that an arrest warrant is in force anywhere in Canada or that grounds for a warrantless arrest exist. This provision and the companion provisions in ss. 529.1 to 529.5 were apparently enacted in response to the decision of the Supreme Court of Canada in *R. v. Feeney*, [1997] 2 S.C.R. 13, 115 C.C.C. (3d) 129, noted below.

ANNOTATIONS

It was held in *R. v. Feeney*, [1997] 2 S.C.R. 13, 115 C.C.C. (3d) 129, that the common law right to make a warrantless arrest on private premises must now be adjusted to comport with Charter values. In general, the privacy interest in a dwelling-house now outweighs the interests of the police and warrantless arrests in dwelling-houses are prohibited. An arrest warrant alone is insufficient protection of a suspect's privacy rights. [**Note:** This case was decided prior to the enactment of this section and the companion provisions of ss. 529 and 529.2 to 529.5. This section and s. 529 now provide for judicial authorization of entry into a dwelling-house to effect an arrest. In addition, s. 529.2 now gives statutory authority for a warrantless entry in exigent circumstances.]

REASONABLE TERMS AND CONDITIONS

529.2 Subject to section 529.4, the judge or justice shall include in a warrant referred to in section 529 or 529.1 any terms and conditions that the judge or justice considers advisable to ensure that the entry into the dwelling-house is reasonable in the circumstances. 1997, c. 39, s. 2.

CROSS-REFERENCES

"Justice" is defined in s. 2. A warrant to arrest may be issued under various provisions of this Act. The most important provision is s. 507. Sections 511 and 512 set out the contents of the arrest warrant. Section 514 contains other provisions concerning execution of an arrest warrant. Under s. 20, a warrant may be executed on a holiday. A warrant is executed in accordance with ss. 29 and 10 of the Charter. For protection of persons executing warrants, see ss. 25 to 28. Section 528 deals with endorsing the warrant where it cannot be executed in accordance with s. 514. Section 529 permits a justice or judge to include a term in an arrest warrant authorizing a peace officer to enter a dwelling-house for the purpose of arresting or apprehending a person. An authorization granted under s. 529 is subject to the condition that the peace officer may not enter the dwelling-house unless the officer has, immediately before entering the dwelling-house, reasonable grounds to believe that the person to be arrested is present in the dwelling-house. Section 529.1 permits a justice or judge to issue a warrant authorizing a peace officer to enter a dwelling-house for the purpose of arresting or apprehending a person, where a warrant is already in force anywhere in Canada or where there exists grounds for a warrantless arrest. Section 529.3 allows for warrantless entry to effect an arrest in exigent circumstances. Section 529.4 sets out the circumstances in which a peace officer may enter without prior announcement. Section 529.5 permits application for a telewarrant where it is impracticable to appear personally before a judge or justice to obtain a warrant to enter a dwelling-house or the authorization to enter or enter without announcement under s. 529 or s. 529.4. The provisions respecting issuance of a telewarrant are set out in s. 487.1.

Section 34.1 of the *Interpretation Act*, R.S.C. 1985, c. I-21, provides that any person who may issue a warrant to arrest or apprehend a person under any other Act of Parliament may also authorize entry into a dwelling-house to effect the arrest and without prior announcement.

For notes on warrantless search of the home, see annotations following s. 529.3. For notes with respect to prior announcement, see annotations following s. 529.4.

Section 489(2) gives the officer power to seize without warrant anything that the officer believes on reasonable grounds has been obtained by the commission of an offence, has been used in the commission of an offence or will afford evidence in respect of any offence under the *Criminal Code* or other federal statute, provided that the officer is lawfully present in the place pursuant to a warrant or in the execution of duties.

SYNOPSIS

This section requires the justice or judge to include terms and conditions in the warrant to ensure that the entry is reasonable in the circumstances.

AUTHORITY TO ENTER DWELLING WITHOUT WARRANT / Exigent circumstances

529.3 (1) Without limiting or restricting any power a peace officer may have to enter a dwelling-house under this or any other Act or law, the peace officer may enter the dwelling-house for the purpose of arresting or apprehending a person, without a warrant referred to in section 529 or 529.1 authorizing the entry, if the peace officer has reasonable grounds to believe that the person is present in the dwelling-house, and the conditions for obtaining a warrant under section 529.1 exist but by reason of exigent circumstances it would be impracticable to obtain a warrant.

(2) For the purposes of subsection (1), exigent circumstances include circumstances in which the peace officer

(*a*) has reasonable grounds to suspect that entry into the dwelling-house is necessary to prevent imminent bodily harm or death to any person; or

(*b*) has reasonable grounds to believe that evidence relating to the commission of an indictable offence is present in the dwelling-house and that entry into the dwelling-house is necessary to prevent the imminent loss or imminent destruction of the evidence. 1997, c. 39, s. 2.

CROSS-REFERENCES

"Peace officer" and "dwelling-house" are defined in s. 2. Section 495 is the most important provision setting out the circumstances in which a peace officer may make an arrest without warrant. A warrantless arrest must conform to the dictates of s. 10 of the Charter. A warrant to arrest may be issued under various provisions of this Act. The most important provision is s. 507. Sections 511 and 512 set out the contents of the arrest warrant. Section 514 contains other provisions concerning execution of an arrest warrant. Under s. 20, a warrant may be executed on a holiday. A warrant is executed in accordance with ss. 29 and 10 of the Charter. For protection of persons executing warrants, see ss. 25 to 28. Section 528 deals with endorsing the warrant where it cannot be executed in accordance with s. 514. Section 529 permits a justice or judge to include a term in an arrest warrant authorizing a peace officer to enter a dwelling-house for the purpose of arresting or apprehending a person. Section 529.1 permits a justice or judge to issue a warrant authorizing a peace officer to enter a dwelling-house for the purpose of arresting or apprehending a person, where a warrant is already in force anywhere in Canada or where grounds exist for a warrantless arrest. Section 529.2 requires the justice or judge to include terms and conditions in the warrant to ensure that the entry is reasonable in the circumstances. Section 529.4 sets out the circumstances in which a peace officer may enter without prior announcement. Section 529.5 permits application for a telewarrant where it is impracticable to appear personally before a judge or justice to obtain a warrant to enter a dwelling-house or the authorization to enter or enter without announcement under s. 529 or s. 529.4.

For notes with respect to prior announcement, see annotations following s. 529.4.

SYNOPSIS

This section provides statutory authority for a peace officer to enter a dwelling-house to effect an arrest although the officer does not have a warrant or specific authorization from a judicial official to enter. This section defines some of the circumstances in which the warrantless entry may be made. Subsection (2) defines certain exigent circumstances justifying the warrantless entry. They include where the officer has reasonable grounds to suspect that entry is necessary to prevent imminent bodily harm or death or where the officer has reasonable grounds to believe that entry is necessary to prevent the imminent loss or destruction of evidence. Note the different standard of belief depending on the reason for entry. This section is in addition to any other warrantless entry powers that may be given to an officer either by statute or common law. This provision and the companion provisions in ss. 529, 529.1, 529.2, 529.4 and 529.5 were apparently enacted in response to the decision of the Supreme Court of Canada in *R. v. Feeney*, [1997] 2 S.C.R. 13, 115 C.C.C. (3d) 129, noted below and under s. 529.

ANNOTATIONS

Note: Some of the following cases were decided prior to the enactment of this section.

In *R. v. Macooh*, [1993] 2 S.C.R. 802, 82 C.C.C. (3d) 481, the court held that the police have the power to enter private premises to effect an arrest where they are in hot pursuit and they have a warrant for an arrest or have the power to make an arrest without a warrant. It was also held that the power to enter private premises to make an arrest while in hot pursuit is not limited to an arrest for an indictable offence. Nor is it necessary that the offence had been committed in the presence of the police. The essence of hot or fresh pursuit is that it must be continuous pursuit conducted with reasonable diligence so that the pursuit and capture along with the commission of the offence may be considered as forming part of a single transaction.

In the subsequent case of *R. v. Feeney*, [1997] 2 S.C.R. 13, 115 C.C.C. (3d) 129, the court held that warrantless entry to effect an arrest was ordinarily inconsistent with s. 8 of the Charter. However, there may be exigent circumstances were warrantless entry is reasonable. At least one exception is where the officer is in hot pursuit as recognized in *R. v. Macooh, supra.*

The warrantless search of a home incident to arrest is generally prohibited subject to exceptional circumstances where the law enforcement interest is so compelling that it overrides the individual's right to privacy within the home. The risk of physical harm to those at the scene of the arrest constitutes exceptional circumstances justifying the warrantless entry and search of a residence. If the circumstances of an arrest give rise to a legitimate cause for concern with respect to the safety of those at the scene, reasonable steps to allay that concern may be taken. The nature of the apprehended risk, the potential consequences of not taking protective measures, the availability of alternative measures and the likelihood of the contemplated danger actually existing, must all be considered: *R. v.*

Golub (1997), 117 C.C.C. (3d) 193 (Ont. C.A.), leave to appeal to S.C.C. refused 128 C.C.C. (3d) vi.

In *R. v. Godoy*, [1999] 1 S.C.R. 311, 131 C.C.C. (3d) 129, the Supreme Court of Canada held that forced entry into a dwelling house in response to a disconnected 911 call did not violate s. 8. The common law duty of police to preserve life is engaged whenever it may be inferred that the 911 caller may be in distress. In this case, the accused had refused entry to the police responding to the 911 call. The forced entry of the apartment to locate the caller and determine the reason for the call constituted a justifiable use of police powers. The police do not, however, have a further authority to search the premises or otherwise intrude on a resident's privacy or property. The court did not consider the applicability of the plain view doctrine in such circumstances.

Exigent circumstances include reasonable grounds to believe that entry was necessary to prevent the imminent loss or destruction of evidence: *R. v. Duong* (2002), 162 C.C.C. (3d) 242 (B.C.C.A.), leave to appeal to S.C.C. refused [2002] 3 S.C.R. vii, 167 C.C.C. (3d) vi.

"Any person" in subsec. (2)(*a*) includes the accused. In this case, therefore, the police were in lawful execution of their duty when entering the accused's home without a warrant, on the basis that he was suicidal and needed to be returned to hospital: *R. v. Phillips* (2006), 219 C.C.C. (3d) 252 (N.S.C.A.).

OMITTING ANNOUNCEMENT BEFORE ENTRY / Execution of authorization / Exception.

529.4 (1) A judge or justice who authorizes a peace officer to enter a dwelling-house under section 529 or 529.1, or any other judge or justice, may authorize the peace officer to enter the dwelling-house without prior announcement if the judge or justice is satisfied by information on oath that there are reasonable grounds to believe that prior announcement of the entry would

(*a*) expose the peace officer or any other person to imminent bodily harm or death; or

(*b*) result in the imminent loss or imminent destruction of evidence relating to the commission of an indictable offence.

(2) An authorization under this section is subject to the condition that the peace officer may not enter the dwelling-house without prior announcement despite being authorized to do so unless the peace officer has, immediately before entering the dwelling-house,

(*a*) reasonable grounds to suspect that prior announcement of the entry would expose the peace officer or any other person to imminent bodily harm or death; or

(*b*) reasonable grounds to believe that prior announcement of the entry would result in the imminent loss or imminent destruction of evidence relating to the commission of an indictable offence.

(3) A peace officer who enters a dwelling-house without a warrant under section 529.3 may not enter the dwelling-house without prior announcement unless the peace officer has, immediately before entering the dwelling-house,

(*a*) reasonable grounds to suspect that prior announcement of the entry would expose the peace officer or any other person to imminent bodily harm or death; or

(*b*) reasonable grounds to believe that prior announcement of the entry would result in the imminent loss or imminent destruction of evidence relating to the commission of an indictable offence. R.S. 1985, c. 27 (1st Supp.), s. 203; 1997, c. 39, s. 2.

CROSS-REFERENCES

"Justice", "dwelling-house" and "peace officer" are defined in s. 2. A warrant to arrest may be issued under various provisions of this Act. The most important provision is s. 507. Sections 511 and 512 set out the contents of the arrest warrant. Section 514 contains other provisions concerning execution of an arrest warrant. Under s. 20, a warrant may be executed on a holiday. A warrant is executed in accordance with ss. 29 and 10 of the Charter. For protection of persons executing warrants see, ss. 25 to 28. Section 528 deals with endorsing the warrant where the warrant cannot be executed in accordance with s. 514. Section 529 permits a justice or judge to include a term in an arrest warrant authorizing a peace officer to enter a dwelling-house for the purpose of arresting or apprehending a person. Section 529.1 permits a justice or judge to issue a warrant authorizing a peace officer to enter a dwelling-house for the purpose of arresting or apprehending a person, where a warrant is already in force anywhere in Canada or where grounds exist for a warrantless arrest. Section 529.2 requires the justice or judge to include terms and conditions in the warrant to ensure that the entry is reasonable in the circumstances. Section 529.3 allows for warrantless entry to effect an arrest in exigent circumstances. Section 529.5 permits application for a telewarrant where it is impracticable to appear personally before a judge or justice to obtain a warrant to enter a dwelling-house or the authorization to enter or enter without announcement under s. 529 or 529.4. The provisions respecting issuance of a telewarrant are set out in s. 487.1.

Section 34.1 of the *Interpretation Act*, R.S.C. 1985, c. I-21, provides that any person who may issue a warrant to arrest or apprehend a person under any other Act of Parliament may also authorize entry into a dwelling-house to effect the arrest and without prior announcement.

For notes on warrantless search of the home, see annotations following s. 529.3.

SYNOPSIS

This section sets out the circumstances in which a peace officer may enter a dwelling-house without prior announcement. The section contemplates two different circumstances. A judicial official when granting authorization to enter a dwelling-house may also authorize entry to effect an arrest without prior announcement. This authorization is dependent upon the judge or justice being satisfied by information on oath in writing that there are reasonable grounds to believe that prior announcement would expose the officer or another person to imminent bodily harm or death or result in the imminent loss or destruction of evidence relating to the commission of an indictable offence. Nevertheless, the warrant must include a condition that the officer only enter the dwelling-house if the officer has, immediately before entering, reasonable grounds to suspect that prior announcement would expose the officer or another person to imminent bodily harm or death or the officer has reasonable grounds to believe that prior announcement would result in the imminent loss or destruction of evidence relating to the commission of an indictable offence. The second circumstance contemplated by this section is where the officer is making a warrantless entry as authorized by s. 529.3 as a result of the exigent circumstances there set out. The officer may only enter the dwelling-house if the officer has, immediately before entering, reasonable grounds to suspect that prior announcement would expose the officer or another person to imminent bodily harm or death or the officer has reasonable grounds to believe that prior announcement would result in the imminent loss or destruction of evidence relating to the commission of an indictable offence. It would seem that, in enacting this section, Parliament did not necessarily intend to exclude other circumstances where, at common law and consistent with the Charter, entry without prior announcement is authorized. This provision and the companion provisions in ss. 529 to 529.2 and s. 529.5 were apparently enacted in response to the decision of the Supreme Court of Canada in *R. v. Feeney*, [1997] 2 S.C.R. 13, 115 C.C.C. (3d) 129, noted above under s. 529.

ANNOTATIONS

Note: the following cases were decided prior to the enactment of this section.

At common law, except in exigent circumstances, the requirements of prior announcement by police officers include giving notice of presence by knocking or ringing the doorbell, giving notice of authority by identifying themselves as law enforcement police officers and giving notice of purpose by stating a lawful reason for entry. Further, before forcing entry, police should, at a minimum, request admission and have admission denied: *R. v. Feeney*, [1997] 2 S.C.R. 13, 115 C.C.C. (3d) 129.

The requirement of prior announcement is not limited to a forcible entry and applies even where the officers enter private premises through an open door for the purpose of effecting an arrest, unless in the circumstances the open door can be construed as an invitation to enter: *R. v. Delong* (1989), 47 C.C.C. (3d) 402 (Ont. C.A.).

TELEWARRANT

529.5 If a peace officer believes that it would be impracticable in the circumstances to appear personally before a judge or justice to make an application for a warrant under section 529.1 or an authorization under section 529 or 529.4, the warrant or authorization may be issued on an information submitted by telephone or other means of telecommunication and, for that purpose, section 487.1 applies, with any modifications that the circumstances require, to the warrant or authorization. 1997, c. 39, s. 2.

CROSS-REFERENCES

"Justice" and "peace officer" are defined in s. 2. A warrant to arrest may be issued under various provisions of this Act. The most important provision is s. 507. Sections 511 and 512 set out the contents of the arrest warrant. Section 514 contains other provisions concerning execution of an arrest warrant. Under s. 20, a warrant may be executed on a holiday. A warrant is executed in accordance with ss. 29 and 10 of the Charter. For protection of persons executing warrants, see ss. 25 to 28. Section 528 deals with endorsing the warrant where the warrant cannot be executed in accordance with s. 514. Section 529 permits a justice or judge to include a term in an arrest warrant authorizing a peace officer to enter a dwelling-house for the purpose of arresting or apprehending a person. Section 529.1 permits a justice or judge to issue a warrant authorizing a peace officer to enter a dwelling-house for the purpose of arresting or apprehending a person, where a warrant is already in force anywhere in Canada or where grounds exist for a warrantless arrest. Section 529.2 requires the justice or judge to include terms and conditions in the warrant to ensure that the entry is reasonable in the circumstances. Section 529.3 allows for warrantless entry to effect an arrest in exigent circumstances. Section 529.4 sets out the circumstances in which a peace officer may enter without prior announcement. The provisions respecting issuance of a telewarrant are set out in s. 487.1.

Section 34.1 of the *Interpretation Act*, R.S.C. 1985, c. I-21, provides that any person who may issue a warrant to arrest or apprehend a person under any other Act of Parliament may also authorize entry into a dwelling-house to effect the arrest and without prior announcement.

SYNOPSIS

This section permits application for a telewarrant where it is impracticable to appear personally before a judge or justice to obtain a warrant to enter a dwelling-house or the authorization to enter or enter without announcement under s. 529 or s. 529.4.

Part XVII / LANGUAGE OF ACCUSED

LANGUAGE OF ACCUSED / Idem / Accused to be advised of right / Remand / Variation of order / Circumstances warranting order directing trial in both official languages.

530. (1) On application by an accused whose language is one of the official languages of Canada, made not later than

(*a*) the time of the appearance of the accused at which his trial date is set, if

(i) he is accused of an offence mentioned in section 553 or punishable on summary conviction, or

(ii) the accused is to be tried on an indictment preferred under section 577,

(*b*) the time of the accused's election, if the accused elects under section 536 to be tried by a provincial court judge or under section 536.1 to be tried by a judge without a jury and without having a preliminary inquiry, or

(*c*) the time when the accused is ordered to stand trial, if the accused

(i) is charged with an offence listed in section 469,

(ii) has elected to be tried by a court composed of a judge or a judge and jury, or

(iii) is deemed to have elected to be tried by a court composed of a judge and jury,

a justice of the peace, provincial court judge or judge of the Nunavut Court of Justice shall grant an order directing that the accused be tried before a justice of the peace, provincial court judge, judge or judge and jury, as the case may be, who speak the official language of Canada that is the language of the accused or, if the circumstances warrant, who speak both official languages of Canada.

(2) On application by an accused whose language is not one of the official languages of Canada, made not later than whichever of the times referred to in paragraphs (1)(*a*) to (*c*) is applicable, a justice of the peace or provincial court judge may grant an order directing that the accused be tried before a justice of the peace, provincial court judge, judge or judge and jury, as the case may be, who speak the official language of Canada in which the accused, in the opinion of the justice or provincial court judge, can best give testimony or, if the circumstances warrant, who speak both official languages of Canada.

(3) The justice of the peace or provincial court judge before whom an accused first appears shall ensure that they are advised of their right to apply for an order under subsection (1) or (2) and of the time before which such an application must be made.

(4) Where an accused fails to apply for an order under subsection (1) or (2) and the justice of the peace, provincial court judge or judge before whom the accused is to be tried, in this Part referred to as "the court", is satisfied that it is in the best interests of justice that the accused be tried before a justice of the peace, provincial court judge, judge or judge and jury who speak the official language of Canada that is the language of the accused or, if the language of the accused is not one of the official languages of Canada, the official language of Canada in which the accused, in the opinion of the court, can best give testimony, the court may, if it does not speak that language, by order remand the accused to be tried by a justice of the peace, provincial court judge, judge or judge and jury, as the case may be, who speak that language or, if the circumstances warrant, who speak both official languages of Canada.

(5) An order under this section that a trial be held in one of the official languages of Canada may, if the circumstances warrant, be varied by the court to require that it be held in both official languages of Canada, and vice versa.

(6) The facts that two or more accused who are to be tried together are each entitled to be tried before a justice of the peace, provincial court judge, judge or judge and jury who speak one of the official languages of Canada and that those official languages are different may constitute circumstances that warrant that an order be granted directing that they be tried before a justice of the peace, provincial court judge, judge or judge and jury who speak both official languages of Canada. 1977-78, c. 36, s. 1; R.S.C. 1985, c. 27 (1st Supp.), s. 94; 1999, c. 3, s. 34; 2008, c. 18, s. 18.

CROSS-REFERENCES

The terms "justice" and "provincial court judge" are defined in s. 2.

The procedure respecting conduct of the proceedings is set out in s. 530.1. Change of venue where necessary to facilitate the trial where an order is made under this section is provided for in s. 531. This Part does not derogate from other rights which may be afforded by provincial legislation, by virtue of s. 532. Provision for making regulations to carry out the provisions of this Part is provided for in s. 533. Where an order is made under this section, s. 530.01 requires the public prosecutor, on application of the accused, to provide a copy of the information or indictment translated into the official language used by the accused. Under s. 530.2, if an order is made for a bilingual proceeding, the judicial officer may make an order setting out the circumstances in which the prosecutor, justice and judge may use each official language. The order shall, to the extent possible, respect the right of the accused to use their official language. Section 531 provides for a change of venue, other than in New Brunswick, if the order under this section cannot be conveniently complied with in the territorial division in which the offence would ordinarily be tried.

Also see s. 841(3) which requires that any preprinted portions of a form set out in Part XXVIII shall be printed in both official languages.

SYNOPSIS

This section sets out the procedure whereby an accused can elect to be tried before a court (including a jury) which speaks one *or both* official languages.

Subsection (1), which deals with an accused whose mother tongue is either French or English, provides that the application in this regard shall be made not later than the time a trial date is fixed where: (a) the offence is indictable, but within the absolute jurisdiction of a provincial court judge; (b) the offence is a summary conviction matter; (c) proceedings are commenced by way of a "direct" indictment (s. 577), or (d) the accused "elects" to be tried before a provincial court judge. In cases where there is a preliminary inquiry, the application need not be made until the accused has been ordered to stand trial.

Under subsec. (2) a similar application can be made by an accused whose mother tongue is not one of the two official languages but who is able to testify in one, or both, of them.

Subsection (3) imposes upon the justice of the peace or provincial court judge before whom the accused first appears an obligation to ensure that the accused is advised of his or her rights in this regard.

Even if no application is made by the accused under this provision, subsec. (4) empowers the trial court to make the necessary order if it is satisfied that to do so would be in the best interests of the administration of justice. If the justice of the peace or judge who makes the order does not speak the necessary language(s), he can remand the accused to appear before someone who does.

Subsection (5) provides that any order made under this provision for a trial in only one official language can, if circumstances warrant, be varied to encompass both languages and vice versa. Under subsec. (6), one basis for making such an order is that accused who are to be tried together speak different official languages.

ANNOTATIONS

Constitutional considerations – In the companion cases of *Manitoba (Attorney General) v. Forest*, [1979] 2 S.C.R. 1032, 49 C.C.C. (2d) 353 (7:0), and *Quebec (Attorney General) v. Blaikie; Quebec (Attorney General) v. Laurier*, [1979] 2 S.C.R. 1016, 49 C.C.C. (2d) 359 (7:0), provincial legislation in Manitoba and Quebec respectively making English in the former and French in the latter the official language of, *inter alia,* the courts was held *ultra vires* as being in conflict with the *Manitoba Act, 1870* (Can.), c. 3, as confirmed by the *British North America Act, 1871*, in the case of Manitoba and in conflict with s. 133 of the *British North America Act, 1867*, in the case of Quebec. In both those provinces use of either official language in the courts is an entrenched right.

Section 16(3) of the Charter does not have the effect of constitutionalizing this provision: *R. v. Schneider* (2004), 192 C.C.C. (3d) 1, 247 D.L.R. (4th) 693 (N.S.C.A.), leave to appeal to S.C.C. refused [2005] 2 S.C.R. xi, 198 C.C.C. (3d) vi.

Sections 530 and 530.1 are intended to ensure equal access to the courts by accused persons who speak either official language. Those sections must be given a large and liberal interpretation in order to achieve that objective: *R. v. Munkonda* (2015), 324 C.C.C. (3d) 9 (Ont. C.A.).

"language of the accused" – The term "language of the accused" in this section is either official language to which the accused has a sufficient connection. It does not have to be the dominant language. If the accused has sufficient knowledge of an official language to instruct counsel, he or she will be able to assert that language is his or her language, regardless of his or her ability to speak the official language: *R. v. Beaulac*, [1999] 1 S.C.R. 768, 134 C.C.C. (3d) 481.

Circumstances where order to be made – The combined effect of this section and s. 530.1 is to permit the ordering of a bilingual trial being a trial before a judge and jury who speak both official languages but in which both English and French are used interchangeably as the working languages, depending upon who is speaking and in what context, and interpretation and translation are available if needed. Thus, where different accused, who are alleged to have participated in a common enterprise or conspiracy seek to be tried in different official languages of choice, severance is not mandatory and it would be open to the judge to order a joint bilingual trial: *R. v. Sarrazin* (2005), 195 C.C.C. (3d) 257, 75 O.R. (3d) 485 (Ont. C.A.). Similarly: *R. v. Garcia* (1990), 58 C.C.C. (3d) 43 (Que. S.C.). [And now see subsec. (6) which confirms the appropriateness of a bilingual trial in such circumstances.]

Duty to advise unrepresented accused [subsec. (3)] – It is not necessary for unrepresented accused to identify themselves as French speaking or state a preference for French prior to the judge notifying them of the right to apply for a trial in either official language. This provision, however, did not constitute a Charter violation as ss. 16 and 19 of the Charter do not apply to provincial courts which are established by provincial legislation rather than Parliament: *R. v. MacKenzie* (2004), 181 C.C.C. (3d) 485, 221 N.S.R. (2d) 51 (C.A.), leave to appeal to S.C.C. refused 191 C.C.C. (3d) vi.

Subsection (4) – Where a new trial has been ordered, the application is made under subsec. (4), rather than subsec. (1), and thus the order is discretionary. There is, however, a strong presumption in favour of granting the order because of the similarity between that situation and the one contemplated by subsec. (1): *R. v. Beaulac*, [1999] 1 S.C.R. 768, 134 C.C.C. (3d) 481.

In the context of subsec. (4), the term "best interests of justice" requires that the foremost consideration be the reasons for the delay in making the application. The trial judge must then consider other factors including whether the accused is represented by counsel, the language in which the evidence is available, the language of witnesses, whether a jury has been empanelled, whether witnesses have already testified, whether they are still available, whether proceedings can continue in a different language, the fact that there may be co-accused (which would indicate the need for separate trials), the need for counsel for the accused or the Crown to change, and the language ability of the judge. However, neither trial fairness nor mere administrative inconvenience is a relevant factor. Generally, the best interests of justice will be served by accepting the application of the accused to be tried in his official language. It was an error to refuse the order solely because the accused was fluent in the majority language (in this case English): *R. v. Beaulac, supra.*

Procedure on trial – The accused having requested a trial of a drinking and driving offence to be in the French language, the trial judge did not err in refusing to admit into evidence a breathalyzer certificate which was only in the English language. The Crown had made no attempt at trial to have the certificate translated: *R. v. Boudreau* (1990), 59 C.C.C. (3d) 436, 25 M.V.R. (2d) 103 (N.B.C.A.).

While there may be circumstances in which a court before trial would order translation of a document to enable the accused to make full answer and defence and to have a fair trial, the mere fact that the accused has chosen to have his trial in the French language pursuant to s. 530 does not thereby entitle him to have disclosure from the Crown and police provided to him in the French language: *R. v. Rodrigue* (1994), 91 C.C.C. (3d) 455 (Y.T.S.C.), affd 95 C.C.C. (3d) 129, 26 C.R.R. (2d) 175 (Y.T.C.A.), leave to appeal to S.C.C. refused 99 C.C.C. (3d) vi, 112 W.A.C. 240*n*.

Once an order is made that a trial shall proceed solely in the official language of the accused, the trial should comply with the terms of the order. In this case, the accused was denied the benefit of a trial in French, as the trial judge and Crown continued to speak English and simply provided the accused with a translator. The judge and prosecutor must communicate in the official language of the accused's choice so that the accused can understand the remarks of the judge and prosecutor in the original language spoken by them at trial: *R. v. Potvin* (2004), 186 C.C.C. (3d) 257, 69 O.R. (3d) 641 (C.A.).

The accused is not required to bring a formal application under this provision in order to have a trial in his official language of choice: *R. v. Dow* (2009), 245 C.C.C. (3d) 368 (Que. C.A.), leave to appeal to S.C.C. refused 245 C.C.C. (3d) vi.

Where one accused requested a trial in English and the other requested a trial in French, the trial judge did not err in ordering a bilingual trial with an interpretor in the circumstances: *R. v. Schneider* (2004), 188 C.C.C. (3d) 137, 226 N.S.R. (2d) 110 (C.A.), leave to appeal to S.C.C. refused 194 C.C.C. (3d) vi.

An order that a trial or preliminary inquiry be held before a judge or justice of the peace who speaks both official languages is an exception to the rule that an accused has an absolute right to a trial before a judge who speaks the official language of the accused. An order that a trial or preliminary inquiry be held before a bilingual judge will be made only "if the circumstances warrant". However, in the case of two or more accused who are to be tried together and who speak different official languages, the trial or preliminary inquiry is really a bilingual trial or preliminary inquiry, in the sense that there are accused who have the right to a trial in each of the two official languages and both rights operate within a single trial. In such cases, the accused retain their right to equal access to proceedings in their language notwithstanding the imposition of a bilingual proceeding, and the court and the prosecution must be bilingual and must not favour either of the official languages: *R. v. Munkonda*, 2015 ONCA 309.

The effect of an order for a bilingual trial or preliminary inquiry under s. 530 is that all court personnel whose presence is necessary to the proper conduct of the proceeding must be bilingual. To the extent that the presence of the court reporter is necessary for the proper conduct of the inquiry or the trial, the judge must ensure that the reporter is bilingual: *R. v. Mukonda, supra.*

TRANSLATION OF DOCUMENTS / Original version prevails.

530.01 (1) If an order is granted under section 530, a prosecutor — other than a private prosecutor — shall, on application by the accused,

(*a*) cause any portion of an information or indictment against the accused that is in an official language that is not that of the accused or that in which the accused can best give testimony to be translated into the other official language; and

(*b*) provide the accused with a written copy of the translated text at the earliest possible time.

(2) In the case of a discrepancy between the original version of a document and the translated text, the original version shall prevail. 2008, c. 18, s. 19.

SYNOPSIS

This section requires that a public prosecution provide translated copies of the indictment or information. If there is a discrepancy, the original prevails.

IF ORDER GRANTED.

530.1 If an order is granted under section 530,

(a) the accused and his counsel have the right to use either official language for all purposes during the preliminary inquiry and trial of the accused;

(b) the accused and his counsel may use either official language in written pleadings or other documents used in any proceedings relating to the preliminary inquiry or trial of the accused;

(c) any witness may give evidence in either official language during the preliminary inquiry or trial;

(c.1) the presiding justice or judge may, if the circumstances warrant, authorize the prosecutor to examine or cross-examine a witness in the official language of the witness even though it is not that of the accused or that in which the accused can best give testimony;

(d) the accused has a right to have a justice presiding over the preliminary inquiry who speaks the official language of the accused or both official languages, as the case may be;

(e) the accused has a right to have a prosecutor — other than a private prosecutor — who speaks the official language of the accused or both official languages, as the case may be;

(f) the court shall make interpreters available to assist the accused, his counsel or any witness during the preliminary inquiry or trial;

(g) the record of proceedings during the preliminary inquiry or trial shall include

(i) a transcript of everything that was said during those proceedings in the official language in which it was said,

(ii) a transcript of any interpretation into the other official language of what was said, and

(iii) any documentary evidence that was tendered during those proceedings in the official language in which it was tendered; and

(h) any trial judgment, including any reasons given therefor, issued in writing in either official language, shall be made available by the court in the official language that is the language of the accused. R.S.C. 1985, c. 31 (4th Supp.), s. 94; 2008, c. 18, s. 20.

CROSS-REFERENCES

The terms "justice" and "provincial court judge" are defined in s. 2.

Change of venue, where necessary to facilitate the trial where an order is made under s. 530, is provided for in s. 531. This Part does not derogate from other rights which may be afforded by provincial legislation, by virtue of s. 532. Provision for making regulations to carry out the provisions of this Part is provided for in s. 533.

Also see s. 841(3) which requires that any preprinted portions of a form set out in Part XXVIII shall be printed in both official languages.

Where an order is made under s. 530, s. 530.01 requires the public prosecutor, on application of the accused, to provide a copy of the information or indictment translated into the official language used by the accused. Under s. 530.2, if an order is made for a bilingual proceeding, the judicial officer may make an order setting out the circumstances in which the prosecutor, justice and judge may use each official language. The order shall, to the extent possible, respect the right of the accused to use their official language. Section 531 provides for a change of venue, other than in New Brunswick, if the order under s. 530 cannot be conveniently complied with in the territorial division in which the offence would ordinarily be tried.

SYNOPSIS

This section deals with the effect of an order made under s. 530. Where there is such an order, this section provides that: (a) the accused and defence counsel have the right to use either official language during the preliminary inquiry or trial; (b) the accused and defence counsel may use pleadings and documents in either official language during such proceedings; (c) any witness may give evidence in either official language; (c.1) the justice or judge may authorize the prosecutor to examine or cross-examine the witness, in the witness's official language; (d) the accused has the right to have a justice presiding over the preliminary inquiry who speaks the official language of the accused; (e) except in the case of private prosecutions, the accused has the right to a prosecutor who speaks the official language of the accused or is bilingual as the case may be; (f) interpreters shall be made available as required to the accused, defence counsel and witnesses during the preliminary inquiry or trial (this is also required by s. 14 of the *Canadian Charter of Rights and Freedoms*); (g) the record of the proceedings will be in the official language which was spoken, and will contain any interpretation which was given in the other official language, documents will be in the official language in which they were tendered; and (h) any written reasons will be made available in the official language of the accused.

ANNOTATIONS

This section is valid and applicable in Quebec. Where an order is made under s. 530, this section imposes an obligation on the Attorney General to choose a Crown counsel who is capable and agrees to conduct the trial in the official language of the accused. If it happens that during the trial this Crown counsel feels unable to proceed with the case in the language of the accused, s. 133 of the *Constitution Act, 1867* permits the counsel in Quebec to speak in French or English as the case may be. However, in such circumstances the judge should adjourn the trial to permit the Attorney General to find a replacement ready to continue the case in the language of the accused: *R. v. Cross* (1998), 128 C.C.C. (3d) 161, 165 D.L.R. (4th) 288 (Que. C.A.), leave to appeal to S.C.C. granted 132 C.C.C. (3d) vi, 169 D.L.R. (4th) vi.

This section applies to a bilingual trial, *i.e.* where the trial is ordered to be before a trier or triers who speak both official languages: *R. v. Beaulac*, [1999] 1 S.C.R. 768, 134 C.C.C. (3d) 481.

All Crown prosecutors in a bilingual trial must be bilingual and capable of participating fully in the trial in both languages: *R. v. Munkonda* (2015), 324 C.C.C. (3d) 9 (Ont. C.A.).

The accused could not be said to have waived his rights where on two occasions the judge asked the accused if it was agreeable if he spoke with counsel about certain legal matters in French and the accused gave his consent: *R. v. Dow* (2009), 245 C.C.C. (3d) 368 (Que. C.A.), leave to appeal to S.C.C. refused 245 C.C.C. (3d) vi.

Where the accused had received an order under s. 530 that he be tried in French, the Crown's use of English during an adjournment application violated the accused's right under s. 530.1(*e*). However, the violation was relatively minor and did not warrant setting aside the conviction: *R. v. Bujold* (2011), 276 C.C.C. (3d) 442 (N.B.C.A.).

Section 530.1(*b*) gives the accused the right to use either official language in written pleadings or other documents at the preliminary inquiry and trial. The Crown is not given the same right and must provide the documents in the accused's language. The obligation to make judgments available in the official language of the accused as set out in para. (*h*) applies to all judgments, including interlocutory and oral judgments. A summary or synopsis is not sufficient: *R. v. Munkonda, supra.*

LANGUAGE USED IN PROCEEDING / Right of the accused.

530.2 (1) If an order is granted directing that an accused be tried before a justice of the peace, provincial court judge, judge or judge and jury who speak both official languages, the justice or judge presiding over a preliminary inquiry or trial may, at the start of the proceeding, make an order setting out the circumstances in which, and the extent to which, the prosecutor and the justice or judge may use each official language.

(2) Any order granted under this section shall, to the extent possible, respect the right of the accused to be tried in his or her official language. 2008, c. 18, s. 21.

CROSS-REFERENCES

See Cross-References under s. 530.

SYNOPSIS

This section gives the judge or justice presiding at a bilingual proceeding to make an order setting out the circumstances in which, and the extent to which, the prosecutor, justice or judge may use each official language. The order shall, to the extent possible, respect the right of the accused to be tried in their official language.

ANNOTATIONS

In a bilingual trial or preliminary inquiry, the language rights of each of the accused must be respected to the extent possible, and provided that it is reasonable. The equality of the two official languages is a governing principle that is particularly important in a bilingual trial or preliminary inquiry since both languages, English and French, have the same official status in the proceeding. This means, for example, that, if an accused or his or her counsel addresses the court or the prosecution in the language of that accused, the prosecution or the court should interact with that accused or his or her counsel in that language. The duty to deal with each accused in his or her own language is not diminished if the proceeding becomes a bilingual proceeding. The rights of the accused and the obligation of the state and the court to provide the service are not reduced or diminished by the fact that an accused understands and speaks the language of the majority: *R. v. Munkonda* (2015), 324 C.C.C. (3d) 9 (Ont. C.A.).

CHANGE OF VENUE.

531. Despite any other provision of this Act but subject to any regulations made under section 533, if an order made under section 530 cannot be conveniently complied with in the territorial division in which the offence would otherwise be tried, the court shall, except if that territorial division is in the Province of New Brunswick, order that the trial of the accused be held in another territorial division in the same province. 1977-78, c. 36, s. 1; R.S. 1985, c. 27 (1st Supp.), s. 203; 2008, c. 18, s. 21.

CROSS-REFERENCES

The terms "justice", "provincial court judge" and "territorial division" are defined in s. 2. Procedure for an order for a trial in the official language of the accused is in s. 530. The procedure respecting conduct of the proceedings is set out in s. 530.1. This Part does not derogate from other rights which may be afforded by provincial legislation, by virtue of s. 532. Provision for making regulations to carry out the provisions of this Part is provided for in s. 533.

Also see s. 841(3) which requires that any preprinted portions of a form set out in Part XXVIII shall be printed in both official languages.

Provision for change of venue in other circumstances is provided for in ss. 599 and 600.

SYNOPSIS

This section provides that, except in New Brunswick, subject to any regulations made pursuant to s. 533, the court must make an order changing the venue of the trial of an accused to another location within the province where an order has been made under s. 530, and that order cannot be conveniently complied with in the territorial division in which the offence would otherwise be tried.

It is expected that such orders will be made only in jury trials. In all other situations, court officials will be able to arrange for a justice of the peace or judge fluent in the required language(s) to travel to the area where proceedings would normally be held.

SAVING.

532. Nothing in this Part or the *Official Languages Act* derogates from or otherwise adversely affects any right afforded by a law of a province in force on the coming into force of this Part in that province or thereafter coming into force relating to the language of proceedings or testimony in criminal matters that is not inconsistent with this Part or that Act. 1977-78, c. 36, s. 1.

CROSS-REFERENCES

Procedure for an order for a trial in the official language of the accused is in s. 530.

The procedure respecting conduct of the proceedings is set out in s. 530.1. Change of venue where necessary to facilitate the trial where an order is made under s. 530 is provided for in s. 531. Provision for making regulations to carry out the provisions of this Part is provided for in s. 533.

Also see s. 841(3) which requires that any preprinted portions of a form set out in Part XXVIII shall be printed in both official languages.

ANNOTATIONS

As a result of pre-Confederation legislation still in force in Alberta an accused and his counsel have the right to use the French language for all purposes during his preliminary hearing and trial but the presiding judge or the jury need not be able to comprehend the French language without an interpreter: *R. v. Paquette* (1987), 38 C.C.C. (3d) 333, [1988] 1 W.W.R. 97 (Alta. C.A.). The same pre-Confederation legislation was also considered in Saskatchewan in *R. v. Mercure*, [1988] 1 S.C.R. 234, 39 C.C.C. (3d) 385 (6:2), in relation, however, to a trial of a provincial offence. It was there held that while the defendant was entitled to use French and to have his plea entered in French the defendant did not have the right to insist on a trial before a judge who understood that language without an interpreter.

REGULATIONS.

533. The Lieutenant Governor in Council of a province may make regulations generally for carrying into effect the purposes and provisions of this Part in the province and the Commissioner of Yukon, the Commissioner of the Northwest Territories and the Commissioner of Nunavut may make regulations generally for carrying into effect the purposes and provisions of this Part in Yukon, the Northwest Territories and Nunavut, respectively. 1977-78, c. 36, s. 1; 1993, c. 28, Sch. III, s. 33; 2002, c. 7, s. 144.

CROSS-REFERENCES

Procedure for an order for a trial in the official language of the accused is in s. 530. The procedure respecting conduct of the proceedings is set out in s. 530.1. This Part does not derogate from other rights which may be afforded by provincial legislation, by virtue of s. 532. Change of venue, where necessary to facilitate the trial where an order is made under s. 530, is provided for in s. 531.

Also see s. 841(3) which requires that any preprinted portions of a form set out in Part XXVIII shall be printed in both official languages.

---

534. [*Repealed*, 1997, c. 18, s. 63.]

Part XVIII / PROCEDURE ON PRELIMINARY INQUIRY

Jurisdiction

INQUIRY BY JUSTICE.

535. If an accused who is charged with an indictable offence is before a justice and a request has been made for a preliminary inquiry under subsection 536(4) or 536.1(3), the justice shall, in accordance with this Part, inquire into the charge and any other indictable offence, in respect of the same transaction, founded on the facts that are disclosed by the evidence taken in accordance with this Part. R.S., c. C-34, s. 463; R.S.C. 1985, c. 27 (1st Supp.), s. 96; 2002, c. 13, s. 24.

CROSS-REFERENCES

The term "justice" is defined in s. 2. As a matter of practice preliminary inquiries are usually conducted by provincial court judges. For further discussion re procedure on preliminary inquiries see *Note on procedure at preliminary inquiry* under s. 537.

SYNOPSIS

This provision confers general jurisdiction on a "justice" to deal with accused persons, in accordance with Part XVIII, who are charged with indictable offences.

Section 2 defines "justice" as including justices of the peace and provincial court judges. Local practice will determine which functions are carried out by a justice and which by a judge. For the most part, it is the provincial court judge who will deal with matters of bail and election, and preside over preliminary inquiries.

ANNOTATIONS

In *R. v. Mairs* (1961), 130 C.C.C. 361, 35 C.R. 265 (B.C.S.C.), it was held, following *R. v. Hughes* (1879), 4 Q.B.D. 614, and *R. v. Shaw* (1865), 10 Cox. C.C. 66, that process is not necessary to the jurisdiction of the justices to hear and adjudicate and that when a person is before justices who have jurisdiction to try the case they need not inquire how he came there but may try it.

If the justice is of the opinion that the charge does not reveal an offence known to law and is an absolute nullity, the accused is not "charged with an indictable offence" and the justice may discharge him without taking evidence: *R. v. Bolduc* (1980), 60 C.C.C. (2d) 357, 20 C.R. (3d) 372 (Que. C.A.), affd [1982] 1 S.C.R. 573, 68 C.C.C. (2d) 413 (7:0).

Aside from determining whether the charge in the information is valid on its face, the justice presiding at a preliminary inquiry has no jurisdiction to inquire into the validity of the allegation contained in the information itself, by embarking on an inquiry as to whether or not the informant had reasonable grounds for swearing the information: *R. v. Hislop* (1983), 7 C.C.C. (3d) 240, 36 C.R. (3d) 29 (Ont. C.A.), leave to appeal to S.C.C. refused November 7, 1983.

REMAND BY JUSTICE TO PROVINCIAL COURT JUDGE IN CERTAIN CASES / Election before justice in certain cases / Procedure where accused elects trial by provincial court judge / Request for preliminary inquiry / Endorsement on the information / Preliminary inquiry if two or more accused / When no request for preliminary inquiry / Jurisdiction.

536. (1) Where an accused is before a justice other than a provincial court judge charged with an offence over which a provincial court judge has absolute jurisdiction under section 553, the justice shall remand the accused to appear before a provincial

court judge having jurisdiction in the territorial division in which the offence is alleged to have been committed.

(2) If an accused is before a justice charged with an indictable offence, other than an offence listed in section 469, and the offence is not one over which a provincial court judge has absolute jurisdiction under section 553, the justice shall, after the information has been read to the accused, put the accused to an election in the following words:

> **You have the option to elect to be tried by a provincial court judge without a jury and without having had a preliminary inquiry; or you may elect to be tried by a judge without a jury; or you may elect to be tried by a court composed of a judge and jury. If you do not elect now, you are deemed to have elected to be tried by a court composed of a judge and jury. If you elect to be tried by a judge without a jury or by a court composed of a judge and jury or if you are deemed to have elected to be tried by a court composed of a judge and jury, you will have a preliminary inquiry only if you or the prosecutor requests one. How do you elect to be tried?**

(3) Where an accused elects to be tried by a provincial court judge, the justice shall endorse on the information a record of the election and shall

- **(*a*) where the justice is not a provincial court judge, remand the accused to appear and plead to the charge before a provincial court judge having jurisdiction in the territorial division in which the offence is alleged to have been committed; or**
- **(*b*) where the justice is a provincial court judge, call on the accused to plead to the charge and if the accused does not plead guilty, proceed with the trial or fix a time for the trial.**

(4) If an accused elects to be tried by a judge without a jury or by a court composed of a judge and jury or does not elect when put to the election or is deemed under paragraph 565(1)(*b*) to have elected to be tried by a court composed of a judge and jury or is charged with an offence listed in section 469, the justice shall, subject to section 577, on the request of the accused or the prosecutor made at that time or within the period fixed by rules of court made under section 482 or 482.1 or, if there are no such rules, by the justice, hold a preliminary inquiry into the charge.

(4.1) If an accused elects to be tried by a judge without a jury or by a court composed of a judge and jury or does not elect when put to the election or is deemed under paragraph 565(1)(*b*) to have elected to be tried by a court composed of a judge and jury or is charged with an offence listed in section 469, the justice shall endorse on the information and, if the accused is in custody, on the warrant of remand, a statement showing

- **(*a*) the nature of the election or deemed election of the accused or that the accused did not elect, as the case may be; and**
- **(*b*) whether the accused or the prosecutor has requested that a preliminary inquiry be held.**

(4.2) If two or more persons are jointly charged in an information and one or more of them make a request for a preliminary inquiry under subsection (4), a preliminary inquiry must be held with respect to all of them.

(4.3) If no request for a preliminary inquiry is made under subsection (4), the justice shall fix the date for the trial or the date on which the accused must appear in the trial court to have the date fixed.

(5) Where a justice before whom a preliminary inquiry is being or is to be held has not commenced to take evidence, any justice having jurisdiction in the province where the offence with which the accused is charged is alleged to have been committed has jurisdiction for the purposes of subsection (4). R.S., c. C-34, s. 464; R.S.C. 1985, c. 27 (1st Supp.), s. 96; 2002, c. 13, s. 25; 2004, c. 12, s. 9.

CROSS-REFERENCES

The terms "justice", "provincial court judge" and "territorial division" are defined in s. 2. Territorial jurisdiction is generally dealt with in Part XIV. The pleas that the accused may enter are set out in ss. 606 to 613. Validity of an information is dealt with in ss. 580 to 601. The jurisdiction of the provincial court judge to try the accused is set out in Part XIX. Where the accused refuses to elect under this section then by virtue of s. 565(1)(*c*) the accused is deemed to have elected trial by judge and jury. The accused may, however, re-elect in accordance with s. 561. Where accused who are jointly charged fail to elect the same mode of trial, pursuant to s. 567, the justice may decline to record the elections and the accused are deemed to have elected trial by judge and jury under s. 565(1)(*b*). Where the accused or the prosecutor request a preliminary inquiry the party making the request is to identify the issues and the witnesses required under s. 536.3. The justice may hold a hearing under s. 536.4 to assist in managing the conduct of the hearing. Under s. 536.5 the parties may agree to limit the scope of the preliminary inquiry and the agreement is then filed with the court. An election or re-election by an accused in respect of mode of trial may be made in writing without the accused's attendance.

For further discussion regarding procedure on preliminary inquiries, see Note on procedure at preliminary inquiry under s. 537.

Note on mode of trial – The scheme of the *Criminal Code* is to classify offences as pure indictable [*e.g.*, robbery, s. 344], purely summary [*e.g.*, soliciting, s. 213] or hybrid, *i.e.*, the prosecution may elect whether to proceed by way of summary conviction or by indictment [*e.g.*, assault, s. 266]. The effect of s. 468 is that the superior court of criminal jurisdiction may try any purely indictable offence or any hybrid offence where the prosecution elects to proceed by way of indictment. Other courts of criminal jurisdiction (defined in s. 2) may, however, try indictable offences except those offences listed in s. 469 [*e.g.*, murder, s. 235]. The offences listed in s. 469 may only be tried by the superior court of criminal jurisdiction with a jury subject to a re-election in conformity with s. 473. Indictable offences not listed in s. 469 fall into two categories. For the majority of the indictable offences not listed in s. 469 the accused may elect his mode of trial as set out in s. 536(2) and within limits may change his election [see, *e.g.*, s. 561]. While the Attorney General is given a narrow discretion to override this election and require a jury trial under s. 568 in the circumstances defined therein and in addition a provincial court judge has a discretion to override or not record an accused's election for trial by provincial court judge and hold a preliminary inquiry [see for example ss. 555 and 567] the thrust of the provisions is to give the accused the right to determine the manner of trial. [In those provinces which still maintain two levels of courts in addition to the provincial court, it is in the discretion of the Crown whether to place the indictment in the superior court or the other court, however described, *e.g.*, county court, where the accused elects trial other than by provincial court judge.] The other group of offences are those offences listed in s. 553 [*e.g.*, keeping common bawdy house, s. 210(1)] which fall within the absolute jurisdiction of a provincial court judge, meaning that the accused does not have a normal election as to the mode of trial under s. 536(2). Nevertheless, the other courts with jurisdiction to try indictable offences have jurisdiction to try the offences listed in s. 553 if the provincial court judge elects not to try the offence and requires that the case proceed by way of preliminary inquiry pursuant to s. 555(1), or in the course of the trial it is disclosed that in fact the offence is not one over which the provincial court judge has absolute jurisdiction, in which case the accused must then be put to his election under s. 536(2) [for example a charge of theft of goods of a value not exceeding $5,000 where the evidence discloses that the value of the goods exceeds $5,000].

For all summary conviction offences meaning purely summary conviction or hybrid offences where the prosecution elects to proceed by way of summary conviction only the summary conviction court (defined in s. 785) may try the accused. The procedure for trial of summary conviction offences generally resembles trial of an indictable offence by a provincial court judge but that procedure including special rights of appeal is set out in Part XXVII.

As to procedures in Nunavut, see ss. 536.1, 554(2), 555.1, 561.1, 562.1, 565(1.1), 566.1, 567.1, 569 and Part XIX.1.

SYNOPSIS

This section sets out the general procedures to be followed in the provincial court in dealing with an accused charged with an indictable offence.

If the accused appears before a justice of the peace and the offence is one within the absolute jurisdiction of a provincial court judge, the justice must, under subsec. (1), remand the accused to appear before a judge in the territorial division in which the offence is alleged to have occurred.

Subsection (2) sets out the language to be used where the offence is one for which the accused has an "election" as to the mode of trial (*i.e.*, provincial court judge, judge alone or judge and jury). This will occur where the offence is not one within the absolute jurisdiction of a provincial court judge (s. 533), or is one that must proceed before a superior court (s. 469).

Under subsec. (3), where the election for trial in provincial court is made before a justice, the accused will be remanded to appear before a judge for the taking of a plea and the fixing of a date for hearing. Of course, if the accused is already before a judge, he or she can deal with these matters. There is no requirement that the "election" be put at the accused's first appearance before a justice or judge. Often this will be deferred until the accused has had sufficient time to retain and be advised by counsel.

Where the election is for trial other than before a provincial court judge, or the accused is deemed to have elected judge and jury or is charged with an offence listed in s. 469, such as murder, a preliminary inquiry will be held only if the accused or the prosecutor requests one (subsec. (4)). If one of several jointly charged accused requests a preliminary inquiry, a preliminary inquiry must be held with respect to all of them (subsec. (4.2)). If no request is made for a preliminary inquiry, the justice either fixes a trial date or a date for the accused to appear in the trial court (subsec. (4.3)).

If no evidence has yet been called, subsec. (5) permits the hearing to be conducted by a justice or judge other than the one before whom the accused elected. (Also see s. 547.1 — justice unable to continue.)

ANNOTATIONS

Form of election – The form of election should be put to the accused substantially in the form in which it is set out in this subsection and in fact courts should follow the precise language of the subsection. In particular, merely asking the accused: "How do you elect to be tried?" is not sufficient to give the court jurisdiction to hold a preliminary hearing where counsel replies that he elects to be tried by "judge alone": *R. v. Leske*, [1968] 1 C.C.C. 347 (Alta. S.C. App. Div.).

Election by accused – In *R. v. Karpuk* (1962), 133 C.C.C. 108 (Ont. C.A.), a conviction was quashed when it appeared that the reply of the accused, when asked to elect, left no doubt that he was considering trial forthwith as against trial at a later date, rather than the alternative modes of trial open to him.

It was held in *R. v. Bobyk*, [1963] 2 C.C.C. 91 (Alta. S.C. App. Div.), that the consent by which the accused foregoes the privilege of trial by jury must be given in a manner that makes it clear beyond doubt that he has consented to forego that right. The consent cannot be inferred from the conduct of the accused nor given otherwise than by an express consent given openly in court.

Despite the fact that the election does not appear in the transcript the endorsement on the information as to the accused's election constitutes sufficient proof of the compliance with this section in the absence of evidence to the contrary: *R. v. Squires* (1977), 35 C.C.C. (2d) 325 (Nfld. C.A.).

Absent a valid waiver, the failure to put the accused to his election in terms which at least substantially comply with the section is a procedural error resulting in a loss of jurisdiction. In this case, the Crown's request that the accused make an election and defence counsel's indication that the accused elected a trial by provincial court judge constituted a valid waiver of the requirement that the accused be formally put to his election: *R. v. Mitchell* (1997), 121 C.C.C. (3d) 139 (Ont. C.A.). See also: *R. v. Shia* (2015), 320 C.C.C. (3d) 111 (Ont. C.A.).

Defence counsel's statement when setting a date that he intended to elect a provincial court trial did not on its own amount to a waiver of s. 536(2). Subsequent appearances where no mention of election was made were sufficient to conclude that the formal election had been waived. Every action taken by the accused, through his counsel, was consistent with an election to proceed with a provincial court trial and inconsistent with any equivocation as to that choice: *R. v. Vuong* (2010), 264 C.C.C. (3d) 39 (Ont. C.A.).

In *R. v. Varcoe* (2007), 219 C.C.C. (3d) 397, however, the Ontario Court of Appeal held that, although an unrepresented accused was advised that he could be tried by judge and jury, judge of the Superior Court or provincial court judge, he was not informed of the right to a preliminary inquiry. The failure to do so constituted a loss of jurisdiction, which could not be cured on appeal.

Where there was virtually a complete failure to comply with these procedural requirements including a failure to read the information to the accused, no election as to the mode of trial and no plea taken, the proceedings were defective to the point of amount to a miscarriage of justice: *R. v. Spence* (2001), 46 C.R. (5th) 387 (B.C.C.A.).

Where the accused receives no advice from counsel as to his options in respect of election, the accused has effectively been denied his right to choose his mode of trial. Proceeding against the accused without allowing him to make an informed election constitutes a miscarriage of justice, and the accused need not establish further prejudice: *R. v. Stark* (2017), 347 C.C.C. (3d) 73 (Ont. C.A.).

Delay in putting to election – In *R. v. Doyle*, [1977] 1 S.C.R. 597, 29 C.C.C. (2d) 177 (9:0), it was held that what would have amounted to a delay of almost eight months before the accused was put to his election involved a loss of jurisdiction over the accused. Ritchie J., referring to [now] s. 536 stated as follows:

> In my view, the whole structure of the procedural provisions of the *Code* which deal with the treatment of persons immediately after they have been arrested is designed to provide a speedy disposition of their cases. As I have said, the arresting officer is required to bring such a person before a Magistrate within 24 hours, and the duties with which a Magistrate is thereafter seized are all phrased in mandatory langauge so that I am unable to agree with the view expressed in the Newfoundland Court of Appeal which culminates in the present case in authorization of a delay of eight months between the arrest and the opportunity to elect for trial. In my view, the failure of both Magistrates to put the accused to his election as required by the *Code* was a clear error which of itself involved the loss of jurisdiction over the accused.

In *R. v. Aiello* (1977), 33 C.C.C. (2d) 280 (Ont. H.C.J.), it was held that under s. 537(1)(*a*) the Magistrate has power to adjourn the inquiry for any sufficient reason which would include an adjournment to enable the accused to retain counsel so that an intelligent election under this subsection can be made. Further, even if the failure to put the accused to his election resulted in a loss of jurisdiction it was only loss of jurisdiction over the person which would be regained when the accused appeared in court again on the charge.

The mere failure to put the accused to his election at the first or any particular subsequent appearance will not result in loss of jurisdiction but the refusal to put the accused to his election when he so requests will result in a loss of jurisdiction over the accused: *R. v. Chaisson* (1984), 15 C.C.C. (3d) 50 (Ont. H.C.J.).

In *R. v. Geszthelyi* (1977), 33 C.C.C. (2d) 543 (B.C.C.A.), this section was interpreted as merely prescribing the order which is to be followed in the proceedings but does not fix the time for making the election. Thus jurisdiction was not lost where the accused was not put to his election on his first appearance. Further, the power of adjournment under s. 537(1)(*a*) exists throughout the proceedings and is not dependent on the accused having been given his election at the outset.

Failure to endorse election [subsec. (4)] – It was held in relation to the predecessor to this subsection that failure to endorse the nature of the election was fatal to the conviction: *R. v.*

MacDonald (1974), 18 C.C.C. (2d) 136 (N.S.S.C. App. Div.); but the justice need not set out the entire subsec. (2). This subsection is sufficiently complied with if a memorandum as to how the accused elected is endorsed on the information: *R. v. Squires* (1977), 35 C.C.C. (2d) 325 (Nfld. C.A.). And in *R. v. Sagutch* (1991), 63 C.C.C. (3d) 569 (B.C.C.A.), it was held that, while the failure of the judge to endorse the election was a jurisdictional error, the accused's appeal from the dismissal of an application to quash the order to stand trial could be dismissed pursuant to s. 686(1)(*b*)(iv).

REMAND BY JUSTICE — NUNAVUT / Election before justice in certain cases — Nunavut / Request for preliminary inquiry — Nunavut / Endorsement on the information / Preliminary inquiry if two or more accused / Procedure if accused elects trial by judge — Nunavut / Jurisdiction — Nunavut / Application to Nunavut.

536.1 (1) If an accused is before a justice of the peace charged with an indictable offence mentioned in section 553, the justice of the peace shall remand the accused to appear before a judge.

(2) If an accused is before a justice of the peace or a judge charged with an indictable offence, other than an offence mentioned in section 469 or 553, the justice of the peace or judge shall, after the information has been read to the accused, put the accused to an election in the following words:

> **You have the option to elect to be tried by a judge without a jury or to be tried by a court composed of a judge and jury. If you do not elect now, you are deemed to have elected to be tried by a court composed of a judge and jury. If you elect to be tried by a judge without a jury or by a court composed of a judge and jury or if you are deemed to have elected to be tried by a court composed of a judge and jury, you will have a preliminary inquiry only if you or the prosecutor requests one. How do you elect to be tried?**

(3) If an accused elects to be tried by a judge without a jury or by a court composed of a judge and jury or does not elect when put to the election or is deemed under paragraph 565(1)(*b*) to have elected to be tried by a court composed of a judge and jury or is charged with an offence listed in section 469, the justice or judge shall, subject to section 577, on the request of the accused or the prosecutor made at that time or within the period fixed by rules of court made under section 482 or 482.1 or, if there are no such rules, by the judge or justice, hold a preliminary inquiry into the charge.

(4) If an accused elects to be tried by a judge without a jury or by a court composed of a judge and jury or does not elect when put to the election or is deemed under paragraph 565(1)(*b*) to have elected to be tried by a court composed of a judge and jury or is charged with an offence listed in section 469, the justice or judge shall endorse on the information and, if the accused is in custody, on the warrant of remand, a statement showing

(*a*) the nature of the election or deemed election of the accused or that the accused did not elect, as the case may be; and

(*b*) whether the accused or the prosecutor has requested that a preliminary inquiry be held.

(4.1) If two or more persons are jointly charged in an information and one or more of them make a request for a preliminary inquiry under subsection (3), a preliminary inquiry must be held with respect to all of them.

(4.2) If no request for a preliminary inquiry is made under subsection (3),

(*a*) if the accused is before a justice of the peace, the justice of the peace shall remand the accused to appear and plead to the charge before a judge; or

(*b*) if the accused is before a judge, the judge shall

(i) if the accused elects to be tried by a judge without a jury, call on the accused to plead to the charge and if the accused does not plead guilty, proceed with the trial or fix a time for the trial, or

(ii) if the accused elects or is deemed to have elected to be tried by a court composed of a judge and jury, fix a time for the trial.

(5) If a justice of the peace before whom a preliminary inquiry is being or is to be held has not commenced to take evidence, any justice of the peace having jurisdiction in Nunavut has jurisdiction for the purpose of subsection (3).

(6) This section, and not section 536, applies in respect of criminal proceedings in Nunavut. 1999, c. 3, s. 35; 2002, c. 13, s. 26; 2004, c. 12, s. 10.

CROSS-REFERENCES

In view of the unique court system established for Nunavut, special provision has been made for elections and trial in that territory as well as for review of certain interlocutory orders. These provisions must be read with the provisions of the *Nunavut Act* that establish the Nunavut Court of Justice and the Court of Appeal of Nunavut as a superior court (s. 32 of the *Nunavut Act*).

The judges of the Nunavut Court of Justice not only exercise the jurisdiction of a superior court but may also exercise or perform the powers, duties and functions given by the *Criminal Code* to a provincial court judge or justice of the peace. However, when exercising such functions, the judge does so as a judge of a superior court except that when presiding at a preliminary inquiry, the judge has no jurisdiction to grant a remedy under s. 24 of the *Canadian Charter of Rights and Freedoms* (s. 34 of the *Nunavut Act* and s. 573 of the Code). Certain of those decisions are nevertheless reviewable under Part XIX.1, in accordance with s. 573.1, by a single judge of the Court of Appeal of Nunavut in the same manner that a decision or order of a provincial court judge or justice in the rest of Canada would be reviewable by a judge of the superior court. The decisions or orders that may be reviewed relate to a warrant or summons, the conduct of a preliminary inquiry, a subpoena, publication of the proceedings or access to the courtroom, refusal to quash an information or detention, and disposal or forfeiture of any thing seized under a warrant or order. Section 573.1(3) sets out the grounds for granting relief in respect of such an order or decision and are similar to the grounds developed at common law in relation to the extraordinary remedies. The relief that may be granted under s. 573.1(4) is similar to relief that may be granted by superior court judges in the rest of Canada on similar applications and may include a remedy under s. 24(1) of the *Canadian Charter of Rights and Freedoms*. Section 573.2 also preserves *habeas corpus* in relation to certain proceedings in the Nunavut Court of Justice. The application is made to a single judge of the Court of Appeal. An appeal lies to the full court of appeal from orders made under Part XIX.1 (ss. 573.1(7) and 573.2(3)). Section 536.1 sets out the normal right of an election for indictable offences tried in Nunavut. If the offence would be within the absolute jurisdiction of a provincial court judge in the rest of Canada, it is tried by a judge of the Nunavut Court of Justice without a jury in accordance with s. 553. Where the accused has an election under subsec. (2), the trial, whether or not the accused had a preliminary inquiry, will be before a judge of the Nunavut Court of Justice (s. 554) and a jury, if the accused so elects. If the accused elects to have a preliminary inquiry, that inquiry may be before either a justice of the peace or a judge of the Nunavut Court of Justice. A judge of the Nunavut Court of Justice conducting a trial under s. 553 or 554 in circumstances where the trial would have been before a provincial court judge in the rest of Canada may decide to hold a preliminary inquiry and in some circumstances may be required to put the accused to his election in accordance with s. 555.1. Sections 561.1, 562.1 and 563.1 set out the accused's rights of re-election and the procedure following a re-election in Nunavut. The case of multiple accused making different elections is dealt with in s. 567.1. Where the trial is before a judge alone of the Nunavut Court of Justice in circumstances where in the rest of Canada the trial would be by a superior court judge alone, the trial, as in the rest of Canada, is on an indictment rather than an information (s. 566.1). Section 565(1.1) sets out circumstances where the accused is deemed to have elected trial by a judge of the Nunavut Court of Justice and a jury, as where the judge decided to hold a preliminary inquiry under s. 555.1. Further, under s. 569 the Attorney

General may require a jury trial where the accused is charged with an offence punishable by more than five years.

Section 686(5.01), (5.1) and (5.2) deal with the procedure on a new trial ordered by the Court of Appeal of Nunavut.

With respect to summary convictions proceedings, where the summary conviction trial was conducted by a judge of the Nunavut Court of Justice, the appeal under s. 813 or s. 830 is to a single judge of the Court of Appeal of Nunavut (ss. 812(2) and 829(2)). In such a case, a further appeal lies to the full Court of Appeal with leave (s. 839(1.1)). Aside from these differences, the summary conviction procedure in Nunavut is the same as in the rest of Canada.

ELECTIONS AND RE-ELECTIONS IN WRITING.

536.2 An election or a re-election by an accused in respect of a mode of trial may be made by submission of a document in writing without the personal appearance of the accused. 2002, c. 13, s. 27.

Procedures before Preliminary Inquiry

STATEMENT OF ISSUES AND WITNESSES.

536.3 If a request for a preliminary inquiry is made, the prosecutor or, if the request was made by the accused, counsel for the accused shall, within the period fixed by rules of court made under section 482 or 482.1 or, if there are no such rules, by the justice, provide the court and the other party with a statement that identifies

(*a*) the issues on which the requesting party wants evidence to be given at the inquiry; and

(*b*) the witnesses that the requesting party wants to hear at the inquiry. 2002, c. 13, s. 27.

CROSS-REFERENCES

See *Note on procedure at preliminary inquiry* under s. 537.

ANNOTATIONS

This provision does not apply to an unrepresented accused: *R. v. LeBlanc* (2009), 250 C.C.C. (3d) 29, 352 N.B.R. (2d) 333 (C.A.).

ORDER FOR HEARING / Agreement to be recorded.

536.4 (1) The justice before whom a preliminary inquiry is to be held may order, on application of the prosecutor or the accused or on the justice's own motion, that a hearing be held, within the period fixed by rules of court made under section 482 or 482.1 or, if there are no such rules, by the justice, to

(*a*) assist the parties to identify the issues on which evidence will be given at the inquiry;

(*b*) assist the parties to identify the witnesses to be heard at the inquiry, taking into account the witnesses' needs and circumstances; and

(*c*) encourage the parties to consider any other matters that would promote a fair and expeditious inquiry.

(2) When the hearing is completed, the justice shall record any admissions of fact agreed to by the parties and any agreement reached by the parties. 2002, c. 13, s. 27.

CROSS-REFERENCES

See *Note on procedure at preliminary inquiry* under s. 537.

AGREEMENT TO LIMIT SCOPE OF PRELIMINARY INQUIRY.

536.5 Whether or not a hearing is held under section 536.4 in respect of a preliminary inquiry, the prosecutor and the accused may agree to limit the scope of the preliminary inquiry to specific issues. An agreement shall be filed with the court or recorded under subsection 536.4(2), as the case may be. 2002, c. 13, s. 27.

CROSS-REFERENCES

See *Note on procedure at preliminary inquiry* under s. 537.

Powers of Justice

POWERS OF JUSTICE / Section 715 / Inappropriate questioning / Change of venue.

537. (1) A justice acting under this Part may

(*a*) adjourn an inquiry from time to time and change the place of hearing, where it appears to be desirable to do so by reason of the absence of a witness, the inability of a witness who is ill to attend at the place where the justice usually sits or for any other sufficient reason;

(*b*) remand the accused to custody for the purposes of the *Identification of Criminals Act;*

(*b*) [*Repealed* (old provision). 1991, c. 43, s. 9.]

(*c*) except where the accused is authorized pursuant to Part XVI to be at large, remand the accused to custody in a prison by warrant in Form 19;

(*d*) resume an inquiry before the expiration of a period for which it has been adjourned with the consent of the prosecutor and the accused or his counsel;

(*e*) order in writing, in Form 30, that the accused be brought before him, or any other justice for the same territorial division, at any time before the expiration of the time for which the accused has been remanded;

(*f*) grant or refuse permission to the prosecutor or his counsel to address him in support of the charge, by way of opening or summing up or by way of reply on any evidence that is given on behalf of the accused;

(*g*) receive evidence on the part of the prosecutor or the accused, as the case may be, after hearing any evidence that has been given on behalf of either of them;

(*h*) order that no person other than the prosecutor, the accused and their counsel shall have access to or remain in the room in which the inquiry is held, where it appears to him that the ends of justice will be best served by so doing;

(*i*) regulate the course of the inquiry in any way that appears to the justice to be consistent with this Act and that, unless the justice is satisfied that to do so would be contrary to the best interests of the administration of justice, is in accordance with any admission of fact or agreement recorded under subsection 536.4(2) or agreement made under section 536.5;

(*j*) where the prosecutor and the accused so agree, permit the accused to appear by counsel or by closed-circuit television or any other means that allow the court and the accused to engage in simultaneous visual and oral communication, for any part of the inquiry other than a part in which the evidence of a witness is taken;

(*j*.1) permit, on the request of the accused, that the accused be out of court during the whole or any part of the inquiry on any conditions that the justice considers appropriate; and

(*k*) for any part of the inquiry other than a part in which the evidence of a witness is taken, require an accused who is confined in prison to appear by closed-circuit television or any other means that allow the court and the accused to engage in simultaneous visual and oral communication, if the accused is given

the opportunity to communicate privately with counsel, in a case in which the accused is represented by counsel.

(1.01) Where a justice grants a request under paragraph (1)(*j*.1), the Court must inform the accused that the evidence taken during his or her absence could still be admissible under section 715.

(1.1) A justice acting under this Part shall order the immediate cessation of any part of an examination or cross-examination of a witness that is, in the opinion of the justice, abusive, too repetitive or otherwise inappropriate.

(2) [*Repealed* [old provision], 1991, c. 43, s. 9.]

(2) Where a justice changes the place of hearing under paragraph (1)(*a*) to a place in the same province, other than a place in a territorial division in which the justice has jurisdiction, any justice who has jurisdiction in the place to which the hearing is changed may continue the hearing. R.S., c. C-34, s. 465; R.S.,. c. 2 (2nd Supp.), s. 6; 1972, c. 13, s. 38; 1974-75-76, c. 93, s. 58; 1991, c. 43, s. 9; 1994, c. 44, s. 53; 1997, c. 18, s. 64; 2002, c. 13, s. 28; 2008, c. 18, s. 22.

(3) and (4) [*Repealed*, 1991, c. 43, s. 9.].

CROSS-REFERENCES

The term "justice" is defined in s. 2. As a matter or practice preliminary inquiries are usually conducted by provincial court judges.

Note on procedure at preliminary inquiry – This section, in general, sets out the powers of the justice or provincial court judge presiding at a preliminary inquiry and, in particular, deals with adjournment of the inquiry and orders directing that the accused attend for observation or be remanded for observation. Where an issue of fitness to stand trial arises at the preliminary inquiry, then the procedure to be followed is set out in ss. 672.11 to 672.2 and 672.22 to 672.33. Section 523(2) gives the justice a power to vary a release or detention order for non-s. 469 offences where cause is shown, where the Crown and defence consent to the justice exercising that jurisdiction (not necessarily consenting that the order should be made). In addition, at the completion of the preliminary inquiry, the justice without consent of the parties but upon cause being shown may vary the release or detention order in relation to a non-s. 469 offence.

The procedure for conducting the preliminary inquiry is set out in this Part and may briefly be described as follows. A preliminary inquiry for a non-s. 469 offence is not always held even if the accused has elected trial other than before a provincial court judge. The request for a preliminary inquiry is made in accordance with s. 536 or s. 536.1 (Nunavut). Under s. 536.3, the party requesting the preliminary inquiry must provide the court and the other party with a statement of the issues on which the party wants evidence to be given and the witnesses. Under s. 536.4, the justice on his or her own motion or at the request of the party may hold a pre-inquiry hearing to assist in identifying the issues, the witnesses to be heard and for managing the inquiry. The justice makes a record of any admissions of fact agreed upon and any agreement reached by the parties. Under s. 536.5, the parties may agree to limit the scope of the inquiry and the agreement is filed with the court. Under s. 549(1.1), where the parties have agreed to limit the scope of the inquiry, the justice, without recording further evidence, may order the accused to stand trial.

At the preliminary inquiry, while the accused is arraigned on the charge, he is not called upon to plead. Section 539 permits an application to be made to prohibit the publication, broadcast or transmission in any way of the proceedings until the accused is discharged, or if ordered to stand trial, until the trial is ended. The order is mandatory when applied for by the accused at the opening of the inquiry. The order is discretionary when applied for by the prosecutor. Where the accused is not represented by counsel, the justice is to inform the accused of his right to apply for the order under s. 539. It is a summary conviction offence (s. 539(3)) to violate the order. It is not unusual, in addition, to apply for an order excluding witnesses until they have testified. While not specifically provided for in this Part, it would seem that s. 537(1)(*h*) or (*i*) is wide enough to permit the making of such an order. In a proper case, the judge can hold the inquiry *in camera* pursuant to

s. 537(1)(*h*). By reason of s. 485(1.1), jurisdiction over the person is not lost where the accused was to appear by counsel under subsec. (1)(*j*). Subsection (1)(*k*) allows the court to require an accused who is confined in prison to appear by closed-circuit television or other similar means, except when the evidence of a witness is taken. Note s. 848 that provides that if an accused who is in prison does not have access to legal advice, the court shall, before permitting the accused to appear by means of communication that allows the court and the accused to engage in simultaneous visual and oral communication, be satisfied that the accused will be able to understand the proceedings and that any decisions made by the accused during the proceedings will be voluntary. Under s. 539(1)(*j*.1), the justice may permit the accused to be out of court during the whole or any part of the inquiry on appropriate conditions. Section 539(1.1) allows the justice to regulate the inquiry by preventing questioning that is abusive, too repetitive or otherwise inappropriate.

The taking of evidence commences with the calling of evidence by the prosecutor which is taken under oath (or affirmation) in accordance with s. 540 and the provisions of ss. 14 to 16 of the *Canada Evidence Act*, R.S.C. 1985, c. C-5. While s. 540 provides for the evidence to be taken in the form of a deposition, this provision is virtually never resorted to now and evidence is usually taken verbatim by a court reporter or through the use of sound-recording equipment as contemplated by ss. 540(1)(*b*)(ii) and (5). The record is then in the form of a transcript. Sections 540(7) and (8) allow for the reception of evidence, such as hearsay, that, while credible and trustworthy, might otherwise be inadmissible under the strict rules of evidence. The justice does, however, have the power to require a declarant to attend to testify under s. 540(9). Section 715 provides for the admission of evidence taken at the preliminary inquiry where the witness is unavailable for the reasons set out therein at the trial, except for evidence received under s. 540(7). Section 715.1 provides for admission of a videotape at the preliminary inquiry, made within a reasonable time after the alleged offence in the case of an accused charged with certain sexual offences, where the complainant is under 18 years of age. As to other provisions that govern admission of evidence in sexual offence cases, see the notes under the particular section with which the accused is charged or the cross-references under s. 150.1. Sections 709 to 714 provide a means for obtaining the evidence of a witness through appointment of a commissioner to take the evidence. Provisions for securing the presence of witnesses through subpoena and material witness warrant are set out in Part XXII. Procedure for procuring the attendance of a witness who is in custody or the attendance of the accused himself where he is in custody is set out in s. 527. Where a witness refuses to be sworn or to answer questions or to produce documents requested, the justice may adjourn the inquiry and remand the witness to custody for successive periods each not exceeding eight days, pursuant to s. 545. Where the accused absconds in the course of the preliminary inquiry, the justice may continue the preliminary inquiry in his absence under s. 544. Pursuant to s. 549, the preliminary inquiry may be waived at any stage where the accused and the Crown consent to an order to stand trial. This may be done at any stage of the proceedings and even before any evidence has been taken. Under s. 549(1.1), where the parties have agreed to limit the scope of the inquiry, the justice, without recording further evidence, may order the accused to stand trial.

The accused has the right to cross-examine any prosecution witnesses by virtue of s. 540(1)(*a*), although note the justice's right to limit cross-examination under s. 537(1.1). Section 542 makes it clear that the prosecution may introduce a confession by an accused. However, the common law voluntariness rule applies at the preliminary inquiry as at trial. It is a summary conviction offence to publish, broadcast or transmit in any way a report concerning a confession or admission by the accused unless the accused was discharged or the trial has been completed (s. 542(2)). After the prosecution has called its evidence, s. 541 provides that the accused is to be addressed in the terms set out in s. 541(1) and anything he says is taken down pursuant to s. 541(2) and is admissible in evidence in accordance with s. 657, subject to possible application of s. 13 of the Charter. Having been addressed, the accused is then entitled to call witnesses pursuant to s. 541(3) and their evidence is taken in the same manner as the prosecution evidence (s. 541(4)). At the conclusion of all the evidence, the accused and probably the prosecutor are entitled to make submissions as to whether or not the accused should be ordered to stand trial pursuant to s. 548. Section 548 gives the justice the power to order that the accused stand trial for the offence charged or any other indictable offence (including a hybrid offence) in respect of the same transaction. Following an order to stand trial, an indictment will be presented in accordance with s. 574, except that if the accused was discharged, or no preliminary inquiry was held, the provisions of s. 577 must be complied with.

Certain other miscellaneous provisions govern the conduct of the inquiry. Section 538 incorporates s. 556 respecting appearance of a corporate accused. Section 543 provides for the transfer of the proceedings to another jurisdiction where it appears that the offence was committed outside the limits of the jurisdiction in which the accused has been charged. Section 546 provides that certain irregularities, defects or variances do not affect the validity of the preliminary inquiry or subsequent proceedings. Section 547 provides for adjournment where the accused has been misled by the irregularity, defect or variance. Section 547.1 provides for the continuation of the preliminary inquiry before another justice where the initial justice is unable to continue. Section 550 is a little-used provision permitting the justice to require a material witness to enter into a recognizance and for committal of the witness if he fails to comply with the recognizance. Section 551 provides for the transmission of the record to the trial court. After the order to stand trial, s. 603 gives the accused the right to inspect the record and to receive copies upon payment of a fee. It is customary in any event to order a copy of the preliminary inquiry. The evidence taken on the preliminary inquiry constitutes a prior statement reduced to writing for the purposes of ss. 9 and 10 of the *Canada Evidence Act*.

Section 715 provides that evidence given at the preliminary inquiry may be admissible at the accused's trial if, for example, the witness is too ill to attend the trial.

SYNOPSIS

This section sets out the powers of a justice or provincial court judge in conducting an inquiry under Part XVIII. It contains general provisions dealing with adjournments (subsecs. (1)(*a*) and (2)), remanding the accused in custody (subsec. (1)(*c*), (*e*)), resuming the proceedings (subsec. (1)(*d*)), hearing from counsel (subsec. (1)(*f*)), receiving evidence (subsec. (1)(*g*)), holding proceedings *in camera* (subsec. (1)(*h*)), and otherwise regulating the course of the inquiry (subsec. (1)(*i*)).

By reason of subsec. (1)(*j*), on consent, an accused may appear by counsel or television, etc., and under subsec. (1)(*k*) the accused can be required to appear by television, provided no evidence of a witness is taken. The justice may permit the accused to be absent from court in accordances with subsec. (1)(*j*.1). If the justice makes an order under subsec. (1)(*j*.1) permitting the accused to be absent, the court must inform the accused that the evidence taken may nevertheless be admissible at the trial under s. 715. Subsection (1.1) gives the justice the power to halt abusive, repetitive or inappropriate examination.

ANNOTATIONS

Jurisdiction generally to control process – It was held in *R. v. Doyle*, [1977] 1 S.C.R. 597, 29 C.C.C. (2d) 177 (9:0), that the power and jurisdiction of a magistrate [now provincial court judge] acting under the Code are circumscribed by the provisions contained therein and must be found to have been confirmed thereby either expressly or by necessary implication. The court disapproved of the opinion expressed in *R. v. Keating* (1973), 11 C.C.C. (2d) 133, 21 C.R.N.S. 217 (Ont. C.A.), that the court has an inherent jurisdiction to control its own process. Rather, "the careful and detailed procedural directions mentioned in the *Code* are of necessity exhaustive . . . the power of a magistrate or justice acting under the *Criminal Code* [are] entirely statutory".

The power given the judge under this section includes the power to order that counsel be disqualified from continuing to act where necessary to prevent the lawyer from placing himself in a conflict of interest: *R. v. Robillard* (1986), 28 C.C.C. (3d) 22 (Ont. C.A.).

Whether the accused should be physically restrained during the course of the preliminary inquiry is a matter within the jurisdiction of the preliminary inquiry judge: *R. v. McNeill* (1996), 108 C.C.C. (3d) 364, 49 C.R. (4th) 131 (Ont. C.A.). See also *R. v. Jones* (1996), 107 C.C.C. (3d) 517, 49 C.R. (4th) 136 (Ont. Ct. (Gen. Div.)).

Right to adjourn – Until the Crown elects otherwise a Crown option offence is deemed to be indictable and the court has power to adjourn the proceedings under this subsection: *R. v. Gougeon; R. v. Haesler; R. v. Gray* (1980), 55 C.C.C. (2d) 218 (Ont. C.A.), leave to appeal to S.C.C. refused 35 N.R. 83*n*.

Right to make submissions [subsec. (1)(*f*)] – The justice has no discretion to refuse counsel for the accused the right to make submissions and such a refusal is a denial of natural justice which will lead to the committal for trial being quashed: *R. v. Taillefer* (1978), 42 C.C.C. (2d) 282, 3 C.R. (3d) 357 (Ont. C.A.).

Evidence and Crown right to call witnesses [As to defence evidence, see s. 541] – The Crown has a discretion to present only that evidence which makes out a *prima facie* case: *R. v. Caccamo*, [1976] 1 S.C.R. 786, 21 C.C.C. (2d) 257 (7:2).

The Crown has a discretion to call whatever witnesses it requires and the presiding justice has no power to direct the Crown to call certain witnesses: *R. v. Brass* (1981), 64 C.C.C. (2d) 206 (Sask. Q.B.).

Conversely, the judge has no power to prevent the prosecution from calling certain witnesses although he is satisfied there is sufficient evidence to order that the accused stand trial: *R. v. Schreder* (1987), 36 C.C.C. (3d) 216, 59 C.R. (3d) 183 (N.W.T.S.C.).

The Crown has the right during a preliminary inquiry to withdraw the charge against one accused and call him as a witness against the other accused: *R. v. Dick*, [1969] 1 C.C.C. 147, 4 C.R.N.S. 102 *sub nom. Re Dick* (Ont. H.C.J.).

Exclusion of public [subsec. (1)(*h*)] – If possible a hearing should be conducted by the judge on the question as to whether he should exercise his discretion and limit the public's access to his court, but in any event the record should contain both his order and his reasons therefor: *Armstrong v. State of Wisconsin* (1972), 7 C.C.C. (2d) 331, [1972] 3 O.R. 229 (Ont. H.C.J.).

The justice has no power to limit the exclusion order to certain members of the public such as foreign journalists who have indicated they intend to publish details of the evidence despite a publication ban under s. 539. Thus, it may be that to secure a fair trial for the accused all members of the public must be excluded: *R. v. Sayegh (No. 1)* (1982), 66 C.C.C. (2d) 430 (Ont. Prov. Ct.), and *R. v. Sayegh (No. 2)* (1982), 66 C.C.C. (2d) 432 (Ont. Prov. Ct.).

The mere possibility that spectators might talk to prospective witnesses is not a ground to order exclusion of the public. Further, while the judge is, in some circumstances, entitled to make the order excluding the public on the basis of submissions of counsel, where those submissions, to the effect that certain spectators might intimidate witnesses, are challenged and it is clear that counsel did not purport to speak from personal knowledge nor to convey instructions that he had received on the matter, then the submissions are nothing but speculation and not a basis for an order of exclusion: *R. v. Vaudrin* (1982), 2 C.C.C. (3d) 214, 32 C.R. (3d) 162 (B.C.S.C.).

Exclusion of witnesses – Upon counsel's request an order for exclusion of witnesses must be made unless grounds are shown why the justice should not make the order: *R. v. Learn* (1981), 63 C.C.C. (2d) 191 (Ont. H.C.J.).

Further, there is virtually no case where credibility is in issue and witnesses will be testifying as to fact and the application is unopposed, that the justice would be justified in refusing to make the requested order: *R. v. Collette; R. v. Richard* (1983), 6 C.C.C. (3d) 300 (Ont. H.C.J.), affd 7 C.C.C. (3d) 574*n* (C.A.), leave to appeal to S.C.C. refused February 7, 1984.

The power to make an exclusion order does not include the power to order that there be no communication between counsel and the witnesses: *R. v. O'Callaghan* (1982), 65 C.C.C. (2d) 459, 25 C.R. (3d) 68 (Ont. H.C.J.).

Absence of accused – In an identification case, the judge has a discretion to permit the accused to sit in the body of the court. However, refusal to exercise the discretion is not a jurisdictional matter and is therefore not reviewable by the superior court: *R. v. Vaudrin* (1982), 2 C.C.C. (3d) 214 (B.C.S.C.).

Full answer and defence – The accused is entitled to make full answer and defence at his preliminary inquiry: *R. v. Pearson* (1957), 117 C.C.C. 249, 25 C.R. 342 (Alta. S.C. App. Div.).

The accused was deprived of his right to full answer and defence when he attended for his preliminary inquiry and found that the Crown had substituted numerous charges within the exclusive jurisdiction of a provincial court judge who refused to allow him an adjournment: *R. v. Carter* (1972), 7 C.C.C. (2d) 49, [1972] 3 O.R. 50 (H.C.J.).

While the primary function of the preliminary inquiry is to determine whether there is sufficient evidence for committal, there is no jurisdictional limitation that precludes a preliminary inquiry judge from allowing defence counsel to pursue discovery within reasonable bounds. Further, s. 541(5) does not limit defence witnesses only to those relevant to the issue of committal: *R. v. McGrath* (2007), 225 C.C.C. (3d) 1, 258 N.S.R. (2d) 11 (S.C.).

Application of Charter – A provincial court judge presiding at a preliminary inquiry is not a court of competent jurisdiction under s. 24 of the *Canadian Charter of Rights and Freedoms* and therefore has no power to order a stay of proceedings by reason of unreasonable delay under s. 11(*b*) of the Charter: *R. v. Mills*, [1986] 1 S.C.R. 863, 26 C.C.C. (3d) 481 (4:3).

Nor can a preliminary inquiry judge order costs as a remedy for late disclosure: *R. v. Howard* (2009), 250 C.C.C. (3d) 102, 292 Nfld. & P.E.I.R. 6 (P.E.I.C.A.).

A preliminary inquiry judge is not a "court of competent jurisdiction" for the purpose of excluding evidence under s. 24(2) of the Charter. Accordingly, while a preliminary inquiry judge may determine the admissibility of statements based on the common law confessions rule, the judge has no jurisdiction to exclude the statement as a remedy for any Charter violations under s. 24(2): *R. v. Hynes*, [2001] 3 S.C.R. 623, 159 C.C.C. (3d) 359.

Nor does a judge presiding at a preliminary inquiry have jurisdiction to determine the constitutionality of an evidentiary provision of the *Criminal Code* under s. 52 of the *Constitution Act, 1982*: *R. v. Seaboyer*, [1991] 2 S.C.R. 577, 66 C.C.C. (3d) 321 (7:2).

Review of crown disclosure decisions is not incidental to a justice's power to regulate the course of the preliminary inquiry. Where the Crown has not provided sufficient disclosure to allow the accused to make a reasonably informed election and the Crown requests further time to make that disclosure, a justice should adjourn the taking of the election and allow the Crown a reasonable time to fulfill its disclosure obligations. If the time needed to make proper disclosure is inordinate, any delay in the proceedings will count against the Crown. Where there is a dispute in respect of the disclosure, a justice may adjourn the taking of the election to allow the accused to seek the appropriate remedy in the superior court. If it is determined that the Crown has improperly withheld disclosure, any delay caused by the bringing of that application in the superior court will count against the Crown: *R. v. Girimonte* (1997), 121 C.C.C. (3d) 33, 12 C.R. (5th) 332 (Ont. C.A.).

Notwithstanding the preference for alleged violations of s. 11(*b*) of the Charter being heard by the trial court, in a proper case, the superior court should grant an order staying proceedings by reason of violation of s. 11(*b*) of the Charter due to unreasonable delay in commencing the preliminary inquiry. Where the application is brought to the superior court in advance of the preliminary inquiry, that court may properly consider the entire period of time up to the date set for the hearing where the date for the preliminary inquiry was fixed and could not, at the behest of the accused, be moved up: *R. v. Smith*, [1989] 2 S.C.R. 1120, 52 C.C.C. (3d) 97 (9:0).

While preliminary inquiry judges have no jurisdiction to remedial jurisdiction pursuant to s. 24(1) of the Charter, they may balance Charter values in exercising their statutory powers. The power to regulate the inquiry, conferred by s. 537(1)(*i*), includes the power to make orders directed at witnesses, such as whether a niqab may be worn: *R. v. S. (N.)* (2010), 262 C.C.C. (3d) 4 (Ont. C.A.), affd (2012), 290 C.C.C. (3d) 404 (S.C.C.).

ORGANIZATION.

538. Where an accused is an organization, subsections 556(1) and (2) apply with such modifications as the circumstances require. R.S., c. C-34, s. 466; 2003, c. 21, s. 8

CROSS-REFERENCES

For a discussion of the procedure on preliminary inquiries and cross-references, see *Note on procedure at preliminary inquiry* under s. 537. "Organization" is defined in s. 2.

SYNOPSIS

Under s. 556, an organization shall appear at the preliminary inquiry into charges against it by counsel or by agent. Where the organization has been served with a summons and does not appear, the judge shall set a date for trial.

Taking Evidence of Witnesses

ORDER RESTRICTING PUBLICATION OF EVIDENCE TAKEN AT PRELIMINARY INQUIRY / Accused to be informed of right to apply for order / Failure to comply with order / Definition of "newspaper".

539. (1) Prior to the commencement of the taking of evidence at a preliminary inquiry, the justice holding the inquiry

(*a*) may, if application therefor is made by the prosecutor, and

(*b*) shall, if application therefor is made by any of the accused,

make an order directing that the evidence taken at the inquiry shall not be published in any document or broadcast or transmitted in any way before such time as, in respect of each of the accused,

(*c*) he or she is discharged, or

(*d*) if he or she is ordered to stand trial, the trial is ended.

(2) Where an accused is not represented by counsel at a preliminary inquiry, the justice holding the inquiry shall, prior to the commencement of the taking of evidence at the inquiry, inform the accused of his right to make application under subsection (1).

(3) Everyone who fails to comply with an order made pursuant to subsection (1) is guilty of an offence punishable on summary conviction. R.S., c. C-34, s. 467; R.S.C. 1985, c. 27 (1st Supp.), s. 97; 2005, c. 32, s. 18.

(4) [*Repealed*, 2005, c. 32, s. 18(2).]

CROSS-REFERENCES

The trial of the offence under s. 539(3) is conducted by a summary conviction court in accordance with Part XXVII. For a discussion of the procedure on preliminary inquiries and cross-references, see *Note on procedure at preliminary inquiry* under s. 537.

SYNOPSIS

This section authorizes the justice conducting the preliminary inquiry to make an order, prior to the commencing of the taking of evidence, banning the publication, broadcast or transmission in any way of the evidence called at the inquiry until such time as the accused is either discharged (subsec. (1)(*c*)) or, where there is an order to stand trial, until the trial has ended (subsec. (1)(*d*)). Its purpose is to protect the accused's right to a fair trial. Such an order is mandatory if sought by the accused (subsec. (1)(*b*)), and discretionary if sought by the Crown (subsec. (1)(*c*)).

If the accused is not represented by counsel at the preliminary inquiry, the justice holding the inquiry must inform the accused of his right to make application under subsec. (1) prior to the commencement of the taking of evidence.

It is a summary conviction offence to breach an order made under subsec. (1) (subsec. (3)).

ANNOTATIONS

Subsection (1) – This subsection, which is directed at ensuring a fair trial for the accused as guaranteed by s. 11(*d*) of the *Charter of Rights and Freedoms*, does not constitute an unconstitutional infringement on the guarantee to freedom of the press as guaranteed by s. 2(*b*) of the Charter: *R. v. Banville* (1983), 3 C.C.C. (3d) 312, 34 C.R. (3d) 20 (N.B.Q.B.).

Where the application for a ban on publication is made only during the course of the preliminary inquiry the justice has a discretion whether or not to make the order and he is also entitled to lift the ban in proper circumstances: *R. v. Harrison* (1984), 14 C.C.C. (3d) 549 (Que. Ct. Sess.).

When the Crown stayed the proceedings after the accused was committed to stand trial, the trial was "ended" within the meaning of subsec. (1)(*d*) and the publication ban no longer applied: *British Columbia College of Teachers v. British Columbia (Ministry of the Attorney General)* (2010), 256 C.C.C. (3d) 345 (B.C.S.C.).

Subsection (3) – A reporter for a United States newspaper who submitted a story containing a report of evidence at a preliminary inquiry notwithstanding an order under subsec. (1) could be tried in Canadian courts for the offence under this subsection where the United States newspaper was circulated in Canada: *R. v. Banville* (1983), 3 C.C.C. (3d) 312, 34 C.R. (3d) 20 (N.B.Q.B.).

TAKING EVIDENCE / Reading and signing depositions / Authentication by justice / Stenographer to be sworn / Authentication of transcript / Transcription of record taken by sound recording apparatus / Evidence / Notice of intention to tender / Appearance for examination.

540. (1) Where an accused is before a justice holding a preliminary inquiry, the justice shall

(*a*) take the evidence under oath of the witnesses called on the part of the prosecution and allow the accused or counsel for the accused to cross-examine them; and

(*b*) cause a record of the evidence of each witness to be taken

(i) in legible writing in the form of a deposition, in Form 31, or by a stenographer appointed by him or pursuant to law, or

(ii) in a province where a sound recording apparatus is authorized by or under provincial legislation for use in civil cases, by the type of apparatus so authorized and in accordance with the requirements of the provincial legislation.

(2) Where a deposition is taken down in writing, the justice shall, in the presence of the accused, before asking the accused if he wishes to call witnesses,

(*a*) cause the deposition to be read to the witness;

(*b*) cause the deposition to be signed by the witness; and

(*c*) sign the deposition himself.

(3) Where depositions are taken down in writing, the justice may sign

(*a*) at the end of each deposition; or

(*b*) at the end of several or of all the depositions in a manner that will indicate that his signature is intended to authenticate each deposition.

(4) Where a stenographer appointed to take down the evidence is not a duly sworn court stenographer, he shall make oath that he will truly and faithfully report the evidence.

(5) Where the evidence is taken down by a stenographer appointed by the justice or pursuant to law, it need not be read to or signed by the witnesses, but, on request of the justice or of one of the parties, shall be transcribed, in whole or in part, by the stenographer and the transcript shall be accompanied by

(*a*) an affidavit of the stenographer that it is a true report of the evidence; or

(*b*) a certificate that it is a true report of the evidence if the stenographer is a duly sworn court stenographer.

(6) Where, in accordance with this Act, a record is record taken in any proceedings under this Act by a sound recording apparatus, the record so taken shall, on request of the justice or of one of the parties, be dealt with and transcribed, in whole or in part, and the transcription certified and used in accordance with the provincial legislation, with such modifications as the circumstances require mentioned in subsection (1).

(7) A justice acting under this Part may receive as evidence any information that would not otherwise be admissible but that the justice considers credible or trustworthy in the circumstances of the case, including a statement that is made by a witness in writing or otherwise recorded.

(8) Unless the justice orders otherwise, no information may be received as evidence under subsection (7) unless the party has given to each of the other parties reasonable notice of his or her intention to tender it, together with a copy of the statement, if any, referred to in that subsection.

(9) The justice shall, on application of a party, require any person whom the justice considers appropriate to appear for examination or cross-examination with respect to information intended to be tendered as evidence under subsection (7). R.S., c. C-34, s. 468; R.S.C. 1985, c. 27 (1st Supp.), s. 98; 1997, c. 18, s. 65; 2002, c. 13, s. 29.

CROSS-REFERENCES

For a discussion of the procedure on preliminary inquiries and cross-references, see *Note on procedure at preliminary inquiry* under s. 537. As to taking evidence of children and persons whose competency is objected, see s. 16 of the *Canada Evidence Act*.

SYNOPSIS

This section requires that a permanent record be made of the evidence called at a preliminary inquiry. This is usually done by either a court stenographer or through the use of sound recording equipment approved under provincial legislation. In either case a transcript of the evidence will be produced.

Subsection (1)(*a*) provides that the accused has a right to cross-examine any witness called by the Crown.

Although written depositions are provided for, such are rarely used.

For the most part, the normal rules of evidence apply. However, a justice has the power to admit credible or trustworthy evidence, such as hearsay, that would otherwise be inadmissible under subsec. (7). Such evidence is not admissible at trial under s. 715. The justice may require the declarant to attend to be examined under subsec. (9). As the Supreme Court of Canada has held that a justice or judge presiding at a preliminary inquiry is not "a court of competent jurisdiction" for the purpose of granting Charter remedies, there is no power to exclude evidence obtained in a manner which breached one of its provisions (*e.g.*, s. 8 — unreasonable search or seizure) under s. 24(2) of the Charter.

ANNOTATIONS

Recalling of witnesses – A justice may allow a witness to be recalled to correct any wrong evidence that he has given: *R. v. Jones, ex p. Ponak*, [1970] 1 C.C.C. 250, 7 D.L.R. (3d) 381 (B.C.C.A.).

Right to cross-examine – The arbitrary fixing of a time limitation on cross-examination of a witness constituted a refusal to exercise jurisdiction and was cured by a *mandamus* order to allow counsel to continue: *R. v. Roulette* (1972), 7 C.C.C. (2d) 244, [1972] 4 W.W.R. 508 (Man. Q.B.).

The right of cross-examination contemplated by this subsection is that of full, detailed and careful cross-examination based on a known examination-in-chief; and thus where counsel for accused was delayed in attending the preliminary hearing because of attendance in another court, so that he was not present for the examination-in-chief of the principal Crown witness, the committal for trial was quashed: *R. v. Durette* (1979), 47 C.C.C. (2d) 170 (Ont. H.C.J.).

Although the accused has counsel he may personally exercise the right to cross-examine all or some of the witnesses. The justice does not have a discretion to decide who will cross-examine: *R. v. Zaor* (1984), 12 C.C.C. (3d) 265 (Que. C.A.).

Questions necessary to establish an evidentiary foundation for an application for third party records are permissible at a preliminary inquiry. Not every question regarding the substantive contents of a private record is presumptively precluded. The purpose and reach of each question must be assessed to evaluate whether the question elicits information touching upon the private or personal domain or intensely private aspects of the life or recordings of the author of the record. Questions relating to whether any particular topic is covered should be permitted but the complainant may not be asked about a recollection of the exact contents of an entry: *R. v. B. (E.)* (2002), 162 C.C.C. (3d) 451, 2 C.R. (6th) 178 (Ont. C.A.), leave to appeal to S.C.C. refused [2003] 1 S.C.R. xvi, 169 C.C.C. (3d) vi.

This provision confers on the preliminary inquiry judge a broader discretion, allowing him or her to take into account, not the relevance of the evidence in the strict sense, but rather the appropriateness of having the witness appear. Cross-examination at a preliminary inquiry is not an exceptional procedure. The accused is not required to show justiciable cause for cross-examining the complainant or contradictions in the complainant's statement. In determining whether to allow cross-examination, the judge should consider the accused's legitimate interest in preparing his defence and bringing out the insufficiency or weaknesses in the Crown's evidence: *R. v. M. (P.)* (2007), 222 C.C.C. (3d) 393 (Que. C.A.), leave to appeal to S.C.C. refused 222 C.C.C. (3d) vi.

Review of evidentiary rulings – *Mandamus* with *certiorari* in aid will not lie to supervise a justice's conduct of a preliminary inquiry as where review is sought of a justice's refusal to allow certain cross-examination: *R. v. Depagie* (1976), 32 C.C.C. (2d) 89, [1976] 6 W.W.R. 1 (Alta. S.C. App. Div.) (2:1).

The decision of the justice concerning the admissibility of evidence even if erroneous, does not affect jurisdiction and is therefore not reviewable on *certiorari*: *Quebec (Attorney General) v. Cohen*, [1979] 2 S.C.R. 305, 46 C.C.C. (2d) 473 (7:0).

The decision of a justice refusing to order production of a police witness' notebook to defence counsel is not reviewable on *certiorari*. The refusal does not amount to a denial of natural justice or of the right to cross-examine: *R. v. Martin, Simard and Desjardins; R. v. Nichols* (1977), 41 C.C.C. (2d) 308, 87 D.L.R. (3d) 634 (Ont. C.A.).

Admissibility of statement of facts or evidence from another proceeding – A statement of facts agreed to by defence counsel and Crown counsel may be admitted without calling *viva voce* evidence and constitutes evidence upon which the justice may base his decision as to committal: *R. v. Ulrich* (1977), 38 C.C.C. (2d) 1, [1978] 1 W.W.R. 422 (Alta. S.C.T.D.).

The accused may waive strict compliance with the requirement that evidence be adduced through witnesses who have been sworn or affirmed and heard at the trial before the trier of fact, but this requires that the consent to the procedure of both the accused and the Crown be conveyed to the court and that for example, the evidence taken on a previous proceeding enter the record during the trial: *R. v. Matheson*, [1981] 2 S.C.R. 214, 59 C.C.C. (2d) 289 (7:0).

Interpreter – An interpreter is like an expert witness and should be sworn prior to interpreting for a witness testifying in a foreign language. The accused may, however, waive compliance with this requirement and in certain circumstances counsel's acquiescence can constitute a waiver: *R. v. Hilts* (1984), 14 C.C.C. (3d) 187 (Ont. H.C.J.).

Power to order production [Also see notes under s. 603] – A preliminary inquiry is not a trial, so s. 10(1) of the *Canada Evidence Act* is not applicable and the presiding judge does not have the power to order production for the defence of a Crown witness' previous written statement: *R. v. Patterson*, [1970] S.C.R. 409, 2 C.C.C. (2d) 227 (5:2). Also see *R. v. Girimonte* (1997), 121 C.C.C. (3d) 33, 12 C.R. (5th) 332 (Ont. C.A.), noted under s. 537.

While the preliminary inquiry protects the accused from a needless and improper exposure to a public trial it is also a forum where the accused is afforded an opportunity to discover and to appreciate the case to be made against him at trial: *R. v. Skogman*, [1984] 2 S.C.R. 93, 13 C.C.C. (3d) 161 (4:3).

A provincial court judge presiding at a preliminary hearing has power to order a police officer to produce notes from which he refreshed his memory prior to testifying which were relevant to the evidence given by the officer and to the issues in the case: *R. v. Monfils* (1971), 4 C.C.C. (2d) 163, [1972] 1 O.R. 11 (C.A.).

A judge presiding at a preliminary inquiry has no jurisdiction to order the Crown to make disclosure: *R. v. Hynes*, [2001] 3 S.C.R. 623, 159 C.C.C. (3d) 359.

A judge presiding at a preliminary inquiry is competent to make all evidentiary rulings, including rulings on claims of privilege. It may, however, be necessary to follow certain procedural steps to bring the relevant evidence before the court, as where the records sought by the accused are kept in accordance with provincial legislation: *R. v. R. (L.)* (1995), 100 C.C.C. (3d) 329, 39 C.R. (4th) 390 (Ont. C.A.). [Also now see ss. 278.1 to 278.9.]

Requirement that record of evidence be taken – [**Note:** These cases were decided prior to the amendment of s. 540(5) and (6), which no longer automatically require that a transcript be made.]

The provisions for the examination of witnesses and the taking of evidence are mandatory and non-compliance therewith is fatal to a conviction: *R. v. Lacasse* (1972), 8 C.C.C. (2d) 270, [1972] 5 W.W.R. 198 (B.C.C.A.).

Similarly, where the recording device used at the accused's preliminary hearing failed and no transcript was available, the mandatory provisions of this subsection have not been complied with and the committal for trial must be quashed: *R. v. Boylan* (1979), 46 C.C.C. (2d) 415, 8 C.R. (3d) 36 (Sask. C.A.). *Contra: R. v. Rupert* (1978), 43 C.C.C. (2d) 34, 3 C.R. (3d) 351 (Ont. H.C.J.), affd without written reasons, January 23, 1979 (Ont. C.A.), where it was held the provisions are directory only and loss of the recording before a transcript could be made was not grounds for quashing the committal for trial.

Malfunctioning of the sound recording equipment at the preliminary inquiry is not necessarily fatal to the validity of the order to stand trial and where that portion of the evidence which has been transcribed supports the order there has not been a failure to comply with the provisions of this subsection: *R. v. Rayer* (1981), 61 C.C.C. (2d) 331 (B.C.S.C.).

Provisions of this type are directory and the judge's failure to abide by them will not result in his loss of jurisdiction. Where, however, his notes under Form 31 fail to establish whether the witnesses had sworn to or affirmed their evidence a new trial was ordered: *R. v. Czyszczon*, [1963] 3 C.C.C. 106, 41 C.R. 17 (Alta. S.C. App. Div.).

Subsection (6) does not apply to absolute jurisdiction trials: *R. v. L'Espinay* (2008), 228 C.C.C. (3d) 129, 54 C.R. (6th) 357 (B.C.C.A.).

Reception of credible and trustworthy evidence [subsecs. (7) - (9)] – Videotaped and audiotaped statements of the complainants were admissible under subsec. (7) where the

Crown had given the notice required by subsec. (8) and written statements were available to assist the judge and the parties in following the video and audio statements. By calling the officer who interviewed the complainants, the Crown had established that the evidence was credible and trustworthy: *R. v. I. (S.P.)* (2005), 193 C.C.C. (3d) 240, 27 C.R. (6th) 112 (Nunavut C.J.).

In *R. v. McFadden* (2012), 288 C.C.C. (3d) 507 (B.C.C.A.), the court held that the preliminary inquiry judge had erred in permitting the Crown to file its entire case in paper form without permitting the appellant to cross-examine any Crown witnesses. Although the Crown's case can be placed before the court in paper form pursuant to s. 540(7), the Crown's right to tender its case in this form does not detract from the right of the defence to apply, pursuant to s. 540(9), to examine or cross-examine witnesses. The preliminary inquiry judge acted without jurisdiction when she denied a defence request to cross-examine witnesses whose evidence formed part of the paper record, without regard to s. 540(9). The court held that the preliminary inquiry judge also exceeded her jurisdiction in ruling that she would not have allowed him to call evidence under s. 541(5) in any event, because discovery was not a purpose relevant to the inquiry. The words "relevant to the inquiry" in s. 541(5) mean more than "relevant to committal". Discovery remains a valid function of preliminary inquiries.

Application of Charter – A provincial court judge presiding at a preliminary inquiry is not a court of competent jurisdiction under s. 24 of the *Canadian Charter of Rights and Freedoms* and therefore has no power to grant a remedy under that section, including exclusion of evidence, for violation of a Charter right: *R. v. Mills*, [1986] 1 S.C.R. 863, 26 C.C.C. (3d) 481, 52 C.R. (3d) 1 (4:3); *R. v. Hynes* (2001), 159 C.C.C. (3d) 359, 47 C.R. (5th) 278, 206 D.L.R. (4th) 483, 208 Nfld. & P.E.I.R. 181, 88 C.R.R. (2d) 222, 278 N.R. 299 (S.C.C.).

The accused has the right to cross-examine a police officer as to the basis for obtaining a search warrant to establish a foundation for submissions at trial relevant to his rights under ss. 8 and 24(2) of the *Charter of Rights and Freedoms: R. v. Cover* (1988), 44 C.C.C. (3d) 34 (Ont. H.C.J.). Also see: *R. v. Dawson* (1998), 123 C.C.C. (3d) 385, 15 C.R. (5th) 201 (Ont. C.A.), respecting wiretap affidavits.

An accused is entitled to cross-examine Crown witnesses at a preliminary inquiry relating to Charter defences which are not of concern to the judge conducting the inquiry. However, the refusal of the provincial court judge to allow certain questions relating to a Charter issue will not amount to jurisdictional error so as to require that the order to stand trial be quashed: *R. v. George* (1991), 69 C.C.C. (3d) 148, 5 O.R. (3d) 144 (C.A.).

HEARING OF WITNESSES / Contents of address to accused / Statement of accused / Witnesses for accused / Depositions of such witnesses.

541. (1) When the evidence of the witnesses called on the part of the prosecution has been taken down and, where required by this Part, has been read, the justice shall, subject to this section, hear the witnesses called by the accused.

(2) Before hearing any witness called by an accused who is not represented by counsel, the justice shall address the accused as follows or to the like effect:

"Do you wish to say anything in answer to these charges or to any other charges which might have arisen from the evidence led by the prosecution? You are not obliged to say anything, but whatever you do say may be given in evidence against you at your trial. You should not make any confession or admission of guilt because of any promise or threat made to you but if you do make any statement it may be given in evidence against you at your trial in spite of the promise or threat."

(3) Where the accused who is not represented by counsel says anything in answer to the address made by the justice pursuant to subsection (2), the answer shall be taken down in writing and shall be signed by the justice and kept with the evidence of the witnesses and dealt with in accordance with this Part.

(4) Where an accused is not represented by counsel, the justice shall ask the accused if he or she wishes to call any witnesses after subsections (2) and (3) have been complied with.

(5) The justice shall hear each witness called by the accused who testifies to any matter relevant to the inquiry, and for the purposes of this subsection, section 540 applies with such modifications as the circumstances require. R.S., c. C-34, s. 469; R.S.C. 1985, c. 27 (1st Supp.), s. 99; 1994, c. 44, s. 54.

CROSS-REFERENCES

For a discussion of the procedure on preliminary inquiries and cross-references, see *Note on procedure at preliminary inquiry* under s. 537.

SYNOPSIS

This section sets out the procedure to be followed after the Crown has closed its case at a preliminary inquiry.

Subsection (1) contains the "address" to be read by the justice to an unrepresented accused. It essentially advises the accused that he is not obliged to answer to the charge but that anything that the accused does say may be given in evidence at any subsequent trial. It is rare that an accused will make a statement or give evidence at this stage of a matter.

The accused has the right to call witnesses and an unrepresented accused must be advised of this right.

ANNOTATIONS

Giving of warning – After the Crown has closed its case and the accused has been given the warning under this subsection, *semble,* the Crown may not then be permitted to reopen its case to call additional evidence: *R. v. Ulrich* (1977), 38 C.C.C. (2d) 1, [1978] 1 W.W.R. 442 (Alta. S.C.T.D.).

This provision is only engaged by the prosecutor's decision not to call further evidence. The preliminary inquiry judge erred, therefore, in cautioning the accused prior to the completion of the prosecutor's case upon deciding that the evidence adduced by the prosecutor amounted to a *prima facie* case: *R. v. Jenkins* (1996), 108 C.C.C. (3d) 565 (Ont. Ct. (Gen. Div.)).

The accused may move for discharge after the Crown's case on the ground that the evidence is insufficient either before or after the warning is given under this subsection but before he elects whether or not to call evidence: *R. v. Hardy; R. v. Johnston* (1979), 50 C.C.C. (2d) 34 (Que. Ct. Sess.).

However, in *Quebec (Attorney General) v. Beauchemin J.S.P.* (1980), 30 C.R. (3d) 51 (Que. S.C.), Hugessen A.C.J.S.C. expressed the view that it would have been better for the Judge to comply with the provisions of this section and give the accused the warning prior to ruling on a motion for dismissal.

This section requires that the judge inform the accused in general terms that he is liable to be ordered to stand trial for additional offences in respect of the same transaction. Thus, the fact that the judge provides the accused with more specific information, by indicating the charges which he feels may arise from the Crown's case, is not improper where there is nothing to indicate that the judge had predetermined the issue before hearing defence evidence and submissions: *R. v. Melaragni* (1990), 73 C.C.C. (3d) 356 (Ont. H.C.J.).

However, where all the counts are contained in one information, it is not necessary to address the accused separately with respect to each count: *R. v. Eusler* (1978), 43 C.C.C. (2d) 501, 23 N.B.R. (2d) 643 (C.A.).

Right of accused to call witnesses – Despite the fact that the Crown need only present sufficient evidence to make out a *prima facie* case to obtain an order that the accused stand trial, this subsection is mandatory and the justice does not have a discretion to order that the accused stand trial without giving the accused an opportunity to call witnesses notwithstanding at the time of the Crown's case the justice is satisfied there is sufficient evidence to order that the accused stand trial: *R. v. Ward* (1976), 31 C.C.C. (2d) 466, 35 C.R.N.S. 117 (Ont. H.C.J.), affd 31 C.C.C. (2d) 466*n* (C.A.).

This section does not require the presiding judge to grant an adjournment in all cases in order to obtain the attendance of a material witness. Ordinarily, where an application is made for an adjournment to call a witness, it must be shown that the applicant has been guilty of no neglect in procuring the attendance of the witness and that there is a reasonable expectation that the witness' attendance can be procured for the future time to which it is sought to put off the case: *R. v. McKenzie* (1989), 51 C.C.C. (3d) 285 (B.C.S.C.).

Failure to allow the accused to call witnesses constitutes jurisdictional error. In this case, the judge had refused the defence an adjournment to call witnesses where the location of the preliminary inquiry had been changed to accommodate police concerns for security and at the end of the single day set for the inquiry, the accused sought an adjournment to call its own witnesses: *R. v. Lena* (2001), 158 C.C.C. (3d) 415 (B.C.C.A.).

While the primary function of the preliminary inquiry is to determine whether there is sufficient evidence for committal, there is no jurisdictional limitation that precludes a preliminary inquiry judge from allowing defence counsel to pursue discovery within reasonable bounds. Further, s. 541(5) does not limit defence witnesses only to those relevant to the issue of committal: *R. v. McGrath* (2007), 225 C.C.C. (3d) 1, 258 N.S.R. (2d) 11 (S.C.).

Effect of Adducing Defence Evidence – The test for committal is the same whether the evidence is direct or circumstantial. Where there is direct evidence as to each element of the offence, the accused must be committed to stand trial. If the Crown's case is based on direct evidence, the case must proceed to trial even if the accused adduces exculpatory evidence under s. 541 of the *Criminal Code*. If the Crown's case consists of circumstantial evidence, however, the judge must engage in a limited weighing of the evidence because there is an inferential gap between the evidence and the matter to be established. The judge must determine whether the evidence is reasonably capable of supporting the inferences that the Crown asks the jury to draw. Where the accused adduces exculpatory evidence in these circumstances, the judge must engage in a limited weighing of the whole of the evidence to determine whether a jury properly instructed could return a verdict of guilty. The judge cannot draw inferences from facts nor assess credibility. The judge must merely make an assessment of the reasonableness of the inferences to be drawn from the circumstantial evidence: *R. v. Arcuri*, [2001] 2 S.C.R. 828, 157 C.C.C. (3d) 21, 44 C.R. (5th) 213, 203 D.L.R. (4th) 20.

CONFESSION OR ADMISSION OF ACCUSED / Restriction of publication of reports of preliminary inquiry / Definition of "newspaper".

542. (1) Nothing in this Act prevents a prosecutor giving in evidence at a preliminary inquiry any admission, confession or statement made at any time by the accused that by law is admissible against him.

(2) Every one who publishes in any document, or broadcasts or transmits in any way, a report that any admission or confession was tendered in evidence at a preliminary inquiry or a report of the nature of such admission or confession so tendered in evidence unless

(*a*) the accused has been discharged, or

(*b*) if the accused has been ordered to stand trial, the trial has ended,

is guilty of an offence punishable on summary conviction. R.S., c. C-34, s. 470; R.S.C. 1985, c. 27 (1st Supp.), s. 101(2)(*c*); 2005, c. 32, s. 19.

(3) [*Repealed*, 2005, c. 32, s. 19(2).]

CROSS-REFERENCES

The trial of the offence under s. 542(2) is conducted by a summary conviction court in accordance with Part XXVII. For a discussion of the procedure on preliminary inquiries and cross-references, see *Note on procedure at preliminary inquiry* under s. 537.

SYNOPSIS

This section codifies the Crown's right to introduce into evidence a statement made by the accused. The normal rules of admissibility apply and, therefore, the "voluntariness" of the statement must be proven beyond a reasonable doubt.

Subsection (2) makes it an offence, punishable on summary conviction, to publish, broadcast or transmit in any way any confession tendered in evidence until the accused has been discharged or the trial has ended. (Also see s. 539.)

ANNOTATIONS

Burden of proof of voluntariness – An accused's statement may only be admitted on the same basis as it would before a trial judge who must be satisfied beyond a reasonable doubt as to its voluntary nature: *R. v. Pickett* (1975), 28 C.C.C. (2d) 297, 31 C.R.N.S. 239 (Ont. C.A.).

On this latter point it should be noted that in *R. v. Leboeuf* (1979), 57 C.C.C. (2d) 257 (Que. C.A.), the court adopted a standard requiring proof that was "sufficiently strong and conclusive" to satisfy the trial judge as to the voluntariness of the statement, rather than proof beyond a reasonable doubt.

Waiver of *voir dire* – An accused or his counsel may waive the necessity of a *voir dire* to determine the voluntariness of a confession: *R. v. Park*, [1981] 2 S.C.R. 64, 59 C.C.C. (2d) 385, 21 C.R. (3d) 182 (9:0).

Right to inquire into circumstances of taking statement – Although the Crown has a discretion not to introduce a statement made by the accused to the police, counsel for the accused is entitled to fully cross-examine the officers as to the circumstances surrounding the taking of the statement: *R. v. Williams, ex p. Barnett* (1970), 2 C.C.C. (2d) 298, [1971] 1 O.R. 703 (H.C.J.). Also see *R. v. Poirier, Prov. J.* (1988), 68 C.R. (3d) 67, [1989] R.L. 6 (Que. C.A.).

Constitutional considerations – While a judge presiding at a preliminary inquiry has the power to exclude a confession under the common law voluntariness rule, the judge has no power to exclude a confession for a violation of the *Charter of Rights and Freedoms* as the judge is not a court of competent jurisdiction within the meaning of s. 24 of the Charter: *R. v. Hynes*, [2001] 3 S.C.R. 623, 159 C.C.C. (3d) 359, 47 C.R. (5th) 278.

Remand Where Offence Committed in Another Jurisdiction

ORDER THAT ACCUSED APPEAR OR BE TAKEN BEFORE JUSTICE WHERE OFFENCE COMMITTED / Transmission of transcript and documents and effect of order or warrant.

543. (1) Where an accused is charged with an offence alleged to have been committed out of the limits of the jurisdiction in which he has been charged, the justice before whom he appears or is brought may, at any stage of the inquiry after hearing both parties,

(*a*) order the accused to appear, or

(*b*) if the accused is in custody, issue a warrant in Form 15 to convey the accused

before a justice having jurisdiction in the place where the offence is alleged to have been committed, who shall continue and complete the inquiry.

(2) Where a justice makes an order or issues a warrant pursuant to subsection (1), he shall cause the transcript of any evidence given before him in the inquiry and all documents that were then before him and that are relevant to the inquiry to be transmitted to a justice having jurisdiction in the place where the offence is alleged to have been committed and

(*a*) any evidence the transcript of which is so transmitted shall be deemed to have been taken by the justice to whom it is transmitted; and

(*b*) any appearance notice, promise to appear, undertaking or recognizance issued to or given or entered into by the accused under Part XVI shall be deemed to have been issued, given or entered into in the jurisdiction where the offence is alleged to have been committed and to require the accused to appear before the justice to whom the transcript and documents are transmitted at the time provided in the order made in respect of the accused under paragraph (1)(*a*). R.S., c. C-34, s. 471; R.S., c. 2 (2nd Supp.), s. 7.

CROSS-REFERENCES

As to territorial jurisdiction generally see ss. 470, 476 to 481. For a discussion of the procedure on preliminary inquiries and cross-references, see *Note on procedure at preliminary inquiry* under s. 537.

SYNOPSIS

An accused charged in one jurisdiction may be arrested in another and brought before a justice sitting in the latter location. In these circumstances, the court can deal with bail (under Part XVI) and order that the accused appear, or be conveyed in custody, before a justice in the jurisdiction where the matter arose. Provision is also made in subsec. (2) for the transferability of transcript evidence and obligations relating to such matters as undertakings.

ANNOTATIONS

Even if an information was defective in that it failed to indicate where the offence occurred, the refusal of the provincial court judge to quash or order particulars would not be reviewable by way of *certiorari* unless the evidence adduced revealed that the alleged offence took place outside the court's jurisdiction. In that event, *certiorari* would lie if the judge persisted in continuing to exercise a jurisdiction he did not have: *R. v. Webster*, [1993] 1 S.C.R. 3, 78 C.C.C. (3d) 302, 17 C.R. (4th) 393 (7:0).

Absconding Accused

ACCUSED ABSCONDING DURING INQUIRY / Adverse inference / Accused not entitled to re-opening / Counsel for accused may continue to act / Accused calling witnesses.

544. (1) Notwithstanding any other provision of this Act, where an accused, whether or not he is charged jointly with another, absconds during the course of a preliminary inquiry into an offence with which he is charged,

(*a*) he shall be deemed to have waived his right to be present at the inquiry, and

(*b*) the justice

(i) may continue the inquiry and, when all the evidence has been taken, shall dispose of the inquiry in accordance with section 548, or

(ii) if a warrant is issued for the arrest of the accused, may adjourn the inquiry to await his appearance,

but where the inquiry is adjourned pursuant to subparagraph (*b*)(ii), the justice may continue it at any time pursuant to subparagraph (*b*)(i) if he is satisfied that it would no longer be in the interests of justice to await the appearance of the accused.

(2) Where the justice continues a preliminary inquiry pursuant to subsection (1), he may draw an inference adverse to the accused from the fact that he has absconded.

(3) Where an accused reappears at a preliminary inquiry that is continuing pursuant to subsection (1), he is not entitled to have any part of the proceedings that was conducted in his absence re-opened unless the justice is satisfied that because of exceptional circumstances it is in the interests of justice to re-open the inquiry.

(4) Where the accused has absconded during the course of a preliminary inquiry and the justice continues the inquiry, counsel for the accused is not thereby deprived of any authority he may have to continue to act for the accused in the proceedings.

(5) Where, at the conclusion of the evidence on the part of the prosecution at a preliminary inquiry that has been continued pursuant to subsection (1), the accused is absent but counsel for the accused is present, he or she shall be given an opportunity to call witnesses on behalf of the accused and subsection 541(5) applies with such modifications as the circumstances require. 1974-75-76, c. 93, s. 59; 1994, c. 44, s. 55.

CROSS-REFERENCES

A similar provision where the accused absconds during trial is found in s. 475. In addition an accused who fails to appear for his jury trial may forfeit the right to trial by jury by virtue of s. 598. For a discussion of the procedure on preliminary inquiries and cross-references, see *Note on procedure at preliminary inquiry* under s. 537.

SYNOPSIS

This section deals with the situation where an accused, having "elected" for trial in a higher court, fails to appear at the preliminary inquiry. If the justice is satisfied that the accused has absconded, he can either continue the hearing (subsec. (1)(*b*)(i)) or issue a warrant and adjourn the proceedings (subsec. (1)(*b*)(ii)). If the latter course is followed the proceedings can be resumed if the court is of the opinion that it is no longer in the interests of justice to await the accused's appearance. The adjournment need only be for a few minutes.

Subsection (2) permits the court to draw an adverse inference from the fact that the accused has absconded (*e.g.*, consciousness of guilt).

Counsel for the accused may continue to act and retains the right to call witnesses on the accused's behalf (subsecs. (4), (5)).

An accused who reappears does not have the right to have reopened that portion of the proceedings conducted in his or her absence (subsec. (3)). The proceedings will only be reopened where the justice finds that there are exceptional circumstances and that it is in the interests of justice to do so. (Also see s. 475 — absconding at trial.)

ANNOTATIONS

An accused may be found to have absconded "during the course of a preliminary inquiry" where having elected trial by judge and jury he fails to appear on the return date of an adjournment: *R. v. Plummer* (1983), 5 C.C.C. (3d) 17, [1983] 4 W.W.R. 351 (B.C.C.A.).

Procedure Where Witness Refuses to Testify

WITNESS REFUSING TO BE EXAMINED / Further commitment / Saving.

545. (1) Where a person, being present at a preliminary inquiry and being required by the justice to give evidence,

(*a*) refuses to be sworn,

(*b*) having been sworn, refuses to answer the questions that are put to him,

(*c*) fails to produce any writings that he is required to produce, or

(*d*) refuses to sign his deposition,

without offering a reasonable excuse for his failure or refusal, the justice may adjourn the inquiry and may, by warrant in Form 20, commit the person to prison for a period not exceeding eight clear days or for the period during which the inquiry is adjourned, whichever is the lesser period.

(2) Where a person to whom subsection (1) applies is brought before the justice upon the resumption of the adjourned inquiry and again refuses to do what is required of him, the justice may again adjourn the inquiry for a period not exceeding eight clear days and commit him to prison for the period of adjournment or any part thereof, and may adjourn the inquiry and commit the person to prison from time to time until the person consents to do what is required of him.

(3) Nothing in this section shall be deemed to prevent the justice from sending the case for trial on any other sufficient evidence taken by him. R.S., c. C-34, s. 472.

CROSS-REFERENCES

For a discussion of the procedure on preliminary inquiries and cross-references, see *Note on procedure at preliminary inquiry* under s. 537.

SYNOPSIS

This section sets out the powers of a justice or judge in dealing with a witness who, without a reasonable excuse, refuses to be sworn, answer questions or otherwise properly participate in a preliminary inquiry. The ability to punish for contempt of court is not available.

Where this situation arises, the court may adjourn the inquiry and commit the witness to prison for no longer than eight clear days (subsec. (1)). If, upon the resumption of the hearing, the witness persists in this course of conduct, he can be recommitted for a further eight days. In theory, this process can be repeated until such time as the witness agrees to co-operate (subsec. (2)).

ANNOTATIONS

This section limits the power of the justice, who may not resort to contempt of court proceedings for refusal to testify: *R. v. Bubley* (1976), 32 C.C.C. (2d) 79, [1976] 6 W.W.R. 179 (Alta. S.C. App. Div.).

Similarly, a superior court has no jurisdiction to punish for contempt a witness who refuses to testify at a preliminary hearing: *R. v. Marsden* (1977), 37 C.C.C. (2d) 107, 40 C.R.N.S. 11 *sub nom. Re Kenney, R. v. Marsden* (Que. Sup. Ct.).

Nor may the witness be proceeded against by way of indictment for contempt of court: *R. v. McKenzie* (1978), 41 C.C.C. (2d) 394, [1978] 4 W.W.R. 582 (Alta. S.C. App. Div.).

However, it would seem that at least where the witness was not committed to prison under this section, a charge of attempting to obstruct justice would lie under s. 139(2) for the witness' refusal to testify: *R. v. Lacroix*, [1987] 1 S.C.R. 244, 34 C.C.C. (3d) 94, 59 C.R. (3d) 92 (5:0), revg 15 C.C.C. (3d) 265, 41 C.R. (3d) 163 (Que. C.A.); *R. v. Mercer* (1988), 43 C.C.C. (3d) 347, 65 C.R. (3d) 275 (Alta. C.A.).

The words "reasonable excuse" grant a discretion to the justice to refuse to send a person to jail even if the person in law is required to answer the question: *R. v. Abko Medical Laboratories Ltd.* (1977), 35 C.C.C. (2d) 65, 77 D.L.R. (3d) 295 (Ont. H.C.J.). In this case the witness, a member of the legislature, had been called as a defence witness but refused to answer questions as to how he received certain information. It was held that the justice had the authority to consider whether the witness had a reasonable excuse, by virtue of his position, to refuse to answer the question. [**Note:** in a subsequent reference to the Ontario Court of Appeal *Reference Re Legislative Privilege* (1978), 39 C.C.C. (2d) 226, 18 O.R. (2d) 529, it was held that a member of the legislature has no privilege to refuse to disclose the sources of his information assuming the information to be relevant and admissible evidence.]

Remedial Provisions

IRREGULARITY OR VARIANCE NOT TO AFFECT VALIDITY.

546. The validity of any proceeding at or subsequent to a preliminary inquiry is not affected by

- **(*a*) any irregularity or defect in the substance or form of the summons or warrant;**
- **(*b*) any variance between the charge set out in the summons or warrant and the charge set out in the information; or**
- **(*c*) any variance between the charge set out in the summons, warrant or information and the evidence adduced by the prosecution at the inquiry. R.S., c. C-34, s. 473.**

CROSS-REFERENCES

As to provisions governing the sufficiency of informations and powers of amendment see ss. 581 to 601. For a discussion of the procedure on preliminary inquiries and cross-references, see *Note on procedure at preliminary inquiry* under s. 537.

SYNOPSIS

This section provides that irregularities or defects in the process by which the accused is brought before the court (*i.e.*, the summons or warrant) shall not affect the validity of any proceedings.

ADJOURNMENT IF ACCUSED MISLED.

547. Where it appears to the justice that the accused has been deceived or misled by any irregularity, defect or variance mentioned in section 546, he may adjourn the inquiry and may remand the accused or grant him interim release in accordance with Part XVI. R.S., c. C-34, s. 474; 1974-75-76, c. 93, s. 59.1.

CROSS-REFERENCES

The general adjournment and remand power is found in s. 537. For a discussion of the procedure on preliminary inquiries and cross-references, see *Note on procedure at preliminary inquiry* under s. 537.

SYNOPSIS

If an accused has been deceived or misled by any irregularity or defect in a summons or warrant, the justice may adjourn the inquiry and, if appropriate, deal with the question of bail.

INABILITY OF JUSTICE TO CONTINUE.

547.1 Where a justice acting under this Part has commenced to take evidence and dies or is unable to continue for any reason, another justice may

- **(*a*) continue taking the evidence at the point at which the interruption in the taking of the evidence occurred, where the evidence was recorded pursuant to section 540 and is available; or**
- **(*b*) commence taking the evidence as if no evidence had been taken, where no evidence was recorded pursuant to section 540 or where the evidence is not available. R.S.C. 1985, c. 27 (1st Supp.), s. 100.**

CROSS-REFERENCES

A similar provision, where the trial judge is unable to continue, is found in s. 669.2. For a discussion of the procedure on preliminary inquiries and cross-references, see *Note on procedure at preliminary inquiry* under s. 537.

SYNOPSIS

Where the justice presiding at a preliminary inquiry dies or is unable to continue, another justice may continue with the hearing. If a record of the evidence previously called is available that evidence need not be recalled. However, if no record is available, the inquiry shall start again as if no evidence had yet been heard.

Adjudication and Recognizances

ORDER TO STAND TRIAL OR DISCHARGE / Endorsing charge / Where accused ordered to stand trial / Defect not to affect validity.

548. (1) When all the evidence has been taken by the justice, he shall

(*a*) if in his opinion there is sufficient evidence to put the accused on trial for the offence charged or any other indictable offence in respect of the same transaction, order the accused to stand trial; or

(*b*) discharge the accused, if in his opinion on the whole of the evidence no sufficient case is made out to put the accused on trial for the offence charged or any other indictable offence in respect of the same transaction.

(2) Where the justice orders the accused to stand trial for an indictable offence, other than or in addition to the one with which the accused was charged, the justice shall endorse on the information the charges on which he orders the accused to stand trial.

(2.1) A justice who orders that an accused is to stand trial has the power to fix the date for the trial or the date on which the accused must appear in the trial court to have that date fixed.

(3) The validity of an order to stand trial is not affected by any defect apparent on the face of the information in respect of which the preliminary inquiry is held or in respect of any charge on which the accused is ordered to stand trial unless, in the opinion of the court before which an objection to the information or charge is taken, the accused has been misled or prejudiced in his defence by reason of that defect. R.S., c. C-34, s. 475; R.S., c. 2 (2nd Supp.), s. 8; R.S.C. 1985, c. 27 (1st Supp.), s. 101(1); 1994, c. 44, s. 56.

CROSS-REFERENCES

Procedure for waiver of the preliminary inquiry is set out in s. 549. After the accused has been ordered to stand trial the justice may vary the release or detention order where cause is shown provided the accused is not ordered to stand trial for a s. 469 offence such as murder. For a discussion of the procedure on preliminary inquiries and cross-references, see *Note on procedure at preliminary inquiry* under s. 537.

SYNOPSIS

Subsection (1) sets out the test to be applied at a preliminary inquiry. The standard which the Crown must meet to obtain a committal (*i.e*, "sufficient evidence") is the same as that which applies when a "no evidence" motion is made at trial. In other words, there must be evidence before the court upon which a reasonable jury properly instructed could convict. If the evidence is insufficient, the accused will be discharged.

Where the information contains a number of counts, the test is applied separately to each charge.

In addition to the charge(s) in the information, the court can consider whether there is evidence of the commission of other indictable offences "in respect of the same transaction". If there is, the accused can be ordered to stand trial on these matters (subsecs. (1)(*a*), and (2)).

The justice may also set the date for trial in the trial court.

Once there has been an order to stand trial, any defects apparent on the face of the information will not affect subsequent proceedings unless the accused can show that he or she has been misled or prejudiced in some way (subsec. (3)).

ANNOTATIONS

Test for order to stand trial – In *The United States of America v. Sheppard*, [1977] 2 S.C.R. 1067, 30 C.C.C. (2d) 424, 34 C.R.N.S. 207, the judgment of the majority (5:4) was given by Ritchie J. (Martland, Judson, Pigeon and de Grandpré JJ. concurring), who wrote:

> I agree that the duty imposed upon a "justice" under s. 475(1) [now s. 548(1)] is the same as that which governs a trial judge sitting with a jury in deciding whether the evidence is "sufficient" to justify him in withdrawing the case from the jury and this is to be determined according to whether or not there is any evidence upon which a reasonable jury properly instructed could return a verdict of guilty. The "justice", in accordance with this principle, is, in my opinion, required to commit an accused person for trial in any case in which there is admissible evidence which could, if it were believed, result in a conviction.

The test for committal is the same whether the evidence is direct or circumstantial. Where there is direct evidence as to each element of the offence, the accused must be committed to stand trial. If the Crown's case is based on direct evidence, the case must proceed to trial even if the accused adduces exculpatory evidence under s. 541 of the *Criminal Code*. If the Crown's case consists of circumstantial evidence, however, the judge must engage in a limited weighing of the evidence because there is an inferential gap between the evidence and the matter to be established. The judge must determine whether the evidence is reasonably capable of supporting the inferences that the Crown asks the jury to draw. Where the accused adduces exculpatory evidence in these circumstances, the judge must engage in a limited weighing of the whole of the evidence to determine whether a jury properly instructed could return a verdict of guilty. The judge cannot draw inferences from facts nor assess credibility. The judge must merely make an assessment of the reasonableness of the inferences to be drawn from the circumstantial evidence: *R. v. Arcuri*, [2001] 2 S.C.R. 828, 157 C.C.C. (3d) 21, 44 C.R. (5th) 213, 203 D.L.R. (4th) 20.

Order to stand trial on other indictable offences – An accused may be ordered to stand trial on a lesser and included offence over which a provincial court judge has absolute jurisdiction: *Ex p. Walker* (1974), 20 C.C.C. (2d) 539 (Ont. H.C.J.).

The test for whether the justice may order the accused to stand trial for other offences "in respect of the same transaction" is whether the other offences form part of the series of connected acts extending over a period of time which, the Crown alleges, prove the commission of the offence charged in the information. The other offence will of necessity be closely interwoven with or related to the offence charged in the information: *R. v. Goldstein* (1988), 42 C.C.C. (3d) 548, 64 C.R. (3d) 360 (Ont. C.A.); *R. v. Stewart* (1988), 44 C.C.C. (3d) 109 (Ont. C.A.).

Merely because the additional offence relates to a different victim, it does not mean that it cannot be in respect of the same transaction where it was a component part or constituent element of the transaction relating to the offence charged in the information: *R. v. Brown* (1990), 54 C.C.C. (3d) 561 (Ont. H.C.J.).

The power to order that the accused stand trial for other offences may be exercised even where the accused consents to an order that he stand trial without the taking of further evidence pursuant to s. 549: *R. v. Cancor Software Corp.* (1990), 58 C.C.C. (3d) 53, 79 C.R. (3d) 22 (Ont. C.A.).

The power to order the accused to stand trial for other indictable offences in respect of the same transaction does not infringe the guarantee in s. 11(*a*) of the Charter: *R. v. Cancor Software Corp., supra*.

Although the accused was discharged on the charge of conspiracy, it was open to the judge to order the accused to stand trial on substantive charges in respect of the same transaction. The judge had to consider whether there was sufficient evidence to commit the accused on the offence charge and then consider independently whether there was sufficient evidence to order the accused to stand trial on any other offence in respect of the same transaction: *R. v. Do* (2005), 196 C.C.C. (3d) 210, 257 Sask. R. 260 (Sask. C.A.).

Review by superior court – Where the record of the preliminary inquiry does not include evidence relating to each essential element of the charge then an order to stand trial may be brought forward by way of *certiorari* to a superior court and can be quashed: *R. v. Skogman*, [1984] 2 S.C.R. 93, 13 C.C.C. (3d) 161, 41 C.R. (3d) 1 (4:3).

An order discharging the accused may also be quashed on *certiorari* when there has been jurisdictional error as where the judge does not merely apply the wrong test for sufficiency of evidence but arrogates to himself the decision on the issue reserved to the trial court by purporting to dismiss the charge after applying the reasonable doubt standard: *R. v. Dubois*, [1986] 1 S.C.R. 366, 25 C.C.C. (3d) 221, 51 C.R. (3d) 193.

However, an error by the judge as to the elements of the offence is one made within the scope of his jurisdiction, and *certiorari* does not lie to quash the discharge: *R. v. Tremblay*, (1988), 47 C.C.C. (3d) 88, [1988] 2 S.C.R. 254 *sub nom. Quebec (Attorney General) v. Girouard* (4:0).

The authority to order an accused to stand trial following a preliminary inquiry is reserved to a justice under this section. "Justice" does not include a superior court judge and thus, where the judge allows an application by the Crown to quash an order discharging the accused, the judge must remit the matter to the preliminary inquiry judge to decide whether to order the accused to stand trial: *R. v. Thomson* (2005), 74 O.R. (3d) 721, 196 O.A.C. 39 (C.A.).

The failure of the preliminary inquiry judge, in discharging the accused, to consider "the whole of the evidence" may constitute a jurisdictional error giving rise to *certiorari* at the instance of the Crown to quash the discharge: *R. v. Deschamplain* (2004), 196 C.C.C. (3d) 1, 252 D.L.R. (4th) 289 (S.C.C.); *R. v. Sazant*, [2004] 3 S.C.R. 635, 208 C.C.C. (3d) 225.

Double jeopardy – The defence of *res judicata* and the special pleas of *autrefois* are not available at the preliminary hearing stage: *R. v. Schmidt* (1984), 10 C.C.C. (3d) 564, 44 O.R. (2d) 777 (C.A.), affd on other grounds [1987] 1 S.C.R. 500, 33 C.C.C. (3d) 193.

A preliminary inquiry judge's decision is reviewable where it is alleged that the conduct did not fall within the scope of s. 231(5). Even though this provision is a sentence-classification provision, the same right of review applies to the absence of evidence on an essential condition of a sentence-classification provision: *R. v. Russell*, [2001] 2 S.C.R. 804, 157 C.C.C. (3d) 1, 44 C.R. (5th) 231.

ORDER TO STAND TRIAL AT ANY STAGE OF INQUIRY WITH CONSENT / Limited preliminary inquiry / Procedure.

549. (1) Notwithstanding any other provision of this Act, the justice may, at any stage of a preliminary inquiry, with the consent of the accused and the prosecutor, order the accused to stand trial in the court having criminal jurisdiction, without taking or recording any evidence or further evidence.

(1.1) If the prosecutor and the accused agree under section 536.5 to limit the scope of a preliminary inquiry to specific issues, the justice, without recording evidence on any other issues, may order the accused to stand trial in the court having criminal jurisdiction.

(2) If an accused is ordered to stand trial under this section, the justice shall endorse on the information a statement of the consent of the accused and the prosecutor, and the accused shall after that be dealt with in all respects as if ordered to stand trial under section 548. R.S., c. C-34, s. 476; R.S.C. 1985, c. 27 (1st Supp.), s. 101(3); 2002, c. 13, s. 30.

CROSS-REFERENCES

For a discussion of the procedure on preliminary inquiries and cross-references, see *Note on procedure at preliminary inquiry* under s. 537.

SYNOPSIS

With the prosecutor's concurrence, the accused, at any stage of a preliminary inquiry, can consent to being ordered to stand trial. Under subsec. (1.1), where the parties have agreed to limit the scope of the inquiry, the justice, without recording further evidence, may order the accused to stand trial.

ANNOTATIONS

An undertaking by Crown counsel to disclose witnesses and evidence in advance of trial in return for defence counsel waiving the preliminary inquiry could not reasonably be interpreted to include evidence of which Crown counsel was not then aware and which he might be required not to disclose in the interests of the administration of justice. However, in this case, when the evidence was disclosed in the course of the trial and the accused were surprised by it, the trial judge adjourned the case to permit the accused to consider their position and their conduct of the defence and offered to recall any witnesses for further cross-examination. In the result, the accused were not prejudiced by the late disclosure: *R. v. Mitchell* (1989), 70 C.R. (3d) 71, 33 O.A.C. 360 (C.A.).

RECOGNIZANCE OF WITNESS / Form / Sureties or deposit for appearance of witness / Witness refusing to be bound / Discharge.

550. (1) Where an accused is ordered to stand trial, the justice who held the preliminary inquiry may require any witness whose evidence is, in his opinion, material to enter into a recognizance to give evidence at the trial of the accused and to comply with such reasonable conditions prescribed in the recognizance as the justice considers desirable for securing the attendance of the witness to give evidence at the trial of the accused.

(2) A recognizance entered into pursuant to this section may be in Form 32, and may be set out at the end of a deposition or be separate therefrom.

(3) A justice may, for any reason satisfactory to him, require any witness entering into a recognizance pursuant to this section

(*a*) to produce one or more sureties in such amount as he may direct; or

(*b*) to deposit with him a sum of money sufficient in his opinion to ensure that the witness will appear and give evidence.

(4) Where a witness does not comply with subsection (1) or (3) when required to do so by a justice, he may be committed by the justice, by warrant in Form 24, to a prison in the territorial division where the trial is to be held, there to be kept until he does what is required of him or until the trial is concluded.

(5) Where a witness has been committed to prison pursuant to subsection (4), the court before which the witness appears or a justice having jurisdiction in the territorial division where the prison is situated may, by order in Form 39, discharge the witness from custody when the trial is concluded. R.S., c. C-34, s. 477; 1974-75-76, c. 39, s. 60; R.S.C. 1985, c. 27 (1st Supp.), s. 101(3).

CROSS-REFERENCES

Procedure for enforcement of recognizances is set out in Part XXV. For a discussion of the procedure on preliminary inquiries and cross-references, see *Note on procedure at preliminary inquiry* under s. 537.

SYNOPSIS

This section deals with what may otherwise be referred to as "material" witnesses. If, following committal, the justice considers it necessary, he can order that a witness enter into a recognizance, with or without sureties, conditions or deposit, for the purpose of securing that person's attendance at the trial. A witness who fails to comply with such an order may be incarcerated.

Transmission of Record

TRANSMITTING RECORD.

551. Where a justice orders an accused to stand trial, he shall forthwith send to the clerk or other proper officer of the court by which the accused is to be tried, the information, the evidence, the exhibits, the statement if any of the accused taken down in writing under section 541, any promise to appear, undertaking or recognizance given or entered into in accordance with Part XVI, or any evidence taken before a coroner, that is in the possession of the justice. R.S., c. C-34, s. 478; R.S., c. 2 (2nd Supp.), s. 9; R.S.C. 1985, c. 27 (1st Supp.), s. 102.

CROSS-REFERENCES

The accused has the right to inspect the record which is transmitted to the trial court under this section, by virtue of s. 603. For a discussion of the procedure on preliminary inquiries and cross-references, see *Note on procedure at preliminary inquiry* under s. 537.

SYNOPSIS

Following the order to stand trial, the complete file is transferred from the Provincial Court to the court before which the trial is to be held. The obligation of the accused to appear is also transferred.

Editor's Note: CASE MANAGEMENT JUDGE – Part XVIII.1 creates the position of Case Management Judge to assist in the management of jury and judge alone trials. A case management judge will not be appointed in all cases, only where the Chief Justice or Chief Judge or their designate is of the view that the appointment is, in the words of s. 551.1(1), "necessary for the proper administration of justice". The scheme of the legislation is as follows. Under s. 551.1, the appointment of the case management judge is made by the Chief Justice or Chief Judge or their designate. The appointment must be made before jury selection in the case of a jury trial and otherwise before evidence on the merits is presented. Where the trial is not being held in the provincial court, the appointment can only be made after the indictment is preferred in the superior court. The appointment can be made on application by the prosecutor or the accused or on their own motion by the Chief Justice or Chief Judge or their designate. If necessary the Chief Justice or Chief Judge or their designate can order a conference between the prosecutor and the accused or the accused's lawyer for the purpose of deciding whether the appointment should be made. Alternatively, a hearing can be ordered for that purpose, presumably to be held before the Chief Justice or Chief Judge or their designate. The case management judge can also be the trial judge.

Section 551.2 sets out the role of the case management judge, namely, to promote a fair and efficient trial and to ensure that the evidence on the merits is presented with as few interruptions as possible.

Section 551.3 sets out the powers of the case management judge in dealing with issues before the presentation of the evidence on the merits, in the normal case, that is other than a case governed by s. 551.7, where there are separate but related trials. The powers are extensive and fall into roughly three categories: powers to encourage or assist the parties for a fair and efficient trial; the power to hear a guilty plea and impose sentence; and powers to adjudicate on specific matters, some of which, prior to enactment of Part XVIII.1, could only be dealt with by the trial judge hearing the trial on the merits. The powers related to ensuring a fair and efficient trial on the merits include assisting in identify, the witnesses to be heard, making admissions and other agreements, establishing schedules and imposing deadlines, and identifying the issues in the case.

The matters upon which the case management judge may adjudicate are set out in s. 551.3(1)(*g*) and include any matters that can be decided before the hearing of evidence on the merits. Some of the matters listed are those relating to disclosure, admissibility of evidence, the *Charter of Rights and Freedoms*, expert evidence, and severance of counts and accused. Section 551.3(2) provides that the case management judge will hold a hearing to determine these matters. Pursuant to s. 551.3(3), the case management judge is acting as the trial judge in making these rulings. It follows that any appeal from a ruling would follow the normal appeal route following conviction or acquittal as the case may be. The decision on these matters is binding on the parties, even if the case management judge does not turn out to be the judge on the trial itself "unless the court is satisfied that it would not be in the interests of justice because, among other considerations, fresh evidence has been adduced".

Under s. 551.4, where the case management judge is not the trial judge, there must be a record made of the various decisions that have been made in case management. Subsection (1) lists some of the matters that are to be included in the record, such as the names of witness, any admissions, estimated time requirements, any orders or decisions and any issues identified by the parties to be dealt with at the trial on the merits.

Section 551.5 provides that the trial "shall proceed continuously, subject to adjournment by the court". The powers of adjournment are set out in ss. 571 and 645.

Section 551.6 provides that the trial judge, during the trial on the merits, can refer matters to the case management judge, who can exercise the powers of a trial judge. It is unclear what matters would need to be referred to a case management judge in the course of a trial, but presumably it would be matters that might interrupt the flow of the trial.

Section 551.7 deals with cases requiring a case management judge where there are separate but related proceedings in the province before courts of the same jurisdiction. The Chief Justice or Chief Judge or their designate must decide whether it is in the interests of justice to appoint a single case management judge to conduct a joint hearing for some or all of those trials. Subsection (2) sets out the considerations that the Chief Justice or Chief Judge or their designate will take into account in deciding whether to have a joint hearing. The balance of the section sets out the procedural steps to be taken to ensure the joint hearing. As with the orders and decisions made under s. 551.3, the judge conducting the joint hearing acts as a trial judge.

In addition to the provisions of Part XVIII.1, other amendments that are part of this legislation found in other Parts of the *Criminal Code* may impact on trial management. Thus, s. 591(4.1) and (4.2) allow a judge to make a severance order under that section that will only take effect later in the proceedings. Thus, decisions made after the severance order would be binding in the severed trial. More generally, unless the court is satisfied that it would not be in the interests of justice, the decisions relating to the disclosure or admissibility of evidence or the *Canadian Charter of Rights and Freedoms* that are made before any severance order takes effect continue to bind the parties if the decisions are made or could have been made before the stage at which the evidence on the merits is presented.

Also note s. 653.1, which provides that, in the case of a mistrial, unless the court is satisfied that it would not be in the interests of justice, rulings relating to the disclosure or admissibility of evidence or the *Charter of Rights and Freedoms* that were made during the trial are binding on the parties in any new trial, if the rulings are made — or could have been made — before the stage at which the evidence on the merits is presented (in other words, could have been made under Part XVIII.1).

Finally, other amendments have been made to the jury selection process allowing for a jury of 13 or 14 members to hear the case up to the end of the charge to the jury. This will make it less likely that there will be a mistrial because the number of jurors has fallen below ten persons. However, prior to deliberations, the judge reduces the jury to 12 members by discharging one or two members, as the case may be, if the number of jurors has remained at 13 or 14.

PART XVIII.1 / CASE MANAGEMENT JUDGE

APPOINTMENT / Conference or hearing / Timing of application or appointment / Same judge.

551.1 (1) On application by the prosecutor or the accused or on his or her own motion, the Chief Justice or the Chief Judge of the court before which a trial is to be or is being held or the judge that the Chief Justice or the Chief Judge designates may, if he or she is of the opinion that it is necessary for the proper administration of justice, appoint a judge as the case management judge for that trial at any time before the jury selection, if the trial is before a judge and jury, or before the stage at which the evidence on the merits is presented, if the trial is being heard by a judge without a jury or a provincial court judge.

(2) The Chief Justice or the Chief Judge or his or her designate may order that a conference between the prosecutor and the accused or counsel for the accused or a hearing be held for the purpose of deciding if it is necessary for the proper administration of justice to proceed with the appointment.

(3) In the case of a trial for an indictable offence, other than a trial before a provincial court judge, the application or appointment may only be made after the prosecution prefers the indictment.

(4) The appointment of a judge as the case management judge does not prevent him or her from becoming the judge who hears the evidence on the merits. 2011, c. 16, s. 4.

See **Editor's Note** before s. 551.1.

ROLE.

551.2 The case management judge shall assist in promoting a fair and efficient trial, including by ensuring that the evidence on the merits is presented, to the extent possible, without interruption. 2011, c. 16, s. 4.

See **Editor's Note** before s. 551.1.

POWERS BEFORE EVIDENCE ON MERITS PRESENTED / Hearing / Power exercised at trial / Decision binding.

551.3 (1) In performing his or her duties before the stage of the presentation of the evidence on the merits, the case management judge, as a trial judge, may exercise the powers that a trial judge has before that stage, including

- **(*a*) assisting the parties to identify the witnesses to be heard, taking into account the witnesses' needs and circumstances;**
- **(*b*) encouraging the parties to make admissions and reach agreements;**
- **(*c*) encouraging the parties to consider any other matters that would promote a fair and efficient trial;**
- **(*d*) establishing schedules and imposing deadlines on the parties;**
- **(*e*) hearing guilty pleas and imposing sentences;**
- **(*f*) assisting the parties to identify the issues that are to be dealt with at the stage at which the evidence on the merits is presented; and**
- **(*g*) subject to section 551.7, adjudicating any issues that can be decided before that stage, including those related to**
  - **(i) the disclosure of evidence,**

(ii) the admissibility of evidence,
(iii) the *Canadian Charter of Rights and Freedoms*,
(iv) expert witnesses,
(v) the severance of counts, and
(vi) the separation of trials on one or more counts when there is more than one accused.

(2) The case management judge shall order that a hearing be held for the purpose of exercising the power referred to in paragraph (1)(*g*).

(3) When the case management judge exercises the power referred to in paragraph (1)(*g*), he or she is doing so at trial.

(4) A decision that results from the exercise of the power referred to in paragraph (1)(*g*) is binding on the parties for the remainder of the trial — even if the judge who hears the evidence on the merits is not the same as the case management judge — unless the court is satisfied that it would not be in the interests of justice because, among other considerations, fresh evidence has been adduced. 2011, c. 16, s. 4.

See **Editor's Note** before s. 551.1.

INFORMATION RELEVANT TO PRESENTATION OF EVIDENCE ON MERITS TO BE PART OF COURT RECORD / Exception.

551.4 (1) When the case management judge is of the opinion that the measures to promote a fair and efficient trial that can be taken before the stage of the presentation of the evidence on the merits have been taken — including adjudicating the issues that can be decided — he or she shall ensure that the court record includes information that, in his or her opinion, may be relevant at the stage of the presentation of the evidence on the merits, including

(*a*) the names of the witnesses to be heard that have been identified by the parties;
(*b*) any admissions made and agreements reached by the parties;
(*c*) the estimated time required to conclude the trial;
(*d*) any orders and decisions; and
(*e*) any issues identified by the parties that are to be dealt with at the stage of the presentation of the evidence on the merits.

(2) This section does not apply to a case management judge who also hears the evidence on the merits. 2011, c. 16, s. 4.

See **Editor's Note** before s. 551.1.

TRIAL CONTINUOUS.

551.5 Even if the judge who hears the evidence on the merits is not the same as the case management judge, the trial of an accused shall proceed continuously, subject to adjournment by the court. 2011, c. 16, s. 4.

See **Editor's Note** before s. 551.1.

ISSUES REFERRED TO CASE MANAGEMENT JUDGE / Powers at stage of presentation of evidence on merits.

551.6 (1) During the presentation of the evidence on the merits, the case management judge shall adjudicate any issue referred to him or her by the judge hearing the evidence on the merits.

(2) For the purposes of adjudicating an issue, the case management judge may exercise the powers of a trial judge. 2011, c. 16, s. 4.

See **Editor's Note** before s. 551.1.

DECISION WHETHER TO HOLD JOINT HEARING / Considerations / Order for joint hearing / Limitation — indictable offence / Order in court record and transmission to parties / Transmission of court record / Order to appear at joint hearing / Removal of prisoner / Powers of judge / Adjudication at trial / Decision in court records and return of documents.

551.7 (1) If an issue referred to in any of subparagraphs 551.3(1)(*g*)(i) to (iii) is to be adjudicated in related trials that are to be or are being held in the same province before a court of the same jurisdiction, the Chief Justice or the Chief Judge of that court or his or her designate may, on application by the prosecutor or the accused or on his or her own motion, determine if it is in the interests of justice, including ensuring consistent decisions, to adjudicate that issue at a joint hearing for some or all of those trials.

(2) To make the determination, the Chief Justice or the Chief Judge or his or her designate

- **(*a*) shall take into account, among other considerations, the degree to which the evidence relating to the issue is similar in the related trials; and**
- **(*b*) may order that a conference between the prosecutor and the accused or counsel for the accused or a hearing be held.**

(3) If the Chief Justice or the Chief Judge or his or her designate determines that it is in the interests of justice to adjudicate the issue at a joint hearing for some or all of the related trials, he or she shall issue an order

- **(*a*) declaring that a joint hearing be held to adjudicate the issue in the related trials that he or she specifies;**
- **(*b*) naming the parties who are to appear at the hearing;**
- **(*c*) appointing a judge to adjudicate the issue; and**
- **(*d*) designating the territorial division in which the hearing is to be held, if the trials are being held in different territorial divisions.**

(4) However, the order may only be made in respect of a trial for an indictable offence, other than a trial before a provincial court judge, if the indictment has been preferred.

(5) The Chief Justice or the Chief Judge or his or her designate shall cause a copy of the order to be included in the court record of each of the trials specified in the order and to be provided to each of the parties named in it.

(6) If one of the specified trials is being held in a territorial division other than the one in which the joint hearing will be held, the officer in that territorial division who has custody of the indictment or information and the writings relating to the trial shall, when he or she receives the order, transmit the indictment or information and the writings without delay to the clerk of the court before which the joint hearing is to be held.

(7) The judge appointed under the order shall require the parties who are named in it to appear at the joint hearing.

(8) The order made under subsection (2) or (3) is sufficient warrant, justification and authority to all sheriffs, keepers of prisons and peace officers for an accused's removal, disposal and reception in accordance with the terms of the order, and the sheriff may appoint and authorize any peace officer to convey the accused to a prison for the territorial division in which the hearing, as the case may be, is to be held.

(9) The judge appointed under the order may, as a trial judge and for the purpose of adjudicating the issue at the joint hearing, exercise the powers of a trial judge.

(10) When the judge adjudicates the issue, he or she is doing so at trial.

(11) Once the judge has adjudicated the issue, he or she shall cause his or her decision, with reasons, to be included in the court record of each of the related trials in respect of which the joint hearing was held and, in the case of a trial for which an indictment,

CR. CODE

information or writings were transmitted by an officer under subsection (6), the judge shall have the documents returned to the officer. 2011, c. 16, s. 4.

See **Editor's Note** before s. 551.1.

Part XIX / INDICTABLE OFFENCES — TRIAL WITHOUT JURY

Interpretation

DEFINITIONS / "Judge".

552. In this Part,

"judge" means,

(*a*) in the Province of Ontario, a judge of the superior court of criminal jurisdiction of the Province,

(*b*) in the Province of Quebec, a judge of the Court of Quebec,

(*c*) in the Province of Nova Scotia, a judge of the superior court of criminal jurisdiction of the Province,

(*d*) in the Province of New Brunswick, a judge of the Court of Queen's Bench,

(*e*) in the Province of British Columbia, the Chief Justice or a puisne judge of the Supreme Court,

(*f*) in the Province of Prince Edward Island, a judge of the Supreme Court,

(*g*) in the Province of Manitoba, the Chief Justice or a puisne judge of the Court of Queen's Bench,

(*h*) in the Provinces of Saskatchewan and Alberta, a judge of the superior court of criminal jurisdiction of the province,

(*h*.1) in the Province of Newfoundland and Labrador, a judge of the Trial Division of the Supreme Court,

(*i*) in Yukon and the Northwest Territories, a judge of the Supreme Court, and

(*j*) in Nunavut, a judge of the Nunavut Court of Justice. R.S., c. C-34, s. 482; 1972, c. 13, s. 39, c. 17, s. 2; 1974-75-76, c. 48, s. 25, c. 93, s. 61; 1978-79, c. 11, s. 10; R.S.C. 1985, c. 11 (1st Supp.), s. 2, c. 27 (1st Supp.), s. 103(1); c. 27 (2nd Supp.), s. 10; c. 40 (4th Supp.), s. 2; 1990, c. 16, s. 6; 1990, c. 17, s. 13; 1992, c. 51, s. 38; 1993, c. 28, Sch. III, s. 34 (repealed 1999, c. 3, s. 12); 1999, c. 3, ss. 12, 36; 2002, c. 7, s. 145; 2015, c. 3, s. 53.

"magistrate". [*Repealed*, R.S.C. 1985, c. 27 (1st Supp.), s. 103(2).]

CROSS-REFERENCES

The term "superior court of criminal jurisdiction" is defined in s. 2. In addition to the definitions in this section, see s. 2 and notes to that section.

SYNOPSIS

This section defines "judge" for the purposes of Part XIX. It includes all federally appointed judges to the provincial trial courts and members of the Court of Quebec.

JURISDICTION OF PROVINCIAL COURT JUDGES

Absolute Jurisdiction

ABSOLUTE JURISDICTION.

553. The jurisdiction of a provincial court judge, or in Nunavut, of a judge of the Nunavut Court of Justice, to try an accused is absolute and does not depend on the consent of the accused where the accused is charged in an information

(*a*) with

(i) theft, other than theft of cattle,

(ii) obtaining money or property by false pretences,

(iii) unlawfully having in his possession any property or thing or any proceeds of any property or thing knowing that all or a part of the property or thing or of the proceeds was obtained by or derived directly or indirectly from the commission in Canada of an offence punishable by indictment or an act or omission anywhere that, if it had occurred in Canada, would have constituted an offence punishable by indictment,

(iv) having, by deceit, falsehood or other fraudulent means, defrauded the public or any person, whether ascertained or not, of any property, money or valuable security, or

(v) mischief under subsection 430(4),

where the subject-matter of the offence is not a testamentary instrument and the alleged value of the subject-matter of the offence does not exceed five thousand dollars;

(*b*) with counselling or with a conspiracy or attempt to commit or with being an accessory after the fact to the commission of

(i) any offence referred to in paragraph (*a*) in respect of the subject-matter and value thereof referred to in that paragraph, or

(ii) any offence referred to in paragraph (*c*); or

(*c*) with an offence under

(i) section 201 (keeping gaming or betting house),

(ii) section 202 (betting, pool-selling, book-making, etc.),

(iii) section 203 (placing bets),

(iv) section 206 (lotteries and games of chance),

(v) section 209 (cheating at play),

(vi) section 210 (keeping common bawdy-house),

(vii) [*Repealed*, 2000, c. 25, s. 4.]

(viii) section 393 (fraud in relation to fares),

(viii.01) section 490.031 (failure to comply with order or obligation),

(viii.02) section 490.0311 (providing false or misleading information),

(viii.1) section 811 (breach of recognizance),

(ix) subsection 733.1(1) (failure to comply with probation order), or

(x) paragraph 4(4)(*a*) of the *Controlled Drugs and Substances Act*. R.S., c. C-34, s. 483; 1972, c. 13, s. 40; 1974-75-76, c. 93, s. 62; R.S.C. 1985, c. 27 (1st Supp.), s. 104; 1992, c. 1, s. 58; 1994, c. 44, s. 57; 1995, c. 22, s. 2; 1996, c. 19, s. 72; 1997, c. 18, s. 66; 1999, c. 3, s. 37; 2000, c. 25, s. 4; 2010, c. 17, s. 25; 2012, c. 1, s. 33, 2018, c. 16, s. 219.

(xi) [*Repealed*, 2018, c. 16, s. 219.]

CROSS-REFERENCES

The terms "provincial court judge" and "testamentary instrument" are defined in s. 2. Note that s. 3 provides that the descriptions in parenthesis after the section number are inserted for convenience of reference only and are no part of the provision.

Note on mode of trial – The scheme of the *Criminal Code* is to classify offences as pure indictable [*e.g.*, robbery, s. 344], purely summary [*e.g.*, soliciting, s. 213] or hybrid, *i.e.*, the prosecution may elect whether to proceed by way of summary conviction or by indictment [*e.g.*, assault, s. 266]. The effect of s. 468 is that the superior court of criminal jurisdiction may try any purely indictable offence or any hybrid offence where the prosecution elects to proceed by way of indictment. Other courts of criminal jurisdiction (defined in s. 2) may, however, try indictable offences except those offences listed in s. 469 [*e.g.*, murder, s. 235]. The offences listed in s. 469 may only be tried by the superior court of criminal jurisdiction with a jury subject to a re-election in conformity with s. 473.

Indictable offences not listed in s. 469 fall into two categories. For the majority of the indictable offences not listed in s. 469 the accused may elect the mode of trial as set out in s. 536(2) and within limits may change an election [see, *e.g.*, s. 561]. While the Attorney General is given a narrow discretion to override this election and require a jury trial under s. 568 in the circumstances defined therein and in addition a provincial court judge has a discretion to override or not record an accused's election for trial by provincial court judge and hold a preliminary inquiry [see for example ss. 555 and 567] the thrust of the provisions is to give the accused the right to determine the manner of trial. Where the accused elects trial by provincial court judge, jurisdiction is given to such judge to try the case by virtue of s. 554. The trial takes place on the basis of the information. Where the case is tried in a court other than the provincial court, the trial is conducted on the basis of an indictment preferred in accordance with ss. 574 and 577, usually following an order to stand trial. For notes on conduct of the preliminary inquiry see s. 537.

The other group of indictable offences are those offences listed in s. 553 [*e.g.*, keeping common bawdy house, s. 210(1)] which fall within the absolute jurisdiction of a provincial court judge, meaning that the accused does not have a normal election as to the mode of trial under s. 536(2). Nevertheless, the other courts with jurisdiction to try indictable offences have jurisdiction to try the offences listed in s. 553, if the provincial court judge elects not to try the offence and requires that the case proceed by way of preliminary inquiry pursuant to s. 555(1): see *R. v. Scherbank*, [1967] 2 C.C.C. 279, 50 C.R. 170 (Ont. C.A.); *R. v. Coupland* (1978), 45 C.C.C. (2d) 437 (Alta. C.A.). In that case the accused is deemed to have elected trial by judge and jury by virtue of s. 565(1)(*a*). If in the course of the trial before the provincial court judge pursuant to s. 553 it is disclosed that in fact the offence is not one over which the provincial court judge has absolute jurisdiction, then the accused must then be put to his election under s. 536(2) [for example a charge of theft of goods of a value not exceeding $5,000 where the evidence discloses that the value of the goods exceeds $5,000]. If he fails to elect then he is deemed to have elected trial by judge and jury under s. 565(1)(*c*). The accused may re-elect in accordance with s. 561.

For all summary conviction offences meaning purely summary conviction or hybrid offences where the prosecution elects to proceed by way of summary conviction only the summary conviction court (defined in s. 785) may try the accused. The procedure for trial of summary conviction offences generally resembles trial of an indictable offence by a provincial court judge but that procedure including special rights of appeal is set out in Part XXVII.

As to the mode of trial for offences tried in Nunavut, see ss. 536.1, 554(2), 555.1, 561.1, 562.1, 565(1.1), 566.1, 569 and Part XIX.1.

For cross-references and a note on procedure in Nunavut, see the cross-references under s. 536.1.

SYNOPSIS

The accused does not have an "election" as to mode of trial for the indictable offences listed in this section (see s. 536(2)), which are normally tried by a provincial court judge (or a judge of the Nunavut Court of Justice).

The offences listed in this section fall into three categories. Those in para. (*a*) are classified by reason of the value of the goods taken or damaged, *i.e.*, value does not exceed $5,000 and is not a testamentary instrument (not theft of cattle). Offences in para. (*c*) being certain relatively minor indictable offences, mostly in Part VII relating to disorderly houses and gaming but also including offences relating to obligations to report under the *Sex*

Offender Information Registration Act, S.C. 2004, c. 10. Offences in para. (*b*) being an attempt, accessory after the fact or counselling of the offence in paras. (*a*) or (*c*).

ANNOTATIONS

Paragraph (*a*) – In order to vest absolute jurisdiction in the provincial court judge the information must contain the statement that the alleged value of the property in question is less than the prescribed limit: *R. v. Miller and Newman* (1973), 14 C.C.C. (2d) 370, (Ont. C.A.).

Provincial Court Judge's Jurisdiction with Consent

TRIAL BY PROVINCIAL COURT JUDGE WITH CONSENT / Nunavut.

554. (1) Subject to subsection (2), if an accused is charged in an information with an indictable offence other than an offence that is mentioned in section 469, and the offence is not one over which a provincial court judge has absolute jurisdiction under section 553, a provincial court judge may try the accused if the accused elects to be tried by a provincial court judge.

(2) With respect to criminal proceedings in Nunavut, if an accused is charged in an information with an indictable offence other than an offence that is mentioned in section 469 and the offence is not one over which a judge of the Nunavut Court of Justice has absolute jurisdiction under section 553, a judge of the Nunavut Court of Justice may try the accused if the accused elects to be tried by a judge without a jury. R.S., c. C-34, s. 484; R.S.C. 1985, c. 27 (1st Supp.), s. 105; 1999, c. 3, s. 38; 2002, c 13, s. 31.

CROSS-REFERENCES

The term "provincial court judge" is defined in s. 2. For procedure respecting election for mode of trial, including trial by provincial court judge, see *Note on mode of trial* under s. 553.

For cross-references and a note on procedure in Nunavut, see the cross-references under s. 536.1.

SYNOPSIS

This section is a companion provision to s. 536. An accused charged with an indictable offence that is not one which is to be tried before a superior court of criminal jurisdiction (see s. 469) or before a provincial court judge (see s. 553) may "elect" to be tried in provincial court. Where this occurs there will not be a preliminary inquiry.

ANNOTATIONS

Jurisdiction – Notwithstanding the accused elects trial by provincial court judge he is tried under the provisions of this Part and not the summary conviction provisions of Part XXVII: *R. v. Edmunds*, [1981] 1 S.C.R. 233, 58 C.C.C. (2d) 485 (4:1).

A provincial court judge before whom an accused elects to be tried and pleads not guilty is not seised of exclusive jurisdiction and accordingly the accused may later be tried by another judge: *R. v. Wiseberg* (1973), 15 C.C.C. (2d) 26 (Ont. C.A.); *R. v. Gillis*, [1967] 1 C.C.C. 266 (Sask. C.A.).

Arraignment – Even though the accused was not deceived or misled by the substantial differences between the information and the charge upon which he was arraigned, his conviction must be set aside: *R. v. Arnott and St. James*, [1970] 5 C.C.C. 190 (Ont. C.A.).

Joint trial of summary and indictable offences – A provincial court judge may jointly try summary and indictable offences even where they are contained on separate informations, provided that the accused has not elected trial by a higher court in respect of the indictable offence. In the event of any conflict as to the applicable procedure, indictable offence procedures would apply. Where, following the trial, both charges have gone for appeal, the summary conviction appeal court should await the decision of the court of appeal in the indictable proceeding: *R. v. Clunas*, [1992] 1 S.C.R. 595, 70 C.C.C. (3d) 115 (5:0).

Joint trial of summary conviction and provincial offence charges – At least in Ontario, a provincial court judge has jurisdiction to conduct a joint trial of provincial charges and summary conviction criminal charges. The two-part common law test for joinder set out in *R. v. Clunas*, *supra*, applies to joinder in this context: *R. v. Sciascia*, [2017] 2 S.C.R. 539, 355 C.C.C. (3d) 553.

Failure of Crown to elect on hybrid offence – Where the accused is charged with a Crown option offence and the Crown fails to elect the mode of procedure the Crown is deemed to proceed on a summary conviction basis if the case proceeds in a summary conviction court: *R. v. Robert* (1973), 13 C.C.C. (2d) 43 (Ont. C.A.).

On arraignment for a Crown-election offence the prosecution failed to elect and then the magistrate [now provincial court judge] failed to put the accused to his complete election with the result that although the accused had indicated that he wished to be tried by the magistrate, that judge did not obtain jurisdiction under this Part of the Code and accordingly the magistrate is deemed to have been sitting as a summary conviction court. Accordingly, no appeal from conviction lay to the Court of Appeal: *R. v. Hawryluk* (1975), 29 C.C.C. (2d) 41 (N.B.S.C. App. Div.) (2:1). Limerick J.A., dissenting, held that, where the Crown fails to elect, the magistrate has the option of determining the mode of trial and, in this case, by commencing to give the accused his election under subsec. (2), the magistrate indicated he was treating the offence as indictable. The failure to give the complete election resulted in a lack of jurisdiction to try the case and the conviction should be quashed.

PROVINCIAL COURT JUDGE MAY DECIDE TO HOLD PRELIMINARY INQUIRY / Where subject-matter is a testamentary instrument or exceeds $5,000 in value / Continuing proceedings.

555. (1) Where in any proceedings under this Part an accused is before a provincial court judge and it appears to the provincial court judge that for any reason the charge should be prosecuted by indictment, he may, at any time before the accused has entered on his defence, decide not to adjudicate and shall thereupon inform the accused of his decision and continue the proceedings as a preliminary inquiry.

(2) Where an accused is before a provincial court judge charged with an offence mentioned in paragraph 553(*a*) or subparagraph 553(*b*)(i), and, at any time before the provincial court judge makes an adjudication, the evidence establishes that the subject-matter of the offence is a testamentary instrument or that its value exceeds five thousand dollars, the provincial court judge shall put the accused to his or her election in accordance with subsection 536(2).

(3) Where an accused is put to his election pursuant to subsection (2), the following provisions apply, namely,

(*a*) if the accused elects to be tried by a judge without a jury or a court composed of a judge and jury or does not elect when put to his or her election, the provincial court judge shall continue the proceedings as a preliminary inquiry under Part XVIII and, if the provincial court judge orders the accused to stand trial, he or she shall endorse on the information a record of the election; and

(*b*) if the accused elects to be tried by a provincial court judge, the provincial court judge shall endorse on the information a record of the election and continue with the trial. R.S., c. C-34, s. 485; 1972, c. 13, s. 41; R.S.C. 1985, c. 27 (1st Supp.), s. 106; 1994, c. 44, s. 58; 2002, c. 13, s. 32.

CROSS-REFERENCES

The term "provincial court judge" is defined in s. 2. Where the judge continues the case as a preliminary inquiry under subsec. (1) then the accused is deemed to have elected trial by judge and jury pursuant to s. 565(1)(*a*), but may re-elect by complying with s. 561. Where the accused refuses to elect under subsec. (1) then again he is deemed to have elected trial by judge and jury pursuant to s. 565(1)(*c*), but may re-elect by complying with s. 561. Where accused are jointly charged and do not all elect the same mode of trial then the judge may refuse to record the election pursuant to s. 567 and by virtue of s. 565(1)(*b*) they are all deemed to have elected trial by judge and jury pursuant to s. 565(1)(*c*), but may re-elect by complying with s. 561. For procedure respecting election for mode of trial, including trial by provincial court judge, see *Note on mode of trial* under s. 553. For procedure respecting conduct of preliminary inquiry, see the note following s. 537.

In Nunavut, see s. 555.1.

SYNOPSIS

This section deals with situations where a trial in the provincial court may be transformed into a preliminary inquiry, even when the accused has elected to be tried in that forum or, by virtue of s. 553, the offence is within the absolute jurisdiction of the provincial court judge.

Where, before the accused has been called upon to enter a defence, a provincial court judge presiding at the trial of an indictable offence under Part XIX is of the opinion that the matter should be tried in a higher court, he can convert the proceedings into a preliminary inquiry. Should this occur, the accused will be deemed to have elected to be tried by a judge sitting with a jury (see s. 565(1)(*a*)).

Where the trial is in relation to an offence within the absolute jurisdiction of the provincial court, on the basis that the subject-matter of the charge does not exceed $5,000 (see s. 553), and before the conclusion of the proceedings the evidence establishes a greater value, the accused will be asked to elect the mode of trial (see s. 536(2)). Depending on the election, the matter will continue as either a trial or become a preliminary inquiry. If the accused refuses to elect, the proceedings will convert to an inquiry. The election is endorsed on the information.

ANNOTATIONS

Subsection (1) – Completion of an unsuccessful motion for dismissal at the conclusion of the Crown's case is a proceeding before the accused has entered upon his defence and at that point the court may continue the proceedings as a preliminary inquiry: *R. v. Nadeau* (1971), 3 C.C.C. (2d) 276 (N.B.S.C. App. Div.).

This subsection only applies to indictable proceedings under Part XIX and therefore could have no application to a trial commenced as a summary conviction trial under Part XXVII. Thus, a judge having commenced a trial under Part XXVII for assault, the Crown having elected to proceed by way of summary conviction, could not invoke this subsection and continue the proceedings as a preliminary inquiry: *R. v. Turton* (1988), 44 C.C.C. (3d) 49 (Alta. C.A.).

While the language of this section is very broad, unless there is a judicial reason for overruling the accused's election to be tried by a provincial court judge then the accused should be entitled to proceed in that way: *R. v. Babcock* (1989), 68 C.R. (3d) 285, 31 O.A.C. 354 (Ont. C.A.).

An order under subsec. (1) may be made after the commencement of a trial for an absolute jurisdiction offence: *R. v. Baldasaro* (2006), 213 C.C.C. (3d) 89, 216 O.A.C. 68 *sub nom. R. v. Tucker* (C.A.), leave to appeal to S.C.C. refused [2007] 1 S.C.R. xvi, 215 C.C.C. (3d) vi.

DECISION TO HOLD PRELIMINARY INQUIRY — NUNAVUT / If subject-matter is a testamentary instrument or exceeds $5,000 in value — Nunavut / Continuation as preliminary inquiry — Nunavut / Continuing proceedings — Nunavut / Application to Nunavut.

555.1 (1) If in any criminal proceedings under this Part an accused is before a judge of the Nunavut Court of Justice and it appears to the judge that for any reason the charge should be prosecuted by indictment, the judge may, at any time before the accused has entered a defence, decide not to adjudicate and shall then inform the accused of the decision and continue the proceedings as a preliminary inquiry.

(2) If an accused is before a judge of the Nunavut Court of Justice charged with an indictable offence mentioned in paragraph 553(*a*) or subparagraph 553(*b*)(i), and, at any time before the judge makes an adjudication, the evidence establishes that the subject-matter of the offence is a testamentary instrument or that its value exceeds five thousand dollars, the judge shall put the accused to an election in accordance with subsection 536.1(2).

(3) A judge shall continue the proceedings as a preliminary inquiry under Part XVIII if the accused is put to an election under subsection (2) and elects to be tried by a judge without a jury and requests a preliminary inquiry under subsection 536.1(3) or elects to be tried by a court composed of a judge and jury or does not elect when put to the election.

(4) If an accused is put to an election under subsection (2) and elects to be tried by a judge without a jury and does not request a preliminary inquiry under subsection 536.1(3), the judge shall endorse on the information a record of the election and continue with the trial.

(5) This section, and not section 555, applies in respect of criminal proceedings in Nunavut. 1999, c. 3, s. 39; 2002, c. 13, s. 33.

CROSS-REFERENCES

For cross-references and a note on procedure in Nunavut, see the cross-references under s. 536.1.

ORGANIZATION / Non-appearance / Preliminary inquiry not requested / Preliminary inquiry not requested — Nunavut.

556. (1) An accused organization shall appear by counsel or agent.

(2) Where an accused organization does not appear pursuant to a summons and service of the summons on the organization is proved, the provincial court judge or, in Nunavut, the judge of the Nunavut Court of Justice

(*a*) may, if the charge is one over which the judge has absolute jurisdiction, proceed with the trial of the charge in the absence of the accused organization; and

(*b*) shall, if the charge is not one over which the judge has absolute jurisdiction, fix the date for the trial or the date on which the accused organization must appear in the trial court to have that date fixed.

(3) If an accused organization appears and a preliminary inquiry is not requested under subsection 536(4), the provincial court judge shall fix the date for the trial or the date on which the organization must appear in the trial court to have that date fixed.

(4) If an accused organization appears and a preliminary inquiry is not requested under subsection 536.1(3), the justice of the peace or the judge of the Nunavut Court of Justice shall fix the date for the trial or the date on which the organization must appear in the trial court to have that date fixed. R.S., c. C-34, s. 486; R.S.C. 1985, c. 27 (1st Supp.), s. 107; 1999, c. 3, s. 40; 2002, c. 13, s. 34; 2003, c. 21, ss. 9, 22.

CROSS-REFERENCES

The terms "organization" and "provincial court judge" are defined in s. 2. Service on an organization is effected pursuant to s. 703.2.

SYNOPSIS

An accused organization charged with an offence must appear either by counsel or agent (usually an officer of the company). Where an accused organization does not appear pursuant to a summons, and service of the summons is proved, a provincial court judge may proceed to trial in the absence of the accused if the charge is within the judge's absolute discretion (subsec. (2)(*a*)). Where the charge is not one over which the provincial court judge has absolute jurisdiction, the judge shall fix a date for the trial or the date upon which the organization must appear in the trial court to have the trial date fixed (subsec. (2)(*b*)). If the organization appears but has not requested a preliminary inquiry, the justice or judge, as the case may be, will set a date for trial or a date when the organization is to appear in the trial court to fix a trial date.

ANNOTATIONS

An amalgamated company is responsible for the criminal acts of its amalgamating companies: *R. v. Black & Decker Manufacturing Co.*, [1975] 1 S.C.R. 411, 15 C.C.C. (2d) 193, 43 D.L.R. (3d) 393 (9:0).

TAKING EVIDENCE.

557. If an accused is tried by a provincial court judge or a judge of the Nunavut Court of Justice in accordance with this Part, the evidence of witnesses for the prosecutor and the accused must be taken in accordance with the provisions of Part XVIII, other than subsections 540(7) to (9), relating to preliminary inquiries. R.S., c. C-34, s. 487; 1999, c. 30, s. 41; 2002, c. 13, s. 35.

CROSS-REFERENCES

The term "provincial court judge" is defined in s. 2. The principle provision respecting taking of evidence in Part XVIII is s. 540.

SYNOPSIS

At a provincial court trial the evidence shall be taken down in the same manner as prescribed in relation to preliminary inquiries by Part XVIII.

JURISDICTION OF JUDGES

Judge's Jurisdiction with Consent

TRIAL BY JUDGE WITHOUT A JURY.

558. If an accused who is charged with an indictable offence, other than an offence mentioned in section 469, elects under section 536 or 536.1 or re-elects under section 561 or 561.1 to be tried by a judge without a jury, the accused shall, subject to this Part, be tried by a judge without a jury. R.S., c. C-34, s. 488; R.S.C. 1985, c. 27 (1st Supp.), s. 108; 1999, c. 3, s. 41.

CROSS-REFERENCES

By virtue of s. 566 the trial before a judge without a jury, other than before a provincial court judge, shall be on an indictment preferred in accordance with ss. 574 and 577. An accused may re-elect his mode of trial by complying with s. 561. Where accused are jointly charged but have not re-elected the same mode of trial then the judge may decline to record the re-election pursuant to s. 567 and they are deemed to have elected trial by judge and jury, by virtue of s. 565(1)(*b*). For procedure respecting election for mode of trial generally, see *Note on mode of trial* under s. 553. For procedure respecting conduct of preliminary inquiry, see the note following s. 537. For cross-references respecting trial by judge alone, see s. 559.

SYNOPSIS

This section provides the statutory authority for trial by judge alone as permitted by this Part in accordance with the procedure in this Part.

COURT OF RECORD / Custody of records.

559. (1) A judge who holds a trial under this Part shall, for all purposes thereof and proceedings connected therewith or relating thereto, be a court of record.

(2) The record of a trial that a judge holds under this Part shall be kept in the court over which the judge presides. R.S., c. C-34, s. 489.

CROSS-REFERENCES

For notes on power of a court of record to find a person in contempt of court, see notes following ss. 9 and 10. Where the judge has not commenced to hear evidence then any judge having jurisdiction to try the accused has jurisdiction for purpose of the hearing and adjudication by virtue of s. 669.1. Where the trial judge is unable to continue, see s. 669.2. Where the accused absconds during his trial, the trial may be continued in his absence under s. 475. The procedure respecting conduct of trial is generally found in Part XX, made applicable to trials under this Part by s. 572. Appeals in indictable proceedings are governed by Part XXI. Sentence is imposed in accordance with Part XXIII, except in the case of dangerous-offender proceedings, in which case, see Part XXIV.

SYNOPSIS

Judges who conduct trials under this Part are courts of record, and the records of such trials are to be kept in the court of the judge who conducts the trial.

ANNOTATIONS

A provincial court judge acting under this Part has the power in appropriate circumstances to impose a ban on publication of the proceedings before him where publication could impair the actual or apparent fairness of the trials of co-accused thereafter taking place: *R. v. Church of Scientology (No. 6)* (1986), 27 C.C.C. (3d) 193 (Ont. H.C.J.).

Election

DUTY OF JUDGE / Notice by sheriff, when given / Duty of sheriff when date set for trial / Duty of accused when not in custody.

560. (1) If an accused elects, under section 536 or 536.1, to be tried by a judge without a jury, a judge having jurisdiction shall

(*a*) on receiving a written notice from the sheriff or other person having custody of the accused stating that the accused is in custody and setting out the nature of the charge against him, or

(*b*) on being notified by the clerk of the court that the accused is not in custody and of the nature of the charge against him,

fix a time and place for the trial of the accused.

(2) The sheriff or other person having custody of the accused shall give the notice mentioned in paragraph (1)(*a*) within twenty-four hours after the accused is ordered to stand trial, if the accused is in custody pursuant to that order or if, at the time of the order, he is in custody for any other reason.

(3) Where, pursuant to subsection (1), a time and place is fixed for the trial of an accused who is in custody, the accused

- **(*a*) shall be notified forthwith by the sheriff or other person having custody of the accused of the time and place so fixed, and**
- **(*b*) shall be produced at the time and place so fixed.**

(4) Where an accused is not in custody, the duty of ascertaining from the clerk of the court the time and place fixed for the trial, pursuant to subsection (1), is on the accused, and he shall attend for his trial at the time and place so fixed. R.S., c. C-34, s. 490; R.S.C. 1985, c. 27 (1st Supp.), ss. 101(3), 109(1); 1999, c. 3, s. 42; 2002, c. 13, s. 36.

(5) [*Repealed.* R.S.C. 1985, *c.*27 (1st Supp.), *s.* 109(2).]

CROSS-REFERENCES

The term "clerk of the court" is defined in s. 2. For notes respecting trial by judge alone see cross-references under s. 559. Power to issue a bench warrant where the accused fails to attend for trial is found in s. 597. The attendance of an accused who is in custody may be procured by compliance with s. 527. Where the accused absconds during his trial the trial may be continued in his absence under s. 475.

SYNOPSIS

This section deals with the fixing of trial dates where the accused has been committed following a preliminary inquiry and has elected to be tried by a judge sitting without a jury. Local practices will govern how arrangements are made to set the matter down, having regard to the court's rota and the availability of counsel and the witnesses. The person having custody of an incarcerated accused is required to initiate the setting of a trial date within 24 hours of the accused being ordered to stand trial.

Where the accused is in custody, he will have to be brought to court for trial (subsec. (3)). An accused who is not in custody is responsible for ascertaining the date which has been set and for appearing at the required time and place (subsec. (4)).

RIGHT TO RE-ELECT / Idem / Notice / Idem / Notice and transmitting record / Time and place for re-election / Proceedings on re-election.

561. (1) An accused who elects or is deemed to have elected a mode of trial other than trial by a provincial court judge may re-elect

- **(*a*) at any time before or after the completion of the preliminary inquiry, with the written consent of the prosecutor, to be tried by a provincial court judge;**
- **(*b*) at any time before the completion of the preliminary inquiry or before the fifteenth day following the completion of the preliminary inquiry, as of right, another mode of trial other than trial by a provincial court judge; and**
- **(*c*) on or after the fifteenth day following the completion of the preliminary inquiry, any mode of trial with the written consent of the prosecutor.**

(2) An accused who elects to be tried by a provincial court judge or who does not request a preliminary inquiry under subsection 536(4) may, not later than 14 days before the day first appointed for the trial, re-elect as of right another mode of trial, and may do so after that time with the written consent of the prosecutor.

(3) Where an accused wishes to re-elect under subsection (1) before the completion of the preliminary inquiry, the accused shall give notice in writing that he wishes to re-elect, together with the written consent of the prosecutor, where such consent is

required, to the justice presiding at the preliminary inquiry who shall on receipt of the notice,

(*a*) in the case of a re-election under paragraph (1)(*b*), put the accused to his re-election in the manner set out in subsection (7); or

(*b*) where the accused wishes to re-elect under paragraph (1)(*a*) and the justice is not a provincial court judge, notify a provincial court judge or clerk of the court of the accused's intention to re-elect and send to the provincial court judge or clerk the information and any promise to appear, undertaking or recognizance given or entered into in accordance with Part XVI, or any evidence taken before a coroner, that is in the possession of the justice.

(4) Where an accused wishes to re-elect under subsection (2), the accused shall give notice in writing that he wishes to re-elect together with the written consent of the prosecutor, where such consent is required, to the provincial court judge before whom the accused appeared and pleaded or to a clerk of the court.

(5) Where an accused wishes to re-elect under subsection (1) after the completion of the preliminary inquiry, the accused shall give notice in writing that he wishes to re-elect, together with the written consent of the prosecutor, where that consent is required, to a judge or clerk of the court of his original election who shall, on receipt of the notice, notify the judge or provincial court judge or clerk of the court by which the accused wishes to be tried of the accused's intention to re-elect and send to that judge or provincial court judge or clerk the information, the evidence, the exhibits and the statement, if any, of the accused taken down in writing under section 541 and any promise to appear, undertaking or recognizance given or entered into in accordance with Part XVI, or any evidence taken before a coroner, that is in the possession of the first-mentioned judge or clerk.

(6) Where a provincial court judge or judge or clerk of the court is notified under paragraph (3)(*b*) or subsection (4) or (5) that the accused wishes to re-elect, the provincial court judge or judge shall forthwith appoint a time and place for the accused to re-elect and shall cause notice thereof to be given to the accused and the prosecutor.

(7) The accused shall attend or, if he is in custody, shall be produced at the time and place appointed under subsection (6) and shall, after

(*a*) the charge on which he has been ordered to stand trial or the indictment, where an indictment has been preferred pursuant to section 556, 574 or 577 or is filed with the court before which the indictment is to be preferred pursuant to section 577, or

(*b*) in the case of a re-election under subsection (1) before the completion of the preliminary inquiry or under subsection (2), the information

has been read to the accused, be put to his re-election in the following words or in words to the like effect:

> **You have given notice of your wish to re-elect the mode of your trial. You now have the option to do so. How do you wish to re-elect? R.S., c. C-34, s. 491; R.S.C. 1985, c. 27 (1st Supp.), s. 110; 2002, c. 13, s. 37.**

CROSS-REFERENCES

Where the accused re-elects under s. 561(1) for trial by provincial court judge or judge alone then s. 562(1) sets out the procedure to be followed. Where the accused re-elects under s. 561(1)(*b*) or (2) then the justice proceeds with the preliminary inquiry under s. 562(2). Where the accused re-elects trial by provincial court judge then, pursuant to s. 563, the trial takes place on the information and the re-election is to be endorsed on the information. Section 565 sets out the circumstances when the accused is deemed to have elected judge and jury. Note s. 567 giving the judge or justice power not to record the re-election where jointly charged accused do not all re-elect the same mode of trial. Under s. 568, the Attorney General may override an election or re-election and require a jury trial except where the offence is punishable by five years or less. For offences listed in s. 469, the right of re-election is limited according to s. 473. An accused, against whom a direct indictment has been preferred under s. 577, may re-elect only with the consent of the prosecutor under s. 565(2). Under s. 536.2, an accused may make a re-election in writing without personal attendance.

For procedure in Nunavut, see s. 561.1.

SYNOPSIS

This section sets out the procedure to be followed when an accused wishes to change his or her election (or deemed election) as to the mode of trial.

Where the accused has chosen to be tried other than before a provincial court judge, the consent of the Crown is required to re-elect for trial in the provincial court (subsec. (1)(*a*)).

Where the accused wishes to change from judge alone to judge and jury, or vice versa, he has a "right" to do so for up to two weeks following the completion of the preliminary inquiry (subsec. (1)(*b*)). Afterwards the written consent of the prosecutor is required (subsec. (1)(*c*)).

Where the election is for trial before a provincial court judge or where the accused has not requested a preliminary inquiry, the accused can exercise a "right" of re-election up to 14 days before the first trial date that has been fixed. Thereafter, the written consent of the prosecutor is needed (subsec. (2)).

Written notice of a desire to re-elect must be given to the court and the prosecutor in accordance with subsecs. (3), (4) and (5). The procedure to be followed by the court is set out in subsecs. (6) and (7). In cases where the matter is before the provincial court (*i.e.*, because the accused has elected trial in that forum or where a preliminary inquiry has not yet been completed) the re-election shall take place before a provincial court judge.

Where there has been a committal for trial and the accused wishes to re-elect "down", the procedure will take place in the provincial court. A change from judge alone to judge and jury, or vice versa, will occur before a judge of the trial court.

Where the Crown has proceeded by way of "direct" indictment, s. 565(2) applies.

ANNOTATIONS

It was held in relation to the predecessor to this section that the accused, personally or through his counsel, may waive the procedural requirements which were enacted for his benefit. However, the Judge has a paramount right to require compliance. The validity of any waiver depends upon it being clear and unequivocal that the person is waiving the procedural safeguard and is doing so with full knowledge of the right which the procedure was enacted to protect and of the effect the waiver will have on those rights: *Korponey v. Canada (Attorney General)*, [1982] 1 S.C.R. 41, 65 C.C.C. (2d) 65 (9:0).

The requirement of Crown consent to re-election in the course of preliminary inquiry does not offend ss. 7 and 15 of the *Charter of Rights and Freedoms*: *R. v. Koleff* (1987), 33 C.C.C. (3d) 460 (Man. Q.B.).

To avoid a violation of s. 11(*f*) of the Charter, this section must be interpreted so as to give the accused the right to re-elect trial by judge and jury within 15 days of learning of a substantial change in the Crown's case, even though this is beyond 15 days following the completion of the preliminary inquiry: *R. v. Ruston* (1991), 63 C.C.C. (3d) 419 (Man. C.A.).

Absent conduct on the part of the Crown amounting to an abuse of process, the court has no power to override the Crown's decision refusing to consent to a re-election for trial by judge alone: *R. v. E. (L.)* (1994), 94 C.C.C. (3d) 228 (Ont. C.A.). There is no requirement for the Crown to provide reasons for refusing to consent and the failure to provide reasons for such a refusal is not a basis for judicial intervention. The exercise of prosecutorial discretion must be arbitrary, capricious or motivated by improper considerations to constitute an abuse of process: *R. v. Ng* (2003), 173 C.C.C. (3d) 349 (Alta. C.A.), leave to appeal to S.C.C. refused 183 C.C.C. (3d) vi.

It will only be in unusual circumstances that the discretionary power, given to the Crown under this section, to refuse to consent to a re-election after expiration of the 15-day period from the date of the order to stand trial, will be subject to judicial review. The accused, it would seem, must establish improper motives or some other factor amounting to an abuse of process. The mere fact that the Crown perceived a tactical advantage from a trial by judge alone is not an improper motive or an abuse of process: *R. v. Mohammed* (1990), 60 C.C.C. (3d) 296 (Man. Q.B.).

Where an indictment has been preferred under s. 574(1)(*b*) containing additional counts founded on the evidence at the preliminary inquiry, the accused, if he wishes to re-elect his mode of trial, must re-elect in respect of the entire indictment. He does not have the right to "elect" his mode of trial in relation to the additional counts: *R. v. Puric* (1990), 54 C.C.C. (3d) 373 (Sask. Q.B.).

RIGHT TO RE-ELECT WITH CONSENT — NUNAVUT / Right to re-elect before trial — Nunavut / Right to re-elect at preliminary inquiry — Nunavut / Notice of re-election under subsection (1) or (3) — Nunavut / Notice at preliminary inquiry — Nunavut / Notice when no preliminary inquiry or preliminary inquiry completed — Nunavut / Time and place for re-election — Nunavut / Proceedings on re-election — Nunavut / Application to Nunavut.

561.1 (1) An accused who has elected or is deemed to have elected a mode of trial may re-elect any other mode of trial at any time with the written consent of the prosecutor.

(2) An accused who has elected or is deemed to have elected a mode of trial but has not requested a preliminary inquiry under subsection 536.1(3) may, as of right, re-elect to be tried by any other mode of trial at any time up to 14 days before the day first appointed for the trial.

(3) An accused who has elected or is deemed to have elected a mode of trial and has requested a preliminary inquiry under subsection 536.1(3) may, as of right, re-elect to be tried by the other mode of trial at any time before the completion of the preliminary inquiry or before the 15th day after its completion.

(4) If an accused wishes to re-elect under subsection (1) or (3), before the completion of the preliminary inquiry, the accused shall give notice in writing of the wish to re-elect, together with the written consent of the prosecutor, if that consent is required, to the justice of the peace or judge presiding at the preliminary inquiry who shall on receipt of the notice put the accused to a re-election in the manner set out in subsection (9).

(5) If at a preliminary inquiry an accused wishes to re-elect under subsection (1) or (3) to be tried by a judge without a jury but does not wish to request a preliminary inquiry under subsection 536.1(3), the presiding justice of the peace shall notify a judge or a clerk of the Nunavut Court of Justice of the accused's intention to re-elect and send to the judge or clerk the information and any promise to appear, undertaking or recognizance given or entered into in accordance with Part XVI, or any evidence taken before a coroner, that is in the possession of the justice of the peace.

(6) If an accused who has not requested a preliminary inquiry under subsection 536.1(3) or who has had one wishes to re-elect under this section, the accused shall give notice in writing of the wish to re-elect together with the written consent of the prosecutor, if that consent is required, to the judge before whom the accused appeared and pleaded or to a clerk of the Nunavut Court of Justice.

(7) [*Repealed*, 2002, c. 13, s. 38.]

(8) On receipt of a notice given under any of subsections (4) to (7) that the accused wishes to re-elect, a judge shall immediately appoint a time and place for the accused to re-elect and shall cause notice of the time and place to be given to the accused and the prosecutor.

(9) The accused shall attend or, if in custody, shall be produced at the time and place appointed under subsection (8) and shall, after

(*a*) the charge on which the accused has been ordered to stand trial or the indictment, if an indictment has been preferred pursuant to section 566, 574 or 577 or is filed with the court before which the indictment is to be preferred pursuant to section 577, or

(*b*) in the case of a re-election under subsection (1) or (3), before the completion of the preliminary inquiry or under subsection (2), the information has been read to the accused, be put to a re-election in the following words or in words to the like effect:

You have given notice of your wish to re-elect the mode of your trial. You now have the option to do so. How do you wish to re-elect?

(10) This section, and not section 561, applies in respect of criminal proceedings in Nunavut. 1999, c. 3, s. 43; 2002, c. 13, s. 38.

CROSS-REFERENCES

For cross-references and a note on procedure in Nunavut, see the cross-references under s. 536.1. Under s. 536.2, an accused may make a re-election in writing without personal attendance.

PROCEEDINGS FOLLOWING RE-ELECTION / Idem.

562. (1) Where the accused re-elects under paragraph 561(1)(*a*) before the completion of the preliminary inquiry or under subsection 561(1) after the completion of the preliminary inquiry, the provincial court judge or judge, as the case may be, shall proceed with the trial or appoint a time and place for the trial.

(2) Where the accused re-elects under paragraph 561(1)(*b*) before the completion of the preliminary inquiry or under subsection 561(2), the justice shall proceed with the preliminary inquiry. R.S., c. C-34, s. 492; R.S.C. 1985, c. 27 (1st Supp.), s. 110.

CROSS-REFERENCES

Where the accused re-elects trial by provincial court judge, see s. 563. For circumstances where the accused may not re-elect, see s. 561, cross-reference. The companion provision for re-election in Nunavut is set out in s. 562.1.

SYNOPSIS

This section provides that after re-election by the accused under s. 561(1) or (2), the trial or preliminary inquiry, as the case may be, shall proceed. In the case of a trial, the judge or provincial court judge may also set a time and place for trial.

PROCEEDINGS FOLLOWING RE-ELECTION — NUNAVUT / Proceedings following re-election — Nunavut / Application to Nunavut.

562.1 (1) If the accused re-elects under subsection 561.1(1) to be tried by a judge without a jury and does not request a preliminary inquiry under subsection 536.1(3), the judge shall proceed with the trial or appoint a time and place for the trial.

(2) If the accused re-elects under section 561.1 before the completion of the preliminary inquiry to be tried by a judge without a jury or by a court composed of a judge and jury, and requests a preliminary inquiry under subsection 536.1(3), the justice of the peace or judge shall proceed with the preliminary inquiry.

(3) This section, and not section 562, applies in respect of criminal proceedings in Nunavut. 1999, c. 3, s. 44; 2002, c. 13, s. 39.

CROSS-REFERENCES

For cross-references and a note on procedure in Nunavut, see the cross-references under s. 536.1.

PROCEEDINGS ON RE-ELECTION TO BE TRIED BY PROVINCIAL COURT JUDGE WITHOUT JURY.

563. Where an accused re-elects under section 561 to be tried by a provincial court judge,

(*a*) the accused shall be tried on the information that was before the justice at the preliminary inquiry, subject to any amendments thereto that may be allowed by the provincial court judge by whom the accused is tried; and

(*b*) the provincial court judge before whom the re-election is made shall endorse on the information a record of the re-election. R.S., c. C-34, s. 493; R.S.C. 1985, c. 27 (1st Supp.), s. 110.

CROSS-REFERENCES

The terms "justice" and "provincial court judge" are defined in s. 2. The term "judge" is defined in s. 552. For circumstances where the accused may not re-elect, see s. 561.

For proceedings in Nunavut, see s. 563.1.

SYNOPSIS

This section sets the procedure where an accused re-elects under s. 561 to be tried before a provincial court judge. Its principal effect is to confirm that the trial takes place on the original information that was before the justice conducting the preliminary inquiry. The fact of the re-election is enclosed in the information.

ANNOTATIONS

Where the accused re-elects trial by provincial court judge and intends to have the evidence taken on the preliminary inquiry apply at the trial, both he and the Crown must consent to such procedure and their consent must be conveyed to the court and then the evidence must in some way, be it by the filing of transcripts or by some reference to the previous judicial proceedings, enter the record during the trial: *R. v. Matheson*, [1981] 2 S.C.R. 214, 59 C.C.C. (2d) 289 (7:0).

PROCEEDINGS ON RE-ELECTION TO BE TRIED BY JUDGE WITHOUT JURY — NUNAVUT / Application to Nunavut.

563.1 (1) If an accused re-elects under section 561.1 to be tried by a judge without a jury and does not request a preliminary inquiry under subsection 536.1(3),

(*a*) the accused shall be tried on the information that was before the justice of the peace or judge at the preliminary inquiry, subject to any amendments that may be allowed by the judge by whom the accused is tried; and

(*b*) the judge before whom the re-election is made shall endorse on the information a record of the re-election.

(2) This section, and not section 563, applies in respect of criminal proceedings in Nunavut. 1999, c. 3, s. 45; 2002, c. 13, s. 40.

CROSS-REFERENCES

For cross-references and a note on procedure in Nunavut, see the cross-references under s. 536.1.

564. [*Repealed*, R.S.C. 1985, c. 27 (1st Supp.), s. 110.]

ELECTION DEEMED TO HAVE BEEN MADE / Nunavut / When direct indictment preferred / Notice of re-election / Application.

565. (1) Subject to subsection (1.1), if an accused is ordered to stand trial for an offence that, under this Part, may be tried by a judge without a jury, the accused shall, for the

purposes of the provisions of this Part relating to election and re-election, be deemed to have elected to be tried by a court composed of a judge and jury if

(*a*) the accused was ordered to stand trial by a provincial court judge who, pursuant to subsection 555(1), continued the proceedings before him as a preliminary inquiry;

(*b*) the justice, provincial court judge or judge, as the case may be, declined pursuant to section 567 to record the election or re-election of the accused; or

(*c*) the accused does not elect when put to an election under section 536.

(1.1) With respect to criminal proceedings in Nunavut, if an accused is ordered to stand trial for an offence that, under this Part, may be tried by a judge without a jury, the accused shall, for the purposes of the provisions of this Part relating to election and re-election, be deemed to have elected to be tried by a court composed of a judge and jury if

(*a*) the accused was ordered to stand trial by a judge who, under subsection 555.1(1), continued the proceedings as a preliminary inquiry;

(*b*) the justice of the peace or judge, as the case may be, declined pursuant to subsection 567.1(1) to record the election or re-election of the accused; or

(*c*) the accused did not elect when put to an election under section 536.1.

(2) If an accused is to be tried after an indictment has been preferred against the accused pursuant to a consent or order given under section 577, the accused is, for the purposes of the provisions of this Part relating to election and re-election, deemed both to have elected to be tried by a court composed of a judge and jury and not to have requested a preliminary inquiry under subsection 536(4) or 536.1(3) and may re-elect to be tried by a judge without a jury without a preliminary inquiry.

(3) Where an accused wishes to re-elect under subsection (2), the accused shall give notice in writing that he wishes to re-elect to a judge or clerk of the court where the indictment has been filed or preferred who shall, on receipt of the notice, notify a judge having jurisdiction or clerk of the court by which the accused wishes to be tried of the accused's intention to re-elect and send to that judge or clerk the indictment and any promise to appear, undertaking or recognizance given or entered into in accordance with Part XVI, any summons or warrant issued under section 578, or any evidence taken before a coroner, that is in the possession of the first-mentioned judge or clerk.

(4) Subsections 561(6) and (7), or subsections 561.1(8) and (9), as the case may be, apply to a re-election made under subsection (3). R.S., c. C-34, s. 495; R.S.C. 1985, c. 27 (1st Supp.), s. 111; 1999, c. 3, s. 46; 2002, c. 13, s. 41; 2008; c. 18, s. 23.

CROSS-REFERENCES

The terms "justice", "clerk of the court" and "provincial court judge" are defined in s. 2. The term "judge" is defined in s. 552.

For cross-references and a note on procedure in Nunavut, see the cross-references under s. 536.1.

SYNOPSIS

Subsection (1) sets out the circumstances where an accused will be "deemed" to have elected trial by judge and jury. This will be the case where: (a) a provincial court judge acting under s. 555(1) has converted a trial into a preliminary inquiry (subsec. (1)(*a*)); (b) the accused's election has not been recorded as provided for in s. 567 (subsec. (1)(*b*)), and (c) the accused has stood mute and refused to enter an election (subsec. (1)(*c*)).

Where the Crown has proceeded by way of "direct" indictment (see s. 577), the trial will be before a jury unless the accused re-elects to be tried by a judge alone (subsec. (2)).

Written notice is required; the procedure to be followed is set out in subsecs. (3) and (4).

Trial

INDICTMENT / Preferring indictment / What counts may be included and who may prefer indictment.

566. (1) The trial of an accused for an indictable offence, other than a trial before a provincial court judge, shall be on an indictment in writing setting forth the offence with which he is charged.

(2) Where an accused elects under section 536 or re-elects under section 561 to be tried by a judge without a jury, an indictment in Form 4 may be preferred.

(3) Section 574 and subsection 576(1) apply, with such modifications as the circumstances require, to the preferring of an indictment pursuant to indictment subsection (2). R.S., c. C-34, s. 496; R.S.C. 1985, c. 27 (1st Supp.), s. 111; 1997, c. 18, s. 67.

CROSS-REFERENCES

The term "provincial court judge" is defined in s. 2. The term "judge" is defined in s. 552. As to trial before a provincial court judge, see s. 563. For proceedings in Nunavut, see s. 566.1.

SYNOPSIS

This section provides that trial by judge alone shall be on an indictment in writing, other than in a trial before a provincial court judge (in which case, the trial is on an information) (subsec. (1)). The procedure to prefer indictments in jury trials is adopted for the purposes of this Part (see ss. 574 and 576).

INDICTMENT — NUNAVUT / Preferring indictment — Nunavut / What counts may be included and who may prefer indictment — Nunavut / Application to Nunavut.

566.1 (1) The trial of an accused for an indictable offence, other than an indictable offence referred to in section 553 or an offence in respect of which the accused has elected or re-elected to be tried by a judge without a jury and in respect of which no party has requested a preliminary inquiry under subsection 536.1(3), must be on an indictment in writing setting out the offence with which the accused is charged.

(2) If an accused elects under section 536.1 or re-elects under section 561.1 to be tried by a judge without a jury and one of the parties requests a preliminary inquiry under subsection 536.1(3), an indictment in Form 4 may be preferred.

(3) Section 574 and subsection 576(1) apply, with any modifications that the circumstances require, to the preferring of an indictment under subsection (2).

(4) This section, and not section 566, applies in respect of criminal proceedings in Nunavut. 1999, c. 3, s. 47; 2002, c. 13, s. 42.

CROSS-REFERENCES

For cross-references and a note on procedure in Nunavut, see the cross-references under s. 536.1.

General

MODE OF TRIAL WHEN TWO OR MORE ACCUSED.

567. Despite any other provision of this Part, if two or more persons are jointly charged in an information, unless all of them elect or re-elect or are deemed to have elected the same mode of trial, the justice, provincial court judge or judge may decline to record any election, re-election or deemed election for trial by a provincial court judge or a

judge without a jury. R.S., c. C-34, s. 497; R.S.C. 1985, c. 27 (1st Supp.), s. 111; 2002, c. 13, s. 43.

CROSS-REFERENCES

The terms "justice" and "provincial court judge" are defined in s. 2. The term "judge" is defined in s. 552. Where the justice or judge declines to record the election or re-election then the accused is deemed to have elected trial by judge and jury pursuant to s. 565(1)(*b*). As to right to re-elect, see s. 561. For proceedings in Nunavut, see s. 567.1.

SYNOPSIS

This section gives a provincial court judge jurisdiction to decline to record an election for other than trial by jury where there is more than one accused and all do not elect the same mode of trial. Where this occurs, the election will be deemed to be for a judge sitting with a jury (see s. 565(1)(*b*)), and the hearing shall continue as a preliminary inquiry. This provision is designed to enable the court to avoid jointly charged accused obtaining severance by selecting different methods of trial.

ANNOTATIONS

It was held in relation to the predecessor to this section that even where there is no objection to the procedure by the accused a provincial court judge has no power to simultaneously conduct the trial of one accused who has elected trial by provincial court judge, and the preliminary hearing of another who has elected trial by judge: *R. v. Niedzwieki* (1980), 57 C.C.C. (2d) 184, [1981] 3 W.W.R. 151 (B.C.S.C.).

MODE OF TRIAL IF TWO OR MORE ACCUSED — NUNAVUT / Application to Nunavut.

567.1 (1) Despite any other provision of this Part, if two or more persons are jointly charged in an information, unless all of them elect or re-elect or are deemed to have elected the same mode of trial, the justice of the peace or judge may decline to record any election, re-election or deemed election for trial by a judge without a jury.

(2) This section, and not section 567, applies in respect of criminal proceedings in Nunavut. 1999, c. 3, s. 48; 2002, c. 13, s. 43.

CROSS-REFERENCES

For cross-references and a note on procedure in Nunavut, see the cross-references under s. 536.1.

ATTORNEY GENERAL MAY REQUIRE TRIAL BY JURY.

568. Even if an accused elects under section 536 or re-elects under section 561 or subsection 565(2) to be tried by a judge or provincial court judge, as the case may be, the Attorney General may require the accused to be tried by a court composed of a judge and jury unless the alleged offence is one that is punishable with imprisonment for five years or less. If the Attorney General so requires, a judge or provincial court judge has no jurisdiction to try the accused under this Part and a preliminary inquiry must be held if requested under subsection 536(4), unless one has already been held or the reelection was made under subsection 565(2). R.S., c. C-34, s. 498; R.S.C. 1985, c. 27 (1st Supp.), s. 111; 2002, c. 13, s. 43; 2008, c. 18, s. 24.

CROSS-REFERENCES

The terms "Attorney General", "justice" and "provincial court judge" are defined in s. 2. The term "judge" is defined in s. 552. The similar provision for proceedings in Nunavut is set out in s. 569.

SYNOPSIS

Unless the offence is punishable with imprisonment for five years or less, the Attorney General has the right to require that an accused be tried by a jury. Once this provision has been invoked, the accused cannot select another mode of trial.

An example of a situation where this provision might be used is where jointly charged accused select different methods of trial, a provincial court judge having chosen not to exercise the power in s. 567 to decline to record the non-jury elections. In these circumstances, the Attorney General may act so that all are tried before the same court. Of course, this in no way precludes the trial court from ordering severance if such is determined appropriate (see s. 591(3)(*b*)).

ANNOTATIONS

The Attorney General may exercise his jurisdiction under this section notwithstanding the accused has previously re-elected trial by judge alone with the consent of counsel for the Attorney General: *R. v. Pontbriand* (1978), 39 C.C.C. (2d) 145, 1 C.R. (3d) 97 (Que. S.C.).

Where the Attorney General has exercised his power under this section, then the accused has no right to re-elect trial by judge alone, even with the consent of Crown counsel: *R. v. Thompson* (1987), 40 C.C.C. (3d) 365 (N.S.C.A.).

The exercise of his power under this section by the Attorney General is not subject to review by the courts: *R. v. M.* (1982), 1 C.C.C. (3d) 465, 143 D.L.R. (3d) 487 (Ont. H.C.J.).

This section does not infringe the rights to fundamental justice and equality guaranteed by ss. 7 and 15 of the *Canadian Charter of Rights and Freedoms*: *R. v. Hanneson* (1987), 31 C.C.C. (3d) 560, 27 C.R.R. 278 (Ont. H.C.J.).

569. [*Repealed*, R.S.C. 1985, c. 27 (1st Supp.), s. 111 (old provision).]

ATTORNEY GENERAL MAY REQUIRE TRIAL BY JURY — NUNAVUT / Application to Nunavut.

569. (1) Even if an accused elects under section 536.1 or re-elects under section 561.1 or subsection 565(2) to be tried by a judge without a jury, the Attorney General may require the accused to be tried by a court composed of a judge and jury unless the alleged offence is one that is punishable with imprisonment for five years or less. If the Attorney General so requires, a judge has no jurisdiction to try the accused under this Part and a preliminary inquiry must be held if requested under subsection 536.1(3), unless one has already been held or the re-election was made under subsection 565(2).

(2) This section, and not section 568, applies in respect of criminal proceedings in Nunavut. 1999, c. 3, s. 49; 2002, c. 13, s. 44; 2008, c. 18, s. 24.1.

CROSS-REFERENCES

"Attorney General" is defined in s. 2. For other cross-references and a note on procedure in Nunavut, see the cross-references under s. 536.1.

RECORD OF CONVICTION OR ORDER / Acquittal and record of acquittal / Transmission of record / Proof of conviction, order or acquittal / Warrant of committal / Admissibility of certified copy.

570. (1) Where an accused who is tried under this Part is determined by a judge or provincial court judge to be guilty of an offence on acceptance of a plea of guilty or on a finding of guilt, the judge or provincial court judge, as the case may be, shall endorse the information accordingly and shall sentence the accused or otherwise deal with the accused in the manner authorized by law and, on request by the accused, the prosecutor, a peace officer or any other person, shall cause a conviction in Form 35 and

a certified copy of it, or an order in Form 36 and a certified copy of it, to be drawn up and shall deliver the certified copy to the person making the request.

(2) Where an accused who is tried under this Part is found not guilty of an offence with which he is charged, the judge or provincial court judge, as the case may be, shall immediately acquit the accused in respect of that offence and shall cause an order in Form 37 to be drawn up, and on request shall make out and deliver to the accused a certified copy of the order.

(3) Where an accused elects to be tried by a provincial court judge under this Part, the provincial court judge shall transmit the written charge, the memorandum of adjudication and the conviction, if any, into such custody as the Attorney General may direct.

(4) A copy of a conviction in Form 35 or of an order in Form 36 or 37, certified by the judge or by the clerk or other proper officer of the court, or by the provincial court judge, as the case may be, or proved to be a true copy, is, on proof of the identity of the person to whom the conviction or order relates, sufficient evidence in any legal proceedings to prove the conviction of that person or the making of the order against him or his acquittal, as the case may be, for the offence mentioned in the copy of the conviction or order.

(5) Where an accused other than an organization is convicted, the judge or provincial court judge, as the case may be, shall issue or cause to be issued a warrant of committal in Form 21, and section 528 applies in respect of a warrant of committal issued under this subsection.

(6) Where a warrant of committal is issued by a clerk of a court, a copy of the warrant of committal, certified by the clerk, is admissible in evidence in any proceeding. R.S., c. C-34, s. 500; R.S.C. 1985, c. 27 (1st Supp.), s. 112; 1994, c. 44, s. 59; 2003, c. 21, s. 10.

CROSS-REFERENCES

The terms "justice", "clerk of the court", "organization" and "provincial court judge" are defined in s. 2. The term "judge" is defined in s. 552. Procedure with respect to pleas is set out in ss. 606 to 613. Previous convictions may be proved in accordance with ss. 665 to 667. Also see s. 12 of the *Canada Evidence Act*, R.S.C. 1985, c. C-5. An accused found guilty is entitled to speak to sentence, s. 668.

SYNOPSIS

This section sets out the forms to be used for the recording of convictions, acquittals, warrants and orders under this Part. A certified or proved copy of such forms is proof of the result referred to therein.

ANNOTATIONS

Where there were two informations each charging a separate fraud offence it was wrong for the convicting court to impose one joint sentence for both offences and embody it on one conviction certificate: *R. v. Pretty* (1971), 5 C.C.C. (2d) 332, 2 Nfld. & P.E.I.R. 10 (P.E.I.S.C.).

A minute of conviction, setting out all the essential ingredients of a warrant of committal, is a document satisfactory to authorize an accused's confinement for sentence: *Ex P. Leclerc* (1973), 21 C.C.C. (2d) 16 (Que. C.A.).

The ministerial act of signing a warrant of committal may be committed by a rubber stamp facsimile: *R. v. Bellefontaine* (1975), 27 C.C.C. (2d) 200, 37 C.R.N.S. 100 (N.S. Co. Ct.).

A driving prohibition order made in summary conviction proceedings is not admissible pursuant to subsec. (4): *R. v. Tatomir* (1989), 51 C.C.C. (3d) 321, [1990] 1 W.W.R. 470, 99 A.R. 188 (C.A.).

Until the trial judge has endorsed the indictment he retains jurisdiction to correct an error made in pronouncing sentence and to ensure that the judgment of the court as recorded accurately reflects the court's intentions: *R. v. Maider* (1991), 64 C.C.C. (3d) 62 (B.C.C.A.).

ADJOURNMENT.

571. A judge or provincial court judge acting under this Part may from time to time adjourn a trial until it is finally terminated. R.S., c. C-34, s. 501.

CROSS-REFERENCES
The term "provincial court judge" is defined in s. 2. The term "judge" is defined in s. 552. As to curative provisions respecting adjournments, see ss. 485 and 485.1. For procedure respecting continuation of trial before any evidence has been taken, see s. 669.1 and where the trial judge is unable to continue, see s. 669.2.

ANNOTATIONS
Where a judge was unable to attend court it was held that the court clerk acting under a judge's instruction could adjourn the case: *R. v. Pattyson* (1974), 19 C.C.C. (2d) 537, [1975] 1 W.W.R. 91 (Sask. Q.B.).

In *R. v. Pickett* (1971), 5 C.C.C. (2d) 371 (Ont. C.A.), a conviction was quashed where the accused was refused an adjournment although his counsel was unavoidably engaged in another court. The trial had proceeded with the accused being represented by an inexperienced solicitor who had virtually no knowledge of the facts of the case and had been sent by counsel to request the adjournment. The trial proceeding in this manner lacked the appearance of justice. [Also see notes re "Right to counsel" under s. 650, *infra*.]

APPLICATION OF PARTS XVI, XVIII, XX and XXIII.

572. The provisions of Part XVI, the provisions of Part XVIII relating to transmission of the record by a provincial court judge where he holds a preliminary inquiry, and the provisions of Parts XX and XXIII, in so far as they are not inconsistent with this Part, apply, with such modifications as the circumstances require, to proceedings under this Part. R.S., c. C-34, s. 502; R.S., c. 2 (2nd Supp.), s. 10.

CROSS-REFERENCES
The term "provincial court judge" is defined in s. 2.

SYNOPSIS
This section provides that Part XVI (compelling appearance of accused), Part XX (jury trials) and Part XXIII (punishment) apply to this Part, *mutatis mutandis*. The provisions of Part XVIII relating to transmission of the record by a provincial court judge after a preliminary inquiry also apply.

ANNOTATIONS
By virtue of this section a provincial court judge has power to take a view as provided in s. 652: *R. v. Prentice,* [1965] 4 C.C.C. 118, 47 C.R. 231 (B.C.C.A.).

573. [*Repealed*, R.S.C. 1985, c. 27 (1st Supp.), s. 113 (old provision).]

Part XIX.1 / NUNAVUT COURT OF JUSTICE

NUNAVUT COURT OF JUSTICE / Status when exercising power / Interpretation.

573. (1) The powers to be exercised and the duties and functions to be performed under this Act by a court of criminal jurisdiction, a summary conviction court, a judge, a provincial court judge, a justice or a justice of the peace may be exercised or performed by a judge of the Nunavut Court of Justice.

(2) A power exercised or a duty or function performed by a judge of the Nunavut Court of Justice under subsection (1) is exercised or performed by that judge as a judge of a superior court.

(3) Subsection (2) does not authorize a judge of the Nunavut Court of Justice who is presiding at a preliminary inquiry to grant a remedy under section 24 of the *Canadian Charter of Rights and Freedoms*. 1999, c. 3, s. 50.

CROSS-REFERENCES
The terms "superior court of justice", "court of criminal jurisdiction", "provincial court judge", and "justice" are defined in s. 2. "Summary conviction court" is defined in s. 785. For other cross-references and a note on procedure in Nunavut, see the cross-references under s. 536.1.

APPLICATION FOR REVIEW — NUNAVUT / Limitation / Grounds of review / Powers of judge / Interim orders / Rules / Appeal.

573.1 (1) An application for review may be made by the Attorney General or the accused, or by any person directly affected by the decision or order, to a judge of the Court of Appeal of Nunavut in respect of a decision or order of a judge of the Nunavut Court of Justice

- **(*a*) relating to a warrant or summons;**
- **(*b*) relating to the conduct of a preliminary inquiry, including an order under subsection 548(1);**
- **(*c*) relating to a subpoena;**
- **(*d*) relating to the publication or broadcasting of information or access to the court room for all or part of the proceedings;**
- **(*e*) to refuse to quash an information or indictment; or**
- **(*f*) relating to the detention, disposal or forfeiture of any thing seized under a warrant or order.**

(2) A decision or order may not be reviewed under this section if

- **(*a*) the decision or order is of a kind that could only be made in a province or a territory other than Nunavut by a superior court of criminal jurisdiction or a judge as defined in section 552; or**
- **(*b*) another statutory right of review is available.**

(3) The judge of the Court of Appeal of Nunavut may grant relief under subsection (4) only if the judge is satisfied that

- **(*a*) in the case of any decision or order mentioned in subsection (1),**
  - **(i) the judge of the Nunavut Court of Justice failed to observe a principle of natural justice or failed or refused to exercise the judge's jurisdiction, or**
  - **(ii) the decision or order was made as a result of an irrelevant consideration or for an improper purpose;**
- **(*b*) in the case of a decision or order mentioned in paragraph (1)(*a*), that**
  - **(i) the judge failed to comply with a statutory requirement for the making of the decision or order,**
  - **(ii) the decision or order was made in the absence of any evidence that a statutory requirement for the making of the decision or order was met,**

(iii) the decision or order was made as a result of reckless disregard for the truth, fraud, intentional misrepresentation of material facts or intentional omission to state material facts,

(iv) the warrant is so vague or lacking in particularity that it authorizes an unreasonable search, or

(v) the warrant lacks a material term or condition that is required by law;

(*c*) in the case of a decision or order mentioned in paragraph (1)(*b*), that the judge of the Nunavut Court of Justice

(i) failed to follow a mandatory provision of this Act relating to the conduct of a preliminary inquiry,

(ii) ordered the accused to stand trial when there was no evidence adduced on which a properly instructed jury acting reasonably could convict, or

(iii) discharged the accused when there was some evidence adduced on which a properly instructed jury acting reasonably could convict;

(*d*) in the case of a decision or order mentioned in paragraph (1)(*c*) or (*d*), that the judge of the Nunavut Court of Justice erred in law;

(*e*) in the case of a decision or order mentioned in paragraph (1)(*e*), that

(i) the information or indictment failed to give the accused notice of the charge,

(ii) the judge of the Nunavut Court of Justice did not have jurisdiction to try the offence, or

(iii) the provision creating the offence alleged to have been committed by the accused is unconstitutional; or

(*f*) in the case of a decision or order mentioned in paragraph (1)(*f*), that

(i) the judge failed to comply with a statutory requirement for the making of the decision or order,

(ii) the decision or order was made in the absence of any evidence that a statutory requirement for the making of the decision or order was met, or

(iii) the decision or order was made as a result of reckless disregard for the truth, fraud, intentional misrepresentation of material facts or intentional omission to state material facts.

(4) On the hearing of the application for review, the judge of the Court of Appeal of Nunavut may do one or more of the following:

(*a*) order a judge of the Nunavut Court of Justice to do any act or thing that the judge or any other judge of that court failed or refused to do or has delayed in doing;

(*b*) prohibit or restrain a decision, order or proceeding of a judge of the Nunavut Court of Justice;

(*c*) declare invalid or unlawful, quash or set aside, in whole or in part, a decision, order or proceeding of a judge of the Nunavut Court of Justice;

(*d*) refer back for determination in accordance with any directions that the judge considers to be appropriate, a decision, order or proceeding of a judge of the Nunavut Court of Justice;

(*e*) grant any remedy under subsection 24(1) of the *Canadian Charter of Rights and Freedoms*;

(*f*) refuse to grant any relief if the judge is of the opinion that no substantial wrong or miscarriage of justice has occurred or that the subject-matter of the application should be determined at trial or on appeal; and

(*g*) dismiss the application.

(5) If an application for review is made, a judge of the Court of Appeal of Nunavut may make any interim order that the judge considers appropriate pending the final disposition of the application for review.

(6) A person who proposes to make an application for review shall do so in the manner and within the period that may be directed by rules of court, except that a judge of the Court of Appeal of Nunavut may at any time extend any period specified in the rules.

(7) An appeal lies to the Court of Appeal of Nunavut against a decision or order made under subsection (4). The provisions of Part XXI apply, with any modifications that the circumstances require, to the appeal. 1999, c. 3, s. 50.

CROSS-REFERENCES

"Attorney General" and "indictment" are defined in s. 2. For notes of cases concerning the review of orders of inferior courts through extraordinary remedies in the rest of Canada see Part XXVI. For other cross-references and a note on procedure in Nunavut, see the cross-references under s. 536.1.

HABEAS CORPUS / Exception / Provisions apply.

573.2 (1) *Habeas corpus* proceedings may be brought before a judge of the Court of Appeal of Nunavut in respect of an order made or warrant issued by a judge of the Nunavut Court of Justice, except where

- **(*a*) the order or warrant is of a kind that could only be made or issued in a province or a territory other than Nunavut by a superior court of criminal jurisdiction or a judge as defined in section 552; or**
- **(*b*) another statutory right of review or appeal is available.**

(2) Despite subsection (1), *habeas corpus* proceedings may be brought before a judge of the Court of Appeal of Nunavut with respect to an order or warrant of a judge of the Nunavut Court of Justice if the proceedings are brought to challenge the constitutionality of a person's detention or confinement.

(3) Subsections 784(2) to (6) apply in respect of any proceedings brought under subsection (1) or (2). 1999, c. 3, s. 50.

CROSS-REFERENCES

For cross-references and a note on procedure in Nunavut, see the cross-references under s. 536.1. For notes on the availability of *habeas corpus* in the rest of Canada see the notes following s. 774.

Part XX / PROCEDURE IN JURY TRIALS AND GENERAL PROVISIONS

Preferring Indictment

PROSECUTOR MAY PREFER INDICTMENT / Preferring indictment when no preliminary inquiry requested / Preferring single indictment / Consent to inclusion of other charges / Private prosecutor requires consent.

574. (1) Subject to subsection (3), the prosecutor may, whether the charges were included in one information or not, prefer an indictment against any person who has been ordered to stand trial in respect of

- **(*a*) any charge on which that person was ordered to stand trial; or**
- **(*b*) any charge founded on the facts disclosed by the evidence taken on the preliminary inquiry, in addition to or in substitution for any charge on which that person was ordered to stand trial.**

(1.1) If a person has not requested a preliminary inquiry under subsection 536(4) or 536.1(3) into the charge, the prosecutor may, subject to subsection (3), prefer an indictment against a person in respect of a charge set out in an information or

informations, or any included charge, at any time after the person has made an election, re-election or deemed election on the information or informations.

(1.2) If indictments may be preferred under both subsections (1) and (1.1), the prosecutor may prefer a single indictment in respect of one or more charges referred to in subsection (1) combined with one or more charges or included charges referred to in subsection (1.1).

(2) An indictment preferred under any of subsections (1) to (1.2) may, if the accused consents, include a charge that is not referred to in those subsections, and the offence charged may be dealt with, tried and determined and punished in all respects as if it were an offence in respect of which the accused had been ordered to stand trial. However, if the offence was committed wholly in a province other than that in which the accused is before the court, subsection 478(3) applies.

(3) In a prosecution conducted by a prosecutor other than the Attorney General and in which the Attorney General does not intervene, an indictment may not be preferred under any of subsections (1) to (1.2) before a court without the written order of a judge of that court. R.S., c. C-34, s. 504; R.S.C. 1985, c. 27 (1st Supp.), s. 113; 2002, c. 13, s. 45.

CROSS-REFERENCES

The terms "prosecutor", "Attorney General" and "indictment" are defined in s. 2. Where no preliminary inquiry has been held or the accused has been discharged following a preliminary inquiry, see s. 577. The formal requirements of an indictment are set forth in ss. 581 to 593. The Attorney General may direct a stay of an indictment pursuant to s. 579. Pursuant to s. 580, an indictment is sufficient if it is on paper and in Form 4. An indictment preferred under this part is required whenever the accused is to be tried in a court other than the provincial court, whether by a judge alone or a judge with a jury. Section 597 provides that where an indictment has been preferred against the person who is at large and the person does not appear or remain in attendance for his trial the court may issue a warrant for his arrest.

SYNOPSIS

This section deals with the drafting and preferring of indictments.

Where, following a preliminary inquiry, there has been an order to stand trial, the prosecutor may include in the indictment not only the charge(s) on which the accused has been ordered to stand trial (subsec. (1)(*a*)), but also any other charge(s) disclosed by the evidence taken at the inquiry (subsec. (1)(*b*)).

If no party has requested a preliminary inquiry, the prosecutor may prefer an indictment included charges set out in the information or any included offences (subsec. (1.1)).

By reason of subsec. (2), the accused can consent to adding to the indictment charges other than those referred to in subsec. (1) and (1.1). The only limitation is that the offences must have been committed within the province in which the indictment is being preferred, otherwise the transfer provisions of the Code must be used (see s. 478(3)). An accused may wish to use this provision as a means of bringing a number of charges before one judge for disposition by way of a guilty plea.

Subsection (3) precludes an indictment being preferred in a "private prosecution" without the approval of a judge of the court in which the trial will occur.

ANNOTATIONS

Editor's Note: Some of the decisions noted below although decided under the predecessor legislation were felt to be relevant to these provisions.

It is after the presentment of the indictment that the indictment becomes the foundation of any further proceedings and the accused is precluded from attacking the regularity of the order to stand trial by way of *certiorari*. However, such an indictment is not preferred or presented until it is lodged with the trial court at the opening of the accused's trial with a court ready to proceed with the trial: *R. v. Chabot*, [1980] 2 S.C.R. 985, 55 C.C.C. (2d) 385, 18 C.R. (3d) 258 (7:0).

The agent of the Attorney General who signed the indictment is not also required to conduct the trial: *R. v. Alward* (1976), 32 C.C.C. (2d) 416, 73 D.L.R. (3d) 290 (N.B.C.A.).

The accused's election and any subsequent re-election apply to offences added to the indictment pursuant to subsec. (1)(*b*): *R. v. Garcia* (1990), 75 C.R. (3d) 250 (B.C.C.A.).

The prosecutor has no power under this section to prefer an indictment including a charge which was before the judge presiding at the preliminary inquiry but upon which the judge did not order the accused to stand trial. When the judge presiding at the preliminary hearing has heard all of the evidence, the judge's refusal to order the accused to stand trial for an offence charged in an information amounts to a judicial determination that that charge is not founded on the facts disclosed by the evidence for the purpose of this section. In order to proceed with the original charge, a new charge would have to be laid either by a new information or by a preferred indictment under s. 577. However, since s. 577 does not apply to trials by judge alone under Part XIX, to prefer an indictment under that section, the Attorney General would also have to make a direction under s. 568: *R. v. Tapaquon*, [1993] 4 S.C.R. 535, 87 C.C.C. (3d) 1, 26 C.R. (4th) 193.

The refusal of the judge presiding at the preliminary inquiry to order the accused to stand trial on another offence, disclosed by the evidence pursuant to s. 548, does not mean that the accused was discharged on that other offence within the meaning of s. 577(*b*) and, therefore, an indictment may be preferred under this section including the charges upon which the accused was ordered to stand trial and other offences disclosed by the evidence, and s. 577 need not be complied with: *R. v. Hyde* (1990), 55 C.C.C. (3d) 251 (Man. C.A.).

The error in the labelling of the offence with which the accused was charged as sexual assault [an offence which did not exist at the time of the offence] rather than indecent assault was voidable and thus, when the error was detected, it was open to the Crown to prefer a new indictment, without the consent of the Attorney General [as required by s. 577], based on the evidence adduced at the preliminary inquiry the validity of which was never directly challenged by the accused: *R. v. Barbeau*, [1992] 2 S.C.R. 845, 75 C.C.C. (3d) 129, 15 C.R. (4th) 169.

The Crown's power to prefer an indictment is an exercise of core prosecutorial discretion and therefore not subject to judicial review except for abuse of process: *R. v. Johnson* (2011), 285 C.C.C. (3d) 191 (Ont. S.C.J.).

---

575. [*Repealed*, R.S.C. 1985, c. 27 (1st Supp.), s. 113.]

INDICTMENT / Criminal information and bill of indictment / Coroner's inquisition.

576. (1) Except as provided in this Act, no indictment shall be preferred.

(2) No criminal information shall be laid or granted and no bill of indictment shall be preferred before a grand jury.

(3) No person shall be tried on a coroner's inquisition. R.S., c. C-34, s. 506; R.S.C. 1985, c. 27 (1st Supp.), s. 114.

CROSS-REFERENCES

The term "indictment" is defined in s. 2. An indictment is preferred pursuant to ss. 574 and 577. Pursuant to s. 529, where a person is alleged, by a verdict on a coroner's inquest, to have committed murder or manslaughter but he has not been charged with the offence, the coroner shall direct, by warrant, that the person be taken into custody and taken before a justice or direct that the person enter into a recognizance to appear before a justice.

SYNOPSIS

This section, in effect, abolishes certain archaic, mostly common law, modes of proceeding and confirms that an accused may only be tried upon indictment as provided for in the *Criminal Code*.

ANNOTATIONS

In *R. v. Hemlock Park Co-Operative Farm Ltd.*, [1974] S.C.R. 123, 6 C.C.C. (2d) 189, 24 D.L.R. (3d) 688, it was held (5:0) that a criminal information referred to the historic laying of a charge by the Attorney General or some other authorized person directly before a Superior Court of Criminal Jurisdiction instead of being preferred to a Grand Jury or presented by a Grand Jury.

DIRECT INDICTMENTS.

577. Despite section 574, an indictment may be preferred even if the accused has not been given the opportunity to request a preliminary inquiry, a preliminary inquiry has been commenced but not concluded or a preliminary inquiry has been held and the accused has been discharged, if

(*a*) in the case of a prosecution conducted by the Attorney General or one in which the Attorney General intervenes, the personal consent in writing of the Attorney General or Deputy Attorney General is filed in court; or

(*b*) in any other case, a judge of the court so orders. R.S., c. C-34, s. 507; 1974-75-76, c. 93, s. 63; 1984, c. 40, s. 20(2); R.S.C. 1985, c. 27 (1st Supp.), s. 115; 2002, c. 13, s. 46.

CROSS-REFERENCES

The preliminary inquiry is held pursuant to Part XVIII. In particular, s. 548 sets out the test for determining whether or not the accused should be ordered to stand trial or discharged. This section is complementary to s. 574 which represents the ordinary procedure for preferring an indictment, *i.e.*, where the accused has been ordered to stand trial. The term "indictment" is defined in s. 2. The term "Attorney General" is also defined in s. 2 but as this section indicates, the full definition of that term is not applicable since the "personal consent" of the Attorney General or the Deputy Attorney General is required. Where an indictment has been preferred pursuant to s. 577, the court, by virtue of s. 578, may issue a summons addressed to or warrant for the arrest of the accused to compel his attendance to answer the charge in the indictment. While, by virtue of s. 566(3), a direct indictment may not be preferred under s. 577 for trial by judge alone, the accused may, pursuant to s. 565(2), re-elect trial by judge alone with the written consent of the prosecutor. Absent the re-election, the accused will be tried by judge and jury. The Attorney General may direct a stay of proceedings pursuant to s. 579.

SYNOPSIS

Where the accused has not had the opportunity to request a preliminary inquiry, one has been conducted but not concluded, or the accused discharged, the Crown can only prefer an indictment with the personal written consent of the Attorney General or the Deputy Attorney General. Such consent is also required to proceed on a new information.

In "private prosecutions" the written consent of a judge is required in these circumstances.

ANNOTATIONS

Editor's Note: Some of the decisions noted below, although decided under the predecessor legislation, were felt to be relevant to these provisions.

Formalities of preferring indictment – Where the Attorney General consents to the preferring of the indictment it is sufficient that the Attorney General has personally signed the indictment and he is not required to be present in court when the indictment is actually preferred: *R. v. Philbin and Henderson* (1977), 37 C.C.C. (2d) 528 (Alta. S.C. App. Div.); *R. v. Dwyer and Lauzon* (1978), 42 C.C.C. (2d) 83 (Ont. C.A.), revd on other grounds [1980] 1 S.C.R. 481, 47 C.C.C. (2d) 1; *R. v. Balderstone* (1982), 2 C.C.C. (3d) 37 (Man. Q.B.), affd 8 C.C.C. (3d) 532 (Man. C.A.).

An indictment signed by the then Attorney General some months before the trial at which time the indictment is preferred is valid notwithstanding that by the time of trial a new Attorney General has been appointed: *R. v. Rooke* (1988), 40 C.C.C. (3d) 484 (B.C.C.A.).

The refusal of the judge presiding at the preliminary inquiry to order the accused to stand trial on another offence, disclosed by the evidence pursuant to s. 548, does not mean that the accused was discharged on that other offence and, therefore, an indictment may be preferred under s. 574 including the charges upon which the accused was ordered to stand trial and other offences disclosed by the evidence. This section need not be complied with: *R. v. Hyde* (1990), 55 C.C.C. (3d) 251 (Man. C.A.).

Where the accused has been discharged on the full offence but ordered to stand trial on an included offence, in order to prefer an indictment for the full offence, the provisions of this section must be complied with. The prosecutor cannot simply rely upon the provisions of s. 574(1)(*b*): *R. v. Tapaquon*, [1993] 4 S.C.R. 535, 87 C.C.C. (3d) 1.

The Crown may prefer a direct indictment where the order to stand trial has been quashed: *R. v. Charlie* (1998), 126 C.C.C. (3d) 513 (B.C.C.A.); *R. v. Ewen* (2000), 144 C.C.C. (3d) 277, *sub nom. R. v. E. (S.W.)* (Sask. C.A.).

The quashing of an indictment for failure to comply with the provisions of s. 581(3) does not result in the accused being "discharged" so as to require the consent of the Attorney General to the preferring of a subsequent indictment. The term "discharged" in para. (*b*) refers to an order made at the conclusion of the preliminary inquiry where the justice finds that there is insufficient evidence to order the accused to stand trial. Preferring of a subsequent indictment to cure the supposed defect does not amount to an abuse of process: *R. v. D. (A.)* (1990), 60 C.C.C. (3d) 407 (Ont. C.A.).

A direct indictment can include counts for which the accused has been committed after a preliminary inquiry. Accordingly, a direct indictment could be used to join two accused together for trial where the Crown decided to proceed against one accused at a preliminary inquiry because the case against the co-accused had to be adjourned: *R. v. Benji* (2002), 161 C.C.C. (3d) 479 (S.C.C.).

Where the accused was ordered to stand trial for the offence charged of sexual assault, an offence which, however, did not exist at the time alleged, it was open to the Crown to prefer an indictment charging indecent assault without the consent of the Attorney General, this latter offence having been disclosed by the evidence at the preliminary inquiry within the meaning of s. 574: *R. v. B. (A.)* (1991), 64 C.C.C. (3d) 104 (Que. C.A.).

Where the Crown has directed an indictment pending preliminary inquiry proceedings, the Crown should seek a hearing in respect of the detention order pursuant to s. 515 of the *Criminal Code*. Where the Crown directed an indictment and then stayed the preliminary inquiry, the result was to vacate the original detention order. The failure to accord the accused a s. 515 review was a technical oversight and the Crown should be afforded a reasonable opportunity, having directed an indictment, to seek the continued detention of the accused pursuant to s. 515: *R. v. Jones* (1997), 113 C.C.C. (3d) 225 (Ont. C.A.).

A direct indictment under this section is available even where the accused has already elected trial by judge alone in provincial court: *Canada (Attorney General) v. Sher* (2012), 291 C.C.C. (3d) 1 (Ont. S.C.J.).

Right to hearing before Attorney General – In exercising his power under this subsection the Attorney General is not required to afford the accused a hearing even where the Attorney General proposes to prefer the indictment part way through the accused's preliminary hearing: *R. v. Saikaly* (1979), 48 C.C.C. (2d) 192 (Ont. C.A.).

Review of Attorney General's consent generally – The courts have no jurisdiction to review a decision of the Attorney General under this subsection to prefer an indictment despite the discharge of the accused at his preliminary inquiry: *R. v. Balderstone* (1983), 8 C.C.C. (3d) 532 (Man. C.A.), leave to appeal to S.C.C. refused C.C.C. *loc. cit.*; *R. v. Moore* (1986), 26 C.C.C. (3d) 474 (Man. C.A.), or where no preliminary inquiry has been held: *R. v. Stolar* (1983), 4 C.C.C. (3d) 333 (Man. C.A.), leave to appeal to S.C.C. refused 21 Man. R. (2d) 240*n*, 50 N.R. 396*n*.

A superior court judge had no power to compel potential Crown witnesses to attend to be questioned by defence counsel because the Attorney General had preferred a direct indictment: *R. v. Sterling* (1993), 84 C.C.C. (3d) 65 (Sask. C.A.).

As to the scope of judicial review generally of the exercise of the powers of the Attorney General, see *Krieger v. Law Society of Alberta*, [2002] 3 S.C.R. 372, 168 C.C.C. (3d) 97, and *R. v. Regan*, [2002] 1 S.C.R. 297, 161 C.C.C. (3d) 97. In summary, within the core of prosecutorial discretion, the courts cannot interfere except in circumstances of flagrant impropriety. Prosecutorial discretion refers to decisions regarding the nature and extent of the prosecution and the Attorney General's participation in it. Decisions that govern a Crown prosecutor's tactics or conduct before the court, do not fall within the scope of prosecutorial discretion and are governed by the inherent jurisdiction of the court to control its own processes once the Attorney General has elected to enter into that forum.

Constitutional considerations – This section does not infringe ss. 7, 9 and 15 of the *Charter of Rights and Freedoms*. However, the exercise of the power by the Attorney General to override a discharge and prefer a direct indictment could be reviewed by a court of competent jurisdiction if in the particular case it resulted in a denial or infringement of a constitutionally protected right: *R. v. Ertel* (1987), 35 C.C.C. (3d) 398 (Ont. C.A.), leave to appeal to S.C.C. refused 36 C.C.C. (3d) vi. Also see: *Patrick v. Canada (Attorney General)* (1986), 28 C.C.C. (3d) 417 (B.C.S.C.) [**Note:** an appeal to the B.C.C.A. was quashed, 35 C.C.C. (3d) 551, and leave to appeal to S.C.C. was refused 80 N.R. 160]; *R. v. Andrew*, [1986] 6 W.W.R. 323 (B.C.S.C.); *R. v. Ahmad* (2008), 256 C.C.C. (3d) 552 (Ont. S.C.J.).

The statutory right to a preliminary hearing is not a constitutional right and therefore where the accused has been given complete disclosure of the Crown's case, the preferring of a direct indictment where a preliminary inquiry has not been held, does not constitute a violation of the right to fundamental justice in s. 7 of the *Canadian Charter of Rights and Freedoms: R. v. Arviv* (1985), 19 C.C.C. (3d) 395 (Ont. C.A.), leave to appeal to S.C.C. refused C.C.C. *loc. cit.*; *R. v. Sterling* (1993), 84 C.C.C. (3d) 65 (Sask. C.A.).

Order of judge where private complaint [para. (*b*)] – In two cases, *Johnson v. Inglis* (1980), 52 C.C.C. (3d) 385 (Ont. H.C.J.), and *Garton v. Whelan* (1984), 14 C.C.C. (3d) 449 (H.C.J.), decided prior to the amendment to this section, Evans C.J.H.C. considered the role of a judge in consenting to private prosecution where no preliminary inquiry had been held or the accused had been discharged. In the *Johnson* case it was held that a distinction must be drawn between cases where a preliminary hearing has and has not been held. In either case, however, in deciding whether to exercise his discretion the judge must consider the nature of the offence, whether it is of a "public" nature such as murder, or of a "private" nature such as criminal libel, and he should also consider the position of the Crown in the matter. Where a preliminary hearing has been held, the judge's consent should be granted only where it is necessary to prevent a miscarriage of justice. Thus, consent will not automatically be granted simply because a *prima facie* case was made out at the preliminary hearing. Where no preliminary hearing has been held a much stricter test is appropriate, consent being granted only where some urgency or other strongly persuasive reasons exist so as to require depriving the person of a preliminary hearing to which he would otherwise be entitled under the law. In *Garton*, it was held that the judge should not give his consent merely because of an error of law made by the judge presiding at the preliminary inquiry. Rather, the court will only give its consent where it is necessary to prevent a miscarriage of justice. In making that determination a relevant consideration is the fact that the Attorney General's Department has on two occasions reviewed the sufficiency of the evidence. It is open to the court in its discretion to hear new evidence on an application pursuant to s. 577.

SUMMONS OR WARRANT / Part XVI to apply.

578. (1) Where notice of the recommencement of proceedings has been given pursuant to subsection 579(2) or an indictment has been filed with the court before which the proceedings are to commence or recommence, the court, if it considers it necessary, may issue

(*a*) a summons addressed to, or

(*b*) a warrant for the arrest of,

the accused or defendant, as the case may be, to compel him to attend before the court to answer the charge described in the indictment.

(2) The provisions of Part XVI apply with such modifications as the circumstances require where a summons or warrant is issued under subsection (1). 1974-75-76, c. 93, s. 64; R.S.C. 1985, c. 27 (1st Supp.), s. 116.

CROSS-REFERENCES

The term "indictment" is defined in s. 2. The terms "summons" and "warrant" are defined for the purposes of Part XVI in s. 493.

The ordinary power to issue a bench warrant is found in s. 597 where the accused does not appear or remain in attendance for his trial.

SYNOPSIS

This section provides for compelling the appearance of the accused where the Attorney General has recommenced proceedings following a stay of proceedings (see s. 579(2)), or the matter is being dealt with by way of "direct" indictment (see s. 577). The normal rules governing the issuance of process and judicial interim release apply.

ANNOTATIONS

A direct indictment starts new proceedings and triggers the judicial interim release provisions of Part XVI of the *Criminal Code*. The signing of a direct indictment does not invalidate an earlier detention order or bail order in relation to the same charges. The original order remains in effect until the charges in the information are disposed of according to law. However, where the Crown stays the original information, the bail order or detention order is no longer in effect and the accused is entitled to a bail hearing pursuant to s. 515 before a judge of the trial court. An accused who is in custody and is the subject of a direct indictment may be brought before the court by a judge's order pursuant to s. 527. An accused who is out of custody may be brought before the court through the issuance of a summons or warrant for arrest pursuant to s. 578 by the trial judge or may be arrested by pursuant to s. 503: *R. v. Jones* (1997), 113 C.C.C. (3d) 225 (Ont. C.A.).

The judge need not hear evidence before issuing a warrant under this section: *R. v. Denbigh* (1988), 45 C.C.C. (3d) 86 (B.C.S.C.).

ATTORNEY GENERAL MAY DIRECT STAY / Recommencement of proceedings.

579. (1) The Attorney General or counsel instructed by him for that purpose may, at any time after any proceedings in relation to an accused or a defendant are commenced and before judgment, direct the clerk or other proper officer of the court to make an entry on the record that the proceedings are stayed by his direction, and such entry shall be made forthwith thereafter, whereupon the proceedings shall be stayed accordingly and any recognizance relating to the proceedings is vacated.

(2) Proceedings stayed in accordance with subsection (1) may be recommenced, without laying a new information or preferring a new indictment, as the case may be, by the Attorney General or counsel instructed by him for that purpose giving notice of the recommencement to the clerk of the court in which the stay of the proceedings was entered, but where no such notice is given within one year after the entry of the stay of

proceedings, or before the expiration of the time within which the proceedings could have been commenced, whichever is the earlier, the proceedings shall be deemed never to have been commenced. R.S., c. C-34, s. 508; 1972, c. 13, s. 43; R.S.C. 1985, c. 27 (1st Supp.), s. 117.

CROSS-REFERENCES

The terms "Attorney General", "indictment" and "clerk of the court" are defined in s. 2. The procedure for enforcement of recognizance is in Part XXV.

Section 579.01 permits the Attorney General to intervene in the proceedings by calling witnesses and examining and cross-examining witnesses without actually taking over the prosecution.

SYNOPSIS

This section governs the Attorney General's ability to stay and recommence proceedings.

The Attorney General or his counsel has the right to direct a stay after proceedings have been commenced (*i.e.*, after an information has been laid or an indictment has been filed) and before a verdict has been rendered.

In the case of an indictable offence the proceedings can be recommenced within one year of the stay. For summary conviction matters the Crown must act before the expiration of the limitation period. Where notice of recommencement is given within these time limits the proceedings will be continued on the original indictment or information.

After the one-year period has elapsed the Crown, if it wishes to proceed on an indictable matter, will have to start afresh.

ANNOTATIONS

Procedure in directing stay – In *R. v. Dowson*, [1983] 2 S.C.R. 144, 7 C.C.C. (3d) 527 (7:0), it was held in relation to the predecessor to this section that an information charging an indictable offence could not be stayed until the justice had determined whether or not to issuc process pursuant to s. 518. However, in reaching this conclusion the court appeared to accept that this created an anomaly in that under former s. 732.1 summary conviction proceedings could be stayed as soon as the information was laid. With the amendment to this section and the repeal of s. 732.1, this section now covers both summary and indictable proceedings and in terms similar to former s. 732.1. Accordingly, it would appear that all charges can be stayed as soon as the information is laid.

This view was confirmed in *R. v. Pardo* (1990), 62 C.C.C. (3d) 371 (Que. C.A.), where it was held that the Attorney General may direct a stay of proceedings prior to the decision of the justice whether or not to issue process.

An agent of the Attorney General may exercise his power under this section under his general authority as such an agent and does not require specific instructions from the Attorney General: *R. v. McKay* (1979), 9 C.R. (3d) 378, [1979] 4 W.W.R. 90 (Sask. C.A.).

Effect of entering of stay – Subsequent to proceedings being stayed a new information in identical terms may be laid and proceeded upon: *R. v. Judge of the Provincial Court, Ex p. McLeod,* [1970] 5 C.C.C. 128, 74 W.W.R. 319 *sub nom. R. v. McLeod* (B.C.S.C.).

By virtue of this section, the pre-existing right of the Crown to withdraw charges with leave of the Court after the proceedings have been commenced and a plea taken has been abolished by Parliament and this section governs the procedure and the effect of the discontinuance. A stay, however, does not prevent a new information from being laid, and the Crown still has the right to withdraw charges prior to a plea being taken: *R. v. Grocutt* (1977), 35 C.C.C. (2d) 76 (Alta. S.C.T.D.).

The vacating of the recognizance upon entering of a stay of proceedings does not render the recognizance void *ab initio* and if prior to the stay being entered the accused failed to comply with its terms a court has jurisdiction under s. 770 to endorse such default: *Purves v. Canada (Attorney General)* (1990), 54 C.C.C. (3d) 355 (B.C.C.A.).

The Crown is entitled to stay proceedings on one indictment while replacing it with another. The filing of a motion of intention to stay proceedings does not have the effect of staying all proceedings against the accused: *R. v. Pawluk* (2002), 170 C.C.C. (3d) 163 (Sask. C.A.).

The Crown preferred a direct indictment which was stayed at the request of the Crown under subsec. (1) and subsequently recommenced under subsec. (2). Because the accused had elected trial by judge alone prior to the stay, that election remained binding when the proceeding was recommenced. No statutory provision or legal principle provides an accused who has elected to be tried by a judge alone the right to re-elect to be tried by a judge and jury when a proceeding under a direct indictment that has been stayed is recommenced within one year: *R. v. Scott* (2014), 310 C.C.C. (3d) 143 (B.C.C.A.).

Right of Attorney General to intervene – Once the Attorney General intervenes in a prosecution, then he assumes control of the prosecution and has the right to stay those proceedings despite the wishes of the informant. At least in the absence of flagrant impropriety on the part of the Crown officers, such action does not constitute a violation of the informant's rights under s. 7 of the *Charter of Rights and Freedoms*: *R. v. Hamilton* (1986), 30 C.C.C. (3d) 65 (B.C.S.C.). Similarly: *R. v. Osiowy* (1989), 50 C.C.C. (3d) 189 (Sask. C.A.).

Except perhaps where there is a flagrant impropriety on the part of the Attorney General, the courts may not review the exercise of discretion under this section: *Campbell v. Ontario (Attorney General)* (1987), 31 C.C.C. (3d) 289 (Ont. H.C.J.), affd 35 C.C.C. (3d) 480 (Ont. C.A.), leave to appeal to S.C.C. refused 43 D.L.R. (4th) vii. Similarly: *Quebec (Attorney General) v. Chartrand* (1987), 40 C.C.C. (3d) 270 (Que. C.A.), where it was held that while by reason of enactment of the Charter the exercise of the discretion under this section is subject to review, the private complainant's rights under s. 15 of the Charter were not infringed because a stay of proceedings was entered to bar prosecution of abortion charges.

The fact that the Attorney General has broad powers of intervention, including the right to stay proceedings initiated by a private informant, does not violate the equality rights under s. 15 of the *Canadian Charter of Rights and Freedoms*: *R. v. Baker* (1986), 26 C.C.C. (3d) 123 (B.C.S.C.).

Section 7 of the Charter does not give a private prosecutor the right to continue a criminal prosecution in the face of an intervention by the Attorney General: *Kostuch (Informant) v. Alberta (Attorney General)* (1995), 101 C.C.C. (3d) 321 (Alta. C.A.), leave to appeal to S.C.C. refused 105 C.C.C. (3d) vi.

Also now see ss. 579.01 and 579.1.

Withdrawal of charge – It was held in *R. v. Osborne* (1975), 25 C.C.C. (2d) 405 (N.B.C.A.), that the trial judge should not have refused the Crown's request prior to plea to withdraw one charge so as to lay a more serious charge.

Prior to the preferring of an indictment or the entering of a plea and the tendering of evidence an information may be withdrawn by the Crown without the leave of the court. Where the Crown has tendered evidence after taking of a plea then the trial judge is seized with jurisdiction and the information cannot be withdrawn without his consent. Accordingly, where, prior to plea, the Crown states that an information is withdrawn the court has no jurisdiction to proceed with trial or preliminary hearing: *R. v. Blasko* (1975), 29 C.C.C. (2d) 321 (Ont. H.C.J.).

The Crown may withdraw an information on which an election of summary conviction has been made, file a new information and proceed by way of indictment, despite a plea of not guilty having been entered. The exercise of prosecutorial discretion does not offend the principles of fundamental justice unless there is bad faith or some improper motive or arbitrary purpose: *R. v. McArthur* (1995), 102 C.C.C. (3d) 84 (Sask. C.A.).

Once evidence has been heard on a preliminary hearing the prosecutor has the right to "withdraw the charges" in the sense that he does not wish to prosecute the proceedings any further but this decision does not eliminate the proceedings and the court should continue the preliminary hearing until completion, either by discharge or committal of the accused, or until the prosecutor directs a stay under this section. Further, where the prosecutor is counsel for the Attorney General his verbal assurance that he has the necessary instructions from the Attorney General to direct a stay be entered is all that is required: *R. v. Mastroianni* (1976), 36 C.C.C. (2d) 97 (Ont. Prov. Ct.).

Abuse of process – Courts have a residual discretion to remedy an abuse of process by a stay of proceedings only in the "clearest of cases" which requires proof of conduct which shocks the conscience of the community and is so detrimental to the proper administration of justice that it warrants judicial intervention. There must be "overwhelming" evidence that the proceedings are unfair to the point that they are contrary to the interest of justice. Courts must be careful not to attempt to second-guess the Attorney General and to intervene only where there is "conspicuous evidence of improper motives or of bad faith or of an act so wrong that it violates the conscience of the community, such that it would genuinely be unfair and indecent to proceed": *R. v. Power*, [1994] 1 S.C.R. 601, 89 C.C.C. (3d) 1. Also see the earlier cases of: *R. v. Jewitt*, [1985] 2 S.C.R. 128, 21 C.C.C. (3d) 7, and *R. v. Keyowski*, [1988] 1 S.C.R. 657, 40 C.C.C. (3d) 481.

Crown counsel acted properly and in good faith in staying proceedings when the trial judge ordered that the identity of a confidential informer be disclosed. In the circumstances, the Crown was not required to offer no evidence and then proceed through an appeal against acquittal to challenge the correctness of the ruling. Subsequent to the stay of proceedings, the Crown acted at the first reasonable opportunity to recommence the proceedings. There was no abuse of process in the circumstances: *R. v. Scott*, [1990] 3 S.C.R. 979, 61 C.C.C. (3d) 300.

Abuse of process arises where the individual's right to a fair trial is implicated as where the prosecution is conducted in such a manner as to contravene the community's basic sense of decency and fair play and thereby call into question the integrity of the system. There is also a residual category not affecting the fairness of the trial addressing other circumstances in which the prosecution is conducted in such a manner as to connote unfairness and vexatiousness of such a degree that it contravenes fundamental notions of justice and thus undermine the integrity of the judicial process. Even where there has been an abuse of process a stay of proceedings will only be appropriate where the prejudice caused by the abuse in question will be manifested, perpetuated or aggravated through the conduct of the trial, or by its outcome; and no other remedy is reasonably capable of removing that prejudice. Generally speaking, a stay of proceedings is appropriate only where the abuse is likely to continue or to be carried forward. Exceptionally, a stay of proceedings will be appropriate because the past misconduct was so egregious that the mere fact of going forward in the light of it will be offensive. Any likelihood of continuing abuse must be considered in relation to possible remedies less drastic than a stay. Where uncertainty persists about whether the abuse is sufficient to justify the drastic remedy of a stay there must be a balancing of interests that would be served by granting the stay against the interest that society has in a final decision on the merits: *R. v. Regan*, [2002] 1 S.C.R. 297, 161 C.C.C. (3d) 97. Also see *R. v. O'Connor*, [1995] 4 S.C.R. 411, 103 C.C.C. (3d) 1; *Canada (Minister of Citizenship and Immigration) v. Tobiass*, [1997] 3 S.C.R. 391, 118 C.C.C. (3d) 443; *R. v. Conway*, [1989] 1 S.C.R. 1659, 49 C.C.C. (3d) 289.

In *R. v. Orysiuk* (1977), 37 C.C.C. (2d) 445 (5:0) (Alta. S.C. App. Div.), the court was unanimous in holding that the laying of criminal charges following a public inquiry into the same matter as were the subject of the charges did not give rise to grounds for staying the proceedings. Also see *Phillips v. Nova Scotia (Commission of Inquiry into the Westray Mine Tragedy)*, [1995] 2 S.C.R. 97, 98 C.C.C. (3d) 20, *sub nom. Phillips v. Nova Scotia (Commissioner, Public Inquiries Act); Phillips v. Richard, J.*, and *R. v. Kenny* (1996), 108 C.C.C. (3d) 349 (Nfld. C.A.), leave to appeal to S.C.C. refused 112 C.C.C. (3d) vii.

One ground for staying proceedings as an abuse of process is where the criminal proceedings have been instituted to collect a debt or realize on some civil claim. However, this must amount to more than merely evidence that the victim asked the accused for repayment and agreed on cross-examination that had he had been repaid he would not have contacted the police: *R. v. Laird* (1983), 4 C.C.C. (3d) 92 (Ont. H.C.J.).

In *R. v. B.* (1986), 29 C.C.C. (3d) 365 (Ont. C.A.), the court reviewed the circumstances in which the act of the prosecution in splitting the case by laying a second charge, resting upon some of the same facts as underlay a charge of which the accused had been acquitted, amounted to an abuse of process. Abuse of process has been found where the second trial is such that it will, in effect, force the accused to answer for the same delinquency twice; where the second trial is such that it will, in effect, relitigate matters that have already been decided on the merits, raising the spectre of inconsistent verdicts; or where the second trial is brought because of malice or spite so as to harass the accused and not for any proper purpose.

An abuse of process can also arise in a case of multiple re-trials that fail to produce a definitive result. Courts have sometimes posited a presumptive limit of three trials: see *R. v. Jack*, [1997] 2 S.C.R. 334, 117 C.C.C. (3d) 43, and the cases reviewed in *R. v. Badgerow* (2014), 311 C.C.C. (3d) 26 (Ont. C.A.), leave to appeal to S.C.C. refused [2014] 3 S.C.R. v.

Note: Section 579.001 enacted, to come after s. 579, 2017, c. 27, s. 62 (to come into force by order of the Governor in Council):

Instruction to stay / Stay / Recommencement / Proceedings deemed never commenced / Definition of "Agreement".

579.001 (1) The Attorney General or counsel instructed by him or her for that purpose shall, at any time after proceedings in relation to an act or omission of a "preclearance officer", as defined in section 5 of the *Preclearance Act, 2016*, are commenced and before judgment, direct the clerk or other proper officer of the court to make an entry on the record that the proceedings are stayed by direction of the Attorney General if the Government of the United States has provided notice of the exercise of primary criminal jurisdiction under paragraph 14 of Article X of the Agreement.

(2) The clerk or other officer of the court shall make the entry immediately after being so directed, and on the entry being made the proceedings are stayed and any recognizance relating to the proceedings is vacated.

(3) The proceedings may be recommenced without laying a new information or preferring a new indictment, if the Attorney General or counsel instructed by him or her gives notice to the clerk or other officer of the court that

(*a*) the Government of the United States has provided notice of waiver under paragraph 15 of Article X of the Agreement; or

(*b*) the Government of the United States has declined, or is unable, to prosecute the accused and the accused has returned to Canada.

(4) However, if the Attorney General or counsel does not give notice under subsection (3) on or before the first anniversary of the day on which the stay of proceedings was entered, the proceedings are deemed never to have been commenced.

(5) In this section, "Agreement" means the Agreement on Land, Rail, Marine, and Air Transport Preclearance between the Government of Canada and the Government of the United States of America, done at Washington on March 16, 2015.

WHEN ATTORNEY GENERAL DOES NOT STAY PROCEEDINGS.

579.01 If the Attorney General intervenes in proceedings and does not stay them under section 579, he or she may, without conducting the proceedings, call witnesses, examine and cross-examine witnesses, present evidence and make submissions. 2002, c. 13, s. 47.

CROSS-REFERENCES

"Attorney General" is defined in s. 2. Section 507.1 sets out the special procedure to be followed before a summons or warrant may be issued in a private prosecution.

SYNOPSIS

This section allows the Attorney General to intervene in a private prosecution without having to actually take carriage of the prosecution.

INTERVENTION BY ATTORNEY GENERAL OF CANADA / Section 579 to apply.

579.1 (1) The Attorney General of Canada or counsel instructed by him or her for that purpose may intervene in proceedings in the following circumstances:

- **(*a*) the proceedings are in respect of a contravention of, a conspiracy or attempt to contravene or counselling the contravention of an Act of Parliament or a regulation made under that Act, other than this Act or a regulation made under this Act;**
- **(*b*) the proceedings have not been instituted by an Attorney General;**
- **(*c*) judgment has not been rendered; and**
- **(*d*) the Attorney General of the province in which the proceedings are taken has not intervened.**

(2) Section 579 applies, with such modifications as the circumstances require, to proceedings in which the Attorney General of Canada intervenes pursuant to this section. 1994, c. 44, s. 60.

SYNOPSIS

This section allows the Attorney General of Canada to intervene in proceedings for an offence other than an offence under this Act, even though the proceedings were not commenced at the instance of the Government of Canada within the meaning of "Attorney General" in s. 2, except where, *inter alia*, the proceedings were instituted by a provincial Attorney General or the provincial Attorney General intervened. Having intervened, the federal Attorney General may then stay the proceedings under s. 579.

ANNOTATIONS

When the accused is charged with conspiracy under the Code and the object of the conspiracy charged was to violate the *Controlled Drugs and Substances Act*, S.C. 1996, c. 19, the Attorney General of Canada has the right to intervene in the proceeding: *Roberts v. Canada (Attorney General)* (2010), 262 C.C.C. (3d) 507 (B.C.C.A.).

FORM OF INDICTMENT.

580. An indictment is sufficient if it is on paper and is in Form 4. R.S., c. C-34, s. 509; R.S.C. 1985, c. 27 (1st Supp.), s. 117.

CROSS-REFERENCES

The term "indictment" is defined in s. 2. Section 841(3) provides that any pre-printed portions of the form shall be printed in both official languages. The other formal requirements for an indictment are set out in ss. 581 to 593 and the power to amend an indictment is in s. 601.

General Provisions Respecting Counts

SUBSTANCE OF OFFENCE / Form of statement / Details of circumstances / Indictment for treason / Reference to section / General provisions not restricted.

581. (1) Each count in an indictment shall in general apply to a single transaction and shall contain in substance a statement that the accused or defendant committed an offence therein specified.

(2) The statement referred to in subsection (1) may be

(*a*) in popular language without technical averments or allegations of matters that are not essential to be proved;

(*b*) in the words of the enactment that describes the offence or declares the matters charged to be an indictable offence; or

(*c*) in words that are sufficient to give to the accused notice of the offence with which he is charged.

(3) A count shall contain sufficient detail of the circumstances of the alleged offence to give to the accused reasonable information with respect to the act or omission to be proved against him and to identify the transaction referred to, but otherwise the absence or insufficiency of details does not vitiate the count.

(4) If an accused is charged with an offence under section 47 or sections 50 to 53, every overt act that is to be relied on shall be stated in the indictment.

(5) A count may refer to any section, subsection, paragraph or subparagraph of the enactment that creates the offence charged, and for the purpose of determining whether a count is sufficient, consideration shall be given to any such reference.

(6) Nothing in this Part relating to matters that do not render a count insufficient shall be deemed to restrict or limit the application of this section. R.S., c. C-34, s. 510; R.S.C. 1985, c. 27 (1st Supp.), s. 118; 2018, c. 29, s. 63.

CROSS-REFERENCES

The terms "indictment" and "count" are defined in s. 2. The other formal requirements with respect to sufficiency of counts in an information or indictment are found in ss. 582 to 586. Under s. 587, particulars may be ordered. Joinder and severance are dealt with in ss. 589 to 591. Under s. 592, an accessory after the fact may be indicted whether or not the principal has been indicted or convicted. Section 593 provides that any number of persons may be charged in the same indictment with the offences under s. 354 or s. 356(1)(*b*). Provision for amending a defective indictment is found in s. 601. The accused is entitled to inspect without charge the indictment pursuant to s. 603. Special provision for delivery of documents including a copy of the indictment in cases of treason is found in s. 604. Pursuant to s. 580, an indictment is sufficient if it is on paper and is in Form 4. Pursuant to s. 841(3), any pre-printed parts of a form are to be in both official languages.

SYNOPSIS

This section sets out the rules which govern the drafting of charges. The purpose of these provisions is to ensure that an accused is reasonably informed of the offence alleged and is thus able to properly defend the matter.

Subsection (1), in general, restricts a count to a "single transaction". This, however, is not synonymous with a single incident or occurrence. A "transaction" may be made up of a series of events or involve a number of victims.

Subsection (3) permits several methods of stating the offence: (a) popular language; (b) the words of the enactment that describe the offence or declares the matters charged to be an offence, and (c) words sufficient to give the accused notice of the offence. Most charges are drafted using the language of the offence-creating provision.

To be valid, a charge must contain sufficient detail to enable the accused to identify the transaction in issue (subsec. (3)). This requires that the count raise the matter from the general to the particular and specify "time, place and subject-matter".

Where the offence charged is high treason (s. 47), alarming Her Majesty (s. 49), assisting alien enemy (s. 50), intimidating Parliament (s. 51), sabotage (s. 52) or mutiny (s. 53), all of the overt acts relied upon by the Crown must be set out (subsec. (4)).

It is permissible (and certainly advisable) to refer in the body of a charge to the section number of the offence-creating provision (subsec. (5)).

While subsequent provisions, such as s. 583, provide that omissions of certain details do not render the information or indictment insufficient, those provisions, by virtue of subsec. (6), do not limit the application of the mandatory minimum conditions for validity and sufficiency set out in this section.

ANNOTATIONS

Review of judge's decision re validity – Where an information falls within a trial court's jurisdiction the judge has exclusive jurisdiction to determine its validity and his decision upholding it is not subject to either a motion to quash or extraordinary remedy proceedings but only to an appeal against his disposition of the case: *R. v. Jarman* (1972), 10 C.C.C. (2d) 426 (Ont. C.A.); *R. v. Pouliot* (1978), 41 C.C.C. (2d) 93 (Que. C.A.).

Single transaction rule (subsec. (1)) – In *R. v. Zamal,* [1964] 1 C.C.C. 12 (Ont. C.A.), where five accused were charged jointly with rape and the evidence was that each had successively raped the complainant, although there were separate offences, they were all one transaction and the indictment was not therefore void for duplicity or uncertainty.

The single transaction rule was not offended where the accused was charged with a single count of indecent assault in relation to four different incidents. The trial judge was not required to instruct the jury that they must be unanimous in their finding as to which incident or incidents had occurred. The unanimity requirement applies only to the essential ingredients of the offence, not the facts that establish them. The four sexual touchings were facts which supplied proof of the essential ingredient and, accordingly, it did not matter which factual route each juror took to arrive at a conclusion: *R. v. M. (G.L.)* (1999), 138 C.C.C. (3d) 383 (B.C.C.A.).

An indictment which charged that the accused, over a two and a half year period at specified premises, committed sexual assault by touching the very young victim in specified areas of her body did not offend the single transaction rule set out in subsec. (1): *R. v. German* (1989), 51 C.C.C. (3d) 175 (Sask. C.A.).

An indictment covering a period of time for a sexual offence for which there was an issue of consent for part of the period of indictment violates this provision. The jury may have split on the reasons for conviction so as to undermine the requirement of jury unanimity. While jurors can rely on two different factual paths in deciding whether each element of an offence is made out, they cannot convict on differing elements or ingredients of that offence. The count must be framed so that there is a single set of elements upon which the jury can be unanimous. In this case, consent became a live issue when the complainant turned 14 years of age. The indictment as framed would allow some jurors to convict the accused on the basis that indecent acts were performed when the complainant was 13 years old and consent was no defence, while others could have had a reasonable doubt on this issue but concluded that the complainant did not consent to the acts when he was 14 years old: *R. v. Sharpe* (2007), 219 C.C.C. (3d) 187 (B.C.C.A.).

Contrast *Sharpe* with the situation in *R. v. Chamot* (2012), 296 C.C.C. (3d) 91 (Ont. C.A.), where the trial judge's jury charge did not distinguish between conduct before and after the complainant's fourteenth birthday. The accused denied any sexual activity with the complainant and there was no suggestion of consensual sex. The jury was not given two paths to conviction. Therefore, even on the analysis in *Sharpe*, the single transaction rule was not offended in these circumstances.

An agreement to commit a number of different indictable offences is only one conspiracy transaction: *R. v. Addison, ex p. Mooney*, [1970] 1 C.C.C. 127 (Ont. C.A.).

Where it is alleged that the accused over several months attempted to procure a number of different women to have illicit sexual intercourse, more than one transaction is involved, and each woman should be the subject of a separate count: *R. v. Deutsch* (1983), 5 C.C.C. (3d) 41 (Ont. C.A.), affd on other grounds [1986] 2 S.C.R. 2, 27 C.C.C. (3d) 385.

In determining the validity of a charge a single transaction may include a general scheme of operation constituting one continuing offence: *R. v. Kisinger and Voszler* (1972), 6 C.C.C. (2d) 212 (Alta. C.A.).

Although no objection was made at trial it is permissible to object on appeal that an indictment violated subsec. (1). Where a fraudulent scheme includes different representations made to separate complainants a count alleging fraud cannot be said to apply in general to a single transaction: *R. v. Rafael* (1972), 7 C.C.C. (2d) 325 (Ont. C.A.).

A triple, instant death situation may result in a single count indictment, even though three separate counts are quite permissible: *R. v. Porter* (1976), 33 C.C.C. (2d) 215 (Ont. C.A.).

Duplicity rule / *Common law* – In *R. v. Cotroni; R. v. Papalia*, [1979] 2 S.C.R. 256, 45 C.C.C. (2d) 1 (7:0), while the court unanimously dismissed a Crown appeal against C's acquittal and P's appeal against his conviction on a charge of conspiracy the court divided on whether where the evidence reveals two separate conspiracies this renders the indictment duplicitous. Dickson J. (Spence, Beetz and Pratte JJ., concurring), was of the view that where the count charges one conspiracy but the evidence at trial proves more than one conspiracy this did not render the charge duplicitous and the only issue is which conspiracy was envisaged by the indictment. Pigeon J. (Ritchie J., concurring), was of the view that as the indictment covered two separate conspiracies to which P was a party it was duplicitous. However, by virtue of s. 590(1)(*b*) this did not render the indictment void and "transaction" in s. 581(1) is not to be equated with "offence". As no prejudice was occasioned to P his appeal was dismissed. Martland J., agreed with Dickson and Pigeon JJ. that P's appeal should be dismissed.

An indictment alleging a course of conduct commencing with an initial theft by taking of a cheque and then theft by conversion and theft by failing to account for the cheque and its proceeds does not violate the duplicity rule nor the single transaction rule: *R. v. Fischer* (1987), 31 C.C.C. (3d) 303 (Sask. C.A.).

An indictment of three separate conspiracy counts of importing, trafficking and exporting narcotics in effect sets out three different objects of a single subject-matter and accordingly while the accused should be found guilty on no more than one count the indictment is valid: *R. v. Bloomfield, Cormier and Ettinger* (1973), 10 C.C.C. (2d) 398 (N.B.C.A.).

Sufficiency of notice of offence charged (subsecs. (1), (2)) – Where the fraud indictment charged payments of about $400 received through false medical treatment claims rendered over a specific six-month period and the trial judge found that the Crown had failed to prove its general theory of a continued course of conduct constituting a fraudulent scheme of operation, it was still open to him, as he did, to find the accused guilty of the count where he was satisfied beyond a reasonable doubt that fraud had been committed by the accused in connection with nine of the seventy medical treatment claims adduced in evidence by the Crown: *R. v. Barnes* (1975), 26 C.C.C. (2d) 112 (N.S.S.C. App. Div.).

A theft by a person required to account, charged against a taxi-driver who withheld fares from the vehicle's owner, which read "unlawfully did commit theft of the approximate sum of sixteen dollars and fifty cents the property of Dominic Louis Christian" was valid as declaring the matter to be an indictable offence in the words of the general theft section: *R. v. McKenzie*, [1972] S.C.R. 409, 4 C.C.C. (2d) 296.

A defective information is not a nullity if it gives fair notice of the offence to the accused. Only if a charge is so badly drawn up as to fail even to give the accused notice of the charge will it fail the minimum test required by para. (*c*). Otherwise, the charge is capable of amendment under s. 601 and should not be quashed: *R. v. Moore*, [1988] 1 S.C.R. 1097, 41 C.C.C. (3d) 289 (4:3).

Sufficiency of identification of offence (subsec. (3)) – An information that not only charges an offence, but does so in the exact wording of the section, is valid, despite its lack of particularity: *R. v. Rowley* (1972), 7 C.C.C. (2d) 230 (Ont. C.A.) (2:1).

It was held in *R. v. Cochrane* (1976), 33 C.C.C. (2d) 549 (B.C.C.A.), that there is a distinction between an imperfectly stated averment and the total omission of an essential allegation. An averment imperfectly stated cannot be raised after verdict if that verdict could not have been found without proof of that averment stated as it ought to have been. A further appeal to the Supreme Court of Canada was allowed, 38 C.C.C. (2d) 175*n* (9:0), on other grounds without consideration of this particular issue.

In *R. v. WIS Developments Corp. Ltd.*, [1984] 1 S.C.R. 485, 12 C.C.C. (3d) 129 (4:0), the court appeared to affirm the continuing vitality of its prior decision in *R. v. Brodie*, [1936] S.C.R. 188, 65 C.C.C. 289, where the predecessor to this section was described as requiring that the indictment identify with reasonable precision the act charged in order that the accused know the particular offence alleged against him and prepare his defence accordingly; that it is not sufficient to charge an offence in the abstract, rather, concrete facts of a nature to identify the particular act which is charged and to give the accused notice of it are necessary ingredients of the indictment; that the indictment must specify time, place and matter, and describe the offence in such a way "as to lift it from the general to the particular". It would seem that the absence of sufficient details so as to comply with this section will vitiate the count. However, the further holding in *Wis Developments* that the information cannot be cured by amendment or the delivery of particulars where objection is taken prior to plea, must be read in light of the fact that this was a summary conviction matter and decided under the former ss. 729(2) and 732 which contained only limited powers of amendment prior to plea. With the repeal of those sections, and ss. 587 and 601 applying in both indictable and summary conviction matters, it may well be that in a proper case an indictment which fails to comply with this section can be cured by amendment or delivery of particulars.

While the circumstances in which acts of care or control of a motor vehicle may be found will vary widely, it cannot be said that the allegation of the care or control offence under s. 253 could relate to a multitude of activities so as to require that the information contain greater detail than allegations that "on or about" a particular date and "at or near" a named district, the accused had "care or control" of a motor vehicle while his ability to drive a motor vehicle was impaired by alcohol or a drug: *R. v. Fox* (1986), 24 C.C.C. (3d) 366 (B.C.C.A.).

The offences of keeping a common betting house and keeping a common gaming house contrary to s. 201 can embrace a number of separate and distinct activities in view of the definition of those houses in s. 197 and so a count simply charging that the accused did unlawfully keep a common betting house or common gaming house at a specific address does not comply with this subsection: *R. v. Wilson* (1986), 26 C.C.C. (3d) 8 (Man. Q.B.); *R. v. Bingo Enterprises Ltd.* (1984), 15 C.C.C. (3d) 261 (Man. C.A.).

Charging the offence in the words of the statute will be insufficient if the offence as so described is capable of covering a multitude of diverse and unrelated acts. However the offence of keeping a common bawdy house is not of that kind: *R. v. Milberg* (1987), 35 C.C.C. (3d) 45 (Ont. C.A.), leave to appeal to S.C.C. refused 79 N.R. 398; not following *R. v. Bingo Enterprises Ltd., supra*. Similarly: *R. v. Billon-Rey* (1990), 57 C.C.C. (3d) 223 (Que. C.A.).

Sufficiency of identification of transaction (subsec. (3)) – A count charging merely conspiracy to commit fraud which did not identify the transaction complained of was quashed in *Shumiatcher v. Saskatchewan (Attorney General)* (1962), 133 C.C.C. 69 (Sask. C.A.). The new information, which contained details of the various overt acts in connection with the conspiracy was unsuccessfully attacked as being void for multiplicity: *Shumiatcher v. Saskatchewan (Attorney General)*, [1963] 2 C.C.C. 319 (Sask. C.A.).

A count of break and enter and to commit theft therein was upheld on the basis that while a simple charge of theft alone would require reference to the property which was the subject of the offence, the allegation of theft here is lifted from the general to the particular by its association with the particular break and entry in this compounded offence: *R. v. Wixalbrown and Schmidt*, [1964] 1 C.C.C. 29 (B.C.C.A.) (3:2).

The test as to whether there has been compliance with the requirements of subsec. (3) is whether the information contains sufficient detail to give to the accused reasonable information with respect to the charge and to identify the transaction referred to therein. The kind of information that would be necessary to satisfy this test will vary depending on the nature of the offence charged. Thus, the necessity for an information to specify the time and place of the offence does not require that an information charging offences contrary to s. 253 specify the exact time in terms of hour and minute or the exact location of the offence: *R. v. Ryan; R. v. Charbonneau* (1985), 23 C.C.C. (3d) 1 (Ont. C.A.), leave to appeal to S.C.C. refused with respect to *Ryan* February 24, 1986; *R. v. Fox* (1986), 24 C.C.C. (3d) 366 (B.C.C.A.), leave to appeal to S.C.C. refused May 22, 1986.

The information in the possession of the accused, other than through the language of the indictment, such as material contained in the Crown brief to which the accused had been given access, is relevant in considering the sufficiency of the indictment: *R. v. C. (R.I.)* (1986), 32 C.C.C. (3d) 399 (Ont. C.A.).

An information charging an accused with sexual assault of a young child was sufficient, although the period of time specified extended for many months. These are the kinds of cases in which, because of the age of the alleged victim, full particularity with respect to, for example, dates, is likely impossible and to require it would make prevention of a serious social problem exceedingly difficult: *R. v. R.I.C.*, *supra*; *R. v. German*, *supra*. In both these cases, it should be noted that the court appeared to take into account the sufficiency of the disclosure made by the prosecution.

If an information states the time of the offence (even a lengthy period), the place, the victim and the offence (in the language of the enactment) then, except where there is a possibility of prejudice to accused, it will not be quashed prior to plea: *R. v. MacLean* (1988), 45 C.C.C. (3d) 185 (B.C.C.A.).

As to time of offence, see notes under s. 601.

Reference to section number (subsec. (5)) – The omission of certain words from an indictment will not be fatal if it still has set forth the offence requirements, particularly where it is expressed to be contrary to the relevant specific subsection of the Code: *R. v. Lessard* (1970), 6 C.C.C. (2d) 239 (Ont. C.A.).

Where the information fully and adequately sets out an offence, an erroneous section reference, which even if correct is mere surplusage, will not affect its validity: *R. v. Sourwine* (1970), 10 C.R.N.S. 380 (Alta. D.C.).

Specific reference to the offence section will cure the omission of the words "without reasonable excuse" in an information charging a refusal to provide a breath sample as the section reference complies with the rule of reasonably informing the defendant of the transaction alleged against him: *R. v. Cote*, [1978] 1 S.C.R. 8, 33 C.C.C. (2d) 353 (6:2).

Subsection (6) – Parliament enacted this subsection to ensure that neither subsec. (2)(*b*) nor s. 590(1)(*a*) or (*b*) could be invoked to answer a valid complaint of multiplicity: *R. v. Toth* (1959), 123 C.C.C. 292 (Ont. C.A.).

See also cases noted under s. 789.

HIGH TREASON AND FIRST DEGREE MURDER.

582. No person shall be convicted for the offence of high treason or first degree murder unless in the indictment charging the offence he is specifically charged with that offence. R.S., c. C-34, s. 511; 1973-74, c. 38, s. 4; 1974-75-76, c. 105, s. 6.

CROSS-REFERENCES

The term "indictment" is defined in s. 2. High treason is defined in s. 46 and first degree murder is defined in s. 231. Both of these offences are within the exclusive jurisdiction of the superior court of criminal jurisdiction (defined in s. 2) by virtue of ss. 468 and 469 and an accused charged with these offences may only be released by a judge of the superior court of criminal jurisdiction by virtue of s. 522. Section 604 makes special provision for delivery of documents including a copy of the indictment in cases of treason. For other cross-references respecting these offences, see the notes under sections creating the offences. Note in particular, however, s. 589 providing that no count that charges an offence other than murder shall be joined in an indictment to a count that charges murder.

SYNOPSIS

This section requires that an indictment specifically charge first degree murder or high treason if an accused is to be convicted of these offences. Thus, an indictment, charging the accused with "murder", would be deemed to be second degree murder.

CERTAIN OMISSIONS NOT GROUNDS FOR OBJECTION.

583. No count in an indictment is insufficient by reason of the absence of details where, in the opinion of the court, the count otherwise fulfils the requirements of section 581 and, without restricting the generality of the foregoing, no count in an indictment is insufficient by reason only that

(*a*) it does not name the person injured or intended or attempted to be injured;

(*b*) it does not name the person who owns or has a special property or interest in property mentioned in the count;

(*c*) it charges an intent to defraud without naming or describing the person whom it was intended to defraud;

(*d*) it does not set out any writing that is the subject of the charge;

(*e*) it does not set out the words used where words that are alleged to have been used are the subject of the charge;

(*f*) it does not specify the means by which the alleged offence was committed;

(*g*) it does not name or describe with precision any person, place or thing; or

(*h*) it does not, where the consent of a person, official or authority is required before proceedings may be instituted for an offence, state that the consent has been obtained. R.S., c. C-34, s. 512.

CROSS-REFERENCES

The terms "count" and "indictment" are defined in s. 2. Other provisions respecting sufficiency of indictment are found in ss. 581, 582 and 584 to 586. Section 587 provides for the ordering of particulars. Section 588 makes provision with respect to ownership of property and s. 601 permits amendment of a defective indictment. Note s. 581(6) which provides that nothing in this part relating to matters that do not render a count insufficient shall be deemed to restrict or limit the application of the requirements in s. 581.

SYNOPSIS

This section provides that a charge which otherwise complies with the minimum requirements of s. 581 is not insufficient by reason only of the fact that it does not: (a) name the person injured or intended or attempted to be injured; (b) name the owner of an interest in property; (c) name the victim of a fraud; (d) set out the writing which is the subject of the charge; (e) set out the words which are the subject of the charge; (f) specify the means by which an offence was committed; (h) fully name or describe any person, place or thing, or (h) state that, where required, a consent to the prosecution has been obtained.

ANNOTATIONS

Victim of offence generally (paras. (*a*), (*b*), (*g*)) – An information not naming a person or persons affected by a criminal act is not *per se* insufficient: *R. v. Kozodoy* (1957), 117 C.C.C. 315 (Ont. C.A.), but once the victim is named the name is a material part of the charge and must be proved: *R. v. Austin* (1955), 113 C.C.C. 95 (Ont. C.A.).

In *R. v. Vogelle and Reid,* [1970] 3 C.C.C. 171 (Man. C.A.), the court agreed that if the owner's name is unknown the Crown could charge ownership to person or persons unknown, but divided on the method of proving the theft of the goods.

In *R. v. Little*, [1976] 1 S.C.R. 20, 19 C.C.C. (2d) 385 (5:0), an appeal from conviction for theft was dismissed where although the owner of the goods allegedly stolen was named in the indictment as "Westwood Jewellers Limited" the only evidence was that the goods were stolen from "Westwood Jewellers" which was owned and managed by one of the witnesses. The court divided on the effect of this apparent failure to prove ownership in the entity named in the indictment. de Grandpré J., for the majority held that

> . . . if the owner of the object allegedly stolen is mentioned in the indictment and if his ownership is not proven and there are no circumstances to indicate to the accused the true nature of the charge, an acquittal should be entered. However, when, as in the present case there cannot be any possibility for the accused to fail to identify the transaction about which they are charged, there is no reason to discharge the accused for the sole reason that the owner mentioned in the indictment has not been mentioned in the evidence.

Dickson J., for himself and Beetz J., while agreeing that the conviction was proper held that except in exceptional circumstances as where the theft can be inferred from the suspicious circumstances of the accused's possession, an allegation of ownership is not mere surplusage. However, the identity of the owner is sufficiently established, in instances in which the owner is named in the indictment, when:

> . . . (i) the evidence adduced by the Crown reasonably identifies the owner with the person named in the indictment as owner, and (ii) it is clear that failure to prove the identity of the owner with greater precision has not misled or prejudiced the accused in preparation or presentation of his defence.

In this case, both (i) and (ii) were met and therefore the conviction was proper.

Person defrauded (para. (*c*)) – While the identification of a victim in a charge of fraud is surplusage, the rule that particulars which are surplusage need not be proved is subject to the proviso that the accused not be prejudiced in his defence: *R. v. Vezina; R. v. Cote*, [1986] 1 S.C.R. 2, 23 C.C.C. (3d) 481 (7:0).

Means of commission of offence (para. (*f*)) – On a charge of committing an act of gross indecency under former s. 157 the failure to specify the detail of what act was alleged to constitute the act of gross indecency was nothing more than a failure to specify the means by which the offence is alleged to have been committed and by virtue of this paragraph the charge is not rendered insufficient: *R. v. Dugdale and Leullier* (1979), 47 C.C.C. (2d) 555 (B.C.C.A.), approving the "modern approach" to the question of sufficiency of indictments in *R. v. Borek,* [1979] 1 W.W.R. 709 (B.C.C.A.), that "now technical omissions that have no real substance should not be considered as cause for rejection of the charges asserted".

Place of offence (para. (*g*)) – The place of the offence must be both alleged and proven: *R. v. Budovitch* (1969), 8 C.R.N.S. 280 (N.B.S.C. App. Div.).

Consent to prosecution (para. (*h*)) – The consent must be exact and refer to one specific matter: *R. v. Whyte Avenue Hotel Co.; R. v. Wakalich* (1962), 39 C.R. 40 (Alta. S.C.).

In exercising his power to consent, the Attorney General is under no duty that can be enforced by the courts to act fairly and is not required to afford the accused a hearing before deciding whether or not to consent to the prosecution: *R. v. Warren* (1981), 61 C.C.C. (2d) 65 (Ont. H.C.J.).

Consent of the Attorney General is presumed to exist absent a challenge during the trial by the accused to the jurisdiction of the court: *R. v. E. (M.)* (2015), 319 C.C.C. (3d) 352 (B.C.C.A.); *R. v. Minot* (2011), 266 C.C.C. (3d) 74 (N.L.C.A.).

An objection to the validity of the form of consent, in this case consent required by s. 477(2), cannot be raised for the first time near the conclusion of the trial just prior to the charge to the jury: *R. v. Sunila* (1987), 35 C.C.C. (3d) 289 (S.C. App. Div.).

Special Provisions Respecting Counts

SUFFICIENCY OF COUNT CHARGING LIBEL / Specifying sense / Proof.

584. (1) No count for publishing a seditious or defamatory libel, or for selling or exhibiting an obscene book, pamphlet, newspaper or other written matter, is insufficient by reason only that it does not set out the words that are alleged to be libellous or the writing that is alleged to be obscene.

(2) A count for publishing a libel may charge that the published matter was written in a sense that by innuendo made the publication thereof criminal, and may specify that sense without any introduction assertion to show how the matter was written in that sense.

(3) It is sufficient, on the trial of a count for publishing a libel, to prove that the matter published was libellous, with or without innuendo. R.S., c. C-34, s. 513; 2018, c. 29, s. 64.

CROSS-REFERENCES

The term "count" is defined in s. 2. Section 587 provides for the ordering of particulars. Note s. 581(6) which provides that nothing in this part relating to matters that do not render a count insufficient shall be deemed to restrict or limit the application of that section which sets out the minimum requirements for sufficiency. Provision for amending an indictment is made in s. 601.

SYNOPSIS

This section provides that a count for publishing or selling a libel or an obscenity does not need to contain the specific words complained of (subsec. (1)). A count for publishing a libel can claim libel by innuendo without giving the mechanism of the innuendo (subsec. (2)). Proof that published material was libellous is sufficient in a trial for publishing libel (subsec. (3)).

ANNOTATIONS

Even though the count does not set out the specific words it will be sufficient, particularly if it is clear that the accused knew what the count referred to: *Pratte v. Maher*, [1965] 1 C.C.C. 77 (Que. C.A.).

SUFFICIENCY OF COUNT CHARGING PERJURY, ETC.

585. No count that charges

(*a*) perjury,

(*b*) the making of a false oath or a false statement,

(*c*) fabricating evidence, or

(*d*) procuring the commission of an offence mentioned in paragraph (*a*), (*b*) or (*c*),

is insufficient by reason only that it does not state the nature of the authority of the tribunal before which the oath or statement was taken or made, or the subject of the inquiry, or the words used or the evidence fabricated, or that it does not expressly negative the truth of the words used. R.S., c. C-34, s. 514.

CROSS-REFERENCES

The term "count" is defined in s. 2. Section 587 makes provision for the ordering of particulars, *inter alia*, in para. (*a*) of what is relied on in support of a charge of perjury, the making of a false oath or of a false statement, fabricating evidence or counselling the commission of any of those offences. Section 587(1)(*e*) provides that particulars may be ordered further describing any "writing or words" that are the subject of the charge. Note section 581(6) which provides that nothing in this part relating to matters that do not render a count insufficient shall limit or restrict the application of s. 581 which sets out the minimum sufficiency requirements. A defective indictment may be amended pursuant to s. 601.

SYNOPSIS

This section states that a count for perjury or related offences need not contain: (a) the nature of the authority of the tribunal; (b) the subject of the inquiry; (c) the words or evidence at issue; or (d) an express negation of the truth of such words.

SUFFICIENCY OF COUNT RELATING TO FRAUD.

586. No count that alleges false pretences, fraud or an attempt or conspiracy by fraudulent means is insufficient by reason only that it does not set out in detail the nature of the false pretence, fraud or fraudulent means. R.S., c. C-34, s. 515.

CROSS-REFERENCES

The term "count" is defined in s. 2. Section 587 provides for the ordering of particulars and, in particular, s. 587(1)(*b*) provides for the ordering of particulars of any false pretence or fraud that is alleged and para. (*c*) provides for provision of particulars of any alleged attempt or conspiracy by fraudulent means. Section 581(6) provides that nothing in this part relating to matters that do not render a count insufficient shall be deemed to restrict or limit the application of s. 581 which sets out the minimum sufficiency requirements for a count in an indictment.

Particulars

WHAT MAY BE ORDERED / Regard to evidence / Particular.

587. (1) A court may, where it is satisfied that it is necessary for a fair trial, order the prosecutor to furnish particulars and, without restricting the generality of the foregoing, may order the prosecutor to furnish particulars

(*a*) of what is relied on in support of a charge of perjury, the making of a false oath or of a false statement, fabricating evidence or counselling the commission of any of those offences;

(*b*) of any false pretence or fraud that is alleged;

(*c*) of any alleged attempt or conspiracy by fraudulent means;

(*d*) setting out the passages in a book, pamphlet, newspaper or other printing or writing that are relied on in support of a charge of selling or exhibiting an obscene book, pamphlet, newspaper, printing or writing;

(*e*) further describing any writing or words that are the subject of a charge;

(*f*) further describing the means by which an offence is alleged to have been committed; or

(*g*) further describing a person, place or thing referred to in an indictment.

(2) For the purpose of determining whether or not a particular is required, the court may give consideration to any evidence that has been taken.

(3) Where a particular is delivered pursuant to this section,

(*a*) a copy shall be given without charge to the accused or his counsel;

(*b*) the particular shall be entered in the record; and

(*c*) the trial shall proceed in all respects as if the indictment had been amended to conform with the particular. R.S., c. C-34, s. 516; R.S.C. 1985, c. 27 (1st Supp.), s. 7(2)(*c*).

CROSS-REFERENCES

The terms "count" and "indictment" are defined in s. 2. Section 581 defines the minimum requirements for sufficiency of a count in an indictment. Section 601 provides for amending an indictment or count therein or a particular that is furnished under this section. Any objection to the sufficiency of an indictment is to be taken pursuant to a motion to quash prior to plea by virtue of s. 601(1). Other provisions respecting sufficiency of indictment are found in ss. 582 to 586.

SYNOPSIS

This section gives the trial court the authority to order the Crown to furnish "particulars" where it is satisfied that the same are necessary for an accused to receive a fair trial. Particulars, once provided, are treated as part of the indictment (subsec. (2)). They further define the charge by providing more detailed information with respect to what is alleged.

Although not restricted to these matters, particulars may be ordered in regard to: (a) what is alleged in support of a charge of perjury, the making of a false oath, the fabrication of evidence or counselling the commission of an offence; (b) any false pretence or fraud; (c) an attempt or conspiracy by fraudulent means; (d) the passage relied upon in a charge relating to selling or exhibiting an obscene publication; (e) the description of the writing or words relied on in a charge; (f) further describing the means by which an offence was committed, and (g) further describing any person, place or thing referred to in the charge.

In considering whether to order particulars, the court will have regard to any evidence which has been taken (at either the preliminary inquiry or trial).

ANNOTATIONS

When particulars ordered – A judge presiding at a preliminary inquiry has no power to order the Crown to provide particulars: *R. v. Hynes*, [2001] 3 S.C.R. 623, 159 C.C.C. (3d) 359, 47 C.R. (5th) 278.

Any judge of the court in which an indictment has been filed, not necessarily the trial judge, has jurisdiction to order particulars: *R. v. Pope* (1978), 45 C.C.C. (2d) 348 (B.C. Co. Ct.); *R. v. Cole* (1980), 70 C.C.C. (2d) 460 (Ont. H.C.J.).

Purpose of particulars – Particulars are to give the accused exact and reasonable information to enable him to establish fully his defence and to facilitate the administration of justice by defining the issues to assist the trial judge in rulings on admissibility of evidence: *R. v. Canadian General Electric Co. (No. 1)* (1974), 17 C.C.C. (2d) 433, 16 C.P.R. (2d) 175 (Ont. H.C.J.).

Effect of Crown's opening address – The purpose of Crown counsel's opening address to the jury is to assist the jury in following the evidence by informing them of the theory of the Crown and what the various witnesses may say, to inform defence counsel as to the evidence which he may not know is going to be adduced, and to alert the trial judge of possible legal questions, but it does not constitute particulars of the indictment: *R. v. Bengert (No. 5)* (1980), 53 C.C.C. (2d) 481, 15 C.R. (3d) 114 (B.C.C.A.), leave to appeal to S.C.C. refused C.C.C. *loc. cit.*, 34 N.R. 350*n sub nom. R. v. Robertson.*

Failure to prove charge as particularized – In *R. v. Vezina; R. v. Cote*, [1986] 1 S.C.R. 2, 23 C.C.C. (3d) 481, 25 D.L.R. (4th) 82 (7:0), the court adopted the following description of the so-called "surplusage rule": "If the particular, whether as originally drafted or as subsequently supplied, is not essential to constitute the offence, it will be treated as surplusage, *i.e.*, a non-necessary which need not be proved." However, that rule is subject to the proviso that the accused not be prejudiced in his defence.

It is a fundamental principle of criminal law that the offence, as particularized in the indictment, must be proved. Thus, although the gravamen of the offence of conspiracy to import narcotics is the agreement to import narcotics rather than a particular narcotic, where the Crown has chosen to particularize the narcotic, in this case heroin, then it was required to prove that offence and not some other conspiracy. To allow the Crown to prove some other offence characterized by different particulars would be to undermine the purpose of providing particulars: that purpose is to permit the accused to be reasonably informed of the transaction alleged against him, thus giving him the possibility of a full defence and a fair trial. In this case, it was not appropriate to amend the indictment on appeal to remove reference to the term "heroin". No such amendment was sought at trial and the trial had proceeded originally on the basis that the Crown must prove a conspiracy relating to heroin and on this basis one of the accused took the stand and testified that he was only involved in a conspiracy relating to cocaine. It would be unfair and prejudicial to the accused after that course of events to permit an amendment fundamentally and retroactively changing the nature of what the Crown must prove: *R. v. Saunders*, [1990] 1 S.C.R. 1020, 56 C.C.C. (3d) 220, 77 C.R. (3d) 397.

Where the "particulars" were really no more than information as to the major overt acts relied upon by the Crown to prove the accused's participation in the conspiracy, their effect is not to amend the indictment so as to charge more than one conspiracy: *R. v. May* (1984), 13 C.C.C. (3d) 257 (Ont. C.A.), leave to appeal to S.C.C. refused [1984] 2 S.C.R. vii, 56 N.R. 239*n*.

The Crown is not required to particularize its theory as to the manner in which the crime was alleged to have been committed. It may change its theory in accordance with the evidence adduced at trial, including the testimony of the accused. Where the accused testified and admitted to having trafficked cocaine hours prior to the incident that had been the focus of the evidence — but still within the time frame covered by the indictment — there was no unfairness in the Crown inviting the judge to convict on the conduct admitted: *R. v. Heaton* (2014), 318 C.C.C. (3d) 115 (Sask. C.A.).

Ownership of Property

OWNERSHIP.

588. The real and personal property of which a person has, by law, the management, control or custody shall, for the purposes of an indictment or proceeding against any other person for an offence committed on or in respect of the property, be deemed to be the property of the person who has the management, control or custody of it. R.S., c. C-34, s. 517.

CROSS-REFERENCES

The terms "property", "person" and "indictment" are defined in s. 2. The minimum requirements respecting sufficiency of an indictment are set out in s. 581. Section 587 provides for the ordering of particulars. Section 601 sets out the procedure for objecting to the sufficiency of an indictment and for amendment of an indictment. Section 583(*b*) provides that an indictment which otherwise fulfills the sufficiency requirements of s. 581 is not insufficient by reason only that it does not name the person who owns or has the special property or interest in property mentioned in the count.

SYNOPSIS

A person having the management, control or custody of property is deemed to own that property for the purposes of an indictment or proceeding against another person for an offence committed on or in respect of the property.

ANNOTATIONS

The phrase "by law" in this section limits its application to situations where a person is entrusted with property by statute or common law and accordingly this section cannot be invoked to remedy the failure of the Crown to prove the actual ownership alleged in a theft information: *R. v. Scott,* [1970] 3 C.C.C. 109, 6 C.R.N.S. 17 (Alta. C.A.).

However, an employee of a store could be found to be the custodian of the goods in the store and thus properly named in an indictment for robbery as the person with property in the stolen goods: *R. v. Wright* (1990), 60 C.C.C. (3d) 321, 110 A.R. 28 (C.A.).

If the imprecision of the count is only that it names as the owner of the property its bailee then as he has a special property interest the count will stand: *R. v. Allen and Gray* (1972), 7 C.C.C. (2d) 506, 19 C.R.N.S. 239 (Alta. C.A.).

Joinder or Severance of Counts

COUNT FOR MURDER.

589. No count that charges an indictable offence other than murder shall be joined in an indictment to a count that charges murder unless

(*a*) the count that charges the offence other than murder arises out of the same transaction as a count that charges murder; or

(*b*) the accused signifies consent to the joinder of the counts. R.S., c. C-34, s. 518; 1991, c. 4, s. 2.

CROSS-REFERENCES

The terms "count" and "indictment" are defined in s. 2. This section limits the general right of the prosecution to join any number of offences subject to power of the court to sever charges as provided in s. 591. Note s. 582 which provides that no person shall be convicted of the offence of first degree murder unless in the indictment charging the offence he specifically is charged with that offence. The offence of murder is defined in ss. 229 to 231.

SYNOPSIS

This section provides that no count charging murder shall be joined with any count other than another murder count, unless the other offences arise out of the same transaction or the accused consents.

ANNOTATIONS

The phrase "arises out of the same transaction" is not to be given the somewhat restrictive interpretation that a similar phrase "in respect of the same transaction" in s. 548(1) has been given. Thus, the accused was properly jointly indicted with his co-accused who was charged with murder, where the offences arose out of the identical set of circumstances and were closely related in both time and space, although there was no allegation that either accused was a party to the other's offences: *R. v. Melaragni* (1991), 72 C.C.C. (3d) 339 (Ont. Ct. (Gen. Div.)).

The test for joinder of counts must be applied more stringently when the accused is to be tried in respect of different murders. The test for joinder of counts requires a nexus between the offences in time, place and offence. As the deaths occurred three years apart and were not properly admissible as similar fact evidence, the jury should have been discharged in relation to one of the counts, a mistrial declared or a warning to the jury provided: *R. v. Khan* (1996), 108 C.C.C. (3d) 108 (Man. C.A.).

In considering whether joinder should be allowed, the court should consider the factual and legal nexus of the charges; any general prejudice to the accused; the effect on the accused's ability to testify; whether the joiner will lead to undue complexity; and whether severance will lead to a multiplicity of hearings: *R. v. Giroux* (2002), 318 A.R. 201 (Q.B.). See also *R. v. Riley* (2008), 229 C.C.C. (3d) 266 (Ont. S.C.J.).

This provision is an exception to the general rule of joinder in s. 591(1) that any number of counts for any number of offences may be joined in the same indictment. The purpose of the "same transaction" carve-out in para. (*a*) is to permit the inclusion of other offences, such as sexual assault and robbery, during the commission of which a person was killed. "Transaction" is not confined to a single event or occurrence; it can embrace a series of connected acts or events that extend over a period of time. Where the deceased had been punched repeatedly by one accused (charged with murder) then knocked out some time later by the second accused (charged with manslaughter) it was permissible to try the two accused together because the events amounted to a single transaction: *R. v. Manasseri* (2016), 344 C.C.C. (3d) 281 (Ont. C.A.), leave to appeal to S.C.C. refused 2017 CarswellOnt 5288.

OFFENCES MAY BE CHARGED IN THE ALTERNATIVE / Application to amend or divide counts / Order.

590. (1) A count is not objectionable by reason only that

(*a*) it charges in the alternative several different matters, acts or omissions that are stated in the alternative in an enactment that describes as an indictable offence the matters, acts or omissions charged in the count; or

(*b*) it is double or multifarious.

(2) An accused may at any stage of his trial apply to the court to amend or to divide a count that

(*a*) charges in the alternative different matters, acts or omissions that are stated in the alternative in the enactment that describes the offence or declares that the matters, acts or omissions charged are an indictable offence, or

(*b*) is double or multifarious,

on the ground that, as framed, it embarrasses him in his defence.

(3) The court may, where it is satisfied that the ends of justice require it, order that a count be amended or divided into two or more counts, and thereupon a formal commencement may be inserted before each of the counts into which it is divided. R.S., c. C-34, s. 519.

CROSS-REFERENCES

The term "count" is defined in s. 2. Minimum requirements respecting sufficiency of a count on an information are set out in s. 581. Note in particular s. 581(1) which requires that an indictment shall in general apply to a single transaction. The general power to sever counts in an indictment is found in s. 591. Procedure for objecting to the sufficiency of an indictment and for amendment of an indictment is found in s. 601.

SYNOPSIS

Subsection (1) provides that a count is not objectionable because it: (a) charges in the alternative several different acts or omissions where the same are referred to in the offence-creating provision as the various ways in which the offence may be committed, or (b) encompasses two or more separate occurrences of the offence.

However, in such circumstances an accused, to be better able to defend the matter, can apply to the trial judge for an order either amending the count or dividing it into separate counts with respect to each occurrence (subsecs. (2), (3)). The trial judge is to grant such an order where the ends of justice require it.

ANNOTATIONS

Subsection (3) – Once the accused, who was charged in a single count of theft, testified that there were two groups of transactions with a different defence for the two sets it would be preferable to divide the count: *R. v. Lilly*, [1983] 1 S.C.R. 794, 5 C.C.C. (3d) 1 (7:0).

Only the trial judge has jurisdiction to divide or sever counts. However, the application may be brought prior to trial, once a trial judge has been assigned: *R. v. Litchfield*, [1993] 4 S.C.R. 333, 86 C.C.C. (3d) 97.

Where at the end of the Crown's case, particulars were orders and the indictment was severed into the particularized counts, the failure to file a new indictment did not vitiate the proceedings: *R. v. H. (J.A.)* (1998), 124 C.C.C. (3d) 221 (B.C.C.A.).

JOINDER OF COUNTS / Each count separate / Severance of accused and counts / Order for severance / Delayed enforcement / Decisions binding on parties / Subsequent procedure / Idem.

591. (1) Subject to section 589, any number of counts for any number of offences may be joined in the same indictment, but the counts shall be distinguished in the manner shown in Form 4.

(2) Where there is more than one count in an indictment, each count may be treated as a separate indictment.

(3) The court may, where it is satisfied that the interests of justice so require, order

(*a*) that the accused or defendant be tried separately on one or more of the counts; and

(*b*) where there is more than one accused or defendant, that one or more of them be tried separately on one or more of the counts.

(4) An order under subsection (3) may be made before or during the trial but, if the order is made during the trial, the jury shall be discharged from giving a verdict on the counts

(*a*) on which the trial does not proceed; or

(*b*) in respect of the accused or defendant who has been granted as separate trial.

(4.1) The court may make an order under subsection (3) that takes effect either at a specified later date or on the occurrence of a specified event if, taking into account, among other considerations, the need to ensure consistent decisions, it is satisfied that it is in the interests of justice to do so.

(4.2) Unless the court is satisfied that it would not be in the interests of justice, the decisions relating to the disclosure or admissibility of evidence or the *Canadian Charter of Rights and Freedoms* that are made before any order issued under subsection (3) takes effect continue to bind the parties if the decisions are made — or could have been made — before the stage at which the evidence on the merits is presented.

(5) The counts in respect of which a jury is discharged pursuant to paragraph (4)(*a*) may subsequently be proceeded on in all respects as if they were contained in a separate indictment.

(6) Where an order is made in respect of an accused or defendant under paragraph (3)(*b*), the accused or defendant may be tried separately on the counts in relation to which the order was made as if they were contained in a separate indictment. R.S., c. C-34, s. 520; R.S.C. 1985, c. 27 (1st Supp.), s. 119; 2011, c. 16, s. 5.

CROSS-REFERENCES

The terms "count" and "indictment" are defined in s. 2. Provision for dividing a count which is double or multifarious is found in s. 590. Notwithstanding this section, no count that charges an offence other than murder shall be joined in an indictment to a count that charges murder by virtue of s. 589. Section 574(1) provides that counts originally charged in separate informations may be joined in the same indictment. Under s. 593, any number of persons may be charged in the same indictment with an offence under s. 354 or s. 356(1)(*b*) notwithstanding that the property was held in possession at different times or the person by whom the property was obtained is not indicted with them or is not in custody or amenable to justice.

SYNOPSIS

This section deals with indictments in respect of more than one count or accused and the powers of a court to order separate trials.

Other than an indictment alleging murder (see s. 589), any number of counts for any number of offences may be included in an indictment (subsec. (1)). The court can, if the interests of justice require, order that certain counts and/or accused be tried separately (*i.e.*, severance) (subsec. (3)).

Severance can be ordered either before or during a trial. Where the order is made during the course of a jury trial, no verdict will be returned with respect to the severed counts and/or accused which may be proceeded with at a later time as if on a separate indictment (subsecs. (4), (5) and (6)).

ANNOTATIONS

Jurisdiction – Only the trial judge has jurisdiction to divide or sever counts. However, the application for severance may be brought prior to trial, once a trial judge has been assigned: *R. v. Litchfield*, [1993] 4 S.C.R. 333, 86 C.C.C. (3d) 97.

Review of discretion – The appellate court should interfere with the trial judge's discretion to sever counts only if the trial judge did not act judicially or the ruling resulted in an injustice: *R. v. Litchfield, supra*; *R. v. Cuthbert*, [1997] 1 S.C.R. 8, 112 C.C.C. (3d) 96. In *R. v. Last*, [2009] 3 S.C.R. 146, 247 C.C.C. (3d) 449 *sub nom. R. v. L. (G.E.)*, the Supreme Court of Canada held that determining whether the judge acted unjudicially calls for an inquiry into the circumstances prevailing at the time it was made. The review of whether the ruling resulted in an injustice will usually entail scrutiny that includes the unfolding of the trial and of the verdicts.

The interests of justice in subsec. (3) include the accused's right to be tried on the evidence admissible against him, as well as society's interest in seeing that justice is done in a reasonably efficient and cost-effective manner. The court should consider the general prejudice to the accused, the legal and factual nexus between the counts, the complexity of the evidence, whether the accused intends to testify on one count but not another, the possibility of inconsistent verdicts, the desire to avoid a multiplicity of proceedings, the use of similar fact evidence at trial, the length of the trial having regard to the evidence to be called, the potential prejudice to the accused with respect to the right to be tried within a reasonable time, and the existence of antagonistic defences as between co-accused. In assessing the accused's testimonial intention on a severance application, the underlying concern is for the accused's ability to control his defence and his right to decide whether or not to testify with respect to each of the counts unimpaired by inappropriate constraints. The accused's expression should have both a subjective and an objective component. The trial judge must be satisfied that the circumstances objectively establish a rationale for testifying on some counts but not others. The burden on the accused is to provide the trial judge with sufficient information to convey that, objectively, there is substance to his testimonial intention. The information could consist of the type of potential defences open to the accused or the nature of his testimony. The accused, ultimately, however, is not bound by his stated intention: *R. v. Last*, *supra*.

A multiplicity of counts, some of which did not involve the two accused, is not *per se* a ground for separate trials: *R. v. Kestenberg & McPherson* (1959), 126 C.C.C. 387 (Ont. C.A.), leave to appeal to S.C.C. refused [1960] S.C.R. x.

Generally – Where the application for severance of counts is made during the course of the trial, it should rest on some prejudice that has arisen in the trial and was not apparent at the beginning of the trial. While the failure to make an application at the earliest opportunity does not constitute a waiver, the failure to do so makes it difficult to rest the application solely on factors which were apparent from the beginning and whose character has not changed: *R. v. Cuthbert* (1996), 106 C.C.C. (3d) 28 (B.C.C.A.), appeal dismissed [1997] 1 S.C.R. 8, 112 C.C.C. (3d) 96.

While the accused is entitled to wait until the close of the Crown's case to bring a motion for severance, the burden on the accused is very heavy at this stage and cannot be met by merely advancing his desire not to testify on certain counts and to testify on others. The trial judge's consideration of the proper administration of justice is more important where the motion for separate trials is brought at the close of the Crown's case, particularly in the case of a jury trial. The trial judge must consider the practical consequences of a separate trial and the potential prejudice to other co-accused: *R. v. Cross* (1996), 112 C.C.C. (3d) 410 (Que. C.A.), leave to appeal to S.C.C. refused 114 C.C.C. (3d) vi.

Where the essence of the charge is common enterprise all accused should be jointly tried except for anyone who would be prejudiced in his defence or denied the opportunity of a fair trial. The mere allegation that one accused may give evidence for another is not *per se* sufficient to disturb the trial Judge's discretionary refusal for severance: *R. v. Quiring and Kuipers* (1974), 19 C.C.C. (2d) 337 (Sask. C.A.).

Considering the interests of justice as well as the interests of the accused, and provided that there was no improper prejudice to the accused, where there was a common intention to commit a crime a joint trial with all of its characteristics was the proper course: *R. v. Miller and Cockriell* (1975), 24 C.C.C. (2d) 401 (B.C.C.A.), at p. 422 (5:0).

In *R. v. McCaw* (1971), 5 C.C.C. (2d) 416 (Ont. C.A.), it was held that where the appellant was the only one of three accused who raised a defence of alibi he should not have been tried jointly with the others nor should he have been represented by the same counsel.

Antagonistic defences – Where each co-accused has made a statement blaming the other for the murder, the fact that their defences are apparently antagonistic is not an overriding factor for granting separate trials, which will not be done in this particular case: *R. v. Lane and Ross*, [1970] 1 C.C.C. 196 (Ont. H.C.J.).

To call co-accused as defence witness – *Prima facie*, accused who are jointly indicted should be jointly tried if it is alleged that they acted in concert, an appeal court will only interfere with the trial judge's decision refusing severance when such refusal has resulted in a miscarriage of justice: *R. v. Agawa and Mallett* (1975), 28 C.C.C. (2d) 379 (Ont. C.A.). In this case severance was refused although one accused had given a statement, which the Crown was not tendering, exculpating the other. It was held that severance was properly refused although in the result this accused was not a compellable witness for the other, especially since the accused who had given the statement indicated he would deny its truth if it were brought out.

In the subsequent case of *R. v. Torbiak and Gillis* (1978), 40 C.C.C. (2d) 193 (Ont. C.A.), the test for severance in this type of situation was stated to be whether the evidence of the co-accused sought to be elicited on behalf of another is such that, when considered in the light of the other evidence, it might reasonably affect the verdict of the jury by creating a reasonable doubt as to the guilt of the latter. If so, then if a joint trial would preclude him from having the benefit of that evidence a separate trial may be required. In and of itself it is no ground for refusal of severance that the evidence is merely corroborative of other evidence.

The accused must establish that there is a reasonable possibility that the co-accused will testify and that his testimony could affect the verdict by creating a reasonable doubt in order to obtain severance. In this case, the trial judge erred in engaging in a detailed study of the co-accused's reliability and credibility as this was solely within the purview of the jury in determining the issue of severance: *R. v. Savoury* (2005), 200 C.C.C. (3d) 94 (Ont. C.A.). See also *R. v. Bradley* (1980), 57 C.C.C. (2d) 542 (Que. S.C.).

In the absence of decisive evidence to the contrary the court must assume that counsel is acting in good faith in seeking severance in order to call a co-accused, who he asserts has evidence which would support the defence. Severance will be necessary where required for the accused to fully defend himself, as where the evidence of the co-accused is likely to raise a reasonable doubt: *R. v. Boulet* (1987), 40 C.C.C. (3d) 38 (Que. C.A.).

Where inadmissible evidence would be adduced – Where the evidence is substantially stronger against one of two co-conspirators the better course is to direct separate trials, particularly where the Crown intends to tender in evidence a damaging statement made by one accused under circumstances which make it inadmissible against the other: *R. v. Guimond*, [1979] 1 S.C.R. 960, 44 C.C.C. (2d) 481.

Even where each accused gives a statement incriminating the others where the evidence suggests a joint venture, the accused are properly tried together: *R. v. Puffer, McFall and*

Kizyma (1976), 31 C.C.C. (2d) 81 (Man. C.A.), affd as to *McFall*, [1980] 1 S.C.R. 321, 48 C.C.C. (2d) 225 (6:3).

Similar fact evidence – In deciding whether counts should be severed, the admissibility of similar acts alleged as part of a multi-count indictment must be taken into account. Admissibility should not, however, be confused with severance. Despite a refusal to sever counts, it is open to the trial judge as the evidence progresses to determine that evidence on one count is not admissible as similar fact evidence on the other count. A link between the alleged similar acts is also a precondition to admissibility in that there must be some evidence linking the accused to the alleged similar acts disclosing more than a mere possibility that the similar act is the act of the accused. Where similar fact evidence is admitted to prove identity in a multi-count indictment, the judge should charge the jury as follows: (1) they may find from the evidence, although they are not required to do so, that the manner of commission of the offences is so similar that it is likely they were committed by the same person; (2) the judge should review the similarities between the offences; (3) if the jury concludes that it is likely the same person committed more than one of the offences, then the evidence on each of those counts may assist them in deciding whether the accused committed the other similar count or counts; (4) the jury must be instructed that if it accepts the evidence of the similar acts, it is relevant for the limited purpose for which it was admitted; (5) the evidence on one count cannot be used to infer that the accused is a person whose character or disposition is such that he is likely to have committed the offence or offences charged in the other count or counts; (6) if the jury does not conclude that it is likely the same person committed the similar offences, they must reach their verdict by considering the evidence related to each count separately and put out of their minds the evidence on any other count or counts; (7) the trial judge must make it clear that the accused must not be convicted on any count unless the jury is satisfied beyond a reasonable doubt that he is guilty of that offence: *R. v. Arp*, [1998] 3 S.C.R. 339, 129 C.C.C. (3d) 321.

To call evidence prejudicial to co-accused – The trial judge erred in refusing an application for severance by one accused where in the result that accused was not able to make full answer and defence by reason of rulings designed to protect the co-accused. Thus the accused had been prevented from cross-examining his co-accused on prior, possibly involuntary, statements and from leading evidence of the co-accused's disposition for violence: *R. v. Kendall and McKay* (1987), 35 C.C.C. (3d) 105 (Ont. C.A.). But also see *R. v. Crawford*, [1995] 1 S.C.R. 858, 96 C.C.C. (3d) 481.

Where the effect of the joint trial of the accused was to prevent one accused from being able to cross-examine a co-accused on testimony that she gave in a prior proceeding [by reason of s. 13 of the Charter] thus resulting in real prejudice to the accused, then the trial judge should have granted an application for severance: *R. v. Zurlo* (1990), 57 C.C.C. (3d) 407 (Que. C.A.).

Grounds for severance of counts – Although it has been frowned upon, the Crown may join with a count of the commission of a substantive offence a count of conspiracy to commit it: *R. v. Kelly*, [1967] 1 C.C.C. 215 (B.C.C.A.).

In *R. v. Jefferson and Five Others* (1971), 6 C.C.C. (2d) 33 (Ont. H.C.J.), severance of counts was granted where the indictment charged six accused with 15 counts and the trial judge was of the opinion that the jury would have great difficulty segregating the evidence legally admissible against each accused on each count. It was also held that while the Crown has a right to join counts charging conspiracy and the substantive offence which was allegedly the object of the conspiracy in the same indictment, it is generally undesirable to do so and in the absence of unusual circumstances the trial judge should exercise his discretion to order severance of the counts.

On an application by an accused for severance of counts the onus is on the accused to show on the balance of probabilities that the ends of justice require severance. Even when a joint trial will be very long a judge may properly dismiss the application although the facts fall short of demonstrating that a joint trial is required as a matter of absolute necessity: *R. v. McNamara (No. 1)* (1981), 56 C.C.C. (2d) 193 (Ont. C.A.), at pp. 264-6.

When deciding whether to sever counts, courts balance the risk of prejudice to the accused and the public's interest in a single trial. Factors that may be weighed when deciding whether or not to sever include prejudice to the accused, the legal and factual nexus between the counts, the complexity of the evidence, whether the accused intends to testify on one count but not another, the possibility of inconsistent verdicts, the desire to avoid a multiplicity of proceedings, the use of similar fact evidence at trial, the length of the trial having regard to the evidence to be called, the potential prejudice to the accused with respect to the right to be tried within a reasonable time and the existence of antagonistic defences as between co-accused persons: *R. v. Last*, [2009] 3 S.C.R. 146, *sub nom. R. v. L. (G.E.)*, 247 C.C.C. (3d) 449.

The absence of similar fact evidence between counts militates against severance. The trial judge erred in failing to sever to murder charges given the seriousness of the offences and the likelihood of propensity reasoning: *R. v. Jeanvenne* (2010), 261 C.C.C. (3d) 462 (Ont. C.A.).

The Crown is not precluded from joining a charge of breach of probation with other counts in an information despite that in so doing, evidence of the accused's criminal record would be adduced: *R. v. Colby* (2002), 165 C.C.C. (3d) 312 (Sask. C.A.), leave to appeal to S.C.C. refused [2003] 1 S.C.R. viii, 170 C.C.C. (3d) vi.

Joint trial of separate informations – A court has jurisdiction to jointly try separate informations. Where joinder of offences or of accused is being considered, then the court should seek the consent of the accused and the prosecution. If consent is withheld, then the reasons should be explored. Whether the accused consents or not, joinder should only occur when, in the opinion of the court, it is in the interests of justice and the offences or accused could initially have been jointly charged. Where the accused wishes to testify in respect to only one of the informations, then consent to a joint trial would be withheld and the judge should not order a joint trial. The procedure to be followed should, to the extent possible, follow the procedure for a trial of an information containing multiple accused or charges. Where the separate informations involve two accused, the Crown may not compel one accused to testify against the other: *R. v. Clunas*, [1992] 1 S.C.R. 595, 70 C.C.C. (3d) 115 (5:0).

Joint trial of summary and indictable offences – A provincial court judge may jointly try summary and indictable offences even where they are contained on separate informations, provided that the accused has not elected trial by a higher court in respect of the indictable offence. In the event of any conflict as to the applicable procedure, indictable offence procedures would apply. Where, following the trial, both charges have gone for appeal, the summary conviction appeal court should await the decision of the court of appeal in the indictable proceeding: *R. v. Clunas, supra.*

Joint trial of summary conviction and provincial offence charges – At least in Ontario, a provincial court judge has jurisdiction to conduct a joint trial of provincial charges and summary conviction criminal charges. The two-part common law test for joinder set out in *R. v. Clunas*, *supra*, applies to joinder in this context: *R. v. Sciascia*, [2017] 2 S.C.R. 539, 355 C.C.C. 553.

Other notes – An accused has an absolute right to cross-examine a co-accused who testifies at their joint trial, whether the latter's evidence is favourable or unfavourable to him: *R. v. McLaughlin* (1974), 15 C.C.C. (2d) 562 (Ont. C.A.).

An information may include an offence upon which the Crown intends to proceed summarily and an offence under provincial legislation where the applicable provincial legislation does not prohibit such a procedure: *R. v. Massick* (1985), 21 C.C.C. (3d) 128 (B.C.C.A.).

Joinder of Accused in Certain Cases

ACCESSORIES AFTER THE FACT.

592. Any one who is charged with being an accessory after the fact to any offence may be indicted, whether or not the principal or any other party to the offence has been indicted or convicted or is or is not amenable to justice. R.S., c. C-34, s. 521.

CROSS-REFERENCES

Accessory after the fact is defined in s. 23. Section 23.1 provides that s. 23 applies in respect of an accused notwithstanding the fact that the person whom the accused received, comforted or assisted could not be convicted of the offence. A party to the offence is defined by ss. 21 and 22. Section 463 sets out the punishment for persons convicted of being an accessory after the fact except for certain offences such as an accessory after the fact to murder (see s. 240).

SYNOPSIS

This section states that a person may be indicted as an accessory after the fact even though no other person has been indicted for or convicted of the principal offence.

ANNOTATIONS

See notes under s. 23.

TRIAL OF PERSONS JOINTLY / Conviction of one or more.

593. (1) Any number of persons may be charged in the same indictment with an offence under section 354 or 355.4 or paragraph 356(1)(*b*), even though

(*a*) the property was had in possession at different times; or

(*b*) the person by whom the property was obtained

(i) is not indicted with them, or

(ii) is not in custody or is not amenable to justice.

(2) Where, pursuant to subsection (1), two or more persons are charged in the same indictment with an offence referred to in that subsection, any one or more of those persons who separately committed the offence in respect of the property or any part of it may be convicted. R.S., c. C-34, s. 522; 2010, c. 14, s. 11.

CROSS-REFERENCES

The term "indictment" is defined in s. 2. The minimum requirements respecting sufficiency of an indictment are set out in s. 581. Provision respecting charging of ownership of property is found in s. 588. Section 591 gives the court power to sever counts and accused in an indictment. The term "property" is defined in s. 2. Possession is defined in s. 4(3).

SYNOPSIS

Subsection (1) provides that all persons alleged to have been in possession of property obtained by crime may be jointly charged even though: (a) they may have had possession at different times, or (b) the person who illegally obtained the property in the first instance is not charged or within the court's jurisdiction.

One or more of several jointly charged accused may be convicted, notwithstanding they are proven to have separately committed the offence (subsec. (2)).

594-596. [*Repealed*, R.S.C. 1985, c. 27 (1st Supp.), s. 120.]

Proceedings when Person Indicted is at Large

BENCH WARRANT / Execution / Interim release / Discretion to postpone execution / Deemed execution of warrant.

597. (1) Where an indictment has been preferred against a person who is at large, and that person does not appear or remain in attendance for his trial, the court before which the accused should have appeared or remained in attendance may issue a warrant in Form 7 for his arrest.

(2) A warrant issued under subsection (1) may be executed anywhere in Canada.

(3) Where an accused is arrested under a warrant issued under subsection (1), a judge of the court that issued the warrant may order that the accused be released on his giving an undertaking that he will do any one or more of the following things as specified in the order, namely,

- **(*a*) report at times to be stated in the order to a peace officer or other person designated in the order;**
- **(*b*) remain within a territorial jurisdiction specified in the order;**
- **(*c*) notify the peace officer or other person designated under paragraph (*a*) of any change in his address or his employment or occupation;**
- **(*d*) abstain from communicating with any witness or other person expressly named in the order except in accordance with such conditions specified in the order as the judge deems necessary;**
- **(*e*) where the accused is the holder of a passport, deposit his passport as specified in the order; and**
- **(*f*) comply with such other reasonable conditions specified in the order as the judge considers desirable.**

(4) A judge who issues a warrant may specify in the warrant the period before which the warrant shall not be executed, to allow the accused to appear voluntarily before a judge having jurisdiction in the territorial division in which the warrant was issued.

(5) Where the accused appears voluntarily for the offence in respect of which the accused is charged, the warrant is deemed to be executed. R.S., c. C-34, s. 526; R.S., c. 2 (2nd Supp.), s. 11; 1974-75-76, c. 93, s. 64.1; R.S.C. 1985, c. 27 (1st Supp.), s. 121; 1997, c. 18, s. 68.

CROSS-REFERENCES

Section 841(3) provides that any preprinted portions of a form are to be printed in both official languages. Failure to appear for trial is an offence under s. 145. Under s. 598, a person to whom s. 597(1) applies may lose his right to trial by jury. Section 475 provides that the trial may continue where the accused absconds in the course of the trial.

SYNOPSIS

The court may issue a warrant, executable throughout Canada, for the apprehension of an accused who is at large (*i.e.*, not in custody) but who does not appear for trial or remain in attendance at the trial on an indictment (subsecs. (1) and (2)). The judge may order that the warrant be held for a specified time to allow the accused to appear voluntarily (subsecs. (4) and (5)).

An accused, arrested on such a warrant, shall be brought before a judge of the court which issued it for a bail hearing. The judge may either order that the accused remain in custody or be released on an undertaking, with or without conditions.

ANNOTATIONS

Review under subsec. (3) is not limited to one judge nor is the accused required to wait 30 days before making a further application: *R. v Rodrigues* (1998), 123 C.C.C. (3d) 93 (Man. C.A.).

ELECTION DEEMED TO BE WAIVED / Idem.

598. (1) Notwithstanding anything in this Act, where a person to whom subsection 597(1) applies has elected or is deemed to have elected to be tried by a court composed of a judge and jury and, at the time he failed to appear or to remain in attendance for his trial, he had not re-elected to be tried by a court composed of a judge without a jury or provincial court judge without a jury, he shall not be tried by a court composed of a judge and jury unless

(*a*) he establishes to the satisfaction of a judge of the court in which he is indicted that there was a legitimate excuse for his failure to appear or remain in attendance for his trial; or

(*b*) the Attorney General requires pursuant to section 568 or 569 that the accused be tried by a court composed of a judge and jury.

(2) An accused who, under subsection (1), may not be tried by a court composed of a judge and jury is deemed to have elected under section 536 or 536.1 to be tried without a jury by a judge of the court where the accused was indicted and section 561 or 561.1, as the case may be, does not apply in respect of the accused. 1974-75-76, c. 93, s. 65; R.S.C. 1985, c. 27 (1st Supp.), s. 122; 1999, c. 3, s. 51; 2002, c. 13, s. 48.

CROSS-REFERENCES

The term "Attorney General" is defined in s. 2. Section 475 provides that a trial may continue where the accused has absconded in the course of the trial and the accused is deemed to have waived his right to be present at the trial. Failure to appear or remain in attendance at trial is an offence under s. 145.

SYNOPSIS

This section sets out the rules which apply to an accused who does not appear for, or remain in attendance at, a jury trial.

In such circumstances, the right to a jury will have been lost, unless the accused can satisfy a judge of the trial court that he or she had a "legitimate excuse" for not appearing (subsec. (1)(*a*)). The Attorney General, however, can still require a jury, pursuant to s. 568 or s. 569 (subsec. (1)(*b*)).

An accused who has forfeited the right to a jury is deemed to have elected to be tried by a judge alone and has no right to "re-elect" (subsec. (2)).

ANNOTATIONS

Although this section infringes the right to a jury trial as guaranteed by s. 11(*f*) of the Charter, it constitutes a reasonable limit on that right within the meaning of s. 1 of the Charter and, accordingly, is valid legislation: *R. v. Lee*, [1989] 2 S.C.R. 1384, 52 C.C.C. (3d) 289 (5:2).

This section is mandatory and operates as an exception to the provisions of Part XIX and therefore an accused indicted in Quebec Superior Court who has failed to appear without legitimate excuse must be tried by a judge of that court without a jury notwithstanding that in Quebec a judge of the Superior Court is not included in the definition of "judge" for the purposes of Part XIX: *R. v. Voisard* (1978), 43 C.C.C. (2d) 570 (Que. C.A.).

An honest mistake as to the date when the trial was to commence is a legitimate excuse within the meaning of this section, even if the accused did not exercise due diligence. Nothing less than an intentional avoidance of appearing at trial for the purpose of impeding or frustrating the trial or with the intention of avoiding its consequences, or failure to appear because of a mistake resulting from wilful blindness, should deprive an accused of his right to a jury trial: *R. v. Harris* (1991), 66 C.C.C. (3d) 536 (Ont. C.A.).

A hearing under this section may be before a superior court judge who is not the trial judge and the accused has no right to have the trial judge review the determination. A further application, however, may be brought by the accused where there has been a change in circumstances: *R. v. Brown* (2000), 146 C.C.C. (3d) 401 (Ont. C.A.).

Change of Venue

REASONS FOR CHANGE OF VENUE / Reasons to be stated / Conditions as to expense / Transmission of record / Idem.

599. (1) A court before which an accused is or may be indicted, at any term or sittings thereof, or a judge who may hold or sit in that court, may at any time before or after an indictment is found, on the application of the prosecutor or the accused, order the trial to be held in a territorial division in the same province other than that in which the offence would otherwise be tried if

(*a*) it appears expedient to the ends of justice, or

(*b*) a competent authority has directed that a jury is not to be summoned at the time appointed in a territorial division where the trial would otherwise by law be held.

(2) [*Repealed*, R.S.C. 1985, c. 1 (4th Supp.), s. 16.]

(3) The court or judge may, in an order made on an application by the prosecutor under subsection (1), prescribe conditions that he thinks proper with respect to the payment of additional expenses caused to the accused as a result of the change of venue.

(4) Where an order is made under subsection (1), the officer who has custody of the indictment, if any, and the writings and exhibits relating to the prosecution, shall transmit them forthwith to the clerk of the court before which the trial is ordered to be held, and all proceedings in the case shall be held or, if previously commenced, shall be continued in that court.

(5) Where the writings and exhibits referred to in subsection (4) have not been returned to the court in which the trial was to be held at the time an order is made to change the place of trial, the person who obtains the order shall serve a true copy thereof on the person in whose custody they are and that person shall thereupon transmit them to the clerk of the court before which the trial is to be held. R.S., c. C-34, s. 527; 1974-75-76, c. 93, s. 66; R.S.C. 1985, c. 1 (4th Supp.), s. 16.

CROSS-REFERENCES

The terms "indictment", "prosecutor" and "territorial division" are defined in s. 2. Territorial jurisdiction is generally dealt with in ss. 470 and 476 to 481. Also note s. 7 which gives courts territorial jurisdiction in certain circumstances as where offence is committed on aircraft or outside Canada. Where an order is made changing the venue of trial then s. 600 provides for the removal, disposal and reception of an accused pursuant to such order for change of venue. Section 531 provides for change of venue where necessary for the purpose of a trial in the official language of the accused.

SYNOPSIS

Subsection (1) provides that an application to change the venue of a trial may be made at any time, by either the prosecutor or the accused, to a judge of the court before which the trial is to take place. Where the judge is satisfied that: (a) the ends of justice so require; or (b) that a jury panel will not be available, he or she can order that the matter be transferred to another territorial division within the same province.

Where the order is made upon the application of the prosecution, the court may require the prosecutor to pay any additional expenses incurred by the accused (subsec. (3)).

The record will be transmitted to the court where the trial is to be held (subsecs. (4) and (5)).

ANNOTATIONS

Jurisdiction – The superior court of one province has no power to change the venue of an offence, committed entirely in that province, to another province: *R. v. Threinen* (1976), 30 C.C.C. (2d) 42 (Sask. Q.B.).

General – Placing the onus on the accused to demonstrate that a change of venue is "expedient to the ends of justice" does not violate s. 11(*d*) of the Charter: *R. v. Suzack* (2000), 141 C.C.C. (3d) 449 (Ont. C.A.), leave to appeal to S.C.C. refused [2001] 1 S.C.R. xvi *sub nom. R. v. Pennett*, 152 C.C.C. (3d) vi.

Procedure – An accused has no right to bring successive applications before different judges for a change of venue unless new grounds have arisen since the previous application. On any subsequent application the judge hears the matter *de novo: R. v. Hutchison* (1975), 26 C.C.C. (2d) 423 (N.B. S.C. App. Div.), affd [1977] 2 S.C.R. 717 *sub nom. R. v. Ambrose; R. v. Hutchison*, 30 C.C.C. (2d) 97.

Where the prejudice which caused a change of venue to be ordered has been eradicated, a return to the original venue should be ordered as *prima facie* the accused should be tried in the jurisdiction where the offence was alleged to have been committed: *R. v. Kellar* (1973), 24 C.R.N.S. 71 (Ont. Co. Ct.).

No interlocutory appeal lies from a superior court's judgment in respect of an application for a change of venue or the requirement that the Attorney General pay counsel a *per diem* fee over and above that being paid by legal aid: *R. v. Noel* (1996), 110 C.C.C. (3d) 168, [1996] R.J.Q. 1182 (C.A.).

Principles – The test is whether it has been made to appear that there is a fair and reasonable probability of partiality or prejudice against the accused: *R. v. Beaudry,* [1966] 3 C.C.C. 51 (B.C.S.C.).

The test to be applied on an application for a change of venue is whether it is necessary in order to ensure that the accused has a fair trial with an impartial jury. A fair trial can be conducted only in a reasonably serene environment. The test enunciated in *R. v. Beaudry, supra*, requiring the accused to establish that a jury would not render a true verdict free of bias or partiality, is too narrow: *R. v. Charest* (1990), 57 C.C.C. (3d) 312 (Que. C.A.).

For a change of venue the accused must present evidence that a fair and impartial trial cannot be held. Where the only prejudice likely to exist arises out of the very nature of the offence the application will be refused: *R. v. Turvey* (1970), 1 C.C.C. (2d) 90 (N.S.S.C.).

The fundamental consideration in determining an application to grant a change of venue is whether it is necessary to ensure that the accused has a fair trial with an impartial jury. Where most of the pretrial publicity was over a year prior to the trial and the accused was given an unrestricted right to challenge potential jurors for cause, it could not be said that the trial judge improperly exercised his discretion against a change of venue: *R. v. Collins* (1989), 48 C.C.C. (3d) 343 (Ont. C.A.). See also *R. v. Suzack, supra.*

In *R. v. Lafferty* (1977), 35 C.C.C. (2d) 183 (N.W.T.S.C.), a change of venue on application by the Crown was granted where all the potential jurors in the area either knew the accused or the victim and evidence was tendered that there was a reasonable probability of prejudice and that most members of a jury would be reluctant to return a verdict for fear of retaliation. It was held that in administering justice the court should not sanction a course of action which will cause or aggravate devisiveness or hostility in a small settlement.

Subsequent to an appeal in relation to a trial in which a change of venue had originally been granted, the test to return the trial to the district where the offence was committed is not as high as the test for granting a change of venue: *R. v. Eng (No. 2)* (1999), 138 C.C.C. (3d) 188 (B.C.C.A.).

The test for a change of venue for a parole eligibility hearing is not as stringent as for a trial: *Thatcher v. Saskatchewan (Attorney General)* (2003), 175 C.C.C. (3d) 567 (Sask. Q.B.), leave to appeal to S.C.C. refused April 1, 2004.

ORDER IS AUTHORITY TO REMOVE PRISONER.

600. An order that is made under section 599 is sufficient warrant, justification and authority to all sheriffs, keepers of prisons and peace officers for the removal, disposal and reception of an accused in accordance with the terms of the order, and the sheriff may appoint and authorize any peace officer to convey the accused to a prison in the territorial division in which the trial is ordered to be held. R.S., c. C-34, s. 528.

CROSS-REFERENCES

The terms "prison", "peace officer" and "territorial division" are defined in s. 2. The order for a change of venue is made pursuant to s. 599.

SYNOPSIS

This section provides that an order under s. 599 to change venues is also a sufficient authority to provide for the transfer and imprisonment, if relevant, of the accused.

Amendment

AMENDING DEFECTIVE INDICTMENT OR COUNT / Amendment where variance / Amending indictment / Matters to be considered by the court / Variance not material / Adjournment if accused prejudiced / Question of law / Endorsing indictment / Mistakes not material / Limitation / Definition of "court" / Application.

601. (1) An objection to an indictment preferred under this Part or to a count in an indictment, for a defect apparent on its face, shall be taken by motion to quash the indictment or count before the accused enters a plea, and, after the accused has entered a plea, only by leave of the court before which the proceedings take place. The court before which an objection is taken under this section may, if it considers it necessary, order the indictment or count to be amended to cure the defect.

(2) Subject to this section, a court may, on the trial of an indictment, amend the indictment or a count therein or a particular that is furnished under section 587, to make the indictment, count or particular conform to the evidence, where there is a variance between the evidence and

(*a*) a count in the indictment as preferred; or

(*b*) a count in the indictment

(i) as amended, or

(ii) as it would have been if it had been amended in conformity with any particular that has been furnished pursuant to section 587.

(3) Subject to this section, a court shall, at any stage of the proceedings, amend the indictment or a count therein as may be necessary where it appears

(*a*) that the indictment has been preferred under a particular Act of Parliament instead of another Act of Parliament;

(*b*) that the indictment or a count thereof

(i) fails to state or states defectively anything that is requisite to constitute the offence,

(ii) does not negative an exception that should be negatived,

(iii) is in any way defective in substance,

and the matters to be alleged in the proposed amendment are disclosed by the evidence taken on the preliminary inquiry or on the trial; or

(*c*) that the indictment or a count thereof is in any way defective in form.

(4) The court shall, in considering whether or not an amendment should be made to the indictment or a count in it, consider

(*a*) the matters disclosed by the evidence taken on the preliminary inquiry;

(*b*) the evidence taken on the trial, if any;

(*c*) the circumstances of the case;

(*d*) whether the accused has been misled or prejudiced in his defence by any variance, error or omission mentioned in subsection (2) or (3); and

(*e*) whether, having regard to the merits of the case, the proposed amendment can be made without injustice being done.

(4.1) A variance between the indictment or a count therein and the evidence taken is not material with respect to

(*a*) the time when the offence is alleged to have been committed, if it is proved that the indictment was preferred within the prescribed period of limitation, if any; or

(*b*) the place where the subject-matter of the proceedings is alleged to have arisen, if it is proved that it arose within the territorial jurisdiction of the court.

(5) Where, in the opinion of the court, the accused has been misled or prejudiced in his defence by a variance, error or omission in an indictment or a count therein, the court may, if it is of the opinion that the misleading or prejudice may be removed by an adjournment, adjourn the proceedings to a specified day or sittings of the court and may make such an order with respect to the payment of costs resulting from the necessity for amendment as it considers desirable.

(6) The question whether an order to amend an indictment or a count thereof should be granted or refused is a question of law.

(7) An order to amend an indictment or a count therein shall be endorsed on the indictment as part of the record and the proceedings shall continue as if the indictment or count had been originally preferred as amended.

(8) A mistake in the heading of an indictment shall be corrected as soon as it is discovered but, whether corrected or not, is not material.

(9) The authority of a court to amend indictments does not authorize the court to add to the overt acts stated in an indictment for high treason or treason or for an offence against any provision in sections 50, 51 and 53.

(10) In this section, "court" means a court, judge, justice or provincial court judge acting in summary conviction proceedings or in proceedings on indictment.

(11) This section applies to all proceedings, including preliminary inquiries, with such modifications as the circumstances require. R.S., c. C-34, s. 529; 1974-75-76, c. 105, s. 29; R.S.C. 1985, c. 27 (1st Supp.), s. 123; 1999, c. 5, s. 23; 2011, c. 16, s. 6; 2018, c. 29, s. 65.

CROSS-REFERENCES

The terms "count", "indictment", "justice" and "provincial court judge" are defined in s. 2. Section 581 sets out the minimum sufficiency requirements with respect to a count in an indictment or information. Other provisions respecting sufficiency of counts in an indictment are found in ss. 582 to 586. Provision for ordering particulars is made in s. 587 and any such particular may be amended pursuant to this section. Provision for amending a count which is double or multifarious is found in s. 590. Section 591 permits a judge to sever jointly charged accused and to order severance of counts. Under s. 683(1)(*g*), an appellate court may amend an indictment.

SYNOPSIS

This section governs applications to quash or amend an indictment.

Where a defect is apparent on the face of an indictment, subsec. (1) directs that a motion to quash shall be made prior to plea. Thereafter, leave of the court is required.

Where evidence has been called, the court can amend the indictment, or any particular, to conform with the evidence (subsec. (2)).

At any stage of the proceedings, the court can amend a charge which, although otherwise properly drawn, refers to the wrong statute (subsec. (3)(*a*)) or is in any way defective in form (subsec. (3)(*c*)).

In cases where the need for the proposed amendment has been disclosed by the evidence called at either the preliminary inquiry or the trial, the indictment may be amended where it: (a) fails to state or defectively states an essential averment (subsec. (3)(*b*)(i); (b) fails to negative an exception (subsec. (3)(*b*)(ii); (c) is in any way defective in substance (subsec. (3)(*b*)(iii).

Subsection (4) directs the trial judge to consider the following in deciding whether an amendment ought to be made: (a) the evidence from the preliminary inquiry; (b) any evidence adduced at trial; (c) the circumstances of the case; (d) whether the accused has been misled or prejudiced by the defect in the charge; and (e) whether the amendment would cause an injustice.

By reason of subsec. (4.1), a variation between the evidence and the time of the offence is not material if the indictment was preferred within the limitation period. Similarly, a variation between the evidence and the location of the offence is not material if the matter arose within the territorial jurisdiction of the court.

The court may, pursuant to subsec. (5), adjourn the trial (and order costs if appropriate) where necessary, to remove any prejudice caused by an error in the wording of the charge.

A decision with respect to amending an indictment is a question of law (subsec. (6)). This is important for the purposes of appeals.

This section does not authorize amendments with respect to the overt acts which must be set out in treason charges or in charges of alarming Her Majesty (s. 49), assisting an alien or omitting to prevent treason (s. 50), intimidating Parliament (s. 51), sabotage (s. 52) or mutiny (s. 53).

The powers of amendment set out in this section also apply to summary conviction proceedings (subsec. (10)) and to preliminary inquiries (subsec. (11)).

ANNOTATIONS

Amendment on court's own motion – It was held in *R. v. Powell,* [1965] 4 C.C.C. 349 (B.C.C.A.), that a trial judge may *ex mero motu,* upon a motion for dismissal at the conclusion of the Crown's case, amend the information to conform with the evidence.

Procedure – In *R. v. Bouchard,* [1970] 5 C.C.C. 95 (N.B.S.C. App. Div.), it was held that an objection to a defect apparent on the face of the indictment cannot be entertained initially upon appeal unless the accused has been misled or prejudiced by that defect.

Where the accused refuses to plead and stands mute, then, although a plea of not guilty is entered, the accused has never actually pleaded and therefore does not require leave to raise an objection to the indictment in the course of the trial: *R. v. Wilson* (1986), 26 C.C.C. (3d) 8 (Man. Q.B.).

An information charging a summary conviction offence may be amended by the trial judge and resworn to properly state the grounds for belief by the informant, *i.e.*, reasonable grounds rather than personal knowledge, notwithstanding the six-month limitation period has expired by that time: *R. v. Canadian Industries Ltd.* (1982), 69 C.C.C. (2d) 533 (N.B.C.A.).

An accused may move at his preliminary inquiry to quash an information for failure to comply with s. 581(3): *Dallas v. Cassidy* (1986), 25 C.C.C. (3d) 287 (Ont. C.A.).

An application to quash an information on the basis that it fails to comply with s. 581(3) may be brought prior to the accused's election as to mode of trial: *Volpi v. Lanzino* (1987), 34 C.C.C. (3d) 1 (Ont. C.A.); *R. v. Itt Industries of Canada* (1987), 39 C.C.C. (3d) 268 (B.C.C.A.).

Where an information falls within a trial court's jurisdiction the Judge has exclusive jurisdiction to determine its validity and his decision upholding it is not subject to either a motion to quash or extraordinary remedy proceedings but only to an appeal against his disposition of the case: *R. v. Jarman* (1972), 10 C.C.C. (2d) 426 (Ont.C.A.).

An information not being an absolute nullity, in deciding whether or not to quash it, the provincial court judge presiding at the accused's preliminary inquiry was acting within his jurisdiction and *certiorari* was not available to review that decision. However, there may be very rare and highly exceptional circumstances where *certiorari* was available, as where the judge refused to quash an information which was an absolute nullity in that it failed even to give the accused notice of the charge. The existence of some charge of an offence known to the law, albeit very imperfectly described, is the basis of the judge's jurisdiction: *R. v. Webster*, [1993] 1 S.C.R. 3, 78 C.C.C. (3d) 302 (7:0).

Nature of amendments which may be made – On the second trial (this time for wounding), following an acquittal of attempted murder, the trial judge refused the special plea of *autrefois acquit*. In affirming this decision it was held in *R. v. Rinnie,* [1970] 3 C.C.C. 218 (Alta. C.A.), that an included offence, which can only be found by definition of the crime, or by statutory prescription, or by the inclusion of apt words of description cognate to the offence, may be pleaded to by this special plea where there has been an acquittal of the principal offence. Furthermore, as the Crown is not to be permitted to amend a count at trial to include a lesser and included offence, because such amendment is not envisaged by this section, the accused cannot argue that a proper amendment might have been made at the former trial to entitle him subsequently to plea *autrefois acquit*.

Circumstances where amendment should be made generally – An amendment during a trial which fundamentally changes the Crown's case is an injustice to the accused: *R. v. Charlton and Ostere* (1976), 30 C.C.C. (2d) 372 (B.C.C.A.).

An information which is duplicitous or multifarious is not null or void but merely contains a defect apparent on its face within this section, and may be amended: *R. v. Sault Ste. Marie (City)* (1976), 30 C.C.C. (2d) 257 (Ont. C.A.), affd on other grounds [1978] 2 S.C.R. 1299, 40 C.C.C. (2d) 353 (9:0).

Amendment to conform with evidence [subsec. (2)] – A trial continues until the charge is disposed of so that until that point a judge may amend the charge to conform with the evidence: *R. v. Clark* (1974), 19 C.C.C. (2d) 445 (Alta. C.A.).

It would seem that the test to be applied as to whether the indictment is to be amended to conform to the evidence is whether or not the amendment can be made without causing irreparable prejudice to the accused: *R. v. Morozuk*, [1986] 1 S.C.R. 31, 24 C.C.C. (3d) 257 (7:0); *R. v. Campbell And Kotler*, [1986] 2 S.C.R. 376, 29 C.C.C. (3d) 97.

Thus it was held that this subsection authorizes an amendment that substitutes a new charge provided that the accused will not be prejudiced: *R. v. Irwin* (1998), 123 C.C.C. (3d) 316 (Ont. C.A.).

Amendments to cure defects in form and substance [subsec. (3)] – An amendment clarifying a count by including particulars was not one of substance, but in any event subsec. (3) gave the trial judge an unqualified right to amend: *R. v. Denis,* [1970] 1 C.C.C. 86 (Ont. C.A.).

It would seem that the test to be applied as to whether the indictment is to be amended rather than quashed is a test of irreparable prejudice. Absent absolute nullity, if the defect to be cured by the amendment has misled or prejudiced the accused then the judge must determine whether the misleading or prejudice can be removed by an adjournment. If it can, then the judge must make the amendment and adjourn and thereafter proceed. Only if the amendment cannot be made without injustice being done, it is open to the judge to quash the charge: *R. v. Moore*, [1988] 1 S.C.R. 1097, 41 C.C.C. (3d) 289 (4:3).

Where it was shown that the officer who swore the information had no knowledge whatsoever of the offence despite having sworn that she had reasonable grounds to believe the accused had committed it, the information was a nullity. Lack of reasonable grounds is neither a defect in form nor substance and cannot give rise to an amendment under this provision: *R. v. Awad* (2015), 321 C.C.C. (3d) 107 (N.S.C.A.).

An information which lacks an essential averment is not thereby rendered a nullity, but rather may be amended: *R. v. Stewart* (1979), 7 C.R. (3d) 165 (B.C.C.A.) (5:0).

The Crown should have been permitted to amend the indictment at the close of its case to add another person as a named, but unindicted, co-conspirator. It was clear from the outset of the trial that this person, although not named in the original indictment, was known to be a co-conspirator in the conspiracy charged. However, because no preliminary inquiry had been held, an evidentiary basis was necessary for the proposed amendment. There was no suggestion that the Crown deliberately omitted the name, acted in bad faith or that there was any prejudice to the accused as a result of the amendment: *R. v. Callocchia* (2000), 149 C.C.C. (3d) 215 (Que. C.A.).

The erroneous description of the accused's vehicle was not a defect in form or substance within the meaning of subsec. (3)(*b*)(iii) or (3)(*c*). Accordingly, without the accused's consent, the information could not be amended until some evidence as to the correct description had been given at the trial. At that point, the information could be amended in accordance with subsec. (2) or (3)(*b*)(i) to conform with the evidence: *R. v. McConnell* (2005), 196 C.C.C. (3d) 28 (Ont. C.A.).

Factors to be considered under [subsec. (4)] – These requirements are mandatory and the failure of the trial judge to observe them vitiates an amendment made to the charge by him: *R. v. Geary* (1960), 126 C.C.C. 325 (Alta. S.C. App. Div.).

The effect of this subsection is not that a preliminary inquiry must have been held before an amendment can be made. If the preliminary inquiry has been waived by the accused the result is that there is nothing for the trial judge to consider under para. (*a*) in following the directions under the subsection: *R. v. Smith* (1961), 131 C.C.C. 14 (Ont. C.A.), revd on other grounds [1962] S.C.R. 215, 131 C.C.C. 403.

Time and place of offence [subsec. (4.1)] – While time must be specified in an information in order to provide an accused with reasonable information about the charges brought against him and to ensure the possibility of a full defence and a fair trial, exact time need not be specified. The individual circumstances of the particular case may, however, be such that greater precision as to time is required, as where there is a lack of other factual information available with which to identify the transaction. If the time specified in the information is inconsistent with the evidence, there is conflicting evidence as to the time of the offence or the date cannot be established with precision, the information need not be quashed and conviction may result, provided that time is not an essential element of the offence or crucial to the defence: *R. v. B. (G.)*, [1990] 2 S.C.R. 30, 56 C.C.C. (3d) 161 (5:0). See also: *R. v. D. (S.)*, [2011] 1 S.C.R. 527, 270 C.C.C. (3d) 287, affirming the dissent of Duval Hesler J.A. in *R. v. D. (S.)* (2010), 270 C.C.C. (3d) 289 (Que. C.A.).

While a variance between the date of the offence as set out in the indictment and as shown in the evidence is not material, it was held to constitute misdirection to instruct the jury to disregard any variance. While the dates on the indictment alleging sexual assault may have had several sources, the jury was entitled to assume that the adult complainant must have been consulted before the charges were laid. The direction to the jury may have led the jury to disregard evidence which was material in assessing the credibility of the complainant: *R. v. C. (M.H.)*, [1991] 1 S.C.R. 763, 63 C.C.C. (3d) 385 (5:0).

In *R. v. P. (M.B.)*, [1994] 1 S.C.R. 555, 89 C.C.C. (3d) 289, it was held that, particularly with respect to sexual offences against young children, absolute precision with respect to the timing of the alleged offence will often be unrealistic and unnecessary. The fact that an accused may have an alibi for part of the period described in the indictment does not necessarily or automatically freeze the dates specified in that indictment. The alibi evidence must respond to the case as presented by the Crown. However, at the time the Crown closed its case there was no occasion for an amendment to the indictment, the testimony of the complainant and her mother as to the date of the offence corresponding to the dates set out in the indictment. The Crown should not have been allowed to reopen its case after the accused had declared his intention to call evidence of an alibi in order to justify the subsequent amendment to the indictment. The fundamental principle in determining whether the Crown should be permitted to reopen its case is whether the accused will suffer prejudice in his defence. Whether or not the Crown should be permitted to reopen its case will depend on the stage at which the application is made and the nature of the evidence to be called. Before the Crown has closed its case, the trial judge has considerable latitude to permit the Crown to recall a witness to correct earlier testimony. Any prejudice to the accused can generally be cured by an adjournment, cross-examination of the recalled witness and other crown witnesses and a review by the trial judge of the record in order to determine whether certain portions should be struck. Once the Crown actually closes its case, the trial judge's discretion will narrow with reopening being permitted to correct some oversight or inadvertent omission by the Crown in the presentation of its case, provided that justice requires it and there will be no prejudice to the defence. Where the Crown has closed its case and as, in this case, the defence has started to answer the case against him, the trial judge's discretion is very restricted and it will only be in the narrowest of circumstances that the Crown will be permitted to reopen its case.

Review of decision of trial judge [subsec. (6)] – Failure to make an amendment to the information which had merely misdescribed the allegedly stolen property, which amendment would not have prejudiced the accused, is an error of law which the Crown may appeal to the Court of Appeal: *R. v. Cousineau* (1982), 1 C.C.C. (3d) 293 (Ont. C.A.).

While the decision to refuse an amendment is a question of law and reviewable by the Court of Appeal, the decision of the trial judge, when based on a finding of irreparable prejudice should not be interfered with lightly and the trial judge's privileged position as regards the effect on the fairness of a trial should be borne in mind: *R. v. Vezina*; *R. v. Cote*, [1986] 1 S.C.R. 2, 23 C.C.C. (3d) 481 (7:0).

602. [*Repealed*, R.S.C. 1985, c. 27 (1st Supp.), s. 124.]

Inspection and Copies of Documents

RIGHT OF ACCUSED.

603. An accused is entitled, after he has been ordered to stand trial or at his trial,

(*a*) to inspect without charge the indictment, his own statement, the evidence and the exhibits, if any; and

(*b*) to receive, on payment of a reasonable fee determined in accordance with a tariff of fees fixed or approved by the Attorney General of the province, a copy

(i) of the evidence,

(ii) of his own statement, if any, and

(iii) of the indictment;

but the trial shall not be postponed to enable the accused to secure copies unless the court is satisfied that the failure of the accused to secure them before the trial is not attributable to lack of diligence on the part of the accused. R.S., c. C-34, s. 531; 1974-75-76, c. 93, s. 67; R.S.C. 1985, c. 27 (1st Supp.), s. 101(2)(*d*).

CROSS-REFERENCES

The terms "indictment" and "Attorney General" are defined in s. 2. Following the order to stand trial, s. 551 provides that the record is to be transmitted to the trial court. As to disclosure of records containing personal information at the trial of certain sexual offences, see ss. 278.1 to 278.91.

SYNOPSIS

This section sets out the material which an accused is entitled to examine, or obtain copies of. Accused persons may inspect the indictment, their own statements and any evidence or exhibits tendered at the preliminary inquiry.

Upon payment of a prescribed fee, the accused can obtain copies of the evidence, his or her own statements and the indictment. A trial should not be adjourned until the accused receives copies, if the failure to obtain copies is due to lack of diligence on the part of the accused.

ANNOTATIONS

Disclosure generally – At least in the case of indictable offences, the Crown is required to produce to the defence all relevant information whether or not the Crown intends to introduce it into evidence and whether it is inculpatory or exculpatory. The Crown does have a discretion to withhold information and as to the timing of the disclosure where necessary to protect the identity of an informer or a continuing investigation. A discretion must also be exercised with respect to the relevance of information. The exercise of this discretion is reviewable by the trial judge who will be guided by the general principle that information ought not to be withheld if there is a reasonable possibility that the withholding of information will impair the right of the accused to make full answer and defence, unless the non-disclosure is justified by the law of privilege. Even then, the trial judge might conclude that the recognition of an existing privilege does not constitute a reasonable limit on the constitutional right to make full answer and defence and thus require disclosure in spite of the law of privilege. Initial disclosure should occur before the accused is called upon to elect the mode of trial or to plead. The obligation to disclose will be triggered by a request by or on behalf of the accused. In the case of an unrepresented accused, the trial judge should not take a plea unless satisfied that the accused has been informed of his right to disclosure: *R. v. Stinchcombe*, [1991] 3 S.C.R. 326, 68 C.C.C. (3d) 1 (7:0).

Production of witness' statement – Subject to the discretion discussed above under the heading "Disclosure generally", the Crown must disclose any statements in its possession of witnesses the Crown proposes to call and all statements obtained from persons who have provided relevant information to the authorities notwithstanding that they are not proposed as Crown witnesses. Where statements are not in existence, other information such as notes should be produced, and, if there are no notes, then in addition to the name, address and occupation of the witness, all information in the possession of the prosecution relating to any relevant evidence that the person could give should be disclosed: *R. v. Stinchcombe, supra*.

Production of accused's statement – The phrase "his own statement" in para. (*a*) includes the accused's statement to the police and not merely the statement given pursuant to s. 541 at the preliminary hearing. Further, even apart from this section, the trial judge has a discretion which, absent some cogent reason, he should exercise to order the Crown to produce the accused's statement for the defence even if the Crown has no intention of introducing the statement as part of its case: *R. v. Savion and Mizrahi* (1980), 52 C.C.C. (2d) 276 (Ont. C.A.). Folld: *R. v. Gonneville* (1982), 69 C.C.C. (2d) 269 (Que. S.C.).

For other notes on disclosure, see notes following s. 650.

---

604. [*Repealed*, 1997, c. 18, s. 69.]

RELEASE OF EXHIBITS FOR TESTING / Disobeying orders.

605. (1) A judge of a superior court of criminal jurisdiction or a court of criminal jurisdiction may, on summary application on behalf of the accused or the prosecutor, after three days notice to the accused or prosecutor, as the case may be, order the release of any exhibit for the purpose of a scientific or other test or examination, subject to such terms as appear to be necessary or desirable to ensure the safeguarding of the exhibit and its preservation for use at the trial.

(2) Every one who fails to comply with the terms of an order made under subsection (1) is guilty of contempt of court and may be dealt with summarily by the judge or provincial court judge who made the order or before whom the trial of the accused takes place. R.S., c. C-34, s. 533; R.S.C. 1985, c. 27 (1st Supp.), s. 203.

CROSS-REFERENCES

In addition to the power in this section, note s. 258(4) which provides for a court order releasing samples of blood taken from the accused pursuant to ss. 254 and 256. Under s. 603, an accused is entitled to inspect exhibits which have been transmitted to the trial court pursuant to s. 551. The rights of appeal in cases of contempt of court are set out in s. 10.

SYNOPSIS

This section authorizes a trial judge to release an item which has been marked as an exhibit for scientific testing or other examination. Either the Crown or the accused can apply, upon giving three days notice to the other party. A court making such an order can impose terms to safeguard the item and to ensure its preservation for use at trial.

Failure to comply with the order is punishable as a contempt of court.

ANNOTATIONS

This section would permit the release for testing of a tape recording which was ordered produced by the trial judge although not made an exhibit: *R. v. Savion and Mizrahi* (1980), 52 C.C.C. (2d) 276 (Ont. C.A.).

On the trial of a narcotics offence the fact that the entire amount of the alleged narcotic was used up in scientific analysis so that the accused was rendered unable to exercise his right to apply under this section does not deprive the accused of his right to make full answer and defence: *R. v. O'Quinn* (1976), 36 C.C.C. (2d) 364 (B.C.C.A.); *Canada (Attorney General) v. Ross* (1971), 15 C.R.N.S. 71 (Que. C.A.).

An accused charged with a narcotics offence may apply under this section for an order releasing the narcotics for the purpose of scientific testing. But an order should be granted only where the intended analysis can be characterized as quantitatively and qualitatively different from the one initially carried out by the government analyst: *R. v. Bryers and Mueller* (1975), 28 C.C.C. (2d) 466 (Ont. Co. Ct.).

This section will permit release of narcotics for scientific testing which have been made exhibits, even to persons not otherwise authorized by the *Narcotic Control Act* or Regulations to possess narcotics: *R. v. Vales* (1979), 46 C.C.C. (2d) 269 (Ont. H.C.J.).

Where there is an "air of reality" to the production and examination sought and if the production and examination sought have any meaningful capacity to advance any available defence then the order should be made: *R. v. Rhab* (1985), 21 C.C.C. (3d) 97 (Ont. H.C.J.).

A justice presiding at a preliminary inquiry has no power to order the release of exhibits for scientific testing under this section: *R. v. Walsh* (1981), 59 C.C.C. (2d) 554 (Ont. Ct. (Prov. Div.)). *Contra: R. v. McGee* (1973), 15 Crim. L.Q. 468 (B.C. Prov. Ct.).

The word "exhibit" in this provision should be read broadly to allow the trial court to make an order in respect of forensic DNA extracts which were before the court but not formally entered as exhibits at the preliminary inquiry: *R. v. Oland* (2015), 334 C.C.C. (3d) 553 (N.B.Q.B.).

For notes on the power of the court to control release of exhibits following the trial see notes under s. 683, **Powers of court of appeal generally [subsec. (3)].**

Pleas

PLEAS PERMITTED / Conditions for accepting guilty plea / Validity of plea / Refusal to plead / Allowing time / Included or other offence / Inquiry of court — murder and serious personal injury offences / Inquiry of court — certain indictable offences / Duty to inform / Validity of plea / Video links.

606. (1) An accused who is called on to plead may plead guilty or not guilty, or the special pleas authorized by this Part and no others.

(1.1) A court may accept a plea of guilty only if it is satisfied that the accused

(*a*) is making the plea voluntarily; and

(*b*) understands

(i) that the plea is an admission of the essential elements of the offence,

(ii) the nature and consequences of the plea, and

(iii) that the court is not bound by any agreement made between the accused and the prosecutor.

(1.2) The failure of the court to fully inquire whether the conditions set out in subsection (1.1) are met does not affect the validity of the plea.

(2) Where an accused refuses to plead or does not answer directly, the court shall order the clerk of the court to enter a plea of not guilty.

(3) An accused is not entitled as of right to have his trial postponed but the court may, if it considers that the accused should be allowed further time to plead, move to quash, or prepare for his defence or for any other reason, adjourn the trial to a later time in the session or sittings of the court, or to the next of any subsequent session or sittings of the court, on such terms as the court considers proper.

(4) Notwithstanding any other provision of this Act, where an accused or defendant pleads not guilty of the offence charged but guilty of any other offence arising out of the same transaction, whether or not it is an included offence, the court may, with the consent of the prosecutor, accept that plea of guilty and, if such plea is accepted, the court shall find the accused or defendant not guilty of the offence charged and find him guilty of the offence in respect of which the plea of guilty was accepted and enter those findings in the record of the court.

(4.1) If the accused is charged with a serious personal injury offence, as that expression is defined in section 752, or with the offence of murder, and the accused and the prosecutor have entered into an agreement under which the accused will enter a plea of guilty of the offence charged — or a plea of not guilty of the offence charged but guilty of any other offence arising out of the same transaction, whether or not it is an included offence — the court shall, after accepting the plea of guilty, inquire of the prosecutor if reasonable steps were taken to inform the victims of the agreement.

(4.2) If the accused is charged with an offence, as defined in section 2 of the *Canadian Victims Bill of Rights*, that is an indictable offence for which the maximum punishment is imprisonment for five years or more, and that is not an offence referred to in subsection (4.1), and the accused and the prosecutor have entered into an agreement referred to in subsection (4.1), the court shall, after accepting the plea of guilty, inquire of the prosecutor whether any of the victims had advised the prosecutor of their desire to be informed if such an agreement were entered into, and, if so, whether reasonable steps were taken to inform that victim of the agreement.

(4.3) If subsection (4.1) or (4.2) applies, and any victim was not informed of the agreement before the plea of guilty was accepted, the prosecutor shall, as soon as

feasible, take reasonable steps to inform the victim of the agreement and the acceptance of the plea.

(4.4) Neither the failure of the court to inquire of the prosecutor, nor the failure of the prosecutor to take reasonable steps to inform the victims of the agreement, affects the validity of the plea.

(5) For greater certainty, subsections 650(1.1) and (1.2) apply, with any modifications that the circumstances require, to pleas under this section if the accused has agreed to use a means referred to in those subsections. R.S., c. C-34, s. 534; 1974-75-76, c. 105, s. 7; R.S.C. 1985, c. 27 (1st Supp.), s. 125; 2002, c. 13, s. 49; 2015, c. 13, s. 21.

CROSS-REFERENCES

The rules respecting included offences are set out in ss. 660 to 662. The special pleas are provided for in ss. 607 to 610. The special plea of justification in cases of libel is set out in ss. 611 and 612. Any ground of defence for which a special plea is not provided for in this part may be relied upon under the plea of not guilty pursuant to s. 613. Thus, for example, the defence of insanity as defined in s. 16 is tried pursuant to a plea of not guilty entered pursuant to s. 606(1).

Under s. 848, if an accused who is in prison does not have access to legal advice, the court shall, before permitting the accused to appear by means of communication that allows the court and the accused to engage in simultaneous visual and oral communication, be satisfied that the accused will be able to understand the proceedings and that any decisions made by the accused during the proceedings will be voluntary.

A plea of guilty may be made by counsel in the absence of the accused only if the court orders in accordance with s. 650.01.

SYNOPSIS

The only pleas recognized by Canadian law are guilty, not guilty and the "special pleas" referred to in s. 607, *viz.*, *autrefois acquit*, *autrefois convict*, and pardon (subsec. (1)).

Subsection (1.1) sets out the procedure to be followed before the court accepts a guilty plea. The court must be satisfied that the plea is voluntary, that the accused understands the nature and consequences of the plea and that the court is not bound by any agreement with the prosecutor. However, the failure of the court to "fully" comply with this procedure does not invalidate the plea.

A plea of not guilty will be entered if the accused refuses to plead to a charge (subsec. (2)).

The judge can adjourn a trial if he or she feels it is appropriate to allow the accused more time to consider what plea to enter or for any other reason related to the preparation and conduct of the defence (subsec. (3)).

With the consent of the Crown, the court may accept a plea of guilty to another offence arising out of the same transaction, whether or not it is an included offence. In such a case, the accused will be found not guilty of the offence charged, but guilty of the offence in respect of which the plea was accepted (subsec. (4)).

In accordance with subsec. (5), the court may accept the plea using the procedures set out in s. 650(1.1) or (1.2) such as video conferencing.

ANNOTATIONS

Guilty plea / Procedure – [**Note:** the following cases were decided before the enactment of subsec. (1.1)] In *R. v. Adgey*, [1975] 2 S.C.R. 426, 13 C.C.C. (2d) 177 (3:2), the majority held that a trial judge has a discretion with respect to accepting a plea of guilty, first, when the charge is read and a plea of guilty is entered and, second, following the hearing of evidence if the judge chooses to hear evidence. The trial judge is not bound as a matter of law in all cases to conduct an inquiry after a guilty plea has been entered. If he chooses to hear evidence it may indicate the accused never intended to admit to an essential fact of the offence charged or may have misapprehended the effect of the plea or may never have intended to plead guilty at all. In such cases the judge may, in his discretion, permit the accused to withdraw the plea or direct the entry of a plea of not guilty. The discretion of the trial judge if exercised judicially will not be lightly interfered with. The court's right to permit withdrawal of a guilty plea is not limited to matters arising from "admitted facts" but can be based upon any statements made in the course of the inquiry following a guilty plea. **Editor's Note:** Now see subsec. (1.1).

A plea of guilty may be entered by counsel on behalf of the accused in the presence of the accused: *R. v. Sommerfeldt* (1984), 14 C.C.C. (3d) 445 (B.C.C.A.).

While there is no plea of *nolo contendre*, the procedure followed in the instant case was not barred by statute or common law. Here, experienced counsel obtained detailed written instructions and the accused entered a plea of not guilty but did not contest the facts as read in by the Crown. The finding of guilt was inevitable and the accused was fully aware of this fact given the absence of any challenge to the facts alleged by the Crown: *R. v. P. (R.)* (2013), 295 C.C.C. (3d) 28 (Ont. C.A.), leave to appeal to S.C.C. refused 2013 CarswellOnt 7980.

Qualified or conditional plea – When a qualified or conditional plea is given the court should not accept it as a plea of guilty unless the court is satisfied, after due inquiry, that the qualification or condition does not derogate from the accused's intention to enter an unequivocal plea of guilty: *R. v. McNabb* (1971), 4 C.C.C. (2d) 316 (Sask. C.A.). In this case on appeal the accused was permitted to withdraw his guilty plea when at trial he pleaded "guilty with an explanation" and the trial judge did not make the inquiry which would justify his acceptance of the plea.

A plea of guilty must be an admission by the accused of all the legal ingredients necessary to constitute the crime charged thus dispensing with the necessity of proof of those ingredients. The accused may not enter a conditional plea of guilty, for example, in a homicide case, conditional on the Crown establishing the cause of death: *R. v. Lucas* (1983), 9 C.C.C. (3d) 71 (Ont. C.A.), leave to appeal to S.C.C. refused C.C.C. *loc. cit.*

The acceptance of a plea of guilty to a lesser and included offence means that there is a concurrent acquittal on the offence with which the accused was charged. Where the accused was charged with sexual assault and pleaded guilty to the lesser and included offence of assault, the Crown was precluded from relying on the sexual nature of the offence at a dangerous offender hearing: *R. v. Miller* (2000), 147 C.C.C. (3d) 156 (B.C.C.A.).

In *R. v. G. (D.M.)* (2011), 275 C.C.C. (3d) 295 (Ont. C.A.), the court held that it is not proper procedure for the accused to enter a plea of not guilty, allow the prosecutor to read a summary of the allegations into the record, provide no submissions or evidence in response, and invite the judge to convict based on the Crown's submissions. In absence of express agreement, the Crown's submissions were not formal admissions of fact under s. 655. Rather, this was the functional equivalent of a guilty plea and required the trial judge to undertake an inquiry to ensure that the accused understood the nature and effect of the procedure and voluntarily participated in it.

However, the same court approved a similar procedure where it was accompanied by detailed written instructions to defence counsel which clearly exhibited the accused's understanding of the uncontested facts and the potential consequences. Even though a plea of *nolo contender* is not available by virtue of s. 606(1), the procedure adopted here after a plea of not guilty was not barred by statute or common law principle, and did not cause a miscarriage of justice or lead to an unreliable verdict: *R. v. P. (R.)* (2013), 295 C.C.C. (3d) 28 (Ont. C.A.), leave to appeal to S.C.C. refused 2013 CarswellOnt 7980.

Grounds for withdrawing plea – An accused person seeking to withdraw a guilty plea on the basis that he or she was unaware of legally relevant consequences at the time of the plea must establish subjective prejudice. Therefore, the accused must file an affidavit establishing a reasonable possibility that he or she would have either: (1) opted for a trial and pleaded not guilty; or (2) pleaded guilty, but with different conditions. However, the accused need not show a viable defence to the charge: *R. v. Wong* (2018), 364 C.C.C. (3d) 1 (S.C.C.).

On appeal the accused was permitted to withdraw his guilty plea and a new trial was ordered where a statement by the trial judge may have been construed by the accused as meaning he was liable as a party to the offence though he was only present. Further, on the facts as disclosed by the Crown there was no evidence that would make the accused a party to the offence and the trial judge having heard the facts was under a duty to stop the proceedings and permit a change of plea: *R. v. Voorwinde* (1975), 29 C.C.C. (2d) 413 (B.C.C.A.).

In *R. v. Hansen* (1977), 37 C.C.C. (2d) 371 (Man. C.A.) (3:2), the accused on appeal was permitted to withdraw his plea of guilty to second degree murder and a new trial was ordered where evidence adduced on the appeal showed that the accused was in a disturbed state of mind at the time and was under the false impression that if he did not plead guilty the Crown would proceed on a charge of first degree murder.

A plea of guilty must always be a free and voluntary act by the accused himself, untainted by any threats or promises to induce the accused to admit that he committed the offence when he does not wish or intend to do so. While counsel has a duty to advise and this advice may sometimes have to be firmly given, counsel has no right to pressure the accused into pleading guilty: *R. v. Lamoureux* (1984), 13 C.C.C. (3d) 101 (Que. C.A.).

The accused was allowed to withdraw his guilty plea on appeal where it was shown that he pleaded guilty to avoid spending a week in jail awaiting trial after he was remanded in custody after failing to appear for the original trial date: *R. v. Cesari* (1986), 50 C.R. (3d) 93 (Que. C.A.).

The court allowed a guilty plea to be withdrawn on appeal where the accused was able to show that his decision was based on a misapprehension of audiotape disclosure by his counsel, which counsel had only listened to on the morning of the plea. Counsel's mishearing of a key passage had led him to the erroneous conclusion that a Charter challenge to the admissibility of the evidence against the accused would be fruitless. Had the true state of affairs been communicated to the appellant, there was a realistic likelihood that he would have run the risk of a trial: *R. v. Henry* (2011), 277 C.C.C. (3d) 293 (Ont. C.A.).

Where the accused pleaded guilty to dangerous driving without understanding that his driver's licence would be suspended indefinitely pursuant to provincial law, the plea was found to be uninformed: *R. v. Quick* (2016), 128 W.C.B. (2d) 100, [2016] O.J. No. 582 (C.A.).

It is not a ground for allowing an accused on appeal to withdraw his guilty plea that the sentence imposed by the trial judge was substantially greater than the submission by Crown and defence counsel, there being no evidence that the accused did not understand the charges nor any evidence that the plea was equivocal: *R. v. Rubenstein* (1987), 41 C.C.C. (3d) 91 (Ont. C.A.).

It was not a valid ground for withdrawal of a guilty plea that, subsequent to the plea, the co-accused was acquitted at a trial where the facts adduced at the plea indicated that the appellant was convicted as a principal. The acquittal of the co-accused determined nothing in respect of the appellant's conviction: *R. v. Hick*, [1991] 3 S.C.R. 383, 67 C.C.C. (3d) 573.

The limited cognitive capacity test, as applied in fitness determinations, is an appropriate standard to assess whether a mental disorder affected the voluntariness of a plea. In this case, the accused, who was suffering from depression, nonetheless met the requisite voluntariness threshold as he understood the process and made a conscious volitional decision that he considered appropriate: *R. v. W. (M.A.)* (2008), 237 C.C.C. (3d) 560 (Ont. C.A.).

Appeal from refusal to traverse trial – There is no right of appeal from a refusal to traverse a trial: *R. v. Lahosky* (1972), 7 C.C.C. (2d) 407 (Man. C.A.).

Plea of guilty to included or other offence [subsec. (4)] – Where an accused pleads guilty to a lesser count the court may proceed with the trial of the more serious count, and if he is acquitted on that count, can sentence him on the plea of guilty: *R. v. St. Jean* (1970), 15 C.R.N.S. 194 (Que. C.A.). *Contra: R. v. MacDonald* (1974), 21 C.C.C. (2d) 87 (Ont. C.A.), affd [1977] 2 S.C.R. 832, 34 C.C.C. (2d) 1, where it was held that once the guilty plea to the included offence is not accepted the only plea that is deemed to have been made is that of not guilty of the primary offence.

During a joint trial for murder the trial judge may accept a plea of guilty to manslaughter from one or more of the accused, directing a verdict in respect of those accused at that stage and then continuing with the trial of the other accused: *R. v. MacGregor* (1981), 64 C.C.C. (2d) 353 (Ont. C.A.), leave to appeal to S.C.C. refused 42 N.R. 349*n*.

An accused may plead guilty to and be convicted of second degree murder on an indictment for first degree murder without intervention of a jury: *R. v. Bennett*, [1982] 2 S.C.R. 582, 70 C.C.C. (2d) 575 (7:0), and without re-electing trial by judge alone pursuant to s. 473: *R. v. Luis* (1989), 50 C.C.C. (3d) 398 (Ont. H.C.J.).

The proper practice, after an accused has been given in charge to the jury and wishes to plead guilty with prosecutorial consent pursuant to subsec. (4), is for the trial judge, in the absence of the jury, to consider the appropriateness of the plea and rule whether it is acceptable. If the plea is acceptable, then the jury may be discharged and the "court" now consisting of the judge alone may record the verdict of not guilty to the offence charged and guilty to the lesser offence admitted: *R. v. Rowbotham*, [1994] 2 S.C.R. 463, 90 C.C.C. (3d) 449.

It was not an abuse of process for the Crown to attach as a condition to its agreement to a plea of guilty by the accused to the included offence of manslaughter that the accused agree to a joint submission as to sentence. This subsection recognizes the Crown's discretion to refuse a plea of guilty to an offence other than the offence charged, and the exercise of this discretion will amount to an abuse of process only in exceptional cases: *R. v. Conway*, [1989] 1 S.C.R. 1659, 49 C.C.C. (3d) 289.

Section 10(*b*) of the Charter mandates that the Crown or police, when offering a plea bargain to a detainee, tender that offer either to counsel or to the detainee while in the presence of counsel, unless the detainee has expressly waived the right to counsel: *R. v. Burlingham*, [1995] 2 S.C.R. 206, 97 C.C.C. (3d) 385.

The trial judge should, in most cases, give substantial weight to the decision of the prosecutor to accept a plea to the lesser offence, but the judge has a discretion to refuse to accept the guilty plea as where the facts relied upon support the full offence. This is not to say that the judge would be wrong in accepting a plea to the lesser offence although the facts supported the full offence where a case is made out that the result reflects a reasonable exercise of prosecutorial discretion having regard to the public interest in the effective administration of justice: *R. v. Naraindeen* (1990), 80 C.R. (3d) 66 (Ont. C.A.).

The words "any other offence arising out of the same transaction" include provincial offences: *R. v. Garnett* (1995), 15 M.V.R. (3d) 198 (B.C.S.C.).

SPECIAL PLEAS / In case of libel / Disposal / Pleading over / Statement sufficient / Exception: foreign trials *in absentia*.

607. (1) An accused may plead the special pleas of

(*a*) *autrefois acquit*,

(*b*) *autrefois convict*,

(*c*) pardon; and

(*d*) an expungement order under the *Expungement of Historically Unjust Convictions Act*.

(2) An accused who is charged with defamatory libel may plead in accordance with sections 611 and 612.

(3) The pleas of *autrefois acquit*, *autrefois convict*, pardon and an expungement order under the *Expungement of Historically Unjust Convictions Act* shall be disposed of by the judge without a jury before the accused is called on to plead further.

(4) When the pleas referred to in subsection (3) are disposed of against the accused, he may plead guilty or not guilty.

(5) Where an accused pleads *autrefois acquit* or *autrefois convict*, it is sufficient if he

(*a*) states that he has been lawfully acquitted, convicted or discharged under subsection 730(1), as the case may be, of the offence charged in the count to which the plea relates; and

(*b*) indicates the time and place of the acquittal, conviction or discharge under subsection 730(1).

(6) A person who is alleged to have committed an act or omission outside Canada that is an offence in Canada by virtue of any of subsections 7(2) to (3.1) or (3.7), or an offence under the *Crimes Against Humanity and War Crimes Act*, and in respect of which the person has been tried and convicted outside Canada, may not plead *autrefois convict* with respect to a count that charges that offence if

(*a*) at the trial outside Canada the person was not present and was not represented by counsel acting under the person's instructions, and

(*b*) the person was not punished in accordance with the sentence imposed on conviction in respect of the act or omission.

notwithstanding that the person is deemed by virtue of subsection 7(6), or subsection 12(1) of the *Crimes Against Humanity and War Crimes Act*, as the case may be, to have been tried and convicted in Canada in respect of the act or omission. R.S., c. C-34, s. 535; 1974-75-76, c. 105, s. 8; R.S.C. 1985, c. 27 (1st Supp.), s. 126, c. 30 (3rd Supp.), s. 2; 1995, c. 22, s. 10; 2000, c. 24, s. 45; 2013, c. 13, s. 9; 2018, c. 11, s. 29.

CROSS-REFERENCES

Sections 608 to 610 assist in determining when the plea of *autrefois* is made out. Also see ss. 660 to 662 which define circumstances in which an offence is included in another. For notes respecting the "defence" of *res judicata* and issue estoppel see notes under s. 613. For abuse of process, see notes under s. 579. Also see notes under s. 11(*h*) of the Charter which defines a limited constitutional protection against double jeopardy.

SYNOPSIS

This section sets out the "special pleas" which are recognized in Canadian law, *viz., autrefois acquit, autrefois convict* and pardon (subsec. (1)). Justification may be pleaded to a charge of defamatory libel (subsec. (2)).

The trial judge will decide whether such a plea should be accepted. If it is not, the accused will be called upon to plead guilty or not guilty (subsecs. (3) and (4)).

In pleading *autrefois*, an accused must state whether the earlier disposition was an acquittal, conviction or discharge and, further, where and when it occurred (subsec. (5)).

With respect to offences tried under s. 7 or the *Crimes Against Humanity and War Crimes Act*, an accused cannot plead *autrefois convict* with respect to an act or omission outside of Canada if: (a) the earlier trial was outside of Canada and the accused was not present and was not represented by counsel; and (b) the accused did not actually serve the sentence which was imposed (subsec. (6)).

ANNOTATIONS

[For notes on *res judicata* and issue estoppel, see s. 613.]

Availability where earlier charge withdrawn or quashed – In *R. v. Karpinski*, [1957] S.C.R. 343, 117 C.C.C. 241 (4:1), the accused was charged with a Crown option offence. The information had been laid over six months after the offence allegedly occurred, however the Crown elected to proceed summarily. When the accused pleaded not guilty and raised the defence that the prosecution was statute barred the magistrate permitted the Crown to withdraw the charge. In subsequent proceedings on an identical information upon which the Crown proceeded by way of indictment the special plea of *autrefois acquit* was refused. Kerwin C.J.C., and Taschereau J., held that the Crown had the right to change its election and to withdraw the information and the fact of the withdrawal did not amount to an acquittal when there was no adjudication by the magistrate. Fauteux and Abbott JJ. held that as the information showed on its face that there could be no trial by way of summary conviction the judge had no jurisdiction either to take an election or receive a plea and both were void. Therefore the issue of *autrefois acquit* never arose. Cartwright J., dissenting, held that s. 786 constituted a defence and that the withdrawal was equivalent to a dismissal which gave rise to a successful plea of *autrefois acquit*.

It was held, applying *R. v. Karpinski, supra*, that the plea of *autrefois acquit* was not available where the information upon which the Crown elected to proceed by way of summary conviction was quashed prior to plea for being laid outside the six-month limitation period. Further, the relaying of the charge and the Crown electing to proceed by indictment did not, in the circumstances, constitute an abuse of process: *R. v. Belair* (1988), 41 C.C.C. (3d) 329, 64 C.R. (3d) 179 (Ont. C.A.).

It was held in *R. v. Petersen*, [1982] 2 S.C.R. 493, 69 C.C.C. (2d) 385 (7:0), that the summary conviction court was free of jurisdictional error where the judge dismissed the charge, after the accused had entered a plea, apparently because it was not shown that several previous adjournments which exceeded eight days had been with the accused's consent as required by s. 803. In deciding he lacked jurisdiction to continue the trial the judge simply made an error in law but as long as that disposition stood it was a bar to subsequent proceedings on any new information even where the Crown proceeds by way of indictment on the relaid charge. The plea of *autrefois acquit* must be given effect on the trial of this new charge.

The erroneous decision of a trial judge, following the accused's plea of not guilty, quashing charges which, though defective, could have been cured by an amendment under s. 601, is tantamount to an acquittal and gives rise to a valid plea of *autrefois acquit* should the Crown relay the same charges: *R. v. Moore*, [1988] 1 S.C.R. 1097, 41 C.C.C. (3d) 289 (4:3).

However, where the Crown is permitted by the trial judge to withdraw the charges following a plea of not guilty, the plea of *autrefois acquit* is not available in answer to a subsequent identical charge, at least where the withdrawal flowed from purely technical considerations before any evidence was adduced: *R. v. Selhi* (1985), 18 C.C.C. (3d) 131, 32 M.V.R. 299 (Sask. C.A.), affd [1990] 1 S.C.R. 277, 53 C.C.C. (3d) 576.

Nor is the plea available where the charge is quashed prior to plea for failure to comply with s. 581(3): *R. v. Pretty* (1989), 47 C.C.C. (3d) 70 (B.C.C.A.); *R. v. D. (A.)* (1990), 60 C.C.C. (3d) 407, 75 O.R. (2d) 762 (C.A.).

The quashing of the order to stand trial and the setting aside of the indictment is not an acquittal which will support a plea of *autrefois acquit: R. v. Gould*, [1984] 5 W.W.R. 430 (Sask. C.A.).

Availability where earlier charge stayed – The plea is not available where the proceedings were stayed by the Crown part way through the first trial: *R. v. Tateham* (1982), 70 C.C.C. (2d) 565 (B.C.C.A.).

A foreign acquittal may be the basis for a plea of *autrefois acquit* provided that the accused was in jeopardy at the time of the earlier proceeding, which proceeding terminated in an acquittal or an order tantamount to an acquittal. Thus the dismissal of an indictment by a United States magistrate who had no jurisdiction to try the accused which was the equivalent of a stay of proceedings could not give rise to a plea of *autrefois* when the accused was subsequently charged with the same offence in Canada: *R. v. Frisbee* (1989), 48 C.C.C. (3d) 386 (B.C.C.A.), leave to appeal to S.C.C. refused 50 C.C.C. (3d) vi.

Availability where no evidence offered on previous trial – On a trial before a provincial court judge, once the accused has been arraigned and pleaded to the charge he has been "given in charge" and placed in jeopardy and if the Crown, because of a refusal to grant an adjournment by the court, elects then not to call any evidence, the disposition of the charge by dismissal will give rise to a successful plea of *autrefois acquit* to a subsequent identical charge. There is no requirement of a trial "on the merits" of the first charge. Generally the only requirements are that the previous dismissal must have been made by a court of competent jurisdiction whose proceedings were free from jurisdictional error and which rendered judgment on the charge: *R. v. Riddle, supra.*

Availability where jury unable to reach verdict – The accused was convicted of aggravated sexual assault but the jury was unable to reach a verdict on attempted murder arising out of the same circumstances. The trial judge refused to stay the conviction on aggravated assault pending retrial on the attempted murder but adjourned the sentencing. The plea of "autrefois convict" had no application to the new trial for attempted murder because there had not been a conviction for the purposes of autrefois convict. In context, a conviction means a complete adjudication including a verdict and sentence and there had been no sentencing for the aggravated sexual assault: *R. v. Melanson* (2001), 152 C.C.C. (3d) 375, 142 O.A.C. 184 (C.A.), leave to appeal to S.C.C. refused 158 C.C.C. (3d) vi.

Requirement of identity of charges *[Also see notes under s. 609]* – Assuming that the plea of *autrefois acquit* was available to an accused on the basis of his acquittal of the same offence in the United States, the plea was not made out in this case. The accused must show that: (1), the matter is the same, in whole or in part and (2), that the new count is the same as at the first trial or be implicitly included in that of the first trial, either in law or on account of the evidence presented if it had been legally possible at that time to make the necessary amendments. If the differences between the charges at the first and second trials are such that it must be concluded that the charges are different in nature, the plea is not appropriate. However, the mere availability of a defence in the foreign jurisdiction which is not available in Canada would not prevent the principle of *autrefois acquit* from applying. In this case, however, the Canadian charges were limited to events which occurred in Canada and the conduct referred to in the charges was different: *R. v. Van Rassel*, [1990] 1 S.C.R. 225, 53 C.C.C. (3d) 353 (7:0).

To maintain the plea of *autrefois acquit* the accused must prove that he was acquitted previously for the same offence before a court having proper jurisdiction: *R. v. Suleyman Sanver* (1973), 12 C.C.C. (2d) 105, 28 C.R.N.S. 10 (N.B.C.A.).

In *R. v. Ko and Yip* (1977), 36 C.C.C. (2d) 32, 38 C.R.N.S. 243 (B.C.C.A.), it was held that the trial judge erred in rejecting a plea of *autrefois convict* where the second trial took place on an identical indictment charging the offence of trafficking narcotics. Substantially the same evidence was led at both trials although the Crown stated in his opening at the first trial that it only involved the delivery of a sample of the larger quantity of narcotics which was to be the subject of the second trial. It was held that while these two transactions could constitute two separate offences justifying two convictions this could only be done if the Crown alleged in the indictment or in particulars properly given, the acts alleged so that the two acts could be isolated. The mere accusation by the Crown that the first trial was limited to the sample would not suffice.

In determining the validity of a plea of *autrefois acquit* the true test is whether the offence charged is substantially identical to the offence of which the accused was previously acquitted. This may be compared with the common law defence of *res judicata* where the onus is upon the accused to show that in the former proceedings there was a determination of a question of fact in favour of the accused which is vital to the present offence: *R. v. Feeley, McDermott and Wright*, [1963] 1 C.C.C. 254, 38 C.R. 321 (Ont. C.A.). Affirmed as to the first issue (5:0) and as to the second issue (3:2), [1963] S.C.R. 539, [1963] 3 C.C.C. 201.

Summary conviction proceedings – The procedure in s. 808 does not supplant the common law right to raise the special plea of *autrefois acquit* in summary conviction proceedings: *R. v. Riddle*, [1980] 1 S.C.R. 380, 48 C.C.C. (2d) 365 (7:0).

New trial – On a new trial ordered by the Court of Appeal the accused may be permitted to enter one of the special pleas: *R. v. Moore* (1980), 52 C.C.C. (2d) 202, [1980] 4 W.W.R. 511 (B.C.C.A.).

EVIDENCE OF IDENTITY OF CHARGES.

608. Where an issue on a plea of *autrefois acquit* or *autrefois convict* is tried, the evidence and adjudication and the notes of the judge and official stenographer on the former trial and the record transmitted to the court pursuant to section 551 on the charge that is pending before that court are admissible in evidence to prove or to disprove the identity of the charges. R.S., c. C-34, s. 536.

CROSS-REFERENCES

Other provisions respecting the plea of *autrefois* are set out in ss. 607, 609 and 610. Thus, see the notes following s. 607.

SYNOPSIS

This section makes the record of the proceedings at the earlier trial, including the judge's notes, admissible in the determination of a plea of *autrefois*.

ANNOTATIONS

In *R. v. Gee* (1973), 14 C.C.C. (2d) 538 (Ont. C.A.), a Crown appeal was allowed where the trial judge allowed the plea of *autrefois convict* after simply comparing the information on the first trial with the indictment presented on the second trial. It was held that the trial judge erred in allowing the plea without receiving evidence pursuant to this section on the question whether the second charge and the charge on which the accused was convicted were found in the same transaction.

WHAT DETERMINES IDENTITY / Allowance of special plea in part.

609. (1) Where an issue on a plea of *autrefois acquit* or *autrefois convict* to a count is tried and it appears

(*a*) that the matter on which the accused was given in charge on the former trial is the same in whole or in part as that on which it is proposed to give him in charge, and

(*b*) that on the former trial, if all proper amendments had been made that might then have been made, he might have been convicted of all the offences of which he may be convicted on the count to which the plea of *autrefois acquit* or *autrefois convict* is pleaded,

the judge shall give judgment discharging the accused in respect of that count.

(2) The following provisions apply where an issue on a plea of *autrefois acquit* or *autrefois convict* is tried:

(*a*) where it appears that the accused might on the former trial have been convicted of an offence of which he may be convicted on the count in issue, the judge shall direct that the accused shall not be found guilty of any offence of which he might have been convicted on the former trial, and

(*b*) where it appears that the accused may be convicted on the count in issue of an offence of which he could not have been convicted on the former trial, the accused shall plead guilty or not guilty with respect to that offence. R.S., c. C-34, s. 537.

CROSS-REFERENCES

Other provisions respecting the plea of *autrefois* are found in ss. 607, 608 and 610. Section 601 defines the circumstances in which an indictment may be amended. Sections 660 to 662 define cases in which one offence is included in another. Also see notes following s. 11(*h*) which defines a limited constitutional right against double jeopardy. For notes on *res judicata* and issue estoppel, see the notes following s. 613. Also see s. 12 which provides that where an act or omission is an offence under more than one act of Parliament unless a contrary intention appears, the person, although subject to proceedings under any of those acts, is not liable to be punished more than once for the same offence.

SYNOPSIS

This section establishes what is required to successfully advance a plea of *autrefois*.

An accused will be discharged if it is shown that: (a) the earlier trial was on a charge which was, in whole or in part, the same as the later one; and (b) he or she was in jeopardy of being convicted at the earlier trial of the offence now before the court.

ANNOTATIONS

On the second trial (this time for wounding), following an acquittal of attempted murder, the trial judge refused the special plea of *autrefois acquit*. In affirming this decision it was held in *R. v. Rinnie,* [1970] 3 C.C.C. 218, 9 C.R.N.S. 81 (Alta. C.A.), that an included offence, which can only be found by definition of the crime, or by statutory prescription, or by the inclusion of apt words of description cognate to the offence, may be pleaded to by this special plea where there has been an acquittal of the principal offence. Because of the manner in which the indictment was worded on the first trial, however, wounding was not an included offence. Furthermore, an amendment to that indictment could only have been made under s. 601 and that section did not apply to the first trial as the indictment was not defective nor was there a variance between the indictment and the evidence adduced. An amendment to include a charge of wounding would have constituted the adding of a fresh count in the indictment rather than the curing of a defect.

In *R. v. Plank* (1986), 28 C.C.C. (3d) 386, 40 M.V.R. 298 (Ont. C.A.), it was held that the accused could rely on the plea of *autrefois acquit* to a charge of care or control of a motor vehicle while his blood alcohol level exceeded .08 as a result of his earlier acquittal of the driving offence. The judge at the first trial had properly refused to amend the information to charge the separate care or control offence. While the judge erred in failing to go on to consider whether the accused should be convicted of that offence pursuant to s. 662 as an included offence, since the accused was acquitted, that acquittal stood as a final disposition of both offences.

The plea of "autrefois acquit" requires that the previous verdict arise from the same transaction on which it is later purported to try the accused. Consequently, the plea of *autrefois acquit* was not available where the accused had been previously acquitted of keeping a common bawdy house in relation to two similar operations at other locations. The "matter" before the judge on the previous trial was not the same as that before the trial judge in this case because the matters involved different factual transactions. Multiple prosecutions under the same statutory provision are permitted if each prosecution arises from a different physical act or from separate transactions: *R. v. Turmel* (1996), 109 C.C.C. (3d) 162 (Ont. C.A.).

CIRCUMSTANCES OF AGGRAVATION / Effect of previous charge of murder or manslaughter / Previous charges of first degree murder / Effect of previous charge of infanticide or manslaughter.

610. (1) Where an indictment charges substantially the same offence as that charged in an indictment on which an accused was previously convicted or acquitted, but adds a statement of intention or circumstances of aggravation tending, if proved, to increase the punishment, the previous conviction or acquittal bars the subsequent indictment.

(2) A conviction or an acquittal on an indictment for murder bars a subsequent indictment for the same homicide charging it as manslaughter or infanticide, and a conviction or acquittal on an indictment for manslaughter or infanticide bars a subsequent indictment for the same homicide charging it as murder.

(3) A conviction or an acquittal on an indictment for first degree murder bars a subsequent indictment for the same homicide charging it as second degree murder, and

a conviction or acquittal on an indictment for second degree murder bars a subsequent indictment for the same homicide charging it as first degree murder.

(4) A conviction or an acquittal on an indictment for infanticide bars a subsequent indictment for the same homicide charging it as manslaughter, and a conviction or acquittal on an indictment for manslaughter bars a subsequent indictment for the same homicide charging it as infanticide. R.S., c. C-34, s. 538; 1973-74, c. 38, s. 5; 1974-75-76, c. 105, s. 9.

CROSS-REFERENCES

Sections 607 to 609 also set out the circumstances in which the plea of *autrefois* is available and thus see notes under those sections for other cross-references.

SYNOPSIS

A plea of *autrefois* is available where the subsequent charge merely adds a statement of intention or circumstances of aggravation to the earlier charge (subsec. (1)).

A conviction or acquittal on a homicide related charge (*i.e.*, murder, manslaughter or infanticide) bars further proceedings on a subsequent homicide related charge (subsecs. (2), (3) and (4)).

ANNOTATIONS

In *R. v. Hemmingway, Ewert and Benford* (1971), 5 C.C.C. (2d) 127 (B.C. Co. Ct.), the plea of *autrefois convict* for one accused was allowed to a charge of possession of narcotics for the purpose of trafficking, the accused having been previously convicted of simple possession. The accused was found on a boat in which there were quantities of narcotics, as well he had narcotics on his person. On the plea of guilty to the simple possession charge, no evidence was led as to the quantities found on the boat. It was held that to distinguish between the materials found on the accused's person and the materials found in the boat would be an unreal distinction. There was one possession of the prohibited substances at a specific time and place.

Subsection (1) did not bar the accused from being charged with second degree murder where the victim had died after the accused had pleaded guilty to break and enter and aggravated assault of the victim, as the indictment charging murder was not substantially the same offence as the prior offences: *R. v. Hall* (1999), 134 C.C.C. (3d) 256, 242 A.R. 85 (Q.B.).

LIBEL, PLEA OF JUSTIFICATION / Where more than one sense alleged / Plea in writing / Reply.

611. (1) An accused who is charged with publishing a defamatory libel may plead that the defamatory matter published by him was true, and that it was for the public benefit that the matter should have been published in the manner in which and at the time when it was published.

(2) A plea that is made under subsection (1) may justify the defamatory matter in any sense in which it is specified in the count, or in the sense that the defamatory matter bears without being specified, or separate pleas justifying the defamatory matter in each sense may be pleaded separately to each count as if two libels had been charged in separate counts.

(3) A plea that is made under subsection (1) shall be in writing, and shall set out the particular facts by reason of which it is alleged to have been for the public good that the matter should have been published.

(4) The prosecutor may in his reply deny generally the truth of a plea that is made under this section. R.S., c. C-34, s. 539.

CROSS-REFERENCES

The offence of defamatory libel and procedure respecting the trial of that offence is set out in ss. 297 to 317. As to circumstances in which the plea of justification is necessary, see s. 612. Also note ss. 728 and 729 respecting the awarding of costs in libel cases.

SYNOPSIS

This section sets out the procedure with respect to a plea of justification on a charge of defamatory libel.

A plea of justification shall be in writing. The accused may plead that the matter published was true and that its publication was for the public benefit. The prosecutor is entitled to deny the truth of such a plea.

PLEA OF JUSTIFICATION NECESSARY / Not guilty, in addition / Effect of plea on punishment.

612. (1) The truth of the matters charged in an alleged libel shall not be inquired into in the absence of a plea of justification under section 611 unless the accused is charged with publishing the libel knowing it to be false, in which case evidence of the truth may be given to negative the allegation that the accused knew that the libel was false.

(2) The accused may, in addition to a plea that is made under section 611, plead not guilty and the pleas shall be inquired into together.

(3) Where a plea of justification is pleaded and the accused is convicted, the court may, in pronouncing sentence, consider whether the guilt of the accused is aggravated or mitigated by the plea. R.S., c. C-34, s. 540.

CROSS-REFERENCES

Provision for the plea that the defamatory matter published was true and that it was for the public benefit is set out in s. 611. The offence of defamatory libel and procedure for trial of the offence is generally set out in ss. 297 to 317. Also note ss. 728 and 729 respecting awarding of costs in libel cases.

SYNOPSIS

Unless an accused is charged with publishing a libel knowing it to be false, the truth of the alleged libel shall not be an issue, except when there has been a plea of justification. On a charge of knowingly publishing false information, evidence as to the truth of the statements may be given to negative the allegation that the accused knew that the libel was false (subsec. (1)).

In addition to justification, a plea of not guilty may be entered (subsec. (2)).

The fact that the accused pleaded justification may be considered on the question of sentence (subsec. (3)).

PLEA OF NOT GUILTY.

613. Any ground of defence for which a special plea is not provided by this Act may be relied on under the plea of not guilty. R.S., c. C-34, s. 541.

CROSS-REFERENCES

The pleas which are permitted are defined in ss. 606 to 612. Most defences including the insanity defence are not specially pleaded but are simply raised under the plea of not guilty.

ANNOTATIONS

***Res judicata* [Kienapple rule]** – In *R. v. Kienapple*, [1975] 1 S.C.R. 729, 15 C.C.C. (2d) 524 (5:4), Laskin J., for the majority stated that:

. . . the term *res judicata* best expresses the theory of precluding multiple convictions for the same delict, although the matter is the basis of two separate offences . . . Where there has been a previous conviction of an accused, whether in a former trial or on one count of a multicount indictment, issue estoppel is obviously an inappropriate term to urge against a further conviction of another offence. So, too, would be *autrefois convict* in its strict connotation; hence the utility of *res judicata*.

The proper procedure where a case calls for the application of the rule precluding multiple convictions is for the trial judge to enter a conviction for the more serious charge and enter a conditional stay with respect to the alternative charge. This stay is conditional on the final disposition of the charge of which the accused has been convicted. If the accused's appeal from conviction arising from the same delict is eventually dismissed or the accused does not appeal within the specified time then the conditional stay becomes a permanent stay and is tantamount to a verdict of acquittal. If, however, the accused's appeal from conviction is successful, the conditional stay dissolves and the appellate court, while allowing the appeal, can make an order remitting to the trial judge the count which was conditionally stayed by reason of the application of the rule against multiple convictions, notwithstanding that no appeal was taken by the Crown from the conditionally stayed count: *R. v. P. (D.W.)*, [1989] 2 S.C.R. 3, 49 C.C.C. (3d) 417 (5:0).

In *R. v. Loyer and Blouin*, [1978] 2 S.C.R. 631, 40 C.C.C. (2d) 291 (9:0), the court considered the proper application of the principle laid down in *R. v. Kienapple, supra*, and held, *inter alia*, that if the accused pleads guilty to the less serious charge the plea is held in abeyance pending the trial on the more serious charge.

In *R. v. Prince*, [1986] 2 S.C.R. 480, 30 C.C.C. (3d) 35 (7:0), the court considered at length the application of the rule in *R. v. Kienapple, supra*. That judgment may be summarized as follows: The rule against multiple convictions applies only where there is a sufficient factual nexus between the charges and a legal nexus between the offences themselves. The requirement of a factual nexus will be satisfied usually if the same act of the accused grounds each of the charges. Subject to a clearly expressed parliamentary intention to the contrary, the sufficient nexus between the offences will be satisfied if there is no additional and distinguishing element that goes to guilt contained in the offence for which a conviction is sought to be precluded by the rule against multiple convictions. As a corollary, where the offences are of unequal gravity the rule may bar a conviction for a lesser offence for which a conviction has been registered, provided that there are no distinct additional elements in the lesser offence. There are at least three ways in which sufficient correspondence between elements can be found. First, an element may be a particularization of another element. Second, there may be more than one method, embodied in more than one offence, to prove a single delict. Third, Parliament, in effect, may deem a particular element to be satisfied by proof of a different nature, not necessarily because logic compels that conclusion, but because of social policy or inherent difficulties of proof. However, in applying these criteria, it is important not to frustrate the intent of Parliament or to lose sight of the overarching question whether the same cause, matter or delict underlies both charges. Thus, there exist offences aimed at a particular evil which, in certain circumstances, contain as an element the commission of some other offence directed toward an entirely different wrong and in which case the *Kienapple* case would have no application.

The requirement of sufficient proximity between the offences will be satisfied only if there is no additional and distinguishing element contained in the offence for which a conviction is sought to be precluded by this principle. Thus conviction of an accused for both break and enter and commit robbery and attempted murder was not barred by the rule in *Kienapple*: *R. v. Wigman*, [1987] 1 S.C.R. 246, 33 C.C.C. (3d) 97 (6:0).

The doctrine precluding multiple convictions for the same cause or matter does not preclude an accused's conviction for conspiracy to traffic in narcotics and trafficking in narcotics although the latter transaction was one of several overt acts relied upon by the Crown to prove the conspiracy: *R. v. Sheppe*, [1980] 2 S.C.R. 22, 51 C.C.C. (2d) 481 (7:0).

The rule against multiple convictions did not preclude a conviction for extortion and sexual assault where the accused had extorted sexual activity by threatening to reveal nude photos of the complainants as the convictions arose out of different factual transactions: *R. v. Davis*, [1999] 3 S.C.R. 759, 139 C.C.C. (3d) 193.

This doctrine does not preclude conviction for obstruction of a peace officer in the execution of his duty where the obstruction is based on the accused's conduct in attempting to conceal narcotics when searched by the police. The obstruction constitutes a separate act from that of possession of narcotics: *R. v. Bennett* (1996), 108 C.C.C. (3d) 175 (Que. C.A.).

The rule against multiple convictions does not preclude conviction for criminal negligence causing death and impaired driving causing death. Intoxication is not required to establish criminal negligence causing death and the accused could be found guilty of criminal negligence causing death because of evidence other than intoxication, such as speed: *R. v. Plante* (1997), 120 C.C.C. (3d) 323, 33 M.V.R. (3d) 235 (Que. C.A.).

Issue estoppel – In *R. v. Gushue*, [1980] 1 S.C.R. 798, 50 C.C.C. (2d) 417 (7:0), the accused had previously been acquitted of murder which had occurred in the course of a robbery. The accused testified that he did not shoot the deceased. He later confessed to the killing and was charged with robbery and perjury; and later, under s. 136, for giving contradictory evidence as the result of an admission under oath at the preliminary hearing. The court held that issue estoppel is available in criminal proceedings in Canada (unlike in Britain: *D.P.P. v. Humphreys,* [1976] 2 All E.R. 497 (H.L.)), but the doctrine did not apply in this case. As to the s. 124 charge and the perjury charge it was held that unless the subsequent prosecution is an attempt by the Crown to retry the accused on the original charge then the preferable policy is to exclude issue estoppel. That was not the case here since, *inter alia,* the Crown could rely on the accused's own statements made subsequent to the acquittal. As to the robbery charge the court held that only if a finding in the accused's favour on the relevant issue at the first trial was the only rational explanation of the jury's verdict can issue estoppel avail. In this case the court from examining the charge to the jury considered that a finding that the accused did not participate in the robbery was not necessary for the acquittal on the murder charge.

In the subsequent case *R. v. Grdic*, [1985] 1 S.C.R. 810, 19 C.C.C. (3d) 289 (5:4), the court upheld the defence of issue estoppel to a perjury charge arising out of the accused's testimony at his own trial on a motor vehicle offence of which he was acquitted. An acquittal even if only by reason of the trier of fact having a reasonable doubt is equivalent to a finding of innocence, and any issue the resolution of which had to be in favour of the accused as a prerequisite to the acquittal is irrevocably deemed to have been found conclusively in his favour. While fraud, including perjury, is an exception to the application of issue estoppel, the Crown is not entitled to merely relitigate the issues at the first trial and therefore a subsequent perjury charge must be founded on additional evidence. This additional evidence must, however, be evidence which was not available to the Crown at the first trial using reasonable diligence. In this case, the accused had relied on the defence of alibi at the first trial and was acquitted. On the perjury charge the Crown called the same evidence and several other police officers to establish that the accused was driving the vehicle at the time of the motor vehicle offence. This evidence was available at the first trial by exercise of reasonable diligence and could have been called at the first trial in rebuttal.

Issue estoppel does have application in criminal law. Issue estoppel does not prevent the Crown from leading evidence on any issue raised in a previous trial resulting in an acquittal. It does preclude the Crown from adducing evidence that is inconsistent with determinations of issues which were finally resolved in the accused's favour at a previous trial, on the basis of either a positive factual finding or reasonable doubt. The accused bears the onus in establishing that the issue has been conclusively decided in her or her favour: *R. v. Mahalingan*, [2008] 3 S.C.R. 316, 237 C.C.C. (3d) 417.

Where the prior proceeding was before a jury, the question is whether a finding in favour of the accused was logically necessary to the verdict of acquittal, not whether the general circumstances of the case tend to indicate that the jury resolved the issue in favour of the accused. Further, a factual finding made by a sentencing judge following a jury trial does not bind a judge sitting on a subsequent motion based on issue estoppel: *R. v. Punko*, [2012] 2 S.C.R. 396, 284 C.C.C. (3d) 285.

The fact that an alleged co-conspirator had previously been acquitted of the charge did not create an issue estoppel preventing the Crown from treating him as an unindicted co-conspirator and attempting to adduce his out-of-court statements under the co-conspirator exception to the hearsay rule: *R. v. Tran* (2014), 316 C.C.C. (3d) 270 (B.C.C.A.).

In *R. v. Smith* (1997), 119 C.C.C. (3d) 547, 9 C.R. (5th) 337 (Ont. C.A.), supp. reasons 119 C.C.C. (3d) 547 at p. 560 (Ont. C.A.), the court held that issue estoppel and *res judicata* should be narrowly applied in the context of criminal litigation. Accordingly, where the accused had been acquitted of public mischief for falsely reporting a vehicle stolen, the principles of *res judicata* and issue estoppel did not prevent his trial on five charges of perjury which related to collateral questions of fact that had been canvassed at the accused's public mischief trial. The acquittal in respect of the mischief charge cannot be extended by inference to a finding in favour of the accused on collateral matters.

In *R. v. Wright,* [1965] 3 C.C.C. 160, 50 D.L.R. (2d) 498 (Ont. C.A.), the accused had previously been acquitted of conspiracy to commit bribery and convicted of conspiracy to effect an unlawful purpose. It was held that the combined effect of these verdicts was to create an estoppel against the Crown with respect to charges for the substantive offences of bribery. In this case it was admitted by the Crown that there was only one conspiracy. As the jury found this was not a conspiracy to commit bribery but was a conspiracy to effect an unlawful purpose all the elements of the charges in the substantive counts were *res judicata.*

In *R. v. Quinn* (1905), 10 C.C.C. 412, 11 O.R. 242 (C.A.), the defence of *res judicata* was allowed to a charge of perjury following the accused's acquittal on a charge of personation. In that case the accused allegedly impersonated another at a polling station which gave rise to the personation charge and also at the same time swore an oath of identity, giving rise to the perjury charge. The majority held that while *autrefois acquit* was not available the common law defence of *res judicata* was a bar to conviction on the second charge. In this case the main issue was identity but the acquittal in the first case established that it was not the accused who had committed the personation and this had become *res judicata* as between the Crown and the accused. The issue of identity having been determined adversely to the Crown by the decision in the first case, while that decision stood it was not open to the Crown to have it tried a second time.

An acquittal on a charge of perjury did not gives rise to issue estoppel to a charge of attempting to obstruct justice contrary to s. 139 although the giving of false evidence was common to both charges. The jury could well have acquitted on the perjury charge, although they found that the accused's testimony was false, because of the absence of corroboration which is required as a matter of law (s. 133) for a conviction for perjury, but not attempting to obstruct justice: *R. v. Moore* (1980), 52 C.C.C. (2d) 202 (B.C.C.A.).

A decision declining to revoke a conditional sentence is not a final decision capable of giving rise to the operation of *issue estoppel* in a subsequent criminal trial: *R. v. Thompson* (2014), 305 C.C.C. (3d) 218 (Ont. C.A.), leave to appeal to S.C.C. refused 2014 CarswellOnt 13166.

Interlocutory rulings – The doctrine of *res judicata* does not operate so as to preclude the Crown from relitigating the admissibility of a confession held inadmissible in a previous trial of the accused on another charge, or ruled inadmissible at a preliminary inquiry: *R. v. Duhamel*, [1984] 2 S.C.R. 555, 15 C.C.C. (3d) 491 (5:0).

Availability at preliminary inquiry – The defence of *res judicata* and the special pleas of *autrefois* are not available at the preliminary hearing stage: *R. v. Schmidt* (1984), 10 C.C.C. (3d) 564, 44 O.R. (2d) 777 (C.A.), affd on other grounds [1987] 1 S.C.R. 500, 33 C.C.C. (3d) 193.

---

614. [*Repealed* (with heading), 1991, c. 43, s. 3.]

Transitional provision

1991, c. 43, s. 10 provides as follows:

10. (1) Any order for the detention of an accused or accused person made under section 614, 615 or 617 of the *Criminal Code* or section 200 or 201 of the *National Defence Act*, as those sections read immediately before the coming into force of section 3 or 18 of this Act, shall continue in force until the coming into force of section 672.64 of the *Criminal Code*, subject to any order made by a court or Review Board under section 672.54 of the *Criminal Code*.

(2) The Review Board of a province shall, within twelve months after the coming into force of this section, review the case of every person detained in custody in the province by virtue of an order of detention referred to in subsection (1).

615. [*Repealed*, 1991, c. 43, s. 3.]

Transitional provision

1991, c. 43, s. 10 provides as follows:

10. (1) Any order for the detention of an accused or accused person made under section 614, 615 or 617 of the *Criminal Code* or section 200 or 201 of the *National Defence Act*, as those sections read immediately before the coming into force of section 3 or 18 of this Act, shall continue in force until the coming into force of section 672.64 of the *Criminal Code*, subject to any order made by a court or Review Board under section 672.54 of the *Criminal Code*.

(2) The Review Board of a province shall, within twelve months after the coming into force of this section, review the case of every person detained in custody in the province by virtue of an order of detention referred to in subsection (1).

616. [*Repealed*, 1991, c. 43, s. 3.]

617. [*Repealed*, 1991, c. 43, s. 3.]

Transitional provision

1991, c. 43, s. 10 provides as follows:

10. (1) Any order for the detention of an accused or accused person made under section 614, 615 or 617 of the *Criminal Code* or section 200 or 201 of the *National Defence Act*, as those sections read immediately before the coming into force of section 3 or 18 of this Act, shall continue in force until the coming into force of section 672.64 of the *Criminal Code*, subject to any order made by a court or Review Board under section 672.54 of the *Criminal Code*.

(2) The Review Board of a province shall, within twelve months after the coming into force of this section, review the case of every person detained in custody in the province by virtue of an order of detention referred to in subsection (1).

618. [*Repealed*, 1991, c. 43, s. 3.]

619. [*Repealed*, 1991, c. 43, s. 3.]

Organizations

APPEARANCE BY ATTORNEY.

620. Every organization against which an indictment is filed shall appear and plead by counsel or agent. R.S., c. C-34, s. 548; 1997, c. 18, s. 70; 2003, c. 21, s. 11.

CROSS-REFERENCES

The terms "counsel" and "organization" are defined in s. 2. Pursuant to s. 621, where an indictment has been filed against an organization, the clerk of the court is to cause notice of the indictment to be served on the organization. Service on an organization is effected pursuant to s. 703.2. Punishment of an organization is by way of probation (s. 732.1(3.1)) and/or a fine pursuant to s. 735. Enforcement of fines on organizations is provided for in ss. 735(2) and 734.6. The organization also appears by counsel or agent at a preliminary inquiry pursuant to s. 538 and for trial by provincial court judge pursuant to s. 556 and indictable matters similarly with respect to summary conviction proceedings, see s. 800(3). Where the organization fails to appear then the procedure is as set out in s. 622. Where the organization appears and pleads to the indictment or a plea of not guilty is entered then the court shall proceed with the trial of an indictment pursuant to s. 623.

NOTICE TO ORGANIZATION / Contents of notice.

621. (1) The clerk of the court or the prosecutor may, where an indictment is filed against an organization, cause a notice of the indictment to be served on the organization.

(2) A notice of an indictment referred to in subsection (1) shall set out the nature and purport of the indictment and advise that, unless the organization appears on the date set out in the notice or the date fixed under subsection 548(2.1), and enters a plea, a plea of not guilty will be entered for the accused by the court, and that the trial of the indictment will be proceeded with as though the organization had appeared and pleaded. R.S., c. C-34, s. 549; 1997, c. 18, s. 71; 2003, c. 21, s. 11.

CROSS-REFERENCES

"Clerk of the court", "counsel", "organization" and "prosecutor" are defined in s. 2. An organization appears by counsel or agent pursuant to s. 620. Procedure where the organization does not appear pursuant to the notice referred to in this section is set out in s. 622. Where the organization appears and pleads or a plea of not guilty is entered pursuant to s. 622 then the trial proceeds as directed by s. 623. Upon conviction, the organization is fined in accordance with s. 735 and/or placed on probation (s. 732.1(3.1)). Service upon an organization is effected pursuant to s. 703.2.

SYNOPSIS

This section sets out a notice requirement where an organization is to be prosecuted on indictment, and specifies that the organization must be advised in the notice of the provisions of s. 622, which deals with default of appearance.

PROCEDURE ON DEFAULT OF APPEARANCE.

622. Where an organization does not appear in accordance with the notice referred to in section 621, the presiding judge may, on proof of service of the notice, order the clerk of the court to enter a plea of not guilty on behalf of the organization, and the plea has the same force and effect as if the organization had appeared by its counsel or agent and pleaded that plea. R.S., c. C-34, s. 550; 1997, c. 18, s. 72; 2003, c. 21, s. 11.

CROSS-REFERENCES

"Clerk of the court", "counsel" and "organization" are defined in s. 2. An organization appears and pleads by counsel or agent pursuant to s. 620. Service on an organization is effected in accordance with s. 703.2. By virtue of s. 623, where a plea of not guilty is entered pursuant to this section, the court shall proceed with the trial. Upon conviction, an organization is fined in accordance with the provisions of s. 735, which fine may be enforced pursuant to s. 734.6.

SYNOPSIS

This section provides that where an organization being prosecuted on indictment fails to appear and plead within the time specified in the notice referred to in s. 621, on proof of service, a plea of not guilty will be entered on the organization's behalf and the trial will proceed as if the organization had appeared and pleaded.

TRIAL OF ORGANIZATION.

623. Where an organization appears and pleads to an indictment or a plea of not guilty is entered by order of the court under section 622, the court shall proceed with the trial of the indictment and, where the organization is convicted, section 735 applies. R.S., c. C-34, s. 551; 1995, c. 22, s. 10; 2003, c. 21, s. 11.

CROSS-REFERENCES

"Organization" is defined in s. 2. An organization appears by counsel or agent by virtue of s. 620. After an indictment has been filed against an organization, the clerk of the court must cause a notice of indictment to be served on the organization. Section 735 provides that an organization is punished by way of a fine which may be enforced pursuant to s. 734.6. An organization may also be placed on probation (s. 732.1(3.1)). Note s. 727(4) which provides that where the trial proceeds pursuant to this section but the organization has not appeared or pleaded then the court may, whether or not the organization was notified that a greater punishment would be sought by reason of a previous conviction, make inquiries and hear evidence with respect to previous convictions of the organization and, if any such conviction is proved, may impose a greater punishment by reason thereof. Service on an organization is effected in accordance with s. 703.2.

SYNOPSIS

This section notes that s. 735 applies to the trial of an organization, regardless of whether the organization appears and pleads or a plea is entered under s. 622. Section 735 provides for a fine in lieu of imprisonment for an organization, with no maximum, except where otherwise provided, where the conviction is for an indictable offence.

Record of Proceedings

HOW RECORDED / Record of proceedings.

624. (1) It is sufficient, in making up the record of a conviction or acquittal on an indictment, to copy the indictment and the plea that was pleaded, without a formal caption or heading.

(2) The court shall keep a record of every arraignment and of proceedings subsequent to arraignment. R.S., c. C-34, s. 552.

CROSS-REFERENCES

The term "indictment" is defined in s. 2. Note s. 667 which sets out the procedure for proving a previous conviction through a certificate of that conviction. Pursuant to s. 625, where it is necessary to draw up a formal record of proceedings in which the indictment has been amended, the record shall be drawn up in the form in which the indictment remained after the amendment without reference to the fact that the indictment was amended. The power to amend is found in s. 601.

SYNOPSIS

The formal record of a conviction or acquittal may be made by copying the indictment and plea and the same need not have a formal heading (subsec. (1)). A record is required to be kept of the arraignment and all subsequent proceedings (subsec. (2)).

FORM OF RECORD IN CASE OF AMENDMENT.

625. Where it is necessary to draw up a formal record in proceedings in which the indictment has been amended, the record shall be drawn up in the form in which the indictment remained after the amendment, without reference to the fact that the indictment was amended. R.S., c. C-34, s. 553.

CROSS-REFERENCES

The term "indictment" is defined in s. 2. Provision for amendment of an indictment is made in ss. 590, 591 and, in particular, s. 601.

SYNOPSIS

This section provides that, if the indictment is amended, the formal record shall reflect only the amended version, and not the fact that there was an amendment.

Pre-hearing Conference

PRE-HEARING CONFERENCE / Mandatory pre-trial hearing for jury trials.

625.1 (1) Subject to subsection (2), on application by the prosecutor or the accused or on its own motion, the court, or a judge of the court, before which, or the judge, provincial court judge or justice before whom, any proceedings are to be held may order that a conference between the prosecutor and the accused or counsel for the accused, to be presided over by the court, judge, provincial court judge or justice, be held prior to the proceedings to consider the matters that, to promote a fair and expeditious hearing, would be better decided before the start of the proceedings, and other similar matters, and to make arrangements for decisions on those matters.

(2) In any case to be tried with a jury, a judge of the court before which the accused is to be tried shall, before the trial, order that a conference between the prosecutor and the accused or counsel for the accused, to be presided over by a judge of that court, be held in accordance with the rules of court made under sections 482 and 482.1 to consider any matters that would promote a fair and expeditious trial. R.S.C. 1985, c. 27 (1st Supp.), s. 127; 1997, c. 18, s. 73; 2002, c. 13, s. 50.

CROSS-REFERENCES

The terms "provincial court judge", "justice", "prosecutor" are defined in s. 2.

SYNOPSIS

To facilitate the expeditious hearing of trials, a judge, with the consent of the parties, may order a pre-trial conference. Either the Crown, the defence or the judge may initiate the motion for such a meeting. Conferences are mandatory for all jury trials.

Courts have the authority to promolgate rules in this regard.

ANNOTATIONS

A pre-hearing conference judge does not have the jurisdiction to review Crown disclosure decisions or to order disclosure: *R. v. S. (S.S.)* (1999), 136 C.C.C. (3d) 477 (Ont. S.C.J.).

The fact that a pre-trial conference has been held in accordance with subsec. (2) does not provide any basis for the trial court interfering with the proper exercise of prosecutorial discretion. Thus, the trial judge erred in entering a stay of proceedings when the Crown preferred two new indictments to replace the single indictment that was before the court at the time of the pre-trial conference. Crown counsel was not bound to apply to the court to sever the joint indictment: *R. v. Derksen* (1999), 140 C.C.C. (3d) 184 (Sask. C.A.), leave to appeal to S.C.C. refused 142 C.C.C. (3d) vi.

No appeal lies from the decision of the judge setting aside the order: *R. v. Derksen, supra*.

Juries

QUALIFICATION OF JURORS / No disqualification based on sex.

626. (1) A person who is qualified as a juror according to, and summoned as a juror in accordance with, the laws of a province is qualified to serve as a juror in criminal proceedings in that province.

(2) Notwithstanding any law of a province referred to in subsection (1), no person may be disqualified, exempted or excused from serving as a juror in criminal proceedings on the grounds of his or her sex. R.S., c. C-34, s. 554; 1972, c. 13, s. 46; R.S.C. 1985, c. 27 (1st Supp.), s. 128.

CROSS-REFERENCES

The precedure for selecting a jury is found in ss. 629 to 644. Note s. 530 which provides for an order that the accused be tried by a jury which speaks the official language of the accused or speaks both official languages.

Note s. 670 which provides that judgment shall not be stayed or reversed after verdict on an indictment by reason of any irregularity in the summoning or empanelling of the jury or for the reason that a person who served on the jury was not returned as a juror by a sheriff or other officer. Under s. 671, no omission to observe the directions contained in any Act with respect to the qualification, the preparation of the jurors book, the selecting of jury lists or the drafting of panels from the jury lists is a ground for impeaching or quashing a verdict rendered in criminal proceedings.

SYNOPSIS

This section states that jurors in criminal proceedings are qualified if they are qualified and summoned as jurors under the laws of the relevant province. No person may be disqualified, exempted or excused as a juror on the grounds of gender.

ANNOTATIONS

None of ss. 15, 25 nor 27 of the *Canadian Charter of Rights and Freedoms*, which refer respectively to equality and aboriginal rights and Canada's multicultural heritage, entitle an accused to a jury composed entirely or proportionately of persons belonging to the same race as the accused, in this case, native Indians: *R. v. Kent, Sinclair and Gode* (1986), 27 C.C.C. (3d) 405 (Man. C.A.).

The accused's right to a representative jury roll as guaranteed by s. 11 of the Charter was not violated by provincial legislation which made non-citizens ineligible to serve as jurors. The right to a representative jury roll is not absolute in the sense that the accused is entitled to a roll representative of all the many groups that make up Canadian society. What is required is a process that provides a platform for the selection of a competent and impartial petit jury, ensures confidence in the jury's verdict, and contributes to the community's support for the criminal justice system. Also required is a representative cross-section of society, honestly and fairly chosen. There is no characteristic that persons bring to the fact-finding process of the jury based solely on their immigration status. Exclusion of non-citizens also did not infringe the accused's rights under s. 7 of the Charter: *R. v. Church of Scientology of Toronto* (1997), 116 C.C.C. (3d) 1 (Ont. C.A.), leave to appeal to S.C.C. refused 122 C.C.C. (3d) vi.

PRESIDING JUDGE.

626.1 The judge before whom an accused is tried may be either the judge who presided over matters pertaining to the selection of a jury before the commencement of a trial or another judge of the same court. 2002, c. 13, s. 51.

CROSS-REFERENCES

The other provisions respecting replacing the trial judge are set out in ss. 669.1, 669.2 and 669.3.

SYNOPSIS

This section permits a judge other than the trial judge to preside over jury selection.

627. [*Repealed*, R.S.C. 1985, c. 2 (1st Supp.), s. 1.]

SUPPORT FOR JUROR WITH PHYSICAL DISABILITY.

627. The judge may permit a juror with a physical disability who is otherwise qualified to serve as a juror to have technical, personal, interpretative or other support services. 1998, c. 9, s. 4.

CROSS-REFERENCES

Section 153.1 creates the offence of sexual exploitation of a person with a mental or physical disability. Section 486.2 provides that, where a witness may have difficulty communicating the evidence by reason of a mental or physical disability, the presiding judge or justice may order that the witness testify outside the courtroom or behind a screen or other device that would allow the witness not to see the accused. Further, such a witness may have a support person present pursuant to s. 486.1. Sections 709 and 711 provide for the taking of commission evidence from a witness who is, by reason of physical disability arising out of illness, not likely to be able to attend at the time of the trial. Section 715.2 provides that, in proceedings for certain sexual offences, a videotape, made within a reasonable time after the alleged offence, in which the complainant describes the acts complained of, is admissible in evidence if the complainant adopts its contents and if the complainant may have difficulty communicating the evidence by reason of a mental or physical disability. Section 6 of the *Canada Evidence Act* provides that the court may order that a witness who has difficulty communicating, by reason of a physical or mental disability, be permitted to give evidence by any means that enables the evidence to be intelligible. Under s. 6.1 of the Act, a witness may give evidence as to the identity of an accused whom the witness is able to identify visually or in any other sensory manner.

SYNOPSIS

This section is part of a package of amendments to permit persons with physical disabilities to participate in the trial. Thus under this section the trial judge may permit a juror to have support services. Those services may apparently include the assistance of another person. Thus, see s. 649.

ANNOTATIONS

Despite this provision, a trial judge's decision to discharge pursuant to s. 644 a juror whose health problems seemed to compromise his ability to carry out his duties did not amount to impermissible discrimination. In any event, the accused had no entitlement on appeal to assert the rights of a juror: *R. v. Kossyrine* (2017), 348 C.C.C. (3d) 508 (Ont. C.A.).

628. [*Repealed*, R.S.C. 1985, c. 27 (1st Supp.), s. 129.]

CHALLENGING THE JURY PANEL / In writing / Form.

629. (1) The accused or the prosecutor may challenge the jury panel only on the ground of partiality, fraud or wilful misconduct on the part of the sheriff or other officer by whom the panel was returned.

(2) A challenge under subsection (1) shall be in writing and shall state that the person who returned the panel was partial or fraudulent or that he wilfully misconducted himself, as the case may be.

(3) A challenge under this section may be in Form 40. R.S., c. C-34, s. 558; R.S.C. 1985, c. 27 (1st Supp.), s. 130.

CROSS-REFERENCES

This section sets out what is commonly referred to as the challenge to the array. The challenge is to be tried by the trial judge pursuant to s. 630. Procedure for challenging individual jurors is set out in ss. 631 to 641. Note s. 670 which provides that judgment shall not be stayed or reversed after verdict on an indictment by reason of any irregularity in the summoning or empanelling of the jury or for the reason that a person who served on the jury was not returned as a juror by a sheriff or other officer. Under s. 671, no omission to observe directions contained in any Act with respect to the qualification, selection, balloting or distribution of jurors, the preparation of the jurors book, the selecting of jury lists or the drafting of panels from the jury lists is a ground for impeaching or quashing a verdict rendered in criminal proceedings.

SYNOPSIS

Either the Crown or the accused can challenge the entire jury panel, otherwise known as the array, on the grounds that improper procedures were employed by the sheriff in preparing the jury list. Challenges must be in writing and allege either partiality, fraud or wilful misconduct (*e.g.*, the deliberate exclusion of persons of a particular race or ethnic background).

ANNOTATIONS

In *R. v. Diabo* (1974), 27 C.C.C. (2d) 411 (Que. C.A.), it was held that a challenge to the array by an accused treaty Indian, based on the absence of persons from his reservation on the jury panel, was properly dismissed. The accused argued that the *Jury Act* (Que.) was inoperative by reason of the *Canadian Bill of Rights* prohibition of discrimination on the basis of race. Under the *Jury Act* only persons on the valuation role are eligible for jury duty and there are no valuation roles on the reservations. It was held that assuming the *Jury Act* was subject to the supervision of the Bill of Rights by virtue of its incorporation by reference in s. 626(1), the Act was not inoperative as the exclusion of Indians arose on the basis of geography not race.

In a similar case, *R. v. Laforte* (1975), 25 C.C.C. (2d) 75 (Man. C.A.), a challenge based on the small number of women and band Indians was held to have been properly dismissed there being no evidence of misconduct by the Sheriff in returning the panel.

When evidence came to light in the course of a trial of two native Indians that there was a policy of the sheriff to exclude Indians from all jury panels then the matter should have been investigated. Such deliberate exclusion would amount to partiality on the part of the sheriff within the meaning of this section. The trial judge not having investigated the matter, the appeal by the accused was allowed and a new trial ordered. The privative provisions of ss. 670 and 671 could not apply to preclude a new trial where there has been a failure to observe a fundamental principle of jury selection: *R. v. Butler* (1984), 63 C.C.C. (3d) 243 (B.C.C.A.).

In the absence of evidence to the contrary the doctrine of *omnia praesumuntur* applies to a statutory official such as the Sheriff in the performance of his statutory duties. The mere fact that there were no black persons on the panel summoned for a trial of two black accused on a charge of rape was not proof of partiality on the part of the Sheriff and the challenge was therefore dismissed: *R. v. Bradley and Martin (No. 1)* (1973), 23 C.R.N.S. 33 (Ont. H.C.J.). It was also held that the absence of black jurors in this case did not offend the Canadian Bill of Rights: *R. v. Bradley and Martin (No. 2)* (1973), 23 C.R.N.S. 39 (Ont. H.C.J.).

TRYING GROUND OF CHALLENGE.

630. Where a challenge is made under section 629, the judge shall determine whether the alleged ground of challenge is true or not, and where he is satisfied that the alleged ground of challenge is true, he shall direct a new panel to be returned. R.S., c. C-34, s. 559.

CROSS-REFERENCES

This section deals with trial of what is commonly referred to as a challenge to the array. The grounds upon which the jury panel may be challenged are set out in s. 629. Note, however, the saving provisions in ss. 670 to 672.

SYNOPSIS

This section provides that where a challenge to the jury panel is made under s. 629, the issue will be determined by the trial judge who shall, if he upholds the challenge, direct a new empanelment.

Empanelling Jury

NAMES OF JURORS ON CARDS / To be placed in box / Additional jurors / Alternate jurors / Cards to be drawn by clerk of court / Exception / Juror and other persons to be sworn / Drawing additional cards if necessary / Ban on publication, limitation to access or use of information.

631. (1) The name of each juror on a panel of jurors that has been returned, his number on the panel and his address shall be written on a separate card, and all the cards shall, as far as possible, be of equal size.

(2) The sheriff or other officer who returns the panel shall deliver the cards referred to in subsection (1) to the clerk of the court who shall cause them to be placed together in a box to be provided for the purpose and to be thoroughly shaken together.

(2.1) If the judge considers it advisable in the interests of justice to have one or two alternate jurors, the judge shall so order before the clerk of the court draws out the cards under subsection (3).

(2.2) If the judge considers it advisable in the interests of justice, he or she may order that 13 or 14 jurors, instead of 12, be sworn in accordance with this Part before the clerk of the court draws out the cards under subsection (3) or (3.1).

(3) If the array of jurors is not challenged or the array of jurors is challenged but the judge does not direct a new panel to be returned, the clerk of the court shall, in open court, draw out one after another the cards referred to in subsection (1), call out the number on each card as it is drawn and confirm with the person who responds that he or she is the person whose name appears on the card drawn, until the number of persons who have answered is, in the opinion of the judge, sufficient to provide a full jury and any alternate jurors ordered by the judge after allowing for orders to excuse, challenges and directions to stand by.

(3.1) The court, or a judge of the court, before which the jury trial is to be held may, if the court or judge is satisfied that it is necessary for the proper administration of justice, order the clerk of the court to call out the name and the number on each card.

(4) The clerk of the court shall swear each member of the jury, and any alternate jurors, in the order in which the names of the jurors were drawn and shall swear any other person providing technical, personal, interpretative or other support services to a juror with a physical disability.

(5) If the number of persons who answer under subsection (3) or (3.1) is not sufficient to provide a full jury and the number of alternate jurors ordered by the judge, the clerk of the court shall proceed in accordance with subsections (3), (3.1) and (4) until 12 jurors — or 13 or 14 jurors, as the case may be, if the judge makes an order under subsection (2.2) — and any alternate jurors are sworn.

(6) On application by the prosecutor or on its own motion, the court or judge before which a jury trial is to be held may, if the court or judge is satisfied that such an order is necessary for the proper administration of justice, make an order

(*a*) directing that the identity of a juror or any information that could disclose their identity shall not be published in any document or broadcast or transmitted in any way; or

(*b*) limiting access to or the use of that information. R.S. c. C-34, s. 560; R.S.C. 1985, c. 27 (1st Supp.), s. 131; 1992, c. 41, s. 1; 1998, c. 9, s. 5; 2001, c. 32, s. 38; 2002, c. 13, s. 52; 2005, c. 32, s. 20; 2011, c. 16, s. 7.

Note: S.C. 2002, c. 13, s. 52(2) replaced the portion of 631(3) after paragraph (*b*); however subsection 631(3) was previously amended by 2001, c. 32, s. 38 which re-enacted the subsection so that it read as it does above, without the portion following paragraph (*b*). This inconsistency will be corrected at a later date by the Legislature.

CROSS-REFERENCES

The term "clerk of the court" is defined in s. 2. The challenge to array referred to in this section is dealt with under ss. 629 and 630. Sections 632 to 635 and 638 to 643 set out the procedure for jury selection. Section 632 permits a judge, before the commencement of the trial, to order that a juror be excused because of personal interest in the matter, a relationship with the judge, the parties, their counsel or a prospective witness or personal hardship or any other reasonable cause. Section 633 permits the judge to direct a juror to stand by for reasons of personal hardship or any other reasonable cause. Under s. 641, those jurors may be called again if a full jury has not been selected and no names remain. The number of peremptory challenges that the accused and the prosecutor may exercise, that is a challenge where the party is not required to provide a reason, is set out in s. 634. Challenge for cause is dealt with in accordance with ss. 638 to 641. Section 642 provides a procedure for summoning further jurors where the panel has been exhausted. Note ss. 670 to 672 which set out saving provisions respecting defects in the jury selection procedure; also consider the application of s. 686(1)(*b*)(iv). Note also s. 643(3), which provides that no omission to follow the directions of this section affects the validity of a proceeding.

The trial judge who presided at the selection of the jury need not be the trial judge (s. 626.1). In accordance with s. 634(2.1), if the judge orders the selection of alternate jurors, the number of peremptory challenges is increased by one for each alternate juror. The alternate jurors attend at the commencement of the trial and are substituted if a full jury is not present. Otherwise, they are then excused pursuant to s. 642.1. If the judge decides that the jury will consist of 13 or 14 jurors in accordance with s. 634(2.01), the number of peremptory challenges is increased by one for each additional juror. Pursuant to s. 652.1, if after the charge to the jury, there are 13 or 14 jurors present, the trial judge will select the names of the one or two jurors, as the case may be, to be discharged to bring the jury down to 12 persons.

SYNOPSIS

This section sets out the general procedure followed in empanelling a jury.

Each juror's name, number and address will be on a card in a box. The clerk of the court will then proceed as follows: (1) cards will be selected at random; (2) the number, or if the judge is satisfied that the proper administration of justice requires, the name and number of each juror selected will be called out; (3) when the judge is satisfied that sufficient members of the panel have been called forward, the clerk will go through the names in the order that the cards were selected; (4) as each juror steps forward the parties will declare any challenges or, in the case of the Crown, whether it wishes to "stand aside" a person; (5) if both parties are content, then the juror will be sworn and take a seat in the jury box; (6) if the initial number of persons is not sufficient to provide a full jury, the process will be repeated as many times as is necessary. The judge may prohibit publication, broadcast or transmission in any way of the juror's identity where necessary for the proper administration of justice and may also limit access to or the use of information that could disclose the identity of a juror.

Subsection (2.1) permits the judge to have up to two alternate jurors selected. The participation of the alternate jurors is governed by s. 642.1. Subsection (2.2) provides that, if the judge considers it advisable in the interest of justice, the size of the jury may be increased to 13 or 14. In accordance with s. 652.1, the additional jurors participate in the trial until after the charge to the jury, at which time the additional jurors are discharged by the judge.

ANNOTATIONS

General – Prior to the empanelling of the jury, the Crown had improperly interfered with prospective jurors by distributing a questionnaire which asked prospective jurors for their views on various issues relevant to the case. The actions of the Crown constituted a flagrant abuse of process and interference with the administration of justice: *R. v. Latimer*, [1997] 1 S.C.R. 217, 112 C.C.C. (3d) 193.

Subsection (3) – The judge should not depart from the procedure set out in this subsection by, for example, directing the clerk to only draw four cards at a time: *R. v. Alward* (1976), 32 C.C.C. (2d) 416 (N.B.S.C. App. Div.).

Where, because of the large array required to select a jury, it is not feasible to strictly comply with the requirements of this section without causing intolerable inconvenience to potential jurors, the judge has an inherent jurisdiction to adopt a process that is consistent with the spirit of this section. Thus, it was open to the trial judge in this case to divide the array into groups of 25 and have those groups attend on successive days for the selection procedures, which included challenge for cause. The judge did not require the consent of the parties to proceed in this manner. The judge should not, however, have determined the order in which the groups of 25 attended based on the number of persons of colour in the group, albeit the judge was attempting to ensure that the black accused had access to persons of colour for their jury: *R. v. Brown* (2006), 215 C.C.C. (3d) 330 (Ont. C.A.).

The practice whereby the judge addresses a few preliminary questions to the jury panel is not a substitute for a challenge for cause and the procedure laid down in s. 640(2) which requires the determination as to partiality to be made by two triers, not the trial judge: *R. v. Guérin and Pimparé* (1984), 13 C.C.C. (3d) 231 (Que. C.A.).

EXCUSING JURORS.

632. The judge may, at any time before the commencement of a trial, order that any juror be excused from jury service, whether or not the juror has been called pursuant to subsection 631(3) or (3.1) or any challenge has been made in relation to the juror, for reasons of

(*a*) personal interest in the matter to be tried;

(*b*) relationship with the judge presiding over the jury selection process, the judge before whom the accused is to be tried, the prosecutor, the accused, the counsel for the accused or a prospective witness; or

(*c*) personal hardship or any other reasonable cause that, in the opinion of the judge, warrants that the juror be excused. R.S., c. C-34, s. 561; 1992, c. 41, s. 2; 2001, c. 32, s. 39; 2002, c. 13, s. 53.

CROSS-REFERENCES

Section 631 sets out the procedure for selecting the potential jury members. The number and order of challenges is prescribed by ss. 634 and 635 respectively. In addition to the power in the judge in this section to excuse jurors, s. 633 gives the judge the power [which formerly resided in the Crown] to stand jurors aside. Once the accused has been given in charge to the jury then the procedure for discharge of jurors is governed by s. 644. As to the procedure for replacement of jurors prior to commencement of the trial, see the notes under s. 644.

SYNOPSIS

This section codifies a practice which had developed at common law of permitting the judge to excuse potential jurors by reason of manifest bias or personal hardship. The practice at common law, which will no doubt be continued, was for the judge, prior to the commencement of jury selection, to direct a question or questions to the panel as a whole as to whether they had any connection to the parties.

ANNOTATIONS

The pre-screening procedure in which the trial judge directs questions to the jury panel to deal with cases of obvious partiality, as where the juror is related to the accused or a witness, is part of the trial and must be done in the presence of the accused: *R. v. Barrow*, [1987] 2 S.C.R. 694, 38 C.C.C. (3d) 193 (5:2).

As this initial procedure goes only to such clear-cut cases of partiality, the consent of counsel is and can be presumed. Once out of obvious situations of non-indifference, the consent can no longer be presumed and the procedure must conform to that set out in the *Criminal Code*, including the procedure for challenge for cause. The trial judge has no right to take over the challenge process by deciding controversial questions of partiality. If there exist legitimate grounds for a challenge for cause, outside of the obvious cases, it must proceed in accordance with the Code: *R. v. Sherratt*, [1991] 1 S.C.R. 509, 63 C.C.C. (3d) 193 (5:0), approving *R. v. Guérin and Pimparé* (1984), 13 C.C.C. (3d) 231 (Que. C.A.). See also *R. v. Betker* (1997), 115 C.C.C. (3d) 421, 7 C.R. (5th) 238, *sub nom. R. v. B. (A.)* (Ont. C.A.), leave to appeal to S.C.C. refused 121 C.C.C. (3d) vi, noted under s. 638.

This provision does not allow the judge to delegate the power to excuse jurors. Furthermore, potential jurors should not be excused in private as the accused and the public must be able to know the reasons for any decision to excuse. Consequently, the trial judge erred when he asked the sheriff to pre-screen additional jurors in the absence of the accused when the jury panel had been exhausted: *R. v. Mid Valley Tractor Sales Ltd.* (1995), 101 C.C.C. (3d) 253 (N.B.C.A.).

The trial judge was entitled to dismiss the juror where the triers of cause were unable to agree on a challenge for cause in respect of a prospective juror: *R. v. Gayle* (2001), 154 C.C.C. (3d) 221 (Ont. C.A.), leave to appeal to S.C.C. refused 159 C.C.C. (3d) vi.

The inquiry into hardship must occur prior to the challenge for cause process and exercise of peremptory challenges: *R. v. Douglas* (2002), 170 C.C.C. (3d) 126 (Ont. C.A.).

STAND BY.

633. The judge may direct a juror who has been called pursuant to subsection 631(3) or (3.1) to stand by for reasons of personal hardship or any other reasonable cause. R.S., c. C-34, s. 562; 1974-75-76, c. 105, s. 10; 1992, c. 41, s. 2; 2001, c. 32, s. 40.

CROSS-REFERENCES

This provision is in addition to the power in the judge under s. 632 to excuse jurors. If after the panel is exhausted but a full jury has not been sworn, then jurors who have been ordered to stand by under this section are called back in accordance with the procedure set out in s. 641.

ANNOTATIONS

The trial judge must wait until the juror's name has been drawn before the juror can be directed to stand aside under this section: *R. v. Krugel* (2000), 143 C.C.C. (3d) 367 (Ont. C.A.).

The term "any other reasonable cause" includes the subject of juror partiality and thus would permit the trial judge to stand jurors aside because of a possible connection to a witness or the accused: *R. v. Krugel, supra.*

PEREMPTORY CHALLENGES / Maximum number / If 13 or 14 jurors / If alternate jurors / Supplemental peremptory challenges / Where there are multiple counts / Where there are joint trials.

634. (1) A juror may be challenged peremptorily whether or not the juror has been challenged for cause pursuant to section 638.

(2) Subject to subsections (2.1) to (4), the prosecutor and the accused are each entitled to

- **(*a*) twenty peremptory challenges, where the accused is charged with high treason or first degree murder;**
- **(*b*) twelve peremptory challenges, where the accused is charged with an offence, other than an offence mentioned in paragraph (*a*), for which the accused may be sentenced to imprisonment for a term exceeding five years; or**
- **(*c*) four peremptory challenges, where the accused is charged with an offence that is not referred to in paragraph (*a*) or (*b*).**

(2.01) If the judge orders under subsection 631(2.2) that 13 or 14 jurors be sworn in accordance with this Part, the total number of peremptory challenges that the prosecutor and the accused are each entitled to is increased by one in the case of 13 jurors or two in the case of 14 jurors.

(2.1) If the judge makes an order for alternate jurors, the total number of peremptory challenges that the prosecutor and the accused are each entitled to is increased by one for each alternate juror.

(2.2) For the purposes of replacing jurors under subsection 644(1.1), the prosecutor and the accused are each entitled to one peremptory challenge for each juror to be replaced.

(3) Where two or more counts in an indictment are to be tried together, the prosecutor and the accused are each entitled only to the number of peremptory challenges provided in respect of the count for which the greatest number of peremptory challenges is available.

(4) Where two or more accused are to be tried together,

- **(*a*) each accused is entitled to the number of peremptory challenges to which the accused would be entitled if tried alone; and**
- **(*b*) the prosecutor is entitled to the total number of peremptory challenges available to all the accused. R.S., c. C-34, s. 563; 1992, c. 41, s. 2; 2002, c. 13, s. 54; 2008, c. 18, s. 25; 2011, c. 16, s. 8.**

CROSS-REFERENCES

The order of challenges is set out in s. 635. The procedure for challenge for cause is governed by ss. 638 to 640. For jurors who have been ordered to stand by under s. 633, see s. 641. The procedure for selecting talesmen is set out in s. 642. Jurors may be excused by the trial judge in accordance with s. 632. Section 631 sets out the procedure for drawing the names of potential jurors.

SYNOPSIS

This section prescribes the number of peremptory challenges (*i.e.*, challenges for which no reason need be given) for both the accused and the prosecutor. The number of challenges for the accused depends on the offence. Where the accused is charged with a number of offences, then the accused is only entitled to the number of challenges for the one offence which carries the largest number of challenges. The number of challenges for the prosecutor depends on the offence with which the accused is charged and the number of accused. Thus, for example, if two accused were charged with forgery and fraud under $1000 (maximum penalties 14 years and 2 years respectively), each accused would be entitled to 12 challenges and the prosecutor would be entitled to 24 challenges.

In accordance with subsecs. (2.1) and (2.2), the number of peremptory challenges is increased by one for each alternate or replacement juror to be selected.

ANNOTATIONS

This section sets out the maximum number of peremptory challenges to which the parties are entitled and the trial judge has no jurisdiction to increase the number by "restoring" challenges because, before the complete panel was chosen, a juror was discharged and replaced: *R. v. Brown* (2005), 194 C.C.C. (3d) 76 (Ont. C.A.).

This section, which limits to 12 the number of peremptory challenges of an accused charged with second degree murder, does not violate the principles of fundamental justice as guaranteed by s. 7 of the *Canadian Charter of Rights and Freedoms*, although an accused charged with first degree murder is entitled to 20 peremptory challenges. The seriousness of the charge is a valid basis upon which to distinguish accused for the purpose of allocating peremptory challenges: *R. v. Oliver* (2005), 194 C.C.C. (3d) 92 (Ont. C.A.), leave to appeal to S.C.C. refused 203 C.C.C. (3d) vi.

635. [*Repealed* (old provision), R.S.C. 1985, c. 2 (1st Supp.), s. 2.]

ORDER OF CHALLENGES / Where there are joint trials.

635. (1) The accused shall be called on before the prosecutor is called on to declare whether the accused challenges the first juror, for cause or peremptorily, and thereafter the prosecutor and the accused shall be called on alternately, in respect of each of the remaining jurors, to first make such a declaration.

(2) Subsection (1) applies where two or more accused are to be tried together, but all of the accused shall exercise the challenges of the defence in turn, in the order in which their names appear in the indictment or in any other order agreed on by them,

(*a*) in respect of the first juror, before the prosecutor; and

(*b*) in respect of each of the remaining jurors, either before or after the prosecutor, in accordance with subsection (1). 1992, c. 41, s. 2.

CROSS-REFERENCES

The number of peremptory challenges is goverend by s. 634. Procedure for challenge for cause is set out in ss. 638 to 640. Section 641 governs procedure for calling back jurors who have been stood by under s. 633.

SYNOPSIS

This section in effect prescribes that the accused and the prosecutor shall alternate in the exercise of challenges. Where there are two or more accused, then all of the accused will challenge at the same time. For example, the order of challenges will proceed as follows: Juror #1 — Accused "A", Accused "B", Prosecutor; Juror #2 — Prosecutor, Accused "A", Accused "B", etc. As to who of the accused must go first, this section provides that the accused will go in the order of the names as set out in the indictment or some other order as may be decided amongst the accused.

ANNOTATIONS

Where it is the accused who seeks to challenge jurors for cause, then he may be called upon to declare the challenge for cause first with respect to each juror. The Crown and defence would, however, alternate peremptory challenges: *R. v. Aguilera* (1993), 87 C.C.C. (3d) 474 (Ont. Ct. (Gen. Div.)).

Subsection (2), which requires co-accused to exercise their challenges in the order in which their names appear on the indictment does not violate s. 11(*d*) of the Charter: *R. v. Suzack* (2000), 141 C.C.C. (3d) 449 (Ont. C.A.), leave to appeal to S.C.C. refused [2001] 1 S.C.R. xvi *sub nom. R. v. Pennett*, 152 C.C.C. (3d) vi.

---

636. [*Repealed*, 1992, c. 41, s. 2.]

---

637. [*Repealed*, 1992, c. 41, s. 2.]

CHALLENGE FOR CAUSE / No other ground.

638. (1) A prosecutor or an accused is entitled to any number of challenges on the ground that

(*a*) the name of a juror does not appear on the panel, but no misnomer or misdescription is a ground of challenge where it appears to the court that the description given on the panel sufficiently designates the person referred to;

(*b*) a juror is not indifferent between the Queen and the accused;

(*c*) a juror has been convicted of an offence for which he was sentenced to death or to a term of imprisonment exceeding twelve months;

(*d*) a juror is an alien;

(*e*) a juror, even with the aid of technical, personal, interpretative or other support services provided to the juror under section 627, is physically unable to perform properly the duties of a juror; or

(*f*) a juror does not speak the official language of Canada that is the language of the accused or the official language of Canada in which the accused can best give testimony or both official languages of Canada, where the accused is required by reason of an order under section 530 to be tried before a judge and jury who speak the official language of Canada that is the language of the accused or the official language of Canada in which the accused can best give testimony or who speak both official languages of Canada, as the case may be.

(2) No challenge for cause shall be allowed on a ground not mentioned in subsection (1). R.S., c. C-34, s. 567; 1977-78, c. 36, ss. 5, 6; R.S.C. 1985, c. 27 (1st Supp.), s. 132; c. 31 (4th) Supp.), s. 96; 1997, c. 18, s. 74; 1998, c. 9, s. 6.

(3) [*Repealed*, 1997, c. 18, s. 74.]

(4) [*Repealed*, 1997, c. 18, s. 74.].

CROSS-REFERENCES

The terms "prosecutor" and "Attorney General" are defined in s. 2. Section 639 provides that the judge may require that the challenge be put in writing and that such challenge may be in Form 41. Under s. 639(3), a challenge may be denied by the other party to the proceedings on the grounds that it is not true. Where the ground of the challenge is that the name of the juror does not appear on the panel, the issue is to be tried by the judge pursuant to s. 640. Any other ground of challenge for cause is tried in accordance with s. 640(2) by the two jurors who were last sworn or, if no jurors have been sworn, two persons present whom the court may appoint for the purpose. Procedure for trial of the issue is then as set out in s. 640(3) and (4). Procedure for challenge to the array is set out is ss. 629 and 630, for excusing jurors in s. 632, for standing jurors by in s. 633, and for peremptory challenges in s. 634. Note the saving provisions respecting jury selection in ss. 670 to 672.

SYNOPSIS

This section specifies the bases upon which individual jurors may be challenged for cause. The grounds for such a challenge are that: (a) the juror's name does not appear on the list; (b) the juror is not unbiased; (c) the juror has previously been sentenced to death or to more than 12 months in prison; (d) the juror is an alien; (e) the juror is physically unable to properly carry out his or her duties; and (f) the juror is not proficient in the official language of the accused (see s. 530).

ANNOTATIONS

Procedure – The jury panel must be properly instructed in respect of the nature of their task with respect to a challenge for cause. They must be instructed that they are to decide the question on the balance of probabilities, that the decision had to be that of both of them, that they could retire to the jury room in order to deliberate or discuss the matter where they were and that if they could not agree within a reasonable time, they were to say so. In addition, the jury should be given assistance in understanding the meaning of partiality or acceptability and the importance of the challenge for cause process. *R. v. Moore-McFarlane* (2001), 160 C.C.C. (3d) 493 (Ont. C.A.); see also *R. v. Douglas* (2002), 170 C.C.C. (3d) 126 (Ont. C.A.).

While the first two triers were given preliminary instructions in the presence of the rest of the panel, it cannot be assumed that the subsequent triers listened to the instructions or knew to apply them. While it may not be necessary to fully instruct each trier, there was a substantial danger that at least some of the triers received virtually no instruction. In addition, the trial judge must instruct the triers as to the meaning of partiality and acceptability, that they were to decide the issue on a balance of probabilities, that the decision had to be by both of them, that they had the right to disagree and the right to retire to consider their decision: *R. v. Li* (2004), 183 C.C.C. (3d) 48 (Ont. C.A.).

In *R. v. Hubbert* (1975), 29 C.C.C. (2d) 279 (Ont. C.A.) (5:0), the court considered at length the scope of the challenge for cause and the procedure to be followed. It was held that the presumption is that a juror not disqualified by statute will perform his duties in accordance with his oath. Accordingly, the purpose of a challenge of a prospective juror for cause is to eliminate from the jury those persons who come within the categories listed therein, not to find out what type of person the prospective juror is or to aid counsel in deciding whether to exercise his peremptory challenge. The trial judge has a wide discretion in controlling the challenge process, to prevent its abuse, to ensure it is fair to the prospective juror as well as the accused and to provide that the trial is not unnecessarily prolonged by suspect challenges for cause. Possible grounds for a challenge for cause on the ground that a juror is not "indifferent between the Queen and the accused" would include prior association with the accused, direct connection with the prosecution and pre-trial publicity surrounding the case. As to the latter ground, in an extreme case the publication of the facts of a case can give rise to the degree of partiality that should lead to the right to challenge for cause, but the mere fact that the prospective juror has prior information about the case or even that he holds a tentative opinion about it does not render him partial.

Where counsel seeks to challenge for cause the challenge need not be in writing though in certain circumstances, as where the challenge may cause embarrassment to the prospective juror, it may be desirable and the trial judge may require it.

Although the challenge itself may be simply in the words of subsec. (1) and Form 41 and need not be particularized, counsel must have a reason for the challenge, and the trial judge must be made aware of it so that he may properly control the trial of the truth of the challenge. If counsel refuses to state the reason then the trial judge may refuse to permit the trial of the issue. Where the challenge is taken under subsec. (1)(*b*) and the basis for the alleged non-indifference appears "far-fetched" the judge may in his discretion require further elucidation or the tendering of evidence before permitting the trial of the issue. The other party may deny the challenge, in which case the issue is tried, admit the challenge, in which case the juror is excused, or make submissions that the ground for the challenge is not in law a valid ground of challenge for cause. For example, a challenge on the basis that the prospective juror and a prospective witness are of the same racial origin would not in law be a proper challenge.

On the trial of the issue the party challenging for cause may call the prospective juror as a witness without having to establish first through other evidence a *prima facie* case as to the truth of the challenge. The questioning of the juror is not strictly characterized as either direct or cross-examination, but it must be relevant, succinct and fair. The other party may then question the witness, or call his own witness and the challenging party may with leave call other reply evidence. The judge in his discretion may allow counsel to address the jurors and may himself "charge" them in terms he considers sufficient. If the challenge is not found to be true either party may exercise the further right of peremptory challenge and the Crown may stand the juror aside.

An appeal by the accused to the Supreme Court of Canada was dismissed, [1977] 2 S.C.R. 267, 33 C.C.C. (2d) 207*n*, in brief oral reasons. However, the court stated the procedures outlined by the Court of Appeal provides a useful guide for the trial judges.

When two triers have been called and sworn, the trial judge should explain briefly to them what is happening and what their function is. The judge should tell them they are to decide "whether the challenged juror is indifferent — that is, is impartial — between the Crown and the accused", that they are to decide the question on the balance of probabilities, that the decision must be that of both of them, that they may retire to the jury room or discuss it right where they are, and that if they cannot agree within a reasonable time, they are to say so: *R. v. Hubbert, supra.*

It is also desirable that the trial judge assist the jury in understanding the importance and purpose of the challenge for cause process and the meaning of partiality: *R. v. Moore-McFarlane* (2001), 160 C.C.C. (3d) 493 (Ont. C.A.); *R. v. Douglas* (2002), 170 C.C.C. (3d) 126 (Ont. C.A.).

However, the failure of the judge to precisely follow the guidelines in *R. v. Hubbert, supra*, in instructing the jury panel and the triers will not be fatal. On appeal where the accused alleges that the instructions were deficient, the issue to be determined is whether the circumstances of the particular case reveal a reasonable likelihood that the triers misunderstood the nature of their task and the procedure they were to follow: *R. v. Brown* (2005), 194 C.C.C. (3d) 76 (Ont. C.A.).

As the trial judge must be able to retain a reasonable degree of control over the challenge for cause procedure, there is some burden placed upon the challenger to ensure that sufficient information is provided to the trial judge so that the trial of the issue is contained within permissible bounds. There must, therefore, be an "air of reality" to the ground for the challenge. There must exist a realistic potential for the existence of partiality, on a ground sufficiently articulated in the application, before the challenger should be allowed to proceed. The right to challenge for cause is, however, an important one designed to ensure a fair trial and is not limited to extraordinary or exceptional cases. In cases of pre-trial publicity, the question is whether the particular publicity and notoriety of the accused could potentially have the effect of destroying the prospective juror's indifference: *R. v. Sherratt*, [1991] 1 S.C.R. 509, 63 C.C.C. (3d) 193 (5:0).

In *R. v. Zundel* (1987), 31 C.C.C. (3d) 97 (Ont. C.A.), leave to appeal to S.C.C. refused 61 O.R. (2d) 588, the court considered the issue of challenge for cause in a case where there had been extensive pre-trial publicity, much of it adverse to the accused. The court held that the trial judge erred in failing to permit challenge for cause and ought to have advised defence counsel that while the questions which he proposed to ask were improper, some could be rephrased so as to be the basis for a proper challenge for cause. Further, there is no prerequisite to challenge for cause on the grounds of pre-trial publicity that there had been a particular notorious episode and the fact that the accused's own conduct attracted notoriety is not sufficient to disallow the challenged. The issue is whether the particular publicity and notoriety of the accused could potentially have the effect of destroying the prospective jurors' indifference between the Crown and the accused. Whether or not there is then any evidentiary connection between the publicity and the particular juror's lack of indifference is for the triers, not the judge. There is a denial of a fundamental right to a fair trial where the accused is not allowed to challenge any number of jurors for cause when the grounds of challenge are properly specified in accordance with this section.

Grounds – Although there is a presumption that a jury pool is composed of persons who can serve impartially, challenges for cause are permitted where the accused establishes that there is a realistic potential for partiality. Evidence of widespread racial prejudice may, depending on the nature of the evidence and the circumstances of the case, lead to the conclusion that there is a realistic potential for partiality. While the potential for partiality is irrefutable where the prejudice can be linked to specific aspects of the trial, it may be made out in the absence of such links. Racial prejudice against the accused may be detrimental to an accused in a variety of ways. The link between prejudice and verdict is clearest where there is an "interracial element" to the crime or a perceived link between those of the accused's race and the particular crime. Racial prejudice, however, may also play a role in various less obvious ways. Absent specific links to the trial, it is within the discretion of the trial judge to determine whether widespread racial prejudice in the community is sufficient to give an air of reality to the challenge in the particular circumstances of each case: *R. v. Williams, infra.*

This section requires two stages of inquiry. In the first stage of inquiry to determine whether challenges for cause should be permitted, the test is whether there is a realistic potential for partiality, not whether anyone in the jury pool will in fact be unable to set aside his or her racial prejudices. The question at this stage is whether there is reason to suppose that the jury pool may contain people who are prejudiced and whose prejudice may not be capable of being set aside on direction from the judge. It is not always necessary for the accused to present evidence in respect of the first stage. Absent evidence to the contrary, where widespread prejudice against people of the accused's race is demonstrated at a national or provincial level, it will often be reasonable to infer that such prejudice is replicated at the community level. Widespread racial prejudice may be established by evidence and by judicial notice. Once a finding of fact of widespread racial prejudice in the community is made on evidence by a judge, judges in subsequent cases may be able to take judicial notice of the fact. A reasonable generous approach may be taken at the first stage of inquiry. The second stage of the inquiry requires a determination of whether the candidate in question will be able to act impartially. At this stage, the issue of how any prejudice may play out in the context of the trial comes to the forefront. The defence may question potential jurors as to whether they harbour prejudices against people of the accused's race and, if so, whether they are able to set those prejudices aside and act as impartial jurors. Alternatively, it may be concluded that the juror's beliefs are highly indicative of partiality. The challenge procedure is a summary procedure and the trial judge has a wide discretion in controlling the process to prevent its abuse, to ensure that it is fair to the prospective juror as well as to the accused and to avoid the trial being unnecessarily prolonged: *R. v. Williams*, [1998] 1 S.C.R. 1128, 124 C.C.C. (3d) 481.

Parties are entitled to adduce evidence to support a challenge for cause under subsec. (1)(*c*). Accordingly, the police were entitled to investigate whether prospective jurors had criminal records. The Crown has an obligation to disclose any positive results of such inquiries: *R. v. Yumnu* (2010), 260 C.C.C. (3d) 421 (Ont. C.A.), affd (2012), 290 C.C.C. (3d) 323 (S.C.C.). See also *R. v. Emms* (2010), 264 C.C.C. (3d) 402 (Ont. C.A.), leave to appeal to S.C.C. granted 2011 CarswellOnt 5138; *R. v. Davey* (2010), 264 C.C.C. (3d) 465 (Ont. C.A.), affd (2012), 293 C.C.C. (3d) 265 (S.C.C.).

While the trial judge permitted prospective jurors to be asked about the potential for partiality due to the accused's race, there was no error in refusing to permit broader questioning, including the potential for partiality due to the victim's ethnicity. Jury partiality requires the accused to establish that a widespread bias existed in the community and that some jurors might be incapable of setting aside this bias to render an impartial decision. If it was demonstrated that there was widespread prejudice in the community, it would be reasonable to infer that the jury pool would include some individuals that harbored such prejudice. The accused then must establish that there was a realistic possibility that such bias could not be set aside on instructions from the trial judge. While courts have taken judicial notice of the widespread existence of racism and the likelihood that anti-black racism was aggravated where the alleged victim was white, the suggestion that there was race-based sympathy for victims or partiality in favour of certain witnesses was not so notorious so as to be capable of judicial notice: *R. v. Spence* (2005), 202 C.C.C. (3d) 1 (S.C.C.).

In *R. v. Koh* (1998), 131 C.C.C. (3d) 257 (Ont. C.A.), it was held that judicial notice could be taken of the history of discrimination against visible minorities and/or racism, and that challenge for cause should be permitted when requested by any accused of a visible minority (in this case Chinese).

The trial judge did not err in refusing to permit the jurors to be challenged as to whether they would be more likely to believe the testimony of a police officer than that of an ordinary witness. These concerns could be adequately met by the question relating to racial prejudice. As a general rule, the refusal to permit such a question would not impinge upon an accused's right to be tried by an impartial jury. There are two aspects to the threshold test for partiality: attitudinal and behavioural. In satisfying the threshold test for partiality, it must be shown that individuals who might be inclined to believe the testimony of police officers over that of an ordinary witness would also not be able to set aside their bias on instructions from the judge. Apart from cases where racial prejudice is a live issue, there was no evidence from which it could be inferred that potential jurors who hold the police in high regard might not be capable of setting aside their beliefs on directions from the trial judge: *R. v. Barnes* (1999), 138 C.C.C. (3d) 500 (Ont. C.A.).

The trial judge did not err in refusing to allow jurors to be asked whether they believed that a white woman is less likely to consent to sex with an Aboriginal as opposed to a Caucasian man: *R. v. Hummel* (2002), 166 C.C.C. (3d) 30 (Y.T.C.A.).

An accused should not have to establish a realistic potential for partiality in the community if he asks for the right to challenge for cause based on race or based on other enumerated factors prohibited by s. 15 of the Charter. Such a challenge should be available to an accused as a matter of right: *R. v. Sinclair* (2009), 245 C.C.C. (3d) 203 (Ont. S.C.J.).

The nature of the charge standing alone is generally not a basis for a challenge for cause. Strong attitudes about a particular crime will rarely if ever translate into partiality in respect of an accused. A trial judge may alert the entire panel as to the nature of the charges and invite those prospective jurors who would find it too difficult to sit as a juror to identify themselves and they may be excused on the basis of personal hardship. However, the trial judge does not have any authority to prescreen prospective jurors by making opening remarks to the panel at large inviting prospective jurors to identify themselves if they felt that they might not be able to decide the case with an open, fair and impartial mind as a result of the nature of the allegations against the accused: *R. v. Betker* (1997), 115 C.C.C. (3d) 421 (Ont. C.A.), leave to appeal to S.C.C. refused 121 C.C.C. (3d) vi.

In *R. v. Find*, [2001] 1 S.C.R. 863, 154 C.C.C. (3d) 97, it was held that absent proof, the courts could not simply assume that strong beliefs and emotions about the type of offence translate into a realistic potential for partiality, grounding a right to challenge for cause on the basis of the offence with which the accused was charged. Thus, it was held that the trial judge did not err in refusing to permit the accused to challenge for cause because of the nature of the offences with which he was charged, offences involving sexual abuse of children. The case for widespread bias arising from the nature of charges of sexual assault on children is tenuous and, in any event, its link to actual juror behaviour is speculative, leaving the presumption that any bias would be cleansed by the trial process firmly in place.

The precise nature of the questions falls within the discretion of the trial judge and is to be determined in light of the circumstances of the case and evidence called on the issues. While the attitudinal and behavioural components of partiality are distinct, there is no requirement that discrete questions be allowed on each aspect and a "rolled-up" question may be sufficient: *R. v. Gayle* (2001), 154 C.C.C. (3d) 221 (Ont. C.A.), leave to appeal to S.C.C. refused 159 C.C.C. (3d) vi.

The trial judge was entitled to dismiss the juror where the triers of cause were unable to agree on a challenge for cause in respect of a prospective juror: *R. v. Gayle*, *supra*.

Absent an order under s. 530(1), language competency of potential jurors can be ascertained by the trial judge in the normal vetting process and is not a proper subject of a challenge for cause: *R. v. Leon* (2012), 283 C.C.C. (3d) 243 (Ont. S.C.J.).

Jury vetting, particularly if it went beyond eligibility criteria, raised serious concerns for the administration of justice. Any scrutiny of prospective jurors using government or police databases should be limited to criminal record checks for the purpose of determining juror eligibility under provincial legislation or acceptability under this provision. Any information obtained relevant to the selection process must be disclosed. Informal consultation with police officers should be approached with caution. The Crown should not engage in systematic consultations with police services regarding the suitability of jurors given the real risk that such inquiries could represent access to an informal database of the contacts that a juror has had with the criminal justice system. The Crown was, however, permitted to ask the opinion of someone who was part of the prosecution team, including officers, regarding concerns relating to partiality, eligibility or suitability. Provided that any relevant information was disclosed, consultation was not inappropriate. General impressions, personal or public knowledge in the community, rumours or hunches need not be disclosed. Any underlying material upon which the opinion was based, including information derived from a police officer's role as an officer or as a member of the community, must be disclosed: *R. v. Davey*, [2012] 3 S.C.R. 828, 293 C.C.C. (3d) 265.

CHALLENGE IN WRITING / Form / Denial.

639. (1) Where a challenge is made on a ground mentioned in section 638, the court may, in its discretion, require the party that challenges to put the challenge in writing.

(2) A challenge may be in Form 41.

(3) A challenge may be denied by the other party to the proceedings on the ground that it is not true. R.S., c. C-34, s. 568.

CROSS-REFERENCES

The challenge for cause is tried in accordance with s. 640.

SYNOPSIS

This section provides that challenges for cause may be required by the court to be in writing and may be in Form 41. The other party is free to argue that the grounds given for the challenge are untrue.

ANNOTATIONS

"Other party" refers to the party on the opposite side of the litigation and does not include a co-accused: *R. v. Sandham* (2009), 248 C.C.C. (3d) 46 (Ont. S.C.J.).

OBJECTION THAT NAME NOT ON PANEL / Other grounds / Challenge for cause / Exclusion order / If challenge not sustained, or if sustained / Disagreement of triers.

640. (1) Where the ground of a challenge is that the name of a juror does not appear on the panel, the issue shall be tried by the judge on the *voir dire* by the inspection of the panel, and such other evidence that the judge thinks fit to receive.

(2) If the ground of a challenge is one that is not mentioned in subsection (1) and no order has been made under subsection (2.1), the two jurors who were last sworn — or, if no jurors have been sworn, two persons present who are appointed by the court for the purpose — shall be sworn to determine whether the ground of challenge is true.

(2.1) If the challenge is for cause and if the ground of the challenge is one that is not mentioned in subsection (1), on the application of the accused, the court may order the exclusion of all jurors — sworn and unsworn — from the court room until it is determined whether the ground of challenge is true, if the court is of the opinion that such an order is necessary to preserve the impartiality of the jurors.

(2.2) If an order is made under subsection (2.1), two unsworn jurors, who are then exempt from the order, or two persons present who are appointed by the court for that purpose, shall be sworn to determine whether the ground of challenge is true. Those persons so appointed shall exercise their duties until 12 jurors — or 13 or 14 jurors, as the case may be, if the judge makes an order under subsection 631(2.2) — and any alternate jurors are sworn.

(3) Where the finding, pursuant to subsection (1), (2) or (2.2) is that the ground of challenge is not true, the juror shall be sworn, but if the finding is that the ground of challenge is true, the juror shall not be sworn.

(4) Where, after what the court considers to be a reasonable time, the two persons who are sworn to determine whether the ground of challenge is true are unable to agree, the court may discharge them from giving a verdict and may direct two other persons to be sworn to determine whether the ground of challenge is true. R.S., c. C-34, s. 569; 2008, c. 18, s. 26; 2011, c. 16, s. 9.

CROSS-REFERENCES

The grounds for challenge for cause are set out in s. 638. Pursuant to s. 639, the judge may require that the challenge be in writing and may be in Form 41. Under s. 639(3), a challenge may be denied by the other party in the proceedings on the ground that it is not true. Procedure for challenge to array is set out in ss. 629 and 630. Procedure for challenge to the array is set out in ss. 629 and 630, for excusing jurors in s. 632, for standing jurors by in s. 633, and for peremptory challenges in s. 634. Note the saving provisions respecting jury selection in ss. 670 to 672.

The procedure for selecting alternate jurors and additional jurors is set out in s. 631(2.1) and (2.2).

SYNOPSIS

This section sets out the procedures for dealing with challenges for cause (see s. 638).

A challenge based on the fact that the juror's name is not on the list is heard and determined by the trial judge (subsec. (1)).

Other challenges for cause are determined in a mini-trial. The issue will be tried by the last two jurors who have been sworn. If no jurors have been selected the judge will appoint two persons for this purpose (subsec. (2)). Subsections (2.1) and (2.2) set out the procedure for choosing the triers where it is necessary to exclude jurors during the selection process.

If the two appointed persons are unable to agree on a decision within a reasonable time the judge may discharge them and appoint two new persons to act (subsec. (4)).

It should be noted that if a challenge for cause does not succeed a prospective juror may still be peremptorily challenged.

ANNOTATIONS

The proper procedure under subsec. (2) is that the two persons appointed by the court try the challenge for cause with respect to the first two jurors. It is only after two jurors have been sworn that they replace the appointed triers. Further, by virtue of subsec. (4), where the triers are unable to agree they are to be discharged and two other triers selected. It is not proper for the judge to simply excuse the juror when the triers are unable to agree: *R. v. Brigham* (1988), 44 C.C.C. (3d) 379 (Que. C.A.).

An exclusion order made under subsec. (2.1) makes it impossible to use sworn jurors as rotating triers during the challenge for cause process because sworn jurors cannot simultaneously be excluded from the courtroom during the challenge for cause process and act as triers of the challenge. Subsection (2.2) solves that dilemma by requiring the judge, if he makes an order under subsec. (2.1), to use static triers, who do not become part of the jury. Absent an application by the accused under subsec. (2.1), the use of static triers is illegal and means that the trial court has not been properly constituted: *R. v. Noureddine* (2015), 332 C.C.C. (3d) 114 (Ont. C.A.); *R. v. Husbands* (2017), 353 C.C.C. (3d) 317 (Ont. C.A.), leave to appeal to S.C.C. refused 2018 CarswellOnt 2060.

However, trial judges retain a discretion to exclude only prospective jurors from the courtroom, while using rotating triers during the challenge for cause proceedings. Before exercising the discretion to exclude only unsworn jurors to preserve impartiality, a trial judge is entitled to insist on a sufficient reason or reasons for doing so. What is sufficient will vary from case to case: *R. v. Grant* (2016), 342 C.C.C. (3d) 514 (Ont. C.A.).

Where defence counsel's stated position could reasonably be construed as an application to exclude all jurors from the courtroom and use static triers to try the challenge for cause, the court was properly constituted despite the absence of an explicit application under subsec. (2.1): *R. v. Kossyrine* (2017), 348 C.C.C. (3d) 508 (Ont. C.A.); *R. v. Mansingh* (2017), 136 W.C.B. (2d) 16, [2017] O.J. No. 379 (C.A.).

There is no requirement that the first two triers should initially be questioned to determine their impartiality: *R. v. English* (1993), 84 C.C.C. (3d) 511 (Nfld. C.A.), leave to appeal to S.C.C. refused 87 C.C.C. (3d) vi.

Once his challenge for cause is lost the challenger may still then exercise one of his remaining peremptory challenges against a prospective juror: *R. v. Cloutier*, [1979] 2 S.C.R. 709, 48 C.C.C. (2d) 1.

The inadequacy of instructions to the jury can constitute an error of law. In this case, the trial judge was required to explain to the jury partiality and acceptability as well as an explanation of the importance and purpose of the process of challenging for cause on the basis of race: *R. v. Brown* (2002), 166 C.C.C. (3d) 570 (Ont. C.A.).

CALLING PERSONS WHO HAVE STOOD BY / Other persons becoming available.

641. (1) If a full jury and any alternate jurors have not been sworn and no cards remain to be drawn, the persons who have been directed to stand by shall be called again in the order in which their cards were drawn and shall be sworn, unless excused by the judge or challenged by the accused or the prosecutor.

(2) If, before a person is sworn as a juror under subsection (1), other persons in the panel become available, the prosecutor may require the cards of those persons to be put into and drawn from the box in accordance with section 631, and those persons shall be challenged, directed to stand by, excused or sworn, as the case may be, before the persons who were originally directed to stand by are called again. R.S., c. C-34, s. 570; 1992, c. 41, s. 3; 2001, c. 32, s. 41; 2002, c. 13, s. 55; 2011, c. 16, s. 10.

CROSS-REFERENCES

Jurors may be ordered to stand by for reasons of personal hardship or other reasonable cause by the judge under s. 633. Once the panel has been exhausted but a full jury has not been selected, then these jurors are subject to selection. They may, however, be excused by the judge under s. 632 and are subject to peremptory challenge in accordance with s. 634 or challenge for cause in accordance with ss. 638 to 640. If after the stand by jurors have been exhausted and a full jury has not been selected, then talesmen may be obtained in accordance with s. 642.

SYNOPSIS

Under subsection (1), jurors who have been stood by under s. 633 are dealt with in the same manner as the other members of the panel except that the juror cannot be stood aside again. However, if prior to a previously stood by juror being sworn other members of the panel become available, then the prosecutor may ask that their names be drawn before the jurors who have been stood aside.

ANNOTATIONS

After a number of stand asides resulting in the exhaustion of the whole panel and with one jury vacancy remaining, instead of following the predecessor to this section, the court incorrectly proceeded under s. 642(1) with the result that it was held that the appellant was not tried by a lawfully constituted jury; the curative provision, s. 643, could not be applied to such a defect because the procedure constituted an omission to follow the procedure in s. 642 which authorizes the addition of *talesmen* only where a full jury cannot be provided in spite of compliance with the provisions of this Part, including s. 641: *R. v. James,* [1969] 1 C.C.C. 278 (B.C.C.A.).

This section had no application where a full jury was sworn but it then became necessary to select a new juror because a juror had to be excused. Since the balance of the jury panel had been discharged before it became necessary to excuse the juror and before the accused had been put in the charge of the jury, it was not improper for the trial judge to instruct the sheriff to assemble talesmen and then select a new juror from among them: *R. v. Ladouceur* (1998), 124 C.C.C. (3d) 269 (Ont. C.A.).

SUMMONING OTHER JURORS WHEN PANEL EXHAUSTED / Orally / Adding names to panel.

642. (1) If a full jury and any alternate jurors considered advisable cannot be provided notwithstanding that the relevant provisions of this Part have been complied with, the court may, at the request of the prosecutor, order the sheriff or other proper officer to summon without delay as many persons, whether qualified jurors or not, as the court directs for the purpose of providing a full jury and alternate jurors.

(2) Jurors may be summoned under subsection (1) by word of mouth, if necessary.

(3) The names of the persons who are summoned under this section shall be added to the general panel for the purposes of the trial, and the same proceedings shall be taken with respect to calling and challenging those persons, excusing them and directing them to stand by as are provided in this Part with respect to the persons named in the original panel. R.S., c. C-34, s. 571; 1992, c. 41, s. 4; 2002, c. 13, s. 56.

CROSS-REFERENCES

The term "prosecutor" is defined in s. 2. This section sets out a procedure for the summonsing of talesmen where the jury panel has been exhausted.

SYNOPSIS

If the original panel has been exhausted and a full jury has not been selected the trial judge may, at the request of the Crown, direct the sheriff to summons other persons (known as "talesmen") for jury service. In carrying out this order the sheriff may notify prospective jurors by word of mouth (*e.g.*, by simply going out onto the streets adjacent to the court-house). Persons summoned in this fashion are added to the list and thereafter are dealt with in the normal way.

ANNOTATIONS

Subsection (1) requires that where the judge orders a *tales* he shall specify the number of persons the sheriff is to summon. Where that number has been exhausted and a full jury not yet selected, then before ordering that a further number of jurors be summoned the *talesman* added to the panel and directed to stand by must be called again and sworn unless challenged: *R. v. Rowbotham* (1988), 41 C.C.C. (3d) 1 (Ont. C.A.).

The approach of the sheriff in summonsing talesmen has to be one which attempts to preserve the randomness and representativeness of the jury. The sheriff should not undertake his own pre-screening of potential jurors; that authority lies with the judge. However, the sheriff has a limited discretion to refrain from serving individuals whom he is satisfied cannot attend because of prior commitments: *R. v. Blackduck* (2014), 313 C.C.C. (3d) 238 (N.W.T.S.C.), leave to appeal to S.C.C. refused 2015 CarswellNWT 17.

SUBSTITUTION OF ALTERNATE JURORS / Excusing of alternate jurors.

642.1 (1) Alternate jurors shall attend at the commencement of the presentation of the evidence on the merits and, if there is not a full jury present, shall replace any absent juror, in the order in which their cards were drawn under subsection 631(3).

(2) An alternate juror who is not required as a substitute shall be excused. 2002, c. 13, s. 57; 2011, c. 16, s. 11.

CROSS-REFERENCES

The procedure for selecting alternate jurors is set out in s. 631(2.1).

The procedure for selecting alternate jurors is set out in s. 631(2.1) and for selecting additional jurors is set out in s. 631(2.2). The distinction is that alternate jurors are used to bring the jury back up to 12 members at the commencement of the trial. If they are not needed, they are discharged. Additional jurors remain throughout the trial and are discharged only after the charge to the jury before the jury begins deliberations.

SYNOPSIS

This section allows the trial judge to use alternate jurors, selected in accordance with s. 631(2.1), to bring the jury up to 12 members at the commencement of the trial.

WHO SHALL BE THE JURY / Names of jurors / Same jury may try another issue by consent / Sections directory.

643. (1) The 12, 13 or 14 jurors who are sworn in accordance with this Part and present at the commencement of the presentation of the evidence on the merits shall be the jury to hear the evidence on the merits.

(1.1) The name of each juror, including alternate jurors, who is sworn shall be kept apart until the juror is excused or the jury gives its verdict or is discharged, at which time the name shall be returned to the box as often as occasion arises, as long as an issue remains to be tried before a jury.

(2) The court may try an issue with the same jury in whole or in part that previously tried or was drawn to try another issue, without the jurors being sworn again, but if the prosecutor or the accused objects to any of the jurors or the court excuses any of the jurors, the court shall order those persons to withdraw and shall direct that the required number of cards to make up a full jury be drawn and, subject to the provisions of this Part relating to challenges, orders to excuse and directions to stand by, the persons whose cards are drawn shall be sworn.

(3) Failure to comply with the directions of this section or section 631, 635 or 641 does not affect the validity of a proceeding. R.S., c. C-34, s. 572; 1992, c. 41, s. 5; 2001, c. 32, s. 42; 2002, c. 13, s. 58; 2011, c. 16, s. 12.

CROSS-REFERENCES

The terms "prosecutor" and "indictment" are defined in s. 2. Sections 670 to 672 set out other saving provisions with respect to jury selection and other defects in the jury process. Also consider the application of s. 686(1)(*b*)(iv). A juror may be discharged pursuant to s. 644. Ordinarily jurors are not required to be sequestered until time for them to retire to consider their verdict pursuant to s. 647.

If the jury has been increased pursuant to s. 631(2.2) to 13 or 14 members, after the charge to the jury, s. 652.1 provides that the number of jurors will be reduced to 12 by the judge discharging the one or two extra jurors.

SYNOPSIS

A jury panel or list is often prepared for use in a number of trials. Local practice governs whether a juror will be available for service on more than one trial as is permitted by subsec. (1.1)

Subsection (1) provides that that the jury (usually 12 persons, but can be 13 or 14 persons in accordance with s. 631(2.2)), is the jury to try the case.

Subsection (2) permits the court, with the consent of the parties, to try another matter with all or some of the jurors who have already been sworn. In practice, this provision is not utilized.

Subsection (3) provides that certain irregularities in the selection process will not affect the validity of the proceedings.

ANNOTATIONS

Subsection (3) – This provision and the predecessor of s. 686(1)(*b*)(iii) were applied where, through inadvertence, the balance of the jury was selected from persons originally stood aside despite the fact there remained a member of the panel who had not yet been called: *R. v. McLachlan* (1923), 41 C.C.C. 249, 56 N.S.R. 413 (S.C.), leave to appeal to P.C. 42 C.C.C. 86, [1924] 1 D.L.R. 1109. Also see: *R. v. James*, [1969] 1 C.C.C. 278 (B.C.C.A.), noted under s. 641.

This subsection applies only to irregularities and has no application where the error is such that the accused has been deprived of a statutory right, or where the error deprived the accused of the right to a trial by a jury lawfully constituted: *R. v. Rowbotham* (1988), 41 C.C.C. (3d) 1 (Ont. C.A.).

DISCHARGE OF JUROR / Replacement of juror / Trial may continue.

644. (1) Where in the course of a trial the judge is satisfied that a juror should not, by reason of illness or other reasonable cause, continue to act, the judge may discharge the juror.

(1.1) A judge may select another juror to take the place of a juror who by reason of illness or other reasonable cause cannot continue to act, if the jury has not yet begun to hear evidence, either by drawing a name from a panel of persons who were summoned to act as jurors and who are available at the court at the time of replacing the juror or by using the procedure referred to in section 642.

(2) Where in the course of a trial a member of the jury dies or is discharged pursuant to subsection (1), the jury shall, unless the judge otherwise directs and if the number of jurors is not reduced below ten, be deemed to remain properly constituted for all purposes of the trial and the trial shall proceed and a verdict may be given accordingly. R.S., c. C-34, s. 573; 1972, c. 13, s. 47; 1980-81-82-83, c. 47, s. 53; 1992, c. 41, s. 6; 1997, c. 18, s. 75.

CROSS-REFERENCES

The procedure for jury selection is set out in ss. 626 to 643. Ordinarily jurors are permitted to separate pursuant to s. 647.

If the jury has been increased pursuant to s. 631(2.2) to 13 or 14 members, after the charge to the jury, in accordance with s. 652.1, the number of jurors will be reduced to 12 by the judge discharging the one or two extra jurors.

SYNOPSIS

Subsection (1) permits a trial judge to discharge a juror who by reason of illness or other reasonable cause (*e.g.*, lack of impartiality) is unable to continue to act. Subsection (1.1) allows a judge to replace a juror if the jury has not yet begun to hear evidence.

A trial must commence with 12 jurors. However, a verdict can be rendered by as few as 10 (subsec. (2)). Less than this will result in a mistrial.

ANNOTATIONS

Note: the cases noted under this section were decided prior to the procedure set out in ss. 631(2.1) and 642.1 for the selection and use of alternate jurors.

Grounds for discharge of juror – Where it appears that a juror might not be manifestly impartial there may be a cause for his discharge: *R. v. Tsoumas* (1973), 11 C.C.C. (2d) 344 (Ont. C.A.).

"Other reasonable cause" means any cause that the trial judge deems reasonable to ensure a competent and impartial jury: *R. v. Holcomb* (1973), 12 C.C.C. (2d) 417 (N.B.S.C. App. Div.), affd [1973] S.C.R. vi, 15 C.C.C. (2d) 239 (7:0).

In *R. v. Giroux* (2006), 207 C.C.C. (3d) 512 (Ont. C.A.), leave to appeal to S.C.C. refused 212 C.C.C. (3d) vi, the court held that a hostile juror causing internal strife amongst jurors could constitute "other reasonable cause" to discharge the juror.

However, care must be taken to ensure that a majority of jurors are not able to achieve unanimity merely by alleging impropriety and having their dissenting colleagues discharged. In *R. v. Kum* (2015), 320 C.C.C. (3d) 190 (Ont. C.A.), two jurors were discharged after allegations by their colleagues of obstinate behaviour were confirmed on an inquiry held by the trial judge. The remaining jurors convicted but the Court of Appeal ordered a new trial, holding that there was an appearance of unfairness.

It is not grounds for discharge of a juror that he was previously convicted of a Crown option offence and fined. Although by virtue of provincial legislation, applicable to the proceedings under s. 626, such a person was not qualified to serve on the jury, the presence of such a person would not affect the validity of the verdict and such a record is not even grounds for a challenge for cause under s. 638(1)(*c*): *R. v. Lessard (No. 2)* (1986), 33 C.C.C. (3d) 561 (Que. S.C.).

There would be serious consequences for the jury system if an accused were entitled to a mistrial as of right whenever there was an attempt to bribe a member of the jury. The test to be applied in determining whether or not the trial judge should continue the trial is whether there was a real danger that the accused's position had been prejudiced in the circumstances. The trial judge is in the best position to assess the impact on the jury of the bribery attempt. The judge will take into account the general atmosphere in which the trial took place, the specific circumstances of the case, what the judge had observed during the stages of the trial and the reactions of the members of the jury at the time of his comments on the incident. The judge is also in the best position to find a solution to neutralize the effect of the incident: *R. v. Lessard* (1992), 74 C.C.C. (3d) 552 (Que. C.A.).

Procedure – Where circumstances arise during the course of a trial requiring resort to this section the course to be followed lies in the discretion of the trial judge after consideration of counsel's statements and any evidence there may be, and an appellate court will not lightly interfere with the exercise of this discretion. The course of action, for example, whether or not to give an explanation for the discharge to the remaining jurors, must have regard for the fundamental necessity to avoid any significant risk of his decision resulting in a trial which is unfair or prejudicial to the accused or to the Crown: *R. v. MacKay* (1980), 53 C.C.C. (2d) 366 (B.C.C.A.).

Excusing a juror for reasons of illness or hardship cannot reasonably be said to have a bearing on the substantive conduct of the trial or on guilt or innocence of the accused which is fundamental and thus constitutes part of the trial so as to trigger the accused's right to be present as provided for in s. 650. Thus, neither a report by the sheriff to the trial judge nor the call to the judge by the juror's physician constituted part of the trial which required the presence of the accused. Nevertheless, due to the importance of the step in discharging the juror, it would be preferable for a trial judge to advise counsel, in court and in the presence of the accused, of the nature of the health or hardship problem and to invite counsel to make submissions: *R. v. Chambers*, [1990] 2 S.C.R. 1293, 59 C.C.C. (3d) 321 (6:1).

Normally an inquiry into whether or not a juror should continue should take place in open court. The normal rules of the adversarial system, however, do not apply and counsel have no right to put questions directly to the juror. Counsel may suggest questions which the judge may put to the juror and then make submissions on the issue: *R. v. Hanna* (1993), 80 C.C.C. (3d) 289 (B.C.C.A.), leave to appeal to S.C.C. refused 91 C.C.C. (3d) vi.

The judge has no power under this section to discharge a juror and commence the trial with less than 12 jurors where the accused has not yet been given in charge of the jury: *R. v. Basarabas*, [1982] 2 S.C.R. 730, 2 C.C.C. (3d) 257 (7:0). The consent of the accused cannot cure this jurisdictional defect: *R. v. Wellman* (1996), 108 C.C.C. (3d) 372 (B.C.C.A.).

Since the balance of the jury panel had been discharged before it became necessary to excuse a juror and before the accused had been put in the charge of the jury, it was not improper for the trial judge to instruct the sheriff to assemble talesmen and then select a new juror from among them: *R. v. Ladouceur* (1998), 124 C.C.C. (3d) 269 (Ont. C.A.).

Where the accused have pleaded not guilty, the jury empanelled, and the accused placed in charge of the jury, then the proceedings have reached the stage of being "in the course of a trial" and a juror may be discharged under this section and the trial continued with 11 jurors: *R. v. Andrews, Farrant and Kerr* (1984), 13 C.C.C. (3d) 207, 41 C.R. (3d) 82 (B.C.C.A.); *R. v. Richardson* (1987), 39 C.C.C. (3d) 262 (N.S.C.A.); *R. v. Varcoe* (1996), 104 C.C.C. (3d) 449, 88 O.A.C. 127 (C.A.); *R. v. Socobasin* (1996), 110 C.C.C. (3d) 535, 154 N.S.R. (2d) 118, *sub nom. R. v. S. (R.J.)* (C.A.), leave to appeal to S.C.C. refused 113 C.C.C. (3d) vi. [However, now see subsec. (1.1) allowing the judge to replace a juror if no evidence has been heard by the jury.]

Similarly, *R. v. Ladouceur* (1998), 124 C.C.C. (3d) 269, 108 O.A.C. 321 (C.A.), where it was held that it was proper to proceed with 11 jurors in accordance with subsec. (2). The balance of the jury panel had been discharged, the accused had been put in the charge of the jury, the judge had given his introductory comments and the Crown counsel had delivered his opening address.

Where three jurors had been discharged and replaced after the jury had been selected but before evidence had been heard, both the Crown and the accused should have been afforded three additional peremptory challenges: *R. v. Cazzetta* (2003), 173 C.C.C. (3d) 144 (Que. C.A.). *Contra R. v. Brown* (2005), 194 C.C.C. (3d) 76, 28 C.R. (6th) 315 (Ont. C.A.), noted under s. 634.

Constitutional considerations – The right to a jury trial as guaranteed by s. 11(*f*) of the Charter is not the right as envisaged at common law or at the time of Confederation, namely a jury composed of 12 men. Thus, this section, which permits the trial judge to discharge up to two jurors, does not violate s. 11(*f*): *R. v. Genest* (1990), 61 C.C.C. (3d) 251, [1990] R.J.Q. 2387 (C.A.).

Trial

TRIAL CONTINUOUS / Adjournment / Formal adjournment unnecessary / Questions reserved for decision / Questions reserved for decision in a trial with a jury.

645. (1) The trial of an accused shall proceed continuously subject to adjournment by the court.

(2) The judge may adjourn the trial from time to time in the same sittings.

(3) No formal adjournment of trial or entry thereof is required.

(4) A judge, in any case tried without a jury, may reserve final decision on any question raised at the trial, or any matter raised further to a pre-hearing conference, and the decision, when given, shall be deemed to have been given at the trial.

(5) In any case to be tried with a jury, the judge before whom an accused is or is to be tried has jurisdiction, before any juror on a panel of jurors is called pursuant to subsection 631(3) or (3.1) and in the absence of any such juror, to deal with any matter that would ordinarily or necessarily be dealt with in the absence of the jury after it has been sworn. R.S., c. C-34, s. 574; R.S.C. 1985, c. 27 (1st Supp.), s. 133; 1997, c. 18, s. 76; 2001, c. 32, s. 43.

CROSS-REFERENCES

Under s. 474, the trial may be adjourned where panel of jurors was not summoned for the sittings of the court. Under s. 475, the trial may proceed in the absence of the accused where the accused has absconded in the course of the trial. Discharge of jurors is governed by s. 644. Jurors are ordinarily permitted to separate by virtue of s. 647 until they have retired to consider their verdict. It is an offence under s. 648 to publish information regarding any portion of the trial at which the jury is not present where the jury has not been sequestered. Under s. 650, the accused is to be present during the whole of his trial subject to certain narrow exceptions in s. 650(2). The order of jury addresses is set out in s. 651. In s. 652, the court may order that a view be taken outside the courtroom. Where the jury is unable to agree on its verdict then, pursuant to s. 653, the jury may be discharged. Pursuant to s. 654, the taking of the verdict of a jury and any proceeding incidental thereto is not invalid by reason only that it is done on a Sunday or on a holiday.

SYNOPSIS

This section provides that, subject to adjournments being granted from time to time, a trial shall proceed continuously.

In non-jury trials subsec. (4) permits a judge to reserve final judgment on a point. When reasons are delivered they are deemed to have been given at trial. In other words, the judge can decide a matter during the course of the trial with "reasons to follow".

Subsection (5) allows the trial judge to deal with questions that would ordinarily be dealt with in the absence of the jury, before the jury is empanelled (*e.g.*, a *voir dire* with respect to the admissibility of evidence). This facilitates the calling of evidence in a more orderly and continuous manner as the jury will not have to be excused to enable such matters to be decided.

ANNOTATIONS

When trial commences – The course of a trial commences when the members of the jury are sworn and the accused is given in charge of the jury: *R. v. Emkeit* (1971), 3 C.C.C. (2d) 309, 14 C.R.N.S. 290 (Alta. S.C. App. Div.).

Adjournment *[Also see notes under ss. 571 and 650]* – Absent unconstitutional conduct, there will be no loss of jurisdiction when a trial court, acting on an indictment, fails to proceed at the time set for trial: *R. v. Franklin*, [1985] 1 S.C.R. 293, 18 C.C.C. (3d) 97 (7:0).

Chambers discussions – In *R. v. Johnson* (1977), 35 C.C.C. (2d) 439, 2 B.C.L.R. 193 (C.A.), the court stated that the practice of counsel discussing certain aspects of the case in the judge's chambers during a jury trial should be discouraged. There may be exceptions but, if so, the substance of the discussion in Chambers should be reviewed in open court and recorded and the assent of counsel should also appear on the record.

In *R. v. Roy* (1976), 32 C.C.C. (2d) 97 (Ont. C.A.), a conviction by a judge alone was set aside where part way through the case the trial judge invited counsel into his Chambers and suggested a range of sentence should the accused plead guilty to a lesser offence, an offer which the accused declined. A judge sitting without a jury cannot initiate such discussions after having heard the evidence and still preserve the appearance of impartiality.

Grounds for declaring mistrial *[Also see notes under s. 653]* – In *R. v. Browning* (1976), 34 C.C.C. (2d) 200 (Ont. C.A.), it was held that the trial judge did not err in failing to declare a mistrial where the Crown in cross-examination of a defence witness referred to an unproved threat by the accused on the deceased. The trial judge had immediately told the jury that there was no evidence of such a threat.

The ruling of the trial judge on such matters as to whether or not to declare a mistrial where police are seen talking to a Crown witness at a break, before the completion of his evidence, are within the trial judge's discretion and are not subject to review by way of a prerogative writ: *Stewart v. Dalton* (1977), 36 C.C.C. (2d) 5 (Ont. C.A.).

Pre-trial motions [subsec. (5)] – Subject to s. 669.2, the judge hearing motions under this subsection is seized with the trial: *R. v. Curtis* (1991), 66 C.C.C. (3d) 156 (Ont. Ct. (Gen. Div.)).

Evidentiary rulings made prior to jury selection are not invalidated by the subsequent declaration of a mistrial: *R. v. Wu* (2002), 170 C.C.C. (3d) 225, 167 O.A.C. 141 (C.A.). See, however, *R. v. Reashore* (2002), 170 C.C.C. (3d) 246, 211 N.S.R. (2d) 130 (C.A.), leave to appeal to S.C.C. refused [2003] 1 S.C.R. xvi, 172 C.C.C. (3d) vi, in which the court held that the incorporation of evidentiary rulings made after the discharge of the first jury and before the commencement of the second trial may be have been erroneous.

Other notes – Even where there is no jury the evidence on a *voir dire*, unless so specifically consented to by the parties, is not a part of the trial evidence: *R. v. Gauthier*, [1977] 1 S.C.R. 441, 27 C.C.C. (2d) 14 (6:2).

At least in the absence of objection by counsel the trial judge may permit jurors to take notes during the testimony. He also has a discretion to permit jurors to put questions to witnesses following conclusion of the witness' testimony: *R. v. Andrade* (1985), 18 C.C.C. (3d) 41 (Ont. C.A.).

TAKING EVIDENCE.

646. On the trial of an accused for an indictable offence, the evidence of the witnesses for the prosecutor and the accused and the addresses of the prosecutor and the accused or counsel for the accused by way of summing up shall be taken in accordance with the provisions of Part XVIII, other than subsections 540(7) to (9), relating to the taking of evidence at preliminary inquiries. R.S., c. C-34, s. 575; 2002, c. 13, s. 59.

CROSS-REFERENCES

The section of Part XVIII referred to in this section is s. 540. In addition to the *Canada Evidence Act*, R.S.C. 1985, c. C-5, provisions of the *Criminal Code* itself deal with the admissibility of evidence. For example, s. 655 provides that counsel for an accused may admit any fact alleged against him for the purpose of dispensing with proof thereof. Section 657.1 provides a simple method for proof of ownership and value of property with respect to certain property offences. Proof of age where material may be proved under s. 658. Section 667 provides a means of proving previous convictions. Sections 709 to 714 provide for the taking of evidence on commission. Section 715 permits evidence taken on a previous proceeding, such as the preliminary inquiry, to be admitted. Under s. 715.1, in some circumstances a videotape in which the complainant describes the acts complained of may be admitted on the trial of certain sexual offences. For other notes respecting trial of sexual offences, see the notes after the offence charged or the notes under s. 150.1.

SYNOPSIS

This section states that the evidence of the witnesses for the prosecution and the defence and the addresses of the prosecution and the defence must be recorded in a trial by indictment in the same way in which they are recorded on a preliminary inquiry. The special provisions relating to hearsay at a preliminary inquiry do not apply.

ANNOTATIONS

The provisions of this section are mandatory and the failure to record addresses by counsel will result in a new trial: *R. v. Robillard,* [1969] 4 C.C.C. 120, [1968] Que. Q.B. 255*n* (C.A.).

SEPARATION OF JURORS / Keeping in charge / Non-compliance with subsection (2) / Empanelling new jury in certain cases / Refreshment and accommodation.

647. (1) The judge may, at any time before the jury retires to consider its verdict, permit the members of the jury to separate.

(2) Where permission to separate under subsection (1) cannot be given or is not given, the jury shall be kept under the charge of an officer of the court as the judge directs, and that officer shall prevent the jurors from communicating with anyone other than himself or another member of the jury without leave of the judge.

(3) Failure to comply with subsection (2) does not affect the validity of the proceedings.

(4) Where the fact that there has been a failure to comply with this section or section 648 is discovered before the verdict of the jury is returned, the judge may, if he considers that the failure to comply might lead to a miscarriage of justice, discharge the jury and

- **(*a*) direct that the accused be tried with a new jury during the same session or sittings of the court; or**
- **(*b*) postpone the trial on such terms as justice may require.**

(5) The judge shall direct the sheriff to provide the jurors who are sworn with suitable and sufficient refreshment, food and lodging while they are together until they have given their verdict. R.S., c. C-34, s. 576; 1972, c. 13, s. 48.

CROSS-REFERENCES

It is an offence under s. 648 to publish any information regarding any portion of the trial at which the jury is not present where the jury has not been sequestered, before the jury retires to consider its verdict. It is also an offence subject to limited exceptions for any member of the jury to disclose information relating to the proceedings of the jury when it was absent from the courtroom pursuant to s. 649. Under s. 652, the judge may order that a view be taken of any place, thing or person in accordance with s. 652. Where the jury is unable to agree on its verdict then the jury may be discharged under s. 653. A juror may be discharged in accordance with the provisions of s. 644.

SYNOPSIS

This section deals with the sequestering of the jury. Once they begin their deliberations the jurors will be in the charge of a court officer and will not be permitted to communicate with outside persons. Before this time the trial judge has a discretion to allow them to separate (subsecs. (1), (2)).

Where a failure to comply with the provisions of this section or that dealing with publication bans (see s. 648) is discovered before a verdict is returned, the trial judge can discharge the jury or postpone the trial and make such order as may be required (subsec. (4)). Subsection (5) provides for the food and lodging of the jurors.

ANNOTATIONS

Grounds for sequestration of jury – The decision of the trial judge refusing to sequester the jury is discretionary and does not involve a question of law alone which the accused may appeal to the Supreme Court of Canada: *R. v. Demeter*, [1978] 1 S.C.R. 538, 34 C.C.C. (2d) 137 (9:0).

The fact that inflammatory newspaper articles are circulated in the district where the accused is to be tried does not afford grounds for setting aside the conviction if there is nothing in the record or the evidence to show that the members of the jury had any knowledge of the contents of such articles or that they did not give a free unbiased verdict: *R. v. Koufis*, [1941] S.C.R. 481, 76 C.C.C. 161.

Proceedings concerning jury – Where there has been a potentially prejudicial communication to a juror the trial judge should conduct an inquiry himself by personally examining the juror to determine whether the communication has affected the impartiality of the juror. This function cannot be delegated to some other official such as the sheriff. As well, counsel should be informed of the incident so that they can participate in the inquiry: *R. v. Hertrich, Stewart and Skinner* (1982), 67 C.C.C. (2d) 510, 137 D.L.R. (3d) 400 (Ont. C.A.), leave to appeal to S.C.C. refused 45 N.R. 629*n*. [Also see note of this case under s. 650, *infra*.]

In view of the importance of the step of excusing a juror, even on account of illness, it would be preferable for the trial judge to advise counsel, in court and in the presence of the accused, of the nature of the health or hardship problem and to invite counsel to make submissions if they wish to: *R. v. Chambers*, [1990] 2 S.C.R. 1293, 59 C.C.C. (3d) 321, 80 C.R. (3d) 235.

Subsection (5) cannot reasonably be interpreted as permitting an unsworn constable to take a sequestered juror to a hotel bar for several drinks: *R. v. Cameron* (1991), 64 C.C.C. (3d) 96, 2 O.R. (3d) 633 (C.A.).

The duty of the sworn constables is to provide contact between a sequestered jury and the outside world and to make certain that no unauthorized persons have contact with the jury. It was unacceptable to allow unsworn constables and a police officer who was a relative of the deceased in a murder case, to dine with the jury which had been sequestered for their deliberations. It was also improper to allow an unsworn constable to take a sequestered jury to a hotel bar for several drinks. These incidents were so blatantly irregular that a new trial must be ordered, even in the absence of proof by the accused of actual prejudice: *R. v. Cameron, supra.*

Giving jury excerpts from *Criminal Code* – There is some division in the case law about the propriety of giving the jurors excerpts from the *Criminal Code* for use during their deliberations. Earlier decisions tended to discourage the practice: *R. v. Schimanowsky* (1973), 15 C.C.C. (2d) 82, 25 C.R.N.S. 332 (Sask. C.A.); *R. v. Crothers* (1978), 43 C.C.C. (2d) 27 (Sask. C.A.). Other authorities have approved the practice provided it is done with sufficient safeguards, for example instructing the jury that the sections have only a limited use to help them remember the elements of the offence, and they are not to engage in their own interpretation of the sections but must take the law from the trial judge: *R. v. Tennant* (1975), 23 C.C.C. (2d) 80, 31 C.R.N.S. 1 (Ont. C.A.); *R. v. Vawryk* (1979), 46 C.C.C. (2d) 290, [1979] 3 W.W.R. 50 (Man. C.A.); *R. v. Stanford* (1975), 27 C.C.C. (2d) 520 (Que. C.A.). It would seem that now in light of *R. v. Menard*, [1998] 2 S.C.R. 109, 125 C.C.C. (3d) 416, there is no legal impediment to providing the sections and other written instructions to the jury provided that the procedures set out in that case are followed. The judge should not give an annotated version of the *Code* sections to the jury. *R. v. Menard* is noted under s. 650.1.

Procedure in answering jury questions generally – Where the trial judge receives a question from the jury he should read it in open court in the presence of the parties and give counsel an opportunity to make submissions in open court before answering the question for the jury in open court in the presence of the parties: *R. v. Dunbar and Logan* (1982), 68 C.C.C. (2d) 13, 28 C.R. (3d) 324 (Ont. C.A.). Folld: *R. v. Hay* (1982), 70 C.C.C. (2d) 286, 30 C.R. (3d) 37 (Sask. C.A.); *R. v. Parnell* (1983), 9 C.C.C. (3d) 353 (Ont. C.A.), leave to appeal to S.C.C. refused C.C.C. *loc. cit.*

Questions from the jury require careful consideration and must be clearly, correctly and comprehensively answered. The question presented by the jury gives the clearest possible indication of the particular problem that the jury is confronting and upon which it seeks further instructions. Even where the question relates to a matter that has been carefully reviewed in the main charge, it still must be answered in a complete, accurate and careful manner. The longer the delay between the question and the charge, the more important it will be that the recharge is correct and comprehensive. As a general rule, an error in the recharge on the question presented will not be saved by a correct charge which was given earlier: *R. v. S. (W.D.)*, [1994] 3 S.C.R. 521, 93 C.C.C. (3d) 1.

Where, after being properly charged, a jury remained in doubt and asked a question about the standard of proof, the trial judge had to attempt to answer that question in an effort to assist them in understanding what was required of them. While the trial judge's written charge correctly instructed the jury on reasonable doubt, the jury remained unclear. The judge did not assist by merely repeating the original instructions. Further, the judge's comments at the end of her recharge implied that she could not assist the jury with their apparent confusion and there was no reason for them to return with another question or to try to clarify more precisely what was causing the confusion. The trial judge failed to provide a responsive answer and discouraged further questions on the standard of proof: *R. v. Layton*, [2009] 2 S.C.R. 540, 244 C.C.C. (3d) 417.

It is open to the jury to withdraw a question and the trial judge may take the jury's verdict without having answered the question: *R. v. Sit* (1989), 47 C.C.C. (3d) 45, 31 O.A.C. 21 (C.A.).

Where the jury's question is unclear, the trial judge must take steps to clarify it, if necessary by questioning the jury to ascertain the nature of the difficulty. To avoid disclosure of the jury's deliberations, it may be necessary for the trial judge to ask leading questions: *R. v. Mohamed* (1991), 64 C.C.C. (3d) 1 (B.C.C.A.).

Once the jury has begun to deliberate, the Crown should not be permitted to adduce further evidence, even in answer to a question from the jury: *R. v. Templeman* (1994), 88 C.C.C. (3d) 254, 65 W.A.C. 76 (B.C.C.A.).

With the jury having asked to hear the tape recording of defence counsel's address, the trial judge should have acceded to the joint submission of counsel and permitted the jury to listen again to the addresses of all counsel: *R. v. Hajian* (1998), 124 C.C.C. (3d) 440 (Que. C.A.).

To maintain a balance in the deliberative process, the trial judge must give the jury a copy of the transcripts of both the defence and Crown closing arguments, even if the jury only requests Crown counsel's jury address: *R. v. Ferguson* (2000), 142 C.C.C. (3d) 353, 130 O.A.C. 253 (C.A.), revd [2001] 1 S.C.R. 281, 152 C.C.C. (3d) 95.

Right of jury to have evidence read back – A jury is entitled to have read to them excerpts of evidence upon which their recollection is not clear: *R. v. Mace* (1975), 25 C.C.C. (2d) 121 (Ont. C.A.). Accordingly, the fact that the trial judge had reviewed the evidence only a few hours earlier was not a basis upon which to refuse to allow the jury to review the evidence of a witness. The form of assistance provided to the jury through the reading of the evidence or the provision of a summary, however, is within the discretion of the trial judge: *R. v. A. (J.)* (1996), 112 C.C.C. (3d) 528, 95 O.A.C. 383 (C.A.).

While the jury is entitled to have read to them excerpts of the testimony in order to clarify the evidence on any point, it is not wrong for the trial judge to inform the jury that it was not possible to accede to their request to provide them with a transcript of the entire evidence. The judge should, however, remind the jury of their right to have portions of the evidence read back by the reporter or to have the matter clarified by the judge by reference to his notes: *R. v. Andrade* (1985), 18 C.C.C. (3d) 41 (Ont. C.A.).

The trial judge is required to assist the jury where they express concern about an area of the evidence and it is important that the jury not be misled as to the availability of that assistance in the form of reference to the trial judge's notes or the notes of the court reporter: *R. v. Corriveau* (1985), 19 C.C.C. (3d) 238 (Ont. C.A.).

Where the jury requests that the evidence of a witness be read back, it is incumbent upon the trial judge not to permit the jury to hear a part only of the evidence without also hearing those portions of the evidence of the witness which qualify the part read: *R. v. Olbey*, [1980] 1 S.C.R. 1008, 50 C.C.C. (2d) 257 (6:1), approving authorities such as *R. v. Stewart and Johnson*, [1969] 2 C.C.C. 244, 5 C.R.N.S. 75 (B.C.C.A.); *R. v. Wydryk and Wilkie* (1971),

5 C.C.C. (2d) 473, 17 C.R.N.S. 336 (B.C.C.A.); and *R. v. Bell, Christiansen, Coolen and MacDonald* (1973), 14 C.C.C. (2d) 225, 28 C.R.N.S. 55 (S.C. App. Div.).

Length of deliberations – Save in exceptional circumstances the jury should not be permitted to deliberate into the early morning hours and where such circumstances exist they should be fully set out on the record: *R. v. Kulak* (1979), 46 C.C.C. (2d) 30, 7 C.R. (3d) 304 (Ont. C.A.); *R. v. Robertson* (1979), 50 C.C.C. (2d) 127 (Ont. C.A.); *R. v. Martin* (1980), 53 C.C.C. (2d) 250 (Ont. C.A.); *R. v. Owen* (1983), 4 C.C.C. (3d) 538, 56 N.S.R. (2d) 541 (S.C. App. Div.); *R. v. Mohamed* (1991), 64 C.C.C. (3d) 1 (B.C.C.A.).

Effect of unauthorized publication or communication with jury ***[Also see notes under s. 649]*** – The Appeal Court will not interfere with the judge's discretion under this subsection refusing a mistrial unless he has acted on a wrong principle: *R. v. Demeter* (1975), 25 C.C.C. (2d) 417, 10 O.R. (2d) 321 (C.A.).

Not every communication by a witness with a member of a jury will result in a mistrial. When such communication has taken place, but it is clear after inquiry that there is no real prejudice to the accused or the Crown, then a trial judge has the discretion to continue with the trial. Where the communication takes place after the jury has been sequestered to consider their verdict, there is a presumption of prejudice. However, where the communication takes place prior to the deliberations and thus the extent of the prejudice to the accused can be determined on a *voir dire* of the jurors and the offending witness, there is no such presumption: *R. v. Horne* (1987), 35 C.C.C. (3d) 427, 78 A.R. 144 (C.A.), leave to appeal to S.C.C. refused 36 C.C.C. (3d) vi.

RESTRICTION ON PUBLICATION / Offence / Definition of "newspaper".

648. (1) After permission to separate is given to members of a jury under subsection 647(1), no information regarding any portion of the trial at which the jury is not present shall be published in any document or broadcast or transmitted in any way before the jury retires to consider its verdict.

(2) Every one who fails to comply with subsection (1) is guilty of an offence punishable on summary conviction. 1972, c. 13, s. 49; 2005, c. 32, s. 21.

(3) [*Repealed*, 2005, c. 32, s. 21(2).]

CROSS-REFERENCES

The offence under subsec. (2) is tried in accordance with Part XXVII by a summary conviction court defined in s. 785.

SYNOPSIS

Unless the jurors have been sequestered, it is an offence, punishable on summary conviction, to publish, broadcast or transmit in any way any part of the trial that was heard in their absence.

ANNOTATIONS

A violation of this section must be shown to have resulted in a miscarriage of justice before an appellate court will interfere with the jury's verdict: *R. v. Demeter* (1975) 25 C.C.C. (2d) 417 at p. 448, 10 O.R. (2d) 321 at p. 352 (5:0) (C.A.).

Section 648(1) combined with s. 645(5) automatically bans publication of any pre-trial motion that ordinarily must be dealt with in the absence of the jury. Motions and applications that do not involve the admissibility of evidence and would not necessarily be dealt with in the absence of the jury are not captured by subsec. (1): *R. v. Stobbe* (2011), 284 C.C.C. (3d) 123 (Man. Q.B.).

It was doubtful whether an incident which occurred between the accused and a member of the public, after the jury had left the courtroom, during a break in the proceedings could constitute "any portion of the trial" so as to invoke the prohibition against publication in this section: *R. v. Dobson* (1985), 19 C.C.C. (3d) 93 (Ont. C.A.).

While the ban on publication imposed by this section lapses once the jury has retired to begin its deliberations the trial judge, who was a superior court judge, had power to ban publication of evidence admitted on a *voir dire* in the course of controlling the proceedings in his court. Thus in an extortion case an order was justified in the public interest prohibiting publication of evidence which would identify persons involved with the accused, persons who might be potential blackmail victims or persons who were simply accidentally involved: *Toronto Sun Publishing Corp. v. Alberta (Attorney General)*, [1985] 6 W.W.R. 36 (Alta. C.A.).

The section is applicable to motions heard before jury selection. The mandatory publication ban should be interpreted to minimally impair the freedom of the press. The ban applies only to information that would reasonably be expected to taint a juror's impression of the accused: *R. v. Regan* (1997), 124 C.C.C. (3d) 77 (N.S.S.C.). See also *R. v. Sandham* (2008), 248 C.C.C. (3d) 543 (Ont. S.C.J.), and *R. v. Valentine* (2009), 251 C.C.C. (3d) 120 (Ont. S.C.J.).

In *R. v. Cheung* (2000), 150 C.C.C. (3d) 192 (Alta. Q.B.), the court held that this provision did not apply to proceedings prior to empanelling the jury. The fairness of the trial could be protected, however, by a partial publication ban pursuant to the court's common law jurisdiction.

In *Canadian Broadcasting Corp. v. Millard* (2015), 338 C.C.C. (3d) 227 (Ont. S.C.J.), the court held that it was not appropriate to subdivide pre-trial motions into categories for the purposes of applying this provision. The statutory ban applies to all pre-trial motions adjudicated by the trial judge, whether litigated before or after the jury is selected.

Discussion of "housekeeping matters", such as the place where the in-custody accused would be incarcerated during an adjournment of the trial, is part of the trial and within the prohibition in this section: *R. v. CHBC Television* (1999), 132 C.C.C. (3d) 390 (B.C.C.A.).

DISCLOSURE OF JURY PROCEEDINGS.

649. Every member of a jury, and every person providing technical, personal, interpretative or other support services to a juror with a physical disability, who, except for the purposes of

(*a*) an investigation of an alleged offence under subsection 139(2) in relation to a juror, or

(*b*) giving evidence in criminal proceedings in relation to such an offence,

discloses any information relating to the proceedings of the jury when it was absent from the courtroom that was not subsequently disclosed in open court is guilty of an offence punishable on summary conviction. 1972, c. 13, s. 49; 1998, c. 9, s. 7.

CROSS-REFERENCES

The offence under this section is tried in accordance with Part XXVII by summary conviction court defined in s. 785. The limitation period is as set out in s. 786(2) and the penalty is as set out in s. 787(1).

SYNOPSIS

It is an offence, punishable on summary conviction, for a juror to disclose matters which arose in the jury room when the same were not disclosed in open court (*e.g.*, what was discussed during the jury's deliberations). An exception exists where the disclosure is made for the purpose of an investigation into, or criminal proceedings on, a charge of obstructing justice (see s. 139(2)).

ANNOTATIONS

The slightest communication with jurors about the case they are trying has always been prohibited. Thus it constituted contempt of court for the accused, a member of a firm of lawyers one of whom was defending a case, to attempt to elicit from a juror discharged under s. 644 what the other jurors thought of the case: *R. v. Papineau* (1980), 58 C.C.C. (2d) 72, 16 C.R. (3d) 56 *sub nom. Re Papineau; R. v. Varin* (Que. S.C.).

The words "proceedings of jury" in this section have the same meaning as the deliberation process for the common law rule of jury secrecy. Both refer to the deliberation process which includes opinions expressed, arguments advanced and votes cast by individual jurors. The common law rule does not render inadmissible evidence of facts, statements or events extrinsic to the deliberation process. Evidence indicating that the jury has been exposed to some information or influence from outside the jury is admissible in considering whether there is a reasonable possibility that this information or influence had an effect upon the jury's verdict. While jurors may testify as to whether or not they were exposed to extrinsic information, they cannot testify as to what effect it had upon their deliberations: *R. v. Pan; R. v. Sawyer*, [2001] 2 S.C.R. 344, 155 C.C.C. (3d) 97.

This section is consistent with the common law rule of jury secrecy that itself meets the constitutional requirements of fairness embodied in s. 7 of the *Canadian Charter of Rights and Freedoms*. Since this section does not prevent a juror from revealing any information that would be admissible in proceedings to impeach the jury's verdict, the section does not violate the accused's rights under s. 7: *R. v. Pan; R. v. Sawyer, supra.*

A juror, although a competent witness on a Crown appeal from the accused's acquittal, cannot be compelled to testify and therefore cannot be ordered to attend to be examined under s. 683(1)(*b*): *R. v. Budai* (1999), 140 C.C.C. (3d) 1, 30 C.R. (5th) 399 (B.C.C.A.).

Where it is revealed after trial that extraneous information was brought into the jury room, the appellate court must determine, within the bounds of the jury secrecy rule, whether there is a reasonable possibility that the information had an effect on the jury's verdict: *R. v. Bains* (2015), 328 C.C.C. (3d) 149 (Ont. C.A.), leave to appeal to S.C.C. refused 2016 CarswellOnt 4117, leave to appeal to S.C.C. refused 2016 CarswellOnt 4119; *R. v. Farinacci* (2015), 328 C.C.C. (3d) 101 (Ont. C.A.).

Out-of-court conduct of a juror can rebut the presumption of juror impartiality only if a reasonable observer would conclude that the juror's conduct made it more likely than not that the juror, whether consciously or unconsciously, would not decide the case fairly: *R. v. Dowholis* (2016), 341 C.C.C. (3d) 443 (Ont. C.A.).

ACCUSED TO BE PRESENT / Video links / Video links / Exceptions / To make defence.

650. (1) Subject to subsections (1.1) to (2) and section 650.01, an accused, other than an organization, shall be present in court during the whole of his or her trial.

(1.1) Where the court so orders, and where the prosecutor and the accused so agree, the accused may appear by counsel or by closed-circuit television or any other means that allow the court and the accused to engage in simultaneous visual and oral communication, for any part of the trial other than a part in which the evidence of a witness is taken.

(1.2) Where the court so orders, an accused who is confined in prison may appear by closed-circuit television or any other means that allow the court and the accused to engage in simultaneous visual and oral communication, for any part of the trial other than a part in which the evidence of a witness is taken, if the accused is given the opportunity to communicate privately with counsel, in a case in which the accused is represented by counsel.

(2) The court may

(*a*) cause the accused to be removed and to be kept out of court, where he misconducts himself by interrupting the proceedings so that to continue the proceedings in his presence would not be feasible;

(*b*) permit the accused to be out of court during the whole or any part of his trial on such conditions as the court considers proper; or

(*c*) cause the accused to be removed and to be kept out of court during the trial of an issue as to whether the accused is unfit to stand trial, where it is satisfied that failure to do so might have an adverse effect on the mental condition of the accused.

(3) An accused is entitled, after the close of the case for the prosecution, to make full answer and defence personally or by counsel. R.S., c. C-34, s. 577; 1972, c. 13, s. 50; 1991, c. 43, s. 9; 1994, c. 44, s. 61; 1997, c. 18, s. 77; 2002, c. 13, s. 60; 2003, c. 21, s. 12.

CROSS-REFERENCES

"Counsel", "organization" and "prosecutor" are defined in s. 2. An organization appears by counsel or agent pursuant to s. 620. Sections 622 and 623 provide for trial of an organization which does not appear by counsel or agent. Note s. 475 which provides that the trial may proceed in the absence of the accused where the accused has absconded in the course of the trial. Also note s. 486(2.1) which provides that in the case of trial of certain sexual offences specified therein, the judge may order that the complainant testify outside the courtroom or behind a screen or other device that would allow the complainant not to see the accused. Jurisdiction over the person is not lost where the accused was to appear by counsel under subsec. (1.1), see s. 485(1.1).

Sections 650.01 and 650.02 allow an accused to appear by designated counsel without being present in certain circumstances. Under s. 848, if an accused who is in prison does not have access to legal advice, the court shall, before permitting the accused to appear by means of communication that allows the court and the accused to engage in simultaneous visual and oral communication, be satisfied that the accused will be able to understand the proceedings and that any decisions made by the accused during the proceedings will be voluntary.

Appearance of an organization is dealt with in s. 556.

SYNOPSIS

Unless the court orders otherwise an accused, other than an organization, is required to be present throughout the trial. If the trial judge considers it proper the accused may be permitted to be absent (*e.g.*, during lengthy submissions on the admissibility of evidence) (subsec. (2)(*b*)).

An accused who interrupts the proceedings and interferes with the conduct of the trial may be removed from the court-room (subsec. (2)(*a*)). As well, a fitness hearing may be held in the absence of the accused if the judge feels that the accused's mental health might be adversely affected by his or her presence (subsec. (2)(*c*)).

Subsection (3) is a codification of the accused's right to make "full answer and defence" at the close of the Crown's case.

Provision is also made in subsec. (1.1) for appearance by counsel or through closed-circuit television or similar means. The accused who is a prisoner may be required to appear by closed-circuit television or similar means pursuant to subsec. (1.2).

ANNOTATIONS

Right of accused to be present [subsec. (1)] – Without the authority of his client, counsel cannot, even with permission from the court, proceed in his absence: *R. v. Page,* [1969] 1 C.C.C. 90 (B.C.C.A.).

The right of an accused to be present in court during the whole of his trial as provided by this subsection includes the right to have direct knowledge of anything that transpires in the course of the trial which could involve his vital interests. This would include not only proceedings which are part of the normal trial process for determining the guilt or innocence of the accused but also proceedings conducted by the judge during the trial for the purpose of investigating matters which have occurred outside the trial but which may affect its fairness. If on the facts of a particular case the trial judge receives a communication from a juror and is uncertain whether the accused's vital interests are involved, the judge may, in the absence of the accused, investigate the matter. This would include the questioning of jurors and if the judge determines that the vital interests of the accused are not in issue that ends the matter, subject to a record being kept of the proceedings in order to determine whether the trial judge erred as regards there being uncertainty of what was in issue at the outset and as regards his final determination of the matter. However, at the moment that it appears that the accused's vital interests are in issue, as where it is an issue as to the partiality of one of the jurors, then the matter must be determined in the presence of the accused: *R. v. Vezina*, [1986] 1 S.C.R. 2, 23 C.C.C. (3d) 481 (7:0).

It is not everything that occurs during a trial that is part of the trial for the purposes of this section. Thus, things may occur which cannot reasonably be considered part of the trial for the purposes of the principle because they cannot reasonably be said to have a bearing on the substantive conduct of the trial, or the issue of guilt or innocence. However, an accused is entitled to be present at his trial not only so that he can hear the case made out against him, and having heard it, have the opportunity of answering it, but also because his presence at all stages of his trial affords him the opportunity of acquiring first-hand knowledge of the proceedings leading to the eventual result of the trial. Thus, an accused was entitled to be present during an inquiry conducted by the trial Judge concerning certain anonymous telephone calls made to members of the jury: *R. v. Hertrich, Stewart and Skinner* (1982), 67 C.C.C. (2d) 510 (Ont. C.A.), leave to appeal to S.C.C. refused 45 N.R. 629*n*. Similarly: *R. v. Fenton* (1984), 11 C.C.C. (3d) 109 (B.C.C.A.).

This subsection is to be given expansive interpretation. The examination following arraignment of potential jurors by the trial judge to determine claims for exemptions on grounds including partiality is part of the trial at which the accused is entitled to be present: *R. v. Barrow*, [1987] 2 S.C.R. 694, 38 C.C.C. (3d) 193 (5:2).

Aside from breaching this subsection, proceeding in the absence of the accused may violate the accused's rights under ss. 7 and 11(*d*) of the Charter: *R. v. Dedam* (2018), 364 C.C.C. (3d) 360 (N.B.C.A.).

The provisions of subsec. (1.1) were not satisfied where the trial judge delivered his reasons for judgment over the telephone: *R. v. Gates* (2002), 163 C.C.C. (3d) 274 (B.C.C.A.), leave to appeal to S.C.C. refused [2004] 4 S.C.R. v, 168 C.C.C. (3d) vi.

A severance application was part of the trial and should not have been conducted in the absence of the accused: *R. v. T. (L.W.)* (2008), 230 C.C.C. (3d) 220 (Sask. C.A.).

The trial judge interrupted the complainant's cross-examination and commented on the problems of her evidence during an in-chambers discussion. On the basis of this discussion as reported by counsel, the accused decided not to testify. The trial judge breached the accused's right to be present at his trial and affected his vital interests: *R. v. James* (2009), 244 C.C.C. (3d) 330 (Ont. C.A.).

The trial judge convened a mid-trial conference with counsel in his chambers during which he expressed some views on the strengths and weaknesses of the evidence and urged counsel to try to resolve the case. While not every in-chambers discussion is prohibited, this one had a profound effect on the appearance of fairness and required the conviction to be quashed: *R. v. Schofield* (2012), 286 C.C.C. (3d) 555 (Ont. C.A.).

A new dangerous offender hearing was ordered where the trial judge refused to entertain oral argument at the end of a dangerous offender hearing, relying on written submissions instead: *R. v. McDonald* (2018), 360 C.C.C. (3d) 494 (Ont. C.A.).

In *R. v. Simon* (2010), 263 C.C.C. (3d) 59 (Ont. C.A.), leave to appeal to S.C.C. refused 265 C.C.C. (3d) iv, the court held that to determine whether a breach of s. 650(1) may be salvaged by the application of the proviso, requires a consideration of all the relevant factors, which may include: (i) the nature and extent of the exclusion, including whether it was inadvertent or deliberate; (ii) the role or position of the defence counsel in initiating or concurring in the exclusion; (iii) whether any subjects discussed during the exclusion were repeated on the record or otherwise reported to the accused; (iv) whether any discussions in the accused's absence were preliminary in nature or involved decisions about procedural, evidentiary or substantive matters; (v) the effect, if any, of the discussions on the apparent fairness of trial proceedings; and (vi) the effect, if any, of the discussions on decisions about the conduct of the defence.

Discussion outside presence of accused *[Also see notes under s. 647]* – Communications between a sheriff's officer and the trial judge and then between the judge and a juror's doctor concerning the juror's illness are not part of trial and therefore the accused's rights were not violated although he was absent during those discussions: *R. v. Chambers*, [1990] 2 S.C.R. 1293, 59 C.C.C. (3d) 321.

An accused is not present within the meaning of this section where the proceedings although conducted in court take place out of earshot of the accused and his counsel: *R. v. Barrow, supra.*

An *in camera* meeting between the judge, the Crown and an R.C.M.P. officer to discuss a claim of privilege pursuant to s. 37 of the *Canada Evidence Act* on consent of all counsel was not part of the accused's trial and accordingly, there was no right to be present at the meeting: *R. v. Pilotte* (2002), 163 C.C.C. (3d) 225 (Ont. C.A.).

Likewise, holding an *in camera, ex parte* hearing for the sole purpose of determining whether two police informants referred to in the ITO were protected by confidential informer privilege did not violate the accused's right to be present: *R. v. Lucas*, [2014] O.J. No. 3471 (C.A.).

Where the trial judge met with counsel during which she expressed her opinion about the case and asked whether plea bargaining was being pursued, this section was contravened as the accused's vital interests were engaging during the meeting: *R. v. Walker* (2010), 258 C.C.C. (3d) 36 (Sask. C.A.).

This section was not breached by an in-chambers discussion, prior to trial and in the absence of the accused, about the wording of the challenge for cause question. The discussions were preliminary in nature and summarized by the trial judge in open court: *R. v. Sinclair* (2013), 300 C.C.C. (3d) 69 (Ont. C.A.).

During jury selection, several potential jurors had "private conversations" with the trial judge in the courtroom after their names were called and they came forward from the body of the courtroom. The "private conversations" between the trial judge and the jurors were part of the accused's trial. Absent waiver, he was entitled to hear the conversations. However, in this case, the procedural error caused no prejudice to the accused: *R. v. Kakegamic* (2010), 265 C.C.C. (3d) 420 (Ont. C.A.). See also *R. v. Sinclair, supra.*

It was a breach of this provision for the trial judge to receive an oral request from the sheriff on behalf of the jury to provide it with a typewritten list of the elements of the offence, and to provide it to the jury outside of court without consulting the parties. Notwithstanding the judge's view that the request was "innocuous", it affected the accused's vital interests and the error required a new trial: *R. v. L. (D.P.)* (2008), 309 C.C.C. (3d) 529 (N.W.T.C.A.).

While it is acceptable for the trial judge to provide a draft jury charge to counsel via email, substantive submissions on the charge should be conducted in court in the presence of the accused, not via email: *R. v. Hassanzada* (2016), 335 C.C.C. (3d) 1 (Ont. C.A.).

Removal of accused [subsec. (2)] – A trial judge's belief that the accused might tailor his evidence if he heard the argument as to the admissibility of a portion of his testimony is not an adequate basis for his exclusion from the courtroom and if something transpires which is part of the trial, during the time when the accused is improperly excluded then this subsection has been contravened and the conviction must be quashed. Matters such as the adducing of evidence, presentation of argument, ruling on evidentiary points and addresses to the jury all constitute part of the trial, or advance the case, and if the accused is improperly excluded during those parts of the trial, then this subsection has been contravened: *R. v. Grimba* (1980), 56 C.C.C. (2d) 570 (Ont. C.A.). Similarly, *R. v. Dunbar* (1982), 68 C.C.C. (2d) 13 (Ont. C.A.).

Where it becomes necessary to remove the accused under para. (*a*) and the accused is unrepresented by counsel then there is an obligation on the trial judge to cross-examine the Crown witnesses in an attempt to assist him: *R. v. Pawliw* (1985), 23 C.C.C. (3d) 14 (B.C.S.C.).

Paragraph (*a*) of subsec. (2) is not an unconstitutional infringement of the legal rights guaranteed by the *Canadian Charter of Rights and Freedoms*: *R. v. Pawliw, supra.*

The accused's absence from court initially because of his refusal to attend court and subsequently pursuant to subsec. (2)(*c*), while his fitness to stand trial is determined, cannot vitiate his subsequent plea of guilty: *R. v. Lefebvre* (1989), 71 C.R. (3d) 213 (Que. C.A.), leave to appeal to S.C.C. refused 27 Q.A.C. 234*n*.

Subsection (2)(*b*) involves an element of waiver by the accused, and for there to be a waiver, the accused must be fully aware of his right to present in court and freely give up his right without pressure of any kind, including the pressure of custodial expediency: *R. v. Fecteau*, (1989), 49 C.C.C. (3d) 534 (Ont. H.C.J.).

The accused may be permitted to be absent for the arraignment and plea: *R. v. Butler* (1993), 81 C.C.C. (3d) 248 (Man. Q.B.).

The court has the discretion to allow the accused to be absent from the whole or any part of the trial where the accused is fully aware of the consequences of the decision to be absent and is content that counsel will represent his interests: *R. v. Drabinsky* (2008), 235 C.C.C. (3d) 350 (Ont. S.C.J.).

The accused's rights had not been infringed by his counsel's continued representation of him after the accused withdrew from the proceedings and had no intention of participating in the process: *R. v. Zarubin* (2001), 157 C.C.C. (3d) 115 (Sask. C.A.).

Right to interpreter – When an accused is deprived of his interpreter for the judge's charge he in effect is denied the right to be present at his trial: *R. v. Reale* (1973), 13 C.C.C. (2d) 345 (Ont. C.A.), affd [1975] 2 S.C.R. 624, 22 C.C.C. (2d) 571 (7:2).

However, accidental contravention of the right to an interpreter during the sentence proceedings does not vitiate the conviction itself following a trial which is otherwise untainted by jurisdictional error: *R. v. Petrovic* (1984), 13 C.C.C. (3d) 416 (Ont. C.A.), leave to appeal to S.C.C. refused [1985] 1 S.C.R. xi.

As a general rule, s. 14 of the Charter requires that the court appoint an interpreter when it becomes apparent to the judge that an accused is, for language reasons, having difficulty expressing himself or understanding the proceedings and that the assistance of an interpreter would be helpful; or the accused or counsel for the accused requests the services of an interpreter and the judge is of the opinion that the request is justified. There is, however, no requirement that the courts inform all accused appearing before them of the existence of the right to interpreter assistance. Where the accused at trial claims the Charter right to an interpreter, assistance should not be denied unless there is cogent and compelling evidence that the accused's request is not made in good faith but rather for an oblique motive. The quality of interpretation must be high but the standard is not one of perfection. The interpretation of the proceedings should be continuous, precise, impartial, competent and contemporaneous. Summaries of the testimony are unlikely to meet the general standard of interpretation required: *R. v. Tran*, [1994] 2 S.C.R. 951, 92 C.C.C. (3d) 218. [Also see notes of this case under s. 14 of the Charter, *infra*.]

Crown's discretion to call witnesses – There is no duty on the Crown to call particular witnesses including the complainant. References in case law to the Crown calling all witnesses who are "essential to the narrative" refers only to the burden of proof in that where the narrative of the case is not adequately set forth, the elements of the offence might not be properly proven and the Crown risks losing its case. Furthermore, the absence of witnesses may become a factor for an appellate court considering the reasonableness of the verdict. In the rare case where the tactical disadvantage to the defence calling a potentially hostile witness would be manifestly unfair, the trial judge is entitled to consider this factor in determining whether to call the witness him or herself. The loss of the right to not call evidence and thus address the jury last is a factor in determining whether the judge should call the witness. The testimony of the complainant or victim is not different from any other witness. In a situation where the failure to have the complainant testify is completely unexplained, it would be open to the trial judge to instruct the jury that they could adversely consider this absence of testimony in deciding upon whether or not the Crown had proved its case. While an inquiry into the reasons for which the Crown decided not to call the witness might be appropriate in a given case, that is a matter for the discretion of the trial judge: *R. v. Cook*, [1997] 1 S.C.R. 1113, 114 C.C.C. (3d) 481.

Directed verdict – In *R. v. Vander-Beek and Albright*, [1971] S.C.R. 260, 2 C.C.C. (2d) 45, at trial the motion of the two appellants for dismissal at the conclusion of the Crown's case on the ground that there was no evidence upon which they could be convicted was dismissed, and their immediately succeeding motion that they be acquitted on the ground that there was insufficient evidence for conviction was reserved by the judge until he heard all of the evidence. Their counsel took no further part in the evidence, even when the third accused testified to raise a reasonable doubt on his part at the expense of his other two co-accused. The trial judge acquitted the third accused on his evidence and excluding his evidence as against the two co-accused, acquitted them. It was held (9:0), that the case was not concluded until all of the evidence was in and that all testimony heard was evidence for or against each accused. Further, *per* Laskin J., the accused's closing of his case at the conclusion of the Crown's case does not allow a co-accused to separate his trial from the joint trial.

The application for a directed verdict must be determined before the accused is called upon to elect whether or not he intends to call evidence: *R. v. Boissonneault* (1986), 29 C.C.C. (3d) 345 (Ont. C.A.).

In *R. v. Mezzo*, [1986] 1 S.C.R. 802, 27 C.C.C. (3d) 97 (7:2), the majority of the court reaffirmed its adherence to the statement of the test set out in *United States of America v. Sheppard*, [1977] 2 S.C.R. 1067, 30 C.C.C. (2d) 424 [noted under s. 548] for determining whether the evidence is sufficient to justify the trial judge putting the case to the jury. That test, whether there is any evidence upon which a reasonable jury, properly instructed, could return a verdict of guilty, employs as the measure of the sufficiency the concept of a *prima facie* case, that is, a case containing evidence on all essential points of a charge which, if believed by the trier of fact and unanswered, would warrant a conviction. Questions of credibility and the quality, in the sense of the weight to be attached to the evidence, are for the jury to decide after appropriate directions from the trial judge.

If there is admissible evidence, whether direct or circumstantial, which if believed by a properly instructed jury acting reasonably would justify a conviction, then the case must be left to the jury. The trial judge on an application for a directed verdict is not entitled to weigh the evidence, test its quality or reliability, or draw inferences of fact from that evidence: *R. v. Monteleone*, [1987] 2 S.C.R. 154, 35 C.C.C. (3d) 193 (7:0). Furthermore, where the evidence is purely circumstantial, the question of whether or not there is a rational explanation for the evidence other than the guilt of the accused is a question for the jury: *R. v. Charemski*, [1998] 1 S.C.R. 679, 123 C.C.C. (3d) 225.

On a trial by judge and jury, where the trial judge rules that there is no evidence upon which a jury properly instructed may convict and so allows an application for a directed verdict of acquittal, then the trial judge should withdraw the case from the jury and enter the verdict of acquittal: *R. v. Rowbotham*, [1994] 2 S.C.R. 463, 90 C.C.C. (3d) 449.

Right to make full answer and defence generally – The seating and location of the accused is within the sole discretion of the trial judge and his decision refusing to permit the accused to sit outside the prisoner's dock will not be interfered with on appeal unless the decision manifestly precluded the accused from making full answer and defence: *R. v. Faid* (1981), 61 C.C.C. (2d) 28 (Alta. C.A.), revd on other grounds [1983] 1 S.C.R. 265, 2 C.C.C. (3d) 513.

In *R. v. Lovie* (1995), 100 C.C.C. (3d) 68 (Ont. C.A.), the accused refused to return to the witness-stand to complete his cross-examination. After several adjournments to permit examinations by psychiatrists, the trial judge rejected an application for a mistrial when the accused still refused to return to the witness-stand. In the circumstances, the trial judge could direct the jury that if they found the refusal was deliberate, or was based on symptoms of mental disorder that were simulated, the jury was entitled to consider that circumstance not only in assessing what weight they should give to the accused's testimony-in-chief, but they could also use it in assessing the accused's reliability as a witness. His refusal to complete the cross-examination could not, however, be considered evidence of consciousness of guilt.

Right to counsel – Where there is a conflict of interest between two accused the same counsel should not act for both, even at separate trials for the same offence: *R. v. Depatie* (1970), 2 C.C.C. (2d) 339 (Ont. C.A.).

A trial judge's order refusing to allow defence counsel to withdraw was, in its peculiar circumstances of delaying manoeuvres and the equivocal discharge, upheld: *R. v. Spataro*, [1974] S.C.R. 253, 7 C.C.C. (2d) 1 (3:2).

An accused has the right to make full answer and defence personally, and counsel cannot be forced upon an unwilling accused. Where an accused wishes to discharge counsel part way through his trial he must be permitted to do so: *R. v. Bowles and Danylak* (1985), 21 C.C.C. (3d) 540 (Alta. C.A.).

In *R. v. Barrette*, [1977] 2 S.C.R. 121, 29 C.C.C. (2d) 189, the accused's case was called for trial some five months after that date was set on consent. His counsel improperly was not present and he was forced on and gave evidence. It was held (6:3) that even though the accused was treated with consideration by the Crown, the trial judge erred in visiting upon the accused the sins of his counsel's non-appearance and the congested court system particularly where the accused himself was without fault. While a decision for adjournment is in the judge's discretion, it is a judicial discretion which may be reviewed on appeal if it is based on reasons which are not well-founded in law. Accordingly, where it cannot be said on a review of the proceedings that the accused had a fair trial his conviction should be quashed and a new trial ordered.

Representation of the accused by counsel is generally essential to a fair trial. Where the accused desires to be defended by counsel then, unless the accused has deliberately failed to retain counsel or has discharged counsel with the intent of delaying the process of the court, the court should afford the accused a reasonable opportunity to retain counsel: *R. v. Smith* (1989), 52 C.C.C. (3d) 90 (Ont. C.A.).

Where following the withdrawal of his counsel the accused was given over a month and a half and two adjournments in order to obtain a new lawyer, and on the date set for trial on the last occasion the court was satisfied that the accused had not retained a lawyer and was attempting to delay the trial, there was no error in refusing a further request for an adjournment: *R. v. Manhas* (1978), 17 C.R. (3d) 331 (B.C.C.A.), affd [1980] 1 S.C.R. 591 (7:0).

While the Constitution has not expressly constitutionalized the right of an indigent accused to be provided with counsel, in cases not falling within the provincial legal aid plans, ss. 7 and 11(*d*) of the *Charter of Rights and Freedoms*, which guarantee an accused a fair trial in accordance with the principles of fundamental justice, require funded counsel to be provided if the accused wishes counsel, but cannot pay a lawyer, and representation of the accused by counsel is essential to a fair trial. Where a trial judge is confronted with a case where legal aid has been refused to an indigent accused in circumstances where representation by counsel is essential, then the judge may stay the proceedings until the necessary funding of counsel is available. An accused, however, who has the means to pay the costs of her defence but refuses to retain counsel may properly be considered to have chosen to defend herself and there would be no breach of the Charter if the trial proceeded without counsel being appointed: *R. v. Rowbotham* (1988), 41 C.C.C. (3d) 1 (Ont. C.A.).

Before staying proceedings, however, the trial judge must determine whether the accused is incapable of self-representation because of the seriousness and complexity of the case: *R. v. Wilson* (1997), 121 C.C.C. (3d) 92 (N.S.C.A.).

An accused, entitled to receive the assistance of counsel in order to make full answer and defence, is entitled to effective assistance and it is generally recognized that a lawyer representing more than one accused in a joint criminal trial is potentially in a position of conflict such that he will not be able to provide effective assistance. In a case of joint representation of conflicting interests, defence counsel's basic duty of undivided loyalty and effective assistance is jeopardized and his performance may be adversely affected since he may refrain from doing certain things for one client by reason of his concern that his action might adversely affect his other client: *R. v. Silvini* (1991), 68 C.C.C. (3d) 251 (Ont. C.A.).

A provincial court judge has the power to appoint counsel in an appropriate case: *R. v. White* (1976), 32 C.C.C. (2d) 478 (Alta. S.C.T.D.).

In principle, the accused's trial counsel is a compellable witness but it would only be in extraordinary circumstances that Crown counsel should, without prior warning, call defence counsel, with the result that counsel would be forced out of the case. Thus, in *R. v. St. Laurent* (1984), 11 C.C.C. (3d) 74 (Que. C.A.), a new trial was ordered where Crown counsel had insisted on calling defence counsel although it was totally unnecessary. In the circumstances justice was not seen to be done by the accused.

Although the accused had discharged his counsel and attempted to cross-examine the Crown witnesses himself, he should have been permitted to have his former counsel re-enter the case and complete cross-examination when the accused found he was unable to properly conduct the case: *R. v. Long* (1983), 9 C.C.C. (3d) 229 (Que. C.A.).

Assistance to unrepresented accused – Consistent with the trial judge's duty to ensure that an unrepresented accused has a fair trial, the judge is required within reason to provide assistance to him, to aid him in the proper conduct of his defence, and to guide him throughout the trial in such a way that his defence is brought out with its full force and effect. The judge is not, however, required to become the accused's advocate and, for example, search through the preliminary inquiry transcript for inconsistencies in the evidence of the Crown witnesses. The judge, having explained to the accused how he could cross-examine on the preliminary inquiry transcript, was not obliged to go any further: *R. v. McGibbon* (1988), 45 C.C.C. (3d) 334 (Ont. C.A.).

Moreover, it is not open to the trial judge to conduct an extensive cross-examination of the Crown witnesses as would be expected from defence counsel and which goes beyond merely assisting the accused: *R. v. Turlon* (1989), 49 C.C.C. (3d) 186 (Ont. C.A.).

Where the accused is unrepresented and there is admissible uncontradicted evidence of a Charter breach, the trial judge has an obligation to raise the issue and conduct a hearing: *R. v. Travers* (2001), 154 C.C.C. (3d) 426 (N.S.C.A.); *R. v. Richards* (2017), 349 C.C.C. (3d) 284 (Ont. C.A.); *R. v. Bialski* (2018), 364 C.C.C. (3d) 485 (Sask. C.A.), leave to appeal to S.C.C. refused 2019 CarswellSask 89; *R. v. Breton* (2018), 366 C.C.C. (3d) 281 (Ont. C.A.).

Accused's right to call witnesses – The accused has an absolute right to call any Crown witness, who has previously testified and been cross-examined by him, as a defence witness: *R. v. Cook* (1960), 127 C.C.C. 287 (3:2) (Alta. S.C. App. Div.).

A trial judge should not make any order as to the sequence of the defence witnesses and where he indicated that if the accused did not precede his witnesses he would not consider his evidence too strongly a new trial was ordered: *R. v. Smuk* (1971), 3 C.C.C. (2d) 457 (B.C.C.A.). Nor can he simply direct the order in which the accused will testify: *R. v. Angelantoni* (1975), 28 C.C.C. (2d) 179 (Ont. C.A.).

In an earlier case, *R. v. Archer* (1972), 26 C.R.N.S. 225 (Ont. C.A.), the court held that the trial judge did not err in requiring the defence to call the accused first when the defence raised was alibi as it was to the accused's benefit that he do so.

In *R. v. Sparre* (1977), 37 C.C.C. (2d) 495 (Ont. Co. Ct.), the trial judge considered *R. v. Archer, supra,* and held that no special rule applies where the defence is alibi and that defence counsel may call witnesses in any order that counsel sees fit and the accused need not be called first.

Right to make submissions – The failure of the trial judge to invite an unrepresented accused to make submissions at the close of the evidence constitutes a deprivation of the right to make full answer and defence and will result in the conviction being set aside: *R. v. Aucoin*, [1979] 1 S.C.R. 554; *R. v. Gronka* (1979), 45 C.C.C. (2d) 573 (Ont. C.A.).

Surrebuttal evidence – It is open to a court to grant leave to the accused to call evidence in surrebuttal to reply evidence: *R. v. Demeter* (1975), 25 C.C.C. (2d) 417 at p. 473, 10 O.R. (2d) 321 at p. 377 (C.A.) (5:0), affd [1978] 1 S.C.R. 538, 34 C.C.C. (2d) 137.

Subsection (3), which gives the accused the right "after the close of the case for the prosecution" to make full answer and defence, must apply to evidence given by way of rebuttal as well as to that given during the Crown's case-in-chief. Accordingly, it was held in *R. v. Ewert* (1989), 52 C.C.C. (3d) 280 (B.C.C.A.), that the rules regarding the permissible scope of surrebuttal must be applied liberally in favour of the accused where the accused relied on the defence of insanity and evidence to rebut that defence was first given by the Crown in rebuttal.

Reopening the case – The fundamental principle, in determining whether the Crown should be permitted to reopen its case, is whether the accused will suffer prejudice in his defence and this will depend on the stage at which the application is made and the nature of the evidence to be called. Before the Crown has closed its case, the trial judge has considerable latitude to permit the Crown to recall a witness to correct earlier testimony. Once the Crown actually closes its case, the trial judge's discretion will be narrow with reopening being permitted to correct some oversight or inadvertent omission, provided that justice requires it and there will be no prejudice to the defence. Where the Crown has closed its case and the defence has started to answer the case, then the trial judge's discretion is very restricted and it will only be in the narrowest of circumstances that the Crown will be permitted to reopen its case: *R. v. P. (M.B.)*, [1994] 1 S.C.R. 555, 89 C.C.C. (3d) 289.

The test to permit the defence to re-open the case varies according to the stage of proceedings reached when the application is made. Where the application is made after a finding of guilt has been entered, the test is more rigorous. In addition to the criteria set out in *R. v. Palmer*, [1980] 1 S.C.R. 759, dealing with the admissibility of fresh evidence, the trial judge must consider whether the application to re-open is in reality an attempt to reverse a tactical decision made at trial: *R. v. Arabia* (2008), 235 C.C.C. (3d) 354 (Ont. C.A.).

The decision of a trial judge to allow the Crown to re-open its case is discretionary and will generally be accorded great deference. It must be exercised judicially and in the interests of justice. The discretion is broadest during the first phase where the Crown has not yet closed its case. At the second phase, which arises when the Crown has just closed its case but the defence has not yet elected whether or not to call evidence, the discreiton is more limited. In the third phase, where the defence has already begun to answer the Crown's case, the discretion of the trial judge is extremely narrow. The emphasis during this last phase is the protection fo the accused's interests. There are limited circumstances where the Crown will be entitled to re-open its case even during this phase; for example, where the conduct of the defence directly or indirectly contributes to the Crown's failure to lead the particular evidence before the close of its case or where the Crown has made an omission or mistake on a non-controversial issue that was purely formal or technical and had nothing to do with the substance of the case. Re-opening during the third phase of the trial should only be permitted in those very exceptional cases that are closely analogous to these two examples. At the third stage of the trial, the opportunity to re-call Crown witnesses and to re-open the case for the defence can never completely cure the resulting harm to the defence. The accused is almost inevitably prejudiced where the re-opening will require the accused to take the stand for a second time and undergo further cross-examination. The court should not speculate as to whether the defence would have changed if the evidence had been adduced in the proper order. If the trial judge refuses the Crown's application to re-open, the Crown may either elect to proceed without the witness or may enter a stay of proceedings and recommence the trial within the requisite time period under s. 579 of the *Criminal Code*. If the Crown elects to recommence the trial, it will be for the judge presiding at the new trial to determine whether this procedure has created an abuse of process or such unfairness that the rights of the accused have been violated: *R. v. G. (S.G.)*, [1997] 2 S.C.R. 716, 116 C.C.C. (3d) 193.

Where during his address to the jury counsel for the accused, who had called no evidence, argued that the Crown had failed to prove the identity of the accused as the person referred to by the same name in the evidence of a Crown witness read in at trial, the trial judge had a discretion where the interest of justice so required and the accused was not in danger of being taken by surprise, to allow the Crown to reopen its case for the purpose of formal identification, an inference that the jury would have been entitled to assume in any event: *R. v. Robillard* (1975), 24 C.C.C. (2d) 36, 30 C.R.N.S. 351 (Que. C.A.) (2:1), affd [1978] 2 S.C.R. 728, 41 C.C.C. (2d) 1 (9:0).

A judge sitting without a jury is not *functus officio* following a finding of guilt until he has imposed sentence or otherwise finally disposed of the case. Accordingly, he may in his discretion, following a finding of guilt, vacate that finding, reopen the case, and permit the accused to tender further evidence. However, this power should be exercised only in exceptional circumstances and where its exercise is clearly called for. It should be noted, however, that a judge has no power to reopen a case following an acquittal since the proceeding has been terminated by such a verdict. Further, when sitting with a jury, under no circumstances has a judge power to set aside the jury's verdict: *R. v. Lessard* (1976), 30 C.C.C. (2d) 70, 33 C.R.N.S. 16 (Ont. C.A.).

A judge does, however, have power to reopen an acquittal where the acquittal was not on the merits but solely on the basis of application of the rule against multiple convictions as set out in *R. v. Kienapple*, [1975] 1 S.C.R. 729, 15 C.C.C. (2d) 524; *R. v. Schmidt, Able and Medeiros* (1982), 66 C.C.C. (2d) 366, 35 O.R. (2d) 784 (C.A.), leave to appeal to S.C.C. refused C.C.C. *loc. cit.*, 42 N.R. 179*n*.

Disclosure to defence – [**Note:** As to records containing personal information of the complainant or a witness in sexual assault offences, now see ss. 278.1 to 278.9.]

At least in the case of indictable offences, the Crown is required to produce to the defence all relevant information whether or not the Crown intends to introduce it into evidence and whether it is inculpatory or exculpatory. The Crown does have a discretion to withhold information and as to the timing of the disclosure where necessary to protect the identity of an informer or a continuing investigation. A discretion must also be exercised with respect to the relevance of information. The exercise of this discretion is reviewable by the trial judge who will be guided by the general principle that information ought not to be withheld if there is a reasonable possibility that the withholding of information will impair the right of the accused to make full answer and defence, unless the non-disclosure is justified by the law of privilege. Even then, the trial judge might conclude that the recognition of an existing privilege does not constitute a reasonable limit on the constitutional right to make full answer and defence and thus require disclosure in spite of the law of privilege. Initial disclosure should occur before the accused is called upon to elect the mode of trial or to plead. The obligation to disclose will be triggered by a request by or on behalf of the accused. In the case of an unrepresented accused, the trial judge should not take a plea unless satisfied that the accused has been informed of his right to disclosure: *R. v. Stinchcombe*, [1991] 3 S.C.R. 326, 68 C.C.C. (3d) 1 (7:0).

Where the Crown disputes the existence of material which the defence alleges is relevant, the defence must establish a basis which could enable the presiding judge to conclude that there is in existence further material which is potentially relevant. Relevance in this context means that there is a reasonable possibility of being useful to the accused in making full answer and defence. The existence of the disputed material must be sufficiently identified to reveal its nature and enable the judge to determine that it may meet the test for requiring disclosure as set out in *R. v. Stinchcombe, supra*. In most cases, this preliminary issue can be determined on the basis of submissions. If the defence meets this preliminary test, then the Crown must justify a continuing refusal to disclose and is entitled to call relevant evidence on the issue: *R. v. Chaplin*, [1995] 1 S.C.R. 727, 96 C.C.C. (3d) 225.

CR. CODE

There is no absolute right to have originals of documents or tape recordings produced. If the Crown has the originals, it should either produce them or allow them to be inspected. If, however, the originals are not available and if they have been in the Crown's possession then it should explain their absence. If the explanation is satisfactory, the Crown has discharged its obligations unless the conduct which resulted in the absence or loss of the original is itself such that it may warrant a remedy under the Charter: *R. v. Stinchcombe*, [1995] 1 S.C.R. 754, 96 C.C.C. (3d) 318.

The disclosure requirements upon the Crown did not put a duty on the Crown to obtain the prison records of a Crown witness. This was an ordinary criminal prosecution being conducted by a prosecutor in the department of the provincial Attorney General. The federal penitentiary authorities were strangers to the proceedings and there could not be any onus on the Crown to seek out such material which had nothing to do with the crime or the matters at issue in the case, but, at most, might bear on the credibility of a prospective Crown witness: *R. v. Gingras* (1992), 71 C.C.C. (3d) 53, 120 A.R. 300 (C.A.).

The Crown's duty to disclose is triggered whenever there is a reasonable possibility of the information being useful to the accused in making full answer and defence. The Crown's duty to disclose gives rise to a corresponding constitutional right to the disclosure of all material which meets the threshold for disclosure. The right to disclosure is violated where the accused demonstrates a reasonable possibility that the undisclosed information could have been used in meeting the case for the Crown, advancing a defence or otherwise making a decision which could have affected the conduct of the defence. Although the right to disclosure may be violated, the right to make full answer and defence may not be impaired as a result of that violation. Different principles and standards apply in determining whether disclosure should be made before conviction and in determining the effect of a failure to disclose after conviction. When non-disclosure is raised on appeal from a conviction, the accused must, as a threshold matter, establish a violation of the right to disclosure and must demonstrate on the balance of probabilities that the right to make full answer and defence was impaired as a result of the failure to disclose. Where a stay of proceedings is sought, the accused must establish on the balance of probabilities that the right to make full answer and defence is irreparably prejudiced. Where the remedy sought is a new trial, that burden is discharged where an accused demonstrates there is a reasonable possibility that the non-disclosure affected the outcome at trial or the overall fairness of the trial process. The reasonable possibility must be based on reasonably possible uses of the non-disclosed evidence or reasonably possible avenues of investigation that were closed to the accused as a result of the non-disclosure. In order to determine whether the right to make full answer and defence was impaired, a two-step analysis must be undertaken. First, in order to assess the reliability of the conviction, the undisclosed information must be examined to determine the impact it might have had on the decision to convict. A new trial should be ordered if the appellate court is satisfied that there is a reasonable possibility that, on its face, the undisclosed information affects the reliability of the conviction. Even if the undisclosed information does not itself affect the reliability of the conviction, the effect of the non-disclosure on the overall fairness of the trial process must be considered at the second stage of the analysis by assessing, on the basis of a reasonable possibility, the lines of inquiry with witnesses or the opportunities to garner additional evidence that could have been available to the defence if the relevant information had been disclosed. Defence counsel's diligence in pursuing disclosure from the Crown must be taken into account in considering the overall fairness of the trial process. The lack of due diligence is a significant factor in determining whether the Crown's non-disclosure affected the fairness of the trial process. The fairness of the trial process will not be affected where defence counsel knew or ought to have known on the basis of other disclosures that through inadvertence the Crown had failed to disclose information, yet remained passive as a result of a tactical decision or lack of due diligence: *R. v . Dixon*, [1998] 1 S.C.R. 244, 122 C.C.C. (3d) 1.

In applying the *Dixon* test, the issue is not whether the undisclosed evidence *would* have made a difference, but rather whether it *could* have made a difference. The appellate court must determine whether there is a reasonable possibility that the additional evidence could have created a reasonable doubt in the jury's mind. This must be assessed having regard to the evidence in its entirety. With respect to the second prong of the *Dixon* test, the appellant need only establish a reasonable possibility that the overall fairness of the trial process was impaired. This burden can be discharged by showing that the undisclosed evidence could have been used to impeach the credibility of a prosecution witness, could have assisted the defence in its pre-trial investigations and preparations or in its tactical decisions at trial: *R. v. Illes*, [2008] 3 S.C.R. 134, 236 C.C.C. (3d) 129.

Where evidence that should have been disclosed has been lost, the Crown has a duty to explain the loss. Where the Crown's explanation satisfies the trial judge that the evidence has not been destroyed or lost owing to unacceptable negligence, the duty to disclose has not been breached. In considering whether the explanation is satisfactory, the court should review the circumstances surrounding the loss of the evidence. The main consideration is whether the Crown or the police took reasonable steps in the circumstances to preserve the evidence for disclosure. One circumstance that must be considered is the relevance that the evidence was perceived to have had at the time. The police cannot be expected to preserve everything and even the loss of relevant evidence will not result in a breach of the duty to disclose the conduct of the police is reasonable. As the relevance of the evidence increases, however, so does the degree of care for its preservation that is expected of the police. Note that the court left open the issue of a remedy in the extraordinary case in which a satisfactory explanation is given for the loss of the evidence and no abuse of process is found but the evidence is so important that its loss renders a fair trial problematic: *R. v. La*, [1997] 2 S.C.R. 680, 116 C.C.C. (3d) 97.

The Crown is under a duty at common law to disclose to the defence all material evidence whether favourable to the accused or not. Failure to disclose may constitute grounds for appeal where it results in an unfair trial. Thus, on a charge of sexual assault, a new trial was ordered where the prosecution failed to disclose to the defence the existence of a witness who had questioned the complainant about sexual abuse. The complainant had denied being abused and, had the defence been aware of the statement, it might have been used to support the defence that the evidence of the complainant was fabricated: *R. v. C. (M.H.)*, [1991] 1 S.C.R. 763, 63 C.C.C. (3d) 385 (5:0).

The Crown was required to disclose evidence in its possession that could rebut evidence of good character the accused proposed to call. That evidence could reasonably be used by the accused in advancing a defence and in making a decision which could affect the conduct of the defence, such as whether or not to call evidence: *R. v. Hutter* (1993), 86 C.C.C. (3d) 81, 16 O.R. (3d) 145 (C.A.), leave to appeal to S.C.C. refused 87 C.C.C. (3d) vi, 72 O.A.C. 140*n*.

Counsel for the accused is required to bring any lack of disclosure to the attention of the trial judge at the earliest opportunity. At least in the case of a trial by judge alone this includes a lack of disclosure that comes to counsel's attention after conviction and before sentence. During this period, the trial judge is still seized of the trial and would have the discretion to reopen the trial proceedings or to order a mistrial: *R. v. McAnespie*, [1993] 4 S.C.R. 501, 86 C.C.C. (3d) 191*n*.

The principles of fundamental justice as guaranteed by the Charter reflect and accommodate the nature of the common law doctrine of abuse of process. Issues relating to disclosure by the Crown would normally fall within ss. 7 and 11(*d*) of the Charter. Therefore, a challenge based on non-disclosure will generally require a showing of actual prejudice to the ability to make full answer and defence. The accused must establish that the impugned non-disclosure has, on the balance of probabilities, prejudiced or had an adverse effect on the accused's ability to make full answer and defence. Such a determination requires a reasonable inquiry into the materiality of the non-disclosed information. The propriety of the Crown's conduct or intention are not necessarily relevant to whether or not the accused's right to a fair trial has been infringed. Once a violation is made out, the remedy will typically be a disclosure order and an adjournment. There may be some extreme cases, however, where the prejudice to the accused's ability to make full answer and defence or to the integrity of the justice system is irremediable. In those clearest of cases, a stay of proceedings will be appropriate. Other remedies would include permitting the defence to recall certain witnesses for examination or cross-examination, adjournments to permit the defence to subpoena additional witnesses or even, in extreme cases, declaring a mistrial. When considering the appropriate remedy, the court should consider whether the Crown's breach of its disclosure obligations has also violated fundamental principles underlying the community's sense of decency and fair play, and thereby caused prejudice to the integrity of the judicial system. For these purposes, among the most relevant considerations are the conduct and intention of the Crown. However, a demonstration of *mala fides* on the part of the Crown is not a necessary pre-condition to a finding of flagrant and intentional Crown misconduct which might lead to a stay of proceedings: *R. v. O'Connor*, [1995] 4 S.C.R. 411, 103 C.C.C. (3d) 1 (5:3).

In *R. v. 974649 Ontario Inc.*, [2001] 3 S.C.R. 575, 159 C.C.C. (3d) 321, the court held that a provincial offences court was a court of competent jurisdiction within the meaning of s. 24(1) of the *Canadian Charter of Rights and Freedoms* with the power to award costs for breach of the defendant's right to disclosure. The reasoning in that case would apply to a trial court acting under the *Criminal Code*.

Records relating to findings of serious misconduct by police officers involved in the investigation against the accused are first party disclosure where the police misconduct is either related to the investigation, or the finding of misconduct could reasonably impact on the case against the accused. The Crown does not encompass all state authorities and, accordingly, the *Stinchcombe* disclosure regime only extends to material relating to the accused's case in the possession or control of the prosecuting Crown entity. There is a corollary duty on the police to disclose all material pertaining to the investigation of an accused to the prosecuting Crown. Production of disciplinary records and criminal investigation files in the possession of the police that do not fall within the scope of first party disclosure are governed by the *R. v. O'Connor* regime for third party production. The *O'Connor* likely relevance threshold differs significantly from the statutory likely relevance threshold set out in s. 278.3 of the *Criminal Code*. Under the *O'Connor* regime, likely relevant means a reasonable possibility that the information is logically probative to an issue at trial or the competence of a witness to testify. An issue at trial includes not only material issues concerning the unfolding of events but also evidence relating to credibility of witnesses and reliability of other evidence in the case. Once the court has ascertained that the records are truly relevant, the third party records are in the same category for disclosure purposes as the fruits of the investigation. While privacy interests may require redactions of the disclosure, it is unlikely that, in the context of investigative files or disciplinary records, a third party privacy interest can defeat an application for production: *R. v. McNeil*, [2009] 1 S.C.R. 66, 238 C.C.C. (3d) 353.

[**Note:** The following cases were decided prior to the recent amendments adding ss. 278.1 to 278.9 which set out a statutory scheme for production and disclosure of records containing personal information of the complainant or a witness at the trial of specified sexual offences. This scheme applies to a wide range of records, including records in possession of the Crown.]

The accused's entitlement to production from third parties or the Crown constitutes a constitutional right. Where interview notes with the complainant about the sexual assault were destroyed by a crisis center, the appropriate remedy was a stay of proceedings. The proof of actual or additional prejudice relates to the appropriate remedy under s. 24(1) of the Charter. If the material which was destroyed met the threshold test for disclosure or production, the accused's Charter rights were breached without the requirement of showing additional prejudice. There was sufficient evidence before the trial judge to support the conclusion that there was a reasonable possibility that the information contained in the notes that were destroyed was logically probative to an issue at trial as to the credibility of the complainant thereby satisfying the test for disclosure and the higher test for production from third parties. In this case, the material met the requisite test for disclosure as the Crown, the complainant, and the centre had consented to a disclosure order at trial and consequently, the Crown was required to disclose the file. Even if the somewhat higher standard relating to production from third parties applied, it would have been met in this case as the notes related to the complainant's initial disclosure of the alleged incidents and constituted the first written record of the complainant's allegations. The accused could have made use of the information in the notes although it was difficult to specify the precise manner in which the information would have been used without knowing the contents of the notes. In considering the appropriate remedy, the lack of availability of an alternative remedy and irreparable prejudice to the integrity of the judicial system if the prosecution were continued are alternative factors. The presence of either one justifies the exercise of discretion in favour of a stay: *R. v. Carosella*, [1997] 1 S.C.R. 80, 112 C.C.C. (3d) 289. However, also now see: *R. v. Buric*, [1997] 1 S.C.R. 535, 114 C.C.C. (3d) 95.

Also see notes under s. 603.

Right of jury to ask questions of witnesses – While jurors may ask questions of witnesses, the judge should refrain from inviting such questioning. Where jurors seek to ask questions they should be instructed that the conduct of the case, including lines of questioning, is in the hands of the parties. The questions should not transform the nature of the trial and it is preferable that any questions be reduced to writing and asked at the conclusion of the examination by both counsel: *R. v. Nordyne* (1998), 17 C.R. (5th) 393 (Que. C.A.), leave to appeal to S.C.C. refused 232 N.R. 195*n*.

Intervention by trial judge – While examination and cross-examination of witnesses are primarily the responsibility of counsel, the judge is not required to remain silent and may question witnesses to clear up ambiguities, explore some matter which the answers of a witness have left vague and he may put questions which should have been put to bring out some relevant matter, but which have been omitted. Generally speaking, the questions by the judge should be put after counsel has completed his examination, and the witnesses should not be cross-examined by the judge during their examination-in-chief. The judge also has a duty to intervene to clear the innocent. He has the duty to ensure that the accused is afforded the right to make full answer and defence, but he has the right and the duty to prevent the trial from being unnecessarily protracted by questions directed to irrelevant matters. This power must however be exercised with caution so as to leave unfettered the right of an accused to subject any witness' testimony to the test of cross-examination. The judge must not improperly curtail cross-examination that is relevant to the issues or the credibility of witnesses, but he has power to protect a witness from harassment by questions that are repetitious or are irrelevant: *R. v. Valley* (1986), 26 C.C.C. (3d) 207 (Ont. C.A.).

The trial judge may not question the accused or his witnesses to such an extent or in such a manner that he conveys the impression of placing his authority on the side of the prosecution or the impression of disbelief of the defence evidence: *R. v. Brouillard*, [1985] 1 S.C.R. 39, 17 C.C.C. (3d) 193.

Mere discourtesy to counsel by the trial judge is not itself ground for quashing a conviction. Where, however, the trial judge suggests that counsel is acting in a professionally unethical manner for the purpose of misleading the jury, the integrity and good faith of the defence may be denigrated and the appearance of an unfair trial created: *R. v. Turkiewicz, Barrow and MacNamara* (1979), 50 C.C.C. (2d) 406 (Ont. C.A.).

DESIGNATION OF COUNSEL OF RECORD / Contents of designation / Effect of designation / When court orders presence of accused.

650.01 (1) An accused may appoint counsel to represent the accused for any proceedings under this Act by filing a designation with the court.

(2) The designation must contain the name and address of the counsel and be signed by the accused and the designated counsel.

(3) If a designation is filed,

(*a*) the accused may appear by the designated counsel without being present for any part of the proceedings, other than

(i) a part during which oral evidence of a witness is taken,

(ii) a part during which jurors are being selected, and

(iii) an application for a writ of habeas corpus;

(*b*) an appearance by the designated counsel is equivalent to the accused's being present, unless the court orders otherwise; and

(*c*) a plea of guilty may be made, and a sentence may be pronounced, only if the accused is present, unless the court orders otherwise.

(4) If the court orders the accused to be present otherwise than by appearance by the designated counsel, the court may

(*a*) issue a summons to compel the presence of the accused and order that it be served by leaving a copy at the address contained in the designation; or

(*b*) issue a warrant to compel the presence of the accused. 2002, c. 13, s. 61.

CROSS-REFERENCES

"Counsel" is defined in s. 2. Section 650.02 permits the designated counsel to appear by technological means. Where this section does not apply and the accused does not wish to be present, he or she must apply to the trial judge for an order in accordance with s. 650(2)(*b*).

SYNOPSIS

This section permits the accused to designate a counsel to appear on behalf of the accused without the accused being present for certain proceedings. Notwithstanding the accused has filed a designation under this section, the judge may require the accused to be present and issue a summons or warrant for that purpose.

ANNOTATIONS

This provision does not allow counsel to elect the mode of trial for an accused without the accused's presence or a written document. In addition, only counsel named in the designation may appear on behalf of the accused and, accordingly, the election by counsel's agent was invalid: *R. v. Trites* (2011), 268 C.C.C. (3d) 206 (N.B.C.A.).

The term "counsel" includes law firms and lawyers specifically named in the designation, as well as other lawyers and articling students who are authorized by the law firm or named lawyer to act as a designated counsel from time-to-time, provided that the designation signed by the defendant specifically permits such use of articling students: *R. v. Golyanik* (2003), 173 C.C.C. (3d) 307 (Ont. S.C.J.).

Paralegals are included in the definition of "counsel" in this provision and can appear on an administrative remand for an accused charged with an indictable offence, pursuant to a proper designation: *R. v. L. (G.Y.)* (2009), 246 C.C.C. (3d) 112 (Ont. S.C.J.).

An inmate serving a sentence in a federal penitentiary is not an "accused" within the meaning of subsec. (3)(*b*)(iii): *R. v. Gustavson* (2005), 193 C.C.C. (3d) 545 (B.C.C.A.).

A court may permit an accused to enter a guilty plea and obtain sentence by designated counsel. An application under subsec. (3)(*c*) requires the court to balance the public interest in having the accused physically present in the courtroom against the inconvenience, or other reasons advanced by the accused, for not being present in the courtroom. Due to the serious nature of a guilty plea and sentencing, the accused must support his or her application with factors that show significant hardship to him or herself if required to physically attend. Factors that may support the court allowing for designated counsel to appear on a guilty plea and/or sentencing include: serious illness or infirmity, deplorable conditions in jail, family considerations, financial hardship, and excessive travel. Factors that may support requiring the accused to physically attend include: nature of the proceeding, seriousness of the offence, engagement of community in the matter, respect for the courts, and maintaining the repute of the administration of justice. If the accused does appear through designated counsel, appropriate safeguards should be put in place to alleviate societal concerns: *R. v. Walker* (2014), 313 C.C.C. (3d) 467 (Ont. C.J.).

TECHNOLOGICAL APPEARANCE.

650.02 The prosecutor or the counsel designated under section 650.01 may appear before the court by any technological means satisfactory to the court that permits the court and all counsel to communicate simultaneously. 2002, c. 13, s. 61.

PRE-CHARGE CONFERENCE.

650.1 A judge in a jury trial may, before the charge to the jury, confer with the accused or counsel for the accused and the prosecutor with respect to the matters that should be explained to the jury and with respect to the choice of instructions to the jury. 1997, c. 18, s. 78.

ANNOTATIONS

As a general proposition, the format of the charge to the jury is a matter of discretion for the trial judge and judges should not be discouraged from taking new approaches in an effort to make their instructions more accessible to the jury. Instructing the jury in segments throughout the trial does not constitute error, and may in fact be beneficial in some circumstances. However, it does increase the risk that the jury might be confused by erroneous statements of law at the outset of the trial or by instructions that are not ultimately related to any of the evidence introduced in the case. Where the trial judge decides to provide the jury with a transcript of the instructions, including instructions given throughout the course of the trial, the judge must ensure that the entire charge is provided to the jury in a clear and legible form, and that all members of the jury are capable of reading the materials. It may well be that the dangers associated with such an approach outweigh the potential benefits: *R. v. Menard*, [1998] 2 S.C.R. 109, 125 C.C.C. (3d) 416.

The reference in *R. v. Menard, supra*, to the "entire charge" should be interpreted as meaning all of the instructions on the topic or topics to which the written material is directed. For example, if a judge decides to give a jury a written copy of the instructions relating to the applicable legal principles, that written material should contain all of the instructions referable to those principles. This requirement guards against two dangers. Juries may be misled by written instructions that tell them only part of what they have to know, and incomplete written instructions may be skewed in favour of one side or the other. If a trial judge decides to give a jury a written copy of part of the instructions, he or she should clearly identify the topics to be addressed in the written material and ensure that the written material contains a complete and balanced instruction on those topics. If the aim of written material is to assist the jury in arriving at a true verdict by improving its comprehension, recall and application of the oral instructions, that aim is best served by targeting for written reproduction those parts of the instructions that will prove difficult for the jury. Where the trial judge provides the jury with a written copy of the applicable legal principles care must be taken to ensure that the written material contains all the instructions referable to those principles including instructions on the presumption of innocence and reasonable doubt: *R. v. Poitras* (2002), 1 C.R. (6th) 366 (Ont. C.A.).

In *R. v. Poitras, supra*, the court found that the procedure followed by the trial judge was appropriate. Before giving the jury written material, the trial judge vetted the material with counsel and made several changes to the material in response to counsel's submissions. The trial judge alerted the jury to the fact that they would receive written instructions. The document he gave to the jury was very "reader friendly". It was well-spaced, made extensive use of headings, used straightforward, plain language and simple, declarative sentences. It also presented a balanced and accurate statement of the applicable legal principles.

In *R. v. Pan* (2014), 318 C.C.C. (3d) 54 (Ont. S.C.J.), the court considered the evolving practice with respect to allowing materials beyond trial exhibits and the judge's charge to go into the jury room. At issue here was a PowerPoint presentation prepared by a police analyst and relied on by the Crown in its closing address, which was intended to assist the jury in comprehending a large body of cell phone evidence. The court held that it was appropriate to provide this material to the jury, accompanied by a caution to guard against overemphasis or misuse. See also: *R. v. Basi* (2010), 90 W.C.B. (2d) 706, [2010] B.C.J. No. 2219 (S.C.); *R. v. Sandham* (2009), 85 W.C.B. (2d) 907, [2009] O.J. No. 4517 (S.C.J.); *R. v. Belcourt* (2012), 107 W.C.B. (2d) 675, [2012] B.C.J. No. 2966 (S.C.).

The trial judge, in order to avoid recalling the jury for further instructions, erred in permitting counsel to address the jury on factual issues after the charge to the jury was complete. Neither counsel should be permitted to comment to the jury after the judge's charge: *R. v. C. (J.D.)* (2003), 172 C.C.C. (3d) 268 (Ont. C.A.).

The practice of sending and receiving counsel's submissions on a draft jury charge via email is discouraged, as it risks contravening the accused's right to be present for his or her trial pursuant to s. 650. The pre-charge conference should be held in court, on the record, in the presence of the accused: *R. v. Hassanzada* (2016), 335 C.C.C. (3d) 1 (Ont. C.A.).

SUMMING UP BY PROSECUTOR / Summing up by accused / Accused's right of reply / Prosecutor's right of reply where more than one accused.

651. (1) Where an accused, or any one of several accused being tried together, is defended by counsel, the counsel shall, at the end of the case for the prosecution, declare whether or not he intends to adduce evidence on behalf of the accused for whom he appears and if he does not announce his intention to adduce evidence, the prosecutor may address the jury by way of summing up.

(2) Counsel for the accused or the accused, where he is not defended by counsel, is entitled, if he thinks fit, to open the case for the defence, and after the conclusion of that opening to examine such witnesses as he thinks fit, and when all the evidence is concluded to sum up the evidence.

(3) Where no witnesses are examined for an accused, he or his counsel is entitled to address the jury last, but otherwise counsel for the prosecution is entitled to address the jury last.

(4) Where two or more accused are tried jointly and witnesses are examined for any of them, all the accused or their respective counsel are required to address the jury before it is addressed by the prosecutor. R.S., c. C-34, s. 578.

CROSS-REFERENCES

The term "prosecutor" is defined in s. 2. For notes on the accused's right to counsel and the duty of the prosecution to call witnesses, see the notes following s. 650.

SYNOPSIS

This section contains the rules relating to the order of jury addresses.

By reason of subsecs. (1) and (3), if no defence evidence is called, the prosecutor shall address the jury first.

An accused who wishes to call evidence is entitled to make an opening statement to the jury (subsec. (2)).

Where an accused (or at least one of several accused) elects to call evidence, the Crown will address the jury last (subsec. (4)).

ANNOTATIONS

General – Subsection (2) is a statutory and substantive right to make submissions. The trial judge erred in failing to permit counsel to sum up evidence and state position on law at the end of the case: *R. v. Prior* (2010), 260 C.C.C. (3d) 281 (Nfld. & Lab. C.A.).

Opening addresses – The question whether defence counsel may make an opening statement immediately after Crown counsel's opening has been considered in a number of recent cases. The most restrictive view was taken in *R. v. Vitale* (1987), 40 C.C.C. (3d) 267 (Ont. Dist. Ct.), where it was held that defence counsel's only right to make an opening statement was as provided in this section, at the conclusion of the Crown's case if counsel intends to call evidence for the defence. In *R. v. Edwards* (1986), 31 C.R.R. 343 (Ont. H.C.J.), it was held that this section did not preclude defence counsel making an opening after Crown counsel's opening referring to the evidence counsel intended to call, provided that counsel undertook to call evidence. The most expansive view was taken in *R. v. Barrow* (1989), 48 C.C.C. (3d) 308 (N.S.S.C.), and in *R. v. Morgan* (1997), 125 C.C.C. (3d) 478 (Ont. Ct. (Gen. Div.)), where it was held that counsel could make an opening statement after Crown counsel's opening whether or not counsel had decided to call evidence. If the defence does not intend to call evidence or is unwilling to declare his intention at that time then counsel can tell the jury what evidence he expects to elicit in cross-examination of the Crown witnesses.

In *R. v. D. (A.)* (2003), 180 C.C.C. (3d) 319 (Ont. S.C.J.), the court held that the discretion to allow the defence to open immediately after the Crown should be exercised only in special or unusual circumstances which may include some of the following considerations: the trial is expected to be lengthy; the trial is expected to involve complex factual issues; the defence was not expected to be apparent to the jury during the Crown's lengthy case; there is competing and significant expert evidence; or the Crown has one central witness whose testimony was the focus of the case and from whom the defence expected to raise self-defence, or who would be the subject of significant inconsistencies and admitted perjuries.

Subsection (2) does not give defence counsel the right to make any comment he or she may wish. The trial judge has the authority to prevent counsel from straying into improper territory during the opening. In this case, the trial judge did not err in ordering that defence counsel not inform the jury that a defence witness would admit to confessing to the murder with which the accused was charged. Because of earlier rulings, the trial judge was aware that it was far from clear that the witness would say any such thing. In an opening statement, counsel should not make comments about the facts that will not or cannot be supported by proof: *R. v. Sparvier* (2006), 215 C.C.C. (3d) 555 (Sask. C.A.).

Right to testify – The right to call witnesses and testify is not absolute. In exceptional cases where, despite efforts by the trial judge to avoid the inevitable, an accused still persists in disruptive conduct and abuse of his rights, then he can lose the right to testify and call witnesses: *R. v. Fabrikant* (1995), 97 C.C.C. (3d) 544 (Que. C.A.), leave to appeal to S.C.C. refused 98 C.C.C. (3d) vi.

Order of closing addresses – The order of addresses as prescribed by subsecs. (3) and (4) does not offend the fundamental justice and fair hearing guarantees in ss. 7 and 11(*d*) of the *Canadian Charter of Rights and Freedoms*. However, where the trial judge is of the opinion that an irregularity in counsel's address has jeopardized the fairness of the trial, in most cases, it may be rectified by a specific correcting reference in the charge to the jury. Exceptionally, where the judge is of the opinion that a direction in the charge will not suffice, the judge may grant the prejudiced party a limited opportunity to reply. Such prejudice may arise where the substantive legal theory of liability that the Crown has added or substituted in its closing has so dramatically changed that the accused could not reasonably have been expected to answer such an argument, or where the accused was actually misled by the Crown as to the theory intended to be advanced. It is, however, only in the clearest of cases of unfairness that the trial judge should grant an opportunity to reply. The reply must be confined to those issues improperly dealt with by Crown counsel: *R. v. Rose*, [1998] 3 S.C.R. 262, 129 C.C.C. (3d) 449.

In deciding whether to call a witness essential to the unfolding of the narrative, the trial judge may consider as one factor that if the defence called the witness, it would lose the advantage of being able to address the jury last: *R. v. Finta*, [1994] 1 S.C.R. 701, 88 C.C.C. (3d) 417.

Content of closing addresses – Where Crown counsel addressed the jury on extraneous prejudicial matters not found in the evidence a new trial was ordered: *R. v. Pisani* (1970), 1 C.C.C. (2d) 477 (S.C.C.).

It was held in *R. v. Bengert (No. 5)* (1980), 53 C.C.C. (2d) 481 (B.C.C.A.), leave to appeal to S.C.C. refused 53 C.C.C. (2d) 481*n*, that Crown counsel was properly permitted to give the members of the jury a typed chronology of dates and events to follow during his address after a lengthy and complicated conspiracy trial, and to take this chronology with them into the jury room during deliberations.

While counsel is obligated to comment only on admissible evidence, this responsibility must not be inverted to encourage jurors to make findings in conflict with undisputed facts which did not reach their attention simply because of trial safeguards: *R. v. Clarke* (1981), 63 C.C.C. (2d) 224 (Alta. C.A.), leave to appeal to S.C.C. refused C.C.C. *loc. cit.*

Comments by Crown counsel, which were extremely disparaging of a defence expert who was called to support an insanity defence, were sufficiently prejudicial as to impose a legal duty on the trial judge to comment and thus ensure that the position of the defence was fairly put to the jury. The failure of the trial judge to comment constituted an incorrect decision on a question of law and in this case the proviso in s. 686(1)(*b*)(iii) could not be applied: *R. v. Romeo*, [1991] 1 S.C.R. 86, 62 C.C.C. (3d) 1 (6:1).

VIEW / Directions to prevent communication / Who shall attend.

652. (1) The judge may, where it appears to be in the interests of justice, at any time after the jury has been sworn and before it gives its verdict, direct the jury to have a view of any place, thing or person, and shall give directions respecting the manner in which, and the persons by whom, the place, thing or person shall be shown to the jury, and may for that purpose adjourn the trial.

(2) Where a view is ordered under subsection (1), the judge shall give any directions that he considers necessary for the purpose of preventing undue communication by any person with members of the jury, but failure to comply with any directions given under this subsection does not affect the validity of the proceedings.

(3) Where a view is ordered under subsection (1) the accused and the judge shall attend. R.S., c. C-34, s. 579.

CROSS-REFERENCES

The accused's right to be present during his trial as guaranteed by s. 650 extends to the taking of a view.

SYNOPSIS

Subsection (1) enables the trial judge to give directions with respect to the jury leaving the courtroom for the purpose of viewing any place, person or thing (*e.g.*, the scene of the alleged offence).

A failure to comply with any of the judge's directions relating to communications with the jury does not affect (automatically) the validity of the proceedings (subsec. (2)).

The judge and accused shall also attend the view (subsec. (3)).

ANNOTATIONS

A view of the occurrence is an extension of the trial and if the accused was absent at that time his conviction must be quashed: *R. v. Tanguay and Pilon* (1971), 15 C.R.N.S. 21 (Que. C.A.).

However, this section must be read with s. 650 and the judge has the same power to permit the accused to be absent from the view as from any other part of the trial: *R. v. Auger* (1982), 4 C.C.C. (3d) 282 (Que. C.A.), leave to appeal to S.C.C. refused C.C.C. *loc. cit.*, 48 N.R. 319*n*.

Mere failure on the part of the accused or his counsel to object to the accused being kept handcuffed in a sheriff's vehicle so that he was not present while thc judge conducted the view does not constitute an express waiver of the provisions of subsec. (3). Where something occurred to advance the case such as the hearing of the submissions as to the manner in which the view should be conducted the accused's conviction must be quashed: *R. v. Gavin* (1983), 10 C.C.C. (3d) 92 (B.C.C.A.).

By virtue of s. 572 this section applies to non-jury cases and a provincial court judge has power to take a view: *R. v. Prentice,* [1965] 4 C.C.C. 118, 47 C.R. 231 (B.C.C.A.).

A view may be taken after the jury has commenced their deliberations if it is in the interests of justice to do so: *R. v. Welsh* (1997), 120 C.C.C. (3d) 68, 30 M.V.R. (3d) 168 (B.C.C.A.).

While this section does not authorize evidence by videoconference, the trial judge does have the jurisdiction to admit evidence by videoconference where it is necessary and reliable: *R. v. Dix* (1998), 125 C.C.C. (3d) 377, 16 C.R. (5th) 137 (Alta. Q.B.).

TRYING OF ISSUES OF INDICTMENT BY JURY / Reduction of number of jurors to 12.

652.1 (1) After the charge to the jury, the jury shall retire to try the issues of the indictment.

(2) However, if there are more than 12 jurors remaining, the judge shall identify the 12 jurors who are to retire to consider the verdict by having the number of each juror written on a card that is of equal size, by causing the cards to be placed together in a box that is to be thoroughly shaken together and by drawing one card if 13 jurors remain or two cards if 14 jurors remain. The judge shall then discharge any juror whose number is drawn. 2011, c. 16, s. 13.

CROSS-REFERENCES

The procedure for jury selection is set out in ss. 626 to 643. In particular, s. 631(2.2) provides for the selection of a jury consisting of 13 or 14 persons, rather than the usual 12.

SYNOPSIS

In the normal case, after the charge to the jury, the jury of 12 members (or 11 or 10, if jurors have been discharged under s. 644, will retire to consider their verdict. Where, pursuant to s. 631(2.2), the jury consists of 13 or 14 members, this section directs the judge to discharge the extra jurors by, in effect, drawing lots.

DISAGREEMENT OF JURY / Discretion not reviewable.

653. (1) Where the judge is satisfied that the jury is unable to agree on its verdict and that further detention of the jury would be useless, he may in his discretion discharge that jury and direct a new jury to be empanelled during the sittings of the court, or may adjourn the trial on such terms as justice may require.

(2) A discretion that is exercised under subsection (1) by a judge is not reviewable. R.S., c. C-34, s. 580.

CROSS-REFERENCES

Section 672 preserves the common law power of the court with respect to trials by jury and would permit the discharge of a jury for reasons other than the jury's inability to reach a verdict. Although the jury may be given permission to separate pursuant to s. 647 once they have retired to consider their verdict they must be sequestered. Section 644 provides for the discharge of a juror for cause. Under s. 654, the taking of the verdict of a jury and any proceeding incidental thereto is not invalid by reason only that it is done on a Sunday or on a holiday.

Where there is a mistrial, s. 653.1 provides that the rulings made during the trial are binding in any subsequent retrial unless it would not be in the interests of justice.

SYNOPSIS

If the trial judge is of the opinion that the jurors are unable to reach a unanimous verdict (*i.e.*, the jury is "hung") he or she can declare a mistrial and discharge the jury or, alternatively, adjourn the trial. Where a mistrial occurs there will be a new trial (subsec. (1)).

The exercise of the discretion in this regard is not subject to an appeal (subsec. (2)).

ANNOTATIONS

Direction on right to disagree – A trial judge is not obliged to tell the jury that they may disagree, and accordingly a direction that the verdict returned must be unanimous is not improper, this is particularly so where the trial judge then continued on to tell the jury that they will be "attempting to reach a verdict": *R. v. Harrison*, [1975] 2 S.C.R. 95, 18 C.C.C. (2d) 129 (6:3).

Where a member of the jury might have reasonably concluded from the judge's charge that they cannot disagree a new trial will be ordered: *R. v. Davidson* (1975), 24 C.C.C. (2d) 161 (Ont. C.A.).

In *R. v. Wedge and Three others* (1973), 14 C.C.C. (2d) 490 (Man. C.A.), the court did not find that a particular direction had the effect of leaving the jury with the impression that they must agree. However, the court suggested that the following direction be given: "To render a verdict, you must be unanimous. This does not mean that you must bring in a verdict, juries cannot always agree, but if you do bring in a verdict, it must be the verdict of all of you."

Exhortation to reach verdict – In considering the appropriate exhortation to a deadlocked jury, the following principles were set out in *R. v. G. (R.M.)*, [1996] 3 S.C.R. 362, 110 C.C.C. (3d) 26. Where a jury has reached an impasse, any exhortation given should avoid introducing factors which are extraneous and irrelevant to the task of reaching a verdict and should not encourage a juror by reference to extraneous considerations or by exerting unwanted pressures to abandon an honestly held view of the evidence. The exhortation must not interfere with the right of jurors to deliberate in complete freedom uninfluenced by extraneous pressure. Consequently, it cannot be suggested to a deadlocked jury that they take into account such factors as expense, the inconvenience occasioned by a new trial or the hardship caused to the participants when a trial is left unresolved or to consider carefully only the position of the majority and not the minority. The exhortation must appeal to the individual jurors to once again reason together. Furthermore, a juror should not be encouraged or exhorted to change his or her mind simply for the sake of conformity. Finally, a deadline for reaching a verdict should not be imposed and a jury should never be rushed into returning a verdict.

A trial judge ought not to offer his or her opinion on the facts to a deadlocked jury, in the course of an exhortation, except to the extent that the jury has indicated the need for assistance on some particular point. The purpose of the exhortation is to impress on the jury the need to listen to each other and consider each other's views in order to avoid a disagreement, but is not to suggest to the jury that one view of the evidence may be preferable to another, or that a particular inference should be drawn: *R. v. Sims*, [1992] 2 S.C.R. 858, 75 C.C.C. (3d) 278.

Polling jury – There is no legal requirement that the jury be polled after it has rendered its verdict but a request to poll is usually granted where doubt as to unanimity appears to exist: *R. v. Laforet*, [1980] 1 S.C.R. 869, 50 C.C.C. (2d) 1 (5:2).

Ambiguous verdict – On the return of the jury, if a clear and unambiguous verdict is given, it is the duty of the trial judge to accept the verdict and, in accordance with the practice of his court, cause it to become a part of the record of the court. Where the verdict is one of acquittal, the prisoner is entitled to an immediate discharge unless subject to continued lawful detention for some other reason. Where, however, there is ambiguity in the verdict or where there is reason to doubt that the verdict is unanimous, the trial judge should inquire into the matter to ascertain the true position and where necessary he should give such further directions as may be required and allow further deliberation by the jury to satisfy himself that any verdict given will indeed be unanimous, complete and expressive of the actual findings of the jury. The judge has a discretion in such a case to accept a substituted or second verdict for the first one returned. This discretion, however, is one which must be exercised during the course of the trial in the presence of the accused and his counsel, and prior to the dissolution of the court by the discharge of the jury. It will be too late to make inquiries relating to the true nature of the verdict when the jury is discharged and the court created for the trial of the accused has dissolved. Once the accused and the jury have been discharged the court is wholly functus: *R. v. Head*, [1986] 2 S.C.R. 684, 30 C.C.C. (3d) 481 (7:0).

However, if an irregularity has been detected and the jury has been discharged but the error is not such that it would involve the jury reconsidering its verdict or completing its deliberations, the trial judge has a narrow and exceptional jurisdiction to recall the jury for the purposes of inquiring into the alleged error. This jurisdiction may only be exercised where there is no reasonable apprehension of bias. Whether there is a reasonable apprehension of bias depends on all the circumstances of the case such as the length of time that has elapsed between the original verdict and the moment when the jury express their wish to alter it, the probable reason for the initial mistake, the necessity to ensure that justice is done not only to the accused but also to the prosecution, whether the accused has been discharged from custody, and whether the jury was exposed to an immediate and strong reaction to the recorded verdict by the public and the media. In many cases, a significant element in establishing reasonable apprehension is dispersal. The trial judge should take care to examine the length of time during which the jury was separated, as the jury's absence from the courtroom for a few seconds or minutes is often less indicative of a reasonable apprehension of bias, as compared to a more extended absence. If a jury has dispersed for a relatively lengthy period of time, such as several days, the trial judge would almost always conclude that this extensive degree of dispersal would raise a reasonable apprehension of bias. If the trial judge concludes that there exists a reasonable apprehension of bias, the judge cannot correct the verdict. Nevertheless, the trial judge retains a remedial jurisdiction and has the discretion to declare a mistrial where necessary to prevent a miscarriage of justice having regard to all the circumstances. In making this determination, injustice to the accused is of particular concern. But, this factor should be balanced against other relevant factors, such as the seriousness of the offence, protection of the public and bringing the guilty to justice. Where the trial judge concludes that a reasonable apprehension of bias is not raised, the trial judge can and should correct the error and register the proper verdict: *R. v. Burke*, [2002] 2 S.C.R. 857, 164 C.C.C. (3d) 385.

Upon receipt of a verdict of "guilty with a plea of leniency on account of conflicting evidence" the trial judge acted correctly by recharging on the doctrine of reasonable doubt and sending the jury out to reconsider its verdict: *R. v. Goforth* (1974), 19 C.C.C. (2d) 88, [1974] 6 W.W.R. 119 (2:1) (Sask. C.A.).

Use of "verdict sheet" – There is no objection to use of a "verdict sheet" which sets out the different verdicts available. The sheet must not, however, require the jury to give particulars as to the offences of which they found the accused guilty, as in the case of sexual assault causing bodily harm, of what the assault consisted. Members of the jury must be unanimous in their verdict but may arrive at their verdict for different reasons and on separate evidential bases: *R. v. Tuckey, Baynham and Walsh* (1985), 20 C.C.C. (3d) 502, 46 C.R. (3d) 97 (Ont. C.A.).

Constitutional considerations respecting mistrial – After a mistrial the judge may adjourn the case to the next jury sittings. Where the jurors are unable to agree and the jury is discharged the accused has not been "finally acquitted" within the meaning of s. 11(*h*) of the *Canadian Charter of Rights and Freedoms* so as to prevent his retrial on the same offence: *R. v. Misra* (1985), 18 C.C.C. (3d) 134, 44 C.R. (3d) 179 (Sask. Q.B.).

While a third trial (after juries were unable to agree on two prior occasions) may stretch the limits of the community's sense of fair play it does not of itself exceed them so as to constitute an abuse of process: *R. v. Keyowski*, [1988] 1 S.C.R. 657, 40 C.C.C. (3d) 481 (7:0).

At common law, the power of the trial judge to discharge the jury is discretionary and whether his discretion to discharge the jury was exercised properly or improperly was not subject to review, and the improper exercise of his discretion in discharging the jury did not bar a second trial. However, notwithstanding these common law limitations, the propriety of a decision to declare a mistrial is subject to scrutiny under the *Charter of Rights and Freedoms* where a second trial, after the improper termination of the first trial, would contravene the principles of fundamental justice as guaranteed under s. 7 of the Charter. For example, if upon a breakdown of the Crown's case, a judge were to declare a mistrial in order to give the prosecution an opportunity to strengthen its case against the accused by attempting to find additional witnesses thereby depriving the accused of an acquittal where the Crown's initial preparation had been negligent, a second trial in those circumstances would contravene the principles of fundamental justice: *R. v. D. (T.C.)* (1987), 38 C.C.C. (3d) 434, 61 C.R. (3d) 168 (Ont. C.A.).

MISTRIAL — RULINGS BINDING AT NEW TRIAL.

653.1 In the case of a mistrial, unless the court is satisfied that it would not be in the interests of justice, rulings relating to the disclosure or admissibility of evidence or the *Canadian Charter of Rights and Freedoms* that were made during the trial are binding on the parties in any new trial if the rulings are made — or could have been made — before the stage at which the evidence on the merits is presented. 2011, c. 16, s. 14.

CROSS-REFERENCES

This section complements other case management powers found in Part XVIII.1, which similarly provide for rulings made by the case management judge to be binding during the trial on the merits. For further notes on case management, see the note before s. 551.1. Section 653 provides for the directing of a mistrial where the jury is unable to agree.

SYNOPSIS

This section provides that, in case of a mistrial, certain rulings will be binding at the retrial unless it would not be in the interest of justice. The rulings are those relating to disclosure or admissibility of evidence of the *Charter of Rights and Freedoms*, if the ruling were or could have been made before the stage of the trial at which the evidence on the merits is presented.

ANNOTATIONS

This section represents Parliament's determination to minimize the consequences of a mistrial on court resources by restricting relitigation of certain issues determined in the prior proceedings. It creates a presumption that prior rulings will continue to bind the parties unless the presumption is rebutted by, for example, demonstrating that new issues of fact or law have arisen: *R. v. Victoria* (2018), 359 C.C.C. (3d) 179 (Ont. C.A.).

PROCEEDING ON SUNDAY, ETC., NOT INVALID.

654. The taking of the verdict of a jury and any proceeding incidental thereto is not invalid by reason only that it is done on Sunday or on a holiday. R.S., c. C-34, s. 581.

CROSS-REFERENCES

The term "holiday" is defined in s. 35 of the *Interpretation Act*, R.S.C. 1985, c. I-21. Where the jury is unable to agree on its verdict then it may be discharged pursuant to s. 653.

ANNOTATIONS

In *R. v. Kinch* (1961), 131 C.C.C. 342, it was held that Easter Monday, although included in the definition of "holiday" in the *Interpretation Acts* of Canada and of P.E.I. is not *dies non juridicus*. A plea, conviction and sentence are not invalid because they took place on that day. *Ex p. Cormier* (1907), 12 C.C.C. 339, followed.

The jury being permitted to continue its deliberations on Sunday is also entitled to be assisted by having evidence read back. The whole of this process is incidental to the taking of the verdict: *R. v. Baillie* (1991), 66 C.C.C. (3d) 274 (B.C.C.A.).

Evidence on Trial

ADMISSIONS AT TRIAL.

655. Where an accused is on trial for an indictable offence, he or his counsel may admit any fact alleged against him for the purpose of dispensing with proof thereof. R.S., c. C-34, s. 582.

CROSS-REFERENCES

The term "counsel" is defined in s. 2.

ANNOTATIONS

Admissions – In *R. v. Castellani*, [1970] S.C.R. 310, [1970] 4 C.C.C. 287 (9:0), the purpose of this section was said to be to eliminate the necessity of proof by the Crown of any fact it desires to prove that the accused is prepared to admit and accordingly the accused cannot admit a fact until it is alleged against him by the Crown.

An agreed statement of facts should only be used where the facts are clearly agreed upon and if it becomes apparent during his testimony that the accused's evidence conflicts with the agreed statement of facts the trial judge should require the Crown to call evidence on the points in issue: *R. v. Coburn* (1982), 66 C.C.C. (2d) 463 (Ont. C.A.).

A justice presiding at a preliminary hearing may admit a statement of facts agreed to by the Crown and defence. This statement constitutes evidence upon which the justice may base a decision as to order to stand trial: *R. v. Ulrich* (1977), 38 C.C.C. (2d) 1 (Alta. S.C.T.D.).

Where a mistrial had been declared, the agreed statement of fact was admissible as an ordinary admission at the new trial, but was no longer conclusive such that it could be explained, attacked or countered: *R. v. Baksh* (2005), 199 C.C.C. (3d) 201 (Ont. S.C.J.).

Necessity of *voir dire* to determine voluntariness of confession – It was held in *R. v. Dietrich* (1970), 1 C.C.C. (2d) 49 (Ont. C.A.), that while this section was probably not authority for permitting the accused to waive a *voir dire* as to the voluntariness of a confession, such a right exists apart from any provision of the *Criminal Code*.

This approach was approved in *R. v. Park*, [1981] 2 S.C.R. 64, 59 C.C.C. (2d) 385 (9:0), where the court held that no particular words or formula need be uttered by defence counsel to express the waiver and admission. All that is necessary is that the trial judge be satisfied that counsel understands the matter and has made an informed decision to waive the *voir dire*. It is sufficient for counsel to indicate that no objection is taken to admission of the statement without a *voir dire*, or that voluntariness is not in issue.

In *R. v. Powell*, [1977] 1 S.C.R. 362, 28 C.C.C. (2d) 148 (9:0), the court held that a *voir dire* as to the admissibility of a confession is required even on a trial by a judge alone.

In *R. v. Erven*, [1979] 1 S.C.R. 926, 44 C.C.C. (2d) 76 (6:3), Dickson J., for the plurality held that there is no exception from the rule requiring the holding of a *voir dire* on the basis that the statement is "obviously volunteered" to the person in authority.

Where the defence has not requested a *voir dire* and a statement is admitted into evidence, the trial judge will only have committed reversible error if clear evidence existed in the record that objectively should have alerted the judge to the need for a *voir dire* notwithstanding counsel's silence. Where the evidence clearly demonstrates that the receiver of the statement was closely connected to the authorities, this should alert the judge to the need to hold a *voir dire*. To demonstrate the need for a *voir dire*, the evidence must show that the receiver of the statement was closely associated to the authorities prior to obtaining the statement and that there was, as well, a close connection in time between the contact with the authorities and its receipt. The evidence must suggest that the receiver was acting in concert with the police or prosecutorial authorities, or as their agent, or as part of their team: *R. v. Hodgson*, [1998] 2 S.C.R. 449, 127 C.C.C. (3d) 449, *sub nom. R. v. H. (M.C.)*; *R. v. Wells*, [1998] 2 S.C.R. 517, 127 C.C.C. (3d) 500; *R. v. T. (S.G.)*, [2010] 1 S.C.R. 688, 255 C.C.C. (3d) 1.

The confessions rule does not apply to statements tendered in the context of a *voir dire* under the Charter. Admitting a statement by an accused for the purpose of assessing the constitutionality of state action, as opposed to the purpose of determining the accused's guilt, does not engage the rationale for the confessions rule: *R. v. Paterson*, [2017] 1 S.C.R. 202, 347 C.C.C. (3d) 257.

"Mr. Big" confessions – Where the state recruits an accused into a fictitious criminal organization and seeks to elicit a confession from him, any confession made by the accused to the state during the operation should be treated as presumptively inadmissible. This presumption of inadmissibility is overcome where the Crown can establish, on a balance of probabilities, that the probative value of the confession outweighs its prejudicial effect: *R. v. Hart*, [2014] 2 S.C.R. 544, 312 C.C.C. (3d) 250.

PRESUMPTION — VALUABLE MINERALS.

656. In any proceeding in relation to theft or possession of a valuable mineral that is unrefined, partly refined, uncut or otherwise unprocessed by any person actively engaged in or on a mine, if it is established that the person possesses the valuable mineral, the person is presumed, in the absence of evidence raising a reasonable doubt to the contrary, to have stolen or unlawfully possessed the valuable mineral. R.S., c. C-34, s. 583; 1999, c. 5, s. 24.

CROSS-REFERENCES

The general theft offence is defined in s. 322. Note, however, the exemption in s. 333 for the taking of specimens for the purpose of exploration or scientific investigation. Other offences in relation to minerals and mines are found in ss. 394, 394.1 and 396. "Valuable mineral" is defined in s. 2.

SYNOPSIS

This section establishes a presumption in trials for theft or possession of valuable minerals. Possession of valuable mineral that is unrefined, partly refined, uncut or otherwise unprocessed by a person actively employed in a mine is rebuttable proof that such person stole the material or that the possession was unlawful.

USE IN EVIDENCE OF STATEMENT BY ACCUSED.

657. A statement made by an accused under subsection 541(3) and purporting to be signed by the justice before whom it was made may be given in evidence against the accused at his or her trial without proof of the signature of the justice, unless it is

proved that the justice by whom the statement purports to be signed did not sign it. R.S., c. C-34, s. 584; 1994, c. 44, s. 62.

CROSS-REFERENCES

The term "justice" is defined in s. 2. Section 541(2) refers to the statement made by an accused after he was warned at the conclusion of the evidence adduced by thc prosecutor at his preliminary inquiry. It may be that this section must now be read in light of s. 13 of the Charter.

SYNOPSIS

A statement made by an accused at a preliminary inquiry (see s. 541) may be tendered in evidence by the Crown at trial if signed by the justice of the peace or provincial court judge before whom it was made. The signature need not be proved, but it may be proved to be false.

PROOF OF OWNERSHIP AND VALUE OF PROPERTY / Statements to be made / Notice of intention to produce affidavit or solemn declaration / Attendance for examination.

657.1 (1) In any proceedings, an affidavit or a solemn declaration of a person who claims to be the lawful owner of, or the person lawfully entitled to possession of, property that was the subject-matter of the offence, or any other person who has specialized knowledge of the property or of that type of property, containing the statements referred to in subsection (2), shall be admissible in evidence and, in the absence of evidence to the contrary, is evidence of the statements contained in the affidavit or solemn declaration without proof of the signature of the person appearing to have signed the affidavit or solemn declaration.

(2) For the purposes of subsection (1), a person shall state in an affidavit or a solemn declaration

- **(*a*) that the person is the lawful owner of, or is lawfully entitled to possession of, the property, or otherwise has specialized knowledge of the property or of property of the same type as the property;**
- **(*b*) the value of the property;**
- **(*c*) in the case of a person who is the lawful owner of or is lawfully entitled to possession of the property, that the person has been deprived of the property by fraudulent means or otherwise without the lawful consent of the person,**
- **(*c*.1) in the case of proceedings in respect of an offence under section 342, that the credit card had been revoked or cancelled, is a false document within the meaning of section 321 or that no credit card that meets the exact description of that credit card was ever issued; and**
- **(*d*) any facts within the personal knowledge of the person relied on to justify the statements referred to in paragraphs (*a*) to (*c*.1).**

(3) Unless the court orders otherwise, no affidavit or solemn declaration shall be received in evidence pursuant to subsection (1) unless the prosecutor has, before the trial or other proceeding, given to the accused a copy of the affidavit or solemn declaration and reasonable notice of intention to produce it in evidence.

(4) Notwithstanding subsection (1), the court may require the person who appears to have signed an affidavit or solemn declaration referred to in that subsection to appear before it for examination or cross-examination in respect of the issue of proof of any of the statements contained in the affidavit or solemn declaration. R.S.C. 1985, c. 23 (4th Supp.), s. 3; 1997, c. 18, s. 79.

CROSS-REFERENCES
Note s. 4(6) which provides for proof of service by way of affidavit or solemn declaration. Also note s. 491.2 which provides for the admissibility of photographic evidence of property that would otherwise be required to be produced for the purposes of a preliminary inquiry, trial or other proceedings.

SYNOPSIS
The purpose of this section is to obviate the need for the Crown to call *viva voce* evidence to prove ownership, value of property, loss of property or that a credit card is invalid.

Proof of such matters may be given by way of affidavit or declaration wherein the affiant/declarant states: (a) that he or she is the lawful owner of the property or the person entitled to possession; (b) the value of the property; and (c) how the person was deprived of the property; and (d) the credit card has been revoked etc. (subsec. (2)).

The Crown must give the accused a copy of the document and reasonable notice of its intention to tender it. The court can order the affiant/declarant to attend for cross-examination (subsecs. (3), (4)).

THEFT AND POSSESSION / Accessory after the fact.

657.2 (1) Where an accused is charged with possession of any property obtained by the commission of an offence, evidence of the conviction or discharge of another person of theft of the property is admissible against the accused, and in the absence of evidence to the contrary is proof that the property was stolen.

(2) Where an accused is charged with being an accessory after the fact to the commission of an offence, evidence of the conviction or discharge of another person of the offence is admissible against the accused, and in the absence of evidence to the contrary is proof that the offence was committed. 1997, c. 18, s. 80.

CROSS-REFERENCES
The offence of possession of property obtained by crime is described in s. 354 and punishable under s. 355. Bringing property obtained by crime into Canada is an offence under s. 357. Other special evidentiary provisions for proof of the offence of possession of property obtained by crime are set out in ss. 358 to 360. The theft offences are set out in ss. 322 to 327, 328 and 330 to 332.

Liability of an accessory after the fact is set out in s. 23. Punishment of an accessory after the fact generally is set out in s. 463. Accessory after the fact to murder is punishable in accordance with s. 240.

SYNOPSIS
This section facilitates the proof of two types of offences. Subsection (1) makes the conviction or discharge of another person for theft admissible at the accused's trial for possession of that property. The subsection also creates the presumption from that conviction or discharge that in the absence of evidence to the contrary the property was stolen. Subsection (2) similarly facilitates proof of the offence of accessory after the fact by making the conviction or discharge of the principal offender admissible at the accessory's trial. As well, in the absence of evidence to the contrary, the conviction or discharge is proof that the offence was committed.

ANNOTATIONS
Even aside from subsec. (2), the principal's conviction is admissible on the accessory's trial as evidence that the principal committed the crime. This rule does not offend Charter notions of fairness. The rule does not place any persuasive or even evidentiary burden on the accused to disprove a fact in issue. It also does not foreclose a full exploration of the principal's guilt on the trial of the accessory. Finally, the fact that the principal was appealing his conviction

did not render evidence of that conviction inadmissible at the accessory's trial. However, in the circumstances it was appropriate to adjourn the accessory's appeal to await the outcome of the principal's appeal: *R. v. Duong* (1998), 124 C.C.C. (3d) 392, 15 C.R. (5th) 209 (Ont. C.A.). *Contra*: *R. v. Hamel* (1993), 20 C.R. (4th) 68, [1993] R.J.Q. 999 (C.A.).

EXPERT TESTIMONY / Attendance for examination / Notice for expert testimony / If notices not given / Additional court orders / Use of material by prosecution / No further disclosure.

657.3 (1) In any proceedings, the evidence of a person as an expert may be given by means of a report accompanied by the affidavit or solemn declaration of the person, setting out, in particular, the qualifications of the person as an expert if

- **(*a*) the court recognizes that person as an expert; and**
- **(*b*) the party intending to produce the report in evidence has, before the proceeding, given to the other party a copy of the affidavit or solemn declaration and the report and reasonable notice of the intention to produce it in evidence.**

(2) Notwithstanding subsection (1), the court may require the person who appears to have signed an affidavit or solemn declaration referred to in that subsection to appear before it for examination or cross-examination in respect of the issue of proof of any of the statements contained in the affidavit or solemn declaration or report.

(3) For the purpose of promoting the fair, orderly and efficient presentation of the testimony of witnesses,

- **(*a*) a party who intends to call a person as an expert witness shall, at least thirty days before the commencement of the trial or within any other period fixed by the justice or judge, give notice to the other party or parties of his or her intention to do so, accompanied by**
  - **(i) the name of the proposed witness,**
  - **(ii) a description of the area of expertise of the proposed witness that is sufficient to permit the other parties to inform themselves about that area of expertise, and**
  - **(iii) a statement of the qualifications of the proposed witness as an expert;**
- **(*b*) in addition to complying with paragraph (*a*), a prosecutor who intends to call a person as an expert witness shall, within a reasonable period before trial, provide to the other party or parties**
  - **(i) a copy of the report, if any, prepared by the proposed witness for the case, and**
  - **(ii) if no report is prepared, a summary of the opinion anticipated to be given by the proposed witness and the grounds on which it is based; and**
- **(*c*) in addition to complying with paragraph (*a*), an accused, or his or her counsel, who intends to call a person as an expert witness shall, not later than the close of the case for the prosecution, provide to the other party or parties the material referred to in paragraph (*b*).**

(4) If a party calls a person as an expert witness without complying with subsection (3), the court shall, at the request of any other party,

- **(*a*) grant an adjournment of the proceedings to the party who requests it to allow him or her to prepare for cross-examination of the expert witness;**
- **(*b*) order the party who called the expert witness to provide that other party and any other party with the material referred to in paragraph (3)(*b*); and**
- **(*c*) order the calling or recalling of any witness for the purpose of giving testimony on matters related to those raised in the expert witness's testimony, unless the court considers it inappropriate to do so.**

(5) If, in the opinion of the court, a party who has received the notice and material referred to in subsection (3) has not been able to prepare for the evidence of the proposed witness, the court may do one or more of the following:

(*a*) adjourn the proceedings;

(*b*) order that further particulars be given of the evidence of the proposed witness; and

(*c*) order the calling or recalling of any witness for the purpose of giving testimony on matters related to those raised in the expert witness's testimony.

(6) If the proposed witness does not testify, the prosecutor may not produce material provided to him or her under paragraph (3)(*c*) in evidence without the consent of the accused.

(7) Unless otherwise ordered by a court, information disclosed under this section in relation to a proceeding may only be used for the purpose of that proceeding. 1997, c. 18, s. 80; 2002, c. 13, s. 62.

CROSS-REFERENCES

For other notes with respect to expert evidence, see the notes following ss. 16 and 150.1 of the *Criminal Code*, and s. 7 of the *Canada Evidence Act*. Section 7 of the *Canada Evidence Act* sets limits on the number of expert witnesses. Section 8 of that Act deals with the admissibility of evidence to prove whether handwriting samples are genuine. Also see s. 258 permitting certificates from experts to be admitted respecting breathalyzer and blood test results for certain drinking and driving offences. Section 4(6) and (7) facilitate proof of service of documents and notice.

SYNOPSIS

Subsections (1) and (2) operate as an exception to the rule against hearsay and allow for admission of the report of an expert. The report must be accompanied by an affidavit or solemn declaration of the expert setting out the expert's qualifications. The court may admit the report as evidence if the court recognizes the person as an expert and the party intending to produce the report has given to the other side the affidavit, the report and reasonable notice of the intention to produce it. Nevertheless, the court may require the expert to appear before the court for examination or cross-examination.

Subsection (3) requires the party intending to call an expert to give notice to the other party of the intention to do so together with the name of the witness, a description of the witness's expertise and of the witness's qualifications. The notice is to be given 30 days before trial or such other period as fixed by the judge. The prosecutor must also provide a copy of the expert's report or a summary of the expert's opinion before trial. The accused must provide the same material but only by the close of the prosecution's case. Under subsec. (6), the prosecutor may not produce the material provided by the accused if the accused's expert does not testify, without the consent of the accused. Subsection (4) sets out the consequences of the failure to comply with these notice requirements. Even where subsec. (3) has been complied with, if the party requires additional time to prepare, subsec. (5) permits the court to make further orders.

Subsection (7) provides that the material disclosed under this section may only be used for the purpose of this section, unless ordered by a court.

ANNOTATIONS

Subsection (4) does not give the trial judge the jurisdiction to refuse to allow an expert witness to testify. The section is a trial management provision that authorizes the trial judge to order compliance, an adjournment or particulars: *R. v. Horan* (2008), 237 C.C.C. (3d) 514, 60 C.R. (6th) 46 (Ont. C.A.).

The remedies for the failure to comply with the requisite notice provisions are an adjournment, the provision of further details of the expert's proposed evidence, or an order to call or recall a witness to testify to matters raised by the expert's testimony. The more drastic remedies of exclusion or a mistrial should be considered in the context of the Crown's constitutional disclosure obligations. The defence must establish a violation of the right to make full answer and defence under s. 7 of the Charter warranting a stay of proceedings or mistrial pursuant to s. 24(1): *R. v. Perjalian* (2011), 274 C.C.C. (3d) 432 (B.C.C.A.).

Children and Young Persons

TESTIMONY AS TO DATE OF BIRTH / Testimony of a parent / Proof of age / Other evidence / Inference from appearance.

658. (1) In any proceedings to which this Act applies, the testimony of a person as to the date of his or her birth is admissible as evidence of that date.

(2) In any proceedings to which this Act applies, the testimony of a parent as to the age of a person of whom he or she is a parent is admissible as evidence of the age of that person.

(3) In any proceedings to which this Act applies,

- **(*a*) a birth or baptismal certificate or a copy of such a certificate purporting to be certified under the hand of the person in whose custody the certificate is held is evidence of the age of that person; and**
- **(*b*) an entry or record of an incorporated society or its officers who have had the control or care of a child or young person at or about the time the child or young person was brought to Canada is evidence of the age of the child or young person if the entry or record was made before the time when the offence is alleged to have been committed.**

(4) In the absence of any certificate, copy, entry or record mentioned in subsection (3), or in corroboration of any such certificate, copy, entry or record, a jury, judge, justice or provincial court judge, as the case may be, may receive and act on any other information relating to age that they consider reliable.

(5) In the absence of other evidence, or by way of corroboration of other evidence, a jury, judge, justice or provincial court judge, as the case may be, may infer the age of a child or young person from his or her appearance. R.S., c. C-34, s. 585; 1994, c. 44, s. 64.

CROSS-REFERENCES

Age is determined in accordance with s. 30 of the *Interpretation Act*, R.S.C. 1985, c. I-21. As to the taking of evidence of children, see ss. 16 and 16.1 of the *Canada Evidence Act*, R.S.C. 1985, c. C-5.

SYNOPSIS

This section deals with some of the methods by which the age of a person may be proven and most conveniently allows the witness to testify to his or her own age, although technically that evidence would be hearsay.

Where an incorporated society was involved in the child's immigration to Canada and had custody or care of the child, a record of the society made before the commission of the alleged offence is receivable as to the child's age (subsec. (2)(*b*)).

In the absence of any other evidence, either direct or corroborative, the court may infer the age of a child from his or her appearance (subsec. (5)).

659. [*Repealed* (old provision), R.S.C. 1985, c. 19 (3rd Supp.), s. 15.]

CR. CODE

Corroboration

CHILDREN'S EVIDENCE.

659. Any requirement whereby it is mandatory for a court to give the jury a warning about convicting an accused on the evidence of a child is abrogated. 1993, c. 45, s. 9.

SYNOPSIS

Prior to recent decisions of the Supreme Court of Canada [see notes under s. 150.1] there was some common law authority requiring the trial judge to warn the jury as to the danger of convicting the accused on the evidence of a child. Any such *mandatory* rules are now abrogated.

Verdicts

FULL OFFENCE CHARGED, ATTEMPT PROVED.

660. Where the complete commission of an offence charged is not proved but the evidence establishes an attempt to commit the offence, the accused may be convicted of the attempt. R.S., c. C-34, s. 587.

CROSS-REFERENCES

The definition of attempt is found in s. 24. For most offences, the attempt to commit an offence is punished in accordance with s. 463. However, attempted murder, for example, is punished under s. 239. Section 661 provides for the case where an attempt to commit an offence is charged by the evidence discloses the commission of the complete offence. With respect to other included offences, see s. 662.

SYNOPSIS

This section provides that in a trial for a complete offence, proof only of an attempt can result in a conviction for an attempt.

ATTEMPT CHARGED, FULL OFFENCE PROVED / Conviction a bar.

661. (1) Where an attempt to commit an offence is charged but the evidence establishes the commission of the complete offence, the accused is not entitled to be acquitted, but the jury may convict him of the attempt unless the judge presiding at the trial, in his discretion, discharges the jury from giving a verdict and directs that the accused be indicted for the complete offence.

(2) An accused who is convicted under this section is not liable to be tried again for the offence that he was charged with attempting to commit. R.S., c. C-34, s. 588.

CROSS-REFERENCES

Attempt to commit an offence is defined in s. 24. The general provisions respecting the pleas of *autrefois convict* are found in ss. 607 to 610.

SYNOPSIS

Where the accused has been charged with an attempt, but the Crown proves the full offence, the trial judge can direct that there be a trial for the full offence or record the conviction for the attempt (subsec. (1)).

If the accused is convicted of an attempt he or she cannot subsequently be charged with the full offence (subsec. (2)).

ANNOTATIONS

This section also applies to a judge or provincial court judge sitting without a jury: *R. v. Doiron* (1960), 129 C.C.C. 283, 34 C.R. 188 (B.C.C.A.).

OFFENCE CHARGED, PART ONLY PROVED / First degree murder charged / Conviction for infanticide or manslaughter on charge of murder / Conviction for concealing body of child where murder or infanticide charged / Conviction for dangerous operation when another offence charged / Conviction for break and enter with intent.

662. (1) A count in an indictment is divisible and where the commission of the offence charged, as described in the enactment creating it or as charged in the count, includes the commission of another offence, whether punishable by indictment or on summary conviction, the accused may be convicted

- **(*a*) of an offence so included that is proved, notwithstanding that the whole offence that is charged is not proved; or**
- **(*b*) of an attempt to commit an offence so included.**

(2) For greater certainty and without limiting the generality of subsection (1), where a count charges first degree murder and the evidence does not prove first degree murder but proves second degree murder or an attempt to commit second degree murder, the jury may find the accused not guilty of first degree murder but guilty of second degree murder or an attempt to commit second degree murder, as the case may be.

(3) Subject to subsection (4), where a count charges murder and the evidence proves manslaughter or infanticide but does not prove murder, the jury may find the accused not guilty of murder but guilty of manslaughter or infanticide, but shall not on that count find the accused guilty of any other offence.

(4) Where a count charges the murder of a child or infanticide and the evidence proves the commission of an offence under section 243 but does not prove murder or infanticide, the jury may find the accused not guilty of murder or infanticide, as the case may be, but guilty of an offence under section 243.

(5) For greater certainty, when a count charges an offence under section 220, 221 or 236 arising out of the operation of a conveyance, and the evidence does not prove that offence but proves an offence under section 320.13, the accused may be convicted of an offence under that section.

(6) Where a count charges an offence under paragraph 98(1)(*b*) or 348(1)(*b*) and the evidence does not prove that offence but does prove an offence under, respectively, paragraph 98(1)(*a*) or 348(1)(*a*), the accused may be convicted of an offence under that latter paragraph. R.S., c. C-34, s. 589; 1973-74, c. 38, s. 6; 1974-75-76, c. 105, s. 11; R.S.C. 1985, c. 27 (1st Supp.), s. 134; 2000, c. 2, s. 3; 2008, c. 6, s. 38; 2018, c. 21, s. 20.

CROSS-REFERENCES

The term "indictment" is defined in s. 2. The offence of murder is defined in ss. 229 and 231. The offence of infanticide is defined in s. 233, although see s. 663 which enacts special rules where an accused is charged with infanticide but the evidence does not prove that offence.

SYNOPSIS

This section deals with situations where an accused may be convicted on less than the full offence charged. Subsection (1) provides that if the full offence is not proven the accused may still be found guilty of a lesser included offence or an attempt to commit the full offence.

For greater certainty murder is partially dealt with in subsec. (2). An accused charged with first degree murder may be convicted of second degree murder or an attempt to commit second degree murder.

Subsection (3) provides that on a charge of murder the accused may be convicted of manslaughter or infanticide. Where the victim is a child, and the charge is murder or infanticide, it is open to the trier of fact to convict of the offence of concealing the body of a child (see s. 243) (subsec. (4)).

For greater certainty, subsec. (5) provides that where the charge is criminal negligence causing death (see s. 220), criminal negligence causing bodily harm (see s. 221) or manslaughter (see s. 236) arising out of the operation of a motor vehicle, vessel or aircraft, the accused may be convicted of dangerous operation of a motor vehicle, etc. (see s. 249).

By reason of subsec. (6) it is open to convict a person of breaking and entering with intent to commit an indictable offence (see ss. 98(1)(*a*) and 348(1)(*a*)) on a charge of breaking and entering and committing an indictable offence (see ss. 91(1)(*b*) and 348(1)(*a*)).

ANNOTATIONS

Definition of included offence – An included offence is one that an accused committed in the commission of the offence charged: *R. v. Foote* (1974), 16 C.C.C. (2d) 44 (N.B. S.C. App. Div.).

It was held in *R. v. McDowell* (1976), 32 C.C.C. (2d) 309, [1977] 1 W.W.R. 97 (Alta. S.C. App. Div.), that there are three ways in which an offence may be included in another:

1. Where the Code prescribes that certain offences are included offences such as in subsecs. (2) to (6) of this section.
2. Where the description of the offence as described in the enactment creating it includes the commission of that other offence as provided by this subsection.
3. Where the description of the offence as charged in the count includes the commission of another offence.

An offence is included in the enactment creating the offence charged where the essential elements of the offence are part of the offence charged. Thus, if the whole offence charge can be committed without committing another offence, that other offence is not included. Therefore, sexual assault and sexual interference are not included in the offence of incest. Incest can be committed without any assault and sexual interference is related to the age of the victim, whereas incest is indifferent to the age of the victim. Further, where the indictment merely charged the accused with incest with his daughter, neither sexual assault nor sexual interference became included by the wording of the indictment. The fact that the accused father must have known that his daughter was under the age of 14 and thus incapable of consenting did not make either offence included in the charge of incest. The Crown cannot supplement the indictment by resort to the personal knowledge of the accused: *R. v. R. (G.)*, [2005] 2 S.C.R. 371, 198 C.C.C. (3d) 161.

To come within the words "as described in the enactment creating it" the lesser offence must be included in the offence charged as described in the enactment, albeit not in all the subsections and it is sufficient if the other offence is included in the enactment creating it. Thus on a charge that the accused "did commit robbery" common assault is an included offence since it is a lesser offence in at least one, albeit not all, the descriptions of the offence of robbery under s. 343: *R. v. Luckett*, [1980] 1 S.C.R. 1140, 50 C.C.C. (2d) 489 (7:0).

It was held in *R. v. Fergusson*, [1962] S.C.R. 229, 132 C.C.C. 112, that:

> The count must therefore include but not necessarily mention the commission of another offence, but the latter must be a lesser offence than the offence charged. The expression "lesser offence" is a "part of an offence" which is charged, and it must necessarily include some elements of the "major offence", but be lacking in some of the essentials, without which the major offence would be incomplete . . .

In *R. v. Simpson (No. 2)* (1981), 58 C.C.C. (2d) 122, 20 C.R. (3d) 36 (Ont. C.A.), the court considered *R. v. Luckett, supra*, but held that a charge in an indictment simply that the accused "did attempt to cause the death of [the victim] and did thereby attempt to commit murder, contrary to s. 222" did not include the offences of causing bodily harm with intent to wound, assault causing bodily harm or unlawfully causing bodily harm. Such an indictment does not charge any of these offences as included offences and s. 222 [now s. 239] either alone or read with ss. 24, 222, 229 or 230 does not describe the various ways in which attempted murder can be committed so as to include these ways as included offences within the meaning of this subsection.

For an offence to be included by the addition of apt words of description to the principal charge the charge must be so worded that the accused is afforded reasonable notice of the offence or offences alleged to be included in the principal offence charged. Moreover, the offence must be one which is properly included in the count: *R. v. Harmer and Miller* (1976), 33 C.C.C. (2d) 17, 75 D.L.R. (3d) 20 (Ont. C.A.). In this case on a charge of robbery in that the accused did steal and at the same time used violence which caused bodily harm to the victim the offence of assault causing bodily harm was an included offence. See also *R. v. Doliente*, [1997] 2 S.C.R. 11, 115 C.C.C. (3d) 352, affg dissenting reasons of Harradence J.A., 108 C.C.C. (3d) 137, 122 W.A.C. 131 (C.A.).

Application of provision – In *R. v. Rickard*, [1970] S.C.R. 1022, 1 C.C.C. (2d) 153, both the majority and the minority held that subsec. (5) is also applicable to proceedings by way of summary conviction.

Duty to direct jury on included offences – In *R. v. Longson* (1976), 31 C.C.C. (2d) 421, [1976] 6 W.W.R. 534 (B.C.C.A.), it was held that where there is evidence upon which a jury could convict of an included offence the judge is under a duty to properly instruct the jury on that included offence. A conviction for attempted murder was set aside and a new trial ordered where the judge failed to instruct the jury on the included offences of discharging a firearm with intent to wound or endanger life contrary to s. 244(*a*) and (*b*) and dangerous use of a firearm contrary to the former s. 86(*b*). In this case the indictment charged that the accused "did attempt to murder [the victim] by discharging a firearm at him".

A trial judge does not have an untrammelled discretion to decide whether or not to charge the jury on included offences. He must be governed by the issues raised in the evidence: *R. v. Smith*, [1979] 1 S.C.R. 215, 43 C.C.C. (2d) 417 (9:0).

Included offences in murder case – The mere verdict of "guilty of manslaughter" is not in accordance with subsec. (2): *R. v. Vincent* (1957), 119 C.C.C. 188, [1957] O.W.N. 577 (C.A.).

Where the accused is charged with murder and the means are not particularized, the accused may be convicted of the included offence of manslaughter based on either an unlawful act or on criminal negligence. However, where the case was prosecuted and defended on the basis of an unlawful act and the theory of criminal negligence emerged for the first time only in Crown counsel's closing address, the accused was deprived of the right to make full answer and defence: *R. v. McCune* (1998), 131 C.C.C. (3d) 152, 21 C.R. (5th) 247 (B.C.C.A.).

It would appear that the accused may properly apply at the close of the Crown's case for a directed verdict of acquittal on the charge of first degree murder, where for example there is no evidence of planning and deliberation, with the case then proceeding on the charge of second degree murder: *R. v. Titus*, [1983] 1 S.C.R. 259, 2 C.C.C. (3d) 321 (7:0); *R. v. Talbot (No. 3)* (1977), 38 C.C.C. (2d) 562 (Ont. H.C.J.). *Contra: R. v. Andrews, Elton and Van Amerongen* (1979), 8 C.R. (3d) 1 (B.C.C.A.), leave to appeal to S.C.C. refused June 15, 1979.

The words of subsec. (3) are clear and unambiguous and on a trial on a charge of murder the court may not return a verdict such as assault causing bodily harm: *R. v. Chichak* (1978), 38 C.C.C. (2d) 489 (Alta. S.C. App. Div.). *Contra, R. v. Sandhu* (1973), 29 C.R.N.S. 126, [1975] 1 W.W.R. 204 (B.C.S.C.).

Attempted murder is an available verdict on a murder charge. Nothing in s. 662 addresses an accused's potential liability for attempting to commit the murder with which he is charged or limits the application of s. 660 to that situation: *R. v. Sarrazin* (2010), 259 C.C.C. (3d) 293 (Ont. C.A.), affd [2011] 3 S.C.R. 505, 276 C.C.C. (3d) 210.

NO ACQUITTAL UNLESS ACT OR OMISSION NOT WILFUL.

663. Where a female person is charged with infanticide and the evidence establishes that she caused the death of her child but does not establish that, at the time of the act or omission by which she caused the death of the child,

(*a*) she was not fully recovered from the effects of giving birth to the child or from the effect of lactation consequent on the birth of the child, and

(*b*) the balance of her mind was, at that time, disturbed by reason of the effect of giving birth to the child or of the effect of lactation consequent on the birth of the child,

she may be convicted unless the evidence establishes that the act or omission was not wilful. R.S., c. C-34, s. 590.

CROSS-REFERENCES

The offence of infanticide is defined in s. 233 and punished pursuant to s. 237. As to cause of death, see the notes under s. 233.

SYNOPSIS

This section states that a female accused may be convicted of infanticide (see s. 233) if the evidence *establishes* that she caused the death of her child and if both elements of the defence outlined in s. 233 are not made out. The accused must not have recovered from the effects of giving birth or consequent lactation, and must have been of disturbed mind due to these effects at the time the infant was killed. However, it is still a defence that the killing was not wilful. In effect, the section prevents acquittal of the accused of infanticide, because she had a greater *mens rea* than that prescribed by s. 233.

Previous Convictions

NO REFERENCE TO PREVIOUS CONVICTION.

664. No indictment in respect of an offence for which, by reason of previous convictions, a greater punishment may be imposed shall contain any reference to previous convictions. R.S., c. C-34, s. 591.

CROSS-REFERENCES

The term "indictment" is defined in s. 2. Section 727 sets out the procedure where an accused is convicted of an offence for which a greater punishment may be imposed by reason of previous convictions. Section 667 provides a method of proving the prior conviction.

SYNOPSIS

Certain offences (such as impaired operation, s. 255) carry a greater minimum or maximum penalty, depending on whether the accused has previously been convicted of the same (or sometimes a related) offence. This section provides, however, that there shall be no reference to such previous convictions in the information or indictment.

665. [*Repealed*, 1995, c. 22, s. 3.]

EVIDENCE OF CHARACTER.

666. Where, at a trial, the accused adduces evidence of his good character, the prosecutor may, in answer thereto, before a verdict is returned, adduce evidence of the previous conviction of the accused for any offences, including any previous conviction by reason of which a greater punishment may be imposed. R.S., c. C-34, s. 593.

CROSS-REFERENCES

The term "prosecutor" is defined in s. 2. Also note s. 12 of the *Canada Evidence Act*, R.S.C. 1985, c. C-5 which permits cross-examination of an accused on a prior criminal record. Section 667 provides a method of proof of a prior conviction.

SYNOPSIS

This section permits the Crown to lead evidence as part of its case of the accused's criminal record where the accused has put his or her character in issue.

ANNOTATIONS

The evidence of good character is not some personal attributes of the accused brought out on cross-examination of a Crown witness but is an expression of the accused's reputation in the community: *R. v. Demyen (No. 2)* (1976), 31 C.C.C. (2d) 383, [1976] 5 W.W.R. 324 (Sask. C.A.).

This section lets in only evidence of previous convictions and does not deal with previous misconduct not resulting in convictions. Further, the evidence of good character must be adduced at trial and does not include a statement to the police: *R. v. Drysdale,* [1969] 2 C.C.C. 141, 66 W.W.R. 664 (Man. C.A.).

Whenever the accused puts his character in issue, it is open to the Crown to prove his bad character, *i.e.,* that his general reputation or moral disposition is bad. Resort to this section is not the only method open to the Crown to prove the accused's bad character but was enacted rather to avoid the rule that bad character cannot generally be proven by specific acts of misconduct. Where an accused in examination-in-chief testified that he had never been convicted nor arrested he put his character in issue: *R. v. Morris*, [1979] 1 S.C.R. 405, 43 C.C.C. (2d) 129 (5:4).

Therefore, although evidence of an absolute or conditional discharge does not constitute a conviction within the meaning of this section, the prosecutor may none the less rebut evidence of good character by cross-examining the accused to establish that a prior relevant offence for which the accused received a discharge had been committed: *R. v. Deyardin* (1997), 119 C.C.C. (3d) 365, [1997] R.J.Q. 2367 *sub nom. Bombiski-Deyardin (Re)* (C.A.).

An accused does not put his character in issue merely by denying his guilt and repudiating the allegations against him, nor by giving an explanation of matters which are essential to his defence. However, he may not, without putting his character in issue, assert expressly or implicitly that he would not have done the acts alleged against him because he is a person of good character. Thus an accused may during his own testimony put his character in issue. It is not merely by adducing evidence of general reputation that he does so. Evidence of good character may be rebutted by the Crown by extrinsic evidence of bad reputation, extrinsic evidence of similar facts and cross-examination of the accused as to specific past acts of disreputable conduct, subject to a possible discretion in the trial judge to exclude cross-examination on acts which did not result in a conviction, were of little probative value or remote in time, and gravely prejudicial: *R. v. McNamara (No. 1)* (1981), 56 C.C.C. (2d) 193 (Ont. C.A.), at pp. 342-54.

Similarly, in *R. v. P. (N.A.)* (2002), 171 C.C.C. (3d) 70, 8 C.R. (6th) 186, the Ontario Court of Appeal held that the accused had not put his character into issue where the Crown's case included evidence of an unfavourable family relationship as a backdrop to the charges. The line between permissible repudiation of the Crown's case and putting one's character into issue was not crossed where the accused testified about his parenting skills and his relationships with his children, who were not the subject of the criminal charges in response to the case led by the Crown.

This section permits the Crown to lead evidence of convictions registered either before or after the incident giving rise to the charge upon which the accused is being tried provided that convictions after the incident relate to offences which are so closely related in time to the charge as to show his disposition at that time: *R. v. Close* (1982), 68 C.C.C. (2d) 105, 137 D.L.R. (3d) 655 (Ont. C.A.).

PROOF OF PREVIOUS CONVICTION / Idem / Proof of identity / Attendance and right to cross-examine / Notice of intention to produce certificate / Definition of "fingerprint examiner".

667. (1) In any proceedings,

(*a*) a certificate setting out with reasonable particularity the conviction or discharge under section 730, the finding of guilt under the *Young Offenders Act*, chapter Y-1 of the Revised Statutes of Canada, 1985, the finding of guilt under the *Youth Criminal Justice Act* or the conviction and sentence or finding of guilt and sentence in Canada of an offender is, on proof that the accused or defendant is the offender referred to in the certificate, evidence that the accused or defendant was so convicted, so discharged or so convicted and sentenced or found guilty and sentenced, without proof of the signature or the official character of the person appearing to have signed the certificate, if it is signed by

(i) the person who made the conviction, order for the discharge or finding of guilt,

(ii) the clerk of the court in which the conviction, order for the discharge or finding of guilt was made, or

(iii) a fingerprint examiner;

is, on proof that the accused or defendant is the offender referred to in the certificate, evidence that the accused or defendant was so convicted, so discharged or so convicted and sentenced or found guilty and sentenced, or that a judicial determination was made against the accused or defendant, without proof of the signature or the official character of the person appearing to have signed the certificate;

(*b*) evidence that the fingerprints of the accused or defendant are the same as the fingerprints of the offender whose fingerprints are reproduced in or attached to a certificate issued under subparagraph (*a*)(iii) is, in the absence of evidence to the contrary, proof that the accused or defendant is the offender referred to in that certificate;

(*c*) a certificate of a fingerprint examiner stating that he has compared the fingerprints reproduced in or attached to that certificate with the fingerprints reproduced in or attached to a certificate issued under subparagraph (*a*)(iii) and that they are those of the same person is evidence of the statements contained in the certificate without proof of the signature or the official character of the person appearing to have signed the certificate; and

(*d*) a certificate under subparagraph (*a*)(iii) may be in Form 44, and a certificate under paragraph (*c*) may be in Form 45.

(2) In any proceedings, a copy of the summary conviction or discharge under section 730 in Canada of an offender, signed by the person who made the conviction or order for the discharge or by the clerk of the court in which the conviction or order for the discharge was made, is, on proof that the accused or defendant is the offender referred to in the copy of the summary conviction, evidence of the conviction or discharge under section 730 of the accused or defendant, without proof of the signature or the official character of the person appearing to have signed it.

(2.1) In any summary conviction proceedings, where the name of a defendant is similar to the name of an offender referred to in a certificate made under subparagraph (1)(*a*)(i) or (ii) in respect of a summary conviction or referred to in a copy of a summary conviction mentioned in subsection (2), that similarity of name is, in the absence of evidence to the contrary, evidence that the defendant is the offender referred to in the certificate or the copy of the summary conviction.

(3) An accused against whom a certificate issued under subparagraph (1)(*a*)(iii) or paragraph (1)(*c*) is produced may, with leave of the court, require the attendance of the person who signed the certificate for the purposes of cross-examination.

(4) No certificate issued under subparagraph (1)(*a*)(iii) or paragraph (1)(*c*) shall be received in evidence unless the party intending to produce it has given to the accused reasonable notice of his intention together with a copy of the certificate.

(5) In this section, "fingerprint examiner" means a person designated as such for the purposes of this section by the Minister of Public Safety and Emergency Preparedness. R.S., c. C-34, s. 594; 1972, c. 13, s. 51; R.S.C. 1985, c. 27 (1st Supp.), s. 136; 1995, c. 22, s. 10; 2002, c. 1, s. 181; 2005, c. 10, s. 34(1)(*f*)(xii); 2012, c. 1, s. 200.

CROSS-REFERENCES

This section does not displace other means of proving previous convictions either by application of the common law or provisions of the *Canada Evidence Act*, R.S.C. 1985, c. C-5. Note s. 727 which requires that where an accused is convicted of an offence for which a greater punishment may be imposed by reason of previous convictions, no greater punishment shall be imposed on him by reason thereof unless the prosecutor has given notice of intention to seek the greater punishment. Such notice is not, however, required in the case of an accused convicted of second degree murder who has previously been convicted of culpable homicide that is murder and who is sentenced in accordance with s. 745(*b*). Note s. 841(3) which provides that any pre-printed portions of forms must be in both official languages.

A certificate under subsec. (1)(*a*) is to accompany an application for authorization to take samples of bodily substances for forensic DNA analysis from certain offenders under s. 487.055.

SYNOPSIS

This section deals with the methods available to prove a previous conviction.

Subsection (1)(*a*) provides for the issuance and admissibility of a certificate of conviction which may be signed by a judge, clerk of the court or a "fingerprint examiner" designated by the Solicitor General of Canada. In the absence of evidence to the contrary, evidence that the fingerprints of the accused are the same as those which form part of that certificate is evidence that the accused is the person referred to in the certificate (subsec. (1)(*b*)). A "fingerprint examiner" may also issue a certificate which links fingerprints attached to that certificate to those in the certificate of conviction (subsec. (1)(*c*)). The signature and official character of the person signing any of the above mentioned certificates is presumed and need not be proven (subsec. (1)(*a*), (*c*)).

With respect to summary conviction proceedings a copy of the summary conviction or discharge signed by either the judge or clerk of the court may be used to prove that the accused has previously been convicted. The signature and official character of the person signing the document need not be proven (subsec. (2)).

In summary conviction proceedings similarity of name will be sufficient, in the absence of evidence to the contrary, to connect the accused to a judge's or clerk's certificate, or to the copy of a summary conviction (subsec. (2.1)). (**Note**: In many cases a person convicted of a summary conviction offence will not have been fingerprinted in connection with that matter.)

The court may grant leave to require the "fingerprint examiner" to attend for cross-examination (subsec. (3)).

The Crown must give an accused reasonable notice of its intention to produce the certificate of a "fingerprint examiner" together with a copy of the certificate (subsec. (4)).

ANNOTATIONS

Proof of previous conviction – Since subsec. (1)(*c*) provides a convenient shortcut for the Crown its provisions must be strictly followed and accordingly a certificate referring to the section's previous number prior to the coming into force of R.S.C.1970, with no S.C. 1953-54 reference is inadmissible: *R. v. Gordon* (1972), 8 C.C.C. (2d) 132 (B.C.C.A.).

In view of the definition of "clerk of the court" in s. 2, there is no requirement that the person performing the duties of a clerk of the court has been appointed as such under the provincial legislation for that person to sign a copy of the summary conviction under subsec. (2): *R. v. Hughes* (1981), 60 C.C.C. (2d) 16, 31 Nfld. & P.E.I.R. 349 (P.E.I.S.C. *in banco*).

Circumstances in which accused liable to greater penalty – In the absence of explicit and unqualified language to the contrary the increased penalty for a subsequent offence may only be imposed where there was a prior conviction at the time the subsequent offence was committed. Thus the accused was not liable to the increased minimum penalty prescribed by s. 85(1)(*d*) [old provision] in the case of a "second or subsequent offence" of using a firearm while committing an indictable offence where all offences were committed prior to the first conviction: *R. v. Cheetham* (1980), 53 C.C.C. (2d) 109, 17 C.R. (3d) 1 (Ont. C.A.), leave to appeal to S.C.C. refused 33 N.R. 539*n*. Folld: *R. v. Oswald* (1981), 57 C.C.C. (2d) 484 (B.C.C.A.).

The same principle was applied in *R. v. Negridge* (1980), 54 C.C.C. (2d) 304, 17 C.R. (3d) 14 (Ont. C.A.), a case involving the drinking and driving provisions.

Similarly, the accused was not liable to the increased penalty for a third offence under s. 236(1)(*c*) [now s. 255(1)(*a*)(iii)] where his two prior convictions for the offences contrary to ss. 234 [now s. 253] and 235 [now s. 254] were registered on the same day. In such circumstances he has had only one "warning" and is therefore only liable to be sentenced for a second offence under s. 236(1)(*b*) [now s. 255(1)(*a*)(ii)]: *R. v. Skolnick*, [1982] 2 S.C.R. 47, 68 C.C.C. (2d) 385 (9:0).

A copy of a previous conviction certified in accordance with this section is admissible without compliance with the notice provisions of s. 28 of the *Canada Evidence Act*: *R. v. Jonasson* (1980), 56 C.C.C. (2d) 121, 5 Sask. R. 154 (C.A.).

Since proof of prior convictions is part of the sentencing hearing, the common law rule which permits the admission of evidence, even hearsay evidence, which is credible and trustworthy at a sentence hearing applies. Thus an extract of a provincial driving record although hearsay would be admissible. However, if the accuracy of the certificate is seriously put in issue, then it would be incumbent upon the Crown to call whoever signed the certificate and make him available for cross-examination: *R. v. Albright*, [1987] 2 S.C.R. 383, 37 C.C.C. (3d) 105 (5:0).

An admission by the accused during his testimony in the trial proper, as to his prior criminal record is proof of that record for the purposes of sentencing: *R. v. Protz* (1984), 13 C.C.C. (3d) 107, [1984] 5 W.W.R. 263 (Sask. C.A.).

Proof of previous conviction must establish that the conviction was in Canada: *R. v. Marois*, [1969] 4 C.C.C. 208, [1968] Que. Q.B. 797*n* (C.A.).

It is the number of previous convictions, and not the number of times that s. 665 has been resorted to by the Crown that will determine the minimum penalty: *R. v. Bohnet* (1976), 31 C.C.C. (2d) 253, [1976] 6 W.W.R. 176 (N.W.T.C.A.).

---

668. [*Repealed*, R.S.C. 1985, c. C-34; 1995, c. 22, s. 4.]

---

669. [*Repealed*, R.S.C. 1985, c. C-34; 1995, c. 22, s. 4.]

Jurisdiction

JURISDICTION / Adjournment.

669.1 (1) Where any judge, court or provincial court judge by whom or which the plea of the accused or defendant to an offence was taken has not commenced to hear evidence, any judge, court or provincial court judge having jurisdiction to try the accused or defendant has jurisdiction for the purpose of the hearing and adjudication.

(2) Any court, judge or provincial court judge having jurisdiction to try an accused or a defendant, or any clerk or other proper officer of the court, or in the case of an offence punishable on summary conviction, any justice, may, at any time before or after the plea of the accused or defendant is taken, adjourn the proceedings. R.S.C. 1985, c. 27 (1st Supp.), s. 137.

CROSS-REFERENCES

Where the trial has actually commenced with the taking of evidence but the judge has been unable to continue, see s. 669.2.

Section 626.1 permits a judge other than the trial judge to preside over jury selection.

SYNOPSIS

Provided that no evidence has been called the judge before whom the accused has entered a plea is not "seized" of the matter and, therefore, another member of that court has jurisdiction to hear and decide the case (*e.g.*, where the first judge is unavailable due to illness) (subsec. (1)).

Adjournments may be granted not only by a judge but also by the court clerk or other proper officer. Justices of the peace may adjourn summary conviction proceedings (subsec. (2)).

ANNOTATIONS

This section does not apply so as to give a judge other than the trial judge jurisdiction to hear a pre-trial application for an order allowing a defence expert access to the breathalyzer machine and to analyze samples of the accused's breath: *R. v. Delaney* (1989), 48 C.C.C. (3d) 276, 89 N.S.R. (2d) 253 (N.S.C.A.).

This section applies to proceedings on a guilty plea. However, the judge has "commenced to hear evidence" when she hears the Crown's version of the facts prior to deciding whether or not to accept the plea and thus, absent the circumstances set out in s. 669.2, the judge who took the plea and heard the evidence must also impose the sentence: *R. v. Cataract* (1994), 93 C.C.C. (3d) 483, 35 C.R. (4th) 186 *sub nom. Saskatchewan (Attorney General) v. Saskatchewan (Provincial Court Judge)* (Sask. C.A.).

An agreed statement of facts filed on a guilty plea is an admission under s. 655 and constitutes evidence. By directing it be marked as an exhibit, the judge ruled on its admissibility. Accordingly, he was seized with the sentencing. Section 669.2(1) did not allow another judge to conduct the sentencing because there was no evidence that the judge was unable to continue: *R. v. Magbanua* (2013), 301 C.C.C. (3d) 225 (Alta. Prov. Ct.).

CONTINUATION OF PROCEEDINGS / Where adjudication is made / If no adjudiction made / If no adjudication made — jury trials / Where trial continued.

669.2 (1) Subject to this section, where an accused or a defendant is being tried by

(*a*) a judge or provincial court judge,

(*b*) a justice or other person who is, or is a member of, a summary conviction court, or

(*c*) a court composed of a judge and jury,

as the case may be, and the judge, provincial court judge, justice or other person dies or is for any reason unable to continue, the proceedings may be continued before another judge, provincial court judge, justice or other person, as the case may be, who has jurisdiction to try the accused or defendant.

(2) Where a verdict was rendered by a jury or an adjudication was made by a judge, provincial court judge, justice or other person before whom the trial was commenced, the judge, provincial court judge, justice or other person before whom the proceedings

are continued shall, without further election by an accused, impose the punishment or make the order that is authorized by law in the circumstances.

(3) Subject to subsections (4) and (5), if the trial was commenced but no adjudication was made or verdict rendered, the judge, provincial court judge, justice or other person before whom the proceedings are continued shall, without further election by an accused, commence the trial again as if no evidence on the merits had been taken.

(4) If a trial that is before a court composed of a judge and a jury was commenced but no adjudication was made or verdict rendered, the judge before whom the proceedings are continued may, without further election by an accused, continue the trial or commence the trial again as if no evidence on the merits had been taken.

(5) Where a trial is continued under paragraph (4)(*a*), any evidence that was adduced before a judge referred to in paragraph (1)(*c*) is deemed to have been adduced before the judge before whom the trial is continued but, where the prosecutor and the accused so agree, any part of that evidence may be adduced again before the judge before whom the trial is continued. R.S.C. 1985, c. 27 (1st Supp.), s. 137; 1994, c. 44, s. 65; 2011, c. 16, s. 15.

CROSS-REFERENCES

Where the plea has been taken from the accused but the judge has not commenced to hear evidence than the provisions of s. 669.1 apply. As regards the preliminary inquiry, see s. 547.1.

SYNOPSIS

This section deals with the continuation of proceedings where the trial judge dies or for any reason is unable to carry on with the proceedings.

Where a verdict has been rendered by a jury, or a finding of guilt has been made by a judge sitting alone, another judge may continue the proceedings and impose sentence (subsec. (2)).

If the trial has commenced but a verdict or decision has not yet been rendered, another judge may recommence the trial, without further election by the accused, as if no evidence on the merits had been taken (subsec. (3)). In essence, the original proceedings will be considered a mistrial. However, if the trial was a jury trial, the judge has the discretion to simply continue the trial.

ANNOTATIONS

Editor's Note: Some of the decisions noted below, although decided under the predecessor legislation, were felt to be relevant to these provisions.

Unless the situation falls precisely within one of the enumerated instances a judge has no jurisdiction after the commencement of trial to waive jurisdiction to another judge: *R. v. Ramsey* (1972), 8 C.C.C. (2d) 188 (N.B.C.A.).

Application – This provision also applies where the judge is appointed to another court: *R. v. Shrubsall* (2000), 148 C.C.C. (3d) 425 (N.S.S.C.).

This provision permits the transfer of jurisdiction from a trial judge to another judge when a trial judge is unable to continue to preside as a result of a reasonable apprehension of bias. In this case, the accused brought a stay application during the course of the trial. The issue of bias arose in the context of the stay of proceedings application. While normally a mistrial should have been declared, in the unusual circumstances of the case, the trial judge was entitled to have another superior court judge determine the stay application: *R. v. Leduc* (2003), 176 C.C.C. (3d) 321 (Ont. C.A.), leave to appeal to S.C.C. refused [2004] 1 S.C.R. xi, 179 C.C.C. (3d) vi.

Where a new judge takes jurisdiction under this provision, he or she becomes the trial judge for all purposes and is not bound by evidentiary rulings made by the prior judge. The new judge has the same power to reconsider prior rulings that the prior judge possessed, where it is in the interests of justice to do so: *R. v. R.V.* (2018), 362 C.C.C. (3d) 434 (Ont. C.A.), leave to appeal to S.C.C. allowed 2018 CarswellOnt 21618.

Jurisdiction to declare mistrial / *Also see notes under s. 653* – It would offend the principles of fundamental justice for a judge upon breakdown of the Crown's case to declare a mistrial in order to give the prosecution an opportunity to strengthen its case against the accused by endeavouring to find additional evidence thereby depriving the accused of an acquittal: *R. v. D. (T.C.)* (1987), 38 C.C.C. (3d) 434 (Ont. C.A.).

A judge sitting without a jury has jurisdiction to declare a mistrial. The power of a judge to disqualify himself for good and sufficient reason is one which exists aside from this section: *R. v. Bucholz* (1976), 32 C.C.C. (2d) 331 (Ont. C.A.); *R. v. Jassman* (1975), 27 C.C.C. (2d) 271 (B.C.S.C.). In both these cases the courts refused to follow the case of *R. v. McRitchie* (1974), 23 C.C.C. (2d) 255 (B.C.S.C.), which held that a judge sitting alone has no power to declare a mistrial.

A provincial court judge who has made a finding of guilt still has power to declare a mistrial prior to imposition of sentence where he feels he must disqualify himself as where the police sent the judge certain information about the accused which was not disclosed to the defence and considered prejudicial: *R. v. Bertucci* (1984), 11 C.C.C. (3d) 83 (Sask. C.A.).

There was no jurisdiction for the trial judge to hear a mistrial application where the jury had rendered a verdict and was discharged: *R. v. Halcrow* (2008), 236 C.C.C. (3d) 363 (Alta. C.A.), leave to appeal to S.C.C. refused 238 C.C.C. (3d) vi.

Delay due to illness – Where the trial judge falls ill and is expected to return, the Crown must balance two competing factors in considering whether to bring a motion to replace the judge. The first factor is the need to proceed with the utmost care and caution when considering removal of a judge seized with a case to protect judicial independence and fairness to the accused. The second factor is the need to protect the accused's right to a trial within a reasonable time, including the right to be sentenced within a reasonable time, as guaranteed by s. 11(*b*) of the *Canadian Charter of Rights and Freedoms* and prevent undue prejudice to the accused: *R. v. MacDougall*, [1998] 3 S.C.R. 45, 128 C.C.C. (3d) 483.

JURISDICTION WHEN APPOINTMENT TO ANOTHER COURT.

669.3 Where a court composed of a judge and a jury, a judge or a provincial court judge is conducting a trial and the judge or provincial court judge is appointed to another court, he or she continues to have jurisdiction in respect of the trial until its completion. 1994, c. 44, s. 66.

SYNOPSIS

This section confirms the jurisdiction of a judge who has been appointed to another court to complete any trial that the judge was presiding over.

Formal Defects in Jury Process

JUDGMENT NOT TO BE STAYED ON CERTAIN GROUNDS.

670. Judgment shall not be stayed or reversed after verdict on an indictment

(*a*) by reason of any irregularity in the summoning or empanelling of the jury; or

(*b*) for the reason that a person who served on the jury was not returned as a juror by a sheriff or other officer. R.S., c. C-34, s. 598.

CROSS-REFERENCES

This section is one of several saving provisions respecting jury proceedings and thus, also see ss. 643(3), 671 and 672 and also consider the application of s. 686(1)(*b*)(iv).

SYNOPSIS

This section provides that formal defects in jury proceedings on indictment shall not be grounds for overturning or staying judgment. The "formal defects" identified in this section are irregularities in summoning or empanelling the jury and the presence on the jury of a person not returned by an appropriate officer.

ANNOTATIONS

Paragraph (*a*) of this section applies only to irregularities and has no application where the error is such that the accused has been deprived of a statutory right, or to an error depriving an accused of the right to a trial by a jury lawfully constituted. Thus it could not apply to a case where the trial judge, instead of following the procedure prescribed in s. 642 for summonsing of *talesmen*, purported to continuously expand the jury panel by adding additional members with the result that these potential jurors who were directed by the Crown to stand by were never called again to be sworn, unless challenged: *R. v. Rowbotham* (1988), 41 C.C.C. (3d) 1 (Ont. C.A.).

DIRECTIONS RESPECTING JURY OR JURORS DIRECTORY.

671. No omission to observe the directions contained in any Act with respect to the qualification, selection, balloting or distribution of jurors, the preparation of the jurors' book, the selecting of jury lists, or the drafting of panels from the jury lists, is a ground for impeaching or quashing a verdict rendered in criminal proceedings. R.S., c. C-34, s. 599.

CROSS-REFERENCES

See the notes following s. 670, *supra*.

SYNOPSIS

This section provides that a failure to observe statutory procedural directions regarding juries is not grounds for quashing a jury's verdict.

ANNOTATIONS

The presence of an exempt person on a jury is not a ground for disturbing its legal verdict: *R. v. Rushton* (1974), 20 C.C.C. (2d) 297 (Ont. C.A.).

This section was applied where the jury panel was selected from the municipal electoral list and not the provincial electoral list as required by the *Jury Act*, R.S.N.B. 1973, c. J-3. The qualifications for both lists were the same: *R. v. Arseneau* (1977), 36 C.C.C. (2d) 65 (N.B.S.C. App. Div.), applying *Reference re: R. v. Coffin*, [1956] S.C.R. 191, 114 C.C.C. 1.

SAVING POWERS OF COURT.

672. Nothing in this Act alters, abridges or affects any power or authority that a court or judge had immediately before April 1, 1955, or any practice or form that existed immediately before April 1, 1955, with respect to trials by jury, jury process, juries or jurors, except where the power or authority, practice or form is expressly altered by or is inconsistent with this Act. R.S., c. C-34, s. 600.

CROSS-REFERENCES

Also note s. 8 which preserves the criminal law of England that was in force in the province immediately before April 1, 1955, except as altered, varied, modified or affected by this Act or an Act of Parliament. Section 8(3) also preserves common law justifications, excuses and defences. The common law authority of the court to punish for contempt of court is preserved by s. 9.

SYNOPSIS

This section preserves powers held by judges prior to April 1, 1955, with respect to juries, except as altered by or inconsistent with the current *Criminal Code*.

ANNOTATIONS

This section preserves the common law power of a court to arrest judgment and discharge the accused, as where following verdict and the discharge of the jury the trial judge discovers that the accused was found guilty of an offence not known to law at the time of the incident. In this case, through an error in the drafting of the indictment, the accused was found guilty of dangerous driving causing death arising out of an incident prior to the enactment of that offence in December, 1985: *R. v. Jacobson* (1988), 46 C.C.C. (3d) 50 (Sask. C.A.).

Part XX.1 / MENTAL DISORDER

Transitional provision

Note: 1991, c. 43, s. 10 (in force except subsec. (8)) provides as follows:

10. (1) Any order for the detention of an accused or accused person made under section 614, 615 or 617 of the *Criminal Code* or section 200 or 201 of the *National Defence Act*, as those sections read immediately before the coming into force of section 3 or 18 of this Act, shall continue in force until the coming into force of section 672.64 of the *Criminal Code*, subject to any order made by a court or Review Board under section 672.54 of the *Criminal Code*.

(2) The Review Board of a province shall, within twelve months after the coming into force of this section, review the case of every person detained in custody in the province by virtue of an order of detention referred to in subsection (1).

(3) Sections 672.5 to 672.85 of the *Criminal Code* apply, with such modifications as the circumstances require, to a review under subsection (2) as if

(*a*) the review were a review of a disposition conducted pursuant to section 672.81 of that Act;

(*b*) the warrant issued by the lieutenant governor pursuant to which the person is being detained in custody were a disposition made under section 672.54 of that Act;

(*c*) there were included in the definition "designated offence" in subsection 672.64(1) of that Act a reference to any offence under any Act of Parliament, as that Act read at the time of the commission of the alleged offence for which the person is in custody, involving violence or a threat of violence to a person or danger to the safety or security of the public, including, without limiting the generality of the foregoing, a reference to the following sections of the *Criminal Code*, as those sections read immediately before January 4, 1983, namely,

(i) section 144 (rape),

(ii) section 145 (attempt to commit rape),

(iii) section 149 (indecent assault on female),

(iv) section 156 (indecent assault on male),

(v) section 245 (common assault),

(vi) section 246 (assault with intent); and

(*d*) there were included in the offences mentioned in paragraph 672.64(3)(*a*) a reference to any of the following offences under any Act of Parliament, as that Act read at the time of the commission of the alleged offence for which the person is in custody, namely,

(i) murder punishable by death or punishable by imprisonment for life, capital murder, non-capital murder and any offence of murder, however it had been described or classified by the provisions of the *Criminal Code* that were in force at that time, and

(ii) any other offence under any Act of Parliament for which a minimum punishment of imprisonment for life had been prescribed by law.

(4) The Attorney General of Canada shall appoint a Commissioner from among the judges of superior courts of criminal jurisdiction to review and determine, before the coming into force of section 672.64 of the *Criminal Code*, whether any person detained in custody by virtue of an order of detention described in subsection (1) would have been a dangerous mentally disordered accused under section 672.65 of the *Criminal Code*, if that section were in force at the time the order of detention was made.

(5) Where an order of detention referred to in subsection (1) was issued against a person found not guilty by reason of insanity of an offence that is a designated offence as defined in subsection 672.64(1) of the *Criminal Code* or that is included as a designated offence under paragraph (3)(*c*), the Attorney General of the province where the order was made, or of the province where the person is detained in custody, may apply to the Commissioner for review and determination of whether the person would be a dangerous mentally disordered accused.

(6) Sections 672.65 and 672.66 of the *Criminal Code* apply to an application made under subsection (5) with such modifications as the circumstances require, and

(*a*) in addition to the evidence described in paragraph 672.65(3)(*a*), the Commissioner shall consider any relevant evidence subsequent to the detention of the person in respect of whom the application is made; and

(*b*) where the Commissioner determines that the person would be a dangerous mentally disordered accused, the Commissioner may make an order that the person be detained in custody for a maximum of life.

(7) An order made by the Commissioner in respect of an application under this section shall have effect on the coming into force of section 672.64 of the *Criminal Code* and be subject to the rights of appeal described in sections 672.79 and 672.8 as if the order were an order of a court under section 672.65 of that Act.

(8) Where, before the coming into force of section 5 of this Act, a person has committed an offence but a sentence has not been imposed on that person for that offence, that person may be detained in accordance with section 736.11 of the *Criminal Code*, as enacted by section 6 of this Act.

Interpretation

DEFINITIONS / "Accused" / "Assessment" / "Chairperson" / "Court" / "Disposition" / "Dual status offender" / "Hospital" / "Medical practitioner" / "Party" / "Placement decision" / "Prescribed" / "Review Board" / "Verdict of not criminally responsible on account of mental disorder".

672.1 (1) In this Part,

"accused" includes a defendant in summary conviction proceedings and an accused in respect of whom a verdict of not criminally responsible on account of mental disorder has been rendered;

"assessment" means an assessment by a medical practitioner or any other person who has been designated by the Attorney General as being qualified to conduct an assessment of the mental condition of the accused under an assessment order made under section 672.11 or 672.121, and any incidental observation or examination of the accused;

"chairperson" includes any alternate that the chairperson of a Review Board may designate to act on the chairperson's behalf;

"court" includes a summary conviction court as defined in section 785, a judge, a justice and a judge of the court of appeal as defined in section 673;

"disposition" means an order made by a court or Review Board under section 672.54, an order made by a court under section 672.58 or a finding made by a court under subsection 672.64(1);

"dual status offender" means an offender who is subject to a sentence of imprisonment in respect of one offence and a custodial disposition under paragraph 672.54(*c*) in respect of another offence;

"high-risk accused" means an accused who is found to be a high-risk accused by a court under subsection 672.64(1);

"hospital" means a place in a province that is designated by the Minister of Health for the province for the custody, treatment or assessment of an accused in respect of whom an assessment order, a disposition or a placement decision is made.

"medical practitioner" means a person who is entitled to practise medicine by the laws of a province;

"party" in relation to proceedings of a court or Review Board to make or review a disposition, means

(*a*) the accused,

(*b*) the person in charge of the hospital where the accused is detained or is to attend pursuant to an assessment order or a disposition,

(*c*) an Attorney General designated by the court or Review Board under subsection 672.5(3),

(*d*) any interested person designated by the court or Review Board under subsection 672.5(4), or

(*e*) where the disposition is to be made by a court, the prosecutor of the charge against the accused;

"placement decision" means a decision by a Review Board under subsection 672.68(2) as to the place of custody of a dual status offender;

"prescribed" means prescribed by regulations made by the Governor in Council under section 672.95;

"Review Board" means the Review Board established or designated for a province pursuant to subsection 672.38(1);

"verdict of not criminally responsible on account of mental disorder" means a verdict that the accused committed the act or made the omission that formed the basis of the offence with which the accused is charged but is not criminally responsible on account of mental disorder.

(2) For the purposes of subsections 672.5(3) and (5), paragraph 672.86(1)(*b*) and subsections 672.86(2) and (2.1), 672.88(2) and 672.89(2), in respect of a territory or proceedings commenced at the instance of the Government of Canada and conducted by or on behalf of that Government, a reference to the Attorney General of a province shall be read as a reference to the Attorney General of Canada. 1991, c. 43, s. 4; 2005, c. 22, s. 1; 2014, c. 6, s. 2.

CROSS-REFERENCES

Reference should be had to the specific provisions of Part XX.1 of the *Criminal Code*. In particular, "electro-convulsive therapy" is defined in s. 672.61(2); "psychosurgery" is defined in s. 672.61(2); "protected statement" is defined in s. 672.21; and "Minister" is defined in s. 672.68(1).

Reference should also be made to s. 2 of the *Criminal Code* which includes definitions of "mental disorder" and "unfit to stand trial".

Assessment Orders

ASSESSMENT ORDER.

672.11 A court having jurisdiction over an accused in respect of an offence may order an assessment of the mental condition of the accused, if it has reasonable grounds to believe that such evidence is necessary to determine

(*a*) whether the accused is unfit to stand trial;

(*b*) whether the accused was, at the time of the commission of the alleged offence, suffering from a mental disorder so as to be exempt from criminal responsibility by virtue of subsection 16(1);

(*c*) whether the balance of the mind of the accused was disturbed at the time of commission of the alleged offence, where the accused is a female person charged with an offence arising out of the death of her newly-born child;

(*d*) the appropriate disposition to be made, where a verdict of not criminally responsible on account of mental disorder or unfit to stand trial has been rendered in respect of the accused;

(*d*.1) whether a finding that the accused is a high-risk accused should be revoked under subsection 672.84(3); or

(*e*) whether an order should be made under section 672.851 for a stay of proceedings, where a verdict of unfit to stand trial has been rendered against the accused. 1991, c. 43, s. 4; 1995, c. 22, s. 10; 2005, c. 22, s. 2; 2014, c. 6, s. 3.

CROSS-REFERENCES

The terms "accused", "assessment", "high-risk accused" and "verdict of not criminally responsible on account of insanity" are defined in s. 672.1. The terms "newly-born child", "unfit to stand trial" and "mental disorder" are defined in s. 2. Paragraph (*c*) refers to the offence of infanticide, thus see s. 233. For further cross-references respecting the making of assessment orders, see the references under s. 672.12.

SYNOPSIS

The court is afforded a broad discretion to require an assessment of the accused's mental condition where the court has jurisdiction over the accused in the course of a preliminary hearing, indictable trial, indictable appeal, summary conviction trial and summary conviction appeal.

An assessment order may be issued to determine: (1) fitness to stand trial; (2) exemption from criminal responsibility as a result of mental disorder; (3) mental condition with respect to infanticide; (4) the appropriate disposition where the accused is found unfit to stand trial or not criminally responsible on account of mental disorder; (5) whether a finding that the offender is a high-risk offender should be revoked; and (6) whether an order pursuant to s. 672.851 for a stay of proceedings, where a verdict of unfit to stand trial has been rendered.

Unlike the previous *Criminal Code* provisions, s. 672.11 does not require medical evidence in order to support the assessment order. An assessment order may be issued simply if the court has "reasonable ground to believe such evidence is necessary" to determine the aforementioned issues. Therefor, while medical evidence may be adduced, it would appear that the observations of the accused's behavior by lay witnesses or the court would be sufficient to constitute reasonable grounds to require an assessment order.

ANNOTATIONS

This provision exhaustively sets out the circumstances in which a judge may make an assessment order. Thus, the judge has no power to make an assessment order for the purposes of psychiatric assessment prior to sentencing: *R. v. Snow* (1992), 76 C.C.C. (3d) 43 (Ont. Gen. Div.). See also *R. v. Gray* (2002), 169 C.C.C. (3d) 194 (B.C.S.C.).

An accused who was deaf and unable to speak could not be said to suffer from a mental disorder: *R. v. Isaac* (2009), 250 C.C.C. (3d) 565 (Ont. C.J.).

A trial judge has the authority to remand an accused in custody pending sentence pursuant to s. 523(1)(*b*)(ii). The judge can also order a pre-sentence report and make use of provincial mental health legislation that permits a psychiatric facility to accept an offender remanded to custody for observation and requires the senior physician to report in writing to the trial judge. The provincial legislation provides a mechanism to furnish the court with information that may assist in sentencing: *R. v. Lenart* (1998), 123 C.C.C. (3d) 353, 158 D.L.R. (4th) 508 (Ont. C.A.).

Furthermore, the result of a psychiatric assessment relating to fitness to stand trial is admissible at a sentencing hearing provided the accused is given an opportunity to challenge the report: *R. v. Roussel* (1996), 112 C.C.C. (3d) 538, 183 N.B.R. (2d) 364 (C.A.).

A Crown application for an assessment during the course of a sentence appeal was dismissed on the basis that an assessment is relevant to a conviction appeal but not to a sentence appeal: *R. v. Resler* (2011), 270 C.C.C. (3d) 162 (Alta. C.A.).

WHERE COURT MAY ORDER ASSESSMENT / Limitation on prosecutor's application for assessment fitness / Limitation on prosecutor's application for assessment.

672.12 (1) The court may make an assessment order at any stage of proceedings against the accused of its own motion, on application of the accused or, subject to subsections (2) and (3), on application of the prosecutor.

(2) Where the prosecutor applies for an assessment in order to determine whether the accused is unfit to stand trial for an offence that is prosecuted by way of summary conviction, the court may only order the assessment if

(*a*) the accused raised the issue of fitness; or

(*b*) the prosecutor satisfies the court that there are reasonable grounds to doubt that the accused is fit to stand trial.

(3) Where the prosecutor applies for an assessment in order to determine whether the accused was suffering from a mental disorder at the time of the offence so as to be exempt from criminal responsibility, the court may only order the assessment if

(*a*) the accused puts his or her mental capacity for criminal intent into issue; or

(*b*) the prosecutor satisfies the court that there are reasonable grounds to doubt that the accused is criminally responsible for the alleged offence, on account of mental disorder. 1991, c. 43, s. 4.

CROSS-REFERENCES

The terms "accused", "assessment", "court" and "verdict of not criminally responsible on account of insanity" are defined in s. 672.1. The term "prosecutor" is defined in ss. 2 and 785; and "unfit to stand trial" and "mental disorder" are defined in s. 2. The assessment order is in Form 48, see s. 672.13. As to grounds for making the order, see s. 672.11 and for the length of time that order may be in force, see ss. 672.14 and 672.15. The assessment order may require that the accused also be detained pursuant to s. 672.16 in which case the accused is not eligible for bail, s. 672.17. The court has power to vary the terms of the detention or interim release order under s. 672.18 but no assessment order may direct that the accused submit to treatment, s. 672.19. The accused shall appear before the court as soon as practicable after the assessment is completed and not later than the last day of the order for the assessment, s. 672.191. The order may require that a report be submitted, s. 672.2. Statements made by accused for the purposes of preparation of an assessment report are admissible in limited circumstances referred to in s. 672.21.

SYNOPSIS

The court may make an assessment order at any stage of the proceedings either on its own motion or on the application of the accused or the prosecutor.

The provision restricts, however, the availability of the application to the Crown in the context of summary conviction proceedings. In a summary conviction offence, the prosecutor may not make an application for an assessment order relating to the issue of fitness unless the accused has raised the issue of fitness or the prosecutor establishes that there are reasonable grounds to doubt the accused's fitness. There are no similar restrictions on the Crown raising the issue of fitness in the context of an indictable offence.

Where the issue of the accused's exemption from criminal responsibility as a result of a mental disorder is raised either in the context of a summary or indictable offence, the Crown may raise the issue only if the accused puts their mental capacity for criminal intent into issue or reasonable grounds to question the accused's responsibility as a result of a mental disorder are established.

ANNOTATIONS

A prosecutor's statements without affidavit or *viva voce* evidence and medical opinion are insufficient to establish that there are reasonable grounds to doubt that the accused is criminally responsible. In this case, a letter from a psychiatrist which was prepared for the purpose of a bail hearing and which focused on the possibility of harm to others was also insufficient to determine the need for an assessment. Even the consent of the accused cannot dispose of the requirement that sufficient evidence be adduced to provide a basis for concluding that there are reasonable grounds to order an assessment: *R. v. Muschke* (1997), 121 C.C.C. (3d) 51 (B.C.S.C.).

The Crown was not precluded from applying for an assessment order during the course of the accused's testimony even though the defence had an expert available for presentation. It is for the trial judge to determine whether the issue of mental disorder can be determined properly without a clinical assessment of the mental condition of the accused by an expert other than the defence expert: *R. v. Walker* (2002), 163 C.C.C. (3d) 29 (B.C.C.A.), leave to appeal to S.C.C. refused [2004] 4 S.C.R. vii, 169 C.C.C. (3d) vi.

REVIEW BOARD MAY ORDER ASSESSMENT.

672.121 The Review Board that has jurisdiction over an accused found not criminally responsible on account of mental disorder or unfit to stand trial may order an assessment of the mental condition of the accused of its own motion or on application of the prosecutor or the accused, if it has reasonable grounds to believe that such evidence is necessary to

(*a*) make a recommendation to the court under subsection 672.851(1);

(*b*) make a disposition under section 672.54 in one of the following circumstances:

(i) no assessment report on the mental condition of the accused is available,

(ii) no assessment of the mental condition of the accused has been conducted in the last twelve months, or

(iii) the accused has been transferred from another province under section 672.86; or

(*c*) determine whether to refer to the court for review under subsection 672.84(1) a finding that an accused is a high-risk accused. 2005, c. 22, s. 3; 2014, c. 6, s. 4.

CROSS-REFERENCES

The terms "accused", "assessment", "court", "high-risk accused", "Review Board" and "verdict of not criminally responsible on account of insanity" are defined in s. 672.1. The term "prosecutor" is defined in ss. 2 and 785; and "unfit to stand trial" and "mental disorder" are defined in s. 2. The assessment order is in Form 48.1 (see s. 672.13). The similar power of the court to order an assessment is set out in ss. 672.11 and 672.12. For the length of time the order may be in force, see ss. 672.14 and 672.15. The assessment order may not require that the accused also be detained pursuant to s. 672.16 unless the accused is subject to an order detaining the accused in a hospital, the Review Board is satisfied that custody is necessary to carry out the assessment, or custody is required in respect of any other matter or by virtue of any other provision of the *Criminal Code*. No assessment order may direct that the accused submit to treatment (s. 672.19). The accused shall appear before the Review Board as soon as practicable after the assessment is completed and not later than the last day of the order for the assessment (s. 672.191). The order may require that a report be submitted, (s. 672.2). Statements made by the accused for the purposes of preparation of an assessment report are admissible in limited circumstances referred to in s. 672.21.

A peace officer may arrest an accused without warrant under s. 672.91 where the officer has reasonable grounds to believe that the accused has contravened or wilfully failed to comply with an assessment order.

SYNOPSIS

This section gives the Review Board discretion to require an assessment of the accused's mental condition where the accused has been found not criminally responsible on account of mental disorder or unfit to stand trial. The board may make the order on its own motion or on application by the accused or the prosecutor.

An assessment order may be made to make a recommendation to the court concerning a stay of proceedings in relation to an accused who is not fit to stand trial or where evidence from such an assessment is necessary to make a disposition under s. 672.54 if no assessment report on the mental condition of the accused is available, no assessment has been conducted in the last 12 months, or the accused has been transferred from another province. And the Board may make an assessment order to determine whether to refer to the court whether the accused is a high-risk accused or whether to revoke such a finding.

ANNOTATIONS

It would appear that this section was enacted in response to *R. v. Demers*, [2004] 2 S.C.R. 489, 185 C.C.C. (3d) 257, where the court held, in part, that the inability of a review board to order a psychiatric assessment of the accused after the initial evaluation made it impossible to ensure that the disposition under s. 672.54 or a review under s. 672.81(1) was tailored to the unfit accused's current circumstances.

CONTENTS OF ASSESSMENT ORDER / Form.

672.13 (1) An assessment order must specify

- **(*a*) the service that or the person who is to make the assessment, or the hospital where it is to be made;**
- **(*b*) whether the accused is to be detained in custody while the order is in force; and**
- **(*c*) the period that the order is to be in force, including the time required for the assessment and for the accused to travel to and from the place where the assessment is to be made.**

(2) An assessment order may be in Form 48 or 48.1. 1991, c. 43, s. 4; 2005, c. 22, s. 4.

CROSS-REFERENCES

The terms "accused", "assessment" and "hospital" are defined in s. 672.1. The length of time that an assessment order may be in force is governed by ss. 672.14 and 672.15. For further cross-references respecting the making of assessment orders, see the references under s. 672.12.

SYNOPSIS

The assessment order must specify the service or person who is to make the assessment or the hospital in which the assessment is to be conducted, whether the assessment is to be conducted in custody and the period of the order. An assessment order may be in the prescribed Form 48 which also provides the assessment officer with the reason for the assessment.

GENERAL RULE FOR PERIOD / Exception in fitness cases / Exception for compelling circumstances.

672.14 (1) An assessment order shall not be in force for more than thirty days.

(2) No assessment order to determine whether the accused is unfit to stand trial shall be in force for more than five days, excluding holidays and the time required for the accused to travel to and from the place where the assessment is to be made, unless the accused and the prosecutor agree to a longer period not exceeding thirty days.

(3) Despite subsections (1) and (2), a court or Review Board may make an assessment order that remains in force for sixty days if the court or Review Board is satisfied that compelling circumstances exist that warrant it. 1991, c. 43, s. 4; 2005, c. 22, s. 5.

CROSS-REFERENCES

The terms "accused", "assessment", "Review Board" and "hospital" are defined in s. 672.1. An assessment order may be extended pursuant to s. 672.14. For further cross-references respecting the making of assessment orders, see the references under s. 672.12 (court-ordered assessments) and s. 672.121 (assessment ordered by the Review Board).

SYNOPSIS

This provision provides a 30-day limitation for assessment orders despite the purpose of the assessment except in the case of a fitness assessment, in which case the order is limited to five days, unless the parties consent. Notwithstanding these time limitations, however, the court or the Review Board does have the discretion to make an assessment order for a period of not more than 60 days where the court or Review Board is satisfied that "compelling circumstances" exist to do so.

EXTENSION / Maximum duration of extensions.

672.15 (1) Subject to subsection (2), a court or Review Board may extend an assessment order, of its own motion or on the application of the accused or the prosecutor made during or at the end of the period during which the order is in force, for any further period that is required, in its opinion, to complete the assessment of the accused.

(2) No extension of an assessment order shall exceed thirty days, and the period of the initial order together with all extensions shall not exceed sixty days. 1991, c. 43. s. 4; 2005, c. 22, s. 6.

CROSS-REFERENCES

The terms "Review Board", "accused" and "assessment" are defined in s. 672.1. The term "prosecutor" is defined in s. 2. The limitations on the length of time for the initial order are set out in s. 672.14. For further cross-references respecting the making of assessment orders, see the references under s. 672.12 (court-ordered assessments) and s. 672.121 (assessment ordered by the Review Board).

SYNOPSIS

A court or the Review Board has the discretion to extend an assessment order either of its own motion or on the application of the accused or the prosecutor at any time during the force of the assessment order for a period of not more than 30 days at a time. However, this provision limits the extensions so that the period of the initial order together with all of the extensions shall not exceed 60 days.

PRESUMPTION AGAINST CUSTODY / Presumption against custody — Review Board / Residency as a condition of disposition / Report of medical practitioner / Presumption of custody in certain circumstances.

672.16 (1) Subject to subsection (3), an accused shall not be detained in custody under an assessment order of a court unless

- **(*a*) the court is satisfied that on the evidence custody is necessary to assess the accused, or that on the evidence of a medical practitioner custody is desirable to assess the accused and the accused consents to custody;**
- **(*b*) custody of the accused is required in respect of any other matter or by virtue of any other provision of this Act; or**
- **(*c*) the prosecutor, having been given a reasonable opportunity to do so, shows that detention of the accused in custody is justified on either of the grounds set out in subsection 515(10).**

(1.1) If the Review Board makes an order for an assessment of an accused under section 672.121, the accused shall not be detained in custody under the order unless

- **(*a*) the accused is currently subject to a disposition made under paragraph 672.54(*c*);**
- **(*b*) the Review Board is satisfied on the evidence that custody is necessary to assess the accused, or that on the evidence of a medical practitioner custody is desirable to assess the accused and the accused consents to custody; or**
- **(*c*) custody of the accused is required in respect of any other matter or by virtue of any other provision of this Act.**

(1.2) Subject to paragraphs (1.1)(*b*) and (*c*), if the accused is subject to a disposition made under paragraph 672.54(*b*) that requires the accused to reside at a specified place, an assessment ordered under section 672.121 shall require the accused to reside at the same place.

(2) For the purposes of paragraphs (1)(*a*) and (1.1)(*b*), if the prosecutor and the accused agree, the evidence of a medical practitioner may be received in the form of a report in writing.

(3) An assessment order made in respect of an accused who is detained under subsection 515(6) or 522(2) shall order that the accused be detained in custody under the same circumstances referred to in that subsection, unless the accused shows that custody is not justified under the terms of that subsection. 1991, c. 43, s. 4; 2005, c. 22, s. 7.

CROSS-REFERENCES

The terms "Review Board", "accused" and "assessment" are defined in s. 672.1. The term "prosecutor" is defined in s. 2. Section 672.17 provides that, during the time that the court-ordered assessment order is in force, no application may be made for interim release or detention in respect of the offence for which the order is made. However, provision is made to vary the terms of the detention or release order under s. 672.18. For further cross-references respecting the making of assessment orders, see the references under s. 672.12 (court-ordered assessments) and s. 672.121 (assessment ordered by the Review Board).

SYNOPSIS

An assessment order is presumed to be conducted out of custody unless, in the case of a court-ordered assessment, custody is necessary or custody is desirable in view of the evidence of a medical practitioner and the accused consents to custody. In addition, an in-custody assessment will be conducted where the accused is required to be in custody in respect of any other matter, or by virtue of any other provision of the Act, or where the prosecutor shows that the detention of the accused is just on either the primary or secondary grounds set out in s. 515(10).

There is a presumption of in-custody assessment, however, where the accused is charged with an offence described in any of s. 515(6)(*a*) to (*d*) or s. 522(2). In these circumstances, the accused must bear the burden of proof that an in-custody assessment is not just under the terms of that paragraph or subsection.

Similarly, where the assessment is ordered by the Review Board, the accused shall not be detained in custody unless the accused is under a detention order made under s. 672.54(*c*), the board is satisfied that custody is necessary to assess the accused, or that, on the evidence of a medical practitioner, custody is desirable and the accused consents, or the accused's custody is required in respect of another matter or by virtue of some other provision of the *Criminal Code*. If the accused is under a disposition (conditional discharge) made under s. 672.54(*b*) to reside at a specified place, the assessment order shall require the accused to reside at the same place.

The court or Review Board may receive the evidence of the medical practitioner in the form of a written report, if the accused and the prosecutor agree.

ASSESSMENT ORDER TAKES PRECEDENCE OVER BAIL HEARING.

672.17 During the period that an assessment order made by a court in respect of an accused charged with an offence is in force, no order for the interim release or detention of the accused may be made by virtue of Part XVI or section 679 in respect of that offence or an included offence. 1991, c. 43, s. 4; 2005, c. 22, s. 8.

CROSS-REFERENCES

The terms "accused" and "assessment" are defined in s. 672.1. Provision for detention of an accused for the purposes of making the detention order is in s. 672.16 and to vary the terms of release or custody, see s. 672.18. For further cross-references respecting the making of assessment orders, see the references under s. 672.12.

SYNOPSIS

An assessment order takes priority over an interim release order and consequently, no interim release order or detention order may be issued during the period of the assessment order.

APPLICATION TO VARY ASSESSMENT ORDER.

672.18 Where at any time while an assessment order made by a court is in force the prosecutor or an accused shows cause, the court may vary the terms of the order respecting the interim release or detention of the accused in such manner as it considers appropriate in the circumstances. 1991, c. 43, s. 4.

CROSS-REFERENCES

The terms "accused" and "assessment" are defined in s. 672.1. "Prosecutor" is defined in s. 2. Provision for detention of an accused for the purposes of making the detention order is in s. 672.16 and for limitation on application for interim release or detention during the currency of the order, see s. 672.17. For further cross-references respecting the making of assessment orders see the references under s. 672.12.

SYNOPSIS

Notwithstanding s. 672.17, this provision authorizes the variation of an interim release order while an assessment order is in force.

NO TREATMENT ORDER ON ASSESSMENT.

672.19 No assessment order may direct that psychiatric or any other treatment of the accused be carried out, or direct the accused to submit to such treatment. 1991, c. 43, s. 4.

CROSS-REFERENCES

The terms "accused" and "assessment" are defined in s. 672.1. For further cross-references respecting the making of assessment orders, see the references under s. 672.12.

SYNOPSIS

Under this section, the scope of the assessment order is limited to examination and cannot direct treatment or that the accused submit to such treatment subject to the provisions of s. 672.58 which allow a treatment order to issue for a period of not more than 60 days where forced treatment will render the accused fit to stand trial.

WHEN ASSESSMENT COMPLETED.

672.191 An accused in respect of whom an assessment order is made shall appear before the court or Review Board that made the order as soon as practicable after the assessment is completed and not later than the last day of the period that the order is to be in force. 1997, c. 18, s. 81; 2005, c. 22, s. 10.

CROSS-REFERENCES

The terms "assessment order", "accused" and "Review Board" are defined in s. 672.1. For further cross-references respecting the making of assessment orders, see the references under s. 672.12 (court-ordered assessments) and s. 672.121 (assessment ordered by the Review Board).

Assessment Reports

ASSESSMENT REPORT / Assessment report to be filed / Court to send assessment report to Review Board / Copies of reports to accused and prosecutor.

672.2 (1) An assessment order may require the person who makes the assessment to submit in writing an assessment report on the mental condition of the accused.

(2) An assessment report shall be filed with the court or Review Board that ordered it, within the period fixed by the court or Review Board, as the case may be.

(3) The court shall send to the Review Board without delay a copy of any report filed with it pursuant to subsection (2), to assist in determining the appropriate disposition to be made in respect of the accused.

(4) Subject to subsection 672.51(3), copies of any report filed with a court or Review Board under subsection (2) shall be provided without delay to the prosecutor, the accused and any counsel representing the accused. 1991, c. 43, s. 4; 2005, c. 22, s. 11.

CROSS-REFERENCES

The terms "accused", "assessment" and "Review Board" are defined in s. 672.1. "Prosecutor" is defined in s. 2. A limitation on the use of statements made by an accused in the course of preparation of the assessment report is set out in s. 672.21. For further cross-references respecting the making of assessment orders, see the references under s. 672.12 (court-ordered assessments) and s. 672.121 (assessment ordered by the Review Board).

SYNOPSIS

The court or Review Board may require a written assessment report within a time period fixed by the court. Where such a report is received, a copy shall be provided to the prosecutor, the accused, any counsel to the accused and shall also be forwarded to the Review Board to assist in the determination of the disposition relating to the accused.

It is important to note, however, that this provision is subject to the restrictions imposed in the disclosure of disposition information contained in s. 672.51. An assessment report may be withheld from the accused where its disclosure would endanger the safety of another person or would seriously impair the treatment or recovery of the accused.

Protected Statements

DEFINITION OF "PROTECTED STATEMENT" / Protected statements not admissible against accused / Exceptions.

672.21 (1) In this section, "protected statement" means a statement made by the accused during the course and for the purposes of an assessment or treatment directed by a disposition, to the person specified in the assessment order or the disposition, or to anyone acting under that person's direction.

(2) No protected statement or reference to a protected statement made by an accused is admissible in evidence, without the consent of the accused, in any proceeding before a court, tribunal, body or person with jurisdiction to compel the production of evidence.

(3) Notwithstanding subsection (2), evidence of a protected statement is admissible for the purpose of

(*a*) determining whether the accused is unfit to stand trial;

(*b*) making a disposition or placement decision respecting the accused;

(*c*) determining, under section 672.84, whether to refer to the court for review a finding that an accused is a high-risk accused or whether to revoke such a finding;

(*d*) determining whether the balance of the mind of the accused was disturbed at the time of commission of the alleged offence, where the accused is a female person charged with an offence arising out of the death of her newly-born child;

(*e*) determining whether the accused was, at the time of the commission of an alleged offence, suffering from automatism or a mental disorder so as to be exempt from criminal responsibility by virtue of subsection 16(1), if the accused puts his or her mental capacity for criminal intent into issue, or if the prosecutor raises the issue after verdict;

(*f*) challenging the credibility of an accused in any proceeding where the testimony of the accused is inconsistent in a material particular with a protected statement that the accused made previously; or

(*g*) establishing the perjury of an accused who is charged with perjury in respect of a statement made in any proceeding. 1991, c. 43, s. 4; 2005, c. 22, s. 12; 2014, c. 6, s. 5.

CROSS-REFERENCES

The terms "accused", "assessment" and "verdict of not criminally responsible on account of insanity" are defined in s. 672.1. The terms "newly-born child", "prosecutor", "unfit to stand trial" and "mental disorder" are defined in s. 2. Subsection (3)(*d*) refers to the offence of infanticide, thus see s. 233.

SYNOPSIS

This provision, in effect, establishes a narrow patient-doctor privilege in criminal law. The statutory privilege, however, applies only to "protected statements" which are defined as: (1) statements made by the accused in the course and for the purpose of an assessment or treatment directed by a disposition; and (2) statements must be made to a person specified in the assessment order or the disposition or to anyone acting under that persons's direction. Statements not made pursuant to compliance with a disposition or assessment order, therefore, do not fall within the scope of "protected statements" as defined by this privilege. It is important to note that this provision does not erode the solicitor-client privilege which attaches to assessments or examinations conducted independent of the court by a solicitor's agent.

In addition, the privilege is circumscribed by subsec. (3), which permits the admission of evidence of a protected statement for the following purposes: (a) to determine fitness; (b) at a determination of a disposition or placement decision; (c) to determine whether the balance of the mind of the accused was disturbed where the offence is infanticide; (d) at a trial to determine if the accused is suffering from automatism or a mental disorder where the issue is raised either by the accused or by the prosecutor subsequent to the rendering of the verdict; (e) for the limited purpose of an inconsistent statement in a material issue; or (f) to establish a charge of perjury.

ANNOTATIONS

Subsection (3)(*f*) must be read in light of the common law voluntariness rule that has been given constitutional expression in s. 7 of the *Canadian Charter of Rights and Freedoms*. Where a protected statement is inadmissible by reason of that rule and s. 7 of the Charter, it cannot be used for any purpose and thus cannot be used to challenge the credibility of the accused under subsec. (3)(*f*): *R. v. G. (B.)*, [1999] 2 S.C.R. 475, 135 C.C.C. (3d) 303, 24 C.R. (5th) 266.

Although the accused consented to an assessment order to determine fitness and criminal responsibility, the statements made during the course of the assessment are protected and cannot be used by the Crown to establish intent, planning or deliberation. The consent of the accused to the assessment did not constitute a consent to the gathering of evidence against him on a psychiatric remand. The accused's statements were admissible solely for the purpose of addressing the issue of fitness and criminal responsibility: *R. v. Genereux* (2000), 154 C.C.C. (3d) 362, 140 O.A.C. 165 (C.A.).

Where the Crown tenders the accused's statements through their expert for a non-hearsay purpose to show the basis of the expert's opinion, the statements are not admissible for the truth of their contents pursuant to the admissions exception to the hearsay rule: *R. v. Palma* (2000), 149 C.C.C. (3d) 338 (Ont. S.C.J.).

Statements made by an accused in the course of his psychiatric assessments or references to such statements are inadmissible at a sentencing hearing: *R. v. Bennight* (2010), 261 C.C.C. (3d) 386 (B.C.S.C.), affd (2012), 104 W.C.B. (2d) 613 (B.C.C.A.).

In *R. v. Paul* (2010), 262 C.C.C. (3d) 490 (Ont. C.A.), it was held that the sentencing judge did not contravene this provision by relying on a dangerous offender assessment pursuant to s. 752.21, which, in turn, referred to statements made by the accused as part of his fitness and criminally responsible assessment. The protected statement provisions in s. 672.21 apply to an accused and not to an offender.

Fitness to Stand Trial

PRESUMPTION OF FITNESS.

672.22 An accused is presumed fit to stand trial unless the court is satisfied on the balance of probabilities that the accused is unfit to stand trial. 1991, c. 43, s. 4.

CROSS-REFERENCES

References should be made to s. 2 of the *Criminal Code* which defines "unfit to stand trial" and s. 672.1 which defines "accused". For further cross-references in respect of fitness to stand trial, see the references under s. 672.23.

SYNOPSIS

This provision entrenches a general presumption of fitness unless the court is satisfied on the balance of probabilities that the accused is unfit to stand trial.

COURT MAY DIRECT ISSUE TO BE TRIED / Burden of proof.

672.23 (1) Where the court has reasonable grounds, at any stage of the proceedings before a verdict is rendered, to believe that the accused is unfit to stand trial, the court may direct, of its own motion or on application of the accused or the prosecutor, that the issue of fitness of the accused be tried.

(2) An accused or a prosecutor who makes an application under subsection (1) has the burden of proof that the accused is unfit to stand trial. 1991, c. 43, s. 4.

CROSS-REFERENCES

To assist in the determination of the fitness issue, the court may make an assessment order which can include preparation of an assessment report. Thus, see ss. 672.11 to 672.21. Note in particular that the limitation on use of statements made by the accused in the course of the assessment does not apply to proceedings to determine fitness. Section 672.24 provides for the appointment of counsel for the purposes of the fitness hearing. Section 672.25 allows the court to postpone the fitness hearing and if the accused is acquitted then the issue is never tried, s. 672.3. Section 672.26 governs the procedure where the accused is to be tried by jury. Otherwise, pursuant to s. 672.27, the issue is tried by the "court" defined in s. 672.1 and, in particular, may be tried at the preliminary inquiry stage. The terms "unfit to stand trial" and "prosecutor" are defined in s. 2. If the accused is found to be fit to stand trial, then the trial proceeds in accordance with s. 672.28, although, under s. 672.29 provision may be made to permit the accused to remain in custody in a hospital where there is reason to believe that the accused may otherwise become unfit. If the accused is found unfit, then the proceedings are conducted in accordance with ss. 672.31 to 672.33. Note, in particular, provision for review every two years of the sufficiency of the evidence to put the accused on trial. While the accused is unfit, his or her case is reviewed by the Review Board, defined in s. 672.1 in accordance with ss. 672.38 to 672.53. Note, however, that the court which found the accused unfit may hold a disposition hearing itself in accordance with s. 672.45 and may also vacate any interim release or detention order in accordance with s. 672.46. Under s. 672.851, the court may stay proceedings where the accused is unlikely to become fit, does not pose a signigicant threat to public safety and a stay is in the interests of the proper administration of justice.

SYNOPSIS

The court may order the trial of the issue of fitness at any stage in the proceedings provided it is before a verdict is rendered either on its own motion or on the application of the accused or prosecutor. The court must be satisfied that there are reasonable grounds to believe that the issue of fitness should be tried and the party raising the issue of fitness bears the burden of proof in establishing there are reasonable grounds to try the issue.

ANNOTATIONS

Section 2 gives a statutory definition of "unfit to stand trial" in the following terms:

"unfit to stand trial" means unable on account of mental disorder to conduct a defence at any stage of the proceedings before a verdict is rendered or to instruct counsel to do so, and, in particular, unable on account of mental disorder to

(a) understand the nature or object of the proceedings,

(b) understand the possible consequences of the proceedings, or

(c) communicate with counsel

Some of the following cases were decided under the predecessor legislation [former s. 615] which, however, did not contain a statutory definition of unfitness. Nevertheless, it is suggested that many of the following cases will be applicable to the interpretation of this section.

Where the accused became unfit after conviction but prior to sentence, the failure to provide for a fitness hearing after a verdict has been rendered violates s. 7 of the Charter. The appropriate remedy is to read in words permitting the court to conduct a fitness hearing before sentence is imposed: *Canada (Attorney General) v. Balliram* (2003), 173 C.C.C. (3d) 547 (Ont. S.C.J.).

Even after the entry of a guilty plea, the court has the discretion to direct a fitness inquiry on its own motion: *R. v. Proulx* (2011), 273 C.C.C. (3d) 367 (Sask. Prov. Ct.).

Procedure on fitness hearing – The trial judge has a discretion as to whether or not he will submit the issue of the accused's capacity to instruct counsel to the jury and furthermore, where there was no evidence to support such a request his refusal was justified: *R. v. Wolfson*, [1965] 3 C.C.C. 304, 46 C.R. 8 (Alta. S.C. App. Div.). See also *R. v. Kolbe* (1974), 27 C.R.N.S. 1, [1974] 4 W.W.R. 579 (Alta. S.C. App. Div.), where approval was given to the trial judge's discretionary refusal when the issue was first raised after the accused had given evidence.

The predecessor to this section was held to envisage a two-stage process. The first stage is for the judge alone to decide whether there is sufficient reason to doubt that the accused is, on account of insanity, capable of conducting his defence. The second stage, which is only pursued if the first stage is answered affirmatively, is for the jury to determine whether the accused is fit to stand trial. In the first stage, it is not for the judge to determine any conflict of evidence. There is, however, a discretionary element and where the trial judge, who had the advantage of hearing the expert witnesses and observing the accused, determined that there was nothing in the evidence to support a finding that the accused was incapable of conducting his defence, then the appellate court will not interfere: *R. v. McLeod, Pinnock and Farquharson* (1983), 6 C.C.C. (3d) 29, 66 N.R. 309 (Ont. C.A.), affd as to *Farquharson*, [1986] 1 S.C.R. 703*n*, 27 C.C.C. (3d) 383*n*.

The term "may", as used in former s. 615(1) was held to intend to confer authority, rather than to vest in the trial judge a discretion. Where a doubt as to fitness arises, the accused has a statutory right to have the issue directed. A statement by counsel as to the fitness of the accused is entitled to very serious consideration. There is a discretion only in the limited sense that a court is not bound to try the issue where there is no real basis for the request and under subsec. (5)(*a*), the judge is expressly permitted to postpone the trial of the issue up to the opening of the case for the defence where it arises in the course of the Crown's case: *R. v. Steele* (1991), 63 C.C.C. (3d) 149, 4 C.R. (4th) 53 (Que. C.A.).

In the first stage of the inquiry, where the judge must determine whether or not there is sufficient reason to doubt that the accused is, on account of insanity, capable of conducting his defence and therefore, whether he should direct an inquiry into the accused's fitness to stand trial, the judge may act on the material placed before him by Crown and defence or direct that a further assessment of the accused be made. It may in some cases be necessary to hear psychiatrists and other witnesses: *R. v. McIlvride* (1986), 29 C.C.C. (3d) 348 (B.C.C.A.).

The trial of the issue as to whether the accused is fit to stand trial is a separate issue prior to trial, and accordingly, without the consent of the accused, medical evidence given in that prior proceeding cannot be automatically considered at trial without the doctor being recalled: *R. v. Curran* (1974), 21 C.C.C. (2d) 23, 9 N.B.R. (2d) 683 (C.A.).

Test for fitness to stand trial – The test of whether an accused is fit to stand trial is not whether or not he is able to act in his own best interests. The fact that the accused is emotionally unwilling to accept a defence of insanity and therefore refused to allow his counsel to advance this defence did not render him unfit. *Reference Re: R. v. Gorecki (No. 1)* (1976), 32 C.C.C. (2d) 129, 14 O.R. (2d) 212 (C.A.).

The test to be applied is one of limited cognitive ability, whether the accused understands the nature and object of the proceedings, understands the possible consequences, and can recount to counsel the necessary facts relating to the offence in such a way that counsel can then properly present a defence. It is not necessary that the accused be able to meet some higher test of analytic capacity or capacity to make rational decisions beneficial to himself: *R. v. Taylor* (1992), 77 C.C.C. (3d) 551, 17 C.R. (4th) 371 (Ont. C.A.).

An accused is incapable of conducting his defence if he cannot distinguish between available pleas; does not understand the nature or purpose of the proceedings, including the respective roles of the judge, jury and counsel; is unable to communicate with counsel rationally or make critical decisions on counsel's advice; or is unable to take the stand to testify if necessary: *R. v. Steele, supra.*

Testimonial competence is not a condition precedent to fitness to stand trial. The requirement that the accused be able to recount the necessary facts relating to the offence in such a way that counsel can properly present a defence must be interpreted in a purposive and functional manner. It refers more broadly to the accused person's ability to recount the facts generally relating to the offence with which he is charged. It is not intended to narrow the inquiry solely to the ability to relate the immediate facts pertaining to the particular incident giving rise to the crime: *R. v. Morrissey* (2007), 227 C.C.C. (3d) 1, 54 C.R. (6th) 313 (Ont. C.A.), leave to appeal to S.C.C. refused 231 C.C.C. (3d) vi.

COUNSEL / Counsel fees and disbursements / Taxation of fees and disbursements.

672.24 (1) Where the court has reasonable grounds to believe that an accused is unfit to stand trial and the accused is not represented by counsel, the court shall order that the accused be represented by counsel.

(2) Where counsel is assigned pursuant to subsection (1) and legal aid is not granted to the accused pursuant to a provincial legal aid program, the fees and disbursements of counsel shall be paid by the Attorney General to the extent that the accused is unable to pay them.

(3) Where counsel and the Attorney General cannot agree on the fees or disbursements of counsel, the Attorney General or the counsel may apply to the registrar of the court and the registrar may tax the disputed fees and disbursements. 1991, c. 43, s. 4; 1997, c. 18, s. 82.

CROSS-REFERENCES

For further cross-references respecting fitness to stand trial, see references under s. 672.23.

SYNOPSIS

Unlike the previous provision, which afforded the court some discretion in the appointment of counsel, under these provisions, where the issue of fitness arises with respect to an unrepresented accused, the court *must* appoint counsel for the accused. Provisions for payment of counsel are set out in subsecs. (2) and (3).

ANNOTATIONS

The entitlement to counsel applies prior to the fitness hearing at the time that an assessment is being considered by the court: *R. v. Waranuk* (2010), 89 W.C.B. (2d) 235, [2010] Y.J. No. 81 (C.A.).

POSTPONING TRIAL OF ISSUE / Idem.

672.25 (1) The court shall postpone directing the trial of the issue of fitness of an accused in proceedings for an offence for which the accused may be prosecuted by indictment or that is punishable on summary conviction, until the prosecutor has elected to proceed by way of indictment or summary conviction.

(2) The court may postpone directing the trial of the issue of fitness of an accused

- **(*a*) where the issue arises before the close of the case for the prosecution at a preliminary inquiry, until a time that is not later than the time the accused is called on to answer to the charge; or**
- **(*b*) where the issue arises before the close of the case for the prosecution at trial, until a time not later than the opening of the case for the defence or, on motion of the accused, any later time that the court may direct. 1991, c. 43, s. 4.**

ANNOTATIONS

Although subsec. (2) implies that the trial of the issue can be held at any time prior to the opening of the defence, in exercising this discretion the judge must consider whether there is any dispute as to the Crown's ability to demonstrate that the accused committed the offence. If there is a dispute, the trial judge should not decide the question of fitness without being satisfied that the Crown is in a position to establish that the accused committed the acts alleged. The trial judge may thus proceed with the trial proper or at least require the Crown to demonstrate at the outset of the fitness hearing that it is in a position to establish that the accused committed the acts alleged: *R. v. Taylor* (1992), 77 C.C.C. (3d) 551, 17 C.R. (4th) 371 (Ont. C.A.).

Pursuant to subsec. (2)(*a*), the preliminary inquiry judge has the jurisdiction, prior to the commencement of the preliminary inquiry, to postpone the fitness determination until the close of the Crown's case: *R. v. L. (B.V.)* (2004), 187 C.C.C. (3d) 283 (Ont. C.J.).

TRIAL OF ISSUE BY JUDGE AND JURY.

672.26 Where an accused is tried or is to be tried before a court composed of a judge and jury,

- **(*a*) if the judge directs that the issue of fitness of the accused be tried before the accused is given in charge to a jury for trial on the indictment, a jury composed of the number of jurors required in respect of the indictment in the province where the trial is to be held shall be sworn to try that issue and, with the consent of the accused, the issues to be tried on the indictment; and**
- **(*b*) if the judge directs that the issue of fitness of the accused be tried after the accused has been given in charge to a jury for trial on the indictment, the jury shall be sworn to try that issue in addition to the issues in respect of which it is already sworn. 1991, c. 43, s. 4.**

TRIAL OF ISSUE BY COURT.

672.27 The court shall try the issue of fitness of an accused and render a verdict where the issue arises

- **(*a*) in respect of an accused who is tried or is to be tried before a court other than a court composed of a judge and jury; or**
- **(*b*) before a court at a preliminary inquiry or at any other stage of the proceedings. 1991, c. 43, s. 4.**

PROCEEDING CONTINUES WHERE ACCUSED IS FIT.

672.28 Where the verdict on trial of the issue is that an accused is fit to stand trial, the arraignment, preliminary inquiry, trial or other stage of the proceeding shall continue as if the issue of fitness of the accused had never arisen. 1991, c. 43, s. 4.

WHERE CONTINUED DETENTION IN CUSTODY.

672.29 Where an accused is detained in custody on delivery of a verdict that the accused is fit to stand trial, the court may order the accused to be detained in a hospital until the completion of the trial, if the court has reasonable grounds to believe that the accused would become unfit to stand trial if released. 1991, c. 43, s. 4.

ACQUITTAL.

672.3 Where the court has postponed directing the trial of the issue of fitness of an accused pursuant to subsection 672.25(2) and the accused is discharged or acquitted before the issue is tried, it shall not be tried. 1991, c. 43, s. 4.

CROSS-REFERENCES

Reference should be made to s. 672.25(2) which affords the judge the discretion to postpone the trial of the issue of fitness if the issue arises before the close of the prosecution's case at a preliminary inquiry or trial until the accused is called on to answer the charge, until the opening of the accused's case or on motion of the accused until any later time that the court may direct. For further cross-references respecting fitness to stand trial, see references under s. 672.23.

SYNOPSIS

The issue of fitness is not to be tried where it has been postponed pursuant to s. 672.25(2) and the accused is discharged at the preliminary hearing or acquitted before the opening of the defence's case or until any later time as the court may direct.

VERDICT OF UNFIT TO STAND TRIAL.

672.31 Where the verdict on trial of the issue is that an accused is unfit to stand trial, any plea that has been made shall be set aside and any jury shall be discharged. 1991, c. 43, s. 4.

CROSS-REFERENCES

Where the accused is found unfit, then the procedure to be followed is set out in s. 672.45 *et seq*. For further cross-references respecting fitness to stand trial, see references under s. 672.23.

SYNOPSIS

This section requires that where the verdict in a trial turns on the issue of fitness to stand trial, any plea by the accused must be struck and any jury which has been empanelled must be discharged.

SUBSEQUENT PROCEEDINGS / Burden of proof.

672.32 (1) A verdict of unfit to stand trial shall not prevent the accused from being tried subsequently where the accused becomes fit to stand trial.

(2) The burden of proof that the accused has subsequently become fit to stand trial is on the party who asserts it, and is discharged by proof on the balance of probabilities. 1991, c. 43, s. 4.

CROSS-REFERENCES

Although the accused is found fit, the court may order that he or she be detained in a hospital if there is reason to believe the accused may become unfit otherwise, s. 672.29.

For further cross-references respecting fitness to stand trial, see references under s. 672.23.

SYNOPSIS

An accused who subsequently becomes fit to stand trial must be tried provided that the party asserting fitness establishes fitness on the balance of probabilities.

PRIMA FACIE CASE TO BE MADE EVERY TWO YEARS / Extension of time for holding inquiry / Court may order inquiry to be held / Burden of proof / Admissible evidence at an inquiry / Conduct of inquiry / Where _prima facie_ case not made.

672.33 (1) The court that has jurisdiction in respect of the offence charged against an accused who is found unfit to stand trial shall hold an inquiry, not later than two years after the verdict is rendered and every two years thereafter until the accused is acquitted pursuant to subsection (6) or tried, to decide whether sufficient evidence can be adduced at that time to put the accused on trial.

(1.1) Despite subsection (1), the court may extend the period for holding an inquiry where it is satisfied on the basis of an application by the prosecutor or the accused that the extension is necessary for the proper administration of justice.

(2) On application of the accused, the court may order an inquiry under this section to be held at any time if it is satisfied, on the basis of the application and any written material submitted by the accused, that there is reason to doubt that there is a _prima facie_ case against the accused.

(3) At an inquiry under this section, the burden of proof that sufficient evidence can be adduced to put the accused on trial is on the prosecutor.

(4) In an inquiry under this section, the court shall admit as evidence

(_a_) any affidavit containing evidence that would be admissible if given by the person making the affidavit as a witness in court; or

(_b_) any certified copy of the oral testimony given at a previous inquiry or hearing held before a court in respect of the offence with which the accused is charged.

(5) The court may determine the manner in which an inquiry under this section is conducted and may follow the practices and procedures in respect of a preliminary inquiry under Part XVIII where it concludes that the interests of justice so require.

(6) Where, on the completion of an inquiry under this section, the court is satisfied that sufficient evidence cannot be adduced to put the accused on trial, the court shall acquit the accused. 1991, c. 43, s. 4; 2005, c. 22, s. 13.

CROSS-REFERENCES

Reference should be made to s. 2 of the *Criminal Code* which defines "unfit to stand trial" and s. 672.1 which defines "accused" and "Review Board". While the accused is unfit, his or her case is reviewed by the Review Board in accordance with ss. 672.38 to 672.53.

For further cross-references in respect of fitness to stand trial, see the references under s. 672.23.

SYNOPSIS

This provision imposes a continuing obligation on the Crown, with respect to an unfit accused, to demonstrate its case every two years such that no individual declared unfit to stand trial may continue to be held where the Crown is unable to prove the charge against the accused if required to do so. However, pursuant to subsec. (1.1), on application by the prosecutor or the accused, the court may extend the period for holding the inquiry where the extension is necessary for the proper administration of justice.

In addition, the accused may apply for a review of the case at any time pursuant to s. 672.33(2) provided it is established that there is reason to doubt that there is a *prima facie* case against the accused. In either case, the Crown bears the burden of establishing that a *prima facie* case still exists against the accused. If on completion of an inquiry under this section, the court is satisfied that a *prima facie* does not exist, the court shall acquit the accused.

The procedure prescribed by the provisions with respect to such an inquiry allows the court to consider evidence in the form of oral testimony at a previous hearing in respect of the same offence or affidavit evidence containing admissible evidence of a person who would be a witness in court. In addition, s. 672.33(5) also allows the procedure in respect of a preliminary inquiry under Part XVIII to be adopted where the court concludes that the interests of justice so require.

ANNOTATIONS

Constitutional Considerations – This provision violates s. 7 of the Charter and accordingly, was declared of no force or effect as it applied to accused persons who are found unfit to stand trial. The declaration of invalidity was suspended for 12 months to allow Parliament to amend the legislation: *R. v. Demers*, [2004] 2 S.C.R. 489, 185 C.C.C. (3d) 257, 20 C.R. (6th) 241.

Subsection (5) – The accused has the right to cross-examine in proceedings under this section: *R. v. Pawlivsky* (1998), 130 C.C.C. (3d) 465, [1999] 2 W.W.R. 543 (Alta. Q.B.).

Verdict of Not Criminally Responsible on Account of Mental Disorder

VERDICT OF NOT CRIMINALLY RESPONSIBLE ON ACCOUNT OF MENTAL DISORDER.

672.34 Where the jury, or the judge or provincial court judge where there is no jury, finds that an accused committed the act or made the omission that formed the basis of the offence charged, but was at the time suffering from mental disorder so as to be exempt from criminal responsibility by virtue of subsection 16(1), the jury or the judge shall render a verdict that the accused committed the act or made the omission but is not criminally responsible on account of mental disorder. 1991, c. 43, s. 4.

CROSS-REFERENCES

The term "mental disorder" is defined in s. 2 and "verdict of not criminally responsible on account of mental disorder" is defined in s. 672.1. Reference should be made to s. 16 which contains the defence of not criminally responsible on account of mental disorder.

Reference should also be made to s. 672.54(*a*) authorizing the court or Review Board to either discharge the accused absolutely subsequent to a finding of not criminally responsible on account of mental disorder or direct the accused to be detained where the accused is a significant threat to the safety of the public.

SYNOPSIS

This provision replaces the previous terminology of "not guilty by reason of insanity" with "not criminally responsible on account of mental disorder". The verdict is defined to mean that the person committed the act or omission but is not criminally responsible on account of mental disorder.

ANNOTATIONS

The procedural rights accorded to an accused at trial apply to a finding that the accused is not criminally responsible on account of mental disorder. Thus, the accused had the right to cross-examine the author of reports relied upon by the Crown in seeking to have the accused found not criminally responsible: *R. v. Langlois* (2005), 195 C.C.C. (3d) 152 (B.C.C.A.).

The following cases were decided under the predecessor legislation, s. 614 but may be of assistance in applying these new provisions.

It was held that former s. 614(1) was mandatory and a new trial was ordered on a Crown appeal where the trial judge failed to direct the jury that if they found the accused not guilty by reason of insanity they must so state in their verdict: *R. v. Potvin* (1971), 16 C.R.N.S. 233 (Que. C.A.).

In *R. v. Conkie* (1978), 39 C.C.C. (2d) 408, 3 C.R. (3d) 7 (Alta. S.C. App. Div.), the court considered whether the trial judge should inform the jury of the consequences of an insanity verdict. Leiberman J.A. was of the view that he should in certain circumstances where a possible misapprehension that the accused would go free if found not guilty by reason of insanity could affect the jury's verdict. Such a case would be where the evidence discloses the accused is a dangerous individual and defence counsel has not referred to this subsection in his jury address. Moir J.A. considered that the judge was not required to so inform the jury, the practice in Alberta being that defence counsel could enforce the jury in his jury address. Haddad J.A., while leaning to the view that the judge should inform the jury of the provisions of this subsection, did not feel that in this case it was necessary to decide the issue.

EFFECT OF VERDICT OF NOT CRIMINALLY RESPONSIBLE ON ACCOUNT OF MENTAL DISORDER.

672.35 Where a verdict of not criminally responsible on account of mental disorder is rendered, the accused shall not be found guilty or convicted of the offence, but

- **(*a*) the accused may plead *autrefois acquit* in respect of any subsequent charge relating to that offence;**
- **(*b*) any court may take the verdict into account in considering an application for judicial interim release or in considering what dispositions to make or sentence to impose for any other offence; and**
- **(*c*) the Parole Board of Canada or any provincial parole board may take the verdict into account in considering an application by the accused for parole or for a record suspension under the *Criminal Records Act* in respect of any other offence. 1991, c. 43, s. 4; 2012, c. 1, s. 145; 2012, c. 1, s. 160(*c*)(ii).**

CROSS-REFERENCES

The term "mental disorder" is defined in s. 2. The term "verdict of not criminally responsible on account of mental disorder" is defined in s. 672.1. Reference should also be made to s. 672.36 excluding the verdict of not criminally responsible on account of mental disorder from the meaning of a previous conviction for the purpose of any offence under any Act of Parliament for which an increased penalty is provided by reason of a previous conviction.

SYNOPSIS

Although the verdict of not criminally responsible on account of mental disorder is not a previous conviction for the purpose of any offence for which a greater punishment is provided by reason of previous convictions (see s. 672.36), the verdict may be used as a basis for the accused to plead *autrefois acquit* in respect of a subsequent charge relating to the offence, for the purpose of judicial interim release, disposition or sentence with respect to any other offence and by the National Parole Board or any provincial parole board for the purpose of considering an application for parole or pardon with respect to any other offence.

VERDICT NOT A PREVIOUS CONVICTION.

672.36 A verdict of not criminally responsible on account of mental disorder is not a previous conviction for the purposes of any offence under any Act of Parliament for which a greater punishment is provided by reason of previous convictions. 1991, c. 43, s. 4.

CROSS-REFERENCES

The term "mental disorder" is defined in s. 2. The term "verdict of not criminally responsible on account of mental disorder" is defined in s. 672.1.

Reference should be made to s. 672.35 which states that a verdict of not criminally responsible on account of mental disorder may be relied on in the following circumstances: (1) by the accused to plead *autrefois acquit* [s. 672.35(*a*)]; (2) by the court in an application for judicial interim release [s. 672.35(*b*)]; (3) by the court in considering the sentence or disposition in another offence [s. 672.35(*b*)]; and (4) by the National Parole Board or any provincial parole board in considering an application for a parole or pardon in respect of any other offence [s. 672.35(*c*)].

SYNOPSIS

A finding of not criminally responsible on account of mental disorder cannot be used as a previous conviction in a subsequent proceeding under any federal act for which a greater punishment is provided by reason of previous convictions such as the offence of impaired driving.

DEFINITION OF "APPLICATION FOR FEDERAL EMPLOYMENT" / Application for federal employment / Punishment.

672.37 (1) In this section, "application for federal employment" means an application form relating to

- **(*a*) employment in any department, as defined in section 2 of the *Financial Administration Act*;**
- **(*b*) employment by any Crown corporation as defined in subsection 83(1) of the *Financial Administration Act*;**
- **(*c*) enrollment in the Canadian Forces; or**
- **(*d*) employment in connection with the operation of any work, undertaking or business that is within the legislative authority of Parliament.**

(2) No application for federal employment shall contain any question that requires the applicant to disclose any charge or finding that the applicant committed an offence that resulted in a finding or a verdict of not criminally responsible on account of mental disorder if the applicant was discharged absolutely or is no longer subject to any disposition in respect of that offence.

(3) Any person who uses or authorizes the use of an application for federal employment that contravenes subsection (2) is guilty of an offence punishable on summary conviction. 1991, c. 43, s. 4.

CROSS-REFERENCES

The term "mental disorder" is defined in s. 2. The term "verdict of not criminally responsible on account of mental disorder" is defined in s. 672.1. Reference should be made to s. 2 of the *Financial Administration Act* defining "department" and s. 83(1) of the Act defining "Crown corporation".

SYNOPSIS

This provision creates the summary conviction offence of use or authorizing the use of an application for federal employment that contains a question requiring the applicant to disclose a charge or finding regarding the commission of an offence that resulted in a finding of not criminally responsible on account of mental disorder where the applicant was discharged or is not subject to any disposition.

An "application for federal employment" is defined as an application relating to employment in the following: any department as defined in s. 2 of the *Financial Administration Act*; any Crown corporation as defined in s. 83(1) of the *Financial*

Administration Act; enrollment in the Canadian Forces or in the operation of any work, undertaking or business that is within the legislative authority of Parliament.

Review Boards

REVIEW BOARDS TO BE ESTABLISHED / Treated as provincial Board / Personal liability.

672.38 (1) A Review Board shall be established or designated for each province to make or review dispositions concerning any accused in respect of whom a verdict of not criminally responsible by reason of mental disorder or unfit to stand trial is rendered, and shall consist of not fewer than five members appointed by the lieutenant governor in council of the province.

(2) A Review Board shall be treated as having been established under the laws of the province.

(3) No member of a Review Board is personally liable for any act done in good faith in the exercise of the member's powers or the performance of the member's duties and functions or for any default or neglect in good faith in the exercise of those powers or the performance of those duties and functions. 1991, c. 43, s. 4; 1997, c. 18, s. 83.

CROSS-REFERENCES

The terms "unfit to stand trial" and "mental disorder" are defined in s. 2. The terms "accused", "not criminally responsible on account of mental disorder", "chairperson", "medical practitioner" and "Review Board" are defined in s. 672.1.

The constitution of the Review Board is outlined in ss. 672.39 to 672.44. In particular, the board must have at least one member who is entitled to practise psychiatry in that province and where there is only one member qualified in psychiatry, the board must have another member entitled to practice medicine or psychology by virtue of s. 672.39. The chairperson of the board must be a judge or a person who is so qualified or has retired as a judge of the Federal Court or of a superior, district or county court [s. 672.4(1)]. Where the board is established prior to the coming into force of s. 672.4(1), the existing chairperson who is not a judge may continue to act until the end of his term if at least one other member of the board is a judge or person referred to in subsection (1) or a member of the bar of the province. Pursuant to s. 672.41, a quorum is constituted by a chairperson, a psychiatrist and any other member unless the board pre-existed the new provisions in which case the quorum may be composed of a chairperson, a psychiatrist and a member who is referred to in that subsection or a member of the bar. A decision of the majority is a decision of the Review Board [s. 672.42]. Pursuant to s. 672.43, the chairperson has all the powers of a commissioner conferred by ss. 4 and 5 of the *Inquiries Act* in disposition or review hearings held by the board. In addition, the Review Board is entitled to makes rules relating to practice and procedure before the board, subject to the approval of the lieutenant governor in council of the province [s. 672.44].

As to disposition hearings before the Review Board, see ss. 672.46 to 672.49. As to the procedure on disposition hearings before the Review Board, see s. 672.5. As to the release of disposition information by the Review Board, see ss. 672.51 to 672.52. As to the power of the Review Board to make dispositions in relation to an accused, see ss. 672.54 to 672.57 and 672.63. As to appeals from a decision of the Review Board, see ss. 672.72 to 672.8 and as to the review of dispositions of a court or Review Board, see ss. 672.81 to 672.85.

SYNOPSIS

This provision requires the establishment of Review Boards by the province. In addition, subsec. (2) provides that the Review Board is treated as having been established under provincial law thus excluding the application of the *Federal Courts Act* to the actions of the Review Board.

The Review Board must consist of at least five members who are appointed by the lieutenant governor in council of the province.

Protection of Review Board members is provided by subsec. (3) for acts done in good faith.

MEMBERS OF REVIEW BOARD.

672.39 A Review Board must have at least one member who is entitled under the laws of a province to practise psychiatry and, where only one member is so entitled at least one other member must have training and experience in the field of mental health, and be entitled under the laws of a province to practise medicine or psychology. 1991, c. 43, s. 4.

CROSS-REFERENCES

The terms "chairperson", "medical practitioner" and "Review Board" are defined in s. 672.1. Reference should also be made to s. 672.4 which requires the chairperson of the Review Board to be a judge, or a person who is qualified or retired from judicial office. If the Review Board pre-exists the new provisions, however, the chairperson may continue to act until the end of his term provided that another member of the board is a judge, a person qualified for or retired from judicial office or a member of the bar.

For further cross-references respecting the Review Board, see references under s. 672.38.

SYNOPSIS

Section 672.39 prescribes the composition of the Review Board which must have at least one member of the board who is a psychiatrist. Where there is only one member trained in psychiatry, at least one other member of the Review Board must be trained in the practise of medicine or psychology.

CHAIRPERSON OF A REVIEW BOARD / Transitional.

672.4 (1) Subject to subsection (2), the chairperson of a Review Board shall be a judge of the Federal Court or of a superior, district or county court of a province, or a person who is qualified for appointment to, or has retired from, such a judicial office.

(2) Where the chairperson of a Review Board that was established before the coming into force of subsection (1) is not a judge or other person referred to therein, the chairperson may continue to act until the expiration of his or her term of office if at least one other member of the Review Board is a judge or other person referred to in subsection (1) or is a member of the bar of the province. 1991, c. 43, s. 4.

CROSS-REFERENCES

The terms "chairperson" and "Review Board" are defined in s. 672.1. For further cross-references respecting Review Boards, see references under s. 672.38.

SYNOPSIS

The chairperson of a Review Board must be a judge, retired judge, or qualified to be a judge of the Federal Court or of a superior, district or county court of a province. Where, however, the Review Board pre-exists the new provisions, a chairperson who is not a judge may continue to act until the end of his term provided that at least one member of the Review Board is a judge or member of the bar of that province.

QUORUM OF REVIEW BOARD / Transitional.

672.41 (1) Subject to subsection (2), the quorum of a Review Board is constituted by the chairperson, a member who is entitled under the laws of a province to practise psychiatry, and any other member.

(2) Where the chairperson of a Review Board that was established before the coming into force of this section is not a judge or other person referred to in subsection 672.4(1), the quorum of the Review Board is constituted by the chairperson, a member who is entitled under the laws of a province to practise psychiatry, and a member who is a person referred to in that subsection or a member of the bar of the province. 1991, c. 43, s. 4.

CROSS-REFERENCES

The term "Review Board" and "chairperson" are defined in s. 672.1. For further cross-references respecting Review Boards, see references under s. 672.38.

SYNOPSIS

A Review Board must have a quorum of three persons composed of the chairperson, a psychiatrist and any other member.

Where the Review Board pre-exists the new provisions, however, the quorum must be constituted of the chairperson, a psychiatrist and a judge or member of the bar of the province.

MAJORITY VOTE.

672.42 A decision of a majority of the members present and voting is a decision of a Review Board. 1991, c. 43, s. 4.

CROSS-REFERENCES

"Review Board" is defined in s. 672.1. For further cross-references respecting Review Boards, see references under s. 672.38.

SYNOPSIS

A decision of the majority governs the Review Board.

POWERS OF REVIEW BOARDS.

672.43 At a hearing held by a Review Board to make a disposition or review a disposition in respect of an accused, the chairperson has all the powers that are conferred by sections 4 and 5 of the *Inquiries Act* on persons appointed as commissioners under Part I of that Act. 1991, c. 43, s. 4.

CROSS-REFERENCES

The terms "accused", "Review Board", "chairperson" and "disposition" are defined in s. 672.1. In addition, reference should be made to ss. 4 and 5 of the *Inquiries Act* which outline the powers of a person appointed as a commissioner. For further cross-references respecting "Review Boards", see references under s. 672.38.

SYNOPSIS

A chairperson of the Review Board has all the powers of a commissioner conferred by ss. 4 and 5 of the *Inquiries Act*.

ANNOTATIONS

While the Review Board does have the implied power to compel the accused to attend a fitness hearing, it does not have the jurisdiction to compel the accused to testify: *Boucher v. New Brunswick (Review Board)* (1999), 141 C.C.C. (3d) 221 (N.B.C.A.).

RULES OF REVIEW BOARD / Application and publication of rules / Regulations.

672.44 (1) A Review Board may, subject to the approval of the lieutenant governor in council of the province, make rules providing for the practice and procedure before the Review Board.

(2) The rules made by a Review Board under subsection (1) apply to any proceeding within its jurisdiction, and shall be published in the *Canada Gazette*.

(3) Notwithstanding anything in this section, the Governor in Council may make regulations to provide for the practice and procedure before Review Boards, in particular to make the rules of Review Boards uniform, and all regulations made under this subsection prevail over any rules made under subsection (1). 1991, c. 43, s. 4.

CROSS-REFERENCES

"Review Board" is defined in s. 672.1. The procedures to be followed by a Review Board with respect to a disposition hearing are outlined in s. 672.5. With respect to procedures of the Review Board to be followed in the review of dispositions, see s. 672.83. For further cross-references respecting Review Boards, see references under s. 672.38.

SYNOPSIS

A Review Board has the authority to make rules as to the practice of the Review Board subject to the approval of the lieutenant governor. The Governor in Council, however, may also make rules for practice and procedure in order to make Review Board practices uniform. The Federal rules take precedence over any rules established by the provincial Review Board.

Disposition Hearings

HEARING TO BE HELD BY A COURT / Transmittal of transcript to Review Board / Disposition to be made.

672.45 (1) Where a verdict of not criminally responsible on account of mental disorder or unfit to stand trial is rendered in respect of an accused, the court may of its own motion, and shall on application by the accused or the prosecutor, hold a disposition hearing.

(1.1) If the court does not hold a hearing under subsection (1), it shall send without delay, following the verdict, in original or copied form, any transcript of the court proceedings in respect of the accused, any other document or information related to the proceedings, and all exhibits filed with it, to the Review Board that has jurisdiction in respect of the matter, if the transcript, document, information or exhibits are in its possession.

(2) At a disposition hearing, the court shall make a disposition in respect of the accused, if it is satisfied that it can readily do so and that a disposition should be made without delay. 1991, c. 43, s. 4; 2005, c. 22, s. 14.

CROSS-REFERENCES

The terms "mental disorder", "prosecutor" and "unfit to stand trial" are defined in s. 2. The terms "accused", "court", "disposition" and "verdict of not criminally responsible on account of mental disorder" are defined in s. 672.1.

The court may choose not to exercise its discretion to hold a disposition hearing, in which case, a disposition hearing must be held by the Review Board within 45 days subsequent to the verdict unless there are exceptional circumstances warranting a court to extend the time limit. See s. 672.47(1) and (2). In addition, pursuant to s. 672.47(3), even if the court has rendered a disposition subsequent to a hearing, the Review Board must hold a review hearing not less than 90 days subsequent to the disposition. Where the court does not make a disposition, the accused's release or detention order continues in force until the Review Board renders a disposition [s. 672.46(1)]. It is important to note that, notwithstanding this subsection, a court may vary or vacate any order or detain the accused until the disposition hearing if the court considers it appropriate to do so. The procedures to be followed in a review hearing are set out in s. 672.5. See also s. 672.52 requiring a record of the proceedings of the hearing to be kept. Pursuant to s. 672.53, any procedural irregularity in a disposition hearing does not render the hearing a nullity unless the accused is caused substantial prejudice as a result of the irregularity. Pursuant to s. 672.48, where the Review Board either holds a disposition hearing or a review hearing and finds the accused fit to stand trial subsequent to a finding of unfitness, the board must order that the accused be sent to trial. The Review Board has the power to detain the accused pursuant to s. 672.49 subsequent to a finding of fitness if there are grounds to believe that, if the accused were released, he would subsequently become unfit. Reference should also be had to s. 672.51 which provides a definition for "disposition information" and under what circumstances this information may be released to the accused, a party or a non-party.

As to the power of the Review Board to make dispositions in relation to an accused, see ss. 672.54 to 672.57 and 672.63. As to appeals from a decision of the Review Board, see ss. 672.72 to 672.8 and as to the review of dispositions of a court or Review Board, see ss. 672.81 to 672.85. Pursuant to s. 672.541, in determining the disposition of an accused found not criminally responsible, the court shall take into consideration any victim impact statement filed in accordance with s. 672.5(14).

SYNOPSIS

Subsequent to a finding of unfitness or not criminally responsible on account of mental disorder, the court has the discretion on its own motion to hold a disposition hearing. Where the application to hold a disposition hearing is brought by the accused or the prosecutor, however, the provision requires that the court hold a disposition hearing. If the court does not hold a disposition hearing then, pursuant to subsec. (1.1), the court is to transmit to the Review Board a transcript of the court proceedings and any other document or information and all exhibits in its possession.

Section 672.45(2) establishes a test for the jurisdiction of the court in disposition hearings. The court is required to make a disposition only if it is satisfied that it can readily do so and that the disposition should be made without delay.

ANNOTATIONS

In *R. v. Swain*, [1991] 1 S.C.R. 933, 63 C.C.C. (3d) 481, 5 C.R. (4th) 253, the court held that the predecessor legislation, which also provided for the confinement of persons found to be not guilty by reason of insanity, was a valid exercise of Parliament's criminal law power under s. 91(27) of the *Constitution Act, 1867*. There is no reason to believe that this legislation would not also be held to be valid criminal law. [The predecessor legislation was, however, held to violate ss. 7 and 9 of the Charter.]

STATUS QUO PENDING REVIEW BOARD HEARING / Variation of order.

672.46 (1) Where the court does not make a disposition in respect of the accused at a disposition hearing, any order for the interim release or detention of the accused or any appearance notice, promise to appear, summons, undertaking or recognizance in respect of the accused that is in force at the time the verdict of not criminally responsible on account of mental disorder or unfit to stand trial is rendered continues in force, subject to its terms, until the Review Board makes a disposition.

(2) Notwithstanding subsection (1), a court may, on cause being shown, vacate any order, appearance notice, promise to appear, summons, undertaking or recognizance referred to in that subsection and make any other order for the interim release or detention of the accused that the court considers to be appropriate in the circumstances,

including an order directing that the accused be detained in custody in a hospital pending a disposition by the Review Board in respect of the accused. 1991, c. 43, s. 4.

CROSS-REFERENCES

The terms "accused", "court" and "disposition" are defined in s. 672.1. Reference should also be made to Part XVI of the *Criminal Code* as to compelling the appearance of the accused by way of order for interim release, detention, appearance notice, promise to appear, summons or undertaking or recognizance. For further cross-references respecting disposition hearing, see references under s. 672.45.

SYNOPSIS

Where the court does not make a disposition, the accused's release or detention order continues in force until the review board renders a disposition. [s. 672.46(1)].

Notwithstanding subsection (1), however, a court may vary or vacate any order or detain the accused until the disposition hearing if the court considers it appropriate to do so.

REVIEW BOARD TO MAKE DISPOSITION WHERE COURT DOES NOT / Extension of time for hearing / Disposition made by court / Exception — high-risk accused / Extension of time for hearing.

672.47 (1) Where a verdict of not criminally responsible on account of mental disorder or unfit to stand trial is rendered and the court makes no disposition in respect of an accused, the Review Board shall, as soon as is practicable but not later than forty-five days after the verdict was rendered, hold a hearing and make a disposition.

(2) Where the court is satisfied that there are exceptional circumstances that warrant it, the court may extend the time for holding a hearing under subsection (1) to a maximum of ninety days after the verdict was rendered.

(3) Where a court makes a disposition under section 672.54 other than an absolute discharge in respect of an accused, the Review Board shall, not later than ninety days after the disposition was made, hold a hearing and make a disposition in respect of the accused.

(4) Despite subsections (1) to (3), if the court makes a disposition under subsection 672.64(3), the Review Board shall, not later than 45 days after the day on which the disposition is made, hold a hearing and make a disposition under paragraph 672.54(c), subject to the restrictions set out in that subsection.

(5) If the court is satisfied that there are exceptional circumstances that warrant it, the court may extend the time for holding a hearing under subsection (4) to a maximum of 90 days after the day on which the disposition is made. 1991, c. 43, s. 4; 2005, c. 22, s. 15; 2014, c. 6, s. 6(2).

CROSS-REFERENCES

The terms "mental disorder", "prosecutor" and "unfit to stand trial" are defined in s. 2. The terms "accused", "court", "disposition", "Review Board" and "verdict of not criminally responsible on account of mental disorder" are defined in s. 672.1. A disposition other than an absolute discharge is an order discharging the accused with conditions or an order detaining the accused in custody in a hospital (see s. 672.54(*b*) and (*c*)). As to the procedures to be followed at a disposition hearing before the Review Board, see s. 672.5. As to the review of dispositions made by the Review Board, see s. 672.81, which sets out the times for holding a review. For further cross-references respecting disposition hearings, see references under s. 672.45. Pursuant to s. 672.541, in determining the disposition of an accused found not criminally responsible, the Review Board shall take into consideration any victim impact statement filed in accordance with s. 672.5(14).

SYNOPSIS

If the court does not exercise its discretion to make a disposition after the accused is found to be unfit or not criminally responsible on account of mental disorder pursuant to s. 672.4, the Review Board must hold a disposition hearing not later than 45 days subsequent to the verdict unless the court is satisfied that there are exceptional circumstances warranting an extension of the time period.

Where the court has made a disposition pursuant to s. 672.54 other than an absolute discharge, the Review Board must hold a hearing not later than 90 days subsequent to the court disposition and make a disposition.

If the court finds the accused to be a high-risk accused, the court is required to make a detention order with limits on absence from the hospital. Under subsec. (4), the Review Board must within 45 days hold a hearing and make a detention order under s. 672.54(*c*), subject to the restrictions set out in that section. In exceptional circumstances, the time for holding the hearing may be extended to 90 days.

ANNOTATIONS

The failure to hold the hearing within the time-limits in this section does not affect the validity of the hearing or the order made unless the delay causes substantial prejudice to the accused: *Doucet v. British Columbia (Adult Forensic Psychiatric Services)* (2000), 143 C.C.C. (3d) 445, 185 D.L.R. (4th) 313 (B.C.C.A.).

REVIEW BOARD TO DETERMINE FITNESS / Review Board shall send accused to court / Chairperson may send accused to court.

672.48 (1) Where a Review Board holds a hearing to make or review a disposition in respect of an accused who has been found unfit to stand trial, it shall determine whether in its opinion the accused is fit to stand trial at the time of the hearing.

(2) If a Review Board determines that the accused is fit to stand trial, it shall order that the accused be sent back to court, and the court shall try the issue and render a verdict.

(3) The chairperson of a Review Board may, with the consent of the accused and the person in charge of the hospital where an accused is being detained, order that the accused be sent back to court for trial of the issue of whether the accused is unfit to stand trial, where the chairperson is of the opinion that

(*a*) the accused is fit to stand trial; and

(*b*) the Review Board will not hold a hearing to make or review a disposition in respect of the accused within a reasonable period. 1991, c. 43, s. 4.

CROSS-REFERENCES

Reference should be made to s. 2 of the *Criminal Code* which defines "unfit to stand trial" and to s. 672.1 which defines "accused", "chairperson", "court", "hospital" and "Review Board". If the accused is found to be fit to stand trial, then the trial proceeds in accordance with s. 672.28, although under s. 672.29, provision may be made to permit the accused to remain in custody in a hospital where there is reason to believe that the accused may otherwise become unfit. For further references as to the issue of fitness, see cross-references under s. 672.23 and for further cross-references respecting the disposition hearings, see s. 672.45.

SYNOPSIS

This provision requires the Review Board, during the course of the making or review of a disposition of unfitness where he is subsequently found fit, to send the accused back to trial. In addition, the chairperson may, with the consent of the accused and the person in charge of the hospital, dispense with the hearing and send the accused back to trial where the chairperson is of the opinion that the accused is presently fit to stand trial. For further cross-references respecting disposition hearings, see references under s. 672.44.

There is no right of appeal from a Review Board's decision regarding fitness to stand trial: *R. v. Pare* (2001), 159 C.C.C. (3d) 222, 151 O.A.C. 103 (C.A.).

CONTINUED DETENTION IN HOSPITAL / Copy of disposition to be sent to court.

672.49 (1) In a disposition made pursuant to section 672.47 the Review Board or chairperson may require the accused to continue to be detained in a hospital until the court determines whether the accused is fit to stand trial, if the Review Board or chairperson has reasonable grounds to believe that the accused would become unfit to stand trial if released.

(2) The Review Board or chairperson shall send a copy of a disposition made pursuant to section 672.47 without delay to the court having jurisdiction over the accused and to the Attorney General of the province where the accused is to be tried. 1991, c. 43, s. 4.

CROSS-REFERENCES

Section 2 of the *Criminal Code* defines "unfit to stand trial". The terms "accused", "chairperson", "disposition", "hospital" and "Review Board" are defined in s. 672.1. See also s. 672.29 which accords the court the same power to detain the accused where the release of the accused could render the accused unfit. Further cross-references respecting disposition hearings may be found in references under s. 672.45.

SYNOPSIS

The Review Board or the chairperson has the discretion to detain the accused until the court determines the issue of fitness if there are reasonable grounds to believe that the accused would become unfit if released.

Subsection (2) provides for notice requiring the Review Board or chairperson to send a copy of the disposition to the court having jurisdiction over the accused and the Attorney General of the province in which the accused is to be tried.

PROCEDURE AT DISPOSITION HEARING / Hearing to be informal / Attorneys General may be parties / Interested person may be a party / Notice of hearing / Notice / Notice of discharge and intended place of residence / Order excluding the public / Right to counsel / Assigning counsel / Counsel fees and disbursements / Taxation of fees and disbursements / Right of accused to be present / Removal or absence of accused / Rights of parties at hearing / Request to compel attendance of witnesses / Video links / Adjournment / Determination of mental condition of the accused / Notice to victims — referral of finding to court / Victim impact statement / Copy of statement / Presentation of victim statement / Inquiry by court or Review Board / Adjournment / Definition of "victim".

672.5 (1) A hearing held by a court or Review Board to make or review a disposition in respect of an accuse, including a hearing referred to in subsection 672.84(1) or (3), shall be held in accordance with this section.

(2) The hearing may be conducted in as informal a manner as is appropriate in the circumstances.

(3) On application, the court or Review Board shall designate as a party the Attorney General of the province where the disposition is to be made and, where an accused is transferred from another province, the Attorney General of the province from which the accused is transferred.

(4) The court or Review Board may designate as a party any person who has a substantial interest in protecting the interests of the accused, if the court or Review Board is of the opinion that it is just to do so.

(5) Notice of the hearing shall be given to the parties, the Attorney General of the province where the disposition is to be made and, where the accused is transferred to another province, the Attorney General of the province from which the accused is transferred, within the time and in the manner prescribed, or within the time and in the manner fixed by the rules of the court or Review Board.

(5.1) At the victim's request, notice of the hearing and of the relevant provisions of the Act shall be given to the victim within the time and in the manner fixed by the rules of the court or Review Board.

(5.2) If the accused is discharged absolutely under paragraph 672.54(*a*) or conditionally under paragraph 672.54(*b*), a notice of the discharge and accused's intended place of residence shall, at the victim's request, be given to the victim within the time and in the manner fixed by the rules of the court or Review Board.

(6) Where the court or Review Board considers it to be in the best interests of the accused and not contrary to the public interest, the court or Review Board may order the public or any members of the public to be excluded from the hearing or any part of the hearing.

(7) The accused or any other party has the right to be represented by counsel.

(8) If an accused is not represented by counsel, the court or Review Board shall, either before or at the time of the hearing, assign counsel to act for any accused

- **(*a*) who has been found unfit to stand trial; or**
- **(*b*) wherever the interests of justice so require.**

(8.1) Where counsel is assigned pursuant to subsection (8) and legal aid is not granted to the accused pursuant to a provincial legal aid program, the fees and disbursements of counsel shall be paid by the Attorney General to the extent that the accused is unable to pay them.

(8.2) Where counsel and the Attorney General cannot agree on the fees or disbursements of counsel, the Attorney General or the counsel may apply to the registrar of the court and the registrar may tax the disputed fees and disbursements.

(9) Subject to subsection (10), the accused has the right to be present during the whole of the hearing.

(10) The court or the chairperson of the Review Board may

- **(*a*) permit the accused to be absent during the whole or any part of the hearing on such conditions as the court or chairperson considers proper; or**
- **(*b*) cause the accused to be removed and barred from re-entry for the whole or any part of the hearing**
  - **(i) where the accused interrupts the hearing so that to continue in the presence of the accused would not be feasible,**
  - **(ii) on being satisfied that failure to do so would likely endanger the life or safety of another person or would seriously impair the treatment or recovery of the accused, or**
  - **(iii) in order to hear, in the absence of the accused, evidence, oral or written submissions, or the cross-examination of any witness concerning whether grounds exist for removing the accused pursuant to subparagraph (ii).**

(11) Any party may adduce evidence, make oral or written submissions, call witnesses and cross-examine any witness called by any other party and, on application, cross-examine any person who made an assessment report that was submitted to the court or Review Board in writing.

(12) A party may not compel the attendance of witnesses, but may request the court or the chairperson of the Review Board to do so.

(13) Where the accused so agrees, the court or the chairperson of the Review Board may permit the accused to appear by closed-circuit television or any other means that

allow the court or Review Board and the accused to engage in simultaneous visual and oral communication, for any part of the hearing.

(13.1) The Review Board may adjourn the hearing for a period not exceeding thirty days if necessary for the purpose of ensuring that relevant information is available to permit it to make or review a disposition or for any other sufficient reason.

(13.2) On receiving an assessment report, the court or Review Board shall determine whether, since the last time the disposition in respect of the accused was made or reviewed there has been any change in the mental condition of the accused that may provide grounds for the discharge of the accused under paragraph 672.54(*a*) or (*b*) and, if there has been such a change, the court or Review Board shall notify every victim of the offence that they are entitled to file a statement in accordance with subsection (14).

(13.3) If the Review Board refers to the court for review under subsection 672.84(1) a finding that an accused is a high-risk accused, it shall notify every victim of the offence that they are entitled to file a statement with the court in accordance with subsection (14).

(14) A victim of the offence may prepare and file with the court or Review Board a written statement describing the physical or emotional harm, property damage or economic loss suffered by the victim as the result of the commission of the offence and the impact of the offence on the victim. Form 48.2 in Part XXVIII, or a form approved by the lieutenant governor in council of the province in which the court or Review Board is exercising its jurisdiction, must be used for this purpose.

(15) The court or Review Board shall ensure that a copy of any statement filed in accordance with subsection (14) is provided to the accused or counsel for the accused, and the prosecutor, as soon as practicable after a verdict of not criminally responsible on account of mental disorder is rendered in respect of the offence.

(15.1) The court or Review Board shall, at the request of a victim, permit the victim to read a statement prepared and filed in accordance with subsection (14), or to present the statement in any other manner that the court or Review Board considers appropriate, unless the court or Review Board is of the opinion that the reading or presentation of the statement would interfere with the proper administration of justice.

(15.2) The court or Review Board shall, as soon as practicable after a verdict of not criminally responsible on account of mental disorder is rendered in respect of an offence and before making a disposition under section 672.45, 672.47 or 672.64, inquire of the prosecutor or a victim of the offence, or any person representing a victim of the offence, whether the victim has been advised of the opportunity to prepare a statement referred to in subsection (14).

(15.3) On application of the prosecutor or a victim or of its own motion, the court or Review Board may adjourn the hearing held under section 672.45, 672.47 or 672.64 to permit the victim to prepare a statement referred to in subsection (14) if the court or Review Board is satisfied that the adjournment would not interfere with the proper administration of justice. 1991, c. 43, s. 4; 1997, c. 18, s. 84; 1999, c. 25, s. 11; 2005, c. 22, s. 16; 2014, c. 6, s. 7(1)-(3), (5); 2015, c. 13, s. 22.

(16) [*Repealed*, 2015, c. 13, s. 22(2).]

CROSS-REFERENCES

The terms "Attorney General" and "unfit to stand trial" are defined in s. 2. "Victim" is defined in s. 722(4) for the purpose of this section. Also see s. 672.541 respecting the use of victim impact statements following a finding of not criminally responsible on account of mental disorder and s. 672.542 which requires the court or Review Board to consider imposing conditions respecting communication and safety of victims, witnesses or other persons identified in the disposition. The terms "accused", "court", "disposition", "party" and "Review Board" are defined in s. 672.1. For the purposes of subsec. (14) of this section, "victim" is defined in s. 722(4).

Pursuant to s. 672.84, the Review Board shall hold a review hearing under s. 672.81 or 672.82 in accordance with the procedures described in s. 672.5. Where the court is exercising its review power pursuant to s. 672.33 to determine whether there is sufficient evidence to put the accused on trial after a verdict of unfit to stand trial has been rendered, the court does not follow the procedures outlined in s. 672.5 but, pursuant to s. 672.33 (5), the court may determine the manner in which the inquiry is conducted and has the discretion to incorporate the procedures in respect of a preliminary inquiry under Part XVIII. Reference should be made to s. 672.51(8) regulating the disclosure of "disposition information" obtained at disposition hearings during which the accused was excluded from the proceedings. Disposition information is defined in s. 672.51. In particular, note that no information may be disclosed to either the accused or a non-party where the accused has been excluded from the proceedings pursuant to s. 672.5(10)(*b*)(ii) or (iii). For further cross-references respecting disposition hearings, see references under s. 672.45.

SYNOPSIS

This section sets out the procedures to be followed at disposition hearings by courts and review boards. The court or Review Board may designate, as a party on an application, the Attorney General of the province where the disposition was made or, where the accused is transferred from another province, the Attorney General of the province from which the accused is transferred. In addition, the court or Review Board has the power to designate any person as a party if they have a substantial interest in protecting the interests of the accused, provided that it is satisfied that it is just to so designate the party.

General notice provisions provide that notice of the hearing be given to the parties and the Attorney General of the province where the disposition is made or the Attorney General of the province from which the accused has been transferred whether or not the Attorney General has been made a party to the proceedings. The specific time period within which notice is to be provided is not specified in the section but is to be fixed by the rules of the court or Review Board [s. 672.5(5)]. The proceedings are conducted in an open forum subject to the right of the court or review board to exclude the public where it is in the best interests of the accused *and* not contrary to the public interest to do so [s. 672.5(6)].

The provisions allow for the hearings to be conducted in an informal manner [s. 672.5(2)]. A party is entitled to adduce evidence, make oral or written submissions, call and cross-examine witnesses and on application, cross-examine any person who made an assessment report which is submitted to the court or Review Board. However, no party has the authority to compel the attendance of any witness. The attendance of a witness may be compelled, only, by the court or chairperson of the Review Board on the request of a party [s. 672.5(11), (12)].

Section 672.5(7) creates the right of the accused or any other party to the proceedings to be represented by counsel. Where the accused is not represented, the court or Review Board must assign counsel to act for an accused who has been found unfit to stand trial or wherever the interests of justice so require. Payment of counsel is provided for in subsecs. (8.1) and (8.2).

The accused has the *prima facie* right to be present at a disposition hearing. The accused may be permitted to be absent on such conditions as the court or chairperson deems appropriate. The court or chairperson of the Review Board also has the authority to bar the accused from the hearing if the accused interrupts the hearing to the point that continuation is not feasible, where it is necessary so as not to endanger the life or safety of another person, where continued attendance would seriously impair the treatment or recovery of the accused or in order to hear evidence relating to the grounds for removing the accused pursuant to s. 672.5(10)(*b*)(ii). The accused may consent to appear by closed-circuit television or other means under subsec. (13). A victim of an offence, as defined in s. 722(4), may file a victim impact statement before the court or Review Board as the case may be.

This section also gives the victim of the accused's offence certain rights. Thus, under subsec. (5.1), at the victim's request, the victim is to be given notice of the hearing and of the relevant provisions of the *Criminal Code*. Under subsec. (5.2), if the accused is discharged absolutely or conditionally, a notice of the discharge and the accused's intended place of residence must be given to the victim, at the victim's request. Under subsec. (13.2), if the court or Review Board is of the view that there has been a change in the mental condition of the accused that may provide grounds for an absolute or conditional discharge, it is to notify the victims that they are entitled to file a statement under subsec. (14). If the Review Board refers to the court for review of a finding that the accused is a high-risk accused, it shall notify every victim of their right to file a statement with the court. Subsection (14) gives every victim the right to file a form of victim impact statement. The accused and the prosecutor are to be provided with copies of the statements and, under subsec. (15.1), the victims have the right to read the statement or present them in some other way that the court or Review Board considers appropriate unless the reading or presentation would interfere with the proper administration of justice. Subsection (15.2) requires the court or Review Board to inquire of the prosecutor whether the victims have been advised of their right to prepare statements under subsec. (14) as soon as practicable after the finding of not criminally responsible. Where it is necessary, the court or the Review Board may adjourn the hearing pursuant to subsec. (15.3) to permit the victim to prepare a statement if the adjournment would not interfere with the proper administration of justice.

ANNOTATIONS

Subsection (6) does not infringe ss. 7 and 15 of the Charter. It is appropriate that the board be required to take into account the public interest in determining whether or not to exclude the public: *Blackman v. British Columbia (Review Board)* (1995), 95 C.C.C. (3d) 412 (B.C.C.A.).

The Crown is accorded certain statutory rights of participation in relation to Board hearings. There is no broader common law duty of procedural fairness owed to the Crown in this context. Therefore, the Board did not err in adding a community access condition to those proposed by the parties in their joint submission without first providing the Attorney General with the opportunity to make submissions on that condition: *Kachkar (Re)* (2014), 309 C.C.C. (3d) 1 (Ont. C.A.).

ORDER RESTRICTING PUBLICATION — SEXUAL OFFENCES / Order restricting publication — child pornography / Order restricting publication — other offences / Order restricting publication / Application and notice / Grounds / Hearing may be held / Factors to be considered / Conditions / Publication of application prohibited / Offence / Application of order.

672.501 (1) Where a Review Board holds a hearing referred to in section 672.5 in respect of an accused who has been declared not criminally responsible on account of mental disorder or unfit to stand trial for an offence referred to in subsection 486.4(1), the Review Board shall make an order directing that any information that could identify a victim, or a witness who is under the age of eighteen years, shall not be published in any document or broadcast or transmitted in any way.

(2) Where a Review Board holds a hearing referred to in section 672.5 in respect of an accused who has been declared not criminally responsible on account of mental disorder or unfit to stand trial for an offence referred to in section 163.1, a Review Board shall make an order directing that any information that could identify a witness who is under the age of eighteen years, or any person who is the subject of a representation, written material or a recording that constitutes child pornography within the meaning of section 163.1, shall not be published in any document or broadcast or transmitted in any way.

(3) Where a Review Board holds a hearing referred to in section 672.5 in respect of an accused who has been declared not criminally responsible on account of mental disorder or unfit to stand trial for an offence other than the offences referred to in subsection (1) or (2), on application of the prosecutor, a victim or a witness, the Review Board may make an order directing that any information that could identify the victim or witness shall not be published in any document or broadcast or transmitted in any way if the Review Board is satisfied that the order is necessary for the proper administration of justice.

(4) An order made under any of subsections (1) to (3) does not apply in respect of the disclosure of information in the course of the administration of justice if it is not the purpose of the disclosure to make the information known in the community.

(5) An applicant for an order under subsection (3) shall

(*a*) apply in writing to the Review Board; and

(*b*) provide notice of the application to the prosecutor, the accused and any other person affected by the order that the Review Board specifies.

(6) An applicant for an order under subsection (3) shall set out the grounds on which the applicant relies to establish that the order is necessary for the proper administration of justice.

(7) The Review Board may hold a hearing to determine whether an order under subsection (3) should be made, and the hearing may be in private.

(8) In determining whether to make an order under subsection (3), the Review Board shall consider

(*a*) the right to a fair and public hearing;

(*b*) whether there is a real and substantial risk that the victim or witness would suffer significant harm if their identity were disclosed;

(*c*) whether the victim or witness needs the order for their security or to protect them from intimidation or retaliation;

(*d*) society's interest in encouraging the reporting of offences and the participation of victims and witnesses in the criminal justice process;

(*e*) whether effective alternatives are available to protect the identity of the victim or witness;

(*f*) the salutary and deleterious effects of the proposed order;

(*g*) the impact of the proposed order on the freedom of expression of those affected by it; and

(*h*) any other factor that the Review Board considers relevant.

(9) An order made under subsection (3) may be subject to any conditions that the Review Board thinks fit.

(10) Unless the Review Board refuses to make an order under subsection (3), no person shall publish in any document or broadcast or transmit in any way

(*a*) the contents of an application;

(*b*) any evidence taken, information given or submissions made at a hearing under subsection (7); or

(*c*) any other information that could identify the person to whom the application relates as a victim or witness in the proceedings.

(11) Every person who fails to comply with an order made under any of subsections (1) to (3) is guilty of an offence punishable on summary conviction.

(12) For greater certainty, an order referred to in subsection (11) also prohibits, in relation to proceedings taken against any person who fails to comply with the order, the publication in any document or the broadcasting or transmission in any way of information that could identify a victim or witness whose identity is protected by the order. 2005, c. 22, ss. 17 and 64(2).

CROSS-REFERENCES

"Accused" and "Review Board" are defined in s. 672.1. "Victim", "prosecutor", "unfit to stand trial" and "mental disorder" are defined in s. 2. Age is determined by reference to s. 30 of the *Interpretation Act*, R.S.C. 1985, c. I-21. Similar provisions respecting ban on publication, broadcast or transmission in any way of information that would identify witnesses and other persons are found in ss. 486.4 to 486.6.

SYNOPSIS

This section creates a code of procedure for the making of non-publication orders in proceedings before the Review Board. The section contemplates three different situations. Under subsec. (1), the order is mandatory in respect of any victim or witness who is under the age of 18 years. Similarly, under subsec. (2), the order is mandatory in proceedings relating to the offence of child pornography under s. 163.1 in relation to information that could identify a witness who is under the age of 18 years or any person who is the subject of a representation, written material or a recording that constitutes child pornography within the meaning of s. 163.1. In all other cases, the order is made under subsec. (3) on application of the victim or a witness. The basis for making the order under that subsection is whether the board is satisfied that the order is necessary for the proper administration of justice. Where the order is made, it applies to prohibit publication, broadcast or transmission in any way of any information that could identify the person.

Subsection (4) provides an exception for disclosure in the course of the administration of justice, where disclosure is not for the purpose of making the information known to the community.

Subsection (5) requires the applicant for the order under subsec. (3) to apply in writing to the Review Board. The application must be on notice to the accused, prosecutor and any other person affected by the order as required by the board and, pursuant to subsec. (6), must set out the grounds for the making of the order. The board may hold a hearing, which may be *in camera*. The factors the board must consider are set out in subsec. (8). The board may include conditions in the order. Unless the board refuses to make the order, the contents of the application, the proceedings at the hearing and any other information that would identify the person shall also not be published, broadcasted or transmitted in any way. It is an offence to fail to comply with the order made under this section. The orders made under this section also apply to protect the identity of the persons named in the orders in proceedings under this section.

DEFINITION OF "DISPOSITION INFORMATION" / Disposition information to be made available to parties / Exception where disclosure dangerous to any person / Idem / Exception where disclosure unnecessary or prejudicial / Exclusion of certain persons from hearing / Prohibition of disclosure in certain cases / Idem / Information to be made available to specified persons / Disclosure for research or statistical purposes / Prohibition on publication / Powers of courts not limited.

672.51 (1) In this section, "disposition information" means all or part of an assessment report submitted to the court or Review Board and any other written information before the court or Review Board about the accused that is relevant to making or reviewing a disposition.

(2) Subject to this section, all disposition information shall be made available for inspection by, and the court or Review Board shall provide a copy of it to, each party and any counsel representing the accused.

(3) The court or Review Board shall withhold some or all of the disposition information from an accused where it is satisfied, on the basis of that information and the evidence or report of the medical practitioner responsible for the assessment or treatment of the accused, that disclosure of the information would be likely to endanger the life or safety of another person or would seriously impair the treatment or recovery of the accused.

(4) Notwithstanding subsection (3), the court or Review Board may release some or all of the disposition information to an accused where the interests of justice make disclosure essential in its opinion.

(5) The court or Review Board shall withhold disposition information from a party other than the accused or an Attorney General, where disclosure to that party, in the opinion of the court or Review Board, is not necessary to the proceeding and may be prejudicial to the accused.

(6) A court or Review Board that withholds disposition information from the accused or any other party pursuant to subsection (3) or (5) shall exclude the accused or the other party, as the case may be, from the hearing during

- **(*a*) the oral presentation of that disposition information; or**
- **(*b*) the questioning by the court or Review Board or the cross-examination of any person concerning that disposition information.**

(7) No disposition information shall be made available for inspection or disclosed to any person who is not a party to the proceedings

- **(*a*) where the disposition information has been withheld from the accused or any other party pursuant to subsection (3) or (5); or**
- **(*b*) where the court or Review Board is of the opinion that disclosure of the disposition information would be seriously prejudicial to the accused and that, in the circumstances, protection of the accused takes precedence over the public interest in disclosure.**

(8) No part of the record of the proceedings in respect of which the accused was excluded pursuant to subparagraph 672.5(10)(*b*)(ii) or (iii) shall be made available for inspection to the accused or to any person who is not a party to the proceedings.

(9) Notwithstanding subsections (7) and (8), the court or Review Board may make any disposition information, or a copy of it, available on request to any person or member of a class of persons

- **(*a*) that has a valid interest in the information for research or statistical purposes, where the court or Review Board is satisfied that disclosure is in the public interest;**
- **(*b*) that has a valid interest in the information for the purposes of the proper administration of justice; or**
- **(*c*) that the accused requests or authorizes in writing to inspect it, where the court or Review Board is satisfied that the person will not disclose or give to the accused a copy of any disposition information withheld from the accused pursuant to subsection (3), or of any part of the record of proceedings referred to in subsection (8), or that the reasons for withholding that information from the accused no longer exist.**

(10) A person to whom the court or Review Board makes disposition information available under paragraph (9)(*a*) may disclose it for research or statistical purposes, but not in any form or manner that could reasonably be expected to identify any person to whom it relates.

(11) No person shall publish in any document or broadcast or transmit in any way

- **(*a*) any disposition information that is prohibited from being disclosed pursuant to subsection (7); or**
- **(*b*) any part of the record of the proceedings in respect of which the accused was excluded pursuant to subparagraph 672.5(10)(*b*)(ii) or (iii).**

(12) Except as otherwise provided in this section, nothing in this section limits the powers that a court may exercise apart from this section. 1991, c. 43, s. 4; 1997, c. 18, s. 85; 2005, c. 22, s. 18; 2005, c. 32, s. 22; 2014, c. 6, s. 8.

CROSS-REFERENCES

The terms "accused", "court", "disposition" and "Review Board" are defined in s. 672.1 of the *Criminal Code*. Pursuant to s. 672.5(10)(*b*)(ii) and (iii), an accused may be excluded from the court if failure to do so would endanger the life or safety of another person, impair the treatment or recovery of the accused or to hear submissions and witnesses as to the grounds which exist for removing the accused. Information obtained during these hearings may not be released to the accused. For further cross-references respecting disposition hearings, see references under s. 672.45.

SYNOPSIS

This provision sets out the circumstances in which "disposition information" may be disclosed to or withheld from parties to the disposition hearing as well as non-parties. Section 672.51(1) broadly defines "disposition information" to include all or part of any assessment and any other written information that is before the court or Review Board and is relevant to making a disposition.

The provision entrenches the general principle that any party or counsel representing the accused is entitled to a copy of all disposition information. Pursuant to s. 672.51(3), information may be withheld from the accused in one of two circumstances: (1) where disclosure would endanger the life or safety of another person; or (2) where disclosure would seriously impair either the treatment or recovery of the accused. The discretion to withhold disposition information, however, is subject to s. 672.51(4) which mandates the disclosure of the information notwithstanding subsec. (3) where the interests of justice make disclosure necessary. Nonetheless, evidence of proceedings pursuant to s. 672.5(10)(*b*)(ii) or (iii) relating to the exclusion of the accused from the hearing may not be disclosed to either the accused or any non-party.

Where disclosure is to a party who is not the accused or the Attorney General, the provision set out a different test. Pursuant to s. 672.51(5), disposition information may be withheld where disclosure is not necessary and would be prejudicial to the accused.

In determining the issue of disclosure, the court or review board must exclude either the accused or other party while hearing evidence relating to the disposition information in question.

A non-party is not entitled to any disposition information either where the disposition information has been withheld from the accused or another party, where the disclosure would be seriously prejudicial to the accused and in the circumstances, protection of the accused takes precedence over public interest in disclosure. No person is entitled to publish in any newspaper or broadcast any disposition information that is withheld or any part of the record of the proceedings in relation to the exclusion of the accused from the hearing pursuant to s. 672.5(10)(*b*)(ii) or (iii). Notwithstanding the general prohibition on disclosure of disposition information to non-parties, the court or Review Board has the discretion to disclose the information to persons performing research or statistical work where disclosure is in the public interest, to individuals having a valid interest in the information for the purpose of the proper administration of justice, and to persons authorized or requested by the accused to inspect the information where the court or Review Board is satisfied that the person will not disclose or give the accused a copy of the information withheld from the accused.

Pursuant to s. 672.51(12), the power of the court is not limited in the disclosure of information beyond the provisions of this section.

It is an offence under subsec. (11) to publish, broadcast or transmit in any way any disposition information that is prohibited from being disclosed under subsec. (7) or any part of the record of the proceedings in respect of which the accused was excluded under s. 672.5(10)(*b*)(ii) or (iii).

RECORD OF PROCEEDINGS / Transmittal of transcript to Review Board / Reasons for disposition and copies to be provided.

672.52 (1) The court or Review Board shall cause a record of the proceedings of its disposition hearings to be kept, and include in the record any assessment report submitted.

(2) If a court holds a disposition hearing under subsection 672.45(1), whether or not it makes a disposition, it shall send without delay to the Review Board that has jurisdiction in respect of the matter, in original or copied form, a transcript of the hearing, any other document or information related to the hearing, and all exhibits filed with it, if the transcript, document, information or exhibits are in its possession.

(3) The court or Review Board shall state its reasons for making a disposition in the record of the proceedings, and shall provide every party with a copy of the disposition and those reasons. 1991, c. 43, s. 4; 2005, c. 22, s. 19.

CROSS-REFERENCES

The terms "court", "party" and "Review Board" are defined in s. 672.1. As to the material to be filed on appeal of a disposition or placement decision of the court or Review Board, see s. 672.73 requiring that an appeal is to be based on a transcript of proceedings. As to the review of dispositions by the Review Board, see ss. 672.81 to 672.85. For further references respecting disposition hearings, see references under s. 672.45.

SYNOPSIS

This provision establishes several requirements on the court or Review Board with respect to the preservation of a record for appeal purposes. Pursuant to subsec. (1), the court or Review Board must ensure that a record of the proceedings including any assessment report is kept. Where the court holds a disposition hearing, it shall send a transcript of the hearing and any other relevant documentation, including exhibits in its possession, to the Review Board that has jurisdiction (subsec. (2)).

In addition, there is a requirement that the court or Review Board provide reasons for the disposition on the record and provide each party with a copy of those reasons [s. 672.52(3)].

ANNOTATIONS

Tapes of the hearing prepared by a private court reporting service are considered part of the board's record: *Ontario (Criminal Code Review Board) v. Ontario (Freedom of Information and Protection of Privacy Act, Inquiry Officer)* (1999), 180 D.L.R. (4th) 657, 140 C.C.C. (3d) 400 (Ont. C.A.).

PROCEEDINGS NOT INVALID.

672.53 Any procedural irregularity in relation to a disposition hearing does not affect the validity of the hearing unless it causes the accused substantial prejudice. 1991, c. 43, s. 4.

CROSS-REFERENCES

As to the procedures to be followed at a disposition hearing, see s. 672.5. For further cross-references respecting disposition hearings, see s. 672.45.

SYNOPSIS

Minor procedural irregularities do not vitiate the hearing unless the breach has caused the accused *substantial* prejudice.

DISPOSITIONS BY A COURT OR REVIEW BOARD

Terms of Dispositions

DISPOSITIONS THAT MAY BE MADE.

672.54 When a court or Review Board makes a disposition under subsection 672.45(2), section 672.47, subsection 672.64(3) or section 672.83 or 672.84, it shall, taking into account the safety of the public, which is the paramount consideration, the mental condition of the accused, the reintegration of the accused into society and the other needs of the accused, make one of the following dispositions that is necessary and appropriate in the circumstances:

(*a*) where a verdict of not criminally responsible on account of mental disorder has been rendered in respect of the accused and, in the opinion of the court or Review Board, the accused is not a significant threat to the safety of the public, by order, direct that the accused be discharged absolutely;

(*b*) by order, direct that the accused be discharged subject to such conditions as the court or Review Board considers appropriate; or

(*c*) by order, direct that the accused be detained in custody in a hospital, subject to such conditions as the court or Review Board considers appropriate. 1991, c. 43, s. 4; 2005, c. 22, s. 20; 2014, c. 6, s. 9.

CROSS-REFERENCES

The terms "mental disorder", "prosecutor" and "unfit to stand trial" are defined in s. 2 of the *Criminal Code*. The terms "accused", "court", "disposition", "hospital", "Review Board" and "verdict of not criminally responsible on account of mental disorder" are defined in s. 672.1. Section 672.5401 defines "significant threat to the safety of the public".

A disposition under s. 672.54 cannot include a requirement that the accused submit to treatment without the accused's consent (s. 672.55), subject to s. 672.58 which allows the court to order that the accused submit to such treatment as is not excluded by s. 672.61 where doing so is likely to render the accused fit. See also ss. 672.59 and 672.6 which define the conditions under which such a disposition can be made. A disposition comes into force the day it is made or any later day that the court or Review Board specifies and shall remain in force until the day it expires. A court cannot order a disposition requiring the accused to be detained in custody or in a hospital pursuant to s. 672.54 for more than 90 days after which the Review Board must hold a hearing and make a disposition in respect of the accused by virtue of s. 672.47. Where the court chooses not to hold a disposition hearing, the Review Board must hold a hearing within 45 days subject to the court's discretion to extend this time period for not more than 90 days (ss. 672.45 and 672.46). A disposition detaining the accused requires the Review Board to issue a warrant of committal which may be in Form 49 (s. 672.57). Reference should also be made to s. 672.56 which allows the Review Board to make a disposition which delegates a person in charge of the hospital authorized to increase or decrease the liberty of the accused. Where increased restrictions on the accused's liberty exceed seven days, the Review Board must be notified and pursuant to s. 672.81(2)(*b*), the Review Board must hold a hearing to review the disposition of the accused.

As to appeals from a decision of the Review Board, see ss. 672.72 to 672.8 and as to the review of dispositions of a court or Review Board, see ss. 672.81 to 672.85. For further cross-references with respect to disposition hearings, see references under s. 672.45.

The process to initiate review of a finding that the accused is a high-risk accused is set out in s. 672.84.

SYNOPSIS

This provision establishes both the test for a disposition and the forms of dispositions which may be issued by a court or Review Board.

In making a disposition, the court or Review Board is to take into account the safety of the public as the paramount consideration, and the mental condition of the accused, reintegration of the accused into society and the other needs of the accused.

The Review Board may either discharge the accused with respect to such conditions as are appropriate, detain the accused in a hospital or, where the verdict of not criminally responsible on account of mental disorder is rendered and the accused is not a significant threat to the safety of the public, discharge the accused absolutely. The court has similar powers, except that the detention order continues in force for no longer than 90 days [s. 672.55].

This section also applies where the Review Board makes a disposition under s. 672.83 in respect of a person found unfit to stand trial.

ANNOTATIONS

The Board has no jurisdiction to order costs as a remedy pursuant to s. 24(1) of the Charter: *Re Chaudry* (2015), 324 C.C.C. (3d) 281 (Ont. C.A.), leave to appeal to S.C.C. refused 2017 CarswellOnt 1053.

Note: The following cases were decided prior to the amendment to this section that changed the nature of the test to be applied by the court or the Review Board. The court or Review Board is to consider safety of the public as the paramount consideration. Further, the statutory requirement that the court was to make the disposition that was the least onerous and least restrictive for the accused has been removed. Section 672.5401 defines "significant threat to the safety of the public" to include a risk of serious physical or psychological harm resulting from conduct that is criminal in nature but not necessarily violent. Thus, these cases must be read with care and bearing in mind the amendments to this section and s. 672.5401.

Constitutional Considerations – This provision does not violate s. 7 of the Charter: *Penetanguishene Mental Health Centre v. Ontario (Attorney General)*, [2004] 1 S.C.R. 498, 182 C.C.C. (3d) 193.

The Review Board has s. 24(1) jurisdiction and was entitled to decide constitutional questions that arose in the course of its proceedings. The board did not have statutory jurisdiction to grant an absolute discharge to an NCR patient found to be dangerous or an order direction that a hospital provide a NCR patient with particular treatment: *C. (P.) v. Ontario*, [2010] 1 S.C.R. 765, 255 C.C.C. (3d) 506 *sub nom. R. v. Conway*.

Test to be applied – The duties of a court or review board acting under this section may be summarized as follows. A "significant threat to the safety of the public" means a real risk of physical or psychological harm to members of the public that is serious in the sense of going beyond the merely trivial or annoying. The conduct giving rise to the harm must be criminal in nature. There is no presumption that the accused poses a significant threat. Restrictions to the accused's liberty can only be justified if, at the time of the hearing, the evidence shows that the accused actually constitutes such a threat. If the court or the board cannot come to a decision with any certainty, it has not found that the accused poses a significant threat to the safety of the public. The proceeding is not adversarial and if the parties do not present sufficient information, it is up to the court or the board to seek out the evidence it requires. There is never any legal burden on the accused to show that he or she does not pose a significant threat to the safety of the public. The court or board may have recourse to a broad range of evidence in making its determination. A past offence committed while the accused suffered from a mental illness is not, by itself, evidence that the accused continues to pose a significant risk to the safety of the public. However, that fact may be considered together with other circumstances where it is relevant to identifying a pattern of behaviour, and hence to the issue of whether the accused presents a significant threat. If the accused is not a significant risk, he or she must be absolutely discharged. If the accused is a significant risk, the court or board may order the accused be discharged subject to conditions considered necessary, or it may order that the accused be detained in custody in a hospital, again subject to appropriate conditions. When deciding to make an order for conditional discharge or for detention, the court or board must consider the matters set out in subsec. (1) and make the order that is the least onerous and least restrictive to the accused. So interpreted, this section does not violate ss. 7 and 15 of the *Canadian Charter of Rights and Freedoms*: *Winko v. British Columbia (Forensic Psychiatric Institute)*, [1999] 2 S.C.R. 625, 135 C.C.C. (3d) 129; *R. v. LePage*, [1999] 2 S.C.R. 744, 135 C.C.C. (3d) 205; *Orlowski v. British Columbia (Forensic Psychiatric Institute)*, [1999] 2 S.C.R. 733, 135 C.C.C. (3d) 220; and *Bese v. British Columbia (Forensic Psychiatric Institute)*, [1999] 2 S.C.R. 722, 135 C.C.C. (3d) 212.

It was an error for the board to proceed on the basis that if it was not satisfied that the accused did not constitute a significant risk to public safety, it must continue to impose restrictive conditions. Restrictions to the accused's liberty can only be justified if, at the time of the hearing, the evidence shows that the accused actually constitutes such a threat: *Orlowski v. British Columbia (Forensic Psychiatric Institute), supra*, and *Bese v. British Columbia (Forensic Psychiatric Institute), supra.*

The liberty interests of NCR detainees must be taken into account at all stages of a Review Board's consideration in reconciling the twin goals of treatment and public protection. The "least onerous and least restrictive" regime applies not only to the place or mode of detention but also to the conditions governing it. The conditions under which an NCR accused is detained can have serious ramifications on his or her liberty interests. A review board may impose conditions on the detainee's access to hospital grounds or to the host community. The use of the term "appropriate" does not mean "unfettered". The conditions must be appropriate having regard to the rest of the section. On review, the conditions must be evaluated in the context of the entire package of provisions of which it forms a part: *Penetanguishene Mental Health Centre v. Ontario (Attorney General)*, [2004] 1 S.C.R. 498, 182 C.C.C. (3d) 193; *Pinet v. St. Thomas Psychiatric Hospital*, [2004] 1 S.C.R. 528, 182 C.C.C. (3d) 214.

Proper consideration of the appropriate placement, reintegration into society and the other needs of the accused would, in some circumstances, require the board to advert to the unique circumstances and background of an aboriginal NCR accused. In addition, the board's duty to search out evidence pertinent to the factors identified in this section would apply to ensure that the board had adequate information about the accused's aboriginal background where that information would be relevant to its determination: *Sim v. Ontario (Review Board)* (2005), 201 C.C.C. (3d) 482 (Ont. C.A.).

Proof of need for continued detention or supervision – It was not open to the Board to accept the recommendation of the hospital and order that the accused be released unconditionally where his basic condition was untreatable and it was clear that, since he had consistently refused treatment, the accused's problems remained unresolved. The accused was a nuisance and the administrators of the hospital sought to get rid of him either by proposing that he be sent to some other institution or that he be released unconditionally so that when he ran afoul of the law, as it was conceded that he would, he could be dealt with by the criminal justice system. The question the review board should have asked itself was how it could effectively supervise a reintegration of the accused into society when he wilfully refused to abide by the conditions of release that were imposed earlier. For the accused to be discharged absolutely, the Board had to form the opinion that the accused was not a significant threat to the safety of the public: *R. v. Jones* (1994), 87 C.C.C. (3d) 350 (Ont. C.A.).

In considering the "mental condition" of the accused, the Board is required to consider the accused's mental condition at the time of the hearing. There is nothing in this section suggesting that the Board must first decide whether the mental condition which first led to the finding that the accused is not criminally responsible still exists: *Peckham v. Ontario (Attorney General)* (1994), 93 C.C.C. (3d) 443 (Ont. C.A.), leave to appeal to S.C.C. refused 94 C.C.C. (3d) vi.

Order to be made – The Review Board did not act unreasonably in rejecting the medical evidence supporting the accused's transfer from a maximum to a minimum-security hospital.

The Review Board ordered the transfer to a medium-security facility because the accused had undergone a short period of treatment and did not have a complete understanding of his mental condition. The ease of access to the community was the only meaningful difference in the treatment available to the accused at the medium-secure unit. While the Review Board did not err or act unreasonably in not imposing a time limit for the accused's transfer, transfer orders must be implemented within a reasonable time: *Beauchamp v. Penetanguishene Mental Health Centre (Administrator)* (1999), 138 C.C.C. (3d) 172 (Ont. C.A.), leave to appeal to S.C.C. refused 134 C.C.C. (3d) vi.

The Review Board has jurisdiction to make orders binding on parties other than the accused and thus could impose conditions binding on hospital authorities and, in particular, the Director of the hospital, regarding or supervising medical treatment, but it could not prescribe or impose specific treatment: *Mazzei v. British Columbia (Adult Forensic Psychiatric Services, Director)* (2006), 206 C.C.C. (3d) 161 (S.C.C.).

It is not for the court to micromanage the conditions attached to a detention order under which the accused is permitted to leave the hospital. Since it was not unreasonable for the board to find that the accused represented a significant threat to the safety of the public, the court should not be too quick to overturn the board's expert opinion about how that risk is to be managed: *R. v. Owen*, [2003] 1 S.C.R. 779, 174 C.C.C. (3d) 1.

The imposition of a drug testing condition does not violate s. 8 of the *Canadian Charter of Rights and Freedoms*: *Mazzei v. British Columbia (Adult Forensic Services, Director)* (2006), 210 C.C.C. (3d) 367 (B.C.C.A.).

Evidence – The board has an inquisitorial function and, accordingly, has a duty to search out and consider evidence on both sides of the case, even where the accused refused to participate in or appear before the Review Board: *Lepage v. Ontario* (2006), 214 C.C.C. (3d) 105, 217 O.A.C. 82 *sub nom. R. v. Lepage* (C.A.). See also *R. v. Baker* (2001), 155 C.C.C. (3d) 202 (Ont. C.A.).

The hearing before the Review Board is an administrative proceeding and the board may therefore take into account any reliable material that has some probative value. Given that there was evidence of a possible nexus between the accused's overall mental condition and the threat of sexual assault, the board was entitled to consider evidence concerning his ongoing pattern of conduct, including unproven sexual assaults, as evidence of a propensity to pose a continuing significant threat to the public. Such conduct may be established on the balance of probabilities and need not be measured on the criminal standard of proof beyond a reasonable doubt: *R. v. Wodajio* (2005), 194 C.C.C. (3d) 133 (Alta. C.A.).

Joint submissions – The Board has an obligation to give the accused notice if it is considering rejecting a joint submission and to provide the opportunity to all parties to lead further evidence or make submissions to address the Board's concerns: *Osawe, Re* (2015), 323 C.C.C. (3d) 405 (Ont. C.A.).

SIGNIFICANT THREAT TO SAFETY OF PUBLIC.

672.5401 For the purposes of section 672.54, a significant threat to the safety of the public means a risk of serious physical or psychological harm to members of the public — including any victim of or witness to the offence, or any person under the age of 18 years — resulting from conduct that is criminal in nature but not necessarily violent. 2014, c. 6, s. 10.

SYNOPSIS

This section defines significant threat to the safety of the public for the purposes of making a disposition under s. 672.54.

VICTIM IMPACT STATEMENT.

672.541 If a verdict of not criminally responsible on account of mental disorder has been rendered in respect of an accused, the court or Review Board shall

- **(*a*) at a hearing held under section 672.45, 672.47, 672.64, 672.81 or 672.82 or subsection 672.84(5), take into consideration any statement filed by a victim in accordance with subsection 672.5(14) in determining the appropriate disposition or conditions under section 672.54, to the extent that the statement is relevant to its consideration of the criteria set out in section 672.54;**
- **(*b*) at a hearing held under section 672.64 or subsection 672.84(3), take into consideration any statement filed by a victim in accordance with subsection 672.5(14), to the extent that the statement is relevant to its consideration of the criteria set out in subsection 672.64(1) or 672.84(3), as the case may be, in deciding whether to find that the accused is a high-risk accused, or to revoke such a finding; and**
- **(*c*) at a hearing held under section 672.81 or 672.82 in respect of a high-risk accused, take into consideration any statement filed by a victim in accordance with subsection 672.5(14) in determining whether to refer to the court for review the finding that the accused is a high-risk accused, to the extent that the statement is relevant to its consideration of the criteria set out in subsection 672.84(1). 1999, c. 25, s. 12; 2005, c. 22, s. 21; 2014, c. 6, s. 10.**

CROSS-REFERENCES

The terms "accused", "court", "disposition", "high-risk accused", "Review Board" and "verdict of not criminally responsible on account of mental disorder" are defined in s. 672.1. "Victim" is defined in s. 672.5(16) to have the same meaning as in s. 722(4). Section 672.5 sets out the rights of the victim at a disposition hearing. Section 672.542 requires the court or Review Board to consider imposing conditions respecting communication with victim, witness or any other person and any other conditions necessary to ensure the safety and security of those persons.

SYNOPSIS

This section directs the court or Review Board to take into consideration any statement filed by a victim in accordance with s. 672.5(14). This requirement applies at any hearing held that will lead to a disposition or condition under s. 672.54, in deciding whether the accused should be found to be a high-risk offender or whether that finding should be revoked, and at a hearing to determine whether to refer to the court that the accused is a high-risk accused. The statement must be relevant to the issues to be considered.

ADDITIONAL CONDITIONS — SAFETY AND SECURITY.

672.542 When a court or Review Board holds a hearing referred to in section 672.5, the court or Review Board shall consider whether it is desirable, in the interests of the safety and security of any person, particularly a victim of or witness to the offence or a justice system participant, to include as a condition of the disposition that the accused

- **(*a*) abstain from communicating, directly or indirectly, with any victim, witness or other person identified in the disposition, or refrain from going to any place specified in the disposition; or**
- **(*b*) comply with any other condition specified in the disposition that the court or Review Board considers necessary to ensure the safety and security of those persons. 2014, c. 6, s. 10.**

CROSS-REFERENCES

The term "justice system participant" is defined in s. 2. The terms "accused", "court", "disposition", and "Review Board" are defined in s. 672.1. "Victim" is defined in s. 672.5(16) to have the same meaning as in s. 722(4). Other provisions respecting victims under this Part are found in ss. 672.14 and 672.541.

SYNOPSIS

This section requires the court or Review Board, when holding a hearing under s. 672.5, to consider inclusion of conditions in a disposition requiring the accused not to communicate with a victim, witness, justice system participant or other person identified in the disposition or to comply with any other condition necessary to ensure the safety and security of those persons.

TREATMENT NOT A CONDITION.

672.55 (1) No disposition made under section 672.54 shall direct that any psychiatric or other treatment of the accused be carried out or that the accused submit to such treatment except that the disposition may include a condition regarding psychiatric or other treatment where the accused has consented to the condition and the court or Review Board considers the condition to be reasonable and necessary in the interests of the accused. 1991, c. 43, s. 4; 1997, c. 18, s. 86; 2005, c. 22, s. 22.

(2) [*Repealed*, 2005, c. 22, s. 22.]

CROSS-REFERENCES

Pursuant to s. 672.58, the court can issue an order directing that the accused submit to treatment for a period of not more than 90 days, where a verdict of unfit to stand trial has been rendered and the treatment is rendered for the purpose of making the accused fit. Section 672.59 outlines the necessary evidence required to obtain a treatment order and s. 672.61 precludes the use of electro-convulsive therapy or psychosurgery as part of the treatment order. "Electro-convulsive therapy" and "psychosurgery" are defined in s. 672.61(2). The term "unfit to stand trial" is defined in s. 2 of the *Criminal Code*.

SYNOPSIS

The power of the court or Review Board cannot encompass an order for psychiatric or other treatment of the accused or an order requiring the accused to submit to such treatment unless the accused consents and the court or Review Board considers the condition to be reasonable and necessary in the interests of the accused.

ANNOTATIONS

This section does not require the accused him or herself to have the capacity to consent under relevant provincial law to the treatment in the condition. Rather, the section presumes that valid consent to treatment has been, or will be, otherwise obtained. To consent to the condition, the accused must understand all information relevant to the operation of the condition and appreciate the reasonably foreseeable consequences of agreeing to the condition. Generally, this would not require the accused to have insight into his or her medical condition: *Ohenhen (Re)* (2018), 359 C.C.C. (3d) 154 (Ont. C.A.).

DELEGATED AUTHORITY TO VARY RESTRICTIONS ON LIBERTY OF ACCUSED / Exception — high-risk accused / Notice to accused and Review Board of increase in restrictions.

672.56 (1) A Review Board that makes a disposition in respect of an accused under paragraph 672.54(*b*) or (*c*) may delegate to the person in charge of the hospital authority to direct that the restrictions on the liberty of the accused be increased or decreased within any limits and subject to any conditions set out in that disposition, and any direction so made is deemed for the purposes of this Act to be a disposition made by the Review Board.

(1.1) If the accused is a high-risk accused, any direction is subject to the restrictions set out in subsection 672.64(3).

(2) A person who increases the restrictions on the liberty of the accused significantly pursuant to authority delegated to the person by a Review Board shall

(*a*) make a record of the increased restrictions on the file of the accused; and

(*b*) give notice of the increase as soon as is practicable to the accused and, if the increased restrictions remain in force for a period exceeding seven days, to the Review Board. 1991, c. 43, s. 4; 2014, c. 6, s. 11(2).

CROSS-REFERENCES

The terms "accused", "disposition", "hospital" and "Review Board" are defined in s. 672.1. Where the Review Board receives notice of increased restrictions on the accused's liberty for a period of more than seven days, s. 672.81(2)(*a*) requires the board to hold a hearing to review the disposition. For further cross-references as to dispositions, see references under s. 672.54. "High-risk accused" is defined in s. 672.64(1).

SYNOPSIS

The Review Board may direct that the restrictions on the liberty of the accused be increased or decreased where the accused is discharged with conditions or detained in a hospital. Although the facility has the discretion to increase the restrictions on the accused's liberty, these increased restrictions must be recorded and notice must be given to the accused. Where the restrictions remain in force for a period of more than seven days, notice must be provided to the Review Board which, by virtue of s. 672.81(2)(*a*), will be required to hold a review hearing. Finally, if the accused is a high-risk accused, any change in restrictions must comply with s. 672.64(3), which limits the accused's absence from the hospital.

ANNOTATIONS

The purpose of this provision is to act as a final safeguard of liberty, allowing for a second look at restrictions that significantly impact the accused's liberty. Only where the change in liberty status clearly deviates from the accused's prior established liberty norm must the hospital notify the Board, thus triggering a mandatory hearing under s. 672.81(2.1): *Campbell (Re)* (2018), 359 C.C.C. (3d) 466 (Ont. C.A.).

WARRANT OF COMMITTAL.

672.57 Where the court or Review Board makes a disposition under paragraph 672.54(*c*), it shall issue a warrant of committal of the accused, which may be in Form 49. 1991, c. 43, s. 4.

CROSS-REFERENCES

For further references with respect to dispositions, see references under s. 672.54.

SYNOPSIS

This provision requires the issuance of a warrant of committal which may be in Form 49 where the accused is detained in custody by order of the Review Board in a hospital pursuant to s. 672.54(*c*).

TREATMENT DISPOSITION.

672.58 Where a verdict of unfit to stand trial is rendered and the court has not made a disposition under section 672.54 in respect of an accused, the court may, on application by the prosecutor, by order, direct that treatment of the accused be carried out for a specified period not exceeding sixty days, subject to such conditions as the court

considers appropriate and, where the accused is not detained in custody, direct that the accused submit to that treatment by the person or at the hospital specified. 1991, c. 43, s. 4.

CROSS-REFERENCES

The term "unfit to stand trial" and "prosecutor" are defined in s. 2 of the *Criminal Code*. The terms "accused", "court", "disposition" and "hospital" are defined in s. 672.1. A treatment order requires the consent of the person in charge of the hospital treating the accused and the person assigned to treat the accused but does not require the consent of the accused or a person authorized to consent to treatment on the accused's behalf (s. 672.62). The prosecutor must give the accused notice of the application and the accused must be allowed to adduce evidence challenging the application (s. 672.6). The test which must be met and the type of evidence adduced for the court to issue a treatment order is set out in s. 672.59 and requires a medical doctor to have assessed the accused and concluded that: (1) at the time of the assessment, the accused was unfit; (2) the medical or psychiatric treatment will render the accused fit within 60 days; (3) the risk of harm to the accused from the treatment is not disproportionate to the expected benefit; and (4) the treatment is the least restrictive and intrusive method available to render the accused fit to stand trial. The treatment order cannot include the performance of psychosurgery or electro-convulsive therapy which are defined in s. 672.61(2). For further references as to fitness to stand trial, see references under s. 672.23.

SYNOPSIS

Where the issue is the fitness of the accused, the prosecutor may apply to the court for an order directing that the accused submit to treatment for a period not exceeding 60 days whether the accused is or is not in custody. The application for a treatment order must be made subsequent to a verdict of unfit to stand trial but prior to the court making a disposition in the matter.

CRITERIA FOR DISPOSITION / Evidence required.

672.59 (1) No disposition may be made under section 672.58 unless the court is satisfied, on the basis of the testimony of a medical practitioner, that a specific treatment should be administered to the accused for the purpose of making the accused fit to stand trial.

(2) The testimony required by the court for the purposes of subsection (1) shall include a statement that the medical practitioner has made an assessment of the accused and is of the opinion, based on the grounds specified, that

(*a*) the accused, at the time of the assessment, was unfit to stand trial;

(*b*) the psychiatric treatment and any other related medical treatment specified by the medical practitioner will likely make the accused fit to stand trial within a period not exceeding sixty days and that without that treatment the accused is likely to remain unfit to stand trial;

(*c*) the risk of harm to the accused from the psychiatric and other related medical treatment specified is not disproportionate to the benefit anticipated to be derived from it; and

(*d*) the psychiatric and other related medical treatment specified is the least restrictive and least intrusive treatment that could, in the circumstances, be specified for the purpose referred to in subsection (1), considering the opinions referred to in paragraphs (*b*) and (*c*). 1991, c. 43, s. 4.

CROSS-REFERENCES

The term "unfit to stand trial" and "prosecutor" are defined in s. 2 of the *Criminal Code*. The terms "accused", "court", "disposition" and "hospital" are defined in s. 672.1. The application must be brought by the prosecutor and served upon the accused and cannot extend for a period of more than 60 days, see s. 672.58 and 672.6. In addition, a treatment order cannot include electro-convulsive therapy or psychosurgery as defined in s. 672.61(2).

SYNOPSIS

The court may not make a treatment order unless it is satisfied on the basis of medical testimony that the treatment is required to render the accused fit to stand trial. The medical doctor must have assessed the accused and concluded that: (1) at the time of the assessment, the accused was unfit; (2) the medical or psychiatric treatment will render the accused fit within 60 days; (3) the risk of harm to the accused from the treatment is not disproportionate to the expected benefit; and (4) the treatment is the least restrictive and intrusive available to render the accused fit to stand trial.

NOTICE REQUIRED / Challenge by accused.

672.6 (1) The court shall not make a disposition under section 672.58 unless the prosecutor notifies the accused, in writing and as soon as practicable, of the application.

(2) On receiving the notice referred to in subsection (1), the accused may challenge the application and adduce evidence for that purpose. 1991, c. 43, s. 4; 1997, c. 18, s. 87.

CROSS-REFERENCES

As to the application for a treatment order, the prescribed requirements, see ss. 672.58 and 672.59. As to prohibited treatments, see s. 672.61. The court may not issue a treatment order without the consent of the person in charge of the hospital where the accused is to be treated and the person treating the accused, but the accused's consent to treatment is not required. See s. 672.62.

SYNOPSIS

This provision requires that the accused be given notice by the prosecutor of the treatment application and allowed the opportunity to adduce evidence challenging the application.

EXCEPTION / Definitions / "electro-convulsive therapy" / "psychosurgery".

672.61 (1) The court shall not direct, and no disposition made under section 672.58 shall include, the performance of psychosurgery or electro-convulsive therapy or any other prohibited treatment that is prescribed.

(2) In this section,

"electro-convulsive therapy" means a procedure for the treatment of certain mental disorders that induces, by electrical stimulation of the brain, a series of generalized convulsions;

"psychosurgery" means any procedure that by direct or indirect access to the brain removes, destroys or interrupts the continuity of histologically normal brain tissue, or inserts indwelling electrodes for pulsed electrical stimulation for the purpose of altering behaviour or treating psychiatric illness, but does not include neurological procedures used to diagnose or treat intractable physical pain, organic brain conditions, or epilepsy, where any of those conditions is clearly demonstrable. 1991, c. 43, s. 4.

CROSS-REFERENCES

As to the application for a treatment order and the prescribed requirements, see ss. 672.58 and 672.59. The court may not issue a treatment order without the consent of the person in charge of the hospital where the accused is to be treated and the person treating the accused, but the accused's consent to treatment is not required. See. s. 672.62.

SYNOPSIS

This provision outlines the boundaries of a treatment order. The order may not include psychosurgery or electro-convulsive therapy as defined in subsec. (2).

CONSENT OF HOSPITAL REQUIRED FOR TREATMENT / Consent of accused not required for treatment.

672.62 (1) No court shall make a disposition under section 672.58 without the consent of

- **(*a*) the person in charge of the hospital where the accused is to be treated; or**
- **(*b*) the person to whom responsibility for the treatment of the accused is assigned by the court.**

(2) The court may direct that treatment of an accused be carried out pursuant to a disposition made under section 672.58 without the consent of the accused or a person who, according to the laws of the province where the disposition is made, is authorized to consent for the accused. 1991, c. 43, s. 4.

CROSS-REFERENCES

Although the accused's consent is not required, the prosecutor is required to notify the accused of the application and the accused is entitled to challenge the application and adduce evidence to this effect (s. 672.6). Reference should be made to ss. 672.58 and 672.59 which set out the test required to obtain a treatment order. Section 672.61 defines the prohibited treatments of "electro-convulsive therapy" and "psychosurgery".

SYNOPSIS

Treatment orders require the consent of the person in charge of the hospital treating the accused and the person assigned by the court who is responsible for the treatment.

In addition, subsec. (2) clarifies the power of the court to make a treatment order pursuant to s. 672.58 without the consent of the accused or a person authorized to consent to the treatment on behalf of the accused.

ANNOTATIONS

The hospital or person in charge of treatment must consent to all of the terms of a disposition ordering treatment and, if there is no consent, the order cannot be made. Therefore, a court may not make a disposition order directing that treatment begin immediately if the hospital or treating physician does not consent to that disposition, unless the situation is a rare case in which a delay in treatment would breach the accused's rights under the Charter and an order for immediate treatment is an appropriate and just remedy for that breach: *Centre for Addiction and Mental Health v. R.* (2014), 316 C.C.C. (3d) 182 (S.C.C.).

EFFECTIVE DATE OF DISPOSITION.

672.63 A disposition shall come into force on the day on which it is made or on any later day that the court or Review Board specifies in it, and shall remain in force until the Review Board holds a hearing to review the disposition and makes another disposition. 1991, c. 43, s. 4; 2005, c. 22, s. 23.

CROSS-REFERENCES

The terms "disposition" and "Review Board" are defined in s. 672.1. Where no disposition is made by the court, the Review Board must hold a disposition hearing not more than 45 days after the verdict, although the court can extend the time period to a maximum of 90 days. See s. 672.47(1) and (2). Pursuant to s. 672.47(3), a court ordered disposition made under s. 672.54 cannot remain in effect for more than 90 days after which the Review Board is required to hold a hearing to review the disposition. As to review hearings, see ss. 672.81 to 672.85.

SYNOPSIS

A disposition is effective as of the date it is made or any later day that the court or Review Board specifies. The disposition remains in force until the Review Board holds a hearing to review the disposition or makes another disposition.

High-Risk Accused

FINDING / Factors to consider / Detention of high-risk accused / Appeal / For greater certainty.

672.64 (1) On application made by the prosecutor before any disposition to discharge an accused absolutely, the court may, at the conclusion of a hearing, find the accused to be a high-risk accused if the accused has been found not criminally responsible on account of mental disorder for a serious personal injury offence, as defined in subsection 672.81(1.3), the accused was 18 years of age or more at the time of the commission of the offence and

(*a*) the court is satisfied that there is a substantial likelihood that the accused will use violence that could endanger the life or safety of another person; or

(*b*) the court is of the opinion that the acts that constitute the offence were of such a brutal nature as to indicate a risk of grave physical or psychological harm to another person.

(2) In deciding whether to find that the accused is a high-risk accused, the court shall consider all relevant evidence, including

(*a*) the nature and circumstances of the offence;

(*b*) any pattern of repetitive behaviour of which the offence forms a part;

(*c*) the accused's current mental condition;

(*d*) the past and expected course of the accused's treatment, including the accused's willingness to follow treatment; and

(*e*) the opinions of experts who have examined the accused.

(3) If the court finds the accused to be a high-risk accused, the court shall make a disposition under paragraph 672.54(*c*), but the accused's detention must not be subject to any condition that would permit the accused to be absent from the hospital unless

(*a*) it is appropriate, in the opinion of the person in charge of the hospital, for the accused to be absent from the hospital for medical reasons or for any purpose that is necessary for the accused's treatment, if the accused is escorted by a person who is authorized by the person in charge of the hospital; and

(*b*) a structured plan has been prepared to address any risk related to the accused's absence and, as a result, that absence will not present an undue risk to the public.

(4) A decision not to find an accused to be a high-risk accused is deemed to be a disposition for the purpose of sections 672.72 to 672.78.

(5) For greater certainty, a finding that an accused is a high-risk accused is a disposition and sections 672.72 to 672.78 apply to it. 2014, c. 6, s. 12.

CROSS-REFERENCES

The terms "accused", "court", "disposition", "high-risk accused", "Review Board" and "verdict of not criminally responsible on account of mental disorder" are defined in s. 672.1. The term "prosecutor" is defined in s. 2. Under s. 672.81, the review of a disposition of a high-risk accused may be extended to 36 months. Under s. 672.84, the Review Board on a review hearing may refer to the superior court of justice the finding that the accused is a high-risk accused. Under that section, the court may revoke the finding.

SYNOPSIS

This section sets out the process for finding that an accused is a high-risk accused and the limits on the detention of such a person. The application may be made by a prosecutor to a court before any disposition to discharge an accused absolutely if the accused has been found not criminally responsible on account of mental disorder for a serious personal injury offence as defined in s. 672.81, the accused was 18 years of age or more at the time of the commission of the offence, and the court is satisfied that there is a substantial likelihood that the accused will use violence that could endanger the life or safety of another person, or the acts that constitute the offence were of such a brutal nature as to indicate a risk of grave physical or psychological harm to another person. Subsection (2) sets out the evidence to be considered by the court. If the finding of a high-risk accused is made, the court shall make a disposition of detention in a hospital. In addition, the accused's detention must not be subject to any condition that would permit the accused to be absent from hospital unless the circumstances in subsec. (3) are complied with. A decision to not find or find an accused to be a high-risk offender is a disposition that may be appealed in accordance with ss. 672.72 to 672.78.

This provision operates retrospectively to acts committed before it came into force: *R. v. Schoenborn* (2015), 333 C.C.C. (3d) 189 (B.C.S.C.).

"Substantial likelihood" of violence under subsec. (1)(*a*) refers to a level of risk greater than that of "significant threat" in s. 672.5401: *R. v. Schoenborn* (2017), 354 C.C.C. (3d) 393 (B.C.S.C.).

Note: Sections 672.65 and 672.66 and their headings, as enacted by 1991, c. 43, s. 4, have never been brought into force and have since been repealed by 2005, c. 22, s. 24.

Dual Status Offenders

WHERE COURT IMPOSES A SENTENCE / Custodial disposition by court.

672.67 (1) Where a court imposes a sentence of imprisonment on an offender who is, or thereby becomes, a dual status offender, that sentence takes precedence over any prior custodial disposition, pending any placement decision by the Review Board.

(2) Where a court imposes a custodial disposition on an accused who is, or thereby becomes, a dual status offender, the disposition takes precedence over any prior sentence of imprisonment pending any placement decision by the Review Board. 1991, c. 43, s. 4; 1995, c. 22, s. 10; 2005, c. 22, s. 25.

CROSS-REFERENCES

Section 672.1 defines "dual status offender", "court", "hospital", "placement decision", and "Review Board". Note that, at this time, the provisions for making a hospital order are not yet in force.

SYNOPSIS

This section and the following provisions deal with so-called "dual status" offenders being prisoners who are or become subject to sentences of imprisonment as well as custodial dispositions under s. 672.54(*c*) [*i.e.*, detention in a hospital upon a finding of unfitness or a verdict of not criminally responsible]. The effect of this section is that the last disposition be it a sentence of imprisonment or a custodial disposition takes precedence until the Review Board has the opportunity to make the appropriate placement decision under s. 672.68.

DEFINITION OF "MINISTER" / Placement decision by Review Board / Idem / Time for making placement decision / Effects of placement decision.

672.68 (1) In this section and in sections 672.69 and 672.7, "Minister" means the Minister of Public Safety and Emergency Preparedness or the Minister responsible for correctional services of the province to which a dual status offender may be sent pursuant to a sentence of imprisonment.

(2) On application by the Minister or of its own motion, where the Review Board is of the opinion that the place of custody of a dual status offender pursuant to a sentence or custodial disposition made by the court is inappropriate to meet the mental health needs of the offender or to safeguard the well-being of other persons, the Review Board shall, after giving the offender and the Minister reasonable notice, decide whether to place the offender in custody in a hospital or in a prison.

(3) In making a placement decision, the Review Board shall take into consideration

- **(*a*) the need to protect the public from dangerous persons;**
- **(*b*) the treatment needs of the offender and the availability of suitable treatment resources to address those needs;**
- **(*c*) whether the offender would consent to or is a suitable candidate for treatment;**
- **(*d*) any submissions made to the Review Board by the offender or any other party to the proceedings and any assessment report submitted in writing to the Review Board; and**
- **(*e*) any other factors that the Review Board considers relevant.**

(4) The Review Board shall make its placement decision as soon as practicable but not later than thirty days after receiving an application from, or giving notice to, the Minister under subsection (2), unless the Review Board and the Minister agree to a longer period not exceeding sixty days.

(5) Where the offender is detained in a prison pursuant to the placement decision of the Review Board, the Minister is responsible for the supervision and control of the offender. 1991, c. 43, s. 4; 2005, c. 10, s. 34(1)(*f*)(xiii).

CROSS-REFERENCES

The terms "court", "disposition", "dual status offender" and "Review Board" are defined in s. 672.1. Reference should be made to s. 672.69 which authorizes the Review Board to conduct a review of the placement decision on application of the Minister, the dual status offender or on its own motion where there has been a change in circumstances. Note that, although the Minister is responsible for the supervision of the offender while he is detained in prison pursuant to the placement decision of the Review Board, s. 672.69(1) entitles the Review Board to access to any dual status offender for the purpose of conducting a review of the disposition. In addition, the Minister is automatically a party in any proceedings relating to the placement of a dual status offender. See s. 672.69(4).

SYNOPSIS

On application by the Minister or of its own motion, the Review Board has the discretion to make a placement decision where it is of the opinion that the sentence or custodial disposition will not protect the mental health needs of the offender or safeguard other persons. "Minister" is defined to mean any Solicitor General of Canada or the Minister responsible for correctional services in the province in which the dual status offender may be sent pursuant to a sentence of imprisonment [s. 672.68(1)].

The Review Board must consider the following factors in making a placement decision: (1) need to protect the public from dangerous persons; (2) treatment and availability of treatment to the offender; (3) consent of the offender to treatment; (4) whether the offender is a suitable candidate for treatment; (5) submissions by the offender; (6) submissions by other parties; (7) any written assessment report submitted to the board; (8) any other relevant factors. Notice must be provided to the offender and the Minister. The decision is to be rendered within 30 days after receiving the application, although this may be extended to a maximum of 60 days with the consent of the Review Board and the Minister. In addition, subsec. (5) clarifies that the Minister is responsible for the dual status offender while he is detained in prison pursuant to a Review Board placement decision.

MINISTER AND REVIEW BOARD ENTITLED TO ACCESS / Review of placement decisions / Idem / Minister shall be a party.

672.69 (1) The Minister and the Review Board are entitled to have access to any dual status offender in respect of whom a placement decision has been made, for the purpose of conducting a review of the sentence or disposition imposed.

(2) The Review Board shall hold a hearing as soon as is practicable to review a placement decision, on application by the Minister or the dual status offender who is the subject of the decision, where the Review Board is satisfied that a significant change in circumstances requires it.

(3) The Review Board may of its own motion hold a hearing to review a placement decision after giving the Minister and the dual status offender who is subject to it reasonable notice.

(4) The Minister shall be a party in any proceedings relating to the placement of a dual status offender. 1991, c. 43, s. 4.

CROSS-REFERENCES

The terms "dual status offender" and "Review Board" are defined in s. 672.1. "Minister" is defined in s. 672.68(1). Reference should be made to s. 672.68 as to the relevant considerations with respect to a placement decision. For further cross-references with respect to dual status offenders, see references under s. 672.68. Placement decisions are also appealable under s. 672.72 *et seq.*

SYNOPSIS

A placement decision may be reviewed on application by the Minister or the offender where the Review Board is satisfied that there has been a significant change in circumstances. In addition, the Review Board may choose to review the placement decision on its own motion provided that notice is given to the Minister and the dual status offender. Note that the Minister is automatically a party to any proceedings relating to the placement of a dual status offender. The Minister and the Review Board are entitled to access to the dual status offender in order to review the placement decision. The provision does not prescribe any substantive or procedural requirements for the exercise of the Review Board's discretion apart from requiring that the review be conducted "as soon as practicable".

NOTICE OF DISCHARGE / Warrant of committal.

672.7 (1) Where the Minister or the Review Board intends to discharge a dual status offender from custody, each shall give written notice to the other indicating the time, place and conditions of the discharge.

(2) A Review Board that makes a placement decision shall issue a warrant of committal of the accused, which may be in Form 50. 1991, c. 43, s. 4.

CROSS-REFERENCES

The terms "dual status offender" and "Review Board" are defined in s. 672.1. "Minister" is defined in s. 672.68(1). For further cross-references with respect to dual status offenders, see references under s. 672.68.

SYNOPSIS

This provision requires notice to be given to the Minister or the Review Board where either party wishes to discharge the dual status offender from custody.

A warrant of committal must be issued which may be in Form 50 by the Review Board once a placement decision is determined.

DETENTION TO COUNT AS SERVICE OF TERM / Disposition takes precedence over probation orders.

672.71 (1) Each day of detention of a dual status offender pursuant to a placement decision or a custodial disposition shall be treated as a day of service of the term of imprisonment, and the accused shall be deemed, for all purposes, to be lawfully confined in a prison.

(2) When a dual status offender is convicted or discharged on the conditions set out in a probation order made under section 730 in respect of an offence but is not sentenced to a term of imprisonment, the custodial disposition in respect of the accused comes into force and, notwithstanding subsection 732.2(1), takes precedence over any probation order made in respect of the offence. 1991, c. 43, s. 4; 1995, c. 22, s. 10.

CROSS-REFERENCES

The terms "accused", "disposition" and "dual status offender" are defined in s. 672.1. Reference should be made to s. 672.67 which states that in the case of a dual status offender, the latter disposition, whether it be a sentence or a custodial disposition pursuant to s. 672.54(*c*) prevails pending any placement decision by the Review Board. For further cross-references pertaining to dual status offenders, see references under s. 672.68.

SYNOPSIS

Where a dual status offender is detained pursuant either to a placement decision or custodial disposition, each day served in the facility is treated as a day served of the term of imprisonment. If a dual status offender is given a conditional discharge or a suspended sentence, the custodial disposition takes precedence and the probation order is deemed to come into effect after the custodial disposition is completed notwithstanding s. 738(1) which states that a probation order comes into force on the date that the order is made.

Appeals

GROUNDS FOR APPEAL / Limitation period for appeal / Appeal to be heard expeditiously.

672.72 (1) Any party may appeal against a disposition made by a court or a Review Board, or a placement decision made by a Review Board, to the court of appeal of the province where the disposition or placement decision was made on any ground of appeal that raises a question of law or fact alone or of mixed law and fact.

(2) An appellant shall give notice of an appeal against a disposition or placement decision in the manner directed by the applicable rules of court within fifteen days after the day on which the appellant receives a copy of the placement decision or disposition and the reasons for it or within any further time that the court of appeal, or a judge of that court, may direct.

(3) The court of appeal shall hear an appeal against a disposition or placement decision in or out of the regular sessions of the court, as soon as practicable after the day on which the notice of appeal is given, within any period that may be fixed by the court of appeal, a judge of the court of appeal, or the rules of that court. 1991, c. 43, s. 4; 1997, c. 18, s. 88.

CROSS-REFERENCES

The term "court of appeal" is defined in s. 2 of the *Criminal Code*. See s. 672.1 for definition of "disposition", "party" and "Review Board".

Rights of appeal are conferred by the *Criminal Code* which also defines the authority of the court to hear and determine the appeal from a disposition or placement decision by a court or Review Board under s. 672.78. The powers of the court of appeal in respect of disposition or placement orders are defined in s. 672.76. An appeal shall be determined based on the transcript subject to the power of the court to admit any other evidence pursuant to s. 683(1). See s. 672.73. Note also that upon receiving the notice of the appeal, the clerk of the court must notify the court or Review Board responsible for the decision so that all exhibits and other materials are forwarded to the court of appeal. See s. 672.74. In addition to the rights of appeal contained in s. 672.72, the Attorney General has a right of appeal against the dismissal of an application to find the accused is a dangerous mentally disordered accused on a ground of law alone. See s. 672.8. The accused may appeal from a finding that the accused is a dangerous mentally disordered accused and increasing the cap on a question of law, fact or mixed fact and law. See 672.79.

Reference should be made to ss. 672.75 to 672.77 which outline the powers of the court of appeal with respect to the accused pending appeal. Upon filing of the notice of appeal, an absolute discharge or treatment order is automatically stayed subject to the court of appeal's authority to require that the discharge or treatment order be carried out pending the determination of the appeal. See s. 672.75. Where the order is not automatically stayed, any party may apply to the court to stay or enforce a disposition order or placement decision pending the appeal and the court of appeal may require the order to be carried out, suspended and make any other disposition which is appropriate. See s. 672.76. Note that, if the court of appeal simply suspends the disposition or placement order, any disposition, interim release or detention order, that was in place prior to the disposition or placement decision appealed from took effect, is in force. See s. 672.77.

Reference should also be made to s. 672.82 which allows the accused or other party to request that the Review Board review a disposition, however, such a request is deemed to be an abandonment of any appeal against disposition pursuant to s. 672.72. There are no analogous provisions with respect to placement decisions.

SYNOPSIS

Subsection (1) creates a right of appeal from a disposition or placement order by a court or Review Board for *any party* on a question of law, fact or mixed fact and law to the court of appeal. A notice of appeal must be filed within 15 days from the date when the appellant is provided with reasons for the disposition. This period may be extended by the court of appeal or a judge of the court of appeal. The provision requires that the court of appeal must hear the appeal as soon as practicable within any period that is fixed by the court, a judge of the court of appeal or the rules of that court. The effect of this section is that all appeals from dispositions of placement decisions are to the court of appeal, even those made in respect of summary conviction matters. Appeals in respect of the verdict of not criminally responsible and the finding of unfitness, however, follow the normal appeal routes under Parts XXI and XXVII, as the case may be.

ANNOTATIONS

No appeal lies from the decision of the Review Board refusing to make a recommendation for transfer of the accused out of the province pursuant to s. 672.86: *Krueger v. Ontario (Criminal Code Review Board)* (1994), 95 C.C.C. (3d) 88 (Ont. C.A.).

No appeal lies from the decision of the Review Board regarding fitness to stand trial: *R. v. Pare* (2001), 159 C.C.C. (3d) 222 (Ont. C.A.).

A court of appeal has jurisdiction to hear an appeal from a Board decision rendered after a restriction of liberty hearing: *Re Chaudry* (2015), 324 C.C.C. (3d) 281 (Ont. C.A.), leave to appeal to S.C.C. refused 2017 CarswellOnt 1053.

APPEAL ON THE TRANSCRIPT / Additional evidence.

672.73 (1) An appeal against a disposition by a court or Review Board or placement decision by a Review Board shall be based on a transcript of the proceedings and any other evidence that the court of appeal finds necessary to admit in the interests of justice.

(2) For the purpose of admitting additional evidence under this section, subsections 683(1) and (2) apply, with such modifications as the circumstances require. 1991, c. 43, s. 4.

CROSS-REFERENCES

"Court of appeal" is defined in s. 2 of the *Criminal Code*. The terms "court" and "Review Board" are defined in s. 672.1. As to the powers of the court of appeal to admit evidence other than the transcripts, see s. 683(1) and (2). For further cross-references with respect to appeals, see references under s. 672.72.

SYNOPSIS

In most instances, the court will make the determination of the appeal based on the transcript of the proceedings. Note that the appellant must provide the court of appeal and the respondent with a transcript by virtue of s. 672.74(4). The court of appeal, however, has the discretion pursuant to s. 683(1) of the *Criminal Code* to admit any other evidence which is necessary in the interests of justice.

ANNOTATIONS

The admission of fresh evidence "in the interests of justice" in this context includes both justice to the accused and justice to the public whose protection is sought to be assured. It is generally desirable for an appellate court to admit fresh evidence that is trustworthy and touches on the issue of risk to public safety. In addition, appellate courts should provide reasons for the decision to admit or reject fresh evidence: *R. v. Owen*, [2003] 1 S.C.R. 779, 174 C.C.C. (3d) 1.

NOTICE OF APPEAL TO BE GIVEN TO COURT OR REVIEW BOARD / Transmission of records to court of appeal / Record to be kept by court of appeal / Appellant to provide transcript of evidence / Saving.

672.74 (1) The clerk of the court of appeal, on receiving notice of an appeal against a disposition or placement decision, shall notify the court or Review Board that made the disposition.

(2) On receipt of notification under subsection (1), the court or Review Board shall transmit to the court of appeal, before the time that the appeal is to be heard or within any time that the court of appeal or a judge of that court may direct,

(*a*) a copy of the disposition or placement decision;

(*b*) all exhibits filed with the court or Review Board or a copy of them; and

(*c*) all other material in its possession respecting the hearing.

(3) The clerk of the court of appeal shall keep the material referred to in subsection (2) with the records of the court of appeal.

(4) Unless it is contrary to an order of the court of appeal or any applicable rules of court, the appellant shall provide the court of appeal and the respondent with a transcript of any evidence taken before a court or Review Board by a stenographer or a sound recording apparatus, certified by the stenographer or in accordance with subsection 540(6), as the case may be.

(5) An appeal shall not be dismissed by the court of appeal by reasons only that a person other than the appellant failed to comply with this section. 1991, c. 43, s. 4.

CROSS-REFERENCES

For further cross-references with respect to appeals, see references under s. 672.72.

SYNOPSIS

Upon receiving the notice of appeal, the clerk of the court of appeal must notify the court or Review Board responsible for the decision and upon receipt of the notice, the court or Review Board shall forward to the court of appeal a copy of the decision, exhibits and other material with respect to the hearing. The appellant must provide the court of appeal and the respondent with a transcript of the evidence. Non-compliance by a person other than an appellant is not grounds for dismissing the appeal.

AUTOMATIC SUSPENSION OF CERTAIN DISPOSITIONS.

672.75 The filing of a notice of appeal against a disposition made under section 672.58 suspends the application of the disposition pending the determination of the appeal. 1991, c. 43, s. 4; 2014, c. 6, s. 13.

CROSS-REFERENCES

"Court of appeal" is defined in s. 2. "Court", "disposition" and "Review Board" are defined in s. 672.1. Reference should also be had to s. 672.76 allowing any party to apply to the court to stay or enforce a disposition order or placement disposition pending an appeal. In addition, where a disposition or placement decision is suspended, any pre-existing dispositions, detention orders or interim release orders are deemed to be in effect by virtue of s. 672.77. For further cross-references respecting appeals, see references under s. 672.72.

SYNOPSIS

A treatment order pursuant to s. 672.58 is automatically stayed upon filing of a notice of appeal. Notwithstanding this provision, however, the Court of Appeal has the authority pursuant to s. 672.76(2)(*a*) to require that treatment order be carried out pending the determination of the appeal.

APPLICATION RESPECTING DISPOSITIONS UNDER APPEAL / Discretionary powers respecting suspension of dispositions / Copy of order to parties.

672.76 (1) Any party who gives notice to each of the other parties, within the time and in the manner prescribed, may apply to a judge of the court of appeal for an order under this section respecting a disposition or placement decision that is under appeal.

(2) On receipt of an application made pursuant to subsection (1) a judge of the court of appeal may, if satisfied that the mental condition of the accused justifies it,

(*a*) by order, direct that a disposition made under section 672.58 be carried out pending the determination of the appeal, notwithstanding section 672.75;

(*a*.1) by order, direct that a disposition made under paragraph 672.54(*a*) be suspended pending the determination of the appeal;

(*b*) by order, direct that the application of a placement decision or a disposition made under paragraph 672.54(*b*) or (*c*) be suspended pending the determination of the appeal;

(*c*) where the application of a disposition is suspended pursuant to section 672.75 or paragraph (*b*), make any other disposition in respect of the accused that is appropriate in the circumstances, other than a disposition under paragraph 672.54(*a*) or section 672.58, pending the determination of the appeal;

(*d*) where the application of a placement decision is suspended pursuant to an order made under paragraph (*b*), make any other placement decision that is appropriate in the circumstances, pending the determination of the appeal; and

(*e*) give any directions that the judge considers necessary for expediting the appeal.

(3) A judge of the court of appeal who makes an order under this section shall send a copy of the order to each of the parties without delay. 1991, c. 43, s. 4; 2014, c. 6, s. 14.

CROSS-REFERENCES

"Court" and "disposition" defined in s. 672.1. Reference should be made to s. 672.75 providing for an automatic stay of an absolute discharge subsequent to a verdict of not criminally responsible on account of mental disorder or a treatment order. For further cross-references respecting appeals, see references under s. 672.72.

SYNOPSIS

Where the treatment order is not automatically stayed pursuant to s. 672.75, any party may apply to a judge of the Court of Appeal to stay enforcement of the order pending appeal. The judge may also direct that a disposition of an absolute discharge under s. 672.54(*a*) be suspending pending the appeal. The judge may, if satisfied that the mental condition of the accused so justifies, do any of the following: (1) order that a treatment order under s. 672.58 be carried out notwithstanding s. 672.75; (2) suspend a placement decision or a disposition made under s. 672.54(*a*), (*b*) or (*c*) until the determination of the appeal; (3) make any other disposition or placement decision (with some exceptions) where the disposition or placement decision is suspended pending appeal; or (4) give directions expediting the appeal. Copies of the order must be given to all parties without delay.

ANNOTATIONS

This provision is intended to suspend dispositions in light of changes in circumstances that may make compliance with an earlier disposition pending appeal inappropriate. Before suspending a disposition, the court must be satisfied that the mental condition of the accused justifies it and the moving party bears the burden of proof: *Penetanguishene Mental Health Centre (Administrator) v. Ontario (Attorney General)* (2001), 154 C.C.C. (3d) 187, 142 O.A.C. 244 (C.A.).

EFFECT OF SUSPENSION OF DISPOSITION.

672.77 Where the application of a disposition or placement decision appealed from is suspended, a disposition, or in the absence of a disposition any order for the interim release or detention of the accused, that was in effect immediately before the disposition or placement decision appealed from took effect, shall be in force pending the determination of the appeal, subject to any disposition made under paragraph 672.76(2)(*c*). 1991, c. 43, s. 4.

CROSS-REFERENCES

For further cross-references relating to appeals, see references under s. 672.72.

SYNOPSIS

Where a disposition or placement decision is suspended and no order for the interim release or detention of the accused is issued by the court of appeal, any disposition, interim release or detention order, that was in place prior to the disposition or placement decision appealed from took effect, is in force.

ANNOTATIONS

A suspension should be granted only in extraordinary or rare circumstances. There must be compelling evidence that demonstrates that the Board's decision is unsound or invalid. The onus is on the moving party to meet these requirements: *Northeast Mental Health Centre v. Rogers* (2007), 287 C.C.C. (3d) 389 (Ont. C.A. [In Chambers]).

POWERS OF COURT OF APPEAL / Idem / Orders that the court may make.

672.78 (1) The court of appeal may allow an appeal against a disposition or placement decision and set aside an order made by the court or Review Board, where the court of appeal is of the opinion that

(*a*) it is unreasonable or cannot be supported by the evidence;

(*b*) it is based on a wrong decision on a question of law; or

(*c*) there was a miscarriage of justice.

(2) The court of appeal may dismiss an appeal against a disposition or placement decision where the court is of the opinion

(*a*) that paragraphs (1)(*a*), (*b*) and (*c*) do not apply; or

(*b*) that paragraph (1)(*b*) may apply, but the court finds that no substantial wrong or miscarriage of justice has occurred.

(3) Where the court of appeal allows an appeal against a disposition or placement decision, it may

(*a*) make any disposition under section 672.54 or any placement decision that the Review Board could have made;

(*b*) refer the matter back to the court or Review Board for rehearing, in whole or in part, in accordance with any directions that the court of appeal considers appropriate; or

(*c*) make any other order that justice requires. 1991, c. 43, s. 4; 1997, c. 18, s. 89.

CROSS-REFERENCES

"Court of appeal" is defined in s. 2. The terms "court", "disposition" and "Review Board" are defined in s. 672.1. For further cross-references respecting appeals, see references under s. 672.72.

SYNOPSIS

This provision sets out the powers of the court of appeal with respect to a disposition or placement decision and incorporates the appeal powers contained in the *Criminal Code*. The court may set aside the order on the grounds that it is unreasonable and cannot be supported by evidence, is based on a mistake of law or there was a miscarriage of justice. Alternatively, the court may dismiss the appeal where these conditions are not met or where there is no substantial wrong or miscarriage of justice. If the court allows the appeal, it may make any disposition or placement decision that is appropriate, order a new hearing in the court or Review Board or make any other order that justice requires.

ANNOTATIONS

While there are some parallels with the unreasonable verdict test in s. 686, the appellate standard of review of a board decision should not be raised higher than reasonableness *simpliciter*. The appellate court should consider whether the board's risk assessment and disposition order was unreasonable in the sense of not being supported by reasons that can bear even a somewhat probing examination. The medical expertise and generalized knowledge of the board mandate deference. If the board's decision could reasonably be the subject of disagreement among board members properly informed of the facts and instructed on the applicable law, the court should generally decline to intervene: *R. v. Owen*, [2003] 1 S.C.R. 779, 174 C.C.C. (3d) 1.

In determining whether a disposition by the board is unreasonable, the Court of Appeal must recognize that the board enjoys several advantages not available on appellate review especially as a result of the board's special medical expertise and knowledge of the various facilities available within the mental health system *Peckham v. Ontario (Attorney General)*

(1994), 93 C.C.C. (3d) 443, 34 C.R. (4th) 227, 19 O.R. (3d) 766 (C.A.), leave to appeal to S.C.C. refused 94 C.C.C. (3d) vi, 37 C.R. (4th) 399*n*.

See also: *Penetanguishene Mental Health Centre v. Ontario (Attorney General)* (1999), 131 C.C.C. (3d) 473, 116 O.A.C. 291 (C.A.).

Whether or not the Review Board is a court of competent jurisdiction for the purposes of the *Canadian Charter of Rights and Freedoms* and s. 52 of the *Constitution Act, 1982*, on appeal from a disposition by the board, the Court of Appeal had jurisdiction to deal with constitutional issues and, pursuant to subsec. (3)(*c*), the ability to fashion an appropriate remedy: *R. v. Hoeppner* (1999), 25 C.R. (5th) 91, 193 W.A.C. 163 (Man. C.A.).

672.79 [*Repealed*, 2005, c. 22, s. 26].

672.8 [*Repealed*, 2005, c. 22, s. 26.]

Review of Dispositions

MANDATORY REVIEW OF DISPOSITIONS / Extension on consent / Extension for serious personal violence offence / Definition of "serious personal injury offence" / Extension on consent — high-risk accused / Extension — no likely improvement / Notice / Appeal / Additional mandatory reviews in custody cases / Review in case of increase on restrictions on liberty / Idem.

672.81 (1) A Review Board shall hold a hearing not later than twelve months after making a disposition and every twelve months thereafter for as long as the disposition remains in force, to review any disposition that it has made in respect of an accused, other than an absolute discharge under paragraph 672.54(*a*).

(1.1) Despite subsection (1), the Review Board may extend the time for holding a hearing to a maximum of twenty-four months after the making or reviewing of a disposition if the accused is represented by counsel and the accused and the Attorney General consent to the extension.

(1.2) Despite subsection (1), at the conclusion of a hearing under this section the Review Board may, after making a disposition, extend the time for holding a subsequent hearing under this section to a maximum of twenty-four months if

(*a*) the accused has been found not criminally responsible for a serious personal injury offence;

(*b*) the accused is subject to a disposition made under paragraph 672.54(*c*); and

(*c*) the Review Board is satisfied on the basis of any relevant information, including disposition information within the meaning of subsection 672.51(1) and an assessment report made under an assessment ordered under paragraph 672.121(*a*), that the condition of the accused is not likely to improve and that detention remains necessary for the period of the extension.

(1.3) For the purposes of subsection (1.2), "serious personal injury offence" means

(*a*) an indictable offence involving

(i) the use or attempted use of violence against another person, or

(ii) conduct endangering or likely to endanger the life or safety of another person or inflicting or likely to inflict severe psychological damage upon another person; or

(*b*) an indictable offence referred to in section 151, 152, 153, 153.1, 155, 160, 170, 171, 172, 271, 272 or 273 or an attempt to commit such an offence.

(1.31) Despite subsections (1) to (1.2), the Review Board may extend the time for holding a hearing in respect of a high-risk accused to a maximum of 36 months after making or reviewing a disposition if the accused is represented by counsel and the accused and the Attorney General consent to the extension.

(1.32) Despite subsections (1) to (1.2), at the conclusion of a hearing under subsection 672.47(4) or this section in respect of a high-risk accused, the Review Board may, after making a disposition, extend the time for holding a subsequent hearing under this section to a maximum of 36 months if the Review Board is satisfied on the basis of any relevant information, including disposition information as defined in subsection 672.51(1) and an assessment report made under an assessment ordered under paragraph 672.121(*c*), that the accused's condition is not likely to improve and that detention remains necessary for the period of the extension.

(1.4) If the Review Board extends the time for holding a hearing under subsection (1.2) or (1.32), it shall provide notice of the extension to the accused, the prosecutor and the person in charge of the hospital where the accused is detained.

(1.5) A decision by the Review Board to extend the time for holding a hearing under subsection (1.2) or (1.32) is deemed to be a disposition for the purpose of sections 672.72 to 672.78.

(2) The Review Board shall hold a hearing to review any disposition made under paragraph 672.54(*b*) or (*c*) as soon as practicable after receiving notice that the person in charge of the place where the accused is detained or directed to attend requests the review.

(2.1) The Review Board shall hold a hearing to review a decision to significantly increase the restrictions on the liberty of the accused, as soon as practicable after receiving the notice referred to in subsection 672.56(2).

(3) Where an accused is detained in custody pursuant to a disposition made under paragraph 672.54(*c*) and a sentence of imprisonment is subsequently imposed on the accused in respect of another offence, the Review Board shall hold a hearing to review the disposition as soon as is practicable after receiving notice of that sentence. 1991, c. 43, s. 4; 2005, c. 22, s. 27(2); 2014, c. 6, s. 15.

CROSS-REFERENCES

The terms "disposition" and "Review Board" are defined in s. 672.71. The term "high-risk accused" is defined in s. 672.1. An application to refer to a superior court of justice a finding that the accused is a high-risk accused may be made under s. 672.84. Reference should be made to s. 672.93 which requires the Review Board to review the disposition where the accused has been arrested as a result of a breach of a disposition or any condition of the disposition. The Review Board sitting in review of a prior disposition is empowered to make any other disposition or variation that is considered appropriate. See s. 672.83. The procedural rules for disposition hearings contained in s. 672.5 apply to review hearings. Note that, although any party may request the review of a disposition, the request is deemed to be an abandonment of any pending appeal by the party against the disposition. See s. 672.82.

SYNOPSIS

This section deals with the review of dispositions. Pursuant to subsec. (1), the Review Board must conduct a review hearing every 12 months that the disposition remains in force subject to the accused being absolutely discharged. However, under subsec. (1.1), if the accused has counsel and the accused and the prosecutor consent, the Review Board may extend the time for holding a hearing for up to 24 months. Under subsec. (1.2), the Review Board may also extend the time for up to 24 months if the accused has been found not criminally responsible for a serious personal injury offence, the accused is subject to a detention order under s. 672.54(*c*) and the board is satisfied that the condition of the accused is not likely to improve and that detention remains necessary for the period of the detention.

Subsection (1.3) defines the term "personal injury offence". Subsection (1.31) allows the Review Board to extend the time for holding a hearing in respect of a high-risk accused to 36 months if the accused is represented by counsel, and the accused and the Attorney General consent to the extensions. Further, under subsec. (1.32), where a disposition in relation to a high-risk offender has been made by a court under s. 672.64(3) or this section, the Review Board may extend the time for the next hearing for up to 36 months if the Review Board is satisfied on the basis of evidence referred to in this subsection that the accused's condition is not likely to improve and that detention remains necessary for the period of the extension. Under subsec. (1.4), the Review Board is required to give notice to the accused, the prosecutor and the person in charge of the hospital of its decision to extend the time for holding a hearing under subsec. (1.2). Pursuant to subsec. (1.5), a decision to extend the time under subsec. (1.2) or (1.32) is deemed to be a disposition for appeal purposes.

The Review Board is also required to hold a review hearing as soon as is practicable subsequent to receiving notice where the place that the accused is detained has significantly increased restrictions on the liberty of the accused for more than seven days, or where the hospital requests a review.

ANNOTATIONS

Any disposition made under this section must be made applying the criteria and scheme created by s. 672.54: *Pinet v. Ontario* (1995), 100 C.C.C. (3d) 343 (Ont. C.A.).

Failure to comply with the 12 months' requirement, while allowing for other remedies to compel the hearing to take place, does not deprive the board of jurisdiction to hold a hearing and make any further dispositions: *Runnalls v. Ontario* (2007), 217 C.C.C. (3d) 515 (Ont. C.A.).

Nor does failure to hold the hearing within the statutory time frame necessarily infringe the accused's s. 7 Charter rights: *Re Starz* (2015), 324 C.C.C. (3d) 228 (Ont. C.A.), leave to appeal to S.C.C. refused 2017 CarswellOnt 1014.

Confinement pursuant to the *Mental Health Act*, R.S.O. 1990, c. M.7, was not a restriction on liberty made pursuant to any authority delegated to hospital personnel by the Review Board and is not subject to the requirement of subsec. (2.1): *Centre for Addiction and Mental Health v. Young* (2011), 273 C.C.C. (3d) 512 (Ont. C.A.).

Where no appeal was filed by the hospital or Crown from the board's order of discharge, it was not an abuse of process for the hospital to request an early review of the disposition pursuant to subsec. (2). The scheme is intended to allow the board to respond quickly to changing circumstances: *Re Katzav* (2013), 311 C.C.C. (3d) 413 (Ont. C.A.).

DISCRETIONARY REVIEW / Review Board to provide notice / Review cancels appeal.

672.82 (1) A Review Board may hold a hearing to review any of its dispositions at any time, of its own motion or at the request of the accused or any other party.

(1.1) Where a Review Board holds a hearing under subsection (1) of its own motion, it shall provide notice to the prosecutor, the accused and any other party.

(2) Where a party requests a review of a disposition under this section, the party is deemed to abandon any appeal against the disposition taken under section 672.72. 1991, c. 43, s. 4; 2005, c. 22, s. 28.

CROSS-REFERENCES

The terms "accused", "disposition", "party" and "Review Board" are defined in s. 672.1. As to appeals from dispositions, see s. 672.72. For further cross-references respecting review hearings, see references under s. 672.81.

SYNOPSIS

An accused or other party may request that the Review Board review the disposition at any time. A request for a review of a disposition, however, is deemed to be an abandonment of any appeal against disposition pursuant to s. 672.72. The board may also on its own motion decide to hold a review hearing, in which case it must give notice to the accused, the prosecutor and any other party.

DISPOSITION BY REVIEW BOARD.

672.83 (1) At a hearing held pursuant to section 672.81 or 672.82, the Review Board shall, except where a determination is made under subsection 672.48(1) that the accused is fit to stand trial, review the disposition made in respect of the accused and make any other disposition that the Review Board considers to be appropriate in the circumstances. 1991, c. 43, s. 4; 1997, c. 18, s. 90; 2005, c. 43, s. 29.

(2) [*Repealed*, 2005, c. 22, s. 29.]

CROSS-REFERENCES

The term "unfit to stand trial" is defined in s. 2. The terms "Review Board" and "disposition" are defined in s. 672.1. Reference should be made to ss. 672.52(2), 672.64, 672.71 and 672.82. Reference should also be made to s. 672.48(1) which requires a Review Board which holds a hearing to review a disposition in respect of an accused who has been found unfit to stand trial to determine whether the accused is not fit. Where the accused is found fit to stand trial, the accused shall be sent back to court to try the issue.

In making a disposition under this section, the Review Board is to apply the provisions of s. 672.54.

SYNOPSIS

Except where the accused is determined to be fit to stand trial, the Review Board sitting in review of a prior disposition is empowered to make any other disposition or variation that is considered appropriate.

REVIEW OF FINDING — HIGH-RISK ACCUSED / Review of finding — high-risk accused / Review of finding by court / Hearing and disposition / Review of conditions / Appeal.

672.84 (1) If a Review Board holds a hearing under section 672.81 or 672.82 in respect of a high-risk accused, it shall, on the basis of any relevant information, including disposition information as defined in subsection 672.51(1) and an assessment report made under an assessment ordered under paragraph 672.121(*c*), if it is satisfied that there is not a substantial likelihood that the accused — whether found to be a high-risk accused under paragraph 672.64(1)(*a*) or (*b*) — will use violence that could endanger the life or safety of another person, refer the finding for review to the superior court of criminal jurisdiction.

(2) If the Review Board is not so satisfied, it shall review the conditions of detention imposed under paragraph 672.54(*c*), subject to the restrictions set out in subsection 672.64(3).

(3) If the Review Board refers the finding to the superior court of criminal jurisdiction for review, the court shall, at the conclusion of a hearing, revoke the finding if the court is satisfied that there is not a substantial likelihood that the accused will use violence that could endanger the life or safety of another person, in which case the court or the Review Board shall make a disposition under any of paragraphs 672.54(*a*) to (*c*).

(4) Any disposition referred to in subsection (3) is subject to sections 672.45 to 672.47 as if the revocation is a verdict.

(5) If the court does not revoke the finding, it shall immediately send to the Review Board, in original or copied form, a transcript of the hearing, any other document or information related to the hearing, and all exhibits filed with it, if the transcript, document, information or exhibits are in its possession. The Review Board shall, as soon

as practicable but not later than 45 days after the day on which the court decides not to revoke the finding, hold a hearing and review the conditions of detention imposed under paragraph 672.54(*c*), subject to the restrictions set out in subsection 672.64(3).

(6) A decision under subsection (1) about referring the finding to the court for review and a decision under subsection (3) about revoking the finding are deemed to be dispositions for the purpose of sections 672.72 to 672.78. 2014, c. 6, s. 16.

CROSS-REFERENCES

The term "superior court of jurisdiction" is defined in s. 2. The terms "assessment", "disposition", "high-risk accused" and "Review Board" are defined in s. 672.71. If the Review Board refers to the court for review under this section, s. 672.5(13.3) requires the Review Board to notify every victim of the offence that they are entitled to file a statement with the court.

SYNOPSIS

This section sets out the procedure where the Review Board can initiate a process for reviewing a finding that the accused is a high-risk accused. If the Review Board holds a mandatory or discretionary review under either s. 672.81 or s. 672.82 in respect of a high-risk accused and is satisfied based on the information set out in subsec. (1) that there is not a substantial likelihood that the accused will use violence that could endanger the life or safety of another person, it can refer the finding for review to the superior court of criminal jurisdiction. If the Review Board is not satisfied, it holds a review of the conditions of detention under s. 672.54(*c*) subject to the restrictions on absence from the hospital as set out in s. 672.64(3). If the Review Board refers the matter to the superior court of criminal jurisdiction for review, the court shall revoke the finding if the court is satisfied that there is not a substantial likelihood that the accused will use violence that could endanger the life or safety of another person, in which case the court or the Review Board can make a disposition under s. 672.54. Any disposition is subject to the provisions in ss. 672.45 to 672.47, which deal with disposition hearings. If the court does not revoke the finding, it is required to send its materials, including a transcript of the hearing, to the Review Board. The Review Board under subsec. (5) is required to hold a hearing and review the conditions of detention, subject to the restrictions set out in s. 672.64(3). Referring the finding to the court for review and a decision made under subsec. (3) about revoking the finding of high-risk accused are dispositions for the purpose of appeals.

Power to Compel Appearance

BRINGING ACCUSED BEFORE REVIEW BOARD.

672.85 For the purpose of bringing the accused in respect of whom a hearing is to be held before the Review Board, including in circumstances in which the accused did not attend a previous hearing in contravention of a summons or warrant, the chairperson

(*a*) shall order the person having custody of the accused to bring the accused to the hearing at the time and place fixed for it; or

(*b*) may, if the accused is not in custody, issue a summons or warrant to compel the accused to appear at the hearing at the time and place fixed for it. 1991, c. 43, s. 4; 2005, c. 22, ss. 31 (heading) and 32.

CROSS-REFERENCES

The terms "accused", "chairperson" and "Review Board" are defined in s. 672.1. For further cross-references as to review of dispositions, see references under s. 672.81.

SYNOPSIS

The chairperson of the Review Board must compel the accused to attend court either by ordering the person having custody of the accused to bring the accused forth or by issuing a summons or warrant to the accused where the accused is not in custody.

Stay of Proceedings

RECOMMENDATION BY REVIEW BOARD / Notice / Inquiry / Court may act on own motion / Assessment order / Application / Stay / Proper administration of justice / Effect of stay.

672.851 (1) The Review Board may, of its own motion, make a recommendation to the court that has jurisdiction in respect of the offence charged against an accused found unfit to stand trial to hold an inquiry to determine whether a stay of proceedings should be ordered if

(*a*) the Review Board has held a hearing under section 672.81 or 672.82 in respect of the accused; and

(*b*) on the basis of any relevant information, including disposition information within the meaning of subsection 672.51(1) and an assessment report made under an assessment ordered under paragraph 672.121(*a*), the Review Board is of the opinion that

(i) the accused remains unfit to stand trial and is not likely to ever become fit to stand trial, and

(ii) the accused does not pose a significant threat to the safety of the public.

(2) If the Review Board makes a recommendation to the court to hold an inquiry, the Review Board shall provide notice to the accused, the prosecutor and any party who, in the opinion of the Review Board, has a substantial interest in protecting the interests of the accused.

(3) As soon as practicable after receiving the recommendation referred to in subsection (1), the court may hold an inquiry to determine whether a stay of proceedings should be ordered.

(4) A court may, of its own motion, conduct an inquiry to determine whether a stay of proceedings should be ordered if the court is of the opinion, on the basis of any relevant information, that

(*a*) the accused remains unfit to stand trial and is not likely to ever become fit to stand trial; and

(*b*) the accused does not pose a significant threat to the safety of the public.

(5) If the court holds an inquiry under subsection (3) or (4), it shall order an assessment of the accused.

(6) Section 672.51 applies to an inquiry of the court under this section.

(7) The court may, on completion of an inquiry under this section, order a stay of proceedings if it is satisfied

(*a*) on the basis of clear information, that the accused remains unfit to stand trial and is not likely to ever become fit to stand trial;

(*b*) that the accused does not pose a significant threat to the safety of the public; and

(*c*) that a stay is in the interests of the proper administration of justice.

(8) In order to determine whether a stay of proceedings is in the interests of the proper administration of justice, the court shall consider any submissions of the prosecutor, the accused and all other parties and the following factors:

(*a*) the nature and seriousness of the alleged offence;

(*b*) the salutary and deleterious effects of the order for a stay of proceedings, including any effect on public confidence in the administration of justice;
(*c*) the time that has elapsed since the commission of the alleged offence and whether an inquiry has been held under section 672.33 to decide whether sufficient evidence can be adduced to put the accused on trial; and
(*d*) any other factor that the court considers relevant.

(9) If a stay of proceedings is ordered by the court, any disposition made in respect of the accused ceases to have effect. If a stay of proceedings is not ordered, the finding of unfit to stand trial and any disposition made in respect of the accused remain in force, until the Review Board holds a disposition hearing and makes a disposition in respect of the accused under section 672.83. 2005, c. 22, s. 33.

CROSS-REFERENCES

"Accused" and "Review Board" are defined in s. 672.1. The term "unfit to stand trial" is defined in s. 2. Section 579 sets out the statutory power of the Attorney General to stay charges. The Review Board may order an assessment under s. 672.121 for the purposes of making a recommendation to the court under this section. An appeal from an order staying proceedings lies to the Court of Appeal in accordance with s. 672.852.

SYNOPSIS

This section, enacted in response to *R. v. Demers*, [2004] 2 S.C.R. 489, 185 C.C.C. (3d) 257, sets out the procedure for a court staying proceedings against an unfit accused. Under subsec. (1), the Review Board may make a recommendation to the court to hold an inquiry to determine whether the proceedings should be stayed because the accused is not likely to ever become fit and does not pose a significant threat to the safety of the public. If the Review Board makes such a recommendation, it is to give notice to the accused, the prosecutor and other affected parties in accordance with subsec. (2). The court may then hold a hearing under subsec. (3). Alternatively, the court itself may initiate the process pursuant to subsec. (4). In either case, it is to order an assessment pursuant to subsec. (5). The court may order a stay of proceedings where the criteria in subsec. (7) are met because there is clear evidence that the accused will not likely ever become fit, the accused does not pose a significant threat to the public and a stay is in the interest of the proper administration of justice. The factors to be considered as to the proper administration of justice are set out in subsec. (8). The effect of the stay as set out in subsec. (9) is that any disposition in respect of the accused ceases to have effect. (The stay would, of course, have the effect of staying the proceedings on the underlying charge.)

APPEAL / Effect.

672.852 (1) The Court of Appeal may allow an appeal against an order made under subsection 672.851(7) for a stay of proceedings, if the Court of Appeal is of the opinion that the order is unreasonable or cannot be supported by the evidence.

(2) If the Court of Appeal allows the appeal, it may set aside the order for a stay of proceedings and restore the finding that the accused is unfit to stand trial and the disposition made in respect of the accused. 2005, c. 22, s. 33.

CROSS-REFERENCES

"Court of appeal" and "unfit to stand trial" are defined in s. 2. Section 676 gives the Attorney General the right to appeal against an order of a trial court that stays proceedings on an indictment.

SYNOPSIS

This section sets out the powers of the Court of Appeal where an appeal is taken from a stay of proceedings ordered under s. 672.851. The appeal may be allowed on the basis that the order is unreasonable or cannot be supported by the evidence. If the court of appeal allows the appeal, it may set aside the stay of proceedings and restore the finding of unfitness.

Interprovincial Transfers

INTERPROVINCIAL TRANSFERS / Transfer where accused in custody / Transfer if accused not in custody / Order.

672.86 (1) An accused who is detained in custody or directed to attend at a hospital pursuant to a disposition made by a court or Review Board under paragraph 672.54(*c*) or a court under section 672.58 may be transferred to any other place in Canada where

(*a*) the Review Board of the province where the accused is detained or directed to attend recommends a transfer for the purpose of the reintegration of the accused into society or the recovery, treatment or custody of the accused; and

(*b*) the Attorney General of the province to which the accused is being transferred, or an officer authorized by that Attorney General, and the Attorney General of the province from which the accused is being transferred, or an officer authorized by that Attorney General, give their consent.

(2) Where an accused who is detained in custody is to be transferred, an officer authorized by the Attorney General of the province where the accused is being detained shall sign a warrant specifying the place in Canada to which the accused is to be transferred.

(2.1) An accused who is not detained in custody may be transferred to any other place in Canada where

(*a*) the Review Board of the province from which the accused is being transferred recommends a transfer for the purpose of the reintegration of the accused into society or the recovery or treatment of the accused; and

(*b*) the Attorney General of the province to which the accused is being transferred, or an officer authorized by that Attorney General, and the Attorney General of the province from which the accused is being transferred, or an officer authorized by that Attorney General, give their consent.

(3) Where an accused is being transferred in accordance with subsection (2.1), the Review Board of the province from which the accused is being transferred shall, by order,

(*a*) direct that the accused be taken into custody and transferred pursuant to a warrant under subsection (2); or

(*b*) direct that the accused attend at a specified place in Canada, subject to any conditions that the Review Board of the province to or from which the accused is being transferred considers appropriate. 1991, c. 43, s. 4; 2005, c. 22, s. 34.

CROSS-REFERENCES

"Attorney General" is defined in s. 2. The terms "accused", "court", "hospital", and "Review Board" are defined in s. 672.1. As to inter-provincial jurisdiction of the Review Boards over the accused, the Attorneys General of the two provinces may enter an agreement allowing the Review Board of the province from which the accused has been transferred to retain jurisdiction. In addition, where the accused is transferred to another province other than by virtue of s. 672.86, such as where the accused is a dual status offender and offences occurred in different provinces, the Review Board from which the accused is transferred has exclusive jurisdiction over the accused. See s. 672.89. Similar to s. 672.88, the Attorneys General may derogate from this provision by agreement. Pursuant to s. 672.87, a warrant signed by the Attorney General constitutes sufficient authority for the person in charge of the accused to transfer the accused and for the person specified in the warrant to take charge of the accused.

SYNOPSIS

An accused who is detained in custody or directed to attend at a hospital may be transferred to another province on the recommendation of the Review Board, where the transfer is necessary for the purpose of the accused's reintegration into society, recovery, treatment or custody of the accused. However, where the accused is in custody, the transfer requires the consent of the Attorneys General of both the province from which and to which the accused is being transferred. The Attorney General in the province from where the accused is to be transferred must sign a warrant specifying the place of transfer where the accused is in custody. If the accused is not in custody, the consent of the Attorneys General or their authorized officers is required. In such cases, the Review Board will direct that the accused be taken into custody and transferred or direct the accused to attend at the specified place subject to any conditions that are appropriate.

DELIVERY AND DETENTION OF ACCUSED.

672.87 A warrant described in subsection 672.86(2) is sufficient authority

(*a*) for any person who is responsible for the custody of an accused to have the accused taken into custody and conveyed to the person in charge of the place specified in the warrant; and

(*b*) for the person specified in the warrant to detain the accused in accordance with any disposition made in respect of the accused under paragraph 672.54(*c*). 1991, c. 43, s. 4.

CROSS-REFERENCES

"Attorney General" is defined in s. 2. The terms "accused", "court", "hospital", and "Review Board" are defined in s. 672.1. As to further cross-references respecting interprovincial transfers, see references under s. 672.86.

SYNOPSIS

A warrant signed by the Attorney General constitutes sufficient authority for the person in charge of the accused's custody to convey the accused to the person in charge of the place specified in the warrant and for the person specified in the warrant to detain the accused in accordance with any disposition outstanding against the accused.

REVIEW BOARD OF RECEIVING PROVINCE / Agreement.

672.88 (1) The Review Board of the province to which an accused is transferred under section 672.86 has exclusive jurisdiction over the accused, and may exercise the powers and shall perform the duties mentioned in sections 672.5 and 672.81 to 672.84 as if that Review Board had made the disposition in respect of the accused.

(2) Notwithstanding subsection (1), the Attorney General of the province to which an accused is transferred may enter into an agreement subject to this Act with the Attorney General of the province from which the accused is transferred, enabling the Review Board of that province to exercise the powers and perform the duties referred to in subsection (1) in respect of the accused, in the circumstances and subject to the terms and conditions set out in the agreement. 1991, c. 43, s. 4; 2014, c. 6, s. 17.

CROSS-REFERENCES

"Attorney General" is defined in s. 2. The terms "accused", "court", "hospital", and "Review Board" are defined in s. 672.1. Note that where the accused is transferred to another province other than by virtue of s. 672.86, for example, where the accused is a dual status offender and the offences occurred in different provinces, the Review Board from which the accused is transferred has exclusive jurisdiction over the accused. The Attorneys General may, however, enter into an agreement to transfer jurisdiction to the receiving Review Board. As to further cross-references respecting interprovincial transfers, see references under s. 672.86.

SYNOPSIS

This provision confers exclusive jurisdiction over the accused to the Review Board of the province to which the accused has been transferred. This general power, however, may be superseded by the agreement of the Attorney General of the province to which the accused has been transferred and the Attorney General from which the accused has been transferred. The Attorneys General may enter into an agreement authorizing the Review Board from which the accused has been transferred to retain jurisdiction over the accused.

OTHER INTERPROVINCIAL TRANSFERS / Agreement.

672.89 (1) If an accused who is detained in custody under a disposition made by a Review Board is transferred to another province otherwise than under section 672.86, the Review Board of the province from which the accused is transferred has exclusive jurisdiction over the accused and may continue to exercise the powers and shall continue to perform the duties mentioned in sections 672.5 and 672.81 to 672.84.

(2) Notwithstanding subsection (1), the Attorneys General of the provinces to and from which the accused is to be transferred as described in that subsection may, after the transfer is made, enter into an agreement subject to this Act, enabling the Review Board of the province to which an accused is transferred to exercise the powers and perform the duties referred to in subsection (1) in respect of the accused, subject to the terms and conditions and in the circumstances set out in the agreement. 1991, c. 43, s. 4; 2014, c. 6, s. 18.

CROSS-REFERENCES

"Attorney General" is defined in s. 2. The terms "accused", "court", "hospital", and "Review Board" are defined in s. 672.1. Note that where the accused is transferred pursuant to s. 672.86, the Review Board in the province to which the accused is transferred retains exclusive jurisdiction over the accused. The Attorneys General may enter into an agreement to require that the Review Board of the province from which the accused is transferred retains exclusive jurisdiction over the accused. See s. 672.88. As to further cross-references respecting interprovincial transfers, see references under s. 672.86.

SYNOPSIS

Where the accused is transferred to another province other than by virtue of s. 672.86, for example where the accused is a dual status offender and the offences occurred in different provinces, the Review Board from which the accused is transferred has exclusive jurisdiction over the accused. Notwithstanding this provision, however, the Attorneys General of the respective provinces may enter into an agreement enabling the Review Board of the province to which the accused has been transferred to obtain jurisdiction over the accused.

Enforcement of Orders and Regulations

EXECUTION OF WARRANT ANYWHERE IN CANADA.

672.9 Any warrant or process issued in relation to an assessment order or disposition made in respect of an accused may be executed or served in any place in Canada outside the province where the order or disposition was made as if it had been issued in that province. 1991, c. 43, s. 4; 1997, c. 18, s. 91.

CROSS-REFERENCES

Reference should be made to s. 672.92 which authorizes a peace officer to make a warrantless arrest anywhere in Canada where there are reasonable and probable grounds that the accused has failed to comply with a disposition or a condition thereof or is about to commit a breach. Upon arrest, the accused must be taken before a justice within 24 hours or as soon as practicable and the accused must be released unless the justice has grounds to believe that the accused did in fact contravene the disposition. See ss. 672.92 and 672.93. Upon notice of the detention, the Review Board must hold a hearing to review the disposition in accordance with s. 672.5. See s. 672.94.

SYNOPSIS

A warrant or process issued in relation to an assessment or disposition order is valid anywhere in Canada outside the province in which the order or disposition had been made.

ARREST WITHOUT WARRANT FOR CONTRAVENTION OF DISPOSITION.

672.91 A peace officer may arrest an accused without a warrant at any place in Canada if the peace officer has reasonable grounds to believe that the accused has contravened or wilfully failed to comply with the assessment order or disposition or any condition of it, or is about to do so. 1991, c. 43, s. 4; 2005, c. 22, s. 36.

CROSS-REFERENCES

The term "peace officer" is defined in s. 2. Reference should be made to s. 672.92 which provides that, if the accused is subject to a conditional discharge or an assessment order, the peace officer may release the accused from custody. If the accused is not released by the peace officer, that section requires the accused to be taken before a justice within 24 hours of the arrest or as soon as practicable and the accused may not be detained unless the justice is satisfied that the accused has contravened or failed to comply with a disposition. If the justice releases the accused, notice is to be given to the court or the Review Board that made the disposition or assessment order. See ss. 672.92 and 672.93. If the Review Board receives the notice it may exercise the powers and perform the duties set out in ss. 672.5 (hold a disposition hearing) and 672.81 to 672.83 (review the disposition).

Reference should also be made to the following arrest provisions contained in the *Criminal Code*. Section 28 protects the peace officer in case of arrest of the wrong person when executing a warrant. Section 29(1) requires the person executing the warrant to have it with him where feasible and to produce it upon request, and s. 29(2) imposes a duty on a person making an arrest to give notice of the warrant under which he makes the arrest and the reason for the arrest.

SYNOPSIS

This section provides peace officers with arrest powers, including the power to make a warrantless arrest anywhere in Canada where there are reasonable grounds to believe that the accused has failed to comply with an assessment order disposition or a condition of the disposition or is about to commit a breach.

RELEASE OR DELIVERY OF ACCUSED SUBJECT TO PARAGRAPH 672.54(*b*) DISPOSITION ORDER / No release / Accused to be brought before justice / Accused subject to paragraph 672.54(*c*) disposition order / Justice not available.

672.92 (1) If a peace officer arrests an accused under section 672.91 who is subject to a disposition made under paragraph 672.54(*b*) or an assessment order, the peace officer, as soon as practicable, may release the accused from custody and

(*a*) issue a summons or appearance notice compelling the accused's appearance before a justice; and

(*b*) deliver the accused to the place specified in the disposition or assessment order.

(2) A peace officer shall not release an accused under subsection (1) if the peace officer believes, on reasonable grounds,

(*a*) that it is necessary in the public interest that the accused be detained in custody having regard to all the circumstances, including the need to

(i) establish the identity of the accused,

(ii) establish the terms and conditions of a disposition made under section 672.54 or of an assessment order,

(iii) prevent the commission of an offence, or

(iv) prevent the accused from contravening or failing to comply with the disposition or assessment order;

(*b*) that the accused is subject to a disposition or an assessment order of a court, or Review Board, of another province; or

(*c*) that, if the accused is released from custody, the accused will fail to attend, as required, before a justice.

(3) If a peace officer does not release the accused, the accused shall be taken before a justice having jurisdiction in the territorial division in which the accused is arrested, without unreasonable delay and in any event within twenty-four hours after the arrest.

(4) If a peace officer arrests an accused under section 672.91 who is subject to a disposition under paragraph 672.54(*c*), the accused shall be taken before a justice having jurisdiction in the territorial division in which the accused is arrested without unreasonable delay and, in any event, within twenty-four hours.

(5) If a justice described in subsection (3) or (4) is not available within twenty-four hours after the arrest, the accused shall be taken before a justice as soon as practicable. 1991, c. 43, s. 4; 2005, c. 22, s. 36.

CROSS-REFERENCES

The terms "peace officer" and "justice" are defined in s. 2. An accused may be detained by the justice pursuant to s. 672.93 where the justice is satisfied that there are reasonable grounds to believe that the accused has contravened or failed to comply with a disposition or assessment order. Where the accused is detained, notice must be given to the Review Board pursuant to s. 672.93(2). Pursuant to s. 672.94, upon receipt of notice of detention, a Review Board may exercise its powers under s. 672.5 to hold a hearing in order to review the disposition under ss. 672.81 to 672.83.

Presumably the appearance notice and summons referred to in this section are the documents provided for in Part XVI.

SYNOPSIS

This section sets out the procedure the peace officer is to follow after an arrest under s. 672.91. If the accused is subject to a conditional discharge disposition or an assessment order, the peace officer is to release the accused as soon as possible and issue a summons or appearance notice compelling the accused to appear before a justice and deliver the accused to the place specified in the disposition or assessment order. The peace officer is to refuse release if the officer believes on reasonable grounds that any of the conditions set out in subsec. (2) apply, for example, that the accused may commit other offences or will fail to attend before a justice. If the officer refuses to release the accused, the accused is to be brought before a justice without unreasonable delay and in any event within 24 hours (subsec. (3)).

If, however, the accused is subject to a disposition detaining him or her in a hospital under s. 672.54(*c*), the accused is to be taken before a justice, again without unreasonable delay and, in any event, within 24 hours.

If a justice is not available within 24 hours, the accused is to be taken before a justice as soon as practicable (subsec. (5)).

WHERE JUSTICE TO RELEASE ACCUSED / Notice / Order of justice pending decision of Review Board.

672.93 (1) A justice shall release an accused who is brought before the justice under section 672.92 unless the justice is satisfied that there are reasonable grounds to believe that the accused has contravened or failed to comply with a disposition or an assessment order.

(1.1) If the justice releases the accused, notice shall be given to the court or Review Board, as the case may be, that made the disposition or assessment order.

(2) If the justice is satisfied that there are reasonable grounds to believe that the accused has contravened or failed to comply with a disposition or an assessment order, the justice, pending a hearing of a Review Board with respect to the disposition or a hearing of a court or Review Board with respect to the assessment order, may make an order that is appropriate in the circumstances in relation to the accused, including an order that the accused be returned to a place that is specified in the disposition or assessment order. If the justice makes an order under this subsection, notice shall be given to the court or Review Board, as the case may be, that made the disposition or assessment order. 1991, c. 43, s. 4; 2005, c. 22, s. 36.

CROSS-REFERENCES

"Justice" is defined in s. 2 of the *Criminal Code*. "Review Board" and "accused" are defined in s. 672.1. Pursuant to s. 672.94, upon receipt of notice of detention, a Review Board may exercise its powers under s. 672.5 to hold a hearing in order to review the disposition under ss. 672.81 to 672.83.

SYNOPSIS

This section sets out the powers and duties of the justice before whom an accused has been brought following an arrest under s. 672.92. The justice is to release the accused unless there are reasonable grounds to believe that the accused has contravened or failed to comply with a disposition or assessment order. If the justice releases the accused, notice is to be given to the court or Review Board that made the disposition or assessment order (subsec. (1.1)). If, however, there are reasonable grounds to believe that the accused has contravened or failed to comply with the order, the justice may make an appropriate order pending a hearing by the Review Board or court, as the case may be. One order that the justice may make is to return the accused to the place specified in the assessment order or disposition. Notice is to be given to the Review Board or the court that made the order.

POWERS OF REVIEW BOARD.

672.94 Where a Review Board receives a notice given under subsection 672.93(1.1) or (2), it may exercise the powers and shall perform the duties mentioned in sections 672.5 and 672.81 to 672.83 as if the Review Board were reviewing a disposition. 1991, c. 43, s. 4; 2005, c. 22, s. 36.

CROSS-REFERENCES

"Review Board" is defined in s. 672.1. Reference should be made to s. 672.5 and the cross-references contained therein with respect to the procedures followed at a Review Board hearing. Reference should also be had to ss. 672.81 to 672.83, which outline the powers the board may exercise in the review of any disposition.

SYNOPSIS

Upon receiving notice of detention, the Review Board must hold a hearing in accordance with the provisions of s. 672.5 in order to review the disposition as prescribed by s. 672.81 to 672.83.

REGULATIONS.

672.95 The Governor in Council may make regulations

(*a*) prescribing anything that may be prescribed under this Part; and

(*b*) generally to carry out the purposes and provisions of this Part. 1991, c. 43, s. 4.

SYNOPSIS

This provision permits the Governor in Council to make any regulations regarding Part XX.1 of the *Criminal Code.*

SCHEDULE TO PART XX.1

[***Repealed***, 2005, c. 22, s. 37.]

Part XXI / APPEALS – INDICTABLE OFFENCES

Interpretation

DEFINITIONS / "court of appeal" / "indictment" / "registrar" / "sentence" / "trial court".

673. In this Part

"court of appeal" means the court of appeal, as defined by the definition "court of appeal" in section 2, for the province or territory in which the trial of a person by indictment is held;

"indictment" includes an information or charge in respect of which a person has been tried for an indictable offence under Part XIX;

"registrar" means the registrar or clerk of the court of appeal;

"sentence" includes

(*a*) a declaration made under subsection 199(3),

(*b*) an order made under subsection 109(1) or 110(1), section 161, subsection 164.2(1) or 194(1), section 320.24 or 462.37, subsection 491.1(2), 730(1) or 737(3) or section 738, 739, 742.1, 742.3, 743.6, 745.4 or 745.5,

(*c*) a disposition made under section 731 or 732 or subsection 732.2(3) or (5), 742.4(3) or 742.6(9),

(*d*) an order made under subsection 16(1) of the *Controlled Drugs and Substances Act*, and

(*e*) an order made under subsection 94(1) of the *Cannabis Act*;

"trial court" means the court by which an accused was tried and includes a judge or a provincial court judge acting under Part XIX. R.S., c. C-34, s. 601; 1972, c. 13, s. 52; 1973-74, c. 38, s. 6.1, c. 50, s. 3; 1974-75-76, c. 93, s. 72; 1976-77, c. 53, s. 4; R.S.C. 1985, c. 27 (1st Supp.), s. 138; c. 23 (4th Supp.), s. 4; c. 42 (4th Supp.), s. 4; 1991, c. 43, s. 5; 1992, c. 1, s. 58; 1993, c. 45, s. 10, 16 and 19; 1995, c. 22, s. 5, c. 39, ss. 155, 190(*a*), (*b*); 1996, c. 19, s. 74(1); 1999, c. 5, ss. 25, 51 (s. 51 replaced by 2005, c. 22, s. 45; c. 25, ss. 13, 31(5); 2002, c. 13, s. 63; 2005, c. 22, s. 38; 2006, c. 14, s. 6; 2013, c. 11, s. 2; 2018, c. 16, s. 220; 2018, c. 21, s. 21.

CROSS-REFERENCES
See s. 2 for the general definition section of the *Criminal Code* and references cited thereunder for other sources of definitions of words and phrases used in the Code.

SYNOPSIS
This section sets out the definitions that apply to this Part.

Note in particular that by reason of the definition of "sentence", appeals are available in indictable matters from not only the imposition of jail terms, fines, etc., but also from: an order made under s. 161 prohibiting the offender from attending near certain places or obtaining employment where children are expected to be present; firearms etc. prohibition orders (ss. 109, 110); a declaration of forfeiture following a seizure made under s. 199; punitive damages awarded following conviction for unlawful interception or disclosure of information in respect of private communications (s. 194(1)); forfeiture orders with respect to seized property (s. 199(3)); driving prohibitions (ss. 259(1) and (2), 261); forfeiture orders with respect to the proceeds of crime (s. 462.37); orders for the restitution or forfeiture of property obtained by crime (s. 491.1(2)); conditional and absolute discharges (s. 730(1)); probation orders and variation of such orders (ss. 731, 732.2(3) or (5)); intermittent sentence and probation (s. 732); victim fine surcharges in excess of the statutory minimums (s. 737(3)); restitution orders (s. 738); restitution to *bona fide* purchasers (s. 739); conditional sentence order and variation of such order (ss. 742.1, 742.3); and a forfeiture order made under subsection 16(1) of the *Controlled Drugs and Substances Act*. Reference should also be made to ss. 675 and 676, which provide rights of appeal from other types of sentence orders, namely parole ineligibility. Also note s. 676.1, which gives a right of appeal from a costs order. While the definition of "sentence" in this section no longer contains reference to orders for delay in parole eligibility, appeals in respect of such orders are provided for in ss. 675(2) and (2.1) and 676(4) and (5).

ANNOTATIONS
The Court of Appeal has jurisdiction to hear a Crown appeal from orders made under ss. 742.6(14) or 742.6(16): *R. v. Buggins* (2004), 182 C.C.C. (3d) 418 (Alta. C.A.).

A finding that there has been no breach of a conditional sentence is neither an acquittal nor a disposition under s. 742.6(9) and accordingly, the Crown has no right of appeal: *R. v. Cross* (2004), 192 C.C.C. (3d) 415, 229 N.S.R. (2d) 89 (C.A.). There is, however, a right of appeal from a finding of a breach and the termination of a conditional sentence order: *R. v. Carpentier* (2005), 203 C.C.C. (3d) 251 (Man. C.A.).

Right of Appeal

PROCEDURE ABOLISHED.

674. No proceedings other than those authorized by this Part and Part XXVI shall be taken by way of appeal in proceedings in respect of indictable offences. R.S., c. C-34, s. 602.

CROSS-REFERENCES
See ss. 812 to 839 of Part XXVII "Summary Convictions" for appeals in summary convictions proceedings. Sections 675 to 676 contain rights of appeal in proceedings by indictment and ss. 678 to 685 govern procedure on appeals. Sections 686 to 689 prescribe powers of a court of appeal. Sections 691 to 696 govern appeals to the Supreme Court of Canada.

Appellate rights in respect of an appeal from a disposition or placement decision or a finding that the accused is a dangerous mentally disordered accused made under Part XX.1 are contained in ss. 672.72 to 672.78.

Recourse to the extraordinary remedies of Part XXVI is restricted to matters involving jurisdictional error.

SYNOPSIS

By virtue of this section, no appeal lies in respect of indictable proceedings except as provided for in this Part or Part XXVI [extraordinary remedies].

ANNOTATIONS

In *R. v. Laba*, [1994] 3 S.C.R. 965, 94 C.C.C. (3d) 385, the Court of Appeal allowed the Crown's appeal from a stay of proceedings entered when the trial judge held the provision under which the accused was charged was of no force and effect. However, the Court of Appeal held that a portion of the provision was still unconstitutional. While no appeal lay to the Supreme Court at the instance of the Crown under this Act, it was open to the Crown to apply for leave to appeal under s. 40 of the *Supreme Court Act*. An appeal against a ruling on the constitutionality of a law that cannot be piggy backed onto any proceedings set out in the *Criminal Code* is a judgment of the highest court of final resort in a province in which judgment can be had in the particular case for the purposes of s. 40(1). Also see: *R. v. Keegstra*, [1995] 2 S.C.R. 381, 98 C.C.C. (3d) 1.

For a third party, such as the media, who have been affected by a publication ban, where the ban has been imposed by a provincial court judge then the third party may apply to the superior court by way of *certiorari* and may then follow the appellate routes prescribed in the *Criminal Code*. When the order has been made by a superior court judge, then the third party may apply for leave to appeal to the Supreme Court of Canada under s. 40 of the *Supreme Court Act*: *Dagenais v. Canadian Broadcasting Corp.*, [1994] 3 S.C.R. 835, 94 C.C.C. (3d) 289.

See also *R. v. Beharriell*, [1995] 4 S.C.R. 536 *sub nom. A. (L.L.) v. B. (A.)*, 103 C.C.C. (3d) 92, 44 C.R. (4th) 91, where it was held that a complainant and sexual assault victim organization had a right to apply for leave to appeal from an order compelling production pursuant to s. 40(1) of the *Supreme Court Act*.

No appeal lies from the decision of a superior court judge removing the accused's counsel as counsel of record. The decision to remove counsel is to be reviewed after the trial through the normal appeal process: *R. v. Druken*, [1998] 1 S.C.R. 978, 126 C.C.C. (3d) 1.

There is no right to appeal a sentencing judge's dismissal of defence counsel's motion to withdraw: *R. v. Deschamps* (2003), 179 C.C.C. (3d) 174, 19 C.R. (6th) 311 (Man. C.A.).

Courts of appeal are divided on whether there is jurisdiction to entertain an appeal, prior to trial, from a refusal to grant a "*Rowbotham*" order for state funding of counsel. On one view, the application should be characterized as civil in nature, avoiding the prohibition on interlocutory appeals in criminal matters: *R. v. Pardy* (2014), 315 C.C.C. (3d) 217 (N.L.C.A.); *R. v. Hennessey* (2017), 347 C.C.C. (3d) 412 (N.L.C.A.). However, other authority holds that such appeals are barred by s. 674: *R. v. Dunkers* (2010), 505 W.A.C. 47 (B.C.C.A. [In Chambers]); *R. v. Hales* (2009), 331 Sask. R. 102 (C.A.).

The *Code* does not permit an appeal from a judge's discretionary decision to decline to hear a matter on the basis that there was another reasonably effective way to address the issue raised. Thus, the court declined to hear an appeal against a superior court's refusal to hear an application for a declaration of constitutional invalidity by an accused who was facing trial before the provincial court and had the ability to challenge the relevant provisions in that venue: *R. v. Jonathan Craig Gaudet* (2018), 364 C.C.C. (3d) 257 (P.E.I.C.A.), leave to appeal to S.C.C. refused 2018 CarswellPEI 106.

The Crown's decision to call no evidence, invite an acquittal and then appeal against an adverse interlocutory decision may constitute an abuse of process. The Crown should not be entitled to gain the advantage of circumventing the rule against interlocutory appeals, an advantage not available to the accused. Halting the proceedings and launching an appeal is only permissible where the Crown can clearly demonstrate that it had no reasonable alternative, for instance where the interlocutory ruling excluded evidence essential to the

Crown's case or where the interlocutory order raised a reasonable prospect of harm to an interest worthy of the court's protection such as a class privilege: *R. v. Tingley* (2015), 330 C.C.C. (3d) 227 (N.B.C.A.), leave to appeal to S.C.C. refused 2016 CarswellNB 28. In the extradition context, see *United States v. Fafalios* (2012), 284 C.C.C. (3d) 432 (Ont. C.A.).

RIGHT OF APPEAL OF PERSON CONVICTED / Summary conviction appeals / Appeal against absolute term in excess of ten years / Appeal against s. 743.6 order / Persons under 18 / Appeal against s. 745.51(1) order / Appeals against verdicts based on mental disorder / Where application for leave to appeal refused by judge.

675. (1) A person who is convicted by a trial court in proceedings by indictment may appeal to the court of appeal

(*a*) against his conviction

(i) on any ground of appeal that involves a question of law alone,

(ii) on any ground of appeal that involves a question of fact or a question of mixed law and fact, with leave of the court of appeal or a judge thereof or on the certificate of the trial judge that the case is a proper case for appeal, or

(iii) on any ground of appeal not mentioned in subparagraph (i) or (ii) that appears to the court of appeal to be a sufficient ground of appeal, with leave of the court of appeal; or

(*b*) against the sentence passed by the trial court, with leave of the court of appeal or a judge thereof unless that sentence is one fixed by law.

(1.1) A person may appeal, pursuant to subsection (1), with leave of the court of appeal or a judge of that court, to that court in respect of a summary conviction or a sentence passed with respect to a summary conviction as if the summary conviction had been a conviction in proceedings by indictment if

(*a*) there has not been an appeal with respect to the summary conviction;

(*b*) the summary conviction offence was tried with an indictable offence; and

(*c*) there is an appeal in respect of the indictable offence.

(2) A person who has been convicted of second degree murder and sentenced to imprisonment for life without eligibility for parole for a specified number of years in excess of ten may appeal to the court of appeal against the number of years in excess of ten of his imprisonment without eligibility for parole.

(2.1) A person against whom an order under section 743.6 has been made may appeal to the court of appeal against the order.

(2.2) A person who was under the age of eighteen at the time of the commission of the offence for which the person was convicted of first degree murder or second degree murder and sentenced to imprisonment for life without eligibility for parole until the person has served the period specified by the judge presiding at the trial may appeal to the court of appeal against the number of years in excess of the minimum number of years of imprisonment without eligibility for parole that are required to be served in respect of that person's case. [as enacted by 1997, c. 18, s. 92]

(2.3) A person against whom an order under subsection 745.51(1) has been made may appeal to the court of appeal against the order.

(3) Where a verdict of not criminally responsible on account of mental disorder or unfit to stand trial is rendered in respect of a person, that person may appeal to the court of appeal against that verdict on any ground of appeal, mentioned in subparagraph (1)(*a*)(i), (ii) or (iii) and subject to the conditions described therein.

(4) Where a judge of the court of appeal refuses leave to appeal under this section otherwise than under paragraph (1)(*b*), the appellant may, by filing notice in writing with the court of appeal within seven days after the refusal, have the application for leave to appeal determined by the court of appeal. R.S., c. C-34, s. 603; 1974-75-76, c.

105, s. 13; 1991, c. 43, s. 9; 1995, c. 42, s. 73; 1997, c. 18, s. 92; 1999, c. 31, s. 68; 2002, c. 13, s. 64; 2011, c. 5, s. 2.

CROSS-REFERENCES

See s. 673 for definition of "court of appeal", "indictment", "sentence" and "trial court". See s. 672.1 for definition of "verdict of not criminally responsible on account of mental disorder" and s. 2 for definition of "unfit to stand trial".

Rights of appeal are conferred by the *Criminal Code*, which also defines the authority of the court to hear and determine the appeal under ss. 686 to 687. Under s. 482(1), appeal procedure is governed by rules of the court established by a majority of the judges of the court of appeal which vary from one jurisdiction to another. Sections 676 and 696 govern rights of appeal of the Attorney General from dispositions made in proceedings by indictment. Section 759 confers rights of appeal in dangerous offender proceedings and s. 784 applies to applications for the extraordinary remedies of *mandamus, habeas corpus, certiorari* and prohibition.

Appellate rights are determined by the nature of proceedings in the trial court, not the nature of the conviction or the level of the trial court. Where proceedings must be or have been taken by indictment before a provincial court judge or judge alone under Part XIX or a court composed of judge and jury under Part XX, upon indictment or information, Part XXI is applicable.

Appellate rights in respect of an appeal from a disposition or placement decision or a finding that the accused is a dangerous mentally disordered accused made under Part XX.1 are contained in ss. 672.72 to 672.79. Appeals respecting dangerous and long-term offenders, s. 759.

An order to pay costs may be appealed with leave under s. 676.1.

A determination to make or refuse to make an order under s. 278.5(1) or s. 278.7(1) is deemed to be a question of law pursuant to s. 278.91.

An order of forfeiture of offence-related property may be appealed as if the appeal were one against sentence pursuant to s. 490.1(3).

SYNOPSIS

This section sets out the matters which an accused convicted of an indictable offence may appeal to the court of appeal.

A conviction may be appealed on: (a) grounds of law alone; (b) grounds of fact or mixed law and fact, with leave of the court of appeal or a judge thereof or with a certificate of the trial judge; and (c) any other ground, with leave of the court of appeal (subsec. (1)(*a*)).

The trial judge's certificate is now virtually never used as a means of bringing an appeal. Local practice will dictate whether the question of leave needs to be spoken to independently of the appeal itself. In some jurisdictions grounds which technically require leave are simply argued as part of the appeal.

An accused may also appeal a "sentence" (see s. 673) unless the same is fixed by law. Leave of a judge or the court is required (subsec. (1)(*b*)). Local practice will again determine whether a separate leave hearing will be held.

A person convicted of second degree murder may appeal against the period of parole ineligibility, in excess of the mandatory 10 years (subsec. (2)). A person who was under the age of 18 at the time of the offence and was convicted of murder may appeal against the period of parole ineligibility that exceeds the minimum period. The person may also appeal against an order made under s. 745.51(1) requiring that the period of parole ineligibility be consecutive to a period of parole ineligibility imposed for another murder.

Findings of unfitness, or not criminally responsible on account of mental disorder, may be appealed (subsec. (3)).

With the exception of sentence appeals, the refusal of leave to appeal by a single judge may be appealed to the court of appeal within seven days of the dismissal of the original application (subsec. (4)).

Where a summary conviction offence was tried with an indictable offence that is under appeal, then with leave the summary conviction and sentence may also be appealed to the court of appeal, pursuant to subsec. (1.1).

ANNOTATIONS

Application of provisions – It is not the nature of the conviction but the nature of the proceedings that determines the forum for appeal. Thus in *R. v. Yaworski* (1959), 124 C.C.C. 151 (Man. C.A.), an accused convicted of a summary conviction offence in proceedings originally charging an indictable offence may only appeal under Part XXI of the Code.

Where the Crown purported to elect summarily on an exclusively indictable offence, the election was a nullity and the accused's appeal lay under Part XXI to the Court of Appeal: *R. v. Shia* (2015), 320 C.C.C. (3d) 111 (Ont. C.A.).

Where the Crown failed to state its election on the record but proceeded to trial in provincial court on a hybrid offence, the deemed indictable election (s. 34(1) of the *Interpretation Act*) was displaced by the manner in which the proceedings were actually conducted. The Crown's intention to proceed summarily was clear. Therefore, the Court of Appeal lacked jurisdiction to hear the appeal: *R. v. Matthews* (2015), 321 C.C.C. (3d) 463 (N.S.C.A.).

When an appellant dies, the court retains jurisdiction to proceed with the appeal, but it is a jurisdiction that should be sparingly exercised. When an interested party seeks to continue an appeal notwithstanding the death of the appellant (or, in the case of a Crown appeal, the respondent), a motion should be made for substitution of the personal representative or another interested party for the deceased. In considering whether to proceed with an appeal rendered moot by the death of the appellant (or, in a Crown appeal, the respondent), the general test is whether there exists special circumstances that make it in the interests of justice to proceed. The court may have regard to the particular circumstances of the case including the following:

1. whether the appeal will proceed in a proper adversarial context;
2. the strength of the grounds of the appeal;
3. whether there are special circumstances that transcend the death of the individual appellant/respondent, including:
   a. a legal issue of general public importance, particularly if it is otherwise evasive of appellate review;
   b. a systemic issue related to the administration of justice;
   c. collateral consequences to the family of the deceased or to other interested persons or to the public;
4. whether the nature of the order that could be made by the appellate court justifies the expenditure of limited judicial (or court) resources to resolve a moot appeal;
5. whether continuing the appeal would go beyond the judicial function of resolving concrete disputes and involve the court in free-standing, legislative-type pronouncements more properly left to the legislature itself.

In the end, the court must determine whether in the particular case, notwithstanding the general rule favouring abatement, it is in the interests of justice to proceed: *R. v. Smith*, [2004] 1 S.C.R. 385, 181 C.C.C. (3d) 225.

Where the accused's first trial ended in a mistrial and second trial ended in a conviction, the court of appeal lacked jurisdiction under subsec. (1)(*a*) to entertain an appeal of the mistrial declaration: *R. v. Hahn* (2018), 365 C.C.C. (3d) 149 (Sask. C.A.).

There is no jurisdiction to reopen an appeal where the appeal has been disposed of on its merits: *R. v. H. (E.F.)* (1997), 115 C.C.C. (3d) 89 (Ont. C.A.), leave to appeal to S.C.C. refused 117 C.C.C. (3d) vi. See also *R. v. Purdy* (2010), 261 C.C.C. (3d) 33 (B.C.C.A.), leave to appeal to S.C.C. refused (2012), 322 B.C.A.C. 320*n.*

Although the trial judge applied the evidence of the indictable offence to the summary conviction offences on the consent of both parties, the offences were nonetheless tried separately. Accordingly, there was no jurisdiction for the Court of Appeal to hear the summary conviction appeal: *R. v. Pelletier* (2003), 180 C.C.C. (3d) 560 (N.B.C.A.).

Subsection (1.1) applies where the summary conviction and indictable offences were tried together, even if the indictable appeal pending in the Court of Appeal is brought by the co-accused: *R. v. Thiboutot* (1999), 143 C.C.C. (3d) 283 (Que. C.A.).

The existence of reasonable and probable grounds to make a breathalyzer demand pursuant to s. 254(3) raises a question of law pertaining to the application of a legal standard to the facts of the case. Although the trial judge's factual findings are entitled to deference, the trial judge's ultimate ruling is subject to review for correctness: *R. v. Shepherd* (2009), 245 C.C.C. (3d) 137 (S.C.C.).

Sentence appeal / *Also see notes under s. 687* – In *R. v. Clifford,* [1969] 2 C.C.C. 363 (Ont. C.A.), it was held that an appellant may abandon his appeal before it comes on for hearing and the Crown, although having submitted in its factum that the sentence should be varied upwards, not having proceeded by its own notice of appeal, cannot contest the abandonment, which prevented the hearing of the sentence appeal. However, in *R. v. Mahon,* [1969] 2 C.C.C. 179 (B.C.C.A.), the accused appealed the quantum of a sentence illegally imposed as concurrent rather than consecutive to his unexpired parole term and the court, holding that the disposition of a sentence appeal was in its hands, and not in the control of the appellant, refused to allow him to abandon and corrected the illegality of sentence.

No appeal lies to the Court of Appeal from the determination of the jury under former s. 745 [now s. 745.63] refusing to reduce the period of years of parole ineligibility: *R. v. Vaillancourt* (1989), 49 C.C.C. (3d) 544 (Ont. C.A.), leave to appeal to S.C.C. refused 76 C.C.C. (3d) 384*n*.

"Sentence" does not include a provincial suspension of a driver's licence: *R. v. Sull* (2003), 176 C.C.C. (3d) 46 (B.C.C.A.).

Pursuant to subsec. (1)(*b*), an appeal, with leave, lies from a firearms forfeiture order made under s. 491: *R. v. Montague* (2014), 312 C.C.C. (3d) 1 (S.C.C.).

Pre-sentence custody was not a sentence passed by the trial judge and, therefore, did not afford a right to seek leave to appeal: *R. v. Mizen* (2009), 244 C.C.C. (3d) 395 (B.C.C.A.).

RIGHT OF ATTORNEY GENERAL TO APPEAL / Summary conviction appeals / Acquittal / Appeal against verdict of unfit to stand trial / Appeal against ineligible parole period / Appeal against decision not to make s. 743.6 order / Appeal against decision not to make s. 745.51(1) order.

676. (1) The Attorney General or counsel instructed by him for the purpose may appeal to the court of appeal

(*a*) against a judgment or verdict of acquittal or a verdict of not criminally responsible on account of mental disorder of a trial court in proceedings by indictment on any ground of appeal that involves a question of law alone;

(*b*) against an order of a superior court of criminal jurisdiction that quashes an indictment or in any manner refuses or fails to exercise jurisdiction on an indictment;

(*c*) against an order of a trial court that stays proceedings on an indictment or quashes an indictment; or

(*d*) with leave of the court of appeal or a judge thereof, against the sentence passed by a trial court in proceedings by indictment, unless that sentence is one fixed by law.

(1.1) The Attorney General or counsel instructed by the Attorney General may appeal, pursuant to subsection (1), with leave of the court of appeal or a judge of that court, to that court in respect of a verdict of acquittal in a summary offence proceeding or a sentence passed with respect to a summary conviction as if the summary offence proceeding was a proceeding by indictment if

(*a*) there has not been an appeal with respect to the summary conviction;

(*b*) the summary conviction offence was tried with an indictable offence; and

(*c*) there is an appeal in respect of the indictable offence.

(2) For the purposes of this section, a judgment or verdict of acquittal includes an acquittal in respect of an offence specifically charged where the accused has, on the trial thereof, been convicted or discharged under section 730 of any other offence.

(3) The Attorney General or counsel instructed by the Attorney General for the purpose may appeal to the court of appeal against a verdict that an accused is unfit to stand trial, on any ground of appeal that involves a question of law alone.

(4) The Attorney General or counsel instructed by him for the purpose may appeal to the court of appeal in respect of a conviction for second degree murder, against the number of years of imprisonment without eligibility for parole, being less than twenty-five, that has been imposed as a result of that conviction.

(5) The Attorney General or counsel instructed by the Attorney General for the purpose may appeal to the court of appeal against the decision of the court not to make an order under section 743.6.

(6) The Attorney General or counsel instructed by the Attorney General for the purpose may appeal to the court of appeal against the decision of the court not to make an order under subsection 745.51(1). R.S., c. C-34, s. 605; 1974-75-76, c. 105, s. 15; R.S.C. 1985, c. 27 (1st Supp.), s. 139; 1991, c. 43, s. 9; 1995, c. 22, s. 10; 1995, c. 42, s. 74; 1997, c. 18, s. 93; 2002, c. 13, s. 65; 2008, c. 18, s. 28; 2011, c. 5, s. 3.

CROSS-REFERENCES

The Attorney General of Canada has equivalent rights of appeal under s. 696, in proceedings instituted by the Government of Canada and conducted by or on behalf of the government, as has the Attorney General of the province under Part XXI.

Appellate rights in respect of an appeal from a disposition or placement decision made under Part XX.1 are contained in ss. 672.72 to 672.78. Appellate rights respecting long-term and dangerous offenders, s. 759. The right of appeal by the Attorney General from dismissal of an application for a finding that the accused is a dangerous mentally disordered accused is provided for in s. 672.8. An order for costs may be appealed with leave under s. 676.1.

See s. 2 for definitions of "Attorney General" and "unfit to stand trial". Definition of Attorney General includes his lawful deputy for the purposes of s. 676.

A number of provisions deem certain determinations by a judge to be questions of law, including the decision as to admissibility of sexual conduct evidence in the trial of a sexual offence [s. 276.5], determination to make or refuse to make an order under s. 278.5(1) or s. 278.7(1) [s. 278.91], and whether or not to permit an amendment to an information or indictment [s. 601(6)]. The failure to make an order of forfeiture of offence-related property may be appealed as if the appeal were one against sentence pursuant to s. 490.1(3).

See also references cited under s. 675.

SYNOPSIS

This section sets out what the Crown may appeal to the court of appeal in respect of indictable matters. These are: (a) an acquittal or finding of not criminally responsible on account of mental disorder on grounds of law alone (grounds of fact or mixed law and fact are not open to the Crown); (b) an order of a superior court quashing an indictment or refusing to exercise jurisdiction; (c) an order by a trial judge staying or quashing an indictment; and (d) sentence (with leave of a judge or the court), unless the punishment is fixed by law (subsec. (1)).

An appeal may be taken where the accused, although acquitted of the offence charged, has been found guilty of an included offence (subsec. (2)).

A finding that the accused is unfit to stand trial may be appealed on grounds of law alone (subsec. (3)).

In cases of second degree murder the Crown can appeal the length of the parole ineligibility period if it is less than the maximum 25 years (subsec. (4)). The Attorney

General may also appeal against the refusal to make an order under s. 745.51(1) that the period of parole ineligibility be consecutive to a period of parole ineligibility imposed for another murder.

Under subsec. (1.1) a summary conviction matter tried with an indictable matter may be appealed to the court of appeal if there is an appeal of the indictable matter.

ANNOTATIONS

Constitutional considerations – The right of the Crown to appeal against an acquittal as provided by this subsection does not offend the guarantee against double jeopardy in s. 11(*h*) of the *Canadian Charter of Rights and Freedoms*: *R. v. Morgentaler, Smoling and Scott*, [1988] 1 S.C.R. 30, 37 C.C.C. (3d) 449.

Exercise of Crown right to appeal – Duties of an Attorney General may be exercised under his authority by a responsible subordinate official who may instruct counsel to appeal: *R. v. Harrison*, [1977] 1 S.C.R. 238, 28 C.C.C. (2d) 279 (9:0).

A notice of appeal signed by a person as "agent" of the Attorney General is proper: *R. v. Badall*, [1975] 2 S.C.R. 503, 17 C.C.C. (2d) 420 (9:0).

An undertaking by the trial Crown not to appeal cannot constitute a bar to the Attorney General's right to appeal: *R. v. Ryazanov* (2008), 237 C.C.C. (3d) 19 (Ont. C.A.).

Right of appeal – A Crown appeal from acquittal cannot succeed on the abstract or purely hypothetical possibility that the accused would have been convicted but for the error of law. It is the duty of the Crown in order to obtain a new trial to satisfy the appellate court that the error of the trial judge might reasonably be thought, in the concrete reality of the case at hand, to have had a material bearing on the acquittal. The Crown is not required, however, to establish that the verdict would necessarily have been different: *R. v. Graveline*, [2006] 1 S.C.R. 609, 207 C.C.C. (3d) 481.

An abstract or purely hypothetical possibility of materiality is below the threshold for appellate intervention while an error that would necessarily have been material is above the threshold. An error about which there is a reasonable degree of certainty of its materiality is at the required threshold: *R. v. George*, [2017] 1 S.C.R. 1021, 349 C.C.C. (3d) 371.

An order declaring a mistrial is not a judgment or verdict of acquittal giving the Crown a right of appeal: *R. v. Holliday* (1973), 12 C.C.C. (2d) 56 (Alta. C.A.).

Dismissal of an information upon the plea of *autrefois acquit* is appealable by the Crown: *R. v. Suleyman Sanver* (1973), 12 C.C.C. (2d) 105 (N.B.S.C. App. Div.).

A default hearing pursuant to s. 734.7 is not appealable by the Crown: *R. v. Druet* (2001), 159 C.C.C. (3d) 445 (N.B.C.A.).

There is no right of appeal from a finding that an offender did not breach a term of a conditional sentence: *R. v. Cross* (2004), 192 C.C.C. (3d) 415 (N.S.C.A.).

A trial judge's quashing of an indictment on his interpretation of the governing substantive offence section, rather than for some procedural or technical defect, such as duplicity, misjoinder or omission of an essential ingredient in the indictment, is tantamount to a judgment of acquittal to permit the Attorney General to appeal under subsec. (1)(*a*): *R. v. Sheets*, [1971] S.C.R. 614, 1 C.C.C. (2d) 508 (9:0).

Where after plea the defendant successfully argued that the offence was not known to law and the trial judge then ruled that he did not have jurisdiction, that result amounted to a verdict of acquittal: *Cheyenne Realty Ltd. v. Thompson*, [1975] 1 S.C.R. 87, 15 C.C.C. (2d) 49 (5:0).

A finding by the trial judge prior to plea that the charge is a nullity because the federal enactment under which it was laid is *ultra vires* Parliament is tantamount to an acquittal under subsec. (1)(*a*): *R. v. Kripps Pharmacy Ltd. and Kripps* (1981), 60 C.C.C. (2d) 332, [1981] 5 W.W.R. 190 *sub nom. Canada (Attorney General) v. Wetmore Co. Ct. J.* (B.C.C.A.), leave to appeal to S.C.C. refused 38 N.R. 180*n sub nom. R. v. Wetmore*.

It was held, prior to the amendment of this section which added subsec. (1)(*c*), that quashing an indictment is tantamount to an acquittal where (a) the decision to quash is not based on defects in the indictment or technical procedural irregularities, and (b) the decision is a final decision resting on a question of law alone, such that if the accused were charged subsequently with the same offence he or she could plead *autrefois acquit*. Similarly, if the order of the court, whatever the terminology used, effectively brings the proceedings to a final conclusion in favour of the accused, then it is tantamount to a judgment or verdict of acquittal. This would include a stay of proceedings ordered after a plea of not guilty upon the basis of a successful "defence" of entrapment: *R. v. Jewitt*, [1985] 2 S.C.R. 128, 21 C.C.C. (3d) 7 (7:0).

The Crown may appeal a pre-trial order by a judge of the provincial court that stays proceedings on an indictment if the judge was acting under Part XIX of the *Criminal Code.* In this case, an appeal was unavailable as the judge had not put the accused to his election before entering a stay of proceedings and, accordingly, it could not be said that the provincial court judge entered a stay while acting under Part XIX: *R. v. Waugh* (2009), 246 C.C.C. (3d) 116 (N.B.C.A.).

The Crown and the affected witnesses had a right to appeal an order of a chambers judge requiring that the witnesses attend to be questioned by defence counsel. The order was made because the Attorney General had preferred a direct indictment but was made without notice to the witnesses. The right of appeal exists either under provincial statute or through application of the doctrine of *ex debito justitiae*: *R. v. Sterling* (1993), 84 C.C.C. (3d) 65, [1993] 8 W.W.R. 623 (Sask. C.A.).

In *R. v. H. (J.M.)* (2011), 421 N.R. 76 (S.C.C.), the court held that there are at least four types of cases in which alleged mishandling of the evidence may constitute an error of law alone giving rise to a Crown appeal of an acquittal: (1) it is an error of law to make a finding of fact for which there is no evidence (however, a conclusion that the trier of fact has a reasonable doubt is not a finding of fact for the purposes of this rule); (2) the legal effect of findings of fact or of undisputed facts may raise a question of law; (3) an assessment of the evidence based on a wrong legal principle is an error of law; (4) the trial judge's failure to consider all of the evidence in relation to the ultimate issue of guilt or innocence is an error of law, but this error will be found to have been committed only if the reasons demonstrate that this was not done. See also: *R. v. Rudge* (2011), 283 C.C.C. (3d) 3 (Ont. C.A.), leave to appeal to S.C.C. refused (2012), 436 N.R. 400*n*.

Question of law – Even though the reasons for acquittal were couched in terms of reasonable doubt, where the trial judge sitting alone has misdirected himself as to the legal effect of facts found by him, an appeal on a question of law is open to the Crown: *R. v. Davis and Sokoloski* (1973), 14 C.C.C. (2d) 517 (Ont. C.A.), affd [1977] 2 S.C.R. 523, 33 C.C.C. (2d) 496 (5:4).

An error of law by a trial judge in assessing the facts as they apply to the law so as to found a Crown appeal may arise in three ways: (1) the trial judge finds all the facts necessary to reach a conclusion in law but the court of appeal disagrees with the conclusion reached, the disagreement being with respect to the law not the facts nor the inferences to be drawn from the facts; (2) failure by the trial judge to appreciate the evidence, provided that failure is based on a misapprehension of some legal principle; (3) where the reasons of the trial judge demonstrate a failure to consider all of the evidence in relation to the ultimate issue [however, the mere failure by the trial judge to record the fact of having taken into account all of the evidence is not a proper basis for concluding that there was an error of law in this last respect]: *R. v. Morin*, [1992] 3 S.C.R. 286, 76 C.C.C. (3d) 193 (8:0).

Whether an error is "legal" generally turns on its character, not its severity. It was an error for the Court of Appeal to translate its strong opposition to the trial judge's factual inferences (severity) into supposed legal errors (character). Such an approach disregards the restraint required by Parliament's choice to limit Crown appeals from acquittals in proceedings by indictment to questions of law alone: *R. v. George, supra.*

A judge's assessment of evidence does not constitute an error of law when the appeal is from an acquittal premised on reasonable doubt. The Crown cannot appeal the reasonableness of the verdict: *R. v. B. (R.G.)* (2012), 287 C.C.C. (3d) 463 (Man. C.A.).

The interpretation or application of a legal standard constitutes a question of law. Accordingly, the Court of Appeal had jurisdiction to hear a Crown appeal regarding the combined interpretation and application of a legal standard of investigative necessity and the standard of review for a judge reviewing a wiretap authorization: *R. v. Araujo*, [2000] 2 S.C.R. 992, 149 C.C.C. (3d) 449.

The manner in which the trial judge used counselling records in assessing the complainant's credibility did not raise a question of law: *R. v. J. (G.P.)* (2001), 151 C.C.C. (3d) 382, 41 C.R. (5th) 307 (Man. C.A.).

A finding by a trial judge that the Crown had failed to prove that a confession was voluntary is essentially a finding of fact and not appealable by the Crown unless the trial judge had misdirected himself as to the governing principles or his reasons for judgment disclose that he failed to appreciate, or disregarded, relevant evidence: *R. v. Moreau* (1986), 26 C.C.C. (3d) 359, 51 C.R. (3d) 209 (Ont. C.A.).

No evidence to support acquittal – While a finding of fact that is made in the absence of any supportive evidence is an error of law, such an error will occur with respect to an acquittal only if there has been a transfer to the accused by law of the burden of proof of the given fact. Absent a shifting of the burden of proof upon the accused there is always some evidence upon which to make a finding of fact favourable to the accused, and such a finding, if an error, is an error of fact: *R. v. Schuldt*, [1985] 2 S.C.R. 592, 23 C.C.C. (3d) 225 (7:0).

The trial judge's reasonable doubt does not have to be based on the evidence; it could arise from the absence of evidence or a simple failure of the evidence to persuade him to the requisite level of beyond reasonable doubt: *R. v. H. (J.M.)*, 2011 SCC 45.

The finding of a trial judge that an inference cannot be drawn because its foundation has not been proven is not a question of law alone: *R. v. Weir*, [1970] 3 C.C.C. 254 (B.C.C.A.).

In *R. v. Sunbeam Corp. (Canada) Ltd.*, [1969] S.C.R. 221, [1969] 2 C.C.C. 189, it was held (4:3) that "a question of law" does not include whether the trial verdict was unreasonable or could not be supported by the evidence. The matter of sufficiency of proof is a question of fact for the trial judge and not a question of law.

Accordingly, the failure of the trial judge to infer guilt, even in the face of compelling evidence, is a question of fact no matter how wrong that failure is regarded by the appellate court: *R. v. Poirier* (1997), 147 Nfld. & P.E.I.R. 195 (P.E.I.C.A.), affd [1998] 1 S.C.R. 24, 121 C.C.C. (3d) 486.

Finding of lack of intent – In *R. v. Lampard*, [1969] S.C.R. 373, [1969] 3 C.C.C. 249, the full court (9:0) followed *Sunbeam, supra,* holding that an inquiry as to the commission of certain acts with a certain intent involved a question of fact.

The failure of the trial judge to draw the appropriate inference of intent from the facts found by him is an error of fact, not law: *R. v. Sorrell and Bondett* (1978), 41 C.C.C. (2d) 9 (Ont. C.A.).

Right of accused to uphold acquittal on other grounds – On a Crown appeal against acquittal, while the Crown is restricted to questions of law alone, the accused, in an effort to uphold the acquittal, may raise error of fact allegedly made by the trial judge which if properly decided would have resulted in an acquittal notwithstanding the errors of law relied upon by the Crown: *R. v. Atlantic Sugar Refineries Co.* (1978), 41 C.C.C. (2d) 209 (Que. C.A.).

Change of position by Crown on appeal – The Crown may not use its right of appeal to secure a retrial based on a theory or legal argument not advanced at the first trial: *R. v. Suarez-Noa* (2017), 350 C.C.C. (3d) 267 (Ont. C.A.), leave to appeal to S.C.C. refused [2018] S.C.C.A. No. 142; *R. v. Wexler*, [1939] S.C.R. 350, 72 C.C.C. 1.

Crown Appeal under subsec. (1)(*b*) – Subsequent to a jury's guilty verdict, the trial judge granted a mistrial on the basis of the Crown's lack of disclosure. The Crown had a right of appeal as the trial judge had failed to carry out his statutory jurisdiction under s. 720 of the

Criminal Code to sentence the accused: *R. v. Henderson* (2004), 189 C.C.C. (3d) 447 (Ont. C.A.), leave to appeal to S.C.C. refused [2005] 2 S.C.R. viii, 196 C.C.C. (3d) vi.

Intervention by third party – A third party will not be given leave to intervene in a Crown appeal to raise a ground of appeal not being raised by the Attorney General in his appeal: *R. v. Morgentaler, Smoling and Scott* (1985), 19 C.C.C. (3d) 573 (Ont. C.A.).

Crown appeal against sentence generally – The Attorney General may appeal against a disposition of a discharge as of right on a question of law alone or with leave of the Court of Appeal as a sentence appeal under this subsection: *R. v. Hunt*, [1979] 2 S.C.R. 73, 45 C.C.C. (2d) 257.

In view of the definition of "sentence" in s. 673, the Attorney General may appeal from the decision of a trial judge refusing to make an order of forfeiture under s. 462.37(1): *R. v. Pawlyk* (1991), 65 C.C.C. (3d) 63 (Man. C.A.).

On a Crown appeal against sentence it will not be permitted to introduce new evidence unless there is something which trial counsel could not have reasonably been expected to introduce, or, perhaps in a case where the accused constitutes a real danger to the public: *R. v. Irwin* (1979), 48 C.C.C. (2d) 423 (Alta. S.C. App. Div.).

Similarly, in *R. v. Hogan* (1979), 50 C.C.C. (2d) 439 (N.S.S.C. App. Div.), the Crown was refused leave to introduce fresh evidence as to aggravating circumstances of the offence as it would be unfair to the accused and not in the interests of the proper administration of justice.

Where the sentence originally imposed has already been served the Court of Appeal will not allow a Crown appeal against that sentence which would have the effect of sending or returning the accused to jail unless it is satisfied that the sentence is so manifestly wrong that it must intervene in the interests of justice: *R. v. Richards* (1979), 49 C.C.C. (2d) 517 (Ont. C.A.); *R. v. Bartkow* (1978), 1 C.R. (3d) S-36, 24 N.S.R. (2d) 518 (S.C. App. Div.).

The court should be reluctant to vary a non-custodial sentence to a custodial sentence on a Crown appeal even where it finds error in principle, unless it is also satisfied that the sentence imposed was outside of the acceptable range: *R. v. Russo* (1998), 130 C.C.C. (3d) 339 (Ont. C.A.).

Where the final sentencing of an accused has been delayed by a lengthy appellate process and the accused has served the sentence imposed at trial, the imposition of a "just sanction" demands that these factors be taken into account, especially where the accused has made demonstrable progress in rehabilitation: *R. v. Smickle* (2014), 306 C.C.C. (3d) 351 (Ont. C.A.).

APPEAL RE COSTS.

676.1 A party who is ordered to pay costs may, with leave of the court of appeal or a judge of a court of appeal, appeal the order or the amount of costs ordered. 1997, c. 18, s. 94.

ANNOTATIONS

"Costs" extends beyond a punitive order for costs or costs already incurred to include those fees payable in consideration of services to be provided in the future. An appeal of a costs order, made directly to the provincial appellate court rather than to the Supreme Court of Canada through s. 40 of the *Supreme Court Act*, was dismissed: *C. (R.) v. Quebec (Attorney General)*, [2002] 2 S.C.R. 762, 164 C.C.C. (3d) 423 *sub nom. R. v. C. (R.)*.

While an appeal from a costs award should not be heard while a trial is ongoing, the appellate court considered the Crown appeal in circumstances where the trial judge ordered costs during the course of the trial to be paid within 30 days. A stay of proceedings, including a remedy of an award of costs, as a result of an abuse of process should generally not be determined until the end of the trial: *R. v. Clement* (2002), 166 C.C.C. (3d) 219, 159 O.A.C. 323 (C.A.).

Where the Crown alleged that the motions judge had erred in considering an *R. v. Rowbotham* (1988), 41 C.C.C. (3d) 1 (Ont. C.A.) application, the appropriate avenue was an appeal pursuant to this provision rather than review on *certiorari*: *R. v. Innocente* (2004), 183 C.C.C. (3d) 215 (N.S.C.A.).

The application judge had no jurisdiction to review the reasonableness of the legal aid plan's decision and was limited to determining whether the accused's right to a fair trial was infringed because of the conditions under which he was being defended. In this case, the refusal of legal aid to authorize junior counsel and to pay travel expenses did not infringe the right to a fair trial. There was no positive obligation for the state to fund counsel of choice. There was no evidence on the application that other competent counsel was not available to take the case on the conditions imposed by the legal aid plan, notwithstanding that the trial was imminent. Furthermore, the order, if properly made, should be made against the Crown, not the legal aid plan: *R. v. Peterman* (2004), 185 C.C.C. (3d) 352 (Ont. C.A.).

Costs awards should not be made against the Ontario Review Board in the absence of egregious misconduct constituting a marked and unacceptable departure from the reasonable standards expected of a review board: *Leyshon-Hughes v. Ontario Review Board* (2009), 240 C.C.C. (3d) 181 (Ont. C.A.).

SPECIFYING GROUNDS OF DISSENT.

677. Where a judge of the court of appeal expresses an opinion dissenting from the judgment of the court, the judgment of the court shall specify any grounds in law on which the dissent, in whole or in part, is based. R.S., c. C-34, s. 606; 1994, c. 44, s. 67.

CROSS-REFERENCES

Under ss. 691(1)(*a*), 692(3)(*a*) and 693(1)(*a*), a dissent on a question of law may found an appeal to the Supreme Court of Canada, as of right.

SYNOPSIS

This section requires that the reasons in law of any dissenting judgment must be specified in the formal judgment of the court.

ANNOTATIONS

The irregularity of the formal judgment in not formally specifying the grounds for dissent will not be fatal to the appellant's right of appeal under s. 691(1)(*a*) particularly as the points of law upon which the minority judge dissented were clearly set out in his reasons for judgment: *R. v. Warkentin, Hanson and Brown*, [1977] 2 S.C.R. 355, 30 C.C.C. (2d) 1 (5:4).

Procedure on Appeals

NOTICE OF APPEAL / Extension of time.

678. (1) An appellant who proposes to appeal to the court of appeal or to obtain the leave of that court to appeal shall give notice of appeal or notice of his application for leave to appeal in such manner and within such period as may be directed by rules of court.

(2) The court of appeal or a judge thereof may at any time extend the time within which notice of appeal or notice of an application for leave to appeal may be given. R.S., c. C-34, s. 607; 1972, c. 13, s. 53; 1974-75-76, c. 105, s. 16.

CROSS-REFERENCES

The court of appeal may make rules relating to criminal appeals which are consistent with the Code. Under s. 678.1, substitutional service of a notice of appeal or notice of application for leave to appeal may be made on a respondent who has not been located after reasonable efforts.

See also references cited under s. 675.

SYNOPSIS

This section provides that an appellant shall give notice of appeal, or apply for leave to appeal, according to the rules of court. The Court of Appeal or a judge of that court may extend the time for notice.

ANNOTATIONS

Service of notice of appeal – In *Kipnes v. Alberta (Attorney General)*, [1966] 4 C.C.C. 387 (Alta. C.A.), it was held (2:1), that in the absence of a specific rule under the Alberta Rules of Court, the rule governing civil matters would apply for service of a notice of appeal under this section.

Trial counsel in filing a notice of appeal to preserve the accused's appeal rights cannot be required to proceed with the appeal at his own expense where Legal Aid is subsequently refused and in such circumstances he should be permitted to withdraw from the case: *R. v. Dorion* (1978), 40 C.C.C. (2d) 549 (Man. C.A.).

Pursuant to s. 683(3), the Court of Appeal may authorize the service of a notice of appeal out of the jurisdiction. Accordingly, the accused was properly served with the Crown's notice of appeal in the United States: *R. v. Smith* (1999), 141 C.C.C. (3d) 421 (B.C.C.A.).

Extension of time / *Application of subsection* – In *R. v. Stokes and Stevenson* (1966), 49 C.R. 97 (Man. C.A.), it was held that this subsection does not empower the Registrar to make an order extending the time for appeal.

Grounds for granting extension of time – Where the Crown has demonstrated a *bona fide* intention to appeal within the appeal period, has exercised reasonable diligence in attempting to locate the accused for service of the notice of appeal and has shown there are arguable grounds for appeal, then the extension of time should be granted. Moreover, the Crown is not required to establish that the appeal would probably succeed: *R. v. Gruener* (1979), 46 C.C.C. (2d) 88 (Ont. C.A. in chambers). See also *R. v. Antonangeli* (2000), 146 C.C.C. (3d) 90 (Ont. C.A.).

It is a cardinal principle that the party seeking the extension must have displayed a *bona fide* intention to appeal within the time limit. The Crown was refused an extension of time where although it was clear that the Crown intended to continue the prosecution against the accused there was no intention to do so by appealing the decision dismissing the charges, within the statutory time. In this case the Crown had originally proceeded by relaying the information but these informations were stayed as an abuse of process: *R. v. Scheller (No. 2)* (1976), 32 C.C.C. (2d) 286 (Ont. C.A. in chambers).

However, in *R. v. Hetsberger* (1979), 47 C.C.C. (2d) 154 (Ont. C.A. in chambers), an extension of time was granted notwithstanding the absence of an intention to appeal within the time limit where the consequences of the conviction (deportation) were out of all proportion to the penalty imposed and it was arguable that in law no offence was committed. See also *R. v. W. (G.)* (1999), 137 C.C.C. (3d) 194 (Nfld. C.A.), in which an extension of time to appeal a sentence was granted because of the unusual circumstances, despite an absence of an intention to appeal within the prescribed time limit.

An extension of time was granted to appeal a dangerous offender designation, despite the absence of a *bona fide* intention to appeal, having regard to the fact that subsequent decisions clarified the law and demonstrated that the trial judge had erred in refusing to consider the long-term offender provisions. In addition, the dangerous offender designation was extremely onerous, the accused was mentally handicapped and the Crown would not be unduly prejudiced as a result of the extension: *R. v. G. (M.A.)* (2002), 167 C.C.C. (3d) 435 (B.C.C.A.).

Subsection (2) gives the judge a very full discretionary power to grant an extension of time and there are no absolute rules for when the application should be granted. However, some of the criteria applied are whether the applicant has shown a *bona fide* intention to appeal within the appeal period, whether the applicant has accounted for the delay and has shown that the other side was not seriously prejudiced, that the applicant has not taken the benefits of the judgment he seeks to appeal and that the appeal has a reasonable chance of success. The relevance and relative importance of each of these criteria are for the judge to determine. It is also incumbent on the applicant to provide the judge with sufficient material upon which he can exercise his discretion. Facts accounting for the delay would ordinarily be placed before the judge by way of affidavit evidence. Facts concerning the merits of the appeal could be by way of affidavit or through counsel's statement to the court, except that if there is any disagreement between counsel as to what the record will contain then it should be resolved by evidence as to what occurred in the court below: *R. v. Henry* (1989), 52 C.C.C. (3d) 470 (Man. C.A.).

There is no absolute rule to be applied in the exercise of the discretion whether or not to grant an extension of time. The court will, however, usually consider the following three factors: (i) whether the applicant has shown a *bona fide* intention to appeal within the appeal period; (ii) whether the applicant has accounted for or explained the delay; and (iii) whether there is merit to the proposed appeal. Depending on the case, the court may take into consideration other factors such as whether the consequences of the conviction are out of all proportion to the penalty imposed, whether the Crown will be prejudiced and whether the applicant has taken the benefit of the judgment. In the end, the main consideration is whether the applicant has demonstrated that justice requires that the extension of time be granted: *R. v. Menear* (2002), 162 C.C.C. (3d) 233 (Ont. C.A.), leave to appeal refused [2002] 3 S.C.R. ix, 164 C.C.C. (3d) vi.

As a general rule, an offender whose sentence was the product of the law in force at the time it was imposed should not be granted an extension of time to appeal so that he or she can take advantage of a new legal landscape: *R. v. Letiec* (2015), 322 C.C.C. (3d) 306 (Alta. C.A.). See also: *R. v. Canto* (2015), 329 C.C.C. (3d) 169 (Alta. C.A.). Nonetheless, the British Columbia Court of Appeal has taken a more generous approach to cases in which the offender was sentenced prior to *R. v. Summers*, [2014] 1 S.C.R. 575, 308 C.C.C. (3d) 471, routinely granting extensions of time to appellants seeking the benefit of enhanced credit for pre-sentence custody: see, e.g., *R. v. Sagastume* (2015), 119 W.C.B. (2d) 311, [2015] B.C.J. No. 272 (C.A.).

In *R. v. Ansari* (2015), 328 C.C.C. (3d) 439 (Ont. C.A.), the court granted a lengthy extension of the time within which to appeal sentence, due to the coming into force (after sentencing) of a law allowing the minister to revoke the citizenship of people like the appellant convicted of terrorism offences.

Jurisdiction to rescind order refusing extension – A Court of Appeal has jurisdiction to rescind a previous order, even one made by a full court of three judges, refusing an extension of time to appeal where the interests of justice so require: *R. v. Audy (No. 1)* (1977), 34 C.C.C. (2d) 228 (Ont. C.A.).

Further, a single judge of the Court of Appeal has jurisdiction to rescind his own order previously made refusing an extension of time: *R. v. Dunbrook* (1978), 44 C.C.C. (2d) 264 (Ont. C.A. in chambers).

An application for an extension of time, previously refused by a single judge, may be renewed before the full court where conditions have changed since the initial refusal: *R. v. Walker* (1978), 46 C.C.C. (2d) 124 (Que. C.A.), or there are other special circumstances: *R. v. Coulombe* (1988), 64 C.R. (3d) 58 (Que. C.A.). See also *R. v. O'Malley* (1997), 119 C.C.C. (3d) 360 (B.C.C.A.), leave to appeal to S.C.C. refused 127 C.C.C. (3d) vi. In *R. v. G. (E.H.)* (2008), 237 C.C.C. (3d) 203, the Manitoba Court of Appeal held that there was no right of appeal or review from the decision of a single judge except where the judge made demonstrable and decisive error.

SERVICE WHERE RESPONDENT CANNOT BE FOUND.

678.1 Where a respondent cannot be found after reasonable efforts have been made to serve the respondent with a notice of appeal or notice of an application for leave to appeal, service of the notice of appeal or the notice of the application for leave to appeal may be effected substitutionally in the manner and within the period directed by a judge of the court of appeal. R.S.C. 1985, c. 27 (1st Supp.), s. 140.

CROSS-REFERENCES

An order for substitutional service should include the date of hearing and determination of the appeal and should attempt to ensure receipt of notification by the respondent.

SYNOPSIS

This section allows for substituted service on a respondent of notice of appeal, or application for leave to appeal, as directed by a judge of the Court of Appeal.

ANNOTATIONS

In *R. v. Gruener* (1979), 46 C.C.C. (2d) 88 (Ont. C.A. in chambers), a case decided prior to the enactment of this section, the judge, while prepared to assume that there was jurisdiction to make an order for substitutional service under the rules of the court, held that the order should only be made where personal service upon the accused is demonstrably not possible through no fault of the Crown authorities and where if such an order is made it will, in all probability, if not certainly, be effective to bring notice to the accused. A relevant factor in deciding whether to make the order is whether the accused dropped out of sight to avoid service because he was aware of a firm intention by the Crown to appeal the acquittal.

Substituted service is also available in summary conviction appeals where provided for in rules of court enacted pursuant to s. 482(1): *R. v. Marton* (2016), 340 C.C.C. (3d) 472 (Ont. C.A.).

RELEASE PENDING DETERMINATION OF APPEAL / Notice of application for release / Circumstances in which appellant may be released / Idem / Conditions of order / Conditions / Application of certain provisions of s. 525 / Release or detention pending hearing of reference / Release or detention pending new trial or new hearing / Application to appeals on summary conviction proceedings / Form of undertaking or recognizance / Directions for expediting appeal, new trial, etc.

679. (1) A judge of the court of appeal may, in accordance with this section, release an appellant from custody pending the determination of his appeal if,

(*a*) in the case of an appeal to the court of appeal against conviction, the appellant has given notice of appeal or, where leave is required, notice of his application for leave to appeal pursuant to section 678;

(*b*) in the case of an appeal to the court of appeal against sentence only, the appellant has been granted leave to appeal; or

(*c*) in the case of an appeal or an application for leave to appeal to the Supreme Court of Canada, the appellant has filed and served his notice of appeal or, where leave is required, his application for leave to appeal.

(2) Where an appellant applies to a judge of the court of appeal to be released pending the determination of his appeal, he shall give written notice of the application to the prosecutor or to such other person as a judge of the court of appeal directs.

(3) In the case of an appeal referred to in paragraph (1)(*a*) or (*c*), the judge of the court of appeal may order that the appellant be released pending the determination of his appeal if the appellant establishes that

(*a*) the appeal or application for leave to appeal is not frivolous;

(*b*) he will surrender himself into custody in accordance with the terms of the order; and

(*c*) his detention is not necessary in the public interest.

(4) In the case of an appeal referred to in paragraph (1)(*b*), the judge of the court of appeal may order that the appellant be released pending the determination of his appeal or until otherwise ordered by a judge of the court of appeal if the appellant establishes that

(*a*) the appeal has sufficient merit that, in the circumstances, it would cause unnecessary hardship if he were detained in custody;

(*b*) he will surrender himself into custody in accordance with the terms of the order; and

(*c*) his detention is not necessary in the public interest.

(5) Where the judge of the court of appeal does not refuse the application of the appellant, he shall order that the appellant be released

(*a*) on his giving an undertaking to the judge, without conditions or with such conditions as the judge directs, to surrender himself into custody in accordance with the order, or

(*b*) on his entering into a recognizance

(i) with one or more sureties,

(ii) with deposit of money or other valuable security,

(iii) with both sureties and deposit, or

(iv) with neither sureties nor deposit,

in such amount, subject to such conditions, if any, and before such justice as the judge directs,

and the person having the custody of the appellant shall, where the appellant complies with the order, forthwith release the appellant.

(5.1) The judge may direct that the undertaking or recognizance referred to in subsection (5) include the conditions described in subsections 515(4), (4.1) and (4.2) that the judge considers desirable.

(6) The provisions of subsections 525(5), (6) and (7) apply with such modifications as the circumstances require in respect of a person who has been released from custody under subsection (5) of this section.

(7) If, with respect to any person, the Minister of Justice gives a direction or makes a reference under section 696.3, this section applies to the release or detention of that person pending the hearing and determination of the reference as though that person were an appellant in an appeal described in paragraph (1)(*a*).

(7.1) Where, with respect to any person, the court of appeal or the Supreme Court of Canada orders a new trial, section 515 or 522, as the case may be, applies to the release or detention of that person pending the new trial or new hearing as though that person were charged with the offence for the first time, except that the powers of a justice under section 515 or of a judge under section 522 are exercised by a judge of the court of appeal.

(8) This section applies to applications for leave to appeal and appeals to the Supreme Court of Canada in summary conviction proceedings.

(9) An undertaking under this section may be in Form 12 and a recognizance under this section may be in Form 32.

(10) A judge of the court of appeal, where on the application of an appellant he does not make an order under subsection (5) or where he cancels an order previously made

under this section, or a judge of the Supreme Court of Canada on application by an appellant in the case of an appeal to that Court, may give such directions as he thinks necessary for expediting the hearing of the appellant's appeal or for expediting the new trial or new hearing or the hearing of the reference, as the case may be. R.S., c. C-34, s. 608; R.S., c. 2 (2nd Supp.), s. 12; R.S.C. 1985, c. 27 (1st Supp.), s. 141; 1997, c. 18, s. 95; 1999, c. 25, s. 14; 2002, c. 13, s. 66.

CROSS-REFERENCES

Authority for the review of a decision of a judge of the court of appeal under s. 679 may be found in s. 680. An undertaking and a recognizance may be in Forms 12 and 32 respectively. A release order will usually include terms governing the appellant's conduct pending the appeal, breach of which may result in dismissal of the appeal. Also, liability under s. 145(2) and (3) may be attracted by a breach of a term of the undertaking or recognizance.

Reference should also be had to s. 683 regarding the power of a judge or the court to suspend various types of orders including the payment of a fine, forfeiture order, probation orders or conditional sentence orders. A driving prohibition may be stayed pursuant to s. 261.

Note that s. 672.1 defines "court" for the purposes of Part XX.1 [Mental Disorder] to include a judge of the court of appeal and, thus, a judge of the court of appeal may make the various orders provided for in that Part including an assessment order under s. 672.11. Under s. 672.17, no order may be made under this section during the period that an assessment order of an accused is in force. The assessment may, however, be varied under s. 672.18.

SYNOPSIS

This section provides for the granting of bail pending an appeal to the Court of Appeal or the Supreme Court of Canada.

A judge of the court of appeal may make an order releasing an appellant from custody where: (a) an appeal from conviction/application for leave has been filed; (b) leave to appeal sentence has been granted; or (c) in the case of appeals to the Supreme Court, the notice of appeal or application for leave to appeal has been filed and served (subsec. (1)).

Notice must be given to the Crown (subsec. (2)).

On applications relating to conviction appeals to the court of appeal or appeals/ applications to the Supreme Court the appellant must establish that: (a) the appeal is not frivolous (*i.e.*, it is arguable); (b) he or she will surrender into custody as and when required; and (c) detention is not necessary in the public interest (subsec. (3)).

On applications relating to sentence appeals the appellant, having obtained leave, must establish that: (a) the appeal has sufficient merit that hardship would result if bail was not granted (*e.g.*, the sentence would be served before the appeal could be heard); (b) the appellant will surrender into custody as and when required; and (c) detention is not necessary in the public interest (subsec. (4)).

The order for release may require that the appellant give an undertaking, or enter into a recognizance, with such terms and conditions as the judge sees fit to impose (subsec. (5)).

An appellant who breaches his or her bail may be arrested, with or without warrant, and dealt with in the same way as an accused who is awaiting trial (subsec. (6)).

A judge of the court of appeal also has jurisdiction to grant bail where the Minister of Justice directs a new trial or hearing. In such cases the application shall proceed as if the appellant was appealing a conviction (subsec. (7)). A judge of the court of appeal also has jurisdiction to grant bail where a new trial is ordered by the court of appeal or the Supreme Court of Canada, in which case the application proceeds as if the applicant was charged with the offence (subsec. (8)).

Bail may also be granted in connection with summary conviction matters before the Supreme Court of Canada (see *Supreme Court Act*, s. 40) (subsec. (8)).

Where bail is refused a judge of the court of appeal may give directions for expediting the hearing of the appeal, new trial, etc. Where the appeal is to the Supreme Court of Canada a judge of that court may give similar directions (subsec. (10)).

ANNOTATIONS

Jurisdiction to order release – The Court of Appeal has jurisdiction to grant release pending appeal of an accused who has been convicted and has filed a notice of appeal against conviction, though the accused had not yet been sentenced and was remanded into custody for sentencing: *R. v. Smale* (1979), 51 C.C.C. (2d) 126 (Ont. C.A.).

However, the order for release can only apply to the custody to which the accused is then subject and must provide that it expires at the time of sentencing or the disposition of the appeal, whichever is earlier: *R. v. Morris* (1985), 21 C.C.C. (3d) 242 (Ont. C.A.). See also: *R. v. Ururyar* (2016), 132 W.C.B. (2d) 445, [2016] O.J. No. 4293 (S.C.J.).

Further, an order releasing the appellant pending sentence should only be made where the accused demonstrates that there are unusual circumstances that warrant interfering with the trial judge's discretion remanding the accused into custody: *R. v. Hart* (1998), 128 C.C.C. (3d) 221 (N.S.C.A.).

The Court of Appeal has jurisdiction to grant release where the accused has been released on day parole: *R. v. Wood* (1999), 139 C.C.C. (3d) 475 (N.S.C.A.).

The court has no jurisdiction to grant release pending appeal to an offender who has not been sentenced unless he or she is incarcerated. Courts do not grant bail prospectively: *R. v. Barbour* (2016), 336 C.C.C. (3d) 542 (Alta. C.A.).

Under the *Corrections and Conditional Release Act*, S.C. 1992, c. 20, an offender on parole continues to serve his or her sentence and is therefore under a form of custody. Thus, the offender may apply for bail pending appeal under this section: *R. v. Walsh* (2005), 193 C.C.C. (3d) 517 (Ont. C.A.).

This provision allows for successive applications before a single judge without seeking a review pursuant to s. 680 where the correctness of the dismissal of the first application is conceded but the circumstances have changed. Although it is preferable that the judge who heard the initial application hear the subsequent application, there is no such hard and fast rule. While in some situations, fairness to the parties will require the same judge to hear the application, in other situations this may not be necessary. The judge before whom the second application is brought must exercise his or her discretion and determine whether justice requires that the second application be heard by the judge who heard the first application. In this case, the restatement [of legal argument] in a more comprehensive form and one additional legal argument constituted a material change in circumstances justifying release: *R. v. Daniels* (1997), 119 C.C.C. (3d) 413 (Ont. C.A.). Also see *R. v. D'Agostino* (1998), 127 C.C.C. (3d) 209 (Alta. C.A.).

A single judge had the jurisdiction to consider an application to vary a previous order made by that judge or a colleague: *R. v. Knockwood* (2009), 246 C.C.C. (3d) 547 (N.S.C.A.).

A judge only has jurisdiction to deal with the merits on a subsequent original application, as permitted by *R. v. Daniels, supra*, if the judge is satisfied that there has been a material change in circumstances. A material change in circumstances requires additional information that could alter the assessment of one or more of the statutory factors governing release pending appeal. If there is a material change in circumstances, the judge must consider all of the statutory grounds and be satisfied that the appellant has met the onus in subsec. (3). Since this application is not a review under s. 680, the parties must accept the correctness of the decision of the first judge: *R. v. Baltovich* (2000), 144 C.C.C. (3d) 233 (Ont. C.A.).

Subsection (3) applies to the extradition context with the necessary modifications. Subsection (3)(*a*) requires the fugitive to show that the application is neither vexatious nor frivolous in that there are issues warranting the Minister's consideration. The public interest criterion applies with less force in extradition in that the need to enforce the committal order weighs less heavily than does the public interest in immediate enforcement of a sentence: *Trinidad and Tobago (Republic) v. Raghoonanan* (2003), 173 C.C.C. (3d) 294, 63 O.R. (3d) 465, *sub nom. Canada (Attorney General) v. Raghoonon* (C.A.). In *T. (S.J.) v. United States of America* (2003), 174 C.C.C. (3d) 373, 220 Nfld. & P.E.I.R. 312, however, the Newfoundland Court of Appeal held that only subsec. (3)(*b*) and (*c*) were relevant in the extradition context. Subsection (3)(*a*), requiring the fugitive to demonstrate that the appeal was not frivolous, was not a proper consideration in the extradition context.

Burden of proof – The appellant has the burden of establishing or proving on a balance of probabilities the requirements of this subsection: *R. v. Ponak and Gunn*, [1972] 4 W.W.R. 316 (B.C.C.A. in chambers).

Grounds for granting release – The public interest criterion of subsec. (3)(*c*) consists of two components: public safety and public confidence in the administration of justice. In accordance with *R. v. Farinacci, infra*, the public confidence component involves the weighing of two competing interests: enforceability and reviewability. Seriousness of the offence and apparent strength of the grounds of appeal are the most important factors in assessing enforceability and reviewability, respectively. Public confidence is to be measured through the eyes of a reasonable member of the public who is thoughtful and dispassionate. Where the applicant has been convicted of murder or some other very serious crime, the public interest in enforceability will be high and will often outweigh the reviewability interest, particularly where there are lingering public safety or flight concerns, or the grounds of appeal appear to be weak. Where public safety or flight concerns are negligible, and where the grounds of appeal clearly surpass the "not frivolous" criterion, the public interest in reviewability may well overshadow the enforceability interest, even in the case of murder or other very serious offences: *R. v. Oland*, [2017] 1 S.C.R. 250, 347 C.C.C. (3d) 257.

The "public interest" ground in subsec. (3)(*c*) for detention pending appeal is not unconstitutional. In the context of bail pending appeal, the public interest provides a clear standard relating both to the protection and safety of the public and to the need to maintain a balance between the competing dictates of enforceability of judgments and reviewability for correction of errors. Thus, there will be cases where the hearing of the appeal will be so delayed and the probability of success so strong that it would be contrary to the public interest to refuse release even for a serious offence. On the other hand, the public interest may require that a person convicted of a very serious offence, particularly a repeat offender who is advancing grounds of appeal that are arguable but weak, be denied bail: *R. v. Farinacci* (1993), 86 C.C.C. (3d) 32 (Ont. C.A.). Similarly: *R. v. Branco* (1993), 87 C.C.C. (3d) 71 (B.C.C.A.), leave to appeal to S.C.C. refused 90 C.C.C. (3d) vi. Also see: *R. v. Parsons* (1994), 30 C.R. (4th) 169, 117 Nfld. & P.E.I.R. 69 (Nfld. C.A., Marshall J.A.) [affd 30 C.R. (4th) 189, 117 Nfld. & P.E.I.R. 69], where, however, the constitutional issue was not raised.

Release should be granted unless there is some factor which would cause ordinary, reasonable, fair-minded members of society or persons informed about the philosophy of legislative provisions, Charter values and the actual circumstances of the case to believe that detention is necessary to maintain public confidence in the administration of justice: *R. v. Nguyen* (1997), 119 C.C.C. (3d) 269 (B.C.C.A.).

The greater the seriousness of the offence, the stronger the grounds required to shift the balance from enforceability to reviewability: *R. v. Gingras* (2012), 293 C.C.C. (3d) 100 (B.C.C.A.).

However, even an accused convicted of a horrendous crime is entitled to release pending appeal where he has clearly arguable grounds of appeal and there is no real risk of non-compliance. A reasonable member of the public would conclude that release is consistent with the just and proper functioning of the justice system: *R. v. Papasotiriou* (2018), 366 C.C.C. (3d) 298 (Ont. C.A.).

The applicant need only show that the ground of appeal would not necessarily fail in order to establish that the appeal is not frivolous: *R. v. Passey* (1997), 121 C.C.C. (3d) 444 (Alta. C.A.).

There is no burden on the Crown to adduce evidence that the accused will not surrender into the custody. The burden is upon the applicant to establish all three criteria in subsec. (3): *R. v. Allen* (2001), 158 C.C.C. (3d) 225 (Nfld. C.A.).

Where the principal ground of appeal depends upon the admission of fresh evidence, the appellant must demonstrate an arguable case that he can satisfy the test in *R. v. Palmer* (1979), [1980] 1 S.C.R. 759, 50 C.C.C. (2d) 193: *R. v. Manasseri* (2013), 312 C.C.C. (3d) 132 (Ont. C.A.).

When seeking bail on a sentence appeal, obtaining leave is a prerequisite to obtaining bail. However, the "leave" standard is clearly a less onerous threshold to satisfy than the "sufficient merit" standard in subsec. (4)(*a*). The analysis of "sufficient merit" takes into consideration whether the time the appellant will spend in jail pending a sentence appeal is greater than the time spent in jail under a fit sentence: *R. v. Mauger* (2017), 359 C.C.C. (3d) 131 (N.S.C.A.).

Revocation of release order [subsec. (6)] – There is no power to issue a warrant under s. 525(5) where the violation of the appellant's release order was not discovered until after that order had expired and the appellant was released on a new order. However, where the new order was obtained by fraud, by reason of the false assertion in the material in support of the application for the new order that the appellant had not violated the terms of his previous release order, then the court has an inherent power to set aside the new order and any subsequent release order. A warrant may therefore issue for the arrest of the appellant. The appellant will then be dealt with pursuant to s. 525(7): *R. v. Stoltz* (1993), 84 C.C.C. (3d) 422, 53 W.A.C. 147 (B.C.C.A.). *Contra:* See *R. v. Dosch* (2000), 145 C.C.C. (3d) 348 (Ont. C.A.), in which the court concluded that the power to issue a warrant pursuant to s. 525(5) is not affected by the fact that the recognizance that is the subject of the breach has been superseded by a new recognizance.

Where the accused was already in custody in respect of new charges, there was no need to obtain a warrant in separate proceedings prior to a determination of the application for revocation. The justice may, however, delay consideration of the endorsement of a certificate of default until the determination of the outstanding charges: *R. v. Dallaire* (2001), 40 C.R. (5th) 385, 141 O.A.C. 65 (C.A.).

Release pending new trial – Where a new trial is ordered following a successful Crown appeal a judge of the trial court has jurisdiction to deal with release of the accused pending that new trial: *R. v. Graham* (1986), 30 C.C.C. (3d) 176 (Ont. H.C.J.); *R. v. Schwartz* (1996), 113 C.C.C. (3d) 220 (B.C.S.C.).

Where the accused is released pursuant to an order of the Court of Appeal pending a new trial, a single judge of the Court of Appeal has jurisdiction to hear an application to revoke the release order: *R. v. Parsons* (1997), 124 C.C.C. (3d) 92 (Nfld. C.A.).

The principal purpose of subsec. (7.1) is to bridge the temporal gap from the time the new trial is ordered to the accused's appearance in the trial court. During that period, only a judge of the Court of Appeal has jurisdiction to release the accused on bail pending the new trial. However, once the accused has appeared in the court before which the new trial is to be had, even if the Court of Appeal and the trial court have concurrent jurisdiction, a bail application should be brought in the trial court: *R. v. Barbeau* (1998), 131 C.C.C. (3d) 350 (Que. C.A.).

Where concurrent jurisdiction exists, all relevant factors should be considered to determine the most appropriate forum for the hearing and determination of the application. Factors may include the geographic location of the applicant, sureties, and counsel; the need for familiarity with the appellate record; the likely need for *viva voce* evidence; and the anticipated length of the hearing: *R. v. Manasseri*, 2017 ONCA 226.

A review of an order denying release pending a new trial may be brought either before a trial court pursuant to s. 520 or before the appellate court pursuant to s. 680: *R. v. Fleming* (1999), 141 C.C.C. (3d) 391 (Nfld. C.A.).

Release pending appeal to Supreme Court of Canada – A judge of the court of appeal has jurisdiction to order the release of an accused pending his application for leave to appeal to the Supreme Court, where a notice of motion for leave to appeal has been filed with the court, even if all the documents necessary to perfect the leave application have not yet been filed: *R. v. Zundel* (1990), 54 C.C.C. (3d) 400 (Ont. C.A.).

On an application to review a release order made by a judge of the Court of Appeal, the reviewing court has the authority to substitute its opinion for that of the single judge after considering the record, the principles that govern the grant of bail and the conclusions and findings made by the judge. The nature of the review is correctness, not reasonableness. The court may also receive and consider additional evidence that bears upon the application, provided the evidence is relevant and arose subsequent to the time the bail order was granted. While a judge has a wide discretion in determining what the public interest is, that discretion does not extend to exclude the public interest as a criterion of equal weight and importance with the other two criteria of merit of the appeal and likelihood of surrender into custody. In determining whether it is contrary to the public interest to release the accused, the court should consider a number of factors including the nature of the offence, the age of the victim, the circumstances surrounding the commission of the offence and the public attitude to such an offence: *R. v. Benson* (1992), 73 C.C.C. (3d) 303, 14 C.R. (4th) 245, *sub nom. R. v. B. (F.F.)* (N.S.C.A.).

REVIEW BY COURT OF APPEAL / Single judge acting / Enforcement of decision.

680. (1) A decision made by a judge under section 522 or subsection 524(4) or (5) or a decision made by a judge of the court of appeal under section 320.25 or 679 may, on the direction of the chief justice or acting chief justice of the court of appeal, be reviewed by that court and that court may, if it does not confirm the decision,

(*a*) vary the decision; or

(*b*) substitute such other decision as, in its opinion, should have been made.

(2) On consent of the parties, the powers of the court of appeal under subsection (1) may be exercised by a judge of that court.

(3) A decision as varied or substituted under this section shall have effect and may be enforced in all respects as though it were the decision originally made. R.S., c. 2 (2nd Supp.), s. 12; 1974-75-76, c. 93, s. 73; R.S.C. 1985, c. 27 (1st Supp.), s. 142; 1994, c. 44, s. 68; 2018, c. 21, s. 22.

CROSS-REFERENCES

While misconduct may attract liability under s. 145(2) and (3), there is no express provision authorizing misconduct hearings.

The discretionary substitution authority of s. 680(1)(*b*) incorporates s. 679(10), thus permitting an order expediting the hearing of an appeal.

SYNOPSIS

This section gives the court of appeal jurisdiction to entertain applications to review certain bail decisions.

Where bail has been granted or refused by a Supreme Court judge in connection with an offence listed in s. 469 (*e.g.*, treason, murder) (see ss. 522, 524(4), (5)) or pending appeal, by a judge of the court of appeal (see s. 679), an application can be made to the chief justice of the court of appeal (or acting chief justice) for an order directing the hearing of an appeal from the earlier ruling (subsec. (1)). The similar procedure must be followed where an order is made under s. 261 respecting a stay of a driving prohibition.

The parties can consent to the review being heard by a single judge of the court of appeal (subsec. (2)).

A decision on such a review is treated, for all intents and purposes, as a decision of the court of first instance.

ANNOTATIONS

A panel conducting a review under subsec. (1) must show deference to the judge's findings of fact, but may substitute its decision for that of the judge where it is satisfied that the judge erred in law or in principle, and the error was material to the outcome. In the absence of legal error, the panel may intervene and substitute its decision for that of the judge where it concludes that the decision was clearly unwarranted. Accordingly, the chief justice should consider directing a review under subsec. (1) where it is arguable that the judge committed material errors of fact or law in arriving at the impugned decision, or that the decision was clearly unwarranted in the circumstances: *R. v. Oland*, [2017] 1 S.C.R. 250, 347 C.C.C. (3d) 257.

Where an accused is detained pursuant to a charge for an offence listed in s. 469, the appropriate procedure for challenging the denial of bail turns on the nature of the applicant's grievance. Where the applicant disputes the correctness of a bail decision of a Superior Court or Court of Appeal judge, the proper course is to seek review by a Court of Appeal under s. 680. Where an applicant concedes the validity of the bail decision but seeks a review on the basis of a change in circumstances, the normal course is to bring a second bail application in Superior Court. This second avenue reflects the common sense in returning to the originating court, creating an evidentiary record and obtaining the views of a judge of first instance on the impact of the new or changed information on the issue of interim release. However, the availability of this second procedure does not foreclose consideration of a change in circumstances on a s. 680 application. In other words, the Superior Court of Justice and the Court of Appeal have concurrent jurisdiction to decide whether there has been a material change of circumstances warranting judicial interim release: *R. v. Whyte* (2014), 310 C.C.C. (3d) 335 (Ont. C.A.).

This section does not apply where the original decision detaining the accused for an offence listed in s. 469 is admittedly correct, but the accused seeks to overturn that decision on the basis of a change in circumstances. In such a case, the accused must apply to the Superior Court under s. 522: *R. v. Turner* (1999), 133 C.C.C. (3d) 180, 171 Nfld. & P.E.I.R. 333 (Nfld. C.A.). See also *R. v. Dempsey* (2001), 153 C.C.C. (3d) 311 (B.C.C.A.).

The requirement to obtain leave of the Chief Justice or designate serves as a screening function to exclude those applications that cannot succeed. The standard applied at this stage is whether the proposed application has a reasonable prospect of success: *R. v. Gale*, [2011] O.J. No. 6410 (C.A.); *R. v. McRae* (unreported, Strathy C.J.O. in chambers, February 2, 2016, File No. M45877).

An application should be dismissed if the applicant would have no hope of success on a review or there was no possibility that the reviewing judge or panel would interfere with the decision: *R. v. Allen* (2001), 158 C.C.C. (3d) 225, 45 C.R. (5th) 242 (Nfld. C.A.).

A review under this section should take the general form of an ordinary appeal and is not a hearing *de novo* in which either side has the right to submit additional materials. However, the court, as in appeals, can grant leave in the usual way and upon the usual grounds to a party to produce new evidence: *R. v. West* (1972), 9 C.C.C. (2d) 369 (Ont. C.A.).

This provision is not restricted to the review of release or detention and includes the jurisdiction to review and vary the conditions of release: *R. v. Hardiman* (2003), 172 C.C.C. (3d) 211 (N.S.C.A.). The duty of the court under this section is to examine the record below and render the decision that "should have been made" by the judge below giving proper regard to his findings of fact and the inferences which he has drawn: *R. v. Smith* (1973), 13 C.C.C. (2d) 374 (N.B.S.C. App. Div.).

A review of the jurisprudence indicates that, while this section confirms an ordinary appellate jurisdiction, nonetheless it is a broad jurisdiction to be exercised not necessarily with the same amount of deference normally applied on appeal. The court has jurisdiction to review an order where a ground of appeal is a material change in circumstances, but, where that is the sole ground for review, the better course is to have the matter dealt with by a judge of the court that dealt with the original bail, and preferably the same judge: *R. v. Massan* (2012), 289 C.C.C. (3d) 285 (Man. C.A.).

In *R. c. Turcotte* (2014), 328 C.C.C. (3d) 119 (C.A. Que.), the court affirmed a "hybrid" standard which affords deference to the bail judge's findings of fact and limits intervention to where an error of law was committed, where clear errors in the weighing of evidence occurred, where significant new evidence must be considered, and where the bail judge's discretion was not exercised judiciously.

This provision has no application where a direct indictment has been preferred and the applicant has been denied bail under s. 515. The appropriate appeal is to a superior court judge by virtue of s. 520: *R. v. Garoufalis* (1996), 107 C.C.C. (3d) 173 (Man. C.A.).

681. [*Repealed*, 1991, c. 43, s. 9.]

REPORT BY JUDGE / Transcript of evidence / Notes of proceedings / Copies to interested parties / Copy for Minister of Justice.

682. (1) Where, under this Part, an appeal is taken or an application for leave to appeal is made, the judge or provincial court judge who presided at the trial shall, at the request of the court of appeal or a judge thereof, in accordance with rules of court, furnish it or him with a report on the case or on any matter relating to the case that is specified in the request.

(2) A copy or transcript of

- **(*a*) the evidence taken at the trial,**
- **(*b*) any charge to the jury and any objections that were made to a charge to the jury,**
- **(*c*) the reasons for judgment, if any, and**
- **(*d*) the addresses of the prosecutor and the accused, if a ground for the appeal is based on either of the addresses,**

shall be furnished to the court of appeal, except in so far as it is dispensed with by order of a judge of that court.

(3) [*Repealed*, 1997, c. 18, s. 96(2).]

(4) A party to an appeal is entitled to receive, on payment of any charges that are fixed by rules of court, a copy or transcript of any material that is prepared under subsections (1) and (2).

(5) The Minister of Justice is entitled, on request, to receive a copy or transcript of any material that is prepared under subsections (1) and (2). R.S., c. C-34, s. 609; 1972, c. 13, s. 55; 1974-75-76, 105, s. 17; R.S.C. 1985, c. 27 (1st Supp.), s. 143; 1997, c. 18, s. 96.

CROSS-REFERENCES

In most instances, the court of appeal will make a determination based on a transcript, agreed statement of facts, charge to the jury or reasons for judgment and any additional proceedings, together with a report of the trial judge.

SYNOPSIS

This section deals with some of the material which is required for the purposes of an appeal (see also the court of appeal rules).

Pursuant to subsec. (1) the court of appeal can request a report from the trial judge concerning the proceedings in that forum.

Subsection (2) allows a judge of the court of appeal to dispense with the filing of portions of the trial record which are not needed for the purposes of the appeal.

Subsection (3) directs that the transcript of a jury charge, and any objections thereto, be certified by the trial judge before the same is filed. If the trial judge is of the opinion that the transcript is inaccurate he or she shall so indicate to the court of appeal and shall provide a correct version of the charge and any objections.

Material filed for use on an appeal is available to the parties at a cost specified in the rules of court (subsec. (4)). The same shall be provided to the Minister of Justice upon request (subsec. (5)).

ANNOTATIONS

Subsection (1) – To a large extent this provision is an historical anachronism. There should not be a standing request from the courts of appeal to trial judges to routinely make a report. The request should only be made in rare cases where something has occurred which is not reflected on the record upon which opposing counsel cannot agree. In those cases, trial counsel ought probably to be afforded an opportunity to appear before the trial judge in order to make submissions with regard to the requested report. When the report is made, copies should be provided to counsel appearing on the appeal. An unsolicited report by the trial judge expressing the opinion that the verdict of the jury was unsafe and indicating that, had he felt entitled to do so the judge would have commented on the testimony of the complainant, should not have been considered by the court of appeal: *R. v. E. (A.W.)*, [1993] 3 S.C.R. 155, 83 C.C.C. (3d) 462.

Subsection (2) – Where one ground of appeal is based upon the address of Crown counsel for which no stenographic notes were taken a conviction for non-capital murder was quashed and a new trial ordered: *R. v. Robillard*, [1969] 4 C.C.C. 120, [1968] Que. Q.B. 255*n* (C.A.). See also *R. v. Gregoire* (1996), 139 Nfld. & P.E.I.R. 294 (Nfld. C.A.).

Merely because there is a gap in the transcript due to malfunctioning of the recording equipment does not in every case require that there be a new trial, even where a portion of the charge to the jury is missing. As a general rule there must be a serious possibility that there was an error in the missing portion of the charge, or that the omission deprived the appellant of a ground of appeal: *R. v. Hayes*, [1989] 1 S.C.R. 44, 48 C.C.C. (3d) 161 (4:3).

An indigent appellant has no absolute right guaranteed by the Charter to have the transcript supplied to him by the state: *R. v. Robinson* (1989), 51 C.C.C. (3d) 452 (Alta. C.A.).

Subsection (3) – Where there is no dispute between the parties as to the accuracy of the transcript of his charge the death of the trial judge preventing his certification will not affect the hearing of the appeal: *R. v. Johnston* (1975), 28 C.C.C. (2d) 222 (N.B. S.C. App. Div.).

POWERS OF COURT OF APPEAL / Parties entitled to adduce evidence and be heard / Virtual presence of parties / Virtual presence of witnesses / Other powers / Execution of process / Power to order suspension / Undertaking or recognizance / Revocation of suspension order / Undertaking or recognizance to be taken into account.

683. (1) For the purposes of an appeal under this Part, the court of appeal may, where it considers it in the interests of justice,

(*a*) order the production of any writing, exhibit, or other thing connected with the proceedings;

(*b*) order any witness who would have been a compellable witness at the trial, whether or not he was called at the trial,

(i) to attend and be examined before the court of appeal, or

(ii) to be examined in the manner provided by rules of court before a judge of the court of appeal, or before any officer of the court of appeal or justice of the peace or other person appointed by the court of appeal for the purpose;

(*c*) admit, as evidence, an examination that is taken under subparagraph (*b*)(ii);

(*d*) receive the evidence, if tendered, of any witness, including the appellant, who is a competent but not compellable witness;

(*e*) order that any question arising on the appeal that

(i) involves prolonged examination of writings or accounts, or scientific or local investigation, and

(ii) cannot in the opinion of the court of appeal conveniently be inquired into before the court of appeal,

be referred for inquiry and report, in the manner provided by rules of court, to a special commissioner appointed by the court of appeal;

(*f*) act on the report of a commissioner who is appointed under paragraph (*e*) in so far as the court of appeal thinks fit to do so, and

(*g*) amend the indictment, unless it is of the opinion that the accused has been misled or prejudiced in his defence or appeal.

(2) In proceedings under this section, the parties or their counsel are entitled to examine or cross-examine witnesses and, in an inquiry under paragraph (1)(*e*), are entitled to be present during the inquiry, and to adduce evidence and to be heard.

(2.1) In proceedings under this section, the court of appeal may order that the presence of a party may be by any technological means satisfactory to the court that permits the court and the other party or parties to communicate simultaneously.

(2.2) Sections 714.1 to 714.8 apply, with any modifications that the circumstances require, to examinations and cross-examinations of witnesses under this section.

(3) A court of appeal may exercise, in relation to proceedings in the court, any powers not mentioned in subsection (1) that may be exercised by the court on appeals in civil matters, and may issue any process that is necessary to enforce the orders or sentences of the court, but no costs shall be allowed to the appellant or respondent on the hearing and determination of an appeal or on any proceedings preliminary or incidental thereto.

(4) Any process that is issued by the court of appeal under this section may be executed anywhere in Canada.

(5) If an appeal or an application for leave to appeal has been filed in the court of appeal, that court, or a judge of that court, may, when the court, or the judge, considers it to be in the interests of justice, order that any of the following be suspended until the appeal has been determined:

(*a*) an obligation to pay a fine;

(*b*) an order of forfeiture or disposition of forfeited property;

(*c*) an order to make restitution under section 738 or 739;

(*d*) an obligation to pay a victim surcharge under section 737;

(*e*) a probation order under section 731; and

(*f*) a conditional sentence order under section 742.1.

(5.1) Before making an order under paragraph (5)(*e*) or (*f*), the court of appeal, or a judge of that court, may order the offender to enter into an undertaking or recognizance.

(6) The court of appeal may revoke any order it makes under subsection (5) where it considers such revocation to be in the interests of justice.

(7) If the offender has been ordered to enter into an undertaking or recognizance under subsection (5.1), the court of appeal shall, in determining whether to vary the sentence of the offender, take into account the conditions of that undertaking or recognizance and the period during which they were imposed. R.S., c. C-34, s. 610; R.S.C. 1985, c. 27 (1st Supp.), s. 144; c. 23 (4th Supp.), s. 5; 1995, c. 22, s. 10; 1997, c. 18, ss. 97, 141; 1999, c. 25, s. 15; 2002, c. 13, s. 67; 2008, c. 18, s. 29.

CROSS-REFERENCES

Authorization for the determination or disposition of an appeal on its merits may be found in s. 687. Section 695(1) confers similar authority upon the Supreme Court of Canada in an appeal brought under ss. 691 to 694 and 696.

Section 688(2.1) permits the court of appeal to order that an inmate appear through technological means for certain parts of the proceedings, including the hearing of the appeal if the conditions set out in that subsection are complied with. Under s. 848, if an accused who is in prison does not have access to legal advice, the court shall, before permitting the accused to appear by means of communication that allows the court and the accused to engage in simultaneous visual and oral communication, be satisfied that the accused will be able to understand the proceedings and that any decisions made by the accused during the proceedings will be voluntary.

SYNOPSIS

This section sets out some of the powers which may be exercised by a court of appeal.

Pursuant to subsec. (1) the court can: (a) order the production of any writing, exhibit, etc., connected with the proceeding; (b) admit "fresh evidence"; (c) refer matters to a special commission for examination; (d) act on the report of a special commissioner; and (e) amend the indictment.

Where witnesses appear, the parties are entitled to examine or cross-examine. In a commissioner's inquiry the parties are entitled to be present to adduce evidence and to be heard (subsec. (2)).

In addition, the court generally can exercise the incidental powers it has in connection with civil matters. However, no costs are to be awarded (subsec. (3)). Any process issued by the court may be executed anywhere in Canada (subsec. (4)).

The court or a judge may suspend the payment of a fine, forfeiture order, restitution order, obligation to pay a victim surcharge, a probation order, or a conditional sentence pending the outcome of an appeal (subsec. (5)). The court or judge may require the appellant to enter into an undertaking or recognizance where they stay a probation order or conditional sentence. Any such order may be revoked if the circumstances warrant (subsec. (6)). Under subsec. (7), in determining whether to vary the sentence, the appellate court may take into account the conditions of the undertaking or recognizance and the period during which they were imposed. A driving prohibition may be stayed pursuant to s. 261.

Subsections (2.1) and (2.2) permit the court of appeal to order that a party be present by technological means and for the taking of evidence through technological means as set out in ss. 714.1 to 714.8.

ANNOTATIONS

Admission of evidence wrongfully excluded at trial – Where the trial judge incorrectly refused to admit a document into evidence, it was accepted upon appeal by the appellate court and considered in allowing the appeal and entering a verdict of acquittal: *R. v. Partridge* (1973), 15 C.C.C. (2d) 434, 5 Nfld. & P.E.I.R. 420 (P.E.I.S.C.).

Rather than simply ordering a new trial because of the error by the trial judge in refusing to permit access to the sealed packet containing the affidavit used to obtain an authorization to intercept private communications, the court of appeal ordered that the accused be given the affidavit and provided with an opportunity to cross-examine the affiant before a person designated by the Chief Justice. The transcript of the cross-examination would then be filed into the record and the court of appeal would be able to determine whether the error required a new trial: *R. v. Hiscock* (1991), 68 C.C.C. (3d) 182 (Que. C.A.).

Admission of evidence to complete the record – Approval was given to an appellate court receiving *viva voce* evidence of analysts whose certificates had been admitted as evidence at trial: *R. v. Kissick*, [1952] 1 S.C.R. 343, 102 C.C.C. 129 (4:1).

In order to obtain the remedy of an examination of a witness during the appeal process, the applicant must satisfy the court that there is at least a reasonable possibility that the proposed examination will produce meaningful evidence to assist the court in fulfilling its role: *R. v. Hobbs* (2010), 253 C.C.C. (3d) 364 (N.S.C.A.).

Where the trial judge refused to allow a deceased preliminary inquiry witness' evidence to be read in because the Crown had overlooked first proving that the accused had been present there, an appellate court allowed this technical defect to be cured before it: *R. v. Huluszkiw* (1962), 133 C.C.C. 244 (Ont. C.A.).

Those cases where the Crown has been permitted to tender further evidence are, generally speaking, cases where the appellate court is doing nothing more than what would clearly have happened at trial had the error or omission been noted and rectified at trial. Where, however, it was not clear that the course of the trial would not have been in any respect different if the error had been discovered at trial, then the application by the Crown should be refused: *R. v. Cheung* (1990), 56 C.C.C. (3d) 381 (B.C.C.A.).

Although the court of appeal has no jurisdiction to remit a matter to the trial court for re-sentencing, it does have jurisdiction pursuant to subsec. (1)(*c*) to appoint a lower court judge to conduct a "Gardiner" hearing in the role of a special commissioner. The commissioner would then report back to the court of appeal on aggravating and mitigating factors that should guide the appellate court's assessment of a fit sentence: *R. v. Pahl* (2016), 336 C.C.C. (3d) 221 (B.C.C.A.), additional reasons 2016 BCCA 493.

Test for admission of fresh evidence – The Court of Appeal's power under this section is limited to admitting as fresh evidence admissible evidence only and manifestly does not authorize a Court of Appeal to dispense with the law of hearsay evidence: *R. v. O'Brien*, [1978] 1 S.C.R. 591, 35 C.C.C. (2d) 209 (9:0).

In *R. v. Palmer and Palmer*, [1980] 1 S.C.R. 759, 50 C.C.C. (2d) 193 (9:0), the court reviewed the principles upon which fresh evidence should be admitted as follows: (1) the evidence should generally not be admitted if, by due diligence, it could have been adduced at trial, although this principle is not applied with the same strictness in a criminal trial as in a civil trial; (2) the evidence must be relevant in that it bears upon a decisive or potentially decisive issue; (3) the evidence must be credible; and (4) it must be such that if believed, it could have affected the result. In that case the accused's appeal was dismissed, the court holding that the Court of Appeal did not err in rejecting the fresh evidence, which concerned the dealings of the chief Crown witness with the Crown and police, on the basis that it was not credible. Also see: *R. v. McAnespie*, [1993] 4 S.C.R. 501, 86 C.C.C. (3d) 191*n*.

Due diligence is not an essential requirement of the fresh evidence test and its importance varies from case to case. The due diligence criterion must yield where a miscarriage of justice would otherwise result. In determining whether due diligence has been met, the reason that the evidence was not available at trial must be determined: *R. v. B. (G.D.)*, [2000] 1 S.C.R. 520, 143 C.C.C. (3d) 289.

Due diligence is only one factor in determining the admissibility of fresh evidence and its absence, particularly in criminal cases, should be assessed in light of other circumstances. If the evidence is compelling and the interests of justice require that it be admitted, then the failure to meet the test should yield to permit its admission. While the failure to meet the due diligence requirement is serious and in many circumstances would be fatal, as held in *R. v. C. (R.)* (1989), 47 C.C.C. (3d) 84 (Ont. C.A.), that failure should not override accomplishing a just result. The Court of Appeal also has the discretion to permit fresh evidence in respect of a defence of not criminally responsible that was not raised at trial: *R. v. Warsing*, [1998] 3 S.C.R. 579, 130 C.C.C. (3d) 259.

Even where the proffered evidence clearly could have been adduced at trial, due diligence should not trump the other criteria, particularly in circumstances where trial counsel's strategy was not unreasonable given the nature of the anticipated Crown evidence. Here, neither the Crown nor the defence had contemplated calling expert evidence about the nature of the injury in question, and the trial judge relied on lay opinion later shown by expert fresh evidence to have been erroneous. Admission was therefore justified: *R. v. A. (J.)*, [2011] 1 S.C.R. 628, 268 C.C.C. (3d) 135.

The fact that the evidence which is tendered neither confirms nor corroborates the testimony of the accused does not mean that it could not have had an impact on the verdict and thus be capable of constituting fresh evidence: *R. v. D'Amours*, [1990] 1 S.C.R. 115.

When deciding whether or not to exercise the broad discretion under this section, the overriding consideration is the interests of justice. This discretion should be exercised to permit the adducing of evidence of the fact that, following the trial, the accused was acquitted of a charge which had formed the basis of similar act evidence at the earlier trial. The acquittal was the equivalent of a finding of innocence and there would be a clear miscarriage of justice if allegations of conduct, of which the accused was innocent, played a part in his conviction for other offences: *R. v. G. (K.R.)* (1991), 68 C.C.C. (3d) 268 (Ont. C.A.).

The traditional criteria for the admission of fresh evidence do not apply, where an accused who has been convicted seeks to place before an appellate court additional material relevant to a factual or legal determination made at trial, where the material sought to be admitted challenges the very validity of the trial process. Where an appellant contends that trial counsel's conduct resulted in a miscarriage of justice, the interests of justice will generally require that the court receive otherwise admissible evidence relevant to that claim, assuming that the material sought to be adduced provides a basis upon which the court could conclude that a miscarriage of justice occurred, and that the opposing party has had adequate notice of the material, an opportunity to challenge it by cross-examination, and an opportunity to offer additional material relevant to the issue: *R. v. W. (W.)* (1995), 100 C.C.C. (3d) 225 (Ont. C.A.). See also *R. v. Strauss* (1995), 100 C.C.C. (3d) 303 (B.C.C.A.). See also *R. v. Gumbly* (1996), 112 C.C.C. (3d) 61 (N.S.C.A.).

Consequently, in *R. v. Barbeau* (1996), 110 C.C.C. (3d) 69 (Que. C.A.), the court admitted fresh evidence relating to the issue of conflict of interest. Where the attack on the validity of the trial process is based on conflict of interest arising out of the joint representation by the same counsel, the accused must demonstrate an actual conflict of interest by pointing to specific instances where the interests of the co-accused diverged and counsel was required to choose between them and by establishing that there was some impairment of counsel's ability to represent the accused effectively as a result of that conflict.

Where an accused seeks to tender evidence on appeal challenging the jurisdiction of the trial court, a stringent standard for admission is applied because of the strong onus on an accused to advance jurisdictional challenges at the outset of trial, especially those which lie within the accused's own peculiar knowledge like the accused's age: *R. v. Shafia* (2016), 341 C.C.C. (3d) 354 (Ont. C.A.), leave to appeal to S.C.C. refused 2017 CarswellOnt 5290.

Where the appellant seeks a new trial as a result of inadvertent non-disclosure by the Crown, it must be established that: (1) there is a reasonable possibility that the undisclosed information could have been used in meeting the Crown's case, advancing a defence or otherwise making a decision that could have affected the conduct of the defence; and (2) that, on a balance of probabilities, the right to make full answer and defence was impaired as a result of the failure to disclose by showing that there is a reasonable possibility that the non-disclosure affected the outcome at trial or the overall fairness of the trial process: *R. v. Babinski* (1999), 135 C.C.C. (3d) 1 (Ont. C.A.).

Procedure for admission of fresh evidence – On an application to adduce fresh evidence the motion should be heard and, if not dismissed, then judgment reserved and the appeal heard. The court can then consider the question of the fresh evidence in light of the background of the case and of the other evidence and then dismiss the application; admit the evidence as conclusive of the issues and dispose of the matter immediately; or admit evidence that may have sufficient probative force, if accepted by the trier of fact, to affect the verdict and direct a new trial: *R. v. Stolar*, [1988] 1 S.C.R. 480, 40 C.C.C. (3d) 1 (5:0).

The phrase "connected with the proceedings" in subsec. (1)(*a*) is not wide enough to give the court power to compel production of papers in the possession of the Crown relating to a crime with which the accused was not charged: *R. v. Evans* (1988), 45 C.C.C. (3d) 523 (B.C.C.A.).

A juror, although a competent witness on a Crown appeal from the accused's acquittal, cannot be compelled to testify and therefore cannot be ordered to attend to be examined under subsec. (1)(*b*) of this section: *R. v. Budai* (1999), 140 C.C.C. (3d) 1 (B.C.C.A.).

The witness sought to have an examination on his affidavit conducted through written interrogatories rather than orally before a special examiner. The limitations of written interrogatories including delay and the curtailment of spontaneous responses rendered oral examination preferable: *R. v. Wolf*, [2007] O.J. No. 1666 (C.A.).

Statistical and other statements of social and economic facts proffered by the Crown to justify, under s. 1 of the Charter, a violation of the Charter would not seem to be admissible under subsec. (1)(*d*). However, provided the other party is given notice of the materials and an opportunity to reply, an appeal court should take notice of relevant matters of social and economic facts, whether or not they have been available to the trial judge: *R. v. Bonin* (1989), 47 C.C.C. (3d) 230 (B.C.C.A.), leave to appeal to S.C.C. refused 50 C.C.C. (3d) vi.

Order for production (subsec. (1)(*a*)) – When production is sought in support of an anticipated fresh evidence application, the applicant must demonstrate: (1) a connection between the request for production and the proposed fresh evidence application, meaning a reasonable possibility that production will assist the applicant in developing or obtaining information that will be admissible as fresh evidence, and (2) that there is some reasonable possibility that the evidence to which the production request is linked may be received as fresh evidence on appeal: *R. v. Trotta* (2004), 23 C.R. (6th) 261 (Ont. C.A.).

However, where the appellant sought disclosure of material over which the Crown claimed informer privilege, the court held that the motion was more properly described as a motion for directions with respect to the scope of Crown disclosure. The more rigourous *Trotta* test did not have to be satisfied at this point, as the appellant had yet to see the material that could possibly give rise to a fresh evidence application: *R. v. Cook* (2014), 307 C.C.C. (3d) 495 (Ont. C.A.).

Where a ground of appeal was that the trial judge erred by denying a third-party records motion at the first stage ("likely relevance"), it was appropriate for the Court of Appeal to obtain the records in question from the lower court file to determine what if any portion of the records should have been disclosed to the defence: *R. v. B. (P.)* (2015), 331 C.C.C. (3d) 511 (Ont. C.A.).

Amendment of indictment [subsec. (1)(*g*)] – There being reversible error in relation to the accused's conviction for attempted murder, it was open to the Court of Appeal, with the consent of the Crown, to amend the indictment so that it included the offence contrary to s. 245, and then dismiss the accused's appeal and substitute a conviction for the s. 245 offence pursuant to s. 686(1)(*b*)(i) and (3). The accused was in no way prejudiced, since he had originally been charged with the s. 245 offence but that charge had in effect been stayed by reason of the rules against multiple convictions: *R. v. Symes* (1989), 49 C.C.C. (3d) 81 (Ont. C.A.).

It is an extraordinary step for an appellate court to amend the charge materially and then to enter a conviction on the basis of the charge as amended. In this case, the court of appeal should not have done so, the accused having conducted their case, including the calling of expert evidence, based on the information as it was initially framed: *R. v. Tremblay*, [1993] 2 S.C.R. 932, 84 C.C.C. (3d) 97 (3:2).

The Court of Appeal should proceed cautiously in amending a charge on appeal, where the effect of the proposed amendment is to materially change the charge against the appellant, even if the amendment does not substitute one charge for another: *R. v. B. (A.L.)* (1998), 128 C.C.C. (3d) 87 (B.C.C.A.), leave to appeal to S.C.C. refused 130 C.C.C. (3d) vi.

The Court of Appeal has power under this subsection to amend the indictment where the amendment cures a variance between the charge laid and the evidence led at trial regardless of whether the amendment materially changes the charge, substitutes a new charge for the initial charge, or adds an additional charge. However, particularly where the effect of the amendment is to substitute a new charge, the court must adopt a cautious approach and give thorough consideration of the potential prejudice to the accused flowing from the amendment: *R. v. Irwin* (1998), 123 C.C.C. (3d) 316 (Ont. C.A.). See also *R. v. Brownson* (2013), 301 C.C.C. (3d) 453 (Ont. C.A.).

The court refused to amend a charge of anal intercourse to charge sexual assault. The original count charged an offence found to be unconstitutional and was therefore a nullity not subject to amendment. In any event, bearing in mind the distinctions between the two offences this was not one of the rare cases where an amendment should be made on appeal:

R. v. S. (A.) (1998), 130 C.C.C. (3d) 320 (Ont. C.A.), leave to appeal to S.C.C. refused 137 C.C.C. (3d) vi.

Powers of Court of Appeal generally (subsec. (3)) – Curtailment of public accessibility to the courts, including trial exhibits, is justified where there is a need to protect the innocent. There is a distinction between records produced by the court or pleadings and similar documents, and exhibits which are frequently the property of non-parties. While such exhibits remain in its custody, the court has a duty to entertain any request for access. This duty includes the right to inquire into the use that is to be made of the exhibits, and the court is fully entitled to regulate that use by securing appropriate undertakings and assurances if those be advisable to protect competing interests. An accused who has been acquitted on appeal must be considered to be innocent. In this case, the media sought access to the audio and video tapes of a confession which were admitted at trial but later held to be inadmissible on appeal because the accused's constitutional rights had been violated. A person, charged and convicted of a serious crime on the basis of self-incriminating evidence obtained in violation of the Charter, should not be made to bear the stigma resulting from unrestricted repetition of the very same illegally obtained evidence. His privacy interests, in this case, outweighed the interest in unrestricted access: *Vickery v. Nova Scotia Supreme Court (Prothonotary)*, [1991] 1 S.C.R. 671, 64 C.C.C. (3d) 65 (6:3).

The combined operation of subsec. (3) and the relevant civil rules gives the court power to make an order providing for the disposition of documents seized during execution of a search warrant quashed by the Court of Appeal, even after the formal order allowing the appeal has been entered: *R. v. Dobney Foundry Ltd. (No. 3)* (1986), 29 C.C.C. (3d) 285 (B.C.C.A.).

The Court of Appeal has ancillary jurisdiction, not necessarily dependent on this subsection, to make an order necessary to prevent frustration of an appeal pending before it. Thus in this case the court ordered that documents, seized during execution of a search warrant and alleged to be privileged, remain sealed until the appeal against the refusal to quash the warrant had been disposed of. However, since there is no specific statutory basis for exercise of this jurisdiction by a single judge the "court", meaning three members of the Court of Appeal, must make the order: *R. v. Church of Scientology; R. v. Zaharia* (1986), 25 C.C.C. (3d) 149 (Ont. C.A.).

In considering an interim measure such as an impoundment order preventing the authorities from having access to the seized material until the validity of the underlying law is determined in the face of a challenge under the Charter, a court must consider three factors. The first, is whether a serious question of law is raised. The second, is whether irreparable harm will be occasioned to the applicant if the interim order is refused. The third, requires the court to consider and weigh in the balance the inconveniences caused to the parties by the interim order: *143471 Canada Inc. v. Quebec (Attorney General); Tabah v. Québec (Procureur Général)*, [1994] 2 S.C.R. 339, 90 C.C.C. (3d) 1.

There is no jurisdiction to stay a DNA order pending an appeal from conviction: *R. v. Zurowski* (2003), 175 C.C.C. (3d) 494 (Alta. C.A.), motion to quash dismissed 183 C.C.C. (3d) 448 (S.C.C.). *Contra*: *R. v. Briggs* (2001), 53 O.R. (3d) 124 (Ont. C.A.), leave to appeal to S.C.C. refused 154 O.A.C. 198*n*.

Stay of order to pay fine or of forfeiture [subsec. (5)] – The interests of justice do not refer exclusively to the merits of the appeal and include, *inter alia*, the interests of the state, the public's confidence in and respect for the court in its administration of the criminal law: *R. v. Chek TV Ltd.* (1986), 27 C.C.C. (3d) 380 (B.C.C.A.).

There is no inherent jurisdiction to stay a compliance order made under s. 238(2) of the *Income Tax Act* pending appeal to the court of appeal: *R. v. Lin* (1997), 117 C.C.C. (3d) 438 (B.C.C.A.).

The Court of Appeal has no jurisdiction to stay aspects of the sentence not mentioned in subsec. (5), for example a firearms prohibition and DNA order: *R. v. Doiron* (2011), 285 C.C.C. (3d) 413 (N.B.C.A.).

Stay of conditional sentence order (subsec. (5)(*f*)) – An application to stay a conditional sentence should be brought under this provision and not under s. 679, which deals with release from custody. However, because the ultimate question is whether the order sought is in the interests of justice, the inquiry shares much in common with that carried out under the "public interest" test in s. 679(4)(*c*): *R. v. Kuzyk* (2015), 329 C.C.C. (3d) 15 (Man. C.A.).

On a Crown appeal of a conditional sentence, the Crown sought an order under subsec. (5)(*f*) suspending the sentence while the appeal was being processed in order to prevent the offender from defending the appeal by pointing to the fact that the sentence had already been substantially served. The court held that the Crown's claim of prejudice was untenable and the interests of justice were clearly against granting the order sought: *R. v. Steward* (2014), 306 C.C.C. (3d) 162 (Alta. C.A.).

LEGAL ASSISTANCE FOR APPELLANT / Counsel fees and disbursements / Taxation of fees and disbursements.

684. (1) A court of appeal or a judge of that court may, at any time, assign counsel to act on behalf of an accused who is a party to an appeal or to proceedings preliminary or incidental to an appeal where, in the opinion of the court or judge, it appears desirable in the interests of justice that the accused should have legal assistance and where it appears that the accused has not sufficient means to obtain that assistance.

(2) Where counsel is assigned pursuant to subsection (1) and legal aid is not granted to the accused pursuant to a provincial legal aid program, the fees and disbursements of counsel shall be paid by the Attorney General who is the appellant or respondent, as the case may be, in the appeal.

(3) Where subsection (2) applies and counsel and the Attorney General cannot agree on fees or disbursements of counsel, the Attorney General or the counsel may apply to the registrar of the court of appeal and the registrar may tax the disputed fees and disbursements. R.S., c. C-34, s. 611; R.S.C. 1985, c. 34 (3rd Supp.), s. 9.

CROSS-REFERENCES

Where the accused is a party to an appeal to the Supreme Court of Canada or related proceedings to such an appeal, s. 694.1 applies with similar effect. No such provision exists at the trial level.

Section 672.24 prescribes the assignment of counsel for an accused who is unrepresented and where an issue of fitness is being directed.

An accused will be afforded the protection of s. 10(*b*) of the Charter and the right to retain and instruct counsel without delay and to be informed of such right, upon arrest or detention.

SYNOPSIS

This section provides that the Court of Appeal, or a judge thereof, can appoint counsel for an appellant or respondent who is without means to retain such assistance independently (subsec. (1)). Such an application will generally be made only after Legal Aid has refused to assist in this connection.

In the absence of Legal Aid funding, costs are paid by the Attorney General who is a party to the appeal (subsec. (2)). In the event of a dispute with respect to fees and disbursements the registrar of the Court of Appeal may tax the account submitted by counsel.

ANNOTATIONS

The Charter does not guarantee an indigent accused an absolute right to be provided with legal counsel to argue his appeal. Thus, this section which gives the court a discretion whether or not to assign counsel where it appears desirable in the interests of justice is valid. The court may consider the merit of the proposed appeal in considering whether or not an order should be made under this section: *R. v. Robinson* (1989), 51 C.C.C. (3d) 452 (Alta.

C.A.). See also *R. v. C. (P.)* (2014), 314 C.C.C. (3d) 43 (Ont. C.A.), leave to appeal to S.C.C. refused (January 15, 2015), Doc. 36129.

This section must be read with the provisions for legal aid. It does not give the court power to assign counsel where the accused have apparently been offered but refused legal aid. The accused had applied to have the Attorney General pay for their counsel at rates beyond those paid by legal aid. The *Canadian Charter of Rights and Freedoms* does not require the provision of paid counsel on the scale requested by the accused or any other scale beyond what had been offered: *R. v. Johal* (1998), 127 C.C.C. (3d) 273, 178 W.A.C. 146 (B.C.C.A.).

The "interests of justice" involve a consideration of the appellant's age, education, ability to understand and to express oneself, experience with the criminal process and the complexity of the appeal: *R. v. M. (A.)* (1996), 30 O.R. 313, 92 O.A.C. 381 (C.A.). See also *R. v. Baig* (1990), 58 C.C.C. (3d) 156 (B.C.C.A.), leave to appeal to S.C.C. refused 60 C.C.C. (3d) vi, 129 N.R. 240*n*.

The court may exercise its jurisdiction to appoint counsel notwithstanding a refusal of a prior application by a single judge. Counsel should be appointed where the accused cannot effectively present the appeal without the assistance of a lawyer or where the court cannot properly decide the issue without the assistance of counsel. The merits of the appeal should be considered to determine whether the appeal is arguable. If the appeal is arguable, the appellant's need for assistance must be determined by considering the complexity of the arguments which is a product of the grounds of appeal, the length and content of the record on appeal, the legal principles engaged and the application of those principles to the facts of the case. The ability of the accused to make oral argument must also be considered having regard to the accused's ability to understand the written word, comprehend the applicable legal principles, relate those principles to the facts of the case and articulate the end product of that process before the court: *R. v. Bernardo* (1997), 121 C.C.C. (3d) 123, 12 C.R. (5th) 310 (Ont. C.A.).

The court has the authority to preclude a lay person from representing a party as part of the power to control its own process: *R. v. Gouchie* (2006), 213 C.C.C. (3d) 250, 248 N.S.R. (2d) 167 (C.A.).

The court should not entertain a motion to fix an hourly rate for counsel appointed under subsec. (1) where the provincial legal aid plan has confirmed that a certificate would be granted. Only when legal aid is denied following an order under subsec. (1) does the obligation to pay fall upon the Attorney General, which then leads to the taxation referred to in subsec. (3): *R. v. Roussin* (2011), 277 C.C.C. (3d) 223 (Man. C.A.).

SUMMARY DETERMINATION OF FRIVOLOUS APPEALS / Summary determination of appeals filed in error.

685. (1) Where it appears to the registrar that a notice of appeal, which purports to be on a ground of appeal that involves a question of law alone, does not show a substantial ground of appeal, the registrar may refer the appeal to the court of appeal for summary determination, and, where an appeal is referred under this section, the court of appeal may, if it considers that the appeal is frivolous or vexatious and can be determined without being adjourned for a full hearing, dismiss the appeal summarily, without calling on any person to attend the hearing or to appear for the respondent on the hearing.

(2) If it appears to the registrar that a notice of appeal should have been filed with another court, the registrar may refer the appeal to a judge of the court of appeal for summary determination, and the judge may dismiss the appeal summarily without calling on any person to attend the hearing or to appear for the respondent on the hearing. R.S., c. C-34, s. 612; 2008, c. 18, s. 30.

CROSS-REFERENCES

This section is probably included in the general incorporation of appellate authority under s. 695(1), without express reference to appeals to the Supreme Court of Canada. The provisions are applicable to summary conviction appeals brought under s. 813, pursuant to s. 822(1).

SYNOPSIS

Subsection (1) provides for summary dismissal of appeals where the court of appeal, on the application of the registrar, determines that the appeal is frivolous or vexatious, based on the legal grounds advanced in the notice of appeal. This section only applies where the notice of appeal refers to questions of law alone. Subsection (2) provides for summary dismissal if the appeal was filed in the wrong court.

Powers of the Court of Appeal

POWERS / Order to be made / Substituting verdict / Appeal from acquittal / New trial under Part XIX / New trial under Part XIX — Nunavut / Election where new trial a jury trial / Election if new trial a jury trial — Nunavut / Where appeal allowed against verdict of unfit to stand trial / Appeal court may set aside verdict of unfit to stand trial / Additional powers.

686. (1) On the hearing of an appeal against a conviction or against a verdict that the appellant is unfit to stand trial or not criminally responsible on account of mental disorder, the court of appeal

- **(*a*) may allow the appeal where it is of the opinion that**
  - **(i) the verdict should be set aside on the ground that it is unreasonable or cannot be supported by the evidence,**
  - **(ii) the judgment of the trial court should be set aside on the ground of a wrong decision on a question of law, or**
  - **(iii) on any ground there was a miscarriage of justice;**
- **(*b*) may dismiss the appeal where**
  - **(i) the court is of the opinion that the appellant, although he was not properly convicted on a count or part of the indictment, was properly convicted on another count or part of the indictment,**
  - **(ii) the appeal is not decided in favour of the appellant on any ground mentioned in paragraph (*a*),**
  - **(iii) notwithstanding that the court is of the opinion that on any ground mentioned in subparagraph (*a*)(ii) the appeal might be decided in favour of the appellant, it is of the opinion that no substantial wrong or miscarriage of justice has occurred, or**
  - **(iv) notwithstanding any procedural irregularity at trial, the trial court had jurisdiction over the class of offence of which the appellant was convicted and the court of appeal is of the opinion that the appellant suffered no prejudice thereby;**
- **(*c*) may refuse to allow the appeal where it is of the opinion that the trial court arrived at a wrong conclusion respecting the effect of a special verdict, may order the conclusion to be recorded that appears to the court to be required by the verdict and may pass a sentence that is warranted in law in substitution for the sentence passed by the trial court, or**
- **(*d*) may set aside a conviction and find the appellant unfit to stand trial or not criminally responsible on account of mental disorder and may exercise any of the powers of the trial court conferred by or referred to in section 672.45 in any manner deemed appropriate to the court of appeal in the circumstances.**

(2) Where a court of appeal allows an appeal under paragraph (1)(*a*), it shall quash the conviction and

(*a*) direct a judgment or verdict of acquittal to be entered; or
(*b*) order a new trial.

(3) Where a court of appeal dismisses an appeal under subparagraph (1)(*b*)(i), it may substitute the verdict that in its opinion should have been found and

(*a*) affirm the sentence passed by the trial court; or
(*b*) impose a sentence that is warranted in law or remit the matter to the trial court and direct the trial court to impose a sentence that is warranted in law.

(4) If an appeal is from an acquittal or verdict that the appellant or respondent was unfit to stand trial or not criminally responsible on account of mental disorder, the court of appeal may

(*a*) dismiss the appeal; or
(*b*) allow the appeal, set aside the verdict and
(i) order a new trial, or
(ii) except where the verdict is that of a court composed of a judge and jury, enter a verdict of guilty with respect to the offence of which, in its opinion, the accused should have been found guilty but for the error in law, and pass a sentence that is warranted in law, or remit the matter to the trial court and direct the trial court to impose a sentence that is warranted in law.

(5) Subject to subsection (5.01), if an appeal is taken in respect of proceedings under Part XIX and the court of appeal orders a new trial under this Part, the following provisions apply:

(*a*) if the accused, in his notice of appeal or notice of application for leave to appeal, requested that the new trial, if ordered, should be held before a court composed of a judge and jury, the new trial shall be held accordingly;
(*b*) if the accused, in his notice of appeal or notice of application for leave to appeal, did not request that the new trial, if ordered, should be held before a court composed of a judge and jury, the new trial shall, without further election by the accused, be held before a judge or provincial court judge, as the case may be, acting under Part XIX, other than a judge or provincial court judge who tried the accused in the first instance, unless the court of appeal directs that the new trial be held before the judge or provincial court judge who tried the accused in the first instance;
(*c*) if the court of appeal orders that the new trial shall be held before a court composed of a judge and jury, the new trial shall be commenced by an indictment in writing setting forth the offence in respect of which the new trial was ordered; and
(*d*) notwithstanding paragraph (*a*), if the conviction against which the accused appealed was for an offence mentioned in section 553 and was made by a provincial court judge, the new trial shall be held before a provincial court judge acting under Part XIX, other than the provincial court judge who tried the accused in the first instance, unless the court of appeal directs that the new trial be held before the provincial court judge who tried the accused in the first instance.

(5.01) If an appeal is taken in respect of proceedings under Part XIX and the Court of Appeal of Nunavut orders a new trial under Part XXI, the following provisions apply:

(*a*) if the accused, in the notice of appeal or notice of application for leave to appeal, requested that the new trial, if ordered, should be held before a court composed of a judge and jury, the new trial shall be held accordingly;
(*b*) if the accused, in the notice of appeal or notice of application for leave to appeal, did not request that the new trial, if ordered, should be held before a court composed of a judge and jury, the new trial shall, without further election by the accused, and without a further preliminary inquiry, be held before a judge, acting under Part XIX, other than a judge who tried the accused in the

first instance, unless the Court of Appeal of Nunavut directs that the new trial be held before the judge who tried the accused in the first instance;

(*c*) if the Court of Appeal of Nunavut orders that the new trial shall be held before a court composed of a judge and jury, the new trial shall be commenced by an indictment in writing setting forth the offence in respect of which the new trial was ordered; and

(*d*) despite paragraph (*a*), if the conviction against which the accused appealed was for an indictable offence mentioned in section 553, the new trial shall be held before a judge acting under Part XIX, other than the judge who tried the accused in the first instance, unless the Court of Appeal of Nunavut directs that the new trial be held before the judge who tried the accused in the first instance.

(5.1) Subject to subsection (5.2), if a new trial ordered by the court of appeal is to be held before a court composed of a judge and jury,

(*a*) the accused may, with the consent of the prosecutor, elect to have the trial heard before a judge without a jury or a provincial court judge;

(*b*) the election shall be deemed to be a re-election within the meaning of subsection 561(5); and

(*c*) subsection 561(5) applies, with such modifications as the circumstances require, to the election.

(5.2) If a new trial ordered by the Court of Appeal of Nunavut is to be held before a court composed of a judge and jury, the accused may, with the consent of the prosecutor, elect to have the trial heard before a judge without a jury. The election shall be deemed to be a re-election within the meaning of subsection 561.1(1), and subsection 561.1(6) applies, with any modifications that the circumstances require, to the election.

(6) Where a court of appeal allows an appeal against a verdict that the accused is unfit to stand trial, it shall, subject to subsection (7), order a new trial.

(7) Where the verdict that the accused is unfit to stand trial was returned after the close of the case for the prosecution, the court of appeal may, notwithstanding that the verdict is proper, if it is of the opinion that the accused should have been acquitted at the close of the case for the prosecution, allow the appeal, set aside the verdict and direct a judgment or verdict of acquittal to be entered.

(8) Where a court of appeal exercises any of the powers conferred by subsection (2), (4), (6) or (7), it may make any order, in addition, that justice requires. R.S., c. C-34, s. 613; 1974-75-76, c. 93, s. 75; R.S.C. 1985, c. 27 (1st Supp.), s. 145; 1991, c. 43, s. 9; 1997, c. 18, s. 98; 1999, c. 3, s. 52; c. 5, s. 26.

CROSS-REFERENCES

Section 687 authorizes the determination of sentence appeals. Orders for compensation or restitution made at trial may be varied or annulled under the courts plenary authority under s. 689(2). The Supreme Court of Canada may, under s. 695(1), make any order that the Court of Appeal might have made on an appeal under Part XXII. A summary conviction appeal court has similar authority under s. 822(1) relating to s. 813 appeals.

Part XXI provisions are applicable to appeals from the determination of application for extraordinary remedies under Part XXVI, s. 784(2). The provisions of Part XX also apply, under s. 839(2), to appeals to the court of appeal from decisions in summary conviction proceedings under ss. 822 and 834. The court of appeal has been given broad authority under s. 683 for the purposes of Part XXI appeals.

See s. 672.1 for definition of "verdict of not criminally responsible on account of mental disorder" and s. 2 for definitions of "mental disorder" and "unfit to stand trial".

SYNOPSIS

This section sets out the orders which may be made by the Court of Appeal in disposing of an appeal.

Subsection (1) relates to appeals by an accused from conviction, a finding of unfitness, or a verdict of not guilty on account of insanity. Such appeals may succeed where it is shown that (a) the verdict is not reasonably supported by the evidence, (b) an error of law was made by the trial judge, or (c) there has been a miscarriage of justice (subsec. (1)(*a*)). An appeal may be dismissed where (a) the accused was properly convicted on part of the indictment (*e.g.*, an included offence), (b) the grounds raised have not been made out, (c) any error of law did not occasion a substantial wrong or miscarriage of justice (*i.e.*, the verdict would necessarily have been the same), or (d) the error at trial was a procedural irregularity which did not prejudice the accused (subsec. (1)(*b*)).

The court can dismiss an appeal and sentence the accused where it concludes that the trial court erred by arriving at a wrong conclusion respecting the effect of a special verdict (subsec. (1)(*c*)).

If the court finds that the appellant was insane at the time of the commission of the offence it may set aside the conviction and remand the appellant into the custody of the lieutenant governor (subsec. (1)(*d*)). Similarly, the accused may be remanded if the court finds that he was unfit to stand trial (subsec. (1)(*e*)).

Where a conviction appeal is allowed the court can, depending on the circumstances, enter an acquittal or order a new trial (subsec. (2)). However, where an acquittal is not appropriate the court is under no obligation to order a retrial and can set aside the conviction without making any other order.

Where the court is of the opinion that the appellant was properly convicted on part of the indictment it can either affirm the sentence imposed at trial, impose a new sentence, or remit the matter to the trial judge for a hearing on the matter (subsec. (3)).

On an appeal by the Crown from acquittal the court, if it does not dismiss the appeal can (a) order a new trial, or (b) except where the case was tried by a jury, enter a conviction and either impose sentence or refer that issue to the trial judge. If the trial was with a jury the court is limited to ordering a new trial (subsec. (4)).

Subsection (5) permits an accused appealing a conviction in proceedings before a judge sitting alone (other than for an offence within the absolute jurisdiction of the provincial court: see s. 553) to request that a new trial be with a jury. Normally a retrial in a case heard by a judge alone will be before other than the original judge unless the Court of Appeal specifically directs otherwise. Subsection (5.01) enacts similar provisions in respect of Nunavut. Subsection (5.1) provides for a re-election as to mode of trial with consent of the prosecutor.

Where a verdict of unfit to stand trial or not criminally responsible on account of mental disorder is rendered, the Court of Appeal will order a new trial. However, if no defence evidence was called and the court is of the opinion that the accused should have been acquitted at the close of the prosecution case, a judgment to that effect will be entered (subsecs. (6), (7)).

Pursuant to subsec. (8) the court of appeal may, in disposing of an appeal, make any ancillary order which it feels justice requires.

ANNOTATIONS

Stare decisis – A provincial appellate court is not obliged as a matter of either law or practice to follow a decision of another provincial appellate court unless it is persuaded that it should do so on its merits or for other independent reasons. The only required uniformity among provincial appellate courts is that which is the result of the decisions of the Supreme Court of Canada: *R. v. Wolf*, [1975] 2 S.C.R. 107, 17 C.C.C. (2d) 425, 27 C.R.N.S. 150 (9:0).

Although *obiter dicta* from the Supreme Court should generally be followed by lower courts, all *obiter* are not intended to have the same weight. The weight decreases as one moves from the dispositive *ratio decidendi* to a wider circle of analysis which is obviously intended for guidance and which should be accepted as authoritative. Beyond that, there will be commentary, examples or exposition that are intended to be helpful and may be found to be persuasive, but are certainly not "binding": *R. v. Henry*, [2005] 3 S.C.R. 609, 202 C.C.C. (3d) 449.

The Court of Appeal is not bound by one of its previous decisions where the liberty of the subject is in issue and the Court is convinced that the prior decision is wrong: *R. v. Santeramo* (1976), 32 C.C.C. (2d) 35, 36 C.R.N.S. 1 (Ont. C.A.).

Moot appeal – An appeal rendered moot by the death of the appellant or, in a Crown appeal, the respondent, should proceed only where there exists special circumstances that make it "in the interests of justice" to proceed. Although not exhaustive, the court should have regard to the following: whether the appeal will proceed in a proper adversarial context; the strength of the grounds of the appeal; whether there are special circumstances that transcend the death of the individual including a legal issue of general public importance, a systemic issue related to the administration of justice or a collateral consequence to the family of the deceased or to other interested persons or the public; whether the nature of the order which could be made justifies the expenditure of limited judicial resources to resolve a moot appeal; and whether continuing the appeal would go beyond the judicial function of resolving concrete disputes and involve the court in free-standing, legislative type pronouncements more properly left to the legislature itself: *R. v. Smith*, [2004] 1 S.C.R. 385, 181 C.C.C. (3d) 225, 17 C.R. (6th) 203.

New issues raised by appellate court – An appellate court has the jurisdiction to raise new issues and invite submissions on an issue neither party has raised. However, this discretion should be exercised only in rare circumstances. Where there is good reason to believe that the result would realistically have differed had the error not been made, this risk of injustice warrants the court of appeal's intervention. Procedurally, the court of appeal must make the parties aware that it has discerned a potential issue and ensure that they are sufficiently informed so they may prepare and respond: *R. v. Mian*, [2014] 2 S.C.R. 689, 315 C.C.C. (3d) 453.

Unreasonable verdict (subsec. (1)(*a*)(i)) – The test to be applied under this paragraph is whether the verdict is one that a properly instructed jury acting judicially could reasonably have rendered. The Court of Appeal's function goes beyond merely finding that there is evidence to support a conviction. While the Court of Appeal must not merely substitute its view for that of the jury, in order to apply the test the court must re-examine and to some extent reweigh and consider the effect of the evidence: *R. v. Yebes*, [1987] 2 S.C.R. 168, 36 C.C.C. (3d) 417 (6:0).

Where the appeal relates to a judge alone trial, the appellate court should identify the defects in the judge's analysis that led to an unreasonable conclusion. If the appeal relates to a jury trial, the reviewing court must still articulate the basis upon which it finds that the conclusion reached by the jury was unreasonable. A lurking or lingering doubt without further articulation of the basis for such doubt is not a proper basis upon which to interfere with the findings of a jury. If the jury returns a finding that the reviewing court finds to be unreasonable, then the only inference is that the jury was not acting judicially. "Acting judicially" means not only acting dispassionately, applying the law and adjudicating on the basis of the record and nothing else; it also means arriving at a conclusion that does not conflict with the bulk of judicial experience. The reviewing court must, therefore, articulate as precisely as possible what features of the case suggested that the verdict was unreasonable: *R. v. Biniaris*, [2000] 1 S.C.R. 381, 143 C.C.C. (3d) 1.

The test to be applied by a court of appeal in considering an allegation that the verdict was unreasonable is whether the trier of fact could reasonably have reached the conclusion that the accused was guilty beyond a reasonable doubt. In making this determination, the court of appeal must re-examine, and to some extent at least, reweigh and consider the effect of the evidence. This rule applies to verdicts based on findings of credibility except that, in applying the test, the court of appeal should show great deference to findings of credibility made at trial. An appellate court does, however, have the power to overturn verdicts based on findings of credibility where, after considering all of the evidence and having due regard to the advantages afforded to the trial judge, it concluded that the verdict is unreasonable: *R. v. W. (R.)*, [1992] 2 S.C.R. 122, 74 C.C.C. (3d) 134. Consequently, this provision is applicable where the assessment of credibility made at trial is not supported by the evidence: *R. v. Burke*, [1996] 1 S.C.R. 474, 105 C.C.C. (3d) 205. See also: *R. v. H. (W.)*, [2013] 2 S.C.R. 180, 297 C.C.C. (3d) 4; *R. v. M. (N.)* (2012), 284 C.C.C. (3d) 555 (Ont. C.A.).

While vague unease about the adequacy of the evidence is not a sufficient basis for an appellate court to intervene, the court conducting a reasonableness analysis should nonetheless bring to bear the knowledge gained through its broad exposure to the criminal process. This judicial experience provides insights into credibility assessments and fact-finding not available to jurors whose experience is generally limited to a single case: *R. v. M. (N.), supra*.

Where the trial was by judge alone, even where the verdict was available on the evidence, it may still be unreasonable under s. 686(1)(*a*)(i) if the judge reached the verdict by an illogical or irrational reasoning process. This ground addresses the reasonableness of the judge's verdict by scrutinizing the logic of the judge's findings of fact or inferences drawn from the evidence admitted at trial. For instance, a verdict is unreasonable where the judge draws an inference or makes a finding of fact essential to the verdict that is plainly contradicted by the very evidence from which it was drawn, or upon which it has been made to rest. Another example is where the judge draws an inference or makes a finding of fact essential to the verdict if that inference or finding of fact is demonstrably incompatible with evidence that is neither contradicted by other evidence, nor rejected by the trial judge. This is to be distinguished from a case in which the judge misapprehends critical evidence, which is assessed under s. 686(1)(*a*)(iii) pursuant to *R. v. Lohrer*, [2004] 3 S.C.R. 732, 193 C.C.C. (3d) 1. See: *R. v. Beaudry*, [2007] 1 S.C.R. 190, 216 C.C.C. (3d) 353, as clarified in *R. v. Sinclair* (2011), 270 C.C.C. (3d) 421 (S.C.C.).

The test to be applied by courts of appeal in reviewing jury verdicts for unreasonableness does not involve the reviewing court attempting to put itself in the place of an imaginary trial judge and on a review of the written record asking whether that imaginary judge could have articulated legally adequate reasons for conviction. Such an approach fails to take a sufficiently deferential approach to the findings of the jury viewed, as they must be, in the context of the whole of the evidence: *R. v. H. (W.) supra*.

The court's jurisdiction to set aside a finding of not criminally responsible on account of mental disorder on the basis that it was unreasonable is the same as the court's power to set aside a conviction for that reason. The appellant must demonstrate that a trier of fact acting reasonably and properly applying the law could not have arrived at the finding of not criminally responsible on account of mental disorder: *R. v. Fraser* (1997), 6 C.R. (5th) 420 (Ont. C.A.).

Concern about the reasonableness of a verdict based on identification evidence is particularly high were the person identified is a stranger to the witness, the circumstances of the identification processes are flawed and where there is no other evidence tending to confirm or support the identiifcation evidence. Review under this section, however, is not limited exclusively to questions of the reliability of the evidence. The entire record must be considered and to a limited degree, the credibility of witnesses must be assessed. In this case, the trial judge had erred in admitting evidence of a witness's prior, out-of-court, identification of the accused as original evidence given the witness's denial of the truth of the prior statement. The circumstances in which out-of-court statements of identification are admitted do not involve a hearsay use of the statements. Out-of-court statements regarding prior identiifcation may be admitted in two circumstances: first, where the identifying witness identifies the accused at trial, the prior identification is admissible to allow the trier of fact to make an informed determination of the probative value of the purported identification. Second, where the identifying witness is unable to identify the accused at trial but can testify that they previously gave an accurate description or made an accurate identification, the prior statement is admissble as original evidence to show who it was that the identifying witness previously identified. Where the witness denies the truth of the prior statement, however, the evidence of the prior identification is not admissible unless the statement satisfies the criteria generally applicable for the substantive admissibility of prior inconsistent statements: *R. v. Tat* (1997), 117 C.C.C. (3d) 481 (Ont. C.A.).

Inconsistent verdicts (subsec. (1)(*a*)(i) – Where, on any realistic view of the evidence, the verdicts cannot be reconciled on any rational or logical basis, the illogicality of the verdict tends to indicate that the jury must have been confused as to the evidence or must have reached some unjustifiable compromise. On this basis, the verdict is unreasonable and a basis for allowing the appeal: *R. v. McShannock* (1980), 55 C.C.C. (2d) 53 (Ont. C.A.).

In the case of a single accused charged with multiple offences, different verdicts may be reconcilable because the offences are temporally distinct, or are qualitatively different, or dependent on the credibility of different complainants or witnesses. However, where the evidence on one count is so wound up with the evidence on the other count that it is not logically separable, inconsistent verdicts may be held to be unreasonable: *R. v. Pittiman* (2006), 206 C.C.C. (3d) 6 (S.C.C.).

Even where the verdict sheet raised a likelihood that the jury merely miscommunicated the verdict it meant to render, it is the verdict as announced in open court that governs: *R. v. Catton* (2015), 319 C.C.C. (3d) 99 (Ont. C.A.).

Similarly, in the case of multiple accused charged with the same offence, the jury may accept the complainant's testimony in respect of one accused but not the other; the strength of the evidence relating to each accused may be different. As a practical matter, the test may be harder for an appellant to meet where there are multiple accused since the evidence will almost always be different against different accused. The test is whether the verdicts are irreconcilable such that no reasonable jury, properly instructed, could possibly have rendered them on the evidence. Moreover, it was open to the jury to reject the prosecution's position that the case was "all or nothing" and find one accused guilty and the other not guilty: *R. v. Pittiman, supra.*

Where the basis for finding the verdict unreasonable is that the verdicts are inconsistent, but the evidence against the appellant supported the conviction, the appropriate remedy is a new trial rather than entering an acquittal: *R. v. Pittiman, supra.*

However, in *R. v. F. (J.)*, [2008] 3 S.C.R. 215, 236 C.C.C. (3d) 421, the court held that to order a new trial in a case of inconsistent verdicts where the acquittal was not appealed would be to put the accused in jeopardy with respect to an allegation on which he had already been definitively acquitted. See also: *R. v. Catton, supra.*

An acquittal for sexual assault and conviction for sexual interference in respect of the same incident with an underage complainant were not necessarily inconsistent. The jury likely misunderstood the "force" requirement for sexual assault and gave the accused an undeserved windfall: *R. v. Tremblay* (2016), 334 C.C.C. (3d) 520 (Alta. C.A.), leave to appeal to S.C.C. refused 2016 CarswellAlta 1260; *R. v. L. (S.)* (2013), 300 C.C.C. (3d) 100 (Ont. C.A.), leave to appeal to S.C.C. refused (2013), 333 O.A.C. 402*n.*

Where a trial judge renders inconsistent verdicts and it is clear that the acquittal rather than the conviction is predicated on a legal error, it is appropriate to uphold the conviction despite the inconsistency: *R. v. Plein* (2018), 365 C.C.C. (3d) 437 (Ont. C.A.).

Reopening Appeal (subsec. (1)(*a*)(i)) – An appellate court may reopen an appeal prior to the entry of a formal judgment. The applicant bears a significant burden and must make out a clear and compelling case to justify reopening. If the case has been heard on the merits, the applicant must establish that the court overlooked or misapprehended the evidence or an argument: *R. v. Hummel* (2003), 175 C.C.C. (3d) 1 (Y.T.C.A.), leave to appeal to S.C.C. refused [2003] 3 S.C.R. vi, 179 C.C.C. (3d) vi.

An application may not be made after an accused's appeal has been dismissed to reopen the appeal on the ground of the discovery of new evidence: *R. v. Liscomb* (1961), 131 C.C.C. 418 (Alta. C.A.).

An accused may in Quebec invoke the civil rules of procedure and apply to revoke the order dismissing his appeal, even where the appeal was originally dismissed on other merits following an appeal to the Court of Appeal. However, the conditions for revoking the original order are similar to the conditions which would apply in the case of a civil appeal and the accused must show that such an order is necessary to remedy a serious injustice not due to the gross negligence of the affected party or that there are exceptional circumstances: *R. v. Vaudry* (1989), 51 C.C.C. (3d) 410 (Que. C.A.).

However, in a subsequent case, *R. v. Tenorio* (1991), 66 C.C.C. (3d) 429 (Que. C.A.), leave to appeal to S.C.C. refused 67 C.C.C. (3d) vi, the court held that it would not revoke a judgment which had been dismissed on the merits where there was some other useful recourse available, such as an application to the Minister of Justice under [former] s. 690.

The dismissal of an appeal by an appellate court upon receipt of an appellant's notice of abandonment is not an adjudication upon the merits and thus the court is entitled upon his subsequent application to rescind its order and extend the time within which to appeal: *R. v. Watson* (1975), 23 C.C.C. (2d) 366 (Ont. C.A.). However, there is no power to reopen an appeal that has been disposed of on its merits: *R. v. H. (E.F.)* (1997), 115 C.C.C. (3d) 89 (Ont. C.A.), leave to appeal to S.C.C. refused 117 C.C.C. (3d) vi.

The court may set aside an order dismissing the appeal for want of prosecution for failure of counsel to provide the necessary transcripts: *R. v. Blaker* (1983), 6 C.C.C. (3d) 385, 46 B.C.L.R. 344 (C.A.).

Failure of trial judge to give reasons – Not every failure or deficiency in the reasons provides a ground of appeal. Reasons perform an important function in the appellate process. Where the functional needs are not satisfied, the appellate court may conclude that it is a case of unreasonable verdict, an error of law, or a miscarriage of justice within the scope of para. (1)(*a*), depending on the circumstances of the case and the nature and importance of the trial decision being rendered. Reasons acquire particular importance when a trial judge is called upon to address troublesome principles of unsettled law, or to resolve confused and contradictory evidence on a key issue, unless the basis of the trial judge's conclusion is apparent from the record, even without being articulated. The trial judge's duty is satisfied by reasons that are sufficient to serve the purpose for which the duty is imposed, *i.e.*, a decision which, having regard to the particular circumstances of the case, is reasonably intelligible to the parties and provides the basis for meaningful appellate review of the correctness of the trial judge's decision. Where the trial decision is deficient in explaining the result to the parties, but the appeal court considers itself able to do so, the appeal court's explanation in its own reasons is sufficient. There is no need in such a case for a new trial. The error of law, if it is so found, would be cured under the para. (1)(*b*)(iii): *R. v. Sheppard*, [2002] 1 S.C.R. 869, 162 C.C.C. (3d) 298. See also *R. v. G. (L.)*, [2006] 1 S.C.R. 621, 207 C.C.C. (3d) 353.

Where a case turns largely on determinations of credibility, the sufficiency of the reasons should be considered in light of the deference afforded to trial judges on credibility findings. Deficiencies will rarely merit intervention on appeal. However, a failure to sufficiently articulate how credibility concerns were resolved may constitute reversible error. The reasons are particularly important where the trial judge must resolve confused and contradictory testimony on a key issue unless the basis of the trial judge's conclusion is apparent from the record. If the reasons are deficient, the reviewing court must examine the evidence and determine whether the reasons for conviction are patent on the record. This is not, however, an invitation to appellate courts to engage in a reassessment of aspects of the case not resolved by the trial judge. Where the trial judge's reasons are not apparent from the reasons or on the record, the appeal court ought not to substitute its own analysis for that of the trial judge. In this case, the trial judge erred in failing to explain how he reconciled the inconsistencies in the complainant's testimony on whether she invented the allegations and the failure to do so prejudiced the accused's right to an appeal: *R. v. Dinardo*, [2008] 1 S.C.R. 788, 231 C.C.C. (3d) 177.

In *R. v. M. (R.E.)*, [2008] 3 S.C.R. 3, 235 C.C.C. (3d) 290, the Supreme Court of Canada once again considered the sufficiency of trial judge's reasons. A trial judge's reasons must be sufficient to fulfill their functions of explaining why the accused was convicted or acquitted, providing public accountability and permitting effective appellate review. Reasons should be read as a whole, in the context of the evidence, the arguments and the trial, with an appreciation of the purposes or functions for which they are delivered. A logical connection between the verdict and the basis for the verdict must be apparent but a detailed description of the judge's process in arriving at the verdict is unnecessary. The reasons are sufficient if, viewed in light of the record and counsel's submissions on the live issues presented by the case, they explain why the decision was reached, by establishing a logical connection between the evidence and the law on the one hand and the verdict on the other. Detailed recitations of the evidence or the law are not required. Assessing credibility is a difficult matter that does not always lend itself to precise and complete verbalization. Accordingly, the degree of detail required in explaining findings on credibility may also vary with the evidentiary record and the dynamic of the trial. An appellate court, proceeding with deference, must look at the reasons in their entire context and determine whether the trial judge has seized the substance of the critical issues on the trial. There is no requirement to reconcile every frailty in the evidence or allude to every principle of law.

While the trial judge's duty to give reasons applies generally to acquittals as much as convictions, the content of the reasons necessary to give full effect to the right of appeal is governed by the different issues to which the reasons are directed on an acquittal and a conviction. The Crown does not have a right of appeal from an unreasonable acquittal. Accordingly, the Crown's limited right to appeal only on a question of law alone must inform an assessment of whether the reasons are so deficient as to preclude meaningful appellate review: *R. v. Walker*, [2008] 2 S.C.R. 245, 231 C.C.C. (3d) 289.

Miscarriage of justice (subsec. (1)(*a*)(iii)) – In order to attack a verdict on the basis of the incompetence of counsel, the accused must establish that counsel was incompetent and that a miscarriage of justice resulted. In assessing such a claim, there is a performance component determined by a reasonableness standard that includes a strong presumption that counsel's conduct fell within the wide range of reasonable professional assistance and a prejudice component that requires the accused to establish that a miscarriage of justice resulted. Where there is no prejudice, it is usually undesirable for the appellate courts to consider the performance component of the analysis. In this case, the court concluded that defence counsel had the implied authority to make a tactical decision not to introduce a tape recording of the complainant denying any assault by the accused: *R. v. B. (G.D.)*, [2000] 1 S.C.R. 520, 143 C.C.C. (3d) 289. Also see: *R. v. B. (L.C.)* (1996), 104 C.C.C. (3d) 353 (Ont. C.A.); *R. v. Joanisse* (1995), 102 C.C.C. (3d) 35 (Ont. C.A.), leave to appeal to S.C.C. refused 111 C.C.C. (3d) vi, and *R. v. Silvini* (1991), 68 C.C.C. (3d) 251 (Ont. C.A.).

Where ineffective assistance of counsel is raised, the appellant must establish that counsel's acts or omissions constituted incompetence and that a miscarriage of justice resulted. The acts or omissions of counsel cannot have been the result of reasonable professional judgment. The first issue is whether a miscarriage of justice occurred which may be established by a procedural unfairness or unreliable verdict. In this case, there was no miscarriage of justice based on the fact that counsel was suspended from the Law Society at the time of the trial. The disqualification was not based on counsel's competency. Accordingly, there was no appearance of unfairness arising from counsel's disqualification from practice: *R. v. Prebtani* (2008), 240 C.C.C. (3d) 237 (Ont. C.A.), leave to appeal to S.C.C. refused 243 C.C.C. (3d) vi. See also *R. v. Weagle* (2008), 240 C.C.C. (3d) 311 (N.S.C.A.).

To establish ineffective assistance based on trial counsel's conflict of interest, the appellant must demonstrate an actual conflict of interest on the part of counsel, and that the conflict impaired counsel's ability to effectively represent him or her. The appellant need not demonstrate that, but for the ineffective assistance, the verdict would have been different: *R. v. Baharloo* (2017), 348 C.C.C. (3d) 64 (Ont. C.A.).

Where an appellant claims ineffective assistance of counsel as a result of a conflict of interest on the part of trial counsel that was recognized at trial, the question is whether the accused validly waived his right to a mistrial. Here, the accused legitimately believed that saving the trial gave him the best opportunity for an acquittal, and so was not entitled to a remedy on appeal: *R. v. Yellowhead* (2015), 329 C.C.C. (3d) 216 (B.C.C.A.).

Where improper contact with the jury during its deliberations, which is discovered after the verdict, is such as to taint the administration of justice, then a miscarriage of justice has occurred and there is no need for the accused to prove any actual prejudice. Confidence in the administration of justice is equally as shaken by the appearance as by the fact of an unfair trial: *R. v. Cameron* (1991), 64 C.C.C. (3d) 96 (Ont. C.A.).

The failure of the trial judge to make a preliminary determination as to the admissibility of evidence constitutes an error of law. In these circumstances, the appellate court is required to determine what the right conclusion in law would have been. If applying the correct legal principles, the evidence would have been admitted, then the trial judge's error had no effect on the verdict. Where however the preliminary matter is one of fact or mixed law and fact, the general rule is that the accused is entitled to a decision from the trial judge. In such circumstances, the appellate court cannot simply decide the matter. The process of reasoning is to ask whether the issue of fact would inevitably have been decided in favour of admissibility. If the answer is in the affirmative, then the error had no effect. If the answer is in the negative, then it might reasonably have affected the verdict because the evidence might have been excluded: *R. v. Rockey* (1995), 99 C.C.C. (3d) 31 (Ont. C.A.), affd [1996] 3 S.C.R. 829, 110 C.C.C. (3d) 481.

While a trial judge's misapprehension of evidence and failure to appreciate relevant evidence may not be errors of law, they are errors of fact or mixed fact and law and, if they deprive the accused of a fair trial, may result in a miscarriage of justice within the meaning of this subsection. An accused whose conviction rests on findings tainted by error has been denied a fair trial: *R. v. G. (G.)* (1995), 97 C.C.C. (3d) 362 (Ont. C.A.); *R. v. Morrissey* (1995), 97 C.C.C. (3d) 193 (Ont. C.A.).

Where a trial judge was mistaken as to the substance of material parts of evidence and those errors played an essential part in the reasoning process, then the accused could establish that he had not received a fair trial. The misapprehension of evidence has to go to the substance rather than to detail and had to be material rather than peripheral to the reasoning of the trial judge, such that the errors played an essential part, not just in the narrative of the judgment, but also in the reasoning process resulting in conviction: *R. v. Lohrer* (2004), 193 C.C.C. (3d) 1 (S.C.C.).

Dismissal of appeal where conviction proper in part [subsecs. (1)(*b*)(i) and (3)] – Where the court is of the view that the conviction for the full offence cannot stand but that it should substitute a conviction for an included offence, the proper procedure is to *dismiss* the appeal and substitute such a verdict: *R. v. Nantais,* [1966] 4 C.C.C. 108 (Ont. C.A.).

An appellate court dismissing an appeal pursuant to subsec. (1)(*b*)(i) has the power to amend the conviction to conform with the evidence: *R. v. Lake,* [1969] S.C.R. 49, [1969] 2 C.C.C. 224.

Thus the court was entitled to amend an indictment charging possession of *cannabis* marihuana for the purpose of trafficking to conform to the evidence showing the narcotic to be *cannabis* resin, by deleting the word "marihuana", inserting the word "resin" and dismissing the appeal: *R. v. Morozuk*, [1986] 1 S.C.R. 31, 24 C.C.C. (3d) 257 (7:0).

It was held in *R. v. Kent* (1986), 27 C.C.C. (3d) 405 (Man. C.A.), that by reason of the combined operation of subsec. (3) and subsec. (1)(*b*)(i) it is open to the court to substitute a conviction for an included offence, even in the case of misdirection below in respect of the conviction under appeal, where it is of the opinion that no properly instructed jury acting reasonably could have reached a conclusion more favourable to the accused than that he was guilty of the lesser included offence. To the contrary are *R. v. Popoff* (1960), 129 C.C.C. 250 (B.C.C.A.), and *R. v. Morris* (1975), 29 C.C.C. (2d) 540 (N.B.C.A.), where it was held that subsec. (3) is not available where the appeal is based on grounds of misdirection and it cannot be said that a conviction for the full offence ought not to have been found on the evidence.

In *R. v. Wigman*, [1987] 1 S.C.R. 246, 33 C.C.C. (3d) 97 (6:0), the court substituted a conviction for an included offence where there had been misdirection in relation to the offence of which the accused was convicted. The Crown however was not seeking a new trial if the conviction for the full offence could not be maintained.

If the court, after substituting the conviction, merely affirms the original sentence then that sentence runs from the date of its imposition by the trial judge. If, however, the court imposes a new sentence it may provide that the sentence runs from the date of its imposition by the court of appeal or, *semble*, from the date of imposition of the original sentence: *R. v. Boyd* (1979), 47 C.C.C. (2d) 369 (Ont. C.A.).

In *R. v. Conway* (1997), 121 C.C.C. (3d) 397 (Ont. C.A.), the court held that in light of s. 719(1), where the Court of Appeal exercises its jurisdiction to impose sentence, the sentence runs from the date imposed by the Court of Appeal. The court should therefore take into account time spent by the accused serving the sentence originally imposed by the trial court pending the appeal.

Where the court of appeal exercises its jurisdiction under subsec. (3) and substitutes a conviction for second degree murder it may also set the period of parole non-eligibility, which period may exceed the minimum 10 years: *R. v. Kjeldsen* (1980), 53 C.C.C. (2d) 55 (Alta. C.A.).

Application of rule precluding multiple convictions – Although the trial judge has purported to enter an acquittal on a lesser charge by reason of the doctrine precluding multiple convictions, the Court of Appeal may deal with that charge on the accused's appeal from conviction, even in the absence of a Crown appeal from that acquittal. Where the Court of Appeal allows the accused's appeal from conviction and enters an acquittal, the court may then make an order in respect of the charge upon which the accused was acquitted. However, rather than entering a conviction on that charge, the appropriate order is to remit the matter back to the trial judge to enter a conviction and sentence the accused. This then preserves the accused's right to launch an appeal from that conviction if he so desires: *R. v. P. (D.W.)*, [1989] 2 S.C.R. 3 *sub nom. R. v. Provo*, 49 C.C.C. (3d) 417 (5:0).

To a similar effect, see *R. v. Pringle*, [1989] 1 S.C.R. 1645, 48 C.C.C. (3d) 449 (5:0).

Dismissal of appeal as no substantial wrong or miscarriage of justice [subsec. (1)(*b*)(iii)] – The test under this subsection has been expressed as whether the verdict would necessarily have been the same if the error had not occurred or whether there is any possibility that, if the error had not been committed, a judge or properly instructed jury would have acquitted the accused. Under either approach, the task of the appellate court is to determine whether "there is any reasonable possibility that the verdict would have been different had the error at issue not been made": *R. v. Bevan*, [1993] 2 S.C.R. 599, 82 C.C.C. (3d) 310.

There are two classes of errors which result in the application of the proviso: a "harmless error" or error of a minor nature having no impact on the verdict and causing no prejudice to the accused and serious errors which would justify a new trial but for the fact that the evidence adduced was seen as so overwhelming that the reviewing court concludes that there was no substantial wrong or miscarriage of justice: *R. v. Khan*, [2001] 3 S.C.R. 823, 160 C.C.C. (3d) 1.

The application of the curative proviso must be considered in the context of the evidence heard by the jury, not by the evidence it might have heard had the trial judge made different rulings. An appellant who has demonstrated an entitlement to a new trial should not be deprived of it based on assumptions about the probative force of evidence he was never called upon to answer at trial. Therefore the Crown cannot rely on prosecution evidence excluded (even wrongly excluded) at trial to meet the "overwhelming case" threshold: *R. v. James* (2011), 283 C.C.C. (3d) 212 (Ont. C.A.).

The curative proviso should not be watered down. The burden on the Crown to establish a harmless error or overwhelming evidence cannot be relaxed: *R. v. Sarrazin*, [2011] 3 S.C.R. 505, 276 C.C.C. (3d) 210.

It is an error of law for an appellate court to apply the curative proviso on its own motion. It can only be applied upon submissions from a party: *R. v. G. (P.)* (2017), 348 C.C.C. (3d) 368 (Ont. C.A.); *R. c. Pétel,* [1994] 1 S.C.R. 3, 87 C.C.C. (3d) 97.

There is no appearance of unfairness amounting to a miscarriage of justice so as to preclude resort to subsec. (1)(*b*)(iii) where, although inadmissible evidence was improperly admitted, the trial judge in his reasons for conviction expressly arrives at his conclusion without reliance on such evidence: *R. v. Leaney*, [1989] 2 S.C.R. 393, 50 C.C.C. (3d) 289 (4:1).

When the error of law is the exclusion of exculpatory evidence then the determination of whether the verdict would necessarily have been the same if the error had not been made must be made having regard to the entirety of the evidence, the exculpatory evidence having been included, and in the light of the effect the excluded evidence could, within reason, possibly have had on the evidence that did go to the jury. Any reasonable effect that the excluded evidence could have had on the jury should, in applying this paragraph, enure to the benefit of the accused. *R. v. Wildman*, [1984] 2 S.C.R. 311, 14 C.C.C. (3d) 321 (7:0).

The correct explanation of the requisite burden of proof is necessary to ensure a fair trial and there is a very real concern whether the proviso would ever be available to cure an erroneous instruction which may have misled a jury into improperly applying the burden of proof or reasonable doubt standard. Reasonable doubt should not be described as an ordinary concept as jurors should not be invited to apply to the determination of guilt in a criminal trial the same standard of proof that they would apply to the decisions they are required to make in their every day lives or even to the most important of these decisions. Reasonable doubt should not be described as proof to a moral certainty nor is it essential to instruct the jury that reasonable doubt is a doubt for which a reason can be supplied. The jury should be instructed that a reasonable doubt is a doubt based on reason and common sense which must be logically based on the evidence and it must not be based on sympathy or prejudice and must not be imaginary or frivolous. The jury must be advised that the Crown is not required to prove its case to an absolute certainty and that proof establishing a probability of guilt is not sufficient to establish guilt beyond a reasonable doubt: *R. v. Lifchus*, [1997] 3 S.C.R. 20, 118 C.C.C. (3d) 1. See also *R. v. Bisson*, [1998] 1 S.C.R. 306, 121 C.C.C. (3d) 449.

The assessment of the sufficiency of a charge requires a detailed review of the charge as a whole in the full context of the trial including: the complexity of the factual issues, their degree of contentiousness, the nature and quality of the evidence, the positions of the parties and any questions from the jury: *R. v. Russell*, [2000] 2 S.C.R. 731, 149 C.C.C. (3d) 66. See also *R. v. Beauchamp*, [2000] 2 S.C.R. 720, 149 C.C.C. (3d) 58; and *R. v. Avetysan*, [2000] 2 S.C.R. 745, 149 C.C.C. (3d) 77. In *R. v. Rhee* (2001), 158 C.C.C. (3d) 129, the Supreme Court of Canada stated that it will not interfere when an appellate court has exercised its judgment in evaluating substantial compliance of a pre-*Lifchus* jury charge.

There is no legal requirement for a special instruction on circumstantial evidence. The essential component is to instill in the jury that they must be satisfied beyond a reasonable doubt that the only rational inference that can be drawn from the circumstantial evidence is that the accused is guilty. Imparting the necessary message to the jury may be achieved in different ways. The trial judge did not err in instructing the jury that "if there is an equally reasonable inference" which would indicate an innocent purpose, they could acquit. Read in context, the phrases "equally rational" and "as reasonable" were not used as measure of the comparative value or weight of a non-guilty inference, but rather to describe the quality of any inference, guilty or otherwise, which might be drawn from the circumstantial evidence: *R. v. Griffin*, [2009] 2 S.C.R. 42, 244 C.C.C. (3d) 289.

The Court of Appeal, having found an error of law by the trial judge in the admission of evidence, was obliged to allow the appeal unless, on a consideration of the admissible evidence, the court was able to conclude that a conviction was inevitable. The Court of Appeal is not to substitute itself for the trial judge and determine the guilt or innocence of the accused. The appropriate inquiry was not whether this particular trial judge would have convicted but whether there was any possibility that a trial judge would have a reasonable doubt on the admissible evidence: *R. v. S. (P.L.)*, [1991] 1 S.C.R. 909, 64 C.C.C. (3d) 193 (4:3).

Notwithstanding the jury was properly charged as to the mental state required for murder, a new trial following conviction for murder was required where there was clearly evidence to support the accused's liability as a party to manslaughter and the basis for manslaughter had not been properly explained to the jury. A person charged with murder has the right to have the issue of manslaughter left to the jury if there is any evidence upon which such a verdict can be found and it cannot be said that no miscarriage of justice results from the failure to do so: *R. v. Jackson*, [1993] 4 S.C.R. 573, 86 C.C.C. (3d) 385, affg 68 C.C.C. (3d) 385 (Ont. C.A.).

In considering the application of this subsection, the findings of the jury may be a factor. However, where an included offence has erroneously not been left with the jury, a conviction for the more serious offence cannot generally be relied on since the verdict may have been a reaction against a complete acquittal: *R. v. Haughton*, [1994] 3 S.C.R. 516, 93 C.C.C. (3d) 99.

While counsel's failure to object to the judge's charge to the jury does not preclude the allegation of error on appeal it is a circumstance which the appellate court will consider particularly where the complaint is the trial judge's failure to place before the jury matters which the party alleges were essential matters to be included in the charge: *R. v. Imrich*, [1978] 1 S.C.R. 622, 34 C.C.C. (2d) 143 (8:1).

This paragraph can only relieve against errors of law and where the court finds that by reason of an error of mixed fact and law the accused has been unfairly prejudiced then the appeal must be allowed under subsec. (1)(*a*)(iii): *R. v. Fanjoy*, [1985] 2 S.C.R. 233, 21 C.C.C. (3d) 312 (7:0).

There is no basis for treating errors of law made in the course of an exhortation to the jury any differently from errors committed in any other part of the instructions to the jury, or during the trial. Not every improper reference in an exhortation will lead to a new trial. Once it is determined, however, that the exhortation may have improperly coerced the jury to reach a verdict, it cannot be said that the verdict would necessarily have been the same in the absence of the error and it would not be appropriate to apply the curative provision: *R. v. G. (R.M.)*, [1996] 3 S.C.R. 362, 110 C.C.C. (3d) 26.

It was held in *R. v. Nygaard and Schimmens*, [1989] 2 S.C.R. 1074, 51 C.C.C. (3d) 417 (8:1), that the court, having allowed the appeal of the accused alleged to be the principal on a charge of first degree murder as a result of improper admission of evidence, should also allow the appeal of the co-accused who was alleged to be a party to the offence. This was necessary to avoid the potentially incongruous and unacceptable result that the prime mover in the crime might on the new trial be only convicted of second degree murder whereas the party to the offence would have remained convicted of first degree murder.

Dismissal of appeal where procedural irregularities [subsec. (1)(*b*)(iv)] – The following principles apply in the context of a procedural irregularity: where a procedural irregularity amounts to or is based on an error of law, it falls under s. 686(1)(*a*)(ii) or (1)(*b*)(iii); if the procedural irregularity was prior to 1985 classified as an irregularity causing a loss of jurisdiction, subsec. (1)(*b*)(iv) provides that this is no longer fatal to the conviction and an analysis of prejudice must be undertaken in accordance with the principles set out in subsec. (1)(*b*)(iii); if the procedural error did not amount to or originate in an error of law, which is rare, subsec. (1)(*a*)(iii) applies and the reviewing court must consider whether a miscarriage of justice has occurred; or if it is determined that a miscarriage of justice has occurred, there are no remedial provisions that can cure such a defect and the appeal must be allowed and either an acquittal entered or a new trial ordered: *R. v. Khan* (2001), 160 C.C.C. (3d) 1 (S.C.C.).

Subsection (1)(*b*)(iv) could not apply to an error in the jury selection process where the trial judge instead of following the procedure prescribed in the *Criminal Code* for summonsing of *talesmen*, purported to continuously expand the jury panel by adding additional members with the result that those potential jurors who were directed by the

Crown to stand by were never called again to be sworn unless challenged: *R. v. Rowbotham* (1988), 41 C.C.C. (3d) 1 (Ont. C.A.).

This provision likewise had no application where the trial judge used "static" triers for a challenge for cause in circumstances where the Code required the use of "rotating" triers. This error prevented a properly constituted trial court from coming into existence, rendering recourse to this curative proviso unavailable: *R. v. Noureddine* (2015), 332 C.C.C. (3d) 114 (Ont. C.A.). See also: *R. v. Swite* (2011), 268 C.C.C. (3d) 184 (B.C.C.A.).

Subsection (1)(*b*)(iv) could apply and the appeal of an inmate from the refusal to issue a writ of *habeas corpus* dismissed where the Court of Appeal, having held that the superior court judge erred in refusing to issue the writ, went on to consider the merits of the inmate's application, with the participation of the inmate, and held that the application should have been dismissed: *R. v. Olson*, [1989] 1 S.C.R. 296, 47 C.C.C. (3d) 491 (5:0).

It was held in *R. v. Tran*, [1994] 2 S.C.R. 951, 92 C.C.C. (3d) 218, that, where there has been a violation of s. 14 of the Charter, it was for the court to fashion an appropriate and just remedy tailored to the particular circumstances of the case under s. 24(1) of the Charter. Neither s. 686(1)(*b*)(iii) nor s. 686(1)(*b*)(iv) have any application in such circumstances. A breach of the Charter cannot be characterised as minor or harmless or a mere procedural irregularity. As a matter of law, a violation of s. 14 of the Charter precludes application of these curative provisions. As a general rule, however, the appropriate remedy under s. 24(1) of the Charter for breach of s. 14 will be the same as it would be under the common law and under statutory guarantees, namely a rehearing of the issue or proceeding in which the violation occurred. [Also see note of this case under s. 24 of the Charter *infra*.]

Subsection (1)(*b*)(iv) could not apply to a situation where the judge had effectively deprived the accused of the opportunity to make submissions at the close of evidence: *R. v. Prior* (2010), 260 C.C.C. (3d) 281 (Nfld. & Lab. C.A.).

Absent exceptional circumstances, subsec. (1)(*b*)(iv) will not save a breach of the s. 650(1) right to be present caused by the trial judge conducting the pre-charge conference in chambers in the absence of the accused: *R. v. E. (F.E.)* (2011), 282 C.C.C. (3d) 552 (Ont. C.A.).

Although there is no jurisdiction to try a criminal and provincial offence jointly, subsec. (1)(*b*)(iv) can cure the irregularity where there was no prejudice to the defence: *R. v. Sciascia* (2016), 336 C.C.C. (3d) 419 (Ont. C.A.), affd [2017] 2 S.C.R. 539, 355 C.C.C. (3d) 553.

Power to set aside conviction and substitute not criminally responsible verdict [subsec. (1)(*d*)] – In *R. v. Mailloux*, [1988] 2 S.C.R. 1089, 45 C.C.C. (3d) 193 (6:0), the court explained the effect of the combined operation of the predecessor to subsec. (1)(*d*) and subsec. (1)(*a*) as follows:

1. When the issue is raised for the first time on appeal, the court will examine the evidence and, if it is satisfied that the appellant was insane at the time of the wrongful act, it will exercise its power under para. (*d*) to quash the conviction and to substitute the special verdict of not guilty by reason of insanity.
2. If insanity [now mental disorder] has been raised at trial and there has been an error of law in the form of a misdirection on the issue, and
   - (*a*) if the court is satisfied that a proper direction would have resulted in a verdict of not guilty by reason of insanity, it will substitute that verdict;
   - (*b*) if the court is not satisfied that, absent the misdirection, the inevitable verdict would have been not guilty by reason of insanity, it will decline to act under para. (*d*) but will order a new trial.
3. If there has been no misdirection, but the verdict is either unreasonable or cannot be supported by the evidence, the court will set aside the conviction and substitute the special verdict provided for under para. (*d*).
4. If there has been no error of law and the verdict cannot be said to be unreasonable or unsupported by the evidence, the court will decline to interfere with the verdict. Thus

para. (*d*) does not give the Court of Appeal an unfettered jurisdiction to substitute an insanity verdict without regard to the reasonableness of the jury's verdict.

It was held, prior to the amendment of subsec. (4) which now expressly refers to a person found unfit or not criminally responsible on account of mental disorder, that this paragraph is not exhaustive of the court's power where not criminally responsible is raised for the first time on appeal. It is also open to the Court of Appeal to order a new trial through the combined operation of subsecs. (1)(*a*) and (2)(*b*). At least where the appeal was from a jury verdict, the new trial must be a full new trial, not one limited to the issue of not criminally responsible: *R. v. Warsing*, [1998] 3 S.C.R. 579, 130 C.C.C. (3d) 259.

Even where the defence of not criminally responsible was not raised at trial, the appellate court may substitute such a verdict where there are sufficient facts to make a determination. In this case, the fact that the accused was not fit to conduct the appeal but was assisted by an *amicus curiae* was not a bar to imposing a not criminally responsible verdict in the circumstances: *R. v. Ta* (2002), 164 C.C.C. (3d) 97 (Ont. C.A.).

Power to set aside conviction and substitute finding of unfitness [subsec. (1)(*e*)] – In the absence of misdirection or other fault in the trial of the issue as to fitness to stand trial, the issue is properly one to be decided by the jury and, unless the Court of Appeal is satisfied the jury erred in its finding, the court cannot substitute its opinion for that of the jury: *R. v. Hubach*, [1966] 4 C.C.C. 114 (Alta. S.C. App. Div.) (3:2).

Order to be made when appeal from conviction allowed [subsec. (2)] – Where it cannot be said that there was no evidence to go to the jury the proper disposition is to order a new trial: *R. v. Woodward* (1975), 23 C.C.C. (2d) 508 (Ont. C.A.).

Service of a portion of an intermittent gaol term prior to a successful appeal is a factor making it appropriate to order that an acquittal be entered: *R. v. Dillabough* (1975), 28 C.C.C. (2d) 482 (Ont. C.A.). *Contra: R. v. O'Brien* (1987), 41 C.C.C. (3d) 86 (Que. C.A.).

The accused's conviction following a third trial for trafficking in narcotics having been quashed as a result of, *inter alia*, misdirection of the jury and improper admission of evidence, the appropriate order was to enter a verdict of acquittal rather than order a new trial: *R. v. Jamieson* (1989), 48 C.C.C. (3d) 287 (N.S.C.A.).

In the absence of a Crown appeal against the accused's acquittal of the full offence charged, Court of Appeal if it allows the accused's appeal against conviction for the included offence is limited to ordering a new trial on the included offence and cannot order that the new trial be on the full offence: *R. v. Guillemette*, [1986] 1 S.C.R. 356, 26 C.C.C. (3d) 1 (7:0).

Similarly, except in cases where the rule precluding multiple convictions applies [see notes *supra*], in the absence of a Crown appeal from an acquittal, the Court of Appeal has no jurisdiction to substitute a conviction for the offence of which the accused was acquitted when it allows an appeal from conviction for a related offence. Thus, in this case, the accused were charged with criminal negligence causing bodily harm [the victim being the mother] and criminal negligence causing death [the victim being the unborn child]. They were acquitted on the merits on the former offence and convicted on the latter offence. Since there was no appeal by the Crown from the acquittal, the Court of Appeal had no jurisdiction to substitute a conviction for that offence when it determined that the appeal on the latter offence must be allowed because the unborn child was not a "person": *R. v. Sullivan*, [1991] 1 S.C.R. 489, 63 C.C.C. (3d) 97 (8:1).

Appeal by Crown from acquittal [subsec. (4)] / Burden on Crown – It is the duty of the Crown in order to obtain a new trial to satisfy the appellate court that the verdict would not necessarily have been the same if the trial judge had properly directed the jury: *R. v. Vezeau*, [1977] 2 S.C.R. 277, 28 C.C.C. (2d) 81 (9:0).

Where the Crown appeals from a directed verdict of acquittal, the Crown has the burden to demonstrate that the legal error may have impacted the verdict of acquittal. It will only be in rare cases that the Crown will not be able to demonstrate that the verdict may be different after a new trial. Appellate courts cannot speculate as to what might have occurred if the trial had proceeded. It will be rare, therefore, that an appellate court will not order a new trial after determining that a directed verdict of acquittal was an error of law, particularly when the trial was with a jury: *R. v. O'Kane* (2012), 292 C.C.C. (3d) 222 (Man. C.A.).

Before the Court of Appeal may exercise its jurisdiction under subsec. (4)(*b*)(ii) and enter a conviction rather than order a new trial, it must be shown that all the findings necessary to support a verdict of guilty must have been made either explicitly or implicitly or not be in issue: *R. v. Cassidy*, [1989] 2 S.C.R. 345, 50 C.C.C. (3d) 193 (7:0).

Once an appellate court has concluded that the trial judge erred in law, the Crown appellant, before a new trial will be ordered, must discharge the onus of satisfying the appellate court that had the trial judge properly instructed himself, his judgment of acquittal would not necessarily have been the same: *R. v. Anthes Business Forms Ltd.* (1975), 26 C.C.C. (2d) 349 (Ont. C.A.).

However, the test to be applied is an objective one and not whether the particular trial judge who erroneously granted a directed verdict would have acquitted the accused: *R. v. Melo* (1986), 29 C.C.C. (3d) 173 (Ont. C.A.).

Procedure – Prior to the imposition of sentence under this subsection the appeal court must give the accused an opportunity to make submissions: *R. v. Lowry and Lepper*, [1974] S.C.R. 195, 6 C.C.C. (2d) 531.

In an unusual case, the court of appeal, on a Crown appeal, concluded that the trial judge erred in entering a stay of proceedings by reason of the delay in instituting the proceedings. Thus, while the proper order was to set aside the stay of proceedings, nevertheless the court entered an acquittal, since, based on the findings of fact by the trial judge, the accused was not guilty of the offences charged. This order was proper, notwithstanding no provision is made for entering an acquittal under subsec. (4): *R. v. Fraillon* (1990), 62 C.C.C. (3d) 474 (Que. C.A.).

Effect of failure of Crown to object, advance theory or offer further evidence – It is not open to the Crown to seek a new trial following the accused's acquittal in order to submit to the jury a basis of liability not raised at the original trial: *R. v. Wexler*, [1939] S.C.R. 350, 72 C.C.C. 1 (7:0); *R. v. Merson* (1983), 4 C.C.C. (3d) 251 (B.C.C.A.). Similarly, where the appellate court finds that there is no evidence to support the conviction on the basis of liability relied upon by the Crown at trial, the court will enter an acquittal rather than order a new trial which would enable the Crown to place before the jury a new theory of liability not relied upon at trial: *R. v. Savard and Lizotte*, [1946] S.C.R. 20, 85 C.C.C. 254 (5:0).

On the other hand the failure of Crown counsel to object to misdirection at trial will not necessarily preclude an appeal from an acquittal based on such misdirection as where the trial judge was led into error by defence counsel's address to the jury and the accused did not testify and called no witnesses: *R. v. Cullen*, [1949] S.C.R. 658, 94 C.C.C. 337 (4:1).

Beyond the court's general power to control its process in case of abuse, subsec. (4) confers no discretion on the court of appeal to refuse to order a new trial where a reversible error of law is found in the trial judge's decision. The court's residual discretion to remedy an abuse of the court's process can be exercised only in the clearest of cases where the conduct shocks the conscience of the community and is so detrimental to the proper administration of justice that it warrants judicial intervention. There must be overwhelming evidence that the proceedings under scrutiny are unfair to the point that they are contrary to the interests of justice. It may be, however, that a court of appeal might find an abuse of process in a case where the Crown refuses to continue a trial, despite sufficient evidence to found a verdict, for the sole purpose of obtaining an interlocutory appeal on an adverse ruling: *R. v. Power*, [1994] 1 S.C.R. 601, 89 C.C.C. (3d) 1.

Power of Court of Appeal – The power of the Court of Appeal to substitute a guilty verdict for an acquittal on appeal from trial by judge alone but not on trial by judge and jury does not violate s. 7 of the Charter: *R. v. Skalbania*, [1997] 3 S.C.R. 995, 120 C.C.C. (3d) 217.

The power of the court of appeal to order a new trial means an order for a full new trial and not merely resumption of the original trial before the trial judge: *R. v. Gunn*, [1982] 1 S.C.R. 522, 66 C.C.C. (2d) 294.

Procedure on new trial – It was held, prior to the recent amendment to s. 491 [now s. 561], that where the court of appeal orders a new trial under this subsection an accused who has, pursuant to his previous election or re-election, been tried by a magistrate, he has no right to re-elect trial by a court composed of a judge and jury on the new trial: *R. v. Sagliocco* (1979), 45 C.C.C. (2d) 493 (B.C.S.C.), affd 51 C.C.C. (2d) 188 (B.C.C.A.).

It has also been held that the fact that the accused in such circumstances could not re-elect trial by jury did not offend. s. 11(*f*) of the *Canadian Charter of Rights and Freedoms*: *R. v. Switzer* (1985), 22 C.C.C. (3d) 60 (B.C.S.C.); *R. v. Leaney*, [1991] 6 W.W.R. 314, 82 Alta. L.R. (2d) 63 (C.A.).

The power of the Court of Appeal under para. (*b*) of this subsection is to enter a verdict of guilty and although the order of the court is expressed as a "verdict of conviction", the trial court, to whom the matter of sentence had been remitted, is not precluded from granting a discharge under s. 736: *R. v. Stewart (No. 2)* (1983), 11 C.C.C. (3d) 92 (Ont. H.C.J.).

Request for new trial by jury [subsec. (5) and (5.1) – In *R. v. Budic (No. 2)* (1977), 35 C.C.C. (2d) 333 (Alta. S.C. App. Div.), the accused was allowed to amend his notice of appeal to request that the new trial be before a judge and jury, the original trial having been before a judge alone.

Subsection (5.1) applies to a new trial ordered by the Supreme Court of Canada: *R. v. Cook* (2002), 164 C.C.C. (3d) 540 (B.C.C.A.).

This provision has no application to a dangerous offender appeal: *R. v. Kelly* (2005), 199 C.C.C. (3d) 336 (B.C.C.A.).

Additional order under subsec. (8) – While this subsection gives the Court of Appeal power to make a considerable range of orders, those orders must be ancillary in nature and not in direct variance with the court's underlying judgment. At least in the case of an appeal from conviction by a jury, the court having decided to allow the appeal and order a new trial, has no jurisdiction under this subsection to limit the new trial, for example, to whether the accused is guilty of second degree murder or manslaughter: *R. v. Thomas*, [1998] 3 S.C.R. 535, 130 C.C.C. (3d) 225. Nor can the new trial be limited to whether the defence of not criminally responsible has been made out: *R. v. Warsing*, [1998] 3 S.C.R. 579, 130 C.C.C. (3d) 259.

Notwithstanding *Warsing*, in two "sexsomnia" cases, the Ontario Court of Appeal held that it had jurisdiction under subsec. (8) to limit the scope of a new trial where such an order does not interfere with any of the accused's rights and is otherwise consistent with the demands of justice in the circumstances: *R. v. Luedecke* (2008), 236 C.C.C. (3d) 317 (Ont. C.A.); *R. v. Hartman* (2015), 326 C.C.C. (3d) 263 (Ont. C.A.).

However, given the unique nature of an entrapment proceeding after a verdict of guilty, where the errors related only to the trial judge's ruling on entrapment, the Court of Appeal may quash the formal order of conviction, affirm the verdict of guilty and order a new trial limited to the post-verdict entrapment motion: *R. v. Pearson*, [1998] 3 S.C.R. 620, 130 C.C.C. (3d) 293.

Where on an appeal by the accused the Court of Appeal quashes the conviction and orders a new trial, it may also order a new trial on an alternative charge which was dismissed at trial solely because of the application of the doctrine precluding multiple convictions notwithstanding the Crown has not appealed the latter acquittal: *R. v. Letendre* (1979), 46 C.C.C. (2d) 398 (B.C.C.A.). Similarly: *R. v. McLeod* (1983), 6 C.C.C. (3d) 29 (Ont. C.A.), affd [1986] 1 S.C.R. 703*n*, 27 C.C.C. (3d) 383*n*. Also see *R. v. Terlecki* (1983), 4 C.C.C. (3d) 522 (Alta. C.A.), affd [1985] 2 S.C.R. 483, 22 C.C.C. (3d) 224*n* (7:0) noted, *supra*, under s. 613.

Where the Court of Appeal allows a new trial because of misdirection by the trial judge, it may order that the new trial be on an included offence or an attempt where it is of the view that in any event the full offence had not been made out: *R. v. Cook* (1979), 47 C.C.C. (2d) 186 (Ont. C.A.); *R. v. Ruptash* (1982), 68 C.C.C. (2d) 182 (Alta. C.A.).

The Court of Appeal has a residual discretion to stay the charge where any further proceedings would constitute an abuse of process: *R. v. Power*, [1994] 1 S.C.R. 601, 89 C.C.C. (3d) 1; *R. v. Hinse*, [1995] 4 S.C.R. 597, 102 C.C.C. (3d) 289; *R. v. Rain* (1998), 130 C.C.C. (3d) 167 (Alta. C.A.), leave to appeal to S.C.C. refused 132 C.C.C. (3d) vi; and *R. v. Codina* (1999), 132 C.C.C. (3d) 338 (Ont. C.A.). However, where there was no evidence upon which a properly instructed jury could convict the appropriate order is to direct a verdict of acquittal, not a stay of proceedings: *R. v. Hinse*, [1997] 1 S.C.R. 3, 112 C.C.C. (3d) 383.

The Court of Appeal has the discretion, where appropriate, to order the continuation of a trial before the same trial judge where the Crown has been successful in setting aside a stay of proceedings. To do otherwise where there had already been several months of evidence adduced would harm the reputation of the administration of justice: *R. v. Yelle* (2006), 213 C.C.C. (3d) 20 (Alta. C.A.). *Contra R. v. Kelly* (2002), 213 C.C.C. (3d) 385 (N.S.C.A.).

A court of appeal has jurisdiction, under subsec. (8), to remit a matter to the summary conviction appeal court in order to consider a ground of appeal not disposed of below: *R. v. Lange* (2016), 337 C.C.C. (3d) 379 (Sask. C.A.).

POWERS OF COURT ON APPEAL AGAINST SENTENCE / Effect of judgment.

687. (1) Where an appeal is taken against sentence, the court of appeal shall, unless the sentence is one fixed by law, consider the fitness of the sentence appealed against, and may on such evidence, if any, as it thinks fit to require or to receive,

(*a*) vary the sentence within the limits prescribed by law for the offence of which the accused was convicted; or

(*b*) dismiss the appeal.

(2) A judgment of a court of appeal that varies the sentence of an accused who was convicted has the same force and effect as if it were a sentence passed by the trial court. R.S., c. C-34, s. 614.

CROSS-REFERENCES

See s. 673 for the definition of "sentence". Sections 675(1)(*b*) and 676(1)(*d*) confer rights of appeal respecting sentences. Under s. 689(2), the court has jurisdiction to consider appropriate terms of orders of restitution. Section 687(1) permits the court to receive new or "fresh" evidence on an appeal against sentence. This avoids the more onerous standards applicable under s. 683(1)(*d*).

Under s. 683(7), in determining whether to vary the sentence, the appellate court may take into account the conditions of the undertaking or recognizance and the period during which they were imposed, when the court suspends a probation order or conditional sentence order pending appeal.

SYNOPSIS

On a sentence appeal where the sentence is not fixed by law, the court of appeal will consider the "fitness" of the sentence imposed at trial. It can either vary the sentence within the limits prescribed by law or dismiss the appeal. If the sentence is varied the judgment of the court of appeal has the same force and effect as an order of the trial court.

Note: For notes respecting sentencing principles see ss. 718, 718.1 and 718.2.

ANNOTATIONS

Powers of Court of Appeal – The clause "vary the sentence within the limits prescribed by law" plainly fixes the scope of the power of an appellate court by reference to the maximum prescribed penalty irrespective of the penalty imposed at trial, and accordingly where the Crown has given reasonable notice in its factum an appellate court may increase the sentence on the accused's sentence appeal. Furthermore on any appeal against sentence an appellate court has jurisdiction to vary either way as it deems proper: *R. v. Hill (No. 2)*, [1977] 1 S.C.R. 827, 25 C.C.C. (2d) 6 (5:4).

Thus the court may on its own motion upon notice to the accused impose a sentence of life imprisonment where the accused has appealed against a definite sentence: *R. v. Kempton* (1980), 53 C.C.C. (2d) 176, 12 Alta. L.R. (2d) 258 (C.A.).

The Court of Appeal has no inherent jurisdiction to consider sentence on its own motion in the absence of an appeal from sentence. However, in rare circumstances, the court in the course of oral argument on the conviction appeal could ask about a sentence appeal where the sentence is so clearly unreasonable or demonstrably unfit as to indicate possible oversight on the part of counsel or an unrepresented accused: *R. v. W. (G.)*, [1999] 3 S.C.R. 597, 138 C.C.C. (3d) 23.

On an appeal from sentence, the Court of Appeal has no power to remit the matter to the trial court, notwithstanding that serious errors in procedure and admission of evidence at the sentence hearing would make this the preferrable course to follow. The court's only power is to consider the fitness of the sentence, taking into account evidence which was properly admissible: *R. v. Pelletier* (1989), 52 C.C.C. (3d) 340 (Que. C.A.).

Where a conditional sentence order is set aside, the accused is entitled to be given credit for the time spent serving the conditional sentence: *R. v. Birchall* (2001), 158 C.C.C. (3d) 340 (B.C.C.A.).

Admission of fresh evidence – While the rules concerning the sources and types of evidence are more flexible in respect of a sentence appeal, the criteria for admitting fresh evidence are the same in respect of an appeal from conviction or sentence: (1) the evidence should generally not be admitted if, by due diligence, it could have been adduced at trial provided that this general principle will not be applied as strictly in criminal cases as in civil cases; (2) the evidence must be relevant in the sense that it bears upon a decisive or potentially decisive issue in the trial; (3) the evidence must be credible in the sense that it is reasonably capable of belief; and (4) it must be such that if believed it could reasonably, when taken with the other evidence adduced at trial, be expected to have affected the result. Due diligence is not a necessary prerequisite but is an important factor in determining whether it is in the interests of justice to admit the fresh evidence. Before admitting new opinion evidence on appeal, it may be necessary to determine the basis of that opinion and to establish whether the facts on which the opinion is based have been proven and are credible. While evidence relating to events subsequent to sentence or regarding an accused's rehabilitation process normally meet the due diligence criterion, the evidence must also satisfy the other criteria, particularly the likelihood that the result would be affected. The Court of Appeal may properly consider the Crown's consent to admission of the evidence or that admission is uncontested particularly when assessing the relevance, credibility and probative value of fresh evidence: *R. v. Levesque*, [2000] 2 S.C.R. 487, 148 C.C.C. (3d) 193.

In dangerous offender appeals, the appellate courts are frequently confronted with evidence about the offender's rehabilitation efforts and prospects long after the initial sentencing. While the *Levesque* test sets out the applicable legal framework for admitting this sort of evidence, appellate courts generally take a very cautious approach to intervening solely on the basis of evidence of this nature. Evidence about the offender's post-sentencing rehabilitative efforts and prospects will only exceptionally meet this threshold. Such developments are, generally speaking, matters for the correctional authorities to consider in the course of administering the offender's indeterminate sentence: *R. v. S. (J.P.)*, [2014] 2 S.C.R. 423, 311 C.C.C. (3d) 121.

Standard of review – A variation in the sentence should only be made if the Court of Appeal is convinced it is not fit in the sense that the sentence is clearly unreasonable. The Court of Appeal must determine if the sentencing judge applied wrong principles or if the sentence was clearly excessive or inadequate. Unreasonableness in the sentence process involves the sentencing order falling outside the acceptable range of orders: *R. v. Shropshire*, [1995] 4

S.C.R. 227, 102 C.C.C. (3d) 193. Absent an error in principle, failure to consider a relevant factor, or an overemphasis of the appropriate factors, a Court of Appeal should only intervene to vary a sentence if it is demonstrably unfit. Furthermore, an appellate court should only intervene to minimize the disparity of sentences where the sentence imposed by the trial judge is a substantial, marked departure from the sentences customarily imposed for similar offenders committing similar crimes: *R. v. M. (C.A.)*, [1996] 1 S.C.R. 500, 105 C.C.C. (3d) 327.

On review of the imposition of a maximum sentence, the appellate court must determine whether the sentence was reasonable having regard to the circumstances and the objectives of sentencing: *R. v. M. (L.)*, [2008] 2 S.C.R. 163, 231 C.C.C. (3d) 310.

A sentence that falls outside an established range is not necessarily unfit. Sentencing ranges are nothing more than summaries of the minimum and maximum sentences imposed in the past, which serve in any given case as guides for the application of all the relevant sentencing principles and objectives. However, they should not be considered "averages", let alone straitjackets, but should instead be seen as historical portraits for the use of sentencing judges: *R. c. Lacasse*, [2015] 3 S.C.R. 1089, 333 C.C.C. (3d) 450.

The framework for appellate review of sentence is disjunctive in that where there is an error in principle that impacts the sentence, the sentence need not also be demonstrably unfit in order to warrant intervention. A sentence that has been impacted by error is not a judicial exercise of discretion, which is why it is not owed the usual deference: *R. v. Agin* (2018), 361 C.C.C. (3d) 258 (B.C.C.A.).

While there is no presumption in favour of a conditional sentence, if the statutory prerequisites in s. 742.1 have been satisfied, serious consideration should be given to the imposition of a conditional sentence in all cases where these statutory prerequisites are satisfied. Failure to advert to the possibility, where there are reasonable grounds for finding that the prerequisites have been met, may constitute reversible error. However, the deference due trial judges in imposing sentence generally applies to the decision whether or not to impose a conditional sentence. Although an appellate court might entertain a different opinion as to what objectives should be pursued and the best way to do so, that difference will generally not constitute an error of law justifying intervention: *R. v. Proulx*, [2000] 1 S.C.R. 61, 140 C.C.C. (3d) 449.

The same level of deference does not apply where the law changes and the accused may be entitled to the benefit of the more lenient disposition, such as a conditional sentence, which came into force in 1996, after the accused's sentencing but prior to his appeal: *R. v. S. (R.N.)*, [2000] 1 S.C.R. 149, 140 C.C.C. (3d) 553. The Court of Appeal need not, therefore, defer to all of the trial judge's findings, and can proceed to re-sentence the accused in light of the new principles: *R. v. Bunn*, [2000] 1 S.C.R. 183, 140 C.C.C. (3d) 505.

A decision to make a DNA order pursuant to s. 487.051 with respect to a primary designated offence is entitled to deference. Absent an error in principle, a failure to consider a relevant factor or an over-emphasis of the appropriate factors, an appellate court should only intervene to vary a decision respecting a DNA order if the decision was clearly unreasonable: *R. v. C. (R.W.)*, [2005] 3 S.C.R. 99, 201 C.C.C. (3d) 321.

Where the court is asked to consider a sentencing option that was not available to the sentencing judge, such as a conditional sentence, material should be provided indicating the basis for the submission that the appellant would be a suitable candidate for a conditional sentence, including the conditions that might be imposed to ensure that the community will not be put at risk and that the other principles and objectives of sentencing will be met by such a disposition: *R. v. Fleet* (1997), 120 C.C.C. (3d) 457 (Ont. C.A.).

The period of parole ineligibility imposed by a trial judge is entitled to deference on appeal. An appellate court should interfere only if there is an error in principle or the period of parole ineligibility was unreasonable because it was outside the acceptable range. Although overemphasizing a relevant factor or failing to give enough weight to a relevant factor may amount to an error in principle, an appellate court cannot interfere with the trial judge's discretion merely because it would have given different weight or emphasis to a factor relevant to the sentence: *R. v. McKnight* (1999), 135 C.C.C. (3d) 41 (Ont. C.A.).

The sentencing judge's departure from the starting point established by the appellate court may be a factor to consider in determining whether the sentence is demonstrably unfit and a wide disparity between the starting-point for the offence and the sentence imposed may suggest but is not determinative of unfitness. Absent another reason to interfere, however, a sentence cannot be altered on appeal solely as a result of a deviation from the starting-point: *R. v. McDonnell*, [1997] 1 S.C.R. 948, 114 C.C.C. (3d) 436. Also see *R. v. Stone*, [1999] 2 S.C.R. 290, 134 C.C.C. (3d) 353, noted under s. 718.2.

Absent an error in principle, the trial judge's decision as to whether the sentence is concurrent or consecutive should be treated with the same deference as that accorded the trial judge's discretion as to the length of the sentence: *R. v. McDonnell, supra.*

Evidence of the appellant's progress in the penitentiary was relevant and admissible on his appeal from sentence where the Court of Appeal had concluded that the sentence was so excessive that it must be reviewed: *R. v. Lemay* (1998), 127 C.C.C. (3d) 528 (Que. C.A.).

Position taken by counsel at trial / *Also see notes under s. 676* – Absent exceptional circumstances, the Crown upon appeal against a sentence cannot repudiate its position taken at trial: *R. v. Brewer* (1999), 141 C.C.C. (3d) 290, 182 Nfld. & P.E.I.R. 14 (Nfld. C.A.). See also *R. v. Agozzino*, [1970] 1 C.C.C. 380, [1970] 1 O.R. 480 (C.A.). *Contra*, *R. v. Wood* (1975), 26 C.C.C. (2d) 100, [1976] 2 W.W.R. 135 (Alta. C.A.).

However, an undertaking by Crown counsel at trial that he would not recommend an appeal, but that he could not bind the Attorney General, does not in fact prevent the Attorney General from exercising his right to appeal against the sentence imposed by the trial judge, which sentence was below that which Crown counsel sought at trial: *R. v. Dubien* (1982), 67 C.C.C. (2d) 341 (Ont. C.A.).

To permit the Crown to repudiate its position at trial is destructive of the orderly administration of justice and the Crown will therefore only be permitted to do so where it can be shown that the public interest in the orderly administration of justice is outweighed by the gravity of the offence and the gross insufficiency of the sentence: *R. v. MacArthur* (1978), 39 C.C.C. (2d) 158 (P.E.I.S.C. App. Div.); *R. v. Smith* (1981), 25 C.R. (3d) 190 (Alta. C.A.).

While generally speaking, the Crown will not be entitled to repudiate a position taken at trial by Crown counsel as to the appropriate sentence, a greater latitude is given the accused in that he is not generally bound to the same extent by the submission of his counsel as to sentence. Where the sentence imposed by the trial judge as a result of a joint submission by Crown and defence counsel, having regard to all the circumstances, is not a fit sentence, the Court of Appeal will reduce it accordingly: *R. v. Wood* (1988), 43 C.C.C. (3d) 570 (Ont. C.A.).

The court will pay a great deal of attention to a joint recommendation and the parties should not lightly be heard to repudiate on appeal the positions that were taken before the sentencing judge. Where, however, the joint recommendation was based, in part, on a psychological report which the "psychologist" was not qualified to make, then the court will not attach much weight either to the report or to the joint submission. In this case, a lengthy sentence for manslaughter was substantially reduced on appeal by the accused where the court was provided with more accurate information in the report of a qualified psychiatrist as to the accused's background and her state of mind at the time of the offence: *R. v. Valiquette* (1990), 60 C.C.C. (3d) 325 (Que. C.A.).

Sentencing after retrial – The judge sentencing a person after a retrial should be alive to the accused's justified sense of grievance if, without apparent reason, the second judge imposes a much longer sentence than the first. Accordingly, where an accused has been convicted of an offence a second time after retrial, the sentencing judge should first consider the fitness of the original sentence. If the judge does not accept the fitness of the original sentence, either because it was inordinately low or because new facts have emerged, the judge may impose a longer sentence. But, where no new facts have emerged, the judge should avoid imposing a sentence which is so much longer than the first as to cause a reasonable person to think that the accused was penalized for his successful appeal: *R. v. W. (R.S.)* (1992), 74 C.C.C. (3d) 1 (Man. C.A.).

Effect of variation of sentence [subsec. (2)] – Violation of a probation order imposed by an appeal court in substitution for the trial court's penalty is to be dealt with by the trial court as the substituted sentence of that court: *R. v. Keller* (1971), 14 C.R.N.S. 234 (Sask. Q.B.). Also see *R. v. H.* (1983), 6 C.C.C. (3d) 382, [1983] 5 W.W.R. 94 *sub nom. Alberta (Attorney General) v. H.* (Alta. C.A.), noted, *infra*, under s. 738.

RIGHT OF APPELLANT TO ATTEND / Appellant represented by counsel / Manner of appearance / Argument may be oral or in writing / Sentence in absence of appellant.

688. (1) Subject to subsection (2), an appellant who is in custody is entitled, if he desires, to be present at the hearing of the appeal.

(2) An appellant who is in custody and who is represented by counsel is not entitled to be present

- **(*a*) at the hearing of the appeal, where the appeal is on a ground involving a question of law alone,**
- **(*b*) on an application for leave to appeal, or**
- **(*c*) on any proceedings that are preliminary or incidental to an appeal,**

unless rules of court provide that he is entitled to be present or the court of appeal or a judge thereof gives him leave to be present.

(2.1) In the case of an appellant who is in custody and who is entitled to be present at any proceedings on an appeal, the court may order that, instead of the appellant personally appearing,

- **(*a*) at an application for leave to appeal or at any proceedings that are preliminary or incidental to an appeal, the appellant appear by means of any suitable telecommunication device, including telephone, that is satisfactory to the court; and**
- **(*b*) at the hearing of the appeal, if the appellant has access to legal advice, he or she appear by means of closed-circuit television or any other means that permits the court and all parties to engage in simultaneous visual and oral communication.**

(3) An appellant may present his case on appeal and his argument in writing instead of orally, and the court of appeal shall consider any case of argument so presented.

(4) A court of appeal may exercise its power to impose sentence notwithstanding that the appellant is not present. R.S., c. C-34, s. 615; 2002, c. 13, s. 68.

CROSS-REFERENCES

See s. 694.2 for a similar provision respecting appeals to the Supreme Court of Canada. These provisions are incorporated by s. 822(1) into summary conviction appeals under s. 812.

Also, see s. 683(2.1) and (2.2), which provide that the court may order a party to appear by technological means and for use of technological means to take evidence on an appeal. Under s. 848, if an accused who is in prison does not have access to legal advice, the court shall, before permitting the accused to appear by means of communication that allows the court and the accused to engage in simultaneous visual and oral communication, be satisfied that the accused will be able to understand the proceedings and that any decisions made by the accused during the proceedings will be voluntary.

SYNOPSIS

This section deals with when an appellant, who is in custody, is entitled to be present for the hearing of his or her appeal.

An "in person" appellant has a right to appear at the hearing. However, an appellant who has retained counsel has no right to attend (a) the hearing of an appeal on a question of law alone; (b) an application for leave to appeal, or (c) a proceeding preliminary or incidental to an appeal. This is subject to any rules of court or an order of a judge (subsec. (1), (2)).

Arguments may be presented in written form instead of orally (subsec. (3)).

The appellant need not be present for the court to impose sentence (subsec. (4)).

Subsection (2.1) provides that the court may order the inmate to appear through technological means for certain preliminary parts of the proceedings and for the hearing of the appeal, if the inmate has counsel, through closed-circuit television or similar means provided the accused has access to counsel.

ANNOTATIONS

In *R. v. Smith*, [1965] S.C.R. 658, [1966] 1 C.C.C. 162, it was held that an appeal cannot proceed in the absence of an appellant who has signified his desire to be present at the hearing.

In *R. v. Trecroce* (1980), 55 C.C.C. (2d) 202 (Ont. C.A.), the accused who was present during his appeal pursuant to this section sought to discharge his counsel. The court being possessed of certain psychiatric evidence raised the question of the accused's competency to discharge his counsel and appoint other counsel. The court thereupon directed that the accused be examined by psychiatrists who then gave evidence as to the accused's fitness to instruct counsel. The court held that the accused was competent to instruct counsel based on the evidence that he understood the nature of the proceedings and the function of the persons involved and knew the issues and the possible outcomes notwithstanding he might misinterpret some of the evidence and might not only disagree with his counsel but might not act with good judgment.

The discretion under subsec. (2.1) to order the appellant appear remotely by video involves a balancing of the interests affected. While the benefits of an appellant's physical presence may be less pressing on appeal than at trial, an appellant who has an intimate knowledge of the factual material can reasonably consider it important to be able to speak with counsel during the appeal hearing: *R. v. Flynn* (2018), 366 C.C.C. (3d) 321 (N.L.C.A.).

Subsection (4) – The term "appellant" is to be construed as equivalent to the accused even though he is the respondent on the appeal: *R. v. Krawetz* (1974), 20 C.C.C. (2d) 173 (Man. C.A.).

RESTITUTION OR FORFEITURE OF PROPERTY / Annulling or varying order.

689. (1) If the trial court makes an order for compensation or for the restitution of property under section 738 or 739 or an order of forfeiture of property under subsection 164.2(1) or 462.37(1) or (2.01), the operation of the order is suspended

- **(*a*) until the expiration of the period prescribed by rules of court for the giving of notice of appeal or of notice of application for leave to appeal, unless the accused waives an appeal; and**
- **(*b*) until the appeal or application for leave to appeal has been determined, where an appeal is taken or application for leave to appeal is made.**

(2) The court of appeal may by order annul or vary an order made by the trial court with respect to compensation or the restitution of property within the limits prescribed by the provision under which the order was made by the trial court, whether or not the conviction is quashed. R.S., c. C-34, s. 616; R.S.C. 1985, c. 42 (4th Supp.), s. 5; 1995, c. 22, s. 10; 2002, c. 13, s. 69; 2005, c. 44, s. 12.

CROSS-REFERENCES

A comprehensive code governing the limitations on the authorization of restitution orders may be found in ss. 738 to 741.2. The definition of "sentence" in s. 673 includes such orders. Those orders are reviewable on an appeal against sentence under ss. 675(1)(*b*) and 676(1)(*d*). The incorporation of these provisions by s. 822(1) renders them applicable to summary conviction appeals under s. 812.

If the authority of s. 689 is not limited to proceedings where fitness of sentence is in issue, the Supreme Court of Canada would seem to have equivalent jurisdiction.

SYNOPSIS

Subsection (1) provides for the automatic stay of compensation, restitution or forfeiture orders until either the expiration of the appeal period or the resolution of any appeal or application for leave which is taken (subsec. (1)).

The court can annul or vary any compensation or restitution orders even if it does not quash the underlying conviction (subsec. (2)).

ANNOTATIONS

Notwithstanding this section, in a proper case, the superior court may grant an interim injunction to a victim to prevent an accused from disposing of assets which were the fruits of crime so that those assets would be available to satisfy a compensation order made under former s. 725 [now s. 738], should the accused's appeal from conviction be dismissed: *Oerlikon Aerospatiale Inc. v. Ouellete* (1989), 54 C.C.C. (3d) 403 (Que. C.A.).

Powers of Minister of Justice

690. [*Repealed*, 2002, c. 13, s. 70.]

Appeals to the Supreme Court of Canada

APPEAL FROM CONVICTION / Appeal where acquittal set aside.

691. (1) A person who is convicted of an indictable offence and whose conviction is affirmed by the court of appeal may appeal to the Supreme Court of Canada

(*a*) on any question of law on which a judge of the court of appeal dissents; or

(*b*) on any question of law, if leave to appeal is granted by the Supreme Court of Canada.

(2) A person who is acquitted of an indictable offence other than by reason of a verdict of not criminally responsible on account of mental disorder and whose acquittal is set aside by the court of appeal may appeal to the Supreme Court of Canada

(*a*) on any question of law on which a judge of the court of appeal dissents;

(*b*) on any question of law, if the Court of Appeal enters a verdict of guilty against the person; or

(*c*) on any question of law, if leave to appeal is granted by the Supreme Court of Canada. R.S., c. C-34, s. 618; 1974-75-76, c. 105, s. 18; R.S.C. 1985, c. 34 (3rd Supp.), s. 10; 1991, c. 43, s. 9; 1997, c. 18, s. 99.

CROSS-REFERENCES

Similar rights of appeal to the Supreme Court of Canada from a verdict of not criminally responsible on account of mental disorder or a finding of unfit to stand trial are authorized in s. 692. See ss. 693 and 696 for the rights of appeal of the Attorney General. The Supreme Court of Canada has the authority to determine appeals under Part XXI, equivalent to that of provincial courts of appeal whose authority is incorporated by reference under s. 695(1).

See s. 672.1 for definition of "verdict of not criminally responsible on account of mental disorder".

SYNOPSIS

This section governs appeals to the Supreme Court of Canada by a person convicted of an indictable offence. Such appeals are restricted to "questions of law".

Where an appeal by the accused has been dismissed by the Court of Appeal an appeal may be taken "as of right" on any question of law upon which a judge of the Court of Appeal has dissented. Absent such a dissent, leave to appeal must be obtained from the Supreme Court (subsecs. (1)(*a*), (*b*)). (**Note**: Where an appeal is taken on the basis of a dissent, leave is required to raise other issues.)

An appeal "as of right" lies from a judgment of the Court of Appeal allowing a Crown appeal from acquittal on a dissent in law (subsec. (2)(*a*)).

Where the Court of Appeal allows a Crown appeal from acquittal and enters a verdict of guilty, the accused may appeal "as of right" (subsec. (2)(*b*)), otherwise the accused requires leave to appeal to appeal to the Supreme Court.

(**Note**: Appeals with respect to summary conviction matters and prerogative writs are governed by s. 40 of the *Supreme Court Act*.)

ANNOTATIONS

Dissent in law (subsec. 1(*a*)) – To proceed under this paragraph there must be a strict question of law, not one of mixed fact and law, which is involved in the *ratio decidendi* and upon which there was a disagreement in the provincial appellate court: *R. v. Demenoff*, [1964] S.C.R. 79, [1964] 2 C.C.C. 305 (5:0).

In *R. v. Mahoney*, [1982] 1 S.C.R. 834, 67 C.C.C. (2d) 197, the majority of the court appears to have adopted the view that the application of s. 686(1)(*b*)(iii) is a question of law which is reviewable by the Supreme Court of Canada.

Whether a verdict of guilty is unreasonable or is unsupported by the evidence pursuant to s. 686(1)(*a*)(i) raises a question of law: *R. v. Biniaris*, [2000] 1 S.C.R. 381, 143 C.C.C. (3d) 1.

In view of s. 27(5) of the [former] *Young Offenders Act*, no appeal lies as of right under this section in matters governed by the *Young Offenders Act*. Thus, even if there is a dissent in law, leave to appeal must be obtained: *R. v. C. (T.L.)*, [1994] 2 S.C.R. 1012, 92 C.C.C. (3d) 444. [Similarly, now see s. 37(10) of the *Youth Criminal Justice Act*.]

Leave to appeal (subsec. (1)(*b*)) – With the literal interpretation of s. 40 of the *Supreme Court Act*, R.S.C. 1985, c. S-26, particularly the words "convicting" and "conviction" in subsec. (3) thereof jurisdiction to entertain an appeal against the principle, not the fitness, of a sentence from an appellate court's order was confirmed in *R. v. Hill*, [1977] 1 S.C.R. 830, 23 C.C.C. (2d) 321 (8:0). It should be noted that while six members of the court agreed with the reasons for judgment of Pigeon J., Laskin C.J.C., concurred in the conclusion, not by applying a rule of interpretation, but by proceeding on the basis that he would only exclude from the leave jurisdiction of the court those appeals which are quite plainly excluded by statute.

Where the court grants leave to appeal without restriction, the appellant was entitled to bring into question the validity of his conviction on a question of law, other than the question of law upon which leave to appeal was sought, which arose as a result of a decision of the Supreme Court intervening between the order granting leave and the hearing of the appeal: *R. v. Wigman*, [1987] 1 S.C.R. 246, 33 C.C.C. (3d) 97 (6:0).

The granting of leave does not preclude the court from later deciding that the question does not raise a ground of law: *R. v. Demeter*, [1978] 1 S.C.R. 538, 34 C.C.C. (2d) 137 (9:0).

An appellant who seeks to raise the invalidity of a law, under which he was convicted on grounds arising out of a subsequent decision of the Supreme Court, must still be in the judicial system in that an appeal has been launched to the court, an application for leave has been made within time or an application for an extension of time is granted, based on the criteria that normally apply in such cases, including demonstration of an intention to appeal within the appeal period and an adequate explanation of the delay: *R. v. Thomas*, [1990] 1 S.C.R. 713 (3:0).

Acquittal set aside by Court of Appeal (subsec. (2)(*a*)) – An accused may appeal under subsec. (2)(*a*) where the trial judge "quashed" the charges against him on the basis of a violation of s. 11(*b*) of the *Charter of Rights and Freedoms*. The judge should have stayed the proceedings, which order is tantamount to an acquittal: *R. v. Kalanj*, [1989] 1 S.C.R. 1594, 48 C.C.C. (3d) 459.

Where the Court of Appeal dismisses the accused's appeal and substitutes a conviction for another offence, both the Crown and the accused have rights of appeal from the order for a substituted verdict: *R. v. Biniaris*, [2000] 1 S.C.R. 381, 143 C.C.C. (3d) 1.

Verdict of guilty entered by Court of Appeal (subsec. (2)(*b*)) – The accused and the Crown both appealed a second degree murder conviction to the Court of Appeal. The accused's appeal was dismissed, the Crown's appeal was allowed, and a verdict of guilty of first degree murder substituted. The accused's appeal as of right under this provision was limited to grounds relating to the substituted conviction for first degree murder. Grounds relating to the conviction for second degree murder required leave pursuant to subsec. (1)(*b*): *R. v. Magoon* (2018), 361 C.C.C. (3d) 1 (S.C.C.).

APPEAL AGAINST AFFIRMATION OF VERDICT OF NOT CRIMINALLY RESPONSIBLE ON ACCOUNT OF MENTAL DISORDER / Appeal against affirmation of verdict of unfit to stand trial / Grounds of appeal.

692. (1) A person who has been found not criminally responsible on account of mental disorder and

- **(*a*) whose verdict is affirmed on that ground by the court of appeal, or**
- **(*b*) against whom a verdict of guilty is entered by the court of appeal under subparagraph 686(4)(*b*)(ii),**

may appeal to the Supreme Court of Canada.

(2) A person who is found unfit to stand trial and against whom that verdicit is affirmed by the court of appeal may appeal to the Supreme Court of Canada.

(3) An appeal under subsection (1) or (2) may be

- **(*a*) on any question of law on which a judge of the court of appeal dissents, or**
- **(*b*) on any question of law, if leave to appeal is granted by the Supreme Court of Canada. R.S., c. C-34, s. 620; R.S.C. 1985, c. 34 (3rd Supp.), s. 11; 1991, c. 43, s. 9.**

CROSS-REFERENCES

See s. 2 for definition of "unfit to stand trial" and s. 672.1 for definition of "verdict of not criminally responsible".

Section 675(3) governs an accused's right of appeal from a finding of unfitness or a verdict of not guilty by reason of insanity. In these circumstances, leave to appeal is not required respecting such grounds. Such an appeal is not restricted to questions of law alone. Under s. 676(1)(*a*) and (3), the right of appeal of the prosecutor in respect of similar findings is restricted to questions of law alone. For the authority of the court of appeal to hear such appeals, see s. 686(1) to (4), (6) and (7). See s. 695(1) for the equivalent authority of the Supreme Court of Canada.

SYNOPSIS

This section governs appeals to the Supreme Court of Canada by an accused who has been found unfit or not criminally responsible on account of mental disorder. These may be brought, on questions of law: (a) "as of right" on the basis of a dissent in the court of appeal; or (b) with leave of the Supreme Court (subsec. (3)).

An appeal lies where a verdict of not criminally responsible is either: (a) affirmed on appeal (subsec. (1)(*a*)); or (b) is set aside and a conviction entered by the court of appeal (subsec. (1)(*b*)). A finding of unfitness which is affirmed on appeal may also be appealed (subsec. (2)).

APPEAL BY ATTORNEY GENERAL / Terms.

693. (1) Where a judgment of a court of appeal sets aside a conviction pursuant to an appeal taken under section 675 or dismisses an appeal taken pursuant to paragraph 676(1)(*a*), (*b*) or (*c*) or subsection 676(3), the Attorney General may appeal to the Supreme Court of Canada

(*a*) on any question of law on which a judge of the court of appeal dissents; or

(*b*) on any question of law, if leave to appeal is granted by the Supreme Court of Canada.

(2) Where leave to appeal is granted under paragraph (1)(*b*), the Supreme Court of Canada may impose such terms as it sees fit. R.S., c. C-34, s. 621; R.S.C. 1985, c. 27 (1st Supp.), s. 146, c. 34 (3rd Supp.), s. 12.

CROSS-REFERENCES

See s. 2 for definition of "Attorney General". The Attorney General of Canada has equivalent rights of appeal to those of a provincial Attorney General under Part XXII, respecting proceedings instituted at the instance of and conducted by or on behalf of the Government of Canada. Section 695(1) authorizes the Supreme Court of Canada to determine appeals by the Attorney General. Section 695(1) incorporates the dispositive authority of the court of appeal. See the Supreme Court Act and Rules for procedure in appeals to the Supreme Court of Canada.

SYNOPSIS

This section governs appeals by the Crown to the Supreme Court of Canada in indictable matters. Such appeals may be brought, on questions of law: (a) "as of right" on thc basis of a dissent in the court of appeal; or (b) with leave of the Supreme Court (subsec. (1)).

Where the Crown is granted leave to appeal, the court can impose such conditions as it sees fit (*e.g.*, in a "test" case, the Crown may be ordered to pay the respondent's costs) (subsec. (2)).

Note: Appeals with respect to summary conviction matters and prerogative writs are governed by s. 40 of the *Supreme Court Act*.

ANNOTATIONS

Subsection (1)(*b*) – Where the provincial appellate court had to weigh the evidence in coming to its decision, it cannot be said that the decision was a pure question of law: *R. v. Fergusson*, [1962] S.C.R. 229, 132 C.C.C. 112 (5:0).

A finding by the Court of Appeal that there was no evidence to go to the jury raises a question of law alone: *R. v. Olan, Hudson and Hartnett*, [1978] 2 S.C.R. 1175, 41 C.C.C. (2d) 145; *R. v. Cotroni; R. v. Papalia*, [1979] 2 S.C.R. 256, 45 C.C.C. (2d) 1.

Under this section, the Crown right of appeal is limited to a case where the court of appeal "dismisses an appeal". Thus, where the court of appeal had allowed the Crown appeal on some grounds, but not others, the Crown had no right to cross-appeal with respect to that part of the decision of the court of appeal with respect to those latter grounds although the accused was appealing to the Supreme Court of Canada pursuant to s. 691(2): *R. v. MacKenzie*, [1993] 1 S.C.R. 212, 78 C.C.C. (3d) 193.

Where the Court of Appeal dismisses the accused's appeal and substitutes a conviction for another offence, both the Crown and the accused have rights of appeal appeal from the order for a substituted verdict: *R. v. Biniaris*, [2000] 1 S.C.R. 381, 143 C.C.C. (3d) 1.

The reasonableness of a verdict within the meaning of s. 686(1)(*a*)(i) is a question of law for the purposes of this section: *R. v. Biniaris supra*.

The application of the curative proviso raises a question of law: *R. v. Jolivet*, [2000] 1 S.C.R. 751, 144 C.C.C. (3d) 97.

NOTICE OF APPEAL.

694. No appeal lies to the Supreme Court of Canada unless notice of appeal in writing is served by the appellant on the respondent in accordance with the *Supreme Court Act*. R.S., c. C-34, s. 622; R.S.C. 1985, c. 34 (3rd Supp.), s. 13.

CROSS-REFERENCES

Section 678 contains a similar provision respecting appeals to the provincial court of appeal. See the *Supreme Court Act* and the Supreme Court of Canada Rules for applicable rules relating to service and filing of the notice of appeal.

SYNOPSIS

This section states that the appellant on an appeal to the Supreme Court of Canada must give notice to the respondent in accordance with the *Supreme Court Act*.

LEGAL ASSISTANCE FOR ACCUSED / Counsel fees and disbursements / Taxation of fees and disbursements.

694.1 (1) The Supreme Court of Canada or a judge thereof may, at any time, assign counsel to act on behalf of an accused who is a party to an appeal to the Court or to proceedings preliminary or incidental to an appeal to the Court where, in the opinion of the Court or judge, it appears desirable in the interests of justice that the accused should have legal assistance and where it appears that the accused has not sufficient means to obtain that assistance.

(2) Where counsel is assigned pursuant to subsection (1) and legal aid is not granted to the accused pursuant to a provincial legal aid program, the fees and disbursements of counsel shall be paid by the Attorney General who is the appellant or respondent, as the case may be, in the appeal.

(3) Where subsection (2) applies and where counsel and the Attorney General cannot agree on fees or disbursements of counsel, the Attorney General or the counsel may apply to the Registrar of the Supreme Court of Canada, and the Registrar may tax the disputed fees and disbursements. R.S.C. 1985, c. 34 (3rd Supp.), s. 13.

CROSS-REFERENCES

Section 684 contains similar provisions applicable where accused is a party to an appeal to the provincial court of appeal or proceedings related thereto. For a similar provision applicable at trial, see s. 672.24 which prescribes the assignment of counsel where the accused is unrepresented and an issue of fitness is being directed.

SYNOPSIS

This section provides that the Supreme Court of Canada, or a judge thereof, can appoint counsel for an appellant or respondent who is without means to independently retain such assistance (subsec. (1)). Such an application will generally be made only after Legal Aid has refused to assist in this regard.

In the absence of legal aid, funding costs are paid by the Attorney General who is a party to the appeal (subsec. (2)). In the event of a dispute with respect to fees and disbursements, the Registrar of the Supreme Court may tax the account submitted by counsel.

ANNOTATIONS

The determination under subsec. (3) is not limited by the Legal Aid Tariff and should be based on a broader assessment of what is fair and reasonable in the circumstances, including the recognition of the limits of state funding, but having regard to counsel's experience, the importance of the issues raised, and the complexity of the case: *R. v. White*, [2010] 3 S.C.R. 374, 265 C.C.C. (3d) 1.

RIGHT OF APPELLANT TO ATTEND / Appellant represented by counsel.

694.2 (1) Subject to subsection (2), an appellant who is in custody and who desires to be present at the hearing of the appeal before the Supreme Court of Canada is entitled to be present at it.

(2) An appellant who is in custody and who is represented by counsel is not entitled to be present before the Supreme Court of Canada

(*a*) on an application for leave to appeal,

(*b*) on any proceedings that are preliminary or incidental to an appeal, or

(*c*) at the hearing of the appeal,

unless rules of court provide that entitlement or the Supreme Court of Canada or a judge thereof gives the appellant leave to be present. R.S.C. 1985, c. 34 (3rd Supp.), s. 13.

CROSS-REFERENCES

For a similar and more extensive provision applicable in appeals to the Supreme Court of Canada, see s. 688.

SYNOPSIS

This section deals with when an appellant, who is in custody, is entitled to be present for a hearing before the Supreme Court of Canada.

An "in person" appellant has a right to attend. However, an appellant who has retained counsel has no right to attend: (a) an application for leave to appeal; (b) a proceeding preliminary or incidental to an appeal; or (c) the hearing of an appeal. This is subject to any rules of court or an order of a judge (subsec. (1), (2)).

ORDER OF SUPREME COURT OF CANADA / Election if new trial / Nunavut.

695. (1) The Supreme Court of Canada may, on an appeal under this Part, make any order that the court of appeal might have made and may make any rule or order that is necessary to give effect to its judgment.

(2) Subject to subsection (3), if a new trial ordered by the Supreme Court of Canada is to be held before a court composed of a judge and jury, the accused may, with the consent of the prosecutor, elect to have the trial heard before a judge without a jury or a provincial court judge. The election is deemed to be a re-election within the meaning of subsection 561(5) and subsections 561(5) to (7) apply to it with any modifications that the circumstances require.

(3) If a new trial ordered by the Supreme Court of Canada is to be held before a court composed of a judge and jury in Nunavut, the accused may, with the consent of the prosecutor, elect to have the trial heard before a judge without a jury. The election is deemed to be a re-election within the meaning of subsection 561.1(6) and subsections 561.1(6) to (9) apply to it with any modifications that the circumstances require. R.S., c. C-34, s. 623; 1999, c. 5, s. 27; 2008, c. 18, s. 31.

CROSS-REFERENCES

See the *Supreme Court Act* and Rules of Court for procedure on appeal to the Supreme Court of Canada.

See also the references cited under ss. 683, 686 and 689 for the scope of authority conferred by each of these sections.

SYNOPSIS

This section provides that the Supreme Court of Canada may make any order that the court of appeal might have made on appeal, and any other necessary order, and gives the accused rights of re-election.

ANNOTATIONS

Where the Appeal Court allowed the accused's main ground of appeal and accordingly did not consider his other grounds, the Supreme Court of Canada upon reversing the Appeal Court on that main ground is empowered to deal with and dispose of the other grounds: *R. v. Borg*, [1969] S.C.R. 551, [1969] 4 C.C.C. 262 (9:0).

The respondent can raise any argument which supports the order of the court below, including grounds on which the respondent was successful in the court below, re-arguing grounds which were unsuccessful or not dealt with below, and even making new arguments. The Supreme Court of Canada has a discretion not to hear arguments which lack an appropriate evidentiary basis below, but that decision is not related to the court's jurisdiction: *R. v. Keegstra*, [1995] 2 S.C.R. 381, 98 C.C.C. (3d) 1; *R. v. Perka*, [1984] 2 S.C.R. 232, 14 C.C.C. (3d) 385.

This section gives the Supreme Court the power to make any order that the Court of Appeal might have made under its broad powers under s. 686(8): *R. v. P. (D.W.)*, [1989] 2 S.C.R. 3, 49 C.C.C. (3d) 417 (5:0).

This section should be read to encompass the leave application process. A panel of the court hearing an application for leave to appeal had the jurisdiction to make an order pursuant to s. 683(1)(*a*) for the release of trial exhibits for forensic testing, in anticipation of a fresh evidence application supplemental to the application for leave to appeal: *R. v. Hay*, [2010] 3 S.C.R. 206, 264 C.C.C. (3d) 129.

Appeals by Attorney General of Canada

RIGHT OF ATTORNEY GENERAL OF CANADA TO APPEAL.

696. The Attorney General of Canada has the same rights of appeal in proceedings instituted at the instance of the Government of Canada and conducted by or on behalf of that Government as the Attorney General of a province has under this Part. R.S., c. C-34, s. 624.

CROSS-REFERENCES

See s. 2 for definition of "Attorney General". Section 676 describes the right of the Attorney General to appeal in proceedings by indictment.

The Attorney General of Canada has equivalent rights of appeal to those of the provincial Attorney General under Part XXVII, respecting summary conviction proceedings instituted at the instance of and conducted by or on behalf of the Government of Canada.

SYNOPSIS

This section gives the Attorney General of Canada the same rights on appeal as the provincial Attornies General, where the proceedings were originated by the Government of Canada.

Part XXI.1 / APPLICATIONS FOR MINISTERIAL REVIEW — MISCARRIAGES OF JUSTICE

APPLICATION / Form of application.

696.1 (1) An application for ministerial review on the grounds of miscarriage of justice may be made to the Minister of Justice by or on behalf of a person who has been convicted of an offence under an Act of Parliament or a regulation made under an Act of Parliament or has been found to be a dangerous offender or a long-term offender under Part XXIV and whose rights of judicial review or appeal with respect to the conviction or finding have been exhausted.

(2) The application must be in the form, contain the information and be accompanied by any documents prescribed by the regulations. 2002, c. 13, s. 71.

CROSS-REFERENCES

The remedy under this section is only available after the offender has exhausted all other remedies. Those appellate remedies are set out in Part XXI in relation to indictable matters and Part XXVII in relation to summary conviction matters. The extension of the royal prerogative of mercy is authorized under ss. 749 to 751. These provisions also authorize the Governor in Council to grant a free or conditional pardon or order relief from any penalty, fine or forfeiture. Pursuant to s. 53(2) of the *Supreme Court Act*, R.S.C. 1985, c. S-26, the Governor in Council may direct references to the Supreme Court of Canada.

SYNOPSIS

This section permits a person to apply to the federal Minister of Justice for review of a conviction or a finding that they were a dangerous or long-term offender. The person may only apply after they have exhausted all of their normal appellate remedies. Section 696.2 sets out the procedure to be followed by the Minister once an application has been made under this section. The Minister is to proceed in accordance with the regulations made under s. 696.1. The Minister has and may exercise certain of the powers of a commissioner under the *Inquiries Act*, R.S.C. 1985, c. I-11, and may also delegate certain of those powers to a lawyer, retired judge or other individual. Under s. 696.3, the Minister may at any time refer a question in relation to an application to the court of appeal as defined in s. 2. If the Minister is satisfied that "there is a reasonable basis to conclude that a miscarriage of justice likely occurred", the Minister may direct a new trial or a new dangerous offender or long-term offender hearing or direct a reference to the court of appeal. The Minister's decision is final and is not subject to appeal. Section 696.4 sets out the matters the Minister is to take into account in making the decision under s. 696.3. In particular, the section indicates that the remedy under this Part is extraordinary and not intended to serve as a further appeal. The Minister is required to take into account all relevant matters, including whether the application is supported by new matters of significance and the relevance and reliability of the information presented in connection with the application. Section 696.5 requires the Minister to annually table a report in Parliament in relation to applications under this section.

ANNOTATIONS

It is the duty of the Minister of Justice to determine whether or not the applicant has exhausted his or her rights of judicial review or appeal with respect to the conviction as a pre-condition to conducting a ministerial review beyond a preliminary assessment of the application, subject to review by the courts. The Minister is not precluded from determining that the applicant has exhausted his or her rights of judicial review or appeal despite the fact that the applicant has not applied for leave to appeal to the Supreme Court of Canada with respect to the conviction: *McArthur v. Ontario (Attorney General)* (2013), 302 C.C.C. (3d) 177 (Ont. C.A.), leave to appeal to S.C.C. refused 2014 CarswellOnt 4927.

REVIEW OF APPLICATIONS / Powers of investigation / Delegation.

696.2 (1) On receipt of an application under this Part, the Minister of Justice shall review it in accordance with the regulations.

(2) For the purpose of any investigation in relation to an application under this Part, the Minister of Justice has and may exercise the powers of a commissioner under Part I of the Inquiries Act and the powers that may be conferred on a commissioner under section 11 of that Act.

(3) Despite subsection 11(3) of the Inquiries Act, the Minister of Justice may delegate in writing to any member in good standing of the bar of a province, retired judge or any other individual who, in the opinion of the Minister, has similar background or experience the powers of the Minister to take evidence, issue subpoenas, enforce the attendance of witnesses, compel them to give evidence and otherwise conduct an investigation under subsection (2). 2002, c. 13, s. 71.

CROSS-REFERENCES

See notes under s. 696.1.

SYNOPSIS

See notes under s. 696.1.

DEFINITION OF "COURT OF APPEAL" / Power to refer / Powers of Minister of Justice / No appeal.

696.3 (1) In this section, "the court of appeal" means the court of appeal, as defined by the definition "court of appeal" in section 2, for the province in which the person to whom an application under this Part relates was tried.

(2) The Minister of Justice may, at any time, refer to the court of appeal, for its opinion, any question in relation to an application under this Part on which the Minister desires the assistance of that court, and the court shall furnish its opinion accordingly.

(3) On an application under this Part, the Minister of Justice may

(*a*) if the Minister is satisfied that there is a reasonable basis to conclude that a miscarriage of justice likely occurred,

(i) direct, by order in writing, a new trial before any court that the Minister thinks proper or, in the case of a person found to be a dangerous offender or a long-term offender under Part XXIV, a new hearing under that Part, or

(ii) refer the matter at any time to the court of appeal for hearing and determination by that court as if it were an appeal by the convicted person or the person found to be a dangerous offender or a long-term offender under Part XXIV, as the case may be; or

(*b*) dismiss the application.

(4) A decision of the Minister of Justice made under subsection (3) is final and is not subject to appeal. 2002, c. 13, s. 71.

CROSS-REFERENCES

See notes under s. 696.1.

SYNOPSIS

See notes under s. 696.1.

ANNOTATIONS

The power of referral in subsec. (2) may only be exercised personally by the Minister, not by his or her delegate. Accordingly, a letter from a Department of Justice lawyer apparently purporting to broaden the terms of a Ministerial reference had no legal effect: *R. v. Ross* (2017), 355 C.C.C. (3d) 21 (Man. C.A.).

Note: The following cases were decided in relation to the Minister's power under the former s. 690 on an application for the mercy of the Crown but may be of assistance in interpreting this section.

The rules as to the admissibility of fresh evidence on appeal should be borne in mind on a reference. The appellate court will determine each such situation on its merits and, where the circumstances are unusual, the appellate court should not refuse to hear fresh evidence where the interests of justice require that it be heard: *R. v. Gorecki* (1976), 32 C.C.C. (2d) 135, 14 O.R. (2d) 218 (C.A.).

In *Reference re: Milgaard (Can.)*, [1992] 1 S.C.R. 866, 71 C.C.C. (3d) 260, the Governor in Council had referred the accused's case to the Supreme Court of Canada to determine whether the continued conviction of the accused for murder constituted a miscarriage of justice. The court considered a number of instances where the continued conviction would constitute a miscarriage of justice and thus require that the Governor in Council be advised to exercise powers under s. 749. As well, if the court was satisfied on a preponderance of evidence that the accused was innocent of the murder, then it would be open to the accused to apply to reopen his application for leave to appeal to the Supreme Court of Canada with a view to determining whether the conviction should be quashed and a verdict of acquittal entered, in which case, the Minister would be advised to take no steps pending final determination of those proceedings. The continued conviction of the accused would also constitute a miscarriage of justice if there were reasonably believable new evidence which was relevant to the issue of the accused's guilt and which, taken together with the evidence adduced at trial, could reasonably be expected to have affected the verdict. In that case, the Minister of Justice would be advised to quash the conviction and direct a new trial. It would then be for the provincial Attorney General to determine whether or not to enter a stay in all the circumstances.

It was held that there is no appeal to the Supreme Court of Canada from a decision made on a reference ordered under former s. 690(*c*): *R. v. Kelly*, [2001] 1 S.C.R. 741, 153 C.C.C. (3d) 45.

Neither a superior court judge nor a commission of inquiry, appointed by the province with the powers of a superior court judge, has the power to compel another judge to testify on how and why he arrived at a particular judicial decision and why a certain judge sat on a particular panel of the court of appeal to hear a reference under para. (*b*) of this section. It is an essential element of judicial independence that judges be immune from testifying with respect to their grounds for decision and the reasons for composition of a given panel: *MacKeigan v. Hickman*, [1989] 2 S.C.R. 796, 50 C.C.C. (3d) 449.

The Minister is not required to be personally involved in each step of the review process. As long as the Minister acts in accordance with s. 7 of the Charter, there is no fixed procedure which must be followed: *Bonamy v. Canada (Attorney General)* (2001), 156 C.C.C. (3d) 110, 201 D.L.R. (4th) 761 (F.C.T.D.). [However, now see s. 696.2.]

CONSIDERATIONS

696.4 In making a decision under subsection 696.3(3), the Minister of Justice shall take into account all matters that the Minister considers relevant, including

(*a*) whether the application is supported by new matters of significance that were not considered by the courts or previously considered by the Minister in an application in relation to the same conviction or finding under Part XXIV;

(*b*) the relevance and reliability of information that is presented in connection with the application; and

(*c*) the fact that an application under this Part is not intended to serve as a further appeal and any remedy available on such an application is an extraordinary remedy. 2002, c. 13, s. 71.

CROSS-REFERENCES

See notes under s. 696.1.

SYNOPSIS

See notes under s. 696.1.

ANNUAL REPORT.

696.5 The Minister of Justice shall within six months after the end of each financial year submit an annual report to Parliament in relation to applications under this Part. 2002, c. 13, s. 71.

CROSS-REFERENCES

See notes under s. 696.1.

SYNOPSIS

See notes under s. 696.1.

REGULATIONS.

696.6 The Governor in Council may make regulations

(*a*) prescribing the form of, the information required to be contained in and any documents that must accompany an application under this Part;

(*b*) prescribing the process of review in relation to applications under this Part, which may include the following stages, namely, preliminary assessment, investigation, reporting on investigation and decision; and

(*c*) respecting the form and content of the annual report under section 696.5. 2002, c. 13, s. 71.

CROSS-REFERENCES

See notes under s. 696.1.

SYNOPSIS

See notes under s. 696.1.

Part XXII / PROCURING ATTENDANCE

Application

APPLICATION.

697. Except where section 527 applies, this Part applies where a person is required to attend to give evidence in a proceeding to which this Act applies. R.S., c. C-34, s. 625; R.S.C. 1985, c. 27 (1st Supp.), s. 147.

CROSS-REFERENCES

Section 527 concerns procedure to procure the attendance of a prisoner for a preliminary inquiry, for trial or to give evidence in any other proceeding to which the *Criminal Code* applies.

The content and circumstances of issue of a subpoena or warrant to compel attendance of a witness are governed by ss. 698 to 700.

The execution or service of process on a person and a corporation and the jurisdictional application of a subpoena, as well as the jurisdictional application of a warrant and a summons, are addressed in ss. 701 to 703.2.

Sections 704 to 708 govern procedure and sanctions in respect of defaulting or absconding witnesses.

Procedure in respect of commission evidence is governed by ss. 709 to 714. Section 715 provides for the reading in of testimony given at an investigation, preliminary inquiry or previous trial on the same charge where the witness is unavailable to the present trial. Section 715.1 provides for the admission, in certain circumstances, of videotape evidence.

SYNOPSIS

This section clarifies that Part XXII is to apply where a person is required to give evidence, except where s. 527 applies because the person is a prisoner.

Process

SUBPOENA / Warrant in Form 17 / Subpoena issued first.

698. (1) Where a person is likely to give material evidence in a proceeding to which this Act applies, a subpoena may be issued in accordance with this Part requiring that person to attend to give evidence.

(2) Where it is made to appear that a person who is likely to give material evidence

(*a*) will not attend in response to a subpoena if a subpoena is issued, or

(*b*) is evading service of a subpoena,

a court, justice or provincial court judge having power to issue a subpoena to require the attendance of that person to give evidence may issue a warrant in Form 17 to cause that person to be arrested and to be brought to give evidence.

(3) Except where paragraph (2)(*a*) applies, a warrant in Form 17 shall not be issued unless a subpoena has first been issued. R.S., c. C-34, s. 626.

CROSS-REFERENCES

"Justice" and "provincial court judge" are defined in s. 2.

See s. 699 for the form of a subpoena and the authority by whom it may be issued, and s. 700 for its content. Under s. 699(6), a subpoena may be in Form 16. It may be in the form of a *subpoena ad testificandum* — a requirement to attend and give evidence, or a *subpoena duces tecum* — a requirement that the witness attend, give evidence and bring anything in his possession or control that relates to the charge or any document or thing specified in the subpoena.

The service of a subpoena and execution of a warrant are governed by ss. 701 to 703.2.

Sections 704 to 708 prescribe procedure and sanctions in respect of defaulting or absconding witnesses.

Under s. 705, a warrant for the arrest of an elusive witness may be issued in Form 17. Under s. 706, where the witness is brought before a court as a consequence of a warrant, the court may detain him in custody or release him on recognizance in Form 32.

SYNOPSIS

Under Part XXII of the Code a person who is likely to have material evidence to give may be the subject of either a subpoena or an arrest warrant. A warrant may be issued where it appears that the person will not respond to a subpoena or is evading service of a subpoena that has already been issued (subsecs. (2), (3)).

ANNOTATIONS

A trial judge has jurisdiction to quash a subpoena issued by another judge of the same court where the subpoena should never have been issued or its issue amounted to an abuse of process. A subpoena may issue only where the witness has material evidence in the proceedings and not to authorize a pure fishing expedition: *R. v. Gingras* (1992), 71 C.C.C. (3d) 53, 120 A.R. 300 (C.A.). In this case, it was also held that the subpoena was irregular in that it required the person named in the subpoena not to produce evidence in court, but to produce it to the party seeking the subpoena.

The provincial Superior Court has jurisdiction to quash a subpoena issued out of that Court or any other Court of provincial jurisdiction in the Province where the witness would not be able to give any material evidence: *R. v. Baldwin and Bauer* (1980), 54 C.C.C. (2d) 85 (Ont. H.C.J.).

Notwithstanding that a subpoena is regular on its face the subpoena power can still be abused if some form of abuse were shown or the witness's interests under s. 7 of the Charter infringed, the superior court would have jurisdiction to grant an appropriate remedy. In this case, shortly before a police informer was to testify, protection was withdrawn from his parents, allegedly in breach of an agreement that the witness had with the police. Even if the subpoena were not quashed, the superior court must consider whether to exercise the inherent jurisdiction of the court and grant an appropriate remedy, even though the witness's parents were outside the country: *R. v. A.*, [1990] 1 S.C.R. 995, 55 C.C.C. (3d) 562 (7:2).

It is implicit in this section that before issuing the subpoena the justice or other person having power to issue a subpoena should conduct some inquiry to be satisfied that the proposed witness has material evidence to give. The type of inquiry is within the discretion of the justice who may choose not to insist upon evidence on oath but may nevertheless want to conduct an oral examination, if only a cursory one, of some person who has knowledge of the circumstances. The extent of such an examination will depend on the circumstances but, if he takes no steps whatever to satisfy himself that the person is likely to give material evidence, then the justice is abusing his power and discretion and the decision to issue the subpoena may be set aside on *certiorari*: *Foley v. Gares* (1989), 53 C.C.C. (3d) 82, 74 C.R. (3d) 386 (Sask. C.A.). Folld: *R. v. Singh* (1990), 57 C.C.C. (3d) 444, 108 A.R. 233 (Q.B.).

The applicant must make it clear to the trial judge that the proposed witness is likely to give material evidence before he will consider whether or not to issue a bench warrant: *R. v. Kinzie* (1956), 25 C.R. 6, [1956] O.W.N. 896 (C.A.).

In issuing subpoenas for a preliminary hearing, the evidence is "likely material" for the purposes of a preliminary inquiry if it is relevant to the purposes of the preliminary inquiry. Materiality must be interpreted in light of the requirement in s. 541 of the *Criminal Code* that the preliminary inquiry judge must hear witnesses called by the defence testifying to any matter relevant to the inquiry: *R. v. Regan* (1997), 113 C.C.C. (3d) 237, 144 D.L.R. (4th) 456 (N.S.C.A.), leave to appeal to S.C.C. refused 113 C.C.C. (3d) vi, 158 N.S.R. (2d) 240*n*.

A justice presiding at a preliminary inquiry, having no jurisdiction to order disclosure pursuant to *R. v. Stinchcombe*, [1991] 3 S.C.R. 326, 68 C.C.C. (3d) 1, or *R. v. O'Connor*, [1995] 4 S.C.R. 411, 103 C.C.C. (3d) 1, cannot issue a *subpoena duces tecum* for first- or third-party disclosure purposes. The accused must instead bring the proper application before the trial judge: *Ontario Provincial Police Commisioner v. Mosher* (2015), 330 C.C.C. (3d) 149 (Ont. C.A.).

In determining the compellability of an expert who is totally unconnected to the proceedings, the court should consider the following non-exhaustive factors: the entitlement of the court to every person's evidence whether fact or opinion; whether the expert has some connection with the case in question; whether the expert is willing to come provided his image is protected by the issuance of a subpoena; whether attendance in court will disrupt or impede other important work that the expert has to do; whether and to what extent the expert will be required to expend time and effort preparing evidence for the court; and whether another expert of equal caliber is available: *R. v. Blais* (2008), 238 C.C.C. (3d) 434, 60 C.R. (6th) 330 (B.C.C.A.).

WHO MAY ISSUE / Order of judge / Order of judge / Seal / Signature / Sexual offences / Form of subpoena / Form of subpoena in sexual offences.

699. (1) If a person is required to attend to give evidence before a superior court of criminal jurisdiction, a court of appeal, an appeal court or a court of criminal jurisdiction other than a provincial court judge acting under Part XIX, a subpoena directed to that person shall be issued out of the court before which the attendance of that person is required.

(2) If a person is required to attend to give evidence before a provincial court judge acting under Part XIX or a summary conviction court under Part XXVII or in proceedings over which a justice has jurisdiction, a subpoena directed to the person shall be issued

(*a*) by a provincial court judge or a justice, where the person whose attendance is required is within the province in which the proceedings were instituted; or

(*b*) by a provincial court judge or out of a superior court of criminal jurisdiction of the province in which the proceedings were instituted, where the person whose attendance is required is not within the province.

(3) A subpoena shall not be issued out of a superior court of criminal jurisdiction pursuant to paragraph (2)(*b*), except pursuant to an order of a judge of the court made on application by a party to the proceedings.

(4) A subpoena or warrant that is issued by a court under this Part shall be under the seal of the court and shall be signed by a judge of the court or by the clerk of the court.

(5) A subpoena or warrant that is issued by a justice or provincial court judge under this Part shall be signed by the justice or provincial court judge.

(5.1) Notwithstanding anything in subsections (1) to (5), in the case of an offence referred to in subsection 278.2(1), a subpoena requiring a witness to bring to the court a record, the production of which is governed by sections 278.1 to 278.91, must be issued and signed by a judge.

(6) Subject to subsection (7), a subpoena issued under this Part may be in Form 16.

(7) In the case of an offence referred to in subsection 278.2(1), a subpoena requiring a witness to bring anything to the court shall be in Form 16.1. R.S., c. C-34, s. 627; 1994, c. 44, s. 69; 1997, c. 30, s. 2; 1999, c. 5, s. 28.

CROSS-REFERENCES

The terms "superior court of criminal jurisdiction", "court of appeal", "court of criminal jurisdiction", "provincial court judge" and "justice" are defined in s. 2.

The definitions of "appeal court" and "summary conviction court" in Part XXVII are restricted to that Part and do not have application to Part XXII.

See s. 701(2) for the requirement that a subpoena issued pursuant to s. 699(2)(*b*) be personally served on the witness. See s. 698 for corresponding notes on other related provisions.

SYNOPSIS

This section deals with the manner in which subpoenas (and warrants under s. 698) are issued.

Except in summary conviction proceedings, proceeding by a provincial court judge under Part XIX or proceedings over which a justice of the peace has jurisdiction, a subpoena shall be issued out of the court before which the witness is required to attend (subsec. (1)).

Where the matter is summary conviction, a proceeding by a provincial court judge under Part XIX, or is a proceeding over which a justice of the peace has jurisdiction, subpoenas may only be issued by a justice of the peace if the witness is within the province (subsec. (2)(*a*)). Out-of-province subpoenas must be sought from a provincial court judge, or by order of a judge out of the superior court (subsec. (2)(*b*), (3)).

ANNOTATIONS

It was held in *R. v. Medicine Hat Greenhouses Ltd. and German (No. 2)* (1977), 34 C.C.C. (2d) 339 (Alta. S.C. App. Div.), by two of the judges that while no appeal is provided from an order under this section by a superior court judge, the superior court has an inherent right to inquire into the regularity of its process and this right can be exercised by the appeal division of the court as well as the trial division. However, it would be a remarkable case that warranted intervention by the appeal court of an order made by a justice of the trial division.

It is implicit in this section that before issuing the subpoena the justice or other person having power to issue a subpoena should conduct some inquiry to be satisfied that the proposed witness has material evidence to give. The type of inquiry is within the discretion of the justice who may choose not to insist upon evidence on oath but may nevertheless want to conduct an oral examination, if only a cursory one, of some person who has knowledge of the circumstances. The extent of such an examination will depend on the circumstances, but if he takes no steps whatever to satisfy himself that the person is likely to give material evidence, then the justice is abusing his power and discretion and the decision to issue the subpoena may be set aside on *certiorari*: *Foley v. Gares* (1989), 53 C.C.C. (3d) 82 (Sask. C.A.).

CONTENTS OF SUBPOENA / Witness to appear and remain.

700. (1) A subpoena shall require the person to whom it is directed to attend, at a time and place to be stated in the subpoena, to give evidence and, if required, to bring with him anything that he has in his possession or under his control relating to the subject-matter of the proceedings.

(2) A person who is served with a subpoena issued under this Part shall attend and shall remain in attendance throughout the proceedings unless he is excused by the presiding judge, justice or provincial court judge. R.S., c. C-34, s. 628; R.S.C. 1985, c. 27 (1st Supp.), s. 148.

CROSS-REFERENCES

Form 16 is used for both types of subpoenas described in this section: the *subpoena ad testificandum*, which compels attendance to give evidence; and the *subpoena duces tecum*, which compels attendance as well as requires the witness to bring documents or other material relevant to the subject-matter of the proceedings.

See s. 698 for corresponding notes on other related provisions.

Section 701.1 allows for service and proof of service in accordance with the laws of the province.

Section 708.1 allows for use of electronically transmitted copies.

SYNOPSIS

A subpoena requires that a witness attend court as directed. It may also direct the witness to bring documents or other material relating to the proceedings (subsec. (1)).

A person served with a subpoena shall remain in attendance throughout the proceedings unless excused by the presiding judge or justice (subsec. (2)).

ANNOTATIONS

Where the trial judge concludes that the witness is not compellable he has the power under this section to excuse him. At least since the proclamation of the *Charter of Rights and Freedoms*, a trial judge in a proper case is not precluded from permitting counsel to be heard on behalf of the witness: *R. v. Chase* (1982), 1 C.C.C. (3d) 188, 142 D.L.R. (3d) 507 (B.C.S.C.).

The issuance of a *subpoena duces tecum* is not an order for production or disclosure of the documents the witness is required to bring with him or her. In other words, without more it is not a disclosure order or its functional equivalent, and cannot be used to circumvent the established procedures for first- and third-party disclosure and production: *Ontario Provincial Police Commisioner v. Mosher* (2015), 330 C.C.C. (3d) 149 (Ont. C.A.).

VIDEO LINKS, ETC. / Sections of *Criminal Code*.

700.1 (1) If a person is to give evidence under section 714.1 or 714.3 or under subsection 46(2) of the *Canada Evidence Act* — or is to give evidence or a statement pursuant to an order made under section 22.2 of the *Mutual Legal Assistance in Criminal Matters Act* — at a place within the jurisdiction of a court referred to in subsection 699(1) or (2) where the technology is available, a subpoena shall be issued out of the court to order the person to give that evidence at such a place.

(2) Sections 699, 700 and 701 to 703.2 apply, with any modifications that the circumstances require, to a subpoena issued under this section. 1999, c. 18, s. 94.

CROSS-REFERENCES

"Court" is defined in s. 699(1) and (2). Reference should also be made to ss. 714.1 and 714.3, which relate to the taking of evidence by video or audio. For other cross-references with respect to such evidence, see the cross-references under s. 714.1.

SYNOPSIS

A subpoena must be issued by a court as defined in s. 699(1) or (2) where a person is to give evidence by video or audio pursuant to sections 714.1 or 714.3, s. 46(2) of the *Canada Evidence Act* or pursuant to an order under s. 22.2 of the *Mutual Legal Assistance in Criminal Matters Act*.

Execution or Service of Process

SERVICE / Personal service.

701. (1) Subject to subsection (2), a subpoena shall be served in a province by a peace officer or any other person who is qualified in that province to serve civil process, in accordance with subsection 509(2), with such modifications as the circumstances require.

(2) A subpoena that is issued pursuant to paragraph 699(2)(*b*) shall be served personally on the person to whom it is directed. R.S., c. C-34, s. 629; 1972, c. 13, s. 56; 1994, c. 44, s. 70; 2008, c. 18, s. 32.

(3) [*Repealed.* 2008, c. 18, s. 32.]

CROSS-REFERENCES

See s. 2 for the definition of "peace officer".

See s. 698 for corresponding notes on other related sections.

SYNOPSIS

This section specifies how a subpoena is to be served.

A subpoena issued for service out of province (see s. 699(2)(*b*)) must be personally served on the person to whom it is directed (subsec. (2)). In all other cases a subpoena may be served personally or, if the person to whom it is directed cannot conveniently be found, left at his or her last known or usual place of residence with someone who appears to be at least 16 years old (see s. 509(2)) (subsec. (1)).

Service and proof of service may also be made in accordance with s. 4 or in accordance with the laws of the province relating to provincial offences, s. 701.1. An electronic copy has the same probative force as the original, s. 708.1.

SERVICE IN ACCORDANCE WITH PROVINCIAL LAWS.

701.1 Despite section 701, in any province, service of a document may be made in accordance with the laws of the province relating to offences created by the laws of that province. 1997, c. 18, s. 100; 2008, c. 18, s. 33.

ANNOTATIONS

This provision does not permit service of a summons on a person or corporation outside Canada. In this case, service of the summons on a foreign corporation by mail was held to be invalid: *R. v. R.J. Reynolds Tobacco Co. (Delaware)* (2007), 230 C.C.C. (3d) 72 (Ont. C.A.).

SUBPOENA EFFECTIVE THROUGHOUT CANADA / Subpoena effective throughout province.

702. (1) A subpoena that is issued by a provincial court judge or out of a superior court of criminal jurisdiction, a court of appeal, an appeal court or a court of criminal jurisdiction has effect anywhere in Canada according to its terms.

(2) A subpoena that is issued by a justice has effect anywhere in the province in which it is issued. R.S., c. C-34, s. 630; 1994, c. 44, s. 71.

CROSS-REFERENCES

The terms "superior court of criminal jurisdiction", "court of appeal", "court of criminal jurisdiction" and "provincial court judge" are defined in s. 2. The definitions of "appeal court" and "summary conviction court" in Part XXVII are restricted to that part and do not have application to Part XXII.

Under s. 701(2), a subpoena issued under s. 699(2)(*b*) must be personally served on the witness. The territorial jurisdiction of a warrant or summons is described in ss. 703 and 703.1.

See s. 698 for corresponding notes on other related provisions.

SYNOPSIS

This section states that a subpoena issued by a justice has effect in the province in which it is issued, but any other subpoena has effect throughout Canada.

WARRANT EFFECTIVE THROUGHOUT CANADA / Warrant effective in a province.

703. (1) Notwithstanding any other provision of this Act, a warrant of arrest or committal that is issued out of a superior court of criminal jurisdiction, a court of appeal, an appeal court within the meaning of section 812 or a court of criminal jurisdiction other than a provincial court judge acting under Part XIX may be executed anywhere in Canada.

(2) Despite any other provision of this Act but subject to subsections 487.0551(2) and 705(3), a warrant of arrest or committal that is issued by a justice or provincial court judge may be executed anywhere in the province in which it is issued. R.S., c. C-34, s. 631; R.S.C. 1985, c. 27 (1st Supp.), s. 149; 2007, c. 22, s. 22.

CROSS-REFERENCES

Forms 17 to 20 are used for warrants of arrest or committal in respect of witnesses.

The terms "superior court of criminal jurisdiction", "court of criminal jurisdiction", "provincial court judge", "court of appeal" and "justice" are defined in s. 2. The definition of "appeal court" is in s. 812. Warrants issued to compel attendance of a defaulting or absconding witness are described in ss. 704 and 705.

See ss. 706 to 708 for the procedure to be followed on default.

See s. 514 for the execution of a warrant issued under s. 703(2).

SYNOPSIS

This section provides that a warrant for arrest or committal issued by a justice or provincial court judge has effect in the province in which it was issued, or throughout Canada if it was issued for a defaulting or absconding witness under s. 705(3). Other warrants for arrest or committal have effect throughout Canada under any circumstances.

SUMMONS EFFECTIVE THROUGHOUT CANADA.

703.1 A summons may be served anywhere in Canada and, if served, is effective notwithstanding the territorial jurisdiction of the authority that issued the summons. R.S.C. 1985, c. 27 (1st Supp.), s. 149.

CROSS-REFERENCES

The content and service of a summons are described in s. 509. The potential consequences of failure to appear in response to a summons are described in ss. 510 and 145(4). Probative value of electronically transmitted copy, s. 708.1.

SYNOPSIS

This section provides that a summons may be served and is effective throughout Canada.

ANNOTATIONS

This provision does not permit service of a summons outside Canada: *R. v. R.J. Reynolds Tobacco Co. (Delaware)* (2007), 230 C.C.C. (3d) 72 (Ont. C.A.).

SERVICE OF PROCESS ON AN ORGANIZATION.

703.2 Where any summons, notice or other process is required to be or may be served on an organization, and no other method of service is provided, service may be effected by delivery

(*a*) in the case of a municipality, to the mayor, warden, reeve or other chief officer of the municipality, or to the secretary, treasurer or clerk of the municipality; and

(*b*) in the case of any other organization, to the manager, secretary or other senior officer of the organization or one of its branches. R.S.C. 1985, c. 27 (1st Supp.), s. 149; 2003, c. 21, s. 13.

CROSS-REFERENCES

"Organization" is defined in s. 2. See ss. 620, 622 and 623 for the trial of an organization for an indictable offence. Section 800 governs the appearance of an organization in respect of summary conviction proceedings. See s. 621 for provision for notice of an indictment to be served on an organization.

SYNOPSIS

This section provides that service on a municipal corporation may be effected by serving certain named officers thereof and service on any other organization may be effected by serving any executive officer thereof.

Defaulting or Absconding Witness

WARRANT FOR ABSCONDING WITNESS / Endorsement of warrant / Copy of information.

704. (1) Where a person is bound by recognizance to give evidence in any proceedings, a justice who is satisfied on information being made before him in writing and under oath that the person is about to abscond or has absconded may issue his warrant in Form 18 directing a peace officer to arrest that person and to bring him before the court, judge, justice or provincial court judge before whom he is bound to appear.

(2) Section 528 applies, with such modifications as the circumstances require, to a warrant issued under this section.

(3) A person who is arrested under this section is entitled, on request, to receive a copy of the information on which the warrant for his arrest was issued. R.S., c. C-34, s. 632.

CROSS-REFERENCES

See s. 2 for definitions of "justice", "peace officer" and "provincial court judge".

The territorial jurisdiction of a warrant for arrest is defined in s. 703.

While s. 704 applies to a witness who is bound by recognizance to give evidence and who has absconded or is about to abscond, s. 705 applies to a witness who has been served with a subpoena or bound by a recognizance and fails to attend the hearing. A witness may be either required to enter into a recognizance or, under s. 706, be released on a recognizance following arrest. A warrant issued in respect of an absconding witness is in Form 18. See s. 706 for the procedure to be followed in the case of a witness arrested by warrant and brought before court. Section 707 governs his detention thereafter.

SYNOPSIS

This section authorizes a justice of the peace to issue a warrant for the arrest of a person bound by a recognizance to give evidence where he or she is satisfied, by information on oath, that the witness has absconded or is about to abscond (subsec. (1)). Anyone arrested on such a warrant is entitled to receive a copy of the information (subsec. (3)).

A warrant may be endorsed (pursuant to s. 528) with respect to the terms of release (subsec. (2)).

WARRANT WHEN WITNESS DOES NOT ATTEND / Warrant where witness bound by recognizance / Warrant effective throughout Canada.

705. (1) Where a person who has been served with a subpoena to give evidence in a proceeding does not attend or remain in attendance, the court, judge, justice or provincial court judge before whom that person was required to attend may, if it is established

(*a*) that the subpoena has been served in accordance with this Part, and

(*b*) that the person is likely to give material evidence,

issue or cause to be issued a warrant in Form 17 for the arrest of that person.

(2) Where a person who has been bound by a recognizance to attend to give evidence in any proceeding does not attend or does not remain in attendance, the court, judge, justice or provincial court judge before whom that person was bound to attend may issue or cause to be issued a warrant in Form 17 for the arrest of that person.

(3) A warrant that is issued by a justice or provincial court judge pursuant to subsection (1) or (2) may be executed anywhere in Canada. R.S., c. C-34, s. 633.

CROSS-REFERENCES

See s. 2 for definitions of "justice" and "provincial court judge".

See s. 704 for the issuance of a warrant for the arrest of an absconding witness.

See ss. 701(1) and 509(2) for service of a subpoena. A subpoena issued under s. 699(2)(*b*) must be served personally on the person to whom it is directed. A warrant issued pursuant to this section is in Form 17.

See s. 703(2) for the general rule that a warrant of arrest issued by a justice or provincial court judge may be executed only in the province in which it is issued; s. 705(3) is the only exception to this rule.

See s. 706 for the procedure to be followed in the case of a witness arrested by warrant and brought before court. Section 707 governs his detention thereafter. By s. 708, failure to attend or remain in attendance to give evidence when required by law to do so is punishable as contempt.

SYNOPSIS

This section provides for the issuance of an arrest warrant for a witness who does not attend after having either been served with a subpoena or released on a recognizance on the condition that he or she appear to give evidence. Such warrants are issued by the court, judge or justice of the peace before whom the witness was to have appeared and are valid throughout Canada.

ANNOTATIONS

A provincial court judge has the power to issue a warrant under this section requiring that the witness be brought before him and to reserve for himself the exclusive jurisdiction to deal with the witness: *Pigeau v. Crowell* (1990), 57 C.C.C. (3d) 45, 96 N.S.R. (2d) 412 (C.A.).

Issuance of a warrant to procure the attendance of a witness is within the discretion of the hearing judge and will only be reviewable on *certiorari* where the judge exercises that discretion injudiciously: *R. v. Earhart* (2007), 272 C.C.C. (3d) 400 (B.C.C.A.).

ORDER WHERE WITNESS ARRESTED UNDER WARRANT.

706. Where a person is brought before a court, judge, justice or provincial court judge under a warrant issued pursuant to subsection 698(2) or section 704 or 705, the court, judge, justice or provincial court judge may order that the person

(*a*) be detained in custody, or

(*b*) be released on recognizance in Form 32, with or without sureties,

to appear and give evidence when required. R.S., c. C-34, s. 634.

CROSS-REFERENCES

See s. 2 for definitions of "justice" and "provincial court judge".

A warrant of arrest of a witness may be issued in the circumstances of ss. 698(2), 704 and 705. Release on recognizance under this section is in Form 32.

The maximum period for which a witness may be detained as a witness is prescribed by s. 707. By s. 708, failure to attend or remain in attendance in accordance with a recognizance may attract liability for contempt. See s. 145(2) for the consequences of breach of recognizance. Execution of a warrant under s. 514 is conducted within the territorial jurisdictions permitted by ss. 703 and 705(3).

SYNOPSIS

This section provides that when a witness is brought before any court under a warrant pursuant to s. 698(2) (witness not likely to appear), s. 704 (witness absconding) or s. 705 (witness failing to appear), that court may order the witness detained or released on recognizance.

ANNOTATIONS

A provincial court judge has the power to issue a warrant under s. 705 requiring that the witness be brought before him and to reserve for himself the exclusive jurisdiction to deal with the witness. Where the warrant is issued in that form then a justice of the peace before whom the witness is originally brought has no jurisdiction under this section to deal with her: *Pigeau v. Crowell* (1990), 57 C.C.C. (3d) 45, 96 N.S.R. (2d) 412 (C.A.).

MAXIMUM PERIOD FOR DETENTION OF WITNESS / Application by witness to judge / Review of detention.

707. (1) No person shall be detained in custody under the authority of any provision of this Act, for the purpose only of appearing and giving evidence when required as a witness, for any period exceeding thirty days unless prior to the expiration of those thirty days he has been brought before a judge of a superior court of criminal jurisdiction in the province in which he is being detained.

(2) Where at any time prior to the expiration of the thirty days referred to in subsection (1), a witness being detained in custody as described in that subsection applies to be brought before a judge of a court described therein, the judge before whom the application is brought shall fix a time prior to the expiration of those thirty days for the hearing of the application and shall cause notice of the time so fixed to be given to the witness, the person having custody of the witness and such other persons as the judge may specify, and at the time so fixed for the hearing of the application the person having custody of the witness shall cause the witness to be brought before a judge of the court for that purpose.

(3) If the judge before whom a witness is brought under this section is not satisfied that the continued detention of the witness is justified, he shall order him to be discharged, or to be released on recognizance in Form 32, with or without sureties, to appear and to give evidence when required, but if the judge is satisfied that the continued detention of the witness is justified, he may order his continued detention until the witness does what is required of him pursuant to section 550 or the trial is concluded, or until the witness appears and gives evidence when required, as the case may be, except that the total period of detention of the witness from the time he was first detained in custody shall not in any case exceed ninety days. R.S., c. C-34, s. 635.

CROSS-REFERENCES

Authorization to detain a witness arrested by warrant issued pursuant to ss. 698(2), 704 or 705 is found in s. 706.

Liability for contempt under s. 708 or for having breached a recognizance under s. 145(2) could result if a witness without lawful execuse fails to attend or remain to give evidence.

Release on recognizance under this section is in Form 32. See s. 550 for an order of continued detention.

SYNOPSIS

This section sets out the procedures to be followed in dealing with a witness who has been ordered detained.

A person imprisoned as a material witness may not be held for more than 30 days unless brought before a judge of a superior court (subsec. (1)). Such a person may, in any event, apply within the 30-day period to be taken before a superior court judge for a hearing (subsec. (2)).

The judge may release the witness, with or without a recognizance, or order that he or she remain in custody until the evidence has been given or the trial concluded. A witness may not be held for more than 90 days (subsec. (3)).

CONTEMPT / Punishment / Form.

708. (1) A person who, being required by law to attend or remain in attendance for the purpose of giving evidence, fails, without lawful excuse, to attend or remain in attendance accordingly is guilty of contempt of court.

(2) A court, judge, justice or provincial court judge may deal summarily with a person who is guilty of contempt of court under this section and that person is liable to a fine not exceeding one hundred dollars or to imprisonment for a term not exceeding ninety days or to both, and may be ordered to pay the costs that are incident to the service of any process under this Part and to his detention, if any.

(3) A conviction under this section may be in Form 38 and a warrant of committal in respect of a conviction under this section may be in Form 25. R.S., c. C-34, s. 636.

CROSS-REFERENCES

The terms "justice" and "provincial court judge" are defined in s. 2.

See s. 145(2) and (3) for potential liability where a witness fails to comply with the terms of a recognizance.

A conviction under this section may be in Form 38, and a warrant of committal in respect of conviction under this section may be in Form 25.

An appeal from conviction and sentence of contempt is authorized by s. 10(1). Such an appeal is governed by Part XXI.

SYNOPSIS

A witness who, without lawful excuse, fails to attend court as required is guilty of contempt and may be dealt with summarily. The maximum penalty is a fine of $100 and/or imprisonment for 90 days, plus costs (subsecs. (1), (2)).

Electronically Transmitted Copies

ELECTRONICALLY TRANSMITTED COPIES.

708.1 A copy of a summons, warrant or subpoena transmitted by a means of telecommunication that produces a writing has the same probative force as the original for the purposes of this Act. 1997, c. 18, s. 101.

Evidence on Commission

ORDER APPOINTING COMMISSIONER / Idem.

709. (1) A party to proceedings by way of indictment or summary conviction may apply for an order appointing a commissioner to take the evidence of a witness who

(*a*) is, by reason of

(i) physical disability arising out of illness, or

(ii) some other good and sufficient cause,

not likely to be able to attend at the time the trial is held; or

(*b*) is out of Canada.

(2) A decision under subsection (1) is deemed to have been made at the trial held in relation to the proceedings mentioned in that subsection. R.S., c. C-34, s. 637; R.S.C. 1985, c. 27 (1st Supp.), s. 150; 1994, c. 44, s. 72.

CROSS-REFERENCES

An application under s. 709 is made pursuant to the provisions of s. 710. See s. 712(1) in respect of a proposed witness who is out of Canada. Section 711 governs the reception of evidence taken under s. 709(1)(*a*) and s. 710. The evidence of a witness out of Canada is governed by ss. 709(1)(*b*), 712(2) and 713.1.

See s. 713(1) for an order that an accused be present or represented by counsel when commission evidence is taken.

Sections 714.1 and 714.3 provide that a court may make an order that a witness in Canada testify through video links or audio links, if the prerequisites in those provisions are met. Similarly, ss. 714.2 and 714.4 give the court the power to receive such evidence where the witness is outside Canada. Sections 700.1 and 714.5 to 714.7 set out the procedure for procuring the attendance of the witness, the administering of an oath or affirmation and its effect, and payment of costs associated with the use of the technology. Section 714.8 accommodates the use of such technology on consent.

SYNOPSIS

A commissioner may be appointed to take the evidence of a witness who is out of Canada or, because of illness or some other reason, is likely to be unable to attend the trial. It would appear that subsec. (2) was added to overcome the problem identified in *R.* v. *Pawlowski*, *infra*, that, under the former provision, no appeal lay from a decision refusing to make an order for commission evidence. In that case, the judge had also made an order for costs against the Crown which could not be appealed.

ANNOTATIONS

Where a witness is outside of Canada, the Crown is not required to establish that all other avenues for obtaining the witness's attendance have been exhausted. In this case, information that the witness was out of Canada by reason of imprisonment in a foreign state and not likely to be able to attend satisfied the requirements of this section: *R.* v. *Beck* (1996), 108 C.C.C. (3d) 385, 127 W.A.C. 56, 187 A.R. 56 (C.A.).

As an appeal is a proceeding a judge of the Court of Appeal may make an order for evidence on commission to be taken out of Canada: *R.* v. *Lester* (1972), 6 C.C.C. (2d) 227, [1972] 2 O.R. 330 (C.A. in Chambers).

An application under this section may be made during the trial. However, in deciding whether to grant the application the trial judge is entitled to consider such factors as whether the trial will be seriously disrupted, the possible prejudice to the opposite party resulting therefrom, as well as the consequence that the trier of fact will not have the advantage of observing the demeanour of the witness: *R.* v. *Bulleyment* (1979), 46 C.C.C. (2d) 429 (Ont. C.A.).

Evidence on commission as opposed to *viva voce* evidence at trial particularly where it goes to the root of the defence is unsatisfactory, but the seriousness of the charge and the accused's pre-trial detention require that his request for this order be granted: *R. v. Banton* (1976), 30 C.C.C. (2d) 253 (Ont. H.C.J.).

The court has no power to dictate to the Crown the manner in which it presents its case and thus cannot refuse an order for commission evidence until the completion of the preliminary inquiry. On the other hand, the courts have the right to ensure basic principles of a fair trial and if the defence is severly prejudiced by the decision to take commission evidence before the preliminary inquiry then an application may have to be brought to reopen the commission at the Crown's expense: *R. v. Buchanan* (1991), 65 C.C.C. (3d) 336 (Alta. Q.B.).

A superior court judge to whom an application is made under this section may make an order awarding costs against the Crown, not only where there has been serious misconduct by the Crown, but where there has been an infringement of the Charter: *R. v. Pawlowski* (1993), 79 C.C.C. (3d) 353, 20 C.R. (4th) 233, 101 D.L.R. (4th) 267 (Ont. C.A.) , leave to appeal to S.C.C. refused September 23, 1993.

While this section does not authorize evidence by videoconference, the trial judge does have the jurisdiction to admit evidence by videoconference where it is necessary and reliable: *R. v. Dix* (1998), 125 C.C.C. (3d) 377, 16 C.R. (5th) 157 (Alta. Q.B.).

While live video conferencing via s. 714.2 will often be preferable to recorded commission evidence, that other possible route of securing the evidence does not deprive the Crown of recourse to this provision: *R. v. Stevenson* (2012), 289 C.C.C. (3d) 315 (B.C.S.C.).

Evidence taken on commission outside of Canada does not become part of the court record until tendered at trial and therefore the commission is not a public proceeding within the meaning of s. 486. The court acceded to the host country's request to bar the media from the proceeding: *R. v. Magnotta* (2014), 309 C.C.C. (3d) 520 (Que. S.C.).

APPLICATION WHERE WITNESS IS ILL / Evidence of medical practitioner.

710. (1) An application under paragraph 709(1)(*a*) shall be made

- **(*a*) to a judge of a superior court of the province in which the proceedings are taken; or**
- **(*b*) to a judge of a county or district court in the territorial division in which the proceedings are taken; or**
- **(*c*) to a provincial court judge, where**
  - **(i) at the time the application is made, the accused is before a provincial court judge presiding over a preliminary inquiry under Part XXVIII, or**
  - **(ii) the accused or defendant is to be tried by a provincial court judge acting under Part XIX or XXVII.**

(2) An application under subparagraph 709(1)(*a*)(i) may be granted on the evidence of a registered medical practitioner. R.S., c. C-34, s. 638; R.S.C. 1985, c. 27 (1st Supp.), s. 151; 1994, c. 44, s. 73.

CROSS-REFERENCES

See s. 711 for the circumstances in which the evidence of a witness taken under ss. 709(1)(*a*) and 710 may be read in evidence in the proceedings.

See the corresponding note to s. 709 for other related provisions.

SYNOPSIS

An application for the appointment of a commissioner with respect to a witness who is in Canada shall be made to a Supreme, County or District Court judge except where the proceedings are before the Provincial Court, in which case it will be made to a judge of that court (subsec. (1)). The application may be supported by the evidence of a doctor (subsec. (2)).

READING EVIDENCE OF WITNESS WHO IS ILL.

711. Where the evidence of a witness mentioned in paragraph 709(1)(*a*) is taken by a commissioner appointed under section 710, it may be admitted in evidence in the proceedings if

(*a*) it is proved by oral evidence or by affidavit that the witness is unable to attend by reason of death or physical disability arising out of illness or some other good and sufficient cause;

(*b*) the transcript of the evidence is signed by the commissioner by or before whom it purports to have been taken; and

(*c*) it is proved to the satisfaction of the court that reasonable notice of the time for taking the evidence was given to the other party, and that the accused or his counsel, or the prosecutor or his counsel, as the case may be, had or might have had full opportunity to cross-examine the witness. R.S., c. C-34, s. 639; R.S.C. 1985, c. 27 (1st Supp.), s. 152; 1994, c. 44, s. 74; 1997, c. 18, s. 102.

CROSS-REFERENCES

See ss. 709(1)(*a*) and 710 for application to appoint a commissioner to take the evidence of a witness too ill to attend trial.

The requirements governing the reading in of evidence under this section may be contrasted with the absence of such requirements under s. 712(2) in respect of the evidence of a witness out of Canada.

SYNOPSIS

This section deals with the use of evidence taken by a commissioner from a witness in Canada. The party seeking to admit the testimony must establish: (a) that the witness is unable to attend (this may be done by affidavit); (b) that the transcript purports to be signed by the commissioner; and (c) that the other party had reasonable notice of the taking of the evidence and had, or could have had, an opportunity to cross-examine the witness.

APPLICATION FOR ORDER WHEN WITNESS OUT OF CANADA / Admitting evidence of witness out of Canada.

712. (1) An application that is made under paragraph 709(1)(*b*) shall be made

(*a*) to a judge of a superior court of criminal jurisdiction or of a court of criminal jurisdiction before which the accused is to be tried; or

(*b*) to a provincial court judge, where the accused or defendant is to be tried by a provincial court judge acting under Part XIX or XXVII.

(2) Where the evidence of a witness is taken by a commissioner appointed under this section, it may be admitted in evidence in the proceedings. R.S., c. C-34, s. 640; R.S.C. 1985, c. 27 (1st Supp.), s. 153(1); 1994, c. 44, s. 75; 1997, c. 18, s. 103; 1997, c. 23, s. 17.

(3) [*Repealed*, R.S.C. 1985, c. 27 (1st Supp.), s. 153(2).]

CROSS-REFERENCES

The term "superior court of criminal jurisdiction" is defined in s. 2.

See s. 709(1)(*b*) for an application to appoint a commissioner to take the evidence of a witness who is out of Canada.

See s. 711 governing the reading in of evidence of a witness who is ill; s. 712(2) does not contain similar conditions precedent.

See s. 713.1 respecting admission of evidence taken out of Canada.

SYNOPSIS

An application for the appointment of a commissioner with respect to a witness who is out of Canada shall be made to a judge of a superior court or to a judge of the court before which the trial is to take place, except where the trial is before the Provincial Court, in which case it will be made to a judge of that court (subsec. (1)). Evidence so taken may be admitted at the trial.

ANNOTATIONS

Where the trial has commenced before the provincial court judge an application by the accused to take commission evidence should be made to that judge rather than to the superior court. It is inappropriate, however, to name the trial judge as the commissioner as the accused may later choose not to tender the evidence at the trial. The disadvantage of the trial judge not being able to see the witness can be met by use of audio-visual equipment: *R. v. Nunus* (1985), 19 C.C.C. (3d) 522 (Ont. H.C.J.).

PROVIDING FOR PRESENCE OF ACCUSED COUNSEL / Return of evidence.

713. (1) A judge or provincial court judge who appoints a commissioner may make provision in the order to enable an accused to be present or represented by counsel when the evidence is taken, but failure of the accused to be present or to be represented by counsel in accordance with the order does not prevent the admission of the evidence in the proceedings if the evidence has otherwise been taken in accordance with the order and with this Part.

(2) An order for the taking of evidence by commission shall indicate the officer of the court to whom the evidence that is taken under the order shall be returned. R.S., c. C-34, s. 641; 1997, c. 18, s. 104.

CROSS-REFERENCES

The appointment of a commissioner to take the evidence of a person unable or unlikely to attend at trial is governed by ss. 709, 710, 712 and 713.1.

Section 714 establishes that, except where the provisions of Part XXII provide otherwise, the practice and procedure relating to the appointment of commissioners under this Part shall be that which governs like matters in civil proceedings in the superior court of the province in which the proceedings are taken.

SYNOPSIS

An order for the appointment of a commissioner may make provision to enable the accused or defence counsel to be present when the evidence is taken (*e.g.*, ordering the Crown to pay reasonable expenses). However, the fact that the accused is not present or represented when the evidence is taken will not, in and of itself, prevent the evidence being used (subsec. (1)).

The order shall specify the officer of the court to whom the transcript is to be returned (subsec. (2)).

ANNOTATIONS

An order made under this section may properly include provision that the Crown as applicant pay reasonable expenses of the accused's counsel including a counsel fee for the time spent travelling to and from the foreign jurisdiction: *R. v. Nicholson and Murphy* (1981), 62 C.C.C. (2d) 477 (B.C.S.C.).

This section does not authorize the judge appointing a commission to refuse, without justifiable excuse, permission to the accused to attend the commission. Rather, this section contemplates a situation in which the accused either voluntarily absents himself from the taking of the commission evidence or is unable to attend for reasons beyond the control of the court: *R. v. Branco* (1988), 41 C.C.C. (3d) 248, 62 C.R. (3d) 371 (Ont. C.A.).

This provision does not violate the accused's rights under ss. 7 and 11(*d*) of the Charter. Evidence taken by a commissioner in the absence of an accused may be read in only where the accused is voluntarily absent from the proceedings or is otherwise disqualified from misbehaviour from the right to attend: *R. v. Beck* (1996), 108 C.C.C. (3d) 385, 127 W.A.C. 56, 187 A.R. 56 (C.A.).

It is not a valid objection to the making of an order for commission evidence that the accused is unwilling to attend on the commission because he might be arrested in the jurisdiction and the Crown is not bound to attempt to obtain assurances from the foreign government that the accused would not be arrested: *R. v. Buchanan* (1991), 65 C.C.C. (3d) 336 (Alta. Q.B.). And the admission of evidence obtained in such circumstances did not violate the accused's rights under ss. 7 and 11(*d*) of the Charter: *R. v. Buchanan* (1992), 76 C.C.C. (3d) 236, 133 A.R. 321 (Q.B.). See also *R. v. Beck, supra.*

Even though evidence has been taken in accordance with an order made under s. 709 it is still for the trial judge to determine its admissibility. Thus, where the accused was improperly barred from attending on the taking of the commission evidence, his absence at the commission amounted to absence at trial once the evidence was tendered at the trial, and the evidence should not have been admitted: *R. v. Branco* (1988), 41 C.C.C. (3d) 248, 62 C.R. (3d) 371 (Ont. C.A.).

This provision is applicable to both the voluntary and involuntary absence of the accused. In this case, the accused was precluded from attending the commission because the Canadian authorities were unable to obtain sufficient guarantees that the accused would remain in prison upon entering the foreign jurisdiction: *R. v. Neverson* (1998), 124 C.C.C. (3d) 468, 17 C.R. (5th) 381 (Que. C.A.).

EVIDENCE NOT EXCLUDED.

713.1 Evidence taken by a commissioner appointed under section 712 shall not be excluded by reason only that it would have been taken differently in Canada, provided that the process used to take the evidence is consistent with the law of the country where it was taken and that the process used to take the evidence was not contrary to the principles of fundamental justice. 1994, c. 44, s. 76.

CROSS-REFERENCES

The application for a commission to take the evidence of a witness out of Canada is made under ss. 709(1)(*b*) and 712. The evidence is admitted pursuant to s. 712(2) and this section. Presence of the accused and representation by counsel at the commission are governed by s. 713. Rules and practice at the commission are governed by the civil rules pursuant to s. 714.

SYNOPSIS

This section provides that evidence is admissible although the process was different than would be the procedure in Canada, provided that the procedure used conformed with the law of the country where it was taken and was not contrary to the principles of fundamental justice.

RULES AND PRACTICE SAME AS IN CIVIL CASES.

714. Except where otherwise provided by this Part or by rules of court, the practice and procedure in connection with the appointment of commissioners under this Part, the taking of evidence by commissioners, the certifying and return thereof and the use of the evidence in the proceedings shall, as far as possible, be the same as those that govern like matters in civil proceedings in the superior court of the province in which the proceedings are taken. R.S., c. C-34, s. 642.

CROSS-REFERENCES
The appointment of a commissioner to take the evidence of a person unable or unlikely to attend at trial is governed by ss. 709, 710 and 712.

Section 713 makes provision for an accused or his counsel to be present at the giving of commission evidence. The reading in of commission evidence is governed by ss. 711 and 712(2).

SYNOPSIS
This section states that procedures with respect to commissioners under this Part shall be the same as those in the superior civil court of the jurisdiction, unless otherwise provided for in this Part or the rules of court.

ANNOTATIONS
Subject to objections as to admissibility of its contents evidence taken *ex juris* on commission for a preliminary inquiry may also be read in at trial: *R. v. Crux* (1972), 6 C.C.C. (2d) 330 (B.C.S.C.).

To obtain the evidence of an unwilling witness in a foreign jurisdiction the party seeking the examination requires the assistance of the appropriate Court in the foreign jurisdiction to compel the witness to attend, answer questions and apply sanctions if the witness does not comply. Further, an order from the Court of the foreign jurisdiction appointing the commission with full authority to do everything necessary to accomplish the purpose of the order including prescribing the practice and procedure, gives the commissioner power to rule on objections to relevancy. However, ultimate admissibility of the evidence will be determined by the trial judge in Canada: *R. v. Robertson* (1982), 66 C.C.C. (2d) 210, 31 C.R. (3d) 383 (B.C.C.A.), leave to appeal to S.C.C. refused C.R. *loc. cit.*, 43 N.R. 619*n*.

Video and Audio Evidence

VIDEO LINKS, ETC. — WITNESS IN CANADA.

714.1 A court may order that a witness in Canada give evidence by means of technology that permits the witness to testify elsewhere in Canada in the virtual presence of the parties and the court, if the court is of the opinion that it would be appropriate in all the circumstances, including

(*a*) the location and personal circumstances of the witness;

(*b*) the costs that would be incurred if the witness had to be physically present; and

(*c*) the nature of the witness' anticipated evidence. 1999, c. 18, s. 95.

CROSS-REFERENCES
Section 700.1 provides for the issuance of a subpoena to procure the attendance of the witness at the place within the jurisdiction of the court where the technology is available. Section 714.3 allows a judge to make an order similar to the order under this section, but to obtain the evidence by way of an audio link. Section 714.2 provides that the court shall receive evidence given by video link of a witness outside Canada unless one of the parties satisfies the court that the reception of such testimony would be contrary to the principles of fundamental justice. Section 714.4 similarly allows for reception of evidence given by an audio link of a witness outside Canada. In either case, pursuant to s. 714.5, the evidence is to be given under oath or affirmation in accordance with Canadian law, the law of the place where the witness is, or in any other manner that demonstrates that the witness understands that they must tell the truth. Section 714.6 deems the evidence to be given in Canada for the purposes of laws relating to evidence, procedure, perjury or contempt of court. The costs of the use of technology under this section or ss. 714.2 to 714.4 are to be borne by the party who wishes to call the witness (s. 714.7). These sections do not preclude the use of technology on consent (s. 714.8).

Pursuant to s. 136(1.1), evidence given under this section and ss. 714.2 to 714.3 is deemed to be evidence given by a witness in a judicial proceeding for the purposes of the offence under s. 136(1) [witness giving contradictory evidence].

A more limited use of technology at the preliminary inquiry and the trial is provided for in ss. 537(1)(*j*), (*k*) [preliminary inquiry], 650(1.1), (1.2) [trial] to allow for the accused to appear by closed-circuit television for certain parts of the proceedings. Also note s. 486(2.1) to (2.3), which allow the judge to make an order that the complainant and witnesses in certain cases testify outside of court by means of closed-circuit television.

SYNOPSIS

A witness in Canada may give evidence by video link provided that it is appropriate having regard to all of the circumstances including: the location and personal circumstances of the witness; the costs that would be incurred if the witness had to be physically present; and the nature of the witness' anticipated evidence.

ANNOTATIONS

An application to have a witness residing in British Columbia video-conferenced for a trial in Saskatchewan was dismissed on the basis that there was no evidence that the witness would be inconvenienced or that he was not fully accessible for attendance at the trial: *R. v. Young* (2000), 150 C.C.C. (3d) 317, 201 Sask. R. 158 (Q.B.).

Where credibility is at issue, the court should authorize video testimony under this section only in the face of exceptional circumstances that impact the proposed witness. Mere inconvenience should not suffice: *R. v. S.D.L.* (2017), 352 C.C.C. (3d) 159 (N.S.C.A.).

VIDEO LINKS, ETC. — WITNESS OUTSIDE CANADA / Notice.

714.2 (1) A court shall receive evidence given by a witness outside Canada by means of technology that permits the witness to testify in the virtual presence of the parties and the court unless one of the parties satisfies the court that the reception of such testimony would be contrary to the principles of fundamental justice.

(2) A party who wishes to call a witness to give evidence under subsection (1) shall give notice to the court before which the evidence is to be given and the other parties of their intention to do so not less than ten days before the witness is scheduled to testify. 1999, c. 18, s. 95.

CROSS-REFERENCES

Section 714.1 provides that a court may make an order that a witness in Canada may give evidence by means of video links. For other cross-references see notes under s. 714.1.

SYNOPSIS

A witness who is outside of Canada may testify by means of video unless it is established that the reception of such testimony would be contrary to the principles of fundamental justice. Pursuant to subsec. (2), the party seeking to call a witness to testify by video must provide notice of not less than 10 days before the witness is scheduled to testify.

AUDIO EVIDENCE — WITNESS IN CANADA.

714.3 The court may order that a witness in Canada give evidence by means of technology that permits the parties and the court to hear and examine the witness elsewhere in Canada, if the court is of the opinion that it would be appropriate, considering all the circumstances including

(*a*) the location and personal circumstances of the witness;

(*b*) the costs that would be incurred if the witness had to be physically present;

(*c*) the nature of the witness' anticipated evidence; and

(*d*) any potential prejudice to either of the parties caused by the fact that the witness would not be seen by them. 1999, c. 18, s. 95.

CROSS-REFERENCES
Section 700.1 provides for the issuance of a subpoena to procure the attendance of the witness at the place within the jurisdiction of the court where the technology is available. Section 714.1 provides that a court may make an order that a witness in Canada may give evidence by means of video links. For other cross-references see notes under s. 714.1.

SYNOPSIS
A witness in Canada may give evidence by audio where the court concludes that it would be appropriate having regard to all of the circumstances including the location and personal circumstances of the witness; the costs that would be incurred if the witness had to be physically present; the nature of the witness' anticipated evidence; and any potential prejudice to either of the parties caused by the fact that the witness would not be seen by them.

AUDIO EVIDENCE — WITNESS OUTSIDE CANADA.

714.4 The court may receive evidence given by a witness outside Canada by means of technology that permits the parties and the court in Canada to hear and examine the witness, if the court is of the opinion that it would be appropriate, considering all the circumstances including

(*a*) the nature of the witness' anticipated evidence; and

(*b*) any potential prejudice to either of the parties caused by the fact that the witness would not be seen by them. 1999, c. 18, s. 95.

CROSS-REFERENCES
Section 714.1 provides that a court may make an order that a witness in Canada may give evidence by means of video links. For other cross-references see notes under s. 714.1.

SYNOPSIS
A witness outside of Canada may give evidence by audio if it is established that it is appropriate considering all the circumstances including the nature of the witness' anticipated evidence and any potential prejudice to either party caused by the fact that the witness would not be seen by them.

OATH OR AFFIRMATION.

714.5 The evidence given under section 714.2 or 714.4 shall be given

(*a*) under oath or affirmation in accordance with Canadian law;

(*b*) under oath or affirmation in accordance with the law in the place in which the witness is physically present; or

(*c*) in any other manner that demonstrates that the witness understands that they must tell the truth. 1999, c. 18, s. 95.

CROSS-REFERENCES
Section 714.1 provides that a court may make an order that a witness in Canada may give evidence by means of video links. For other cross-references see notes under s. 714.1.

SYNOPSIS
Evidence given by a witness outside of Canada through video or audio link must be under oath or affirmation in accordance with Canadian law; under oath or affirmation in

accordance with the law in the place in which the witness is physically present; or in any other manner that demonstrates that the witness understands that they must tell the truth.

OTHER LAWS ABOUT WITNESSES TO APPLY.

714.6 When a witness who is outside Canada gives evidence under section 714.2 or 714.4, the evidence is deemed to be given in Canada, and given under oath or affirmation in accordance with Canadian law, for the purposes of the laws relating to evidence, procedure, perjury and contempt of court. 1999, c. 18, s. 95.

CROSS-REFERENCES

Section 714.1 provides that a court may make an order that a witness in Canada may give evidence by means of video links. For other cross-references see notes under s. 714.1.

SYNOPSIS

Evidence that is given outside of Canada pursuant to s. 714.2 or s. 714.4 is deemed to be given in Canada for the purposes of laws relating to evidence, procedure, perjury and contempt of court.

COSTS OF TECHNOLOGY.

714.7 A party who wishes to call a witness to give evidence by means of the technology referred to in section 714.1, 714.2, 714.3 or 714.4 shall pay any costs associated with the use of the technology. 1999, c. 18, s. 95.

CROSS-REFERENCES

Section 714.1 provides that a court may make an order that a witness in Canada may give evidence by means of video links. For other cross-references see notes under s. 714.1.

SYNOPSIS

The costs incurred in giving video or audio evidence must be paid by the party calling the witness.

CONSENT.

714.8 Nothing in sections 714.1 to 714.7 is to be construed as preventing a court from receiving evidence by means of the technology referred to in sections 714.1 to 714.4 if the parties so consent. 1999, c. 18, s. 95.

CROSS-REFERENCES

Section 714.1 provides that a court may make an order that a witness in Canada may give evidence by means of video links. For other cross-references see notes under s. 714.1.

SYNOPSIS

The provisions of sections 714.1 to 714.7, which authorize the making of orders for reception of evidence given in Canada by way of a video or audio link or permit the reception of such evidence given outside Canada do not preclude the reception of evidence by means of that technology on consent.

Evidence Previously Taken

EVIDENCE AT PRELIMINARY INQUIRY MAY BE READ AT TRIAL IN CERTAIN CASES / Admission of evidence / Admission of evidence / Absconding accused deemed present / Exception.

715. (1) Where, at the trial of an accused, a person whose evidence was given at a previous trial on the same charge, or whose evidence was taken in the investigation of the charge against the accused or on the preliminary inquiry into the charge, refuses to be sworn or to give evidence, or if facts are proved on oath from which it can be inferred reasonably that the person

(*a*) is dead,

(*b*) has since become and is insane,

(*c*) is so ill that he is unable to travel or testify, or

(*d*) is absent from Canada,

and where it is proved that the evidence was taken in the presence of the accused, it may be admitted as evidence in the proceedings without further proof, unless the accused proves that the accused did not have full opportunity to cross-examine the witness.

(2) Evidence that has been taken on the preliminary inquiry or other investigation of a charge against an accused may be admitted as evidence in the prosecution of the accused for any other offence on the same proof and in the same manner in all respects, as it might, according to law, be admitted as evidence in the prosecution of the offence with which the accused was charged when the evidence was taken.

(2.1) Despite subsections (1) and (2), evidence that has been taken at a preliminary inquiry in the absence of the accused may be admitted as evidence for the purposes referred to in those subsections if the accused was absent further to the permission of a justice granted under paragraph 537(1)(*j*.1).

(3) For the purposes of this section, where evidence was taken at a previous trial or preliminary hearing or other proceeding in respect of an accused in the absence of the accused, who was absent by reason of having absconded, the accused is deemed to have been present during the taking of the evidence and to have had full opportunity to cross-examine the witness.

(4) Subsections (1) to (3) do not apply in respect of evidence received under subsection 540(7). R.S., c. C-34, s. 643; 1974-75-76, c. 93, s. 76; 1994, c. 44, s. 77; 1997, c. 18, s. 105; 2002, c. 13, s. 72; 2008, c. 18, s. 34.

CROSS-REFERENCES

The term "justice" is defined in s. 2.

The order and receipt of evidence taken on commission is provided for in ss. 709 to 714.

SYNOPSIS

This section provides for the admissibility at trial of the transcript of the evidence given at a preliminary inquiry, or previous trial, where the witness refuses to be sworn; is dead; insane; unable due to illness to attend, or absent from Canada.

To use a transcript one of the above conditions must be established together with the fact that the evidence was taken in the presence of the accused unless the accused was given permission to be absent from the preliminary hearing under s. 537(1)(*j*.1). The onus is on the accused to prove that he or she was denied a full opportunity to cross-examine (subsec. (1)). (**Note**: Even if the statutory preconditions have been met, the Supreme Court of Canada has held that a trial judge has a discretion not to admit the evidence.)

Subsection (2) provides that transcript evidence is admissible at the trial of a charge other than the one which was the subject of the earlier proceedings.

An accused who absconded during an earlier trial is deemed to have had a full opportunity to cross-examine the witness (subsec. (3)). (**Note**: Section 544(1)(*a*) provides that an accused who absconds at a preliminary inquiry is deemed to have waived his or her right to be present.)

This section does not apply to hearsay evidence received under s. 540(7) at the preliminary inquiry.

ANNOTATIONS

Application of provision – Compliance with this section does not require proof that the witness' absence or refusal to testify is unavoidable and justified. Further, the right to full opportunity to cross-examine the witness refers to the procedure at the preliminary hearing and does not include a right to cross-examination of events which have occurred since the preliminary hearing: *R. v. Cole* (1980), 53 C.C.C. (2d) 269 (Ont. C.A.); *R. v. Rogers and Thurber*, *infra*.

Illness in this section includes mental illness and is not confined to physical illness: *R. v. Novalinga* (1985), 19 C.C.C. (3d) 190 (Ont. H.C.J.).

This section is applicable although the witness is only temporarily absent from Canada: *R. v. Rogers and Thurber* (1987), 35 C.C.C. (3d) 50, 55 Sask. R. 198 (C.A.).

Where the accused had married his spouse subsequent to the preliminary inquiry but prior to trial, the spouse's preliminary inquiry evidence was not admissible under this provision. The marriage of the accused to the spouse does not represent a refusal to give evidence but rather, the common law rule of spousal incompetency disqualified the spouse from giving evidence regardless of the spouse's choice. The evidence, however, could be admitted under the principled approach to the hearsay rule: *R. v. Hawkins*, [1996] 3 S.C.R. 1043, 111 C.C.C. (3d) 129. See also *R. v. Menard* (1996), 108 C.C.C. (3d) 424 (Ont. C.A.), affd [1998] 2 S.C.R. 109, 125 C.C.C. (3d) 416.

Principles to be applied generally – In *R. v. Waucash* (1966), 1 C.R.N.S. 262 (Ont. H.C.J.), Grant J., at trial, decided (affirmed without written reasons by the Ontario Court of Appeal, April 25, 1967), that where the accused had been committed to custody at the pleasure of the Lieutenant Governor in Council 10 years previously just after his preliminary inquiry at which he had been represented by experienced counsel, the evidence which was taken of three witnesses, since deceased, could not be now admitted, as at that time the accused, because of his mental condition, was at a disadvantage in advising his counsel and was unable to avail himself of his full opportunity to cross-examine those witnesses.

This section does not infringe an accused's rights to fundamental justice and a fair trial under ss. 7 and 11(*d*) of the *Charter of Rights and Freedoms*, although the accused would have a constitutional right to have the prior evidence excluded if he did not have a full opportunity to cross-examine as where he was deprived of the right to counsel or where improper restrictions were placed by the court on the cross-examination by counsel. However, properly interpreted, it gives the trial judge a discretion to depart from the purely mechanical application of this section and to exclude evidence where the testimony was obtained in a manner which was unfair to the accused or where its admission at the trial would not be fair to the accused. The discretion should be exercised only after weighing the competing interests of fair treatment of the accused and society's interest in the admission of probative evidence. The importance of the evidence is not the determinative factor in deciding whether to exercise the discretion and in fact the purpose of this provision was to ensure that evidence, even important and highly probative evidence, is not lost because of the unavailability of a witness at trial. Where the trial judge does admit the evidence then it is highly desirable that he remind the jury that they have not had the benefit of observing the witness giving the testimony. This is particularly the case where the unavailability arises from the witness's deliberate refusal to testify before the jury: *R. v. Potvin*, [1989] 1 S.C.R. 525, 47 C.C.C. (3d) 289, 68 C.R. (3d) 193 (5:0).

Although there was a thorough cross-examination of the complainant, the admission of the complainant's preliminary inquiry evidence would violate the accused's right to make full answer and defence where the Crown had not disclosed information to the defence which could have been used in the cross-examination of the complainant to attack credibility: *R. v. Barembruch* (1997), 119 C.C.C. (3d) 185, 155 W.A.C. 215 (B.C.C.A.).

The discovery of potentially useful information after a witness has testified does not deprive the accused of the full opportunity to cross-examine within the meaning of this section nor does it result in any unfairness in the trial. A denial or restriction of cross-examination occurs if the intention to pursue certain questions was present and was frustrated: *R. v. Michaud* (2000), 144 C.C.C. (3d) 62, 224 N.B.R. (2d) 371 (C.A.).

Where the Crown proposed to tender the preliminary inquiry testimony of an alleged accomplice who had been tried separately but refused to testify at the accused's trial, the trial judge erred by failing to consider the witness' manifest unreliability in deciding whether to exercise his discretion to exclude the evidence under this section. The judge also erred in failing to consider the unfairness produced by the inability of the defence to confront the witness with significant new information obtained after he had testified at the preliminary inquiry: *R. v. Saleh* (2013), 303 C.C.C. (3d) 431 (Ont. C.A.).

Where the cross-examination of an important Crown witness at the preliminary inquiry by counsel for the co-accused seriously weakened admissions obtained by counsel for the accused, the trial judge should consider whether fairness required that the transcript of the cross-examination by the co-accused's counsel be deleted now that the co-accused having pleaded guilty was no longer on trial: *R. v. Ingraham* (1991), 66 C.C.C. (3d) 27, 46 O.A.C. 216 (C.A.).

In considering the exercise of the discretion under this section, the trial judge should have considered that the complainant's absence from the jurisdiction was unexplained with no suggestion that it was through threats or duress from the accused: *R. v. Harris* (1991), 66 C.C.C. (3d) 536 (Ont. C.A.).

The evidence given by an expert at the first trial of the accused was properly read in under this section on the retrial. In exercising the discretion under this section, in the circumstances of this case, the issue was whether there was a need for further cross-examination of the expert in light of the publication by him of a second treatise after the first trial. Any question as to the expert's honesty or the weight to be given his opinion was effectively dealt with in other ways and, accordingly, the evidence was admissible. *R. v. Zundel* (1990), 53 C.C.C. (3d) 161 (Ont. C.A.).

As to circumstances where it was held that the admission of the preliminary inquiry testimony of an expert witness would operate unfairly see: *R. v. F. (D.M.)* (1999), 139 C.C.C. (3d) 144, 179 D.L.R. (4th) 492 (Alta. C.A.).

Reading this section together with the provisions in ss. 714.2 and 714.4 for taking the evidence of a witness outside Canada, the court concluded that it is incumbent on a trial judge hearing an application under this section to consider the possibility of taking the evidence in a live manner via audio or video technology: *R. v. Li* (2012), 284 C.C.C. (3d) 207 (Ont. C.A.).

Procedure – Notwithstanding a witness' preliminary hearing testimony has been read in pursuant to this section because of his refusal to testify, where the witness then changes his mind and agrees to testify, it is open to the trial judge to permit defence counsel to cross-examine the witness: *R. v. Valence* (1982), 5 C.C.C. (3d) 552 (Que. C.A.), leave to appeal to S.C.C. granted C.C.C. *loc. cit.*, 46 N.R. 628*n*.

There were no grounds for interfering with the trial judge's discretion permitting the Crown to reopen its case and prove that the accused was the person referred to in the testimony given at the preliminary hearing which was read in at the accused's trial pursuant to this section: *R. v. Robillard*, [1978] 2 S.C.R. 728, 41 C.C.C. (2d) 1, 85 D.L.R. (3d) 449 (9:0).

Evidence of statements by the missing witness as to his intention to leave the jurisdiction, even if hearsay, are admissible to prove the absence of the witness from Canada, if such evidence is surrounded by circumstantial guarantees of trustworthiness: *R. v. Kaddoura* (1987), 60 C.R. (3d) 393 (Alta. C.A.), leave to appeal to S.C.C. refused 42 C.C.C. (3d) vi, 87 A.R. 160*n*, 89 N.R. 397*n*.

Where a witness who was called at the preliminary hearing is not called at trial and his evidence is not read in under this section and his evidence is not admissible under some exception to the hearsay rule then it is improper to place before the jury the witness' preliminary hearing testimony by referring to such evidence and asking the accused on cross-examination if he remembers the witness giving that evidence: *R. v. McNamara (No. 1)* (1981), 56 C.C.C. (2d) 193 (Ont. C.A.), at pp. 381-4.

Video-recorded Evidence

EVIDENCE OF VICTIM OR WITNESS UNDER 18 / Order prohibiting use.

715.1 (1) In any proceeding against an accused in which a victim or other witness was under the age of eighteen years at the time the offence is alleged to have been committed, a video recording made within a reasonable time after the alleged offence, in which the victim or witness describes the acts complained of, is admissible in evidence if the victim or witness, while testifying, adopts the contents of the video recording, unless the presiding judge or justice is of the opinion that admission of the video recording in evidence would interfere with the proper administration of justice.

(2) The presiding judge or justice may prohibit any other use of a video recording referred to in subsection (1). R.S.C. 1985, c. 19, (3rd supp.), s. 16; 1997, c. 16, s. 7; 2005, c. 32, s. 23.

CROSS-REFERENCES

"Victim" is defined in s. 2. See ss. 486 to 486.5 for procedures for the reception of evidence of complainants and witnesses under 18 years of age. Age is determined by reference to s. 30 of the *Interpretation Act*, R.S.C. 1985, c. I-21.

See ss. 16 and 16.1 of the *Canada Evidence Act*, R.S.C. 1985, c. C-5, for the manner in which evidence of a witness under 14 years of age or of diminished mental capacity may be received.

Also see notes under s. 150.1.

As to admission of videotaped evidence of a witness with mental or physical disability, see s. 715.2.

SYNOPSIS

This section allows for the admission of videotaped testimony where the victim or other witness was under 18 years of age at the time of the alleged offence. The video recording must describe the acts complained of, must be adopted in the testimony of the witness at trial and must have been taped within a reasonable time after the alleged offence. The judge or justice may exclude the video recording if admission of it into evidence would interfere with the proper administration of justice. The judge or justice may prohibit any other use of a video recording.

ANNOTATIONS

Note: Some of the cases noted below were decided under the predecessor to this section, which limited the right to use a video recording to proceedings involving certain named sexual offences.

Procedure – The videotape is not an exhibit that goes to the jury room during the jury's deliberations: *R. v. Kilabuk* (1990), 60 C.C.C. (3d) 413 (N.W.T.S.C.).

A judge's decision to allow the jury to have the complainant's videotaped evidence during deliberations is reviewable if the exercise of the discretion deprived the accused of a fair trial: *R. v. Noftall* (2004), 181 C.C.C. (3d) 470, 182 O.A.C. 150 *sub nom. R. v. R.W.N.* (Ont. C.A.), leave to appeal to S.C.C. refused 189 C.C.C. (3d) vi.

A *voir dire* must be held prior to the admission of a videotaped statement: *R. v. F. (C.C.)* (1996), 88 O.A.C. 397 (C.A.), revd [1997] 3 S.C.R. 1183, 120 C.C.C. (3d) 225, 11 C.R. (5th) 209 *sub nom. R. v. F. (C.)*.

The Crown bears the onus of proving the preconditions of subsec. (1) and it is an error of law to reverse the onus on this issue: *R. v. H. (R.A.)* (2017), 348 C.C.C. (3d) 248 (P.E.I.C.A.).

Defence counsel's admission that the requirements of subsec. (1) are met is not an admission of fact binding on the trial judge. The trial judge has an independent obligation to ensure that the requirements are met before admitting a videotaped statement: *R. v. P.W.M.* (2018), 366 C.C.C. (3d) 374 (P.E.I.C.A.).

Discretion to exclude video recording – The trial judge has a discretion to exclude the videotaped statement if prejudice from its admission would outweigh its probative value. However, this discretion is limited to circumstances where its admission would outweigh its probative value. If there is conflicting evidence as to how useful the videotaped statement may be in providing an honest and complete account of the complainant's story, the statement should be admitted unless the trial judge is satisfied that it could interfere with the truth-finding process. For example, the fact that the police conduct a pre-video interview will be relevant to weight, not admissibility: *R. v. F. (C.C.), supra.* [Note, that subsec. (1) now specifies circumstances in which the video recording may be excluded as whether admission of it into evidence would interfere with the proper administration of justice. It is not clear whether inclusion of this phrase was intended to capture all of the circumstances in which the judge has a discretion to exclude the video recording.]

Conditions for admissibility of video recording, generally – A statement is "adopted" within the meaning of this section where the witness recalls giving the statement and testifies that they were attempting to be honest and truthful when they gave the statement. A videotaped statement is admissible even if a witness has an independent present memory of the events or if the witness cannot remember the events discussed in the videotape. In the latter case, there are several factors in this provision which guarantee the reliability of the videotaped statement, including the requirement that the statement be made within a reasonable time, that the trier of fact will have an opportunity to observe the demeanour and assess the personality and intelligence of the child in the videotape, and that the child attest that she was attempting to be truthful at the time that the statement was made. The test for adoption is not a final determination of reliability, but rather a test for determining the threshold degree of reliability required for the admission of the video. Once a trial judge rules that the statement has been adopted, the videotaped statement together with the viva voce evidence given at trial comprises the whole of the evidence-in-chief. Even if evidence that contradicts the videotaped statement is elicited in cross-examination, this does not render those parts of the videotape inadmissible. The circumstances in which the video was made, the veracity of the witness's statements and the overall reliability of the evidence are factors which are relevant to weight rather than the admissibility of the statement: *R. v. F. (C.C.), supra.*

The videotaped statement becomes part of the witness's examination-in-chief and does not constitute a prior consistent statement nor corroboration: *R. v. Aksidan* (2006), 209 C.C.C. (3d) 423 (B.C.C.A.).

However, while *mere* consistency between the videotaped statement and in-court testimony cannot corroborate the complainant's account, this does not mean that consistencies cannot be considered in the overall assessment of credibility and reliability. Rather, the whole of the complainant's evidence, including internal consistencies between the videotaped statement and trial evidence, should be scrutinized to determine whether inconsistencies relied on by the defence give rise to a reasonable doubt: *R. v. Untinen* (2017), 355 C.C.C. (3d) 371 (B.C.C.A.), leave to appeal to S.C.C. refused [2017] S.C.C.A. No. 485.

Conditions for admissibility of video recording, meaning of "within a reasonable time" – In *R. v. L. (D.O.)*, [1993] 4 S.C.R. 419, 85 C.C.C. (3d) 289, the court held that the trial judge did not err in admitting a videotaped interview under this section, notwithstanding the delay of five months from the time disclosure was first made by the nine-year-old complainant. In her concurring opinion, L'Heureux-Dubé J. held that what is a reasonable time depends entirely on the circumstances of the case and that, in making the determination, the judge may take into consideration the fact that children often delay disclosure. As well, it may be necessary to conduct a prior investigation to ensure the seriousness of the allegations. On the other hand, such determination must also take into account empirical data indicating that recollection decreases in accuracy with time and that children's memories fade faster than those of adults. There is thus a clear advantage to gathering evidence from a child as early as possible.

In considering whether or not a videotape statement was made within a reasonable time after the alleged offence, the court should consider the totality of circumstances. One consideration in particular is the fact that children, for a number of reasons, are often likely to delay disclosure, as where the child has been severely traumatized by the assault: *R. v. Scott* (1993), 87 C.C.C. (3d) 327 (Ont. C.A.).

Even though there was a very lengthy delay between the date of the offence and the time of the taping, it was open to the judge to find that the delay was reasonable and that the videotape was admissible. The delay arose because of the natural reluctance of the complainant, and perhaps of the mother, to make a report to the authorities: *R. v. M. (S.)* (1995), 98 C.C.C. (3d) 526 (Alta. C.A.).

A four-year delay was held not to be "within a reasonable time", given the likely effect of the passage of time on the complainant's memory, a concern borne out by the brevity of her statement and inability to recall collateral facts: *R. v. B. (A.G.)* (2011), 280 C.C.C. (3d) 85 (Alta. Prov. Ct.).

A three-year delay was "within a reasonable time of the alleged offence", having regard to the reasons for the delay and the impact of the delay on the child's ability to accurately recall the events: *R. v. G. (S.)* (2007), 221 C.C.C. (3d) 439 (Ont. S.C.J.).

Meaning of "acts complained of" – The phrase "the acts complained of" does not include additional assaults which may be introduced as similar fact evidence but are not charged in the indictment: *R. v. A. (J.F.)* (1993), 82 C.C.C. (3d) 295 (Ont. C.A.).

It does, however, include a description given by the complainant of her assailant and statements made by the attacker during the offence: *R. v. Scott, supra.*

Application of common law – A videotaped statement that does not meet the requirements of this section may nevertheless be admissible under the common law, provided that the principles of necessity and reliability are met: *R. v. F. (W.J.)*, [1999] 3 S.C.R. 569, 138 C.C.C. (3d) 1; *R. v. Burk* (1999), 139 C.C.C. (3d) 266 (Ont. C.A.).

Constitutional considerations – The predecessor to this section was held to violate neither s. 7 nor s. 11 of the Charter. Incorporation of a judicial discretion to edit or refuse to admit videotaped evidence where its prejudicial effect outweighs its probative value ensures that the section is consistent with fundamental principles of justice and the right to a fair trial: *R. v. L. (D.O.), supra.* [Note, that subsec. (1) now specifies circumstances in which the video recording may be excluded as whether admission of it into evidence would interfere with the proper administration of justice.]

EVIDENCE OF VICTIM OR WITNESS WHO HAS A DISABILITY / Order prohibiting use.

715.2 (1) In any proceeding against an accused in which a victim or other witness is able to communicate evidence but may have difficulty doing so by reason of a mental or physical disability, a video recording made within a reasonable time after the alleged offence, in which the victim or witness describes the acts complained of, is admissible in

evidence if the victim or witness, while testifying, adopts the contents of the video recording, unless the presiding judge or justice is of the opinion that admission of the video recording in evidence would interfere with the proper administration of justice.

(2) The presiding judge or justice may prohibit any other use of a video recording referred to in subsection (1). 1998, c. 9, s. 8; 2005, c. 32, s. 23.

CROSS-REFERENCES

"Victim" is defined in s. 2. See ss. 486 to 486.5 for procedures for the reception of evidence of complainants and witnesses under a mental or physical disability. See ss. 16 and 16.1 of the *Canada Evidence Act*, R.S.C. 1985, c. C-5, for the manner in which evidence of a witness under 14 years of age or of diminished mental capacity may be received.

As to admission of videotaped evidence of witnesses under the age of 18 years, see s. 715.1.

SYNOPSIS

This section allows for the admission of a video recording where the victim or other witness who is able to communicate evidence but may have difficulty doing so by reason of a mental or physical disability. The video recording must describe the acts complained of, must be adopted in the testimony of the witness at trial and must have been taped within a reasonable time after the alleged offence. The judge or justice may exclude the video recording if admission of it into evidence would interfere with the proper administration of justice. The judge or justice may prohibit any other use of a video recording.

ANNOTATIONS

This section is similar to s. 715.1 and thus reference should be made to the cases noted under that section, bearing in mind that those cases were decided under a predecessor to s. 715.1.

"Adopts" in this section has the same meaning as in s. 715.1. Therefore, it does not require the witness to be able to confirm the truth of the video-recorded statement based on present memory of the events in question: *R. v. Osborne* (2017), 346 C.C.C. (3d) 77 (Ont. C.A.), leave to appeal to S.C.C. refused 2017 CarswellOnt 19579.

PART XXII.1 / REMEDIATION AGREEMENTS **2018, c. 12, s. 404.**

DEFINITIONS / Acting on victim's behalf.

715.3 (1) The following definitions apply in this Part.

"court" means a superior court of criminal jurisdiction but does not include a court of appeal.

"offence" means any offence listed in the schedule to this Part.

"organization" has the same meaning as in section 2 but does not include a public body, trade union or municipality.

"remediation agreement" means an agreement, between an organization accused of having committed an offence and a prosecutor, to stay any proceedings related to that offence if the organization complies with the terms of the agreement.

"victim" has the same meaning as in section 2 but, with respect to an offence under section 3 or 4 of the *Corruption of Foreign Public Officials Act*, it includes any person outside Canada.

(2) For the purposes of this Part, a third party not referred to in section 2.2 may also act on a victim's behalf when authorized to do so by the court, if the victim requests it or the prosecutor deems it appropriate. 2018, c. 12, s. 404.

PURPOSE.

715.31 The purpose of this Part is to establish a remediation agreement regime that is applicable to organizations alleged to have committed an offence and that has the following objectives:

(*a*) to denounce an organization's wrongdoing and the harm that the wrongdoing has caused to victims or to the community;

(*b*) to hold the organization accountable for its wrongdoing through effective, proportionate and dissuasive penalties;

(*c*) to contribute to respect for the law by imposing an obligation on the organization to put in place corrective measures and promote a compliance culture;

(*d*) to encourage voluntary disclosure of the wrongdoing;

(*e*) to provide reparations for harm done to victims or to the community; and

(*f*) to reduce the negative consequences of the wrongdoing for persons — employees, customers, pensioners and others — who did not engage in the wrongdoing, while holding responsible those individuals who did engage in that wrongdoing. 2018, c. 12, s. 404.

CONDITIONS FOR REMEDIATION AGREEMENT / Factors to consider / Factors not to consider.

715.32 (1) The prosecutor may enter into negotiations for a remediation agreement with an organization alleged to have committed an offence if the following conditions are met:

(*a*) the prosecutor is of the opinion that there is a reasonable prospect of conviction with respect to the offence;

(*b*) the prosecutor is of the opinion that the act or omission that forms the basis of the offence did not cause and was not likely to have caused serious bodily harm or death, or injury to national defence or national security, and was not committed for the benefit of, at the direction of, or in association with, a criminal organization or terrorist group;

(*c*) the prosecutor is of the opinion that negotiating the agreement is in the public interest and appropriate in the circumstances; and

(*d*) the Attorney General has consented to the negotiation of the agreement.

(2) For the purposes of paragraph (1)(*c*), the prosecutor must consider the following factors:

(*a*) the circumstances in which the act or omission that forms the basis of the offence was brought to the attention of investigative authorities;

(*b*) the nature and gravity of the act or omission and its impact on any victim;

(*c*) the degree of involvement of senior officers of the organization in the act or omission;

(*d*) whether the organization has taken disciplinary action, including termination of employment, against any person who was involved in the act or omission;

(*e*) whether the organization has made reparations or taken other measures to remedy the harm caused by the act or omission and to prevent the commission of similar acts or omissions;

(*f*) whether the organization has identified or expressed a willingness to identify any person involved in wrongdoing related to the act or omission;

(*g*) whether the organization — or any of its representatives — was convicted of an offence or sanctioned by a regulatory body, or whether it entered into a previous remediation agreement or other settlement, in Canada or elsewhere, for similar acts or omissions;

(*h*) whether the organization — or any of its representatives — is alleged to have committed any other offences, including those not listed in the schedule to this Part; and

(*i*) any other factor that the prosecutor considers relevant.

(3) Despite paragraph (2)(*i*), if the organization is alleged to have committed an offence under section 3 or 4 of the *Corruption of Foreign Public Officials Act*, the prosecutor must not consider the national economic interest, the potential effect on relations with a state other than Canada or the identity of the organization or individual involved. 2018, c. 12, s. 404.

NOTICE TO ORGANIZATION — INVITATION TO NEGOTIATE / **Admissions not admissible in evidence.**

715.33 (1) If the prosecutor wishes to negotiate a remediation agreement, they must give the organization written notice of the offer to enter into negotiations and the notice must include

(*a*) a summary description of the offence to which the agreement would apply;

(*b*) an indication of the voluntary nature of the negotiation process;

(*c*) an indication of the legal effects of the agreement;

(*d*) an indication that, by agreeing to the terms of this notice, the organization explicitly waives the inclusion of the negotiation period and the period during which the agreement is in force in any assessment of the reasonableness of the delay between the day on which the charge is laid and the end of trial;

(*e*) an indication that negotiations must be carried out in good faith and that the organization must provide all information requested by the prosecutor that the organization is aware of or can obtain through reasonable efforts, including information enabling the identification of any person involved in the act or omission that forms the basis of the offence or any wrongdoing related to that act or omission;

(*f*) an indication of how the information disclosed by the organization during the negotiations may be used, subject to subsection (2);

(*g*) a warning that knowingly making false or misleading statements or knowingly providing false or misleading information during the negotiations may lead to the recommencement of proceedings or prosecution for obstruction of justice;

(*h*) an indication that either party may withdraw from the negotiations by providing written notice to the other party;

(*i*) an indication that reasonable efforts must be made by both parties to identify any victim as soon as practicable; and

(*j*) a deadline to accept the offer to negotiate according to the terms of the notice.

(2) No admission, confession or statement accepting responsibility for a given act or omission made by the organization during the negotiations is admissible in evidence against that organization in any civil or criminal proceedings related to that act or omission, except those contained in the statement of facts or admission of responsibility referred to in paragraphs 715.34(1)(*a*) and (*b*), if the parties reach an agreement and it is approved by the court. 2018, c. 12, s. 404.

MANDATORY CONTENTS OF AGREEMENT / **Admissions not admissible in evidence / Optional content of agreement.**

715.34 (1) A remediation agreement must include

(*a*) a statement of facts related to the offence that the organization is alleged to have committed and an undertaking by the organization not to make or condone any public statement that contradicts those facts;

(*b*) the organization's admission of responsibility for the act or omission that forms the basis of the offence;

(*c*) an indication of the obligation for the organization to provide any other information that will assist in identifying any person involved in the act or omission, or any wrongdoing related to that act or omission, that the organization becomes aware of, or can obtain through reasonable efforts, after the agreement has been entered into;

(*d*) an indication of the obligation for the organization to cooperate in any investigation, prosecution or other proceeding in Canada — or elsewhere if the prosecutor considers it appropriate — resulting from the act or omission, including by providing information or testimony;

(*e*) with respect to any property, benefit or advantage identified in the agreement that was obtained or derived directly or indirectly from the act or omission, an obligation for the organization to

(i) forfeit it to Her Majesty in right of Canada, to be disposed of in accordance with paragraph 4(1)(*b*.2) of the *Seized Property Management Act*,

(ii) forfeit it to Her Majesty in right of a province, to be disposed of as the Attorney General directs, or

(iii) otherwise deal with it, as the prosecutor directs;

(*f*) an indication of the obligation for the organization to pay a penalty to the Receiver General or to the treasurer of a province, as the case may be, for each offence to which the agreement applies, the amount to be paid and any other terms respecting payment;

(*g*) an indication of any reparations, including restitution consistent with paragraph 738(1)(*a*) or (*b*), that the organization is required to make to a victim or a statement by the prosecutor of the reasons why reparations to a victim are not appropriate in the circumstances and an indication of any measure required in lieu of reparations to a victim;

(*h*) an indication of the obligation for the organization to pay a victim surcharge for each offence to which the agreement applies, other than an offence under section 3 or 4 of the *Corruption of Foreign Public Officials Act*, the amount to be paid and any other terms respecting payment;

(*i*) an indication of the obligation for the organization to report to the prosecutor on the implementation of the agreement and an indication of the manner in which the report is to be made and any other terms respecting reporting;

(*j*) an indication of the legal effects of the agreement;

(*k*) an acknowledgement by the organization that the agreement has been made in good faith and that the information it has provided during the negotiation is accurate and complete and a commitment that it will continue to provide accurate and complete information while the agreement is in force;

(*l*) an indication of the use that can be made of information obtained as a result of the agreement, subject to subsection (2);

(*m*) a warning that the breach of any term of the agreement may lead to an application by the prosecutor for termination of the agreement and a recommencement of proceedings;

(*n*) an indication of the obligation for the organization not to deduct, for income tax purposes, the costs of any reparations or other measures referred to in paragraph (*g*) or any other costs incurred to fulfil the terms of the agreement;

(*o*) a notice of the prosecutor's right to vary or terminate the agreement with the approval of the court; and

(*p*) an indication of the deadline by which the organization must meet the terms of the agreement.

(2) No admission, confession or statement accepting responsibility for a given act or omission made by the organization as a result of the agreement is admissible in evidence against that organization in any civil or criminal proceedings related to that act or omission, except those contained in the statement of facts and admission of

responsibility referred to in paragraphs (1)(*a*) and (*b*), if the agreement is approved by the court.

(3) A remediation agreement may include, among other things,

(*a*) an indication of the obligation for the organization to establish, implement or enhance compliance measures to address any deficiencies in the organization's policies, standards or procedures — including those related to internal control procedures and employee training — that may have allowed the act or omission;

(*b*) an indication of the obligation for the organization to reimburse the prosecutor for any costs identified in the agreement that are related to its administration and that have or will be incurred by the prosecutor; and

(*c*) an indication of the fact that an independent monitor has been appointed, as selected with the prosecutor's approval, to verify and report to the prosecutor on the organization's compliance with the obligation referred to in paragraph (*a*), or any other obligation in the agreement identified by the prosecutor, as well as an indication of the organization's obligations with respect to that monitor, including the obligations to cooperate with the monitor and pay the monitor's costs. 2018, c. 12, s. 404.

INDEPENDENT MONITOR — CONFLICT OF INTEREST.

715.35 A candidate for appointment as an independent monitor must notify the prosecutor in writing of any previous or ongoing relationship, in particular with the organization or any of its representatives, that may have a real or perceived impact on the candidate's ability to provide an independent verification. 2018, c. 12, s. 404.

DUTY TO INFORM VICTIMS / Interpretation / Reasons.

715.36 (1) After an organization has accepted the offer to negotiate according to the terms of the notice referred to in section 715.33, the prosecutor must take reasonable steps to inform any victim, or any third party that is acting on the victim's behalf, that a remediation agreement may be entered into.

(2) The duty to inform any victim is to be construed and applied in a manner that is reasonable in the circumstances and not likely to interfere with the proper administration of justice, including by causing interference with prosecutorial discretion or compromising, hindering or causing excessive delay to the negotiation of an agreement or its conclusion.

(3) If the prosecutor elects not to inform a victim or third party under subsection (1), they must provide the court, when applying for approval of the agreement, with a statement of the reasons why it was not appropriate to do so in the circumstances. 2018, c. 12, s. 404.

APPLICATION FOR COURT APPROVAL / Coming into force / Consideration of victims / Victim or community impact statement / Victim surcharge / Approval order / Stay of proceedings / Other proceedings / Limitation period.

715.37 (1) When the prosecutor and the organization have agreed to the terms of a remediation agreement, the prosecutor must apply to the court in writing for an order approving the agreement.

(2) The coming into force of the agreement is subject to the approval of the court.

(3) To determine whether to approve the agreement, the court hearing an application must consider

(*a*) any reparations, statement and other measure referred to in paragraph 715.34(1)(*g*);

(*b*) any statement made by the prosecutor under subsection 715.36(3);
(*c*) any victim or community impact statement presented to the court; and
(*d*) any victim surcharge referred to in paragraph 715.34(1)(*h*).

(4) For the purpose of paragraph (3)(*c*), the rules provided for in sections 722 to 722.2 apply, other than subsection 722(6), with any necessary modifications and, in particular,

(*a*) a victim or community impact statement, or any other evidence concerning any victim, must be considered when determining whether to approve the agreement under subsection (6);
(*b*) the inquiry referred to in subsection 722(2) must be made at the hearing of the application; and
(*c*) the duty of the clerk under section 722.1 or subsection 722.2(5) is deemed to be the duty of the prosecutor to make reasonable efforts to provide a copy of the statement to the organization or counsel for the organization as soon as feasible after the prosecutor obtains it.

(5) For the purpose of paragraph 715.34(1)(*h*), the amount of the victim surcharge is 30% of any penalty referred to in paragraph 715.34(1)(*f*), or any other percentage that the prosecutor deems appropriate in the circumstances, and is payable to the treasurer of the province in which the application for approval referred to in section 715.37 is made.

(6) The court must, by order, approve the agreement if it is satisfied that

(*a*) the organization is charged with an offence to which the agreement applies;
(*b*) the agreement is in the public interest; and
(*c*) the terms of the agreement are fair, reasonable and proportionate to the gravity of the offence.

(7) As soon as practicable after the court approves the agreement, the prosecutor must direct the clerk or other proper officer of the court to make an entry on the record that the proceedings against the organization in respect of any offence to which the agreement applies are stayed by that direction and that entry must be made immediately, after which time the proceedings shall be stayed accordingly.

(8) No other proceedings may be initiated against the organization for the same offence while the agreement is in force.

(9) The running of a limitation period in respect of any offence to which the agreement applies is suspended while the agreement is in force. 2018, c. 12, s. 404.

VARIATION ORDER.

715.38 On application by the prosecutor, the court must, by order, approve any modification to a remediation agreement if the court is satisfied that the agreement continues to meet the conditions set out in subsection 715.37(6). On approval, the modification is deemed to form part of the agreement. 2018, c. 12, s. 404.

TERMINATION ORDER / Recommencement of proceedings / Stay of proceedings.

715.39 (1) On application by the prosecutor, the court must, by order, terminate the agreement if it is satisfied that the organization has breached a term of the agreement.

(2) As soon as the order is made, proceedings stayed in accordance with subsection 715.37(7) may be recommenced, without a new information or a new indictment, as the case may be, by the prosecutor giving notice of the recommencement to the clerk of the court in which the stay of the proceedings was entered.

(3) If no notice is given within one year after the order is made under subsection (1), or before the expiry of the time within which the proceedings could have been commenced,

whichever is earlier, the proceedings are deemed never to have been commenced. 2018, c. 12, s. 404.

ORDER DECLARING SUCCESSFUL COMPLETION / **Stay of proceedings.**

715.4 (1) On application by the prosecutor, the court must, by order, declare that the terms of the agreement were met if it is satisfied that the organization has complied with the agreement.

(2) The order stays the proceedings against the organization for any offence to which the agreement applies, the proceedings are deemed never to have been commenced and no other proceedings may be initiated against the organization for the same offence. 2018, c. 12, s. 404.

DEADLINE / **Deeming.**

715.41 (1) The prosecutor must, as soon as practicable after the deadline referred to in paragraph 715.34(1)(*p*), apply to the court in writing for a variation order under section 715.38, including to extend the deadline, an order terminating the agreement under section 715.39 or an order under section 715.4 declaring that its terms were met and the court may issue any of these orders as it deems appropriate.

(2) The agreement is deemed to remain in force until a court issues an order terminating it or declaring that its terms were met. 2018, c. 12, s. 404.

PUBLICATION / **Decision not to publish / Factors to be considered / Conditions / Review of decision.**

715.42 (1) Subject to subsection (2), the following must be published by the court as soon as practicable:

(*a*) the remediation agreement approved by the court;

(*b*) an order made under any of sections 715.37 to 715.41 and the reasons for that order or the reasons for the decision not to make that order; and

(*c*) a decision made under subsection (2) or (5) and the reasons for that decision.

(2) The court may decide not to publish the agreement or any order or reasons referred to in paragraph (1)(*b*), in whole or in part, if it is satisfied that the non-publication is necessary for the proper administration of justice.

(3) To decide whether the proper administration of justice requires making the decision referred to in subsection (2), the court must consider

(*a*) society's interest in encouraging the reporting of offences and the participation of victims in the criminal justice process;

(*b*) whether it is necessary to protect the identity of any victims, any person not engaged in the wrongdoing and any person who brought the wrongdoing to the attention of investigative authorities;

(*c*) the prevention of any adverse effect to any ongoing investigation or prosecution;

(*d*) whether effective alternatives to the decision referred to in subsection (2) are available in the circumstances;

(*e*) the salutary and deleterious effects of making the decision referred to in subsection (2); and

(*f*) any other factor that the court considers relevant.

(4) The court may make its decision subject to any conditions that it considers appropriate, including a condition related to the duration of non-publication.

(5) On application by any person, the court must review the decision made under subsection (2) to determine whether the non-publication continues to be necessary for the proper administration of justice. If the court is satisfied that the non-publication is

no longer necessary, it must publish the agreement, order or reasons, as the case may be, in whole or in part, as soon as practicable. 2018, c. 12, s. 404; 2018, c. 27, s. 686.

REGULATIONS / Amendment of schedule / Deleting offence.

715.43 (1) On the recommendation of the Minister of Justice, the Governor in Council may make regulations generally for the purposes of carrying out this Part, including regulations respecting

- **(*a*) the form of the remediation agreement; and**
- **(*b*) the verification of compliance by an independent monitor, including**
  - **(i) the qualifications for monitors,**
  - **(ii) the process to select a monitor,**
  - **(iii) the form and content of a conflict of interest notification, and**
  - **(iv) reporting requirements.**

(2) On the recommendation of the Minister of Justice, the Governor in Council may, by order, amend the schedule by adding or deleting any offence to which a remediation agreement may apply.

(3) If the Governor in Council orders the deletion of an offence from the schedule to this Part, this Part continues to apply to an organization alleged to have committed that offence if a notice referred to in section 715.33 respecting that offence was sent to the organization before the day on which the order comes into force. 2018, c. 12, s. 404.

PART XXIII / PUNISHMENT (old provision)

Repealed 1995, c. 22, s. 6 (in force Sept. 3, 1996).

PART XXIII / SENTENCING

Interpretation

DEFINITIONS / "Accused" / "Alternative measures" / "Court" / "Fine".

716. In this Part,

"accused" includes a defendant;

"alternative measures" means measures other than judicial proceedings under this Act used to deal with a person who is eighteen years of age or over and alleged to have committed an offence;

"court" means

- **(*a*) a superior court of criminal jurisdiction,**
- **(*b*) a court of criminal jurisdiction,**
- **(*c*) a justice or provincial court judge acting as a summary conviction court under Part XXVII, or**
- **(*d*) a court that hears an appeal;**

"fine" includes a pecuniary penalty or other sum of money, but does not include restitution. 1999, c. 5, s. 29.

CROSS-REFERENCES

Age is determined by s. 30 of the *Interpretation Act*, R.S.C. 1985, c. I-21. Extrajudicial measures for persons under 18 years of age are dealt with under ss. 4 to 10 of the *Youth Criminal Justice Act*.

CR. CODE

Alternative Measures

WHEN ALTERNATIVE MEASURES MAY BE USED / Restriction on use / Admissions not admissible in evidence / No bar to proceedings / Laying of information, etc.

717. (1) Alternative measures may be used to deal with a person alleged to have committed an offence only if it is not inconsistent with the protection of society and the following conditions are met:

(*a*) the measures are part of a program of alternative measures authorized by the Attorney General or the Attorney General's delegate or authorized by a person, or a person within a class of persons, designated by the lieutenant governor in council of a province;

(*b*) the person who is considering whether to use the measures is satisfied that they would be appropriate, having regard to the needs of the person alleged to have commited the offence and the interests of society and of the victim;

(*c*) the person, having been informed of the alternative measures, fully and freely consents to participate therein;

(*d*) the person has, before consenting to participate in the alternative measures, been advised of the right to be represented by counsel;

(*e*) the person accepts responsibility for the act or omission that forms the basis of the offence that the person is alleged to have committed;

(*f*) there is, in the opinion of the Attorney General or the Attorney General's agent, sufficient evidence to proceed with the prosecution of the offence; and

(*g*) the prosecution of the offence is not in any way barred at law.

(2) Alternative measures shall not be used to deal with a person alleged to have committed an offence if the person

(*a*) denies participation or involvement in the commission of the offence; or

(*b*) expresses the wish to have any charge against the person dealt with by the court.

(3) No admission, confession or statement accepting responsibility for a given act or omission made by a person alleged to have committed an offence as a condition of the person being dealt with by alternative measures is admissible in evidence against that person in any civil or criminal proceedings.

(4) The use of alternative measures in respect of a person alleged to have committed an offence is not a bar to proceedings against the person under this Act, but, if a charge is laid against that person in respect of that offence,

(*a*) where the court is satisfied on a balance of probabilities that the person has totally complied with the terms and conditions of the alternative measures, the court shall dismiss the charge; and

(*b*) where the court is satisfied on a balance of probabilities that the person has partially complied with the terms and conditions of the alternative measures, the court may dismiss the charge if, in the opinion of the court, the prosecution of the charge would be unfair, having regard to the circumstances and that person's performance with respect to the alternative measures.

(5) Subject to subsection (4), nothing in this section shall be construed as preventing any person from laying an information, obtaining the issue or confirmation of any process, or proceeding with the prosecution of any offence, in accordance with law. 1995, c. 22, s. 6.

CROSS-REFERENCES

"Alternative measures" are defined in s. 716. "Attorney General" is defined in s. 2. Sections 717.1 to 717.4 deal with the keeping and disclosure of records of the person's involvement in alternative measures. Where the person is found guilty of an offence then pursuant to s. 721(3)(*c*), the pre-sentence report should make reference to any history of use of alternative measures.

SYNOPSIS

This section gives statutory recognition to alternative measure or diversion programmes for adult accused. Alternative measures are means of dealing with persons alleged to have committed offences where it is appropriate not to invoke the judicial procedure provided for by the *Criminal Code*. Where the person fully complies with the alternative measures, any charges based on the same offence will be dismissed. Where the person has only partially complied with the alternative measures, the court is to dismiss the charge if it is of the opinion that prosecution would be unfair. This sections sets out the pre-conditions for invoking alternative measures.

In summary, the use of alternative measures must be in accordance with a programme approved by the Attorney General or the Attorney General's delegate or by a person or class of persons designated by the Lieutenant Governor in Council.

The accused's participation in the programme is to be voluntary; thus the accused must fully and freely consent to the programme and be informed of the right to consult counsel. The accused must accept responsibility for the act that formed the basis of the offence alleged to have been committed. In determining whether the use of alternative measures is appropriate, the Attorney General's delegate must have regard to the interests of the victim and society and the needs of the accused. The delegate must be satisifed that there would have been sufficient evidence to prosecute the offence were alternative measures not invoked and that there is no legal bar to the prosecution such as a limitation period. If the accused denies participation in the offence or wishes to have the charges dealt with in court, alternative measures may not be used.

Subsection (3) provides that any statement made by the accused is inadmissible in evidence in civil or criminal proceedings if the statement was made "as a condition for the person being dealt with by alternative measures".

ANNOTATIONS

The Crown's decision to deny an accused entry to an alternative measures program established under this section is generally not subject to judicial review: *Okimow v. Saskatchewan (Attorney General)*, 2000 SKQB 311. On the limited scope of judicial review of discretionary prosecutorial decisions generally, see: *R. v. Anderson*, [2014] 2 S.C.R. 167, 311 C.C.C. (3d) 1.

RECORDS OF PERSONS DEALT WITH.

717.1 Sections 717.2 to 717.4 apply only in respect of persons who have been dealt with by alternative measures, regardless of the degree of their compliance with the terms and conditions of the alternative measures. 1995, c. 22, s. 6.

CROSS-REFERENCES

"Alternative measures" are defined in s. 716. Section 717 sets out when alternative measures may be used and the consequences of full or partial compliance with the measures on any charges laid in respect of the offence for which the alternative measures were invoked. Sections 717.2 to 717.4 set out the circumstances under which records of a person's participation in alternative measures may be kept and disclosed. Where the person is found guilty of an offence then pursuant to s. 721(3)(*c*), the pre-sentence report should make reference to any history of use of alternative measures.

POLICE RECORDS / Disclosure by peace officer / Idem.

717.2 (1) A record relating to any offence alleged to have been committed by a person, including the original or a copy of any fingerprints or photographs of the person, may be kept by any police force responsible for, or participating in, the investigation of the offence.

(2) A peace officer may disclose to any person any information in a record kept pursuant to this section that it is necessary to disclose in the conduct of the investigation of an offence.

(3) A peace officer may disclose to an insurance company any information in a record kept pursuant to this section for the purpose of investigating any claim arising out of an offence committed or alleged to have been committed by the person to whom the record relates. 1995, c. 22, s. 6.

CROSS-REFERENCES

"Alternative measures" are defined in s. 716. Section 717 sets out when alternative measures may be used and the consequences of full or partial compliance with the measures on any charges laid in respect of the offence for which the alternative measures were invoked. Sections 717.3 and 717.4 set out the circumstances under which records of a person's participation in alternative measures may be kept and disclosed by the government. Where the person is subsequently found guilty of an offence then pursuant to s. 721(3)(*c*), the pre-sentence report should make reference to any history of use of alternative measures.

SYNOPSIS

This section applies to records kept by the police in relation to any offence alleged to have been committed by a person who has been dealt with by way of alternative measures in relation to that offence. Subsection (1) authorizes the police to keep records, including fingerprint records and photographs of the accused. The police may disclose these records to any person where it is necessary for the investigation of an offence, and may disclose the records to an insurance company for the purpose of investigating a claim arising out of an offence allegedly committed by the person who was subject to the alternative measures.

GOVERNMENT RECORDS / Private records.

717.3 (1) A department or agency of any government in Canada may keep records containing information obtained by the department or agency

(*a*) for the purposes of an investigation of an offence alleged to have been committed by a person;

(*b*) for use in proceedings against a person under this Act; or

(*c*) as a result of the use of alternative measures to deal with a person.

(2) Any person or organization may keep records containing information obtained by the person or organization as a result of the use of alternative measures to deal with a person alleged to have committed an offence. 1995, c. 22, s. 6.

CROSS-REFERENCES

"Alternative measures" are defined in s. 716. Section 717 sets out when alternative measures may be used and the consequences of full or partial compliance with the measures on any charges laid in respect of the offence for which the alternative measures were invoked. Sections 717.2 and 717.4 set out the circumstances under which police records may be kept and disclosed and when police and government records kept pursuant to s. 717.2 and this section may be disclosed. Where the person is found guilty of an offence then pursuant to s. 721(3)(*c*), the pre-sentence report should make reference to any history of use of alternative measures.

SYNOPSIS

This section authorizes government agencies to keep records relating to a person involved in an alternative measures programme. Subsection (2) authorizes non-governmental agencies to also keep such records. Presumably this subsection relates to organizations that participate in alternative measures programmes.

DISCLOSURE OF RECORDS / Subsequent disclosure / Information, copies / Evidence / Idem.

717.4 (1) Any record that is kept pursuant to section 717.2 or 717.3 may be made available to

(*a*) any judge or court for any purpose relating to proceedings relating to offences committed or alleged to have been committed by the person to whom the record relates;

(*b*) any peace officer

(i) for the purpose of investigating any offence that the person is suspected on reasonable grounds of having committed, or in respect of which the person has been arrested or charged, or

(ii) for any purpose related to the administration of the case to which the record relates;

(*c*) any member of a department or agency of a government in Canada, or any agent thereof, that is

(i) engaged in the administration of alternative measures in respect of the person, or

(ii) preparing a report in respect of the person pursuant to this Act; or

(*d*) any other person who is deemed, or any person within a class of persons that is deemed, by a judge of a court to have a valid interest in the record, to the extent directed by the judge, if the judge is satisfied that the disclosure is

(i) desirable in the public interest for research or statistical purposes, or

(ii) desirable in the interest of the proper administration of justice.

(2) Where a record is made available for inspection to any person under subparagraph (1)(*d*)(i), that person may subsequently disclose information contained in the record, but may not disclose the information in any form that would reasonably be expected to identify the person to whom it relates.

(3) Any person to whom a record is authorized to be made available under this section may be given any information contained in the record and may be given a copy of any part of the record.

(4) Nothing in this section authorizes the introduction into evidence of any part of a record that would not otherwise be admissible in evidence.

(5) A record kept pursuant to section 717.2 or 717.3 may not be introduced into evidence, except for the purposes set out in paragraph 721(3)(*c*), more than two years after the end of the period for which the person agreed to participate in the alternative measures. 1995, c. 22, s. 6.

CROSS-REFERENCES

"Alternative measures" and "court" are defined in s. 716. Section 717 sets out when alternative measures may be used and the consequences of full or partial compliance with the measures on any charges laid in respect of the offence for which the alternative measures were invoked. Sections 717.2 and 717.3 authorize the police, government agencies and non-governmental organizations to keep records in relation to persons dealt with through alternative measures programmes. Where the person is found guilty of an offence then pursuant to s. 721(3)(*c*), the pre-sentence report should make reference to any history of use of alternative measures.

SYNOPSIS

This section sets out the circumstances under which records relating to persons who have been dealt with by alternative measures may be disclosed. Such records may be disclosed to a court for "any purpose" relating to proceedings relating to offences committed or allegedly committed by the person to whom the record relates. The records may also be disclosed to peace officers for certain specified purposes and to government agencies involved in administering the alternative measures programme for that person, or preparing a report under the *Criminal Code* in respect of that person such as a pre-sentence report under s. 721. Subsection (1)(*d*) gives a court residual discretion to authorize disclosure of records to a person with a valid interest in the record if disclosure is in the interest of the proper administration of justice, or it is in the public interest to disclose for research or statistical purposes.

If the disclosure order is made for these latter purposes, any subsequent disclosure of information by the researcher cannot identify the person to whom the record relates. While this section authorizes disclosure of records it does not otherwise alter the rules of evidence.

Subsection (5) sets out a limitation on the admissibility of these records. They may not be introduced into evidence more than two years after the end of the period for which the person agreed to participate in the alternative measures. There is one exception to this limitation period, that is, where the record is included as part of a pre-sentence report prepared in accordance with s. 721(3)(*c*).

Purpose and Principles of Sentencing

PURPOSE.

718. The fundamental purpose of sentencing is to protect society and to contribute, along with crime prevention initiatives, to respect for the law and the maintenance of a just, peaceful and safe society by imposing just sanctions that have one or more of the following objectives:

(*a*) to denounce unlawful conduct and the harm done to victims or to the community that is caused by unlawful conduct;

(*b*) to deter the offender and other persons from committing offences;

(*c*) to separate offenders from society, where necessary;

(*d*) to assist in rehabilitating offenders;

(*e*) to provide reparations for harm done to victims or to the community; and

(*f*) to promote a sense of responsibility in offenders, and acknowledgment of the harm done to victims or to the community. 1995, c. 22, s. 6; 2015, c. 13, s. 23.

CROSS-REFERENCES

Some of the principles that the court are to apply in attempting to carry out the purpose and objectives set out in this section are listed in ss. 718.1 and 718.2.

Section 718.01 provides that, in cases of abuse of persons under the age of 18 years, the primary considerations are denunciation and deterrence.

SYNOPSIS

This sections sets out the fundamental purpose of sentencing and the objectives which the sentence should attempt to achieve. These objectives are denunciation, general and specific deterrence, separation of offenders, rehabilitation, making reparations and promotion of a sense of responsibility in the offender.

ANNOTATIONS

In enacting this section, Parliament has mandated that expanded use be made of restorative principles in sentencing because of the general failure of incarceration to rehabilitate offenders and reintegrate them into society. Because it is served in the community, a conditional sentence imposed under s. 742.1 will generally be more effective than incarceration at achieving the restorative objectives of rehabilitation: *R. v. Proulx*, [2000] 1 S.C.R. 61, 140 C.C.C. (3d) 449.

OBJECTIVES — OFFENCES AGAINST CHILDREN.

718.01 When a court imposes a sentence for an offence that involved the abuse of a person under the age of eighteen years, it shall give primary consideration to the objectives of denunciation and deterrence of such conduct. 2005, c. 32, s. 24.

CROSS-REFERENCES

The other objectives of sentencing are set out in s. 718. Age is determined by reference to s. 30 of the *Interpretation Act*, R.S.C. 1985, c. I-21. Under s. 718.2(*a*)(ii), evidence the offender abused a person under the age of 18 years is deemed to be an aggravating circumstance.

SYNOPSIS

This section enacts a special rule for sentencing in child abuse cases, that is, abuse of persons under the age of 18 years. In such cases, denunciation and deterrence are to be the primary objectives.

ANNOTATIONS

Giving "primary consideration" to denunciation and deterrence requires a meaningful assessment of how the facts of the offence and the circumstances of the offender relate to denunciation and deterrence and an acknowledgment that substantial weight must be given to these objectives so that they are properly vindicated in the sentencing process: *R. v. Branton* (2013), 301 C.C.C. (3d) 408 (N.L.C.A.). See also *R. v. Allen* (2012), 293 C.C.C. (3d) 455 (B.C.C.A.).

OBJECTIVES — OFFENCE AGAINST PEACE OFFICER OR OTHER JUSTICE SYSTEM PARTICIPANT.

718.02 When a court imposes a sentence for an offence under subsection 270(1), section 270.01 or 270.02 or paragraph 423.1(1)(*b*), the court shall give primary consideration to the objectives of denunciation and deterrence of the conduct that forms the basis of the offence. 2009, c. 22, s. 18.

CROSS-REFERENCES

The purpose and objectives of sentencing are set out in s. 718. Section 718.01 requires the court to give primary consideration to the objectives of denunciation and deterrence for offences involving abuse of a person under the age of 18 years. The fundamental principle of sentencing, proportionality, is given statutory recognition by s. 718.1. The procedure for determining whether the various mitigating or aggravating factors apply is set out in ss. 723 to 729. Other provisions of the Code deem certain circumstances to be considered aggravating factors, such as s. 163.1(4.3), committing child pornography offence with intent to profit; s. 255.1, blood alcohol level in excess of .16 for various vehicle operating offences; and s. 264(4), person committing criminal harassment while in breach of court order. Section 348.1 enacts the "home invasion" aggravating circumstance for the offences under ss. 279(2), 343, 346 and 348.

SYNOPSIS

This section enacts a special rule for sentencing in cases of assaulting a peace officer with a weapon or causing bodily harm (s. 270.01); aggravated assault of a peace officer (s. 270.02); and intimidation of a justice system participant to impede that person in the performance of their duty (s. 423.1(1)(*b*)). In accordance with this section, the judge is to give primary consideration to the objectives of denunciation and deterrence.

OBJECTIVES — OFFENCE AGAINST CERTAIN ANIMALS.

718.03 When a court imposes a sentence for an offence under subsection 445.01(1), the court shall give primary consideration to the objectives of denunciation and deterrence of the conduct that forms the basis of the offence. 2015, c. 34, s. 4.

CROSS-REFERENCES

The purpose and objectives of sentencing are set out in s. 718. The other statutory principles of sentencing are set out in s. 718.2.

SYNOPSIS

This section enacts a special rule for sentencing in cases of killing or injuring law enforcement or military animals aiding in the course of duty, or doing the same to service animals. In accordance with this section, the judge is to give primary consideration to the objectives of denunciation and deterrence.

FUNDAMENTAL PRINCIPLE.

718.1 A sentence must be proportionate to the gravity of the offence and the degree of responsibility of the offender. 1995, c. 22, s. 6.

CROSS-REFERENCES

The fundamental purpose and objectives of sentencing are set out in s. 718. The other statutory principles of sentencing are set out in s. 718.2.

SYNOPSIS

This section sets out the fundamental principle of proportionality.

ANNOTATIONS

The proportionality principle in this section requires that full consideration be given to both the gravity of the offence and the moral blameworthiness of the offender. Thus, any offence that meets the statutory prerequisites in s. 742.1 is eligible for a conditional sentence of imprisonment. There is no presumption that certain violent offences are not eligible: *R. v. Proulx*, [2000] 1 S.C.R. 61, 140 C.C.C. (3d) 449.

Proportionality is the cardinal principle that must guide appellate courts in considering the fitness of a sentence imposed on an offender. The more serious the crime and its consequences, or the greater the offender's degree of responsibility, the heavier the sentence will be: *R. c. Lacasse*, [2015] 3 S.C.R. 1089, 333 C.C.C. (3d) 450.

Note: The following cases were decided prior to the enactment of this section.

The fundamental nature of the proportionality principle arises out of the general principle in our law that criminal liability can only be imposed on persons who possess a morally culpable state of mind. At the outer limits this proportionality principle has a constitutional dimension. A sentence that is grossly disproportionate in the sense that it is so excessive as to outrage standards of decency will violate the prohibition against cruel and unusual punishment in s. 12 of the *Canadian Charter of Rights and Freedoms*: *R. v. M. (C.A.)*, [1996] 1 S.C.R. 500, 105 C.C.C. (3d) 327. In this case the court assimilated retribution into the principle of proportionality and distinugished it from vengeance.

> Retribution in a criminal context, by contrast, represents an objective, reasoned and measured determination of an appropriate punishment which properly reflects the *moral culpability* of the offender; having regard to the intentional risk-taking of the offender; the consequential harm caused by the offender; and the normative character of the offender's conduct. Furthermore, unlike

vengeance, retribution incorporates a principle of restraint; retribution requires the imposition of a just and appropriate punishment and *nothing more.* (at pp. 557-558 S.C.R.).

A useful review of the modern authorities on the principles of sentencing is found in *R. v. Mellstrom* (1975), 22 C.C.C. (2d) 472 (Alta. S.C. App. Div.), where it was also held that the sentence should be within the range of those contemporaneously imposed for similar offences and that the enormity of the tragic consequences of an offence should not be allowed to unduly distort the consideration of the court as to the appropriate penalty.

Where guilt depends upon the probable, not the actual result of an act, and it is clear that at the time of the act the probability of the actual results of the act would not have been on the accused's mind, it is an error for the trial judge on sentence to give undue weight to the actual rather than to the probable results of the act: *R. v. Griffin* (1975), 23 C.C.C. (2d) 11 (P.E.I.S.C.).

To consider judicially created guidelines as constituting a *de facto* minimum sentence is inconsistent with the fundamental principle of proportionality: *R. v. Jacko* (2010), 256 C.C.C. (3d) 113 (Ont. C.A.).

OTHER SENTENCING PRINCIPLES.

718.2 A court that imposes a sentence shall also take into consideration the following principles:

(*a*) a sentence should be increased or reduced to account for any relevant aggravating or mitigating circumstances relating to the offence or the offender, and, without limiting the generality of the foregoing,

(i) evidence that the offence was motivated by bias, prejudice or hate based on race, national or ethnic origin, language, colour, religion, sex, age, mental or physical disability, sexual orientation, or gender orientation or expression, or on any other similar factor,

(ii) evidence that the offender, in committing the offence, abused the offender's spouse or common-law partner,

(ii.1) evidence that the offender, in committing the offence, abused a person under the age of eighteen years,

(iii) evidence that the offender, in committing the offence, abused a position of trust or authority in relation to the victim,

(iii.1) evidence that the offence had a significant impact on the victim, considering their age and other personal circumstances, including their health and financial situation,

(iv) evidence that the offence was committed for the benefit of, at the direction of or in association with a criminal organization,

(v) evidence that the offence was a terrorism offence; or

(vi) evidence that the offence was committed while the offender was subject to a conditional sentence order made under section 742.1 or released on parole, statutory release or unescorted temporary absence under the *Corrections and Conditional Release Act*;

shall be deemed to be aggravating circumstances;

(*b*) a sentence should be similar to sentences imposed on similar offenders for similar offences committed in similar circumstances;

(*c*) where consecutive sentences are imposed, the combined sentence should not be unduly long or harsh;

(*d*) an offender should not be deprived of liberty, if less restrictive sanctions may be appropriate in the circumstances; and

(*e*) all available sanctions, other than imprisonment, that are reasonable in the circumstances and consistent with the harm done to victims or to the community should be considered for all offenders, with particular attention to the circumstances of Aboriginal offenders. 1995, c. 22, s. 6; 1997, c. 23, s. 17;

2000, c. 12, s. 95(*c*); 2001, c. 41, s. 20; 2005, c. 32, s. 25; 2012, c. 29, s. 2; 2015, c. 13, s. 24; c. 23, s. 16; 2017, c. 13, s. 4.

CROSS-REFERENCES

The terms "criminal organization", "common-law partner" and "terrorism offence" are defined in s. 2. Age is determined by reference to s. 30 of the *Interpretation Act*, R.S.C. 1985, c. I-21. The purpose and objectives of sentencing are set out in s. 718. Section 718.02 requires the court to give primary consideration to the objectives of denunciation and deterrence for offences of assaulting a peace officer with a weapon or causing bodily harm (s. 270.01); aggravated assault of a peace officer (s. 270.02); and intimidation of a justice system participant to impede that person in the performance of their duty (s. 423.1(1)(*b*)). Section 718.01 requires the court to give primary consideration to the objectives of denunciation and deterrence for offences involving abuse of a person under the age of 18 years. The fundamental principle of sentencing, proportionality, is given statutory recognition by s. 718.1. The procedure for determining whether the various mitigating or aggravating factors apply is set out in ss. 723 to 729. Section 10 of the *Controlled Drugs and Substances Act* sets out certain principles of particular application to sentencing in drug cases. Other provisions of the Code deem certain circumstances to be considered aggravating factors such as s. 163.1(4.3), committing child pornography offence with intent to profit; s. 255.1, blood alcohol level in excess of .16 for various vehicle operating offences; and s. 264(4), person committing criminal harassment while in breach of court order. Section 348.1 enacts the "home invasion" aggravating circumstance for the offences under ss. 279(2), 343, 346 and 348.

Sentencing principles for an organization are set out in s. 718.21.

SYNOPSIS

In attempting to carry out one or more of the objectives set out in s. 718 the court is to apply the principles set out in this section and s. 718.1. This section first directs the court to take into account the various relevant aggravating and mitigating circumstances, some of which are set out in this section. The court must then take into account the principle that like offenders should be treated alike and thus avoid unjustified disparity (para. (*b*)); the totality principle (para. (*c*)); the principle of restraint in use of incarceration and other sanctions that deprive the offender of liberty (para. (*d*)); and the principle that imprisonment should, within reason, be seen as a last resort, especially for aboriginal offenders (para. (*e*)).

Paragraph (*a*) sets out certain deemed aggravating factors. This section is not meant to be exhaustive in its list of aggravating factors, such as breach of a position of trust. Other aggravating factors developed by the courts still apply. Presumably, this section does not purport to be an an exhaustive list of sentencing principles.

ANNOTATIONS

Note: Some of the following cases were decided prior to the enactment of this section but were considered to be of assistance in applying this section.

Offences motivated by bias, prejudice or hate (para. (*a*)(i)) – An accused who commits offences of mischief to property which are motivated by racial or religious hatred cannot be sentenced for his beliefs. Those beliefs are, however, relevant in so far as they explain his actions and an offence which is directed against a particular racial or religious group is more heinous, as it attacks the very fabric of society and invites imitation and incites retaliation. Moreover, where the offence involves desecration of a place of worship, it is even more serious, especially where it is done to cause emotional upset and injury to the members of the congregation. Such offences require a more severe penalty than mischief which is done merely to damage property: *R. v. Lelas* (1990), 58 C.C.C. (3d) 568 (Ont. C.A.).

An assault which is racially motivated renders the offence more heinous and the sentence to be imposed in such a case must be one which expresses the public abhorrence for such conduct and their refusal to countenance it: *R. v. Ingram and Grimsdale* (1977), 35 C.C.C.

(2d) 376 (Ont. C.A.). In this case reformatory sentences for an unprovoked racially motivated assault which caused serious injury to the victim were raised to penitentiary terms.

Similarly, *R. v. Simms* (1990), 60 C.C.C. (3d) 499 (Alta. C.A.), where sentences for assault were substantially increased to take into account that the assaults were racially inspired by the accused who were adherents to or sympathizers with neo-Nazi organizations.

Paragraph (*a*)(i) can be seen as an expression of Canadian social values of respect for diversity and preservation and promotion of multiculturalism. It is more than simply a reaffirmation of existing sentencing principles but a direction to judges to give substantial weight to this aggravating factor. Nevertheless, the maximum sentence of life imprisonment for manslaughter was not appropriate given the offenders' relative youth, that all but one was a first offender and that the offence did not involve extended acts of brutality or torture. The offenders were, however, sentenced to periods of imprisonment ranging from 12 years to 15 years after taking into account credit for 18 months of pre-trial custody for the beating death of Sikh man on the grounds of his Temple. The offenders were members of a loosely knit Neo-Nazi, skinhead racist group: *R. v. Miloszewski*, [1999] B.C.J. No. 2710 (Prov. Ct.). An appeal by two of the offenders was dismissed: 264 W.A.C. 57 (B.C.C.A.), the court noting that, in this kind of gang crime committed together by like-minded persons motivated by hate carrying out a co-ordinated activity in pursuit of the aims of the gang, there is no room to make nice distinctions about degrees of participation.

Abuse of offender's spouse or child (para. (*a*)(ii)) – Where there is a serious offence involving violence to the person, then general and individual deterrence must be the paramount consideration in sentencing. This principle is also applicable to domestic violence and while not every incident requires imposition of a custodial term, such a term should be normal where significant bodily harm has been inflicted. Where the offence is even graver, involving persistent or repetitious and escalating violence towards the spouse, a longer term may be justified: *R. v. Inwood* (1989), 48 C.C.C. (3d) 173 (Ont. C.A.).

In domestic assaults, jail terms will usually be imposed unless the assault is very minor in nature or there are strong extenuating circumstances. Nevertheless, even on a charge of assault causing bodily harm, a discharge may be an appropriate disposition as where the accused was subjected to provocation by the victim, the incident was an isolated one and there was no significant bodily harm: *R. v. Mullin* (1990), 56 C.C.C. (3d) 476 (P.E.I.C.A.).

Domestic violence is a profound problem and when cases of beatings of a wife by a husband result in prosecution and conviction, then the courts have an opportunity, by their sentencing policy, to denounce such offences in clear terms and attempt to deter its recurrence on the part of the accused and on the part of other men. The starting point in sentencing in such cases would be to determine what would be a fit sentence if the man had assaulted a woman on the street or in a bar. The court must then examine circumstances which are peculiar because of the relationship. When a man assaults his wife or other female partner, his violence toward her constitutes a breach of a position of trust and is an agrravating factor. The paramount considerations in imposing sentence must be general deterrence and denunciation. The desire of the victim that the accused be returned to her and that she not be further victimized by being deprived of his income should not readily be permitted to prevail over the general sentencing policy that requires imprisonment of a man as not only an instrument of deterrence of other persons, but as a means of breaking the cycle of violence in the accused's home: *R. v. Brown; R. v. Highway; R. v. Umpherville* (1992), 73 C.C.C. (3d) 242 (Alta. C.A.); *R. v. Bonneteau* (1994), 93 C.C.C. (3d) 385 (Alta. C.A.). [**Note:** These decisions must now be read in light of the comments of the Supreme Court in *R. v. McDonnell, infra.*]

Position of trust or authority (para. (*a*)(iii)) – Theft by a person such as a bank manager who is in a position of trust requires imposition of a custodial sentence except in exceptional circumstances: *R. v. McEachern* (1978), 42 C.C.C. (2d) 189 (Ont. C.A.).

In a special situation where the accused upon conviction would lose his business position and benefits of 25 years an absolute discharge will be granted in lieu of a suspended sentence: *R. v. Tanguay* (1975), 24 C.C.C. (2d) 77 (Que. C.A.).

The breach of a position of trust for personal gain requires imposition of a deterrent sentence and, absent exceptional circumstances, some period of imprisonment is required. The offender's addiction to gambling is neither an exceptional circumstance justifying the imposition of a non-custodial sentence, nor a mitigating factor warranting a lesser sentence than would otherwise be required: *R. v. McIvor* (1996), 106 C.C.C. (3d) 285 (Alta. C.A.).

For sentencing purposes, a major sexual assault of a child by a parent or by a person who because of his relationship with the child is in a position of control and trust with respect to the child, should constitute a separate category of sexual assault. The starting point in those cases where there is a single major sexual assault upon a child should be four years. Sentencing in these cases is based mainly on the objectives of general deterrence and denunciation. The fact that there is a very real risk of very real psychological harm to the child is one which can be relied upon, even when there is no expert or non-expert evidence called in the particular case to establish that the child has suffered some specific traumatic effect. Factors such as repetition of the assaults, protracted confinement or kidnapping, gratuitous violence and injuries, threats to kill or hurt the child, extreme youth of the child, parental use of the child for the carnal pleasure of other adults, exposure of the child to pornography, transmission of venereal or other sexually-transmitted disease or pregnancy of the child resulting from the sexual assault will constitute aggravating factors. There may be mitigating factors such as a guilty plea: *R. v. S. (W.B.); R. v. P. (M.)* (1992), 73 C.C.C. (3d) 530 (Alta. C.A.). [**Note:** This case must now be read in light of the decision of the Supreme Court of Canada in *R. v. McDonnell, infra.*]

The Court of Appeal erred in substituting a conditional sentence for a sentence of imprisonment imposed upon the accused following his convictions for sexual assault and assault, given the gravity of the offences, which were violent and demeaning, and the accused's moral blameworthiness given his abuse of a position of authority over the complainant, a naive and vulnerable employee. The Court of Appeal failed to take sufficient account of the key aggravating factor, the accused's abuse of his position of authority by assaulting the complainant in the workplace: *R. v. R. (R.A.)*, [2000] 1 S.C.R. 1163, 140 C.C.C. (3d) 523. Similarly, *R. v. S. (R.N.)*, [2000] 1 S.C.R. 149, 140 C.C.C. (3d) 553, where the accused sexually assaulted his step-granddaughter over a period of years when she was five and eight years old.

Similarly, in *R. v. D. (D.)* (2002), 163 C.C.C. (3d) 471 (Ont. C.A.), the Ontario Court of Appeal held that sexual abuse of children by adult offenders in a position of trust on a regular basis over a substantial period of time warrants incarceration in the mid to upper single digit penitentiary range. Where full intercourse is accompanied by violence and threats, upper single digit to low double digit penitentiary range is appropriate. Where the conduct also involves psychological, emotional and physical brutalization, higher penalties are warranted.

Also see *R. v. Bunn*, [2000] 1 S.C.R. 183, 140 C.C.C. (3d) 505, where the accused lawyer was in a position of trust but a lengthy conditional sentence was imposed. The ruin and humiliation that the accused brought down on himself and his family, together with the loss of professional status could provide sufficient denunciation and deterrence when coupled with house arrest and community service. There were also mitigating circumstances relating to the circumstances of the appellant's family.

Benefit to criminal organization (para. (*a*)(iv)) – When sentencing an offender for an offence involving assistance to a criminal organization, the focus should be on the offender's intent to assist the organization. The fact that the conduct did not actually have the *effect* of assisting the organization is not mitigating: *R. v. Mastop* (2013), 303 C.C.C. (3d) 411 (B.C.C.A.), leave to appeal to S.C.C. refused 2014 CarswellBC 877.

It was an error of law to make a finding of criminal organization membership as an aggravating factor where there was no evidence that the offenders were a group with any structure or any degree of continuity beyond one incident of drug importation: *R. v. Kwok* (2015), 320 C.C.C. (3d) 212 (B.C.C.A.).

Membership in a criminal organization is not an aggravating factor unless the offence is either gang-sanctioned or related to membership in a gang: *R. v. Kirton* (2007), 219 C.C.C. (3d) 485 (Man. C.A.).

Disparity (para. (*b*)) – In a case decided prior to the enactment of this section the Supreme Court has emphasized that courts of appeal must exercise a measure of deference before intervening in the exercise of discretion by the trial judge on the basis of disparity. As the court pointed out, there is "no such thing as a uniform sentence for a particular crime." Sentencing is an individualized process and in any event, "sentences for a particular offence should be expected to vary some degree across various communities and regions in this country, as the 'just and appropriate' mix of accepted sentencing goals will depend on the needs and current conditions of and in the particular community where the crime occurred": *R. v. M. (C.A.)*, [1996] 1 S.C.R. 500, 105 C.C.C. (3d) 327.

As part of its duty to give guidance to the trial courts, the Alberta Court of Appeal is committed to the "starting-point approach" to sentencing whereby the court states with precision the appropriate sentence for a typical case while acknowledging that each actual case presents differences which might mitigate or aggravate. The advantage of such an approach is that it attempts to prevent unjustified disparity while taking into account the immense variety of circumstances which can be found in different cases involving a conviction for the same offence: *R. v. Sandercock* (1985), 22 C.C.C. (3d) 79 (Alta. C.A.). In this case, the court set the starting-point for a major sexual assault at three years' imprisonment.

In *R. v. Arcand* (2010), 264 C.C.C. (3d) 134, a five-judge panel of the Alberta Court of Appeal re-affirmed its commitment to the starting-point approach, again in the context of major sexual assaults. Judicial categorization of offences and starting point sentences remain important tools that sentencing judges must respect. The majority (3:2) held that unexplained deviation from a starting point sentence can, in itself, constitute an error in principle. See also *R. v. Hajar* (2016), 338 C.C.C. (3d) 477 (Alta. C.A.), where the court again re-inforced this approach and adopted a new starting point sentence of three years for "major sexual interference".

In *R. v. McDonnell*, [1997] 1 S.C.R. 948, 114 C.C.C. (3d) 436, the court extensively reviewed the starting-point approach adopted by several appellate courts, and, in particular, by the Alberta Court of Appeal. The court held that appellate courts may set out starting-point sentences as guides to trial judges. The sentencing judge's departure from the starting point established by the appellate court may be a factor to consider in determining whether the sentence is demonstrably unfit. A wide disparity between the starting-point for the offence and the sentence imposed, assuming that the Court of Appeal has set a reasonable starting-point, may suggest, but is not determinative of, unfitness. However, it is not open to the appellate court to create a category of offence within a statutory offence for the purposes of sentencing. In particular, it was not open to the Court of Appeal to create a category of "major sexual offence" based on a presumption of the likelihood of psychological harm from certain kinds of sexual acts.

In carrying out the function of minimizing disparity of sentences, appellate courts may fix ranges for particular categories of offences as guidelines for trial courts. The description of the category created and the logic behind the starting point must be stated with clarity. The appellate court must not, however, interfere with the duty of the sentencing judge to consider all relevant circumstances in sentencing: *R. v. Stone*, [1999] 2 S.C.R. 290, 134 C.C.C. (3d) 353.

In *R. v. Phun* (1997), 120 C.C.C. (3d) 560 (Alta. C.A.), the court considered the decision in *R. v. McDonnell, supra*, in the course of an extensive review of narcotic trafficking sentences in the province. The court held that the starting-point for low-level commercial trafficking in heroin should be five years' imprisonment. However, it was not open to the court to interfere with the sentence imposed by the trial judge, which was below this starting-point, unless the trial judge made an error in principle, failed to consider a relevant factor, overemphasized a relevant factor or imposed a sentence that was clearly unreasonable.

The imposition of an excessively lenient sentence on one co-accused by one trial court will not bind the other trial court to make the same error in principle against the second co-accused: *R. v. Hunter* (1970), 16 C.R.N.S. 12 (Ont. C.A.).

Generally speaking, the court should try to make a sentence conform with that imposed upon a co-accused for the same offence by some other court not merely to achieve equality of treatment but to avoid bitterness and resentment. Nevertheless, less severe treatment may be warranted for an accused in view of a difference in material circumstances, as where he suffers from a severe personality disorder which was a form of mental illness but which did not afflict the co-accused: *R. v. Chisholm* (1985), 18 C.C.C. (3d) 518 (N.S.S.C. App. Div.), leave to appeal to S.C.C. refused *loc. cit.*

The principle of disparity requires that the sentence imposed on one accused should not be unduly disparate with that received by his co-accused, except that where the sentence to which it is being compared is considered to be wholly inadequate a sentence will not be reduced by the appellate court: *R. v. Fait* (1982), 68 C.C.C. (2d) 367 (Alta. C.A.).

However, if the offender's sentence was pursuant to a joint submission, he will not generally succeed in having his sentence reduced on appeal on the grounds that his co-accused subsequently received a lesser sentence: *R. v. Omoth* (2011), 270 C.C.C. (3d) 337 (Sask. C.A.).

Totality (para. (*c*)) – The totality principle requires a sentencing judge who orders an offender to serve consecutive sentences for multiple offences to ensure that the cumulative sentence does not exceed the overall culpability of the offender: *R. v. M. (C.A.)*, [1996] 1 S.C.R. 500, 105 C.C.C. (3d) 327. In this case, the court adopted the following articulation of the principle from D.A. Thomas, *Principles of Sentencing*, 2nd ed. (London: Heinemann, 1979) at p. 56:

> The effect of the totality principle is to require a sentencer who has passed a series of sentences, each properly calculated in relation to the offence for which it is imposed and each properly made consecutive in accordance with the principles governing consecutive sentences, to review the aggregate sentence and consider where the aggregate sentence is "just and appropriate".

There is no pre-fixed outer limit such as 20 or 25 years for fixed-term sentences. Whether a fixed-term sentence beyond 20 years is imposed for a single offence where life imprisonment is available or as a cumulative sentence for multiple offences where life imprisonment is not available, there is no ceiling on fixed-term sentence under this Act, however, at a certain point the goals of sentencing will eventually begin to exhaust themselves once the sentence starts to surpass the offender's likely remaining life span. Thus the judge should generally avid imposing a fixed-term sentence that so greatly exceeds the expected life span that the traditional objectives of sentencing such as deterrence and denunciation have lost their value: *R. v. M. (C.A.)*, *supra.*

The principle of totality requires a consideration of the total of all of the sentences, not the totality of groups of offences within charges: *R. v. Hicks* (2007), 221 C.C.C. (3d) 458 (Nfld. & Lab. C.A.).

When sentencing for multiple offences, it may be an error in principle to work backwards from a global disposition rather than first determining the appropriate sentence for each offence: *R. v. Adams* (2010), 255 C.C.C. (3d) 150 (N.S.C.A.).

It is an error in principle to first give consideration to totality before determining appropriate sentences for the individual offences: *R. v. Hutchings* (2012), 282 C.C.C. (3d) 104 (Nfld. & Lab. C.A.).

In *R. v. Taylor* (2010), 263 C.C.C. (3d) 307 (Man. C.A.), the court provided a usefully concise outline of the proper approach to sentencing on multiple offences. The judge must first determine whether any or all of the sentences will be served concurrently or consecutively. This has to do with the nexus between the offences, not the overall length of sentence. If concurrent sentences are warranted for a set of offences, the judge will determine the fit sentence for the most serious offence and make the other sentences lesser in length, or determine the fit penalty for this set of offences. Where consecutive sentences are appropriate, the judge will determine a fit sentence for each offence, then total them up and give that total sentence a "last look" in accordance with the totality principle. Where some sentences are to be imposed consecutively and others concurrently, the judge will apply each approach to each set of offences, then combine them before applying the principle of totality to ensure that the resultant sentence is not unduly harsh.

Where the accused had been sentenced the previous day for a separate crime committed against the same victim, it was an error in principle for the sentencing judge to fail to consider the totality principle in relation to the other sentence. The sentencing judge should have considedered whether an additional consecutive sentence would offend the principle of proportionality: *R. v. MacArthur* (2018), 362 C.C.C. (3d) 205 (P.E.I.C.A.).

Restraint (paras. (*d*) and (*e*)) – It is unrealistic to believe that persons coming from extremely disadvantaged backgrounds can be rehabilitated, once the cycle of crime starts, by successive and increased periods of imprisonment, especially when, upon release, they are returned to the same environment and lifestyle which contributed to their misfortune in the first place. What is required, in such a case, is intensive guidance, encouragement, training and supervision while on probation, preferably on a daily basis by a person in whom the accused has confidence. In the case of a native Canadian, it may be essential that any program include support of his indigenous community: *R. v. M. (R.B.)* (1990), 54 C.C.C. (3d) 132 (B.C.C.A.).

Paragraph (*e*) is not simply a codification of existing sentence principles but was intended to be remedial. As a general principle, it applies to all offenders, and states that imprisonment should be the penal sanction of last resort. Prison is to be used only where no other sanction or combination of sanctions is appropriate to the offence and the offender. Paragraph (*e*) and other provisions in this Part have placed a new emphasis upon decreasing the use of incarceration: *R. v. Gladue*, [1999] 1 S.C.R. 688, 133 C.C.C. (3d) 385. As to the meaning of the phrase "with particular attention to the circumstances of aboriginal offenders", see below.

Particularly, when regard is had to the French version of this section, it is apparent that para. (*e*) does have a bearing on whether an immediate sentence of imprisonment or a conditional sentence of imprisonment should be imposed. To the extent that both punitive and restorative objectives can be achieved in a given case, a conditional sentence is likely a better sanction than incarceration. Where the need for punishment is particularly pressing and there is little opportunity to achieve restorative objectives, incarceration will likely be the more attractive sanction. However, even if restorative objectives cannot be readily satisfied, a conditional sentence will still be preferable where a conditional sentence can achieve the objectives of denunciation and deterrence as effectively as incarceration, in view of the principle of restraint in paras. (*d*) and (*e*): *R. v. Proulx*, [2000] 1 S.C.R. 61, 140 C.C.C. (3d) 449.

In view of the principle of restraint as reflected in paras. (*d*) and (*e*), it is possible that a judge who would have sentenced an offender to a short penitentiary term prior to the proclamation of this Part, would find that a sentence of less than two years was appropriate in which case a conditional sentence under the new s. 742.1 would be available: *R. v. Bunn*, [2000] 1 S.C.R. 183, 140 C.C.C. (3d) 505.

It is an error in principle to impose a jail term instead of a fine for an offence because the defendant is a man of means, for to do so is to discriminate against an economic class rather than dispensing equal treatment before the law: *R. v. Johnson* (1971), 5 C.C.C. (2d) 541 (N.S.S.C. App. Div.).

Even though it was imposed with the best of intentions an extended sentence to provide an opportunity for treatment for drug abuse will not be maintained where there is no connection between the accused's addiction and the commission of the crime: *R. v. Luther* (1971), 5 C.C.C. (2d) 354 (Ont. C.A.) (2:1). Similarly, in *R. v. Wilson* (1996), 109 C.C.C. (3d) 184 (Alta. C.A.), the court concluded that rehabilitation cannot be used to take the sentence beyond what is appropriate for the offence in the circumstances. Consequently, although the accused suffered from a psychiatric illness, incarceration could not be used as a substitute for mental health care.

It was an error in principle for the sentencing judge to impose a life sentence and then suggest an appropriate alternative sentence of 16 years ostensibly for the benefit of a reviewing court. Having identified two fit sentences that reflecting all the applicable sentencing principles, the trial judge should have imposed the least onerous one: *R. v. Tasew* (2011), 282 C.C.C. (3d) 260 (Alta. C.A.).

Aboriginal offenders (para. (*e*)) – Paragraph (*e*) is not simply a codification of existing jurisprudence. Its purpose is to ameliorate the serious problem of overrepresentation of aboriginal people in prison, and to encourage sentencing judges to have recourse to a restorative approach to sentencing. It directs sentencing judges to undertake the sentencing of aboriginal offenders individually, but also differently, because the circumstances of aboriginal people are unique. The judge must therefore consider the unique systemic or background factors that may have played a part in bringing the offender before the court and the types of sentencing procedures and sanctions that may be appropriate in the circumstances because of the offender's heritage or connection. While judges may take judicial notice of the broad systemic and background factors and the priority given to restorative justice, the court should be provided with case-specific information by counsel or in the pre-sentence report. Whether the offender resides on a reserve, in a rural or an urban area, the judge must be made aware of alternatives to incarceration that exist whether inside or outside the aboriginal community. This paragraph should not, however, be taken as a means of automatically reducing the prison sentence of aboriginal offenders. The sentence imposed will depend upon all the factors that must be taken into account in each individual case. It is unreasonable to assume that aboriginal people themselves do not believe in the importance of the objectives of denunciation, deterrence and separation. Generally, the more violent and serious the offence the more likely it is as a practical reality that the terms of imprisonment for aboriginals and non-aboriginals will be close to each other or the same. The class of aboriginal people who come within this paragraph must be, at least, all who come within the scope of s. 25 of the Charter and s. 35 of the *Constitution Act, 1982* and this paragraph applies to all aboriginal offenders, not just those residing on a reserve: *R. v. Gladue*, [1999] 1 S.C.R. 688, 133 C.C.C. (3d) 385.

In *R. v. Ipeelee*, [2012] 1 S.C.R. 433, 280 C.C.C. (3d) 265, the Supreme Court of Canada reaffirmed the special sentencing approach in respect of aboriginal offenders and, in particular, addressed the application of those principles to the breach of a long-term supervision order. This provision requires the court to use a different method of analysis in determining a fit sentence for Aboriginal offenders. A judge must consider: (a) the unique systemic or background factors which may have played a part in bringing the particular Aboriginal offender before the courts; and (b) the types of sentencing procedures and sanctions which may be appropriate in the circumstances for the offender because of his or her particular Aboriginal heritage or connection. Judges may take judicial notice of the broad systemic and background factors affecting Aboriginal people generally, but additional case-specific information must come from counsel and from the pre-sentence report. Courts must take judicial notice of such matters as the history of colonialism, displacement and residential schools and how that history continues to translate into lower educational attainment, lower incomes, higher unemployment, higher rates of substance abuse and suicide, and higher levels of incarceration for Aboriginal peoples. While these factors, on their own, do not necessarily justify a different sentence for an Aboriginal offender, they provide the requisite context for considering the case-specific information. Failing to take these circumstances into account would violate the fundamental principle of sentencing that requires the sentence to be proportionate to the gravity of the offence and the degree of responsibility of the offender. To the extent that the application of the *Gladue* principles leads to different sanctions for Aboriginal offenders, thereby implicating the parity principle contained in s. 718.2, those differences will be justified based on the unique Aboriginal circumstances. These principles apply equally in considering the breach of a long-term supervision order. The failure to consider the *Gladue* principles constitutes an error justifying appellate intervention.

The restorative approach which is premised on the assumption that there is no place for punishment in the sentencing process has much value. In borrowing from the restorative justice approach, however, it must be determined when and in what manner it can be applied in any given case. The restorative sentence must be more individualized and more comprehensive, based on a realistic assessment of the offenders needs from his own point of view as well as his future relationship with the victims and the community. The disposition must protect the community from future short-term and long-term harm. The offender must want to participate and the representatives of the community at large should also express a willingness to assume at least part of the responsibility for the healing process. The victims should also play an important part either by direct participation or having their interests be given prominence as part of the healing community. There must also be an infrastructure in place which can provide the holistic approach required and which will at the same time ensure the requisite protection of the public during the healing process: *R. v. J. (C.)* (1997), 119 C.C.C. (3d) 444, 155 Nfld. & P.E.I.R. 197 *sub nom. R. v. Jacobish (Tshakapesh)* (Nfld. C.A.). [**Note:** this case must now be read in light of *R. v. Gladue, supra.*]

Notwithstanding what may well be different approaches to sentencing as between aboriginal and non-aboriginal conceptions of sentencing, for some aboriginal offenders, and depending on the nature of the offence, the goals of denunciation and deterrence are fundamentally relevant to the offender's community. Thus, the more violent and serious the offence, the more likely as a practical matter that the appropriate sentence will not differ as between aboriginal and non-aboriginal offenders. Paragraph (*e*) requires a different methodology for assessing a fit sentence for an aboriginal offender; it does not mandate, necessarily, a different result. Nor does that paragraph require that the principles of restorative justice must be given the greatest weight. On the other hand, a judge may accord the greatest weight to the concept of restorative justice, notwithstanding that an aboriginal offender has committed a serious crime: *R. v. Wells*, [2000] 1 S.C.R. 207, 141 C.C.C. (3d) 368.

While, as a general rule, the more serious and violent the offence, the less difference there will be on sentences imposed on aboriginal and non-aboriginal offenders, in some such instances, the sentence of an aboriginal offender may be less than that imposed on a non-aboriginal offender. Restorative justice may predominate in the sentencing of an aboriginal offender even for a serious or violent crime: *R. v. Jacko* (2010), 256 C.C.C. (3d) 113 (Ont. C.A.).

It is an error to proceed on the basis that *Gladue* factors do not justify departing from a proportionate sentence in a given case. Rather, the point of the *Gladue* analysis itself is to achieve a proportionate sentence: *R. v. Swampy* (2017), 347 C.C.C. (3d) 105 (Alta. C.A.).

It is an error in principle to discount *Gladue* principles because the offender was raised in a non-Aboriginal community or to require a link between the offender's Aboriginal heritage and the offence: *R. v. J.L.M.* (2017), 353 C.C.C. (3d) 40 (B.C.C.A.), leave to appeal to S.C.C. refused 2018 CarswellBC 680.

Gladue reports should provide information about the writer including relevant background and experience so that the weight given to the report may be assessed: *R. v. Lawson* (2012), 294 C.C.C. (3d) 369 (B.C.C.A.).

Failure to take into account *Gladue* principles in deciding whether to make a dangerous or long-term offender designation in respect of an aboriginal offender constitutes an error in principle: *R. v. Moise* (2015), 322 C.C.C. (3d) 400 (Sask. C.A.).

Counsel has a duty to assist the sentencing judge by presenting relevant *Gladue* evidence, failing which the obligation rests with the sentencing judge to acquire such Aboriginal-specific information as is necessary to properly apply *Gladue* principles: *R. v. Wolfleg* (2018), 363 C.C.C. (3d) 168 (Alta. C.A.).

Systemic racism – In *R. v. Borde* (2003), 172 C.C.C. (3d) 225, the Ontario Court of Appeal held that the status of an accused as an African-Canadian was of little relevance in respect of violent and serious offences.

The fact that an offender is a member of a group that has historically been subject to systemic racial and gender bias does not in and of itself justify any mitigation of sentence. A sentencing judge is, however, required to take into account all factors that are germane to the gravity of the offence and the personal culpability of the offender. That inquiry can encompass systemic racial and gender bias. If racial and gender bias suffered by the offender helps explain why the offender committed the crime, those factors can be said to have played a role in the commission of the offence: *R. v. Hamilton* (2004), 186 C.C.C. (3d) 129 (Ont. C.A.).

OTHER PRINCIPLES

Effect of accused having left jurisdiction – The accused's demonstrated successful rehabilitation as a result of his having "jumped bail" many years before is entitled to little consideration as a mitigating factor. The courts cannot impose a light sentence in such circumstances and thus appear to reward accused for breaching their bail conditions. On the other hand, the courts may properly take into account the accused's voluntary surrender and guilty plea as a mitigating circumstance: *R. v. Thompson* (1989), 50 C.C.C. (3d) 126 (Alta. C.A.).

Effect of guilty plea – A factor in mitigation of sentence is the plea of guilty which saves the community the expense of a trial: *R. v. Johnston and Tremayne*, [1970] 4 C.C.C. 64 (Ont. C.A.).

The accused's offer to plead guilty to a lesser offence is a mitigating factor only if the accused is ultimately convicted of the lesser offence rather than the offence as charged: *R. v. Shyback* (2018), 366 C.C.C. (3d) 197 (Alta. C.A.).

Terrorism (para. (*a*)(v)) – In cases of acts of politically motivated terrorism, the paramount consideration is general deterrence: *R. v. Atwal* (1990), 57 C.C.C. (3d) 143 (B.C.C.A.); *R. v. Balian* (1988), 29 O.A.C. 387 (C.A.).

Joint submissions – Joint submissions on sentence — that is, when Crown and defence counsel agree to recommend a particular sentence to the trial judge, in exchange for the accused entering a plea of guilty — are vitally important to the well-being of the criminal justice system, as well as the justice system at large. A sentencing judge should only depart from a joint submission where the proposed sentence would be viewed by reasonable and informed persons as a breakdown in the proper functioning of the justice system. The sentencing judge should notify counsel of any concerns and invite further submissions on those concerns. If the court's concerns are not alleviated, it may allow the accused to withdraw his or her guilty plea. Finally, if the judge remains unsatisfied by counsel's submissions, he or she should provide clear and cogent reasons for departing from the joint submission: *R. v. Anthony-Cook*, [2016] 2 S.C.R. 204, 342 C.C.C. (3d) 1.

Frequency of offence – An unusually high frequency of a particular offence in the area is only one factor to be considered in imposing sentence. The paramount question is always: "What should this offender receive for this offence, committed in the circumstances under which it was committed?": *R. v. Sears* (1978), 39 C.C.C. (2d) 199 (Ont. C.A.).

Maximum sentence – In *R. v. Cheddesingh*, [2004] 1 S.C.R. 433, 182 C.C.C. (3d) 37, the court held that, in considering whether the maximum sentence is appropriate, terms such as "stark horror", "worst offence" and "worst offender" add nothing to the analysis and should be avoided. All relevant factors must be considered. A maximum penalty of any kind will, by its very nature, be imposed only rarely and is only appropriate if the offence is of sufficient gravity and the offender displays sufficient blameworthiness. The inquiry must proceed on a case-by-case basis.

The maximum sentence is not to be reserved for the abstract case of the worst crime committed in the worst circumstances. Comparisons to hypothetical worst case scenarios should be avoided. The decision must be dictated by the principle of proportionality which is achieved by means of a complicated calculus whose elements the trier of fact understands best: *R. v. M. (L.)*, [2008] 2 S.C.R. 163, 231 C.C.C. (3d) 310. See also *R. v. S. (K.S.T.)*, [2008] 3 S.C.R. 309, 237 C.C.C. (3d) 129.

The "worst case" means the worst offender and offence and would thus not apply to an accused who has a great potential for rehabilitation: *R. v. Pruner* (1979), 9 C.R. (3d) S-8 (Ont. C.A.).

The types of acts that attract a life sentence are those where it can be said that a specific outrage has been premeditated and/or repeated needlessly many times, indicating a degree of callousness and a lack of feeling amounting virtually to a deliberate intent at terrorization, leading frequently to permanent injuries. There must usually be not only an intent to do the act but an intent to do it in a sadistic way that will cause terror to the victim. The case must be such that the necessity of punishing, denouncing and exacting retribution from the offender justifies minimizing the interests of the offender himself when considering the factors applicable to sentencing. Where the seriousness of the crime would not in itself justify the sentence, future dangerousness should rarely if ever be sufficient in itself: *R. v. Cooper* (1997), 117 C.C.C. (3d) 249 (Nfld. C.A.).

In determining the fitness of a sentence the maximum sentence provided by Parliament is an important consideration and where the Crown proceeds summarily on a Crown option offence it is the maximum provided for a summary conviction which must be considered: *R. v. Sanatkar* (1981), 64 C.C.C. (2d) 325 (Ont. C.A.).

Corporations/Organizations – See notes under ss. 718.21 and 735.

Youthful offenders – Particularly, in the case of a youthful first offender the first sentence of imprisonment should focus on the particular offender, including requirements of individual deterrence. Its length ought not to be governed by the factor of general deterrence: *R. v. Vandale and Maciejewski* (1974), 21 C.C.C. (2d) 250 (Ont. C.A.).

The length of a first penitentiary sentence for a youthful offender should rarely be determined solely by the objectives of denunciation and general deterrence: *R. v. Borde* (2003), 172 C.C.C. (3d) 225 (Ont. C.A.).

In *R. v. Demeter and Whitmore* (1976), 32 C.C.C. (2d) 379 (Ont. C.A.), custodial sentences for robbery were reduced (2:1) to time served and probation; the majority being of the view that for youthful first offenders the paramount consideration must be rehabilitation, while Houlden J.A., felt that for such a serious crime, unless there were extraordinary circumstances, a substantial reformatory term is required.

Where, however, violence or a serious crime is involved this principle does not apply and particularly where careful planning is involved a lengthy reformatory sentence may be imposed: *R. v. Gonidis, McCullough and Stevenson* (1980), 57 C.C.C. (2d) 90 (Ont. C.A.); *R. v. Campbell* (1981), 64 C.C.C. (2d) 336 (B.C.C.A.).

A judge is entitled to take a chance with a convicted person, particularly a youthful one, by exercising leniency in circumstances where leniency might not otherwise appear to be called for, provided there is some factor present in the case that is sufficient to warrant a reasonable belief on the part of the trial judge, going beyond a mere hope, that the leniency proposed to be extended holds some prospect of succeeding where other dispositions available to the trial judge might fail. Such a factor might be the indication of remorse, a glimpsed change in attitude on the part of the accused, or some other sign that the accused may have learned something beneficial from his past and present encounters with the criminal justice system: *R. v. Quesnel and Smith* (1984), 14 C.C.C. (3d) 254 (Ont. C.A.).

Juvenile antecedents – Juvenile antecedents should be considered in the preparation of an offender's pre-sentence report, and in the case of a youthful offender a custodial sentence should generally be avoided, but if it is necessary it is undesirable that it should be very long: *R. v. Beacon and Modney* (1976), 31 C.C.C. (2d) 56 (Alta. C.A.).

However, the court is not entitled to consider the juvenile delinquencies as in the case of an adult's criminal record: *R. v. Denault* (1981), 20 C.R. (2d) 154 (Ont. C.A.).

First offender – The primary objectives in sentencing a first offender are individual deterrence and rehabilitation. The sentence should constitute the minimum necessary intervention that is adequate in the particular circumstances. Community-based dispositions must be considered and more serious forms of punishment should be imposed only when necessary. Furthermore, a trial judge should have either a pre-sentence report or a very clear statement with respect to the accused's background and circumstances before imposing a sentence of imprisonment on a first offender: *R. v. Priest* (1996), 110 C.C.C. (3d) 289 (Ont. C.A.). Furthermore, the transition from a statutorily-defined young person to an adult should not be marked by an immediate abandonment of rehabilitation as a primary goal where the prospect of successful rehabilitation is real: *R. v. Leask* (1996), 112 C.C.C. (3d) 400 (Man. C.A.).

In the case of a first offender, whether or not he is a young offender all other methods available to the court of punishing the accused must be carefully considered before a term of imprisonment is imposed. Moreover, before a prison term is imposed there should be a pre-sentence report or some very clear statement with respect to the accused's background and circumstances: *R. v. Bates* (1977), 32 C.C.C. (2d) 493 (Ont. C.A.).

Criminal record – Pursuant to the Coke principle, a harsher sentence with respect to a second offence cannot be imposed unless the offender was convicted for the first offence prior to the commission of the second. This rule is limited to provisions that provide harsher penalties for second and subsequent offences. The judge has the discretion to consider the prior conviction as an aggravating factor: *R. v. Andrade* (2010), 260 C.C.C. (3d) 353 (N.B.C.A.).

Where a criminal record shows repeated related criminal conduct, the principles of sentencing require the judge to impose a sentence that is greater than what the accused received for past conduct. While the judge cannot punish an accused again for previous convictions, a prior criminal record can assist the judge in determining the normative character of the accused and, where repeated related behaviour is revealed, it is an aggravating factor causing the sentence to be increased: *R. v. Wright* (2010), 261 C.C.C. (3d) 333 (Man. C.A.).

Dangerous offender – In *R. v. Pontello* (1977), 38 C.C.C. (2d) (Ont. C.A.), the court considered the propriety of a life sentence in a case of rape. The accused was convicted of two counts of rape and psychiatric evidence indicated he was a very dangerous person. The court held that in a case of rape unaccompanied by acts of unusual violence, brutality or cruelty the evidence of a psychiatrist with respect to the accused's continuing or potential danger to the physical safety of others would not justify a court in categorizing the offence as one calling for a sentence outside the usual range of sentences for such offences. In this case the nature of the offences indicated a serious personality disorder and required that the expert evidence be taken into consideration and the life sentence was upheld. The court stated however that a life sentence may not be sought by the Crown so as to avoid the protective provisions of the dangerous offenders legislation, Part XXIV of the Code.

A sentence of life imprisonment for attempted murder was upheld having regard to the uncertainty as to when the accused might be cured or cease to be dangerous, the cruelty and callousness of his act and the severity of his personality disorder which made him a continuing danger to others. Cases in which a sentence of life imprisonment is appropriate are not necessarily confined to cases in which the facts could be described as "stark horror" or to cases which form part of a pattern of violent behaviour: *R. v. Simpson (No. 3)* (1981), 58 C.C.C. (2d) 308 (Ont. C.A.).

While the court can, in effect, impose a sentence of preventive detention by sentencing the accused to life imprisonment although the Crown has not proceeded under Part XXIV, it should do so only where it is shown that the accused is dangerous and not merely incorrigible: *R. v. Hastings* (1985), 19 C.C.C. (3d) 86 (Alta. C.A.). See also *R. v. Robinson* (1997), 121 C.C.C. (3d) 240 (B.C.C.A.).

Effect of parole – In imposing sentence it is the duty of the court to punish in accordance with the established principles and to disregard any policies of the Parole Board whose only function is to determine when the punishment may be safely alleviated: *R. v. Holden,* [1963] 2 C.C.C. 394 (B.C.C.A.).

The court's function of imposing sentence and the Parole Board's subsequent review of the punishment for parole purposes are intended by Parliament to be complementary one to the other in the field of corrections. The deliberate imposition of a long sentence to support the policies of the Parole Board would amount to an improper abandonment and delegation of the court's duties to the board. However, a court may in determining an appropriate prison term quite properly take into consideration the powers and duties of the Parole Board: *R. v. Wilmott,* [1967] 1 C.C.C. 171 (Ont. C.A.).

In *R. v. Jackson* (1975), 23 C.C.C. (2d) 147 (N.S.C.A.), only MacDonald J.A. followed *R. v. Evans* (1975), 24 C.C.C. (2d) 300 (N.S.S.C. App. Div.), and held that where a forfeiture of parole has occurred as a result of the offence then the sentence should to some degree reflect that additional punishment.

In *R. v. Keeble* (1977), 37 C.C.C. (2d) 387 (P.E.I.S.C. in *banco*), the court preferred the minority view in *R. v. Evans, supra,* and held that the court should not reduce an otherwise proper sentence to mitigate against the forfeiture of parole. Similarly: *R. v. Labuik* (1984), 42 C.R. (3d) 185 (Man. C.A.).

Risk of deportation – Immigration consequences may be taken into account in sentencing as personal circumstances of the offender. They are not, strictly speaking, aggravating or mitigating factors. Their relevance flows from the application of the principles of individualization and parity. Relevance may also flow from the sentencing objective of rehabilitation. Where the court takes collateral immigration consequences into account, the sentence that is ultimately imposed must still be proportionate to the gravity of the offence and the degree of responsibility of the offender. The flexibility of the sentencing process should not be misused by imposing inappropriate and artificial sentences in order to avoid collateral consequences which may flow from a statutory scheme, thus circumventing Parliament's will: *R. v. Pham,* [2013] 1 S.C.R. 739, 293 C.C.C. (3d) 530.

Effect of state misconduct – Where the state misconduct in the context of a Charter breach relates to the circumstances of the offence or the offender, the sentencing judge may properly take the relevant facts into account in crafting a fit sentence. State misconduct which does not amount to a Charter breach but which impacts the offender may also be a relevant factor in crafting a fit sentence. In such cases, the offender need not prove that the conduct amounted to a Charter breach. The remedial power of the court under s. 24(1) of the Charter need not be resorted to, although there may be some exceptional cases in which a sentence reduction outside the statutory limits may be the sole effective remedy for some particularly egregious form of misconduct by state agents in relation to the offence and the offender: *R. v. Nasogaluak,* [2010] 1 S.C.R. 206, 251 C.C.C. (3d) 293.

Conduct of and co-operation with authorities – In *R. v. Burke,* [1968] 2 C.C.C. 124, [1967] 2 O.R. 562, the Court of Appeal in considering a possible inference of unfairness where the police obviously must have originally known of both similar offences and had just prior to the accused's release from prison from serving his sentence on the second offence arrested him for the first offence, accordingly reduced the second sentence to time served until the appeal.

Co-operation with the authorities leading to the conviction of the accused's confederates is a proper consideration to be taken into account in mitigation of sentence: *R. v. Laroche* (1983), 6 C.C.C. (3d) 268 (Que. C.A.).

Safety of inmate – The safety of inmates is the responsibility of the prison authorities and the alleged risk to the safety of the offender is not a relevant factor to be taken into account in imposing a fit sentence: *R. v. Rafuse* (2004), 193 C.C.C. (3d) 234 (Sask. C.A.).

Mistake of law – Although no defence to a criminal charge, mistake of law can be a mitigating factor on sentence, because offenders who honestly but mistakenly believe in the lawfulness of their actions are less morally blameworthy than offenders who are unsure about the lawfulness of their actions or know that their actions are unlawful: *R. v. Suter* (2018), 363 C.C.C. (3d) 1 (S.C.C.).

Vigilante violence – Violence committed against an offender for his or her role in the commission of the offence — whether by a fellow inmate, or by a vigilante group — necessarily form part of the personal circumstances of that offender, and should be taken into account on sentence: *R. v. Suter, supra*.

Remorse – While remorse is a mitigating factor, the accused's failure to express remorse is not an aggravating factor: *R. v. Cormier* (1999), 140 C.C.C. (3d) 87 (N.B.C.A.).

Lack of remorse is not, ordinarily, an aggravating circumstance and should only be considered aggravating in very unusual circumstances as where the accused's attitude toward the crime demonstrates a substantial likelihood of future dangerousness. Even then the trial judge must be careful not to increase the sentence beyond what is proportionate having regard to the circumstances of the particular offence: *R. v. Valentini* (1999), 132 C.C.C. (3d) 262 (Ont. C.A.).

The failure to express remorse following conviction is not an aggravating factor and the expression of sincere remorse is a mitigating one. In very unusual circumstances, however, the lack of remorse can be viewed as an aggravating factor, where, for example, the offender's attitude toward the crime demonstrates a substantial likelihood of future dangerousness. The failure to express remorse following a guilty plea should be treated as an aggravating factor unless there is a rational explanation for the failure: *R. v. Nash* (2009), 240 C.C.C. (3d) 421 (N.B.C.A.), leave to appeal to S.C.C. refused 243 C.C.C. (3d) vi.

Age and health – The accused's advanced age and poor health are factors that should be considered in determining a fit sentence, not merely considered after the fact when applying the totality principle: *R. v. A.E.S.* (2018), 369 C.C.C. (3d) 92 (B.C.C.A.).

Provocation – To give full effect to s. 232, which reduces murder to manslaughter where provocation is made out, provocation must be considered as well at the sentencing stage and may be considered as a mitigating factor: *R. v. Stone*, [1999] 2 S.C.R. 290, 134 C.C.C. (3d) 353.

Conditional sentence – While aggravating circumstances relating to the offence or the offender increase the need for denunciation and deterrence, a conditional sentence may be imposed even if such factors are present. Each case must be considered individually: *R. v. Proulx*, [2000] 1 S.C.R. 61, 140 C.C.C. (3d) 449.

Notwithstanding the presence of aggravating factors, the trial judge's decision to impose a 21-month conditional sentence with restrictive conditions for offences of gross indecency and indecent assault committed by the accused on his younger cousin some 25 years earlier, was entitled to deference. The trial judge was well positioned to assess the degree of denunciation and deterrence required in the circumstances and that would be provided by the conditional sentence he imposed: *R. v. W. (L.F.)*, [2000] 1 S.C.R. 132, 140 C.C.C. (3d) 539.

In the vast majority of cases, a conditional sentence will not reflect the gravity of cocaine importation, nor will it send the requisite denunciatory and deterrent message. Cocaine importation is viewed as a violent and serious offence requiring a range of sentence from three to five years' imprisonment for approximately a kilogram of cocaine. A conditional sentence, however, is available for importers of less than a kilogram: *R. v. Hamilton* (2004), 186 C.C.C. (3d) 129 (Ont. C.A.).

Pre-trial bail conditions – Time spent on stringent pre-sentence bail conditions, especially house arrest, is a relevant mitigating factor in determining the length of sentence. The amount of credit to be given is within the discretion of the trial judge and there is no formula that the judge is required to apply. The amount of credit will depend upon a number of factors, including the length of time spent on bail under house arrest, the stringency of the conditions, the impact on the offender's liberty, the ability of the offender to carry on normal relationships, employment and activity. The failure of a trial judge to explain why time spent on bail under house arrest has not been taken into account is an error in principle. Where the offender seeks to rely on the pre-sentence bail conditions, the offender should supply the judge with information as to the impact of the conditions. If there is a dispute as to the impact of the conditions, the onus is on the offender to establish those facts on a balance of probabilities in accordance with s. 724(2) of the *Criminal Code*: *R. v. Downes* (2006), 205 C.C.C. (3d) 488 (Ont. C.A.).

While a judge should explain why he or she has decided whether or not to take predisposition house arrest into account on sentencing, the amount of credit to be given, if any, lies within the judge's discretion: *R. v. Adamson* (2018), 364 C.C.C. (3d) 41 (Ont. C.A.).

A curfew is not the same as house arrest. Here, the sentencing judge erred by using this pre-trial bail condition as a mitigating factor on sentence, especially given that the accused never applied to vary the condition now claimed to be an undue hardship: *R. v. H. (R.J.)* (2012), 295 C.C.C. (3d) 301 (N.L.C.A.).

Organizations

ADDITIONAL FACTORS.

718.21 A court that imposes a sentence on an organization shall also take into consideration the following factors:

(*a*) any advantage realized by the organization as a result of the offence;

(*b*) the degree of planning involved in carrying out the offence and the duration and complexity of the offence;

(*c*) whether the organization has attempted to conceal its assets, or convert them, in order to show that it is not able to pay a fine or make restitution;

(*d*) the impact that the sentence would have on the economic viability of the organization and the continued employment of its employees;

(*e*) the cost to public authorities of the investigation and prosecution of the offence;

(*f*) any regulatory penalty imposed on the organization or one of its representatives in respect of the conduct that formed the basis of the offence;

(*g*) whether the organization was — or any of its representatives who were involved in the commission of the offence were — convicted of a similar offence or sanctioned by a regulatory body for similar conduct;

(*h*) any penalty imposed by the organization on a representative for their role in the commission of the offence;

(*i*) any restitution that the organization is ordered to make or any amount that the organization has paid to a victim of the offence; and

(*j*) any measures that the organization has taken to reduce the likelihood of it committing a subsequent offence. 2003, c. 21, s. 14.

CROSS-REFERENCES

The terms "organization" and "representative" are defined in s. 2. Terms of probation for an organization are set out in subsecs. 732.1(3.1) and (3.2). Fines on an organization are set out in s. 735. Enforcement of the fine is set out in ss. 735(2) and 734.6.

SYNOPSIS

While ss. 718.1 and 718.2 set out the general principles of sentencing, this section sets out special principles that apply to offences committed by organizations.

ANNOTATIONS

A sentencing judge has no jurisdiction to order that only part of a sentence be served consecutively to another term of imprisonment: *R. v. Sadykov*, 2018 ONCA 296; *R. v. Tam* (1994), 76 W.A.C. 238 (B.C.C.A.).

Note: Some of the following cases were decided prior to the enactment of this section, but may still be of assistance.

In *R. v. McNamara (No. 2)* (1981), 56 C.C.C. (2d) 516 (Ont. C.A.), the court upheld fines imposed on corporations for conspiracy to defraud government agencies in the rigging of bids on dredging contracts, which ranged from $50,000 to $2 million. The court dealt with the various factors that governed the size of the fines which, to be an effective general deterrent, would have to be substantial and exemplary. In particular, the court was of the view that it could properly consider the anticipated profits (rather than the actual profits or profits shown on the accused's books) in determining the size of the fine.

In another case involving sentencing of a corporation, the court considered that, while it was a relevant factor that the corporation was now owned by persons who had had no knowledge of the commission of the offence by former employees, this did not warrant the imposition of merely a nominal penalty. A fine of some magnitude was required as a matter of general deterrence and to make clear to corporations the duty to properly supervise employees: *R. v. Adam Clark Co.* (1982), 3 C.C.C. (3d) 323 (Ont. C.A.).

It is an error to impose a reduced fine in order to prevent a corporate defendant from facing bankruptcy. While bankruptcy is a factor, it is not necessarily preclusive. Here, the more important objective was to deliver a message on the importance of worker safety: *R. v. Metron Construction Corp.* (2013), 300 C.C.C. (3d) 212 (Ont. C.A.).

In a case under the *Fisheries Act*, the court considered the principles to be applied to the sentencing of a municipal corporation. Municipal corporations should not be treated more leniently than commercial corporations when sentenced for environmental offences, and in particular, for offences under the *Fisheries Act*. A municipal corporation may, however, be treated differently in recognition of its different size, organizational structure, objectives and responsibilities. Whether the defendant is a municipal or commercial corporation, the primary sentencing objectives should be to correct any harm to the environment and to ensure that the corporation takes all necessary steps to make certain that the offence is not repeated. In this case, it was appropriate to impose only a modest fine but make an order that the city construct a sewage treatment plant that would remedy or avoid any harm to fish or the fish habitat: *R. v. Dawson (City)* (2003), 50 C.E.L.R. (N.S.) 99 (Y.T. Terr. Ct.).

Punishment Generally

DEGREES OF PUNISHMENT / Discretion respecting punishment / Imprisonment in default where term not specified / Cumulative punishments / Cumulative punishments — fines / Cumulative punishments — youth / Cumulative punishments — sexual offences against children.

718.3 (1) Where an enactment prescribes different degrees or kinds of punishment in respect of an offence, the punishment to be imposed is, subject to the limitations prescribed in the enactment, in the discretion of the court that convicts a person who commits the offence.

(2) Where an enactment prescribes a punishment in respect of an offence, the punishment to be imposed is, subject to the limitations prescribed in the enactment, in the discretion of the court that convicts a person who commits the offence, but no punishment is a minimum punishment unless it is declared to be a minimum punishment.

(3) Where an accused is convicted of an offence punishable with both fine and imprisonment and a term of imprisonment in default of payment of the fine is not specified in the enactment that prescribes the punishment to be imposed, the imprisonment that may be imposed in default of payment shall not exceed the term of imprisonment that is prescribed in respect of the offence.

(4) The court that sentences an accused shall consider directing

(*a*) that the term of imprisonment that it imposes be served consecutively to a sentence of imprisonment to which the accused is subject at the time of sentencing; and

(*b*) that the terms of imprisonment that it imposes at the same time for more than one offence be served consecutively, including when

(i) the offences do not arise out of the same event or series of events,

(ii) one of the offences was committed while the accused was on judicial interim release, including pending the determination of an appeal, or

(iii) one of the offences was committed while the accused was fleeing from a peace officer.

(5) For the purposes of subsection (4), a term of imprisonment includes imprisonment that results from the operation of subsection 734(4).

(6) For the purposes of subsection (4), a sentence of imprisonment includes

(*a*) a disposition made under paragraph 20(1)(*k*) or (*k*.1) of the *Young Offenders Act*, chapter Y-1 of the Revised Statutes of Canada, 1985;

(*b*) a youth sentence imposed under paragraph 42(2)(*n*), (*o*), (*q*) or (*r*) of the *Youth Criminal Justice Act*; and

(*c*) a sentence that results from the operation of subsection 743.5(1) or (2).

(7) When a court sentences an accused at the same time for more than one sexual offence committed against a child, the court shall direct

(*a*) that a sentence of imprisonment it imposes for an offence under section 163.1 be served consecutively to a sentence of imprisonment it imposes for a sexual offence under another section of this Act committed against a child; and

(*b*) that a sentence of imprisonment it imposes for a sexual offence committed against a child, other than an offence under section 163.1, be served consecutively to a sentence of imprisonment it imposes for a sexual offence committed against another child other than an offence under section 163.1.

1995, c. 22, s. 6; 1997, c. 18, s. 141(*c*); 1999, c. 5, s. 30; 2002, c. 1, s. 182; 2015, c. 23, s. 17.

CROSS-REFERENCES

Disposition and enforcement of fines are governed by ss. 734 to 738. The terms "fine" and "court" are defined in s. 716. The other rules respecting conditional sentence of imprisonment are set out in ss. 742 to 742.7. The place and manner for serving a sentence of imprisonment are governed by ss. 743 to 743.6. Under s. 83.27(1), if the act or omission also constitutes a terrorist activity, the offender is liable to imprisonment for life if the prosecutor proves that the offender was notified the application of that subsection would be sought.

Consecutive sentences for terrorist offences, see s. 83.26, for possession of explosives for criminal organization, s. 82.1, for using firearm, s. 85.4 and criminal organization offences, s. 467.14.

SYNOPSIS

This section deals with certain of the discretionary aspects of sentencing. Where different degrees or kinds of punishment are provided, the judge, subject to any specific statutory limitations, has a discretion as to the penalty to be imposed (*e.g.*, a fine and/or imprisonment) (subsec. (1)). There are no "minimum" sentences unless the legislation so provides (subsec. (2)).

Where an offence is punishable by both a fine and imprisonment, the maximum term in default of payment of a fine, unless otherwise provided, shall not exceed the maximum term that is prescribed for that offence (subsec. (3)).

The court shall consider imposing "consecutive" jail sentences in any case where: (a) the offender is already subject to a sentence of imprisonment at the time of sentencing; or (b) the offender is being sentenced to terms of imprisonment for more than one offence. If being sentenced for multiple offences, a consecutive sentence may be appropriate where the offences do not arise out of the same event or series of events, where one of the offences was committed while the offender was out on bail, or where one of the offences was committed while fleeing a peace officer (subsec. (4)).

Subsection (4) applies to a deemed period of imprisonment for default of payment of a fine under s. 734(4) (subsec. (5)). It also applies to sentences imposed by a youth court (subsec. (6)).

A consecutive sentence shall be imposed where an offender is sentenced at the same time for: (a) a child pornography offence (s. 163.1) and another sexual offence committed against the same child; or (b) sexual offences other than child pornography offences committed against more than one child (subsec. (7)).

ANNOTATIONS

A sentencing judge has no jurisdiction to order that only part of a sentence be served consecutively to another term of imprisonment: *R. v. Sadykov*, 2018 ONCA 296; *R. v. Tam* (1994), 76 W.A.C. 238 (B.C.C.A.).

Note: The following cases were decided prior to the enactment of this section and the amendments to subsecs. (4) to (7), but were considered to be of assistance in applying this section.

Subsection (1) – This subsection explicitly vests in the sentencing judge a discretion to determine the appropriate degree and kind of punishment. Thus, absent an error in principle, failure to consider a relevant factor, or an overemphasis of the apropriate factors, a court of appeal should only intervene to vary a sentence if it demonstrably unfit. Furthermore, an appellate court should only intervene to minimize the disparity of sentences where the sentence imposed by the trial judge is a substantial and marked departure from the sentences customarily imposed for similar offenders committing similar crimes: *R. v. M. (C.A.)*, [1996] 1 S.C.R. 500, 105 C.C.C. (3d) 327.

A variation in the sentence should only be made if the court of appeal is convinced it is not fit in the sense that the sentence is clearly unreasonable. The court of appeal must determine if the sentencing judge applied wrong principles or if the sentence was clearly excessive or inadequate. Unreasonableness in the sentence process involves the sentencing order falling outside the acceptable range of orders: *R. v. Shropshire*, [1995] 4 S.C.R. 227, 102 C.C.C. (3d) 193.

Consecutive sentences / *Procedure [subsec. (4)]* – In *R. v. Dean* (1977), 35 C.C.C. (2d) 217 (Ont. C.A.), the accused had been sentenced to a number of consecutive sentences. He was then given a sentence to run "consecutive with sentence now serving" and argued that this latter sentence, while consecutive to the first of the sentences earlier imposed, was concurrent to the other consecutive sentences because he was not then serving those sentences. It was held, dismissing his application for *habeas corpus,* that by virtue of former s. 14(1) of the *Parole Act*, R.S.C. 1970, c. P-2, as amended by R.S.C. 1970, c. 31 (1st Supp.) [now s. 139(1) of the *Corrections and Conditional Release Act*, S.C. 1992, c. 20], where a person is sentenced to two or more terms of imprisonment such terms "shall, for all purposes of this Act, the *Penitentiary Act* and the *Prisons and Reformatories Act,* be deemed to constitute one sentence". Once the accused was in the custody of the penitentiary services it was those three statutes which governed the time to be served and in the result, at the time he was given the last sentence he was then serving one sentence to which the final sentence was consecutive, and not a series of consecutive sentences. Section 14 abrogates the effect of the earlier decision in *Ex p. McCaud,* [1970] 1 C.C.C. 293 (Ont. H.C.J.).

A fixed sentence cannot be made consecutive to a sentence of life imprisonment: *R. v. Sinclair* (1972), 6 C.C.C. (2d) 523 (Ont. C.A.); *R. v. Cooney* (1981), 62 C.C.C. (2d) 95 (Que. C.A.); *R. v. Camphaug* (1986), 28 C.C.C. (3d) 125 (B.C.C.A.). Nor to a sentence of preventive detention in a penitentiary for an indeterminate period: *R. v. Robillard* (1985), 22 C.C.C. (3d) 505 (Que. C.A.).

Consecutive sentences / *Principles* – In *R. v. Chisholm,* [1965] 4 C.C.C. 289 (Ont. C.A.), it was held that where there was no relationship between the separate commissions of criminal offences the court should, bearing in mind the total term, impose consecutive sentences.

A second crime committed while in flight from a first crime should be punished with a consecutive punishment: *R. v. McCaw, Warnholtz, Frame and Morrison* (1974), 15 C.C.C. (2d) 321 (Ont. C.A.).

In considering the appropriate sentence, where the accused has been convicted of more than one offence arising out of the same general circumstances, the proper approach is to first identify the gravamen of the conduct giving rise to all of the criminal offences. The trial judge should next determine the total sentence to be imposed. Having determined the appropriate total sentence, the judge should, with respect to each offence, impose sentences which result in that total sentence and appropriately reflect the gravamen of the overall criminal conduct, considering not only the appropriate sentence for each offence but whether, in light of totality concerns, a particular sentence should be consecutive or concurrent to the other sentences imposed: *R. v. Jewell* (1995), 100 C.C.C. (3d) 270 (Ont. C.A.).

A sentencing judge may take into account offences committed after an accused has been convicted but prior to sentencing in order to assess the character of the accused and the degree to which he may be on the road to rehabilitation but such offences do not carry the same weight as a prior criminal record where the accused having been convicted and punished commits new criminal offences. Further, if a consecutive sentence could not be imposed directly because of this subsection, it could not be imposed indirectly in the guise of an improper concurrent sentence: *R. v. Paquin* (1989), 70 C.R. (3d) 39 (Que. C.A.).

The appellate court should treat the decision to order concurrent or consecutive sentences with the same deference owed to the decision concerning the length of the sentence. The appellate court is not entitled to intervene absent an error in principle, unless the sentencing judge ignored factors or imposed a sentence which, considered in its entirety, is demonstrably unfit: *R. v. McDonnell,* [1997] 1 S.C.R. 948, 114 C.C.C. (3d) 436.

See also notes respecting "totality" under s. 718.2(*c*).

COMMENCEMENT OF SENTENCE / Time at large excluded from term of imprisonment / Determination of sentence / Exception / Reasons / Record of proceedings / Validity not affected / When time begins to run / When fine imposed / Application for leave to appeal.

719. (1) A sentence commences when it is imposed, except where a relevant enactment otherwise provides.

(2) Any time during which a convicted person is unlawfully at large or is lawfully at large on interim release granted pursuant to any provision of this Act does not count as part of any term of imprisonment imposed on the person.

(3) In determining the sentence to be imposed on a person convicted of an offence, a court may take into account any time spent in custody by the person as a result of the offence but the court shall limit any credit for that time to a maximum of one day for each day spent in custody.

(3.1) Despite subsection (3), if the circumstances justify it, the maximum is one and one-half days for each day spent in custody.

(3.2) The court shall give reasons for any credit granted and shall cause those reasons to be stated in the record.

(3.3) The court shall cause to be stated in the record and on the warrant of committal the offence, the amount of time spent in custody, the term of imprisonment that would have been imposed before any credit was granted, the amount of time credited, if any, and the sentence imposed.

(3.4) Failure to comply with subsection (3.2) or (3.3) does not affect the validity of the sentence imposed by the court.

(4) Notwithstanding subsection (1), a term of imprisonment, whether imposed by a trial court or the court appealed to, commences or shall be deemed to be resumed, as the case may be, on the day on which the convicted person is arrested and taken into custody under the sentence.

(5) Notwithstanding subsection (1), where the sentence that is imposed is a fine with a term of imprisonment in default of payment, no time prior to the day of execution of the warrant of committal counts as part of the term of imprisonment.

(6) An application for leave to appeal is an appeal for the purposes of this section. 1995, c. 22, s. 6; 2009, c. 29, s. 3; 2018, c. 29, s. 66.

CROSS-REFERENCES

Note that special rules for dealing with pre-trial custody of persons later sentenced to life imprisonment are dealt with in s. 746.

Section 687 authorizes the determination of sentence appeals by the court of appeal. Sentences imposed under s. 686(1)(*b*)(i) and (3) by the court of appeal, may run from the date of imposition or, alternatively, the date of the original sentence. The latter date will prevail in the event that the appeal court affirms the original sentence. Time spent by the accused in custody as a result of the offence may be considered by the appeal court in determining the imposition of a sentence, pursuant to subsec. (3).

See ss. 743 to 743.6 for the location and manner of serving a sentence of imprisonment.

Section 515(9.1) provides that, if the justice orders that the accused be detained pending trial primarily because of a previous conviction, that fact is to be recorded in writing. Section 524 deals with the detention of accused alleged to have breached the conditions of their release.

SYNOPSIS

Unless otherwise provided for by statute, a sentence commences when it is imposed (subsec. (1)). However, a term of imprisonment, whether imposed at trial or on appeal, commences or resumes (*e.g.*, where the accused is on bail pending appeal) when the accused is taken into custody (subsec. (4)).

Time spent on bail or while unlawfully at large does not count as part of any sentence (subsec. (2)). Subsection (3) sets out the general rule that the sentencing court may give credit for time spent in custody awaiting sentence at not more than 1:1. However, if the circumstances justify it, the court may, under subsec. (3.1) increase the credit to one and a half days for each day spent in pre-sentence custody. The court may not give enhanced credit where the justice, in ordering the accused detained, stated in writing in the record in accordance with s. 515(9.1) that the primary reason for detention was a previous conviction. Enhanced credit may also not be given where the accused was ordered detained under s. 524 for having breached a release order. Subsections (3.2) and (3.3) impose duties on the sentencing court in respect of reasons. The former requires the sentencing court to give reasons for any credit granted. The latter requires the court to state in the record and on the warrant of committal: (1) the amount of time spent in pre-sentence custody; (2) the term of imprisonment that would have been imposed but for the credit for pre-sentence custody; (3)

the amount of time credited towards pre-sentence custody; and (4) the actual sentence imposed. (Note that Form 21, the warrant of committal, has been amended accordingly.) However, failure to comply with these requirements does not affect the validity of the sentence (subsec. (3.4)).

No time prior to the day on which a warrant of committal for non-payment of a fine is executed shall count as part of the default term (subsec. (5)).

ANNOTATIONS

Note: Some of the cases noted below were decided under the predecessor to this section [former s. 721] but were considered to be of assistance in applying this section. Note, however, the change in wording of subsec. (2) to refer to time while the convict was "unlawfully at large".

Commencement of sentence (subsec. (1)) – Once a conviction is set aside, the term of imprisonment imposed for that conviction is also set aside and a sentence originally made consecutive to that sentence begins to run from the date it was imposed: *R. v. Zitek* (1986), 30 C.C.C. (3d) 60 (Ont. C.A.).

Time spent at large (subsec. (2)) – [**Note:** These cases must be read in light of the change in wording from former s. 721(2), which made no reference to "unlawfully at large"].

The mere fact that a mistake has been made in the administration of sentence cannot be taken to justify a premature release and protect the prisoner from re-arrest to serve the full sentence when the mistake is discovered: *R. v. Law* (1981), 63 C.C.C. (2d) 412, 24 C.R. (3d) 332 (Ont. C.A.). In that case the error resulted because the appropriate authorities were never informed that the accused had abandoned his appeal from a conviction which had resulted in a penitentiary sentence when he was re-incarcerated in a reformatory for an offence committed while on bail pending appeal. The court however appeared to recognize that special circumstances, such as perhaps existed in *R. v. Stanton* (1979), 49 C.C.C. (2d) 177 (Ont. H.C.J.), could require the court to order an accused's release following his re-arrest. In *R. v. Stanton* the accused had been released due to an error in calculation by prison authorities. The accused, who believed he had been released on parole, had in no way contributed to the error and had lived openly in the community. The court released the accused on *habeas corpus* holding that in the circumstances the time spent at large counted against the sentence.

Time spent by the accused on probation pending a Crown appeal against a suspended sentence does not count against the sentence of imprisonment imposed by the Court of Appeal: *R. v. Roach* (1982), 2 C.C.C. (3d) 73 (B.C.S.C.), approved in *R. v. Roach (No. 2)* (1983), 5 C.C.C. (3d) 90 (B.C.C.A.).

Nor does the time that the accused was at large following his release on *habeas corpus* count against the sentence when on appeal it is found that the judge erred in releasing him and orders his re-arrest: *R. v. Law (No. 2)* (1981), 64 C.C.C. (2d) 181 (Ont. H.C.J.), affd 65 C.C.C. (2d) 512*n* (Ont. C.A.).

In *R. v. Lachance* (1985), 22 C.C.C. (3d) 119 (Que. S.C.), the court held that resort could be had to ss. 7, 12 and 24(1) of the *Canadian Charter of Rights and Freedoms* to relieve against the unfairness of requiring an inmate to serve the remainder of a sentence which would have expired much earlier but for the incompetence of the authorities in failing to execute an outstanding warrant of committal.

To a similar effect is *R. v. Lawrence* (1989), 47 C.C.C. (3d) 462 (Nfld. S.C.), where the court quashed a committal order, the accused having done everything in his power to surrender to prison upon dismissal of his appeal and it was only six months later that arrangements were finally made so that the prison authorities would accept the accused so he could serve the balance of a five-month sentence which would have been served but for the error of the penal system administrators.

Pre-trial custody – The "circumstances" justifying enhanced credit under subsec. (3.1) need not be exceptional or unique to the offender. The loss of early release, taken alone, will generally be a sufficient basis to award credit at the rate of 1.5 to 1, even if the conditions of detention are not particularly harsh, and parole is unlikely. A rule that resulted in longer sentences for offenders who do not obtain bail compared to otherwise identical offenders would be incompatible with the sentencing principles of parity and proportionality: *R. v. Summers* (2014), 308 C.C.C. (3d) 471 (S.C.C.); and *R. v. Carvery* (2014), 308 C.C.C. (3d) 375 (S.C.C.).

The fact of pre-sentence custody is generally sufficient to give rise to an inference that an offender has lost eligibility for parole or early release, thereby justifying enhanced credit. It then falls to the Crown to challenge this inference, for instance by demonstrating that the offender's bad conduct in jail renders it unlikely that he or she will be granted parole or early release: *R. v. Slack* (2015), 321 C.C.C. (3d) 474 (Ont. C.A.).

The denial of enhanced credit for pre-sentence custody to offenders who are denied bail primarily because of a prior conviction pursuant to subsec. (3.1) is constitutionally overbroad because it denies credit in ways that have nothing to do with the subsection's legislative purpose, which is to enhance public safety and security. Section 719(3.1) thus violates s. 7 of the Charter, and is not justified pursuant to s. 1: *R. v. Safarzadeh-Markhali*, [2016] 1 S.C.R. 180, 334 C.C.C. (3d) 1.

Additionally, subsec. (3.1) is unconstitutional to the extent that it denies enhanced credit to offenders who were detained for breach of recognizance pursuant to s. 524: *R. v. Dinardo* (2015), 321 C.C.C. (3d) 525 (Ont. S.C.J.). See also *R. v. Norman* (2015), 331 C.C.C. (3d) 550 (Ont. S.C.J.); *R. v. Meads* (2016), 343 C.C.C. (3d) 279 (Ont. S.C.J.); *R. v. Taylor* (2017), 346 C.C.C. (3d) 540 (Y.T. Terr. Ct.); *R. v. Romanchych* (2018), 359 C.C.C. (3d) 316 (B.C.C.A.).

Subsection (3.1) is unconstitutional to the extent that it denies enhanced credit to offenders whose release was cancelled pursuant to s. 524 because of alleged misconduct while on bail: *R. v. Meads*, 2018 ONCA 146; *R. v. Romanchych*, *supra*; *R. v. Kovich* (2016), 333 C.C.C. (3d) 1 (Man. C.A.).

To the extent that it applies to offenders who committed their offence before it came into force, subsec. (3.1) violates the s. 11(*i*) Charter right to the benefit of the lesser punishment available between the commission of the offence and the time of sentencing: *R. v. S. (R.)* (2015), 20 C.R. (7th) 336 (Ont. C.A.). See also *R. v. Clarke* (2013), 293 C.C.C. (3d) 369 (Ont. C.A.), affirmed, reasons in full [2014] 1 S.C.R. 612, 308 C.C.C. (3d) 299, where (in absence of a constitutional challenge) it was held that the new credit regime applies retrospectively to offences committed prior to February 22, 2010, as long as the offender was charged after that date.

A court is not entitled under subsec. (3.1) to credit an accused for time spent serving a sentence previously imposed on an unrelated offence which happens to coincide with the time the accused is in pre-trial custody on the offence for which he is being sentenced: *R. v. Keepness* (2014), 317 C.C.C. (3d) 267 (Sask. C.A.), leave to appeal to S.C.C. refused 2015 CarswellSask 167.

It is an error in principle for the sentencing judge to fail to comply with subsecs. (3.2) and (3.3). Such an error entitles the appellate court to intervene and determine the appropriate remand credit: *R. v. Murphy* (2015), 318 C.C.C. (3d) 296 (N.S.C.A.).

It is an error to deny enhanced credit on the basis of the accused's moral culpability in relation to the offence: *R. v. Colt* (2015), 324 C.C.C. (3d) 1 (B.C.C.A.).

It was an error in principle for the sentencing judge to deny even one-to-one credit based on the accused's breaches of recognizance, given that the accused had been sentenced for those very breaches: *R. v. Stewart* (2016), 334 C.C.C. (3d) 295 (N.S.C.A.).

Subsections (3) and (3.1) do not strictly limit consideration of pre-sentence custody to time served with respect to the offence that was the immediate trigger of the detention. Rather, the court must assess whether a sufficient link exists between the detention for which credit is sought and the offence for which the offender is being sentenced so as to meet the "as a result of" requirement in subsec. (3): *R. v. Barnett* (2017), 356 C.C.C. (3d) 480 (Ont. C.A.). See also *R. v. Wilson* (2008), 236 C.C.C. (3d) 285 (Ont. C.A.).

The sentencing judge erred by denying the accused credit for a period spent in pre-trial custody on the basis of other charges that were subsequently stayed. It was reasonable to assume that the accused was prevented from being released on bail on those other charges as a result of the pending charges for which the accused was sentenced. Therefore, the period in custody was substantially as a result of the charges before the court and the accused was eligible for credit: *R. v. Hoelscher* (2017), 357 C.C.C. (3d) 409 (Alta. C.A.).

Note: The following cases were decided before the amendments to this section imposed limits on the amount of credit for pre-sentence custody. Prior to these amendments, judges had a broad discretion in fixing the amount of credit, although a guideline had emerged that credit would usually be two days' credit for each day spent in custody. (See *R. v. Wust*, [2000] 1 S.C.R. 455, 143 C.C.C. (3d) 129; *R. v. Arrance*, [2000] 1 S.C.R. 488, 143 C.C.C. (3d) 154; and *R. v. Arthurs*, [2000] 1 S.C.R. 481, 143 C.C.C. (3d) 149.) The cases noted below must be read taking these amendments into account.

The sentencing judge may deduct the time spent in pre-sentence custody even if the resulting sentence is less than the minimum period of imprisonment prescribed by the enactment, such as the four-year minimum provided for in s. 344(*a*) (robbery with a firearm): *R. v. Wust, supra.*

In determining a sentence, including a minimum sentence, time spent in custody or detention may be considered. Time spent out of custody or on bail cannot be counted. Strict bail does not constitute a "punishment of imprisonment" and cannot be taken into account in the imposition of a minimum sentence: *R. v. Panday* (2007), 226 C.C.C. (3d) 349 (Ont. C.A.), leave to appeal to S.C.C. refused [2008] 1 S.C.R. xiv, 228 C.C.C. (3d) vi.

It is not mandatory that sentencing judges consider stringent bail conditions as a mitigating factor, and a failure to refer to this factor does not necessarily constitute an error in principle. The weight to be given to bail conditions as a mitigating factor depends on the circumstances of the case and is within the discretion of the sentencing judge: *R. v. Ijam* (2007), 226 C.C.C. (3d) 376 (Ont. C.A.).

The failure to give credit for pre-trial custody without good reason is an error in principle: *R. v. Rezaie* (1996), 112 C.C.C. (3d) 97 (Ont. C.A.); *R. v. Mills* (1999), 133 C.C.C. (3d) 451 (B.C.C.A.).

Subsection (3.1) does not set out what circumstances would justify enhanced credit for pre-sentence custody beyond the 1:1 rule set out in subsec. (3). Prior to enactment of these sections, courts had considered particularly difficult jail conditions as reasons for enhanced credit. See: *R. v. Pangman* (2001), 154 C.C.C. (3d) 193 (Man. C.A.).

The dangerousness of the accused is a factor to be reflected by increasing the sentence, but is not a proper basis to deny credit for pre-trial custody: *R. v. Orr* (2008), 228 C.C.C. (3d) 432 (B.C.C.A.).

Except for cases where the sentence is life imprisonment and s. 746 applies, a sentencing judge may deny credit for pre-sentence custody, provided that the aggregate of the pre-sentence detention and the sentence imposed does not exceed the maximum sentence allowed for the offence: *R. v. LeBlanc* (2005), 193 C.C.C. (3d) 387 (N.B.C.A.).

Where the judge considers that the gravity of the offence and the offender's moral blameworthiness requires imposition of a penitentiary sentence, a conditional sentence is not available under s. 742.1, even though the judge imposes a sentence of less than two years after taking into account pre-sentence custody: *R. v. Fice*, [2005] 1 S.C.R. 742, 196 C.C.C. (3d) 97.

Denunciation is not a relevant consideration in considering pre-trial custody: *R. v. Calder Berg* (2007), 221 C.C.C. (3d) 449 (B.C.C.A.).

This provision does not apply to time spent in custody as a result of the suspension of a long-term supervision order: *R. v. Wilson* (2010), 252 C.C.C. (3d) 117 (B.C.C.A.), leave to appeal to S.C.C. refused [2010] 2 S.C.R. ix, 256 C.C.C. (3d) iv.

Pre-trial custody and statutory maximums – A sentence is illegal if the sentence imposed plus time spent in pre-trial custody exceeds the statutory maximum: *R. v. Walker* (2017), 345 C.C.C. (3d) 497 (Ont. C.A.); *R. v. Rotman* (2015), 339 O.A.C. 266 (Ont. C.A.); *R. v. Severight* (2014), 306 C.C.C. (3d) 197 (Alta. C.A.), leave to appeal to S.C.C. refused [2014] S.C.C.A. No. 184; *R. v. LeBlanc* (2005), 193 C.C.C. (3d) 387 (N.B.C.A.).

Subsection (4) – A conviction for escaping lawful custody was imposed where the accused was present in court when a sentence of incarceration was imposed but then left the court after a recess when the officer in charge briefly left the room. He was in custody within the meaning of s. 145 as he was present when sentence was pronounced and submitted to arrest by asking permission of the officer to do various things, notwithstanding he was never placed in a prisoner's dock, handcuffed or otherwise physically placed under arrest. The court, considering subsec. (4), held that there is a distinction between the arrest of a person before trial or the arrest of a person who is tried *in absentia* and therefore not present upon pronouncement of sentence, and this case of an accused who is present in court, being in custody at the time of his sentence: *R. v. Zajner* (1977), 36 C.C.C. (2d) 417 (Ont. C.A.).

Imprisonment in default of payment of fine (subsec. (5)) – Although a warrant of committal in default of payment could have been executed earlier on the accused, an accused is validly held under such warrant even though had the warrant in fact been executed earlier the term of imprisonment could have been served concurrently to other sentences he was serving at the time: *R. v. Goyette,* [1982] 1 S.C.R. 688 (5:0).

Procedure and Evidence

SENTENCING PROCEEDINGS / Court-supervised programs.

720. (1) A court shall, as soon as practicable after an offender has been found guilty, conduct proceedings to determine the appropriate sentence to be imposed.

(2) The court may, with the consent of the Attorney General and the offender and after considering the interests of justice and of any victim of the offence, delay sentencing to enable the offender to attend a treatment program approved by the province under the supervision of the court, such as an addiction treatment program or a domestic violence counseling program. 1995, c. 22, s. 6; 2008, c. 18, s. 35.

CROSS-REFERENCES

"Court" is defined in s. 716. Sections 721 to 729 set out the procedure to be followed at the sentence proceedings.

SYNOPSIS

This section requires that the sentence proceedings be conducted as soon as practicable after the accused has been found guilty. However, subsec. (2) allows the court to delay sentencing with the consent of the Attorney General and the offender to permit the offender to attend a treatment program approved by the province under the supervision of the court.

ANNOTATIONS

The "as soon as practicable" requirement in subsec. (1) entails that information relevant to an Aboriginal offender's background should be brought before the court in a comprehensive and timely manner. Here, the "shameful" delay in production of the *Gladue* report warranted the reduction of sentence as a remedy: *R. v. Knockwood* (2012), 286 C.C.C. (3d) 36 (Ont. S.C.J.).

Note: The cases noted below were decided before the addition of subsec. (2), which gives the court authority to continue a practice that had developed in the so-called problem-solving courts, such as the drug treatment courts, of delaying sentence while the offender attends an approved treatment or counselling program under court supervision.

In a number of cases prior to the enactment of this section, the appellate courts have held that it is improper for the trial court to delay imposition of sentence for a collateral purpose such as to see how the accused behaves. Thus in *R. v. Urton*, [1974] 5 W.W.R. 476 (Sask. C.A.), it was held that a lengthy delay to consider matters not in existence at the time of the offence is improper and unfair to the accused. Most recently, the same court in *R. v. Taylor* (1995), 104 C.C.C. (3d) 346, held that it was improper for the trial judge, in order to implement the recommendations of a sentencing circle, to adjourn the sentencing of the accused for a year on certain conditions, including a condition that the accused spend the year in isolation on an island to work towards his rehabilitation. The trial judge was empowered to adjourn the sentencing for reasonable periods of time for the purpose of conducting the sentence hearing and obtaining information about the offender as would be contained in expert and pre-sentence reports and receiving a victim impact statement. The purpose of the adjournment to give effect to the recommendations of the sentencing circle was beyond anything contemplated by the law.

In *R. v. Nunner* (1976), 30 C.C.C. (2d) 199 (Ont. C.A.) (2:1), it was held that postponement of sentence for more than one or two months must be regarded as *prima facie* evidence of the exercise of the judicial discretion to delay sentence for an illegal purpose. However, in this case the court refused to interfere with a trial judge's discretion, delaying for five months the imposition of sentence on a charge of robbery in the case of a 16-year-old, to see how the accused responded to probation imposed for other less serious offences. Having regard to the youth of the accused and the objectives sought to be achieved by the trial judge, it could not be said that the postponement of five months was an illegal exercise of his discretion.

REPORT BY PROBATION OFFICER / Provincial regulations / Content of report / Idem / Copy of report.

721. (1) Subject to regulations made under subsection (2), where an accused, other than an organization, pleads guilty to or is found guilty of an offence, a probation officer shall, if required to do so by a court, prepare and file with the court a report in writing relating to the accused for the purpose of assisting the court in imposing a sentence or in determining whether the accused should be discharged under section 730.

(2) The lieutenant governor in council of a province may make regulations respecting the types of offences for which a court may require a report, and respecting the content and form of the report.

(3) Unless otherwise specified by the court, the report must, wherever possible, contain information on the following matters:

(*a*) the offender's age, maturity, character, behaviour, attitude and willingness to make amends;

(*b*) subject to subsection 119(2) of the *Youth Criminal Justice Act*, the history of previous dispositions under the *Young Offenders Act*, chapter Y-1 of the Revised Statutes of Canada, 1985, the history of previous sentences under the *Youth Criminal Justice Act*, and of previous findings of guilt under this Act and any other Act of Parliament;

(*c*) the history of any alternative measures used to deal with the offender, and the offender's response to those measures; and

(*d*) any matter required, by any regulation made under subsection (2), to be included in the report.

(4) The report must also contain information on any other matter required by the court, after hearing argument from the prosecutor and the offender, to be included in the report, subject to any contrary regulation made under subsection (2).

(5) The clerk of the court shall provide a copy of the report, as soon as practicable after filing, to the offender or counsel for the offender, as directed by the court, and to the prosecutor. 1995, c. 22, s. 6; 1999, c. 25, s. 16; 2002, c. 1, s. 183; 2003, c. 21, s. 15.

CROSS-REFERENCES

"Court" and "alternative measures" are defined in s. 716. Where there is a dispute as to any of the facts in the pre-sentence report, the procedure prescribed in s. 724 is to be followed.

SYNOPSIS

This section is the statutory authorization for the preparation of a pre-sentence report by a probation officer. The Lieutenant Governor in Council may make regulations prescribing the types of offences for which a court may require a report and respecting the content and form of the report. Subsection (3) sets out the mandatory contents of the report unless otherwise ordered by the judge. Subsection (3)(*a*) is particularly broad since it requires *inter alia* information on the offender's "character". In addition to the matters specified in subsec. (3), the judge may require the probation officer to report on any other matter, after hearing argument from the prosecutor and the offender. This power is, however, subject to any regulation made under subsec. (2). Under subsec. (5), the clerk of the court is to provide copies of the report to the offender or counsel for the offender, as directed by the court, and to the prosecutor.

ANNOTATIONS

Note: Some of the cases noted below were decided under the predecessor to this section but were considered of assistance in applying this section. Note, however, that the predecessor to this section [former s. 735(1)] did not set out the mandatory contents of a pre-sentence report, nor provide for the making of regulations as to the form and content of the report.

Where the accused challenges or denies a statement in the pre-sentence report which the judge considers relevant, then proof of this information should be given, with the onus being upon the Crown to prove the accuracy of the information. Otherwise, the challenged information must be disregarded. A statement in the pre-sentence report that the accused is suspected of other crimes which were not the subject of charges should not be considered by the trial court: *R. v. Morelli* (1977), 37 C.C.C. (2d) 392 (Ont. Prov. Ct.). (For notes of other cases respecting the use of evidence of other offences see s. 725, *infra*.).

A statement by the accused, who did not testify, that the commission of the offence was accidental, was not properly included in the pre-sentence report. Further, statements in the report are not evidence and not admissible to set aside the conviction: *R. v. Urbanovitch and Brown* (1985), 19 C.C.C. (3d) 43 (Man. C.A.).

The purpose of the report is to supply a picture of the offender as a person in society. The sentencing court may properly take into account negative information about the offender to which no objection was taken, including his drug use and lack of remorse, so as to relate the offence to the individual: *R. v. Riley* (1996), 107 C.C.C. (3d) 278 (N.S.C.A.).

However, a pre-sentence report is intended to be an accurate, independent, and balanced assessment of an offender, his background, and prospects for the future. Probation officers must be thorough and fair and should canvass the relevant information before commenting on an issue. While cross-examination may neutralize the prejudice of an unfair pre-sentence report for sentencing purposes, the danger is that the Parole Board may later be misled: *R. v. Junkert* (2010), 259 C.C.C. (3d) 14 (Ont. C.A.).

Section 718.2(*e*) requires the sentencing court to consider the unique systemic or background factors that may have played a part in bringing the aboriginal offender before the court and the types of sentencing procedures and sanctions that may be appropriate in the circumstances because of the offender's heritage or connection. While judges may take judicial notice of the broad systemic and background factors and the priority given to restorative justice, the court should be provided with case-specific information by counsel or in the pre-sentence report. Whether the offender resides on a reserve, in a rural or an urban area, the judge must be made aware of alternatives to incarceration that exist whether inside or outside the aboriginal community: *R. v. Gladue*, [1999] 1 S.C.R. 688, 133 C.C.C. (3d) 385.

Subsection (4) authorizes the court, on its own motion, to order a non-consensual psychiatric assessment for sentencing purposes: *R. v. Blackwell* (2007), 227 C.C.C. (3d) 275 (B.C.S.C.).

Where media outlets sought access to pre-sentence reports filed on a sentencing hearing, the court allowed access subject to redactions to protect third-party privacy interests and the court's ability to gain access to the best evidence available to discharge its obligations: *R. v. Blackmore* (2018), 364 C.C.C. (3d) 559 (B.C.S.C.).

VICTIM IMPACT STATEMENT / Inquiry by court / Adjournment / Form / Presentation of statement / Photograph / Conditions of exclusion / Consideration of statement / Evidence concerning victim admissible.

722. (1) When determining the sentence to be imposed on an offender or determining whether the offender should be discharged under section 730 in respect of any offence, the court shall consider any statement of a victim prepared in accordance with this section and filed with the court describing the physical or emotional harm, property damage or economic loss suffered by the victim as the result of the commission of the offence and the impact of the offence on the victim.

(2) As soon as feasible after a finding of guilt and in any event before imposing sentence, the court shall inquire of the prosecutor if reasonable steps have been taken to provide the victim with an opportunity to prepare a statement referred to in subsection (1).

(3) On application of the prosecutor or a victim or on its own motion, the court may adjourn the proceedings to permit the victim to prepare a statement referred to in subsection (1) or to present evidence in accordance with subsection (9), if the court is satisfied that the adjournment would not interfere with the proper administration of justice.

(4) The statement must be prepared in writing, using Form 34.2 in Part XXVIII, in accordance with the procedures established by a program designated for that purpose by the lieutenant governor in council of the province in which the court is exercising its jurisdiction.

(5) The court shall, on the request of a victim, permit the victim to present the statement by

(*a*) reading it;

(*b*) reading it in the presence and close proximity of any support person of the victim's choice;

(*c*) reading it outside the court room or behind a screen or other device that would allow the victim not to see the offender; or

(*d*) presenting it in any other manner that the court considers appropriate.

(6) During the presentation

(*a*) the victim may have with them a photograph of themselves taken before the commission of the offence if it would not, in the opinion of the court, disrupt the proceedings; or

(*b*) if the statement is presented by someone acting on the victim's behalf, that individual may have with them a photograph of the victim taken before the commission of the offence if it would not, in the opinion of the court, disrupt the proceedings.

(7) The victim shall not present the statement outside the court room unless arrangements are made for the offender and the judge or justice to watch the

presentation by means of closed-circuit television or otherwise and the offender is permitted to communicate with counsel while watching the presentation.

(8) In considering the statement, the court shall take into account the portions of the statement that it considers relevant to the determination referred to in subsection (1) and disregard any other portion.

(9) Whether or not a statement has been prepared and filed in accordance with this section, the court may consider any other evidence concerning any victim of the offence for the purpose of determining the sentence to be imposed on the offender or whether the offender should be discharged under section 730. 1995, c. 22, s. 6; 1999, c. 25, s. 17; 2000, c. 12, s. 95(*d*); 2015, c. 13, s. 25.

CROSS-REFERENCES

"Court" is defined in s. 716. "Common-law partner" is defined in s. 2. Under s. 722.1, the clerk of the court is to provide copies of the statement to the offender or counsel for the offender and to the prosecutor. Where there is a dispute as to any of the facts in the statement, then presumably the procedure prescribed in s. 724 is to be followed. Section 718 sets out various objectives of sentencing. Section 722.2 requires the court to inquire of the prosecutor or victim or any person representing the victim of the opportunity to prepare a statement under this section. The court may adjourn the proceedings to permit the victim to prepare a statement or present evidence.

Section 718(*e*) and (*f*) make particular reference to victims. Victims may also provide victim impact statements at disposition hearings for an accused found not criminally responsible on account of a mental disorder (ss. 672.5(14) to (15) and 672.541) and at the parole review hearing under s. 745.63.

Section 380.4 provides for the court to consider a community impact statement in the case of the offence of fraud under s. 380(1).

SYNOPSIS

This section sets out the circumstances under which a victim impact statement is admissible. Where a statement is properly before the court, then the court "shall" consider the statement in determining the sentence. The court may, however, take into account any other evidence concerning the victim, for example, evidence given by the victim during the trial proper, in accordance with s. 724. The statement is to be prepared in writing and in the form and in accordance with the procedures established by a program designated by the Lieutenant Governor in Council. Pursuant to subsec. (2.1), the victim is entitled to read, or present in any other manner, the victim impact statement that has been prepared and filed in accordance with this section. The term "victim" is defined in subsec. (4) and means a person to whom harm was done or who suffered physical or emotional loss as a result of the commission of the offence. Where that person is dead, ill or otherwise incapacitated, then subsec. (4)(*b*) describes the class of persons who may provide a victim impact statement.

ANNOTATIONS

"Victim" includes both the direct recipient of the harm and the victim who is directly affected in an emotional or physical way including members of the direct victim's family: *R. v. Duffus* (2000), 40 C.R. (5th) 350 (Ont. S.C.J.).

Where information is not available from the enumerated list of victims, others may seek leave of the court to file statements. The statements that are almost exclusively tributes to the victim, criticism of the offender, comments amounting to offender bashing, assertions as to the facts of the offence, recommendations as to the severity of punishments and statement addressed to the offender do not accord with the legislation: *R. v. McDonough* (2006), 209 C.C.C. (3d) 547 (Ont. S.C.J.).

Fairness in the sentencing process was adversely affected by the admission of victim impact statements containing inappropriate material including recommendations as to the length of sentence, statements sought to achieve personal revenge and the use of psychiatric diagnostic terms in reference to the accused: *R. v. Bremner* (2000), 146 C.C.C. (3d) 59 (B.C.C.A.).

Subsequent to sentencing submissions, a police officer testified and expressed an opinion about firearms and the facts of the offence. The evidence was inadmissible both procedurally and substantively on sentencing. Subsection (3) did not allow for an alternative method of placing victim impact evidence before the court. In addition, the contents of the statement exceeded that which is permissible: *R. v. Jackson* (2002), 163 C.C.C. (3d) 451 (Ont. C.A.).

There is no automatic right of cross-examination on a victim impact statement. Where an issue is raised, the court must be satisfied that there was an air of reality to the claim that there were disputable facts in the statement before cross-examination is permitted: *R. v. W. (V.)* (2008), 229 C.C.C. (3d) 344 (Ont. C.A.).

There is no discretion to refuse a victim the right to read a statement provided it conforms with subsec. (2): *R. v. Cook* (2009), 250 C.C.C. (3d) 248 (Que. C.A.), leave to appeal to S.C.C. refused 253 C.C.C. (3d) vi.

The amendments to this section brought about by the *Victims Bill of Rights Act*, S.C. 2015, c. 13, do not effect a substantial change to the role of victims in the sentencing process. The accepted restrictions on victim impact statements — for instance, prohibiting sentence recommendations and expressions of vengeance — continue to apply: *R. v. P. (B.)* (2015), 325 C.C.C. (3d) 300 (N.S. Prov. Ct.).

COPY OF STATEMENT.

722.1 The clerk of the court shall provide a copy of a statement referred to in subsection 722(1), as soon as practicable after a finding of guilt, to the offender or counsel for the offender, and to the prosecutor. 1995, c. 22, s. 6; 1999, c. 25, s. 18.

CROSS-REFERENCES

"Clerk of the court" and "prosecutor" are defined in s. 2. Section 722 refers to the victim impact statement.

SYNOPSIS

This section requires that the clerk of the court supply copies of the victim impact statement to the offender or counsel for the offender and the prosecutor as soon as practicable after the report and statement have been filed with the court.

COMMUNITY IMPACT STATEMENT / Form / Presentation of statement / Conditions of exclusion / Copy of statement.

722.2 (1) When determining the sentence to be imposed on an offender or determining whether the offender should be discharged under section 730 in respect of any offence, the court shall consider any statement made by an individual on a community's behalf that was prepared in accordance with this section and filed with the court describing the harm or loss suffered by the community as the result of the commission of the offence and the impact of the offence on the community.

(2) The statement must be prepared in writing, using Form 34.3 in Part XXVIII, in accordance with the procedures established by a program designated for that purpose by the lieutenant governor in council of the province in which the court is exercising its jurisdiction.

(3) The court shall, on the request of the individual making the statement, permit the individual to present the statement by

(*a*) reading it;

(*b*) reading it in the presence and close proximity of any support person of the individual's choice;

(*c*) reading it outside the court room or behind a screen or other device that would allow the individual not to see the offender; or

(*d*) presenting it in any other manner that the court considers appropriate.

(4) The individual making the statement shall not present it outside the court room unless arrangements are made for the offender and the judge or justice to watch the presentation by means of closed-circuit television or otherwise and the offender is permitted to communicate with counsel while watching the presentation.

(5) The clerk of the court shall, as soon as feasible after a finding of guilt, provide a copy of the statement to the offender or counsel for the offender, and to the prosecutor. 1999, c. 25, s. 18; 2015, c. 13, s. 26.

CROSS-REFERENCES

"Victim" is defined in s. 722(4).

SYNOPSIS

The court is required to inquire of the prosecutor or the victim or a person representing a victim whether the victim has been advised of the opportunity to prepare a victim impact statement and the court may adjourn the sentencing to permit the victim to prepare a statement or present evidence.

SUBMISSIONS ON FACTS / Submission of evidence / Production of evidence / Compel appearance / Hearsay evidence.

723. (1) Before determining the sentence, a court shall give the prosecutor and the offender an opportunity to make submissions with respect to any facts relevant to the sentence to be imposed.

(2) The court shall hear any relevant evidence presented by the prosecutor or the offender.

(3) The court may, on its own motion, after hearing argument from the prosecutor and the offender, require the production of evidence that would assist it in determining the appropriate sentence.

(4) Where it is necessary in the interests of justice, the court may, after consulting the parties, compel the appearance of any person who is a compellable witness to assist the court in determining the appropriate sentence.

(5) Hearsay evidence is admissible at sentencing proceedings, but the court may, if the court considers it to be in the interests of justice, compel a person to testify where the person

(*a*) has personal knowledge of the matter;

(*b*) is reasonably available; and

(*c*) is a compellable witness. 1995, c. 22, s. 6.

CROSS-REFERENCES

"Court" is defined in s. 716. Section 724 also sets out the procedure for determing the facts upon which the sentence will be based, particularly when the facts are in dispute. Section 726.1 requires the court to take into account any other relevant information placed before it, including submissions by or on behalf of the offender and the prosecutor, before imposing sentence.

SYNOPSIS

This section together with s. 724 set out most of the powers and procedures for determining the facts upon which the sentence will be based. The court is required to give the parties an opportunity to make submissions and to present relevant evidence. The court also has the power (subsec. (3)) on its own motion to require the production of evidence and (subsec. (4))

may compel the appearance of any person who is a compellable witness. These powers are to be exercised, however, only after giving the parties an opportunity to make submissions. Subsection (5) confirms that while hearsay evidence is admissible at the sentence hearing, the court in a proper case may compel a person with personal knowledge of the matter to testify. The person must be reasonably available and a compellable witness.

ANNOTATIONS

Note: Some of the cases noted below were decided prior to the enactment of this section but were considered to be of continuing relevance.

Since proof of prior convictions is part of the sentencing hearing, the common law rule which permits the admission of evidence, even hearsay evidence, which is credible and trustworthy at a sentence hearing applies. Thus an extract of a provincial driving record, although hearsay, would be admissible. However, if the accuracy of the certificate is seriously put in issue, then it would be incumbent upon the Crown to call whoever signed the certificate and make him available for cross-examination: *R. v. Albright*, [1987] 2 S.C.C. 383, 37 C.C.C. (3d) 105 (5:0).

A psychiatric assessment which had been obtained for dangerous offender proceedings subsequently abandoned by the Crown was admissible at the sentencing hearing of the offender: *R. v. N. (R.A.)* (2001), 160 C.C.C. (3d) 571 (Alta. C.A.).

There is no jurisdiction to order a psychiatric assessment of a non-consenting offender: *R. v. Gettliffe-Grant* (2006), 217 C.C.C. (3d) 474 (B.C.S.C.). *Contra*: *R. v. Blackwell* (2007), 227 C.C.C. (3d) 275 (B.C.S.C.).

Despite the mandatory language of subsec. (2) requiring the court to hear all relevant evidence, as well as similar language in s. 726.1, the court should nevertheless exclude otherwise relevant evidence proffered by the Crown on sentence where its prejudicial effect outweighs its probative value. Here, the sentencing judge made no error in declining to view a video of the offender sexually assaulting his daughter: *R. v. M. (P.)* (2012), 282 C.C.C. (3d) 450 (Ont. C.A.).

It was an error in principle for the sentencing judge to accept the accused's coercion-based explanation for why he committed the offence on the basis of a psychologist's report and submissions of counsel. Although subsec. (5) renders hearsay evidence admissible, it must be credible and trustworthy. The accused's out-of-court statement to his counsel and psychologist did not meet this threshold: *R. v. Pahl* (2016), 336 C.C.C. (3d) 221 (B.C.C.A.), additional reasons 2016 BCCA 493. However, see *R. v. Kunicki* (2014), 307 C.C.C. (3d) 233 (Man. C.A.), where the court took a more permissive approach to the offender advancing his version of the facts through counsel's submissions.

INFORMATION ACCEPTED / Jury / Disputed facts.

724. (1) In determining a sentence, a court may accept as proved any information disclosed at the trial or at the sentence proceedings and any facts agreed on by the prosecutor and the offender.

(2) Where the court is composed of a judge and jury, the court

(*a*) shall accept as proven all facts, express or implied, that are essential to the jury's verdict of guilty; and

(*b*) may find any other relevant fact that was disclosed by evidence at the trial to be proven, or hear evidence presented by either party with respect to that fact.

(3) Where there is a dispute with respect to any fact that is relevant to the determination of a sentence,

(*a*) the court shall request that evidence be adduced as to the existence of the fact unless the court is satisfied that sufficient evidence was adduced at the trial;

(*b*) the party wishing to rely on a relevant fact, including a fact contained in a presentence report, has the burden of proving it;

(*c*) either party may cross-examine any witness called by the other party;

(*d*) subject to paragraph (*e*), the court must be satisfied on a balance of probabilities of the existence of the disputed fact before relying on it in determining the sentence; and

(*e*) the prosecutor must establish, by proof beyond a reasonable doubt, the existence of any aggravating fact or any previous conviction by the offender. 1995, c. 22, s. 6.

CROSS-REFERENCES

"Court" is defined in s. 716. Section 723 also sets out the procedure for determing the facts upon which the sentence will be based. Section 726.1 requires the court to take into account any other relevant information placed before it, including submissions by or on behalf of the offender and the prosecutor, before imposing sentence. Also see s. 729, which sets out a procedure for admission of a certificate of an analyst on a prosecution for failing to comply with a probation order or a condition of a conditional sentence respecting possession or use of drugs.

SYNOPSIS

This section, together with s. 723, sets out most of the procedure to be followed in determining the facts upon which the sentence is to be based. Subsection (1) permits the court to rely upon facts proved during the trial proper as well as any other facts agreed on by the parties. Subsection (2) deals with the difficult issue where the judge is not the finder of fact. In a jury trial the judge *shall* accept as proven any of the facts that were essential to the jury's verdict. The judge *may* also find any other relevant fact disclosed by the evidence to be proven or hear other evidence that the parties may present. Subsection (3) sets out the procedure to be followed where there is a dispute as to a relevant fact. If there is a dispute concerning any fact relevant to determination of sentence, then the party seeking to rely on that fact has the burden of proving it. Where the fact is an aggravating fact, then the Crown must prove it beyond a reasonable doubt. Otherwise the burden of proof is a balance of probabilities.

ANNOTATIONS

Note: Some of the cases noted below were decided prior to the enactment of this section but were felt to be of assistance in applying this section.

Information disclosed during trial (subsec. (1)) – An admission by the accused during his testimony in the trial proper, as to his prior criminal record is proof of that record for the purposes of sentencing: *R. v. Protz* (1984), 13 C.C.C. (3d) 107 (Sask. C.A.).

Interpreting jury's verdict (subsec. (2)) – The sentencer is bound by the express and implied factual implications of the jury's verdict but, *semble*, where the factual implication is ambiguous, the sentencer should not attempt to follow the logical processes of the jury, but may come to an independent determination of the relevant facts. Thus, where the accused charged with dangerous driving causing death was convicted only of dangerous driving, *simpliciter*, the consequence of death cannot be taken into account in imposing sentence: *R. v. Brown*, [1991] 2 S.C.R. 518, 66 C.C.C. (3d) 1.

Where the trial judge failed to make the necessary sentencing findings, the Court of Appeal was unable to assess the fitness of the sentence. In the circumstances, the proper order was to remit the matter to the trial judge, pursuant to s. 683(3) and the applicable rules of court, to make those findings so that the Court of Appeal would then be in a position to determine the sentence appeal: *R. v. Englehart* (1998), 124 C.C.C. (3d) 505 (N.B.C.A.).

Disputed facts (subsec. (3)) – Where following a plea of guilty there is conflicting evidence with respect to factors going to the gravity of the offence, the onus is on the Crown to prove the aggravating facts beyond a reasonable doubt: *R. v. Gardiner*, [1982] 2 S.C.R. 368, 68 C.C.C. (2d) 477.

However, the court is not to assume all mitigating factors in favour of the accused merely because of an absence of proof beyond a reasonable doubt of the contrary: *R. v. Holt* (1983), 4 C.C.C. (3d) 32 (Ont. C.A.), leave to appeal to S.C.C. refused C.C.C. *loc. cit.*, 47 N.R. 240*n*.

In *R. v. Boulet* (1990), 58 C.C.C. (3d) 178 (Sask. C.A.), the majority of the court held that it did not need to consider the principles to be applied respecting the conduct of a sentence hearing where there are disputed facts as to the circumstances of the commission of the offence, since, even on the version of the facts most favourable to the accused, the sentence originally imposed was inadequate and thus the Crown appeal must be allowed. Bayda C.J.S., however, in his dissenting opinion, gave extensive consideration to the issue and held that the judge does not have the power to accept the prosecution's version of material disputed facts unless he first holds a formal sentence hearing at which evidence is called. Where the accused's version of the facts is so manifestly false as to be incapable of belief or is not within the bounds of reasonable possibility, the judge is entitled to reject that version, in which case, the prosecution's version is deemed not to be in dispute. Where the accused's version, however, is not manifestly false and is reasonable, the judge may accept the accused's version at an informal hearing and without the necessity of a formal hearing. The onus is primarily on the Crown to request the formal hearing, where it disputes the accused's version of events, although the trial judge may on his own motion hold a formal sentence hearing.

In *R. v. Poorman* (1991), 66 C.C.C. (3d) 82 (Sask. C.A.), the court returned to this issue and held that where there is a conflict between the Crown and the accused's version of facts, which are not crucial for the determination of guilt or innocence, then, in an informal sentence hearing, the trial judge is required so far as possible to accept the version of the accused. If the judge is of the view that the matter cannot be resolved in that way, then he must hear sworn evidence.

The requirement in subsec. (3) to hear evidence on disputed facts must be read together with s. 723(5) which makes hearsay admissible at sentencing hearings. Therefore, the sentencing judge was entitled to accept defence counsel's submissions as evidence that the accused was a street-level trafficker notwithstanding expert evidence tendered by the Crown suggesting that he was a higher-level trafficker: *R. v. Kunicki* (2014), 307 C.C.C. (3d) 233 (Man. C.A.).

In *R. v. Pahl* (2016), 336 C.C.C. (3d) 221 (B.C.C.A.), additional reasons 2016 BCCA 493, however, the court rejected the approach in *Kunicki*, holding that an accused is not entitled to put his or her disputed version of events in "evidence" through submissions of counsel. The court held that, while different burdens of proof apply to the Crown and offender at a sentencing hearing, the evidentiary rules are the same for both.

The factual foundation, including aggravating factors, should be determined before a sentencing circle determines the sanction: *R. v. Labelle* (2002), 163 C.C.C. (3d) 404, [2002] 6 W.W.R. 602 *sub nom. R. v. L. (B.)* (Alta. C.A.).

OTHER OFFENCES / Attorney General's consent / No further proceedings.

725. (1) In determining the sentence, a court

(*a*) shall consider, if it is possible and appropriate to do so, any other offences of which the offender was found guilty by the same court, and shall determine the sentence to be imposed for each of those offences;

(*b*) shall consider, if the Attorney General and the offender consent, any outstanding charges against the offender to which the offender consents to plead guilty and pleads guilty, if the court has jurisdiction to try those charges, and shall determine the sentence to be imposed for each charge unless the court is of the opinion that a separate prosecution for the other offence is necessary in the public interest;

(*b*.1) shall consider any outstanding charges against the offender, unless the court is of the opinion that a separate prosecution for one or more of the other offences is necessary in the public interest, subject to the following conditions:

(i) the Attorney General and the offender consent,

(ii) the court has jurisdiction to try each charge,

(iii) each charge has been described in open court,

(iv) the offender has agreed with the facts asserted in the description of each charge, and

(v) the offender has acknowledged having committed the offence described in each charge; and

(*c*) may consider any facts forming part of the circumstances of the offence that could constitute the basis for a separate charge.

(1.1) For the purpose of paragraphs (1)(*b*) and (*b*.1), the Attorney General shall take the public interest into account before consenting.

(2) The court shall, on the information or indictment, note

(*a*) any outstanding charges considered in determining the sentence under paragraph (1)(*b*.1), and

(*b*) any facts considered in determining the sentence under paragraph (1)(*c*),

and no further proceedings may be taken with respect to any offence described in those charges or disclosed by those facts unless the conviction for the offence of which the offender has been found guilty is set aside or quashed on appeal. 1995, c. 22, s. 6; 1999, c. 5, s. 31.

CROSS-REFERENCES

"Court" is defined in s. 716. The procedure for determining the facts upon which the sentence will be based is set out in ss. 723 and 724. The procedure where the offender actually pleads guilty to other offences is set out in Part XX. In addition, note ss. 478 and 479 which provide a procedure for transferring charges from another part of the province and from other provinces for the purpose of the accused pleading guilty to those additional offences.

SYNOPSIS

This section gives the sentencing court jurisdiction to take other offences, of which the accused is guilty, into account in sentencing the accused. The section appears to contemplate four different situations. Subsection (1)(*a*) deals with the usual case where the accused is found guilty of several offences by the same court. Subsection (1)(*b*) allows the court, with the consent of the parties, to take other offences into account even if the offender has not been found guilty of those offences by the same court, if the offender consents to and pleads guilty. The only conditions for invoking this paragraph are that the charges are outstanding at the time and the offender and the Attorney General consent. The court may refuse to invoke this procedure if it is of the opinion that a separate prosecution for the other offences is necessary in the public interest. The relationship between this section and the formal procedure for transferring charges from another part of the province or from other provinces as set out in ss. 478 and 479 is unclear. Subsection (1)(*b*.1) contemplates a procedure similar to that considered in cases such as *R. v. Garcia and Silva,* [1970] 3 C.C.C. 124 (Ont. C.A.), to have other outstanding charges taken into account although the accused did not plead guilty to those other offences. Subsection (1)(*c*) allows the court to take into consideration in imposing sentence any facts forming part of the circumstances of the offence, even though those facts could themselves have formed the subject of separate charges. Where the procedure under this paragraph is followed and these other facts taken into account then, pursuant to subsec. (2) the court is to note any of those facts on the information or indictment and no further proceedings may be taken in respect of those other offences, unless the conviction for the predicate offence is set aside or quashed on appeal.

ANNOTATIONS

Note: Some of the cases noted below were decided prior to the enactment of this section but were felt to be of assistance in interpreting this provision.

Evidence of other offences – Outstanding offences under subsec. (1)(*b*) and (*b*.1) may be considered only if they are separately charged offences (1) with the accused's consent, and (2) if they agree to plead guilty or agree with the facts asserted and acknowledge having committed the offence. In *R. v. Edwards* (2001), 155 C.C.C. (3d) 473, the Ontario Court of Appeal held that evidence of untried offences is admissible at a sentencing hearing for the purpose of showing the offender's background and character as it relates to the objectives of sentencing. The trial judge has the discretion to exclude this evidence where necessary to ensure that the accused has a fair hearing. In determining the admissibility of untried offences, the judge should consider the nexus between the evidence and the offence, the similarity between the evidence and the offence, the difficulty the offender may have in properly defending against the allegations, the danger that the sentencing hearing will be prolonged, whether the accused has adduced good character evidence and the cogency of the proposed evidence. See also *R. v. Roberts* (2006), 208 C.C.C. (3d) 454 (Alta. C.A.), leave to appeal to S.C.C. refused [2007] 2 S.C.R. vii, 208 C.C.C. (3d) vi.

While a sentencing judge cannot consider uncharged offences under subsec. (1)(*b*) and (*b*.1) without the consent of both the Crown and the offender, there is no such requirement contained in subsec. (1)(*c*). The sentencing judge may consider uncharged offences over the objections of the Crown. Accordingly, where the facts form part of the circumstances of the offence that could constitute the basis for a separate charge, the sentencing judge has the discretion to take these facts into account. Where the accused does not consent to the application of this provision, the Crown bears the burden of proving the uncharged offence beyond a reasonable doubt. "Part of the circumstances of the offence" require a nexus or connexity between the uncharged criminal conduct and the offence for which the offender has been convicted. Therefore, this provision encompasses the facts of a single transaction and also the broader category of related facts that inform the court about the circumstances of the offence more generally. This provision contains two important safeguards: (1) unrelated offences are excluded, and (2) the judge can decline to consider the uncharged offences if this would result in unfairness to the accused or to the Crown: *R. v. Larche*, [2006] 2 S.C.R. 762, 214 C.C.C. (3d) 289. See also *R. v. Angelillo*, [2006] 2 S.C.R. 728, 214 C.C.C. (3d) 309.

Under subsec. (1)(*c*), where the uncharged offence was committed abroad, the facts that form "part of the circumstances of the offence" must also have a real and substantial connection to Canada: *R. v. Larche, supra.*

At his sentence hearing on a charge of robbery the accused was entitled to lead psychiatric evidence to show he was not a danger to the community but it was also open to the Crown to lead evidence in reply as to the circumstances surrounding the accused's arrest which showed the accused was planning a further robbery, the money from the first robbery having run out: *R. v. Lees*, [1979] 2 S.C.R. 749, 46 C.C.C. (2d) 385 (7:0).

OFFENDERS MAY SPEAK TO SENTENCE.

726. Before determining the sentence to be imposed, the court shall ask whether the offender, if present, has anything to say. 1995, c. 22, s. 6.

CROSS-REFERENCES

"Court" is defined in s. 716. Section 726.1 requires the court to consider any relevant information placed before it including submissions made by or on behalf of the parties.

SYNOPSIS

This section requires the court to give the offender an opportunity to make a statement before sentence is imposed.

ANNOTATIONS

Note: Some of the cases noted below were decided under the predecessor to this section [former s. 668] but were considered of assistance in interpreting this provision. Note, however, that former s. 668 contained a proviso that the failure to give the accused an opportunity to make a statement before sentencing did not affect the validity of the proceedings.

The deliberate refusal of the trial judge to comply with former s. 668 constituted a violation of the accused's rights under s. 7 of the Charter. While the error did not invalidate the earlier proceedings leading to conviction, it was not a sufficient remedy on appeal to merely give the accused an opportunity to make the submissions that he would have made befor ehte trial judge. Rather, the appellate court should reduce the length of what otherwise was a fit sentence: *R. v. Dennison* (1990), 60 C.C.C. (3d) 342 (N.B.C.A.).

However, where the failure of the trial judge to comply with this provision was merely due to an oversight, the sentencing proceedings were not invalidated. In this case, no evidence was submitted on appeal indicating that the accused had anything to add to the submissions of his counsel at trial: *R. v. Senek* (1998), 130 C.C.C. (3d) 473 (Man. C.A.).

RELEVANT INFORMATION.

726.1 In determining the sentence, a court shall consider any relevant information placed before it, including any representations or submissions made by or on behalf of the prosecutor or the offender. 1995, c. 22, s. 6.

CROSS-REFERENCES

"Court" is defined in s. 716. Sections 723 and 724 set out the procedure to be followed in determining the facts of the offence which form the basis for the sentence. Section 721 provides that the court may order a pre-sentence report. Section 722 requires the court to take into account any victim impact statement. Section 726 requires the court to give the offender an opportunity to say anything prior to sentence.

SYNOPSIS

This section requires the court to take into account any relevant information placed before it. This information may come in the form of evidence or submissions by the prosecutor and the offender.

ANNOTATIONS

Aboriginal offenders – While it is open to the trial judge to use a sentencing circle to assist in developing the appropriate sentence, the power and duty to impose a fit sentence remains vested exclusively in the trial judge. Where a sentencing circle recommends a sentence which is not fit, the judge is duty-bound to ignore the recommendation to the extent that it varies from what is a fit sentence. The duty of the court of appeal in reviewing the fitness of a sentence is the same. The very purpose of sentencing circles is to fashion sentences that will differ in some mix or measure from those which the courts have up to now imposed in order to take into account aboriginal culture and traditions, and to permit and take into account direct community participation both in imposition and administration of the sentence. The possibility of rehabilitation is a factor which must be taken into account in any sentence and departure from the normal range of sentences for a given offence may be permitted where there are circumstances out of the ordinary to justify the departure. This leaves substantial room for the use of sentencing circles. However, it would not be appropriate to use a sentencing circle in those cases where it was clear that the circumstances required a penitentiary term. If a sentence exceeds two years imprisonment, the court is without power to impose any condition on the accused after the sentence has been served and there is no means of enforcing any obligations undertaken by an accused as a result of the recommendations of the community through a sentencing circle: *R. v. Morin* (1995), 101 C.C.C. (3d) 124 (Sask. C.A.).

The sentencing court's obligation to make inquiries into the circumstances of an aboriginal offender, beyond what might be contained in the pre-sentence report, is limited to appropriate circumstances and where such inquiries are practicable. The trial judge's assessment of whether further inquiries are either appropriate or practicable is entitled to deference by the Court of Appeal: *R. v. Wells*, [2000] 1 S.C.R. 207, 141 C.C.C. (3d) 368.

Where a not guilty plea is entered, the accused will have to demonstrate his or her remorse, sincerity and acceptance of responsibility in some other way before a sentencing circle will be held. The fact that the offence was a serious sexual assault did not automatically rule out a sentencing circle. However, the community must be willing to help to restore and reintegrate the offender. Before using a sentencing circle, the trial judge must consult with the community and obtain confirmation from the victim that they are prepared to participate in the circle proceedings: *R. v. Taylor* (1997), 122 C.C.C. (3d) 376 (Sask. C.A.).

Use of statistics – Evidence of statistics compiled by a police department based on police investigations during a certain period without regard to population growth and presented to the court by a police employee untrained in statistics is insufficient and inherently unreliable for use at a sentence hearing: *R. v. Petrovic* (1984), 13 C.C.C. (3d) 416 (Ont. C.A.). Compare *R. v. Richards* noted, *supra*, under s. 718.2.

The trial judge erred in taking judicial notice of the prevalence of break and enters in a local area and imposing a deterrent sentence. The error was compounded by the failure to notify the accused ahead of time so as to allow him an opportunity to respond: *R. v. Mallory* (2004), 189 C.C.C. (3d) 345 (N.B.C.A.).

Disclosure by accused – It would not be proper to increase the sentence which would otherwise be appropriate because of the voluntary disclosure by the accused of information to a psychiatrist which gave the acts committed a more serious character. The disclosure of this information was necessary if treatment of the accused was to be effective and it should not be used to impose a sentence which would not otherwise be warranted: *R. v. Henderson* (1990), 56 C.C.C. (3d) 413 (B.C.C.A.).

Conduct of defence – Conduct of the defence at trial, including suspected perjury by the accused in testifying or defence tactics in cross-examination of the complainant, cannot be taken into account as aggravating circumstances in sentencing the accused. The accused's conduct in his defence can only be used to negate any other evidence of remorse which might have mitigated the fit sentence: *R. v. Kozy* (1990), 58 C.C.C. (3d) 500 (Ont. C.A.).

REASONS FOR SENTENCE.

726.2 When imposing a sentence, a court shall state the terms of the sentence imposed, and the reasons for it, and enter those terms and reasons into the record of the proceedings. 1995, c. 22, s. 6.

CROSS-REFERENCES

"Court" is defined in s. 716.

SYNOPSIS

The court is required to provide reasons for imposing the sentence and to state the terms of the sentence. The terms and the reasons are to be included in the record.

PREVIOUS CONVICTION / Procedure / Where hearing *ex parte* / Organizations / Section does not apply.

727. (1) Subject to subsections (3) and (4), where an offender is convicted of an offence for which a greater punishment may be imposed by reason of previous convictions, no greater punishment shall be imposed on the offender by reason thereof unless the prosecutor satisfies the court that the offender, before making a plea, was notified that a greater punishment would be sought by reason thereof.

(2) Where an offender is convicted of an offence for which a greater punishment may be imposed by reason of previous convictions, the court shall, on application by the prosecutor and on being satisfied that the offender was notified in accordance with subsection (1), ask whether the offender was previously convicted and, if the offender does not admit to any previous convictions, evidence of previous convictions may be adduced.

(3) Where a summary conviction court holds a trial pursuant to subsection 803(2) and convicts the offender, the court may, whether or not the offender was notified that a greater punishment would be sought by reason of a previous conviction, make inquiries and hear evidence with respect to previous convictions of the offender and, if any such conviction is proved, may impose a greater punishment by reason thereof.

(4) If, under section 623, the court proceeds with the trial of an organization that has not appeared and pleaded and convicts the organization, the court may, whether or not the organization was notified that a greater punishment would be sought by reason of a previous conviction, make inquiries and hear evidence with respect to previous convictions of the organization and, if any such conviction is proved, may impose a greater punishment by reason of that conviction.

(5) This section does not apply to a person referred to in paragraph 745(*b*). 1995, c. 22, s. 6; 2003, c. 21, s. 16.

CROSS-REFERENCES

Section 667 provides a method of proof of a prior conviction. The reference in subsec. (5) to s. 745(*b*) is to an accused convicted of second degree murder who has previously been convicted of murder. Section 745 sets the period of parole eligibility for such person at 25 years. The reference in subsec. (3) to s. 803(2) is to the case where the defendant has been tried *ex parte* on a summary conviction offence. Reference in subsec. (4) to s. 623 is to the trial of a corporation that has failed to appear by counsel or agent. A verdict of not criminally responsible on account of mental disorder is not a "previous conviction" (s. 672.36).

SYNOPSIS

This section deals with the procedures to be followed where the Crown seeks a higher range of sentence by reason of the accused's previous criminal record.

Except where a trial has proceeded *ex parte* (see subsecs. (3), (4)), no greater punishment can be imposed unless the Crown proves that it notified the accused of its intention to seek an increased sentence before the accused entered a plea (subsec. (1)). This is commonly referred to as giving notice of greater punishment.

If, having been duly notified, the accused does not admit the earlier convictions proof of the same may be given (subsec. (2)).

Notice is not required in cases where the sentence for second degree murder is increased as a result of an earlier murder conviction (see s. 745.6).

ANNOTATIONS

Some of the cases noted below were decided under the predecessors to this section, former ss. 665 and 740(1), but were considered to be of assistance in applying this section, which is similarly worded.

When notice required – This section also applies where the Crown seeks the longer firearms prohibition provided for in [former] s. 100(1)(*b*) [now s. 109(3)] by reason of the accused's prior conviction for an offence involving violence: *R. v. Jobb* (1988), 43 C.C.C. (3d) 476 (Sask. C.A.). See also *R. v. King* (1996), 107 C.C.C. (3d) 542 (P.E.I.S.C.); *R. v. Ellis* (2001), 143 O.A.C. 43 (C.A.).

This provision applies where the Crown seeks a longer driving prohibition pursuant to s. 259(1)(*c*): *R. v. Tabor* (2004), 184 C.C.C. (3d) 262 (B.C.C.A.).

Reviewability – The Crown's decision to file a notice under this section is not an exercise of core prosecutorial discretion, and, because it has a direct impact on the liberty interests of the accused, it is reviewable by the courts for compliance with s. 7 principles of fundamental justice. The prosecutor's decision will run contrary to the principles of fundamental justice if it undermines the integrity of the administration of justice, operates in a manner that renders the sentencing proceedings fundamentally unfair, is arbitrary, or results in a limit on the accused's liberty that is grossly disproportionate to the state interest in proving the notice. The courts cannot review the decision for substantive "reasonableness", since there is no such principle of fundamental justice: *R. v. Gill* (2012), 96 C.R. (6th) 172 (Ont. C.A.).

The decision in *Gill*, *supra*, must be read in light of *R. v. Anderson*, [2014] 2 S.C.R. 167, 311 C.C.C. (3d) 1, which makes clear that conduct falling short of abuse of process may not form a basis for reviewing prosecutorial discretion.

Sufficiency of notice – Since subsec. (1) does not specify written notice, verbal notice may be given: *R. v. Bolley*, [1966] 3 C.C.C. 57, 47 C.R. 247 *sub nom. R. ex rel. Perry v. Bolley* (B.C.S.C.); *R. v. Collini* (1979), 3 M.V.R. 218 (Ont. H.C.J.).

The accused is not entitled to "reasonable" notice of the Crown's intention to seek a higher penalty and thus notification the morning of the accused's trial is scheduled to commence is sufficient. If the accused has been prejudiced by the short notice he may apply for an adjournment: *R. v. Boufford* (1988), 46 C.C.C. (3d) 116 (Ont. Dist. Ct.).

As long as the error in it did not mislead or prejudice the defendant, a notice reasonably identifying the previous conviction and the Crown's intention is sufficient: *R. v. Reid*, [1970] 5 C.C.C. 368 (B.C.C.A.).

In *R. v. Thunderblanket* (1979), 2 Sask. R. 199 (C.A.), the court held that a notice is valid although given to the accused prior to the charge being laid.

A notice to the effect that the Crown would seek a greater punishment by reason of a previous conviction or convictions without specifying the previous convictions intended to be proved is sufficient compliance with this section: *R. v. Pidlubny* (1973), 10 C.C.C. (2d) 178 (Ont. C.A.).

The notice of intent to seek greater punishment need not refer specifically to the offence for which the greater punishment would be sought: *R. v. Duncan* (1982), 1 C.C.C. (3d) 444 (B.C.C.A.).

Similarly, a notice which referred to the accused as having been convicted of "offence(s)" is sufficient. There is no requirement that the notice specify the number of convictions or whether the Crown intends to proceed by way of a second or third conviction: *R. v. Monk* (1981), 62 C.C.C. (2d) 6 (Ont. C.A.).

A notice which inaccurately refers to the accused as having been charged with several drinking and driving offences could not have prejudiced or misled the accused. Further, a notice need not specifically identify the offence with which the accused was charged, nor the alleged previous offences. Finally, the prosecution at the time of serving the notice need not have a reasonable belief that the accused has previous convictions: *R. v. Kelly* (1986), 40 M.V.R. 50 (N.B.Q.B.).

A notice which merely indicates that if he has previously been convicted the accused "may" receive a greater punishment does not comply with this section: *R. v. Riley* (1982), 69 C.C.C. (2d) 245 (Ont. H.C.J.).

There is no requirement that the nature or character of the greater punishment being sought be set out in the notice. Thus it is not necessary to set out that a jail term will be sought: *R. v. Bear* (1979), 47 C.C.C. (2d) 462 (Sask. C.A.).

This section and s. 667 constitute a complete code of procedure by which a greater punishment may be sought and there is no requirement that s. 28 of the *Canada Evidence Act* be complied with: *R. v. Jonasson* (1980), 56 C.C.C. (2d) 121 (Sask. C.A.).

Sufficiency of service of notice – The notice must be given to the accused personally and service of the notice on a member of the accused's family is not sufficient: *R. v. Boileau; R. v. Lepine* (1979), 50 C.C.C. (2d) 189 (Que. S.C.).

In *R. v. Godon* (1984), 12 C.C.C. (3d) 446 (Sask. C.A.), the court distinguished *R. v. Boileau; R. v. Lepine, supra*, and held that service on the accused's mother was sufficient as she had appeared as agent for the accused pursuant to s. 800(2).

However, it was held in *R. v. Fowler* (1982), 2 C.C.C. (3d) 227 (N.S.S.C. App. Div.), that this section does not require personal service and service on the accused's counsel was sufficient. Similarly: *R. v. Simms* (1986), 31 C.C.C. (3d) 350 (Nfld. C.A.).

Effect of failure to give notice – The trial judge is entitled to take into account the accused's previous record in determining the appropriate sentence even if notice has not been given pursuant to this section. The giving or not giving of notice merely fixes the bottom limit to the judge's power to sentence for an offence such as "over 80" which, as a result of s. 255, has a different minimum depending on the number of prior convictions. However, failure to give notice does not require that the accused be treated as a first offender: *R. v. Norris* (1988), 41 C.C.C. (3d) 441 (N.W.T.C.A.).

SENTENCE JUSTIFIED BY ANY COUNT.

728. Where one sentence is passed on a verdict of guilty on two or more counts of an indictment, the sentence is good if any of the counts would have justified the sentence. 1995, c. 22, s. 6.

CROSS-REFERENCES

Section 718.3 sets out the general discretion of the court in imposing sentence, including imposition of consecutive sentences. Section 725 provides a procedure for imposing sentence in respect of other offences.

SYNOPSIS

Notwithstanding the provisions of this section, it is the general practice to impose sentence in respect of each count upon which the offender has been found guilty, even if those sentences are simply made concurrent to each other.

ANNOTATIONS

Note: The cases noted below were decided under the predecessor to this section (former s. 669) but were considered to be of assistance in applying this section.

Although the imposition of a single sentence for two offences is permitted by this section, it is preferable that one sentence be imposed for each conviction and the sentences may, of course, be made concurrent: *R. v. Thorpe* (1976), 32 C.C.C. (2d) 46 (Man. C.A.).

This section does not authorize the imposition of concurent fines. A separate fine must be imposed with respect to each count: *R. v. Stubel* (1990), 25 M.V.R. (2d) 118 (Alta. C.A.).

PROOF OF CERTIFICATE OF ANALYST / Definition of "analyst" / Notice of intention to produce certificate / Requiring attendance of analyst.

729. (1) In

(*a*) a prosecution for failure to comply with a condition in a probation order that the accused not have in possession or use drugs, or

(*b*) a hearing to determine whether the offender breached a condition of a conditional sentence order that the offender not have in possession or use drugs,

a certificate purporting to be signed by an analyst stating that the analyst has analyzed or examined a substance and stating the result of the analysis or examination is admissible in evidence and, in the absence of evidence to the contrary, is proof of the statements contained in the certificate without proof of the signature or official character of the person appearing to have signed the certificate.

(2) In this section, "analyst" means a person designated as an analyst under the *Controlled Drugs and Substances Act* or the *Cannabis Act*.

(3) No certificate shall be admitted in evidence unless the party intending to produce it has, before the trial or hearing, as the case may be, given reasonable notice and a copy of the certificate to the party against whom it is to be produced.

(4) and (5) [*Repealed*, 2008, c. 18, s. 36.]

(6) The party against whom a certificate of an analyst is produced may, with leave of the court, require the attendance of the analyst for cross-examination. 1995, c. 22, s. 6; 1999, c. 31, s. 69; 2004, c. 12, s. 11; 2008, c. 18, s. 36; 2018, c. 16, s. 221.

CROSS-REFERENCES

The companion provisions for proof by way of certificate of the nature of a drug or narcotic during the trial proper can be found in s. 35 of the Food and Drugs Act, R.S.C. 1985, c. F-27 and s. 9 of the *Narcotic Control Act*, R.S.C. 1985, c. N-1. Breach of probation is an offence under s. 733.1. The hearing to determine whether the offender breached a condition of a conditional sentence is conducted under s. 742.6.

SYNOPSIS

This section provides a method of proof by way of analyst's certificate of the nature of the substance found in the offender's possession allegedly in breach of a condition of probation or conditional sentence that the offender not use or possess drugs. The analyst's certificate is proof of the facts stated therein, in the absence of evidence to the contrary. The court may, however, require the analyst to attend for cross-examination. The party intending to rely upon the certificate must give reasonable notice of the intention to rely on the certificate together with a copy of the certificate. Proof of notice may be made in accordance with s. 4(6) and (6.1). The court may, however, require the person who gave the affidavit, solemn declaration or declaration to attend for examination or cross-examination in respect of the issue of proof of service pursuant to s. 4(7).

PROOF OF CERTIFICATE OF ANALYST — BODILY SUBSTANCE / Definition of "analyst" / Notice of intention to produce certificate / Requiring attendance of analyst.

729.1 (1) In a prosecution for failure to comply with a condition in a probation order that the accused not consume drugs, alcohol or any other intoxicating substance, or in a hearing to determine whether the offender breached such a condition of a conditional sentence order, a certificate purporting to be signed by an analyst that states that the analyst has analyzed a sample of a bodily substance and that states the result of the analysis is admissible in evidence and, in the absence of evidence to the contrary, is proof of the statements contained in the certificate without proof of the signature or official character of the person who appears to have signed the certificate.

(2) In this section, "analyst" has the same meaning as in section 320.11.

(3) No certificate shall be admitted in evidence unless the party intending to produce it has, before the trial or hearing, as the case may be, given reasonable notice and a copy of the certificate to the party against whom it is to be produced.

(4) The party against whom a certificate of an analyst is produced may, with leave of the court, require the attendance of the analyst for cross-examination. 2011, c. 7, s. 2; 2018, c. 21, s. 23.

Absolute and Conditional Discharges

CONDITIONAL AND ABSOLUTE DISCHARGE / Period for which appearance notice, etc., continues in force / Effect of discharge / Where person bound by probation order convicted of offence.

730. (1) Where an accused, other than an organization, pleads guilty to or is found guilty of an offence, other than an offence for which a minimum punishment is prescribed by law or an offence punishable by imprisonment for fourteen years or for life, the court before which the accused appears may, if it considers it to be in the best interests of the accused and not contrary to the public interest, instead of convicting the accused, by order direct that the accused be discharged absolutely or on the conditions prescribed in a probation order made under subsection 731(2).

(2) Subject to Part XVI, where an accused who has not been taken into custody or who has been released from custody under or by virtue of any provision of Part XVI pleads guilty of or is found guilty of an offence but is not convicted, the appearance notice, promise to appear, summons, undertaking or recognizance issued to or given or entered into by the accused continues in force, subject to its terms, until a disposition in respect of the accused is made under subsection (1) unless, at the time the accused pleads guilty or is found guilty, the court, judge or justice orders that the accused be taken into custody pending such a disposition.

(3) Where a court directs under subsection (1) that an offender be discharged of an offence, the offender shall be deemed not to have been convicted of the offence except that

- **(*a*) the offender may appeal from the determination of guilt as if it were a conviction in respect of the offence;**
- **(*b*) the Attorney General and, in the case of summary conviction proceedings, the informant or the informant's agent may appeal from the decision of the court not to convict the offender of the offence as if that decision were a judgment or verdict of acquittal of the offence or a dismissal of the information against the offender; and**
- **(*c*) the offender may plead autrefois convict in respect of any subsequent charge relating to the offence.**

(4) Where an offender who is bound by the conditions of a probation order made at a time when the offender was directed to be discharged under this section is convicted of an offence, including an offence under section 733.1, the court that made the probation order may, in addition to or in lieu of exercising its authority under subsection 732.2(5), at any time when it may take action under that subsection, revoke the discharge, convict the offender of the offence to which the discharge relates and impose any sentence that could have been imposed if the offender had been convicted at the time of discharge, and no appeal lies from a conviction under this subsection where an appeal was taken from the order directing that the offender be discharged. 1995, c. 22, s. 6; 1997, c. 18, s. 141; 2003, c. 21, s. 17.

CROSS-REFERENCES
The accused's right of appeal from conviction in proceedings by indictment are governed by s. 675(1)(*a*) and in summary conviction proceedings by ss. 813(*a*) and 830(1). The Crown's right of appeal from acquittal in proceedings by indictment is governed by s. 676(1)(*a*) and in summary conviction proceedings by ss. 813(*b*) and 830(1). Sections 673 and 785 define an order under subsec. (1) as a "sentence". Parts XXI and XXVII, deal with appeals.

Section 607(1)(*b*) permits the special plea of *autrefois convict* with its use determined by ss. 607 to 610.

See s. 732.1 for the contents and form of the probation order and s. 732.2 for the coming into force of the order. Section 733 governs the transfer of orders. Under s. 733.1, failure or refusal to comply with the order constitutes a summary conviction offence. The court discharging the offender must consider the imposition of a victim fine surcharge (s. 737).

SYNOPSIS
This section provides the court with a sentencing option which results in the accused not having a criminal record in connection with the offence in question.

If an accused other than a corporation is convicted of an offence for which no minimum punishment is prescribed, or for which the maximum is less than 14 years, the court can, if it considers it to be in the best interests of the accused and not contrary to the public interest, discharge the accused either absolutely or on conditions (subsec. (1)).

An absolute discharge takes effect immediately and the accused is deemed not to have been convicted. A conditional discharge requires that the accused enter into a probation order for a period of time and does not become absolute until that time has passed. If the accused breaches the terms of the probation order he or she may be brought back before the court which can then formally enter a conviction and impose sentence (subsecs. (3), (4)). Such a conviction may not be appealed if an appeal has already been taken from the order directing a discharge (subsec. (4)).

Both the accused and the Crown (and the informant in summary conviction matters) have the right to appeal a discharge (subsec. (3)(*a*), (*b*)).

A discharge will support a plea of *autrefois convict* (subsec. (3)(*c*)).

Subsection (2) provides that until discharged an accused who remains at large following a finding of guilt, will continue to be bound by the terms and conditions of his or her release.

ANNOTATIONS
Principles in imposing discharge – In *R. v. Sanchez-Pino* (1973), 11 C.C.C. (2d) 53 (Ont. C.A.), the court gave some guidelines as to when a discharge is appropriate, as follows:

> The granting of some form of discharge must be "in the best interests of the accused". I take this to mean that deterrence of the offender himself is not a relevant consideration, in the circumstances, except to the extent required by conditions in a probation order. Nor is his rehabilitation through correctional or treatment centres, except to the same extent. Normally he will be a person of good character, or at least of such character that the entry of a conviction against him may have significant repercussions. It must not be "contrary to the public interest" to grant some form of discharge. One element thereby brought in will be the necessity or otherwise of a sentence which will be a deterrent to others who may be minded to commit a like offence — a standard part of the criteria for sentencing.

In *R. v. Fallofield* (1973), 13 C.C.C. (2d) 450 (B.C.C.A.), the court draws the following conclusions as to the application of this section:

(1) The section may be used in respect of *any* offence other than an offence for which a minimum punishment is prescribed by law or the offence is punishable by imprisonment for 14 years or for life or by death.
(2) The section contemplates the commission of an offence. There is nothing in the language that limits it to a technical or trivial violation.

(3) Of the two conditions precedent to the exercise of the jurisdiction, the first is that the court must consider that it is in the best interests of the accused that he should be discharged either absolutely or upon condition. If it is not in the best interests of the accused, that, of course, is the end of the matter. If it is decided that it is in the best interests of the accused, then that brings the next consideration into operation.
(4) The second condition precedent is that the court must consider that a grant of discharge is not contrary to the public interest.
(5) Generally, the first condition would presuppose that the accused is a person of good character, without previous conviction, that it is not necessary to enter a conviction against him in order to deter him from future offences or to rehabilitate him, and that the entry of a conviction against him may have significant adverse repercussions.
(6) In the context of the second condition the public interest in the deterrence of others, while it must be given due weight, does not preclude the judicious use of the discharge provisions.
(7) The powers given by s. 662.1 [now s. 730] should not be exercised as an alternative to probation or suspended sentence.
(8) Section 662.1 [now s. 730] should not be applied routinely to any particular offence. This may result in an apparent lack of uniformity in the application of the discharge provisions. This lack will be more apparent than real and will stem from the differences in the circumstances of cases.

In considering whether a discharge should be granted the court may consider whether the accused has been granted a discharge on a previous occasion: *R. v. Tan* (1974), 22 C.C.C. (2d) 184 (B.C.C.A.).

However, a previous experience with a diversion programme which did not entail any finding or admission of guilt is not the equivalent of a previous discharge and does not of itself disqualify the accused from receiving a discharge: *R. v. Drew* (1978), 45 C.C.C. (2d) 212 (B.C.C.A.).

A discharge should not be granted where it would otherwise clearly not be mandated merely because it is urged by the accused that the immigration authorities might not be sympathetic to his situation: *R. v. Melo* (1975), 26 C.C.C. (2d) 510 (Ont. C.A.). However, consideration must be given to the effect of a conviction on the rights of an accused including the right to emigrate and immigrate. In this case, it was an appropriate consideration that a conviction would result in the deportation of the accused who was on a student visa: *R. v. Abouabedellah* (1996), 109 C.C.C. (3d) 477 (Que. C.A.).

In *R. v. Myers* (1977), 37 C.C.C. (2d) 182 (Ont. C.A.), it was held that the trial judge adopted too narrow a test when he refused a discharge because the registering of a conviction would have no immediate effect upon the accused's employment.

In *R. v. Culley* (1977), 36 C.C.C. (2d) 433 (Ont. C.A.), it was held that the trial judge erred in refusing a discharge to a mature accused because he was of the view that the discharge provisions are primarily applicable to young offenders and on appeal a discharge was granted to a 26-year-old accused for possession of a small quantity of marihuana where the registering of conviction would have serious repercussions to his future employment.

Procedure – The formal oral conviction by the trial judge upon the jury's verdict of guilty being rendered does not preclude the court from granting a discharge to the accused. Further, the phrase "in the proceedings commenced against him" relates to the proceedings only in respect of which he was found guilty and therefore, where an accused is found guilty of possession of a narcotic only, after a trial on a charge of possession for the purpose of trafficking, the accused can be discharged upon the charge of possession notwithstanding that the offence originally charged carries a maximum penalty of life imprisonment: *R. v. Sampson* (1975), 23 C.C.C. (2d) 65 (Ont. C.A.).

It is not possible to include as a condition of a probation order that the accused pay a fine: *R. v. Carroll* (1995), 38 C.R. (4th) 238 (B.C.C.A.).

Constitutional considerations – The subsequent conviction and sentence of an accused initially granted a conditional discharge, as a result of his commission of an offence while on probation, does not violate the guarantee against double jeopardy in s. 11(*h*) of the *Charter of Rights and Freedoms*: *R. v. Elendiuk* (1986), 27 C.C.C. (3d) 94 (Alta. C.A.).

Probation

MAKING OF PROBATION ORDER / Idem.

731. (1) Where a person is convicted of an offence, a court may, having regard to the age and character of the offender, the nature of the offence and the circumstances surrounding its commission,

(*a*) if no minimum punishment is prescribed by law, suspend the passing of sentence and direct that the offender be released on the conditions prescribed in a probation order; or

(*b*) in addition to fining or sentencing the offender to imprisonment for a term not exceeding two years, direct that the offender comply with the conditions prescribed in a probation order.

(2) A court may also make a probation order where it discharges an accused under subsection 730(1). 1995, c. 22, s. 6.

CROSS-REFERENCES

Section 732.1 sets out the mandatory and optional conditions for a probation order and the procedure for making the order. Section 732.2 prescribes when the order comes into effect, the procedure for varying the order, and the court's power to change the order where the offender is convicted of an offence while on probation. The maximum period of probation is three years [s. 732.2(2)(*b*)]. Section 732.2(5)(*d*) gives the court power to revoke a suspended sentence where the offender was convicted of an offence while on probation. Section 733 provides a procedure for transferring the order where the offender becomes a resident of another territorial division. The offence of failing to comply with probation is set out in s. 733.1. The definition of "sentence" in ss. 673 and 785 for the purpose of appeal in indictable and summary conviction proceedings includings dispositions made under this section. Under s. 683(5), a judge of the Court of Appeal may suspend the probation order pending appeal.

SYNOPSIS

This section provides the authority to place the offender on probation. Under subsec. (1)(*a*) the court may impose a suspended sentence together with probation, provided there is no minimum punishment prescribed in the enactment creating the offence. Under subsec. (1)(*b*) the court may join probation to some other disposition such as a fine, conditional imprisonment, or imprisonment. Probation may only be imposed in addition to imprisonment if the sentence of imprisonment is two years or less. Under subsec. (2), probation may also be joined with a conditional discharge imposed under s. 730(1). Pursuant to s. 732.2, the maximum period of probation is three years.

ANNOTATIONS

Note: Some of the cases noted below were decided under the predecessor to this section [former s. 737(1)(*a*) and (*b*)].

Suspended sentence (subsec. 1(*a*)) – The court has no power to suspend sentence under subsec. (1)(*a*) and impose a fine in addition to probation: *R. v. St. James* (1981), 20 C.R. (3d) 389 (Que. C.A.); *R. v. Polywjanyj* (1982), 1 C.C.C. (3d) 161 (Ont. C.A.); *R. v. Kelly* (1995), 104 C.C.C. (3d) 95, 136 Nfld. & P.E.I.R. 279 (Nfld. C.A.).

As it is not the sentence itself, but its passing that is suspended a court in exercising this power should not mention any fixed term of proposed incarceration, for in addition, to do so would place the court in the position of binding itself should the accused be subsequently brought before it for sentence: *R. v. Sangster* (1973), 21 C.R.N.S. 339 (Que. C.A.).

The $1,000 court costs ordered to be paid as a term of probation was tantamount to the levying of a fine and as such was illegal as the trial court had decreed the suspension of the passing of sentence: *R. v. Pawlowski* (1971), 5 C.C.C. (2d) 87, 16 C.R.N.S. 313 (Man. C.A.).

Power to make probation order (subsec. (1)*(b)*) – In *R. v. Knott*, [2012] 2 S.C.R. 470, 284 C.C.C. (3d) 176, affg 258 C.C.C. (3d) 470 (B.C.C.A.), the court held that the phrase "imprisonment for a term not exceeding two years" in subsec. (1)(*b*) relates only to the actual term of imprisonment imposed by a sentencing court at a single sitting. It does not refer to the aggregate of the custodial term imposed by the sentencing court and all other sentences then being served or later imposed on the offender. Older cases to contrary effect (often relying on s. 139 of the *Corrections and Conditional Release Act*, S.C. 1992, c. 20) have been superseded. There is additionally no rule that a probation order must come into force within two years of being made. However, a probation order may not be attached to a sentence that does not exceed two years' imprisonment if that sentence results in continuous custody for more than two years when combined with other sentences imposed at the same sentencing session.

Probation may be imposed in addition to either a fine or imprisonment, but not in addition to both: *R. v. Smith* (1972), 7 C.C.C. (2d) 468 (N.W.T.T.C.); *R. v. Blacquiere* (1975), 24 C.C.C. (2d) 168 (Ont. C.A.); *R. v. St. James* (1981), 20 C.R. (3d) 389 (Que. C.A.).

Where, however, the court imposes an intermittent sentence under subsec. (1)(*c*), it may impose a fine, in addition to the mandatory probation order prescribed by that paragraph, for the times when the accused is not in confinement: *R. v. Cartier* (1990), 57 C.C.C. (3d) 569 (Que. C.A.).

While probation may not be imposed if the sentence exceeds two years, the calculation of the term of imprisonment does not include pre-trial custody: *R. v. Mathieu* (2008), 231 C.C.C. (3d) 1, 56 C.R. (6th) 1 (S.C.C.).

Where a judge imposes consecutive terms of imprisonment, the total term must not exceed two years if the judge also intends to impose a term of probation: *R. v. Amaralik* (1984), 16 C.C.C. (3d) 22 (N.W.T.C.A.).

One probation order may not be made consecutive to another: *R. v. Hunt* (1982), 2 C.C.C. (3d) 126, 55 N.S.R. (2d) 68 (S.C. App. Div.).

FIREARM, ETC., PROHIBITIONS / Application of s. 109 or 110.

731.1 (1) Before making a probation order, the court shall consider whether section 109 or 110 is applicable.

(2) For greater certainty, a condition of a probation order referred to in paragraph 732.1(3)(d) does not affect the operation of section 109 or 110. 1995, c. 22, s. 6; 2002, c. 13, s. 73.

CROSS-REFERENCES

Section 731 sets out the court's power to make a probation order. Section 732.1 sets out the conditions that may be included in the order.

INTERMITTENT SENTENCE / Application to vary intermittent sentence / Court may vary intermittent sentence if subsequent offence.

732. (1) Where the court imposes a sentence of imprisonment of ninety days or less on an offender convicted of an offence, whether in default of payment of a fine or otherwise, the court may, having regard to the age and character of the offender, the nature of the offence and the circumstances surrounding its commission, and the

availability of appropriate accommodation to ensure compliance with the sentence, order

(*a*) that the sentence be served intermittently at such times as are specified in the order; and

(*b*) that the offender comply with the conditions prescribed in a probation order when not in confinement during the period that the sentence is being served and, if the court so orders, on release from prison after completing the intermittent sentence.

(2) An offender who is ordered to serve a sentence of imprisonment intermittently may, on giving notice to the prosecutor, apply to the court that imposed the sentence to allow it to be served on consecutive days.

(3) Where a court imposes a sentence of imprisonment on a person who is subject to an intermittent sentence in respect of another offence, the unexpired portion of the intermittent sentence shall be served on consecutive days unless the court otherwise orders. 1995, c. 22, s. 6.

CROSS-REFERENCES

The other provisions respecting imposition of a term of imprisonment are set out in ss. 743 to 744. The provisions respecting imposition of fines are set out in ss. 734 to 737 and see in particular s. 734 and 734.7 dealing with imprisonment in default of payment of a fine. The definition of "sentence" in ss. 673 and 785 for the purpose of appeal in indictable and summary conviction proceedings includings dispositions made under this section.

SYNOPSIS

This section allows a court that imposes a sentence of imprisonment of 90 days or less to permit the offender to serve the sentence on an intermittent basis. This form of sentence is often imposed to permit the offender to continue employment, and for example will permit the offender to live at home during the week and serve the sentence on weekends. In determining whether or not to permit the offender to serve the sentence on an intermittent basis the court is to consider the character of the offender, the circumstances of the offence and the availability of appropriate accomodation to ensure compliance with the sentence. The court must include in the order a direction that the offender be on probation when not serving the sentence. The court may also include a period of probation to take effect after the sentence has been served.

Subsection (2) allows the offender to apply to the court, upon notice to the prosecutor, for permission to serve the sentence on consecutive days.

Subsection (3) provides that where the offender is sentenced to a term of imprisonment while serving an intermittent sentence then the intermittent sentence is automatically converted to a sentence to be served on consecutive days, unless the court otherwise orders.

ANNOTATIONS

Note: Some of the cases noted below were decided under the predecessor to this section [former s. 737(1)(*c*)] but were considered of some assistance in applying this section.

The judge must clearly and definitely set out those periods when the accused is to be incarcerated and may not merely order that the sentence be served on days of the accused's own choosing: *R. v. Downe, Smith and Dow* (1978), 44 C.C.C (2d) 468, 17 Nfld. & P.E.I.R. 87 (P.E.I.S.C. *in banco*).

The limit of 90 days is the length of the sentence, not the time period within which it must be served: *R. v. Lyall* (1974), 18 C.C.C. (2d) 381, [1974] 6 W.W.R. 479 (B.C.C.A.).

Pre-sentence custody is a factor to be taken into account but does not form part of the sentence itself. Accordingly, the "ninety days or less" refers to the sentence imposed after taking into account any credit for pre-sentence custody: *R. v. Peebles* (2010), 254 C.C.C. (3d) 559 (Man. C.A.).

There is no power to impose consecutive 90-day sentences to be served intermittently: *R. v. Fletcher* (1982), 2 C.C.C. (3d) 221 (Ont. C.A.); *R. v. Aubin* (1992), 72 C.C.C. (3d) 189 (Que. C.A.); *R. v. Drost* (1996), 104 C.C.C. (3d) 389 (N.B.C.A.).

Where the court imposes an intermittent sentence, it may also pose a fine, in addition to the mandatory probation order for the times when the accused is not in confinement: *R. v. Cartier* (1990), 57 C.C.C. (3d) 569 (Que. C.A.).

A conditional sentence is not a "sentence of imprisonment" for the purposes of this section. Accordingly, where a conditional sentence was imposed, the accused was not required to serve a 90-day intermittent sentence on consecutive days. However, the combination of an intermittent sentence and a conditional sentence was not objectionable, even when the aggregate duration of the sentences exceeded 90 days. The trial judge, therefore, did not err in imposing a 90-day intermittent sentence and a concurrent 18-month conditional sentence: *R. v. Middleton*, [2009] 1 S.C.R. 674, 244 C.C.C. (3d) 52.

It was impermissible for the sentencing judge to effectively circumvent the 90-day limit on intermittent sentences by imposing an intermittent sentence of 90 days in respect of one count, adjourning sentencing in respect of the other counts, and then imposing 60-day sentences on the other counts: *R. v. Clouthier*, [2016] O.J. No. 1232 (C.A.).

Where an accused serving both an intermittent and conditional sentence was committed to custody for the remainder of his conditional sentence after a finding of breach, this had the effect of collapsing the intermittent sentence pursuant to subsec. (3) and requiring the collapsed conditional sentence be served consecutively to the collapsed intermittent sentence pursuant to s. 742.7(2): *R. v. Marcelli* (2012), 281 C.C.C. (3d) 130 (N.S.S.C.).

DEFINITIONS / "Change" / "Optional conditions" / Compulsory conditions of probation order / Consent / Reasons / Optional conditions of probation order / Optional conditions — organization / Consideration — organizations / Form and period of order / Obligations of court / For greater certainty / Notice — samples at regular intervals / Designations and specifications / Further designations / Restriction / Destruction of samples / Regulations.

732.1 (1) In this section and section 732.2,

"change", in relation to optional conditions, includes deletions and additions;

"optional conditions" means the conditions referred to in subsection (3) or (3.1).

(2) The court shall prescribe, as conditions of a probation order, that the offender do all of the following:

(*a*) keep the peace and be of good behaviour;

(*a*.1) abstain from communicating, directly or indirectly, with any victim, witness or other person identified in the order, or refrain from going to any place specified in the order, except in accordance with the conditions specified in the order that the court considers necessary, unless

(i) the victim, witness or other person gives their consent or, if the victim, witness or other person is a minor, the parent or guardian, or any other person who has the lawful care or charge of them, gives their consent, or

(ii) the court decides that, because of exceptional circumstances, it is not appropriate to impose the condition;

(*b*) appear before the court when required to do so by the court; and

(*c*) notify the court or the probation officer in advance of any change of name or address, and promptly notify the court or the probation officer of any change of employment or occupation.

(2.1) For the purposes of subparagraph (2)(*a*.1)(i), the consent is valid only if it is given in writing or in the manner specified in the order.

(2.2) If the court makes the decision described in subparagraph (2)(*a*.1)(ii), it shall state the reasons for the decision in the record.

(3) The court may prescribe, as additional conditions of a probation order, that the offender do one or more of the following:

(*a*) report to a probation officer;

(i) within two working days, or such longer period as the court directs, after the making of the probation order, and

(ii) thereafter, when required by the probation officer and in the manner directed by the probation officer;

(*b*) remain within the jurisdiction of the court unless written permission to go outside that jurisdiction is obtained from the court or the probation officer;

(*c*) abstain from the consumption of drugs except in accordance with a medical prescription, of alcohol or of any other intoxicating substance;

(*c*.1) provide, for the purpose of analysis, a sample of a bodily substance prescribed by regulation on the demand of a peace officer, a probation officer or someone designated under subsection (9) to make a demand, at the place and time and on the day specified by the person making the demand, if that person has reasonable grounds to believe that the offender has breached a condition of the order that requires them to abstain from the consumption of drugs, alcohol or any other intoxicating substance;

(*c*.2) provide, for the purpose of analysis, a sample of a bodily substance prescribed by regulation at regular intervals that are specified by a probation officer in a notice in Form 51 served on the offender, if a condition of the order requires the offender to abstain from the consumption of drugs, alcohol or any other intoxicating substance;

(*d*) abstain from owning, possessing or carrying a weapon;

(*e*) provide for the support or care of dependants;

(*f*) perform up to 240 hours of community service over a period not exceeding eighteen months;

(*g*) if the offender agrees, and subject to the program director's acceptance of the offender, participate actively in a treatment program approved by the province;

(*g*.1) where the lieutenant governor in council of the province in which the probation order is made has established a program for curative treatment in relation to the consumption of alcohol or drugs, attend at a treatment facility, designated by the lieutenant governor in council of the province, for assessment and curative treatment in relation to the consumption by the offender of alcohol or drugs that is recommended pursuant to the program;

(*g*.2) where the lieutenant governor in council of the province in which the probation order is made has established a program governing the use of an alcohol ignition interlock device by an offender and if the offender agrees to participate in the program, comply with the program; and

(*h*) comply with such other reasonable conditions as the court considers desirable, subject to any regulations made under subsection 738(2), for protecting society and for facilitating the offender's successful reintegration into the community.

(3.1) The court may prescribe, as additional conditions of a probation order made in respect of an organization, that the offender do one or more of the following:

(*a*) make restitution to a person for any loss or damage that they suffered as a result of the offence;

(*b*) establish policies, standards and procedures to reduce the likelihood of the organization committing a subsequent offence;

(*c*) communicate those policies, standards and procedures to its representatives;

(*d*) report to the court on the implementation of those policies, standards and procedures;

(*e*) identify the senior officer who is responsible for compliance with those policies, standards and procedures;

(*f*) provide, in the manner specified by the court, the following information to the public, namely,

(i) the offence of which the organization was convicted,

(ii) the sentence imposed by the court, and

(iii) any measures that the organization is taking — including any policies, standards and procedures established under paragraph (*b*) — to reduce the likelihood of it committing a subsequent offence; and

(*g*) comply with any other reasonable conditions that the court considers desirable to prevent the organization from committing subsequent offences or to remedy the harm caused by the offence.

(3.2) Before making an order under paragraph (3.1)(*b*), a court shall consider whether it would be more appropriate for another regulatory body to supervise the development or implementation of the policies, standards and procedures referred to in that paragraph.

(4) A probation order may be in Form 46, and the court that makes the probation order shall specify therein the period for which it is to remain in force.

(5) The court that makes a probation order shall

(*a*) cause a copy of the order to be given to the offender and, on request, to the victim;

(*b*) explain the conditions of the order set under subsections (2) to (3.1) and the substance of section 733.1 to the offender;

(*c*) cause an explanation to be given to the offender of the procedure for applying under subsection 732.2(3) for a change to the optional conditions and of the substance of subsections 732.2(3) and (5); and

(*d*) take reasonable measures to ensure that the offender understands the order and the explanations.

(6) For greater certainty, a failure to comply with subsection (5) does not affect the validity of the probation order.

(7) The notice referred to in paragraph (3)(*c*.2) must specify the places and times at which and the days on which the offender must provide samples of a bodily substance under a condition described in that paragraph. The first sample may not be taken earlier than 24 hours after the offender is served with the notice, and subsequent samples must be taken at regular intervals of at least seven days.

(8) For the purposes of paragraphs (3)(*c*.1) and (*c*.2) and subject to the regulations, the Attorney General of a province or the minister of justice of a territory shall, with respect to the province or territory,

(*a*) designate the persons or classes of persons that may take samples of bodily substances;

(*b*) designate the places or classes of places at which the samples are to be taken;

(*c*) specify the manner in which the samples are to be taken;

(*d*) specify the manner in which the samples are to be analyzed;

(*e*) specify the manner in which the samples are to be stored, handled and destroyed;

(*f*) specify the manner in which the records of the results of the analysis of the samples are to be protected and destroyed;

(*g*) designate the persons or classes of persons that may destroy the samples; and

(*h*) designate the persons or classes of persons that may destroy the records of the results of the analysis of the samples.

(9) For the purpose of paragraph (3)(*c*.1) and subject to the regulations, the Attorney General of a province or the minister of justice of a territory may, with respect to the province or territory, designate persons or classes of persons to make a demand for a sample of a bodily substance.

(10) Samples of bodily substances referred to in paragraphs (3)(*c*.1) and (*c*.2) may not be taken, analyzed, stored, handled or destroyed, and the records of the results of the analysis of the samples may not be protected or destroyed, except in accordance with the designations and specifications made under subsection (8).

(11) The Attorney General of a province or the minister of justice of a territory, or a person authorized by the Attorney General or minister, shall cause all samples of bodily substances provided under a probation order to be destroyed within the periods prescribed by regulation unless the samples are reasonably expected to be used as evidence in a proceeding for an offence under section 733.1.

(12) The Governor in Council may make regulations

(*a*) prescribing bodily substances for the purposes of paragraphs (3)(*c*.1) and (*c*.2);

(*b*) respecting the designations and specifications referred to in subsections (8) and (9);

(*c*) prescribing the periods within which samples of bodily substances are to be destroyed under subsection (11); and

(*d*) respecting any other matters relating to the samples of bodily substances. 1995, c. 22, s. 6; 1999, c. 32, s. 6; 2003, c. 21, s. 18; 2008, c. 18, s. 37; 2011, c. 7, s. 3; 2014, c. 21, s. 2; 2015, c. 13, s. 27.

CROSS-REFERENCES

"Organization" is defined in s. 2. Section 731 sets out the circumstances in which a probation order may be made. Section 732.2 prescribes when the order comes into effect, the procedure for varying the order, and the court's power to change the order where the offender is convicted of an offence while on probation. The maximum period of probation is three years [s. 732.2(2)(*b*)]. Section 732.2(5)(*d*) gives the court power to revoke a suspended sentence where the offender was convicted of an offence while on probation. Section 733 provides a procedure for transferring the order where the offender becomes a resident of another territorial division. The offence of failing to comply with probation is set out in s. 733.1. It should be noted that unlike former s. 737, this section does not list restitution as one of the specified optional conditions and pursuant to s. 738(2) the lieutenant governor may make regulations precluding the inclusion of provisions on enforcement of restitution orders as an option condition of a probation order. The making of restitution orders is provided for in ss. 738 to 741.2. Where a weapons prohibition order is made a condition of probation under subsec. (3)(d), pursuant to s. 113, the judge may make an order authorizing a chief firearms officer or the Registrar to issue, in accordance with such terms and conditions as is considered appropriate, an authorization, a licence or a registration certificate, as the case may be, to the accused for sustenance or employment purposes. Under s. 114, the prohibition order may require the accused to surrender anything the possession of which is prohibited by the order and every authorization, licence and registration certificate relating to any such thing. Unless the prohibition order provides otherwise, everything the possession of which is prohibited by the order is forfeited to the Crown pursuant to s. 115, subject to the true owner making an application under s. 117. Under s. 116, every authorization, licence and registration certificate relating to anything the possession of which is prohibited by a prohibition order and issued to the accused is, on the commencement of the prohibition order, revoked, or amended, as the case may be, to the extent of the prohibitions in the order.

SYNOPSIS

This section sets out the mandatory conditions to be included in a probation order [subsec. (2)] and the optional conditions that the court may impose [subsec. (3)]. In addition to the particularized optional conditions such as reporting to a probation order, para. (3)(*h*) gives the court a broad discretion to order the offender to comply with other reasonable conditions for protecting society and for facilitating the offender's reintergration into the community. Note that there are restrictions in respect of certain of the optional conditions. Thus the maximum amount of community service that may be ordered is 240 hours to be completed over a period not exceeding 18 months. A term that the offender take part in a treatment programme may only be ordered if the offender agrees and is subject to the acceptance of the offender by the programme director. Subsection (2.1) provides for the optional conditions where a probation order is made in relation to an organization. Pursuant to subsec. (4) the court must specify the length of the probation order. The maximum term is three years [s. 732.2(2)(*b*)]. Subsection (5) requires the court to cause the offender to be given a copy of the order and an explanation of the procedure for applying to vary the optional conditions under s. 732.2, and to give an explanation of the terms of the probation and the consequences for breaching the order as set out in s. 733.1. The court shall also take reasonable measures to ensure that the offender understands the order and these explanations. However, a failure to comply with subsec. (5) does not affect the validity of the order.

ANNOTATIONS

Note: Some of the cases noted below were decided under the predecessor to this section [s. 737] but were considered to be of assistance in applying this provision. However, there has been a significant change in certain of the provisions. In particular there is now explicit statutory authority to impose community service and participation in a treatment programme requires the offender's consent. Finally, subsec. (3)(*h*), which allows for imposition of other reasonable conditions, has been significantly amended. The former provision limited the court's power under that provision to conditions considered desirable "for securing the good conduct of the accused and for preventing a repetition by him of the same offence or the commission of other offences". The new subsec. (3)(*h*) may provide a broader discretion especially as it refers to the protection of society.

Statutory conditions (subsec. (2)) – The obligation to keep the peace and be of good behaviour imposes separate and distinct conditions that may overlap in certain circumstances. A breach of the peace is a violent disruption or disturbance of public tranquility, peace and order: *R. v. S. (S.)* (1999), 138 C.C.C. (3d) 430 (Nfld. C.A.).

Failure to be of good behaviour is limited to non-compliance with federal, provincial or municipal statutes and regulations and obligations imposed by court orders specifically applicable to the accused: *R. v. R. (D.)* (1999), 138 C.C.C. (3d) 405 (Nfld. C.A.).

Community service – Community service has an inherent quality of guidance or rehabilitation and thus a person who has developed a proclivity toward crime, may benefit from the lessons learned by spending time and effort on more worthy causes: *R. v. Brand* (1996), 105 C.C.C. (3d) 225 (B.C.S.C.).

Charitable donation – The imposition of a charitable donation condition in a probation order was considered punitive in nature and therefore not a valid sentencing option. If charitable donations are to be considered a valid sentencing option, Parliament should enact an appropriate regime to avoid the negative impact on the administration of justice that may arise when judges make such orders on an *ad hoc* basis: *R. v. Choi* (2013), 301 C.C.C. (3d) 390 (Man. C.A.). Contra: see *R. v. Prokos* (1998), 127 C.C.C. (3d) 190 (Que. C.A.).

Treatment – A probation order requiring the accused to reside at a community training residence and participate in the programme at the residence does not constitute the unlawful imposition of a term of imprisonment, notwithstanding the residence is designated as a correctional facility and the rules of the residence do not permit the person to be absent without permission: *R. v. Degan* (1985), 20 C.C.C. (3d) 293 (Sask. C.A.).

While a term that the young accused attend for treatment, for a severe personality disorder and a serious drug problem, at a particular treatment centre was a reasonable condition within the meaning of para. (*h*), where the centre is outside of Canada such a condition should only be imposed in exceptional cases. Moreover, as there might be some doubt as to the legality of such a condition since it could be viewed as imposing a term of exile on the accused, the condition can only be imposed where the accused consents: *R. v. Chisholm* (1985), 18 C.C.C. (3d) 518 (N.S.S.C. App. Div.), leave to appeal to S.C.C. refused *loc. cit.*

A term of a probation order, compelling an accused to take psychiatric treatment or medication, is an unreasonable restraint upon the liberty or security of the person and contrary to the principles of fundamental justice as guaranteed by s. 7 of the Charter a probation order could contain terms requiring the accused to take reasonable steps to maintain himself in such a condition that his mental illness will not likely cause him to be a danger to himself or to others or to commit other offences; such an order could require the accused to attend for recommended medical counselling and treatment, though he need not submit to any treatment or medication to which he does not consent: *R. v. Rogers* (1990), 61 C.C.C. (3d) 481 (B.C.C.A.). [now see para. (*g*)].

A condition that the accused take medication as prescribed by a psychiatrist is unlawful: *R. v. L. (J.J.)* (2001), 152 C.C.C. (3d) 572 (Man. C.A.).

A condition requiring the offender to attend a batterers treatment program which compels the offender to make admissions or statements against his will or conscience is contrary to s. 7 of the Charter. The condition was modified to require the offender to comply with the program to the extent that it did not require any admissions contrary to his or her personal beliefs or conscience and to provide that the offender would be released from the condition in the event that this resulted in the offender's exclusion from the program: *R. v. Sookochoff* (1999), 133 C.C.C. (3d) 532 (Sask. Q.B.).

Banishment and similar terms – Banishment should be the exception rather than the rule. Banishment from an entire province is an extreme measure that could be justified only in exceptional circumstances even in cases of domestic violence: *R. v. Rowe* (2006), 212 C.C.C. (3d) 254 (Ont. C.A.).

In *R. v. Malboeuf* (1982), 68 C.C.C. (2d) 544 (Sask. C.A.), the court considered a term of probation which had the effect of banishing the accused from his home community. In the result, the court quashed the term but stated *obiter* that while such terms should not be encouraged they might not be inappropriate in every case. There should, however, at least be an indication that communities have entered into arrangements sanctioning or providing for an exchange of undesirable individuals. Subsequently, in *R. v. Taylor* (1997), 122 C.C.C. (3d) 376 (Sask. C.A.), the court upheld a term of a probation order requiring banishment. While there may be a punitive aspect to banishment, the central purpose is that it is an individualized measure designed to influence the offender's future behaviour. See also: *R. v. Adam* (2014), 316 C.C.C. (3d) 343 (B.C.S.C.).

It was not inappropriate to impose a term of probation on a young accused, with a record for drug offences, that he refrain from entering an area of the city which was notorious for drug trafficking: *R. v. Pedersen* (1986), 31 C.C.C. (3d) 574 (B.C. Co. Ct.).

A condition removing the accused from his home and office for a lengthy period may be necessary for the protection of society but should be imposed only after all relevant evidence is heard and considered. In this case, the judge imposed the term to prevent contact between the accused and his neighbour but failed to consider that the immediate cause of the offence of mischief was the accused's anger at the police, not his neighbour. The term was therefore struck out on appeal: *R. v. Griffith* (1998), 128 C.C.C. (3d) 178 (B.C.C.A.).

Other terms – There is no jurisdiction to impose a term of probation requiring the offender to submit to urinalysis, blood tests or breathalyzer tests on the demand of a peace or probation officer. The residual discretion to impose additional conditions under subsec. (3)(*h*) is the same as the listed conditions and does not include conditions designed to facilitate the gathering of evidence for enforcement purposes: *R. v. Shoker*, [2006] 2 S.C.R. 399, 212 C.C.C. (3d) 417.

A curfew has punitive aspects, but if the evidence reveals a connection between the curfew and the legitimate goals of a probation order — namely, rehabilitation and community protection — then the condition will be reasonable: *R. v. Singh* (2016), 334 C.C.C. (3d) 423 (Man. C.A.).

It is inappropriate to impose what is in effect a custodial term as a condition of probation, for example that the accused attend at the local jail for a number of consecutive hours on a certain number of days in a month: *R. v. L.* (1986), 50 C.R. (3d) 398 (Alta. C.A.).

In a proper case, it was open to the court to make it a term of probation that the accused be strictly confined to his home except for absences for employment or otherwise as may be approved by a probation officer. Such a term may be an appropriate alternative to imprisonment: *R. v. M. (D.E.S.)* (1993), 80 C.C.C. (3d) 371 (B.C.C.A.). [Although now see s. 742.3].

Parliament amended the residual clause in subsec. (3)(*h*), to read "for protecting society and for facilitating the offender's successful reintegration into the community" to make clear the rehabilitative purpose of probation: *R. v. Proulx*, [2000] 1 S.C.R. 61, 140 C.C.C. (3d) 449.

In *R. v. McLeod* (1993), 81 C.C.C. (3d) 83 (Sask. C.A.), the court discussed the principles which should apply in imposing terms of intensive probation and electronic monitoring where the need for general deterrence did not require a sentence of imprisonment.

In *R. v. Caja and Billings* (1977), 36 C.C.C. (2d) 401 (Ont. C.A.), it was held that a term of probation that the accused, who were convicted of theft, not apply for unemployment insurance was not authorized by the *Criminal Code* and the term was struck out. As well a term that the accused not take drugs or associate with drug users was also struck out, there being no indication that drugs were involved in the commission of the offence or that the accused used drugs.

The condition deferring the imposition of optional probation conditions until the accused had completed his or her jail sentence, at which time it would be determined whether the conditions were necessary, is invalid. In addition, a condition directing a review of the probation order is invalid as such a review may only be brought on the application of the offender, probation officer or prosecutor: *R. v. H. (P.A.)* (1999), 134 C.C.C. (3d) 251 (B.C.C.A.).

The sentencing judge was not entitled to take judicial notice that the Hells Angels was a criminal organization. A term requiring the accused to refrain from associating or communicating with members of gangs was so vague and uncertain as to be unreasonable: *R. v. Kirton* (2007), 219 C.C.C. (3d) 485 (Man. C.A.).

Formalities in probation order (subsecs. (3) and (4)) – An accused is not bound by a probation order which does not specify within it the period for which it is to remain in force: *R. v. Foulston* (1983), 6 C.C.C. (3d) 236 (Sask. Q.B.).

A probation order was not illegal when it was imposed while the accused was in pre-trial custody on other charges and where, subsequent to the imposition of probation, the accused was sentenced to a period of custody on another charge. The probation order did not come into effect until the accused was released from prison on the sentence subsequently imposed: *R. v. Ivan* (2000), 148 C.C.C. (3d) 295 (B.C.C.A.).

PROHIBITION ON USE OF BODILY SUBSTANCE / Prohibition on use or disclosure of result / Exception / Offence.

732.11 (1) No person shall use a bodily substance provided under a probation order except for the purpose of determining whether an offender is complying with a condition of the order that they abstain from the consumption of drugs, alcohol or any other intoxicating substance.

(2) Subject to subsection (3), no person shall use, disclose or allow the disclosure of the results of the analysis of a bodily substance provided under a probation order.

(3) The results of the analysis of a bodily substance provided under a probation order may be disclosed to the offender to whom they relate, and may also be used or disclosed in the course of an investigation of, or in a proceeding for, an offence under section 733.1 or, if the results are made anonymous, for statistical or other research purposes.

(4) Every person who contravenes subsection (1) or (2) is guilty of an offence punishable on summary conviction. 2011, c. 7, s. 4.

COMING INTO FORCE OF ORDER / Duration of order and limit on term of order / Changes to probation order / Judge may act in chambers / Where person convicted of offence / Compelling appearance of person bound.

732.2 (1) A probation order comes into force

(*a*) on the date on which the order is made;

(*b*) where the offender is sentenced to imprisonment under paragraph 731(1)(*b*) or was previously sentenced to imprisonment for another offence, as soon as the offender is released from prison or, if released from prison on conditional release, at the expiration of the sentence of imprisonment; or

(*c*) where the offender is under a conditional sentence order, at the expiration of the conditional sentence order.

(2) Subject to subsection (5),

(*a*) where an offender who is bound by a probation order is convicted of an offence, including an offence under section 733.1, or is imprisoned under paragraph 731(1)(*b*) in default of payment of a fine, the order continues in force except in so far as the sentence renders it impossible for the offender for the time being to comply with the order; and

(*b*) no probation order shall continue in force for more than three years after the date on which the order came into force.

(3) A court that makes a probation order may at any time, on application by the offender, the probation officer or the prosecutor, require the offender to appear before it and, after hearing the offender and one or both of the probation officer and the prosecutor,

(*a*) make any changes to the optional conditions that in the opinion of the court are rendered desirable by a change in the circumstances since those conditions were prescribed,

(*b*) relieve the offender, either absolutely or on such terms or for such period as the court deems desirable, of compliance with any optional condition, or

(*c*) decrease the period for which the probation order is to remain in force,

and the court shall thereupon endorse the probation order accordingly and, if it changes the optional conditions, inform the offender of its action and give the offender a copy of the order so endorsed.

(4) All the functions of the court under subsection (3) may be exercised in chambers.

(5) Where an offender who is bound by a probation order is convicted of an offence, including an offence under section 733.1, and

(*a*) the time within which an appeal may be taken against that conviction has expired and the offender has not taken an appeal,

(*b*) the offender has taken an appeal against that conviction and the appeal has been dismissed, or

(*c*) the offender has given written notice to the court that convicted the offender that the offender elects not to appeal the conviction or has abandoned the appeal, as the case may be,

in addition to any punishment that may be imposed for that offence, the court that made the probation order may, on application by the prosecutor, require the offender to appear before it and, after hearing the prosecutor and the offender,

(*d*) where the probation order was made under paragraph 731(1)(*a*), revoke the order and impose any sentence that could have been imposed if the passing of sentence had not been suspended, or

(*e*) make such changes to the optional conditions as the court deems desirable, or extend the period for which the order is to remain in force for such period, not exceeding one year, as the court deems desirable,

and the court shall thereupon endorse the probation order accordingly and, if it changes the optional conditions or extends the period for which the order is to remain in force, inform the offender of its action and give the offender a copy of the order so endorsed.

(6) The provisions of Parts XVI and XVIII with respect to compelling the appearance of an accused before a justice apply, with such modifications as the circumstances require, to proceedings under subsections (3) and (5). 1995, c. 22, s. 6; 2004, c. 12, s. 12.

CROSS-REFERENCES

Sections 731 sets out the circumstances in which a probation order may be made and in particular provides for the imposition of a suspended sentence and probation [para. 731(1)(*a*)]. Pursuant to s. 731.1, before making a probation order the court must consider whether s. 100 is applicable and requires the court to impose a firearms prohibition. Section 732.1 sets out the mandatory and optional conditions for a probation order, the procedure for making the order and requires the court that makes the order to cause the offender to be informed of the provisions of this section. Section 733 provides a procedure for transferring the order where the offender becomes a resident of another territorial division. The offence of failing to comply with probation is set out in s. 733.1. The definition of "sentence" in ss. 673 and 785 for the purpose of appeal in indictable and summary conviction proceedings includings dispositions made under subsec. (3) and (5) of this section.

SYNOPSIS

This section deals with matters such as the duration of probation orders and modifications thereto. Subsection (1) provides that the order takes effect when it is made except when the offender is sentenced to a term of imprisonment, in which case the order takes effect when the offender is released from imprisonment or, if the offender is released from prison on conditional release, at the expiration of the sentence of imprisonment. If the offender has been sentenced to a conditional sentence, then the order takes effect at the expiration of the conditional sentence order. Where the offender is convicted of an offence while on probation, or imprisoned for non-payment of a fine the order continues in effect except in so far as the sentence renders it impossible for the offender, for the time being, to comply with the order.

The maximum term of probation is three years [subsec. (2)(*b*)], except that where the offender is convicted of an offence while on probation the court may impose an additional year of probation pursuant to subsec. (5)(*e*). The court that made the order may, on application by the offender, the prosecutor or the probation officer, pursuant to subsec. (3) vary the optional terms, relieve the offender from compliance with the optional terms and decrease the period for which the order is to remain in force. The powers granted by subsec. (3) may be exercised in chambers. Subsection (5) deals with the procedure where the offender commits an offence while on probation. The court may, on application by the prosecutor, vary the optional conditions and increase the period to a maximum of one year. Where the offender had previously been given a suspended sentence under s. 731(1)(*a*), the court may revoke the suspended sentence and impose any sentence that could have been imposed. The procedures set out in Parts XVI an XVIII may be used to compel the offender's appearance before the court for the purposes of subsecs. (3) and (5).

ANNOTATIONS

Note: Some of the cases noted below were decided under the predecessor to this section [former s. 738] but were considered to be of assistance in interpreting this section which is similarly worded.

Variations of terms of probation [subsec. (3)] – In *R. v. Muise* (1980), 56 C.C.C. (2d) 191, 44 N.S.R. (2d) 324 (S.C. App. Div.), an order varying the terms was set aside on appeal by the Crown where the variation was made by the trial judge on an *ex parte* application by the accused without the Crown being given an opportunity to make representations.

Where the probation order is made by the Court of Appeal on a sentence appeal pursuant to s. 687 then both the Court of Appeal and by virtue of s. 687(2) the original sentencing judge has jurisdiction to vary the order. Where the application to vary is made to the Court of Appeal any panel of judges of that court may make the variation not necessarily the same panel which heard the original appeal: *R. v. H.* (1983), 6 C.C.C. (3d) 382, [1983] 5 W.W.R. 94 *sub nom. Alberta (Attorney General) v. H.* (Alta. C.A.).

On an application by the accused to vary the terms of probation it is not open to the judge to revoke the suspended sentence and impose a term of imprisonment. Prior to revocation of the suspended sentence there must be an application by the prosecutor so as to give the accused notice and enable him to make proper answer and defence: *R. v. Lake* (1986), 27 C.C.C. (3d) 305 (N.S.C.A.).

Optional conditions of a probation order should be prospective in nature, focusing on rehabilitation, rather than focusing retrospectively on the circumstances of the offence. Conditions must be reasonable. A condition which sets up a person for failure, such as prohibiting an alcoholic from drinking, is not a reasonable condition. Accordingly, the probation officer's application for an order that the accused, a drug addict, abstain from the consumption of drugs was rejected as it was unreasonable and would have resulted in a breach. Requiring the accused to take treatment and counselling would be a more appropriate condition in the circumstances: *R. v. Coombs* (2004), 189 C.C.C. (3d) 397, 369 A.R. 215 (Q.B.).

This provision is not meant to displace an accused's right to appeal a probation order that is outside the sentencing judge's discretion or is otherwise unlawful: *R. v. Etifier* (2009), 246 C.C.C. (3d) 448 (B.C.C.A.).

Revocation of probation [subsec. (5)] – A probationee's conviction of a provincial offence must be proven either by his admission or in the normal manner and he must be given an opportunity to present his case and give his explanation before the court may adjudicate upon a breach of probation complaint: *R. v. Borland,* [1970] 2 C.C.C. 172, 5 C.R.N.S. 251 (N.W.T.T.C.).

Unless there is proper transfer procedure only the original convicting court should revoke a suspended sentence and impose sentence: *R. v. Graham* (1975), 27 C.C.C. (2d) 475 (Ont. C.A.).

Where an application is made by a prosecutor under subsec. (5) the basic principles of natural justice apply. Accordingly, although the *Criminal Code* does not require an information on oath, the minimum requirement is that the accused, before being brought before the judge, should be given reasonable notice in writing of the Crown's intention to take such proceedings, which notice should clearly articulate the nature of the proceedings, the grounds upon which the Crown intends to rely in support of its application, the nature of the order sought, and the hearing date. As well, the accused must be given a fair opportunity to make full answer and defence. Further, in imposing sentence under this subsection the judge must consider that although it may be that the accused by his conduct has forfeited his right to leniency the function of the trial judge is then to impose a sentence proportionate to the offence which the accused had committed. It is wrong therefore for the judge at the time he suspends the passing of sentence to indicate that if the probation is breached he will be given any particular term, such as a penitentiary term of imprisonment: *R. v. Tuckey* (1977), 34 C.C.C. (2d) 572 (Ont. C.A.).

Where the court revokes the probation order because of commission of an offence while on probation it has no power to make the sentence consecutive to the sentence imposed for the offence which brought about the termination of the probation: *R. v. Oakes* (1977), 37 C.C.C. (2d) 84 (Ont. C.A.), and *Ex p. Risby* (1975), 24 C.C.C. (2d) 211, [1975] W.W.D. 880

(B.C.S.C.); *R. v. Clermont* (1986), 30 C.C.C. (3d) 571 (Que. C.A.), affd [1988] 2 S.C.R. 171, 45 C.C.C. (3d) 480 (5:0).

Once the probation order has expired the court has no jurisdiction to revoke it and impose sentence, even where the act giving rise to the Crown's application occurred during the currency of the probation order: *Re R. and Paquette* (1980), 53 C.C.C. (2d) 281 (Alta. Q.B.). On the other hand, if the probation is revoked prior to its expiration, the judge may adjourn the imposition of sentencing and impose sentence at a time beyond the period when the probation order would have expired had it not been revoked: *R. v. Montanaro* (1980), 55 C.C.C. (2d) 143, 15 C.R. (3d) 346 (Que. C.A.).

At least where the original probation order only contained the statutory terms and terms requiring the accused to abstain from consumption of alcohol, to report to a probation officer and to notify the officer and the court of change of address or employment, then revocation of the order and imposition of a sentence of imprisonment under para. (*d*) would not violate the protection against double punishment in s. 11(*h*) of the *Charter of Rights and Freedoms*: *R. v. Linklater* (1983), 9 C.C.C. (3d) 217 (Y.T.C.A.).

TRANSFER OF ORDER / Attorney General's consent / Where court unable to act.

733. (1) Where an offender who is bound by a probation order becomes a resident of, or is convicted or discharged under section 730 of an offence including an offence under section 733.1 in, a territorial division other than the territorial division where the order was made, on the application of a probation officer, the court that made the order may, subject to subsection (1.1), transfer the order to a court in that other territorial division that would, having regard to the mode of trial of the offender, have had jurisdiction to make the order in that other territorial division if the offender had been tried and convicted there of the offence in respect of which the order was made, and the order may thereafter be dealt with and enforced by the court to which it is so transferred in all respects as if that court had made the order.

(1.1) The transfer may be granted only with

(*a*) the consent of the Attorney General of the province in which the probation order was made, if the two territorial divisions are not in the same province; or

(*b*) the consent of the Attorney General of Canada, if the proceedings that led to the issuance of the probation order were instituted by or on behalf of the Attorney General of Canada.

(2) Where a court that has made a probation order or to which a probation order has been transferred pursuant to subsection (1) is for any reason unable to act, the powers of that court in relation to the probation order may be exercised by any other court that has equivalent jurisdiction in the same province. 1995, c. 22, s. 6; 1999, c. 5, s. 32.

CROSS-REFERENCES

See cross-references under s. 732.2.

SYNOPSIS

This section provides a mechanism for transferring probation orders from one jurisdiction to another. Where it is sought to transfer the order from one province to another, consent must be obtained from the Attorney General of the province in which the order was made or the Attorney General of Canada if the proceedings were instituted by the Attorney General of Canada (subsec. (1.1)).

If the judge who made the order or the one to whom it has been transferred is unable to act, the court's powers may be exercised by any other court that has equivalent jurisdiction in the same province (subsec. (2)).

FAILURE TO COMPLY WITH PROBATION ORDER / Where accused may be tried and punished.

733.1 (1) An offender who is bound by a probation order and who, without reasonable excuse, fails or refuses to comply with that order is guilty of

(*a*) an indictable offence and is liable to imprisonment for a term of not more than four years; or

(*b*) an offence punishable on summary conviction and is liable to imprisonment for a term of not more than 18 months, or to a fine of not more than $5000, or to both.

(2) An accused who is charged with an offence under subsection (1) may be tried and punished by any court having jurisdiction to try that offence in the place where the offence is alleged to have been committed or in the place where the accused is found, is arrested or is in custody, but where the place where the accused is found, is arrested or is in custody is outside the province in which the offence is alleged to have been committed, no proceedings in respect of that offence shall be instituted in that place without the consent of the Attorney General of that province. 1995, c. 22, s. 6; 2015, c. 23, s. 18.

CROSS-REFERENCES

Section 731 sets out the circumstances under which a probation order may be made. Section 732.1 sets out the mandatory and optional terms of a probation order. Under s. 732.1(5) the court that makes the probation order must cause the offender to be informed of the provisions of this section. Section 729 allows for the use of an analyst's certificate at a prosecution for an offence under this section where it is alleged that the offender breached a condition of a probation that the offender not have in possession or use drugs. Section 732.1(6) provides that a failure to comply with the requirements for giving the offender a copy of the probation order, notifying the offender of the terms of the probation order and the consequences of failing to comply does not affect the validity of the order.

SYNOPSIS

This section creates the crown option offence of failing or refusing to comply with a probation order. Where the prosecutor proceeds by way of indictment, the maximum sentence is four years' imprisonment. Where the prosecutor proceeds by way of summary conviction, the maximum sentence is 18 months' imprisonment and/or a fine of $5,000.

Unlike former s. 740, the predecessor to this section, the offence under this section does not expressly require proof that the failure or refusal to comply was done "wilfully". Rather, the term "wilfully" has been replaced by the phrase "without reasonable excuse". Under former s. 740, it had been held in *R. v. Docherty*, [1989] 2 S.C.R. 941, 51 C.C.C. (3d) 1, that where the Crown, in order to prove the offence of breach of probation, relies on the commission of a criminal offence, proof of commission of that offence constitutes the *actus reus* of breach of probation but is not itself even *prima facie* proof of an intent to breach the probation order. Thus, an honest but mistaken belief that the accused was not committing the criminal offence alleged to constitute the breach means that the accused could not be convicted of "wilfully" failing to comply with the probation order. It is unclear whether the same reasoning would be applied with the change in wording.

Under subsec. (2) any court having jurisdiction to try the offence in the place where the offence was alleged to have been committed or where the accused is found, is arrested, or is in custody has jurisdiction to try the offence under this section. However, where the place where the accused is found, arrested or is in custody is outside of the province where the offence was alleged to have been committed, the Attorney General of the province must consent to the institution of the proceedings. [The wording of this section does not make it entirely clear whether the Attorney General of the province where the offence was committed or of the province where the accused is found must consent. Since subsec. (2)

constitutes an exception to the general rule in s. 478 that a court in one province has no jurisdiction to try an offence committed entirely in another province, it is suggested that the most sensible meaning is that it is the Attorney General where the offence was committed must consent. This is consistent with s. 478(3), which permits the transfer of charges from one province to another if the accused intends to plead guilty, with the consent of the Attorney General of the province where the offence was committed.]

ANNOTATIONS

Note: The cases noted under this section were decided under the predecessor to this section [former s. 740] but were considered to be of assistance in interpreting this section. Note, however, that under former s. 740 the offence required proof that the accused had "wilfully" failed or refused to comply. The term "wilfully" has now been replaced with the phrase "without reasonable excuse".

Proof of breach of probation order – Breach of the statutory term that the accused "keep the peace and be of good behaviour" so as to amount to an offence under this section may include conduct not amounting to a criminal offence. This would include conduct which might violate a provincial or municipal enactment: *R. v. Stone* (1985), 22 C.C.C. (3d) 249 (Nfld. S.C.T.D.).

Proof of validity of probation order ***[Also see notes under s. 732.1]*** – The mere filing of a notice of appeal does not operate to stay or suspend the operation of the sentence imposed at trial and thus an accused may be convicted of this offence notwithstanding that at the time of the alleged failure to comply the underlying conviction was under appeal: *R. v. Trabulsey* (1993), 84 C.C.C. (3d) 240 (Ont. Ct. (Gen. Div.)).

Double jeopardy – The rule against multiple convictions enunciated in *R. v. Kienapple*, [1975] 1 S.C.R. 729, 15 C.C.C. (2d) 524, has no application although the accused was previously convicted of an offence which was alleged to be the foundation for the charge under this section: *R. v. Pinkerton* (1979), 46 C.C.C. (2d) 284 (B.C.C.A.).

The double jeopardy guarantee in s. 11(*h*) of the *Canadian Charter of Rights and Freedoms* is not offended by the accused's conviction for the offence under this section although it is based on his conviction for another offence, break and enter, under the *Criminal Code*: *R. v. Daniels* (1985), 44 C.R. (3d) 184 (Sask. Q.B.).

Sentencing – Where an accused has been convicted of an offence while on probation and the fact that he was on probation was taken into account at that time the trial Judge in imposing sentence for breach of probation arising out of the same circumstances is bound to consider the punishment imposed previously for the same conduct and accordingly does not err by imposing a nominal sentence for the breach of probation charge. Any sentence other than a nominal one would come close to violating the fundamental principle that no one is to undergo double punishment: *R. v. Chinn* (1977), 38 C.C.C. (2d) 45 (Alta. Dist. Ct.).

Jurisdiction – By virtue of subsec. (2), notwithstanding the probation order had never been transferred to Saskatchewan, the courts of that province had jurisdiction to try an offence under this section where the breach took place in Saskatchewan although the probation order was made in Manitoba: *R. v. Michelle* (1986), 28 C.C.C. (3d) 572 (Sask. Q.B.).

A Canadian court has the jurisdiction to try an accused for breach of a probation order even if the breaching acts occurred in a foreign country. There is no rule of international law depriving a judge of jurisdiction to make a probation order binding on the conduct of a probationer abroad. Absent a term to the contrary, probation orders are meant to apply to probationers at all times and extraterritorially. *R. v. Greco* (2001), 159 C.C.C. (3d) 146 (Ont. C.A.), leave to appeal to S.C.C. refused 162 C.C.C. (3d) vi.

Fines and Forfeiture

POWER OF COURT TO IMPOSE FINE / Offender's ability to pay / Meaning of default of payment / Imprisonment in default of payment / Determination of term / Moneys found on offender / Provincial regulations / Application to other law.

734. (1) Subject to subsection (2), a court that convicts a person, other than an organization, of an offence may fine the offender by making an order under section 734.1

(*a*) if the punishment for the offence does not include a minimum term of imprisonment, in addition to or in lieu of any other sanction that the court is authorized to impose; or

(*b*) if the punishment for the offence includes a minimum term of imprisonment, in addition to any other sanction that the court is required or authorized to impose.

(2) Except when the punishment for an offence includes a minimum fine or a fine is imposed in lieu of a forfeiture order, a court may fine an offender under this section only if the court is satisfied that the offender is able to pay the fine or discharge it under section 736.

(3) For the purposes of this section and sections 734.1 to 737, a person is in default of payment of a fine if the fine has not been paid in full by the time set out in the order made under section 734.1.

(4) Where an offender is fined under this section, a term of imprisonment, determined in accordance with subsection (5), shall be deemed to be imposed in default of payment of the fine.

(5) The term of imprisonment referred to in subsection (4) is the lesser of

(*a*) the number of days that corresponds to a fraction, rounded down to the nearest whole number, of which

(i) the numerator is the unpaid amount of the fine plus the costs and charges of committing and conveying the defaulter to prison, calculated in accordance with regulations made under subsection (7), and

(ii) the denominator is equal to eight times the provincial minimum hourly wage, at the time of default, in the province in which the fine was imposed, and

(*b*) the maximum term of imprisonment that the court could itself impose on conviction or, if the punishment for the offence does not include a term of imprisonment, five years in the case of an indictable offence or six months in the case of a summary conviction offence.

(6) All or any part of a fine imposed under this section may be taken out of moneys found in the possession of the offender at the time of the arrest of the offender if the court making the order, on being satisfied that ownership of or right to possession of those moneys is not disputed by claimants other than the offender, so directs.

(7) The lieutenant governor in council of a province may make regulations respecting the calculation of the costs and charges referred to in subparagraph (5)(*a*)(i) and in paragraph 734.8(1)(*b*).

(8) This section and sections 734.1 to 734.8 and 736 apply to a fine imposed under any Act of Parliament, except that subsections (4) and (5) do not apply if the term of imprisonment in default of payment of the fine provided for in that Act or regulation is

(*a*) calculated by a different method; or

(*b*) specified, either as a minimum or a maximum. 1995, c. 22, s. 6; 1999, c. 5, s. 33; 2003, s. 21, s. 19; 2008, c. 18, s. 38.

CROSS-REFERENCES

"Court" and "fine" are defined in s. 716. Section 734.1 prescribes the terms of the order imposing a fine. Section 734.2 sets out the procedure for making the order under s. 734.1. Under s. 734.3 the offender may apply to the court to change the terms of the order, except the amount of the fine. Sections 734.5 to 734.8 deal with the consequences of failure to pay the fine. Section 734.5 allows the province or the federal government as the case may be to refuse to issue or renew any licence, permit or other similar instrument until the fine is paid. Section 734.6 allows for civil enforcement of the fine by filing the order in any civil court. Section 734.7 sets out the procedure for issuing a warrant of committal where time for paying the fine has expired and the fine is in default. Section 734.8 sets out the procedure for paying all or part of the fine after the offender has been imprisoned for failing to pay the fine. Section 735 sets out the maximum fine where the accused is a corporation. Except where otherwise provided, where the proceedings are by indictment then the amount of the fine is unlimited and where the proceedings are by way of summary conviction then the maximum fine is $25,000. A fine imposed on a corporation may be enforced through s. 734.6. Section 736 provides for the establishing of a fine-option programme, allowing the offender to discharge the fine by earning credits for work performed. Section 736 only applies where the Lieutenant Governor has established a programme for that purpose. Section 737 requires the court imposing sentence on or discharging the offender to order that the offender pay a victim fine surcharge, except if the offender establishes that undue hardship to the offender or the offender's dependants would result from the making of the order. Under s. 748.1 the Governor in Council may remit only fine or forfeiture. Subsections (3) to (7) of this section also apply to the victim surcharge imposed under s. 737.

SYNOPSIS

Under this section the court may impose a fine in lieu of (except where there is a minimum term of imprisonment), or in addition to, another punishment such as probation, conditional imprisonment or imprisonment. A fine may be imposed in addition to a term of imprisonment where the enactment prescribes a minimum term of imprisonment. Before imposing the fine the court must be satisfied that the offender is ablc to pay the fine or discharge it through a fine option programme under s. 736. A term of imprisonment is deemed to be imposed in default of payment of the fine. The length of the term of imprisonment is determined in accordance with a formula set out in subsec. (5). The length of the term of imprisonment in default is the product of the sum of the amount of the unpaid fine plus the costs of committing and conveying the defaulter to prison divided by the sum of eight times the provincial minimum wage. This number is then rounded down to the nearest whole number of days. This number cannot exceed the maximum term of imprisonment that the court itself could impose on conviction. The Lieutenant Governor in Council may make regulations respecting the calculation of the costs and charges under subsec. (5). Under subsec. (6) all or part of the fine may be taken out of money found in the possession of the offender at the time of the offender's arrest, provided the court is satisfied that ownership of or right to possession of those moneys is not disputed by claimants other than the offender and the court so directs.

ANNOTATIONS

There is no authority to impose concurrent fines upon conviction of two separate offences: *R. v. Ward* (1980), 56 C.C.C. (2d) 15 (Ont. C.A.).

A conditional sentence is not available for imprisonment in default of payment of a fine. The Crown has a number of options available for collection in the event of default. Where an individual has defaulted because of an inability to pay, notwithstanding time to pay, the court should not issue a warrant of committal unless, pursuant to s. 734.7(*b*)(ii), the offender has, without reasonable excuse, refused to pay: *R. v. Wu*, [2003] 3 S.C.R. 530, 180 C.C.C. (3d) 97.

The imposition of substantial fines in addition to a penitentiary term where the accused had been convicted of a large scale misleading advertising scam was appropriate. The purpose of a fine in economic crimes is to ensure that the accused did not retain a significant profit from the crime and that the fine was more than a mere licence fee or part of the cost of doing business: *R. v. Benlolo* (2006), 209 C.C.C. (3d) 232 (Ont. C.A.).

The legislative purpose of s. 734(2) is to prevent offenders from incurring fines they truly cannot afford to pay, and to reduce the number of offenders who are incarcerated in default. Accordingly, this section requires the court to make an affirmative finding on a balance of probabilities that the offender is able to pay before imposing a fine. While past receipt of illegally obtained funds will often support an inference of ability to pay (absent a reasonable explanation to the contrary from the offender), the sentencing judge is not bound as a matter of law to make such a finding: *R. v. Topp*, [2011] 3 S.C.R. 119, 272 C.C.C. (3d) 417.

TERMS OF ORDER IMPOSING FINE.

734.1 A court that fines an offender under section 734 shall do so by making an order that clearly sets out

(*a*) the amount of the fine;

(*b*) the manner in which the fine is to be paid;

(*c*) the time or times by which the fine, or any portion thereof, must be paid; and

(*d*) such other terms respecting the payment of the fine as the court deems appropriate. 1995, c. 22, s. 6.

CROSS-REFERENCES

See cross-references under s. 734.

SYNOPSIS

This section requires the court that imposes the fine to make an order clearly setting out the amount of the fine, the manner in which it is to be paid, the time or times by which the fine is to be paid and such other terms as the court considers appropriate.

ANNOTATIONS

Where a court has determined that a conditional sentence for the offence is proper, it is inconsistent and inappropriate to put the offender in jeopardy of imprisonment for failure to pay a fine imposed as part of the sentence: *R. v. Grimberg* (2002), 163 C.C.C. (3d) 310, 155 O.A.C. 296 (C.A.).

OBLIGATIONS OF COURT / For greater certainty.

734.2 (1) A court that makes an order under section 734.1 shall

(*a*) cause a copy of the order to be given to the offender;

(*b*) explain the substance of sections 734 to 734.8 and 736 to the offender;

(*c*) cause an explanation to be given to the offender of the procedure for applying under section 734.3 for a change to the optional conditions and of any available fine option programs referred to in section 736 as well as the procedure to apply for admission to them; and

(*d*) take reasonable measures to ensure that the offender understands the order and the explanations.

(2) For greater certainty, a failure to comply with subsection (1) does not affect the validity of the order. 1995, c. 22, s. 6; 2008, c. 18, s. 39.

CROSS-REFERENCES

See cross-references under s. 734.

SYNOPSIS

This section requires the court that imposes a fine to cause a copy of the order to be given to the offender. In addition, the offender is to be informed of the consequences of failure to comply with the order, the procedure for varying the terms of the order as set out in ss. 734 to 734.8 and s. 736.

The offender is also to be informed of available fine-option programmes. The court is to take reasonable measures to ensure that the offender understands the order and these explanations. A failure to comply with these notice requirements does not affect the validity of the order.

CHANGE IN TERMS OF ORDER.

734.3 A court that makes an order under section 734.1, or a person designated either by name or by title of office by that court, may, on application by or on behalf of the offender, subject to any rules made by the court under section 482 or 482.1, change any term of the order except the amount of the fine, and any reference in this section and sections 734, 734.1, 734.2 and 734.6 to an order shall be read as including a reference to the order as changed under this section. 1995, c. 22, s. 6; 2002, c. 13, s. 74.

CROSS-REFERENCES

See cross-references under s. 734. This section also applies to a victim surcharge imposed under s. 737.

SYNOPSIS

Under this provision an offender may apply to a court or to a person designated by the court to change any of the terms of the order imposing the fine, except the amount of the fine.

ANNOTATIONS

It was held in relation to the former s. 722(10) [which then applied to summary conviction proceedings] that even after the termination of an extension of time to pay a fine the sentencing court is not *funtus* to grant another further extension of time. Furthermore, even though the trial judge's warrant of committal had been executed and he had since died, his ministerial, not judicial, issuance of the warrant, which is nothing maore than a written direction to carry out a sentence, may in effect be rescinded by another judge's order granting a further extension of time to pay the fine: *R. v. Yamelst* (1975), 22 C.C.C. (2d) 502, [1975] 3 W.W.R. 546 (B.C.S.C.).

PROCEEDS TO GO TO PROVINCIAL TREASURER / Proceeds to go to Receiver General for Canada / Direction for payment to municipality.

734.4 (1) Where a fine or forfeiture is imposed or a recognizance is forfeited and no provision, other than this section, is made by law for the application of the proceeds thereof, the proceeds belong to Her Majesty in right of the province in which the fine or forfeiture was imposed or the recognizance was forfeited, and shall be paid by the person who receives them to the treasurer of that province.

(2) Where

(*a*) a fine or forfeiture is imposed

(i) in respect of a contravention of a revenue law of Canada,

(ii) in respect of a breach of duty or malfeasance in office by an officer or employee of the Government of Canada, or

(iii) in respect of any proceedings instituted at the instance of the Government of Canada in which that government bears the costs of prosecution, or

(*b*) a recognizance in connection with proceedings mentioned in paragraph (*a*) is forfeited,

the proceeds of the fine, forfeiture or recognizance belong to Her Majesty in right of Canada and shall be paid by the person who receives them to the Receiver General.

(3) Where a provincial, municipal or local authority bears, in whole or in part, the expense of administering the law under which a fine or forfeiture is imposed or under which proceedings are taken in which a recognizance is forfeited,

- **(*a*) the lieutenant governor in council of a province may direct that the proceeds of a fine, forfeiture or recognizance that belongs to Her Majesty in right of the province shall be paid to that authority; and**
- **(*b*) the Governor in Council may direct that the proceeds of a fine, forfeiture or recognizance that belongs to Her Majesty in right of Canada shall be paid to that authority. 1995, c. 22, s. 6.**

CROSS-REFERENCES

See cross-references under s. 734.

SYNOPSIS

This section provides that the proceeds of any fine or forfeiture are to be paid to the provincial treasurer except in the circumstances set out in subsec. (2), in which case the proceeds are paid to the Receiver General of Canada. Subsection (3) makes provision for the Lieutenant Governor in Council or the Governor in Council as the case may, be to direct that the proceeds be paid to the authority, be it provincial, municipal or local that incurred expenses in administering the law under which a fine or forfeiture is imposed.

LICENCES, PERMITS, ETC.

734.5 If an offender is in default of payment of a fine,

- **(*a*) where the proceeds of the fine belong to Her Majesty in right of a province by virtue of subsection 734.4(1), the person responsible, by or under an Act of the legislature of the province, for issuing, renewing or suspending a licence, permit or other similar instrument in relation to the offender may refuse to issue or renew or may suspend the licence, permit or other instrument until the fine is paid in full, proof of which lies on the offender; or**
- **(*b*) where the proceeds of the fine belong to Her Majesty in right of Canada by virtue of subsection 734.4(2), the person responsible, by or under an Act of Parliament, for issuing or renewing a licence, permit or other similar instrument in relation to the offender may refuse to issue or renew or may suspend the licence, permit or other instrument until the fine is paid in full, proof of which lies on the offender. 1995, c. 22, s. 6; 1999, c. 5, s. 34.**

CROSS-REFERENCES

See cross-references under s. 734. This section also applies to a victim surcharge imposed under s. 737.

SYNOPSIS

This section is one of a number of provisions that are available to enforce payment of a fine. Under this section the provincial or federal government, as the case may be, may refuse to issue or renew a licence, permit or other instrument until the fine is paid in full. The burden of proving that the fine has been paid is on the offender.

CIVIL ENFORCEMENT OF FINES FORFEITURE / Effect of filing order.

734.6 (1) Where

- **(*a*) an offender is in default of payment of a fine, or**

(*b*) a forfeiture imposed by law is not paid as required by the order imposing it,

then, in addition to any other method provided by law for recovering the fine or forfeiture,

(*c*) the Attorney General of the province to whom the proceeds of the fine or forfeiture belong, or

(*d*) the Attorney General of Canada, where the proceeds of the fine or forfeiture belong to Her Majesty in right of Canada.

may, by filing the order, enter as a judgment the amount of the fine or forfeiture, and costs, if any, in any civil court in Canada that has jurisdiction to enter a judgment for that amount.

(2) An order that is entered as a judgment under this section is enforceable in the same manner as if it were a judgment obtained by the Attorney General of the province or the Attorney General of Canada, as the case may be, in civil proceedings. 1995, c. 22, s. 6.

CROSS-REFERENCES

"Attorney General" is defined in s. 2. Also see cross-references under s. 734.

SYNOPSIS

This section provides the mechanism for civil enforcement of fines and forfeitures. The Attorney General of the province or the Attorney General of Canada, as the case may be, may file the order imposing the fine in the civil court. The order and costs, is then a judgment that may be enforced in the same manner as any other civil judgment.

Section 9 of the *Mutual Legal Assistance in Criminal Matters Act*, R.S.C. 1985, c. 30 (4th Supp.), provides that a foreign order including a "fine" may be enforced as if it had been imposed by a Canadian court. Fine under s. 9 is to be interpreted to include a restitution order and thus a restitution order imposed in the United States is enforceable in civil proceedings under this provision: *United States of America v. Zschiegner* (2001), 154 C.C.C. (3d) 547, 194 N.S.R. (2d) 30 (C.A.).

WARRANT OF COMMITTAL / Reasons for committal / Period of imprisonment / Compelling appearance of person bound / Effect of imprisonment.

734.7 (1) Where time has been allowed for payment of a fine, the court shall not issue a warrant of committal in default of payment of the fine

(*a*) until the expiration of the time allowed for payment of the fine in full; and

(*b*) unless the court is satisfied

(i) that the mechanisms provided by sections 734.5 and 734.6 are not appropriate in the circumstances, or

(ii) that the offender has, without reasonable excuse, refused to pay the fine or discharge it under section 736.

(2) Where no time has been allowed for payment of a fine and a warrant committing the offender to prison for default of payment of the fine is issued, the court shall state in the warrant the reason for immediate committal.

(2.1) The period of imprisonment in default of payment of the fine shall be specified in a warrant of committal referred to in subsection (1) or (2).

(3) The provisions of Parts XVI and XVIII with respect to compelling the appearance of an accused before a justice apply, with such modifications as the circumstances require, to proceedings under paragraph (1)(*b*).

(4) The imprisonment of an offender for default of payment of a fine terminates the operation of sections 734.5 and 734.6 in relation to that fine. 1995, c. 22, s. 6; 1999, c. 5, s. 35.

CROSS-REFERENCES

Section 734.8 sets out the manner in which the offender who has been imprisoned for non-payment of a fine may reduce the period of imprisonment by paying all or a portion of the fine. This section should also be read with s. 734 which sets out the formula for calculating the deemed length of imprisonment depending upon the amount of the fine. Also see cross-references under s. 734. This section also applies to a victim surcharge imposed under s. 737.

SYNOPSIS

Pursuant to this section an offender who has failed to pay the fine imposed may be committed to prison. There are, however, a number of important safeguards to attempt to ensure that the offender is not imprisoned merely because of an inability to pay the fine. A warrant of committal *shall not* be issued until the time for payment has expired and only where the court is satisfied that the less intrusive measures in ss. 734.5 [refusal to issue licence etc.] and 734.6 [civil enforcement] are not appropriate in the circumstances, or that the offender has "without reasonable excuse" *refused* to pay the fine or discharge it through a fine option programme. Subsection (2) appears to assume that the general rule is that the court should give the offender time to pay the fine since where no time is allowed the court shall state in the warrant of committal the reason for immediate committal to prison. Where the offender is imprisoned pursuant to this section then the enforcement mechanisms in ss. 734.5 and 734.6 are terminated.

ANNOTATIONS

It was held, considering the former s. 722(7) the equivalent of subsec. (2), that the absence of the endorsement on the warrant of the reason for immediate committal was more than a mere irregularity and invalidates the warrant: *Ex p. Andrews* (1973), 15 C.C.C. (2d) 43, [1974] 2 W.W.R. 481 (B.C.S.C.).

A default hearing is not a "sentence passed by a trial court" pursuant to s. 676(1) and accordingly, cannot be the subject of a Crown appeal: *R. v. Druet* (2001), 159 C.C.C. (3d) 445, 243 N.B.R. (2d) 117 (C.A.).

A conditional sentence is not available in default of a fine, even where the offender is given no time to pay. Genuine inability to pay a fine is not a proper basis for imprisonment. Since a conditional sentence is a form of imprisonment, a conditional sentence is not an appropriate sentence to impose on an offender simply because he or she has no means to pay a fine: *R. v. Wu*, [2003] 3 S.C.R. 530, 180 C.C.C. (3d) 97, 16 C.R. (6th) 289, 234 D.L.R. (4th) 87.

This section is procedural and applies retrospectively: *R. v. Bourque* (2005), 193 C.C.C. (3d) 485, 194 O.A.C. 280 (C.A.).

DEFINITION OF "PENALTY" / Reduction of imprisonment on part payment / Minimum that can be accepted / To whom payment made / Application of money paid.

734.8 (1) In this section, "penalty" means the aggregate of

(*a*) the fine, and

(*b*) the costs and charges of committing and conveying the defaulter to prison, calculated in accordance with regulations made under subsection 734(7).

(2) The term of imprisonment in default of payment of a fine shall, on payment of a part of the penalty, whether the payment was made before or after the execution of a warrant of committal, be reduced by the number of days that bears the same proportion to the number of days in the term as the part paid bears to the total penalty.

(3) No amount offered in part payment of a penalty shall be accepted after the execution of a warrant of committal unless it is sufficient to secure a reduction of sentence of one day, or a whole number multiple of one day, and no part payment shall be accepted until any fee that is payable in respect of the warrant or its execution has been paid.

(4) Payment may be made under this section to the person that the Attorney General directs or, if the offender is imprisoned, to the person who has lawful custody of the prisoner or to any other person that the Attorney General directs.

(5) A payment under this section shall be applied firstly to the payment in full of costs and charges, secondly to the payment in full of any victim surcharge imposed under section 737, and then to payment of any part of the fine that remains unpaid. 1995, c. 22, s. 6; 1999, c. 5, s. 36; c. 25, s. 19.

CROSS-REFERENCES

See cross-references under s. 734. This section also applies to a victim surcharge imposed under s. 737.

SYNOPSIS

This section sets out the procedure by which an offender who has been imprisoned for non-payment of a fine, may reduce the length of imprisonment by paying all or part of the fine. To secure release the offender must pay the "penalty" being the sum of the amount of the fine then outstanding plus the costs and charges of committing and conveying the defaulter to prison as calculated in accordance with regulations made under s. 734(7). Where the offender only pays a part of the penalty then the number of days is reduced by the proportion that the partial payment bears to the total penalty. In other words, if the offender pays one-half of the penalty then the number of days is reduced by half. No part payment may be accepted unless it is sufficient to at least reduce the period of imprisonment by one day or a multiple thereof. Further, where a warrant of committal has been issued, the defaulter must first pay any fee that is payable in respect of the warrant or its execution. Subsection (5) sets out the priority of the proceeds of the part payment. The proceeds are to be first applied to the costs and charges of committing and conveying the defaulter to prison, then to pay the victim fine surcharge and then payment of the fine. Payments under this section may be made to the gaoler or to any other person as the Attorney General directs.

FINES ON ORGANIZATIONS / Application of certain provisions — fines / Effect of filing order.

735. (1) An organization that is convicted of an offence is liable, in lieu of any imprisonment that is prescribed as punishment for that offence, to be fined in an amount, except where otherwise provided by law,

(*a*) that is in the discretion of the court, where the offence is an indictable offence; or

(*b*) not exceeding one hundred thousand dollars, where the offence is a summary conviction offence.

(1.1) A court that imposes a fine under subsection (1) or under any other Act of Parliament shall make an order that clearly sets out

(*a*) the amount of the fine;

(*b*) the manner in which the fine is to be paid;

(*c*) the time or times by which the fine, or any portion of it, must be paid; and

(*d*) any other terms respecting the payment of the fine that the court deems appropriate.

(2) Section 734.6 applies, with any modifications that are required, when an organization fails to pay the fine in accordance with the terms of the order. 1995, c. 22, s. 6; 1999, c. 5, s. 37; 2003, c. 21, s. 20.

CROSS-REFERENCES

"Organization" is defined in s. 2. Special principles of sentencing applicable to organizations are set out in s. 718.21. An organization may also be placed on probation on terms set out in s.

732.1(3.1). For provisions respecting the trial of an organization, see ss. 620 to 623. For other cross-references respecting fines, see notes under s. 734.

SYNOPSIS

This section sets out the maximum penalty that may be imposed on an organization in lieu of imprisonment. Except where otherwise provided by law the maximum fine in summary conviction proceedings is $100,000 and in indictable proceedings is unlimited. In default of payment the court may resort to the civil enforcement mechanism provided by s. 734.6.

ANNOTATIONS

The superior court has jurisdiction to issue a *Mareva*-type injunction in support of the criminal law to preserve the assets of the accused for the payment of a possible fine should it be convicted. This jurisdiction, however, is to be exercised only in exceptional circumstances and the Crown must demonstrate (i) that the accused has assets within the jurisdiction of the court; (ii) that there exists a strong *prima facie* case the accused will likely be convicted of the offence with which it is charged, and that the amount of the fine will likely equal or exceed the value of the assets sought to be attached; and (iii) that the accused is or has been dissipating, removing or disposing of its assets for the improper purpose of making them unavailable to pay a fine in the event of conviction. Finally, the Crown must give the usual undertaking respecting damages: *R. v. Consolidated Fastfrate Transport Inc.* (1995), 99 C.C.C. (3d) 143, 125 D.L.R. (4th) 1, 24 O.R. (3d) 564 (C.A.).

FINE OPTION PROGRAM / Credits and other matters / Deemed payment / Federal-provincial agreement.

736. (1) An offender who is fined under section 734 may, whether or not the offender is serving a term of imprisonment imposed in default of payment of the fine, discharge the fine in whole or in part by earning credits for work performed during a period not greater than two years in a program established for that purpose by the lieutenant governor in council

(*a*) of the province in which the fine was imposed, or

(*b*) of the province in which the offender resides, where an appropriate agreement is in effect between the government of that province and the government of the province in which the fine was imposed.

if the offender is admissible to such a program.

(2) A program referred to in subsection (1) shall determine the rate at which credits are earned and may provide for the manner of crediting any amounts earned against the fine and any other matters necessary for or incidental to carrying out the program.

(3) Credits earned for work performed as provided by subsection (1) shall, for the purposes of this Act, be deemed to be payment in respect of a fine.

(4) Where, by virtue of subsection 734.4(2), the proceeds of a fine belong to Her Majesty in right of Canada, an offender may discharge the fine in whole or in part in a fine option program of a province pursuant to subsection (1), where an appropriate agreement is in effect between the government of the province and the Government of Canada. 1995, c. 22, s. 6.

CROSS-REFERENCES

By virtue of s. 737(6) the program established under this section is not available to discharge a victim fine surcharge imposed under s. 737. Also see cross-references under s. 734.

SYNOPSIS

This section provides for the establishment of fine-option programs by the Lieutenant Governor in Council. Where such a program is in effect the offender may discharge the fine by earning credits for work performed during a period of not greater than two years. The program determines the rate at which credits are earned. Where there is an agreement between provinces or between the province and the federal government as the case may be, the offender may be able to enter a fine-option program in one province to earn credits against a fine imposed in another province, or in respect of a fine where the proceeds would ordinarily go to the federal Crown.

VICTIM SURCHARGE / Amount of surcharge / Increase in surcharge / Time for payment / Amounts applied to aid victims / Notice / Enforcement.

737. (1) An offender who is convicted, or discharged under section 730, of an offence under this Act, the *Controlled Drugs and Substances Act* or the *Cannabis Act* shall pay a victim surcharge, in addition to any other punishment imposed on the offender.

(2) Subject to subsection (3), the amount of the victim surcharge in respect of an offence is

(*a*) 30 per cent of any fine that is imposed on the offender for the offence; or

(*b*) if no fine is imposed on the offender for the offence,

(i) $100 in the case of an offence punishable by summary conviction, and

(ii) $200 in the case of an offence punishable by indictment.

(3) The court may order an offender to pay a victim surcharge in an amount exceeding that set out in subsection (2) if the court considers it appropriate in the circumstances and is satisfied that the offender is able to pay the higher amount.

(4) The victim surcharge imposed in respect of an offence is payable within the time established by the lieutenant governor in council of the province in which the surcharge is imposed. If no time has been so established, the surcharge is payable within a reasonable time after its imposition.

(5) [*Repealed*, 2013, c. 11, s. 3(3).]

(6) [*Repealed*, 2013, c. 11, s. 3(3).]

(7) A victim surcharge imposed under subsection (1) shall be applied for the purposes of providing such assistance to victims of offences as the lieutenant governor in council of the province in which the surcharge is imposed may direct from time to time.

(8) The court shall cause to be given to the offender a written notice setting out

(*a*) the amount of the victim surcharge;

(*b*) the manner in which the victim surcharge is to be paid;

(*c*) the time by which the victim surcharge must be paid; and

(*d*) the procedure for applying for a change in any terms referred to in paragraphs (*b*) and (*c*) in accordance with section 734.3.

(9) Subsections 734(3) to (7) and sections 734.3, 734.5, 734.7, 734.8 and 736 apply, with any modifications that the circumstances require, in respect of a victim surcharge imposed under subsection (1) and, in particular,

(*a*) a reference in any of those provisions to "fine", other than in subsection 734.8(5), must be read as if it were a reference to "victim surcharge"; and

(*b*) the notice provided under subsection (8) is deemed to be an order made under section 734.1. 1995, c. 22, s. 6; 1996, c. 19, s. 75 [amended 1995, c. 22, s. 18 (Sched. IV, item 15]; 1999, c. 5, s. 38; c. 25, s. 20; 2013, c. 11, s. 3; 2015, c. 13, s. 28; 2018, c. 16, s. 222.

(10) [*Repealed*, 2013, c. 11, s. 3(5).]

Note: If Bill C-28, introduced in the 1st session of the 42nd Parliament and entitled *An Act to amend the Criminal Code (victim surcharge)*, receives Royal Assent, then, on the first day on which both subsec. 2(1) of that Act and s. 222 of 2018, c. 16 are in force, s. 737 is amended by replacing subsec. (1), 2018, c. 16, s. 190:

Victim surcharge

737 (1) Subject to subsection (1.1), an offender who is convicted, or discharged under section 730, of an offence under this Act, the *Controlled Drugs and Substances Act* or the *Cannabis Act* shall pay a victim surcharge for each offence, in addition to any other punishment imposed on the offender.

CROSS-REFERENCES

The definition of "sentence" in ss. 673 and 785 for the purpose of appeal in indictable and summary conviction proceedings includes an order made under this section. "Court" is defined in s. 716. Pursuant to s. 734.8, where a person who has been imprisoned for default in payment of the fine makes a part payment, then the proceeds are to first be applied to payment in full of costs and charges of committing the defaulter, and then to pay the victim fine surcharge imposed pursuant to this section. Also see cross-references under s. 734.

SYNOPSIS

This section authorizes the imposition of victim surcharges in addition to any other penalty. Where the offender is convicted or discharged of an offence under this Act or the *Controlled Drugs and Substances Act*, the court imposing sentence or discharging the offender "shall" order the offender to pay a victim surcharge. The victim surcharge is 30% of any fine imposed or $100 or $200 where no fine is imposed in the case of a summary or indictable offence respectively. The court, however, has the discretion under subsec. (3) to order the offender to pay a victim surcharge for a greater amount. The proceeds of the victim surcharge are to be applied for the purpose of providing assistance to victims as directed by the Lieutenant Governor in Council. The enforcement provisions of ss. 734.5 and 734.7 apply and thus an offender who fails to pay the victim surcharge may be committed to prison in accordance with s. 734.7. The court must cause the offender to be given a notice setting out the amount of the surcharge, the manner of payment and procedure for changing any of the terms of payment.

ANNOTATIONS

This provision infringes s. 12 of the Charter and is not saved by s. 1 because in its application to vulnerable and impecunious offenders, it creates circumstances that are grossly disproportionate to what would otherwise be a fit sentence. It is therefore of no force or effect: *R. v. Boudreault*, 2018 SCC 58.

Restitution

COURT TO CONSIDER RESTITUTION ORDER / Inquiry by court / Adjournment / Form / Reasons.

737.1 (1) If an offender is convicted or is discharged under section 730 of an offence, the court that sentences or discharges the offender, in addition to any other measure imposed on the offender, shall consider making a restitution order under section 738 or 739.

(2) As soon as feasible after a finding of guilt and in any event before imposing the sentence, the court shall inquire of the prosecutor if reasonable steps have been taken to provide the victims with an opportunity to indicate whether they are seeking restitution for their losses and damages, the amount of which must be readily ascertainable.

(3) On application of the prosecutor or on its own motion, the court may adjourn the proceedings to permit the victims to indicate whether they are seeking restitution or to

establish their losses and damages, if the court is satisfied that the adjournment would not interfere with the proper administration of justice.

(4) Victims and other persons may indicate whether they are seeking restitution by completing Form 34.1 in Part XXVIII or a form approved for that purpose by the lieutenant governor in council of the province in which the court is exercising its jurisdiction or by using any other method approved by the court, and, if they are seeking restitution, shall establish their losses and damages, the amount of which must be readily ascertainable, in the same manner.

(5) If a victim seeks restitution and the court does not make a restitution order, it shall include in the record a statement of the court's reasons for not doing so. 2015, c. 13, s. 29.

RESTITUTION TO VICTIMS OF OFFENCES / Regulations.

738. (1) Where an offender is convicted or discharged under section 730 of an offence, the court imposing sentence on or discharging the offender may, on application of the Attorney General or on its own motion, in addition to any other measure imposed on the offender, order that the offender make restitution to another person as follows:

(*a*) in the case of damage to, or the loss or destruction of, the property of any person as a result of the commission of the offence or the arrest or attempted arrest of the offender, by paying to the person an amount not exceeding the replacement value of the property as of the date the order is imposed, less the value of any part of the property that is returned to that person as of the date it is returned, where the amount is readily ascertainable;

(*b*) in the case of bodily or psychological harm to any person as a result of the commission of the offence or the arrest or attempted arrest of the offender, by paying to the person an amount not exceeding all pecuniary damages incurred as a result of the harm, including loss of income or support, if the amount is readily ascertainable;

(*c*) in the case of bodily harm or threat of bodily harm to the offender's spouse or common-law partner or child, or any other person, as a result of the commission of the offence or the arrest or attempted arrest of the offender, where the spouse or common-law partner, child or other person was a member of the offender's household at the relevant time, by paying to the person in question, independently of any amount ordered to be paid under paragraphs (*a*) and (*b*), an amount not exceeding actual and reasonable expenses incurred by that person, as a result of moving out of the offender's household, for temporary housing, food, child care and transportation, where the amount is readily ascertainable;

(*d*) in the case of an offence under section 402.2 or 403, by paying to a person who, as a result of the offence, incurs expenses to reestablish their identity, including expenses to replace their identity documents and to correct their credit history and credit rating, an amount that is not more than the amount of those expenses, to the extent that they are reasonable, if the amount is readily ascertainable; and

(*e*) in the case of an offence under subsection 162.1(1), by paying to a person who, as a result of the offence, incurs expenses to remove the intimate image from the Internet or other digital network, an amount that is not more than the amount of those expenses, to the extent that they are reasonable, if the amount is readily ascertainable.

(2) The lieutenant governor in council of a province may make regulations precluding the inclusion of provisions on enforcement of restitution orders as an optional condition of a probation order or of a conditional sentence order. 1995, c. 22, s. 6; 2000, c. 12, s. 95(*e*); 2005, c. 43, s. 7; 2009, c. 28, s. 11; 2014, c. 31, s. 24.

CROSS-REFERENCES

"Property", "common-law partner" and "Attorney General" are defined in s. 2. "Court" is defined in s. 716. Pursuant to paras. 718(*e*) and (*f*), two of the objectives of sentencing are to provide "reparations for harm done to victims or to the community" and to promote a sense of responsibility in offenders and "acknowledgment of the harm done to victims and to the community." Optional conditions for probation are set out in s. 732.1 and for a conditional sentence set out in s. 742.3. The procedure for restitution, where the property has been transferred or conveyed to a person acting in good faith or where the offender has borrowed money on the security of that property from a person acting in good faith, is set out in s. 739. Section 740 provides that an order for restitution has priority over other monetary penalties that might be imposed. The procedure for enforcing a restitution order is set out in s. 741. Section 741.1 requires the court to cause notice of any restitution order to be given to the person in whose favour the order was made. Pursuant to s. 741.2 a civil remedy is not affected by reason only that a resitution order was made. The definition of "sentence" in ss. 673 and 785 for the purpose of appeal in indictable and summary conviction proceedings includes an order made under this section.

Section 380.3 expressly directs the court to consider making an order under this section where the person was found guilty of the general fraud offence in s. 380(1). That section also requires the court to inquire of the prosecutor whether steps have been taken to provide the victims with an opportunity to indicate whether they are seeking restitution. The court must provide reasons for refusing to make a restitution order where a victim has applied for one.

SYNOPSIS

This section authorizes the making of an order, in addition to any other measure imposed upon an offender including a discharge, requiring the offender to make restitution to another person. The order may be made following an application by the Attorney General or by the court on its own motion.

Restitution may be ordered in three circumstances. Under para. (1)(*a*), the offender can be required to pay to persons whose property was lost or destroyed the replacement value of the property, provided that the damage or loss or destruction of the property was the result of the commission of the offence or the arrest or attempted arrest of the offender. The amount to be paid cannot exceed the replacement value of the property at the time the order is made less the value of any of the property that has been returned to the person. Under para. (1)(*b*) the offender may be required to pay an amount not exceeding all pecuniary damages, including loss of income and support, to any person who suffered bodily harm as a result of the commission of the offence or the arrest or attempted arrest of the offender. Paragraph (1)(*c*) allows the court to order the offender to pay an amount not exceeding the actual and reasonable expenses incurred by a spouse, child or other person who was a member of the offender's household, as a result of moving out of the offender's household, for temporary housing, food, child care and transportation. Paragraph (1)(*c*) only applies in the case of bodily harm or threat of bodily harm to the offender's spouse, child or any other person as a result of the commission of the offence or the arrest or attempted arrest of the offender. In all cases the amount must be "readily ascertainable".

Under subsec. (2) the lieutenant governor in council may make regulations that preclude the court from including a restitution order as part of a probation order or conditional sentence order.

ANNOTATIONS

Note: Some of the cases noted below were decided prior to the enactment of this section but were considered of assistance in applying this section. Where the offender was found guilty of the offence of fraud in s. 380(1), s. 380.3 sets out a procedure to assist a victim in applying for an order under this section, including use of a form that requires the victim to establish their losses, "the amount of which must be readily ascertainable".

In *R. v. Zelensky*, [1978] 2 S.C.R. 940, 41 C.C.C. (2d) 97, it was held that the predecessor to this section is *intra vires* Parliament being in pith and substance part of the sentencing process. It should be noted, however, that the predecessor did not provide for compensation as a result of bodily harm. In the same case the court held that an order for compensation should only be made with restraint and caution and in particular should not be made where there is any serious contest on legal or factual issues or on whether the person alleging himself to be aggrieved is so in fact. An order under this section is by virtue of the definition of "sentence" in s. 673 appealable as provided under the *Criminal Code*. The filing of the order in the provincial superior court as provided in [now] s. 741 does not put in motion any civil proceedings other than those relating to enforcement. Only the accused has the right of appeal against a compensation order, and not the person in whose favour the compensation order was made.

A restitution order constitutes part of punishment and must be included in considering the totality of the punishment imposed. The means of the offender and the impact of a restitution order upon the chances or rehabilitation must be considered. A restitution order is more likely to be appropriate with a short period of imprisonment. The amount of the order need not be for the full amount of the loss. No restitution order should be made where it is difficult to determine the amount of the loss or difficult to apportion restitution among multiple victims: *R. v. Siemens* (1999), 136 C.C.C. (3d) 353 (Man. C.A.). See also *R. v. Biegus* (1999), 141 C.C.C. (3d) 245 (Ont. C.A.).

A restitution order should not be made mechanically. Care must be taken not to simply add a restitution order to a sentence of imprisonment which, in itself, is a fit punishment for the crime, as this can amount to excessive punishment and offend the totality principle: *R. v. Castro* (2010), 261 C.C.C. (3d) 304 (Ont. C.A.).

It is permissible for a court to make restitution orders against multiple offenders that exceed the total value of the property, as long as the orders are properly structured via joint and several liability to avoid over-compensation of the victim and inequity among the perpetrators: *R. v. Fast-Carlson* (2015), 329 C.C.C. (3d) 239 (Sask. C.A.).

It was held that the predecessor to this section does not permit the making of a compensation order for legal costs incurred to recover property lost or damaged as a result of a criminal offence. The order under that section was limited to an amount representing the actual loss of the property: *R. v. Devgan* (1999), 136 C.C.C. (3d) 238 (Ont. C.A.), leave to appeal to S.C.C. refused 142 C.C.C. (3d) vi, and 143 C.C.C. (3d) vi. Similarly, in *R. v. Bullen* (2001), 48 C.R. (5th) 110 (Y.T. Terr. Ct.), the court held that restitution is limited to the loss and cost of repairing property and does not extend to costs incurred in preparing for the case.

An insurance company could obtain an order under subsec. (1)(*a*) where it had paid out monies in respect of an arson. The court will have to consider the issue of quantification and it cannot be assumed that the restitution order can be made for any and all monies paid out by the insurance company: *R. v. Popert* (2010), 251 C.C.C. (3d) 30 (Ont. C.A.).

The mere fact that the claim is disputed is not a sufficient basis for refusing to make the order where the amount of money involved and the nature of the claim indicate that the claim could be dealt with reasonably and expeditiously: *R. v. Ghislieri* (1980), 56 C.C.C. (2d) 4 (Alta. C.A.).

The accused's inability to pay a large compensation order is not determinative against an order under this section as where the making of such an order is the most expeditious way for the victim to fulfil a pre-condition entitling them to compensation from another source, in this case the Law Society Compensation Fund. Unlike a restitution order made as a term of a probation order, an order under this section is enforceable as a civil judgment and so entirely different considerations apply. Where there is no dispute as to the amounts payable it would not assist the accused's rehabilitation to permit him to put the victims to additional expense by launching civil actions: *R. v. Scherer* (1984), 16 C.C.C. (3d) 30 (Ont. C.A.), leave to appeal to S.C.C. refused C.C.C. *loc. cit.*

The means of the offender will not always be the controlling factor in determining whether a compensation order should be made. Thus, in *R. v. Fitzgibbon*, [1990] 1 S.C.R. 1005, 55 C.C.C. (3d) 449, it was held appropriate to make a compensation order against the accused, an undischarged bankrupt, who, while a lawyer, had defrauded his clients. The claims of the victims of the fraudulent acts should be paramount. Further, the Law Society, which through its compensation fund had paid back many of the accused's victims, was a person aggrieved within the meaning of this section and a compensation order could properly be made in its favour, provincial legislation providing that the Law Society was to be subrogated to the rights of the victim to whom it paid money from its compensation fund. Finally, a victim who was only given partial repayment by the Law Society was entitled to an order under this section against the offender for the balance of the amount of which he was defrauded.

With respect to some offences such as breach of trust, the accused's ability to pay, including future ability to pay, is not determinative: *R. v. Yates* (2002), 169 C.C.C. (3d) 506 (B.C.C.A.).

Although the accused is an undischarged bankrupt, leave of the bankruptcy court is not required before a court in criminal proceedings makes a compensation order under this section. It is only when the compensation order is filed with the superior court that it becomes enforceable against the person and property of the accused. When the victim sought to enforce the order then the trustee in bankruptcy must be notified and the consent of the bankruptcy court obtained: *R. v. Fitzgibbon, supra.*

A restitution order may be particularly appropriate to deter acts of vandalism and can and should be used either to replace or reduce what would otherwise be a fit sentence of imprisonment: *R. v. Hoyt* (1992), 77 C.C.C. (3d) 289 (B.C.C.A.).

It was held that the predecessor to subsec. (1)(*a*) did not authorize an order representing loss of rents or profits from the loss of property. The order must be limited to the replacement value of the thing: *R. v. Brunner* (1995), 97 C.C.C. (3d) 31 (Alta. C.A.).

There is no jurisdiction to order bail monies forfeited in order to satisfy a restitution order: *R. v. Dodson* (2000), 142 C.C.C. (3d) 134 (Ont. C.A.).

A third party, in this case a lawyer acting for the U.S. Department of Justice, did not have standing on the issue of the penalty and in particular had no standing to apply for an order that any fine paid by the offender be remitted to a receiver appointed by the U.S. court. Furthermore, there was no jurisdiction to make a restitution order in a case where the applicant, as here, was not directly aggrieved: *R. v. Levy* (2004), 184 C.C.C. (3d) 427 (Ont. S.C.J.).

RESTITUTION TO PERSONS ACTING IN GOOD FAITH.

739. Where an offender is convicted or discharged under section 730 of an offence and

(*a*) any property obtained as a result of the commission of the offence has been conveyed or transferred for valuable consideration to a person acting in good faith and without notice, or

(*b*) the offender has borrowed money on the security of that property from a person acting in good faith and without notice.

the court may, where that property has been returned to the lawful owner or the person who had lawful possession of that property at the time the offence was committed, order the offender to pay as restitution to the person referred to in paragraph (*a*) or (*b*) an amount not exceeding the amount of consideration for that property or the total amount outstanding in respect of the loan, as the case may be. 1995, c. 22, s. 6.

CROSS-REFERENCES

The definition of "sentence" in ss. 673 and 785 for the purpose of appeal in indictable and summary conviction proceedings includes an order made under this section. Also see cross-references under s. 738.

Section 380.3 expressly directs the court to consider making an order under this section where the person was found guilty of the general fraud offence in s. 380(1). That section also requires the court to inquire of the prosecutor whether steps have been taken to provide the victims with an opportunity to indicate whether they are seeking restitution.

SYNOPSIS

This section authorizes the court to make an order requiring the offender to pay an amount to a person who has purchased property in good faith and without notice that was obtained as the result of the commission of the offence and where the property has been returned to the lawful owner or the person who had lawful possession at the time of the offence. The court may also make a similar order in favour of a person who has loaned money to the offender on the security of that property provided that the person was acting in good faith and without notice. The amount to be ordered may not exceed the amount of consideration for the property or the amount outstanding in respect of the loan.

ABILITY TO PAY.

739.1 The offender's financial means or ability to pay does not prevent the court from making an order under section 738 or 739. 2015, c. 13, s. 30.

PAYMENT UNDER ORDER.

739.2 In making an order under section 738 or 739, the court shall require the offender to pay the full amount specified in the order by the day specified in the order, unless the court is of the opinion that the amount should be paid in installments, in which case the court shall set out a periodic payment scheme in the order. 2015, c. 13, s. 30.

MORE THAN ONE PERSON.

739.3 An order under section 738 or 739 may be made in respect of more than one person, in which case the order must specify the amount that is payable to each person. The order may also specify the order of priority in which those persons are to be paid. 2015, c. 13, s. 30.

PUBLIC AUTHORITY / Orders.

739.4 (1) On the request of a person in whose favour an order under section 738 or 739 would be made, the court may make the order in favour of a public authority, designated by the regulations, who is to be responsible for enforcing the order and remitting to the person making the request all amounts received under it.

(2) The lieutenant governor in council of a province may, by order, designate any person or body as a public authority for the purpose of subsection (1). 2015, c. 13, s. 30.

PRIORITY TO RESTITUTION.

740. Where the court finds it applicable and appropriate in the circumstances of a case to make, in relation to an offender, an order of restitution under section 738 or 739, and

(*a*) an order of forfeiture under this or any other Act of Parliament may be made in respect of property that is the same as property in respect of which the order of restitution may be made, or

(*b*) the court is considering ordering the offender to pay a fine and it appears to the court that the offender would not have the means or ability to comply with both the order of restitution and the order to pay the fine,

the court shall first make the order of restitution and shall then consider whether and to what extent an order of forfeiture or an order to pay a fine is appropriate in the circumstances. 1995, c. 22, s. 6.

CROSS-REFERENCES

See cross-references under s. 738.

SYNOPSIS

This section sets out the order of priority of the various types of orders that may be made against an offender where the order for restitution and a forfeiture order would apply to the same property [para. (*a*)], or where the offender would not have the means or ability to comply with both an order of restitution and an order to pay a fine. The court is to first make the order of restitution and then consider whether and to what extent an order for forfeiture or an order to pay a fine is appropriate.

ENFORCING RESTITUTION ORDER / Moneys found on offender.

741. (1) An offender who fails to pay all of the amount that is ordered to be paid under section 732.1, 738, 739 or 742.3 by the day specified in the order or who fails to make a periodic payment required under the order is in default of the order and the person to whom the amount, or the periodic payment, as the case may be, was to be made may, by filing the order, enter as a judgment any amount ordered to be paid that remains unpaid under the order in any civil court in Canada that has jurisdiction to enter a judgment for that amount, and that judgment is enforceable against the offender in the same manner as if it were a judgment rendered against the offender in that court in civil proceedings.

(2) All or any part of an amount that is orderd to be paid under section 738 or 739 may be taken out of moneys found in the possession of the offender at the time of the arrest of the offender if the court making the order, on being satisfied that ownership of or right to possession of those moneys is not disputed by claimants other than the offender, so directs. 1995, c. 22, s. 6; 2004, c. 12, s. 13; 2015, c. 13, s. 31.

CROSS-REFERENCES

See cross-references under s. 738.

SYNOPSIS

This section sets out two ways in which a restitution order to victims under s. 738 or to persons acting in good faith under s. 739 may be enforced. The person in whose favour the order was made may file the order in a civil court. The order may then be enforced as a civil judgment [subsec. (1)]. As well, all or any part of the order may be satisfied out of moneys found in the possession of the offender at the time of the offender's arrest, where there is no dispute as to the ownership of those moneys.

Where the order is made under ss. 732.1 or 742.3, the person in whose favour the order was made may file the order in a civil court. The order may then be enforced as a civil judgment.

ANNOTATIONS

It was held that to invoke the predecessor of subsec. (1) that the victim at the time of filing the order in the Superior Court should present evidence as to the amount of the order still outstanding and the court clerk may require such evidence before issuing a writ of execution or other civil process for enforcement of the order: *103956 Canada Ltd. v. Moniuk* (1981), 61 C.C.C. (2d) 285, 23 C.R. (3d) 87 (N.W.T.S.C.).

NOTICE OF ORDERS OF RESTITUTION.

741.1 If a court makes an order of restitution under section 738 or 739, it shall cause notice of the content of the order, or a copy of the order, to be given to the person to

whom the restitution is ordered to be paid, and if it is to be paid to a public authority designated by regulations made under subsection 739.4(2), to the public authority and the person to whom the public authority is to remit amounts received under the order. 1995, c. 22, s. 6; 2015, c. 13, s. 32.

CROSS-REFERENCES

See cross-references under s. 738.

SYNOPSIS

The court that makes a restitution order to victims under s. 738 or to persons acting in good faith under s. 739 is to cause notice of the contents of the order to be given to the person in whose favour the order was made.

CIVIL REMEDY NOT AFFECTED.

741.2 A civil remedy for an act or omission is not affected by reason only that an order for restitution under section 738 or 739 has been made in respect of that act or omission. 1995, c. 22, s. 6.

CROSS-REFERENCES

See cross-references under s. 738.

SYNOPSIS

The making of an order of restitution to victims under s. 738 or to persons acting in good faith under s. 739 does not of itself affect any civil remedy that the person may have.

ANNOTATIONS

Prior to the enactment of this section it was held that a compensation order cannot bar resort to civil suit to recover the moneys owed to the victim. Double recovery would be prevented by the jurisdiction of the civil court to require a proper accounting for any sums recovered under rhe compensation order: *London Life Insurance Co. v. Zavitz* (1992), 12 C.R. (4th) 267 (B.C.C.A.).

Similarly, it was held that the fact the victim has obtained a civil judgment against the accused was not a bar to a criminal court making an order under former s. 725 [now s. 738]: *R. v. Devgan* (1999), 136 C.C.C. (3d) 238 (Ont. C.A.), leave to appeal to S.C.C. refused 142 C.C.C. (3d) vi, 143 C.C.C. (3d) vi.

Conditional Sentence of Imprisonment

DEFINITIONS / "Change" / "Optional conditions" / "Supervisor".

742. In sections 742.1 to 742.7,

"change", in relation to optional conditions, includes deletions and additions;

"optional conditions" means the conditions referred to in subsection 742.3(2);

"supervisor" means a person designated by the Attorney General, either by name or by title of office, as a supervisor for the purposes of sections 742.1 to 742.7. 1995, c. 22, s. 6.

CROSS-REFERENCES

"Attorney General" is defined in s. 2. For cross-references on conditional sentence of imprisonment see notes under s. 742.1.

IMPOSING OF CONDITIONAL SENTENCE.

742.1 If a person is convicted of an offence and the court imposes a sentence of imprisonment of less than two years, the court may, for the purpose of supervising the offender's behaviour in the community, order that the offender serve the sentence in the community, subject to the conditions imposed under section 742.3, if

(*a*) the court is satisfied that the service of the sentence in the community would not endanger the safety of the community and would be consistent with the fundamental purpose and principles of sentencing set out in sections 718 to 718.2;

(*b*) the offence is not an offence punishable by a minimum term of imprisonment;

(*c*) the offence is not an offence, prosecuted by way of indictment, for which the maximum term of imprisonment is 14 years or life;

(*d*) the offence is not a terrorism offence, or a criminal organization offence, prosecuted by way of indictment, for which the maximum term of imprisonment is 10 years or more;

(*e*) the offence is not an offence, prosecuted by way of indictment, for which the maximum term of imprisonment is 10 years, that

(i) resulted in bodily harm,

(ii) involved the import, export, trafficking or production of drugs, or

(iii) involved the use of a weapon; and

(*f*) the offence is not an offence, prosecuted by way of indictment, under any of the following provisions:

(i) section 144 (prison breach),

(ii) section 264 (criminal harassment),

(iii) section 271 (sexual assault),

(iv) section 279 (kidnapping),

(v) section 279.02 (trafficking in persons — material benefit),

(vi) section 281 (abduction of person under fourteen),

(vii) section 333.1 (motor vehicle theft),

(viii) paragraph 334(*a*) (theft over $5000),

(ix) paragraph 348(1)(*e*) (breaking and entering a place other than a dwelling-house),

(x) section 349 (being unlawfully in a dwelling-house), and

(xi) section 435 (arson for fraudulent purpose). 1995, c. 22, s. 6; 1997, c. 18, s. 107.1; 2007, c. 12, s. 1; 2012, c. 1, s. 34.

CROSS-REFERENCES

Section 718(*c*) provides that an objective of sentencing is to separate offenders from society "where necessary". It is a principle of sentence under s. 718.2(*d*) that an offender should not be deprived of liberty if less restrictive sanctions may be appropriate, and under para. (*e*) that "all available sanctions other than imprisonment that are reasonable in the circumstances should be considered for all offenders, with particular attention to the circumstances of aboriginal offenders."

"Court" is defined in s. 716. Pursuant to s. 742.2, the court, before imposing a conditional sentence under this section, is to consider whether a firearms prohibition must or should be imposed under s. 100. The requirement for such an order is not affected by the fact that the court may also make it an optional condition under s. 742.3(2)(*b*) that the offender abstain from owning, possessing or carrying a weapon.

The mandatory and optional conditions of a conditional sentence order are set out in s. 742.3. Section 742.3 also sets out the procedure for notifying the offender of the consequences of failure to comply with the conditions and of the possibility of changing the conditions. Pursuant to s. 742 "change" includes deletions and additions. Section 742.3 requires *inter alia* that the offender report to a supervisor while on a conditional sentence. "Supervisor" is defined in s. 742. Section 742.4 allows the supervisor to apply to the court to change the optional conditions of the order.

Section 742.5 provides a mechanism to transfer the order to a court in another territorial division where the offender becomes a resident of the other territiorial division. The transfer can only be made on application of a supervisor and with the consent of the Attorney General of the province in which the order was made. "Attorney General" is defined in s. 2.

Section 742.6 sets out the procedure for holding a hearing where it is alleged that the offender is in breach of the conditions of the conditional sentence. Under s. 742.6, where the court is satisfied that the offender has without reasonable excuse breached a condition, it may take no action, change the optional conditions, suspend the conditional sentence for a period of time and require the offender to serve a portion of the term in custody, or terminate the conditional sentence and direct that the offender be committed to custody until expiration of the sentence.

Section 742.7 deals with the case of an offender who is imprisoned for another offence while at large under a conditional sentence.

"Criminal organization offence" and "terrorism offence" are defined in s. 2.

Under s. 683(5), a judge of the Court of Appeal may suspend the conditional sentence order pending appeal.

Note that s. 3 provides that the descriptions in parenthesis after the section number are inserted for convenience of reference only and are no part of the provision.

Under s. 718.2(*a*)(vi), it is deemed an aggravating factor if an offender commits an offence while subject to a conditional sentence order.

SYNOPSIS

This section authorizes a court to make an order for a conditional sentence. Unlike the suspended sentence under s. 731(1)(*a*), the court acting under this section actually imposes a sentence of imprisonment. That sentence must be less than two years. The sentence, however, is served in the community subject to the conditions prescribed in an order made under s. 742.3. The conditional sentence may be made where the court is satisfied that serving the sentence in the community would not endanger the safety of the community, and would be consistent with the fundamental purpose and principles of sentencing in ss. 718 to 718.2.

A conditional sentence is unavailable where the enactment prescribes a minimum term of imprisonment. A conditional sentence is also not available for an offence prosecuted by indictment for which the maximum term is 14 years or life; or a terrorism offence and a criminal organization offence where the maximum punishment is 10 years' or more. A conditional sentence is not available for offences prosecuted by indictment and punishable by a maximum of ten years' imprisonment committed in the circumstances set out in para. (*e*). Finally, the conditional sentence is not available for the offences prosecuted by indictment and listed in para. (*f*).

ANNOTATIONS

Note: Some of the cases noted below were decided prior to recent amendments to this section that broadened the number of offences for which a conditional sentence is not available.

In several cases released at the same time, the Supreme Court of Canada considered the principles to be applied under this section. The lead judgment was given in *R. v. Proulx*, [2000] 1 S.C.R. 61, 140 C.C.C. (3d) 449. The principles set out in that decision may be summarized as follows:

(i) Unlike probation, which is primarily a rehabilitative sentencing tool, a conditional sentence is intended to address both punitive and rehabilitative objectives. Accordingly, conditional sentences should generally include punitive conditions that restrict the offender's liberty. Therefore, conditions such as house arrest or strict curfews should be the norm.

(ii) In deciding whether to impose a conditional sentence, the judge will not proceed by way of a rigid two-step process whereby the length of the term is fixed and then the decision made whether to impose a conditional sentence. While a two-stage process is involved, the judge at the first stage merely considers whether to exclude the two possibilities of a penitentiary term or a non-custodial term. In making this preliminary determination, the judge need only consider the fundamental purpose and principles of sentencing to the extent necessary to narrow the range of sentences for this offender. At the second stage, the judge will consider the principles of sentencing in a comprehensive way in determining whether to impose a conditional sentence. Thus, the judge may properly conclude that the term of the conditional sentence should be longer than it would have been if the offender were sentenced to immediate imprisonment.

(iii) That the safety of the community would not be endangered is merely one of the three prerequisites for imposing a conditional sentence and is not the primary consideration. "Safety of the community" refers only to the threat posed by the specific offender and not to a broader risk of undermining respect for the law. It includes consideration of the risk of any criminal activity, including property offences. In considering the danger to the community, the judge must consider the risk of the offender re-offending and the gravity of the damage that could ensue. Particularly in the case of violent offenders, a small risk of very harmful future crime may warrant a finding that this prerequisite has not been met. The risk should be assessed in light of the conditions that could be attached to the sentence. Thus, the danger that the offender might pose may be reduced to an acceptable level through imposition of appropriate conditions.

(iv) A conditional sentence is available for all offences in which the statutory prerequisites are satisfied. There is no presumption that conditional sentences are inappropriate for specific offences. Nevertheless, the gravity of the offence is clearly relevant to determining whether a conditional sentence is appropriate in the circumstances.

(v) There is also no presumption in favour of a conditional sentence if the prerequisites have been satisfied. However, serious consideration should be given to the imposition of a conditional sentence in all cases where these statutory prerequisites are satisfied.

(vi) A conditional sentence can provide a significant amount of denunciation particularly when onerous conditions are imposed and the term of the sentence is longer than would have been imposed as a jail sentence. Generally, the more serious the offence, the longer and more onerous the conditional sentence should be.

(vii) A conditional sentence can also provide significant deterrence if sufficiently punitive conditions are imposed and judges should be wary of placing too much weight on deterrence when choosing between a conditional sentence and incarceration. Nevertheless, there may be circumstances in which the need for deterrence will warrant incarceration. Offences such as dangerous driving and impaired driving may be offences for which harsh sentences plausibly provide general deterrence.

(viii) When the objectives of rehabilitation, reparation and promotion of a sense of responsibility may realistically be achieved, a conditional sentence will likely be the appropriate sanction, subject to considerations of denunciation and deterrence.

(ix) While aggravating circumstances relating to the offence or the offender increase the need for denunciation and deterrence, a conditional sentence may be imposed even if such factors are present.

(x) Neither party has the onus of establishing that the offender should or should not receive a conditional sentence. However, the offender will usually be best situated to convince the judge that such a sentence is appropriate and it will be in his or her interests to make submissions and provide information establishing those elements militating in favour of such a disposition.

(xi) The deference due trial judges in imposing sentence generally applies to the decision whether or not to impose a conditional sentence. Although an appellate court might entertain a different opinion as to what objectives should be pursued and the best way to do so, that difference will generally not constitute an error of law justifying intervention.

In circumstances where either a sentence of incarceration or a conditional sentence would be appropriate, a conditional sentence should generally be imposed, even if it would be longer than the appropriate sentence of incarceration. However, there may be circumstances where a short, sharp sentence of incarceration is preferable to a lengthy conditional sentence: *R. v. S. (R.N.)*, [2000] 1 S.C.R. 149, 140 C.C.C. (3d) 553.

Where the judge considers that the gravity of the offence and the offender's moral blameworthiness requires imposition of a penitentiary sentence, a conditional sentence is not available, even though the judge imposes a sentence of less than two years after taking into account pre-sentence custody. Pre-sentence custody is part of the total punishment imposed and is not a mitigating factor that can affect the range of sentence and the availability of a conditional sentence: *R. v. Fice*, [2005] 1 S.C.R. 742, 196 C.C.C. (3d) 97.

In determining whether a conditional sentence should be imposed, a starting point sentence may be considered at the initial stage of determining whether a penitentiary term can be rejected: *R. v. Rahime* (2001), 156 C.C.C. (3d) 349 (Alta. C.A.).

A conditional sentence cannot be combined with imprisonment: *R. v. Kopf* (1997), 6 C.R. (5th) 305 (Que. C.A.); and *R. v. Hirtle* (1999), 136 C.C.C. (3d) 419 (N.S.C.A.). The trial judge erred in principle by effectively imposing penitentiary sentence, a portion of which was to be served as a conditional sentence where a conditional sentence of two years less one day for charges of indecent assault was combined with a jail sentence of nine months for sexual assault: *R. v. Alfred* (1998), 122 C.C.C. (3d) 213 (Ont. C.A.).

A so-called blended sentence whereby the accused serves a portion of the sentence in prison and the balance of the sentence in the community under a conditional sentence order is illegal: *R. v. Monkman* (1999), 132 C.C.C. (3d) 89 (Man. C.A.). Similarly, *R. v. Wey* (1999), 142 C.C.C. (3d) 556 (Alta. C.A.); and *R. v. Fisher* (2000), 143 C.C.C. (3d) 413 (Ont. C.A.).

It is legally permissible to blend a conditional sentence for one offence with a custodial sentence for another offence as long as the total sentence does not exceed two years less one day in length and the preconditions in para. (*b*) have been met in respect of one of the offences but not the other: *R. v. Ploumis* (2000), 150 C.C.C. (3d) 424 (Ont. C.A.), leave to appeal to S.C.C. refused 153 C.C.C. (3d) vi. See also *R. v. Davies* (2005), 199 C.C.C. (3d) 389 (Ont. C.A.). See also *R. v. Lyver* (2007), 229 C.C.C. (3d) 535 (Alta. C.A.).

Consecutive conditional sentences cannot exceed the two-year maximum: *R. v. Frechette* (2001), 154 C.C.C. (3d) 191 (Man. C.A.).

A conditional sentence is not available in default of a fine, even where the offender is given no time to pay. Genuine inability to pay a fine is not a proper basis for imprisonment. Since a conditional sentence is a form of imprisonment, a conditional sentence is not an appropriate sentence to impose on an offender simply because he or she has no means to pay a fine: *R. v. Wu*, [2003] 3 S.C.R. 530, 180 C.C.C. (3d) 97.

An earlier version of this section which made a conditional sentence unavailable for a "serious personal injury offence" was found not to violate ss. 7, 9, or 12 of the *Charter of Rights and Freedoms*: *R. c. Perry* (2013), 302 C.C.C. (3d) 531 (Que. C.A.), leave to appeal to S.C.C. refused 2013 CarswellQue 11263.

FIREARM, ETC., PROHIBITIONS / Application of s. 109 or 110.

742.2 (1) Before imposing a conditional sentence under section 742.1, the court shall consider whether section 109 or 110 is applicable.

(2) For greater certainty, a condition of a conditional sentence order referred to in paragraph 742.3(2)(*b*) does not affect the operation of section 109 or 110. 1995, c. 22, s. 6; 2002, c. 13, s. 75; 2004, c. 12, s. 14.

CROSS-REFERENCES

Section 742.3(2)(*b*) gives the court the option of including a condition in a conditional sentence that the offender abstain from owning, possessing or carrying a weapon. For other cross-references see notes under s. 742.1.

SYNOPSIS

Before imposing a conditional sentence, the court is required to consider whether it is also necessary to make an order under ss. 109 or 110 prohibiting the offender from possessing any firearm, or other weapons, ammunition or explosive substance. The fact that the court also imposes a condition under s. 742.3(2)(*b*), that the offender abstain from owning, possessing or carrying a weapon as part of the conditional sentence, does not affect the operation of the order made under ss. 100 or 110.

COMPULSORY CONDITIONS OF CONDITIONAL SENTENCE ORDER / Abstain from communicating / Consent / Reasons / Optional conditions of conditional sentence order / Obligations of court / For greater certainty / Notice — samples at regular intervals / Designations and specifications / Further designations / Restriction / Destruction of samples / Regulations.

742.3 (1) The court shall prescribe, as conditions of a conditional sentence order, that the offender do all of the following:

(*a*) keep the peace and be of good behaviour;

(*b*) appear before the court when required to do so by the court;

(*c*) report to a supervisor

(i) within two working days, or such longer period as the court directs, after the making of the conditional sentence order, and

(ii) thereafter, when required by the supervisor and in the manner directed by the supervisor;

(*d*) remain within the jurisdiction of the court unless written permission to go outside that jurisdiction is obtained from the court or the supervisor; and

(*e*) notify the court or the supervisor in advance of any change of name or address, and promptly notify the court or the supervisor of any change of employment or occupation.

(1.1) The court shall prescribe, as a condition of a conditional sentence order, that the offender abstain from communicating, directly or indirectly, with any victim, witness or other person identified in the order, or refrain from going to any place specified in the order, except in accordance with the conditions specified in the order that the court considers necessary, unless

(*a*) the victim, witness or other person gives their consent or, if the victim, witness or other person is a minor, the parent or guardian, or any other person who has the lawful care or charge of them, gives their consent; or

(*b*) the court decides that, because of exceptional circumstances, it is not appropriate to impose the condition.

(1.2) For the purposes of paragraph (1.1)(*a*), the consent is valid only if it is given in writing or in the manner specified in the order.

(1.3) If the court makes the decision described in paragraph (1.1)(*b*), it shall state the reasons for the decision in the record.

(2) The court may prescribe, as additional conditions of a conditional sentence order, that the offender do one or more of the following:

(*a*) abstain from the consumption of drugs except in accordance with a medical prescription, of alcohol or of any other intoxicating substance;

(*a*.1) provide, for the purpose of analysis, a sample of a bodily substance prescribed by regulation on the demand of a peace officer, the supervisor or someone designated under subsection (7) to make a demand, at the place and time and on the day specified by the person making the demand, if that person has reasonable grounds to suspect that the offender has breached a condition of the order that requires them to abstain from the consumption of drugs, alcohol or any other intoxicating substance;

(*a*.2) provide, for the purpose of analysis, a sample of a bodily substance prescribed by regulation at regular intervals that are specified by the supervisor in a notice in Form 51 served on the offender, if a condition of the order requires the offender to abstain from the consumption of drugs, alcohol or any other intoxicating substance;

(*b*) abstain from owning, possessing or carrying a weapon;

(*c*) provide for the support or care of dependants;

(*d*) perform up to 240 hours of community service over a period not exceeding eighteen months;

(*e*) attend a treatment program approved by the province; and

(*f*) comply with such other reasonable conditions as the court considers desirable, subject to any regulations made under subsection 738(2), for securing the good conduct of the offender and for preventing a repetition by the offender of the same offence or the commission of other offences.

(3) A court that makes an order under this section shall

(*a*) cause a copy of the order to be given to the offender and, on request, to the victim;

(*b*) explain the substance of subsection (1) and sections 742.4 and 742.6 to the offender;

(*c*) cause an explanation to be given to the offender of the procedure for applying under section 742.4 for a change to the optional conditions; and

(*d*) take reasonable measures to ensure that the offender understands the order and the explanations.

(4) For greater certainty, a failure to comply with subsection (3) does not affect the validity of the order.

(5) The notice referred to in paragraph (2)(*a*.2) must specify the places and times at which and the days on which the offender must provide samples of a bodily substance under a condition described in that paragraph. The first sample may not be taken earlier than 24 hours after the offender is served with the notice, and subsequent samples must be taken at regular intervals of at least seven days.

(6) For the purposes of paragraphs (2)(*a*.1) and (*a*.2) and subject to the regulations, the Attorney General of a province or the minister of justice of a territory shall, with respect to the province or territory,

(*a*) designate the persons or classes of persons that may take samples of bodily substances;

(*b*) designate the places or classes of places at which the samples are to be taken;

(*c*) specify the manner in which the samples are to be taken;

(*d*) specify the manner in which the samples are to be analyzed;

(*e*) specify the manner in which the samples are to be stored, handled and destroyed;

(*f*) specify the manner in which the records of the results of the analysis of the samples are to be protected and destroyed;

(*g*) designate the persons or classes of persons that may destroy the samples; and
(*h*) designate the persons or classes of persons that may destroy the records of the results of the analysis of the samples.

(7) For the purpose of paragraph (2)(*a*.1) and subject to the regulations, the Attorney General of a province or the minister of justice of a territory may, with respect to the province or territory, designate persons or classes of persons to make a demand for a sample of a bodily substance.

(8) Samples of bodily substances referred to in paragraphs (2)(*a*.1) and (*a*.2) may not be taken, analyzed, stored, handled or destroyed, and the records of the results of the analysis of the samples may not be protected or destroyed, except in accordance with the designations and specifications made under subsection (6).

(9) The Attorney General of a province or the minister of justice of a territory, or a person authorized by the Attorney General or minister, shall cause all samples of bodily substances provided under a conditional sentence order to be destroyed within the periods prescribed by regulation, unless the samples are reasonably expected to be used as evidence in proceedings under section 742.6.

(10) The Governor in Council may make regulations
(*a*) prescribing bodily substances for the purposes of paragraphs (2)(*a*.1) and (*a*.2);
(*b*) respecting the designations and specifications referred to in subsections (6) and (7);
(*c*) prescribing the periods within which samples of bodily substances are to be destroyed under subsection (9); and
(*d*) respecting any other matters relating to the samples of bodily substances. 1995, c. 22, s. 6; 2008, c. 18, s. 40; 2011, c. 7, s. 5; 2014, c. 21, s. 3; 2015, c. 13, s. 33.

CROSS-REFERENCES

Section 738(2) gives the Lieutenant Governor in Council the power to make regulations precluding the inclusion of provisions on enforcement of a restitution order as an optional condition of a conditional sentence. The definition of "sentence" in ss. 673 and 785 for the purpose of appeal in indictable and summary conviction proceedings includes an order made under this section. For other cross-references, see notes under s. 742.1.

SYNOPSIS

This section sets out the mandatory and optional conditions for a conditional sentence imposed under s. 742.1 and imposes an obligation on the court to ensure that the offender has notice of the terms of the sentence and the consequences of breaching the conditions. Subsection (1) sets out the mandatory conditions of a conditional sentence. The order requires the offender to keep the peace and be of good behaviour, attend court when required, report to a supervisor, remain within the jurisdiction unless given written permission by the court or the supervisor, notify the court or the supervisor in advance of any change of name or address and promptly notify the court or supervisor of any change of employment or occupation.

Subsection (2) sets out the optional conditions. These conditions are similar to the conditions that may be included in a probation order. Note, however, that under para. (*e*) the court may order the offender to attend a treatment programme. There is no statutory requirement for the offender's consent as there is under s. 732.1(3)(*g*). Paragraph (*f*) gives the court a broad discretion to impose such other reasonable conditions as the court considers desirable for securing the good conduct of the offender and for preventing a repetition by the offender of the same offence or committing another offence.

Subsection (3) requires the court to cause the offender to be given a copy of the order and an explanation of the procedure for changing the optional conditions and the consequences of breaching the conditions. The court must take reasonable measures to ensure that the offender understands the order and the explanations.

Where a weapons prohibition order is made a condition of probation under subsec. (2)(*b*), pursuant to s. 113, the judge may make an order authorizing a chief firearms officer or the Registrar to issue, in accordance with such terms and conditions as is considered appropriate, an authorization, a licence or a registration certificate, as the case may be, to the accused for sustenance or employment purposes. Under s. 114, the prohibition order may require the accused to surrender anything the possession of which is prohibited by the order and every authorization, licence and registration certificate relating to any such thing. Unless the prohibition order provides otherwise, everything the possession of which is prohibited by the order is forfeited to the Crown pursuant to s. 115, subject to the true owner making an application under s. 117. Under s. 116, every authorization, licence and registration certificate relating to anything the possession of which is prohibited by a prohibition order and issued to the accused is, on the commencement of the prohibition order, revoked, or amended, as the case may be, to the extent of the prohibitions in the order.

ANNOTATIONS

Unlike the similar residual clause for probation in s. 732.1(3)(*h*), the wording of subsec. (2)(*f*) of this section does not focus principally on the rehabilitation and reintegration of the offender and therefore authorizes the imposition of punitive conditions such as house arrest or strict curfews. Such conditions should be the norm subject to appropriate exceptions for employment, schooling, community service, treatment, medical emergencies, religious observance and the like. The conditions must be realistically enforceable. This section gives the trial judge a wide discretion in the drafting of appropriate conditions: *R. v. Proulx*, [2000] 1 S.C.R. 61, 140 C.C.C. (3d) 449.

Conditions that would promote the restorative objectives of rehabilitation, reparations, and promotion of a sense of responsibility include mandatory treatment orders, house arrest, restitution orders, community service and speaking in public about the unfortunate consequences of the conduct: *R. v. Proulx*, *supra*.

The alternative to incarceration contemplated by the conditional sentence regime is the alternative to a regime of detention, program and release governed by legislation such as the *Corrections and Conditional Release Act*. Resort may be made to community-based facilities, even residential ones such as mental health facilities that have a custodial aspect, as long as they can be seen as a genuine alternative to incarceration. In this case, the accused advocated the imposition of a term in a lock-up, psychiatric facility. It is important to note, however, that the court did not decide whether a lock-up in a mental institution could be imposed as a condition against the will of the accused: *R. v. Knoblauch*, [2000] 2 S.C.R. 780, 149 C.C.C. (3d) 1.

A condition requiring the offender to attend a batterers treatment program which compels the offender to make admissions or statements against his or her will or conscience is contrary to s. 7 of the Charter. The condition was modified to require the offender to comply with the program to the extent that it did not require any admissions contrary to his personal beliefs or conscience and to provide that the offender would be released from the condition in the event that this resulted in the offender's exclusion from the program: *R. v. Sookochoff* (1999), 133 C.C.C. (3d) 532 (Sask. Q.B.).

A properly crafted conditional sentence order should require the offender to work full-time at a job, or schooling, or treatment, assuming that it is not appropriate to confine the offender to an institution or place the offender under house arrest. The defence, in asking for a conditional sentence, should be in a position to suggest an imaginative and realistic set of conditions that reflect available resources, that would bar all actual dangers and that would likely cure all addictions, mental problems or criminal habits: *R. v. Brady* (1998), 121 C.C.C. (3d) 504 (Alta. C.A.).

A judge is functus after sentencing and, accordingly, cannot impose a condition requiring the accused to report back to the judge to provide progress reports: *R. v. Ermine* (2010), 254 C.C.C. (3d) 192 (Sask. C.A.).

PROHIBITION ON USE OF BODILY SUBSTANCE / Prohibition on use or disclosure of result / Exception / Offence.

742.31 (1) No person shall use a bodily substance provided under a conditional sentence order except for the purpose of determining whether an offender is complying with a condition of the order that they abstain from the consumption of drugs, alcohol or any other intoxicating substance.

(2) Subject to subsection (3), no person shall use, disclose or allow the disclosure of the results of the analysis of a bodily substance provided under a conditional sentence order.

(3) The results of the analysis of a bodily substance provided under a conditional sentence order may be disclosed to the offender to whom they relate, and may also be used or disclosed in the course of proceedings under section 742.6 or, if the results are made anonymous, for statistical or other research purposes.

(4) Every person who contravenes subsection (1) or (2) is guilty of an offence punishable on summary conviction. 2011, c. 7, s. 6.

SUPERVISOR MAY PROPOSE CHANGES TO OPTIONAL CONDITIONS / Hearing / Decision at hearing / Where no hearing requested or ordered / Changes proposed by offender or prosecutor / Judge may act in chambers.

742.4 (1) Where an offender's supervisor is of the opinion that a change in circumstances makes a change to the optional conditions desirable, the supervisor shall give written notification of the proposed change, and the reasons for it, to the offender, to the prosecutor and to the court.

(2) Within seven days after receiving a notification referred to in subsection (1),

(*a*) the offender or the prosecutor may request the court to hold a hearing to consider the proposed change, or

(*b*) the court may, of its own initiative, order that a hearing be held to consider the proposed change,

and a hearing so requested or ordered shall be held within thirty days after the receipt by the court of the notification referred to in subsection (1).

(3) At a hearing held pursuant to subsection (2), the court

(*a*) shall approve or refuse to approve the proposed change; and

(*b*) may make any other change to the optional conditions that the court deems appropriate.

(4) Where no request or order for a hearing is made within the time period stipulated in subsection (2), the proposed change takes effect fourteen days after the receipt by the court of the notification referred to in subsection (1), and the supervisor shall so notify the offender and file proof of that notification with the court.

(5) Subsections (1) and (3) apply, with such modifications as the circumstances require, in respect of a change proposed by the offender or the prosecutor to the optional conditions, and in all such cases a hearing must be held, and must be held within thirty days after the receipt by the court of the notification referred to in subsection (1).

(6) All the functions of the court under this section may be exercised in chambers. 1995, c. 22, s. 6; 1999, c. 5, s. 39.

CROSS-REFERENCES
The terms "change", "optional conditions" and "supervisor" are defined in s. 742.1. Subsection 742.5(2) provides for the case where the court that imposed the conditional sentence or the court to which the order was transferred is unable to act. In such a case the powers of the court in relation to the conditional sentence may be exercised by any other court of equivalent jurisdiction in the province. The definition of "sentence" in ss. 673 and 785 for the purpose of appeal in indictable and summary conviction proceedings includes a dispostion made under subsec. (3).

Also see cross-references under s. 742.1.

SYNOPSIS
This section sets out a procedure for changing the optional conditions on application by the supervisor. The supervisor must give written notice to the offender, the prosecutor and to the court. If no party requests a hearing within seven days of receiving the notice and the court on its own motion does not require a hearing, then the proposed change takes effect 14 days after the court received notice. The offender is to be given notice of the change by the supervisor. Where a hearing is required the court may approve the change, refuse to make the change and may make any other change to the optional conditions that the court deems appropriate. The application by the supervisor depends upon the supervisor forming an opinion that a change in circumstances makes a change in the optional conditions desirable. Where the application for a change is made by the offender or the prosecutor there must be a hearing and the hearing must be held within 30 days after the court receives notice of the application.

All the functions of the court under this section may be exercised in chambers.

ANNOTATIONS
Subsection (1) should be used sparingly and should propose technical rather than substantive amendments. A proposed change in the length of the house arrest portion is a substantive amendment which should proceed pursuant to subsec. (5). In addition, where the offender wishes the change, recourse should be had to subsec. (5): *R. v. Kobsar* (2004), 192 C.C.C. (3d) 224 (Alta. Q.B.).

Recourse to this provision should be reserved for situations in which there has been a material change in the offender's circumstances making the proposed change desirable and where the supervisor actively supports the amendment: *R. v. Pavlovich* (2011), 269 C.C.C. (3d) 571 (Ont. C.J.).

While the Court of Appeal and trial court have concurrent jurisdiction to vary an optional condition, the trial court is a more appropriate forum to hear evidence on a variation: *R. v. Barrett* (2008), 237 C.C.C. (3d) 37 (Nfld. & Lab. C.A.).

TRANSFER OF ORDER / Attorney General's consent / Where court unable to act.
742.5 (1) Where an offender who is bound by a conditional sentence order becomes a resident of a territorial division, other than the territorial division where the order was made, on the application of a supervisor, the court that made the order may, subject to subsection (1.1), transfer the order to a court in that other territorial division that would, having regard to the mode of trial of the offender, have had jurisdiction to make the order in that other territorial division if the offender had been tried and convicted there of the offence in respect of which the order was made, and the order may thereafter be dealt with and enforced by the court to which it is so transferred in all respects as if that court had made the order.

(1.1) The transfer may be granted only with

(*a*) the consent of the Attorney General of the province in which the conditional sentence order was made, if the two territorial divisions are not in the same province; or

(*b*) the consent of the Attorney General of Canada, if the proceedings that led to the issuance of the conditional sentence order were instituted by or on behalf of the Attorney General of Canada.

(2) Where a court that has made a conditional sentence order or to which a conditional sentence order has been transferred pursuant to subsection (1) is for any reason unable to act, the powers of that court in relation to the conditional sentence order may be exercised by any other court that has equivalent jurisdiction in the same province. 1995, c. 22, s. 6; 1999, c. 5, s. 40.

CROSS-REFERENCES
"Attorney General" and "territorial division" are defined in s. 2. "Court" is defined in s. 716. "Supervisor" is defined in s. 742.

SYNOPSIS

This section provides the procedure for transferring an order to a court in another jurisdiction where the offender becomes a resident of that other territorial jurisdiction. The transfer requires the consent of the supervisor and, if the transfer is to another province, the consent of the Attorney General of the province in which the conditional sentence was imposed or the Attorney General of Canada if the proceedings were instituted on behalf of the Attorney General of Canada.

Subsection (2) also provides for the case where the court that imposed the conditional sentence or the court to which the order was transferred is unable to act. In such a case the powers of the court in relation to the conditional sentence may be exercised by any other court of equivalent jurisdiction in the province.

PROCEDURE ON BREACH OF CONDITION / Interim release / Hearing / Place / Attorney General's consent / Adjournment / Report of supervisor / Admission of report on notice of intent / Requiring attendance of supervisor or witness / Powers of court / Warrant or arrest — suspension of running of conditional sentence / Conditions continue / Detention under s. 515(6) / Earned remission does not apply / Unreasonable delay in execution / Allegation dismissed or reasonable excuse / Powers of court / Considerations.

742.6 (1) For the purpose of proceedings under this section,

(*a*) the provisions of Parts XVI and XVIII with respect to compelling the appearance of an accused before a justice apply, with any modifications that the circumstances require, and any reference in those Parts to committing an offence shall be read as a reference to breaching a condition of a conditional sentence order;

(*b*) the powers of arrest for breach of a condition are those that apply to an indictable offence, with any modifications that the circumstances require, and subsection 495(2) does not apply;

(*c*) despite paragraph (*a*), if an allegation of breach of condition is made, the proceeding is commenced by

(i) the issuance of a warrant for the arrest of the offender for the alleged breach,

(ii) the arrest without warrant of the offender for the alleged breach, or

(iii) the compelling of the offender's appearance in accordance with paragraph (*d*);

(*d*) if the offender is already detained or before a court, the offender's appearance may be compelled under the provisions referred to in paragraph (*a*);

(*e*) if an offender is arrested for the alleged breach, the peace officer who makes the arrest, the officer in charge or a judge or justice may release the offender

and the offender's appearance may be compelled under the provisions referred to in paragraph (*a*); and

(*f*) any judge of a superior court of criminal jurisdiction or of a court of criminal jurisdiction or any justice of the peace may issue a warrant to arrest no matter which court, judge or justice sentenced the offender, and the provisions that apply to the issuance of telewarrants apply, with any modifications that the circumstances require, as if a breach of condition were an indictable offence.

(2) For the purpose of the application of section 515, the release from custody of an offender who is detained on the basis of an alleged breach of a condition of a conditional sentence order shall be governed by subsection 515(6).

(3) The hearing of an allegation of a breach of condition shall be commenced within thirty days, or as soon thereafter as is practicable, after

(*a*) the offender's arrest; or

(*b*) the compelling of the offender's appearance in accordance with paragraph (1)(*d*).

(3.1) The allegation may be heard by any court having jurisdiction to hear that allegation in the place where the breach is alleged to have been committed or the offender is found, arrested or in custody.

(3.2) If the place where the offender is found, arrested or in custody is outside the province in which the breach is alleged to have been committed, no proceedings in respect of that breach shall be instituted in that place without

(*a*) the consent of the Attorney General of the province in which the breach is alleged to have been committed; or

(*b*) the consent of the Attorney General of Canada, if the proceedings that led to the issuance of the conditional sentence order were instituted by or on behalf of the Attorney General of Canada.

(3.3) A judge may, at any time during a hearing of an allegation of breach of condition, adjourn the hearing for a reasonable period.

(4) An allegation of a breach of condition must be supported by a written report of the supervisor, which report must include, where appropriate, signed statements of witnesses.

(5) The report is admissible in evidence if the party intending to produce it has, before the hearing, given the offender reasonable notice and a copy of the report.

(6) and (7) [*Repealed*, 2008, c. 18, s. 41.]

(8) The offender may, with leave of the court, require the attendance, for cross-examination, of the supervisor or of any witness whose signed statement is included in the report.

(9) Where the court is satisfied, on a balance of probabilities, that the offender has without reasonable excuse, the proof of which lies on the offender, breached a condition of the conditional sentence order, the court may

(*a*) take no action;

(*b*) change the optional conditions;

(*c*) suspend the conditional sentence order and direct

(i) that the offender serve in custody a portion of the unexpired sentence, and

(ii) that the conditional sentence order resume on the offender's release from custody, either with or without changes to the optional conditions; or

(*d*) terminate the conditional sentence order and direct that the offender be committed to custody until the expiration of the sentence.

(10) The running of a conditional sentence order imposed on an offender is suspended during the period that ends with the determination of whether a breach of condition had occurred and begins with the earliest of

(*a*) the issuance of a warrant for the arrest of the offender for the alleged breach,
(*b*) the arrest without warrant of the offender for the alleged breach, and
(*c*) the compelling of the offender's appearance in accordance with paragraph (1)(*d*).

(11) If the offender is not detained in custody during any period referred to in subsection (10), the conditions of the order continue to apply, with any changes made to them under section 742.4, and any subsequent breach of those conditions may be dealt with in accordance with this section.

(12) A conditional sentence order referred to in subsection (10) starts running again on the making of an order to detain the offender in custody under subsection 515(6) and, unless section 742.7 applies, continues running while the offender is detained under the order.

(13) Section 6 of the *Prisons and Reformatories Act* does not apply to the period of detention in custody under subsection 515(6).

(14) Despite subsection (10), if there was unreasonable delay in the execution of a warrant, the court may, at any time, order that any period between the issuance and execution of the warrant that it considers appropriate in the interests of justice is deemed to be time served under the conditional sentence order unless the period has been so deemed under subsection (15).

(15) If the allegation is withdrawn or dismissed or the offender is found to have had a reasonable excuse for the breach, the sum of the following periods is deemed to be time served under the conditional sentence order:
(*a*) any period for which the running of the conditional sentence order was suspended; and
(*b*) if subsection (12) applies, a period equal to one half of the period that the conditional sentence order runs while the offender is detained under an order referred to in that subsection.

(16) If a court is satisfied, on a balance of probabilities, that the offender has without reasonable excuse, the proof of which lies on the offender, breached a condition of the conditional sentence order, the court may, in exceptional cases and in the interests of justice, order that some or all of the period of suspension referred to in subsection (10) is deemed to be time served under the conditional sentence order.

(17) In exercising its discretion under subsection (16), a court shall consider
(*a*) the circumstances and seriousness of the breach;
(*b*) whether not making the order would cause the offender undue hardship based on the offender's individual circumstances; and
(*c*) the period for which the offender was subject to conditions while the running of the conditional sentence order was suspended and whether the offender complied with those conditions during that period. 1995, c. 22, s. 6; 1999, c. 5, s. 41; 2004, c. 12, s. 15; 2008, c. 18, s. 41.

CROSS-REFERENCES

The reference to s. 515 is to the provisions respecting a show cause hearing for a person who is detained. Section 515(6) reverses the normal burden of proof and requires the accused to show cause why the the accused should be released.

"Attorney General" and "territorial division" are defined in s. 2. "Court" is defined in s. 716. "Supervisor" is defined in s. 742.

Section 729 allows for the use of an analyst's certificate at a hearing conducted under this section where it is alleged that the offender breached a condition of a conditional sentence that the offender not have in possession or use drugs.

Section 742.7 and 718.3(5) govern the serving of the conditional sentence where the offender is imprisoned for another offence while under conditional sentence. The definition of "sentence" in ss. 673 and 785 for the purpose of appeal in indictable and summary conviction proceedings includes a disposition made under subsec. (9). For other cross-references, see notes under s. 742.1.

Under s. 718.2(*a*)(vi), it is deemed an aggravating factor if an offender commits an offence while subject to a conditional sentence order.

SYNOPSIS

This section governs the procedure where it is alleged that the offender has breached the terms of a conditional sentence. The provisions in Part XVI [compelling appearance] and part XVIII [preliminary inquiry] apply with the necessary changes. Thus the warrant and release provisions of Part XVI apply. In particular, the provisions of s. 515(6) apply and thus the burden is on the offender to show cause why the offender should be released pending the hearing of the allegation. The hearing of an allegation of a breach may be held by any court having jurisdiction in the place where the breach is alleged to have been committed or in the place where the accused is found, is arrested or is in custody. However, where the place where the accused is found, is arrested or is in custody is outside the province in which the breach is alleged to have been committed, the Attorney General of the place where the breach allegedly occurred must consent to the institution of the proceedings. The allegation of the breach shall be commenced within 30 days of the offender's arrest or so soon thereafter as is practicable.

This section contemplates that the allegation of the breach may be made out by documentary evidence. The allegation must be supported by a written report of the supervisor including, where possible, signed witness statements. The report shall not be admitted in evidence unless the offender has been given reasonable notice of the intention to produce the report and a copy of the report. Notice may be proved by oral evidence or by way of affidavit or solemn declaration, although the court may require the person who made the affidavit or solemn declaration attend the hearing for examination and cross-examination. The offender may also, with leave of the court, require the attendance of the supervisor or persons who gave statements included in the report, for the purpose of cross-examination [subsec. (8)].

Subsection (9) sets out the options where the court is satisfied that the breach of condition was made out. The breach must be proved only on a balance of probabilities. The burden is then on the offender to show a reasonable excuse. Where the breach is made out the court may take no action, change the optional conditions, suspend the conditional sentence for a period of time and require the offender to serve a portion of the sentence and then resume the conditional sentence with or without changes to the optional conditions, or terminate the conditional sentence and require the offender to serve the balance of the sentence in custody.

Subsections (10) to (16) enact rules for the running of the conditional sentence order pending determination of the breach allegation.

ANNOTATIONS

General – Where an offender breaches a condition without reasonable excuse, there should be a presumption that the offender serve the remainder of the sentence in jail: *R. v. Proulx*, [2000] 1 S.C.R. 61, 140 C.C.C. (3d) 449.

The time period set out in subsec. (3)(*a*) refers to the arrest of the offender for having allegedly breached a condition of the conditional sentence order, rather than an arrest for any new offence which was allegedly committed: *R. v. Kabosos* (2008), 238 C.C.C. (3d) 428 (Ont. C.A.).

As a general rule, a breach of a conditional sentence should be heard in the trial court that imposed the sentence: *R. v. Tomic* (2000), 147 C.C.C. (3d) 567 (Alta. C.A.).

While there is a presumption of termination, not every unexpected breach need result in the termination of the conditional sentence. A disposition appropriate to each offender and the circumstances of the breach must be fashioned so that the purposes of sentencing can be achieved and the public protected from further criminal activity: *R. v. L. (T.E.)* (2005), 202 C.C.C. (3d) 431 (B.C.C.A.).

The 30-day time period for the hearing in subsec. (3)(*a*) is triggered upon the execution of the warrant of arrest for the charge of breach of condition: *R. v. Kabosos* (2008), 238 C.C.C. (3d) 428 (Ont. C.A.).

An offender facing an allegation of a breach of a conditional sentence order is not charged with an offence within the meaning of s. 11 of the *Canadian Charter of Rights and Freedoms* and thus the reversal of the burden of proof under subsec. (9) does not violate s. 11(*d*) of the Charter. Similarly, there is no violation of the double jeopardy protection in s. 11(*h*). Finally, the procedure set out in this section does not violate the principles of fundamental justice as guaranteed by s. 7 of the Charter: *R. v. Casey* (2000), 141 C.C.C. (3d) 506 (Ont. C.A.), leave to appeal to S.C.C. refused 149 C.C.C. (3d) vi.

The principles that govern Crown disclosure obligations at trial do not apply to a conditional sentence breach hearing. Once the supervisor's report and statements have been served, disclosure should be considered *prima facie* complete unless the offender requests more. Upon request, however, any further information in the Crown's control supporting the report or statements should be provided: *R. v. Sitaram* (2011), 277 C.C.C. (3d) 421 (Ont. C.J.).

Pursuant to subsec. (4), the contents of the supervisor's report and any witness statements are limited to what the author of the report or statement could testify to if called to give *viva voce* evidence. This need not be confined to firsthand knowledge. For example, the report may include a summary of evidence expected to be non-contentious or relevant information about the offender to assist the court in determining an appropriate sanction in the event of a finding that the conditional sentence order has been breached. While the hearing is to proceed in a more expedited fashion, the requirement of signed witness statements ensures a minimum reliability. Personal authentication of the material facts alleged to constitute the breach is required. Further, pursuant to subsec. (8), the offender bears the burden of showing that cross-examination may serve a useful purpose: *R. v. McIvor*, [2008] 1 S.C.R. 285, 229 C.C.C. (3d) 1.

Subsection (9), which requires proof of a breach only on the balance of probabilities, unless the accused proves a reasonable excuse, does not violate ss. 7 or 11(*d*) or (*h*) of the Charter: *R. v. Whitty* (1999), 135 C.C.C. (3d) 77 (Nfld. C.A.). Nor does it require the application of a more stringent standard than that required in civil cases: *R. v. Filippelli* (2002), 169 C.C.C. (3d) 217 (Ont. C.A.). See also *R. v. Carpentier* (2005), 203 C.C.C. (3d) 251 (Man. C.A.).

An intermittent sentence is not an available sanction for a breach of a conditional sentence: *R. v. Bailey* (2012), 289 C.C.C. (3d) 279 (Alta. C.A.).

Subsection (4) does not preclude the Crown from calling *viva voce* evidence: *R. v. Balaj* (2010), 252 C.C.C. (3d) 560 (B.C.S.C.). See also: *R. v. Laporte* (2011), 279 C.C.C. (3d) 500 (Man. C.A.).

Upon revocation of a conditional sentence order, the judge is bound by the length of the conditional sentence that has not been served. Accordingly, the trial judge must either partially suspend the conditional sentence by ordering that part of the sentence be served in custody followed by the resumption of the conditional sentence or terminate the conditional sentence completely and require the accused to serve the rest of the unexpired term in custody: *R. v. Love* (2001), 155 C.C.C. (3d) 196 (Que. C.A.).

A decision declining to revoke a conditional sentence is not a final decision capable of giving rise to the operation of *issue estoppel* in a subsequent criminal trial: *R. v. Thompson* (2014), 305 C.C.C. (3d) 218 (Ont. C.A.), leave to appeal to S.C.C. refused 2014 CarswellOnt 13165.

An intermittent sentence is not available where the offender breaches a term of the conditional sentence order: *R. v. Pierre* (2004), 187 C.C.C. (3d) 560 (B.C.S.C.). See also *R. v. Langmaier* (2009), 245 C.C.C. (3d) 252 (Sask. C.A.).

An accused is not bound by the conditions of a conditional sentence order while in custody: *R. v. Bollig* (1999), 136 C.C.C. (3d) 345 (Ont. C.J.).

There is a presumption that a termination order pursuant to subsec. (9) is to be imposed where there has been a breach of the conditional sentence order: *R. v. White* (2008), 241 C.C.C. (3d) 175 (Nfld. & Lab. Prov. Ct.).

The conditional sentence of imprisonment stops running between the issuance of the warrant, arrest without warrant or service of process, and the time when the adjudication of the breach is complete. The sentence starts running again immediately upon the accused being detained by a justice pending a hearing under s. 515(6) or after a hearing under that section in which the accused is detained: *R. v. Atkinson* (2003), 174 C.C.C. (3d) 144 (Ont. C.A.). See also *R. v. Vromans*, [2007] A.J. No. 85 (C.A.).

Orders made under subsecs. (14) and (16) may be appealed to the Court of Appeal pursuant to s. 673 of the *Criminal Code*: *R. v. Buggins* (2004), 182 C.C.C. (3d) 418 (Alta. C.A.).

IF PERSON IMPRISONED FOR NEW OFFENCE / Breach of condition / Multiple sentences / Conditional sentence order resumes.

742.7 (1) If an offender who is subject to a conditional sentence order is imprisoned as a result of a sentence imposed for another offence, whenever committed, the running of the conditional sentence order is suspended during the period of imprisonment for that other offence.

(2) If an order is made under paragraph 742.6(9)(*c*) or (*d*) to commit an offender to custody, the custodial period ordered shall, unless the court considers that it would not be in the interests of justice, be served consecutively to any other period of imprisonment that the offender is serving when that order is made.

(3) If an offender is serving both a custodial period referred to in subsection (2) and any other period of imprisonment, the periods shall, for the purpose of section 743.1 and section 139 of the *Corrections and Conditional Release Act*, be deemed to constitute one sentence of imprisonment.

(4) The running of any period of the conditional sentence order that is to be served in the community resumes upon the release of the offender from prison on parole, on statutory release, on earned remission, or at the expiration of the sentence. 1995, c. 22, s. 6; 1999, c. 5, s. 42; 2004, c. 12, s. 16.

CROSS-REFERENCES

For cross-references see notes under s. 742.1

SYNOPSIS

This section, together with s. 742.6, deals with the offender who is imprisoned while serving a conditional sentence.

Where the offender is imprisoned for another offence, whenever committed, the running of the conditional sentence order is suspended during the sentence of imprisonment for the other offence, unless the court otherwise orders under s. 742.4(3) [change in optional conditions] or under s. 742.6(9) [change in optional conditions, suspension or termination of conditional sentence for breach of conditions].

Imprisonment

IMPRISONMENT WHEN NO OTHER PROVISION.

743. Every one who is convicted of an indictable offence for which no punishment is specially provided is liable to imprisonment for a term not exceeding five years. 1995, c. 22, s. 6.

CROSS-REFERENCES

Where an offence is punishable by five years' imprisonment or more, the accused is entitled to trial by jury under the guarantee of s. 11(*f*) of the Charter.

See ss. 126 and 127 for general punishment provisions for disobedience of a statute or lawful court order.

Those sections do not apply to orders respecting money payments. Maximum punishment prescribed in ss. 126 and 127 is two years, subject to specific contrary provisions.

IMPRISONMENT FOR LIFE OR MORE THAN TWO YEARS / Subsequent term less than two years / Imprisonment for term less than two years / Long-term supervision / Sentence to penitentiary of person serving sentence elsewhere / Transfer to penitentiary / Newfoundland.

743.1 (1) Except where otherwise provided, a person who is sentenced to imprisonment for

- **(*a*) life,**
- **(*b*) a term of two years or more, or**
- **(*c*) two or more terms of less than two years each that are to be served one after the other and that, in the aggregate, amount to two years or more,**

shall be sentenced to imprisonment in a penitentiary.

(2) Where a person who is sentenced to imprisonment in a penitentiary is, before the expiration of that sentence, sentenced to imprisonment for a term of less than two years, the person shall serve that term in a penitentiary, but if the previous sentence of imprisonment in a penitentiary is set aside, that person shall serve that term in accordance with subsection (3).

(3) A person who is sentenced to imprisonment and who is not required to be sentenced as provided in subsection (1) or (2) shall, unless a special prison is prescribed by law, be sentenced to imprisonment in a prison or other place of confinement, other than a penitentiary, within the province in which the person is convicted, in which the sentence of imprisonment may be lawfully executed.

(3.1) Despite subsection (3), an offender who is subject to long-term supervision under Part XXIV and is sentenced for another offence during the period of the supervision shall be sentenced to imprisonment in a penitentiary.

(4) Where a person is sentenced to imprisonment in a penitentiary while the person is lawfully imprisoned in a place other than a penitentiary, that person shall, except where otherwise provided, be sent immediately to the penitentiary, and shall serve in the penitentiary the unexpired portion of the term of imprisonment that that person was serving when sentenced to the penitentiary as well as the term of imprisonment for which that person was sentenced to the penitentiary.

(5) Where, at any time, a person who is imprisoned in a prison or place of confinement other than a penitentiary is subject to two or more terms of imprisonment, each of which is for less than two years, that are to be served one after the other, and the aggregate of the unexpired portions of those terms at that time amounts to two years or more, the person shall be transferred to a penitentiary to serve those terms, but if any one or more of such terms is set aside or reduced and the unexpired portions of the remaining term or terms on the day on which that person was transferred under this section amounted to less than two years, that person shall serve that term or terms in accordance with subsection (3).

(6) For the purposes of subsection (3), "penitentiary" does not, until a day to be fixed by order of the Governor in Council, include the facility mentioned in subsection 15(2) of the *Corrections and Conditional Release Act*. 1995, c. 22, s. 6; 1997, c. 17, s. 1; 2008, c. 6, s. 39.

CROSS-REFERENCES

See s. 2 for definition of "prison". Section 144 makes prison-break an indictable offence. See ss. 145(1), 146 and 147 for escape offences. Service of sentences for escape are governed by s. 149.

The Solicitor General of Canada may contract with provincial authorities for the confinement of persons sentenced to less than two years in federal institutions, under the *Corrections and Conditional Release Act*, S.C. 1992, c. 20, s. 16(1)(*b*). Inmates in a federal institution may be transferred to a provincial institution upon agreement between the Solicitor General and the provincial government under s. 16(1)(*a*) of the Act.

See the *Corrections and Conditional Release Act*, s. 15 dealing with the provincial penitentiary at St. John's, Newfoundland referred to in subsec. (6).

A convicted person is delivered to the keeper of a prison under s. 744, following sentencing and the issuance and execution of a warrant of committal.

Correctional statutes and regulations, made under s. 743.3, govern the actual institution and manner of service of a sentence.

Under s. 743.21, the sentencing judge may make an order prohibiting the offender from communicating with any victim, witness or other person identified in the order during the custodial period of the sentence.

SYNOPSIS

This section sets out the rules used to determine whether a prisoner will be incarcerated in a federal or provincial institution.

Single or aggregate sentences of two years or more, including life sentences, will normally be served in the federal penitentiary system (subsecs. (1), (2), (5)). (**Note**: A sentence of two years less one day is sometimes imposed for the purpose of keeping an inmate in the provincial system, *i.e.*, "provincial time" (subsec. (3)).

Where a prisoner in a prison other than a penitentiary is sentenced to a term in a penitentiary that prisoner shall be transferred forthwith to a penitentiary, where he or she shall serve both the unexpired portion of the previous sentence and the present sentence (subsec. (4)). Also a long-term offender who is sentenced for another offence while under supervision shall be sentenced to a penitentiary (subsec. (3.1)).

ANNOTATIONS

Subsection (1) – By virtue of this subsection a person given a sentence of two years or more must be sentenced to a penitentiary and the court has no power to direct that the sentence be served at a provincial mental health centre such as the centre at Penetanguishene in Ontario. Where the trial judge wishes an accused to receive treatment at such a centre he should impose the sentence pursuant to this subsection and recommend in the certificate of sentence that the prisoner receive treatment at the centre: *R. v. Deans* (1977), 37 C.C.C. (2d) 221 (Ont. C.A.). Folld: *Re R. and McCullough* (1983), 3 C.C.C. (3d) 423 (Alta. C.A.).

Except where he is considering imposing the minimum penitentiary sentence, the trial judge is not required to impose a reformatory sentence because the accused might be the object of reprisals in the penitentiary: *R. v. Demers* (1981), 63 C.C.C. (2d) 351 (Que. C.A.).

Subsection (2) – An accused while serving the remanet of a sentence in a penitentiary who is sentenced to a term of imprisonment of less than two years is properly imprisoned in a penitentiary to serve the latter sentence as well: *R. v. Olson*, [1980] 1 S.C.R. 808, 50 C.C.C. (2d) 275.

This subsection applies and requires the additional term of imprisonment to be served in the penitentiary even where it is imposed for violations of provincial statutes: *Durand v. Forget* (1980), 24 C.R. (3d) 119 (Que. S.C.).

Moreover, the penitentiary authorities are required to accept the warrants of committal for provincial offences which a peace officer attempts to execute. The calculation of the sentence to be served for those offences however depends on the applicable provincial legislation and may result in a consecutive sentence for those offences: *Dempsey v. Canada (Attorney General)* (1986), 25 C.C.C. (3d) 193 (F.C.A.).

The sentence of an accused on mandatory supervision has not expired and if he is sentenced to imprisonment while on mandatory supervision then this sentence must be served in the penitentiary even if the new sentence is less than two years and the accused's mandatory supervision remains unrevoked: *R. v. Dinardo* (1982), 67 C.C.C. (2d) 505 (Ont. C.A.).

In determining whether the aggregate of the sentences is two years or more, the amount of earned remission standing to the inmate's credit must be taken into account: *R. v. Shiminousky* (1981), 64 C.C.C. (2d) 187 (B.C.S.C.).

Subsection (3) – A trial judge may recommend or refuse to recommend the accused's eligibility for release on a temporary absence programme established under provincial legislation but he cannot make an order denying the accused such release. That is a decision to be made by an official designated under applicable provincial legislation: *R. v. Laycock* (1989), 51 C.C.C. (3d) 65 (Ont. C.A.).

REPORT BY COURT TO CORRECTIONAL SERVICE.

743.2 A court that sentences or commits a person to penitentiary shall forward to the Correctional Service of Canada its reasons and recommendation relating to the sentence or committal, any relevant reports that were submitted to the court, and any other information relevant to administering the sentence or committal. 1995, c. 22, s. 6.

CROSS-REFERENCES

Section 726.2 requires the court to give reasons for the sentence imposed and to enter the terms of the sentence and the reasons into the record of the proceedings.

NON-COMMUNICATION ORDER / Failure to comply with order.

743.21 (1) The sentencing judge may issue an order prohibiting the offender from communicating, directly or indirectly, with any victim, witness or other person identified in the order during the custodial period of the sentence, except in accordance with any conditions specified in the order that the sentencing judge considers necessary.

(2) Every person who fails, without lawful excuse, to comply with the order

(*a*) is guilty of an indictable offence and liable to imprisonment for a term not exceeding two years; or

(*b*) is guilty of an offence punishable on summary conviction and liable to imprisonment for a term not exceeding eighteen months. 2008, c. 18, s. 42; 2018, c. 29, s. 67.

SYNOPSIS

This section gives the sentencing court the power to make an order prohibiting the offender from communicating with any victim, witness or other person identified in the order during the custodial period of the sentence, except in accordance with conditions specified in the order. Failure to comply with the order is a hybrid offence.

SENTENCE SERVED ACCORDING TO REGULATIONS.

743.3 A sentence of imprisonment shall be served in accordance with the enactments and rules that govern the institution to which the prisoner is sentenced. 1995, c. 22, s. 6.

CROSS-REFERENCES

A sentence is served in either a federal penitentiary or a provincial correctional institution depending on the determination in s. 743.1.

Also see references cited under s. 743.1.

SYNOPSIS

The predecessor to this section [former s. 732] explicitly eliminates judicial impositions of hard labour in sentences, and provided that, as here, terms are to be served in accordance with the regulations of the institution with respect to employment of prisoners. However, a sentence which does refer to hard labour shall not be invalid, but shall be amended.

743.4 [*Repealed*, 2002, c. 1, s. 184.]

TRANSFER OF JURISDICTION WHEN PERSON ALREADY SENTENCED UNDER *YOUTH CRIMINAL JUSTICE ACT* / Transfer of jurisdiction when youth sentence imposed under *Youth Criminal Justice Act* / Sentences deemed to constitute one sentence — section 743.1.

743.5 (1) If a young person or an adult is or has been sentenced to a term of imprisonment for an offence while subject to a disposition made under paragraph 20(1)(*k*) or (*k*.1) of the *Young Offenders Act*, chapter Y-1 of the Revised Statutes of Canada, 1985, or a youth sentence imposed under paragraph 42(2)(*n*), (*o*), (*q*) or (*r*) of the *Youth Criminal Justice Act*, the remaining portion of the disposition or youth sentence shall be dealt with, for all purposes under this Act or any other Act of Parliament, as if it had been a sentence imposed under this Act.

(2) If a disposition is made under paragraph 20(1)(*k*) or (*k*.1) of the *Young Offenders Act*, chapter Y-1 of the Revised Statutes of Canada, 1985, with respect to a person or a youth sentence is imposed on a person under paragraph 42(2)(*n*), (*o*), (*q*) or (*r*) of the *Youth Criminal Justice Act* while the young person or adult is under sentence of imprisonment imposed under an Act of Parliament other than the *Youth Criminal Justice Act*, the disposition or youth sentence shall be dealt with, for all purposes under this Act or any other Act of Parliament, as if it had been a sentence imposed under this Act.

(3) For greater certainty, the following are deemed to constitute one sentence of imprisonment for the purposes of section 139 of the *Corrections and Conditional Release Act*:

(*a*) for the purposes of subsection (1), the remainder of the youth sentence or disposition and the subsequent term of imprisonment; and

(*b*) for the purposes of subsection (2), the term of imprisonment and the subsequent youth sentence or disposition. 1995, c. 22, s. 6; 2002, c. 1, s. 184; 2008, c. 18, s. 43.

CROSS-REFERENCES

Sections 20(1)(*k*) and (*k*.1) of the former *Young Offenders Act* refer to custodial dispositions. Similarly, ss. 42(2)(*n*), (*o*), (*q*) and (*r*) under the *Youth Criminal Justice Act* refer to custody and supervision orders.

SYNOPSIS

This section deals with situations where a person subject to a custodial sentence imposed under the former *Young Offenders Act* or the *Youth Criminal Justice Act* is sentenced to a term of imprisonment under the *Criminal Code* or other federal Act and the reverse, where the person while serving a term of imprisonment under the *Criminal Code* or other federal legislation is given a custodial sentence under the former *Young Offenders Act* or the *Youth Criminal Justice Act*. The solution adopted in this section to deal with the interaction between the two systems is that the offender is dealt with as if the sentence had been imposed under the *Criminal Code*. The disposition and sentences then merge for the purposes of s. 139 of the *Corrections and Conditional Release Act*, subsec. (1) of which provides as follows:

(1) Where a person who is subject to a sentence that has not expired receives an additional sentence, the person is, for the purposes of the *Criminal Code*, the *Prisons and Reformatories Act* and this Act, deemed to have been sentenced to one sentence commencing at the beginning of the first of those sentences to be served and ending on the expiration of the last of them to be served.

Eligibility for Parole

POWER OF COURT TO DELAY PAROLE / Principles that are to guide the court.

743.6 (1) Notwithstanding subsection 120(1) of the *Corrections and Conditional Release Act*, where an offender receives, on or after November 1, 1992, a sentence of imprisonment of two years or more, including a sentence of imprisonment for life imposed otherwise than as a minimum punishment, on conviction for an offence set out in Schedules I and II to that Act that was prosecuted by way of indictment, the court may, if satisfied, having regard to the circumstances of the commission of the offence and the character and circumstances of the offender, that the expression of society's denunciation of the offence or the objective of specific or general deterrence so requires, order that the portion of the sentence that must be served before the offender may be released on full parole is one half of the sentence or ten years, whichever is less.

(1.1) Notwithstanding section 120 of the *Corrections and Conditional Release Act*, where an offender receives a sentence of imprisonment of two years or more, including a sentence of imprisonment for life imposed otherwise than as a minimum punishment, on conviction for a criminal organization offence other than an offence under section 467.11, 467.111, 467.12 or 467.13, the court may order that the portion of the sentence that must be served before the offender may be released on full parole is one half of the sentence or ten years, whichever is less.

(1.2) Notwithstanding section 120 of the *Corrections and Conditional Release Act*, where an offender receives a sentence of imprisonment of two years or more, including a sentence of imprisonment for life, on conviction for a terrorism offence or an offence under ss. 467.11, 467.111, 467.12 or 467.13, the court shall order that the portion of the sentence that must be served before the offender may be released on full parole is one half of the sentence or ten years, whichever is less, unless the court is satisfied, having regard to the circumstances of the commission of the offence and the character and circumstances of the offender, that the expression of society's denunciation of the offence and the objectives of specific and general deterrence would be adequately served by a period of parole ineligibility determined in accordance with the *Corrections and Conditional Release Act*.

(2) For greater certainty, the paramount principles which are to guide the court under this section are denunciation and specific or general deterrence, with rehabilitation of the offender, in all cases, being subordinate to those paramount principles. 1995, c. 22, s. 6; 1995, c. 42, s. 86(*b*); 1997, c. 23, s. 18; 2001, c. 32, s. 45; 2001, c. 41, ss. 21, 133(18); 2014, c. 17, ss. 15, 16.

CROSS-REFERENCES

The terms "criminal organization offence" and "terrorism offence" are defined in s. 2. Section 120 of the *Corrections and Conditional Release Act* sets out the normal periods of parole eligibility which, in most circumstances, will be one-third of the sentence or seven years, whichever is the lesser. Section 120 of the Act set out the manner for calculating parole ineligibility where an offender while serving sentence for one offence, for which no order has been made under this section, is sentenced for a further offence in which an order is made under this section.

Schedules I and II to the *Corrections and Conditional Release Act* are as follows:

Schedule I (Subsections 107(1), 129(1) and (2), 130(3) and (4), 133(4.1) and 156(3))

1. An offence under any of the following provisions of the Criminal Code, that was prosecuted by way of indictment:

(*a*) sections 46 and 47 (high treason);
(*a*.01) section 75 (piratical acts);
(*a*.1) section 76 (hijacking);
(*a*.2) section 77 (endangering safety of aircraft or airport);
(*a*.3) section 78.1 (seizing control of ship or fixed platform);
(*a*.4) paragraph 81(1)(a), (b) or (d) (use of explosives);
(*a*.5) paragraph 81(2)(a) (causing injury with intent);
(*a*.6) section 83.18 (participation in activity of terrorist group);
(*a*.7) section 83.19 (facilitating terrorist activity);
(*a*.8) section 83.2 (commission of offence for terrorist group);
(*a*.9) section 83.21 (instructing to carry out activity for terrorist group);
(*a*.91) section 83.22 (instructing to carry out terrorist activity);
(*a*.92) subsection 83.221(1) (advocating or promoting commission of terrorism offences);
(*b*) subsection 85(1) (using firearm in commission of offence);
(*b*.1) subsection 85(2) (using imitation firearm in commission of offence);
(*c*) section 87 (pointing a firearm);
(*c*.1) section 98 (breaking and entering to steal firearm);
(*c*.2) section 98.1 (robbery to steal firearm);
(*d*) section 144 (prison breach);
(*e*) section 151 (sexual interference);
(*f*) section 152 (invitation to sexual touching);
(*g*) section 153 (sexual exploitation);
(*g*.1) section 153.1 (sexual exploitation of person with disability);
(*h*) section 155 (incest);
(*i*) section 159 (anal intercourse);
(*j*) section 160 (bestiality, compelling, in presence of or by child);
(*j*.1) section 163.1 (child pornography);
(*k*) section 170 (parent or guardian procuring sexual activity by child);
(*l*) section 171 (householder permitting sexual activity by or in presence of child);
(*m*) section 172 (corrupting children);
(*m*.1) section 172.1 (luring a child);
(*n*) [Repealed 2014, c. 25, s. 42(1).]
(*n*.1) [Repealed 2014, c. 25, s. 42(1).]
(*o*) [Repealed 2014, c. 25, s. 42(1).]
(*o*.1) section 220 (causing death by criminal negligence);
(*o*.2) section 221 (causing bodily harm by criminal negligence);
(*p*) section 236 (manslaughter);
(*q*) section 239 (attempt to commit murder);
(*r*) section 244 (discharging firearm with intent);
(*r*.1) section 244.1 (causing bodily harm with intentair gun or pistol);
(*r*.2) section 244.2 (discharging firearm — recklessness);
(*r*.3) section 245 (administering noxious thing);
(*s*) section 246 (overcoming resistance to commission of offence);
(*s*.01) section 247 (traps likely to cause bodily harm);
(*s*.02) section 248 (interfering with transportation facilities);
(*s*.*1*) subsections 249(3) and (4) (dangerous operation causing bodily harm and dangerous operation causing death);
(*s*.11) subsections 249.1(3) and (4) (flight causing bodily harm or death);
(*s*.12) section 249.2 (causing death by criminal negligence (street racing));
(*s*.13) section 249.3 (causing bodily harm by criminal negligence (street racing));

(*s*.14) section 249.4 (dangerous operation of motor vehicle while street racing);
(*s*.2) subsections 255(2) and (3) (impaired driving causing bodily harm and impaired driving causing death);
(*s*.3) section 264 (criminal harassment);
(*s*.4) section 264.1 (uttering threats);
(*t*) section 266 (assault);
(*u*) section 267 (assault with a weapon or causing bodily harm);
(*v*) section 268 (aggravated assault);
(*w*) section 269 (unlawfully causing bodily harm);
(*w*.1) section 269.1 (torture);
(*x*) section 270 (assaulting a peace officer);
(*x*.1) section 270.01 (assaulting peace officer with weapon or causing bodily harm);
(*x*.2) section 270.02 (aggravated assault of peace officer);
(*y*) section 271 (sexual assault);
(*z*) section 272 (sexual assault with a weapon, threats to a third party or causing bodily harm);
(*z*.1) section 273 (aggravated sexual assault);
(*z*.11) section 273.3 (removal of child from Canada);
(*z*.2) section 279 (kidnapping and forcible confinement);
(*z*.201) section 279.011 (trafficking — person under 18 years);
(*z*.202) subsection 279.02(2) (material benefit — trafficking of person under 18 years);
(*z*.203) subsection 279.03(2) (withholding or destroying documents — trafficking of person under 18 years);
(*z*.21) section 279.1 (hostage taking);
(*z*.22) subsection 286.1(2) (obtaining sexual services for consideration from person under 18 years);
(*z*.23) subsection 286.2(2) (material benefit from sexual services provided by person under 18 years);
(*z*.24) subsection 286.3(2) (procuring — person under 18 years);
(*z*.3) sections 343 and 344 (robbery);
(*z*.301) section 346 (extortion);
(*z*.31) subsection 430(2) (mischief that causes actual danger to life);
(*z*.32) section 431 (attack on premises, residence or transport of internationally protected person);
(*z*.33) section 431.1 (attack on premises, accommodation or transport of United Nations or associated personnel);
(*z*.34) subsection 431.2(2) (explosive or other lethal device);
(*z*.4) section 433 (arson — disregard for human life);
(*z*.5) section 434.1 (arson — own property);
(*z*.6) section 436 (arson by negligence); and
(*z*.7) paragraph 465(1)(a) (conspiracy to commit murder).

2. An offence under any of the following provisions of the *Criminal Code*, as they read immediately before July 1, 1990, that was prosecuted by way of indictment:
(*a*) section 433 (arson);
(*b*) section 434 (setting fire to other substance); and
(*c*) section 436 (setting fire by negligence).

3. An offence under any of the following provisions of the *Criminal Code*, chapter C-34 of the Revised Statutes of Canada, 1970, as they read immediately before January 4, 1983, that was prosecuted by way of indictment:
(*a*) section 144 (rape);
(*b*) section 145 (attempt to commit rape);
(*c*) section 149 (indecent assault on female);
(*d*) section 156 (indecent assault on male);
(*e*) section 245 (common assault); and
(*f*) section 246 (assault with intent).

4. An offence under any of the following provisions of the *Criminal Code*, chapter C-34 of the Revised Statutes of Canada, 1970, as they read immediately before January 1, 1988, that was prosecuted by way of indictment:
(*a*) section 146 (sexual intercourse with a female under 14);
(*b*) section 151 (seduction of a female between 16 and 18);
(*c*) section 153 (sexual intercourse with step-daughter);
(*d*) section 155 (buggery or bestiality);
(*e*) section 157 (gross indecency);
(*f*) section 166 (parent or guardian procuring defilement); and
(*g*) section 167 (householder permitting defilement).
5. The offence of breaking and entering a place and committing an indictable offence therein, as provided for by paragraph 348(1)(*b*) of the *Criminal Code*, where the indictable offence is an offence set out in sections 1 to 4 of this Schedule and its commission
(*a*) is specified in the warrant of committal;
(*b*) is specified in the Summons, Information or Indictment on which the conviction has been registered;
(*c*) is found in the reasons for judgment of the trial judge; or
(*d*) is found in a statement of facts admitted into evidence pursuant to section 655 of the *Criminal Code*.
5.1 If prosecuted by way of indictment, the offence of pointing a firearm, as provided for by subsection 86(1) of the *Criminal Code*, as it read immediately before December 1, 1998.
5.2 An offence under any of the following provisions of the *Criminal Code*, as they read from time to time before the day on which this section comes into force, that was prosecuted by way of indictment:
(*a*) subsection 212(2) (living on the avails of prostitution of person under 18 years);
(*b*) subsection 212(2.1) (aggravated offence in relation to living on the avails of prostitution of person under 18 years); and
(*c*) subsection 212(4) (prostitution of person under 18 years).
6. An offence under any of the following provisions of the *Crimes Against Humanity and War Crimes Act*:
(*a*) section 4 (genocide, etc., committed in Canada);
(*b*) section 5 (breach of responsibility committed in Canada by military commanders or other superiors);
(*c*) section 6 (genocide, etc., committed outside Canada); and
(*d*) section 7 (breach of responsibility committed outside Canada by military commanders or other superiors). 1992, c. 20, Sch. 1; 1995, c. 39, s. 165; 1995, c. 42, ss. 65-67; 2000, c. 24, s. 41; 2001, c. 41, ss. 91-93; 2008, c. 6, s. 57; 2011, c. 11, s. 8; 2012, c. 1, ss. 103, 104; 2014, c. 25, s. 42; 2015, c. 20, s. 30.

Schedule II (Subsections 107(1), 129(1), (2) and (9), 130(3) and (4) and 156(3))

1. An offence under any of the following provisions of the *Narcotic Control Act*, as it read immediately before the day on which section 64 of the *Controlled Drugs and Substances Act* came into force, that was prosecuted by way of indictment:
(*a*) section 4 (trafficking);
(*b*) section 5 (importing and exporting);
(*c*) section 6 (cultivation);
(*d*) section 19.1 (possession of property obtained by certain offences); and
(*e*) section 19.2 (laundering proceeds of certain offences).
2. An offence under any of the following provisions of the *Food and Drugs Act*, as it read immediately before the day on which section 64 of the *Controlled Drugs and Substances Act* came into force, that was prosecuted by way of indictment:
(*a*) section 39 (trafficking in controlled drugs);
(*b*) section 44.2 (possession of property obtained by trafficking in controlled drugs);
(*c*) section 44.3 (laundering proceeds of trafficking in controlled drugs);

(*d*) section 48 (trafficking in restricted drugs);
(*e*) section 50.2 (possession of property obtained by trafficking in restricted drugs); and
(*f*) section 50.3 (laundering proceeds of trafficking in restricted drugs).

3. An offence under any of the following provisions of the *Controlled Drugs and Substances Act* that was prosecuted by way of indictment:
(*a*) section 5 (trafficking);
(*b*) section 6 (importing and exporting);
(*c*) section 7 (production);
(*d*) [Repealed 2001, c. 32, s. 57.]
(*e*) [Repealed 2001, c. 32, s. 57.]

4. The offence of conspiring, as provided by paragraph 465(1)(c) of the *Criminal Code*, to commit any of the offences referred to in items 1 to 3 of this Schedule. 1995, c. 42, s. 68; 1996, c. 19, s. 64; 2001, c. 32, s. 57; 2011, c. 11, s. 9.

SYNOPSIS

This section gives the court the power to set the period of parole ineligibility for certain specified offences. Those offences, generally speaking, are the various sexual offences, crimes of violence and various drug offences. The period of parole ineligibility can only be increased to one-half of the sentence imposed, or 10 years whichever is less.

An order may also be made under this section with respect to an accused convicted of a criminal organization offence and who receives a sentence of two years or more, subsec. (1.1). The order is mandatory under subsec. (1.2) for the offences under ss. 467.11 to 467.13 and terrorism offences unless the court is satisfied that denunciation and deterrence do not require it.

ANNOTATIONS

In view of s. 11(*i*) of the Charter, this section does not apply to offences committed prior to the effective date of this section [November 1, 1992]: *R. v. Boone* (1993), 88 Man. R. (2d) 110 (C.A.); *R. v. C. (T.J.)* (1993), 86 C.C.C. (3d) 181 (Man. C.A.); *R. v. Lambert* (1994), 93 C.C.C. (3d) 88 (Nfld. C.A.), leave to appeal to S.C.C. refused 94 C.C.C. (3d) vii; *R. v. Ferris* (1994), 93 C.C.C. (3d) 497 (N.B.C.A.); *R. v. Richard* (1994), 94 C.C.C. (3d) 285 (N.S.C.A.); *R. v. Mesgun* (1997), 121 C.C.C. (3d) 439 (Ont. C.A.).

This section does not apply to the offence of breaking and entering and committing an indictable offence pursuant to s. 348(1)(*b*) even if the indictable offence committed, which in this case was aggravated assault, is a listed offence as s. 348(1)(*b*) is not a listed offence: *R. v. Nichol* (1995), 102 C.C.C. (3d) 441 (Ont. C.A.).

The word "trafficking" following the phrase "section 4" in s. 1(*a*) of Schedule II to the *Corrections and Conditional Release Act* is inserted for ease of reference only and Parliament clearly intended that both the trafficking offence and possession for the purpose of trafficking contrary to [former] s. 4 of the *Narcotic Control Act* be subject to the same penalty, including the possibility of an order under this section: *R. v. Dankyi* (1993), 86 C.C.C. (3d) 368 (Que. C.A.).

The scope of permissible sentences for an offence such as possession of narcotics for the purpose of trafficking is itself wide enough to accommodate the best and the worst cases and thus an order under this section can only be justified as an exceptional measure reserved for particular circumstances requiring an additional form of denunciation, deterrence or incapacitation. The trial judge must clearly enunciate the specific reasons for increasing the ordinary period of ineligibility for parole: *R. v. Dankyi, supra*.

The phrase "the expression of society's denunciation of the offence" is not so vague as to offend principles of fundamental justice: *R. v. Warren* (1994), 95 C.C.C. (3d) 86 (Sask. C.A.).

Subsection (1.2) does not apply at all to sentences of less than 24 months. A judge may not add sentences imposed on different counts to conclude that the two-year threshold for the application of that provision has been reached. This provision applies only in respect of individual counts, taken separately, and only in respect of a sentence imposed for one of the offences referred to in the subsection. The sentence does not include a consideration of pre-trial custody but only the actual term of imprisonment imposed by the court after taking into account any time spent in pre-trial custody: *R. v. Mathieu* (2008), 231 C.C.C. (3d) 1 (S.C.C.).

In *R. v. Zinck*, [2003] 1 S.C.R. 41, 171 C.C.C. (3d) 1, the Supreme Court of Canada considered the case law as to the circumstances in which delayed parole should be invoked. Delayed parole is a decision that remains out of the ordinary and must be used in a manner that is fair to the offender. The sentencing judge must engage in a double weighing exercise. First, they must evaluate the facts of the case in light of the factors set out in s. 718 of the Code in order to impose the appropriate sentence. The issue of parole eligibility is not considered at this stage. The sentencing judge must then review the same facts primarily from the perspective of the requirements of deterrence and denunciation which are given priority at this stage. The prosecution has the burden of demonstrating that the additional punishment of increased parole ineligibility is required. The procedure is not a distinct two-stage process that requires a special and separate hearing. Delayed parole should not be exercised in a mechanical or automatic way, nor should it be invoked in connection with every jail term imposed for an offence covered by this provision.

The issue of increased parole ineligibility should be raised in a fair and timely manner so as to allow the offender to respond effectively. While there is no mandatory requirement that written notice be provided, where possible, the Crown may give notice in writing or verbally before the hearing. If the issue is raised at the sentencing hearing itself by the judge, the offender must be allowed to make submissions and introduce additional evidence in response to the request for delayed parole. Courts should be generous if adjournments are requested for this purpose. Written reasons must be given at the end of the process. The reasons must state with sufficient clarity the reasons for the delayed parole order. *R. v. Zinck, supra.*

Where all of the offences qualify for an order deferring full parole until half of the sentence has been served, it is permissible to order that parole eligibility be deferred until one-half of the global sentence has been served: *R. v. Smith* (2008), 232 C.C.C. (3d) 176 (Sask. C.A.).

While denunciation and deterrence have been considered in arriving at the appropriate sentence, they must also be considered in respect of the period of parole ineligibility. This provision allows the court to consider the length of sentence as well as the time actually served in custody: *R. v. Smith, supra.*

Delivery of Offender to Keeper of Prison

EXECUTION OF WARRANT OF COMMITTAL.

744. A peace officer or other person to whom a warrant of committal authorized by this or any other Act of Parliament is directed shall arrest the person named or described therein, if it is necessary to do so in order to take that person into custody, convey that person to the prison mentioned in the warrant and deliver that person, together with the warrant, to the keeper of the prison who shall thereupon give to the peace officer or other person who delivers the prisoner a receipt in Form 43 setting out the state and condition of the prisoner when delivered into custody. 1995, c. 22, s. 6.

CROSS-REFERENCES

Depending on the circumstances, warrants for committal may be in Form 8 or Forms 19 to 27.

See ss. 25 to 31 for protection of law enforcement and administration personnel.

SYNOPSIS

This section gives a peace officer who has received a warrant of committal the power to arrest the person named in the warrant, if necessary, and the power to convey that person to the prison named in the warrant. The keeper of the prison shall receive the prisoner, along with the warrant, and provide the peace officer with a receipt which sets out the state and condition of the prisoner on delivery.

Imprisonment for Life

SENTENCE OF LIFE IMPRISONMENT.

745. Subject to section 745.1, the sentence to be pronounced against a person who is to be sentenced to imprisonment for life shall be

(*a*) in respect of a person who has been convicted of high treason or first degree murder, that the person be sentenced to imprisonment for life without eligibility for parole until the person has served twenty-five years of the sentence;

(*b*) in respect of a person who has been convicted of second degree murder where that person has previously been convicted of culpable homicide that is murder, however described in this Act, that that person be sentenced to imprisonment for life without eligibility for parole until the person has served twenty-five years of the sentence;

(*b*.1) in respect of a person who has been convicted of second degree murder where that person has previously been convicted of an offence under section 4 or 6 of the *Crimes Against Humanity and War Crimes Act* that has as its basis an intentional killing, whether or not it was planned and deliberate, that that person be sentenced to imprisonment for life without eligibility for parole until the person has served twenty-five years of the sentence;

(*c*) in respect of a person who has been convicted of second degree murder, that the person be sentenced to imprisonment for life without eligibility for parole until the person has served at least ten years of the sentence or such greater number of years, not being more than twenty-five years, as has been substituted therefor pursuant to section 745.4; and

(*d*) in respect of a person who has been convicted of any other offence, that the person be sentenced to imprisonment for life with normal eligibility for parole. 1995, c. 22, s. 6; 2000, c. 24, s. 46.

CROSS-REFERENCES

See s. 46(1) for the definition of "high treason" and s. 47(1) for its punishment. Sections 229 and 230 define "murder", with s. 231 providing the classification of murder for the purpose of sentencing. Under s. 745.2, where a jury finds the accused guilty of second degree murder, the judge presiding at the trial must put to the jury the statutory questions concerning their recommendations as to parole ineligibility. The judge then applies s. 744 to set the period of ineligibility for parole. At the time of sentencing, the judge is required to read out a notice respecting the availability for judicial review, except where s. 745.6(2) applies (no judicial review for a person who has been convicted of more than one murder).

An accused may apply for judicial review under s. 745.6 if the period of ineligibility is greater than 15 years and the person has served at least 15 years of the sentence, except where the person has been convicted of more than one murder.

In calculating the period of imprisonment for the purposes of ss. 745, 745.4 and 745.6, any time spent in custody before sentencing and after the date of arrest is to be included by s. 746.

See s. 746.1, which limits parole for those offenders serving a sentence including a period of parole ineligibility.

In the case of a young person transferred to ordinary courts, a different sentencing regime applies; see ss. 745.1, 745.3 and 745.5.

SYNOPSIS

The parole ineligibility periods with respect to life sentences are: (a) 25 years for persons convicted of high treason or first degree murder (para. (*a*)); (b) 25 years for persons convicted of second degree murder who have previously been convicted of murder (para. (*b*)) or genocide, crimes against humanity or war crimes based on murder (para. (*b*.1)); (c) 10 years for persons convicted of second degree murder, unless the court has substituted a greater period not to exceed 25 years (para. (*c*); and (d) the normal periods in all other cases (para. (*d*)).

ANNOTATIONS

The mandatory minimum sentence prescribed by para. (*a*) for a planned and deliberate murder does not infringe s. 12 of the *Charter of Rights and Freedoms*: *R. v. Cairns* (1989), 51 C.C.C. (3d) 90 (B.C.C.A.).

The combined effect of s. 231(5) and para. (*a*), requiring that a person convicted of first degree murder where the murder is committed while committing one of the offences, such as kidnapping, specified in s. 231(5) must be sentenced to life imprisonment without eligibility for parole for 25 years, does not infringe ss. 7, 9 and 12 of the Charter: *R. v. Luxton*, [1990] 2 S.C.R. 711, 58 C.C.C. (3d) 449, 79 C.R. (3d) 193 (7:0).

To a similar effect, see *R. v. Bowen* (1990), 59 C.C.C. (3d) 515, 2 C.R. (4th) 225, [1991] 1 W.W.R. 466 (C.A.), and *R. v. Lefebvre* (1992), 72 C.C.C. (3d) 162, 45 Q.A.C. 47 (C.A.), leave to appeal to S.C.C. refused 72 C.C.C. (3d) vi, 139 N.R. 399*n*, upholding the validity of these provisions in relation to the first degree murder of a police officer as prescribed by s. 231(4).

Paragraph (*b*) applies only where the accused was convicted of the earlier murder prior to commission of the murder for which he is now being sentenced: *R. v. Harris* (1993), 86 C.C.C. (3d) 284, 25 C.R. (4th) 389 (Que. C.A.); *R. v. Okkuatsiak* (1994), 91 C.C.C. (3d) 83, 120 Nfld. & P.E.I.R. 79 (Nfld. S.C.).

Paragraph (*b*) does not violate ss. 7 or 9 of the Charter: *R. v. Falkner* (2004), 188 C.C.C. (3d) 406, 122 C.R.R. (2d) 240 (B.C.S.C.).

The mandatory sentence prescribed by para. (*c*) does not offend s. 12 of the *Charter of Rights and Freedoms*: *R. v. Mitchell* (1987), 39 C.C.C. (3d) 141, 81 N.S.R. (2d) 57 (S.C. App. Div.); *R. v. Latimer* (1995), 99 C.C.C. (3d) 481, 126 D.L.R. (4th) 203, [1995] 8 W.W.R. 609 (Sask. C.A.).

As the minimum sentence for second degree murder was not in the particular circumstances grossly disproportionate and therefore did not violate s. 12 of the *Canadian Charter of Rights and Freedoms* where the accused killed his seriously disabled daughter, the accused was not entitled to a constitutional exemption: *R. v. Latimer*, [2001] 1 S.C.R. 3, 150 C.C.C. (3d) 129, 39 C.R. (5th) 1.

INFORMATION IN RESPECT OF PAROLE / Exception.

745.01 (1)Except where subsection 745.6(2) applies, at the time of sentencing under paragraph 745(*a*), (*b*) or (*c*), the judge who presided at the trial of the offender shall state the following, for the record:

The offender has been found guilty of (state offence) and sentenced to imprisonment for life. The offender is not eligible for parole until (state date). However, after serving at least 15 years of the sentence, the offender may apply under section 745.6 of the *Criminal Code* for a reduction in the number of years of imprisonment without eligibility for parole. If the jury hearing the application reduces the period of parole ineligibility, the offender may then make an application for parole under the *Corrections and Conditional Release Act* at the end of that reduced period.

(2) Subsection (1) does not apply if the offender is convicted of an offence committed on or after the day on which this subsection comes into force. 1999, c. 25, s. 21; 2011, c. 2, s. 2.

CROSS-REFERENCES

Section 745.6(2) provides that there can be no judicial review under that section for a person who has been convicted of more than one murder.

SYNOPSIS

This section requires the judge to read out a notice respecting the availability of judicial review of the period of parole ineligibility. This section does not apply where the person has been convicted of more than one murder in the circumstances set out in s. 745.6(2), or was convicted of a murder that was committed after the date subsec. (2) came into force: December 2, 2011.

PERSONS UNDER EIGHTEEN.

745.1 The sentence to be pronounced against a person who was under the age of eighteen at the time of the commission of the offence for which the person was convicted of first degree murder or second degree murder and who is to be sentenced to imprisonment for life shall be that the person be sentenced to imprisonment for life without eligibility for parole until the person has served

(*a*) such period between five and seven years of the sentence as is specified by the judge presiding at the trial, or if no period is specified by the judge presiding at the trial, five years, in the case of a person who was under the age of sixteen at the time of the commission of the offence;

(*b*) ten years, in the case of a person convicted of first degree murder who was sixteen or seventeen years of age at the time of the commission of the offence; and

(*c*) seven years, in the case of a person convicted of second degree murder who was sixteen or seventeen years of age at the time of the commission of the offence. 1995, c. 22, ss. 6, 21.

SYNOPSIS

This section sets out the sentence for a young person who is to be given an adult sentence in accordance with the *Youth Criminal Justice Act* having been found guilty of first degree or second degree murder. The provisions of this section apply to such young persons, rather than the provisions of s. 745. In the case of a trial by jury of an offender who was under 16 years of age at the time of the commission of the offence, the judge is required to put a question to the jury in the terms set out in s. 745.3. The judge then takes the jury's recommendation into account in fixing the period of parole ineligibility between five and seven years pursuant to s. 745.5. Under this section, for an offender under the age of 16 years, the period of parole ineligibility is fixed between five and seven years as specified by the judge, or five years if no period is specified. For an offender who was 16 or 17 years of age at the time of the offence, then the parole ineligibility is fixed at 10 years if the offender was convicted of first degree murder (para. (*b*)), and seven years if the offender was convicted of second degree murder (para. (*c*)). Note that if the young person is given a youth sentence the provisions of s. 42(2)(*q*) apply.

RECOMMENDATION BY JURY.

745.2 Subject to section 745.3, where a jury finds an accused guilty of second degree murder, the judge presiding at the trial shall, before discharging the jury, put to them the following question:

You have found the accused guilty of second degree murder and the law requires that I now pronounce a sentence of imprisonment for life against the accused. Do you wish to make any recommendation with respect to the number of years that the accused must serve before the accused is eligible for release on parole? You are not required to make any recommendation but if you do, your recommendation will be considered by me when I am determining whether I should substitute for the ten year period, which the law would otherwise require the accused to serve before the accused is eligible to be considered for release on parole, a number of years that is more than ten but not more than twenty-five. 1995, c. 22, s. 6.

CROSS-REFERENCES

In setting the parole ineligibility period under s. 745.4, the judge is to take into consideration the recommendation of the jury. Judicial review under s. 745.6 is available when the ineligibility period is set at more than 15 years.

See s. 746.1 for limits on parole during the ineligibility period.

In the case of a young person given an adult sentence, a different sentencing regime applies. See ss. 745.1, 745.3 and 745.5. For young persons given a youth sentence, see s. 42(2)(*q*) of the *Youth Criminal Justice Act*.

ANNOTATIONS

The jury is only to be asked for a recommendation where it finds the accused guilty after hearing all the evidence and counsels' addresses, not where it returns a verdict following the accused's guilty plea in the course of the trial: *R. v. Larter and Burt* (1982), 2 C.C.C. (3d) 240, 39 Nfld. & P.E.I.R. 178 (P.E.I.S.C. App. Div.); *R. v. Kivell* (1985), 21 C.C.C. (3d) 299 (B.C.C.A.). *Contra*: *R. v. Oughton* (unreported, February 11, 1985, Ont. C.A.).

The jury's recommendation under this section is to be based solely on the evidence leading to the conviction and the jury should hear no further evidence or argument for the purposes of a recommendation under this section. This section in effect constitutes a complete code: *R. v. Nepoose* (1988), 46 C.C.C. (3d) 421, 69 C.R. (3d) 59 (Alta. C.A.); *R. v. Poirier* (2005), 193 C.C.C. (3d) 303, 195 O.A.C. 301 (C.A.).

The fact that the jury makes no recommendation under this section is a factor to be taken into account but the judge is still faced with the responsibility of imposing a fit sentence having regard to the factors set out in s. 745.4: *R. v. Jordan* (1983), 7 C.C.C. (3d) 143 (B.C.C.A.), leave to appeal to S.C.C. refused 52 N.R. 319*n*.

The jury's recommendation under this section need not be unanimous and the trial judge ought not to express to the jury a preference for a unanimous recommendation: *R. v. Brenn* (1989), 8 W.C.B. (2d) 822 (Ont. C.A.).

To the contrary is *R. v. Ameeriar* (1990), 60 C.C.C. (3d) 431 (Que. C.A.), where the court held that the trial judge properly directed the jury that any recommendation must be unanimous and that, if they failed to make a recommendation, the jury should indicate whether this was because they were not unanimous or because they all agreed not to make any recommendation. Where the jury failed to make a recommendation because they were not unanimous, then the trial judge was not required to treat that finding as if it were a recommendation that the period of parole ineligibility ought not to be increased.

The accused does not have any right to make submissions to the jury: *R. v. Cruz* (1998), 124 C.C.C. (3d) 157, 16 C.R. (5th) 136 (B.C.C.A.), leave to appeal to S.C.C. refused 130 C.C.C. (3d) vi, 58 C.R.R. (3d) 376*n*. This does not infringe s. 7 of the Charter. Further, since the jury is merely making a recommendation, they need not be unanimous: *R. v. Okkuatsiak* (1993), 80 C.C.C. (3d) 251, 20 C.R. (4th) 400 (Nfld. C.A.).

RECOMMENDATION BY JURY — MULTIPLE MURDERS / Application.

745.21 (1) Where a jury finds an accused guilty of murder and that accused has previously been convicted of murder, the judge presiding at the trial shall, before discharging the jury, put to them the following question:

> **You have found the accused guilty of murder. The law requires that I now pronounce a sentence of imprisonment for life against the accused. Do you wish to make any recommendation with respect to the period without eligibility for parole to be served for this murder consecutively to the period without eligibility for parole imposed for the previous murder? You are not required to make any recommendation, but if you do, your recommendation will be considered by me when I make my determination.**

(2) Subsection (1) applies to an offender who is convicted of murders committed on a day after the day on which this section comes into force and for which the offender is sentenced under this Act, the *National Defence Act* or the *Crimes Against Humanity and War Crimes Act*. 2011, c. 5, s. 4.

CROSS-REFERENCES

The question to be asked of the jury respecting parole eligibility where the offender was not previously convicted of murder is set out in s. 745.2. Section 745.4 sets out the judge's power to set the period of parole ineligibility for an offender convicted of second degree murder. Where the offender has previously been convicted of murder, s. 745.51 provides that the trial judge may order that the periods of parole ineligibility be served consecutively.

PERSONS UNDER SIXTEEN.

745.3 Where a jury finds an accused guilty of first degree murder or second degree murder and the accused was under the age of sixteen at the time of the commission of the offence, the judge presiding at the trial shall, before discharging the jury, put to them the following question:

> **You have found the accused guilty of first degree murder (or second degree murder) and the law requires that I now pronounce a sentence of imprisonment for life against the accused. Do you wish to make any recommendation with respect to the period of imprisonment that the accused must serve before the accused is eligible for release on parole? You are not required to make any recommendation but if you do, your recommendation will be considered by me when I am determining the period of imprisonment that is between five years and seven years that the law would require the accused to serve before the accused is eligible to be considered for release on parole. 1995, c. 22, ss. 6, 22.**

SYNOPSIS

This section sets out the question to be asked of the jury which has found a young person who was under the age of 16 years at the time of the offence, guilty of first degree or second degree murder. The provisions of this section apply to such young persons, rather than the provisions of s. 745.2. The judge then takes the jury's recommendation into account in fixing the period of parole ineligibility between five and ten years pursuant to s. 745.5. The sentence itself is life imprisonment as prescribed by s. 745. Note that if the young person is given a youth sentence, the provisions of s. 42(2)(*q*) of the *Youth Criminal Justice Act* apply.

INELIGIBILITY FOR PAROLE.

745.4 Subject to section 745.5, at the time of the sentencing under section 745 of an offender who is convicted of second degree murder, the judge who presided at the trial of the offender or, if that judge is unable to do so, any judge of the same court may,

having regard to the character of the offender, the nature of the offence and the circumstances surrounding its commission, and to the recommendation, if any, made pursuant to section 745.2, by order, substitute for ten years a number of years of imprisonment (being more than ten but not more than twenty-five) without eligibility for parole, as the judge deems fit in the circumstances. 1995, c. 22, s. 6.

CROSS-REFERENCES

See s. 745.2 for the statutory question which the judge addresses to the jury in order to obtain the jury's recommendation. Also see references cited under ss. 745 and 745.2.

In the case of a young person transferred to ordinary courts, a different sentencing regime applies, see ss. 745.1, 745.3 and 745.5.

SYNOPSIS

In sentencing an accused convicted of second degree murder, the trial judge or, if necessary, another judge of the same court, may increase the mandatory 10-year parole ineligibility period up to 25 years. (See s. 745.2 with respect to asking the jury for a recommendation in this regard.)

ANNOTATIONS

Jurisdiction and procedure – In *R. v. Leahy* (1978), 44 C.C.C. (2d) 479 (Ont. C.A.), the court in setting aside the order of parole non-eligibility stated that the case was of a type in which the specific reasons of the trial judge should have been clearly enunciated.

Notwithstanding there is no jury recommendation under s. 745.2 where the Court of Appeal substitutes a conviction of second degree murder on an appeal by the accused from his conviction for first degree murder the Court of Appeal has power to set a period of parole non-eligibility which exceeds 10 years: *R. v. Kjeldsen* (1980), 53 C.C.C. (2d) 55, [1980] 3 W.W.R. 411 (Alta. C.A.).

A judge also has jurisdiction to increase the number of years of parole ineligibility where the accused pleads guilty to a charge of second degree murder: *R. v. O'Brien* (1982), 66 C.C.C. (2d) 374 (B.C.C.A.), and *semble, R. v. Bennett*, [1982] 2 S.C.R. 582, 70 C.C.C. (2d) 575.

Principles in setting period of parole ineligibility – As a general rule, the period of parole ineligibility shall be for 10 years but this can be ousted by a determination of the trial judge that, according to the criteria set out in this section, the accused should wait a longer period before having his suitability to be released into the general public assessed. Denunciation, future dangerousness and general as well as specific deterrence are relevant criteria in making the determination. An extension of the period of parole ineligibility would not be unusual, although it may well be that, in the median number of cases, a period of 10 years might still be imposed. The power to extent the period of parole ineligibility need not be used sparingly: *R. v. Shropshire*, [1995] 4 S.C.R. 227, 102 C.C.C. (3d) 193.

The failure of the jury to make a recommendation is not the equivalent of a recommendation that the minimum period be imposed: *R. v. Cerra* (2004), 192 C.C.C. (3d) 78 (B.C.C.A.).

The judge may take into account prior uncharged conduct of the accused in determining the period of parole ineligibility as it is relevant to the accused's background and character: *R. v. Roberts* (2006), 208 C.C.C. (3d) 454 (Alta. C.A.), leave to appeal to S.C.C. refused [2007] 2 S.C.R. vii, 208 C.C.C. (3d) vi. Reference should also be had to annotations under s. 725 of the *Criminal Code*.

Rehabilitation potential is relevant to the character of the offender, although it does not have the same scope that it would have in other sentencing situations: *R. v. Armstrong* (1995), 218 C.C.C. (3d) 1 (Ont. C.A.), leave to appeal to S.C.C. refused November 16, 1995.

In *R. v. Ryan* (2015), 329 C.C.C. (3d) 285 (Alta. C.A.), leave to appeal to S.C.C. refused [2016] S.C.C.A. No. 52, Wakeling J.A. undertook a comprehensive review of the jurisprudence and proposed a structured approach to determining parole ineligibility which encompasses three categories of cases. However, this approach was not endorsed by the other members of the panel, so it is informative rather than binding.

IDEM.

745.5 At the time of the sentencing under section 745.1 of an offender who is convicted of first degree murder or second degree murder and who was under the age of sixteen at the time of the commission of the offence, the judge who presided at the trial of the offender or, if that judge is unable to do so, any judge of the same court, may, having regard to the age and character of the offender, the nature of the offence and the circumstances surrounding its commission, and to the recommendation, if any, made pursuant to section 745.3, by order, decide the period of imprisonment the offender is to serve that is between five years and seven years without eligibility for parole, as the judge deems fit in the circumstances. 1995, c. 22, s. 6.

SYNOPSIS

This section sets out the factors to be considered by the judge in sentencing a young person who is to be given an adult sentence for first degree or second degree murder and was under the age of 16 years at the time of the offence. The provisions of this section apply to such young persons, rather than the provisions of s. 745.4. In the case of a trial by jury, the judge is required to put a question to the jury in the terms set out in s. 745.3. The judge then takes the jury's recommendation into account in fixing the period of parole ineligibility between five and seven years. Note that if the young person is given a youth sentence then the provisions of s. 42(2)(*q*) of the *Youth Criminal Justice Act* apply.

INELIGIBILITY FOR PAROLE — MULTIPLE MURDERS / Reasons / Application.

745.51 (1) At the time of the sentencing under section 745 of an offender who is convicted of murder and who has already been convicted of one or more other murders, the judge who presided at the trial of the offender or, if that judge is unable to do so, any judge of the same court may, having regard to the character of the offender, the nature of the offence and the circumstances surrounding its commission, and the recommendation, if any, made pursuant to section 745.21, by order, decide that the periods without eligibility for parole for each murder conviction are to be served consecutively.

(2) The judge shall give, either orally or in writing, reasons for the decision to make or not to make an order under subsection (1).

(3) Subsections (1) and (2) apply to an offender who is convicted of murders committed on a day after the day on which this section comes into force and for which the offender is sentenced under this Act, the *National Defence Act* or the *Crimes Against Humanity and War Crimes Act*. 2011, c. 5, s. 5.

CROSS-REFERENCES

Section 745.21 sets out the wording of the question to be read to the jury in a case where the offender was previously convicted of murder. The offender may appeal from an order made under this section (s. 675(2.3)). The Attorney General may appeal from the refusal of a judge to make the order (s. 676(6)).

SYNOPSIS

This section gives the judge power to make the period of parole ineligibility consecutive to the parole ineligibility imposed for an offender who has already been convicted of one or more murders. The judge is required to give reasons for the order. Under subsec. (3), this section only applies "to an offender who is convicted of murders" committed on a day after the section came into force (December 2, 2011). The wording suggests that the previous murder and the murder for which the offender is not being sentenced must have been committed after December 2, 2011.

ANNOTATIONS

This provision violates neither ss. 7 nor 12 of the Charter. Because it is permissive, not mandatory, it does not authorize the imposition of grossly disproportionate sentences: *R. v. Husbands* (2015), 122 W.C.B. (2d) 21, [2015] O.J. No. 2673 (S.C.J.); *R. v. Granados-Arana* (2017), 356 C.C.C. (3d) 340 (Ont. S.C.J.).

APPLICATION FOR JUDICIAL REVIEW / Exception — multiple murders / Less than 15 years of sentence served / At least 15 years of sentence served / Non-application of subsection (2.2) / Further five-year period if no application made / Subsequent applications / Subsequent applications / Definition of "appropriate Chief Justice".

745.6 (1) Subject to subsections (2) to (2.6), a person may apply, in writing, to the appropriate Chief Justice in the province in which their conviction took place for a reduction in the number of years of imprisonment without eligibility for parole if the person

(*a*) has been convicted of murder or high treason;

(*a*.1) committed the murder or high treason before the day on which this paragraph comes into force;

(*b*) has been sentenced to imprisonment for life without eligibility for parole until more than fifteen years of their sentence has been served; and

(*c*) has served at least fifteen years of their sentence.

(2) A person who has been convicted of more than one murder may not make an application under subsection (1), whether or not proceedings were commenced in respect of any of the murders before another murder was committed.

(2.1) A person who is convicted of murder or high treason and who has served less than 15 years of their sentence on the day on which this subsection comes into force may, within 90 days after the day on which they have served 15 years of their sentence, make an application under subsection (1).

(2.2) A person who is convicted of murder or high treason and who has served at least 15 years of their sentence on the day on which this subsection comes into force may make an application under subsection (1) within 90 days after

(*a*) the end of five years after the day on which the person was the subject of a determination made under subsection 745.61(4) or a determination or conclusion to which subsection 745.63(8) applies; or

(*b*) the day on which this subsection comes into force, if the person has not made an application under subsection (1).

(2.3) Subsection (2.2) has no effect on a determination or decision made under subsection 745.61(3) or (5) or 745.63(3), (5) or (6) as it read immediately before the day on which this subsection comes into force. A person in respect of whom a time is set under paragraph 745.61(3)(*a*) or 745.63(6)(*a*) as it read immediately before that day may make an application under subsection (1) within 90 days after the end of that time.

(2.4) If the person does not make an application in accordance with subsection (2.1), (2.2) or (2.3), as the case may be, they may make an application within 90 days after the day on which they have served a further five years of their sentence following the 90-day period referred to in that subsection, as the case may be.

(2.5) A person who makes an application in accordance with subsection (2.1), (2.2) or (2.3), as the case may be, may make another application under subsection (1) within 90 days after

(*a*) **the end of the time set under paragraph 745.61(3)(*a*) or 745.63(6)(*a*), if a time is set under that paragraph; or**

(*b*) **the end of five years after the day on which the person is the subject of a determination made under subsection 745.61(4) or a determination or conclusion to which subsection 745.63(8) applies, if the person is the subject of such a determination or conclusion.**

(2.6) A person who had made an application under subsection (1) as it read immediately before the day on which this subsection comes into force, whose application was finally disposed of on or after that day and who has then made a subsequent application may make a further application in accordance with subsection (2.5), if either paragraph (2.5)(*a*) or (*b*) is applicable.

(2.7) The 90-day time limits for the making of any application referred to in subsections (2.1) to (2.5) may be extended by the appropriate Chief Justice, or his or her designate, to a maximum of 180 days if the person, due to circumstances beyond their control, is unable to make an application within the 90-day time limit.

(2.8) If a person convicted of murder does not make an application under subsection (1) within the maximum time period allowed by this section, the Commissioner of Correctional Service Canada, or his or her designate, shall immediately notify in writing a parent, child, spouse or common-law partner of the victim that the convicted person did not make an application. If it is not possible to notify one of the aforementioned relatives, then the notification shall be given to another relative of the victim. The notification shall specify the next date on which the convicted person will be eligible to make an application under subsection (1).

(3) For the purposes of this section and sections 745.61 to 745.64, the "appropriate Chief Justice" is

(*a*) **in relation to the Province of Ontario, the Chief Justice of the Ontario Court;**

(*b*) **in relation to the Province of Quebec, the Chief Justice of the Superior Court;**

(*c*) **in relation to the Province of Newfoundland and Labrador, the Chief Justice of the Supreme Court, Trial Division;**

(*d*) **in relation to the Provinces of New Brunswick, Manitoba, Saskatchewan and Alberta, the Chief Justice of the Court of Queen's Bench;**

(*e*) **in relation to the Provinces of Nova Scotia, British Columbia and Prince Edward Island, the Chief Justice of the Supreme Court; and**

(*f*) **in relation to Yukon, the Northwest Territories and Nunavut, the Chief Justice of the Court of Appeal. 1993, c. 28, Sch. III, s. 35; 1995, c. 22, s. 6; 1996, c. 34, s. 2(2); 2002, c. 7, s. 146; 2011, c. 2, s. 3; 2015, c. 3, s. 55.**

CROSS-REFERENCES

Ineligibility orders can be appealed under ss. 675(2) and 676(4).

Also see references cited under ss. 745 and 745.4.

SYNOPSIS

This section provides for a review of the parole ineligibility period with respect to the offences of high treason and murder where the sentence has been imprisonment for life without eligibility for parole for more than 15 years and the inmate has served at least 15 years of the sentence.

Pursuant to subsec. (2), a person who has been convicted of more than one murder may not make an application to review their parole ineligibility period. And, by virtue of para. (1)(*a*.1), the procedure set out in this section only applies to an offender who committed the murder or high treason before that paragraph came into force, namely, December 2, 2011. Subsections (2.1) and (2.2) set out the times for making an application for offenders who are still eligible. Where the person has served less than 15 years before December 2, 1011, the application may be made within 90 days after the day on which they have served 15 years. If the person has already served 15 years on December 2, 2011, they may make their application within 90 days after December 2, 2011 unless they have had a previous application dealt with. In the latter case, the application may be made within 90 days after the end of five years after the day on which the decision was made under s. 745.61 by the Chief Justice or their designate not to permit the application for review, or if there was a review hearing but the jury hearing the review did not make an order setting the time for a further review under s. 745.63(8), within 90 days after the end of five years after the day on which the decision was made. Under subsec. (2.3), where dates were set by the Chief Justice or their designate or by the jury, a further application may be made within 90 days after the end of the dates set by the Chief Justice or their designate or the jury, as the case may be. By virtue of subsec. (2.4), where the person does not make an application in accordance with these provisions, they may not make an application until they have served another five years. The application may be made within 30 days after the end of that time.

Where an applicant has previously made an application, which has been refused either at the judicial screening stage (s. 745.61) or the jury stage (s. 745. 63), the applicant may make another application after 90 days of the date set by the judge or the jury for reapplication or, if no date was set, after the end of five years from the decision refusing the application (subsec. (2.5)).

Subsection (2.6) is a transitional provision for persons who made an application under subsec. (1) before December 2, 2011. Subsection (2.7) gives the Chief Justice or their designate power to extend the 90-day time limit to 180 days. The test, however, is a rigorous one: only if the person was unable to make the application due to circumstances beyond the person's control.

Subsection (2.8) requires the Commissioner of Correctional Service Canada to inform the victim's family that the person did not make an application and of the date of eligibility for a further application.

ANNOTATIONS

The purpose of the review procedure under this section is to re-examine a decision in light of new information or factors which could not have been known initially. It follows that the primary purpose of the hearing is to call attention to changes which have occurred in the applicant's situation and which might justify imposing a less harsh penalty upon the applicant. The jury's decision is not essentially different from the ordinary decision regarding length of a sentence. The section gives the jury a broad discretionary power. Accordingly, there is no need to analyze the judge's charge to the jury in the detail that would be appropriate in the case of a trial. The Supreme Court's function is essentially to determine whether the applicant was given a fair hearing at trial. Since the jury's duty is to make a discretionary decision, the concepts of burden of proof, proof on the balance of probabilities, or proof beyond a reasonable doubt are of very limited value in such a hearing. The jury must instead make what, in its discretion, it deems to be the best decision on the evidence. For the applicant to obtain a reduction in the period of parole ineligibility, the applicant need not succeed with respect to all three factors set out in subsec. (2). It was improper for Crown counsel in questioning witnesses and in his closing address to attempt to discredit the review process by calling attention to the fact that the deceased had no opportunity as the applicant did to have her suffering reduced and because the 25 years ineligibility period was a bargain compared with the death penalty. The possible reduction of the ineligibility period after 15 years is a choice made by Parliament which the jury must accept. It is not open to the prosecution to call this choice into question by suggesting to the jury that it is an abnormal procedure, excessively indulgent and contrary to what it argues was Parliament's intent. It was also improper to invite the jury to consider isolated cases in which prisoners committed murder after being paroled. The jury must consider only the applicant's case and must not try the cases of other inmates or determine whether the existing system of parole is effective. While it is possible to invite the jury to take the deterrent aspect of the penalty into account, this should be done in the context of a general submission on the various functions performed by the penalty. It was also an error in this case for the judge to limit his discussion of the applicant's character to matters prior to or contemporaneous with the murder: *R. v. Swietlinski*, [1994] 3 S.C.R. 481, 92 C.C.C. (3d) 449.

On this hearing, the offender is no longer a person charged with an offence within the meaning of s. 11 of the *Charter of Rights and Freedoms* and therefore the legal rights set out therein have no application. As well, since the procedure does not involve a deprivation of liberty, the offender already being deprived of his liberty, s. 7 of the Charter does not apply. In any event, it was held that rules established by the Chief Justice of Ontario pursuant to subsec. (5) provided for a fair hearing of the issue *R. v. Vaillancourt* (1988), 43 C.C.C. (3d) 238 (Ont. H.C.J.).

On an application under this section, there is no basis for departing from the general rule that criminal cases should be heard in the territorial division where the offence was committed: *R. v. Nicholson* (2012), 283 C.C.C. (3d) 254 (B.C.S.C.).

JUDICIAL SCREENING / Criteria / Decision re new application / If no decision re new application / Designation of judge to empanel jury.

745.61 (1) On receipt of an application under subsection 745.6(1), the appropriate Chief Justice shall determine, or shall designate a judge of the superior court of criminal jurisdiction to determine, on the basis of the following written material, whether the applicant has shown, on a balance of probabilities, that there is a substantial likelihood that the application will succeed:

- **(*a*) the application;**
- **(*b*) any report provided by the Correctional Service of Canada or other correctional authorities; and**
- **(*c*) any other written evidence presented to the Chief Justice or judge by the applicant or the Attorney General.**

(2) In determining whether the applicant has shown that there is a substantial likelihood that the application will succeed, the Chief Justice or judge shall consider the criteria set out in paragraphs 745.63(1)(*a*) to (*e*), with any modifications that the circumstances require.

(3) If the Chief Justice or judge determines that the applicant has not shown that there is a substantial likelihood that the application will succeed, the Chief Justice or judge may

- **(*a*) set a time, no earlier than five years after the date of the determination, at or after which the applicant may make another application under subsection 745.6(1); or**
- **(*b*) decide that the applicant may not make another application under that subsection.**

(4) If the Chief Justice or judge determines that the applicant has not shown that there is a substantial likelihood that the application will succeed but does not set a time for another application or decide that such an application may not be made, the applicant may make another application no earlier than five years after the date of the determination.

(5) If the Chief Justice or judge determines that the applicant has shown that there is a substantial likelihood that the application will succeed, the Chief Justice shall designate a judge of the superior court of criminal jurisdiction to empanel a jury to hear the application. 1995, c. 22, s. 6; 1996, c. 34, s. 2(2); 2011, c. 2, s. 4.

CROSS-REFERENCES

There is a right of appeal from determinations made under this section pursuant to s. 745.62. The pre-requisites for making an application under this section are set out in s. 745.6. Note that, as a result of a number of amendments, particularly those in force as of December 2, 2011, eligibility for judicial review of a parole ineligibility exceeding 15 years has been restricted, essentially to persons who committed a single murder prior to December 2, 2011. However, the applicant must carefully review that section because of the relatively strict timelines. If the Chief Justice or their designate permit the application to proceed, it is heard in accordance with the procedures in s. 745.63. Also note the transitional provisions in S.C. 2011, c. 2, s. 7 governing applications already in the system when the December 2, 2011 amendments came into force.

SYNOPSIS

The Chief Justice or a superior court judge designated by the Chief Justice, must make a preliminary determination as to whether the applicant has shown on the balance of probabilities that there is a substantial likelihood that the application for review will succeed having regard to the criteria set out in s. 745.63(1)(*a*) to (*e*). If the application is dismissed for lack of a substantial likelihood of success, the Chief Justice or judge may set a time for a further application not earlier than five years after the decision or decide that the inmate will not be entitled to make another application. Where no such determination is made pursuant to subsec. (3), the inmate is entitled to make another application five years after the date of the preliminary determination.

If the Chief Justice determines that the application has a substantial likelihood of success, a judge will be assigned to hear the matter with a jury.

ANNOTATIONS

The "substantial likelihood" test is an augmented, stringent threshold requiring the screening judge to consider the evidence in greater depth: *R. v. Morrison* (2012), 293 C.C.C. (3d) 416 (Alta. Q.B.).

The retroactive application of this provision to people who committed murder prior to January 9, 1997, unjustifiably infringes s. 11(*i*) of the Charter. Such offenders are entitled to a hearing before a jury: *R. v. Dell* (2018), 364 C.C.C. (3d) 419 (Ont. C.A.), leave to appeal to S.C.C. refused 2019 CarswellOnt 1404. *Contra*: *R. v. Simmonds* (2018), 362 C.C.C. (3d) 215 (B.C.C.A.), holding that the infringement of s. 11(*i*) was justified under s. 1.

APPEAL / Documents to be considered / Sections to apply.

745.62 (1) The applicant or the Attorney General may appeal to the Court of Appeal from a determination or a decision made under section 745.61 on any question of law or fact or mixed law and fact.

(2) The appeal shall be determined on the basis of the documents presented to the Chief Justice or judge who made the determination or decision, any reasons for the determination or decision and any other documents that the Court of Appeal requires.

(3) Sections 673 to 696 apply, with such modifications as the circumstances require. 1995, c. 22, s. 6; 1996, c. 34, s. 2(2).

HEARING OF APPLICATION / Information provided by victim / Definition of "victim" / Reduction / No reduction / Where determination to reduce number of years / Decision re new application / Two-thirds decision / If no decision re new application.

745.63 (1) The jury empanelled under subsection 745.61(5) to hear the application shall consider the following criteria and determine whether the applicant's number of years of imprisonment without eligibility for parole ought to be reduced:

(*a*) the character of the applicant;

(*b*) the applicant's conduct while serving the sentence;

(*c*) the nature of the offence for which the applicant was convicted;

(*d*) any information provided by a victim at the time of the imposition of the sentence or at the time of the hearing under this section; and

(*e*) any other matters that the judge considers relevant in the circumstances.

(1.1) Information provided by a victim referred to in paragraph (1)(*d*) may be provided either orally or in writing, at the discretion of the victim, or in any other manner that the judge considers appropriate.

(2) [*Repealed*, 2015, c. 13, s. 34.]

(3) The jury hearing an application under subsection (1) may determine that the applicant's number of years of imprisonment without eligibility for parole ought to be reduced. The determination to reduce the number of years must be by unanimous vote.

(4) The applicant's number of years of imprisonment without eligibility for parole is not reduced if

(*a*) the jury hearing an application under subsection (1) determines that the number of years ought not to be reduced;

(*b*) the jury hearing an application under subsection (1) concludes that it cannot unanimously determine that the number of years ought to be reduced; or

(*c*) the presiding judge, after the jury has deliberated for a reasonable period, concludes that the jury is unable to unanimously determine that the number of years ought to be reduced.

(5) If the jury determines that the number of years of imprisonment without eligibility for parole ought to be reduced, the jury may, by a vote of not less than two thirds of the members of the jury,

(*a*) substitute a lesser number of years of imprisonment without eligibility for parole than that then applicable; or

(*b*) terminate the ineligibility for parole.

(6) If the applicant's number of years of imprisonment without eligibility for parole is not reduced, the jury may

(*a*) set a time, no earlier than five years after the date of the determination or conclusion under subsection (4), at or after which the applicant may make another application under subsection 745.6(1); or

(*b*) decide that the applicant may not make another application under that subsection.

(7) The decision of the jury under paragraph (6)(*a*) or (*b*) must be made by not less than two thirds of its members.

(8) If the jury does not set a date on or after which another application may be made or decide that such an application may not be made, the applicant may make another application no earlier than five years after the date of the determination or conclusion under subsection (4). 1996, c. 34, s. 2(2); 1999, c. 25, s. 22; 2011, c. 2, s. 5; 2015, c. 13, s. 34.

CROSS-REFERENCES

A hearing under this section is held only if the applicant has been successful at the judicial screening stage as described in s. 745.61 by showing a substantial likelihood that the application will be successful. There are strict time limits for making the application as set out in s. 745.6 and only certain persons are now eligible to apply as set out in that section. There is no provision under this Part for an appeal from the jury's decision. The only route of appeal appears to be directly to the Supreme Court of Canada through s. 40 of the *Supreme Court Act*.

SYNOPSIS

In determining whether the period of parole ineligibility should be reduced, the jury should consider: the character of the applicant; conduct while serving the sentence; the nature of the offence; information provided by the victim at the time of sentence or the hearing; and any other matters considered relevant by the judge. The victim (as defined in s. 722(4)) may provide information at the hearing either orally or in writing or in any other manner that the judge considers appropriate. The jury must be unanimous with respect to a determination to reduce the parole ineligibility. However, the actual number of years of reduction is determined by a two-thirds majority. The jury may determine the number of years until the person is eligible or terminate the parole ineligibility.

If the application is dismissed, the jury may, by a majority of two-thirds, either set a time not earlier than five years after the determination for the inmate to make another application, or decide that the inmate will not be entitled to make any further applications. If the jury does not set a date for when another application may be made, the applicant may not make another application for five years.

ANNOTATIONS

No appeal lies to the Court of Appeal from the determination made by the jury under this section: *R. v. Vaillancourt* (1989), 49 C.C.C. (3d) 544 (Ont. C.A.), leave to appeal to S.C.C. refused 76 C.C.C. (3d) 384*n*.

However, the inmate may apply directly to the Supreme Court of Canada for leave to appeal pursuant to s. 40 of the *Supreme Court Act*, R.S.C. 1985, c. S-26: *R. v. Vaillancourt, supra* (S.C.C.).

The first step in an application requires a determination of whether it is appropriate to empanel a jury. At this stage, the applicant is required to establish on a balance of probabilities that there is a reasonable probability that a jury, applying the factors set out in subsec. (1), could conclude that the parole ineligibility period should be reduced: *R. v. Ryan* (2010), 251 C.C.C. (3d) 114 (Alta. Q.B.).

The prohibition on comment as to the accused's failure to testify in s. 4 of the *Canada Evidence Act* does not apply to proceedings under this section and the prosecutor may invite the jury to draw an adverse inference from the prisoner's silence at the hearing: *Poulin v. Quebec (Attorney General)* (1991), 68 C.C.C. (3d) 472 (Que. S.C.).

The procedural provisions pertaining to jury selection should be applied in selecting a jury under this section, including the procedure for challenge for cause: *R. v. Nichols* (1992), 71 C.C.C. (3d) 385 (Alta. Q.B.). In *R. v. Serplus* (1999), 27 C.R. (5th) 306 (Ont. S.C.J.), the court held that this includes the right to challenge for cause on the ground of prejudice about parole and parole ineligibility.

A change of venue was granted in this case because while an impartial jury could be selected, the hearing of the application in the community that the accused hoped to join if paroled would give the fullest effect to the intention of Parliament with respect to such applications: *Thatcher v. Saskatchewan (Attorney General)* (1999), 141 C.C.C. (3d) 33 (Sask. Q.B.).

The enactment of subsec. (4) to provide that the jury must be unanimous in order to reduce the number of years of imprisonment without parole eligibility was expressly stated to be retrospective, unless the applicant had, before January 6, 1997, made an application under s. 745.1. This change in the law does not violate the principles of fundamental justice: *R. v. Chaudhary* (1999), 139 C.C.C. (3d) 547 (Ont. S.C.J.), leave to appeal to S.C.C. refused 144 C.C.C. (3d) vi.

RULES / Territories.

745.64 (1) The appropriate Chief Justice in each province or territory may make such rules as are required for the purposes of sections 745.6 to 745.63.

(2) When the appropriate Chief Justice is designating a judge of the superior court of criminal jurisdiction, for the purpose of a judicial screening under subsection 745.61(1) or to empanel a jury to hear an application under subsection 745.61(5), in respect of a conviction that took place in Yukon, the Northwest Territories or Nunavut, the appropriate Chief Justice may designate the judge from the Court of Appeal of Yukon, the Northwest Territories or Nunavut, or the Supreme Court of Yukon or the

Northwest Territories or the Nunavut Court of Justice, as the case may be. 1993, c. 28, Sch. III, s. 35.1 (repealed 1999, c. 3, s. 12); 1996, c. 34, s. 2(2); 1999, c. 3, ss. 12, 53; 2002, c. 7, s. 147.

TIME SPENT IN CUSTODY.

746. In calculating the period of imprisonment served for the purposes of section 745, 745.1, 745.4, 745.5 or 745.6, there shall be included any time spent in custody between

(*a*) in the case of a sentence of imprisonment for life after July 25, 1976, the day on which the person was arrested and taken into custody in respect of the offence for which that person was sentenced to imprisonment for life and the day the sentence was imposed; or

(*b*) in the case of a sentence of death that has been or is deemed to have been commuted to a sentence of imprisonment for life, the day on which the person was arrested and taken into custody in respect of the offence for which that person was sentenced to death and the day the sentence was commuted or deemed to have been commuted to a sentence of imprisonment for life. 1995, c. 22, s. 6.

CROSS-REFERENCES

See s. 719(3) which allows the judge, in determining sentence, to consider the time spent in custody prior to sentencing.

Also see references cited under ss. 745 and 745.2.

SYNOPSIS

This section provides that for the purposes of parole proceedings with respect to persons sentenced to life imprisonment, the calculation of time served shall include time spent in custody prior to sentence or, in the case of those sentenced to death, prior to commutation or deemed commutation of sentence. The former provision only applies to those sentenced to life imprisonment after July 25, 1976.

ANNOTATIONS

Where there has been a delay in execution of the arrest warrant, although the police were aware of the accused's whereabouts and the warrant was capable of being executed, then the judge, in setting the period of parole ineligibility, should take that into account. Where this delay was not taken into account and the circumstances demonstrate an abuse of process and infringement of s. 7 of the Charter, it is open to a court to subsequently grant a remedy under s. 24(1) of the Charter by, for example, treating the accused as if he had been arrested on the date on which the warrant was issued and calculating the date of eligibility for judicial review under s. 745 accordingly: *Parker v. Canada (Solicitor General)* (1990), 57 C.C.C. (3d) 68, 73 O.R. (2d) 193, 78 C.R. (3d) 209 (H.C.J.).

This provision has no applicability to the determination of the period of parole ineligibility: *R. v. Toor* (2005), 199 C.C.C. (3d) 155 (B.C.C.A.).

PAROLE PROHIBITED / Absence with or without escort and day parole / Young offenders.

746.1 (1) Unless Parliament otherwise provides by an enactment making express reference to this section, a person who has been sentenced to imprisonment for life without eligibility for parole for a specified number of years pursuant to this Act shall not be considered for parole or released pursuant to a grant of parole under the *Corrections and Conditional Release Act* or any other Act of Parliament until the expiration or termination of the specified number of years of imprisonment.

(2) Subject to subsection (3), in respect of a person sentenced to imprisonment for life without eligibility for parole for a specified number of years pursuant to this Act, until the expiration of all but three years of the specified number of years of imprisonment,

(*a*) no day parole may be granted under the *Corrections and Conditional Release Act*;

(*b*) no absence without escort may be authorized under that Act or the *Prisons and Reformatories Act*; and

(*c*) except with the approval of the Parole Board of Canada, no absence with escort otherwise than for medical reasons or in order to attend judicial proceedings or a coroner's inquest may be authorized under either of those Acts.

(3) In the case of any person convicted of first degree murder or second degree murder who was under the age of eighteen at the time of the commission of the offence and who is sentenced to imprisonment for life without eligibility for parole for a specified number of years pursuant to this Act, until the expiration of all but one fifth of the period of imprisonment the person is to serve without eligibility for parole,

(*a*) no day parole may be granted under the *Corrections and Conditional Release Act*;

(*b*) no absence without escort may be authorized under that Act or the *Prisons and Reformatories Act*; and

(*c*) except with the approval of the Parole Board of Canada, no absence with escort otherwise than for medical reasons or in order to attend judicial proceedings or a coroner's inquest may be authorized under either of those Acts. 1995, c. 22, s. 6; 1995, c. 42, s. 87; 1997 c. 17, s. 2; 2012, c. 1, s. 160(*c*)(iii).

CROSS-REFERENCES

Section 746 states that parole ineligibility for the purposes of ss. 745, 745.4 and 745.6 includes the time spent in custody before sentencing. As this section is not included, there is some question as to how the ineligibility period is to be calculated.

Section 745.6 may be used to vary the original period of parole ineligibility.

Also see the *Corrections and Conditional Release Act*, especially s. 119.

SYNOPSIS

This section states that no prisoner sentenced to life imprisonment shall be paroled under any other Act prior to the expiry of his or her term of ineligibility for parole under the Code, unless an enactment of Parliament referring to this section provides for such parole (subsec. (1)). In the case of an adult, there shall be no day parole, no absence without escort prior to three years before the expiry of the ineligibility period. However, there may be absence with escort for medical reasons, and no absence with escort, except with the approval of the National Parole Board.

Where the prisoner was under 18 years of age at the time of the offence there shall be no day parole, no absence without escort and, except with the approval of the National Parole Board, no absence with escort until the expiration of all but one-fifth of the specified period of parole ineligibility. The only exceptions are that the prisoner may be absent with escort for medical reasons or to attend judicial proceedings or a coroner's inquest (subsec. (3)).

747. [*Repealed*, 1995, c. 22, s. 6.]

Note: Sections 747 to 747.8, with heading, as enacted by 1995, c. 22, s. 6, have never been brought into force and have since been repealed by 2005, c. 22, s. 39.

Pardons and Remissions

TO WHOM PARDON MAY BE GRANTED / Free or conditional pardon / Effect of free pardon / Punishment for subsequent offence not affected.

748. (1) Her Majesty may extend the royal mercy to a person who is sentenced to imprisonment under the authority of an Act of Parliament, even if the person is imprisoned for failure to pay money to another person.

(2) The Governor in Council may grant a free pardon or a conditional pardon to any person who has been convicted of an offence.

(3) Where the Governor in Council grants a free pardon to a person, that person shall be deemed thereafter never to have committed the offence in respect of which the pardon is granted.

(4) No free pardon or conditional pardon prevents or mitigates the punishment to which the person might otherwise be lawfully sentenced on a subsequent conviction for an offence other than that for which the pardon was granted. 1995, c. 22, s. 6.

CROSS-REFERENCES

Application may also be made to the Solicitor General of Canada for a pardon pursuant to the *Criminal Records Act*, R.S.C. 1985, c. C-47. The effect of the pardon is contained by s. 5 of the Act with revocation of the pardon governed by s. 7.

Remission of pecuniary penalties, fines or forfeiture by the Governor in Council is dealt with by s. 748.1.

By s. 749, there is no limit in this Act on Her Majesty's royal prerogative of mercy.

In the case of disabilities under s. 750, before the granting of a pardon, the Governor in Council may allow, by s. 748(4), the restoration of any capacities lost by virtue of that section.

See s. 690 which allows the Minister of Justice, on an application for mercy by a person convicted in proceedings by indictment or sentenced to preventative detention under Part XXIV, to order a new trial or hearing or to refer the matter to the Court of Appeal or to direct a reference.

SYNOPSIS

This section states that Her Majesty may extend the royal mercy and the Governor in Council may grant free or conditional pardons to those imprisoned or convicted under this Act. Where there is a free pardon, the person is deemed never to have committed the offence, but a free or conditional pardon does not mitigate any sentence the person might receive on conviction for another offence.

ANNOTATIONS

Where an accused has been previously pardoned and is then convicted of a further offence, for the purposes of sentencing he is to be treated as a first offender: *R. v. Spring* (1977), 35 C.C.C. (2d) 308 (Ont. C.A.). [However, now see s. 7.2 of the *Criminal Records Act*, R.S.C. 1985, c. C-47.]

An inmate who seeks to review the validity of revocation of his conditional pardon by way of *habeas corpus* may be admitted to bail pending the hearing of the application. The onus is on the Crown to show cause why the inmate should not be admitted to bail. The onus would also ultimately be on the Crown to show breach of the conditions and that the pardon was terminated thereby, or the Governor in Council was justified on the facts in confirming that the pardon was at an end, as a result of the breach: *R. v. Reddekopp* (1983), 6 C.C.C. (3d) 241 (Ont. H.C.J.).

In *Reference re: Milgaard (Can.)*, [1992] 1 S.C.R. 866, 71 C.C.C. (3d) 260, the Governor in Council had referred the accused's case to the Supreme Court of Canada to determine whether the continued conviction of the accused for murder constituted a miscarriage of justice. The court held that the continued conviction of the accused would constitute a miscarriage of justice if, on the basis of the judicial record, the reference case and such further evidence as the court in its discretion received, the court was satisfied beyond a reasonable doubt that the accused was innocent. If the court was of that view, then it would consider advising the Governor in Council to exercise his power under subsec. (2) to grant a free pardon to the accused. Even if the record did not establish that there had been a miscarriage of justice, the court might still consider advising the Minister of Justice that granting of a conditional pardon under subsec. (2) may be warranted, having regard to all the circumstances. [Also see note of this case under s. 690, *supra.*]

In view of subsec. (3), a Crown witness may not be cross-examined by defence counsel on convictions for which a pardon has been granted: *R. v. Paterson* (1998), 122 C.C.C. (3d) 254 (B.C.C.A.), leave to appeal to S.C.C. refused 134 C.C.C. (3d) vi.

REMISSION BY GOVERNOR IN COUNCIL / Terms of remission.

748.1 (1) The Governor in Council may order the remission, in whole or in part, of a fine or forfeiture imposed under an Act of Parliament, whoever the person may be to whom it is payable or however it may be recoverable.

(2) An order for remission under subsection (1) may include the remission of costs incurred in the proceedings, but no costs to which a private prosecutor is entitled shall be remitted. 1995, c. 22, s. 6.

CROSS-REFERENCES

Section 748(2) to (4) govern the granting of pardons by the Governor in Council. Application may also be made to the Solicitor General of Canada for a pardon pursuant to the *Criminal Records Act*, R.S.C. 1985, c. C-47.

By virtue of s. 748(1), mercy under the royal prerogative, may be extended to persons sentenced to imprisonment under any federal Act.

ROYAL PREROGATIVE.

749. Nothing in this Act in any manner limits or affects Her Majesty's royal prerogative of mercy. 1995, c. 22, s. 6.

CROSS-REFERENCES

See s. 748(1) which allows mercy under the royal prerogative to be extended to persons sentenced to imprisonment.

Pardons may also be granted by the Governor in Council under s. 748(2) to (4) and by the Solicitor General pursuant to the *Criminal Records Act*, R.S.C. 1985, c. C-47, for the granting of pardons.

See s. 748.1 which allows the Governor in Council to order the remission of pecuniary penalties, fines or forfeitures.

Disabilities

PUBLIC OFFICE VACATED FOR CONVICTION / When disability ceases / Disability to contract / Application for restoration of privileges / Order of restoration / Removal of disability.

750. (1) Where a person is convicted of an indictable offence for which the person is sentenced to imprisonment for two years or more and holds, at the time that person is convicted, an office under the Crown or other public employment, the office or employment forthwith becomes vacant.

(2) A person to whom subsection (1) applies is, until undergoing the punishment imposed on the person or the punishment substituted therefor for competent authority

or receives a free pardon from Her Majesty, incapable of holding any office under the Crown or other public employment, or of being elected or sitting or voting as a member of Parliament or of a legislature or of exercising any right of suffrage.

(3) No person who is convicted of

(*a*) an offence under section 121, 124 or 418,

(*b*) an offence under section 380 committed against Her Majesty, or

(*c*) an offence under paragraph 80(1)(*d*), subsection 80(2) or section 154.01 of the *Financial Administration Act*,

has, after that conviction, capacity to contract with Her Majesty or to receive any benefit under a contract between Her Majesty and any other person or to hold office under Her Majesty.

(4) A person to whom subsection (3) applies may, at any time before a record suspension for which he or she has applied is ordered under the *Criminal Records Act*, apply to the Governor in Council for the restoration of one or more of the capacities lost by the person by virtue of that subsection.

(5) Where an application is made under subsection (4), the Governor in Council may order that the capacities lost by the applicant by virtue of subsection (3) be restored to that applicant in whole or in part and subject to such conditions as the Governor in Council considers desirable in the public interest.

(6) Where a conviction is set aside by competent authority, any disability imposed by this section is removed. 1995, c. 22, s. 6; 2000, c. 1, s. 9; 2006, c. 9, s. 246; 2012, c. 1, s. 146.

CROSS-REFERENCES

See s. 748 for the granting of pardons by the Governor in Council. Under s. 748.1, the Governor in Council may order the remission of all or part of a pecuniary penalty, fine or forfeiture. The royal mercy may be granted by Her Majesty and is not limited by anything in the *Criminal Code* under s. 749.

SYNOPSIS

This section provides that no person shall assume or hold public office or employment, or vote, if they have been sentenced to a term of imprisonment exceeding five years until they have served that term or been given a free pardon. Also, a person convicted of certain corrupt crimes against the Crown is disqualified from ever contracting with (directly or indirectly) or being employed by the Crown again, unless, on application, a restoration of capacity is granted by the Governor in Council.

Miscellaneous Provisions

COSTS TO SUCCESSFUL PARTY IN CASE OF LIBEL.

751. The person in whose favour judgment is given in proceedings by indictment for defamatory libel is entitled to recover from the opposite party costs in a reasonable amount to be fixed by order of the court. 1995, c. 22, s. 6.

CROSS-REFERENCES

See ss. 297 to 317 respecting defamatory libel. In the absence of a general authority in proceedings upon indictment, costs may be awarded under s. 599(3) as a condition of a change of venue on application by the prosecutor or upon an adjournment under s. 601(5). Under s. 683(3), costs are not allowable on appeals of conviction for indictable offences. Sections 684 and 694.1 permit costs relating to legal assistance.

For award of costs provisions in summary conviction proceedings, see s. 809 for trials and ss. 826, 834(1) and 839(3) on appeal.

The definition of "sentence" in s. 673 does not include an award of costs under s. 728. Section 751.1 governs recovery of costs under s. 728.

SYNOPSIS

This section provides for costs to be paid to the successful party by the other party in proceedings by indictment for defamatory libel. The court shall fix reasonable costs.

HOW RECOVERED.

751.1 Where costs that are fixed under section 751 are not paid forthwith, the party in whose favour judgment is given may enter judgment for the amount of the costs by filing the order in any civil court of the province in which the trial was held that has jurisdiction to enter a judgment for that amount, and that judgment is enforceable against the opposite party in the same manner as if it were a judgment rendered against that opposite party in that court in civil proceedings. 1995, c. 22, s. 6.

CROSS-REFERENCES

For similar recovery or enforcement mechanisms, see ss. 734 to 736 for fines; see ss. 738 to 741.2 for restitution orders and s. 737 for "victim fine surcharges".

The definition of "sentence" in s. 673 does not include an award of costs under s. 728.

SYNOPSIS

This section provides that costs to a successful party in a prosecution for defamatory libel may be enforced and collected in the same manner as a civil judgment of the superior court of the province.

Part XXIV / DANGEROUS OFFENDERS AND LONG-TERM OFFENDERS

1997, c. 17, s. 3.

Interpretation

DEFINITIONS / "court" / "designated offence" / "long-term supervision" / "primary designated offence" / "serious personal injury offence".

752. In this Part,

"court" means the court by which an offender in relation to whom an application under this Part is made was convicted, or a superior court of criminal jurisdiction;

"designated offence" means

- **(*a*) a primary designated offence,**
- **(*b*) an offence under any of the following provisions:**
  - **(i) paragraph 81(1)(*a*) (using explosives),**
  - **(ii) paragraph 81(1)(*b*) (using explosives),**
  - **(iii) section 85 (using firearm or imitation firearm in commission of offence),**
  - **(iv) section 87 (pointing firearm),**
  - **(iv.1) section 98 (breaking and entering to steal firearm),**
  - **(iv.2) section 98.1 (robbery to steal firearm),**
  - **(v) section 153.1 (sexual exploitation of person with disability),**
  - **(vi) section 163.1 (child pornography),**
  - **(vii) section 170 (parent or guardian procuring sexual activity),**

(viii) section 171 (householder permitting sexual activity by or in presence of child),
(ix) section 172.1 (luring child),
(ix.1) section 172.2 (agreement or arrangement — sexual offence against child),
(x) [*Repealed*, 2014, c. 25, s. 29(1).]
(x.1) [*Repealed*, 2014, c. 25, s. 29(1).]
(xi) [*Repealed*, 2014, c. 25, s. 29(1).]
(xii) [*Repealed*, 2014, c. 25, s. 29(1).]
(xiii) section 245 (administering noxious thing),
(xiv) section 266 (assault),
(xv) section 269 (unlawfully causing bodily harm),
(xvi) section 269.1 (torture),
(xvii) paragraph 270(1)(*a*) (assaulting peace officer),
(xviii) section 273.3 (removal of child from Canada),
(xix) subsection 279(2) (forcible confinement),
(xx) section 279.01 (trafficking in persons),
(xx.1) section 279.011 (trafficking of a person under the age of eighteen years),
(xx.2) section 279.02 (material benefit — trafficking),
(xx.3) section 279.03 (withholding or destroying documents — trafficking),
(xxi) section 279.1 (hostage taking),
(xxii) section 280 (abduction of person under age of 16),
(xxiii) section 281 (abduction of person under age of 14),
(xxiii.1) subsection 286.1(2) (obtaining sexual services for consideration from person under 18 years),
(xxiii.2) section 286.2 (material benefit from sexual services),
(xxiii.3) section 286.3 (procuring),
(xxiii.4) section 320.13 (dangerous operation),
(xxiii.5) subsections 320.14(1), (2) and (3) (operation while impaired),
(xxiii.6) section 320.15 (failure or refusal to comply with demand),
(xxiii.7) section 320.16 (failure to stop after accident),
(xxiii.8) section 320.17 (flight from peace officer),
(xxiv) section 344 (robbery), and
(xxv) section 348 (breaking and entering with intent, committing offence or breaking out),

(*c*) an offence under any of the following provisions of the *Criminal Code*, chapter C-34 of the Revised Statutes of Canada, 1970, as they read from time to time before January 1, 1988:
(i) subsection 146(2) (sexual intercourse with female between ages of 14 and 16),
(ii) section 148 (sexual intercourse with feeble-minded),
(iii) section 166 (parent or guardian procuring defilement), and
(iv) section 167 (householder permitting defilement),

(*c*.1) an offence under any of the following provisions of this Act, as they read from time to time before the day on which this paragraph comes into force:
(i) subsection 212(1) (procuring),
(ii) subsection 212(2) (living on the avails of prostitution of person under 18 years),
(iii) subsection 212(2.1) (aggravated offence in relation to living on the avails of prostitution of person under 18 years), and
(iv) subsection 212(4) (prostitution of person under 18 years); or

(*d*) an attempt or conspiracy to commit an offence referred to in paragraph (*b*), (*c*) or (*c*.1);

"long-term supervision" means long-term supervision ordered under subsection 753(4), 753.01(5) or (6) or 753.1(3) or subparagraph 759(3)(*a*)(i);

"primary designated offence" means

(*a*) an offence under any of the following provisions:

(i) section 151 (sexual interference),

(ii) section 152 (invitation to sexual touching),

(iii) section 153 (sexual exploitation),

(iv) section 155 (incest),

(v) section 239 (attempt to commit murder),

(vi) section 244 (discharging firearm with intent),

(vii) section 267 (assault with weapon or causing bodily harm),

(viii) section 268 (aggravated assault),

(ix) section 271 (sexual assault),

(x) section 272 (sexual assault with weapon, threats to third party or causing bodily harm),

(xi) section 273 (aggravated sexual assault), and

(xii) subsection 279(1) (kidnapping),

(*b*) an offence under any of the following provisions of the *Criminal Code*, chapter C-34 of the Revised Statutes of Canada, 1970, as they read from time to time before January 4, 1983:

(i) section 144 (rape),

(ii) section 145 (attempt to commit rape),

(iii) section 149 (indecent assault on female),

(iv) section 156 (indecent assault on male),

(v) subsection 245(2) (assault causing bodily harm), and

(vi) subsection 246(1) (assault with intent) if the intent is to commit an offence referred to in any of subparagraphs (i) to (v) of this paragraph,

(*c*) an offence under any of the following provisions of the *Criminal Code*, chapter C-34 of the Revised Statutes of Canada, 1970, as enacted by section 19 of *An Act to amend the Criminal Code in relation to sexual offences and other offences against the person and to amend certain other Acts in relation thereto or in consequence thereof*, chapter 125 of the Statutes of Canada, 1980-81-82-83:

(i) section 246.1 (sexual assault),

(ii) section 246.2 (sexual assault with weapon, threats to third party or causing bodily harm), and

(iii) section 246.3 (aggravated sexual assault),

(*d*) an offence under any of the following provisions of the *Criminal Code*, chapter C-34 of the Revised Statutes of Canada, 1970, as they read from time to time before January 1, 1988:

(i) subsection 146(1) (sexual intercourse with female under age of 14), and

(ii) paragraph 153(1)(*a*) (sexual intercourse with step-daughter), or

(*e*) an attempt or conspiracy to commit an offence referred to in any of paragraphs (*a*) to (*d*);

"serious personal injury offence" means

(*a*) an indictable offence, other than high treason, treason, first degree murder or second degree murder, involving

(i) the use or attempted use of violence against another person, or

(ii) conduct endangering or likely to endanger the life or safety of another person or inflicting or likely to inflict severe psychological damage on another person,

and for which the offender may be sentenced to imprisonment for ten years or more, or

(*b*) an offence or attempt to commit an offence mentioned in section 271 (sexual assault), 272 (sexual assault with a weapon, threats to a third party or causing bodily harm) or 273 (aggravated sexual assault). R.S., c. C-34, s. 687; 1976-77,

c. 53, s. 14; 1980-81-82-83, c. 125, s. 26; 2008, c. 6, s. 40; 2012, c. 1, s. 35; 2014, c. 25, s. 29; 2018, c. 21, s. 25.

Note: By virtue of s. 179(1)(*b*) of the *Criminal Code*, as re-enacted by R.S.C. 1985, c. 27 (1st Supp.), s. 22, proclaimed in force December 4, 1985, para. (*b*) of the above definition, as it read immediately before January 4, 1983 (the date upon which 1980-81-82, c. 125, s. 26 came into force, amending para. (*b*)) is now relevant to determining whether the offence of vagrancy has been committed. The text of para. (*b*), as it read immediately before January 4, 1983, is as follows:

"(*b*) an offence mentioned in section 144 (rape) or 145 (attempted rape) or an offence or attempt to commit an offence mentioned in section 146 (sexual intercourse with a female under fourteen or between fourteen and sixteen), 149 (indecent assault on a female), 156 (indecent assault on a male) or 157 (gross indecency)."

CROSS-REFERENCES

See s. 2 for definition of "superior court of criminal jurisdiction".

The *Interpretation Act*, R.S.C. 1985, c. I-21, s. 34(1)(*a*), defines indictable offence as any offence which may be prosecuted on indictment. The reference to "indictable offence" in para. (*a*) of the definition may include offences triable either way, if the other required elements of the definition are present.

A person who fears on reasonable grounds that another person will commit a serious personal injury offence, as defined by this section, may, with the consent of the Attorney General, lay an information pursuant to s. 810.2 seeking an order that the person enter into a recognizance.

ANNOTATIONS

The definitions contained in paras. (a) and (b) are not mutually exclusive and consequently, sexual assault may constitute a "serious personal injury offence" under either paragraph: *R. v. Yanoshewski* (1996), 104 C.C.C. (3d) 512 (Sask. C.A.).

The level of violence or endangerment must be objectively serious for an offence to constitute a serious personal injury offence. In this case, the fact that a robbery involved some degree of violence was insufficient to make it a serious personal injury offence: *R. v. Neve* (1999), 137 C.C.C. (3d) 97 (Alta. C.A.). *Contra*: *R. v. Goforth* (2005), 193 C.C.C. (3d) 354 (Sask. C.A.), leave to appeal to S.C.C. refused December 22, 2005, holding that there is no requirement of proof that the predicate offence involves objectively serious violence or endangerment. There is nothing in para. (*a*) that invites a qualitative assessment of the degree of violence or endangerment in the predicate offence.

A threat of violence that suffices to ground a conviction for robbery under s. 343(*a*) does constitute the use of violence against another person within the meaning of subpara. (*a*)(i) of the definition of a "serious personal injury offence" set out in s. 752. Subparagraph (*a*)(i) of the definition in s. 752 does not invite a court to assess the seriousness of the violence the offender used or attempted to use; any level of violence is sufficient: *R. v. Steele*, [2014] 3 S.C.R. 138, 316 C.C.C. (3d) 315.

There is no requirement that the predicate offence be an offence that, by definition in the *Criminal Code*, is an offence against the person to meet the definition of serious personal injury offence in para. (*a*)(ii). Thus, depending on the particular circumstances, the offence of attempting to obstruct justice could fall within this definition: *R. v. Morgan* (2005), 195 C.C.C. (3d) 408 (Ont. C.A.), leave to appeal to S.C.C. refused 199 C.C.C. (3d) vi.

An accused is entitled to the benefit of the amended provisions, including the addition of the long-term offender designation, even if the predicate offences occurred prior to the 1997 amendments. However, the accused is also entitled to the benefit of lesser punishment by being eligible for parole after three years under the former provisions rather than seven years under the new provisions: *R. v. Johnson* (2001), 158 C.C.C. (3d) 155 (B.C.C.A.), affd [2003] 2 S.C.R. 357, 177 C.C.C. (3d) 97; *contra*, *R. v. Yanoshewski*, *supra*.

Where the Crown applies to have the accused declared a dangerous or long-term offender on the basis of a sexual assault, the seriousness of the offence is determined by statutory criteria, not by the facts surrounding the commission of the offence. There is no requirement that the facts surrounding the sexual assault clear any threshold of seriousness to engage the dangerous offender or long-term offender designations. The issue is whether the totality of the accused's conduct in sexual matters showed a failure to control sexual impulses and, pursuant to s. 753(1)(*b*), "a likelihood of causing injury, pain or other evil to other persons through failure in the future to control his or her sexual impulses": *R. v. H. (M.B.)* (2004), 186 C.C.C. (3d) 62, 70 O.R. (3d) 257 *sub nom. R. v. Hall* (C.A.).

PROSECUTOR'S DUTY TO ADVISE COURT.

752.01 If the prosecutor is of the opinion that an offence for which an offender is convicted is a serious personal injury offence that is a designated offence and that the offender was convicted previously at least twice of a designated offence and was sentenced to at least two years of imprisonment for each of those convictions, the prosecutor shall advise the court, as soon as feasible after the finding of guilt and in any event before sentence is imposed, whether the prosecutor intends to make an application under subsection 752.1(1). 2008, c. 6, s. 41.

CROSS-REFERENCES

"Prosecutor" is defined in s. 2. "Court", "designated offence" and "serious personal injury offence" are defined in s. 752. By virtue of s. 754, the consent of the Attorney General is not required before the prosecutor applies for an assessment under s. 752.1. Under s. 753(1.1), on dangerous offender application where the person was convicted of a primary designated offence and was previously twice convicted of a primary designated offence and sentenced to at least two years' imprisonment, the conditions for a finding that the person is a dangerous offender are presumed.

SYNOPSIS

This section requires the prosecutor to advise the court as soon as feasible and at least before sentencing whether the prosecutor will be making an application for a remand for assessment under s. 752.1, where the offender has been convicted of a designated offence and it would be appropriate to impose a sentence of imprisonment of two years or more, and the offender was convicted previously at least twice of a designated offence and was sentenced to at least two years of imprisonment for each of those convictions.

APPLICATION FOR REMAND FOR ASSESSMENT / Report / Extension of time.

752.1 (1) On application by the prosecutor, if the court is of the opinion that there are reasonable grounds to believe that an offender who is convicted of a serious personal injury offence or an offence referred to in paragraph 753.1(2)(*a*) might be found to be a dangerous offender under section 753 or a long-term offender under section 753.1, the court shall, by order in writing, before sentence is imposed, remand the offender, for a period not exceeding 60 days, to the custody of a person designated by the court who can perform an assessment or have an assessment performed by experts for use as evidence in an application under section 753 or 753.1.

(2) The person to whom the offender is remanded shall file a report of the assessment with the court not later than 30 days after the end of the assessment period and make copies of it available to the prosecutor and counsel for the offender.

(3) On application by the prosecutor, the court may extend the period within which the report must be filed by a maximum of 30 days if the court is satisfied that there are reasonable grounds to do so. 1997, c. 17, s. 4; 2008, c. 6, s. 41.

CROSS-REFERENCES

"Serious personal injury offence" and "court" are defined in s. 752. Procedure for and criteria for finding a person to be a dangerous offender are set out in ss. 753, 754 and 757. Procedure, criteria for and consequences of finding a person to be a long-term offender are set out in ss. 753.1 to 753.4, 754 and 757. Rights of appeal are set out in s. 759. By virtue of s. 754, the consent of the Attorney General is not required before the prosecutor applies for an assessment under this section.

SYNOPSIS

This section requires the court to remand the offender for a period not exceeding 60 days for the purpose of obtaining an assessment for use on an application to find the offender to be a dangerous offender under s. 753 or a long-term offender under s. 753.1. The report is to be filed within 30 days after the end of the assessment period, although this time may be extended for up to 30 days on application to the prosecution.

ANNOTATIONS

This provision is properly characterized as being procedural rather than substantive: *R. v. Albert* (2001), 154 C.C.C. (3d) 286 (Sask. C.A.).

A psychiatric assessment which had been obtained for dangerous offender proceedings subsequently abandoned by the Crown was admissible at the sentencing hearing of the offender: *R. v. N. (R.A.)* (2001), 160 C.C.C. (3d) 571 (Alta. C.A.).

Similarly, in *R. v. Bouvier* (2011), 274 C.C.C. (3d) 406 (Sask. C.A.), there is no jurisdiction to order an assessment for sentencing purposes subject to ss. 752.1 and 753.01 of the *Criminal Code*.

Subsection (2) – A report is "filed" within the meaning of this section when handed to the proper official or registry clerk: *R. v. Small* (2000), 147 C.C.C. (3d) 302 (B.C.C.A.).

Subsection (3) – The effect of non-compliance with the 60-day assessment period results in a nullity of the proceedings regarding the prosecutor's request for a long-term offender designation: *R. v. Gow* (2010), 259 C.C.C. (3d) 364 (Alta. Q.B.).

APPLICATION FOR FINDING THAT AN OFFENDER IS A DANGEROUS OFFENDER / Presumption / Time for making application / Application for remand for assessment after imposition of sentence / If offender found to be dangerous offender / Sentence for dangerous offender / If application made after sentencing / If offender not found to be dangerous offender.

753. (1) On application made under this Part after an assessment report is filed under subsection 752.1(2), the court shall find the offender to be a dangerous offender if it is satisfied

(*a*) that the offence for which the offender has been convicted is a serious personal injury offence described in paragraph (*a*) of the definition of that expression in section 752 and the offender constitutes a threat to the life, safety or physical or mental well-being of other persons on the basis of evidence establishing

(i) a pattern of repetitive behaviour by the offender, of which the offence for which he or she has been convicted forms a part, showing a failure to restrain his or her behaviour and a likelihood of causing death or injury to other persons, or inflicting severe psychological damage on other persons, through failure in the future to restrain his or her behaviour,

(ii) a pattern of persistent aggressive behaviour by the offender, of which the offence for which he or she has been convicted forms a part, showing a substantial degree of indifference on the part of the offender respecting the reasonably foreseeable consequences to other persons of his or her behaviour, or

(iii) any behaviour by the offender, associated with the offence for which he or she has been convicted, that is of such a brutal nature as to compel the

conclusion that the offender's behaviour in the future is unlikely to be inhibited by normal standards of behavioural restraint; or

(*b*) that the offence for which the offender has been convicted is a serious personal injury offence described in paragraph (*b*) of the definition of that expression in section 752 and the offender, by his or her conduct in any sexual matter including that involved in the commission of the offence for which he or she has been convicted, has shown a failure to control his or her sexual impulses and a likelihood of causing injury, pain or other evil to other persons through failure in the future to control his or her sexual impulses.

(1.1) If the court is satisfied that the offence for which the offender is convicted is a primary designated offence for which it would be appropriate to impose a sentence of imprisonment of two years or more and that the offender was convicted previously at least twice of a primary designated offence and was sentenced to at least two years of imprisonment for each of those convictions, the conditions in paragraph (1)(*a*) or (*b*), as the case may be, are presumed to have been met unless the contrary is proved on a balance of probabilities.

(2) An application under subsection (1) must be made before sentence is imposed on the offender unless

(*a*) before the imposition of sentence, the prosecutor gives notice to the offender of a possible intention to make an application under section 752.1 and an application under subsection (1) not later than six months after that imposition; and

(*b*) at the time of the application under subsection (1) that is not later than six months after the imposition of sentence, it is shown that relevant evidence that was not reasonably available to the prosecutor at the time of the imposition of sentence became available in the interim.

(3) Notwithstanding subsection 752.1(1), an application under that subsection may be made after the imposition of sentence or after an offender begins to serve the sentence in a case to which paragraphs (2)(*a*) and (*b*) apply.

(4) If the court finds an offender to be a dangerous offender, it shall

(*a*) impose a sentence of detention in a penitentiary for an indeterminate period;

(*b*) impose a sentence for the offence for which the offender has been convicted — which must be a minimum punishment of imprisonment for a term of two years — and order that the offender be subject to long-term supervision for a period that does not exceed 10 years; or

(*c*) impose a sentence for the offence for which the offender has been convicted.

(4.1) The court shall impose a sentence of detention in a penitentiary for an indeterminate period unless it is satisfied by the evidence adduced during the hearing of the application that there is a reasonable expectation that a lesser measure under paragraph (4)(*b*) or (*c*) will adequately protect the public against the commission by the offender of murder or a serious personal injury offence.

(4.2) If the application is made after the offender begins to serve the sentence in a case to which paragraphs (2)(*a*) and (*b*) apply, a sentence imposed under paragraph (4)(*a*), or a sentence imposed and an order made under paragraph 4(*b*), replaces the sentence that was imposed for the offence for which the offender was convicted.

(5) If the court does not find an offender to be a dangerous offender,

(*a*) the court may treat the application as an application to find the offender to be a long-term offender, section 753.1 applies to the application and the court may either find that the offender is a long-term offender or hold another hearing for that purpose; or

(b) the court may impose sentence for the offence for which the offender has been convicted. R.S., c. C-34, s. 688; 1976-77, c. 53, s. 14; 1997, c. 17, s. 4; 2008, c. 6, s. 42.

(6) [*Repealed*, 2008, c. 6, s. 42(5).]

CROSS-REFERENCES

Section 754 describes the procedural steps in an application to have a person declared a dangerous offender. The subject may be compelled to attend the hearing pursuant to s. 758. By virtue of s. 755, the court is not to order the offender to be subject to long-term supervision if they have been sentenced to life imprisonment. And, the period of long-term supervision to which an offender is subject at any particular time must not exceed a total of 10 years.

See s. 757 for rules governing evidence at the hearing. Right of appeal is conferred by s. 759 including appeal from a dismissal of an application for an order under Part XXIV. Procedure on appeal generally parallels the procedure in indictable appeals under Part XXI.

SYNOPSIS

This section sets out what findings are required to be made before an accused can be declared a "dangerous offender". If such a declaration is made, the court has three options under subsec. (4): detention in a penitentiary term for an indeterminate period; impose a sentence of at least two years and make a long-term supervision order not to exceed ten years; or impose a sentence for the offence for which the offender was convicted. By virtue of subsec. (4.1), the presumption is that the indeterminate sentence will be imposed unless the court is satisfied by the evidence adduced during the hearing of the application that there is a reasonable expectation that a lesser measure will adequately protect the public against the commission by the offender of murder or a serious personal injury offence.

Depending on the nature of the underlying offence, the court will consider whether the evidence establishes: (a) a pattern of repetitive or aggressive behaviour such that the accused constitutes a threat to the safety of the public; or (b) that the inability of the accused to control his or her sexual impulses will likely cause injury or pain to other persons. However, subsec. (1.1) provides a presumption that the person is a dangerous offender if the offender is convicted of a primary designated offence (defined in s. 752), and it would be appropriate to impose a sentence of imprisonment of two years or more, and the offender was convicted previously at least twice of a primary designated offence and was sentenced to at least two years of imprisonment for each of those convictions. The onus is on the offender to rebut the presumption on a balance of probabilities.

Ordinarily, the application to have the offender found to be a dangerous offender must be made before the offender is sentenced on the predicate offence. However, subsecs. (2), (3) and (4.2) provide a procedure for making the application after sentencing for the predicate offence if (a) at the time of the sentencing for the predicate offence the prosecutor gives notice of a possible intention to apply to have the offender declared a dangerous offender, and (b) it is shown on the application that relevant evidence was not reasonably available to the prosecution at the time of sentencing for the predicate offence.

Under subsec. (5), if the court does not find the offender to be a dangerous offender, it may treat the application under this section as an application to find the offender to be a long-term offender in accordance with s. 753.1.

ANNOTATIONS

Note: Also see notes of cases under s. 753.1, which may be of assistance in determining whether it is appropriate to order long-term supervision rather than an order for indeterminate detention in a penitentiary.

Constitutional considerations – The imposition of a sentence of indeterminate detention as authorized by the predecessor provisions does not offend ss. 7, 9, and 12 of the *Charter of Rights and Freedoms*: *R. v. Lyons*, [1987] 2 S.C.R. 309, 37 C.C.C. (3d) 1 (5:2).

Pursuant to s. 11(*i*) of the Charter, an accused is entitled to the benefit of the new dangerous and long-term offender provisions. Although the criteria for the dangerous offender status are the same, it is not clear that every person designated as a dangerous offender under the predecessor legislation would necessarily be declared a dangerous offender under the new provision in light of the availability of the new long-term offender designation: *R. v. Johnson*, [2003] 2 S.C.R. 357, 177 C.C.C. (3d) 97.

Section 753(1) does not preclude a sentencing judge from considering future treatment prospects before designating an offender as dangerous and therefore is not overbroad under s. 7 of the Charter: *R. v. Boutilier*, [2017] 2 S.C.R. 936.

Section 753(4.1) does not lead to a grossly disproportionate sentence, contrary to s. 12 of the Charter, by presumptively imposing indeterminate detention and preventing the sentencing judge from imposing a fit sentence. Properly applied, subsec. (4.1) merely provides guidance on how a sentencing judge can properly exercise his or her discretion in accordance with the applicable objectives and principles of sentencing: *R. v. Boutilier*, *supra*. Nor is subsec. (4.1) overbroad contrary to s. 7: *R. v. Boutilier*, *supra*.

Subsection (1.1) violates s. 7 of the Charter by unjustifiably reversing the burden of proof and requiring the offender to prove that he does not meet the dangerous offender criteria: *R. v. Hill* (2012), 291 C.C.C. (3d) 321 (Ont. S.C.J.).

General – To make out a finding that the accused is a dangerous offender, the Crown need not prove absolute intractability. Although the trial judge was of the view that there was at least a possibility of successful treatment, and since he was also satisfied that such treatment was highly unlikely to occur within the time contemplated by the long-term offender provisions, he was right to find that the accused was a dangerous offender: *R. v. Pedden* (2005), 194 C.C.C. (3d) 476 (B.C.C.A.), leave to appeal to S.C.C. refused 203 C.C.C. (3d) vi.

The 2008 amendments removed the discretion that existed under the previous legislation not to find the person to be a dangerous offender even though he or she met the criteria of subsec. (1). It also removed any doubt that intractability is not a necessary element to find a person to be a dangerous offender. However, intractability remains an important consideration in deciding what disposition to impose: *R. v. Szostak* (2014), 306 C.C.C. (3d) 68 (Ont. C.A.), leave to appeal to S.C.C. refused 2014 CarswellOnt 16347.

A dangerous offender designation is not restricted to offenders who commit the gravest of crimes. There is no requirement that the serious personal injury offence required to trigger a dangerous offender application meet a specified threshold of seriousness. Rather, a dangerous offender designation and an indeterminate sentence are properly imposed in cases where the offender meets the statutory criteria and his or her future risk cannot be controlled through a determinate sentence or the imposition of a long-term supervision order: *R. v. Solano* (2014), 309 C.C.C. (3d) 386 (Ont. C.A.).

Violent offence (para. (*a*)) – The pattern of repetitive behaviour referred to in subpara. (i) may be made out where there is only one other incident but both incidents display elements of similarity in the accused's behaviour. With respect to the element of future conduct, the Crown need only establish beyond a reasonable doubt an existing likelihood of causing death, injury or severe psychological damage through the accused's failure in the future to restrain his behaviour: *R. v. Langevin* (1984), 11 C.C.C. (3d) 336 (Ont. C.A.).

Two convictions, including the predicate offence, can constitute a "pattern" within the meaning of subsec. (1)(*a*)(i). However, the fewer the incidents, the more similar they must be. If there are only two incidents, they must be remarkably similar: *R. v. Walsh* (2017), 348 C.C.C. (3d) 1 (B.C.C.A.).

Conduct which involved the rape of a 12-year-old girl and performances of other sexual acts and which can be described as coarse, savage and cruel properly comes within the term "brutal" in subpara. (iii): *R. v. Langevin, supra*.

Subparagraphs (i), (ii) and (iii) are disjunctive and the finding of dangerous offender may be supported by any of the definitions alone: *R. v. Lewis* (1984), 12 C.C.C. (3d) 353 (Ont. C.A.), appeal to S.C.C. abandoned 25 C.C.C. (3d) 288*n*.

A finding that one of the past conduct thresholds has been met does not automatically lead to the finding that the accused is a threat. The type of behaviour encompassed by subpara. (i) or (ii) must involve some degree of actual or attempted violence or endangerment. Repetitive behaviour pursuant to subpara. (i) or persistent behaviour pursuant to subpara. (ii) can be established by similarities either in the kind of offences or in the degree of violence or aggression inflicted. The fewer the incidents, the more similar they must be to constitute a pattern. In addition, to satisfy the pattern requirement, the conduct must also demonstrate a relatively high level of intractability in that the reasons for the behaviour should militate against any reasonable prospect for meaningful change in the future. The context of the past criminal conduct will therefore be relevant: *R. v. Neve* (1999), 137 C.C.C. (3d) 97 (Alta. C.A.).

The pattern of aggressive behaviour referred to in subpara. (ii) must include a consideration of the social realities relevant to the accused. In this case, the accused's aboriginal status and disadvantaged background required a differentiation in considering childhood aggression as opposed to adult criminality for the purpose of determining the pattern of aggressive behaviour. Furthermore, the accused's "indifference" must include a consideration not only of the conduct at the time of the offence but also any genuine expressions of remorse after the crime: *R. v. George* (1998), 126 C.C.C. (3d) 384 (B.C.C.A.).

The term "conduct" in subsec. (1)(*a*)(iii) is broad enough to include the sexually sadistic writings of the accused: *R. v. Melanson* (2001), 152 C.C.C. (3d) 375 (Ont. C.A.), leave to appeal to S.C.C. refused 158 C.C.C. (3d) vi. See also *R. v. Leopold* (2001), 155 C.C.C. (3d) 251 (B.C.C.A.), leave to appeal to S.C.C. refused 161 C.C.C. (3d) vi.

Sexual offences (para. (*b*)) / *Pedophile* – It was held in *R. v. Roestad* (1971), 5 C.C.C. (2d) 564 (Ont. Co. Ct.), considering the former s. 687 which was in substantially the same language that the words "other evil" are not necessarily related to injury and pain and accordingly damage caused by an accused to the morals of children which could lead them to male prostitution or some other form of exploitive behaviour is a form of that evil.

In another case under the former provisions, which also involved a homosexual pedophile, it was held that "evil" in the context of the young male victims must be taken to mean evil consequent on the commission of any offence within the category of offences such as gross indecency, which do not necessarily involve violence as a constituent element. In this case although the accused had not permanently harmed any of the boys in the past there was evidence from which the trial judge could find that evil would likely be caused to a young boy by subjection to such experiences: *R. v. Dwyer* (1977), 34 C.C.C. (2d) 293 (Alta. C.A.).

In concluding that an untreatable pedophile was not a dangerous offender, the trial judge did not err in considering that various factors, conditions and opportunities for reoffending would not exist in the future. The trial judge examined the risk of reoffending in light of past behaviour but with the knowledge of present facts as interpreted by skilled professionals: *R. v. Bakker* (1999), 133 C.C.C. (3d) 75 (B.C.C.A.).

The statutory criteria set out in s. 753 do not preclude consideration of all of the principles of sentencing in determining whether to impose a determinate or indeterminate sentence: *R. v. Bakker*, *supra*.

Evidence and procedure – In *R. v. Knight* (1975), 27 C.C.C. (2d) 343 (Ont. H.C.J.), the psychiatrists were shown certain police reports as to other offences allegedly committed by the offender. However, no evidence was led as to those other offences. The court held that it could not rely on the psychiatrists' evaluation of what factual inference should be drawn from the reports, for it is not within their area of competence to make such findings, and even if it were, those facts would have to be independently proved before the court could rely on any consequent opinion based on inferences drawn therefrom. In this case the application was dismissed as one psychiatrist was unable to give an opinion on the future likelihood without taking into account data of which the court could not take cognizance and the other psychiatrist may have been influenced by that information in forming his opinion. In the result, the Crown had not met the burden of proof. Specifically, with respect to the burden of proof of likelihood, His Lordship held that proof beyond a reasonable doubt is not required since in the nature of things that would be impossible in almost every case but His Lordship stated "I do refer to the quality and strength of the evidence of past and present facts together with the expert opinion thereon, as an existing basis for finding present likelihood of future conduct".

A "pattern of behaviour" cannot be established on the basis of unproven allegations. The trial judge erred in relying on unproven allegations of sexual offences referred to in the materials filed before the court and in expert opinions that were not part of the pattern of behaviour established by the evidence beyond a reasonable doubt: *R. v. Pike* (2010), 260 C.C.C. (3d) 68 (B.C.C.A.). See also *R. v. Lewis* (1984), 12 C.C.C. (3d) 353 (Ont. C.A.).

While previous convictions for sexual offences is relevant evidence the accused must be permitted to adduce evidence of the circumstances of those convictions to show that they were not the result of his failure to control his sexual impulses: *R. v. Dawson*, [1970] 3 C.C.C. 212 (B.C.C.A.).

Facts relating to offences committed in the United States, which were resolved through a dispute resolution process in which the accused apologized to the victim, and offences for which the Crown stayed or withdrew proceedings in Canada were admissible: *R. v. Shrubsall* (2001), 163 C.C.C. (3d) 110 (N.S.S.C.).

The trial judge need not focus on the objective seriousness of a predicate offence in order to conclude that a dangerous offender designation is warranted. The conviction for a "serious personal injury offence" merely triggers the application of para. (*b*) and accordingly, the fact that the accused's most recent offences were less serious than his prior record did not preclude a finding of dangerousness. As long as some conduct of the accused in any sexual matter demonstrates a likelihood that his sexual urges will cause future injury, pain or other evil, there is no conceptual need to pay any attention to the predicate offence: *R. v. Currie*, [1997] 2 S.C.R. 260, 115 C.C.C. (3d) 205.

The burden on the Crown is to establish beyond a reasonable doubt all the necessary elements contained in this section before the accused may be found to be a dangerous offender: *R. v. Jackson* (1981), 61 C.C.C. (2d) 540 (N.S.S.C. App. Div.).

The court must be satisfied of a likelihood that the accused will be a danger to others. A mere possibility of dangerousness is insufficient. *R. v. H. (J.T.)* (2002), 170 C.C.C. (3d) 405 (N.S.C.A.).

The requirements for a finding that the accused is a dangerous offender within the meaning of this paragraph are: (1) whether the accused by his conduct in sexual matters has shown a failure to control his sexual impulses; (2) is the accused likely in the future to show a similar failure; and (3) if so, is he likely to cause injury, pain or other evil to any persons? While psychiatric evidence is relevant to all three issues the trial judge may also properly base her findings on the first and third issues by an analysis of the facts surrounding the predicate offence and other previous offences committed by the accused: *R. v. Sullivan* (1987), 37 C.C.C. (3d) 143 (Ont. C.A.).

Expert evidence may be relevant at all stages of an inquiry under this provision. In considering psychiatric evidence, however, the court should consider: (1) the expert's qualifications and practice; (2) the expert's opportunity to assess the person; (3) the unique features of the doctor-patient relationship; (4) the documents reviewed by the doctor; (5) the nature and scope of the consultations; (6) precisely what the expert relied upon in coming to an opinion; and (7) the strengths and weaknesses of the information and material relied upon: *R. v. Neve*, *supra*.

Where a statement has been ruled inadmissible at trial because of a breach of the accused's rights under s. 10 of the *Canadian Charter of Rights and Freedoms*, its contents cannot be relied upon at the sentencing process and, thus, the statement should not have formed part of the materials provided to the psychiatrist in making his assessment of the accused: *R. v. Archer* (2005), 193 C.C.C. (3d) 376 (Ont. C.A.).

A provincial court judge before whom an application is made to have an accused found to be a dangerous offender has jurisdiction under s. 523(2)(*a*) to release the accused pending the hearing: *R. v. Davidson* (1999), 140 C.C.C. (3d) 166 (B.C.S.C.).

The trial judge's refusal to entertain oral argument at the end of a dangerous offender hearing, relying on written submissions from the parties instead, resulted in procedural unfairness and breached s. 650(1): *R. v. McDonald* (2018), 360 C.C.C. (3d) 494 (Ont. C.A.).

Subsection (5) – The sole purpose of this section is to increase efficiency so that the Crown is not required to bring a dangerous offender application and, should it fail, a separate application seeking a long-term designation. This provision does not, however, limit the scope of factors that a sentencing judge might properly take into account when determining whether or not to declare an offender a dangerous offender: *R. v. Johnson, supra*.

Subsection (4) – In determining the length of a fixed term custodial component of a composite sentence under subsec. (4)(*b*), the court is not restricted to imposing a custodial term that would be appropriate on a conviction for the predicate offence in absence of a dangerous offender designation. Public protection concerns may make a lengthier sentence appropriate: *R. v. Spilman* (2018), 362 C.C.C. (3d) 415 (Ont. C.A.).

Subsection (4.1) – The balance of authority suggests that the "reasonable expectation" standard under this subsection constitutes a new and higher threshold than the "reasonable possibility" of eventual control standard that formerly determined whether an offender would be subject to an indeterminate sentence: *R. v. Osborne* (2014), 314 C.C.C. (3d) 57 (Man. C.A.); *R. v. Bunn* (2014), 446 Sask. R. 184 (C.A.); *R. v. S. (D.J.)* (2015), 635 W.A.C. 57 (B.C.C.A.), leave to appeal to S.C.C. refused 2015 CarswellBC 2583. However, in *R. v. Sawyer* (2015), 328 C.C.C. (3d) 523 (Ont. C.A.), the Ontario Court of Appeal declined to decide the issue.

Other notes – A definite sentence of imprisonment may not be made consecutive to a sentence of indeterminate detention imposed under this Part: *R. v. Martin* (1982), 65 C.C.C. (2d) 376 (Que. C.A.).

APPLICATION FOR REMAND FOR ASSESSMENT — LATER CONVICTION / Report / Extension of time / Application for new sentence or order / Sentence of indeterminate detention / New long-term supervision

753.01 (1) If an offender who is found to be a dangerous offender is later convicted of a serious personal injury offence or an offence under subsection 753.3(1), on application by the prosecutor, the court shall, by order in writing, before sentence is imposed, remand the offender, for a period not exceeding 60 days, to the custody of a person designated by the court who can perform an assessment or have an assessment performed by experts for use as evidence in an application under subsection (4).

(2) The person to whom the offender is remanded shall file a report of the assessment with the court not later than 30 days after the end of the assessment period and make copies of it available to the prosecutor and counsel for the offender.

(3) On application by the prosecutor, the court may extend the period within which the report must be filed by a maximum of 30 days if the court is satisfied that there are reasonable grounds to do so.

(4) After the report is filed, the prosecutor may apply for a sentence of detention in a penitentiary for an indeterminate period, or for an order that the offender be subject to a new period of long-term supervision in addition to any other sentence that may be imposed for the offence.

(5) If the application is for a sentence of detention in a penitentiary for an indeterminate period, the court shall impose that sentence unless it is satisfied by the evidence adduced during the hearing of the application that there is a reasonable expectation that a sentence for the offence for which the offender has been convicted — with or without a new period of long-term supervision — will adequately protect the public against the commission by the offender of murder or a serious personal injury offence.

(6) If the application is for a new period of long-term supervision, the court shall order that the offender be subject to a new period of long-term supervision in addition to a sentence for the offence for which they have been convicted unless it is satisfied by the evidence adduced during the hearing of the application that there is a reasonable expectation that the sentence alone will adequately protect the public against the commission by the offender of murder or a serious personal injury offence. 2008, c. 6, s. 43.

CROSS-REFERENCES

"Prosecutor" is defined in s. 2. The terms "long-term supervision" and "serious personal injury offence" are defined in s. 752. Under s. 753.02, any evidence given during the hearing of an application made under s. 753(1) by a victim of an offence for which the offender was convicted is deemed also to have been given during any hearing held with respect to a hearing under subsecs. (5) or (6) of this section. Under s. 754, the Attorney General's consent is not required for the application for a remand for an assessment. By virtue of s. 755, the court is not to order the offender to be subject to long-term supervision if they have been sentenced to life imprisonment. And, the period of long-term supervision to which an offender is subject at any particular time must not exceed a total of 10 years.

SYNOPSIS

This section deals with dangerous offenders who are later convicted of another serious personal injury offence or breach of a long-term supervision order contrary to s. 753.3. On application by the prosecutor, the offender is remanded for an assessment. The person providing the assessment is to file a report within 30 days although, under subsec. (3), an extension of up to 30 days may be obtained. After the report is filed, the prosecutor may apply for a sentence of detention in a penitentiary for an indeterminate detention, or for a new period of long-term supervision in addition to any other sentence that may be imposed for the predicate offence. Where the prosecutor applies for indeterminate detention, the presumption is that that sentence will be imposed unless the court is satisfied that there is a reasonable expectation that a sentence for the offence for which the offender has been convicted — with or without a new period of long-term supervision — will adequately protect the public against the commission by the offender of murder or a serious personal injury offence. Similarly, if the application is for long-term supervision, the court shall order that the offender be subject to a new period of long-term supervision in addition to a sentence for the offence for which the offender has been convicted, unless it is satisfied that there is a reasonable expectation that the determinate sentence alone will adequately protect the public against the commission by the offender of murder or a serious personal injury offence.

ANNOTATIONS

This provision transforms the import of the dangerousness designation stage. It is no longer a mere introduction to the penalty stage. Rather, it establishes a separate regime for offenders who have previously been designated as dangerous and exposes them to the prospect of an indeterminate sentence in circumstances that would not otherwise fall within the s. 753 regime: *R. v. Boutilier* (2014), 317 C.C.C. (3d) 1 (B.C.S.C.).

VICTIM EVIDENCE.

753.02 Any evidence given during the hearing of an application made under subsection 753(1) by a victim of an offence for which the offender was convicted is deemed also to have been given during any hearing held with respect to the offender under paragraph 753(5)(*a*) or subsection 753.01(5) or (6). 2008, c. 6, s. 43.

APPLICATION FOR FINDING THAT AN OFFENDER IS A LONG-TERM OFFENDER / Substantial risk / Sentence for long-term offender / Exception — if application made after sentencing / If offender not found to be long-term offender.

753.1 (1) The court may, on application made under this Part following the filing of an assessment report under subsection 752.1(2), find an offender to be a long-term offender if it is satisfied that

(*a*) it would be appropriate to impose a sentence of imprisonment of two years or more for the offence for which the offender has been convicted;

(*b*) there is a substantial risk that the offender will reoffend; and

(*c*) there is a reasonable possibility of eventual control of the risk in the community.

(2) The court shall be satisfied that there is a substantial risk that the offender will reoffend if

(*a*) the offender has been convicted of an offence under section 151 (sexual interference), 152 (invitation to sexual touching) or 153 (sexual exploitation), subsection 163.1(2) (making child pornography), 163.1(3) (distribution, etc., of child pornography), 163.1(4) (possession of child pornography) or 163.1(4.1) (accessing child pornography), section 170 (parent or guardian procuring sexual activity), 171 (householder permitting sexual activity), 171.1 (making sexually explicit material available to child), 172.1 (luring a child) or 172.2 (agreement or arrangement — sexual offence against child), subsection 173(2) (exposure) or section 271 (sexual assault), 272 (sexual assault with a weapon) 273 (aggravated sexual assault) or 279.011 (trafficking — person under 18 years) or subsection 279.02(2) (material benefit — trafficking of person under 18 years), 279.03(2) (withholding or destroying documents — trafficking of person under 18 years), 286.1(2) (obtaining sexual services for consideration from person under 18 years), 286.2(2) (material benefit from sexual services provided by person under 18 years) or 286.3(2) (procuring — person under 18 years), or has engaged in serious conduct of a sexual nature in the commission of another offence of which the offender has been convicted; and

(*b*) the offender

(i) has shown a pattern of repetitive behaviour, of which the offence for which he or she has been convicted forms a part, that shows a likelihood of the offender's causing death or injury to other persons or inflicting severe psychological damage on other persons, or

(ii) by conduct in any sexual matter including that involved in the commission of the offence for which the offender has been convicted, has shown a likelihood of causing injury, pain or other evil to other persons in the future through similar offences.

(3) If the court finds an offender to be a long-term offender, it shall

(*a*) impose a sentence for the offence for which the offender has been convicted, which must be a minimum punishment of imprisonment for a term of two years; and

(*b*) order that the offender be subject to long-term supervision for a period that does not exceed 10 years.

(3.1) The court may not impose a sentence under paragraph (3)(*a*) and the sentence that was imposed for the offence for which the offender was convicted stands despite the offender's being found to be a long-term offender, if the application was one that

- **(*a*) was made after the offender begins to serve the sentence in a case to which paragraphs 753(2)(*a*) and (*b*) apply; and**
- **(*b*) was treated as an application under this section further to the court deciding to do so under paragraph 753(5)(*a*).**

(4) and (5) [*Repealed*, 2008, c. 6, s. 44(2).]

(6) If the court does not find an offender to be a long-term offender, the court shall impose sentence for the offence for which the offender has been convicted. 1997, c. 17, s. 4; 2002, c. 13, s. 76; 2006, c. 6, s. 44; 2012, c. 1, s. 36; 2014, c. 25, s. 30.

CROSS-REFERENCES

"Court" and "long-term supervision" are defined in s. 752. The assessment report is prepared in accordance with s. 752.1. Pursuant to s. 753(4) although the court finds the offender to be a dangerous offender it may make a long-term supervision order. The procedure on an application under this section are set out in ss. 754 and 757. In particular, s. 754 requires notice to the offender and consent to the application by the Attorney General. Pursuant to s. 758, the offender must be present for the hearing subject to certain narrow exceptions. The consequences of a finding that the offender is a long-term offender are set out in ss. 753.2 and 753.4. The period of supervision may be reduced on an application to a superior court pursuant to s. 753.2(3). Failure or refusal to comply with an order made under this section is an offence under s. 753.3. Rights of appeal from a finding under this section are set out in s. 759. Where an offender commits a further offence while under supervision he or she is to be sentenced to a penitentiary pursuant to s. 743.1(3.1). By virtue of s. 755, the court is not to order the offender to be subject to long-term supervision if they have been sentenced to life imprisonment. And, the period of long-term supervision to which an offender is subject at any particular time must not exceed a total of 10 years. Breach of long-term supervision is an offence under s. 753.3.

Also see the *Corrections and Conditional Release Act*, especially ss. 134.1, 135.1 and 157.1.

SYNOPSIS

This section sets out the circumstances in which the offender may be found to be a long-term offender. The court must be satisfied that there is a substantial risk that the offender will reoffend and that there is a reasonable possibility of eventual control of the risk in the community. "Substantial risk that the offender will reoffend" is defined in subsec. (2) and focuses on the likelihood of causing death or injury or inflicting severe psychological harm [(2)(*b*)(i)] or likelihood of causing injury, pain or other evil through similar sexual offences [(2)(*b*)(ii)]. The court must also find that it would be appropriate to impose a sentence of imprisonment of two years or more.

If the offender is found to be a long-term offender, the court will impose a sentence of two years or more for the predicate offence and order that the offender be supervised in the community for a further period not exceeding 10 years [subsec. (3)]. Subsection (3.1) sets out the procedure in the unusual situation where the application was commenced as a dangerous offender application under s. 753 after the offender had been sentenced for the predicate offence. In effect, the sentence for the predicate offence stands and the court will add the appropriate supervision order.

No period of long-term supervision is imposed if the offender is already serving a life sentence.

Under s. 755(2), where the offender is found to be a long-term offender while already under supervision any additional period of supervision when added to the remaining period of supervision previously imposed cannot exceed 10 years.

Under subsec. (6), if the person is not found to be a long-term offender, the court will simply proceed to impose sentence for the predicate offence.

ANNOTATIONS

The two specific objectives of a long-term supervision order as a form of conditional release are: (1) protecting the public from the risk of re-offence; and (2) rehabilitating the offender and reintegrating him or her into the community. Rehabilitation is an appropriate sentencing objective and has a significant role to play in the status of a long-term offender. Rehabilitation is a key feature of the long-term offender regime that distinguishes it from the dangerous offender regime: *R. v. Ipeelee*, [2012] 1 S.C.R. 433, 280 C.C.C. (3d) 265.

The risk of re-offending in subsec. (1)(*b*) must be a risk of *violent* re-offending to justify a long-term offender designation: *R. v. Piapot* (2017), 355 C.C.C. (3d) 239 (Sask. C.A.).

The Crown need not prove beyond a reasonable doubt that there was no possibility that the offender will eventually be manageable in the community: *R. v. Wormell* (2005), 198 C.C.C. (3d) 252 (B.C.C.A.), leave to appeal to S.C.C. refused 203 C.C.C. (3d) vi. Followed: *R. v. M. (L.W.)* (2008), 239 C.C.C. (3d) 362 (Sask. C.A.); *R. v. Bouillon* (2006), 71 W.C.B. (2d) 532 (Que. C.A.); *R. v. D. (F.E.)* (2007), 222 C.C.C. (3d) 373 (Ont. C.A.), leave to appeal to S.C.C. refused 228 C.C.C. (3d) vi.

The Crown is not required to prove beyond a reasonable doubt that there was no reasonable possibility for eventual control of the risk that the accused presented in the community. This is not an issue requiring either party to satisfy a burden of proof. Rather, the sentencing judge must be satisfied, having regard to the whole of the evidence, that the public threat could be reduced to an acceptable level through either the long-term offender provisions or a determinate sentence. The use of the word "satisfied" does not connote a standard of proof beyond a reasonable doubt: *R. v. D. (F.E.)* (2007), 222 C.C.C. (3d) 373 (Ont. C.A.), leave to appeal to S.C.C. refused 228 C.C.C. (3d) vi.

"Control" connotes the containment or management of risk, rather than the eradication of risk. Further, there only needs to be a "reasonable possibility" of control rather than a certainty. Where the determination that an offender's risk may be safely controlled in the community rests on adequate community supervision, rather than treatment, the availability of the resources necessary to implement such supervision effectively cannot be uncertain and must be considered. In addition, where the supervision effectively replicates in the community the form of monitoring and supervision that the state provides in custodial settings, the dangerous offender provisions of the *Criminal Code* are engaged and the protection of the public is paramount: *R. v. Little* (2007), 225 C.C.C. (3d) 20, 87 O.R. (3d) 683 *sub nom. R. v. L. (G.)* (C.A.), leave to appeal to S.C.C. refused 228 C.C.C. (3d) vi.

The existence of certain contingencies, including the offender's own motivation to follow through with the contemplated treatment, does not negate a reasonable possibility of control in the community: *R. v. Lawson* (2015), 328 C.C.C. (3d) 395 (Ont. S.C.J.).

Subsection (2) does not restrict the scope of subsec. (1) only to offenders who are convicted of one or more of the sexual offences listed, but rather sets out the circumstances in which the court must find that there is a substantial risk that the offender will reoffend: *R. v. McLeod* (1999), 136 C.C.C. (3d) 492 (B.C.C.A.).

Subsection (2)(*a*) does not provide an exhaustive list of offences and, accordingly, the trial judge did not err in granting a long-term designation where the accused pleaded guilty to attempted murder of a common law partner and had a history of violence offences: *R. v. D. (D.)* (2006), 221 C.C.C. (3d) 57 (Que. C.A.).

Subsection (2) does not define "substantial risk" but, rather, creates a conclusive presumption of "substantial risk" in those circumstances to which paras. (*a*) and (*b*) apply. Furthermore, the long-term offender provisions are not limited to sexual offenders listed in para. (*a*) as the predicate offence: *R. v. McLean* (2009), 241 C.C.C. (3d) 538 (N.S.C.A.).

Subsection (3) is not a pre-requisite to the determination of an accused's status as a long-term offender. Rather, this provision establishes a minimum sentence, from which pre-trial custody can be deducted, once the accused has been found to be a long-term offender: *R. v. W. (H.P.)* (2001), 159 C.C.C. (3d) 91 (Alta. C.A.). Similarly, *R. v. H. (M.B.)* (2004), 186 C.C.C. (3d) 62, 70 O.R. (3d) 257 *sub nom. R. v. Hall* (C.A.).

It is an error of law not to impose a dangerous offender designation on the basis that the possibility of treatment, albeit remote, was an absolute bar to the dangerous offender designation: *R. v. Dagenais* (2003), 181 C.C.C. (3d) 332 (Alta. C.A.), leave to appeal to S.C.C. refused [2004] 3 S.C.R. vii, 188 C.C.C. (3d) vi.

To achieve the goal of protection of the public under the dangerous offender and long-term offender provisions, there must be evidence of treatability that is more than an expression of hope and that indicates that the specific offender can be treated within a definite period of time: *R. v. Higginbottom* (2001), 156 C.C.C. (3d) 178 (Ont. C.A.); *R. v. M. (J.S.)* (2003), 173 C.C.C. (3d) 75, 12 C.R. (6th) 354 *sub nom. R. v. Muir* (B.C.C.A.).

Evidence that amounted to no more than a hope that the accused would either be amenable to treatment or that, if amenable, would be treatable within a definite period of time, cannot meet the requirement in subsec. (1)(*c*) of a reasonable possibility of eventual control to justify making a long-term offender rather than dangerous offender designation: *R. v. M. (N.J.)* (2005), 201 C.C.C. (3d) 541 (Ont. C.A.).

If persons who are otherwise highly dangerous cannot meet the requirements of subsec. (1)(*c*) within the allotted ten-year time frame, they should be declared dangerous offenders. Ongoing monitoring of the accused by a s. 810.2 recognizance is not a solution in these circumstances. In the instant case, the trial judge did not err in concluding that there was no reasonable possibility of eventual control of the accused in the community after the termination of a ten-year supervision order: *R. v. B. (D.V.)* (2010), 254 C.C.C. (3d) 221 (Ont. C.A.), leave to appeal to S.C.C. refused 2011 CarswellOnt 9794.

LONG-TERM SUPERVISION / Sentence served concurrently with supervision / Application for reduction in period of long-term supervision.

753.2 (1) Subject to subsection (2), an offender who is subject to long-term supervision shall be supervised in the community in accordance with the *Corrections and Conditional Release Act* when the offender has finished serving

(*a*) the sentence for the offence for which the offender has been convicted; and

(*b*) all other sentences for offences for which the offender is convicted and for which sentence of a term of imprisonment is imposed on the offender, either before or after the conviction for the offence referred to in paragraph (*a*).

(2) A sentence imposed on an offender referred to in subsection (1), other than a sentence that requires imprisonment, is to be served concurrently with the long-term supervision.

(3) An offender who is required to be supervised, a member of the Parole Board of Canada or, on approval of that Board, the offender's parole supervisor, as defined in subsection 99(1) of the *Corrections and Conditional Release Act*, may apply to a superior court of criminal jurisdiction for an order reducing the period of long-term supervision or terminating it on the ground that the offender no longer presents a substantial risk of reoffending and thereby being a danger to the community. The onus of proving that ground is on the applicant.

(4) The applicant must give notice of an application under subsection (3) to the Attorney General at the time the application is made. 1997, c. 17, s. 4; 2008, c. 6, s. 45; 2012, c. 1, s. 147; 2012, c. 1, s. 160(*c*)(iv).

CROSS-REFERENCES

"Attorney General" and "superior court of criminal jurisdiction" are defined in s. 2. Section 752.1 provides for a remand of the offender for the purpose of preparing an assessment report for use on an application to find the offender to be a long-term offender. The criteria for finding an offender to be a long-term offender are set out in s. 753.1. Under s. 753.3 it is an offence to fail or refuse to comply with the long-term supervision order. Section 753.4 provides that the long-term supervision is interrupted while the offender is serving sentence for other offences. The procedure for finding the offender to be a long-term offender are set out in ss. 754, 757 and 758. Rights of appeal from a finding under this section are set out in s. 759. Where an offender commits a further offence while under supervision he or she is to be sentenced to a penitentiary pursuant to s. 743.1(3.1). Also see the *Corrections and Conditional Release Act*, especially ss. 134.1, 135.1 and 157.1.

SYNOPSIS

This section provides that the period of long-term supervision takes effect after the offender has finished serving the sentence for the predicate offence and any other sentences of imprisonment that the offender is serving. Non-custodial sentences for other offences are served concurrent to the long-term supervision [subsec. (2)]. Under subsec. (3), the offender, the National Parole Board or the offender's supervisor, with the consent of the Parole Board, may apply to a superior court to reduce the period of long-term supervision on the basis that the offender no longer presents a substantial risk of reoffending and thereby being a danger to the community. Pursuant to subsec. (4) this application must be on notice to the Attorney General.

BREACH OF LONG-TERM SUPERVISION / Where accused may be tried and punished.

753.3 (1) An offender who, without reasonable excuse, fails or refuses to comply with long-term supervision is guilty of an indictable offence and liable to imprisonment for a term not exceeding 10 years.

(2) An accused who is charged with an offence under subsection (1) may be tried and punished by any court having jurisdiction to try that offence in the place where the offence is alleged to have been committed or in the place where the accused is found, is arrested or is in custody, but if the place where the accused is found, is arrested or is in custody is outside the province in which the offence is alleged to have been committed, no proceedings in respect of that offence shall be instituted in that place without the consent of the Attorney General of that province. 1997, c. 17, s. 4; 2008, c. 6, s. 46.

CROSS-REFERENCES

"Attorney General" is defined in s. 2. Section 752.1 provides for a remand of the offender for the purpose of preparing an assessment report for use on an application to find the offender to be a long-term offender. The criteria for finding an offender to be a long-term offender are set out in s. 753.1. Section 753.2 sets out the procedure for serving the period set out in the long-term supervision order. Section 753.4 provides that the long-term supervision is interrupted while the offender is serving sentence for other offences. The procedure for finding the offender to be a long-term offender are set out in ss. 754 and 757. Rights of appeal from a finding under this section are set out in s. 759. Where an offender commits a further offence while under supervision he or she is to be sentenced to a penitentiary pursuant to s. 743.1(3.1). Also see the *Corrections and Conditional Release Act*, especially ss. 134.1, 135.1 and 157.1.

SYNOPSIS

This section makes it an indictable offence, punishable by up to 10 years, to fail or refuse without lawful excuse to comply with long-term supervision. The accused may be tried for this offence in the place where the offence is alleged to have been committed or where the accused is found, arrested or in custody. The consent of the Attorney General of the province in which the offence was committed is required if the offence was committed outside the province where the accused is found, arrested or in custody.

ANNOTATIONS

All of the principles set out in ss. 718.1 and 718.2, including the principle of rehabilitation, are to be considered in fashioning a sentence for the breach of a condition of a long-term supervision order. The severity of a breach will ultimately depend on all of the circumstances, including the nature of the condition breached, how that condition is tied to managing the particular offender's risk of re-offence and the circumstances of the breach. Notwithstanding the lengthy maximum penalty available for a breach, the mere existence of a high statutory maximum penalty does not mandate that a significant period of imprisonment must be imposed for any breach. It is the judge's obligation to consider the entire range of sentencing options available, including non-custodial sentences where appropriate. The sentencing judge must consider, within this open range of sentencing options, which sentence will be proportionate to both the gravity of the offence and the degree of responsibility of the offender. The severity of a particular breach will depend, in part, on the circumstances of the breach, the nature of the condition breached, and the role that the condition plays in managing the offender's risk of re-offence in the community. The guide for determining a fit sentence is the well-established principles and objectives of sentencing set out in the *Criminal Code*: *R. v. Ipeelee*, [2012] 1 S.C.R. 433, 280 C.C.C. (3d) 265.

A person charged with breach of a long-term supervision order under subsec. (1) is not entitled to collaterally attack the validity of the Parole Board order in defence of the charge. Rather, the proper route is to ask the Board to vary or remove the condition or, if judicial review in the Federal Court would not provide an effective remedy, apply for *habeas corpus*: *R. v. Bird*, 2019 SCC 7.

NEW OFFENCE / Reduction in term of long-term supervision.

753.4 (1) If an offender who is subject to long-term supervision commits one or more offences under this or any other Act and a court imposes a sentence of imprisonment for the offence or offences, the long-term supervision is interrupted until the offender has finished serving all the sentences, unless the court orders its termination.

(2) A court that imposes a sentence of imprisonment under subsection (1) may order a reduction in the length of the period of the offender's long-term supervision. 1997, c. 17, s. 4; 2008, c. 6, s. 47.

CROSS-REFERENCES

Section 752.1 provides for a remand of the offender for the purpose of preparing an assessment report for use on an application to find the offender to be a long-term offender. The criteria for imposing long-term supervision are set out in ss. 753(4), (4.1) and 753.1. Section 753.2 sets out the procedure for serving the long-term supervision. Under s. 753.2(3), the offender may apply to a superior court to reduce the period of long-term supervision. Under s. 753.3 it is an offence to fail or refuse to comply with the long-term supervision order. The procedure for finding the offender to be a long-term offender are set out in ss. 754 and 757. Rights of appeal from a finding under this section are set out in s. 759. Where an offender commits a further offence while under supervision he or she is to be sentenced to a penitentiary pursuant to s. 743.1(3.1). Also see the *Corrections and Conditional Release Act*, especially ss. 134.1, 135.1 and 157.1.

SYNOPSIS

Under subsec. (1), the period of long-term supervision is interrupted while the offender is serving another sentence of imprisonment, unless the court that imposes these other sentences orders that the order be terminated. Under subsec. (2), the court that imposes the other sentence may reduce the length of the long-term supervision.

HEARING OF APPLICATION / By court alone / When proof unnecessary / Proof of consent.

754. (1) With the exception of an application for remand for assessment, the court may not hear an application made under this Part unless

(a) the Attorney General of the province in which the offender was tried has, either before or after the making of the application, consented to the application;
(b) at least seven days notice has been given to the offender by the prosecutor, following the making of the application, outlining the basis on which it is intended to found the application; and
(c) a copy of the notice has been filed with the clerk of the court or the provincial court judge, as the case may be.

(2) An application under this Part shall be heard and determined by the court without a jury.

(3) For the purposes of an application under this Part, where an offender admits any allegations contained in the notice referred to in paragraph (1)(*b*), no proof of those allegations is required.

(4) The production of a document purporting to contain any nomination or consent that may be made or given by the Attorney General under this Part and purporting to be signed by the Attorney General is, in the absence of any evidence to the contrary, proof of that nomination or consent without proof of the signature or the official character of the person appearing to have signed the document. R.S., c. C-34, s. 689; 1976-77, c. 53, s. 14; R.S.C. 1985, c. 27 (1st Supp.), s. 203; 2008, c. 6, s. 48(1).

CROSS-REFERENCES

The subject of a dangerous offender application hearing must be present with certain narrow exceptions. Section 757 allows character evidence to be adduced. Presence of the accused is governed by s. 758.

Section 753 describes the ground upon which a person may be found to be a dangerous offender and sentenced to an indeterminate period instead of being sentenced for the original serious personal injury offence. Right of appeal is conferred by s. 759 including appeal from a dismissal of an application for an order under this part.

SYNOPSIS

An application for a declaration that an accused is a "dangerous offender" or "long-term offender" requires the consent of the Attorney General of the province in which the order is sought. Proper notice (at least seven days) must be given (subsec. (1)). However, the Attorney General's consent and notice are not required for the application for a remand for an assessment.

The issue is determined by a judge sitting alone (subsec. (2)).

It is open to the offender to admit any of the allegations set out in the Crown's notice, eliminating the need to prove the allegations (subsec. (3)).

ANNOTATIONS

General – This provision requires four procedural steps: (i) an application must be made under the specific circumstances set forth in ss. 752 and 753; (ii) the Attorney General must consent pursuant to s. 754(1)(*a*); (iii) at least seven days notice must be given to the accused in relation to the basis for the application; (iv) a copy of the application must be filed with the court: *R. v. Van Boeyen* (1996), 107 C.C.C. (3d) 135 (B.C.C.A.), leave to appeal to S.C.C. refused 114 C.C.C. (3d) vi.

Subsection (1)(*a*) – The consent need not be provided in any prescribed form and can be given either before or after the application to have the offender declared a dangerous offender has been made, but before the hearing of the application: *R. v. Bedard* (2009), 247 C.C.C. (3d) 275 (Ont. C.A.).

Subsection (1)(*b*) – There is no minimum period of time for giving notice of the intention to seek an order under this Part. It is sufficient if the application is made in court in the presence of the accused. Thereafter the court should adjourn the proceedings to permit the Crown to give the accused the notice in writing as required by this paragraph outlining the basis upon which it is intended to found the application: *R. v. Currie* (1984), 12 C.C.C. (3d) 28 (Ont. C.A.).

The seven days' notice refers to the time between the date upon which the notice of application is given to the offender and the date upon which the hearing of the application is commenced. This provision does not require personal service upon the accused. It is sufficient to have effected personal service upon counsel for the accused: *R. v. Van Boeyen, supra.*

The Crown is required to give notice to the accused of any untried criminal allegations that will form evidence of a pattern: *R. v. Neve* (1999), 137 C.C.C. (3d) 97 (Alta. C.A.).

The notice must outline in a general way the allegations providing the foundation or starting point for the pleaded grounds, but the prosecution is not required to plead the manner of proof or the evidence to be adduced. The Crown is required to provide the accused with disclosure sufficient to allow meaningful defence to the allegations, including allegations of untried criminal conduct: *R. v. Campbell* (2003), 180 C.C.C. (3d) 543 (Ont. S.C.J.).

Subsection (2) – This subsection is not inconsistent with the guarantee in s. 11(*f*) of the *Charter of Rights and Freedoms* to a jury trial: *R. v. Lyons*, [1987] 2 S.C.R. 309, 37 C.C.C. (3d) 1 (5:2).

The following cases were decided under the predecessor legislation.

Admissibility of confessions – It was held in *R. v. Wilband*, [1967] S.C.R. 14, [1967] 2 C.C.C. 6 (5:0), that a psychiatrist appointed under the former s. 689 is not a person in authority and therefore the rule with respect to confessions does not apply to statements given by the offender to such a psychiatrist. Further, the court held that the confession rule would also not apply to such evidence as these proceedings do not involve the conviction of an offence but the determination of the sentence. "The confession rule . . . is a rule which has been designed for proceedings where, broadly speaking, the guilt or innocence of a person charged with an offence is the matter in issue. The rule has not been established for proceedings related to the determination of a sentence." Finally, the psychiatrist's opinion is not inadmissible because it is based partly on hearsay according to recognized psychiatric procedures. The value of the opinion may be affected to the extent that it rests on secondhand source material but that goes only to weight, not admissibility.

The ruling in *R. v. Wilband, supra,* was applied to hold that the Crown was not required to prove the voluntariness of the accused's statements to the police concerning previous sexual offences committed by him: *R. v. Boyd* (1983), 8 C.C.C. (3d) 143 (B.C.C.A.).

Application of other rules of evidence – Evidence to be admissible on the hearing must be adduced in accordance with the regular rules of evidence: *R. v. Jackson* (1981), 61 C.C.C. (2d) 540 (N.S.S.C. App. Div.).

"Other evidence" may include evidence of other incidents which did not result in convictions: *R. v. MacInnis* (1981), 64 C.C.C. (2d) 553, 49 N.S.R. (2d) 393 *sub nom. R. v. MacInnis (No. 2)* (N.S.S.C. App. Div.); *R. v. Lewis* (1984), 12 C.C.C. (3d) 353 (Ont. C.A.), appeal to S.C.C. abandoned 25 C.C.C. (3d) 288*n*.

It would seem that where the hearing is before the court by which the accused was convicted, the judge may take into consideration the evidence adduced at the trial of the substantive offence: *R. v. McGrath*, [1962] S.C.R. 739, 133 C.C.C. 57 (5:0). However, where a judge other than the trial judge hears the application (which is possible by reason of the definition of "court" in s. 752), it is not sufficient to simply file a transcript of the previous proceedings; rather, the evidence must be adduced in the form of sworn testimony: *R. v. Canning,* [1966] 4 C.C.C. 379 (B.C.C.A.).

Constitutional considerations – The use of psychiatric evidence does not violate the guarantee in s. 7 of the Charter to fundamental justice: *R. v. Lyons*, [1987] 2 S.C.R. 309, 37

C.C.C. (3d) 1 (5:2), nor infringe the guarantee against self-incrimination in s. 11(*c*). In particular at this stage of the proceedings the offender is no longer a "person charged with an offence" under s. 11. In any event, the offender is not compelled to testify at the hearing nor required to cooperate with the psychiatrists. The psychiatrist is under no duty to caution the accused as to the possible uses of his examination even where the examination is prior to trial: *R. v. Langevin* (1984), 11 C.C.C. (3d) 336 (Ont. C.A.).

Evidence legally obtained on a remand under former s. 537(1)(*b*) [now see ss. 672.11 and 672.21] is admissible in proceedings under this Part. The evidence is not being used to incriminate the accused at this stage and the constitutional protection against self-incrimination as guaranteed by s. 7 of the Charter is not engaged: *R. v. Jones*, [1994] 2 S.C.R. 229, 89 C.C.C. (3d) 353 (5:4).

755. (old provision) [*Repealed*, 1997, c. 17, s. 5.]

EXCEPTION TO LONG-TERM SUPERVISION — LIFE SENTENCE / Maximum length of long-term supervision.

755. (1) The court shall not order that an offender be subject to long-term supervision if they have been sentenced to life imprisonment.

(2) The periods of long-term supervision to which an offender is subject at any particular time must not total more than 10 years. 2008, c. 6, s. 49.

756. [*Repealed*, 1997, c. 17, s. 5.]

EVIDENCE OF CHARACTER.

757. Without prejudice to the right of the offender to tender evidence as to their character and repute, if the court thinks fit, evidence of character and repute may be admitted

(*a*) on the question of whether the offender is or is not a dangerous offender or a long-term offender; and

(*b*) in connection with a sentence to be imposed or an order to be made under this Part. R.S., c. C-34, s. 692; 1976-77, c. 53, s. 14; 1997, c. 17, s. 5; 2008, c. 6, s. 50.

CROSS-REFERENCES

Relevance is the principle requirement for evidence in dangerous offender proceedings as in criminal proceedings generally. Admission of allegations contained in a s. 754(1) notice are permitted by s. 754(3).

SYNOPSIS

With the permission of the court, the Crown may introduce evidence of character and repute, with respect to whether or not the accused is a dangerous or long-term offender, or in connection with any sentence to be imposed or any order to be made. This provision operates without prejudice to the accused's right to tender evidence respecting their character and repute.

ANNOTATIONS

Character and reputation witnesses need not confine their evidence to their personal knowledge of the accused's reputation and are entitled to provide background information for holding that opinion: *R. v. Gregoire* (1998), 130 C.C.C. (3d) 65, 180 W.A.C. 261 (Man. C.A.).

PRESENCE OF ACCUSED AT HEARING OF APPLICATION / Exception.

758. (1) The offender shall be present at the hearing of the application under this Part and if at the time the application is to be heard

(*a*) he is confined in a prison, the court may order, in writing, the person having the custody of the accused to bring him before the court; or

(*b*) he is not confined in a prison, the court shall issue a summons or a warrant to compel the accused to attend before the court and the provisions of Part XVI relating to summons and warrant are applicable with such modifications as the circumstances require.

(2) Notwithstanding subsection (1), the court may

(*a*) cause the offender to be removed and to be kept out of court, where he misconducts himself by interrupting the proceedings so that to continue the proceedings in his presence would not be feasible; or

(*b*) permit the offender to be out of court during the whole or any part of the hearing on such conditions as the court considers proper. R.S., c. C-34, s. 693; 1976-77, c. 53, s. 14.

CROSS-REFERENCES

Section 650 prescribes the general rule regarding the presence of an accused in criminal proceedings. Exceptions to the general rule may be found in s. 650(2) and in ss. 475 and 598 (accused absconding during trial) and s. 544 (accused absconding during preliminary inquiry).

SYNOPSIS

Unless the accused is granted leave not to be present or is removed by order of the court, he or she shall be present for the hearing of the application. The court can issue any order or process required to secure the attendance of the accused.

APPEAL — OFFENDER / Appeal — Attorney General / Disposition of appeal / Effect of decision / Commencement of sentence / Part XXI applies.

759. (1) An offender who is found to be a dangerous offender or a long-term offender may appeal to the court of appeal from a decision made under this Part on any ground of law or fact or mixed law and fact.

(2) The Attorney General may appeal to the court of appeal from a decision made under this Part on any ground of law.

(3) The court of appeal may

(*a*) allow the appeal and

(i) find that an offender is or is not a dangerous offender or a long-term offender or impose a sentence that may be imposed or an order that may be made by the trial court under this Part, or

(ii) order a new hearing, with any directions that the court considers appropriate; or

(*b*) dismiss the appeal.

(4) A decision of the court of appeal has the same force and effect as if it were a decision of the trial court.

(5) [*Repealed*, 2008, c. 6, s. 51.]

(6) Notwithstanding subsection 719(1), a sentence imposed on an offender by the court of appeal pursuant to this section shall be deemed to have commenced when the offender was sentenced by the court by which he was convicted.

(7) The provisions of Part XXI with respect to procedure on appeals apply, with such modifications as the circumstances require, to appeals under this section. R.S., c. C-34, s. 694; 1976-77, c. 53, s. 14; 1995, c. 22, s. 10; 1997, c. 17, s. 6; 2008, c. 6, s. 51.

CROSS-REFERENCES

Right of appeal to the Supreme Court of Canada is given in ss. 691 to 696, Part XXI, in indictable matters. Section 759 provides no more express right. See s. 41 of the *Supreme Court Act*, R.S.C. 1985, c. S-26, for governing provisions in appeal to the Supreme Court of Canada. Although the general rule is that a sentence commences when imposed (s. 721(1)), s. 759(6) provides an exception.

See s. 2 for definition of "court of appeal". No leave of the court or of a judge is required for the rights of appeal under subsecs. (1) and (2).

SYNOPSIS

This section governs appeals under this part. A person found to be a dangerous offender or a long-term offender may appeal a decision made under this Part to the Court of Appeal on any ground of law, fact, or mixed law and fact. The Attorney General may appeal against any decision under this Part, but only on a ground of law.

The Court of Appeal is given broad powers on such an appeal. It may dismiss the appeal, or allow the appeal and find that the offender is or is not a dangerous offender or a long-term offender, or impose a sentence that may be imposed or an order that may be made by the trial court under this Part. It may also direct a new hearing with any directions that it considers appropriate. The procedure on appeals under this section are governed by the procedure for indictable appeals set out in Part XXI.

Under subsecs. (4) and (6), a decision of the Court of Appeal has the same effect as if it were a finding by a trial court and a sentence imposed pursuant to this section is deemed to have commenced when the offender was sentenced by the court by which he or she was convicted.

ANNOTATIONS

Subsection (1) – It was held, considering the predecessor to this subsection, that the appellant need not show that the decision of the sentencing judge was manifestly wrong or demonstrably unfit. Nevertheless, some deference to the findings of a trial judge is warranted and, absent an error of law, the crucial question on appeal is whether the trial judge's findings were reasonable: *R. v. Currie*, [1997] 2 S.C.R. 260, 115 C.C.C. (3d) 205.

While deference is owed to the factual and credibility findings of the sentencing judge, appellate review of a dangerous offender designation is more robust than on a regular sentence appeal: *R. v. Sipos*, [2014] 2 S.C.R. 423, 311 C.C.C. (3d) 121; *R. v. Sawyer* (2015), 328 C.C.C. (3d) 523 (Ont. C.A.). This standard of review applies equally to the dangerous offender designation and the imposition of an indeterminate sentence: *R. v. Bragg* (2015), 332 C.C.C. (3d) 145 (B.C.C.A.).

Subsection (2) – It was held under the predecessor to this section that where the application is dismissed upon insufficiency of the form of notice the Crown may appeal: *R. v. Galbraith* (1971), 5 C.C.C. (2d) 37 (B.C.C.A.), affd [1972] S.C.R. xi, 6 C.C.C. (2d) 188*n*.

Subsection (3) – It was held, considering the predecessor to this subsection, that the Court of Appeal may order a new hearing for sentence on the predicate offence: *R. v. George* (1998), 126 C.C.C. (3d) 384 (B.C.C.A.).

In determining whether to make a dangerous offender finding, the Court of Appeal must consider the nature of the error in law, the evidence and any relevant findings of fact by the trial judge that are not contaminated by the error: *R. v. Dow* (1999), 134 C.C.C. (3d) 323 (B.C.C.A.), leave to appeal to S.C.C. refused 137 C.C.C. (3d) v.

The appeal may be dismissed if an error in law has caused the appellant no substantial wrong or miscarriage of justice. The curative proviso is limited to those circumstances in which there is no reasonable possibility that the verdict would have been any different had the error in law not been made: *R. v. Bedard* (2009), 247 C.C.C. (3d) 275 (Ont. C.A.).

DISCLOSURE TO CORRECTIONAL SERVICE OF CANADA.

760. Where a court finds an offender to be a dangerous offender or a long-term offender, the court shall order that a copy of all reports and testimony given by psychiatrists, psychologists, criminologists and other experts and any observations of the court with respect to the reasons for the finding, together with a transcript of the trial of the offender, be forwarded to the Correctional Service of Canada for information. R.S., c. C-34, s. 695; 1976-77, c. 53, s. 14; 1997, c. 17, s. 7.

CROSS-REFERENCES

No specific use to which the Solicitor General may put this information is indicated by s. 760.

See s. 761(1) for parole review eligibility.

SYNOPSIS

This section provides for the forwarding of a copy of all evidence, records, transcripts and reasons from a proceeding in which a person is declared a dangerous offender to the Solicitor General of Canada.

REVIEW FOR PAROLE / Idem.

761. (1) Subject to subsection (2), where a person is in custody under a sentence of detention in a penitentiary for an indeterminate period, the Parole Board of Canada shall, as soon as possible after the expiration of seven years from the day on which that person was taken into custody and not later than every two years after the previous review, review the condition, history and circumstances of that person for the purpose of determining whether he or she should be granted parole under Part II of the *Corrections and Conditional Release Act* and, if so, on what conditions.

(2) Where a person is in custody under a sentence of detention in a penitentiary for an indeterminate period that was imposed before October 15, 1977, the Parole Board of Canada shall, at least once in every year, review the condition, history and circumstances of that person for the purpose of determining whether he should be granted parole under Part II of the *Corrections and Conditional Release Act* and, if so, on what conditions. 1976-77, c. 53, s. 14; 1992, c. 20, s. 215; 1997, c. 17, s. 8; 2012, c. 1, s. 160(*c*)(v).

CROSS-REFERENCES

Parole eligibility is largely governed by the *Parole Act*, R.S.C. 1985, c. P-2, and regulations thereto.

See ss. 742 to 744, 746 and 747, for parole ineligibility periods in cases of high treason, treason and murder.

SYNOPSIS

This section provides that, where a person is in custody as a dangerous offender, his or her case shall be reviewed for parole seven years after custody commenced and at least every two years thereafter. Where a person has been incarcerated for an indefinite term prior to October 15, 1977, that person's case is to be reviewed for parole at least once a year.

ANNOTATIONS

While the initial sentencing of an offender to an indeterminate term as a criminal sexual psychopath under the predecessor legislation is valid and does not contravene s. 12 of the Charter, his continued incarceration may become unlawful as a result of errors committed by the Parole Board in conducting the review mandated by this section according to the criteria set out in s. 16(1)(*a*) of the *Parole Act*. It is only by a careful consideration and application of these criteria that the indeterminate sentence can be made to fit the circumstances of the individual offender and not violate his rights under s. 12. If it is clear on the face of the record that the Parole Board has misapplied or disregarded those criteria over a period of years with the result that an offender remains incarcerated far beyond the time that he should have been properly paroled resulting in a length of incarceration which is grossly disproportionate to the circumstances of the offence then the board's decision may violate s. 12: *Steele v. Mountain Institution*, [1990] 2 S.C.R. 1385, 60 C.C.C. (3d) 1 (7:0).

Where an inmate sentenced to an indeterminate term seeks to challenge the validity of his continued incarceration on the basis that his rights under s. 12 of the Charter have been infringed, it is preferable that the challenge be by way of judicial review of the decision of the Parole Board refusing to release him, rather than by way of *habeas corpus: Steel v. Mountain Institution, supra.*

An inmate serving an indeterminate sentence as a result of a finding that he was a dangerous offender who has not acquired the status of a parolee cannot review his detention by *habeas corpus*, and the additional claim of Charter relief cannot give the provincial courts jurisdiction. The appropriate mechanism to review the inmate's continued detention lay in the Federal Court: *R. v. Latham* (1997), 113 C.C.C. (3d) 222 (Ont. C.A.), leave to appeal to S.C.C. refused 154 C.C.C. (3d) vi.

PART XXV / EFFECT AND ENFORCEMENT OF RECOGNIZANCES

APPLICATIONS FOR FORFEITURE OF RECOGNIZANCES / Definitions / "clerk of the court" / "schedule".

762. (1) Applications for the forfeiture of recognizances shall be made to the courts, designated in column II of the schedule, of the respective provinces designated in column I of the schedule.

(2) In this Part,

"clerk of the court" means the officer designated in column III of the schedule in respect of the court designated in column II of the schedule;

"schedule" means the schedule to this Part. R.S., c. C-34, s. 696.

CROSS-REFERENCES

This section deals with applications for forfeiture of a recognizance for non-compliance with the conditions thereof. Reference should be made to s. 145(1) and (3) which establish the elements of the default.

Sections 766 to 769 outline the rights of a surety for a person bound by a recognizance to render that person into custody. The judicial interim release provisions of Parts XVI, XXI and XXVII are made applicable by s. 769. No procedure for enforcing a recognizance in default cases is outlined in ss. 770 to 773.

See s. 2 for further definition of "clerk of the court".

SYNOPSIS

This section describes the use of the schedule to this Part. The schedule indicates to whom applications for the forfeiture of recognizances should be made in each province.

RECOGNIZANCE BINDING.

763. Where a person is bound by recognizance to appear before a court, justice or provincial court judge for any purpose and the session or sittings of that court or the proceedings are adjourned or an order is made changing the place of trial, that person and his sureties continue to be bound by the recognizance in like manner as if it had

been entered into with relation to the resumed proceedings or the trial at the time and place at which the proceedings are ordered to be resumed or the trial is ordered to be held. R.S., c. C-34, s. 697; R.S.C. 1985, c. 27 (1st Supp.), s. 203.

CROSS-REFERENCES

See s. 523 for the period for which a recognizance continues in effect.

SYNOPSIS

A recognizance continues to bind the accused and any sureties, notwithstanding that the proceedings have been adjourned or an order changing the venue has been made.

RESPONSIBILITY OF SURETIES / Committal or new sureties / Effect of committal / Endorsement on recognizance.

764. (1) Where an accused is bound by recognizance to appear for trial, his arraignment or conviction does not discharge the recognizance, but it continues to bind him and his sureties, if any, for his appearance until he is discharged or sentenced, as the case may be.

(2) Notwithstanding subsection (1), the court, justice or provincial court judge may commit an accused to prison or may require him to furnish new or additional sureties for his appearance until he is discharged or sentenced, as the case may be.

(3) The sureties of an accused who is bound by recognizance to appear for trial are discharged if he is committed to prison pursuant to subsection (2).

(4) The provisions of section 763 and subsections (1), (2) and (3) of this section shall be endorsed on any recognizance entered into pursuant to this Act. R.S., c. C-34, s. 698.

CROSS-REFERENCES

See s. 523 for the period during which recognizances are in force. Where a defendant is arrested for another offence during a recognizance, s. 765 becomes applicable.

Authorization for a surety to render into custody a person bound by a recognizance is found in ss. 766 to 768. The judicial interim release provisions of Parts XVI, XXI and XXVII are made applicable by s. 769.

Sections 770 to 773 deal with the enforcement of a recognizance in the event of a default by the defendant.

SYNOPSIS

A recognizance continues in effect until the accused is either acquitted or sentenced (subsec. (1)). The court, however, does have the power to commit the accused to prison or require new or additional sureties (subsec. (2)). If the accused is so committed, the existing sureties are discharged (subsec. (3)).

EFFECT OF SUBSEQUENT ARREST.

765. Where an accused is bound by recognizance to appear for trial, his arrest on another charge does not vacate the recognizance, but it continues to bind him and his sureties, if any, for his appearance until he is discharged or sentenced, as the case may be, in respect of the offence to which the recognizance relates. R.S., c. C-34, s. 699.

CROSS-REFERENCES

A defendant arrested for another offence while under recognizance will be held in custody pending trial on the later charge under ss. 515(6)(*a*) or (*c*) and 522(2) unless reasons to the contrary are established by the defendant. Section 524 deals with the circumstances and procedures in the event of misconduct on the part of a defendant or judicial interim release.

Section 524(4) or (8) provide for the cancellation of a recognizance unless the defendant establishes reasons to the contrary under s. 515(10).

See also s. 145(2) and (3), ss. 766 to 769 and ss. 770 to 773.

SYNOPSIS

This section clarifies that an arrest on another charge during the duration of a recognizance relating to a previous charge does not affect that recognizance, which continues in force until the previous charge is dealt with.

RENDER OF ACCUSED BY SURETIES / Arrest / Certificate and entry of render / Discharge of sureties.

766. (1) A surety for a person who is bound by recognizance to appear may, by an application in writing to a court, justice or provincial court judge, apply to be relieved of his obligation under the recognizance, and the court, justice or provincial court judge shall thereupon issue an order in writing for committal of that person to the prison nearest to the place where he was, under the recognizance, bound to appear.

(2) An order under subsection (1) shall be given to the surety and on receipt thereof he or any peace officer may arrest the person named in the order and deliver that person with the order to the keeper of the prison named therein, and the keeper shall receive and imprison that person until he is discharged according to law.

(3) Where a judge, justice or provincial court judge who issues an order under subsection (1) receives from the sheriff a certificate that the person named in the order has been committed to prison pursuant to subsection (2), the court, justice or provincial court judge shall order an entry of the committal to be endorsed on the recognizance.

(4) An endorsement under subsection (3) vacates the recognizance and discharges the sureties. R.S., c. C-34, s. 700.

CROSS-REFERENCES

The judicial interim release provisions of Parts XVI, XXI and XXVII are made applicable by s. 769 to a defendant rendered into custody by a surety. A defendant bound by a recognizance may be rendered into custody under s. 767.

Section 767.1 provides for the substitution of another surety for the one who had made a s. 766(1) application.

See ss. 770 to 773 for default proceedings.

SYNOPSIS

This section provides the means by which a surety can apply to the court to be relieved of his or her obligations under a recognizance.

Upon receipt of the written application of the surety the court shall issue an order for the committal of the accused. Such order is authority for the arrest and detention of the accused (subsecs. (1) and (2)). Once the accused has been committed the recognizance shall be duly endorsed and the surety's obligations will be at an end (subsecs. (3) and (4)).

RENDER OF ACCUSED IN COURT BY SURETIES.

767. A surety for a person who is bound by recognizance to appear may bring that person into the court at which he is required to appear at any time during the sittings thereof and before his trial and the surety may discharge his obligation under the recognizance by giving that person into the custody of the court, and the court shall

thereupon commit that person to prison until he is discharged according to law. R.S., c. C-34, s. 701.

CROSS-REFERENCES

The surety substitute procedure in s. 767.1 is applicable to s. 767 circumstances. See also s. 766 regarding a surety rendering a defendant bound by a recognizance into custody.

Section 769 makes the judicial interim release provision of Parts XVI, XXI and XXVII applicable to s. 767 proceedings. See ss. 770 to 773 for default proceedings.

SYNOPSIS

This section allows sureties to discharge their obligation under a recognizance by delivering the accused into the custody of the relevant court during a sitting thereof prior to the accused's trial.

SUBSTITUTION OF SURETY / Signing of recognizance by new sureties.

767.1 (1) Notwithstanding subsection 766(1) and section 767, where a surety for a person who is bound by a recognizance has rendered the person into the custody of a court pursuant to section 767 or applies to be relieved of his obligation under the recognizance pursuant to subsection 766(1), the court, justice or provincial court judge, as the case may be, may, instead of committing or issuing an order for the committal of the person to prison, substitute any other suitable person for the surety under the recognizance.

(2) Where a person substituted for a surety under a recognizance pursuant to subsection (1) signs the recognizance, the original surety is discharged, but the recognizance and the order for judicial interim release pursuant to which the recognizance was entered into are not otherwise affected. R.S.C. 1985, c. 27 (1st Supp.), s. 167.

CROSS-REFERENCES

Particular persons may be named as sureties by the court under s. 515(2.1).

For review of bail generally, see note under ss. 515 and 522 and provisions of ss. 520, 521, 523 and 524. These provisions may used instead of ss. 766(1) and 767.

SYNOPSIS

This section provides that where an existing surety wishes to be relieved of his or her obligations the court may, instead of issuing an order for the accused's committal (see s. 766(1)), permit the accused to obtain a new surety (subsec. (1)). Once the new surety has signed the recognizance the previous one is discharged (subsec. (2)).

RIGHTS OF SURETY PRESERVED.

768. Nothing in this Part limits or restricts any right that a surety has of taking and giving into custody any person for whom, under a recognizance, he is a surety. R.S., c. C-34, s. 702.

CROSS-REFERENCES

Section 766(1) provides for application for relief from obligations under a recognizance by the surety. Section 767 provides for such release upon the release of the defendant into the custody of the court.

See s. 767.1 for substitution of sureties.

SYNOPSIS

This section preserves common law rights of a surety to deliver the person for whom they are a surety into custody. See Note: E. Armour, "Bail in Criminal Cases", 47 C.C.C. 1 at pages 8 and 9.

APPLICATION OF JUDICIAL INTERIM RELEASE PROVISIONS.

769. Where a surety for a person has rendered him into custody and that person has been committed to prison, the provisions of Parts XVI, XXI and XXVII relating to judicial interim release apply, with such modifications as the circumstances require in respect of him and he shall forthwith be taken before a justice or judge as an accused charged with an offence or as an appellant, as the case may be, for the purposes of those provisions. R.S., c. C-34, s. 703; R.S., c. 2 (2nd Supp.), s. 14.

CROSS-REFERENCES

Section 515 governs the release of accused charged with an indictable offence not listed in s. 469. Section 522 applies where the offence is listed in s. 469.

Section 795 incorporates the provisions of Parts XVI and XVIII in compelling the defendant to appear before a judge. See ss. 816 to 818 and 831 and 832 for applicable appeal provisions.

SYNOPSIS

A new bail hearing is required when an accused has been rendered by a surety and committed to prison.

ANNOTATIONS

Where an accused has been committed to jail pursuant to s. 766 he is to be brought before a justice for a new judicial interim release hearing notwithstanding he has already been committed for trial or that the original release order was made by a judge under s. 520 on a bail review: *R. v. Whalen* (1980), 57 C.C.C. (2d) 10 (Ont. Dist. Ct.).

DEFAULT TO BE ENDORSED / Transmission to clerk of court / Certificate is evidence / Transmission of deposit.

770. (1) Where, in proceedings to which this Act applies, a person who is bound by recognizance does not comply with a condition of the recognizance, a court, justice or provincial court judge having knowledge of the facts shall endorse or cause to be endorsed on the recognizance a certificate in Form 33 setting out

- **(*a*) the nature of the default,**
- **(*b*) the reason for the default, if it is known;**
- **(*c*) whether the ends of justice have been defeated or delayed by reason of the default; and**
- **(*d*) the names and addresses of the principal and sureties.**

(2) A recognizance that has been endorsed pursuant to subsection (1) shall be sent to the clerk of the court and shall be kept by him with the records of the court.

(3) A certificate that has been endorsed on a recognizance pursuant to subsection (1) is evidence of the default to which it relates.

(4) Where, in proceedings to which this section applies, the principal or surety has deposited money as security for the performance of a condition of a recognizance, that money shall be sent to the clerk of the court with the defaulted recognizance, to be dealt with in accordance with this Part. R.S., c. C-34, s. 704; 1997, c. 18, s. 108.

CROSS-REFERENCES
Sections 771 to 773 govern the proceedings taken against the principal and sureties upon a default in a recognizance. Under s. 145(2) and (3), the principal may incur criminal liability for failing to appear or comply.

SYNOPSIS

This section sets out the first step in the bail estreatment process.

Where an accused has breached the terms of a recognizance, a court with knowledge of the facts (usually the court which is otherwise dealing with the matter) will endorse the recognizance setting out: (a) the nature of the breach; (b) the reason for the breach, if known; (c) whether justice has been delayed or defeated; and (d) the name and address of the accused and those of any sureties (subsec. (1)).

The recognizance shall then be forwarded to the clerk of the court (see s. 762(2)) to be dealt with under s. 771 (subsec. (2)). Any moneys deposited as security will also be sent to the clerk (subsec. (4)).

ANNOTATIONS

In *R. v. Mackie* (1977), 38 C.C.C. (2d) 385 (Man. Q.B.), the accused acknowledged in the recognizance that he owed "nil" amount to the Queen if he failed to comply with the conditions while the sureties each acknowledged that they owed $1,000 if the accused failed in any of the conditions. It was held that to be bound by a recognizance the person must acknowledge that he owes a sum of money to the Queen and accordingly the accused was not bound by the recognizance. However, as the sureties did acknowledge their indebtedness and were thus bound by the recognizance and having failed to ensure that the accused attend for his trial they failed to comply with a condition of recognizance and it was ordered forfeited.

Merely endorsing on the certificate the words "fail to comply" does not meet the requirement in subsec. (1)(*a*): *R. v. Gabrielson* (1991), 62 C.C.C. (3d) 571 (Ont. Ct. (Gen. Div.)).

A separate certificate of default of appearance, although not actually endorsed on the back of the recognizance, was held to be adequate in *Re Ingebrigtson* (1961), 37 C.R. 21 (Man. Q.B.).

The recognizance need not be physically in court at the precise time the accused is required to appear and the endorsement under this section may be made at a later time when the recognizance is obtained: *R. v. Wolf* (1982), 65 C.C.C. (2d) 331 (Alta. Q.B.).

Provided that the accused was bound by the recognizance at the time of the non-compliance therewith, the court has jurisdiction under this section to make the endorsement in Form 33, even if the information was stayed by the Crown after the act of non-compliance: *Purves v. Canada (Attorney General)* (1990), 54 C.C.C. (3d) 355 (B.C.C.A.).

The court has some discretion in determining whether a finding of default should be made. The manner in which the issue arises and the degree of the sureties' involvement are proper considerations: *R. v. Parsons* (1997), 124 C.C.C. (3d) 92, 161 Nfld. & P.E.I.R. 145 (Nfld. C.A.).

PROCEEDINGS IN CASE OF DEFAULT / Order of judge / Judgment debtors of the Crown / Order may be filed / Transfer of deposit.

771. (1) Where a recognizance has been endorsed with a certificate pursuant to section 770 and has been received by the clerk of the court pursuant to that section,

(*a*) a judge of the court shall, on the request of the clerk of the court or the Attorney General or counsel acting on his behalf, fix a time and place for the hearing of an application for the forfeiture of the recognizance; and

(*b*) the clerk of the court shall, not less than ten days before the time fixed under paragraph (*a*) for the hearing, send by registered mail, or have served in the manner directed by the court or prescribed by the rules of court, to each

principal and surety named in the recognizance, directed to the principal or surety at the address set out in the certificate, a notice requiring the person to appear at the time and place fixed by the judge to show cause why the recognizance should not be forfeited.

(2) Where subsection (1) has been complied with, the judge may, after giving the parties an opportunity to be heard, in his discretion grant or refuse the application and make any order with respect to the forfeiture of the recognizance that he considers proper.

(3) Where, pursuant to subsection (2), a judge orders forfeiture of a recognizance, the principal and his sureties become judgment debtors of the Crown, each in the amount that the judge orders him to pay.

(3.1) An order made under subsection (2) may be filed with the clerk of the superior court and if an order is filed, the clerk shall issue a writ of *fieri facias* in Form 34 and deliver it to the sheriff of each of the territorial divisions in which the principal or any surety resides, carries on business or has property.

(4) Where a deposit has been made by a person against whom an order for forfeiture of a recognizance has been made, no writ of *fieri facias* shall issue, but the amount of the deposit shall be transferred by the person who has custody of it to the person who is entitled by law to receive it. R.S., c. C-34, s. 705; 1972, c. 13, s. 60; R.S.C. 1985, c. 27 (1st Supp.), s. 168; 1994, c. 44, s. 78; 1999, c. 5, s. 43.

CROSS-REFERENCES

Section 772 deals with execution of a writ of *fieri facias*. Section 773 provides for committal in the event of an insufficiency of property found to satisfy the court.

SYNOPSIS

This section sets out the procedures to be followed after a recognizance has been "marked for estreatment" pursuant to s. 770.

At the request of the clerk of the court (see s. 762(2)) or the Crown a judge shall fix a date for the hearing of a forfeiture application. Notice will then be sent, by registered mail, to the accused and any sureties at least 10 days before the hearing (subsec. (1)).

After giving the parties an opportunity to be heard the judge may grant or refuse the application. If forfeiture is ordered the amount is within the judge's discretion (subsec. (2)).

If all or any part of the recognizance is ordered forfeited the accused/sureties become judgment debtors of the Crown and civil action may be taken to collect the amount owing (subsecs. (3), (3.1), s. 772). Any moneys ordered forfeited are delivered to the Crown (subsec. (4)).

(Note: The *Criminal Code* does not provide an appeal from the decision on a forfeiture application.)

ANNOTATIONS

The onus is on the surety to show why the recognizance should not be forfeited. A rule of total forfeiture absent exceptional circumstances is not necessary. In the vast majority of cases, however, involving relatively small sums, nothing less than total forfeiture will normally suffice. The judge must balance various relevant factors, including: the amount of the recognizance; the circumstances under which the surety entered into the recognizance, especially whether there was any duress or coercion; the surety's means; the surety's diligence; any significant change in the surety's financial position after the recognizance was entered into, especially after the breach; the surety's post-breach conduct, especially attempts to assist the authorities in locating the accused; and the relationship between the surety and the accused. Sureties asserting that they should be relieved from forfeiture of any amount have the obligation to adduce credible evidence to support their position. It is not open to the surety to mount a collateral attack on the appropriateness of the order. In addition, it is open to the court to make a conditional order that the recognizance be forfeited unless the accused is taken into custody by a certain date: *Canada (Minister of Justice) v. Mirza* (2009), 248 C.C.C. (3d) 1 (Ont. C.A.).

In determining that all or part of the recognizance should not be forfeited the court may take into acount that the surety had not properly understood the nature of the obligations he assumed and that the terms of the recognizance had been varied without the knowledge of the surety: *R. v. Sandhu* (1984), 38 C.R. (3d) 56 (Que. S.C.).

Subsection (2) grants the judge a broad discretion to make any order with respect to the forfeiture of the recognizance that he or she considers proper. Though broad, the discretion is to be exercised in a manner consistent with the statutory scheme. Ensuring that defence counsel gets paid is not an appropriate factor to consider: *R. v. Flanders* (2015), 319 C.C.C. (3d) 240 (B.C.C.A.).

It would appear that where a potential surety's property is wholly outside the province in which the release order is made such a surety is not put at risk of having his property taken in execution in the event of default. Accordingly such a person could not be taken as a sufficient surety: *R. v. Martin (No. 2)* (1980), 57 C.C.C. (2d) 31 (Ont. C.A. in Chambers).

A person who lent the accused the money which he deposited in order to comply with the terms of his recognizance has no standing when the Crown seeks to forfeit the recognizance: *R. v. Cochrane* (1981), 60 C.C.C. (2d) 329 (Sask. Dist. Ct.); *R. v. Frenette* (1982), 30 C.R. (3d) 123 (B.C. Co. Ct.). In addition, a surety who has loaned money to the accused for a cash deposit has no standing to seek the return of the monies prior to any actual default by the accused of the conditions of the recognizance: *W. (J.) v. M. (S.)* (1999), 137 C.C.C. (3d) 571 (Alta. Q.B.).

The normal practice is to have money deposited for bail returned to the accused or to the surety who deposited it. The third parties who lent the accused money for use as a deposit were not sureties and it would be improper for the court to make an order returning the money to those third parties, particularly if all of the potentially interested parties were not present on the application by the accused: *R. v. Dodson* (2000), 142 C.C.C. (3d) 134 (Ont. C.A.).

There is no right of appeal from an order of forfeiture made under this section: *R. v. Coles* (1982), 2 C.C.C. (3d) 65 (B.C.C.A.).

Where the accused has not deliberately absented himself and in fact is, to the knowledge of the judge, in custody at the time of the estreatment proceedings then the judge cannot proceed without giving the accused an opportunity to make submissions: *R. v. Gabrielson* (1991), 62 C.C.C. (3d) 571 (Ont. Ct. (Gen. Div.)).

Lawyers, to whom bail moneys have been assigned by their client, are entitled to step into the shoes of the accused. They are not, however, entitled to a more favourable position than that of the accused and, in particular, are not entitled to the treatment of a surety. An accused who has not surrendered to justice has no standing to ask for the return of the recognizance: *R. v. Webster* (1994), 94 C.C.C. (3d) 562, 159 A.R. 278 (Q.B.).

When a lawyer becomes an assignee of bail monies, the lawyer steps into the shoes of the accused in terms of the accused's entitlement to those bail monies. Where the accused absconded, he had no entitlement to the bail monies and defence counsel's entitlement as assignee can be no greater: *R. v. Estephan* (2004), 195 C.C.C. (3d) 94 (Ont. S.C.J.).

LEVY UNDER WRIT / Costs.

772. (1) Where a writ of *fieri facias* is issued pursuant to section 771, the sheriff to whom it is delivered shall execute the writ and deal with the proceeds thereof in the same manner in which he is authorized to execute and deal with the proceeds of writs of *fieri facias* issued out of superior courts in the province in civil proceedings.

(2) Where this section applies the Crown is entitled to the costs of execution and of proceedings incidental thereto that are fixed, in the Province of Quebec, by any tariff applicable in the Superior Court in civil proceedings, and in any other province, by any

tariff applicable in the superior court of the province in civil proceedings, as the judge may direct. R.S., c. C-34, s. 706.

CROSS-REFERENCES

Section 773 provides for committal when writ of *fieri facias* is not satisfied.

SYNOPSIS

This section provides that a writ issued under s. 771 to enforce a forfeiture of a recognizance may be enforced in the same manner as a writ issued civilly through the superior court of the province (subsec. (1)). The costs of executing the writ are also recoverable according to the provincial superior court tariff (subsec. (2)).

COMMITTAL WHEN WRIT NOT SATISFIED / Notice / Hearing / Warrant to committal / Definition of "Attorney General".

773. (1) Where a writ of *fieri facias* has been issued under this Part and it appears from a certificate in a return made by the sheriff that sufficient goods and chattels, lands and tenements cannot be found to satisfy the writ, or that the proceeds of the execution of the writ are not sufficient to satisfy it, a judge of the court may, upon the application of the Attorney General or counsel acting on his behalf, fix a time and place for the sureties to show cause why a warrant of committal should not be issued in respect of them.

(2) Seven clear days notice of the time and place fixed for the hearing pursuant to subsection (1) shall be given to the sureties.

(3) The judge shall, at the hearing held pursuant to subsection (1), inquire into the circumstances of the case and may in his discretion

- **(*a*) order the discharge of the amount for which the surety is liable; or**
- **(*b*) make any order with respect to the surety and to his imprisonment that he considers proper in the circumstances and issue a warrant of committal in Form 27.**

(4) A warrant of committal issued pursuant to this section authorizes the sheriff to take into custody the person in respect of whom the warrant was issued and to confine him in a prison in the territorial division in which the writ was issued or in the prison nearest to the court, until satisfaction is made or until the period of imprisonment fixed by the judge has expired.

(5) In this section and in section 771, "Attorney General" means, where subsection 734.4(2) applies, the Attorney General of Canada. R.S., c. C-34, s. 707; 1995, c. 22, s. 10.

CROSS-REFERENCES

The court in which a show cause hearing shall be heard is prescribed in the Schedule, col. II.

SYNOPSIS

This section provides for the committal of a surety where the amount owing cannot be satisfied through the collection processes of the court (*e.g.*, a writ of execution). The sheriff must certify such inability to satisfy the amount owing. The surety must be given seven clear days notice of the Crown's application in this regard (subsecs. (1) and (2)).

The judge hearing the matter may discharge the obligation or make an order for the imprisonment of the surety (subsec. (3)). Imprisonment shall be for the term imposed by the judge or until the surety is satisfied (subsec. (4)).

ANNOTATIONS

Except where the accused is released by the Court of Appeal, in Ontario application for forfeiture of recognizance is to the Court of the General Sessions of the Peace [now the Superior Court of Justice] and not, for example, to the provincial Court although the failure to appear was in that court: *R. v. Moffatt* (1981), 21 C.R. (3d) 372 (Ont. H.C.J.).

SCHEDULE TO PART XXII.1

(Section 715.3 and subsections 715.32(2) and 715.43(2) and (3))

1. An offence under any of the following provisions of this Act:

(*a*) section 119 or 120 (bribery of officers);
(*b*) section 121 (frauds on the government);
(*c*) section 123 (municipal corruption);
(*d*) section 124 (selling or purchasing office);
(*e*) section 125 (influencing or negotiating appointments or dealing in offices);
(*f*) subsection 139(3) (obstructing justice);
(*g*) section 322 (theft);
(*h*) section 330 (theft by person required to account);
(*i*) section 332 (misappropriation of money held under direction);
(*j*) section 340 (destroying documents of title);
(*k*) section 341 (fraudulent concealment);
(*l*) section 354 (property obtained by crime);
(*m*) section 362 (false pretence or false statement);
(*n*) section 363 (obtaining execution of valuable security by fraud);
(*o*) section 366 (forgery);
(*p*) section 368 (use, trafficking or possession of forged document);
(*q*) section 375 (obtaining by instrument based on forged document);
(*r*) section 378 (offences in relation to registers);
(*s*) section 380 (fraud);
(*t*) section 382 (fraudulent manipulation of stock exchange transactions);
(*u*) section 382.1 (prohibited insider trading);
(*v*) section 383 (gaming in stocks or merchandise);
(*w*) section 389 (fraudulent disposal of goods on which money advanced);
(*x*) section 390 (fraudulent receipts under *Bank Act*);
(*y*) section 392 (disposal of property to defraud creditors);
(*z*) section 397 (books and documents);
(*z*.1) section 400 (false prospectus);
(*z*.2) section 418 (selling defective stores to Her Majesty); and
(*z*.3) section 426 (secret commissions);
(*z*.4) section 462.31 (laundering proceeds of crime).

2. An offence under any of the following provisions of the *Corruption of Foreign Public Officials Act*:

(*a*) section 3 (bribing a foreign public official); and
(*b*) section 4 (maintenance or destruction of books and records to facilitate or hide the bribing of a foreign public official).

3. A conspiracy or an attempt to commit, being an accessory after the fact in relation to, or any counselling in relation to, an offence referred to in section 1 or 2. 2018, c. 12, s. 405 (Sched. 6).

SCHEDULE TO PART XXV

(Section 762)

Column I	Column II	Column III
Ontario	A judge of the Court of Appeal in respect of a recognizance for the appearance of a person before the Court	The Registrar of the Court of Appeal
	The Superior Court of Justice in respect of all other recognizances	A Registrar of the Superior Court of Justice
Quebec	The Court of Quebec Criminal and Penal Division	The Clerk of the Court
Nova Scotia	The Supreme Court	A Prothonotary of the Supreme Court
New Brunswick	The Court of Queen's Bench	The Registrar of the Court of Queen's Bench
British Columbia	The Supreme Court in respect of a recognizance for the appearance of a person before that Court or the Court of Appeal.	The District Registrar of the Supreme Court
	A Provincial Court in respect of a recognizance for the appearance of a person before a judge of that Court or a justice.	The Clerk of the Provincial Court
Prince Edward Island	The Supreme Court	The Prothonotory
Manitoba	The Court of Queen's Bench	The registrar or a deputy registrar of the Court of Queen's Bench
Saskatchewan	The Court of Queen's Bench	The Local Registrar of the Court of Queen's Bench
Alberta	The Court of Queen's Bench	The Clerk of the Court of Queen's Bench
Newfoundland and Labrador	The Trial Division of the Supreme Court	The Registrar of the Supreme Court
Yukon	The Supreme Court	The Clerk of the Supreme Court
Northwest Territories	The Supreme Court	The Clerk of the Supreme Court
Nunavut	The Nunavut Court of Justice	The Clerk of the Nunavut Court of Justice

R.S., c. C-46, Sch. to Part XXV; 1985, c. 11, (1st Supp.), s. 2; R.S. 1985, c. 27 (2nd Supp.), s. 10; 1992, c. 1, s. 58; 1992, c. 51, ss. 40 to 42; 1993, c. 28, Sch. III, s. 35.2 (repealed 1999, c. 3, s. 12); 1998, c. 30, s. 14(*d*); 1999, c. 3, ss. 12, 54; c. 5, s. 44; 2002, c. 7, s. 148; 2015, c. 3, ss. 57-59.

PART XXVI / EXTRAORDINARY REMEDIES

APPLICATION OF PART.

774. This Part applies to proceedings in criminal matters by way of *certiorari, habeas corpus, mandamus, procedendo* and prohibition. R.S., c. C-34, s. 708; R.S.C. 1985, c. 27 (1st Supp.), s. 169.

CROSS-REFERENCES

This part is chiefly concerned with the extraordinary remedies of *certiorari* and *habeas corpus*, and the extent of their applications. The sole reference to *mandamus* or prohibition occurs in s. 784(1). The single reference to *procedendo* occurs in this section. Section 780 provides a parallel procedure.

Extraordinary remedies are generally only available in respect of jurisdictional errors. In a case of excess of jurisdiction, *certiorari* is available to quash an order, and prohibition lies to prevent proceedings or their continuance. *Mandamus* and *procedendo* require a tribunal of limited jurisdiction to exercise that jurisdiction. Detention may be challenged on grounds of authority and jurisdiction through *habeas corpus*. Also see s. 10(*c*) of the Charter and pre-Confederation legislation which may still be in force in the province and the rules of court enacted pursuant to s. 482.

With respect to proceedings in Nunavut, see ss. 573.1 and 573.2.

In accordance with s. 774.1, a person who is the subject of a writ of *habeas corpus* must appear personally in court.

ANNOTATIONS

Applications under the Charter of Rights – In *R. v. Mills*, [1986] 1 S.C.R. 863, 26 C.C.C. (3d) 481 (4:3), the court considered some of the problems raised by the Charter in relation to claims for prerogative relief. The plurality (McIntyre, Beetz and Chouinard JJ.) held that while the provincial superior court is a court of competent jurisdiction within the meaning of s. 24(1) of the *Canadian Charter of Rights and Freedoms* where a Charter violation arises in the context of the court exercising its supervisory jurisdiction over the inferior courts, not all Charter violations are jurisdictional and thus reviewable by way of the prerogative remedies. LaForest J. appeared to envisage a somewhat wider role for the superior court to fill the gap which could arise when a remedy is required and no other court, such as the trial court, is in a position to exercise an effective remedy. The dissenting members of the court (Dickson C.J.C., Lamer and Wilson JJ.) were of the view that original application may be made to the superior court under s. 24(1) and that while the court had a discretion to refuse the application where a more appropriate forum exists, the court could grant a remedy for Charter violations which are jurisdictional in nature.

Certiorari – The court ought not to refuse *certiorari* because of alternative remedies other than appeal unless it is clearly satisfied that those other remedies are more appropriate: *R. v. Dubois, infra*.

Receiving information – The act of a justice in receiving an information under s. 498 is ministerial and accordingly the information is not subject to *certiorari: McDonald v. Alberta (Attorney General)* (1968), 4 C.R.N.S. 362, 66 W.W.R. 111 (Alta. C.A.).

Preliminary inquiry *[Also see notes under s. 548]* – *Certiorari* lies against a justice holding a preliminary hearing only for lack of jurisdiction and a decision concerning the admissibility of evidence, even if erroneous does not affect jurisdiction: *Quebec (Attorney General) v. Cohen*, [1979] 2 S.C.R. 305, 46 C.C.C. (2d) 473 (7:0), revg 32 C.C.C. (2d) 446, 34 C.R.N.S. 362 *sub nom. R. v. Cohen* (Que. C.A.).

Lack of jurisdiction in this context means not merely lack of initial jurisdiction but loss of jurisdiction which can occur where the justice presiding at the preliminary hearing fails to observe a mandatory provision of this Act or where there has been a denial of natural justice. However, mere disallowance of some questions on cross-examination does not result in a loss of jurisdiction: *R. v. Forsythe*, [1980] 2 S.C.R. 268, 53 C.C.C. (2d) 225 (7:0).

Certiorari alone lies to review orders made by a justice on a preliminary hearing only where the grounds relate to the justice's jurisdiction. With respect to quashing a committal for trial on the basis that there was no evidence to support the committal for trial it was held that it cannot be said that the justice acted without jurisdiction unless he commits the accused "without any evidence at all, in the sense of an entire absence of proper material as a basis for the formation of a judicial opinion that the evidence was sufficient to put the accused on trial. That is quite a different question from the question "whether in the opinion of the reviewing tribunal there was evidence upon which a properly instructed jury acting judicially could convict": *R. v. Martin; R. v. Nichols* (1977), 41 C.C.C. (2d) 308 (Ont. C.A.), affd [1978] 2 S.C.R. 511, 41 C.C.C. (2d) 342.

Certiorari also lies to quash an order discharging the accused following a preliminary inquiry where there has been jurisdictional error, as where the judge assumed the jurisdiction of the trial court and applying the standard of proof beyond reasonable doubt purported to dismiss the charge: *R. v. Dubois*, [1986] 1 S.C.R. 366, 25 C.C.C. (3d) 221.

Although there has been a jurisdictional error in the form of a denial of natural justice because the judge presiding at the preliminary inquiry refused to permit the accused to make submissions on certain issues, the superior court judge has the discretion to refuse to issue *certiorari* to quash the order to stand trial because the accused suffered no prejudice since the order to stand trial was inevitable: *R. v. Papadopoulos* (2005), 201 C.C.C. (3d) 363, 196 O.A.C. 335 (C.A.), leave to appeal to S.C.C. refused 201 C.C.C. (3d) vi.

The authority to order an accused to stand trial following a preliminary inquiry is reserved to a justice under s. 548. "Justice" does not include a superior court judge and thus, where the judge allows an application by the Crown to quash an order discharging the accused, the judge must remit the matter to the preliminary inquiry judge to decide whether to order the accused to stand trial: *R. v. Thomson* (2005), 74 O.R. (3d) 721, 196 O.A.C. 39 (C.A.).

Trial rulings – Where a trial judge has embarked upon a trial in the proper exercise of his jurisdiction the superior court will accord him the widest latitude in the conduct of the trial without prerogative intervention, the proper remedy if he errs being by way of appeal at the conclusion of the trial. Once having properly embarked on a trial in which he has jurisdiction, the trial judge has a further jurisdiction to decide all matters of law, including questions as to the admissibility of evidence, necessary for the conduct of the trial and the final disposition of the charge, and the superior court will not exercise its discretion to grant a prerogative remedy: *R. v. Madden* (1977), 35 C.C.C. (2d) 381 (Ont. H.C.J.).

A superior court will intervene by way of prerogative remedies in the course of a trial only in an extraordinary case. Short of conducting himself in a manner that shocks the judicial conscience, a trial judge who has embarked upon a trial, over which he has jurisdiction, is to be left free to complete it and challenges to decisions made by him in the course of the trial must be initiated by way of appeal: *R. v. Madden (No. 2)* (1977), 35 C.C.C. (2d) 385 (Ont. H.C.J.).

An erroneous decision to order disclosure of records in an impaired driving trial was not jurisdictional in nature and therefore should not have been reviewed on *certiorari*: *R. v. Awashish* (2018), 367 C.C.C. (3d) 377 (S.C.C.).

Where the accused had been convicted, *certiorari* was not available to the Crown seeking to overturn a pre-trial ruling of a provincial court judge declaring certain provisions of the *Criminal Code* unconstitutional. The appropriate remedy was a reference pursuant to the

Constitutional Questions Act, R.S.B.C. 1996, c. 68: *R. v. Bhudda* (1998), 128 C.C.C. (3d) 80, 55 C.R.R. (2d) 133 (B.C.S.C.).

***Habeas Corpus* / Procedure** – The application for a writ of *habeas corpus* is actually a two-stage process. In the first stage the judge to whom the application is made must determine whether probable and reasonable grounds for the complaint exist as provided, for example, in Ontario, in s. 1 of the pre-Confederation *Habeas Corpus Act*, S.C. 1866, c. 45. If such grounds are present, the writ issues and merits are determined on the return of the writ. The usual practice, however, in most provinces where the prisoner is represented by counsel, is to collapse both stages into one. However, where a written application is made by a prisoner then the judge must determine whether or not to issue the writ, although usually the formality of issuing the writ is dispensed with, the judge simply ordering the prisoner to be brought before the court to make submissions. In this case the Court of Appeal concluded that the motions court judge erred in refusing to consider the merits of the application made by a prisoner. However, rather than remitting the matter to that judge, it was open to the Court of Appeal to examine the merits itself, the prisoner being present in the Court of Appeal and participating in the argument: *R. v. Olson*, [1989] 1 S.C.R. 296, 47 C.C.C. (3d) 491.

On an application for *habeas corpus* without *certiorari* in aid affidavit evidence is admissible to establish jurisdictional error. The only limitation on the admissibility of extrinsic evidence on an application for *habeas corpus* arises from the conclusive character of the record of courts of superior or general common law jurisdiction: *R. v. Miller* (1985), 23 C.C.C. (3d) 97, 49 C.R. (3d) 1 (S.C.C.) (7:0).

Prerequisites for invoking *habeas corpus* – An accused who is at liberty on interim release on his own recognizance and who has complied with the terms thereof and has not surrendered into custody for the purposes of the application cannot invoke the preconfederation *Habeas Corpus Act* of 1866 (still in force in Ontario) to review his committal for trial: *R. v. Martin; R. v. Nichols* (1977), 41 C.C.C. (2d) 308, 87 D.L.R. (3d) 634 (Ont. C.A.), affd on other grounds [1978] 2 S.C.R. 511, 41 C.C.C. (2d) 342. [Also, see note under s. 548, *supra*.]

Before a writ of *habeas corpus* may issue, the applicant must establish that he is in detention; assert the cause or basis for his detention; complain that his detention is unlawful and establish that there are probable and reasonable grounds for his complaint: *Idziak v. Canada (Minister of Justice)* (1989), 53 C.C.C. (3d) 464, 63 D.L.R. (4th) 267 (Ont. H.C.J.).

Availability of other remedies – *Habeas corpus* was refused where the inmate sought to quash his conviction and sentence made in adult court on the basis that that court lacked jurisdiction since he was a juvenile at the time of the offence. It was held that the accused could appeal the conviction and appeal was thus the appropriate remedy: *R. v. Johnson* (1982), 68 C.C.C. (2d) 65, 31 C.R. (3d) 329 *sub nom. A.-G. B.C. v. Johnson (McLean)* (B.C.C.A.).

Prohibition / General considerations – On an application for prohibition only judicial dignity would require the trial judge to adjourn the case pending disposition of the prohibition application. In the particular circumstances it was not inconsistent with judicial dignity for the trial judge to proceed with the accused's jury trial where the trial was almost at an end when the judge was served with the notice of motion, the matters referred to could be raised on appeal in the event of conviction and a long interruption in the trial would be undesirable: *R. v. Turkiewicz, Barrow and MacNamara* (1979), 50 C.C.C. (2d) 406, 10 C.R. (3d) 352 (Ont. C.A.).

Bias – Where there is no proof of actual bias in the sense, for example, of financial gain, the test is whether the circumstances give rise to a reasonable apprehension, which reasonably well-informed persons could properly have, of a biased appraisal and judgment of the issues to be determined by the tribunal: *Committee for Justice and Liberty v. National Energy Board*, [1978] 2 S.C.R. 369, 68 D.L.R. (3d) 716 (5:3).

Validity of information – Where prohibition is sought on the ground that the information does not disclose a criminal offence, it will be refused unless the statute under which the charge was laid is *ultra vires*: *R. v. Layton, Ex p. Thodas*, [1970] 5 C.C.C. 260, 10 C.R.N.S. 290, *sub nom. Re Thodas* (B.C.C.A.) (2:1).

Where an information falls within a trial court's jurisdiction the judge has exclusive jurisdiction to determine its validity and his decision upholding it is not subject to either a motion to quash or to extraordinary remedy proceedings but only to an appeal against his disposition of the case: *R. v. Jarman* (1972), 10 C.C.C. (2d) 426 (Ont. C.A.).

A trial judge's refusal to quash an information charging an offence within his jurisdiction, is not reviewable by prohibition proceedings: *R. v. Acme Bedding & Felt Co.* (1974), 16 C.C.C. (2d) 292, [1974] 3 W.W.R. 66 (Man. Q.B.).

The correctness of a trial judge's ruling on his interpretation of certain Code sections such as the scope of jury challenge for cause is not reviewable by an extraordinary remedy application: *Re Regina and Jones (Nos. 1 and 2); Re Regina and Daley (Nos. 1 and 2)* (1974), 16 C.C.C. (2d) 338, 2 O.R. (2d) 741 (C.A.) (3:2).

Rulings of trial judge – Where an information shows on its face that an applicable limitation period has expired then the court has no jurisdiction to receive it. The proper remedy is to move by way of motion to quash before the trial judge and prohibition, being a discretionary remedy, should be refused. However, where the expiration of the limitation period is not apparent on the face of the information the accused may move by way of prohibition and attempt to show, by adducing evidence, that the trial judge is without jurisdiction to receive the information: *R. v. Medicine Hat Greenhouses Ltd. (No. 3)* (1977), 37 C.C.C. (2d) 287, [1977] 5 W.W.R. 532 (Alta. S.C.T.D.); affd, but without reference to the point: 45 C.C.C. (2d) 27, [1979] 1 W.W.R. 296 (Alta. S.C. App. Div.), leave to appeal to S.C.C. refused C.C.C. *loc. cit.*

The rulings of a trial judge in such matters as to whether or not to declare a mistrial, as where a Crown witness was seen talking to police officers during a break in his testimony, are within his jurisdiction and prohibition will not lie to review the decision: *R. v. Stewart* (1977), 36 C.C.C. (2d) 5 (Ont. C.A.).

Mandamus / Availability generally – Where an inferior court makes an error in law in the course of actually exercising its jurisdiction *mandamus* will not lie, but where the inferior court makes an error in law which leads it away from exercising lawful jurisdiction this remedy may be invoked: *R. v. Mann* (1971), 4 C.C.C. (2d) 319, [1971] 5 W.W.R. 84 (B.C.S.C.).

This extraordinary remedy, available to require an inferior court to accept its jurisdiction and discharge its duty will not lie where there is another remedy by appeal available: *Cheyenne Realty Ltd. v. Thompson*, [1975] 1 S.C.R. 87, 15 C.C.C. (2d) 49 (5:0).

A finding by the trial judge that the charge is a nullity as the provision of the federal enactment under which it was laid was *ultra vires* Parliament is tantamount to an acquittal and the Crown must therefore appeal to the Court of Appeal rather than apply for *mandamus*: *R. v. Kripps Pharmacy Ltd.* (1981), 60 C.C.C. (2d) 332, [1981] 5 W.W.R. 190, *sub nom. Canada (Attorney General) v. Wetmore Co. Ct. J.* (B.C.C.A.), leave to appeal to S.C.C. refused 38 N.R. 180*n*.

Mandamus is available to review the decision of a judge staying the charges or quashing the information on the basis that the accused's right to trial within a reasonable time as guaranteed by s. 11(*b*) of the *Charter of Rights and Freedoms* has been infringed: *R. v. Thompson* (1983), 8 C.C.C. (3d) 127, 3 D.L.R. (4th) 642 (B.C.C.A.). On the other hand it was held in *R. v. Beason* (1983), 7 C.C.C. (3d) 20, 36 C.R. (3d) 73 (Ont. C.A.), that such a ruling could also be appealed by the Crown under s. 676 and the latter was the preferable route of review.

In exceptional cases the Court of Appeal has original jurisdiction to make an order of *mandamus* but this jurisdiction should be exercised sparingly, the normal practice being to take the matter to the Court of Queen's Bench first: *Re Forest and Registrar of Court of Appeal of Manitoba* (1977), 35 C.C.C. (2d) 497, 77 D.L.R. (3d) 445 (Man. C.A.).

Preliminary inquiry – It was held in *R. v. Depagie* (1976), 32 C.C.C. (2d) 89, 1 Alta. L.R. (2d) 30 (S.C. App. Div.) (2:1), that the principles limiting applications for *certiorari* to cases where the justice conducting the preliminary hearing has lost jurisdiction are equally applicable to an application for *mandamus* with *certiorari* in aid. Assuming a justice was wrong in disallowing certain questions, such error did not cause the court to lose jurisdiction and *mandamus* with *certiorari* in aid would not lie. In cases where the accused desires to question a ruling by the justice, the proper procedure is to conclude the preliminary hearing and then apply for *certiorari* if the defence feels it is available.

Mandamus will not lie at the instance of the Crown to review the decision of a justice ruling inadmissible certain evidence at the accused's preliminary hearing: *R. v. Commisso (No. 2)* (1977), 35 C.C.C. (2d) 237 (B.C.S.C.).

APPEARANCE IN PERSON — HABEAS CORPUS.

774.1 Despite any other provision of this Act, the person who is the subject of a writ of habeas corpus must appear personally in court. 2002, c. 13, s. 77.

CROSS-REFERENCES

For other provisions respecting *habeas corpus*, see s. 782 (defects in form) and s. 784 (appeals).

ANNOTATIONS

Traditionally, the habeas corpus procedure involves two steps. At the first step, the judge considers the inmate's application and decides whether the writ should issue. A person is not the subject of a writ of habeas corpus until the writ has been issued and, thus, has no right to attend at the first stage by virtue of this section. However, it offends the *audi alteram partem* principle to have Crown counsel present making oral submissions in the absence of the inmate. Accordingly, either the application should be dealt with in a single stage (as is permitted by the *Criminal Rules of the Supreme Court of British Columbia*, SI/97-140) with the inmate present or the parties only permitted to file written submissions at the first stage: *R. v. Gustavson* (2005), 193 C.C.C. (3d) 545, 27 C.R. (6th) 159 (B.C.C.A.). Also see *R. v. Olson*, [1989] 1 S.C.R. 296, 47 C.C.C. (3d) 491, noted under s. 774.

DETENTION ON INQUIRY TO DETERMINE LEGALITY OF IMPRISONMENT.

775. Where proceedings to which this Part applies have been instituted before a judge or court having jurisdiction, by or in respect of a person who is in custody by reason that he is charged with or has been convicted of an offence, to have the legality of his imprisonment determined, the judge or court may, without determining the question, make an order for the further detention of that person and direct the judge, justice or provincial court judge under whose warrant he is in custody, or any other judge, justice or provincial court judge, to take any proceedings, hear such evidence or do any other thing that, in the opinion of the judge or court, will best further the ends of justice. R.S., c. C-34, s. 709.

CROSS-REFERENCES

See s. 776 for the special circumstances where a conviction or order can not be removed by *certiorari*. In certain cases of procedural defects made at first instance, ss. 777 and 778 grant the superior court of criminal jurisdiction remedial authority.

See s. 781 for the operation of judicial notice of statutory Acts and rules in place of formal proof so as not to invalidate orders, convictions or other proceedings. See s. 782 for the circumstances in which certain formal defects do not invalidate a warrant of committal.

SYNOPSIS

This section permits the court to take remedial action on an application for *habeas corpus*, even though that detention is unlawful. The judge hearing the matter may order the continued detention of the applicant and direct the judge or other judicial officer under whose process the applicant is detained to do such other thing or hear such evidence as will best further the ends of justice.

ANNOTATIONS

This section is not inoperative by reason of s. 2(*c*) of the Canadian Bill of Rights and may be resorted to although s. 525 of the *Criminal Code* has not been complied with: *Ex p. Gooden* (1975), 27 C.C.C. (2d) 161 (Ont. H.C.J.); *Kenny v. Canada (Attorney General)*, [1977] 5 W.W.R. 393 (B.C.S.C.).

In *R. v. Pomfret* (1990), 53 C.C.C. (3d) 56 (Man. C.A.), while the court did not reach a settled conclusion on the matter, it queried whether this section would violate ss. 9 and 10(*c*) of the Charter if the court, having found that the accused was not lawfully held, nevertheless ordered that the accused continue to be detained.

Notwithstanding the court determines that the accused's detention is unlawful, as where it is demonstrated that the review procedure in s. 525 has not been complied with, the court may still exercise the power under this section and make an order for the further detention of the accused: *R. v. Ferreira* (1981), 58 C.C.C. (2d) 147 (B.C.C.A.).

In *R. v. Demerais* (1978), 42 C.C.C. (2d) 287, 5 C.R. (3d) 229 (Ont. C.A.), the court found that there was no evidence of planning and deliberation and therefore quashed the accused's committal for trial on charges of first degree murder. However, rather than ordering the accused's discharge the court invoked the provisions of this section and remitted the matter back to the magistrate to permit the Crown to call further evidence, if any, on the charges of first degree murder.

This provision does not permit the delegation of powers of the superior court to the lower court: *R. v. Rosete* (2007), 225 C.C.C. (3d) 548 (Ont. C.A.).

WHERE CONVICTION OR ORDER NOT REVIEWABLE.

776. No conviction or order shall be removed by *certiorari*

(*a*) where an appeal was taken, whether or not the appeal has been carried to a conclusion; or

(*b*) where the defendant appeared and pleaded and the merits were tried, and an appeal might have been taken, but the defendant did not appeal. R.S., c. C-34, s. 710.

CROSS-REFERENCES

See ss. 777 and 778 for the circumstances in which a conviction or order cannot, because of irregularity or insufficiency, be held to be invalid on removal by *certiorari.*

See s. 781 for the operation of judicial notice in place of formal proof. See s. 782 for the circumstances in which particular formal defects do not invalidate a warrant of committal.

SYNOPSIS

This section prohibits the removal by *certiorari* of a conviction or order where: (a) an appeal has been taken (regardless of whether it has been carried to a conclusion); or (b) the defendant appeared and pleaded, the merits were tried, and the defendant did not appeal.

ANNOTATIONS

In *R. v. Sanders*, [1970] S.C.R. 109, [1970] 2 C.C.C. 57, 10 D.L.R. (3d) 638, the accused made a second application for *habeas corpus ad subjiciendum* with *certiorari* in aid to direct his release from a sentence of preventive detention following a finding that he was a criminal sexual psychopath. It was held (5:4) that s. 776(*b*) was a bar to the removal by *certiorari* of the preventive detention order. The majority were of the view that Parliament provided in clear terms by s. 776 that in any case falling within its provisions rectification of an error must be by way of appeal only and furthermore the so-called "exceptional cases" involving absence of jurisdiction or denial of natural justice constitute an erroneous refusal to apply this section. Folld: *R. v. Stewart* (1979), 7 C.R. (3d) 165, [1979] 3 W.W.R. 177 (B.C.C.A.).

The limitations of s. 776 do not, by virtue of s. 17 of the *Interpretation Act*, R.S.C. 1985, c. I-21, apply to the Crown: *R. v. Eross,* [1970] 5 C.C.C. 169, 73 W.W.R. 398 (B.C.C.A.). Folld: *R. v. Conley* (1979), 47 C.C.C. (2d) 359, [1979] 5 W.W.R. 692 (Alta. S.C. App. Div.). Similarly: *R. v. Moodie* (1984), 13 C.C.C. (3d) 264 (Ont. H.C.J.).

Only in very rare cases would expediency be sufficient reason for the superior court to grant prerogative relief in a situation where Parliament has created a right of appeal. Thus, even where different aspects of a single order for forfeiture of offence-related property required appeals to different courts, the superior court declined to treat part of the appeal as an application for *certiorari* in order to consolidate the appeal in one court: *R. v. Smith* (2018), 359 C.C.C. (3d) 550 (Ont. S.C.J.).

Once the accused has appeared and entered a plea, even if the judge lost jurisdiction because of a subsequent refusal of an adjournment, the defendant's remedy is by way of appeal and not by *certiorari*: *R. v. Mearns; R. v. Kreutziger,* [1970] 5 C.C.C. 226, 73 W.W.R. 435, *sub nom. R. v. Kreutziger,* 73 W.W.R. 447 *sub nom. R. v. Mearns* (B.C.C.A.) (2:1). Branca J.A., dissented on the ground that the refusal of the requested adjournment resulted in an *ex parte* trial at which the merits of the defendant's case were not tried, resulting in a complete and total nullity of proceedings.

In *R. v. Gallicano* (1978), 42 C.C.C. (2d) 113, [1978] 3 W.W.R. 452 (B.C.C.A.), following a plea of guilty the trial judge imposed a fine but upon learning the accused had a record, imposed a jail sentence. The accused did not appeal but rather applied for *certiorari.* The court in dismissing the application held that whether the second sentence was a nullity, invalid or otherwise ineffective, para. (*b*) of this section precluded resort to *certiorari.* A plea of guilty still constituted a trial on the merits.

Even where the section under which the accused was convicted was later held to be *ultra vires,* this section precludes resort to *certiorari* to quash the conviction: *R. v. Beaupre* (1981), 61 C.C.C. (2d) 92, [1981] 5 W.W.R. 278 (Man. C.A.).

A warrant of committal is not a conviction or order within the meaning of this section: *R. v. Carleton* (1982), 2 C.C.C. (3d) 310 (B.C.C.A.).

CONVICTION OR ORDER REMEDIABLE, WHEN / Correcting punishment / Amendment / Sufficiency of statement.

777. (1) No conviction, order or warrant for enforcing a conviction or order shall, on being removed by *certiorari*, be held to be invalid by reason of any irregularity, informality or insufficiency therein, where the court before which or the judge before whom the question is raised, on perusal of the evidence, is satisfied

(*a*) that an offence of the nature described in the conviction, order or warrant, as the case may be, was committed,

(*b*) that there was jurisdiction to make the conviction or order or issue the warrant, as the case may be, and

(*c*) that the punishment imposed, if any, was not in excess of the punishment that might lawfully have been imposed,

but the court or judge has the same powers to deal with the proceedings in the manner that he considers proper that are conferred on a court to which an appeal might have been taken.

(2) Where, in proceedings to which subsection (1) applies, the court or judge is satisfied that a person was properly convicted of an offence but the punishment that was imposed is greater than the punishment that might lawfully have been imposed, the court or judge

(*a*) shall correct the sentence,

(i) where the punishment is a fine, by imposing a fine that does not exceed the maximum fine that might lawfully have been imposed,

(ii) where the punishment is imprisonment, and the person has not served a term of imprisonment under the sentence that is equal to or greater than the term of imprisonment that might lawfully have been imposed, by imposing a term of imprisonment that does not exceed the maximum term of imprisonment that might lawfully have been imposed, or

(iii) where the punishment is a fine and imprisonment, by imposing a punishment in accordance with subparagraph (i) or (ii), as the case requires; or

(*b*) shall remit the matter to the convicting judge, justice or provincial court judge and direct him to impose a punishment that is not greater than the punishment that may be lawfully imposed.

(3) Where an adjudication is varied pursuant to subsection (1) or (2), the conviction and warrant of committal, if any, shall be amended to conform to the adjudication as varied.

(4) Any statement that appears in a conviction and is sufficient for the purpose of the conviction is sufficient for the purposes of an information, summons, order or warrant in which it appears in the proceedings. R.S., c. C-34, s. 711.

CROSS-REFERENCES

This section is deemed to apply in the circumstances set out in s. 778. Section 781 provides that no order, conviction or other proceeding shall be set aside for reason that evidence which by s. 781(2) shall be judicially noticed has not been given. See s. 782 for the circumstances in which defects in form will not invalidate a warrant of committal in proceedings on *certiorari* and *habeas corpus*.

SYNOPSIS

This section permits a judge hearing an application for prerogative relief to make certain remedial orders.

Subsection (1) provides that a conviction, warrant or order will not be invalidated on purely technical grounds and confers on the court the same curative powers as those exercisable in appeal proceedings.

Pursuant to subsec. (2) corrective steps may be taken with respect to a sentence which exceeds the maximum provided for by law, including remitting the matter to the trial judge.

ANNOTATIONS

This section empowers a court to amend a carelessly recorded conviction to meet a technical objection first raised upon application for *certiorari*: *R. v. Holuboff* (1961), 130 C.C.C. 414 (B.C.S.C.). Folld: *R. v. Ringheim,* [1965] 3 C.C.C. 219 (B.C.S.C.).

The court may on *certiorari* remove a warrant of committal and correct the warrant under subsec. (2) where it appears on the face of the warrant that an illegal sentence was imposed. The imposition of a consecutive sentence in circumstances where there is no power to do so falls within the meaning of subsec. (2): *R. v. Carleton* (1982), 2 C.C.C. (3d) 310 (B.C.C.A.).

Under s. 149, a term of imprisonment imposed for escaping custody may be made concurrent to the sentence the accused was serving at the time of the escape or consecutive to such sentence, but not consecutive to a sentence imposed for some further offence. Where the trial judge mistakenly made an order that the escape sentence be consecutive to the sentence for new offences imposed on that day, then on an application in the nature of *certiorari*, rather than simply quashing the illegal sentence, the court, pursuant to this section, may carry out the obvious intention of the trial judge and reverse the sequence of sentences so that the escape sentence runs consecutive to the time remaining unserved and the new sentences run consecutive to the escape sentence: *R. v. Easton* (1989), 8 W.C.B. (2d) 206 (Ont. C.A.), affd [1991] 2 S.C.R. 209.

IRREGULARITIES WITHIN SECTION 777.

778. Without restricting the generality of section 777, that section shall be deemed to apply where

(*a*) the statement of the adjudication or of any other matter or thing is in the past tense instead of in the present tense;

(*b*) the punishment imposed is less than the punishment that might by law have been imposed for the offence that appears by the evidence to have been committed; or

(*c*) there has been an omission to negative circumstances, the existence of which would make the act complained of lawful, whether those circumstances are stated by way of exception or otherwise in the provision under which the offence is charged or are stated in another provision. R.S., c. C-34, s. 712.

CROSS-REFERENCES

See the cross-references under s. 777.

SYNOPSIS

This section is a non-exhaustive set of examples of cases in which the remedial powers created by s. 777 may be used. These examples are: (a) where a document is in the past tense as opposed to the present tense; (b) where a punishment is imposed which is less than the maximum; and (c) where there has been a failure to negative circumstances which would have made the act complained of lawful.

GENERAL ORDER FOR SECURITY BY RECOGNIZANCE / Provisions of Part XXV.

779. (1) A court that has authority to quash a conviction, order or other proceeding on *certiorari* may prescribe by general order that no motion to quash any such conviction, order or other proceeding removed to the court by *certiorari* shall be heard unless the defendant has entered into a recognizance with one or more sufficient sureties, before one or more justices of the territorial division in which the conviction or order was made or before a judge or other officer, or has made a deposit to be prescribed with a condition that the defendant will prosecute the writ of *certiorari* at his own expense, without wilful delay, and, if ordered, will pay to the person in whose favour the conviction, order or other proceeding is affirmed his full costs and charges to be taxed according to the practice of the court where the conviction, order or proceeding is affirmed.

(2) The provisions of Part XXV relating to forfeiture of recognizances apply to a recognizance entered into under this section. R.S., c. C-34, s. 713.

CROSS-REFERENCES

"Justice" and "territorial division" are defined in s. 2.

By s. 482(1) and (3)(*c*), every superior court of criminal jurisdiction and every court of appeal, respectively, may make rules of court to regulate, *inter alia*, proceedings with respect to *mandamus, certiorari, habeas corpus,* prohibition and *procedendo*.

Procedure in respect of the forfeiture of recognizances is governed by s. 770 to 773 of Part XXV.

SYNOPSIS

This section makes provision for an order requiring that an applicant for *certiorari* agree to prosecute the matter, at his own expense and without wilful delay, by entering into a recognizance with a condition to that effect. The recognizance may also contain conditions with respect to costs.

EFFECT OF ORDER DISMISSING APPLICATION TO QUASH.

780. Where a motion to quash a conviction, order or other proceeding is refused, the order of the court refusing the application is sufficient authority for the clerk of the court forthwith to return the conviction, order or proceeding to the court from which or the person from whom it was removed, and for proceedings to be taken with respect thereto for the enforcement thereof. R.S., c. C-34, s. 714.

CROSS-REFERENCES

This is a parallel procedure to the old remedy of *procedendo*. The issuance of process to compel reattendance is affected by s. 507(8).

SYNOPSIS

This section provides that when a motion to quash is refused, the court order indicating the refusal is sufficient authority for the return forthwith of the original proceeding to the original court or official for enforcement thereof.

ANNOTATIONS

This section makes it unnecessary to invoke the old procedure of *procedendo* returning the proceedings back to the inferior court upon dismissal of the motion to quash: *R. v. Batchelor*, [1978] 2 S.C.R. 988, 38 C.C.C. (2d) 113, 81 D.L.R. (3d) 241 (9:0).

Once the application has been dismissed and the record returned to the lower court pursuant to this section no particular form of notice is required to secure the accused's attendance in the lower court. Thus a summons may properly be used for this purpose and should the accused fail to attend court having been given notice then the judge may issue a warrant for his arrest: *R. v. Batchelor* (1980), 56 C.C.C. (2d) 20, 17 C.R. (3d) 349 (Ont. H.C.J.). [Also now see s. 507(8).]

WANT OF PROOF OF ORDER IN COUNCIL / Judicial notice.

781. (1) No order, conviction or other proceeding shall be quashed or set aside, and no defendant shall be discharged, by reason only that evidence has not been given

- **(*a*) of a proclamation or order of the Governor in Council or the lieutenant governor in council;**
- **(*b*) of rules, regulations or by-laws made by the Governor in Council under an Act of Parliament or by the lieutenant governor in council under an Act of the legislature of the province; or**
- **(*c*) of the publication of a proclamation, order, rule, regulation or by-law in the *Canada Gazette* or in the official gazette for the province.**

(2) Proclamations, orders, rules, regulations and by-laws mentioned in subsection (1) and the publication thereof shall be judicially noticed. R.S., c. C-34, s. 715.

CROSS-REFERENCES

Judicial notice must be taken of all Acts of the Imperial Parliament and Parliament of Canada, pursuant to ss. 17 and 18 of the *Canada Evidence Act*, R.S.C. 1985, c. C-5, which obviates the need for their formal proof. Documentary proof of certain types of proclamation, order, regulation and appointment made under federal or provincial enabling legislation is permitted by ss. 20 to 22 and 24 of the *Canada Evidence Act*.

By s. 782, a warrant of committal is not invalidated by its formal defects.

SYNOPSIS

This section provides that no conviction, order or other proceeding will be set aside or quashed solely by reason of the fact that evidence was not given with respect to proclamations, orders, rules, regulations or by-laws made by the Governor in Council or the Lieutenant Governor in Council, or of matters published in the official government Gazettes (subsec. (1)). Judicial notice is to be taken of such matters (subsec. (2)).

ANNOTATIONS

In *R. v. Steam Tanker "Evgenia Chandris"*, [1977] 2 S.C.R. 97, 27 C.C.C. (2d) 241, 65 D.L.R. (3d) 553 (7:2), the majority of the court held that by virtue of s. 23(1) of the *Statutory Instruments Act, 1970-71-72* (Can.), c. 38 the trial judge was required to take judicial notice of certain regulations published in the *Canada Gazette* and therefore there was no need to consider the Crown's alternative submission that s. 715(2) [now s. 781(2)] required that judicial notice be taken of such regulations. Laskin C.J.C., dissenting as to the effect of s. 23 went on to consider s. 715 [now s. 781] and held that by virtue of s. 708 [now s. 774], s. 715(2) [now s. 781(2)] applied only on proceedings for the prerogative remedies and was not a provision of general application.

DEFECT IN FORM.

782. No warrant of committal shall, on *certiorari* or *habeas corpus*, be held to be void by reason only of any defect therein, where

(*a*) it is alleged in the warrant that the defendant was convicted; and

(*b*) there is a valid conviction to sustain the warrant. R.S., c. C-34, s. 716.

CROSS-REFERENCES

By s. 781, judicial notice must be taken of federal and provincial proclamations, orders, rules, regulations and by-laws, and no order, conviction or other proceeding shall be quashed or set aside and no defendant discharged by reason only that evidence of such matters has not been given.

See the note to s. 781 for other related provisions.

SYNOPSIS

This section states that a warrant of committal is immune from challenge on grounds of defect in form as long as it alleges a valid conviction which exists and which can sustain the warrant.

ANNOTATIONS

In general, on a *habeas corpus* application, the court should only determine whether the face of the warrant discloses lawful authority for detaining a person, and if so, any technical objections should then be dismissed under this section: *Fischer v. Warden of the Manitoba Penitentiary* (1961), 131 C.C.C.101, 35 C.R. 191 (Man. Q.B.).

While it is not an order of the court, a warrant of committal, unless it is invalid on its face, must be considered valid until it is set aside. An error in a warrant of committal having been brought to the attention of the court, the clerk of the court has the power to amend the warrant to conform with the sentence as it was imposed by the trial judge: *Ewing v. Mission Institution* (1994), 92 C.C.C. (3d) 484 (B.C.C.A.).

NO ACTION AGAINST OFFICIAL WHEN CONVICTION, ETC., QUASHED.

783. Where an application is made to quash a conviction, order or other proceeding made or held by a provincial court judge acting under Part XIX or a justice on the ground that he exceeded his jurisdiction, the court to which or the judge to whom the application is made may, in quashing the conviction, order or other proceeding, order that no civil proceedings shall be taken against the justice or provincial court judge or against any officer who acted under the conviction, order or other proceeding or under any warrant issued to enforce it. R.S., c. C-34, s. 717.

CROSS-REFERENCES

"Provincial court judge" and "justice" are defined in s. 2.

See generally ss. 25 to 31 regarding the protection of persons administering and enforcing the law.

SYNOPSIS

This section gives a judge who grants an application for *certiorari* quashing the order of a provincial court judge or justice of the peace the power to make a further order protecting the person who made the order and anyone acting under it from civil proceedings in that connection.

ANNOTATIONS

In making a determination under this section the court should consider where there was clear jurisdiction for the justice of the peace to act whether he acted with bad faith, malice or ulterior motive. Furthermore, where the law required the justice to act, and particularly since his decision involved questions of some difficulty and nicety, an order should be made for his protection: *Royal Canadian Legion (Branch 177) v. Mount Pleasant Branch 177 Savings Credit Union*, [1964] 3 C.C.C. 381, 44 C.R. 35 (B.C.S.C.).

As a general rule a protection order should be made in the absence of misconduct, malice or an oblique motive by the judge of the inferior court: *Mayrand v. Cronier* (1981), 63 C.C.C. (2d) 561, 23 C.R. (3d) 114 (Que. C.A.).

A protection order should not be made where there is some reasonable basis upon which a person complaining of police action might succeed in a civil action: *R. v. Sieger* (1982), 65 C.C.C. (2d) 449, 27 C.R. (3d) 91 *sub nom. Sieger v. Barker* (B.C.S.C.).

APPEAL IN MANDAMUS ETC. / Application of Part XXI / Refusal of application, and appeal / Where writ granted / Appeal from judgment on return of writ / Hearing of appeal.

784. (1) An appeal lies to the court of appeal from a decision granting or refusing the relief sought in proceedings by way of *mandamus, certiorari* or prohibition.

(2) Except as provided in this section, Part XXI applies, with such modifications as the circumstances require, to appeals under this section.

(3) Where an application for a writ of *habeas corpus ad subjiciendum* is refused by a judge of a court having jurisdiction therein, no application may again be made on the same grounds, whether to the same or to another court or judge, unless fresh evidence is adduced, but an appeal from that refusal shall lie to the court of appeal, and where on the appeal the application is refused a further appeal shall lie to the Supreme Court of Canada, with leave of that Court.

(4) Where a writ of *habeas corpus ad subjiciendum* is granted by any judge, no appeal therefrom shall lie at the instance of any party including the Attorney General of the province concerned or the Attorney General of Canada.

(5) Where a judgment is issued on the return of a writ of *habeas corpus ad subjiciendum*, an appeal therefrom lies to the court of appeal, and from a judgment of the court of appeal to the Supreme Court of Canada, with the leave of that Court, at the instance of the applicant or the Attorney General of the province concerned or the Attorney General of Canada, but not at the instance of any other party.

(6) An appeal in *habeas corpus* matters shall be heard by the court to which the appeal is directed at an early date, whether in or out of the prescribed sessions of the court. R.S., c. C-34, s. 719; 1997, c. 18, s. 109.

CROSS-REFERENCES

"Court of appeal" is defined in s. 2.

See s. 675 for the rights of appeal of a person convicted in proceedings by indictment.

See s. 676 for the Crown's rights of appeal.

SYNOPSIS

This section provides for appeals from the granting or refusal of prerogative relief.

Decisions or applications for *certiorari, mandamus*, and prohibition may be appealed to the Court of Appeal (subsec. (1)). (**Note**: Leave to appeal to the Supreme Court of Canada must be obtained under s. 40 of the *Supreme Court Act*.)

Specific rules are set out with respect to *habeas corpus*. (**Note**: The case-law draws a distinction between an application for the writ and a judgment on the merits after the writ has issued. Although historically a two-stage process there is now generally only one hearing at which the merits are determined.)

Where an application for the writ has been dismissed a further application cannot be made on the same grounds unless fresh evidence is adduced. An appeal from such a dismissal lies to the Court of Appeal and, if refused, the matter may be appealed with leave to the Supreme Court of Canada (subsec. (3)). No appeal lies from the simple issuance of the writ (subsec. (4)).

A decision on the merits with respect to an application for *habeas corpus* may be appealed to the Court of Appeal and thereafter, with leave, to the Supreme Court of Canada (subsec. (5)). Such appeals are to be heard as soon as possible (subsec. (6)).

ANNOTATIONS

Subsection (1) – Although this subsection gives an accused a right to appeal from dismissal of an application for *certiorari* including an application to quash an order to stand trial, the accused does not have a right to a stay of the trial proceedings pending the appeal. The power to grant a stay is discretionary, the test being whether the accused can show the existence of a serious question, that unless the stay were granted he would suffer irreparable harm and that the balance of convenience favours granting the stay: *R. v. Boutin* (1990), 58 C.C.C. (3d) 237 (Que. C.A.).

An accused's right to appeal pursuant to subsec. (1) from a decision granting or refusing prerogative relief is not limited by ss. 674 and 675 to appeals following convictions but applies equally to appeals of interlocutory matters. Therefore, the fact that the accused was criminally charged following the filing of his notice of appeal did not deprive the court of jurisdiction to hear his appeal of a decision refusing to quash a search warrant by way of *certiorari*: *R. v. Douglas* (2016), 341 C.C.C. (3d) 314 (Man. C.A.).

A provincial court judge whose ruling is quashed via prerogative writ by the superior court has no standing to appeal the order: *Alberta (Attorney General) v. Malin* (2016), 344 C.C.C. (3d) 420 (Alta. C.A.).

Where an affected party sought to revoke a production order under s. 487.0193(4) and set aside a sealing order under s. 487.3(4), and also sought prerogative relief in the nature of *certiorari*, an appeal to the Court of Appeal lay under this section: *R. v. Vice Media Canada Inc.* (2017), 352 C.C.C. (3d) 355 (Ont. C.A.), affd 2018 SCC 53.

Subsection (2) – In *Kipnes v. Alberta (Attorney General)*, [1966] 4 C.C.C. 387 (Alta. S.C. App. Div.), it was held (2:1) that there being no rule which specifically deals with service of the notice of appeal in this case, it would follow that service in accordance with Rule 39 of the Rules of Court in civil matters would apply.

Subsection (3) – Where the Court of Appeal finds that the superior court judge erred in refusing to issue the writ it need not remit the application to the original judge but rather may deal with application on the merits itself as if the writ had issued, the inmate being present and participating in the application: *R. v. Olson*, [1989] 1 S.C.R. 296, 47 C.C.C. (3d) 491 (5:0).

Subsection (5) – Although costs of a *certiorari* application may be ordered under s. 779, there is no such other substantive authority under the *Criminal Code* for a *habeas corpus* application: *Re Ange,* [1970] 5 C.C.C. 371 (Ont. C.A.).

Where the accused's application for *habeas corpus* had been heard on the merits, treating the writ as having been issued, and dismissed, the appeal procedure is provided by subsec. (5) and the prisoner has no right of appeal to the Supreme Court of Canada. This is the case even where the superior court thereafter refuses to issue a writ on further applications. The prisoner cannot invoke the appeal procedure under subsec. (3). He cannot argue that the application for a writ was "refused' when an earlier application was heard on the merits: *United States of America v. Desfosses*, [1997] 2 S.C.R. 462, 115 C.C.C. (3d) 257.

Part XXVII / SUMMARY CONVICTIONS

Interpretation

DEFINITIONS / "clerk of the appeal court" / "informant" / "information" / "order" / "proceedings" / "prosecutor" / "sentence" / "summary conviction court" / "trial".

785. In this Part,

"clerk of the appeal court" includes a local clerk of the appeal court;

"informant" means a person who lays an information;

"information" includes

(*a*) a count in an information, and

(*b*) a complaint in respect of which a justice is authorized by an Act of Parliament or an enactment made thereunder to make an order;

"order" means any order, including an order for the payment of money;

"proceedings" means

(*a*) proceedings in respect of offences that are declared by an Act of Parliament or an enactment made thereunder to be punishable on summary conviction, and

(*b*) proceedings where a justice is authorized by an Act of Parliament or an enactment made thereunder to make an order;

"prosecutor" means the Attorney General or, where the Attorney General does not intervene, the informant, and includes counsel or an agent acting on behalf of either of them;

"sentence" includes

(*a*) a declaration made under subsection 199(3),

(*b*) an order made under subsection 109(1) or 110(1), section 320.24, subsection 730(1) or 737(3) or section 738, 739, 742.1 or 742.3,

(*c*) a disposition made under section 731 or 732 or subsection 732.2(3) or (5), 742.4(3) or 742.6(9),

(*d*) an order made under subsection 16(1) of the *Controlled Drugs and Substances Act*; and

(*e*) an order made under subsection 94(1) of the *Cannabis Act*;

"summary conviction court" means a person who has jurisdiction in the territorial division where the subject-matter of the proceedings is alleged to have arisen and who

(*a*) is given jurisdiction over the proceedings by the enactment under which the proceedings are taken,

(*b*) is a justice or provincial court judge, where the enactment under which the proceedings are taken does not expressly give jurisdiction to any person or class of persons, or

(*c*) is a provincial court judge, where the enactment under which the proceedings are taken gives jurisdiction in respect thereof to two or more justices;

"trial" includes the hearing of a complaint.

R.S., c. C-34, s. 720; 1972, c. 13, s. 61; 1974-75-76, c. 93, s. 85; 1976-77, c. 53, s. 4; R.S.C. 1985, c. 27 (1st Supp.), s. 170; 1992, c. 1, s. 58; 1995, c. 22, s. 7(1); c. 39, s. 156; 1996, c. 19, s. 76; 1999, c. 25, s. 23; 2002, c. 13, s. 78; 2006, c. 14, s. 7; 2013, c. 11, s. 4; 2018, c. 16, s. 223; 2018, c. 21, s. 26.

CROSS-REFERENCES

Whether an offence is exclusively indictable, prosecutable by summary conviction alone or triable either way (hybrid) is determined by the section creating or prescribing the punishment for the offence.

By virtue of s. 34(1)(*a*) of the *Interpretation Act*, R.S.C. 1985, c. I-21, hybrid offences are "indictable" until the prosecution elects to proceed by summary conviction. Part XXVII applies to the trial of a summary conviction offence as well as to any appeal from a summary conviction trial.

ANNOTATIONS

"prosecutor" – While counsel may not in the same prosecution and at the same time be agent of both the provincial and federal Attorneys General, he can be duly authorized by both so that his authority cannot be disputed: *R. v. Thomas* (1979), 53 C.C.C. (2d) 472 (B.C.C.A.).

The definition in this section applies only to the trial of summary conviction offences and has no application to indictable offences although the accused has elected to be tried by provincial court judge: *R. v. Edmunds*, [1981] 1 S.C.R. 233, 58 C.C.C. (2d) 485 (4:1).

A police officer who was not the informant could only be "agent" for the Attorney General if he were appointed as such by the Attorney General. His superior officer could not appoint him. However, prosecution by a police officer properly appointed by the Attorney General does not offend the fair hearing guarantees in s. 11(*d*) of the *Canadian Charter of Rights and Freedoms*: *R. v. Hart* (1986), 26 C.C.C. (3d) 438 (Nfld. C.A.).

Nor does it offend the fundamental justice and equality guarantees in ss. 7 and 15 of the Charter: *R. v. White* (1988), 41 C.C.C. (3d) 236, 69 Nfld. & P.E.I.R. 91 (Nfld. C.A.).

Further, the court has no discretion to refuse a right of audience to an agent who has been properly designated: *R. v. Maher* (1986), 27 C.C.C. (3d) 476 (Nfld. C.A.).

"summary conviction court" – By virtue of para. (*b*) a justice has jurisdiction to try a Crown option offence where the Crown elects to proceed by way of summary conviction: *R. v. Ashoona; R. v. Jonah* (1985), 19 C.C.C. (3d) 377 (N.W.T.S.C.).

APPLICATION OF PART / Limitation.

786. (1) Except where otherwise provided by law, this Part applies to proceedings as defined in this Part.

(2) No proceedings shall be instituted more than six months after the time when the subject-matter of the proceedings arose, unless the prosecutor and the defendant so agree. R.S., c. C-34, 721; 1997, c. 18, s. 110.

CROSS-REFERENCES

There exists no limitation provision of general application in respect of proceedings on indictment. An accused will have the benefit of s. 11(*b*) of the Charter in terms of being tried within a reasonable time and s. 7 protection against undue delays in the prosecutional process warranting a stay of proceedings or abuse of process.

Summary conviction proceedings are commenced by laying an information in Form 2, pursuant to s. 788(1).

See s. 789 for the formalities of the information. Proceedings against an accused in respect of an offence are instituted by the issuance of process to compel the accused's appearance or by the confirmation of the already issued process.

SYNOPSIS

This section limits the application of this Part to summary conviction proceedings as defined, unless otherwise provided for by law (subsec. (1)). This section also sets the summary conviction offence limitation period of six months from the arising of the subject-matter of the proceedings unless the prosecutor and defendant agree (subsec. (2)).

ANNOTATIONS

Subsection (2) – In *Dressler v. Tallman Gravel & Sand Supply Ltd.*, [1963] 2 C.C.C. 25, 36 D.L.R. (2d) 398 (Man. C.A.), it was held that where a continuing offence was charged, part of which was outside the six-month period of limitation, the information was not void but could be amended by striking the part that was out of time.

An information in respect of a continuing offence which commenced more than six months before the information was laid but continued into the six-month period is valid: *R. v. Belgal Holdings Ltd.*, [1967] 3 C.C.C. 34, [1967] 1 O.R. 405 (H.C.J.).

A summons issued more than six months after the time when the subject-matter of the proceedings arose on the presentment of an information laid within the six months is valid: *R. v. Southwick, ex p. Gilbert Steel Ltd.*, [1968] 1 C.C.C. 356, 2 C.R.N.S. 46 (Ont. C.A.).

It is not open to the court to convict an accused out of a summary conviction offence included in an indictable offence where the information was laid outside the six-month limitation period: *R. v. Chausse* (1986), 28 C.C.C. (3d) 412, 51 C.R. (3d) 332 (Que. C.A.); *R. v. Hoskins* (1929), 52 C.C.C. 365, [1930] 1 W.W.R. 85 (Alta. S.C.); *R. v. Halcrow* (1993), 80 C.C.C. (3d) 320 (B.C.C.A.), affd [1995] 1 S.C.R. 440, 95 C.C.C. (3d) 94.

An election by the Crown to proceed by way of summary conviction on a hybrid offence is a nullity where the information was laid outside the six-month limitation period: *R. v. Phelps* (1993), 79 C.C.C. (3d) 550 (Ont. C.A.). However, in *R. v. Dudley* (2008), 231 C.C.C. (3d) 80, the Alberta Court of Appeal held that, where the Crown has erroneously elected to proceed summarily, the Crown can re-elect on the original information once the error is discovered, unless an abuse of process through improper Crown motive is established (leave to appeal to S.C.C. granted 233 C.C.C. (3d) vi).

In calculating the six-month limitation period, the day of the alleged offence is excluded and the entire day with the same calendar number is included: *Society for the Prevention of Cruelty to Animals (Newfoundland and Labrador) v. Harding* (2002), 163 C.C.C. (3d) 547 (Nfld. & Lab. C.A.).

The information itself, however, is not void and remains a valid information charging an indictable offence. Even though due to a mistake the trial had initially proceeded as a summary conviction matter, the Crown could change its election and the matter could proceed by way of indictment. Since the accused was never in jeopardy *autrefois acquit*, had no application and the trial judge could only stay the proceedings as an abuse of process if it was one of the clearest of cases in that there was overwhelming evidence that the proceedings were unfair to the point that they were contrary to the interests of justice: *R. v. Kelly* (1998), 128 C.C.C. (3d) 206 (Ont. C.A.).

At least with the accused's consent, the Crown may re-elect to proceed by way of summary conviction even though the preliminary inquiry has commenced. The judge would, however, have the ultimate decision to permit or deny such a re-election. Rare and exceptional cases may arise where a joint request to permit the Crown to re-elect to proceed summarily should be refused in view of the judge's overall responsibility to safeguard the integrity of the judicial process: *R. v. Linton* (1994), 90 C.C.C. (3d) 528 (Ont. Ct. (Gen. Div.)).

This section does not require that the defendant personally signify his agreement to extend the limitation period and the judge need not conduct an inquiry to ensure that the defendant is fully aware of his or her rights before accepting the communication from counsel. The defendant is bound by such a communication unless the court record discloses that some issue or question was raised in court that signalled a lack of understanding by the defendant: *R. v. Chern* (2005), 194 C.C.C. (3d) 431 (Alta. C.A.), leave to appeal to S.C.C. refused 196 C.C.C. (3d) vi.

Where a trial in respect of a hybrid offence proceeds before summary conviction court, there is a presumption that the Crown has elected to proceed summarily. If proceedings are instituted more than six months after the date of the commission of the offence, and the parties do not waive the limitation period, the appropriate remedy is to declare a mistrial. The Crown may then reinstitute proceedings by way of indictment, except where this would amount to an abuse of process. Where the accused does not consent to prosecution of a summary conviction offence outside the limitation period, the proceedings are a nullity and do not operate as a bar on the Crown's ability to then proceed by indictment: *R. v. Dudley* (2009), 249 C.C.C. (3d) 421 (S.C.C.).

Punishment

GENERAL PENALTY / Imprisonment in default where not otherwise specified.

787. (1) Unless otherwise provided by law, everyone who is convicted of an offence punishable on summary conviction is liable to a fine of not more than five thousand dollars or to a term of imprisonment not exceeding six months or to both.

(2) Where the imposition of a fine or the making of an order for the payment of money is authorized by law, but the law does not provide that imprisonment may be imposed in default of payment of the fine or compliance with the order, the court may order that in default of payment of the fine or compliance with the order, as the case may be, the defendant shall be imprisoned for a period not exceeding six months. R.S., c. C-34, s. 722; R.S.C. 1985, c. 27 (1st Supp.), s. 171(1); 2008, c. 18, s. 44.

(3) to (11) [*Repealed*, R.S.C. 1985, c. 27 (1st Supp.), s. 171(2).]

CROSS-REFERENCES

The formula for calculating the amount of time to be imposed in default of payment of a fine is set out in ss. 734 and 734.8. The procedure for making an order imposing a fine is set out in ss. 734.1 and 734.2. Procedures for enforcing payment of a fine short of imprisonment are set out in ss. 734.5 (refusing or suspension of licences, permits, etc.) and 734.6 (civil enforcement).

Section 735(1)(*b*) imposes a maximum fine not exceeding $100,000 for organizations convicted of summary conviction offences subject to exceptions.

Section 736 sets out a fine-option program under which an individual accused may discharge a fine wholly or in part. Such programs are not provided for in all provinces.

Unless the offender establishes that undue hardship would result, the court is required to impose a victim surcharge in accordance with s. 737.

SYNOPSIS

Unless otherwise provided, the maximum penalty for a summary conviction offence is a fine of $5000 and/or six months' imprisonment (subsec. (1)).

Unless otherwise provided, the maximum period of imprisonment for non-payment of a fine is six months (subsec. (2)).

ANNOTATIONS

Subsection (1) – In determining a fit sentence for a hybrid offence prosecuted summarily, the principle of the worst offence and worse offence no longer operate as a constraint on the imposition of a maximum sentence where it is otherwise appropriate: *R. v. S. (K.S.T.)*, [2008] 3 S.C.R. 309, 237 C.C.C. (3d) 129.

This section does not limit the sentence for criminal contempt by summary procedure to six months, because criminal contempt is a common law offence preserved by s. 9 of the Code: *R. v. Krawczyk* (2010), 264 C.C.C. (3d) 511 (B.C.C.A.), leave to appeal to S.C.C. refused 264 C.C.C. (3d) iv.

Subsection (2) – It is open to the court to pass a sentence that does not provide for imprisonment in default of payment of a fine, leaving recovery thereof to civil process. This section does not offend the *Canadian Bill of Rights*: *R. v. Natrall* (1972), 9 C.C.C. (2d) 390 (B.C.C.A.) (2:1).

This subsection should not be used routinely as a practical method for the Crown to enforce the collection of its financial penalties. Rather, the court should consider what, if any, rehabilitation or deterrence will occur if the accused is required to serve a term of imprisonment if he is unable to pay the fine within the time specified: *R. v. Yamelst* (1975), 22 C.C.C. (2d) 502 (B.C.S.C.). Similarly: *R. v. Deeb*; *R. v. Wilson* (1986), 28 C.C.C. (3d) 257 (Ont. Prov. Ct.).

Information

COMMENCEMENT OF PROCEEDINGS / One justice may act before the trial.

788. (1) Proceedings under this Part shall be commenced by laying an information in Form 2.

(2) Notwithstanding any other law that requires an information to be laid before or to be tried by two or more justices, one justice may

(*a*) receive the information;

(*b*) issue a summons or warrant with respect to the information; and

(*c*) do all other things preliminary to the trial. R.S., c. C-34, s. 723.

CROSS-REFERENCES

Proceedings must be instituted within six months of the occurrence of the subject matter of the proceedings, under s. 786(2).

An information in Form 2 may charge more than one offence or relate to more than one matter of complaint as long as each is set out in a separate count. The information must be in writing and under oath. The Rules of criminal pleadings in ss. 581 to 593 and s. 601 of Part XX apply to summary conviction proceedings under s. 795 with modifications. There is no need to set out any exception, exemption, proviso, excuse or qualification in an information in summary conviction proceedings under s. 794.

SYNOPSIS

This section prescribes the form for the information which commences the proceedings under this Part and provides that a single justice may receive that information, issue a summons or warrant or do any other preliminary thing, notwithstanding any requirement, as is found in some other federal legislation, that two or more justices be present.

ANNOTATIONS

An information includes the face and back thereof and where the title of the person taking the information is set out on the back of the information but not under his signature on the jurat the information is valid. Such deviation from Form 2 is one permitted by s. 841: *R. v. Deal* (1978), 38 C.C.C. (2d) 425 (N.S.S.C. App. Div.).

Pursuant to this section, an information charging an offence contrary to the *Excise Act*, R.S.C. 1985, c. 15, which Act requires that a prosecution be brought before a police or stipendiary magistrate or "before any two justices of the peace", may be laid before a single justice: *R. v. Keefe* (1990), 57 C.C.C. (3d) 573 (P.E.I.S.C.).

FORMALITIES OF INFORMATION / No reference to previous convictions.

789. (1) In proceedings to which this Part applies, the information

(*a*) shall be in writing and under oath; and

(*b*) may charge more than one offence or relate to more than one matter of complaint, but where more than one offence is charged or the information relates to more than one matter of complaint, each offence or matter of complaint, as the case may be, shall be set out in a separate count.

(2) No information in respect of an offence for which, by reason of previous convictions, a greater punishment may be imposed shall contain any reference to previous convictions. R.S., c. C-34, s. 724.

CROSS-REFERENCES

The rules of criminal pleadings in ss. 581 to 593 and s. 601 of Part XX apply to summary conviction proceedings under s. 795 with modifications. There is no need to set out any exception, exemption, proviso, excuse or qualification in an information or count in summary conviction proceedings under s. 794. See s. 664 for similar provision to s. 789(2).

Sections 665 to 667 permit the introduction of evidence of previous convictions. Such evidence applies to summary conviction proceedings under s. 795. Also see *Canada Evidence Act*, R.S.C. 1985, c. C-5, s. 12.

SYNOPSIS

This section provides that informations are to be written and under oath and shall divide charges or complaints into separate counts (subsec. (1)). It also provides that no information shall contain references to previous convictions where such convictions might result in a greater punishment (subsec. (2)).

ANNOTATIONS

Signature of justice of the peace [Also see notes under s. 504] – In *R. v. Welsford,* [1968] 1 C.C.C. 1 (Ont. C.A.), it was held that a rubber-stamped facsimile of the signature of a justice of the peace on the jurat invalidated an information on the ground that the use of such a facsimile, which could be applied by anyone, instead of his own signature, which has characteristics that could hardly be denied by him, was an insufficient method of evidencing the administration of a solemn oath on an information: affd [1969] S.C.R. 438, [1969] 4 C.C.C. 1 (9:0).

Defects in jurat [Also see notes under s. 504] – A typographical error in the jurat so that the year in which the information was sworn is not shown cannot operate to nullify the information. The insertion of the date in the jurat is merely evidence that the oath was administered on a certain date and the date is only relevant and material where the issue of a limitation period arises: *R. v. Dean* (1985), 17 C.C.C. (3d) 410 (Alta. Q.B.).

Belief of informant – Failure of the informant, who did not have personal knowledge of the alleged offence, to employ the alternative phrase "reasonable and probable grounds to believe and does believe" in his information constitutes a failure to comply with the Code and in the absence of the appropriate amendment before the evidence was heard, the conviction must be quashed: *R. v. Lepage,* [1969] 1 C.C.C. 187 (Ont. H.C.J.).

The word "oath" includes a solemn affirmation. Accordingly, an information which is affirmed is valid: *R. v. Netley,* [1983] 5 W.W.R. 508 (B.C.S.C.).

There must not be a wilful disregard of the statutory requirements of laying an information; there need only be reasonable compliance with those provisions. Accordingly, where the informant's belief was conclusive within the bounds of reasonableness an information sworn on positive, rather than reasonable and probable grounds, was upheld: *R. v. McGuffey* (1972), 17 C.R.N.S. 393, [1972] 2 W.W.R. 462 (Sask. Dist. Ct.).

An information regular on its face is presumed to be valid and if the defendant claims a latent defect such that the informant did not have reasonable and probable grounds to believe the alleged offence had been committed, then the onus is upon him to demonstrate his claim upon a balance of probabilities: *R. v. Peavoy* (1974), 15 C.C.C. (2d) 97 (Ont. H.C.J.).

Where it was shown that the officer who swore the information had no knowledge whatsoever of the offence despite having sworn that she had reasonable grounds to believe the accused had committed it, the information was a nullity. Lack of reasonable grounds is neither a defect in form nor substance and cannot give rise to an amendment under s. 601: *R. v. Awad* (2015), 321 C.C.C. (3d) 107 (N.S.C.A.).

Duplicity – The primary test for duplicity is "does the accused know the case he has to meet, or is he prejudiced in the preparation of his defence by ambiguity in the charge?" A charge that the accused "did discharge, or cause to be discharged, or permitted to be discharged, or deposited materials" into a river contrary to s. 32(1) of the *Ontario Water Resources Act*, R.S.O. 1970, c. 332, is not duplicitous within this test. There is nothing ambiguous or uncertain in the charge and the accused knows the case it has to meet. The gist of the offence is pollution which may be committed in one or more of several modes: *R. v. City of Sault Ste. Marie*, [1978] 2 S.C.R. 1299, 40 C.C.C. (2d) 353 (9:0).

Where an information is defective by reason of duplicity it is not null and void *ab initio* but is capable even after the expiry of a limitation period of being amended and resworn to cure the defect: *R. v. Baldassara* (1973), 11 C.C.C. (2d) 17 (Ont. H.C.J.).

Presence of information in court – There is no requirement that the information be physically present in court during every step of the proceedings: *R. v. Perrault* (1982), 65 C.C.C. (2d) 279 (Sask. C.A.); *Veltri and Veltri Stamping Co. (Re)* (1986), 17 O.A.C. 81 (C.A.).

Subsection (2) – The inadvertent reference by a Crown witness to the fact that the accused had been served with a notice seeking a greater penalty by reason of a previous conviction is not grounds to dismiss the charge: *R. v. Peters* (1991), 35 M.V.R. (2d) 14, 96 Sask. R. 177 (Q.B.).

Other notes – The date of the offence in an information is only an allegation and may not be treated as evidence by a court: *R. v. Walker,* [1968] 2 C.C.C. 150 (B.C.S.C.).

Although the use of a stamped signature of the informant in an information is to be deprecated, his manual signature is not required: *R. v. Burton,* [1970] 3 C.C.C. 381 (Ont. H.C.J.).

The prefacing of two separate counts with a common date and place of the offence does not invalidate the information: *R. v. Schille* (1976), 28 C.C.C. (2d) 230 (B.C.C.A.).

ANY JUSTICE MAY ACT BEFORE AND AFTER TRIAL / Two or more justices.

790. (1) Nothing in this Act or any other law shall be deemed to require a justice before whom proceedings are commenced or who issues process before or after the trial to be the justice or one of the justices before whom the trial is held.

(2) Where two or more justices have jurisdiction with respect to proceedings, they shall be present and act together at the trial, but one justice may thereafter do anything that is required or is authorized to be done in connection with the proceedings. R.S., c. C-34, s. 725; 1974-75-76, c. 93, s. 86.

(3) and (4) [*Repealed*, R.S.C. 1985, c. 27 (1st Supp.), s. 172.]

CROSS-REFERENCES

Subsection (1) permits different justices to receive the information, issue process and adjourn the matter from time to time until trial in the application of ss. 798 to 803. Another summary conviction court may continue summary conviction proceedings under ss. 669.1 and 669.2 rendered applicable to Part XXVII by s. 795. Trials by two or more justices of the peace seem anachronistic in light of s. 483 and para. (*c*) of the definition "summary conviction court" in s. 785.

SYNOPSIS

This section states that the justice who issues process, before or after trial or before whom the trial is commenced, need not be the justice before whom the trial is held (subsec. (1)). Also, where two or more justices are required, they must act together at trial, but any one of them may deal with post-trial matters (subsec. (2)).

791. [*Repealed*, R.S.C. 1985, c. 27 (1st Supp.), s. 173.]

792. [*Repealed* (with heading), R.S.C. 1985, c. 27 (1st Supp.), s. 174.]

793. [*Repealed*, R.S.C. 1985, c. 27 (1st Supp.), s. 175.]

NO NEED TO NEGATIVE EXCEPTION, ETC.

794. (1) No exception, exemption, proviso, excuse or qualification prescribed by law is required to be set out or negatived, as the case may be, in an information. R.S., c. C-34, s. 730; 2018, c. 29, s. 68.

(2) [*Repealed*, 2018, c. 29, s. 68.]

CROSS-REFERENCES

The rules of criminal pleadings in ss. 581 to 593 and s. 601 of Part XX apply to summary conviction proceedings under s. 795, with modifications. No comparable provision exists for proceedings upon indictment.

SYNOPSIS

This section provides that an exemption, or other proviso under which the accused might have a defence, need not be negatived or referred to in the information (subsec. (1)). The onus of proving the applicability of the exculpatory proviso rests on the accused, and the prosecutor need not prove the inapplicability even if the proviso *is* negatived in the information (subsec. (2)).

ANNOTATIONS

It is only necessary in an information for the Crown to allege the unlawful commission of an offence at a time and place, and the inclusion of any clauses negativing any exceptions to the offence, as enumerated in the offence section, is surplusage and does not cast any further onus of proof upon the Crown: *R. v. Hundt* (1971), 3 C.C.C. (2d) 279 (Alta. S.C. App. Div.).

Subsection (2) applies in narrow circumstances, usually regulatory offences, where a status in law has been conferred upon the accused who otherwise would be culpable. It has no application to a defence similar to the defence of duress set out in s. 335(1.1): *R. v. H. (P.)* (2000), 143 C.C.C. (3d) 223 (Ont. C.A.).

By virtue of subsec. (2), an accused who asserts a "reasonable excuse" for failing or refusing to comply with a breathalyzer demand bears the burden of proving the factual foundation for that excuse on a balance of probabilities: *R. v. Goleski* (2014), 307 C.C.C. (3d) 1 (B.C.C.A.), affirmed [2015] 1 S.C.R. 399, 320 C.C.C. (3d) 433.

It has been held that the provincial equivalent of this subsection does not offend the guarantee to the presumption of innocence in s. 11(*d*) of the *Canadian Charter of Rights and Freedoms*: *R. v. Lee's Poultry Ltd.* (1985), 17 C.C.C. (3d) 539 (Ont. C.A.).

R. v. Lee's Poultry Ltd., supra was followed in *R. v. Daniels* (1990), 60 C.C.C. (3d) 392 (B.C.C.A.), a prosecution under the *Fisheries Act* (Can.) where it was held that the Crown need not prove that the accused did not have a Minister's permit to take shellfish in a contaminated area.

Application

APPLICATION OF PARTS XVI, XVIII, XVIII.1, XX and XX.1.

795. The provisions of Parts XVI and XVIII with respect to compelling the appearance of an accused before a justice, and the provisions of Parts XVIII.1, XX and XX.1, in so far as they are not inconsistent with this Part, apply, with any necessary modifications, to proceedings under this Part. R.S.C. 1985, c. 27 (1st Supp.), s. 176; 1991, c. 43, s. 7; 2011, c. 16, s. 16.

CROSS-REFERENCES

For the provisions of Part XX which are incorporated, see ss. 581 to 593 for rules of pleading and joinder, ss. 601, 794, 606 to 610 and 613 regarding pleas.

SYNOPSIS

This section imports the procedures for compelling the appearance of the accused from Parts XVI, XVIII, XX and XX.1 into summary conviction proceedings.

796. [*Repealed*, R.S.C. 1985, c. 27 (1st Supp.), s. 176.]

797. [*Repealed*, R.S.C. 1985, c. 27 (1st Supp.), s. 176.]

Trial

JURISDICTION.

798. Every summary conviction court has jurisdiction to try, determine and adjudge proceedings to which this Part applies in the territorial division over which the person who constitutes that court has jurisdiction. R.S., c. C-34, s. 733.

CROSS-REFERENCES

Terms of the appointment of the court will determine the territorial jurisdiction in which a summary conviction court has jurisdiction. See ss. 476 to 481 for examples of *Criminal Code* provisions extending territorial jurisdiction.

ANNOTATIONS

A case is deemed to have properly proceeded in the summary conviction court where the Crown, on an ambivalent offence, failed to make its election as to mode of procedure: *R. v. Robert* (1973), 13 C.C.C. (2d) 43 (Ont. C.A.).

Once the accused is convicted and sentenced the summary conviction court is *functus officio* and has no jurisdiction to declare a mistrial: *R. v. Conley* (1979), 47 C.C.C. (2d) 359 (Alta. S.C. App. Div.).

Nor does the court have power to issue a warrant for arrest of an accused who fails to comply with a term of a probation order that he appear before the court on a specified day: *R. v. Langlois* (1985), 25 C.C.C. (3d) 191 (Que. S.C.).

No judge of the summary conviction court has jurisdiction to hear a pre-trial application, such as an application for an order allowing a defence expert access to the breathalyzer machine used to analyze samples of the accused's breath: *R. v. Delaney* (1989), 48 C.C.C. (3d) 276 (N.S.C.A.) *sub nom. R. v. How*.

The phrase "territorial division" should be broadly interpreted to mean the entire province of Ontario. Accordingly, there is no jurisdictional impediment to hearing a matter that is alleged to have occurred in a nearby judicial region: *R. v. Ponnuthurai* (2002), 170 C.C.C. (3d) 440 (Ont. C.J.).

A superior court of criminal jurisdiction is not a "summary conviction court" as defined in s. 785 and therefore has no authority to try summary conviction offences: *R. v. E. (D.M.)* (2014), 313 C.C.C. (3d) 70 (Ont. C.A.).

NON-APPEARANCE OF PROSECUTOR.

799. Where, in proceedings to which this Part applies, the defendant appears for the trial and the prosecutor, having had due notice, does not appear, the summary conviction court may dismiss the information or may adjourn the trial to some other time upon such terms as it considers proper. R.S., c. C-34, s. 734.

CROSS-REFERENCES

Section 803 contains the general authority to adjourn summary conviction proceedings. See s. 840 for scale of fees. A summary conviction court may award and order such costs as it considers reasonable and consistent with the scale of fees, pursuant to s. 809.

The informant, Attorney General or his agent may appeal to the appeal court from an order dismissing an information, under s. 813(*b*)(i).

See s. 812 for definition of "appeal court".

SYNOPSIS

This section allows for dismissal of the information or adjournment of the trial by the summary conviction court where, on due notice, the defendant appears and the prosecutor does not.

ANNOTATIONS

Where the prosecutor gives evidence of a merely formal nature, such as to prove service of a subpoena, this does not result in the prosecutor's case being vacant and does not constitute grounds for dismissal of the Crown's case for want of prosecution: *R. v. Hayward* (1981), 59 C.C.C. (2d) 134, 32 Nfld. & P.E.I.R. 465 (Nfld. C.A.).

This provision and s. 803(4) set out when an information may be dismissed. Both refer to a "trial". Therefore, a provincial court judge does not have jurisdiction to dismiss an information for want of prosecution on a remand appearance that is not a trial date: *R. v. Sauve* (2016), 340 C.C.C. (3d) 377 (Sask. C.A.).

WHEN BOTH PARTIES APPEAR / Counsel or agent / Video links / Appearance by organization.

800. (1) Where the prosecutor and defendant appear for the trial, the summary conviction court shall proceed to hold the trial.

(2) A defendant may appear personally or by counsel or agent, but the summary conviction court may require the defendant to appear personally and may, if it thinks fit, issue a warrant in Form 7 for the arrest of the defendant and adjourn the trial to await his appearance pursuant thereto.

(2.1) Where the court so orders and the defendant agrees, the defendant who is confined in prison may appear by closed-circuit television or any other means that allow the court and the defendant to engage in simultaneous visual and oral communication, if the defendant is given the opportunity to communicate privately with counsel, in a case in which the defendant is represented by counsel.

(3) Where the defendant is an organization, it shall appear by counsel or agent and, if it does not appear, the summary conviction court may, on proof of service of the summons, proceed *ex parte* to hold the trial. R.S., c. C-34, s. 735; 1997, c. 18, s. 111; 2003, c. 21, s. 21.

CROSS-REFERENCES

"Organization" is defined in s. 2. The procedure in summary conviction trials is governed by the provisions of ss. 801 to 803 and those of Part XX, incorporated in summary conviction proceedings by s. 795 to the extent they are consistent with Part XXVII.

A summary conviction trial of either an individual or organization may be held *ex parte* where either has been properly served and has failed to appear or remain in attendance as required.

Sections 804 to 809 outline the adjudicative powers and authority of the summary conviction court. See ss. 812 to 838 for appeal procedures.

Under s. 848, if an accused who is in prison does not have access to legal advice, the court shall, before permitting the accused to appear by means of communication that allows the court and the accused to engage in simultaneous visual and oral communication, be satisfied that the accused will be able to understand the proceedings and that any decisions made by the accused during the proceedings will be voluntary.

SYNOPSIS

This section provides that, where both defendant and prosecutor appear, the trial should be held (subsec. (1)). A defendant may appear by counsel or agent, but the court may require the defendant's personal appearance and enforce this requirement through warrant (subsec. (2)). If a defendant who is confined in prison agrees, then he or she may appear by closed-circuit television or similar means. In the case of an organization, a counsel or agent must appear, and if such a person does not, the court may proceed *ex parte*, on proof of service.

ANNOTATIONS

Subsection (2) – It was held in *R. v. Fedoruk,* [1966] 3 C.C.C. 118 (Sask. C.A.), that a plea can only be entered on behalf of the person named in the information. Once counsel had done this, it was no longer open for him to argue either that the person named in the information had not been served with the summons, or that he was not appearing for that person named in the information.

The warrant itself should not be issued until there is non-compliance of the court's direction that the defendant appear personally: *R. v. Richard* (1974), 27 C.R.N.S. 337 (Que. S.C.). In *R. v. Sidorov* (2001), 160 C.C.C. (3d) 122 (Alta. C.A.), leave to appeal to S.C.C. refused loc. cit. C.C.C. vi, the Alberta Court of Appeal held that the jurisdiction to issue an arrest warrant is not limited to situations where the defendant has been previously directed to appear in person.

Although this subsection gives the court power to require the accused to appear personally, it is improper to issue a bench warrant where the accused has appeared by counsel: *R. v. Okanee* (1981), 59 C.C.C. (2d) 149 (Sask. C.A.).

A provincial court judge has power to appoint counsel to represent an indigent accused in summary conviction proceedings: *R. v. White* (1976), 32 C.C.C. (2d) 478 (Alta. S.C.T.D.).

While the requisite inquiry will depend on the circumstances, where a defendant is represented by an agent who is not a lawyer, the trial judge should: (1) make inquiries to determine whether the defendant has made an informed choice to forego representation by counsel; (2) ensure that the defendant is aware that the agent is not a lawyer and that the defendant will not have recourse to various remedies which might be available if the agent were a lawyer who performed inadequately; (3) inform the defendant as to the absence of any provincially imposed restrictions that persons receive any training or demonstrate any level of expertise before representing people in criminal matters; and (4) inform the defendant that while minimum competence standards are imposed on lawyers, no such standards are imposed on non-lawyer agents. While there is no requirement that the trial judge inquire into the competence of the agents, the trial judge does have the authority to disqualify the agent where the agent's appearance would be inconsistent with the proper administration of justice. The competence of the agent may be raised by the Crown, third parties such as the Law Sociey or by the judge: *R. v. Romanowicz* (1999), 138 C.C.C. (3d) 225 (Ont. C.A.).

Subsection (3) – The court may adjourn a case for an *ex parte* trial and such adjournment although made in the absence of the accused may be for more than eight days: *R. v. Saskatoon Custom Drywall (1978) Ltd.* (1982), 69 C.C.C. (2d) 441 (Sask. Q.B.).

Once counsel appears on behalf of the corporation identified as the defendant in the information as amended and enters a plea it is not open to the corporation to argue that the Crown has failed to serve a summons on that company: *R. v. Westmin Resources Ltd. (Western Mines Ltd.)*, [1985] 1 W.W.R. 30 (B.C.C.A.), leave to appeal to S.C.C. refused 56 N.R. 240.

ARRAIGNMENT / Finding of guilt, conviction or order if charge admitted / Procedure if charge not admitted.

801. (1) Where the defendant appears for the trial, the substance of the information laid against him shall be stated to him, and he shall be asked,

(*a*) whether he pleads guilty or not guilty to the information, where the proceedings are in respect of an offence that is punishable on summary conviction; or

(*b*) whether he has cause to show why an order should not be made against him, in proceedings where a justice is authorized by law to make an order.

(2) Where the defendant pleads guilty or does not show sufficient cause why an order should not be made against him, as the case may be, the summary conviction court shall convict the defendant, discharge the defendant under section 730 or make an order against him accordingly.

(3) Where the defendant pleads not guilty or states that he has cause to show why an order should not be made against him, as the case may be, the summary conviction court shall proceed with the trial, and shall take the evidence of witnesses for the prosecutor and the defendant in accordance with the provisions of Part XVIII relating to preliminary inquiries. R.S., c. C-34, s. 736; R.S.C. 1985, c. 27 (1st Supp.), s. 177(1); 1995, c. 22, s. 10.

(4) and (5) [*Repealed*, R.S.C. 1985, c. 27 (1st Supp.), s. 177(2).]

CROSS-REFERENCES

No reference is made in subsec. (1) to the availability of the special pleas. The incorporation of the provisions of Part XX by s. 795 to the extent they are consistent with Part XXVII, include the special plea provisions in ss. 607 to 610. Also, the procedure followed at trial under Part XXVII is substantially the same as under Part XX, subject to some specific provisions in the former. There is no authorization in this section for the trial of separate informations together. The section does not permit the joint trial of summary conviction and indictable offences by a provincial court judge sitting under Part XIX and XXVII. The prosecution should elect the mode of procedure before opting for summary conviction or indictment in cases triable either way.

SYNOPSIS

This section states the procedure on arraignment. The defendant is to be asked for a plea or to show cause why an order against him should not be made, as the case may be. Where the plea is guilty or no cause is shown, the court shall convict, discharge or make the order. Where the plea is not guilty, or intent to show cause is indicated, the trial shall proceed according to the provisions of Part XVIII relating to preliminary inquiries.

ANNOTATIONS

Special pleas [subsec. (1)] – The special pleas to an indictment are also available to a defendant upon an information: *R. v. Riddle* (1977), 36 C.C.C. (2d) 391, [1977] 5 W.W.R. 58 (Alta. S.C. App. Div.), affd [1980] 1 S.C.R. 380, 48 C.C.C. (2d) 365, 100 D.L.R. (3d) 577 (7:0).

Arraignment and plea – Since in British Columbia it has been the practice of counsel in summary conviction trials to enter a plea vicariously on behalf of the defendant, where the Crown enters the plea in the presence of counsel and the defendant no error has been committed. Furthermore, the stating of the substance of the information to the defendant is a statutory requirement going to jurisdiction, and as such as a special jurisdiction over the defendant it may be, as it was in the facts of this case, waived: *R. v. Franiek* (1970), 13 C.R.N.S. 230, [1971] 1 W.W.R. 104 (B.C.S.C.).

The arraignment of the defendant to identify him to the judge and the members of the public is an established procedure, and the power of the court under s. 800(2) to require the personal appearance of the defendant includes the power to require him to identify himself in open court: *R. v. Conrad* (1973), 12 C.C.C. (2d) 405 (N.S.S.C.).

A judge may decline to accept a plea until the defendant appears before him at the commencement of trial: *R. v. Jones* (1973), 26 C.R.N.S. 398, [1974] 2 W.W.R. 396 (B.C.S.C.).

Joint trial of information ***[Also see notes under s. 591]*** – A provincial court judge may jointly try summary and indictable offences, even where they are contained on separate informations, provided that the accused has not elected trial by a higher court in respect of the indictable offence. In the event of any conflict as to the applicable procedure, indictable offences procedures would apply. Where joinder of offences or accused are being considered, the court should seek the consent of both of the accused and the prosecution. If consent is withheld, the reasons should be explored. Whether the accused consents or not, joinder should only occur when, in the opinion of the court, it is in the interests of justice to proceed jointly and the offences or the accused could initially have been jointly charged. Where the accused wishes to testify in respect of only one of the informations, then consent to a joint trial would be withheld. Furthermore, where the separate informations involve two accused, the Crown may not compel one accused to testify against the other: *R. v. Clunas*, [1992] 1 S.C.R. 595, 70 C.C.C. (3d) 115, 11 C.R. (4th) 238 (5:0).

Recording of evidence [subsec. (3)] – Where the summary conviction court fails to record the evidence in accordance with s. 540 the superior court judge, upon motion for *certiorari*, will be unable to review the evidence pursuant to s. 804 and accordingly must quash the conviction: *R. v. Lichty, ex p. Zerawsky* (1970), 2 C.C.C. (2d) 581, [1971] 2 O.R. 193 (H.C.J.).

In *R. v. Boylan* (1979), 46 C.C.C. (2d) 415, 8 C.R. (3d) 36, [1979] 3 W.W.R. 435 (Sask. C.A.), Culliton C.J.S., held that the provisions of s. 540 are mandatory, and in *obiter* expressed the opinion that failure to comply with those provisions in a summary conviction trial is the failure to carry out a basic requirement of the trial, in the absence of which a verdict rendered cannot stand and on appeal the court would order a new trial.

RIGHT TO MAKE FULL ANSWER AND DEFENCE / Examination of witnesses / On oath.

802. (1) The prosecutor is entitled personally to conduct his case and the defendant is entitled to make his full answer and defence.

(2) The prosecutor or defendant, as the case may be, may examine and cross-examine witnesses personally or by counsel or agent.

(3) Every witness at a trial in proceedings to which this Part applies shall be examined under oath. R.S., c. C-34, s. 737.

CROSS-REFERENCES

The general order in which evidence is addressed on indictment is followed in summary conviction proceedings. The incorporation by s. 795 of s. 655 applicable in trials upon indictment permits admissions to be made in summary conviction proceedings.

Reception of evidence given by affirmation under the *Canada Evidence Act*, R.S.C. 1985, c. C-5, s. 14, is permissible notwithstanding the "under oath" provision in subsec. (3). The general adjectival rules of evidence apply in summary conviction procedures, including evidentiary provisions in Part XX, incorporated by reference in s. 795. See s. 785 for definition of "prosecutor" as "the Attorney General or where the Attorney General does not intervene, the informant and including counsel or an agent acting on behalf of either of them". Pursuant to s. 801(3), the evidence given at trial is taken in accordance with the provisions of Part XVIII regarding preliminary inquiries.

SYNOPSIS

This section sets further rules for summary conviction proceedings. The prosecutor is entitled to conduct the case personally and the accused is entitled to make full answer and defence (subsec. (1)). The prosecutor and the accused may examine and cross-examine through counsel or agent (subsec. (2)) and every witness shall testify under oath (subsec. (3)).

ANNOTATIONS

While inability to make full answer and defence is a substantive defence, it would seem that delay in laying the charge, provided it is laid within the statutory limitation period in s. 786(2), does not give rise to such a defence: *R. v. Field* (1983), 6 C.C.C. (3d) 182, 57 N.S.R. (2d) 35 (S.C. App. Div.).

This section is not inconsistent with the right of a provincial Crown Attorney to intervene in the prosecution of an offence: *R. v. Bradley* (1975), 24 C.C.C. (2d) 482, 335 C.R.N.S. 192 (Ont. C.A.).

It is a fatal error for the court to convict and sentence the defendant without giving him an opportunity to make his defence: *R. v. Pestell* (1976), 31 C.C.C. (2d) 436 (Ont. H.C.J.).

See also cases under s. 650(3), *supra*.

LIMITATION ON THE USE OF AGENTS.

802.1 Despite subsections 800(2) and 802(2), a defendant may not appear or examine or cross-examine witnesses by agent if he or she is liable, on summary conviction, to imprisonment for a term of more than six months, unless the defendant is a corporation or the agent is authorized to do so under a program approved by the lieutenant governor in council of the province. 2002, c. 13, s. 79.

ANNOTATIONS

This provision applies only where the offence charged exposed the accused to the liability of imprisonment for more than six months. It has no application where the accused was charged with two summary conviction offences, each with a maximum penalty of six months' imprisonment, on the same information, notwithstanding that, if convicted of both, the accused was liable for a total imprisonment of more than six months: *R. v. May* (2008), 244 C.C.C. (3d) 268 (Alta. Prov. Ct.).

ADJOURNMENT / Non-appearance of defendant / Consent of Attorney General required / Non-appearance of prosecutor.

803. (1) The summary conviction court may, in its discretion, before or during the trial, adjourn the trial to a time and place to be appointed and stated in the presence of the parties or their counsel or agents.

(2) If a defendant who is tried alone or together with others does not appear at the time and place appointed for the trial after having been notified of that time and place, or does not appear for the resumption of a trial that has been adjourned in accordance with subsection (1), the summary conviction court

(*a*) may proceed *ex parte* to hear and determine the proceedings in the absence of that defendant as if they had appeared; or

(*b*) may, if it thinks fit, issue a warrant in Form 7 for the arrest of that defendant and adjourn the trial to await their appearance under the warrant.

(3) If the summary conviction court proceeds in the manner described in paragraph (2)(*a*), no proceedings under section 145 arising out of the defendant's failure to appear at the time and place appointed for the trial or for the resumption of the trial shall, without the consent of the Attorney General, be instituted or be proceeded with.

(4) Where the prosecutor does not appear at the time and place appointed for the resumption of an adjourned trial, the summary conviction court may dismiss the information with or without costs. R.S., c. C-34, s. 738; R.S., c. 2 (2nd Supp.), s. 15; 1972, c. 13, s. 63; 1974-75-76, c. 93, s. 87; 1994, c. 44, s. 79; 1997, c. 18, s. 112; 2008, c. 18, s. 45.

(5) [*Repealed*, 1991, c. 43, s. 9.]

(6) [*Repealed*, 1991, c. 43, s. 9.]

(7) [*Repealed*, 1991, c. 43, s. 9.]

(8) [*Repealed*, 1991, c. 43, s. 9.]

CROSS-REFERENCES

The laying of an information under s. 505 is required procedure to confirm an appearance notice issued by a police officer. See s. 508 regarding the conduct of the hearing. Liability may be attracted under s. 145(2), (4) or (5) and the issuance of a warrant of arrest under subsec. (2)(*b*) of this section, in the event the accused fails to appear or reattend a trial in response to a confirmed appearance notice or summons. Section 475 provides the authority to proceed with trial of an indictable offence where the accused absconds during the course of the trial. Section 475 is not made applicable to summary conviction proceedings under s. 795. See s. 544 for similar provision regarding preliminary inquiries. Section 799 permits the court to dismiss the information or adjourn the trial in the event that the prosecution fails to appear for trial.

Note that s. 672.1 defines "court" for the purposes of Part XX.1 [Mental Disorder] to include a summary conviction court and, thus, a judge of that court may make the various orders provided for in that Part including an assessment order under s. 672.11. Further, s. 672.1 defines "accused" for the purposes of Part XX.1 to include a defendant in summary conviction proceedings and, thus, the procedures respecting fitness to stand trial are governed by Part XX.1 as are the consequences of a verdict of not criminally responsible on account of mental disorder.

SYNOPSIS

The court may adjourn the proceedings from time to time (subsec. (1)).

If the defendant does not appear or remain in attendance for the trial, the matter can be continued on an *ex parte* basis. Alternatively, an arrest warrant can be issued and the proceedings adjourned (subsec. (2)). In the event the trial proceeds in the absence of the accused, a failure to appear charge (see s. 145) cannot be laid without the consent of the Attorney General (subsec. (3)).

An information may be dismissed, with or without costs, if the prosecutor does not appear (subsec. (4)).

ANNOTATIONS

Adjournment [subsec. (1)] – An adjournment verbally correct, but recorded in error as to the date causes a loss of jurisdiction over the defendant only, and may be remedied by his counsel's right to correct this error: *R. v. Wick* (1974), 20 C.C.C. (2d) 203, [1974] 6 W.W.R. 335 *sub nom. R. ex rel. Seale v. Wick* (Sask. Q.B.).

A case adjourned to a holiday which being a non-juridical day, is a *dies non,* shall be considered as being adjourned to the following day: *R. v. Brand* (1974), 20 C.C.C. (2d) 253, [1975] 2 W.W.R. 356 (Alta. S.C.).

A court will not lose jurisdiction by adjourning a case in the absence of the defendant or his representative: *R. v. Szoboszloi,* [1970] 5 C.C.C. 366, [1970] 3 O.R. 485 (C.A.).

Dismissal of information [subsec. (4)] – This provision and s. 799 set out when an information may be dismissed. Both refer to a "trial". A provincial court judge does not have jurisdiction to dismiss an information for want of prosecution on a remand appearance that is not a trial date: *R. v. Sauve* (2016), 340 C.C.C. (3d) 377 (Sask. C.A.).

***Ex parte* trial** – The trial does not commence before a plea is entered and, therefore, there can be no "resumption" of a trial unless there has been a plea: *R. v. Grimwood* (1984), 15 C.C.C. (3d) 318 (B.C. Co. Ct.).

The court should not proceed *ex parte* under para. (*a*) where the accused has been prevented from attending court by reasons beyond his control, such as weather conditions: *R. v. McLeod* (1983), 36 C.R. (3d) 378, 49 A.R. 321 (N.W.T.S.C.).

The judge is not precluded from proceeding *ex parte* under this subsection although he has earlier issued a warrant for the accused's arrest: *R. v. Tarrant* (1984), 13 C.C.C. (3d) 219, 10 D.L.R. (4th) 751 (B.C.C.A.).

Provision for an *ex parte* trial does not offend the rights guaranteed in ss. 7 and 11(*d*) of the *Charter of Rights and Freedoms*: *R. v. Tarrant* (1984), 13 C.C.C. (3d) 219, 10 D.L.R. (4th) 751 (B.C.C.A.); *R. v. Rogers*, [1984] 6 W.W.R. 89, 34 Sask. R. 284 (C.A.).

Adjudication

FINDING OF GUILT, CONVICTION, ORDER OR DISMISSAL.

804. When the summary conviction court has heard the prosecutor, defendant and witnesses, it shall, after considering the matter, convict the defendant, discharge him under section 730, make an order against the defendant or dismiss the information, as the case may be. R.S., c. C-34, s. 739; R.S.C. 1985, c. 27 (1st Supp.), s. 178.

CROSS-REFERENCES

Section 806 requires a minute or memorandum of the order of the court be made where a conviction is recorded of an order made. An accused may request an order of dismissal under s. 808.

See s. 809 for costs. See ss. 813 and 830 for rights of appeal in summary conviction matters and ss. 812 to 838 for procedure.

SYNOPSIS

This section states the options of the summary conviction court after hearing the prosecutor, defendant and witnesses. It shall convict, discharge, make an order or dismiss the information.

ANNOTATIONS

Motion for dismissal / directed verdict [Also see notes under s. 650] – In *R. v. Vander-Beek*, [1971] S.C.R. 260, 2 C.C.C. (2d) 45, at trial the motion of the two appellants for dismissal at the conclusion of the Crown's case on the ground that there was no evidence upon which they could be convicted was dismissed and their immediately succeeding motion that they be acquitted on the ground that there was insufficient evidence for conviction was reserved by the judge until he heard all of the evidence. Their counsel took no further part in the evidence, even when the third accused testified to raise a reasonable doubt on his part at the expense of his other two co-accused. The trial judge acquitted Ellsworth on his evidence and, excluding his evidence as against the two co-accused, acquitted them. It was held (9:0) that the case was not concluded until all of the evidence was in and that all the testimony heard was evidence for or against each accused. Further, *per* Laskin J., the accused's closing of his case at the conclusion of the Crown's case does not allow a co-accused to separate his trial from the joint trial.

At the close of the Crown's case the trial judge, if requested by the defendant, must rule whether or not a *prima facie* case has been established: *R. v. Kennedy* (1973), 11 C.C.C. (2d) 263, 21 C.R.N.S. 251 (Ont. C.A.), apld *R. v. Snyder* (1974), 16 C.C.C. (2d) 331, [1974] 3 W.W.R. 372 (Sask. Q.B.).

A trial judge must dispose of a motion for dismissal before he may put the defendant to his election as to calling evidence: *R. v. Angelatoni* (1975), 28 C.C.C. (2d) 179, 31 C.R.N.S. 342 (Ont. C.A.).

Charter remedies – In addition to the dispositions set out in this section, the summary conviction court may enter a stay of proceedings pursuant to s. 24(1) of the *Charter of Rights and Freedoms* where such a remedy is appropriate for violation of a provision of the Charter: *R. v. Cutforth*, [1988] 1 W.W.R. 274 (Alta. C.A.). Also see *R. v. 974649 Ontario Inc.*, [2001] 3 S.C.R. 575, 159 C.C.C. (3d) 321, noted under s. 809.

Other notes – Failure of the Crown to notify a defendant, who neither himself nor by agent or counsel was present for the verdict, of his conviction constitutes a denial of natural justice: *R. v. Welsh*, [1968] 4 C.C.C. 243 (Sask. Q.B.).

---

805. [*Repealed*, R.S.C. 1985, c. 27 (1st Supp.), s. 179.]

MEMO OF CONVICTION OR ORDER / Warrant of committal / Admissibility of certified copy.

806. (1) Where a defendant is convicted or an order is made in relation to the defendant, a minute or memorandum of the conviction or order shall be made by the summary conviction court indicating that the matter was dealt with under this Part and, on request by the defendant, the prosecutor or any other person, the court shall cause a conviction or order in Form 35 or 36, as the case may be, and a certified copy of the conviction or order to be drawn up and shall deliver the certified copy to the person making the request.

(2) Where a defendant is convicted or an order is made against him, the summary conviction court shall issue a warrant of committal in Form 21 or 22, and section 528 applies in respect of a warrant of committal issued under this subsection.

(3) Where a warrant of committal in Form 21 is issued by a clerk of a court, a copy of the warrant of committal, certified by the clerk, is admissible in evidence in any proceeding. R.S., c. C-34, s. 741; 1972, c. 13, s. 64; 1994, c. 44, s. 80.

CROSS-REFERENCES

Section 734 deals with execution of warrant of committal. The accused is taken, together with the warrant, to the prison named therein. The delivering officer is given a receipt in Form 43 detailing the state and condition of accused upon delivery.

The accused may request an order of dismissal under s. 808. See s. 809 for costs. Also see references cited under s. 804.

SYNOPSIS

This section provides that upon a conviction or the making of an order by the summary conviction court, there shall be a memo recording same made up, and that a party is entitled to a certified copy of the conviction or order on request (subsec. (1)). In these circumstances, there shall also be a warrant of committal issued, which may be enforced by endorsement as provided for in s. 528 (subsec. (2)).

DISPOSAL OF PENALTIES WHEN JOINT OFFENDERS.

807. Where several persons join in committing the same offence and on conviction each is adjudged to pay an amount to a person aggrieved, no more shall be paid to that person than an amount equal to the value of the property destroyed or injured or the amount of the injury done, together with costs, if any, and the residue of the amount adjudged to be paid shall be applied in the manner in which other penalties imposed by law are directed to be applied. R.S., c. C-34, s. 742.

CROSS-REFERENCES

Section 741.1 governs restitution payments to aggrieved persons.

Sections 722(4), 737 and 734.8 deal with application of money penalties. A V.F.S. under s. 737 is a payment to a fund to assist victims as prescribed by the Governor in Council, not a payment to a person aggrieved, and does not fall within s. 807.

SYNOPSIS

This section provides that the total of multiple payments made to the victim by multiple convicted accused shall not exceed the damage done to that victim, plus costs, and that any excess shall be applied against other penalties imposed by law.

ORDER OF DISMISSAL / Effect of certificate.

808. (1) Where the summary conviction court dismisses an information, it may, if requested by the defendant, draw up an order of dismissal and shall give to the defendant a certified copy of the order of dismissal.

(2) A copy of an order of dismissal, certified in accordance with subsection (1) is, without further proof, a bar to any subsequent proceedings against the defendant in respect of the same cause. R.S., c. C-34, s. 743.

CROSS-REFERENCES

Section 570 governs records of conviction, acquittal and orders in non-jury trials.

Under s. 795, special pleas in ss. 607 to 610 apply in summary conviction proceedings. See s. 11(*h*) of the Charter for relation to provisions of subsec. (2).

Rights of appeal of informant, Attorney General or his agent are dealt with in ss. 813(*b*) and 830(1). See s. 809 for costs.

SYNOPSIS

This section gives a defendant for whom an information has been dismissed the right to request and receive a certified copy of the order of dismissal, and such copy acts, absent other proof, as a bar to subsequent proceedings on the same subject-matter.

ANNOTATIONS

The procedure under this section does not supplant the common law right to raise the special pleas of *autrefois* but merely serves to supplement those rights and provide a second and convenient method of proving a previous acquittal to bar subsequent proceedings. Further, the plea of *autrefois acquit* is available where following a plea of not guilty the Crown offers no evidence: *R. v. Riddle*, [1980] 1 S.C.R. 380, 48 C.C.C. (2d) 365 (7:0).

It was also held in *R. v. Riddle, supra,* that the drawing up of the order of dismissal and the giving of a certified copy of the order to the accused is a purely administrative act which may be performed at any time subsequent to the trial. The doctrine of *functus officio* has no application to such acts.

An order of dismissal under this section is not a bar to further proceedings where the magistrate was without jurisdiction to hear the charge because the information was not sworn: *R. v. Nazaroff* (1959), 123 C.C.C. 134 (B.C.S.C.).

An order of dismissal obtained after the dismissal of an information because the offence charged was *ultra vires* Parliament is not a bar to a subsequent charge under valid provincial legislation for the same conduct: *R. v. Logan* (1981), 64 C.C.C. (2d) 238, 25 C.R. (3d) 35 (N.S.S.C. App. Div.).

Further, the dismissal of a private information for want of prosecution as a result of the failure of the complainant to attend and the issuance of a certificate of dismissal was not a bar to a subsequent charge of assault causing bodily harm by indictment. The plea of *autrefois acquit* was not available as the accused had not pleaded and therefore was not "in jeopardy" in the prior proceedings: *R. v. Walsh* (1996), 106 C.C.C. (3d) 462, 47 C.R. (4th) 184 (N.S.C.A.).

Where the accused has pleaded not guilty and the Crown, because it was refused an adjournment, offered no evidence so that the charge was dismissed the accused is entitled to request a certificate under this section: *R. v. Canadian Pacific Ltd.* (1976), 32 C.C.C. (2d) 14, [1977] 1 W.W.R. 203 (Alta. S.C. App. Div.) (5:0), and *semble, R. v. Davis and Lakehead Bag Co.* (1977), 34 C.C.C. (2d) 388, 37 C.R.N.S. 302 (Ont. C.A.).

Similarly, where the Crown, having been refused an amendment to the charge, offered no evidence the magistrate properly dismissed the charge and issued the certificate under this section: *R. v. Pirri* (1978), 41 C.C.C. (2d) 499, 27 N.S.R. (2d) 41 (S.C. App. Div.).

COSTS / Order set out / Costs are part of fine / Where no fine imposed / Definition of "costs".

809. (1) The summary conviction court may in its discretion award and order such costs as it considers reasonable and not inconsistent with such of the fees established by section 840 as may be taken or allowed in proceedings before that summary conviction court, to be paid

(*a*) to the informant by the defendant, where the summary conviction court convicts or makes an order against the defendant; or

(*b*) to the defendant by the informant, where the summary conviction court dismisses an information.

(2) An order under subsection (1) shall be set out in the conviction, order or order of dismissal, as the case may be.

(3) Where a fine or sum of money or both are adjudged to be paid by a defendant and a term of imprisonment in default of payment is imposed, the defendant is, in default of payment, liable to serve the term of imprisonment imposed, and for the purposes of this

subsection, any costs that are awarded against the defendant shall be deemed to be part of the fine or sum of money adjudged to be paid.

(4) Where no fine or sum of money is adjudged to be paid by a defendant, but costs are awarded against the defendant or informant, the person who is liable to pay them is, in default of payment, liable to imprisonment for one month.

(5) In this section, "costs" includes the costs and charges, after they have been ascertained, of committing and conveying to prison the person against whom costs have been awarded. R.S., c. C-34, s. 744.

CROSS-REFERENCES

See ss. 826, 834(1) and 839(3) for other costs provisions in summary conviction proceedings. Specific costs provisions in indictable matters include s. 599(3) for change of venue granted at prosecution's request, ss. 728 to 729 for defamatory libel, and s. 601(5) and (6) for adjournment granted because accused was misled by the form of the indictment.

SYNOPSIS

Costs may be ordered in summary conviction proceedings (subsec. (1), s. 840).

If the accused is ordered to pay both a fine and costs the latter will be deemed to be part of the fine for the purposes of any term of imprisonment that is imposed for non-payment of the fine (subsec. (3)).

If the accused is not fined, but is ordered to pay costs, the maximum period of incarceration in default of payment that can be imposed is 2 months (subsec. (4)).

ANNOTATIONS

The summary conviction court has no power to grant an adjournment conditional on the party requesting it paying the costs of the day and has no power to award costs to the defendant's counsel: *R. v. Cross* (1978), 42 C.C.C. (2d) 277 (P.E.I.S.C. *in banco*).

In *R. v. 974649 Ontario Inc.*, [2001] 3 S.C.R. 575, 159 C.C.C. (3d) 321, 47 C.R. (5th) 316 *sub nom. Ontario v. 974649 Ontario Inc.*, the court held that a provincial offences court was a court of competent jurisdiction within the meaning of s. 24(1) of the *Charter of Rights and Freedoms* with the power to award costs for breach of the defendant's right to disclosure. The reasoning in that case would apply to a summary conviction court acting under this Part. Also see the earlier decision in *R. v. Pang* (1994), 95 C.C.C. (3d) 60 (Alta. C.A.).

Sureties to Keep the Peace

IF INJURY OR DAMAGE FEARED / Duty of justice / Adjudication / Refusal to enter into recognizance / Conditions in recognizance / Conditions / Surrender, etc. / Reasons / Idem / Forms / Modification of recognizance / Procedure.

810. (1) An information may be laid before a justice by or on behalf of any person who fears on reasonable grounds that another person

(*a*) will cause personal injury to him or her or to his or her spouse or common-law partner or child or will damage his or her property; or

(*b*) will commit an offence under section 162.1.

(2) A justice who receives an information under subsection (1) shall cause the parties to appear before him or before a summary conviction court having jurisdiction in the same territorial division.

(3) If the justice or summary conviction court before which the parties appear is satisfied by the evidence adduced that the person on whose behalf the information was laid has reasonable grounds for the fear, the justice or court may order that the

defendant enter into a recognizance, with or without sureties, to keep the peace and be of good behaviour for a period of not more than 12 months.

(3.01) The justice or summary conviction court may commit the defendant to prison for a term of not more than 12 months if the defendant fails or refuses to enter into the recognizance.

(3.02) The justice or summary conviction court may add any reasonable conditions to the recognizance that the justice or court considers desirable to secure the good conduct of the defendant, including conditions that require the defendant

(*a*) to abstain from the consumption of drugs except in accordance with a medical prescription, of alcohol or of any other intoxicating substance;

(*b*) to provide, for the purpose of analysis, a sample of a bodily substance prescribed by regulation on the demand of a peace officer, a probation officer or someone designated under paragraph 810.3(2)(*a*) to make a demand, at the place and time and on the day specified by the person making the demand, if that person has reasonable grounds to believe that the defendant has breached a condition of the recognizance that requires them to abstain from the consumption of drugs, alcohol or any other intoxicating substance; or

(*c*) to provide, for the purpose of analysis, a sample of a bodily substance prescribed by regulation at regular intervals that are specified, in a notice in Form 51 served on the defendant, by a probation officer or a person designated under paragraph 810.3(2)(*b*) to specify them, if a condition of the recognizance requires the defendant to abstain from the consumption of drugs, alcohol or any other intoxicating substance.

(3.1) Before making an order under subsection (3), the justice or the summary conviction court shall consider whether it is desirable, in the interests of the safety of the defendant or of any other person, to include as a condition of the recognizance that the defendant be prohibited from possessing any firearm, crossbow, prohibited weapon, restricted weapon, prohibited device, ammunition, prohibited ammunition or explosive substance, or all such things, for any period specified in the recognizance and, where the justice or summary conviction court decides that it is so desirable, the justice or summary conviction court shall add such a condition to the recognizance.

(3.11) Where the justice or summary conviction court adds a condition described in subsection (3.1) to a recognizance order, the justice or summary conviction court shall specify in the order the manner and method by which

(*a*) the things referred to in that subsection that are in the possession of the accused shall be surrendered, disposed of, detained, stored or dealt with; and

(*b*) the authorizations, licences and registration certificates held by the person shall be surrendered.

(3.12) Where the justice or summary conviction court does not add a condition described in subsection (3.1) to a recognizance order, the justice or summary conviction court shall include in the record a statement of the reasons for not adding the condition.

(3.2) Before making an order under subsection (3), the justice or the summary conviction court shall consider whether it is desirable, in the interests of the safety of the informant, of the person on whose behalf the information was laid or of that person's spouse or common-law partner or child, as the case may be, to add either or both of the following conditions to the recognizance, namely, a condition

(*a*) prohibiting the defendant from being at, or within a distance specified in the recognizance from, a place specified in the recognizance where the person on whose behalf the information was laid or that person's spouse or common-law partner or child, as the case may be, is regularly found; and

(*b*) prohibiting the defendant from communicating, in whole or in part, directly or indirectly, with the person on whose behalf the information was laid or that person's spouse or common-law partner or child, as the case may be.

(4) A recognizance and a committal to prison in default of recognizance may be in Forms 32 and 23, respectively.

(4.1) The justice or the summary conviction court may, on application of the informant or the defendant, vary the conditions fixed in the recognizance.

(5) The provisions of this Part apply, with such modifications as the circumstances require, to proceedings under this section. R.S., c. C-34, s. 745; 1974-75-76, c. 93, s. 88; 1980-81-82-83, c. 125, s. 28; 1991, c. 40, s. 33; 1994, c. 44, s. 81; 1995, c. 22, s. 8, c. 39, s. 157; 2000, c. 12, s. 95(*f*), (*g*); 2011, c. 7, s. 7; 2014, c. 31, s. 25.

CROSS-REFERENCES

An information laid before a justice under this section does not contain a formal charge. Under s. 524, a similar procedure without laying an information initiates a misconduct hearing. The inquiry is to determine whether evidence indicates the informant had reasonable grounds for fear, not guilt or innocence of accused. Committal is for failure or refusal to enter recognizance. No plea is entered.

With respect to a prohibition order under subsec. (3.1), note that pursuant to s. 113, the judge may make an order authorizing a chief firearms officer or the Registrar to issue, in accordance with such terms and conditions as is considered appropriate, an authorization, a licence or a registration certificate, as the case may be, to the accused for sustenance or employment purposes. Under s. 114, the prohibition order may require the accused to surrender anything the possession of which is prohibited by the order and every authorization, licence and registration certificate relating to any such thing. Under s. 116, every authorization, licence and registration certificate relating to anything the possession of which is prohibited by a prohibition order and issued to the accused is, on the commencement of the prohibition order, revoked, or amended, as the case may be, to the extent of the prohibitions in the order.

Breach of recognizance is a hybrid offence under s. 811.

An accused under Part XXVII proceedings may appeal an order against him pursuant to s. 813(*b*). A party to Part XXVII proceedings may appeal against determination of a summary conviction court under s. 830(1), on specified grounds.

SYNOPSIS

This section authorizes a provincial court judge or justice of the peace to require an individual to enter into a recognizance (sometimes known as a "peace bond") where grounds exist to believe that he or she will cause injury to, or damage the property of another person, will injure the spouse or child of the other person or will commit an offence under s. 162.1. The application must be supported by an information and there must be a hearing (subsecs. (1) and (2)).

The recognizance can be for a period of up to 12 months and may contain such conditions as the judge considers desirable for ensuring the defendant's good conduct, including requirements that the defendant abstain from consuming alcohol or drugs, or submit samples of a bodily substance for analysis. If the defendant refuses to sign the recognizance he or she can be imprisoned for up to 12 months (subsec. (3)). Subsections (3.1) and (3.2) require the justice to consider inclusion of specific terms respecting possession of firearms, ammunition or explosives, non-attendance at certain premises and non-communication. On application, the judge may vary the conditions in the recognizance (subsec. (4.1)).

ANNOTATIONS

Subsection (1) – The provisions respecting the sufficiency of informations apply to an information under this section: *R. v. Boyko* (1978), 43 C.C.C. (2d) 408 (Ont. Prov. Ct.).

This section is *intra vires* Parliament, being a valid exercise of the criminal law power although it is directed at prevention of harm and does not create an offence: *R. v. Dhesi* (1983), 9 C.C.C. (3d) 149 (B.C.S.C.).

Subsection (3) – In addition to the authority of subsec. (3)(*a*) a judge has common law jurisdiction on facts established to his satisfaction to bind anyone over to keep the peace: *R. v. White, ex p. Chohan,* [1969] 1 C.C.C. 19 (B.C.S.C.).

Along with his common law jurisdiction the judge must have before him sufficient evidence and he must first accord any person who might be affected by such jurisdiction an opportunity to be fully heard: *R. v. Shaben* (1972), 8 C.C.C. (2d) 422 (Ont. H.C.J.).

The judge's common law jurisdiction to dispense "preventative justice" must not be exercised arbitrarily or unfairly and without giving the person bound over notice and an opportunity to be heard. It is a denial of natural justice resulting in a loss of jurisdiction to make an order against the petitioner on an application under this section when she has been given no notice that she, as well as the defendant, would be bound over: *R. v. Compton* (1978), 42 C.C.C. (2d) 163 (B.C.S.C.).

Peace bonds can have serious implications for an individual; it is therefore imperative that procedural safeguards be observed. Here, a peace bond was quashed because the judge did not give the subject an opportunity to be heard before he imposed it: *R. v. Petre* (2013), 299 C.C.C. (3d) 246 (Ont. S.C.J.).

A defendant on a charge of assault need not be specifically warned that the judge intends to dismiss that charge but exercise his common law jurisdiction to bind the defendant over to keep the peace: *R. v. Broomes* (1984), 12 C.C.C. (3d) 220 (Ont. H.C.J.).

The ordinary rules precluding admission of evidence of an accused's disposition for violence do not apply to proceedings under subsec. (3). The actions of the defendant in the past may well assist the court in determining the reasonableness of the informant's fears and the likelihood that the defendant will carry out his threats: *R. v. Patrick* (1990), 75 C.R. (3d) 222 (B.C. Co. Ct.).

On a charge of breach of a term of a recognizance made under this section, it is not open to the accused to defend the charge by questioning the validity of the term. This would amount to an impermissible collateral attack: *R. v. Pheiffer* (1999), 139 C.C.C. (3d) 552 (B.C.C.A.).

Subsection (5) – One line of authority holds that a person against whom an information has been laid under this section may be dealt with according to the provisions of Part XVI including s. 515. Therefore, the judge may issue a warrant of arrest and order the release of the accused on conditions pending determination of the peace bond proceedings: *R. v. Wakelin* (1992), 71 C.C.C. (3d) 115 (Sask. C.A.); *R. v. Cachine* (2001), 154 C.C.C. (3d) 376 (B.C.C.A.); *R. v. Budreo* (2000), 142 C.C.C. (3d) 225 (Ont. C.A.), leave to appeal to S.C.C. refused [2001] 1 S.C.R. vii, 153 C.C.C. (3d) vi. A contrary line of authority holds that Part XVI has no application to peace bond proceedings, given Parliament's recognition that a defendant in a peace bond proceeding stands in a very different position from a criminal accused: *R. v. Penunsi* (2018), 357 C.C.C. (3d) 539 (N.L.C.A.), leave to appeal to S.C.C. allowed [2018] S.C.C.A. No. 73; *MacAusland v. Pyke* (1995), 96 C.C.C. (3d) 373 (N.S.S.C.).

FEAR OF CERTAIN OFFENCES / Appearances / Adjudication / Duration extended / Refusal to enter into recognizance / Conditions in recognizance / Conditions — firearms / Surrender, etc. / Reasons / Variance of conditions / Other provisions to apply / Definition of "Attorney General".

810.01 (1) A person who fears on reasonable grounds that another person will commit an offence under section 423.1 or a criminal organization offence may, with the Attorney General's consent, lay an information before a provincial court judge.

(2) A provincial court judge who receives an information under subsection (1) may cause the parties to appear before a provincial court judge.

(3) If the provincial court judge before whom the parties appear is satisfied by the evidence adduced that the informant has reasonable grounds for the fear, the judge

may order that the defendant enter into a recognizance to keep the peace and be of good behaviour for a period of not more than 12 months.

(3.1) However, if the provincial court judge is also satisfied that the defendant was convicted previously of an offence referred to in subsection (1), the judge may order that the defendant enter into the recognizance for a period of not more than two years.

(4) The provincial court judge may commit the defendant to prison for a term not exceeding twelve months if the defendant fails or refuses to enter into the recognizance.

(4.1) The provincial court judge may add any reasonable conditions to the recognizance that the judge considers desirable for preventing the commission of an offence referred to in subsection (1), including conditions that require the defendant

(*a*) to participate in a treatment program;

(*b*) to wear an electronic monitoring device, if the Attorney General makes the request;

(*c*) to remain within a specified geographic area unless written permission to leave that area is obtained from the judge;

(*d*) to return to and remain at their place of residence at specified times;

(*e*) to abstain from the consumption of drugs, except in accordance with a medical prescription, of alcohol or of any other intoxicating substance;

(*f*) to provide, for the purpose of analysis, a sample of a bodily substance prescribed by regulation on the demand of a peace officer, a probation officer or someone designated under paragraph 810.3(2)(*a*) to make a demand, at the place and time and on the day specified by the person making the demand, if that person has reasonable grounds to believe that the defendant has breached a condition of the recognizance that requires them to abstain from the consumption of drugs, alcohol or any other intoxicating substance; or

(*g*) to provide, for the purpose of analysis, a sample of a bodily substance prescribed by regulation at regular intervals that are specified, in a notice in Form 51 served on the defendant, by a probation officer or a person designated under paragraph 810.3(2)(*b*) to specify them, if a condition of the recognizance requires the defendant to abstain from the consumption of drugs, alcohol or any other intoxicating substance.

(5) The provincial court judge shall consider whether it is desirable, in the interests of the defendant's safety or that of any other person, to prohibit the defendant from possessing any firearm, cross-bow, prohibited weapon, restricted weapon, prohibited device, ammunition, prohibited ammunition or explosive substance, or all of those things. If the judge decides that it is desirable to do so, the judge shall add that condition to the recognizance and specify the period during which the condition applies.

(5.1) If the provincial court judge adds a condition described in subsection (5) to a recognizance, the judge shall specify in the recognizance how the things referred to in that subsection that are in the defendant's possession shall be surrendered, disposed of, detained, stored or dealt with and how the authorizations, licences and registration certificates that are held by the defendant shall be surrendered.

(5.2) If the provincial court judge does not add a condition described in subsection (5) to a recognizance, the judge shall include in the record a statement of the reasons for not adding the condition.

(6) A provincial court judge may, on application of the informant, the Attorney General or the defendant, vary the conditions fixed in the recognizance.

(7) Subsections 810(4) and (5) apply, with any modifications that the circumstances require, to recognizances made under this section.

(8) With respect to proceedings under this section, "Attorney General" means either the Attorney General of Canada or the Attorney General of the province in which those

proceedings are taken and includes the lawful deputy of any of them. 1997, c. 23, ss. 19, 26; 2001, c. 32, s. 46 [amended 2001, c. 41, s. 133(21)]; 2001, c. 41, s. 22, 133(19); 2002, c. 13, s. 80; 2009, c. 22, s. 19; 2011, c. 7, s. 8; 2015, c. 20, s. 24.

CROSS-REFERENCES

The terms "criminal organization offence", "provincial court judge", and "terrorism offence" are defined in s. 2. Breach of a recognizance made under this section is an offence under s. 811. Sections 490.1 to 490.9 set out a scheme for the forfeiture of offence-related property. "Offence-related property" is defined in s. 2 and, in essence, refers to property used for, or obtained in, the commission of a criminal organization offence. Related offences include: possession of explosives for the benefit of a criminal organization [s. 82(2)]; first degree murder where death is caused while committing the using explosive offence in s. 81 for the benefit of a criminal organization [s. 231(6.1)]; and participation in a criminal organization [s. 467.1].

Also see ss. 810, 810.1 and 810.2, which allow a judge to order the person to enter into a recognizance where grounds exist to believe the defendant will cause injury to another person or damage property; will commit a sexual offence against a child; or commit a serious personal injury offence as defined in s. 752.

Where a weapons prohibition order is made a condition of a recognizance under subsec. (5), pursuant to s. 113, the judge may make an order authorizing a chief firearms officer or the Registrar to issue, in accordance with such terms and conditions as is considered appropriate, an authorization, a licence or a registration certificate, as the case may be, to the accused for sustenance or employment purposes. Under s. 114, the prohibition order may require the accused to surrender anything the possession of which is prohibited by the order and every authorization, licence and registration certificate relating to any such thing. Unless the prohibition order provides otherwise everything the possession of which is prohibited by the order is forfeited to the Crown pursuant to s. 115, subject to the true owner making an application under s. 117. Under s. 116, every authorization, licence and registration certificate relating to anything the possession of which is prohibited by a prohibition order and issued to the accused is, on the commencement of the prohibition order, revoked, or amended, as the case may be, to the extent of the prohibitions in the order.

Also see the special provision for terrorist activity in s. 83.3.

Pursuant to s. 2.1, the terms "cross-bow", "prohibited weapon", "restricted weapon", "prohibited device", "ammunition", and "prohibited ammunition" have the same meaning as in s. 84(1).

SYNOPSIS

This section allows anyone, with the consent of the Attorney General, to lay an information before a provincial court judge for the purpose of having the defendant enter into a recognizance where there are reasonable grounds to believe the defendant may commit a criminal organization offence or the offence under s. 423.1. The recognizance can be for a period of up to 12 months, unless the person was previously convicted of one of the offences set out in subsec. (1), in which case the recognizance can be for a period of up to two years. The judge may add any reasonable conditions to the recognizance including conditions set out in subsec. (4.1), such as participation in a treatment program and electronic monitoring. Subsection (5) specifically directs the judge to consider whether a weapons and explosives prohibition is desirable. Subsection (5.1) requires the judge to specify how the weapons, authorizations, licences and registration certificates that the defendant possessed or held are to be disposed of. If the judge does not add a weapons and explosives prohibition, the judge is to provide reasons (subsec. (5.2)).

FEAR OF TERRORISM OFFENCE / Appearances / Adjudication / Duration extended / Refusal to enter into recognizance / Conditions in recognizance / Conditions — firearms / Surrender, etc. / Condition — passport / Condition — specified geographic area / Reasons / Variance of conditions / Other provisions to apply / Definition of "Attorney General".

810.011 (1) A person who fears on reasonable grounds that another person may commit a terrorism offence may, with the Attorney General's consent, lay an information before a provincial court judge.

(2) The provincial court judge who receives an information under subsection (1) may cause the parties to appear before a provincial court judge.

(3) If the provincial court judge before whom the parties appear is satisfied by the evidence adduced that the informant has reasonable grounds for the fear, the judge may order that the defendant enter into a recognizance, with or without sureties, to keep the peace and be of good behaviour for a period of not more than 12 months.

(4) However, if the provincial court judge is also satisfied that the defendant was convicted previously of a terrorism offence, the judge may order that the defendant enter into the recognizance for a period of not more than five years.

(5) The provincial court judge may commit the defendant to prison for a term of not more than 12 months if the defendant fails or refuses to enter into the recognizance.

(6) The provincial court judge may add any reasonable conditions to the recognizance that the judge considers desirable to secure the good conduct of the defendant, including conditions that require the defendant

(*a*) to participate in a treatment program;

(*b*) to wear an electronic monitoring device, if the Attorney General makes that request;

(*c*) to return to and remain at their place of residence at specified times;

(*d*) to abstain from the consumption of drugs, except in accordance with a medical prescription, of alcohol or of any other intoxicating substance;

(*e*) to provide, for the purpose of analysis, a sample of a bodily substance prescribed by regulation on the demand of a peace officer, a probation officer or someone designated under paragraph 810.3(2)(*a*) to make a demand, at the place and time and on the day specified by the person making the demand, if that person has reasonable grounds to believe that the defendant has breached a condition of the recognizance that requires them to abstain from the consumption of drugs, alcohol or any other intoxicating substance; or

(*f*) to provide, for the purpose of analysis, a sample of a bodily substance prescribed by regulation at regular intervals that are specified, in a notice in Form 51 served on the defendant, by a probation officer or a person designated under paragraph 810.3(2)(*b*) to specify them, if a condition of the recognizance requires the defendant to abstain from the consumption of drugs, alcohol or any other intoxicating substance.

(7) The provincial court judge shall consider whether it is desirable, in the interests of the defendant's safety or that of any other person, to prohibit the defendant from possessing any firearm, cross-bow, prohibited weapon, restricted weapon, prohibited device, ammunition, prohibited ammunition or explosive substance, or all of those things. If the judge decides that it is desirable to do so, the judge shall add that condition to the recognizance and specify the period during which it applies.

(8) If the provincial court judge adds a condition described in subsection (7) to a recognizance, the judge shall specify in the recognizance how the things referred to in that subsection that are in the defendant's possession shall be surrendered, disposed of, detained, stored or dealt with and how the authorizations, licences and registration certificates that are held by the defendant shall be surrendered.

(9) The provincial court judge shall consider whether it is desirable, to secure the good conduct of the defendant, to include in the recognizance a condition that the defendant deposit, in the specified manner, any passport or other travel document issued in their name that is in their possession or control. If the judge decides that it is desirable, the judge shall add the condition to the recognizance and specify the period during which it applies.

(10) The provincial court judge shall consider whether it is desirable, to secure the good conduct of the defendant, to include in the recognizance a condition that the defendant remain within a specified geographic area unless written permission to leave that area is obtained from the judge or any individual designated by the judge. If the judge decides that it is desirable, the judge shall add the condition to the recognizance and specify the period during which it applies.

(11) If the provincial court judge does not add a condition described in subsection (7), (9) or (10) to a recognizance, the judge shall include in the record a statement of the reasons for not adding it.

(12) A provincial court judge may, on application of the informant, the Attorney General or the defendant, vary the conditions fixed in the recognizance.

(13) Subsections 810(4) and (5) apply, with any modifications that the circumstances require, to recognizances made under this section.

(14) With respect to proceedings under this section, "Attorney General" means either the Attorney General of Canada or the Attorney General of the province in which those proceedings are taken and includes the lawful deputy of any of them. 2015, c. 20, s. 25.

CROSS-REFERENCES

The recognizance made under this section is similar to the recognizance under s. 810 and so reference should be made to the cases noted under that section. Breach of the recognizance is an offence under s. 811.

"Provincial court judge" and "terrorism offence" are defined in s. 2. Pursuant to s. 2.1, the terms "cross-bow", "prohibited weapon", "restricted weapon", "prohibited device", "ammunition", and "prohibited ammunition" have the same meaning as in s. 84(1).

SYNOPSIS

This section allows anyone, with the consent of the Attorney General, to lay an information before a provincial court judge for the purpose of having the defendant enter into a recognizance where there are reasonable grounds to believe the defendant may commit a terrorism offence. The recognizance can be for a period of up to 12 months, unless the defendant was previously convicted of a terrorism offence, in which case the recognizance may be for a period of up to five years. The judge may impose a term of imprisonment of up to 12 months if the defendant fails or refuses to enter the recognizance. Subsection (6) provides a non-exhaustive list of conditions that may be imposed to secure the good conduct of the defendant. Subsection (7) requires the court to consider imposing a weapons prohibition. Subsection (8) requires the judge to specify how the weapons, authorizations, licences and registration certificates that the defendant possessed or held are to be disposed of. Subsection (9) requires the court to consider whether to order the defendant to surrender his or her passport as a condition of the recognizance. Subsection (10) requires the court to consider whether to order the defendant to remain within a specified geographic area as a condition of the recognizance. A judge who declines to add one of the conditions described in subsecs. (7), (9) or (10) to the recognizance must give reasons for the refusal. Under subsec. (12), the conditions of the recognizance may be varied by the judge on application of the informant or the defendant.

ANNOTATIONS

In view of the significant curtailment of liberty and lifelong stigma that will attached to an order under this section, such an order should not be made lightly. Here, the defendant's behavior in the community was disturbing but, especially given his mental illness, it was not reasonable to conclude there was any imminent possibility that he would commit a terrorism offence: *R. v. Ibrahim* (2018), 359 C.C.C. (3d) 95 (B.C. Prov. Ct.).

FEAR OF FORCED MARRIAGE OR MARRIAGE UNDER AGE OF 16 YEARS / Appearances / Adjudication / Duration extended / Refusal to enter into recognizance / Conditions in recognizance / Conditions — firearms / Surrender, etc. / Variance of conditions.

810.02 (1) A person who fears on reasonable grounds that another person will commit an offence under paragraph 273.3(1)(*d*) or section 293.1 or 293.2 may lay an information before a provincial court judge.

(2) The judge who receives the information may cause the parties to appear before a provincial court judge.

(3) If the provincial court judge before whom the parties appear is satisfied by the evidence adduced that the informant has reasonable grounds for the fear, the judge may order that the defendant enter into a recognizance to keep the peace and be of good behaviour for a period of not more than 12 months.

(4) However, if the provincial court judge is also satisfied that the defendant was convicted previously of an offence referred to in subsection (1), the judge may order that the defendant enter into the recognizance for a period of not more than two years.

(5) The provincial court judge may commit the defendant to prison for a term not exceeding 12 months if the defendant fails or refuses to enter into the recognizance.

(6) The provincial court judge may add any reasonable conditions to the recognizance that the judge considers desirable to secure the good conduct of the defendant, including conditions that

(*a*) prohibit the defendant from making agreements or arrangements for the marriage, whether in or outside Canada, of the person in respect of whom it is feared that the offence will be committed;

(*b*) prohibit the defendant from taking steps to cause the person in respect of whom it is feared that the offence will be committed to leave the jurisdiction of the court;

(*c*) require the defendant to deposit, in the specified manner, any passport or any other travel document that is in their possession or control, whether or not such passport or document is in their name or in the name of any other specified person;

(*d*) prohibit the defendant from communicating, directly or indirectly, with any specified person, or refrain from going to any specified place, except in accordance with any specified conditions that the judge considers necessary;

(*e*) require the defendant to participate in a treatment program, including a family violence counselling program;

(*f*) require the defendant to remain within a specified geographic area unless written permission to leave that area is obtained from the provincial court judge; and

(*g*) require the defendant to return to and remain at their place of residence at specified times.

(7) The provincial court judge shall consider whether it is desirable, in the interests of the defendant's safety or that of any other person, to prohibit the defendant from possessing any firearm, cross-bow, prohibited weapon, restricted weapon, prohibited device, ammunition, prohibited ammunition or explosive substance, or all of those

things. If the judge decides that it is desirable to do so, the judge shall add that condition to the recognizance and specify the period during which the condition applies.

(8) If the provincial court judge adds a condition described in subsection (7) to a recognizance, the judge shall specify in the recognizance how the things referred to in that subsection that are in the defendant's possession are to be surrendered, disposed of, detained, stored or dealt with and how the authorizations, licences and registration certificates that are held by the defendant are to be surrendered.

(9) A provincial court judge may, on application of the informant or the defendant, vary the conditions fixed in the recognizance. 2015, c. 29, s. 11.

CROSS-REFERENCES

The recognizance made under this section is similar to the recognizance under s. 810 and so reference should be made to the cases noted under that section. Breach of the recognizance is an offence under s. 811.

"Attorney General" and "provincial court judge" are defined in s. 2. Pursuant to s. 2.1, the terms "cross-bow", "prohibited weapon", "restricted weapon", "prohibited device", "ammunition", and "prohibited ammunition" have the same meaning as in s. 84(1).

SYNOPSIS

This section allows anyone to lay an information before a provincial court judge for the purpose of having the defendant enter into a recognizance where there are reasonable grounds to fear that the defendant will commit the offences of forced marriage (s. 293.1), marriage under the age of 16 years (s. 293.2), or doing anything for the purpose of removing a person under the age of 18 years from Canada with the intention of committing a ss. 293.1 or 293.2 offence (s. 273.3(1)(*d*)). The judge makes the order where satisfied on evidence that the informant has reasonable grounds for the fear. The maximum duration of the order is 12 months, unless the defendant was previously convicted of one of the specified offences, in which case the recognizance may be for a period of up to two years. The judge may impose a term of imprisonment of up to two years if the defendant fails or refuses to enter the recognizance. Subsection (6) provides a non-exhaustive list of conditions that may be imposed to secure the good conduct of the defendant. Subsection (7) requires the court to consider imposing a weapons prohibition. Subsection (8) requires the judge to specify how the weapons, authorizations, licences and registration certificates that the defendant possessed or held are to be disposed of. Under subsec. (9), the conditions of the recognizance may be varied by the judge on application of the informant or the defendant.

WHERE FEAR OF SEXUAL OFFENCE / Appearances / Adjudication / Duration extended / Conditions in recognizance / Conditions — firearms / Surrender, etc. / Condition — reporting / Refusal to enter into recognizance / Judge may vary recognizance / Other provisions to apply.

810.1 (1) Any person who fears on reasonable grounds that another person will commit an offence under section 151 or 152, subsection 153(1), section 155 or 159, subsection 160(2) or (3), section 163.1, 170, 171, 171.1, 172.1 or 172.2, subsection 173(2), section 271, 272, 273 or 279.011, subsection 279.02(2) or 279.03(2), section 280 or 281 or subsection 286.1(2), 286.2(2) or 286.3(2), in respect of one or more persons who are under the age of 16 years, may lay an information before a provincial court judge, whether or not the person or persons in respect of whom it is feared that the offence will be committed are named.

(2) A provincial court judge who receives an information under subsection (1) may cause the parties to appear before a provincial court judge.

(3) If the provincial court judge before whom the parties appear is satisfied by the evidence adduced that the informant has reasonable grounds for the fear, the judge

may order that the defendant enter into a recognizance to keep the peace and be of good behaviour for a period that does not exceed 12 months.

(3.01) However, if the provincial court judge is also satisfied that the defendant was convicted previously of a sexual offence in respect of a person who is under the age of 16 years, the judge may order that the defendant enter into the recognizance for a period that does not exceed two years.

(3.02) The provincial court judge may add any reasonable conditions to the recognizance that the judge considers desirable to secure the good conduct of the defendant, including conditions that

(*a*) prohibit the defendant from having any contact — including communicating by any means — with a person under the age of 16 years, unless the defendant does so under the supervision of a person whom the judge considers appropriate;

(*a*.1) prohibit the defendant from using the Internet or other digital network, unless the defendant does so in accordance with conditions set by the judge;

(*b*) prohibit the defendant from attending a public park or public swimming area where persons under the age of 16 years are present or can reasonably be expected to be present, or a daycare centre, schoolground or playground;

(*b*.1) prohibit the defendant from communicating, directly or indirectly, with any person identified in the recognizance, or refrain from going to any place specified in the recognizance, except in accordance with the conditions specified in the recognizance that the judge considers necessary;

(*c*) require the defendant to participate in a treatment program;

(*d*) require the defendant to wear an electronic monitoring device, if the Attorney General makes the request;

(*e*) require the defendant to remain within a specified geographic area unless written permission to leave that area is obtained from the provincial court judge;

(*f*) require the defendant to return to and remain at his or her place of residence at specified times;

(*g*) require the defendant to abstain from the consumption of drugs except in accordance with a medical prescription, of alcohol or of any other intoxicating substance;

(*h*) require the defendant to provide, for the purpose of analysis, a sample of a bodily substance prescribed by regulation on the demand of a peace officer, a probation officer or someone designated under paragraph 810.3(2)(*a*) to make a demand, at the place and time and on the day specified by the person making the demand, if that person has reasonable grounds to believe that the defendant has breached a condition of the recognizance that requires them to abstain from the consumption of drugs, alcohol or any other intoxicating substance; or

(*i*) require the defendant to provide, for the purpose of analysis, a sample of a bodily substance prescribed by regulation at regular intervals that are specified, in a notice in Form 51 served on the defendant, by a probation officer or a person designated under paragraph 810.3(2)(*b*) to specify them, if a condition of the recognizance requires the defendant to abstain from the consumption of drugs, alcohol or any other intoxicating substance.

(3.03) The provincial court judge shall consider whether it is desirable, in the interests of the defendant's safety or that of any other person, to prohibit the defendant from possessing any firearm, cross-bow, prohibited weapon, restricted weapon, prohibited device, ammunition, prohibited ammunition or explosive substance, or all of those things. If the judge decides that it is desirable to do so, the judge shall add that condition to the recognizance and specify the period during which the condition applies.

(3.04) If the provincial court judge adds a condition described in subsection (3.03) to a recognizance, the judge shall specify in the recognizance how the things referred to in

that subsection that are in the defendant's possession should be surrendered, disposed of, detained, stored or dealt with and how the authorizations, licences and registration certificates that are held by the defendant should be surrendered.

(3.05) The provincial court judge shall consider whether it is desirable to require the defendant to report to the correctional authority of a province or to an appropriate police authority. If the judge decides that it is desirable to do so, the judge shall add that condition to the recognizance.

(3.1) The provincial court judge may commit the defendant to prison for a term not exceeding twelve months if the defendant fails or refuses to enter into the recognizance.

(4) A provincial court judge may, on application of the informant or the defendant, vary the conditions fixed in the recognizance.

(5) Subsections 810(4) and (5) apply, with such modifications as the circumstances require, to recognizances made under this section. 1993, c. 45, s. 11; 1997, c. 18, s. 113; 2002, c. 13, s. 81; 2008, c. 6, s. 54; 2008, c. 6, ss. 52, 54(*j*); 2012, c. 1, s. 37; 2011, c. 7, s. 9; 2014, c. 21, s. 4; 2014, c. 25, s. 31.

CROSS-REFERENCES

Also see s. 161 which allows for the making of a prohibition order where the accused is actually found guilty of one of the offences named in this section. The recognizance made under this section is similar to the recognizance under s. 810 and so reference should be made to cases noted under that section.

"Provincial court judge" is defined in s. 2. Pursuant to s. 2.1, the terms "cross-bow", "prohibited weapon", "restricted weapon", "prohibited device", "ammunition", and "prohibited ammunition" have the same meaning as in s. 84(1).

SYNOPSIS

This section allows anyone to lay an information before a provincial court judge for the purpose of having the defendant enter into a recognizance including conditions that he not engage in activity that involves contact with persons under 16 years of age and prohibiting him from attending certain places where persons under 16 years of age are likely to be present. The informant must fear, on reasonable grounds, that the defendant will commit one of the specified sexual offences in respect of children under 16 years of age. The judge makes the order where satisfied on evidence that the informant has reasonable grounds for the fear. The maximum duration of the order is 12 months, except if the defendant was previously convicted of a sexual offence in respect of a child under the age of 16 years, in which case the recognizance may be for a period of up to two years. Subsection (3.02) provides a non-exhaustive list of conditions that may be imposed to secure the good conduct of the defendant. Subsection (3.03) requires the court to consider imposing a weapons prohibition, and subsec. (3.05) requires the court to consider whether the defendant should report to a correctional authority or police authority. Under subsec. (4), the conditions may be varied by the judge on application of the informant or the defendant.

ANNOTATIONS

The principles of fundamental justice in s. 7 of the Charter require that there be a residual discretion to issue process. Subsection (2) must therefore be read down so that the word "may" should replace the word "shall": *R. v. Budreo* (1996), 104 C.C.C. (3d) 245 (Ont. Ct. (Gen. Div.)), affd 142 C.C.C. (3d) 225 (Ont. C.A.), leave to appeal to S.C.C. refused 153 C.C.C. (3d) vi.

By virtue of subsec. (5), which incorporates s. 810(5) into this section and thus the provisions of this Part, including s. 795 which incorporates Part XVI, ss. 507(4) and 515 apply to proceedings under this section. Thus, the court has the power to issue a warrant for the arrest of the defendant and require that he be detained in custody or to make a release order under s. 515. However, because a hearing under this section can only result in the defendant being required to enter into a recognizance, the circumstances in which it would be necessary in the public interest to issue an arrest warrant will be limited to cases where that process is necessary to preserve the integrity of these proceedings. The justice will require the informant to make out a case that the defendant will not otherwise attend court or that the defendant poses an imminent risk to the safety of children, which this section is designed to protect. If the justice does issue an arrest warrant, s. 515 directs the justice to release the defendant on a simple undertaking without conditions, unless the prosecutor shows cause why some more intrusive order — such as a recognizance with conditions — is required. The discretion under s. 515 must be exercised judicially and bearing in mind the limited conditions that can be imposed following a successful application. Although s. 515 provides that the justice may order the detention of the defendant pending the hearing, that discretion is circumscribed by the provisions of s. 515(10). In light of the limited consequences of a successful application under this section, only in unusual circumstances will the justice be entitled to order the detention of the defendant pending the hearing: *R. v. Budreo* (2000), 142 C.C.C. (3d) 225 (Ont. C.A.).

However, a contrary line of authority holds that Part XVI has no application to peace bond proceedings, given Parliament's recognition that a defendant in a peace bond proceeding stands in a very different position from a criminal accused: *R. v. Penunsi* (2018), 357 C.C.C. (3d) 539 (N.L.C.A.), leave to appeal to S.C.C. allowed [2018] S.C.C.A. No. 73; *MacAusland v. Pyke* (1995), 96 C.C.C. (3d) 373 (N.S.S.C.).

The inclusion of the term "community centre" in the restrictions imposed under subsec. (3), without a requirement that children be reasonably expected to be there, is overly broad and therefore a violation of s. 7 of the Charter. The appropriate remedy is to declare the term "community centre" inoperative. The provision is otherwise valid: *R. v. Budreo, supra.*

The judicial interim release provisions are not applicable where a person is summonsed to court for proceedings under this section because a summons does not put the person in custody. Further, a condition that the person submit to searches of his home and computer are beyond the scope of the conditions authorized under subsec. (3.02): *R. v. Nowazek* (2018), 366 C.C.C. (3d) 389 (Y.T.C.A.).

Given the different issues involved, the doctrines of *res judicata* and issue *estoppel* did not preclude the prosecution on a hearing under this section from leading evidence of acts that had been the subject of previous criminal charges and which had been stayed or even resulted in acquittals: *R. v. C. (C.J.)* (1999), 140 C.C.C. (3d) 159 (Man. Q.B.).

WHERE FEAR OF SERIOUS PERSONAL INJURY OFFENCE / Appearances / Adjudication / Duration extended / Refusal to enter into recognizance / Conditions in recognizance / Condition — firearms / Surrender, etc. / Reasons / Conditions — reporting / Variance of conditions / Other provision to apply.

810.2 (1) Any person who fears on reasonable grounds that another person will commit a serious personal injury offence, as that expression is defined in section 752, may, with the consent of the Attorney General, lay an information before a provincial court judge, whether or not the person or persons in respect of whom it is feared that the offence will be committed are named.

(2) A provincial court judge who receives an information under subsection (1) may cause the parties to appear before a provincial court judge.

(3) If the provincial court judge before whom the parties appear is satisfied by the evidence adduced that the informant has reasonable grounds for the fear, the judge may order that the defendant enter into a recognizance to keep the peace and be of good behaviour for a period that does not exceed 12 months.

(3.1) However, if the provincial court judge is also satisfied that the defendant was convicted previously of an offence referred to in subsection (1), the judge may order

that the defendant enter into the recognizance for a period that does not exceed two years.

(4) The provincial court judge may commit the defendant to prison for a term not exceeding twelve months if the defendant fails or refuses to enter into the recognizance.

(4.1) The provincial court judge may add any reasonable conditions to the recognizance that the judge considers desirable to secure the good conduct of the defendant, including conditions that require the defendant

(*a*) to participate in a treatment program;

(*b*) to wear an electronic monitoring device, if the Attorney General makes the request;

(*c*) to remain within a specified geographic area unless written permission to leave that area is obtained from the provincial court judge;

(*d*) to return to and remain at his or her place of residence at specified times;

(*e*) to abstain from the consumption of drugs except in accordance with a medical prescription, of alcohol or of any other intoxicating substance;

(*f*) to provide, for the purpose of analysis, a sample of a bodily substance prescribed by regulation on the demand of a peace officer, a probation officer or someone designated under paragraph 810.3(2)(*a*) to make a demand, at the place and time and on the day specified by the person making the demand, if that person has reasonable grounds to believe that the defendant has breached a condition of the recognizance that requires them to abstain from the consumption of drugs, alcohol or any other intoxicating substance; or

(*g*) to provide, for the purpose of analysis, a sample of a bodily substance prescribed by regulation at regular intervals that are specified, in a notice in Form 51 served on the defendant, by a probation officer or a person designated under paragraph 810.3(2)(*b*) to specify them, if a condition of the recognizance requires the defendant to abstain from the consumption of drugs, alcohol or any other intoxicating substance.

(5) The provincial court judge shall consider whether it is desirable, in the interests of the defendant's safety or that of any other person, to prohibit the defendant from possessing any firearm, cross-bow, prohibited weapon, restricted weapon, prohibited device, ammunition, prohibited ammunition or explosive substance, or all of those things. If the judge decides that it is desirable to do so, the judge shall add that condition to the recognizance and specify the period during which the condition applies.

(5.1) If the provincial court judge adds a condition described in subsection (5) to a recognizance, the judge shall specify in the recognizance how the things referred to in that subsection that are in the defendant's possession should be surrendered, disposed of, detained, stored or dealt with and how the authorizations, licences and registration certificates that are held by the defendant should be surrendered.

(5.2) If the provincial court judge does not add a condition described in subsection (5) to a recognizance, the judge shall include in the record a statement of the reasons for not adding the condition.

(6) The provincial court judge shall consider whether it is desirable to require the defendant to report to the correctional authority of a province or to an appropriate police authority. If the judge decides that it is desirable to do so, the judge shall add that condition to the recognizance.

(7) A provincial court judge may, on application of the informant, of the Attorney General or of the defendant, vary the conditions fixed in the recognizance.

(8) Subsections 810(4) and (5) apply, with such modifications as the circumstances require, to recognizances made under this section. 1997, c. 17, s. 9; 2002, c. 13, s. 82; 2008, c. 6, s. 53; 2011, c. 7, s. 10.

CROSS-REFERENCES

The recognizance made under this section is similar to the recognizance under ss. 810 and 810.1. Breach of the recognizance is an offence under s. 811. Where a weapons prohibition order is made a condition of probation under subsec. (5), pursuant to s. 113, the judge may make an order authorizing a chief firearms officer or the Registrar to issue, in accordance with such terms and conditions as is considered appropriate, an authorization, a licence or a registration certificate, as the case may be, to the accused for sustenance or employment purposes.

"Provincial court judge" is defined in s. 2. Pursuant to s. 2.1, the terms "cross-bow", "prohibited weapon", "restricted weapon", "prohibited device", "ammunition", and "prohibited ammunition" have the same meaning as in s. 84(1).

SYNOPSIS

This section allows anyone to lay an information before a provincial court judge with the consent of the Attorney General, for the purpose of having the defendant enter into a recognizance where there are reasonable grounds to fear that the defendant may commit a serious personal injury offence as defined in s. 752. The maximum duration of the order is 12 months, except if the defendant was previously convicted of a serious personal injury offence, in which case the recognizance may be for a period of up to two years. Subsection (4) provides a non-exhaustive list of conditions that may be imposed to secure the good conduct of the defendant. Subsection (5) requires the court to consider imposing a weapons prohibition and, under subsec. (5.2), the judge must provide reasons for not imposing such a condition. Subsection (6) requires the court to consider whether the defendant should report to a correctional authority or police authority. Under subsec. (4), the conditions may be varied by the judge on application of the informant or the defendant, including conditions prohibiting the defendant from being in possession of firearms or ammunition (subsec. (5)) and requiring the offender to report to police or a correctional authority (subsec. (6)). If the defendant fails or refuses to enter into the recognizance, the judge may commit the offender to prison for up to 12 months. The recognizance may be for a period not exceeding 12 months. Under subsec. (7), an application may be made to vary the conditions in the recognizance.

ANNOTATIONS

The judicial interim release provisions under s. 515 and the ability to issue an arrest warrant pursuant to s. 507 release apply to peace bond proceedings: *R. v. Cachine* (2001), 154 C.C.C. (3d) 376 (B.C.C.A.).

This provision does not create a continuing proceeding nor is it akin to a bail hearing. Once the recognizance is entered into or a jail term is ordered, the judge is *functus officio*. Accordingly, where a jail term had been imposed and prior to the expiration of that term, a new proceeding under this provision was initiated, the judge who heard the first application was *functus officio*: *R. v. Ferrier* (2001), 155 C.C.C. (3d) 521 (Ont. S.C.J.).

VIDEO CONFERENCE.

810.21 If a defendant is required to appear under any of sections 83.3 and 810 to 810.2, a provincial court judge may, on application of the prosecutor, order that the defendant appear by video conference if the judge is satisfied that it would serve the proper administration of justice, including by ensuring a fair and efficient hearing and enhancing access to justice. 2015, c. 20, s. 26.

TRANSFER OF ORDER / Attorney General's consent / If judge unable to act.

810.22 (1) If a person who is bound by an order under any of sections 83.3 and 810 to 810.2 becomes a resident of — or is charged with, convicted of or discharged under section 730 of an offence, including an offence under section 811, in — a territorial division other than the territorial division in which the order was made, on application

of a peace officer or the Attorney General, a provincial court judge may, subject to subsection (2), transfer the order to a provincial court judge in that other territorial division and the order may then be dealt with and enforced by the provincial court judge to whom it is transferred in all respects as if that provincial court judge had made the order.

(2) The transfer may be granted only with

(*a*) the consent of the Attorney General of the province in which the order was made, if the two territorial divisions are not in the same province; or

(*b*) the consent of the Attorney General of Canada, if the information that led to the issuance of the order was laid with the consent of the Attorney General of Canada.

(3) If the judge who made the order or a judge to whom an order has been transferred is for any reason unable to act, the powers of that judge in relation to the order may be exercised by any other judge of the same court. 2015, c. 20, s. 26.

SAMPLES — DESIGNATIONS AND SPECIFICATIONS / Further designations / Restriction / Destruction of samples / Regulations / Notice — samples at regular intervals.

810.3 (1) For the purposes of sections 810, 810.01, 810.011, 810.1 and 810.2 and subject to the regulations, the Attorney General of a province or the minister of justice of a territory shall, with respect to the province or territory,

(*a*) designate the persons or classes of persons that may take samples of bodily substances;

(*b*) designate the places or classes of places at which the samples are to be taken;

(*c*) specify the manner in which the samples are to be taken;

(*d*) specify the manner in which the samples are to be analyzed;

(*e*) specify the manner in which the samples are to be stored, handled and destroyed;

(*f*) specify the manner in which the records of the results of the analysis of the samples are to be protected and destroyed;

(*g*) designate the persons or classes of persons that may destroy the samples; and

(*h*) designate the persons or classes of persons that may destroy the records of the results of the analysis of the samples.

(2) Subject to the regulations, the Attorney General of a province or the minister of justice of a territory may, with respect to the province or territory, designate the persons or classes of persons

(*a*) to make a demand for a sample of a bodily substance for the purposes of paragraphs 810(3.02)(*b*), 810.01(4.1)(*f*), 810.011(6)(*e*), 810.1(3.02)(*h*) and 810.2(4.1)(*f*); and

(*b*) to specify the regular intervals at which a defendant must provide a sample of a bodily substance for the purposes of paragraphs 810(3.02)(*c*), 810.01(4.1)(*g*), 810.011(6)(*f*), 810.1(3.02)(*i*) and 810.2(4.1)(*g*).

(3) Samples of bodily substances referred to in sections 810, 810.01, 810.011, 810.1 and 810.2 may not be taken, analyzed, stored, handled or destroyed, and the records of the results of the analysis of the samples may not be protected or destroyed, except in accordance with the designations and specifications made under subsection (1).

(4) The Attorney General of a province or the minister of justice of a territory, or a person authorized by the Attorney General or minister, shall cause all samples of bodily substances provided under a recognizance under section 810, 810.01, 810.011, 810.1 or 810.2 to be destroyed within the period prescribed by regulation unless the samples are reasonably expected to be used as evidence in a proceeding for an offence under section 811.

(5) The Governor in Council may make regulations

(*a*) prescribing bodily substances for the purposes of sections 810, 810.01, 810.011, 810.1 and 810.2;

(*b*) respecting the designations and specifications referred to in subsections (1) and (2);

(*c*) prescribing the periods within which samples of bodily substances are to be destroyed under subsection (4); and

(*d*) respecting any other matters relating to the samples of bodily substances.

(6) The notice referred to in paragraph 810(3.02)(*c*), 810.01(4.1)(*g*), 810.011(6)(*f*), 810.1(3.02)(*i*) or 810.2(4.1)(*g*) must specify the places and times at which and the days on which the defendant must provide samples of a bodily substance under a condition described in that paragraph. The first sample may not be taken earlier than 24 hours after the defendant is served with the notice, and subsequent samples must be taken at regular intervals of at least seven days. 2011, c. 7, s. 11; 2015, c. 20, s. 34(2)(*a*)-(*e*).

PROHIBITION ON USE OF BODILY SUBSTANCE / Prohibition on use or disclosure of result / Exception / Offence.

810.4 (1) No person shall use a bodily substance provided under a recognizance under section 810, 810.01, 810.011, 810.1 or 810.2 except for the purpose of determining whether a defendant is complying with a condition in the recognizance that they abstain from the consumption of drugs, alcohol or any other intoxicating substance.

(2) Subject to subsection (3), no person shall use, disclose or allow the disclosure of the results of the analysis of a bodily substance provided under a recognizance under section 810, 810.01, 810.011, 810.1 or 810.2.

(3) The results of the analysis of a bodily substance provided under a recognizance under section 810, 810.01, 810.011, 810.1 or 810.2 may be disclosed to the defendant to whom they relate, and may also be used or disclosed in the course of an investigation of, or in a proceeding for, an offence under section 811 or, if the results are made anonymous, for statistical or other research purposes.

(4) Every person who contravenes subsection (1) or (2) is guilty of an offence punishable on summary conviction. 2011, c. 7, s. 11; 2015, c. 20, s. 34(2)(*f*).

BREACH OF RECOGNIZANCE.

811. A person bound by a recognizance under any of sections 83.3 and 810 to 810.2 who commits a breach of the recognizance is guilty of

(*a*) an indictable offence and is liable to imprisonment for a term of not more than four years; or

(*b*) an offence punishable on summary conviction and is liable to imprisonment for a term of not more than 18 months. R.S., c. C-34, s. 746; 1993, c. 45, s. 11; 1994, c. 44, s. 82; 1997, c. 17, s. 10; c. 23, ss. 20, 27; 2001, c. 41, s. 23; 2015, c. 20, s. 27(1); c. 23, s. 19; c. 29, s. 12.

SYNOPSIS

This section creates the Crown option offence of breaching a recognizance under ss. 83.3, 810, 810.01, 810.02, 810.1 or 810.2, and when proceeded with by indictment is within the absolute jurisdiction of a provincial court judge pursuant to s. 553.

ANNOTATIONS

An allegation that the defendant violated the terms of a recognizance made under s. 810 must be charged under this section. The general provisions in s. 145 respecting breach of recognizance are not applicable: *R. v. Simanek* (1993), 82 C.C.C. (3d) 576 (Ont. C.A.).

The validity of the recognizance cannot be collaterally challenged on the trial under this section: *R. v. Bourque* (1999), 140 C.C.C. (3d) 435 (N.B.C.A.); *R. v. Walsh* (2016), 345 C.C.C. (3d) 298 (Sask. C.A.).

PROOF OF CERTIFICATE OF ANALYST — BODILY SUBSTANCE / Definition of "analyst" / Notice of intention to produce certificate / Requiring attendance of analyst.

811.1 (1) In a prosecution for breach of a condition in a recognizance under section 810, 810.01, 810.011, 810.1 or 810.2 that a defendant not consume drugs, alcohol or any other intoxicating substance, a certificate purporting to be signed by an analyst that states that the analyst has analyzed a sample of a bodily substance and that states the result of the analysis is admissible in evidence and, in the absence of evidence to the contrary, is proof of the statements contained in the certificate without proof of the signature or official character of the person who appears to have signed the certificate.

(2) In this section, "analyst" has the same meaning as in section 320.11.

(3) No certificate shall be admitted in evidence unless the party intending to produce it has, before the trial, given reasonable notice and a copy of the certificate to the party against whom it is to be produced.

(4) The party against whom a certificate of an analyst is produced may, with leave of the court, require the attendance of the analyst for cross-examination. 2011, c. 7, s. 12; 2015, c. 20, s. 34(3); 2018, c. 21, s. 27.

Appeal

DEFINITION OF "APPEAL COURT".

812. (1) For the purposes of sections 813 to 828 "appeal court" means

- **(*a*) in the Province of Ontario, the Superior Court of Justice sitting in the region, district or county or group of counties where the adjudication was made;**
- **(*b*) in the Province of Quebec, the Superior Court;**
- **(*c*) in the Provinces of Nova Scotia, British Columbia and Prince Edward Island, the Supreme Court;**
- **(*d*) in the Provinces of New Brunswick, Manitoba, Saskatchewan and Alberta, the Court of Queen's Bench;**
- **(*e*) [*Repealed*, 1992, c. 51, s. 43(2).]**
- **(*f*) [*Repealed*. 2015, c. 3, s. 56(2).]**
- **(*g*) in the Province of Newfoundland and Labrador, the Trial Division of the Supreme Court;**
- **(*h*) in Yukon and the Northwest Territories, a judge of the Supreme Court; and**
- **(*i*) in Nunavut, a judge of the Nunavut Court of Justice.**

(2) A judge of the Court of Appeal of Nunavut is the appeal court for the purposes of sections 813 to 828 if the appeal is from a conviction, order, sentence or verdict of a summary conviction court consisting of a judge of the Nunavut Court of Justice. R.S., c. C-34, s. 747; 1972, c. 13, s. 65, c. 17, s. 2; 1974-75-76, c. 19, s. 1; 1978-79, c. 11, s. 10; R.S.C. 1985, c. 11 (1st Supp.), s. 2; c. 27 (2nd Supp.), s. 10.; 1990, c. 16, s. 7; 1990, c. 17, s. 15; 1992, c. 51, s. 43; 1993, c. 28, Sch. III, s. 36 (repealed 1999, c. 3, s. 12); 1998, c. 30, s. 14(*d*); 1999, c. 3, ss. 12, 55; 2002, c. 7, s. 149; 2015, c. 3, s. 56.

CROSS-REFERENCES

Section 813 confers rights of appeal. Section 815 deals with filing of notice of appeal. Appeal procedures are governed by ss. 821 to 823 and s. 482(2). Sections 816 and 819 authorize the judicial interim release of an appellant who was a defendant in summary conviction proceedings.

Sections 817 and 818 govern appeals by a prosecutor other than the Attorney General or counsel acting on his behalf. Appeals under s. 813 are determined on the record in accordance with ss. 683 and 689, except for ss. 683(3) and 686(5), made applicable to summary conviction appeals by s. 822(1). An appeal may be determined by a trial *de novo* under s. 822(4) to (7) in certain circumstances. Further appeal lies under s. 839(1)(*a*).

SYNOPSIS

This section defines "appeal court" for each of the provinces and territories for the purposes of appeals from summary conviction.

ANNOTATIONS

Paragraph (*c*) – A county court judge who has heard summary conviction appeals in criminal proceedings has jurisdiction to deliver judgment after his resignation on reserved appeals if provincial legislation so provides. Such legislation is validly enacted under the province's power to legislate with respect to the constitution, maintenance and organization of the courts pursuant to s. 92(14) of the *British North America Act, 1867*: *R. v. Ritcey*, [1980] 1 S.C.R. 1077, 50 C.C.C. (2d) 481 (7:0).

APPEAL BY DEFENDANT, INFORMANT OR ATTORNEY GENERAL.

813. Except where otherwise provided by law,

(*a*) the defendant in proceedings under this Part may appeal to the appeal court

(i) from a conviction or order made against him,

(ii) against a sentence passed on him, or

(iii) against a verdict of unfit to stand trial or not criminally responsible on account of mental disorder; and

(*b*) the informant, the Attorney General or his agent in proceedings under this Part may appeal to the appeal court

(i) from an order that stays proceedings on an information or dismisses an information,

(ii) against a sentence passed on a defendant, or

(iii) against a verdict of not criminally responsible on account of mental disorder or unfit to stand trial,

and the Attorney General of Canada or his agent has the same rights of appeal in proceedings instituted at the instance of the Government of Canada and conducted by or on behalf of that Government as the Attorney General of a province or his agent has under this paragraph. R.S., c. C-34, s. 748; R.S.C. 1985, c. 27 (1st Supp.), s. 180; 1991, c. 43, s. 9.

CROSS-REFERENCES

See s. 812 for definition of "appeal court", s. 785 for "informant" and "proceedings" and s. 2 for "Attorney General". "Prosecutor" as used throughout Part XXVII does not appear in s. 813. See ss. 675 and 676 for corresponding rights of appeal in proceedings by indictment by accused and Attorney General respectively. Also see reference cited under s. 812.

See s. 672.1 for definition of "verdict of not criminally responsible on account of mental disorder" and s. 2 for definition of "unfit to stand trial".

SYNOPSIS

This section gives rights of appeal, except where otherwise provided by law, to defendants against conviction, order, sentence, finding of unfitness or verdict of not criminally responsible and to informants or the Crown (provincial or federal) against stay, dismissal or sentence.

ANNOTATIONS

Right of appeal (para. (*a*)(i)) – It is the nature of the trial proceedings, and not the ultimate conviction that determines the appeal procedure so where a summary conviction is the result of an indictable offence trial, appeal only lies under Part XXI of the Code: *R. v. Yaworski* (1959), 124 C.C.C. 151 (Man. C.A.).

Imposition of sentence is not a prerequisite to the hearing of an appeal against conviction: *R. v. Benson* (1978), 40 C.C.C. (2d) 271 (B.C.C.A.); *R. v. MacNeil* (1979), 46 C.C.C. (2d) 383 (Ont. C.A.). *Contra: R. v. Hofer* (1977), 36 C.C.C. (2d) 426 (Man. Co. Ct.).

Procedure (para. (*a*)(ii)) – Unless an appeal is specifically lodged against sentence the appeal court has no jurisdiction to deal with it: *R. v. Praisley,* [1965] 1 C.C.C. 316 (B.C.C.A.), and *R. v. Ferencsik,* [1970] 4 C.C.C. 166 (Ont. C.A.).

Crown appeal generally (para. (*b*)(i)) – The unqualified language that appears in s. 813(*b*)(i) compels the conclusion that an appeal by the Attorney General from dismissal of an information in summary conviction proceedings may be based on grounds of fact, mixed fact and law or law alone: *R. v. Labadie* (2011), 275 C.C.C. (3d) 75 (Ont. C.A.).

Where a summary conviction court refuses to dispose of a case on the ground that it lacks jurisdiction the only remedy is for the informant to *mandamus* the court into dismissing the information and then appeal that dismissal: *R. ex rel. Hickman v. Marshall* (1960), 127 C.C.C. 76 (Ont. C.A.). [However, also see s. 830.]

Similarly where before plea objections are raised to an information and the summary conviction court endorses it "no jurisdiction" no appeal lies under this section: *R. ex rel. Lees v. Wacker* (1958), 121 C.C.C. 185 (Ont. C.A.).

A notice of appeal styled as "Her Majesty the Queen, (Informant) Appellant" and signed on her behalf by the Attorney General's Agent as her solicitor is proper: *R. v. Genser & Sons Ltd.*, [1969] 3 C.C.C. 87 (Man. C.A.).

It was held prior to the amendment of this paragraph permitting an appeal against a stay of proceedings as well as a dismissal that this paragraph gives the Crown a right of appeal only where the disposition by the summary conviction court is in the nature of a judgment or verdict of acquittal or what is tantamount to an acquittal, that is, a disposition made after the issue raised in the information has been tried on the merits, in law or on the facts. An order quashing an information on an objection being taken to its form does not give a right of appeal. Dispositions which would give rise to a right of appeal are, for example, where the charge is dismissed on the ground that the information does not disclose an offence known to law, where the offence alleged is *ultra vires,* or where the prosecutor fails to appear. Where the summary conviction court dismisses an information for failure of the Crown to supply particulars as previously ordered, such disposition gives the Crown a right of appeal only where the failure to provide particulars left the information in a state where it disclosed no offence known to law. Otherwise, the order is not an acquittal or tantamount to an acquittal as it does not purport to dispose of the issue raised in the information on the merits, in law or on the facts, and the Crown's remedy is by way of *mandamus: R. v. Canadian Pacific Ltd.* (1976), 32 C.C.C. (2d) 14 (Alta. S.C. App. Div.) (5:0).

An order quashing an information for failure to comply with s. 581 does not constitute an order dismissing an information and the appeal should be taken pursuant to s. 830: *R. v. Moore* (1987), 38 C.C.C. (3d) 471 (Ont. C.A.).

Whether undisputed facts in a case have the legal effect of infringing an accused's constitutional rights is a question of law: *R. v. Burke* (1997), 118 C.C.C. (3d) 59 (Nfld. C.A.).

Crown appeal from dismissal of information – An order dismissing an information for want of prosecution is an appealable order: *R. v. Allen* (1960), 128 C.C.C. 409 (B.C. Co. Ct.); *R. v. Yanke* (1983), 4 C.C.C. (3d) 26 (Sask. C.A.).

It is not necessary for appeal purposes that a formal dismissal order be taken out; it is sufficient if the trial court made a finding of not guilty: *R. v. Leblanc,* [1964] 3 C.C.C. 40 (N.S. Co. Ct.).

Where a piece of evidence essential to the success of the prosecution is ruled inadmissible the Crown may elect to call no further evidence and proceed immediately to appeal upon dismissal of the charge: *R. v. Aleksich* (1979), 50 C.C.C. (2d) 62 (B.C.C.A.); *R. v. Croquet* (1973), 12 C.C.C. (2d) 331 (B.C.C.A.); and similarly *R. v. Davis and Lakehead Bag Co.* (1977), 34 C.C.C. (2d) 388 (Ont. C.A.), where as a result of certain rulings the verdict was a "foregone conclusion".

Dismissal of a charge prior to plea on the basis that the enactment under which the charge was laid is *ultra vires* is a dismissal within the meaning of this paragraph against which the Crown may appeal: *R. v. Miracle Mart Inc.* (1982), 68 C.C.C. (2d) 242 (Que. S.C.).

An appeal from a curative discharge pursuant to s. 255(5) is an appeal from the dismissal of an information: *R. v. Ahenakew* (2005), 200 C.C.C. (3d) 527 (Sask. C.A.).

Appeal by informant – An appellant is not entitled to be represented by an agent: *R. v. Hammond* (1972), 24 C.R.N.S. 309 (Ont. Co. Ct.).

An appeal against dismissal brought by the informant does not abate with his death: *R. v. Fillmore* (1974), 17 C.C.C. (2d) 66 (N.S. Co. Ct.).

While the informant has an unfettered right to appeal to the summary conviction appeal court from an order staying proceedings on an information or dismissing an information whether or not the prosecution at trial was conducted by an agent of the Attorney General, the Attorney General or his agent may intervene, either by taking carriage of the appeal itself or by indicating that he does not wish that the matter be further prosecuted by way of appeal. Where there is such active opposition by the Attorney General or his agent, then the appeal by the informant must be dismissed: *Bouree v. Parsons* (1986), 29 C.C.C. (3d) 126 (Ont. Dist. Ct.).

MANITOBA AND ALBERTA / Saskatchewan / British Columbia / Territories.

814. (1) In the Provinces of Manitoba and Alberta, an appeal under section 813 shall be heard at the sittings of the appeal court that is held nearest to the place where the cause of the proceedings arose, but the judge of the appeal court may, on the application of one of the parties, appoint another place for the hearing of the appeal.

(2) In the Province of Saskatchewan, an appeal under section 813 shall be heard at the sittings of the appeal court at the judicial centre nearest to the place where the adjudication was made, but the judge of the appeal court may, on the application of one of the parties, appoint another place for the hearing of the appeal.

(3) In the Province of British Columbia, an appeal under section 813 shall be heard at the sittings of the appeal court that is held nearest to the place where the adjudication was made, but the judge of the appeal court may, on the application of one of the parties, appoint another place for the hearing of the appeal.

(4) In Yukon, the Northwest Territories and Nunavut, an appeal under section 813 shall be heard at the place where the cause of the proceedings arose or at the place nearest to it where a court is appointed to be held. R.S., c. C-34, s. 749; 1984, c. 41, s. 2; 1993, c. 28, Sch. III, s. 37; 2002, c. 7, s. 150.

CROSS-REFERENCES

Section 822(4) to (7) is authority to have appeal heard and determined as trial *de novo*. Also see references cited under s. 812.

SYNOPSIS

This section sets the rules with respect to the venue of the appeal for the provinces west of Ontario and the territories.

NOTICE OF APPEAL / Extension of time.

815. (1) An appellant who proposes to appeal to the appeal court shall give notice of appeal in such manner and within such period as may be directed by rules of court.

(2) The appeal court or a judge thereof may at any time extend the time within which notice of appeal may be given. R.S., c. C-34, s. 750; 1972, c. 13, s. 66; 1974-75-76, c. 93, s. 89.

CROSS-REFERENCES

Section 482(2) is authority for the appeal court to pass rules consistent with the *Criminal Code* or other federal Acts governing procedures on appeals under s. 813. These rules determine the form of the notice of appeal, filing and service provisions.

An order, conviction or sentence must be appealed to challenge its validity under s. 820(2) and the onus is on the accused to establish appeal. Under s. 813, payment of fine does not waive accused's right of appeal.

Payment of a fine or other pecuniary penalty may be suspended by the court pending the determination of the appeal as authorized by the incorporation of s. 683(5) by s. 822(1). Section 689 authorizes stay in respect of restitution orders and is available to summary conviction appeals under s. 822(1).

SYNOPSIS

This section states that the appellant shall give notice of appeal according to the rules of court and that the appeal court or a judge thereof may extend the time for notice to be given.

ANNOTATIONS

Notice of appeal [subsec. (1)] – Failure to include the appellant's address for service as required by the rule of court is not fatal to hearing of the appeal. The proper procedure is to permit amendment of the notice and proceed with the hearing of the appeal: *R. v. Saad* (1978), 45 C.C.C. (2d) 318 (Que. C.A.).

Extension of time generally / Extension of time sought by Crown – The court has no power to grant the Crown an extension of time *ex parte* without notice to the accused whether the application for the extension is made after expiration of the appeal period: *Neal v. Saskatchewan (Attorney General)*, [1977] 2 S.C.R. 624, 56 C.C.C. (2d) 128, 115 D.L.R. (3d) 20 (9:0); or before expiration of the appeal period: *R. v. Taylor* (1980), 56 C.C.C. (2d) 86, 28 N.B.R. (2d) 704 (Q.B.).

In *R. v. Ruffo* (1982), 1 C.C.C. (3d) 358 (Ont. C.A.), the court considered *Neal, supra,* but held that in exceptional circumstances the court could grant the Crown an extension of time on an *ex parte* application as where it was impossible to give notice of the application because the respondent could not be found. In the absence of the most unusual circumstances there must be evidence by way of affidavit, documentary evidence or *viva voce* testimony as to the basis for the *ex parte* application. On the other hand, where objection to an order for an extension of time is taken at the hearing of the appeal it would be open to the appeal court to grant an extension, on notice at that time, in which event the notice of appeal could then be re-served.

The order extending time for service on the accused/respondent must also provide for an extension of time in which to file the notice of appeal. A judge on an application for extension of time has no power to validate the prior service of a notice of appeal made out of time. Where the notice of appeal is served out of time it must be re-served within the extended time: *R. v. Holmes* (1982), 2 C.C.C. (3d) 471, 18 M.V.R. 92 (Ont. C.A.). *Contra*: *R. v. Fenrich*, [1985] 6 W.W.R. 269 (Sask. Q.B.), where it was held that the court has power to grant an order *nunc pro tunc* to validate service already made.

There being no evidence that the Crown had an intention to appeal within the appeal period and no explanation having been offered for the long delay an extension of time should not be granted: *R. v. Osgoode Sand & Gravel Ltd.* (1978), 41 C.C.C. (2d) 503 (Ont. Div. Ct.).

Principles in granting extension of time – There is no absolute rule to be applied in the exercise of the discretion whether or not to grant an extension of time. The court will, however, usually consider the following three factors: (i) whether the applicant has shown a *bona fide* intention to appeal within the appeal period; (ii) whether the applicant has accounted for or explained the delay; and (iii) whether there is merit to the proposed appeal. Depending on the case, the court may take into consideration other factors such as whether the consequences of the conviction are out of all proportion to the penalty imposed, whether the Crown will be prejudiced and whether the applicant has taken the benefit of the judgment. In the end, the main consideration is whether the applicant has demonstrated that justice requires that the extension of time be granted: *R. v. Menear*, [2002] 3 S.C.R. ix, 162 C.C.C. (3d) 233 (Ont. C.A.), leave to appeal to S.C.C. refused [2002] 3 S.C.R. ix, 164 C.C.C. (3d) vi.

Setting aside dismissal of appeal – The appeal court has a discretionary jurisdiction to rescind a notice of abandonment filed by the accused, set aside the dismissal of his appeal and restore the appeal for hearing on the merits: *R. v. Robertson* (1978), 45 C.C.C. (2d) 344 (Ont. C.A.).

Interim Release of Appellant

UNDERTAKING OR RECOGNIZANCE OF APPELLANT / Application of certain provisions of section 525.

816. (1) A person who was the defendant in proceedings before a summary conviction court and by whom an appeal is taken under section 813 shall, if he is in custody, remain in custody unless the appeal court at which the appeal is to be heard orders that the appellant be released

(*a*) on his giving an undertaking to the appeal court, without conditions or with such conditions as the appeal court directs, to surrender himself into custody in accordance with the order,

(*b*) on his entering into a recognizance without sureties in such amount, with such conditions, if any, as the appeal court directs, but without deposit of money or other valuable security, or

(*c*) on his entering into a recognizance with or without sureties in such amount, with such conditions, if any, as the appeal court directs, and on his depositing with that appeal court such sum of money or other valuable security as the appeal court directs,

and the person having the custody of the appellant shall, where the appellant complies with the order, forthwith release the appellant.

(2) The provisions of subsections 525(5), (6) and (7) apply with such modifications as the circumstances require in respect of a person who has been released from custody under subsection (1). R.S., c. C-34, s. 752; R.S., c. 2 (2nd Supp.), s. 16; 1974-75-76, c. 39, s. 91; R.S.C. 1985, c. 27 (1st Supp.), s. 181.

CROSS-REFERENCES

Section 819 permits the hearing of an appeal to be expedited if not commenced within 30 days of the notice of appeal. There is no statutory right of review of an order made under s. 816 nor under subsec. (2) in the application of the provisions of s. 525(7).

Section 679(3) and (4) govern judicial interim release in indictable appeal proceedings.

Where the appellant under s. 813 is a private prosecutor, he is required by s. 817 to give an undertaking or enter into a recognizance. A private prosecutor must appear personally or by counsel at the sittings of the appeal court. Section 818 governs review by the court of appeal of an order of a justice under s. 817.

SYNOPSIS

This section provides for the granting of bail pending appeal to an accused appealing the decision of a summary conviction court. The court can order that the accused be released from custody on an undertaking or recognizance with or without sureties on deposit.

ANNOTATIONS

Bearing in mind that, generally, summary conviction offences are less serious, the principles governing release pending appeal on indictable matters as set out in s. 679 apply on an application under this section. Further, in Ontario, no rules having been adopted as to the proper procedure to be followed on the application, the provisions of the Criminal Rules relating to bail pending appeal in indictable matters should be applied by analogy: *R. v. Simpson* (1978), 44 C.C.C. (2d) 109 (Ont. Co. Ct.).

A judge of the summary conviction appeal Court has an inherent jurisdiction to stay the terms of a probation order pending an appeal to that court: *R. v. Anderson* (1982), 70 C.C.C. (2d) 253 (Ont. Co. Ct.).

UNDERTAKING OR RECOGNIZANCE OF PROSECUTOR / Condition / Appeals by Attorney General / Form of undertaking or recognizance.

817. (1) The prosecutor in proceedings before a summary conviction court by whom an appeal is taken under section 813 shall, forthwith after filing the notice of appeal and proof of service thereof in accordance with section 815, appear before a justice, and the justice shall, after giving the prosecutor and the respondent a reasonable opportunity to be heard, order that the prosecutor

(*a*) give an undertaking as prescribed in this section; or

(*b*) enter into a recognizance in such amount, with or without sureties and with or without deposit of money or other valuable security, as the justice directs.

(2) The condition of an undertaking or recognizance given or entered into under this section is that the prosecutor will appear personally or by counsel at the sittings of the appeal court at which the appeal is to be heard.

(3) This section does not apply in respect of an appeal taken by the Attorney General or by counsel acting on behalf of the Attorney General.

(4) An undertaking under this section may be in Form 14 and a recognizance under this section may be in Form 32. R.S., c. 2 (2nd Supp.), s. 16.

CROSS-REFERENCES

An order of a justice is reviewable by the court of appeal under s. 818.

See s. 785 for definition of "prosecutor", "proceedings" and "summary conviction court" which apply strictly to Part XXVII. Section 816 contains the judicial interim release provisions where the appellant is the accused.

See also references cited under s. 816.

SYNOPSIS

Where the prosecutor, other than the Attorney General, is the appellant an undertaking or recognizance, with or without sureties or deposit containing a condition with respect to appearing for the hearing must be entered into before a justice of the peace. Both the prosecutor and the respondent must be given the opportunity to be heard before the justice.

ANNOTATIONS

The failure to give the respondent an opportunity to be heard is a substantive, not procedural, error and a loss of the appeal court's jurisdiction follows: *R. v. Esam Construction Ltd.* (1974), 15 C.C.C. (2d) 335, 2 O.R. (2d) 344 (H.C.J.).

In *R. v. Broadfoot* (1977), 35 C.C.C. (2d) 493 (Ont. C.A.), it was held that this section is mandatory and while compliance therewith is not a condition precedent to the right of appeal it is a condition precedent to the hearing of the appeal.

APPLICATION TO APPEAL COURT FOR REVIEW / Disposition of application by appeal court / Effect of order.

818. (1) Where a justice makes an order under section 817, either the appellant or the respondent may, before or at any time during the hearing of the appeal, apply to the appeal court for a review of the order made by the justice.

(2) On the hearing of an application under this section, the appeal court, after giving the appellant and the respondent a reasonable opportunity to be heard, shall

(*a*) dismiss the application; or

(*b*) if the person applying for the review shows cause, allow the application, vacate the order made by the justice and make the order that in the opinion of the appeal court should have been made.

(3) An order made under this section shall have the same force and effect as if it had been made by the justice. R.S., c. 2 (2nd Supp.), s. 16; 1974-75-76, c. 93, s. 91.1.

CROSS-REFERENCES

No similar right of review exists where a judicial interim release order has been determined respecting an accused who is an appellant under s. 819.

See references cited under s. 816.

SYNOPSIS

This section provides that either party may apply to the summary conviction appeal court to review the order made by a justice of the peace with respect to the undertaking or recognizance of the appellant/prosecutor (see s. 817).

APPLICATION TO FIX DATE FOR HEARING OF APPEAL / Order fixing date.

819. (1) Where, in the case of an appellant who has been convicted by a summary conviction court and who is in custody pending the hearing of his appeal, the hearing of his appeal has not commenced within thirty days from the day on which notice of his appeal was given in accordance with the rules referred to in section 815, the person having the custody of the appellant shall, forthwith on the expiration of those thirty days, apply to the appeal court to fix a date for the hearing of the appeal.

(2) On receiving an application under subsection (1), the appeal court shall, after giving the prosecutor a reasonable opportunity to be heard, fix a date for the hearing of the appeal and give such directions as it thinks necessary for expediting the hearing of the appeal. R.S., c. 2 (2nd Supp.), s. 16; 1974-75-76, c. 93, s. 92.

CROSS-REFERENCES

See s. 525 for similar provision regarding delays in trial proceedings where accused is charged with an offence not listed in s. 469.

Section 526 is authority for expediting proceedings where accused appears before a court under Part XVI. Section 679(10) confers authority on a judge of the court of appeal in indictable matters.

SYNOPSIS

If the appeal of an appellant who is in custody has not commenced within 30 days of the filing of the notice of appeal the person who has custody of the appellant shall apply forthwith for a hearing date (subsec. (1)).

The court, in setting the date, may give such directions as are necessary to expedite the matter. The prosecutor must be given a reasonable opportunity to be heard before the date is set (subsec. (2)).

PAYMENT OF FINE NOT A WAIVER OF APPEAL / Presumption.

820. (1) A person does not waive his right of appeal under section 813 by reason only that he pays the fine imposed on conviction, without in any way indicating an intention to appeal or reserving the right to appeal.

(2) A conviction, order or sentence shall be deemed not to have been appealed against until the contrary is shown. R.S., c. C-34, s. 753.

CROSS-REFERENCES

Section 683(5) permits the suspension of pecuniary penalty obligations pending appeal.

Section 689 permits the suspension, pending appeal, of a restitution order under ss. 725 to 727. The appeal court has, under s. 822(1), similar authority in summary conviction appeals under s. 813.

SYNOPSIS

This section provides that the payment of a fine does not act as a waiver of the right to appeal (subsec. (1)). An appeal is deemed not to be taken until the contrary is shown (subsec. (2)).

Procedure on Appeal

NOTIFICATION AND TRANSMISSION OF CONVICTION, ETC. / Saving / Appellant to furnish transcript of evidence.

821. (1) Where a notice of appeal has been given in accordance with the rules referred to in section 815, the clerk of the appeal court shall notify the summary conviction court that made the conviction or order appealed from or imposed the sentence appealed against of the appeal and on receipt of the notification that summary conviction court shall transmit the conviction, order or order of dismissal and all other material in its possession in connection with the proceedings to the appeal court before the time when the appeal is to be heard, or within such further time as the appeal court may direct, and the material shall be kept by the clerk of the appeal court with the records of the appeal court.

(2) An appeal shall not be dismissed by the appeal court by reason only that a person other than the appellant failed to comply with the provisions of this Part relating to appeals.

(3) Where the evidence on a trial before a summary conviction court has been taken by a stenographer duly sworn or by a sound recording apparatus, the appellant shall, unless the appeal court otherwise orders or the rules referred to in section 815 otherwise provide, cause a transcript thereof, certified by the stenographer or in accordance with subsection 540(6), as the case may be, to be furnished to the appeal court and the respondent for use on the appeal. R.S., c. C-34, s. 754; 1972, c. 13, s. 67; 1974-75-76, c. 93, s. 93.

CROSS-REFERENCES

Evidence of witnesses in summary conviction proceedings is governed by the provisions relating to preliminary inquiries in Part XVIII, under s. 801(3).

Section 822 provides the authority of the appeal court to hear appeals under s. 813. The appeal is usually determined on the record of the lower court but a trial *de novo* under s. 822(4) to (7) may be necessary. Under s. 825, the appeal court may dismiss an appeal for appellant's failure to comply with orders under ss. 816 and 817 or failure to prosecute the appeal. See ss. 826 to 828 for cost provisions.

SYNOPSIS

This section deals with the transfer of the record from the trial court to the summary conviction appeal court. The appellant will not be held responsible if another person fails to comply with these provisions (subsecs. (1) and (2)).

Unless the appeal court orders otherwise it is the appellant's responsibility to obtain, file and serve transcripts of the evidence, if available (subsec. (3)).

CERTAIN SECTIONS APPLICABLE TO APPEALS / New trial / Order of detention or release / Trial *de novo* / Former evidence / Appeal against sentence / General provisions re appeals.

822. (1) Where an appeal is taken under section 813 in respect of any conviction, acquittal, sentence, verdict or order, sections 683 to 689, with the exception of subsections 683(3) and 686(5), apply, with such modifications as the circumstances require.

(2) Where an appeal court orders a new trial, it shall be held before a summary conviction court other than the court that tried the defendant in the first instance, unless the appeal court directs that the new trial be held before the summary conviction court that tried the accused in the first instance.

(3) Where an appeal court orders a new trial, it may make such order for the release or detention of the appellant pending the trial as may be made by a justice pursuant to section 515 and the order may be enforced in the same manner as if it had been made by a justice under that section, and the provisions of Part XVI apply with such modifications as the circumstances require to the order.

(4) Despite subsections (1) to (3), if an appeal is taken under section 813 and because of the condition of the record of the trial in the summary conviction court or for any other reason, the appeal court, on application of the defendant, the informant, the Attorney General or the Attorney General's agent, is of the opinion that the interests of justice would be better served by hearing and determining the appeal by holding a trial de novo, the appeal court may order that the appeal shall be heard by way of trial de novo in accordance with any rules that may be made under section 482 or 482.1, and for that purpose the provisions of sections 793 to 809 apply, with any modifications that the circumstances require.

(5) The appeal court may, for the purpose of hearing and determining an appeal under subsection (4), permit the evidence of any witness taken before the summary conviction court to be read if that evidence has been authenticated in accordance with section 540 and if

(*a*) the appellant and respondent consent,

(*b*) the appeal court is satisfied that the attendance of the witness cannot reasonably be obtained, or

(*c*) by reason of the formal nature of the evidence or otherwise the court is satisfied that the opposite party will not be prejudiced,

and any evidence that is read under the authority of this subsection has the same force and effect as if the witness had given the evidence before the appeal court.

(6) Where an appeal is taken under subsection (4) against sentence, the appeal court shall, unless the sentence is one fixed by law, consider the fitness of the sentence appealed against and may, on such evidence, if any, as it thinks fit to require or receive, by order,

(*a*) dismiss the appeal, or

(*b*) vary the sentence within the limits prescribed by law for the offence of which the defendant was convicted,

and in making any order under paragraph (*b*) the appeal court may take into account any time spent in custody by the defendant as a result of the offence.

(7) The following provisions apply in respect of appeals under subsection (4):

(*a*) where an appeal is based on an objection to an information or any process, judgment shall not be given in favour of the appellant

(i) for any alleged defect therein in substance or in form, or

(ii) for any variance between the information or process and the evidence adduced at the trial,

unless it is shown

(iii) that the objection was taken at the trial, and

(iv) that an adjournment of the trial was refused notwithstanding that the variance referred to in subparagraph (ii) had deceived or misled the appellant; and

(*b*) where an appeal is based on a defect in a conviction or an order, judgment shall not be given in favour of the appellant, but the court shall make an order curing the defect. R.S., c. C-34, s. 755; R.S., c. 2 (2nd Supp.), s. 17; 1974-75-76, c. 93, s. 94; 1984, c. 40, s. 20; 1991, c. 43, s. 9; 2002, c. 13, s. 83.

CROSS-REFERENCES

Section 482(2) contains authority for the appeal court to make rules under s. 813. Such rules require the approval of the Lieutenant Governor in Council and must be consistent with the *Criminal Code* and other federal Acts. The nature of the rules passed under s. 482(2) prescribes the procedure to be followed. Procedure on trial *de novo* imitates that prescribed in trial proceedings before a summary conviction court and includes the provisions of Parts XVI and XVIII (compelling accused's appearance), as well as those of Parts XX and XX.1 provided they are consistent with Part XXVII, which are incorporated by s. 795 with modifications.

An accused who is an appellant may be remanded or directed to attend for observation in accordance with s. 681 under s. 823. Costs may be awarded under s. 826. Appeal may be dismissed under s. 825 for failure to appear or want of prosecution.

SYNOPSIS

The provisions apply to verdicts which include a verdict of unfit to stand trial or not criminally responsible on account of mental disorder.

Certain of the provisions applicable to appeals in indictable matters apply to appeals under s. 813 (subsec. (1)).

Unless the appeal court directs otherwise a new trial is to be heard by a different judge (subsec. (2)).

The appeal court can grant bail or continue detention pending a new trial (subsec. (3)).

If it determines that such would be in the interests of justice an appeal court can hear an appeal by way of a trial *de novo*, on application of one of the parties (subsec. (4)). For this purpose the court can permit evidence from the trial to be "read in" (subsec. (5)).

On a sentence appeal, the court will consider the fitness of the sentence imposed and may vary the same within the limits prescribed by law (subsec. (6)).

Technical objections to the information or process will not succeed unless (a) the objection in question was raised at trial, and (b) in the case of a variance between the information or process and the evidence, an adjournment of the trial was refused. The appeal court may cure any defect in the formal conviction or order (subsec. (7)).

ANNOTATIONS

Representation by counsel [subsec. (1)] – In *R. v. Chmilar,* [1963] 3 C.C.C. 373, 40 C.R. 105 (B.C.C.A.), it was held that attendance of counsel at the date set for hearing a summary conviction appeal does not constitute waiver of objection to jurisdiction.

An appellant may not be represented by an agent: *R. v. Duggan* (1976), 31 C.C.C. (2d) 167 (Ont. C.A.).

Procedure – While the mere filing of the appeal does not stay or suspend the operation of the conviction, order or sentence appealed against the appeal court does have the power to stay or suspend the operation of an order which is subject to review on an appeal pending before the court: *R. v. Borger Industries Ltd. and Ladco Co.* (1979), 49 C.C.C. (2d) 527, [1979] 6 W.W.R. 474 (Man. Co. Ct.).

The summary conviction appeal court erred where the accused's appeal from conviction for driving "over 80" was allowed but the appeal court entered a conviction and sentenced the accused on a charge of impaired driving on the basis of the trial judge's findings. The charge of impaired driving should have been remitted to the trial judge for entry of a conviction and the imposition of sentence so as to preserve the accused's appeal rights: *R. v. Bjarnason* (1998), 130 C.C.C. (3d) 219, 173 W.A.C. 308 (Sask. C.A.).

A summary conviction appeal court has no authority to remit the case to the trial court for further consideration together "with the opinion of the appeal court". Section 822(1) contains no express provision that authorizes this remedy, and the incorporated sections of Part XXI include no such authority: *R. v. Labadie* (2011), 275 C.C.C. (3d) 75 (Ont. C.A.).

Nature of jurisdiction to review findings of fact – The summary convictions appeal court has no jurisdiction to retry the case. Its jurisdiction is limited to determining whether the evidence is so weak that a verdict of guilty was unreasonable: *R. v. Colbeck* (1978), 42 C.C.C. (2d) 117 (Ont. C.A.); *R. v. Arthur* (1981), 63 C.C.C. (2d) 117, [1982] 1 W.W.R. 122 (B.C.C.A.), leave to appeal to S.C.C. refused December 21, 1981. However, this jurisdiction is not limited to cases where there is no evidence but like the Court of Appeal in indictable matters under s. 686(1)(*a*)(i), includes the power to allow an appeal where the verdict cannot be supported by the evidence or is unreasonable: *R. v. Ponsford* (1978), 41 C.C.C. (2d) 433, 6 Alta. L.R. (2d) 370 (S.C. App. Div.). And even where the conviction turns on questions of credibility, if the court is satisfied that the basis for a finding of credibility is so tenuous that it would be an unreasonable basis for a conviction: *R. v. Saikaley* (1979), 52 C.C.C. (2d) 191 (Ont. C.A.).

Crown appeal on issues of fact – Despite the changes in procedure governing summary conviction appeals so that the primary procedure is an appeal on the record rather than by way of trial *de novo,* the Crown may appeal the dismissal of a charge on a question of fact alone. The amendments change the procedure on appeal but not the jurisdiction of the appeal court: *R. v. Antonelli* (1977), 38 C.C.C. (2d) 206 (B.C.C.A.); *R. v. Purves and Purves* (1979), 50 C.C.C. (2d) 211, 12 C.R. (3d) 362, [1980] 1 W.W.R. 148 (Man. C.A.); *R. v. Wilke* (1980), 56 C.C.C. (2d) 61 (Ont. C.A.); *R. v. Nelson,* [1979] 3 W.W.R. 97, 3 Sask. R. 45 (C.A.); *R. v. Sall* (1990), 54 C.C.C. (3d) 48 (Nfld. C.A.).

At least where the Crown appeal proceeds on the record in the lower court rather than by way of trial *de novo*, the availability of an appeal on questions of fact does not violate the *Charter of Rights and Freedoms* guarantees to fundamental justice, equality and protection against double jeopardy: *R. v. Century 21 Ramos Realty Inc. and Ramos* (1987), 32 C.C.C. (3d) 353, 56 C.R. (3d) 150, 37 D.L.R. (4th) 649 (Ont. C.A.), leave to appeal to S.C.C. refused 44 D.L.R. (4th) vii, 22 O.A.C. 319*n*, 80 N.R. 313*n*.

Although the Crown has a right of appeal on questions of fact the limitations on the appeal court's jurisdiction in appeals by the accused also apply to Crown appeals and, in particular, the appeal court has no right to retry the case: *R. v. Sall, supra*.

It may be that where the Crown appeal is not on a question of law alone the appeal court's only power is to order a new trial, and that the court would have no power to enter a conviction in view of the wording of s. 686(4)(*b*)(ii) which is applicable *mutatis mutandis* and which founds the court's jurisdiction to enter a conviction on a Crown appeal on the error in law: *R. v. Medicine Hat Greenhouses Ltd. and German* (1981), 59 C.C.C. (2d) 257, [1981] 3 W.W.R. 587 (Alta. C.A.), leave to appeal to S.C.C. refused 30 A.R. 360*n*, 38 N.R. 180*n*. Also see the discussion of this point in *R. v. Century 21 Ramos Realty Inc. and Ramos, supra*, and *R. v. Sall, supra*, where however the court left the issue open.

Trial *de novo* [subsec. (4)] – The words "or for any other reason" should be given a restrictive interpretation and the trial *de novo* procedure should be resorted to only where there was a denial of natural justice in the summary conviction court or a deficiency in the transcript of the trial. In particular a trial *de novo* should not be ordered solely because the accused, having elected to call no evidence in the summary conviction court, wishes to present a defence on appeal. Nor should the court allow such evidence to be called on the appeal under the power to hear fresh evidence pursuant to s. 683 of the *Criminal Code* made applicable to summary conviction appeals to subsec. (1): *R. v. Faulkner* (1977), 37 C.C.C. (2d) 26, 39 C.R.N.S. 331 (N.S. Co. Ct.).

Although the circumstances did not warrant the ordering of a trial *de novo* the accused may still be entitled to have evidence admitted on the appeal as fresh evidence pursuant to s. 683: *R. v. Winters* (1981), 59 C.C.C. (2d) 454, 21 C.R. (3d) 230 (B.C.C.A.).

However, in appropriate circumstances the discovery of fresh evidence may be grounds for allowing an application under subsec. (4): *R. v. Steinmiller* (1979), 47 C.C.C. (2d) 151 (Ont. C.A.).

On the hearing of an application under subsec. (4) the judge has no jurisdiction to dispose of the appeal itself and allow a new trial: *R. v. Steinmiller, supra*.

Where, because of the state of the record, the court has ordered that the accused's appeal proceed by way of trial *de novo*, the court may allow the appeal and enter an acquittal when neither the informant nor his counsel appear on the date set for the trial *de novo*: *R. v. Lacasse* (1979), 55 C.C.C. (2d) 337 (Que. C.A.).

It has now been held that provincial legislation which gave the Crown a right of appeal by way of trial *de novo* from an acquittal for a provincial offence was of no force and effect by reason of s. 11(*h*) of the *Charter of Rights and Freedoms*: *Corporation Professionnelles des Medecins du Quebec v. Thibault*, [1988] 1 S.C.R. 1033, 42 C.C.C. (3d) 1, 63 C.R. (3d) 273 (6:0). It may well be that similar reasoning would apply to preclude an application by the Crown under this subsection.

Where the transcript is unavailable due to a malfunctioning of the recording equipment an application for a trial *de novo* on a Crown appeal against an acquittal should be granted: *R. v. Street* (1981), 60 C.C.C. (2d) 376, 10 Sask. R. 266 (Dist. Ct.).

Sentence appeals [subsec. (6)] – In *R. v. Sproule* (1978), 39 C.C.C. (2d) 430 (Ont. C.A), a case decided under the former s. 755(3) which is worded in a similar manner to this subsection the Court of Appeal held that the summary conviction appeal court had no jurisdiction on an appeal by the accused against his sentence to increase the sentence, at least in the absence of notice by the Crown that it would be seeking such an increase. This decision accords generally with the decision of the Supreme Court of Canada in *R. v. Hill (No. 2)*, [1977] 1 S.C.R. 827, 25 C.C.C. (2d) 6, 62 D.L.R. (3d) 193, which considered an appeal against sentence in an indictable offence under s. 687 and is therefore likely applicable to an ordinary sentence appeal pursuant to subsec. (1).

Defects in information [subsec. (7)] – Where a charge omits or makes a defective statement of an essential element, but contains in substance a statement that the defendant committed the offence, an appellate court may, if the absence of the correct averment did not cause any substantial wrong or miscarriage of justice, amend the information and affirm the conviction: *R. v. Major* (1975), 25 C.C.C. (2d) 62, 10 N.S.R. (2d) 348 (S.C. App. Div.), revd on other grounds [1977] 1 S.C.R. 826, 27 C.C.C. (2d) 239*n*, 40 C.R.N.S. 298 (9:0). In any event inclusion of the offence section number will provide a reasonable description of the transaction alleged: *R. v. Cote*, [1978] 1 S.C.R. 303, 33 C.C.C. (2d) 353, 73 D.L.R. (3d) 752 (6:2).

An information that is duplicitous or multifarious contains a defect apparent on its face and must be raised at trial. Where no objection is taken at trial this subsection prevents the raising of the matter on appeal. Nor may the objection be raised on a further appeal to the Court of Appeal under s. 839(1)(*a*): *R. v. City of Sault Ste. Marie* (1976), 30 C.C.C. (2d) 257, 70 D.L.R. (3d) 430 (Ont. C.A.). On further appeal, [1978] 2 S.C.R. 1299, 40 C.C.C. (2d) 353, 85 D.L.R. (3d) 161 (9:0), the court found that the information was not duplicitous and therefore did not find it necessary to deal with this issue.

823. [*Repealed*, 1991, c. 43, s. 9.]

ADJOURNMENT.

824. The appeal court may adjourn the hearing of the appeal from time to time as may be necessary. R.S., c. C-34, s. 756.

CROSS-REFERENCES

The hearing of an appeal may be ordered expedited where accused is in custody and the appeal is not commenced within 30 days of notice of appeal, under s. 819(2).

Under s. 825, an appeal may be dismissed for failure to appear or want of prosecution.

ANNOTATIONS

An adjournment for judgment may be made *sine die: Hawryluk v. McLellan* (1967), 3 C.R.N.S. 66 (Sask. Q.B.).

DISMISSAL FOR FAILURE TO APPEAR OR WANT OF PROSECUTION.

825. The appeal court may, on proof that notice of an appeal has been given and that

(*a*) the appellant has failed to comply with any order made under section 816 or 817 or with the conditions of any undertaking or recognizance given or entered into as prescribed in either of those sections, or

(*b*) the appeal has not been proceeded with or has been abandoned,

order that the appeal be dismissed. R.S., c. C-34, s. 757; R.S., c. 2 (2nd Supp.), s. 18.

CROSS-REFERENCES

The appeal court may summarily determine frivolous appeals under s. 795. A similar provision is s. 685 in indictable matters. The court is not given the added authority of s. 825 in indictable matters. Formal notice of the applicable rules passed under s. 482(2) may be abandoned by the provisions of those rules.

SYNOPSIS

This section provides that failure to proceed or failure to comply with the terms of recognizances or undertakings may, on proof of notice, result in the dismissal of the appeal.

ANNOTATIONS

It is open to the appeal court to find that the appeal has not been proceeded with within the meaning of para. (*b*) where the appellant has failed to comply with the Rules of the Court requiring the filing of a memorandum at a certain time prior to the hearing: *R. v. Clarke* (1981), 62 C.C.C. (2d) 442, [1981] 6 W.W.R. 289 (Alta. C.A.).

COSTS.

826. Where an appeal is heard and determined or is abandoned or is dismissed for want of prosecution, the appeal court may make any order with respect to costs that it considers just and reasonable. R.S., c. C-34, s. 758.

CROSS-REFERENCES

Section 827 provides for remedies in the event of non-payment of costs and directions as to whom costs are payable.

Costs may be awarded under s. 809 in summary conviction trial proceedings if they are consistent with the s. 840 provisions. Section 826 has no similar limitation.

Costs may be awarded under s. 839(3) where a further appeal is brought under s. 839(1)(*a*).

SYNOPSIS

This section gives the appeal court wide powers with respect to orders as to costs.

ANNOTATIONS

This provision allows for three types of costs awards: (1) judicial costs at trial and appeal; (2) extra-judicial costs including solicitor-client costs in exceptional cases if it is unfair that a single person incur a significant expense where the Crown has pursued a valid social objective by appealing or solicitor-client costs if the conduct of the Crown has been unfair or oppressive; and (3) costs fixed at an arbitrary amount which the court, in the exercise of its discretion, awards a party who has succeeded on appeal: *R. v. Gagnon* (2000), 147 C.C.C. (3d) 184 (Que. C.A.).

The power to award costs under this section includes the power to award costs against the Crown: *R. v. Ouellette* (1979), 50 C.C.C. (2d) 346 (Que. C.A.), affd [1980] 1 S.C.R. 568, 52 C.C.C. (2d) 336, 15 C.R. (3d) 372 (7:0).

The appeal court has the power to order imprisonment of the appellant in default of payment of costs: *R. v. Duguay* (1990), 57 C.C.C. (3d) 309 (Que. C.A.).

An award of costs for or against the Crown in summary conviction appeal matters will be the exception and not the rule. Costs will be ordered against the Crown generally in two sets of circumstances. The first consists of cases where the conduct of the prosecution is said to merit sanction in the form of an award of costs against the Crown. The second are cases where there is no Crown misconduct, but other exceptional circumstances exist such that fairness requires that the individual litigant not carry the financial burden flowing from his or her involvement in the litigation. The mere fact that a Crown appeal raises a legal issue of general importance whose resolution will affect other cases cannot suffice to make the appeal an exceptional case warranting a costs order against the Crown. In deciding whether the public interest at stake in an appeal justifies a costs order against the Crown, the court must consider both the public importance of the legal issue raised on the appeal and the significance of the outcome of the appeal to the individual respondent. Where the public interest is high and the appeal has little or no significance to the particular defendant, a costs order against the Crown may be appropriate regardless of the outcome of the appeal. Where, however, there is a significant public interest in the legal issue raised on the appeal and the defendant has a significant personal interest, it is not unfair to follow the general rule and require each side to bear its own costs: *R. v. Garcia* (2005), 194 C.C.C. (3d) 361, 29 C.R. (6th) 127, 195 O.A.C. 64 (C.A.).

TO WHOM COSTS PAYABLE, AND WHEN / Certificate of non-payment of costs / Committal.

827. (1) Where the appeal court orders the appellant or respondent to pay costs, the order shall direct that the costs be paid to the clerk of the court, to be paid by him to the person entitled to them, and shall fix the period within which the costs shall be paid.

(2) Where costs are not paid in full within the period fixed for payment and the person who has been ordered to pay them has not been bound by a recognizance to pay them, the clerk of the court shall, on application by the person entitled to the costs, or by any person on his behalf, and on payment of any fee to which the clerk of the court is entitled, issue a certificate in Form 42 certifying that the costs or a part thereof, as the case may be, have not been paid.

(3) A justice having jurisdiction in the territorial division in which a certificate has been issued under subsection (2) may, on production of the certificate, by warrant in Form 26, commit the defaulter to imprisonment for a term not exceeding one month, unless the amount of the costs and, where the justice thinks fit so to order, the costs of the committal and of conveying the defaulter to prison are sooner paid. R.S., c. C-34, s. 759.

CROSS-REFERENCES

Section 809 governs the awarding and enforcement of costs at a summary conviction trial. Authorization for the award of costs on an appeal under s. 813 may be found in s. 826. For similar provisions relating to appeals under s. 830, see s. 834(1) and for costs on further summary conviction appeals, see s. 839(3).

SYNOPSIS

This section makes the clerk of the court the administrator of the enforcement of cost orders under s. 826 (subsecs. (1) and (2)). On failure to pay such costs, a justice may order the defaulter imprisoned for up to one month, unless costs and costs of committal, if ordered, are paid sooner.

ENFORCEMENT OF CONVICTION OR ORDER BY COURT OF APPEAL / Enforcement by justice / Duty of clerk of court.

828. (1) A conviction or order made by the appeal court may be enforced

(*a*) in the same manner as if it had been made by the summary conviction court; or

(*b*) by process of the appeal court.

(2) Where an appeal taken against a conviction or order adjudging payment of a sum of money is dismissed, the summary conviction court that made the conviction or order or a justice for the same territorial division may issue a warrant of committal as if no appeal had been taken.

(3) Where a conviction or order that has been made by an appeal court is to be enforced by a justice, the clerk of the appeal court shall send to the justice the conviction or order and all writings relating thereto, except the notice of intention to appeal and any recognizance. R.S., c. C-34, s. 760.

CROSS-REFERENCES

Sections 701 to 708 of Part XXII provide for the service and execution of process to compel the attendance of witnesses. See Part XXV regarding enforcement of recognizances. The enforcement of sentences is described in Part XXIII, which applies without the need for express incorporation in Part XXVII proceedings. A court of appeal decision under s. 839(1) is enforceable under s. 839(4) in the same manner as if made in summary conviction trial proceedings. See s. 835 for a similar provision regarding s. 830 appeals.

SYNOPSIS

This section provides that a conviction or order of the appeal court may be enforced by that court or the original court, and in the event of a dismissal the original court may proceed by way of warrant of committal as if there had been no appeal (subsecs. (1) and (2)). Where a conviction or order of the appeal court is to be enforced by a justice, the clerk of the court shall forward to that justice the documentary record except the notice of appeal and recognizances (subsec. (3)).

ANNOTATIONS

In *R. v. Green,* [1967] 2 C.C.C. 95, 50 C.R. 281 (Sask. Dist. Ct.), it was held that "process of the appeal court" includes processes available to enforce judgments in civil proceedings, so that where imprisonment for default is not ordered, judgment may be enforced by the Crown.

Summary Appeal on Transcript or Agreed Statement of Facts

DEFINITION OF "APPEAL COURT" / Nunavut.

829. (1) Subject to subsection (2), for the purposes of sections 830 to 838, "appeal court" means, in any province, the superior court of criminal jurisdiction for the province.

(2) If the appeal is from a conviction, judgment, verdict or other final order or determination of a summary conviction court consisting of a judge of the Nunavut Court of Justice, "appeal court" means a judge of the Court of Appeal of Nunavut. R.S.C. 1985, c. 27 (1st Supp.), s. 182; 1999, c. 3, s. 56.

CROSS-REFERENCES

See s. 812 for the definition of "appeal court" for the purposes of ss. 813 to 828. It contains territorial limitations respecting provinces where the "appeal court" is not also the superior court of criminal jurisdiction. Section 829 has no such limitation.

Section 830 deals with the right of appeal and the form and manner for commencement, hearing and determination of such appeals. Pursuant to s. 836, an appeal under s. 830 precludes an appeal under s. 813 from the same decision.

Section 830 creates no right of appeal if none is otherwise provided by law.

Sections 816 and 819 govern the judicial interim release of an appellant who was the defendant at trial, made applicable by s. 831. Under ss. 831 and 832, an appeal by a private prosecutor requires compliance with s. 817. See s. 834 for the authority of the court of appeal to make determinations under s. 830 and for consequential enforcement provisions under s. 835.

SYNOPSIS

This section defines "appeal court" as the superior criminal court of the province for the purposes of summary appeals.

APPEALS / Form of appeal / Rules for appeals / Rights of Attorney General of Canada.

830. (1) A party to proceedings to which this Part applies or the Attorney General may appeal against a conviction, judgment, verdict of acquittal or verdict of not criminally responsible on account of mental disorder or of unfit to stand trial or other final order or determination of a summary conviction court on the ground that

(*a*) it is erroneous in point of law;
(*b*) it is in excess of jurisdiction; or
(*c*) it constitutes a refusal or failure to exercise jurisdiction.

(2) An appeal under this section shall be based on a transcript of the proceedings appealed from unless the appellant files with the appeal court, within fifteen days of the filing of the notice of appeal, a statement of facts agreed to in writing by the respondent.

(3) An appeal under this section shall be made within the period and in the manner directed by any applicable rules of court and where there are no such rules otherwise providing, a notice of appeal in writing shall be served on the respondent and a copy thereof, together with proof of service, shall be filed with the appeal court within thirty days after the date of the conviction, judgment or verdict of acquittal or other final order or determination that is the subject of the appeal.

(4) The Attorney General of Canada has the same rights of appeal in proceedings instituted at the instance of the Government of Canada and conducted by or on behalf of that Government as the Attorney General of a province has under this section. R.S.C. 1985, c. 27 (1st Supp.), s. 182; 1991, c. 43, s. 9.

CROSS-REFERENCES

The "Attorney General", as defined in s. 2, retains a right of appeal under s. 830(1), even where he did not intervene at trial and thereby become the prosecution and a party to the trial proceedings.

See s. 672.1 for definition of "verdict of not criminally responsible on account of mental disorder" and s. 2 for definition of "unfit to stand trial".

Also see references cited under s. 829.

SYNOPSIS

This section provides for summary conviction appeals, to a superior court of criminal jurisdiction, on points of law or jurisdiction. Such are argued on the trial transcript unless an agreed statement of facts is filed within 15 days of the filing of the notice of appeal (subsecs. (1) and (2)).

Unless the rules of court otherwise provide the notice of appeal must be served on the respondent and filed within 30 days of the decision under appeal (subsec. (3)).

ANNOTATIONS

Subsection (1) – Note: Some of the following cases were decided under former s. 762 which determined the availability of an appeal by way of stated case. These cases were considered to be of continuing relevancy to issues which may arise on summary appeals, but the differences in wording and procedure must be borne in mind, particularly the change from "conviction, order, determination or other proceeding" and the broadening of the grounds to include a "refusal or failure to exercise jurisdiction".

It was held in *R. v. Canadian Pacific Ltd.* (1976), 32 C.C.C. (2d) 14, [1977] 1 W.W.R. 203 (Alta. S.C. App. Div.), that an appeal by way of stated case lies only from a final judgment, that is, one that determines the issue raised on the information. Thus no appeal lies where the information is dismissed for failure of the Crown to supply particulars as ordered by the court. The Crown's remedy is by way of *mandamus*. The correctness of the holding, that the decision must be "final" in the sense of determining the issue raised in the information rather than merely "final" in the sense that it brings to an end that particular proceeding was doubted in *R. v. B & B Stone Ltd. (No. 2)* (1977), 34 C.C.C. (2d) 464 (Ont. C.A.), where it was held that the quashing of an information in summary conviction proceedings on the grounds of duplicity is a final order or determination and an appeal by way of stated case under this section is the appropriate remedy, not an application by way of *mandamus*. However, where the judge finds the information is a nullity and so declines jurisdiction the proper remedy is by way of *mandamus*.

A stay of proceedings as an abuse of process is a "determination" within the meaning of subsec. (1) from which the Crown may appeal by way of stated case: *R. v. Kathis* (1977), 36 C.C.C. (2d) 551 (Ont. H.C.J.).

An interlocutory order dismissing an application to quash an information is not a final order and hence is not appealable by way of stated case: *R. v. Goldrick* (1974), 17 C.C.C. (2d) 74, 25 C.R.N.S. 389 (Ont. H.C.J.), and *R. v. Appleby* (1974), 21 C.C.C. (2d) 282, 18

C.P.R. (2d) 194 (N.B.S.C. App. Div.). *Contra*: *R. v. Chisholm* (1973), 21 C.R.N.S. 181 (Que. S.C.).

The existence of reasonable and probable grounds to make a breathalyzer demand pursuant to s. 254(3) raises a question of law pertaining to the application of a legal standard to the facts of the case. Although the trial judge's factual findings are entitled to deference, the trial judge's ultimate ruling is subject to review for correctness: *R. v. Shepherd* (2009), 245 C.C.C. (3d) 137 (S.C.C.).

The decision of a judge quashing an information prior to plea, because the signature of the justice of the peace who took the information was illegible, was a refusal or failure to exercise jurisdiction within the meaning of para. (*c*) against which the Crown may appeal: *R. v. Kapoor* (1989), 52 C.C.C. (3d) 41 (Ont. H.C.J.).

This section gives a right of appeal only to a party, which would include the informant, and the Attorney General. Thus, in a prosecution under the *Canada Elections Act* while the police officer who laid the charge would have a right of appeal, the Commissioner of Elections would not, even though the police officer in laying the charge was acting on the Commissioner's instructions: *R. v. Trimarchi* (1987), 40 C.C.C. (3d) 433, 62 C.R. (3d) 204, 49 D.L.R. (4th) 382 (Ont. C.A.).

The accused has no right to file a notice of cross-appeal challenging various rulings made by the trial judge where the Crown appeals an acquittal: *R. v. Wilcox* (2001), 152 C.C.C. (3d) 157 (N.S.C.A.).

Subsection (3) – It was held with respect to the former procedure by way of stated case that where the *Criminal Code* is silent as to the method of service then resort may be had to the Criminal Rules promulgated by the provincial Supreme Court: *R. v. Hummell* (1972), 9 C.C.C. (2d) 380, [1973] 1 W.W.R. 663 (B.C.C.A.).

APPLICATION.

831. The provisions of sections 816, 817, 819 and 825 apply, with such modifications as the circumstances require, in respect of an appeal under section 830, except that on receiving an application by the person having the custody of an appellant described in section 819 to appoint a date for the hearing of the appeal, the appeal court shall, after giving the prosecutor a reasonable opportunity to be heard, give such directions as it thinks necessary for expediting the hearing of the appeal. R.S.C. 1985, c. 27 (1st Supp.), s. 182.

CROSS-REFERENCES

These provisions should apply in conjunction with s. 832 which permits the appeal court to order the appellant to appear before a justice to enter into a recognizance or give an undertaking under ss. 816 or 817.

Also see references cited under ss. 816, 817, 819, 825 and 829.

SYNOPSIS

This section states that the provisions with respect to recognizances (ss. 816 and 817), applications by persons having custody (s. 819) and dismissal for failure to comply or proceed (s. 825) apply to summary appeals, with the exception that no date for hearing need be fixed.

UNDERTAKING OR RECOGNIZANCE / Attorney General.

832. (1) When a notice of appeal is filed pursuant to section 830, the appeal court may order that the appellant appear before a justice and give an undertaking or enter into a recognizance as provided in section 816 where the defendant is the appellant, or as provided in section 817, in any other case.

(2) Subsection (1) does not apply where the appellant is the Attorney General or counsel acting on behalf of the Attorney General. R.S.C. 1985, c. 27 (1st Supp.), s. 182.

CROSS-REFERENCES

The provisions of ss. 816 and 817 to appeals under s. 830 are incorporated by s. 831.

Also see references cited under ss. 816, 817, 819, 825 and 829.

SYNOPSIS

This section states that ss. 816 and 817 relating to undertakings and recognizances may be applied by the appeal court upon receipt of a notice of appeal, but that these provisions do not apply to the Attorney General or his counsel.

NO WRIT REQUIRED.

833. No writ of *certiorari* or other writ is required to remove any conviction, judgment, verdict or other final order or determination of a summary conviction court for the purpose of obtaining the judgment, determination or opinion of the appeal court. R.S.C. 1985, c. 27 (1st Supp.), s. 182; 1991, c. 43, s. 9.

CROSS-REFERENCES

Section 830 appeals are characterized as "summary appeal on transcript or agreed statement of facts" indicating the rationale for the section. A provision, similar to s. 821 and applicable to s. 825 appeals, requires the summary conviction court to transmit the record to the "appeal court" under s. 829.

See Part XXVI for the "Extraordinary Remedies" of *certiorari, habeas corpus, mandamus, procedendo* and prohibition.

SYNOPSIS

This section states that no writ is required to obtain the reversal of a summary conviction court from a court on summary appeal.

POWERS OF APPEAL COURT / Authority of judge.

834. (1) When a notice of appeal is filed pursuant to section 830, the appeal court shall hear and determine the grounds of appeal and may

- **(*a*) affirm, reverse or modify the conviction, judgment, verdict or other final order or determination, or**
- **(*b*) remit the matter to the summary conviction court with the opinion of the appeal court,**

and may make any other order in relation to the matter or with respect to costs that it considers proper.

(2) Where the authority and jurisdiction of the appeal court may be exercised by a judge of that court, such authority and jurisdiction may, subject to any applicable rules of court, be exercised by a judge of the court sitting in chambers as well in vacation as in term time. R.S.C. 1985, c. 27 (1st Supp.), s. 182; 1991, c. 43, s. 9.

CROSS-REFERENCES

The authority of the appeal court over s. 830 appeals is much more restrictive than that given to the appeal court by s. 822(1) over s. 813 appeals. None of the disposition or ancillary powers of the court of appeal in indictable matters are incorporated under s. 834.

Section 835 contains enforcement provisions for decisions of the court in s. 830 appeals.

SYNOPSIS

The appeal court has the power to affirm, reverse or modify the decision under appeal. In addition, it can remit the matter to the trial judge to continue the proceedings in a manner consistent with the opinion expressed on the appeal and may make any other order, including an order with respect to costs. These powers may be exercised in chambers.

ANNOTATIONS

The following cases were decided under former s. 768 which contained the powers of the appeal court in relation to an appeal by way of stated case. The wording of this section is similar, however, to former s. 768 and therefore these cases were considered to be of continuing relevancy to issues which may arise under this section.

The superior court has no power to dismiss an appeal merely because the error at trial did not result in a substantial wrong or miscarriage of justice: *R. v. Tunke* (1975), 25 C.C.C. (2d) 518 (Alta. S.C.).

In *R. v. McMullen* (1979), 47 C.C.C. (2d) 499, 100 D.L.R. (3d) 671 (Ont. C.A.), the court remitted the matter to the summary conviction court under para. (*c*) [now (*b*)] and therefore left open the question whether under this section the appeal court has power to order a new trial rather than merely a resumption of the impugned trial.

However, in the subsequent case of *R. v. Giambalvo* (1982), 70 C.C.C. (2d) 324, 39 O.R. (2d) 588 (C.A.), the court held that s. 771(2) [now s. 839] did not give the Court of Appeal any wider powers than the Superior Court hearing the initial appeal possessed under this section. The court noted that there did not appear to be any case where a new trial had been ordered such as may be ordered under s. 686(2)(*b*).

An extension of time was granted to the Crown where it launched an application for *mandamus* within 30 days of the decision quashing an information but realized later that an appeal lay under s. 830. The Crown had established a *bona fide* intention to impeach the correctness of the decision of the judge within the appeal period: *R. v. Kapoor* (1989), 52 C.C.C. (3d) 41 (Ont. H.C.J.).

ENFORCEMENT / Idem.

835. (1) Where the appeal court renders its decision on an appeal, the summary conviction court from which the appeal was taken or a justice exercising the same jurisdiction has the same authority to enforce a conviction, order or determination that has been affirmed, modified or made by the appeal court as the summary conviction court would have had if no appeal had been taken.

(2) An order of the appeal court may be enforced by its own process. R.S.C. 1985, c. 27 (1st Supp.), s. 182.

CROSS-REFERENCES

Section 828(1) contains a similar provision which applies to appeals under s. 813.

See also references cited under s. 828.

SYNOPSIS

This section provides that the appeal court, the original court or a justice with the same jurisdiction as the original court may enforce the decision of the summary appeal court.

APPEAL UNDER SECTION 830.

836. Every person who appeals under section 830 from any conviction, judgment, verdict or other final order or determination in respect of which that person is entitled to an appeal under section 813 shall be taken to have abandoned all the person's rights of appeal under section 813. R.S.C. 1985, c. 27 (1st Supp.), s. 182; 1991, c. 43, s. 9.

CROSS-REFERENCES

Section 813 rights of appeal permit appeals from conviction, orders made against a defendant, staying proceedings or dismissing an information and sentence. The grounds of appeal are not restricted. An appeal may be taken against a conviction, judgment or verdict of acquittal or other final order or decision, under s. 830, upon questions of law or allegations of jurisdictional error.

SYNOPSIS

This section provides that an appellant who proceeds by way of summary appeal (s. 830) is deemed to have given up his rights of regular appeal (s. 813).

APPEAL BARRED.

837. Where it is provided by law that no appeal lies from a conviction or order, no appeal under section 830 lies from such a conviction or order. R.S.C. 1985, c. 27 (1st Supp.), s. 182.

CROSS-REFERENCES

There is no similar provision relating to s. 813 appeals.

SYNOPSIS

This section bars summary appeals where the law states that there is no appeal from a conviction or order.

EXTENSION OF TIME.

838. The appeal court or a judge thereof may at any time extend any time period referred to in section 830, 831 or 832. R.S.C. 1985, c. 27 (1st Supp.), s. 182.

CROSS-REFERENCES

The criteria used in determining whether to order an extension of time is not contained in this section. The statutory provision may be supplemented by rules of court passed under s. 482(1).

A judge of the appeal court, as defined in s. 812, may extend the time within which notice of appeal is to be given, under s. 815(2).

Rights of appeal to the "appeal court", as defined in s. 829, are conferred under s. 830 which establishes time limits for the service and filing of notice of appeal and agreed statement of facts. Time limits relating to service and filing of notice of appeal apply only where no applicable rules of court provide to the contrary.

Interim release of a defendant who is an appellant under s. 830 is dealt with in ss. 831 and 832, as well as the obligation of a private prosecutor to give an undertaking or enter into a recognizance to prosecute an appeal in which he is the appellant.

SYNOPSIS

This section gives the appeal court or a judge thereof the power to extend time with respect to summary appeal proceedings, including undertakings and recognizances.

Appeals to Court of Appeal

APPEAL ON QUESTION OF LAW / Nunavut / Sections applicable / Costs / Enforcement of decision / Right of Attorney General of Canada to appeal.

839. (1) Subject to subsection (1.1), an appeal to the court of appeal as defined in section 673 may, with leave of that court or a judge thereof, be taken on any ground that involves a question of law alone, against

(*a*) a decision of a court in respect of an appeal under section 822; or
(*b*) a decision of an appeal court under section 834, except where that court is the court of appeal.

(1.1) An appeal to the Court of Appeal of Nunavut may, with leave of that court or a judge of that court, be taken on any ground that involves a question of law alone, against a decision of a judge of the Court of Appeal of Nunavut acting as an appeal court under subsection 812(2) or 829(2).

(2) Sections 673 to 689 apply with such modifications as the circumstances require to an appeal under this section.

(3) Notwithstanding subsection (2), the court of appeal may make any order with respect to costs that it considers proper in relation to an appeal under this section.

(4) The decision of the court of appeal may be enforced in the same manner as if it had been made by the summary conviction court before which the proceedings were originally heard and determined.

(5) The Attorney General of Canada has the same rights of appeal in proceedings instituted at the instance of the Government of Canada and conducted by or on behalf of that Government as the Attorney General of a province has under this Part. R.S., c. C-34, s. 771; R.S.C. 1985, c. 27 (1st Supp.), s. 183; 1999, c. 3, s. 57.

CROSS-REFERENCES
The *Supreme Court Act*, R.S.C. 1985, c. S-26, s. 41, governs appeals to the Supreme Court of Canada in summary conviction matters.

See references cited under ss. 673 to 689, incorporated by subsec. (2) for discussion of those provisions.

SYNOPSIS

The decision of a summary conviction appeal court may be appealed, with leave, to the court of appeal. Such appeals are restricted to questions of law alone. However, no such appeal is available where the first appeal was heard by a court of appeal sitting as a superior court of criminal jurisdiction (see ss. 2 and 829) (subsec. (1)).

Costs may be awarded on the appeal (subsec. (3)).

(**Note**: Leave to appeal to the Supreme Court of Canada must be obtained under s. 40 of the *Supreme Court Act*.)

ANNOTATIONS

Determinations from which appeal lies [subsec. (1)] – The refusal of a trial *de novo* court [now summary conviction appeal court], upon a preliminary objection, to hear an appeal is a decision of that court which may be appealed: *R. v. Dennis*, [1960] S.C.R. 286, 125 C.C.C. 321 (7:0).

It was held in *R. v. Canadian Pacific Ltd.* (1976), 32 C.C.C. (2d) 14, [1977] 1 W.W.R. 203 (Alta. S.C. App. Div.), that an appeal lies under this section only where the order made by the court below has the effect of disposing of the appeal. Thus in that case it was held that no appeal lay from an order setting down for hearing the appeal (which at that time was an appeal by way of trial *de novo*). Folld: *R. v. Hunt* (1978), 39 C.C.C. (2d) 135, 25 N.S.R. (2d) 1 (S.C. App. Div.).

Thus an appeal under this section *did* lie where the judge refused to set the appeal down for hearing: *R. v. Cuthill* (1976), 32 C.C.C. (2d) 495, 73 D.L.R. (3d) 720 (Alta. S.C. App. Div.).

An appeal to the Court of Appeal is from the judgment of the Summary Conviction Appeal Court, not the trial judge: *R. v. Emery* (1981), 61 C.C.C. (2d) 84 (B.C.C.A.), leave to appeal to S.C.C. refused 40 N.R. 358*n*.

An appeal cannot be initiated until a finding guilt and the imposition of sentence: *R. v. Payne* (2002), 170 C.C.C. (3d) 145, [2003] 5 W.W.R. 76 (Man. C.A.).

Right of appeal – Even if a question of law alone is raised on a Crown application the court may refuse leave to appeal: *R. v. Giftwares Wholesale Co. (No. 2)* (1980), 53 C.C.C. (2d) 380, [1980] 3 W.W.R. 573 (Man. C.A.).

Leave to appeal should be granted sparingly. Where the question of law is significant to the general administration of justice, then leave to appeal may be granted even if the merits are not particularly strong. If the case does not raise a question of general importance, leave to appeal may be granted where the merits appear very strong, particularly if the accused is facing a significant deprivation of liberty in light of the convictions: *R. v. R. (R.)* (2008), 234 C.C.C. (3d) 463, 59 C.R. (6th) 258 (Ont. C.A.).

Leave to appeal should only be granted if the issue or questions of law have a reasonable possibility of success, or if the questions of law have significance to the administration of justice beyond the implications of the case before the court: *R. v. Dorgan* (2009), 248 C.C.C. (3d) 181 (P.E.I.C.A.).

The informant as well as the Attorney General may appeal to the court of appeal from the decision of the summary conviction appeal court: *Scullion v. Canadian Breweries Transport Ltd.*, [1956] S.C.R. 512, 114 C.C.C. 337; *R. v. Lacasse* (1979), 55 C.C.C. (2d) 337 (Que. C.A.).

There is no right of appeal from the decision of a single judge granting or refusing leave to appeal: *R. v. Johnson* (2001), 155 C.C.C. (3d) 506, 281 A.R. 368 (C.A.); *R. v. Scherba* (2001), 155 C.C.C. (3d) 512, 54 O.R. (3d) 555 (C.A.), *R. v. B.C. Tel* (2002), 165 C.C.C. (3d) 470, 214 D.L.R. (4th) 729 (B.C.C.A).

The decision of a Superior Court Judge extending or refusing to extend time for the filing of a notice of appeal from sentence in a summary conviction court can be appealed on a question of law alone: *R. v. Belaroui* (2004), 186 C.C.C. (3d) 386 (Que. C.A.).

Question of law – While the question whether there is any evidence to support a conviction is a question of law, the question whether on the evidence an inference of guilt should be drawn cannot be said to involve a question of law alone: *R. v. Waite,* [1965] 1 C.C.C. 301, 46 C.R. 23 (N.B.S.C. App. Div.).

An inference to be drawn from proved facts is in itself a question of fact, and not of law: *R. v. Hook* (1955), 113 C.C.C. 248, 22 C.R. 378 (Ont. C.A.) (2:1).

The failure of the summary conviction appeal judge to give adequate reasons for dismissing the appeal constitutes an error of law. The appropriate remedy is for the Court of Appeal to consider the grounds raised before the appeal judge and determine whether the appeal to the appeal judge was bound to be dismissed. If not, the proviso could not be applied such that a new trial should be ordered or an acquittal entered: *R. v. Minuskin* (2003), 181 C.C.C. (3d) 542, 68 O.R. (3d) 577 (C.A.).

The application of the *de minimis* doctrine to undisputed facts raises a question of law: *R. v. Kubassek* (2004), 188 C.C.C. (3d) 307, 25 C.R. (6th) 340 (Ont. C.A.).

Sentence appeal – The failure of the summary conviction appeal court judge to recognize that the trial judge failed to consider relevant evidence with respect to the imposition of sentence constitutes an error of law alone: *R. v. Griffith* (1998), 128 C.C.C. (3d) 178 (B.C.C.A.). Also see *R. v. Paterson*, [1963] 2 C.C.C. 369 and 375, 39 C.R. 156 and 195 (B.C.C.A.).

Where a judge in refusing a discharge holds that the discharge provisions are primarily applicable to young offenders he errs in law and since the sentence imposed is inextricably bound up in this error an appeal lies to the court of appeal as a question of law alone is involved. The Court of Appeal may therefore grant leave to appeal and consider the fitness of the sentence: *R. v. Culley* (1977), 36 C.C.C. (2d) 433 (Ont. C.A.).

It was held in *R. v. S. S. Kresge Co.* (1975), 27 C.C.C. (2d) 420, 65 D.L.R. (3d) 628 (P.E.I.C.A.), considering the former s. 755(3) [now s. 822(6)] that as the summary conviction appeal court is required to consider the "fitness of the sentence appealed against" whether or not the sentence was proper in the circumstances is a question of law upon which an appeal lies under this section to the Court of Appeal.

It was held, however, in *R. v. Thomas (No. 2)* (1980), 53 C.C.C. (2d) 285 (B.C.C.A.), that fitness of sentence *per se* does not raise a question of law alone.

To a similar effect is *R. v. Guida* (1989), 51 C.C.C. (3d) 305 (Que. C.A.), where a majority of the court held that whether or not the sentence is too severe, whether or not it is a fit sentence, does not raise a question of law alone. Also see *R. v. Loughery* (1992), 73 C.C.C. (3d) 411 (Alta. C.A.).

Procedure – Where the court of appeal restores a conviction, but the respondent had also appealed his sentence to the summary conviction appeal court, the case must be remitted to that court to complete the sentence appeal. The Court of Appeal may only impose sentence on a Crown appeal where no sentence was imposed by the trial court, by invoking s. 686(4)(*b*)(ii): *R. v. Broda* (1983), 7 C.C.C. (3d) 161, [1983] 5 W.W.R. 747 (Sask. C.A.); *R. v. Devitt* (1999), 139 C.C.C. (3d) 187, 124 O.A.C. 348 (C.A.).

The Court of Appeal has no jurisdiction to review the decision of a single judge of the Court of Appeal under subsec. (1) refusing leave to appeal: *R. v. Gelz* (1990), 55 C.C.C. (3d) 425 (B.C.C.A.). See also *R. v. Gillespie* (1997), 115 C.C.C. (3d) 461 (Man. C.A.), leave to appeal to S.C.C. refused 117 C.C.C. (3d) vi; *R. v. Wadhams* (2014), 308 C.C.C. (3d) 102 (B.C.C.A.).

There is no authority to stay, pending appeal to the court of appeal, the judgment of the summary conviction appeal court dismissing a Crown appeal from the dismissal of a charge. In effect, what the Crown sought was a stay of the reasons of the court underlying a dismissal of the charge: *R. v. P. (J.)* (2003), 175 C.C.C. (3d) 449, 228 D.L.R. (4th) 225 (Ont. C.A.).

The registrar of the court of appeal does not have authority to refuse to accept a notice of appeal purportedly filed under subsec. (1) on the grounds that the matter is not within the court's jurisdiction. Such a refusal is tantamount to an order quashing the notice for want of jurisdiction, an authority reserved to a judge or panel of the court: *R. v. Verma* (2016), 341 C.C.C. (3d) 78 (B.C.C.A.).

Costs [subsec. (3)] – In *R. v. Danyleyko* (1962), 39 W.W.R. 576 (B.C.C.A.), it was held that the case was one in which appellant ought to have costs of the appeal.

The court's power under this subsection includes the power to award costs against the Crown: *R. v. Ouellette*, [1980] 1 S.C.R. 568, 52 C.C.C. (2d) 336 (7:0).

Costs should be awarded in criminal matters only in special circumstances as in the case of a successful appeal by the accused where the prosecution was frivolous, conducted for an oblique motive or taken by the Crown as a test case: *R. v. King* (1986), 26 C.C.C. (3d) 349 (B.C.C.A.).

An appellant who successfully appeals his conviction to the Supreme Court of Canada is not automatically entitled to costs: *R. v. Trask*, [1987] 2 S.C.R. 304, 37 C.C.C. (3d) 92 (6:0).

Fees and Allowances

FEES AND ALLOWANCES / Order of lieutenant governor in council.

840. (1) Subject to subsection (2), the fees and allowances mentioned in the schedule to this Part are the fees and allowances that may be taken or allowed in proceedings before summary conviction courts and justices under this Part.

(2) The lieutenant governor in council of a province may order that all or any of the fees and allowances mentioned in the schedule to this Part shall not be taken or allowed in proceedings before summary conviction courts and justices under this Part in that province and, when the lieutenant governor in council so orders, he or she may fix any other fees and allowances for any items similar to those mentioned in the schedule, or any other items, to be taken or allowed instead. R.S., c. C-34, s. 772; 1994, c. 44, s. 83; 1997, c. 18, s. 114.

SCHEDULE
(Section 840)

FEES AND ALLOWANCES THAT MAY BE CHARGED BY SUMMARY CONVICTION COURTS AND JUSTICES

1.	Information	$1.00
2.	Summons or warrant	0.50
3.	Warrant where summons issued in first instance	0.30
4.	Each necessary copy of summons or warrant	0.30
5.	Each subpoena or warrant to or for witnesses	0.30
	(A subpoena may contain any number of names. Only one subpoena may be issued on behalf of a party in any proceeding, unless the summary conviction court or the justice considers it necessary or desirable that more than one subpoena be issued.)	
6.	Information for warrant for witness and warrant for witness	1.00
7.	Each necessary copy of subpoena to or warrant for witness	0.20
8.	Each recognizance	1.00
9.	Hearing and determining proceeding	1.00
10.	Where hearing lasts more than two hours	2.00
11.	Where two or more justices hear and determine a proceeding, each is entitled to the fee authorized by item 9.	
12.	Each warrant of committal	0.50
13.	Making up record of conviction or order on request of a party to the proceedings	1.00
14.	Copy of a writing other than a conviction or order, on request of a party to the proceedings; for each folio of one hundred words	0.10
15.	Bill of costs, when made out in detail upon request of a party to the proceedings	0.20
	(Items 14 and 15 may be charged only where there has been an adjudication.)	
16.	Attending to remand prisoner	1.00
17.	Attending to take recognizance of bail	1.00

FEES AND ALLOWANCES THAT MAY BE ALLOWED TO PEACE OFFICERS

18.	Arresting a person on a warrant or without a warrant	$1.50
19.	Serving summons or subpoena	0.50
20.	Mileage to serve summons or subpoena or to make an arrest, both ways, for each mile	0.10
	(Where a public conveyance is not used, reasonable costs of transportation may be allowed.)	
21.	Mileage where service cannot be effected, on proof of a diligent attempt to effect service, each way, for each mile	0.10
22.	Returning with prisoner after arrest to take him before a summary conviction court or justice at a place different from the place where the peace officer received the warrant to arrest, if the journey is of necessity over a route different from that taken by the peace officer to make the arrest, each way, for each mile	0.10
23.	Taking a prisoner to prison on remand or committal, each way, for each mile	0.10
	(Where a public conveyance is not used, reasonable costs of transportation may be allowed. No charge may be made under this item in respect of a service for which a charge is made under item 22.)	
24.	Attending summary conviction court or justice on summary conviction proceedings, for each day necessarily employed	2.00

(No more than $2.00 may be charged under this item in respect of any day notwithstanding the number of proceedings that the peace officer attended on that day before that summary conviction court or justice.)

FEES AND ALLOWANCES THAT MAY BE ALLOWED TO WITNESSES

25.	**Each day attending trial ....**	**$4.00**
26.	**Mileage travelled to attend trial, each way, for each mile ....**	**0.10**

FEES AND ALLOWANCES THAT MAY BE ALLOWED TO INTERPRETERS

27.	**Each half day attending trial ....**	**$2.50**
28.	**Actual living expenses when away from ordinary place of residence, not to exceed per day ....**	**10.00**
29.	**Mileage travelled to attend trial, each way, for each mile ....**	**0.10**

R.S., c. C-34, Sch. to Part XXIV.

CROSS-REFERENCES

See ss. 809, 826, 830(1) and 839(3) for authority to award costs in summary conviction trial and appeal proceedings.

ANNOTATIONS

It was held in *Lockett v. City of Kingston,* [1966] 2 O.R. 843, 58 D.L.R. (2d) 689, that this section does not entitle a justice of the peace who issues summonses and warrants and receives informations to charge the municipality for all such services, but rather sets out a limitation on the costs that may be awarded against an informant or defendant in such proceedings.

This schedule has no application once an appeal has been launched and thus in particular the appellant must pay for the transcript on the basis of the fees set by the appeal court rules not at the rate provided for in para. 14: *R. v. Dubuc* (1978), 49 C.C.C. (2d) 54 (Que. S.C.).

While there have been some minor amendments to this section and the companion provision s. 809 since the decision of the court in *A.- G. Que. v. A.- G. Can.*, [1945] S.C.R. 600, 84 C.C.C. 369, it would still appear to be the case as there held that only the fees and allowances set out in this schedule may be awarded by a summary conviction court. Thus the court has no power to award a counsel fee: *R. v. Abram* (1945), 1 C.R. 151 (Ont. Co. Ct.); *R. v. Cross* (1978), 42 C.C.C. (2d) 277 (P.E.I.S.C. *in banco*).

Part XXVIII / MISCELLANEOUS

Electronic Documents

DEFINITIONS / "data" / "electronic document".

841. The definitions in this section apply in this section and in sections 842 to 847.

"data" means representations of information or concepts, in any form.

"electronic document" means data that is recorded or stored on any medium in or by a computer system or other similar device and that can be read or perceived by a person or a computer system or other similar device. It includes a display, print-out or other output of the data and any document, record, order, exhibit, notice or form that contains the data.

DEALING WITH DATA IN COURT.

842. Despite anything in this Act, a court may create, collect, receive, store, transfer, distribute, publish or otherwise deal with electronic documents if it does so in accordance with an Act or with the rules of court.

CROSS-REFERENCES

"Electronic document" is defined in s. 841. Rules of court are made under ss. 482 and 482.1. Section 843 provides that a court may accept the transfer of data by electronic means and for the filing of documents by electronic means. Under s. 844, making the document in electronic form can satisfy a requirement that a document be made in writing. Section 845 allows for use of electronic signatures. Section 846 makes provision for oaths and solemn declarations in electronic documents. A person may obtain printed copies of electronic documents in accordance with s. 847.

TRANSFER OF DATA / Time of filing.

843. (1) Despite anything in this Act, a court may accept the transfer of data by electronic means if the transfer is made in accordance with the laws of the place where the transfer originates or the laws of the place where the data is received.

(2) If a document is required to be filed in a court and the filing is done by transfer of data by electronic means, the filing is complete when the transfer is accepted by the court.

CROSS-REFERENCES

"Data" is defined in s. 841. Also, see Cross-references under s. 842.

DOCUMENTS IN WRITING.

844. A requirement under this Act that a document be made in writing is satisfied by the making of the document in electronic form in accordance with an Act or the rules of court.

CROSS-REFERENCES

See Cross-references under s. 842.

SIGNATURES.

845. If this Act requires a document to be signed, the court may accept a signature in an electronic document if the signature is made in accordance with an Act or the rules of court.

CROSS-REFERENCES

"Electronic document" is defined in s. 841. Also, see Cross-references under s. 842.

OATHS.

846. If under this Act an information, an affidavit or a solemn declaration or a statement under oath or solemn affirmation is to be made by a person, the court may accept it in the form of an electronic document if

- **(*a*) the person states in the electronic document that all matters contained in the information, affidavit, solemn declaration or statement are true to his or her knowledge and belief;**
- **(*b*) the person before whom it is made or sworn is authorized to take or receive informations, affidavits, solemn declarations or statements and he or she states in the electronic document that the information, affidavit, solemn declaration**

or statement was made under oath, solemn declaration or solemn affirmation, as the case may be; and

(*c*) the electronic document was made in accordance with the laws of the place where it was made.

CROSS-REFERENCES

"Electronic document" is defined in s. 841. Also, see Cross-references under s. 842.

COPIES.

847. Any person who is entitled to obtain a copy of a document from a court is entitled, in the case of a document in electronic form, to obtain a printed copy of the electronic document from the court on payment of a reasonable fee determined in accordance with a tariff of fees fixed or approved by the Attorney General of the relevant province.

CROSS-REFERENCES

"Attorney General" is defined in s. 2. Also, see Cross-references under s. 842.

Remote Appearance by Incarcerated Accused

CONDITION FOR REMOTE APPEARANCE.

848. Despite anything in this Act, if an accused who is in prison does not have access to legal advice during the proceedings, the court shall, before permitting the accused to appear by a means of communication that allows the court and the accused to engage in simultaneous visual and oral communication, be satisfied that the accused will be able to understand the proceedings and that any decisions made by the accused during the proceedings will be voluntary.

CROSS-REFERENCES

A number of provisions now allow an accused to make a "virtual appearance" through electronic means. Thus, see s. 537(1)(*k*) [preliminary inquiry]; s. 606 [plea]; s. 650 [indictable trial]; s. 800 [summary conviction trial]; ss. 683 and 688 [indictable appeals].

Forms

FORMS / Seal not required / Official languages.

849. (1) The forms set out in this Part, varied to suit the case, or forms to the like effect are deemed to be good, valid and sufficient in the circumstances for which they are provided.

(2) No justice is required to attach or affix a seal to any writing or process that he or she is authorized to issue and in respect of which a form is provided by this Part.

(3) Any pre-printed portions of a form set out in this Part, varied to suit the case, or of a form to the like effect shall be printed in both official languages. R.S., c. C-34, s. 773; R.S.C. 1985, c. 31 (4th Supp.), s. 97; 2002, c. 13, s. 84.

ANNOTATIONS

The provisions of s. 26(5) [now s. 32] of the *Interpretation Act*, R.S.C. 1970, c. I-23, which provide that "where a form is prescribed, deviations therefrom, not affecting the substance or calculated to mislead, do not invalidate the form used" apply to these forms: *R. v. Crawford* (1981), 23 C.R. (3d) 83 (B.C.S.C.).

The failure of the Crown to comply with the provisions of subsec. (3) in respect of an information in Form 2 does not render the information a nullity and does not necessitate the quashing of the information: *R. v. Goodine* (1992), 71 C.C.C. (3d) 146 (N.S.C.A.). Failure of the Crown to translate the preprinted portions of the form is a defect within the meaning of s. 601(3)(*c*) which is capable of amendment when the omission has not caused irreparable prejudice to the accused. The proper course is for the trial judge to order that the preprinted portions of the information be translated into the other official language: *R. v. Sorensen* (1990), 59 C.C.C. (3d) 211 (Ont. Ct. (Gen. Div.)).

Failure to employ the French language in the pre-printed portions of Form 35 was not a matter of substance and therefore did not invalidate the form: *R. v. Langlois* (1991), 67 C.C.C. (3d) 375 (B.C.S.C.).

FORM 1

(*Sections 320.29 and 487*)

Information to obtain a search warrant

Canada,
Province of ....,
(*territorial division*).

This is the information of A.B., of .... in the said (*territorial division*), (*occupation*), hereinafter called the informant, taken before me.

The informant says that (*describe things to be searched for and offence in respect of which search is to be made*), and that he believes on reasonable grounds that the said things, or some part of them, are in the (*dwelling-house, etc.*) of C.D., of .... in the said (*territorial division*). (*Here add the grounds of belief, whatever they may be.*)

Wherefore the informant prays that a search warrant may be granted to search the said (*dwelling-house, etc.*) for the said things.

Sworn before me this .... day of ...., A.D. ...., at ....

..
(Signature of Informant)

...
A Justice of the Peace in and for **.....................................**

2018, c. 21, s. 28(*a*).

FORM 2

(*Sections 506 and 788*)

Information

Canada,
Province of ....,
(*territorial division*).

This is the information of C.D., of ...., (*occupation*), hereinafter called the informant.

The informant says that (*if the informant has no personal knowledge state that he believes on reasonable grounds and state the offence.*)

Sworn before me this .... day of ....
....................., A.D. ...., *(Signature of Informant)*
at ....

...
A Justice of the Peace in and
***for* ....**

***Note*: The date of birth of the accused may be mentioned on the information or indictment.**

FORM 3

[*Repealed*, R.S.C. 1985, c. 27 (1st Supp.), s. 184(2).]

FORM 4

(*Sections 566, 566.1, 580 and 591*)

Heading of Indictment

Canada,
Province of ....,
(*territorial division*).

In the (*set out name of the court*)

Her Majesty the Queen

against

(name of accused)

(*Name of accused*) stands charged

1. That he (*state offence*).

2. That he (*state offence*).

Dated this .... day of .... A.D. ...., at ....

..
(*Signature of signing officer, Agent of Attorney General, etc., as the case may be*)

***Note*: The date of birth of the accused may be mentioned on the information or indictment.**

1999, c. 3, s. 58.

FORM 5

(*Sections 320.29 and 487*)

Warrant to search

Canada,
Province of ....,
(*territorial division*).

To the peace officers in the said (*territorial division*) or to the (*named public officers*):

Whereas it appears on the oath of A.B., of ..... that there are reasonable grounds for believing that (*describe things to be searched for and offence in respect of which search is to be made*) are in .... at ...., hereinafter called the premises;

This is, therefore, to authorize and require you between the hours of (*as the justice may direct*) to enter into the said premises and to search for the said things and to bring them before me or some other justice.

Dated this .... day of .... A.D. ...., at ....

..
A Justice of the Peace in and for ....

1999, c. 5, s. 45; 2018, c. 21, s. 28(*b*).

FORM 5.001

Preservation Demand

(*Subsection 487.012(1)*)

Canada,
Province of ....
(*territorial division*)

To (*name of person*), of ....:

Because I have reasonable grounds to suspect that the computer data specified below is in your possession or control and that that computer data will assist in the investigation of an offence that has been or will be committed under (*specify the provision of the Criminal Code or other Act of Parliament*),

(*or*)

will assist in the investigation of an offence that has been committed under (*specify the provision of the law of the foreign state*) that is being conducted by a person or authority, (*name of person or authority*), with responsibility in (*specify the name of the foreign state*) for the investigation of such offences,

you are required to preserve (*specify the computer data*) that is in your possession or control when you receive this demand until (*insert date*) unless, before that date, this demand is revoked or a document that contains that data is obtained under a warrant or an order.

This demand is subject to the following conditions:

If you contravene this demand without lawful excuse, you may be subject to a fine.

You are required to destroy the computer data that would not be retained in the ordinary course of business, and any document that is prepared for the purpose of preserving the computer data, in accordance with section 487.0194 of the *Criminal Code*. If you contravene that provision without lawful excuse, you may be subject to a fine, to imprisonment or to both.

..
(*Signature of peace officer or public officer*)

2014, c. 31, s. 26.

FORM 5.002

Information to Obtain a Preservation Order

(*Subsection 487.013(2)*)

Canada,
Province of ....
(*territorial division*)

This is the information of (*name of peace officer or public officer*), of .... ("the informant").

The informant says that they have reasonable grounds to suspect that an offence has been or will be committed under (*specify the provision of the Criminal Code or other Act of Parliament*) (*or* has been committed under (*specify the provision of the law of the foreign state*)) and that (*specify the computer data*) is in the possession or control of (name of the person) and will assist in the investigation of the offence.

The informant also says that a peace officer or public officer intends to apply or has applied for a warrant or order in connection with the investigation to obtain a document that contains the computer data (*and, if applicable*, and that (*name of person or authority*) is conducting the investigation and has responsibility for the investigation of such offences in (*insert the name of the foreign state*)).

The reasonable grounds are: (*including, if applicable, whether a preservation demand was made under section 487.012 of the Criminal Code*)

The informant therefore requests that (*name of the person*) be ordered to preserve (*specify the computer data*) that is in their possession or control when they receive the order for 90 days after the day on which the order is made.

Sworn before me on (*date*), at (*place*).

...
(*Signature of informant*)

...
(*Signature of justice or judge*)

2014, c. 31, s. 26.

FORM 5.003

Preservation Order

(*Subsection 487.013(4)*)

Canada,
Province of ....
(*territorial division*)

To (name of person), of ....:

Whereas I am satisfied by information on oath of (*name of peace officer or public officer*), of ....,

(*a*) that there are reasonable grounds to suspect that an offence has been or will be committed under (*specify the provision of the Criminal Code or other Act of Parliament*) (*or* has been committed under (*specify the provision of the law of the foreign state*)) and that (*specify the computer data*) is in your possession or control and will assist in the investigation of the offence; and

(*b*) that a peace officer or public officer intends to apply or has applied for a warrant or order to obtain a document that contains the computer data (*and, if applicable*, and that (*name of person or authority*) is conducting the investigation and has responsibility for the investigation of such offences in (*insert the name of the foreign state*));

Therefore, you are required to preserve the specified computer data that is in your possession or control when you receive this order until (*insert date*) unless, before that date, this order is revoked or a document that contains that data is obtained under a warrant or an order.

This order is subject to the following conditions:

If you contravene this order without lawful excuse, you may be subject to a fine, to imprisonment or to both.

You are required to destroy the computer data that would not be retained in the ordinary course of business, and any document that is prepared for the purpose of preserving the computer data, in accordance with section 487.0194 of the *Criminal Code*. If you contravene that provision without lawful excuse, you may be subject to a fine, to imprisonment or to both.

Dated (*date*), at (*place*).

..

(*Signature of justice or judge*)

2014, c. 31, s. 26.

FORM 5.004

Information to Obtain a Production Order

(*Subsections 487.014(2), 487.015(2), 487.016(2), 487.017(2) and 487.018(3)*)

Canada,
Province of ....
(*territorial division*)

This is the information of (*name of peace officer or public officer*), of .... ("the informant").

The informant says that they have reasonable grounds to suspect (*or, if the application is for an order under section 487.014 of the Criminal Code*, reasonable grounds to believe)

(*a*) that an offence has been or will be committed under (*specify the provision of the Criminal Code or other Act of Parliament*); and

(*b*) (*if the application is for an order under section 487.014 of the Criminal Code*) that (*specify the document or data*) is in the possession or control of (*name of the person*) and will afford evidence respecting the commission of the offence.

(*or*)

(*b*) (*if the application is for an order under section 487.015 of the Criminal Code*) that the identification of a device or person involved in the transmission of (*specify the communication*) will assist in the investigation of the offence and that (*specify the transmission data*) that is in the possession or control of one or more persons whose identity is unknown will enable that identification.

(*or*)

(*b*) (*if the application is for an order under section 487.016 of the Criminal Code*) that (*specify the transmission data*) is in the possession or control of (*name of the person*) and will assist in the investigation of the offence.

(*or*)

(*b*) (*if the application is for an order under section 487.017 of the Criminal Code*) that (*specify the tracking data*) is in the possession or control of (*name of the person*) and will assist in the investigation of the offence.

(*or*)

(*b*) (*if the application is for an order under section 487.018 of the Criminal Code*) that (*specify the data*) is in the possession or control of (*name of the financial institution, person or entity*) and will assist in the investigation of the offence.

The reasonable grounds are:

The informant therefore requests

(*if the application is for an order under section 487.014 of the Criminal Code*) that (*name of the person*) be ordered to produce a document that is a copy of (*specify the document*) that is in their possession or control when they receive the order (*and/or* to prepare and produce a document containing (*specify the data*) that is in their possession or control when they receive the order).

(*or*)

(*if the application is for an order under section 487.015 of the Criminal Code*) that a person who is served with the order in accordance with subsection 487.015(4) of the *Criminal Code* be ordered to prepare and produce a document containing (*specify the transmission data*) that is in their possession or control when they are served with the order.

(*or*)

(*if the application is for an order under section 487.016 of the Criminal Code*) that (*name of the person*) be ordered to prepare and produce a document containing (*specify the transmission data*) that is in their possession or control when they receive the order.

(*or*)

(*if the application is for an order under section 487.017 of the Criminal Code*) that (*name of the person*) be ordered to prepare and produce a document containing (*specify the tracking data*) that is in their possession or control when they receive the order.

(*or*)

(*if the application is for an order under section 487.018 of the Criminal Code*) that (*name of the financial institution, person or entity*) be ordered to prepare and produce a document setting out (*specify the data*) that is in their possession or control when they receive the order.

Sworn before me on (*date*), at (*place*).

...
(*Signature of informant*)

...
(*Signature of justice or judge*)

2014, c. 31, s. 26.

FORM 5.005

Production Order for Documents

(*Subsection 487.014(3)*)

Canada,
Province of ....
(*territorial division*)

To (*name of person*), of ....:

Whereas I am satisfied by information on oath of (*name of peace officer or public officer*), of ...., that there are reasonable grounds to believe that an offence has been or will be committed under (*specify the provision of the Criminal Code or other Act of Parliament*) and that (*specify the document or data*) is in your possession or control and will afford evidence respecting the commission of the offence;

Therefore, you are ordered to

produce a document that is a copy of (*specify the document*) that is in your possession or control when you receive this order

(*and/or*)

prepare and produce a document containing (*specify the data*) that is in your possession or control when you receive this order.

The document must be produced to (*name of peace officer or public officer*) within (*time*) at (*place*) in (*form*).

This order is subject to the following conditions:

You have the right to apply to revoke or vary this order.

If you contravene this order without lawful excuse, you may be subject to a fine, to imprisonment or to both.

Dated (*date*), at (*place*).

...
(*Signature of justice or judge*)

2014, c. 31, s. 26.

FORM 5.006

Production Order to Trace a Communication

(*Subsection 487.015(3)*)

Canada,
Province of ....
(*territorial division*)

Whereas I am satisfied by information on oath of (*name of peace officer or public officer*), of ...., that there are reasonable grounds to suspect that an offence has been or will be committed under (*specify the provision of the Criminal Code or other Act of Parliament*), that the identification of a device or person involved in the transmission of (*specify the communication*) will assist in the investigation of the offence and that one or more persons whose identity was unknown when the application was made have possession or control of (*specify the transmission data*) that will enable that identification;

Therefore, on being served with this order in accordance with subsection 487.015(4) of the *Criminal Code*, you are ordered to prepare and produce a document containing (*specify the transmission data*) that is in your possession or control when you are served with this order.

The document must be produced to (*name of peace officer or public officer*) as soon as feasible at (*place*) in (*form*).

This order is subject to the following conditions:

You have the right to apply to revoke or vary this order.

If you contravene this order without lawful excuse, you may be subject to a fine, to imprisonment or to both.

Dated (*date*), at (*place*).

....
(*Signature of justice or judge*)

Served on (*name of person*) on (*date*), at (*place*).

....
(*Signature of peace officer or public officer*)

....
(*Signature of person served*)

2014, c. 31, s. 26.

FORM 5.007

Production Order for Transmission Data or Tracking Data

(*Subsections 487.016(3) and 487.017(3)*)

Canada,
Province of ....
(*territorial division*)

To (*name of person*), of ....:

Whereas I am satisfied by information on oath of (*name of peace officer or public officer*), of ...., that there are reasonable grounds to suspect that an offence has been or will be committed under (*specify the provision of the Criminal Code or other Act of Parliament*) and that (*if the order is made under section 487.016 of the Criminal Code, specify the transmission data*) (*or, if the order is made under section 487.017 of the Criminal Code, specify the tracking data*) is in your possession or control and will assist in the investigation of the offence;

Therefore, you are ordered to prepare and produce a document containing the data specified that is in your possession or control when you receive this order.

The document must be produced to (*name of peace officer or public officer*) within (*time*) at (*place*) in (*form*).

This order is subject to the following conditions:

You have the right to apply to revoke or vary this order.

If you contravene this order without lawful excuse, you may be subject to a fine, to imprisonment or to both.

Dated (*date*), at (*place*).

....
(*Signature of justice or judge*)

2014, c. 31, s. 26.

FORM 5.008

Production Order for Financial Data

(*Subsection 487.018(4)*)

Canada,
Province of ....
(*territorial division*)

To (*name of financial institution, person or entity*), of ....:

Whereas I am satisfied by information on oath of (*name of peace officer or public officer*), of ...., that there are reasonable grounds to suspect that an offence has been or will be committed under (*specify the provision of the Criminal Code or other Act of Parliament*) and that (*specify the data*) is in your possession or control and will assist in the investigation of the offence;

Therefore, you are ordered to prepare and produce a document setting out (*specify the data*) that is in your possession or control when you receive this order.

The document must be produced to (*name of the peace officer or public officer*) within (*time*) at (*place*) in (*form*).

This order is subject to the following conditions:

You have the right to apply to revoke or vary this order.

If you contravene this order without lawful excuse, you may be subject to a fine, to imprisonment or to both.

Dated (*date*), at (*place*).

....
(*Signature of justice or judge*)

2014, c. 31, s. 26.

FORM 5.0081

Information to Revoke or Vary an Order Made under Any of Sections 487.013 to 487.018 of the *Criminal Code*

(*Subsection 487.019(3)*)

Canada,
Province of ....
(*territorial division*)

This is the information of (*name of peace officer or public officer*), of .... ("the informant").

The informant says that on or after (*insert date*) the informant became aware of the following facts that justify the revocation (*or variation*) of an order made on (*insert date*) under (*specify the provision of the Criminal Code*):

....

The informant therefore requests that the order be revoked (*or* be varied as follows: ....).

Sworn before me on (*date*), at (*place*).

....

(*Signature of informant*)

....

(*Signature of justice or judge*)

2014, c. 31, s. 26.

FORM 5.009

Information to Obtain a Non-Disclosure Order

(*Subsection 487.0191(2)*)

Canada,
Province of ....
(*territorial division*)

This is the information of (*name of peace officer or public officer*), of .... ("the informant").

The informant says that they have reasonable grounds to believe that the disclosure of the existence (or any of the contents or any of the following portion or portions) of (*identify the preservation demand made under section 487.012 of the Criminal Code, the preservation order made under section 487.013 of that Act or the production order made under any of sections 487.014 to 487.018 of that Act, as the case may be*) during (*identify the period*) would jeopardize the conduct of the investigation of the offence to which it relates:

(*specify portion or portions*)

The reasonable grounds are:

The informant therefore requests an order prohibiting (*name of the person*, financial institution or entity) from disclosing the existence (*or* any of the contents or any of the specified portion or portions) of the demand (*or* the order) during a period of (*identify the period*) after the day on which the order is made.

Sworn before me on (*date*), at (*place*).

....

(*Signature of informant*)

....

(*Signature of justice or judge*)

2014, c. 31, s. 26.

FORM 5.0091

Non-Disclosure Order

(*Subsection 487.0191(3)*)

Canada,
Province of ....

(*territorial division*)

To (*name of person, financial institution or entity*), of ....:

Whereas I am satisfied by information on oath of (*name of peace officer or public officer*), of ...., that there are reasonable grounds to believe that the disclosure of the existence (*or* any of the contents or any of the portion or portions, specified in the information,) of (*identify the preservation demand made under section 487.012 of the Criminal Code, the preservation order made under section 487.013 of that Act or the production order made under any of sections 487.014 to 487.018 of that Act, as the case may be*) during (*identify the period*) would jeopardize the conduct of the investigation of the offence to which it relates;

Therefore, you are prohibited from disclosing the existence (*or* any of the contents or any of the following portion or portions) of the demand (*or* the order) during a period of (*identify the period*) after the day on which this order is made.

(*specify portion or portions*)

You have the right to apply to revoke or vary this order.

If you contravene this order without lawful excuse, you may be subject to a fine, to imprisonment or to both.

Dated (*date*), at (*place*).

..
(*Signature of justice or judge*)

2014, c. 31, s. 26.

FORM 5.01

(*Subsection 487.05(1)*)

Information to Obtain a Warrant to take Bodily Substances for Forensic DNA Analysis
Canada,
Province of ....,
(*territorial division*).

This is the information of (*name of peace officer*), (*occupation*), of .... in the said (*territorial division*), hereinafter called the informant, taken before me.

The informant says that he or she has reasonable grounds to believe

(*a*) that (*offence*), a designated offence within the meaning of section 487.04 of the *Criminal Code*, has been committed;

(*b*) that a bodily substance has been found

(i) at the place where the offence was committed,

(ii) on or within the body of the victim of the offence,

(iii) on anything worn or carried by the victim at the time when the offence was committed, or

(iv) on or within the body of any person or thing or at any place associated with the commission of the offence;

(*c*) that (*name of person*) was a party to the offence; and

(*d*) that forensic DNA analysis of a bodily substance from (name of person) will provide evidence about whether the bodily substance referred to in paragraph (*b*) was from that person.

The reasonable grounds are:

The informant therefore requests that a warrant be issued authorizing the taking from (*name of person*) of the number of samples of bodily substances that are reasonably required for forensic DNA analysis, provided that the person taking the samples is able by virtue of training or experience to take them by means of the investigative procedures described in subsection 487.06(1) of the *Criminal Code* and provided that, if the person taking the samples is not a peace officer, he or she take the samples under the direction of a peace officer.

Sworn to before me

this .... day of ...., A.D. ...., at ....

...
(Signature of informant)

...
(*Signature of provincial court judge*)

1998, c. 37, s. 24.

FORM 5.02

(*Subsection 487.05(1)*)

Warrant Authorizing the Taking of Bodily Substances for Forensic DNA Analysis

Canada,
Province of ....,
(*territorial division*).

To the peace officers in (*territorial division*):

Whereas it appears on the oath of (name of peace officer) of .... in the said (*territorial division*), that there are reasonable grounds to believe

(*a*) that (*offence*), a designated offence within the meaning of section 487.04 of the *Criminal Code*, has been committed,

(*b*) that a bodily substance has been found

(i) at the place where the offence was committed,

(ii) on or within the body of the victim of the offence,

(iii) on anything worn or carried by the victim at the time when the offence was committed, or

(iv) on or within the body of any person or thing or at any place associated with the commission of the offence,

(*c*) that (*name of person*) was a party to the offence, and

(*d*) that forensic DNA analysis of a bodily substance from (*name of person*) will provide evidence about whether the bodily substance referred to in paragraph (*b*) was from that person;

And whereas I am satisfied that it is in the best interests of the administration of justice to issue this warrant;

This is therefore to authorize and require you to take from (name of person) or cause to be taken by a person acting under your direction, the number of samples of bodily substances that are reasonably required for forensic DNA analysis, provided that the person taking the samples is able by virtue of training or experience to take them by means of the investigative procedures described in subsection 487.06(1) of the *Criminal Code* and provided that, if the person taking the samples is not a peace officer, he or she take the samples under the direction of a peace officer. This warrant is subject to the following terms and conditions that I consider advisable to ensure that the taking of the samples is reasonable in the circumstances:

Dated this .... day of .... A.D. ...., at ....

...
(*Signature of provincial court judge*)

1998, c. 37, s. 24.

FORM 5.03

(*Subsections 487.051(1) and (2)*)

ORDER AUTHORIZING THE TAKING OF BODILY SUBSTANCES FOR FORENSIC DNA ANALYSIS

Canada
Province of ....
(*territorial division*)

To the peace officers in (*territorial division*):

Whereas (*name of offender*) has been convicted under the *Criminal Code*, discharged under section 730 of that Act or, in the case of a young person, found guilty under the *Young Offenders Act*, chapter Y-1 of the Revised Statutes of Canada, 1985, or the *Youth Criminal Justice Act* of (*offence*), which, on the day on which the offender was sentenced or discharged, was a primary designated offence within the meaning of section 487.04 of the *Criminal Code*;

Therefore, you are authorized to take or cause to be taken from (*name of offender*) the number of samples of bodily substances that is reasonably required for forensic DNA analysis, provided that the person taking the samples is able, by virtue of training or experience, to take them by means of the investigative procedures described in subsection 487.06(1) of the *Criminal Code* and that, if the person taking the samples is not a peace officer, they take them under the direction of a peace officer.

This order is subject to the following terms and conditions that I consider advisable to ensure that the taking of the samples is reasonable in the circumstances:

Dated this .... day of ...., A.D. ...., at ....

...
(*Signature of judge of the court*)
Canada

1998, c. 37, s. 24; 2002, c. 1, s. 185; 2005, c. 25, s. 12; 2007, c. 22, s. 23.

FORM 5.04

(*Subsection 487.051(3)*)

ORDER AUTHORIZING THE TAKING OF BODILY SUBSTANCES FOR FORENSIC DNA ANALYSIS

Canada
Province of ....
(*territorial division*)

To the peace officers in (*territorial division*):

Whereas (*name of offender*), in this order called the "offender",

(*a*) has been found not criminally responsible on account of mental disorder for (*offence*), which, on the day on which the finding was made, was a primary designated offence within the meaning of section 487.04 of the *Criminal Code*, or

(*b*) has been convicted under the *Criminal Code*, discharged under section 730 of that Act or, in the case of a young person, found guilty under the *Young Offenders Act*, chapter Y-1 of the Revised Statutes of Canada, 1985, or the *Youth Criminal Justice Act*, of, or has been found not criminally responsible on account of mental disorder for, (*offence*), which, on the day on which the offender was sentenced or discharged or the finding was made, was one of the following secondary designated offences within the meaning of section 487.04 of the *Criminal Code* (*check applicable box*):

[ ] (i) an offence under the *Criminal Code* for which the maximum punishment is imprisonment for five years or more and that was prosecuted by indictment,

[ ] (i.01) an offence under any of sections 9 to 14 of the *Cannabis Act* for which the maximum punishment is imprisonment for five years or more and that was prosecuted by indictment,

[ ] (ii) an offence under any of sections 5 to 7 of the *Controlled Drugs and Substances Act* for which the maximum punishment is imprisonment for five years or more and that was prosecuted by indictment,

[ ] (iii) an offence under any of sections 145 to 148, subsection 173(1), sections 264, 264.1, 266 and 270, subsections 286.1(1) and 320.16(1), paragraph 348(1)(*e*) and sections 349 and 423 of the *Criminal Code*,

[ ] (iv) an offence under section 433 or 434 of the *Criminal Code* as that section read from time to time before July 1, 1990,

[ ] (iv.1) an offence under section 252 of the *Criminal Code*, as it read from time to time before the day on which section 14 of *An Act to amend the Criminal Code (offences relating to conveyances) and to make consequential amendments to other Acts* comes into force, or

[ ] (v) an attempt or a conspiracy to commit an offence referred to in any of subparagraphs (i) to (ii) that was prosecuted by indictment (*or, if applicable*, an attempt or a conspiracy to commit an offence referred to in subparagraph (iii) or (iv));

Whereas I have considered the offender's criminal record, the nature of the offence, the circumstances surrounding its commission, whether the offender was previously found not criminally responsible on account of mental disorder for a designated offence, and the impact that this order would have on the offender's privacy and security of the person;

And whereas I am satisfied that it is in the best interests of the administration of justice to make this order;

Therefore, you are authorized to take or cause to be taken from (*name of offender*) the number of samples of bodily substances that is reasonably required for forensic DNA analysis, provided that the person taking the samples is able, by virtue of training or experience, to take them by means of the investigative procedures described in subsection 487.06(1) of the *Criminal Code* and that, if the person taking the samples is not a peace officer, they take them under the direction of a peace officer.

This order is subject to the following terms and conditions that I consider advisable to ensure that the taking of the samples is reasonable in the circumstances:

Dated this .... day of .... , A.D. ...., at ....

..
(*Signature of judge of the court*)
Canada

1998, c. 37, s. 24; 2002, c. 1, s. 186; 2005, c. 25, s. 12; 2007, c. 22, s. 23; 2012, c. 1, s. 38; 2014, c. 25, s. 32; 2018, c. 16, s. 224; 2018, c. 21, s. 29.

FORM 5.041

(*Subsections 487.051(4) and 487.055(3.11)*)

ORDER TO A PERSON TO HAVE BODILY SUBSTANCES TAKEN FOR FORENSIC DNA ANALYSIS

Canada
Province of ....
(*territorial division*)

To A.B., of ....,

Whereas an order has been made under section 487.051, or an authorization has been granted under section 487.055, of the *Criminal Code*, to take from you the number of samples of bodily substances that is reasonably required for forensic DNA analysis;

This is therefore to command you, in Her Majesty's name, to appear on ...., the .... day of ...., A.D. ...., at .... o'clock, at ...., for the purpose of the taking of bodily substances by means of the investigative procedures set out in subsection 487.06(1) of the *Criminal Code*.

You are warned that failure to appear in accordance with this order may result in a warrant being issued for your arrest under subsection 487.0551(1) of the *Criminal Code*. You are also warned that failure to appear, without reasonable excuse, is an offence under subsection 487.0552(1) of that Act.

Subsection 487.0551(1) of the *Criminal Code* states as follows:

487.0551 (1) If a person fails to appear at the place, day and time set out in an order made under subsection 487.051(4) or 487.055(3.11) or in a summons referred to in subsection 487.055(4) or 487.091(3), a justice of the peace may issue a warrant for their arrest in Form 5.062 to allow samples of bodily substances to be taken.

Subsection 487.0552(1) of the *Criminal Code* states as follows:

487.0552 (1) Every person who, without reasonable excuse, fails to comply with an order made under subsection 487.051(4) or 487.055(3.11) of this Act or under subsection 196.14(4) or 196.24(4) of the *National Defence Act*, or with a summons referred to in subsection 487.055(4) or 487.091(3) of this Act, is guilty of

(*a*) an indictable offence and liable to imprisonment for a term of not more than two years; or

(*b*) an offence punishable on summary conviction.

Dated this .... day of .... , A.D. ...., at ....

...
(*Signature of judge of the court*)
Canada

2005, c. 25, s. 12; 2007, c. 22, s. 23.

FORM 5.05

(*Subsection 487.055(1)*)

APPLICATION FOR AN AUTHORIZATION TO TAKE BODILY SUBSTANCES FOR FORENSIC DNA ANALYSIS

Canada
Province of ....
(*territorial division*)

I (*name of peace officer*), (*occupation*), of .... in (*territorial division*), apply for an authorization to take bodily substances for forensic DNA analysis. A certificate referred to in paragraph 667(1)(*a*) of the *Criminal Code* is filed with this application.

Whereas (*name of offender*), before June 30, 2000,

(*a*) had been declared a dangerous offender under Part XXIV of the *Criminal Code*,

(*b*) had been declared a dangerous offender or a dangerous sexual offender under Part XXI of the *Criminal Code*, chapter C-34 of the Revised Statutes of Canada, 1970, as it read from time to time before January 1, 1988,

(*c*) had been convicted of murder,

(*c*.1) had been convicted of attempted murder or conspiracy to commit murder or to cause another person to be murdered and is currently serving a sentence of imprisonment for that offence,

(*d*) had been convicted of a sexual offence within the meaning of subsection 487.055(3) of the *Criminal Code* and is currently serving a sentence of imprisonment for that offence, or

(*e*) had been convicted of manslaughter and is currently serving a sentence of imprisonment for that offence;

Therefore, I request that an authorization be granted under subsection 487.055(1) of the *Criminal Code* to take from (*name of offender*) the number of samples of bodily substances that is reasonably required for forensic DNA analysis, provided that the person taking the samples is able, by virtue of training or experience, to take them by means of the investigative procedures described in subsection 487.06(1) of the *Criminal Code* and that, if the person taking the samples is not a peace officer, they take them under the direction of a peace officer.

Dated this .... day of .... , A.D. ...., at ....

..
(*Signature of applicant*)
Canada

1998, c. 37, s. 24; 2005, c. 25, s. 12; 2007, c. 22, s. 23.

FORM 5.06

(*Subsection 487.055(1)*)

AUTHORIZATION TO TAKE BODILY SUBSTANCES FOR FORENSIC DNA ANALYSIS

Canada
Province of ....
(*territorial division*)

To the peace officers in (*territorial division*):

Whereas (*name of peace officer*), a peace officer in (*territorial division*), has applied for an authorization to take the number of samples of bodily substances from (*name of offender*) that is reasonably required for forensic DNA analysis by means of the investigative procedures described in subsection 487.06(1) of the *Criminal Code*;

Whereas (*name of offender*), before June 30, 2000,

(*a*) had been declared a dangerous offender under Part XXIV of the *Criminal Code*,

(*b*) had been declared a dangerous offender or a dangerous sexual offender under Part XXI of the *Criminal Code*, chapter C-34 of the Revised Statutes of Canada, 1970, as it read from time to time before January 1, 1988,

(*c*) had been convicted of murder,

(*c*.1) had been convicted of attempted murder or conspiracy to commit murder or to cause another person to be murdered and, on the date of the application, was serving a sentence of imprisonment for that offence,

(*d*) had been convicted of a sexual offence within the meaning of subsection 487.055(3) of the *Criminal Code* and, on the date of the application, was serving a sentence of imprisonment for that offence, or

(*e*) had been convicted of manslaughter and, on the date of the application, was serving a sentence of imprisonment for that offence;

And whereas I have considered the offender's criminal record, the nature of the offence, the circumstances surrounding its commission and the impact that this authorization would have on the offender's privacy and security of the person;

Therefore, you are authorized to take those samples or cause them to be taken from (*name of offender*), provided that the person taking the samples is able, by virtue of training or experience, to take them by means of the investigative procedures described in subsection 487.06(1) of the *Criminal Code* and that, if the person taking the samples is not a peace officer, they take them under the direction of a peace officer.

This authorization is subject to the following terms and conditions that I consider advisable to ensure that the taking of the samples is reasonable in the circumstances:

Dated this .... day of ...., A.D. ...., at ....

..
(Signature of provincial court judge)
Canada

1998, c. 37, s. 24; 2005, c. 25, s. 12; 2007, c. 22, s. 23.

FORM 5.061

(Subsections 487.055(4) and 487.091(3))

SUMMONS TO A PERSON TO HAVE BODILY SUBSTANCES TAKEN FOR FORENSIC DNA ANALYSIS

Canada
Province of ....
(*territorial division*)

To A.B., of ....,

Whereas an authorization has been granted under section 487.055 or 487.091 of the *Criminal Code* to take from you the number of samples of bodily substances that is reasonably required for forensic DNA analysis;

This is therefore to command you, in Her Majesty's name, to appear on ...., the .... day of ...., A.D. ...., at .... o'clock, at ...., for the purpose of the taking of bodily substances by means of the investigative procedures set out in subsection 487.06(1) of the *Criminal Code*. A peace officer, or a person who is acting under a peace officer's direction, who takes the samples of bodily substances may use as much force as necessary to do so.

You are warned that failure to appear in accordance with this summons may result in a warrant being issued for your arrest under subsection 487.0551(1) of the *Criminal Code*. You are also warned that failure to appear, without reasonable excuse, is an offence under subsection 487.0552(1) of that Act.

Subsection 487.0551(1) of the *Criminal Code* states as follows:

487.0551 (1) If a person fails to appear at the place, day and time set out in an order made under subsection 487.051(4) or 487.055(3.11) or in a summons referred to in subsection 487.055(4) or 487.091(3), a justice of the peace may issue a warrant for their arrest in Form 5.062 to allow samples of bodily substances to be taken.

Subsection 487.0552(1) of the *Criminal Code* states as follows:

487.0552 (1) Every person who, without reasonable excuse, fails to comply with an order made under subsection 487.051(4) or 487.055(3.11) of this Act or under subsection 196.14(4) or 196.24(4) of the *National Defence Act*, or with a summons referred to in subsection 487.055(4) or 487.091(3) of this Act, is guilty of

(*a*) an indictable offence and liable to imprisonment for a term of not more than two years; or

(*b*) an offence punishable on summary conviction.

Dated this .... day of ...., A.D. ...., at ....

....
(***Signature of judge of the court***)
Canada

2005, c. 25, s. 12; 2007, c. 22, s. 23.

FORM 5.062

(*Subsection 487.0551(1)*)

WARRANT FOR ARREST

Canada
Province of ....
(*territorial division*)

To the peace officers in (*territorial division*):

This warrant is issued for the arrest of A.B., of ...., (*occupation*), in this warrant called the "offender".

Whereas the offender failed to appear at the place, day and time set out in an order made under subsection 487.051(4) or 487.055(3.11), or in a summons referred to in subsection 487.055(4) or 487.091(3), of the *Criminal Code* to submit to the taking of samples of bodily substances;

This is, therefore, to command you, in Her Majesty's name, to arrest the offender without delay in order to allow the samples of bodily substances to be taken.

Dated this .... day of .... , A.D. ...., at ....

....
A Justice of the Peace in and for ....
Canada

2005, c. 25, s. 12; 2007, c. 22, s. 23.

FORM 5.07

(Subsection 487.057(1))

REPORT TO A PROVINCIAL COURT JUDGE OR THE COURT

Canada
Province of ....
(*territorial division*)

[ ] To (*name of judge*), a judge of the provincial court who issued a warrant under section 487.05 or granted an authorization under section 487.055 or 487.091 of the *Criminal Code* or to another judge of that court:

[ ] To the court that made an order under section 487.051 of the *Criminal Code*:

I (*name of peace officer*), declare that (*state here whether the samples were taken under a warrant issued under section 487.05, an order made under section 487.051 or an authorization granted under section 487.055 or 487.091 of the Criminal Code*).

I have (*state here whether you took the samples yourself or caused them to be taken under your direction*) from (*name of offender*) the number of samples of bodily substances that I believe is reasonably required for forensic DNA analysis, in accordance with (*state*

whether the samples were taken under a warrant issued or an authorization granted by the judge or another judge of the court or an order made by the court).

The samples were taken on the .... day of ...., A.D. ...., at .... o'clock.

I (*or state the name of the person who took the samples*) took the following samples from (*name of offender*) in accordance with subsection 487.06(1) of the *Criminal Code* and was able, by virtue of training or experience, to do so (*check applicable box*):

[ ] individual hairs, including the root sheath

[ ] epithelial cells taken by swabbing the lips, tongue or inside cheeks of the mouth

[ ] blood taken by pricking the skin surface with a sterile lancet

Any terms or conditions in the (*warrant, order or authorization*) have been complied with.

Dated this .... day of .... , A.D. ...., at ....

..
(*Signature of peace officer*)

1998, c. 37, s. 24; 2007, c. 22, s. 24.

FORM 5.08
(*Subsection 487.091(1)*)

APPLICATION FOR AN AUTHORIZATION TO TAKE ADDITIONAL SAMPLES OF BODILY SUBSTANCES FOR FORENSIC DNA ANALYSIS

Canada
Province of ....
(*territorial division*)

I (*name of peace officer*), (*occupation*), of .... in (*territorial division*), apply for an authorization to take additional samples of bodily substances for forensic DNA analysis.

Whereas samples of bodily substances were taken from (*name of offender*) for the purpose of forensic DNA analysis under an order made under section 487.051, or an authorization granted under section 487.055, of the *Criminal Code* (*attach a copy of the order or authorization*);

And whereas on (*day/month/year*) it was determined that

(*a*) a DNA profile could not be derived from the samples for the following reasons:
(*b*) the information or bodily substances required by regulations made under the *DNA Identification Act* were not transmitted in accordance with the requirements of the regulations or were lost for the following reasons:

Therefore, I request that an authorization be granted under subsection 487.091(1) of the *Criminal Code* to take from (*name of offender*) the number of additional samples of bodily substances that is reasonably required for forensic DNA analysis, provided that the person taking the samples is able, by virtue of training or experience, to take them by means of the investigative procedures described in subsection 487.06(1) of the *Criminal Code* and that, if the person taking the samples is not a peace officer, they take them under the direction of a peace officer.

Dated this .... day of ...., A.D. ...., at ....

...

(*Signature of applicant*)

Canada

1998, c. 37, s. 24; 2005, c. 25, s. 13; 2007, c. 22, s. 25.

FORM 5.09

(*Subsection 487.091(1)*)

AUTHORIZATION TO TAKE ADDITIONAL SAMPLES OF BODILY SUBSTANCES FOR FORENSIC DNA ANALYSIS

Canada
Province of ....
(*territorial division*)

To the peace officers in (*territorial division*):

Whereas samples of bodily substances were taken from (*name of offender*) for the purpose of forensic DNA analysis under an order made under section 487.051 or an authorization granted under section 487.055, of the *Criminal Code*;

Whereas on (*day/month/year*) it was determined that

(*a*) a DNA profile could not be derived from the samples for the following reasons:

(*b*) the information or bodily substances required by regulations made under the *DNA Identification Act* were not transmitted in accordance with the requirements of the regulations or were lost for the following reasons:

And whereas (*name of peace officer*), a peace officer in (*territorial division*), has applied for an authorization to take the number of additional samples of bodily substances from (*name of offender*) that is reasonably required for forensic DNA analysis by means of the investigative procedures described in subsection 487.06(1) of the *Criminal Code*;

Therefore, you are authorized to take those additional samples, or cause them to be taken, from (*name of offender*), provided that the person taking the samples is able, by virtue of training or experience, to take them by means of the investigative procedures described in subsection 487.06(1) of the *Criminal Code* and that, if the person taking the samples is not a peace officer, they take them under the direction of a peace officer.

This authorization is subject to the following terms and conditions that I consider advisable to ensure that the taking of the samples is reasonable in the circumstances:

Dated this .... day of ...., A.D. ...., at ....

...

(*Signature of provincial court judge*)

Canada

1998, c. 37, s. 24; 2005, c. 25, s. 13; 2007, c. 22, s. 25.

FORM 5.1

(*Sections 320.29 and 487.1*)

Warrant to search

Canada,
Province of [*specify province*].

To A.B. and other peace officers in the [*territorial division in which the warrant is intended for execution*]:

Whereas it appears on the oath of A.B., a peace officer in the [*territorial division in which the warrant is intended for execution*], that there are reasonable grounds for dispensing with an information presented personally and in writing; and that there are reasonable grounds for believing that the following things

[*describe things to be searched for*]

relevant to the investigation of the following indictable offence

[*describe offence in respect of which search is to be made*]

are to be found in the following place or premises

[*describe place or premises to be searched*]:

This is, therefore, to authorize you to enter the said place or premises between the hours of [*as the justice may direct*] and to search for and seize the said things and to report thereon as soon as practicable but within a period not exceeding seven days after the execution of the warrant to the clerk of the court for the [*territorial division in which the warrant is intended for execution*].

Issued at [*time*] on the [*day*] of [*month*] A.D. [*year*], at [*place*].

....
A Judge of the Provincial Court in and for the Province of [*specify province*].

***To the Occupant*: This search warrant was issued by telephone or other means of telecommunication. If you wish to know the basis on which this warrant was issued, you may apply to the clerk of the court for the territorial division in which the warrant was executed, at [*address*], to obtain a copy of the information on oath.**

You may obtain from the clerk of the court a copy of the report filed by the peace officer who executed this warrant. That report will indicate the things, if any, that were seized and the location where they are being held.

R.S.C. 1985, c. 27 (1st Supp.), s. 184(3); R.S.C. 1985, c. 1 (4th Supp.), s. 17; 2018, c. 1, s. 30.

FORM 5.2

(*Section 489.1*)

REPORT TO A JUSTICE

Canada,
Province of ....,
(*territorial division*).

To the justice who issued a warrant to the undersigned under section 320.29, 487 or 487.1 of the *Criminal Code* (*or another justice for the same territorial division or, if no warrant was issued, any justice having jurisdiction in respect of the matter*).

I, (*name of the peace officer or other person*) have (*state here whether you have acted under a warrant issued under section 320.29, 487 or 487.1 of the Criminal Code or under section 489 of the Criminal Code or otherwise in the execution of duties under the Criminal Code or other Act of Parliament to be specified*)

1 searched the premises situated at ....; and

2 seized the following things and dealt with them as follows:

Property Seized (*describe each thing seized*)	**Disposition (*state, in respect of each thing seized, whether*** ***(a) it was returned to the person lawfully entitled to its possession, in which case the receipt for it shall be attached to this report; or*** ***(b) it is being detained to be dealt with according to law, in which case indicate the location and manner in which or, if applicable, the person by whom, it is being detained.*)**
1.	**........**
2.	**........**
3.	**........**
4.	**........**

In the case of a warrant issued by telephone or other means of telecommunication, the statements referred to in subsection 487.1(9) of the *Criminal Code* shall be specified in the report.

Dated (*date*), at (*place*).

....

Signature of the peace officer or other person

R.S.C. 1985, c. 27 (1st Supp.), s. 184(3); R.S.C. 1985, c. 1 (4th Supp.), s. 17; 2018, c. 21, s. 31.

FORM 5.3

(*Section 462.32*)

REPORT TO A JUDGE OF PROPERTY SEIZED

Canada,
Province of ....,
(*territorial division*).

To a judge of the court from which the warrant was issued (*specify court*):

I, (*name of the peace officer or other person*) have acted under a warrant issued under section 462.32 of the *Criminal Code* and have

1. searched the premises situated at ....; and

2. seized the following property:

Property Seized (*describe each item of property seized*)	Location (*state, in respect of each item of property seized, the location where it is being detained*).
1.	....
2.	....
3.	....
4.	....

Dated this .... day of .... A.D. ...., at ....

...

Signature of peace officer or other person

R.S.C. 1985, c. 42 (4th Supp.), s. 6.

FORM 6

(*Sections 493, 508 and 512*)

Summons to a person charged with an offence

Canada,
Province of ....,
(*territorial division*).

To A.B., of ...., (*occupation*):

Whereas you have this day been charged before me that (*set out briefly the offence in respect of which the accused is charged*);

This is therefore to command you, in Her Majesty's name:

(*a*) to attend court on ...., the .... day of .... A.D........., at .... o'clock in the .... noon, at .... or before any justice for the said (*territorial division*) who is there, and to attend thereafter as required by the court, in order to be dealt with according to law; and

(*b*) to appear on ...., the .... day of .... A.D........., at .... o'clock in the ....noon, at ...., for the purposes of the *Identification of Criminals Act*. (*Ignore, if not filled in.*)

You are warned that failure without lawful excuse to attend court in accordance with this summons is an offence under subsection 145(4) of the *Criminal Code*.

Subsection 145(4) of the *Criminal Code* states as follows:

"(4) Every person who is served with a summons and who fails, without lawful excuse, to appear at a time and place stated in it for the purposes of the *Identification of Criminals Act* or to attend court in accordance with it, is guilty of

(*a*) an indictable offence and is liable to imprisonment for a term not exceeding two years; or

(*b*) an offence punishable on summary conviction."

Section 510 of the *Criminal Code* states as follows:

"510 Where an accused who is required by a summons to appear at a time and place stated therein for the purposes of the *Identification of Criminals Act* does not appear at that time and place, a justice may issue a warrant for the arrest of the accused for the offence with which he is charged."

Dated this .... day of .... A.D. ...., at ....

....
A Justice of the Peace in and
for .... *or* Judge

2018, c. 29, s. 69(1).

FORM 7

(*Sections 475, 493, 597, 800 and 803*)

Warrant for Arrest

Canada,
Province of ....,
(*territorial division*).

To the peace officers in the said (*territorial division*):

This warrant is issued for the arrest of A.B., of ...., (*occupation*), hereinafter called the accused.

Whereas the accused has been charged that (*set out briefly the offence in respect of which the accused is charged*);

And whereas:*

(*a*) there are reasonable grounds to believe that it is necessary in the public interest to issue this warrant for the arrest of the accused [507(4), 512(1)];

(*b*) the accused failed to attend court in accordance with the summons served on him [512(2)];

(*c*) (an appearance notice *or* a promise to appear *or* a recognizance entered into before an officer in charge) was confirmed and the accused failed to attend court in accordance therewith [512(2)];

(*d*) it appears that a summons cannot be served because the accused is evading service [512(2)];

(*e*) the accused was ordered to be present at the hearing of an application for a review of an order made by a justice and did not attend the hearing [520(5), 521(5)];

(*f*) there are reasonable grounds to believe that the accused has contravened or is about to contravene the (promise to appear or undertaking or recognizance) on which he was released [524(1), 525(5), 679(6)];

(*g*) there are reasonable grounds to believe that the accused has since his release from custody on (a promise to appear or an undertaking or a recognizance) committed an indictable offence [524(1), 525(5), 679(6)];

(*h*) the accused was required by (an appearance notice or a promise to appear or a recognizance entered into before an officer in charge or a summons) to attend at a time and place stated therein for the purposes of the *Identification of Criminals Act* and did not appear at that time and place [502, 510];

(*i*) an indictment has been found against the accused and the accused has not appeared or remained in attendance before the court for his trial [597];

(*j*) **

This is, therefore, to command you, in Her Majesty's name, forthwith to arrest the said accused and to bring him before (*state court, judge or justice*), to be dealt with according to law.

(*Add where applicable*) Whereas there are reasonable grounds to believe that the accused is or will be present in (*here describe dwelling-house*);

This warrant is also issued to authorize you to enter the dwelling-house for the purpose of arresting or apprehending the accused, subject to the condition that you may not enter the dwelling-house unless you have, immediately before entering the dwelling-house, reasonable grounds to believe that the person to be arrested or apprehended is present in the dwelling-house.

Dated this .... day of .... A.D. ...., at ....

...
Judge, Clerk of the Court,
Provincial Court Judge or Justice

---

* *Initial applicable recital.*

** *For any case not covered by recitals (a) to (i), insert recital in the words of the statute authorizing the warrant.*

1997, c. 39, s. 3; 1999, c. 5, s. 46.

FORM 7.1

(*Section 529.1*)

Warrant to Enter Dwelling House

Canada,
Province of ....,
(*territorial division*).

To the peace officers in the said (*territorial division*):

This warrant is issued in respect of the arrest of A.B., or a person with the following description ( ), of ...., (*occupation*).

Whereas there are reasonable grounds to believe:*

(*a*) a warrant referred to in this or any other Act of Parliament to arrest or apprehend the person is in force anywhere in Canada;

(*b*) grounds exist to arrest the person without warrant under paragraph 495(1)(*a*) or (*b*) or section 672.91 of the *Criminal Code*; or

(*c*) grounds exist to arrest or apprehend without warrant the person under an Act of Parliament, other than this Act;

And whereas there are reasonable grounds to believe that the person is or will be present in (*here describe dwelling-house*);

This warrant is issued to authorize you to enter the dwelling-house for the purpose of arresting or apprehending the person.

Dated this .... day of .... A.D. ...., at ....

....

Judge, Clerk of the Court, Provincial Court Judge *or* Justice

* *Initial applicable recital.*

1997, c. 39, s. 3; 2002, c. 13, s. 85.

FORM 8

(*Sections 493 and 515*)

Warrant for committal

Canada,
Province of ....,
(*territorial division*).

To the peace officers in the said (*territorial division*) and to the keeper of the (*prison*) at ....:

This warrant is issued for the committal of A.B., of ...., (*occupation*), hereinafter called the accused.

Whereas the accused has been charged that (*set out briefly the offence in respect of which the accused is charged*);

And whereas:*

(*a*) the prosecutor has shown cause why the detention of the accused in custody is justified [515(5)];

(*b*) an order has been made that the accused be released on (giving an undertaking *or* entering into a recognizance) but the accused has not yet complied with the order [519(1); 520(9); 521(10); 524(12); 525(8)];**

(*c*) the application by the prosecutor for a review of the order of a justice in respect of the interim release of the accused has been allowed and that order has been

vacated, and the prosecutor has shown cause why the detention of the accused in custody is justified [521];

(*d*) the accused has contravened or was about to contravene his (promise to appear *or* undertaking *or* recognizance) and the same was cancelled, and the detention of the accused in custody is justified or seems proper in the circumstances [524(4); 524(8)];

(*e*) there are reasonable grounds to believe that the accused has after his release from custody on (a promise to appear *or* an undertaking *or* a recognizance) committed an indictable offence and the detention of the accused in custody is justified or seems proper in the circumstances [524(4); 524(8)];

(*f*) the accused has contravened or was about to contravene the (undertaking *or* recognizance) on which he was released and the detention of the accused in custody seems proper in the circumstances [525(7); 679(6)];

(*g*) there are reasonable grounds to believe that the accused has after his release from custody on (an undertaking *or* a recognizance) committed an indictable offence and the detention of the accused in custody seems proper in the circumstances [525(7); 679(6)];

(*h*) ***

This is, therefore, to command you, in Her Majesty's name, to arrest, if necessary, and take the accused and convey him safely to the (*prison*) at ...., and there deliver him to the keeper thereof, with the following precept:

I do thereby command you the said keeper to receive the accused in your custody in the said prison and keep him safely there until he is delivered by due course of law.

Dated this .... day of .... A.D. ...., at ....

...
Judge, Clerk of the Court, Provincial Court Judge *or* Justice

---

* *Initial applicable recital.*

** *If the person having custody of the accused is authorized under paragraph 519(1)(b) to release him on his complying with an order, endorse the authorization on this warrant and attach a copy of the order.*

*** *For any case not covered by recitals* **(*a*) to (*g*), insert recital in the words of the statute authorizing the warrant.**

FORM 9

(*Section 493*)

APPEARANCE NOTICE ISSUED BY A PEACE OFFICER TO A PERSON NOT YET CHARGED WITH AN OFFENCE

Canada,
Province of ....,
(*territorial division*).

To A.B., of ...., (*occupation*):

You are alleged to have committed (*set out substance of offence*).

1. You are required to attend court on .... day, the .... day of .... A.D. ...., at .... o'clock in the .... noon, in courtroom No. ...., at .... court, in the municipality of ...., and to attend thereafter as required by the court, in order to be dealt with according to law.

2. You are also required to appear on .... day, the .... day of .... A.D. ...., at .... o'clock in the .... noon, at .... (*police station*), (*address*), for the purposes of the *Identification of Criminals Act*. (*Ignore if not filled in.*)

You are warned that failure to attend court in accordance with this appearance notice is an offence under subsection 145(5) of the *Criminal Code*.

Subsections 145(5) and (6) of the *Criminal Code* state as follows:

"(5) Every person who is named in an appearance notice or promise to appear, or in a recognizance entered into before an officer in charge or another peace officer, that has been confirmed by a justice under section 508 and who fails, without lawful excuse, to appear at the time and place stated in it for the purposes of the *Identification of Criminals Act*, or to attend court in accordance with it, is guilty of

(*a*) an indictable offence and liable to imprisonment for a term not exceeding two years; or

(*b*) an offence punishable on summary conviction.

(6) For the purposes of subsection (5), it is not a lawful excuse that an appearance notice, promise to appear or recognizance states defectively the substance of the alleged offence."

Section 502 of the *Criminal Code* states as follows:

"502. Where an accused who is required by an appearance notice or promise to appear or by a recognizance entered into before an officer in charge or another peace officer to appear at a time and place stated therein for the purposes of the *Identification of Criminals Act* does not appear at that time and place, a justice may, where the appearance notice, promise to appear or recognizance has been confirmed by a justice under section 508, issue a warrant for the arrest of the accused for the offence with which the accused is charged."

Issued at .... a.m./p.m. this .... day of .... A.D. ...., at ....

...

(*Signature of peace officer*)

...

(*Signature of accused*)

1994, c. 44, s. 84; 1997, c. 18, s. 115; 2018, c. 29, s. 70(1).

FORM 10

(*Section 493*)

PROMISE TO APPEAR

Canada,
Province of ....,
(*territorial division*).

I, A.B., of ...., (*occupation*), understand that it is alleged that I have committed (*set out substance of offence*).

In order that I may be released from custody,

1. I promise to attend court on .... day, the .... day of .... A.D. ...., at .... o'clock in the .... noon, in courtroom No. ...., at .... court, in the municipality of ...., and to attend thereafter as required by the court, in order to be dealt with according to law.

2. I also promise to appear on .... day, the .... day of .... A.D. ...., at .... o'clock in the .... noon, at .... (*police station*), (*address*), for the purposes of the *Identification of Criminals Act*. (*Ignore if not filled in*.)

I understand that failure without lawful excuse to attend court in accordance with this promise to appear is an offence under subsection 145(5) of the *Criminal Code*.

Subsections 145(5) and (6) of the *Criminal Code* state as follows:

"(5) Every person who is named in an appearance notice or promise to appear, or in a recognizance entered into before an officer in charge or another peace officer, that has been confirmed by a justice under section 508 and who fails, without lawful excuse, to appear at the time and place stated in it for the purposes of the *Identification of Criminals Act*, or to attend court in accordance with it, is guilty of

(*a*) an indictable offence and liable to imprisonment for a term not exceeding two years; or

(*b*) an offence punishable on summary conviction.

(6) For the purposes of subsection (5), it is not a lawful excuse that an appearnce notice, promise to appear or recognizance states defectively the substance of the alleged offence."

Section 502 of the *Criminal Code* states as follows:

"502. Where an accused who is required by an appearance notice or promise to appear or by a recognizance entered into before an officer in charge or another peace officer to appear at a time and place stated therein for the purposes of the *Identification of Criminals Act* does not appear at that time and place, a justice may, where the appearance notice, promise to appear or recognizance has been confirmed by a justice under section 508, issue a warrant for the arrest of the accused for the offence with which the accused is charged."

Dated this .... day of .... A.D. ...., at ....

...
(*Signature of accused*)

1994, c. 44, s. 84; 1997, c. 18, s. 115; 2018, c. 29, s. 70(1).

FORM 11

(*Section 493*)

RECOGNIZANCE ENTERED INTO BEFORE AN OFFICER IN CHARGE OR OTHER PEACE OFFICER

Canada,
Province of ....,
(*territorial division*).

I, A.B., of ...., (*occupation*), understand that it is alleged that I have committed (*set out substance of offence*).

In order that I may be released from custody, I hereby acknowledge that I owe $ (*not exceeding $500*) to Her Majesty the Queen to be levied on my real and personal property if I fail to attend court as hereinafter required.

(*or, for a person not ordinarily resident in the province in which the person is in custody or within two hundred kilometres of the place in which the person is in custody*)

In order that I may be released from custody, I hereby acknowledge that I owe $ (*not exceeding $500*) to Her Majesty the Queen and deposit herewith (*money or other valuable security not exceeding in amount or value $500*) to be forfeited if I fail to attend court as hereinafter required.

1. I acknowledge that I am required to attend court on .... day, the .... day of .... A.D. ...., at .... o'clock in the .... noon, in courtroom No. ...., at .... court, in the municipality of ...., and to attend thereafter as required by the court, in order to be dealt with according to law.

2. I acknowledge that I am also required to appear on .... day, the .... day of .... A.D. ...., at .... o'clock in the .... noon, at .... (*police station*), (*address*), for the purposes of the *Identification of Criminals Act*. (*Ignore if not filled in.*)

I understand that failure without lawful excuse to attend court in accordance with this recognizance to appear is an offence under subsection 145(5) of the *Criminal Code*.

Subsections 145(5) and (6) of the *Criminal Code* state as follows:

"(5) Every person who is named in an appearance notice or promise to appear, or in a recognizance entered into before an officer in charge or another peace officer, that has been confirmed by a justice under section 508 and who fails, without lawful excuse, to appear at the time and place stated in it for the purposes of the *Identification of Criminals Act* or to attend court in accordance with it, is guilty of

(*a*) an indictable offence and liable to imprisonment for a term not exceeding two years; or

(*b*) an offence punishable on summary conviction.

(6) For the purposes of subsection (5), it is not a lawful excuse that an appearance notice, promise to appear or recognizance states defectively the substance of the alleged offence."

Section 502 of the *Criminal Code* states as follows:

"502. Where an accused who is required by an appearance notice or promise to appear or by a recognizance entered into before an officer in charge or another peace officer to appear at a time and place stated therein for the purposes of the *Identification of Criminals Act* does not appear at that time and place, a justice may, where the appearance notice, promise to appear or recognizance has been confirmed by a justice under section 508, issue a warrant for the arrest of the accused for the offence with which the accused is charged."

Dated this .... day of .... A.D. ...., at ....

...
(*Signature of accused*)

1992, c. 1, s. 58; 1994, c. 44, s. 84; 1997, c. 18, s. 115; 2018, c. 29, s. 70(1).

FORM 11.1

(*Sections 493, 499 and 503*)

UNDERTAKING GIVEN TO A PEACE OFFICER OR AN OFFICER IN CHARGE

Canada,
Province of ....,
(*territorial division*).

I, A.B., of ...., (*occupation*), understand that it is alleged that I have committed (*set out substance of the offence*).

In order that I may be released from custody by way of (a promise to appear or a recognizance), I undertake to (*insert any conditions that are directed*):

(*a*) remain within (*designated territorial jurisdiction*);

(*b*) notify (*name of peace officer or other person designated*) of any change in my address, employment or occupation;

(*c*) abstain from communicating, directly or indirectly, with (*identification of victim, witness or other person*) or from going to (*name or description of place*) except in accordance with the following conditions: (*as the peace officer or other person designated specifies*);

(*d*) deposit my passport with (*name of peace officer or other person designated*).

(*e*) to abstain from possessing a firearm and to surrender to (*name of peace officer or other person designated*) any firearm in my possession and any authorization, licence or registration certificate or other document enabling the acquisition or possession of a firearm;

(*f*) report at (*state times*) to (*name of peace officer or other person designated*);

(*g*) to abstain from

(i) the consumption of alcohol or other intoxicating substances, or

(ii) the consumption of drugs except in accordance with a medical prescription.

(*h*) comply with any other conditions that the peace officer or officer in charge considers necessary to ensure the safety and security of any victim of or witness to the offence.

I understand that I am not required to give an undertaking to abide by the conditions specified above, but that if I do not, I may be kept in custody and brought before a justice so that the prosecutor may be given a reasonable opportunity to show cause why I should not be released on giving an undertaking without conditions.

I understand that if I give an undertaking to abide by the conditions specified above, then I may apply, at any time before I appear, or when I appear, before a justice pursuant to (*a promise to appear or a recognizance entered into before an officer in charge or another peace officer*), to have this undertaking vacated or varied and that my application will be considered as if I were before a justice pursuant to section 515 of the *Criminal Code*.

I also understand that this undertaking remains in effect until it is vacated or varied.

I also understand that failure without lawful excuse to abide by any of the conditions specified above is an offence under subsection 145(5.1) of the *Criminal Code*.

Subsection 145(5.1) of the *Criminal Code* states as follows:

"(5.1) Every person who, without lawful excuse, fails to comply with any condition of an undertaking entered into pursuant to subsection 499(2) or 503(2.1)

(*a*) is guilty of an indictable offence and is liable to imprisonment for a term not exceeding two years; or

(*b*) is guilty of an offence punishable on summary conviction."

Dated this .... day of .... A.D. ...., at ....

..
(*Signature of accused*)

1994, c. 44, s. 84; 1997, c. 18, s. 115; 1999, c. 25, s. 24; 2018, c. 29, s. 71.

FORM 12

(*Sections 493 and 679*)

UNDERTAKING GIVEN TO A JUSTICE OR A JUDGE

Canada,
Province of.....................................,
(*territorial division*).

I, A.B., of ...., (*occupation*), understand that I have been charged that (*set out briefly the offence in respect of which accused is charged*).

In order that I may be released from custody, I undertake to attend court on .... day, the .... day of .... A.D. ...., and to attend after that as required by the court in order to be dealt with according to law (*or, where date and place of appearance before court are not known at the time undertaking is given*, to attend at the time and place fixed by the court and after that as required by the court in order to be dealt with according to law).
(*and, where applicable*)

I also undertake to (*insert any conditions that are directed*)

(*a*) report at (*state times*) to (*name of peace officer or other person designated*);

(*b*) remain within (*designated territorial jurisdiction*);

(*c*) notify (*name of peace officer or other person designated*) of any change in my address, employment or occupation;

(*d*) abstain from communicating, directly or indirectly, with (*identification of victim, witness or other person*) except in accordance with the following conditions: (*as the justice or judge specifies*);

(*e*) deposit my passport (*as the justice or judge directs*); and

(*f*) (*any other reasonable conditions*).

I understand that failure without lawful excuse to attend court in accordance with this undertaking is an offence under subsection 145(2) of the *Criminal Code*.

Subsections 145(2) and (3) of the *Criminal Code* state as follows:

"(2) Every person is guilty of an indictable offence and liable to imprisonment for a term of not more than two years or is guilty of an offence punishable on summary conviction who,

(*a*) being at large on their undertaking or recognizance given to or entered into before a justice or judge, fails, without lawful excuse, to attend court in accordance with the undertaking or recognizance, or

(*b*) having appeared before a court, justice or judge, fails, without lawful excuse, to attend court as subsequently required by the court, justice or judge or to surrender themselves in accordance with an order of the court, justice or judge, as the case may be.

(3) Every person who is at large on an undertaking or recognizance given to or entered into before a justice or judge and is bound to comply with a condition of that undertaking or recognizance, and every person who is bound to comply with a direction under subsection 515(12) or 522(2.1) or an order under subsection 516(2), and who fails, without lawful excuse, the proof of which lies on them, to comply with the condition, direction or order is guilty of

(*a*) an indictable offence and liable to imprisonment for a term not exceeding two years; or

(*b*) an offence punishable on summary conviction."

Dated this .... day of .... A.D. ...., at ....

..
(*Signature of accused*)
1994, c. 44, s. 84; 1999, c. 25, s. 25.; 2008, c. 18, s. 45.1; 2018, c. 29, s. 72.

FORM 13

(*Sections 816, 832 and 834*)

Undertaking by appellant (defendant)

Canada,
Province of ....,
(*territorial division*).

I, A.B., of ...., (*occupation*), being the appellant against conviction (*or* against sentence *or* against an order *or* by way of stated case) in respect of the following matter (*set out the offence, subject-matter of order or question of law*) undertake to appear personally at the sittings of the appeal court at which the appeal is to be heard.
(*and where applicable*)

I also undertake to (*insert any conditions that are directed*)

(*a*) report at (*state times*) to (*name of peace officer or other person designated*);

(*b*) remain within (*designated territorial jurisdiction*);

(*c*) notify (*name of peace officer or other person designated*) of any change in my address, employment or occupation;

(*d*) abstain from communicating, directly or indirectly, with (*identification of victim, witness or other person*) except in accordance with the following conditions: (*as the justice or judge specifies*);

(*e*) deposit my passport (*as the justice or judge directs*); and

(*f*) (*any other reasonable conditions*).

Dated this .... day of .... A.D. ...., at ....

..
(*Signature of appellant*)
1999, c. 25, s. 26.

FORM 14

(*Section 817*)

Undertaking by appellant (prosecutor)

Canada,
Province of ....,
(*territorial division*).

I, A.B., of ...., (*occupation*), being the appellant against an order of dismissal (*or* against sentence) in respect of the following charge (*set out the name of the defendant and the offence, subject-matter of order or question of law*) undertake to appear personally or by counsel at the sittings of the appeal court at which the appeal is to be heard.

Dated this .... day of .... A.D. ...., at ....

...
(*Signature of appellant*)

FORM 15

(*Section 543*)

Warrant to convey accused before justice of another territorial division

Canada,
Province of ....,
(*territorial division*).
To the peace officers in the said (*territorial division*):

Whereas A.B., of .... hereinafter called the accused, has been charged that (*state place of offence and charge*);

And Whereas I have taken the deposition of X.Y. in respect of the said charge;

And Whereas the charge is for an offence committed in the (*territorial division*):

This is to command you, in Her Majesty's name, to convey the said A.B., before a justice of the (*last mentioned territorial division*).

Dated this .... day of .... A.D. ...., at ....

...
A Justice of the Peace in and for ....

FORM 16

(*Section 699*)

Subpoena to a Witness

Canada,
Province of ....,
(*territorial division*).

To E.F., of ...., (*occupation*);

Whereas A.B. has been charged that (*state offence as in the information*), and it has been made to appear that you are likely to give material evidence for (*the prosecution or the defence*);

This is therefore to command you to attend before (set out court or justice), on .... the .... day of .... A.D. ...., at .... o'clock in the .... noon at .... to give evidence concerning the said charge.*

*** Where a witness is required to produce anything, add the following: and to bring with you anything in your possession or under your control that relates to the said charge, and more particularly the following: (*specify any documents, objects or other things required*).**

Dated this .... day of .... A.D. ...., at ....

..
A Judge, Justice or Clerk of the court
(*Seal, if required*)

1999, c. 5, s. 47.

FORM 16.1
(*Subsections 278.3(5) and 699(7)*)

SUBPOENA TO A WITNESS IN THE CASE OF PROCEEDINGS IN RESPECT OF AN OFFENCE REFERRED TO IN SUBSECTION 278.2(1) OF THE CRIMINAL CODE

Canada,
Province of ....,
(*territorial division*).

To E.F., of ...., (*occupation*);

Whereas A.B. has been charged that (*state offence as in the information*), and it has been made to appear that you are likely to give material evidence for (*the prosecution or the defence*);

This is therefore to command you to attend before (*set out court or justice*), on .... the .... day of .... A.D. ...., at .... o'clock in the .... noon at .... to give evidence concerning the said charge, and to bring with you anything in your possession or under your control that relates to the said charge, and more particularly the following: (*specify any documents, objects or other things required*).

TAKE NOTE

You are only required to bring the things specified above to the court on the date and at the time indicated, and you are not required to provide the things specified to any person or to discuss their contents with any person unless and until ordered by the court to do so.

If anything specified above is a "record" as defined in section 278.1 of the *Criminal Code*, it may be subject to a determination by the court in accordance with sections 278.1 to 278.91 of the *Criminal Code* as to whether and to what extent it should be produced.

If anything specified above is a "record" as defined in section 278.1 of the *Criminal Code*, the production of which is governed by sections 278.1 to 278.91 of the *Criminal Code*, this subpoena must be accompanied by a copy of an application for the production of the record made pursuant to section 278.3 of the *Criminal Code*, and you will have an opportunity to make submissions to the court concerning the production of the record.

If anything specified above is a "record" as defined in section 278.1 of the *Criminal Code*, the production of which is governed by sections 278.1 to 278.91 of the *Criminal Code*, you are not required to bring it with you until a determination is made in accordance with those sections as to whether and to what extent it should be produced.

As defined in section 278.1 of the *Criminal Code*, "record" means any form of record that contains personal information for which there is a reasonable expectation of privacy and includes, without limiting the generality of the foregoing, medical, psychiatric, therapeutic, counselling, education, employment, child welfare, adoption and social services records, personal journals and diaries, and records containing personal information the

production or disclosure of which is protected by any other Act of Parliament or a provincial legislature, but does not include records made by persons responsible for the inves tigation or prosecution of the offence.

Dated this .... day of .... A.D. ...., at ....

..
Judge, Clerk of the Court,
Provincial Court Judge *or* Justice
(*Seal, if required*)

1997, c. 30, s. 3.

FORM 17

(*Sections 698 and 705*)

Warrant for witness

Canada,
Province of ....,
(*territorial division*).

To the peace officers in the (*territorial division*):

Whereas A.B. of ...., has been charged that (*state offence as in the information*);

And Whereas it has been made to appear that E.F. of ...., hereinafter called the witness, is likely to give material evidence for (the prosecution *or* the defence) and that*
****Insert whichever of the following is appropriate*:**

(*a*) the said E.F. will not attend unless compelled to do so;

(*b*) the said E.F. is evading service of a subpoena;

(*c*) the said E.F. was duly served with a subpoena and has neglected (to attend at the time and place appointed therein *or* to remain in attendance);

(*d*) the said E.F. was bound by a recognizance to attend and give evidence and has neglected (to attend *or* to remain in attendance).

This is therefore to command you, in Her Majesty's name, to arrest and bring the witness forthwith before (*set out court or justice*) to be dealt with in accordance with section 706 of the *Criminal Code*.

Dated this .... day of .... A.D. ...., at ....

..
A Justice *or* Clerk of the Court

(*Seal if required*)

FORM 18

(*Section 704*)

Warrant to arrest an absconding witness

Canada,
Province of ....,
(*territorial division*).

To the peace officers in the (*territorial division*):

Whereas A.B., of ...., has been charged that (*state offence as in the information*);

And Whereas I am satisfied by information in writing and under oath that C.D., of ...., hereinafter called the witness, is bound by recognizance to give evidence on the trial of the accused on the said charge, and that the witness (has absconded *or* is about to abscond);

This is therefore to command you, in Her Majesty's name, to arrest the witness and bring him forthwith before (*the court, judge, justice or provincial court judge before whom the witness is bound to appear*) to be dealt with in accordance with section 706 of the *Criminal Code*.

Dated this .... day of .... A.D. ...., at ....

..
A Justice of the Peace in and for ....

FORM 19

(*Sections 516 and 537*)

Warrant remanding a prisoner

Canada,
Province of ....,
(*territorial division*).

To the peace officers in the (*territorial division*):

You are hereby commanded forthwith to arrest, if necessary, and convey to the (*prison*) at .... the persons named in the following schedule each of whom has been remanded to the time mentioned in the schedule:

Person charged	Offence	Remanded to

And I hereby command you, the keeper of the said prison, to receive each of the said persons into your custody in the prison and keep him safely until the day when his remand expires and then to have him before me or any other justice at .... at .... o'clock in the .... noon of the said day, there to answer to the charge and to be dealt with according to law, unless you are otherwise ordered before that time.

Dated this .... day of .... A.D. ...., at ....

..
A Justice of the Peace in and for ....

FORM 20

(*Section 545*)

Warrant of committal of witness for refusing to be sworn or to give evidence

Canada,
Province of ....,
(*territorial division*).

To the peace officers in the (*territorial division*):

Whereas A.B. of ...., hereinafter called the accused, has been charged that (*set out offence as in the information*);

And Whereas E.F. of ...., hereinafter called the witness, attending before me to give evidence for (the prosecution *or* the defence) concerning the charge, against the accused (refused to be sworn *or* being duly sworn as a witness refused to answer certain questions concerning the charge that were put to him *or* refused or neglected to produce the following writings, namely .... *or* refused to sign his deposition) having been ordered to do so, without offering any just excuse for such refusal or neglect;

This is therefore to command you, in Her Majesty's name, to arrest, if necessary, and take the witness and convey him safely to the prison at ...., and there deliver him to the keeper thereof, together with the following precept:

I do hereby command you, the said keeper, to receive the said witness into your custody in the said prison and safely keep him there for the term of .... days, unless he sooner consents to do what was required of him, and for so doing this is a sufficient warrant.

Dated this .... day of .... A.D. ...., at ....

..

A Justice of the Peace in and for ....

FORM 21

(*Sections 570 and 806*)

WARRANT OF COMMITTAL ON CONVICTION

Canada,
Province of ....,
(*territorial division*).

To the peace officers in (*territorial division*) and to the keeper of (*prison*) at ....:

Whereas (*name*), in this Form called the offender, was, on the .... day of .... 20..............., convicted by (*name of judge and court*) of having committed the following offence(s) and it was adjudged that the offender be sentenced as follows:

Offence	Sentence	Remarks
(*state offence of which offender was convicted*)	(*state term of imprisonment for the offence and, in case of imprisonment for default of payment of fine, so indicate together with the amount of it and applicable costs and whether payable immediately or within a time fixed*)	(*state the amount of time spent in custody before sentencing, the term of imprisonment that would have been imposed before any credit was granted under subsection 719(3) or (3.1), the amount of time credited, if any, and whether the sentence is consecutive or concurrent, and specify consecutive to or concurrent with what other sentence*)

1. ....
2. ....
3. ....
4. ....

You are hereby commanded, in Her Majesty's name, to arrest the offender if it is necessary to do so in order to take the offender into custody, and to take and convey him or her safely to (*prison*) at .... and deliver him or her to its keeper, who is hereby commanded to receive the accused into custody and to imprison him or her there for the term(s) of his or her imprisonment, unless, if a term of imprisonment was imposed only in default of payment of a fine or costs, those amounts and the costs and charges of the committal and of conveying the offender to that prison are paid sooner, and this is a sufficient warrant for so doing.

Dated this .... day of .... 20 .... , at ....

..
Clerk of the Court, Justice, Judge *or* Provincial Court Judge

1995, c. 22, s. 9; 2009, c. 29, s. 4.

FORM 22

(*Section 806*)

Warrant of committal on an order for the payment of money

Canada,
Province of ....,
(*territorial division*).

To the peace officers in the (*territorial division*) and to the keeper of the (*prison*) at ....:

Whereas A.B., hereinafter called the defendant, was tried on an information alleging that (*set out matter of complaint*), and it was ordered that (*set out the order made*), and in default that the defendant be imprisoned at the (*prison*) at .... for a term of ....;

I hereby command you, in Her Majesty's name, to arrest, if necessary, and take the defendant and convey him safely to the (*prison*) at ...., and deliver him to the keeper thereof, together with the following precept:

I hereby command you, the keeper of the said prison, to receive the defendant into your custody in the said prison and imprison him there for the term of ...., unless the said amounts and the costs and charges of the committal and of conveying the defendant to the prison are sooner paid, and for so doing this is a sufficient warrant.

Dated this .... day of .... A.D. ...., at ....

..
A Justice of the Peace in and for ....

FORM 23

(*Sections 810 and 810.1*)

Warrant of committal for failure to furnish recognizance to keep the peace

Canada,
Province of ....,
(*territorial division*).

To the peace officers in the (*territorial division*) and to the keeper of the (*prison*) at ....:

Whereas A.B., hereinafter called the accused, has been ordered to enter into a recognizance to keep the peace and be of good behaviour, and has (refused *or* failed) to enter into a recognizance accordingly;

You are hereby commanded, in Her Majesty's name, to arrest, if necessary, and take the accused and convey him safely to the (*prison*) at .... and deliver him to the keeper thereof, together with the following precept:

You, the said keeper, are hereby commanded to receive the accused into your custody in the said prison and imprison him there until he enters into a recognizance as aforesaid or until he is discharged in due course of law.

Dated this .... day of .... A.D. ...., at ....

..
Clerk of the Court, Justice *or* Provincial Court Judge

(*Seal, if required*) **1993, c. 45, s. 12.**

FORM 24

(*Section 550*)

Warrant of committal of witness for failure to enter into recognizance

Canada,
Province of ....,
(*territorial division*).

To the peace officers in the (*territorial division*) and to the keeper of the (*prison*) at ....:

Whereas A.B., hereinafter called the accused, was committed for trial on a charge that (*state offence as in the information*);

And Whereas E.F., hereinafter called the witness, having appeared as a witness on the preliminary inquiry into the said charge, and being required to enter into a recognizance to appear as a witness on the trial of the accused on the said charge, has (failed *or* refused) to do so;

This is therefore to command you, in Her Majesty's name, to arrest, if necessary, and take and safely convey the said witness to the (*prison*) at .... and there deliver him to the keeper thereof, together with the following precept:

I do hereby command you, the said keeper, to receive the witness into your custody in the said prison and keep him there safely until the trial of the accused upon the said charge, unless before that time the witness enters into the said recognizance.

Dated this .... day of .... A.D. ...., at ....

..
A Justice of the Peace in and for ....

FORM 25

(*Section 708*)

Warrant of committal for contempt

Canada,
Province of ....,
(*territorial division*).

To the peace officers in the said (*territorial division*) and to the keeper of the (*prison*) at ....:

Whereas E.F. of ...., hereinafter called the defaulter, was on the .... day of .... A.D. ...., at ...., convicted before .... for contempt in that he did not attend before .... to give evidence on the trial of a charge that (*state offence as in the information*) against A.B. of ...., although (duly subpoenaed *or* bound by recognizance to appear and give evidence in that behalf, *as the case may be*) and did not show any sufficient excuse for his default;

And Whereas in and by the said conviction it was adjudged that the defaulter (*set out punishment adjudged*);

And Whereas the defaulter has not paid the amounts adjudged to be paid; (*delete if not applicable*)

This is therefore to command you, in Her Majesty's name, to arrest, if necessary, and take the defaulter and convey him safely to the (*prison*) at .... and there deliver him to the keeper thereof, together with the following precept:

I do hereby command you, the said keeper, to receive the defaulter into your custody in the said prison and imprison him there* and for so doing this is a sufficient warrant.
****Insert whichever of the following is applicable*:**

(*a*) for the term of ....;

(*b*) for the term of .... unless the said sums and the costs and charges of the committal and of conveying the defaulter to the said prison are sooner paid;

(*c*) for the term of .... and for the term of (*if consecutive so state*) unless the said sums and the costs and charges of the committal and of conveying the defaulter to the said prison are sooner paid.

Dated this .... day of .... A.D. ...., at ....

..
A Justice *or* Clerk of the Court

(*Seal, if required*)

FORM 26

(*Section 827*)

Warrant of committal in default of payment of costs of an appeal

Canada,
Province of ....,
(*territorial division*).

To the peace officers of (*territorial division*) and to the keeper of the (*prison*) at ....:

Whereas it appears that on the hearing of an appeal before the (*set out court*) it was adjudged that A.B., of ...., hereinafter called the defaulter, should pay to the Clerk of the Court the sum of .... dollars inrespect of costs;

And Whereas the Clerk of the Court has certified that the defaulter has not paid the sum within the time limited therefor;

I do hereby command you, the said peace officers, in Her Majesty's name, to take the defaulter and safely convey him to the (*prison*) at .... and deliver him to the keeper thereof, together with the following precept:

I do hereby command you, the said keeper, to receive the defaulter into your custody in the said prison and imprison him for the term of ...., unless the said sum and the costs and charges of the committal and of conveying the defaulter to the said prison are sooner paid, and for so doing this is a sufficient warrant.

Dated this .... day of .... A.D. ...., at ....

..
A Justice of the Peace in and for ....

FORM 27

(*Section 773*)

Warrant of committal on forfeiture of a recognizance

Canada,
Province of ....,
(*territorial division*).

To the sheriff of (*territorial division*) and to the keeper of the (*prison*) at ....:

You are hereby commanded to arrest, if necessary, and take (A.B. and C.D. *as the case may be*) hereinafter called the defaulters, and to convey them safely to the (*prison*) at .... and deliver them to the keeper thereof, together with the following precept:

You, the said keeper, are hereby commanded to receive the defaulters into your custody in the said prison and imprison them for a period of .... or until satisfaction is made of a judgment debt of .... dollars due to Her Majesty the Queen in respect of the forfeiture of a recognizance entered into by .... on the .... day of .... A.D. ....

Dated this .... day of .... A.D. ...., at ....

Clerk of the ....

(*Seal*)

FORM 28

(*Sections 487 and 528*)

Endorsement of warrant

Canada,
Province of ....,
(*territorial division*).

Pursuant to application this day made to me, I hereby authorize the arrest of the accused (*or* defendant) (*or* execution of this warrant, *in the case of a warrant issued pursuant to section 487*), within the said (*territorial division*).

Dated this .... day of .... A.D. ...., at ....

...
A Justice of the Peace in and for ....

FORM 28.1

(*Subsection 487.03(2)*)

[*Repealed*, 2007, c. 22, s. 26.]

FORM 29

(*Section 507*)

Endorsement of warrant

Canada,
Province of ....,
(*territorial division*).

Whereas this warrant is issued under section 507, 508 or 512 of the *Criminal Code* in respect of an offence other than an offence mentioned in section 522 of the *Criminal Code*, I hereby authorize the release of the accused pursuant to section 499 of that Act.

Dated this .... day of .... A.D. ...., at ....

...
A Justice of the Peace in and for ....

1994, c. 44, s. 84.

FORM 30

(*Section 537*)

Order for accused to be brought before justice prior to expiration of period of remand

Canada,
Province of ....,
(*territorial division*).

To the keeper of the (*prison*) at ....:

Whereas by warrant dated the .... day of .... A.D. ...., I committed A.B., hereinafter called the accused, to your custody and required you safely to

keep until the .... day of .... A.D. ...., and then to have him before me or any other justice at .... at .... o'clock in the .... noon to answer to the charge against him and to be dealt with according to law unless you should be ordered otherwise before that time;

Now, therefore, I order and direct you to have the accused before .... at .... at .... o'clock in the .... noon to answer to the charge against him and to be dealt with according to law.

Dated this .... day of .... A.D. ...., at ....

..
A Justice of the Peace in and for ....

FORM 31

(*Section 540*)

Deposition of a witness

Canada,
Province of ....,
(*territorial division*).

These are the depositions of X.Y., of ...., and M.N., of ...., taken before me, this .... day of .... A.D., at ...., in the presence and hearing of A.B., hereinafter called the accused, who stands charged (*state offence as in the information*).

X.Y., having been duly sworn, deposes as follows: (*insert deposition as nearly as possible in words of witness*).

M.N., having been duly sworn, deposes as follows:

I certify that the depositions of X.Y., and M.N., written on the several sheets of paper hereto annexed to which my signature is affixed, were taken in the presence and hearing of the accused (and signed by them respectively, in his presence *where they are required to be signed by witness*). In witness whereof I have hereto signed my name.

..
A Justice of the Peace in and for ....

FORM 32

(*Sections 493, 550, 679, 706, 707, 810, 810.1 and 817*)

Recognizance

Canada,
Province of ....,
(*territorial division*).

Be it remembered that on this day the persons named in the following schedule personally came before me and severally acknowledged themselves to owe to Her Majesty the Queen the several amounts set opposite their respective names, namely,

Name	Address	Occupation	Amount
A.B.			
C.D.			
E.F.			

to be made and levied of their several goods and chattels, lands and tenements, respectively, to the use of Her Majesty the Queen, if the said A.B. fails in any of the conditions hereunder written.

Taken and acknowledged before me on the .... day of .... A.D. ...., at ....

..
Judge, Clerk of the Court, Provincial Court Judge *or* Justice

1. Whereas the said ...., hereinafter called the accused, has been charged that (*set out the offence in respect of which the accused has been charged*);

Now, therefore, the condition of this recognizance is that if the accused attends court on .... day, the .... day of .... A.D. ...., at .... o'clock in the .... noon and attends thereafter as required by the court in order to be dealt with according to law (*or, where date and place of appearance before court are not known at the time recognizance is entered into* if the accused attends at the time and place fixed by the court and attends thereafter as required by the court in order to be dealt with according to law) [515; 520; 521; 522; 523; 524; 525; 680];

And further, if the accused (*insert in Schedule of Conditions any additional conditions that are directed*),
the said recognizance is void, otherwise it stands in full force and effect,

2. Whereas the said ...., hereinafter called the appellant, is an appellant against his conviction (*or* against his sentence) in respect of the following charge (*set out the offence for which the appellant was convicted*) [679; 680]:

Now, therefore, the condition of this recognizance is that if the appellant attends as required by the court in order to be dealt with according to law;

And further, if the appellant (*insert in Schedule of Conditions any additional conditions that are directed*),
the said recognizance is void, otherwise it stands in full force and effect.

3. Whereas the said ...., hereinafter called the appellant, is an appellant against his conviction (*or* against his sentence *or* against an order *or* by way of stated case) in respect of the following matter (*set out offence, subject-matter of order or question of law*) [816; 831; 832; 834];

Now, therefore, the condition of this recognizance is that if the appellant appears personally at the sittings of the appeal court at which the appeal is to be heard;

And further, if the appellant (*insert in Schedule of Conditions any additional conditions that are directed*),
the said recognizance is void, otherwise it stands in full force and effect.

4. Whereas the said ...., hereinafter called the appellant, is an appellant against an order of dismissal (*or* against sentence) in respect of the following charge (*set out the name of the defendant and the offence, subject-matter of order or question of law*) [817; 831; 832; 834];

Now, therefore, the condition of this recognizance is that if the appellant appears personally or by counsel at the sittings of the appeal court at which the appeal is to be heard the said recognizance is void, otherwise it stands in full force and effect.

5. Whereas the said ...., hereinafter called the accused, was ordered to stand trial on a charge that (*set out the offence in respect of which the accused has been charged*);

And whereas A.B. appeared as a witness on the preliminary inquiry into the said charge [550; 706; 707];

Now, therefore, the condition of this recognizance is that if the said A.B. appears at the time and place fixed for the trial of the accused to give evidence on the indictment that is found against the accused, the said recognizance is void, otherwise it stands in full force and effect.

6. The condition of the above written recognizance is that if A.B. keeps the peace and is of good behaviour for the term of .... commencing on ...., the said recognizance is void, otherwise it stands in full force and effect [810 and 810.1].

7. Whereas a warrant was issued under section 462.32 or a restraint order was made under subsection 462.33(3) of the *Criminal Code* in relation to any property (*set out a description of the property and its location*);

Now, therefore, the condition of this recognizance is that A.B. shall not do or cause anything to be done that would result, directly or indirectly, in the disappearance, dissipation or reduction in value of the property or otherwise affect the property so that all or a part thereof could not be subject to an order of forfeiture under section 462.37 or 462.38 of the *Criminal Code* or any other provision of the *Criminal Code* or any other Act of Parliament [462.34].

Schedule of Conditions

(*a*) reports at (*state times*) to (*name of peace officer or other person designated*);

(*b*) remains within (*designated territorial jurisdiction*);

(*c*) notifies (*name of peace officer or other person designated*) of any change in his address, employment or occupation;

(*d*) abstains from communicating, directly or indirectly, with (*identification of victim, witness or other person*) except in accordance with the following conditions: (*as the justice or judge specifies*);

(*e*) deposits his passport (*as the justice or judge directs*); and

(*f*) (*any other reasonable conditions*).

***Note*: Section 763 and subsections 764(1) to (3) of the *Criminal Code* state as follows:**

"763. Where a person is bound by recognizance to appear before a court, justice or provincial court judge for any purpose and the session or sittings of that court or the proceedings are adjourned or an order is made changing the place of trial, that person and his sureties continue to be bound by the recognizance in like manner as if it had been entered into with relation to the resumed proceedings or the trial at the time and place at which the proceedings are ordered to be resumed or the trial is ordered to be held.

764. (1) Where an accused is bound by recognizance to appear for trial, his arraignment or conviction does not discharge the recognizance, but it continues to bind him and his sureties, if any, for his appearance until he is discharged or sentenced, as the case may be.

(2) Notwithstanding subsection (1), the court, justice or provincial court judge may commit an accused to prison or may require him to furnish new or additional sureties for his appearance until he is discharged or sentenced, as the case may be.

(3) The sureties of an accused who is bound by recognizance to appear for trial are discharged if he is committed to prison pursuant to subsection (2)."

R.S.C. 1985, c. 42 (4th Supp.), s. 7; 1993, c. 45, ss. 13, 14; 1999, c. 25, s. 27.

FORM 33

(*Section 770*)

CERTIFICATE OF DEFAULT TO BE ENDORSED ON RECOGNIZANCE

I hereby certify that A.B. (has not appeared as required by this recognizance *or* has not complied with a condition of this recognizance) and that by reason thereof the ends of justice have been (defeated *or* delayed, *as the case may be*).

The nature of the default is .... and the reason for the default is .... (*state reason if known*).

The names and addresses of the principal and sureties are as follows:

Dated this .... day of .... A.D. ...., at ....

..
(Signature of justice, judge, provincial court judge, clerk of the court, peace officer or other person, as the case may be)

(*Seal, if required*)

1994, c. 44, s. 84.

FORM 34

(*Section 771*)

Writ of fieri facias

Elizabeth II by the Grace of God, etc.

To the sheriff of (*territorial division*), GREETING.

You are hereby commanded to levy of the goods and chattels, lands and tenements of each of the following persons the amount set opposite the name of each:

Name Address Occupation Amount

And you are further commanded to make a return of what you have done in execution of this writ.

Dated this .... day of .... A.D. ...., at ....

..
Clerk of the..................

(*Seal*)

FORM 34.1

(*Subsection 737.1(4)*)

STATEMENT ON RESTITUTION

Canada,
Province of ....,
(*territorial division*).

To the court that is sentencing (*name the offender*) who was convicted, or was discharged under section 730 of the *Criminal Code*, of an offence under that Act.

I, (*name of declarant*), declare that (*check the appropriate box*):

[ ] (i) I am not seeking restitution for the losses and damages I suffered as the result of the commission of the offence.

[ ] (ii) I am seeking restitution in the amount of $......... for the following losses and damages I suffered as the result of the commission of the offence.

I declare that I have suffered the following losses and damages as the result of the commission of the offence:

(*Complete the following table if seeking restitution.*)

Description	**Amount of loss and damage**
(*describe each loss and damage*)	**(*state the amount of each loss and damage*)**
1.	**......................**
2.	**......................**
3.	**......................**
4.	**......................**

I understand that the amount of my losses and damages must be readily ascertainable by the court. For that purpose, I am responsible for providing the court with all necessary documents, including bills, receipts and estimates, in support of my claim for restitution.

Dated this .... day of .... 20 ...., at ....

Signature of declarant

2011, c. 6, s. 5; 2015, c. 13, s. 35.

FORM 34.2

(*Subsection 722(4)*)

VICTIM IMPACT STATEMENT

This form may be used to provide a description of the physical or emotional harm, property damage or economic loss suffered by you as the result of the commission of an offence, as well as a description of the impact of the offence on you. You may attach additional pages if you need more space.

Your statement must not include

- **any statement about the offence or the offender that is not relevant to the harm or loss you suffered;**
- **any unproven allegations;**

- **any comments about any offence for which the offender was not convicted;**
- **any complaint about any individual, other than the offender, who was involved in the investigation or prosecution of the offence; or**
- **except with the court's approval, an opinion or recommendation about the sentence.**

You may present a detailed account of the impact the offence has had on your life. The following sections are examples of information you may wish to include in your statement. You are not required to include all of this information.

Emotional impact

Describe how the offence has affected you emotionally. For example, think of

- **your lifestyle and activities;**
- **your relationships with others such as your spouse, family and friends;**
- **your ability to work, attend school or study; and**
- **your feelings, emotions and reactions as they relate to the offence.**

____

____

____

____

Physical impact

Describe how the offence has affected you physically. For example, think of

- **ongoing physical pain, discomfort, illness, scarring, disfigurement or physical limitation;**
- **hospitalization or surgery you have had because of the offence;**
- **treatment, physiotherapy or medication you have been prescribed;**
- **the need for any further treatment or the expectation that you will receive further treatment; and**
- **any permanent or long-term disability.**

____

____

____

____

Economic impact

Describe how the offence has affected you financially. For example, think of

- **the value of any property that was lost or damaged and the cost of repairs or replacement;**
- **any financial loss due to missed time from work;**
- **the cost of any medical expenses, therapy or counselling;**
- **any costs or losses that are not covered by insurance.**

Please note that this is not an application for compensation or restitution.

Fears for security

Describe any fears you have for your security or that of your family and friends. For example, think of

- **concerns with respect to contact with the offender; and**
- **concerns with respect to contact between the offender and members of your family or close friends.**

Drawing, poem or letter

You may use this space to draw a picture or write a poem or letter if it will help you express the impact that the offence has had on you.

I would like to present my statement in court.

To the best of my knowledge, the information contained in this statement is true.

Dated this .... day of .... 20.........., at.......... .

Signature of declarant

If you completed this statement on behalf of the victim, please indicate the reasons why you did so and the nature of your relationship with the victim.

Dated this .... day of .... 20.........., at.......... .

Signature of declarant

2015, c. 13, s. 35.

FORM 34.3

(*Subsection 722.2(2)*)

COMMUNITY IMPACT STATEMENT

This form may be used to provide a description of the harm or loss suffered by a community as the result of the commission of an offence, as well as a description of the impact of the offence on the community. You may attach additional pages if you need more space.

Your statement must not include

- **any statement about the offence or the offender that is not relevant to the harm or loss suffered by the community;**
- **any unproven allegations;**
- **any comments about any offence for which the offender was not convicted;**
- **any complaint about any individual, other than the offender, who was involved in the investigation or prosecution of the offence; or**
- **except with the court's approval, an opinion or recommendation about the sentence.**

Name of community on whose behalf the statement is made: ....

Explain how the statement reflects this community's views:

____

____

____

____

You may present a detailed account of the impact the offence has had on the community.

The following sections are examples of information you may wish to include in your statement. You are not required to include all of this information.

Emotional impact

Describe how the offence has affected community members emotionally. For example, think of

- **community members' lifestyles and activities;**
- **community members' relationships with others in the community and outside it;**
- **community members' ability to work, attend school or study;**
- **community members' feelings, emotions and reactions as they relate to the offence; and**
- **the community's sense of belonging to the region.**

____

____

____

____

Physical impact

Describe how the offence has affected community members physically. For example, think of

- **the ability of community members to access services; and**
- **changes in transportation and routes taken to and from school, work, shopping, etc.**

____

____

Economic impact

Describe how the offence has affected the community financially. For example, think of

- **any reduction in the number of visitors or tourists to the region;**
- **the value of any property that was lost or damaged and the cost of repairs or replacement; and**
- **any costs or losses that are not covered by insurance.**

Please note that this is not an application for compensation or restitution.

Fears for security

Describe any fears that community members have for their security or that of their family and friends. For example, think of concerns with respect to contact with the offender.

Drawing, poem or letter

You may use this space to draw a picture or write a poem or letter if it will help you express the impact that the offence has had on the community.

☐ I would like to present this statement in court.

To the best of my knowledge, the information contained in this statement is true.

Dated this .... day of .... 20.........., at.......... .

Signature of declarant

2015, c. 13, s. 35.

FORM 35

(*Sections 570 and 806*)

Conviction

Canada,
Province of ....,
(*territorial division*).

Be it remembered that on the .... day of .... at ...., A.B., (*date of birth*) hereinafter called the accused, was tried under Part (XIX *or* XXVII) of the *Criminal Code* on the charge that (*state fully the offence of which accused was convicted*), was convicted of the said offence and the following punishment was imposed upon him, namely,*

****Use whichever of the following forms of sentence is applicable*:**

(*a*) that the said accused be imprisoned in the (*prison*) at .... for the term of ....;

(*b*) that the said accused forfeit and pay the sum of .... dollars to be applied according to law and also pay to .... the sum of .... dollars in respect of costs and in default of payment of the said sums forthwith (*or within a time fixed, if any*), to be imprisoned in the (*prison*) at .... for the term of .... unless the said sums and the costs and charges of the committal and of conveying the accused to the said prison are sooner paid;

(*c*) that the said accused be imprisoned in the (*prison*) at .... for the term of .... and in addition forfeit and pay the sum of .... dollars to be applied according to law and also pay to .... the sum of .... dollars in respect of costs and in default of payment of the said sums (forthwith *or within a time fixed, if any*), to be imprisoned in the (*prison*) at .... for the term of .... (*if sentence to be consecutive, state accordingly*) unless the said sums and the costs and charges of the committal and of conveying the accused to the said prison are sooner paid.

Dated this .... day of .... A.D. ...., at ....

....

Clerk of the Court, Justice *or* Provincial Court Judge

(*Seal, if required*)

FORM 36

(*Sections 570 and 806*)

Order against an offender

Canada,
Province of ....,
(*territorial division*).

Be it remembered that on the .... day of .... A.D. ...., at ...., A.B., (*date of birth*) of ...., was tried on an information (*indictment*) alleging that (*set out matter of complaint or alleged offence*), and it was ordered and adjudged that (*set out the order made*).

Dated this .... day of .... A.D. ...., at ....

....

Justice *or* Clerk of the Court

FORM 37

(*Section 570*)

Order acquitting accused

Canada,
Province of ....,
(*territorial division*).

Be it remembered that on the .... day of .... A.D. ...., at .... A.B., of ...., (*occupation*), (*date of birth*), was tried on the charge that (*state fully the offence of which accused was acquitted*) and was found not guilty of the said offence.

Dated this .... day of .... A.D. ...., at ....

...
Provincial Court Judge *or* Clerk of the Court

(*Seal, if required*)

FORM 38

(*Section 708*)

Conviction for contempt

Canada,
Province of ....,
(*territorial division*).

Be it remembered that on the .... day of .... A.D. ...., at .... in the (*territorial division*), E.F. of ...., hereinafter called the defaulter, is convicted by me for contempt in that he did not attend before (*set out court or justice*) to give evidence on the trial of a charge that (*state fully offence with which accused was charged*), although (duly subpoenaed *or* bound by recognizance to attend to give evidence, *as the case may be*) and has not shown before me any sufficient excuse for his default;

Wherefore I adjudge the defaulter for his said default, (*set out punishment as authorized and determined in accordance with section 708 of the Criminal Code*).

Dated this .... day of .... A.D. ...., at ....

...
A Justice *or* Clerk of the Court

(*Seal, if required*)

FORM 39

(*Sections 519 and 550*)

Order for discharge of a person in custody

Canada,
Province of ....,
(*territorial division*).
To the keeper of the (*prison*) at ....:

I hereby direct you to release E.F., detained by you under a (warrant of committal *or* order) dated the .... day of .... A.D. ...., if the said E.F. is detained by you for no other cause.

...
A Judge, Justice *or* Clerk of the Court

(*Seal, if required*)

FORM 40

(*Section 629*)

Challenge to array

Canada,
Province of ....,
(*territorial division*).

The Queen
v.
C.D.

The (prosecutor *or* accused) challenges the array of the panel on the ground that X.Y., (sheriff *or* deputy sheriff), who returned the panel, was guilty of (partiality *or* fraud *or* wilful misconduct) on returning it.

Dated this .... day of .... A.D. ...., at ....

...
Counsel for (prosecutor *or* accused)

FORM 41

(*Section 639*)

Challenge for cause

Canada,
Province of ....,
(*territorial division*).

The Queen
v.
C.D.

The (prosecutor *or* accused) challenges G.H. on the ground that (*set out ground of challenge in accordance with subsection 638(1) of the Criminal Code*).

...
Counsel for (prosecutor *or* accused)

FORM 42

(*Section 827*)

Certificate of non-payment of costs of appeal

In the Court of ....

(*Style of Cause*)

I hereby certify that A.B. (the appellant *or* respondent, *as the case may be*) in this appeal, having been ordered to pay costs in the sum of .... dollars, has failed to pay the said costs within the time limited for the payment thereof.

Dated this .... day of .... A.D. ...., at ....

...
Clerk of the Court of.................

(*Seal*)

FORM 43

(*Section 734*)

Jailer's receipt to peace officer for prisoner

I hereby certify that I have received from X.Y., a peace officer for (*territorial division*), one A.B., together with a (warrant *or* order) issued by (*set out court or justice, as the case may be*).*

****Add a statement of the condition of the prisoner***

Dated this .... day of .... A.D. ...., at ....

..
Keeper of (*prison*)

1995, c. 22, s. 18.

FORM 44

(*Section 667*)

I, (*name*), a fingerprint examiner designated as such for the purposes of section 667 of the *Criminal Code* by the Minister of Public Safety and Emergency Preparedness, do hereby certify that (*name*) also known as (*aliases if any*), FPS Number ...., whose fingerprints are shown reproduced below (*reproduction of fingerprints*) or attached hereto, has been convicted, discharged under section 736 of the *Criminal Code* or convicted and sentenced in Canada as follows:

(*record*)

Dated this .... day of .... A.D. ...., at ....

..
Fingerprint Examiner

1995, c. 22, s. 18; 2005, c. 10, s. 34(1)(*f*)(xiv).

FORM 45

(*Section 667*)

I, (*name*), a fingerprint examiner designated as such for the purposes of section 667 of the *Criminal Code* by the Minister of Public Safety and Emergency Preparedness, do hereby certify that I have compared the fingerprints reproduced in or attached to exhibit A with the fingerprints reproduced in or attached to the certificate in Form 44 marked exhibit B and that they are those of the same person.

Dated this .... day of .... A.D. ...., at ....

..
Fingerprint Examiner

2005, c. 10, s. 34(1)(*f*)(xiv).

FORM 46

(*Section 732.1*)

PROBATION ORDER

Canada,
Province of ....,
(*territorial division*).

Whereas on the .... day of .... at ...., A.B., hereinafter called the offender, (pleaded guilty to *or* was tried under (*here insert Part XIX, XX or XXVII, as the case may be*) of the *Criminal Code* and was (*here insert convicted or found guilty, as the case may be*) on the charge that (*here state the offence to which the offender pleaded guilty or for which the offender was convicted or found guilty, as the case may be*);

And whereas on the .... day of .... the court adjudged*

***Use whichever of the following forms of disposition is applicable:**

(*a*) that the offender be discharged on the following conditions:

(*b*) that the passing of sentence on the offender be suspended and that the said offender be released on the following conditions:

(*c*) that the offender forfeit and pay the sum of .... dollars to be applied according to law and in default of payment of the said sum without delay (*or within a time fixed, if any*), be imprisoned in the (*prison*) at .... for the term of .... unless the said sum and charges of the committal and of conveying the said offender to the said prison are sooner paid, and in addition thereto, that the said offender comply with the following conditions:

(*d*) that the offender be imprisoned in the (*prison*) at .... for the term of .... and, in addition thereto, that the said offender comply with the following conditions:

(*e*) that following the expiration of the offender's conditional sentence order related to this or another offence, that the said offender comply with the following conditions:

(*f*) that following the expiration of the offender's sentence of imprisonment related to another offence, that the said offender comply with the following conditions:

(*g*) when the offender is ordered to serve the sentence of imprisonment intermittently, that the said offender comply with the following conditions when not in confinement:

Now therefore the said offender shall, for the period of .... from the date of this order (*or, where paragraph (d), (e) or (f) is applicable*, the date of expiration of the offender's sentence of imprisonment or conditional sentence order) comply with the following conditions, namely, that the said offender shall keep the peace and be of good behaviour, appear before the court when required to do so by the court and notify the court or probation officer in advance of any change of name or address and promptly notify the court or probation officer of any change of employment or occupation, and, in addition,

(here state any additional conditions prescribed pursuant to subsection 732.1(3) of the Criminal Code).

Dated this .... day of .... A.D. .... , at ....

...
Clerk of the Court,
Justice *or* Provincial Court Judge

1995, c. 22, s. 10; 2004, c. 12, s. 17.

FORM 47

(*Section 462.48*)

ORDER TO DISCLOSE INCOME TAX INFORMATION

Canada,
Province of ....,
(*territorial division*).

To A.B., of ...., (*office or occupation*):

Whereas, it appears on the oath of C.D., of ...., that there are reasonable grounds for believing that E.F., of ...., has committed or benefited from the commission of the offence of .... and that the information or documents (*describe information or documents*) are likely to be of substantial value to an investigation of that offence or a related matter; and

Whereas there are reasonable grounds for believing that it is in the public interest to allow access to the information or documents, having regard to the benefit likely to accrue to the investigation if the access is obtained;

This is, therefore, to authorize and require you between the hours of (*as the judge may direct*), during the period commencing on .... and ending on ...., to produce all the above-mentioned information and documents to one of the following police officers, namely, (*here name police officers*) and allow the police officer to remove the information or documents, or to allow the police officer access to the above-mentioned information and documents and to examine them, *as the judge directs*, subject to the following conditions (*state conditions*): ....

Dated this .... day of .... A.D. ...., at ....

...
Signature of judge

FORM 48

(*Section 672.13*)

ASSESSMENT ORDER OF THE COURT

Canada,
Province of ....,
(*territorial division*).

Whereas I have reasonable grounds to believe that evidence of the mental condition of (*name of accused*), who has been charged with ...., may be necessary to determine *

[ ] whether the accused is unfit to stand trial

[ ] whether the accused suffered from a mental disorder so as to exempt the accused from criminal responsibility by virtue of subsection 16(1) of the *Criminal Code* at the time of the act or omission charged against the accused

[ ] whether the balance of the mind of the accused was disturbed at the time of commission of the alleged offence, if the accused is a female person charged with an offence arising out of the death of her newly-born child

[ ] if a verdict of unfit to stand trial or a verdict of not criminally responsible on account of mental disorder has been rendered in respect of the accused, the appropriate disposition to be made in respect of the accused under section 672.54, 672.58 or 672.64 of the *Criminal Code* or whether the court should, under subsection 672.84(3) of that Act, revoke a finding that the accused is a high-risk accused

[ ] if a verdict of unfit to stand trial has been rendered in respect of the accused, whether the court should order a stay of proceedings under section 672.851 of the *Criminal Code*

I hereby order an assessment of the mental condition of (*name of accused*) to be conducted by/at (*name of person or service by whom or place where assessment is to be made*) for a period of .... days.

This order is to be in force for a total of .... days, including travelling time, during which time the accused is to remain ⋆

[ ] in custody at (*place where accused is to be detained*)

[ ] out of custody, on the following conditions:

(*set out conditions, if applicable*)

⋆ Check applicable option.

Dated this .... day of .... A.D. ...., at ....

...
(*Signature of justice or judge or clerk of the court, as the case may be*)

1991, c. 43, s. 8; 1995, c. 22, s. 10; 2005, c. 22, s. 40; 2014, c. 6, s. 19.

FORM 48.1

(*Section 672.13*)

ASSESSMENT ORDER OF THE REVIEW BOARD

Canada,
Province of ....,
(*territorial division*).

Whereas I have reasonable grounds to believe that evidence of the mental condition of (*name of accused*), who has been charged with ...., may be necessary to ⋆

[ ] if a verdict of unfit to stand trial or a verdict of not criminally responsible on account of mental disorder has been rendered in respect of the accused, make a disposition under section 672.54 of the *Criminal Code* or determine whether the Review Board should, under subsection 672.84(1) of that Act, refer to the superior court of criminal jurisdiction for review a finding that the accused is a high-risk accused

[ ] if a verdict of unfit to stand trial has been rendered in respect of the accused, determine whether the Review Board should make a recommendation to the court

that has jurisdiction in respect of the offence charged against the accused to hold an inquiry to determine whether a stay of proceedings should be ordered in accordance with section 672.851 of the *Criminal Code*

I hereby order an assessment of the mental condition of (*name of accused*) to be conducted by/at (*name of person or service by whom or place where assessment is to be made*) for a period of .... days.

This order is to be in force for a total of .... days, including travelling time, during which time the accused is to remain ⋆

[ ] in custody at (*place where accused is to be detained*)

[ ] out of custody, on the following conditions:

(*set out conditions, if applicable*)

⋆ Check applicable option.

⋆ Check applicable option.

Dated this .... day of .... A.D. ...., at ....

...

(*Signature of Chairperson of the Review Board*)

2005, c. 22, s. 40; 2014, c. 6, s. 20.

FORM 48.2

(*Subsection 672.5(14)*)

VICTIM IMPACT STATEMENT — NOT CRIMINALLY RESPONSIBLE

This form may be used to provide a description of the physical or emotional harm, property damage or economic loss suffered by you arising from the conduct for which the accused person was found not criminally responsible on account of mental disorder, as well as a description of the impact that the conduct has had on you. You may attach additional pages if you need more space.

Your statement must not include

- **any statement about the conduct of the accused that is not relevant to the harm or loss suffered by you;**
- **any unproven allegations;**
- **any comments about any conduct for which the accused was not found not criminally responsible;**
- **any complaint about any individual, other than the accused, who was involved in the investigation or prosecution of the offence; or**
- **except with the court's or Review Board's approval, an opinion or recommendation about the disposition.**

The following sections are examples of information you may wish to include in your statement. You are not required to include all of this information.

Emotional impact

Describe how the accused's conduct has affected you emotionally. For example, think of

- **your lifestyle and activities;**
- **your relationships with others such as your spouse, family and friends;**
- **your ability to work, attend school or study; and**
- **your feelings, emotions and reactions as these relate to the conduct.**

____

____

____

____

Physical impact

Describe how the accused's conduct has affected you physically. For example, think of

- **ongoing physical pain, discomfort, illness, scarring, disfigurement or physical limitation;**
- **hospitalization or surgery you have had because of the conduct of the accused;**
- **treatment, physiotherapy or medication you have been prescribed;**
- **the need for any further treatment or the expectation that you will receive further treatment; and**
- **any permanent or long-term disability.**

____

____

____

____

Economic impact

Describe how the accused's conduct has affected you financially. For example, think of

- **the value of any property that was lost or damaged and the cost of repairs or replacement;**
- **any financial loss due to missed time from work;**
- **the cost of any medical expenses, therapy or counselling; and**
- **any costs or losses that are not covered by insurance.**

Please note that this is not an application for compensation or restitution.

____

____

____

____

Fears for security

Describe any fears you have for your security or that of your family and friends. For example, think of

- **concerns with respect to contact with the accused; and**
- **concerns with respect to contact between the accused and members of your family or close friends.**

____

____

____

____

Drawing, poem or letter

You may use this space to draw a picture or write a poem or letter if it will help you express the impact that the accused's conduct has had on you.

☐ **I would like to read or present my statement (in court or before the Review Board).**

To the best of my knowledge, the information contained in this statement is true.

Dated this .... day of .... 20.........., at.......... .

Signature of declarant

2015, c. 13, s. 36.

FORM 49

(*Section 672.57*)

WARRANT OF COMMITTAL

DISPOSITION OF DETENTION

Canada,
Province of ....,
(*territorial division*).

To the peace officers in the said (*territorial division*) and to the keeper (*administrator, warden*) of the (*prison, hospital or other appropriate place where the accused is detained*).

This warrant is issued for the committal of A.B., of ...., (*occupation*), hereinafter called the accused.

Whereas the accused has been charged that (*set out briefly the offence in respect of which the accused was charged*);

And whereas the accused was found*

☐ **..unfit to stand trial**

☐ **................................. not criminally responsible on account of mental disorder**

This is, therefore, to command you, in Her Majesty's name, to take the accused in custody and convey the accused safely to the (*prison, hospital or other appropriate place*) at ...., and there deliver the accused to the keeper (*administrator, warden*) with the following precept:

I do therefore command you the said keeper (*administrator, warden*) to receive the accused in your custody in the said (*prison, hospital or other appropriate place*) and to keep the accused safely there until the the accused is delivered by due course of law.

The following are the conditions to which the accused shall be subject while in your (*prison, hospital or other appropriate place*):

The following are the powers regarding the restrictions (*and the limits and conditions on those restrictions*) on the liberty of the accused that are hereby delegated to you the said keeper (*administrator, warden*) of the said (*prison, hospital or other appropriate place*):

***Check applicable option.**

Dated this .... day of .... A.D. ...., at ....

...
(Signature of judge, clerk of the court, provincial court judge or chairperson of the Review Board)
1991, c. 43, s. 8.

FORM 50

(*Section 672.7(2)*)

WARRANT OF COMMITTAL

PLACEMENT DECISION

Canada,
Province of ....,
(*territorial division*).

To the peace officers in the said (*territorial division*) and to the keeper (*administrator, warden*) of the (*prison, hospital or other appropriate place where the accused is detained*).

This warrant is issued for the committal of A.B., of ...., (*occupation*), hereinafter called the accused.

Whereas the accused has been charged that (*set out briefly the offence in respect of which the accused was charged*);

And whereas the accused was found*

☐ ....unfit to stand trial

☐ .... not criminally responsible on account of mental disorder

And whereas the Review Board had held a hearing and decided that the accused shall be detained in custody;

And whereas the accused is required to be detained in custody pursuant to a warrant of committal issued by (*set out the name of the Judge, Clerk of the Court, Provincial Court Judge or Justice as well as the name of the court and territorial division*), dated the .... day of ...., in respect of the offence that (*set out briefly the offence in respect of which the accused was charged or convicted*);

This is, therefore, to command you, in Her Majesty's name, to*

☐ ....execute the warrant of committal issued by the court, according to its terms

☐ ....execute the warrant of committal issued herewith by the Review Board

*Check applicable option.

Dated this .... day of .... A.D. ...., at ....

....

(Signature of chairperson of the Review Board)

1991, c. 43, s. 8.

FORM 51

(Paragraphs 732.1(3)(c.2), 742.3(2)(a.2), 810(3.02)(c), 810.01(4.1)(g), 810.011(6)(f), 810.1(3.02)(i) and 810.2(4.1)(g))

NOTICE OF OBLIGATION TO PROVIDE SAMPLES OF BODILY SUBSTANCE

To A.B., of ...., (*occupation*), (*address in Canada*), (*date of birth*), (*gender*):

Because, on (*date*), you were ordered, under (*applicable provision*) of the *Criminal Code*, to provide samples of a bodily substance prescribed by regulation at regular intervals for the purpose of analysis;

You are provided with this notice to inform you of your obligations with respect to providing samples.

1. **On (*specify a day not earlier than 24 hours after the day on which the notice is served*), you must report, at any time from (*time*) to (*time*), at (*address of place at which sample to be taken, as designated by the Attorney General of the province or Minister of Justice of the territory*), to provide a sample of your (*specify type of bodily substance prescribed by regulation*).**

2. **Every (*specify a number not less than seven*) days after you first report to provide a sample, you must report, at any time from (*time*) to (*time*), at (*address of place at which sample to be taken, as designated by the Attorney General of the province or Minister of Justice of the territory*), to provide a sample of your (*specify type of bodily substance prescribed by regulation*).**

3. **You have the right to apply to a court to terminate the obligation to provide samples, and the right to appeal any decision of that court.**

4. **If you are found to have not complied with your obligation to provide samples as set out in this notice, you may be subject to a fine or imprisonment, or to both (*or, in the case of a conditional sentence*, you may be subject to proceedings under section 742.6 of the *Criminal Code*, the consequences of which may include imprisonment).**

5. **The results of the analysis of the bodily substances may be used or disclosed in accordance with the *Criminal Code*, including in proceedings against you, the result of which may be that you are subject to a fine or imprisonment, or to both (*or, in the case of a conditional sentence*, including in proceedings under section 742.6 of the *Criminal Code*, the consequences of which may include imprisonment).**

Served on (*date*), at (*place the notice is served*).

....

(*Signature of probation officer, supervisor or person designated by the Attorney General or Minister of Justice, as the case may be*)

2005, c. 22, s. 41; 2011, c. 7, s. 13; 2015, c. 20, s. 34(4).

FORM 52

(*Section 490.012*)

ORDER TO COMPLY WITH SEX OFFENDER INFORMATION REGISTRATION ACT

Canada,
Province of ....,
(*territorial division*)

To A.B., of ...., (*occupation*), (*address or address of court if no fixed address*), (*date of birth*), (*gender*):

You have been convicted of or found not criminally responsible on account of mental disorder for (*description of offence(s)*) under (*applicable designated offence provision(s) of the Criminal Code*), a designated offence (*or* designated offences) within the meaning of subsection 490.011(1) of the *Criminal Code*.

1. You must report for the first time to the registration centre referred to in section 7.1 of the *Sex Offender Information Registration Act*, whenever required under subsection 4(1) of that Act.

2. You must subsequently report to the registration centre referred to in section 7.1 of the *Sex Offender Information Registration Act*, whenever required under section 4.1 or 4.3 of that Act, for a period of .... years after this order is made (*or if paragraph 490.013(2)(c) or any of subsections 490.013(2.1) to (5) of the Criminal Code applies*, for life).

3. Information relating to you will be collected under sections 5 and 6 of the *Sex Offender Information Registration Act* by a person who collects information at the registration centre.

4. Information relating to you will be registered in a database, and may be consulted, disclosed and used in the circumstances set out in the *Sex Offender Information Registration Act*.

5. If you believe that the information registered in the database contains an error or omission, you may ask a person who collects information at the registration centre referred to in section 7.1 of the *Sex Offender Information Registration Act* or, if applicable, the Canadian Forces Provost Marshal, to correct the information.

6. You have the right to apply to a court to terminate this order, and the right to appeal the decision of that court.

7. If you are found to have contravened this order, you may be subject to a fine or imprisonment, or to both.

8. If you are found to have provided false or misleading information, you may be subject to a fine or imprisonment, or to both.

Dated this .... day of ...., at ....

..
(*Signature of judge or clerk and name of court*)

..
(*Signature of person subject to order*)

2004, c. 10, s. 21; 2007, c. 5, s. 30; 2010, c. 17, s. 26.

FORM 53

(*Sections 490.019 and 490.032*)

NOTICE OF OBLIGATION TO COMPLY WITH SEX OFFENDER INFORMATION REGISTRATION ACT

Canada,
Province of ....
(*territorial division*).

To A.B., of ...., (*occupation*), a person referred to in subsection 490.02(1) of the *Criminal Code*:

Because, on .... (*insert date(s)*), you were convicted of, or found not criminally responsible on account of mental disorder for, ... (*insert description of offence(s)*), one or more offences referred to in paragraph (*a*), (*c*), (*c*.1), (*d*), (*d*.1) or (*e*) of the definition "designated offence" in subsection 490.011(1) of the *Criminal Code* or in paragraph (*a*) or (*c*) of the definition "designated offence" in section 227 of the *National Defence Act*, under .... (*insert the applicable offence provision(s)*), this is provided to give you notice that you are required to comply with the *Sex Offender Information Registration Act*.

1. You must report for the first time to the registration centre referred to in section 7.1 of the *Sex Offender Information Registration Act*, whenever required under subsection 4(2) of that Act.

2. You must subsequently report to the registration centre referred to in section 7.1 of the *Sex Offender Information Registration Act*, whenever required under section 4.1 or 4.3 of that Act, for a period of .... years after you were sentenced, or found not criminally responsible on account of mental disorder, for the offence (*or if paragraph 490.022(3)(c) or (d) of the Criminal Code applies*, for life) or for any shorter period set out in subsection 490.022(2) of the *Criminal Code*.

3. Information relating to you will be collected under sections 5 and 6 of the *Sex Offender Information Registration Act* by a person who collects information at the registration centre.

4. Information relating to you will be registered in a database, and may be consulted, disclosed and used in the circumstances set out in the *Sex Offender Information Registration Act*.

5. If you believe that the information registered in the database contains an error or omission, you may ask a person who collects information at the registration centre referred to in section 7.1 of the *Sex Offender Information Registration Act* or, if applicable, the Canadian Forces Provost Marshal, to correct the information.

6. You have the right to apply to a court to exempt you from the obligation to comply with the *Sex Offender Information Registration Act*, and the right to appeal any decision of that court.

7. You have the right to apply to a court to terminate the obligation, and the right to appeal any decision of that court.

8. If you are found to have contravened the obligation, you may be subject to a fine or imprisonment, or to both.

9. If you are found to have provided false or misleading information, you may be subject to a fine or imprisonment, or to both.

Dated this .... day of ...., at ....

2004, c. 10, s. 21; 2007, c. 5, s. 31; 2014, c. 25, s. 33.

FORM 54

(*Sections 490.02901 to 490.02903, 490.02905 and 490.032*)

OBLIGATION TO COMPLY WITH SEX OFFENDER INFORMATION REGISTRATION ACT

To A.B., of ...., (*occupation*), (*address in Canada*), (*date of birth*), (*gender*):

Because, on (*date*), you were convicted of or found not criminally responsible on account of mental disorder for an offence (*or* offences) in (*location of offence(s)*) that the Attorney General of the province, or the minister of justice of the territory, has identified as being equivalent to (*description of offence(s)*) under (*applicable provision(s) of the Criminal Code*), a designated offence (*or* designated offences) as defined in subsection 490.011(1) of the *Criminal Code*;

You are provided with this to inform you that you are required to comply with the *Sex Offender Information Registration Act*.

1. You must report for the first time to the registration centre referred to in section 7.1 of the *Sex Offender Information Registration Act*, whenever required under subsection 4(2) of that Act.

2. You must subsequently report to the registration centre referred to in section 7.1 of the *Sex Offender Information Registration Act*, whenever required under section 4.1 or 4.3 of that Act, for a period of .... years after the day on which you were sentenced or found not criminally responsible on account of mental disorder for the offence (*or if paragraph 490.02904(3)(c) or (d) of the Criminal Code applies*, for life because you were convicted of or found not criminally responsible on account of mental disorder for (*description of offence(s)*) under (*applicable designated offence provision(s) of the Criminal Code*), a designated offence (or designated offences) within the meaning of subsection 490.011(1) of the *Criminal Code*) or for any shorter period determined under subsection 490.02904(2) of the *Criminal Code*.

3. Information relating to you will be collected under sections 5 and 6 of the *Sex Offender Information Registration Act* by a person who collects information at the registration centre.

4. Information relating to you will be registered in a database, and may be consulted, disclosed and used in the circumstances set out in the *Sex Offender Information Registration Act*.

5. If you believe that the information registered in the database contains an error or omission, you may ask a person who collects information at the registration centre referred to in section 7.1 of the *Sex Offender Information Registration Act* to correct the information.

6. You have the right to apply to a court to exempt you from the obligation to comply with the *Sex Offender Information Registration Act*, and the right to appeal the decision of that court.

7. You have the right to apply to a court to terminate the obligation to comply with the *Sex Offender Information Registration Act* and the right to appeal the decision of that court.

8. If you are found to have not complied with the *Sex Offender Information Registration Act*, you may be subject to a fine or imprisonment, or to both.

9. If you are found to have provided false or misleading information, you may be subject to a fine or imprisonment, or to both.

Served on (*date*).

***For administrative use only*:**

Sentence imposed or verdict of not criminally responsible on account of mental disorder rendered on (*date*).

2010, c. 17, s. 27.

CANADA EVIDENCE ACT

R.S.C. 1985, Chap. C-5

Amended R.S.C. 1985, c. 27 (1st Supp.), s. 203(1)
Amended R.S.C. 1985, c. 19 (3rd Supp.), ss. 17 and 18
Amended 1992, c. 1, s. 142(1); Sch. V, item 9(1) in force February 28, 1992; Sch. V, item 9(2) in force September 2, 1994 as provided by s. 142(2)
Amended 1992, c. 47, s. 66; brought into force August 1, 1996 by SI/96-56, *Can. Gaz., Part II*, October 7, 1996
Amended 1993, c. 28, Sch. III, s. 8; in force April 1, 1999
Amended 1993, c. 34, s. 15; in force June 23, 1993
Amended 1994, c. 44, ss. 85 to 93; brought into force February 15, 1995
Amended 1995, c. 28, s. 47; in force July 13, 1995
Amended 1997, c. 18, ss. 116 to 118; in force June 16, 1997
Amended 1998, c. 9, s. 1; brought into force June 30, 1998 by SI/98-79, *Can. Gaz., Part II*, June 24, 1998
Amended 1999, c. 18, ss. 89 to 91; in force June 17, 1999
Amended 1999, c. 28, ss. 149 and 150; brought into force June 28, 1999 by SI/99-70
Amended 2000, c. 5, ss. 52 to 57; brought into force May 1, 2000 by para. (*a*) of SI/2000-29
Amended 2001, c. 41, ss. 43, 44, 124(2) and (3), 140(1), 141(3)(b) and 141(4) to (7); ss. 43 and 44 brought into force December 24, 2001 by SI/2002-16, *Can. Gaz., Part II*, January 2, 2002; s. 141(3)(b) brought into force March 27, 2002 as provided by this section; s. 124(2) and (3) in force June 28, 2002 as provided by this section; ss. 140(1) and 141(4) to (7) in force July 2, 2003 as provided by these sections
Amended 2002, c. 1, s. 166; brought into force April 1, 2003 by SI/2002-91, *Can. Gaz., Part II*, June 19, 2002
Amended 2002, c. 7, s. 96; brought into force April 1, 2003 by SI/2003-48, *Can. Gaz., Part II*, April 9, 2003
Amended 2002, c. 8, ss. 118, 119 and 183(1)(*b*); s. 119 since repealed by 2001, c. 41, s. 141(3)(*b*); remainder brought into force July 2, 2003 by SI/2003-109, *Can. Gaz.*, June 4, 2003
Amended 2003, c. 22, ss. 104 and 105; brought into force April 6, 2005 by SI/2005-24, *Can. Gaz.*, April 6, 2005
Amended SOR/2004-19, s. 1, in force February 12, 2004
Amended 2004, c. 12, ss. 18 and 19, in force on Royal Assent, April 22, 2004
Amended 2005, c. 32, ss. 26 and 27, in force January 2, 2006 as provided by para. (*b*) of SI/2005-104, *Can. Gaz.*, Part II, November 16, 2005
Amended 2005, c. 46, s. 56; brought into force April 15, 2007 by SI/2007-43, *Can. Gaz., Part II*, April 4, 2007
Amended SOR/2006-80, s. 1, in force May 1, 2006 as provided by s. 2
Amended 2006, c. 9, s. 222; in force December 12, 2006
Amended SOR/2006-335, s. 1, *Can. Gaz., Part II*, December 27, 2006, in force December 11, 2006 as provided by s. 2
Amended 2008, c. 3, s. 11; brought into force February 22, 2008, by SI/2008-24, *Can. Gaz., Part II*, March 5, 2008
Amended SOR/2012-220, *Can. Gaz., Part II*, October 24, 2012, s. 1; in force October 5, 2012 as provided by s. 2
Amended 2013, c. 9, ss. 17, and 19 to 24; in force July 15, 2013 by SI/2013-67, *Can. Gaz., Part II*, June 19, 2013

Amended 2013, c. 18, ss. 45, 85; in force November 28, 2014 by SI/2014-104, *Can. Gaz., Part II*, December 17, 2014
Amended 2013, c. 40, s. 448; in force November 1, 2014 by SI/2014-84, *Can. Gaz., Part II*, November 5, 2014
Amended 2014, c. 2, s. 5; in force April 1, 2014 by SI/2014-34, *Can. Gaz., Part II*, April 9, 2014
Amended 2014, c. 25, s. 34; in force December 6, 2014
Amended 2014, c. 31, s. 27; in force March 9, 2015
Amended 2015, c. 13, ss. 52 and 53; in force July 22, 2015
Amended 2015, c. 20, s. 13; brought into force August 1, 2015 by SI/2015-64, *Can. Gaz., Part II*, July 15, 2015
Amended 2015, c. 23, s. 20; repealed before coming into force 2015, c. 13, s. 57(2)
Amended 2015, c. 36, s. 43; in force June 23, 2015
Amended 2017, c. 9, s. 41; in force June 19, 2017
Amended 2017, c. 22, s. 2; in force on Royal Assent, October 18, 2017

An Act respecting witnesses and evidence

SHORT TITLE

SHORT TITLE.

1. This Act may be cited as the *Canada Evidence Act*. R.S., c. E-10, s. 1.

Part I / *Application*

APPLICATION.

2. This Part applies to all criminal proceedings and to all civil proceedings and other matters whatever respecting which Parliament has jurisdiction. R.S., c. E-10, s. 2.

Witnesses

INTEREST OR CRIME.

3. A person is not incompetent to give evidence by reason of interest or crime. R.S., c. E-10, s. 3.

ANNOTATIONS

While an accomplice who is separately charged from the accused and has not yet been sentenced is a competent and compellable witness at the instance of the Crown, a trial judge does have a discretion to exclude his evidence if satisfied that it is in the interests of justice to do so. That discretion however can only be exercised with knowledge of the evidence to be tendered and after inquiry into all the surrounding circumstances. It was not proper for the trial judge to simply refuse to hear the witness: *R. v. Piercey* (1988), 42 C.C.C. (3d) 475, 70 Nfld. & P.E.I.R. 271 (Nfld. C.A.). See also *R. v. Williams* (1974), 21 C.C.C. (2d) 1 (Ct. Mart. App. Ct.), leave to appeal to S.C.C. refused C.C.C. *loc. cit.*, and *R. v. Caulfield* (1972), 10 C.C.C. (2d) 539, 10 C.R. (3d) 383 (Alta. C.A.). Also see *R. v. Buric* (1996), 106 C.C.C. (3d) 97, 48 C.R. (4th) 149 (Ont. C.A.), affd [1997] 1 S.C.R. 535, 114 C.C.C. (3d) 95, 32 O.R. (3d) 320*n*.

The fact that the accomplice has not yet been sentenced for his involvement in the offence does not affect the admissibility of the witness's evidence and admission of such evidence does not infringe the accused's rights under s. 7 of the Charter: *R. v. Cruikshanks* (1990), 58 C.C.C. (3d) 26 (B.C.C.A.).

ACCUSED AND SPOUSE / Spouse of accused / Communications during marriage / Offences against young persons / Saving / Failure to testify.

4. (1) Every person charged with an offence, and, except as otherwise provided in this section, the wife or husband, as the case may be, of the person so charged, is a competent witness for the defence, whether the person so charged is charged solely or jointly with any other person.

(2) No person is incompetent, or uncompellable, to testify for the prosecution by reason only that they are married to the accused.

(3) No husband is compellable to disclose any communication made to him by his wife during their marriage, and no wife is compellable to disclose any communication made to her by her husband during their marriage.

(4) [*Repealed*, 2015, c. 13, s. 52(2).]

(5) [*Repealed*, 2015, c. 13, s. 52(2).]

(6) The failure of the person charged, or of the wife or husband of that person, to testify shall not be made the subject of comment by the judge or by counsel for the prosecution. R.S., c. E-10, s. 4; 1980-81-82-83, c. 110, s. 71, c. 125, s. 29; 1984, c. 40, s. 27; R.S.C. 1985, c. 19 (3rd Supp.), s. 17; 2002, c. 1, s. 166; 2014, c. 25, s. 34; 2014, c. 31, s. 27; 2015, c. 13, s. 52.

SYNOPSIS

Of particular importance, the new subsec. (2) abolishes the long-standing rule of spousal incompetency and non-compellability. This provision is procedural rather than substantive and accordingly, has retrospective application. Thus, a witness married to the accused is competent and compellable despite not having been so at the time that the offence was committed: *R. v. Grewal* (2017), 140 W.C.B. (2d) 529, 2017 ONSC 4099 (S.C.J.).

ANNOTATIONS

Compellability of accused [subsec. (1)] – The Review Board has no power to compel the accused to testify at a review hearing with respect to the accused's fitness to stand trial. Although s. 672.43 of the *Criminal Code* gives the chairperson of the board the powers under ss. 4 and 5 of the *Inquiries Act*, R.S.C. 1985, c. I-11, that section must be interpreted in harmony with the whole of the relevant legislation, including this subsection: *Boucher v. New Brunswick (Review Board)* (1999), 141 C.C.C. (3d) 221 (N.B.C.A.).

Competency of employees of corporation – An officer or employee of an accused corporation although he is determined to be the directing mind and will of the corporation is a compellable witness at the instance of the Crown: *R. v. N. M. Paterson and Sons Ltd.*, [1980] 2 S.C.R. 679, 55 C.C.C. (2d) 289 (7:0). And compelling the officer or employee to testify does not violate s. 11(*c*) of the *Canadian Charter of Rights and Freedoms: R. v. Amway Corp. of Canada Ltd.*, [1989] 1 S.C.R. 21, 68 C.R. (3d) 97 (7:0).

Spousal communications privilege [subsec. (3)] – It would seem that once the marriage has been dissolved by divorce the marital privilege with respect to communication between spouses may not be claimed: *R. v. Marchand* (1980), 55 C.C.C. (2d) 77 (N.S.C.A.).

The spouse cannot be compelled to disclose marital communications even if a compellable witness at the instance of the Crown: *R. v. Jean and Piesinger* (1979), 46 C.C.C. (2d) 176 (Alta. C.A.), affd [1980] 1 S.C.R. 400, 51 C.C.C. (2d) 192*n*; *R. v. Zylstra* (1995), 99 C.C.C. (3d) 477, 41 C.R. (4th) 130 (Ont. C.A.). *Contra*: *R. v. St. Jean* (1976), 32 C.C.C. (2d) 438 (Que. C.A.).

The spouse is required to assert the privilege in the presence of the jury. However, a special instruction would be required that at least informs the jury that the privilege is that of the witness and that the decision whether or not to assert the privilege lies with the witness, not the accused: *R. v. Zylstra, supra.*

The spouse during cross-examination should be advised of spousal privilege and the right to withhold evidence of such communications. There is no waiver where such questions are answered without objection and without advising the testifying spouse of the privilege: *R. v. E. (G.V.)* (2014), 118 W.C.B. (2d) 229, [2014] O.J. No. 6158 (S.C.J.).

By virtue of subsec. (3) when combined with s. 189(5) of the *Criminal Code*, which preserves the privilege of information obtained by an interception of a private communication, the intercepted private communications between spouses are inadmissible in evidence at the instance of the Crown (except, *semble*, with the consent of the spouse enjoying the privilege): *R. v. Lloyd and Lloyd*, [1981] 2 S.C.R. 645, 64 C.C.C. (2d) 169 (6:3).

However, the privilege does not prevent the admission into evidence of communications intercepted prior to the marriage even if the parties to the communication are married by the time of the trial: *R. v. Andrew* (1986), 26 C.C.C. (3d) 111 (B.C.S.C.).

Spousal communication privilege has no impact on the admissibility of historical text messages between spouses seized pursuant to a production order: *R. v. Cuthill* (2018), 368 C.C.C. (3d) 261 (Alta. C.A.).

The privilege codified in s. 4(3) does not apply to the communications between the accused and his wife which were intercepted and recorded by corrections officials. This section provides only a testimonial immunity and does not prevent a third party who overheard the conversation from giving evidence as to its contents. This general proposition is qualified only in respect of private communications intercepted pursuant to authorizations under Part VI of the *Criminal Code*: *R. v. Siniscalchi* (2010), 257 C.C.C. (3d) 329 (B.C.C.A.).

The privilege in subsec. (3) is testimonial only and does not prevent the introduction into evidence of a document written by the accused and sent to his wife which is later found by police in a search of the accused's home: *R. v. Kotapski* (1981), 66 C.C.C. (2d) 78 (Que. S.C.), affd 13 C.C.C. (3d) 185 (C.A.), leave to appeal to S.C.C. refused 57 N.R. 318*n*.

In *R. v. Nguyen* (2015), 323 C.C.C. (3d) 240 (Ont. C.A.), leave to appeal to S.C.C. refused (2016), [2015] S.C.C.A. No. 365, the court held that the exclusion of common law spouses from the ambit of spousal incompetency infringed s. 15(1) of the Charter, but that the infringement was justified under s. 1. Common law spouses are competent and compellable witnesses for the Crown in a criminal prosecution.

Comment by trial judge [subsec. (6)] – The silence of the accused may not be used against the accused in establishing guilt beyond a reasonable doubt. Silence is neither inculpatory nor exculpatory evidence. Silence may indicate, for example, that there is no evidence to support speculative explanations of the Crown's evidence offered by defence counsel, or it may indicate that the accused has not put forward any evidence that would require the Crown to negate an affirmative defence. In this limited sense, silence may be used by the trier of fact. If there is a rational explanation which is consistent with innocence and which may raise a reasonable doubt, however, the silence of the accused cannot be used to remove that doubt. There is an exception to this rule where the accused advances a defence of alibi. Where the defence of alibi is advanced, the trier of fact may draw an adverse inference from the failure of the accused to testify and subject himself to cross-examination: *R. v. Noble*, [1997] 1 S.C.R. 874, 114 C.C.C. (3d) 385.

Subsection (6) does not violate ss. 7 and 11(*c*) and (*d*) of the Charter. While the prosecutor and the trial judge are precluded from commenting on the failure of the accused to testify, his own counsel may make an appropriate comment and explain that the accused is under no duty to testify. Further, neither s. 11(*c*) nor (*d*) of the Charter requires that a trial judge specifically instruct jurors that no adverse inference can be drawn from the failure of the accused to testify: *R. v. Boss* (1988), 46 C.C.C. (3d) 523, 68 C.R. (3d) 123 (Ont. C.A.).

This section does not prohibit comment by counsel for the co-accused on an accused's failure to testify. Further, such comment does not violate s. 11(*c*) of the Charter. This does not mean, however, that counsel has free rein to encourage the jury to speculate or draw unwarranted inferences: *R. v. Naglik* (1991), 65 C.C.C. (3d) 272, 3 O.R. (3d) 385 (C.A.), revd on other grounds [1993] 3 S.C.R. 122, 83 C.C.C. (3d) 526.

The accused having been cross-examined by his co-accused, whom he incriminated in his testimony, as to his failure to give a statement to the police, the trial judge was required to direct the jury that the accused had a right to pre-trial silence. Further, the judge should have instructed the jury that the exercise of this right was not evidence as to guilt or innocence but merely went to credibility: *R. v. Crawford*, [1995] 1 S.C.R. 858, 96 C.C.C. (3d) 481.

Subsection (6) does not prohibit a trial judge from commenting affirmatively in a jury charge on the accused's right to silence. Statements to the contrary in *R. v. Noble* and *R. v. Crawford*, *infra*, should now be disregarded. However, the trial judge need not affirm the accused's right in every case, only where there is a realistic concern that the jury may place evidential value on an accused's decision not to testify. In such a case, the trial judge should make it clear to the jury that an accused's silence is not evidence and cannot be used as a makeweight in deciding whether the Crown has proved its case: *R. v. Prokofiew*, [2012] 2 S.C.R. 639, 290 C.C.C. (3d) 280; *R. v. Deol* (2017), 352 C.C.C. (3d) 343 (Ont. C.A.).

Advising the unrepresented accused in the course of his jury address that, since he had not testified, he could not do so now and advising the jury to disregard the accused's statement of matters that were not in evidence did not violate subsec. (6). The purpose of this subsection is to prevent a trial judge from telling a jury directly or in effect that they could draw an adverse inference from the accused's failure to testify. The trial judge's comments did not suggest that the accused's failure to testify was a source of an adverse inference: *R. v. Assoun* (2006), 207 C.C.C. (3d) 372 (N.S.C.A.), leave to appeal to S.C.C. refused [2006] 2 S.C.R. v, 210 C.C.C. (3d) vi.

When the jury asked the trial judge whether they could draw an inference from the failure of the accused to testify, it was appropriate for the trial judge to simply respond by reading subsec. (6) to them: *R. v. Trevor* (2006), 206 C.C.C. (3d) 370 (B.C.C.A.), leave to appeal to S.C.C. refused [2006] 2 S.C.R. xiii, 210 C.C.C. (3d) vi.

Where defence counsel, in his closing address, indicated that the decision not to call evidence was counsel's decision and not the accused's, the trial judge did not violate this section by instructing the jury that the decision not to testify could only be made by the accused and not by counsel: *R. v. Smith* (1997), 120 C.C.C. (3d) 500 (Ont. C.A.).

The statement by the trial judge at the opening of the trial in outlining trial procedure that at the close of the Crown's case defence counsel may open to the jury and outline the evidence to be called does not infringe this section even where in fact no defence evidence is called: *R. v. Agawa and Mallet* (1975), 28 C.C.C. (2d) 379 (Ont. C.A.); *R. v. Sherman* (1979), 47 C.C.C. (2d) 521 (B.C.C.A.).

This section did not prohibit the trial judge from correcting any misperception, if created in the judge's opening address, that the accused would or must testify: *R. v. C. (R.C.)* (1996), 107 C.C.C. (3d) 362 (N.S.C.A.).

Where the accused's wife was alleged to have been present for some of the accused's alleged confessions, the trial judge was not obliged to tell the jury that the wife was under no obligation to testify and that they should draw no negative inferences from her failure to testify. The trial judge also refused to tell the jury that the wife was not a compellable witness for the Crown. This approach struck the right balance: *R. v. St-Germain* (2009), 262 C.C.C. (3d) 366 (Que. C.A.), leave to appeal to S.C.C. refused [2010] 1 S.C.R. xv.

Comment by prosecutor [subsec. (6)] – An explanation by Crown counsel as to why he did not call the accused's wife, that is, that as a matter of law he was prohibited from doing so, was held not to constitute a comment prohibited by this subsection: *R. v. Wildman* (1981), 60 C.C.C. (2d) 289 (Ont. C.A.), revd on other grounds [1985] 2 S.C.R. 311, 14 C.C.C. (3d) 321.

A statement by the prosecutor of the obvious fact that the jury had not heard from the accused's wife in a case where the accused's defence was that he was asleep at home at the time of the offence, would seem not to constitute a comment prohibited by this subsection, and in any event did not result in any miscarriage of justice: *R. v. Gray* (1986), 25 C.C.C. (3d) 145 (B.C.C.A.).

A statement by the prosecutor that only the accused, alleged to have killed his common law spouse, knew what really happened and "now the rest of us know", and that the jury should consider the evidence put before them "as well as the evidence not put before you", when considered in context, did not violate this subsection: *R. v. Emile* (1988), 42 C.C.C. (3d) 408, 65 C.R. (3d) 135 (N.W.T.C.A.).

Crown counsel's comment to the jury that the accused had a constitutional right not to testify and did not have to prove anything was made in the context of a submission urging the jury not to speculate and not to use the failure to testify as a "cloak for his guilt". Thus, while the comment should not have been made, it did not violate subsec. (6): *R. v. Knox* (2006), 209 C.C.C. (3d) 76, 80 O.R. (3d) 515 (C.A.).

Crown counsel's jury address, taken as a whole, which included repeated references to the fact that there was no version of events other than the complainant's and including the comment in relation to the question of the accused's knowledge: "but he didn't testify, so he can't be asked directly what he thought at the time or what he construed or what he knew", did violate this subsection. The comments strongly implied that the jury could and should infer that the accused's silence and refusal to expose himself to cross-examination were indicia of his guilt: *R. v. Biladeau* (2008), 241 C.C.C. (3d) 374 (Ont. C.A.).

Subsection (6) does not apply to proceedings under s. 745 [now s. 745.63] to review the period of parole ineligibility of a prisoner serving sentence for murder: *Poulin v. Quebec (Attorney General)* (1991), 68 C.C.C. (3d) 472 (Que. S.C.).

INCRIMINATING QUESTIONS / Answer not admissible against witness.

5. (1) No witness shall be excused from answering any question on the ground that the answer to the question may tend to criminate him, or may tend to establish his liability to a civil proceeding at the instance of the Crown or of any person.

(2) Where with respect to any question a witness objects to answer on the ground that his answer may tend to criminate him, or may tend to establish his liability to a civil proceeding at the instance of the Crown or of any person, and if but for this Act, or the Act of any provincial legislature, the witness would therefore have been excused from answering the question, then although the witness is by reason of this Act or the provincial Act compelled to answer, the answer so given shall not be used or admissible in evidence against him in any criminal trial or other criminal proceeding against him thereafter taking place, other than a prosecution for perjury in the giving of that evidence or for the giving of contradictory evidence. R.S., c. E-10, s. 5; 1997, c. 18, s. 116.

ANNOTATIONS

Effect of provision on common law right – This section and comparable provincial legislation have abolished the common law right of a witness to refuse to answer a question on the grounds that it may incriminate him and the witness must answer questions put to him, notwithstanding he was then facing criminal charges in a foreign jurisdiction: *Summa Corp v. Meier* (1981), 127 D.L.R. (3d) 238, 30 B.C.L.R. 69 (C.A.), leave to appeal to S.C.C. refused D.L.R. *loc. cit.* 39 N.R. 538.

Absent conduct on the part of the Crown amounting to an abuse of process, a witness who is charged in separate proceedings with the same offence as the accused is a compellable witness at the instance of the Crown at the accused's trial. However, s. 7 of the Charter provides protection to the witness in addition to the protection afforded by this section and s. 13 of the Charter. Thus, derivative evidence which could not have been obtained, or the significance of which could not have been appreciated, but for the testimony of the witness ought generally to be excluded under s. 7 of the Charter at the witness' subsequent trial since its admission would tend to affect the fairness of the trial: *R. v. S. (R.J.)*, [1995] 1 S.C.R. 451, 96 C.C.C. (3d) 1. [Also see notes under ss. 7 and 13 of the Charter.]

Admission of evidence of refusal to comply with investigative tests – There is no general privilege against self-incrimination. The privilege in its modern form means only the right of a witness as qualified by this section to refuse to answer certain questions, if the answer will tend to incriminate the witness, and the absolute right of the accused to refuse to go into the witness-box. Thus, in particular, evidence may be led of the accused's refusal to see a Crown psychiatrist where the accused relies on the defence of insanity: *R. v. Sweeney (No. 2)* (1977), 35 C.C.C. (2d) 245, 76 D.L.R. (3d) 211 (Ont. C.A.).

While there is no legal obligation to participate in a line-up, failure to do so may have legal consequences in respect of the evidence that may be admitted at trial. For example, in circumstances where the Crown must explain the omission of a line-up, the accused's refusal may be both relevant and admissible: *R. v. Ross*, [1989] 1 S.C.R. 3, 46 C.C.C. (3d) 129; *R. v. Marcoux* (1975), [1976] 1 S.C.R. 763, 24 C.C.C. (2d) 1.

However, in *R. v. Henry* (2010), 262 C.C.C. (3d) 307 (B.C.C.A.), it was held that the trial judge at the accused's 1983 trial committed reversible error by instructing the jury that the accused's resistance to participating in a line-up could be used as consciousness of guilt evidence. There was no statutory authority for the police to force the accused to participate in the line-up and his refusal to do so could not properly support an inference of guilt.

Where it can be reasonably anticipated that defence counsel would challenge the adequacy of the police identification procedures the Crown may anticipate that the trial judge or the defence would make adverse comments on the unexplained absence of an identification parade and the danger of a "one on one" or courtroom identification and lead evidence as to the accused's refusal to attend for a line-up or provide a photograph for a photo line-up. The evidence is admissible however for a limited purpose, to explain the absence of an identification parade, and not admissible as evidence of a consciousness of guilt: *R. v. Shortreed* (1990), 54 C.C.C. (3d) 292 (Ont. C.A.).

Where, however, the suspect's conduct goes beyond a mere refusal to participate in a line-up or provide a photograph and he takes extraordinary efforts to prevent the taking of a photograph by altering or concealing his facial appearance then, in the absence of a plausible explanation, the jury is entitled to draw an inference that he has something to conceal and that this is evidence of a consciousness of guilt: *R. v. Shortreed, supra.*

The accused's after-the-fact conduct in offering to provide DNA samples and taking a lie detector test were relevant and admissible. There are policy concerns and fundamental constitutional principles at play where the Crown seeks to tender evidence of a refusal to cooperate which are not engaged when the defence tenders evidence of an accused's cooperation with the police. There is no logical inconsistency between the admission of evidence that a person cooperated with the police and the exclusion of evidence that a person did not cooperate with the police. The freedom to choose whether to assist the state in the investigation of an alleged crime would be illusory if the failure to render assistance could, standing alone, be used as evidence against a person at trial. Similarly, the right to maintain the integrity of one's body against unauthorized state intrusion would lose its force if the exercise of that right could take on an incriminatory connotation at trial: *R. v. B. (S.C.)* (1997), 119 C.C.C. (3d) 530 (Ont. C.A.). See also *R. v. Baltrusaitis* (2002), 162 C.C.C. (3d) 539 (Ont. C.A.).

Application of subsec. (2) – The trial judge before whom this section is invoked has a duty to ensure that the witnesses are properly placing themselves within the ambit of the section. The answer to which the witnesses object must be ones that but for this Act they would have been entitled at common law to refuse to answer on the ground that they could tend to incriminate them. Beyond this limited function, the judge must simply take note that the witnesses have claimed the statutory protection: *R. v. Noël*, [2002] 3 S.C.R. 433, 168 C.C.C. (3d) 193.

CAN. EV.

The objection may only be made after the question is asked but in practice a trial judge may permit a general objection for the ensuing series of questions to follow: *R. v. Mottola* (1959), 124 C.C.C. 288, 31 C.R. 4 (Ont. C.A.); *R. v. Cote* (1979), 50 C.C.C. (2d) 564, 8 C.R. (3d) 171 *sub nom. A.-G. Que. v. Cote* (Que. C.A.).

However, where the objection is made only part way through the witness' testimony the presiding officer, such as a coroner, has no power to extend the protection of this section retroactively back to the commencement of the testimony: *R. v. Vigeant* (1982), 3 C.C.C. (3d) 445 (Que. C.A.), leave to appeal to S.C.C. refused C.C.C. *loc. cit.*.

It was held in *R. v. Kuldip*, [1990] 3 S.C.R. 618, 61 C.C.C. (3d) 385, that this section does not prevent cross-examination of an accused on testimony given in an earlier trial on the same indictment, notwithstanding an objection under subsec. (2). And, in *R. v. Henry* (2005), 202 C.C.C. (3d) 449 (S.C.C.), the court held that cross-examination is permissible whether the purpose of the cross-examination is to impeach the accused's credibility or to incriminate the accused. The court pointed out that a witness who was also the accused at the first trial is, at both trials, a voluntary rather than a compelled witness. In such a case, the *quid pro quo* that lies at the heart of this subsection is absent. (The *quid pro quo* being that, when a witness who is compelled to give evidence in a court proceeding is exposed to the risk of self-incrimination, the state offers protection against the subsequent use of that evidence against the witness in exchange for his or her full and frank testimony.)

The testimony of an accused on the *voir dire* as to the admissibility of his confession in answer to questions as to whether the confession is true is inadmissible on the trial proper even if the accused does not claim the protection under this subsection. In fact it is doubtful whether this subsection can apply in such circumstances: *R. v. Magdish, Bennett and Sweet* (1978), 41 C.C.C. (2d) 449, 3 C.R. (3d) 377 (Ont. H.C.J.). Support for this view may be found in the statement of Dickson J., for the plurality in *R. v. Erven*, [1979] 1 S.C.R. 926, 44 C.C.C. (2d) 76 (6:3), that the "accused may testify on the *voir dire* while remaining silent during the trial. Evidence on the *voir dire* cannot be used in the trial itself".

Whatever the scope of this subsection, at least where the statement is ruled inadmissible, the accused may not be cross-examined by the Crown at the trial proper on his testimony given at the *voir dire*: *R. v. Coughlin and Nicholson* (1982), 3 C.C.C. (3d) 259 (Ont. C.A.), applying *R. v. Wong Kam-ming*, [1979] 2 W.L.R. 81, [1979] 1 All E.R. 939 (P.C.).

While refusal to testify does not fall within the protection provided by this section, cross-examination of an accused as to why he refused to testify at the preliminary inquiry of a separately charged co-accused would produce evidence of only marginal relevancy that could carry substantial prejudice. The cross-examination was therefore not permitted: *R. v. Hines* (2001), 154 C.C.C. (3d) 158 (Ont. S.C.J.).

Evidence that the accused gave as a compelled witness at the trial of another person, in which he admitted a number of criminal acts, was not admissible at the accused's subsequent sentence hearing in relation to other offences: *R. v. Duhamel* (2013), 278 C.R.R. (2d) 52 (Ont. S.C.J.).

Evidence the accused gave at his own trial, in which he admitted to criminal acts that were not the ones charged, may be admitted in a subsequent forfeiture application on the same trial. The court held that the forfeiture application was not "other proceedings", but part of the sentencing phase of the trial and accordingly, the evidence was admissible: *R. v. Chu* (2016), 337 C.C.C. (3d) 548 (Sask. Q.B.).

Effect of s. 13 of the Charter of Rights [subsec. (2)] – Cases under this subsection must now be considered in light of s. 13 of the *Canadian Charter of Rights and Freedoms*. Cases decided prior to *R. v. Nedelcu*, [2012] 3 S.C.R. 311, 290 C.C.C. (3d) 153, must be read in light of its relatively narrow holding discussed below. In *R. v. Dubois*, [1985] 2 S.C.R. 350, 22 C.C.C. (3d) 513 (6:1), the court held that: (1) section 13 applies although the first proceeding took place prior to the Charter's proclamation; (2) section 13 applies to a technically voluntary witness such as the accused at his own trial and its protection does not depend on an objection, unlike this subsection; (3) the evidence need not have been incriminating in the first proceedings; (4) the retrial of the same offence following an appeal is another proceeding and the accused's testimony at the first trial can therefore not be tendered at the second trial as part of the Crown's case.

In *R. v. Henry*, [2005] 3 S.C.R. 609, 202 C.C.C. (3d) 449, the court overruled its earlier decision in *R. v. Mannion*, [1986] 2 S.C.R. 272, 28 C.C.C. (3d) 544, and held that s. 13 is not available to an accused who chooses to testify at his or her retrial on the same indictment.

In *R. v. Nedelcu, supra*, the court (6:3) held that the Crown was entitled to cross-examine the accused on the *non-incriminatory* portions of his civil discovery transcript for impeachment purposes at his criminal trial. Incriminating evidence is evidence given by the witness at the prior proceeding that the Crown could use at the subsequent proceeding, if it were permitted to do so, to prove guilt, *i.e.*, to prove or assist in proving one or more of the essential elements of the offence for which the witness is being tried. Where the evidence given by the witness at the prior proceeding could not be used by the Crown at the subsequent proceeding to prove the witness's guilt on the charge for which he or she is being tried, the prior evidence is not "incriminating evidence" and can be used to test the accused's credibility.

Section 13 of the Charter is violated by testimony of a police officer that he was able to identify the accused as a result of hearing him testify in another proceeding: *R. v. Skinner* (1988), 42 C.C.C. (3d) 575 (Ont. C.A.).

A witness's knowledge of immunity from the use of testimony to incriminate them is rarely relevant to credibility. Inquiries into a witness's knowledge of this provision may deflect the jury's attention away from the real issues and may impinge upon confidential solicitor-client communications. Without further evidence of a motive for falsely testifying, a witness's knowledge of s. 13 standing alone does not constitute a motive to lie and cannot affect the witness's credibility: *R. v. Jabarianha*, [2001] 3 S.C.R. 430, 159 C.C.C. (3d) 1.

In *R. v. Jabarianha, supra*, the court approved *R. v. Swick* (1997), 118 C.C.C. (3d) 33, 150 D.L.R. (4th) 566 (Ont. C.A.), and held that the probative value of a witness's knowledge of s. 13 of the Charter will generally be overborne by its prejudicial effect. Crown counsel should rarely be permitted to cross-examine on a witness's knowledge of s. 13. A witness's knowledge of the law is not co-extensive with a tendency to lie. Without other evidence of a motive for testifying falsely, evidence of a witness's knowledge of s. 13 of the Charter should not affect his or her credibility. In rare circumstances, cross-examination of a witness's knowledge of s. 13 may be permitted. If the Crown provided some evidence of a plot to lie or to obtain favours, the probative value of a witness's knowledge of s. 13 could outweigh its prejudicial effect whereas evidence of mere friendship between the accused and witness will not. Similarly, *R. v. Noël*, [2002] 3 S.C.R. 433, 168 C.C.C. (3d) 193.

EVIDENCE OF PERSON WITH PHYSICAL DISABILITY / Evidence of person with mental disability / Inquiry.

6. (1) If a witness has difficulty communicating by reason of a physical disability, the court may order that the witness be permitted to give evidence by any means that enables the evidence to be intelligible.

(2) If a witness with a mental disability is determined under section 16 to have the capacity to give evidence and has difficulty communicating by reason of a disability, the court may order that the witness be permitted to give evidence by any means that enables the evidence to be intelligible.

(3) The court may conduct an inquiry to determine if the means by which a witness may be permitted to give evidence under subsection (1) or (2) is necessary and reliable. R.S., c. E-10, s. 6; 1998, c. 9, s. 1.

ANNOTATIONS

To ensure that persons with mental and physical disabilities receive the equal protection of the law, it may be necessary that their evidence be presented with the evidence of others who are able to explain, support and supplement it so that as far as possible the court will receive the account that the witness would have given had he or she not been disabled. In this case, the trial judge could properly find that statements the mentally and physically disabled complainant made to his mother on several occasions after the alleged offence met the necessity and reliability requirements for admission of hearsay evidence, even though the complainant testified: *R. v. Pearson* (1994), 95 C.C.C. (3d) 365, 36 C.R. (4th) 343 (B.C.C.A.).

Where the deaf and non-oral witnesses were of normal intelligence and over the age of 14 years, s. 16 of this Act had no application. This section applied and the evidence of the witnesses was admissible notwithstanding they used a unique form of sign language. An interpreter was available who could make the testimony intelligible: *R. v. Carlick* (1999), 42 W.C.B. (2d) 326 (B.C.S.C.).

Given the applicable provincial legislation that is incorporated into criminal proceedings pursuant to s. 540 of the *Criminal Code*, it was not an error in law for the trial judge not to have a video recording made of the testimony that included sign language: *R. v. Titchener* (2013), 333 B.C.A.C. 234 (C.A.).

Subsection (3) is permissive and it is not mandatory for the judge to conduct an inquiry, for example, into the competency of the sign-language interpreter. When, during the course of the trial, a problem did arise with the interpretation, the trial judge dealt with it properly by giving directions as to how the evidence would be given to ensure accuracy of the interpretation: *R. v. Titchener, supra.*

IDENTIFICATION OF ACCUSED.

6.1 For greater certainty, a witness may give evidence as to the identity of an accused whom the witness is able to identify visually or in any other sensory manner. 1998, c. 9, s. 1.

EXPERT WITNESSES.

7. Where, in any trial or other proceeding, criminal or civil, it is intended by the prosecution or the defence, or by any party, to examine as witnesses professional or other experts entitled according to the law or practice to give opinion evidence, not more than five of such witnesses may be called on either side without the leave of the court or judge or person presiding. R.S., c. E-10, s. 7.

ANNOTATIONS

Where the opinion evidence played a minor and insignificant part of the evidence the failure of the Crown to obtain leave to call over five experts was excused: *R. v. Vincent* (1963), 40 C.R. 365, 42 W.W.R. 638 (Man. C.A.).

This section was intended, in part, to limit the number of experts to prevent abuse, expense and delay caused by excessive use of expert evidence. Where there would not be unnecessary duplication and the hearing of the other two witnesses would not unduly prolong the trial, leave was granted: *Canada (Commissioner of Competition) v. Chatr Wireless Inc.* (2013), 232 A.C.W.S. (3d) 688, 2013 ONSC 5385.

The common law rule, applied in, *inter alia*, maritime cases, that where the judge sits with assessors the parties may not call expert evidence is out of step with modern trial practice which permits expert evidence on matters of opinion at issue on a trial. This section confirms the modern practice, imposing limits only on the number of expert witnesses each side may call. The rule is also at variance with the principles of natural justice. Accordingly, the rule should no longer be followed. Assessors function to assist the trial judge in understanding and explaining technical evidence which the parties put before the court. The parties are not, however, precluded from calling expert evidence and the trial judge retains the sole responsibility for making the necessary findings of fact and applying the law to them. In addition, there may be cases where it is useful to employ a limited version of the old admiralty rule of appointing assessors to assist the judge with findings of fact and fact-related opinions, provided precautions, including disclosure and right of response, are taken to avoid breach of the principles of natural justice: *Porto Seguro Companhia De Seguros Gerais v. Belcan S.A.*, [1997] 3 S.C.R. 1278, 153 D.L.R. (4th) 577.

Properly interpreted, this section permits each defendant to call five expert witnesses without leave: *Eli Lilly and Co. v. Novopharm Ltd.* (1997), 147 D.L.R. (4th) 673, 130 F.T.R. 1 (T.D.).

HANDWRITING COMPARISON.

8. Comparison of a disputed writing with any writing proved to the satisfaction of the court to be genuine shall be permitted to be made by witnesses, and such writings, and the evidence of witnesses respecting those writings, may be submitted to the court and jury as proof of the genuineness or otherwise of the writing in dispute. R.S., c. E-10, s. 8.

ANNOTATIONS

A witness may be competent to prove a person's handwriting through having carried on regular correspondence or having frequently seen the person's handwriting: *R. v. Pitre*, [1933] S.C.R. 69, 59 C.C.C. 148.

Particularly in light of the possibility of calling a witness under this section a judge ought not himself become a witness by attempting to compare signatures, in this case the signature of the accused on the appearance notice with a signature of a certificate of business name and style which the Crown relied upon to prove the accused's connection with premises alleged to have contained gaming devices: *R. v. Boudreau* (1987), 81 N.B.R. (2d) 148 (C.A.).

This provision does not displace the common law rule allowing a trier of fact to undertake a comparative analysis of handwriting specimens without the need of witnesses interpreting or identifying the relevant writing. In so doing, the trier of fact must exercise caution having regard to a number of factors that can impact the assessment, including, *inter alia*, the quality of the handwriting exemplar, the lack of expertise and experience in performing the task and the lack of access to specialized equipment: *R. v. Cunsolo* (2011), 277 C.C.C. (3d) 435 (Ont. S.C.J.), affd (2014), 319 O.A.C. 278 (C.A.).

It does not follow from this section that proof of handwriting may only be accomplished by way of comparison. In this case, it was admissible for the complainant and her mother to testify that a diary adduced into evidence looked like it contained the accused's handwriting: *R. v. V. (L.)* (2016), [2017] 1 W.W.R. 439 (Sask. C.A.).

ADVERSE WITNESSES / Previous statements by witness not proved adverse.

9. (1) A party producing a witness shall not be allowed to impeach his credit by general evidence of bad character, but if the witness, in the opinion of the court, proves adverse, the party may contradict him by other evidence, or, by leave of the court, may prove that the witness made at other times a statement inconsistent with his present testimony, but before the last mentioned proof can be given the circumstances of the supposed statement, sufficient to designate the particular occasion, shall be mentioned to the witness, and he shall be asked whether or not he did make the statement.

(2) Where the party producing a witness alleges that the witness made at other times a statement in writing, reduced to writing, or recorded on audio tape or video tape or otherwise, inconsistent with the witness' present testimony, the court may, without proof that the witness is adverse, grant leave to that party to cross-examine the witness as to the statement and the court may consider the cross-examination in determining whether in the opinion of the court the witness is adverse. R.S., c. E-10, s. 9; 1994, c. 44, s. 85.

ANNOTATIONS

Proof of statement of adverse witness [subsec. (1)] – The meaning of the word "adverse" has been considered by a number of courts. The majority of the court in *Wawanesa Mutual Ins. Co. v. Hanes*, [1963] 1 C.C.C. 176, 28 D.L.R. (2d) 386 (Ont. C.A.), vard [1963] S.C.R. 154, [1963] 1 C.C.C. 321, held in relation to the comparable provision of the *Ontario Evidence Act*, R.S.O. 1950, c. 119, that "adverse" was not limited to hostility but included a witness who, though not hostile, was unfavourable in the sense of assuming by his testimony a position opposite to that of the party calling him. This position has been accepted in Ontario as representing the law with respect to this subsection: *R. v. Cassibo* (1982), 70 C.C.C. (2d) 498 (Ont. C.A.); *R. v. Johnson* (2002), 166 C.C.C. (3d) 44 (Ont. C.A.). The narrower view that "adverse" means "hostile" is represented by the dissenting judgment of Roach J.A., in *Wawanesa Mutual Ins. Co. v. Hanes*, following the judgment of the court in *Greenough v. Eccles* (1859), 28 L.J.C.P. 160 in relation to a similar provision in the *Common Law Procedure Act, 1854* (U.K.), c. 125. This narrower view has been adopted by several courts, see: *R. v. Wyman* (1958), 122 C.C.C. 65, 28 C.R. 371 (N.B.S.C. App. Div.), and *R. v. McIntyre*, [1963] 2 C.C.C. 380, 43 C.R. 262 (N.S.S.C. *in banco*). In this latter case reference was made by Ilsley C.J., to *Wawanesa Mutual Ins. Co. v. Hanes* and to a passage in *Reference re R. v. Coffin*, [1956] S.C.R. 191 at p. 213, 114 C.C.C. 1 at p. 24, where Kellock J. appeared to equate adversity with hostility which he defined as "not giving her evidence fairly and with a desire to tell the truth because of a hostile animus towards the prosecution".

On the *voir dire* to determine adversity the trial judge may receive evidence of both oral and written statements by the witness which are alleged to be inconsistent with his present testimony. However, the judge after hearing evidence with respect to the making of a previous oral statement may refuse to declare the witness adverse or may refuse to grant leave to prove the statement at the trial proper because the evidence with respect to its making is too conflicting, unsatisfactory or the words allegedly spoken are ambiguous. In some circumstances a judge may find a witness adverse solely on the basis of a previous inconsistent statement. On the *voir dire* the witness should only be examined, not cross-examined, on the prior inconsistent oral statement: *R. v. Cassibo, supra.*

A declaration of adversity under s. 9(1), unlike a declaration of hostility at common law, does not entitle a party to cross-examine the witness at large. Rather, the party is restricted to cross-examining the witness on his prior inconsistent statements and the circumstances surrounding them: *R. v. Figliola* (2011), 272 C.C.C. (3d) 518 (Ont. C.A.). See also: *R. v. Vivar* (2004), 60 W.C.B. (2d) 53, [2004] O.J. No. 9 (Ont. S.C.J.).

In some circumstances, to preclude an accused by mechanical application of the adverse witness requirement of this subsection from cross-examining a witness whom he has called with respect to a prior confession made by the witness that he, rather than the accused, had committed the crime might deprive the accused of his constitutional right to a fair trial as guaranteed by the *Canadian Charter of Rights and Freedoms*, and a court has a residual discretion to relax in favour of the accused a strict rule of evidence where it is necessary to prevent a miscarriage of justice and where the danger against which an exclusionary rule aims to provide a safeguard does not exist. However, there should be some indication of the reliability of the alleged prior confession as a basis for holding that the refusal, without a finding that the witness is adverse, to permit cross-examination on the witness's prior confession by an accused calling a witness, will deprive the accused of his constitutional right to a fair trial: *R. v. Williams* (1985), 18 C.C.C. (3d) 356, 44 C.R. (3d) 351 (Ont. C.A.), leave to appeal to S.C.C. refused [1985] 1 S.C.R. xiv, C.C.C. and C.R. *loc. cit.*

A witness may be allowed to refresh his memory by reference to his earlier deposition, such as the preliminary hearing transcript, unless the object of the examination is to discredit or contradict the party's own witness in which case the procedure under this section must be followed: *Reference re R. v. Coffin, supra.* Also *R. v. Muise* (2013), 332 N.S.R. (2d) 106 (C.A.).

Cross-examination without proof of adversity [subsec. (2)] – In *R. v. Milgaard* (1971), 2 C.C.C. (2d) 206, [1971] 2 W.W.R. 266 (Sask. C.A.), leave to appeal to S.C.C. refused [1971]

S.C.R. x, 4 C.C.C. (2d) 566*n*, at the trial for non-capital murder, in the absence of the jury, the Crown in making an application under this subsection produced a statement in writing allegedly inconsistent with a witness' evidence-in-chief. The trial judge read the statement, ruled that he was satisfied that it was inconsistent, and recalled the jury and allowed Crown counsel to cross-examine her on it. She admitted signing the pages but could not remember the contents. Upon application by the Crown she was declared hostile and upon further cross-examination on that statement she admitted remembering the events referred to in it. It was held (5:0) that the trial judge's error in declaring, without hearing evidence, that the previous statement was inconsistent, and allowing her to be cross-examined on it, was in those particular circumstances not prejudicial to the appellant, and applied the present s. 686(1)(*b*)(iii) to dismiss the appeal. In its reasons for judgment the court recommended the procedure for an application under this subsection where a jury is trying the case at pp. 221-2 C.C.C.:

(1) Counsel should advise the Court that he desires to make an application under s. 9(2) of the *Canada Evidence Act*.

(2) When the Court is so advised, the Court should direct the jury to retire.

(3) Upon retirement of the jury, counsel should advise the learned trial Judge of the particulars of the application and produce for him the alleged statement in writing, or the writing to which the statement has been reduced.

(4) The learned trial Judge should read the statement, or writing, and determine whether, in fact, there is an inconsistency between such statement or writing and the evidence the witness has given in Court. If the learned trial Judge decides there is no inconsistency, then that ends the matter. If he finds there is an inconsistency, he should call upon counsel to prove the statement or writing.

(5) Counsel should then prove the statement, or writing. This may be done by producing the statement or writing to the witness. If the witness admits the statement, or the statement reduced to writing, such proof would be sufficient. If the witness does not so admit, counsel then could provide the necessary proof by other evidence.

(6) If the witness admits making the statement, counsel for the opposing party should have the right to cross-examine as to the circumstances under which the statement was made. A similar right to cross-examine should be granted if the statement is proved by other witnesses. It may be that he will be able to establish that there were circumstances which would render it improper for the learned trial Judge to permit the cross-examination, notwithstanding the apparent inconsistencies. The opposing counsel, too, should have the right to call evidence as to factors relevant to obtaining the statement, for the purpose of attempting to show that cross-examination should not be permitted.

(7) The learned trial Judge should then decide whether or not he will permit the cross-examination. If so, the jury should be recalled.

This procedure was referred to with apparent approval in *R. v. McInroy, infra.*

While it may be appropriate to attempt to refresh the memory of an honest but forgetful witness by showing him the previous statement, where the Crown witness was an accomplice whose testimony was inconsistent with the previous statement and who even Crown counsel considered was not acting honestly then the trial judge should hold a *voir dire* following the procedure set out in *R. v. Milgaard, supra.* The trial judge ought not to put the prior statement to the witness himself and conduct a cross-examination before the conclusion of that procedure: *R. v. Booth* (1984), 15 C.C.C. (3d) 237 (B.C.C.A.).

While it was open to Crown counsel to use the preliminary inquiry transcript to refresh a difficult witness's memory, when the questioning became more persistent and involved leading questions and reminding the witness of the punishment for perjury, counsel was required to comply with the provisions of this section. The cross-examination had crossed the line from controlled examination into cross-examination and impeachment: *R. v. Situ* (2005), 200 C.C.C. (3d) 9 (Alta. C.A.).

The notes of a police officer as to his interview with a witness which the witness has never confirmed prior to testifying do not constitute a statement in writing or reduced to writing within the meaning of this subsection: *R. v. Handy* (1978), 45 C.C.C. (2d) 232, 5 C.R. (3d) 97 (B.C.C.A.).

However, a conversation in the form of questions and answers recorded by the officer at the time although translated in the process from French to English is a statment reduced to writing within the meaning of this subsection: *R. v. Carpenter (No. 2)* (1982), 1 C.C.C. (3d) 149, 31 C.R. (3d) 261 (Ont. C.A.).

A trial judge has a residual discretion to refuse to permit cross-examination on a prior inconsistent statement, even when the requirements of s. 9(1) and (2) have been met. Here, the circumstances in which the statement was taken were problematic. A private conversation was improperly recorded without the witness's knowledge or consent. Refusing the Crown's application to cross-examine the witness on the prior statement was necessary to protect the integrity of the justice system: *R. v. D. (C.)* (2010), 257 C.C.C. (3d) 427 (Ont. S.C.J.).

A trial judge may first direct how the witness should be examined before deciding whether or not to grant leave to counsel to cross-examine: *R. v. Stewart*, [1977] 2 S.C.R. 748, 31 C.C.C. (2d) 497 (9:0).

The trial judge has a discretion whether or not to permit cross-examination on the prior inconsistent statement, depending on whether the ends of justice would be best attained by allowing it: *R. v. Carpenter (No. 2), supra.*

In *R. v. Soobrian* (1995), 96 C.C.C. (3d) 208 (Ont. C.A.), Crown counsel, before calling the witness, a friend of the accused, was aware that he would testify in conformity to a second statement he had given to the police and as he had testified at the preliminary inquiry, and thereby exculpate the accused. Crown counsel should not have been permitted to cross-examine his own witness on an earlier statement where the admitted purpose of the cross-examination was to provide a foundation to argue that the accused were not telling the truth, because the Crown witness was not telling the truth in his testimony. Absent an evidentiary foundation to support the Crown's contention that the witness was acting in collusion with the accused, the cross-examination should not have been permitted. See also: *R. v. Figliola* (2011), 272 C.C.C. (3d) 518 (Ont. C.A.).

It was open to Crown counsel to cross-examine the witness under this subsection as to why he had changed his account of the events and, in particular, whether he had done so to protect the accused: *R. v. Dayes* (2013), 301 C.C.C. (3d) 337 (Ont. C.A.).

While there may be cases where allowing cross-examination of one's own witness would bring the administration of justice into disrepute, the fact that the statement was taken in circumstances of inducements, intimidation and the denial of legal counsel did not necessarily preclude its use for the purpose of cross-examination: *R. v. Aitkenhead* (2001), 154 C.C.C. (3d) 79 (Man. C.A.), leave to appeal to S.C.C. refused 157 C.C.C. (3d) vi.

When he was confronted by the police with what purported to be a complaint by the accused, a witness made a statement implicating the accused. At trial, the witness resiled from the statement and the Crown sought to cross-examine the witness on the statement. The "complaint" had been fabricated by a police officer and although not signed, was a false document and the officer probably committed the offence of forgery. In those circumstances, the trial judge should not have permitted the Crown to cross-examine the witness on his statement: *R. v. McMillan* (2003), 176 O.A.C. 215 (C.A.).

There is no requirement that the witness be proved adverse before cross-examination may be permitted under this subsection. Further, even where the witness simply claims he has no recollection of the matters which are contained in the prior statement it is open to the judge, having heard the witness, to find that he is lying about his lack of recollection and that there is therefore an inconsistency within the meaning of this section: *R. v. McInroy and Rouse*, [1979] 1 S.C.R. 588, 42 C.C.C. (2d) 481 (7:0).

The party opposing the cross-examination bears the burden of establishing that there were circumstances that would render it improper to permit the cross-examination. While the voluntariness of the statement is a relevant factor, it is not the deciding factor. Accordingly, a statement found to have been involuntary when the witness was an accused in another proceeding, is not necessarily unavailable for cross-examination under this provision: *R. v. S. (C.L.)* (2011), 266 C.C.C. (3d) 360 (Man. Q.B.).

In a proper case the court may grant a party leave to cross-examine his own witness on a prior inconsistent statement even at the stage of re-examination where the witness in cross-examination has given evidence on a material matter which is contrary to the prior statement: *R. v. Moore* (1984), 15 C.C.C. (3d) 541 (Ont. C.A.), leave to appeal to S.C.C. refused [1985] 1 S.C.R. x, C.C.C. *loc. cit.*

There is no duty on the Crown to call particular witnesses including the complainant. It is always open to the accused to call the complainant and resort to the provisions of this section if she or he did not testify in a manner consistent with any pre-trial exculpatory statements and gave evidence adverse to the accused. In the rare case where the tactical disadvantage to the defence calling a potentially hostile witness would be manifestly unfair, the trial judge is entitled to consider this factor in determining whether to call the witness him or herself: *R. v. Cook*, [1997] 1 S.C.R. 1113, 114 C.C.C. (3d) 481.

It is not an error to permit cross-examination on a statement found to be unreliable on a *K.G.B.* application. The test for admissibility does not apply to the question of whether cross-examination should be permitted on a prior inconsistent statement: *R. v. Tran* (2010), 257 C.C.C. (3d) 18 (Ont. C.A.).

Refreshing memory – Witnesses may refresh their memory from a previous statement, even one not made contemporaneous with the events about which the witnesses seek to testify. Thus, in this case it was proper for the witnesses to have refreshed their memory prior to court from statements that they gave to the police several years after the events. It was of course open to defence counsel to attempt to demonstrate through cross-examination that the witnesses, in fact, had no present memory of the events or that the memory was unreliable: *R. v. B. (K.G.)* (1998), 125 C.C.C. (3d) 61 (Ont. C.A.).

Evidentiary value of prior statement – Where a witness is cross-examined pursuant to this subsection on a prior inconsistent statement and does not adopt the statement then it merely goes to the witness' credibility and is not admissible for the truth of its contents: *R. v. Deacon*, [1947] S.C.R. 531, 89 C.C.C. 1 (5:0).

For the statement to be admissible for its truth, the party tendering the statement must establish the following: The party must show on a balance of probabilities that there are sufficient *indicia* of reliability, namely, "(i) the statement is made under oath or solemn affirmation following a warning as to the existence of sanctions and the significance of the oath or affirmation, (ii) the statement is videotaped in its entirety, and (iii) the opposing party, whether the Crown or defence, has a full opportunity to cross-examine the witness respecting the statement . . . Alternatively, other circumstantial guarantees of reliability may suffice to render such statements substantively admissible, provided that the judge is satisfied that the circumstances provide adequate assurances of reliability". In addition, where the prior statement was made to a person in authority, the judge must be satisfied that the statement was made voluntarily and that there are no factors which would tend to bring the administration of justice into disrepute if the statement were admitted for its truth. Even if the statement is admitted as substantive evidence, the trial judge must direct the jury to consider carefully the circumstances in assessing the credibility of the prior inconsistent statement relative to the witness' testimony at trial: *R. v. B. (K.G.)*, [1993] 1 S.C.R. 740, 79 C.C.C. (3d) 257 (7:0).

In *R. v. Biscette* (1995), 99 C.C.C. (3d) 326 (Alta. C.A.), affd [1996] 3 S.C.R. 599, 110 C.C.C. (3d) 285, it was held that it was open to the judge to make substantive use of the witness' preliminary hearing testimony when she recanted that testimony at the accused's trial. The inability of the defence to conduct a complete cross-examination due to the witness' failure of memory is only a factor to be considered in respect to the weight to be

CAN. EV.

accorded to the prior statement. This fact alone, however, cannot bar the admission of the prior inconsistent statement for its substantive use.

In *R. v. Bradshaw*, [2017] 1 S.C.R. 865, 349 C.C.C. (3d) 429, the Supreme Court of Canada reconciled the jurisprudence on threshold reliability. Corroborative evidence may be used to assess threshold reliability of hearsay statements if it overcomes the specific hearsay dangers presented by the statement. Hearsay dangers can be overcome by showing that: (1) there are adequate substitutes for testing truth and accuracy (procedural reliability); or (2) there are sufficient circumstantial or evidentiary guarantees that the statement is inherently trustworthy (substantive reliability). Procedural reliability is established where there are adequate substitutes for the testing of the evidence such as a video recording, the presence of an oath and a warning about the consequences of lying. However, some form of cross-examination of the declarant such as preliminary inquiry testimony or cross-examination of a recanting witness at trial is usually required. The standard for substantive reliability is high and requires the judge to be satisfied that the statement is so reliable that contemporaneous cross-examination of the declarant would add little if anything to the process. Procedural reliability and substantive reliability are not mutually exclusive and may work in tandem in establishing threshold reliability. However, the threshold reliability standard always remains high to ensure that the combined approach does not lead to the admission of statements despite insufficient procedural safeguards and guarantees of inherent trustworthiness.

In considering substantive reliability, a trial judge can only rely on corroborative evidence if it shows, when considered as a whole and in the circumstances of the case, that the only likely explanation for the hearsay statement is the declarant's truthfulness about or the accuracy of the material aspects of the statements. The material aspects are those relied on by the moving party for the truth of their contents. The function of corroborative evidence at the threshold reliability stage is to mitigate the need for cross-examination not generally but on the point that the hearsay is tendered to prove. At the threshold reliability stage, corroborative evidence must work in conjunction with the circumstances to overcome the specific hearsay dangers raised by the tendered statement. Corroborative evidence must show that the material aspects of the statement are unlikely to change under cross-examination. In assessing substantial reliability, the trial judge must identify alternative, even speculative explanations for the hearsay statements. Corroborative evidence that is "equally consistent" with the truthfulness and accuracy of the statement as well as another hypothesis is of no assistance as it does not add to the statement's inherent trustworthiness. Accordingly, when considering corroborative evidence, the trial judge should: (1) identify the material aspects of the hearsay statement that are tendered for their truth; (2) identify the specific hearsay dangers raised by those aspects of the statement in the particular circumstances of the case; (3) based on the circumstances and these dangers, consider alternative, even speculative, explanations for the statement; and (4) determine whether, given the circumstances of the case, the corroborative evidence led at the *voir dire* rules out these alternative explanations such that the only remaining likely explanation is the declarant's truthfulness about or the accuracy of the material aspects of the statement.

It is on the basis of the evidence on the *voir dire* alone that the trial judge must look to determine the threshold issue of reliability, not the part of the trial preceding the *voir dire*. Counsel can, however, agree that certain trial evidence is to be taken into account on the *voir dire*: *R. v. Conway* (1997), 121 C.C.C. (3d) 397 (Ont. C.A.); *R. v. Szpala* (1998), 124 C.C.C. (3d) 430 (Ont. C.A.).

Concerns arise in relation to the admission under *K.G.B.* of facts acknowledged as "substantially correct" on a guilty plea. Where an accused has merely acknowledged the facts through counsel and has made a deal with the Crown to plead guilty and implicate others, reliability is suspect and admission of the facts against other accused persons on a *K.G.B.* application at a later trial should be refused in all but the most exceptional cases: *R. v. Tran* (2010), 257 C.C.C. (3d) 18 (Ont. C.A.).

In *R. v. Youvarajah*, [2013] 2 S.C.R. 720, 300 C.C.C. (3d) 1, the Supreme Court of Canada considered the admissibility of the witness's guilty plea Agreed Statement of Facts as a prior inconsistent statement. A prior inconsistent statement of a non-accused witness may be admitted for the truth of its contents if the following reliability indicia are met: (1) the statement is made under oath or solemn affirmation after a warning as to possible sanctions if the person is untruthful; (2) the statement is videotaped or recorded in its entirety; and (3) the opposing party has a full opportunity to cross-examine the witness on the statement. Threshold reliability may also be established by: (1) the presence of adequate substitutes for testing truth and accuracy (procedural reliability); and (2) sufficient circumstantial guarantees of reliability or an inherent trustworthiness (substantive reliability). In this case, the witness invoked solicitor-client privilege which curtailed significantly the cross-examination available to assess the threshold reliability of the prior inconsistent statement. The Crown could not have probed the conversations between the witness and his counsel about legal advice in connection with his decision to plead guilty or to accept the facts as set out in the ASF.

CROSS-EXAMINATION AS TO PREVIOUS STATEMENTS / Deposition of witness in criminal investigation.

10. (1) On any trial a witness may be cross-examined as to previous statements that the witness made in writing, or that have been reduced to writing, or recorded on audio tape or video tape or otherwise, relative to the subject-matter of the case, without the writing being shown to the witness or the witness being given the opportunity to listen to the audio tape or view the video tape or otherwise take cognizance of the statements, but, if it is intended to contradict the witness, the witness' attention must, before the contradictory proof can be given, be called to those parts of the statement that are to be used for the purpose of so contradicting the witness, and the judge, at any time during the trial, may require the production of the writing or tape or other medium for inspection, and thereupon make such use of it for the purposes of the trial as the judge thinks fit.

(2) A deposition of a witness, purporting to have been taken before a justice on the investigation of a criminal charge and to be signed by the witness and the justice, returned to and produced from the custody of the proper officer shall be presumed, in the absence of evidence to the contrary, to have been signed by the witness. R.S., c. E-10, s. 10; 1994, c. 44, s. 86.

ANNOTATIONS

Production of statements or notes – A preliminary inquiry is not a trial, so subsec. (1) is not applicable and the presiding judge does not have the power to order production for the defence of a Crown witness' previous written statement: *R. v. Patterson*, [1970] S.C.R. 409, 2 C.C.C. (2d) 227 (5:2).

Where the defence has obtained a statement from a witness and wishes to cross-examine on it, the defence may be required to produce it to the Crown prior to cross-examination: *R. v. Howe*, 2016 NSSC 328.

As to disclosure of statements, aside from this section, to defence, see notes under ss. 603 and 650 of the *Criminal Code*.

Meaning of previous statement in writing or reduced to writing – A report prepared by a police officer from notes of a conversation with the witness the contents of which the witness has never seen, read nor otherwise verified is not a statement within the meaning of this subsection: *R. v. Cherpak* (1978), 42 C.C.C. (2d) 166 (Alta. C.A.), leave to appeal to S.C.C. refused C.C.C. *loc. cit.*

A "will say" statement which was based on a transcript of the witness' videotaped statements was a statement reduced to writing within the meaning of s. 10 if the document was an accurate transcript of the things said by the witness during the interviews, whether or not the witness was involved in the actual preparation of the document: *R. v. Morgan* (1993), 80 C.C.C. (3d) 16 (Ont. C.A.), leave to appeal to S.C.C. refused 87 C.C.C. (3d) vi.

Where the witness has not previously signed or acknowledged the contents of the document, there must be a corresponding assurance of reliability from the circumstances demonstrating that the maker has attempted to record the words of the witness: *R. v. B. (S.)* (1996), 28 O.R. (3d) 409 (Gen. Div.).

Procedure – As this section makes clear, at least where it is not intended to contradict the witness by proof of the statement, there is no requirement that it be shown to the witness: *R. v. Valley* (1986), 26 C.C.C. (3d) 207, 3 O.A.C. 39 (C.A.).

The distinction between this section and s. 9 must be kept in mind. In particular, the trial judge has no right to determine whether the previous statement is inconsistent before permitting it to be put to the witness in cross-examination: *R. v. Cormier* (1973), 25 C.R.N.S. 94 (5:0) (Que. C.A.); *R. v. Savion and Mizrahi* (1980), 52 C.C.C. (2d) 276 (Ont. C.A.).

It was held in *R. v. Peebles* (1989), 49 C.C.C. (3d) 168 (B.C.C.A.), that the accused could not be cross-examined on statements made by his counsel in the course of a show cause hearing.

On a joint trial counsel for the co-accused may cross-examine another accused on a previous statement whether or not it is shown to be voluntary. The only limitation is that the trial judge has a very significant discretion to hold in balance fairness to the witness in his role as an accused and fairness to the accused whose counsel is cross-examining: *R. v. Ma, Ho and Lai* (1978), 44 C.C.C. (2d) 537 (B.C.C.A.).

Where one accused voluntarily enters the witness box and gives evidence which incriminates his co-accused, much as a Crown witness might have done, then justice requires that he be liable to impeachment by counsel for the co-accused on a previous inconsistent statement even if that statement was to a person in authority and was not proved voluntary. Such an accused is not entitled to the same rights he would have as an accused if the Crown were adducing the statement as part of its case or was seeking to cross-examine the accused on it: *R. v. Logan* (1988), 46 C.C.C. (3d) 354 (Ont. C.A.), affd on other grounds [1990] 2 S.C.R. 731.

Evidentiary value of statement [subsec. (1)] – A prior statement by a witness, even if sworn, is, if not adopted by the witness, not evidence of the truth of its contents but rather is only admissible with respect to the credibility of the witness. Further, the fact that the trial judge requires its production pursuant to this subsection and has it marked as an exhibit does not make the statement evidence of the truth of its contents: *R. v. Campbell* (1977), 38 C.C.C. (2d) 6, 1 C.R. (3d) 309, 17 O.R. (2d) 673 (C.A.).

It would be open to an adverse party to invoke the exception to the hearsay rule developed in *R. v. B. (K.G.),* [1993] 1 S.C.R. 740, 79 C.C.C. (3d) 257, noted above under s. 9. However, as with a statement introduced under s. 9, the party must comply with the procedure laid down in that case and, in particular, notify the court of the intention to rely on the reformed rule so that the trial judge can decide on a *voir dire* whether it is a proper case to leave the statement to the jury for its truth: *R. v. Beriault* (1997), 6 C.R. (5th) 382, [1997] R.J.Q. 1171 (C.A.). To a similar effect, see *R. v. Eisenhauer* (1998), 123 C.C.C. (3d) 37, 14 C.R. (5th) 35 (N.S.C.A.), leave to appeal to S.C.C. refused 126 C.C.C. (3d) vi, 230 N.R. 400*n*, where the court noted that in fact the reliability threshold may be somewhat relaxed where a party seeks to make substantive use of a prior inconsistent statement of the adversary's witness.

It is open to the trial judge to mark the written statement as an exhibit. Further, while counsel has the right to contradict the witness by the statement, the witness has the right to show that the writing generally, not merely those parts referred to by counsel, does not necessarily contradict his testimony. This may be done in re-examination or by reference to the writing generally: *R. v. Smith* (1983), 35 C.R. (3d) 86, 45 B.C.L.R. 286 (C.A.); *R. v. Newall* (1983), 9 C.C.C. (3d) 519, [1984] 2 W.W.R. 131 (B.C.C.A.).

A statement upon which a witness has been cross-examined under this section and re-examined is not evidence and should not be made an exhibit which goes to the jury room during the jury's deliberations: *R. v. Rowbotham* (1988), 41 C.C.C. (3d) 1, 63 C.R. (3d) 113 (Ont. C.A.).

As indicated by the decisions in *R. v. Smith, R. v. Newall* and *R. v. Rowbotham, supra*, there is a division of opinion as to the use to be made of a prior inconsistent written statement. In *R. v. Rodney* (1988), 46 C.C.C. (3d) 323, 33 B.C.L.R. (2d) 80 (C.A.), affd [1990] 2 S.C.R. 687, 58 C.C.C. (3d) 408, the court reaffirmed its view that in a proper case the trial judge may permit the statement to go to the jury as an exhibit. However, if the cross-examination has not been extensive the proper exercise of the discretion might lead the trial judge to permit none or only edited parts of the writing to be marked as an exhibit. To a similar effect, see: *R. v. Campbell* (1990), 57 C.C.C. (3d) 200, 106 A.R. 308 (C.A.).

CROSS-EXAMINATION AS TO PREVIOUS ORAL STATEMENTS.

11. Where a witness, on cross-examination as to a former statement made by him relative to the subject-matter of the case and inconsistent with his present testimony, does not distinctly admit that he did make the statement, proof may be given that he did in fact make it, but before that proof can be given the circumstances of the supposed statement, sufficient to designate the particular occasion, shall be mentioned to the witness, and he shall be asked whether or not he did make the statement. R.S., c. E-10, s. 11.

ANNOTATIONS

This section applies to proof of both oral and written prior inconsistent statements and applies where the prior inconsistent statement was allegedly made by the accused and the prosecution seeks to prove the statement in reply. Where counsel seeks to prove a prior inconsistent statement, counsel must during cross-examination, to the extent possible, advise the witness of the time and place where the statement was made. Counsel must advise the witness of the person involved in the prior statement and advise the witness of the substance of the statement. Finally, the witness must be asked if he or she made the statement. In a proper case, a trial judge would have the discretion to permit proof of the prior inconsistent statement notwithstanding that there has not been strict compliance with these prerequisites: *R. v. P. (G.)* (1996), 112 C.C.C. (3d) 263, 4 C.R. (5th) 36 (Ont. C.A.).

The predominant view seems to be that where the witness does not distinctly admit making the statement, the proof of the statement should be offered as part of the case of the party seeking to prove the statement: *R. v. Eisenhauer* (1998), 123 C.C.C. (3d) 37, 14 C.R. (5th) 35 (N.S.C.A.), leave to appeal to S.C.C. refused 126 C.C.C. (3d) vi, 230 N.R. 400*n*.

Where the Crown sought to re-open its case to adduce a prior inconsistent statement of a defence witness, the appropriate procedure was to allow the Crown to re-call the witness and lay the foundation for proof of the statement before any extrinsic evidence is adduced. In failing to do so, it was difficult for the jury to assess the impact of the prior inconsistent statement on the credibility of the witness in the absence of any direct evidence from the witness who allegedly made the statement. Failure to comply with s. 11, however, is not necessarily fatal. In this case, there was no prejudice resulting from this procedure as the defence called the witness and allowed her an opportunity to explain the prior inconsistent statement: *R. v. Sylvester* (1997), 114 C.C.C. (3d) 364, 97 O.A.C. 380 (C.A.).

Where at trial a hostile witness is confronted with previous inconsistent preliminary inquiry answers which she either refuses to acknowledge or denies the truth of, the jury must be instructed that those previous answers only are to be considered in assessing the credibility of her trial testimony and may not be accepted as being truthful unless she specifically accepts or adopts them as being true: *R. v. Hamelin* (1972), 10 C.C.C. (2d) 114 (B.C.C.A.).

It is essential that a jury be instructed that those discrepancies between a witness's previous statement and his evidence at trial may only be considered to assess the witness's credibility and not as evidence of the truth of the previous statement: *R. v. Blunden* (1976), 30 C.C.C. (2d) 122 (Ont. C.A.).

This section is confined to allowing the leading of evidence to rebut testimony shown to be inconsistent with a former statement made by the witness: *R. v. Krause* (1984), 12 C.C.C. (3d) 392 (B.C.C.A.), revd on other grounds [1986] 2 S.C.R. 466, 29 C.C.C. (3d) 385.

It was held in *R. v. Grant* (1989), 49 C.C.C. (3d) 410, 71 C.R. (3d) 231 (Man. C.A.), that counsel for the accused need not have complied with the provisions of this section in order to prove a statement by the complainant, in a sexual assault case, that she had agreed to accept and had accepted payment of money for a sexual act. This statement constituted an admission by a party and was admissible as such and not merely as a prior inconsistent statement. While not formally a party, the complainant is in the position of a party for the purposes of the admissions exception to the hearsay rule. It was therefore sufficient that counsel complied with the common law rule that requires before contradicting a witness that, in fairness, the witness be given notice of the allegation being made against her and an opportunity to explain herself.

If what the Crown witness said to another person is relevant then the jury ought to be allowed to hear the statement even if the procedure set out in this section was not followed. It would then be open to the judge to allow the Crown to call the witness in rebuttal: *R. v. Demerchant* (1991), 66 C.C.C. (3d) 49, 116 N.B.R. (2d) 247 (C.A.).

In *R. v. McNeill* (2000), 144 C.C.C. (3d) 551, 33 C.R. (5th) 390 (Ont. C.A.), the court considered the proper procedure where defence counsel has failed to cross-examine a witness on a matter upon which counsel intends to call contradictory evidence, in breach of the so-called rule in *Browne v. Dunn* (1893), 6 R. 67 (H.L.). Although the case was not dealt with as if there had been a breach of this section, the court's suggestions may be of some assistance in applying this section. Where the concern lies in a witness's inability to present his or her side of the story, the first option worth exploring is whether the witness is available for recall. If so, then assuming the trial judge is otherwise satisfied that recall is appropriate, the aggrieved party can either take up the opportunity or decline it. If the opportunity is declined, no special instruction to the jury is required beyond the normal instruction that the jury is entitled to believe all, part or none of a witness's evidence, regardless of whether the evidence is uncontradicted. The mechanics of when the witness should be recalled and by whom should be left to the discretion of the trial judge. Where it is impossible or highly impracticable to have the witness recalled or where the trial judge otherwise determines that recall is inappropriate, it should be left to the trial judge to decide whether a special instruction should be given to the jury. If one is warranted, the jury should be told that in assessing the weight to be given to the uncontradicted evidence, they may properly take into account the fact that the opposing witness was not questioned about it. The jury should also be told that they might take this into account in assessing the credibility of the opposing witness. Depending on the circumstances, there may be other permissible ways of rectifying the problem.

EXAMINATION AS TO PREVIOUS CONVICTION / Proof of previous convictions / How conviction proved.

12. (1) A witness may be questioned as to whether the witness has been convicted of any offence, excluding any offence designated as a contravention under the *Contraventions Act*, but including such an offence where the conviction was entered after a trial on an indictment.

(1.1) If the witness either denies the fact or refuses to answer, the opposite party may prove the conviction.

(2) A conviction may be proved by producing

(*a*) a certificate containing the substance and effect only, omitting the formal part, of the indictment and conviction, if it is for an indictable offence, or a copy of the summary conviction, if it is for an offence punishable on summary conviction, purporting to be signed by the clerk of the court or other officer

having the custody of the records of the court in which the conviction, if on indictment, was had, or to which the conviction, if summary, was returned; and

(*b*) **proof of identity. R.S., c. E-10, s. 12; 1992, c. 47, s. 66.**

ANNOTATIONS

Meaning of "conviction" and "any offence" [subsec. (1)] – A "conviction" includes sentence so that a cross-examination as to credibility on a previous conviction may include the penalty imposed: *R. v. Boyce* (1975), 23 C.C.C. (2d) 16 (Ont. C.A.); *R. v. Poitras* (2002), 1 C.R. (6th) 366 (Ont. C.A.).

It was held in *R. v. Sheik-Qasim* (2007), 230 C.C.C. (3d) 531 (Ont. S.C.J.), that, by reason of s. 82 of the *Youth Criminal Justice Act*, a witness may not be cross-examined on a youth record where, by operation of that section, the young person is deemed not to have been found guilty or convicted of an offence, in the absence of an order for disclosure of the record made by a youth court judge. In *R. v. Hammerstrom* (2018), 363 C.C.C. (3d) 430 (B.C.C.A.), the court agreed that cross-examination on a youth criminal record was impermissible without complying with the legislative provisions governing access to such records. *Contra*: *R. v. U. (D.A.)* (2008), 239 C.C.C. (3d) 409 (N.S.S.C.), holding that, properly interpreted, s. 82 of the *Youth Criminal Justice Act* expressly permits cross-examination under this section on a youth record. Further, at common law an accused was permitted to cross-examine a Crown witness on prior discreditable conduct and it should not matter that the conduct resulted in a conviction under the *Youth Criminal Justice Act*.

The words "any offence" may include conviction for offences outside of Canada. However, only the process of adjudication of guilt of a character which would constitute a conviction under Canadian law should be considered a conviction for impeachment purposes. The accused would be entitled to explain the circumstances surrounding the conviction and it may be that if the circumstances surrounding the "conviction" in another jurisdiction were so oppressive then the judge would be justified in ruling that the adjudication was not a conviction at all: *R. v. Stratton* (1978), 42 C.C.C. (2d) 449 (Ont. C.A.).

The term "any offence" in this section is wide enough to permit cross-examination on any offence under a federal statute and not merely offences which truly relate to the criminal law power of the federal government. Thus, the accused could be cross-examined on her previous convictions under the *Unemployment Insurance Act* (Can.): *R. v. Watkins* (1992), 70 C.C.C. (3d) 341 (Ont. C.A.).

Disciplinary proceedings do not constitute "convictions for offences" within the meaning of this section: *R. v. Stevely* (2001), 152 C.C.C. (3d) 538 (Sask. Q.B.).

Cross-examination of the accused on parole violations is not permitted by this section since parole violations are not convictions: *R. v. Latoski* (2005), 200 C.C.C. (3d) 361 (Ont. C.A.).

A witness may not be cross-examined under this section on a conditional or absolute discharge: *R. v. Conway* (1985), 17 C.C.C. (3d) 481 (Ont. C.A.); *R. v. Danson* (1982), 66 C.C.C. (2d) 369 (Ont. C.A.); *R. v. Sark* (2004), 182 C.C.C. (3d) 530 (N.B.C.A.).

A Crown witness may not be cross-examined by defence counsel on convictions for which a pardon has been granted: *R. v. Paterson* (1998), 122 C.C.C. (3d) 254 (B.C.C.A.), leave to appeal to S.C.C. refused 134 C.C.C. (3d) vi. Since *R. v. Paterson*, *supra*, s. 5 of the *Criminal Records Act*, which defines the effect of a pardon issued under that Act, has been amended. In light of those amendments, a Crown witness may be cross-examined on an offence for which the witness has received an administrative pardon from the National Parole Board under that Act: *R. v. Gyles*, [2003] O.J. No. 1924 (S.C.J.).

In *R. v. Hewson*, [1979] 2 S.C.R. 82, 42 C.C.C. (2d) 507 (5:4), the majority held that an accused's previous conviction was admissible under s. 360 of the *Criminal Code* although that conviction was then under appeal. There would seem to be no reason why the same principle should not apply where this section is invoked and in fact the minority dealt with the problem without apparently distinguishing between s. 360 and this section, the previous conviction having been elicited during cross-examination of the accused.

A non-accused witness may be cross-examined on the facts underlying a previous criminal conviction subject to the bounds of relevance and propriety: *R. v. Miller* (1998), 131 C.C.C. (3d) 141, 21 C.R. (5th) 178 (Ont. C.A.).

Cross-examination of accused on other misconduct – Subject to cross-examination on previous convictions as permitted by this section an accused may not be cross-examined upon past misconduct or discreditable associations for the purpose of attacking his credibility, unless such cross-examination is relevant to prove the falsity of his own evidence: *R. v. Davison, Derosie and MacArthur* (1974), 20 C.C.C. (2d) 424 (Ont. C.A.), leave to appeal to S.C.C. refused [1974] S.C.R. viii, C.C.C. *loc. cit.*

If an accused puts his or her character in issue during examination-in-chief, the scope of cross-examination on the criminal record permitted by s. 666 of the *Criminal Code* goes beyond that allowed under this section. Further, since the cross-examination under s. 666 is predicated on the accused having put his or her character in issue, the accused may also be questioned about the specifics underlying the criminal convictions: *R. v. W. (L.K.)* (1999), 138 C.C.C. (3d) 449 (Ont. C.A.), leave to appeal to S.C.C. refused 148 C.C.C. (3d) vi; *R. v. Deyardin* (1997), 119 C.C.C. (3d) 365 (Que. C.A.); *R. v. P. (N.A.)* (2002), 171 C.C.C. (3d) 70 (Ont. C.A.).

Procedure – A Crown witness may disclose his previous record during his examination-in-chief: *R. v. Boyko* (1975), 28 C.C.C. (2d) 193 (B.C.C.A.).

Similarly, defence counsel may lead the accused's criminal record during his examination-in-chief and whether the criminal record is brought out in direct or in cross-examination it goes only to the accused's credibility: *R. v. St. Pierre* (1974), 17 C.C.C. (2d) 489 (Ont. C.A.).

It is permissible to simply ask the witness a general question, as in this case, whether he has ever been convicted of an offence in the United States. There is no need to specify the prior conviction in the question: *R. v. Clark* (1977), 41 C.C.C. (2d) 561 (B.C.C.A.).

An application with respect to the admissibility of evidence concerning an accused's prior criminal record in accordance with *R. v. Corbett, infra*, should be made after the close of the Crown's case and dealt with at the time. If the trial judge believes it to be necessary, a *voir dire* may be held in which the defence discloses what evidence it intends to call, so that the judge can make an informed ruling on the application. This ruling may be subject to modification if the defence evidence departs significantly from what was disclosed. It was an error for the trial judge to refuse to make a ruling until after the accused elected to testify and had testified in-chief. Since, as a result of the trial judge's decision, the accused had not testified, a new trial was ordered: *R. v. Underwood,* [1998] 1 S.C.R. 77, 121 C.C.C. (3d) 117.

In the absence of a ruling that such evidence was admissible as similar fact evidence, it was improper for the Crown to cross-examine the accused in an attempt to elicit the details of the facts underlying the convictions: *R. v. Wells* (1998), 127 C.C.C. (3d) 403 (Nfld. C.A.).

Instructions to jury – The fact that a witness has been convicted of a crime is relevant to his trustworthiness as a witness, but the probative value that previous convictions have on the issue will vary not only with the type of convictions but the number and their proximity to the time when the witness gives evidence. A jury might well be justified in concluding that a conviction, even for a serious offence committed many years before was of little, if any, value in relation to credibility and the trial judge in the exercise of his discretion ought so to instruct the jury. However, it is serious misdirection to instruct the jury that the evidence of a defence witness, with a single prior conviction for a crime of dishonesty many years before, must be carefully scrutinized before it is accepted: *R. v. Brown* (1978), 38 C.C.C. (2d) 339 (Ont. C.A.).

It is misdirection to instruct the jury that "having a criminal record brands [the accused] as an unreliable person to give evidence under oath": *R. v. McIlvride* (1979), 10 C.R. (3d) 95,

[1979] 6 W.W.R. 93 (B.C.C.A.). Or, that the accused should be considered to have an unsavoury reputation: *R. v. Lavallee* (2001), 153 C.C.C. (3d) 120 (Sask. C.A.).

It constituted error for the trial judge to direct the jury that the accused's previous convictions for dishonesty were of little or no weight on the issue of the accused's credibility because the value of the goods stolen was less than $200: *R. v. Turlon* (1989), 49 C.C.C. (3d) 186 (Ont. C.A.).

The trial judge erred in charging the jury that because the co-accused were accomplices, had criminal records and a motive to lie, they were unsavoury witnesses and should not be relied upon absent independent evidence supporting their testimony. The accomplice rule does not apply to witnesses giving favourable evidence for the defence: *R. v. Lavallee, supra*.

Interpretation of provision – It was held in *R. v. Corbett*, [1988] 1 S.C.R. 670, 41 C.C.C. (3d) 385 (5:1), that this section does not violate the right to a fair trial as guaranteed by s. 11(*d*) of the Charter nor *semble* of the principles of fundamental justice under s. 7. However, a majority of the court also held that a trial judge does have a discretion to exclude evidence of previous convictions in an appropriate case where a mechanical application of this section would undermine the right to a fair trial. Factors to be considered in exercising this discretion would include the nature of the the conviction, its similarity to the offence with which the accused is presently on trial, the remoteness of the previous conviction and the nature of the defence including whether it consisted of a deliberate attack upon the credibility of Crown witnesses. With respect to this latter factor it will be of importance that exclusion of the accused's criminal record not create a serious imbalance. The court also summarized some of the rules which courts have laid down in respect to treatment of evidence of a prior criminal record as follows: The accused may only be cross-examined as to the fact of the conviction itself and not concerning the conduct which led to the conviction; the accused cannot be cross-examined as to whether he testified on the prior occasion; the Crown is not entitled to go beyond prior convictions to cross-examine an accused as to discreditable conduct or association with disreputable individuals to attack his credibility, and the accused can only be cross-examined on "convictions" strictly construed and not on discharges.

Discretion to exclude record – In determining whether or not to exercise the discretion to preclude the Crown from cross-examining an accused on his prior criminal record, the judge should consider a number of factors including the nature of the offence of which the accused has been convicted, its similarity to the offence charged, and its remoteness in time. A test which would preclude cross-examination on the record only as a "last resort" is too narrow. In this case, where the accused was charged with sexual assault, cross-examination on 15-year-old convictions for rape should not have been permitted. On the other hand, cross-examination on prior convictions for wounding would have been proper: *R. v. P. (G.F.)* (1994), 89 C.C.C. (3d) 176, 29 C.R. (4th) 35 (Ont. C.A.). Also see: *R. v. T. (D.B.)* (1994), 89 C.C.C. (3d) 466, 71 O.A.C. 233 (C.A.). Similarly, in *R. v. Trudel* (1994), 90 C.C.C. (3d) 318, 60 Q.A.C. 138 (C.A.), it was held that the Crown should not have been permitted to cross-examine the accused, who was charged with first degree murder, on a prior conviction for threatening death.

There is a distinction between an attack on the character of Crown witnesses initiated by the defence and attempts by the defence to meet the prosecution's evidence that incidentally impacts on character. If the cross-examination is merely directed to the latter, this would not be a basis for permitting cross-examination of the accused on his or her criminal record. Thus, in a prosecution for sexual assault, questioning the complainant's account and suggesting that the account was not true did not create the potential for the kind of imbalance discussed in *R. v. Corbett, supra*. Further, where the conviction, although recent, relates to events many years earlier, the conviction may have little relevance to credibility. Finally, it would be unusual circumstances that would require cross-examination of an accused on a conviction resulting from a previously severed trial: *R. v. Batte* (2000), 145 C.C.C. (3d) 498, 34 C.R. (5th) 263 (Ont. C.A.).

It is open to a trial judge to "sanitize" the accused's record by editing to limit its prejudicial effect. This may take the form of editing out certain convictions, but could include describing a conviction for a sexual assault as merely an assault: *R. v. Batte*, *supra*.

Although some of the accused's convictions were 16 years old, they were not too remote when it was apparent that his criminal conduct had been virtually continuous since his first conviction. However, on a trial for robbery, the trial judge should have edited the record to remove reference to most of the offences of violence. This approach would have left for the jury a record that demonstrated a continuing disregard for the law, a record containing offences of dishonesty, while at the same time not overwhelming the jury with similar offences to the one before them: *R. v. Madrusan* (2005), 203 C.C.C. (3d) 513, 35 C.R. (6th) 220 (B.C.C.A.).

In balancing the probative value and prejudicial effect of an accused's criminal record, the trial judge may consider the effectiveness of a warning as to the limited use of the evidence on the risk of prejudice. Generally, previous convictions for violent offences such as sexual assault do not directly reflect on honesty and truthfulness and depending on the circumstances of the case, have limited probative value in assessing credibility. However, such records have more than a trifling probative value in the context of a lengthy criminal record because a jury could reasonably conclude that the convictions reflect a disregard for the laws and rules of society, making it more likely that a person who harbours such attitudes would lie. In this case, on a trial of sexual assault, the last entries on the accused's lengthy criminal record included two sexual assault convictions. If the sexual assault convictions were excluded, it would leave the jury with the erroneous impression that the accused had lived a crime-free life for several years: *R. v. Charland* (1996), 110 C.C.C. (3d) 300, 2 C.R. (5th) 318 (Alta. C.A.), affd [1997] 3 S.C.R. 1006, 120 C.C.C. (3d) 481.

Although it is not an offence of dishonesty, which may be probative of deception, attempted murder is such a serious offence that, in itself, it may be taken to indicate that the prospect of a conviction for perjury is unlikely to keep the witness testifying truthfully. It would be open to a jury to find, on all the relevant evidence, that the witness is unlikely to have more respect for the truth than he has shown for human life: *R. v. Saroya* (1994), 36 C.R. (4th) 253, 76 O.A.C. 25 (C.A.). However, on a trial for crimes of violence, cross-examination on such a conviction poses a real risk that the jury could improperly infer guilt either by reasoning that the prior conviction showed the accused to be a bad person who was prone to criminal conduct or by reasoning that the prior conviction for attempted murder was proof that that accused committed the offences charged. In this case, the trial judge did not err in refusing to allow the cross-examination: *R. v. P. (N.A.)* (2002), 171 C.C.C. (3d) 70, 167 O.A.C. 176 (C.A.).

The trial judge having held that cross-examination on parts of the record would be permitted should have allowed defence counsel to introduce the particulars of the convictions that were ruled admissible during examination-in-chief. Once the trial judge ruled that certain convictions were sufficiently probative to warrant their admissibility, it was up to counsel to decide whether to elicit that evidence during examination-in-chief: *R. v. Poitras* (2002), 1 C.R. (6th) 366, 57 O.R. (3d) 538 (C.A.).

An attack on the character of a Crown witness, whether it was through a prior record or as in this case, through vigorous cross-examination designed to establish that the complainant's allegation was false, is a factor to be considered in determining whether to exclude or edit the accused's criminal record: *R. v. Madrusan*, *supra*; *R. v. Laing* (2016), 33 C.R. (7th) 48 (Ont. C.A.).

However, where the defence puts forward a witness with the intention that the jury accept the witness's evidence that he, not the accused, owned the contraband, this is not a basis to permit the Crown to cross-examine the accused on his entire criminal record: *R. v. McManus* (2017), 353 C.C.C. (3d) 493 (Ont. C.A.).

In *R. v. Tremblay* (2006), 209 C.C.C. (3d) 212 (Que. C.A.), the court held that persistent contempt for the law is relevant in assessing a witness's credibility, as it may be inferred that an individual who repeatedly breaks the law has little respect for the truth and is therefore more likely to lie.

Proof of prior conviction – Where the accused is a witness and in cross-examination cannot recall a particular conviction the proper procedure is to prove the conviction pursuant to subsec. (2) rather than embark on a prejudicial line of cross-examination to "refresh" the memory of the accused, for example, by putting to the accused the name of the victim of the offence for which he was allegedly convicted: *R. v. Howard* (1983), 3 C.C.C. (3d) 399 (Ont. C.A.).

Oaths and Solemn Affirmations

WHO MAY ADMINISTER OATHS.

13. Every court and judge, and every person having, by law or consent of parties, authority to hear and receive evidence, has power to administer an oath to every witness who is legally called to give evidence before that court, judge or person. R.S., c. E-10, s. 13.

SOLEMN AFFIRMATION BY WITNESS INSTEAD OF OATH / Effect.

14. (1) A person may, instead of taking an oath, make the following solemn affirmation:

> **I solemnly affirm that the evidence to be given by me shall be the truth, the whole truth and nothing but the truth.**

(2) Where a person makes a solemn affirmation in accordance with subsection (1), his evidence shall be taken and have the same effect as if taken under oath. R.S., c. E-10, s. 14; 1994, c. 44, s. 87.

ANNOTATIONS

Where an objection is taken to the competency of a witness, not just to take an oath, but to give evidence, the trial judge must allow the party objecting an opportunity to call evidence on that issue and then if he dismisses that objection he must by his examination of the witness and such other evidence that he deems appropriate decide whether the witness should be sworn or affirmed: *R. v. Hawke* (1975), 22 C.C.C. (2d) 19 (Ont. C.A.).

In *R. v. Walsh* (1978), 45 C.C.C. (2d) 199 (Ont. C.A.), the court held that the trial judge erred in refusing to permit a "satanist" to affirm. While he was incompetent to take the oath because it would not bind his conscience due to absence of religious belief this did not render him incompetent to affirm. Moral depravity or a disposition to lie does not render a witness incompetent to testify.

A witness who objects to swearing an oath on the Bible may be given the opportunity to swear another form of religious oath and is not required to affirm: *R. v. Kalevar* (1991), 4 C.R. (4th) 114 (Ont. Ct. (Gen. Div.)).

It was held, considering the comparable provisions of the *Manitoba Evidence Act*, C.C.S.M., c. E150, that requiring a witness to choose between affirming or taking an oath does not violate freedom of religion under s. 2(*a*) or the right to equality under s. 15 of the *Charter of Rights and Freedoms*: *R. v. Robinson* (2005), 198 C.C.C. (3d) 105 (Man. C.A.).

An oath or affirmation are equivalent. It is an error of law to consider evidence of a witness's religious beliefs in assessing his or her credibility. While there are some very limited circumstances in which inquiry into the degree to which an oath or affirmation binds a witness's conscience is permissible, these are restricted to circumstances in which there is a reason to believe that the witness's oath or affirmation is not genuine. Such an inquiry is primarily a question of testimonial competence as opposed to credibility: *R. v. Santhosh* (2016), 342 C.C.C. (3d) 41 (Ont. C.A.). See also *R. v. J. (T.R.)* (2013), 6 C.R. (7th) 207 (B.C.C.A.).

SOLEMN AFFIRMATION BY DEPONENT / Effect.

15. (1) Where a person who is required or who desires to make an affidavit or deposition in a proceeding or on an occasion on which or concerning a matter respecting which an oath is required or is lawful, whether on the taking of office or otherwise, does not wish to take an oath, the court or judge, or other officer or person qualified to take affidavits or depositions, shall permit the person to make a solemn afirmation in the words following, namely, "I, ..., do solemnly affirm, etc.", and that solemn affirmation has the same force and effect as if that person had taken an oath.

(2) Any witness whose evidence is admitted or who makes a solemn affirmation under this section or section 14 is liable to indictment and punishment for perjury in all respects as if he had been sworn. R.S., c. E-10, s. 15; 1994, c. 44, s. 88.

WITNESS WHOSE CAPACITY IS IN QUESTION / Testimony under oath or solemn affirmation / Testimony on promise to tell truth / No questions regarding understanding of promise / Inability to testify / Burden as to capacity of witness.

16. (1) If a proposed witness is a person of fourteen years of age or older whose mental capacity is challenged, the court shall, before permitting the person to give evidence, conduct an inquiry to determine

(*a*) whether the person understands the nature of an oath or a solemn affirmation; and

(*b*) whether the person is able to communicate the evidence.

(2) A person referred to in subsection (1) who understands the nature of an oath or a solemn affirmation and is able to communicate the evidence shall testify under oath or solemn affirmation.

(3) A person referred to in subsection (1) who does not understand the nature of an oath or a solemn affirmation but is able to communicate the evidence may, notwithstanding any provision of any Act requiring an oath or solemn affirmation, testify on promising to tell the truth.

(3.1) A person referred to in subsection (3) shall not be asked any questions regarding their understanding of the nature of the promise to tell the truth for the purpose of determining whether their evidence shall be received by the court.

(4) A person referred to in subsection (1) who neither understands the nature of an oath or a solemn affirmation nor is able to communicate the evidence shall not testify.

(5) A party who challenges the mental capacity of a proposed witness of fourteen years of age or more has the burden of satisfying the court that there is an issue as to the capacity of the proposed witness to testify under an oath or a solemn affirmation. R.S., c. E-10, s. 16; R.S.C. 1985, c. 19 (3rd Supp.), s. 18; 1994, c. 44, s. 89; 2005, c. 32, s. 26; 2015, c. 13, s. 53.

ANNOTATIONS

Editor's Note: Some of the following cases were decided under the predecessor to this section but were thought to be of assistance in applying this section.

In applying subsec. (3), the following principles are relevant: (1) the *voir dire* on the competence of a proposed witness is an independent inquiry: it may not be combined with a *voir dire* on other issues, such as the admissibility of the proposed witness's out-of-court statements; (2) although the *voir dire* should be brief, it is preferable to hear all available relevant evidence that can be reasonably considered before preventing a witness from testifying. A witness should not be found incompetent too hastily; (3) the primary source of evidence for a witness's competence is the witness herself. Her examination should be permitted. Questioning an adult with mental disabilities requires consideration and accommodation for her particular needs; questions should be phrased patiently in a clear, simple manner; (4) expert evidence may be adduced if it meets the criteria for admissibility, but preference should always be given to expert witnesses who have had personal and regular contact with the proposed witness; (6) the trial judge must make two inquiries during the *voir dire* on competence: (a) does the proposed witness understand the nature of an oath or affirmation; and (b) can she communicate the evidence? (7) the second inquiry into the witness's ability to communicate the evidence requires the trial judge to explore in a general way whether she can relate concrete events by understanding and responding to questions. It may be useful to ask if she can differentiate between true and false everyday factual statements; (8) the witness testifies under oath or affirmation if she passes both parts of the test and on promising to tell the truth if she passes the second part only: *R. v. I. (D.)*, [2012] 1 S.C.R. 149, 280 C.C.C. (3d) 127.

In the case of an adult whose competence is challenged, the inquiry is not limited to the witness's capacity to communicate at the time of trial but requires inquiry into whether the witness had the capacity to observe what was happening, the capacity to recollect what was observed and the capacity to communicate what he or she remembers. The inquiry is, however, limited to capacity, not whether the witness actually perceived, recollects and can communicate about the events in question and, generally speaking, the best gauge of capacity is the witness's performance at the time of trial: *R. v. Marquard*, [1993] 4 S.C.R. 223, 85 C.C.C. (3d) 193.

The capacity to communicate the evidence means something more than simply the ability to speak and requires proof that the witness has the capacity to relate the contentious parts of her evidence with some independence and not entirely in response to suggestive questions. The witness must be able to relate to the court the essence of what happened to her: *R. v. Caron* (1994), 94 C.C.C. (3d) 466 (Ont. C.A.).

The ability to communicate evidence should not be the subject-matter of expert evidence. The trial judge should form his or her opinion based on direct observations of the witness, unless there were exceptional circumstances, such as evidence that the complainant would be traumatized by an appearance in court even for this limited purpose: *R. v. Parrott*, [2001] 1 S.C.R. 178, 150 C.C.C. (3d) 449.

The testimonial competence of the accused, as contemplated at common law and pursuant to this section is not a condition precedent to the accused being declared fit to stand trial: *R. v. Morrissey* (2007), 227 C.C.C. (3d) 1, 54 C.R. (6th) 313 (Ont. C.A.), leave to appeal to S.C.C. refused 231 C.C.C. (3d) vi.

PERSON UNDER FOURTEEN YEARS OF AGE / No oath or solemn affirmation / Evidence shall be received / Burden as to capacity of witness / Court inquiry / Promise to tell truth / Understanding of promise / Effect.

16.1 (1) A person under fourteen years of age is presumed to have the capacity to testify.

(2) A proposed witness under fourteen years of age shall not take an oath or make a solemn affirmation despite a provision of any Act that requires an oath or a solemn affirmation.

(3) The evidence of a proposed witness under fourteen years of age shall be received if they are able to understand and respond to questions.

(4) A party who challenges the capacity of a proposed witness under fourteen years of age has the burden of satisfying the court that there is an issue as to the capacity of the proposed witness to understand and respond to questions.

(5) If the court is satisfied that there is an issue as to the capacity of a proposed witness under fourteen years of age to understand and respond to questions, it shall, before permitting them to give evidence, conduct an inquiry to determine whether they are able to understand and respond to questions.

(6) The court shall, before permitting a proposed witness under fourteen years of age to give evidence, require them to promise to tell the truth.

(7) No proposed witness under fourteen years of age shall be asked any questions regarding their understanding of the nature of the promise to tell the truth for the purpose of determining whether their evidence shall be received by the court.

(8) For greater certainty, if the evidence of a witness under fourteen years of age is received by the court, it shall have the same effect as if it were taken under oath. 2005, c. 32, s. 27.

ANNOTATIONS

Editor's Note: Some of the following cases were decided under the predecessor to this section but were thought to be of assistance in applying this section.

General – The amendments to the predecessor to this section removing the requirement for corroboration of the unsworn testimony of a child operate retrospectively. Accordingly, no corroboration is required although the offence occurred prior to January 1, 1988, when the corroboration requirement was removed: *R. v. Inkster* (1988), 69 Sask. R. 1 (Q.B.); *R. v. Jack* (1989), 51 C.C.C. (3d) 255, 92 N.S.R. (2d) 177 (S.C.A.D.); *R. v. Bickford* (1989), 51 C.C.C. (3d) 181, 34 O.A.C. 34 (C.A.). Also see *Criminal Code*, s. 659.

It was held in *R. v. Ferguson* (1996), 112 C.C.C. (3d) 342 (B.C.C.A.), that there may be much to recommend conducting the inquiry in the jury's presence. The evidence given by a prospective child witness on the inquiry may very well assist the jury in weighing the child's evidence on the substance of the complaint if she is subsequently found competent to testify. However, the inquiry need not be conducted in the presence of the jury and, in some circumstances, the possibility of prejudice to an accused if the child were found to be incompetent to testify is a relevant factor in making this determination.

In the case of a child witness whose competence is challenged, the inquiry is not limited to the witness's capacity to communicate at the time of trial but requires inquiry into whether the witness had the capacity to observe what was happening, the capacity to recollect what was observed and the capacity to communicate what he or she remembers. The inquiry is, however, limited to capacity, not whether the witness actually perceived, recollects and can communicate about the events in question and, generally speaking, the best gauge of capacity is the witness's performance at the time of trial: *R. v. Marquard*, [1993] 4 S.C.R. 223, 85 C.C.C. (3d) 193.

The capacity to communicate the evidence means something more than simply the ability to speak and requires proof that the witness has the capacity to relate the contentious parts of her evidence with some independence and not entirely in response to suggestive questions. The witness must be able to relate to the court the essence of what happened to her: *R. v. Caron* (1994), 94 C.C.C. (3d) 466, 19 O.R. (3d) 323 (C.A.).

Although the child had been permitted to testify, the judge was required to warn the jury as to the risks of accepting the child's evidence in view of her young age (three and one-half years old at the time of the incident), that she was unable to give much detail about the incident and had told a different story at an earlier time. There is, however, no fixed and precise formula to be followed in warning the jury: *R. v. Marquard*, *supra*.

The ability to communicate evidence should not be the subject-matter of expert evidence. The trial judge should form his or her opinion based on direct observations of the witness, unless there were exceptional circumstances, such as evidence that the complainant would be traumatized by an appearance in court even for this limited purpose: *R. v. Parrott*, [2001] 1 S.C.R. 178, 150 C.C.C. (3d) 449.

The ability to communicate is to be assessed on the basis of age-appropriate questions on matters about which the child might be familiar. Where the child is not responding to the judge's questions, the judge, following submissions from counsel, in a proper case may invite counsel who called the witness to take part in the questioning: *R. v. F. (R.G.)*, [1997] 6 W.W.R. 273 *sub nom. R. v. F. (R.G.)*, 200 A.R. 8 (C.A.), leave to appeal to S.C.C. refused 219 A.R. 104*n*, 228 N.R. 194*n*.

It was held, considering the predecessor to this section, that a promise to tell the truth is a prerequisite to receiving the unsworn testimony of a child witness and where the promise was not obtained, the evidence of the child was wrongly admitted and the accused's conviction must be quashed: *R. v. S. (J.J.)* (1991), 104 N.S.R. (2d) 385 (S.C.A.D.). However, where, in the course of the examination of the child, it was clear that the child understood the duty to tell the truth and undertook to tell the truth, the failure to obtain an explicit promise to tell the truth did not invalidate the conviction: *R. v. Barsoum* (1991), 13 W.C.B. (2d) 382 (N.W.T.C.A.). See also *R. v. Peterson* (1996), 106 C.C.C. (3d) 64, 47 C.R. (4th) 161 (Ont. C.A.), leave to appeal to S.C.C. refused 109 C.C.C. (3d) vi, 96 O.A.C. 79*n*.

No particular words are required to comply with subsec. (6) as long as the witness has clearly committed to tell the truth: *R. v. F. (C.C.)* (2014), 113 W.C.B. (2d) 237, [2014] O.J. No. 1972 (C.A.).

Constitutional considerations – This section and, in particular, the presumption of competency and thus the presumption prohibiting a pre-testimonial inquiry and inquiry into the moral obligation to tell the truth, does not violate ss. 7 and 11(*d*) of the *Charter of Rights and Freedoms*: *R. v. S. (J.)* (2010), 251 C.C.C. (3d) 1 (S.C.C.).

Judicial Notice

IMPERIAL ACTS, ETC.

17. Judicial notice shall be taken of all Acts of the Imperial Parliament, of all ordinances made by the Governor in Council, or the lieutenant governor in council of any province or colony that, or some portion of which, now forms or hereafter may form part of Canada, and of all the Acts of the legislature of any such province or colony, whether enacted before or after the passing of the *Constitution Act, 1867*. R.S., c. E-10, s. 17.

ANNOTATIONS

In *R. v. Markin*, [1970] 1 C.C.C. 14, 7 C.R.N.S. 135 (B.C.C.A.), it was held (2:1) that "ordinances" do not include a proclamation of the Lieutenant Governor of British Columbia.

An Order in Council amending Schedule J to the *Food and Drugs Act* is an ordinance within this section: *R. v. Whalen* (1971), 4 C.C.C. (2d) 560, 15 C.R.N.S. 187 (N.B.S.C. App. Div.).

ACTS OF CANADA.

18. Judicial notice shall be taken of all Acts of Parliament, public or private, without being specially pleaded. R.S., c. E-10, s. 18.

Documentary Evidence

COPIES BY QUEEN'S PRINTER.

19. Every copy of any Act of Parliament, public or private, published by the Queen's Printer, is evidence of that Act and of its contents, and every copy purporting to be published by the Queen's Printer shall be deemed to be so published, unless the contrary is shown. R.S., c. E-10, s. 19; 2000, c. 5, s. 52.

ANNOTATIONS

Where there is a discrepancy between an Act of Parliament as certified by the Clerk of Parliament and the version as printed by the Queen's Printer, the former must govern: *R. v. Welsh (No. 6)* (1977), 32 C.C.C. (2d) 363, 74 D.L.R. (3d) 748 (Ont. C.A.).

IMPERIAL PROCLAMATIONS, ETC.

20. Imperial proclamations, orders in council, treaties, orders, warrants, licences, certificates, rules, regulations, or other Imperial official records, Acts or documents may be proved

- **(*a*) in the same manner as they may from time to time be provable in any court in England;**
- **(*b*) by the production of a copy of the *Canada Gazette*, or a volume of the Acts of Parliament purporting to contain a copy of the same or a notice thereof; or**
- **(*c*) by the production of a copy of them purporting to be published by the Queen's Printer. R.S., c. E-10, s. 20; 2000, c. 5, s. 53.**

PROCLAMATIONS, ETC. OF GOVERNOR GENERAL.

21. Evidence of any proclamation, order, regulation or appointment, made or issued by the Governor General or by the Governor in Council, or by or under the authority of any minister or head of any department of the Government of Canada and evidence of a treaty to which Canada is a party, may be given in all or any of the following ways:

- **(*a*) by the production of a copy of the *Canada Gazette*, or a volume of the Acts of Parliament purporting to contain a copy of the treaty, proclamation, order, regulation or appointment, or a notice thereof;**
- **(*b*) by the production of a copy of the proclamation, order, regulation or appointment, purporting to be published by the Queen's Printer;**
- **(*c*) by the production of a copy of the treaty purporting to be published by the Queen's Printer;**
- **(*d*) by the production, in the case of any proclamation, order, regulation or appointment made or issued by the Governor General or by the Governor in Council, of a copy or extract purporting to be certified to be true by the clerk or assistant or acting clerk of the Queen's Privy Council for Canada; and**
- **(*e*) by the production, in the case of any order, regulation or appointment made or issued by or under the authority of any minister or head of a department of the Government of Canada, of a copy or extract purporting to be certified to be true by the minister, by his deputy or acting deputy, or by the secretary or acting secretary of the department over which he presides. R.S., c. E-10, s. 21; 1976-77, c. 28, s. 14; 2000, c. 5, s. 54.**

ANNOTATIONS

By s. 23 of the *Statutory Instruments Act*, 1970-71-72 (Can.), c. 38, Parliament intended to obviate the necessity of a court requiring formal proof of the publication and text of statutory instruments published in the *Canada Gazette*: *R. v. "Evgenia Chandris" (The)*, [1977] 2 S.C.R. 97, 27 C.C.C. (2d) 241 (9:0).

Thus, while this section provides a means of proving a regulation, there is no need to do so where the regulation has been published in the *Canada Gazette*. Pursuant to the *Statutory Instruments Act*, judicial notice must be taken of such a regulation: *R. v. Phinney* (1998), 173 N.S.R. (2d) 312, 527 A.P.R. 312 (S.C.).

PROCLAMATIONS, ETC., OF LIEUTENANT GOVERNOR / Territories.

22. (1) Evidence of any proclamation, order, regulation or appointment made or issued by a lieutenant governor or lieutenant governor in council of any province, or by or under the authority of any member of the executive council, being the head of any department of the government of the province, may be given in all or any of the following ways:

- **(*a*) by the production of a copy of the official gazette for the province purporting to contain a copy of the proclamation, order, regulation or appointment, or a notice thereof;**

(*b*) by the production of a copy of the proclamation, order, regulation or appointment purporting to be published by the government or Queen's Printer for the province; and

(*c*) by the production of a copy or extract of the proclamation, order, regulation or appointment, purporting to be certified to be true by the clerk or assistant or acting clerk of the executive council, by the head of any department of the government of a province, or by his deputy or acting deputy, as the case may be.

(2) Evidence of any proclamation, order, regulation or appointment made by the Lieutenant Governor or Lieutenant Governor in Council of the Northwest Territories, as constituted prior to September 1, 1905, or by the Legislature of Yukon, of the Northwest Territories or for Nunavut, may be given by the production of a copy of the *Canada Gazette* purporting to contain a copy of the proclamation, order, regulation or appointment, or a notice of it. R.S., c. E-10, s. 22; 1993, c. 28, Sch. III, s. 8; 2000, c. 5, s. 55; 2002, c. 7, s. 96; 2014, c. 2, s. 5.

EVIDENCE OF JUDICIAL PROCEEDINGS, ETC. / Certificate where court has no seal.

23. (1) Evidence of any proceeding or record whatever of, in or before any court in Great Britain, the Supreme Court, the Federal Court of Appeal, the Federal Court or the Tax Court of Canada, any court in a province, any court in a British colony or possession or any court of record of the United States, of a state of the United States or of any other foreign country, or before any justice of the peace or coroner in a province, may be given in any action or proceeding by an exemplification or certified copy of the proceeding or record, purporting to be under the seal of the court or under the hand or seal of the justice, coroner or court stenographer, as the case may be, without any proof of the authenticity of the seal or of the signature of the justice, coroner or court stenographer or other proof whatever.

(2) Where any court, justice or coroner or court stenographer referred to in subsection (1) has no seal, or so certifies, the evidence may be given by a copy purporting to be certified under the signature of a judge or presiding provincial court judge or of the justice or coroner or court stenographer, without any proof of the authenticity of the signature or other proof whatever. R.S., c. E-10, s. 23; 1997, c. 18, s. 117; 2002, c. 8, s. 118.

ANNOTATIONS

This provision is a procedural mechanism whereby evidence of the court proceeding or record may be proved, without having to provide proof of the authenticity of the document by calling the court officer or stenographer who made the record. It does not render the hearsay content of court proceedings or records admissible for the truth of their contents where they would not otherwise be admissible for that purpose in the circumstances. There may be circumstances where transcripts of a court proceeding may be admissible for the truth of their contents, but they will not be admissible for that purpose unless it was the recorder's duty to validate the truth of their contents or unless they are otherwise admissible under the principled exception to the hearsay rule and the prejudice of their admission does not outweigh their probative value: *R. v. Caesar* (2016), 339 C.C.C. (3d) 354 (Ont. C.A.).

A judge who grants an authorization to intercept private communications does so as a judge of the court not as a *persona designata* and a certified copy of the authorization is therefore admissible under this section: *R. v. Cordes*, [1979] 1 S.C.R. 1062, 47 C.C.C. (2d) 46 (7:0).

On the trial of a charge of being an accessory after the fact, a certified copy of the indictment endorsed by the trial judge and indicating that the principal offender had been convicted was admissible under this section to prove the conviction of the principal offender: *R. v. Duong* (1998), 124 C.C.C. (3d) 392, 15 C.R. (5th) 209 (Ont. C.A.).

This section is not the exclusive means by which court documents may be admitted into evidence. Thus, if its requirements are met resort may be had to s. 24 of this Act for admission of copies of court documents: *R. v. P. (A.)* (1992), 75 C.C.C. (3d) 178 (Ont. Ct. (Gen. Div.)), affd 109 C.C.C. (3d) 385, 1 C.R. (5th) 327 (Ont. C.A.).

In addition, this provision co-exists with the common law rule that judicial documents must be provided by the production of the original record or an exemplification under the seal of the court to which the record belongs. The common law rule does not require any notice be given: *R. v. Tatomir* (1989), 51 C.C.C. (3d) 321 (Alta. C.A.), leave to appeal to S.C.C. refused (1990), 53 C.C.C. (3d) vii. See also *R. v. C. (W.B.)* (2000), 142 C.C.C. (3d) 490 (Ont. C.A.), affirmed [2001] 1 S.C.R. 530, 153 C.C.C. (3d) 575.

Although the transcript of the accused's guilty plea on a prior offence was not admissible under this section, for failure to comply with the notice provisions in s. 28, it was open to the court to admit the transcript under the common law exception for records of a judicial proceeding, provided the document is authentic and the criteria for that exception were met: (i) the document must have been made by a public official, that is a person on whom a duty has been imposed by the public; (ii) the public official must have made the document in the discharge of a public duty or function; (iii) the document must have been made with the intention that it serve as a permanent record; and (iv) the document must be available for public inspection (there is some doubt whether this fourth criterion is still required): *R. v. C. (W.B.)* (2000), 142 C.C.C. (3d) 490, 130 O.A.C. 1 (C.A.), affd [2001] 1 S.C.R. 530, 153 C.C.C. (3d) 575.

Also see *R. v. Truong* (2008), 235 C.C.C. (3d) 547 (B.C.S.C.), holding that documents contained in the court's own files may be admissible pursuant to the common law exception to the hearsay rule upon production of the original document or an exemplification under the seal of the court to which the record belongs.

Affidavits from public officials in a separate proceeding do not fall under the public documents exception: *Henco Industries Ltd. v. R.* (2014), 2014 D.T.C. 1161 (Eng.) (T.C.C. [General Procedure]), additional reasons (2014), 2014 D.T.C. 1205 (Eng.) (T.C.C. [General Procedure]).

CERTIFIED COPIES.

24. In every case in which the original record could be admitted in evidence,

(*a*) a copy of any official or public document of Canada or of any province, purporting to be certified under the hand of the proper officer or person in whose custody the official or public document is placed, or

(*b*) a copy of a document, by-law, rule, regulation or proceeding, or a copy of any entry in any register or other book of any municipal or other corporation, created by charter or Act of Parliament or the legislature of any province, purporting to be certified under the seal of the corporation, and the hand of the presiding officer, clerk or secretary thereof,

is admissible in evidence without proof of the seal of the corporation, or of the signature or official character of the person or persons appearing to have signed it, and without further proof thereof. R.S., c. E-10, s. 24.

ANNOTATIONS

A certificate of incorporation of a provincial company is a public document admissible under this section. To determine whether the document was properly certified resort must be had to the relevant provincial legislation by virtue of s. 40 of this Act: *R. v. John and Murray Motors Ltd.* (1979), 47 C.C.C. (2d) 49 (B.C.C.A.).

Aeronautical charts prepared by a department of the Government of Canada which are in regular and everyday use for navigation purposes and are relied upon implicitly by qualified pilots and which are presumably the best evidence available of distances and directions by air are admissible in evidence, although not certified in the manner provided by this section or s.

25; *R. v. Inuvik Coastal Airways Ltd. and McKerral* (1983), 10 C.C.C. (3d) 89, 51 A.R. 353 (N.W.T.S.C.).

While s. 23 makes specific provision for the admission of court documents, copies of court documents may be admissible under para. (*a*) of this section if the original would have been admissible at common law as a public document. The traditional common law requirements for admission of a public document are: (1) the document must have been made by a public official being a person on whom a duty has been imposed by the public; (2) the public official must have made the document in the discharge of a public duty or function; (3) the document must have been made with the intention that it serve as a permanent record; and (4) the document must be available for public inspection [there is some dispute as to whether this last criterion is still required]. The original information and probation order made in proceedings under the [former] *Young Offenders Act*, R.S.C. 1985, c. Y-1, meet all four requirements. In particular, the statutorily controlled access provided for in s. 44.1 of the Act satisfies the fourth requirement. Accordingly, certified copies of these records were admissible at the offenders trial for breach of probation: *R. v. P. (A.)* (1992), 75 C.C.C. (3d) 178 (Ont. Ct. (Gen. Div.)), affd 109 C.C.C. (3d) 385, 1 C.R. (5th) 327 (Ont. C.A.).

BOOKS AND DOCUMENTS.

25. Where a book or other document is of so public a nature as to be admissible in evidence on its mere production from the proper custody, and no other Act exists that renders its contents provable by means of a copy, a copy thereof or extract therefrom is admissible in evidence in any court of justice or before a person having, by law or by consent of parties, authority to hear, receive and examine evidence, if it is proved that it is a copy or extract purporting to be certified to be true by the officer to whose custody the original has been entrusted. R.S., c. E-10, s. 25.

BOOKS KEPT IN OFFICES UNDER GOVERNMENT OF CANADA / Proof of non-issue of licence or document / Proof of mailing departmental matter / Proof of official character.

26. (1) A copy of any entry in any book kept in any office or department of the Government of Canada, or in any commission, board or other branch in the federal public administration, shall be admitted as evidence of that entry, and of the matters, transactions and accounts therein recorded, if it is proved by the oath or affidavit of an officer of the office or department, commission, board or other branch in the federal public administration that the book was, at the time of the making of the entry, one of the ordinary books kept in the office, department, commission, board or other branch in the federal public administration, that the entry was made in the usual and ordinary course of business of the office, department, commission, board or other branch in the federal public administration and that the copy is a true copy thereof.

(2) Where by any Act of Parliament or regulation made under an Act of Parliament provision is made for the issue by a department, commission, board or other branch in the federal public administration of a licence requisite to the doing or having of any act or thing or for the issue of any other document, an affidavit of an officer of the department, commission, board or other branch in the federal public administration, sworn before any commissioner or other person authorized to take affidavits, setting out that he or she has charge of the appropriate records and that after careful examination and search of those records he or she has been unable to find in any given case that any such licence or other document has been issued, shall be admitted in evidence as proof, in the absence of evidence to the contrary, that in that case no licence or other document has been issued.

(3) Where by any Act of Parliament or regulation made under an Act of Parliament provision is made for sending by mail any request for information, notice or demand by a department or other branch in the federal public administration, an affidavit of an

officer of the department or other branch in the federal public administration, sworn before any commissioner or other person authorized to take affidavits, setting out that he or she has charge of the appropriate records, that he or she has a knowledge of the facts in the particular case, that the request, notice or demand was sent by registered letter on a named date to the person or firm to whom it was addressed (indicating that address) and that he or she identifies as exhibits attached to the affidavit the post office certificate of registration of the letter and a true copy of the request, notice or demand, shall, on production and proof of the post office receipt for the delivery of the registered letter to the addressee, be admitted in evidence as proof, in the absence of evidence to the contrary, of the sending and of the request, notice or demand.

(4) Where proof is offered by affidavit pursuant to this section, it is not necessary to prove the official character of the person making the affidavit if that information is set out in the body of the affidavit. R.S., c. E-10, s. 26; 2003, c. 22, s. 104.

ANNOTATIONS

Information gathered in the course of a special commission, the Self-Defence Review, conducted for the federal government and the conclusions of the commission, are not admissible under this section. Information such as interviews and videotapes could not be said to have been made in the usual and ordinary course of business within the meaning of this section: *Reference re: Gruenke* (1998), 131 C.C.C. (3d) 72, [1999] 3 W.W.R. 118 *sub nom. R. v. Fosty* (Man. C.A.), affd 146 C.C.C. (3d) 319, [2000] 6 W.W.R. 201.

A computer is not a "book" within the meaning of this section and therefore a print-out produced by an armed forces computer is not admissible under this section: *R. v. Sunila and Solayman* (1986), 26 C.C.C. (3d) 331 (N.S.S.C.).

While the word "book" does not include any kind of record and did not extend to reports consisting of opinion and interpretation, the documents could be admitted as an exception to the hearsay rule as they met the requirements of reliability and necessity: *Ethier v. Canada (RCMP Commissioner)*, [1993] 2 F.C. 659 (C.A.)

NOTARIAL ACTS IN QUEBEC.

27. Any document purporting to be a copy of a notarial act or instrument made, filed or registered in the Province of Quebec, and to be certified by a notary or prothonotary to be a true copy of the original in his possession as such notary or prothonotary, shall be admitted in evidence in the place and stead of the original and has the same force and effect as the original would have if produced and proved, but it may be proved in rebuttal that there is no such original, that the copy is not a true copy of the original in some material particular or that the original is not an instrument of such nature as may, by the law of the Province of Quebec, be taken before a notary or be filed, enrolled or registered by a notary in that Province. R.S., c. E-10, s. 27.

NOTICE OF PRODUCTION OF BOOK OR DOCUMENT / Not less than 7 days.

28. (1) No copy of any book or other document shall be admitted in evidence, under the authority of section 23, 24, 25, 26 or 27, on any trial, unless the party intending to produce the copy has before the trial given to the party against whom it is intended to be produced reasonable notice of that intention.

(2) The reasonableness of the notice referred to in subsection (1) shall be determined by the court, judge or other person presiding, but the notice shall not in any case be less than seven days. R.S., c. E-10, s. 28.

ANNOTATIONS

Where the statute, such as the *Unemployment Insurance Act*, 1970-71-72 (Can.), c. 48, has its own provisions governing the admissibility of copies of documents there is no need to comply with this section: *R. v. Yerxa* (1978), 42 C.C.C. (2d) 177, 21 N.B.R. (2d) 569 (C.A.).

In determining whether there has been 7 days notice as required by subsec. (2), s. 27(1) of the *Interpretation Act*, R.S.C. 1985, c. I-21, applies and requires exclusion of the date of service and the date of the trial. However, none of the intervening days are to be excluded, although they are Sundays or statutory holidays: *R. v. Bourque* (1991), 66 C.C.C. (3d) 548 (N.S.C.A.).

There is no requirement that the accused be served with a certified copy of the document, here a copy of his probation order, to comply with this section: *R. v. Dixon* (2006) , 304 N.B.R. (2d) 290 (Q.B.); *R. v. Algafori* (2016), 99 M.V.R. (6th) 105 (Ont. S.C.J.).

There is no notice requirement under the common law rule pertaining to the admissibility of court documents: *R. v. Bailey* (2014), 116 W.C.B. (2d) 218, [2014] O.J. No. 4420 (S.C.J.).

CAN. EV.

COPIES OF ENTRIES / Admission in evidence / Cheques, proof of "no account" / Proof of official character / Compulsion of production or appearance / Order to inspect and copy / Warrants to search / Computation of time / Definitions / "court" / "financial institution" / "legal proceeding".

29. (1) Subject to this section, a copy of any entry in any book or record kept in any financial institution shall in all legal proceedings be admitted in evidence as proof, in the absence of evidence to the contrary, of the entry and of the matters, transactions and accounts therein recorded.

(2) A copy of an entry in the book or record described in subsection (1) shall not be admitted in evidence under this section unless it is first proved that the book or record was, at the time of the making of the entry, one of the ordinary books or records of the financial institution, that the entry was made in the usual and ordinary course of business, that the book or record is in the custody or control of the financial institution and that the copy is a true copy of it, and such proof may be given by any person employed by the financial institution who has knowledge of the book or record or the manager or accountant of the financial institution, and may be given orally or by affidavit sworn before any commissioner or other person authorized to take affidavits.

(3) Where a cheque has been drawn on any financial institution or branch thereof by any person, an affidavit of the manager or accountant of the financial institution or branch, sworn before any commissioner or other person authorized to take affidavits, setting out that he is the manager or accountant, that he has made a careful examination and search of the books and records for the purpose of ascertaining whether or not that person has an account with the financial institution or branch and that he has been unable to find such an account, shall be admitted in evidence as proof, in the absence of evidence to the contrary, that that person has no account in the financial institution or branch.

(4) Where evidence is offered by affidavit pursuant to this section, it is not necessary to prove the signature or official character of the person making the affidavit if the official character of that person is set out in the body of the affidavit.

(5) A financial institution or officer of a financial institution is not in any legal proceedings to which the financial institution is not a party compellable to produce any book or record, the contents of which can be proved under this section, or to appear as a witness to prove the matters, transactions and accounts therein recorded unless by order of the court made for special cause.

(6) On the application of any party to a legal proceeding, the court may order that that party be at liberty to inspect and take copies of any entries in the books or records of a financial institution for the purposes of the legal proceeding, and the person whose

account is to be inspected shall be notified of the application at least two clear days before the hearing thereof, and if it is shown to the satisfaction of the court that he cannot be notified personally, the notice may be given by addressing it to the financial institution.

(7) Nothing in this section shall be construed as prohibiting any search of the premises of a financial institution under the authority of a warrant to search issued under any other Act of Parliament, but unless the warrant is expressly endorsed by the person under whose hand it is issued as not being limited by this section, the authority conferred by any such warrant to search the premises of a financial institution and to seize and take away anything in it shall, with respect to the books or records of the institution, be construed as limited to the searching of those premises for the purpose of inspecting and taking copies of entries in those books or records, and section 490 of the *Criminal Code* does not apply in respect of the copies of those books or records obtained under a warrant referred to in this section.

(8) Holidays shall be excluded from the computation of time under this section.

(9) In this section

"court" means the court, judge, arbitrator or person before whom a legal proceeding is held or taken;

"financial institution" means the Bank of Canada, the Business Development Bank of Canada and any institution that accepts in Canada deposits of money from its members or the public, and includes a branch, agency or office of any of those Banks or institutions;

"legal proceeding" means any civil or criminal proceeding or inquiry in which evidence is or may be given, and includes an arbitration. R.S., c. E-10, s. 29; 1974-75-76, c. 14, s. 57; 1994, c. 44, s. 90; 1995, c. 28, s. 47; 1999, c. 28, s. 149.

ANNOTATIONS

The notice provisions of s. 30 do not apply to copies of records admissible under this section. Such documents are admissible without notice to the other party: *R. v. Best* (1978), 43 C.C.C. (2d) 236, [1978] 5 W.W.R. 421 (B.C.C.A.).

Subsection (1) – A computer print-out of entries stored in a bank's computer falls within the phrase "a copy of any entry in any book on record" in this subsection and therefore may be admissible under this section: *R. v. McMullen* (1978), 42 C.C.C. (2d) 67, 6 C.R. (3d) 218 (Ont. H.C.J.), affd 47 C.C.C. (2d) 499, 100 D.L.R. (3d) 671 (Ont. C.A.).

"Entry" in this subsection means an ordinary financial or bookkeeping entry and would not cover such things as inter-office memos or written reports between branches: *M.N.R. v. Furnasman Ltd.*, [1973] F.C. 1327, [1973] C.T.C. 830 (T.D.), or memoranda of conversations or meetings between a bank employee and the bank's customers: *I.T.L. Industries Ltd. v. Winterbottom* (1980), 106 D.L.R. (3d) 577, 27 O.R. (2d) 496 (C.A.), *R. v. Bell and Bruce*, [1985] 2 S.C.R. 287, 55 O.R. (2d) 287*n* [considering the comparable provision of the *Ontario Evidence Act*, s. 34].

Subsection (2) – Proof of compliance with this subsection may be given by persons other than the manager or accountant, such as the bank employee in charge of the records: *R. v. McGrayne* (1979), 46 C.C.C. (2d) 63 (Ont. C.A.).

In *R. v. Bell and Bruce* (1982), 65 C.C.C. (2d) 377, 35 O.R. (2d) 164 (C.A.), affd as to Bruce [1985] 2 S.C.R. 287, the court gave further consideration to the application of this section to computerized bank records. It was held that: a "record" may be in any, even in an illegible, form; the form in which the information is recorded may change from time to time; a "record" may be a compilation or collation of other records; and the "record" must have been produced for the bank's purposes as a reference source, or as part of its internal audit system and, at the relevant time, must be kept for that purpose. It was also possible for the bank to have more than one record at any one time, for example, the record stored in the computer and a monthly statement prepared by the computer which the bank retained for a number of years.

Entries shown on prints of cheques made from microfiche would be admissible as *prima facie* proof of the entries and of the transactions recorded if "(i) the entries shown on the cheques in the prints were true copies of entries, (ii) made in the ordinary course of the Bank's business, (iii) in records kept in a bank, (iv) that at the time the entries were made, (v) were one of the Bank's ordinary records, (vi) in its custody or control". In this case, however, the prints were made by a private company to which the bank outsourced the clearing and recording of cheques and were never in the custody or control of the bank. There was also no evidence that the company was an agent of the bank. The prints were therefore not admissible under this section. The evidence was, however, admissible at common law as an exception to the hearsay rule. The prosecution had shown that the evidence met the requirements of necessity and reliability: *R. v. Lemay* (2004), 191 C.C.C. (3d) 497, 25 C.R. (6th) 17 (B.C.C.A.), at para. 28.

Printouts of electronic banking transactions captured on so-called Prism Screens are copies of records admissible under this section: *R. v. Tewolde*, [2007] O.J. No. 4568, 2007 ONCJ 555.

Subsection (5) – "Special cause" refers both to documents that would be used to prove a crime and those documents which are necessary to make full answer and defence: *R. v. Moisan* (1999), 141 C.C.C. (3d) 213, 75 Alta. L.R. (3d) 110 (Q.B.).

BUSINESS RECORDS TO BE ADMITTED IN EVIDENCE / Inference where information not in business record / Copy of records / Where record kept in form requiring explanation / Court may order other part of record to be produced / Court may examine record and hear evidence / Notice of intention to produce record or affidavit / Not necessary to prove signature and official character / Examination on record with leave of court / Evidence inadmissible under this section / Construction of this section / Definitions / "business" / "copy" and "photographic film" / "court" / legal proceeding" / "record".

30. (1) Where oral evidence in respect of a matter would be admissible in a legal proceeding, a record made in the usual and ordinary course of business that contains information in respect of that matter is admissible in evidence under this section in the legal proceeding on production of the record.

(2) Where a record made in the usual and ordinary course of business does not contain information in respect of a matter the occurrence or existence of which might reasonably be expected to be recorded in that record, the court may on production of the record admit the record for the purpose of establishing that fact and may draw the inference that the matter did not occur or exist.

(3) Where it is not possible or reasonably practicable to produce any record described in subsection (1) or (2), a copy of the record accompanied by two documents, one that is made by a person who states why it is not possible or reasonably practicable to produce the record and one that sets out the source from which the copy was made, that attests to the copy's authenticity and that is made by the person who made the copy, is admissible in evidence under this section in the same manner as if it were the original of the record if each document is

(*a*) an affidavit of each of those persons sworn before a commissioner or other person authorized to take affidavits; or

(*b*) a certificate or other statement pertaining to the record in which the person attests that the certificate or statement is made in conformity with the laws of a foreign state, whether or not the certificate or statement is in the form of an affidavit attested to before an official of the foreign state.

(4) Where production of any record or of a copy of any record described in subsection (1) or (2) would not convey to the court the information contained in the record by reason of its having been kept in a form that requires explanation, a transcript of the explanation of the record or copy prepared by a person qualified to make the explanation is admissible in evidence under this section in the same manner as if it were the original of the record if it is accompanied by a document that sets out the person's qualifications to make the explanation, attests to the accuracy of the explanation, and is

(*a*) an affidavit of that person sworn before a commissioner or other person authorized to take affidavits; or

(*b*) a certificate or other statement pertaining to the record in which the person attests that the certificate or statement is made in conformity with the laws of a foreign state, whether or not the certificate or statement is in the form of an affidavit attested to before an official of the foreign state.

(5) Where part only of a record is produced under this section by any party, the court may examine any other part of the record and direct that, together with the part of the record previously so produced, the whole or any part of the other part thereof be produced by that party as the record produced by him.

(6) For the purpose of determining whether any provision of this section applies, or for the purpose of determining the probative value, if any, to be given to information contained in any record admitted in evidence under this section, the court may, on production of any record, examine the record, admit any evidence in respect thereof given orally or by affidavit including evidence as to the circumstances in which the information contained in the record was written, recorded, stored or reproduced, and draw any reasonable inference from the form or content of the record.

(7) Unless the court orders otherwise, no record or affidavit shall be admitted in evidence under this section unless the party producing the record or affidavit has, at least seven days before its production, given notice of his intention to produce it to each other party to the legal proceeding and has, within five days after receiving any notice in that behalf given by any such party, produced it for inspection by that party.

(8) Where evidence is offered by affidavit under this section, it is not necessary to prove the signature or official character of the person making the affidavit if the official character of that person is set out in the body of the affidavit.

(9) Subject to section 4, any person who has or may reasonably be expected to have knowledge of the making or contents of any record produced or received in evidence under this section may, with leave of the court, be examined or cross-examined thereon by any party to the legal proceeding.

(10) Nothing in this section renders admissible in evidence in any legal proceeding

(*a*) such part of any record as is proved to be

(i) a record made in the course of an investigation or inquiry,

(ii) a record made in the course of obtaining or giving legal advice or in contemplation of a legal proceeding,

(iii) a record in respect of the production of which any privilege exists and is claimed, or

(iv) a record of or alluding to a statement made by a person who is not, or if he were living and of sound mind would not be, competent and compellable to disclose in the legal proceeding a matter disclosed in the record;

(*b*) any record the production of which would be contrary to public policy; or

(*c*) any transcript or recording of evidence taken in the course of another legal proceeding.

(11) The provisions of this section shall be deemed to be in addition to and not in derogation of

(*a*) any other provision of this or any other Act of Parliament respecting the admissibility in evidence of any record or the proof of any matter; or

(*b*) any existing rule of law under which any record is admissible in evidence or any matter may be proved.

(12) In this section,

"business" means any business, profession, trade, calling, manufacture or undertaking of any kind carried on in Canada or elsewhere whether for profit or otherwise, including any activity or operation carried on or performed in Canada or elsewhere by any government, by any department, branch, board, commission or agency of any government, by any court or other tribunal or by any other body or authority performing a function of government;

"copy", in relation to any record, includes a print, whether enlarged or not, from a photographic film of the record, and "photographic film" includes a photographic plate, microphotographic film or photostatic negative;

"court" means the court, judge, arbitrator or person before whom a legal proceeding is held or taken;

"legal proceeding" means any civil or criminal proceeding or inquiry in which evidence is or may be given, and includes an arbitration;

"record" includes the whole or any part of any book, document, paper, card, tape or other thing on or in which information is written, recorded, stored or reproduced, and, except for the purposes of subsections (3) and (4), any copy or transcript admitted in evidence under this section pursuant to subsection (3) or (4). R.S., c. E-10, s. 30; 1994, c. 44, s. 91.

ANNOTATIONS

Subsection (1) – An inventory sheet made contemporaneously by employees with personal knowledge of the matters then being recorded and under a duty to make the record is admissible through the employees and *prima facie* proof of the truth of its contents at common law or in the alternative is admissible as a business record under this section: *R. v. Penno* (1977), 35 C.C.C. (2d) 266, 76 D.L.R. (3d) 529 (B.C.C.A.).

Fingerprint records kept by the United States Federal Bureau of Investigation are admissible under this subsection. An official of the F.B.I. who has knowledge of the contents of the records kept by the agency based on his experience, although he has no original knowledge of their contents, is competent to give evidence as to the contents of the documents: *R. v. Grimba and Wilder* (1977), 38 C.C.C. (2d) 469 (Ont. Co. Ct.).

Records containing double hearsay are admissible under this provision: *R. v. Martin* (1997), 8 C.R. (5th) 246, [1997] 6 W.W.R. 62 (Sask. C.A.).

Records made in the usual and ordinary course of an escort agency business and relied upon in the day-to-day operation of the agency were admissible under this section. Further, statements from other persons recorded in those records were admissible for their truth since this information was admissible under the co-conspirators exception to the hearsay rule: *R. v. Lukacko* (2002), 164 C.C.C. (3d) 550, 1 C.R. (6th) 309 (Ont. C.A.).

It was open to the Crown to adduce evidence from an auditor who had performed mathematical calculations based upon documents properly admitted under this section. The evidence was admissible to assist the trier of fact with a task that would otherwise pose some degree of difficulty: *R. v. Martin*, *supra.*

Documents compiled by correctional prison authorities which in part contained double hearsay are business records within the meaning of this provision. The authors of the documents had acquired extensive personal knowledge of the accused as part of their job to acquire such information and make reports about the accused's activities and progress within the prison system. *R. v. Gregoire* (1998), 130 C.C.C. (3d) 65, 180 W.A.C. 261 (Man. C.A.).

So-called "war documents" being directives or orders originating in central or field offices of the German armed forces or of the police made during the Second World War and kept in archives maintained by governments were admissible under this section. The evidence of archivists and historians could establish that the documents were produced in the usual and ordinary course of business. It was not necessary that persons with first-hand knowledge of the manner in which the documents were produced give such evidence: *Canada (Minister of Citizenship and Immigration) v. Oberlander*, [1999] 1 F.C. 88, 153 F.T.R. 11 (T.D.). See also *Canada (Minister of Citizenship and Immigration) v. Skomatchuk* (2006), 293 F.T.R. 150, [2006] F.C.J. No. 926 (F.C.).

Unlike the common law business records exception, there is no requirement under this section that the maker of the record be under a duty to make it. Nevertheless, there was considerable doubt that this section was intended to apply to the records in this case — private records kept by an employee against the employer's instructions, even though the employee relied upon the records for the purpose of carrying out his duties. Where, as in this case, admission of a record under this section is seriously debatable, it is preferable to determine admissibility by application of the principled approach to hearsay: *R. v. Wilcox* (2001), 152 C.C.C. (3d) 157, 192 N.S.R. (2d) 159 (C.A.).

The notes made by a visa officer during an interview of the applicant for admission as a permanent resident do not fall within this section. The officer can be required to act as a decision maker. The discharge of that kind of function is not a business contemplated by subsec. (1): *Walia v. Canada (Minister of Citizenship and Immigration)* (2000), 195 F.T.R. 261, 10 Imm. L.R. (3d) 95 (T.D.).

A toxicology report admitted under this provision was capable of constituting proof beyond a reasonable doubt. The Crown is not limited to using s. 254 to adduce a toxicology report. Simply because the *Criminal Code* provides another route for the admission of hearsay evidence does not compel the use of that option. Each provision has different safeguards available to the accused: *R. v. Smith* (2011), 273 C.C.C. (3d) 525 (Alta. C.A.), leave to appeal to S.C.C. refused (2012), 432 N.R. 400*n*.

Subsection (2) – In order to prove that a certain item had not been imported by the accused the proper procedure is to produce the customs records under this section giving rise to the inference under this subsection of the non-occurrence of the importation from the fact that there was no entry of it in the records, rather than merely call an officer who had inspected the records: *R. v. Garofoli* (1988), 41 C.C.C. (3d) 97, 64 C.R. (3d) 193 (Ont. C.A.), revd on other grounds [1990] 2 S.C.R. 1421, 60 C.C.C. (3d) 161.

Subsection (3) – An air way-bill is a document made in the usual and ordinary course of business a copy of which would be admissible if this subsection were complied with. In determining which parts of the way-bill are originals and which are merely copies the court must resort to the *Carriage By Air Act*, R.S.C. 1970, c. C-14. That Act provides that an air way-bill consists of three originals and therefore any other part such as a delivery receipt is a copy whose admissibility is governed by the provisions of this subsection: *R. v. Cloutier*, [1979] 2 S.C.R. 709, 48 C.C.C. (3d) 1 (6:3).

The technical requirements laid down by provincial legislation for the swearing of an affidavit had no application to an affidavit tendered under subsec. (3) in a prosecution for violation of a federal statute: *R. v. Nickerson* (1991), 106 N.S.R. (2d) 300 (C.A.).

Despite the reference to "two documents", the information as to why the original cannot be produced and the authenticity of the copy may be combined into one document made by a person with knowledge relating to both issues: *R. v. Jahanrakhshan* (2013), 296 C.C.C. (3d) 553 (B.C.C.A.), additional reasons (2013), 301 C.C.C. (3d) 334 (B.C.C.A.), affd (2013), 582 W.A.C. 69 (B.C.C.A.).

The subsequent destruction of the original file after the copies were made and affidavits prepared in accordance with this subsection does not affect the admissibility of the copies: *R. v. MacMullin* (2013), 579 A.R. 205 (Q.B.).

Subsection (6) – Affidavit evidence is admissible not only to prove the matters referred to in subsecs. (3) and (4) but to prove that the record was one made in the usual and ordinary course of business: *R. v. Parker* (1984), 16 C.C.C. (3d) 478 (Ont. C.A.). *Contra*: *California (State) v. Meier and Hazelwood (No. 2)* (1982), 69 C.C.C. (2d) 180, 40 B.C.L.R. 297 (S.C.).

Subsection (7) – The notice required by this subsection need not be written or formal. Introduction of the record at the accused's preliminary hearing is sufficient compliance with this subsection where it is sought to tender the document at the accused's trial: *R. v. Penno* (1977), 35 C.C.C. (2d) 266, 76 D.L.R. (3d) 529 (B.C.C.A.).

Similarly, the document is produced for inspection within the meaning of this subsection where it is entered as an exhibit at the preliminary inquiry and is thereafter available for inspection as provided for in the *Criminal Code*: *R. v. Voykin* (1986), 29 C.C.C. (3d) 280, 71 A.R. 241 (C.A.).

Subsection (10) – Notes made by an investigator with the fire marshall's office, who is conducting an investigation into a fire at the accused's premises are inadmissible in view of para. (*a*)(i) of this subsection: *R. v. Laverty (No. 2)* (1979), 47 C.C.C. (2d) 60, 9 C.R. (3d) 288 (Ont. C.A.). Similarly, logs kept by police officers monitoring intercepted private communications are inadmissible: *R. v. Biasi (No. 2)* (1981), 66 C.C.C. (2d) 563 (B.C.S.C.). *Contra*: *R. v. McLarty (No. 3)* (1978), 45 C.C.C. (2d) 184 (Ont. Co. Ct.), where a narrow interpretation was given to para. (*a*), the court holding that "investigation or inquiry" is the type of inquiry contemplated by the *Inquiries Act*, R.S.C. 1970, c. I-13. Thus records kept by the R.C.M.P. to account for the whereabouts of exhibits were admitted.

Reports made by a police officer in the course of an investigation into allegations of sexual assault was also inadmissible by reasons of this subsection. The defence tendered the records to support a claim by the accused, who was charged with murder and advancing a defence of not criminally responsible on account of mental disorder, that he had been sexually assaulted as a child: *R. v. Palma* (2000), 149 C.C.C. (3d) 169 (Ont. S.C.J.).

While computer print-outs made by detection equipment on board armed forces aircraft could otherwise qualify as business records within the meaning of this section, where, as in this case, the records are made in the course of surveillance operations conducted to assist law enforcement personnel in tracking alleged narcotics smugglers, then the records are not admissible by virtue of subpara. (i): *R. v. Sunila* (1986), 26 C.C.C. (3d) 331, 73 N.S.R. (2d) 308 (S.C.). However, in this case, the court did admit these records relying on a common-law business records exception.

Subsection (10) does not apply to screen capture evidence: *R. v. Mills* (2014), 359 Nfld. & P.E.I.R. 336 (N.L. Prov. Ct.), vard on other grounds 2017 NLCA 12, leave to appeal to S.C.C. requested.

Reports prepared by the Correctional Service of Canada including a decision of the National Parole Board are admissible under this section and are not excluded by this subsection in proceedings to determine whether the former inmate should be required to enter into a recognizance under s. 810.2 of the *Criminal Code*: *R. v. Flett* (2013), 419 Sask. R. 193 (Sask. Q.B.).

A Booking Summary Report, including a photograph ("mug shot") taken at the time the accused was booked into the police station, is not excluded by this subsection: *R. v. Farhan* (2013), 110 W.C.B. (2d) 714, [2013] O.J. No. 5519 (S.C.J.).

This subsection does not prohibit the retrieval, from a stock of previously recorded information such as cell phone records, a subset of that information that is useful for purposes of litigation, provided that the information was not itself recorded in contemplation of litigation: *R. v. Marini*, [2006] O.J. No. 4057 (S.C.J.).

The case of *R. v. Scheel* (1978), 42 C.C.C. (2d) 31, 3 C.R. (3d) 359 (Ont. C.A.), is of note although not directly related to this section. It was held in that case that summaries, prepared by an accountant retained by the Crown, from the accused's records are admissible in evidence at least where the summaries are based on evidence which had been properly admitted at the trial.

A spreadsheet summarizing information from a bank's client records is admissible under this section even without the source documents. It is open to the accused to apply for production of the source documents, which may be edited to protect the privacy interests of the clients: *R. v. Agyei*, 2007 ONCJ 459.

While a record made in the course of an investigation is inadmissible, this provision does not prevent information contained in the record of the Requesting State's case from being admitted as direct evidence in an extradition hearing: *United States of America v. New* (2017), 140 W.C.B. (2d) 154, 2017 BCCA 249, leave to appeal to S.C.C. refused 2018 CarswellBC 712.

Subsection (11) – This section is neither mandatory nor exclusive and it was open to the court to admit business records under the common law exception to the hearsay rule. Further, it was open to the court to modify the common law criteria (one of which required proof that the maker of the document was since deceased). In *R. v. Monkhouse* (1987), 61 C.R. (3d) 343, [1988] 1 W.W.R. 725 (Alta. C.A.), the court set down the following criteria for admissibility under the modified common law exception: a record containing (1) an original entry (2) made contemporaneously (3) in the routine (4) of business (5) by a recorder who has a duty to make the record and (6) who had no motive to misrepresent. There is no requirement that the recorder have personal knowledge of the thing recorded if he is functioning in the usual and ordinary course of a system in effect for the preparation of business records. The court warned however that this exception should only be applied where the circumstances make the records inherently trustworthy; where there is an established system in the business which produces records which are regarded as reliable and customarily relied upon by those affected by them. Also see: *R. v. Keats* (2016), 345 C.C.C. (3d) 139 (N.S.C.A.).

As to admission of expert's reports, see *Criminal Code*, s. 657.3.

Subsection (12) – A computer generated print-out produced by an employee of the telephone company showing calls to and from a particular telephone number is a "record" within the meaning of this section not merely a copy of a record: *R. v. Bicknell* (1988), 41 C.C.C. (3d) 545 (B.C.C.A.).

DEFINITIONS / "corporation" / "government" / "photographic film" / When print admissible in evidence / Evidence of compliance with conditions / Proof by notarial copy.

31. (1) In this section,

"corporation" means any bank, including the Bank of Canada and the Business Development Bank of Canada, any authorized foreign bank within the meaning of section 2 of the *Bank Act* and each of the following carrying on business in Canada, namely, every railway, express, telegraph and telephone company (except a street railway and tramway company), insurance company or society, trust company and loan company;

"government" means the government of Canada or of any province and includes any department, commission, board or branch of any such government;

"photographic film" includes any photographic plate, microphotographic film and photostatic negative.

(2) A print, whether enlarged or not, from any photographic film of

- **(*a*) an entry in any book or record kept by any government or corporation and destroyed, lost or delivered to a customer after the film was taken,**
- **(*b*) any bill of exchange, promissory note, cheque, receipt, instrument or document held by any government or corporation and destroyed, lost or delivered to a customer after the film was taken, or**

(*c*) any record, document, plan, book or paper belonging to or deposited with any government or corporation,

is admissible in evidence in all cases in which and for all purposes for which the object photographed would have been admitted on proof that

(*d*) while the book, record, bill of exchange, promissory note, cheque, receipt, instrument or document, plan, book or paper was in the custody or control of the government or corporation, the photographic film was taken thereof in order to keep a permanent record thereof, and

(*e*) the object photographed was subsequently destroyed by or in the presence of one or more of the employees of the government or corporation, or was lost or was delivered to a customer.

(3) Evidence of compliance with the conditions prescribed by this section may be given by any one or more of the employees of the government or corporation, having knowledge of the taking of the photographic film, of the destruction, loss, or delivery to a customer, or of the making of the print, as the case may be, either orally or by affidavit sworn in any part of Canada before any notary public or commissioner for oaths.

(4) Unless the court otherwise orders, a notarial copy of an affidavit under subsection (3) is admissible in evidence in lieu of the original affidavit. R.S., c. E-10, s. 31; 1974-75-76, c. 14, s. 57; 1992, c. 1, s. 142(1) (Sch. V, item 9(1)); 1995, c. 28, s. 47; 1999, c. 28, s. 150.

ANNOTATIONS

A private organization controlled and entrusted by a provincial government to administer a provincial medical care insurance scheme is included within the definition of "government": *R. v. Sanghi* (1971), 6 C.C.C. (2d) 123, 3 N.S.R. (2d) 70 (S.C. App. Div.).

In a case where the prosecution relies upon prints of cheques made from microfiche, there must be evidence from an employee of the bank having knowledge of (i) the cheques being microphotographed, (ii) the cheques being destroyed, lost, or delivered to the customer, or (iii) the making of the prints. It would seem that the required proof could have been given by one employee of the bank having knowledge of the requirements for admissibility, or by more than one employee who between them had such knowledge. However, a private corporation to which the bank outsourced the clearing and recording of cheques is not part of the bank for the purpose of this section and its employee could not give the requisite evidence to comply with this section. The evidence was, however, admissible at common law as an exception to the hearsay rule. The prosecution had shown that the evidence met the requirements of necessity and reliability: *R. v. Lemay* (2004), 191 C.C.C. (3d) 497, 25 C.R. (6th) 17 (B.C.C.A.).

AUTHENTICATION OF ELECTRONIC DOCUMENTS.

31.1 Any person seeking to admit an electronic document as evidence has the burden of proving its authenticity by evidence capable of supporting a finding that the electronic document is that which it is purported to be. 2000, c. 5, s. 56.

ANNOTATIONS

Authentication is not an onerous requirement and does not involve a consideration of the integrity and reliability of the electronic document. The party seeking to adduce an electronic document must prove through direct or circumstantial evidence that the document is what it purports to be: *R. v. Hirsch* (2017), 353 C.C.C. (3d) 230 (Sask. C.A.).

APPLICATION OF BEST EVIDENCE RULE — ELECTRONIC DOCUMENTS / Printouts.

31.2 (1) The best evidence rule in respect of an electronic document is satisfied

(*a*) on proof of the integrity of the electronic documents system by or in which the electronic document was recorded or stored; or

(*b*) if an evidentiary presumption established under section 31.4 applies.

(2) Despite subsection (1), in the absence of evidence to the contrary, an electronic document in the form of a printout satisfies the best evidence rule if the printout has been manifestly or consistently acted on, relied on or used as a record of the information recorded or stored in the printout. 2000, c. 5, s. 56.

ANNOTATIONS

A computer printout of a record is admissible as an original document and need not be shown to meet the requirements for admissibility of a copy under s. 30(3) of this Act: *R. v. Flett* (2013), 419 Sask. R. 193 (Q.B.).

The presumption of integrity in para. (*b*) applies to screen captures adduced from the accused's Facebook page: *R. v. Hirsch* (2017), 353 C.C.C. (3d) 230 (Sask. C.A.).

PRESUMPTION OF INTEGRITY.

31.3 For the purposes of subsection 31.2(1), in the absence of evidence to the contrary, the integrity of an electronic documents system by or in which an electronic document is recorded or stored is proven

(*a*) by evidence capable of supporting a finding that at all material times the computer system or other similar device used by the electronic documents system was operating properly or, if it was not, the fact of its not operating properly did not affect the integrity of the electronic document and there are no other reasonable grounds to doubt the integrity of the electronic documents system;

(*b*) if it is established that the electronic document was recorded or stored by a party who is adverse in interest to the party seeking to introduce it; or

(*c*) if it is established that the electronic document was recorded or stored in the usual and ordinary course of business by a person who is not a party and who did not record or store it under the control of the party seeking to introduce it.

ANNOTATIONS

The presumption of integrity in para. (*b*) applies to screen captures adduced from the accused's Facebook page: *R. v. Hirsch* (2017), 353 C.C.C. (3d) 230 (Sask. C.A.).

PRESUMPTIONS REGARDING SECURE ELECTRONIC SIGNATURES.

31.4 The Governor in Council may make regulations establishing evidentiary presumptions in relation to electronic documents signed with secure electronic signatures, including regulations respecting

(*a*) the association of secure electronic signatures with persons; and

(*b*) the integrity of information contained in electronic documents signed with secure electronic signatures. 2000, c. 5, s. 56.

STANDARDS MAY BE CONSIDERED.

31.5 For the purpose of determining under any rule of law whether an electronic document is admissible, evidence may be presented in respect of any standard, procedure, usage or practice concerning the manner in which electronic documents are to be recorded or stored, having regard to the type of business, enterprise or endeavour that used, recorded or stored the electronic document and the nature and purpose of the electronic document. 2000, c. 5, s. 56.

PROOF BY AFFIDAVIT / Cross-examination.

31.6 (1) The matters referred to in subsection 31.2(2) and sections 31.3 and 31.5 and in regulations made under section 31.4 may be established by affidavit.

(2) A party may cross-examine a deponent of an affidavit referred to in subsection (1) that has been introduced in evidence

- **(*a*) as of right, if the deponent is an adverse party or is under the control of an adverse party; and**
- **(*b*) with leave of the court, in the case of any other deponent. 2000, c. 5, s. 56.**

APPLICATION.

31.7 Sections 31.1 to 31.4 do not affect any rule of law relating to the admissibility of evidence, except the rules relating to authentication and best evidence. 2000, c. 5, s. 56.

DEFINITIONS / "Computer system" / "Data" / "Electronic document" / "Electronic documents system" / "Secure electronic signature".

31.8 The definitions in this section apply in sections 31.1 to 31.6.

"computer system" means a device that, or a group of interconnected or related devices one or more of which,

- **(*a*) contains computer programs or other data; and**
- **(*b*) pursuant to computer programs, performs logic and control, and may perform any other function.**

"data" means representations of information or of concepts, in any form.

"electronic document" means data that is recorded or stored on any medium in or by a computer system or other similar device and that can be read or perceived by a person or a computer system or other similar device. It includes a display, printout or other output of that data.

"electronic documents system" includes a computer system or other similar device by or in which data is recorded or stored and any procedures related to the recording or storage of electronic documents.

"secure electronic signature" means a secure electronic signature as defined in subsection 31(1) of the *Personal Information Protection and Electronic Documents Act*. 2000, c. 5, s. 56.

ORDER SIGNED BY SECRETARY OF STATE / Copies printed in *Canada Gazette*.

32. (1) An order signed by the Secretary of State of Canada and purporting to be written by command of the Governor General shall be admitted in evidence as the order of the Governor General.

(2) All copies of official and other notices, advertisements and documents published in the *Canada Gazette* are admissible in evidence as proof, in the absence of evidence to the contrary, of the originals and of their contents. R.S., c. E-10, s. 32; 2000, c. 5, s. 57.

PROOF OF HANDWRITING OF PERSON CERTIFYING / Printed or written.

33. (1) No proof shall be required of the handwriting or official position of any person certifying, in pursuance of this Act, to the truth of any copy of or extract from any proclamation, order, regulation, appointment, book or other document.

(2) Any copy or extract referred to in subsection (1) may be in print or in writing, or partly in print and partly in writing. R.S., c. E-10, s. 33.

ATTESTING WITNESS / Instrument, how proved.

34. (1) It is not necessary to prove by the attesting witness any instrument to the validity of which attestation is not requisite.

(2) Any instrument referred to in subsection (1) may be proved by admission or otherwise as if there had been no attesting witness thereto. R.S., c. E-10, s. 34.

IMPOUNDING OF FORGED INSTRUMENT.

35. Where any instrument that has been forged or fraudulently altered is admitted in evidence, the court or the judge or person who admits the instrument may, at the request of any person against whom it is admitted in evidence, direct that the instrument shall be impounded and be kept in the custody of an officer of the court or other proper person for such period and subject to such conditions as to the court, judge or person admitting the instrument seem meet. R.S., c. E-10, s. 35.

CONSTRUCTION.

36. This Part shall be deemed to be in addition to and not in derogation of any powers of proving documents given by any existing Act or existing at law. R.S., c. E-10, s. 36.

Interpretation

DEFINITION OF "OFFICIAL".

36.1 In sections 37 to 38.16, "official" has the same meaning as in section 118 of the *Criminal Code*. 2001, c. 41, s. 43.

Specified Public Interest

OBJECTION TO DISCLOSURE OF INFORMATION / Obligation of court, person or body / Objection made to superior court / Objection not made to superior court / Limitation period / Disclosure order / Disclosure order / Prohibition order / Evidence / When determination takes effect / Introduction into evidence / Relevant factors.

37. (1) Subject to sections 38 to 38.16, a Minister of the Crown in right of Canada or other official may object to the disclosure of information before a court, person or body with jurisdiction to compel the production of information by certifying orally or in writing to the court, person or body that the information should not be disclosed on the grounds of a specified public interest.

(1.1) If an objection is made under subsection (1), the court, person or body shall ensure that the information is not disclosed other than in accordance with this Act.

(2) If an objection to the disclosure of information is made before a superior court, that court may determine the objection.

(3) If an objection to the disclosure of information is made before a court, person or body other than a superior court, the objection may be determined, on application, by

(*a*) the Federal Court, in the case of a person or body vested with power to compel production by or under an Act of Parliament if the person or body is not a court established under a law of a province; or

(*b*) the trial division or trial court of the superior court of the province within which the court, person or body exercises its jurisdiction, in any other case.

(4) An application under subsection (3) shall be made within 10 days after the objection is made or within any further or lesser time that the court having jurisdiction to hear the application considers appropriate in the circumstances.

(4.1) Unless the court having jurisdiction to hear the application concludes that the disclosure of the information to which the objection was made under subsection (1) would encroach upon a specified public interest, the court may authorize by order the disclosure of the information.

(5) If the court having jurisdiction to hear the application concludes that the disclosure of the information to which the objection was made under subsection (1) would encroach upon a specified public interest, but that the public interest in disclosure outweighs in importance the specified public interest, the court may, by order, after considering both the public interest in disclosure and the form of and conditions to disclosure that are most likely to limit any encroachment upon the specified public interest resulting from disclosure, authorize the disclosure, subject to any conditions that the court considers appropriate, of all of the information, a part or summary of the information, or a written admission of facts relating to the information.

(6) If the court does not authorize disclosure under subsection (4.1) or (5), the court shall, by order, prohibit disclosure of the information.

(6.1) The court may receive into evidence anything that, in the opinion of the court, is reliable and appropriate, even if it would not otherwise be admissible under Canadian law, and may base its decision on that evidence.

(7) An order of the court that authorizes disclosure does not take effect until the time provided or granted to appeal the order has expired or, if the order is appealed, the time provided or granted to appeal a judgment of an appeal court that confirms the order has expired and no further appeal from a judgment that confirms the order is available.

(8) A person who wishes to introduce into evidence material the disclosure of which is authorized under subsection (5), but who may not be able to do so by reason of the rules of admissibility that apply before the court, person or body with jurisdiction to compel the production of information, may request from the court having jurisdiction under subsection (2) or (3) an order permitting the introduction into evidence of the material in a form or subject to any conditions fixed by that court, as long as that form and those conditions comply with the order made under subsection (5).

(9) For the purpose of subsection (8), the court having jurisdiction under subsection (2) or (3) shall consider all the factors that would be relevant for a determination of admissibility before the court, person or body. 1980-81-82-83, c. 111, s. 4; 2001, c. 41, ss. 43 and 140(1); 2002, c. 8, s. 183(1)(*b*); 2013, c. 9, s. 17.

ANNOTATIONS

The predecessor to this legislation, s. 41 of the *Federal Courts Act*, R.S.C. 1970, c. 10 (2nd Supp.), has been held to be *intra vires* Parliament and not contrary to the *Canadian Bill of Rights: Human Rights Com'n v. A.-G. Can.*, [1982] 1 S.C.R. 215 *sub nom. Com'n des Droits de la Personne v. A.-G. Can.*, 134 D.L.R. (3d) 17.

Even though the trial judge conducts it, the hearing under this section is a separate proceeding and not part of the trial for the purpose of the rule that requires that an accused be present for his trial under s. 650(1) of the *Criminal Code*. Nevertheless, it would have been better had the trial judge presiding at a murder trial not conducted an unrecorded *in camera* hearing with the federal Crown counsel and RCMP officers: *R. v. Pilotte* (2002), 163 C.C.C. (3d) 225, 156 O.A.C. 1 (C.A.), leave to appeal refused 170 C.C.C. (3d) vi (S.C.C.).

In this case the accused alleged that certain documents in the possession of the Parole Board would support his contention that his confession to a murder was the result of improper inducements. The court held that if there was any evidence to support the contention the documents would be disclosed, with the question of their admissibility dealt with by the trial judge. However, since the documents upon examination by the court did not contain any evidence of inducement and in view of the sensitivity of the documents, disclosure would be refused: *R. v. Stewart* (1984), 13 C.C.C. (3d) 278 (B.C.S.C.).

Informer privilege is a matter beyond the discretion of the trial judge. Accordingly, the test set out in *Dagenais v. Canadian Broadcasting Corp.* (1994), 94 C.C.C. (3d) 289 (S.C.C.), and *R. v. Mentuck*, [2001] 3 S.C.R. 442, 158 C.C.C. (3d) 449, has no application to such proceedings. Where informer privilege is raised, the trial judge must proceed *in camera* to determine whether there is sufficient evidence to conclude that the person is a confidential informer. A third party cannot be admitted to the proceedings. Where the judge issues notice or the media become aware of the *in camera* proceedings, the judge should hear submissions to determine the extent of the need for *in camera* proceedings. Where media groups appear to make submissions, no identifying information can be given under any circumstances. Where the judge concludes that only media counsel should receive this information, counsel must agree to be bound by a court order not to disclose the information to their client or anyone else: *Application to Proceed In Camera (Re)*, [2007] 3 S.C.R. 253 *sub nom. Named Person v. Vancouver Sun*, 224 C.C.C. (3d) 1.

Where informer privilege is asserted, the court must operate on the assumption that the privilege applies until it determines that the privilege does not exist or that an exception applies. The court must determine its existence *in camera* at a first stage hearing. Defence counsel cannot be present during an *ex parte* hearing where the identity of the confidential informant cannot otherwise be protected, and only to the extent necessary. In determining whether the privilege exists, the judge must be satisfied on a balance of probabilities that the individual concerned is indeed a confidential informant. Trial judges have broad discretion to craft appropriate procedures to permit defence counsel to make meaningful submissions regarding what occurs in their absence and to propose questions to be put by the trial judge to any witnesses called at the *ex parte* hearing. In appropriate cases, fairness may require the court to provide the defence with a redacted or summarized version of the evidence presented *ex parte*, edited to eliminate any possibility of disclosing the informant's identity, so as to permit the trial judge to receive additional submissions from the defence on whether the privilege applies in the particular circumstances of the case. In particularly difficult cases, the trial judge may appoint an *amicus curiae* to attend the *ex parte* proceeding in order to provide assistance in assessing the claim of privilege: *R. v. Basi* (2009), 248 C.C.C. (3d) 257 (S.C.C.). See also *R. v. Lucas* (2014), 313 C.C.C. (3d) 159 (Ont. C.A.), leave to appeal to S.C.C. refused 2015 CarswellOnt 639.

Police officers accused of criminal offences were not entitled to disclose informer privileged information to their own criminal counsel unless the "innocence at stake" exception were found to apply: *R. v. Brassington* (2018), 365 C.C.C. (3d) 1 (S.C.C.).

While the identity of a police agent is disclosable, the identity of a police informer is not. An informant can be a police agent in one field without losing protection as a police informer in respect of other investigations: *R. v. Babes* (2000), 146 C.C.C. (3d) 465 (Ont. C.A.), leave to appeal to S.C.C. refused 151 C.C.C. (3d) vi.

Informer privilege belongs to the informer, is not qualified by disclosure obligation, is not a legal right that can be balanced against other competing rights or interests, and does not depend on the judge's discretion: *R. v. Omar* (2007), 218 C.C.C. (3d) 242 (Ont. C.A.).

Subsequently, it was discovered that the evidence presented to the Superior Court and the Court of Appeal upon which they found the person to be an informer and not a police agent may have been perjured. In those circumstances, the Superior Court and the Court of Appeal had jurisdiction to set aside the original decision. However, the proper course was to make the application to set aside in the Superior Court: *R. v. Moura* (2003), 172 C.C.C. (3d) 340, 169 O.A.C. 33 *sub nom. R. v. Bogiatzis* (C.A.).

The concept of "Crown" should not be expanded so as to include the Royal Canadian Mounted Police Public Complaints Commission Chairperson so as to permit disclosure to the Chairperson of information that is subject to police informer privilege: *Royal Canadian Mounted Police (Public Complaints Commission) v. Canada (Attorney General)* (2005), 256 D.L.R. (4th) 577 (F.C.A.).

Police reports setting out the relationship between unindicted co-conspirators and the police should not be disclosed where, *inter alia*, it was shown that disclosure of the information would be injurious to the operation of the police and the accused had not demonstrated that the information sought contained evidence that was necessary to establish the innocence of the accused or would establish a fact crucial to their defence: *Bailey v. Royal Canadian Mounted Police* (1990), 43 F.T.R. 73 (T.D.).

The public interest privilege may apply on a case-by-case basis to investigative techniques, ongoing police investigations, material that would affect the safety of individuals, internal police communications and police intelligence: *R. v. Trang* (2002), 168 C.C.C. (3d) 145 (Alta. Q.B.).

In *R. v. Boomer* (2000), 182 N.S.R. (2d) 49 (S.C.), the court upheld a claim made under this section to prevent disclosure of evidence concerning secondary vehicle identification numbers. If criminals knew of the numbers and location, they could remove them precluding vehicles from ever being identified. The primary purpose of the numbers is to determine the true registered owner and to keep the information about the numbers confidential does not inhibit an accused from making full answer and defence.

The location post or surveillance location privilege is similar to, but distinct from, the police informer privilege, and may be raised pursuant to the common law or this provision, although it is preferable that it be dealt with under the common law where the issue arises in the course of a criminal prosecution. The privilege prevents disclosure of the precise location of an observation post used by police in investigating crimes to protect the identity of people who make the post available. As with the police informer privilege, there is an exception where the accused's innocence is at stake. Further, since upholding the privilege may affect the ability of the accused to cross-examine on crucial prosecution evidence, the judge must consider whether the public interest in allowing the accused to make full answer and defence can be overridden by the interest asserted by the Crown. Even if the privilege is upheld, the refusal to disclose the location of the observation post will affect the reliability of the evidence: *R. v. Lam* (2000), 148 C.C.C. (3d) 379 (B.C.C.A.).

In *R. v. Trang* (2001), 46 C.R. (5th) 274, [2002] 2 W.W.R. 317 (Alta. Q.B.), however, the court held that the privilege may be invoked by a police officer or a witness if the Crown does not choose to assert a claim of investigative technique privilege or the protection of the identity of the witness.

An objection may be made under this section to disclosure of information by certifying orally that the information should not be disclosed on the ground of a specified public interest, namely police practices. Where the objection is made, the trial judge may examine or hear the information in circumstances which he considers appropriate, including the absence of the parties, their counsel and the public. In a criminal case, if the trial judge finds that the information could not affect the outcome then the privilege claim should generally be upheld. If, however, the decision to uphold the claim might affect the outcome of the trial, the judge must consider whether upholding the claim of privilege would have the effect of preventing the accused from making full answer and defence. If the trial judge so concludes then he should consider giving the Crown the alternative of either withdrawing the claim of privilege or entering a stay of proceedings. If the Crown refuses to do either then the trial judge may permit the introduction of the evidence, imposing whatever safeguards seem appropriate. In effect, the trial judge must consider whether the public interest, in allowing the accused to make full answer and defence, can be overridden by the interest asserted by the Crown: *R. v. Meuckon* (1990), 57 C.C.C. (3d) 193 (B.C.C.A.).

Where objection was taken to the disclosure of communications between the police and a government lawyer, it is necessary to weigh the importance of the items of information to a defence which may properly be raised by the accused, against a public interest specified in the certificate. Before making the determination, the judge may wish to examine or hear the evidence and will then be able to give consideration to the possibility that other issues bearing on the relevance of the information sought ought to be dealt with first: *R. v. Gray* (1993), 79 C.C.C. (3d) 332 (B.C.C.A.), leave to appeal to S.C.C. refused 83 C.C.C. (3d) vi.

On an application under this section, the trial judge may view the contents of the sealed packet without disclosing the entire contents to the accused: *R. v. Desjardins* (1990), 61 C.C.C. (3d) 376 (Nfld. S.C.).

The requirement that an objection to disclosure which is raised in the provincial court must, pursuant to subsec. (3), be determined in the superior court does not violate an accused's right to a fair trial: *Canada (Attorney General) v. Sander* (1992), 79 C.C.C. (3d) 63 (B.C.S.C.), revd on other grounds 90 C.C.C. (3d) 41 (B.C.C.A.).

This provision, however, does not oust a preliminary inquiry judge's jurisdiction to make evidentiary rulings. Where a claim of public interest privilege arises at a preliminary inquiry, the Crown should normally seek a ruling as to the applicability of privilege before proceeding under this section. Where the public interest claim is based on a substantiated claim of police informant privilege, the preliminary inquiry judge must give effect to the claims since the innocence at stake exception is not operative at the preliminary inquiry stage. Furthermore, the public interest in non-disclosure will outweigh the accused's interest in disclosure at a preliminary inquiry in most cases: *R. v. Richards* (1997), 115 C.C.C. (3d) 377 (Ont. C.A.).

This section does not confer jurisdiction on a superior court judge to review an order of the judge of another court or to entertain an interlocutory appeal from such an order. The application under this section is an independent inquiry which, by statute, may require the attention of a judge other than the trial judge where the trial judge is not a judge of the superior court: *Canada (Attorney General) v. Sander* (1994), 90 C.C.C. (3d) 41 (B.C.C.A.).

A claim of public interest immunity under this section is distinct from an assertion of solicitor-client privilege. Whether a solicitor-client privilege prevails in respect to a particular communication will depend upon the nature of the relationship between the parties, and the purpose for which the communication was made. Cases involving public interest immunity, however, are concerned with a class of documents or their actual content and involve a balancing of the injuries which would be caused by a possible denial of justice as a result of non-disclosure on the one hand and the injury to the public as a result of revelation of government documents which were never intended to be made public. It may be that the proper functioning of government could include a public interest in maintaining the confidentiality of discussions between government lawyers and those government officials that they advise. Legal communications between government investigators and Department of Justice lawyers can be subject to public interest immunity, whether or not a claim at common law of solicitor-client privilege succeeds or fails: *Canada (Attorney General) v. Sander, supra*. See also *R. v. Trang* (2001), 46 C.R. (5th) 274 (Alta. Q.B.).

A certificate filed under this section cannot prevent a court from examining records of an R.C.M.P. investigation in determining an application under s. 41 of the *Privacy Act*, S.C. 1980-81-82, c. 111, (Sch. II): *Davidson v. Canada (Solicitor General)*, [1989] 2 F.C. 341, 47 C.C.C. (3d) 104.

Moreover, this section would not apply where the applicant is seeking the information for his own use and there was no question of disclosure of information before a "court, person, or body with jurisdiction to compel the production of information": *Davidson v. Canada (Solicitor General), supra*.

Other common law privileges may be raised by the Crown outside of the purview of this Act such as police investigative techniques, ongoing police investigations and safety of individuals. This section has not codified all public interest immunity. These common law privileges or immunities must be assessed on a case-by-case basis as to whether the public interest in question outweighs the right of the accused to make full answer and defence: *R. v. Chan* (2002), 164 C.C.C. (3d) 24 (Alta. Q.B.).

On an application for disclosure by the defence, the Crown could assert public interest privilege over investigative techniques, ongoing investigations, material that would affect the safety of individuals, internal police communications, and police intelligence. These were not class privileges, however, and had to be established on a case-by-case basis. Disclosure of investigative techniques might in some cases compromise investigations and put officers or civilians at risk. The Crown could delay disclosure of information relating to an ongoing investigation, but once the investigation had concluded, it would be difficult to justify continued non-disclosure. The safety of individuals could support privilege on a case-by-case basis. Internal police communications should be analyzed on a case-by-case basis to determine whether they met the criteria for privilege. Police intelligence was information gathered in connection with an investigation, a potential investigation, or general public security related to organized crime or terrorism. While no new "police intelligence privilege" should be recognized, police intelligence could be subject to privilege on grounds such as investigative techniques, ongoing investigations, the safety of individuals, or internal police communications. Work product or litigation privilege was a subset of solicitor-client privilege, and work produced by Crown counsel fell within its protection. Work product privilege extended to work produced by the police for the purpose of a criminal trial: *R. v. Trang* (2002), 168 C.C.C. (3d) 145 (Alta. Q.B.).

APPEAL TO COURT OF APPEAL / Limitation period for appeal.

37.1 (1) An appeal lies from a determination under any of subsections 37(4.1) to (6)

(*a*) to the Federal Court of Appeal from a determination of the Federal Court; or

(*b*) to the court of appeal of a province from a determination of a trial division or trial court of a superior court of the province.

(2) An appeal under subsection (1) shall be brought within 10 days after the date of the determination appealed from or within any further time that the court having jurisdiction to hear the appeal considers appropriate in the circumstances. 2001, c. 41, ss. 43 and 141(3)(*b*).

ANNOTATIONS

It was held in *R. v. Archer* (1989), 47 C.C.C. (3d) 567 (Alta. C.A.), considering the similarly worded predecessor to this section that while the appeal must be filed within 10 days, if the objection to disclosure is upheld in the course of a trial it is preferable that, except in exceptional circumstances, the appeal not be disposed of until conclusion of the trial. It is undesirable to adjourn a trial for the purpose of an interlocutory appeal that may turn out to be academic. Similarly: *R. v. McCullough* (2000), 151 C.C.C. (3d) 281 (Sask. C.A.).

Where the accused sought declaratory relief to entitle them to reveal informer privileged material to their own counsel in defending against criminal charges, the Crown properly invoked s. 37 and was entitled to appeal under s. 37.1 against the application judge's adverse decision. The fact the order was declaratory did not deprive the proceeding of its criminal character so as to deprive the Crown of its appeal right under this provision: *R. v. Brassington* (2018), 365 C.C.C. (3d) 1 (S.C.C.).

Where an appeal is brought against a refusal to make a disclosure order, absent exceptional circumstances, the trial should proceed. It is only in cases where a judge orders disclosure that the appeal should proceed prior to trial: *R. v. Tingley* (2011), 266 C.C.C. (3d) 544 (N.B.C.A.), leave to appeal to S.C.C. refused 269 C.C.C. (3d) iv.

The Superior Court made an order under s. 37 to prevent disclosure of the identity of a police informer and that order was upheld on appeal in *R. v. Babes* (2000), 146 C.C.C. (3d) 465, 161 O.A.C. 386 (C.A.), leave to appeal to S.C.C. refused 151 C.C.C. (3d) vi, 149 O.A.C. 391*n*. Subsequently, it was discovered that the evidence presented to the Superior Court and the Court of Appeal upon which they found the person to be an informer and not a police agent may have been perjured. In those circumstances, the Superior Court and the Court of Appeal had jurisdiction to set aside the original decision. However, the proper course was to make the application to set aside in the Superior Court: *R. v. Moura* (2003), 172 C.C.C. (3d) 340, 169 O.A.C. 33 *sub nom. R. v. Bogiatzis* (C.A.).

LIMITATION PERIODS FOR APPEALS TO SUPREME COURT OF CANADA.

37.2 Notwithstanding any other Act of Parliament,

(*a*) an application for leave to appeal to the Supreme Court of Canada from a judgment made under subsection 37.1(1) shall be made within 10 days after the date of the judgment appealed from or within any further time that the court having jurisdiction to grant leave to appeal considers appropriate in the circumstances; and

(*b*) if leave to appeal is granted, the appeal shall be brought in the manner set out in subsection 60(1) of the *Supreme Court Act* but within the time specified by the court that grants leave. 2001, c. 41, s. 43.

37.21 [*Repealed*, 2004, c. 12, s. 18.]

PROTECTION OF RIGHT TO A FAIR TRIAL / Potential orders.

37.3 (1) A judge presiding at a criminal trial or other criminal proceeding may make any order that he or she considers appropriate in the circumstances to protect the right of the accused to a fair trial, as long as that order complies with the terms of any order made under any of subsections 37(4.1) to (6) in relation to that trial or proceeding or any judgment made on appeal of an order made under any of those subsections.

(2) The orders that may be made under subsection (1) include, but are not limited to, the following orders:

(*a*) an order dismissing specified counts of the indictment or information, or permitting the indictment or information to proceed only in respect of a lesser or included offence;

(*b*) an order effecting a stay of the proceedings; and

(*c*) an order finding against any party on any issue relating to information the disclosure of which is prohibited. 2001, c. 41, s. 43.

International Relations and National Defence and Security

DEFINITIONS / "Judge" / "Participant" / "Potentially injurious information" / "Proceeding" / "Prosecutor" / "Sensitive information".

38. The following definitions apply in this section and in sections 38.01 to 38.15.

"judge" means the Chief Justice of the Federal Court or a judge of that Court designated by the Chief Justice to conduct hearings under section 38.04.

"participant" means a person who, in connection with a proceeding, is required to disclose, or expects to disclose or cause the disclosure of, information.

"potentially injurious information" means information of a type that, if it were disclosed to the public, could injure international relations or national defence or national security.

"proceeding" means a proceeding before a court, person or body with jurisdiction to compel the production of information.

"prosecutor" means an agent of the Attorney General of Canada or of the Attorney General of a province, the Director of Military Prosecutions under the *National Defence Act* or an individual who acts as a prosecutor in a proceeding.

"sensitive information" means information relating to international relations or national defence or national security that is in the possession of the Government of Canada, whether originating from inside or outside Canada, and is of a type that the Government of Canada is taking measures to safeguard. 1980-81-82-83, c. 111, s. 4; 2001, c. 41, ss. 43 and 141(4).

ANNOTATIONS

Sections 38 to 38.16 do not violate either s. 96 of the *Constitution Act, 1867*, nor s. 7 of the Charter. Through s. 38.14 and the Charter, the criminal court trial judge possesses the means to safeguard the accused's fair trial rights: *R. v. Ahmad*, [2011] 1 S.C.R. 110, 264 C.C.C. (3d) 345.

This provision does not interfere with the core jurisdiction of the Superior Court: *Abou-Elmaati v. Canada (Attorney General)* (2011), 267 C.C.C. (3d) 1 (Ont. C.A.).

NOTICE TO ATTORNEY GENERAL OF CANADA / During a proceeding / Notice of disclosure from official / During a proceeding / Military proceedings / Exception / Exception / Schedule.

38.01 (1) Every participant who, in connection with a proceeding, is required to disclose, or expects to disclose or cause the disclosure of, information that the participant believes is sensitive information or potentially injurious information shall, as soon as possible, notify the Attorney General of Canada in writing of the possibility of the disclosure, and of the nature, date and place of the proceeding.

(2) Every participant who believes that sensitive information or potentially injurious information is about to be disclosed, whether by the participant or another person, in the course of a proceeding shall raise the matter with the person presiding at the proceeding and notify the Attorney General of Canada in writing of the matter as soon as possible, whether or not notice has been given under subsection (1). In such circumstances, the person presiding at the proceeding shall ensure that the information is not disclosed other than in accordance with this Act.

(3) An official, other than a participant, who believes that sensitive information or potentially injurious information may be disclosed in connection with a proceeding may notify the Attorney General of Canada in writing of the possibility of the disclosure, and of the nature, date and place of the proceeding.

(4) An official, other than a participant, who believes that sensitive information or potentially injurious information is about to be disclosed in the course of a proceeding may raise the matter with the person presiding at the proceeding. If the official raises the matter, he or she shall notify the Attorney General of Canada in writing of the matter as soon as possible, whether or not notice has been given under subsection (3), and the person presiding at the proceeding shall ensure that the information is not disclosed other than in accordance with this Act.

(5) In the case of a proceeding under Part III of the *National Defence Act*, notice under any of subsections (1) to (4) shall be given to both the Attorney General of Canada and the Minister of National Defence.

(6) This section does not apply when

- **(*a*) the information is disclosed by a person to their solicitor in connection with a proceeding, if the information is relevant to that proceeding;**
- **(*b*) the information is disclosed to enable the Attorney General of Canada, the Minister of National Defence, a judge or a court hearing an appeal from, or a review of, an order of the judge to discharge their responsibilities under section 38, this section and sections 38.02 to 38.13, 38.15 and 38.16;**
- **(*c*) disclosure of the information is authorized by the government institution in which or for which the information was produced or, if the information was not produced in or for a government institution, the government institution in which it was first received; or**
- **(*d*) the information is disclosed to an entity and, where applicable, for a purpose listed in the schedule.**

(7) Subsections (1) and (2) do not apply to a participant if a government institution referred to in paragraph (6)(*c*) advises the participant that it is not necessary, in order

to prevent disclosure of the information referred to in that paragraph, to give notice to the Attorney General of Canada under subsection (1) or to raise the matter with the person presiding under subsection (2).

(8) The Governor in Council may, by order, add to or delete from the schedule a reference to any entity or purpose, or amend such a reference. 2001, c. 41, s. 43.

ANNOTATIONS

The open court principle was not violated where the Director of Military Prosecutions required the charge sheet to be sealed and classified as "Secret" pending the appointment of a military judge to preside at the Standing Court Martial. The legislation permitted *in camera* hearings by a court martial where there were public safety or defence concerns: *Canada (Director of Military Prosecutions) v. Canada (Court Martial Administrator)* (2007), 288 D.L.R. (4th) 544 (F.C.A.).

DISCLOSURE PROHIBITED / Entities / Exceptions.

38.02 (1) Subject to subsection 38.01(6), no person shall disclose in connection with a proceeding

- **(*a*) information about which notice is given under any of subsections 38.01(1) to (4);**
- **(*b*) the fact that notice is given to the Attorney General of Canada under any of subsections 38.01(1) to (4), or to the Attorney General of Canada and the Minister of National Defence under subsection 38.01(5);**
- **(*c*) the fact that an application is made to the Federal Court under section 38.04 or that an appeal or review of an order made under any of subsections 38.06(1) to (3) in connection with the application is instituted; or**
- **(*d*) the fact that an agreement is entered into under section 38.031 or subsection 38.04(6).**

(1.1) When an entity listed in the schedule, for any purpose listed there in relation to that entity, makes a decision or order that would result in the disclosure of sensitive information or potentially injurious information, the entity shall not disclose the information or cause it to be disclosed until notice of intention to disclose the information has been given to the Attorney General of Canada and a period of 10 days has elapsed after notice was given.

(2) Disclosure of the information or the facts referred to in subsection (1) is not prohibited if

- **(*a*) the Attorney General of Canada authorizes the disclosure in writing under section 38.03 or by agreement under section 38.031 or subsection 38.04(6); or**
- **(*b*) a judge authorizes the disclosure under subsection 38.06(1) or (2) or a court hearing an appeal from, or a review of, the order of the judge authorizes the disclosure, and either the time provided to appeal the order or judgment has expired or no further appeal is available. 2001, c. 41, ss. 43 and 141(5).**

ANNOTATIONS

In *Ottawa Citizen Group Inc. v. Canada (Attorney General)* (2004), 122 C.R.R. (2d) 359, 255 F.T.R. 173 (F.C.), Lufty C.J. noted some concerns with the operation of these provisions, especially with this section, which gives the Attorney General, who is usually a party to the proceeding, the right to determine whether the fact that an application has been made should be disclosed.

AUTHORIZATION BY ATTORNEY GENERAL OF CANADA / Military proceedings / Notice.

38.03 (1) The Attorney General of Canada may, at any time and subject to any conditions that he or she considers appropriate, authorize the disclosure of all or part of the information and facts the disclosure of which is prohibited under subsection 38.02(1).

(2) In the case of a proceeding under Part III of the *National Defence Act*, the Attorney General of Canada may authorize disclosure only with the agreement of the Minister of National Defence.

(3) The Attorney General of Canada shall, within 10 days after the day on which he or she first receives a notice about information under any of subsections 38.01(1) to (4), notify in writing every person who provided notice under section 38.01 about that information of his or her decision with respect to disclosure of the information. 2001, c. 41, s. 43.

DISCLOSURE AGREEMENT / No application to Federal Court.

38.031 (1) The Attorney General of Canada and a person who has given notice under subsection 38.01(1) or (2) and is not required to disclose information but wishes, in connection with a proceeding, to disclose any facts referred to in paragraphs 38.02(1)(*b*) to (*d*) or information about which he or she gave the notice, or to cause that disclosure, may, before the person applies to the Federal Court under paragraph 38.04(2)(*c*), enter into an agreement that permits the disclosure of part of the facts or information or disclosure of the facts or information subject to conditions.

(2) If an agreement is entered into under subsection (1), the person may not apply to the Federal Court under paragraph 38.04(2)(*c*) with respect to the information about which he or she gave notice to the Attorney General of Canada under subsection 38.01(1) or (2). 2001, c. 41, ss. 43 and 141(6).

APPLICATION TO FEDERAL COURT — ATTORNEY GENERAL OF CANADA / Application to Federal Court — general / Notice to Attorney General of Canada / Court records / Procedure / Disclosure agreement / Termination of Court consideration, hearing, review or appeal.

38.04 (1) The Attorney General of Canada may, at any time and in any circumstances, apply to the Federal Court for an order with respect to the disclosure of information about which notice was given under any of subsections 38.01(1) to (4).

(2) If, with respect to information about which notice was given under any of subsections 38.01(1) to (4), the Attorney General of Canada does not provide notice of a decision in accordance with subsection 38.03(3) or, other than by an agreement under section 38.031, does not authorize the disclosure of the information or authorizes the disclosure of only part of the information or authorizes the disclosure subject to any conditions,

- **(*a*) the Attorney General of Canada shall apply to the Federal Court for an order with respect to disclosure of the information if a person who gave notice under subsection 38.01(1) or (2) is a witness;**
- **(*b*) a person, other than a witness, who is required to disclose information in connection with a proceeding shall apply to the Federal Court for an order with respect to disclosure of the information; and**
- **(*c*) a person who is not required to disclose information in connection with a proceeding but who wishes to disclose it or to cause its disclosure may apply to the Federal Court for an order with respect to disclosure of the information.**

(3) A person who applies to the Federal Court under paragraph (2)(*b*) or (*c*) shall provide notice of the application to the Attorney General of Canada.

(4) Subject to paragraph (5)(*a*.1), an application under this section is confidential. During the period when an application is confidential, the Chief Administrator of the Courts Administration Service may, subject to section 38.12, take any measure that he or she considers appropriate to protect the confidentiality of the application and the information to which it relates.

(5) As soon as the Federal Court is seized of an application under this section, the judge

- **(*a*) shall hear the representations of the Attorney General of Canada and, in the case of a proceeding under Part III of the *National Defence Act*, the Minister of National Defence, with respect to making the application public;**
- **(*a*.1) shall, if he or she decides that the application should be made public, make an order to that effect;**
- **(*a*.2) shall hear the representations of the Attorney General of Canada and, in the case of a proceeding under Part III of the *National Defence Act*, the Minister of National Defence, concerning the identity of all parties or witnesses whose interests may be affected by either the prohibition of disclosure or the conditions to which disclosure is subject, and concerning the persons who should be given notice of any hearing of the matter;**
- **(*b*) shall decide whether it is necessary to hold any hearing of the matter;**
- **(*c*) if he or she decides that a hearing should be held, shall**
  - **(i) determine who should be given notice of the hearing,**
  - **(ii) order the Attorney General of Canada to notify those persons, and**
  - **(iii) determine the content and form of the notice; and**
- **(*d*) if he or she considers it appropriate in the circumstances, may give any person the opportunity to make representations.**

(6) After the Federal Court is seized of an application made under paragraph (2)(*c*) or, in the case of an appeal from, or a review of, an order of the judge made under any of subsections 38.06(1) to (3) in connection with that application, before the appeal or review is disposed of,

- **(*a*) the Attorney General of Canada and the person who made the application may enter into an agreement that permits the disclosure of part of the facts referred to in paragraphs 38.02(1)(*b*) to (*d*) or part of the information, or disclosure of the facts or information subject to conditions; and**
- **(*b*) if an agreement is entered into, the Court's consideration of the application or any hearing, review or appeal shall be terminated.**

(7) Subject to subsection (6), after the Federal Court is seized of an application made under this section or, in the case of an appeal from, or a review of, an order of the judge made under any of subsections 38.06(1) to (3) before the appeal or review is disposed of, if the Attorney General of Canada authorizes the disclosure of all or part of the information or withdraws conditions to which the disclosure is subject, the Court's consideration of the application or any hearing, appeal or review shall be terminated in relation to that information, to the extent of the authorization or the withdrawal. 2001, c. 41, ss. 43 and 141(7); 2013, c. 9, s. 19.

ANNOTATIONS

Note: The provisions of this Act concerning disclosure of information that may be injurious to international relations and national defence and security have been substantially amended. Nevertheless, notes of cases decided under the former provisions may be of assistance in interpreting this and the companion provisions.

Where an objection is made to disclosure of information on the grounds that disclosure would be injurious to international relations or national security, the judge of the Federal Court (formerly the Chief Justice pursuant to former s. 38) has a discretion whether or not to inspect the documents involved and may properly conclude that they should only be inspected if it appears necessary to determine whether disclosure should be made. In determining whether to examine the information the judge may properly consider the apparent balance of the competing public interests and the likelihood that examination could alter the view of that balance and the impression as to whether disclosure should be ordered. Thus, in this case the refusal to order disclosure of the documents was upheld although the judge did not inspect the documents and relied on the certificate of the Solicitor General and a secret affidavit filed to explain why disclosure would be injurious to national security and international relations and identifying the general nature of the documents: *R. v. Goguen*, [1983] 2 F.C. 463, 10 C.C.C. (3d) 492 (C.A.).

Where objection is made to disclosure of documents on the basis of injury to international relations and other grounds such as police informer privilege, the judge has jurisdiction to deal with all of the objections: *R. v. Khan*, [1996] 2 F.C. 316, 110 F.T.R. 81 (T.D.).

In *Jose Pereira E Hijos, S.A. v. Canada (Attorney General)* (2002), 299 N.R. 154, 235 F.T.R. 158*n* (C.A.), the court approved the following factors from *R. v. Khan, supra*, in considering whether, under the former section, disclosure should be made of information alleged to be injurious to international relations: (a) the nature of the public interest sought to be protected by confidentiality; (b) whether the evidence in question will "probably establish a fact crucial to the defence"; (c) the seriousness of the charge or issues involved; (d) the admissibility of the documentation and the usefulness of it; (e) whether the applicants have established that there are no other reasonable ways of obtaining the information; and (f) whether the disclosures sought amount to general discovery or a fishing expedition.

The judge must make a preliminary determination of whether the information is relevant. If it is relevant, the judge must consider whether disclosure would be injurious to international relations, national defence or national security. The Attorney General's submissions regarding this assessment should be given considerable weight having regard to their access to special information. If injury would result, the judge should determine whether the public interest in disclosure outweighed in importance the public interest in non-disclosure. Balancing requires a more stringent test than the usual relevancy rule having regard to the following factors: the nature of the public interest sought to be protected by confidentiality; the seriousness of the charge or issues involved; the admissibility and usefulness of the documentation; whether there were other reasonable ways of obtaining the information and whether the information would probably establish a fact crucial to the defence: *R. v. Ribic* (2003), 185 C.C.C. (3d) 129, [2005] 1 F.C.R. 33 (C.A.), leave to appeal to S.C.C. refused 185 C.C.C. (3d) 129*n*.

It was open to the judge to prohibit the two defence witnesses from testifying at the trial and instead permit disclosure of an edited version of a transcript of their testimony before him on the application under this section. This edited transcript would be available for admission at the accused's trial: *R. v. Ribic, supra*.

The media's concern in keeping the public informed about proceedings under this part is not encompassed within the "interests" protected under subsec. (5). Where the media wishes to exercise its interests, in the legal sense of this term, it may seek to cause the disclosure of the information by initiating an application under subsec. (2)(*c*): *Toronto Star Newspapers Ltd. v. Canada* (2007), 278 D.L.R. (4th) 99 (F.C.).

REPORT RELATING TO PROCEEDINGS.

38.05 If he or she receives notice of a hearing under paragraph 38.04(5)(*c*), a person presiding or designated to preside at the proceeding to which the information relates or, if no person is designated, the person who has the authority to designate a person to preside may, within 10 days after the day on which he or she receives the notice, provide the judge with a report concerning any matter relating to the proceeding that the person considers may be of assistance to the judge. 2001, c. 41, s. 43.

DISCLOSURE ORDER / Disclosure — conditions / Order confirming prohibition / When determination takes effect / Evidence / Introduction into evidence / Relevant factors.

38.06 (1) Unless the judge concludes that the disclosure of the information or facts referred to in subsection 38.02(1) would be injurious to international relations or national defence or national security, the judge may, by order, authorize the disclosure of the information or facts.

(2) If the judge concludes that the disclosure of the information or facts would be injurious to international relations or national defence or national security but that the public interest in disclosure outweighs in importance the public interest in non-disclosure, the judge may by order, after considering both the public interest in disclosure and the form of and conditions to disclosure that are most likely to limit any injury to international relations or national defence or national security resulting from disclosure, authorize the disclosure, subject to any conditions that the judge considers appropriate, of all or part of the information or facts, a summary of the information or a written admission of facts relating to the information.

(3) If the judge does not authorize disclosure under subsection (1) or (2), the judge shall, by order, confirm the prohibition of disclosure.

(3.01) An order of the judge that authorizes disclosure does not take effect until the time provided or granted to appeal the order has expired or, if the order is appealed, the time provided or granted to appeal a judgment of an appeal court that confirms the order has expired and no further appeal from a judgment that confirms the order is available.

(3.1) The judge may receive into evidence anything that, in the opinion of the judge, is reliable and appropriate, even if it would not otherwise be admissible under Canadian law, and may base his or her decision on that evidence.

(4) A person who wishes to introduce into evidence material the disclosure of which is authorized under subsection (2) but who may not be able to do so in a proceeding by reason of the rules of admissibility that apply in the proceeding may request from a judge an order permitting the introduction into evidence of the material in a form or subject to any conditions fixed by that judge, as long as that form and those conditions comply with the order made under subsection (2).

(5) For the purpose of subsection (4), the judge shall consider all the factors that would be relevant for a determination of admissibility in the proceeding. 2001, c. 41, s. 43; 2013, c. 9, s. 20.

ANNOTATIONS

The proceeding under this section concerning disclosure of materials used to obtain a search warrant was premature when the Ontario Court of Justice had not yet made a determination under s. 487.3 of the *Criminal Code* whether or not to unseal the materials. Judicial economy and the scheme envisaged in this section support the view that the *Criminal Code* proceeding should be completed before further pursuing this application: *Ottawa Citizen Group Inc. v. Canada (Attorney General)* (2004), 122 C.R.R. (2d) 359, 255 F.T.R. 173 (F.C.).

Note: The provisions of this Act concerning disclosure of information that may be injurious to international relations and national defence and security have been substantially amended. Nevertheless, notes of cases decided under the former provisions may be of assistance in interpreting this and the companion provisions.

There is a heavy onus on an accused to justify disclosure where objection is taken on the basis of national security and may require that it be established that the evidence sought would probably establish a fact crucial to the defence. Moreover, it is unlikely that a case could ever be made out for disclosure where the evidence is sought for use on a preliminary inquiry, having regard to the function of the preliminary inquiry: *R. v. Kevork*, [1984] 2 F.C. 753, 17 C.C.C. (3d) 426 (T.D.).

It is not necessary for a party seeking documents, concerning which a claim of privilege has been made on the basis of the public interest in national security, to show that production is absolutely essential to the case. Nor is it an established rule that production will be refused if it is merely corroborative evidence or if the matter can otherwise be proved. The courts cannot abdicate their responsibility to balance the public interests involved merely because a claim of national security is made. On the other hand, the designated judge did not err in refusing production without examining the documents, where the information was not required as evidence at trial but merely for general discovery to determine whether any helpful evidence might in fact be available: *Gold v. Canada*, [1986] 2 F.C. 129, 25 D.L.R. (4th) 285 (C.A.).

The three-part test set out in *R. v. Ribic* (2003), 185 C.C.C. (3d) 129, [2005] 1 F.C.R. 33 (F.C.A.) [see note under s. 38.04] applies to an application by the Attorney General for non-disclosure of redacted parts of the final report of the Commission of Inquiry into the Actions of Canadian Officials in Relation to Maher Arar, bearing in mind, however, that the interests at stake in relation to an Inquiry are different from the liberty and security interests of an accused. The court will generally not prohibit disclosure of information already in the public domain and will not prohibit disclosure where the government's sole or primordial purpose for seeking prohibition is to shield itself from criticism or embarrassment: *Canada (Attorney General) v. Canada (Commission of Inquiry)* (2007), 72 Admin. L.R. (4th) 68, 316 F.T.R. 279 (F.C.).

"Information injurious to international relations" refers to information that, if disclosed, would be injurious to Canada's relationship with foreign nations. "National defence" refers to all measures taken by a nation to protect itself against its enemies, including protection of its collective ideals and values and the nation's military establishment. "National security" means, at minimum, the preservation of the Canadian way of life, including the safeguarding of the security of persons, institutions and freedoms in Canada: *Canada (Attorney General) v. Canada (Commission of Inquiry)*, *supra*.

It was open to the judge, in balancing the public interest in a fair trial, which includes the right to full answer and defence, and the public interest in protecting injurious information from disclosure, to disclose a descriptive summary of the documents containing the information at issue: *Canada (Attorney General) v. Khawaja* (2007), 228 C.C.C. (3d) 1 (F.C.A.).

There is no requirement that the judge afford the Attorney General another opportunity to make *ex parte* representations before releasing the decision ordering the disclosure of information. In appropriate cases, however, the Attorney General may bring a motion to reconsider under the *Federal Court Rules*: *Canada (Attorney General) v. Khawaja*, *supra*.

The decision on relevancy is for the judge and the fact that the Crown in the criminal proceedings was of the view that the material was relevant for purposes of its disclosure obligations is not determinative: *Canada (Attorney General) v. Khawaja*, *supra*.

NOTICE OF ORDER.

38.07 The judge may order the Attorney General of Canada to give notice of an order made under any of subsections 38.06(1) to (3) to any person who, in the opinion of the judge, should be notified. 2001, c. 41, s. 43.

AUTOMATIC REVIEW.

38.08 If the judge determines that a party to the proceeding whose interests are adversely affected by an order made under any of subsections 38.06(1) to (3) was not given the opportunity to make representations under paragraph 38.04(5)(*d*), the judge shall refer the order to the Federal Court of Appeal for review. 2001, c. 41, s. 43.

CAN. EV.

APPEAL TO FEDERAL COURT OF APPEAL / Limitation period for appeal.

38.09 (1) An order made under any of subsections 38.06(1) to (3) may be appealed to the Federal Court of Appeal.

(2) An appeal shall be brought within 10 days after the day on which the order is made or within any further time that the Court considers appropriate in the circumstances. 2001, c. 41, s. 43.

ANNOTATIONS

The power to order disclosure and the scope of disclosure is reviewable on the standard of correctness: *R. v. Ribic* (2003), 185 C.C.C. (3d) 129, [2005] 1 F.C.R. 83 (C.A.), leave to appeal to S.C.C. refused October 22, 2003.

LIMITATION PERIODS FOR APPEALS TO SUPREME COURT OF CANADA.

38.1 Notwithstanding any other Act of Parliament,

(*a*) an application for leave to appeal to the Supreme Court of Canada from a judgment made on appeal shall be made within 10 days after the day on which the judgment appealed from is made or within any further time that the Supreme Court of Canada considers appropriate in the circumstances; and

(*b*) if leave to appeal is granted, the appeal shall be brought in the manner set out in subsection 60(1) of the *Supreme Court Act* but within the time specified by the Supreme Court of Canada. 2001, c. 41, s. 43.

SPECIAL RULES — HEARING IN PRIVATE / Special rules — hearing in National Capital Region / *Ex parte* representations / *Ex parte* representations — public hearing.

38.11 (1) The judge conducting a hearing under subsection 38.04(5) or the court hearing an appeal or review of an order made under any of subsections 38.06(1) to (3) may make an order that the hearing be held, or the appeal or review be heard, in private.

(1.1) A hearing under subsection 38.04(5) or an appeal or review of an order made under any of subsections 38.06(1) to (3) shall, at the request of either the Attorney General of Canada or, in the case of a proceeding under Part III of the *National Defence Act*, the Minister of National Defence, be held or heard, as the case may be, in the National Capital Region, as described in the schedule to the *National Capital Act*.

(2) The judge conducting a hearing under subsection 38.04(5) or the court hearing an appeal or review of an order made under any of subsections 38.06(1) to (3) may give any person who makes representations under paragraph 38.04(5)(*d*), and shall give the Attorney General of Canada and, in the case of a proceeding under Part III of the *National Defence Act*, the Minister of National Defence, the opportunity to make representations *ex parte*.

(3) If a hearing under subsection 38.04(5) is held, or an appeal or review of an order made under any of subsections 38.06(1) to (3) is heard, in public, any ex parte representations made in that hearing, appeal or review shall be made in private. 2001, c. 41, s. 43; 2013, c. 9, s. 21.

ANNOTATIONS

Subsection (2), which allows for representations at *ex parte* hearings as of right by the Attorney General and by other parties with leave, does not violate an accused's rights under ss. 7 and 11(*d*) of the *Charter of Rights and Freedoms*: *Canada (Attorney General) v. Khawaja* (2007), 228 C.C.C. (3d) 17, 289 D.L.R. (4th) 260 (F.C.A.), leave to appeal to S.C.C. refused 289 D.L.R. (4th) vii.

PROTECTIVE ORDER / Court records.

38.12 (1) The judge conducting a hearing under subsection 38.04(5) or the court hearing an appeal or review of an order made under any of subsections 38.06(1) to (3) may make any order that the judge or the court considers appropriate in the circumstances to protect the confidentiality of any information to which the hearing, appeal or review relates.

(2) The court records relating to a hearing that is held, or an appeal or review that is heard, in private or to any ex parte representations are confidential. The judge or the court may order that the court records, or any part of them, relating to a private or public hearing, appeal or review be sealed and kept in a location to which the public has no access. 2001, c. 41, s. 43; 2013, c. 9, s. 22.

PROHIBITION CERTIFICATE / Military proceedings / Service of certificate / Filing of certificate / Effect of certificate / *Statutory Instruments Act* does not apply / Publication / Restriction / Expiry.

38.13 (1) The Attorney General of Canada may personally issue a certificate that prohibits the disclosure of information in connection with a proceeding for the purpose of protecting information obtained in confidence from, or in relation to, a foreign entity as defined in subsection 2(1) of the *Security of Information Act* or for the purpose of protecting national defence or national security. The certificate may only be issued after an order or decision that would result in the disclosure of the information to be subject to the certificate has been made under this or any other Act of Parliament.

(2) In the case of a proceeding under Part III of the *National Defence Act*, the Attorney General of Canada may issue the certificate only with the agreement, given personally, of the Minister of National Defence.

(3) The Attorney General of Canada shall cause a copy of the certificate to be served on

- **(*a*) the person presiding or designated to preside at the proceeding to which the information relates or, if no person is designated, the person who has the authority to designate a person to preside;**
- **(*b*) every party to the proceeding;**
- **(*c*) every person who gives notice under section 38.01 in connection with the proceeding;**
- **(*d*) every person who, in connection with the proceeding, may disclose, is required to disclose or may cause the disclosure of the information about which the Attorney General of Canada has received notice under section 38.01;**
- **(*e*) every party to a hearing under subsection 38.04(5) or to an appeal of an order made under any of subsections 38.06(1) to (3) in relation to the information;**
- **(*f*) the judge who conducts a hearing under subsection 38.04(5) and any court that hears an appeal from, or review of, an order made under any of subsections 38.06(1) to (3) in relation to the information; and**
- **(*g*) any other person who, in the opinion of the Attorney General of Canada, should be served.**

(4) The Attorney General of Canada shall cause a copy of the certificate to be filed

- **(*a*) with the person responsible for the records of the proceeding to which the information relates; and**
- **(*b*) in the Registry of the Federal Court and the registry of any court that hears an appeal from, or review of, an order made under any of subsections 38.06(1) to (3).**

(5) If the Attorney General of Canada issues a certificate, then, notwithstanding any other provision of this Act, disclosure of the information shall be prohibited in accordance with the terms of the certificate.

(6) The *Statutory Instruments Act* does not apply to a certificate issued under subsection (1).

(7) The Attorney General of Canada shall, without delay after a certificate is issued, cause the certificate to be published in the *Canada Gazette*.

(8) The certificate and any matters arising out of it are not subject to review or to be restrained, prohibited, removed, set aside or otherwise dealt with, except in accordance with section 38.131.

(9) The certificate expires 10 years after the day on which it is issued and may be reissued. 2001, c. 41, s. 43; 2013, c. 8, s. 23.

APPLICATION FOR REVIEW OF CERTIFICATE / Notice to Attorney General of Canada / Military proceedings / Single judge / Admissible information / Special rules and protective order / Expedited consideration / Varying the certificate / Cancelling the certificate / Confirming the certificate / Determination is final / Publication.

38.131 (1) A party to the proceeding referred to in section 38.13 may apply to the Federal Court of Appeal for an order varying or cancelling a certificate issued under that section on the grounds referred to in subsection (8) or (9), as the case may be.

(2) The applicant shall give notice of the application to the Attorney General of Canada.

(3) In the case of proceedings under Part III of the *National Defence Act*, notice under subsection (2) shall be given to both the Attorney General of Canada and the Minister of National Defence.

(4) Notwithstanding section 16 of the Federal Court Act, for the purposes of the application, the Federal Court of Appeal consists of a single judge of that Court.

(5) In considering the application, the judge may receive into evidence anything that, in the opinion of the judge, is reliable and appropriate, even if it would not otherwise be admissible under Canadian law, and may base a determination made under any of subsections (8) to (10) on that evidence.

(6) Sections 38.11 and 38.12 apply, with any necessary modifications, to an application made under subsection (1).

(7) The judge shall consider the application as soon as reasonably possible, but not later than 10 days after the application is made under subsection (1).

(8) If the judge determines that some of the information subject to the certificate does not relate either to information obtained in confidence from, or in relation to, a foreign entity as defined in subsection 2(1) of the *Security of Information Act*, or to national defence or national security, the judge shall make an order varying the certificate accordingly.

(9) If the judge determines that none of the information subject to the certificate relates to information obtained in confidence from, or in relation to, a foreign entity as defined in subsection 2(1) of the *Security of Information Act*, or to national defence or national security, the judge shall make an order cancelling the certificate.

(10) If the judge determines that all of the information subject to the certificate relates to information obtained in confidence from, or in relation to, a foreign entity as defined in subsection 2(1) of the *Security of Information Act*, or to national defence or national security, the judge shall make an order confirming the certificate.

(11) Notwithstanding any other Act of Parliament, a determination of a judge under any of subsections (8) to (10) is final and is not subject to review or appeal by any court.

(12) If a certificate is varied or cancelled under this section, the Attorney General of Canada shall, as soon as possible after the decision of the judge and in a manner that mentions the original publication of the certificate, cause to be published in the *Canada Gazette*

(*a*) the certificate as varied under subsection (8); or
(*b*) a notice of the cancellation of the certificate under subsection (9). 2001, c. 41, s. 43; 2004, c. 12, s. 19.

PROTECTION OF RIGHT TO A FAIR TRIAL / Potential orders.

38.14 (1) The person presiding at a criminal proceeding may make any order that he or she considers appropriate in the circumstances to protect the right of the accused to a fair trial, as long as that order complies with the terms of any order made under any of subsections 38.06(1) to (3) in relation to that proceeding, any judgment made on appeal from, or review of, the order, or any certificate issued under section 38.13.

(2) The orders that may be made under subsection (1) include, but are not limited to, the following orders:

(*a*) an order dismissing specified counts of the indictment or information, or permitting the indictment or information to proceed only in respect of a lesser or included offence;
(*b*) an order effecting a stay of the proceedings; and
(*c*) an order finding against any party on any issue relating to information the disclosure of which is prohibited. 2001, c. 41, s. 43.

ANNOTATIONS

Note: The provisions of this Act concerning disclosure of information that may be injurious to international relations and national defence and security have been substantially amended. Nevertheless, the note of the following case decided under the former provisions may be of assistance in interpreting this and the companion provisions.

Where the judge (the Chief Justice of the Federal Court or his designate under the former legislation), has refused disclosure to the accused of certain evidence by reason of an objection by the Canadian Security Intelligence Service on the basis of national security, at the subsequent trial of the accused the trial judge would be entitled to grant a stay of proceedings, in view of the breach of the accused's right to fundamental justice brought about by the unavailability of this evidence, only where it is established that the evidence is critical or essential. Such a burden is reasonable in order to avoid fishing expeditions in all cases when it is likely that C.S.I.S. had some hand in gathering information. The burden is on the accused to persuade the trial court that there is evidence being denied that is of a critical nature without which the accused will probably not be able to make full answer and defence. Finally, it may be that where the Federal Court judge has not even inspected the material before making his decision to refuse disclosure, the trial court may be in a position to grant a conditional stay urging inspection of the material: *R. v. Kevork*, [1984] 2 F.C. 753, 17 C.C.C. (3d) 426 (T.D.).

In one of the first cases to consider this section, the court held that the trial judge did not err in refusing to grant a stay of proceedings. While the accused was not able to call two witnesses, that part of their evidence necessary to support the defence was placed before the court in the form of redacted transcripts of testimony that the witnesses had given *in camera* under questioning by counsel for the Attorney General, but in the absence of the accused and his counsel. The courts had adopted sufficient measures to protect the accused's rights: *R. v. Ribic* (2008), 238 C.C.C. (3d) 225 (Ont. C.A.).

Trial judges have the authority to order whatever remedy pursuant to the Charter and s. 38.14 is required to protect the accused's right to a fair trial. If the trial process resulting from the application of the s. 38 scheme becomes unmanageable by virtue of excessive gaps between the hearing of the evidence or other impediments, such that the right of the accused to a fair trial is compromised, the trial judge should not hesitate to use the broad authority Parliament has conferred under s. 38.14 to put an end to the prosecution. The stay of proceedings remedy in s. 38.14 is a statutory remedy to be considered and applied in its own context. It should not be limited by the non-statutory "clearest of cases" test for a stay under the Charter jurisprudence: *R. v. Ahmad*, [2011] 1 S.C.R. 110, 264 C.C.C. (3d) 345.

FIAT / Effect of fiat / Fiat filed in court / Fiat constitutes conclusive proof / Military proceedings.

38.15 (1) If sensitive information or potentially injurious information may be disclosed in connection with a prosecution that is not instituted by the Attorney General of Canada or on his or her behalf, the Attorney General of Canada may issue a fiat and serve the fiat on the prosecutor.

(2) When a fiat is served on a prosecutor, the fiat establishes the exclusive authority of the Attorney General of Canada with respect to the conduct of the prosecution described in the fiat or any related process.

(3) If a prosecution described in the fiat or any related process is conducted by or on behalf of the Attorney General of Canada, the fiat or a copy of the fiat shall be filed with the court in which the prosecution or process is conducted.

(4) The fiat or a copy of the fiat

- **(*a*) is conclusive proof that the prosecution described in the fiat or any related process may be conducted by or on behalf of the Attorney General of Canada; and**
- **(*b*) is admissible in evidence without proof of the signature or official character of the Attorney General of Canada.**

(5) This section does not apply to a proceeding under Part III of the *National Defence Act*. 2001, c. 41, s. 43.

REGULATIONS.

38.16 The Governor in Council may make any regulations that the Governor in Council considers necessary to carry into effect the purposes and provisions of sections 38 to 38.15, including regulations respecting the notices, certificates and the fiat. 2001, c. 41, s. 43.

ANNUAL REPORT.

38.17 Each year the Attorney General of Canada shall prepare and cause to be laid before each House of Parliament a report for the previous year on the operation of sections 38.13 and 38.15 that includes the number of certificates and fiats issued under sections 38.13 and 38.15, respectively. 2013, c. 9, s. 24.

Confidences of the Queen's Privy Council for Canada

OBJECTION RELATING TO A CONFIDENCE OF THE QUEEN'S PRIVY COUNCIL / Definition / Definition of "Council" — Exception.

39. (1) Where a minister of the Crown or the Clerk of the Privy Council objects to the disclosure of information before a court, person or body with jurisdiction to compel the production of information by certifying in writing that the information constitutes a confidence of the Queen's Privy Council for Canada, disclosure of the information shall be refused without examination or hearing of the information by the court, person or body.

(2) For the purpose of subsection (1), "a confidence of the Queen's Privy Council for Canada" includes, without restricting the generality thereof, information contained in

- **(*a*) a memorandum the purpose of which is to present proposals or recommendations to Council;**

(*b*) a discussion paper the purpose of which is to present background explanations, analyses of problems or policy options to Council for consideration by Council in making decisions;

(*c*) an agendum of Council or a record recording deliberations or decisions of Council;

(*d*) a record used for or reflecting communications or discussions between ministers of the Crown on matters relating to the making of government decisions or the formulation of government policy;

(*e*) a record the purpose of which is to brief Ministers of the Crown in relation to matters that are brought before, or are proposed to be brought before, Council or that are the subject of communications or discussions referred to in paragraph (*d*); and

(*f*) draft legislation.

(3) For the purposes of subsection (2), "Council" means the Queen's Privy Council for Canada, committees of the Queen's Privy Council for Canada, Cabinet and committees of Cabinet.

(4) Subsection (1) does not apply in respect of

(*a*) a confidence of the Queen's Privy Council for Canada that has been in existence for more than twenty years; or

(*b*) a discussion paper described in paragraph (2)(*b*)

(i) if the decisions to which the discussion paper relates have been made public, or

(ii) where the decisions have not been made public, if four years have passed since the decisions were made. 1980-81-82-83, c. 111, s. 4; 2001, c. 41, s. 43 (title only).

ANNOTATIONS

To be valid, a certification must be done by the Clerk or a minister, must relate to information within subsec. (2), must be done in a *bona fide* exercise of delegated power, and must be done to prevent disclosure of hitherto confidential information. The certificate must provide a sufficient description of the information to establish on its face that the information is a Cabinet confidence and falls within the categories of subsec. (2) or an analogous category. The kind of description required for claims of solicitor-client privilege under the civil rules will generally suffice and will generally require disclosure of the date, title, author and recipient of the document containing the information. Waiver in the ordinary sense does not apply to information protected by this section. Disclosure of some information does not remove the protection from other, non-disclosed information. However, subsec. (1) cannot be applied retroactively to documents that have already been produced in litigation and if the related information has been disclosed in other documents, this section does not apply and the documents containing the information must be produced. If the related information is contained in documents that have been properly certified, the government is under no obligation to disclose the related information. The refusal to disclose information may permit a court to draw an adverse inference. In this case, this section did not apply to certified documents that were previously disclosed and in the possession of the plaintiffs. As well, the plaintiffs were entitled to cross-examine the affiant on statements in an affidavit previously filed in the proceedings, despite the objection by the government under this section: *Babcock v. Canada (Attorney General)*, [2002] 3 S.C.R. 3.

This section leaves little scope for judicial review of a certification of Cabinet confidentiality. Nevertheless, certification may be challenged where the information does not on its face fall within subsec. (1), or where it can be shown that the Clerk or the minister has improperly exercised the discretion conferred by subsec. (1). The party challenging the certification may present evidence of improper motives in the issue of the certificate, or otherwise present evidence to support the claim of improper issuance. However, the court, person or body reviewing the issuance of the certificate is not entitled to examine the challenged information to make the determination. It would seem that the court, person or body before whom the objection to disclosure is made has jurisdiction to review the certificate and is competent to make orders for disclosure for improperly claimed protection: *Babcock v. Canada (Attorney General)*, *supra*.

This section is constitutional and not inconsistent with unwritten principles of the Canadian Constitution such as the rule of law, the independence of the judiciary and the separation of powers. The section also does not violate s. 96 of the *Constitution Act, 1867* by invading the core jurisdiction of the superior courts: *Babcock v. Canada (Attorney General)*, *supra*.

This section only applies to prevent disclosure of documents. However, where documents, although certified under this section, have been inadvertently disclosed, the Crown may seek a common law remedy requiring their return because of public interest immunity. In this case, the court refused to order return of the documents. The defendant did not allege that the confidential information in the disputed documents involved sensitive policy issues. The court considered, among other things, that the documents also did not appear to contain information from the highest level of government, such as Cabinet itself, and the plaintiffs obtained the information from the documents in a legal manner and received a number of the documents before they were certified under this section. Moreover, they had already received a number of deliberately disclosed documents containing Cabinet confidences. To preclude the admission of the inadvertently disclosed documents could result in an incomplete or misleading evidentiary basis upon which the court must fairly assess the plaintiffs' claims: *Babcock v. Canada (Attorney General)* (2004), 246 D.L.R. (4th) 549 (B.C.S.C.).

While this section can be applied *ex post facto* where a document was mistakenly turned over through inadvertence (see *Pelletier v. Canada*, [2005] 3 F.C.R. 317, 253 D.L.R. (4th) 435 (F.C.A.)), it could not be said that a document, now said to come within this section, was inadvertently disclosed when counsel adverted to whether it should be disclosed and, in fact, provided a redacted version of the document in the course of the discovery process with the approval of the Minister's chief of staff. The Crown could not establish an essential requirement for valid certification, namely, that a calculated disclosure had not already taken place: *Lax Kw'Alaams Indian Band v. Canada (Minister of Western Economic Deversification)* (2006), 294 F.T.R. 233 (F.C.).

While this section is to be strictly construed, it does not impose any specific requirements as to the form of the certificate such as the need for a seal of the Office of the Clerk of the Privy Council. The 20-year-period referred to in subsec. (4)(*a*) is to be calculated as of the date of the application not the date when the trial may take place. On the other hand, a party may be entitled to disclosure of documents if the age of the confidence comes to exceed 20 years before the trial ends: *Samson Indian Band v. Canada* (1996), 110 F.T.R. 1 *sub nom. Buffalo v. Canada (Minister of Indian Affairs and Northern Development)*, [1996] 2 F.C. 483 (T.D.).

As to the form of the certificate under this section see: *Canada (Attorney General) v. Central Cartage Co.* (1988), 23 F.T.R. 174 *sub nom. Canada (Minister of Industry, Trade and Commerce) v. Central Cartage Co.*, 24 C.P.R. (3d) 350 (T.D.), revd 71 D.L.R. (4th) 253, [1990] 2 F.C. 641 (C.A.), leave to appeal to S.C.C. refused 128 D.L.R. (4th) viii.

An objection to disclosure is properly taken under this section in respect of material in the possession of the body whose decision it is sought to review under s. 28 of the *Federal Court Act*. The determination of the validity of the objection is made pursuant to this section by the Chief Justice or a judge designated by him: *Henrie v. Canada (Security Intelligence Review Committee)* (1992), 88 D.L.R. (4th) 575 (F.C.A.).

A memorandum to a single minister of the Crown acting under statutory authority cannot amount to a confidence of the Privy Council within the meaning of this section, since the section makes it clear that only information that concerns the Cabinet in the collegial sense can qualify for the absolute privilege. However, documents which were sent to two ministers because two ministers were responsible for making the single decision did qualify under this section: *Canadian Assn. of Regulated Importers v. Canada (Attorney General)*, [1992] 2 F.C. 130, 87 D.L.R. (4th) 730 (C.A.), leave to appeal to S.C.C. refused 96 D.L.R. (4th) vi.

In *R. v. Carey*, [1986] 2 S.C.R. 637, 30 C.C.C. (3d) 498 (7:0), the court reviewed at length the qustion of state privilege at common law in relation to cabinet documents and held that there is no rule at common law that cabinet documents are absolutely immune from disclosure. While that case must be read with care when applied to the statutory provisions under this Act it may prove of assistance in interpreting those provisions.

To a similar effect see *Nova Scotia (Attorney General) v. Nova Scotia (Royal Commission Into Marshall Prosecution)* (1988), 44 C.C.C. (3d) 330 (N.S.C.A.), affd [1989] 2 S.C.R. 788, 50 C.C.C. (3d) 486, holding that a Royal Commission could properly require cabinet members (the present and former Attorneys General) to testify as to the nature of cabinet discussions concerning the prosecution under investigation by the Royal Commission.

This section does not violate the equality rights in s. 15 of the Charter: *Canadian Assn. of Regulated Importers v. Canada (Attorney General), supra.*

This section gives rise to a separate and distinct proceeding in the superior court of the province or in the Federal Court, Trial Division. Accordingly, the trial judge was entitled to hold an *in camera* meeting with the crown and R.C.M.P. officer, on the consent of all parties, to determine the nature of the claim: *R. v. Pilotte* (2002), 163 C.C.C. (3d) 225 (Ont. C.A.), leave to appeal to S.C.C. refused 170 C.C.C. (3d) vi.

Journalistic Sources

DEFINITIONS / "document" / "journalistic source" / Objection / Former journalist / Power of court, person or body / Objection of court, person or body / Observations / Authorization / Conditions / Burden of proof / Appeal / Limitation period for appeal / Hearing in summary way.

39.1 (1) The following definitions apply in this section.

"document" has the same meaning as in section 487.011 of the *Criminal Code.*

"journalist" means a person whose main occupation is to contribute directly, either regularly or occasionally, for consideration, to the collection, writing or production of information for dissemination by the media, or anyone who assists such a person.

"journalistic source" means a source that confidentially transmits information to a journalist on the journalist's undertaking not to divulge the identity of the source, whose anonymity is essential to the relationship between the journalist and the source.

(2) Subject to subsection (7), a journalist may object to the disclosure of information or a document before a court, person or body with the authority to compel the disclosure of information on the grounds that the information or document identifies or is likely to identify a journalistic source.

(3) For the purposes of subsections (2) and (7), "journalist" includes an individual who was a journalist when information that identifies or is likely to identify the journalistic source was transmitted to that individual.

(4) The court, person or body may raise the application of subsection (2) on their own initiative.

(5) When an objection or the application of subsection (2) is raised, the court, person or body shall ensure that the information or document is not disclosed other than in accordance with this section.

(6) Before determining the question, the court, person or body must give the parties and interested persons a reasonable opportunity to present observations.

(7) The court, person or body may authorize the disclosure of information or a document only if they consider that

(*a*) the information or document cannot be produced in evidence by any other reasonable means; and

(*b*) the public interest in the administration of justice outweighs the public interest in preserving the confidentiality of the journalistic source, having regard to, among other things,

(i) the importance of the information or document to a central issue in the proceeding,

(ii) freedom of the press, and

(iii) the impact of disclosure on the journalistic source and the journalist.

(8) An authorization under subsection (7) may contain any conditions that the court, person or body considers appropriate to protect the identity of the journalistic source.

(9) A person who requests the disclosure has the burden of proving that the conditions set out in subsection (7) are fulfilled.

(10) An appeal lies from a determination under subsection (7)

(*a*) to the Federal Court of Appeal from a determination of the Federal Court;

(*b*) to the court of appeal of a province from a determination of a superior court of the province;

(*c*) to the Federal Court from a determination of a court, person or body vested with power to compel production by or under an Act of Parliament if the court, person or body is not established under a law of a province; or

(*d*) to the trial division or trial court of the superior court of the province within which the court, person or body exercises its jurisdiction, in any other case.

(11) An appeal under subsection (10) shall be brought within 10 days after the date of the determination appealed from or within any further time that the court having jurisdiction to hear the appeal considers appropriate in the circumstances.

(12) An appeal under subsection (10) shall be heard and determined without delay and in a summary way. 2017, c. 22, s. 2.

Provincial Laws of Evidence

HOW APPLICABLE.

40. In all proceedings over which Parliament has legislative authority, the laws of evidence in force in the province in which those proceedings are taken, including the laws of proof of service of any warrant, summons, subpoena or other document, subject to this Act and other Acts of Parliament, apply to those proceedings. R.S., c. E-10, s. 37.

ANNOTATIONS

Provincial procedural enactments, such as one providing for use of another language at trial, are not "laws of evidence" within this section: *R. v. Murphy, ex p. Belisle and Moreau*, [1968] 4 C.C.C. 229, 5 C.R.N.S. 68 (N.B.C.A.).

It was held in *R. v. Marshall*, [1961] S.C.R. 123, 129 C.C.C. 232 (5:0), that provincial legislation, rendering inadmissible an accident report made by a motorist at "any trial", when properly construed applied only to trials of offences within provincial jurisdiction and not for criminal offences. Nor could such legislation apply to the trial of criminal offences by virtue of this section.

However, admission at a trial for a criminal offence of such a statement that is made under statutory compulsion would violate the principle against self-incrimination as protected by s. 7 of the *Canadian Charter of Rights and Freedoms*: *R. v. White*, [1999] 2 S.C.R. 417, 135 C.C.C. (3d) 257.

Similarly, it was held that the combined effect of this section and s. 8(2) of the *Criminal Code* is to incorporate in the criminal law by legislation the common law in effect in a province immediately before April 1, 1955, including for example the rule respecting secrecy of the identities of police informers. Thus, provincial legislation which sought to abrogate that rule would be either *ultra vires* or inoperative: *Bisaillon v. Keable*, [1983] 2 S.C.R. 60, 7 C.C.C. (3d) 385 (7:0).

This section must be given a narrow scope so as to avoid unacceptable differences from province to province on fundamental matters of criminal evidence and thus, for example, should be restricted to the proof of matters within provincial competence: *R. v. Albright*, [1987] 2 S.C.R. 383, 37 C.C.C. (3d) 105 (5:0).

Provincial legislation making admissible a certificate of the Deputy Registrar of Motor Vehicles demonstrating ownership of a motor vehicle is not applicable to trial of federal offences. Such legislation is inconsistent with s. 8(2) of the *Criminal Code* which preserves the common law and the certificate would be inadmissible hearsay at common law: *R. v. Richardson* (1980), 57 C.C.C. (2d) 403, [1981] 2 W.W.R. 755 (Alta. C.A.). *Contra: R. v. Bell* (2001), 152 C.C.C. (3d) 534, 11 M.V.R. (4th) 1 (B.C.C.A.), leave to appeal to S.C.C. refused 155 C.C.C. (3d) vi.

This section is to be given a narrow scope and restricted to matters within provincial competency so as to avoid unacceptable differences between provinces respecting the admissibility of relevant evidence tendered by affidavit under s. 30 in a prosecution under federal legislation: *R. v. Nickerson* (1991), 106 N.S.R. (2d) 300 (C.A.) [prosecution under the *Fisheries Act*]; *R. v. Ducharme* (1999), 182 Sask. R. 138 (Q.B.) [prosecution under the *Excise Tax Act*].

Statutory Declarations

SOLEMN DECLARATION.

41. Any judge, notary public, justice of the peace, provincial court judge, recorder, mayor or commissioner authorized to take affidavits to be used either in the provincial or federal courts, or any other functionary authorized by law to administer an oath in any matter, may receive the solemn declaration of any person voluntarily making the declaration before him, in the following form, in attestation of the execution of any writing, deed or instrument, or of the truth of any fact, or of any account rendered in writing:

> **I, ..., solemnly declare that (*state the fact or facts declared to*), and I make this solemn declaration conscientiously believing it to be true, and knowing that it is of the same force and effect as if made under oath.**
>
> **Declared before me .... at .... this .... day of .... 19 ......**

R.S., c. E-10, s. 38; R.S.C. 1985, c. 27 (1st Supp.), s. 203(1).

Insurance Proofs

AFFIDAVITS, ETC.

42. Any affidavit, solemn affirmation or declaration required by any insurance company authorized by law to do business in Canada, in regard to any loss of or injury to person, property or life insured or assured therein, may be taken before any commissioner or other person authorized to take affidavits, before any justice of the peace or before any notary public for any province, and the commissioner, person, justice of the peace or notary public is required to take the affidavit, solemn affirmation or declaration. R.S., c. E-10, s. 39.

Part II / *Application*

FOREIGN COURTS.

43. This Part applies to the taking of evidence relating to proceedings in courts out of Canada. R.S., c. E-10, s. 40.

Interpretation

DEFINITIONS / "cause" / "court" / "judge" / "oath".

44. In this Part,

"cause" includes a proceeding against a criminal;

"court" means any superior court in any province;

"judge" means any judge of any superior court in any province;

"oath" includes a solemn affirmation in cases in which, by the law of Canada, or of a province, as the case may be, a solemn affirmation is allowed instead of an oath. R.S., c. E-10, s. 41; 1984, c. 40, s. 27.

CONSTRUCTION.

45. This Part shall not be so construed as to interfere with the right of legislation of the legislature of any province requisite or desirable for the carrying out of the objects hereof. R.S., c. E-10, s. 42.

Procedure

ORDER FOR EXAMINATION OF WITNESS IN CANADA / Video links, etc.

46. (1) If, on an application for that purpose, it is made to appear to any court or judge that any court or tribunal outside Canada, before which any civil, commercial or criminal matter is pending, is desirous of obtaining the testimony in relation to that matter of a party or witness within the jurisdiction of the first mentioned court, of the court to which the judge belongs or of the judge, the court or judge may, in its or their discretion, order the examination on oath on interrogatories, or otherwise, before any person or persons named in the order, of that party or witness accordingly, and by the same or any subsequent order may command the attendance of that party or witness for the purpose of being examined, and for the production of any writings or other documents mentioned in the order and of any other writings or documents relating to the matter in question that are in the possession or power of that party or witness.

(2) For greater certainty, testimony for the purposes of subsection (1) may be given by means of technology that permits the virtual presence of the party or witness before the court or tribunal outside Canada or that permits that court or tribunal, and the parties, to hear and examine the party or witness. R.S., c. E-10, s. 43; 1999, c. 18, s. 89.

ANNOTATIONS

Letters rogatory may be enforced by the court of one province with respect to documents then held by an employee of a federal department in another province: *Re Request For International Judicial Assistance* (1979), 49 C.C.C. (2d) 276 (Alta. Q.B.), revd on other grounds 58 C.C.C. (2d) 274 (Alta. C.A.), judgment restored, the court not dealing with this point [1982] 1 S.C.R. 414, *sub nom. District Court of the United States, Middle District of*

Florida v. Royal American Shows Inc.; United States v. Royal American Shows Inc., 66 C.C.C. (2d) 125.

In an unusual case, *Gulf Oil Corp. v. Gulf Canada Ltd.*, [1980] 2 S.C.R. 39, 111 D.L.R. (3d) 74, the Supreme Court of Canada took jurisdiction under this section but refused to exercise its discretion to enforce letters rogatory from United States courts in view of federal government policy which was contrary to disclosure of the documents sought by the United States courts.

A Canadian court may grant a request for production of documents only. The order for production need not be ancillary to an order for examination of a specific witness: *District Court of the United States, Middle District of Florida v. Royal American Shows Inc.; United States of America v. Royal American Shows Inc.*, [1982] 1 S.C.R. 414, 66 C.C.C. (2d) 125 (5:0).

The court's power under this section will not be exercised where the person whose attendance for examination is sought is an accused in pending criminal proceedings in the requesting court and the testimony sought is for the purpose of such proceedings. While Canadian courts in the interest of comity will give judicial assistance whenever possible, comity recognizes that judicial assistance may be denied where its exercise would violate the public policy of the state to which the appeal is made or conflicts with local notions of justice, such as in Canada the right of an accused not to be compelled to testify against himself: *Uszinska v. Republic of France* (1980), 52 C.C.C. (2d) 39 (Ont. H.C.J.).

Courts will not generally exercise their discretion in favour of enforcing letters rogatory merely to provide a basis for corroboration of available evidence. Further, the court will not enforce a request for production of documents which is too wide, too vague and too general to call for production by persons who are strangers to the litigation: *Seminole Electric Co-operative, Inc. v. BBC Brown Boveri, Inc.* (1987), 35 D.L.R. (4th) 102, 80 N.B.R. (2d) 91 (Q.B.).

The court has no power to limit a specific request for production of documents from a foreign court and where the request is too general to be enforced then the request must be refused: *Re Scholnick and Bank of Nova Scotia* (1987), 59 O.R. (2d) 538 (H.C.J.); *Seminole Electric Cooperative Inc. v. BBC Brown Boveri, Inc., supra.*

An order for examination of witnesses may be made under this section even where the proceedings are at a pre-trial stage. Thus an order was made at the request of Swiss authorities where the provisions of this section had been complied with, and the request for assistance had come through the proper diplomatic channels, and if the order were refused the purpose of the Treaty under which Switzerland would conduct a surrogate criminal prosecution in respect of Canadian charges against Swiss citizens would be frustrated: *R. v. Zingre, Wuest and Reiser*, [1981] 2 S.C.R. 392, 61 C.C.C. (2d) 465 (9:0).

An order may be made under this section even if there is no criminal charge pending in the foreign court. It is sufficient that there is a criminal matter pending, as in this case where a judicial officer was conducting the proceeding on the basis of a formal written complaint alleging criminal conduct. The magistrate conducting the proceeding was required to determine whether the accused should stand trial in much the same way as a judge presiding at a preliminary inquiry. With respect to the requirement that the foreign court must be a court of competent jurisdiction, judicial reciprocity is not an element of the requesting court's jurisdictional competence, but may be an element to be considered in the exercise of discretion under this section: *France (Republic) v. De Havilland Aircraft of Canada Ltd.* (1991), 65 C.C.C. (3d) 449 (Ont. C.A.).

Provided that the proceeding in the foreign court has the *indicia* of a criminal proceeding, this section applies even if no actual charges have yet been laid: *Germany (Federal Republic) v. Canadian Imperial Bank of Commerce* (1997), 31 O.R. (3d) 684 (Gen. Div.).

In *Presbyterian Church of Sudan v. Taylor* (2006), 275 D.L.R. (4th) 512, 215 O.A.C. 149 (C.A.), the court adopted the following criteria from *Fecht v. Deloitte & Touche* (1996), 28 O.R. (3d) 188, 47 C.P.C. (3d) 165 (Gen. Div.), affd 32 O.R. (3d) 417, 97 O.A.C. 241 (C.A.), for when an order giving effect to letters rogatory will be made. The evidence (including the letters rogatory) must establish that: (1) the evidence sought is relevant; (2) the evidence sought is necessary for trial and will be adduced at trial, if admissible; (3) the evidence is not otherwise obtainable; (4) the order sought is not contrary to public policy; (5) the documents sought are identified with reasonable specificity; and (6) the order sought is not unduly burdensome, having in mind what the relevant witnesses would be required to do, and produce, were the action to be tried here. Also see: *OPSEU Pension Trust Fund v. Clark* (2006), 270 D.L.R. (4th) 429, 212 O.A.C. 286 *sub nom. Ontario Public Service Employees Union Pension Trust Fund v. Clark* (C.A.); *Monster Energy Co. v. Craig* (2016), 402 D.L.R. (4th) 286 (B.C.C.A.), additional reasons (2016), 273 A.C.W.S. (3d) 258, 2016 BCCA 484.

ENFORCEMENT OF THE ORDER.

47. On the service on the party or witness of an order referred to in section 46, and of an appointment of a time and place for the examination of the party or witness signed by the person named in the order for taking the examination, or, if more than one person is named, by one of the persons named, and on payment or tender of the like conduct money as is properly payable on attendance at a trial, the order may be enforced in like manner as an order made by the court or judge in a cause pending in that court or before that judge. R.S., c. E-10, s. 44.

EXPENSES AND CONDUCT MONEY.

48. Every person whose attendance is required in the manner described is entitled to the like conduct money and payment for expenses and loss of time as on attendance at a trial. R.S., c. E-10, s. 45.

ADMINISTERING OATH.

49. On any examination of parties or witnesses, under the authority of any order made in pursuance of this Part, the oath shall be administered by the person authorized to take the examination, or, if more than one person is authorized, by one of those persons. R.S., c. E-10, s. 46.

RIGHT OF REFUSAL TO ANSWER OR PRODUCE DOCUMENT / Laws about witnesses to apply — video links etc. / Contempt of court in Canada / Nature of right.

50. (1) Any person examined under any order made under this Part has the like right to refuse to answer questions tending to criminate himself, or other questions, as a party or witness, as the case may be, would have in any cause pending in the court by which, or by a judge whereof, the order is made.

(1.1) Despite subsection (1), when a party or witness gives evidence under subsection 46(2), the evidence shall be given as though they were physically before the court or tribunal outside Canada, for the purposes of the laws relating to evidence and procedure but only to the extent that giving the evidence would not disclose information otherwise protected by the Canadian law of non-disclosure of information or privilege.

(1.2) When a party or witness gives evidence under subsection 46(2), the Canadian law relating to contempt of court applies with respect to a refusal by the party or witness to answer a question or to produce a writing or document referred to in subsection 46(1), as ordered under that subsection by the court or judge.

(2) No person shall be compelled to produce, under any order referred to in subsection (1), any writing or other document that he could not be compelled to produce at a trial of such a cause. R.S., c. E-10, s. 47; 1999, c. 18, s. 90.

RULES OF COURT / Letters rogatory.

51. (1) The court may frame rules and orders in relation to procedure and to the evidence to be produced in support of the application for an order for examination of parties and witnesses under this Part, and generally for carrying this Part into effect.

(2) In the absence of any order in relation to the evidence to be produced in support of the application referred to in subsection (1), letters rogatory from a court or tribunal outside Canada in which the civil, commercial or criminal matter is pending, are deemed and taken to be sufficient evidence in support of the application. R.S., c. E-10, s. 48; 1999, c. 18, s. 91.

Part III / *Application*

APPLICATION OF THIS PART.

52. This Part extends to the following classes of persons:

(*a*) officers of any of Her Majesty's diplomatic or consular services while performing their functions in any foreign country, including ambassadors, envoys, ministers, charges d'affaires, counsellors, secretaries, attaches, consuls general, consuls, vice-consuls, pro-consuls, consular agents, acting consuls general, acting consuls, acting vice-consuls and acting consular agents;

(*b*) officers of the Canadian diplomatic, consular and representative services while performing their functions in any foreign country or in any part of the Commonwealth and Dependent Territories other than Canada, including, in addition to the diplomatic and consular officers mentioned in paragraph (*a*), high commissioners, permanent delegates, acting high commissioners, acting permanent delegates, counsellors and secretaries;

(*c*) Canadian Government Trade Commissioners and Assistant Canadian Government Trade Commissioners while performing their functions in any foreign country or in any part of the Commonwealth and Dependent Territories other than Canada;

(*d*) honorary consular officers of Canada while performing their functions in any foreign country or in any part of the Commonwealth and Dependent Territories other than Canada; and

(*e*) judicial officials in a foreign country in respect of oaths, affidavits, solemn affirmations, declarations or similar documents that the official is authorized to administer, take or receive.

(*f*) persons locally engaged and designated by the Deputy Minister of Foreign Affairs or any other person authorized by that Deputy Minister while performing their functions in any foreign country or in any part of the Commonwealth and Dependent Territories other than Canada. R.S., c. E-10, s. 49; 1984, c. 40, s. 27; 1994, c. 44, s. 92; 1997, c. 18, s. 118.

ANNOTATIONS

The term "judicial officials" in para. (*e*) goes to the capacity of the individuals to administer an oath or affirmation, not to their status as a judge. This paragraph is not restricted to judges or high-ranking officials: *R. v. Jahanrakhshan* (2013), 296 C.C.C. (3d) 553 (B.C.C.A.), additional reasons (2013), 301 C.C.C. (3d) 334 (B.C.C.A.), affd (2013), 582 W.A.C. 69 (B.C.C.A.).

Oaths and Solemn Affirmations

OATHS TAKEN ABROAD.

53. Oaths, affidavits, solemn affirmations or declarations administered, taken or received outside Canada by any person mentioned in section 52 are as valid and effectual and are of the like force and effect to all intents and purposes as if they had been administered, taken or received in Canada by a person authorized to administer, take or receive oaths, affidavits, solemn affirmations or declarations therein that are valid and effectual under this Act. R.S., c. E-10, s. 50.

ANNOTATIONS

While it is not clear that this section when taken with s. 40 of this Act was intended to be exclusive and to limit the admissibility of affidavits to those sworn abroad before persons mentioned in s. 52, where the trial is in the Federal Court, s. 53 of the *Federal Court Act*, R.S.C. 1970, c. 10 (2nd Supp.), makes the law of evidence of the province applicable notwithstanding s. 40 of this Act. Thus if the trial is in Ontario an affidavit sworn before a notary public as permitted by the Ontario *Evidence Act* was admissible: *Kemanord AB v. PPG Industries, Inc.* (1980), 49 C.P.R. (2d) 29, [1981] 1 F.C. 567 (T.D.); *Cooper & Beatty Ltd. v. Alpha Graphics Ltd.* (1980), 49 C.P.R. (2d) 145 (F.C.T.D.).

Documentary Evidence

DOCUMENTS TO BE ADMITTED IN EVIDENCE / Status of statements.

54. (1) Any document that purports to have affixed, impressed or subscribed on it or to it the signature of any person authorized by any of paragraphs 52(*a*) to (*d*) to administer, take or receive oaths, affidavits, solemn affirmations or declarations, together with their seal or with the seal or stamp of their office, or the office to which the person is attached, in testimony of any oath, affidavit, solemn affirmation or declaration being administered, taken or received by the person, shall be admitted in evidence, without proof of the seal or stamp or of the person's signature or official character.

(2) An affidavit, solemn affirmation, declaration or other similar statement taken or received in a foreign country by an official referred to in paragraph 52(*e*) shall be admitted in evidence without proof of the signature or official character of the official appearing to have signed the affidavit, solemn affirmation, declaration or other statement. R.S., c. E-10, s. 51; 1994, c. 44, s. 93.

SCHEDULE

(Paragraph 38.01(6)(d) and subsection 38.01(8))

DESIGNATED ENTITIES

1. A judge of the Federal Court, for the purposes of section 21 of *the Canadian Security Intelligence Service Act*

2. A judge of the Federal Court, for the purposes of sections 6 and 7 of the *Charities Registration (Security Information) Act*, except where the hearing is open to the public

3. A judge of the Federal Court, the Federal Court of Appeal or the Immigration Division or Immigration Appeal Division of the Immigration and Refugee Board, for the purposes of sections 77 to 87.1 of the *Immigration and Refugee Protection Act*

4. A judge of the Federal Court, for the purposes of section 16 of the *Secure Air Travel Act*

5. [*Repealed*, 2001, c. 41, s. 124(3).]

6. [*Repealed*, 2001, c. 41, s. 124(3).]

7. [*Repealed*, 2001, c. 41, s. 124(3).]

8. [*Repealed*, 2001, c. 41, s. 124(3).]

9. A board of inquiry convened under section 45 of the *National Defence Act*

10. A service tribunal or a military judge for the purposes of Part III of the *National Defence Act*

11. The Federal Public Sector Labour Relations and Employment Board referred to in subsection 4(1) of the *Federal Public Sector Labour Relations and Employment Board Act*, for the purposes of a grievance process under the *Federal Public Sector Labour Relations Act* with respect to an employee of the Canadian Security Intelligence Service, with the exception of any information provided to the Board by the employee

12. The Information Commissioner, for the purposes of the *Access to Information Act*

13. The Privacy Commissioner, for the purposes of the *Privacy Act*

14. The Privacy Commissioner, for the purposes of the *Personal Information Protection and Electronic Documents Act*

15. A judge of the Federal Court, for the purposes of sections 41 and 42 of the *Access to Information Act*

16. A judge of the Federal Court, for the purpose of sections 41 to 43 of the *Privacy Act*

17. A judge of the Federal Court, for the purpose of sections 14 to 17 of the *Personal Information Protection and Electronic Documents Act*

18. The Security Intelligence Review Committee established by subsection 34(1) of the *Canadian Security Intelligence Service Act*, for the purposes of sections 41 and 42 of that Act, with the exception of any information provided to the committee by the complainant or an individual who has been denied a security clearance

19. The Public Sector Integrity Commissioner, for the purposes of sections 26 to 35 of the *Public Servants Disclosure Protection Act*

20. The Commissioner of the Communications Security Establishment, except where the hearing or proceeding is open to the public

21. A judge of the Federal Court, for the purposes of sections 4 and 6 of the *Prevention of Terrorist Travel Act*

22. The Civilian Review and Complaints Commission for the Royal Canadian Mounted Police, for the purposes of the *Royal Canadian Mounted Police Act*, but only in relation to information that is under the control, or in the possession, of the Royal Canadian Mounted Police. S.C. 2001, c. 41, ss. 44 and 124(2), (3); 2003, c. 22, s. 105; SOR/2004-19; SOR/2006-80, s. 1; SOR/2006-335, s. 1; 2005, c. 46, s. 56; 2006, c. 9, s. 222; SOR/2006-80, s. 1; 2008, c. 3, s. 11; SOR/2012-220, s. 1; 2013, c. 18, ss. 45, 85; c. 40, s. 448; 2015, c. 20, s. 13; c. 36, s. 43; 2017, c. 9, s. 41.

CANADIAN CHARTER OF RIGHTS AND FREEDOMS

Being Part I of the Constitution Act, 1982

Enacted by the *Canada Act 1982* (U.K.) c. 11; proclaimed in force April 17, 1982
Amended by the Constitution Amendment Proclamation, 1983, SI/84-102, effective June 21, 1984
Amended by the Constitution Amendment, 1993 (New Brunswick), SI/93-54, *Can. Gaz., Part II*, April 7, 1993, effective March 12, 1993

Whereas Canada is founded upon principles that recognize the supremacy of God and the rule of law:

Guarantee of Rights and Freedoms

RIGHTS AND FREEDOMS IN CANADA.

1. The *Canadian Charter of Rights and Freedoms* guarantees the rights and freedoms set out in it subject only to such reasonable limits prescribed by law as can be demonstrably justified in a free and democratic society.

ANNOTATIONS

Interpretation – In seeking to justify legislation within the meaning of this section it is not open to the government to rely on a purpose which is outside its legislative jurisdiction. Thus, in the case of the *Lords Day Act*, R.S.C. 1970, c. L-13, Parliament's jurisdiction to enact this legislation depended on its characterization as legislation directed to the preservation of the sanctity of the Christian Sabbath and was therefore a matter within the criminal law power. It was then not open to the government to attempt to justify the legislation under this section against an attack based on the guarantee of freedom of religion in s. 2(*a*), on the basis that the legislation's true purpose was a secular one: *R. v. Big M Drug Mart Ltd.* (1985), 18 C.C.C. (3d) 385, [1985] 1 S.C.R. 295, 18 D.L.R. (4th) 321.

This section has two functions. It constitutionally guarantees the rights and freedoms set out in the following provisions and states explicitly the exclusive justificatory criteria against which limitations on those rights and freedoms must be measured. Accordingly, any inquiry under this section is premised on an understanding that the impugned limit violates the constitutional rights and freedoms which are part of the supreme law of Canada. To establish that a limit is justified under this section two central criteria must be satisfied. First, the objective which the measures responsible for a limit on a Charter right or freedom are designed to serve must be of sufficient importance to warrant overriding a constitutionally protected right or freedom, and secondly, the party invoking this section must show that the means chosen are reasonable and demonstrably justified. The first criterion requires at a minimum that an objective relate to concerns which are pressing and substantial in a free and democratic society. The second requirement involves a form of proportionality test and while the nature of this test will vary, depending on the circumstances, in each case the courts will be required to balance the interests of society with those of the individual and of groups. There are three important components of the proportionality test. First, the measures adopted must be carefully designed to achieve the objective in question. The measures must not be arbitrary, unfair or based on irrational considerations but rather must be rationally connected to the objective. Second, the means, even if rationally connected to the objective, should impair as little as possible the right or freedom in question, and finally, there must be a

CHARTER

proportionality between the effects of the measures which are responsible for limiting the Charter right or freedom and the objective which has been identified as of sufficient importance. The more severe the deleterious effects of a measure, the more important the objective must be if the measure is to be reasonable and demonstrably justified in a free and democratic society: *R. v. Oakes* (1986), 24 C.C.C. (3d) 321, [1986] 1 S.C.R. 103, 50 C.R. (3d) 1.

A reasonable limit within the meaning of this section is one which it was reasonable for the legislature to impose. Courts are not called upon to substitute judicial opinions for legislative ones as to the place at which to draw a precise line. It is open to the legislature to restrict its legislative reforms to sectors in which there appear to be particularly urgent concerns or to constituencies that seem especially needy. Further, legislative choices regarding alternative forms of business regulation do not generally impinge on the values and provisions of the Charter, and the resultant legislation need not be tuned with great precision in order to withstand judicial scrutiny: *R. v. Edwards Books & Art Ltd.; R. v. Nortown Foods Ltd*, [1986] 2 S.C.R. 713, 30 C.C.C. (3d) 385, 55 C.R. (3d) 193.

The various sections of the Charter must not be read in isolation from each other. The Charter protects a complex of interacting values, each more or less fundamental to the free and democratic society that is Canada. Each section must be interpreted in light of the value structure sought to be protected by the Charter as a whole and in light of a content of the other specific rights and freedoms which it embodies: *R. v. Lyons* (1987), 37 C.C.C. (3d) 1, [1987] 2 S.C.R. 309, 61 C.R. (3d) 1.

Legislation may meet the requirement under this section of having been enacted to meet a pressing and substantial objective, notwithstanding the legislation is not confined to protecting the most clearly vulnerable group. In enacting protective legislation, the legislature is required only to exercise a reasonable judgment in specifying the vulnerable group. Whether the means chosen impair the right or freedom in question as little as possible will depend on the government objective and on the means available to achieve it. In matching means to ends and asking whether rights or freedoms are impaired as little as possible, a legislature mediating between the claims of competing groups will be forced to strike a balance without the benefit of absolute certainty concerning how the balance is best struck. The choice of means, like the choice of ends, frequently will require an assessment of conflicting scientific evidence and differing justified demands on scarce resources. As courts review the results of the legislature's deliberations, particularly with respect to the protection of vulnerable groups, they must be mindful of the legislature's representative function. Less certainty may be possible when the government is mediating between different groups than when the government itself is the antagonist of the individual whose right has been infringed. The court will not, in the name of minimal impairment, take a restrictive approach to social science evidence and require legislatures to choose the least ambitious means to protect vulnerable groups. There must, nevertheless, be a sound evidentiary basis for the government's conclusions: *Irwin Toy Ltd. v. Quebec (Attorney General)*, [1989] 1 S.C.R. 927, 58 D.L.R. (4th) 577, 24 Q.A.C. 2.

While context, deference and a flexible and realistic standard of proof are essential aspects of the analysis under this section, these concepts must not be attenuated to the point that they relieve the state of the burden the Charter imposes of demonstrating that the limits imposed on constitutional rights and freedoms are reasonable and justifiable in a free and democratic society. Care must be taken in the first step of a s. 1 analysis not to overstate the objective of the infringing measures: *RJR-MacDonald Inc. v. Canada (Attorney General)*, [1995] 3 S.C.R. 199, 100 C.C.C. (3d) 449, 127 D.L.R. (4th) 1.

Prescribed by law – Limitations on rights cannot be left to the unfettered discretion of administrative bodies: *Reference re: Education Act of Ontario and Minority Language Education Rights* (1984), 10 D.L.R. (4th) 491, 47 O.R. (2d) 1, 11 C.R.R. 17, 27 M.P.L.R. 1 (C.A.).

The term "law" in this section includes common law as well as statute law: *R. v. Canadian Newspapers Company Ltd.* (1984), 16 C.C.C. (3d) 495, 31 Man. R. (2d) 187, 13 C.R.R. 43 (C.A.).

A limit will be prescribed by law within the meaning of this section if it is expressly provided for by statute or regulation, or results by necessary implication from the terms of a statute or regulation or from its operating requirements. The limit may also result from the application of a common law rule: *R. v. Therens*, [1985] 1 S.C.R. 613, 18 C.C.C. (3d) 481, 45 C.R. (3d) 97.

A limit is prescribed by law where the measure falls within the scope of reasonable police authority conferred by necessary implication from the operational requirements of the governing provincial and federal legislative provisions — in this case the right to stop vehicles under provincial highway traffic legislation and in the police duty to enforce s. 254 of the *Criminal Code*: *R. v. Elias; R. v. Orbanski*, [2005] 2 S.C.R. 3, 196 C.C.C. (3d) 481, 29 C.R. (6th) 205.

The test to be applied to determine whether a statute is prescribed by law is whether the law provides an intelligible standard according to which the judiciary must do it work. In determining whether a law does prescribe an intelligible standard, consideration must be given to the manner in which the provision has been judicially interpreted: *R. v. Butler*, [1992] 1 S.C.R. 452, 70 C.C.C. (3d) 129, 11 C.R. (4th) 137.

CHARTER

Burden of proof – The onus of proving that a limit on a right or freedom guaranteed by the Charter is reasonable and demonstrably justified in a free and democratic society rests upon the party seeking to uphold the limitation. While the standard of proof under this section is the civil standard, this test must be applied rigorously and where evidence is required in order to prove the constituent elements of a s. 1 inquiry, and this will generally be the case, it should be cogent and persuasive and made clear to the court the consequences of imposing or not imposing a limit. The court will also need to know what alternative measures for implementing the objective were available to the legislators when they made their decisions. It may be however that there will be cases where certain elements of the analysis under this section are obvious or self-evident: *R. v. Oakes, supra.*

Evidence – It is open to the Court of Appeal to receive evidence in the form of statistical and other statements of social and economic facts, which are the kind of evidence of which the court may take judicial notice in considering the application of this section, notwithstanding that the evidence had not been adduced by the Crown and the courts below. Provided that the other party is given notice of the materials and given an opportunity to reply, the court should take judicial notice of relevant matters of social and economic facts, whether or not they have been available to the trial judge. In this case, the court also noted that it may soon be that judicial notice can be taken of the special problem posed by the drinking driver without materials being adduced before the court: *R. v. Bonin* (1989), 47 C.C.C. (3d) 230, 11 M.V.R. (2d) 31 (B.C.C.A.), leave to appeal to S.C.C. refused 50 C.C.C. (3d) vi, 102 N.R. 400*n*.

Where the basis for legislation is not obvious, the government must, in order to meet its burden under this section, bring forward cogent and persuasive evidence demonstrating that the provisions in issue are justified. In showing that the legislation pursues a pressing and substantial objective, it is not open to the government to assert *post facto* a purpose which did not animate the legislation in the first place. However, in proving that the original objective remains pressing and substantial, the government can and should draw upon the best evidence currently available. Studies subsequent to the enactment of the legislation can be used for the purpose, as well as for the purpose of establishing that the measure is proportional to its objective: *Irwin Toy Ltd. v. Quebec (Attorney General), supra.*

Fundamental Freedoms

FUNDAMENTAL FREEDOMS.

2. Everyone has the following fundamental freedoms:

(*a*) freedom of conscience and religion;

(*b*) freedom of thought, belief, opinion and expression, including freedom of the press and other media of communication;

(*c*) freedom of peaceful assembly; and

(*d*) freedom of association.

ANNOTATIONS

Section 2(*a*): Freedom of religion – The essence of the concept of freedom of religion is the right to entertain such religious beliefs as a person chooses, the right to declare religious beliefs openly and without fear of hindrance or reprisal and the right to manifest religious belief by worship and practice or by teaching and dissemination. The freedom guaranteed by s. 2(*a*) also includes protection against governmental coercion in matters of conscience and religion. Coercion includes not only such blatant forms of compulsion as direct commands to act or refrain from acting on pain of sanction, but also indirect forms of control which determine or limit alternative courses of conduct subject to such limitations as are necessary to protect public safety, order, health or morals or the fundamental rights and freedoms of others, no one is to be forced to act in a way contrary to his belief or his conscience. Whatever else freedom of conscience and religion may mean, it means at the very least that the government may not coerce individuals to affirm a specific religious belief or to manifest a specific religious practice for a sectarian purpose. The Charter protects not only the right to hold and manifest beliefs, but also the right to express and manifest religious non-belief and to refuse to participate in religious practice: *R. v. Big M Drug Mart Ltd.*, [1985] 1 S.C.R. 295, 18 C.C.C. (3d) 385, 18 D.L.R. (4th) 321.

Legislation with a secular inspiration does not abridge the freedom from conformity to religious dogma merely because statutory provisions coincide with the tenets of a religion: *R. v. Edwards Books & Art Ltd.; R. v. Nortown Foods Ltd.*, [1986] 2 S.C.R. 713, 30 C.C.C. (3d) 385, 55 C.R. (3d) 193.

Not every effect of legislation on religious beliefs or practices is offensive to the guarantee provided by s. 2(*a*). That paragraph does not require that the legislature refrain from imposing any burdens on the practice of religion. Legislative or administrative action whose effect on religion is trivial or insubstantial is not a breach of freedom of religion: *R. v. Jones*, [1986] 2 S.C.R. 284, 28 C.C.C. (3d) 513, 31 D.L.R. (4th) 569.

Religious communications are not *prima facie* privileged. However, in a particular case, the court could exclude evidence where the communication between the accused and a religious adviser met the so-called "Wigmore" criteria: (1) the communication must originate in a confidence that it will not be disclosed; (2) this element of confidentiality must be essential to the full and satisfactory maintenance of the relation between the parties; (3) the relation must be one which in the opinion of the community ought to be seduously fostered; (4) the injury that would inure to the relation by the disclosure of the communication must be greater than the benefit thereby gained for the correct disposal of the litigation. However, the fact that the communication was not made to an ordained priest or minister or that it did not constitute a formal confession, will not bar the possibility of the communication being excluded: *R. v. Gruenke*, [1991] 3 S.C.R. 263, 67 C.C.C. (3d) 289, [1991] 6 W.W.R. 673.

Section 2(*b*): Freedom of expression / Interpretation – Section 2(*b*) protects all forms of expression, whether oral, written, pictorial, sculpture, music, dance or film. The freedom of expression referred to, moreover, extends to those engaged in expression for profit and those who wish to express the ideas of others, and to the recipients as well as to the originators of communication: *Ontario Film v. Video Appreciation Society* (1983), 34 C.R. (3d) 73, 147 D.L.R. (3d) 58, 41 O.R. (2d) 583 (Div. Ct.), affd 38 C.R. (3d) 271, 5 D.L.R. (4th) 766*n*, 45

O.R. (2d) 80*n*, 7 C.R.R. 129 (C.A.). Similarly: *R. v. Videoflicks Ltd.* (1984), 15 C.C.C. (3d) 353, 14 D.L.R. (4th) 10, 48 O.R. (2d) 395 (C.A.), affd on other grounds 30 C.C.C. (3d) 385, [1986] 2 S.C.R. 713, 35 D.L.R. (4th) 1, *sub nom. R. v. Edwards Books & Art Ltd.*

Where government action is challenged under s. 2(*b*), the first step which the court must take is to ascertain whether the activity which the person challenging the government action wishes to pursue may properly be characterized as falling within freedom of expression. Where an activity conveys or attempts to convey a meaning, it has expressive content and *prima facie* falls within the scope of the guarantee. Freedom of expression was entrenched in the Charter to ensure that everyone can manifest thoughts, opinions, beliefs and indeed all expressions of the heart and mind however unpopular, distasteful or contrary to the mainstream. Human activity cannot therefore be excluded from the scope of guaranteed free expression on the basis of the content or meaning being conveyed. Once it is determined that the activity in issue comes within the scope of freedom of expression, the next step is to determine whether the purpose or effect of the government action is to restrict freedom of expression. If the government has aimed to control attempts to convey a meaning either by directly restricting the content of expression or by restricting a form of expression tied to content, its purpose trenches upon the guarantee. Where however it aims only to control the physical consequences of particular conduct, its purpose does not trench upon the guarantee. Even if the government's purpose is not to control or restrict attempts to convey a meaning, the court must still decide whether the effect of a government action is to restrict free expression. The burden is on the person challenging government action to demonstrate the existence of such an effect, and to show that the activity in issue promotes at least one of the principles and values underlying the freedom. Those principles and values are: that seeking and attaining the truth is an inherently good activity; that participation in social and political decision-making is to be fostered and encouraged; and that diversity in forms of individual self-fulfillment and human flourishing ought to be cultivated in an essentially tolerant and welcoming environment, not only for the sake of those who convey a meaning, but also for the sake of those to whom it is conveyed: *Irwin Toy Ltd. v. Quebec (Attorney General)*, [1989] 1 S.C.R. 927, 58 D.L.R. (4th) 577.

There is no sound basis on which commercial expression can be excluded from the protection of s. 2(*b*). The guarantee in this paragraph is intended to protect both listeners as well as speakers, and is not confined to political expression. Over and above its intrinsic value as expression, commercial expression plays a significant role in enabling individuals to form economic choices, an important aspect of individual self-fulfillment and personal autonomy: *Ford v. Quebec (Attorney General)*, [1988] 2 S.C.R. 712, 54 D.L.R. (4th) 577, *sub nom. Chaussure Brown's Inc. v. Quebec (Attorney General)*.

Freedom of expression entails the right to say nothing. The combination of the unattributed health warnings and the prohibition against displaying any other information which could allow tobacco manufacturers to express their own views in the *Tobacco Products Control Act*, S.C. 1988, c. 20, thus constitutes an infringement of the right to free expression guaranteed by para. (*b*): *RJR-MacDonald Inc. v. Canada (Attorney General)*, [1995] 3 S.C.R. 199, 100 C.C.C. (3d) 449.

Freedom of expression as guaranteed by s. 2(*b*) includes the freedom to express oneself in the language of one's choice. Language is so intimately related to the form and content of expression that there cannot be true freedom of expression by means of language if one is prohibited from using the language of one's choice: *Ford v. Quebec (Attorney General)*, *supra*.

Activities cannot be excluded from the scope of the guarantee in this paragraph on the basis of the content or meaning conveyed and, thus, the prohibition on communication for the purpose of prostitution or of obtaining the services of a prostitute is a violation of this paragraph. However, eradication of the various forms of social nuisance arising from the public display of the sale of sex is an objective of sufficient importance to warrant a limitation of the freedom of expression and the means chosen by Parliament in s. 212(1)(*c*) of the *Criminal Code* is a proportional response and, thus, a reasonable limit within the meaning of s. 1: *Reference re ss. 193 and 195.1(1)(c) of the Criminal Code*, [1990] 1 S.C.R. 1123, 56 C.C.C. (3d) 65 (4:2).

The term "expression" embraces all content of expression irrespective of the particular meaning or message sought to be conveyed and no matter how invidious and obnoxious the message. While the court has held that expression which is communicated in a physically violent form may not be protected, communications such as hate propaganda cannot be considered as violence nor as analogous to violence so as to fall outside the protection of this subsection. Moreover, even threats of violence fall within the protection of this subsection and their suppression must be justified under s. 1. Further, it would be inappropriate to attenuate the freedom of expression guarantee by attempting to balance it against other protected rights and freedoms such as those in ss. 15 and 27 dealing with equality and multiculturalism. The preferable course is to weigh the various contextual values and factors in the s. 1 analysis: *R. v. Keegstra*, [1990] 3 S.C.R. 397, 61 C.C.C. (3d) 1 (4:3). However, the level of protection to which expression may be entitled will vary with the nature of the expression. The further that expression is from the core values of this right, as with the offence of defamatory libel, the greater will be the ability to justify the state's restrictive action: *R. v. Lucas*, [1998] 1 S.C.R. 439, 123 C.C.C. (3d) 97.

This paragraph does not import any new or additional requirements for the issuance of search warrants at media premises. However, this paragraph does provide a backdrop against which the reasonableness of such a search may be evaluated and there must be a careful consideration as to whether the warrant should issue and also the conditions which might be imposed. Ordinarily, the information to obtain the warrant should disclose whether there are alternative sources from which the information may reasonably be obtained and if there is an alternative source, that it has been investigated and all reasonable efforts to obtain the information have been exhausted. If a search will impede the media from fulfilling its functions of news gatherer and news disseminator, then a warrant should only be issued where a compelling state interest is demonstrated. The fact that the information sought has already been disseminated, in whole or in part, to the public by the media will ordinarily favour the granting of the warrant: *C.B.C. v. New Brunswick (Attorney General)*, [1991] 3 S.C.R. 459, 67 C.C.C. (3d) 544 (6:1); *C.B.C. v. Lessard*, [1991] 3 S.C.R. 421, 67 C.C.C. (3d) 517 (6:1).

Access to judicial proceedings – While public accessibility to the courts is not explicitly guaranteed by the Charter, such access, having regard to its historical origin and necessary purpose, is an integral and implicit part of the guarantee to everyone of freedom of opinion and expression including freedom of the press. The rule of openness in courts fosters the necessary public confidence in the integrity of the court system and an understanding of the administration of justice: *R. v. Southam Inc. (No. 1)* (1983), 3 C.C.C. (3d) 515, 146 D.L.R. (3d) 408 (Ont. C.A.).

The open court principle and the rights conferred by s. 2(*b*) embrace not only the media's right to publish or broadcast information about court proceedings, but also the media's right to gather that information and the right of listeners to receive it. The media's rights are not limited to attending court and reporting on what transpires in the courtroom but, absent some proven countervailing interest, also includes the right to access exhibits and to make copies. When an exhibit is introduced as evidence to be used without restriction in a judicial proceeding, the entire exhibit becomes part of the record. There is, therefore, no principled reason to restrict media access to only those portions played or read in open court: *R. v. Canadian Broadcasting Corp.* (2010), 262 C.C.C. (3d) 455 (Ont. C.A.).

Restrictions on picketing – In any form of picketing there is at least some element of expression. The union is making a statement to the general public that it is involved in a dispute, that it is seeking to impose its will on the object of picketing and that it solicits the assistance of the public in honouring picket lines. While action on the part of the picketers will always accompany the expression, picketing is therefore entitled to protection under this paragraph unless it is accompanied by a form of action, such as threats of violence, disruption of property, assault or other clearly unlawful conduct, that alters the nature of the whole transaction and removes it from Charter protection. Picketing intended to bring about economic pressure and induce a breach of contract nonetheless comes within s. 2(*b*). It is however necessary in the general social interest that picketing be regulated and sometimes limited. However, by virtue of s. 32, the Charter only applies to the legislative, executive and administrative branches of government. It will apply to them whenever their action is invoked in public or private litigation, and whether their action relies on statutory authority or on the authority or justification of a rule of the common law. The Charter will apply to the common law, however, only in so far as it is the basis of some government action alleged to infringe a guaranteed right or freedom. A court order such as an injunction sought to restrict picketing is not an element of government intervention sufficient to invoke the Charter, for otherwise the Charter would apply to all private litigation. The Charter will therefore not apply in an action by one private party relying on the common law of inducing breach of contract to obtain an injunction restraining secondary picketing by another private party: *Retail, Wholesale & Department Union, Local 580 v. Dolphin Delivery Ltd.*, [1986] 2 S.C.R. 573, 33 D.L.R. (4th) 174.

The definition of "picketing" contained in the British Columbia *Labour Relations Code* was overly broad and infringed the guarantee of freedom of expression contained in this paragraph. The effect of the definition was to prohibit consumer leafleting at secondary sites: *UFCW, Local 1518 v. KMart Canada Ltd.*, [1999] 2 S.C.R. 1083, 176 D.L.R. (4th) 607.

Both primary and secondary picketing are forms of expression, even when associated with tortious acts. Limitations on secondary picketing are permitted, but only to the extent that this is shown to be reasonable and demonstrably necessary in a free and democratic society. Although the *Charter* was not directly engaged by the secondary picketing in the course of a labour dispute, the common law must be interpreted in a manner consistent with *Charter* values. Of the possible approaches to the problem of regulating secondary picketing, the one that best conforms to this Charter-mandated methodology is the approach of permitting secondary picketing except where it involves tortious or criminal action: *Pepsi-Cola Canada Beverages (West) Ltd. v. RWDSU, Local 558*, [2002] 1 S.C.R. 156, 208 D.L.R. (4th) 385.

Freedom of the press – Even assuming that s. 2(*b*) enshrines the right to gather news, the witness in this case had not demonstrated that compelling journalists to testify before bodies such as the Labour Relations Board would detrimentally affect journalists' ability to gather information. Accordingly the witness had failed to demonstrate any breach of her right under this section: *Moysa v. Alberta (Labour Relations Board)*, [1989] 1 S.C.R. 1572, 60 D.L.R. (4th) 1.

There is no constitutional immunity for confidential journalistic sources and accordingly, a judicial order compelling disclosure would not violate s. 2(*b*). A journalist-confidential source privilege must be considered on a case-by-case basis having regard to the four Wigmore criteria as informed by the freedom of expression and the rights of the media: *National Post v. Canada*, [2010] 1 S.C.R. 477, 254 C.C.C. (3d) 469.

Freedom of the press is not absolute save for s. 1 limitations: it is circumscribed by the rights of others, inherent in the concept of a democratic freedom. The reconciliation of freedom of the press and the right of the individual to a fair trial does not infringe either right. The press will be free to publish the information after the case has been tried. The accused can have a fair trial only if the trial is not debated publicly, before a verdict is rendered. To the extent that freedom of expression is hindered by the law of contempt, the hindrance is a corollary of the competing right of an accused person to a fair trial. The requirement that the press await the outcome of a trial before publishing information prejudicial to the accused does not infringe the freedom of expression guaranteed by the Charter: *Attorney General for Manitoba v. Groupe Quebecor Inc.* (1987), 37 C.C.C. (3d) 421, 59 C.R. (3d) 1 (Man. C.A.).

A newspaper article concerning accused facing trials is protected by s. 2(*b*), notwithstanding that the publication of the article offends the *sub judice* rule. However the offence of criminal contempt *sub judice* constitutes a reasonable limit within the meaning

CHARTER

of s. 1. While freedom of expression including freedom of the press and other media of communication are vital in a democratic society, the accused also have a right to a fair trial as guaranteed by s. 11(*d*): *R. v. Robinson-Blackmore Printing & Publishing Co*. (1989), 47 C.C.C. (3d) 366, 73 Nfld. & P.E.I.R. 46 (Nfld. S.C.).

Rules preventing media organizations from filming, taking photographs, and conducting interviews in the public areas of courthouses, and preventing them from broadcasting official audio recordings of court proceedings infringe s. 2(*b*) but are justified under s. 1: *Canadian Broadcasting Corp. v. Canada (Attorney General)*, [2011] 1 S.C.R. 19, 264 C.C.C. (3d) 1.

Section 2(*c*): Freedom of assembly – The courts should require that the Crown show a compelling reason why basic rights of an individual to do what is lawful should be curtailed. Thus, a condition of release pending trial that the accused not attend at a demonstration or demonstrate or in any way cause a disturbance within half a mile of a particular factory should not have been imposed upon the accused following his release on bail pending trial on a charge of obstructing police. The rights of an accused cannot be restricted on a speculative concern of danger: *R. v. Collins* (1982), 31 C.R. (3d) 283 (Ont. Co. Ct.).

Section 2(*d*): Freedom of association – The right to strike does not come within the freedom of association as guaranteed by s. 2(*d*). The purpose of freedom of association is to guarantee that activities and goals may be pursued in common. What s. 2(*d*) protects is the exercise in association of such rights as have Charter protection when exercised by the individual, together with the freedom to associate for the purpose of activities which are lawful when performed alone: *Reference re Public Service Employees Relations Act, Labour Relations Act and Police Officers Collective Bargaining Act*, [1987] 1 S.C.R. 313, 38 D.L.R. (4th) 161.

The purpose of this paragraph is to allow the achievement of individual potential through interpersonal relationships and collective action. Ordinarily, this section does not oblige the state to take affirmative action to safeguard or facilitate the exercise of fundamental freedoms. However, it has been recognized in the past that a posture of governmental restraint in the area of labour relations will expose most workers to a range of unfair labour practices and potentially to legal liability because of common law prohibitions. To make the freedom to organize meaningful, this paragraph may impose a positive obligation on the state to extend to protective legislation to unprotected groups. A claim of underinclusion under this section must be grounded in fundamental Charter freedoms. The claimant must demonstrate that exclusion from a statutory regime permits a substantial interference with the exercise of protected activity under this paragraph and the context must be such that the state can be truly held accountable for any inability to exercise a fundamental freedom. In this case, the claimants were agricultural workers who had been excluded from the Ontario *Labour Relations Act*. Their claim to establish and maintain an association of employees fell within the protected ambit of this paragraph. The effective exercise of the freedom in this paragraph required not only the exercise in association of individual constitutional rights but the exercise of certain collective activities. The effect of the exclusion from the legislation was to infringe freedom of association. The evidence showed that these workers would be substantially incapable of exercising their fundamental freedom to organize without the Act's protective regime. This inability can be linked to state action: *Dunmore v. Ontario (Attorney General)*, [2001] 3 S.C.R. 1016, 207 D.L.R. (4th) 193.

The target of s. 213(1)(*c*) of the *Criminal Code*, which prohibits communication in public for the purpose of prostitution, is expressive conduct of a commercial nature and does not attack conduct of an associational nature. Further, the mere fact that an impugned legislative provision limits the possibility of commercial activities or agreements is not sufficient to show a *prima facie* interference with this paragraph. The constitutionality of the provisions was therefore to be determined on the basis of s. 2(*b*) rather than this paragraph. The court, having found that s. 213(1)(*c*) is a reasonable limit on the s. 2(*b*) guarantee, held that provision was valid: *R. v. Skinner*, [1990] 1 S.C.R. 1235, 56 C.C.C. (3d) 1 (4:2).

Democratic Rights

DEMOCRATIC RIGHTS OF CITIZENS.

3. Every citizen of Canada has the right to vote in an election of members of the House of Commons or of a legislative assembly and to be qualified for membership therein.

ANNOTATIONS

Since proclamation of the Charter, the courts have had to consider whether limitations on the rights of inmates to vote in provincial and federal elections infringe this section and if so, whether they constitute reasonable limits within the meaning of s. 1. In *Maltby v. Attorney General of Saskatchewan* (1982), 2 C.C.C. (3d) 153, 143 D.L.R. (3d) 649, 20 Sask. R. 366 (Q.B.) [appeal dismissed as moot appeal 13 C.C.C. (3d) 308, 10 D.L.R. (4th) 745 (C.A.)], it was held that prison inmates on remand were entitled to a declaration that they were entitled to vote in provincial elections. Under the provincial legislation such inmates are not disqualified from voting but have been prevented from exercising their right to vote by reason of an administrative practice within the prison. In *Badger v. Attorney General of Manitoba* (1986), 27 C.C.C. (3d) 158, 51 C.R. (3d) 163 (Man. Q.B.) [appeal to the Court of Appeal 29 C.C.C. (3d) 92, 32 D.L.R. (4th) 310, dismissed due to shortness of time until election], it was held that a provision of the *Provincial Elections Act* disqualifying from voting in a provincial election persons who are in jails, prisons or places of detention serving a sentence infringes this section and cannot be saved by s. 1. However, in view of the uncertain state of the law, the government was not seriously remiss in failing to reconcile the provincial flaw with the Charter. The applicants had asserted their right to vote belatedly and therefore, while entitled to a declaration that the provision of the *Elections Act* was invalid, it would not be appropriate or just to order that the prisoners' names be placed on the voters list or that any other steps be taken to enable convicted prisoners to participate in the impending election. In *Grondin v. Ontario (Attorney General)* (1988), 65 O.R. (2d) 427 (H.C.J.), it was held that a provision of the *Election Act* (Ont.) disqualifying from voting in a provincial election every person who is an inmate in a penal or correctional institution infringes this section and cannot be justified under s. 1.

A provision of the *Election Act* (B.C.), which denies to any person who has been convicted of treason or an indictable offence the right to vote in a provincial election unless he has been pardoned or has served the sentence imposed for the offence, is inconsistent with s. 3 and of no force and effect to the extent that it prohibits from voting persons serving a term of probation: *Reynolds v. Attorney General of British Columbia* (1982), 143 D.L.R. (3d) 365, [1983] 2 W.W.R. 413 (B.C.S.C.); affd 40 C.R. (3d) 393, 11 D.L.R. (4th) 380 (B.C.C.A.).

Section 51(3) of the *Canada Elections Act*, R.S.C. 1985, c. E-2, as amended by S.C. 1993, c. 19, s. 23, which disqualifies every inmate serving a sentence of two years or more in a correctional institution, violates this section and is not a reasonable limit. The provision is therefore of no force and effect: *Sauvé v. Canada (Chief Electoral Officer)*, [2002] 3 S.C.R. 519, 168 C.C.C. (3d) 449.

MAXIMUM DURATION OF LEGISLATIVE BODIES / Continuation in special circumstances.

4. (1) No House of Commons and no legislative assembly shall continue for longer than five years from the date fixed for the return of the writs at a general election of its members.

(2) In time of real or apprehended war, invasion or insurrection, a House of Commons may be continued by Parliament and a legislative assembly may be continued by the legislature beyond five years if such continuation is not opposed by the votes of more

CHARTER

than one-third of the members of the House of Commons or the legislative assembly, as the case may be.

ANNUAL SITTING OF LEGISLATIVE BODIES.

5. There shall be a sitting of Parliament and of each legislature at least once every twelve months.

Mobility Rights

MOBILITY OF CITIZENS / Rights to move and gain livelihood / Limitation / Affirmative action programs.

6. (1) Every citizen of Canada has the right to enter, remain in and leave Canada.

(2) Every citizen of Canada and every person who has the status of a permanent resident of Canada has the right

(*a*) to move to and take up residence in any province; and

(*b*) to pursue the gaining of a livelihood in any province.

(3) The rights specified in subsection (2) are subject to

(*a*) any laws or practices of general application in force in a province other than those that discriminate among persons primarily on the basis of province of present or previous residence; and

(*b*) any laws providing for reasonable residency requirements as a qualification for the receipt of publicly provided social services.

(4) Subsections (2) and (3) do not preclude any law, program or activity that has as its object the amelioration in a province of conditions of individuals in that province who are socially or economically disadvantaged if the rate of employment in that province is below the rate of employment in Canada.

ANNOTATIONS

Interpretation – Subsection (2)(*b*) does not create a separate and distinct right to work divorced from the mobility provisions in which it is found. The rights in paras. (*a*) and (*b*) both relate to movement into another province, either to take up residence or to work without establishing residence: *Law Society of Upper Canada v. Skapinker*, [1984] 1 S.C.R. 357, 11 C.C.C. (3d) 481, 9 D.L.R. (4th) 161.

Section 6 extends to citizens and permanent residents alike the right inherent in citizenship, to reside wherever one wishes in the country and to pursue the gaining of a livelihood without regard for provincial boundaries. Like other individual rights guaranteed by the Charter, it must be interpreted generously to achieve its purpose: to protect the right of citizens and permanent residents to move about the country, to reside where they wish and to pursue their livelihood without regard to provincial boundaries. While the provinces may regulate these rights, they may not do so, subject to the exceptions in this section and s. 1, in terms of provincial boundaries. Section 6(2)(*b*) guarantees not simply the right to pursue a livelihood, but the right to pursue the livelihood of choice to the extent and subject to the same conditions as residents. The right to pursue the livelihood of choice must remain a viable right and cannot be rendered practically ineffective and illusory by provincial regulation. The right to pursue the gaining of a livelihood in the province does not depend on physical movement of the individual to the province. A person can pursue a living in a province without being there personally. This section guarantees the right to offer one's services anywhere in Canada regardless of one's place of residence: *Black v. Law Society of Alberta*, [1989] 1 S.C.R. 591, 58 D.L.R. (4th) 317.

Extradition – While extradition infringes s. 6, the infringement lies at the outer edges of the core values sought to be protected by this provision and extradition constitutes a reasonable limit within the meaning of s. 1. Even where the accused were Canadian citizens and the acts for which their extradition was sought were committed in Canada, their extradition on drug trafficking and importing charges was valid. The extradition of the accused was rationally connected with the objectives sought to be obtained. It would not be appropriate to consider the propriety of extradition on a case by case basis. A general exception from extradition for Canadian citizen who could be charged in Canada would interfere unduly with the objectives of the system of extradition. Moreover, the fact that the Attorney General has a discretion to determine whether a Canadian should be prosecuted in Canada or abroad does not mean that extradition is not a reasonable limit. The authorities must give due weight to the constitutional right of a citizen to remain in Canada and they must in good faith direct their minds to whether prosecution would be equally effective in Canada, given the existing domestic laws in international arrangements. They have an obligation flowing from this section to assure themselves that prosecution in Canada is not a realistic option and if, in a particular case, it was established that the discretion was exercised for improper or arbitrary motives a remedy would lie: *United States of America v. Cotroni*, [1989] 1 S.C.R. 1469, 48 C.C.C. (3d) 193.

The extradition of a fugitive who chose to commit a crime in the United States is not an unjustified denial of the right to remain in Canada. The laying of charges in Canada is not a realistic alternative to extradition when the only justification for dealing with the matter in Canada would be to enable the fugitive to secure a less severe punishment than that likely to be imposed in the place where the fugitive is said to have committed the offence: *Ross v. United States of America* (1994), 93 C.C.C. (3d) 500, 119 D.L.R. (4th) 333 (B.C.C.A.), *per* Taylor J.A., affd for the reasons of Taylor J.A., [1996] 1 S.C.R. 469, 104 C.C.C. (3d) 446.

An extradition judge has no jurisdiction to grant Charter remedies with respect to violations of s. 6 as mobility rights are not engaged at the committal stage. The extradition judge does, however, have the discretion to hear evidence relating to an allegation that mobility rights will be subsequently violated at the ministerial stage by the fugitive's surrender. In considering whether to hear evidence in respect of the Charter breach, the extradition judge must have regard to the need for the expeditious disposition of the issue of committal, the danger of confusion from the reception of irrelevant evidence and waste that will result if the Minister ultimately declines the surrender: *United States of America v. Kwok*, [2001] 1 S.C.R. 532, 152 C.C.C. (3d) 225.

Legal Rights

LIFE, LIBERTY AND SECURITY OF PERSON.

7. Everyone has the right to life, liberty and security of the person and the right not to be deprived thereof except in accordance with the principles of fundamental justice.

ANNOTATIONS

Interpretation – The phrase "principles of fundamental justice" does not describe a protected right itself but rather qualifies the protected right not to be deprived of life, liberty and security of the person. The meaning of the principles of fundamental justice was to be determined having regard to the purpose of the section and its context in the Charter. Thus ss. 8 to 14 of the Charter address specific deprivations of the right to life, liberty and security of the person in breach of the principles of fundamental justice, and as such, violations of this section. They are designed to protect, in a specific manner and setting, the right to life, liberty and security of the person. The term "fundamental justice" was not synonymous merely with natural justice. The principles of fundamental justice are to be found in the basic tenets and principles not only of our judicial process, but also of the other components of the legal system. While many of the principles of fundamental justice are procedural in nature, they are not limited solely to procedural guarantees. Whether any given principle might be said to be a principle of fundamental justice within the meaning of this section will rest upon an analysis of the nature, sources, rationale and essential role of that principle within the judicial process and in the legal system as it evolves: *Reference re Section 94(2) of the Motor Vehicle Act*, [1985] 2 S.C.R. 486, 23 C.C.C. (3d) 289.

The harm principle is not a principle of fundamental justice. While the presence of harm to others may justify legislative action under the criminal law power, the absence of proven harm does not create an unqualified barrier to legislative action. The state may be justified in criminalizing conduct that is either not harmful or harmful only to the accused. The relevant principle of fundamental justice is that the parliamentary response must not be grossly disproportionate to the state interest sought to be protected. The criminalization of the possession of marihuana does not violate the principles of fundamental justice: *R. v. Malmo-Levine; R. v. Caine*, [2003] 3 S.C.R. 571, 179 C.C.C. (3d) 417.

It was not open to a witness, the former manager of a bank in the Bahamas, to allege an infringement of his rights under s. 7 because he was required to testify in Canada about affairs in the Bahamas, in possible violation of Bahamian legislation. Any infringement of the witness's liberty or security did not result from the operation of Canadian law but solely from the operation of Bahamian law in the Bahamas: *R. v. Spencer*, [1985] 2 S.C.R. 278, 21 C.C.C. (3d) 385.

Section 7 does not apply retrospectively and thus an accused charged with an offence allegedly committed prior to the proclamation of the Charter cannot argue that the provision violated his rights as guaranteed by this section because in effect it imposed absolute liability in the circumstances where he was liable to imprisonment: *R. v. Stevens*, [1988] 1 S.C.R. 1153, 41 C.C.C. (3d) 193.

There was no retrospective application of s. 7 in a case where the accused alleged a continuing violation of her liberty interest which was not in accordance with the principles of fundamental justice because of an error made at her pre-Charter trial convicting her of murder, which error affected her period of parole ineligibility. While her claim required the courts to consider pre-Charter history to the extent it explained or contributed to what was alleged to be a current Charter violation, in the circumstances of the case, the court was not being asked to apply s. 7 retrospectively. The crucial issue was to identify the event alleged to be in contravention of s. 7 and the point in time which the event depriving the accused of her liberty occurred. In this case it was the current application of the condition of the accused's sentence that she not be eligible for parole for 25 years which infringed her residual liberty interest: *R. v. Gamble*, [1988] 2 S.C.R. 595, 45 C.C.C. (3d) 204.

The applicant's continued detention following his plea of guilty to second degree murder based on a provision of the *Criminal Code* that was subsequently found to be unconstitutional, did not violate s. 7. The evidence of the accused's involvement was overwhelming and could have supported a conviction for murder under several other *Criminal Code* provisions: *R. v. Sarson*, [1996] 2 S.C.R. 223, 107 C.C.C. (3d) 21.

A corporation cannot avail itself of the protection afforded by this section. A corporation cannot be deprived of life or security of the person. Nor, having regard to the exclusion from this section of a guarantee of a right to property, can the section be regarded as encompassing the economic rights of a corporation so as to protect a corporation against deprivations of economic liberty: *Irwin Toy Ltd. v. Quebec (Attorney General)*, [1989] 1 S.C.R. 927, 58 D.L.R. (4th) 577. [However see notes under s. 52 as to circumstances in which a corporation may allege a violation of this section or other fundamental freedoms when charged with an offence.]

In the criminal context, where a person's liberty is at stake, it is imperative that persons be capable of knowing in advance, with a high degree of certainty, what conduct is prohibited and what is not and, thus, vagueness should be recognized as contrary to the principles of fundamental justice. However, the void for vagueness doctrine is not to be applied to the bare words of the statute, but rather to the provision as interpreted and applied in judicial decisions. In addition, the fact that a particular term is open to varying interpretations by the courts is not fatal. The question is whether the impugned term can be or has been given sensible meaning by the courts: *Reference re ss. 193 and 195.1(1)(c) of the Criminal Code*, [1990] 1 S.C.R. 1123, 56 C.C.C. (3d) 65 (4:2).

The doctrine of vagueness is a principle of fundamental justice under this section and is also part of the s. 1 analysis in that a law may be so vague as to not meet the requirement of "prescribed by law". Vagueness as a principle of fundamental justice is based on the requirements of fair notice to the citizen and limitation on law enforcement discretion. The concept of fair notice includes a formal aspect, that is acquaintance with the actual text of a statute, and a substantive content, that is an understanding that certain conduct is the subject of legal restrictions. The concept of a limitation on law enforcement discretion is based on the principle that a law must not be so devoid of precision in its content that a conviction will automatically flow from the decision to prosecute. Legal rules reach the point of certainty only in particular cases where the law is determined by a competent authority. In the meanwhile, conduct is guided by approximation. Legal dispositions, therefore, delineate a risk zone, and cannot hope to do more, unless they are directed at individual instances. A provision is unconstitutionally vague, therefore, where it does not provide an adequate basis for legal debate, that is for reaching a conclusion as to its meaning by reasoned analysis applying legal criteria. It does not sufficiently delineate any area of risk, and thus can provide neither fair notice to the citizen nor a limitation of enforcement discretion. The courts must, however, be wary of using the doctrine of vagueness to prevent or impede state action and furtherance of valid social objectives, by requiring the law to achieve a degree of precision to which the subject matter does not lend itself: *R. v. Nova Scotia Pharmaceutical Society*, [1992] 2 S.C.R. 606, 74 C.C.C. (3d) 289.

Vagueness must not be considered in the abstract but must be assessed within the larger interpretative context developed through an analysis of considerations such as the purpose, subject matter and nature of the impugned provision, societal values, related legislative provisions, and prior judicial interpretations of the provision. Only after a court has exhausted its interpretative role will it then be in a position to determine whether the provision affords sufficient guidance for legal debate. While it is open to an accused to argue that a statute is unconstitutionally vague even where its conduct clearly falls within the core of the prohibition, reasonable hypotheticals have no place in the vagueness analysis. It would seem, however, that reasonable hypotheticals may be used in an analysis of whether a provision is unconstitutionally overbroad: *R. v. Canadian Pacific Ltd.*, [1995] 2 S.C.R. 1028, 99 C.C.C. (3d) 97.

This section does not protect economic rights *per se* and thus provisions of the *Highway Traffic Act* (Man.), allowing for the seizure of a vehicle driven by a person who was disqualified or prohibited from driving, did not violate this section: *R. v. Werhun*, [1991] 2 W.W.R. 344 (Man. C.A.).

A 90-day administrative suspension of a motorist's driver's licence pursuant to provincial legislation on the basis that a police officer has reasonable grounds to believe that motorist's blood alcohol level exceeded .08 or because the motorist refused to take a breathalyzer test does not violate this section. Driving a motor vehicle on public highways is not a liberty interest protected by this section: *Buhlers v. British Columbia (Superintendent of Motor Vehicles)* (1999), 132 C.C.C. (3d) 478, 170 D.L.R. (4th) 344 (B.C.C.A.), leave to appeal to S.C.C. refused 141 C.C.C. (3d) vi, 181 D.L.R. (4th) vii. Similarly, *Horsefield v. Ontario (Registrar of Motor Vehicles)* (1999), 134 C.C.C. (3d) 161, 172 D.L.R. (4th) 43 (Ont. C.A.); *R. v. MacCormack* (1999), 134 C.C.C. (3d) 351, 180 Nfld. & P.E.I.R. 314 (P.E.I.C.A.).

A non-citizen does not have an unqualified right to enter or remain in Canada and it is open to Parliament to prescribe conditions for them to enter or remain. The removal of a non-citizen who has deliberately violated an essential condition by reason of his conviction for a serious criminal offence does not result in a denial of fundamental justice. Further, the procedure followed by the Security Intelligence Review Committee which was determining whether there were grounds to believe the person was involved in organized crime, in providing the person with a summary of police evidence but barring him from being present while the evidence itself was presented, was in accordance with the principles of fundamental justice. The scope of principles of fundamental justice will vary with the context and the interests at stake: *Chiarelli v. Canada (Minister of Employment and Immigration)*, [1992] 1 S.C.R. 711, 72 C.C.C. (3d) 214.

It now appears that s. 1 can apply to a violation of this section beyond such extreme circumstances as war. At the s. 1 stage, the court is concerned with broader values underlying a free and democratic society, such as respect for the inherent dignity of the human person, commitment to social justice and equality, accommodation of a wide variety of beliefs, respect for cultural and group identity, and faith in social and political institutions which enhance the participation of individuals and groups in society, in contrast to the narrower concerns under this section to be found in the basic tenets of the legal system: *R. v. Mills*, [1999] 3 S.C.R. 668, 139 C.C.C. (3d) 321.

However, in the subsequent decision in *R. v. Ruzic*, [2001] 1 S.C.R. 687, 153 C.C.C. (3d) 1, 41 C.R. (5th) 1, the court, without reference to *R. v. Mills*, *supra*, appeared to adopt the position that exceptional circumstances, such as the outbreak of war or a national emergency, are necessary before an infringement of this section can be saved by s. 1.

The constitutional norm for a fair hearing is procedural fairness. Notice and participation may or may not be required to meet this norm — what is fair depends entirely on the context: *R. v. Rodgers*, [2006] 1 S.C.R. 554, 207 C.C.C. (3d) 225 *sub nom. R. v. Jackpine*.

Self-incrimination – A statutory compulsion to testify engages the witness' liberty interest under this section. However, the liberty interest is affected in accordance with the principles of fundamental justice, since not only is the witness protected from use of his testimony in subsequent proceedings (except for perjury or the giving of contradictory evidence) by virtue of s. 13 of the Charter, but derivative evidence which could not have been obtained, or the significance of which could not have been appreciated, but for the testimony of the witness ought generally to be excluded under this section at the witness' subsequent trial, since its admission would tend to affect the fairness of the trial: *R. v. S. (R.J.)*, [1995] 1 S.C.R. 451, 96 C.C.C. (3d) 1.

Although separately charged as an accused, a witness appearing in another person's criminal trial will ordinarily be compellable in that trial, unless it is established that the predominant purpose in compelling the testimony is incrimination of the witness. A similar test should be applied where the evidence is sought at a preliminary inquiry: *R. v. Primeau*, [1995] 2 S.C.R. 60, 97 C.C.C. (3d) 1. Similar considerations apply where the witness is a suspect in the same offence but has not yet been charged: *R. v. Jobin*, [1995] 2 S.C.R. 78, 97 C.C.C. (3d) 97.

In addition to use immunity guaranteed by s. 13 and limited derivative use immunity guaranteed by this section, in some circumstances the witness cannot be compelled to testify. The test to be applied in determining whether or not the witness can be compelled to testify is whether the predominant purpose for seeking the evidence is to obtain incriminating evidence against the person compelled to testify or rather some legitimate public purpose. In the context of a criminal or *quasi*-criminal prosecution, to qualify as a valid public purpose the compelled testimony must be for the purpose of obtaining evidence in furtherance of that prosecution. If it is established that the predominant purpose is not to obtain relevant evidence for the purpose of the instant proceeding, but rather to incriminate the witness, the party seeking to compel the witness must justify the potential prejudice to the right of the witness against self-incrimination. If it is shown that the only prejudice is the possible subsequent derivative use of the testimony, then the compulsion to testify will occasion no prejudice since the witness will be protected against such use. If, however, the witness can show any other significant prejudice that may arise from the testimony such that his right to a fair trial will be jeopardized, the witness should not be compellable: *British Columbia Securities Commission v. Branch*, [1995] 2 S.C.R. 3, 97 C.C.C. (3d) 505.

Charter protections are engaged when, in light of all relevant circumstances, it is apparent that tax officials are engaged in the determination of penal liability rather than the verification of tax liability. When the purpose of the investigation is penal, the taxpayer must be warned and the powers of compulsion contained in the *Income Tax Act*, R.S.C. 1985, c. 1 (5th Supp.), are not available. Taxpayers have very little privacy interest pursuant to s. 8 of the Charter in materials and records which taxpayers are obliged to keep. Accordingly, there is no reasonable expectation of privacy that prevents auditors from passing their files to investi-gators. There is no principle of use immunity that prevents the investigators in the exercise of their investigative function from making use of evidence obtained through the proper exercise of the CCRA's audit function. In addition, there is no derivative use immunity that would require the trial judge to apply the "but for" test. Where the predominant purpose of a question or inquiry is the determination of penal liability, however, s. 7 of the Charter is clearly engaged. When s. 7 is engaged, no further statements may be compelled from the taxpayer for the purpose of advancing the criminal investigation and no written documents may be inspected or examined except by way of judicial warrant under s. 231.3 of the *Income Tax Act* or s. 487 of the *Criminal Code*, and no documents may be required from the taxpayer or from any third party for the purpose of advancing the criminal investigation: *R. v. Jarvis*, [2002] 3 S.C.R. 757, 169 C.C.C. (3d) 1. See also *R. v. Ling*, [2002] 3 S.C.R. 814, 169 C.C.C. (3d) 46.

The right to remain silent is protected as a principle of fundamental justice and is broader than the common law confession rule and the rule against self-incrimination. The measure of the right to silence resides in the notion that a person whose liberty is placed in jeopardy by the criminal process cannot be required to give evidence against himself, but rather has the right to choose whether to speak or to remain silent. Once it is established that a detained suspect subjectively possesses an operating mind, then the issue is whether the conduct of the authorities, considered on an objective basis, effectively and unfairly deprived the suspect of the right to choose whether to speak to the authorities. Thus, when the police use subterfuge to interrogate an accused after he has advised them that he does not wish to speak to them, they are improperly eliciting information that they are unable to obtain by respecting his constitutional right to silence. However, in the absence of eliciting behaviour on the part of the police, there is no violation of the accused's right. The right as well only applies to a detainee and does not affect the use of undercover police officers prior to detention: *R. v. Hebert*, [1990] 2 S.C.R. 151, 57 C.C.C. (3d) 1.

Questioning of a suspect who was not under arrest, although he has indicated that on the basis of legal advice he does not wish to make a statement, does not violate the right to silence as guaranteed by this section: *R. v. Hicks*, [1990] 1 S.C.R. 120, 54 C.C.C. (3d) 575 (7:0), affg 42 C.C.C. (3d) 394, 64 C.R. (3d) 68 (Ont. C.A.).

The right to silence may be violated not only by the conduct of an undercover police officer, but by any agent of the state such as a prisoner acting as a police informer. In determining who is an agent of the state, the test to be applied is whether the exchange or contact between the accused and the informer would have taken place, in the form and manner in which it did take place, but for the intervention of the state or its agents. If the informer was an agent of the state, there will be a violation of this section if the agent elicited the information. Evidence has been elicited if there is a causal link between the conduct of the state agent and the making of the statement by the accused. This in turn requires consideration of two sets of factors, namely, factors relating to the nature of the exchange between the accused and the agent and factors concerning the nature of the relationship between the agent and the accused: *R. v. Broyles*, [1991] 3 S.C.R. 595, 68 C.C.C. (3d) 308 (7:0).

A breach of the right to silence does not require proof of an atmosphere of oppression or that the accused made a declaration that they do not wish to speak to the police. The right to silence is violated by the use of subterfuge that, in actively eliciting information, deprives the accused of his choice of whether to speak to the police. The mere fact of detention does not render all speech involuntary. The nature of the exchange and the nature of the relationship between the state agent and the accused are considerations in determining whether there was a causal link between the conduct of the state agent and the making of the statement by the accused. In considering the nature of the exchange, the undercover police officer's question about what happened and his statement that his own fingerprints were on the drugs was not a request for any information from the accused nor did it constitute an inducement. The fact that the officer's comment may have directed the conversation into a new area of interest to the Crown did not establish impermissible elicitation. The conduct of the officer was not the equivalent of an interrogation nor did the officer direct the conversation in any manner that prompted, coaxed or cajoled the accused to respond. In this case, the fact that the state agent was posing as a "co-accused" was not sufficient to establish a causal link between his conduct and the accused's statement. There was no relationship of trust between the officer and the accused nor did the undercover officer manipulate the accused to bring about a mental state in which the accused was more likely to talk: *R. v. Liew*, [1999] 3 S.C.R. 227, 137 C.C.C. (3d) 353.

The accused has the right to remain silent at the investigation stage as well as at the trial. This right to silence would, however, be a snare and a delusion if it were open to the Crown to nevertheless put in evidence that the accused remained silent in the face of a question which suggested his guilt. Unless the Crown can establish a real relevance and a proper basis for their admission, neither the questions by investigating officers nor evidence as to the ensuing silence of the accused should be admitted at trial: *R. v. Chambers*, [1990] 2 S.C.R. 1293, 59 C.C.C. (3d) 321.

In *R. v. Singh*, [2007] 3 S.C.R. 405, 225 C.C.C. (3d) 103, the Supreme Court of Canada considered the interplay between the confessions rule and s. 7, as well as whether there is an obligation on the police to cease questioning a detainee who has asserted the right to silence. Where the detainee knows he is speaking to a person in authority, the confessions rule and the s. 7 right to silence are functionally equivalent. Voluntariness requires the court to scrutinize whether the accused was denied his right to silence. A finding of voluntariness, therefore, will be determinative of the s. 7 issues, in that a finding of voluntariness beyond a reasonable doubt precludes a finding of a Charter violation of the right to silence. Conversely, if the accused is able to show on a balance of probabilities a breach of the right to silence, the Crown will not be able to meet the voluntariness test. There is no obligation that the police refrain from questioning a detainee whenever the right to silence is asserted, provided that the detainee's rights are adequately protected, including the freedom to choose whether to speak or not. The use of legitimate means of persuasion by police is permitted but it does not permit the police to ignore a detainee's freedom to choose whether to speak or not. Police persistence in continuing the interview, despite repeated assertions by the detainee that he wishes to remain silent, may raise a strong argument that any subsequently obtained statement was not the product of a free will.

The right to silence applies any time that a individual interacts with a person in authority and is not limited to situations when the accused comes within the power of the state. Voluntary interaction with the police, even one initiated by the individual, and the provision of some information by the accused does not constitute a waiver of the right to silence. Since individuals are generally under no obligation to assist the police, their silence alone cannot be probative of guilt. Evidence of silence is admissible only in limited circumstances if the Crown can establish real relevance and a proper basis. Where it is admitted for a limited purpose, the trial judge must give a proper warning to the jury. In this case, the accused, who was charged with three murders on a ranch, had driven to the police station and requested that the police go to the ranch. He was non-responsive to questions from the police about why they should go to the ranch. The accused's silence at the police station was inadmissible as the evidence was not relevant to the accused's state of mind, nor of post-offence conduct. While in this case, the conduct was arguably admissible as part of the narrative, the trial judge was required to provide the proper limiting instruction to the jury on its use: *R. v. Turcotte*, [2005] 2 S.C.R. 519, 200 C.C.C. (3d) 289, 31 C.R. (6th) 197.

An accused who testifies against a co-accused must accept that his credibility can be fully attacked by the latter. The accused who has incriminated a co-accused by his testimony cannot therefore rely on the right to silence to deprive the accused who is implicated by his testimony of the right to challenge that testimony by a full attack on the credibility of the former including reference to his pre-trial silence. He cannot, however, go further and ask the trier of fact to consider the evidence of the testifying accused's silence as positive evidence of guilt on which the Crown can rely to convict. The accused implicated by the evidence of the co-accused has the right to attack the credibility of the co-accused by reference to the testifying accused's failure to disclose the evidence to the investigating authorities. The jury must, however, be instructed that the evidence could be used as one factor in determining whether the evidence of the co-accused is to be believed: *R. v. Crawford*, [1995] 1 S.C.R. 858, 96 C.C.C. (3d) 481, 37 C.R. (4th) 197.

Section 4(6) of the *Canada Evidence Act* does not prohibit a trial judge from informing the jury about an accused's right to silence. Conversely, the trial judge need not affirm the accused's right in every case, only where there is a realistic concern that the jury may place evidential value on an accused's decision not to testify. In such a case, the trial judge should make it clear to the jury that an accused's silence is not evidence and that it cannot be used as a makeweight for the Crown in deciding whether the Crown has proved its case: *R. v. Prokofiew*, [2012] 2 S.C.R. 639, 290 C.C.C. (3d) 280.

An aspect of the common law confession rule requires that the accused have an operating mind. The operating mind test includes a limited mental component which requires that the accused has sufficient cognitive capacity to understand what he is saying and what is said. This includes the ability to understand a caution that the evidence can be used against the accused. The same standard applies with respect to the right of silence as guaranteed by this section in determining whether a mentally ill accused has the mental capacity to make an active choice: *R. v. Whittle*, [1994] 2 S.C.R. 914, 92 C.C.C. (3d) 11, 32 C.R. (4th) 1.

The general principle against self-incrimination, as applied in the regulatory context, did not require the accused to be granted immunity against Crown use of statutorily compelled reports. In this case, reports which were statutorily compelled pursuant to the *Fisheries Act*, R.S.C. 1985, c. F-14 were held to be admissible in relation to charges under the *Fisheries Act*. The two fundamental purposes behind the principle against self-incrimination are to protect against unreliable confessions and to protect against the abuse of power by the state. Neither of these two rationales was threatened in the circumstances of this case. Little expectation of privacy attached to the documents, since they were produced precisely to be read and relied upon by state officials. Furthermore, the documents were not "compelled" as when an individual decides to participate in a regulated industry, the obligation to submit reports was not an obligation imposed through the denial of free and informed consent: *R. v. Fitzpatrick*, [1995] 4 S.C.R. 154, 102 C.C.C. (3d) 144, 43 C.R. (4th) 343.

R. v. Fitzpatrick, supra, was distinguished in *R. v. White*, [1999] 2 S.C.R. 417, 135 C.C.C. (3d) 257, 24 C.R. (5th) 201, where it was held that admission of a statement made under compulsion of the *Motor Vehicle Act* (B.C.), which requires a motorist to report an accident to the police and furnish the officer with information respecting the accident as required by the officer, does violate this section. A driver who makes a statement pursuant to the statutory duty is entitled, at least, to use immunity in criminal proceedings in relation to the contents of that statement. The spontaneous utterances of a driver, occurring very shortly after an accident, are exactly the type of communication that the principle against self-incrimination is designed to protect.

Right to counsel – While the Constitution has not expressly constitutionalized the right of an indigent accused to be provided with counsel, in cases not falling within the provincial legal aid plans, ss. 7 and 11(*d*) of the Charter require funded counsel to be provided if the accused wishes counsel, but cannot pay a lawyer, and representation of the accused by counsel is essential to a fair trial. Where a trial judge is confronted with a case where legal aid has been refused to an indigent accused in circumstances where representation by counsel is essential, then the judge may stay proceedings until the necessary funding of counsel is available. An accused, however, who has the means to pay the costs of her defence but refuses to retain counsel may properly be considered to have chosen to defend herself and there would be no breach of the Charter if the trial proceeded without counsel being appointed: *R. v. Rowbotham* (1988), 41 C.C.C. (3d) 1, 63 C.R. (3d) 113, 35 C.R.R. 207 (Ont. C.A.).

While the Supreme Court has not directly addressed the question of the right to legal representation in criminal proceedings as a matter of fundamental justice, reference might be made to *New Brunswick (Minister of Health and Community Services) v. G. (J.)*, [1999] 3 S.C.R. 46, 26 C.R. (5th) 203, 177 D.L.R. (4th) 124, where the court held that the right to a fair hearing will not always require an individual to be represented by counsel when a decision is made affecting that individual's right to life, liberty or security of the person. In that case, the court dealt with a parent's right to counsel at child protection proceedings. The court held that the trial judge would have to consider the seriousness and complexity of the hearing and the capacities of the parent. Whether it is necessary for the parent to be represented by counsel is directly proportional to the seriousness and complexity of the proceedings, and inversely proportional to the capacities of the parent. The court noted that similar considerations were taken into account by appellate courts considering this issue in the criminal context in *R. v. Rowbotham, supra; R. v. Robinson* (1989), 51 C.C.C. (3d) 452, 73 C.R. (3d) 81 (Alta. C.A.); and *R. v. Rain* (1998), 130 C.C.C. (3d) 167, [1999] 7 W.W.R. 652 (Alta. C.A.), leave to appeal to S.C.C. refused 132 C.C.C. (3d) vi, 213 W.A.C. 192*n*, 250 A.R. 192*n*.

The duty on a trial judge to ensure that an accused has a fair hearing will generally cast upon the judge an obligation to point out to the accused that he would be at a distinct disadvantage in proceeding without the assistance of competent counsel and that the accused is entitled to have such counsel. Where the accused expressly desires counsel, it is clear that unless the accused has deliberately failed to retain counsel or has discharged counsel with the intent of delaying the process of the court, the trial judge should afford the accused an opportunity to retain counsel either at his expense or through the services of Legal Aid: *R. v. McGibbon* (1988), 45 C.C.C. (3d) 334, 31 O.A.C. 10 (C.A.).

The placing of limits on the number of hours of preparation for which counsel retained through the provincial legal aid plan will be paid does not infringe the accused's right to counsel. There is no constitutional right to require provision of unlimited funding for defence of a case, even a murder case: *R. v. Munroe* (1990), 57 C.C.C. (3d) 421, 97 N.S.R. (2d) 361 (S.C.), affd 59 C.C.C. (3d) 446, 98 N.S.R. (2d) 174 (C.A.).

Delay in taking proceedings – The principles of fundamental justice are not limited to the right to a fair hearing in accordance with the principles of natural justice. Rather, there is a residual discretion in a trial court judge to stay proceedings where compelling an accused to stand trial would violate those fundamental principles of justice which underlie the community sense of fair play and decency, and to prevent the abuse of the court's process through oppressive or vexatious proceedings. It is a power, however, of special application which can only be exercised in the clearest of cases. Thus, specifically with respect to an allegation of delay in the institution of the proceedings, absent any finding that the delay was for the ulterior purpose of depriving an accused of the opportunity of making full answer and defence, delay in itself, even delay resulting in the impairment of the ability to make full answer and defence is not a basis for a stay of proceedings. The courts cannot undertake the supervision of the operation or the efficiency of the police department, and to compel the police or the Crown to institute proceedings before they have reason to believe they will be able to establish the accused's guilt beyond a reasonable doubt, could have a deleterious effect upon the rights of the accused and upon the ability of society to protect itself. However, a distinction is to be drawn between the situation in which the institution of the proceedings is valid and the only issue is delay prejudicial to the accused and that in which the executive acts in leading to the institution of the proceedings is offensive to the principles upon which the administration of justice is conducted by the courts: *R. v. Young* (1984), 13 C.C.C. (3d) 1, 46 O.R. (2d) 520 (C.A.).

Delay in charging and prosecuting an accused for sexual offences cannot in and of itself justify staying of proceedings as an abuse of process either at common law or under this section or s. 11(*d*). Fairness of a trial is not automatically undermined by even a lengthy pre-charge delay. The court cannot assess the fairness of a particular trial without considering the particular circumstances of the case: *R. v. L. (W.K.)*, [1991] 1 S.C.R. 1091, 64 C.C.C. (3d) 321, [1991] 6 C.R. (4th) 1.

While s. 11(*b*) does not apply to appellate delay, this section will provide a remedy when delay of appellate proceedings affects the fairness of the trial. The appellate court is the appropriate forum to determine whether there has been a violation: *R. v. Potvin*, [1993] 2 S.C.R. 880, 83 C.C.C. (3d) 97, 23 C.R. (4th) 10.

Mens rea – The imposition of absolute liability in penal law offends the principles of fundamental justice and therefore a law enacting an absolute liability offence will violate s. 7 if and to the extent that it has the potential of depriving of life, liberty or security of the person. Imprisonment, including probation, deprives persons of their liberty. An offence has that potential as of the moment it is open to the judge to impose imprisonment and there is no need that imprisonment be made mandatory. A combination of imprisonment and of absolute liability violates s. 7 and can only be salvaged if the authorities demonstrate under s. 1 that such deprivation of liberty and breach of those principles of fundamental justice is a reasonable limit: *Reference re: Section 94(2) of the Motor Vehicle Act*, [1985] 2 S.C.R. 486, 23 C.C.C. (3d) 289, 48 C.R. (3d) 289.

Depending upon the provisions of the particular section and the context, the constitutional requirement of *mens rea* may be satisfied by a subjective or objective standard and in appropriate circumstances negligence can be an acceptable basis for liability: *R. v. Hundal*, [1993] 1 S.C.R. 867, 79 C.C.C. (3d) 97, 19 C.R. (4th) 169.

There is no principle of fundamental justice which requires an absolute symmetry between the elements of the *actus reus* and *mens rea*. Thus, there is no requirement that there be proof of *mens rea* in relation to the consequences element of the *actus reus*, such as death in a case of manslaughter: *R. v. Creighton*, [1993] 3 S.C.R. 3, 83 C.C.C. (3d) 346, 23 C.R. (4th) 189.

The development of the doctrine of *mens rea* for criminal offences reflects the conviction that a person should not be punished unless that person knew that he was committing the prohibited act or would have known that he was committing the prohibited act if he had given to his conduct and to the circumstances that degree of attention which the law requires and which he was capable of giving. Thus, this section prohibits the existence of offences that are punishable by imprisonment and that do not allow the accused as a minimum a due diligence defence. Former s. 146(1) of the *Criminal Code*, by removing the defence of mistake of fact as to the age of the complainant on a charge of unlawful intercourse with a girl under the age of 14 years, infringed this section and was not a reasonable limit. The argument in favour of absolute liability is premised primarily on arguments of deterrence. Where, however, a criminal offence allows for a potential penalty of life imprisonment, as did former s. 146(1), it is not good enough to rely on intuition and speculation about the potential deterrent effect of an absolute liability offence. There must be concrete and persuasive evidence to support the argument: *R. v. Nguyen*, [1990] 2 S.C.R. 906, 59 C.C.C. (3d) 161, 79 C.R. (3d) 332 (5:2).

In *R. v. Vaillancourt*, [1987] 2 S.C.R. 636, 39 C.C.C. (3d) 118, 47 D.L.R. (4th) 399, the court was required to consider what degree of *mens rea* is required as a matter of fundamental justice for an offence such as murder. Lamer J., speaking for himself and Dickson C.J.C. and Wilson J., was of the view that there are certain crimes where, because of the special nature of the stigma attached to a conviction therefor or the available penalty, the principles of fundamental justice require a *mens rea* reflecting the particular nature of the crime.

In the subsequent case of *R. v. Martineau*, [1990] 2 S.C.R. 633, 58 C.C.C. (3d) 353, 79 C.R. (3d) 129 (5:2), a majority of the court has now adopted the view that, in view of the stigma and punishment attaching to a conviction for murder, the principles of fundamental justice require a *mens rea* reflecting the particular nature of the crime which, for murder, cannot be anything less than subjective foresight of death. Thus, the constructive murder provisions in s. 230 and imposition of liability on an objective basis in s. 229(*c*) are unconstitutional, since they violated the principle that punishment must be proportionate to the moral blameworthiness of the offender.

It is not a principle of fundamental justice that the guilt for principal offenders and parties must always be the same. Within many offences, there are varying degrees of guilt and it remains the function of the sentencing process to adjust the punishment for each individual offender accordingly. There are, however, a few offences, such as murder and attempted murder, for which this section requires a minimum degree of *mens rea*. In the case of those offences, the constitutionally required minimum applies to both principles and parties: *R. v. Logan*, [1990] 2 S.C.R. 711, 58 C.C.C. (3d) 391, 73 D.L.R. (4th) 40.

Even where imprisonment is available as a penalty for breach of a regulatory statute, negligence is a sufficient level of fault to comport with constitutional standards, provided that the defendant is able to defend the charge by proof of due diligence: *R. v. Wholesale Travel Group Inc.*, [1991] 3 S.C.R. 154, 67 C.C.C. (3d) 193, 8 C.R. (4th) 145.

Criminal procedure – The right to make full answer and defence guaranteed by this section and s. 11(*d*) includes the right of the accused to have before him the full case to meet before answering the Crown's case by adducing defence evidence. In addition, the accused has the right to defend himself against all of the state's efforts to achieve a conviction. The Crown is not entitled to engage in activities aimed at convicting an accused unless that accused is permitted to defend against those state acts. These rights do not, however, guarantee an accused the right to address the jury last: *R. v. Rose*, [1998] 3 S.C.R. 262, 129 C.C.C. (3d) 449, 20 C.R. (5th) 246.

Double jeopardy – Section 7 constitutionalizes a protection against double jeopardy wider than the specific protection in s. 11(*h*). Thus, notwithstanding the common law limitations on the ability to challenge the discretion of a trial judge to declare a mistrial, the propriety of such a decision would be subject to scrutiny under the Charter where a second trial, after the improper termination of the first trial, would contravene the principles of fundamental justice: *R. v. D. (T.C.)* (1987), 38 C.C.C. (3d) 434, 61 C.R. (3d) 168 (Ont. C.A.).

Abuse of process – A trial court has the power to stay proceedings to prevent the abuse of a court's process through oppressive or vexatious proceedings where compelling an accused to stand trial would violate those principles of fundamental justice which underlie the community sense of fair play and decency: *R. v. Jewitt*, [1985] 2 S.C.R. 128, 21 C.C.C. (3d) 7, 20 D.L.R. (4th) 651.

Prosecutorial independence – A prosecutor has a constitutional obligation under s. 7 to act independently of partisan concerns and other improper motives. However, "partisan" in this context is narrowly defined and not synonymous with "political". Decisions to prosecute, or not to prosecute, may have broad social repercussions, and regard for those repercussions properly informs prosecutorial discretion: *R. v. Cawthorne*, [2016] 1 S.C.R. 983, 339 C.C.C. (3d) 263.

Investigative tests – While the common law is not determinative in assessing whether particular practice violates the principles of fundamental justice, it is one of the major repositories of basic tenets of the Canadian legal system and thus of the principles of fundamental justice. It was the common law experience that custodial fingerprinting was not fundamentally unfair and legislation such as found in the *Criminal Code* and the *Identification of Criminals Act* permitting compulsory fingerprinting does not violate s. 7. Further the legislation is not subject to attack because it gives a police officer a discretion whether or not to require the accused to attend for fingerprinting. Discretion in fact is an essential feature of a fair criminal justice system: *R. v. Beare*, [1988] 2 S.C.R. 387, 45 C.C.C. (3d) 57.

Evidentiary rules – A trial court has a residual discretion to relax in favour of the accused a strict rule of evidence where it is necessary to prevent a miscarriage of justice and where the danger against which an exclusionary rule aimed to safeguard does not exist: *R. v. Williams* (1985), 18 C.C.C. (3d) 356 (Ont. C.A.). Similarly *R. v. Rowbotham, supra*, and *semble R. v. Corbett*, [1988] 1 S.C.R. 670, 41 C.C.C. (3d) 385.

It has never been a tenet of fundamental justice that a person has the right to confront any witness before the trier of fact. While it is a basic principle of fundamental justice that the accused has had a full opportunity to cross-examine the witness when previous testimony was taken, if the transcript of such testimony is to be introduced as evidence at a criminal trial for the purpose of convicting the accused, a provision such as s. 715 of the *Criminal Code*, which provides for the admission of evidence taken at the preliminary inquiry where the witness is not available, at trial does not offend s. 7. An accused would however have a constitutional right to have the evidence of prior testimony, obtained in the absence of full opportunity to cross-examine the witness, excluded: *R. v. Potvin*, [1989] 1 S.C.R. 525, 47 C.C.C. (3d) 289.

A law, which prevents the trier of fact from getting at the truth by excluding relevant evidence in the absence of a clear ground of policy or law justifying the exclusion, runs afoul of our fundamental conceptions of justice and what constitutes a fair trial. The fundamental tenet of our system, that the innocent not be convicted, implies that, before a judge may exclude evidence which is relevant to a defence, the potential prejudice to the trial process must substantially outweigh the value of the evidence: *R. v. Seaboyer*, [1991] 2 S.C.R. 577, 66 C.C.C. (3d) 321 (7:2).

Jury availability and selection procedure – The decision of a trial judge to stay proceedings against an R.C.M.P. officer charged with an offence because of certain remarks made by the Premier in the National Assembly was premature. It was only at the stage when the jury was to be selected that it would be possible to determine whether the accused could be tried by an impartial jury. There is an initial presumption that a juror will perform his duties in accordance with his oath. In an extreme case such as this, pretrial publicity should lead to challenge for cause at the trial but it will not be assumed that a person subjected to such publicity will necessarily be biased: *R. v. Vermette*, [1988] 1 S.C.R. 985, 41 C.C.C. (3d) 523.

There is no principle of fundamental justice that requires the right to a jury trial in all cases: *R. v. B. (S.)* (1989), 50 C.C.C. (3d) 34 (Sask. C.A.).

Sentence proceedings – The conduct of a trial in general including the applications of the rule of evidence in a given case must not result in the trial being unfair because the accused has been denied a full opportunity to prepare his case and to challenge and answer the Crown's case. If a rule of statutory or common law were framed in such a way that it would be *per se* a violation of the right to a fair trial, then the statute would be declared inoperative were the common law declared to be otherwise. However, the common law rule which permits a relaxation of the hearsay rule in sentence proceedings is not a violation of s. 7: *R. v. Albright*, [1987] 2 S.C.R. 303, 37 C.C.C. (3d) 105, 60 C.R. (3d) 97.

It is a fundamental rule of law that an accused must be tried and punished under the law in force at the time the offence is committed. Thus it was held in *R. v. Gamble*, [1988] 2 S.C.R. 595, 45 C.C.C. (3d) 204, 66 C.R. (3d) 193, that s. 7 was violated where the accused, prior to proclamation of the Charter, had been convicted and sentenced for first degree murder although the provision in force at the time of commission of her offence was either murder punishable by death or murder punishable by life imprisonment. This represented a significant distinction since it was likely that the accused would only have been convicted of murder punishable by life imprisonment which would have required the judge to fix her parole eligibility date at a period between 10 and 20 years, whereas the conviction for first degree murder carried an automatic minimum period of parole ineligibility of 25 years.

It is not a violation of fundamental justice for Parliament to identify those offenders who in the interests of protecting the public ought to be sentenced according to considerations which are entirely reactive. Thus the imposition of a sentence of indeterminate detention as authorized by Part XXIV of the *Criminal Code* is in accordance with the fundamental purpose of the criminal laws generally and of sentencing in particular, namely, the protection of society. Further, the procedure by which a person is found to be a dangerous offender does not offend s. 7. The principles of fundamental justice do not require that the determination of whether or not the accused is a dangerous offender be made by a jury. Neither the standard proof required for successful application nor the fact that the provisions require the use of psychiatric evidence infringe s. 7. Finally, the failure of the Crown to give the accused notice prior to his election and plea that it was intending to bring an application under Part XXIV did not offend his rights under s. 7. It may be however that in certain circumstances a plea of guilty could be set aside because the court was satisfied the accused did not fully understand the nature of the charge or the potential consequences of a guilty plea: *R. v. Lyons*, [1987] 2 S.C.R. 309, 37 C.C.C. (3d) 1.

While a sentencing scheme must exhibit a proportionality to the seriousness of the offence, it must also take into account other factors that are of significance to the societal interest in punishing wrongdoers. The provisions of the *Criminal Code* which provide for a minimum sentence of life imprisonment without eligibility for parole for certain types of murders, in particular murder while committing an offence such as kidnapping or sexual assault, clearly demonstrate a proportionality between the moral turpitude of the offender and the seriousness of the offence and are in accord with the objectives of a rational system of sentencing: *R. v. Luxton*, [1990] 2 S.C.R. 711, 58 C.C.C. (3d) 449 (7:0); *R. v. Arkell*, [1990] 2 S.C.R. 695, 59 C.C.C. (3d) 65 (7:0).

Proportionality in the sentencing process is not a principle of fundamental justice under s. 7. The principles and purposes for determining a fit sentence, enumerated in s. 718 of the Code and provisions that follow — including the fundamental principle of proportionality in s. 718.1 — do not have constitutional status. The constitutional dimension of proportionality in sentencing is the prohibition of grossly disproportionate sentences in s. 12 of the Charter: *R. v. Safarzadeh-Markhali*, [2016] 1 S.C.R. 180, 334 C.C.C. (3d) 1.

Prison procedure – The standard of procedure required to satisfy s. 7 is not necessarily the most sophisticated, elaborate or perfect procedure imaginable but only a procedure that is fundamentally just. What this may require will vary with the particular situation. An unbiased tribunal, knowledge by the person whose life, liberty and security is in jeopardy of the case to be answered, a fair opportunity to answer and a decision reached on the basis of the material in support of the case and the answer made to it are features of such a procedure. In this context any right a person may have to the assistance of counsel arises from the requirement to afford the person an opportunity to adequately present his case. There is however no absolute right in an inmate to be represented by counsel in a disciplinary court. Whether or not an inmate has such right will depend on the circumstances of the particular case, including its nature, its gravity, its complexity, and the capacity of the inmate to understand the case and present his defence: *Howard v. Stoney Mountain Institution Inmate Disciplinary Court* (1985), 19 C.C.C. (3d) 195, [1984] 2 F.C. 642 (C.A.).

This section does not impose a constitutional obligation on customs officers to provide access to medical supervision of a detainee believed to have swallowed pellets containing heroin during a passive "bedpan vigil" over and above the rejection of medical attention by the detainee: *R. v. Monney*, [1999] 1 S.C.R. 652, 133 C.C.C. (3d) 129.

Extradition and fugitive offender proceeding – The admission of affidavit evidence and depositions at an extradition hearing of an accused fugitive as permitted by the former *Extradition Act* and Treaty does not offend s. 7, notwithstanding the fugitive is not given an opportunity to cross-examine on the affidavits or depositions. The importance of cross-examination varies with the nature of the proceedings and the purpose of an extradition hearing is not to determine guilt or innocence but is merely an inquiry to determine whether there is sufficient evidence to warrant sending the fugitive to the demanding state for trial. The trial and full determination of the fugitive's rights is to take place in the courts of the demanding state and it is a basic assumption of extradition proceedings that the fugitive will receive a fair and just trial in the demanding state: *United States of America v. Smith* (1984), 10 C.C.C. (3d) 540, 38 C.R. (3d) 228, 7 D.L.R. (4th) 12 (Ont. C.A.), leave to appeal to S.C.C. refused 4 O.A.C. 239*n*, 55 N.R. 395*n*; *Decter v. United States of America* (1983),

5 C.C.C. (3d) 364, 148 D.L.R. (3d) 496 (N.S.S.C.), affd 5 C.C.C. (3d) 381*n*, 148 D.L.R. (3d) 512*n* (N.S.C.A.).

While the surrender of a fugitive to a foreign country is subject to Charter scrutiny, notwithstanding that such surrender involves primarily the exercise of executive discretion, in some circumstances the manner in which the foreign state will deal with the fugitive may be such that will violate the principles of fundamental justice to surrender an accused. However, there is nothing unjust to surrendering to a foreign country a person accused of having committed a crime there for trial in the ordinary way in accordance with the system for the administration of justice prevailing in that country simply because that system is substantially different from Canada's with different checks and balances. Thus it was held in *R. v. Schmidt*, [1987] 1 S.C.R. 500, 33 C.C.C. (3d) 193, 58 C.R. (3d) 1, that surrendering the fugitive for trial on state charges, notwithstanding her acquittal on similar federal charges, did not offend fundamental justice. While repeated attempts by the same prosecutorial authorities to prosecute a person for the same offence may in certain circumstances amount to harassment sufficiently oppressive that to surrender such a person would violate the principles of fundamental justice, the court should intervene only in compelling situations and this was not one of those cases.

Even a substantial delay between the time when the demanding state was informed of the presence of the accused in Canada and the request for extradition would not constitute a violation of fundamental justice. To arrive at the conclusion that the surrender of a fugitive would violate the principles of fundamental justice it would be necessary to establish that the fugitive would face a situation that is simply unacceptable. As well, while the courts undoubtedly have the right to review the decision of the executive by virtue of the court's responsibility to uphold the Constitution in extradition matters, this role must be exercised with caution bearing in mind that the discretion to surrender a fugitive to the demanding state is primarily that of the executive. Canada's external obligations are involved and the executive obviously has primary responsibility in this area: *Argentina (Republic) v. Mellino*, [1987] 1 S.C.R. 536, 33 C.C.C. (3d) 334, 40 D.L.R. (4th) 74; *United States of America v. Allard and Charette*, [1987] 1 S.C.R. 564, 33 C.C.C. (3d) 501, 40 D.L.R. (4th) 102.

Extradition does not constitute an abuse of process where the Canadian prosecutor informed the fugitive that if he did not plead guilty to the Canadian charge, he would be extradited and where, in fact, the Canadian charge was stayed on the morning of the accused's trial: *United States of America v. Leon*, [1996] 1 S.C.R. 888, 105 C.C.C. (3d) 385, 47 C.R. (4th) 1.

The failure of the Minister of Justice to request an assurance that the death penalty would not be imposed as a condition of extradition, violated the fugitive's rights. In the absence of exceptional circumstances, assurances in death penalty cases are always constitutionally required: *United States of America v. Burns*, [2001] 1 S.C.R. 283, 151 C.C.C. (3d) 97, 39 C.R. (5th) 205.

The extradition judge does have the jurisdiction to stay an extradition proceeding as an abuse of process where the abuse relates to the extradition hearing: *United States of America v. Tsioubris*, [2001] 1 S.C.R. 613, 152 C.C.C. (3d) 292, 197 D.L.R. (4th) 67, *sub nom. United States of America v. Cobb*; *United States of America v. Shulman*, [2001] 1 S.C.R. 616, 152 C.C.C. (3d) 294, 41 C.R. (5th) 100.

While the extradition judge has the jurisdiction to order disclosure, the disclosure can only relate to the production of materials relevant to issues properly raised at the committal stage of the process, subject to the discretion to expand the scope of the hearing to allow the parties to establish a basis for a subsequent Charter challenge: *United States of America v. Kwok*, [2001] 1 S.C.R. 532, 152 C.C.C. (3d) 225, 41 C.R. (5th) 44.

Defences – In *R. v. Morgentaler, Smoling and Scott*, [1988] 1 S.C.R. 30, 37 C.C.C. (3d) 449, 62 C.R. (3d) 1, the court was required to consider the therapeutic abortion provisions in s. 287 of the *Criminal Code*. Dickson C.J.C. and Lamer J. were of the view that state interference with bodily integrity and serious state-imposed psychological stress at the least in a criminal law context constitutes a breach of security of the person. They held that the breach of the principles of fundamental justice came about by the fact that the requirements of s. 287(4) permitting an abortion where it was approved by hospital committee while seemingly neutral on their face, resulted in abortions being absolutely unavailable in many areas and hospitals, and does not provide a clear legal standard to be applied by the therapeutic abortion committee in reaching its decision as to when to grant a certificate. One of the basic tenets of a criminal justice system is that when Parliament creates a defence to a criminal charge the defence should not be illusory or so difficult to attain as to be practically illusory. While Parliament must be given room to design an appropriate administrative and procedural structure for bringing into operation a particular defence to criminal liability, if that structure is too manifestly unfair, having regard to the decisions it is called upon to make, as to violate the principles of fundamental justice then the structure must be struck down. Beetz and Estey JJ. were of the view that the procedural requirements of s. 287, by significantly delaying a pregnant woman's access to medical treatment, result in additional dangers to her health and thereby deprive her of her rights to security of the person and do so in a manner which does not accord with the principles of fundamental justice. Finally Wilson J. held that the legislative scheme set up in s. 287 not only violates the pregnant woman's rights to security of the person but also the right to liberty as guaranteed by s. 7.

A statutory defence, like any other legislative provision, is not immune from scrutiny under the Charter. Further, there is no basis for the court adopting a position of strong deference in reviewing statutory defences such as compulsion under s. 17 of the *Criminal Code*: *R. v. Ruzic* (2001), 153 C.C.C. (3d) 1, 41 C.R. (5th) 1 (S.C.C.).

This section does not require that a defence such as drunkenness be available for all offences. Thus, it was open to Parliament in creating the offence of impaired driving to preclude drunkenness as a defence. The mental element of voluntary intoxication is a sufficiently guilty mind: *R. v. Penno*, [1990] 2 S.C.R. 865, 59 C.C.C. (3d) 344, 80 C.R. (3d) 97.

The principles of fundamental justice contemplate an accusatorial and adversarial system of criminal justice which is founded on respect for the autonomy and dignity of the person. These principles require that an accused, who is fit to stand trial, have the right to control his own defence. Any common law limit on this right which infringes the life, liberty or security of the person, must be the least intrusive rule which will attain the objectives which are of sufficient importance to override this section of the Charter: *R. v. Swain*, [1991] 1 S.C.R. 933, 63 C.C.C. (3d) 481, 5 C.R. (4th) 253.

Moral involuntariness is a principle of fundamental justice protected by this section. Only voluntary conduct being behaviour that is the product of a free will and controlled body unhindered by external constraints, should attract the penalty and stigma and criminal liability. The defence of compulsion by threats in s. 17 of the *Criminal Code* violates this section because the existence of certain requirements of the defence would allow for the conviction of an individual who acted involuntarily. Those requirements — immediacy (threat of immediate death or bodily harm) and presence (threat from a person who is present when the offence is committed) — infringe this section and must be struck down as unconstitutional: *R. v. Ruzic* (2001), 153 C.C.C. (3d) 1, 41 C.R. (5th) 1 (S.C.C.).

SEARCH OR SEIZURE.

8. Everyone has the right to be secure against unreasonable search or seizure.

ANNOTATIONS

Interpretation generally – Section 8 of the Charter limits the federal and provincial governments' powers of search and seizure. It does not, however, confer any power, even of reasonable search and seizure. These powers are grounded either in the common law or statute. To assess the constitutionality of a search and seizure, or of an authorizing statute, the court must focus on the reasonable or unreasonable impact on its subject, and not simply on its rationality in furtherance of a valid government objective. This section guarantees a broad and general right to be secure from unreasonable search and seizure beyond mere protection of property. Its protections go at least as far as protecting an individual's reasonable expectations of privacy. The court must assess whether, in a particular situation, the public's interest in being left alone by government must give way to the government's interest in intruding on the individual's privacy to advance its goals, notably those of law enforcement: *Hunter v. Southam Inc.*, [1984] 2 S.C.R. 145, 14 C.C.C. (3d) 97.

Protecting individuals from unjustified state intrusions upon their privacy requires preventing unjustified searches before they happen which can only be accomplished by a system of prior authorization, not one of subsequent validation. If it is feasible to obtain prior authorization, such authorization is a pre-condition for a valid search and seizure. Thus, there is a presumption of unreasonableness if the search has taken place without a warrant. The party seeking to justify the warrantless search must rebut this presumption: *Hunter v. Southam Inc., supra.*

Ordinarily, the standard to authorize a search, established on oath, is reasonable and probable grounds to believe that an offence has been committed and that there is evidence to be found at the place of the search: *Hunter v. Southam Inc., supra.*

The person authorizing the search must assess the evidence in an entirely neutral and impartial manner, as to whether the constitutional standard has been met. This person need not be a judge. He or she must at a minimum be capable of acting judicially: *Hunter v. Southam Inc., supra.*

The exercise of a judicial discretion in the decision to grant or withhold authorization for a search warrant is a fundamental aspect of the scheme of prior authorization articulated in *Hunter v. Southam Inc., supra.* The decision to grant or withhold a warrant requires a balancing of the interests of the individual and the state. A section of the *Income Tax Act* was unconstitutional because it required the judge to issue the warrant if the statutory prerequisites were met, removing discretion: *Baron v. Canada*, [1993] 1 S.C.R. 416, 78 C.C.C. (3d) 510.

A claim for relief under s. 24(2) of the Charter can only be made by the person whose Charter rights have been infringed. Section 8 is a personal right which protects people and not places. The right to challenge the legality of a search depends upon the accused establishing that his personal rights to privacy have been violated: *R. v. Edwards*, [1996] 1 S.C.R. 128, 104 C.C.C. (3d) 136.

Privacy is a protean concept, and the difficult issue is where the "reasonableness" line should be drawn. Expectation of privacy is a normative rather than a descriptive standard: *R. v. Tessling*, [2004] 3 S.C.R. 432, 189 C.C.C. (3d) 129.

Requirement of state action – Private security guards were neither agents nor employees of the government and were not subject to government control. Accordingly, their search of a rented locker could not be subject to Charter scrutiny: *R. v. Buhay*, [2003] 1 S.C.R. 631, 174 C.C.C. (3d) 97.

This section did not apply to interceptions made by Bell Canada, at its own initiative, to identify the person using its services to make obscene and harassing telephone calls to subscribers. Bell Canada was not acting as an agent of the state: *R. v. Fegan* (1993), 80 C.C.C. (3d) 356 (Ont. C.A.).

The police and an electricity company established an information-sharing relationship to detect marihuana grow operations that were criminal and that posed a threat to the company's infrastructure. The electricity company always complied with police requests for customer electricity consumption data and also volunteered information. Thus, the police investigation began when the electricity company noticed a suspicious pattern of energy consumption at the accused's residence and forwarded the data to the police: *R. v. Orlandis-Habsburgo* (2017), 352 C.C.C. (3d) 525 (Ont. C.A.).

Onus and burden of proof – The accused bears the burden of persuading the court that her Charter rights or freedoms have been infringed or denied. Once the accused has demonstrated that a warrantless search occurred, however, the Crown has the burden of showing that the search was, on a balance of probabilities, reasonable. A search will be reasonable if: (1) it is authorized by law; (2) the law itself is reasonable; and (3) the manner in which the search was carried out is reasonable: *R. v. Collins*, [1987] 1 S.C.R. 265, 33 C.C.C. (3d) 1.

Extraterritorial application – Subject to the safeguards protecting trial fairness, the Charter does not generally apply to extra-territorial searches. Canadian law can only be enforced on consent of the other state. The court must determine whether the impugned activity falls within s. 32(1) of the Charter, in that a Canadian state actor to whom the Charter applied was involved in the investigation. If the Charter does apply, the court must determine whether the evidence obtained ought to be excluded to preserve trial fairness. In this case, the police officers were government actors, but the foreign state police did not consent to the Charter's application. In addition, the evidence was not conscriptive and the actions of the officers were not unreasonable or unfair, as they were acting under the authority of the foreign state's police. There was nothing to suggest that the searches were conducted in a manner that was inconsistent with the foreign state's law, nor was there any suggestion that the laws of the state failed to meet the requirements accepted by free and democratic societies. Accordingly, the admission of the evidence did not affect trial fairness: *R. v. Hape*, [2007] 2 S.C.R. 292, 220 C.C.C. (3d) 161.

A Canadian official sending a letter to Switzerland's competent legal authority, seeking the Swiss Government's assistance with a Canadian criminal investigation, did not infringe this section. The Swiss authorities' actions in response, including orders to seize documents, were not subject to Charter scrutiny, even though they interfered with the plaintiff's privacy interests. The Canadian government did not undertake any search or seizure — it merely requested that a search and seizure be undertaken: *Schreiber v. Canada (Attorney General)*, [1998] 1 S.C.R. 841, 124 C.C.C. (3d) 129.

Establishing a reasonable expectation of privacy — general – Section 8 of the Charter demands two distinct inquires: (1) whether the accused had a reasonable expectation of privacy in the subject matter of the search; and, if so, (2) whether the search was conducted in a reasonable manner. A reasonable expectation of privacy is to be determined in the totality of the circumstances. In a territorial privacy case, the court considered the following factors in assessing the totality of the circumstances: presence at the time of the search; possession or control of the property or place searched; ownership of the property or place; historical use of the property or item; ability to regulate access to the place; existence of a subjective expectation of privacy; and objective reasonableness of the expectation. In this particular case, the accused did not have a reasonable expectation of privacy in his girlfriend's apartment: *R. v. Edwards*, *supra*.

To establish a subjective expectation of privacy in the subject matter of the search, an accused may rely on the Crown's factual theory to avoid giving self-incriminating testimony at the Charter *voir dire*. An accused mounting a s. 8 Charter claim may ask the court to assume as true any fact the Crown has alleged or will allege in the prosecution against him in lieu of tendering evidence probative of those same facts in the *voir dire*. He or she does not have to formally admit ownership in order to gain s. 8 standing: *R. v. Jones*, [2017] 2 S.C.R. 696, 357 C.C.C. (3d) 350.

The question of whether the accused has a reasonable expectation of privacy in the subject matter of the search, although often treated as a single issue, actually addresses two distinct inquiries. First, whether the police conduct at issue ever amounts to a search or seizure in respect of anyone (the "search inquiry"). If the answer to the search inquiry is "no", the police are able to use the impugned technique absent the judicial supervision that s. 8 imposes. Second, whether the accused, as opposed to some other person, has standing to bring a s. 8 claim (the "standing inquiry"). The question in the standing inquiry is usually whether the accused, as opposed to another more directly interested person, has a sufficient connection with the subject matter of the search to claim a reasonable expectation of privacy: *R. v.*

Marakah, [2017] 2 S.C.R. 608, 357 C.C.C. (3d) 281, *per* Moldaver J., dissent, at paras. 102-110.

The police infringed the accused's Charter rights when they took a family computer from his home, relying on the consent of his estranged wife. Although the computer was shared, the accused maintained a reasonable expectation of privacy in it. The spouse's consent did not nullify his reasonable expectation of privacy, or waive his Charter rights in the computer. The warrantless seizure of the computer and the search of it without a valid warrant were unreasonable, and the admission of the child pornography evidence discovered on it would bring the administration of justice into disrepute: *R. v. Reeves* (2018), 367 C.C.C. (3d) 129 (S.C.C.).

A claim to a reasonable expectation of privacy may relate to the person, a place, information, or any combination of the three: *R. v. Tessling*, [2004] 3 S.C.R. 432, 189 C.C.C. (3d) 129.

Reasonable expectation of privacy — personal – A police officer's demand that a motorist he stopped surrender his driver's licence and insurance card for inspection, as required by provincial legislation, does not offend s. 8 of the Charter. The procedure is not a search, there being no intrusion on a reasonable expectation of privacy by requiring production of a licence, permit, or other documentary evidence of a lawful condition to exercise a right or privilege: *R. v. Hufsky*, [1988] 1 S.C.R. 621, 40 C.C.C. (3d) 398.

The seizure of a blood sample from the accused without his consent and without lawful authority is an unreasonable seizure within the meaning of s. 8 although the sample was taken by a physician. The blood sample was not required for medical purposes and was taken at the direction of the police: *R. v. Pohoretsky*, [1987] 1 S.C.R. 945, 33 C.C.C. (3d) 398.

A police officer seizing a blood sample from a physician violated s. 8. The seizure infringed on the accused's informational, physical and spatial spheres of privacy. Retention of information about oneself is extremely important. People may wish or be compelled to reveal information while reasonably expecting that it shall remain confidential to the persons to whom, and restricted to the purposes for which, it is divulged. The sample was taken by the physician without the accused's consent and then turned over to the police without a warrant or other lawful authority. Although the physician originally took the sample for medical purposes, it was no longer required for those purposes. The physician had a duty to respect the accused's privacy: *R. v. Dyment*, [1988] 2 S.C.R. 417, 45 C.C.C. (3d) 244. See also *R. v. Dersch*, [1993] 3 S.C.R. 768, 85 C.C.C. (3d) 1.

There is no reasonable expectation of privacy in information voluntarily provided by the accused to an emergency room physician regarding drinking and driving. Consequently, the actions of the physician in contacting the police and reporting the information and observations did not attract the application of s. 8 of the Charter: *R. v. Spidell* (1996), 107 C.C.C. (3d) 348 (N.S.C.A.), leave to appeal to S.C.C. refused (1997), 161 N.S.R. (2d) 80*n*.

Reasonable expectation of privacy — informational – As a general proposition, surreptitious electronic surveillance of an individual by an agency of the state constitutes an unreasonable search or seizure. There is no logical reason to distinguish third party electronic surveillance in which neither participant consents, and that in which one participant consents. The rationale for regulating the state's power to record communications that their originator expects will not be intercepted is not grounded in the risk that the intended recipient will divulge communications that are meant to be private. Rather, the regulation of electronic surveillance protects against the more insidious danger inherent in allowing the state, in its unfettered discretion, to record and transmit our words. It is unacceptable in a free society that agents of the state be free to use this technology at their sole discretion: *R. v. Duarte*, [1990] 1 S.C.R. 30, 53 C.C.C. (3d) 1. [Now see ss. 184.1 to 184.4 of the *Criminal Code*.]

Surreptitious video surveillance by agents of the state will sometimes constitute a search and seizure within the meaning of s. 8. In assessing the constitutionality of a search, the court is not to be influenced by the target's illegal activities. Rather, the question is to be framed in

CHARTER

broad and neutral terms. Thus, in the case of video surveillance of a hotel room, the issue was whether, in a society such as ours, persons retiring to a hotel room behind a closed door have a reasonable expectation of privacy. The accused was gambling illegally in a hotel room to which strangers in his community were invited. He nevertheless had a reasonable expectation of privacy and video surveillance of his activities violated s. 8 of the Charter: *R. v. Wong*, [1990] 3 S.C.R. 36, 60 C.C.C. (3d) 460. [Now see s. 487.01 of the *Criminal Code*.]

Both the installation in the accused's car and subsequent monitoring by the police of an electronic "beeper" capable of locating the car constitute searches for the purpose of this section: *R. v. Wise*, [1992] 1 S.C.R. 527, 70 C.C.C. (3d) 193. [Now see s. 492.1 of the *Criminal Code*.]

For constitutional protection to be extended to commercial records relating to the accused, the information seized must be of a personal and confidential nature. This section protects a biographical core of personal information which individuals in a free and democratic society would wish to maintain and control from dissemination to the state. This would include information which tends to reveal intimate details of the lifestyle and personal choices of the individual. The records the utilities commission kept of electricity consumption at the accused's residence, did not fall within the category of protected information. The relationship between the accused and the energy supplier was neither personal nor confidential. Furthermore, the energy consumption data was available to members of the public at large on the energy provider's website: *R. v. Plant*, [1993] 3 S.C.R. 281, 84 C.C.C. (3d) 203.

The power under provincial legislation to make copies of documents authorizes a seizure within the meaning of this section. The powers to examine the work environment and inspect documents are properly characterized as searches: *Comité paritaire de l'industrie de la chemise v. Potash*, [1994] 2 S.C.R. 406, 91 C.C.C. (3d) 315, *sub nom. R. v. Potash*.

Customers of securities-brokers have a reasonable expectation of privacy over documents in the hands of the broker and a police officer cannot enlist the broker's cooperation without executing a search warrant: *R. v. Donaldson* (1990), 58 C.C.C. (3d) 294 (B.C.C.A.).

The police intercepted the accused's telephone conversations while targeting a third party with the authorization. The accused nonetheless had standing to challenge the validity of the authorization: *R. v. Shayesteh* (1996), 111 C.C.C. (3d) 225 (Ont. C.A.).

In *R. v. Patrick*, [2009] 1 S.C.R. 579, 242 C.C.C. (3d) 158, the Supreme Court of Canada emphasized the accused's informational privacy interest in the contents of garbage bags placed at or near his property line for collection. In the reasonable expectation of privacy analysis, the court is required to consider the following: the nature or subject matter of the evidence gathered by the police; whether the accused had a direct interest in the contents; whether there was a subjective expectation of privacy in the informational content of the garbage and, if so, whether the expectation was objectively reasonable. In determining whether the expectation was objectively reasonable, the court should examine: where the alleged search occurred; whether the police trespassed on the accused's property; whether the informational content of the subject matter was in public view; whether the informational content of the subject matter had been abandoned; whether such information was already in the hands of a third party and, if so, whether it was subject to an obligation of confidentiality; whether the police technique was intrusive in relation to the privacy interest; whether the use of this evidence gathering technique was itself objectively unreasonable; and whether the informational content exposed any intimate details of the accused's lifestyle or information of a biographic nature.

In *R. v. Tessling*, *supra*, the Supreme Court of Canada held that the use of an infrared camera to obtain information about the patterns of heat distribution on the external surfaces of a house did not constitute a search within the meaning of s. 8 of the Charter. Information obtained via this technology cannot, by itself, constitute sufficient grounds to obtain a search warrant. The technology, at its current stage of development, was non-intrusive, did not "see" through the wall of a building and did not disclose a biographical core of information or reveal intimate details about the accused's lifestyle. Accordingly, there was no reasonable expectation of privacy in respect of this information.

In *R. v. Gomboc*, [2010] 3 S.C.R. 211, 263 C.C.C. (3d) 383, the court held that the use of a digital recording ammeter (DRA) to record when electrical power was consumed on the accused's property did not constitute a search within the meaning of s. 8. The combined effect of the regulatory scheme and s. 487.014 of the *Criminal Code* established that, not only was there no statutory barrier to the utility company's voluntary cooperation with the police request for DRA information, but no express notice that such cooperation might occur existed.

The accused school teacher had a reasonable, although diminished, expectation of privacy in the laptop computer provided to him by his employer. He was allowed to use the laptop for personal and school-related matters: *R. v. Cole*, [2012] 3 S.C.R. 34, 290 C.C.C. (3d) 247.

An ITO authorizing a search for documents in a residence does not implicitly authorize a search of a computer found in that residence. Specific prior authorization is required for police to search a computer. This is because the privacy interests implicated by computer searches are markedly different from those at stake in searches of receptacles such as cupboards and filing cabinets. Only specific authorization to search a computer ensures that the authorizing justice has considered the distinctive privacy concerns raised by computer searches: *R. v. Vu*, [2013] 3 S.C.R. 657, 302 C.C.C. (3d) 427.

The police infringed s. 8 of the Charter in obtaining subscriber information from an Internet Service Provider (ISP) without prior judicial authorization. The court recognized an informational privacy interest in anonymity that is violated by handing over subscriber information to the police: *R. v. Spencer*, [2014] 2 S.C.R. 212, 312 C.C.C. (3d) 215.

The accused had a reasonable, although diminished, expectation of privacy in hourly electricity consumption data held by their electricity company. The information related to the activities of the accused in their home, favouring the existence of a reasonable expectation of privacy. Their privacy interests were attenuated by the electricity company's legitimate interests, the non-personal character of the information and the substantial qualifications to the accused's control over the data. The contractual relationship with the accused did not contemplate the information-sharing relationship between the company and the police: *R. v. Orlandis-Habsburgo*, *supra*.

The court held (4:3) that, in some circumstances, the sender of an electronic text message has a reasonable expectation of privacy in the copy of that text message recovered from the recipient's electronic device. Relevant factors include: (1) the place where the search occurred, whether it be a real physical place or a metaphorical chat room; (2) the private nature of the subject matter, that is whether the informational content of the electronic conversation revealed details of the accused's lifestyle or information of a biographic nature; and (3) control over the subject matter. Control, although relevant, is not a prerequisite to a reasonable expectation of privacy. Individuals exercise meaningful control over the information that they send by text message by making choices about how, when, and to whom they disclose the information: *R. v. Marakah*, *supra*.

The court held that the sender of a text message has a reasonable expectation of privacy in records of that message stored in the service provider's infrastructure. The court's concern was informational self-determination. An accused may choose to divulge certain information for a limited purpose, or to a limited class of persons, and nonetheless retain a reasonable expectation of privacy, depending on the circumstances. Control and access are not all-or-nothing concepts. Furthermore, the governing federal privacy legislation placed significant limitations on the service provider's ability to disclose information. The production order's targeting of a third party did not defeat the accused's reasonable expectation of privacy: *Jones*, *supra*.

Reasonable expectation of privacy — territorial – The accused was cultivating marihuana on a farm on which he was a trespasser. He did not have any reasonable expectation of privacy in the property and, accordingly, the police did not violate s. 8 of the Charter in attending at the property: *R. v. Lauda*, [1998] 2 S.C.R. 683, 129 C.C.C. (3d) 225, affg (1998), 122 C.C.C. (3d) 74 (Ont. C.A.).

A "perimeter search" in which the police officer trespassed onto the accused's property and attempted to peer into the windows in an effort to confirm suspicions that the accused was cultivating marihuana in his residence, is a search within the meaning of this section. While in *Hunter v. Southam Inc., supra*, the court adopted the view that this section "protects people, not places", this was not intended to inhibit the reasonableness of the individual's expectation of privacy over his activities on private property. The reasonableness of a citizen's expectation of privacy cannot be confined to those situations that involve the enjoyment of property. A warrantless perimeter search, done merely upon suspicion, was not authorized by the search provisions of the former *Narcotics Control Act* and constituted a violation of this section: *R. v. Kokesch*, [1990] 3 S.C.R. 3, 61 C.C.C. (3d) 207.

The warrantless and surreptitious search of a hotel room, upon mere suspicion of criminal activities, when the registered guests are absent and have left a "Do Not Disturb" sign on the door, constitutes an impermissible intrusion by the state on a reasonable expectation of privacy. The police officers' mistaken belief that the management of the hotel had a sufficient possessory or other interest in the room to authorize police entry in the absence and without the consent of the guests, could not render the search valid: *R. v. Mercer; R. v. Kenny* (1992), 70 C.C.C. (3d) 180 (Ont. C.A.), leave to appeal to S.C.C. refused [1992] 2 S.C.R. viii, 74 C.C.C. (3d) vi.

A "knock-on" investigation, in which the police attended at the suspect's door in the hope that, when the suspect opened the door, they would smell marihuana, is a search within the meaning of this section. The occupier of a residential dwelling is deemed to grant the public permission to approach the door and knock. However, the implied invitation to knock extends no further than is required to permit convenient communication with the occupant of the dwelling, and only those activities that are reasonably associated with this purpose are authorized by the implied license to knock: *R. v. Evans*, [1996] 1 S.C.R. 8, 104 C.C.C. (3d) 23.

An accused has a reasonable expectation of privacy in a rental locker. Unless an emergency or other exigent circumstance arose, locker renters could reasonably expect that their lockers would be free from unauthorized search by security guards or the police. The private security guards in this case were not subject to Charter scrutiny. The police, however, were required to obtain a warrant to search the accused's locker. A person's reasonable expectation of privacy in the contents of a rented and locked bus depot locker is not destroyed merely because a private individual invades that privacy by investigating the locker contents. The accused's reasonable expectation of privacy was continuous: *R. v. Buhay, supra.*

All of the relevant facts surrounding a passenger's presence in a vehicle must be considered to determine whether the passenger has a reasonable expectation of privacy. In this case, the passenger did not own or have any control over the vehicle nor was there any evidence that she had used it in the past or had any relationship with the owner or driver which would establish some special access or privilege. Furthermore, she could not demonstrate any reasonable expectation of privacy over the items seized. When asked about the items, she indicated that the other occupants owned them: *R. v. Belnavis*, [1997] 3 S.C.R. 341, 118 C.C.C. (3d) 405.

A warrantless search of an office requires justification to meet the constitutional standard of reasonableness secured by this section. Statutory provisions authorizing searches are subject to challenge. Justification for a warrantless search may be found in the existence of circumstances making it impracticable to obtain a warrant, but where no such circumstances exist and when the obtaining of a warrant would not impede effective law enforcement, the warrantless search of an office, except as an incident of a lawful arrest, cannot be justified and does not meet the constitutional standard of reasonableness proscribed by this section: *R.*

v. Rao (1984), 12 C.C.C. (3d) 97 (Ont. C.A.), leave to appeal to S.C.C. refused (1984), 40 C.R. (3d) xxvi.

Assessing the validity of an information to obtain prior judicial authorization – In considering the validity of a search warrant, facts obtained as a result of an unreasonable search must be excised from the information to obtain. The court must then determine whether the warrant would have been issued without the improperly obtained facts: *R. v. Grant*, [1993] 3 S.C.R. 223, 84 C.C.C. (3d) 173 (9:0).

The legal obligation on anyone seeking an *ex parte* authorization is full and frank disclosure of material facts. It must set out the facts fully and frankly for the authorizing judge in order that he or she can make an assessment of whether these rise to the standard required in the legal test for the authorization. Ideally, an affidavit should be not only full and frank but also clear and concise. It need not include every minute detail of the police investigation: *R. v. Araujo*, [2000] 2 S.C.R. 992, 149 C.C.C. (3d) 449.

Where the police conducted a warrantless search under s. 10(1) of the former *Narcotics Control Act*, the Crown sought to establish the search was reasonable because the officer making the search believed on reasonable grounds that the accused was in possession of narcotics. Evidence as to the officer's belief and the reasonable grounds for that belief was admissible even if those reasonable grounds were based on information received from third parties. The hearsay rule had no application, the evidence not being adduced for its truth but to establish the officer's belief and grounds for belief: *R. v. Collins*, *supra*.

The police searched the accused without a warrant pursuant to the former s. 37(1) of the *Food and Drugs Act*. The Crown sought to establish that the officer had reasonable grounds to believe the accused was in possession of a narcotic. The appropriate standard of proof to establish reasonable grounds for a search is reasonable probability rather than proof beyond a reasonable doubt or a *prima facie* case. The police officer deciding that the suspect should be searched must have reasonable and probable grounds to believe, for example, that the suspect possesses a controlled drug. If another officer conducts the search, then he is entitled to assume that the officer who ordered the search had reasonable and probable grounds for doing so: *R. v. Debot*, [1989] 2 S.C.R. 1140, 52 C.C.C. (3d) 193.

The standard of reasonableness is considered in the totality of the circumstances. The court must consider: (1) whether the information predicting the commission of a criminal offence was compelling; (2) if the police rely on an informer's tip, whether that source was credible; and (3) whether the information was corroborated by a police investigation prior to making the decision to conduct the search. Weaknesses in one of these three areas may to some extent be compensated by strengths in the others. Police are also entitled to take into account the accused's past record and reputation if related to the ostensible reasons for the search. If the suspect's reputation was based on hearsay rather than police familiarity with the suspect, its veracity cannot be assumed. It is not necessary for the police to confirm each detail in an informer's tip so long as the sequence of events actually observed conforms sufficiently to the anticipated pattern to remove the possibility of innocent coincidence. On the other hand, the level of verification required may be higher if the police rely on an informer whose credibility cannot be assessed or if fewer details are provided and the risk of innocent coincidence is greater: *R. v. Debot*, *supra*.

A conclusion that the police had reliable information that the accused was attempting to import narcotics must be based on more than the fact of a subsequent recovery of the drugs. There must be a proper inquiry into the source and reliability of the confidential information to determine whether, "in the totality of the circumstances", there existed reasonable and probable grounds to believe that the accused was carrying the narcotic or whether there was only a suspicion. A rectal examination of the accused, based on the mere suspicion that he was carrying drugs and as an incident to an arrest for outstanding traffic fines, was a serious violation of this section: *R. v. Greffe*, [1990] 1 S.C.R. 755, 55 C.C.C. (3d) 161 (4:3).

In a vehicle search case, the police officer observed garbage bags full of new clothes in the back seat with the price tags on them. The police officer also received conflicting stories about their ownership. An objective observer would find that the police officer had

CHARTER

reasonable and probable grounds to believe that the bags contained stolen property. Furthermore, in light of the crowded back seat, a reasonable person would have good cause to believe that the trunk might contain more stolen clothing: *R. v. Belnavis, supra.*

Interception of private communications – Before an authorization to intercept private communications may be granted, Part VI of the *Criminal Code* requires that a judge must be satisfied other investigative methods would fail or have little likelihood of success and to grant the authorization is in the best interests of the administration of justice. These requirements meet the high standards which s. 8 of the Charter imposes as a prerequisite to electronic surveillance. In particular, the requirement that the authorization could only be granted if it is in the best interests of the administration of justice imports as a minimum requirement that the issuing judge must be satisfied that there are reasonable and probable grounds to believe that an offence has been, or is being, committed and that the authorization sought will afford evidence of that offence: *R. v. Duarte, supra.*

A plurality of the court held that a general warrant was not available to compel a telecommunications company to prospectively provide police with text messages from their computer database on a daily basis for a period of two weeks. According to Abella J., the general warrant was invalid because, contrary to s. 487.01(1)(*c*) of the *Code*, another provision in the *Code* — the Part VI scheme — was available to authorize the technique police used. Moldaver J., taking a substance over form approach, held the general warrant to be invalid because, contrary to s. 487.01(1)(*c*), the investigative technique it authorized was substantively equivalent to an intercept: *R. v. TELUS Communications Co.*, [2013] 2 S.C.R. 3, 294 C.C.C. (3d) 498.

Records of historical text messages – Those already sent and received stored on a service provider's infrastructure were lawfully seized by means of a production order under s. 487.012 of the *Criminal Code*. This investigative technique was not encompassed by the definition of "intercept" in Part VI of the *Criminal Code*. Unlike in *R. v. TELUS Communications Co., supra*, police did not seek an order authorizing the prospective production of text messages: *Jones, supra.*

Searches and seizures in the regulatory context – Powers of inspection in a regulatory context have been deemed reasonable even though the inspector neither required a warrant nor reasonable and probable grounds to inspect. Inspection, especially without notice, is a practical means of encouraging compliance with regulatory standards. An inspection does not carry with it the stigma normally associated with criminal investigations. It may be that, in the course of inspection, violations of the statute will be uncovered, but this possibility does not alter the underling purpose of inspection. The same is true even when the enforcement is prompted by a complaint: *Comité paritaire de l'industrie de la chemise, supra.*

Section 17 of the former *Combines Investigation Act* compelled production of documents without meeting the relatively stringent standard of reasonableness articulated in *Hunter v. Southam Inc., supra*. The court divided as to: whether the legislation was regulatory, quasi-criminal or criminal in nature; thus, whether compelled production amounted to a seizure within the meaning of s. 8 of the Charter; and if so, whether such seizure was unreasonable. La Forest and L'Heureux-Dubé JJ. held that a less strenuous and more flexible standard of reasonableness for administrative or regulatory searches and seizures was fully consistent with a purposive approach to s. 8. Although compelled production of documents may constitute a seizure within the meaning of s. 8, the seizure contemplated by s. 17 was reasonable in light of its limited scope and the limited privacy interests with respect to documents subject to production. Sopinka J., in his concurring judgment, held that an order under s. 17 requiring production of documents did not constitute a seizure within the meaning of s. 8 of the Charter. Lamer and Wilson JJ., dissenting, were of the view that s. 17 did violate the right to be secure against unreasonable seizure as guaranteed by s. 8. Compulsory production of documents in a criminal or quasi-criminal law context fell within the definition of seizure and the seizure was unreasonable because it did not meet the test of reasonableness set out in *Hunter v. Southam Inc., supra*: *Thomson Newspapers Ltd. v. Canada (Director of Investigation and Research, Restrictive Trade Practices Commission)*, [1990] 1 S.C.R. 425, 54 C.C.C. (3d) 417.

In *R. v. McKinlay Transport Ltd.*, [1990] 1 S.C.R. 627, 55 C.C.C. (3d) 530, the court held that the provisions in the *Income Tax Act* providing that the authorities may make a demand for information and the production of documents did not violate s. 8 of the Charter. Lamer and Wilson JJ. held that, while the demand constitutes a seizure, it is not unreasonable. The standard of review of what is "reasonable" in a given context must be flexible. There is a distinction between seizures in the criminal or quasi-criminal context (to which the criteria set out in *Hunter v. Southam Inc., supra*, must apply), and seizures in the administrative or regulatory context (to which a lesser standard may apply). La Forest and L'Heureux-Dube JJ., for the reasons they gave in *Thomson Newspapers Ltd., supra*, held that the demand under the *Income Tax Act*, although it may be a seizure, is not unreasonable. Sopinka J., for the reasons he gave in *Thomson Newspapers Ltd.*, held that the demand does not constitute a seizure within the meaning of s. 8.

Seizure of bodily fluid samples by the coroner would be reasonable and not caught by s. 8 of the Charter only so long as the evidence was being used by the coroner for valid non-criminal purposes. If the evidence, or the information derived from the evidence, was appropriated by the criminal law enforcement arm of the state for use against the person from whom it was seized, the seizure would become unreasonable. Even if a sample was initially properly seized by a coroner pursuant to presumed valid provincial legislation, this does not preclude a finding that the police may also have seized the sample or that the subsequent appropriation of the evidence for use in a criminal prosecution may make the seizure unreasonable. The court must focus on the actions of the police in determining whether or not there has been a violation of this section. The taking of a bodily fluid sample need not be directly from the person whose rights are affected, or even from the medical staff who extracted the sample, to constitute a seizure sufficient to invoke the protection of s. 8: *R. v. Colarusso*, [1994] 1 S.C.R. 20, 87 C.C.C. (3d) 193.

A valid regulatory purpose for a roadside stop, whether predominant or not, would not sanitize or excuse a Charter violation. Random roadside checks of vehicles for highway traffic purposes must be limited to their intended purpose and cannot be turned into an unfounded general inquisition or an unreasonable search. As long as there is a continuing regulatory purpose on which to ground the exercise of the regulatory power, the proper issue is whether the power was exercised in such a way as to violate s. 8 of the Charter by infringing the accused's reasonable expectations of privacy: *R. v. Nolet*, [2010] 1 S.C.R. 851, 256 C.C.C. (3d) 1.

Searches and seizures in schools – Assuming that the Charter applies to the acts of a school official in a public elementary or secondary school, the official, when not acting as an agent of the state, may search a student without a warrant if there are reasonable grounds to believe that a school rule has been or is being violated, and that evidence of the violation will be found in the location or on the person of the student searched. Searches undertaken in situations where the health and safety of students is involved may require different considerations. The search must be authorized by a statutory provision that is reasonable. A provision in provincial legislation placing a responsibility upon teachers and principals to maintain proper order and discipline in the school and to attend to the health and comfort of students by necessary implication authorizes searches of students. The search must be conducted reasonably and must be appropriate in light of the circumstances presented and the nature of the suspected breach of school regulations. The search must be conducted in a sensitive manner and must be minimally intrusive: *R. v. M. (M.R.)*, [1998] 3 S.C.R. 393, 129 C.C.C. (3d) 361.

In *R. v. M. (A.)*, [2008] 1 S.C.R. 569, 230 C.C.C. (3d) 377, the court considered the use of sniffer dogs in schools. The court held that students have an expectation of privacy in the contents of their lockers. In this case, the principal had extended a standing invitation to the

CHARTER

police officers to attend the school with sniffer dogs. The search was unreasonable as there was no reasonable suspicion.

Searches and seizures at international border crossings – The reasonableness of border searches must be treated differently from searches occurring in other circumstances. The degree of personal privacy reasonably expected at customs is lower than most situations. People do not expect to cross international borders free from scrutiny. Routine questioning by customs officers, search of luggage, frisk or pat searches and the requirement to remove in private such articles of clothing as will permit investigation of suspicious bodily bulges as permitted by provisions of the *Customs Act* are not unreasonable. However, a search is not conducted in a reasonable manner if the accused was not informed of the right to counsel at the time that she was detained for a strip search. Had the accused been informed of the right to counsel, she might have had the benefit of legal advice including explanation that the decision to search may be reviewed by a magistrate or chief officer of the court: *R. v. Simmons*, [1988] 2 S.C.R. 495, 45 C.C.C. (3d) 296.

See also *R. v. Jacques* (1993), 143 N.B.R. (2d) 64 (Prov. Ct.), revd (1995), 95 C.C.C. (3d) 238 (N.B.C.A.), affd [1996] 3 S.C.R. 312, 110 C.C.C. (3d) 1, concluding that border-vehicle searches pursuant to s. 99(1)(*f*) of the *Customs Act*, R.S.C. 1985, c. 1 (2nd Supp.), authorizing a police officer who has formed a reasonable suspicion that there is a possibility that the vehicle is being used to smuggle or to attempt to smuggle contrary to the *Customs Act*, and the regulations thereunder, do not violate ss. 8 or 9 of the Charter.

A passive "bedpan vigil" authorized by the *Customs Act* on the basis that there exists a reasonable suspicion that the traveller has ingested narcotics, does not violate this section. Such a procedure, while embarrassing, is analogous to a strip search. It does not interfere with a person's bodily integrity and the legislation strikes a reasonable balance between the individual's privacy interest and the compelling state interest in protecting the integrity of Canada's borders from the importation of dangerous contraband: *R. v. Monney*, [1999] 1 S.C.R. 652, 133 C.C.C. (3d) 129.

Consent searches/waiver – For a waiver of the right to be secure against unreasonable seizure to be effective, the person purporting to consent must have the requisite informational foundation to truly relinquish the right. A right to choose requires not only the volition to prefer one option over another, but also sufficient available information to make the preference meaningful. For the police to rely upon the accused's consent to take a blood sample for use in a sexual assault investigation, the consent form had to make clear the scope of the investigation, *i.e.*, that the blood was sought in relation to two assaults, not just the one upon which the accused had been arrested: *R. v. Borden*, [1994] 3 S.C.R. 145, 92 C.C.C. (3d) 404. Also see *R. v. Wills* (1992), 70 C.C.C. (3d) 529 (Ont. C.A.).

The standard for the waiver of a person's rights under s. 8 is the same as that accorded the statutory procedural guarantees as laid down in *Korponay v. Canada (Attorney General)*, [1982] 1 S.C.R. 41, 65 C.C.C. (2d) 65. The onus is on the Crown, relying upon such a waiver, to establish that the person had full knowledge of his right to be secure against an unreasonable search and that he had full knowledge of the effect the waiver would have on that right: *R. v. Nielsen* (1988), 43 C.C.C. (3d) 548 (Sask. C.A.).

Where more than one person has a privacy right over the place or item at issue, a waiver by one does not amount to a waiver by all. Thus, the police infringed the accused's Charter rights when they took a family computer from his home, relying on the consent of his estranged wife. Although the computer was shared, the accused maintained a reasonable expectation of privacy in it. The spouse's consent did not nullify that reasonable expectation or waive his Charter rights in the computer: *R. v. Reeves, supra*.

The accused consented to provide hair samples in a homicide investigation. The police subsequently seized the samples from a police laboratory pursuant to a search warrant in relation to a different investigation. The accused's rights under this section were not violated. While a valid consent to the seizure of bodily samples must be informed, the police have an obligation to disclose only those anticipated purposes known to them at the time that the consent is obtained. If neither the police nor the consenting person limit the use which may be made of the evidence, as a general rule, there should be no limitation or restriction on the use of that evidence: *R. v. Arp*, [1998] 3 S.C.R. 339, 129 C.C.C. (3d) 321.

While the police are not under a duty to advise a person of the right to refuse to consent to a search, the failure to do so may lead to a violation of this section if the police conduct can only be justified on the basis of an informed consent. A person cannot give an effective consent to a search unless they are aware of the right to refuse consent: *R. v. Lewis* (1998), 122 C.C.C. (3d) 481 (Ont. C.A.).

The fact that guests are aware that cleaning staff will enter their rooms at least daily cannot remove the reasonable expectation of privacy that hotel guests have, at least with respect to objects that are neither left in plain view nor stored in areas that do not require daily maintenance. Hotel management's consent to police officers to enter the accuseds' room, leading to an invasion of the accuseds' privacy, was not an acceptable substitute for prior judicial authorization: *R. v. Mercer; R. v. Kenny*, *supra*.

A person's reasonable expectation of privacy in the contents of a rented and locked bus depot locker is not destroyed merely because a private individual such as a security guard invades that privacy by investigating the locker's contents. The accused's reasonable expectation of privacy was continuous: *R. v. Buhay*, *supra*.

The school board consented to the police searching the accused teacher's school-issued laptop. The court held the consent was invalid, rejecting the U.S. doctrine of third-party consent upon which the Crown relied. The U.S. doctrine was grounded in a risk-based analysis that had previously been rejected in *Duarte*, *supra*, and *Wong*, *supra*. Furthermore, to accept a doctrine of third-party consent would be incompatible with the court's jurisprudence that a first-party consent must be voluntary and informed: *R. v. Cole*, *supra*.

The plain view doctrine – The common law plain view doctrine allows an officer: (i) lawfully positioned; (ii) to seize visible objects; (iii) if discovered inadvertently; and (iv) immediately apparent as constituting evidence of a criminal offence: *R. v. Jones* (2011), 278 C.C.C. (3d) 157 (Ont. C.A.); see also *R. v. Robere* (1999), 181 Nfld. & P.E.I.R. 292 (Nfld. C.A.).

If the police were not lawfully authorized to be in the location in question, the plain view doctrine cannot authorize the seizure: *R. v. Buhay*, *supra*.

Search incident to lawful arrest – Police officers have the power at common law to search an accused incident to a lawful arrest and to seize anything in his possession or immediate surroundings to guarantee the safety of the police and the accused, prevent the accused's escape or provide evidence against him. The existence of reasonable and probable grounds to believe that the accused is in possession of weapons or evidence is not a prerequisite to search incident to arrest, provided that the search is for a valid law enforcement objective. Further, the search must not be conducted in an abusive fashion and the use of physical or psychological constraints should be proportionate to the objective sought and the other circumstances of the situation: *Cloutier c. Langlois*, [1990] 1 S.C.R. 158, 53 C.C.C. (3d) 257.

A search is lawful if: (1) it is authorized by a specific statute or common law rule; (2) the search is carried out in accordance with procedural and substantive requirements provided by the law; and (3) the scope of the search is limited to the area and to those items for which the law has granted the authority to search. For a search to be incident to arrest, the police must be attempting to achieve some valid purpose connected to the arrest. The three main purposes of search incident to arrest are ensuring the safety of the police and public, the protection of evidence from destruction and the discovery of evidence. There are both subjective and objective aspects to this issue. The police must have a valid purpose in mind and the officer's belief must be reasonable. The right to search a car incident to arrest and the scope of that search will depend on a number of factors including the basis for the arrest, the location of the car in relation to the place of arrest, and other relevant circumstances. Furthermore, searches that are truly incidental to arrest will usually occur within a reasonable period of time after the arrest. In this case, the police officer testified that the accused's impounded vehicle was searched solely for the purpose of complying with a police policy requiring an inventory of the contents of an impounded vehicle. Accordingly, the search was not, in the mind of the searching party, consistent with the proper purposes of search incident to arrest: *R. v. Caslake*, [1998] 1 S.C.R. 51, 121 C.C.C. (3d) 97.

The existence of reasonable and probable grounds to arrest does not necessarily result in an automatic right to conduct a strip search even incident to lawful arrest. There must also be reasonable and probable grounds justifying a strip search. Such searches are constitutionally valid only if they are conducted incident to arrest: to discover weapons, to ensure the safety of the police, detainee and other persons; to discover evidence related to the reason for the arrest; or to preserve evidence. Strip searches should generally only be conducted at the police station except if exigent circumstances require that the detainee be searched prior to being transported to the police station: *R. v. Golden*, [2001] 3 S.C.R. 679, 159 C.C.C. (3d) 449.

The common law search incident to arrest power permits the police to search cell phones and similar devices found on the suspect. Because the search of a cell phone has the potential to be a much more significant invasion of privacy than the typical search incident to arrest, four conditions must be met for the search to comply with s. 8 of the Charter: (i) the arrest must be lawful; (ii) the search must be truly incidental to the arrest. This requirement should be strictly applied to permit searches promptly upon arrest to effectively serve law enforcement purposes: protecting the police, the accused or the public; preserving evidence; and, if the investigation will be stymied or significantly hampered absent the ability to promptly conduct the search, discovering evidence; (iii) the nature and the extent of the search must be tailored to its purpose. In practice, this will mean that only recently sent or drafted emails, texts, photos and the call log will, generally, be available, although other searches may, in some circumstances, be justified; and (iv) the police must take detailed notes of what they have examined on the device and how they examined it. The notes should generally include the applications searched, the extent of the search, the time of the search, its purpose and its duration: *R. v. Fearon*, [2014] 3 S.C.R. 621, 318 C.C.C. (3d) 182 (4:3).

A penile swab is a valid search incident to arrest provided the police have reasonable grounds to believe that the swab will reveal and preserve evidence of the offence. Relevant factors include the timing of the arrest in relation to the alleged offence, the nature of the allegation, and whether or not there is evidence that the substance being sought has already been destroyed: *R. v. Saeed*, [2016] 1 S.C.R. 518, 336 C.C.C. (3d) 171.

An acquaintance of the accused informed police that the accused had become involved in a disturbance in a bar, assaulted him and threatened to get even with bar staff that refused to serve the accused more alcohol. The informer said the accused's wife had just left him. The accused had showed him a loaded sub-machine gun and was using cocaine. The police found the accused at his home. The accused complied with officers' demands that he leave his house. He locked his house contrary to police orders and equivocally told police that he did not think anyone was inside the residence. The officer in charge was concerned that someone could be in the residence with a loaded firearm and perhaps an injured person was in the residence. The police conducted a safety sweep of the accused's home and found an illegal firearm under a mattress. In assessing the officers' arrest of the accused, the court held that search warrant cases demanding corroboration of informants were inapposite. The police had a specific and detailed complaint that described the accused committing a serious offence. The safety sweep of the accused's home incident to his arrest was reasonably necessary to secure the scene and preserve the safety of those at the scene: *R. v. Golub* (1997), 117 C.C.C. (3d) 193 (Ont. C.A.), leave to appeal to S.C.C. refused [1998] 1 S.C.R. ix, 128 C.C.C. (3d) vi.

Assuming without deciding that subjecting the accused to a lengthy "bedpan vigil" in an attempt to retrieve contraband secreted in the body cavity could potentially amount to a valid search incident to arrest, it was illegal in this case because it was not carried out in a reasonable manner. The accused was subject to unnecessary physical restraint and the police paid scant attention to the medical risks inherent in the accused's circumstances: *R. v. Poirier* (2016), 342 C.C.C. (3d) 407 (Ont. C.A.).

Search incident to investigative detention – Police have a limited power to detain for investigation where there are reasonable grounds to detain. The detention must be viewed as reasonably necessary on an objective view of the totality of the circumstances, informing the officer's suspicion that there is a clear nexus between the person to be detained and a recent or on-going criminal offence. The officer must have a reasonable suspicion that the particular individual is implicated in the criminal activity under investigation. If the officer has lawfully detained the person for investigation, the officer may undertake a protective pat-down search if the officer believes on reasonable grounds that his or her safety or the safety of others is at risk. The search must be confined in scope to an intrusion reasonably designed to locate weapons. The detention and the pat-down search must be conducted in a reasonable manner: *R. v. Mann*, [2004] 3 S.C.R. 59, 185 C.C.C. (3d) 308.

The court in *R. v. White* (2007), 47 C.R. (6th) 271 (Ont. C.A.), held that an officer may seize an object incident to investigative detention if the officer believes on reasonable grounds that the seizure is necessary to avert a risk to officer safety or the potential loss of evidence. In that case, officers were investigating a suspected drug trafficker. As the officers approached the accused, he pulled out his cellphone and informed an unknown person "Yeah, they're here now." The officers immediately seized the accused's cell phone, believing that the accused was going to tip off accomplices to destroy evidence or send backup.

The power recognized in *Mann* is not necessarily limited to a search of an accused's person. If reasonable concerns for officer safety exist, it may allow for other kinds of searches, for instance the search of a bag for a gun: *R. v. Plummer* (2011), 272 C.C.C. (3d) 172 (Ont. C.A.).

Where the police responded to a 911 call stating that the accused was observed in his car with what the caller believed to be a gun, the police were entitled to search the accused's trunk when no gun was found in the interior of the car: *R. v. Lee* (2017), 351 C.C.C. (3d) 187 (Ont. C.A.). See, however, the concurring reasons of Pardu J.A. sounding a note of caution that the police power to search incidental to investigative detention must be carefully circumscribed so as not to dilute the protection offered by s. 8.

A contrary result was reached in *R. v. Batzer* (2005), 200 C.C.C. (3d) 330 (Ont. C.A.), where a lawful investigative detention of two men connected to a 911 call resulted in an unsuccessful search of their car for a gun but the discovery of cocaine in a small case in the glove compartment. The circumstances lacked the exigency that would warrant such an extensive search incidental to a lawful stop. Likewise, in *R. v. Calderon* (2004), 188 C.C.C. (3d) 481 (Ont. C.A.), a search of a car trunk incident to an investigation was held to violate s. 8 because it exceeded any protective purpose and amounted to an attempt to secure evidence.

The officer was entitled to proceed beyond a mere pat-down search of the accused upon feeling a hard object that was reasonably perceived to be a weapon: *R. v. Duong* (2006), 142 C.R.R. (2d) 261 (B.C.C.A.).

Police roadblocks – The court held that there is a common law police power to establish a reasonably necessary road block at the exit to a public parking lot, to stop all vehicles attempting to leave in order to investigate a 911 caller's report that handguns were being displayed in the parking lot. The court relied upon the analysis in *R. v. Waterfield*, [1963] 3 All E.R. 659, to balance the seriousness of the risk to public or individual safety with the liberty interests of members of the public. The police rapidly responded to the 911 call and had reasonable grounds to believe that there were several handguns in a public place, posing a genuine risk of serious bodily harm to the public: *R. v. Clayton*, [2007] 2 S.C.R. 725, 220 C.C.C. (3d) 449.

Roadside searches of vehicles – A warrantless search of a vehicle, which may move quickly, may be reasonable where there are reasonable grounds to believe that the vehicle contains contraband: *R. v. McComber* (1988), 44 C.C.C. (3d) 241 (Ont. C.A.).

CHARTER

There is no "automobile exception" permitting warrantless search of an automobile because such vehicles are readily moveable. The power to search a vehicle without warrant must be found either in statute or at common law, as, for example, a search incident to a valid arrest: *R. v. Klimchuk* (1991), 67 C.C.C. (3d) 385 (B.C.C.A.).

In *R. v. Mellenthin*, [1992] 3 S.C.R. 615, 76 C.C.C. (3d) 481, it was held that the accused's rights under this section were violated when, after he was stopped at a police check stop, the accused was questioned by the officer about the contents of a bag in the car and, as a result, the accused produced the bag which was found to contain narcotics. When he questioned the accused, the officer did not have any suspicion that the accused was in possession of contraband. The check stop is justified as a means of detecting impaired drivers or dangerous vehicles but not as a means to conduct an unfounded general inquisition or an unreasonable search. In the circumstances, it could be assumed that the accused felt compelled to respond to the police questions and it was not shown that any search resulted from informed consent.

Once the police officer had pulled the car over and the driver indicated that she did not have any ownership information, the police officer was entitled to look for documents pertaining to the ownership or registration of the vehicle including opening the back door and looking into the rear of the vehicle for safety reasons and to speak with the passenger in the back seat: *R. v. Belnavis*, *supra*.

The courts must proceed step by step through the interactions of the police and the accused from the initial stop onwards to determine whether, as the situation developed, the police stayed within their authority, having regard to the information lawfully obtained at each stage of their inquiry. Such information as it emerges may entitle the police to proceed further, or, as the case may be, require them to end their enquiries and allow the vehicle to resume its journey. A valid regulatory purpose, whether predominant or not, would not sanitize or excuse a Charter violation. Random roadside checks of vehicles for highway traffic purposes must be limited to their intended purpose and cannot be turned into an unfounded general inquisition or an unreasonable search. As long as there is a continuing regulatory purpose on which to ground the exercise of the regulatory power, the proper issue is whether the power was exercised in such a way as to violate s. 8 of the Charter by infringing the reasonable expectations of privacy of the accused: *R. v. Nolet*, *supra*.

Sniffer dog searches – In *R. v. Kang-Brown*, [2008] 1 S.C.R. 456, 230 C.C.C. (3d) 289, the court held that use of a sniffer dog, in this case to inspect luggage in a bus station, constituted a search so as to trigger the protection of s. 8 of the Charter. The court was divided, however, on whether the warrantless use of a sniffer dog could be justified absent statutory authorization. A plurality held that it was permissible, and that the constitutional standard was reasonable suspicion. See also, *R. v. Chehil*, *infra*.

In *R. v. Chehil*, [2013] 3 S.C.R. 220, 301 C.C.C. (3d) 157, the court confirmed that deploying a sniffer dog is a search that may be carried out without prior judicial authorization if the police have a reasonable suspicion based on objective, ascertainable facts that evidence of an offence will be discovered. Here, reasonable suspicion was present based on the following factors: the accused was travelling on an overnight flight from Vancouver to Halifax on a one-way ticket, was one of the last passengers to purchase a ticket, was travelling alone, paid for his ticket in cash, and checked one bag.

In the companion case of *R. v. MacKenzie*, [2013] 3 S.C.R. 250, 303 C.C.C. (3d) 281, the court held (5:4) that the threshold was satisfied in the following circumstances: when subject to a routine traffic stop, the accused appeared unusually nervous, gave contradictory details of his trip from Calgary to Regina, and exhibited physical symptoms consistent with marihuana use. He also was travelling along a known "drug pipeline" and had been driving erratically.

Searches to protect police safety – The police responded to a noise complaint at the accused's home. An officer observed an object in the accused's hand, hidden behind his leg.

The officer asked the accused twice what was in his hand but received no response. The officer then pushed the door open a few inches further for a better view. The court, relying upon *Waterfield*, *supra*, held that the safety search, occasioned by pushing the door further open, was reasonably necessary and thus authorized at common law. LeBel J. for the majority held that the safety search was justifiable because the officer had reasonable grounds to believe that the accused posed an imminent threat. Moldaver and Wagner JJ., for the concurring minority, would have held that the common law power to conduct a safety search on a reasonable suspicion standard, established in *Mann*, *supra*, was sufficient authority on the facts of this case: *R. v. MacDonald*, [2014] 1 S.C.R. 37, 303 C.C.C. (3d) 113.

Exigent circumstances – Warrantless entry into a dwelling-house, not authorized by statute even in exigent circumstances, to prevent the destruction of contraband, constituted a violation of this section although the police merely entered to secure the premises and did not actually commence the search for the narcotics until an officer arrived with the search warrant: *R. v. Silveira*, [1995] 2 S.C.R. 297, 97 C.C.C. (3d) 450. [However, now see s. 487.11 of the *Criminal Code*.]

Further, it was held in *R. v. Feeney*, [1997] 2 S.C.R. 13, 115 C.C.C. (3d) 129, that a warrantless entry of a dwelling house to effect an arrest is a violation of this section when the police were not in hot pursuit at the time of the arrest. The court left open whether there was a more general exception to the warrant requirement for exigent circumstances. [Note: Parliament has now enacted ss. 529 to 529.5 to deal with these situations.]

The police officers' warrantless entry into the accused's apartment, following his agreement to surrender several marihuana roaches after representations that he would not be charged, was not justified by the exigent circumstances provision in s. 11(7) of the *Controlled Drugs and Substances Act*. The police, once inside the apartment, observed a bulletproof vest, a firearm and drugs. They arrested the accused and obtained a telewarrant to search his apartment, leading them to discover further contraband. "Exigent circumstances" denotes urgency, not merely convenience, propitiousness or economy. To justify a warrantless search of a residence, the exigent circumstances must render it impracticable to obtain a warrant. The Crown must show that the entry was compelled by urgency posing a serious risk to officer safety, public safety or the ability to preserve evidence: *R. v. Paterson*, [2017] 1 S.C.R. 202, 347 C.C.C. (3d) 280.

The doctrine of abandonment – In *R. v. Patrick*, *supra*, the Supreme Court of Canada considered the right of the police to seize bags of garbage that had been placed for collection. Abandonment is an issue of fact. The question is whether the accused has acted in relation to the subject matter of his privacy claim so as to lead a reasonable and independent observer to conclude that his continued assertion of a privacy interest is unreasonable in the totality of the circumstances. In other words, whether the individual dealt with the items put out for collection so as to forfeit any objective reasonable expectation of keeping the contents of the refuse confidential. In the instant case, the accused had put his garbage at or near his property line and, accordingly, there was no manifestation of a continuing assertion of privacy or control. In so doing, he abandoned his privacy interest in the information contained in the garbage.

The mere fact that the police recover lost or stolen property does not support an inference that the owner has relinquished any expectation of privacy in the item. If the police cannot reasonably conclude that the property has been abandoned, they are limited in their investigation by the owner's privacy interest. Accordingly, police inspection of documents contained in a safe that the accused had reported stolen and that was subsequently recovered by the police violated the accused's expectation of privacy. The inspection of the documents was not justified by the plain view doctrine as the evidence of fraud was neither immediately obvious nor discovered inadvertently: *R. v. Law*, [2002] 1 S.C.R. 227, 160 C.C.C. (3d) 449.

DETENTION OR IMPRISONMENT.

9. Everyone has the right not to be arbitrarily detained or imprisoned.

ANNOTATIONS

The s. 9 guarantee against arbitrary detention is a manifestation of the general principle, enunciated in s. 7, that a person's liberty is not to be curtailed except in accordance with the principles of fundamental justice. Section 9 serves to protect individual liberty against unlawful state interference. A lawful detention is not arbitrary within the meaning of s. 9, unless the law authorizing the detention is itself arbitrary. Conversely, a detention not authorized by law is arbitrary and violates s. 9. Earlier suggestions that an unlawful detention was not necessarily arbitrary (see *R. v. Duguay* (1985), 18 C.C.C. (3d) 289 (Ont. C.A.), affirmed [1989] 1 S.C.R. 93, 46 C.C.C. (3d) 1) are no longer authoritative: *R. v. Grant*, [2009] 2 S.C.R. 353, 245 C.C.C. (3d) 1.

The random stopping of a motorist for the purpose of spot check procedures, to check the driver's licence and proof of insurance and to observe the motorist's condition or sobriety, results in a detention within the meaning of this section. There is no reason to give detention under this section a different meaning than as determined for the purpose of s. 10 in *R. v. Therens*, [1985] 1 S.C.R. 613, 18 C.C.C. (3d) 481 [noted under s. 10]. By the random stop for the purposes of the spot check procedure the officer assumes control over the movement of the motorist by a demand or direction that may have significant legal consequences. Further, detention resulting from a random stop for the purposes of a spot check procedure is arbitrary within the meaning of this section where the provincial legislation empowers the police officer to require the driver of any motor vehicle to stop, but on its face leaves the choice of the drivers to be stopped to the discretion of the officer. A discretion is arbitrary if there are no criteria, express or implied, which govern its exercise. However, the right not to be arbitrarily detained as guaranteed by s. 9 is subject to reasonable limits prescribed by law that are demonstrably justified in a free and democratic society within the meaning of s. 1 and such a reasonable limit could be found in provincial motor vehicle legislation such as s. 189*a*(1) of the *Highway Traffic Act*, R.S.O. 1980, c. 198: *R. v. Hufsky*, [1988] 1 S.C.R. 621, 40 C.C.C. (3d) 398.

Routine check/random stopping of a motorist, as authorized by provincial legislation, violates this section, the officer having assumed control over the movement of the motorist by a demand or direction, even where the detention involved only traffic offences rather than violations of the *Criminal Code*. These offences, however, carried maximum penalties including fine and/or imprisonment. The detention was arbitrary, since the decision as to whether the stop should be made lay in the absolute discretion of the police officers. Such violation can, however, be justified as a reasonable limit to meet the pressing and substantial concern for safety on the highways. The stop must, however, be for legal reasons, to check the driver's licence and insurance, the sobriety of the driver and the mechanical fitness of the vehicle. Once stopped, the only questions which may justifiably be asked are those related to driving offences. Any further, more intrusive procedures could only be undertaken based upon reasonable and probable grounds: *R. v. Ladouceur*, [1990] 1 S.C.R. 1257, 56 C.C.C. (3d) 22.

Stopping of a motorist, as authorized by provincial legislation on grounds which are reasonable and can be clearly expressed, is not random and thus not a violation of this section: *R. v. Wilson*, [1990] 1 S.C.R. 1291, 56 C.C.C. (3d) 142.

Police have a limited power to detain for investigation where there are reasonable grounds to detain. The detention must be viewed as reasonably necessary on an objective view of the totality of the circumstances, informing the officer's suspicion that there is a clear nexus between the person to be detained and a recent or on-going criminal offence. The officer must have a reasonable suspicion that the particular individual is implicated in the criminal activity under investigation. The overall reasonableness of the decision to detain must further be assessed against all of the circumstances, most importantly the extent to which the interference with individual liberty is necessary to perform the officer's duty, the liberty interfered with, and the nature and extent of that interference. The power to detain cannot be exercised on the basis of a hunch, nor can it become a *de facto* arrest. Where the officer has lawfully detained the person for investigation, the officer may undertake a protective pat-down search where the officer believes on reasonable grounds that his or her safety or the safety of others is at risk. The search must be confined in scope to an intrusion reasonably designed to locate weapons. The detention and the pat-down search must be conducted in a reasonable manner: *R. v. Mann*, [2004] 3 S.C.R. 59, 185 C.C.C. (3d) 308. Also see *R. v. Simpson* (1993), 79 C.C.C. (3d) 482, 20 C.R. (4th) 1 (Ont. C.A.).

Police responded to a 911 call reporting black males with guns in a parking lot. Within minutes of the call, the police had blocked the exits of the parking lot and stopped the accused's vehicle. After receiving evasive answers from the accused, the police asked the accused to exit the vehicle, at which time weapons were located. The police were acting in the course of their duty to investigate and prevent crime when they stopped and detained the accused. Both the initial and continuing detentions were justified based on the information available to the police, the nature of the reported offence and the timing and location of the detention. The actions of the police were temporally, geographically and logistically responsive to the circumstances known at the relevant time and were reasonably necessary to respond to the seriousness of the offence and the threat to police and public safety. Accordingly, the initial stop and detention was not contrary to s. 9 of the Charter. In addition, the further detention and search of the accused did not violate s. 8 of the Charter. The information received both prior to the stop and during the brief questioning of the accused constituted a reasonable suspicion that the accused could be in possession of the reported guns and represent a risk to police and public safety. The safety concerns justified the searches incidental to arrest: *R. v. Clayton*, [2007] 2 S.C.R. 725, 220 C.C.C. (3d) 449.

Assuming that the right to attack a sentence under s. 9 is not foreclosed by the fact that it is legislatively prescribed and that the statutory procedures have been judicially complied with, it could not be said that imprisonment resulting from the successful invokation of an application under the *Criminal Code* to have an accused declared a dangerous offender could be considered arbitrary. The legislation narrowly defines the class of offenders with respect to whom it may properly be invoked and prescribes quite specifically the conditions under which an offender may be designated as dangerous. The lack of uniformity in the treatment of dangerous offenders that arises by virtue of prosecutorial discretion to make an application to have an accused declared a dangerous offender does not constitute unconstitutional arbitrariness. In fact, the absence of discretion could render arbitrary the law's application: *R. v. Lyons*, [1987] 2 S.C.R. 309, 37 C.C.C. (3d) 1.

The provisions of the *Criminal Code* which provide for a minimum sentence of life imprisonment without eligibility for parole for certain types of murders, in particular murder while committing an offence such as kidnapping, do not demonstrate arbitrariness on the part of Parliament so as to violate this section. The sentence is statutorily authorized, applies to a narrowly defined class of offenders and prescribes, quite specifically, the conditions under which the offender is liable to be convicted of this offence: *R. v. Luxton*, [1990] 2 S.C.R. 711, 58 C.C.C. (3d) 449 (7:0).

An arrest which is lawfully made, having been made on the basis of reasonable and probable grounds as authorized by s. 495 of the *Criminal Code*, does not become unlawful simply because the police intend to continue their investigation after the arrest. Moreover, in this case the accused's detention for some 18 hours before a formal charge was laid until a lineup could be held did not violate either the *Criminal Code* or s. 9. The delay was necessary to assemble the witnesses in order to hold the lineup and immediately after the accused was positively identified he was taken before a justice as required by the *Criminal Code: R. v. Storrey*, [1990] 1 S.C.R. 241, 53 C.C.C. (3d) 316.

In *R. v. Storrey, supra,* the court also considered what constitutes reasonable and probable grounds so as to constitute a proper arrest without warrant. The requirement of reasonable grounds requires that an arresting officer must subjectively have reasonable and probable grounds on which to base the arrest. These grounds must in addition be justifiable

CHARTER

from an objective point of view. That is, a reasonable person placed in the position the officer, must be able to conclude that there were indeed reasonable and probable grounds for the arrest. On the other hand, the police need not demonstrate anything more than reasonable and probable grounds and specifically are not required to establish a *prima facie* case for conviction before making the arrest.

ARREST OR DETENTION.

10. Everyone has the right on arrest or detention

(*a*) to be informed promptly of the reasons therefor;

(*b*) to retain and instruct counsel without delay and to be informed of that right; and

(*c*) to have the validity of the detention determined by way of *habeas corpus* and to be released if the detention is not lawful.

ANNOTATIONS

Meaning of arrest – An arrest consists of either (i) the actual seizure or touching of a person's body with a view to his or her detention or (ii) the pronouncement of "words of arrest" to a person as long as he or she submits to the arrest: *R. v. Whitfield* (1969), [1970] S.C.R. 46, [1970] 1 C.C.C. 129; *R. v. Latimer*, [1997] 1 S.C.R. 217, 112 C.C.C. (3d) 193; *R. v. Asante-Mensah*, [2003] 2 S.C.R. 3, 174 C.C.C. (3d) 481.

The police need not actually say the word "arrest". In determining whether there was an arrest, the focus is on the substance of what the accused would have reasonably understood and not the formalism of the precise words used: *R. v. Latimer, supra.*

Therefore, a *de facto* arrest of the accused occurred when he was told that he was being detained for an investigation into his daughter's death, was not permitted to enter his house alone to change clothes, and submitted to the authority of the police officers: *R. v. Latimer, supra.*

Meaning of detention – A person is detained where he or she submits or acquiesces to the deprivation of his or her liberty and reasonably believes that there is no choice to do otherwise. The meaning of detention is not limited to situations where the police take explicit control over a person and command obedience. Detention may be effected without the application or threat of application of physical restraint if the person concerned submits in the deprivation of liberty and reasonably believes that the choice to do otherwise does not exist. An individual confronted by state authority can choose to walk away, but he or she is detained when this choice is removed either by physical or psychological compulsion. However, not every trivial or insignificant interference with a person's liberty attracts Charter scrutiny. The meaning of detention does not include any fleeting interference or delay. A detention only arises when the person's liberty is meaningfully constrained: *R. v. Grant*, [2009] 2 S.C.R. 353, 245 C.C.C. (3d) 1, citing *R. v. Therens*, [1985] 1 S.C.R. 613, 18 C.C.C. (3d) 481; *R. v. Dedman*, [1985] 2 S.C.R. 2, 20 C.C.C. (3d) 97; and *R. v. Mann*, [2004] 3 S.C.R. 59, 185 C.C.C. (3d) 308.

Psychological detention arises when an individual is legally required to comply with a direction or demand, such as a demand for a roadside breath sample or where there is no legal obligation to comply with a restrictive or coercive demand, but a reasonable person in the subject's position would feel obligated to comply with the police's requests: *R. v. Grant, supra.* See also *R. v. Suberu*, [2009] 2 S.C.R. 460, 245 C.C.C. (3d) 112; *R. v. Therens, supra*; *R. v. Thomsen*, [1988] 1 S.C.R. 640, 40 C.C.C. (3d) 411.

Even when an encounter ultimately results in a detention, it cannot be assumed that there was a detention from the beginning of the interaction. The police may engage in non-adversarial assistance to the public, such as preliminary questioning of bystanders to a crime, without a detention occurring. The key to determining whether a detention has arisen is to determine the line between general questioning and focussed interrogation amounting to detention. Focussed suspicion is not on its own enough to establish detention; rather, how the police interact with the subject based on that suspicion is what matters: see *R. v. Grant*, *supra*; *R. v. Suberu*, *supra*.

For example, focused suspicion combined with jeopardy for the accused and with something more than a general inquiry from police may be sufficient to give rise to the claimant's reasonable belief that he or she is not permitted to leave: *R. v. Folker* (2016), 332 C.C.C. (3d) 57 (N.L.C.A.), citing *R. v. Koczab* (2013), 309 C.C.C. (3d) 183 (Man. C.A.) (Monnin J.A., dissenting), revd [2014] 1 S.C.R. 138, 309 C.C.C. (3d) 180 (appeal allowed for reasons of Monnin J.A.).

In determining whether there has been a psychological detention, the court should consider the following: (1) the circumstances giving rise to the encounter as would reasonably be perceived by the individual, including whether the police were providing general assistance, maintaining general order, making general inquiries regarding a particular occurrence, or singling out the individual for a focused investigation; (2) the nature of the police conduct including the language used, the use of physical contact, the place where the interaction occurred, the presence of others, and the duration of the encounter; and (3) the particular characteristics or circumstances of the individual where relevant, including age, physical stature, minority status, and level of sophistication. The inquiry is objective and does not require a minute parsing of words and movements. When the police are concerned that their conduct may have a coercive effect, they may inform the subject that he or she is under no obligation to answer questions and is free to go: *R. v. Grant*, *supra*.

In determining whether a person was detained at the time of questioning at a police station, the following factors are relevant: (1) the precise language used by the police in requesting the person to come to the police station and whether the person was given a choice or expressed a preference that the interview be conducted in the police station rather than at his or her home; (2) whether the accused was escorted to the police station by a police officer or came voluntarily in response to a police request; (3) whether the accused left at the conclusion of the interview or whether he or she was arrested; (4) the stage of the investigation, that is, whether the questioning was part of the general investigation of a crime or whether the police had already decided that a crime had been committed and that the accused was the perpetrator or was involved in its commission and the questioning was conducted for the purpose of obtaining an incriminating statement; (5) whether the police had reasonable and probable grounds to believe that the accused had committed the offence; (6) the nature of the questions, whether they were questions of a general nature designed to obtain information or whether the accused was confronted with evidence pointing to his guilt; and (7) the subjective belief by an accused that he was detained. Personal circumstances relating to the accused such as low intelligence, emotional disturbance, youth, and lack of sophistication are factors to be considered in determining whether he or she had a subjective belief that he or she was detained. Additionally, although the accused's subjective belief is relevant, it is not decisive, because the issue is whether the accused reasonably believed that he or she was detained. Note also that the list of factors is not intended to be exhaustive and the absence of any one factor is not determinative in a particular case: *R. v. Moran* (1987), 36 C.C.C. (3d) 225 (Ont. C.A.), leave to appeal to S.C.C. refused [1988] 1 S.C.R. xi. See also *R. v. Voss* (1989), 50 C.C.C. (3d) 58 (Ont. C.A.); *R. v. N.B.* (2018), 362 C.C.C. (3d) 302 (Ont. C.A.).

An accused who, given the choice of whether to attend at the police station or be interviewed at home, agreed to go to the station for the interview was not detained: *R. v. Hawkins*, [1993] 2 S.C.R. 157, 79 C.C.C. (3d) 576. See also: *R. v. Hall* (2004), 193 O.A.C. 7 (C.A.), leave to appeal to S.C.C. refused (2006), 224 O.A.C. 400*n*; *R. v. Pomeroy* (2008), 91 O.R. (3d) 261 (C.A.); *R. v. Tomlinson* (2009), 190 C.R.R. (2d) 28 (B.C.C.A.).

A person attempting to enter Canada who is required to submit to a strip or skin search pursuant to the provisions of the *Customs Act* is detained within the meaning of s. 10. There are three distinct types of border searches. The first is the routine questioning that every traveller undergoes at a port of entry accompanied in some cases by a search of baggage and perhaps a pat or frisk of outer clothing. A person subjected to this type of search could not be said to be detained. The second type of border search is a strip or skin search conducted in a private room after a secondary examination and with the permission of a customs officer in authority. The third and most highly intrusive type of search is a body cavity search in which customs officers have recourse to medical doctors, x-rays, and other highly invasive techniques. A person subjected to the latter two kinds of searches is clearly subject to external restraint and a customs officer, having assumed control over the accused's movements by demands that have significant legal consequences, has detained the accused: *R. v. Simmons*, [1988] 2 S.C.R. 495, 45 C.C.C. (3d) 296.

An accused was detained when he was ordered into an interview room by customs officers who suspected that he was carrying narcotics where he was then questioned and required to empty his pockets on the table, place his hands against the wall, and spread his feet apart: *R. v. Jacoy*, [1988] 2 S.C.R. 548, 45 C.C.C. (3d) 46.

A motorist required to comply with a demand that he provide samples for analysis in a roadside screening device as required pursuant to former s. 234.1 of the *Criminal Code* was detained. The necessary element of compulsion or coercion that constituted detention arises from criminal liability for refusal to comply with a demand or direction or from a reasonable belief that one does not have a choice as to whether or not to comply. Nevertheless, the motorist was not entitled to retain and instruct counsel and to be informed of that right since the provisions of the former s. 234.1 constituted a reasonable limit within the meaning of s. 1: *R. v. Thomsen, supra.*

Similarly, a motorist was not entitled to be informed of the right to counsel and to exercise that right during other roadside screening techniques, such as physical sobriety testing and questioning about prior alcohol consumption, even though the relevant provincial legislation at the time contained no express limit on the right to counsel. Such a limitation was implied by the statutory right to stop vehicles and in the police duty to enforce the former s. 254 of the *Criminal Code*: *R. v. Orbanski*, [2005] 2 S.C.R. 3, 196 C.C.C. (3d) 481.

Onus of establishing a detention – The onus is on the applicant to show that in the circumstances he or she was effectively deprived of his or her liberty of choice: *R. v. Suberu, supra.*

Interpretation generally (s. 10(*a*)) – Individuals who are detained must be advised promptly of the reasons for the detention in clear and simple language: *R. v. Mann, supra.*

Section 10(*a*) is founded most fundamentally on the notion that a person is not obliged to submit to an arrest or detention if he or she does not know the reasons for it. A second purpose of the right to be informed of the reason for a detention or arrest is to complement the right to counsel conferred by s. 10(*b*). An individual can only exercise his or her right to counsel under s. 10(*b*) in a meaningful way if he or she knows the reasons for the detention or arrest. In interpreting s. 10(*a*), the Supreme Court has instructed that regard must be given to the double rationale underlying the right: *R. v. Evans*, [1991] 1 S.C.R. 869, 63 C.C.C. (3d) 289.

An individual can only make an informed choice about whether to exercise the right to counsel, and if so, can obtain sound advice only if he or she knows the extent of his or her jeopardy: *R. v. Borden*, [1994] 3 S.C.R. 145, 92 C.C.C. (3d) 404; *R. v. Black*, [1989] 2 S.C.R. 138, 50 C.C.C. (3d) 1.

In considering whether or not there has been a breach of s. 10(*a*), the substance of what the detainee can reasonably be supposed to have understood must govern, rather than the formalism of the precise words used. The question is whether what the detainee was told, viewed reasonably in all the circumstances of the case, was sufficient to permit him or her to make a reasonable decision to decline to submit to arrest, or alternatively, to decide whether or not to exercise his right to consult counsel: *R. v. Evans, supra.*

Whether s. 10(*a*) has been breached by the authorities is to be tested by asking whether, in "the reality of the total situation", the accused understood generally the sort or extent of jeopardy which he or she faced, so that he or she could make an informed decision on his or her need for legal advice. "Common parlance" may be more useful in communicating the extent of the accused's jeopardy than the language of the *Criminal Code*: *R. v. Wong* (1998), 52 C.R.R. (2d) 89 (B.C.C.A.), citing *R. v. Smith*, [1991] 1 S.C.R. 714, 63 C.C.C. (3d) 313.

Section 10(*a*) was breached when an accused was only cautioned as "an important witness" and not as a suspect (in addition to being breached when the caution was not provided until hours after her detention). The police constantly minimized her actual legal situation to her and kept her ignorant of the information essential to the exercise of her constitutional rights: *R. v. Côté*, [2011] 3 S.C.R. 215, 276 C.C.C. (3d) 42.

Section 10(*a*) was not violated when the police did not tell an accused he was under "arrest" for murder when the accused knew he was being detained for the investigation of his daughter's death, was told by a police officer that the ensuing conversation with the police had "very serious consequences", was prohibited from entering his house without police, and was given his right to counsel. The accused understood the basis of his apprehension by the police and hence the extent of his jeopardy: *R. v. Latimer*, *supra*.

Section 10(*a*) was not breached when it would have been obvious to the detained individual based on the surrounding context that he was being questioned and detained with respect to possible impaired driving: *R. v. Rhodenizer* (2018), 415 C.R.R. (2d) 169 (Alta. C.A.), citing *R. v. Lund* (2008), 440 A.R. 362 (C.A. [In Chambers]).

CHARTER

Timing (s. 10(*a*)) – The term "promptly" in s. 10(*a*) is a functional equivalent of the phrase "without delay", which appears in s. 10(*b*) and is synonymous with "immediately": *R. v. Gonzales* (2017), 354 C.C.C. (3d) 572 (Ont. C.A.). See *R. v. Suberu*, *supra*.

A delay of 22 minutes between the arrest and the provision of the reasons for the arrest breached s. 10(*a*) when there were no exceptional circumstances to justify the delay: *R. v. Mian*, [2014] 2 S.C.R. 689, 315 C.C.C. (3d) 453.

Change in circumstances (s. 10(*a*)) – If the reasons for the arrest or detention change, the police must inform the detainee of the new reasons for his or her detention or arrest. Therefore, an accused's s. 10(*a*) right was breached when he was only informed of his arrest for a single count of sexual assault and was not informed of the police's purpose of detaining him to investigate a second sexual assault. The accused did not have a general knowledge of the events or circumstances that had led to his detention and was given no indication that the police investigations were directed at any offence other than the one for which he had been arrested. Once matters reached a point at which the officers were investigating two offences, the accused was detained in relation to both offences and had the right to be informed of the dual investigative intention: *R. v. Borden*, *supra*.

Interpretation generally (s. 10(*b*)) – Section 10(*b*) imposes both informational and implementational duties on the police. The informational duty requires that the detainee be informed of the right to retain and instruct counsel without delay. The implementational obligation imposed on the police under s. 10(*b*), requires the police to provide the detainee with a reasonable opportunity to retain and instruct counsel. This obligation also requires the police to refrain from eliciting incriminatory evidence from the detainee until he or she has had a reasonable opportunity to reach a lawyer or the detainee has unequivocally waived the right to do so: *R. v. Suberu*, *supra*. See also *R. v. Evans*, *supra*; *R. v. Prosper*, [1994] 3 S.C.R. 236, 92 C.C.C. (3d) 353; *R. v. Bartle*, [1994] 3 S.C.R. 173, 92 C.C.C. (3d) 289; *R. v. Manninen*, [1987] 1 S.C.R. 1233, 34 C.C.C. (3d) 385; *R. v. Brydges*, [1990] 1 S.C.R. 190, 53 C.C.C. (3d) 330.

The purpose of the right to counsel is to allow the detainee not only to be informed of his or her rights and obligations under the law but, equally if not more importantly, to obtain advice as to how to exercise those rights: *R. v. Manninen*, *supra*.

In the context of a custodial interrogation, the right to counsel must be understood as supporting the detainee's right to choose under s. 7 of the Charter whether to cooperate with the investigation or not: *R. v. Sinclair*, [2010] 2 S.C.R. 310, 259 C.C.C. (3d) 443. See also *R. v. McCrimmon*, [2010] 2 S.C.R. 492, [2010] 2 S.C.R. 402.

The right to counsel is constitutionally guaranteed, because when an individual is detained by state authorities, he or she is put in a position of disadvantage relative to the state. Not only has this person suffered a deprivation of liberty, but this person also may be at risk of incriminating himself or herself. Accordingly, a person who is "detained" within the meaning of s. 10 of the Charter is in immediate need of legal advice in order to protect his or her right against self-incrimination and to assist him or her in regaining his or her liberty. The right to counsel protected by s. 10(*b*) is designed to ensure that persons who are arrested or detained are treated fairly in the criminal process: *R. v. Bartle*, *supra*. See also *R. v. Suberu*, *supra*.

Section 10(*b*) must be considered in light of the s. 10(*a*) requirement of advising an individual who is arrested or detained of the reasons for such arrest or detention. The individual can only exercise his or her s. 10(*b*) right in a meaningful way if he or she knows the extent of his or her jeopardy: *R. v. Black*, *supra*.

Since a detainee can only exercise his or her s. 10(*b*) rights in a meaningful way if he or she knows the extent of the jeopardy faced, there must be a close factual connection or linkage relating the warning to the detention and the reasons therefore: *R. v. Schmautz*, [1990] 1 S.C.R. 398, 53 C.C.C. (3d) 556.

While the accused, in order to meaningfully exercise the right to counsel, must possess knowledge of the extent of his or her jeopardy, it is not necessary that the accused be given full information. What is required is that the accused understand generally the jeopardy which he or she faces and appreciate the consequences of deciding for or against counsel. He or she must be possessed of sufficient information to allow him or her to make an informed and appropriate decision as to whether to speak to a lawyer or not. The accused need not be aware of the precise charge faced nor of all the factual details of the case. Moreover, the words of the *Criminal Code* may be less helpful to a lay person than more common parlance in communicating the extent of jeopardy. The emphasis must be on the reality of the total situation as it impacts on the understanding of the accused, rather than on the technical detail of what the accused may or may not have been told: *R. v. Smith*, 1991, *supra*.

Informational component (s. 10(*b*)) – The duty on the police to inform the detainee of his or her right to counsel includes the duty to explain the right in a manner that the detainee can understand. In most cases, one can infer from the circumstances that the accused understands what he or she has been told and, in such cases, the police are required to go no further in explaining the right. Where, however, there is a positive indication that the accused does not understand his or her right to counsel, the police cannot rely on their mechanical recitation of the right to the accused; they must take steps to facilitate that understanding: *R. v. Evans*, *supra*.

In addition to being informed of the existence of their right to counsel, detainees must be informed as a matter of routine of the existence and availability of the applicable systems of duty counsel and legal aid in the relevant jurisdiction and how such advice can be accessed. Imposing this additional duty is consistent with one of the main purposes underlying the s. 10(*b*) right, which is to facilitate contact with counsel since it is upon arrest or detention that the accused is faced with an immediate need for legal advice especially in respect of how to exercise the right to remain silent: *R. v. Brydges*, *supra*. See also *R. v. Bartle*, *supra*; *R. v. Pozniak*, [1994] 3 S.C.R. 310, 92 C.C.C. (3d) 472.

While situations may occasionally arise in which the police officer's duty to make a reasonable effort to inform the detainee of his or her rights will be satisfied even if certain elements of the standard caution are omitted, this will only be the case if the detainee explicitly waives his or her rights to receive the standard caution and if the circumstances reveal a reasonable basis for believing that the detainee in fact knows and has adverted to his or her rights and is aware of the means by which these rights can be exercised. The fact that a detainee merely indicates that he or she knows his or her rights will not by itself provide a reasonable basis for believing that the detainee in fact understands their full extent or the means by which they can be implemented: *R. v. Bartle*, *supra*.

An additional informational obligation on police will be triggered once a detainee, who has previously asserted the right to counsel, indicates that he or she has changed his or her mind and no longer wants legal advice (subsequently waives his or her right to counsel). At this point, the police will be required to tell the detainee of his or her right to be given a reasonable opportunity to contact the lawyer and of the obligation on the part of the police during this time not to take any statements or require the detainee to participate in any potentially incriminating process until he or she has had that reasonable opportunity: *R. v. Prosper*, *supra*.

Implementational component (s. 10(*b*)) – Section 10(*b*) imposes at least two duties on the police in addition to the duty to inform the detainee of his or her rights. First, the police must provide the detainee with a reasonable opportunity to exercise the right to retain and instruct counsel without delay. Second, the police must cease questioning or otherwise attempting to elicit evidence from the detainee until he or she has had a reasonable opportunity to retain and instruct counsel or the detainee has unequivocally waived the right to do so: *R. v. Manninen*, *supra*; *R. v. Suberu*, *supra*.

Under the implementational component, s. 10(*b*) requires that the detainee be given an opportunity, or the means, to "retain and instruct counsel without delay". If the detainee chooses not to contact counsel, no breach results. If the legal system fails to provide the detainee with the opportunity to consult counsel without delay for whatever reason (be it lack of facilities, information, willing counsel, or some other impediment), a breach of s. 10(*b*) is established. If evidence is taken in contravention of this duty, its admissibility falls to be decided under s. 24(2) of the Charter: *R. v. Prosper*, *supra*.

Once a detainee asserts his or her right to counsel, the police cannot in any way compel him or her to make a decision or participate in a process that could ultimately have an adverse effect in the conduct of an eventual trial until that person has had a reasonable opportunity to exercise that right. In other words, the police are obliged to "hold off" from attempting to elicit incriminatory evidence from the detainee until he or she has had a reasonable opportunity to reach counsel. What constitutes a reasonable opportunity to contact counsel will depend on all of the circumstances including the availability of duty counsel services in the jurisdiction where the detention takes place. The non-existence of such services will also affect the determination of what, under the circumstances, is a reasonable opportunity to consult counsel. The absence of duty counsel in a jurisdiction extends the period in which a detainee will have been found to have been duly diligent in exercising his right to counsel. The reasonable opportunity might extend to when the local legal aid office opens, when a private lawyer willing to provide free summary advice can be reached, or when the detainee is brought before a justice of the peace for bail purposes. While during this time detainees would continue to be deprived of their freedom, any deprivation of liberty in the circumstances would be minimal and in accordance with the principles of fundamental justice under s. 7 of the Charter: *R. v. Prosper*, *supra*.

The obligation to "hold off" is contingent on the detainee's reasonable diligence in attempting to contact counsel. What constitutes reasonable diligence in the exercise of the right to contact counsel will depend on the context of the particular circumstances as a whole. If the detainee's chosen lawyer is not immediately available, the detainee has the right to refuse to speak to any other counsel and wait a reasonable amount of time for the lawyer of choice to respond. What amounts to a reasonable period of time depends on the circumstances as a whole and may include factors such as the seriousness of the charge and the urgency of the investigation. The right is not violated by police reminding the detainee of the immediate availability of duty counsel after an unsuccessful attempt to contact counsel of choice, as long as the choice to call duty counsel is not the product of coercion: *R. v. Willier*, [2010] 2 S.C.R. 429, 259 C.C.C. (3d) 536. See also *R. v. McCrimmon*, *supra*; *R. v. Ross*, [1989] 1 S.C.R. 3, 46 C.C.C. (3d) 129; *R. v. Black*, *supra*.

The duty to refrain from engaging with the detainee after he or she asserted the right to counsel restricts the police from compelling, in any way, the detainee to make a decision or participate in a process that could ultimately have an adverse effect in the conduct of an actual trial, including the participation in a police line-up: *R. v. Ross*, *supra*.

The police are also prohibited from pressuring a detainee into accepting a "plea bargain" without the detainee first having the opportunity to consult with a lawyer. Section 10(*b*) mandates that the Crown or police, when offering a plea bargain, tender that offer either to

CHARTER

accused's counsel or to the accused while in the presence of counsel, unless the accused has expressly waived the right to counsel: *R. v. Burlingham*, [1995] 2 S.C.R. 206, 97 C.C.C. (3d) 385.

While the police are under no legal duty to provide their own cell phone to an arrested or detained individual, they do have a duty both to provide phone access at the first reasonable opportunity to avoid self-incrimination and to refrain from eliciting evidence from the individual before access to counsel has been facilitated. Section 10(*b*) does not create a right to use a specific phone, but it does guarantee that the individual will have access to a phone to exercise his right to counsel. Here, where the accused had requested access to counsel while in custody at the hospital, the police had an obligation under s. 10(*b*) to take steps to ascertain whether private access to a phone was in fact available: *R. v. Taylor*, [2014] 2 S.C.R. 495, 311 C.C.C. (3d) 285.

Where the accused had already invoked his right to counsel, the recitation of "do you wish to say anything?" at the conclusion of a standard police caution breached the duty to "hold off" articulated in *R. v. Prosper*, *supra*, and amounted to a violation of the right to counsel: *R. v. G.T.D.*, [2018] 1 S.C.R. 220, 359 C.C.C. (3d) 340.

There is no rule that limits the detainee to a single phone call. A detainee who wishes to make successive phone calls in the exercise and pursuit of the right to retain and instruct counsel must be able to do so unfettered by police questioning. The relevant inquiry after an initial phone call to a law office is not simply whether the detainee spoke to a lawyer but rather whether he had the opportunity to have meaningful contact with and advice from counsel: *R. v. Whitford* (1997), 115 C.C.C. (3d) 52 (Alta. C.A.), leave to appeal to S.C.C. refused [1997] 3 S.C.R. xiii, 117 C.C.C. (3d) vi.

Section 10(*b*) does not confer a constitutional right to have a lawyer present throughout a police interview. In most cases, an initial warning, coupled with a reasonable opportunity to consult counsel when the detainee invokes the right, satisfies s. 10(*b*): *R. v. Sinclair*, *supra*. See also *R. v. McCrimmon*, *supra*.

Section 10(*b*) does not create a constitutional obligation on governments to ensure that free and immediate preliminary legal advice is available to all detainees: *R. v. Matheson*, [1994] 3 S.C.R. 328, 92 C.C.C. (3d) 434.

Timing (s. 10(*b*)) – The words "without delay" in s. 10(*b*) mean "immediately". The immediacy of this obligation is subject only to concerns for officer or public safety or to reasonable limitations that are prescribed by law and justified under s. 1 of the Charter: *R. v. Suberu*, *supra*.

A detainee is advised of the right to retain and instruct counsel without delay because it is upon arrest or detention that an accused is in immediate need of legal advice since one of the main functions of counsel at this early stage of detention is to confirm the existence of the right to remain silent and to advise the detainee about how to exercise that right: *R. v. Brydges*, *supra*.

Section 10(*b*) appears to focus on the rights of an accused to retain and instruct counsel at the time of the initial arrest and detention. It does not give an accused the right to be informed of his or her right to counsel and to be given an opportunity to instruct counsel whenever he or she has a critical encounter (either knowingly or unknowingly) with the police or other authorities. The words "on arrest or detention" indicate a point in time, not a continuum. They do not deal with a continuing right to be instructed before every occasion on which the police obtain a statement from the accused: *R. v. Logan* (1988), 46 C.C.C. (3d) 354 (Ont. C.A.), affd on other grounds [1990] 2 S.C.R. 731, 58 C.C.C. (3d) 391.

The fact that the accused is informed of his or her right to counsel before the actual detention is not determinative of a s. 10(*b*) breach. Section 10(*b*) refers to a factual connection between the detention and the right to a warning rather than a mere coincidence in time. Where an accused was informed at the outset of an interview of his right to counsel, his right to remain silent, and that the police were investigating a hit and run accident, s. 10(*b*) was complied with even though the accused was only actually detained a short time later when given a breathalyzer demand. The situation that arose with respect to the breathalyzer demand was directly connected to the investigation. The demand itself, together with the fact that the accused was advised of the criminal consequences of a refusal to comply, would normally trigger the consideration of the accused as to whether or not to instruct counsel. The demand arose directly and immediately out of the inquiries; it was part of a single incident in which the accused was made fully aware of his rights: *R. v. Schmautz*, *supra*.

A delay of more than 22 minutes between the detention or arrest and the fulfillment of s. 10(*b*) is a breach of s. 10(*b*): *R. v. Mian*, *supra*.

The implementational duties of the police can be suspended in urgent and dangerous circumstances: *R. v. Taylor*, *supra*, citing *R. v. Bartle*, *supra*.

Specific circumstances, such as concerns regarding police safety, public safety, or the preservation of evidence, may justify a delay in providing a detainee access to counsel. For example, s. 10(*b*) was not breached when an accused's right to counsel was delayed for the purpose of allowing the police to properly gain control of the scene of the arrest and search for restricted weapons known to be at the scene. However, s. 10(*b*) was breached when the police failed to provide the accused with his right to counsel after the scene was secured: *R. v. Strachan*, [1988] 2 S.C.R. 980, 46 C.C.C. (3d) 479.

The police may delay access to counsel while a search warrant is being executed only after turning their minds to the specifics of the circumstances and concluding, on some reasonable basis, that police or public safety, or the need to preserve evidence, justifies some delay in granting access to counsel. Even when those circumstances exist, the police must take reasonable steps to minimize the delay in granting access to counsel: *R. v. Rover* (2018), 366 C.C.C. (3d) 103 (Ont. C.A.).

Duty of detainee (s. 10(*b*)) – The accused must be reasonably diligent in attempting to obtain counsel if he wishes to do so. If the accused is not diligent in this regard, then the correlative duties imposed upon the police to refrain from questioning the accused are suspended: *R. v. Tremblay*, [1987] 2 S.C.R. 435, 37 C.C.C. (3d) 565.

The limit on s. 10(*b*) that permits the police to elicit evidence when the detained person is not reasonably diligent in exercising his or her right to counsel is essential because it would otherwise be possible for the accused to delay an investigation needlessly and with impunity and even in certain cases to allow for an essential piece of evidence to be destroyed or rendered impossible to obtain. Thus, s. 10(*b*) was not breached when the police did not implement the right to counsel when an accused who, after being taken back to the police station, refused to attempt to try to contact his lawyer believing that it would be useless to do so having regard to the time of day. It could not be said that it would have been impossible for the accused to contact his lawyer when he was initially arrested or when he was at the police station and given an opportunity to do so. The case would be different if the accused had in fact tried to contact his lawyer but failed in the attempt. However, his decision to not even try to contact his lawyer was fatal and prevented him from establishing that he was reasonably diligent in the exercise of his rights. The burden of proving that it was impossible for him to communicate with his lawyer when the police offered him the opportunity to do so was on the accused. The fact that the accused subsequently reiterated his intention to speak to his lawyer during questioning before saying anything with respect to the charge did not change the legal situation. A detainee who has had a reasonable opportunity to communicate with his counsel but who was not diligent in the exercise of the right cannot, in the absence of exceptional circumstances, subsequently require the police to suspend one more time the investigation or the questioning: *R. v. Smith*, [1989] 2 S.C.R. 368, 50 C.C.C. (3d) 308.

Reasonable diligence in the exercise of the right to choose one's counsel depends upon the context facing the accused or detained person. On being arrested, for example, the detained person is faced with an immediate need for legal advice and must exercise reasonable diligence accordingly. By contrast, when seeking the best lawyer to conduct a trial, the accused person faces no such immediacy. Nevertheless, accused or detained persons have a right to choose their counsel and it is only if the lawyer chosen cannot be available within a

CHARTER

reasonable time that the detainee or the accused should be expected to exercise the right to counsel by calling another lawyer: *R. v. Ross*, *supra*.

Change in circumstances (s. 10(*b*)) – The purpose of s. 10(*b*) normally requires only a single consultation with counsel upon request except when there is a change in circumstances. A further request, without more, is not sufficient to retrigger the s. 10(*b*) right to counsel and to be advised thereof. What is required to retrigger s. 10(*b*) is a change in circumstances that suggests that the choice faced by the accused has been significantly altered, requiring further advice on the new situation. Such changes include new procedures involving the detainee, a change in jeopardy, or a reason to question the detainee's understanding of his s. 10(*b*) right. The categories are not closed. However, the change in circumstances must be objectively observable to trigger the new implementational duties: *R. v. Sinclair*, *supra*. See also *R. v. McCrimmon*, *supra*.

In order to comply with s. 10(*b*), the police must restate and reimplement the accused's right to counsel when there is a fundamental and discrete change in the purpose of the investigation, including investigation of a different and unrelated offence or a significantly more serious offence than that contemplated at the time of the original warning: *R. v. Evans*, *supra*.

Thus, s. 10(*b*) was breached when the accused did not have a general knowledge of the events or circumstances that had led to his detention and was given no indication that the police investigations were directed at any offence other than the one for which he had been arrested. When the nature of the police investigations expanded, the respondent should have been reinformed of his right to counsel: *R. v. Borden*, *supra*.

Additionally, where the accused was originally arrested for attempted murder, but was later informed that the victim had died and that she was under arrest for first degree murder, she should have been reinformed of her right to counsel and given a reasonable opportunity to exercise her rights under s. 10(*b*) again: *R. v. Black*, *supra*.

Onus (s. 10(*b*)) – Absent proof of circumstances indicating that the accused did not understand his or her right to retain counsel when he or she was informed of it, he or she has the onus of proving that he or she asked for the right but it was denied or was denied any opportunity to even ask for it: *R. v. Baig*, [1987] 2 S.C.R. 537, 37 C.C.C. (3d) 181; *R. v. Bain*, [1992] 1 S.C.R. 91, 69 C.C.C. (3d) 481.

However, once a detainee has asserted his or her right to counsel, the burden of establishing a later unequivocal waiver is on the Crown: *R. v. Prosper*, *supra*, citing *R. v. Ross*, *supra*.

Additionally, when there is a delay in performing the implementational duties under s. 10(*b*), the burden is on the Crown to show that a given delay was reasonable in the circumstances: *R. v. Taylor*, *supra*.

Waiver (s. 10(*b*)) – Given the concern for fair treatment of an accused person that underlies such constitutional civil liberties as the right to counsel in s. 10(*b*) of the Charter, it is evident that any alleged waiver of this right by an accused must be carefully considered and that the accused's awareness of the consequences of what he or she was saying is crucial. Any waiver "is dependent upon it being clear and unequivocal that the person is waiving the procedural safeguard and is doing so with full knowledge of the rights the procedure was enacted to protect and of the effect the waiver will have on those rights in the process": *R. v. Clarkson*, [1986] 1 S.C.R. 383, 25 C.C.C. (3d) 207, citing *Korponay v. Canada (Attorney General)*, [1982] 1 S.C.R. 41, 65 C.C.C. (2d) 65.

To establish a valid waiver of the right to counsel, the trial judge must be satisfied that, in all the circumstances revealed by the evidence, the accused generally understood the sort of jeopardy he or she faced when he or she made the decision to dispense with counsel. The accused does not need to be aware of the precise charge faced or of all the factual details of the case. In fact, the words of the *Criminal Code* provision may be less helpful to a lay person than more common parlance in communicating the extent of jeopardy. What is required to establish the validity of the detainee's waiver is that he or she be possessed of sufficient information to allow him or her to make an informed and appropriate decision as to whether to speak to a lawyer or not. The emphasis should be on the reality of the total situation as it impacts on the understanding of the accused, rather than on technical detail of what the accused may or may not have been told: *R. v. Smith*, 1991, *supra.*

Once the detainee has asserted the right to counsel, there must be a clear indication that he or she has changed his or her mind and the burden of establishing an unequivocal waiver will be on the Crown. The waiver must be free and voluntary, and it must not be the product of direct or indirect compulsion. The standard required for an effective waiver of the right to counsel is very high. A person who waives a right must know what he or she is giving up if the waiver is to be valid: *R. v. Prosper*, *supra.*

The accused's understanding of his or her situation is relevant to whether he or she has made a valid and informed waiver. This approach is mandated by s. 10(*a*) and is exemplified by three related concepts: (l) the "tainting" of a warning as to the right to counsel by lack of information; (2) the idea that one is entitled to know "the extent of one's jeopardy"; and (3) the concept of "awareness of the consequences" developed in the context of waiver: *R. v. Smith*, 1991, *supra.*

In circumstances where the detainee has asserted his right to counsel and has been reasonably diligent in exercising it, yet has been unable to reach a lawyer because duty counsel is unavailable at the time of detention, courts must ensure that the Charter-protected right to counsel is not too easily waived: *R. v. Prosper*, *supra.*

In exercising the right to counsel or waiving the right, a mentally ill accused must possess the limited cognitive capacity required for fitness to stand trial. This requires that the accused be capable of understanding the function of counsel, communicating with counsel to instruct counsel, and dispensing with counsel even if this is not in the accused's best interests. It is not necessary that the accused possess analytical ability: *R. v. Whittle*, [1994] 2 S.C.R. 914, 92 C.C.C. (3d) 11.

A person may implicitly waive his rights under s. 10(*b*), but the standard is very high. Responding to questions posed by the police is not an implied waiver of the right to counsel. The detained individual has the right not to be asked questions, and he or she must not be held to have implicitly waived that right simply because he or she answered the questions. Otherwise, the right not to be asked questions would only exist where the detainee refused to answer and, thus, where there is no need for any remedy or exclusionary rule: *R. v. Manninen*, *supra*, citing *R. v. Clarkson*, *supra.*

An accused's response to questions asked by the police did not amount to an implicit waiver of s. 10(*b*) when she was under the influence of alcohol at the time that she gave the statement, was emotionally distraught as is evidenced by her behaviour in the interrogation room, and suffering from certain injuries that required medical attention. The appellant was obviously concerned throughout about her legal rights, both upon her arrival at the police station and upon being advised of the change in the charge. Her initiation of the conversation with the police did not amount to a waiver, because the conversation related to the safety of her child and whether she would have to spend the weekend in jail and it was the police who turned the conversation back to the circumstances of the investigation: *R. v. Black*, *supra.*

The mere fact that an accused did not want to call another lawyer when his counsel was unavailable was not a waiver of his right to retain counsel. Quite the contrary, the accused had asserted his right to counsel and to counsel of his choice: *R. v. Ross*, *supra.*

Participation in a line-up cannot by itself amount to a waiver of the right to counsel. It would contradict the purpose of s. 10(*b*) to conclude that a detained or accused person has waived the right to counsel simply by submitting, before being instructed by counsel, to precisely those attempts to secure the detainee's participation from which the police should refrain. The appellants were unable to make an informed decision about participating in the line-up because they were ignorant of their legal position, not having been advised by their lawyers. In the circumstances, therefore, to conclude that the appellants had waived their rights by participating in the line-up would render the right to counsel nugatory: *R. v. Ross*, *supra.*

Other considerations (s. 10(*b*)) – Paragraph (*b*) prohibits the police from belittling an accused's lawyer with the express goal or effect of undermining the accused's confidence in a relationship with defence counsel: *R. v. Burlingham*, *supra*.

The detainee has the right to consult with counsel in private. It is well-accepted that privacy afforded to a detainee consulting with counsel will be unreasonable where it is established that there has been an actual invasion of privacy such that the police did overhear the detainee's conversation. Additionally, s. 10(*b*) is infringed when the detainee has a reasonable belief that he or she cannot speak to counsel in private, unless it can be shown that the detainee was, in fact, able to speak to counsel in private: *R. v. Coaster* (2014), 317 C.C.C. (3d) 339 (Man. C.A.). See also *R. v. Playford* (1987), 40 C.C.C. (3d) 142 (Ont. C.A.).

Interpretation generally (s. 10(*c*)) – The writ of *habeas corpus* is used to challenge the lawfulness of an individual's detention: *May v. Ferndale Institution*, [2005] 3 S.C.R. 809, 204 C.C.C. (3d) 1.

In an earlier incarnation, *habeas corpus* was a means to ensure that the defendant in an action was brought physically before a court. Over time, however, the writ was transformed into a vehicle for reviewing the justification for a person's imprisonment. In fact, *habeas corpus* is the strongest tool a prisoner has to ensure that the deprivation of his or her liberty is not unlawful: *Mission Institution v. Khela*, [2014] 1 S.C.R. 502, 307 C.C.C. (3d) 427.

Habeas corpus is a crucial remedy in the pursuit of two fundamental rights protected by the Charter: (1) the right to liberty of the person and the right not to be deprived thereof except in accordance with the principles of fundamental justice (s. 7 of the Charter); and (2) the right not to be arbitrarily detained or imprisoned (s. 9 of the Charter). Accordingly, the Charter guarantees the right to *habeas corpus*: *May v. Ferndale Institution*, *supra*.

Section 10(*c*) guarantees the right to a prompt review of an individual's detention: *Charkaoui v. Canada*, [2007] 1 S.C.R. 350.

While the rights conferred by ss. 10(*a*) and 10(*b*) of the Charter only arise at a discrete point in time, the right of *habeas corpus* protected by s. 10(*c*) is self-evidently a continuing right: see *R. v. Sinclair*, *supra*.

In addition to being a free-standing right under s. 10(*c*), the writ of *habeas corpus* is also a remedy under s. 24(1) of the Charter: see *R. v. Gamble*, [1988] 2 S.C.R. 595, 45 C.C.C. (3d) 204; *R. v. Pearson*, [1992] 3 S.C.R. 665, 77 C.C.C. (3d) 124.

Availability of *habeas corpus* (s. 10(*c*)) – Traditionally, the right to seek relief in the nature of *habeas corpus* was not always given to prisoners challenging internal disciplinary decisions. For a long time, at common law, a person convicted of a felony and sentenced to prison was regarded as being devoid of rights. On that basis, courts had refused to review the internal decision-making process of prison officials: *May v. Ferndale Institution*, *supra*.

However, in 1985, the Supreme Court expanded the scope of *habeas corpus* by making the writ available to free inmates from restrictive forms of custody within an institution without releasing the inmate. *Habeas corpus* can therefore free inmates from a "prison within a prison": *May v. Ferndale Institution*, *supra*, referring to *R. v. Miller*, [1985] 2 S.C.R. 613, 23 C.C.C. (3d) 97; *Cardinal v. Kent Institution*, [1985] 2 S.C.R. 643, 23 C.C.C. (3d) 118; and *Morin v. Canada (National Special Handling Unit Review Committee)*, [1985] 2 S.C.R. 662, 23 C.C.C. (3d) 132.

Inmates can apply for *habeas corpus* with respect to decisions that might affect their residual liberty including, but not limited to, administrative segregation, confinement in a special handling unit, and a transfer to a higher security institution: *Mission Institution v. Khela*, *supra*.

Habeas corpus is not limited to incarceration in a custodial facility. An individual's liberty is infringed giving rise to the availability of *habeas corpus* when he or she is released from custody on terms and conditions that included house arrest: see *Wang v. Canada* (2018), 426 D.L.R. (4th) 753 (Ont. C.A.).

Where the applicant is subject to an immigration detention that has become illegal and violates the applicant's ss. 7 and 9 Charter rights, *habeas corpus* is available if the statutory review scheme provides a less efficacious remedy: *Ogiamien v. Ontario (Community Safety and Correctional Services)*, 2017 ONCA 839, citing *Chaudhary v. Canada (Minister of Public Safety & Emergency Preparedness)* (2015), 390 D.L.R. (4th) 598 (Ont. C.A.). See also *Charkaoui v. Canada, supra.*

In the criminal context, *habeas corpus* cannot be used to challenge the legality of a conviction. The remedy of *habeas corpus* is not a substitute for the exercise by prisoners of their right of appeal: *May v. Ferndale Institution, supra*, citing *R. v. Gamble, supra.*

Jurisdiction (s. 10(*c*)) – Although the Federal Court has a general review jurisdiction, it cannot issue the writ of *habeas corpus*. Jurisdiction to grant *habeas corpus* with regard to inmates remains with the provincial superior courts: *Mission Institution v. Khela, supra*, citing *R. v. Miller, supra*. See also *May v. Ferndale Institution, supra.*

Habeas corpus should lie to determine the validity of a particular form of confinement in a penitentiary despite the fact that the same issue may be determined upon *certiorari* in the Federal Court. The proper scope of the availability of *habeas corpus* must be considered first on its own merits, apart from the possible problems arising from concurrent or overlapping jurisdiction. The general importance of this remedy as the traditional means of challenging deprivations of liberty means that its application should not be compromised by concerns about conflicting jurisdiction: *R. v. Miller, supra.*

In other words, *habeas corpus* will remain available to federal inmates in the superior courts regardless of the existence of other avenues for redress: *Mission Institution v. Khela, supra*, citing *R. v. Miller, supra.*

Only in limited circumstances will it be appropriate for a provincial superior court to decline to exercise its *habeas corpus* jurisdiction. In criminal law, where a statute confers jurisdiction on a court of appeal to correct the errors of a lower court and release the applicant if need be, *habeas corpus* will not be available. Jurisdiction should also be declined where a complete, comprehensive, and expert procedure for review of an administrative decision is in place: *May v. Ferndale Institution, supra.*

The writ of *habeas corpus* remains non-discretionary as far as the decision to review the case is concerned. If the applicant raises a legitimate doubt as to the reasonableness of the detention, the provincial superior court judge is required to examine the substance of the decision and determine whether the evidence presented by the detaining authorities is reliable and supports their decision. A provincial superior court hearing a *habeas corpus* application has no inherent discretion to refuse to review the case. However, a residual discretion will come into play at the second stage of the *habeas corpus* proceeding, when the judge must decide whether to discharge the applicant: *Mission Institution v. Khela, supra.*

***Certiorari* in aid (s. 10(*c*))** – Provincial superior courts have the jurisdiction to order *certiorari* in aid of *habeas corpus* to make *habeas corpus* more effective: *R. v. Miller, supra.*

Without *certiorari* in aid, a court hearing a *habeas corpus* application would consider only the facts as they appeared on the "face" of the return or decision. *Certiorari* in aid brings the record before the reviewing judge so that he or she may examine it to determine whether the challenged decision was lawful and, therefore, makes *habeas corpus* more effective: *Mission Institution v. Khela, supra.*

It should be noted that *certiorari* applied for in aid of *habeas corpus* is different from *certiorari* applied for on its own. In the context of a *habeas corpus* application, what is in issue is only the writ of *certiorari* employed to "inform the [c]ourt" and assist it in making the correct determination in a specific case and not the writ of *certiorari* used to bring the record before the decision-maker in order to "have it quashed" as would be done on an application for judicial review in the Federal Court: *Mission Institution v. Khela, supra.*

Onus (s. 10(*c*)) – To be successful, an application for *habeas corpus* must satisfy the following criteria. First, the applicant must establish that he or she has been deprived of liberty. Once a deprivation of liberty is proven, the applicant must raise a legitimate ground upon which to question its legality. If the applicant has raised such a ground, the onus shifts to the respondent authorities to show that the deprivation of liberty was lawful: *Mission Institution v. Khela, supra.*

Shifting the legal burden onto the detaining authorities is compatible with the very foundation of the law of *habeas corpus*, namely that a deprivation of liberty is permissible only if the party effecting the deprivation can demonstrate that it is justified. The shift of the requisite onus differs from applications for judicial review where the onus remains on the individual challenging the impugned decision to show that the decision was unreasonable: *Mission Institution v. Khela, supra.*

Scope of review (s. 10(*c*)) – A decision will not be lawful if the detention is not lawful, if the decision-maker lacks jurisdiction to order the deprivation of liberty, or if there has been a breach of procedural fairness: *Mission Institution v. Khela, supra*, citing *May v. Ferndale Institution, supra*; *R. v. Miller, supra*; and *Cardinal v. Director of Kent Institution, supra.*

Given the flexibility and the importance of the writ, it is clear that a review for lawfulness will sometimes require an assessment of the decision's reasonableness. Superior courts are entitled to review an inmate transfer decision for reasonableness on an application for *habeas corpus* with *certiorari* in aid. If a decision is unreasonable, it will be unlawful. Support for this conclusion can be found in the nature of the writ, in past court decisions regarding the writ, and in the importance of swift access to justice for those who have been unlawfully deprived of their liberty: *Mission Institution v. Khela, supra.*

Limits on remedies available (s. 10(*c*)) – On a *habeas corpus* application, a provincial superior court is limited to determining that the detention is unlawful and then ruling on a motion for discharge (unlike in a judicial review application of a Correctional Services of Canada decision in the Federal Court where a wide array of relief can be sought): *Mission Institution v. Khela, supra.*

PROCEEDINGS IN CRIMINAL AND PENAL MATTERS

11. Any person charged with an offence has the right

(*a*) to be informed without unreasonable delay of the specific offence;

(*b*) to be tried within a reasonable time;

(*c*) not to be compelled to be a witness in proceedings against that person in respect of the offence;

(*d*) to be presumed innocent until proven guilty according to law in a fair and public hearing by an independent and impartial tribunal;

(*e*) not to be denied reasonable bail without just cause;

(*f*) except in the case of an offence under military law tried before a military tribunal, to the benefit of trial by jury where the maximum punishment for the offence is imprisonment for five years or a more severe punishment;

(*g*) not to be found guilty on account of any act or omission unless, at the time of the act or omission, it constituted an offence under Canadian or international law or was criminal according to the general principles of law recognized by the community of nations;

(*h*) if finally acquitted of the offence, not to be tried for it again and, if finally found guilty and punished for the offence, not to be tried or punished for it again; and

(*i*) if found guilty of the offence and if the punishment for the offence has been varied between the time of commission and the time of sentencing, to the benefit of the lesser punishment.

ANNOTATIONS

"Charged with an offence" – This section is limited to criminal or quasi-criminal proceedings or proceedings giving rise to penal consequences. The matter will fall within this section either because, by its very nature, it is a criminal proceeding or because a conviction in respect of the offence may lead to a true penal consequence. The first category of offences are those which involve a matter of public nature, intended to promote public order within a public sphere of activity. Those matters are to be distinguished from private, domestic or disciplinary matters which are regulatory, protective or corrective and which are primarily intended to maintain discipline, professional integrity and professional standards or to regulate conduct within a limited private sphere of activity. Thus all prosecutions for criminal offences under the *Criminal Code* or for quasi-criminal offences under provincial legislation are automatically subject to this section. However, even a private, domestic or disciplinary matter can fall within this section if it involves the imposition of true penal consequences, namely, imprisonment or a fine which by its magnitude would appear to be imposed for the purpose of redressing the wrong done to society at large rather than to the maintenance of internal discipline within the limited sphere: *R. v. Wigglesworth*, [1987] 2 S.C.R. 541, 37 C.C.C. (3d) 385.

The focus of the "criminal in nature" inquiry is not on the nature of the act which is the subject of the proceedings, but on the nature of the proceedings themselves, taking into account their purpose as well as their procedure. A "true penal consequence" is imprisonment or a fine which, having regard to its magnitude and other relevant factors, is imposed to redress the wrong done to society at large rather than simply to secure compliance. A monetary penalty may or may not be a true penal consequence. It will be so when it is, in purpose or effect, punitive. This is assessed by looking at considerations such as the magnitude of the fine, to whom it is paid, whether its magnitude is determined by regulatory considerations rather than principles of criminal sentencing, and whether stigma is associated with the penalty: *Guindon v. R.*, [2015] 3 S.C.R. 3, 327 C.C.C. (3d) 308. See also: *Martineau v. M.N.R.*, [2004] 3 S.C.R. 737, 192 C.C.C. (3d) 129.

A provincial "automatic roadside prohibition" administrative regime for combatting impaired driving did not create an "offence" for Charter purposes. The scheme concerned the licensing of drivers, the enhancement of road safety, and the deterrence of impaired driving: it was not "criminal in nature". Further, the costs and penalties imposed did not amount to "true penal consequences": *Goodwin v. British Columbia (Superintendent of Motor Vehicles)*, [2015] 3 S.C.R. 250, 329 C.C.C. (3d) 545.

Section 11(*a*) – The making of an *ex parte* injunction on the court's own motion restraining picketing of courthouses in the course of a legal strike cannot be said to infringe s. 11(*a*) on the ground that no notice was given to the picketers and they were not afforded an opportunity to be heard. There can be no violation of this paragraph where no person is charged with a specific offence and there is therefore no one to notify of any offence: *B.C.G.E.U. v. British Columbia (Attorney General)*, [1988] 2 S.C.R. 214, 44 C.C.C. (3d) 289.

The right to be informed of the specific offence within the meaning of s. 11(*a*) means the right to be informed of the substantive offence and the acts or conduct which allegedly form the basis of the charge. It does not give an accused charged with a hybrid offence the right to be informed of how the Crown will exercise its discretion with respect to the manner of prosecution: *R. v. Warren* (1983), 35 C.R. (3d) 173, 6 C.R.R. 82 (Ont. H.C.J.).

This paragraph enshrines the rights contained in s. 581(3) of the *Criminal Code* which establishes the minimum requirements of a valid count in an indictment. It was intended to protect the right of an accused to be reasonably informed of the transaction alleged against him, thus giving him the possibility of a full defence and fair trial: *R. v. Lucas* (1983), 6 C.C.C. (3d) 147 (N.S.C.A.).

The purpose of this paragraph is to confirm the right of an accused to be informed of the substantive offence and the acts or conduct which allegedly formed the basis of that charge as is now required by s. 581 of the *Criminal Code*. It is not a right to be charged within a reasonable time of the Crown having knowledge of the offence: *R. v. Cancor Software Corp.* (1990), 58 C.C.C. (3d) 53 (Ont. C.A.).

This section, as well as ss. 7 and 14, entitle the accused to obtain a written translation of an information in the language of the trial, if requested: *R. v. Simard* (1995), 105 C.C.C. (3d) 461 (Ont. C.A.), leave to appeal to S.C.C. refused 108 C.C.C. (3d) vi.

In considering whether there has been an unreasonable delay in informing the accused of the specific offence, the court should consider: (i) the length of the delay, (ii) the waiver of time periods, (iii) the reasons for the delay and (iv) prejudice to the accused. The length of the delay is calculated from the time that the information is sworn to the time that the person is informed of the offence. Proper informing of the accused includes the substance of the offence and the details of the circumstances of its commission. The accused may waive time periods if he acts knowingly in a manner so as to prevent the authorities from informing him of the offence with which he is charged. The reasons for the delay include the inherent time requirements of the case, the actions of the accused, the actions of the Crown and limits on institutional resources. The inherent time requirements should be restrictively defined to include the identification and locating of the accused. The actions of the accused include all actions which may have influenced the delay and the limits on institutional resources relating to the police force involved and the material resources available to them. Prejudice in the context of this provision relates to the violation of the right to a fair trial: *R. v. Delaronde*, [1997] 1 S.C.R. 213, 115 C.C.C. (3d) 355, affg 115 C.C.C. (3d) 355 at p. 370, [1996] R.J.Q. 591 (C.A.). [Note: On appeal to the S.C.C., the court dimsissed the appeal for the reasons of Otis J.A. in the Court of Appeal. However, Lamer C.J.C., in a separate addendum, left open the question of whether economic prejudice could found a remedy under s. 24(1) for a breach of s. 11(*a*).].

Unreasonable delay [s. 11(*b*)] – In *R. v. Jordan*, [2016] 1 S.C.R. 631, 335 C.C.C. (3d) 403, the Supreme Court elaborated a new analytical framework for s. 11(*b*) claims, jettisoning the analysis in *R. v. Morin*, [1992] 1 S.C.R. 771, 71 C.C.C. (3d) 1, which it deemed too unpredictable, confusing, and complex. At the heart of the *Jordan* framework is a presumptive ceiling beyond which delay — from the charge to the actual or anticipated end of trial — is presumed to be unreasonable, unless exceptional circumstances justify it. The presumptive ceiling is 18 months for cases tried in the provincial court, and 30 months for cases in the superior court (or cases tried in the provincial court after a preliminary inquiry, in jurisdiction where this is possible). Delay attributable to or waived by the defence does not count towards the presumptive ceiling. Once the presumptive ceiling is exceeded, the burden is on the Crown to rebut the presumption of unreasonableness on the basis of exceptional circumstances. If the Crown cannot do so, a stay will follow. Exceptional circumstances lie outside the Crown's control in that: (1) they are reasonably unforeseen or reasonably unavoidable; and (2) they cannot reasonably be remedied. This is the only basis upon which the Crown can discharge its burden to justify a delay that exceeds the ceiling. The seriousness or gravity of the offence cannot be relied on, nor can chronic institutional delay. Most significantly, the absence of prejudice can in no circumstances be used to justify delays after the presumptive ceiling is breached. Once so much time has elapsed, only circumstances that are genuinely outside the Crown's control and ability to remedy may furnish a sufficient excuse for the prolonged delay.

Below the presumptive ceiling, the burden is on the defence to show that the delay is unreasonable. To do so, the defence must establish that: (1) it took meaningful steps that demonstrate a sustained effort to expedite the proceedings; and (2) the case took markedly longer than it reasonably should have. Absent these two factors, the s. 11(*b*) application must fail. Stays beneath the presumptive ceiling should only be granted in clear cases.

For cases currently in the system, the new framework applies, subject to two qualifications. First, for cases in which the delay exceeds the ceiling, a transitional exceptional circumstance may arise where the charges were brought prior to the release of this decision. This transitional exceptional circumstance will apply when the Crown satisfies the court that the time the case has taken is justified based on the parties' reasonable reliance on the law as it previously existed. This requires a contextual assessment, sensitive to the manner in which the previous framework was applied. The second qualification applies to cases currently in the system in which the total delay (minus defence delay) falls below the ceiling. For these cases, the two criteria — defence initiative and whether the time the case has taken markedly exceeds what was reasonably required — must also be applied contextually, sensitive to the parties' reliance on the previous state of the law. Specifically, the defence need not demonstrate having taken initiative to expedite matters for the period of delay preceding this decision. Further, if the delay was occasioned by an institutional delay that was, before this decision was released, reasonably acceptable in the relevant jurisdiction under the *Morin* framework, that institutional delay will be a component of the reasonable time requirements of the case for cases currently in the system.

Applying the new framework established in *R. v. Jordan*, *supra*, the accused's right to be tried within a reasonable time was infringed where the total delay between charge and end of trial was about 33.5 months. The accused did not waive any of this delay, and was solely responsible for only one and a half months of it. Subtracting this amount leaves the delay above the 30-month presumptive ceiling. The Crown failed to discharge its burden of showing that the delay was reasonable. The record did not disclose any delay caused by discrete, exceptional circumstances, and the case does not remotely qualify as exceptionally complex. The transitional exceptional circumstance does not apply, in that the *Morin* framework could not justify the nearly three years it took to bring the accused to trial on relatively straightforward charges: *R. v. Williamson*, [2016] 1 S.C.R. 741, 336 C.C.C. (3d) 1.

The exceptionality of the "transitional exceptional circumstance" does not lie in the rarity of its application, but rather in its temporary justification of delay that exceeds the ceiling based on the parties' reasonable reliance on the law as it previously existed. The parties' general level of diligence, the seriousness of the offence and the absence of prejudice are all factors that should be taken into consideration, as appropriate in the circumstances. Where a balancing of factors under the *Morin* framework would have weighed in favour of a stay, the Crown will rarely, if ever, be successful in justifying the delay as a transitional exceptional circumstance under the *Jordan* framework: *R. v. Cody*, [2017] 1 S.C.R. 659, 349 C.C.C. (3d) 488.

Courts must be careful not to miss the forest for the trees in evaluating unreasonable delay claims. Where the accused waited three years for a three-day trial, the court found the delay clearly unreasonable, especially in light of the accused's proactive steps to have his case tried as soon as possible. While the Crown was entitled to insist on a joint trial for all seven co-accused, it was required to ensure that this decision did not compromise the accused's s. 11(*b*) rights: *R. v. Vassell*, [2016] 1 S.C.R. 625, 337 C.C.C. (3d) 1.

The presumptive ceilings established in *R. v. Jordan*, *supra*, do not apply throughout the sentencing process: *R. v. Warring* (2017), 347 C.C.C. (3d) 391 (Alta. C.A.), leave to appeal to S.C.C. refused 2017 CarswellAlta 2547.

Where complexity is relied upon by the Crown as an "exceptional circumstance" justifying a delay above the presumptive ceiling, the court must consider the complexity of the case as a whole. A case that has been streamlined by the time of trial may have been "particularly complex" at earlier stages: *R. v. Picard* (2017), 354 C.C.C. (3d) 212 (Ont. C.A.), leave to appeal to S.C.C. refused [2018] S.C.C.A. No. 135.

An individualized approach to defence-caused delay in a case of jointly-charged accused. Delay caused by one accused does not "count against" all. Rather, delays arising from a joint trial may be considered under the exceptional circumstances analysis, provided that it is in the interests of justice for the charges to proceed jointly: *R. v. Gopie* (2017), 356 C.C.C. (3d) 36 (Ont. C.A.).

In *R. v. Mamouni* (2017), 356 C.C.C. (3d) 153 (Alta. C.A.), leave to appeal to S.C.C. refused [2018] S.C.C.A. No. 176, the members of the panel differed on whether the time taken by a trial judge in rendering reasons for judgment counts as delay for s. 11(*b*) purposes, or whether such delay might amount to "exceptional circumstances" in an appropriate case.

The presumption ceiling does not apply to s. 11(*b*) applications made after conviction. Further, by pleading guilty, the accused waived his right to challenge the pre-conviction delay for unreasonableness: *R. v. S.C.W.* (2018), 367 C.C.C. (3d) 518 (B.C.C.A.), leave to appeal to S.C.C. refused 2019 CarswellBC 702.

Once a trial is imminent or underway, the trial should be completed before a late-breaking s. 11(*b*) application is heard. Where the trial judge erred in granting a stay mid-trial, the proper order was to remit the matter to the trial judge to continue the trial to its conclusion: *R. v. Scher* (2018), 368 C.C.C. (3d) 352 (Alta. C.A.).

Delay caused by the time taken by another government entity outside the control of the prosecuting Crown to respond to defence disclosure requests was not Crown delay for s. 11(*b*) purposes: *R. v. King* (2018), 369 C.C.C. (3d) 1 (N.L.C.A.).

In the context of a re-trial after a successful appeal, the unreasonable delay doctrine must be applied in a manner consistent with the Crown's duty to re-try cases as soon as possible. The 18-month ceiling is far too long for a re-trial: *R. v. MacIsaac* (2018), 365 C.C.C. (3d) 361 (Ont. C.A.).

Editor's note: The following cases were decided before the Supreme Court elaborated a new analytical framework for s. 11(*b*) in *R. v. Jordan*, [2016] 1 S.C.R. 631, 335 C.C.C. (3d) 403. That framework has replaced the analysis in *R. v. Morin*, [1992] 1 S.C.R. 771, 71 C.C.C. (3d) 1. The following cases were decided prior to *Jordan* and should be read with caution, but may continue to be persuasive on discrete analytical points.

A person is only charged with an offence within the meaning of s. 11 when an information is sworn against him alleging an offence or where a direct indictment is laid against him when no information is sworn. Accordingly, the reckoning of time in considering whether a person has been accorded a trial within a reasonable time within the meaning of s. 11(*b*) will commence with the information or indictment, where no information has been laid, and will continue until the completion of the trial. Pre-information delay is not a factor. This does not mean that delays which occur at the pre-charge stage are immune from scrutiny under the law. The *Criminal Code* itself in ss. 650(3) and 802(1) protects the right of the accused to make full answer and defence should he be prejudiced by pre-charge delay and other provisions of the *Criminal Code* provide for the prompt swearing of an information. As well the doctrine of abuse of process may be invoked in an appropriate case. In addition, given the broad wording of s. 7 it is not necessary to distort the words of s. 11(*b*) in order to guard against a pre-charge delay: *R. v. Kalanj*, [1989] 1 S.C.R. 1594, 48 C.C.C. (3d) 459.

Although the primary aim of s. 11(*b*) is the protection of the individual's rights and the provision of fundamental justice for the accused, none the less, there is a community or societal interest implicit in s. 11(*b*). The four factors to be considered in determining whether there has been an unreasonable delay are: (1) the length of the delay; (2) explanation for the delay; (3) waiver; and (4) prejudice to the accused. In considering the explanation for the delay, the court will consider those delays attributable to the Crown, including systemic or institutional delays and those delays attributable to the accused. Delay attributable to the Crown will comprise all of the potential factors causing delay which flow from the nature of the case, the conduct of the Crown, including officers of the state, and the inherent time requirements of the case. The delay attributable to the actions of the Crown or its officers will weigh in favour of the accused. Systemic or institutional limitations will often be the most difficult to assess. The court must pay due deference to political decisions respecting the allocation of funds for courtrooms and Crown attorneys which must be balanced against the duty on the state to provide other services such as health care and highways. The right guaranteed by s. 11(*b*), however, is of such fundamental importance to both the individual and the community that the lack of institutional resources cannot be employed to justify a continuing unreasonable postponement of trials. In all cases, it will be incumbent upon the Crown to show that the institutional delay in question is justifiable. The inquiry into the actions of the accused will be restricted to discovering those situations where the accused's acts either directly caused the delay or the acts of the accused are shown to be a deliberate and calculated tactic employed to delay the trial. Delay caused by factors beyond the control of the accused or a situation where the accused did nothing to prevent a delay caused by the Crown must be distinguished. The burden of proving that the direct acts of the accused caused the delay must fall upon the Crown, except in those cases where the effects of the accused's actions are so clear and readily apparent that the intent of the accused to cause the delay is the inference that must be drawn from the record of his actions. As regards the factor of waiver, it is now well established that any waiver of a Charter right must be clear and unequivocal. The accused is not required to assert explicitly his right to trial within a reasonable time and his failure to assert the right does not give the Crown license to proceed with an unfair trial. Rather, there must be something in the conduct of the accused that is sufficient to give rise to an inference that the accused has understood that he had a guarantee under s. 11(*b*), understood its nature and waived the right provided by that guarantee. As regards prejudice to the accused, it should be inferred that a very long and unreasonable delay has prejudiced the accused. It will, however, be open to the Crown to attempt to demonstrate that the accused has not been prejudiced. In addition, it will be open to an accused who has suffered some additional form of prejudice to adduce evidence of prejudice on his own initiative, in order to strengthen his position in seeking a remedy under s. 24(1): *R. v. Askov*, [1990] 2 S.C.R. 1199, 59 C.C.C. (3d) 449.

In determining whether the right of the accused has been denied, no mere administrative formula can be applied but rather there must be a judicial determination balancing the interests which the section is designed to protect against factors which either inevitably lead to delay or are otherwise the cause of delay. The first factor is the length of the delay and requires the court to examine the period from the charge to the end of the trial. If the length of delay warrants an inquiry into the reasons for the delay, then the court will first consider whether the accused has waived, in whole or in part, her right to complain of the delay. However, any waiver must be clear and unequivocal, with full knowledge of the rights that the procedure was enacted to protect and of the effect that waiver will have on those rights. If the application by the accused is not resolved by reason of principles of waiver, the court will then have to consider other explanations for the delay. This includes consideration of the inherent time requirements which inevitably lead to delay. Thus, the more complex the trial, the more time will be needed to prepare for trial and for the trial to be conducted once it begins. As well, there are inherent requirements which are common to almost all cases. This includes activities such as retention of counsel, bail hearings, police and administrative paperwork, disclosure and similar activities. Another inherent delay that must be taken into account is whether the case proceeds through a preliminary inquiry. The actions of the accused must also be considered as must the actions of the Crown. Another factor is the limits on institutional resources. This period starts to run when the parties are ready for trial but the system cannot accommodate them. While account must be taken of the fact that the state does not have unlimited funds, the court cannot simply accede to the government's allocation of resources and tailor the period of permissible delay accordingly. There is a point in time at which the court will no longer tolerate delay based on the plea of inadequate resources. This period of time may be referred to as an administrative guideline, but is not a limitation period nor is it a fixed ceiling on delay. The application of a guideline will also be influenced by the presence or absence of prejudice. It is appropriate for the court to suggest a period of institutional delay of between eight to ten months as a guide to provincial courts. As regards institutional delay after committal for trial, the range should be an additional six to eight months. The final factor to be considered is prejudice to the accused. In any particular case, prejudice may be inferred simply from the length of the delay. The longer the delay, the more likely that such an inference will be drawn. On the other hand, in circumstances in which prejudice is not inferred and is not otherwise proved, the basis for an enforcement of the accused's right is seriously undermined. The purpose of s. 11(*b*) is to expedite trials and minimize prejudice and not to avoid trials on the merits. Action or non-action by the accused which is inconsistent with a desire for a timely trial is something that the court must consider. Apart, however, from inferred prejudice, either party may rely on evidence to show prejudice or to dispel such a finding. Conduct of the accused falling short of waiver may be relied upon to negative prejudice: *R. v. Morin*, [1992] 1 S.C.R. 771, 71 C.C.C. (3d) 1 (7:0).

A corporate accused charged with a provincial regulatory offence has the right to be tried within a reasonable time. However, in considering the factor of prejudice to the accused, there is no presumption of prejudice in the case of a corporate offender and a corporate accused must be able to establish that its fair trial interest has been irremediably prejudiced: *R. v. CIP Inc.*, [1992] 1 S.C.R. 843, 71 C.C.C. (3d) 129.

The decision in *R. v. Askov, supra*, did not enact a judicially developed limitation period to be mechanically applied whenever there has been a period of systemic delay. In every case, the court is required to weigh the four factors of length of delay, explanation for the delay, waiver and prejudice to the accused: *R. v. Bennett* (1991), 64 C.C.C. (3d) 449, 6 C.R. (4th) 22 (Ont. C.A.), affd [1992] 2 S.C.R. 168, 74 C.C.C. (3d) 384*n*.

A delay of 30 months in a relatively straightforward case substantially exceeded the *Morin* guidelines and warranted a stay of proceedings. Virtually all of the delays were attributable to the Crown. The question of prejudice cannot be considered separately from the length of the delay. Where the delay exceeded the ordinary guidelines by a year or more, even though the case was straightforward, it was reasonable to infer that prolonged exposure to criminal proceedings resulting from the delay gave rise to some prejudice. Proof of actual prejudice to the right to make full answer and defence is not invariably required to establish a s. 11(*b*) violation: *R. v. Godin*, [2009] 2 S.C.R. 3, 245 C.C.C. (3d) 271.

A longer period of delay will be reasonable in a complex case which requires the commitment of substantial preparation time, court time and support services. In considering whether the state has allocated sufficient resources to the preparation of the case, some deference should be given to decisions made by the police in the investigation and it must be recognized that complex cases will often require longer than normal preparation time, greater expenditure of Crown and other resources and the longer use of court-rooms: *R. v. Atkinson* (1991), 68 C.C.C. (3d) 109, 5 O.R. (3d) 301 (C.A.).

Agreement by an accused to a future court date will in most circumstances give rise to an inference that the accused waives his right to subsequently allege that an unreasonable delay has occurred. However, in this case it was held that the actions of defence counsel on behalf of the accused rebutted any possible inference that he waived his s. 11(*b*) rights. When the case had to be adjourned at the request of the Crown in order to convenience the investigating officer defence counsel wrote to Crown counsel indicating his concern and making it clear that he was not waiving his s. 11(*b*) rights. The accused had demonstrated that he neither caused nor acquiesced in the postponement of the preliminary inquiry: *R. v. Smith*, [1989] 2 S.C.R. 1120, 52 C.C.C. (3d) 97.

The trial judge did not err in refusing to attribute to the accused all of the delay occasioned by a defence request for an adjournment. The trial judge held that the system should have had sufficient flexibility to accommodate an earlier trial date after the adjournment: *R. v. Maracle*, [1998] 1 S.C.R. 86, 122 C.C.C. (3d) 104*n*, revg 122 C.C.C. (3d) 97 at p. 97 (Ont. C.A.), and restoring decision of trial judge 122 C.C.C. (3d) 97 (Ont. Ct. (Gen. Div.)).

In *R. v. Smith, supra*, it was also held that it was open to an accused to bring an application in the superior court alleging a violation of s. 11(*b*) several months prior to the date scheduled for the commencement of his preliminary inquiry. The accused's application was anticipatory in the sense that it was brought before the commencement of the preliminary inquiry. However, in the circumstances of the case and since the date for the preliminary inquiry was fixed and could not, at the behest of the accused, be moved up, the superior court judge properly considered the accused's application on the basis that the time had already elapsed. This was also an appropriate case for the superior court to exercise its jurisdiction, notwithstanding the preference for alleged violations of s. 11(*b*) being heard by the trial court. The preliminary inquiry was not scheduled to begin for several months and the provincial court judge would not have jurisdiction to consider an alleged infringement of s. 11(*b*) since he was not a court of competent jurisdiction.

Acquiescence by the accused to a delay that is requested by the judge in whose hands the fate of a motion for directed verdict lies must be assessed differently than acquiescence to those delays and proceedings that are made at the request of the Crown. In this case a substantial delay while the trial judge considered an application for a directed verdict was held to have resulted in an unreasonable delay within the meaning of s. 11(*b*) and in requiring a stay of proceedings. This was also an appropriate case for bringing an application to the superior court as the trial court was implicated in the delay: *R. v. Rahey*, [1987] 1 S.C.R. 588, 33 C.C.C. (3d) 289.

An evidentiary hearing to inquire into the Crown's explanation for delay is not justified by merely pointing out that the discretion of the Crown could have been exercised differently and that this could have entailed different consequences to one or more of the accused. To warrant a hearing, there must be some basis for suspecting the Crown's choice of conduct. The accused bears the burden of making a tenable allegation of bad faith on the part of the Crown, which allegation can be supported by the record before the court or by some offer of proof: *R. v. Durette* (1992), 72 C.C.C. (3d) 421, 54 O.A.C. 81 (C.A.).

While the right to trial within a reasonable time is an individual right, the court cannot ignore the practicalities of what is involved in the prosecution of a conspiracy case and thus an accused's right under this paragraph is not infringed simply because the arranging of a joint trial involving several accused may involve greater delay. To suggest severance as a simple solution ignores the real cost to the Crown and the public from separate trials: *R. v. Koruz; R. Schiewe* (1992), 72 C.C.C. (3d) 353, 125 A.R. 161 (C.A.).

The failure to apply at trial for a stay of proceedings on the ground of a violation of the right to trial within a reasonable time as guaranteed by s. 11(*b*) will normally amount to a waiver depriving the accused of the right to raise the matter for the first time on appeal: *R. v. Rabba* (1991), 64 C.C.C. (3d) 445, 3 O.R. (3d) 238 (C.A.).

The term "charged with an offence", in the context of s. 11(*b*), is not, however, confined to the period before conviction and may extend to the sentencing process. Further, the guarantee to be "tried within a reasonable time" extends to sentencing. However, the inherent time requirements of sentencing do not fall under the time guidelines set out in *R. v. Morin, supra*, and *R. v. Askov, supra*. The inherent time requirements of sentencing must be assessed on a case-by-case basis. Illness of the sentencing judge may be regarded as part of the inherent time required to complete the case up to the point where it is reasonable for the Crown to apply to have the judge replaced. At that point, the inherent delay due to the judge's illness changes to Crown delay. It may also amount to systemic delay where the Crown delays bringing what would be a reasonable motion to replace the judge because the Crown knows there is no other replacement judge available, or where a motion is brought and granted but an unreasonable delay results because no other judge is available: *R. v. MacDougall*, [1998] 3 S.C.R. 45, 128 C.C.C. (3d) 483; *R. v. Gallant*, [1998] 3 S.C.R. 80, 128 C.C.C. (3d) 509.

The right to trial within a reasonable time does not apply to appellate delay. This is the case whether the accused or the Crown is the appellant and whether the appeal by the Crown is from an acquittal or a stay of proceedings: *R. v. Potvin*, [1993] 2 S.C.R. 880, 83 C.C.C. (3d) 97.

For the purposes of characterizing delay, parties should not be deemed to be ready to immediately conduct a hearing as soon as a date is set. Counsel require time to make themselves available, as well as to prepare for the hearing. These time frames are part of the inherent requirements of the case. Institutional delay begins to run only when counsel are ready to proceed but the court is unable to accommodate them: *R. v. Tran* (2012), 288 C.C.C. (3d) 177 (Ont. C.A.).

Non-compellability of accused [s. 11(*c*)] – A corporation cannot be said to be a witness within the meaning of s. 11(*c*) and is therefore not entitled to claim its protection when an officer of the corporation is compelled to testify against it: *R. v. Amway Corp.*, [1989] 1 S.C.R. 21, 68 C.R. (3d) 97.

Neither s. 11(*c*) nor (*d*) requires that a trial judge specifically instruct jurors that no adverse inference can be drawn from the failure of the accused to testify: *R. v. Boss* (1988), 46 C.C.C. (3d) 523, 68 C.R. (3d) 123 (Ont. C.A.).

Comment by counsel for the co-accused that the accused did not testify does not violate s. 11(*c*): *R. v. Naglik* (1991), 65 C.C.C. (3d) 272, 3 O.R. (3d) 385 (C.A.).

A person sued for contempt of court in a civil action cannot be compelled to testify against himself: *Vidéotron Ltée v. Industries Microlect Produits Électriques Inc.* (1990), 56 C.C.C. (3d) 436, 69 D.L.R. (4th) 519 (Que. C.A.).

Compelling a witness to testify against an accused does not violate para. (*c*), notwithstanding the witness is himself accused in a separate indictment of a related offence: *Re Crooks and the Queen* (1982), 2 C.C.C. (3d) 57, 143 D.L.R. (3d) 601 (Ont. H.C.J.), affd *loc. cit.* (C.A.).

However, in *R. v. Zurlo* (1990), 57 C.C.C. (3d) 407, 78 C.R. (3d) 167 (Que. C.A.), the court queried whether, in light of recent decisions of the Supreme Court of Canada, such as *Thomson Newspapers Ltd. v. Canada (Director of Investigation and Research, Restrictive Trade Practices Commission)*, [1990] 1 S.C.R. 425, 54 C.C.C. (3d) 417, a witness could now be compelled to testify at the preliminary inquiry of an accused charged in a separate information with the same offence as the witness, in view of the guarantees in ss. 7, 11 and 13 against self-incrimination.

The applicant commenced an action pursuant to s. 135 of the *Customs Act*, R.S.C. 1985, c. 1 (2nd Supp.), requesting a review of a demand for payment by a customs officer. The Minister of National Revenue filed a notice of motion under Rule 236 of the *Federal Courts Rules, 1998*, SOR/98-106, compelling the applicant to submit to an examination for discovery. This motion did not violate the applicant's rights under s. 11(*c*) because he was not a person charged with an offence. Although an examination for discovery amounts to compelling a person to be a witness, whether proceedings are criminal in nature is not concerned with the nature of the act that gave rise to the proceedings, but the nature of the proceedings themselves. The purpose of these proceedings was to determine the issue of forfeiture not to punish. Ascertaining forfeiture does not attempt to redress a wrong done to society, as it is an administrative measure intended to provide a timely and effective means of enforcing the *Customs Act*: *Martineau v. M.N.R.*, [2004] 3 S.C.R. 737, 192 C.C.C. (3d) 129.

Presumption of innocence [s. 11(*d*)] – At a minimum the right to be presumed innocent as guaranteed by s. 11(*d*) requires that the accused must be proven guilty beyond a reasonable doubt and that it is the state which must bear the burden of proof. The additional requirement in s. 11(*d*) that proof of guilt be "according to law in a fair and public hearing by an independent and impartial tribunal" requires that criminal prosecutions be carried out in accordance with lawful procedures and fairness. A statutory provision which requires an accused to disprove on a balance of probability the existence of a presumed fact, which is an important element of the offence in question violates s. 11(*d*): *R. v. Oakes*, [1986] 1 S.C.R. 103, 24 C.C.C. (3d) 321.

Any uncertainty as to whether reversal of the burden of proof of a defence, as opposed to an element of the offence, infringes the presumption of innocence appears to have been resolved as a result of two decisions in the Supreme Court of Canada: *R. v. Whyte*, [1988] 2 S.C.R. 3, 42 C.C.C. (3d) 97, and *R. v. Keegstra*, [1990] 3 S.C.R. 697, 61 C.C.C. (3d) 1. The combined effect of those two cases is that the distinction between elements of the offence and other aspects of the charge is irrelevant. The real concern is not whether the accused must disprove an element or prove an excuse, but that the accused may be convicted while a reasonable doubt exits. When that possibility exists then the presumption of innocence is infringed. Thus, in the latter case, it was held that s. 319(3)(*a*) of the *Criminal Code*, which requires the accused to prove as a defence to the charge of wilfully promoting hatred that the statements were true, infringes s. 11(*d*). The issue then must be whether the provision can be justified under s. 1. In *Keegstra*, the court held that the reverse onus was a reasonable limit. The objective behind the reverse onus was found to be closely connected with the purpose of the offence itself and if the defence were too easily used, the pressing and substantial objective of Parliament in preventing the harm from hate literature would suffer unduly. It was open to Parliament to use the reverse onus provision to strike a balance between the legitimate concerns of preventing the damage caused by hate literature and the importance of truth in freedom of expression values.

The presumption of innocence is infringed whenever the accused is liable to be convicted, despite the existence of a reasonable doubt and thus only if proof of the basic fact contained in a presumption leads inexorably to proof of the presumed fact will a statutory presumption not infringe this paragraph: *R. v. Downey*, [1992] 2 S.C.R. 10, 72 C.C.C. (3d) 1.

There is no general requirement that, for a reverse onus provision to pass the rational connection part of the s. 1 analysis, that provision be internally rational in the sense that there is a logical connection between the presumed fact and the fact substituted by the presumption. However, the lack of rational connection is a factor to be considered in applying the third stage of the test in *R. v. Oakes, supra*, namely the proportionality requirement: *R. v. Laba*, [1994] 3 S.C.R. 965, 94 C.C.C. (3d) 385.

In a proper case, rather than strike down a reverse onus provision entirely, it was open to the court to read the section down so as to merely place an evidentiary burden on the accused: *R. v. Laba, supra*.

Shifting the burden to the defendant charged with a regulatory offence to prove on a balance of probabilities that he acted with due diligence is a reasonable limit on the guarantee to the presumption of innocence: *R. v. Wholesale Travel Group Inc.*, [1991] 3 S.C.R. 154, 67 C.C.C. (3d) 193.

Provincial legislation which provides that an accused who does not appear in court at the time and place stated in a ticket may be convicted without a trial is valid. The penalties are limited to fines and cannot result in imprisonment. The waiver of the right to be presumed innocent and the right to a hearing may be inferred by the failure of the accused to act provided that he has been fully informed of the consequences and the legislation contains sufficient safeguards to prevent injustices: *R. v. Richard*, [1996] 3 S.C.R. 525, 110 C.C.C. (3d) 385.

The presumption of innocence applies at all stages of the criminal process and is a factor to be considered in considering whether the accused should be released on bail pending trial: *R. v. Lamothe* (1990), 58 C.C.C. (3d) 530, 77 C.R. (3d) 236 (Que. C.A.).

Right to fair hearing [s. 11(*d*)] – The right to a fair hearing does not require that the accused have a full opportunity to cross-examine every witness before the trier of fact. An accused would have a constitutional right to have evidence of prior testimony otherwise admissible under s. 715 of the *Criminal Code* excluded when it is obtained in the absence of a full opportunity to cross-examine the witness at the prior proceeding. The fact that the accused bears the burden of showing that he did not have an adequate opportunity to cross-examine does not infringe the presumption of innocence as guaranteed by s. 11(*d*): *R. v. Potvin*, [1989] 1 S.C.R. 525, 47 C.C.C. (3d) 289.

In considering whether any particular rule of criminal procedure infringes the right to a fair hearing, that rule must be considered in the context of the entire process. Thus while the jury selection procedure prescribed by the *Criminal Code* may in and of itself appear to be unfair or could possibly lead to unfairness, the jury selection process is just one step in the trial and the course of the trial is governed and affected by a large number of rules. It is only an individual rule that is so unfair that it will result in an unfair trial that will be struck down: *R. v. Stoddart* (1987), 37 C.C.C. (3d) 351, 59 C.R. (3d) 134 (Ont. C.A.).

While the Charter does not in express terms guarantee the accused a right to counsel at trial, such right can be inferred from the provisions of s. 11(*d*) and s. 7. The duty on a trial judge to ensure that an accused has a fair hearing will generally cast upon the judge an obligation to point out to the accused that he would be at a distinct disadvantage of proceeding without the assistance of competent counsel and that the accused is entitled to have such counsel: *R. v. McGibbon* (1988), 45 C.C.C. (3d) 334, 31 O.A.C. 10 (C.A.).

In *R. v. Vermette*, [1988] 1 S.C.R. 985, 41 C.C.C. (3d) 523, it was held that a decision by a superior court judge staying proceedings against an accused because of pre-trial publicity following statements by the premier in the National Assembly was premature. It was only at the stage when the jury is to be selected that it would be possible to determine whether the accused could be tried by an impartial jury. There is an initial presumption that a juror will perform his duties in accordance with his oath. In an extreme case pretrial publicity would lead to challenge for cause at the trial but it was not to be assumed that a person subjected to such publicity will necessarily be biased against the accused. Reckless remarks of politicians cannot frustrate the whole judicial process.

This paragraph does not require that a defence such as drunkenness be available for all offences. Thus, it was open to Parliament, in creating the offence of impaired driving, to preclude drunkenness as a defence. The accused's voluntary intoxication provides the guilty mind fundamental to the offence and unavailability of the drunkenness defence does not violate the right to make full answer and defence: *R. v. Penno*, [1990] 2 S.C.R. 865, 59 C.C.C. (3d) 344.

The right to make full answer and defence guaranteed by this paragraph and s. 7 includes the right of the accused to have before him the full case to meet before answering the Crown's case by adducing defence evidence. In addition, the accused has the right to defend himself against all of the state's efforts to achieve a conviction. The Crown is not entitled to engage in activities aimed at convicting an accused unless that accused is permitted to defend against those state acts. These rights do not, however, guarantee an accused the right to address the jury last: *R. v. Rose*, [1998] 3 S.C.R. 262, 129 C.C.C. (3d) 449.

Jury representativeness is captured by both s. 11(*d*) and (*f*) of the Charter, but it plays a different role in these two guarantees. The role of representativeness under s. 11(*d*) is limited to its effect on independence and impartiality. Section 11(*d*) will be violated if the process used to compile the jury roll raises an appearance of bias at the systemic level, even if the petit jury does not appear to be biased. This may occur in two ways: the deliberate exclusion of a particular group, or efforts in compiling the jury roll that are so deficient as to create an appearance of partiality. However, a jury roll containing few individuals of the accused's race or religion is not in itself indicative of bias: *R. v. Kokopenace*, [2015] 2 S.C.R. 398, 321 C.C.C. (3d) 153.

Trial by independent tribunal [s. 11(*d*)] – Generally speaking, where the alleged contemptuous language or actions are insulting and insolent it is preferable that any contempt proceedings be taken before a judge other than the judge to whom the remarks were addressed: *R. v. Martin* (1985), 19 C.C.C. (3d) 248 (Ont. C.A.).

Judicial independence involves both individual and institutional relationships. The individual independence of a judge is reflected in such matters as security of tenure, and the institutional independence of the court or tribunal over which he presides is reflected in its institutional or administrative relationship to the executive and legislative branches of government. The test for independence for the purposes of s. 11(*d*) is whether the tribunal may reasonably be perceived as independent. Both independence and impartiality are fundamental not only to the capacity to do justice in a particular case but also to individual and public confidence in the administration of justice. It is important that a tribunal should be perceived as independent and that the test for independence should include that perception. The perception must however be a perception of whether the tribunal enjoys the essential objective conditions or guarantees of judicial independence, not a perception of how it will in fact act, regardless of whether it enjoys such conditions or guarantees. The standard of judicial independence must necessarily be a standard that reflects what is common to, or at the heart of, various approaches to the essential conditions of judicial independence in Canada and need not be a standard of uniform provisions such as the standard embodied in the *Constitution Act, 1867* for superior court judges: *R. v. Valente*, [1985] 2 S.C.R. 673, 23 C.C.C. (3d) 193.

To meet the requirements of independence, a tribunal must meet three essential conditions, namely: security of tenure, financial security and institutional independence with respect to matters of administration that relate directly to the exercise of the tribunal's judicial function. With respect to this latter, it is unacceptable that an external force be in a position to interfere in matters which are directly and immediately relevant to the adjudicative function. The accused, in challenging the independence of the tribunal for the purposes of this section, need not prove an actual lack of independence. Rather, the test is whether an informed and reasonable person would perceive the tribunal as independent. The independence of a tribunal is to be determined on the basis of the objective status of that tribunal. This objective status is revealed by an examination of the legislative provisions governing the tribunal's constitutional proceedings, irrespective of the actual good faith of the adjudicator. Practice or tradition is not sufficient to support a finding of independence where the status of the tribunal itself does not support such a finding. While the Charter contemplates a separate system of military law, the system of General Court Martial in force at the time of the accused's trial infringed the principle of independence as guaranteed by this section and, in the absence of exceptional circumstances, could not be upheld as a reasonable limit. Recent amendments to the applicable legislation would, however, probably meet the requirements of this section: *R. v. Généreux*, [1992] 1 S.C.R. 259, 70 C.C.C. (3d) 1.

Trial by standing court martial violates the guarantee in this paragraph, at least where the offence is alleged to have been committed in Canada and in the absence of an emergency: *R. v. Ingebrigtson* (1990), 61 C.C.C. (3d) 541 (C.M.A.C.).

Judicial independence is not related solely to independence from government and includes independence from the parties to the litigation. Judicial independence is a safeguard for judicial impartiality. However, this provision does not prohibit the use of part-time judges who are also practicing lawyers where there are sufficient safeguards in place to ensure institutional impartiality. This provision guarantees that part-time judges will not engage in activities which are incompatible with their duties as a judge: *R. v. Lipp*, [1991] 2 S.C.R. 114, 64 C.C.C. (3d) 513.

CHARTER

Reasonable bail [s. 11(*e*)] – There is just cause to deny bail if two factors are present. The denial of bail must occur only in a narrow set of circumstances, and the denial of bail must be necessary to promote the proper functioning of the bail system and must not be undertaken for any purpose extraneous to the bail system: *R. v. Morales*, [1992] 3 S.C.R. 711, 77 C.C.C. (3d) 91; *R. v. Pearson*, [1992] 3 S.C.R. 665, 77 C.C.C. (3d) 124.

The list of grounds that may constitute "just cause" are not frozen, that is limited to the primary [attendance in court] and secondary [protection of the public] grounds for the denial of bail as set out in s. 515(10)(*a*) and (*b*) of the *Criminal Code*. Thus, it was open to Parliament to provide that bail could be refused where necessary to maintain confidence in the administration of criminal justice as set out in s. 515(10)(*c*): *R. v. Hall* (2000), 147 C.C.C. (3d) 279 (Ont. C.A.), affd [2002] 3 S.C.R. 309, 167 C.C.C. (3d) 449.

Right to trial by jury [s. 11(*f*)] – The intent of s. 11(*f*) is to guarantee an accused benefit of a jury trial where a jury trial is in fact, from the accused's perspective, a benefit but not to impose it on the accused when it is not. Implicit in this interpretation is the accused's right to waive a jury trial. Moreover, the accused has the right to waive the right to a jury trial notwithstanding that there may be a substantial pulic interest in a jury trial. In the case of individual constitutional rights an accused cannot be compelled to take advantage of rights intended for his benefit even if such rights may have a public interest aspect. An accused is entitled to weigh the benefit of the s. 11(*f*) right if it is in his interest to do so. However, waiver of a constitutional right such as s. 11(*f*) would not create a corresponding right to a trial by judge alone where there is no statutory framework for such trial. There is nothing in s. 11(*f*) to give the accused a constitutional right to elect their mode of trial or a constitutional right to be tried by judge alone so as to make s. 11(*f*) inconsistent with a provision of the *Criminal Code* mandating a jury trial: *R. v. Turpin*, [1989] 1 S.C.R. 1296, 48 C.C.C. (3d) 8.

A provision of the *Criminal Code* taking away the accused's right to a jury trial where he has failed to appear for court violates s. 11(*f*). It could not be said that by failing to attend court the accused was thereby waiving his right to a jury trial. While the right to a jury trial is a right capable of being waived the standard necessary to achieve such waiver is high. The waiver must be clear and unequivocal and the accused must be fully aware of the consequences of such waiver. Simply failing to show up for one's trial does not amount to an intentional repudiation of the right to a jury trial. However, the *Criminal Code* provision was a reasonable limit within the meaning of s. 1 and therefore valid: *R. v. Lee*, [1989] 2 S.C.R. 1384, 52 C.C.C. (3d) 289.

In *R. v. Ruston* (1991), 63 C.C.C. (3d) 419 (Man. C.A.), it was held that, to avoid a conflict with this paragraph, s. 561(1) of the *Criminal Code* must be interpreted so as to give the accused the right to re-elect trial by judge and jury within 15 says of learning of a substantial change in the Crown's case, even though the provision, read literally, requires the consent of the Crown to any re-election which is beyond 15 days following the completion of the preliminary inquiry.

In *P.P.G. Industries (Canada) Ltd. v. Canada (Attorney General)* (1983), 3 C.C.C. (3d) 97 (B.C.C.A.), it was held that a provision of the former *Combines Investigation Act* removing the right of a corporation to a jury trial did not infringe s. 11(*f*). That decision appears to have been proved in *R. v. Amway Corp.*, *supra*.

The requirement in the *Criminal Code* that an application to have an accused found to be a dangerous offender is to be tried by a judge alone does not infringe s. 11(*f*). The process by which an offender may be designated dangerous is simply part of the sentencing process and does not constitute the charging of an offence. The phrase "any person charged with an offence" in the opening words of s. 11 must be given a constant meaning that harmonizes with the various paragraphs of the section. It would be quite inappropriate to conclude that a convicted person is charged with an offence when confronted with a dangerous offender application: *R. v. Lyons*, [1987] 2 S.C.R. 309, 37 C.C.C. (3d) 1.

The "defence" of entrapment is an aspect of the abuse of process doctrine and is to be determined by the trial judge and not the jury. This procedure does not infringe s. 11(*f*) because the guilt or innocence of the accused is not in issue at the time the entrapment claim is to be decided. It is only if the jury finds that an accused committed the offence that the trial judge must then consider whether or not to enter a stay of proceedings on the basis of entrapment: *R. v. Mack*, [1988] 2 S.C.R. 903, 44 C.C.C. (3d) 513.

The right to a jury trial as guaranteed by this paragraph is not the right as envisaged at common law or at the time of Confederation, namely a jury composed of 12 men. Thus, s. 644(2) of the *Criminal Code*, which permits the trial judge to discharge up to two jurors, does not violate this paragraph: *R. v. Genest* (1990), 61 C.C.C. (3d) 251, [1990] R.J.Q. 2387 (C.A.).

The selection of a jury in a criminal case engages two rights guaranteed by this section. First, the guarantee in para. (*f*) to the benefit of trial by jury implies that the jury will be impartial and representative. Second, para. (*d*) explicitly guarantees the accused the right to be tried by an impartial tribunal. The right to an impartial jury, however, does not mean that an accused has the right to a favourable jury, nor that the selection procedure can be used to thwart the representativeness that is essential to the proper functioning of a jury: *R. v. Sherratt*, [1991] 1 S.C.R. 509, 63 C.C.C. (3d) 193.

Where the judge had directed the jury to return a verdict of guilty, the accused's right to a jury trial had been violated, notwithstanding the overwhelming nature of the case. Although the jury was not entitled to refuse to apply the law, they had the power to do so when their consciences permitted no other recourse: *R. v. Krieger*, [2006] 2 S.C.R. 501, 213 C.C.C. (3d) 303.

The role of representativeness in s. 11(*f*) is broader than under s. 11(*d*): it not only promotes impartiality, it also legitimizes the jury's role as the "conscience of the community" and promotes public trust in the criminal justice system. This broader role creates an important point of distinction: while a problem with representativeness will not necessarily violate s. 11(*d*), its absence will automatically undermine the s. 11(*f*) right to a trial by jury. If the state deliberately excludes a particular subset of the population that is eligible for jury service, it will violate an accused's right to a representative jury, regardless of the size of the group affected. However, if it is a question of unintentional exclusion, it is the quality of the state's efforts in compiling the jury roll that will determine whether an accused's right to a representative jury has been respected. If the state makes reasonable efforts but part of the population is excluded because it declines to participate, the state will nonetheless have met its constitutional obligation. An accused's representativeness right is not the appropriate mechanism for repairing the damaged relationship between particular societal groups and our criminal justice system more generally: *R. v. Kokopenace* (2015), 321 C.C.C. (3d) 153 (S.C.C.).

A potential penalty of five years less a day imprisonment plus a $5 million fine under the Alberta *Securities Act* does not engage the protection of s. 11(*f*) and entitle the accused to a jury trial: *R. v. Peers*, [2017] 1 S.C.R. 196, 346 C.C.C. (3d) 463, affg (2015), 330 C.C.C. (3d) 175 (Alta. C.A.).

Double jeopardy (section 11(*h*)) – Section 11(*h*) is directed at preventing the state from making repeated attempts to convict an individual. It forbids the prosecution of an accused twice for the same offence. In order for it to be operative however there must be two proceedings or trials for the same offence. In *R. v. Shubley*, [1990] 1 S.C.R. 3, 52 C.C.C. (3d) 481, it was held that there was no violation of s. 11(*h*) where the accused was charged with assault although he had previously been subject to prison disciplinary proceedings for the same act. The prison disciplinary proceedings to which the accused was subjected were neither by their very nature criminal proceedings or proceedings involving the imposition of true penal consequences and therefore the accused had not been previously found guilty or punished for an offence within the meaning of s. 11(*h*).

An offence comes within the purview of s. 11(*h*) if either the proceedings are, by their very nature, criminal proceedings or if the punishment invoked involves the imposition of true penal consequences. However, even where the two proceedings involve an offence within the meaning of this section it still must be determined whether or not the accused is being tried and punished for the same offence. In this case the accused R.C.M.P. officer had been convicted of a major service offence under the *Royal Canadian Mounted Police Act* as a result of an alleged assault of a prisoner in his custody. The penalty for such an offence is imprisonment for up to one year and it therefore was an offence involving a true penal consequence thus attracting the application of s. 11. However, the accused was not being tried and punished for the same offence when he was charged with assault in the criminal courts. The offences were quite different. One was an internal disciplinary matter. The accused had been found guilty of a major service offence and therefore accounted to his profession. The other offence is the criminal offence of assault. The accused must now account to society at large for his conduct. He cannot complain as a member of a special group of individuals subject to private internal discipline, that he ought not to account to society for his wrongdoing. His conduct has a double aspect as a member of the R.C.M.P. and as a member of the public at large. The two offences were two different matters totally separate one from the other and were alternative one to the other. While there was only one act of assault there were two distinct delicts, causes or matters which would sustain separate convictions: *R. v. Wigglesworth*, [1987] 2 S.C.R. 541, 37 C.C.C. (3d) 385.

Similarly the accused, a former RCMP officer could not rely on s. 11(*h*) on the basis of acquittals in the United States of charges arising out of disclosure of confidential information gained when he was involved in a joint investigation with United States officials. The U.S. charges and the Canadian charges, also based on the disclosure, were different because they were based on duties of a different nature. The accused's conduct had a double aspect: first, wrongdoing as a Canadian official with a special duty to the Canadian public and second, wrongdoing as an American official temporarily subject to American law. The accused must now account for his conduct to the Canadian public: *R. v. Van Rassel*, [1990] 1 S.C.R. 225, 53 C.C.C. (3d) 353.

Section 11(*h*) does not preclude the Crown's right to appeal against an acquittal in indictable matters on a question of law alone as provided in the *Criminal Code*. The word "finally" in this paragraph must be construed to mean after the appellate procedures have been completed: *R. v. Morgentaler, Smoling and Scott*, [1988] 1 S.C.R. 30, 37 C.C.C. (3d) 449.

However, a provision of the *Summary Convictions Act* (Quebec) giving the Crown a right of appeal by way of trial *de novo* without the requirement of allegation of any error on the part of the trial judge does offend s. 11(*h*) and is of no force and effect. The appeal authorized by the Act does not depend on the party appealing having any ground of appeal, it being sufficient if he thinks himself aggrieved by the decision of the trial judge. The hearing takes the form of a trial, the prosecution being entitled to adduce evidence whether or not it was adduced at the first trial. While an accused has not been finally acquitted within the meaning of s. 11(*h*) until all appeals provided for by law have been exhausted, where the appeal is based on an error by the trial judge, since in such a case there is no real acquittal if the decision rendered was as a result of an error, an appeal by way of *de novo* is merely a new trial disguised as an appeal. This is precisely the type of abuse that s. 11(*h*) was sought to prevent. Further, the accused is entitled to rely on s. 11(*h*) although the original trial took place prior to proclamation of the Charter: *Corporation Professionnele des Médicins du Québec v. Thibault*, [1988] 1 S.C.R. 1033, 42 C.C.C. (3d) 1.

This section has no application to extradition proceedings. The right protected by s. 11(*h*) is the right of a person charged with an offence not to be tried for the offence again if he has already been finally acquitted of the offence. An extradition, however, is not a trial, but simply a hearing similar to a preliminary hearing to determine whether there is sufficient evidence to an alleged extradition crime to warrant the government under its treaty obligations to surrender a fugitive to the demanding state for trial in that state. It may be however that some of the interests protected by s. 11 are protected under other Charter provisions such as s. 7: *R. v. Schmidt*, [1987] 1 S.C.R. 500, 33 C.C.C. (3d) 193.

The retrospective abolition of early parole was found to violate s. 11(*h*). When considering an alleged infringement of s. 11(*h*), the dominant consideration should be the extent to which an offender's expectation of liberty has been thwarted by retrospective legislative action. It is the retrospective frustration of an expectation of liberty that constitutes punishment. Here, the effect of the change was to deprive the claimants of the possibility of being considered for early day parole and to extend their minimum period of incarceration. In this way, it had the effect of punishing them again. The infringement cannot be saved under s. 1: *Canada (Attorney General) v. Whaling*, [2014] 1 S.C.R. 392, 309 C.C.C. (3d) 129.

Where the accused faced regulatory proceedings before the provincial securities commission arising out of her operation of a Ponzi scheme, the right against double jeopardy was not violated by her subsequent criminal prosecution. The penalty imposed by the commission — a disgorgement order and a monetary penalty — was not a true penal consequence: *R. v. Samji* (2017), 357 C.C.C. (3d) 436 (B.C.C.A.), leave to appeal to S.C.C. refused 2018 CarswellBC 1388.

Benefit of lesser punishment [s. 11(*i*)] – This paragraph enshrines the fundamental notion that criminal laws should generally not operate retrospectively. A measure constitutes "punishment" for the purposes of this guarantee if: (1) it is a consequence of conviction that forms part of the arsenal of sanctions to which an accused may be liable in respect of a particular offence; and either (2) it is imposed in furtherance of the purpose and principles of sentencing, or (3) it has a significant impact on an offender's liberty or security interests. To satisfy the third branch of this test, a consequence of conviction must significantly constrain a person's ability to engage in otherwise lawful conduct or impose significant burdens not imposed on other members of the public: *R. v. J. (K.R.)*, [2016] 1 S.C.R. 906, 337 C.C.C. (3d) 285.

The guarantee in this paragraph does not apply to a change in punishment after imposition of sentence but while appellate proceedings are pending: *R. v. Luke* (1994), 87 C.C.C. (3d) 121, 28 C.R. (4th) 93 (Ont. C.A.), leave to appeal to S.C.C. refused 92 C.C.C. (3d) vi, 23 C.R.R. (2d) 384*n*. However, under s. 44(*e*) of the *Interpretation Act*, R.S.C. 1985, c. I-21, an accused is entitled to the benefit of lesser penalty or punishment as a result of amendments which are proclaimed in force following sentence but before the appeal has been decided by the court of appeal: *R. v. Dunn*, [1995] 1 S.C.R. 226, 95 C.C.C. (3d) 289.

"Punishment" as used in this section refers to the punishment fixed by Parliament rather than any range of sentences that may emerge in court decisions within the controlling statutory provisions: *R. v. D. (R.)* (1996), 48 C.R. (4th) 90, 144 Sask. R. 21 (C.A.).

The *Abolition of Early Parole Act*, S.C. 2011, c. 11, was held to violate s. 11(*i*) to the extent it applied to an offender who committed his or her offence before the Act came into effect. The retrospective application of more restrictive parole eligibility rules constitutes punishment. At the time of the offence, the law permitted offenders the benefit of the accelerated parole review system. At the time of sentencing, the system was no longer available. Accordingly, the punishment for the offence had been varied between the time of commission and the time of sentencing, so the offender was constitutionally entitled to the benefit of the lesser punishment, including accelerated parole review: *Liang v. Canada (Attorney General)* (2014), 311 C.C.C. (3d) 159 (B.C.C.A.), leave to appeal to S.C.C. refused 2015 CarswellBC 178; *Canada (Attorney General) v. Lewis* (2015), 323 C.C.C. (3d) 504 (Ont. C.A.), leave to appeal to S.C.C. refused (2016), [2015] S.C.C.A. No. 325.

Where the time period specified in the indictment straddles a change in the law, the court must determine when the crime was "committed" for the purposes of s. 11(*i*). The continuing nature of the offence has no impact on the determination of the time at which liability attaches. If a person engages in the requisite conduct with the specified *mens rea*, the offence has been committed and the protection of s. 11(*i*) attaches as of that point: *Canada (Attorney General) v. Lalonde* (2016), 343 C.C.C. (3d) 423 (Ont. C.A.).

The accused is entitled to the benefit of the least severe sentence regime available during the period between the offence and sentencing, even if there has been only a temporary softening of the sentencing regime between those two dates. Thus, an offender was eligible for a conditional sentence even though conditional sentences did not exist when the offence was committed and were removed as a sentencing option for the offence in question before the accused was sentenced: *R. v. Cadman* (2018), 359 C.C.C. (3d) 427 (B.C.C.A.).

Because it mitigates the harshness of a sentence for murder, the faint hope provisions are an integral element of the sentence itself, subject to scrutiny under this provision. The legislative decision to introduce a judicial screening mechanism as a precondition for a full review increased the punishment for first degree murder because it curtailed the offender's direct access to a jury to ask for clemency. However, the infringement was justified under s. 1 as it was a reasonable way of minimizing the needless re-victimization of victims' families: *R. v. Simmonds* (2018), 362 C.C.C. (3d) 215 (B.C.C.A.). By contrast, in *R. v. Dell* (2018), 364 C.C.C. (3d) 419 (Ont. C.A.), the court held that the infringement caused by the 2011 amendments to the provisions — which imposed a "substantial likelihood" of success threshold at the screening stage — could not be justified under s. 1.

TREATMENT OR PUNISHMENT.

12. Everyone has the right not to be subjected to any cruel and unusual treatment or punishment.

ANNOTATIONS

The criterion which must be applied in order to determine whether a punishment is cruel and unusual is whether the punishment prescribed is so excessive as to outrage standards of decency. The effect of the punishment must not be grossly disproportionate to what would be appropriate. The section is aimed at punishments that are more than merely excessive and are grossly disproportionate. The determination of whether the punishment is necessary to achieve a valid penal purpose, whether it is founded on recognized sentencing principles, and whether there exist valid alternatives to the punishment imposed are all guidelines which without being determinative in themselves help to assess whether the punishment is grossly disproportionate: *R. v. Smith*, [1987] 1 S.C.R. 1045, 34 C.C.C. (3d) 97.

The imposition of indeterminate detention in a penitentiary following a finding under the *Criminal Code* that the accused is a dangerous offender does not violate this section. This section is concerned with the relation between the effects of and reasons for punishment. The

CHARTER

effects of the punishment are to be balanced against the particular circumstances of the offence, the characteristics of the offender and the particular purposes sought to be accomplished in sentencing that person in the manner challenged. If in light of those considerations the punishment is found to be grossly disproportionate, a remedy must be afforded to the accused in the absence of justification under s. 1. However, the dangerous offender provisions apply only to persons convicted of serious personal injury offences, and before the accused can be found to be a dangerous offender it must be established to the satisfaction of the court that the offence for which the accused has been convicted is not an isolated occurrence but part of a pattern of behaviour which has involved violence, aggressive or brutal conduct or failure to control sexual impulses. As well, it must be established that the pattern is very likely to continue. Even then the court has a discretion not to designate the offender as dangerous or to impose an indeterminate sentence. The legislation therefore meets the highest standard of rationality and proportionality that society could reasonably expect of Parliament. Finally, while if the sentence imposed was indeterminate *simpliciter* it could result in sentences grossly disproportionate to what individual offenders deserved, the availability of parole saves the legislation from being successfully challenged under s. 12 as it ensures that incarceration is imposed for only as long as the circumstances of the individual case require: *R. v. Lyons*, [1987] 2 S.C.R. 309, 37 C.C.C. (3d) 1.

However, an indeterminate sentence, which may have been appropriate when it was imposed, may lead to a violation of this section. It is only by a careful consideration and application of the criteria set out in s. 16(1)(*a*) of the *Parole Act* that the indeterminate sentence can be made to fit the circumstances of the individual offender and not violate his rights under this section. If it is clear on the face of the record that the parole board has misapplied or disregarded those criteria over a period of years with the result that an offender remains incarcerated far beyond the time that he should have been properly paroled, resulting in a length of incarceration which is grossly disproportionate to the circumstances of the offence, then the board's decision may violate s. 12: *Steele v. Mountain Institution*, [1990] 2 S.C.R. 1385, 60 C.C.C. (3d) 1.

Confinement of an inmate in administrative or protective segregation at a federal penitentiary is not *per se* cruel and unusual treatment. On the other hand it may become so if it is so excessive as to outrage standards of decency: *R. v. Olson* (1987), 38 C.C.C. (3d) 534 (Ont. C.A.), affd [1989] 1 S.C.R. 296, 47 C.C.C. (3d) 491.

The provisions of the *Criminal Code* which provide for a minimum sentence of life imprisonment without eligibility for parole for certain types of murders, in particular murder while committing an offence such as kidnapping, do not violate this section. The punishment is not excessive and clearly does not outrage our standards of decency. It is within the purview of Parliament, in order to meet the objectives of a rational system of sentencing, to treat the most serious crime with an appropriate degree of certainty and severity. Moreover, even in such a case, Parliament has been sensitive to the particular circumstances of each offender by providing various mechanisms for earlier parole: *R. v. Luxton*, [1990] 2 S.C.R. 711, 58 C.C.C. (3d) 449 (7:0).

There are two aspects to the analysis of alleged invalidity of a statutory minimum penalty. The first aspect involves the assessment of the challenged penalty from the perspective of the person actually subjected to it, balancing the gravity of the offence itself with the particular circumstances of the offence and the personal characteristics of the offender. If it is found that the challenged provision provides for or would actually impose on the offender, a sanction so excessive or grossly disproportionate as to outrage decency in those real and particular circumstances, then it will amount to a *prima facie* violation of this section and must be justified under s. 1. Even if the particular facts do not warrant a finding of gross disproportionality then the court must also consider reasonable hypothetical circumstances to determine whether the provision will authorize the imposition of cruel or unusual punishment: *R. v. Goltz*, [1991] 3 S.C.R. 485, 67 C.C.C. (3d) 481.

A constitutional exemption is not an appropriate remedy for an unconstitutional mandatory minimum sentence. If a minimum sentence is found to be unconstitutional on the facts of a particular case, the law imposing the sentence is inconsistent with the Charter and, therefore, must be declared of no force and effect pursuant to s. 52 of the *Constitution Act, 1982*: *R. v. Ferguson*, [2008] 1 S.C.R. 96, 228 C.C.C. (3d) 385.

This section was of no application to the decision of the Minister to extradite a fugitive to the United States where the fugitive faced the death penalty. The decision to surrender a fugitive does not constitute the imposition of cruel and unusual punishment by a Canadian government. The fugitive may, however, be entitled to rely upon s. 7: *Kindler v. Canada (Minister of Justice)*, [1991] 2 S.C.R. 779, 67 C.C.C. (3d) 1.

In *R. v. Nur*, [2015] S.C.J. No. 15, the Supreme Court of Canada retained the same basic approach, albeit speaking in terms of "reasonably foreseeable cases" in lieu of "reasonable hypotheticals". The court held that, when a mandatory minimum sentencing provision is challenged under s. 12, two questions arise. The first is whether the provision imposes cruel and unusual punishment (*i.e.* a grossly disproportionate sentence) on the particular individual before the court. If the answer is no, the second question is whether the provision's reasonably foreseeable applications would impose cruel and unusual punishment on other offenders. Where mandatory minimum sentencing laws are challenged under s. 12 on the basis of their reasonably foreseeable application to others, the question is what situations may reasonably arise, not whether such situations are likely to arise in the general day-to-day application of the law. Only situations that are remote or far-fetched are excluded. In this case, the three-year mandatory minimum for possession of a loaded prohibited or restricted firearm was held to be grossly disproportionate as applied to reasonably foreseeable cases. The provision casts its net over a wide range of potential conduct, including conduct that resembles a licensing infraction more than a true crime. In this way, the provision foreseeably catches offences that involve little moral fault or danger to the public, rendering the three-year minimum grossly disproportionate. Finally, the majority held that the Crown's ability to proceed summarily and thereby avoid the mandatory minimum did not cure the constitutional defect.

In *R. v. Lloyd*, [2016] 1 S.C.R. 130, 334 C.C.C. (3d) 20, the court made clear that mandatory minimum sentences — at least those for offences that can be committed in various ways, under a broad array of circumstances and by a wide range of people — are constitutionally vulnerable. This is because such provisions will almost inevitably include an acceptable reasonable hypothetical for which the mandatory minimum will be found unconstitutional. The court observed that, if Parliament hopes to maintain mandatory minimum sentences for offences that cast a wide net, it should consider narrowing their reach so that they only catch offenders that merit that mandatory minimum sentence. In the alternative, Parliament could provide for judicial discretion to allow for a lesser sentence where the mandatory minimum would be grossly disproportionate and would constitute cruel and unusual punishment.

The mandatory imposition of a victim fine surcharge on all convicted persons infringes this guarantee and is not saved by s. 1 because its impact and effects create circumstances that are grossly disproportionate to what would otherwise be a fit sentence. The mandatory surcharge imposes deeply disproportionate financial consequences on impecunious offenders unrelated to their moral culpability, creating a *de facto* indeterminate sentence for those who will never be able to pay: *R. v. Boudreault*, 2018 SCC 58.

SELF-CRIMINATION.

13. A witness who testifies in any proceedings has the right not to have any incriminating evidence so given used to incriminate that witness in any other proceedings, except in a prosecution for perjury or for the giving of contradictory evidence.

ANNOTATIONS

A retrial of the same offence or one included therein ordered by a Court of Appeal is an "other proceeding" within the meaning of this section. The purpose of this section when viewed in the context of s. 11(*c*) and (*d*) is to protect the individuals from being indirectly compelled to incriminate themselves, to ensure that the Crown will not be able to do indirectly what s. 11(*c*) prohibits. Further, the right guaranteed by this section inures to an individual at the moment an attempt is made to utilize previous testimony to incriminate him. Therefore, the time at which the previous testimony was given is irrelevant for the purpose of determining who may claim benefit of this section and thus the section would apply notwithstanding that previous testimony had been given prior to proclamation of the Charter. This section unlike s. 5(2) of the *Canada Evidence Act* does not require any objection on the part of the person giving the testimony, nor does it refer to any compulsion to answer and accordingly would apply to a voluntary witness such as an accused at his own trial. The testimony in question need not have been incriminating at the first proceedings. Rather, the use which the Crown seeks to make of the evidence can only be ascertained at the time of the second proceeding and any evidence the Crown tenders as part of its case against the accused is, for the purpose of s. 13, incriminating. Thus an attempt by the Crown to introduce as part of its case in chief the accused's testimony at the first trial would constitute an incriminating use within the meaning of this section: *R. v. Dubois*, [1985] 2 S.C.R. 350, 22 C.C.C. (3d) 513.

This section does not prevent cross-examination of an accused on testimony given in another proceeding, where the purpose of the cross-examination is to impeach the accused's credibility and not to incriminate him. In such a case, however, the previous statement may not be used to establish the truth of its contents and the trial judge must so instruct the jury: *R. v. Kuldip*, [1990] 3 S.C.R. 618, 61 C.C.C. (3d) 385 (4:3).

Kuldip, *supra*, however, should now be considered in light of *R. v. Henry* (2005), 202 C.C.C. (3d) 449, 33 C.R. (6th) 215 (S.C.C.). In *Henry*, the court held that, where a witness was compelled to give evidence and was exposed to the risk of self-incrimination, s. 13 offers protection against the subsequent use of that testimony. Furthermore, where the accused testified at a first trial and a retrial is ordered, the accused may choose not to testify and the Crown cannot simply file the testimony of the accused given at the prior trial. This section does not protect an accused, however, who voluntarily testifies at the first trial and then volunteers inconsistent testimony at the retrial on the same charge. The Crown is fully entitled to cross-examine the accused on the testimony given at the first trial. In addition, if the contradiction reasonably gives rise to an inference of guilt, s. 13 does not preclude the trier of fact from drawing that inference. In addition, as per *R. v. Noël*, *infra*, prior compelled evidence should, under s. 13 and s. 5(2) of the *Canada Evidence Act*, be inadmissible against the accused, even for the purpose of challenging his or her credibility, except in a prosecution for perjury or the giving of contradictory evidence.

In *R. v. Noël*, [2002] 3 S.C.R. 433, 168 C.C.C. (3d) 193, the Supreme Court of Canada considered the scope of both s. 13 of the Charter and s. 5 of the *Canada Evidence Act*. The accused had testified at the preliminary hearing and trial of his brother charged with the same murder and implicated himself. At his own trial, he claimed that he had lied at the previous trial and denied any involvement in the murder. The Crown was precluded from using his evidence at the prior trial for the purpose of cross-examination. Section 13 applies without any requirement that the protection be sought by the witness whereas s. 5 of the *Canada Evidence Act* must be specifically sought. Section 13 protects an accused from the incriminating use of prior evidence. The distinction between credibility-based cross-examination and incriminatory cross-examination disappears when the two purposes are intermingled and the prohibited use is of much greater value to the Crown and irresistible to the jury. Cross-examination can be permitted only when the subsequent use does not incriminate the accused. When the prior evidence was incriminating when it was given, its subsequent use must be totally prohibited even if it is tendered for the limited purpose of testing credibility unless there is no realistic danger of incrimination. If the prior testimony was innocuous, in that it was not incriminatory, it may be used to challenge credibility at another proceeding. Section 5 of the *Canada Evidence Act* can only be invoked in relation to questions thought to be truly incriminating and not in relation to all types of questions. The determination of whether a question is incriminating is not made at the point in time when the testimony is given but rather at the subsequent proceeding when it is tendered.

This section is violated by testimony of a police officer that he was able to identify the accused as a result of hearing him testify in another proceeding: *R. v. Skinner* (1988), 42 C.C.C. (3d) 575 (Ont. C.A.). See also *R. v. Sicurella* (1997), 120 C.C.C. (3d) 403, 47 C.R.R. (2d) 317 (Ont. Ct. (Prov. Div.)).

Evidence given by the accused on discovery at a prior civil trial, while "compelled", was not inadmissible for impeachment purposes at his criminal trial because it was not "incriminating". Section 13 is not directed to "any evidence" the witness may have been compelled to give at the prior proceeding, but to incriminating evidence. Incriminating evidence is evidence given by the witness at the prior proceeding that the Crown could use at the subsequent proceeding, if it were permitted to do so, to prove guilt, *i.e.* to prove or assist in proving one or more of the essential elements of the offence for which the witness is being tried. Where the evidence given by the witness at the prior proceeding could not be used by the Crown at the subsequent proceeding to prove the witness's guilt on the charge for which he or she is being tried, the prior evidence is not "incriminating evidence". Here, it was not incriminating evidence because the accused in his discovery evidence claimed to have no memory of the events at issue. Section 13 therefore did not bar its admission: *R. v. Nedelcu* (2012), 290 C.C.C. (3d) 153 (S.C.C.) (6:3).

Section 13 provides no protection against a charge of attempted obstruction of justice based on courtroom testimony where the testimony itself was the *actus reus* of the offence: *R. v. Schertzer* (2015), 325 C.C.C. (3d) 202 (Ont. C.A.), leave to appeal to S.C.C. refused 2015 CarswellOnt 16493.

A *voir dire* is another proceeding and thus the accused's testimony on the *voir dire* is protected from use by the Crown during the trial proper: *R. v. Tarafa* (1989), 53 C.C.C. (3d) 472, [1990] R.J.Q. 427 (S.C.).

This section does not apply so as to prevent the use, at disciplinary proceedings taken against a nurse, of her testimony at her own criminal trial on a charge of theft: *Knutson v. Sask. Registered Nurses' Assn.*, [1991] 2 W.W.R. 327, 75 D.L.R. (4th) 723 (Sask. C.A.).

This section does not fully define the scope of evidentiary immunity provided to a witness compelled to testify in criminal proceedings against a separately charged co-accused. Section 7 of the Charter provides additional protection to the witness. Thus, derivative evidence which could not have been obtained, or the significance of which could not have been appreciated, but for the testimony of the witness ought generally to be excluded under s. 7 of the Charter at the witness' subsequent trial since its admission would tend to affect the fairness of the trial: *R. v. S. (R.J.)*, [1995] 1 S.C.R. 451, 96 C.C.C. (3d) 1.

A witness's knowledge of immunity from the use of testimony to incriminate them is rarely relevant to credibility. Inquiries into a witness's knowledge of this provision may deflect the jury's attention away from the real issues and may impinge upon confidential solicitor-client communications. Without further evidence of a motive for falsely testifying, a witness's knowledge of s. 13 standing alone does not constitute a motive to lie and cannot affect the witness's credibility: *R. v. Jabarianha*, [2001] 3 S.C.R. 430, 159 C.C.C. (3d) 1.

INTERPRETER.

14. A party or witness in any proceedings who does not understand or speak the language in which the proceedings are conducted or who is deaf has the right to the assistance of an interpreter.

ANNOTATIONS

As a general rule, courts should appoint an interpreter when it becomes apparent to the judge that an accused is, for language reasons, having difficulty expressing himself or understanding the proceedings and that the assistance of an interpreter would be helpful; or the accused or counsel for the accused requests the services of an interpreter and the judge is of the opinion that the request is justified. There is, however, no requirement that the courts inform all accused appearing before them of the existence of the right to interpreter assistance. Where the accused at trial claims the Charter right to an interpreter, assistance should not be denied unless there is cogent and compelling evidence that the accused's request is not made in good faith but rather for an oblique motive. The quality of interpretation must be high under this section but the standard is not one of perfection. The interpretation of the proceedings should be continuous and precise. Summaries of the testimony are unlikely to meet the general standard of interpretation required. The interpretation must be objective and unbiased, although this standard may have to be relaxed where the urgency of the situtation may require the use of a person as interpreter who is closely connected to the events. The interpretation must be of a high enough quality to ensure that justice is done and seen to be done. This means that, at minimum, the accused has a right to competent interpretation. An interpreter must at least be sworn by taking the interpreter's oath before beginning to interpret the proceedings. The interpretation must take place contemporaneously with the proceeding in question. In court proceedings, this will usually mean that the interpretation be consecutive (after the words are spoken) rather than simultaneous (at the same time as the words are spoken): *R. v. Tran*, [1994] 2 S.C.R. 951, 92 C.C.C. (3d) 218.

It is not every deficiency from the protected standard of interpretation which will constitute a violation of this section. The accused must establish that the lapse in interpretation which occurred was in respect of the proceedings themselves, thereby involving the vital interests of the accused, and was not merely in respect of some collateral or extrinsic matter, such as an administrative issue relating to scheduling. In determining whether the alleged deviation in interpretation was part of an occurrence which actually served in some way to advance the case and thus involved the accused's vital interests, the court will consider whether there was an unfolding or development in the proceeding with respect to a point of evidence and/or law. The court is not looking to the effect of the occurence in question. Since the right to interpreter assistance is not only a fundamental constitutional guarantee in its own right but also an important means of ensuring a full, fair public hearing as protected under ss. 7 and 11(*d*), it will be more difficult to waive s. 14 Charter rights than may have been the case under the common law and under statutory enactments. In fact, there will be situations where the rights simply cannot, in the greater public interest, be waived. Where waiver of the right to interpreter assistance is possible, the threshold will be very high. The waiver must be clear and unequivocal and must be done with full knowledge of the rights the procedure was enacted to protect and the effect that the waiver will have on those rights. The waiver should be made personally by the accused, if necessary following an inquiry by the court through an interpreter to ensure that the accused truly understands what he is doing, unless counsel for the accused is fluent in the accused's language or has communicated with the accused through an interpreter before coming to court and satisfies the court that the nature of the right and the effect on the right of waiving it has been explained to the accused: *R. v. Tran*, [1994] 2 S.C.R. 951, 92 C.C.C. (3d) 218.

The accused's rights under this section are not violated merely because the interpreter lacked formal training: *R. v. R. (A.L.)* (1999), 141 C.C.C. (3d) 151 (Man. C.A.). Similarly, in *R. v. Rybak* (2008), 233 C.C.C. (3d) 58, the Ontario Court of Appeal held that neither the presence nor absence of formal accreditation is dispositive of the issue of the competence of the interpreter (leave to appeal to S.C.C. refused 237 C.C.C. (3d) vi).

The lack of an interpreter for the purpose of communicating with counsel does not implicate this provision although it may constitute an aspect of the right to counsel, right to a fair trial or the right to make full answer and defence: *R. v. R. (A.L.)*, *supra*.

Where there were serious problems with the adequacy of interpretation during the testimony of a defence witness, ordering the witness's testimony be re-done rather than directing a stay or a mistrial was an appropriate and just remedy in the circumstances: *R. v. Gill* (2017), 356 C.C.C. (3d) 103 (Sask. C.A.).

The right to an interpreter under this provision entails a right to be understood by the court. The failure of the defence to request an interpreter is not determinative. Where the trial transcript was replete with indications that the trial judge and counsel could not comprehend the accused's testimony, a breach of s. 14 was established: *R. v. Mitroi* (2018), 362 C.C.C. (3d) 374 (B.C.C.A.).

Equality Rights

EQUALITY BEFORE AND UNDER LAW AND EQUAL PROTECTION AND BENEFIT OF LAW / Affirmative action programs.

15. (1) Every individual is equal before and under the law and has the right to the equal protection and equal benefit of the law without discrimination and, in particular, without discrimination based on race, national or ethnic origin, colour, religion, sex, age or mental or physical disability.

(2) Subsection (1) does not preclude any law, program or activity that has as its object the amelioration of conditions of disadvantaged individuals or groups including those that are disadvantaged because of race, national or ethnic origin, colour, religion, sex, age or mental or physical disability.

Note: By s. 32(2) of the *Constitution Act, 1982*, the above section came into force April 17, 1985.

CHARTER

ANNOTATIONS

Section 15(1) is not a general guarantee of equality; it does not provide for equality between individuals or groups within society in a general or abstract sense, and does not impose on individuals or groups an obligation to accord equal treatment to others. It is concerned with the application of the law. The ideal embodied in the section is that a law expressed to bind all should not, because of irrelevant personal differences, have a more burdensome or less beneficial impact on one than another. It is not every distinction or differentiation in treatment at law which will violate the equality guarantee. In order to govern effectively legislatures must treat different individuals and groups in different ways. To achieve true equality it will frequently be necessary to make distinctions. This section spells out four basic rights which apply to all persons whether citizens or not: the right to equality before the law, the right to equality under the law, the right to equal protection of the law and the right to equal benefit of the law. Its purpose is to ensure equality in the formulation and application of the law and the right to equal benefit of the law. All these four rights are granted with the direction that they be without discrimination. Discrimination exists where a distinction, whether intentional or not but based on grounds relating to personal characteristics of the individual group, has the effect of imposing burdens, obligations or disadvantages not imposed upon others, or withholding or limiting access to opportunities, benefits and advantages available to other members of society. Discrimination under this section is limited to discrimination caused by the application or operation of law. The grounds of discrimination enumerated in this section are not exclusive and both they and other possible grounds of discrimination recognized under this section must be interpreted in a broad and generous manner. At a minimum s. 15(1) extends to grounds of discrimination analogous to the enumerated grounds: *Andrews v. Law Society of British Columbia*, [1989] 1 S.C.R. 21.

Equality before the law at a minimum requires that no individual or group of individuals be treated more harshly than another under that law. However, there will only be a violation of s. 15 if the infringement of a right to equality before the law results in discrimination. Discrimination is a distinction based on grounds relating to personal characteristics of the individual or group which has the effect of imposing burdens, obligations or disadvantages on such individual or group not imposed on others. Finding that discrimination exists will in most cases necessarily entail a search for a disadvantage that exists apart from and independent of the particular legal distinction being challenged. Thus, victims of discrimination will often be members of a discrete and insular minority who come within the protection of s. 15. Provisions of the *Criminal Code* which formerly give only residents of Alberta the right to elect trial by judge alone on serious offences such as murder do not violate s. 15. It could not be said that persons resident outside Alberta are members of a discrete and insular minority. There is none of the usual indicia of discrimination such as stereotyping, historical disadvantage or vulnerability to political and social prejudice. While it may be that a person's province of residence or place of trial could in some circumstances be a personal characteristic of the individual or group capable of constituting a ground of discrimination, that was not the case with respect to this *Criminal Code* provision and it is not a fundamental principle under s. 15 that the criminal law apply equally throughout the country: *R. v. Turpin*, [1989] 1 S.C.R. 1296, 48 C.C.C. (3d) 8.

In *Law v. Canada (Minister of Employment and Immigration)*, [1999] 1 S.C.R. 497, Iacobucci J., speaking for the court, set out certain guidelines for analysis under this section. Among other things, he held that a court called upon to determine discrimination under subsec. (1) should make the following three broad inquiries: (1) Does the impugned law draw a distinction between the claimant and others on the basis of one or more personal characteristics, or fail to take into account the claimant's already disadvantaged position resulting in substantively differential treatment on the basis of one or more personal characteristics? (2) Is the claimant subject to differential treatment based on one or more enumerated and analogous grounds? (3) Does the differential treatment discriminate by imposing a burden upon or withholding a benefit from the claimant in a manner that reflects the stereotypical application of presumed group or personal characteristics, or that otherwise has the effect of perpetuating or promoting the view that the individual is less capable or worthy of recognition or value as a human being or as a member of Canadian society, equally deserving of concern, respect, and consideration? The existence of a conflict between the purpose or effect of an impugned law and the purpose of subsec. (1) is essential to found a discrimination claim. The purpose of subsec. (1) is to prevent the violation of essential human dignity and freedom through the imposition of disadvantage, stereotyping, or political or social prejudice, and to promote a society in which all individuals enjoy equal recognition at law, equally capable and equally deserving of concern, respect and consideration. Since the guarantee under this section is a comparative concept, the court must establish one or more relevant comparators.

Merely because a statutory provision addresses a group that is defined by reference to a characteristic, such as sex, that is enumerated in subsec. (1) does not automatically lead to an infringement of this section. There must also be a denial of an equality right that results in discrimination. In the context of the criminal law, a distinction based on sex may legitimately be made where, as a matter of biological fact, the offence can be committed by one sex only. Such an offence was former s. 146(1) of the *Criminal Code* which made it an offence to have sexual intercourse with a girl under the age of 14 years. In view of the *Criminal Code* definitions, it was clear that only males over 14 years are capable of committing the offence. Whether or not a female who commits a similar offence with a young male should be subject to the same societal disapprobation is a matter for Parliament, not the courts: *R. v. Nguyen*, [1990] 2 S.C.R. 906, 59 C.C.C. (3d) 161 (5:2).

The failure of the provincial Attorney General to implement a programme of alternative measures is not "the law" for the purposes of a challenge under this section, and thus a challenge under s. 15 to the exercise of that discretion given the Attorney General by the legislation [the [former] *Young Offenders Act*, s. 4] must fail. The non-exercise of discretion cannot be constitutionally attacked simply because it creates differences as between provinces. To find otherwise would potentially open to Charter scrutiny every jurisdictionally permissible exercise of power by a province, solely on the basis that it creates a distinction in how individuals are treated in different provinces: *R. v. S. (S.)*, [1990] 2 S.C.R. 254, 57 C.C.C. (3d) 115 (7:0).

The word "individual" in this section does not include corporations: *R. v. Paul Magder Furs Ltd.* (1989), 49 C.C.C. (3d) 267 (Ont. C.A.), leave to appeal to S.C.C. refused 51 C.C.C. (3d) vii, 70 O.R. (2d) x.

The Crown cannot be equated with an individual for the purposes of s. 15(1) analysis: *Rudolf Wolff & Co. v. Canada*, [1990] 1 S.C.R. 695.

Official Languages of Canada

OFFICIAL LANGUAGES OF CANADA / Official languages of New Brunswick / Advancement of status and use.

16. (1) English and French are the official languages of Canada and have equality of status and equal rights and privileges as to their use in all institutions of the Parliament and government of Canada.

(2) English and French are the official languages of New Brunswick and have equality of status and equal rights and privileges as to their use in all institutions of the legislature and government of New Brunswick.

(3) Nothing in this Charter limits the authority of Parliament or a legislature to advance the equality of status or use of English and French.

ENGLISH AND FRENCH LINGUISTIC COMMUNITIES IN NEW BRUNSWICK / Role of the legislature and government of New Brunswick.

16.1 (1) The English linguistic community and the French linguistic community in New Brunswick have equality of status and equal rights and privileges, including the right to distinct educational institutions and such distinct cultural institutions as are necessary for the preservation and promotion of those communities.

(2) The role of the legislature and government of New Brunswick to preserve and promote the status, rights and privileges referred to in subsection (1) is affirmed.

PROCEEDINGS OF PARLIAMENT / Proceedings of New Brunswick legislature.

17. (1) Everyone has the right to use English or French in any debates and other proceedings of Parliament.

(2) Everyone has the right to use English or French in any debates and other proceedings of the legislature of New Brunswick.

PARLIAMENTARY STATUTES AND RECORDS / New Brunswick statutes and records.

18. (1) The statutes, records and journals of Parliament shall be printed and published in English and French and both language versions are equally authoritative.

(2) The statutes, records and journals of the legislature of New Brunswick shall be printed and published in English and French and both language versions are equally authoritative.

PROCEEDINGS IN COURTS ESTABLISHED BY PARLIAMENT / Proceedings in New Brunswick courts.

19. (1) Either English or French may be used by any person in, or in any pleading in or process issuing from, any court established by Parliament.

(2) Either English or French may be used by any person in, or in any pleading in or process issuing from, any court of New Brunswick.

CHARTER

COMMUNICATIONS BY PUBLIC WITH FEDERAL INSTITUTIONS / Communications by public with New Brunswick institutions.

20. (1) Any member of the public in Canada has the right to communicate with, and to receive available services from, any head or central office of an institution of the Parliament or government of Canada in English or French, and has the same right with respect to any other office of any such institution where

- **(*a*) there is a significant demand for communications with and services from that office in such language; or**
- **(*b*) due to the nature of the office, it is reasonable that communications with and services from that office be available in both English and French.**

(2) Any member of the public in New Brunswick has the right to communicate with, and to receive available services from, any office of an institution of the legislature or government of New Brunswick in English or French.

CONTINUATION OF EXISTING CONSTITUTIONAL PROVISIONS.

21. Nothing in sections 16 to 20 abrogates or derogates from any right, privilege or obligation with respect to the English and French languages, or either of them, that exists or is continued by virtue of any other provision of the Constitution of Canada.

RIGHTS AND PRIVILEGES PRESERVED.

22. Nothing in sections 16 to 20 abrogates or derogates from any legal or customary right or privilege acquired or enjoyed either before or after the coming into force of this Charter with respect to any language that is not English or French.

Minority Language Educational Rights

LANGUAGE OF INSTRUCTION / Continuity of language instruction / Application where numbers warrant.

23. (1) Citizens of Canada

- **(*a*) whose first language learned and still understood is that of the English or French linguistic minority population of the province in which they reside, or**
- **(*b*) who have received their primary school instruction in Canada in English or French and reside in a province where the language in which they received that instruction is the language of the English or French linguistic minority population of the province,**

have the right to have their children receive primary and secondary school instruction in that language in that province.

(2) Citizens of Canada of whom any child has received or is receiving primary or secondary school instruction in English or French in Canada, have the right to have all their children receive primary and secondary school instruction in the same language.

(3) The right of citizens of Canada under subsections (1) and (2) to have their children receive primary and secondary school instruction in the language of the English or French linguistic minority population of a province

- **(*a*) applies wherever in the province the number of children of citizens who have such a right is sufficient to warrant the provision to them out of public funds of minority language instruction; and**
- **(*b*) includes, where the number of those children so warrants, the right to have them receive that instruction in minority language educational facilities provided out of public funds.**

Enforcement

ENFORCEMENT OF GUARANTEED RIGHTS AND FREEDOMS / Exclusion of evidence bringing administration of justice into disrepute.

24. (1) Anyone whose rights or freedoms, as guaranteed by this Charter, have been infringed or denied may apply to a court of competent jurisdiction to obtain such remedy as the court considers appropriate and just in the circumstances.

(2) Where, in proceedings under subsection (1), a court concludes that evidence was obtained in a manner that infringed or denied any rights or freedoms guaranteed by this Charter, the evidence shall be excluded if it is established that, having regard to all the circumstances, the admission of it in the proceedings would bring the administration of justice into disrepute.

ANNOTATIONS

Standing – A corporation charged with breach of a federal statute, here the *Lords Day Act*, has standing to defend the charge on the basis that the Act violates the guarantee to freedom of conscience and religion and is therefore of no force and effect by reason of s. 52 of the *Constitution Act, 1982*. Section 24(1) sets out a remedy for individuals, whether real persons or artificial ones such as corporations, whose rights under the Charter have been infringed. It is not however the only recourse in the face of unconstitutional legislation. Where the challenge is based on the unconstitutionality of the legislation, recourse to s. 24(1) is unnecessary and the particular effect of the challenging party is irrelevant. Whether a corporation can enjoy or exercise freedom of religion was therefore irrelevant: *R. v. Big M Drug Mart Ltd.*, [1985] 1 S.C.R. 295, 18 C.C.C. (3d) 385.

Similarly it was open to a corporation to challenge a provision of a federal statute on the basis that it imposed absolute liability and thus infringed the provisions of s. 7 of the Charter even though a corporation is not entitled to the protection of s. 7. Although a corporation cannot rely upon s. 7 in circumstances such as an application for a declaration that a law is invalid, it cannot be convicted under a law that violates s. 7. Once charged with an offence a corporation is entitled to submit that the legislation under which it is charged is unconstitutional because it infringes the right to life, liberty and security of the human being and thus violates s. 7: *R. v. Wholesale Travel Group Inc.* (1989), 52 C.C.C. (3d) 9 (Ont. C.A.), revd on other grounds [1991] 3 S.C.R. 154, 67 C.C.C. (3d) 193.

Note: Reference should also be made to the annotations under s. 8 dealing with the circumstances under which a reasonable expectation of privacy can be claimed in respect of a search, thereby potentially entitling the accused to a s. 24 remedy.

Court of competent jurisdiction – The superior court in Ontario was a court of competent jurisdiction under s. 24(1) for the purpose of considering an application by an inmate in Ontario for a remedy by way of *habeas corpus* notwithstanding that the facts underlying the application arose out of her trial in another province. The remedy of *habeas corpus* has traditionally run from the courts of the jurisdiction in which the person seeking review of the legality of her detention is confined: *R. v. Gamble*, [1988] 2 S.C.R. 595, 45 C.C.C. (3d) 204.

A provincial court judge presiding at an accused's preliminary inquiry is not a court of competent jurisdiction for the purpose of an application to stay proceedings for unreasonable delay or for the purpose of excluding evidence on the basis of an alleged infringement of the Charter: *R. v. Mills*, [1986] 1 S.C.R. 863, 26 C.C.C. (3d) 481.

A preliminary inquiry judge is not a "court of competent jurisdiction" for the purpose of excluding evidence under s. 24(2) of the Charter. Accordingly, while a preliminary inquiry judge may determine the admissibility of statements based on the common law confessions rule, the judge has no jurisdiction to consider any Charter violations: *R. v. Hynes*, [2001] 3 S.C.R. 623, 159 C.C.C. (3d) 359.

While the trial court is, as a general rule, a court of competent jurisdiction, the superior court should also have a constant, complete and concurrent jurisdiction for an application under s. 24(1). The superior court should decline to exercise its discretionary jurisdiction however unless in the opinion of that court and given the nature of the violation or any other circumstances it is more suited than is the trial court to assess and grant a remedy that is just and appropriate. An appropriate case where the superior court would exercise its jurisdiction is where an allegation of unreasonable delay is based on the conduct by the trial court: *R. v. Rahey*, [1987] 1 S.C.R. 588, 33 C.C.C. (3d) 289.

Generally speaking, issues, including those with a constitutional dimension, which arise in the context of a criminal prosecution should be raised and resolved within the confines of the established criminal process, rather than by way of an interlocutory application to the superior court. On the other hand, where the circumstances are such that the interests of justice require immediate intervention by the superior court then that jurisdiction can and will be exercised. An issue, however, such as the compellability of a witness [here the common law spouse of the accused] is a matter best left for the trial court which is in the best position to determine issues based on a complete record: *R. v. Duvivier* (1991), 64 C.C.C. (3d) 20 (Ont. C.A.).

Neither s. 24(1) nor s. 52 of the *Constitution Act* have enlarged the jurisdiction of the Court of Appeal. In particular, s. 24(1) does not create courts of competent jurisdiction but merely vests additional powers of courts which are already found to be competent independently of the Charter: *R. v. Meltzer*, [1989] 1 S.C.R. 1781, 49 C.C.C. (3d) 453; *R. v. Heikel*, [1989] 1 S.C.R. 1776, 49 C.C.C. (3d) 462.

The application of s. 24(1) requires an infringement or denial of a Charter-based right. Thus in *Borowski v. Canada (Attorney General)*, [1989] 1 S.C.R. 342, 47 C.C.C. (3d) 1, it was held that the plaintiff's claim that the therapeutic abortion provisions of the *Criminal Code* violated ss. 7 and 15 of the Charter did not meet this requirement as he alleged the rights of a foetus, not his own rights, had been violated.

A summary conviction court is a court of competent jurisdiction with the power to award costs against the Crown in a proper case as a remedy for infringing the defendant's Charter rights: *R. v. Pang* (1994), 95 C.C.C. (3d) 60 (Alta. C.A.).

A bail court, however, has no remedial authority and, accordingly, is not a court of competent jurisdiction for the purpose of granting costs: *R. v. Menard* (2008), 240 C.C.C. (3d) 1 (B.C.C.A.).

The National Parole Board is not a court of competent jurisdiction within the meaning of s. 24: *Mooring v. Canada (National Parole Board)*, [1996] 1 S.C.R. 75, 104 C.C.C. (3d) 97 (5:2).

A provincial offences court is a court of competent jurisdiction to order payment of costs as a remedy for Charter violations arising from disclosure issues: *R. v. 974649 Ontario Inc.* (2001), 159 C.C.C. (3d) 321 (S.C.C.).

A judge presiding at a preliminary inquiry is not a court of competent jurisdiction for the purpose of excluding evidence on that grounds that it was obtained in breach of the Charter: *R. v. Hynes* (2001), 159 C.C.C. (3d) 359 (S.C.C.).

A provincial offences court is a court of competent jurisdiction to determine whether the suspension of a driver's licence without a hearing violates the Charter: *R. v. Giagnocavo* (1995), 99 C.C.C. (3d) 383 (Ont. C.A.).

As a general rule, an action for damages under s. 24(1) cannot be coupled with a declaration of constitutional invalidity: *Guimond v. Québec (Attorney General)* (1995), 123 D.L.R. (4th) 236, [1995] R.J.Q. 380 (C.A.), revd [1996] 3 S.C.R. 347, 110 C.C.C. (3d) 223.

Procedure – An objection to the admissibility of evidence, including an objection based on a Charter infringement, should be made before or when the evidence is proferred and not at the end of the Crown's case. In the interests of conducting an orderly trial, the judge is entitled to insist that defence counsel state his position on possible Charter issues either before or at the outset of the trial. Failing timely notice, a trial judge, having taken into account all relevant circumstances, is entitled to refuse an application to assert a Charter remedy. The trial judge would, however, have a discretion to allow counsel to challenge evidence already received and will do so where the interests of justice so warrant. The accused cannot be required to swear an affidavit in support of the application for relief under the Charter: *R. v. Kutynec* (1992), 70 C.C.C. (3d) 289 (Ont. C.A.).

In *R. v. Cody*, [2017] 1 S.C.R. 659, 349 C.C.C. (3d) 488, the court strongly endorsed the use of the screening procedure established by *Kutynec*, *supra*, and *R. v. Vukelich* (1996), 108 C.C.C. (3d) 193 (B.C.C.A.), leave to appeal to S.C.C. refused [1997] 2 S.C.R. xvi, in order to minimize delay. Before permitting an application to proceed, a trial judge should consider whether it has a reasonable prospect of success. This may entail asking defence counsel to summarize the evidence it anticipates eliciting in the *voir dire* and, where that summary reveals no basis upon which the application could succeed, dismissing the application summarily. Where an application is permitted to proceed, a trial judge should not hesitate to summarily dismiss applications and requests the moment it becomes apparent they are frivolous.

In considering an application to stay proceedings based on undue delay in laying charges thus infringing the accused's right to a fair trial, no particular procedure need be employed. Thus, the parties may be able to agree on a statement of facts or submit evidence by way of affidavit or argue the motion at the end of the Crown's case. However, it was not proper for the trial judge to make findings of fact against the complainants based on credibility when he had not seen them testify and was merely relying upon portions of the transcript of the preliminary inquiry which were drawn to his attention: *R. v. L. (W.K.)*, [1991] 1 S.C.R. 1091, 64 C.C.C. (3d) 321.

CHARTER

Remedies under subsec. (1) – Because of the breadth of the phrase "appropriate and just", a court of competent jurisdiction" has broad discretion to determine what remedy to grant in the circumstances of a particular case. It is improper for courts to reduce this discretion by casting it in a strait-jacket of judicially prescribed conditions. What is appropriate and just will depend on the facts and circumstances of the particular case. An appropriate and just remedy will: (1) meaningfully vindicate the rights and freedoms of the claimants; (2) employ means that are legitimate within the framework of our constitutional democracy; (3) be a judicial remedy which vindicates the right while invoking the function and powers of a court; and (4) be fair to the party against whom the order is made: *Vancouver (City) v. Ward*, [2010] 2 S.C.R. 28.

A stay of proceedings for an abuse of process will only be warranted in the clearest of cases. Two types of state conduct may warrant a stay: conduct that compromises the fairness of an accused's trial (the "main" category); or conduct that risks undermining the integrity of the judicial process (the "residual" category). The test for determining whether a stay of proceedings is warranted is the same for both categories and consists of three requirements: (1) there must be prejudice to the accused's right to a fair trial or to the integrity of the justice system that will be manifested, perpetuated or aggravated through the conduct of the trial, or by its outcome; (2) there must be no alternative remedy capable of redressing the prejudice; and (3) where there is still uncertainty over whether a stay is warranted after steps 1 and 2, the court must balance the interests in favour of granting a stay against the interest that society has in having a final decision on the merits: *R. v. Babos*, [2014] 1 S.C.R. 309, 308 C.C.C. (3d) 445.

It would seem that the trial judge could exclude evidence as a remedy under subsec. (1) where the evidence was not obtained in violation of the Charter (having been obtained outside Canada by officials who were not acting as agents of any Canadian government) but its admission into evidence would result in the trial being unfair. On the other hand, evidence may be obtained in circumstances that would not meet the rigorous standards of the Charter and yet, if admitted into evidence, would not result in the trial being unfair. Canada cannot impose its procedural requirements on proceedings undertaken by other states in their own territories. Canada is not, however, bound by the law of other countries in conducting trials in Canada and the courts must, in determining whether evidence should be admitted, be guided by our sense of fairness as informed by the underlying principles of the Canadian legal system as it applies to the specific context of the case. It was unnecessary in this case to articulate the test to be applied. Thus, for example, it may be that excluding the evidence only where the manner in which it was obtained shocks the conscience sets the standard too low. What is sought is a fair trial in the specific context and it may be that this requirement cannot be satisfied by the rejection of foreign evidence only in the most egregious circumstances: *R. v. Harrer*, [1995] 3 S.C.R. 562, 101 C.C.C. (3d) 193.

The principle in *R. v. Therens*, [1985] 1 S.C.R. 613, 18 C.C.C. (3d) 481, that subsec. (2) represents the sole test for exclusion of evidence applies where it is alleged that evidence was obtained in violation of the accused's Charter rights. It does not apply where evidence was obtained in conformity with the Charter but its admission into evidence would itself violate the Charter. In such a case, the evidence may be excluded pursuant to the trial judge's common law duty to exclude evidence whose admission would render the trial unfair as in *R. v. Harrer, supra*, or as a remedy under subsec. (1): *R. v. White*, [1999] 2 S.C.R. 417, 135 C.C.C. (3d) 257.

A trial judge should exclude evidence as a remedy for late disclosure under s. 24(1) only in exceptional cases where the late disclosure renders the trial process unfair and the unfairness cannot be remedied through an adjournment and disclosure order, or where exclusion is necessary to maintain the integrity of the justice system: *R. v. Bjelland*, [2009] 2 S.C.R. 651, 246 C.C.C. (3d) 129.

In some exceptional cases, a sentence reduction outside statutory limits may be an appropriate remedy under subsec. (1) for some particularly egregious form of misconduct by state agents in relation to the offence and the offender: *R. v. Nasogaluak*, [2010] 1 S.C.R. 206, 251 C.C.C. (3d) 293. It is an error to grant such a remedy where that stringent threshold is not met: *R. v. Donnelly* (2016), 345 C.C.C. (3d) 56 (Ont. C.A.); *R. v. Gowdy* (2016), 345 C.C.C. (3d) 174 (Ont. C.A.), leave to appeal to S.C.C. refused *Kris Gowdy v. Her Majesty the Queen*, 2017 CarswellOnt 11383.

In ordering costs against the Crown, there must be more than a finding of a Charter breach and a causal connection to the costs incurred. A disagreement as to the applicable law, or a technical, unintended or innocent breach is insufficient to support an award of costs against the Crown. A degree of misconduct or an unacceptable degree of negligence must be present before costs are awarded as a remedy: *R. v. Robinson* (1999), 142 C.C.C. (3d) 303 (Alta. C.A.).

While there is no general power to award costs in indictable matters, in a proper case, it would be open to a trial judge to award costs against the Crown as a remedy for violation of an accused's Charter rights. Where, however, an application for costs is joined with an application for damages then both issues should be determined in the same action by way of a civil proceeding: *R. v. McGillivary* (1990), 56 C.C.C. (3d) 304 (N.B.C.A.).

A costs award against the Crown will not be an "appropriate and just remedy" under subsec. (1) absent a finding that the Crown's conduct demonstrated a marked and unacceptable departure from the reasonable standards expected of the prosecution, or something that is rare or unique that must at least result in something akin to an extreme hardship on the defendant: *R. v. Singh* (2016), 334 C.C.C. (3d) 481 (Ont. C.A.).

Where there has been a violation of s. 14, it was for the court to fashion an appropriate and just remedy tailored to the particular circumstances of the case under this section. Neither s. 686(1)(*b*)(iii) nor s. 686(1)(*b*)(iv) of the *Criminal Code* has any application. As a matter of law, a violation of s. 14 of the Charter precludes application of these curative provisions of the Code. To the extent that a particular Charter violation is more or less serious, prejudicing an accused to a greater or lesser degree, this raises remedial issues which fall to be decided under subsec. (1), not under the *Criminal Code*: *R. v. Tran*, [1994] 2 S.C.R. 951, 92 C.C.C. (3d) 218.

A trial judge's order under s. 24(1) should be disturbed on appeal only if the trial judge misdirects himself or if his decision is so clearly wrong as to amount to an injustice. Upon setting aside a stay, the appellate court is entitled to order the continuation of the proceedings before the trial court and was not bound to order a new trial. The trial court to which the matter is remitted, however, retains its discretion to instead order a new trial where resumption of the interrupted proceedings proves to be impractical or unfair: *R. c. Bellusci*, [2012] 2 S.C.R. 509, 293 C.C.C. (3d) 565.

Where the propriety of a remedy granted under subsec. (1) is at issue, appellate intervention is warranted only where a trial judge misdirects him or herself in law, commits a reviewable error of fact, or renders a decision that is so clearly wrong as to amount to an injustice: *R. v. Babos*, [2014] 1 S.C.R. 309, 308 C.C.C. (3d) 445.

Exclusion of evidence under subsec. (2) – In *R. v. Grant* (2009), 245 C.C.C. (3d) 1, the Supreme Court of Canada reconsidered the framework for exclusion as articulated in *R. v. Collins*, [1987] 1 S.C.R. 265, 33 C.C.C. (3d) 1, and *R. v. Stillman*, [1997] 1 S.C.R. 607, 113 C.C.C. (3d) 321. The phrase "bring the administration of justice into disrepute" must be understood in the long-term sense of maintaining the integrity of and public confidence in the justice system. Section 24(2) does not focus on the immediate reaction to an individual case but, rather, whether the overall repute of the justice system, viewed in the long term, will be adversely affected by the admission of the evidence. The inquiry is objective and asks whether a reasonable person, informed of all relevant circumstances and the values underlying the Charter, would conclude that the admission of the evidence would bring the administration of justice into disrepute. The focus is not only long term but also prospective. Section 24(2) starts from the proposition that the breach has caused damage to the administration of justice and seeks to ensure that evidence obtained through the breach does not do further damage to the repute of the justice system. The focus is societal systemic concerns and does not aim to punish the police or provide compensation to the accused. In considering s. 24(2), the court must have regard to the following: (1) the seriousness of the Charter-infringing state conduct (admission may send the message that the justice system condones serious state misconduct); (2) the impact of the breach on the Charter-protected interests of the accused (admission may send the message that individual rights count for little); and (3) society's interest in the adjudication of the case on its merits. The court must balance the assessments under each of these lines of inquiry to determine whether, considering all of the circumstances, admission of the evidence would bring the administration of justice into disrepute.

In considering the seriousness of the Charter-infringing state conduct, the court must consider whether the admission of the evidence would bring the administration of justice into disrepute by sending a message to the public that the courts effectively condone state deviation from the rule of law by failing to dissociate themselves from the fruits of that unlawful conduct. The more severe or deliberate the state conduct that led to the violation, the greater the need for the courts to dissociate themselves from the conduct through exclusion. State conduct varies on a spectrum from inadvertent or minor violations to evidence obtained through willful or reckless disregard of Charter rights. Extenuating circumstance such as the need to prevent the disappearance of evidence may attenuate the seriousness of police conduct. However, ignorance of Charter standards or negligence or willful blindness cannot be equated with good faith. Deliberate police conduct in violation of established Charter standards tends to support exclusion of the evidence. In considering the second criteria of the impact on the Charter-protected interests of the accused, the court must evaluate the extent to which the breach actually undermined the interests protected by the right infringed. The impact may range from fleeting and technical to profoundly intrusive. To determine the seriousness of the infringement from this perspective, the court must look to the interests engaged by the infringed right and examine the degree to which the violation impacted on those interests. With respect to the third criteria, society's interests in an adjudication on the merits, considers whether the truth-seeking function of the criminal process would be better served by the admission of the evidence or by its exclusion. While the reliability of the evidence is not conclusive, it is nonetheless an important consideration. The importance of the evidence to the prosecution's case is another factor that may be considered in that the exclusion of highly reliable evidence may impact more negatively on the repute of the administration of justice where the remedy effectively guts the prosecution.

While the seriousness of the offence may be a valid consideration, it has the potential to cut both ways. The short-term public clamour for a conviction in a particular case must not deafen the s. 24(2) judge to the longer-term repute of the administration of justice. Having considered these three factors, the judge must then determine whether, on balance, the admission of the evidence would bring the administration of justice into disrepute.

In *R. v. Grant*, *supra*, the Supreme Court of Canada considered the admissibility of certain types of evidence. With respect to statements by the accused, the court rejected any notion of automatic exclusion. The three lines of inquiry support the presumptive general, although not the automatic, exclusion of statements obtained in breach of the Charter. Certain circumstances may attenuate the impact of the breach, such as whether the non-compliance with s. 10(*b*) was a technical deficiency, or in the rare circumstances where it can be said that the statement in question would have been made notwithstanding the Charter breach. The heightened concern with proper police conduct in obtaining statements and the centrality of the protected interests affected will, in most cases, favour exclusion of the statements taken in breach of the Charter, while the third factor, obtaining a decision on the merits, may be attenuated by lack of reliability. This, together with the common law's historic tendency to treat statements of the accused differently from other evidence, supports the tendency to exclude statements under s. 24(2).

In *R. v. Grant*, *supra*, the Supreme Court of Canada revisited *R. v. Stillman*, *supra*, and the characterization of all bodily evidence as conscriptive. A flexible and multi-factored approach is required by the wide variation between different kinds of bodily evidence. The seriousness of the police conduct and the impact on the accused's rights of taking the bodily substances varies greatly. The admissibility of bodily samples should not depend solely on whether the evidence is conscriptive. The approach to the admissibility of bodily evidence under s. 24(2) that asks simply whether the evidence was conscripted should be replaced by a flexible test based on all of the circumstances. The seriousness of the Charter-infringing conduct is fact-specific. With respect to the second inquiry, the judge should look at the seriousness of the breach on the accused's protected interests. In the context of bodily evidence obtained in violation of s. 8, this inquiry requires the court to examine the degree to which the search and seizure intruded upon the privacy, bodily integrity and human dignity of the accused. The greater the intrusion, the more important it is that a court exclude the evidence in order to substantiate the Charter rights of the accused. With respect to the third line of inquiry, the court will usually favour admission in cases involving bodily samples given the reliability of the evidence and the risk of error inherent in depriving the trier of fact of the evidence. In general, where an intrusion on bodily integrity is deliberately inflicted and the impact on the accused's privacy, bodily integrity and dignity is high, bodily evidence will be excluded notwithstanding its relevance and reliability. On the other hand, where the violation is less egregious and the intrusion is less severe in terms of privacy, bodily integrity and dignity, reliable evidence may be admitted.

In *R. v. Grant*, *supra*, the court also considered the application of s. 24(2) to derivative evidence. With respect to derivative evidence, discoverability is not determinative of admissibility, although it retains a useful role in assessing the actual impact of the breach on the protected interests of the accused. It allows the court to assess the strength of the causal connection between the Charter-infringing self-incrimination and the resultant evidence. The more likely that the evidence would have been obtained without the statement, the lesser the impact of the breach on the underlying interest against self-incrimination. With respect to the first inquiry, the more serious the state conduct, the more the admission of evidence derived from it tends to undermine public confidence in the rule of law. The second inquiry requires consideration of the extent to which the Charter breach impinged upon that interest in a free and democratic society. In determining the impact of the breach, the discoverability of the derivative evidence may be important as a factor strengthening or attenuating the self-incriminatory character of the evidence. In considering the third inquiry, given the reliability of the evidence, the public interest in having the trial adjudicated on its merits will usually favour admission of derivative evidence.

In *R. v. Harrison* (2009), 245 C.C.C. (3d) 86, the Supreme Court of Canada considered the import of the seriousness of the offence. The seriousness of the offence and the reliability of the evidence cannot overwhelm the s. 24(2) analysis. Police conduct in stopping and searching a vehicle without any reasonable grounds was reprehensible and was aggravated by the officer's misleading testimony in court. The misleading testimony was properly a factor to consider under the first part of the s. 24(2) analysis. The seriousness of the offence, in this case, a significant quantity of cocaine, and the reliability of the evidence did not outweigh the factors pointing to exclusion. To appear to condone willful and flagrant Charter breaches that constituted a significant incursion on the appellant's rights would not enhance the long-term repute of the administration of justice. The fact that a Charter breach is less heinous than the offence charged does not advance the inquiry mandated by s. 24(2).

The seriousness of the offence has the potential to cut both ways and will not always weigh in favour of admission. While society has a greater interest in seeing a serious offence prosecuted, it has an equivalent interest in ensuring that the judicial system is above reproach, particularly when the stakes are high for the accused person. While discoverability may play a useful role in the s. 24(2) analysis, it is not determinative. A finding of discoverability does not necessarily lead to admission. Discoverability is relevant to consider the first and second *Grant* lines of inquiry. In considering the first branch of the *Grant* test, if the officers could have conducted the search legally but failed to turn their minds to obtaining a warrant or proceeded under the view that they could not have demonstrated to a judicial officer that they had reasonable and probable grounds, the seriousness of the state conduct is heightened. A casual attitude towards, or a deliberate flouting of, Charter rights will generally aggravate the seriousness of the Charter-infringing state conduct. Good faith and/or a legitimate reason for not seeking prior judicial authorization will lessen the seriousness of the infringing state conduct. With respect to the second branch of the *Grant* test, the fact that the police could have demonstrated to a judicial officer that they had reasonable and probable grounds to believe that an offence had been committed and that there was evidence to be found at the place of the search will tend to lessen the impact of the illegal search on the accused's privacy and dignity interests. The intrusiveness of such an unauthorized search will be assessed according to the level of privacy that could have reasonably been expected in the given set of circumstances. The greater the expectation of privacy, the more intrusive the unauthorized search will have been. The seriousness of the impact on the accused's Charter-protected interests will not always mirror the seriousness of the breach: *R. v. Côté*, [2011] 3 S.C.R. 215, 276 C.C.C. (3d) 42.

In practical terms, the third inquiry becomes important when one, but not both, of the first two inquiries pushes strongly toward the exclusion of the evidence. If the first and second inquiries make a strong case for exclusion, the third inquiry will seldom, if ever, tip the balance in favour of admissibility. Similarly, if both of the first two inquiries provide weaker support for exclusion of the evidence, the third inquiry will almost certainly confirm the admissibility of the evidence: *R. v. McGuffie* (2016), 336 C.C.C. (3d) 486 (Ont. C.A.). See also: *R. v. Paterson*, [2017] 1 S.C.R. 202, 347 C.C.C. (3d) 280.

The requirement under s. 24(2) that evidence was obtained in a manner that infringed or denied any rights or freedoms guaranteed by the Charter is met where it is established that a Charter violation occurred in the course of obtaining the evidence. It is not necessary that there be a strict causal nexus between the Charter violation and the obtaining of the evidence. A temporal link however between infringement of the Charter and the discovery of the evidence will not always be determinative since situations may arise where the obtaining of the evidence, although following a breach of the Charter, will be too remote from the violation to be obtained in a manner that infringed the Charter: *R. v. Strachan*, [1988] 2 S.C.R. 980, 46 C.C.C. (3d) 479.

In an appropriate case, a court may exclude evidence on the basis of a Charter breach occurring after the evidence was obtained, as long as the connection between the evidence and the breach is not too tenuous or remote: *R. v. Pino* (2016), 337 C.C.C. (3d) 402 (Ont. C.A.).

CHARTER

Note: The following cases were decided prior to the Supreme Court's decision in *R. v. Grant*, [2009] 2 S.C.R. 353, 245 C.C.C. (3d) 1, which substantially revised the governing approach to s. 24(2). They should therefore be approached with caution.

In some cases the harm to the integrity of the judicial system resulting from the excluding of evidence would be so great that exclusion and not admission would bring the administration of justice into disrepute. This would be the case if evidence necessary to substantiate a charge were excluded on the basis of a trivial Charter violation. Evidence as to the finding of narcotics carried by the accused although obtained following a breach of the accused's rights under ss. 8 and 10(*b*) could not affect the fairness of the trial. The accused was in no way conscripted against herself and the customs officers in searching the accused acted in good faith based on accepted customs procedure. The evidence therefore should be admitted: *R. v. Simmons*, [1988] 2 S.C.R. 495, 45 C.C.C. (3d) 296. Similarly, see *R. v. Jacoy*, [1988] 2 S.C.R. 548, 45 C.C.C. (3d) 46.

While the purpose of the rule in s. 24(2) is not to allow an accused to escape conviction, neither should it be interpreted as available only in those circumstances where exclusion of evidence would have no effect at all on the result of the trial. A consideration whether to exclude evidence should not be so closely tied to the ultimate result in a particular case. While the courts must consider the effect on the administration of justice of excluding evidence, that factor alone should not decide a case. Rather in considering whether or not to exclude evidence the court must consider the three groups of factors as set out in *R. v. Collins, supra*. While the purpose of s. 24(2) is not to deter police from unlawful conduct, the court should be reluctant to admit evidence that shows signs of being obtained by an abuse of common law and Charter rights by the police. In this case, although the evidence sought to be excluded was real evidence, it was obtained through serious violations of s. 8 in circumstances that led to the conclusion that the admission of the evidence would bring the administration of justice into disrepute: *R. v. Genest*, [1989] 1 S.C.R. 59, 45 C.C.C. (3d) 385.

Even though a search warrant is held to be valid, if the obtaining of the warrant was preceded by an unreasonable warrantless perimeter search, this provision is triggered and the court must consider whether the admission of the evidence would bring the administration of justice into disrepute: *R. v. Grant*, [1993] 3 S.C.R. 223, 84 C.C.C. (3d) 173 (9:0).

The officer's subjective belief that the accused's rights under s. 8 were not affected does not make the violation less serious, unless the belief was reasonable. Good faith cannot be claimed if based on an unreasonable error or ignorance as to the scope of the officer's authority: *R. v. Buhay*, [2003] 1 S.C.R. 631, 174 C.C.C. (3d) 97.

Any evidence obtained after violation of the Charter by conscripting the accused against himself through a confession or other evidence emanating from him would tend to render the trial process unfair. While the identity of the accused is not evidence emanating from the accused, identification evidence obtained through a lineup is evidence that cannot be obtained but for the participation of the accused and it is not simply pre-existing real evidence. When participating in a lineup, the accused is participating in the construction of credible inculpating evidence and where such evidence has been obtained following violation of the right to counsel its admission would tend to render the trial unfair: *R. v. Ross*, [1989] 1 S.C.R. 3, 46 C.C.C. (3d) 129.

In *R. v. Black*, [1989] 2 S.C.R. 138, 50 C.C.C. (3d) 1, evidence had been obtained following a serious violation of the accused's right to counsel. The court however distinguished between real evidence obtained following a violation and self-incriminating evidence and concluded that her confession and her conduct in leading the police to the murder weapon should be excluded since its admission would tend to render the trial unfair. However, the knife itself was a piece of real evidence and should have been admitted as an exhibit.

Both the temporal link and the causal connection between the Charter breach and the evidence obtained must be examined. The mere existence of a temporal link may not be sufficient. If both the temporal link and the causal link are tenuous, the court may conclude that the evidence was not obtained in a manner that infringes a right or freedom under the

Charter. Alternatively, the temporal connection may be so strong that the Charter breach is an integral part of a single transaction such that a weak or absent causal connection is of no importance. In this case, the causal connection between an unreasonable search and seizure and the *viva voce* evidence of an occupant of the premises who had been arrested and subsequently pleaded guilty, was insufficient. Testimony cannot be treated in the same manner as an inanimate object. In order to find a temporal link , the pertinent event was the witness's decision to co-operate and to testify not his arrest. Any temporal link between the illegal search and the testimony was greatly weakened by the intervening events of the witness's voluntary decision to co-operate with the police, plead guilty and testify. Similarly, the causal connection between the illegal search and the witness's decision to give evidence was extremely tenuous. The nexus between the breach and the impugned evidence was remote: *R. v. Goldhart*, [1996] 2 S.C.R. 463, 107 C.C.C. (3d) 481.

A violation of the sanctity of a person's body is much more serious than search of an office or even a home. Even where a blood sample was taken from an accused by a physician and the police were not directly implicated in the invasion of the accused's body, the dignity of the human being is equally seriously violated when use is made of bodily substances taken by others for medical purposes in a manner that does not respect that limitation. The trust and confidence of the public in the administration of medical facilities would be seriously taxed if an easy and informal flow of information and particularly of bodily substances from hospitals and police were allowed. Such a practice would bring the administration of health services and the administration of justice into disrepute. Accordingly, evidence obtained as a result of the unlawful seizure should be excluded: *R. v. Dyment*, [1988] 2 S.C.R. 417, 45 C.C.C. (3d) 244.

Blood and urine samples initially obtained by hospital staff with the accused's consent for use for medical purposes, without the involvement of the state, were "real evidence" for the purpose of determining whether admission of the results of analysis of the samples would affect the fairness of the trial. The fact that the samples existed independently of the subsequent Charter violations by the authorities was an important consideration favouring admission of the evidence: *R. v. Colarusso*, [1994] 1 S.C.R. 20, 87 C.C.C. (3d) 193.

Notwithstanding the seriousness of the offence with which the accused was charged, importing heroin, the serious nature of the violation of the accused's rights under ss. 8 and 10(*a*), (*b*), which formed part of a pattern of disregard of the accused's rights, required exclusion of real evidence, being the discovery of a quantity of heroin following a rectal examination. The accused had not been informed of his right to counsel when subjected to a search by customs officers and had been told that he was arrested on a traffic warrant. The Crown, not having established that the police had reasonable grounds to arrest the accused for a narcotics offence, the rectal examination as an incident to an arrest for outstanding traffic tickets must be viewed as an extremely serious intrusion. In the circumstances, it was imperative that the court, having regard for the long-term consequences of admitting evidence obtained in these circumstances, disassociate itself from the conduct of the police. The administration of justice would be brought into greater disrepute if the court were to condone the practice of using an arrest for traffic warrants as an artifice to conduct a rectal examination of a person whom the police do not have reasonable and probable grounds to believe is carrying drugs: *R. v. Greffe*, [1990] 1 S.C.R. 755, 55 C.C.C. (3d) 161 (4:3).

In *R. v. Kokesch*, [1990] 3 S.C.R. 3, 61 C.C.C. (3d) 207 (4:3), the court excluded evidence obtained by execution of a *Narcotic Control Act* search warrant at the accused's home. The evidence to obtain the warrant was based on information gathered by a police officer through a warrantless "perimeter search" of the accused's home at a time when the officer merely had a suspicion that the accused was cultivating marihuana on the premises. This was an extremely serious violation of the Charter. The lack of availability of other investigative means was not a mitigating factor. To the contrary, where the police have nothing but suspicion and no legal way to obtain other evidence then they must leave the suspect alone and not proceed to obtain evidence illegally. The illegal intrusion onto the accused's property must be seen as far from trivial and a search conducted in the knowledge that legal search powers are unavailable is not capable of being characterized as demonstrating good faith. The officer either knew or ought to have known that he was trespassing. In either case, this was not good faith. Notwithstanding that the marihuana seized was real evidence whose admission would not affect the fairness of the trial, the evidence must be excluded. The administration of justice would suffer far greater disrepute from its admission than its exclusion. The court must not be seen to condone deliberate unlawful conduct designed to subvert both the legal and constitutional limits of police power to intrude on individual privacy.

In *R. v. Grant*, *supra*, the court held that an important factor in the decision not to exclude the evidence was the fact that the police were acting in good faith reliance upon a provision of a statute which authorized a warrantless search and which had not been struck down in the particular province. Also of significance was that the narcotics offences were serious and exclusion of the evidence would render a conviction an impossibility.

Evidence which has been ruled inadmissible at one stage in a trial pursuant to subsec. (2) may be admitted at another point in the trial only if there has been a material change in circumstances. It will only be in very limited circumstances that a change in use of the evidence will qualify as a material change of circumstances that would warrant the reopening of the issue once evidence has been excluded under this subsection. The admission of statements obtained from the accused in breach of the Charter generally turns on the effect of its admission on the fairness of the trial. The effect on the repute of the administration of justice is to be assessed by reference to the standard of the reasonably well informed citizen who represents community values. The effect of destroying the credibility of an accused who takes the stand in his defence, using evidence obtained from the mouth of the accused in breach of his Charter rights, will usually have the same effect as use of the same evidence when adduced by the Crown in its case-in-chief for the purpose of incrimination. A jury instruction as to the limited use of the evidence does not mean that the admission of the evidence will have a less detrimental effect on the case of the accused. If use of the statement is deemed to be unfair by reason of having been obtained in breach of an accused's Charter rights, it is not likely to be seen to be less unfair because it was only used to destroy credibility. Where the Crown seeks to use the excluded statement for a restricting purpose, a ruling may be obtained either during its case or before cross-examining the accused in a *voir dire*: *R. v. Calder*, [1996] 1 S.C.R. 660, 105 C.C.C. (3d) 1.

In *R. v. Cook*, [1998] 2 S.C.R. 597, 128 C.C.C. (3d) 1, the court gave further consideration to the admission of evidence for the limited purpose of cross-examination going to credibility. The court held that the circumstances in which evidence that was not otherwise admissible could be admitted for a limited purpose would be very rare indeed and that evidence used to incriminate the accused and impeach the accused's credibility should be treated the same for the purposes of subsec. (2).

Although the burden of establishing a violation of a Charter right is upon the accused, this does not mean that the accused must formally prove every single fact upon which the claim of a violation is based, including one which is not in dispute between the parties and is or should be common knowledge amongst members of the criminal bar and those on the bench. For example, the existence of duty counsel services in the province was not a matter which required independent proof by the accused. Duty counsel and legal aid services are an intrinsic part of the practice of criminal law in this country and courts are entitled to take judicial notice of the broad parameters of these services, such as their existence and how they are generally accessed: *R. v. Cobham*, [1994] 3 S.C.R. 360, 92 C.C.C. (3d) 333.

General

ABORIGINAL RIGHTS AND FREEDOMS NOT AFFECTED BY CHARTER.

25. The guarantee in this Charter of certain rights and freedoms shall not be construed so as to abrogate or derogate from any aboriginal, treaty or other rights or freedoms that pertain to the aboriginal peoples of Canada including

(*a*) any rights or freedoms that have been recognized by the Royal Proclamation of October 7, 1763; and

(*b*) any rights or freedoms that now exist by way of land claims agreements or may be so acquired. SI/84-102, Sch.

OTHER RIGHTS AND FREEDOMS NOT AFFECTED BY CHARTER.

26. The guarantee in this Charter of certain rights and freedoms shall not be construed as denying the existence of any other rights or freedoms that exist in Canada.

MULTICULTURAL HERITAGE.

27. This Charter shall be interpreted in a manner consistent with the preservation and enhancement of the multicultural heritage of Canadians.

ANNOTATIONS

In considering whether the hate literature provisions of s. 319(2) of the *Criminal Code* constituted a reasonable limit on freedom of expression, the court took into account the commitment to a multicultural vision. The principle of non-discrimination and the need to prevent attacks on the individual's connection with his or her culture, and, hence, upon the process of self-development, are recognized by s. 27: *R. v. Keegstra*, [1990] 3 S.C.R. 697, 61 C.C.C. (3d) 1.

RIGHTS GUARANTEED EQUALLY TO BOTH SEXES.

28. Notwithstanding anything in this Charter, the rights and freedoms referred to in it are guaranteed equally to male and female persons.

ANNOTATIONS

The guarantee in this provision does not prevent Parliament from creating an offence that, as a matter of biological fact, can only be committed by one sex. The importance of this provision lies in the fact that it is not open to the legislature to deny an accused, who is charged with such an offence, rights and freedoms guaranteed to all persons under the Charter. A person cannot receive less protection under the Charter on account of his or her sex: *R. v. Nguyen*, [1990] 2 S.C.R. 906, 59 C.C.C. (3d) 161 (5:2).

RIGHTS RESPECTING CERTAIN SCHOOLS PRESERVED.

29. Nothing in this Charter abrogates or derogates from any rights or privileges guaranteed by or under the Constitution of Canada in respect of denominational, separate or dissentient schools.

APPLICATION TO TERRITORIES AND TERRITORIAL AUTHORITIES.

30. A reference in this Charter to a province or to the legislative assembly or legislature of a province shall be deemed to include a reference to the Yukon Territory and the Northwest Territories, or to the appropriate legislative authority thereof, as the case may be.

LEGISLATIVE POWERS NOT EXTENDED.

31. Nothing in this Charter extends the legislative powers of any body or authority.

Application of Charter

APPLICATION OF CHARTER / Exception.

32. (1) This Charter applies

(*a*) to the Parliament and government of Canada in respect of all matters within the authority of Parliament including all matters relating to the Yukon Territory and Northwest Territories; and

(*b*) to the legislature and government of each province in respect of all matters within the authority of the legislature of each province.

(2) Notwithstanding subsection (1), section 15 shall not have effect until three years after this section comes into force.

ANNOTATIONS

In *R. v. Harrer*, [1995] 3 S.C.R. 562, 101 C.C.C. (3d) 193, the court left open the question of whether the Charter could have extraterritorial application. The court did point out that automatic exclusion of Charter application outside Canada might unduly restrict the protection Canadians have a right to expect against the interference with their rights by the Canadian governments or their agents. In this case, however, the United States authorities were not acting on behalf of any of the governments of Canada, the provinces or the territories, the state actors to which, by virtue of this section the application of the Charter is confined. The Charter thus had no direct application to the interrogations in the United States. Accordingly, the rights flowing from s. 10(*b*) of the Charter to persons arrested or detained had no application. In those circumstances, the application of the Charter could only be triggered when the Canadian police began proceedings against the accused on her return to Canada. Since the accused did not complain of any improper police action in Canada, the only grounds available to her were that the admission of the evidence would violate the accused's liberty interests in a manner that was not in accordance with the principles of fundamental justice of the Charter or would violate the guarantee of a fair trial. Concepts of fairness and principles of fundamental justice involve a delicate balancing to achieve a just accommodation between the interests of the individual and those of the state in providing a fair and workable system of justice.

Similarly, in *R. v. Terry*, [1996] 2 S.C.R. 207, 106 C.C.C. (3d) 508, the court held that the gathering of evidence by a foreign officer or agency is subject to the rules of that country and none other. Any co-operative investigation involving law enforcement agencies of Canada and a foreign country will be governed by the laws of the jurisdiction in which the activity is undertaken and consequently, the Charter did not apply to an accused detained by American police.

The actions of Canadian police officers in questioning a suspect in the United States about a crime committed in Canada falls within subsec. (1) and therefore the right to counsel guarantees in s. 10(*b*) apply unless the application of the Charter would, in the particular case, interfere with the sovereign authority of the foreign state and thereby generate an objectionable extraterritorial effect. In this case, application of the Charter would not result in an interference with the territorial jurisdiction of the United States. The physical arrest was made by U.S. officials but initiated by a Canadian extradition request and related exclusively to an offence committed in and to be prosecuted in Canada. The U.S. officials did not become involved in any way in the interrogation by the Canadian officers. Unlike *R. v. Terry, supra*, no attempt is being made to impose Canadian criminal law standards on foreign officials and procedures: *R. v. Cook*, [1998] 2 S.C.R. 597, 128 C.C.C. (3d) 1.

The act of a Canadian official in sending a letter of request directed to the competent legal authority of Switzerland, seeking the assistance of the Swiss Government with respect to a Canadian criminal investigation, did not infringe s. 8 of the Charter. Other actions taken by the Swiss authorities, in response to the request, including orders that interfered with the plaintiff's privacy interests, such as orders for the seizure of documents were not subject to Charter scrutiny. The Canadian government did not undertake any search or seizure, it merely requested that a search and seizure be undertaken. However, s. 7 of the Charter may apply to justify excluding evidence obtained abroad through foreign officials where it is necessary to preserve the fairness of the trial: *Schreiber v. Canada (Attorney General)*, [1998] 1 S.C.R. 841, 124 C.C.C. (3d) 129.

The Charter is generally not applicable to extra-territorial searches subject to the safeguards protecting trial fairness. Canadian law can only be enforced on consent of the other state. In order to determine whether the Charter applied to a foreign investigation, the court must first determine whether the activity fell within s. 32(1), in that a Canadian state actor to whom the Charter applied was involved in the investigation. Secondly, if the Charter does apply, the court must determine whether the evidence obtained ought to be excluded to preserve trial fairness. In this case, the police officers were government actors, but the foreign state police did not consent to the application of the Charter. In addition, the evidence was not conscriptive and the actions of the officers were not unreasonable or unfair, as they were acting under the authority of the foreign state's police. There was nothing to suggest that the searches were conducted in a manner that was inconsistent with the foreign state's law, nor was there any suggestion that the laws of the state failed to meet the requirements accepted by free and democratic societies. Accordingly, the admission of the evidence did not affect trial fairness: *R. v. Hape*, [2007] 2 S.C.R. 292, 220 C.C.C. (3d) 161.

CHARTER

EXCEPTION WHERE EXPRESS DECLARATION / Operation of exception / Five year limitation / Re-enactment / Five year limitation.

33. (1) Parliament or the legislature of a province may expressly declare in an Act of Parliament or of the legislature, as the case may be, that the Act or a provision thereof shall operate notwithstanding a provision included in section 2 or sections 7 to 15 of this Charter.

(2) An Act or a provision of an Act in respect of which a declaration made under this section is in effect shall have such operation as it would have but for the provision of this Charter referred to in the declaration.

(3) A declaration made under subsection (1) shall cease to have effect five years after it comes into force or on such earlier date as may be specified in the declaration.

(4) Parliament or the legislature of a province may re-enact a declaration made under subsection (1).

(5) Subsection (3) applies in respect of a re-enactment made under subsection (4).

ANNOTATIONS

This section lays down only requirements of form for the exercise of the override power, and there is no warrant for importing into it grounds for substantive review of the legislative policy in exercising that power. The essential requirement of form is that the override declaration be an express declaration that an Act or a provision of an Act shall operate notwithstanding a provision included in s. 2 or ss. 7 to 15. A declaration is sufficiently expressed if it refers to the number of the section, subsection or paragraph of the Charter which contains the provision or provisions to be overridden. It was not intended by inclusion of the word "expressly" in this section that a legislature should be required to encumber a s. 33 declaration by stating the provision or provisions to be overridden in the words of the Charter. Further, a legislature may validly introduce an override provision into a number of statutes by a single enactment: *Ford v. Quebec (Attorney General)*, [1988] 2 S.C.R. 712, 54 D.L.R. (4th) 577.

Citation

CITATION.

34. This Part may be cited as the *Canadian Charter of Rights and Freedoms*.

. . . . .

CONSTITUTION ACT, 1982
Part VII / GENERAL

PRIMACY OF CONSTITUTION OF CANADA / Constitution of Canada / Amendments to Constitution of Canada.

52. (1) The Constitution of Canada is the supreme law of Canada, and any law that is inconsistent with the provisions of the Constitution is, to the extent of the inconsistency, of no force or effect.

(2) The Constitution of Canada includes

(*a*) the *Canada Act 1982*, including this Act;

(*b*) the Acts and orders referred to in the schedule; and

(*c*) any amendment to any Act or order referred to in paragraph (*a*) or (*b*).

(3) Amendments to the Constitution of Canada shall be made only in accordance with the authority contained in the Constitution of Canada.

ANNOTATIONS

The provincial court, where the accused was being tried, has always had the power to declare legislation invalid in criminal cases and this includes a power to dismiss charges where the legislation is invalid by reason of a violation of the Charter. In dismissing the charge, the provincial court is not called upon to make either a prerogative declaration or an order under s. 24(1) but simply to prevent a violation of a fundamental principle of constitutional law embodied in the section by dismissing the charges: *R. v. Big M Drug Mart*, [1985] 1 S.C.R. 295, 18 C.C.C. (3d) 385.

A judge presiding at a preliminary inquiry does not have jursidiction to determine the constitutionality of an evidentiary provision of the *Criminal Code* under this section: *R. v. Seaboyer*, [1991] 2 S.C.R. 577, 66 C.C.C. (3d) 321 (7:2).

It is open to a corporate accused to defend a charge on the basis that the legislation impaired the rights, such as freedom of religion, of an individual: *R. v. Big M Drug Mart Ltd., supra*, or fundamental justice: *R. v. Wholesale Travel Group Inc.*, [1991] 3 S.C.R. 154, 67 C.C.C. (3d) 193. [Also see notes under s. 24 "standing".]

CONTROLLED DRUGS AND SUBSTANCES ACT

1996, Chap. 19, ss. 1 to 60 (but see ss. 61 to 63); brought into force May 14, 1997 by SI/97-47, *Can. Gaz., Part II*, May 14, 1997

Amended 1996, c. 8, s. 35; brought into force July 12, 1996 by SI/96-69, *Can. Gaz., Part II*, July 24, 1997

Amended 1996, c. 19, s. 93.2; brought into force May 14, 1997 by SI/97-47, *Can. Gaz., Part II*, May 14, 1997

Amended SOR/97-230, *Can. Gaz., Part II*, May 14, 1997

Amended 1997, c. 18, s. 140; brought into force May 14, 1997 by SI/97-62.

Amended SOR/98-157, *Can. Gaz., Part II*, March 12, 1998

Amended SOR/98-173, *Can. Gaz., Part II*, March 19, 1998

Amended 1999, c. 5, ss. 48 and 49; brought into force May 1, 1999 by para. (*b*) of SI/99-24

Amended SOR/99-371, *Can. Gaz., Part II*, September 29, 1999

Amended SOR/99-421, *Can. Gaz., Part II*, October 21, 1999

Amended SOR/2000-220, *Can. Gaz., Part II*, June 1, 2000; in force September 1, 2000 as provided by s. 3

Amended 2001, c. 32, ss. 47 to 56; ss. 47, 49 to 53, 55, 56 brought into force January 7, 2002 by para. (*a*) of SI/2002-17, *Can. Gaz.*, January 16, 2002; ss. 48, 54 brought into force February 1, 2002 by para. (*b*) of SI/2002-17, *Can. Gaz.*, January 16, 2002

Amended SOR/2002-361, *Can. Gaz.*, September 24, 2002, ss. 1 and 2; in force January 9, 2003 as provided by s. 3

Amended SOR/2003-32, *Can. Gaz.*, January 30, 2003, ss. 1 to 3, 5 to 7; in force January 30, 2003 as provided by s. 8

Amended SOR/2003-37, *Can. Gaz.*, January 30, 2003

Amended SOR/2003-412, *Can. Gaz.*, December 11, 2003

Amended 2005, c. 10, ss. 15, 16 and 34(1)(*d*), brought into force April 4, 2005 by SI/2005-29, *Can. Gaz.*, April 20, 2005

Amended SOR/2005-235, *Can. Gaz.*, August 10, 2005

Amended SOR/2005-271, s. 1, *Can. Gaz.*, in force August 31, 2005 as provided by s. 2

Amended SOR/2005-337, s. 1, *Can. Gaz.*, in force November 15, 2005 as provided by s. 2

Amended SOR/2005-364, ss. 1, 2 and 4, *Can. Gaz.*; s. 1 in force November 21, 2005 as provided by s. 5(1); ss. 2 and 4 in force January 31, 2006 as provided by s. 5(2)

Amended 2005, c. 44, s. 13; in force November 25, 2005

Amended 2011, c. 14, s. 1; in force June 23, 2011

Amended 2012, c. 1, ss. 39 to 46; brought into force November 6, 2012 by SI/2012-48, *Can. Gaz, Part II*, July 4, 2012

Amended SOR/2012-66, *Can. Gaz., Part II*, April 11, 2012, s. 1; in force March 30, 2012 as provided by s. 2

Amended SOR/2012-176, *Can. Gaz., Part II*, October 10, 2012, s. 1; in force September 20, 2012

Amended 2015, c. 22, ss. 2 to 5; brought into force June 30, 2015 by SI/2015-63, *Can. Gaz., Part II*, July 15, 2015

Amended SOR/2015-190, *Can Gaz., Part II*, July 29, 2015, s. 1; in force January 13, 2016 as provided by s. 2

Amended SOR/2015-192, *Can Gaz., Part II*, July 29, 2015, ss. 1 and 2; in force July 16, 2015 as provided by s. 3

Amended SOR/2015-209, *Can. Gaz., Part II*, August 12, 2015, s. 1; in force February 9, 2016 as provided by s. 2

Amended SOR/2016-13, *Can. Gaz., Part II*, February 24, 2016, s. 1; in force February 5, 2016, as provided by s. 2

Amended SOR/2016-73, *Can. Gaz., Part II*, May 4, 2016, ss. 1 and 2; in force October 31, 2016 as provided by s. 3

Amended SOR/2016-107, *Can. Gaz., Part II*, June 1, 2016, ss. 1 and 2; in force November 28, 2016 as provided by s. 3

Amended SOR/2016-295, *Can. Gaz., Part II*, November 30, 2016, s. 1; in force November 30, 2016 as provided by s. 2

Amended SOR/2017-13, *Can. Gaz., Part II*, February 2, 2017, ss. 1 to 12; in force February 22, 2017 as provided by s. 13

Amended SOR/2017-44, *Can. Gaz., Part II*, April 5, 2017, s. 1; in force May 5, 2017 as provided by s. 2

Amended 2017, c. 4, s. 2; in force May 4, 2017

Amended 2017, c. 7, ss. 1 to 51; ss. 1(3) to (5), 3(1), (3), (4), 4 to 6, 7(2), (4), 9, 25, 26(1), (3), (4), (5), (6), (7), 27(1), (2), 30, 33, 34, 37, 38, 39, 40(1), (3), (6) to (8) (10) to (12), (14) to (19), 41 to 51 in force May 18, 2017; ss. 1(6), 2, 8, 10 to 24, 26(8), 29 brought into force June 21, 2018 by SI/2018-46, *Can. Gaz., Part II*, July 11, 2018; ss. 1(1), 28, 31, 32, 35, 36, 40(12) and (13) to come into force by order of the Governor in Council as provided by s. 73

Amended SOR/2017-249, *Can. Gaz., Part II*, December 13, 2017; in force December 13, 2017 as provided by s. 3

Amended SOR/2017-275, *Can. Gaz., Part II*, December 27, 2017; in force December 8, 2017 as provided by s. 2

Amended SOR/2017-277, *Can. Gaz., Part II*, December 27, 2017; in force December 27, 2017 as provided by s. 3

Amended SOR/2018-70, *Can. Gaz., Part II*, April 18, 2018; in force April 4, 2018 as provided by s. 5

Amended 2018, c. 16, ss. 194 to 206; ss. 194, 200 to 202, 206 in force on Royal Assent, June 21, 2018; ss. 195 to 198, 203 to 205, 206(6) in force October 17, 2018; if Bill C-37, introduced in the 1st session of the 42nd Parliament and entitled *An Act to amend the Controlled Drugs and Substances Act and to make related amendments to other Acts*, receives royal assent, then, on the first day on which both s. 28 of that Act and s. 199(2) of 2018, c. 16 are in force, s. 199(1) will come into force

Editor's Note: The *Controlled Drugs and Substances Act* creates a new scheme for the regulation of certain dangerous drugs and narcotics, now known as "controlled substances". The Act replaces the *Narcotic Control Act*, R.S.C. 1985, c. N-1 and Part III [Controlled Drugs] and Part IV [Restricted Drugs] of the *Food and Drugs Act*, R.S.C. 1985, c. F-27. The essential scheme of the legislation is similar to the former *Narcotic Control Act* and the *Food and Drugs Act*.

Schedules / An important part of the legislation is the schedules to the Act: Schedule I – includes the most dangerous drugs and narcotics, such as phencyclidine, heroin and cocaine. Schedule II – lists cannabis and its derivatives. Schedule III – includes many of the more dangerous drugs which previously were included in schedules G and H to the *Food and Drugs Act*, such as the amphetamines and lysergic acid diethylamide (LSD). Schedule IV – includes many of the drugs formerly included in Schedule G to the *Food and Drugs Act*. These drugs, such as the barbiturates, while dangerous, have therapeutic uses. As was the case under Part III of the *Food and Drugs Act*, simple possession of Schedule IV drugs is not an offence.

Possession / Under s. 4(1), simple possession of any of the drugs and narcotics listed in Schedules I, II and III of the *Controlled Drugs and Substances Act* is an offence unless the person is authorized to be in possession by the regulations. The offence under s. 4(1) is a

Crown option offence. The penalty for breach of s. 4(1) depends upon the Schedule in which the substance is included. In addition, a special penalty scheme has been included for possession of small quantities of Schedule II [cannabis] offences. Where the subject matter of the offence is a Schedule II substance in an amount that does not exceed the amount set out in Schedule VIII, then the accused is guilty only of a summary conviction offence and the maximum penalty is a $1,000 fine and/or six months' jail. Further, even where the amounts exceed the Schedule VIII amounts and the Crown proceeds by indictment, the offence is within the absolute jurisdiction of the provincial court where the substance is listed in Schedule II.

"Double-doctoring" / Under s. 4(2), it is an offence to seek or obtain any of the scheduled substances from a practitioner, such as a physician, without disclosing particulars relating to the acquisition of any of the scheduled substances within the preceding 30 days. This is the so-called "double-doctoring" offence which was found in both the *Food and Drugs Act* and the *Narcotic Control Act*. Again, this is a Crown option offence. The maximum penalty for the offence where the Crown proceeds by indictment depends upon the schedule in which the substance is found. If the Crown proceeds by way of summary conviction, then the penalty is the same irrespective of the schedule.

Trafficking / Under s. 5(1), it is an offence to traffic in any of the scheduled substances and under s. 5(2) it is an offence to be in possession for the purpose of trafficking. The definition of "traffic", which of course includes sell, when combined with the definition of "sell" is very broad and covers virtually the same activity as was prohibited under the predecessor legislation. These definitions are found in s. 2. The penalty and classification of the offence depend upon the schedule in which the substance is found. For the Schedule I and II substances, it is a pure indictable offence with a maximum punishment of life imprisonment, except where the offence relates to trafficking in smaller amounts of the Schedule II (cannabis) substance. Under s. 5(4), where the amount of the Schedule II substance does not exceed the amount listed in Schedule VII, the maximum penalty is five years less one day. This offence is also listed in s. 553(*c*) of the *Criminal Code* and thus is within the absolute jurisdiction of the provincial court. For the Schedule III and IV offences, the offence is a Crown-option offence with lesser maximum punishments.

Importing / Section 6 creates the importing offence for substances included in Schedules I to VI. Schedules V and VI list chemicals which can be employed in the manufacture of substances listed in the earlier Schedule. Where the substance is listed in Schedules I and II, the offence is indictable and punishable by life imprisonment. Where the substance is listed in the other schedules, the offence is a Crown-option offence with the maximum penalty depending upon the schedule in which the substance is found.

Production / Section 7 prohibits the production of any of the substances in Schedules I to IV except as authorized by regulations. The term "produce" is defined in s. 2 and includes manufacture and cultivation. For Schedule I and II substances, the offence is indictable with a maximum punishment of life imprisonment unless the substance is marihuana in which case the maximum is seven years. Where the substance is listed in Schedule III or IV, the offence is Crown-option with lesser maximum punishments.

Proceeds of Crime / Sections 8 and 9 recreate the proceeds of crime and money-laundering offences in terms similar to the former provisions of the *Narcotic Control Act* and the *Food and Drugs Act*.

Sentencing / Section 10 sets out the principles of sentencing and includes a list of aggravating circumstances such as that the accused used a weapon in relation to the commission of the offence or committed the trafficking offence near a school. Where one of these aggravating circumstances exists but the judge does not impose a prison term, the judge is required to give reasons for that decision.

Search and Seizure / Sections 11 to 13 set out the powers of search and seizure in respect of offences under this Act. The terms are similar to those found in the *Criminal Code*. In addition, special provision is made in s. 11(7) for a warrantless search in exigent circumstances.

Restraint and Forfeiture / Sections 14 to 23 deal with restraint orders and forfeiture orders in terms similar to Part XII.2 of the *Criminal Code*. This is a departure from the scheme under the *Narcotic Control Act* and the *Food and Drugs Act* which had simply adopted the provisions of Part XII.2 with the necessary modifications. A significant difference between the procedure under this Act and the procedure under the *Criminal Code* is that the Attorney General is not required to give an undertaking as to damages and costs when seeking a restraint order under the Act.

Disposal of seized substances / Part III of the Act deals with the disposal of substances seized or found by a peace officer or inspector. Part IV sets out the scheme for appointment of inspectors and the administrative enforcement of the Act and regulations in terms similar to Part II of the *Food and Drugs Act*. Part V sets out a special scheme for enforcement of "designated regulations". Under this Part, the Minister may make an emergency order where there is a substantial risk of immediate danger to the health or safety of any person.

Miscellaneous / Part VI contains a number of miscellaneous provisions. Most important are those relating to the admissibility of certificates of analysis [ss. 51 and 52], continuity of exhibits [s. 53], admissibility of copies of records seized under the Act or regulations [s. 54], and the limitation period of one year where the Crown proceeds by way of summary conviction [s. 47]. Under s. 48, the evidentiary burden is initially upon the accused to show that any certificate, licence, permit or other qualification operates in the accused's favour. Section 55 gives the Governor in Council wide regulation-making powers.

Section 60 permits the Governor in Council to add or delete items from any of the Schedules. An important innovation in this Act is the concept of "analogue" defined in s. 2 as a substance that, in relation to a controlled substance, has "a substantially similar chemical structure". Thus, for example, Schedule III lists amphetamines, their salts, derivatives, isomers and "analogues". This concept was apparently added to attempt to deal with the problem of chemists manufacturing drugs with a slightly different chemical structure than those actually listed in the schedule. Previously, the government would have been required to amend the schedules to prohibit or regulate the trafficking or production of such substances.

"Controlled substance" / It should also be noted that s. 2(2)(*b*) provides that a reference to a "controlled substance" includes a reference to all synthetic and natural forms of the substances. This specifically meets an argument which had been made under the former *Narcotic Control Act* that certain synthetic forms of narcotics were not covered by the Act.

An act respecting the control of certain drugs, their precursors and other substances and to amend certain other Acts and repeal the Narcotic Control Act in consequence thereof

SHORT TITLE

SHORT TITLE.

1. This Act may be cited as the *Controlled Drugs and Substances Act*.

INTERPRETATION

DEFINITIONS / "adjudicator" / "analogue" / "analyst" / "Attorney General" / "controlled substance" / "designated substance offence" / "inspector" / "judge" / "justice" / "Minister" / "offence-related property" / "possession" / "practitioner" / "precursor" / "prescribed" / "produce" / "provide" / "sell" / "traffic" / Interpretation / Idem.

2. (1) In this Act,

"adjudicator" means a person appointed or employed under the *Public Service Employment Act* who performs the duties and functions of an adjudicator under this Act and the regulations;

Note: Subsection 2(1) amended by repealing the definition "adjudicator", 2017, c. 7, s. 1(1) (to come into force by order of the Governor in Council).

"analogue" means a substance that, in relation to a controlled substance, has a substantially similar chemical structure;

"analyst" means a person who is designated as an analyst under section 44;

"Attorney General" means

(*a*) the Attorney General of Canada, and includes their lawful deputy, or

(*b*) with respect to proceedings commenced at the instance of the government of a province and conducted by or on behalf of that government, the Attorney General of that province, and includes their lawful deputy;

"chemical offence-related property" means offence-related property that is a chemical or precursor and includes anything that contains such property or has such property on it;

"controlled substance" means a substance included in Schedule I, II, III, IV or V;

"customs office" has the same meaning as in subsection 2(1) of the *Customs Act*;

"designated device" means a device included in Schedule IX;

"designated substance offence" means

(*a*) an offence under Part I, except subsection 4(1), or

(*b*) a conspiracy or an attempt to commit, being an accessory after the fact in relation to, or any counselling in relation to, an offence referred to in paragraph (*a*);

"inspector" means a person who is designated as an inspector under section 30;

"judge" means a judge as defined in section 552 of the *Criminal Code* or a judge of a superior court of criminal jurisdiction;

"justice" has the same meaning as in section 2 of the *Criminal Code*;

"Minister" means the Minister of Health;

"non-chemical offence-related property" means offence-related property that is not chemical offence-related property;

"offence-related property" means, with the exception of a controlled substance, any property, within or outside Canada,

(*a*) by means of or in respect of which a designated substance offence is committed,

(*b*) that is used in any manner in connection with the commission of a designated substance offence, or

(*c*) that is intended for use for the purpose of committing a designated substance offence;

"organization" has the same meaning as in section 2 of the *Criminal Code*;

"person" means an individual or an organization;

DRUGS

"possession" means possession within the meaning of subsection 4(3) of the *Criminal Code*;

"practitioner" means a person who is registered and entitled under the laws of a province to practise in that province the profession of medicine, dentistry or veterinary medicine, and includes any other person or class or persons prescribed as a practitioner;

"precursor" means a substance included in Schedule VI;

"prescribed" means prescribed by the regulations;

"produce" means, in respect of a substance included in any of Schedules I to V, to obtain the substance by any method or process including

(*a*) manufacturing, synthesizing or using any means of altering the chemical or physical properties of the substance, or

(*b*) cultivating, propagating or harvesting the substance or any living thing from which the substance may be extracted or otherwise obtained,

and includes offer to produce;

"provide" means to give, transfer or otherwise make available in any manner, whether directly or indirectly and whether or not for consideration;

"sell" includes offer for sale, expose for sale, have in possession for sale and distribute, whether or not the distribution is made for consideration;

"traffic" means, in respect of a substance included in any of Schedules I to V,

(*a*) to sell, administer, give, transfer, transport, send or deliver the substance,

(*b*) to sell an authorization to obtain the substance, or

(*c*) to offer to do anything mentioned in paragraph (*a*) or (*b*),

otherwise than under the authority of the regulations.

(2) For the purposes of this Act,

(*a*) a reference to a controlled substance includes a reference to any substance that contains a controlled substance; and

(*b*) a reference to a controlled substance includes a reference to

(i) all synthetic and natural forms of the substance, and

(ii) any thing that contains or has on it a controlled substance and that is used or intended or designed for use

(A) in producing the substance, or

(B) in introducing the substance into a human body.

(3) For the purposes of this Act, where a substance is expressly named in any of Schedules I to VI, it shall be deemed not to be included in any other of those Schedules. 1996, c. 8, s. 35; 2001, c. 32, s. 47; 2017, c. 7, s. 1(3) to (6); 2018, c. 16, s. 194.

ANNOTATIONS

Note: The following cases were decided under the repealed *Narcotic Control Act*, but were considered useful in the interpretation of this section.

"Analyst" – An analyst designated under the *Narcotic Control Act* is deemed to be an analyst under this Act by virtue of s. 44 of the *Interpretation Act*. However, in the absence of evidence that the analyst was actually acting under the *Narcotic Control Act*, the certificate was inadmissible: *R. v. May* (2000), 150 C.C.C. (3d) 122 (Alta. C.A.).

"Controlled substance" – Item 1 [now contained in Schedule 1] which lists opium poppy "its preparations, derivatives, alkaloids and salts, including: . . . (3) morphine . . . and their preparations, derivatives and salts including . . . (10) Diacetylmorphine (heroin)" includes synthetic heroin, that is heroin derived from synthetically produced morphine: *R. v. Rourke* (1980), 54 C.C.C. (2d) 225 (B.C.C.A.).

Item 2 [now contained in Schedule 1] which lists "Coca (Erythroxylon), its preparations, derivatives, alkaloids and salts including: . . . (2) cocaine" includes cocaine whether or not it is proved to have been derived from the coca plant: *R. v. Maskell* (1981), 58 C.C.C. (2d) 408 (Alta. C.A.).

The gravamen of the offence of possession of *cannabis* resin is possession of *cannabis* and the word "resin" is surplusage. When the accused possesses any of the substances set out in item 3 of the Schedule he has committed the offence: *R. v. Barrett* (1980), 54 C.C.C. (2d) 75 (Alta. C.A.).

"Narcotic" does not include a prescription: *R. v. Verma* (1996), 112 C.C.C. (3d) 155 (Ont. C.A.).

It was decided under the predecessor legislation that viable marihuana seeds are a prohibited narcotic: *R. v. Hunter* (2000), 145 C.C.C. (3d) 528 (B.C.C.A.), leave to appeal to S.C.C. refused 149 C.C.C. (3d) vii.

"Offence-related property" – A "significant" change means a consequential, notable or important change to the property. "Modification" means a partial change or alteration of something. In this case, marihuana growing equipment that was attached to the real property by screws and tape could easily have been removed and did not constitute a significant modification which impacted or affected the property in a material way: *R. v. Dupuis* (1998), 130 C.C.C. (3d) 426 (Sask. Q.B.).

"Possession" – Constructive possession requires non-quiescent knowledge and a measure of control. To constitute joint possession, there must be knowledge, consent and a measure of control on the part of the person deemed to be in possession: *R. v. Pham* (2005), 203 C.C.C. (3d) 326 (Ont. C.A.), affd 209 C.C.C. (3d) 351 (S.C.C.).

"Restricted drug" – The drug "Psilocybin" as described in Sch. H [now in Schedule 3] includes the drug as found in its natural form in a mushroom. Thus an accused may be convicted of the trafficking or possession offence although he only has possession of mushrooms containing psilocybin: *R. v. Dunn*, [1982] 2 S.C.R. 677, 1 C.C.C. (3d) 1 (7:0).

DRUGS

INTERPRETATION.

3. (1) Every power or duty imposed under this Act that may be exercised or performed in respect of an offence under this Act may be exercised or performed in respect of a conspiracy, or an attempt to commit, being an accessory after the fact in relation to, or any counselling in relation to, an offence under this Act. 1995, c. 22, s. 18 (Sched. IV, item 26); 2017, c. 7, s. 2.

(2) [*Repealed*, 2017, c. 7, s. 2.]

Part I / OFFENCES AND PUNISHMENT

Particular Offences

POSSESSION OF SUBSTANCE / Obtaining substance / Punishment / Punishment / Punishment / Punishment / Punishment / Determination of amount.

4. (1) Except as authorized under the regulations, no person shall possess a substance included in Schedule I, II or III.

(2) No person shall seek or obtain

(*a*) a substance included in Schedule I, II, III or IV, or

(*b*) an authorization to obtain a substance included in Schedule I, II, III or IV

from a practitioner, unless the person discloses to the practitioner particulars relating to the acquisition by the person of every substance in those Schedules, and of every

authorization to obtain such substances, from any other practitioner within the preceding thirty days.

(3) Every person who contravenes subsection (1) where the subject-matter of the offence is a substance included in Schedule I

(*a*) is guilty of an indictable offence and liable to imprisonment for a term not exceeding seven years; or

(*b*) is guilty of an offence punishable on summary conviction and liable

(i) for a first offence, to a fine not exceeding one thousand dollars or to imprisonment for a term not exceeding six months, or to both, and

(ii) for a subsequent offence, to a fine not exceeding two thousand dollars or to imprisonment for a term not exceeding one year, or to both.

(4) Subject to subsection (5), every person who contravenes subsection (1) where the subject-matter of the offence is a substance included in Schedule II

(*a*) is guilty of an indictable offence and liable to imprisonment for a term not exceeding five years less a day; or

(*b*) is guilty of an offence punishable on summary conviction and liable

(i) for a first offence, to a fine not exceeding one thousand dollars or to imprisonment for a term not exceeding six months, or to both, and

(ii) for a subsequent offence, to a fine not exceeding two thousand dollars or to imprisonment for a term not exceeding one year, or to both.

(5) [*Repealed*, 2018, c. 16, s. 195(1).]

(6) Every person who contravenes subsection (1) where the subject-matter of the offence is a substance included in Schedule III

(*a*) is guilty of an indictable offence and liable to imprisonment for a term not exceeding three years; or

(*b*) is guilty of an offence punishable on summary conviction and liable

(i) for a first offence, to a fine not exceeding one thousand dollars or to imprisonment for a term not exceeding six months, or to both, and

(ii) for a subsequent offence, to a fine not exceeding two thousand dollars or to imprisonment for a term not exceeding one year, or to both.

(7) Every person who contravenes subsection (2)

(*a*) is guilty of an indictable offence and liable

(i) to imprisonment for a term not exceeding seven years, where the subject-matter of the offence is a substance included in Schedule I,

(ii) to imprisonment for a term not exceeding five years less a day, where the subject-matter of the offence is a substance included in Schedule II,

(iii) to imprisonment for a term not exceeding three years, where the subject-matter of the offence is a substance included in Schedule III, or

(iv) to imprisonment for a term not exceeding eighteen months, where the subject-matter of the offence is a substance included in Schedule IV; or

(*b*) is guilty of an offence punishable on summary conviction and liable

(i) for a first offence, to a fine not exceeding one thousand dollars or to imprisonment for a term not exceeding six months, or to both, and

(ii) for a subsequent offence, to a fine not exceeding two thousand dollars or to imprisonment for a term not exceeding one year, or to both. 2018, c. 16, s. 195.

(8) [*Repealed*, 2018, c. 16, s. 195(2).]

ANNOTATIONS

Note: Most of the following cases were decided under the repealed *Narcotic Control Act*, but were considered useful in the interpretation of this section.

Subsection (1) – A minute trace of a narcotic is only an evidence of earlier possession and does not establish present possession: *R. v. McBurney* (1975), 24 C.C.C. (2d) 44 (B.C.C.A.) (4:1). *Contra: R. v. Quigley* (1954), 111 C.C.C. 81 (Alta. C.A.). Also see *R. v. Boyesen* (1982), 75 Cr. App. R. 51 (H.L.), where it was held in relation to s. 5(2) of the *Misuse of Drugs Act* 1971 (U.K.) that the test is not whether the amount is capable of being used but whether it is in possession and can be identified. Quantity is important, however, as the quantity must be sufficient for the court to find that it amounts to something as a matter of fact. But if it is visible, tangible and measurable, it is certainly something. Secondly, quantity may be relevant to the issue of knowledge. If the quantity is so minute, it may be that it cannot be proved that the accused knew it was there.

Where the evidence establishes that the accused had knowledge and control of the drug there is no requirement that the Crown also prove that the amount was usable: *R. v. Brett* (1986), 41 C.C.C. (3d) 190 (B.C.C.A.).

The principle of *de minimum non curat lex* does not apply to the offence under this subsection: *R. v. Keizer* (1990), 98 N.S.R. (2d) 266 (S.C.).

An admission by the accused that he was in possession of "hash" was some evidence that he was in possession of cannabis resin: *R. v. O'Brien* (1987), 41 C.C.C. (3d) 86 (Que. C.A.).

The prohibition against possession of marihuana does not infringe either ss. 15 or 7 of the Charter: *R. v. Hamon* (1993), 85 C.C.C. (3d) 490 (Que. C.A.), leave to appeal to S.C.C. refused 167 N.R. 239*n*.

Constitutionality – The criminalization of the possession of marihuana, even for recreational personal use, does not violate ss. 7 or 15 of the Charter: *R. v. Malmo-Levine; R. v. Caine*, [2003] 3 S.C.R. 571, 179 C.C.C. (3d) 417; *R. v. Clay*, [2003] 3 S.C.R. 735, 179 C.C.C. (3d) 540. The blanket prohibition on the possession of marihuana in this section was held to violate s. 7 of the *Charter of Rights and Freedoms*, since insufficient provision is made for an accused who requires the marihuana for medical purposes. The court struck down the provision but suspended the declaration of invalidity for a period of 12 months. This accused was entitled to a constitutional exemption during the period of suspended invalidity: *R. v. Parker* (2000), 146 C.C.C. (3d) 193 (Ont. C.A.).

The prohibition against marihuana possession is valid when there is a constitutionally acceptable medical exemption regulations in force. If, at the time of the accused's charge, the *Marihuana Medical Access Regulations*, SOR/2001-227, were in force and constitutional, then s. 4 is valid. If the regulations did not solve the constitutional deficiencies, then the possession prohibition, even as modified by the regulations, are of no force and effect: *R. v. P. (J.)* (2003), 177 C.C.C. (3d) 522 (Ont. C.A.). See *R. v. Stavert* (2003), 179 C.C.C. (3d) 117 (P.E.I.T.D.), holding that it was open to the trial judge to conclude that there was no constitutionally valid prohibition in effect for the possession of marihuana given *R. v. Parker*, *supra*, and the absence of constitutionally valid regulations at the time of the offence.

The declaration of invalidity in *R. v. Parker*, *supra*, did not delete marihuana from Schedule II, but simply declared that the reference in s. 4 to Schedule II was of no force or effect for the purpose of a possession charge: *R. v. Turmel* (2003), 177 C.C.C. (3d) 533 (Ont. C.A.).

The exclusion of non-dried forms of marihuana from the lawful possession scheme under the *Marihuana Medical Access Regulations* violates s. 7 of the Charter. It is unconstitutionally arbitrary because there is no connection between the prohibition on non-dried forms of medical marihuana and the health and safety of the patients who qualify for legal access to medical marihuana. However, instead of striking down ss. 4 and 5 of the *Controlled Drugs and Substances Act* in their entirety, the appropriate remedy was a declaration that these provisions are of no force and effect only to the extent that they prohibit a person with a medical authorization from possessing cannabis derivatives for medical purposes: *R. v. Smith*, [2015] 2 S.C.R. 602, 323 C.C.C. (3d) 461.

Possession – Also see cases noted under s. 4 of the *Criminal Code*.

Telephone calls to the accused's phone are admissible as circumstantial evidence of knowledge of the presence of drugs: *R. v. Williams* (2009), 246 C.C.C. (3d) 443 (B.C.C.A.).

DEFINITION OF "MEDICAL EMERGENCY" / Exemption — medical emergency / Exemption — persons at the scene / Exemption — evidence / Deeming.

4.1 (1) For the purposes of this section, "medical emergency" means a physiological event induced by the introduction of a psychoactive substance into the body of a person that results in a life-threatening situation and in respect of which there are reasonable grounds to believe that the person requires emergency medical or law enforcement assistance.

(2) No person who seeks emergency medical or law enforcement assistance because that person, or another person, is suffering from a medical emergency is to be charged or convicted of an offence under subsection 4(1) if the evidence in support of that offence was obtained or discovered as a result of that person having sought assistance or having remained at the scene.

(3) The exemption under subsection (2) also applies to any person, including the person suffering from the medical emergency, who is at the scene on the arrival of the emergency medical or law enforcement assistance.

(4) No person who seeks emergency medical or law enforcement assistance because that person, or another person, is suffering from a medical emergency, or who is at the scene on the arrival of the assistance, is to be charged with an offence concerning a violation of any condition of a pre-trial release or probation order relating to an offence under subsection 4(1) if the evidence in support of that offence was obtained or discovered as a result of that person having sought assistance or having remained at the scene.

(5) Any condition of a person's pre-trial release, probation order, conditional sentence or parole relating to an offence under subsection 4(1) that may be violated as a result of the person seeking emergency medical or law enforcement assistance for their, or another person's, medical emergency, or as a result of having been at the scene on the arrival of the assistance, is deemed not to be violated. 2017, c. 4, s. 2; 2018, c. 16, s. 195.1.

TRAFFICKING IN SUBSTANCE / Possession for purpose of trafficking / Punishment / Punishment in respect of specified substance / Interpretation / Idem.

5. (1) No person shall traffic in a substance included in Schedule I, II, III, IV or V or in any substance represented or held out by that person to be such a substance.

(2) No person shall, for the purpose of trafficking, possess a substance included in Schedule I, II, III, IV or V.

(3) Every person who contravenes subsection (1) or (2)

(*a*) if the subject matter of the offence is a substance included in Schedule I or II, is guilty of an indictable offence and liable to imprisonment for life, and

(i) to a minimum punishment of imprisonment for a term of one year if

(A) the person committed the offence for the benefit of, at the direction of or in association with a criminal organization, as defined in subsection 467.1(1) of the *Criminal Code*,

(B) the person used or threatened to use violence in committing the offence,

(C) the person carried, used or threatened to use a weapon in committing the offence, or

(D) the person was convicted of a designated substance offence, or had served a term of imprisonment for a designated substance offence, within the previous 10 years, or

(ii) to a minimum punishment of imprisonment for a term of two years if

(A) the person committed the offence in or near a school, on or near school grounds or in or near any other public place usually frequented by persons under the age of 18 years,

(B) the person committed the offence in a prison, as defined in section 2 of the *Criminal Code*, or on its grounds, or

(C) the person used the services of a person under the age of 18 years, or involved such a person, in committing the offence;

(*a*.1) [*Repealed*, 2018, c. 16, s. 196(2).]

(*b*) if the subject-matter of the offence is a substance included in Schedule III or V,

(i) is guilty of an indictable offence and liable to imprisonment for a term not exceeding ten years, or

(ii) is guilty of an offence punishable on summary conviction and liable to imprisonment for a term not exceeding eighteen months; and

(*c*) where the subject-matter of the offence is a substance included in Schedule IV,

(i) is guilty of an indictable offence and liable to imprisonment for a term not exceeding three years, or

(ii) is guilty of an offence punishable on summary conviction and liable to imprisonment for a term not exceeding one year.

(4) [*Repealed*. 2012, c. 1, s. 39(2).]

(5) For the purposes of applying subsection (3) in respect of an offence under subsection (1), a reference to a substance included in Schedule I, II, III, IV or V includes a reference to any substance represented or held out to be a substance included in that Schedule. 2012, c. 1, s. 39; 2017, c. 7, s. 3(1), (3), (4); 2018, c. 16, s. 196.

(6) [*Repealed*, 2018, c. 16, s. 196(3).]

DRUGS

ANNOTATIONS

Note: Some of the following cases were decided under the *Narcotic Control Act*, but were considered useful in the interpretation of this section.

Meaning of trafficking generally [subsec. (1)] – Once a person is found to have given or delivered a drug to another the offence of trafficking is proven, and it is not necessary for the Crown to prove that he so acted to promote the distribution of the drug to another: *R. v. Larson* (1972), 6 C.C.C. (2d) 145 (B.C.C.A.).

Nor is profit an element of the offence: *R. v. Drysdelle* (1978), 41 C.C.C. (2d) 238 (N.B.S.C. App. Div.).

The act of an accused in merely giving a narcotic to a friend to hold for him for safekeeping constitutes the offence under this subsection: *R. v. Lauze* (1980), 17 C.R. (3d) 90 (Que. C.A.).

While aiding a buyer is not trafficking if the accused personally committed none of the acts defined as trafficking, where the accused personally committed forbidden acts, it was irrelevant whom he assisted or intended to assist: *R. v. Wood* (2007), 218 C.C.C. (3d) 386 (Alta. C.A.).

The definitions of "sell" and "traffic" cast a very wide net to facilitate the prosecution of those who participate in or contribute to the trafficking of narcotics. Distributing without receiving consideration is selling as is distributing in exchange for consideration. Accordingly, a person who facilitates only the payment for drugs after delivery can be said to have participated in a conspiracy to traffic: *R. v. Neal* (2010), 276 C.C.C. (3d) 294 (Ont. C.A.), leave to appeal to S.C.C. refused [2010] 2 S.C.R. viii *sub nom. R. v. Sansalone.*

Distribution means the allocation to a number of people and accordingly cannot occur where there is only one recipient: *R. v. Christiansen* (1973), 13 C.C.C. (2d) 504 (N.B.S.C. App. Div.).

Where the transportation by the accused of the narcotic is incidental to the accused's own personal use of the narcotic as distinct from transportation as part of a transaction involving others, then the accused does not commit the offence under this subsection: *R. v. Harrington and Scosky*, [1964] 1 C.C.C. 189 (B.C.C.A.); *R. v. Young* (1971), 2 C.C.C. (2d) 560 (B.C.C.A.).

The term "administer" in the former definition of "traffic" in s. 2 of the *Narcotic Control Act* means to apply as a medicine or to give remedially rather than to merely make the narcotic available by giving a prescription: *R. v. Tan* (1984), 15 C.C.C. (3d) 30 (Sask. C.A.).

It was held in *R. v. Dumais* (1979), 51 C.C.C. (2d) 106 (Ont. C.A.), distinguishing *R. v. Maxwell, Watson and Shaw*, *infra,* that the use of the words "jointly traffic" did not preclude the conviction of one accused notwithstanding the acquittal of the other.

The acts of a physician in selling prescriptions for narcotics could constitute trafficking within this section either by selling or administering: *R. v. Rousseau* (1991), 70 C.C.C. (3d) 445 (Que. C.A.), leave to appeal to S.C.C. refused 70 C.C.C. (3d) vi. In *R. v. Verma* (1996), 112 C.C.C. (3d) 155, the Ontario Court of Appeal came to the contrary conclusion. The court concluded that a physician's sale of a prescription for a narcotic does not constitute trafficking as the physician has no control over whether the prescription will be exchanged for drugs. In addition, the doctrine of innocent agency cannot be used to attribute the *actus reus* of the innocent pharmacist in filling the prescript to the physician. Furthermore, the terms "administer" is not broad enough to encompass this type of conduct.

Liability of party to trafficking offence – The civil law concept of "agency" cannot be used to make non-criminal an act which would otherwise be attended by criminal consequences. Thus an accused who is acting on behalf of a purchaser of a narcotic may nevertheless be guilty of trafficking where he does one or more acts which render him liable as a party under s. 21(1) of the *Criminal Code* to the offence committed by the vendor of the narcotic: *R. v. Poitras*, [1974] S.C.R. 649, 12 C.C.C. (2d) 337 (4:1); *R. v. Greenlaw* (1981), 60 C.C.C. (2d) 178 (Ont. C.A.).

Where an accused does nothing more than provide incidental assistance of the sale of a controlled substance through rendering aid to the purchaser, the accused is guilty of the offence of aiding or abetting the possession of a narcotic, not trafficking. Where, however, the accused located the seller, brought the buyer to the site and introduced the parties, negotiated the price of the drugs and passed the money over to the seller, he was not simply a purchaser and he was properly found guilty of trafficking as a party under s. 21(1)(*b*) of the *Criminal Code*: *R. v. Greyeyes*, [1997] 2 S.C.R. 825, 116 C.C.C. (3d) 334. See also *R. v. Meston* (1975), 28 C.C.C. (2d) 497 (Ont. C.A.), *R. v. Schartner* (1977), 38 C.C.C. (2d) 89 (B.C.C.A.).

Trafficking by offer – Once the accused offered to sell a narcotic to the undercover police officer the *actus reus* of the offence of trafficking is complete and the requisite *mens rea* is found in the accused's intention to make an offer to sell the narcotic. Thus it is no defence that the accused knew the purchaser was a police officer and his intention was to "fool" the officer into thinking he would deliver the narcotic in order to cheat the officer: *R. v. Sherman* (1977), 36 C.C.C. (2d) 207 (B.C.C.A.).

The offence of trafficking by offer is made out where the accused offers to traffic in a narcotic and intends to make an offer that will be taken as a genuine offer by the recipient regardless of whether the accused intended to carry out the offer. The words or actions or actions constituting an offer do not, standing alone, constitute the crime. The Crown must prove an intention to make an offer that would be taken as a true and genuine offer to traffic: *R. v. Murdock* (2003), 176 C.C.C. (3d) 232 (Ont. C.A.). See also: *R. v. Crain* (2012), 285 C.C.C. (3d) 235 (Sask. C.A.). Similarly the accused were properly convicted even if they only offered to sell narcotics as part of a scheme to defraud the purchaser of his money and with no intention of actually delivering the narcotics: *R. v. Mancuso* (1989), 51 C.C.C. (3d) 380 (Que. C.A.).

Trafficking by holding out – On a charge of trafficking in a substance held out to be a narcotic it is not material to the proof of the charge that the purchaser believed the substance was a narcotic provided it was represented or held out to be a narcotic by the accused and, therefore, the actual purchaser is not a necessary witness: *R. v. Merritt* (1975), 27 C.C.C. (2d) 156 (N.B.S.C. App. Div.).

Conspiracy to traffic – An accused may be convicted of a conspiracy to commit this offence where the evidence establishes an agreement between the accused and another whereby the co-conspirator would sell narcotics to the accused for the purposes of resale to other persons: *R. v. Genser* (1986), 27 C.C.C. (3d) 264 (Man. C.A.), affd [1987] 2 S.C.R. 685, 39 C.C.C. (3d) 576 (5:0).

Possession for purpose of trafficking generally [subsec. (2)] – The gravamen of the offence under this subsection is possession plus the intent or purpose of physically making the narcotic available to others even if they are owners in common with the accused: *R. v. Taylor* (1974), 17 C.C.C. (2d) 36 (B.C.C.A.).

Under this section the offence requires proof of actual knowledge or wilful blindness as to the presence of the narcotics. Mere recklessness is not sufficient: *R. v. Sandhu* (1989), 50 C.C.C. (3d) 492 (Ont. C.A.).

Transporting for joint use – The doctrine of conjugal unity does not apply to prevent a possession for the purpose of trafficking conviction against a husband for transporting drugs to his wife: *R. v. O'Connor* (1975), 23 C.C.C. (2d) 110 (B.C.C.A.) (5:0).

However, it was held that the driver of a vehicle is not in possession for the purpose of trafficking where he and the joint owner of a quantity of narcotic are both in the vehicle at the time of apprehension and the narcotic is for their own use. The word "transport" in the definition of traffic as formerly defined in s. 2 of the *Narcotic Control Act* contemplates movement of the narcotic for the purpose of promoting its distribution to another person: *R. v. Binkley* (1982), 69 C.C.C. (2d) 169 (Sask. C.A.); *R. v. Gardiner* (1987), 35 C.C.C. (3d) 461 (Ont. C.A.).

DRUGS

Liability of party to possession offence – An accused who assists a narcotics trafficker in concealing the narcotics in the accused's apartment so that the trafficker may avoid detection is liable as party to offence of possession for the purpose of trafficking and is not guilty merely of simple possession: *R. v. Jackson* (1977), 35 C.C.C. (2d) 331 (Ont. C.A.).

An accused is properly convicted as a party to this offence where, although not in possession of the narcotics, she lent the principal offender the money to purchase the narcotics on terms that required him to repay the money and give her a share of the proceeds from the resale of the narcotics: *R. v. Roan* (1985), 17 C.C.C. (3d) 534 (Alta. C.A.).

An accused who set up a commercial cultivation operation and assisted in bringing the crop to maturity can be convicted as a party to the offence under this subsection although he does not own nor have any interest in the disposition of the crop: *R. v. Arason* (1992), 78 C.C.C. (3d) 1 (B.C.C.A.).

While the Regulations do not provide a specific exemption for a person who cohabits with someone who has obtained a narcotic for personal use under a valid prescription, such an exemption must be implied to avoid criminalizing vast swaths of harmless conduct. Where the prescription holder deals with the drugs beyond the scope of permitted use, the cohabiting party can only be liable if he or she knows that the prescription holder is misusing the drugs: *R. v. Pilgrim* (2017), 347 C.C.C. (3d) 141 (Ont. C.A.).

Mistake as to nature of drug – The defence of mistaken belief as to the true identity of the drug must be honest and its reasonableness is only a factor to be considered. This belief must be innocent and accordingly this defence will fail where the evidence establishes that the accused believed that the drug he possessed for sale was mescaline rather than a narcotic: *R. v. Couture* (1976), 33 C.C.C. (2d) 74 (Ont. C.A.).

A genuine though mistaken belief on the part of the accused that the laboratory in which they were employed was authorized to manufacture the controlled drug is a defence to the charge: *R. v. Darquea and Martyn* (1979), 47 C.C.C. (2d) 567 (Ont. C.A.).

Proof of offence charged – The offence under this subsection is possession of a narcotic for the purpose of trafficking. Thus where the Crown particularizes the narcotic as *cannabis* marihuana but proves possession of *cannabis* resin, it is still the same offence and unless there has been irreparable prejudice the indictment may be amended to conform with the evidence: *R. v. Morozuk*, [1986] 1 S.C.R. 31, 24 C.C.C. (3d) 257 (7:0). Where the offence is conspiracy, see note at *R. v. Saunders*, [1990] 1 S.C.R. 1020, 56 C.C.C. (3d) 220, under s. 587.

Where the accused was charged with trafficking "in a substance represented or held to be" cocaine, the Crown is not required to prove that the substance was in fact cocaine but need only prove that the accused represented that the substance was cocaine: *R. v. F. (M.)* (2000), 146 C.C.C. (3d) 187 (Ont. C.A.).

An indictment charging that the accused "being then and there together, did have in their possession a narcotic . . . for the purpose of trafficking" charges the accused jointly with the commission of one offence and will not support a finding of possession by each accused: *R. v. Maxwell, Watson and Shaw* (1978), 39 C.C.C. (2d) 439 (B.C.C.A.); not folld: *R. v. Dalzell and Douglas* (1979), 46 C.C.C. (2d) 193 (Alta. C.A.), where it was held that a charge that the accused "did unlawfully have in their possession a narcotic . . . for the purpose of trafficking" charged the accused jointly and severally with the offence so that even where the joint charge failed the judge could proceed with the trial on the basis that the accused were charged severally with the offence.

In *R. v. Doig* (1980), 54 C.C.C. (2d) 461 (B.C.C.A.), *R. v. Maxwell, Watson and Shaw*, *supra*, was distinguished and the conviction of one of two persons jointly charged with possession of narcotics for the purpose of trafficking upheld. The accused had been jointly charged with one of his employees who had been present when a shipment of barrels later found to contain marihuana was delivered to a warehouse rented by the accused. It was open to the court on these facts to acquit the employee and convict the accused although they were jointly charged.

A charge that the accused trafficked in a narcotic "to wit: 1/4 gram of cocaine" is not made out where the evidence is that the substance was a harmless blend of powder, even though the accused, in giving the substance to her friend, represented that the substance was cocaine: *R. v. C. (N.)* (1991), 64 C.C.C. (3d) 45 (Que. C.A.).

A compassion club, even if faithful to its purpose, is not lawful: *R. v. Wood* (2006), 210 C.C.C. (3d) 526 (N.B.C.A.).

Rule precluding multiple convictions – By reason of the rule precluding multiple convictions laid down in *R. v. Kienapple*, [1975] 1 S.C.R. 729, 15 C.C.C. (2d) 524, an accused who on a single occasion trafficked in two types of narcotics to the same person should be convicted only of one offence under this section: *R. v. Voutsis* (1989), 47 C.C.C. (3d) 451 (Sask. C.A.), leave to appeal to S.C.C. refused 50 C.C.C. (3d) vii.

The doctrine of *res judicata* does not bar a conviction under this subsection where the accused has previously been convicted of the offence of trafficking allegedly occurring on the same date and at the same place where following the sale of the narcotic the accused is still in possession of a quantity of the narcotic: *R. v. Winsor* (1976), 31 C.C.C. (2d) 228 (Nfld. Prov. Ct.).

Included offences – It is the language of the count, and not the evidence that discloses it, that decides whether there is a lesser and included offence therein. The offence of trafficking as statutorily described does not include the offence of possession: *R. v. Shewfelt* (1972), 6 C.C.C. (2d) 304 (B.C.C.A.); *R. v. Drysdelle, supra.*

Constitutional Considerations – The failure to exempt caregivers for individuals who have an exemption certificate for the medicinal use of marihuana does not violate s. 7 of the Charter: *Wakeford v. Canada* (2002), 162 C.C.C. (3d) 51 (Ont. C.A.), leave to appeal to S.C.C. refused [2004] 4 S.C.R. vii, 168 C.C.C. (3d) vi. See also: *R. v. Wood* (2006), 210 C.C.C. (3d) 526 (N.B.C.A.).

Constitutionality of mandatory minimum sentences – The one-year mandatory minimum provided by subsec. (3)(*a*)(i)(D) will be grossly disproportionate in reasonably foreseeable cases and therefore violates the s. 12 guarantee against cruel and unusual punishment. It is not saved by s. 1: *R. v. Lloyd*, [2016] 1 S.C.R. 130, 334 C.C.C. (3d) 20.

The two-year mandatory minimum provided by subsec. (3)(*a*)(ii)(A) and (C) is also contrary to s. 12 and not justified by s. 1: *R. v. Dickey* (2016), 335 C.C.C. (3d) 478 (B.C.C.A.).

IMPORTING AND EXPORTING / Possession for the purpose of exporting / Punishment.

6. (1) Except as authorized under the regulations, no person shall import into Canada or export from Canada a substance included in Schedule I, II, III, IV, V or VI.

(2) Except as authorized under the regulations, no person shall possess a substance included in Schedule I, II, III, IV, V or VI for the purpose of exporting it from Canada.

(3) Every person who contravenes subsection (1) or (2)

(*a*) if the subject matter of the offence is a substance included in Schedule I in an amount that is not more than one kilogram, or in Schedule II, is guilty of an indictable offence and liable to imprisonment for life, and to a minimum punishment of imprisonment for a term of one year if

(i) the offence is committed for the purposes of trafficking,

(ii) the person, while committing the offence, abused a position of trust or authority, or

(iii) the person had access to an area that is restricted to authorized persons and used that access to commit the offence;

(*a*.1) if the subject matter of the offence is a substance included in Schedule I in an amount that is more than one kilogram, is guilty of an indictable offence and liable to imprisonment for life and to a minimum punishment of imprisonment for a term of two years;

(*b*) if the subject matter of the offence is a substance included in Schedule III, V or VI,

(i) is guilty of an indictable offence and liable to imprisonment for a term not exceeding ten years, or

(ii) is guilty of an offence punishable on summary conviction and liable to imprisonment for a term not exceeding eighteen months; and

(*c*) if the subject matter of the offence is a substance included in Schedule IV,

(i) is guilty of an indictable offence and liable to imprisonment for a term not exceeding three years, or

(ii) is guilty of an offence punishable on summary conviction and liable to imprisonment for a term not exceeding one year. 2012, c. 1, s. 40; 2017, c. 7, s. 4.

ANNOTATIONS

Note: Some of the following cases were decided under the *Narcotic Control Act*, but were considered useful in the interpretation of this section.

Meaning of "import" – The word "import" means simply to bring into the country or cause to be brought into the country. The offence of importing is not a continuing one but rather is complete when the goods enter the country. On the other hand an accused need not himself have carried the goods into Canada nor been present at the port of entry and the offence may be committed in whole or in part at more than one location in Canada. Thus, for example, the offence could be tried at the place where the accused made all the arrangements for importation and at the place where the goods entered the country: *R. v. Bell*, [1983] 2 S.C.R. 471, 8 C.C.C. (3d) 97 (5:0).

DRUGS

Further, the offence does not necessarily end when the vessel enters into Canadian waters and persons may properly be convicted of importing who assist in the unloading of a vessel which passed into Canadian waters many hours before: *R. v. Miller* (1984), 12 C.C.C. (3d) 54 (B.C.C.A.).

However, once the narcotic entered a province by crossing an international boundary, the offence was complete and the further transportation of the goods into another province did not give the latter province jurisdiction to try the importing offence: *R. v. Martel* (1986), 55 C.R. (3d) 63 (P.E.I.S.C.).

The fact that the police monitored the voyage of a vessel known to be carrying narcotics and actually assisted the accused at one point when the vessel encountered bad weather did not prevent the offence under this section from being committed. Lack of consent by the police is not an element of the offence: *R. v. Miller, supra.*

The offence of importing was not complete until the accused, arriving at the airport with cocaine secreted on her person, had cleared customs. Therefore, in the context of a duress defence, it was not an error for the judge to instruct the jury that they could consider whether the accused had a "safe avenue of escape" by way of seeking help from Border Services agents: *R. v. Foster* (2018), 360 C.C.C. (3d) 213 (Ont. C.A.), leave to appeal to S.C.C. refused 2018 CarswellOnt 13862.

Mens rea – The offence requires proof of actual knowledge or wilful blindness as to the presence of the narcotics. Mere recklessness is not sufficient: *R. v. Sandhu* (1989), 50 C.C.C. (3d) 492 (Ont. C.A.).

A belief by the accused that he was smuggling goods in violation of the Customs Act would not be sufficient *mens rea* to permit a conviction under this section but an accused may be convicted where he either knew the substance was a narcotic (not necessarily the particular narcotic) or was wilfully blind to that fact: *R. v. Blondin* (1970), 2 C.C.C. (2d) 118 (B.C.C.A.), affd [1971] S.C.R. v, 4 C.C.C. (2d) 566*n*.

Constitutional considerations – The mandatory minimum sentence prescribed by subsec. 3)(*a*)(i) is contrary to s. 12 of the Charter and not justified under s. 1: *R. v. Duffus* (2017), 346 C.C.C. (3d) 121 (Ont. S.C.J.).

PRODUCTION OF SUBSTANCE / Punishment / Factors.

7. (1) Except as authorized under the regulations, no person shall produce a substance included in Schedule I, II, III, IV or V.

(2) Every person who contravenes subsection (1)

(*a*) if the subject matter of the offence is a substance included in Schedule I, is guilty of an indictable offence and liable to imprisonment for life and to a minimum punishment of imprisonment for a term of three years if any of the factors set out in subsection (3) apply and for a term of two years in any other case;

(*a*.1) if the subject matter of the offence is a substance included in Schedule II, is guilty of an indictable offence and liable to imprisonment for life, and to a minimum punishment of imprisonment

(i) for a term of one year if the production is for the purpose of trafficking, or

(ii) for a term of 18 months if the production is for the purpose of trafficking and any of the factors set out in subsection (3) apply;

(*b*) [*Repealed*, 2018, c. 16, s. 197(2).]

(*c*) if the subject matter of the offence is a substance included in Schedule III or V,

(i) is guilty of an indictable offence and liable to imprisonment for a term not exceeding ten years, or

(ii) is guilty of an offence punishable on summary conviction and liable to imprisonment for a term not exceeding eighteen months; and

(*d*) where the subject matter of the offence is a substance included in Schedule IV,
(i) is guilty of an indictable offence and liable to imprisonment for a term not exceeding three years, or
(ii) is guilty of an offence punishable on summary conviction and liable to imprisonment for a term not exceeding one year.

(3) The following factors must be taken into account in applying paragraphs (2)(*a*) and (*a*.1):
(*a*) the person used real property that belongs to a third party in committing the offence;
(*b*) the production constituted a potential security, health or safety hazard to persons under the age of 18 years who were in the location where the offence was committed or in the immediate area;
(*c*) the production constituted a potential public safety hazard in a residential area; or
(*d*) the person set or placed a trap, device or other thing that is likely to cause death or bodily harm to another person in the location where the offence was committed or in the immediate area, or permitted such a trap, device or other thing to remain or be placed in that location or area. 2012, c. 1, s. 41; 2017, c. 7, s. 5; 2018, c. 16, s. 197.

ANNOTATIONS

Note: Some of the following cases were decided under the *Narcotic Control Act*, but were considered useful in the interpretation of this section.

"Produces" is defined in section 2 of this Act.

Cultivation requires that labour and attention be bestowed upon the plants to assist them to grow: *R. v. Busby* (1972), 7 C.C.C. (2d) 234 (Y.T.C.A.).

Cultivating is a continuing offence, commencing when the seeding takes place and continuing until the plants are harvested or the accused abandons the task of raising the crop. A person who undertakes the task of raising the crop to maturity does not cease to cultivate during periods of deliberate inactivity where the crop is left alone to grow and mature in the environment created by that person: *R. v. Arnold* (1990), 74 C.R. (3d) 394 (B.C.C.A.).

The word "cultivate" does not include the mere drying or curing of marihuana plants: *R. v. Gauvreau* (1982), 65 C.C.C. (2d) 316 (Ont. C.A.). Nor does it include acts relating to the harvest of the plants such as the cutting and drying of the plants: *R. v. Couture* (1994), 93 C.C.C. (3d) 540 (Que. C.A.), leave to appeal to S.C.C. refused 94 C.C.C. (3d) vii.

The offence of simple possession is not included in this offence: *R. v. Powell* (1983), 9 C.C.C. (3d) 442 (B.C.C.A.).

To be convicted as a party to production, it is not enough for a person to passively witness the activity and refrain from reporting it to police. Thus, a mother who became aware that her son was cultivating marihuana on her property and failed to report him did not thereby become a party to the offence: *R. v. Rochon* (2011), 299 C.C.C. (3d) 156 (Que. C.A.), affd [2012] 2 S.C.R. 673, 299 C.C.C. (3d) 202.

The prohibition against the cultivation of marihuana does not infringe either ss. 15 or 7 of the Charter: *R. v. Hamon* (1993), 85 C.C.C. (3d) 490 (Que. C.A.), leave to appeal to S.C.C. refused 62 Q.A.C. 139*n*.

The failure to exempt caregivers for individuals who have an exemption certificate for the medicinal use of marihuana does not violate s. 7 of the Charter: *Wakeford v. Canada* (2002), 162 C.C.C. (3d) 51 (Ont. C.A.), leave to appeal to S.C.C. refused [2004] 4 S.C.R. vii, 168 C.C.C. (3d) vi.

Following *Hitzig*, the *Medical Marihuana Access Regulations* were amended to address the concerns of the court. As amended, the current *Regulations* are not unconstitutional. The claimant failed to show that physicians have declined *en masse* to participate in the regime, rendering access to medical marihuana illusory: *R. v. Mernagh* (2013), 295 C.C.C. (3d) 431 (Ont. C.A.), leave to appeal to S.C.C. refused 2013 CarswellOnt 10319.

The six-month minimum sentence mandated by subsec. (2)(*b*)(i) is contrary to the s. 12 Charter guarantee against cruel and unusual punishment and is not justified by s. 1: *R. v. Elliott* (2017), 349 C.C.C. (3d) 1 (B.C.C.A.).

Constitutional considerations – The mandatory minimum sentences provided by subparas. (2)(*b*)(ii) and (2)(*b*)(iv) both violate the s. 12 right against cruel and unusual punishment and are not justified by s. 1: *R. v. Serov* (2017), 358 C.C.C. (3d) 203 (B.C.C.A.).

POSSESSION, SALE, ETC., FOR USE IN PRODUCTION OF OR TRAFFICKING IN SUBSTANCE / Punishment.

7.1 (1) No person shall possess, produce, sell, import or transport anything intending that it will be used

(*a*) to produce a controlled substance, unless the production of the controlled substance is lawfully authorized; or

(*b*) to traffic in a controlled substance.

(2) Every person who contravenes subsection (1)

(*a*) if the subject matter of the offence is a substance included in Schedule I, II, III or V,

(i) is guilty of an indictable offence and liable to imprisonment for a term of not more than 10 years, or

(ii) is guilty of an offence punishable on summary conviction and liable to imprisonment for a term of not more than 18 months; and

(*b*) if the subject matter of the offence is a substance included in Schedule IV,

(i) is guilty of an indictable offence and liable to imprisonment for a term of not more than three years, or

(ii) is guilty of an offence punishable on summary conviction and liable to imprisonment for a term of not more than one year. 2011, c. 14, s. 1; 2017, c. 7, s. 6.

8. [*Repealed*, 2001, c. 32, s. 48.]

9. [*Repealed*, S.C. 2001, c. 32, s. 48.]

NOTICE

NOTICE.

8. The court is not required to impose a minimum punishment unless it is satisfied that the offender, before entering a plea, was notified of the possible imposition of a minimum punishment for the offence in question and of the Attorney General's intention to prove any factors in relation to the offence that would lead to the imposition of a minimum punishment. 2012, c. 1, s. 42.

REPORT TO PARLIAMENT

REVIEW / Report.

9. (1) Within five years after this section comes into force, a comprehensive review of the provisions and operation of this Act, including a cost-benefit analysis of mandatory minimum sentences, shall be undertaken by any committee of the Senate, of the House

of Commons or of both Houses of Parliament that may be designated or established for that purpose.

(2) The committee referred to in subsection (1) shall, within one year after a review is undertaken under that subsection, submit a report to Parliament including a statement of any changes that the committee recommends. 2012, c. 1, s. 42.

Sentencing

PURPOSE OF SENTENCING / Factors to take into consideration / Reasons of court / Drug treatment court program / Minimum punishment.

10. (1) Without restricting the generality of the *Criminal Code*, the fundamental purpose of any sentence for an offence under this Part is to contribute to the respect for the law and the maintenance of a just, peaceful and safe society while encouraging rehabilitation, and treatment in appropriate circumstances, of offenders and acknowledging the harm done to victims and to the community.

(2) If a person is convicted of a designated substance offence for which the court is not required to impose a minimum punishment, the court imposing sentence on the person shall consider any relevant aggravating factors including that the person

(*a*) in relation to the commission of the offence,

(i) carried, used or threatened to use a weapon,

(ii) used or threatened to use violence,

(iii) trafficked in a substance included in Schedule I, II, III, IV or V or possessed such a substance for the purpose of trafficking, in or near a school, on or near school grounds or in or near any other public place usually frequented by persons under the age of 18 years, or

(iv) trafficked in a substance included in Schedule I, II, III, IV or V, or possessed such a substance for the purpose of trafficking, to a person under the age of 18 years;

(*b*) was previously convicted of a "designated substance offence", as defined in subsection 2(1) of this Act, or a "designated offence", as defined in subsection 2(1) of the *Cannabis Act*.

(*c*) used the services of a person under the age of eighteen years to commit, or involved such a person in the commission of, the offence.

(3) If, under subsection (1), the court is satisfied of the existence of one or more of the aggravating factors enumerated in paragraphs (2)(*a*) to (*c*), but decides not to sentence the person to imprisonment, the court shall give reasons for that decision.

(4) A court sentencing a person who is convicted of an offence under this Part may delay sentencing to enable the offender

(*a*) to participate in a drug treatment court program approved by the Attorney General; or

(*b*) to attend a treatment program under subsection 720(2) of the *Criminal Code*.

(5) If the offender successfully completes a program under subsection (4), the court is not required to impose the minimum punishment for the offence for which the person was convicted. 1999, c. 5, s. 49; 2012, c. 1, s. 43; 2017, c. 7, s. 7(2), (4); 2018, c. 16, s. 198.

ANNOTATIONS

Note: Some of these cases were decided under the former *Narcotic Control Act*, Parts III and IV of the *Food and Drugs Act*, and the *Criminal Code*, but were considered useful in dealing with sentencing in this Act.

Drug offences / Principles generally in drug cases – Except in highly unusual cases a custodial sentence is required for narcotic trafficking even in cases involving cannabis. The courts should not, however, attempt to define what can constitute exceptional or highly unusual circumstances: *R. v. Burchnall; R. v. Dumont* (1980), 65 C.C.C. (2d) 490 (Alta. C.A.).

Although the Crown has proceeded on the trafficking offence rather than the importing offence under the *Narcotic Control Act*, R.S.C. 1970, c. N-1, the court may properly take into account the fact that the narcotic was imported by the accused as one of the aggravating circumstances: *R. v. McPartland* (1981), 63 C.C.C. (2d) 88 (Ont. C.A.); *R. v. Ramirez* (1986), 26 C.C.C. (3d) 258 (B.C.C.A.).

In *R. v. Bengert (No. 4)* (1979), 52 C.C.C. (2d) 100 (B.C.S.C.), Berger J., prior to imposing sentence for conspiracy to traffic in cocaine, heard evidence concerning the drug and the danger its use presented to society. In holding that the doctrine of precedent does not apply to evidence he rejected the exaggerated views as to the dangers of cocaine reflected in earlier cases which views were founded on expert testimony which no longer squared with present medical opinion. His Lordship thereupon concluded that cocaine was more properly compared to the amphetamines than heroin. The appeals by the accused and the Crown were either dismissed or abandoned: *R. v. Jefferies* (1981), 61 C.C.C. (2d) 58 (B.C.C.A.); *R. v. Ponak* (1981), 61 C.C.C. (2d) 60 (B.C.C.A.). See also *R. v. Libby* (1980), 63 C.C.C. (2d) 69 (Que. Ct. Sess. of Peace).

While cocaine is an amphetamine-like drug its use can result in a high degree of psychological dependence and psychological damage. Trafficking in cocaine must be dealt with sternly and even first offenders engaged in single transactions will be imprisoned for periods depending on the amount of the narcotic and money involved. Except where there is no profit motivation even a large fine would not be sufficient: *R. v. Merlin* (1984), 13 C.C.C. (3d) 549 (N.S.S.C. App. Div.).

Although deterrence is the major objective in cases of importing and trafficking in hard drugs such as heroin and crack cocaine where addiction is not the cause of the offence, nevertheless it is open to a court to impose a conditional sentence of imprisonment in appropriate circumstances: *R. v. Prokos* (1998), 127 C.C.C. (3d) 190 (Que. C.A.).

In *R. v. Phun* (1997), 120 C.C.C. (3d) 560 (Alta. C.A.), the court extensively reviewed narcotic trafficking sentences in the province. The court held that the starting-point for low-level commercial trafficking in heroin should be five years' imprisonment. However, in light of the decision in *R. v. McDonnell*, [1997] 1 S.C.R. 948, 114 C.C.C. (3d) 436, it was not open to the court to interfere with the sentence imposed by the trial judge, which was below this starting-point, unless the trial judge made an error in principle, failed to consider a relevant factor, overemphasized a relevant factor or imposed a sentence that was clearly unreasonable.

In a high-level trafficking case, the sentencing judge erred in principle by refusing to take into account drug importing cases in his determination of a fit sentence. The fact that importing is considered to be a crime of greater severity does not lead to the conclusion that consideration of sentences for importation are not appropriate when determining a fit sentence for trafficking: *R. v. Bacon* (2013), 301 C.C.C. (3d) 97 (B.C.C.A.).

The presence of weapons in the accused's vehicle, readily accessible to him, at the time of arrest amounts to "carrying" weapons within the meaning of subsec. (2)(*a*)(i) and should have been treated as an aggravating factor on sentencing: *R. v. Oickle* (2015), 330 C.C.C. (3d) 82 (N.S.C.A.).

Effect of addiction – In *R. v. Richards* (1979), 49 C.C.C. (2d) 517 (Ont. C.A.), the court considered at length the principles applicable to sentencing a heroin addict on a charge of possession of heroin. In upholding the disposition of the trial judge against a Crown appeal (suspended sentence and probation with community service order), the court considered the statistics compiled by the Federal Bureau of Dangerous Drugs showing the dispositions with respect to various drug offences. While such statistics should not be given undue weight it was of significance that in a high percentage of cases of simple possession of heroin a non-custodial sentence was imposed. Since the offence, the accused in this case had been cured of his addiction and thus a jail sentence was not required as a matter of rehabilitation and while the offence was serious it was not of such gravity that a jail term was required as a matter of general deterrence. The court also approved the use of a community service order, in this case a benefit concert, the accused being a musician, it being appropriate to tailor the order to the work he is fitted to perform, although an additional term requiring that the accused engage in a programme to point out the dangers of drug use would have been desirable.

In sentencing a heroin addict for possession of narcotics, the principle of deterrence should yield to any reasonable chance of rehabilitation which may show itself to the court imposing sentence. The protection which society derives from incarcerating the addict is transitory at best, whereas, if the addict can be rehabilitated, through attendance at a drug rehabilitation facility as part of a probation order, then society will be permanently protected: *R. v. Preston* (1990), 79 C.R. (3d) 61 (B.C.C.A.).

While trafficking in hard drugs such as morphine is normally dealt with severely, where the accused addict has, since the commission of the offence, controlled his habit and the circumstances are such as to found a reasonable belief that he is no longer a danger to society, a lengthy period of incarceration is no longer required, and in some cases a suspended sentence and probation will be appropriate: *R. v. Lebovitch* (1979), 48 C.C.C. (2d) 539 (Que. C.A.).

On the other hand where the accused addict has not demonstrated an ability to succeed in a drug rehabilitation programme, her willingness to again enter such a programme is not sufficient to prevent the operation of normal sentencing principles in trafficking cases: *R. v. Sabloff* (1979), 13 C.R. (3d) 326 (Que. S.C.).

The fact that the accused is a reformed addict who was not a large scale dealer is not such an exceptional circumstance that would warrant the court to impose a non-custodial sentence for heroin trafficking. There must at least be other factors such as evidence that the trafficking was casual and done solely for the purpose of and limited in quantity sufficient only to support the accused's own dependency: *R. v. Holt* (1983), 4 C.C.C. (3d) 32 (Ont. C.A.), leave to appeal to S.C.C. refused C.C.C. *loc. cit.*

DRUGS

A conditional sentence of imprisonment with a treatment order may be an appropriate disposition for an offender with a drug addiction, notwithstanding the offender has a lengthy record linked to this addiction, provided the judge is confident that there is a good chance of rehabilitation and that the level of supervision will be sufficient to ensure the offender complies with the sentence: *R. v. Proulx*, [2000] 1 S.C.R. 61, 140 C.C.C. (3d) 449.

Importing – In *R. v. Saulnier*, [1988] 2 W.W.R. 546, (1987), 21 B.C.L.R. (2d) 232 (C.A.), the court considered the principles applicable to imposition of sentence for persons found guilty of importing narcotics, since the striking down of the seven-year minimum by the Supreme Court in *R. v. Smith*, [1987] 1 S.C.R. 1045, 34 C.C.C. (3d) 97. The court noted that previous precedents must be carefully considered since it was reasonable to believe that most cases of sentences for 7 to 10 or 12 years were influenced by the minimum. Sentencing was based on the seven-year "floor". Even sentences of 15 or 20 years may have been affected, having been imposed in the climate created by the minimum in which all importing sentences were imposed. Doing away with the minimum permits courts to treat the less serious cases less severely. Distinctions can be made depending on the type of narcotic imported, in view of its nature. As well, a distinction should be drawn between a narcotic such as heroin that can only be obtained outside Canada, and a drug such as marihuana.

To a similar effect is the decision in *R. v. Cirone* (1988), 43 C.C.C. (3d) 228 (Alta. C.A.), where the court pointed out that the striking down of the minimum penalty in no way detracts from the seriousness of the importing offence. In considering an appeal from a sentence imposed prior to the decision in *R. v. Smith, supra*, the court should consider the type and quantity of the drug involved, the position of the offender in the drug distribution hierarchy, the appellant's post-sentence conduct and the effect that the seven-year minimum may have had on the sentence originally imposed.

It was held with respect to an offence under former s. 5 of the *Narcotics Control Act* that there is no rule that an offender convicted of importing narcotics cannot receive a conditional sentence under s. 742.1 of the *Criminal Code*, except in rare or unusual circumstances.

Rather, each case must be approached on the basis that it will be considered on its particular facts taking into account the nature of the offence, the circumstances surrounding the commission of the offence, as well as the personal circumstances of the offender: *R. v. Wellington* (1999), 132 C.C.C. (3d) 470 (Ont. C.A.). Similarly, *R. v. Gagnon* (1998), 130 C.C.C. (3d) 194 (Que. C.A.), where it was held to be an error in principle for the judge to hold that a conditional sentence was simply unavailable in importing cases.

Many aspects of systemic racism and its effects on aboriginal offenders are equally applicable to African-Canadians. The evidence adduced established that a disproportionate number of cocaine importers are black women of poverty. Having regard to this and other factors, a conditional sentence was an appropriate penalty in the circumstances: *R. v. Hamilton* (2003), 172 C.C.C. (3d) 114 (Ont. S.C.J.), affd 186 C.C.C. (3d) 129 (Ont. C.A.).

Part II / ENFORCEMENT

[*Heading repealed*, 2017, c. 7, s. 8.]

INFORMATION FOR SEARCH WARRANT / Application of section 487.1 of the *Criminal Code* / Execution in another province / Effect of endorsement / Search of person and seizure / Seizure of things not specified / Where warrant not necessary / Seizure of additional things.

11. (1) A justice who, on ex parte application, is satisfied by information on oath that there are reasonable grounds to believe that

(*a*) a controlled substance or precursor in respect of which this Act has been contravened,

(*b*) any thing in which a controlled substance or precursor referred to in paragraph (*a*) is contained or concealed,

(*c*) offence-related property, or

(*d*) any thing that will afford evidence in respect of an offence under this Act or an offence, in whole or in part in relation to a contravention of this Act, under section 354 or 462.31 of the *Criminal Code*

is in a place may, at any time, issue a warrant authorizing a peace officer, at any time, to search the place for any such controlled substance, precursor, property or thing and to seize it.

(2) For the purposes of subsection (1), an information may be submitted by telephone or other means of telecommunication in accordance with section 487.1 of the *Criminal Code*, with such modifications as the circumstances require.

(3) A justice may, where a place referred to in subsection (1) is in a province other than that in which the justice has jurisdiction, issue the warrant referred to in that subsection and the warrant may be executed in the other province after it has been endorsed by a justice having jurisdiction in that other province.

(4) An endorsement that is made on a warrant as provided for in subsection (3) is sufficient authority to any peace officer to whom it was originally directed and to all peace officers within the jurisdiction of the justice by whom it is endorsed to execute the warrant and to dispose of or otherwise deal with the things seized in accordance with the law.

(5) Where a peace officer who executes a warrant issued under subsection (1) has reasonable grounds to believe that any person found in the place set out in the warrant has on their person any controlled substance, precursor, property or thing set out in the warrant, the peace officer may search the person for the controlled substance, precursor, property or thing and seize it.

(6) A peace officer who executes a warrant issued under subsection (1) may seize, in addition to the things mentioned in the warrant,

(*a*) any controlled substance or precursor in respect of which the peace officer believes on reasonable grounds that this Act has been contravened;

(*b*) any thing that the peace officer believes on reasonable grounds to contain or conceal a controlled substance or precursor referred to in paragraph (*a*);

(*c*) any thing that the peace officer believes on reasonable grounds is offence-related property; or

(*d*) any thing that the peace officer believes on reasonable grounds will afford evidence in respect of an offence under this Act.

(7) A peace officer may exercise any of the powers described in subsection (1), (5) or (6) without a warrant if the conditions for obtaining a warrant exist but by reason of exigent circumstances it would be impracticable to obtain one.

(8) A peace officer who executes a warrant issued under subsection (1) or exercises powers under subsection (5) or (7) may seize, in addition to the things mentioned in the warrant and in subsection (6), any thing that the peace officer believes on reasonable grounds has been obtained by or used in the commission of an offence or that will afford evidence in respect of an offence. 2005, c. 44, s. 13; 2017, c. 7, s. 9.

ANNOTATIONS

Note: Most of the following cases were decided under the repealed *Narcotic Control Act*, but were considered useful in the interpretation of this section.

General (subsec. (1)) – The justice has no jurisdiction to "amend" a warrant to extend the time for its execution where the warrant had expired without being executed prior to the application for the amendment. Even if the justice had power to amend the warrant he would have to be supplied with further information under oath to show that narcotics were then on the premises to be searched: *R. v. Jamieson* (1989), 48 C.C.C. (3d) 287 (N.S.C.A.).

The guarantee to protection against unreasonable search and seizure in s. 8 of the *Charter of Rights and Freedoms* requires that the justice be unbiased, neutral and detached and that there be no real or apprehended perception of partiality. Where, by reason of the justice's relationship with the police force seeking the warrant, a reasonable person would believe that there was a real danger of bias by reason of a perceived susceptibility of the justice to intimidation or coercion by the police then this requirement is not satisfied. In this case such perception arose from the fact that the justice was also a member of the corps of commissionaires with duties at an airport where she reported to and worked out of the R.C.M.P. offices at the airport, was in daily contact with the R.C.M.P. and was subject to the direct control of a member of that force. The R.C.M.P. was also charged with the enforcement of this Act and a member of that force had applied for the warrant: *R. v. Baylis* (1988), 43 C.C.C. (3d) 514 (Sask. C.A.).

A warrant which has the "wrong" address on it may not be amended by the officer and the justice by simply inserting the correct address, at least if the officer is not placed under oath at the time of the amendment: *R. v. Sieger and Avery* (1982), 65 C.C.C. (2d) 449 (B.C.S.C.).

The failure to specify the place to be searched is a serious defect which not only renders the warrant invalid but the search, pursuant to such warrant, unreasonable within the meaning of s. 8 of the *Charter of Rights and Freedoms*: *R. v. Parent* (1989), 47 C.C.C. (3d) 385 (Y.T.C.A.).

A warrant which specified the dwelling place as the location of the search could not be interpreted to include the search of a vehicle parked outside the house: *R. v. Vu* (2004), 184 C.C.C. (3d) 545 (B.C.C.A.).

This section does not require the warrant to name a specific officer to carry out the search. The warrant was sufficient authority for any peace officer in the jurisdiction of the issuing justice to execute the search: *R. v. Pitre* (2011), 280 C.C.C. (3d) 333 (N.B.C.A.).

There is no prohibition on night-time searches as found in the *Criminal Code* and accordingly, there are no additional requirements for night-time searches: *R. v. Saunders* (2004), 181 C.C.C. (3d) 268 (Nfld. C.A.), affd [2004] 3 S.C.R. 505, 189 C.C.C. (3d) 436. See also *R. v. Dueck* (2005), 200 C.C.C. (3d) 378 (B.C.C.A.).

The police may apply for a warrant under this section or s. 487 of the *Criminal Code*. Where, however, the warrant is obtained under s. 487, the police must execute it in accordance with the *Criminal Code* and cannot resort to the special provisions in this Act: *R. v. Grant*, [1993] 3 S.C.R. 223, 84 C.C.C. (3d) 173 (9:0).

Any factual submissions which are made orally by the police officer supplementing the written information should be made under oath and a record kept of them. The material to obtain the warrant must be current, and appear to be current, and should be sufficient to enable the justice to form an opinion using independent judgment as to whether reasonable grounds exist for believing that there is a narcotic on the premises. The police officer is not required to disclose the identity of a confidential informant: *R. v. Dodge* (1984), 16 C.C.C. (3d) 385 (Nfld. S.C.T.D.).

The validity of a search warrant may properly be raised at trial even if no application has been made prior to trial to have the warrant set aside. In fact, it is preferable that the validity of the warrant be determined by the trial judge where the object of the attack on the warrant is to exclude evidence obtained through its execution by reason of a violation of s. 8 of the Charter, since it is the trial judge alone who has jurisdiction under s. 24(2) to exclude evidence: *R. v. Zevallos* (1987), 37 C.C.C. (3d) 79 (Ont. C.A.); *R. v. Tanner* (1989), 46 C.C.C. (3d) 513 (Alta. C.A.); *R. v. Jamieson* (1989), 48 C.C.C. (3d) 287 (N.S.C.A.). *Contra: R. v. Komadowski* (1986), 27 C.C.C. (3d) 319 (Man. C.A.).

Moreover, the trial judge has jurisdiction to set aside a sealing order, made by the justice at the time the warrant was issued, barring access to the information in support of the warrant: *R. v. Tanner, supra.*

Unlike warrants issued under the *Criminal Code*, there is no statutory presumption that warrants issued under this provision are to be executed before 9:00 p.m. However, the time of execution may factor into the reasonableness of the manner of execution: *R. v. Shivrattan* (2017), 346 C.C.C. (3d) 299 (Ont. C.A.), leave to appeal to S.C.C. refused 2017 CarswellOnt 11385.

A warrant issued under this provision authorizing the police to execute a search "at any time" refers to the lack of a daytime execution requirement and does not confer an open-ended authority to search in perpetuity. An implied time limitation can be inferred from the circumstances: *R. v. Saint* (2017), 353 C.C.C. (3d) 467 (Ont. C.A.).

Search of person – It was held that the power to search under the predecessor to this section depends on the officer having a reasonable belief that the person searched is in possession of a prohibited drug: *R. v. Debot* (1986), 30 C.C.C. (3d) 207 (Ont. C.A.). It should be noted that in this case the court reviewed at length the circumstances in which an officer could have the requisite reasonable grounds, particularly when based on information supplied by an informer, a superior officer and the suspect's reputation in police circles. This case also sanctioned the validity of a warrantless search as an incident of arrest although the search precedes the arrest, provided that the officer had reasonable and probable grounds to make the arrest. A further appeal by the accused to the Supreme Court of Canada was dismissed [1989] 2 S.C.R. 1140, 52 C.C.C. (3d) 193 (5:0). The court agreed that the appropriate standard to establish reasonable grounds for a search is one of "reasonable probability" and in making this determination the court must have regard to the totality of the circumstances. The court also held that the suspect's criminal record and reputation could be taken into account provided that, *inter alia*, the reputation is related to the ostensible reasons for the search. Where the police rely on information from an informer, it is not necessary for the police to confirm each detail in the informer's tip so long as the sequence of events actually observed conforms sufficiently to the anticipated pattern to remove the possibility of innocent coincidence. On the other hand, the level of verification required may be higher where the police rely on an informant whose credibility cannot be assessed or where fewer details are provided and the risk of innocent coincidence is greater. Finally, it was held that in the case of a warrantless search carried out by a police officer pursuant to orders from a superior, it is that officer who must have the requisite reasonable and probable grounds.

A conclusion that the police had reliable information that the accused was attempting to import narcotics must be based on more than the fact of a subsequent recovery of the drugs. There must be a proper inquiry into the source and reliability of the confidential information in order to determine whether, "in the totality of the circumstances", there existed reasonable and probable grounds to believe the accused was carrying the narcotic or whether there was only a suspicion. A rectal examination of the accused, based on the mere suspicion that he was carrying drugs and as an incident to an arrest for outstanding traffic fines, was a serious violation of s. 8 of the Charter and, in the circumstances of the case, required exclusion of the evidence as to the finding of the narcotics: *R. v. Greffe*, [1990] 1 S.C.R. 755, 55 C.C.C. (3d) 161 (4:3).

Immediately upon detention a detainee has the right to be informed of the right to retain and instruct counsel but the police are not obligated to suspend the search incident to arrest until the detainee has the opportunity to retain counsel except in certain circumstances, as where the lawfulness of the search is dependent on the detainee's consent or the statute gives a person a right to seek review of the decision to search: *R. v. Debot, supra.*

In *R. v. Collins*, [1987] 1 S.C.R. 265, 33 C.C.C. (3d) 1 (5:1), the court considered the lawfulness of a search where the accused had been subjected to a throat hold. It was held that for the search to be lawful the Crown must establish that the officer believed on reasonable grounds that there was a narcotic in the place where the person searched was found. The nature of the belief will also determine whether the manner in which the search was carried out was reasonable. For example, if a police officer is told by a reliable source that there are persons in possession of drugs in a certain place, the officer may, depending on the circumstances and the nature and precision of the information given by that source, search persons found in that place, but without very specific information, a seizure by the throat would be unreasonable. However, if he is lawfully searching a person whom he believes on reasonable grounds to be a "drug handler", then the "throat-hold" would not be unreasonable.

Seizure of things not specified in warrant (subsec. (6)) – When a seizure is carried out under the authority of this provision or subsec. (8), there is no requirement that the additional items seized be in plain view and the Crown is not required to establish the components of a "plain view" seizure: *R. v. Mah* (2014), 320 C.C.C. (3d) 294 (Sask. C.A.).

Warrantless search (subsec. (7)) – It was decided under the prior warrant provision that while the fact that the evidence sought is believed to be present in a motor vehicle or other conveyance will often create exigent circumstances, there is no blanket exception to the warrant requirement for such conveyances: *R. v. Grant*, [1993] 3 S.C.R. 223, 84 C.C.C. (3d) 173 (9:0).

The perimeter of a dwelling house is a place within the meaning of this section and thus a so-called "perimeter search" is not authorized unless there are reasonable and probable grounds to believe that a narcotic is present. Where the perimeter search is made purely on the basis of suspicion then the search, which involved approaching the perimeter of the house and attempting to peer into the residence, is unreasonable and constitutes a violation of s. 8 of the Charter. There is no common law right which allows police officers to trespass on private property in order to conduct a search of this kind: *R. v. Kokesch*, [1990] 3 S.C.R. 3, 61 C.C.C. (3d) 207.

In the course of executing a warrant at the residence, the police conducted a safety check in the outbuildings where a grow operation was located. When a warrant has been issued to search one place or premises, the police, in the course of the execution of the warrant, have the authority at common law to inspect and enter other places or premises on that property to the extent reasonably necessary to protect themselves and others. Such action cannot be taken as a matter of course or on the basis of generalized, non-specific concerns. Before acting, they must have a reasonable basis for believing that there is a possibility that their

DRUGS

immediate safety or the safety of others is at risk. While safety concerns can trigger a statutory exigent circumstances exception to a warrant requirement, such concerns will not always satisfy those exceptions. Those concerns must make obtaining a warrant impracticable: *R. v. Chuhaniuk* (2010), 261 C.C.C. (3d) 486 (B.C.C.A.).

Exigent circumstances were found to exist where the police believed that the arrest of the accused had been observed by a third party who may have access to the accused's residence and the ability to destroy evidence: *R. v. McCormack* (2000), 143 C.C.C. (3d) 260 (B.C.C.A.), leave to appeal to S.C.C. refused 147 C.C.C. (3d) vi.

In an unusual case it was held that peace officers were entitled to pursue the accused's ship into international waters and search and seize the ship and arrest the accused for conspiracy to import narcotics. The ship had briefly entered Canadian waters to off-load a cargo of narcotics to another vessel which was used to in fact import the narcotics. The accused's ship had been under continuous surveillance until intercepted by the police. The conduct of the authorities complied with the international law relating to pursuit of ships onto the high seas: *R. v. Sunila* (1986), 26 C.C.C. (3d) 177 (N.S.C.A.). [Now see s. 477.3 of the *Criminal Code*.]

This provision has no application to searches of motor vehicles conducted in the lawful exercise of the common law power to search incident to a driver's arrest: *R. v. Tontarelli* (2009), 247 C.C.C. (3d) 160 (N.B.C.A.).

ASSISTANCE AND USE OF FORCE.

12. For the purpose of exercising any of the powers described in section 11, a peace officer may

(*a*) enlist such assistance as the officer deems necessary; and

(*b*) use as much force as is necessary in the circumstances.

ANNOTATIONS

Note: Some of the following cases were decided under the *Narcotic Control Act*, but were considered useful in the interpretation of this section.

The requirement that the police have information supporting a need for surprise in order for an unannounced entry to be warranted equates to a requirement of exigent circumstances. In this case, risks to officer safety or the possibility of destruction of evidence would support an unannounced entry: *R. v. DeWolfe* (2007), 222 C.C.C. (3d) 491 (N.S.C.A.).

Where there is a risk of loss or destruction of evidence so that rapid action is required or where there is a real threat of violent behaviour whether directed at the police or third parties then the police may be justified in using special procedures in executing the warrant. However, the consideration of the possibility of violence must be carefully limited and should not amount to a *carte blanche* for the police to ignore completely all restrictions on police behaviour. The greater the departure from the standards of behaviour required by the common law and the *Charter of Rights and Freedoms*, then the heavier the onus on the police to show why they thought it necessary to use force in the execution of the warrant: *R. v. Genest*, [1989] 1 S.C.R. 59, 45 C.C.C. (3d) 385, 67 C.R. (3d) 224 (7:0).

The special search provisions in the *Narcotic Control Act* were designed to be a comprehensive set of rules, replacing older common law rules relating to the execution of search warrants. The predecessor section permited the officer to break open any door for the purpose of executing the search warrant and does not impose any requirement of announcement prior to entry. While s. 8 of the *Charter of Rights and Freedoms* imposes limits on the manner in which a search warrant is executed and may in some circumstances require that there be prior announcement, Parliament, in enacting the special entry and search provisions, was well aware of the need for unannounced entry in order to allow the police to surprise the occupants of a dwelling house whom they had reason to believe were dealing in narcotics. In each case the issue will be whether the search was carried out in a reasonable manner; whether it was necessary to resort to the statutory power to force entry. Thus in this case the police had information from a reliable informer that the premises were being used as a retail outlet for cocaine and that the front door was probably barred. In the circumstances they were entitled to force entry without prior announcement: *R. v. Gimson* (1990), 54 C.C.C. (3d) 232, 77 C.R. (3d) 307, 37 O.A.C. 243 (C.A.).

It was held under the predecessor legislation that it was not unreasonable for the officers to force entry into a residence which they had reasonable grounds to believe contained a narcotic. There was no requirement that the officers delay execution until the occupants returned: *R. v. Grenier* (1991), 65 C.C.C. (3d) 76 (Que. C.A.).

REPORT OF SEIZURE, FINDING, ETC.

12.1 Subject to the regulations, every peace officer, inspector or prescribed person who seizes, finds or otherwise acquires a controlled substance, precursor or chemical offence-related property shall, within 30 days,

(*a*) prepare a report setting out

(i) the substance, precursor or property,

(ii) the amount of it that was seized, found or acquired,

(iii) the place where it was seized, found or acquired,

(iv) the date on which it was seized, found or acquired,

(v) the name of the police force, agency or entity to which the peace officer, inspector or prescribed person belongs,

(vi) the number of the file or police report related to the seizure, finding or acquisition, and

(vii) any other prescribed information;

(*b*) cause the report to be sent to the Minister; and

(*c*) in the case of a seizure made under section 11 of this Act, the *Criminal Code* or a power of seizure at common law, cause a copy of the report to be filed with the justice who issued the warrant or another justice for the same territorial division or, if a warrant was not issued, a justice who would have had jurisdiction to issue a warrant. 2017, c. 7, s. 10.

SECTIONS 489.1 AND 490 OF THE *CRIMINAL CODE* APPLICABLE / Sections 489.1 and 490 of *Criminal Code* applicable / Provisions of this Act applicable / Recognizance.

13. (1) Subject to subsections (2) and (3), sections 489.1 and 490 of the *Criminal Code* apply to any thing seized under this Act.

(2) If a thing seized under this Act is non-chemical offence-related property, sections 489.1 and 490 of the *Criminal Code* apply subject to sections 16 to 22 and subsections 31(6) to (9) of this Act.

(3) If a controlled substance, precursor or chemical offence-related property is seized under this Act, any other Act of Parliament or a power of seizure at common law, the provisions of this Act and the regulations apply in respect of that substance, precursor or property.

(4) If, under this section, an order is made in accordance with paragraph 490(9)(*c*) of the *Criminal Code* for the return of any non-chemical offence-related property seized under this Act, the judge or justice making the order may require the applicant for the order to enter into a recognizance before the judge or justice, with or without sureties, in the amount and with any conditions that the judge or justice directs and, if the judge or justice considers it appropriate, require the applicant to deposit with the judge or justice the sum of money or other valuable security that the judge or justice directs. 2017, c. 7, s. 11.

(5) [*Repealed*, 2017, c. 7, s. 11.]

(6) [*Repealed*, 2017, c. 7, s. 11.]

DRUGS

Division 1

Non-chemical Offence-related Property 2017, c. 7, s. 12.

Restraint Orders

APPLICATION FOR RESTRAINT ORDER / Procedure / Restraint order / Property outside Canada / Conditions / Order in writing / Service of order / Registration of order / Order continues in force / Offence.

14. (1) The Attorney General may make an application in accordance with this section for a restraint order in respect of any non-chemical offence-related property.

(2) The application for a restraint order may be made *ex parte* and shall be made in writing to a judge and be accompanied by an affidavit of the Attorney General or any other person deposing to the following matters

(*a*) the offence to which the property relates;

(*b*) the person who is believed to be in possession of the property; and

(*c*) a description of the property.

(3) The judge to whom the application is made may, if satisfied that there are reasonable grounds to believe that the property is non-chemical offence-related property, make a restraint order prohibiting any person from disposing of, or otherwise dealing with any interest in, the property specified in the order other than in the manner that is specified in the order.

(4) A restraint order may be issued under this section in respect of property situated outside Canada, with any modifications that the circumstances require.

(5) A restraint order made by a judge under this section may be subject to such reasonable conditions as the judge thinks fit.

(6) A restraint order made under this section shall be made in writing.

(7) A copy of a restraint order made under this section shall be served on the person to whom the order is addressed in such manner as the judge making the order directs or in accordance with the rules of the court.

(8) A copy of a restraint order made under this section shall be registered against any property in accordance with the laws of the province in which the property is situated.

(9) A restraint order made under this section remains in effect until

(*a*) an order is made under subsection 19(3) or 19.1(3) of this Act or subsection 490(9) or (11) of the *Criminal Code* in relation to the property; or

(*b*) an order of forfeiture of the property is made under subsection 16(1) or 17(2) of this Act or section 490 of the *Criminal Code*.

(10) Any person on whom a restraint order made under this section is served in accordance with this section and who, while the order is in force, acts in contravention of or fails to comply with the order is guilty of an indictable offence or an offence punishable on summary conviction. 1996, c. 16, s. 60; 2001, c. 32, s. 49; 2017, c. 7, s. 13.

ANNOTATIONS

The Court of Appeal has no jurisdiction to entertain an appeal from an order refusing to vary or set aside a restraint order under this section: *Canada (Attorney General) v. 311165 B.C. Ltd.* (2011), 286 C.C.C. (3d) 474 (B.C.C.A.).

14.1 [*Repealed*, 2017, c. 7, s. 14.] 2001, c. 32, s. 50; 2017, c. 7, s. 14.

SECTIONS 489.1 AND 490 OF THE *CRIMINAL CODE* APPLICABLE / Recognizance.

15. (1) Subject to sections 16 to 22, sections 489.1 and 490 of the *Criminal Code* apply, with any modifications that the circumstances require, to any property that is the subject of a restraint order made under section 14.

(2) If, under this section, an order is made in accordance with paragraph 490(9)(*c*) of the *Criminal Code* for the return of any property that is the subject of a restraint order made under section 14, the judge or justice making the order may require the applicant for the order to enter into a recognizance before the judge or justice, with or without sureties, in the amount and with any conditions that the judge or justice directs and, if the judge or justice considers it appropriate, require the applicant to deposit with the judge or justice the sum of money or other valuable security that the judge or justice directs. 2017, c. 7, s. 14.

Management Orders

MANAGEMENT ORDER / Appointment of Minister of Public Works and Government Services / Power to manage / Application for destruction order / Notice required before destruction / Manner of giving notice / Destruction order / Application for forfeiture order / When management order ceases to have effect / For greater certainty / Application to vary conditions.

15.1 (1) On application of the Attorney General or of any other person with the written consent of the Attorney General, a justice in the case of non-chemical offence-related property seized under section 11 of this Act, the *Criminal Code* or a power of seizure at common law, or a judge in the case of property restrained under section 14, may, if they are of the opinion that the circumstances so require,

(*a*) appoint a person to take control of and to manage or otherwise deal with all or part of the property in accordance with the directions of the judge or justice; and

(*b*) require any person having possession of that property to give possession of the property to the person appointed under paragraph (*a*).

(2) If the Attorney General of Canada so requests, a judge or justice appointing a person under subsection (1) shall appoint the Minister of Public Works and Government Services.

(3) The power to manage or otherwise deal with property under subsection (1) includes

(*a*) the power to make an interlocutory sale of perishable or rapidly depreciating property;

(*b*) the power to destroy, in accordance with subsections (4) to (7), property that has little or no value; and

(*c*) the power to have property, other than real property or a conveyance, forfeited to Her Majesty in accordance with subsection (8).

(4) Before a person who is appointed to manage property destroys property that has little or no value, they shall apply to a court for a destruction order.

(5) Before making a destruction order, a court shall require notice in accordance with subsection (6) to be given to and may hear any person who, in the court's opinion, appears to have a valid interest in the property.

(6) A notice shall

(*a*) be given in the manner that the court directs or that may be specified in the rules of the court; and

(*b*) specify the effective period of the notice that the court considers reasonable or that may be set out in the rules of the court.

DRUGS

(7) A court shall order that the property be destroyed if it is satisfied that the property has little or no financial or other value.

(8) On application by a person who is appointed to manage the property, a court shall order that the property, other than real property or a conveyance, be forfeited to Her Majesty to be disposed of or otherwise dealt with in accordance with the law if

- **(*a*) a notice is given or published in the manner that the court directs or that may be specified in the rules of the court;**
- **(*b*) the notice specifies a period of 60 days during which a person may make an application to the court asserting their interest in the property; and**
- **(*c*) during that period, no one makes such an application.**

(9) A management order ceases to have effect when the property that is the subject of the management order is returned in accordance with the law, destroyed or forfeited to Her Majesty.

(10) For greater certainty, if property that is the subject of a management order is sold, the management order applies to the net proceeds of the sale.

(11) The Attorney General may at any time apply to the judge or justice to cancel or vary any condition to which a management order is subject but may not apply to vary an appointment made under subsection (2). 2017, c. 7, s. 14.

Forfeiture

2017, c. 7, s. 15.

FORFEITURE OF PROPERTY / Property related to other offences / Property outside Canada / Appeal.

16. (1) Subject to sections 18 to 19.1, if a person is convicted, or discharged under section 730 of the *Criminal Code*, of a designated substance offence and, on application of the Attorney General, the court is satisfied, on a balance of probabilities, that non-chemical offence-related property is related to the commission of the offence, the court shall

- **(*a*) if the prosecution of the offence was commenced at the instance of the government of a province and conducted by or on behalf of that government, order that the property be forfeited to Her Majesty in right of that province to be disposed of or otherwise dealt with in accordance with the law by the Attorney General or Solicitor General of that province; and**
- **(*b*) in any other case, order that the property be forfeited to Her Majesty in right of Canada to be disposed of or otherwise dealt with in accordance with the law by the member of the Queen's Privy Council for Canada that is designated by the Governor in Council for the purposes of this paragraph.**

(2) Subject to sections 18 to 19.1, if the evidence does not establish to the satisfaction of the court that property in respect of which an order of forfeiture would otherwise be made under subsection (1) is related to the commission of the designated substance offence of which a person is convicted or discharged, but the court is satisfied, beyond a reasonable doubt, that the property is non-chemical offence-related property, the court may make an order of forfeiture under subsection (1) in relation to that property.

(2.1) An order may be issued under this section in respect of property situated outside Canada, with any modifications that the circumstances require.

(3) A person who has been convicted or discharged of a designated substance offence or the Attorney General may appeal to the court of appeal from an order or a failure to make an order under subsection (1) as if the appeal were an appeal against the sentence imposed on the person in respect of the offence. 2001, c. 32, s. 51; 2017, c. 7, s. 16.

ANNOTATIONS

This provision is mandatory. The accused's truck, which was bought through a loan from his parents, was used in the transport of drugs and, accordingly, was properly forfeited: *R. v. Paziuk* (2007), 221 C.C.C. (3d) 518 (Sask. C.A.).

This provision is *intra vires* the federal criminal law power and not contrary to ss. 7, 11(*h*) or 12 of the Charter: *R. v. Fenn* (2013), 295 C.C.C. (3d) 358 (Ont. C.J.). See also: *R. v. Fercan Developments Inc.* (2012), 332 C.C.C. (3d) 396 (Ont. C.J.).

APPLICATION FOR *IN REM* FORFEITURE / Order of forfeiture of property / Accused deemed absconded / Who may dispose of forfeited property / Property outside Canada.

17. (1) Where an information has been laid in respect of a designated substance offence, the Attorney General may make an application to a judge for an order of forfeiture under subsection (2).

(2) Subject to sections 18 to 19.1, where an application is made to a judge under subsection (1) and the judge is satisfied

(*a*) beyond a reasonable doubt that any property is non-chemical offence-related property,

(*b*) that proceedings were commenced in respect of a designated substance offence to which the property referred to in paragraph (*a*) is related, and

(*c*) that the accused charged with the designated substance offence has died or absconded,

the judge shall order that the property be forfeited and disposed of in accordance with subsection (4).

(3) For the purposes of subsection (2), an accused shall be deemed to have absconded in connection with a designated substance offence if

(*a*) an information has been laid alleging the commission of the offence by the accused,

(*b*) a warrant for the arrest of the accused has been issued in relation to that information, and

(*c*) reasonable attempts to arrest the accused pursuant to the warrant have been unsuccessful during a period of six months beginning on the day on which the warrant was issued,

and the accused shall be deemed to have so absconded on the last day of that six month period.

(4) For the purposes of subsection (2),

(*a*) if the proceedings referred to in paragraph (2)(*b*) were commenced at the instance of the government of a province, the judge shall order that the property be forfeited to Her Majesty in right of that province and disposed of or otherwise dealt with in accordance with the law by the Attorney General or Solicitor General of that province, and

(*b*) in any other case, the judge shall order that the property be forfeited to Her Majesty in right of Canada and disposed of or otherwise dealt with in accordance with the law by the member of the Queen's Privy Council for Canada that is designated by the Governor in Council for the purposes of this paragraph.

(5) An order may be issued under this section in respect of property situated outside Canada, with any modifications that the circumstances require. 2001, c. 32, s. 52; 2017, c. 7, s. 17.

DRUGS

VOIDABLE TRANSFERS.

18. A court may, before ordering that property be forfeited under subsection 16(1) or 17(2), set aside any conveyance or transfer of the property that occurred after the property was seized or restrained, unless the conveyance or transfer was for valuable consideration to a person acting in good faith. 2017, c. 7, s. 18.

NOTICE / Manner of giving notice / Order of restoration of property.

19. (1) Before making an order under subsection 16(1) or 17(2) in relation to any property, a court shall require notice in accordance with subsection (2) to be given to, and may hear, any person who, in the opinion of the court, appears to have a valid interest in the property.

(2) A notice shall

(*a*) be given in the manner that the court directs or that may be specified in the rules of the court;

(*b*) specify the period that the court considers reasonable or that may be set out in the rules of the court during which a person may make an application to the court asserting their interest in the property; and

(*c*) set out the designated substance offence charged and a description of the property.

(3) Where a court is satisfied that any person, other than

(*a*) a person who was charged with a designated substance offence, or

(*b*) a person who acquired title to or a right of possession of the property from a person referred to in paragraph (*a*) under circumstances that give rise to a reasonable inference that the title or right was transferred for the purpose of avoiding the forfeiture of the property,

is the lawful owner or is lawfully entitled to possession of any property or any part of any property that would otherwise be forfeited pursuant to an order made under subsection 16(1) or 17(2) and that the person appears innocent of any complicity in an offence referred to in paragraph (*a*) or of any collusion in relation to such an offence, the court may order that the property or part be returned to that person. 2017, c. 7, s. 19.

ANNOTATIONS

A lawful owner may hold property as a joint tenant or a tenant in common, both of which may be the subject of a forfeiture order. The effect of a forfeiture order is to sever the joint tenancy such that the Crown and the other tenant are tenants in common, whereupon the Crown can proceed for partition and sale of the property: *R. v. Ford* (2010), 254 C.C.C. (3d) 442 (B.C.C.A.).

NOTICE / Manner of giving notice / Non-forfeiture of real property / Factors in relation to dwelling-house.

19.1 (1) If all or part of the property that would otherwise be forfeited under subsection 16(1) or 17(2) is a dwelling-house, before making an order of forfeiture, a court shall require notice in accordance with subsection (2) to be given to and may hear any person who resides in the dwelling-house and is a member of the immediate family of the person charged with or convicted, or discharged under section 730 of the *Criminal Code*, of the indictable offence under this Act in relation to which the property would be forfeited.

(2) A notice shall

(*a*) be given in the manner that the court directs or that may be specified in the rules of the court;

(*b*) specify the period that the court considers reasonable or that may be set out in the rules of the court during which a member of the immediate family who resides in the dwelling-house may make themselves known to the court; and

(*c*) set out the offence charged and a description of the property.

(3) Subject to an order made under subsection 19(3), if a court is satisfied that the impact of an order of forfeiture made under subsection 16(1) or 17(2) in respect of real property would be disproportionate to the nature and gravity of the offence, the circumstances surrounding the commission of the offence and the criminal record, if any, of the person charged with or convicted, or discharged under section 730 of the *Criminal Code*, of the offence, as the case may be, it may decide not to order the forfeiture of the property or part of the property and may revoke any restraint order made in respect of that property or part.

(4) Where all or part of the property that would otherwise be forfeited under subsection 16(1) or 17(2) is a dwelling-house, when making a decision under subsection (3), the court shall also consider

(*a*) the impact of an order of forfeiture on any member of the immediate family of the person charged with or convicted or discharged of the offence, if the dwelling-house was the member's principal residence at the time the charge was laid and continues to be the member's principal residence, and

(*b*) whether the member referred to in paragraph (*a*) appears innocent of any complicity in the offence or of any collusion in relation to the offence. 2001, c. 32, s. 53; 2017, c. 7, s. 20.

ANNOTATIONS

The offender has the burden of persuading the court that forfeiture should not be granted. In considering the circumstances surrounding the offence, the following factors are relevant: the offender's role in the commission of the offence; any evidence regarding the offender's motivation for becoming involved in the offence; any aggravating or mitigating factors, particularly those that bear on the nature of the property itself; the nature of the property and the manner in which it was used in the offence; the value of the property itself in comparison to the magnitude of the drug offence; and whether the use of the property to commit the offence detrimentally affected its legitimate uses. In this case, the judge erred in taking into account the sentence imposed on the offender, and over-emphasized the source of the funds and the lack of profit: *R. v. Siek* (2007), 218 C.C.C. (3d) 353 (N.S.C.A.).

A forfeiture order should not be considered together with terms of imprisonment or other sentencing consequences as aspects of an interdependent global punishment. Rather, forfeiture requires a separate inquiry based on the discrete proportionality test set out in subsec. (3). In addition, the provision allows for partial forfeiture such that the court can tailor the amount of property to be forfeited in a way that took into account the relative weight of the factors listed in subsec. (3). Partial forfeiture gives the court greater scope for applying the proportionality test. Accordingly, judges have the discretion to order no forfeiture, partial forfeiture or full forfeiture of offence-related real property depending on the circumstances of the case: *R. v. Craig*, [2009] 1 S.C.R. 762, 244 C.C.C. (3d) 1.

Relief against forfeiture is not restricted to cases in which the offences are minor or technical in nature. In this case, the court considered the fact that a less serious drug was involved, the grow operation was not sophisticated, no alterations had been made to the property and the accused had not organized his affairs so as to avoid detection. The accused was not the mastermind, nor was he responsible for the distribution. The property had been purchased decades before the offence and the vast majority of the residence was used for purposes unrelated to the marihuana grow operation. There was no use of the property in a manner that detrimentally affected its legitimate use and the property posed no risk to the safety or security of the community: *R. v. Van Bemmel* (2010), 253 C.C.C. (3d) 284 (Ont. C.A.).

DRUGS

Subsection (4) is applicable only where the dwelling house was the person's principal residence at the time that the charges were laid and remained so through, to and including, the time of the decision on the forfeiture application: *R. v. Bui* (2010), 88 W.C.B. (2d) 386, [2010] B.C.J. No. 1052 (C.A.), *sub nom. R. v. Tran.*

APPLICATION / Fixing day for hearing / Notice / Order declaring interest not affected by forfeiture / Appeal from order made under subsection (4) / Return of property.

20. (1) If any property is forfeited to Her Majesty under an order made under subsection 16(1) or 17(2), any person who claims an interest in the property, other than

(*a*) in the case of property forfeited under an order made under subsection 16(1), a person who was convicted, or discharged under section 730 of the *Criminal Code*, of the designated substance offence in relation to which the property was forfeited;

(*b*) in the case of property forfeited pursuant to an order made under subsection 17(2), a person who was charged with the designated substance offence in relation to which the property was forfeited, or

(*c*) a person who acquired title to or a right of possession of the property from a person referred to in paragraph (*a*) or (*b*) under circumstances that give rise to a reasonable inference that the title or right was transferred from that person for the purpose of avoiding the forfeiture of the property,

may, within thirty days after the forfeiture, apply by notice in writing to a judge for an order under subsection (4).

(2) The judge to whom an application is made under subsection (1) shall fix a day not less than thirty days after the date of the filing of the application for the hearing of the application.

(3) An applicant shall serve a notice of the application made under subsection (1) and of the hearing of it on the Attorney General at least fifteen days before the day fixed for the hearing.

(4) Where, on the hearing of an application made under subsection (1), the judge is satisfied that the applicant

(*a*) is not a persons referred to in paragraph (1)(*a*), (*b*) or (*c*) and appears innocent of any complicity in any designated substance offence that resulted in the forfeiture of the property or of any collusion in relation to such an offence, and

(*b*) exercised all reasonable care to be satisfied that the property was not likely to have been used in connection with the commission of an unlawful act by the person who was permitted by the applicant to obtain possession of the property or from whom the applicant obtained possession or, where the applicant is a mortgagee or lienholder, by the mortgagor or lien-giver,

the judge may make an order declaring that the interest of the applicant is not affected by the forfeiture and declaring the nature and the extent or value of the interest.

(5) An applicant or the Attorney General may appeal to the court of appeal from an order made under subsection (4), and the provisions of Part XXI of the *Criminal Code* with respect to procedure on appeals apply, with such modifications as the circumstances require, in respect of appeals under this subsection.

(6) The Minister shall, on application made to the Minister by any person in respect of whom a judge has made an order under subsection (4), and where the periods with respect to the taking of appeals from that order have expired and any appeal from that order taken under subsection (5) has been determined, direct that

(*a*) the property, or the part of it to which the interest of the applicant relates, be returned to the applicant; or

(*b*) an amount equal to the value of the interest of the applicant, as declared in the order, be paid to the applicant. 2017, c. 7, s. 21.

ANNOTATIONS

The only right of appeal for a non-accused with an interest in property subject to forfeiture is in relation to proceedings for relief under s. 20. Where the accused's spouse sought to appeal a s. 16 forfeiture order as an interested party, the court quashed the appeal, holding that the spouse needed to bring a s. 20 application in the superior court in order to have any right of appeal: *R. v. Vu* (2011), 284 C.C.C. (3d) 191 (B.C.C.A.).

APPEALS FROM ORDERS UNDER SUBSECTION 17(2).

21. Any person who, in their opinion, is aggrieved by an order made under subsection 17(2) may appeal from the order as if the order were an appeal against conviction or against a judgment or verdict of acquittal, as the case may be, under Part XXI of the *Criminal Code*, and that Part applies, with such modifications as the circumstances require, in respect of such an appeal.

SUSPENSION OF ORDER PENDING APPEAL.

22. Notwithstanding anything in this Act, the operation of an order made in respect of property under subsection 16(1), 17(2) or 20(4) is suspended pending

(*a*) any application made in respect of the property under any of those provisions or any other provision of this or any other Act of Parliament that provides for restoration or forfeiture of the property, or

(*b*) any appeal taken from an order of forfeiture or restoration in respect of the property,

and the property shall not be disposed of or otherwise dealt with until thirty days have expired after an order is made under any of those provisions.

[*Heading repealed*, 2001, c. 32, s. 54.]

Division 2

Controlled Substances, Precursors and Chemical Offence-related Property

RETURN / Receipt / Report by peace officer.

23. (1) A peace officer, inspector or prescribed person who seizes, finds or otherwise acquires a controlled substance, precursor or chemical offence-related property may return it to the person who is its lawful owner or who is lawfully entitled to its possession if the peace officer, inspector or prescribed person is satisfied

(*a*) that there is no dispute as to who is the lawful owner or is lawfully entitled to possession of the substance, precursor or property; and

(*b*) that the continued detention of the substance, precursor or property is not required for the purposes of a preliminary inquiry, trial or other proceeding under this Act or any other Act of Parliament.

(2) When the substance, precursor or property is returned, the peace officer, inspector or prescribed person shall obtain a receipt for it.

(3) In the case of a seizure made under section 11 of this Act, the *Criminal Code* or a power of seizure at common law, the peace officer shall make a report about the return to the justice who issued the warrant or another justice for the same territorial division or, if a warrant was not issued, a justice who would have had jurisdiction to issue a warrant. 2017, c. 7, s. 22.

DRUGS

APPLICATION FOR RETURN / Order to return as soon as practicable / Order to return at specified time / Forfeiture order / Payment of compensation in lieu.

24. (1) If a controlled substance, precursor or chemical offence-related property has been seized, found or otherwise acquired by a peace officer, inspector or prescribed person, any person may, within 60 days after the date of the seizure, finding or acquisition, on prior notification being given to the Attorney General in the prescribed manner, apply, by notice in writing to a justice in the jurisdiction in which it is being detained, for an order to return it to the person.

(2) If, on the hearing of an application made under subsection (1), a justice is satisfied that an applicant is the lawful owner or is lawfully entitled to possession of the substance, precursor or property and the Attorney General does not indicate that it or a portion of it may be required for the purposes of a preliminary inquiry, trial or other proceeding under this Act or any other Act of Parliament, the justice shall, subject to subsection (5), order that it or the portion be returned as soon as practicable to the applicant.

(3) If, on the hearing of an application made under subsection (1), a justice is satisfied that an applicant is the lawful owner or is lawfully entitled to possession of the substance, precursor or property but the Attorney General indicates that it or a portion of it may be required for the purposes of a preliminary inquiry, trial or other proceeding under this Act or any other Act of Parliament, the justice shall, subject to subsection (5), order that it or the portion be returned to the applicant

(*a*) on the expiry of 180 days after the day on which the application was made, if no proceeding in relation to it has been commenced before that time; or

(*b*) on the final conclusion of the proceeding or any other proceeding in relation to it, if the applicant is not found guilty in those proceedings of an offence committed in relation to it.

(4) If, on the hearing of an application made under subsection (1), a justice is not satisfied that an applicant is the lawful owner or is lawfully entitled to possession of the substance, precursor or property, and it or a portion of it is not required for the purposes of a preliminary inquiry, trial or other proceeding under this Act or any other Act of Parliament, the justice shall order that it or the portion be forfeited to Her Majesty to be disposed of or otherwise dealt with in accordance with the regulations or, if there are no applicable regulations, in the manner that the Minister directs.

(5) If, on the hearing of an application made under subsection (1), a justice is satisfied that an applicant is the lawful owner or is lawfully entitled to possession of the substance, precursor or property, but it was disposed of or otherwise dealt with under section 26, the justice shall order that an amount equal to its value be paid to the applicant. 2017, c. 7, s. 22.

FORFEITURE IF NO APPLICATION.

25. If no application for the return of a controlled substance, precursor or chemical offence-related property has been made under subsection 24(1) within 60 days after the date of the seizure, finding or acquisition by a peace officer, inspector or prescribed person and it or a portion of it is not required for the purposes of a preliminary inquiry, trial or other proceeding under this Act or any other Act of Parliament, it or the portion is forfeited to Her Majesty and may be disposed of or otherwise dealt with in accordance with the regulations or, if there are no applicable regulations, in the manner that the Minister directs. 2017, c. 7, s. 22.

EXPEDITED DISPOSITION.

26. If a precursor or chemical offence-related property — whose storage or handling poses a risk to health or safety — or a controlled substance, or a portion of any of them,

is not required for the purposes of a preliminary inquiry, trial or other proceeding under this Act or any other Act of Parliament, it or the portion may be disposed of or otherwise dealt with by the Minister, a peace officer or a prescribed person in accordance with the regulations or, if there are no applicable regulations, in the manner that the Minister directs. 2017, c. 7, s. 22.

DISPOSITION FOLLOWING PROCEEDINGS.

27. Subject to section 24, if, in a preliminary inquiry, trial or other proceeding under this Act or any other Act of Parliament, the court before which the proceedings have been brought is satisfied that any controlled substance, precursor or chemical offence-related property that is the subject of proceedings before the court is no longer required by that court or any other court, the court

(*a*) shall

(i) if it is satisfied that the person from whom the substance, precursor or property was seized came into possession of it lawfully and continued to deal with it lawfully, order that it be returned to the person, or

(ii) if it is satisfied that possession of the substance, precursor or property by the person from whom it was seized is unlawful and the person who is the lawful owner or is lawfully entitled to its possession is known, order that it be returned to the person who is the lawful owner or is lawfully entitled to its possession; and

(*b*) may, if it is not satisfied that the substance, precursor or property should be returned under subparagraph (*a*)(i) or (ii) or if possession of it by the person from whom it was seized is unlawful and the person who is the lawful owner or is lawfully entitled to its possession is not known, order that it be forfeited to Her Majesty to be disposed of or otherwise dealt with in accordance with the regulations or, if there are no applicable regulations, in the manner that the Minister directs. 2017, c. 7, s. 23.

DISPOSITION WITH CONSENT.

28. If a controlled substance, precursor or chemical offence-related property has been seized, found or otherwise acquired by a peace officer, inspector or prescribed person and it or a portion of it is not required for the purposes of a preliminary inquiry, trial or other proceeding under this Act or any other Act of Parliament, the person who is its lawful owner may consent to its disposition, and when that consent is given, it or the portion is forfeited to Her Majesty and may be disposed of or otherwise dealt with in accordance with the regulations or, if there are no applicable regulations, in the manner that the Minister directs. 2017, c. 7, s. 24.

REPORT OF DISPOSITION / Interpretation.

29. (1) Subject to the regulations, every peace officer, inspector or prescribed person who disposes of or otherwise deals with a controlled substance, precursor or chemical offence-related property under this Division shall, within 30 days, prepare a report setting out the following information and cause the report to be sent to the Minister:

(*a*) the substance, precursor or property;

(*b*) the amount of it that was disposed of or otherwise dealt with;

(*c*) the manner in which it was disposed of or otherwise dealt with;

(*d*) the date on which it was disposed of or otherwise dealt with;

(*e*) the name of the police force, agency or entity to which the peace officer, inspector or prescribed person belongs;

(*f*) the number of the file or police report related to the disposition of it or other dealing with it; and

(*g*) any other prescribed information.

DRUGS

(2) For the purposes of subsection (1), dealing with a controlled substance, precursor or chemical offence-related property by a peace officer includes using it to conduct an investigation or for training purposes. 2017, c. 7, s. 24.

Part IV / ADMINISTRATION AND COMPLIANCE

Inspectors

DESIGNATION OF INSPECTORS / Certificate of designation.

30. (1) The Minister may designate, in accordance with the regulations made pursuant to paragraph 55(1)(*n*), any person as an inspector for the purposes of this Act and the regulations.

(2) Every inspector shall be provided with a certificate of designation in a form established by the Minister and, on entering any place under subsection 31(1), shall, on request, produce the certificate to the person in charge of the place. 2015, c. 22, s. 2; 2017, c. 7, s. 25.

POWERS OF INSPECTOR / Place / Means of telecommunication / Limitation — access by means of telecommunication / Person accompanying inspector / Entering private property / Warrant to enter dwelling-house / Authority to issue warrant / Use of force / Assistance to inspector / Storage / Notice / Return by inspector / Return or disposition by Minister.

31. (1) Subject to subsection (2), an inspector may, for a purpose related to verifying compliance or preventing non-compliance with the provisions of this Act or the regulations, enter any place, including a conveyance, referred to in subsection (1.1) and may for that purpose

(*a*) open and examine any receptacle or package found in that place in which a controlled substance, precursor or designated device may be found;

(*b*) examine any thing found in that place that is used or may be capable of being used for the production, preservation, packaging or storage of a controlled substance or a precursor;

(*c*) examine any labels or advertising material or records, books, electronic data or other documents found in that place with respect to any controlled substance, precursor, or designated device other than the records of the medical condition of persons, and make copies thereof or take extracts therefrom;

(*d*) use or cause to be used any computer system at that place to examine any electronic data referred to in paragraph (*c*);

(*e*) reproduce any document from any electronic data referred to in paragraph (*c*) or cause it to be reproduced, in the form of a printout or other output;

(*f*) take the labels or advertising material or records, books or other documents referred to in paragraph (*c*) or the printout or other output referred to in paragraph (*e*) for examination or copying;

(*g*) use or cause to be used any copying equipment at that place to make copies of any document;

(*g*.1) take photographs and make recordings and sketches;

(*h*) examine any substance found in that place and take, for the purpose of analysis, such samples thereof as are reasonably required; and

(*i*) seize and detain, in accordance with this Part, any controlled substance, precursor, designated device or conveyance found in that place the seizure and detention of which the inspector believes on reasonable grounds are necessary;

(*j*) order the owner or person having possession, care or control of any controlled substance, precursor, designated device or other thing to which the provisions

of this Act or the regulations apply that is found in that place to move it or, for any time that may be necessary, not to move it or to restrict its movement;

(*k*) order the owner or person having possession, care or control of any conveyance that is found in that place and that the inspector believes on reasonable grounds contains a controlled substance, precursor or designated device to stop the conveyance, to move it or, for any time that may be necessary, not to move it or to restrict its movement;

(*l*) order any person in that place to establish their identity to the inspector's satisfaction; and

(*m*) order a person who, at that place, conducts an activity to which the provisions of this Act or the regulations apply to stop or start the activity.

(1.1) For the purposes of subsection (1), the inspector may only enter a place in which they believe on reasonable grounds

(*a*) a controlled substance, precursor, designated device or document relating to the administration of this Act or the regulations is located;

(*b*) an activity could be conducted under a licence, permit, authorization or exemption that is under consideration by the Minister;

(*c*) an activity to which the provisions of this Act or the regulations apply is being conducted; or

(*d*) an activity was being conducted under a licence, permit, authorization or exemption before the expiry or revocation of the licence, permit, authorization or exemption, in which case the inspector may enter the place only within 45 days after the day on which it expired or was revoked.

(1.2) For the purposes of subsections (1) and (1.1), an inspector is considered to have entered a place when they access it remotely by a means of telecommunication.

(1.3) An inspector who enters remotely, by a means of telecommunication, a place that is not accessible to the public must do so with the knowledge of the owner or person in charge of the place and only for the period necessary for any purpose referred to in subsection (1).

(1.4) An inspector may be accompanied by any other person that the inspector believes is necessary to help them exercise their powers or perform their duties or functions under this section.

(1.5) An inspector and any person accompanying them may enter and pass through private property, other than a dwelling-house on that property, in order to gain entry to a place referred to in subsection (1.1).

(2) In the case of a dwelling-house, an inspector may enter it only with the consent of an occupant or under the authority of a warrant issued under subsection (3).

(3) A justice may, on *ex parte* application, issue a warrant authorizing the inspector named in it to enter a place and exercise any of the powers mentioned in paragraphs (1)(*a*) to (*m*), subject to any conditions that are specified in the warrant, if the justice is satisfied by information on oath that

(*a*) the place is a dwelling-house but otherwise meets the conditions for entry described in subsections (1) and (1.1);

(*b*) entry to the dwelling-house is necessary for the purpose of verifying compliance or preventing non-compliance with the provisions of this Act or the regulations; and

(*c*) entry to the dwelling-house has been refused or there are reasonable grounds to believe that entry will be refused.

(4) In executing a warrant issued under subsection (3), an inspector shall not use force unless the inspector is accompanied by a peace officer and the use of force is specifically authorized in the warrant.

(5) The owner or other person in charge of a place entered by an inspector and every person found there shall give the inspector all reasonable assistance in that person's power and provide the inspector with any information that the inspector may reasonably require.

(6) Anything that is seized and detained by an inspector under this section may, at the inspector's discretion, be kept or stored at the place where it was seized or, at the inspector's direction, be removed to any other proper place.

(7) An inspector who seizes anything under this section shall take any measures that are reasonable in the circumstances to give to the owner or other person in charge of the place where the seizure occurred notice of the seizure and of the location where the thing is being kept or stored.

(8) If an inspector determines that to verify compliance or prevent non-compliance with the provisions of this Act or the regulations it is no longer necessary to detain anything seized by the inspector under this section, the inspector shall notify in writing the owner or other person in charge of the place where the seizure occurred of that determination and, on being issued a receipt for it, shall return the thing to that person.

(9) If a period of 120 days has elapsed after the date of a seizure under this section and the thing has not been returned, disposed of or otherwise dealt with in accordance with subsection (8) or any of sections 24 to 27, it shall be returned, disposed of or otherwise dealt with in accordance with the regulations or, if there are no applicable regulations, in the manner that the Minister directs. 2015, c. 22, s. 3; 2017, c. 7, s. 26(1), (3) to (8).

OBSTRUCTING INSPECTOR / False statements / Interference.

32. (1) No person shall, by act or omission, obstruct an inspector who is engaged in the exercise of their powers or the performance of their duties or functions under this Act or the regulations.

(2) No person shall knowingly make any false or misleading statement verbally or in writing to an inspector who is engaged in the exercise of their powers or the performance of their duties or functions under this Act or the regulations.

(3) No person shall, without the authority of an inspector, remove, alter or interfere in any way with anything seized, detained or taken under section 31. 2017, c. 7, s. 27(1), (2).

Part V / ADMINISTRATIVE ORDERS FOR CONTRAVENTIONS OF DESIGNATED REGULATIONS

DESIGNATION OF REGULATIONS.

33. The Governor in Council may, by regulation, designate any regulation made under this Act (in this Part referred to as a "designated regulation") as a regulation the contravention of which shall be dealt with under this Part.

CONTRAVENTION OF DESIGNATED REGULATION.

34. Where the Minister has reasonable grounds to believe that a person has contravened a designated regulation, the Minister shall

(*a*) in the prescribed manner, serve a notice to appear on the person; and

(*b*) send a copy of the notice to appear to an adjudicator and direct the adjudicator to conduct a hearing to determine whether the contravention has occurred and to notify the Minister of the adjudicator's determination.

Note: If Bill C-37, introduced in the 1st session of the 42nd Parliament and entitled *An Act to amend the Controlled Drugs and Substances Act and to make related amendments to* *other Acts*, receives royal assent, then, on the first day on which both s. 28 of that Act and s. 199(2) of 2018, c. 16 are in force, s. 34 is amended by enacting subsec. (2), 2018, c. 16, s. 199(1):

Maximum penalty

(2) The maximum penalty for a violation is $1,000,000.

INTERIM ORDER / Idem.

35. (1) Where the Minister has reasonable grounds to believe that a person has contravened a designated regulation and the Minister is of the opinion that, as a result of that contravention, there is a substantial risk of immediate danger to the health or safety of any person, the Minister may, without giving prior notice to the person believed to have contravened the designated regulation, make an interim order in respect of the person

- **(*a*) prohibiting the person from doing anything that the person would otherwise be permitted to do under their licence, permit or authorization, or**
- **(*b*) subjecting the doing of anything under the designated regulation by the person to the terms and conditions specified in the interim order,**

and may, for that purpose, suspend, cancel or amend the licence, permit or authorization issued or granted to the person or take any other measures set out in the regulations.

(2) Where the Minister makes an interim order under subsection (1), the Minister shall forthwith

- **(*a*) in the prescribed manner, serve the interim order on the person;**
- **(*b*) in the prescribed manner, serve a notice to appear on the person; and**
- **(*c*) send a copy of the interim order and the notice to appear to an adjudicator and direct the adjudicator to conduct a hearing to determine whether the contravention has occurred and to notify the Minister of the adjudicator's determination.**

HEARING BY ADJUDICATOR / Change of hearing date / Proceedings on default / Time and place.

36. (1) Where an adjudicator receives from the Minister a copy of a notice to appear under paragraph 34(*b*) or 35(2)(*c*), the adjudicator shall conduct a hearing on a date to be fixed by the adjudicator at the request of the person on whom the notice was served, on two days notice being given to the adjudicator, which hearing date may not

- **(*a*) in the case of a notice served under paragraph 34(*a*), be less than thirty days, or more than forty-five days, after the day of service of the notice; or**
- **(*b*) in the case of a notice served under paragraph 35(2)(*b*), be less than three days, or more than forty-five days, after the day of service of the notice.**

(2) Where the adjudicator is unable to conduct a hearing on the date referred to in subsection (1), the adjudicator shall forthwith notify the person and fix, for the purpose of holding the hearing, the earliest possible date to which the adjudicator and the person agree.

(3) Where an adjudicator has received a copy of a notice to appear referred to in subsection (1) and where the person on whom the notice is served has not requested a date for a hearing within forty-five days after the notice was served on that person, or where the person, having requested a hearing, fails to appear for the hearing, the adjudicator shall proceed to make a determination in the absence of the person.

(4) An adjudicator may, subject to the regulations, determine the time and place of any hearing or other proceeding under this Part.

DRUGS

NOTICE TO APPEAR.

37. A notice to appear served on a person under paragraph 34(*a*) or 35(2)(*b*) shall

(*a*) specify the designated regulation that the Minister believes the person has contravened;

(*b*) state the grounds on which the Minister believes the contravention has occurred;

(*c*) state that the matter has been referred to an adjudicator for a hearing to be conducted on a date within the applicable period described in paragraph 36(1)(*a*) or (*b*); and

(*d*) set out such other information as is prescribed.

PROOF OF SERVICE.

38. Proof of service of any notice, order or interim order under this Part shall be given in the prescribed manner.

POWERS OF ADJUDICATOR.

39. For the purposes of this Act, an adjudicator has and may exercise the powers of a person appointed as a commissioner under Part I of the *Inquiries Act*.

HEARING PROCEDURE.

40. An adjudicator shall deal with all matters as informally and expeditiously as the circumstances and considerations of fairness and natural justice permit.

DETERMINATION BY ADJUDICATOR / Notice of determination / Ministerial orders / Idem.

41. (1) An adjudicator shall, after the conclusion of a hearing referred to in subsection 36(1) or a proceeding referred to in subsection 36(3), within the prescribed time, make a determination that the person who is the subject of the hearing or proceeding contravened or did not contravene the designated regulation.

(2) Where an adjudicator has made a determination under subsection (1), the adjudicator shall

(*a*) forthwith notify the person and the Minister of the adjudicator's determination and the reasons; and

(*b*) where the adjudicator has determined that the person has contravened the designated regulation, notify the person of the opportunity to make representations to the Minister in writing in accordance with the regulations and within the prescribed time.

(3) Where an adjudicator has made a determination referred to in paragraph (2)(*b*) and the Minister has considered the determination and any representations referred to in that paragraph, the Minister shall forthwith make an order

(*a*) prohibiting the person from doing anything that they would, if they were in compliance with the designated regulation, be permitted to do, or

(*b*) subjecting the doing of anything under the designated regulation by the person to the terms and conditions specified in the order,

and may, for that purpose, suspend, cancel or amend any licence, permit or authorization issued or granted to the person under the regulations or take any other measures set out in the regulations.

(4) An order made under subsection (3) shall be served on the person to whom it is directed in the prescribed manner.

EFFECT OF ORDER / Cessation of effect / Application to revoke order / Revocation of order.

42. (1) An interim order made under subsection 35(1) and an order made under subsection 41(3) have effect from the time that they are served on the person to whom they are directed.

(2) An interim order that was made in respect of a person believed to have contravened a designated regulation ceases to have effect

(*a*) where the Minister makes an order under subsection 41(3), at the time the order is served on the person; and

(*b*) where an adjudicator has determined that the person did not contravene the designated regulation, at the time the adjudicator makes the determination.

(3) A person in respect of whom an order was made under subsection 41(3) may make an application in writing to the Minister in accordance with the regulations to revoke the order.

(4) The Minister may, in the prescribed circumstances, revoke, in whole or in part, any order made under subsection 41(3).

OFFENCE FOR CONTRAVENTION OF ORDER.

43. Every person commits an offence who contravenes an order or an interim order made under this Part.

DRUGS

Note: Part V replaced, 2017, c. 7, s. 28 (to come into force by order of the Governor in Council):

Administrative Monetary Penalties

Violation

Commission of violation.

33. Every person who contravenes a provision designated by regulations made under paragraph 34(1)(*a*), or contravenes an order made under section 45.1 or 45.2 or reviewed under section 45.4, commits a violation and is liable to the penalty established in accordance with the provisions of this Act and the regulations.

Powers of the Governor in Council and the Minister

Regulations

34. (1) The Governor in Council may make regulations

(*a*) designating as a violation that may be proceeded with in accordance with this Act the contravention of any specified provision of this Act — except a provision of Part I — or the regulations;

(*b*) fixing a penalty, or a range of penalties, in respect of each violation;

(*c*) classifying each violation as a minor violation, a serious violation or a very serious violation; and

(*d*) respecting the circumstances under which, the criteria by which and the manner in which a penalty may be increased or reduced, including a reduction in the amount that is provided for in a compliance agreement.

Maximum penalty

(2) The maximum penalty for a violation is $30,000.

Criteria for penalty.

35. Unless a penalty is fixed under paragraph 34(1)(*b*), the amount of a penalty shall, in each case, be determined taking into account

(*a*) the history of compliance with the provisions of this Act or the regulations by the person who committed the violation;

(*b*) the harm to public health or safety that resulted or could have resulted from the violation;

(*c*) whether the person made reasonable efforts to mitigate or reverse the violation's effects;

(*d*) whether the person derived any competitive or economic benefit from the violation; and

(*e*) any other prescribed criteria.

Notices of violation

36. The Minister may

(*a*) designate individuals, or classes of individuals, who are authorized to issue notices of violation; and

(*b*) establish, in respect of each violation, a short-form description to be used in notices of violation.

Proceedings

Issuance of notice of violation

37. (1) If a person who is designated under paragraph 36(*a*) believes on reasonable grounds that a person has committed a violation, the designated person may issue, and shall provide the person with, a notice of violation that

(*a*) sets out the person's name;

(*b*) identifies the alleged violation;

(*c*) sets out the penalty for the violation that the person is liable to pay; and

(*d*) sets out the particulars concerning the time and manner of payment.

Summary of rights

(2) A notice of violation shall clearly summarize, in plain language, the named person's rights and obligations under this section and sections 38 to 43.7, including the right to have the acts or omissions that constitute the alleged violation or the amount of the penalty reviewed and the procedure for requesting that review.

Penalties

Payment

38. (1) If the person named in the notice pays, in the prescribed time and manner, the amount of the penalty,

(*a*) they are deemed to have committed the violation in respect of which the amount is paid;

(*b*) the Minister shall accept that amount as complete satisfaction of the penalty; and

(*c*) the proceedings commenced in respect of the violation under section 37 are ended.

Alternatives to payment

(2) Instead of paying the penalty set out in a notice of violation, the person named in the notice may, in the prescribed time and manner,

(*a*) if the penalty is $5,000 or more, request to enter into a compliance agreement with the Minister that ensures the person's compliance with the order or the provision to which the violation relates; or (*b*) request a review by the Minister of the acts or omissions that constitute the alleged violation or the amount of the penalty.

Deeming

(3) If the person named in the notice of violation does not pay the penalty in the prescribed time and manner and does not exercise any right referred to in subsection (2) in the prescribed time and manner, they are deemed to have committed the violation identified in the notice.

Compliance Agreements

Compliance agreements

39. (1) After considering a request under paragraph 38(2)(*a*), the Minister may enter into a compliance agreement, as described in that paragraph, with the person making the request on any terms and conditions that are satisfactory to the Minister. The terms and conditions may

(*a*) include a provision for the giving of reasonable security, in a form and in an amount satisfactory to the Minister, as a guarantee that the person will comply with the compliance agreement; and

(*b*) provide for the reduction, in whole or in part, of the penalty for the violation.

Deeming

(2) A person who enters into a compliance agreement with the Minister is, on doing so, deemed to have committed the violation in respect of which the compliance agreement was entered into.

Notice of compliance

(3) If the Minister is satisfied that a person who has entered into a compliance agreement has complied with it, the Minister shall cause a notice to that effect to be provided to the person, at which time

(*a*) the proceedings commenced in respect of the violation under section 37 are ended; and

(*b*) any security given by the person under the compliance agreement shall be returned to the person.

Notice of default

(4) If the Minister is of the opinion that a person who has entered into a compliance agreement has not complied with it, the Minister shall cause a notice of default to be provided to the person to the effect that

(*a*) instead of the penalty set out in the notice of violation in respect of which the compliance agreement was entered into, the person is liable to pay, in the prescribed time and manner, twice the amount of that penalty, and, for greater certainty, subsection 34(2) does not apply in respect of that amount; or

(*b*) the security, if any, given by the person under the compliance agreement shall be forfeited to Her Majesty in right of Canada.

Effect of notice of default

(5) Once provided with the notice of default, the person may not deduct from the amount set out in the notice any amount that they spent under the compliance agreement and

(*a*) the person is liable to pay the amount set out in the notice; or

(*b*) if the notice provides for the forfeiture of the security given under the compliance agreement, that security is forfeited to Her Majesty in right of Canada and the proceedings commenced in respect of the violation under section 37 are ended.

Effect of payment

(6) If a person pays the amount set out in the notice of default in the prescribed time and manner,

(*a*) the Minister shall accept the amount as complete satisfaction of the amount owing; and

(*b*) the proceedings commenced in respect of the violation under section 37 are ended.

Refusal to enter into compliance agreement

40. (1) If the Minister refuses to enter into a compliance agreement requested under paragraph 38(2)(*a*), the person who made the request is liable to pay the amount of the penalty in the prescribed time and manner.

Effect of payment

(2) If a person pays the amount referred to in subsection (1),

(*a*) they are deemed to have committed the violation in respect of which the payment is made;

(*b*) the Minister shall accept the amount as complete satisfaction of the penalty; and

(*c*) the proceedings commenced in respect of the violation under section 37 are ended.

Deeming

(3) If a person does not pay the amount referred to in subsection (1) in the prescribed time and manner, they are deemed to have committed the violation identified in the notice of violation.

Review by the Minister

Review — facts

41. (1) On completion of a review requested under paragraph 38(2)(*b*) with respect to the acts or omissions that constitute the alleged violation, the Minister shall determine whether the person who requested the review committed the violation. If the Minister determines that the person committed the violation but that the amount of the penalty was not established in accordance with the provisions of this Act and the regulations, the Minister shall correct the amount.

Violation not committed — effect

(2) If the Minister determines under subsection (1) that the person who requested the review did not commit the violation, the proceedings commenced in respect of it under section 37 are ended.

Review — penalty

(3) On completion of a review requested under paragraph 38(2)(*b*) with respect to the amount of the penalty, the Minister shall determine whether the amount of the penalty was established in accordance with the provisions of this Act and the regulations and, if not, the Minister shall correct the amount.

Notice of decision

(4) The Minister shall cause a notice of any decision made under subsection (1) or (3) to be provided to the person who requested the review.

Payment

(5) The person is liable to pay, in the prescribed time and manner, the amount of the penalty that is confirmed or corrected in the Minister's decision made under subsection (1) or (3).

Effect of payment

(6) If a person pays the amount referred to in subsection (5),

- (*a*) the Minister shall accept the amount as complete satisfaction of the penalty; and
- (*b*) the proceedings commenced in respect of the violation under section 37 are ended.

Written evidence and submissions

(7) The Minister shall consider only written evidence and written submissions in determining whether a person committed a violation or whether the amount of a penalty was established in accordance with the provisions of this Act and the regulations.

Enforcement

Debts to Her Majesty

42. (1) The following amounts constitute debts due to Her Majesty in right of Canada that may be recovered in the Federal Court:

- (*a*) the amount of a penalty, from the time the notice of violation setting out the penalty is provided;
- (*b*) every amount set out in a compliance agreement entered into with the Minister under subsection 39(1), from the time the compliance agreement is entered into;
- (*c*) the amount set out in a notice of default referred to in subsection 39(4), from the time the notice is provided; and
- (*d*) the amount of a penalty as set out in a decision of the Minister made under subsection 41(1) or (3), from the time the notice of that decision is provided.

Time limit

(2) No proceedings to recover a debt referred to in subsection (1) may be commenced later than five years after the debt became payable.

Debt final

(3) A debt referred to in subsection (1) is final and not subject to review or to be restrained, prohibited, removed, set aside or otherwise dealt with except to the extent and in the manner provided by sections 38 to 41.

Certificate of default

43. (1) Any debt referred to in subsection 42(1) in respect of which there is a default of payment, or the part of any such debt that has not been paid, may be certified by the Minister.

Judgments

(2) On production to the Federal Court, the certificate shall be registered in that Court and, when registered, has the same force and effect, and all proceedings may be taken on the certificate, as if it were a judgment obtained in that Court for a debt of the amount specified in it and all reasonable costs and charges associated with the registration of the certificate.

Rules About Violations

Certain defences not available

43.1 (1) A person named in a notice of violation does not have a defence by reason that the person

- (*a*) exercised due diligence to prevent the violation; or
- (*b*) reasonably and honestly believed in the existence of facts that, if true, would exonerate the person.

DRUGS

Common law principles

(2) Every rule and principle of the common law that renders any circumstance a justification or excuse in relation to a charge for an offence under this Act applies in respect of a violation to the extent that it is not inconsistent with this Act.

Burden of proof

43.2 In every case when the facts of a violation are reviewed by the Minister, he or she shall determine, on a balance of probabilities, whether the person named in the notice of violation committed the violation identified in the notice.

Violation by corporate officers, etc.

43.3 If a person other than an individual commits a violation under this Act, any of the person's directors, officers, agents or mandataries who directed, authorized, assented to, acquiesced in or participated in the commission of the violation is a party to and liable for the violation whether or not the person who actually committed the violation is proceeded against under this Act.

Vicarious liability — acts of employees and agents

43.4 A person is liable for a violation that is committed by any employee, agent or mandatary of the person acting in the course of the employee's employment or the scope of the agent or mandatary's authority, whether or not the employee, agent or mandatary who actually committed the violation is identified or proceeded against under this Act.

Continuing violation

43.5 A violation that is continued on more than one day constitutes a separate violation in respect of each day on which it is continued.

Other Provisions

Evidence

43.6 In any proceeding in respect of a violation or a prosecution for an offence, a notice of violation purporting to be issued under this Act is admissible in evidence without proof of the signature or official character of the person appearing to have signed the notice of violation.

Time limit

43.7 Proceedings in respect of a violation shall not be commenced later than six months after the Minister becomes aware of the acts or omissions that constitute the alleged violation.

How act or omission may be proceeded with

43.8 If an act or omission may be proceeded with either as a violation or as an offence, proceeding in one manner precludes proceeding in the other.

Certification by Minister

43.9 A document appearing to have been issued by the Minister, certifying the day on which the acts or omissions that constitute the alleged violation became known to the Minister, is admissible in evidence without proof of the signature or official character of the person appearing to have signed the document and, in the absence of evidence to the contrary, is proof that the Minister became aware of the acts or omissions on that day.

Publication of information

43.91 The Minister may, for the purpose of encouraging compliance with the provisions of this Act and the regulations, publish information about any violation after proceedings in respect of it are ended.

Part VI / GENERAL

Analysis

DESIGNATION OF ANALYSTS.

44. The Minister may designate, in accordance with the regulations made pursuant to paragraph 55(1)(*o*), any person as an analyst for the purposes of this Act and the regulations.

ANALYSIS / Report.

45. (1) A peace officer, inspector or prescribed person may submit to an analyst for analysis or examination any substance or sample of it taken by the peace officer, inspector or prescribed person.

(2) An analyst who has made an analysis or examination under subsection (1) may prepare a certificate or report stating that the analyst has analysed or examined a substance or a sample thereof and setting out the results of the analysis or examination. 2017, c. 7, s. 29.

Ministerial Orders

DRUGS

PROVISION OF INFORMATION.

45.1 The Minister may, by order, require a person who is authorized under this Act to conduct activities in relation to controlled substances or precursors or a person who imports designated devices to provide the Minister, in the time and manner that the Minister specifies, with any information respecting those activities that the Minister considers necessary

Note: The portion of s. 45.1 before para. (*a*) replaced, 2017, c. 7, s. 31 (to come into force by order of the Governor in Council):

Provision of information

45.1 Subject to section 24, if, in a preliminary inquiry, trial or other proceeding under this Act or any other Act of Parliament, the court before which the proceedings have been brought is satisfied that any controlled substance, precursor or chemical offence-related property that is the subject of proceedings before the court is no longer required by that court or any other court, the court

(*a*) to verify compliance or prevent non-compliance with the provisions of this Act or the regulations; or

(*b*) to address an issue of public health or safety. 2017, c. 7, s. 30.

MEASURES.

45.2 The Minister may, by order, require a person who is authorized under this Act to conduct activities in relation to controlled substances or precursors to take measures, in the time and manner that the Minister specifies, to prevent non-compliance with the provisions of this Act or the regulations or, if the Minister has reasonable grounds to believe that there is such non-compliance, to remedy it. 2017, c. 7, s. 30.

Note: Section 45.2 replaced, 2017, c. 7, s. 32 (to come into force by order of the Governor in Council):

Measures

45.2 The Minister may, by order, require a person who is authorized under this Act to conduct activities in relation to controlled substances or precursors or who conducts activities referred to in section 46.4 in relation to designated devices, to take measures, in the time and manner that the Minister specifies, to prevent non-compliance with the provisions of this Act or the regulations or, if the Minister has reasonable grounds to believe that there is such non-compliance, to remedy it.

REVIEW OFFICER.

45.3 The Minister may designate any qualified individual or class of qualified individuals as review officers for the purpose of reviewing orders under section 45.4. 2017, c. 7, s. 30.

REQUEST FOR REVIEW / Contents of and time for making request / No authority to review / Reasons for refusal / Review initiated by review officer / Order in effect / Completion of review / Extension of period for review / Reasons for extension / Decision on completion of review / Written notice / Effect of amendment.

45.4 (1) Subject to any other provision of this section, an order that is made under section 45.1 or 45.2 shall be reviewed on the written request of the person who was ordered to provide information or to take measures — but only on grounds that involve questions of fact alone or questions of mixed law and fact — by a review officer other than the individual who made the order.

(2) The request shall state the grounds for review and set out the evidence — including evidence that was not considered by the individual who made the order — that supports those grounds and the decision that is sought. It shall be provided to the Minister within seven days after the day on which the order was provided.

(3) The review is not to be done if the request does not comply with subsection (2) or is frivolous, vexatious or not made in good faith.

(4) The person who made the request shall, without delay, be notified in writing of the reasons for not doing the review.

(5) A review officer — other than the individual who made the order — may review an order, whether or not a request is made under subsection (1).

(6) An order continues to apply during a review unless the review officer decides otherwise.

(7) A review officer shall complete the review no later than 30 days after the day on which the request is provided to the Minister.

(8) The review officer may extend the review period by no more than 30 days if they are of the opinion that more time is required to complete the review. They may extend the review period more than once.

(9) If the review period is extended, the person who made the request shall, without delay, be notified in writing of the reasons for extending it.

(10) On completion of a review, the review officer shall confirm, amend, terminate or cancel the order.

(11) The person who made the request or, if there is no request, the person who was ordered to provide information or to take measures shall, without delay, be notified in writing of the reasons for the review officer's decision under subsection (10).

(12) An order that is amended is subject to review under this section. 2017, c. 7, s. 30.

STATUTORY INSTRUMENTS ACT.

45.5 The *Statutory Instruments Act* does not apply in respect of an order made under section 45.1 or 45.2. 2017, c. 7, s. 30.

Offence and Punishment.

PENALTY.

46. Every person who contravenes a provision of this Act for which punishment is not otherwise provided, a provision of a regulation or an order made under section 45.1 or 45.2

(*a*) is guilty of an indictable offence and liable to a fine of not more than $5,000,000 or to imprisonment for a term not exceeding three years, or to both; or

(*b*) is guilty of an offence punishable on summary conviction and liable, for a first offence, to a fine of not more than $250,000 or imprisonment for a term of not more than six months, or to both, and, for any subsequent offence, to a fine of not more than $500,000 or imprisonment for a term of not more than 18 months, or to both. 2017, c. 7, s. 33; 2018, c. 16, s. 200.

Prohibitions

OFFENCE OF MAKING FALSE OR DECEPTIVE STATEMENTS.

46.1 No person shall knowingly make, or participate in, assent to or acquiesce in the making of, a false or misleading statement in any book, record, return or other document however recorded, required to be maintained, made or furnished under this Act or the regulations. 2017, c. 7, s. 34.

COMPLIANCE WITH TERMS AND CONDITIONS.

46.2 The holder of a licence, permit, authorization or exemption shall comply with its terms and conditions. 2017, c. 7, s. 34.

IMPORTATION OF DESIGNATED DEVICE / Information for registration / Registration / Proof of registration / Refusal or cancellation / Disclosure of information — designated device / Disclosure of information to police force.

46.3 (1) No person shall import into Canada a designated device unless they register the importation with the Minister.

Note: Section 46.3 amended by replacing subsec. (1), 2017, c. 7, s. 35(1) (to come into force by order of the Governor in Council):

Importation of designated device

46.3 (1) No person shall import into Canada a designated device unless they register the importation with the Minister and the person imports it in accordance with the regulations.

(2) The following information shall be submitted to the Minister for the purpose of registering the importation of a designated device:

(*a*) the name of the person importing the designated device or, if the person is a corporation, the corporate name and any other name registered with a province, under which the person carries out its activities or identifies itself;

(*b*) the person's address or, if the person is a corporation, the address of its primary place of business in Canada;

(*c*) a description of the designated device, including the model number, serial number, and the brand name or trademark associated with it, if any;

(*d*) the address where the designated device will be delivered as well as the street address of the premises where it will be used by the person importing it;

(*e*) the name of the customs office where the importation is anticipated; and

(*f*) the anticipated date of importation.

Note: Subsection 46.3(2) amended by striking out "and" at the end of para. (*e*), by adding "and" to the end of para. (*f*) and by enacting para. (*g*), 2017, c. 7, s. 35(2) (to come into force by order of the Governor in Council):

(*g*) any other prescribed information.

(3) After the Minister receives the information, the Minister shall register the importation and provide proof of the registration to the person importing the designated device.

(4) The person importing the designated device shall provide the proof of the registration of its importation to the customs office at the time specified by the regulations or, if no time is specified by the regulations, at the time of importation.

(5) The Minister may refuse to register or cancel the registration of the importation of a designated device if the Minister believes on reasonable grounds that false or misleading information was provided, or it is necessary to do so to protect public health or safety or for any other prescribed reason.

(6) The Minister is authorized to disclose to the Canada Border Services Agency or an officer, as defined in section 2(1) of the *Customs Act*, any information submitted under subsection (2) for the purpose of verifying compliance with the provisions of this Act or the regulations.

(7) The Minister is authorized to disclose any information submitted under subsection (2) to a Canadian police force or a member of a Canadian police force who requests the information in the course of an investigation under this Act. 2017, c. 7, s. 34.

Note: Section 46.4 enacted, 2017, c. 7, s. 36 (to come into force by order of the Governor in Council):

Designated device — prescribed activity

46.4 No person shall conduct a prescribed activity in relation to a designated device except in accordance with the regulations.

Evidence and Procedure

TIME LIMIT / Venue.

47. (1) No summary conviction proceedings in respect of an offence under subsection 4(2) or 32(2) or the regulations or in respect of a contravention of an order made under section 45.1 or 45.2 shall be commenced after the expiry of one year after the time when the subject matter of the proceedings arose.

(2) Proceedings in respect of a contravention of any provision of this Act or the regulations or of an order made under section 45.1 or 45.2 may be held in the place where the offence was committed or where the subject matter of the proceedings arose or in any place where the accused is apprehended or happens to be located. 2017, c. 7, s. 37.

BURDEN OF PROVING EXCEPTION, ETC. / Idem.

48. (1) No exception, exemption, excuse or qualification prescribed by law is required to be set out or negatived, as the case may be, in an information or indictment for an offence under this Act or the regulations or under section 463, 464 or 465 of the *Criminal Code* in respect of such an offence.

(2) In any prosecution under this Act, the prosecutor is not required, except by way of rebuttal, to prove that a certificate, licence, permit or other qualification does not operate in favour of the accused, whether or not the qualification is set out in the information or indictment.

ANNOTATIONS

Note: The following case was decided under the *Narcotic Control Act*, but was considered useful in the interpretation of this section.

It was held that the predecessor section applied only to statutory exceptions, such as possession of a licence, and does not apply to a common law defence such as necessity: *R. v. Perka*, [1984] 2 S.C.R. 232, 14 C.C.C. (3d) 385 (5:0).

COPIES OF DOCUMENTS / Authentication / Evidence inadmissible under this section.

49. (1) A copy of any document filed with a department, ministry, agency, municipality or other body established by or pursuant to a law of a province, or of any statement containing information from the records kept by any such department, ministry, agency, municipality or body, purporting to be certified by any official having custody of that document or those records, is admissible in evidence in any prosecution for an offence referred to in subsection 48(1) and, in the absence of evidence to the contrary, is proof of the facts contained in that document or statement, without proof of the signature or official character of the person purporting to have certified it.

(2) For the purposes of subsection (1), an engraved, lithographed, photocopied, photographed, printed or otherwise electronically or mechanically reproduced facsimile signature of an official referred to in that subsection is sufficient authentication of any copy referred to in that subsection.

(3) Nothing in subsection (1) renders admissible in evidence in any legal proceeding such part of any record as is proved to be a record made in the course of an investigation or inquiry.

CERTIFICATE ISSUED UNDER REGULATIONS / Certificate issued pursuant to regulations.

50. (1) Subject to subsection (2), any certificate or other document issued under regulations made under paragraph 55(2)(*c*) or (2.1)(*c*) is admissible in evidence in a preliminary inquiry, trial or other proceeding under this or any other Act of Parliament and, in the absence of evidence to the contrary, is proof that the certificate or other document was validly issued and of the facts contained in it, without proof of the signature or official character of the person purporting to have certified it.

(2) The defence may, with leave of the court, require that the person who issued the certificate or other document

- **(*a*) produce an affidavit or solemn declaration attesting to any of the matters deemed to be proved under subsection (1); or**
- **(*b*) appear before the court for examination or cross-examination in respect of the issuance of the certificate or other document. 2018, c. 16, s. 201.**

CERTIFICATE OR REPORT OF ANALYST / Attendance of analyst.

51. (1) A certificate or report prepared by an analyst under subsection 45(2) is admissible in evidence in any prosecution for an offence under this Act or any other Act of Parliament and, in the absence of evidence to the contrary, is proof of the statements set out in the certificate or report, without proof of the signature or official character of the person appearing to have signed it.

(2) The party against whom a certificate or report of an analyst is produced under subsection (1) may, with leave of the court, require the attendance of the analyst for the purpose of cross-examination. 2017, c. 7, s. 38.

(3) [*Repealed*, 2017, c. 7, s. 38(2).]

ANNOTATIONS

Note: The following cases were decided under the *Narcotic Control Act*, but were considered useful in the interpretation of this section.

Proof of continuity [subsec. (1)] – A certificate stating that an analysis of a substance sent originally to a federal office in one province was conducted in another province is satisfactory for continuity under the broad provisions of this section: *R. v. Welsh* (1975), 24 C.C.C. (2d) 382 (Ont. C.A.).

The Crown is under no duty to call all persons who handled the drug exhibit envelope from the time it was sealed by the arresting officer until it reached the analyst: *R. v. Oracheski* (1979), 48 C.C.C. (2d) 217 (Alta. S.C. App. Div.). Folld: *R. v. Degraaf* (1981), 60 C.C.C. (2d) 315 (B.C.C.A.).

Proof of nature of substance other than by certificate under this Act – An admission by the accused to the police that he was the owner of the "marihuana" is itself some evidence of the nature of the substance: *R. v. Van Esch* (1975), 24 C.C.C. (2d) 523 (Ont. C.A.).

As well, evidence by a police officer that in his opinion the substance was marihuana because of its odour and appearance, while of little weight, is some evidence of the nature of the substance: *R. v. Woodward* (1975), 23 C.C.C. (2d) 508 (Ont. C.A.).

Meaning of evidence to the contrary – "Evidence to the contrary" is any evidence which tends to put in doubt the probative value Parliament has legislatively conferred upon the statements contained in the certificate. Thus any evidence with respect to the analyst himself, his qualifications, integrity or in regard to the procedures he followed to draw his conclusions which could as a matter of law leave the trier of fact with a reasonable doubt as to the analyst's conclusions had he testified as an expert witness in court may constitute evidence to the contrary: *R. v. Oliver*, [1981] 2 S.C.R. 240, 62 C.C.C. (2d) 97 (9:0).

Sufficiency of analysis – In reaching his conclusion as to the identity of the substance the analyst is entitled to rely on tests performed by others and to make use of standard graphs supplied by other laboratories: *R. v. Jordan* (1984), 11 C.C.C. (3d) 565 (B.C.C.A.).

In the absence of evidence to the contrary, a certificate stood as proof that the material was "cannabis (marihuana)" contrary to Schedule II. The failure to test for the level of THS was irrelevant. The difference in THS levels between "hemp" and "cannabis" was of no significance as the Act proscribed the production and possession of all forms of cannabis, including hemp: *R. v. Agecoutay* (2009), 247 C.C.C. (3d) 75 (Sask. C.A.).

Leave to cross-examine [subsec. (2)] – A time lapse of some 18 days between the date when the substance was submitted and the date it was analyzed is not sufficient reason to grant leave under this subection: *R. v. Dannenbaum and Bevans* (1973), 11 C.C.C. (2d) 299 (B.C.S.C.).

It was held in *R. v. Klippenstein and Isherwood* (1975), 28 C.C.C. (2d) 235 (Man. Q.B.), that a trial judge properly exercised his discretion in refusing to grant leave under this subsection despite affidavit evidence that there existed scientific research casting doubt on the analysis normally used to detect the presence of the species of *cannabis* proscribed by this Act.

Reasonable notice [subsec. (3)] – Where reasonable notice to the accused was proven in a manner that was not strictly admissible, the silence of the accused on that point may be taken as a tacit admission of it: *R. v. Bowles* (1974), 16 C.C.C. (2d) 425 (Ont. C.A.).

The issue of reasonable notice is to be determined before the admission of the certificate, not after it is in the evidence to then determine whether or not a case has been established against the accused: *R. v. M.* (1975), 25 C.C.C. (2d) 507 (Man. Q.B.). *Contra*: *R. v. Braithwaite* (1972), 6 C.C.C. (2d) 257 (Alta. S.C.T.D.).

When the defence first raises the question of reasonableness of notice at the end of the case, the Crown may reopen its case: *R. v. Marcil* (1976), 31 C.C.C. (2d) 172 (Sask. C.A.).

For the Crown to avail itself of this section it must strictly comply with the provisions of notice: *R. v. Henri* (1972), 9 C.C.C. (2d) 52 (B.C.C.A.). Folld: *R. v. Breen* (1975), 30 C.C.C. (2d) 229 (N.B.S.C. App. Div.).

Since a preliminary inquiry is not a trial no notice need be given by the Crown of its intention to introduce a certificate of analysis into evidence: *R. v. Wong and Mar* (1973), 14 C.C.C. (2d) 117 (B.C.S.C.).

However, merely tendering the certificate at the preliminary inquiry without proof of notice does not constitute notice within the meaning of this subsection for the purposes of the trial proper: *R. v. De Vincentis* (1982), 5 C.C.C. (3d) 562 (Que. C.A.). *Contra*: *R. v. Chang* (1996), 106 C.C.C. (3d) 87 (B.C.C.A.).

A notice incorrectly referring to the wrong subsection is still reasonable especially where the accused was not prejudiced or misled by the error: *R. v. Woodward* (1975), 23 C.C.C. (2d) 508 (Ont. C.A.).

An inaccurate reference to the *Criminal Code* rather than this Act did not render the notice void nor unreasonable: *R. v. Taylor* (1983), 5 C.C.C. (3d) 260 (Ont. C.A.). In *R. v. Sturgeon* (2006), 208 C.C.C. (3d) 551 (N.B.C.A.), however, the court held that a notice referencing the *Food and Drugs Act*, R.S.C. 1985, c. F-27, in relation to a different offence did not constitute sufficient notice.

The fact that the certificate referred to a package with a different date on it than testified to by the undercover police officer who placed it in the security envelope was not in any way relevant to the issue of whether the accused was given reasonable notice in compliance with this subsection. This discrepancy went at most to the question of whether the substance sold by the accused was the substance referred to in the certificate. In determining this latter question the court must look at all the circumstances including the correspondence between other writings on the envelope and those contained in the certificate: *R. v. Ebner*, [1979] 2 S.C.R. 996, 47 C.C.C. (2d) 293 (7:0).

The notice provisions were not complied with by service on the accused's mother: *R. v. Lewis* (1972), 6 C.C.C. (2d) 516 (Ont. C.A.).

A new notice is not required where the Crown, prior to trial, withdraws the original information and lays a new information: *R. v. Giesbrecht* (1976), 60 C.C.C. (2d) 135 (B.C.C.A.).

DRUGS

PROOF OF NOTICE / Idem.

52. (1) For the purposes of this Act and the regulations, the giving of any notice, whether orally or in writing, or the service of any document may be proved by the oral evidence of, or by the affidavit or solemn declaration of, the persons claiming to have given that notice or served that document.

(2) Notwithstanding subsection (1), the court may require the affiant or declarant to appear before it for examination or cross-examination in respect of the giving of notice or proof of service.

ANNOTATIONS

Note: The following case was decided under the *Narcotic Control Act*, but were considered useful in the interpretation of this section.

Service of notice – Proof of service of an intention to rely on the certificate may be made by affidavit pursuant to s. 4(6) of the *Criminal Code*: *R. v. Wood* (1991), 64 C.C.C. (3d) 330 (Ont. Gen. Div.).

CONTINUITY OF POSSESSION / Alternative method of proof.

53. (1) In any proceeding under this Act or the regulations, continuity of possession of any exhibit tendered as evidence in that proceeding may be proved by the testimony of,

or the affidavit or solemn declaration of, the person claiming to have had it in their possession.

(2) Where an affidavit or solemn declaration is offered in proof of continuity of possession under subsection (1), the court may require the affiant or declarant to appear before it for examination or cross-examination in respect of the issue of continuity of possession.

COPIES OF RECORDS, BOOKS OR DOCUMENTS.

54. Where any record, book, electronic data or other document is examined or seized under this Act or the regulations, the Minister, or the officer by whom the record, book, electronic data or other document is examined or seized, may make or cause to be made one or more copies thereof, and a copy of any such record, book, electronic data or other document purporting to be certified by the Minister or a person authorized by the Minister is admissible in evidence and, in the absence of evidence to the contrary, has the same probative force as the original record, book, electronic data or other document would have had if it had been proved in the ordinary way.

Technical Assistance

2018, c. 16, 202.

ADVICE OF EXPERTS.

54.1 The Minister may engage the services of persons having technical or specialized knowledge to advise the Minister in respect of his or her powers, duties or functions under this Act and, with the approval of the Treasury Board, fix their remuneration. 2018, c. 16, s. 202.

Regulations and Exemptions

2017, c. 7, s. 39.

REGULATIONS / Exception related to paragraph (1)(*z*) / Regulations / Regulations pertaining to law enforcement / Regulations pertaining to law enforcement under other Acts / Incorporation by reference.

55. (1) The Governor in Council may make regulations for carrying out the purposes and provisions of this Act, including the regulation of the medical, scientific and industrial applications and distribution of controlled substances and precursors and the enforcement of this Act, as well as the regulation of designated devices and, without restricting the generality of the foregoing, may make regulations

(*a*) governing, controlling, limiting, authorizing the importation into Canada, exportation from Canada, production, packaging, sending, transportation, delivery, sale, provision, administration, possession or obtaining of or other dealing in any controlled substances or precursor or any class thereof;

(*b*) respecting the circumstances in which, the conditions subject to which and the persons or classes of persons by whom any controlled substances or precursor or any class thereof may be imported into Canada, exported from Canada, produced, packaged, sent, transported, delivered, sold, provided, administered, possessed, obtained or otherwise dealt in, as well as the means by which and the persons or classes of persons by whom such activities may be authorized;

(*c*) respecting the issuance, suspension, cancellation, duration and terms and conditions of any licence or class of licences for the importation into Canada, exportation from Canada, production, packaging, sale, provision or administration of any substance included in Schedule I, II, III, IV, V or VI or any class of those substances;

(*d*) respecting the issuance, suspension, cancellation, duration and terms and conditions of any permit for the importation into Canada, exportation from Canada or production of a substance included in Schedule I, II, III, IV, V or VI or any class of those substances as well as the amount of those substances or any class of those substances that may be imported, exported or produced under such a permit;

(*d*.1) authorizing the Minister to impose terms and conditions on any licence or any permit including existing licences or permits, and to amend those terms and conditions.

(*e*) prescribing the fees payable on application for any of the licences or permits;

(*f*) respecting the method of production, preservation, testing, packaging or storage of any controlled substance or precursor or any class thereof;

(*g*) respecting the premises, processes or conditions for the production or sale of any controlled substance or any class thereof, and deeming such premises, processes or conditions to be or not to be suitable for the purposes of the regulations;

(*h*) respecting the qualifications of persons who are engaged in the production, preservation, testing, packaging, storage, selling, providing or otherwise dealing in any controlled substance or precursor or any class thereof and who do so under the supervision of a person licensed under the regulations to do any such thing;

(*i*) prescribing standards of composition, strength, concentration, potency, purity or quality or any other property of any controlled substance or precursor;

(*j*) respecting the labelling, packaging, size, dimensions, fill and other specifications of packages used for the importation into Canada, exportation from Canada, sending, transportation, delivery, sale or provision of or other dealing in any substance included in Schedule I, II, III, IV, V or VI or any class thereof;

(*k*) respecting the distribution of samples of any substance included in Schedule I, II, III, IV, V or VI or any class thereof;

(*l*) controlling and limiting the advertising for sale of any controlled substance or precursor or any class thereof;

(*m*) respecting records, reports, electronic data or other documents in respect of controlled substances, precursors or designated devices that are required to be kept and provided by any person or class of persons;

(*n*) respecting the qualifications for inspectors and their powers, duties and functions in relation to verifying compliance or preventing non-compliance with the provisions of this Act or the regulations;

(*o*) respecting the qualifications for analysts and their powers and duties;

(*p*) respecting the detention and disposition of or otherwise dealing with any controlled substance, precursor, designated device, offence-related property or conveyance;

(*q*) [*Repealed*, 2017, c. 7, s. 40(7).];

(*r*) respecting the taking of samples of substances under paragraph 31(1)(*h*);

(*s*) respecting the collection, use, retention, disclosure and disposal of information;

(*t*) respecting the making, serving, filing and manner of proving service of any notice, order, report or other document required or authorized under this Act or the regulations;

(*u*) authorizing the Minister to add to or delete from, by order, a schedule to Part J of the *Food and Drug Regulations* any item or portion of an item included in Schedule V;

(*v*) prescribing forms for the purposes of this Act or the regulations;

(*w*) establishing classes or groups of controlled substances, precursors or designated devices;

(*x*) respecting the provision of information under section 45.1;

DRUGS

(*y*) **respecting the measures referred to in section 45.2.**

(*y*.1) **respecting the review of orders under section 45.4;**

(*z*) **exempting, on any terms and conditions that are specified in the regulations, any person or class of persons or any controlled substance, precursor, designated device or any class of controlled substances, precursors or designated devices from the application of all or any of the provisions of this Act or the regulations;**

(*z*.01) **respecting the registration of the importation of any designated device or class of designated devices, including the time that proof of registration must be provided; and**

Note: Subsection 55.1(1) amended by striking out "and" at the end of para. (*z*.01) and by adding paras. (*z*.02) and (*z*.03), 2017, c. 7, s. 40(12) (to come into force by order of the Governor in Council):

(*z*.02) governing, controlling, limiting, authorizing the importation into Canada, exportation from Canada, sale, provision, possession of or other dealing in any designated device or any class of designated devices;

(*z*.03) respecting the issuance, suspension, cancellation, duration and terms and conditions of any licence or class of licences or of any permit for the importation into Canada, exportation from Canada, sale, provision or possession of any designated device or class of designated devices; and

Note: Subsection 55.1(1) amended by striking out "and" at the end of para. (*z*.03) and by adding paras. (*z*.04) to (*z*.06), 2017, c. 7, s. 40(13) (to come into force by order of the Governor in Council):

(*z*.04) prescribing exportation from Canada, sale, provision, or possession of any designated device or any class of designated devices as activities for the purpose of section 46.4;

(*z*.05) respecting the circumstances in which, the conditions subject to which and the persons or classes of persons by whom any designated device or class of designated devices may be exported from Canada, sold, provided or possessed, as well as the means by which and the persons or classes of persons by whom such activities may be authorized;

(*z*.06) respecting the registration of activities in relation to any designated device or any class of designated devices for the purpose of section 46.4; and

(*z*.1) **prescribing anything that, by this Act, is to be or may be prescribed.**

(1.1) [*Repealed*, 2017, c. 7, s. 40(4).]

(1.2) The Governor in Council may make regulations for carrying out the purposes of section 56.1, including

(*a*) **defining terms for the purposes of that section;**

(*b*) **[*Repealed*, 2017, c. 7, s. 40(15).];**

(*c*) **respecting any information to be submitted to the Minister and the manner in which it is to be submitted;**

(*d*) **respecting the circumstances in which an exemption may be granted;**

(*e*) **respecting requirements in relation to an application for an exemption made under subsection 56.1(1); and**

(*f*) **respecting terms and conditions in relation to an exemption granted under subsection 56.1(1).**

(2) The Governor in Council, on the recommendation of the Minister of Public Safety and Emergency Preparedness, may make regulations that pertain to investigations and other law enforcement activities conducted under this Act by a member of a police force or of the military police and other persons acting under the direction and control of the member and, without restricting the generality of the foregoing, may make regulations

(*a*) **authorizing, for the purposes of this subsection,**

(i) the Minister of Public Safety and Emergency Preparedness or the provincial minister responsible for policing in a province, as the case may be, to designate a police force within their jurisdiction, or

(ii) the Minister of National Defence to designate military police;

(*b*) exempting, on any terms and conditions that are specified in the regulations, a member of a police force or of the military police that has been designated under paragraph (*a*), and other persons acting under the direction and control of the member, from the application of any provision of Part I or the regulations;

(*c*) respecting the issuance, suspension, cancellation, duration and terms and conditions of a certificate, other document or, in exigent circumstances, an approval to obtain a certificate or other document, that is issued to a member of a police force or of the military police that has been designated under paragraph (*a*) for the purpose of exempting the member from the application of any provision of this Act or the regulations;

(*d*) respecting the detention, storage and disposition of or other dealing with any controlled substance or precursor;

(*e*) respecting records, reports, electronic data or other documents in respect of a controlled substance or precursor that are required to be kept and provided by any person or class of persons; and

(*f*) prescribing forms for the purposes of the regulations.

(2.1) The Governor in Council, on the recommendation of the Minister of Public Safety and Emergency Preparedness, may, for the purpose of an investigation or other law enforcement activity conducted under another Act of Parliament, make regulations authorizing a member of a police force or of the military police or other person under the direction and control of the member to commit an act or omission — or authorizing a member of a police force or of the military police to direct the commission of an act or omission — that would otherwise constitute an offence under Part I or the regulations and, without restricting the generality of the foregoing, may make regulations

(*a*) authorizing, for the purposes of this subsection,

(i) the Minister of Public Safety and Emergency Preparedness or the provincial minister responsible for policing in a province, as the case may be, to designate a police force within their jurisdiction, or

(ii) the Minister of National Defence to designate military police;

(*b*) exempting, on any terms and conditions that are specified in the regulations, a member of a police force or of the military police that has been designated under paragraph (*a*), and other persons acting under the direction and control of the member, from the application of any provision of Part I or the regulations;

(*c*) respecting the issuance, suspension, cancellation, duration and terms and conditions of a certificate, other document or, in exigent circumstances, an approval to obtain a certificate or other document, that is issued to a member of a police force or of the military police that has been designated under paragraph (*a*) for the purpose of exempting the member from the application of any provision of Part I or the regulations;

(*d*) respecting the detention, storage and disposition of or other dealing with any controlled substance or precursor;

(*e*) respecting records, reports, electronic data or other documents in respect of a controlled substance or precursor that are required to be kept and provided by any person or class of persons; and

(*f*) prescribing forms for the purposes of the regulations.

(3) Any regulations made under this Act incorporating by reference a classification, standard, procedure or other specification may incorporate the classification, standard, procedure or specification as amended from time to time, and, in such a case, the

DRUGS

reference shall be read accordingly. 2001, c. 32, s. 55; 2005, c. 10, s. 15; 2015, c. 22, s. 4; 2017, c. 7, s. 40(1), (3), (6) to (8), (11), (14) to (19).

EXEMPTION BY MINISTER / Exception.

56. (1) The Minister may, on any terms and conditions that the Minister considers necessary, exempt from the application of all or any of the provisions of this Act or the regulations any person or class of persons or any controlled substance or precursor or any class of either of them if, in the opinion of the Minister, the exemption is necessary for a medical or scientific purpose or is otherwise in the public interest.

(2) The Minister is not authorized under subsection (1) to grant an exemption for a medical purpose that would allow activities in relation to a controlled substance or precursor that is obtained in a manner not authorized under this Act to take place at a supervised consumption site. 2015, c. 22, s. 5; 2017, c. 7, s. 41.

ANNOTATIONS

The possibility of an exemption for medical necessity under this section at the sole discretion of the Minister was not sufficient to save the prohibition on possession of marihuana in s. 4 of this Act. Accordingly, the court struck down the provision but suspended the declaration of invalidity for a period of 12 months. This accused was entitled to a constitutional exemption during the period of suspended invalidity: *R. v. Parker* (2000), 146 C.C.C. (3d) 193 (Ont. C.A.).

The regulatory framework for the possession and cultivation of medical marihuana contained in the *Marihuana Medical Access Regulations*, SOR/2001-227, violate s. 7 of the Charter. In particular, the lack of a legal supply of marihuana requiring individuals entitled to use marihuana to obtain it through black market dealers is inconsistent with principles of fundamental justice. Accordingly, s. 34(2) (a designated-person production licence holder cannot be remunerated for growing marihuana and supplying it to the authorization to possess holder), s. 41(*b*) (a designated-person production licence holder cannot grow marihuana for more than one authorization to possess holder), and s. 54 (a designated-person production licence holder cannot combine his growing with more than two other designated-person production licence holders) of the regulations violate s. 7 of the Charter. In addition, the requirement for a second specialist to support an application for individuals in category 3 as contained in ss. 4(2)(*c*) and 7 of the regulations violates s. 7 of the Charter: *Hitzig v. Canada* (2003), 177 C.C.C. (3d) 449 (Ont. C.A.), leave to appeal to S.C.C. refused [2004] 1 S.C.R. x, 182 C.C.C. (3d) vi.

Following *Hitzig*, the *Medical Marihuana Access Regulations* were amended to address the concerns of the court. As amended, the current *Regulations* are not unconstitutional. The claimant failed to show that physicians have declined *en masse* to participate in the regime, rendering access to medical marihuana illusory: *R. v. Mernagh* (2013), 295 C.C.C. (3d) 431 (Ont. C.A.), leave to appeal to S.C.C. refused 2013 CarswellOnt 10319.

EXEMPTION FOR MEDICAL PURPOSE — SUPERVISED CONSUMPTION SITE / Application / Subsequent application / Notice / Public decision.

56.1 (1) For the purpose of allowing certain activities to take place at a supervised consumption site, the Minister may, on any terms and conditions that the Minister considers necessary, exempt the following from the application of all or any of the provisions of this Act or the regulations if, in the opinion of the Minister, the exemption is necessary for a medical purpose:

- **(*a*) any person or class of persons in relation to a controlled substance or precursor that is obtained in a manner not authorized under this Act; or**
- **(*b*) any controlled substance or precursor or any class of either of them that is obtained in a manner not authorized under this Act;**

(2) An application for an exemption under subsection (1) shall include information, submitted in the form and manner determined by the Minister, regarding the intended public health benefits of the site and information, if any, related to

(*a*) the impact of the site on crime rates;
(*b*) the local conditions indicating a need for the site;
(*c*) the administrative structure in place to support the site;
(*d*) the resources available to support the maintenance of the site; and
(*e*) expressions of community support or opposition.

(3) An application for an exemption under subsection (1) that would allow certain activities to continue to take place at a supervised consumption site shall include any update to the information provided to the Minister since the previous exemption was granted, including any information related to the public health impacts of the activities at the site.

(4) The Minister may give notice, in the form and manner determined by the Minister, of any application for an exemption under subsection (1). The notice shall indicate the period of time — not less than 45 days or more than 90 days — in which members of the public may provide the Minister with comments.

(5) After making a decision under subsection (1), the Minister shall, in writing, make the decision public and, if the decision is a refusal, include the reasons for it. 2015, c. 22, s. 5; 2017, c. 7, s. 42.

56.2 A person who is responsible for the direct supervision, at a supervised consumption site, of the consumption of controlled substances, may offer a person using the site alternative pharmaceutical therapy before that person consumes a controlled substance that is obtained in a manner not authorized under this Act. 2017, c. 7, s. 42.

DRUGS

Miscellaneous

POWERS, DUTIES AND FUNCTIONS OF MINISTER OR MINISTER OF PUBLIC SAFETY AND EMERGENCY PREPAREDNESS.

57. The Minister's powers, duties or functions under this Act or the regulations — and those of the Minister of Public Safety and Emergency Preparedness under the regulations — may be exercised or performed by any person designated, or any person occupying a position designated, for that purpose by the relevant Minister. 2005, c. 10, s. 16.

PARAMOUNTCY OF THIS ACT AND THE REGULATIONS.

58. In the case of any inconsistency or conflict between this Act or the regulations made under it, and the *Food and Drugs Act* or the regulations made under that Act, this Act and the regulations made under it prevail to the extent of the inconsistency or conflict.

OFFENCE OF MAKING FALSE OR DECEPTIVE STATEMENTS.

59. [*Repealed*, 2017, c. 7, s. 44.]

Amendments to Schedules

POWER TO AMEND SCHEDULES.

60. The Governor in Council may, by order, amend any of Schedules I to IV, VI and IX by adding to them or deleting from them any item or portion of an item, if the Governor

in Council considers the amendment to be necessary in the public interest. 2017, c. 7, s. 45; 2018, c. 16, ss. 203, 206(6).

SCHEDULE V / Deletions.

60.1 (1) The Minister may, by order, add to Schedule V any item or portion of an item for a period of up to one year, or extend that period by up to another year, if the Minister has reasonable grounds to believe that it

(*a*) poses a significant risk to public health or safety; or

(*b*) may pose a risk to public health or safety and

(i) is being imported into Canada with no legitimate purpose, or

(ii) is being distributed in Canada with no legitimate purpose.

(2) The Minister may, by order, delete any item or portion of an item from Schedule V. 2017, c. 7, s. 45.

REFERENCES TO PRIOR ENACTMENTS.

61. Any reference in a designation by the Minister of Public Safety and Emergency Preparedness under Part VI of the *Criminal Code* to an offence contrary to the *Narcotic Control Act* or Part III or IV of the *Food and Drugs Act* or any conspiracy or attempt to commit or being an accessory after the fact or any counselling in relation to such an offence shall be deemed to be a reference to an offence contrary to section 5 (trafficking), 6 (importing and exporting) or 7 (production) of this Act, as the case may be, or a conspiracy or attempt to commit or being an accessory after the fact or any counselling in relation to such an offence. 2001, c. 32, s. 56; 2005, c. 10, s. 34(1)(*d*).

SCHEDULE I

(Sections 2, 4 to 7.1, 10, 29, 55 and 60)

1. Opium Poppy (*Papaver somniferum*), its preparations, derivatives, alkaloids and salts, including:

(1) Opium

(2) Codeine (methylmorphine)

(3) Morphine (7,8-didehydro-4,5-epoxy-17-methylmorphinan-3,6-diol)

(4) Thebaine (paramorphine), and the salts, derivatives and salts of derivatives of substances set out in subitems (1) to (4), including:

(5) Acetorphine (acetyletorphine)

(6) Acetyldihydrocodeine (4,5-epoxy-3-methoxy-17-methylmorphinan-6-ol acetate)

(7) Benzylmorphine (7,8-didehydro-4,5-epoxy-17-methyl-3-(phenylmethoxy) morphinan-6-ol)

(8) Codoxime (dihydrocodeinone O-(carboxymethyl) oxime)

(9) Desomorphine (dihydrodeoxymorphine)

(10) Diacetylmorphine (heroin)

(11) Dihydrocodeine (4,5-epoxy-3-methoxy-17-methylmorphinan-6-ol)

(12) Dihydromorphine (4,5-epoxy-17-methylmorphinan-3,6-diol)

(13) Ethylmorphine (7,8-didehydro-4,5-epoxy-3-ethoxy-17-methylmorphinan-6-ol)

(14) Etorphine (tetrahydro-7α-(1-hydroxy-1-methylbutyl)-6,14-endo-thenoori-pavine)

(15) Hydrocodone (dihydrocodeinone)

(16) Hydromorphinol (dihydro-14-hydroxymorphine)

(17) Hydromorphone (dihydromorphinone)

(18) Methyldesorphine (Δ6-deoxy-6-methylmorphine)

(19) Methyldihydromorphine (dihydro-6-methylmorphine)
(20) Metopon (dihydromethylmorphinone)
(21) Morphine-N-oxide (morphine oxide)
(22) Myrophine (benzylmorphine myristate)
(23) Nalorphine (N-allylnormorphine)
(24) Nicocodine (6-nicotinylcodeine)
(25) Nicomorphine (dinicotinylmorphine)
(26) Norcodeine (N-desmethylcodeine)
(27) Normorphine (N-desmethylmorphine)
(28) Oxycodone (dihydrohydroxycodeinone)
(29) Oxymorphone (dihydrohydroxymorphinone)
(30) Pholcodine (3-[2-(4-morpholinyl)ethyl]morphine)
(31) Thebacon (acetyldihydrocodeinone)

but not including

(32) Apomorphine (5,6,6a,7-tetrahydro-6-methyl-4H-dibenzo[de,g] quinoline-10,11-diol) and its salts
(33) Cyprenorphine (N-(cyclopropylmethyl)-6,7,8,14-tetrahydro-7α-(1-hydroxy-1-methylethyl)-6,14-endo-ethenonororipavine) and its salts
(34) Nalmefene (17-(cyclopropylmethyl)-4,5α-epoxy-6-methylenemorphinan-3,14-diol) and its salts
(34.1) Naloxone (4,5α-epoxy-3,14-dihydroxy-17-(2-propenyl)morphinan-6-one) and its salts
(34.2) Naltrexone (17-(cyclopropylmethyl)-4,5α-epoxy-3,14-dihydroxymorphinan-6-one) and its salts
(34.3) Methylnaltrexone (17-(cyclopropylmethyl)4,5α-epoxy-3,14-dihydroxy-17-methyl-6-oxomorphinanium) and its salts
(34.4) Naloxegol (4,5α-epoxy-6α-(3,6,9,12,15,18,21-heptaoxadocos-1-yloxy)-17-(2-propenyl)morphinan-3,14-diol) and its salts
(35) Narcotine (6,7-dimethoxy-3-(5,6,7,8-tetrahydro-4-methoxy-6-methyl-1,3-dioxolos[4,5-g]isoquinolin-5-yl)-1(3H)-isobenzofuranone) and its salts
(36) Papaverine (1-[(3,4-dimethoxyphenyl)methyl]-6,7-dimethoxyisoquinoline) and its salts
(37) Poppy seed

2. Coca (*Erythroxylum*), its preparations, derivatives, alkaloids and salts, including:

(1) Coca leaves
(2) Cocaine (benzoylmethylecgonine)
(3) Ecgonine (3-hydroxy-2-tropane carboxylic acid)

but not including

(4) 123I-ioflupane

3. Phenylpiperidines, their intermediates, salts, derivatives and analogues and salts of intermediates, derivatives and analogues, including:

(1) Allylprodine (3-allyl-1-methyl-4-phenyl-4-piperidinol propionate)
(2) Alphameprodine (α-3-ethyl-1-methyl-4-phenyl-4-piperidinol propionate)
(3) Alphaprodine (α-1,3-dimethyl-4-phenyl-4-piperidinol propionate)
(4) Anileridine (ethyl 1-[2-(p-aminophenyl)-4-phenylpiperidine-4-carboxylate)
(5) Betameprodine B-3-ethyl-1-methyl-4-phenyl-4-piperidinol propionate)
(6) Betaprodine (B-1,3-dimethyl-4-phenyl-4-piperidinol propionate)
(7) Benzethidine (ethyl 1-(2-benzyloxyethyl)-4-phenylpiperidine-4-carboxylate)
(8) Diphenoxylate (ethyl 1-(3-cyano-3,3-diphenylpropyl)-4-phenylpiperidine-4-carboxylate)

DRUGS

(9) Difenoxin (1-(3-cyano-3,3-diphenylpropyl)-4-phenylpiperidine-4-carboxylate)
(10) Etoxeridine (ethyl 1-[2-(2-hydroxyethoxy) ethyl]-4-phenylpiperidine-4-carboxylate)
(11) Furethidine (ethyl 1-(2-tetrahydrofurfury loxyethyl)-4-phenylpiperidine-4-carboxylate)
(12) Hydroxypethidine (ethyl 4-(m-hydroxyphenyl)-1-methylpiperidine-4-carboxylate)
(13) Ketobemidone (1-[4-(m-hydroxyphenyl)-1-methyl-4-piperidyl]-1-propanone)
(14) Methylphenylisonipecotonitrile (4-cyano-1-methyl-4-phenylpiperidine)
(15) Morpheridine (ethyl 1-(2-morpholinoethyl)-4-phenylpiperidine-4-carboxylate)
(16) Norpethidine (ethyl 4-phenylpiperidine-4-carboxylate)
(17) Pethidine (ethyl 1-methyl-4-phenylpiperidine-4-carboxylate)
(18) Phenoperidine (ethyl 1-(3-hydroxy-3-phenylpropyl)-4-phenylpiperidine-4-carboxylate)
(19) Piminodine (ethyl 1-[3-(phenylamino)propyl]-4-phenylpiperidine-4-carboxylate)
(20) Properidine (isopropyl 1-methyl-4-phenylpiperidine-4-carboxylate)
(21) Trimeperidine (1,2,5-trimethyl-4-phenyl-4-piperidinol propionate)
(22) Pethidine Intermediate C (1-methyl-4-phenylpiperidine-4-carboxylate)

but not including

(23) Carperidine (ethyl 1-(2-carbamylethyl)-4-phenylpiperidine-4-carboxylate) and its salts
(24) Oxpheneridine (ethyl 1-(2-hydroxy-2-phenylethyl)-4-phenylpiperidine-4-carboxylate) and its salts

4. Phenazepines, their salts, derivatives and salts of derivatives including:

(1) Proheptazine (hexahydro-1,3-dimethyl-4-phenyl-1H-azepin-4-ol propionate)

but not including

(2) Ethoheptazine (ethyl hexahydro-1-methyl-4-phenyl-azepine-4-carboxylate) and its salts
(3) Metethoheptazine (ethyl hexahydro-1,3-dimethyl-4-phenylazepine-4-carboxylate) and its salts
(4) Metheptazine (ethyl hexahydro-1,2-dimethyl-4-phenylazepine-4-carboxylate) and its salts

5. Amidones, their intermediates, salts, derivatives and salts of intermediates and derivatives including:

(1) Dimethylaminodiphenylbutanonitrile (4-cyano-2-dimethylamino-4,4-diphenylbutane)
(2) Dipipanone (4,4-diphenyl-6-piperidino-3-heptanone)
(3) Isomethadone (6-dimethylamino-5-methyl-4,4-diphenyl-3-hexanone)
(4) Methadone (6-dimethylamino-4,4-diphenyl-3-heptanone)
(5) Normethadone (6-dimethylamino-4,4-diphenyl-3-hexanone)
(6) Norpipanone (4,4-diphenyl-6-piperidino-3-hexanone)
(7) Phenadoxone (6-morpholino-4,4-diphenyl-3-heptanone)

6. Methadols, their salts, derivatives and salts of derivatives including:

(1) Acetylmethadol (6-dimethylamino-4,4-diphenyl-3-heptanol acetate)
(2) Alphacetylmethadol (α-6-dimethylamino-4,4-diphenyl-3-heptanol acetate)
(3) Alphamethadol (α-6-dimethylamino-4,4-diphenyl-3-heptanol)
(4) Betacetylmethadol (B-6-dimethylamino-4,4-diphenyl-3-heptanol acetate)

(5) Betamethadol (B-6-dimethylamino-4,4-diphenyl-3-heptanol)
(6) Dimepheptanol (6-dimethylamino-4,4-diphenyl-3-heptanol)
(7) Noracymethadol (α-6-methylamino-4,4-diphenyl-3-heptanol acetate)

7. Phenalkoxams, their salts, derivatives and salts of derivatives including:
(1) Dimenoxadol (dimethylaminoethyl 1-ethoxy-1,1-diphenylacetate)
(2) Dioxaphetyl butyrate (ethyl 2,2-diphenyl-4-morpholinobutyrate)
(3) Dextropropoxyphene ([S-(R*,S*)]-(α-[2-(dimethylamino)-methylethyl]-(α-phenylbenzene-ethanol, propanoate ester)

8. Thiambutenes, their salts, derivatives and salts of derivatives including:
(1) Diethylthiambutene (N,N-diethyl-1-methyl-3,3-di-2-thienylallylamine)
(2) Dimethylthiambutene (N,N,1-trimethyl-3,3-di-2-thienylallylamine)
(3) Ethylmethylthiambutene (N-ethyl-N,1-dimethyl-3,3-di-2-thienylallylamine)

9. Moramides, their intermediates, salts, derivatives and salts of intermediates and derivatives including:
(1) Dextromoramide (d-1-(3-methyl-4-morpholino-2,2-diphenylbutyryl) pyrrolidine)
(2) Diphenylmorpholinoisovaleric acid (2-methyl-3-morpholino-1,1-diphenylpropionic acid)
(3) Levomoramide (*l*-1-(3-methyl-4-morpholino-2,2-diphenylbutyryl) pyrrolidine)
(4) Racemoramide (d,1-1(3-methyl-4-morpholino-2,2-diphenylbutyryl) pyrrolidine)

10. Morphinans, their salts, derivatives and salts of derivatives including:
(1) Buprenorphine (17-(cyclopropylmethyl)-(α-(1,1-dimethylethyl)-4,5-epoxy-18,19-dihydro-3-hydroxy-6-methoxy-(α-methyl-6,14-ethenomorphinan-7-methanol)
(2) Drotebanol (6(B,14-dihydroxy-3,4-dimethoxy-17-methylmorphinan)
(3) Levomethorphan (1-3-methoxy-17-methylmorphinan)
(4) Levorphanol (1-3-hydroxy-17-methylmorphinan)
(5) Levophenacylmorphan (1-3-hydroxy-17-phenacyl-morphinan)
(6) Norlevorphanol (1-3-hydroxymorphinan)
(7) Phenomorphan (3-hydroxy-17-(2-phenylethyl) morphinan)
(8) Racemethorphan (d,1-3-methoxy-17-methylmorphinan)
(9) Racemorphan (*d, l*-3-hydroxy-N-methylmorphinan)

but not including
(10) Dextromethorphan (d-1,2,3,9,10,10a-hexahydro-6-methoxy-11-methyl-4H-10,4a-iminoethano-phenanthren) and its salts
(11) Dextrorphan (d-1,2,3,9,10,10a-hexahydro-11-methyl-4H-10,4a-iminoethanophenanthren-6-ol) and its salts
(12) Levallorphan (*l*-11-allyl-1,2,3,9,10,10a-hexahydro-4H-10,4a-iminoethanophenanthren-6ol)
(13) Levargorphan (*l*-11-propargyl-1,2,3,9,10,10a-hexahydro-4H-10,4a-iminoethanophenanthren-6-ol) and its salts
(14) Butorphanol (*l*-N-(cyclobutylmethyl)-3,14-dihydroxymorphinan) and its salts
(15) Nalbuphine (N-(cyclobutylmethyl)-4,5-epoxy-morphinan-3,6,14-triol) and its salts

11. Benzazocines, their salts, derivatives and salts of derivatives including:
(1) Phenazocine (1,2,3,4,5,6-hexahydro-6,11-dimethyl-3-phenethyl-2,6-methano-3-benzazocin-8-ol)
(2) Metazocine (1,2,3,4,5,6-hyxahydro-3,6,11-trimethyl-2,6-methano-3-benzazocin-8-ol)

DRUGS

(3) Pentazocine (1,2,3,4,5,6-hexahydro-6,11-dimethyl-3-(3-methyl-2-butenyl)-2,6-methano-3-benzazocin-8-ol)

but not including

(4) Cyclazocine (1,2,3,4,5,6-hexahydro-6,11-dimethyl-3-(cyclopropylmethyl)-2,6-methano-3-benzazocin-8-ol) and its salts

12. Ampromides, their salts, derivatives and salts of derivatives including:

(1) Diampromide (N-[2-(methylphenethylamino) propyl] propionanilide)

(2) Phenampromide (N-(1-methyl-2-piperidino) ethyl) propionanilide)

(3) Propiram (N-(1-methyl-2-piperidinoethyl)-N-2-pyridylpropionamide)

13. Benzimidazoles, their salts, derivatives and salts of derivatives including:

(1) Clonitazene (2-(p-chlorobenzyl)-1-diethylaminoethyl-5-nitrobenzimidazole)

(2) Etonitazene (2-(p-ethoxybenzyl)-1-diethylaminoethyl-5-nitrobenzimidazole)

(3) Bezitramide (1-(3-cyano-3,3-diphenylpropyl)-4-(2-oxo-3-propionyl-1-benzimidazolinyl)-piperidine)

14. Phencyclidine (1-(1-phenylcyclohexyl)piperidine), its salts, derivatives and analogues and salts of derivatives and analogues, including:

(1) Ketamine (2-(2-chlorophenyl)-2-(methylamino)cyclohexanone)

15. Piritramide (1-(3-cyano-3,3-diphenylpropyl)-4-(1-piperidino)piperidine-4-carboxylic acid amide), its salts, derivatives and salts of derivatives

16. Fentanyls, their salts, derivatives, and analogues and salts of derivatives and analogues, including:

(1) Acetyl-α-methylfentanyl (N-[1-(α-methylphenethyl)-4-piperidyl] acetanilide)

(2) Alfentanil (N-[1-[2-(4-ethyl-4,5-dihydro-5-oxo-1H-tetrazol-1-yl) ethyl]-4-(methoxymethyl)-4-piperidyl]propionanilide)

(3) Carfentanil (methyl 4-[(1-oxopropyl)phenylamino]-1-(2-phenethyl)-4-piperidinecarboxylate)

(4) p-Fluorofentanyl (4′fluoro-N-(1-phenethyl-4-piperidyl) propionanilide)

(5) Fentanyl (N-(1-phenethyl-4-piperidyl) propionanilide)

(6) B-Hydroxyfentanyl (N-[1-(B-hydroxyphenethyl)-4-piperidyl] propionanilide)

(7) B-Hydroxy-3-methylfentanyl (N-[1-B-hydroxyphenethyl)-3-methyl-4-piperidyl] propionanilide)

(8) α-Methylfentanyl (N-[1-(α-methylphenethyl)-4-piperidyl] propionanilide)

(9) α-Methylthiofentanyl (N-[1-methyl-2-(2-thienyl) ethyl]-4-piperidyl] propionanilide)

(10) 3-Methylfentanyl (N-(3-methyl-1-phenethyl-4-piperidyl) propionanilide)

(11) 3-Methylthiofentanyl (N-[3-methyl-1-[2-(2-thienyl) ethyl]-4-piperidyl]propionanilide)

(11.1) Remifentanil (dimethyl 4-carboxy-4-(N-phenylpropionamido)-1-piperidinepropionate)

(12) Sufentanil (N-[4-(methoxymethyl)-1-[2-(2-thienyl)ethyl]-4-piperidyl] propionanilide)

(13) Thiofentanyl (N-[1-[2-(2-thienyl)ethyl]-4-piperidyl]propionanilide)

17. Tilidine (ethyl12-(dimethylamino)-1-phenyl-3-cyclohexene-1-carboxylate), its salts, derivatives and salts of derivatives

17.1 Methylenedioxypyrovalerone (MDPV), its salts, derivatives, isomers and analogues and salts of derivatives, isomers and analogues

18. Methamphetamine (N,α-dimethylbenzeneethanamine), its salts, derivatives, isomers and analogues and salts of derivatives, isomers and analogues

19. Amphetamines, their salts, derivatives, isomers and analogues and salts of derivatives, isomers and analogues including:

(1) amphetamine (a-methylbenzene-ethanamine)
(2) N-ethylamphetamine (N-ethyl-a-methylbenzeneethanamine)
(3) 4-methyl-2,5-dimethoxyamphetamine (STP) (2,5-dimethoxy-4,a-dimethylbenzeneethanamine)
(4) 3,4-methylenedioxyamphetamine (MDA) (a-methyl-1,3-benzodioxole-5-ethanamine)
(5) 2,5-dimethoxyamphetamine (2,5-dimethoxy-a-methylbenzene-ethanamine)
(6) 4-methoxyamphetamine (4-methoxy-a-methylbenzeneethanamine)
(7) 2,4,5-trimethoxyamphetamine (2,4,5-trimethoxy-a-methylbenzeneethanamine)
(8) N-methyl-3,4-methylenedioxy-amphetamine (N,a-dimethyl-1,3-benzodioxole-5-ethanamine)
(9) 4-ethoxy-2,5-dimethoxyamphetamine (4-ethoxy-2,5-dimethoxy-a-methylbenzeneethanamine)
(10) 5-methoxy-3,4-methylenedioxy-amphetamine (7-methoxy-a-methyl-1,3-benzodioxole-5-ethanamine)
(11) N,N-dimethyl-3,4-methylenedioxyamphetamine (N,N, a-trimethyl-1,3-benzodioxole-5-ethanamine)
(12) N-ethyl-3,4-methylenedioxyamphetamine (N-ethyl-a-methyl-1,3-benzodioxole-5-ethanamine)
(13) 4-ethyl-2,5-dimethoxyamphetamine (DOET) (4-ethyl-2,5-dimethoxy-a-methylbenzeneethanamine)
(14) 4-bromo-2,5-dimethoxyamphetamine (4-bromo-2,5-dimethoxy-a-methylbenzeneethanamine)
(15) 4-chloro-2,5-dimethoxyamphetamine (4-chloro-2,5-dimethoxy-a-methylbenzeneethanamine)
(16) 4-ethoxyamphetamine (4-ethoxy-a-methylbenzeneethanamine)
(17) Benzphetamine (N-benzyl-N,a-dimethylbenzeneethanamine)
(18) N-Propyl-3,4-methylenedioxy-amphetamine (a-methyl-N-propyl-1,3-benzodioxole-5-ethanamine)
(19) N-(2-Hydroxyethyl)-a-meth-ylbenzene-ethanamine
(20) N-hydroxy-3,4-methylenedioxy-amphetamine (N-[a-methyl-3,4-(methylenedioxy)phenethyl]hydroxyla-mine)
(21) 3,4,5-trimethoxyamphetamine (3,4,5-trimethoxy-a-methylbenzeneethanamine)

20. Flunitrazepam (5-(o-fluorophenyl)-1,3-dihydro-1-methyl-7-nitro-2H-1,4-benzodiazepin-2-one) and any of its salts or derivatives

21. 4-hydroxybutanoic acid (GHB) and any of its salts

22. Tapentadol (3-[(1R,2R)-3-(dimethylamino)-1-ethyl-2-methylpropyl]-phenol), its salts, derivatives and isomers and salts of derivatives and isomers

23. AH-7921 (1-(3,4-dichlorobenzamidomethyl)cyclohexyldimethylamine), its salts, isomers and salts of isomers

24. MT-45 (1-cyclohexyl-4-(1,2-diphenylethyl)piperazine), its salts, derivatives, isomers and analogues and salts of derivatives, isomers and analogues, including
(1) Diphenidine (DEP) (1-(1,2-diphenylethyl)piperidine)
(2) Methoxphenidine (2-MeO-Diphenidine, MXP) (1-[1-(2-methoxyphenyl)-2-phenylethyl]piperidine)
(3) Ephenidine (NEDPA, EPE) (N-ethyl-1,2-diphenylethylamine)
(4) Isophenidine (NPDPA) (N-isopropyl-1,2-diphenylethylamine)

but not including
(5) Lefetamine ((-)-N,N-dimethyl-α-phenylbenzeneethanamine), its salts, derivatives and isomers and salts of derivatives and isomers

25. W-18 (4-chloro-N-[1-[2-(4-nitrophenyl)ethyl]-2-piperidinylidene]benzenesulfonamide), its salts, derivatives, isomers and analogues and salts of derivatives, isomers and analogues

26. U-47700 (3,4-dichloro-N-(2-(dimethylamino)cyclohexyl)-N-methylbenzamide), its salts, derivatives, isomers and analogues, and salts of derivatives, isomers and analogues, including

(1) Bromadoline (4-bromo-N-(2-(dimethylamino)cyclohexyl)benzamide)

(2) U-47109 (3,4-dichloro-N-(2-(dimethylamino)cyclohexyl)benzamide)

(3) U-48520 (4-chloro-N-(2-(dimethylamino)cyclohexyl)-N-methylbenzamide)

(4) U-50211 (N-(2-(dimethylamino)cyclohexyl)-4-hydroxy-N-methylbenzamide)

(5) U-77891 (3,4-dibromo-N-methyl-N-(1-methyl-1-azaspiro[4.5]decan-6-yl)-benzamide). SOR/97-230; SOR/99-371; SOR/99-421; SOR/2005-235, s. 1; SOR/2005-271, s. 1; SOR/2005-337, s. 1; SOR/2012-176, s. 1; 2012, c. 1, s. 44; SOR/2015-190, s. 1; SOR/2016-107, s. 1; SOR/2017-13, ss. 1 to 5; 2017, c. 7, s. 46; SOR/2017-275, s. 1; SOR/2017-277, s. 1; SOR/2018-70, ss. 1, 2.

SCHEDULE II

(Sections 2, 4 to 7.1, 10, 29, 55 and 60)

1. [*Repealed*, 2018, c. 16, s. 204(1).]

2. Synthetic cannabinoid receptor type 1 agonists, their salts, derivatives, isomers, and salts of derivatives and isomers — with the exception of any substance that is identical to any phytocannabinoid and with the exception of ((3S)-2,3-dihydro-5-methyl-3-(4-morpholinylmethyl)pyrrolo[1,2,3-de]-1,4-benzoxazin-6-yl)-1-naphthalenyl-methanone (WIN 55,212-3) and its salts — including those that fall within the following core chemical structure classes:

(1) Any substance that has a 2-(cyclohexyl)phenol structure with substitution at the 1-position of the benzene ring by a hydroxy, ether or ester group and further substituted at the 5-position of the benzene ring, whether or not further substituted on the benzene ring to any extent, and substituted at the 3'-position of the cyclohexyl ring by an alkyl, carbonyl, hydroxyl, ether or ester, and whether or not further substituted on the cyclohexyl ring to any extent, including

(i) Nabilone (±)-trans-3-(1,1-dimethylheptyl)-6,6a,7,8,10,10a-hexahydro-1-hydroxy-6,6-dimethyl-9H-dibenzo[b,d]pyran-9-one)

(ii) Parahexyl (3-hexyl-6,6,9-trimethyl-7,8,9,10-tetrahydro-6H-dibenzo[b,d]-pyran-1-ol)

(iii) 3-(1,2-dimethylheptyl)-7,8,9,10-tetrahydro-6,6,9-trimethyl-6H-dibenzo[b,d]pyran-1-ol (DMHP)

(iv) 5-(1,1-dimethylheptyl)-2-(5-hydroxy-2-(3-hydroxypropyl)cyclohexyl)phenol (CP 55,940)

(v) 5-(1,1-dimethylheptyl)-2-(3-hydroxycyclohexyl)phenol (CP 47,497)

(2) Any substance that has a 3-(1-naphthoyl)indole structure with substitution at the nitrogen atom of the indole ring, whether or not further substituted on the indole ring to any extent and whether or not substituted on the naphthyl ring to any extent, including

(i) 1-pentyl-3-(1-naphthoyl)indole (JWH-018)

(ii) 1-butyl-3-(1-naphthoyl)indole (JWH-073)

(iii) 1-pentyl-3-(4-methyl-1-naphthoyl)indole (JWH-122)

(iv) 1-hexyl-3-(1-naphthoyl)indole (JWH-019)

(v) 1-(4-pentenyl)-3-(1-naphthoyl)indole (JWH-022)

(vi) 1-butyl-3-(4-methoxy-1-naphthoyl)indole (JWH-080)

(vii) 1-pentyl-3-(4-methoxy-1-naphthoyl)indole (JWH-081)

(viii) 1-(2-morpholin-4-ylethyl)-3-(1-naphthoyl)indole (JWH-200)

(ix) 1-pentyl-3-(4-ethyl-1-naphthoyl)indole (JWH-210)
(x) 1-pentyl-3-(2-methoxy-1-naphthoyl)indole (JWH-267)
(xi) 1-[(N-methylpiperidin-2-yl)methyl]-3-(1-naphthoyl)indole (AM-1220)
(xii) 1-(5-fluoropentyl)-3-(1-naphthoyl)indole (AM-2201)
(xiii) 1-(5-fluoropentyl)-3-(4-methyl-1-naphthoyl)indole (MAM-2201)
(xiv) 1-(5-fluoropentyl)-3-(4-ethyl-1-naphthoyl)indole (EAM-2201)
(xv) ((3R)-2,3-dihydro-5-methyl-3-(4-morpholinylmethyl)pyrrolo[1,2,3-de]-1,4-benzoxazin-6-yl)-1-naphthalenyl-methanone (WIN 55,212-2)

(3) Any substance that has a 3-(1-naphthoyl)pyrrole structure with substitution at the nitrogen atom of the pyrrole ring, whether or not further substituted on the pyrrole ring to any extent and whether or not substituted on the naphthyl ring to any extent, including
(i) 1-pentyl-5-(2-fluorophenyl)-3-(1-naphthoyl)pyrrole (JWH-307)

(4) Any substance that has a 3-phenylacetylindole structure with substitution at the nitrogen atom of the indole ring, whether or not further substituted on the indole ring to any extent and whether or not substituted on the phenyl ring to any extent, including
(i) 1-pentyl-3-(2-methoxyphenylacetyl)indole (JWH-250)
(ii) 1-pentyl-3-(2-methylphenylacetyl)indole (JWH-251)
(iii) 1-pentyl-3-(3-methoxyphenylacetyl)indole (JWH-302)

(5) Any substance that has a 3-benzoylindole structure with substitution at the nitrogen atom of the indole ring, whether or not further substituted on the indole ring to any extent and whether or not substituted on the phenyl ring to any extent, including
(i) 1-(1-methylpiperidin-2-ylmethyl)-3-(2-iodobenzoyl)indole (AM-2233)

(6) Any substance that has a 3-methanone(cyclopropyl)indole structure with substitution at the nitrogen atom of the indole ring, whether or not further substituted on the indole ring to any extent and whether or not substituted on the cyclopropyl ring to any extent, including
(i) (1-pentyl-1H-indol-3-yl)(2,2,3,3-tetramethylcyclopropyl)-methanone (UR-144)
(ii) (1-(5-fluoropentyl)-1H-indol-3-yl)(2,2,3,3-tetramethylcyclopropyl)-methanone (5F-UR-144)
(iii) (1-(2-(4-morpholinyl)ethyl)-1H-indol-3-yl)(2,2,3,3-tetramethylcyclopropyl)-methanone (A-796,260)

(7) Any substance that has a quinolin-8-yl 1H-indole-3-carboxylate structure with substitution at the nitrogen atom of the indole ring, whether or not further substituted on the indole ring to any extent and whether or not substituted on the quinolin-8-yl ring to any extent, including
(i) 1-pentyl-8-quinolinyl ester-1H-indole-3-carboxylic acid (PB-22)
(ii) 1-(5-fluoropentyl)-8-quinolinyl ester-1H-indole-3-carboxylic acid (5F-PB-22)

(8) Any substance that has a 3-carboxamideindazole structure with substitution at the nitrogen atom of the indazole ring, whether or not further substituted on the indazole ring to any extent and whether or not substituted at the carboxamide group to any extent, including
(i) N-(adamantan-1-yl)-1-pentyl-1H-indazole-3-carboxamide (AKB48)
(ii) N-(adamantan-1-yl)-1-(5-fluoropentyl)-1H-indazole-3-carboxamide (5F-AKB48)
(iii) N-(1-(aminocarbonyl)-2-methylpropyl)-1-(4-fluorobenzyl)-1H-indazole-3-carboxamide (AB-FUBINACA)
(iv) N-(1-amino-3-methyl-1-oxobutan-2-yl)-1-pentyl-1H-indazole-3-carboxamide (AB-PINACA)

DRUGS

(9) Any substance that has a 3-carboxamideindole structure with substitution at the nitrogen atom of the indole ring, whether or not further substituted on the indole ring to any extent and whether or not substituted at the carboxamide group to any extent, including
(i) N-(adamantan-1-yl)-1-fluoropentylindole-3-carboxamide (STS-135)
(ii) N-(adamantan-1-yl)-1-pentylindole-3-carboxamide (APICA). SOR/98-157; SOR/2003-32; SOR/2015-192, ss. 1, 2; 2017, c. 7, s. 47; 2018, c. 16, s. 204.

SCHEDULE III

(Sections 2. 4 to 7.1, 10, 29, 55 and 60)

1. [*Repealed.* 2012, c. 1, s. 45.]

2. Methylphenidate (methyl 2-phenyl-2-(piperidin-2-yl)acetate), its salts, derivatives, isomers and analogues and salts of derivatives, isomers and analogues, including
(1) Ethylphenidate (ethyl 2-phenyl-2-(piperidin-2-yl)acetate)
(2) Isopropylphenidate (isopropyl 2-phenyl-2-(piperidin-2-yl)acetate)
(3) Propylphenidate (propyl 2-phenyl-2-(piperidin-2-yl)acetate)
(4) 3,4-Dichloromethylphenidate (methyl 2-(3,4-dichlorophenyl)-2-(piperidin2-yl)acetate)
(5) 4-Methylmethylphenidate (methyl 2-(4-methylphenyl)-2-(piperidin2-yl)acetate)
(6) 4-Fluoromethylphenidate (methyl 2-(4-fluorophenyl)-2-(piperidin-2-yl)acetate)
(7) Methylnaphthidate (methyl 2-(naphthalen-2-yl)-2-(piperidin-2-yl)acetate)
(8) Ethylnaphthidate (ethyl 2-(naphthalen-2-yl)-2-(piperidin-2-yl)acetate)

3. Methaqualone (2-methyl-3-(2-methylphenyl)-4(3H)-quinazolinone) and any salt thereof

4. Mecloqualone (2-methyl-3-(2-chlorophenyl)-4(3H)-quinazolinone) and any salt thereof

5. Lysergic acid diethylamide (LSD) (N,N-diethyllysergamide) and any salt thereof

6. N,N-Diethyltryptamine (DET) (3-[2-diethylamino) ethyl]indole) and any salt thereof

7. N,N-Dimethyltryptamine (DMT) (3-[(2-dimethylamino)ethyl]indole) and any salt thereof

8. N-Methyl-3-piperidyl benzilate (3-[(hydroxydiphenylacetyl)oxy]-1-methylpiperidine) and any salt thereof

9. Harmaline (4,9-dihydro-7-methoxy-1-methyl-3H-pyrido(3,4-b)indole) and any salt thereof

10. Harmalol (4,9-dihydro-1-methyl-3H-pyrido (3,4-b)indol-7-ol) and any salt thereof

11. Psilocin (3-[2-(dimethylamino)ethyl]-4-hydroxyindole) and any salt thereof

12. Psilocybin (3-[2-(dimethylamino)ethyl]-4-phosphoryloxyindole) and any salt thereof

13. N-(1-phenylcyclohexyl)ethylamine (PCE) and any salt thereof

14. 1-[1-(2-Thienyl) cyclohexyl]piperidine (TCP) and any salt thereof

15. 1-Phenyl-N-propylcyclohexanamine and any salt thereof

16. Rolicyclidine (1-(1-phenylcyclohexyl) pyrrolidine) and any salt thereof

17. Mescaline (3,4,5-trimethoxybenzeneethanamine) and any salt thereof, but not peyote (lophophora)

18. **[*Repealed.* SOR/2017-249, s. 1.]**

19. **Cathinone ((-)-α-aminopropiophenone) and its salts**

20. **Fenetylline (d,1-3,7-dihydro-1,3-dimethyl-7-(2-[(1-methyl-2-phenethyl)amino]ethyl)-1H-purine-2,6-dione) and any salt thereof**

21. **2-Methylamino-1-phenyl-1-propanone and any salt thereof**

22. **1-[1-(Phenylmethyl)cyclohexyl]piperidine and any salt thereof**

23. **1-[1-(4-Methylphenyl)cyclohexyl]piperidine and any salt thereof**

24. **[*Repealed.* SOR/2016-73, s. 1.]**

25. **[*Repealed.* 2012, c. 1, s. 46.]**

26. **[*Repealed.* 2012, c. 1, s. 46.]**

27. **Aminorex (5-phenyl-4,5-dihydro-1,3-oxazol-2-amine), its salts, derivatives, isomers and analogues and salts of derivatives, isomers and analogues, including**

(1) 4-Methylaminorex (4-methyl-5-phenyl-4,5-dihydro-1,3-oxazol-2-amine)

(2) 4,4'-Dimethylaminorex (4-methyl-5-(4-methylphenyl)-4,5-dihydro-1,3-oxazol-2-amine)

28. **Etryptamine (3-(2-aminobutyl)indole) and any salt thereof**

29. **Lefetamine ((-)-N,N-dimethyl-α-phenylbenzeneethanamine), its salts, derivatives and isomers and salts of derivatives and isomers**

30. **Mesocarb (3-(α-methylphenethyl)-N-(phenylcarbamoyl)sydnone imine) and any salt thereof**

31. **Zipeprol (4-(2-methoxy-2-phenylethyl)-α-(methoxyphenylmethyl)-1-piperazineethanol) and any salt thereof**

32. **Amineptine (7-[(10,11-dihydro-5H-dibenzo[a,d]cyclohepten-5-yl)amino]heptanoic acid) and any salt thereof**

33. **Benzylpiperazine [BZP], namely 1-benzylpiperazine and its salts, isomers and salts of isomers**

34. **Trifluoromethylphenylpiperazine [TFMPP], namely 1-(3-trifluoromethylphenyl)piperazine and its salts, isomers and salts of isomers**

35. **2C-phenethylamines and their salts, derivatives, isomers and salts of derivatives and isomers that correspond to the following chemical description:**

any substance that has a 1-amino-2-phenylethane structure substituted at the 2' and 5' or 2' and 6' positions of the benzene ring by an alkoxy or haloalkoxy group, or substituted at two adjacent carbon atoms of the benzene ring which results in the formation of a furan, dihydrofuran, pyran, dihydropyran or methylenedioxy group — whether or not further substituted on the benzene ring to any extent, whether or not substituted at the amino group by one or two, or a combination of, methyl, ethyl, propyl, isopropyl, hydroxyl, benzyl (or benzyl substituted to any extent) or benzylene (or benzylene substituted to any extent) groups and whether or not substituted at the 2-ethyl (beta carbon) position by a hydroxyl, oxo or alkoxy group — and its salts and derivatives and salts of derivatives, including

(1) 4-bromo-2,5-dimethoxy-N-(2-methoxybenzyl)phenethylamine (25B-NBOMe)

(2) 4-chloro-2,5-dimethoxy-N-(2-methoxybenzyl)phenethylamine (25C-NBOMe)

(3) 4-iodo-2,5-dimethoxy-N-(2-methoxybenzyl)phenethylamine (25I-NBOMe)

(4) 4-bromo-2,5-dimethoxybenzeneethanamine (2C-B). SOR/97-230; SOR/98-173; SOR/2000-220; SOR/2003-32; SOR/2003-412; SOR/2005-235, s. 2; SOR/2012-66, s. 1; 2012, c. 1, ss. 45, 46; SOR/2016-73, ss. 1, 2; SOR/2016-107, s. 2; SOR/2017-13, s. 6; 2017, c. 7, s. 48; SOR/2017-249, ss. 1, 2.

SCHEDULE IV

(Sections 2, 4 to 7.1, 10, 29, 55 and 60)

1. Barbiturates, their salts and derivatives including
(1) Allobarbital (5,5-diallylbarbituric acid)
(2) Alphenal (5-allyl-5-phenylbarbituric acid)
(3) Amobarbital (5-ethyl-5-(3-methylbutyl)barbituric acid)
(4) Aprobarbital (5-allyl-5-isopropylbarbituric acid)
(5) Barbital (5,5-diethylbarbituric acid)
(6) [*Repealed.* SOR/2017-13, s. 7(1).]
(7) Butabarbital (5-sec-butyl-5-ethylbarbituric acid)
(8) Butalbital (5-allyl-5-isobutylbarbituric acid)
(9) Butallylonal (5-(2-bromoallyl)-5-sec-butylbarbituric acid)
(10) Butethal (5-butyl-5-ethylbarbituric acid)
(11) Cyclobarbital (5-(1-cyclohexen-1-yl)-5-ethylbarbituric acid)
(12) Cyclopal (5-allyl-5-(2-cyclopenten-1-yl)barbituric acid)
(13) Heptabarbital (5-(1-cyclohepten-1-yl)-5-ethylbarbituric acid
(14) Hexethal (5-ethyl-5-hexylbarbituric acid)
(15) Hexobarbital (5-(1-cyclohexen-1-yl)-1,5-dimethylbarbituric acid)
(16) Mephobarbital (5-ethyl-1-methyl-5-phenylbarbituric acid)
(17) Methabarbital (5,5-diethyl-1-methylbarbituric acid)
(18) Methylphenobarbital (5-ethyl-1-methyl-5-phenylbarbituric acid)
(19) Propallylonal (5-(2-bromoallyl)-5-isopropylbarbituric acid)
(20) Pentobarbital (5-ethyl-5-(1-methylbutyl)barbituric acid)
(21) Phenobarbital (5-ethyl-5-phenylbarbituric acid)
(22) Probarbital (5-ethyl-5-isopropylbarbituric acid)
(23) Phenylmethylbarbituric Acid (5-methyl-5-phenylbarbituric acid)
(24) Secobarbital (5-allyl-5-(1-methylbutyl)barbituric acid)
(25) Sigmodal (5-(2-bromoallyl)-5-(1-methylbutyl) barbituric acid
(26) Talbutal (5-allyl-5-sec-butylbarbituric acid)
(27) Vinbarbital (5-ethyl-5-(1-methyl-1-butenyl) barbituric acid
(28) Vinylbital (5-(1-methylbutyl)-5-vinylbarbituric acid)

but not including
(29) Barbituric Acid (2,4,6(1H,3H,5H)-pyrimidinetrione) and its salts
(30) 1,3-dimethylbarbituric acid (1,3-dimethyl-2,4,6(1H,3H,5H)-pyrimidinetrione) and its salts

2. Thiobarbiturates, their salts and derivatives including:
(1) Thialbarbital (5-allyl-5-(2-cyclohexen-1-yl)-2-thiobarbituric acid)
(2) Thiamylal (5-allyl-5-(1-methylbutyl)-2-thiobarbituric acid)
(3) Thiobarbituric Acid (2-thiobarbituric acid)
(4) Thiopental (5-ethyl-5-(1-methylbutyl)-2-thiobarbituric acid)

3. Chlorphentermine (1-(p-chlorophenyl)-2-methyl-2-aminopropane) and any salt thereof

4. Diethylpropion (2-(diethylamino)propiophenone) and any salt thereof

5. Phendimetrazine (d-3,4-dimethyl-2-phenylmorpholine) and any salt thereof

6. Phenmetrazine (3-methyl-2-phenylmorpholine) and any salt thereof

7. Pipradol (α,α-diphenyl-2-piperidinemethanol) and its salts

8. Phentermine (α,α-dimethylbenzeneethanamine) and any salt thereof

9. Butorphanol (*l*-N-cyclobutylmethyl-3,14-dihydroxymorphinan) and its salts

10. Nalbuphine (N-cyclobutylmethyl-4,5-epoxy-morphinan-3,6,14-triol) and its salts

11. Gluethimide (2-ethyl-2-phenylglutarimide)

12. Clotiazepam (5-(o-chlorophenyl)-7-ethyl-1,3-dihydro-1-methyl-2H-thieno[2,3-e]-1,4-diazepin-2-one) and any salt thereof

13. Ethchlorvynol (ethyl-2-chlorovinyl ethynyl carbinol)

14. Ethinamate (1-ethynylcyclohexanol carbamate)

15. Mazindol (5-(p-chlorophenyl)-2,5-dihydro-3H-imidazo[2,1-a]isoindol-5-ol)

16. Meprobamate (2-methyl-2-propyl-1,3-propanediol dicarbamate)

17. Methyprylon (3,3-diethyl-5-methyl-2,4-piperidinedione)

18. Benzodiazepines, their salts and derivatives, including:

(1) Alprazolam (8-chloro-1-methyl-6-phenyl-4H-s-triazolo[4,3-a][1,4] benzodiazepine)

(2) Bromazepam (7-bromo-1,3-dihydro-5-(2-pyridyl)-2H-1, 4-benzodiazepin-2-one)

(2.1) Brotizolam (2-bromo-4-(0-chlorophenyl)-9-methyl-6H-thieno[3,2-f]-s-triazolo[4,3-a][1,4]diazepine)

(3) Camazepam (7-chloro-1,3-dihydro-3-(N,N-dimethylcarbamoyl)-1-methyl-5-phenyl-2H-1,4-benzodiazepin-2-one)

(4) Chlordiazepoxide (7-chloro-2-(methylamino)-5-phenyl-3H-1,4-benzodiazepine-4-oxide)

(5) Clobazam (7-chloro-1-methyl-5-phenyl-1H-1,5-benzodiazepine-2,4(3H,5H)-dione)

(6) Clonazepam (5-(o-chlorophenyl)-1,3-dihydro-7-nitro-2H-1,4-benzodiazepin-2-one)

(7) Clorazepate (7-chloro-2,3-dihydro-2,2-dihydroxy-5-phenyl-1H-1,4-benzodiazepine-3-carboxylic acid)

(8) Cloxazolam (10-chloro-11b-(0-chlorophenyl)-2,3,7,11b-tetrahydrooxazolo[3,2-d][1,4]benzodiazepin 6-(5H)-one)

(9) Delorazepam (7-chloro-5-o-chlorophenyl)-1,3-dihydro-2H-1,4-benzodiazepin-2-one)

(10) Diazepam (7-chloro-1,3-dihydro-1-methyl-5-phenyl-2H-1,4-benzodiazepin-2-one)

(11) Estazolam (8-chloro-6-phenyl-4H-s-triazolo[4,3-a][1,4]benzodiazepine)

(12) Ethyl Loflazepate (ethyl 7-chloro-5-(o-fluorophenyl)-2,3-dihydro-2-oxo-1H-1,4-benzodiazepine-3-carboxylate)

(13) Fludiazepam (7-chloro-5-(o-fluorophenyl)-1,3-dihydro-1-methyl-2H-1,4-benzodiazepin-2-one)

(14) [*Repealed*, SOR/98-173, s. 2.]

(15) Flurazepam (7-chloro-1-[2-(diethylamino) ethyl]-5-(o-fluorophenyl)-1,3dihydro-2H-1,4-benzodiazepin-2-one)

(16) Halazepam (7-chloro-1,3-dihydro-5-phenyl-1-(2, 2,2-trifluoroethyl)-2H-1,4-benzodiazepin-2-one)

(17) Haloxazolam (10-bromo-11b-(o-fluorophenyl)-2,3,7,11b-tetrahydrooxazolo[3,2-d][1,4]benzodiazepin-6(5H)-one)

(18) Ketazolam (11-chloro-8,12b-dihydro-2,8-dimethyl-12b-phenyl-4H-[1,3]-oxazino-[3,2-d][1,4] benzodiazepine-4,7(6H)-dione)

(19) Loprazolam (6-(o-chlorophenyl)-2,4-dihydro-2-[(4-methyl-1-piperazinyl)-methylene]-8-nitro-1H-imidazo[1,2-a][1,4]benzodiazepin-1-one)

(20) Lorazepam (7-chloro-5-(o-chlorophenyl)-1,3-dihydro-3-hydroxy-2H-1,4-benzodiazepin-2-one)

(21) Lormetazepam (7-chloro-5-(o-chlorophenyl)-1,3-dihydro-3-hydroxy-1-methyl-2H-1,4-benzodiazepin-2-one)

(22) Medazepam (7-chloro-2,3-dihydro-1-methyl-5-phenyl-1H-1,4-benzodiazepine)

DRUGS

(22.1) Midazolam (8-chloro-6-(0-fluorophenyl)-1-methyl-4H-imidazo[1,5-9][1,4]benzodiazepine)
(23) Nimetazepam (1,3-dihydro-1-methyl-7-nitro-5-phenyl-2H-1,4-benzodiazepin-2-one)
(24) Nitrazepam (1,3-dihydro-7-nitro-5-phenyl-2H-1,4-benzodiazepin-2-one)
(25) Nordazepam (7-chloro-1,3-dihydro-5-phenyl-2H-1,4-benzodiazepin-2-one)
(26) Oxazepam (7-chloro-1,3-dihydro-3-hydroxy-5-phenyl-2H-1,4-benzodiazepin-2-one)
(27) Oxazolam (10-chloro-2,3,7,11b-tetrahydro-2-methyl-11b-phenyloxazolo [3,2-d][1,4]benzodiazepin-6(5H)-one)
(28) Pinazepam (7-chloro-1,3-dihydro-5-phenyl-1-(2-propynyl)-2H-1, 4-benzodiazepin-2-one)
(29) Prazepam (7-chloro-1-(cyclopropylmethyl)-1,3-dihydro-5-phenyl-2H-1,4-benzodiazepin-2-one)
(29.1) Quazepam (7-chloro-5-(0-fluorophenyl)-1,3-dihydro-1-(2,2,2-trifluoroethyl)-2H-1,4-benzodiazepin-2-thione)
(30) Temazepam (7-chloro-1,3-dihydro-3-hydroxy-1-methyl-5-phenyl-2H-1,4-benzodiazepin-2-one)
(31) Tetrazepam (7-chloro-5-(cyclohexen-1-yl)-1,3-dihdyro-1-methyl-2H-1,4-benzodiazepin-2-one)
(32) Triazolam (8-chloro-6-(o-chlorophenyl)-1-methyl-4H-s-triazolo [4,3-a][1,4]benzodiazepine)

but not including

(32.1) Clozapine (8-chloro-11-(4-methyl-1-piperazinyl)-5H-dibenzo[b,e][1,4]diazepine) and any salt thereof
(33) Flunitrazepam (5-(o-fluorophenyl)-1,3-dihydro-1-methyl-7-nitro-2H-1,4-benzodiazepin-2-one) and any salts or derivatives thereof
(34) Olanzapine (2-methyl-4-(4-methyl-1-piperazinyl)-10H-thieno[2,3-b][1,5]benzodiazepine) and its salts
(35) Clozapine N-oxide (8-chloro-11-(4-methyl-4-oxido-1-piperazinyl)-5H dibenzo[b,e][1,4]diazepine) and its salts

19. *Catha edulis* Forsk, its preparations, derivatives, alkaloids and salts, including:
(1) Cathine (d-threo-2-amino-1-hydroxy-1-phenylpropane)

20. Fencamfamin (d,1-N-ethyl-3-phenylbicyclo[2,2,1]heptan-2-amine) and any salt thereof

21. Fenproporex (d,1-3-[(α-methylphenethyl)amino]propionitrile) and any salt thereof

22. Mefenorex (d,1-N(3-chloropropyl)-α-methylbenzeneethanamine) and any salt thereof

23. Anabolic steroids and their derivatives including:
(1) Androisoxazole (17B-hydroxy-17α-methylandrostano[3,2-c]isoxazole)
(2) Androstanolone (17B-hydroxy-5α-androstan-3-one)
(3) Androstenediol (androst-5-ene-3B,17B-diol)
(4) Bolandiol (estr-4-ene-3B,17B-diol)
(5) Bolasterone (17B-hydroxy-7α,17-dimethylandrost-4-en-3-one)
(6) Bolazine (17B-hydroxy-2α-methyl-5B-androstan-3-one azine)
(7) Boldenone (17B-hydroxyandrosta-1,4-dien-3-one)
(8) Bolenol (19-nor-17α-pregn-5-en-17-ol)
(9) Calusterone (17B-hydroxy-7B,17-dimethylandrost-4-en-3-one)
(10) Clostebol (4-chloro-17B-hydroxyandrost-4-en-3-one)
(11) Drostanolone (17B-hydroxy-2α-methyl-5α-androstan-3-one)
(12) Enestebol (4,17B-dihydroxy-17-methylandrosta-1,4-dien-3-one)
(13) Epitiostanol (2α, 3α-epithio-5α-androstan-17B-ol)
(14) Ethylestrenol (19-nor-17α-pregn-4-en-17-ol)

(15) 4-Hydroxy-19-nor testosterone

(16) Fluoxymesterone (9-fluoro-11B,17B-dihydroxy-17-methylandrost-4-en-3-one)

(17) Formebolone (11α,17B-dihydroxy-17-methyl-3-oxoandrosta-1,4 di-2n-2-carboxaldehyde)

(18) Furazabol (17-methol-5α-androstano[2,3-c]furazan-17B-ol)

(19) Mebolazine (17B-hydroxy-2α,17-dimethyl-5α-androstan-3-one azine)

(20) Mesabolone (17B-[(1-methoxycyclohexyl)oxy]-5α-androst-1-en-3-one)

(21) Mesterolone (17B-hydroxy-1α-methyl-5α-androstan-3-one)

(22) Metandienone (17B-hydroxy-17-methylandrosta-1,4-dien-3-one)

(23) Metenolone (17B-hydroxy-1-methyl-5α-androst-1-en-3-one)

(24) Methandriol (17α-methylandrost-5-ene-3B,17B-diol)

(25) Methyltestosterone (17B-hydroxy-17-methylandrost-4-en-3-one)

(26) Metribolone (17B-hydroxy-17-methylestra-4,9,11-trien-3-one)

(27) Mibolerone (17B-hydroxy-7α,170dimethylestr-4-en-3-one)

(28) Nandrolone (17B-hydroxyestr-4-en-3-one)

(29) Norboletone (13-ethyl-17B-hydroxy-18,19-dinorpregn-4-en-3-one)

(30) Norclostebol (4-chloro-17B-hydroxyestr-4-en-3-one)

(31) Norethandrolone (17α-ethyl-17B-hydroxyestr-4-en-3-one)

(32) Oxabolone (4,17B-dihydroxyestr-4-en-3-one)

(33) Oxandrolone (17B-hydroxy-17-methyl-2-oxa-5α-androstan-3-one)

(34) Oxymesterone (4,17B-dihydroxy-17-methylandrost-4-en-3-one)

(35) Oxymetholone (17B-hydroxy-2-(hydroxymethylene)-17-methyl-5α-androstan-3-one)

(36) Prasterone (3B-hydroxyandrost-5-en-17-one)

(37) Quinbolone (17B-(1-cyclopenten-1-yloxy)androsta-1,4-dien-3-one)

(38) Stanozolol (17B-hydroxy-17-methyl-5α-androstano[3,2-c]pyrazole)

(39) Stenbolone (17B-hydroxy-2-methyl-5α-androst-1-en-3-one)

(40) Testosterone (17B-hydroxyandrost-4-en-3-one)

(41) Tibolone ((7α, 17α)-17-hydroxy-7-methyl-19-norpregn-5(10)-en-20-yn-3-one)

(42) Tiomesterone (1α,7α-bis(acetylthio)-17B-hydroxy-17-methylandrost-4-en-3-one)

(43) Trenbolone (17B-hydroxyestra-4,9,11-trien-3-one)

24. Zeranol (3,4,5,6,7,8,9,10,11,12-decahydro-7,14,16-trihydroxy-3-methyl-1H-2-benzoxacyclotetradecin-1-one)

25. Zolpidem (N,N,6-trimethyl-2-(4-methylphenyl)imidazo [1,2-a]pyridine-3-acetamide) and any salt thereof

25.1 Pemoline (2-amino-5-phenyl-oxazolin-4-one) and any salt thereof

26. Pyrovalerone (4′-methyl-2-(1-pyrrolidinyl) valerophenone) and any salt thereof

27. *Salvia divinorum* (*S. divinorum*), its preparations and derivatives, including:

(1) Salvinorin A ((2S,4aR,6aR,7R,9S,10aS,10bR)-9-(acetyloxy)-2-(3-furanyl)dodecahydro-6a,10b-dimethyl-4,10-dioxo-2H-naphtho[2,1-c]pyran-7-carboxylic acid methyl ester). SOR/97-230; SOR/98-173; SOR/99-371; SOR/99-421; SOR/2000-220, s. 2; SOR/2003-32, s. 6; SOR/2003-37, s. 1; SOR/2015-209, s. 1; SOR/2017-13, ss. 7 to 12; 2017, c. 7, s. 49.

SCHEDULE V

(Sections 2, 5 to 7.1, 10, 55 and 60.1)

1. [*Repealed*, SOR/2002-361, s. 1.]

2. [*Repealed*, 2017, c. 7, s. 50 (Sched. 1).]

3. [*Repealed*, SOR/2003-32, s. 7.]

SCHEDULE VI

(Sections 2, 6, 55 and 60)

PART 1
CLASS A PRECURSORS[1]

1. **Acetic anhydride**
2. **N-Acetylanthranilic acid (2-acetamidobenzoic acid) and its salts**
3. **Anthranilic acid (2-aminobenzoic acid) and its salts**
4. **Ephedrine (erythro-2-(methylamino)-1-phenylpropan-1-ol), its salts and any plant containing ephedrine or any of its salts**
5. **Ergometrine (9,10-didehydro-N-(2-hydroxy-1-methylethyl)-6-methylergoline-8-carboxamide) and its salts**
6. **Ergotamine (12-hydroxy-2-methyl-5-(phenylmethyl)ergotaman-3,6,18-trione) and its salts**
7. **Isosafrole (5-(1-propenyl)-1,3-benzodioxole)**
8. **Lysergic acid (9,10-didehydro-6-methylergoline-8-carboxylic acid) and its salts**
9. **3,4-Methylenedioxyphenyl-2-propanone (1-(1,3-benzodioxole)-2-propanone)**
10. **Norephedrine (Phenylpropanolamine) and its salts**
11. **1-Phenyl-2-propanone**
12. **Phenylacetic acid and its salts**
13. **Piperidine and its salts**
14. **Piperonal (1,3-benzodioxole-5-carboxaldehyde)**
15. **Potassium permanganate**
16. **Pseudoephedrine (threo-2-(methylamino)-1-phenylpropan-1-ol), its salts and any plant containing pseudoephedrine or any of its salts**
17. **Safrole (5-(2-propenyl)-1,3-benzodioxole) and any essential oil containing safrole**
18. **Gamma-butyrolactone (dihydro-2(3H)-furanone)**
19. **1,4-butanediol**
20. **Red Phosphorus**
21. **White Phosphorus**
22. **Hypophosphorous acid, its salts and derivatives**
23. **Hydriodic acid**
24. **Alpha-phenylacetoacetonitrile and its salts, isomers and salts of isomers**
25. **Propionyl chloride**
26. **1-Phenethyl-4-piperidone and its salts**
27. **4-Piperidone and its salts**
28. **Norfentanyl (N-phenyl-N-piperidin-4-ylpropanamide) and its salts**
29. **1-Phenethylpiperidin-4-ylidenephenylamine and its salts**
30. **N-Phenyl-4-piperidinamine and its salts**
31. **N1,N1,N2-trimethylcyclohexane-1,2-diamine and its salts**

[1] Each Class A precursor includes synthetic and natural forms.

PART 2
CLASS B PRECURSORS[1]

1. **Acetone**
2. **Ethyl ether**
3. **Hydrochloric acid**
4. **Methyl ethyl ketone**
5. **Sulphuric acid**
6. **Toluene**

[1] Each Class A precursor includes synthetic forms.

PART 3
PREPARATIONS AND MIXTURES

1. **Any preparation or mixture that contains a precursor set out in Part 1, except1 items 20 to 23, or in Part 2. SOR/2002-361, s. 2; SOR/2005-364, ss. 1, 2, 4; SOR/ 2016-13, s. 1; SOR/2016-295, s. 1.**

SCHEDULE VII

[*Repealed,* 2018, c. 16, s. 205.]

SCHEDULE VIII

[*Repealed,* 2018, c. 16, s. 205.]

DRUGS

SCHEDULE IX

(Sections 2 and 60)

1. **Manual, semi-automatic or fully automatic device that may be used to compact or mould powdered, granular or semi-solid material to produce coherent solid tablets**
2. **Manual, semi-automatic or fully automatic device that may be used to fill capsules with any powdered, granular, semi-solid or liquid material. 2017, c. 7, s. 51 (Sched. 2).**

CRIMES AGAINST HUMANITY AND WAR CRIMES ACT

S.C. 2000, c. 24

Amended 2001, c. 32, ss. 59 to 61; brought into force February 1, 2002 by SI/2002-17 by para. (*b*)

An Act respecting genocide, crimes against humanity and war crimes and to implement the Rome Statute of the International Criminal Court, and to make consequential amendments to other Acts

SHORT TITLE

SHORT TITLE.

1. This Act may be cited as the *Crimes Against Humanity and War Crimes Act*.

INTERPRETATION

DEFINITIONS / "Conventional international law" / "International Criminal Court" / "Official" / "Rome Statute" / Words and Expressions.

2. (1) The definitions in this subsection apply in this Act.

"conventional international law" means any convention, treaty or other international agreement

(*a*) that is in force and to which Canada is a party; or

(*b*) that is in force and the provisions of which Canada has agreed to accept and apply in an armed conflict in which it is involved.

"International Criminal Court" means the International Criminal Court established by the Rome Statute.

"official", in respect of the International Criminal Court, means the Prosecutor, Registrar, Deputy Prosecutor and Deputy Registrar, and the staff of the organs of the Court.

"Rome Statute" means the Rome Statute of the International Criminal Court adopted by the United Nations Diplomatic Conference of Plenipotentiaries on the Establishment of an International Criminal Court on July 17, 1998, as corrected by the procès-verbaux of November 10, 1998, July 12, 1999, November 30, 1999 and May 8, 2000, portions of which are set out in the schedule.

(2) Unless otherwise provided, words and expressions used in this Act have the same meaning as in the *Criminal Code*.

HER MAJESTY

BINDING ON HER MAJESTY.

3. This Act is binding on Her Majesty in right of Canada or a province.

OFFENCES WITHIN CANADA

GENOCIDE, ETC., COMMITTED IN CANADA / Conspiracy, attempt, etc. / Punishment / Definitions / Interpretation — customary international law.

4. (1) Every person is guilty of an indictable offence who commits

(*a*) genocide;

(*b*) a crime against humanity; or

(*c*) a war crime.

(1.1) Every person who conspires or attempts to commit, is an accessory after the fact in relation to, or counsels in relation to, an offence referred to in subsection (1) is guilty of an indictable offence.

(2) Every person who commits an offence under subsection (1) or (1.1)

(*a*) shall be sentenced to imprisonment for life, if an intentional killing forms the basis of the offence; and

(*b*) is liable to imprisonment for life, in any other case.

(3) The definitions in this subsection apply in this section.

"crime against humanity" means murder, extermination, enslavement, deportation, imprisonment, torture, sexual violence, persecution or any other inhumane act or omission that is committed against any civilian population or any identifiable group and that, at the time and in the place of its commission, constitutes a crime against humanity according to customary international law or conventional international law or by virtue of its being criminal according to the general principles of law recognized by the community of nations, whether or not it constitutes a contravention of the law in force at the time and in the place of its commission.

"genocide"means an act or omission committed with intent to destroy, in whole or in part, an identifiable group of persons, as such, that, at the time and in the place of its commission, constitutes genocide according to customary international law or conventional international law or by virtue of its being criminal according to the general principles of law recognized by the community of nations, whether or not it constitutes a contravention of the law in force at the time and in the place of its commission.

"war crime" means an act or omission committed during an armed conflict that, at the time and in the place of its commission, constitutes a war crime according to customary international law or conventional international law applicable to armed conflicts, whether or not it constitutes a contravention of the law in force at the time and in the place of its commission.

(4) For greater certainty, crimes described in Articles 6 and 7 and paragraph 2 of Article 8 of the Rome Statute are, as of July 17, 1998, crimes according to customary international law. This does not limit or prejudice in any way the application of existing or developing rules of international law.

ANNOTATIONS

Crimes against humanity – In *Mugesera v. Canada (Minister of Citizenship and Immigration)*, [2005] 2 S.C.R. 100, 197 C.C.C. (3d) 233, 30 C.R. (6th) 39, the court considered the elements of the offence of crime against humanity under former s. 7(3.76) of the *Criminal Code* in the context of deportation proceedings. While the definition under this section is slightly different than the definition under the former section, the court did not find the differences material. The offence requires proof that an enumerated proscribed act such as murder or persecution was committed (this involves showing that the accused committed the criminal act and had the requisite guilty state of mind for the underlying act); that the act was committed as part of a widespread or systematic attack; that the attack was directed against any civilian population or any identifiable group of persons; and that the accused knew of the attack and knew or took the risk that his or her act comprised part of that attack. In defining the acts, the court will have regard to the extensive body of international jurisprudence from the International Criminal Tribunal for the Former Yugoslavia and the International Criminal Tribunal for Rwanda.

While counseling an enumerated act, such as murder, meets the proscribed act requirement (see subsec. (1.1)), counseling an enumerated act that is not committed does not meet the principles of customary international law that are incorporated into the definition: *Mugesera v. Canada (Minister of Citizenship and Immigration), supra.*

"Persecution" as a crime against humanity must constitute a gross or blatant denial, on discriminatory grounds of a fundamental right, laid down in international customary or treaty law, reaching the same level of gravity as the other enumerated acts. The accused must also have been shown to have intended to commit the persecutory acts and with discriminatory intent. A discriminatory intent need not, however, be shown in relation to the other proscribed acts: *Mugesera v. Canada (Minister of Citizenship and Immigration), supra.*

For the purposes of the requirement that the act was committed as part of widespread or systematic attack, a "widespread attack" is a massive, frequent, large scale action, carried out collectively with considerable seriousness and directed against a multiplicity of victims. A systematic attack is one that is thoroughly organized and follows a regular pattern on the basis of a common policy involving substantial public or private resources and is carried out pursuant to a policy or plan. There is, however, no requirement that the policy be an official state policy. Only the attack needs to be widespread or systematic, not the act of the accused. A single act may constitute a crime against humanity as long as the attack it forms a part of is widespread or systematic and is directed against a civilian population. The requirement that the attack be directed against any civilian population means that the civilian population must be the primary object of the attack and that attack must be directed against a relatively large group of people who share distinctive features that identify them as targets of the attack. There must be a link between the accused's act and the widespread or systematic attack. The act must occur as part of the attack in the sense that the accused's acts are objectively part of the attack, as, by their nature or consequences, they are liable to have the effect of furthering the attack: *Mugesera v. Canada (Minister of Citizenship and Immigration), supra.*

In addition to the mental element required for the underlying act, the accused must have knowledge of the attack and must know that his or her acts comprise part of it or takes the risk that his or her acts will comprise part of it. The accused need not intend, however, that the act be directed against the targeted population, and motive is irrelevant once knowledge of the attack has been established, together with knowledge that the act form part of the attack or with recklessness in this regard. In assessing whether an accused had the requisite knowledge, the court will consider the accused's position in a military or other government hierarchy, public knowledge about the existence of the attack, the scale of the violence and the general historical and political environment in which the acts occurred. The accused need not know the details of the attack: *Mugesera v. Canada (Minister of Citizenship and Immigration), supra.*

BREACH OF RESPONSIBILITY BY MILITARY COMMANDER / Breach of responsibility by a superior / Conspiracy, attempt, etc. / Punishment / Definitions.

5. (1) A military commander commits an indictable offence if

(*a*) the military commander

(i) fails to exercise control properly over a person under their effective command and control or effective authority and control, and as a result the person commits an offence under section 4, or

(ii) fails, after the coming into force of this section, to exercise control properly over a person under their effective command and control or effective authority and control, and as a result the person commits an offence under section 6;

WAR

(*b*) the military commander knows, or is criminally negligent in failing to know, that the person is about to commit or is committing such an offence; and

(*c*) the military commander subsequently

(i) fails to take, as soon as practicable, all necessary and reasonable measures within their power to prevent or repress the commission of the offence, or the further commission of offences under section 4 or 6, or

(ii) fails to take, as soon as practicable, all necessary and reasonable measures within their power to submit the matter to the competent authorities for investigation and prosecution.

(2) A superior commits an indictable offence if

(*a*) the superior

(i) fails to exercise control properly over a person under their effective authority and control, and as a result the person commits an offence under section 4, or

(ii) fails, after the coming into force of this section, to exercise control properly over a person under their effective authority and control, and as a result the person commits an offence under section 6;

(*b*) the superior knows that the person is about to commit or is committing such an offence, or consciously disregards information that clearly indicates that such an offence is about to be committed or is being committed by the person;

(*c*) the offence relates to activities for which the superior has effective authority and control; and

(*d*) the superior subsequently

(i) fails to take, as soon as practicable, all necessary and reasonable measures within their power to prevent or repress the commission of the offence, or the further commission of offences under section 4 or 6, or

(ii) fails to take, as soon as practicable, all necessary and reasonable measures within their power to submit the matter to the competent authorities for investigation and prosecution.

(2.1) Every person who conspires or attempts to commit, is an accessory after the fact in relation to, or counsels in relation to, an offence referred to in subsection (1) or (2) is guilty of an indictable offence.

(3) Every person who commits an offence under subsection (1), (2) or (2.1) is liable to imprisonment for life.

(4) The definitions in this subsection apply in this section.

"military commander" includes a person effectively acting as a military commander and a person who commands police with a degree of authority and control comparable to a military commander.

"superior" means a person in authority, other than a military commander.

OFFENCES OUTSIDE CANADA

GENOCIDE, ETC., COMMITTED OUTSIDE CANADA / Conspiracy, attempt, etc. / Punishment / Definitions / Interpretation — customary international law / Interpretation — crimes against humanity.

6. (1) Every person who, either before or after the coming into force of this section, commits outside Canada

(*a*) genocide,

(*b*) a crime against humanity, or

(*c*) a war crime,

is guilty of an indictable offence and may be prosecuted for that offence in accordance with section 8.

(1.1) Every person who conspires or attempts to commit, is an accessory after the fact in relation to, or counsels in relation to, an offence referred to in subsection (1) is guilty of an indictable offence.

(2) Every person who commits an offence under subsection (1) or (1.1)

(*a*) shall be sentenced to imprisonment for life, if an intentional killing forms the basis of the offence; and

(*b*) is liable to imprisonment for life, in any other case.

(3) The definitions in this subsection apply in this section.

"crime against humanity" means murder, extermination, enslavement, deportation, imprisonment, torture, sexual violence, persecution or any other inhumane act or omission that is committed against any civilian population or any identifiable group and that, at the time and in the place of its commission, constitutes a crime against humanity according to customary international law or conventional international law or by virtue of its being criminal according to the general principles of law recognized by the community of nations, whether or not it constitutes a contravention of the law in force at the time and in the place of its commission.

"genocide" means an act or omission committed with intent to destroy, in whole or in part, an identifiable group of persons, as such, that at the time and in the place of its commission, constitutes genocide according to customary international law or conventional international law or by virtue of its being criminal according to the general principles of law recognized by the community of nations, whether or not it constitutes a contravention of the law in force at the time and in the place of its commission.

"war crime" means an act or omission committed during an armed conflict that, at the time and in the place of its commission, constitutes a war crime according to customary international law or conventional international law applicable to armed conflicts, whether or not it constitutes a contravention of the law in force at the time and in the place of its commission.

(4) For greater certainty, crimes described in articles 6 and 7 and paragraph 2 of article 8 of the Rome Statute are, as of July 17, 1998, crimes according to customary international law, and may be crimes according to customary international law before that date. This does not limit or prejudice in any way the application of existing or developing rules of international law.

(5) For greater certainty, the offence of crime against humanity was part of customary international law or was criminal according to the general principles of law recognized by the community of nations before the coming into force of either of the following:

(*a*) the Agreement for the prosecution and punishment of the major war criminals of the European Axis, signed at London on August 8, 1945; and

(*b*) the Proclamation by the Supreme Commander for the Allied Powers, dated January 19, 1946.

ANNOTATIONS

Crimes against humanity – In *Mugesera v. Canada (Minister of Citizenship and Immigration)*, [2005] 2 S.C.R. 100, 197 C.C.C. (3d) 233, 30 C.R. (6th) 39, the court considered the elements of the offence of crime against humanity under former s. 7(3.76) of the *Criminal Code* in the context of deportation proceedings. While the definition under this section is slightly different than the definition under the former section, the court did not find the differences material. The offence requires proof that an enumerated proscribed act such as murder or persecution was committed (this involves showing that the accused committed the criminal act and had the requisite guilty state of mind for the underlying act); that the act

WAR

was committed as part of a widespread or systematic attack; that the attack was directed against any civilian population or any identifiable group of persons; and that the accused knew of the attack and knew or took the risk that his or her act comprised part of that attack. In defining the acts, the court will have regard to the extensive body of international jurisprudence from the International Criminal Tribunal for the Former Yugoslavia and the International Criminal Tribunal for Rwanda.

While counseling an enumerated act, such as murder, meets the proscribed act requirement (see subsec. (1.1)), counseling an enumerated act that is not committed does not meet the principles of customary international law that are incorporated into the definition: *Mugesera v. Canada (Minister of Citizenship and Immigration)*, *supra*.

"Persecution" as a crime against humanity must constitute a gross or blatant denial, on discriminatory grounds of a fundamental right, laid down in international customary or treaty law, reaching the same level of gravity as the other enumerated acts. The accused must also have been shown to have intended to commit the persecutory acts and with discriminatory intent. A discriminatory intent need not, however, be shown in relation to the other proscribed acts: *Mugesera v. Canada (Minister of Citizenship and Immigration)*, *supra*.

For the purposes of the requirement that the act was committed as part of widespread or systematic attack, a "widespread attack" is a massive, frequent, large scale action, carried out collectively with considerable seriousness and directed against a multiplicity of victims. A systematic attack is one that is thoroughly organized and follows a regular pattern on the basis of a common policy involving substantial public or private resources and is carried out pursuant to a policy or plan. There is, however, no requirement that the policy be an official state policy. Only the attack needs to be widespread or systematic, not the act of the accused. A single act may constitute a crime against humanity as long as the attack it forms a part of is widespread or systematic and is directed against a civilian population. The requirement that the attack be directed against any civilian population means that the civilian population must be the primary object of the attack and that attack must be directed against a relatively large group of people who share distinctive features that identify them as targets of the attack. There must be a link between the accused's act and the widespread or systematic attack. The act must occur as part of the attack in the sense that the accused's acts are objectively part of the attack, as, by their nature or consequences, they are liable to have the effect of furthering the attack: *Mugesera v. Canada (Minister of Citizenship and Immigration)*, *supra*.

In addition to the mental element required for the underlying act, the accused must have knowledge of the attack and must know that his or her acts comprise part of it or takes the risk that his or her acts will comprise part of it. The accused need not intend, however, that the act be directed against the targeted population, and motive is irrelevant once knowledge of the attack has been established, together with knowledge that the act form part of the attack or with recklessness in this regard. In assessing whether an accused had the requisite knowledge, the court will consider the accused's position in a military or other government hierarchy, public knowledge about the existence of the attack, the scale of the violence and the general historical and political environment in which the acts occurred. The accused need not know the details of the attack: *Mugesera v. Canada (Minister of Citizenship and Immigration)*, *supra*.

BREACH OF RESPONSIBILITY BY MILITARY COMMANDER / Breach of responsibility by a superior / Conspiracy, attempt, etc. / Jurisdiction / Punishment / Application before coming into force / Definitions.

7. (1) A military commander commits an indictable offence if

(*a*) the military commander, outside Canada,

(i) fails to exercise control properly over a person under their effective command and control or effective authority and control, and as a result the person commits an offence under section 4, or

(ii) fails, before or after the coming into force of this section, to exercise control properly over a person under their effective command and control or

effective authority and control, and as a result the person commits an offence under section 6;

(*b*) the military commander knows, or is criminally negligent in failing to know, that the person is about to commit or is committing such an offence; and

(*c*) the military commander subsequently

(i) fails to take, as soon as practicable, all necessary and reasonable measures within their power to prevent or repress the commission of the offence, or the further commission of offences under section 4 or 6, or

(ii) fails to take, as soon as practicable, all necessary and reasonable measures within their power to submit the matter to the competent authorities for investigation and prosecution.

(2) A superior commits an indictable offence if

(*a*) the superior, outside Canada,

(i) fails to exercise control properly over a person under their effective authority and control, and as a result the person commits an offence under section 4, or

(ii) fails, before or after the coming into force of this section, to exercise control properly over a person under their effective authority and control, and as a result the person commits an offence under section 6;

(*b*) the superior knows that the person is about to commit or is committing such an offence, or consciously disregards information that clearly indicates that such an offence is about to be committed or is being committed by the person;

(*c*) the offence relates to activities for which the superior has effective authority and control; and

(*d*) the superior subsequently

(i) fails to take, as soon as practicable, all necessary and reasonable measures within their power to prevent or repress the commission of the offence, or the further commission of offences under section 4 or 6, or

(ii) fails to take, as soon as practicable, all necessary and reasonable measures within their power to submit the matter to the competent authorities for investigation and prosecution.

(2.1) Every person who conspires or attempts to commit, is an accessory after the fact in relation to, or counsels in relation to, an offence referred to in subsection (1) or (2) is guilty of an indictable offence.

(3) A person who is alleged to have committed an offence under subsection (1), (2) or (2.1) may be prosecuted for that offence in accordance with section 8.

(4) Every person who commits an offence under subsection (1), (2) or (2.1) is liable to imprisonment for life.

(5) Where an act or omission constituting an offence under this section occurred before the coming into force of this section, subparagraphs (1)(*a*)(ii) and (2)(*a*)(ii) apply to the extent that, at the time and in the place of the act or omission, the act or omission constituted a contravention of customary international law or conventional international law or was criminal according to the general principles of law recognized by the community of nations, whether or not it constituted a contravention of the law in force at the time and in the place of its commission.

(6) The definitions in this subsection apply in this section.

"military commander" includes a person effectively acting as a military commander and a person who commands police with a degree of authority and control comparable to a military commander.

"superior" means a person in authority, other than a military commander.

JURISDICTION.

8. A person who is alleged to have committed an offence under section 6 or 7 may be prosecuted for that offence if

- **(*a*) at the time the offence is alleged to have been committed,**
  - **(i) the person was a Canadian citizen or was employed by Canada in a civilian or military capacity,**
  - **(ii) the person was a citizen of a state that was engaged in an armed conflict against Canada, or was employed in a civilian or military capacity by such a state,**
  - **(iii) the victim of the alleged offence was a Canadian citizen, or**
  - **(iv) the victim of the alleged offence was a citizen of a state that was allied with Canada in an armed conflict; or**
- **(*b*) after the time the offence is alleged to have been committed, the person is present in Canada.**

PROCEDURE AND DEFENCES

PLACE OF TRIAL / Presence of accused at trial / Personal consent of Attorney General / Consent of Attorney General.

9. (1) Proceedings for an offence under this Act alleged to have been committed outside Canada for which a person may be prosecuted under this Act may, whether or not the person is in Canada, be commenced in any territorial division in Canada and the person may be tried and punished in respect of that offence in the same manner as if the offence had been committed in that territorial division.

(2) For greater certainty, in a proceeding commenced in any territorial division under subsection (1), the provisions of the *Criminal Code* relating to requirements that an accused appear at and be present during proceedings and any exceptions to those requirements apply.

(3) No proceedings for an offence under any of sections 4 to 7 of this Act, or under section 354 or subsection 462.31(1) of the *Criminal Code* in relation to property or proceeds obtained or derived directly or indirectly as a result of the commission of an offence under this Act, may be commenced without the personal consent in writing of the Attorney General or Deputy Attorney General of Canada, and those proceedings may be conducted only by the Attorney General of Canada or counsel acting on their behalf.

(4) No proceedings for an offence under section 18 may be commenced without the consent of the Attorney General of Canada. 2001, c. 32, s. 59.

EVIDENCE AND PROCEDURE.

10. Proceedings for an offence alleged to have been committed before the coming into force of this section shall be conducted in accordance with the laws of evidence and procedure in force at the time of the proceedings.

DEFENCES.

11. In proceedings for an offence under any of sections 4 to 7, the accused may, subject to sections 12 to 14 and to subsection 607(6) of the *Criminal Code*, rely on any justification, excuse or defence available under the laws of Canada or under international law at the time of the alleged offence or at the time of the proceedings.

WHEN PREVIOUSLY TRIED OUTSIDE CANADA / Exception.

12. (1) If a person is alleged to have committed an act or omission that is an offence under this Act, and the person has been tried and dealt with outside Canada in respect of the offence in such a manner that, had they been tried and dealt with in Canada, they would be able to plead *autrefois acquit, autrefois convict* or pardon, the person is deemed to have been so tried and dealt with in Canada.

(2) Despite subsection (1), a person may not plead *autrefois acquit, autrefois convict* or pardon in respect of an offence under any of sections 4 to 7 if the person was tried in a court of a foreign state or territory and the proceedings in that court

(*a*) were for the purpose of shielding the person from criminal responsibility; or

(*b*) were not otherwise conducted independently or impartially in accordance with the norms of due process recognized by international law, and were conducted in a manner that, in the circumstances, was inconsistent with an intent to bring the person to justice.

CONFLICT WITH INTERNAL LAW.

13. Despite section 15 of the *Criminal Code*, it is not a justification, excuse or defence with respect to an offence under any of sections 4 to 7 that the offence was committed in obedience to or in conformity with the law in force at the time and in the place of its commission.

DEFENCE OF SUPERIOR ORDERS / Interpretation — manifestly unlawful / Limitation — belief of accused.

14. (1) In proceedings for an offence under any of sections 4 to 7, it is not a defence that the accused was ordered by a government or a superior — whether military or civilian — to perform the act or omission that forms the subject-matter of the offence, unless

(*a*) the accused was under a legal obligation to obey orders of the government or superior;

(*b*) the accused did not know that the order was unlawful; and

(*c*) the order was not manifestly unlawful.

(2) For the purpose of paragraph (1)(c), orders to commit genocide or crimes against humanity are manifestly unlawful.

(3) An accused cannot base their defence under subsection (1) on a belief that an order was lawful if the belief was based on information about a civilian population or an identifiable group of persons that encouraged, was likely to encourage or attempted to justify the commission of inhumane acts or omissions against the population or group.

PAROLE ELIGIBILITY

PAROLE ELIGIBILITY / Parole eligibility / Provisions of *Criminal Code* apply / Minimum punishment.

15. (1) The following sentence shall be pronounced against a person who is to be sentenced to imprisonment for life for an offence under section 4 or 6:

(*a*) imprisonment for life without eligibility for parole until the person has served 25 years of the sentence, if a planned and deliberate killing forms the basis of the offence;

(*b*) imprisonment for life without eligibility for parole until the person has served 25 years of the sentence, if an intentional killing that is not planned and deliberate forms the basis of the offence, and

WAR

(i) the person has previously been convicted of an offence under section 4 or 6 that had, as its basis, an intentional killing, whether or not it was planned and deliberate, or

(ii) the person has previously been convicted of culpable homicide that is murder, however described in the *Criminal Code*;

(*c*) imprisonment for life without eligibility for parole until the person has served at least 10 years of the sentence or any greater number of years, not being more than 25, that has been substituted for it under section 745.4 of the *Criminal Code*, if an intentional killing that is not planned and deliberate forms the basis of the offence; and

(*d*) imprisonment for life with normal eligibility for parole, in any other case.

(1.1) The sentence pronounced against a person who is to be sentenced to imprisonment for life for an offence under section 5 or 7 shall be imprisonment for life with normal eligibility for parole.

(2) Sections 745.1 to 746.1 of the *Criminal Code* apply, with any modifications that the circumstances require, to a sentence of life imprisonment imposed under this Act, and, for the purpose of applying those provisions,

(*a*) a reference in sections 745.1, 745.3, 745.5 and 746.1 of the *Criminal Code* to first degree murder is deemed to be a reference to an offence under section 4 or 6 of this Act when a planned and deliberate killing forms the basis of the offence;

(*b*) a reference in sections 745.1 to 745.5 and 746.1 of the *Criminal Code* to second degree murder is deemed to be a reference to an offence under section 4 or 6 of this Act when an intentional killing that is not planned and deliberate forms the basis of the offence;

(*c*) a reference in sections 745.4 and 746 of the *Criminal Code* to section 745 of that Act is deemed to be a reference to subsection (1) or (1.1) of this section;

(*d*) a reference in section 745.6 of the *Criminal Code* to the province in which a conviction took place is deemed, in respect of a conviction that took place outside Canada, to be a reference to the province in which the offender is incarcerated when the offender makes an application under that section; and

(*e*) a reference in section 745.6 of the *Criminal Code* to murder is deemed to be a reference to an offence under section 4 or 6 of this Act when an intentional killing forms the basis of the offence.

(3) For the purpose of Part XXIII of the *Criminal Code*, the sentence of imprisonment for life prescribed by sections 4 and 6 is a minimum punishment when an intentional killing forms the basis of the offence.

OFFENCES AGAINST THE ADMINISTRATION OF JUSTICE

OBSTRUCTING JUSTICE / When deemed to have obstructed justice.

16. (1) Every person who wilfully attempts in any manner to obstruct, pervert or defeat the course of justice of the International Criminal Court is guilty of an indictable offence and liable to imprisonment for a term of not more than 10 years.

(2) Without restricting the generality of subsection (1), every person is deemed wilfully to attempt to obstruct, pervert or defeat the course of justice who in an existing or proposed proceeding of the International Criminal Court

(*a*) dissuades or attempts to dissuade a person by threats, bribes or other corrupt means from giving evidence; or

(*b*) accepts, obtains, agrees to accept or attempts to obtain a bribe or other corrupt consideration to abstain from giving evidence.

OBSTRUCTING OFFICIALS.

17. Every person who resists or wilfully obstructs an official of the International Criminal Court in the execution of their duty or any person lawfully acting in aid of such an official

(*a*) is guilty of an indictable offence and liable to imprisonment for a term of not more than two years; or

(*b*) is guilty of an offence punishable on summary conviction.

BRIBERY OF JUDGES AND OFFICIALS.

18. Every person is guilty of an indictable offence and is liable to imprisonment for a term of not more than 14 years who

(*a*) being a judge or an official of the International Criminal Court, corruptly accepts, obtains, agrees to accept or attempts to obtain for themselves or any other person any money, valuable consideration, office, place or employment

(i) in respect of anything done or omitted or to be done or omitted by them in their official capacity, or

(ii) with intent to interfere in any other way with the administration of justice of the International Criminal Court; or

(*b*) gives or offers, corruptly, to a judge or an official of the International Criminal Court, any money, valuable consideration, office, place or employment

(i) in respect of anything done or omitted or to be done or omitted by them in their official capacity, or

(ii) with intent to interfere in any other way with the administration of justice of the International Criminal Court.

PERJURY / Video links, etc. / Punishment / Application / Application.

19. (1) Subject to subsection (5), every person commits perjury who, with intent to mislead, makes a false statement under oath or solemn affirmation, by affidavit, solemn declaration or deposition or orally, knowing that the statement is false, before a judge of the International Criminal Court or an official of that Court who is authorized by the Court to permit statements to be made before them.

(2) Subject to subsection (5), every person who gives evidence under subsection 46(2) of the *Canada Evidence Act*, or gives evidence or a statement under an order made under section 22.2 of the *Mutual Legal Assistance in Criminal Matters Act*, commits perjury who, with intent to mislead, makes a false statement knowing that it is false, whether or not the false statement was made under oath or solemn affirmation in accordance with subsection (1), so long as the false statement was made in accordance with any formalities required by the law of the place outside Canada in which the person is virtually present or heard.

(3) Every person who commits perjury is guilty of an indictable offence and liable to imprisonment for a term of not more than 14 years.

(4) Subsection (1) applies whether or not a statement is made in a judicial proceeding of the International Criminal Court.

(5) Subsections (1) and (2) do not apply to a statement that is made by a person who is not specially permitted, authorized or required by law to make that statement.

WITNESS GIVING CONTRADICTORY EVIDENCE / Evidence in specific cases / Meaning of "evidence" / Proof of former trial.

20. (1) Every person who, being a witness in a proceeding of the International Criminal Court, gives evidence with respect to any matter of fact or knowledge and who later, in a proceeding of that Court, gives evidence that is contrary to their previous evidence,

WAR

and who, in giving evidence in either proceeding, intends to mislead, is guilty of an indictable offence and liable to imprisonment for a term of not more than 14 years, whether or not the prior or later evidence is true.

(2) Evidence given under section 714.1, 714.2, 714.3 or 714.4 of the *Criminal Code* or subsection 46(2) of the *Canada Evidence Act* or evidence or a statement given under an order made under section 22.2 of the *Mutual Legal Assistance in Criminal Matters Act*, is deemed to be evidence given by a witness in a proceeding for the purpose of subsection (1).

(3) Despite the definition "evidence" in section 118 of the *Criminal Code*, for the purpose of this section, "evidence" does not include evidence that is not material.

(4) If a person is charged with an offence under this section, a certificate that specifies with reasonable particularity the proceeding in which the person is alleged to have given the evidence in respect of which the offence is charged, is evidence that it was given in a proceeding of the International Criminal Court, without proof of the signature or official character of the person by whom the certificate purports to be signed, if it purports to be signed by the Registrar of that Court or another official having the custody of the record of that proceeding or by their lawful deputy.

FABRICATING EVIDENCE.

21. Every person who, with intent to mislead, fabricates anything with intent that it be used as evidence in an existing or proposed proceeding of the International Criminal Court, by any means other than perjury or incitement to perjury, is guilty of an indictable offence and liable to imprisonment for a term of not more than 14 years.

OFFENCES RELATING TO AFFIDAVITS.

22. Every person is guilty of an indictable offence and liable to imprisonment for a term of not more than two years who, in respect of an existing or proposed proceeding of the International Criminal Court,

- **(*a*) signs a writing that purports to be an affidavit or statutory declaration and to have been sworn or declared before them when the writing was not so sworn or declared or when they know that they have no authority to administer the oath or declaration;**
- **(*b*) uses or offers for use any writing purporting to be an affidavit or statutory declaration that they know was not sworn or declared, as the case may be, by the affiant or declarant or before a person authorized to administer the oath or declaration; or**
- **(*c*) signs as affiant or declarant a writing that purports to be an affidavit or statutory declaration and to have been sworn or declared by them, as the case may be, when the writing was not so sworn or declared.**

INTIMIDATION.

23. Every person who, wrongfully and without lawful authority, for the purpose of compelling another person to abstain from doing anything that the person has a lawful right to do, or to do anything that the person has a lawful right to abstain from doing, in relation to a proceeding of the International Criminal Court, causes the person reasonably, in all the circumstances, to fear for their safety or the safety of anyone known to them

- **(*a*) is guilty of an indictable offence and liable to imprisonment for a term of not more than five years; or**
- **(*b*) is guilty of an offence punishable on summary conviction.**

MEANING OF "INTERNATIONALLY PROTECTED PERSON".

24. For greater certainty, the definition "internationally protected person" in section 2 of the *Criminal Code* includes judges and officials of the International Criminal Court.

OFFENCES AGAINST THE INTERNATIONAL CRIMINAL COURT — OUTSIDE CANADA / Offences against the International Criminal Court — outside Canada.

25. (1) Every person who, being a Canadian citizen, commits outside Canada an act or omission in relation to the International Criminal Court that if committed in Canada would be an offence under any of sections 16 to 23, or would be contempt of court by virtue of section 9 of the *Criminal Code*, is deemed to have committed that act or omission in Canada.

(2) Every person who, being a Canadian citizen, commits outside Canada an act or omission that if committed in Canada would constitute conspiring or attempting to commit, being an accessory after the fact in relation to, or counselling in relation to, an act or omission that is an offence or a contempt of court under subsection (1) is deemed to have committed that act or omission in Canada.

RETALIATION AGAINST WITNESSES — OUTSIDE CANADA / Retaliation against witnesses — outside Canada.

26. (1) Every person who, being a Canadian citizen, commits outside Canada an act or omission against a person or a member of the person's family in retaliation for the person having given testimony before the International Criminal Court, that if committed in Canada would be an offence under any of sections 235, 236, 264.1, 266 to 269, 271 to 273, 279 to 283, 430, 433 and 434 of the *Criminal Code*, is deemed to have committed that act or omission in Canada.

(2) Every person who, being a Canadian citizen, commits outside Canada an act or omission that if committed in Canada would constitute conspiring or attempting to commit, being an accessory after the fact in relation to, or counselling in relation to, an act or omission that is an offence under subsection (1) is deemed to have committed that act or omission in Canada.

POSSESSION OF PROPERTY OBTAINED BY CERTAIN OFFENCES.

27. [*Repealed*, 2001, c. 32, s. 60, part]

LAUNDERING PROCEEDS OF CERTAIN OFFENCES.

28. [*Repealed*, 2001, c. 32, s. 60, part]

PART XII.2 OF *CRIMINAL CODE* APPLICABLE.

29. [*Repealed*, 2001, c. 32, s. 60, part]

CRIMES AGAINST HUMANITY FUND

FUND ESTABLISHED / Payment out of Fund / Regulations.

30. (1) There is hereby established a fund, to be known as the Crimes Against Humanity Fund, into which shall be paid

- **(*a*) all money obtained through enforcement in Canada of orders of the International Criminal Court for reparation or forfeiture or orders of that Court imposing a fine;**
- **(*b*) all money obtained in accordance with section 31; and**

(*c*) **any money otherwise received as a donation to the Crimes Against Humanity Fund.**

(2) The Attorney General of Canada may make payments out of the Crimes Against Humanity Fund, with or without a deduction for costs, to the International Criminal Court, the Trust Fund established under article 79 of the Rome Statute, victims of offences under this Act or of offences within the jurisdiction of the International Criminal Court, and to the families of those victims, or otherwise as the Attorney General of Canada sees fit.

(3) The Governor in Council may make regulations respecting the administration and management of the Crimes Against Humanity Fund.

CREDITS TO FUND.

31. The Minister of Public Works and Government Services shall pay into the Crimes Against Humanity Fund

(*a*) **the net amount received from the disposition of any property referred to in subsections 4(1) to (3) of the *Seized Property Management Act* that is**

(i) **proceeds of crime within the meaning of subsection 462.3(1) of the *Criminal Code*, obtained or derived directly or indirectly as a result of the commission of an offence under this Act, and**

(ii) **forfeited to Her Majesty and disposed of by that Minister; and**

(*b*) **any amount paid or recovered as a fine imposed under subsection 462.37(3) of the *Criminal Code* in substitution for the property referred to in paragraph (*a*).**

2001, c. 32, s. 61.

PARTIAL EXCLUSION OF *SEIZED PROPERTY MANAGEMENT ACT.*

32. Paragraphs 9(*d*), (*e*) and (*f*) and sections 10, 11 and 13 to 16 of the *Seized Property Management Act* do not apply in respect of any property, proceeds of property or amounts referred to in section 31.

SCHEDULE
(Subsection 2(1))

PROVISIONS OF ROME STATUTE

ARTICLE 6

Genocide

For the purpose of this Statute, "genocide" means any of the following acts committed with intent to destroy, in whole or in part, a national, ethnical, racial or religious group, as such:

(*a*) **killing members of the group;**

(*b*) **causing serious bodily or mental harm to members of the group;**

(*c*) **deliberately inflicting on the group conditions of life calculated to bring about its physical destruction in whole or in part;**

(*d*) **imposing measures intended to prevent births within the group;**

(*e*) **forcibly transferring children of the group to another group.**

ARTICLE 7

Crimes against humanity

1. For the purpose of this Statute, "crime against humanity" means any of the following acts when committed as part of a widespread or systematic attack directed against any civilian population, with knowledge of the attack:

(*a*) murder;

(*b*) extermination;

(*c*) enslavement;

(*d*) deportation or forcible transfer of population;

(*e*) imprisonment or other severe deprivation of physical liberty in violation of fundamental rules of international law;

(*f*) torture;

(*g*) rape, sexual slavery, enforced prostitution, forced pregnancy, enforced sterilization, or any other form of sexual violence of comparable gravity;

(*h*) persecution against any identifiable group or collectivity on political, racial, national, ethnic, cultural, religious, gender as defined in paragraph 3, or other grounds that are universally recognized as impermissible under international law, in connection with any act referred to in this paragraph or any crime within the jurisdiction of the Court;

(*i*) enforced disappearance of persons;

(*j*) the crime of apartheid;

(*k*) other inhumane acts of a similar character intentionally causing great suffering, or serious injury to body or to mental or physical health.

2. For the purpose of paragraph 1:

(*a*) "attack directed against any civilian population" means a course of conduct involving the multiple commission of acts referred to in paragraph 1 against any civilian population, pursuant to or in furtherance of a State or organizational policy to commit such attack;

(*b*) "extermination" includes the intentional infliction of conditions of life, inter alia the deprivation of access to food and medicine, calculated to bring about the destruction of part of a population;

(*c*) "enslavement" means the exercise of any or all of the powers attaching to the right of ownership over a person and includes the exercise of such power in the course of trafficking in persons, in particular women and children;

(*d*) "deportation or forcible transfer of population" means forced displacement of the persons concerned by expulsion or other coercive acts from the area in which they are lawfully present, without grounds permitted under international law;

(*e*) "torture" means the intentional infliction of severe pain or suffering, whether physical or mental, upon a person in the custody or under the control of the accused; except that torture shall not include pain or suffering arising only from, inherent in or incidental to, lawful sanctions;

(*f*) "forced pregnancy" means the unlawful confinement of a woman forcibly made pregnant, with the intent of affecting the ethnic composition of any population or carrying out other grave violations of international law. This definition shall not in any way be interpreted as affecting national laws relating to pregnancy;

(*g*) "persecution" means the intentional and severe deprivation of fundamental rights contrary to international law by reason of the identity of the group or collectivity;

(*h*) "the crime of apartheid" means inhumane acts of a character similar to those referred to in paragraph 1, committed in the context of an institutionalized

WAR

regime of systematic oppression and domination by one racial group over any other racial group or groups and committed with the intention of maintaining that regime;

(*i*) "enforced disappearance of persons" means the arrest, detention or abduction of persons by, or with the authorization, support or acquiescence of, a State or a political organization, followed by a refusal to acknowledge that deprivation of freedom or to give information on the fate or whereabouts of those persons, with the intention of removing them from the protection of the law for a prolonged period of time.

3. For the purpose of this Statute, it is understood that the term "gender" refers to the two sexes, male and female, within the context of society. The term "gender" does not indicate any meaning different from the above.

PARAGRAPH 2 OF ARTICLE 8

War crimes

2. For the purpose of this Statute, "war crimes" means:

(*a*) grave breaches of the Geneva Conventions of 12 August 1949, namely, any of the following acts against persons or property protected under the provisions of the relevant Geneva Convention:

(i) wilful killing;

(ii) torture or inhuman treatment, including biological experiments;

(iii) wilfully causing great suffering, or serious injury to body or health;

(iv) extensive destruction and appropriation of property, not justified by military necessity and carried out unlawfully and wantonly;

(v) compelling a prisoner of war or other protected person to serve in the forces of a hostile Power;

(vi) wilfully depriving a prisoner of war or other protected person of the rights of fair and regular trial;

(vii) unlawful deportation or transfer or unlawful confinement;

(viii) taking of hostages.

(*b*) other serious violations of the laws and customs applicable in international armed conflict, within the established framework of international law, namely, any of the following acts:

(i) intentionally directing attacks against the civilian population as such or against individual civilians not taking direct part in hostilities;

(ii) intentionally directing attacks against civilian objects, that is, objects which are not military objectives;

(iii) intentionally directing attacks against personnel, installations, material, units or vehicles involved in a humanitarian assistance or peacekeeping mission in accordance with the Charter of the United Nations, as long as they are entitled to the protection given to civilians or civilian objects under the international law of armed conflict;

(iv) intentionally launching an attack in the knowledge that such attack will cause incidental loss of life or injury to civilians or damage to civilian objects or widespread, long-term and severe damage to the natural environment which would be clearly excessive in relation to the concrete and direct overall military advantage anticipated;

(v) attacking or bombarding, by whatever means, towns, villages, dwellings or buildings which are undefended and which are not military objectives;

(vi) killing or wounding a combatant who, having laid down his arms or having no longer means of defence, has surrendered at discretion;

(vii) making improper use of a flag of truce, of the flag or of the military insignia and uniform of the enemy or of the United Nations, as well as of the distinctive emblems of the Geneva Conventions, resulting in death or serious personal injury;

(viii) the transfer, directly or indirectly, by the Occupying Power of parts of its own civilian population into the territory it occupies, or the deportation or transfer of all or parts of the population of the occupied territory within or outside this territory;

(ix) intentionally directing attacks against buildings dedicated to religion, education, art, science or charitable purposes, historic monuments, hospitals and places where the sick and wounded are collected, provided they are not military objectives;

(x) subjecting persons who are in the power of an adverse party to physical mutilation or to medical or scientific experiments of any kind which are neither justified by the medical, dental or hospital treatment of the person concerned nor carried out in his or her interest, and which cause death to or seriously endanger the health of such person or persons;

(xi) killing or wounding treacherously individuals belonging to the hostile nation or army;

(xii) declaring that no quarter will be given;

(xiii) destroying or seizing the enemy's property unless such destruction or seizure be imperatively demanded by the necessities of war;

(xiv) declaring abolished, suspended or inadmissible in a court of law the rights and actions of the nationals of the hostile party;

(xv) compelling the nationals of the hostile party to take part in the operations of war directed against their own country, even if they were in the belligerent's service before the commencement of the war;

(xvi) pillaging a town or place, even when taken by assault;

(xvii) employing poison or poisoned weapons;

(xviii) employing asphyxiating, poisonous or other gases, and all analogous liquids, materials or devices;

(xix) employing bullets which expand or flatten easily in the human body, such as bullets with a hard envelope which does not entirely cover the core or is pierced with incisions;

(xx) employing weapons, projectiles and material and methods of warfare which are of a nature to cause superfluous injury or unnecessary suffering or which are inherently indiscriminate in violation of the international law of armed conflict, provided that such weapons, projectiles and material and methods of warfare are the subject of a comprehensive prohibition and are included in an annex to this Statute, by an amendment in accordance with the relevant provisions set forth in articles 121 and 123;

(xxi) committing outrages upon personal dignity, in particular humiliating and degrading treatment;

(xxii) committing rape, sexual slavery, enforced prostitution, forced pregnancy, as defined in article 7, paragraph 2(f), enforced sterilization, or any other form of sexual violence also constituting a grave breach of the Geneva Conventions;

(xxiii) utilizing the presence of a civilian or other protected person to render certain points, areas or military forces immune from military operations;

(xxiv) intentionally directing attacks against buildings, material, medical units and transport, and personnel using the distinctive emblems of the Geneva Conventions in conformity with international law;

WAR

(xxv) intentionally using starvation of civilians as a method of warfare by depriving them of objects indispensable to their survival, including wilfully impeding relief supplies as provided for under the Geneva Conventions;

(xxvi) conscripting or enlisting children under the age of fifteen years into the national armed forces or using them to participate actively in hostilities.

(*c*) in the case of an armed conflict not of an international character, serious violations of article 3 common to the four Geneva Conventions of 12 August 1949, namely, any of the following acts committed against persons taking no active part in the hostilities, including members of armed forces who have laid down their arms and those placed hors de combat by sickness, wounds, detention or any other cause:

(i) violence to life and person, in particular murder of all kinds, mutilation, cruel treatment and torture;

(ii) committing outrages upon personal dignity, in particular humiliating and degrading treatment;

(iii) taking of hostages;

(iv) the passing of sentences and the carrying out of executions without previous judgement pronounced by a regularly constituted court, affording all judicial guarantees which are generally recognized as indispensable.

(*d*) paragraph 2(c) applies to armed conflicts not of an international character and thus does not apply to situations of internal disturbances and tensions, such as riots, isolated and sporadic acts of violence or other acts of a similar nature.

(*e*) other serious violations of the laws and customs applicable in armed conflicts not of an international character, within the established framework of international law, namely, any of the following acts:

(i) intentionally directing attacks against the civilian population as such or against individual civilians not taking direct part in hostilities;

(ii) intentionally directing attacks against buildings, material, medical units and transport, and personnel using the distinctive emblems of the Geneva Conventions in conformity with international law;

(iii) intentionally directing attacks against personnel, installations, material, units or vehicles involved in a humanitarian assistance or peacekeeping mission in accordance with the Charter of the United Nations, as long as they are entitled to the protection given to civilians or civilian objects under the international law of armed conflict;

(iv) intentionally directing attacks against buildings dedicated to religion, education, art, science or charitable purposes, historic monuments, hospitals and places where the sick and wounded are collected, provided they are not military objectives;

(v) pillaging a town or place, even when taken by assault;

(vi) committing rape, sexual slavery, enforced prostitution, forced pregnancy, as defined in article 7, paragraph 2(f), enforced sterilization, and any other form of sexual violence also constituting a serious violation of article 3 common to the four Geneva Conventions;

(vii) conscripting or enlisting children under the age of fifteen years into armed forces or groups or using them to participate actively in hostilities;

(viii) ordering the displacement of the civilian population for reasons related to the conflict, unless the security of the civilians involved or imperative military reasons so demand;

(ix) killing or wounding treacherously a combatant adversary;

(x) declaring that no quarter will be given;

(xi) subjecting persons who are in the power of another party to the conflict to physical mutilation or to medical or scientific experiments of any kind which are neither justified by the medical, dental or hospital treatment of

the person concerned nor carried out in his or her interest, and which cause death to or seriously endanger the health of such person or persons;

(xii) destroying or seizing the property of an adversary unless such destruction or seizure be imperatively demanded by the necessities of the conflict;

(*f*) paragraph 2(e) applies to armed conflicts not of an international character and thus does not apply to situations of internal disturbances and tensions, such as riots, isolated and sporadic acts of violence or other acts of a similar nature. It applies to armed conflicts that take place in the territory of a State when there is protracted armed conflict between governmental authorities and organized armed groups or between such groups.

YOUTH CRIMINAL JUSTICE ACT

S.C. 2002, c. 1, in force April 1, 2003

Amended 2002, c. 7, s. 274; brought into force April 1, 2003 as provided by the section

Amended 2002, c. 13, s. 91(1); brought into force June 1, 2004, as provided by s. 91(2), by SI/2003-182, *Can. Gaz.*, December 3, 2003

Amended 2004, c. 11, ss. 48 and 49; brought into force May 21, 2004 by SI/2004-58, *Can. Gaz.*, Part II, June 2, 2004

Amended 2005, c. 22, s. 63; brought into force June 30, 2005 by para. (*a*) of SI/2005-56, *Can. Gaz.*, Part II, June 15, 2005

Amended 2012, c. 1, ss. 156 to 159, 160(*l*), 167 to 188(2), 189, 190, and 192 to 195; ss. 156 to 159 in force March 13, 2012; ss. 167 to 188(2), 189 and 190, and 192 to 195 in force October 23, 2012 by SI/2012-48, *Can. Gaz.*, *Part II*, July 4, 2012; s. 160(*l*) brought into force February 28, 2013 by SI/2013-13, *Can. Gaz.*, *Part II*, February 27, 2013

Amended 2014, c. 2, s. 52; in force April 1, 2014 by SI/2014-34, *Can. Gaz.*, *Part II*, April 9, 2014

Amended 2014, c. 25, s. 43; in force December 6, 2014

Amended 2015, c. 20, ss. 32, 33, 36(8) and (9); in force July 18, 2015

Amended 2015, c. 29, ss. 14 and 15; brought into force July 16, 2015 by SI/2015-67, *Can. Gaz.*, *Part II*, July 17, 2015; however, replaced by 2015, c. 20, s. 36(8) and (9)

Amended 2018, c. 16, s. 184; in force October 17, 2018

An Act in respect of criminal justice for young persons and to amend and repeal other Acts

PREAMBLE

WHEREAS members of society share a responsibility to address the developmental challenges and the needs of young persons and to guide them into adulthood;

WHEREAS communities, families, parents and others concerned with the development of young persons should, through multi-disciplinary approaches, take reasonable steps to prevent youth crime by addressing its underlying causes, to respond to the needs of young persons, and to provide guidance and support to those at risk of committing crimes;

WHEREAS information about youth justice, youth crime and the effectiveness of measures taken to address youth crime should be publicly available;

WHEREAS Canada is a party to the United Nations Convention on the Rights of the Child and recognizes that young persons have rights and freedoms, including those stated in the *Canadian Charter of Rights and Freedoms* and the *Canadian Bill of Rights*, and have special guarantees of their rights and freedoms;

AND WHEREAS Canadian society should have a youth criminal justice system that commands respect, takes into account the interests of victims, fosters responsibility and ensures accountability through meaningful consequences and effective rehabilitation and reintegration, and that reserves its most serious intervention for the most serious crimes and reduces the over-reliance on incarceration for non-violent young persons;

NOW, THEREFORE, Her Majesty, by and with the advice and consent of the Senate and House of Commons of Canada, enacts as follows:

EDITOR'S NOTE: In *Quebec (Minister of Justice) v. Canada (Minister of Justice)* (2003), 175 C.C.C. (3d) 321, 10 C.R. (6th) 281, 228 D.L.R. (4th) 63, the Quebec Court of Appeal considered a comprehensive challenge to the Act. The court held that the Act was neither *ultra vires* the federal government, nor was it inconsistent with Canada's international obligations pursuant to the *Convention on the Rights of the Child* and the *International Covenant on Civil and Political Rights*. The new sentencing regime set out in the Act generally did not violate ss. 7, 11(*d*) or 15 of the Charter.

SHORT TITLE

SHORT TITLE.

1. This Act may be cited as the *Youth Criminal Justice Act*.

INTERPRETATION

DEFINITIONS / "adult" / "adult sentence" / "Attorney General" / "child" / "conference" / "confirmed delivery service" / "custodial portion" / "disclosure" / "extrajudicial measures" / "extrajudicial sanction" / "offence" / "parent" / "pre-sentence report" / "provincial director" / "publication" / "record" / "review board" / "serious offence" / "serious violent offence" / "violent offence" / "young person" / "youth custody facility" / "youth justice court" / "youth justice court judge" / "youth sentence" / "youth worker" / Words and expressions / Descriptive cross-references.

2. (1) The definitions in this subsection apply in this Act.

"adult" means a person who is neither a young person nor a child.

"adult sentence", in the case of a young person who is found guilty of an offence, means any sentence that could be imposed on an adult who has been convicted of the same offence.

"Attorney General" means the Attorney General as defined in section 2 of the *Criminal Code*, read as if the reference in that definition to "proceedings" were a reference to "proceedings or extrajudicial measures", and includes an agent or delegate of the Attorney General.

"child" means a person who is or, in the absence of evidence to the contrary, appears to be less than twelve years old.

"conference" means a group of persons who are convened to give advice in accordance with section 19.

"confirmed delivery service" means certified or registered mail or any other method of service that provides proof of delivery.

"custodial portion", with respect to a youth sentence imposed on a young person under paragraph 42(2)(*n*), (*o*), (*q*) or (*r*), means the period of time, or the portion of the young person's youth sentence, that must be served in custody before he or she begins to serve the remainder under supervision in the community subject to conditions under paragraph 42(2)(*n*) or under conditional supervision under paragraph 42(2)(*o*), (*q*) or (*r*).

"disclosure" means the communication of information other than by way of publication.

"extrajudicial measures" means measures other than judicial proceedings under this Act used to deal with a young person alleged to have committed an offence and includes extrajudicial sanctions.

"extrajudicial sanction" means a sanction that is part of a program referred to in section 10.

"offence" means an offence created by an Act of Parliament or by any regulation, rule, order, by-law or ordinance made under an Act of Parliament other than a law of the Legislature of Yukon, of the Northwest Territories or for Nunavut.

"parent" includes, in respect of a young person, any person who is under a legal duty to provide for the young person or any person who has, in law or in fact, the custody or control of the young person, but does not include a person who has the custody or control of the young person by reason only of proceedings under this Act.

"pre-sentence report" means a report on the personal and family history and present environment of a young person made in accordance with section 40.

"presumptive offence" [*Repealed*, 2012, c. 1, s. 167(1).]

"provincial director" means a person, a group or class of persons or a body appointed or designated by or under an Act of the legislature of a province or by the lieutenant governor in council of a province or his or her delegate to perform in that province, either generally or in a specific case, any of the duties or functions of a provincial director under this Act.

"publication" means the communication of information by making it known or accessible to the general public through any means, including print, radio or television broadcast, telecommunication or electronic means.

"record" includes any thing containing information, regardless of its physical form or characteristics, including microform, sound recording, videotape, machine-readable record, and any copy of any of those things, that is created or kept for the purposes of this Act or for the investigation of an offence that is or could be prosecuted under this Act.

"review board" means a review board referred to in subsection 87(2).

"serious offence" means an indictable offence under an Act of Parliament for which the maximum punishment is imprisonment for five years or more.

"serious violent offence" means an offence under one of the following provisions of the *Criminal Code*:

(*a*) section 231 or 235 (first degree murder or second degree murder);
(*b*) section 239 (attempt to commit murder);
(*c*) section 232, 234 or 236 (manslaughter); or
(*d*) section 273 (aggravated sexual assault).

"violent offence" means

(*a*) an offence committed by a young person that includes as an element the causing of bodily harm;
(*b*) an attempt or a threat to commit an offence referred to in paragraph (*a*); or
(*c*) an offence in the commission of which a young person endangers the life or safety of another person by creating a substantial likelihood of causing bodily harm.

"young person" means a person who is or, in the absence of evidence to the contrary, appears to be twelve years old or older, but less than eighteen years old and, if the context requires, includes any person who is charged under this Act with having committed an offence while he or she was a young person or who is found guilty of an offence under this Act.

"youth custody facility" means a facility designated under subsection 85(2) for the placement of young persons and, if so designated, includes a facility for the secure restraint of young persons, a community residential centre, a group home, a child care institution and a forest or wilderness camp.

"youth justice court" means a youth justice court referred to in section 13.

"youth justice court judge" means a youth justice court judge referred to in section 13.

"youth sentence" means a sentence imposed under section 42, 51 or 59 or any of sections 94 to 96 and includes a confirmation or a variation of that sentence.

"youth worker" means any person appointed or designated, whether by title of youth worker or probation officer or by any other title, by or under an Act of the legislature of a province or by the lieutenant governor in council of a province or his or her delegate to perform in that province, either generally or in a specific case, any of the duties or functions of a youth worker under this Act.

(2) Unless otherwise provided, words and expressions used in this Act have the same meaning as in the *Criminal Code*.

(3) If, in any provision of this Act, a reference to another provision of this Act or a provision of any other Act is followed by words in parentheses that are or purport to be descriptive of the subject-matter of the provision referred to, those words form no part of the provision in which they occur but are inserted for convenience of reference only. 2002, c. 7, s. 274; 2012, c. 1, s. 167; 2014, c. 2, s. 52.

ANNOTATIONS

Note: The following cases were decided under the *Young Offenders Act* but were thought to be of assistance in applying this Act.

An accused who, following his 18th birthday, failed to comply with a disposition made by the youth court was no longer a young person and the offence contrary to s. 26 of the *Young Offenders Act* [now see s. 137 of this Act] is properly tried in adult court: *R. v. M. (R.E.)* (1988), 46 C.C.C. (3d) 315 (B.C.S.C.).

Youth justice court – It was open to the Lieutenant Governor in Council to designate the Provincial Court as the Youth Court under the *Young Offenders Act*, although that court is not presided over by judges appointed under s. 96 of the *Constitution Act, 1867*: *Reference re: Young Offenders Act (P.E.I.), s. 2*, [1991] 1 S.C.R. 252, 62 C.C.C. (3d) 385 (7:0).

And it was open to the Lieutenant Governor to designate the Court of Queen's Bench, Family Division as a youth court and a judge of that court as a youth court judge: *Reference re: Young Offenders Act (P.E.I.), supra.*

Violent offence – A home invasion is not necessarily a violent offence within the meaning of subsec. (1)(*a*). Unless an offence is inherently violent so that bodily harm must be assumed, the evidence presented at trial must provide bodily harm that is more than transient or trifling within the meaning of s. 39(1)(*a*): *R. v. C. (J.J.)* (2003), 180 C.C.C. (3d) 137, 230 Nfld. & P.E.I.R. 267 (P.E.I.C.A.).

DECLARATION OF PRINCIPLE

POLICY FOR CANADA WITH RESPECT TO YOUNG PERSONS / Act to be liberally construed.

3. (1) The following principles apply in this Act:

(*a*) the youth criminal justice system is intended to protect the public by

(i) holding young persons accountable through measures that are proportionate to the seriousness of the offence and the degree of responsibility of the young person,

(ii) promoting the rehabilitation and reintegration of young persons who have committed offences, and

(iii) supporting the prevention of crime by referring young persons to programs or agencies in the community to address the circumstances underlying their offending behaviour;

(*b*) the criminal justice system for young persons must be separate from that of adults, must be based on the principle of diminished moral blameworthiness or culpability and must emphasize the following:

(i) rehabilitation and reintegration,

(ii) fair and proportionate accountability that is consistent with the greater dependency of young persons and their reduced level of maturity,

(iii) enhanced procedural protection to ensure that young persons are treated fairly and that their rights, including their right to privacy, are protected,

(iv) timely intervention that reinforces the link between the offending behaviour and its consequences, and

(v) the promptness and speed with which persons responsible for enforcing this Act must act, given young persons' perception of time;

(*c*) within the limits of fair and proportionate accountability, the measures taken against young persons who commit offences should

(i) reinforce respect for societal values,

(ii) encourage the repair of harm done to victims and the community,

(iii) be meaningful for the individual young person given his or her needs and level of development and, where appropriate, involve the parents, the extended family, the community and social or other agencies in the young person's rehabilitation and reintegration, and

(iv) respect gender, ethnic, cultural and linguistic differences and respond to the needs of aboriginal young persons and of young persons with special requirements; and

(*d*) special considerations apply in respect of proceedings against young persons and, in particular,

(i) young persons have rights and freedoms in their own right, such as a right to be heard in the course of and to participate in the processes, other than the decision to prosecute, that lead to decisions that affect them, and young persons have special guarantees of their rights and freedoms,

(ii) victims should be treated with courtesy, compassion and respect for their dignity and privacy and should suffer the minimum degree of inconvenience as a result of their involvement with the youth criminal justice system,

(iii) victims should be provided with information about the proceedings and given an opportunity to participate and be heard, and

(iv) parents should be informed of measures or proceedings involving their children and encouraged to support them in addressing their offending behaviour.

(2) This Act shall be liberally construed so as to ensure that young persons are dealt with in accordance with the principles set out in subsection (1). 2012, c. 1, s. 168.

ANNOTATIONS

Subsection (1)(*a*) – Accountability is achieved through the imposition of meaningful consequences for the offender and sanctions that promote his or her rehabilitation and reintegration into society. The purpose of accountability in this context excludes accountability to society in any larger sense or any notion of deterrence and is the equivalent of the adult sentencing principle of retribution being an objective, reasoned and measured determination of an appropriate punishment which properly reflects the moral culpability of the offender, having regard to the intentional risk-taking of the offender, the consequential harm caused by the offender, and the normative character of the offender's conduct. The need to consider the normative character of an offender's behaviour necessarily requires the court to consider societal values. But the court cannot add on to a youth sentence an element of general deterrence or denunciation: *R. v. O. (A.)* (2007), 218 C.C.C. (3d) 409, 84 O.R. (3d) 561 (C.A.).

In *R. v. P. (B.W.)*, [2006] 1 S.C.R. 941, 209 C.C.C. (3d) 97, the Supreme Court of Canada considered the applicability of the principles of general deterrence and specific deterrence to the sentencing of young persons. The court held that general deterrence is not a principle of youth sentencing under the new regime, nor is there an equivalent concept that can be implied from ss. 3 and 38 of the Act. The court also held that specific deterrence had been excluded as a factor in sentencing a young person. However, in 2012 subsec. (2)(*f*) was added to s. 38 (principles of youth sentencing) as part of Bill C-10 (the *Safe Streets and Communities Act*, S.C. 2012), permitting consideration of the objectives of denouncing unlawful conduct and deterring the young person from committing offences.

Subsection (1)(*b*) – The principle of diminished moral blameworthiness of young persons is a principle of fundamental justice under s. 7 of the Charter, and underlies the *Youth Criminal Justice Act*. The principle recognizes the heightened vulnerability, lack of maturity, and reduced capacity for moral judgment of youth. It has both procedural and substantive consequences: *R. v. B. (D.)*, [2008] 2 S.C.R. 3, 231 C.C.C. (3d) 338.

A consequence of s. 3(1)(*b*) of the *Youth Criminal Justice Act* is that adults and young persons cannot be tried together. The provisions on joint trials in the *Youth Criminal Justice Act* therefore apply only to co-accused young persons: *R. v. L. (S.J.)*, [2009] 1 S.C.R. 426, 242 C.C.C. (3d) 297.

Subsection (1)(*b*)(v) – Though subsec. (1)(*b*) emphasizes the need to act promptly in every case, the Act does not mandate a different substantive approach to the s. 11(*b*) right to be tried within a reasonable time. The appropriate way to take into account the special circumstances of young persons is to acknowledge the potential for heightened prejudice flowing from delay: *R. v. R. (R.)* (2011), 277 C.C.C. (3d) 357 (N.S.C.A.), leave to appeal to S.C.C. refused 250 C.R.R. (2d) 375*n*.

Section 3(1)(*b*)(v) is not a new requirement and was also central to the interpretation of the former *Young Offenders Act*. Accordingly, the guidelines established by the jurisprudence interpreting the *Young Offenders Act* are relevant to the interpretation of this provision. In this case, an intake period of five weeks, a scheduled trial date five weeks later and a brief three-week adjournment could not be said to be unreasonable: *R. v. R. (T.)* (2005), 197 C.C.C. (3d) 14, 75 O.R. (3d) 645, 197 O.A.C. 357 (C.A.).

PART 1 / EXTRAJUDICIAL MEASURES

Principles and Objectives

DECLARATION OF PRINCIPLES.

4. The following principles apply in this Part in addition to the principles set out in section 3:

(*a*) extrajudicial measures are often the most appropriate and effective way to address youth crime;

(*b*) extrajudicial measures allow for effective and timely interventions focused on correcting offending behaviour;

(*c*) extrajudicial measures are presumed to be adequate to hold a young person accountable for his or her offending behaviour if the young person has committed a non-violent offence and has not previously been found guilty of an offence; and

(*d*) extrajudicial measures should be used if they are adequate to hold a young person accountable for his or her offending behaviour and, if the use of

extrajudicial measures is consistent with the principles set out in this section, nothing in this Act precludes their use in respect of a young person who

(i) has previously been dealt with by the use of extrajudicial measures, or

(ii) has previously been found guilty of an offence.

SYNOPSIS

Extrajudicial measures are defined in s. 2 of the Act as being "measures other than judicial proceedings under this Act used to deal with a young person alleged to have committed an offence". *Per* the definition provided in s. 2, extrajudicial measures include extrajudicial sanctions, which are defined separately in s. 2 and delineated in s. 10. Since 2012, s. 115(1.1) of the *Youth Criminal Justice Act* requires the relevant police force to keep a record of the use of extrajudicial measures with a young person.

OBJECTIVES.

5. Extrajudicial measures should be designed to

(*a*) provide an effective and timely response to offending behaviour outside the bounds of judicial measures;

(*b*) encourage young persons to acknowledge and repair the harm caused to the victim and the community;

(*c*) encourage families of young persons — including extended families where appropriate — and the community to become involved in the design and implementation of those measures;

(*d*) provide an opportunity for victims to participate in decisions related to the measures selected and to receive reparation; and

(*e*) respect the rights and freedoms of young persons and be proportionate to the seriousness of the offence.

Warnings, Cautions and Referrals

WARNINGS, CAUTIONS AND REFERRALS / Saving.

6. (1) A police officer shall, before starting judicial proceedings or taking any other measures under this Act against a young person alleged to have committed an offence, consider whether it would be sufficient, having regard to the principles set out in section 4, to take no further action, warn the young person, administer a caution, if a program has been established under section 7, or, with the consent of the young person, refer the young person to a program or agency in the community that may assist the young person not to commit offences.

(2) The failure of a police officer to consider the options set out in subsection (1) does not invalidate any subsequent charges against the young person for the offence.

POLICE CAUTIONS.

7. The Attorney General, or any other minister designated by the lieutenant governor of a province, may establish a program authorizing the police to administer cautions to young persons instead of starting judicial proceedings under this Act.

ANNOTATIONS

Note: The following case was decided under the *Young Offenders Act* but was thought to be of assistance in applying this Act.

The province was not required to establish a programme of alternative measures under the *Young Offenders Act*, and failure of the Attorney General to authorize alternative measures

YOUTH

did not violate s. 15 of the *Charter of Rights and Freedoms*: *R. v. S. (S.)*, [1990] 2 S.C.R. 254, 57 C.C.C. (3d) 115, 77 C.R. (3d) 273.

CROWN CAUTIONS.

8. The Attorney General may establish a program authorizing prosecutors to administer cautions to young persons instead of starting or continuing judicial proceedings under this Act.

ANNOTATIONS

Note: The following case was decided under the *Young Offenders Act* but was thought to be of assistance in applying this Act.

The province was not required to establish a programme of alternative measures under the *Young Offenders Act*, and failure of the Attorney General to authorize alternative measures did not violate s. 15 of the *Charter of Rights and Freedoms*: *R. v. S. (S.)*, [1990] 2 S.C.R. 254, 57 C.C.C. (3d) 115, 77 C.R. (3d) 273.

EVIDENCE OF MEASURES IS INADMISSIBLE.

9. Evidence that a young person has received a warning, caution or referral mentioned in section 6, 7 or 8 or that a police officer has taken no further action in respect of an offence, and evidence of the offence, is inadmissible for the purpose of proving prior offending behaviour in any proceedings before a youth justice court in respect of the young person.

Extrajudicial Sanctions

EXTRAJUDICIAL SANCTIONS / Conditions / Restriction on use / Admissions not admissible in evidence / No bar to judicial proceedings / Laying of information, etc.

10. (1) An extrajudicial sanction may be used to deal with a young person alleged to have committed an offence only if the young person cannot be adequately dealt with by a warning, caution or referral mentioned in section 6, 7 or 8 because of the seriousness of the offence, the nature and number of previous offences committed by the young person or any other aggravating circumstances.

(2) An extrajudicial sanction may be used only if

(*a*) it is part of a program of sanctions that may be authorized by the Attorney General or authorized by a person, or a member of a class of persons, designated by the lieutenant governor in council of the province;

(*b*) the person who is considering whether to use the extrajudicial sanction is satisfied that it would be appropriate, having regard to the needs of the young person and the interests of society;

(*c*) the young person, having been informed of the extrajudicial sanction, fully and freely consents to be subject to it;

(*d*) the young person has, before consenting to be subject to the extrajudicial sanction, been advised of his or her right to be represented by counsel and been given a reasonable opportunity to consult with counsel;

(*e*) the young person accepts responsibility for the act or omission that forms the basis of the offence that he or she is alleged to have committed;

(*f*) there is, in the opinion of the Attorney General, sufficient evidence to proceed with the prosecution of the offence; and

(*g*) the prosecution of the offence is not in any way barred at law.

(3) An extrajudicial sanction may not be used in respect of a young person who

(*a*) denies participation or involvement in the commission of the offence; or

(*b*) expresses the wish to have the charge dealt with by a youth justice court.

(4) Any admission, confession or statement accepting responsibility for a given act or omission that is made by a young person as a condition of being dealt with by extrajudicial measures is inadmissible in evidence against any young person in civil or criminal proceedings.

(5) The use of an extrajudicial sanction in respect of a young person alleged to have committed an offence is not a bar to judicial proceedings under this Act, but if a charge is laid against the young person in respect of the offence,

- **(*a*) the youth justice court shall dismiss the charge if it is satisfied on a balance of probabilities that the young person has totally complied with the terms and conditions of the extrajudicial sanction; and**
- **(*b*) the youth justice court may dismiss the charge if it is satisfied on a balance of probabilities that the young person has partially complied with the terms and conditions of the extrajudicial sanction and if, in the opinion of the court, prosecution of the charge would be unfair having regard to the circumstances and the young person's performance with respect to the extrajudicial sanction.**

(6) Subject to subsection (5) and section 24 (private prosecutions only with consent of Attorney General), nothing in this section shall be construed as preventing any person from laying an information or indictment, obtaining the issue or confirmation of any process or proceeding with the prosecution of any offence in accordance with law.

ANNOTATIONS

Note: The following case was decided under the *Young Offenders Act* but was thought to be of assistance in applying this Act.

The province was not required to establish a programme of alternative measures under the *Young Offenders Act*, and failure of the Attorney General to authorize alternative measures did not violate s. 15 of the *Charter of Rights and Freedoms*: *R. v. S. (S.)*, [1990] 2 S.C.R. 254, 57 C.C.C. (3d) 115.

NOTICE TO PARENT.

11. If a young person is dealt with by an extrajudicial sanction, the person who administers the program under which the sanction is used shall inform a parent of the young person of the sanction.

VICTIM'S RIGHT TO INFORMATION.

12. If a young person is dealt with by an extrajudicial sanction, a police officer, the Attorney General, the provincial director or any organization established by a province to provide assistance to victims shall, on request, inform the victim of the identity of the young person and how the offence has been dealt with.

PART 2 / ORGANIZATION OF YOUTH CRIMINAL JUSTICE SYSTEM

Youth Justice Court

DESIGNATION OF YOUTH JUSTICE COURT / **Deemed youth justice court / Deemed youth justice court / Court of record.**

13. (1) A youth justice court is any court that may be established or designated by or under an Act of the legislature of a province, or designated by the Governor in Council or the lieutenant governor in council of a province, as a youth justice court for the

purposes of this Act, and a youth justice court judge is a person who may be appointed or designated as a judge of the youth justice court or a judge sitting in a court established or designated as a youth justice court.

(2) When a young person elects to be tried by a judge without a jury, the judge shall be a judge as defined in section 552 of the *Criminal Code*, or if it is an offence set out in section 469 of that Act, the judge shall be a judge of the superior court of criminal jurisdiction in the province in which the election is made. In either case, the judge is deemed to be a youth justice court judge and the court is deemed to be a youth justice court for the purpose of the proceeding.

(3) When a young person elects or is deemed to have elected to be tried by a court composed of a judge and jury, the superior court of criminal jurisdiction in the province in which the election is made or deemed to have been made is deemed to be a youth justice court for the purpose of the proceeding, and the superior court judge is deemed to be a youth justice court judge.

(4) A youth justice court is a court of record.

ANNOTATIONS

Conflicting case law exists with respect to whether a provincial court of justice judge or a superior court of justice judge has jurisdiction over an application for judicial interim release where the young person is charged with a s. 469 offence. In *R. v. B. (J.)* (2012), 291 C.C.C. (3d) 43 (Ont. S.C.J.), it was held that, prior to the young person electing his or her mode of trial, the superior court of justice is not deemed a "youth justice court", and therefore lacks jurisdiction. Once an election is made, however, the superior court of justice has exclusive jurisdiction over bail. See also *R. v. W. (E.)* (2004), 188 C.C.C. (3d) 467 (Sask. C.A.). Yet, in other cases it has been held that the provincial court retains exclusive jurisdiction over bail, even in the case of s. 469 offences where the young person has chosen to be tried by a judge and jury: see e.g. *R. v. M. (T.R.)* (2013), 571 A.R. 121 (Q.B.).

EXCLUSIVE JURISDICTION OF YOUTH JUSTICE COURT / Orders / Prosecution prohibited / Continuation of proceedings / Young persons over the age of eighteen years / Powers of youth justice court judge / Powers of a judge of a superior court.

14. (1) Despite any other Act of Parliament but subject to the *Contraventions Act* and the *National Defence Act*, a youth justice court has exclusive jurisdiction in respect of any offence alleged to have been committed by a person while he or she was a young person, and that person shall be dealt with as provided in this Act.

(2) A youth justice court has jurisdiction to make orders against a young person under sections 83.3 (recognizance — terrorist activity), 810 (recognizance — fear of injury or damage), 810.01 (recognizance — fear of certain offences), 810.011 (recognizance — fear of terrorism offence), 810.02 (recognizance — fear of forced marriage or marriage under age of 16 years) and 810.2 (recognizance — fear of serious personal injury offence) of the *Criminal Code*. If the young person fails or refuses to enter into a recognizance referred to in any of those sections, the court may impose any one of the sanctions set out in subsection 42(2) (youth sentences) except that, in the case of an order under paragraph 42(2)(*n*) (custody and supervision order), it shall not exceed 30 days.

(3) Unless the Attorney General and the young person agree, no extrajudicial measures shall be taken or judicial proceedings commenced under this Act in respect of an offence after the end of the time limit set out in any other Act of Parliament or any regulation made under it for the institution of proceedings in respect of that offence.

(4) Extrajudicial measures taken or judicial proceedings commenced under this Act against a young person may be continued under this Act after the person attains the age of eighteen years.

(5) This Act applies to persons eighteen years old or older who are alleged to have committed an offence while a young person.

(6) For the purpose of carrying out the provisions of this Act, a youth justice court judge is a justice and a provincial court judge and has the jurisdiction and powers of a summary conviction court under the *Criminal Code*.

(7) A judge of a superior court of criminal jurisdiction, when deemed to be a youth justice court judge for the purpose of a proceeding, retains the jurisdiction and powers of a superior court of criminal jurisdiction. 2015, c. 20, ss. 32, 36(8); c. 29, s. 14.

ANNOTATIONS

Note: The following cases were decided under the *Young Offenders Act* but were thought to be of assistance in applying this Act.

Except for certain offences the age of the offender is not an element of the offence and need not be proved as part of the prosecution's case: *R. v. R. and C.* (1985), 23 C.C.C. (3d) 11 (B.C.C.A.); it was, however, open to the defence to raise the issue of the youth court's jurisdiction by providing proof that the accused was not a young offender: *R. v. L.* (1984), 17 C.C.C. (3d) 335 (Ont. Prov. Ct.).

Neither the age of the offender nor the fact that he was a "young person" need be set out in the information: *R. v. C. (S.A.)* (1989), 47 C.C.C. (3d) 76 (Alta. C.A.), leave to appeal to S.C.C. refused 50 C.C.C. (3d) vi.

A young offender who has been released on a recognizance but who breaches that recognizance after his 18th birthday is to be tried in adult court with breach of recognizance under the *Criminal Code*: *R. v. Merrick* (1987), 37 C.C.C. (3d) 285 (Man. Q.B.).

There was no jurisdiction to combine a youth court trial with a preliminary inquiry into indictable offences alleged to have been committed while the accused was an adult: *R. v. G. (A.M.)* (2000), 142 C.C.C. (3d) 29, 190 N.S.R. (2d) 196 (C.A.).

CONTEMPT AGAINST YOUTH JUSTICE COURT / Jurisdiction of youth justice court / Concurrent jurisdiction of youth justice court / Youth sentence — contempt.

15. (1) Every youth justice court has the same power, jurisdiction and authority to deal with and impose punishment for contempt against the court as may be exercised by the superior court of criminal jurisdiction of the province in which the court is situated.

(2) A youth justice court has jurisdiction in respect of every contempt of court committed by a young person against the youth justice court whether or not committed in the face of the court, and every contempt of court committed by a young person against any other court otherwise than in the face of that court.

(3) A youth justice court has jurisdiction in respect of every contempt of court committed by a young person against any other court in the face of that court and every contempt of court committed by an adult against the youth justice court in the face of the youth justice court, but nothing in this subsection affects the power, jurisdiction or authority of any other court to deal with or impose punishment for contempt of court.

(4) When a youth justice court or any other court finds a young person guilty of contempt of court, it may impose as a youth sentence any one of the sanctions set out in subsection 42(2) (youth sentences), or any number of them that are not inconsistent with each other, but no other sentence. Section 708 of *Criminal Code* applies in respect of adults (5) Section 708 (contempt) of the *Criminal Code* applies in respect of proceedings under this section in youth justice court against adults, with any modifications that the circumstances require.

ANNOTATIONS

Note: The following case was decided under the *Young Offenders Act* but was thought to be of assistance in applying this Act.

YOUTH

It was permissible to grant youth courts the power to determine contempt of court: *MacMillan Bloedel Ltd. v. Simpson*, [1995] 4 S.C.R. 725, 103 C.C.C. (3d) 225, 44 C.R. (4th) 277.

STATUS OF OFFENDER UNCERTAIN.

16. When a person is alleged to have committed an offence during a period that includes the date on which the person attains the age of eighteen years, the youth justice court has jurisdiction in respect of the offence and shall, after putting the person to their election under section 67 (adult sentence) if applicable, and on finding the person guilty of the offence,

(*a*) if it has been proven that the offence was committed before the person attained the age of eighteen years, impose a sentence under this Act;

(*b*) if it has been proven that the offence was committed after the person attained the age of eighteen years, impose any sentence that could be imposed under the *Criminal Code* or any other Act of Parliament on an adult who has been convicted of the same offence; and

(*c*) if it has not been proven that the offence was committed after the person attained the age of eighteen years, impose a sentence under this Act.

YOUTH JUSTICE COURT MAY MAKE RULES / Rules of court / Publication of rules.

17. (1) The youth justice court for a province may, subject to the approval of the lieutenant governor in council of the province, establish rules of court not inconsistent with this Act or any other Act of Parliament or with any regulations made under section 155 regulating proceedings within the jurisdiction of the youth justice court.

(2) Rules under subsection (1) may be made

(*a*) generally to regulate the duties of the officers of the youth justice court and any other matter considered expedient to attain the ends of justice and carry into effect the provisions of this Act;

(*b*) subject to any regulations made under paragraph 155(b), to regulate the practice and procedure in the youth justice court; and

(*c*) to prescribe forms to be used in the youth justice court if they are not otherwise provided for by or under this Act.

(3) Rules of court that are made under the authority of this section shall be published in the appropriate provincial gazette.

Youth Justice Committees

YOUTH JUSTICE COMMITTEES / Role of committee.

18. (1) The Attorney General of Canada or a province or any other minister that the lieutenant governor in council of the province may designate may establish one or more committees of citizens, to be known as youth justice committees, to assist in any aspect of the administration of this Act or in any programs or services for young persons.

(2) The functions of a youth justice committee may include the following:

(*a*) in the case of a young person alleged to have committed an offence,

(i) giving advice on the appropriate extrajudicial measure to be used in respect of the young person,

(ii) supporting any victim of the alleged offence by soliciting his or her concerns and facilitating the reconciliation of the victim and the young person,

(iii) ensuring that community support is available to the young person by arranging for the use of services from within the community, and enlisting

members of the community to provide short-term mentoring and supervision, and

(iv) when the young person is also being dealt with by a child protection agency or a community group, helping to coordinate the interaction of the agency or group with the youth criminal justice system;

(*b*) advising the federal and provincial governments on whether the provisions of this Act that grant rights to young persons, or provide for the protection of young persons, are being complied with;

(*c*) advising the federal and provincial governments on policies and procedures related to the youth criminal justice system;

(*d*) providing information to the public in respect of this Act and the youth criminal justice system;

(*e*) acting as a conference; and

(*f*) any other functions assigned by the person who establishes the committee.

Conferences

CONFERENCES MAY BE CONVENED / Mandate of a conference / Rules for conferences / Rules to apply.

19. (1) A youth justice court judge, the provincial director, a police officer, a justice of the peace, a prosecutor or a youth worker may convene or cause to be convened a conference for the purpose of making a decision required to be made under this Act.

(2) The mandate of a conference may be, among other things, to give advice on appropriate extrajudicial measures, conditions for judicial interim release, sentences, including the review of sentences, and reintegration plans.

(3) The Attorney General or any other minister designated by the lieutenant governor in council of a province may establish rules for the convening and conducting of conferences other than conferences convened or caused to be convened by a youth justice court judge or a justice of the peace.

(4) In provinces where rules are established under subsection (3), the conferences to which those rules apply must be convened and conducted in accordance with those rules.

Justices of the Peace

CERTAIN PROCEEDINGS MAY BE TAKEN BEFORE JUSTICES / Orders under section 810 of *Criminal Code*.

20. (1) Any proceeding that may be carried out before a justice under the *Criminal Code*, other than a plea, a trial or an adjudication, may be carried out before a justice in respect of an offence alleged to have been committed by a young person, and any process that may be issued by a justice under the *Criminal Code* may be issued by a justice in respect of an offence alleged to have been committed by a young person.

(2) A justice has jurisdiction to make an order under section 810 (recognizance — fear of injury or damage) of the *Criminal Code* in respect of a young person. If the young person fails or refuses to enter into a recognizance referred to in that section, the justice shall refer the matter to a youth justice court.

Clerks of the Court

POWERS OF CLERKS.

21. In addition to any powers conferred on a clerk of a court by the *Criminal Code*, a clerk of the youth justice court may exercise the powers ordinarily exercised by a clerk of a court, and, in particular, may

(*a*) administer oaths or solemn affirmations in all matters relating to the business of the youth justice court; and

(*b*) in the absence of a youth justice court judge, exercise all the powers of a youth justice court judge relating to adjournment.

Provincial Directors

POWERS, DUTIES AND FUNCTIONS OF PROVINCIAL DIRECTORS.

22. The provincial director may authorize any person to exercise the powers or perform the duties or functions of the provincial director under this Act, in which case the powers, duties or functions are deemed to have been exercised or performed by the provincial director.

PART 3 / JUDICIAL MEASURES

Consent to Prosecute

PRE-CHARGE SCREENING / Pre-charge screening program.

23. (1) The Attorney General may establish a program of pre-charge screening that sets out the circumstances in which the consent of the Attorney General must be obtained before a young person is charged with an offence.

(2) Any program of pre-charge screening of young persons that is established under an Act of the legislature of a province or by a directive of a provincial government, and that is in place before the coming into force of this section, is deemed to be a program of pre-charge screening for the purposes of subsection (1).

PRIVATE PROSECUTIONS.

24. No prosecutions may be conducted by a prosecutor other than the Attorney General without the consent of the Attorney General.

Right to Counsel

RIGHT TO COUNSEL / Arresting officer to advise young person of right to counsel / Justice, youth justice court or review board to advise young person of right to counsel / Trial, hearing or review before youth justice court or review board / Appointment of counsel / Release hearing before justice / Young person may be assisted by adult / Counsel independent of parents / Statement of right to counsel / Recovery of costs of counsel / Exception for persons over the age of twenty.

25. (1) A young person has the right to retain and instruct counsel without delay, and to exercise that right personally, at any stage of proceedings against the young person and before and during any consideration of whether, instead of starting or continuing judicial proceedings against the young person under this Act, to use an extrajudicial sanction to deal with the young person.

(2) Every young person who is arrested or detained shall, on being arrested or detained, be advised without delay by the arresting officer or the officer in charge, as the case may be, of the right to retain and instruct counsel, and be given an opportunity to obtain counsel.

(3) When a young person is not represented by counsel

(*a*) at a hearing at which it will be determined whether to release the young person or detain the young person in custody prior to sentencing,

(*b*) at a hearing held under section 71 (hearing — adult sentences),

(*c*) at trial,

(*d*) at any proceedings held under subsection 98(3) (continuation of custody), 103(1) (review by youth justice court), 104(1) (continuation of custody), 105(1) (conditional supervision) or 109(1) (review of decision),

(*e*) at a review of a youth sentence held before a youth justice court under this Act, or

(*f*) at a review of the level of custody under section 87,

the justice or youth justice court before which the hearing, trial or review is held, or the review board before which the review is held, shall advise the young person of the right to retain and instruct counsel and shall give the young person a reasonable opportunity to obtain counsel.

(4) When a young person at trial or at a hearing or review referred to in subsection (3) wishes to obtain counsel but is unable to do so, the youth justice court before which the hearing, trial or review is held or the review board before which the review is held

(*a*) shall, if there is a legal aid program or an assistance program available in the province where the hearing, trial or review is held, refer the young person to that program for the appointment of counsel; or

(*b*) if no legal aid program or assistance program is available or the young person is unable to obtain counsel through the program, may, and on the request of the young person shall, direct that the young person be represented by counsel.

(5) When a direction is made under paragraph (4)(*b*) in respect of a young person, the Attorney General shall appoint counsel, or cause counsel to be appointed, to represent the young person.

(6) When a young person, at a hearing referred to in paragraph (3)(*a*) that is held before a justice who is not a youth justice court judge, wishes to obtain counsel but is unable to do so, the justice shall

(*a*) if there is a legal aid program or an assistance program available in the province where the hearing is held,

(i) refer the young person to that program for the appointment of counsel, or

(ii) refer the matter to a youth justice court to be dealt with in accordance with paragraph (4)(*a*) or (*b*); or

(*b*) if no legal aid program or assistance program is available or the young person is unable to obtain counsel through the program, refer the matter without delay to a youth justice court to be dealt with in accordance with paragraph (4)(*b*).

(7) When a young person is not represented by counsel at trial or at a hearing or review referred to in subsection (3), the justice before whom or the youth justice court or review board before which the proceedings are held may, on the request of the young person, allow the young person to be assisted by an adult whom the justice, court or review board considers to be suitable.

(8) If it appears to a youth justice court judge or a justice that the interests of a young person and the interests of a parent are in conflict or that it would be in the best interests of the young person to be represented by his or her own counsel, the judge or justice shall ensure that the young person is represented by counsel independent of the parent.

YOUTH

(9) A statement that a young person has the right to be represented by counsel shall be included in

(*a*) any appearance notice or summons issued to the young person;

(*b*) any warrant to arrest the young person;

(*c*) any promise to appear given by the young person;

(*d*) any undertaking or recognizance entered into before an officer in charge by the young person;

(*e*) any notice given to the young person in relation to any proceedings held under subsection 98(3) (continuation of custody), 103(1) (review by youth justice court), 104(1) (continuation of custody), 105(1) (conditional supervision) or 109(1) (review of decision); or

(*f*) any notice of a review of a youth sentence given to the young person.

(10) Nothing in this Act prevents the lieutenant governor in council of a province or his or her delegate from establishing a program to authorize the recovery of the costs of a young person's counsel from the young person or the parents of the young person. The costs may be recovered only after the proceedings are completed and the time allowed for the taking of an appeal has expired or, if an appeal is taken, all proceedings in respect of the appeal have been completed.

(11) Subsections (4) to (9) do not apply to a person who is alleged to have committed an offence while a young person, if the person has attained the age of twenty years at the time of his or her first appearance before a youth justice court in respect of the offence; however, this does not restrict any rights that a person has under the law applicable to adults.

ANNOTATIONS

Note: Some of the following cases were decided under the *Young Offenders Act* but were thought to be of assistance in applying this Act.

Sections 25(3) and (4) of the *Youth Criminal Justice Act* make it clear that it is only when the youth is at a certain stage of proceedings and unable to obtain legal counsel through legal aid that the young person may apply for publicly funded counsel. Parliament has specifically provided that it is only when there is a hearing related to the custody of the young person, including sentencing, or when the young person is engaged in a trial that the youth may apply for publicly funded counsel: *R. v. S. (L.)* (2006), 215 C.C.C. (3d) 246 (Ont. C.A.).

The court had no discretion to decline to direct the employment of counsel where the young person had been unable to obtain legal aid. The youth court need only be satisfied that the young person wished to obtain counsel and had been unable to do so because legal aid was not available. An affidavit to that effect, or in the alternative a simple inquiry into those facts alone would suffice. The court had no discretion to determine whether a young person should be provided with a lawyer out of public funds. The issue of payment for those services was to be determined by provincial authorities: *R. v. C. (S.T.); R. v. T. (D.M.)* (1993), 81 C.C.C. (3d) 407, 140 A.R. 259 (Q.B.).

It was held that the mandatory provision of subsec. (4)(*b*) of the *Young Offenders Act*, which is worded similarly to subsec. (4)(*b*) of this section, is triggered only if the youth court judge was satisfied that the young person was legitimately unable to obtain counsel. The trial judge was required to conduct some independent inquiry to ensure that there was actually an inability to obtain counsel. The inquiry would include a consideration of the young person's ability to access the resources normally available to a youth, including having reasonable recourse to the financial resources of their parents: *R. v. M. (B.)* (1999), 139 C.C.C. (3d) 480, 28 C.R. (5th) 129, 180 D.L.R. (4th) 297 (Ont. C.A.), leave to appeal to S.C.C. refused 144 C.C.C. (3d) vi, 185 D.L.R. (4th) vii, 138 O.A.C. 198*n*. [However, now see subsec. (10) of this section.]

The power granted by subsec. (4)(*a*) of the *Young Offenders Act*, which is worded similarly to subsec. (4)(*a*) of this Act, did not include a power to direct legal aid to provide counsel for the young person. The purpose of the provision was merely to refer the young person to determine a possibility of his being represented by legal aid counsel, taking into account the normal criteria applied on such applications. It is only where no legal aid program is available, or the young person is unable to obtain counsel through such program, that the youth court judge, pursuant to subsec. (4)(*b*), may direct that the young person be represented by counsel. Where such direction is made, however, then subsec. (5) applied and the Attorney General of the province must appoint counsel or cause counsel to be appointed to represent the young person. Where an order is made, the process of giving notice of the order by forwarding it to the Attorney General should be initiated by the court: *R. v. F. (S.L.)* (1993), 81 C.C.C. (3d) 268, 106 Nfld. & P.E.I.R. 228 (Nfld. S.C.).

It is open to the court to conclude that a young person has been "unable" to obtain counsel through legal aid where the young person placed several unreturned calls to legal aid but did not submit a formal application: *R. v. P. (C.R.)* (2010), 89 W.C.B. (2d) 457, 2010 ONCJ 313 (C.J.).

Notices to Parents

NOTICE IN CASE OF ARREST OR DETENTION / Notice in other cases / Notice to parent in case of ticket / Notice to relative or other adult / Notice on direction of youth justice court judge or justice / Contents of notice / Notice of ticket under Contraventions Act / Service of notice / Proceedings not invalid / Exception / Where notice is not served / Exception for persons over the age of twenty.

26. (1) Subject to subsection (4), if a young person is arrested and detained in custody pending his or her appearance in court, the officer in charge at the time the young person is detained shall, as soon as possible, give or cause to be given to a parent of the young person, orally or in writing, notice of the arrest stating the place of detention and the reason for the arrest.

(2) Subject to subsection (4), if a summons or an appearance notice is issued in respect of a young person, the person who issued the summons or appearance notice, or, if a young person is released on giving a promise to appear or entering into an undertaking or recognizance, the officer in charge, shall, as soon as possible, give or cause to be given to a parent of the young person notice in writing of the summons, appearance notice, promise to appear, undertaking or recognizance.

(3) Subject to subsection (4), a person who serves a ticket under the *Contraventions Act* on a young person, other than a ticket served for a contravention relating to parking a vehicle, shall, as soon as possible, give or cause to be given notice in writing of the ticket to a parent of the young person.

(4) If the whereabouts of the parents of a young person are not known or it appears that no parent is available, a notice under this section may be given to an adult relative of the young person who is known to the young person and is likely to assist the young person or, if no such adult relative is available, to any other adult who is known to the young person and is likely to assist the young person and who the person giving the notice considers appropriate.

(5) If doubt exists as to the person to whom a notice under this section should be given, a youth justice court judge or, if a youth justice court judge is, having regard to the circumstances, not reasonably available, a justice may give directions as to the person to whom the notice should be given, and a notice given in accordance with those directions is sufficient notice for the purposes of this section.

(6) Any notice under this section shall, in addition to any other requirements under this section, include

(*a*) the name of the young person in respect of whom it is given;

YOUTH

(*b*) the charge against the young person and, except in the case of a notice of a ticket served under the *Contraventions Act*, the time and place of appearance; and

(*c*) a statement that the young person has the right to be represented by counsel.

(7) A notice under subsection (3) shall include a copy of the ticket.

(8) Subject to subsections (10) and (11), a notice under this section that is given in writing may be served personally or be sent by confirmed delivery service.

(9) Subject to subsections (10) and (11), failure to give a notice in accordance with this section does not affect the validity of proceedings under this Act.

(10) Failure to give a notice under subsection (2) in accordance with this section in any case renders invalid any subsequent proceedings under this Act relating to the case unless

(*a*) a parent of the young person attends court with the young person; or

(*b*) a youth justice court judge or a justice before whom proceedings are held against the young person

(i) adjourns the proceedings and orders that the notice be given in the manner and to the persons that the judge or justice directs, or

(ii) dispenses with the notice if the judge or justice is of the opinion that, having regard to the circumstances, the notice may be dispensed with.

(11) Where there has been a failure to give a notice under subsection (1) or (3) in accordance with this section and none of the persons to whom the notice may be given attends court with the young person, a youth justice court judge or a justice before whom proceedings are held against the young person may

(*a*) adjourn the proceedings and order that the notice be given in the manner and to the persons that the judge or justice directs; or

(*b*) dispense with the notice if the judge or justice is of the opinion that, having regard to the circumstances, the notice may be dispensed with.

(12) This section does not apply to a person who is alleged to have committed an offence while a young person, if the person has attained the age of twenty years at the time of his or her first appearance before a youth justice court in respect of the offence.

ANNOTATIONS

Note: The following case was decided under the *Young Offenders Act* but was thought to be of assistance in applying this Act.

A motorist arrested for impaired driving and taken to a police station to comply with a breathalyzer demand was not detained "pending his appearance in court" so as to require compliance with s. 9(1) of the *Young Offenders Act*, which is worded similarly to subsec. (1) of this Act, since, in the normal course following the administration of the test, the offender would be released either on an appearance notice or with the intention of issuing him a summons in which case subsec. (2) would apply: *R. v. T. (R.W.)* (1986), 28 C.C.C. (3d) 193, 73 N.S.R. (2d) 236, 41 M.V.R. 72 (C.A.).

ORDER REQUIRING ATTENDANCE OF PARENT / No order in ticket proceedings / Service of order / Failure to attend / Warrant to arrest parent.

27. (1) If a parent does not attend proceedings held before a youth justice court in respect of a young person, the court may, if in its opinion the presence of the parent is necessary or in the best interests of the young person, by order in writing require the parent to attend at any stage of the proceedings.

(2) Subsection (1) does not apply in proceedings commenced by filing a ticket under the *Contraventions Act*.

(3) A copy of the order shall be served by a peace officer or by a person designated by a youth justice court by delivering it personally to the parent to whom it is directed, unless the youth justice court authorizes service by confirmed delivery service.

(4) A parent who is ordered to attend a youth justice court under subsection (1) and who fails without reasonable excuse, the proof of which lies on the parent, to comply with the order

(*a*) is guilty of contempt of court;

(*b*) may be dealt with summarily by the court; and

(*c*) is liable to the punishment provided for in the *Criminal Code* for a summary conviction offence.

(5) If a parent who is ordered to attend a youth justice court under subsection (1) does not attend when required by the order or fails to remain in attendance as required and it is proved that a copy of the order was served on the parent, a youth justice court may issue a warrant to compel the attendance of the parent.

Detention before Sentencing

APPLICATION OF PART XVI OF CRIMINAL CODE.

28. Except to the extent that they are inconsistent with or excluded by this Act, the provisions of Part XVI (compelling appearance of an accused and interim release) of the *Criminal Code* apply to the detention and release of young persons under this Act.

ANNOTATIONS

Jurisdiction – A youth court judge has jurisdiction to conduct a 90-day review pursuant to s. 525 of the *Criminal Code*: *R. v. O. (A.J.)* (2004), 185 C.C.C. (3d) 120 (S.C.J.).

DETENTION AS SOCIAL MEASURE PROHIBITED / Justification for detention in custody / Onus.

29. (1) A youth justice court judge or a justice shall not detain a young person in custody prior to being sentenced as a substitute for appropriate child protection, mental health or other social measures.

(2) A youth justice court judge or a justice may order that a young person be detained in custody only if

(*a*) the young person has been charged with

(i) a serious offence, or

(ii) an offence other than a serious offence, if they have a history that indicates a pattern of either outstanding charges or findings of guilt;

(*b*) the judge or justice is satisfied, on a balance of probabilities,

(i) that there is a substantial likelihood that, before being dealt with according to law, the young person will not appear in court when required by law to do so,

(ii) that detention is necessary for the protection or safety of the public, including any victim of or witness to the offence, having regard to all the circumstances, including a substantial likelihood that the young person will, if released from custody, commit a serious offence, or

(iii) in the case where the young person has been charged with a serious offence and detention is not justified under subparagraph (i) or (ii), that there are exceptional circumstances that warrant detention and that detention is necessary to maintain confidence in the administration of justice, having regard to the principles set out in section 3 and to all the circumstances, including

YOUTH

(A) the apparent strength of the prosecution's case,
(B) the gravity of the offence,
(C) the circumstances surrounding the commission of the offence, including whether a firearm was used, and
(D) the fact that the young person is liable, on being found guilty, for a potentially lengthy custodial sentence; and

(*c*) the judge or justice is satisfied, on a balance of probabilities, that no condition or combination of conditions of release would, depending on the justification on which the judge or justice relies under paragraph (*b*),
(i) reduce, to a level below substantial, the likelihood that the young person would not appear in court when required by law to do so,
(ii) offer adequate protection to the public from the risk that the young person might otherwise present, or
(iii) maintain confidence in the administration of justice.

(3) The onus of satisfying the youth justice court judge or the justice as to the matters referred to in subsection (2) is on the Attorney General. 2012, c. 1, s. 169.

ANNOTATIONS

Bill C-10 (the *Safe Streets and Communities Act*, S.C. 2012) dramatically altered the law of judicial interim release in relation to young people. The former s. 29(2) of the *Youth Criminal Justice Act* had created a presumption against denial of judicial interim release pursuant to s. 515(10)(*b*) of the *Criminal Code*. Section 29(2) no longer contains this presumption and it creates a comprehensive scheme for judicial interim release: *R. v. B. (R.)* (January 11, 2013), Doc. 1313Y0002 (Nfld. Prov. Ct.).

DESIGNATED PLACE OF TEMPORARY DETENTION / Exception / Detention separate from adults / Transfer to adult facility / When young person is twenty years old or older / Transfer by provincial director / Exception relating to temporary detention / Authorization of provincial authority for detention / Determination by provincial authority of place of detention.

30. (1) Subject to subsection (7), a young person who is arrested and detained prior to being sentenced, or who is detained in accordance with a warrant issued under subsection 59(6) (compelling appearance for review of sentence), shall be detained in any place of temporary detention that may be designated by the lieutenant governor in council of the province or his or her delegate or in a place within a class of places so designated.

(2) A young person who is detained in a place of temporary detention under subsection (1) may, in the course of being transferred from that place to the court or from the court to that place, be held under the supervision and control of a peace officer.

(3) A young person referred to in subsection (1) shall be held separate and apart from any adult who is detained or held in custody unless a youth justice court judge or a justice is satisfied that, having regard to the best interests of the young person,
(*a*) the young person cannot, having regard to his or her own safety or the safety of others, be detained in a place of detention for young persons; or
(*b*) no place of detention for young persons is available within a reasonable distance.

(4) When a young person is detained under subsection (1), the youth justice court may, on application of the provincial director made at any time after the young person attains the age of eighteen years, after giving the young person an opportunity to be heard, authorize the provincial director to direct, despite subsection (3), that the young person be temporarily detained in a provincial correctional facility for adults, if the court considers it to be in the best interests of the young person or in the public interest.

(5) When a young person is twenty years old or older at the time his or her temporary detention under subsection (1) begins, the young person shall, despite subsection (3), be temporarily detained in a provincial correctional facility for adults.

(6) A young person who is detained in custody under subsection (1) may, during the period of detention, be transferred by the provincial director from one place of temporary detention to another.

(7) Subsections (1) and (3) do not apply in respect of any temporary restraint of a young person under the supervision and control of a peace officer after arrest, but a young person who is so restrained shall be transferred to a place of temporary detention referred to in subsection (1) as soon as is practicable, and in no case later than the first reasonable opportunity after the appearance of the young person before a youth justice court judge or a justice under section 503 of the *Criminal Code*.

(8) In any province for which the lieutenant governor in council has designated a person or a group of persons whose authorization is required, either in all circumstances or in circumstances specified by the lieutenant governor in council, before a young person who has been arrested may be detained in accordance with this section, no young person shall be so detained unless the authorization is obtained.

(9) In any province for which the lieutenant governor in council has designated a person or a group of persons who may determine the place where a young person who has been arrested may be detained in accordance with this section, no young person may be so detained in a place other than the one so determined.

ANNOTATIONS

A hearing under s. 30(4) of the *Youth Criminal Justice Act* is not a trial to determine guilt or innocence. The strict rules of evidence which govern a trial do not apply at such a hearing. The court needs as much information as possible about the young person in order to consider what is in his best interest or the public interest. The court should not be denied an opportunity to review relevant information before it including hearsay because of the application of strict rules of evidence. The court may authorize the provincial director to direct a transfer if the court considers the transfer is in the best interests of the young person or in the public interest: *F. (S.D.), Re* (2007), 415 A.R. 367 (Prov. Ct.).

PLACEMENT OF YOUNG PERSON IN CARE OF RESPONSIBLE PERSON / Inquiry as to availability of a responsible person / Condition of placement / Removing young person from care / Order / Effect of arrest.

31. (1) A young person who has been arrested may be placed in the care of a responsible person instead of being detained in custody if a youth justice court or a justice is satisfied that

(*a*) the young person would, but for this subsection, be detained in custody under section 515 (judicial interim release) of the *Criminal Code*;

(*b*) the person is willing and able to take care of and exercise control over the young person; and

(*c*) the young person is willing to be placed in the care of that person.

(2) If a young person would, in the absence of a responsible person, be detained in custody, the youth justice court or the justice shall inquire as to the availability of a responsible person and whether the young person is willing to be placed in that person's care.

(3) A young person shall not be placed in the care of a person under subsection (1) unless

(*a*) that person undertakes in writing to take care of and to be responsible for the attendance of the young person in court when required and to comply with any

YOUTH

other conditions that the youth justice court judge or the justice may specify; and

(*b*) the young person undertakes in writing to comply with the arrangement and to comply with any other conditions that the youth justice court judge or the justice may specify.

(4) A young person, a person in whose care a young person has been placed or any other person may, by application in writing to a youth justice court judge or a justice, apply for an order under subsection (5) if

(*a*) the person in whose care the young person has been placed is no longer willing or able to take care of or exercise control over the young person; or

(*b*) it is, for any other reason, no longer appropriate that the young person remain in the care of the person with whom he or she has been placed.

(5) When a youth justice court judge or a justice is satisfied that a young person should not remain in the custody of the person in whose care he or she was placed under subsection (1), the judge or justice shall

(*a*) make an order relieving the person and the young person of the obligations undertaken under subsection (3); and

(*b*) issue a warrant for the arrest of the young person.

(6) If a young person is arrested in accordance with a warrant issued under paragraph (5)(*b*), the young person shall be taken before a youth justice court judge or a justice without delay and dealt with under this section and sections 28 to 30.

ANNOTATIONS

This section is directed not only to considerations involving the primary and secondary grounds for detention but to tertiary ground cases as well. It contemplates a closer level of supervision than is expected of a surety and imposes a duty to take care of the young person through a written undertaking reinforced by penal consequences. These factors may in some cases meet the public confidence concerns of the tertiary ground and justify release: *R. v. D. (R.)* (2010), 273 C.C.C. (3d) 7 (Ont. C.A.).

Appearance

APPEARANCE BEFORE JUDGE OR JUSTICE / Waiver / Young person not represented by counsel / If youth justice court not satisfied / If youth justice court not satisfied.

32. (1) A young person against whom an information or indictment is laid must first appear before a youth justice court judge or a justice, and the judge or justice shall

(*a*) cause the information or indictment to be read to the young person;

(*b*) if the young person is not represented by counsel, inform the young person of the right to retain and instruct counsel; and

(*c*) if notified under subsection 64(2) (intention to seek adult sentence) or if section 16 (status of accused uncertain) applies, inform the young person that the youth justice court might, if the young person is found guilty, order that an adult sentence be imposed.

(*d*) [*Repealed*, 2012, c. 1, s. 170.]

(2) A young person may waive the requirements of subsection (1) if the young person is represented by counsel and counsel advises the court that the young person has been informed of that provision.

(3) When a young person is not represented by counsel, the youth justice court, before accepting a plea, shall

(*a*) satisfy itself that the young person understands the charge;

(*b*) if the young person is liable to an adult sentence, explain to the young person the consequences of being liable to an adult sentence and the procedure by which the young person may apply for an order that a youth sentence be imposed; and

(*c*) explain that the young person may plead guilty or not guilty to the charge or, if subsection 67(1) (election of court for trial — adult sentence) or (3) (election of court for trial in Nunavut — adult sentence) applies, explain that the young person may elect to be tried by a youth justice court judge without a jury and without having a preliminary inquiry, or to have a preliminary inquiry and be tried by a judge without a jury, or to have a preliminary inquiry and be tried by a court composed of a judge and jury and, in either of the latter two cases, a preliminary inquiry will only be conducted if requested by the young person or the prosecutor.

(4) If the youth justice court is not satisfied that a young person understands the charge, the court shall, unless the young person must be put to his or her election under subsection 67(1) (election of court for trial — adult sentence) or, with respect to Nunavut, subsection 67(3) (election of court for trial in Nunavut — adult sentence), enter a plea of not guilty on behalf of the young person and proceed with the trial in accordance with subsection 36(2) (young person pleads not guilty).

(5) If the youth justice court is not satisfied that a young person understands the matters set out in subsection (3), the court shall direct that the young person be represented by counsel. 2002, c. 13, s. 91(1)(*a*); 2012, c. 1, s. 170.

ANNOTATIONS

Note: The following cases were decided under the *Young Offenders Act* but were thought to be of assistance in applying this Act.

The jurisdiction of the court was dependent on strict compliance with the procedure in subsec. (1)(*a*) of the *Young Offenders Act*, which is worded similarly to subsec. (1)(*a*) of this section, and it was not sufficient that the substance of the information was stated to the young person who at the time of the first appearance was unrepresented by counsel and only assisted by duty counsel: *R. v. H.* (1985), 21 C.C.C. (3d) 396 (B.C.S.C.).

A waiver of the requirement under subsec. (1)(*a*) could be implied by conduct of counsel indicating that counsel was asking for an adjournment as a result of discussions with Crown counsel and the offender's parent: *R. v. J. (J.T.) (No. 2)* (1986), 28 C.C.C. (3d) 62, 42 Man. R. (2d) 271 (Q.B.).

Although the court had a residual discretion to have charges read aloud despite a waiver, the discretion should be exercised only in exceptional cases. Insisting that the charges be read in every first appearance despite a waiver would constitute an abuse of discretion: *R. v. A. (A.)* (2000), 150 C.C.C. (3d) 564 (Ont. S.C.J.). On appeal, 170 C.C.C. (3d) 449 (Ont. C.A.), the court agreed with the reasons of the application judge and added that circumstances where the court might require the charges be read, despite a waiver, include where the presiding officer was concerned about possible miscommunication between counsel and the young person or where it appeared to the court that a young person might fail to appreciate the seriousness of the charges or solemnity of the court process. The decision by the presiding officer to read the charges in the face of an express waiver was an exercise of discretion. As such, it must comply with the legal requirements that prevent an exercise of discretion from being arbitrary. The presiding officer must hear from both sides before coming to a decision but this does not include an inquisitorial approach that requires counsel to disclose a young person's reasons for requesting waiver. This is not to say that a young person's motive or reason is necessarily irrelevant, however, the court does not have the right to invade solicitor-client privilege. The decision, as an exercise of discretion, brings with it an obligation to give reasons. The reading of charges when a young person is represented

YOUTH

cannot be an invariable practice, as that would amount to an improper fetter on discretion. In particular, the reading of charges was not to be done as a form of punishment.

Release from or Detention in Custody

APPLICATION FOR RELEASE FROM OR DETENTION IN CUSTODY / Notice to prosecutor / Notice to young person / Waiver of notice / Application for review under section 520 or 521 of *Criminal Code* / Nunavut / No review / Interim release by youth justice court judge only / Review by court of appeal.

33. (1) If an order is made under section 515 (judicial interim release) of the *Criminal Code* in respect of a young person by a justice who is not a youth justice court judge, an application may, at any time after the order is made, be made to a youth justice court for the release from or detention in custody of the young person, as the case may be, and the youth justice court shall hear the matter as an original application.

(2) An application under subsection (1) for release from custody shall not be heard unless the young person has given the prosecutor at least two clear days notice in writing of the application.

(3) An application under subsection (1) for detention in custody shall not be heard unless the prosecutor has given the young person at least two clear days notice in writing of the application.

(4) The requirement for notice under subsection (2) or (3) may be waived by the prosecutor or by the young person or his or her counsel, as the case may be.

(5) An application under section 520 or 521 of the *Criminal Code* for a review of an order made in respect of a young person by a youth justice court judge who is a judge of a superior court shall be made to a judge of the court of appeal.

(6) Despite subsection (5), an application under section 520 or 521 of the *Criminal Code* for a review of an order made in respect of a young person by a youth justice court judge who is a judge of the Nunavut Court of Justice shall be made to a judge of that court.

(7) No application may be made under section 520 or 521 of the *Criminal Code* for a review of an order made in respect of a young person by a justice who is not a youth justice court judge.

(8) If a young person against whom proceedings have been taken under this Act is charged with an offence referred to in section 522 of the *Criminal Code*, a youth justice court judge, but no other court, judge or justice, may release the young person from custody under that section.

(9) A decision made by a youth justice court judge under subsection (8) may be reviewed in accordance with section 680 of the *Criminal Code* and that section applies, with any modifications that the circumstances require, to any decision so made.

ANNOTATIONS

Where a young person is charged with murder, a Provincial Court judge has exclusive jurisdiction over all proceedings, including bail, before the young person elects the mode of trial. Accordingly, the only right of review of that decision is by the Court of Appeal pursuant to subsec. (9): *R. v. W. (E.E.)* (2004), 188 C.C.C. (3d) 467 (Sask. C.A.).

Notwithstanding subsec. (9), a youth court judge retains jurisdiction to vary a condition of judicial interim release in respect of a s. 522 offence: *R. v. M. (N.)* (2010), 260 C.C.C. (3d) 391 (Man. Prov. Ct.).

A youth court judge has jurisdiction to conduct a 90-day review pursuant to s. 525 of the *Criminal Code*: *R. v. O. (A.J.)* (2004), 185 C.C.C. (3d) 120 (S.C.J.).

Medical and Psychological Reports

MEDICAL OR PSYCHOLOGICAL ASSESSMENT / Purpose of assessment / Custody for assessment / Presumption against custodial remand / Report of qualified person in writing / Application to vary assessment order if circumstances change / Disclosure of report / Cross-examination / Non-disclosure in certain cases / Non-disclosure in certain cases / Exception — interests of justice / Report to be part of record / Disclosure by qualified person/Definition of "qualified person".

34. (1) A youth justice court may, at any stage of proceedings against a young person, by order require that the young person be assessed by a qualified person who is required to report the results in writing to the court,

- **(*a*) with the consent of the young person and the prosecutor; or**
- **(*b*) on its own motion or on application of the young person or the prosecutor, if the court believes a medical, psychological or psychiatric report in respect of the young person is necessary for a purpose mentioned in paragraphs (2)(*a*) to (*g*) and**
  - **(i) the court has reasonable grounds to believe that the young person may be suffering from a physical or mental illness or disorder, a psychological disorder, an emotional disturbance, a learning disability or a mental disability,**
  - **(ii) the young person's history indicates a pattern of repeated findings of guilt under this Act or the *Young Offenders Act*, chapter Y-1 of the Revised Statutes of Canada, 1985, or**
  - **(iii) the young person is alleged to have committed a serious violent offence.**

(2) A youth justice court may make an order under subsection (1) in respect of a young person for the purpose of

- **(*a*) considering an application under section 33 (release from or detention in custody);**
- **(*b*) making its decision on an application heard under section 71 (hearing — adult sentences);**
- **(*c*) making or reviewing a youth sentence;**
- **(*d*) considering an application under subsection 104(1) (continuation of custody);**
- **(*e*) setting conditions under subsection 105(1) (conditional supervision);**
- **(*f*) making an order under subsection 109(2) (conditional supervision); or**
- **(*g*) authorizing disclosure under subsection 127(1) (information about a young person).**

(3) Subject to subsections (4) and (6), for the purpose of an assessment under this section, a youth justice court may remand a young person to any custody that it directs for a period not exceeding thirty days.

(4) A young person shall not be remanded in custody in accordance with an order made under subsection (1) unless

- **(*a*) the youth justice court is satisfied that**
  - **(i) on the evidence custody is necessary to conduct an assessment of the young person, or**
  - **(ii) on the evidence of a qualified person detention of the young person in custody is desirable to conduct the assessment of the young person, and the young person consents to custody; or**
- **(*b*) the young person is required to be detained in custody in respect of any other matter or by virtue of any provision of the *Criminal Code*.**

(5) For the purposes of paragraph (4)(*a*), if the prosecutor and the young person agree, evidence of a qualified person may be received in the form of a report in writing.

YOUTH

(6) A youth justice court may, at any time while an order made under subsection (1) is in force, on cause being shown, vary the terms and conditions specified in the order in any manner that the court considers appropriate in the circumstances.

(7) When a youth justice court receives a report made in respect of a young person under subsection (1),

- **(*a*) the court shall, subject to subsection (9), cause a copy of the report to be given to**
  - **(i) the young person,**
  - **(ii) any parent of the young person who is in attendance at the proceedings against the young person,**
  - **(iii) any counsel representing the young person, and**
  - **(iv) the prosecutor; and**
- **(*b*) the court may cause a copy of the report to be given to**
  - **(i) a parent of the young person who is not in attendance at the proceedings if the parent is, in the opinion of the court, taking an active interest in the proceedings, or**
  - **(ii) despite subsection 119(6) (restrictions respecting access to certain records), the provincial director, or the director of the provincial correctional facility for adults or the penitentiary at which the young person is serving a youth sentence, if, in the opinion of the court, withholding the report would jeopardize the safety of any person.**

(8) When a report is made in respect of a young person under subsection (1), the young person, his or her counsel or the adult assisting the young person under subsection 25(7) and the prosecutor shall, subject to subsection (9), on application to the youth justice court, be given an opportunity to cross-examine the person who made the report.

(9) A youth justice court shall withhold all or part of a report made in respect of a young person under subsection (1) from a private prosecutor, if disclosure of the report or part, in the opinion of the court, is not necessary for the prosecution of the case and might be prejudicial to the young person.

(10) A youth justice court shall withhold all or part of a report made in respect of a young person under subsection (1) from the young person, the young person's parents or a private prosecutor if the court is satisfied, on the basis of the report or evidence given in the absence of the young person, parents or private prosecutor by the person who made the report, that disclosure of the report or part would seriously impair the treatment or recovery of the young person, or would be likely to endanger the life or safety of, or result in serious psychological harm to, another person.

(11) Despite subsection (10), the youth justice court may release all or part of the report to the young person, the young person's parents or the private prosecutor if the court is of the opinion that the interests of justice make disclosure essential.

(12) A report made under subsection (1) forms part of the record of the case in respect of which it was requested.

(13) Despite any other provision of this Act, a qualified person who is of the opinion that a young person held in detention or committed to custody is likely to endanger his or her own life or safety or to endanger the life of, or cause bodily harm to, another person may immediately so advise any person who has the care and custody of the young person whether or not the same information is contained in a report made under subsection (1).

(14) In this section, "qualified person" means a person duly qualified by provincial law to practice medicine or psychiatry or to carry out psychological examinations or assessments, as the circumstances require, or, if no such law exists, a person who is, in the opinion of the youth justice court, so qualified, and includes a person or a member

of a class of persons designated by the lieutenant governor in council of a province or his or her delegate.

Referral to Child Welfare Agency

REFERRAL TO CHILD WELFARE AGENCY.

35. In addition to any order that it is authorized to make, a youth justice court may, at any stage of proceedings against a young person, refer the young person to a child welfare agency for assessment to determine whether the young person is in need of child welfare services.

Adjudication

WHEN YOUNG PERSON PLEADS GUILTY / When young person pleads not guilty.

36. (1) If a young person pleads guilty to an offence charged against the young person and the youth justice court is satisfied that the facts support the charge, the court shall find the young person guilty of the offence.

(2) If a young person charged with an offence pleads not guilty to the offence or pleads guilty but the youth justice court is not satisfied that the facts support the charge, the court shall proceed with the trial and shall, after considering the matter, find the young person guilty or not guilty or make an order dismissing the charge, as the case may be.

ANNOTATIONS

The inquiry and adjudication contemplated by s. 36(1) is additional to the procedural safeguards prescribed under s. 32. The object of s. 36 is to ensure that the young person is convicted and sentenced only for offences he or she has actually committed: *R. v. N. (H.J.P.)* (2010), 254 C.C.C. (3d) 460 (N.B.C.A.).

It is an error of law for a judge dealing with a young person's guilty plea to fail to consider and apply subsec. (1). The judge must consider the facts relating to each charge to determine if they actually support the charge in question. If that is not done, a finding of guilt cannot be made, notwithstanding that the requirements of s. 601(1.1) of the *Criminal Code* have been complied with: *R. v. L. (T.)* (2016), 343 C.C.C. (3d) 396 (Sask. C.A.); *R. v. N. (H.J.P.)*, *supra*.

Appeals

APPEALS / Appeals for contempt of court / Appeal / Appeals heard together / Appeals for summary conviction offences / Appeals where offences are tried jointly / Deemed election / If the youth justice court is a superior court / Nunavut / Appeal to the Supreme Court of Canada / No appeal from youth sentence on review.

37. (1) An appeal in respect of an indictable offence or an offence that the Attorney General elects to proceed with as an indictable offence lies under this Act in accordance with Part XXI (appeals — indictable offences) of the *Criminal Code*, which Part applies with any modifications that the circumstances require.

(2) A finding of guilt under section 15 for contempt of court or a sentence imposed in respect of the finding may be appealed as if the finding were a conviction or the sentence were a sentence in a prosecution by indictment.

(3) Section 10 of the *Criminal Code* applies if a person is convicted of contempt of court under subsection 27(4) (failure of parent to attend court).

YOUTH

(4) An order under subsection 72(1) or (1.1) (adult or youth sentence), 75(2) (lifting of ban on publication) or 76(1) (placement when subject to adult sentence) may be appealed as part of the sentence and, unless the court to which the appeal is taken otherwise orders, if more than one of these is appealed they must be part of the same appeal proceeding.

(5) An appeal in respect of an offence punishable on summary conviction or an offence that the Attorney General elects to proceed with as an offence punishable on summary conviction lies under this Act in accordance with Part XXVII (summary conviction offences) of the *Criminal Code*, which Part applies with any modifications that the circumstances require.

(6) An appeal in respect of one or more indictable offences and one or more summary conviction offences that are tried jointly or in respect of which youth sentences are jointly imposed lies under this Act in accordance with Part XXI (appeals — indictable offences) of the *Criminal Code*, which Part applies with any modifications that the circumstances require.

(7) For the purpose of appeals under this Act, if no election is made in respect of an offence that may be prosecuted by indictment or proceeded with by way of summary conviction, the Attorney General is deemed to have elected to proceed with the offence as an offence punishable on summary conviction.

(8) In any province where the youth justice court is a superior court, an appeal under subsection (5) shall be made to the court of appeal of the province.

(9) Despite subsection (8), if the Nunavut Court of Justice is acting as a youth justice court, an appeal under subsection (5) shall be made to a judge of the Nunavut Court of Appeal, and an appeal of that judge's decision shall be made to the Nunavut Court of Appeal in accordance with section 839 of the *Criminal Code*.

(10) No appeal lies under subsection (1) from a judgment of the court of appeal in respect of a finding of guilt or an order dismissing an information or indictment to the Supreme Court of Canada unless leave to appeal is granted by the Supreme Court of Canada.

(11) No appeal lies from a youth sentence under section 59 or any of sections 94 to 96. 2012, c. 1, s. 171.

ANNOTATIONS

Note: Some of the following cases were decided under the *Young Offenders Act* but was thought to be of assistance in applying this Act.

The Court of Appeal has the jurisdiction to determine whether a young person should remain at a youth facility or an adult facility pending appeal: *R. v. Estacio* (2008), 251 C.C.C. (3d) 257 (Alta. Q.B.).

Although the Crown did not make a formal election in respect of hybrid offences in youth court proceedings, s. 27(2), which is worded similarly to subsec. (7) of this section, had no application where the Crown could not have elected to proceed summarily as the information had been sworn beyond the six-month time limitation prescribed in s. 786(2): *R. v. B. (M.)* (1997), 119 C.C.C. (3d) 570 (B.C.C.A.).

Subsection (7) makes clear that, where the Crown made no election, it was deemed to have elected to proceed summarily for the purposes of an appeal. The right of appeal was therefore to the summary conviction appeal court: *R. v. F. (R.)* (2011), 288 C.C.C. (3d) 224 (N.S.C.A.).

No appeal lies from a sentence review conducted under s. 94. A decision under s. 94 regarding the level of custody is similarly not appealable: *R. v. Z. (A.A.)* (2013), 298 C.C.C. (3d) 59 (Man. C.A.); *R. v. C. (W.J.)* (2008), 230 C.C.C. (3d) 164 (Man. C.A.).

PART 4 / SENTENCING

Purpose and Principles

PURPOSE / Sentencing principles / Factors to be considered.

38. (1) The purpose of sentencing under section 42 (youth sentences) is to hold a young person accountable for an offence through the imposition of just sanctions that have meaningful consequences for the young person and that promote his or her rehabilitation and reintegration into society, thereby contributing to the long-term protection of the public.

(2) A youth justice court that imposes a youth sentence on a young person shall determine the sentence in accordance with the principles set out in section 3 and the following principles:

(*a*) the sentence must not result in a punishment that is greater than the punishment that would be appropriate for an adult who has been convicted of the same offence committed in similar circumstances;

(*b*) the sentence must be similar to the sentences imposed in the region on similar young persons found guilty of the same offence committed in similar circumstances;

(*c*) the sentence must be proportionate to the seriousness of the offence and the degree of responsibility of the young person for that offence;

(*d*) all available sanctions other than custody that are reasonable in the circumstances should be considered for all young persons, with particular attention to the circumstances of aboriginal young persons;

(*e*) subject to paragraph (*c*), the sentence must

(i) be the least restrictive sentence that is capable of achieving the purpose set out in subsection (1),

(ii) be the one that is most likely to rehabilitate the young person and reintegrate him or her into society, and

(iii) promote a sense of responsibility in the young person, and an acknowledgement of the harm done to victims and the community; and

(*f*) subject to paragraph (*c*), the sentence may have the following objectives:

(i) to denounce unlawful conduct, and

(ii) to deter the young person from committing offences.

(3) In determining a youth sentence, the youth justice court shall take into account

(*a*) the degree of participation by the young person in the commission of the offence;

(*b*) the harm done to victims and whether it was intentional or reasonably foreseeable;

(*c*) any reparation made by the young person to the victim or the community;

(*d*) the time spent in detention by the young person as a result of the offence;

(*e*) the previous findings of guilt of the young person; and

(*f*) any other aggravating and mitigating circumstances related to the young person or the offence that are relevant to the purpose and principles set out in this section. 2012, c. 1, s. 172.

YOUTH

ANNOTATIONS

General – The sentencing regime under the *Youth Criminal Justice Act* is completely different from that established under the *Criminal Code*: *R. v. Wobbes* (2008), 235 C.C.C. (3d) 561 (Ont. C.A.).

Section 38 applies only to youth sentences imposed under s. 42 of the *Youth Criminal Justice Act*, not to adult sentences imposed under s. 73: *R. v. Nguyen* (2008), 234 C.C.C. (3d) 67 (B.C.C.A.).

The principles of this Act continue to apply to offenders who have entered an adult facility to serve part or all of a youth sentence: *R. v. K. (C.)* (2008), 233 C.C.C. (3d) 194 (Ont. C.J.).

Subsection (1) – The sentencing provisions establishing numerous principles for approaching the sentencing of young persons, including accountability and proportionality, do not violate s. 15 of the Charter: *Quebec (Minister of Justice) v. Canada (Minister of Justice)* (2003), 175 C.C.C. (3d) 321 (Que. C.A.).

The long-term protection of the public is achieved by addressing the circumstances underlying the offending behaviour, by rehabilitation and reintegration of the young person and by holding the young person accountable through the imposition of meaningful sanctions related to the harm done: *R. v. P. (B.W.)*, [2006] 1 S.C.R. 941, 209 C.C.C. (3d) 97.

For a sentence to hold a young offender "accountable" in the sense of being meaningful it must reflect, as does a retributive sentence, the moral culpability of the offender, having regard to the intentional risk-taking of the offender, the consequential harm caused by the offender, and the normative character of the offender's conduct: *R. v. O. (A.)* (2007), 218 C.C.C. (3d) 409 (Ont. C.A.).

"Accountability" must be understood in part to be concerned with the severity of the sentence in relationship to the seriousness of the offence. Holding a young person "accountable" includes consideration of whether the sentence meets the goal of ensuring the person is rehabilitated and reintegrated into society. This notion of accountability includes consideration of the seriousness of the offence and requires a sentencing judge to balance and match the rehabilitative needs of the young person with the other purposes and principles of sentencing: *R. v. S. (S.N.J.)* (2013), 305 C.C.C. (3d) 160 (B.C.C.A.).

Subsection (2)(*c*) – The proportionality principle contained in subsec. (2)(*c*) does not override the general principles set out in ss. 3 and 4 of the Act which focus on rehabilitation and reintegration into the community: *Quebec (Minister of Justice) v. Canada (Minister of Justice), supra*.

Subsection (2)(*f*) – In *R. v. P. (B.W.)*, [2006] 1 S.C.R. 941, 209 C.C.C. (3d) 97, the Supreme Court of Canada considered the applicability of the principles of general deterrence and specific deterrence to the sentencing of young persons. The court held that general deterrence is not a principle of youth sentencing. The court also held that specific deterrence had been excluded as a factor in sentencing a young person. However, in 2012 subsec. (2)(*f*) was added as part of Bill C-10 (the *Safe Streets and Communities Act*, S.C. 2012), permitting consideration of the objectives of denouncing unlawful conduct and deterring the young person from committing offences.

Subsection (3)(*d*) – In view of subsec. (3)(*d*), the trial judge is required to give credit to the accused for pre-sentence custody. However, the trial judge has a residual discretion, within a certain range, to assess the quantum of credit to be given and may decline to give full credit where to do so would virtually exhaust the custodial term available and result in a sentence contrary to the purposes of the Act. While a 1.5 credit may be the starting point for crediting pre-sentence custody, other considerations may affect the appropriate credit, such as the conditions of the offender's pre-sentence custody, the reasons for that detention, the length of the detention, the reasons for any delay in reaching trial or sentencing, and the offender's need for further custody or community service to meet the purposes of this Act: *R. v. B. (T.)* (2006), 206 C.C.C. (3d) 405 (Ont. C.A.).

In *R. v. W. (M.)* (2017), 346 C.C.C. (3d) 319, the Ontario Court of Appeal held that, although a youth court judge must consider pre-sentence custody in sentencing an offender, the judge's treatment of the pre-sentence custody is discretionary. While s. 38(3)(*d*) of the *Youth Criminal Justice Act* requires the youth court judge to take detention "into account", the judge is not required to actually deduct pre-sentence custody when crafting an appropriate sentence. Whether and to what extent credit is given for pre-sentence custody against a youth sentence is within a youth court judge's discretion, particularly in the context of a Crown application to sentence a youth as an adult. See also *R. v. T. (D.D.)* (2010), 265 C.C.C. (3d) 49 (Alta. C.A.), leave to appeal to S.C.C. refused [2011] 2 S.C.R. x; *R. v. J. (R.R.)* (2009), 250 C.C.C. (3d) 3 (B.C.C.A.); *R. v. P. (N.W.)* (2008), 235 C.C.C. (3d) 125 (Man. C.A.); *R. v. W. (D.)* (2008), 79 W.C.B. (2d) 80, [2008] O.J. No. 1356 (C.A.); *R. v. B. (M.)* (2016), 342 C.C.C. (3d) 34 (Ont. C.A.).

When a youth court judge determines that pre-sentence detention should not be credited against the length of the sentence, the youth court judge is required to articulate reasons for this: *R. v. Z. (A.A.)* (2013), 298 C.C.C. (3d) 59 (Man. C.A.).

The trial judge did not err in considering time spent in custody, where the accused was detained having violated a community supervision order, notwithstanding that the detention was not as a result of the commission of the offences for which he was being sentenced. It was appropriate to consider that the accused did not complete his community supervision order, but that time in detention was more onerous than time spent on community supervision: *R. v. L. (K.E.J.)* (2006), 213 C.C.C. (3d) 326, 208 Man. R. (2d) 185 (C.A.).

COMMITTAL TO CUSTODY / Alternatives to custody / Factors to be considered / Imposition of same sentence / Custody as social measure prohibited / Pre-sentence report / Report dispensed with / Length of custody / Reasons.

39. (1) A youth justice court shall not commit a young person to custody under section 42 (youth sentences) unless

(*a*) the young person has committed a violent offence;

(*b*) the young person has failed to comply with non-custodial sentences;

(*c*) the young person has committed an indictable offence for which an adult would be liable to imprisonment for a term of more than two years and has a history that indicates a pattern of either extrajudicial sanctions or of findings of guilt or of both under this Act or the *Young Offenders Act*, chapter Y-1 of the Revised Statutes of Canada, 1985; or

(*d*) in exceptional cases where the young person has committed an indictable offence, the aggravating circumstances of the offence are such that the imposition of a non-custodial sentence would be inconsistent with the purpose and principles set out in section 38.

(2) If any of paragraphs (1)(*a*) to (*c*) apply, a youth justice court shall not impose a custodial sentence under section 42 (youth sentences) unless the court has considered all alternatives to custody raised at the sentencing hearing that are reasonable in the circumstances, and determined that there is not a reasonable alternative, or combination of alternatives, that is in accordance with the purpose and principles set out in section 38.

(3) In determining whether there is a reasonable alternative to custody, a youth justice court shall consider submissions relating to

(*a*) the alternatives to custody that are available;

(*b*) the likelihood that the young person will comply with a non-custodial sentence, taking into account his or her compliance with previous non-custodial sentences; and

(*c*) the alternatives to custody that have been used in respect of young persons for similar offences committed in similar circumstances.

(4) The previous imposition of a particular non-custodial sentence on a young person does not preclude a youth justice court from imposing the same or any other non-custodial sentence for another offence.

(5) A youth justice court shall not use custody as a substitute for appropriate child protection, mental health or other social measures.

(6) Before imposing a custodial sentence under section 42 (youth sentences), a youth justice court shall consider a pre-sentence report and any sentencing proposal made by the young person or his or her counsel.

(7) A youth justice court may, with the consent of the prosecutor and the young person or his or her counsel, dispense with a pre-sentence report if the court is satisfied that the report is not necessary.

(8) In determining the length of a youth sentence that includes a custodial portion, a youth justice court shall be guided by the purpose and principles set out in section 38, and shall not take into consideration the fact that the supervision portion of the sentence may not be served in custody and that the sentence may be reviewed by the court under section 94.

(9) If a youth justice court imposes a youth sentence that includes a custodial portion, the court shall state the reasons why it has determined that a non-custodial sentence is not adequate to achieve the purpose set out in subsection 38(1), including, if applicable, the reasons why the case is an exceptional case under paragraph (1)(*d*). 2012, c. 1, s. 173.

ANNOTATIONS

Subsection (1) – Subsection (1) does not require categorization of the offence under one of the four specified categories before rejecting a custodial option. Rather, it prohibits a custodial option unless the offence falls within one of those four categories. It was therefore permissible for the sentencing judge to conclude that it was unnecessary for him to consider whether the offence fell within either paras. (*a*) or (*d*) of subsec. (1): *R. v. O. (K.)* (2012), 310 C.C.C. (3d) 64 (N.L.C.A.).

Subsection (1)(*a*) (violent offences) – Bill C-10 (the *Safe Streets and Communities Act*, S.C. 2012) added a definition of "violent offence" in s. 2(1) of the Act. *Per* this definition, "violent offence" means "(a) an offence committed by a young person that includes as an element the causing of bodily harm; (b) an attempt or a threat to commit an offence referred to in paragraph (a); or (c) an offence in the commission of which a young person endangers the life or safety of another person by creating a substantial likelihood of causing bodily harm."

The definition of "violent offence" in ss. 2(1)(*a*) and (*b*) are a reflection of the Supreme Court of Canada's decision in *R. v. D. (C.)*, [2005] 3 S.C.R. 668, 203 C.C.C. (3d) 449. Cases decided following that decision are therefore relevant to a determination of whether an offence constitutes a "violent offence". Section 2(1)(*c*), however, imports a broader definition. The term "bodily harm" is not defined in the *Youth Criminal Justice Act*, but is defined in s. 2 of the *Criminal Code* as meaning "any hurt or injury to a person that interferes with the health or comfort of the person and that is more than merely transient or trifling in nature".

A custodial sentence may be imposed on a young person who has committed a violent offence as a party pursuant to s. 21 of the *Criminal Code*: *R. v. N. (H.T.)* (2006), 209 C.C.C. (3d) 318 (B.C.C.A.).

Subsection (1)(*b*) (failure to comply) – A sentence that includes both a custodial and non-custodial penalty constitutes a non-custodial penalty within the meaning of subsec. (1)(*b*): *R. v. W. (J.B.)* (2004), 186 C.C.C. (3d) 14 (Ont. S.C.J.).

To fall within this subsection, the Crown must prove noncompliance with multiple prior non-custodial sentences; the word "sentences" includes the plural form only: *R. v. D. (R.J.)* (2012), 321 N.S.R. (2d) 1 (S.C.). However, in *R. v. D. (R.J.)* (2011), 279 C.C.C. (3d) 386 (N.S. Prov. Ct.), the court departed from earlier authorities in other provinces and held that multiple breaches of a single probation order can justify custody under subsec. (1)(*b*) (vard 321 N.S.R. (2d) 1 (S.C.)).

Subsection (1)(*b*) does not permit the imposition of a custodial sentence for the breach of a custodial sentence: *R. v. H. (A.D.)* (2004), 190 C.C.C. (3d) 129 (B.C.C.A.).

"Sentences" in subsec. (1)(*b*) includes dispositions under the *Young Offenders Act*. Accordingly, this provision applies to breaches of non-custodial sentences under this Act, as well as breaches of non-custodial sentences under the *Young Offenders Act*: *R. v. A. (E.)* (2003), 178 C.C.C. (3d) 568, 66 O.R. (3d) 265 (C.J.).

Subsection (1)(*c*) (indictable offence and pattern of misbehaviour) – "History" in subsec. (1)(*c*) is limited to findings of guilt that were entered prior to the commission of the offence for which the young person was being sentenced. The relevant period does not extend to the sentencing date. The threshold for demonstrating a "pattern" of findings of guilt is at least three prior convictions unless the sentencing court finds that the offences are so similar that a pattern of findings of guilt can be found in only two prior convictions. The prior findings of guilt do not need to be related to similar or indictable offences, although similarity may be relevant to whether a pattern in fact exists. The threshold is a finding of a pattern of findings of guilt, not a pattern of findings of guilt for the same type of offence: *R. v. C. (S.A.)* (2008), 233 C.C.C. (3d) 417 (S.C.C.).

However, in 2012 this provision was amended to allow consideration not just of prior findings of guilt, but also prior uses of extrajudicial sanctions against the young person in determining whether a custodial term is warranted.

Subsection (1)(*d*) (indictable offence in aggravating circumstances – Subsection (1)(*d*) can be invoked only because of the circumstances of the offence, not the circumstances of the offender, or the offender's history. Exceptional cases are those where any order, other than custody, would undermine the purposes and principles of sentencing set out in s. 38, or where applying the general rule against a custodial disposition would undermine the purpose of this Act. Exceptional cases are limited to the clearest of cases where a custodial disposition is obviously the only disposition that can be justified, as where the circumstances are so shocking as to threaten widely shared community values: *R. v. W. (R.E.)* (2006), 205 C.C.C. (3d) 183, 36 C.R. (6th) 134 (Ont. C.A.).

In *R. v. T. (S.)* (2009), 461 W.A.C. 90 (B.C.C.A.), the British Columbia Court of Appeal did not interpret the Ontario Court of Appeal's holding in *R. v. W. (R.E.)*, *supra*, to mean that the circumstances of the offender are to be completely ignored under s. 39(1)(*d*). In its view, under this subsection, the aggravating circumstances of the offence render a non-custodial sentence inconsistent with the purpose and principles of s. 38 because factors such as proportionality, responsibility and rehabilitation demand a custodial sentence. That determination will necessarily involve an assessment of the young person's circumstances and background. However, in the final analysis, the aggravating circumstances ultimately outweigh those "other relevant considerations" and, in that sense, render them irrelevant in the resulting imposition of a custodial sentence.

Subsection (8) – The purpose of s. 39(8) is to make it clear that youth court judges should not impose a more severe sentence than might be called for on accountability principles in anticipation that the sentence could be reduced at a later time (under s. 94) if circumstances for the young person improved: *R. v. Z. (A.A.)* (2013), 298 C.C.C. (3d) 59 (Man. C.A.).

Subsection (9) – The requirement for reasons under subsec. (9) may be satisfied provided the trial judge's analysis demonstrates that he turned his or her attention to meeting the purposes of the Act: *R. v. H. (A.)* (2011), 276 C.C.C. (3d) 423 (Nfld. & Lab. C.A.).

Pre-sentence Report

PRE-SENTENCE REPORT / Contents of report / Oral report with leave / Report forms part of record / Copies of pre-sentence report / Cross-examination / Report may be withheld from private prosecutor / Report disclosed to other persons / Disclosure by the provincial director / Inadmissibility of statements.

40. (1) Before imposing sentence on a young person found guilty of an offence, a youth justice court

(*a*) shall, if it is required under this Act to consider a pre-sentence report before making an order or a sentence in respect of a young person, and

(*b*) may, if it considers it advisable,require the provincial director to cause to be prepared a pre-sentence report in respect of the young person and to submit the report to the court.

(2) A pre-sentence report made in respect of a young person shall, subject to subsection (3), be in writing and shall include the following, to the extent that it is relevant to the purpose and principles of sentencing set out in section 38 and to the restrictions on custody set out in section 39:

(*a*) the results of an interview with the young person and, if reasonably possible, the parents of the young person and, if appropriate and reasonably possible, members of the young person's extended family;

(*b*) the results of an interview with the victim in the case, if applicable and reasonably possible;

(*c*) the recommendations resulting from any conference referred to in section 41;

(*d*) any information that is applicable to the case, including

(i) the age, maturity, character, behaviour and attitude of the young person and his or her willingness to make amends,

(ii) any plans put forward by the young person to change his or her conduct or to participate in activities or undertake measures to improve himself or herself,

(iii) subject to subsection 119(2) (period of access to records), the history of previous findings of delinquency under the *Juvenile Delinquents Act*, chapter J-3 of the Revised Statutes of Canada, 1970, or previous findings of guilt for offences under the *Young Offenders Act*, chapter Y-1 of the Revised Statutes of Canada, 1985, or under this or any other Act of Parliament or any regulation made under it, the history of community or other services rendered to the young person with respect to those findings and the response of the young person to previous sentences or dispositions and to services rendered to him or her,

(iv) subject to subsection 119(2) (period of access to records), the history of alternative measures under the *Young Offenders Act*, chapter Y-1 of the Revised Statutes of Canada, 1985, or extrajudicial sanctions used to deal with the young person and the response of the young person to those measures or sanctions,

(v) the availability and appropriateness of community services and facilities for young persons and the willingness of the young person to avail himself or herself of those services or facilities,

(vi) the relationship between the young person and the young person's parents and the degree of control and influence of the parents over the young person and, if appropriate and reasonably possible, the relationship between the young person and the young person's extended family and the degree of control and influence of the young person's extended family over the young person, and

(vii) the school attendance and performance record and the employment record of the young person;

(*e*) any information that may assist the court in determining under subsection 39(2) whether there is an alternative to custody; and

(*f*) any information that the provincial director considers relevant, including any recommendation that the provincial director considers appropriate.

(3) If a pre-sentence report cannot reasonably be committed to writing, it may, with leave of the youth justice court, be submitted orally in court.

(4) A pre-sentence report shall form part of the record of the case in respect of which it was requested.

(5) If a pre-sentence report made in respect of a young person is submitted to a youth justice court in writing, the court

(*a*) shall, subject to subsection (7), cause a copy of the report to be given to

(i) the young person,

(ii) any parent of the young person who is in attendance at the proceedings against the young person,

(iii) any counsel representing the young person, and

(iv) the prosecutor; and

(*b*) may cause a copy of the report to be given to a parent of the young person who is not in attendance at the proceedings if the parent is, in the opinion of the court, taking an active interest in the proceedings.

(6) If a pre-sentence report made in respect of a young person is submitted to a youth justice court, the young person, his or her counsel or the adult assisting the young person under subsection 25(7) and the prosecutor shall, subject to subsection (7), on application to the court, be given the opportunity to cross-examine the person who made the report.

(7) If a pre-sentence report made in respect of a young person is submitted to a youth justice court, the court may, when the prosecutor is a private prosecutor and disclosure of all or part of the report to the prosecutor might, in the opinion of the court, be prejudicial to the young person and is not, in the opinion of the court, necessary for the prosecution of the case against the young person,

(*a*) withhold the report or part from the prosecutor, if the report is submitted in writing; or

(*b*) exclude the prosecutor from the court during the submission of the report or part, if the report is submitted orally in court.

(8) If a pre-sentence report made in respect of a young person is submitted to a youth justice court, the court

(*a*) shall, on request, cause a copy or a transcript of the report to be supplied to

(i) any court that is dealing with matters relating to the young person, and

(ii) any youth worker to whom the young person's case has been assigned; and

(*b*) may, on request, cause a copy or a transcript of all or part of the report to be supplied to any person not otherwise authorized under this section to receive a copy or a transcript of the report if, in the opinion of the court, the person has a valid interest in the proceedings.

(9) A provincial director who submits a pre-sentence report made in respect of a young person to a youth justice court may make all or part of the report available to any person in whose custody or under whose supervision the young person is placed or to any other person who is directly assisting in the care or treatment of the young person.

(10) No statement made by a young person in the course of the preparation of a pre-sentence report in respect of the young person is admissible in evidence against any young person in civil or criminal proceedings except those under section 42 (youth

YOUTH

sentences), 59 (review of non-custodial sentence) or 71 (hearing — adult sentences) or any of sections 94 to 96 (reviews and other proceedings related to custodial sentences).

ANNOTATIONS

There is no jurisdiction for a judge to order what information is to be included and excluded in a pre-sentence report. A provincial director is charged with this responsibility, although the trial judge always has the discretion to determine which evidence to rely on in the sentencing proceedings. Subsection (2)(*f*) is sufficiently broad to allow the provincial director to obtain a risk assessment without the informed consent of the young person: *R. v. Q. (K.)* (2007), 229 C.C.C. (3d) 356 (Sask. C.A.).

Youth Sentences

RECOMMENDATION OF CONFERENCE.

41. When a youth justice court finds a young person guilty of an offence, the court may convene or cause to be convened a conference under section 19 for recommendations to the court on an appropriate youth sentence.

CONSIDERATIONS AS TO YOUTH SENTENCE / Youth sentence / Agreement of provincial director / Youth justice court statement / Deferred custody and supervision order / Application of sections 106 to 109 / Intensive rehabilitative custody and supervision order / Safeguard of rights / Determination by court / Appeals / Inconsistency / Coming into force of youth sentence / Consecutive youth sentences / Duration of youth sentence for a single offence / Duration of youth sentence for different offences / Duration of youth sentences made at different times / Sentence continues when adult.

42. (1) A youth justice court shall, before imposing a youth sentence, consider any recommendations submitted under section 41, any pre-sentence report, any representations made by the parties to the proceedings or their counsel or agents and by the parents of the young person, and any other relevant information before the court.

(2) When a youth justice court finds a young person guilty of an offence and is imposing a youth sentence, the court shall, subject to this section, impose any one of the following sanctions or any number of them that are not inconsistent with each other and, if the offence is first degree murder or second degree murder within the meaning of section 231 of the *Criminal Code*, the court shall impose a sanction set out in paragraph (*q*) or subparagraph (*r*)(ii) or (iii) and may impose any other of the sanctions set out in this subsection that the court considers appropriate:

(*a*) reprimand the young person;

(*b*) by order direct that the young person be discharged absolutely, if the court considers it to be in the best interests of the young person and not contrary to the public interest;

(*c*) by order direct that the young person be discharged on any conditions that the court considers appropriate and may require the young person to report to and be supervised by the provincial director;

(*d*) impose on the young person a fine not exceeding $1,000 to be paid at the time and on the terms that the court may fix;

(*e*) order the young person to pay to any other person at the times and on the terms that the court may fix an amount by way of compensation for loss of or damage to property or for loss of income or support, or an amount for, in the Province of Quebec, pre-trial pecuniary loss or, in any other province, special damages,

for personal injury arising from the commission of the offence if the value is readily ascertainable, but no order shall be made for other damages in the Province of Quebec or for general damages in any other province;

(*f*) order the young person to make restitution to any other person of any property obtained by the young person as a result of the commission of the offence within the time that the court may fix, if the property is owned by the other person or was, at the time of the offence, in his or her lawful possession;

(*g*) if property obtained as a result of the commission of the offence has been sold to an innocent purchaser, where restitution of the property to its owner or any other person has been made or ordered, order the young person to pay the purchaser, at the time and on the terms that the court may fix, an amount not exceeding the amount paid by the purchaser for the property;

(*h*) subject to section 54, order the young person to compensate any person in kind or by way of personal services at the time and on the terms that the court may fix for any loss, damage or injury suffered by that person in respect of which an order may be made under paragraph (*e*) or (*g*);

(*i*) subject to section 54, order the young person to perform a community service at the time and on the terms that the court may fix, and to report to and be supervised by the provincial director or a person designated by the youth justice court;

(*j*) subject to section 51 (mandatory prohibition order), make any order of prohibition, seizure or forfeiture that may be imposed under any Act of Parliament or any regulation made under it if an accused is found guilty or convicted of that offence, other than an order under section 161 of the *Criminal Code*;

(*k*) place the young person on probation in accordance with sections 55 and 56 (conditions and other matters related to probation orders) for a specified period not exceeding two years;

(*l*) subject to subsection (3) (agreement of provincial director), order the young person into an intensive support and supervision program approved by the provincial director;

(*m*) subject to subsection (3) (agreement of provincial director) and section 54, order the young person to attend a non-residential program approved by the provincial director, at the times and on the terms that the court may fix, for a maximum of two hundred and forty hours, over a period not exceeding six months;

(*n*) make a custody and supervision order with respect to the young person, ordering that a period be served in custody and that a second period — which is one half as long as the first — be served, subject to sections 97 (conditions to be included) and 98 (continuation of custody), under supervision in the community subject to conditions, the total of the periods not to exceed two years from the date of the coming into force of the order or, if the young person is found guilty of an offence for which the punishment provided by the *Criminal Code* or any other Act of Parliament is imprisonment for life, three years from the date of coming into force of the order;

(*o*) in the case of an offence set out in section 239 (attempt to commit murder), 232, 234 or 236 (manslaughter) or 273 (aggravated sexual assault) of the *Criminal Code*, make a custody and supervision order in respect of the young person for a specified period not exceeding three years from the date of committal that orders the young person to be committed into a continuous period of custody for the first portion of the sentence and, subject to subsection 104(1) (continuation of custody), to serve the remainder of the sentence under conditional supervision in the community in accordance with section 105;

YOUTH

(*p*) subject to subsection (5), make a deferred custody and supervision order that is for a specified period not exceeding six months, subject to the conditions set out in subsection 105(2), and to any conditions set out in subsection 105(3) that the court considers appropriate;

(*q*) order the young person to serve a sentence not to exceed

(i) in the case of first degree murder, ten years comprised of

(A) a committal to custody, to be served continuously, for a period that must not, subject to subsection 104(1) (continuation of custody), exceed six years from the date of committal, and

(B) a placement under conditional supervision to be served in the community in accordance with section 105, and

(ii) in the case of second degree murder, seven years comprised of

(A) a committal to custody, to be served continuously, for a period that must not, subject to subsection 104(1) (continuation of custody), exceed four years from the date of committal, and

(B) a placement under conditional supervision to be served in the community in accordance with section 105;

(*r*) subject to subsection (7), make an intensive rehabilitative custody and supervision order in respect of the young person

(i) that is for a specified period that must not exceed

(A) two years from the date of committal, or

(B) if the young person is found guilty of an offence for which the punishment provided by the *Criminal Code* or any other Act of Parliament is imprisonment for life, three years from the date of committal,

and that orders the young person to be committed into a continuous period of intensive rehabilitative custody for the first portion of the sentence and, subject to subsection 104(1) (continuation of custody), to serve the remainder under conditional supervision in the community in accordance with section 105,

(ii) that is for a specified period that must not exceed, in the case of first degree murder, ten years from the date of committal, comprising

(A) a committal to intensive rehabilitative custody, to be served continuously, for a period that must not exceed six years from the date of committal, and

(B) subject to subsection 104(1) (continuation of custody), a placement under conditional supervision to be served in the community in accordance with section 105, and

(iii) that is for a specified period that must not exceed, in the case of second degree murder, seven years from the date of committal, comprising

(A) a committal to intensive rehabilitative custody, to be served continuously, for a period that must not exceed four years from the date of committal, and

(B) subject to subsection 104(1) (continuation of custody), a placement under conditional supervision to be served in the community in accordance with section 105; and

(*s*) impose on the young person any other reasonable and ancillary conditions that the court considers advisable and in the best interests of the young person and the public.

(3) A youth justice court may make an order under paragraph (2)(*l*) or (*m*) only if the provincial director has determined that a program to enforce the order is available.

(4) When the youth justice court makes a custody and supervision order with respect to a young person under paragraph (2)(*n*), the court shall state the following with respect to that order:

You are ordered to serve (state the number of days or months to be served) in custody, to be followed by (state one-half of the number of days or months stated above) to be served under supervision in the community subject to conditions.

If you breach any of the conditions while you are under supervision in the community, you may be brought back into custody and required to serve the rest of the second period in custody as well.

You should also be aware that, under other provisions of the Youth Criminal Justice Act, a court could require you to serve the second period in custody as well.

The periods in custody and under supervision in the community may be changed if you are or become subject to another sentence.

(5) The court may make a deferred custody and supervision order under paragraph (2)(*p*) if

(*a*) the young person is found guilty of an offence other than one in the commission of which a young person causes or attempts to cause serious bodily harm; and

(*b*) it is consistent with the purpose and principles set out in section 38 and the restrictions on custody set out in section 39.

(6) Sections 106 to 109 (suspension of conditional supervision) apply to a breach of a deferred custody and supervision order made under paragraph (2)(*p*) as if the breach were a breach of an order for conditional supervision made under subsection 105(1) and, for the purposes of sections 106 to 109, supervision under a deferred custody and supervision order is deemed to be conditional supervision.

(7) A youth justice court may make an intensive rehabilitative custody and supervision order under paragraph (2)(*r*) in respect of a young person only if

(*a*) either

(i) the young person has been found guilty of a serious violent offence, or

(ii) the young person has been found guilty of an offence, in the commission of which the young person caused or attempted to cause serious bodily harm and for which an adult is liable to imprisonment for a term of more than two years, and the young person had previously been found guilty at least twice of such an offence;

(*b*) the young person is suffering from a mental illness or disorder, a psychological disorder or an emotional disturbance;

(*c*) a plan of treatment and intensive supervision has been developed for the young person, and there are reasonable grounds to believe that the plan might reduce the risk of the young person repeating the offence or committing a serious violent offence; and

(*d*) the provincial director has determined that an intensive rehabilitative custody and supervision program is available and that the young person's participation in the program is appropriate.

(8) Nothing in this section abrogates or derogates from the rights of a young person regarding consent to physical or mental health treatment or care.

(9) and (10) [*Repealed*, 2012, c. 1, s. 174(4).]

(11) An order may not be made under paragraphs (2)(*k*) to (*m*) in respect of an offence for which a conditional discharge has been granted under paragraph (2)(*c*).

(12) A youth sentence or any part of it comes into force on the date on which it is imposed or on any later date that the youth justice court specifies.

(13) Subject to subsections (15) and (16), a youth justice court that sentences a young person may direct that a sentence imposed on the young person under paragraph (2)(*n*), (*o*), (*q*) or (*r*) be served consecutively if the young person

(*a*) is sentenced while under sentence for an offence under any of those paragraphs; or

(*b*) is found guilty of more than one offence under any of those paragraphs.

(14) No youth sentence, other than an order made under paragraph (2)(*j*), (*n*), (*o*), (*q*) or (*r*), shall continue in force for more than two years. If the youth sentence comprises more than one sanction imposed at the same time in respect of the same offence, the combined duration of the sanctions shall not exceed two years, unless the sentence includes a sanction under paragraph (2)(*j*), (*n*), (*o*), (*q*) or (*r*) that exceeds two years.

(15) Subject to subsection (16), if more than one youth sentence is imposed under this section in respect of a young person with respect to different offences, the continuous combined duration of those youth sentences shall not exceed three years, except if one of the offences is first degree murder or second degree murder within the meaning of section 231 of the *Criminal Code*, in which case the continuous combined duration of those youth sentences shall not exceed ten years in the case of first degree murder, or seven years in the case of second degree murder.

(16) If a youth sentence is imposed in respect of an offence committed by a young person after the commencement of, but before the completion of, any youth sentences imposed on the young person,

(*a*) the duration of the sentence imposed in respect of the subsequent offence shall be determined in accordance with subsections (14) and (15);

(*b*) the sentence may be served consecutively to the sentences imposed in respect of the previous offences; and

(c) the combined duration of all the sentences may exceed three years and, if the offence is, or one of the previous offences was,

(i) first degree murder within the meaning of section 231 of the *Criminal Code*, the continuous combined duration of the youth sentences may exceed ten years, or

(ii) second degree murder within the meaning of section 231 of the *Criminal Code*, the continuous combined duration of the youth sentences may exceed seven years.

(17) Subject to sections 89, 92 and 93 (provisions related to placement in adult facilities) of this Act and section 743.5 (transfer of jurisdiction) of the *Criminal Code*, a youth sentence imposed on a young person continues in effect in accordance with its terms after the young person becomes an adult. 2012, c. 1, s. 174.

ANNOTATIONS

Note: Some of the following cases were decided under the *Young Offenders Act* but were thought to be of assistance in applying this Act.

General – While the sentence to be imposed on both adults and young offenders must be proportional to the offence committed, the principle of proportionality will have greater significance for adults than it will in the disposition of young offenders. For the young offender, a proper disposition must take into account not only the seriousness of the crime but also all relevant factors: *R. v. M. (J.J.)*, [1993] 2 S.C.R. 421, 81 C.C.C. (3d) 487.

The principle of sentencing that the maximum sentence is reserved for the worst case was held to not be fully applicable to dispositions under the *Young Offenders Act* in view of the narrow range of disposition available. The narrow range compresses all serious cases at the top of the range and it would be unrealistic to scale all sentences down from the maximum or to reserve the sentence only for the very worst possible cases: *R. v. H. (A.)* (1991), 65 C.C.C. (3d) 116 (B.C.C.A.). See also *R. v. K. (M.)* (1996), 107 C.C.C. (3d) 149, 28 O.R. (3d) 593 (C.A.).

The court has the power to impose a disposition that is consecutive to a sentence imposed upon the offender by an ordinary court for offences committed by the offender as an adult: *R.*

v. F. (K.R.) (1995), 96 C.C.C. (3d) 469, [1995] 5 W.W.R. 556, 27 Alta. L.R. (3d) 336 (C.A.); *V. (T.) v. Ontario (Attorney General)* (1989), 51 C.C.C. (3d) 155 (Ont. H.C.J.).

Where a number of consecutive dispositions that include periods of custody have been imposed by different judges, the custodial dispositions must be served first before any periods of probation: *R. v. H. (J.)* (1992), 71 C.C.C. (3d) 309, 7 O.R. (3d) 756 (C.A.).

Subsection (2)(*b*) – The best interests of the young person and the public interest are not statutory preconditions to the imposition of a conditional discharge: *R. v. S. (P.J.)* (2008), 240 C.C.C. (3d) 204 (N.S.C.A.).

Subsection (2)(*o*) – A court is not required to impose on a young person guilty of manslaughter two-thirds of the sentence in custody and one-third under supervision. Unlike subsec. (2)(*n*), there is no restriction on what part of the time that can be spent in a custodial sentence and accordingly, the court may impose a lesser proportion of time in actual custody: *R. v. P. (B.W.)*, [2006] 1 S.C.R. 941, 209 C.C.C. (3d) 97.

Subsection (2)(*p*) – Deferred custody and supervision orders under subsec. (2)(*p*) cannot be made consecutive to one another: *R. v. H. (J.P.L.)* (2013), 299 C.C.C. (3d) 32 (B.C.C.A.).

Subsection (7) – Due to amendments to the Act in 2012, the term "serious violent offence" is now defined in s. 2 to include: (1) first degree murder or second degree murder; (2) attempt to commit murder; (3) manslaughter; or (4) aggravated sexual assault.

In the light of the objectives of the *Youth Criminal Justice Act* and s. 42, the term "emotional disturbance" in subsec. (7)(*b*) should have a broad, flexible and inclusive meaning. To fall within the definition of the term "emotional disturbance" there need only be a deviation from, interruption of, or interference with a normal emotional state that can be materially addressed by specialized treatment and rehabilitative service. The young person need not fall within a classified mental illness or psychological disorder to qualify for the IRCS program: *R. v. W. (M.)* (2017), 346 C.C.C. (3d) 319 (Ont. C.A.).

Subsection (14) – A custodial sentence of one year followed by two years of probation is impermissible pursuant to subsec. (14): *R. v. J. (R.R.)* (2009), 250 C.C.C. (3d) 3 (B.C.C.A.).

Subsection (15) – Pursuant to subsec. (15), where more than one youth sentence is imposed in respect of different offences, the continuous combined duration of the sentences shall not exceed three years: *R. v. S. (D.)* (2008), 239 C.C.C. (3d) 426 (Ont. C.A.). See also *R. v. B. (T.)* (2006), 206 C.C.C. (3d) 405 (Ont. C.A.).

Pre-sentence custody – Appellate courts differ on how pre-sentence custody is to be treated in relation to maximum sentences imposed on a youthful offender. In *R. v. S. (D.)*, *supra*, the Ontario Court of Appeal held that pre-sentence custody should be deducted from the maximum sentence. To the same effect, see also *R. v. B. (T.)*, *supra*; *R. v. L. (J.R.)* (2007), 221 C.C.C. (3d) 278 (N.S.C.A.); *R. v. H. (N.L.)* (2009), 457 A.R. 224 (C.A.). In *R. v. W. (M.)*, *supra*, the Ontario Court of Appeal held that, although a youth court judge must consider pre-sentence custody in sentencing an offender, the judge's treatment of the pre-sentence custody is discretionary. While s. 38(3)(*d*) of the *Youth Criminal Justice Act* requires the youth court judge to take detention "into account", the judge is not required to actually deduct pre-sentence custody when crafting an appropriate sentence. Whether and to what extent credit is given for pre-sentence custody against a youth sentence is within a youth court judge's discretion, particularly in the context of a Crown application to sentence a youth as an adult. In such cases, pre-sentence custody can be taken into account as a consideration in determining whether the young person would serve an adult or youth sentence as opposed to through an actual credit to length of sentence imposed. See also *R. v. P. (N.W.)* (2008), 235 C.C.C. (3d) 125 (Man. C.A.); *R. v. J. (R.R.)* (2009), 250 C.C.C. (3d) 3 (B.C.C.A.); *R. v. T. (D.D.)* (2010), 265 C.C.C. (3d) 49 (Alta. C.A.), leave to appeal to S.C.C. refused [2011] 2 S.C.R. x; *R. v. W. (D.)* (2008), 79 W.C.B. (2d) 80, [2008] O.J. No. 1356 (C.A.).

ADDITIONAL YOUTH SENTENCES.

43. Subject to subsection 42(15) (duration of youth sentences), if a young person who is subject to a custodial sentence imposed under paragraph 42(2)(*n*), (*o*), (*q*) or (*r*) that has not expired receives an additional youth sentence under one of those paragraphs, the young person is, for the purposes of the *Corrections and Conditional Release Act*, the *Criminal Code*, the *Prisons and Reformatories Act* and this Act, deemed to have been sentenced to one youth sentence commencing at the beginning of the first of those youth sentences to be served and ending on the expiry of the last of them to be served.

CUSTODIAL PORTION IF ADDITIONAL YOUTH SENTENCE.

44. Subject to subsection 42(15) (duration of youth sentences) and section 46 (exception when youth sentence in respect of earlier offence), if an additional youth sentence under paragraph 42(2)(*n*), (*o*), (*q*) or (*r*) is imposed on a young person on whom a youth sentence had already been imposed under one of those paragraphs that has not expired and the expiry date of the youth sentence that includes the additional youth sentence, as determined in accordance with section 43, is later than the expiry date of the youth sentence that the young person was serving before the additional youth sentence was imposed, the custodial portion of the young person's youth sentence is, from the date the additional sentence is imposed, the total of

(*a*) the unexpired portion of the custodial portion of the youth sentence before the additional youth sentence was imposed, and

(*b*) the relevant period set out in subparagraph (i), (ii) or (iii):

(i) if the additional youth sentence is imposed under paragraph 42(2)(*n*), the period that is two thirds of the period that constitutes the difference between the expiry of the youth sentence as determined in accordance with section 43 and the expiry of the youth sentence that the young person was serving before the additional youth sentence was imposed,

(ii) if the additional youth sentence is a concurrent youth sentence imposed under paragraph 42(2)(*o*), (*q*) or (*r*), the custodial portion of the youth sentence imposed under that paragraph that extends beyond the expiry date of the custodial portion of the sentence being served before the imposition of the additional sentence, or

(iii) if the additional youth sentence is a consecutive youth sentence imposed under paragraph 42(2)(*o*), (*q*) or (*r*), the custodial portion of the additional youth sentence imposed under that paragraph.

SUPERVISION WHEN ADDITIONAL YOUTH SENTENCE EXTENDS THE PERIOD IN CUSTODY / Supervision when additional youth sentence does not extend the period in custody / Supervision when youth sentence additional to supervision.

45. (1) If a young person has begun to serve a portion of a youth sentence in the community subject to conditions under paragraph 42(2)(*n*) or under conditional supervision under paragraph 42(2)(*o*), (*q*) or (*r*) at the time an additional youth sentence is imposed under one of those paragraphs, and, as a result of the application of section 44, the custodial portion of the young person's youth sentence ends on a day that is later than the day on which the young person received the additional youth sentence, the serving of a portion of the youth sentence under supervision in the community subject to conditions or under conditional supervision shall become inoperative and the young person shall be committed to custody under paragraph 102(1)(*b*) or 106(*b*) until the end of the extended portion of the youth sentence to be served in custody.

(2) If a youth sentence has been imposed under paragraph 42(2)(*n*), (*o*), (*q*) or (*r*) on a young person who is under supervision in the community subject to conditions under paragraph 42(2)(*n*) or under conditional supervision under paragraph 42(2)(*o*), (*q*) or (*r*), and the additional youth sentence would not modify the expiry date of the youth sentence that the young person was serving at the time the additional youth sentence was imposed, the young person may be remanded to the youth custody facility that the provincial director considers appropriate. The provincial director shall review the case and, no later than forty-eight hours after the remand of the young person, shall either refer the case to the youth justice court for a review under section 103 or 109 or release the young person to continue the supervision in the community or the conditional supervision.

(3) If a youth sentence has been imposed under paragraph 42(2)(*n*), (*o*), (*q*) or (*r*) on a young person who is under conditional supervision under paragraph 94(19)(*b*) or subsection 96(5), the young person shall be remanded to the youth custody facility that the provincial director considers appropriate. The provincial director shall review the case and, no later than forty-eight hours after the remand of the young person, shall either refer the case to the youth justice court for a review under section 103 or 109 or release the young person to continue the conditional supervision.

EXCEPTION WHEN YOUTH SENTENCE IN RESPECT OF EARLIER OFFENCE.

46. The total of the custodial portions of a young person's youth sentences shall not exceed six years calculated from the beginning of the youth sentence that is determined in accordance with section 43 if

- **(*a*) a youth sentence is imposed under paragraph 42(2)(*n*), (*o*), (*q*) or (*r*) on the young person already serving a youth sentence under one of those paragraphs; and**
- **(*b*) the later youth sentence imposed is in respect of an offence committed before the commencement of the earlier youth sentence.**

COMMITTAL TO CUSTODY DEEMED CONTINUOUS / Intermittent custody / Availability of place of intermittent custody.

47. (1) Subject to subsections (2) and (3), a young person who is sentenced under paragraph 42(2)(*n*) is deemed to be committed to continuous custody for the custodial portion of the sentence.

(2) If the sentence does not exceed ninety days, the youth justice court may order that the custodial portion of the sentence be served intermittently if it is consistent with the purpose and principles set out in section 38.

(3) Before making an order of committal to intermittent custody, the youth justice court shall require the prosecutor to make available to the court for its consideration a report of the provincial director as to the availability of a youth custody facility in which an order of intermittent custody can be enforced and, if the report discloses that no such youth custody facility is available, the court shall not make the order.

REASONS FOR THE SENTENCE.

48. When a youth justice court imposes a youth sentence, it shall state its reasons for the sentence in the record of the case and shall, on request, give or cause to be given a copy of the sentence and the reasons for the sentence to

- **(*a*) the young person, the young person's counsel, a parent of the young person, the provincial director and the prosecutor; and**
- **(*b*) in the case of a committal to custody under paragraph 42(2)(*n*), (*o*), (*q*) or (*r*), the review board.**

ANNOTATIONS

The failure of the trial judge to advert to the imposition of a custodial sentence and to explain why it was rejected constitutes an error of law: *R. v. M. (A.M.)* (2003), 181 C.C.C. (3d) 532, 180 Man. R. (2d) 239 (C.A.).

Section 48 of the *Youth Criminal Justice Act* requires reasons for sentencing, which must communicate the basis for the sentence in a meaningful way: *R. v. T. (T.W.)* (2008), 437 A.R. 321 (C.A.).

WARRANT OF COMMITTAL / Custody during transfer / Subsection 30(3) applies.

49. (1) When a young person is committed to custody, the youth justice court shall issue or cause to be issued a warrant of committal.

(2) A young person who is committed to custody may, in the course of being transferred from custody to the court or from the court to custody, be held under the supervision and control of a peace officer or in any place of temporary detention referred to in subsection 30(1) that the provincial director may specify.

(3) Subsection 30(3) (detention separate from adults) applies, with any modifications that the circumstances require, in respect of a person held in a place of temporary detention under subsection (2).

APPLICATION OF PART XXIII OF CRIMINAL CODE / Section 787 of *Criminal Code* does not apply / Reasons for the prohibition order / Reasons / Application of *Criminal Code.*

50. (1) Subject to section 74 (application of *Criminal Code* to adult sentences), Part XXIII (sentencing) of the *Criminal Code* does not apply in respect of proceedings under this Act except for paragraph 718.2(*e*) (sentencing principle for aboriginal offenders), sections 722 (victim impact statements), 722.1 (copy of statement) and 722.2 (inquiry by court), subsection 730(2) (court process continues in force) and sections 748 (pardons and remissions), 748.1 (remission by the Governor in Council) and 749 (royal prerogative) of that Act, which provisions apply with any modifications that the circumstances require.

(2) Section 787 (general penalty) of the *Criminal Code* does not apply in respect of proceedings under this Act.

ANNOTATIONS

By virtue of s. 50(1) of the *Youth Criminal Justice Act*, the provisions of the *Criminal Code* on sentencing, save certain listed exceptions, do not apply to youth sentencing: *R. v. P. (B.W.)*, [2006] 1 S.C.R. 941, 209 C.C.C. (3d) 97.

MANDATORY PROHIBITION ORDER / Duration of prohibition order / Discretionary prohibition order / Duration of prohibition order / Report.

51. (1) Despite section 42 (youth sentences), when a young person is found guilty of an offence referred to in any of paragraphs 109(1)(*a*) to (*d*) of the *Criminal Code*, the youth justice court shall, in addition to imposing a sentence under section 42 (youth sentences), make an order prohibiting the young person from possessing any firearm, cross-bow, prohibited weapon, restricted weapon, prohibited device, ammunition, prohibited ammunition or explosive substance during the period specified in the order as determined in accordance with subsection (2).

(2) An order made under subsection (1) begins on the day on which the order is made and ends not earlier than two years after the young person has completed the custodial portion of the sentence or, if the young person is not subject to custody, after the time the young person is found guilty of the offence.

(3) Despite section 42 (youth sentences), where a young person is found guilty of an offence referred to in paragraph 110(1)(*a*) or (*b*) of the *Criminal Code*, the youth justice court shall, in addition to imposing a sentence under section 42 (youth sentences), consider whether it is desirable, in the interests of the safety of the young person or of any other person, to make an order prohibiting the young person from possessing any firearm, cross-bow, prohibited weapon, restricted weapon, prohibited device, ammunition, prohibited ammunition or explosive substance, or all such things, and where the court decides that it is so desirable, the court shall so order.

(4) An order made under subsection (3) against a young person begins on the day on which the order is made and ends not later than two years after the young person has completed the custodial portion of the sentence or, if the young person is not subject to custody, after the time the young person is found guilty of the offence.

(5) When a youth justice court makes an order under this section, it shall state its reasons for making the order in the record of the case and shall give or cause to be given a copy of the order and, on request, a transcript or copy of the reasons to the young person against whom the order was made, the counsel and a parent of the young person and the provincial director.

(6) When the youth justice court does not make an order under subsection (3), or when the youth justice court does make such an order but does not prohibit the possession of everything referred to in that subsection, the youth justice court shall include in the record a statement of the youth justice court's reasons.

(7) Sections 113 to 117 (firearm prohibition orders) of the *Criminal Code* apply in respect of any order made under this section.

(8) Before making an order referred to in section 113 (lifting firearms order) of the *Criminal Code* in respect of a young person, the youth justice court may require the provincial director to cause to be prepared, and to submit to the youth justice court, a report on the young person.

ANNOTATIONS

Section 51 provides for a minimum weapons prohibition of two years. Unlike s. 109 of the *Criminal Code*, there is no mandatory lifetime prohibition for a second offence. Another distinction between these provisions is that s. 51(5) requires that reasons be given when an order is made under s. 51: *R. v. W. (D.)* (2011), 269 C.C.C. (3d) 541 (N.L.C.A.).

REVIEW OF ORDER MADE UNDER SECTION 51 / Grounds / Decision of review / New order not to be more onerous / Application of provisions.

52. (1) A youth justice court may, on application, review an order made under section 51 at any time after the end of the period set out in subsection 119(2) (period of access to records) that applies to the record of the offence that resulted in the order being made.

(2) In conducting a review under this section, the youth justice court shall take into account

- **(*a*) the nature and circumstances of the offence in respect of which the order was made; and**
- **(*b*) the safety of the young person and of other persons.**

(3) When a youth justice court conducts a review under this section, it may, after giving the young person, a parent of the young person, the Attorney General and the provincial director an opportunity to be heard,

- **(*a*) confirm the order;**
- **(*b*) revoke the order; or**
- **(*c*) vary the order as it considers appropriate in the circumstances of the case.**

(4) No variation of an order made under paragraph (3)(*c*) may be more onerous than the order being reviewed.

(5) Subsections 59(3) to (5) apply, with any modifications that the circumstances require, in respect of a review under this section.

FUNDING FOR VICTIMS / Victim fine surcharge.

53. (1) The lieutenant governor in council of a province may order that, in respect of any fine imposed in the province under paragraph 42(2)(*d*), a percentage of the fine as fixed by the lieutenant governor in council be used to provide such assistance to victims of offences as the lieutenant governor in council may direct from time to time.

(2) If the lieutenant governor in council of a province has not made an order under subsection (1), a youth justice court that imposes a fine on a young person under paragraph 42(2)(*d*) may, in addition to any other punishment imposed on the young person, order the young person to pay a victim fine surcharge in an amount not exceeding fifteen per cent of the fine. The surcharge shall be used to provide such assistance to victims of offences as the lieutenant governor in council of the province in which the surcharge is imposed may direct from time to time.

WHERE A FINE OR OTHER PAYMENT IS ORDERED / Discharge of fine or surcharge / Rates, crediting and other matters / Representations respecting orders under paragraphs 42(2)(*e*) to (*h*) / Notice of orders under paragraphs 42(2)(*e*) to (*h*) / Consent of person to be compensated / Orders under paragraph 42(2)(*h*), (*i*) or (*m*) / Duration of order for service / Community service order / Application for further time to complete youth sentence.

54. (1) The youth justice court shall, in imposing a fine under paragraph 42(2)(*d*) or in making an order under paragraph 42(2)(*e*) or (*g*), have regard to the present and future means of the young person to pay.

(2) A young person on whom a fine is imposed under paragraph 42(2)(*d*), including any percentage of a fine imposed under subsection 53(1), or on whom a victim fine surcharge is imposed under subsection 53(2), may discharge the fine or surcharge in whole or in part by earning credits for work performed in a program established for that purpose

- **(*a*) by the lieutenant governor in council of the province in which the fine or surcharge was imposed; or**
- **(*b*) by the lieutenant governor in council of the province in which the young person resides, if an appropriate agreement is in effect between the government of that province and the government of the province in which the fine or surcharge was imposed.**

(3) A program referred to in subsection (2) shall determine the rate at which credits are earned and may provide for the manner of crediting any amounts earned against the fine or surcharge and any other matters necessary for or incidental to carrying out the program.

(4) In considering whether to make an order under any of paragraphs 42(2)(*e*) to (*h*), the youth justice court may consider any representations made by the person who would be compensated or to whom restitution or payment would be made.

(5) If the youth justice court makes an order under any of paragraphs 42(2)(*e*) to (*h*), it shall cause notice of the terms of the order to be given to the person who is to be compensated or to whom restitution or payment is to be made.

(6) No order may be made under paragraph 42(2)(*h*) unless the youth justice court has secured the consent of the person to be compensated.

(7) No order may be made under paragraph 42(2)(*h*), (*i*) or (*m*) unless the youth justice court is satisfied that

(*a*) the young person against whom the order is made is a suitable candidate for such an order; and

(*b*) the order does not interfere with the normal hours of work or education of the young person.

(8) No order may be made under paragraph 42(2)(*h*) or (*i*) to perform personal or community services unless those services can be completed in two hundred and forty hours or less and within twelve months after the date of the order.

(9) No order may be made under paragraph 42(2)(*i*) unless

(*a*) the community service to be performed is part of a program that is approved by the provincial director; or

(*b*) the youth justice court is satisfied that the person or organization for whom the community service is to be performed has agreed to its performance.

(10) A youth justice court may, on application by or on behalf of the young person in respect of whom a youth sentence has been imposed under any of paragraphs 42(2)(*d*) to (*i*), allow further time for the completion of the sentence subject to any regulations made under paragraph 155(*b*) and to any rules made by the youth justice court under subsection 17(1).

CONDITIONS THAT MUST APPEAR IN ORDERS / Conditions that may appear in orders.

55. (1) The youth justice court shall prescribe, as conditions of an order made under paragraph 42(2)(*k*) or (*l*), that the young person

(*a*) keep the peace and be of good behaviour; and

(*b*) appear before the youth justice court when required by the court to do so.

(2) A youth justice court may prescribe, as conditions of an order made under paragraph 42(2)(*k*) or (*l*), that a young person do one or more of the following that the youth justice court considers appropriate in the circumstances:

(*a*) report to and be supervised by the provincial director or a person designated by the youth justice court;

(*b*) notify the clerk of the youth justice court, the provincial director or the youth worker assigned to the case of any change of address or any change in the young person's place of employment, education or training;

(*c*) remain within the territorial jurisdiction of one or more courts named in the order;

(*d*) make reasonable efforts to obtain and maintain suitable employment;

(*e*) attend school or any other place of learning, training or recreation that is appropriate, if the youth justice court is satisfied that a suitable program for the young person is available there;

(*f*) reside with a parent, or any other adult that the youth justice court considers appropriate, who is willing to provide for the care and maintenance of the young person;

(*g*) reside at a place that the provincial director may specify;

(*h*) comply with any other conditions set out in the order that the youth justice court considers appropriate, including conditions for securing the young person's good conduct and for preventing the young person from repeating the offence or committing other offences; and

(*i*) not own, possess or have the control of any weapon, ammunition, prohibited ammunition, prohibited device or explosive substance, except as authorized by the order.

ANNOTATIONS

Note: Some of the following cases were decided under the *Young Offenders Act* but were thought to be of assistance in applying this Act.

Subsection (1) – The obligation to keep the peace and be of good behaviour impose separate and distinct conditions that may overlap in certain circumstances. A breach of the peace is a violent disruption or disturbance of public tranquility, peace and order. A young person's disruptive behaviour in the classroom, using foul language and engaging in a physical altercation constituted a breach of the peace: *R. v. S. (S.)* (1999), 138 C.C.C. (3d) 430, 178 Nfld. & P.E.I.R. 219 (Nfld. C.A.).

Failure to be of good behaviour is limited to non-compliance with federal, provincial or municipal statutes and regulations and obligations imposed by court orders specifically applicable to the accused. Running away from a group home did not constitute a statutory offence or breach of a court order so as to constitute a failure to be of good behaviour: *R. v. R. (D.)* (1999), 138 C.C.C. (3d) 405, 27 C.R. (5th) 366, 178 Nfld. & P.E.I.R. 200 (Nfld. C.A.).

Subsection (2) – The conditions imposed under s. 55(2) must be rationally connected to the circumstances of the offence and/or necessary to ensure future good behaviour: *R. v. G. (S.E.)* (2006), 205 Man. R. (2d) 201 (C.A.).

A condition that the accused take medication as prescribed by a psychiatrist is unlawful: *R. v. L. (J.J.)* (2001), 152 C.C.C. (3d) 572, 153 Man. R. (2d) 153 (C.A.). [Also, now see s. 42(8) of this Act.]

A condition requiring the accused to produce bodily samples for drug and alcohol testing is not contrary to law: *R. v. L. (J.R.)* (2007), 221 C.C.C. (3d) 278, 49 C.R. (6th) 1 (N.S.C.A.).

The court has no jurisdiction to direct how a sanction will be administered by the government or how government resources will be used to administer it. Accordingly, there was no jurisdiction for a youth court judge to impose a probation condition requiring that a youth court worker with special training in organic brain impairment be assigned to the accused and that a case plan be submitted subsequent to the disposition for review: *R. v. K. (L.E.)* (2001), 153 C.C.C. (3d) 250, 203 Sask. R. 273 (C.A.).

Similarly, while the court may order a young offender to undergo treatment, the youth court has no jurisdiction to order the government to pay for a specific treatment programme: *R. v. H. (R.J.)* (2000), 145 C.C.C. (3d) 202, 32 C.R. (5th) 241, 186 D.L.R. (4th) 468 (Alta. C.A.).

COMMUNICATION OF ORDER / Copy of order to parent / Endorsement of order by young person / Validity of order / Commencement of order / Effect of order in case of custody / Notice to appear / Warrant in default of appearance.

56. (1) A youth justice court that makes an order under paragraph 42(2)(*k*) or (*l*) shall

- **(*a*) cause the order to be read by or to the young person bound by it;**
- **(*b*) explain or cause to be explained to the young person the purpose and effect of the order, and confirm that the young person understands it; and**
- **(*c*) cause a copy of the order to be given to the young person, and to any parent of the young person who is in attendance at the sentencing hearing.**

(2) A youth justice court that makes an order under paragraph 42(2)(*k*) or (*l*) may cause a copy to be given to a parent of the young person who is not in attendance at the proceedings if the parent is, in the opinion of the court, taking an active interest in the proceedings.

(3) After the order has been read and explained under subsection (1), the young person shall endorse on the order an acknowledgement that the young person has received a copy of the order and had its purpose and effect explained.

(4) The failure of a young person to endorse the order or of a parent to receive a copy of the order does not affect the validity of the order.

(5) An order made under paragraph 42(2)(*k*) or (*l*) comes into force

(*a*) on the date on which it is made; or

(*b*) if a young person receives a sentence that includes a period of continuous custody and supervision, at the end of the period of supervision.

(6) If a young person is subject to a sentence that includes both a period of continuous custody and supervision and an order made under paragraph 42(2)(*k*) or (*l*), and the court orders under subsection 42(12) a delay in the start of the period of custody, the court may divide the period that the order made under paragraph 42(2)(*k*) or (*l*) is in effect, with the first portion to have effect from the date on which it is made until the start of the period of custody, and the remainder to take effect at the end of the period of supervision.

(7) A young person may be given notice either orally or in writing to appear before the youth justice court under paragraph 55(1)(*b*).

(8) If service of a notice in writing is proved and the young person fails to attend court in accordance with the notice, a youth justice court may issue a warrant to compel the appearance of the young person.

ANNOTATIONS

Note: The following cases were decided under the *Young Offenders Act* but were thought to be of assistance in applying this Act.

Subsection (1) – It was held that the duties under s. 23(3)(*c*) of the *Young Offenders Act*, which is worded similarly to para. (1)(*c*) of this section, may be delegated to the clerk of the court. However, in delegating its duties, the court must properly inform the clerk of the need, be it mandatory or discretionary, to inform a parent in accordance with subsecs. (3) and (4) [subsecs. (1) and (2) of this section]. Failure to provide the parent with the order as required by subsec. (3) affects the validity of the order and a charge of breach of probation must be dismissed: *R. v. M. (L.A.)* (1994), 92 C.C.C. (3d) 562, 73 O.A.C. 345 (C.A.). *Contra*: *R. v. A. (D.C.)* (2000), 143 C.C.C. (3d) 302, [2000] 5 W.W.R. 380, 77 Alta. L.R. (3d) 54 (C.A.), leave to appeal to S.C.C. refused 147 C.C.C. (3d) vi, 281 A.R. 247*n*, 263 N.R. 396*n*, holding that non-compliance does not necessarily result in the dismissal of the charge. Where non-compliance is raised, it is must be determined whether, on the balance of probabilities, non-compliance with the provision materially prejudiced the young person's entitlement to guidance and assistance of a parent such that the breach would not have occurred but for the non-compliance. Also see: *R. v. H. (J.)* (2002), 161 C.C.C. (3d) 392, 155 O.A.C. 146 (C.A.), considering s. 20(6) of the *Young Offenders Act* requiring that a copy of the disposition be given to the young person, the young person's parents and counsel.

Subsection (5) – If a deferred custody and supervision order is made in conjunction with a probation order, the probation order commences at the end of the period of the deferred custody and supervision order: *R. v. H. (J.P.L.)* (2013), 299 C.C.C. (3d) 32 (B.C.C.A.).

TRANSFER OF YOUTH SENTENCE / No transfer outside province before appeal completed / Transfer to a province when person is adult.

57. (1) When a youth sentence has been imposed under any of paragraphs 42(2)(*d*) to (*i*), (*k*), (*l*) or (*s*) in respect of a young person and the young person or a parent with whom the young person resides is or becomes a resident of a territorial division outside the jurisdiction of the youth justice court that imposed the youth sentence, whether in the same or in another province, a youth justice court judge in the territorial division in which the youth sentence was imposed may, on the application of the Attorney General or on the application of the young person or the young person's parent, with the consent

of the Attorney General, transfer to a youth justice court in another territorial division the youth sentence and any portion of the record of the case that is appropriate. All subsequent proceedings relating to the case shall then be carried out and enforced by that court.

(2) No youth sentence may be transferred from one province to another under this section until the time for an appeal against the youth sentence or the finding on which the youth sentence was based has expired or until all proceedings in respect of any such appeal have been completed.

(3) When an application is made under subsection (1) to transfer the youth sentence of a young person to a province in which the young person is an adult, a youth justice court judge may, with the consent of the Attorney General, transfer the youth sentence and the record of the case to the youth justice court in the province to which the transfer is sought, and the youth justice court to which the case is transferred shall have full jurisdiction in respect of the youth sentence as if that court had imposed the youth sentence. The person shall be further dealt with in accordance with this Act.

INTERPROVINCIAL ARRANGEMENTS / Youth justice court retains jurisdiction / Waiver of jurisdiction.

58. (1) When a youth sentence has been imposed under any of paragraphs 42(2)(*k*) to (*r*) in respect of a young person, the youth sentence in one province may be dealt with in any other province in accordance with any agreement that may have been made between those provinces.

(2) Subject to subsection (3), when a youth sentence imposed in respect of a young person is dealt with under this section in a province other than that in which the youth sentence was imposed, the youth justice court of the province in which the youth sentence was imposed retains, for all purposes of this Act, exclusive jurisdiction over the young person as if the youth sentence were dealt with within that province, and any warrant or process issued in respect of the young person may be executed or served in any place in Canada outside the province where the youth sentence was imposed as if it were executed or served in that province.

(3) When a youth sentence imposed in respect of a young person is dealt with under this section in a province other than the one in which the youth sentence was imposed, the youth justice court of the province in which the youth sentence was imposed may, with the consent in writing of the Attorney General of that province and the young person, waive its jurisdiction, for the purpose of any proceeding under this Act, to the youth justice court of the province in which the youth sentence is dealt with, in which case the youth justice court in the province in which the youth sentence is dealt with shall have full jurisdiction in respect of the youth sentence as if that court had imposed the youth sentence.

REVIEW OF YOUTH SENTENCES NOT INVOLVING CUSTODY / Grounds for review / Progress report / Subsections 94(10) to (12) apply / Subsections 94(7) and (14) to (18) apply / Compelling appearance of young person / Decision of the youth justice court after review / New youth sentence not to be more onerous / Exception.

59. (1) When a youth justice court has imposed a youth sentence in respect of a young person, other than a youth sentence under paragraph 42(2)(*n*), (*o*), (*q*) or (*r*), the youth justice court shall, on the application of the young person, the young person's parent, the Attorney General or the provincial director, made at any time after six months after the date of the youth sentence or, with leave of a youth justice court judge, at any earlier time, review the youth sentence if the court is satisfied that there are grounds for a review under subsection (2).

(2) A review of a youth sentence may be made under this section

(*a*) on the ground that the circumstances that led to the youth sentence have changed materially;

(*b*) on the ground that the young person in respect of whom the review is to be made is unable to comply with or is experiencing serious difficulty in complying with the terms of the youth sentence;

(*c*) on the ground that the young person in respect of whom the review is to be made has contravened a condition of an order made under paragraph 42(2)(*k*) or (*l*) without reasonable excuse;

(*d*) on the ground that the terms of the youth sentence are adversely affecting the opportunities available to the young person to obtain services, education or employment; or

(*e*) on any other ground that the youth justice court considers appropriate.

(3) The youth justice court may, before reviewing under this section a youth sentence imposed in respect of a young person, require the provincial director to cause to be prepared, and to submit to the youth justice court, a progress report on the performance of the young person since the youth sentence took effect.

(4) Subsections 94(10) to (12) apply, with any modifications that the circumstances require, in respect of any progress report required under subsection (3).

(5) Subsections 94(7) and (14) to (18) apply, with any modifications that the circumstances require, in respect of reviews made under this section and any notice required under subsection 94(14) shall also be given to the provincial director.

(6) The youth justice court may, by summons or warrant, compel a young person in respect of whom a review is to be made under this section to appear before the youth justice court for the purposes of the review.

(7) When a youth justice court reviews under this section a youth sentence imposed in respect of a young person, it may, after giving the young person, a parent of the young person, the Attorney General and the provincial director an opportunity to be heard,

(*a*) confirm the youth sentence;

(*b*) terminate the youth sentence and discharge the young person from any further obligation of the youth sentence; or

(*c*) vary the youth sentence or impose any new youth sentence under section 42, other than a committal to custody, for any period of time, not exceeding the remainder of the period of the earlier youth sentence, that the court considers appropriate in the circumstances of the case.

(8) Subject to subsection (9), when a youth sentence imposed in respect of a young person is reviewed under this section, no youth sentence imposed under subsection (7) shall, without the consent of the young person, be more onerous than the remainder of the youth sentence reviewed.

(9) A youth justice court may under this section extend the time within which a youth sentence imposed under paragraphs 42(2)(*d*) to (*i*) is to be complied with by a young person if the court is satisfied that the young person requires more time to comply with the youth sentence, but in no case shall the extension be for a period of time that expires more than twelve months after the date the youth sentence would otherwise have expired.

PROVISIONS APPLICABLE TO YOUTH SENTENCES ON REVIEW.

60. This Part and Part 5 (custody and supervision) apply with any modifications that the circumstances require to orders made in respect of reviews of youth sentences under sections 59 and 94 to 96.

Adult Sentence and Election

61. [*Repealed.* 2012, c. 1, s. 175.]

ANNOTATIONS

Previous versions of the Act created categories of offences for which, if found guilty, an adult sentence was presumed to apply to the young person. The presumption of adult sentences and reverse onus provisions were found to violate s. 7 of the Charter and could not be justified under s. 1: *R. v. B. (D.)*, [2008] 2 S.C.R. 3, 231 C.C.C. (3d) 338.

62. [*Repealed.* 2012, c. 1, s. 175.]

ANNOTATIONS

Previous versions of the Act created categories of offences for which, if found guilty, an adult sentence was presumed to apply to the young person. The presumption of adult sentences and reverse onus provisions were found to violate s. 7 of the Charter and could not be justified under s. 1: *R. v. B. (D.)*, [2008] 2 S.C.R. 3, 231 C.C.C. (3d) 338.

63. [*Repealed.* 2012, c. 1, s. 175.]

ANNOTATIONS

Previous versions of the Act created categories of offences for which, if found guilty, an adult sentence was presumed to apply to the young person. The presumption of adult sentences and reverse onus provisions were found to violate s. 7 of the Charter and could not be justified under s. 1: *R. v. B. (D.)*, [2008] 2 S.C.R. 3, 231 C.C.C. (3d) 338.

APPLICATION BY ATTORNEY GENERAL / Obligation / Order fixing age / Notice of intention to seek adult sentence / Notice to young person.

64. (1) The Attorney General may, before evidence is called as to sentence or, if no evidence is called, before submissions are made as to sentence, make an application to the youth justice court for an order that a young person is liable to an adult sentence if the young person is or has been found guilty of an offence for which an adult is liable to imprisonment for a term of more than two years and that was committed after the young person attained the age of 14 years.

(1.1) The Attorney General must consider whether it would be appropriate to make an application under subsection (1) if the offence is a serious violent offence and was committed after the young person attained the age of 14 years. If, in those circumstances, the Attorney General decides not to make an application, the Attorney General shall advise the youth justice court before the young person enters a plea or with leave of the court before the commencement of the trial.

(1.2) The lieutenant governor in council of a province may by order fix an age greater than 14 years but not greater than 16 years for the purpose of subsection (1.1).

(2) If the Attorney General intends to seek an adult sentence for an offence by making an application under subsection (1), the Attorney General shall, before the young person enters a plea or with leave of the youth justice court before the commencement of the trial, give notice to the young person and the youth justice court of the intention to seek an adult sentence.

(3) A notice of intention to seek an adult sentence given in respect of an offence is notice in respect of any included offence of which the young person is found guilty for which an adult is liable to imprisonment for a term of more than two years. 2012, c. 1, s. 176.

(4) and (5) [*Repealed.* 2012, c. 1, s. 176(2).]

ANNOTATIONS

Previous versions of the Act created categories of offences for which, if found guilty, an adult sentence was presumed to apply to the young person. The presumption of adult sentences and reverse onus provisions were found to violate s. 7 of the Charter and could not be justified under s. 1: *R. v. B. (D.)*, [2008] 2 S.C.R. 3, 231 C.C.C. (3d) 338.

To succeed on its application pursuant to s. 64(1), *per* s. 72 of the *Youth Criminal Justice Act*, the Crown must (a) rebut the presumption of diminished moral blameworthiness of the young person, and (b) satisfy the court that the sanctions that can be imposed under the *Youth Criminal Justice Act* are inadequate to hold the young person accountable for the two offences: *R. v. L. (B.)* (2013), 292 Man. R. (2d) 51 (Q.B.); *R. v. W. (M.)* (2017), 346 C.C.C. (3d) 319 (Ont. C.A.).

65. [*Repealed.* 2012, c. 1, s. 177.]

66. [*Repealed.* 2012, c. 1, s. 177.]

ELECTION — ADULT SENTENCE / Wording of election / Election — Nunavut / Wording of election / Mode of trial where co-accused are young persons / Attorney General may require trial by jury / Preliminary inquiry / Preliminary inquiry if two or more accused / When no request for preliminary inquiry / Preliminary inquiry provisions of *Criminal Code* / Parts XIX and XX of *Criminal Code*.

67. (1) The youth justice court shall, before a young person enters a plea, put the young person to his or her election in the words set out in subsection (2) if

(*a*) [*Repealed*, 2012, c. 1, s. 178(1).]

(*b*) the Attorney General has given notice under subsection 64(2) of the intention to seek an adult sentence for an offence committed after the young person has attained the age of fourteen years;

(*c*) the young person is charged with having committed first or second degree murder within the meaning of section 231 of the *Criminal Code* before the young person has attained the age of fourteen years; or

(*d*) the person to whom section 16 (status of accused uncertain) applies is charged with having, after attaining the age of fourteen years, committed an offence for which an adult would be entitled to an election under section 536 of the *Criminal Code*, or over which a superior court of criminal jurisdiction would have exclusive jurisdiction under section 469 of that Act.

(2) The youth justice court shall put the young person to his or her election in the following words:

You have the option to elect to be tried by a youth justice court judge without a jury and without having had a preliminary inquiry; or you may elect to be tried by a judge without a jury; or you may elect to be tried by a court composed of a judge and jury. If you do not elect now, you are deemed to have elected to be tried by a court composed of a judge and jury. If you elect to be tried by a judge without a jury or by a court composed of a judge and jury or if you are deemed to have elected to be tried by a court composed of a judge and jury, you will have a preliminary inquiry only if you or the prosecutor requests one. How do you elect to be tried?

(3) In respect of proceedings in Nunavut, the youth justice court shall, before a young person enters a plea, put the young person to his or her election in the words set out in subsection (4) if

(*a*) [*Repealed*, 2012, c. 1, s. 178(2).]

(*b*) the Attorney General has given notice under subsection 64(2) of the intention to seek an adult sentence for an offence committed after the young person has attained the age of fourteen years;

(*c*) the young person is charged with having committed first or second degree murder within the meaning of section 231 of the *Criminal Code* before the young person has attained the age of fourteen years; or

(*d*) the person to whom section 16 (status of accused uncertain) applies is charged with having, after attaining the age of fourteen years, committed an offence for which an adult would be entitled to an election under section 536.1 of the *Criminal Code*.

(4) The youth justice court shall put the young person to his or her election in the following words:

> **You have the option to elect to be tried by a judge of the Nunavut Court of Justice alone, acting as a youth justice court without a jury and without a preliminary inquiry; or you may elect to be tried by a judge of the Nunavut Court of Justice, acting as a youth justice court without a jury; or you may elect to be tried by a judge of the Nunavut Court of Justice, acting as a youth justice court with a jury. If you elect to be tried by a judge without a jury or by a judge, acting as a youth justice court, with a jury or if you are deemed to have elected to be tried by a judge, acting as a youth justice court, with a jury, you will have a preliminary inquiry only if you or the prosecutor requests one. How do you elect to be tried?**

(5) When two or more young persons who are charged with the same offence, who are jointly charged in the same information or indictment or in respect of whom the Attorney General seeks joinder of counts that are set out in separate informations or indictments are put to their election, then, unless all of them elect or re-elect or are deemed to have elected, as the case may be, the same mode of trial, the youth justice court judge

(*a*) may decline to record any election, re-election or deemed election for trial by a youth justice court judge without a jury, a judge without a jury or, in Nunavut, a judge of the Nunavut Court Justice without a jury; and

(*b*) if the judge declines to do so, shall hold a preliminary inquiry, if requested to do so by one of the parties, unless a preliminary inquiry has been held prior to the election, re-election or deemed election.

(6) The Attorney General may, even if a young person elects under subsection (1) or (3) to be tried by a youth justice court judge without a jury or a judge without a jury, require the young person to be tried by a court composed of a judge and jury.

(7) When a young person elects to be tried by a judge without a jury, or elects or is deemed to have elected to be tried by a court composed of a judge and jury, the youth justice court referred to in subsection 13(1) shall, on the request of the young person or the prosecutor made at that time or within the period fixed by rules of court made under section 17 or 155 or, if there are no such rules, by the youth justice court judge, conduct a preliminary inquiry and if, on its conclusion, the young person is ordered to stand trial, the proceedings shall be conducted

(*a*) before a judge without a jury or a court composed of a judge and jury, as the case may be; or

(*b*) in Nunavut, before a judge of the Nunavut Court of Justice acting as a youth justice court, with or without a jury, as the case may be.

(7.1) If two or more young persons are jointly charged in an information and one or more of them make a request for a preliminary inquiry under subsection (7), a preliminary inquiry must be held with respect to all of them.

(7.2) If no request for a preliminary inquiry is made under subsection (7), the youth justice court shall fix the date for the trial or the date on which the young person must appear in the trial court to have the date fixed.

(8) The preliminary inquiry shall be conducted in accordance with the provisions of Part XVIII (procedure on preliminary inquiry) of the *Criminal Code*, except to the extent that they are inconsistent with this Act.

(9) Proceedings under this Act before a judge without a jury or a court composed of a judge and jury or, in Nunavut, a judge of the Nunavut Court of Justice acting as a youth justice court, with or without a jury, as the case may be, shall be conducted in accordance with the provisions of Parts XIX (indictable offences — trial without jury) and XX (procedure in jury trials and general provisions) of the *Criminal Code*, with any modifications that the circumstances require, except that

(*a*) the provisions of this Act respecting the protection of privacy of young persons prevail over the provisions of the *Criminal Code*; and

(*b*) the young person is entitled to be represented in court by counsel if the young person is removed from court in accordance with subsection 650(2) of the *Criminal Code*. 2002, c. 13, s. 91(1)(*b*) to (*e*); 2012, c. 1, s. 178.

ANNOTATIONS

A preliminary inquiry is not mandatory under this Act and accordingly, the Crown can direct an indictment against a youthful offender: *R. v. L. (S.J.)*, [2009] 1 S.C.R. 426, 242 C.C.C. (3d) 297.

A joint trial of a young person with an adult is inconsistent with the governing principles of the Act: *R. v. L. (S.J.), supra.*

The re-election provisions in s. 473 of the *Criminal Code* are inconsistent with this Act and are not applicable. Accordingly, a youth charged with second degree murder has the right to elect trial by judge alone: *R. v. F. (M.)* (2007), 223 C.C.C. (3d) 209 (Ont. S.C.J.). Followed *R. v. H. (K.P.)* (2007), 240 C.C.C. (3d) 115 (Alta. Q.B.).

The power under subsec. (6) must be exercised in a manner consistent with the principles and objectives of the Act. The Crown was required to provide some disclosure of the basis upon which it sought to override the accused's election to be tried by judge alone: *R. v. C. (G.)* (2010), 258 C.C.C. (3d) 550 (Ont. S.C.J.).

Subsection (6) should be read as delegating the authority to impose a jury trial only to the Attorney General or the Deputy Attorney General: *R. v. S-R. (J.)* (2008), 236 C.C.C. (3d) 505 (Ont. S.C.J.).

In *R. v. S.-R. (J.)* (2012), 291 C.C.C. (3d) 394, the Ontario Court of Appeal agreed with the judge in *R. v. C. (G.), supra*, that a decision by the Deputy Attorney General under subsec. (6) to override a young person's decision to be tried by a judge alone is not a core exercise of prosecutorial discretion, and is therefore subject to judicial review for abuse of process on a less deferential standard. However, full administrative law procedural rights should not be read in. In this case, the duty of fairness was satisfied by providing notice to the accused and an opportunity to make submissions. The Crown was not required to provide reasons for the decision.

---

68. [*Repealed.* 2012, c. 1, s. 179.]

INCLUDED OFFENCES.

69. (1) [*Repealed.* 2012, c. 1, s. 180(1).]

(2) If the Attorney General has given notice under subsection 64(2) of the intention to seek an adult sentence and the young person is found guilty of an included offence for which an adult is liable to imprisonment for a term of more than two years, committed after he or she has attained the age of 14 years, the Attorney General may make an application under subsection 64(1) (application for adult sentence). 2012, c. 1, s. 180.

---

70. [*Repealed.* 2012, c. 1, s. 181.]

YOUTH

ANNOTATIONS

Previous versions of the Act created categories of offences for which, if found guilty, an adult sentence was presumed to apply to the young person. The presumption of adult sentences and reverse onus provisions were found to violate s. 7 of the Charter and could not be justified under s. 1: *R. v. B. (D.)*, [2008] 2 S.C.R. 3, 231 C.C.C. (3d) 338.

HEARING — ADULT SENTENCES.

71. The youth justice court shall, at the commencement of the sentencing hearing, hold a hearing in respect of an application under subsection 64(1) (application for adult sentence), unless the court has received notice that the application is not opposed. Both parties and the parents of the young person shall be given an opportunity to be heard at the hearing. 2012, c. 1, s. 182.

ORDER OF ADULT SENTENCE / Order of youth sentence / Onus / Pre-sentence report / Court to state reasons / Appeal.

72. (1) The youth justice court shall order that an adult sentence be imposed if it is satisfied that

(*a*) the presumption of diminished moral blameworthiness or culpability of the young person is rebutted; and

(*b*) a youth sentence imposed in accordance with the purpose and principles set out in subparagraph 3(1)(*b*)(ii) and section 38 would not be of sufficient length to hold the young person accountable for his or her offending behaviour.

(1.1) If the youth justice court is not satisfied that an order should be made under subsection (1), it shall order that the young person is not liable to an adult sentence and that a youth sentence must be imposed.

(2) The onus of satisfying the youth justice court as to the matters referred to in subsection (1) is on the Attorney General.

(3) In making an order under subsection (1) or (1.1), the youth justice court shall consider the pre-sentence report.

(4) When the youth justice court makes an order under this section, it shall state the reasons for its decision.

(5) For the purposes of an appeal in accordance with section 37, an order under subsection (1) or (1.1) is part of the sentence. 2012, c. 1, s. 183.

ANNOTATIONS

Previous versions of the Act created categories of offences for which, if found guilty, an adult sentence was presumed to apply to the young person. The presumption of adult sentences and reverse onus provisions were found to violate s. 7 of the Charter, in particular the principle of fundamental justice that young people are entitled to a presumption of diminished moral blameworthiness or culpability flowing from the fact that, because of their age, they have heightened vulnerability, less maturity and a reduced capacity for moral judgment. The provisions could not be justified under s. 1: *R. v. B. (D.)*, [2008] 2 S.C.R. 3, 231 C.C.C. (3d) 338.

This section does not require that the judge be satisfied beyond a reasonable doubt of the matters referred to in subsec. (1). The section requires the court to weigh and balance the enumerated factors and then to decide whether a youth sentence is sufficiently long to hold a young person accountable for his or her offending behaviour. That type of evaluative decision — making an informed judgment — does not lend itself to proof beyond a reasonable doubt: *R. v. O. (A.)* (2007), 218 C.C.C. (3d) 409 (Ont. C.A.). See also: *R. v. H. (C.T.)* (2015), 318 C.C.C. (3d) 240 (Man. C.A.). The analysis of whether the Crown has overcome the presumption of diminished moral blameworthiness and has satisfied the accountability test are best dealt with as separate inquiries: *R. v. W. (M.)* (2017), 134 O.R. (3d) 1 (C.A.).

With respect to the presumption of diminished moral blameworthiness, the focus must necessarily be on the issue of maturity. The presumption assumes that all young people start from a position of lesser maturity, moral sophistication and capacity for independent judgment than adults. In order to rebut the presumption, the Crown must satisfy the court that, at the time of the offence, the evidence supports a finding that the young person demonstrated the level of maturity, moral sophistication and capacity for independent judgment of an adult such that an adult sentence and adult principles of sentencing should apply to him or her: *R. v. W. (M.)* (2017), 134 O.R. (3d) 1 (C.A.).

Accountability within the meaning of subsec. (1) is achieved through the imposition of meaningful consequences for the offender and sanctions that promote his or her rehabilitation and reintegration into society. The purpose of accountability in this context excludes accountability to society in any larger sense or any notion of deterrence. Accountability in this context is the equivalent of the adult sentencing principle of retribution being an objective, reasoned and measured determination of an appropriate punishment which properly reflects the moral culpability of the offender, having regard to the intentional risk-taking of the offender, the consequential harm caused by the offender, and the normative character of the offender's conduct. The need to consider the normative character of an offender's behaviour necessarily requires the court to consider societal values. But the court cannot add on to a youth sentence an element of general deterrence or denunciation: *R. v. O. (A.), supra*. See also *R. v. W. (M.)* (2017), 134 O.R. (3d) 1 (C.A.).

There is well-settled authority from the Ontario Court of Appeal that, although a youth court judge must consider pre-sentence custody in sentencing an offender, the judge's treatment of the pre-sentence custody is discretionary. While s. 38(3)(*d*) of the *Youth Criminal Justice Act* requires the youth court judge to take detention "into account", the judge is not required to actually deduct pre-sentence custody when crafting an appropriate sentence. Whether and to what extent credit is given for pre-sentence custody against a youth sentence is within a youth court judge's discretion, particularly in the context of a Crown application to sentence a youth as an adult. In such cases, pre-sentence custody can be taken into account as a consideration in determining whether the young person would serve an adult or youth sentence as opposed to through an actual credit to length of sentence imposed: *R. v. W. (M.)* (2017), 346 C.C.C. (3d) 319 (Ont. C.A.). See also *R. v. P. (N.W.)* (2008), 235 C.C.C. (3d) 125 (Man. C.A.); *R. v. J. (R.R.)* (2009), 250 C.C.C. (3d) 3 (B.C.C.A.); *R. v. T. (D.D.)* (2010), 265 C.C.C. (3d) 49 (Alta. C.A.), leave to appeal to S.C.C. refused [2011] 2 S.C.R. x; *R. v. W. (D.)* (2008), 79 W.C.B. (2d) 80, [2008] O.J. No. 1356 (C.A.).

It is not contrary to s. 119(2) of the Act to consider a youth record under this provision: *R. v. Quintana* (2009), 246 C.C.C. (3d) 33 (B.C.C.A.).

COURT MUST IMPOSE ADULT SENTENCE / Court must impose youth sentence.

73. (1) When the youth justice court makes an order under subsection 72(1) in respect of a young person, the court shall, on a finding of guilt, impose an adult sentence on the young person.

(2) When the youth justice court makes an order under subsection 72(1.1) in respect of a young person, the court shall, on a finding of guilt, impose a youth sentence on the young person. 2012, c. 1, s. 184.

ANNOTATIONS

Previous versions of the Act created categories of offences for which, if found guilty, an adult sentence was presumed to apply to the young person. The presumption of adult sentences and reverse onus provisions were found to violate s. 7 of the Charter and could not be justified under s. 1: *R. v. B. (D.)*, [2008] 2 S.C.R. 3, 231 C.C.C. (3d) 338.

APPLICATION OF PARTS XXIII AND XXIV OF CRIMINAL CODE / Finding of guilt becomes a conviction / Interpretation.

74. (1) Parts XXIII (sentencing) and XXIV (dangerous and long-term offenders) of the *Criminal Code* apply to a young person in respect of whom the youth justice court has ordered that an adult sentence be imposed.

(2) A finding of guilt for an offence in respect of which an adult sentence is imposed becomes a conviction once the time allowed for the taking of an appeal has expired or, if an appeal is taken, all proceedings in respect of the appeal have been completed and the appeal court has upheld an adult sentence.

(3) This section does not affect the time of commencement of an adult sentence under subsection 719(1) of the *Criminal Code*.

ANNOTATIONS

An adult sentence is still subject to the ameliorating aspects of the Act, in particular the principles containe in s. 3. While this provision imports the objectives of s. 718 of the *Criminal Code*, the sentencing judge was also required to emphasize the goals of rehabilitation, reintegration and fair and proportionate accountability relevant to youthful offenders: *R. v. P. (D.D.)* (2007), 218 C.C.C. (3d) 298 (B.C.C.A.).

However, the opposite conclusion was reached in *R. v. F. (B.C.)* (2009), 249 C.C.C. (3d) 366 (Sask. C.A.). There, the court held that there are key inconsistencies between the principles set out in s. 3 of the Act and the sentencing principles set out in s. 718 of the *Criminal Code*. The Act establishes a separate regime for the sentencing of young people until such time as that regime fails to allow for a sentence of sufficient length to hold the young person accountable for his offending behaviour and, when that point is reached, the young person is to be sentenced as an adult. There is no "third" sentencing regime creating a hybrid between the sentencing regime in the *Criminal Code* and that contained in the *Youth Criminal Justice Act* where a young person is sentenced as an adult.

DECISION REGARDING LIFTING OF PUBLICATION BAN / Order / Onus / Appeals.

75. (1) When the youth justice court imposes a youth sentence on a young person who has been found guilty of a violent offence, the court shall decide whether it is appropriate to make an order lifting the ban on publication of information that would identify the young person as having been dealt with under this Act as referred to in subsection 110(1).

(2) A youth justice court may order a lifting of the ban on publication if the court determines, taking into account the purpose and principles set out in sections 3 and 38, that the young person poses a significant risk of committing another violent offence and the lifting of the ban is necessary to protect the public against that risk.

(3) The onus of satisfying the youth justice court as to the appropriateness of lifting the ban is on the Attorney General.

(4) For the purposes of an appeal in accordance with section 37, an order under subsection (2) is part of the sentence. 2012, c. 1, s. 185.

ANNOTATIONS

A previous version of this provision was found to violate s. 7 of the *Canadian Charter of Rights and Freedoms* and could not be justified under s. 1 to the extent that it obliged the young person to justify maintaining the publication ban rather than requiring the prosecutor to justify lifting the ban: *R. v. B. (D.)*, [2008] 2 S.C.R. 3, 231 C.C.C. (3d) 338.

PLACEMENT WHEN SUBJECT TO ADULT SENTENCE / Young person under age of 18 / Opportunity to be heard / Report necessary / Appeals / Review / Who may make application / Notice / Limit — age twenty.

76. (1) Subject to subsections (2) and (9) and sections 79 and 80 and despite anything else in this Act or any other Act of Parliament, when a young person who is subject to an adult sentence in respect of an offence is sentenced to a term of imprisonment for the offence, the youth justice court shall order that the young person serve any portion of the imprisonment in

(*a*) a youth custody facility separate and apart from any adult who is detained or held in custody;

(*b*) a provincial correctional facility for adults; or

(*c*) if the sentence is for two years or more, a penitentiary.

(2) No young person who is under the age of 18 years is to serve any portion of the imprisonment in a provincial correctional facility for adults or a penitentiary.

(3) Before making an order under subsection (1), the youth justice court shall give the young person, a parent of the young person, the Attorney General, the provincial director and representatives of the provincial and federal correctional systems an opportunity to be heard.

(4) Before making an order under subsection (1), the youth justice court shall require that a report be prepared for the purpose of assisting the court.

(5) For the purposes of an appeal in accordance with section 37, an order under subsection (1) is part of the sentence.

(6) On application, the youth justice court shall review the placement of a young person under this section and, if satisfied that the circumstances that resulted in the initial order have changed materially, and after having given the young person, a parent of the young person, the Attorney General, the provincial director and the representatives of the provincial and federal correctional systems an opportunity to be heard, the court may order that the young person be placed in

(*a*) a youth custody facility separate and apart from any adult who is detained or held in custody;

(*b*) a provincial correctional facility for adults; or

(*c*) if the sentence is for two years or more, a penitentiary.

(7) An application referred to in this section may be made by the young person, one of the young person's parents, the provincial director, representatives of the provincial and federal correctional systems and the Attorney General, after the time for all appeals has expired.

(8) When an application referred to in this section is made, the applicant shall cause a notice of the application to be given to the other persons referred to in subsection (7).

(9) No young person shall remain in a youth custody facility under this section after the young person attains the age of twenty years, unless the youth justice court that makes the order under subsection (1) or reviews the placement under subsection (6) is satisfied that remaining in the youth custody facility would be in the best interests of the young person and would not jeopardize the safety of others. 2012, c. 1, s. 186.

OBLIGATION TO INFORM — PAROLE / Applicability of Corrections and Conditional Release Act / Appropriate parole board.

77. (1) When a young person is ordered to serve a portion of a sentence in a youth custody facility under paragraph 76(1)(*a*) (placement when subject to adult sentence), the provincial director shall inform the appropriate parole board.

(2) For greater certainty, Part II of the *Corrections and Conditional Release Act* applies, subject to section 78, with respect to a young person who is the subject of an order under subsection 76(1) (placement when subject to adult sentence).

(3) The appropriate parole board for the purposes of this section is

(*a*) if subsection 112(1) of the *Corrections and Conditional Release Act* would apply with respect to the young person but for the fact that the young person was ordered into a youth custody facility, the parole board mentioned in that subsection; and

(*b*) in any other case, the Parole Board of Canada. 2012, c. 1, s. 160(*l*)(i).

RELEASE ENTITLEMENT / **Release entitlement.**

78. (1) For greater certainty, section 6 of the Prisons and Reformatories Act applies to a young person who is ordered to serve a portion of a sentence in a youth custody facility under paragraph 76(1)(*a*) (placement when subject to adult sentence) only if section 743.1 (rules respecting sentences of two or more years) of the *Criminal Code* would direct that the young person serve the sentence in a prison.

(2) For greater certainty, section 127 of the *Corrections and Conditional Release Act* applies to a young person who is ordered to serve a portion of a sentence in a youth custody facility under paragraph 76(1)(a) (placement when subject to adult sentence) only if section 743.1 (rules respecting sentences of two or more years) of the *Criminal Code* would direct that the young person serve the sentence in a penitentiary.

IF PERSON CONVICTED UNDER ANOTHER ACT.

79. If a person who is serving all or a portion of a sentence in a youth custody facility under paragraph 76(1)(*a*) (placement when subject to adult sentence) is sentenced to a term of imprisonment under an Act of Parliament other than this Act, the remainder of the portion of the sentence being served in the youth custody facility shall be served in a provincial correctional facility for adults or a penitentiary, in accordance with section 743.1 (rules respecting sentences of two or more years) of the *Criminal Code*.

IF PERSON WHO IS SERVING A SENTENCE UNDER ANOTHER ACT IS SENTENCED TO AN ADULT SENTENCE.

80. If a person who has been serving a sentence of imprisonment under an Act of Parliament other than this Act is sentenced to an adult sentence of imprisonment under this Act, the sentences shall be served in a provincial correctional facility for adults or a penitentiary, in accordance with section 743.1 (rules respecting sentences of two or more years) of the *Criminal Code*.

PROCEDURE FOR APPLICATION OR NOTICE.

81. An application or a notice to the court under section 64 or 76 must be made or given orally, in the presence of the other party, or in writing with a copy served personally on the other party. 2012, c. 1, s. 187.

Effect of Termination of Youth Sentence

EFFECT OF ABSOLUTE DISCHARGE OR TERMINATION OF YOUTH SENTENCE / **Disqualifications removed / Applications for employment / Finding of guilt not a previous conviction.**

82. (1) Subject to section 12 (examination as to previous convictions) of the Canada Evidence Act, if a young person is found guilty of an offence, and a youth justice court

directs under paragraph 42(2)(*b*) that the young person be discharged absolutely, or the youth sentence, or any disposition made under the *Young Offenders Act*, chapter Y-1 of the Revised Statutes of Canada, 1985, has ceased to have effect, other than an order under section 51 (mandatory prohibition order) of this Act or section 20.1 (mandatory prohibition order) of the *Young Offenders Act*, the young person is deemed not to have been found guilty or convicted of the offence except that

(*a*) the young person may plead autrefois convict in respect of any subsequent charge relating to the offence;

(*b*) a youth justice court may consider the finding of guilt in considering an application under subsection 64(1) (application for adult sentence);

(*c*) any court or justice may consider the finding of guilt in considering an application for judicial interim release or in considering what sentence to impose for any offence; and

(*d*) the Parole Board of Canada or any provincial parole board may consider the finding of guilt in considering an application for conditional release or for a record suspension under the *Criminal Records Act*.

(2) For greater certainty and without restricting the generality of subsection (1), an absolute discharge under paragraph 42(2)(*b*) or the termination of the youth sentence or disposition in respect of an offence for which a young person is found guilty removes any disqualification in respect of the offence to which the young person is subject under any Act of Parliament by reason of a finding of guilt.

(3) No application form for or relating to the following shall contain any question that by its terms requires the applicant to disclose that he or she has been charged with or found guilty of an offence in respect of which he or she has, under this Act or the *Young Offenders Act*, chapter Y-1 of the Revised Statutes of Canada, 1985, been discharged absolutely, or has completed the youth sentence under this Act or the disposition under the *Young Offenders Act*:

(*a*) employment in any department, as defined in section 2 of the *Financial Administration Act*;

(*b*) employment by any Crown corporation, as defined in section 83 of the *Financial Administration Act*;

(*c*) enrolment in the Canadian Forces; or

(*d*) employment on or in connection with the operation of any work, undertaking or business that is within the legislative authority of Parliament.

(4) A finding of guilt under this Act is not a previous conviction for the purposes of any offence under any Act of Parliament for which a greater punishment is prescribed by reason of previous convictions, except for

(*a*) [*Repealed.* 2012, c. 1, s. 188(2).]

(*b*) the purpose of determining the adult sentence to be imposed. 2012, c. 1, s. 156; 2012, c. 1, s. 188; 2012, c. 1, s. 160(*l*)(ii).

ANNOTATIONS

The application of s. 82(4) is affected by the operation of s. 119(9)(a), which prescribes circumstances in which s. 82 does not apply. Section 119 establishes "access periods" during which youth records can be accessible to certain individuals and entities. Following expiration of the access periods, the youth record is generally inaccessible unless access is ordered under s. 123. *Per* s. 119(9), in some instances where a young person is convicted of an offence committed when he or she is an adult during the record access period, the young person loses the benefit of s. 82; the record is dealt with as a record of an adult, and the finding of guilt in respect of the offence for which the record is kept is deemed to be a conviction.

It was held in *R. v. Morris*, [1979] 1 S.C.R. 405, 43 C.C.C. (2d) 129, 6 C.R. (3d) 36, that delinquencies under the *Juvenile Delinquents Act* for acts which, if committed by an adult, would have been punishable under the *Criminal Code*, can be the subject of cross-examination under s. 12 of the *Canada Evidence Act*. On the other hand, it has been held that a discharge under s. 736 of the *Criminal Code* is not a "conviction" for the purposes of s. 12: *R. v. Danson* (1982), 66 C.C.C. (2d) 369, 35 O.R. (2d) 777 (C.A.).

There remains some jurisprudential controversy surrounding the scope of s. 82. In *R. v. Sheik-Qasim* (2007), 230 C.C.C. (3d) 531 (Ont. S.C.J.), it was held that s. 82 does not permit cross-examination on a youth record outside of the access period as defined in s. 119 of the Act. In *R. v. Hammerstrom* (2018), 363 C.C.C. (3d) 430 (B.C.C.A.), it was held that, before cross-examination on a youth criminal record can be conducted, resort must be had to the restrictions, prohibitions and processes governing access to and use of such records as set out in Part 6 of the Act. Simply ordering a publication ban is insufficient. However, in *R. v. U. (D.A.)* (2008), 239 C.C.C. (3d) 409 (N.S.S.C.), the opposite conclusion was reached; there, the court held that nothing in the *Youth Criminal Justice Act* restricts the common law right to cross-examine a witness on matters relating to his or her credibility, and that the expiration of the access period does not prevent access or cross-examination.

PART 5 / CUSTODY AND SUPERVISION

PURPOSE / Principles to be used.

83. (1) The purpose of the youth custody and supervision system is to contribute to the protection of society by

- **(*a*) carrying out sentences imposed by courts through the safe, fair and humane custody and supervision of young persons; and**
- **(*b*) assisting young persons to be rehabilitated and reintegrated into the community as law-abiding citizens, by providing effective programs to young persons in custody and while under supervision in the community.**

(2) In addition to the principles set out in section 3, the following principles are to be used in achieving that purpose:

- **(*a*) that the least restrictive measures consistent with the protection of the public, of personnel working with young persons and of young persons be used;**
- **(*b*) that young persons sentenced to custody retain the rights of other young persons, except the rights that are necessarily removed or restricted as a consequence of a sentence under this Act or another Act of Parliament;**
- **(*c*) that the youth custody and supervision system facilitate the involvement of the families of young persons and members of the public;**
- **(*d*) that custody and supervision decisions be made in a forthright, fair and timely manner, and that young persons have access to an effective review procedure; and**
- **(*e*) that placements of young persons where they are treated as adults not disadvantage them with respect to their eligibility for and conditions of release.**

YOUNG PERSON TO BE HELD APART FROM ADULTS.

84. Subject to subsection 30(3) (pre-trial detention), paragraphs 76(1)(*b*) and (*c*) (placement in adult facilities with adult sentence) and sections 89 to 93 (placement in adult facilities with youth sentence), a young person who is committed to custody shall be held separate and apart from any adult who is detained or held in custody.

LEVELS OF CUSTODY / Designation of youth custody facilities/Provincial director to specify custody level — committal to custody / Provincial director to specify custody level — transfer / Factors / Placement and transfer at appropriate level / Notice.

85. (1) In the youth custody and supervision system in each province there must be at least two levels of custody for young persons distinguished by the degree of restraint of the young persons in them.

(2) Every youth custody facility in a province that contains one or more levels of custody shall be designated by

(*a*) in the case of a youth custody facility with only one level of custody, being the level of custody with the least degree of restraint of the young persons in it, the lieutenant governor in council or his or her delegate; and

(*b*) in any other case, the lieutenant governor in council.

(3) The provincial director shall, when a young person is committed to custody under paragraph 42(2)(*n*), (*o*), (*q*) or (*r*) or an order is made under subsection 98(3), paragraph 103(2)(*b*), subsection 104(1) or paragraph 109(2)(*b*), determine the level of custody appropriate for the young person, after having taken into account the factors set out in subsection (5).

(4) The provincial director may determine a different level of custody for the young person when the provincial director is satisfied that the needs of the young person and the interests of society would be better served by doing so, after having taken into account the factors set out in subsection (5).

(5) The factors referred to in subsections (3) and (4) are

(*a*) that the appropriate level of custody for the young person is the one that is the least restrictive to the young person, having regard to

(i) the seriousness of the offence in respect of which the young person was committed to custody and the circumstances in which that offence was committed,

(ii) the needs and circumstances of the young person, including proximity to family, school, employment and support services,

(iii) the safety of other young persons in custody, and

(iv) the interests of society;

(*b*) that the level of custody should allow for the best possible match of programs to the young person's needs and behaviour, having regard to the findings of any assessment in respect of the young person; and

(*c*) the likelihood of escape.

(6) After the provincial director has determined the appropriate level of custody for the young person under subsection (3) or (4), the young person shall be placed in the youth custody facility that contains that level of custody specified by the provincial director.

(7) The provincial director shall cause a notice in writing of a determination under subsection (3) or (4) to be given to the young person and a parent of the young person and set out in that notice the reasons for it.

YOUTH

PROCEDURAL SAFEGUARDS / Withholding of information.

86. (1) The lieutenant governor in council of a province shall ensure that procedures are in place to ensure that the due process rights of the young person are protected with respect to a determination made under subsection 85(3) or (4), including that the young person be

(*a*) provided with any relevant information to which the provincial director has access in making the determination, subject to subsection (2);

(*b*) given the opportunity to be heard; and

(*c*) informed of any right to a review under section 87.

(2) Where the provincial director has reasonable grounds to believe that providing the information referred to in paragraph (1)(*a*) would jeopardize the safety of any person or the security of a facility, he or she may authorize the withholding from the young person of as much information as is strictly necessary in order to protect such safety or security.

REVIEW / Procedural safeguards / Withholding of information / Factors / Decision is final.

87. (1) A young person may apply for a review under this section of a determination

(*a*) under subsection 85(3) that would place the young person in a facility at a level of custody that has more than a minimal degree of restraint; or

(*b*) under subsection 85(4) that would transfer a young person to a facility at a level of custody with a higher degree of restraint or increase the degree of restraint of the young person in the facility.

(2) The lieutenant governor in council of a province shall ensure that procedures are in place for the review under subsection (1), including that

(*a*) the review board that conducts the review be independent;

(*b*) the young person be provided with any relevant information to which the review board has access, subject to subsection (3); and

(*c*) the young person be given the opportunity to be heard.

(3) Where the review board has reasonable grounds to believe that providing the information referred to in paragraph (2)(*b*) would jeopardize the safety of any person or the security of a facility, it may authorize the withholding from the young person of as much information as is strictly necessary in order to protect such safety or security.

(4) The review board shall take into account the factors referred to in subsection 85(5) in reviewing a determination.

(5) A decision of the review board under this section in respect of a particular determination is final.

FUNCTIONS TO BE EXERCISED BY YOUTH JUSTICE COURT.

88. The lieutenant governor in council of a province may order that the power to make determinations of the level of custody for young persons and to review those determinations be exercised in accordance with the *Young Offenders Act*, chapter Y-1 of the Revised Statutes of Canada, 1985. The following provisions of that Act apply, with any modifications that the circumstances require, to the exercise of those powers:

(*a*) the definitions "review board" and "progress report" in subsection 2(1);

(*b*) section 11;

(*c*) sections 24.1 to 24.3; and

(*d*) sections 28 to 31.

ANNOTATIONS

The four most important factors for a youth court judge to consider when determining the level of custody are: (1) the seriousness and circumstances of the offence; (2) the needs and circumstances of the young person; (3) the safety of other young persons in custody; and (4) the interests of society: *R. v. Z. (A.A.)* (2013), 298 C.C.C. (3d) 59 (Man. C.A.).

EXCEPTION IF YOUNG PERSON IS TWENTY YEARS OLD OR OLDER / If serving youth sentence in a provincial correctional facility / Provisions to apply.

89. (1) When a young person is twenty years old or older at the time the youth sentence is imposed on him or her under paragraph 42(2)(*n*), (*o*), (*q*) or (*r*), the young person

shall, despite section 85, be committed to a provincial correctional facility for adults to serve the youth sentence.

(2) If a young person is serving a youth sentence in a provincial correctional facility for adults pursuant to subsection (1), the youth justice court may, on application of the provincial director at any time after the young person begins to serve a portion of the youth sentence in a provincial correctional facility for adults, after giving the young person, the provincial director and representatives of the provincial and federal correctional systems an opportunity to be heard, authorize the provincial director to direct that the young person serve the remainder of the youth sentence in a penitentiary if the court considers it to be in the best interests of the young person or in the public interest and if, at the time of the application, that remainder is two years or more.

(3) If a young person is serving a youth sentence in a provincial correctional facility for adults or a penitentiary under subsection (1) or (2), the *Prisons and Reformatories Act* and the *Corrections and Conditional Release Act*, and any other statute, regulation or rule applicable in respect of prisoners or offenders within the meaning of those Acts, statutes, regulations and rules, apply in respect of the young person except to the extent that they conflict with Part 6 (publication, records and information) of this Act, which Part continues to apply to the young person.

ANNOTATIONS

Only the custodial portion of a youth sentence is subject to the parole scheme and included in the definition of "sentence" in s. 2(1) of the *Corrections and Conditional Release Act*, S.C. 1992, c. 20: *P. (J.) v. Canada (Attorney General)* (2010), 253 C.C.C. (3d) 425 (F.C.A.).

YOUTH WORKER / Role of youth worker when young person in the community.

90. (1) When a youth sentence is imposed committing a young person to custody, the provincial director of the province in which the young person received the youth sentence and was placed in custody shall, without delay, designate a youth worker to work with the young person to plan for his or her reintegration into the community, including the preparation and implementation of a reintegration plan that sets out the most effective programs for the young person in order to maximize his or her chances for reintegration into the community.

(2) When a portion of a young person's youth sentence is served in the community in accordance with section 97 or 105, the youth worker shall supervise the young person, continue to provide support to the young person and assist the young person to respect the conditions to which he or she is subject, and help the young person in the implementation of the reintegration plan.

REINTEGRATION LEAVE / Renewal of reintegration leave / Revocation of authorization / Arrest and return to custody.

91. (1) The provincial director of a province may, subject to any terms or conditions that he or she considers desirable, authorize, for a young person committed to a youth custody facility in the province further to an order under paragraph 76(1)(*a*) (placement when subject to adult sentence) or a youth sentence imposed under paragraph 42(2)(*n*), (*o*), (*q*) or (*r*),

- **(*a*) a reintegration leave from the youth custody facility for a period not exceeding thirty days if, in the opinion of the provincial director, it is necessary or desirable that the young person be absent, with or without escort, for medical, compassionate or humanitarian reasons or for the purpose of rehabilitating the young person or reintegrating the young person into the community; or**

(*b*) that the young person be released from the youth custody facility on the days and during the hours that the provincial director specifies in order that the young person may
(i) attend school or any other educational or training institution,
(ii) obtain or continue employment or perform domestic or other duties required by the young person's family,
(iii) participate in a program specified by the provincial director that, in the provincial director's opinion, will enable the young person to better carry out employment or improve his or her education or training, or
(iv) attend an out-patient treatment program or other program that provides services that are suitable to addressing the young person's needs.

(2) A reintegration leave authorized under paragraph (1)(*a*) may be renewed by the provincial director for one or more thirty-day periods on reassessment of the case.

(3) The provincial director of a province may, at any time, revoke an authorization made under subsection (1).

(4) If the provincial director revokes an authorization under subsection (3) or if a young person fails to comply with any term or condition of a reintegration leave or a release from custody under this section, the young person may be arrested without warrant and returned to custody.

TRANSFER TO ADULT FACILITY / If serving youth sentence in a provincial correctional facility / Provisions to apply / Placement when adult and youth sentences / Youth sentence and adult sentence.

92. (1) When a young person is committed to custody under paragraph 42(2)(*n*), (*o*), (*q*) or (*r*), the youth justice court may, on application of the provincial director made at any time after the young person attains the age of eighteen years, after giving the young person, the provincial director and representatives of the provincial correctional system an opportunity to be heard, authorize the provincial director to direct that the young person, subject to subsection (3), serve the remainder of the youth sentence in a provincial correctional facility for adults, if the court considers it to be in the best interests of the young person or in the public interest.

(2) The youth justice court may authorize the provincial director to direct that a young person, subject to subsection (3), serve the remainder of a youth sentence in a penitentiary
(*a*) if the youth justice court considers it to be in the best interests of the young person or in the public interest;
(*b*) if the provincial director applies for the authorization at any time after the young person begins to serve a portion of a youth sentence in a provincial correctional facility for adults further to a direction made under subsection (1);
(*c*) if, at the time of the application, that remainder is two years or more; and
(*d*) so long as the youth justice court gives the young person, the provincial director and representatives of the provincial and federal correctional systems an opportunity to be heard.

(3) If the provincial director makes a direction under subsection (1) or (2), the *Prisons and Reformatories Act* and the *Corrections and Conditional Release Act*, and any other statute, regulation or rule applicable in respect of prisoners and offenders within the meaning of those Acts, statutes, regulations and rules, apply in respect of the young person except to the extent that they conflict with Part 6 (publication, records and information) of this Act, which Part continues to apply to the young person.

(4) If a person is subject to more than one sentence, at least one of which is a youth sentence imposed under paragraph 42(2)(*n*), (*o*), (*q*) or (*r*) and at least one of which is a sentence referred to in either paragraph (*b*) or (*c*), he or she shall serve, in a provincial correctional facility for adults or a penitentiary in accordance with section 743.1 (rules respecting sentences of two or more years) of the *Criminal Code*, the following:

(*a*) the remainder of any youth sentence imposed under paragraph 42(2)(*n*), (*o*), (*q*) or (*r*);

(*b*) an adult sentence to which an order under paragraph 76(1)(*b*) or (*c*) (placement in adult facility) applies; and

(*c*) any sentence of imprisonment imposed otherwise than under this Act.

(5) If a young person is committed to custody under a youth sentence under paragraph 42(2)(*n*), (*o*), (*q*) or (*r*) and is also already subject to an adult sentence to which an order under paragraph 76(1)(*a*) (placement when subject to adult sentence) applies, the young person may, in the discretion of the provincial director, serve the sentences, or any portion of the sentences, in a youth custody facility, in a provincial correctional facility for adults or, if the unexpired portion of the sentence is two years or more, in a penitentiary.

WHEN YOUNG PERSON REACHES TWENTY YEARS OF AGE / If serving youth sentence in a provincial correctional facility / Provisions to apply.

93. (1) When a young person who is committed to custody under paragraph 42(2)(*n*), (*o*), (*q*) or (*r*) is in a youth custody facility when the young person attains the age of twenty years, the young person shall be transferred to a provincial correctional facility for adults to serve the remainder of the youth sentence, unless the provincial director orders that the young person continue to serve the youth sentence in a youth custody facility.

(2) If a young person is serving a portion of a youth sentence in a provincial correctional facility for adults pursuant to a transfer under subsection (1), the youth justice court may, on application of the provincial director after the transfer, after giving the young person, the provincial director and representatives of the provincial and federal correctional systems an opportunity to be heard, authorize the provincial director to direct that the young person serve the remainder of the youth sentence in a penitentiary if the court considers it to be in the best interests of the young person or in the public interest and if, at the time of the application, that remainder is two years or more.

(3) If the provincial director makes the direction, the Prisons and Reformatories Act and the Corrections and Conditional Release Act, and any other statute, regulation or rule applicable in respect of prisoners and offenders within the meaning of those Acts, statutes, regulations and rules, apply in respect of the young person except to the extent that they conflict with Part 6 (publication, records and information) of this Act, which Part continues to apply to the young person.

ANNOTATIONS

It is only when the provincial director brings an application, and after the young person, the provincial director and representatives of the provincial and federal correctional systems have had an opportunity to be heard, that a youth court judge may order the remainder of the sentence to be served in a federal penitentiary — and then only if it would be in the best interests of the young person or the public. The *Youth Criminal Justice Act* framework presumes that young persons will serve their sentences in provincial facilities, unless circumstances indicate that a transfer to the federal system is warranted: *R. v. W. (M.)* (2017), 346 C.C.C. (3d) 319 (Ont. C.A.).

YOUTH

ANNUAL REVIEW / Annual review / Optional review / Time for optional review / Review / Grounds for review / No review if appeal pending / Youth justice court may order appearance of young person for review / Progress report / Additional information in progress report / Written or oral report / Subsections 40(4) to (10) to apply / Notice of review from provincial director / Notice of review from person requesting it / Statement of right to counsel / Service of notice / Notice may be waived / If notice not given / Decision of the youth justice court after review.

94. (1) When a young person is committed to custody pursuant to a youth sentence under paragraph 42(2)(*n*), (*o*), (*q*) or (*r*) for a period exceeding one year, the provincial director of the province in which the young person is held in custody shall cause the young person to be brought before the youth justice court without delay at the end of one year from the date of the most recent youth sentence imposed in respect of the offence — and at the end of every subsequent year from that date — and the youth justice court shall review the youth sentence.

(2) When a young person is committed to custody pursuant to youth sentences imposed under paragraph 42(2)(*n*), (*o*), (*q*) or (*r*) in respect of more than one offence for a total period exceeding one year, the provincial director of the province in which the young person is held in custody shall cause the young person to be brought before the youth justice court without delay at the end of one year from the date of the earliest youth sentence imposed — and at the end of every subsequent year from that date — and the youth justice court shall review the youth sentences.

(3) When a young person is committed to custody pursuant to a youth sentence imposed under paragraph 42(2)(*n*), (*o*), (*q*) or (*r*) in respect of an offence, the provincial director may, on the provincial director's own initiative, and shall, on the request of the young person, the young person's parent or the Attorney General, on any of the grounds set out in subsection (6), cause the young person to be brought before a youth justice court to review the youth sentence,

(*a*) when the youth sentence is for a period not exceeding one year, once at any time after the expiry of the greater of

(i) thirty days after the date of the youth sentence imposed under subsection 42(2) in respect of the offence, and

(ii) one third of the period of the youth sentence imposed under subsection 42(2) in respect of the offence; and

(*b*) when the youth sentence is for a period exceeding one year, at any time after six months after the date of the most recent youth sentence imposed in respect of the offence.

(4) The young person may be brought before the youth justice court at any other time, with leave of the youth justice court judge.

(5) If a youth justice court is satisfied that there are grounds for review under subsection (6), the court shall review the youth sentence.

(6) A youth sentence imposed in respect of a young person may be reviewed under subsection (5)

(*a*) on the ground that the young person has made sufficient progress to justify a change in the youth sentence;

(*b*) on the ground that the circumstances that led to the youth sentence have changed materially;

(*c*) on the ground that new services or programs are available that were not available at the time of the youth sentence;

(*d*) on the ground that the opportunities for rehabilitation are now greater in the community; or

(*e*) on any other ground that the youth justice court considers appropriate.

(7) Despite any other provision of this section, no review of a youth sentence in respect of which an appeal has been taken shall be made under this section until all proceedings in respect of any such appeal have been completed.

(8) When a provincial director is required under subsections (1) to (3) to cause a young person to be brought before the youth justice court and fails to do so, the youth justice court may, on application made by the young person, his or her parent or the Attorney General, or on its own motion, order the provincial director to cause the young person to be brought before the youth justice court.

(9) The youth justice court shall, before reviewing under this section a youth sentence imposed in respect of a young person, require the provincial director to cause to be prepared, and to submit to the youth justice court, a progress report on the performance of the young person since the youth sentence took effect.

(10) A person preparing a progress report in respect of a young person may include in the report any information relating to the personal and family history and present environment of the young person that he or she considers advisable.

(11) A progress report shall be in writing unless it cannot reasonably be committed to writing, in which case it may, with leave of the youth justice court, be submitted orally in court.

(12) Subsections 40(4) to (10) (procedures respecting pre-sentence reports) apply, with any modifications that the circumstances require, in respect of progress reports.

(13) When a youth sentence imposed in respect of a young person is to be reviewed under subsection (1) or (2), the provincial director shall cause any notice that may be directed by rules of court applicable to the youth justice court or, in the absence of such a direction, at least five clear days notice of the review to be given in writing to the young person, a parent of the young person and the Attorney General.

(14) When a review of a youth sentence imposed in respect of a young person is requested under subsection (3), the person requesting the review shall cause any notice that may be directed by rules of court applicable to the youth justice court or, in the absence of such a direction, at least five clear days notice of the review to be given in writing to the young person, a parent of the young person and the Attorney General.

(15) A notice given to a parent under subsection (13) or (14) shall include a statement that the young person whose youth sentence is to be reviewed has the right to be represented by counsel.

(16) A notice under subsection (13) or (14) may be served personally or may be sent by confirmed delivery service.

(17) Any of the persons entitled to notice under subsection (13) or (14) may waive the right to that notice.

(18) If notice under subsection (13) or (14) is not given in accordance with this section, the youth justice court may

- **(*a*) adjourn the proceedings and order that the notice be given in the manner and to the persons that it directs; or**
- **(*b*) dispense with the notice if, in the opinion of the court, having regard to the circumstances, notice may be dispensed with.**

(19) When a youth justice court reviews under this section a youth sentence imposed in respect of a young person, it may, after giving the young person, a parent of the young person, the Attorney General and the provincial director an opportunity to be heard, having regard to the needs of the young person and the interests of society,

- **(*a*) confirm the youth sentence;**
- **(*b*) release the young person from custody and place the young person under conditional supervision in accordance with the procedure set out in section 105, with any modifications that the circumstances require, for a period not**

YOUTH

exceeding the remainder of the youth sentence that the young person is then serving; or

(*c*) **if the provincial director so recommends, convert a youth sentence under paragraph 42(2)(*r*) to a youth sentence under paragraph 42(2)(*q*) if the offence was murder or to a youth sentence under paragraph 42(2)(*n*) or (*o*), as the case may be, if the offence was an offence other than murder.**

ANNOTATIONS

Note: Some of the following cases were decided under the *Young Offenders Act* but were thought to be of assistance in applying this Act.

Subsection (1) – A review is designed to monitor and reward rehabilitation and progress, but also to make sure that appropriate treatment and programs are made available to the offender. The review focuses on what can now best advance the needs of the young offender and the interests of society, and requires a balancing of those two considerations: *R. v. K. (C.)* (2008), 233 C.C.C. (3d) 194 (Ont. C.J.). Except, *semble*, where failure to change the venue of the review would result in inconvenience so great as to result in a denial of justice, the review must take place in the judicial district where the original order of committal was made: *R. v. W. (C.)* (1985), 21 C.C.C. (3d) 365 (Ont. Prov. Ct.). For a discussion of the application of s. 94 reviews in the context of IRCS orders, see: *R. v. Z. (A.A.)* (2013), 298 C.C.C. (3d) 59 (Man. C.A.).

Subsection (7) – It was held considering s. 28(5) of the *Young Offenders Act*, which was worded similarly to this subsection, that the limitation on the review provisions does not apply where the appeal is only as to the finding of guilt: *R. v. B. (L.C.)* (1991), 65 C.C.C. (3d) 574 (Ont. Ct. (Prov. Div.)).

ORDERS ARE YOUTH SENTENCES.

95. Orders under subsections 97(2) (conditions) and 98(3) (continuation of custody), paragraph 103(2)(*b*) (continuation of custody), subsections 104(1) (continuation of custody) and 105(1) (conditional supervision) and paragraph 109(2)(*b*) (continuation of suspension of conditional supervision) are deemed to be youth sentences for the purposes of section 94 (reviews).

RECOMMENDATION OF PROVINCIAL DIRECTOR FOR CONDITIONAL SUPERVISION OF YOUNG PERSON / Notice / Application to court for review of recommendation / Subsections 94(7), (9) to (12) and (14) to (19) apply / If no application for review made under subsection (3) / Notice when no release ordered / Provincial director may request review / When provincial director requests a review.

96. (1) When a young person is held in custody pursuant to a youth sentence under paragraph 42(2)(*n*), (*o*), (*q*) or (*r*), the provincial director may, if satisfied that the needs of the young person and the interests of society would be better served by doing so, make a recommendation to the youth justice court that the young person be released from custody and placed under conditional supervision.

(2) If the provincial director makes a recommendation, the provincial director shall cause a notice to be given in writing that includes the reasons for the recommendation and the conditions that the provincial director would recommend be set under section 105 to the young person, a parent of the young person and the Attorney General and give a copy of the notice to the youth justice court.

(3) If notice of a recommendation is made under subsection (2) with respect to a youth sentence imposed on a young person, the youth justice court shall, if an application for review is made by the young person, the young person's parent or the Attorney General within ten days after service of the notice, review the youth sentence without delay.

(4) Subject to subsection (5), subsections 94(7) (no review of appeal pending), (9) to (12) (progress reports) and (14) to (19) (provisions respecting notice and decision of the youth justice court) apply, with any modifications that the circumstances require, in respect of reviews made under this section and any notice required under subsection 94(14) shall also be given to the provincial director.

(5) A youth justice court that receives a notice under subsection (2) shall, if no application for a review is made under subsection (3),

(*a*) order the release of the young person and place the young person under conditional supervision in accordance with section 105, having regard to the recommendations of the provincial director; or

(*b*) if the court considers it advisable, order that the young person not be released.

For greater certainty, an order under this subsection may be made without a hearing.

(6) When a youth justice court orders that the young person not be released under paragraph (5)(*b*), it shall cause a notice of its order to be given to the provincial director without delay.

(7) When the provincial director is given a notice under subsection (6), he or she may request a review under this section.

(8) When the provincial director requests a review under subsection (7),

(*a*) the provincial director shall cause any notice that may be directed by rules of court applicable to the youth justice court or, in the absence of such a direction, at least five clear days notice of the review to be given in writing to the young person, a parent of the young person and the Attorney General; and

(*b*) the youth justice court shall review the youth sentence without delay after the notice required under paragraph (*a*) is given.

CONDITIONS TO BE INCLUDED IN CUSTODY AND SUPERVISION ORDER / Other conditions / Communication of conditions / Provisions to apply.

97. (1) Every youth sentence imposed under paragraph 42(2)(*n*) shall contain the following conditions, namely, that the young person, while serving the portion of the youth sentence under supervision in the community,

(*a*) keep the peace and be of good behaviour;

(*b*) report to the provincial director and then be under the supervision of the provincial director;

(*c*) inform the provincial director immediately on being arrested or questioned by the police;

(*d*) report to the police, or any named individual, as instructed by the provincial director;

(*e*) advise the provincial director of the young person's address of residence and report immediately to the provincial director any change

(i) in that address,

(ii) in the young person's normal occupation, including employment, vocational or educational training and volunteer work,

(iii) in the young person's family or financial situation, and

(iv) that may reasonably be expected to affect the young person's ability to comply with the conditions of the sentence; and

(*f*) not own, possess or have the control of any weapon, ammunition, prohibited ammunition, prohibited device or explosive substance, except as authorized in writing by the provincial director for the purposes of the young person participating in a program specified in the authorization.

(2) The provincial director may set additional conditions that support and address the needs of the young person, promote the reintegration of the young person into the community and offer adequate protection to the public from the risk that the young

YOUTH

person might otherwise present. The provincial director shall, in setting the conditions, take into account the needs of the young person, the most effective programs for the young person in order to maximize his or her chances for reintegration into the community, the nature of the offence and the ability of the young person to comply with the conditions.

(3) The provincial director shall

(*a*) cause the conditions to be read by or to the young person bound by them;

(*b*) explain or cause to be explained to the young person the purpose and effect of the conditions, and confirm that the young person understands them; and

(*c*) cause a copy of the conditions to be given to the young person, and to a parent of the young person.

(4) Subsections 56(3) (endorsement of order by young person) and (4) (validity of order) apply, with any modifications that the circumstances require, in respect of conditions under this section.

ANNOTATIONS

The sentencing judge has no jurisdiction to impose his or her own conditions under this provision: *R. v. S.-L. (L.K.)* (2011), 281 C.C.C. (3d) 213 (B.C.C.A.). See also *R. v. N. (B.)* (2004), 186 C.C.C. (3d) 21 (B.C.C.A.), affd [2006] 1 S.C.R. 941, 209 C.C.C. (3d) 97, affirmed in *R. v. P. (B.W.)*, [2006] 1 S.C.R. 941, 209 C.C.C. (3d) 97; *R. v. N. (H.T.)* (2006), 209 C.C.C. (3d) 318 (B.C.C.A.).

APPLICATION FOR CONTINUATION OF CUSTODY / Continuation of custody / Decision / Factors.

98. (1) Within a reasonable time before the expiry of the custodial portion of a young person's youth sentence, the Attorney General or the provincial director may apply to the youth justice court for an order that the young person remain in custody for a period not exceeding the remainder of the youth sentence.

(2) If the hearing for an application under subsection (1) cannot be completed before the expiry of the custodial portion of the youth sentence, the court may order that the young person remain in custody pending the determination of the application if the court is satisfied that the application was made in a reasonable time, having regard to all the circumstances, and that there are compelling reasons for keeping the young person in custody.

(3) The youth justice court may, after giving both parties and a parent of the young person an opportunity to be heard, order that a young person remain in custody for a period not exceeding the remainder of the youth sentence, if it is satisfied that there are reasonable grounds to believe that

(*a*) the young person is likely to commit a serious violent offence before the expiry of the youth sentence he or she is then serving; and

(*b*) the conditions that would be imposed on the young person if he or she were to serve a portion of the youth sentence in the community would not be adequate to prevent the commission of the offence.

(4) For the purpose of determining an application under subsection (1), the youth justice court shall take into consideration any factor that is relevant to the case of the young person, including

(*a*) evidence of a pattern of persistent violent behaviour and, in particular,

(i) the number of offences committed by the young person that caused physical or psychological harm to any other person,

(ii) the young person's difficulties in controlling violent impulses to the point of endangering the safety of any other person,

(iii) the use of weapons in the commission of any offence,

(iv) explicit threats of violence,
(*v*) behaviour of a brutal nature associated with the commission of any offence, and
(vi) a substantial degree of indifference on the part of the young person as to the reasonably foreseeable consequences, to other persons, of the young person's behaviour;

(*b*) psychiatric or psychological evidence that a physical or mental illness or disorder of the young person is of such a nature that the young person is likely to commit, before the expiry of the youth sentence the young person is then serving, a serious violent offence;

(*c*) reliable information that satisfies the youth justice court that the young person is planning to commit, before the expiry of the youth sentence the young person is then serving, a serious violent offence;

(*d*) the availability of supervision programs in the community that would offer adequate protection to the public from the risk that the young person might otherwise present until the expiry of the youth sentence the young person is then serving;

(*e*) whether the young person is more likely to reoffend if he or she serves his or her youth sentence entirely in custody without the benefits of serving a portion of the youth sentence in the community under supervision; and

(*f*) evidence of a pattern of committing violent offences while he or she was serving a portion of a youth sentence in the community under supervision.

REPORT / Written or oral report / Provisions apply/Notice of hearing / Statement of right to counsel / Service of notice / When notice not given.

99. (1) For the purpose of determining an application under section 98 (application for continuation of custody), the youth justice court shall require the provincial director to cause to be prepared, and to submit to the youth justice court, a report setting out any information of which the provincial director is aware with respect to the factors set out in subsection 98(4) that may be of assistance to the court.

(2) A report referred to in subsection (1) shall be in writing unless it cannot reasonably be committed to writing, in which case it may, with leave of the youth justice court, be submitted orally in court.

(3) Subsections 40(4) to (10) (procedures respecting pre-sentence reports) apply, with any modifications that the circumstances require, in respect of a report referred to in subsection (1).

(4) When an application is made under section 98 (application for continuation of custody) in respect of a young person, the provincial director shall cause to be given, to the young person and to a parent of the young person, at least five clear days notice of the hearing in writing.

(5) Any notice given to a parent under subsection (4) shall include a statement that the young person has the right to be represented by counsel.

(6) A notice under subsection (4) may be served personally or may be sent by confirmed delivery service.

(7) When notice under subsection (4) is not given in accordance with this section, the youth justice court may

(*a*) adjourn the hearing and order that the notice be given in any manner and to any person that it directs; or

(*b*) dispense with the giving of the notice if, in the opinion of the youth justice court, having regard to the circumstances, the giving of the notice may be dispensed with.

YOUTH

REASONS.

100. When a youth justice court makes an order under subsection 98(3) (decision for continued custody), it shall state its reasons for the order in the record of the case and shall provide, or cause to be provided, to the young person in respect of whom the order was made, the counsel and a parent of the young person, the Attorney General and the provincial director

- (*a*) a copy of the order; and
- (*b*) on request, a transcript or copy of the reasons for the order.

REVIEW OF YOUTH JUSTICE COURT DECISION / Extension of time to make application / Notice of application.

101. (1) An order made under subsection 98(3) (decision for continued custody) in respect of a young person, or the refusal to make such an order, shall, on application of the young person, the young person's counsel, the Attorney General or the provincial director made within thirty days after the decision of the youth justice court, be reviewed by the court of appeal, and that court may, in its discretion, confirm or reverse the decision of the youth justice court.

(2) The court of appeal may, at any time, extend the time within which an application under subsection (1) may be made.

(3) A person who proposes to apply for a review under subsection (1) shall give notice of the application in the manner and within the period of time that may be directed by rules of court.

BREACH OF CONDITIONS / Provisions apply.

102. (1) If the provincial director has reasonable grounds to believe that a young person has breached or is about to breach a condition to which he or she is subject under section 97 (conditions to be included in custody and supervision orders), the provincial director may, in writing,

- (*a*) permit the young person to continue to serve a portion of his or her youth sentence in the community, on the same or different conditions; or
- (*b*) if satisfied that the breach is a serious one that increases the risk to public safety, order that the young person be remanded to any youth custody facility that the provincial director considers appropriate until a review is conducted.

(2) Sections 107 (apprehension) and 108 (review by provincial director) apply, with any modifications that the circumstances require, to an order under paragraph (1)(*b*).

ANNOTATIONS

Where a young person breaches the community supervision portion of the custody and supervision order, they are deemed not to be continuing to serve the sentence until apprehended: *R. v. A. (K.P.)* (2005), 204 C.C.C. (3d) 161, 275 Sask. R. 68 (C.A.).

REVIEW BY YOUTH JUSTICE COURT / Order / Provisions apply.

103. (1) When the case of a young person is referred to the youth justice court under section 108 (review by provincial director), the provincial director shall, without delay, cause the young person to be brought before the youth justice court, and the youth justice court shall, after giving the young person an opportunity to be heard,

- (*a*) if the court is not satisfied on reasonable grounds that the young person has breached or was about to breach one of the conditions under which he or she was being supervised in the community, order that the young person continue to serve a portion of his or her youth sentence in the community, on the same or different conditions; or (*b*) if the court is satisfied on reasonable grounds that the young person has breached or was about to breach one of the conditions under which he or she was being supervised in the community, make an order under subsection (2).

(2) On completion of a review under subsection (1), the youth justice court

(*a*) shall order that the young person continue to serve the remainder of the youth sentence the young person is then serving in the community, and when the court does so, the court may vary the existing conditions or impose new conditions; or

(*b*) shall, despite paragraph 42(2)(*n*) (custody and supervision order), order that the young person remain in custody for a period that does not exceed the remainder of the youth sentence the young person is then serving, if the youth justice court is satisfied that the breach of the conditions was serious.

(3) Subsections 109(4) to (8) apply, with any modifications that the circumstances require, in respect of a review under this section.

CONTINUATION OF CUSTODY / Continuation of custody / Factors / Youth justice court to order appearance of young person / Provisions to apply / If application denied.

104. (1) When a young person on whom a youth sentence under paragraph 42(2)(*o*), (*q*) or (*r*) has been imposed is held in custody and an application is made to the youth justice court by the Attorney General, within a reasonable time before the expiry of the custodial portion of the youth sentence, the provincial director of the province in which the young person is held in custody shall cause the young person to be brought before the youth justice court and the youth justice court may, after giving both parties and a parent of the young person an opportunity to be heard and if it is satisfied that there are reasonable grounds to believe that the young person is likely to commit an offence causing the death of or serious harm to another person before the expiry of the youth sentence the young person is then serving, order that the young person remain in custody for a period not exceeding the remainder of the youth sentence.

(2) If the hearing of an application under subsection (1) cannot be completed before the expiry of the custodial portion of the youth sentence, the court may order that the young person remain in custody until the determination of the application if the court is satisfied that the application was made in a reasonable time, having regard to all the circumstances, and that there are compelling reasons for keeping the young person in custody.

(3) For the purpose of determining an application under subsection (1), the youth justice court shall take into consideration any factor that is relevant to the case of the young person, including

(*a*) evidence of a pattern of persistent violent behaviour and, in particular,

(i) the number of offences committed by the young person that caused physical or psychological harm to any other person,

(ii) the young person's difficulties in controlling violent impulses to the point of endangering the safety of any other person,

(iii) the use of weapons in the commission of any offence,

(iv) explicit threats of violence,

(v) behaviour of a brutal nature associated with the commission of any offence, and

(vi) a substantial degree of indifference on the part of the young person as to the reasonably foreseeable consequences, to other persons, of the young person's behaviour;

(*b*) psychiatric or psychological evidence that a physical or mental illness or disorder of the young person is of such a nature that the young person is likely

YOUTH

to commit, before the expiry of the youth sentence the young person is then serving, an offence causing the death of or serious harm to another person;

(*c*) reliable information that satisfies the youth justice court that the young person is planning to commit, before the expiry of the youth sentence the young person is then serving, an offence causing the death of or serious harm to another person; and

(*d*) the availability of supervision programs in the community that would offer adequate protection to the public from the risk that the young person might otherwise present until the expiry of the youth sentence the young person is then serving.

(4) If a provincial director fails to cause a young person to be brought before the youth justice court under subsection (1), the youth justice court shall order the provincial director to cause the young person to be brought before the youth justice court without delay.

(5) Sections 99 to 101 apply, with any modifications that the circumstances require, in respect of an order made, or the refusal to make an order, under this section.

(6) If an application under this section is denied, the court may, with the consent of the young person, the Attorney General and the provincial director, proceed as though the young person had been brought before the court as required under subsection 105(1).

ANNOTATIONS

Subsection (1) does not apply where the youth is not held in custody but is serving a sentence in the community: *R. v. P. (B.W.)* (2004), 187 C.C.C. (3d) 20, 187 Man. R. (2d) 80 (C.A.), affd [2006] 1 S.C.R. 941, 209 C.C.C. (3d) 97.

CONDITIONAL SUPERVISION / Conditions to be included in order / Other conditions / Temporary conditions / Conditions to be set at first opportunity / Report / Provisions apply / Provisions apply.

105. (1) The provincial director of the province in which a young person on whom a youth sentence under paragraph 42(2)(*o*), (*q*) or (*r*) has been imposed is held in custody or, if applicable, with respect to whom an order has been made under subsection 104(1) (continuation of custody), shall cause the young person to be brought before the youth justice court at least one month before the expiry of the custodial portion of the youth sentence. The court shall, after giving the young person an opportunity to be heard, by order, set the conditions of the young person's conditional supervision.

(2) The youth justice court shall include in the order under subsection (1) the following conditions, namely, that the young person

(*a*) keep the peace and be of good behaviour;

(*b*) appear before the youth justice court when required by the court to do so;

(*c*) report to the provincial director immediately on release, and then be under the supervision of the provincial director or a person designated by the youth justice court;

(*d*) inform the provincial director immediately on being arrested or questioned by the police;

(*e*) report to the police, or any named individual, as instructed by the provincial director;

(*f*) advise the provincial director of the young person's address of residence on release and after release report immediately to the clerk of the youth justice court or the provincial director any change

(i) in that address,

(ii) in the young person's normal occupation, including employment, vocational or educational training and volunteer work,

(iii) in the young person's family or financial situation, and

(iv) that may reasonably be expected to affect the young person's ability to comply with the conditions of the order;

(*g*) not own, possess or have the control of any weapon, ammunition, prohibited ammunition, prohibited device or explosive substance, except as authorized by the order; and

(*h*) comply with any reasonable instructions that the provincial director considers necessary in respect of any condition of the conditional supervision in order to prevent a breach of that condition or to protect society.

(3) In setting conditions for the purposes of subsection (1), the youth justice court may include in the order the following conditions, namely, that the young person

(*a*) on release, travel directly to the young person's place of residence, or to any other place that is noted in the order;

(*b*) make reasonable efforts to obtain and maintain suitable employment;

(*c*) attend school or any other place of learning, training or recreation that is appropriate, if the court is satisfied that a suitable program is available for the young person at such a place;

(*d*) reside with a parent, or any other adult that the court considers appropriate, who is willing to provide for the care and maintenance of the young person;

(*e*) reside in any place that the provincial director may specify;

(*f*) remain within the territorial jurisdiction of one or more courts named in the order;

(*g*) comply with conditions set out in the order that support and address the needs of the young person and promote the reintegration of the young person into the community; and

(*h*) comply with any other conditions set out in the order that the court considers appropriate, including conditions for securing the young person's good conduct and for preventing the young person from repeating the offence or committing other offences.

(4) When a provincial director is required under subsection (1) to cause a young person to be brought before the youth justice court but cannot do so for reasons beyond the young person's control, the provincial director shall so advise the youth justice court and the court shall, by order, set any temporary conditions for the young person's conditional supervision that are appropriate in the circumstances.

(5) When an order is made under subsection (4), the provincial director shall bring the young person before the youth justice court as soon after the order is made as the circumstances permit and the court shall then set the conditions of the young person's conditional supervision.

(6) For the purpose of setting conditions under this section, the youth justice court shall require the provincial director to cause to be prepared, and to submit to the youth justice court, a report setting out any information that may be of assistance to the court.

(7) Subsections 99(2) to (7) (provisions respecting reports and notice) and 104(4) (ordering appearance of young person) apply, with any modifications that the circumstances require, in respect of any proceedings held under subsection (1).

(8) Subsections 56(1) to (4) (provisions respecting probation orders), (7) (notice to appear) and (8) (warrant in default) and section 101 (review of youth justice court decision) apply, with any modifications that the circumstances require, in respect of an order made under subsection (1).

ANNOTATIONS

A condition requiring the accused to produce bodily samples for drug and alcohol testing is not contrary to law: *R. v. L. (J.R.)* (2007), 221 C.C.C. (3d) 278, 49 C.R. (6th) 1 (N.S.C.A.).

SUSPENSION OF CONDITIONAL SUPERVISION.

106. If the provincial director has reasonable grounds to believe that a young person has breached or is about to breach a condition of an order made under subsection 105(1), the provincial director may, in writing,

(*a*) suspend the conditional supervision; and

(*b*) order that the young person be remanded to any youth custody facility that the provincial director considers appropriate until a review is conducted under section 108 and, if applicable, section 109.

ANNOTATIONS

A young person remanded under this section does not have the right to a bail hearing until and unless the breach is referred to a youth court justice. The application of s. 503 of the *Criminal Code* would be inconsistent with the very specific procedure prescribed by this section: *R. v. W. (K.T.J.)* (2009), 276 C.C.C. (3d) 542 (B.C. Prov. Ct.).

APPREHENSION / Warrants / Peace officer may arrest / Requirement to bring before provincial director / Release or remand in custody.

107. (1) If the conditional supervision of a young person is suspended under section 106, the provincial director may issue a warrant in writing, authorizing the apprehension of the young person and, until the young person is apprehended, the young person is deemed not to be continuing to serve the youth sentence the young person is then serving.

(2) A warrant issued under subsection (1) shall be executed by any peace officer to whom it is given at any place in Canada and has the same force and effect in all parts of Canada as if it had been originally issued or subsequently endorsed by a provincial court judge or other lawful authority having jurisdiction in the place where it is executed.

(3) If a peace officer believes on reasonable grounds that a warrant issued under subsection (1) is in force in respect of a young person, the peace officer may arrest the young person without the warrant at any place in Canada.

(4) If a young person is arrested under subsection (3) and detained, the peace officer making the arrest shall cause the young person to be brought before the provincial director or a person designated by the provincial director

(*a*) if the provincial director or the designated person is available within a period of twenty-four hours after the young person is arrested, without unreasonable delay and in any event within that period; and

(*b*) if the provincial director or the designated person is not available within that period, as soon as possible.

(5) If a young person is brought before the provincial director or a person designated by the provincial director under subsection (4), the provincial director or the designated person

(*a*) if not satisfied that there are reasonable grounds to believe that the young person is the young person in respect of whom the warrant referred to in subsection (1) was issued, shall release the young person; or

(*b*) if satisfied that there are reasonable grounds to believe that the young person is the young person in respect of whom the warrant referred to in subsection (1) was issued, may remand the young person in custody to await execution of the warrant, but if no warrant for the young person's arrest is executed within a period of forty-eight hours after the time the young person is remanded in custody, the person in whose custody the young person then is shall release the young person.

ANNOTATIONS

This provision applies to a community supervision order and, accordingly, where the Director has obtained a warrant for an alleged breach of the order, the sentence ceases to run until the accused is taken into custody: *R. v. W. (C.K.)* (2005), 204 C.C.C. (3d) 380, [2006] 3 W.W.R. 443, 376 A.R. 107 (C.A.).

REVIEW BY PROVINCIAL DIRECTOR.

108. Without delay after the remand to custody of a young person whose conditional supervision has been suspended under section 106, or without delay after being informed of the arrest of such a young person, the provincial director shall review the case and, within forty-eight hours, cancel the suspension of the conditional supervision or refer the case to the youth justice court for a review under section 109.

ANNOTATIONS

Once the accused is brought into custody, s. 108 requires the Director, without delay, to review the accused's case and, within 48 hours of doing so, to either release him or refer the case to court for review under s. 103. Section 108 does not require the Director to ensure the accused is brought before the court within 48 hours: *R. v. T. (J.D.)* (2009), 242 C.C.C. (3d) 436 (Sask. C.A.).

REVIEW BY YOUTH JUSTICE COURT / Order / Custody and supervision order / Factors to be considered / Reasons / Report / Provisions apply / Provisions apply.

109. (1) If the case of a young person is referred to the youth justice court under section 108, the provincial director shall, without delay, cause the young person to be brought before the youth justice court, and the youth justice court shall, after giving the young person an opportunity to be heard,

(*a*) if the court is not satisfied on reasonable grounds that the young person has breached or was about to breach a condition of the conditional supervision, cancel the suspension of the conditional supervision; or

(*b*) if the court is satisfied on reasonable grounds that the young person has breached or was about to breach a condition of the conditional supervision, review the decision of the provincial director to suspend the conditional supervision and make an order under subsection (2).

(2) On completion of a review under subsection (1), the youth justice court shall order

(*a*) the cancellation of the suspension of the conditional supervision, and when the court does so, the court may vary the conditions of the conditional supervision or impose new conditions;

(*b*) in a case other than a deferred custody and supervision order made under paragraph 42(2)(*p*), the continuation of the suspension of the conditional supervision for any period of time, not to exceed the remainder of the youth sentence the young person is then serving, that the court considers appropriate, and when the court does so, the court shall order that the young person remain in custody; or

(*c*) in the case of a deferred custody and supervision order made under paragraph 42(2)(*p*), that the young person serve the remainder of the order as if it were a custody and supervision order under paragraph 42(2)(*n*).

(3) After a court has made a direction under paragraph (2)(*c*), the provisions of this Act applicable to orders under paragraph 42(2)(*n*) apply in respect of the deferred custody and supervision order.

(4) In making its decision under subsection (2), the court shall consider the length of time the young person has been subject to the order, whether the young person has previously contravened it, and the nature of the contravention, if any.

YOUTH

(5) When a youth justice court makes an order under subsection (2), it shall state its reasons for the order in the record of the case and shall give, or cause to be given, to the young person in respect of whom the order was made, the counsel and a parent of the young person, the Attorney General and the provincial director,

(*a*) a copy of the order; and

(*b*) on request, a transcript or copy of the reasons for the order.

(6) For the purposes of a review under subsection (1), the youth justice court shall require the provincial director to cause to be prepared, and to submit to the youth justice court, a report setting out any information of which the provincial director is aware that may be of assistance to the court.

(7) Subsections 99(2) to (7) (provisions respecting reports and notice) and 105(6) (report for the purpose of setting conditions) apply, with any modifications that the circumstances require, in respect of a review under this section.

(8) Section 101 (review of youth justice court decision) applies, with any modifications that the circumstances require, in respect of an order made under subsection (2).

ANNOTATIONS

Subsection (2)(*c*) should be read in light of subsec. (2)(*a*) so as to afford the sentencing judge the option of releasing the young person on appropriate conditions: *R. v. D. (A.)* (2008), 234 C.C.C. (3d) 413 (N.S.C.A.).

PART 6 / PUBLICATION, RECORDS AND INFORMATION

Protection of Privacy of Young Persons

IDENTITY OF OFFENDER NOT TO BE PUBLISHED / Limitation / Exception / *Ex parte* application for leave to publish / Order ceases to have effect / Application for leave to publish.

110. (1) Subject to this section, no person shall publish the name of a young person, or any other information related to a young person, if it would identify the young person as a young person dealt with under this Act.

(2) Subsection (1) does not apply

(*a*) in a case where the information relates to a young person who has received an adult sentence;

(*b*) in a case where the information relates to a young person who has received a youth sentence for a violent offence and the youth justice court has ordered a lifting of the publication ban under subsection 75(2); and

(*c*) in a case where the publication of information is made in the course of the administration of justice, if it is not the purpose of the publication to make the information known in the community.

(3) A young person referred to in subsection (1) may, after he or she attains the age of eighteen years, publish or cause to be published information that would identify him or her as having been dealt with under this Act or the *Young Offenders Act*, chapter Y-1 of the Revised Statutes of Canada, 1985, provided that he or she is not in custody pursuant to either Act at the time of the publication.

(4) A youth justice court judge shall, on the *ex parte* application of a peace officer, make an order permitting any person to publish information that identifies a young person as having committed or allegedly committed an indictable offence, if the judge is satisfied that

(*a*) there is reason to believe that the young person is a danger to others; and

(*b*) **publication of the information is necessary to assist in apprehending the young person.**

(5) An order made under subsection (4) ceases to have effect five days after it is made.

(6) The youth justice court may, on the application of a young person referred to in subsection (1), make an order permitting the young person to publish information that would identify him or her as having been dealt with under this Act or the *Young Offenders Act*, chapter Y-1 of the Revised Statutes of Canada, 1985, if the court is satisfied that the publication would not be contrary to the young person's best interests or the public interest. 2012, c. 1, s. 189.

ANNOTATIONS

Note: Some of the following cases were decided under the *Young Offenders Act* but were thought to be of assistance in applying this Act.

It was held that s. 38 did not prevent the cross-examination of a youthful witness on his prior record for convictions under the *Young Offenders Act*. Such cross-examination during the trial of an adult accused is not a publication within the meaning of the section: *R. v. Scott* (1984), 16 C.C.C. (3d) 17 (Ont. Gen. Sess.).

The judge did not err in refusing a broadcaster's application permitting it access to videotapes that had been shown in the youth court trial. The open court requirement was satisfied given that the tapes were played in court and transcripts were provided. If the videotapes were broadcast, the public could not be shown an accurate version of the evidence, as the identities of the main participants could not be disclosed through voice modification and the blacking out of their faces. The broadcaster could report what was said without airing the actual videotapes: *R. v. K. (C.)* (2006), 208 C.C.C. (3d) 257 (Ont. S.C.J.).

As the mandatory publication ban in subsec. (1) is inapplicable once the accused receives an adult sentence, there is no legislated presumption that the balance of interests requires a publication ban. In these circumstances, a discretionary ban can only be granted if the two-pronged test in *Dagenais v. Canadian Broadcasting Corp.* (1994), 94 C.C.C. (3d) 289 (S.C.C.), and *R. v. Mentuck* (2001), 158 C.C.C. (3d) 449 (S.C.C.), is met: *R. v. S. (G.D.)* (2007), 226 C.C.C. (3d) 196 (N.S.C.A.), leave to appeal to S.C.C. refused 230 C.C.C. (3d) vi.

IDENTITY OF VICTIM OR WITNESS NOT TO BE PUBLISHED / Exception / Application for leave to publish.

111. (1) Subject to this section, no person shall publish the name of a child or young person, or any other information related to a child or a young person, if it would identify the child or young person as having been a victim of, or as having appeared as a witness in connection with, an offence committed or alleged to have been committed by a young person.

(2) Information that would serve to identify a child or young person referred to in subsection (1) as having been a victim or a witness may be published, or caused to be published, by

(*a*) **that child or young person after he or she attains the age of eighteen years or before that age with the consent of his or her parents; or**

(*b*) **the parents of that child or young person if he or she is deceased.**

(3) The youth justice court may, on the application of a child or a young person referred to in subsection (1), make an order permitting the child or young person to publish information that would identify him or her as having been a victim or a witness if the court is satisfied that the publication would not be contrary to his or her best interests or the public interest.

YOUTH

NON-APPLICATION.

112. Once information is published under subsection 110(3) or (6) or 111(2) or (3), subsection 110(1) (identity of offender not to be published) or 111(1) (identity of victim or witness not to be published), as the case may be, no longer applies in respect of the information.

Fingerprints and Photographs

IDENTIFICATION OF CRIMINALS ACT APPLIES / Limitation.

113. (1) The *Identification of Criminals Act* applies in respect of young persons.

(2) No fingerprint, palmprint or photograph or other measurement, process or operation referred to in the *Identification of Criminals Act* shall be taken of, or applied in respect of, a young person who is charged with having committed an offence except in the circumstances in which an adult may, under that Act, be subjected to the measurements, processes and operations.

ANNOTATIONS

Note: The following case was decided under the *Young Offenders Act* but was thought to be of assistance in applying this Act.

The requirement that a young offender attend for fingerprinting was not a breach of ss. 7, 8 or 9 of the *Canadian Charter of Rights and Freedoms*. Further, s. 44 of the *Young Offenders Act*, which is worded similarly to this section, did not on its face authorize cruel and unusual punishment in violation of s. 12 of the Charter. However, it may be that in a rare case it could be shown that the effect of the fingerprinting process would bring it within s. 12: *R. v. M. (H.) (No. 2)* (1984), 17 C.C.C. (3d) 443, 116 D.L.R. (4th) 542, [1985] 2 W.W.R. 444, *sub nom.* Lunney v. M.H. (Alta. Q.B.), affd 21 C.C.C. (3d) 384*n*, 21 D.L.R. (4th) 767*n* (Alta. C.A.), leave to appeal to S.C.C. granted C.C.C. and D.L.R. *loc. cit.* Also, now see *R. v. Beare; R. v. Higgins*, [1988] 2 S.C.R. 387, 45 C.C.C. (3d) 57, 66 C.R. (3d) 97 (S.C.C.), noted under the *Criminal Code*, s. 509.

Records That May Be Kept

YOUTH JUSTICE COURT, REVIEW BOARD AND OTHER COURTS.

114. A youth justice court, review board or any court dealing with matters arising out of proceedings under this Act may keep a record of any case that comes before it arising under this Act.

POLICE RECORDS / Extrajudicial measures / Police records / Records held by R.C.M.P.

115. (1) A record relating to any offence alleged to have been committed by a young person, including the original or a copy of any fingerprints or photographs of the young person, may be kept by any police force responsible for or participating in the investigation of the offence.

(1.1) The police force shall keep a record of any extrajudicial measures that they use to deal with young persons.

(2) When a young person is charged with having committed an offence in respect of which an adult may be subjected to any measurement, process or operation referred to in the *Identification of Criminals Act*, the police force responsible for the investigation of the offence may provide a record relating to the offence to the Royal Canadian

Mounted Police. If the young person is found guilty of the offence, the police force shall provide the record.

(3) The Royal Canadian Mounted Police shall keep the records provided under subsection (2) in the central repository that the Commissioner of the Royal Canadian Mounted Police may, from time to time, designate for the purpose of keeping criminal history files or records of offenders or keeping records for the identification of offenders. 2012, c. 1, s. 190.

GOVERNMENT RECORDS / Other records.

116. (1) A department or an agency of any government in Canada may keep records containing information obtained by the department or agency

- **(*a*) for the purposes of an investigation of an offence alleged to have been committed by a young person;**
- **(*b*) for use in proceedings against a young person under this Act;**
- **(*c*) for the purpose of administering a youth sentence or an order of the youth justice court;**
- **(*d*) for the purpose of considering whether to use extrajudicial measures to deal with a young person; or**
- **(*e*) as a result of the use of extrajudicial measures to deal with a young person.**

(2) A person or organization may keep records containing information obtained by the person or organization

- **(*a*) as a result of the use of extrajudicial measures to deal with a young person; or**
- **(*b*) for the purpose of administering or participating in the administration of a youth sentence.**

Access to Records

EXCEPTION — ADULT SENTENCE.

117. Sections 118 to 129 do not apply to records kept in respect of an offence for which an adult sentence has been imposed once the time allowed for the taking of an appeal has expired or, if an appeal is taken, all proceedings in respect of the appeal have been completed and the appeal court has upheld an adult sentence. The record shall be dealt with as a record of an adult and, for the purposes of the *Criminal Records Act*, the finding of guilt in respect of the offence for which the record is kept is deemed to be a conviction.

NO ACCESS UNLESS AUTHORIZED / Exception for employees.

118. (1) Except as authorized or required by this Act, no person shall be given access to a record kept under sections 114 to 116, and no information contained in it may be given to any person, where to do so would identify the young person to whom it relates as a young person dealt with under this Act.

(2) No person who is employed in keeping or maintaining records referred to in subsection (1) is restricted from doing anything prohibited under subsection (1) with respect to any other person so employed.

ANNOTATIONS

The access provisions of the Act are a comprehensive scheme designed to carefully control access to young offender records. The language of s. 118 and the comprehensiveness of the scheme itself demonstrate that Parliament intended that access to the records could be gained only through the Act. Parliament in clear and unambiguous terms has placed the responsibility for determining access to records on the shoulders of youth justice court judges: *L. (S.) v. B. (N.)* (2005), 195 C.C.C. (3d) 481 (Ont. C.A.).

PERSONS HAVING ACCESS TO RECORDS / Period of access / Prohibition orders not included / Extrajudicial measures / Exception / Records of assessments or forensic DNA analysis / Introduction into evidence / Disclosures for research or statistical purposes / Application of usual rules / Records of offences that result in a prohibition order.

119. (1) Subject to subsections (4) to (6), from the date that a record is created until the end of the applicable period set out in subsection (2), the following persons, on request, shall be given access to a record kept under section 114, and may be given access to a record kept under sections 115 and 116:

(*a*) the young person to whom the record relates;
(*b*) the young person's counsel, or any representative of that counsel;
(*c*) the Attorney General;
(*d*) the victim of the offence or alleged offence to which the record relates;
(*e*) the parents of the young person, during the course of any proceedings relating to the offence or alleged offence to which the record relates or during the term of any youth sentence made in respect of the offence;
(*f*) any adult assisting the young person under subsection 25(7), during the course of any proceedings relating to the offence or alleged offence to which the record relates or during the term of any youth sentence made in respect of the offence;
(*g*) any peace officer for
(i) law enforcement purposes, or
(ii) any purpose related to the administration of the case to which the record relates, during the course of proceedings against the young person or the term of the youth sentence;
(*h*) a judge, court or review board, for any purpose relating to proceedings against the young person, or proceedings against the person after he or she becomes an adult, in respect of offences committed or alleged to have been committed by that person;
(*i*) the provincial director, or the director of the provincial correctional facility for adults or the penitentiary at which the young person is serving a sentence;
(*j*) a person participating in a conference or in the administration of extrajudicial measures, if required for the administration of the case to which the record relates;
(*k*) a person acting as ombudsman, privacy commissioner or information commissioner, whatever his or her official designation might be, who in the course of his or her duties under an Act of Parliament or the legislature of a province is investigating a complaint to which the record relates;
(*l*) a coroner or a person acting as a child advocate, whatever his or her official designation might be, who is acting in the course of his or her duties under an Act of Parliament or the legislature of a province;
(*m*) a person acting under the *Firearms Act*;
(*n*) a member of a department or agency of a government in Canada, or of an organization that is an agent of, or under contract with, the department or agency, who is
(i) acting in the exercise of his or her duties under this Act,
(ii) engaged in the supervision or care of the young person, whether as a young person or an adult, or in an investigation related to the young person under an Act of the legislature of a province respecting child welfare,
(iii) considering an application for conditional release, or for a record suspension under the *Criminal Records Act*, made by the young person, whether as a young person or an adult,

(iv) administering a prohibition order made under an Act of Parliament or the legislature of a province, or

(v) administering a youth sentence, if the young person has been committed to custody and is serving the custody in a provincial correctional facility for adults or a penitentiary;

(*o*) a person, for the purpose of carrying out a criminal record check required by the Government of Canada or the government of a province or a municipality for purposes of employment or the performance of services, with or without remuneration;

(*p*) an employee or agent of the Government of Canada, for statistical purposes under the *Statistics Act*;

(*q*) an accused or his or her counsel who swears an affidavit to the effect that access to the record is necessary to make a full answer and defence;

(*r*) a person or a member of a class of persons designated by order of the Governor in Council, or the lieutenant governor in council of the appropriate province, for a purpose and to the extent specified in the order; and

(*s*) any person or member of a class of persons that a youth justice court judge considers has a valid interest in the record, to the extent directed by the judge, if the judge is satisfied that access to the record is

(i) desirable in the public interest for research or statistical purposes, or

(ii) desirable in the interest of the proper administration of justice.

(2) The period of access referred to in subsection (1) is

(*a*) if an extrajudicial sanction is used to deal with the young person, the period ending two years after the young person consents to be subject to the sanction in accordance with paragraph 10(2)(*c*);

(*b*) if the young person is acquitted of the offence otherwise than by reason of a verdict of not criminally responsible on account of mental disorder, the period ending two months after the expiry of the time allowed for the taking of an appeal or, if an appeal is taken, the period ending three months after all proceedings in respect of the appeal have been completed;

(*c*) if the charge against the young person is dismissed for any reason other than acquittal, the charge is withdrawn, or the young person is found guilty of the offence and a reprimand is given, the period ending two months after the dismissal, withdrawal, or finding of guilt;

(*d*) if the charge against the young person is stayed, with no proceedings being taken against the young person for a period of one year, at the end of that period;

(*e*) if the young person is found guilty of the offence and the youth sentence is an absolute discharge, the period ending one year after the young person is found guilty;

(*f*) if the young person is found guilty of the offence and the youth sentence is a conditional discharge, the period ending three years after the young person is found guilty;

(*g*) subject to paragraphs (*i*) and (*j*) and subsection (9), if the young person is found guilty of the offence and it is a summary conviction offence, the period ending three years after the youth sentence imposed in respect of the offence has been completed;

(*h*) subject to paragraphs (*i*) and (*j*) and subsection (9), if the young person is found guilty of the offence and it is an indictable offence, the period ending five years after the youth sentence imposed in respect of the offence has been completed;

(*i*) subject to subsection (9), if, during the period calculated in accordance with paragraph (*g*) or (*h*), the young person is found guilty of an offence punishable on summary conviction committed when he or she was a young person, the latest of

YOUTH

(i) the period calculated in accordance with paragraph (*g*) or (*h*), as the case may be, and

(ii) the period ending three years after the youth sentence imposed for that offence has been completed; and

(*j*) subject to subsection (9), if, during the period calculated in accordance with paragraph (*g*) or (*h*), the young person is found guilty of an indictable offence committed when he or she was a young person, the period ending five years after the sentence imposed for that indictable offence has been completed.

(3) Prohibition orders made under an Act of Parliament or the legislature of a province, including any order made under section 51, shall not be taken into account in determining any period referred to in subsection (2).

(4) Access to a record kept under section 115 or 116 in respect of extrajudicial measures, other than extrajudicial sanctions, used in respect of a young person shall be given only to the following persons for the following purposes:

(*a*) a peace officer or the Attorney General, in order to make a decision whether to again use extrajudicial measures in respect of the young person;

(*b*) a person participating in a conference, in order to decide on the appropriate extrajudicial measure;

(*c*) a peace officer, the Attorney General or a person participating in a conference, if access is required for the administration of the case to which the record relates; and

(*d*) a peace officer for the purpose of investigating an offence.

(5) When a youth justice court has withheld all or part of a report from any person under subsection 34(9) or (10) (nondisclosure of medical or psychological report) or 40(7) (nondisclosure of pre-sentence report), that person shall not be given access under subsection (1) to that report or part.

(6) Access to a report made under section 34 (medical and psychological reports) or a record of the results of forensic DNA analysis of a bodily substance taken from a young person in execution of a warrant issued under section 487.05 of the *Criminal Code* may be given only under paragraphs (1)(*a*) to (*c*), (*e*) to (*h*) and (*q*) and subparagraph (1)(*s*)(ii).

(7) Nothing in paragraph (1)(*h*) or (*q*) authorizes the introduction into evidence of any part of a record that would not otherwise be admissible in evidence.

(8) When access to a record is given to a person under paragraph (1)(*p*) or subparagraph (1)(*s*)(i), the person may subsequently disclose information contained in the record, but shall not disclose the information in any form that would reasonably be expected to identify the young person to whom it relates.

(9) If, during the period of access to a record under any of paragraphs (2)(*g*) to (*j*), the young person is convicted of an offence committed when he or she is an adult,

(*a*) section 82 (effect of absolute discharge or termination of youth sentence) does not apply to the young person in respect of the offence for which the record is kept under sections 114 to 116;

(*b*) this Part no longer applies to the record and the record shall be dealt with as a record of an adult; and

(*c*) for the purposes of the *Criminal Records Act*, the finding of guilt in respect of the offence for which the record is kept is deemed to be a conviction.

(10) Despite anything in this Act, when a young person is found guilty of an offence that results in a prohibition order being made, and the order is still in force at the end of the applicable period for which access to a record kept in respect of the order may be given under subsection (2),

(*a*) the record kept by the Royal Canadian Mounted Police pursuant to subsection 115(3) may be disclosed only to establish the existence of the order for purposes of law enforcement; and

(*b*) the record referred to in section 114 that is kept by the youth justice court may be disclosed only to establish the existence of the order in any offence involving a breach of the order. 2012, c. 1, s. 157.

ANNOTATIONS

A superior court judge has no jurisdiction to make an order under the civil rules for production of records kept under this Act although the records are sought in the course of civil litigation in which the young offenders are defendants. Any application for records must be made in accordance with this Act and, where necessary, to a youth justice court judge: *L. (S.) v. B. (N.)* (2005), 195 C.C.C. (3d) 481, 252 D.L.R. (4th) 508, 196 O.A.C. 320 (C.A.).

In *R. v. D. (A.Y.)* (2011), 278 C.C.C. (3d) 136 (Alta. Q.B.), after the charges had been stayed by the Crown, the court granted members of the media access to transcripts of the preliminary inquiry and a video statement of the accused which had been an exhibit at the preliminary inquiry but was ruled inadmissible at trial. Public understanding and scrutiny of the issues raised in the case would benefit the administration of justice. The records could not be published, but they could be quoted subject to the restrictions in the Act.

An application to the court by a victim that is made within the access period does not require a formal motion to the court or notice to any individuals. It involves a simple request to the court office, presumably directed to a court administrator. Similarly a victim may request access to the Crown Attorney's records. Access to those records is not, however, as of right but at the discretion of the Crown. Again, however, the request is an informal one and does not require notice to other parties: *L. (S.) v. B. (N.), supra.*

There is no right of appeal from a decision made under this provision. Civil rights of appeal under provincial legislation have no application to proceedings under the Act. Rather, review may only be obtained by way of an application for *certiorari* under Part XXVI of the *Criminal Code* before a judge of the superior court: *Toronto (Police Service) v. L.D.* (2018), 357 C.C.C. (3d) 1 (Ont. C.A.).

ACCESS TO R.C.M.P. RECORDS / Access for identification purposes / Period of access / Subsequent offences as young person / Disclosure for research or statistical purposes / Subsequent offences as adult.

120. (1) The following persons may, during the period set out in subsection (3), be given access to a record kept under subsection 115(3) in respect of an offence set out in the schedule:

(*a*) the young person to whom the record relates;

(*b*) the young person's counsel, or any representative of that counsel;

(*c*) an employee or agent of the Government of Canada, for statistical purposes under the *Statistics Act*;

(*d*) any person or member of a class of persons that a youth justice court judge considers has a valid interest in the record, to the extent directed by the judge, if the judge is satisfied that access is desirable in the public interest for research or statistical purposes;

(*e*) the Attorney General or a peace officer, when the young person is or has been charged with another offence set out in the schedule or the same offence more than once, for the purpose of investigating any offence that the young person is suspected of having committed, or in respect of which the young person has been arrested or charged, whether as a young person or as an adult;

(*f*) the Attorney General or a peace officer to establish the existence of an order in any offence involving a breach of the order; and

(*g*) any person for the purposes of the *Firearms Act*.

YOUTH

(2) During the period set out in subsection (3), access to the portion of a record kept under subsection 115(3) that contains the name, date of birth and last known address of the young person to whom the fingerprints belong, may be given to a person for identification purposes if a fingerprint identified as that of the young person is found during the investigation of an offence or during an attempt to identify a deceased person or a person suffering from amnesia.

(3) For the purposes of subsections (1) and (2), the period of access to a record kept under subsection 115(3) in respect of an offence is the following:

- **(*a*) if the offence is an indictable offence, other than an offence referred to in paragraph (*b*), the period starting at the end of the applicable period set out in paragraphs 119(2)(*h*) to (*j*) and ending five years later; and**
- **(*b*) if the offence is a serious violent offence for which the Attorney General has given notice under subsection 64(2) (intention to seek adult sentence), the period starting at the end of the applicable period set out in paragraphs 119(2)(*h*) to (*j*) and continuing indefinitely.**

(4) If a young person was found guilty of an offence set out in the schedule is, during the period of access to a record under subsection (3), found guilty of an additional offence set out in the schedule, committed when he or she was a young person, access to the record may be given to the following additional persons:

- **(*a*) a parent of the young person or any adult assisting the young person under subsection 25(7);**
- **(*b*) a judge, court or review board, for a purpose relating to proceedings against the young person under this Act or any other Act of Parliament in respect of offences committed or alleged to have been committed by the young person, whether as a young person or as an adult; or**
- **(*c*) a member of a department or agency of a government in Canada, or of an organization that is an agent of, or is under contract with, the department or agency, who is**
  - **(i) preparing a report in respect of the young person under this Act or for the purpose of assisting a court in sentencing the young person after the young person becomes an adult,**
  - **(ii) engaged in the supervision or care of the young person, whether as a young person or as an adult, or in the administration of a sentence in respect of the young person, whether as a young person or as an adult, or**
  - **(iii) considering an application for conditional release, or for a record suspension under the *Criminal Records Act*, made by the young person after the young person becomes an adult.**

(5) A person who is given access to a record under paragraph (1)(*c*) or (*d*) may subsequently disclose information contained in the record, but shall not disclose the information in any form that would reasonably be expected to identify the young person to whom it relates.

(6) If, during the period of access to a record under subsection (3), the young person is convicted of an additional offence set out in the schedule, committed when he or she was an adult,

- **(*a*) this Part no longer applies to the record and the record shall be dealt with as a record of an adult and may be included on the automated criminal conviction records retrieval system maintained by the Royal Canadian Mounted Police; and**
- **(*b*) for the purposes of the *Criminal Records Act*, the finding of guilt in respect of the offence for which the record is kept is deemed to be a conviction. 2012, c. 1, ss. 158, 192.**

DEEMED ELECTION.

121. For the purposes of sections 119 and 120, if no election is made in respect of an offence that may be prosecuted by indictment or proceeded with by way of summary conviction, the Attorney General is deemed to have elected to proceed with the offence as an offence punishable on summary conviction.

DISCLOSURE OF INFORMATION AND COPIES OF RECORD.

122. A person who is required or authorized to be given access to a record under section 119, 120, 123 or 124 may be given any information contained in the record and may be given a copy of any part of the record.

WHERE RECORDS MAY BE MADE AVAILABLE / Restriction for paragraph (1)(*a*) / Notice / Where notice not required / Use of record / Disclosure for research or statistical purposes.

123. (1) A youth justice court judge may, on application by a person after the end of the applicable period set out in subsection 119(2), order that the person be given access to all or part of a record kept under sections 114 to 116 or that a copy of the record or part be given to that person,

(*a*) if the youth justice court judge is satisfied that

(i) the person has a valid and substantial interest in the record or part,

(ii) it is necessary for access to be given to the record or part in the interest of the proper administration of justice, and

(iii) disclosure of the record or part or the information in it is not prohibited under any other Act of Parliament or the legislature of a province; or

(*b*) if the youth court judge is satisfied that access to the record or part is desirable in the public interest for research or statistical purposes.

(2) Paragraph (1)(*a*) applies in respect of a record relating to a particular young person or to a record relating to a class of young persons only if the identity of young persons in the class at the time of the making of the application referred to in that paragraph cannot reasonably be ascertained and the disclosure of the record is necessary for the purpose of investigating any offence that a person is suspected on reasonable grounds of having committed against a young person while the young person is, or was, serving a sentence.

(3) Subject to subsection (4), an application for an order under paragraph (1)(*a*) in respect of a record shall not be heard unless the person who makes the application has given the young person to whom the record relates and the person or body that has possession of the record at least five days notice in writing of the application, and the young person and the person or body that has possession have had a reasonable opportunity to be heard.

(4) A youth justice court judge may waive the requirement in subsection (3) to give notice to a young person when the judge is of the opinion that

(*a*) to insist on the giving of the notice would frustrate the application; or

(*b*) reasonable efforts have not been successful in finding the young person.

(5) In any order under subsection (1), the youth justice court judge shall set out the purposes for which the record may be used.

(6) When access to a record is given to any person under paragraph (1)(*b*), that person may subsequently disclose information contained in the record, but shall not disclose the information in any form that would reasonably be expected to identify the young person to whom it relates.

ANNOTATIONS

Note: Some of the following cases were decided under the *Young Offenders Act* but were thought to be of assistance in applying this Act.

The accused was entitled to an order under s. 45.1 of the *Young Offenders Act*, which is worded similarly to this section, for disclosure of the youth record of an alleged accomplice who was a witness for the Crown, even though the witness had entered the non-disclosure period as set out in s. 45 of the *Young Offenders Act* [similar to s. 119(2) of this Act]: *R. v. Strain* (1994), 91 C.C.C. (3d) 568, 31 C.R. (4th) 347 (Ont. Ct. (Gen. Div.)).

The expiry periods for disclosure in s. 45(1)(e) and (f) of the *Young Offenders Act* [similar to s. 119(2)(*g*) and (*h*) of this Act] yield to the extent required by a disclosure order under s. 45.1 of the *Young Offenders Act*: *R. v. M. (E.H.B.)* (1996), 106 C.C.C. (3d) 535, 49 C.R. (4th) 370, 125 W.A.C. 130 *sub nom. R. v. McKay* (B.C.C.A.).

The test for applications brought after the expiry of the access period prescribed by the Act is a stringent one. Section 123 rests nothing in "desirability". Access to a record because the interest in it is shown to be valid is not enough under s. 123 of the Act. An interest in a record that is "valid" may or may not rise to the level of an interest that is both "valid" and "substantial". Moreover, the task in an application under s. 123 is to show that it is "necessary" for access to be given to the record or part of it in the interest of the proper administration of justice: *D. (J.), Re* (2009), 182 A.C.W.S. (3d) 57, [2009] O.J. No. 6384 (C.J.).

There is no right of appeal from a decision made under this provision. Civil rights of appeal under provincial legislation have no application to proceedings under the Act. Rather, review may only be obtained by way of an application for *certiorari* under Part XXVI of the *Criminal Code* before a judge of the superior court: *Toronto (Police Service) v. L.D.* (2018), 357 C.C.C. (3d) 1 (Ont. C.A.).

ACCESS TO RECORD BY YOUNG PERSON.

124. A young person to whom a record relates and his or her counsel may have access to the record at any time.

Disclosure of Information in a Record

DISCLOSURE BY PEACE OFFICER DURING INVESTIGATION / Disclosure by Attorney General / Information that may be disclosed to a foreign state / Disclosure to insurance company / Preparation of reports / Schools and others / Information to be kept separate / Time limit.

125. (1) A peace officer may disclose to any person any information in a record kept under section 114 (court records) or 115 (police records) that it is necessary to disclose in the conduct of the investigation of an offence.

(2) The Attorney General may, in the course of a proceeding under this Act or any other Act of Parliament, disclose the following information in a record kept under section 114 (court reports) or 115 (police records):

- **(*a*) to a person who is a co-accused with the young person in respect of the offence for which the record is kept, any information contained in the record; and**
- **(*b*) to an accused in a proceeding, if the record is in respect of a witness in the proceeding, information that identifies the witness as a young person who has been dealt with under this Act.**

(3) The Attorney General or a peace officer may disclose to the Minister of Justice of Canada information in a record that is kept under section 114 (court records) or 115 (police records) to the extent that it is necessary to deal with a request to or by a foreign state under the *Mutual Legal Assistance in Criminal Matters Act*, or for the purposes of any extradition matter under the *Extradition Act*. The Minister of Justice of Canada

may disclose the information to the foreign state in respect of which the request was made, or to which the extradition matter relates, as the case may be.

(4) A peace officer may disclose to an insurance company information in a record that is kept under section 114 (court records) or 115 (police records) for the purpose of investigating a claim arising out of an offence committed or alleged to have been committed by the young person to whom the record relates.

(5) The provincial director or a youth worker may disclose information contained in a record if the disclosure is necessary for procuring information that relates to the preparation of a report required by this Act.

(6) The provincial director, a youth worker, the Attorney General, a peace officer or any other person engaged in the provision of services to young persons may disclose to any professional or other person engaged in the supervision or care of a young person — including a representative of any school board or school or any other educational or training institution — any information contained in a record kept under sections 114 to 116 if the disclosure is necessary

- **(*a*) to ensure compliance by the young person with an authorization under section 91 or an order of the youth justice court;**
- **(*b*) to ensure the safety of staff, students or other persons; or**
- **(*c*) to facilitate the rehabilitation of the young person.**

(7) A person to whom information is disclosed under subsection (6) shall

- **(*a*) keep the information separate from any other record of the young person to whom the information relates;**
- **(*b*) ensure that no other person has access to the information except if authorized under this Act, or if necessary for the purposes of subsection (6); and**
- **(*c*) destroy their copy of the record when the information is no longer required for the purpose for which it was disclosed.**

(8) No information may be disclosed under this section after the end of the applicable period set out in subsection 119(2) (period of access to records).

RECORDS IN THE CUSTODY, ETC., OF ARCHIVISTS.

126. When records originally kept under sections 114 to 116 are under the custody or control of the Librarian and Archivist of Canada or the archivist for any province, that person may disclose any information contained in the records to any other person if

- **(*a*) a youth justice court judge is satisfied that the disclosure is desirable in the public interest for research or statistical purposes; and**
- **(*b*) the person to whom the information is disclosed undertakes not to disclose the information in any form that could reasonably be expected to identify the young person to whom it relates. 2004, c. 11, s. 48.**

DISCLOSURE WITH COURT ORDER / Opportunity to be heard / *Ex parte* application / Time limit.

127. (1) The youth justice court may, on the application of the provincial director, the Attorney General or a peace officer, make an order permitting the applicant to disclose to the person or persons specified by the court any information about a young person that is specified, if the court is satisfied that the disclosure is necessary, having regard to the following circumstances:

- **(*a*) the young person has been found guilty of an offence involving serious personal injury;**
- **(*b*) the young person poses a risk of serious harm to persons; and**
- **(*c*) the disclosure of the information is relevant to the avoidance of that risk.**

YOUTH

(2) Subject to subsection (3), before making an order under subsection (1), the youth justice court shall give the young person, a parent of the young person and the Attorney General an opportunity to be heard.

(3) An application under subsection (1) may be made *ex parte* by the Attorney General where the youth justice court is satisfied that reasonable efforts have been made to locate the young person and that those efforts have not been successful.

(4) No information may be disclosed under subsection (1) after the end of the applicable period set out in subsection 119(2) (period of access to records).

Disposition or Destruction of Records and Prohibition on Use and Disclosure

EFFECT OF END OF ACCESS PERIODS / Disposal of records / Disposal of R.C.M.P. records / Purging CPIC / Exception / Authority to inspect / Definition of "destroy".

128. (1) Subject to sections 123, 124 and 126, after the end of the applicable period set out in section 119 or 120 no record kept under sections 114 to 116 may be used for any purpose that would identify the young person to whom the record relates as a young person dealt with under this Act or the *Young Offenders Act*, chapter Y-1 of the Revised Statutes of Canada, 1985.

(2) Subject to paragraph 125(7)(*c*), any record kept under sections 114 to 116, other than a record kept under subsection 115(3), may, in the discretion of the person or body keeping the record, be destroyed or transmitted to the Librarian and Archivist of Canada or the archivist for any province, at any time before or after the end of the applicable period set out in section 119.

(3) All records kept under subsection 115(3) shall be destroyed or, if the Librarian and Archivist of Canada requires it, transmitted to the Librarian and Archivist, at the end of the applicable period set out in section 119 or 120.

(4) The Commissioner of the Royal Canadian Mounted Police shall remove a record from the automated criminal conviction records retrieval system maintained by the Royal Canadian Mounted Police at the end of the applicable period referred to in section 119; however, information relating to a prohibition order made under an Act of Parliament or the legislature of a province shall be removed only at the end of the period for which the order is in force.

(5) Despite subsections (1), (2) and (4), an entry that is contained in a system maintained by the Royal Canadian Mounted Police to match crime scene information and that relates to an offence committed or alleged to have been committed by a young person shall be dealt with in the same manner as information that relates to an offence committed by an adult for which a record suspension ordered under the *Criminal Records Act* is in effect.

(6) The Librarian and Archivist of Canada may, at any time, inspect records kept under sections 114 to 116 that are under the control of a government institution as defined in section 2 of the *Library and Archives of Canada Act*, and the archivist for a province may at any time inspect any records kept under those sections that the archivist is authorized to inspect under any Act of the legislature of the province.

(7) For the purposes of subsections (2) and (3), "destroy", in respect of a record, means

(*a*) to shred, burn or otherwise physically destroy the record, in the case of a record other than a record in electronic form; and

(*b*) to delete, write over or otherwise render the record inaccessible, in the case of a record in electronic form. 2004, c. 11, s. 49; 2012, c. 1, s. 159.

ANNOTATIONS

A youth court judge has jurisdiction under subsec. (2) to order the destruction of youth court records held by the court where the court was satisfied that taking into account the interests of society and factors relating to the administration of justice, earlier destruction would facilitate the rehabilitation and reintegration of the youth into society: *R. v. C. (L.T.)* (2009), 248 C.C.C. (3d) 98 (N.L.C.A.), leave to appeal to S.C.C. refused (2010), 297 Nfld. & P.E.I.R. 131*n*.

The same is not true of records held by other entities; the youth court judge has no jurisdiction to order such entities to destroy records: *LSJPA - 105* (2010), 253 C.C.C. (3d) 565 (C.A. Que.), leave to appeal to S.C.C. refused (2010), 258 C.C.C. (3d) iv.

NO SUBSEQUENT DISCLOSURE.

129. No person who is given access to a record or to whom information is disclosed under this Act shall disclose that information to any other person unless the disclosure is authorized under this Act.

PART 7 / GENERAL PROVISIONS

Disqualification of Judge

DISQUALIFICATION OF JUDGE / Exception.

130. (1) Subject to subsection (2), a youth justice court judge who, prior to an adjudication in respect of a young person charged with an offence, examines a pre-sentence report made in respect of the young person in connection with that offence or has, after a guilty plea or a finding of guilt, heard submissions as to sentence and then there has been a change of plea, shall not in any capacity conduct or continue the trial of the young person for the offence and shall transfer the case to another judge to be dealt with according to law.

(2) A youth justice court judge may, in the circumstances referred to in subsection (1), with the consent of the young person and the prosecutor, conduct or continue the trial of the young person if the judge is satisfied that he or she has not been predisposed by a guilty plea or finding of guilt, or by information contained in the pre-sentence report or submissions as to sentence.

Substitution of Judge

POWERS OF SUBSTITUTE YOUTH JUSTICE COURT JUDGE / Transcript of evidence already given.

131. (1) A youth justice court judge who acts in the place of another youth justice court judge under subsection 669.2(1) (continuation of proceedings) of the *Criminal Code* shall

(*a*) if an adjudication has been made, proceed to sentence the young person or make the order that, in the circumstances, is authorized by law; or

(*b*) if no adjudication has been made, recommence the trial as if no evidence had been taken.

(2) A youth justice court judge who recommences a trial under paragraph (1)(*b*) may, if the parties consent, admit into evidence a transcript of any evidence already given in the case.

YOUTH

Exclusion from Hearing

EXCLUSION FROM HEARING / Exception / Exclusion after adjudication or during review / Exception.

132. (1) Subject to subsection (2), a court or justice before whom proceedings are carried out under this Act may exclude any person from all or part of the proceedings if the court or justice considers that the person's presence is unnecessary to the conduct of the proceedings and the court or justice is of the opinion that

(*a*) any evidence or information presented to the court or justice would be seriously injurious or seriously prejudicial to

(i) the young person who is being dealt with in the proceedings,

(ii) a child or young person who is a witness in the proceedings, or

(iii) a child or young person who is aggrieved by or the victim of the offence charged in the proceedings; or

(*b*) it would be in the interest of public morals, the maintenance of order or the proper administration of justice to exclude any or all members of the public from the court room.

(2) Subject to section 650 (accused to be present) of the *Criminal Code* and except if it is necessary for the purposes of subsection 34(9) (nondisclosure of medical or psychological report) of this Act, a court or justice may not, under subsection (1), exclude from proceedings under this Act

(*a*) the prosecutor;

(*b*) the young person who is being dealt with in the proceedings, the counsel or a parent of the young person or any adult assisting the young person under subsection 25(7);

(*c*) the provincial director or his or her agent; or

(*d*) the youth worker to whom the young person's case has been assigned.

(3) A youth justice court, after it has found a young person guilty of an offence, or a youth justice court or a review board, during a review, may, in its discretion, exclude from the court or from a hearing of the review board any person other than the following, when it is being presented with information the knowledge of which might, in its opinion, be seriously injurious or seriously prejudicial to the young person:

(*a*) the young person or his or her counsel;

(*b*) the provincial director or his or her agent;

(*c*) the youth worker to whom the young person's case has been assigned; and

(*d*) the Attorney General.

(4) The exception set out in paragraph (3)(*a*) is subject to subsection 34(9) (nondisclosure of medical or psychological report) of this Act and section 650 (accused to be present) of the *Criminal Code*.

ANNOTATIONS

Note: The following case was decided under the *Young Offenders Act* but was thought to be of assistance in applying this Act.

It was held that s. 39 of the *Young Offenders Act*, which is worded similarly to this section, was not an unconstitutional infringement on the right of access to the courts as included in the guarantee to freedom of expression in s. 2(*b*) of the *Charter of Rights and Freedoms*: *R. v. Southam Inc.* (1984), 16 C.C.C. (3d) 262, 42 C.R. (3d) 336, 14 D.L.R. (4th) 683 (Ont. H.C.J.), affd 25 C.C.C. (3d) 119, 50 C.R. (3d) 241, 26 D.L.R. (4th) 479 (Ont. C.A.), leave to appeal to S.C.C. refused C.C.C., D.L.R. *loc. cit.*

Transfer of Charges

TRANSFER OF CHARGES.

133. Despite subsections 478(1) and (3) of the *Criminal Code*, a young person charged with an offence that is alleged to have been committed in one province may, if the Attorney General of the province consents, appear before a youth justice court of any other province and

(*a*) if the young person pleads guilty to that offence and the youth justice court is satisfied that the facts support the charge, the court shall find the young person guilty of the offence alleged in the information or indictment; and

(*b*) if the young person pleads not guilty to that offence, or pleads guilty but the court is not satisfied that the facts support the charge, the young person shall, if he or she was detained in custody prior to the appearance, be returned to custody and dealt with according to law.

Forfeiture of Recognizances

APPLICATIONS FOR FORFEITURE OF RECOGNIZANCES.

134. Applications for the forfeiture of recognizances of young persons shall be made to the youth justice court.

PROCEEDINGS IN CASE OF DEFAULT / Order for forfeiture of recognizance / Judgment debtors of the Crown / Order may be filed / If a deposit has been made / Subsections 770(2) and (4) of *Criminal Code* do not apply / Sections 772 and 773 of *Criminal Code* apply.

135. (1) When a recognizance binding a young person has been endorsed with a certificate under subsection 770(1) of the *Criminal Code*, a youth justice court judge shall

(*a*) on the request of the Attorney General, fix a time and place for the hearing of an application for the forfeiture of the recognizance; and

(*b*) after fixing a time and place for the hearing, cause to be sent by confirmed delivery service, not less than ten days before the time so fixed, to each principal and surety named in the recognizance, directed to his or her latest known address, a notice requiring him or her to appear at the time and place fixed by the judge to show cause why the recognizance should not be forfeited.

(2) When subsection (1) is complied with, the youth justice court judge may, after giving the parties an opportunity to be heard, in his or her discretion grant or refuse the application and make any order with respect to the forfeiture of the recognizance that he or she considers proper.

(3) If, under subsection (2), a youth justice court judge orders forfeiture of a recognizance, the principal and his or her sureties become judgment debtors of the Crown, each in the amount that the judge orders him or her to pay.

(4) An order made under subsection (2) may be filed with the clerk of the superior court or, in the province of Quebec, the prothonotary and, if an order is filed, the clerk or the prothonotary shall issue a writ of fieri facias in Form 34 set out in the *Criminal Code* and deliver it to the sheriff of each of the territorial divisions in which any of the principal and his or her sureties resides, carries on business or has property.

(5) If a deposit has been made by a person against whom an order for forfeiture of a recognizance has been made, no writ of fieri facias shall issue, but the amount of the deposit shall be transferred by the person who has custody of it to the person who is entitled by law to receive it.

(6) Subsections 770(2) (transmission of recognizance) and (4) (transmission of deposit) of the *Criminal Code* do not apply in respect of proceedings under this Act.

(7) Sections 772 (levy under writ) and 773 (committal when writ not satisfied) of the *Criminal Code* apply in respect of writs of fieri facias issued under this section as if they were issued under section 771 (proceedings in case of default) of that Act.

Offences and Punishment

INDUCING A YOUNG PERSON, ETC. / Absolute jurisdiction of provincial court judge.

136. (1) Every person who

(*a*) induces or assists a young person to leave unlawfully a place of custody or other place in which the young person has been placed in accordance with a youth sentence or a disposition imposed under the *Young Offenders Act*, chapter Y-1 of the Revised Statutes of Canada, 1985,

(*b*) unlawfully removes a young person from a place referred to in paragraph (*a*),

(*c*) knowingly harbours or conceals a young person who has unlawfully left a place referred to in paragraph (*a*),

(*d*) wilfully induces or assists a young person to breach or disobey a term or condition of a youth sentence or other order of the youth justice court, or a term or condition of a disposition or other order under the *Young Offenders Act*, chapter Y-1 of the Revised Statutes of Canada, 1985, or

(*e*) wilfully prevents or interferes with the performance by a young person of a term or condition of a youth sentence or other order of the youth justice court, or a term or condition of a disposition or other order under the *Young Offenders Act*, chapter Y-1 of the Revised Statutes of Canada, 1985,

is guilty of an indictable offence and liable to imprisonment for a term not exceeding two years or is guilty of an offence punishable on summary conviction.

(2) The jurisdiction of a provincial court judge to try an adult charged with an indictable offence under this section is absolute and does not depend on the consent of the accused.

FAILURE TO COMPLY WITH SENTENCE OR DISPOSITION.

137. Every person who is subject to a youth sentence imposed under any of paragraphs 42(2)(*c*) to (*m*) or (*s*) of this Act, to a victim fine surcharge ordered under subsection 53(2) of this Act or to a disposition made under any of paragraphs 20(1)(a.1) to (*g*), (*j*) or (*l*) of the *Young Offenders Act*, chapter Y-1 of the Revised Statutes of Canada, 1985, and who wilfully fails or refuses to comply with that sentence, surcharge or disposition is guilty of an offence punishable on summary conviction.

OFFENCES / Provincial court judge has absolute jurisdiction on indictment.

138. (1) Every person who contravenes subsection 110(1) (identity of offender not to be published), 111(1) (identity of victim or witness not to be published), 118(1) (no access to records unless authorized) or 128(3) (disposal of R.C.M.P. records) or section 129 (no subsequent disclosure) of this Act, or subsection 38(1) (identity not to be published), (1.12) (no subsequent disclosure), (1.14) (no subsequent disclosure by school) or (1.15) (information to be kept separate), 45(2) (destruction of records) or 46(1) (prohibition against disclosure) of the *Young Offenders Act*, chapter Y-1 of the Revised Statutes of Canada, 1985,

(*a*) is guilty of an indictable offence and liable to imprisonment for a term not exceeding two years; or

(*b*) is guilty of an offence punishable on summary conviction.

(2) The jurisdiction of a provincial court judge to try an adult charged with an offence under paragraph (1)(*a*) is absolute and does not depend on the consent of the accused.

OFFENCE AND PUNISHMENT / Offence and punishment / Punishment.

139. (1) Every person who wilfully fails to comply with section 30 (designated place of temporary detention), or with an undertaking entered into under subsection 31(3) (condition of placement),

(*a*) is guilty of an indictable offence and liable to imprisonment for a term not exceeding two years; or

(*b*) is guilty of an offence punishable on summary conviction.

(2) Every person who wilfully fails to comply with section 7 (designated place of temporary detention) of the *Young Offenders Act*, chapter Y-1 of the Revised Statutes of Canada, 1985, or with an undertaking entered into under subsection 7.1(2) (condition of placement) of that Act is guilty of an offence punishable on summary conviction.

(3) Any person who uses or authorizes the use of an application form in contravention of subsection 82(3) (application for employment) is guilty of an offence punishable on summary conviction.

Application of *Criminal Code*

APPLICATION OF CRIMINAL CODE.

140. Except to the extent that it is inconsistent with or excluded by this Act, the provisions of the *Criminal Code* apply, with any modifications that the circumstances require, in respect of offences alleged to have been committed by young persons.

SECTIONS OF CRIMINAL CODE APPLICABLE / Notice and copies to counsel and parents / Proceedings not invalid / Exception / No hospital order assessments / Considerations of court or Review Board making a disposition / Cap applicable to young persons / Application to increase cap of unfit young person subject to adult sentence / Consideration of youth justice court for increase in cap / *Prima facie* case to be made every year / Designation of hospitals for young persons / Definition of "Review Board".

141. (1) Except to the extent that they are inconsistent with or excluded by this Act, section 16 (defence of mental disorder) and Part XX.1 (mental disorder) of the *Criminal Code* apply, with any modifications that the circumstances require, in respect of proceedings under this Act in relation to offences alleged to have been committed by young persons.

(2) For the purposes of subsection (1),

(*a*) wherever in Part XX.1 (mental disorder) of the *Criminal Code* a reference is made to a copy to be sent or otherwise given to an accused or a party to the proceedings, the reference shall be read as including a reference to a copy to be sent or otherwise given to

(i) any counsel representing the young person,

(ii) a parent of the young person who is in attendance at the proceedings against the young person, and

(iii) a parent of the young person not in attendance at the proceedings who is, in the opinion of the youth justice court or Review Board, taking an active interest in the proceedings; and

(*b*) wherever in Part XX.1 (mental disorder) of the *Criminal Code* a reference is made to notice to be given to an accused or a party to proceedings, the

YOUTH

reference shall be read as including a reference to notice to be given to a parent of the young person and any counsel representing the young person.

(3) Subject to subsection (4), failure to give a notice referred to in paragraph (2)(*b*) to a parent of a young person does not affect the validity of proceedings under this Act.

(4) Failure to give a notice referred to in paragraph (2)(*b*) to a parent of a young person in any case renders invalid any subsequent proceedings under this Act relating to the case unless

- **(*a*) a parent of the young person attends at the court or Review Board with the young person; or**
- **(*b*) a youth justice court judge or Review Board before whom proceedings are held against the young person**
  - **(i) adjourns the proceedings and orders that the notice be given in the manner and to the persons that the judge or Review Board directs, or**
  - **(ii) dispenses with the notice if the youth justice court or Review Board is of the opinion that, having regard to the circumstances, the notice may be dispensed with.**

(5) [*Repealed*, 2005, c. 22, s. 63(2).]

(6) Before making or reviewing a disposition in respect of a young person under Part XX.1 (mental disorder) of the *Criminal Code*, a youth justice court or Review Board shall consider the age and special needs of the young person and any representations or submissions made by a parent of the young person.

(7) to (9) [*Repealed*, 2005, c. 22, s. 63(3).]

(10) For the purpose of applying subsection 672.33(1) (fitness to stand trial) of the *Criminal Code* to proceedings under this Act in relation to an offence alleged to have been committed by a young person, wherever in that subsection a reference is made to two years, there shall be substituted a reference to one year.

(11) A reference in Part XX.1 (mental disorder) of the *Criminal Code* to a hospital in a province shall be construed as a reference to a hospital designated by the Minister of Health for the province for the custody, treatment or assessment of young persons.

(12) In this section, "Review Board" has the meaning assigned by section 672.1 of the *Criminal Code*. 2005, c. 22, s. 63.

PART XXVII AND SUMMARY CONVICTION TRIAL PROVISIONS OF CRIMINAL CODE TO APPLY / Indictable offences / Attendance of young person / Limitation period / Costs.

142. (1) Subject to this section and except to the extent that they are inconsistent with this Act, the provisions of Part XXVII (summary conviction offences) of the *Criminal Code*, and any other provisions of that Act that apply in respect of summary conviction offences and relate to trial proceedings, apply to proceedings under this Act

- **(*a*) in respect of an order under section 83.3 (recognizance — terrorist activity), 810 (recognizance — fear of injury or damage), 810.01 (recognizance — fear of certain offences), 810.011 (recognizance — fear of terrorism offence), 810.02 (recognizance — fear of forced marriage or marriage under age of 16 years) or 810.2 (recognizance — fear of serious personal injury offence) of that Act or an offence under section 811 (breach of recognizance) of that Act;**
- **(*b*) in respect of a summary conviction offence; and**
- **(*c*) in respect of an indictable offence as if it were defined in the enactment creating it as a summary conviction offence.**

(2) For greater certainty and despite subsection (1) or any other provision of this Act, an indictable offence committed by a young person is, for the purposes of this Act or any other Act of Parliament, an indictable offence.

(3) Section 650 of the *Criminal Code* applies in respect of proceedings under this Act, whether the proceedings relate to an indictable offence or an offence punishable on summary conviction.

(4) In proceedings under this Act, subsection 786(2) of the *Criminal Code* does not apply in respect of an indictable offence.

(5) Section 809 of the *Criminal Code* does not apply in respect of proceedings under this Act. 2015, c. 20, ss. 33, 36(9); c. 29, s. 15.

Procedure

COUNTS CHARGED IN INFORMATION.

143. Indictable offences and offences punishable on summary conviction may under this Act be charged in the same information or indictment and tried jointly.

ISSUE OF SUBPOENA / Service of subpoena.

144. (1) If a person is required to attend to give evidence before a youth justice court, the subpoena directed to that person may be issued by a youth justice court judge, whether or not the person whose attendance is required is within the same province as the youth justice court.

(2) A subpoena issued by a youth justice court and directed to a person who is not within the same province as the youth justice court shall be served personally on the person to whom it is directed.

WARRANT.

145. A warrant issued by a youth justice court may be executed anywhere in Canada.

Evidence

GENERAL LAW ON ADMISSIBILITY OF STATEMENTS TO APPLY / When statements are admissible / Exception in certain cases for oral statements / Waiver of right to consult / Waiver of right to consult / Admissibility of statements / Statements made under duress are inadmissible / Misrepresentation of age / Parent, etc., not a person in authority.

146. (1) Subject to this section, the law relating to the admissibility of statements made by persons accused of committing offences applies in respect of young persons.

(2) No oral or written statement made by a young person who is less than eighteen years old, to a peace officer or to any other person who is, in law, a person in authority, on the arrest or detention of the young person or in circumstances where the peace officer or other person has reasonable grounds for believing that the young person has committed an offence is admissible against the young person unless

- **(*a*) the statement was voluntary;**
- **(*b*) the person to whom the statement was made has, before the statement was made, clearly explained to the young person, in language appropriate to his or her age and understanding, that**
  - **(i) the young person is under no obligation to make a statement,**
  - **(ii) any statement made by the young person may be used as evidence in proceedings against him or her,**
  - **(iii) the young person has the right to consult counsel and a parent or other person in accordance with paragraph (*c*), and**

YOUTH

(iv) any statement made by the young person is required to be made in the presence of counsel and any other person consulted in accordance with paragraph (*c*), if any, unless the young person desires otherwise;

(*c*) the young person has, before the statement was made, been given a reasonable opportunity to consult

(i) with counsel, and

(ii) with a parent or, in the absence of a parent, an adult relative or, in the absence of a parent and an adult relative, any other appropriate adult chosen by the young person, as long as that person is not a co-accused, or under investigation, in respect of the same offence; and

(*d*) if the young person consults a person in accordance with paragraph (*c*), the young person has been given a reasonable opportunity to make the statement in the presence of that person.

(3) The requirements set out in paragraphs (2)(*b*) to (*d*) do not apply in respect of oral statements if they are made spontaneously by the young person to a peace officer or other person in authority before that person has had a reasonable opportunity to comply with those requirements.

(4) A young person may waive the rights under paragraph (2)(*c*) or (*d*) but any such waiver

(*a*) must be recorded on video tape or audio tape; or

(*b*) must be in writing and contain a statement signed by the young person that he or she has been informed of the right being waived.

(5) When a waiver of rights under paragraph (2)(*c*) or (*d*) is not made in accordance with subsection (4) owing to a technical irregularity, the youth justice court may determine that the waiver is valid if it is satisfied that the young person was informed of his or her rights, and voluntarily waived them.

(6) When there has been a technical irregularity in complying with paragraphs (2)(*b*) to (*d*), the youth justice court may admit into evidence a statement referred to in subsection (2), if satisfied that the admission of the statement would not bring into disrepute the principle that young persons are entitled to enhanced procedural protection to ensure that they are treated fairly and their rights are protected.

(7) A youth justice court judge may rule inadmissible in any proceedings under this Act a statement made by the young person in respect of whom the proceedings are taken if the young person satisfies the judge that the statement was made under duress imposed by any person who is not, in law, a person in authority.

(8) A youth justice court judge may in any proceedings under this Act rule admissible any statement or waiver by a young person if, at the time of the making of the statement or waiver,

(*a*) the young person held himself or herself to be eighteen years old or older;

(*b*) the person to whom the statement or waiver was made conducted reasonable inquiries as to the age of the young person and had reasonable grounds for believing that the young person was eighteen years old or older; and

(*c*) in all other circumstances the statement or waiver would otherwise be admissible.

(9) For the purpose of this section, a person consulted under paragraph (2)(*c*) is, in the absence of evidence to the contrary, deemed not to be a person in authority.

ANNOTATIONS

While this section would appear to lay down certain rigorous standards for admission of statements of young people, the courts have always given special consideration to confessions by juveniles. It may be that this extensive case law is still relevant in view of subsec. (1) and subsec. (2)(*a*). In fact, many of the guidelines set out in that case law are now a matter of law under subsec. (2)(*b*). See: *R. v. Jacques* (1958), 29 C.R. 249 (Que. S.W.C.); *R. v. Wilson* (1970), 1 C.C.C. (2d) 14 (B.C.C.A.); *R. v. M. (D.) and P. (J.)* (1980), 58 C.C.C. (2d) 373 (Ont. Prov. Ct.).

Note: Some of the following cases were decided under s. 56 of the *Young Offenders Act*, which is worded similarly to this section, and accordingly were thought to be of assistance in applying this Act.

Subsection (2) (general) – A consultation between a parent and young person in accordance with the predecessor to this section (s. 56 of the *Young Offenders Act*) is privileged to the same extent as would be a consultation between the young person and counsel and should not be admitted at the instance of the Crown: *R. v. K. (K.J.)* (1989), 38 O.A.C. 5 (C.A.). But, s. 56 did not create a class privilege rendering all communications between a parent and child privileged: *R. v. E. (T.K.)* (2005), 194 C.C.C. (3d) 496 (N.B.C.A.), leave to appeal to S.C.C. refused 198 C.C.C. (3d) vi.

There was no requirement under s. 56 of the *Young Offenders Act* that the offender be advised of the possibility that the offender may be raised to adult court. The presence or absence of such a warning was merely an aspect of determining whether or not the statement was voluntary and if the offender waived his right to consult counsel without being aware of the possibility, where it existed, of being raised to adult court, then the waiver would be invalid: *R. v. I. (L.R.)*, [1993] 4 S.C.R. 504, 86 C.C.C. (3d) 289. [Query, whether this holding would apply to a young person facing an adult sentence in accordance with this Act.]

Subsection (2) does not apply to a young person who asserts that they are a witness until they are arrested or detained for the specific matter being investigated or reasonable grounds exist to believe that they are involved in the offence being investigated: *R. v. T. (D.D.)* (2008), 234 C.C.C. (3d) 225 (Alta. Q.B.).

A breathalyzer sample was not a statement within the meaning of s. 56 of the *Young Offenders Act*: *R. v. L. (D.J.)* (1995), 139 Sask. R. 47, 18 M.V.R. 231 (Q.B.), affd 141 Sask. R. 191 (C.A.).

An ambulance attendant rendering first aid to the offender following a serious accident was not a person in authority within the meaning of s. 56: *R. v. B. (M.R.)* (1998), 125 C.C.C. (3d) 335 (B.C.C.A.).

Compliance with subsec. (2) – The test for compliance with the informational requirement is objective. The Crown is not required to prove that a young person in fact understood his or her rights, nor that they were asked to explain back the rights. The Crown's evidentiary burden is discharged by demonstrating that the person in authority took reasonable steps to ensure that the young person was capable of understanding the rights that were explained. The reading of a standardized form will not normally suffice in itself to establish the sufficiency of the caution required. Some insight into the young person's level of comprehension is necessary and the person in authority has to make a reasonable effort to become aware of relevant factors such as learning disabilities and previous experience with the justice system, since the mandatory explanation must be appropriate to the age and understanding of that young person. Adherence to standardized forms can facilitate but will not always constitute compliance with subsec. (2)(*b*). The court must be satisfied that the young person's rights were in fact explained clearly and comprehensively by the person in authority: *R. v. H. (L.T.)*, [2008] 2 S.C.R. 739, 234 C.C.C. (3d) 301.

All of the factors in subsec. (2), as well as the requirements for a valid waiver contained in subsec. (4), must be established beyond a reasonable doubt: *R. v. H. (L.T.), supra*.

The Crown must also prove beyond a reasonable doubt that the preconditions for subsec. (2) do not apply, namely, that the young person was not arrested or detained, and that the officer did not have reasonable grounds for believing that the young person had committed an offence: *R. v. N.B.* (2018), 362 C.C.C. (3d) 302 (Ont. C.A.).

Section 56 was to protect all young people and thus its requirements must be complied with no matter how street-smart or worldly wise the young person may appear. Where the statutory preconditions have not been complied with, then the statement is inadmissible.

Although the offender has been advised of his right to consult with an adult relative or counsel and has availed himself of that opportunity, if the police intend to continue the questioning, they must again advise him of his right to counsel and his right to have either an adult relative or counsel present: *R. v. J. (J.T.)*, [1990] 2 S.C.R. 3, 59 C.C.C. (3d) 1.

The young person must be advised that he may consult both with counsel and with a parent and is entitled to a reasonable opportunity to consult with both and that they may have counsel present, with or without a parent, when giving the statement. The fact that the young person had previously been advised of the right to counsel did not constitute compliance with this aspect of s. 56: *R. v. D. (C.M.)* (1996), 113 C.C.C. (3d) 56 (B.C.C.A.).

While subsec. (2)(*b*)(iii) refers to the "right" to consult with counsel, subsec. (2)(*b*)(iv) refers to the "requirement" that the statement be made in the presence of a consulted person. The officer's failure to inform the accused of the requirement to make the statement in the presence of the consulted person was a breach of that section, which denied the accused access to important information that would have enabled him to decide whether to exercise the right to consult with a third party. The statutory requirement on the police was the same, whether or not the accused had chosen to consult with a third party: *R. v. S. (S.)* (2007), 222 C.C.C. (3d) 545 (Ont. C.A.).

The derived confessions rule has application in the youth context. The police failed to advise the accused in the second interview that he should not be influenced in his decision whether to speak by the fact that he had talked to the police earlier or by what he had said there. In addition, the trial judge failed to consider the effect of the police's failure to tell the accused about the inadmissibility of the prior statement at the outset or at any time during the second interview. The omission left the young person with an incomplete understanding of his jeopardy when deciding whether or not to speak. Such advice was necessary to dispel the taint associated with the first interview: *R. v. D. (M.)* (2012), 293 C.C.C. (3d) 79 (Ont. C.A.).

Spontaneous statement [subsec. (3)] – "Spontaneous" as used in s. 56 of the *Young Offenders Act* means "arising, proceeding, or acting entirely from natural impulse, without any external stimulus or constraint". An external stimulus need not be a question or direction from a person in authority. The mere presence of that authority in certain circumstances could be considered a stimulus giving rise to an unnatural response or reaction although the mere presence of a person in authority cannot, in and of itself, be considered as defeating sponanteity: *R. v. W. (J.)* (1996), 109 C.C.C. (3d) 506, 2 C.R. (5th) 233 (Ont. C.A.).

Even if a statement was made spontaneously, by virtue of s. 56(2)(*c*) of the *Young Offenders Act*, and notwithstanding s. 56(3), it is not admissible if a reasonable opportunity to consult an adult had not been given to the young person, the person in authority to whom the statement was made having had a reasonable opportunity to give the young person the opportunity to do so. Thus, in this case, the officers had a reasonable opportunity when the mother of the offender was present at the police station. For, while the offender's mother was asked if she would like to see her son but declined, there was no evidence that the offender was asked at that time if he would like to see his mother. A young person is entitled to the advice of a parent before he is even questioned by the police if the opportunity for him to have the benefit of that advice is reasonably available, as it was in this case: *R. v. W. (B.C.)* (1986), 27 C.C.C. (3d) 481, 52 C.R. (3d) 201 (Man. C.A.).

A statement was not spontaneous within the meaning of s. 56(3) of the *Young Offenders Act* where it was clear that the offender was a suspect at the time, had been questioned at length and the statement was made in response to an allegation by the police that he had lied: *R. v. J. (J.T.)*, [1990] 2 S.C.R. 3, 59 C.C.C. (3d) 1.

Subsection (4) – A valid waiver under s. 146(4) must be proven beyond a reasonable doubt: *R. v. H. (L.T.)*, [2008] 2 S.C.R. 739, 234 C.C.C. (3d) 301.

To be a fully informed waiver under s. 146(4), the accused must understand the charges against him or her: *R. v. K. (W.C.)* (2012), 288 C.C.C. (3d) 499 (Alta. C.A.).

The validity of the form of waiver will have to be considered in relation to the circumstances of the particular case. However, a waiver which informed the offender that he was not obliged to say anything, but that anything he did say may be given in evidence, sufficiently complied with s. 56(2)(*b*)(ii) of the *Young Offenders Act* where the offender was found to be mature and "street wise": *R. v. G.* (1985), 20 C.C.C. (3d) 289 (B.C.C.A.).

To be valid, a waiver under s. 56(4) of the *Young Offenders Act* must not only have been in writing but also made with full comprehension of what is being waived and the consequences of doing so: *R. v. W. (B.C.)* (1986), 27 C.C.C. (3d) 481, 52 C.R. (3d) 201 (Man. C.A.).

STATEMENTS NOT ADMISSIBLE AGAINST YOUNG PERSON / Exceptions.

147. (1) Subject to subsection (2), if a young person is assessed in accordance with an order made under subsection 34(1) (medical or psychological assessment), no statement or reference to a statement made by the young person during the course and for the purposes of the assessment to the person who conducts the assessment or to anyone acting under that person's direction is admissible in evidence, without the consent of the young person, in any proceeding before a court, tribunal, body or person with jurisdiction to compel the production of evidence.

(2) A statement referred to in subsection (1) is admissible in evidence for the purposes of

- **(*a*) making a decision on an application heard under section 71 (hearing — adult sentences);**
- **(*b*) determining whether the young person is unfit to stand trial;**
- **(*c*) determining whether the balance of the mind of the young person was disturbed at the time of commission of the alleged offence, if the young person is a female person charged with an offence arising out of the death of her newly-born child;**
- **(*d*) making or reviewing a sentence in respect of the young person;**
- **(*e*) determining whether the young person was, at the time of the commission of an alleged offence, suffering from automatism or a mental disorder so as to be exempt from criminal responsibility by virtue of subsection 16(1) of the *Criminal Code*, if the accused puts his or her mental capacity for criminal intent into issue, or if the prosecutor raises the issue after verdict;**
- **(*f*) challenging the credibility of a young person in any proceeding if the testimony of the young person is inconsistent in a material particular with a statement referred to in subsection (1) that the young person made previously;**
- **(*g*) establishing the perjury of a young person who is charged with perjury in respect of a statement made in any proceeding;**
- **(*h*) deciding an application for an order under subsection 104(1) (continuation of custody);**
- **(*i*) setting the conditions under subsection 105(1) (conditional supervision);**
- **(*j*) conducting a review under subsection 109(1) (review of decision); or**
- **(*k*) deciding an application for a disclosure order under subsection 127(1) (information about a young person).**

YOUTH

ANNOTATIONS

Note: The following case was decided under the *Young Offenders Act* but was thought to be of assistance in applying this Act.

It was held considering s. 13.1 of the *Young Offenders Act*, which is worded similarly to this section, that where the young person does not consent and none of the exceptions in subsec. (2) apply, no reference may be made to any statements by the young person during the course and for the purposes of the assessment. The subsection applies to all such statements, not simply those viewed as being inculpatory. Further, where those statements were the foundations of the psychiatrist's opinion and there was no foundation for the opinion without the statements, the opinion is also inadmissible. The section applies even where it is a co-accused and not the Crown seeking to tender the statements and the opinion: *R. v. Spanevello* (1998), 125 C.C.C. (3d) 97, 51 B.C.L.R. (3d) 192 (C.A.), leave to appeal to S.C.C. refused 131 C.C.C. (3d) vi, 207 W.A.C. 320*n*.

TESTIMONY OF A PARENT / Evidence of age by certificate or record / Other evidence / When age may be inferred.

148. (1) In any proceedings under this Act, the testimony of a parent as to the age of a person of whom he or she is a parent is admissible as evidence of the age of that person.

(2) In any proceedings under this Act,

(*a*) a birth or baptismal certificate or a copy of it purporting to be certified under the hand of the person in whose custody those records are held is evidence of the age of the person named in the certificate or copy; and

(*b*) an entry or record of an incorporated society that has had the control or care of the person alleged to have committed the offence in respect of which the proceedings are taken at or about the time the person came to Canada is evidence of the age of that person, if the entry or record was made before the time when the offence is alleged to have been committed.

(3) In the absence of any certificate, copy, entry or record mentioned in subsection (2), or in corroboration of that certificate, copy, entry or record, the youth justice court may receive and act on any other information relating to age that it considers reliable.

(4) In any proceedings under this Act, the youth justice court may draw inferences as to the age of a person from the person's appearance or from statements made by the person in direct examination or cross-examination.

ADMISSIONS / Other party may adduce evidence.

149. (1) A party to any proceedings under this Act may admit any relevant fact or matter for the purpose of dispensing with proof of it, including any fact or matter the admissibility of which depends on a ruling of law or of mixed law and fact.

(2) Nothing in this section precludes a party to a proceeding from adducing evidence to prove a fact or matter admitted by another party.

MATERIAL EVIDENCE.

150. Any evidence material to proceedings under this Act that would not but for this section be admissible in evidence may, with the consent of the parties to the proceedings and if the young person is represented by counsel, be given in such proceedings.

EVIDENCE OF A CHILD OR YOUNG PERSON.

151. The evidence of a child or a young person may be taken in proceedings under this Act only after the youth justice court judge or the justice in the proceedings has

(*a*) if the witness is a child, instructed the child as to the duty to speak the truth and the consequences of failing to do so; and

(*b*) if the witness is a young person and the judge or justice considers it necessary, instructed the young person as to the duty to speak the truth and the consequences of failing to do so.

ANNOTATIONS

Note: The following cases were decided under s. 60 of the *Young Offenders Act*, which is worded similarly to this section.

Compliance with s. 60 was mandatory where it applied and required the judge to instruct the child on the duty to tell the truth, not merely ask the child whether she understands that duty: *R. v. B. (M.)* (1986), 1 W.C.B. (2d) 96 (Sask. C.A.). In *R. v. K. (K.O.)* (2001), 156 C.C.C. (3d) 433, 156 Man. R. (2d) 42, however, the Manitoba Court of Appeal held that this provision was discretionary.

PROOF OF SERVICE / Proof of signature and official character unnecessary.

152. (1) For the purposes of this Act, service of any document may be proved by oral evidence given under oath by, or by the affidavit or statutory declaration of, the person claiming to have personally served it or sent it by confirmed delivery service.

(2) If proof of service of any document is offered by affidavit or statutory declaration, it is not necessary to prove the signature or official character of the person making or taking the affidavit or declaration, if the official character of that person appears on the face of the affidavit or declaration.

SEAL NOT REQUIRED.

153. It is not necessary to the validity of any information, indictment, summons, warrant, minute, sentence, conviction, order or other process or document laid, issued, filed or entered in any proceedings under this Act that any seal be attached or affixed to it.

Forms, Regulations and Rules of Court

FORMS / If forms not prescribed.

154. (1) The forms prescribed under section 155, varied to suit the case, or forms to the like effect, are valid and sufficient in the circumstances for which they are provided.

(2) In any case for which forms are not prescribed under section 155, the forms set out in Part XXVIII of the *Criminal Code*, with any modifications that the circumstances require, or other appropriate forms, may be used.

REGULATIONS.

155. The Governor in Council may make regulations

- **(*a*) prescribing forms that may be used for the purposes of this Act;**
- **(*b*) establishing uniform rules of court for youth justice courts across Canada, including rules regulating the practice and procedure to be followed by youth justice courts; and**
- **(*c*) generally for carrying out the purposes and provisions of this Act.**

YOUTH

Agreements with Provinces

AGREEMENTS WITH PROVINCES.

156. Any minister of the Crown may, with the approval of the Governor in Council, enter into an agreement with the government of any province providing for payments by Canada to the province in respect of costs incurred by the province or a municipality in the province for care of and services provided to young persons dealt with under this Act.

Programs

COMMUNITY-BASED PROGRAMS.

157. The Attorney General of Canada or a minister designated by the lieutenant governor in council of a province may establish the following types of community-based programs:

- **(*a*) programs that are an alternative to judicial proceedings, such as victim-offender reconciliation programs, mediation programs and restitution programs;**
- **(*b*) programs that are an alternative to detention before sentencing, such as bail supervision programs; and**
- **(*c*) programs that are an alternative to custody, such as intensive support and supervision programs, and programs to carry out attendance orders.**

PART 8 / TRANSITIONAL PROVISIONS

PROHIBITION ON PROCEEDINGS.

158. On and after the coming into force of this section, no proceedings may be commenced under the *Young Offenders Act*, chapter Y-1 of the Revised Statutes of Canada, 1985, in respect of an offence within the meaning of that Act, or under the *Juvenile Delinquents Act*, chapter J-3 of the Revised Statutes of Canada, 1970, in respect of a delinquency within the meaning of that Act.

PROCEEDINGS COMMENCED UNDER YOUNG OFFENDERS ACT/Proceedings commenced under *Juvenile Delinquents Act.*

159. (1) Subject to section 161, where, before the coming into force of this section, proceedings are commenced under the *Young Offenders Act*, chapter Y-1 of the Revised Statutes of Canada, 1985, in respect of an offence within the meaning of that Act alleged to have been committed by a person who was at the time of the offence a young person within the meaning of that Act, the proceedings and all related matters shall be dealt with in all respects as if this Act had not come into force.

(2) Subject to section 161, where, before the coming into force of this section, proceedings are commenced under the *Juvenile Delinquents Act*, chapter J-3 of the Revised Statutes of Canada, 1970, in respect of a delinquency within the meaning of that Act alleged to have been committed by a person who was at the time of the delinquency a child as defined in that Act, the proceedings and all related matters shall be dealt with under this Act as if the delinquency were an offence that occurred after the coming into force of this section.

OFFENCES COMMITTED BEFORE THIS SECTION IN FORCE.

160. [*Repealed.* 2012, c. 1, s. 193.]

APPLICABLE SENTENCE / Dispositions under paragraph 20(1)(*k*) or (*k*.1) of *Young Offenders Act* / Review of sentence.

161. (1) A person referred to in section 159 who is found guilty of an offence or delinquency, other than a person convicted of an offence in ordinary court, as defined in subsection 2(1) of the *Young Offenders Act*, chapter Y-1 of the Revised Statutes of Canada, 1985, shall be sentenced under this Act, except that

- **(*a*) paragraph 110(2)(*b*) does not apply in respect of the offence or delinquency; and**

(*b*) paragraph 42(2)(*r*) applies in respect of the offence or delinquency only if the young person consents to its application.

The provisions of this Act applicable to sentences imposed under section 42 apply in respect of the sentence.

(2) Where a young person is to be sentenced under this Act while subject to a disposition under paragraph 20(1)(*k*) or (*k*.1) of the *Young Offenders Act*, chapter Y-1 of the Revised Statutes of Canada, 1985, on the application of the Attorney General or the young person, a youth justice court shall, unless to do so would bring the administration of justice into disrepute, order that the remaining portion of the disposition made under that Act be dealt with, for all purposes under this Act or any other Act of Parliament, as if it had been a sentence imposed under paragraph 42(2)(*n*) or (*q*) of this Act, as the case may be.

(3) For greater certainty, for the purpose of determining when the sentence is reviewed under section 94, the relevant date is the one on which the disposition came into force under the *Young Offenders Act*, chapter Y-1 of the Revised Statutes of Canada, 1985.

COMMENCEMENT OF PROCEEDINGS.

162. For the purposes of sections 158 and 159, proceedings are commenced by the laying of an information or indictment. 2012, c. 1, s. 194.

APPLICATION TO DELINQUENCY AND OTHER OFFENDING BEHAVIOUR.

163. Sections 114 to 129 apply, with any modifications that the circumstances require, in respect of records relating to the offence of delinquency under the *Juvenile Delinquents Act*, chapter J-3 of the Revised Statutes of Canada, 1970, and in respect of records kept under sections 40 to 43 of the *Young Offenders Act*, chapter Y-1 of the Revised Statutes of Canada, 1985.

AGREEMENTS CONTINUE IN FORCE.

164. Any agreement made under the *Young Offenders Act*, chapter Y-1 of the Revised Statutes of Canada, 1985, remains in force until it expires, unless it is amended or a new agreement is made under this Act.

DESIGNATION OF YOUTH JUSTICE COURT / Designation of youth justice court judges / Designation of provincial directors and youth workers / Designation of review boards and youth justice committees / Alternative measures continued as extrajudicial sanctions / Designation of places of temporary detention and youth custody / Exception / Designation of other persons.

165. (1) Any court established or designated as a youth court for the purposes of the *Young Offenders Act*, chapter Y-1 of the Revised Statutes of Canada, 1985, is deemed, as of the coming into force of this section, to have been established or designated as a youth justice court for the purposes of this Act.

(2) Any person appointed to be a judge of the youth court for the purposes of the *Young Offenders Act*, chapter Y-1 of the Revised Statutes of Canada, 1985, is deemed, as of the coming into force of this section, to have been appointed as a judge of the youth justice court for the purposes of this Act.

(3) Any person, group or class of persons or body appointed or designated as a provincial director for the purposes of the *Young Offenders Act*, chapter Y-1 of the Revised Statutes of Canada, 1985, and any person appointed or designated as a youth worker for the purposes of that Act is deemed, as of the coming into force of this section, to have been appointed or designated as a provincial director or youth worker, as the case may be, for the purposes of this Act.

(4) Any review board established or designated for the purposes of the *Young Offenders Act*, chapter Y-1 of the Revised Statutes of Canada, 1985, and any youth justice committee established for the purposes of that Act is deemed, as of the coming into force of this section, to have been established or designated as a review board or a youth justice committee, as the case may be, for the purposes of this Act.

(5) Any program of alternative measures authorized for the purposes of the *Young Offenders Act*, chapter Y-1 of the Revised Statutes of Canada, 1985, is deemed, as of the coming into force of this section, to be a program of extrajudicial sanctions authorized for the purposes of this Act.

(6) Subject to subsection (7), any place that was designated as a place of temporary detention or open custody for the purposes of the *Young Offenders Act*, chapter Y-1 of the Revised Statutes of Canada, 1985, and any place or facility designated as a place of secure custody for the purposes of that Act is deemed, as of the coming into force of this section, to have been designated for the purposes of this Act as

(*a*) in the case of a place of temporary detention, a place of temporary detention; and

(*b*) in the case of a place of open custody or secure custody, a youth custody facility.

(7) If the lieutenant governor in council of a province makes an order under section 88 that the power to make determinations of the level of custody for young persons and to review those determinations be exercised in accordance with the *Young Offenders Act*, chapter Y-1 of the Revised Statutes of Canada, 1985, the designation of any place as a place of open custody or secure custody for the purposes of that Act remains in force for the purposes of section 88, subject to revocation or amendment of the designation.

(8) Any person designated as a clerk of the youth court for the purposes of the *Young Offenders Act*, chapter Y-1 of the Revised Statutes of Canada, 1985, or any person or group of persons who were designated under that Act to carry out specified functions and duties are deemed, as of the coming into force of this section, to have been designated as a clerk of the youth justice court, or to carry out the same functions and duties, as the case may be, under this Act.

Note: Sections 166 to 199 of the *Youth Criminal Justice Act* make consequential amendments to other Acts. These sections are not reproduced here.

COMING INTO FORCE.

200. The provisions of this Act come into force on a day or days to be fixed by order of the Governor in Council.

SCHEDULE

(Subsections 120(1), (4) and (6))

1. An offence under any of the following provisions of the *Criminal Code*:

(*a*) paragraph 81(2)(*a*) (using explosives);

(*b*) subsection 85(1) (using firearm in commission of offence);

(*c*) section 151 (sexual interference);

(*d*) section 152 (invitation to sexual touching);

(*e*) section 153 (sexual exploitation);

(*f*) section 155 (incest);

(*g*) section 159 (anal intercourse);

(*h*) section 170 (parent or guardian procuring sexual activity by child);

(*i*) [*Repealed*, 2014, c. 25, s. 43(1).]

(*j*) [*Repealed*, 2014, c. 25, s. 43(1).]

(*k*) section 231 or 235 (first degree murder or second degree murder within the meaning of section 231);

(*l*) section 232, 234 or 236 (manslaughter);
(*m*) section 239 (attempt to commit murder);
(*n*) section 267 (assault with a weapon or causing bodily harm);
(*o*) section 268 (aggravated assault);
(*p*) section 269 (unlawfully causing bodily harm);
(*q*) section 271 (sexual assault);
(*r*) section 272 (sexual assault with a weapon, threats to a third party or causing bodily harm);
(*s*) section 273 (aggravated sexual assault);
(*t*) section 279 (kidnapping);
(*t*.1) section 279.011 (trafficking — person under 18 years);
(*t*.2) subsection 279.02(2) (material benefit — trafficking of person under 18 years);
(*t*.3) subsection 279.03(2) (withholding or destroying documents — trafficking of person under 18 years);
(*t*.4) subsection 286.1(2) (obtaining sexual services for consideration from person under 18 years);
(*t*.5) subsection 286.2(2) (material benefit from sexual services provided by person under 18 years);
(*t*.6) subsection 286.3(2) (procuring — person under 18 years);
(*u*) section 344 (robbery);
(*v*) section 433 (arson — disregard for human life);
(*w*) section 434.1 (arson — own property);
(*x*) section 436 (arson by negligence); and
(*y*) paragraph 465(1)(*a*) (conspiracy to commit murder).

1.1 An offence under one of the following provisions of the *Criminal Code*, as they read from time to time before the day on which this section comes into force:
(*a*) subsection 212(2) (living on the avails of prostitution of person under 18 years); and
(*b*) subsection 212(4) (prostitution of person under 18 years).

2. An offence under any of the following provisions of the *Criminal Code*, as they read immediately before July 1, 1990:
(*a*) section 433 (arson);
(*b*) section 434 (setting fire to other substance); and
(*c*) section 436 (setting fire by negligence).

3. An offence under any of the following provisions of the *Criminal Code*, chapter C-34 of the Revised Statutes of Canada, 1970, as they read immediately before January 4, 1983:
(*a*) section 144 (rape);
(*b*) section 145 (attempt to commit rape);
(*c*) section 149 (indecent assault on female);
(*d*) section 156 (indecent assault on male); and
(*e*) section 246 (assault with intent).

4. An offence under any of the following provisions of the *Controlled Drugs and Substances Act*:
(*a*) section 5 (trafficking);
(*b*) section 6 (importing and exporting); and
(*c*) section 7 (production of substance).

5. An offence under any of the following provisions of the *Cannabis Act*:
(*a*) section 9 (distribution and possession for purpose of distributing);
(*b*) section 10 (selling and possession for purpose of selling);
(*c*) section 11 (importing and exporting and possession for purpose of exporting);
(*d*) section 12 (production); and
(*e*) section 14 (use of young person). 2014, c. 25, s. 43; 2018, c. 16, s. 184.

OFFENCE GRID

This grid covers offences under the **Criminal Code**. It shows:

- whether an offence is indictable, summary, or hybrid,
- whether an offence is absolute jurisdiction,
- the maximum and minimum sentence,
- available sentencing options,
- illegal sentences,
- orders that you may wish to consider or that are mandatory,
- and more.

DISCLAIMER: The following Offence Grid is provided for convenience only. Users of the Offence Grid should always refer to the official Acts and Regulations of the Government of Canada. This Offence Grid is published on the understanding and basis that none of Thomson Reuters, the author/s or other persons involved in the creation of this Offence Grid shall be responsible for the accuracy or currency of the contents, or for the results of any action taken on the basis of the information contained in this Offence Grid, or for any errors or omissions contained herein. Some uncommonly used offences have been omitted in the interests of space.

CAUTION: The applicability of remarks in the comments column depends upon the circumstances of a particular case. Thus, for example, where the comment "S. 491 mandatory weapon forfeiture order" appears, the order is mandatory only if the requirements of s. 491 are met. Likewise, where the comment "S. 109 mandatory firearms order" appears, the order is mandatory only if the requirements of s. 109 are met. Further, even where it is indicated that the prohibition is discretionary under s. 110, it should be noted that pursuant to s. 109(1)(*d*), where the offence is one that involves, or the subject-matter of which is, a firearm, a cross-bow, a prohibited weapon, a restricted weapon, a prohibited device, any ammunition, any prohibited ammunition or an explosive substance and, at the time of the offence, the person was prohibited by any order made under the *Criminal Code* or any other Act of Parliament from possessing any such thing, the offender is liable to the mandatory firearms prohibition in s. 109. Although referred to as a "firearms order", the order prohibits the person from possessing any firearm, cross-bow, prohibited weapon, restricted weapon, prohibited device, ammunition, prohibited ammunition and explosive substance, unless an order is made under s. 113 allowing the lifting of a prohibition order for certain specified reasons.

GRID

NOTE: A court may impose, in addition to any other measure, a restitution order in the following circumstances:

(1) damage to, or loss or destruction of, property as a result of the commission of an offence, or the arrest or the attempted arrest of the offender (s. 738(1)(*a*));

(2) bodily harm resulting from the commission of an offence, or the arrest or attempted arrest of the offender (s. 738(1)(*b*));
(3) in cases of bodily harm or threat of bodily harm, expenses that are incurred in order to move out of the offender's household (s. 738(1)(*c*));
(4) a person acting in good faith and without notice purchased any property obtained as a result of the commission of an offence, or loaned money to an offender on the security of such property (s. 739).

Further, even where a type of sentence is marked as an option, it may only be available in some circumstances. For example, even where not precluded by a minimum sentence, an intermittent sentence of imprisonment is only available if the sentence imposed is 90 days or less (s. 732). The grid does indicate with an "X" where a conditional sentence is illegal, for example where there is a minimum sentence (s. 742.1(*b*)), the maximum sentence is 14 years or life (s. 742.1(*c*)), or the offence is enumerated as excluded (s. 742.1(*f*)). However, even if an offence does not fit into one of these clearly prescribed categories, a conditional sentence is available only if the sentence imposed is less than two years (s. 742.1(*a*)). A conditional sentence is also not available (even if a sentence of less than two years is imposed) where the Crown proceeds by indictment, the maximum term of imprisonment is ten years, and the offence (i) resulted in bodily harm; (ii) involved the import, export, trafficking or production of drugs; or (iii) involved the use of a weapon (s. 742.1(*e*)).

Sections 487.051 and 487.052 provide that the court may make an order authorizing the taking of samples for forensic DNA analysis if the offender is convicted, discharged, found not guilty by reason of mental disorder or, in the case of a young offender, found guilty of certain offences. The test to be applied depends on whether the offence is a primary or secondary designated offence as defined in s. 487.04. In the "comments" section the application of these provisions is indicated by the letters "PC" (for primary compulsory designated offence, listed in paragraphs (*a*) and (*c*.02) of the definition of "primary designated offence" in s. 487.04 of the Code), "P" (for primary designated offences, listed in paragraphs (*a*.1) to (*c*.01) and (*c*.03) to (*d*) of the definition of "primary designated offence" in s. 487.04 of the Code), or "S" (secondary designated offences, as listed under that definition in s. 487.04 of the Code). Also note that the court may be required to make a *Sex Offender Information Registration Act* order under s. 490.012 if the offence falls within the definition of "designated offence" in s. 490.011. Also see Part XXIV as to circumstances in which the court may impose a dangerous offender or long-term offender disposition.

Acknowledgments

We are indebted to the Provincial Judges' Association of British Columbia, who developed this Offence Grid for their Judges' Handbook and have kindly allowed us to include it here. In particular, we wish to acknowledge, with thanks, the following:

Jim Almstrom (editor)
Judge Lynne Dollis
Judge Jean Lytwyn

Judge Kenneth Scherling
Barbara Schmidt
Judge Thomas Smith (editor-in-chief)
Western Technigraphics (graphics)

We also thank Rachel Young and Lindsay Kromm of the Ontario Bar for their ongoing work in maintaining and updating the Offence Grid.

SECTION	TYPE	MAX/MIN SENTENCE	DISCHARGE s. 730	SUSPENDED SENTENCE s. 731(1)(a)	FINE ALONE s. 734	FINE & PROBATION s. 731(1)(b)	PRISON ss. 718.3, 787	PRISON & PROBATION s. 731(1)(b)	PRISON & FINE s. 734	INTERMITTENT s. 732	FINE, PROB. & INTERMIT s. 732	CONDITIONAL SENTENCE s. 742.1	COMMENTS (applicability depends on circumstances of case)
56.1 Procure etc. identity documents	Hyb-Ind.	5 yrs	✓	✓	✓	✓	✓	✓	✓	✓	✓	✓	S if by indictment
	Hyb-Sum.	6 mth/ 5000*	✓	✓	✓	✓	✓	✓	✓	✓	✓	✓	
57(1) Forge passport or use forged passport	Indictable	14 yrs	×	✓	✓	✓	✓	✓	✓	✓	✓	×	S
57(2) Passport, false statement	Hyb-Ind.	2 yrs	✓	✓	✓	✓	✓	✓	✓	✓	✓	✓	
	Hyb-Sum.	6 mth/ 5000*	✓	✓	✓	✓	✓	✓	✓	✓	✓	✓	
57(3) Possession, forged passport	Indictable	5 yrs	✓	✓	✓	✓	✓	✓	✓	✓	✓	✓	S
58 Fraud, use of citizenship certificate	Indictable	2 yrs	✓	✓	✓	✓	✓	✓	✓	✓	✓	✓	
65(1) Riot	Indictable	2 yrs	✓	✓	✓	✓	✓	✓	✓	✓	✓	✓	
65(2) Riot while masked	Indictable	10 yrs	✓	✓	✓	✓	✓	✓	✓	✓	✓	✓	S
66(1) Unlawful assembly	Summary	6 mth/ 5000*	✓	✓	✓	✓	✓	✓	✓	✓	✓	✓	
66(2) Unlawful assembly while masked	Hyb-Ind.	5 yrs	✓	✓	✓	✓	✓	✓	✓	✓	✓	✓	S. 110 discretionary firearms order. S if by indictment
	Hyb-Sum.	6 mth/5000	✓	✓	✓	✓	✓	✓	✓	✓	✓	✓	
72, 73 Forcible entry	Hyb-Ind.	2 yrs	✓	✓	✓	✓	✓	✓	✓	✓	✓	✓	S. 110 discretionary firearms order.
	Hyb-Sum.	6 mth/ 5000*	✓	✓	✓	✓	✓	✓	✓	✓	✓	✓	
75 Piratical acts	Indictable	14 yrs	×	✓	✓	✓	✓	✓	✓	✓	✓	✓	P
76 Hijacking	Indictable	Life	×	✓	✓	✓	✓	✓	✓	✓	✓	×	P S. 109 mandatory firearms order.
77 Endanger aircraft	Indictable	Life	×	✓	✓	✓	✓	✓	✓	✓	✓	×	P S. 109 mandatory firearms order.
78 Take weapon or explosive on board	Indictable	14 yrs	×	✓	✓	✓	✓	✓	✓	✓	✓	×	S. 109 mandatory firearms order. S. 491 mandatory weapon forfeiture order. S
78.1 Seizing control of ship etc.	Indictable	Life	×	✓	✓	✓	✓	✓	✓	✓	✓	×	S. 109 mandatory firearms order. P

*** $100,000 for organizations for summary conviction offence s. 735.**
***** conditional sentence not available if offence involved use of a weapon.**

✓ Sentence Option   × Illegal Sentence

P = Primary designated offence
S = Secondary designated offence
PC = Primary Compulsory
[see note on p. OG/2]

GRID

SECTION	TYPE	MAX/MIN SENTENCE	DISCHARGE s. 730	SUSPENDED SENTENCE s. 731(1)(a)	FINE ALONE s. 734	FINE & PROBATION s. 731(1)(b)	PRISON ss. 718.3, 787	PRISON & PROBATION s. 731(1)(b)	PRISON & FINE s. 734	INTERMITTENT s. 732	FINE, PROB. & INTERMITS. 732	CONDITIONAL SENTENCE s. 742.1	COMMENTS (applicability depends on circumstances of case)
80(a) Breach of duty of care, explosives, causing death	Indictable	Life	x	✓	✓	✓	✓	✓	✓	✓	✓	x	S. 109 mandatory firearms order. S
80(b) Breach of duty of care, explosives, causing harm	Indictable	14 yrs	x	✓	✓	✓	✓	✓	✓	✓	✓	x	S. 109 mandatory firearms order. S
81(1)(a) & (b) Explosives, intent to cause death or harm	Indictable	Life	x	✓	✓	✓	✓	✓	✓	✓	✓	x	P S. 109 mandatory firearms order.
81(1)(c) & (d) Explosives, placing or making	Indictable	14 yrs	x	✓	✓	✓	✓	✓	✓	✓	✓	x	P S. 109 mandatory firearms order.
82(1) Explosives, possession w/o lawful excuse	Indictable	5 yrs	✓	✓	✓	✓	✓	✓	✓	✓	✓	✓	S
82(2) Explosives, for benefit of criminal organization	Indictable	14 yrs	x	✓	✓	✓	✓	✓	✓	✓	✓	x	S. 82.1 requires sentence to be consecutive to any other sentence. S
82.3 Possession, etc. of nuclear material/ device	Indictable	Life	x	✓	✓	✓	✓	✓	✓	✓	✓	x	P
82.4 Use, etc. of nuclear material/device	Indictable	Life	x	✓	✓	✓	✓	✓	✓	✓	✓	x	P
82.5 Committing indictable offence to obtain nuclear material	Indictable	Life	x	✓	✓	✓	✓	✓	✓	✓	✓	x	P
82.6 Threat to commit nuclear offence	Indictable	14 yrs	x	✓	✓	✓	✓	✓	✓	✓	✓	x	P
83 Prize fight	Summary	6 mth/ 5000*	✓	✓	✓	✓	✓	✓	✓	✓	✓	✓	S. 110 discretionary firearms order.
83.02 Financing terrorism	Indictable	10 yrs	✓	✓	✓	✓	✓	✓	✓	✓	✓	x	S. 83.26 sentence must be consecutive to any other imposed. S
83.03 Providing property for terrorist purpose	Indictable	10 yrs	✓	✓	✓	✓	✓	✓	✓	✓	✓	x	S. 83.26 sentence must be consecutive to any other imposed. S
83.04 Using property for terrorist purposes	Indictable	10 yrs	✓	✓	✓	✓	✓	✓	✓	✓	✓	x	S. 83.26 sentence must be consecutive to any other imposed. S

*** $100,000 for organizations for summary conviction offence s. 735.**

***** conditional sentence not available if offence involved use of a weapon.**

✓ Sentence Option x Illegal Sentence

P = Primary designated offence
S = Secondary designated offence
PC = Primary Compulsory
[see note on p. OG/2]

SECTION	TYPE	MAX/MIN SENTENCE	DISCHARGE s. 730	SUSPENDED SENTENCE s. 731(1)(a)	FINE ALONE s. 734	FINE & PROBATION s. 731(1)(b)	PRISON ss. 718.3, 787	PRISON & PROBATION s. 731(1)(b)	PRISON & FINE s. 734	INTERMITTENT s. 732	FINE, PROB. & INTERMIT s. 732	CONDITIONAL SENTENCE s. 742.1	COMMENTS (applicability depends on circumstances of case)
83.18 Participating in activity of terrorist group	Indictable	10 yrs	✓	✓	✓	✓	✓	✓	✓	✓	✓	✗	S. 83.26 sentence must be consecutive to any other imposed. S. 110 discretionary firearms order. P
83.181 Leaving Canada to participate in activity of terrorist group	Indictable	10 yrs	✓	✓	✓	✓	✓	✓	✓	✓	✓	✗	P
83.19 Facilitating terrorist activity	Indictable	14 yrs	✗	✓	✓	✓	✓	✓	✓	✓	✓	✗	S. 83.26 sentence must be consecutive to any other imposed. S. 110 discretionary firearms order. P
83.191 Leaving Canada to facilitate terrorist activity	Indictable	14 yrs	✗	✓	✓	✓	✓	✓	✓	✓	✓	✗	P
83.2 Committing offence for terrorist group	Indictable	Life	✗	✓	✓	✓	✓	✓	✓	✓	✓	✗	S. 83.26 sentence must be consecutive to any other imposed, except life. S. 110 discretionary firearms order. P
83.201 Leaving Canada to commit offence for terrorist group	Indictable	14 yrs	✗	✓	✓	✓	✓	✓	✓	✓	✓	✗	P
83.202 Leaving Canada to commit offence that is terrorist activity	Indictable	14 yrs	✗	✓	✓	✓	✓	✓	✓	✓	✓	✗	P
83.21 Instructing to carry out activity for terrorist group	Indictable	Life	✗	✓	✓	✓	✓	✓	✓	✓	✓	✗	S. 83.26 sentence must be consecutive to any other imposed, except life. S. 110 discretionary firearms order. P
83.22 Instructing terrorist activity	Indictable	Life	✗	✓	✓	✓	✓	✓	✓	✓	✓	✗	S. 83.26 sentence must be consecutive to any other imposed, except life. S. 110 discretionary firearms order. P
83.221 Advocating or promoting commission of terrorism offences	Indictable	5 yrs	✓	✓	✓	✓	✓	✓	✓	✓	✓	✗	S. 83.221 sentence must be consecutive to any other imposed, except life. S. 110 discretionary firearms order P
83.23(1)(a) Harbouring terrorist, carried out terrorism offence liable to life imprisonment	Indictable	14 yrs	✗	✓	✓	✓	✓	✓	✓	✓	✓	✗	S. 83.26 sentence must be consecutive to any other imposed. P

* $100,000 for organizations for summary conviction offence s. 735.
*** conditional sentence not available if offence involved use of a weapon.

✓ Sentence Option ✗ Illegal Sentence

P = Primary designated offence
S = Secondary designated offence
PC = Primary Compulsory
[see note on p. OG/2]

GRID

SECTION	TYPE	MAX/MIN SENTENCE	DISCHARGE s. 730	SUSPENDED SENTENCE s. 731(1)(a)	FINE ALONE s. 734	FINE & PROBATION s. 731(1)(b)	PRISON ss. 718.3, 787	PRISON & PROBATION s. 731(1)(b)	PRISON & FINE s. 734	INTERMITTENT s. 732	FINE, PROB. & INTERMITS s. 732	CONDITIONAL SENTENCE s. 742.1	COMMENTS (applicability depends on circumstances of case)
83.23(1)(b) Harbouring terrorist, carried out terrorism offence liable to any other punishment	Indictable	10 yrs	✓	✓	✓	✓	✓	✓	✓	✓	✓	×	S. 83.26 sentence must be consecutive to any other imposed. P
83.231(2) Terrorist activity, hoax	Hyb-Ind.	5 yrs	✓	✓	✓	✓	✓	✓	✓	✓	✓	✓	S
	Hyb-Sum.	6 mth/ 5000*	✓	✓	✓	✓	✓	✓	✓	✓	✓	✓	
83.231(3) Terrorism, hoax causing bodily harm	Hyb-Ind.	10 yrs	✓	✓	✓	✓	✓	✓	✓	✓	✓	×	S. 110 discretionary firearms order. S
	Hyb-Sum.	18 mth	✓	✓	✓	✓	✓	✓	✓	✓	✓	✓	
83.231(4) Terrorist hoax, causing death	Indictable	Life	×	✓	✓	✓	✓	✓	✓	✓	✓	×	S. 110 discretionary firearms order. S
85 Use of firearm or imitation, commission of offence	Indictable	14 yrs max. Minimums: 1 yr-1st 3 yrs-2nd	×	×	×	×	✓	**	✓	×	×	×	S S. 109 mandatory firearms order. S. 491 mandatory weapon forfeiture order. Sentence must be consecutive to any other imposed. **Not a possible sentence for a second offence because there is a minimum sentence of three years. Higher penalty for second or subsequent offence requires compliance with s. 727.
86 Firearm, careless use or storage, breach of regulations	Hyb-Ind.	Maximums: 2 yrs-1st 5 yrs-2nd	✓	✓	✓	✓	✓	✓	✓	✓	✓	✓	S. 110 discretionary firearms order. S. 491 mandatory weapon forfeiture order. Higher penalty for second or subsequent offence requires compliance with s. 665.
	Hyb-Sum.	6 mth/ 5000*	✓	✓	✓	✓	✓	✓	✓	✓	✓	✓	S (for secondary or subsequent offence if indictable)
87 Firearm, pointing	Hyb-Ind.	5 yrs	✓	✓	✓	✓	✓	✓	✓	✓	✓	✓	S. 110 discretionary firearms order. S. 491 mandatory weapon forfeiture order. S if by indictment
	Hyb-Sum.	6 mth/ 5000*	✓	✓	✓	✓	✓	✓	✓	✓	✓	✓	
88 Possession for purpose dangerous to the public	Hyb-Ind.	10 yrs	✓	✓	✓	✓	✓	✓	✓	✓	✓	*** ×	S. 109 mandatory firearms order. S. 491 mandatory weapon forfeiture order.
	Hyb-Sum.	6 mth/ 5000*	✓	✓	✓	✓	✓	✓	✓	✓	✓	✓	S. 110 discretionary firearms order. S. 491 mandatory weapon forfeiture order. S if by indictment
89 Weapon at public meeting	Summary	6 mth/ 5000*	✓	✓	✓	✓	✓	✓	✓	✓	✓	✓	S. 110 discretionary firearms order. S. 491 mandatory weapon forfeiture order.

*** $100,000 for organizations for summary conviction offence s. 735.**
***** conditional sentence not available if offence involved use of a weapon.**

✓ Sentence Option | **× Illegal Sentence**

P = Primary designated offence
S = Secondary designated offence
PC = Primary Compulsory
[see note on p. OG/2]

SECTION	TYPE	MAX/MIN SENTENCE	DISCHARGE s. 730	SUSPENDED SENTENCE s. 731(1)(a)	FINE ALONE s. 734	FINE & PROBATION s. 731(1)(b)	PRISON ss. 718.3, 787	PRISON & PROBATION s. 731(1)(b)	PRISON & FINE s. 734	INTERMITTENT s. 732	FINE, PROB. & INTERMITT. s. 732	CONDITIONAL SENTENCE s. 742.1	COMMENTS (applicability depends on circumstances of case)
90 Weapon, concealed	Hyb-Ind.	5 yrs	✓	✓	✓	✓	✓	✓	✓	✓	✓	✓	S. 110 discretionary firearms order. S. 491 mandatory weapon forfeiture order. S if by indictment
	Hyb-Sum.	6 mth/ 5000*	✓	✓	✓	✓	✓	✓	✓	✓	✓	✓	
91 Unauthorized possession of firearm	Hyb-Ind.	5 yrs	✓	✓	✓	✓	✓	✓	✓	✓	✓	✓	S. 110 discretionary firearms order. S. 491 mandatory weapon forfeiture order. S if by indictment
	Hyb-Sum.	6 mth/ 5000*	✓	✓	✓	✓	✓	✓	✓	✓	✓	✓	
92 Possession of firearm knowing possession unauthorized	Indictable	10 yrs max	✓	✓	✓	✓	✓	✓	✓	✓	✓	*** ✗	S. 109 mandatory firearms order. S. 491 mandatory weapon forfeiture order.
		minimums 1 yr-2nd	✗	✗	✗	✗	✓	✓	✓	✗	✗	✗	S. 109 mandatory firearms order. S. 491 mandatory weapon forfeiture order.
		2 yrs less 1 day-3rd	✗	✗	✗	✗	✓	✓	✓	✗	✗	✗	Higher penalty for second or subsequent offence requires compliance with s. 727. S
93 Possession of weapon at unauthorized place	Hyb-Ind.	5 yrs	✓	✓	✓	✓	✓	✓	✓	✓	✓	✓	S. 110 discretionary firearms order. S. 491 mandatory weapon forfeiture order. S if by indictment
	Hyb-Sum.	6 mth/ 5000*	✓	✓	✓	✓	✓	✓	✓	✓	✓	✓	
94 Possession of weapon in motor vehicle	Hyb-Ind.	10 yrs	✓	✓	✓	✓	✓	✓	✓	✓	✓	*** ✗	S. 109 mandatory firearms order. S. 491 mandatory weapon forfeiture order. S if by indictment
	Hyb-Sum.	6 mth/ 5000*	✓	✓	✓	✓	✓	✓	✓	✓	✓	✓	
95 Possession of restricted or prohibited firearm with ammunition	Hyb-Ind.	10 yrs max 3 yrs min-1st 5 yrs min-2nd	✗	✗	✗	✗	✓	✗	✓	✗	✗	✗	S. 109 mandatory firearms order. S. 491 mandatory weapon forfeiture order. S if by indictment **Minimum sentences for indictable offences unconstitutional**
	Hyb-Sum.	1 yr max	✓	✓	✓	✓	✓	✓	✓	✓	✓	✓	
96 Possession of weapon obtained by crime	Hyb-Ind.	10 yrs max 1 yr min	✗	✗	✗	✗	✓	✓	✓	✗	✗	✗	S. 109 mandatory firearms order. S. 491 mandatory weapon forfeiture order. S if by indictment
	Hyb-Sum.	1 yr	✓	✓	✓	✓	✓	✓	✓	✓	✓	✓	
98 Break and enter to steal firearm	Indictable	Life	✗	✓	✓	✓	✓	✓	✓	✓	✓	✗	S. 109 mandatory firearms order. S

*** $100,000 for organizations for summary conviction offence s. 735.**
***** conditional sentence not available if offence involved use of a weapon.**

✓ Sentence Option   ✗ Illegal Sentence

P = Primary designated offence
S = Secondary designated offence
PC = Primary Compulsory
[see note on p. OG/2]

SECTION	TYPE	MAX/MIN SENTENCE	DISCHARGE s. 730	SUSPENDED SENTENCE s. 731(1)(a)	FINE ALONE s. 734	FINE & PROBATION s. 731(1)(b)	PRISON ss. 718.3, 787	PRISON & PROBATION s. 731(1)(b)	PRISON & FINE s. 734	INTERMITTENT s. 732	FINE, PROB. & INTERMIT s. 732	CONDITIONAL SENTENCE s. 742.1	COMMENTS (applicability depends on circumstances of case)
98.1 Robbery to steal firearm	Indictable	Life	✗	✓	✓	✓	✓	✓	✓	✓	✓	✗	S. 109 mandatory firearms order. S
99 Weapons trafficking	Indictable	10 yrs max 1 yr min	✗	✗	✗	✗	✓	✓	✓	✗	✗	✗	S. 109 mandatory firearms order. S. 491 mandatory weapon forfeiture order. S
		Minimums where firearm, prohibited device, ammunition: 3 yrs - 1st	✗	✗	✗	✗	✓	✗	✓	✗	✗	✗	
		5 yrs - 2nd	✗	✗	✗	✗	✓	✗	✓	✗	✗	✗	
100 Possession of weapons for purpose of trafficking	Indictable	10 yrs max 1 yr min	✗	✗	✗	✗	✓	✓	✓	✗	✗	✗	S. 109 mandatory firearms order. S. 491 mandatory weapon forfeiture order. S
		Minimums where firearm, prohibited device, ammunition: 3 yrs - 1st	✗	✗	✗	✗	✓	✗	✓	✗	✗	✗	
		5 yrs - 2nd	✗	✗	✗	✗	✓	✗	✓	✗	✗	✗	
101 Transfer without authority	Hyb-Ind.	5 yrs	✓	✓	✓	✓	✓	✓	✓	✓	✓	✓	S. 110 discretionary firearms order. S. 491 mandatory weapon forfeiture order. S if by indictment
	Hyb-Sum.	6 mth/ 5000*	✓	✓	✓	✓	✓	✓	✓	✓	✓	✓	
102 Making automatic firearm	Hyb-Ind.	10 yrs max 1 yr min	✗	✗	✗	✗	✓	✓	✓	✗	✗	✗	S. 109 mandatory firearms order. S. 491 mandatory weapon forfeiture order. S if by indictment
	Hyb-Sum.	1 yr	✓	✓	✓	✓	✓	✓	✓	✓	✓	✓	
103 Importing or exporting knowing it is unauthorized	Indictable	10 yrs max 1 yr min	✗	✗	✗	✗	✓	✓	✓	✗	✗	✗	S. 109 mandatory firearms order. S. 491 mandatory weapon forfeiture order. S
		Minimums where firearm, prohibited device, ammunition: 3 yrs - 1st	✗	✗	✗	✗	✓	✗	✓	✗	✗	✗	
		5 yrs - 2nd	✗	✗	✗	✗	✓	✗	✓	✗	✗	✗	

*** $100,000 for organizations for summary conviction offence s. 735.**
***** conditional sentence not available if offence involved use of a weapon.**

✓ Sentence Option ✗ Illegal Sentence

P = Primary designated offence
S = Secondary designated offence
PC = Primary Compulsory
[see note on p. OG/2]

SECTION	TYPE	MAX/MIN SENTENCE	DISCHARGE s. 730	SUSPENDED SENTENCE s. 731(1)(a)	FINE ALONE s. 734	FINE & PROBATION s. 731(1)(b)	PRISON ss. 718.3, 787	PRISON & PROBATION s. 731(1)(b)	PRISON & FINE s. 734	INTERMITTENT s. 732	FINE, PROB. & INTERMIT s. 732	CONDITIONAL SENTENCE s. 742.1	COMMENTS (applicability depends on circumstances of case)
104 Unauthorized importing or exporting	Hyb-Ind.	5 yrs	✓	✓	✓	✓	✓	✓	✓	✓	✓	✓	S. 110 discretionary firearms order. S. 491 mandatory weapon forfeiture order. S if by indictment
	Hyb-Sum.	6 mth/ 5000*	✓	✓	✓	✓	✓	✓	✓	✓	✓	✓	
105 Failing to report lost or stolen weapon or documents or found weapons	Hyb-Ind.	5 yrs	✓	✓	✓	✓	✓	✓	✓	✓	✓	✓	S. 110 discretionary firearms order. S. 491 mandatory weapon forfeiture order. S if by indictment
	Hyb-Sum.	6 mth/ 5000*	✓	✓	✓	✓	✓	✓	✓	✓	✓	✓	
106 Failing to report destroyed weapons	Hyb-Ind.	5 yrs	✓	✓	✓	✓	✓	✓	✓	✓	✓	✓	S. 110 discretionary firearms order. S. 491 mandatory weapon forfeiture order. S if by indictment
	Hyb-Sum.	6 mth/ 5000*	✓	✓	✓	✓	✓	✓	✓	✓	✓	✓	
107 Making false statement about loss, theft or destruction	Hyb-Ind.	5 yrs	✓	✓	✓	✓	✓	✓	✓	✓	✓	✓	S if by indictment
	Hyb-Sum.	6 mth/ 5000*	✓	✓	✓	✓	✓	✓	✓	✓	✓	✓	
108 Altering, defacing or removing serial number of firearm	Hyb-Ind.	5 yrs	✓	✓	✓	✓	✓	✓	✓	✓	✓	✓	S. 110 discretionary firearms order. S. 491 mandatory weapon forfeiture order. S if by indictment
	Hyb-Sum.	6 mth/ 5000*	✓	✓	✓	✓	✓	✓	✓	✓	✓	✓	
117.01 Possession contrary to order; failure to surrender documents	Hyb-Ind.	10 yrs	✓	✓	✓	✓	✓	✓	✓	✓	✓	*** ✓	S. 109 mandatory firearms order. S. 491 mandatory weapon forfeiture order S
	Hyb-Sum.	6 mth/ 5000*	✓	✓	✓	✓	✓	✓	✓	✓	✓	✓	
119 Bribery of judicial officers	Indictable	14 yrs	×	✓	✓	✓	✓	✓	✓	✓	✓	×	Written consent of A.G. Canada required to prosecute judge. S. 522 release by superior court judge only where accused is a judge. S. 462.37 proceeds of crime for forfeiture order on Crown application. S. 750(1), (2) conviction may result in loss of office and other disabilities. S
120 Bribery of officers	Indictable	14 yrs	×	✓	✓	✓	✓	✓	✓	✓	✓	×	S. 462.37 proceeds of crime for forfeiture order on Crown application. S. 750(1), (2) conviction may result in loss of office and other disabilities. S

*** $100,000 for organizations for summary conviction offence s. 735.**
***** conditional sentence not available if offence involved use of a weapon.**

✓ Sentence Option × Illegal Sentence

P = Primary designated offence
S = Secondary designated offence
PC = Primary Compulsory
[see note on p. OG/2]

GRID

SECTION	TYPE	MAX/MIN SENTENCE	DISCHARGE s. 730	SUSPENDED SENTENCE s. 731(1)(a)	FINE ALONE s. 734	FINE & PROBATION s. 731(1)(b)	PRISON ss. 718.3, 787	PRISON & PROBATION s. 731(1)(b)	PRISON & FINE s. 734	INTERMITTENT s. 732	FINE, PROB. & INTERMIT s. 732	CONDITIONAL SENTENCE s. 742.1	COMMENTS (applicability depends on circumstances of case)
121 Frauds on the government	Indictable	5 yrs	✓	✓	✓	✓	✓	✓	✓	✓	✓	✓	S. 462.37 proceeds of crime for forfeiture order on Crown application. S. 750(3) conviction bars accused from contracting with Crown or benefiting from contract with Crown unless capacity restored under s. 750(4) and (5). S
121.1 Selling etc., of Tobacoo Products and Raw Leaf Tobacoo	Hyb-Ind.	5 yrs max/ 90 days min, if over 10,000 cigarettes or 10kg tobacco – 2nd/ 80 days min, if over 10,000 cigarettes or 10kg tobacco – 3rd/ 2 yrs less a day, if over 10,000 cigarettes or 10 kg tobacco – 4th or subsequent	† ††	† ††	† ††	† ††	✓	✓	✓	✓ ††	✓ ††	† ††	S. 110 discretionary firearms order. S. 491 mandatory weapon forfeiture order. S if by indictment †These sentences are not available where the Crown proceeds by indictment, the amount of tobacco product is 10,000 cigarettes or more or 10 kg or more of any other tobacco product, or the amount of raw leaf tobacco is 10 kg or more, and the offence is a second or subsequent offence. ††These sentences not available where the Crown proceeds by indictment, the amount of tobacco product is 10,000 cigarettes or more or 10 kg or more of any other tobacco product, or the amount of raw leaf tobacco is 10 kg or more, and the offence is a 3rd or subsequent offence.
	Hyb-Sum.	6 mth/ 5000*	✓	✓	✓	✓	✓	✓	✓	✓	✓	✓	
122 Breach of trust by public officer	Indictable	5 yrs	✓	✓	✓	✓	✓	✓	✓	✓	✓	✓	S. 462.37 proceeds of crime for forfeiture order on Crown application. S. 750(1), (2) conviction may result in loss of office and other disabilities. S
123 Municipal corruption	Indictable	5 yrs	✓	✓	✓	✓	✓	✓	✓	✓	✓	✓	S. 750(1), (2) conviction may result in loss of office and other disabilities. S
125 Influencing or negotiating appointments	Indictable	5 yrs	✓	✓	✓	✓	✓	✓	✓	✓	✓	✓	S. 750(1), (2) conviction may result in loss of office and other disabilities. S
126 Disobeying a statute	Indictable	2 yrs	✓	✓	✓	✓	✓	✓	✓	✓	✓	✓	
127 Disobeying an order of court	Hyb-Ind.	2 yrs	✓	✓	✓	✓	✓	✓	✓	✓	✓	✓	
	Hyb-Sum.	6 mth/ 5000*	✓	✓	✓	✓	✓	✓	✓	✓	✓	✓	

*** $100,000 for organizations for summary conviction offence s. 735.**
***** conditional sentence not available if offence involved use of a weapon.**

✓Sentence Option **× Illegal Sentence**

P = Primary designated offence
S = Secondary designated offence
PC = Primary Compulsory
[see note on p. OG/2]

SECTION	TYPE	MAX/MIN SENTENCE	DISCHARGE s. 730	SUSPENDED SENTENCE s. 731(1)(a)	FINE ALONE s. 734	FINE & PROBATION s. 731(1)(b)	PRISON ss. 718.3,787	PRISON & PROBATION s. 731(1)(b)	PRISON & FINE s. 734	INTERMITTENT s. 732	FINE, PROB. & INTERMIT s. 732	CONDITIONAL SENTENCE s. 742.1	COMMENTS (applicability depends on circumstances of case)
129 Obstructing or resisting peace officer	Hyb-Ind.	2 yrs	✓	✓	✓	✓	✓	✓	✓	✓	✓	✓	S. 110 discretionary firearms order. S. 491 mandatory weapon forfeiture order.
	Hyb-Sum.	6 mth/ 5000*	✓	✓	✓	✓	✓	✓	✓	✓	✓	✓	
130 Personating peace officer	Hyb-Ind.	5 yrs	✓	✓	✓	✓	✓	✓	✓	✓	✓	✓	S. 110 discretionary firearms order. S. 491 mandatory weapon forfeiture order. S if by indictment
	Hyb-Sum.	6 mth/ 5000*	✓	✓	✓	✓	✓	✓	✓	✓	✓	✓	
131, 132 Perjury	Indictable	14 yrs	×	✓	✓	✓	✓	✓	✓	✓	✓	×	S
134 False statement where not required	Summary	6 mth/ 5000*	✓	✓	✓	✓	✓	✓	✓	✓	✓	✓	
136 Contradictory evidence with intent to mislead	Indictable	14 yrs	×	✓	✓	✓	✓	✓	✓	✓	✓	×	Attorney General's consent required. S
137 Fabricating evidence	Indictable	14 yrs	×	✓	✓	✓	✓	✓	✓	✓	✓	×	S
138 Offences relating to affidavits	Indictable	2 yrs	✓	✓	✓	✓	✓	✓	✓	✓	✓	✓	
139(1) Obstructing justice re surety	Hyb-Ind.	2 yrs	✓	✓	✓	✓	✓	✓	✓	✓	✓	✓	
	Hyb-Sum.	6 mth/ 5000*	✓	✓	✓	✓	✓	✓	✓	✓	✓	✓	
139(2) Obstructing justice	Indictable	10 yrs	✓	✓	✓	✓	✓	✓	✓	✓	✓	✓	S
140 Public mischief	Hyb-Ind.	5 yrs	✓	✓	✓	✓	✓	✓	✓	✓	✓	✓	S if by indictment
	Hyb-Sum.	6 mth/ 5000*	✓	✓	✓	✓	✓	✓	✓	✓	✓	✓	
141 Compounding indictable offence	Indictable	2 yrs	✓	✓	✓	✓	✓	✓	✓	✓	✓	✓	
144 Prison breach	Indictable	10 yrs	✓	✓	✓	✓	✓	✓	✓	✓	✓	×	S. 109 mandatory firearms order. S. 491 mandatory weapon forfeiture order. S
145 Escape, failure to appear, etc.	Hyb-Ind.	2 yrs	✓	✓	✓	✓	✓	✓	✓	✓	✓	✓	S. 110 discretionary firearms order. S. 491 mandatory weapon forfeiture order. S
	Hyb-Sum.	6 mth/ 5000*	✓	✓	✓	✓	✓	✓	✓	✓	✓	✓	

*** $100,000 for organizations for summary conviction offence s. 735.**
***** conditional sentence not available if offence involved use of a weapon.**

✓ Sentence Option **× Illegal Sentence**

P = Primary designated offence
S = Secondary designated offence
PC = Primary Compulsory
[see note on p. OG/2]

GRID

SECTION	TYPE	MAX/MIN SENTENCE	DISCHARGE s. 730	SUSPENDED SENTENCE s. 731(1)(a)	FINE ALONE s. 734	FINE & PROBATION s. 731(1)(b)	PRISON ss. 718.3, 787	PRISON & PROBATION s. 731(1)(b)	PRISON & FINE s. 734	INTERMITTENT s. 732	FINE, PROB. & INTERMITS s. 732	CONDITIONAL SENTENCE s. 742.1	COMMENTS (applicability depends on circumstances of case)
146 Permit or assist escape	Indictable	2 yrs	✓	✓	✓	✓	✓	✓	✓	✓	✓	✓	S. 110 discretionary firearms order. S. 491 mandatory weapon forfeiture order. S
147 Rescue or permit escape	Indictable	5 yrs	✓	✓	✓	✓	✓	✓	✓	✓	✓	✓	S. 110 discretionary firearms order. S. 491 mandatory weapon forfeiture order. S
148 Assisting prisoner of war to escape	Indictable	5 yrs max	✓	✓	✓	✓	✓	✓	✓	✓	✓	✓	S
151 Sexual interference	Hyb-Ind.	14 yrs max 1 year min	×	×	×	×	✓	✓	✓	×	✓	×	Indictable, s. 109 mandatory firearms order. Summary conviction, s. 109 discretionary firearms order. S. 491 mandatory weapon forfeiture order. S. 161 discretionary order.
	Hyb-Sum.	2 yrs less a day max/ 90 days min	×	×	×	×	✓	✓	✓	✓	×	×	PC
152 Invite sexual touching, under 16	Hyb-Ind.	14 yrs max 1 year min	×	×	×	×	✓	✓	✓	×	×	×	Indictable, s. 109 mandatory firearms order. Summary conviction, s. 110 discretionary firearms order. S. 491 mandatory weapon forfeiture order. S. 161 discretionary order.
	Hyb-Sum.	2 yrs less a day max/ 90 days min	×	×	×	×	✓	✓	✓	✓	✓	×	PC
153 Sexual exploitation, age 16 to 18	Hyb-Ind.	14 yrs max 1 year min	×	×	×	×	✓	✓	✓	×	×	×	S. 110 discretionary firearms order. S. 491 mandatory weapons forfeiture order.
	Hyb-Sum.	2 yrs less a day max/ 90 days min	×	×	×	×	✓	✓	✓	✓	✓	×	PC
153.1 Sexual exploitation of person with disability	Hyb-Ind.	5 yrs	✓	✓	✓	✓	✓	✓	✓	✓	✓	✓	S. 110 discretionary firearms order. S. 491 mandatory weapons forfeiture order.
	Hyb-Sum.	18 mth/ 5000*	✓	✓	✓	✓	✓	✓	✓	✓	✓	✓	PC

* $100,000 for organizations for summary conviction offence s. 735.
*** conditional sentence not available if offence involved use of a weapon.

✓ Sentence Option   × Illegal Sentence

P = Primary designated offence
S = Secondary designated offence
PC = Primary Compulsory
[see note on p. OG/2]

SECTION	TYPE	MAX/MIN SENTENCE	DISCHARGE s. 730	SUSPENDED SENTENCE s. 731(1)(a)	FINE ALONE s. 734	FINE & PROBATION s. 731(1)(b)	PRISON ss. 718.3, 787	PRISON & PROBATION s. 731(1)(b)	PRISON & FINE s. 734	INTERMITTENT s. 732	FINE, PROB. & INTERMIT s. 732	CONDITIONAL SENTENCE s. 742.1	COMMENTS (applicability depends on circumstances of case)
155 Incest	Indictable	14 yrs max	×	✓	✓	✓	✓	✓	✓	×	✓	×	S. 109 mandatory firearms order. S. 491 mandatory weapon forfeiture order. S. 161 discretionary order.
		14 yrs max 5 yrs min if V under age 16	×	×	×	×		×		×	×	×	PC
160(1), (2) Bestiality	Hyb-Ind.	10 yrs	✓	✓	✓	✓	✓	✓	✓	✓	✓	✓	Indictable, s. 109 mandatory firearms order; summary conviction, s. 110 discretionary firearms order. S. 491 mandatory weapon forfeiture order. No intermittent sentence or conditional sentence (I or S) if V under age 16. S. 161 discretionary prohibition for s. 160(2) or (3) from attending certain public places, taking certain employment where complainant under 16 years, communicating with people under age 16 or using the Internet or other digital network unless in accordance with court conditions.
	Hyb-Sum.	6 mth/ 5000*	✓	✓	✓	✓	✓	✓	✓	✓	✓	✓	S (160(1)) if by indictment. PC (160(2)).
160(3) Bestiality in presence of or by Child	Hyb-Ind.	14 yrs max 1 yr min	×	×	×	×	✓	✓	✓	×	×	×	PC
	Hyb-Sum.	2 yrs less 1 day max 6 mth min	×	×	×	×	✓	✓	✓	×	×	×	
162.1 Publication, etc., of an intimate image without consent	Hyb-Ind.	5 yrs max	✓	✓	✓	✓	✓	✓	✓	✓	✓	✓	S if by indictment
	Hyb-Sum.	6 mth/ 5000*	✓	✓	✓	✓	✓	✓	✓	✓	✓	✓	
163, 169 Corrupting morals (obscenity)	Hyb-Ind.	2 yrs	✓	✓	✓	✓	✓	✓	✓	✓	✓	✓	S. 462.37 proceeds of crime forfeiture order on Crown application.
	Hyb-Sum.	6 mth/ 5000*	✓	✓	✓	✓	✓	✓	✓	✓	✓	✓	
163.1(2), (3) Child pornography	Indictable	14 yrs max 1 yr min	×	×	×	×	✓	✓	✓	×	×	×	S. 462.37 or s. 164.2 discretionary forfeiture order on Crown application. S. 161 discretionary order. PC
163.1(4), (4.1) Possession of or accessing child pornography	Hyb-Ind.	10 yrs max 1 yr min	×	×	×	×	✓	✓	✓	×	×	×	S. 462.37 or S. 164.2 discretionary order.
	Hyb-Sum.	2 yrs less a day max 6 mths min	×	×	×	×	✓	✓	✓	✓	✓	×	P

*** $100,000 for organizations for summary conviction offence s. 735.**
***** conditional sentence not available if offence involved use of a weapon.**

✓ Sentence Option **× Illegal Sentence**

P = Primary designated offence
S = Secondary designated offence
PC = Primary Compulsory
[see note on p. OG/2]

GRID

SECTION	TYPE	MAX/MIN SENTENCE	DISCHARGE s. 730	SUSPENDED SENTENCE s. 731(1)(a)	FINE ALONE s. 734	FINE & PROBATION s. 731(1)(b)	PRISON ss. 718.3, 787	PRISON & PROBATION s. 731(1)(b)	PRISON & FINE s. 734	INTERMITTENT s. 732	FINE, PROB. & INTERMIT s. 732	CONDITIONAL SENTENCE s. 742.1	COMMENTS (applicability depends on circumstances of case)
168 Mailing obscene material	Hyb-Ind.	2 yrs	✓	✓	✓	✓	✓	✓	✓	✓	✓	✓	
	Hyb-Sum.	6 mth/ 5000*	✓	✓	✓	✓	✓	✓	✓	✓	✓	✓	
170 Parent or guardian procuring sexual activity	Indictable	14 yrs max 1 yr min	×	×	×	×	✓	✓	✓	×	×	×	S. 161 discretionary order. PC
171 Householder permitting sexual activity	Indictable	14 yrs max 1 yr min	×	×	×	×	✓	✓	✓	×	×	×	S. 161 discretionary order. S
171.1 Making sexually explicit material available to child	Hyb-Ind.	14 yrs max/ 6 mth min	×	×	×	×	✓	✓	✓	✓	✓	×	S. 161 discretionary order. PC
	Hyb-Sum.	2 yrs less a day max/ 90 days min	×	×	×	×	✓	✓	✓	✓	✓	×	
172 Corrupting children	Indictable	2 yrs	✓	✓	✓	✓	✓	✓	✓	✓	✓	✓	Attorney General's consent may be required, see s. 172(4).
172.1 Child luring	Hyb-Ind.	14 yrs max/ 1 yr min	×	×	×	×	×	✓	✓	×	×	×	S. 161 discretionary order. S. 164(2) discretionary forfeiture order. PC
	Hyb-Sum.	2 yrs less a day max/6 mth min	×	×	×	×	✓	✓	✓	×	×	×	
172.2 Sexual offence against child, agreeing or arranging	Hyb-Ind.	14 yrs max/ 1 yr min	×	×	×	×	✓	✓	✓	×	×	×	S. 161 discretionary order. PC
	Hyb-Sum.	2 yrs less a day max/6 mth min	×	×	×	×	✓	✓	✓	×	×	×	
173(1) Indecent acts	Hyb-Ind.	2 yrs	✓	✓	✓	✓	✓	✓	✓	✓	✓	×	S. 164(2) discretionary forfeiture order S
	Hyb-Sum.	6 mth	✓	✓	✓	✓	✓	✓	✓	✓	✓	×	
173(2) Exposing genitals to person under 16	Hyb-Ind.	2 yrs max/ 90 days min	×	×	×	×	✓	✓	✓	✓	✓	×	
	Hyb-Sum.	6 mth max/ 5000*/30 days min	×	×	×	×	✓	✓	✓	✓	✓	×	S. 161 discretionary order. PC
174 Nudity	Summary	6 mth/ 5000*	✓	✓	✓	✓	✓	✓	✓	✓	✓	✓	S. 174(3) Attorney General's consent required.
175 Disturbance, indecent exhibition, loitering	Summary	6 mth/ 5000*	✓	✓	✓	✓	✓	✓	✓	✓	✓	✓	S. 110 discretionary firearms order. S. 491 mandatory weapon forfeiture order.

*** $100,000 for organizations for summary conviction offence s. 735.**
***** conditional sentence not available if offence involved use of a weapon.**

✓ Sentence Option | **× Illegal Sentence**

P = Primary designated offence
S = Secondary designated offence
PC = Primary Compulsory
[see note on p. OG/2]

SECTION	TYPE	MAX/MIN SENTENCE	DISCHARGE s. 730	SUSPENDED SENTENCE s. 731(1)(a)	FINE ALONE s. 734	FINE & PROBATION s. 731(1)(b)	PRISON ss. 718.3, 787	PRISON & PROBATION s. 731(1)(b)	PRISON & FINE s. 734	INTERMITTENT s. 732	FINE, PROB. & INTERMITS. 732	CONDITIONAL SENTENCE s. 742.1	COMMENTS (applicability depends on circumstances of case)
176(1) Obstructing or violence to clergy	Indictable	2 yrs	✓	✓	✓	✓	✓	✓	✓	✓	✓	✓	S. 110 discretionary firearms order. S. 491 mandatory weapon forfeiture order.
176(2) & (3) Disturbing religious worship, etc.	Summary	6 mth/ 5000*	✓	✓	✓	✓	✓	✓	✓	✓	✓	✓	
177 Trespassing at night	Summary	6 mth/ 5000*	✓	✓	✓	✓	✓	✓	✓	✓	✓	✓	
178 Offensive volatile substance	Summary	6 mth/ 5000*	✓	✓	✓	✓	✓	✓	✓	✓	✓	✓	
179 Vagrancy	Summary	6 mth/ 5000*	✓	✓	✓	✓	✓	✓	✓	✓	✓	✓	
180 Common nuisance	Indictable	2 yrs	✓	✓	✓	✓	✓	✓	✓	✓	✓	✓	S. 110 discretionary firearms order. S. 491 mandatory weapon forfeiture order.
182 Dead body	Indictable	5 yrs	✓	✓	✓	✓	✓	✓	✓	✓	✓	✓	S
184 Interception of communications	Indictable	5 yrs max	✓	✓	✓	✓	✓	✓	✓	✓	✓	✓	S
184.5 Interception of radio-based telephone communications	Indictable	5 yrs max	✓	✓	✓	✓	✓	✓	✓	✓	✓	✓	S
191 Possession, etc. of device for surreptitious interception of private communications	Indictable	2 yrs	✓	✓	✓	✓	✓	✓	✓	✓	✓	✓	S. 192 discretionary forfeiture order.
193 Disclosure of information	Indictable	2 yrs	✓	✓	✓	✓	✓	✓	✓	✓	✓	✓	S. 194 discretionary order of punitive damages to maximum of $5,000 on application of person aggrieved.
193.1 Disclosure of information, radio-based telephone communications	Indictable	2 yrs	✓	✓	✓	✓	✓	✓	✓	✓	✓	✓	S. 194 discretionary order of punitive damages to maximum of $5,000 on application of person aggrieved.
201(1) Keeping gaming or betting house	Indictable **Absolute PCJ**	2 yrs	✓	✓	✓	✓	✓	✓	✓	✓	✓	✓	S. 462.37 proceeds of crime forfeiture order on Crown application.
201(2) Person found in gaming or betting house or owner permitting use	Summary	6 mth/5000	✓	✓	✓	✓	✓	✓	✓	✓	✓	✓	

*** $100,000 for organizations for summary conviction offence s. 735.**
***** conditional sentence not available if offence involved use of a weapon.**

✓ Sentence Option | **× Illegal Sentence**

P = Primary designated offence
S = Secondary designated offence
PC = Primary Compulsory
[see note on p. OG/2]

GRID

SECTION	TYPE	MAX/MIN SENTENCE	DISCHARGE s. 730	SUSPENDED SENTENCE s. 731(1)(a)	FINE ALONE s. 734	FINE & PROBATION s. 731(1)(b)	PRISON ss. 718.3, 787	PRISON & PROBATION s. 731(1)(b)	PRISON & FINE s. 734	INTERMITTENT s. 732	FINE, PROB. & INTERMIT s. 732	CONDITIONAL SENTENCE s. 742.1	COMMENTS (applicability depends on circumstances of case)
202 Betting, pool-selling, book-making, etc.	Indictable **Absolute PCJ**	1st offence: 2 yrs	✓	✓	✓	✓	✓	✓	✓	✓	✓	✓	S. 462.37 proceeds of crime forfeiture order on Crown application. Higher penalty for second or subsequent offence requires compliance with s. 727.
		2nd offence: 14 days min., 2 yrs max.	×	×	×	×	✓	✓	✓	✓	✓	×	
		3rd & subsq: 3 mth min., 2 yrs max.	×	×	×	×	✓	✓	✓	✓	✓	×	
203 Placing bets on behalf of others	Indictable **Absolute PCJ**	1st offence: 2 yrs	✓	✓	✓	✓	✓	✓	✓	✓	✓	✓	
		2nd offence: 14 days min., 2 yrs max.	×	×	×	×	✓	✓	✓	✓	✓	×	
		3rd & subsq: 3 mth min., 2 yrs max.	×	×	×	×	✓	✓	✓	✓	✓	×	
206(1) Lotteries and games of chance	Indictable **Absolute PCJ**	2 yrs	✓	✓	✓	✓	✓	✓	✓	✓	✓	✓	
206(4) Buying, taking or receiving lot, ticket or other device	Summary	6 mth/ 5000*	✓	✓	✓	✓	✓	✓	✓	✓	✓	✓	
210(1) Keep common bawdy house	Indictable **Absolute PCJ**	2 yrs	✓	✓	✓	✓	✓	✓	✓	✓	✓	✓	S. 210(3) notice of conviction to be served on owner, landlord or lessor. S. 462.37 proceeds of crime forfeiture order on Crown application.
210(2) Inmate, etc. of common bawdy house	Summary	6 mth/ 5000*	✓	✓	✓	✓	✓	✓	✓	✓	✓	✓	S. 462.37 proceeds of crime forfeiture order on Crown application.
211 Transport person to bawdy house	Summary	6 mth/ 5000*	✓	✓	✓	✓	✓	✓	✓	✓	✓	✓	
213 Prostitution, or obtaining services	Summary	6 mth/ 5000*	✓	✓	✓	✓	✓	✓	✓	✓	✓	✓	
215 Fail to provide necessaries	Hyb-Ind.	5 yrs	✓	✓	✓	✓	✓	✓	✓	✓	✓	✓	S if by indictment
	Hyb-Sum.	18 mth	✓	✓	✓	✓	✓	✓	✓	✓	✓	✓	
218 Abandon child	Hyb-Ind.	5 yrs	✓	✓	✓	✓	✓	✓	✓	✓	✓	✓	S if by indictment
	Hyb-Sum.	18 mth	✓	✓	✓	✓	✓	✓	✓	✓	✓	✓	

* $100,000 for organizations for summary conviction offence s. 735.
*** conditional sentence not available if offence involved use of a weapon.

✓ Sentence Option × Illegal Sentence

P = Primary designated offence
S = Secondary designated offence
PC = Primary Compulsory
[see note on p. OG/2]

SECTION	TYPE	MAX/MIN SENTENCE	DISCHARGE s. 730	SUSPENDED SENTENCE s. 731(1)(a)	FINE ALONE s. 734	FINE & PROBATION s. 731(1)(b)	PRISON ss. 718.3, 787	PRISON & PROBATION s. 731(1)(b)	PRISON & FINE s. 734	INTERMITTENT s. 732	FINE, PROB. & INTERMIT s. 732	CONDITIONAL SENTENCE s. 742.1	COMMENTS (applicability depends on circumstances of case)
220(a) Cause death by criminal negligence, use of firearm	Indictable	Life Min: 4 yrs	x	x	x	x	✓	x	✓	x	x	x	S. 109 mandatory firearms order. S. 491 mandatory weapon forfeiture order. S
220(b) Cause death by criminal negligence (other)	Indictable	Life	x	✓	✓	✓	✓	✓	✓	✓	✓	x	S. 109 mandatory firearms order. S. 259(2) discretionary driving prohibition (no limit). S. 491 mandatory weapon forfeiture order. S
221 Cause bodily harm by criminal negligence	Indictable	10 yrs	✓	✓	✓	✓	✓	✓	✓	✓	✓	x	S. 109 mandatory firearms order. S. 259(2) discretionary driving prohibition (up to 10 yrs). S. 491 mandatory weapon forfeiture order. S
229-231, 235 Murder	Indictable	Minimum Life See ss.745, 745.1 for parole eligibility	x	x	x	x	✓	x	✓	x	x	x	S. 109 mandatory firearms order. S. 491 mandatory weapon forfeiture order. S. 522, release by Superior Court Judge only. S. 462.37 proceeds of crime forfeiture order on Crown application. PC
234, 236(a) Manslaughter, use of firearm	Indictable	Life Min: 4 yrs	x	x	x	x	✓	x	✓	x	x	x	S. 109 mandatory firearms order. S. 491 mandatory weapon forfeiture order. PC
234, 236(b) Manslaughter (other)	Indictable	Life	x	✓	✓	✓	✓	✓	✓	✓	✓	x	S. 109 mandatory firearms order. S. 259(2) discretionary driving prohibition (no limit). S. 491 mandatory weapon forfeiture order. PC
237 Infanticide	Indictable	5 yrs	✓	✓	✓	✓	✓	✓	✓	✓	✓	✓	S. 110 discretionary firearms order. S. 491 mandatory weapon forfeiture order. P
239(1)(a) Attempt murder, use restricted or prohibited firearm, or any firearm, in committing for criminal organization	Indictable	Life Minimum: 5 yrs-1st 7 yrs-2nd	x	x	x	x	✓	x	✓	x	x	x	S. 109 mandatory firearms order. S. 491 mandatory weapon forfeiture. PC
239(1)(a.1) Attempt murder, use of firearm (other)	Indictable	Life Min: 4 yrs	x	x	x	x	✓	x	✓	x	x	x	S. 109 mandatory firearms order. S. 491 mandatory weapon forfeiture. PC

* $100,000 for organizations for summary conviction offence s. 735.
*** conditional sentence not available if offence involved use of a weapon.

✓ Sentence Option   x Illegal Sentence

P = Primary designated offence
S = Secondary designated offence
PC = Primary Compulsory
[see note on p. OG/2]

GRID

SECTION	TYPE	MAX/MIN SENTENCE	DISCHARGE s. 730	SUSPENDED SENTENCE s. 731(1)(a)	FINE ALONE s. 734	FINE & PROBATION s. 731(1)(b)	PRISON ss. 718.3, 787	PRISON & PROBATION s. 731(1)(b)	PRISON & FINE s. 734	INTERMITTENT s. 732	FINE, PROB. & INTERMIT s. 732	CONDITIONAL SENTENCE s. 742.1	COMMENTS (applicability depends on circumstances of case)
239(1)(b) Attempt murder (other)	Indictable	Life	✗	✓	✓	✓	✓	✓	✓	✓	✓	✗	S. 109 mandatory firearms order. S. 491 mandatory weapon forfeiture order. PC
240 Accessory after fact, murder	Indictable	Life	✗	✓	✓	✓	✓	✓	✓	✓	✓	✗	S. 522, release by Superior Court Judge only. S
244(2)(a) Discharging firearm with intent, use restricted or prohibited firearm, or any firearm, in committing for criminal organization	Indictable	14 yrs Minimum: 5 yrs-1st 7 yrs-2nd	✗	✗	✗	✗	✓	✗	✓	✗	✗	✗	S. 109 mandatory firearms order. S. 491 mandatory weapon forfeiture order. PC
244(2)(b) Discharging firearm (other) with intent	Indictable	14 yrs Minimum - 4 yrs	✗	✗	✗	✗	✓	✗	✓	✗	✗	✗	S. 109 mandatory firearms order. S. 491 mandatory weapon forfeiture order. PC
244.1 Causing bodily harm with intent, use of air gun or pistol	Indictable	14 yrs	✗	✓	✓	✓	✓	✓	✓	✓	✓	✗	S. 109 mandatory firearms order. S. 491 mandatory weapon forfeiture. PC
244.2(3)(a) Discharging firearm recklessness, use	Indictable	14 yrs Minimum: 5 yrs-1st 7 yrs-2nd	✗	✗	✗	✗	✓	✗	✓	✗	✗	✗	S. 109 mandatory firearms order. S. 491 mandatory weapon forfeiture order. PC
244.2(3)(b) Discharging firearm (other) recklessly	Indictable	14 yrs Minimum - 4 yrs	✗	✗	✗	✗	✓	✗	✓	✗	✗	✗	S. 109 mandatory firearms order. S. 491 mandatory weapon forfeiture order. PC
245(a) Administering noxious thing with intent to endanger life or cause bodily harm	Indictable	14 yrs	✗	✓	✓	✓	✓	✓	✓	✓	✓	✗	S. 109 mandatory firearms prohibition. PC
245(b) Administering noxious thing with intent to aggrieve or annoy	Indictable	2 yrs	✓	✓	✓	✓	✓	✓	✓	✓	✓	✓	S. 110 discretionary firearms prohibition.
246 Overcoming resistance to commission of offence	Indictable	Life	✗	✓	✓	✓	✓	✓	✓	✓	✓	✗	S. 109 mandatory firearms prohibition. PC
249(1) Dangerous operation of vehicle, etc., no injury (Repealed as of December 21, 2018)	Hyb-Ind.	5 yrs	✓	✓	✓	✓	✓	✓	✓	✓	✓	✓	S. 259(2) discretionary driving prohibition (up to 3 yrs).
	Hyb-Sum.	6 mth/ 5000*	✓	✓	✓	✓	✓	✓	✓	✓	✓	✓	S if by indictment

* $100,000 for organizations for summary conviction offence s. 735.

*** conditional sentence not available if offence involved use of a weapon.

✓ Sentence Option ✗ Illegal Sentence

P = Primary designated offence
S = Secondary designated offence
PC = Primary Compulsory
[see note on p. OG/2]

SECTION	TYPE	MAX/MIN SENTENCE	DISCHARGE s. 730	SUSPENDED SENTENCE s. 731(1)(a)	FINE ALONE s. 734	FINE & PROBATION s. 731(1)(b)	PRISON ss. 718.3, 787	PRISON & PROBATION s. 731(1)(b)	PRISON & FINE s. 734	INTERMITTENT s. 732	FINE, PROB. & INTERMIT s. 732	CONDITIONAL SENTENCE s. 742.1	COMMENTS (applicability depends on circumstances of case)
249(3) Dangerous operation of vehicle, etc., injury occurs (Repealed as of December 21, 2018)	Indictable	10 yrs	✓	✓	✓	✓	✓	✓	✓	✓	✓	✗	S. 109 mandatory firearms order. S. 259(2) discretionary driving prohibition (up to 10 yrs). S
249(4) Dangerous operation of vehicle, etc., death occurs (Repealed as of December 21, 2018)	Indictable	14 yrs	✗	✓	✓	✓	✓	✓	✓	✓	✓	✗	S. 109 mandatory firearms order. S. 259(2) discretionary driving prohibition (up to 10 yrs). S
249.1(1) Flight (Repealed as of December 21, 2018)	Hyb-Ind.	5 yrs	✓	✓	✓	✓	✓	✓	✓	✓	✓	✓	Discretionary prohibition order under s. 259(2)(c) for a period of not more than 3 yrs. S
	Hyb-Sum.	6 mth/5000	✓	✓	✓	✓	✓	✓	✓	✓	✓	✓	Discretionary prohibition order under s. 259(2)(c) for a period of not more than 3 yrs.
249.1(3) Flight causing bodily harm or death (Repealed as of December 21, 2018)	Indictable	14 yrs if bh/ Life if death	✗	✓	✓	✓	✓	✓	✓	✓	✓	✗	Discretionary prohibition order under s. 259(2)(b) for a period not exceeding 10 yrs for causing bodily harm, or (a) or (a.1) for any duration for causing death. S. 109 mandatory firearms order. S
249.2 Street racing causing death (Repealed as of December 21, 2018)	Indictable	Life	✗	✓	✓	✓	✓	✓	✓	✓	✓	✗	Mandatory driving prohibition of at least 1 yr, under former s. 259(3.3)(a). S. 109 mandatory firearms order S
249.3 Street racing causing bodily harm (Repealed as of December 21, 2018)	Indictable	14 yrs	✗	✓	✓	✓	✓	✓	✓	✓	✓	✗	Mandatory driving prohibition under former s. 259(3.2) for 1-10 yrs-1st, 2-10 yrs-2nd, 3 yrs + period of imprisonment-3rd and subsequent offences. S. 109 mandatory firearms order S
249.4(1) Street racing and dangerous operation (Repealed as of December 21, 2018)	Hyb-Ind.	5 yrs	✓	✓	✓	✓	✓	✓	✓	✓	✓	✓	Mandatory driving prohibition under the former s. 259(3.1), for 1-3 yrs + period of imprisonment-1st; 2-5 yrs-2nd; not less than 3 yrs + period of imprisonment-3rd and subsequent. S
	Hyb-Sum.	6 mth/5000	✓	✓	✓	✓	✓	✓	✓	✓	✓	✓	Mandatory driving prohibition under the former s. 259(3.1), for 1-3 yrs + period of imprisonment-1st; 2-5 yrs-2nd; not less than 3 yrs + period of imprisonment-3rd and subsequent.

*** $100,000 for organizations for summary conviction offence s. 735.**
***** conditional sentence not available if offence involved use of a weapon.**

✓ Sentence Option **✗ Illegal Sentence**

P = Primary designated offence
S = Secondary designated offence
PC = Primary Compulsory
[see note on p. OG/2]

GRID

SECTION	TYPE	MAX/MIN SENTENCE	DISCHARGE s. 730	SUSPENDED SENTENCE s. 731(1)(a)	FINE ALONE s. 734	FINE & PROBATION s. 731(1)(b)	PRISON ss. 718.3, 787	PRISON & PROBATION s. 731(1)(b)	PRISON & FINE s. 734	INTERMITTENT s. 732	FINE, PROB. & INTERMIT s. 732	CONDITIONAL SENTENCE s. 742.1	COMMENTS (applicability depends on circumstances of case)
249.4(3) Street racing and dangerous operation causing bodily harm (Repealed as of December 21, 2018)	Indictable	14 yrs	✗	✓	✓	✓	✓	✓	✓	✓	✓	✗	Mandatory driving prohibition under former s. 259(3.2) for 1-10 yrs-1st, 2-10 yrs-2nd, 3 yrs + period of imprisonment-3rd and subsequent offences S. 109 mandatory firearms order S
249.4(4) Street racing and dangerous operation causing death (Repealed as of December 21, 2018)	Indictable	Life	✗	✓	✓	✓	✓	✓	✓	✓	✓	✗	Mandatory driving prohibition under s. 259(3.3)(b), for 1-10 yrs + period of imprisonment. S. 109 mandatory firearms order S
250 Fail to watch, water skiing at night (Repealed as of December 21, 2018)	Summary	6 mth/ 5000*	✓	✓	✓	✓	✓	✓	✓	✓	✓	✓	S. 259(2) discretionary driving prohibition (up to 3 yrs).
251 Send unsafe vessel or aircraft (Repealed as of December 21, 2018)	Indictable	5 yrs	✓	✓	✓	✓	✓	✓	✓	✓	✓	✓	S. 259(2) discretionary driving prohibition (up to 3 yrs). Prosecution requires consent of A.G. of Canada. S
252 Fail to stop at scene of accident (Repealed as of December 21, 2018)	Hyb-Ind.	5 yrs	✓	✓	✓	✓	✓	✓	✓	✓	✓	✓	S. 259(2) discretionary driving prohibition (up to 3 yrs). S
	Hyb-Sum.	6 mth/ 5000*	✓	✓	✓	✓	✓	✓	✓	✓	✓	✓	
252(1.1) Fail to stop at scene of accident, no injury (Repealed as of December 21, 2018)	Hyb-Ind.	5 yrs	✓	✓	✓	✓	✓	✓	✓	✓	✓	✓	S. 259(2) discretionary driving prohibition (up to 3 yrs). S
	Hyb-Sum.	6 mth/ 5000*	✓	✓	✓	✓	✓	✓	✓	✓	✓	✓	
252(1.2) Fail to stop at scene of accident knowing bodily harm caused (Repealed as of December 21, 2018)	Indictable	10 yrs	✓	✓	✓	✓	✓	✓	✓	✓	✓	✓	S. 259(2) discretionary driving prohibition (up to 5 yrs). S
252(1.3) Fail to stop at scene of accident knowing person is dead; or reckless whether death results (Repealed as of December 21, 2018)	Indictable	Life	✗	✓	✓	✓	✓	✓	✓	✓	✓	✗	S. 259(2) discretionary driving prohibition (up to life). S

*** $100,000 for organizations for summary conviction offence s. 735.**
***** conditional sentence not available if offence involved use of a weapon.**

✓ Sentence Option **✗ Illegal Sentence**

P = Primary designated offence
S = Secondary designated offence
PC = Primary Compulsory
[see note on p. OG/2]

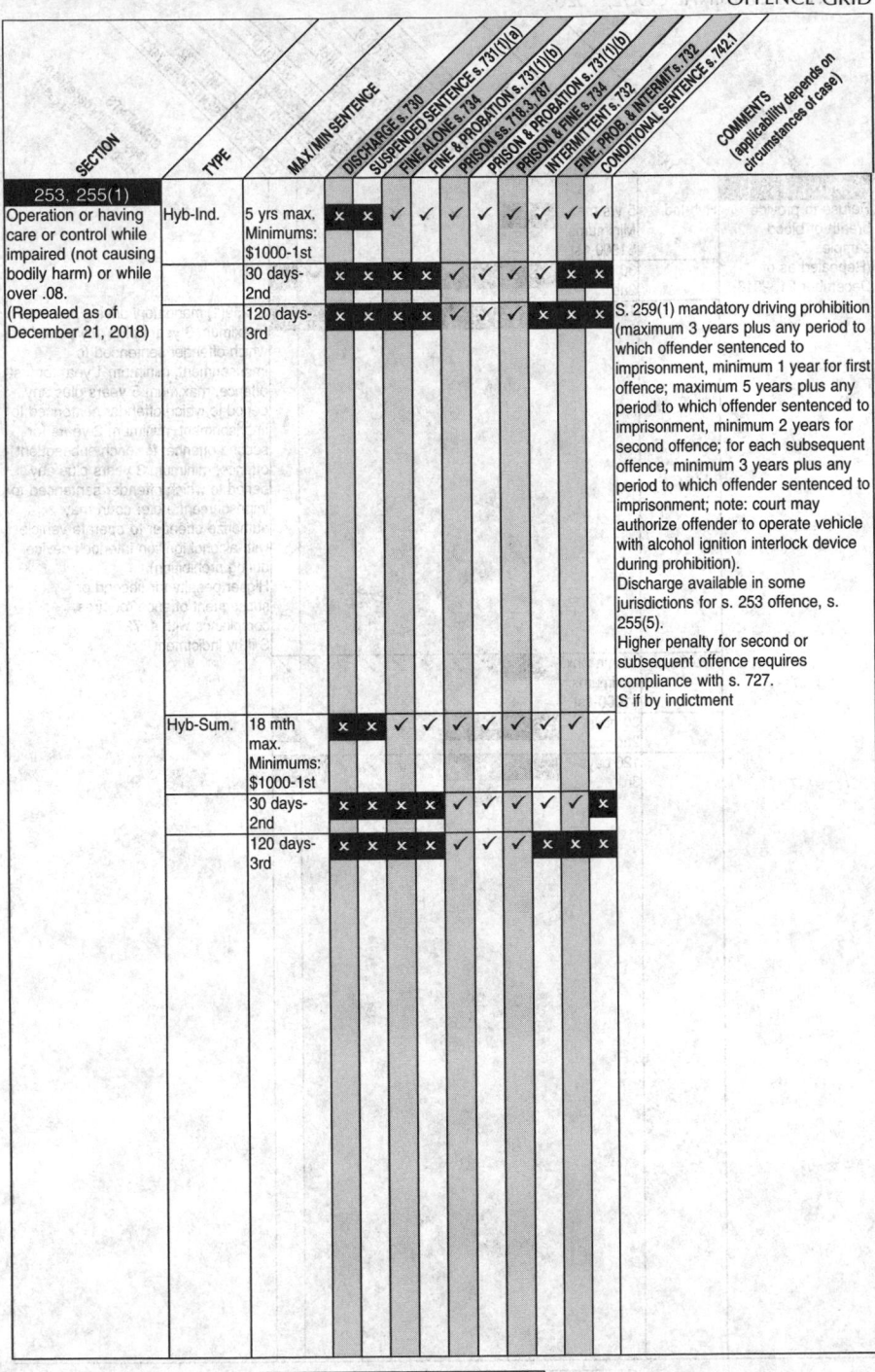

SECTION	TYPE	MAX/MIN SENTENCE	DISCHARGE s. 730	SUSPENDED SENTENCE s. 731(1)(a)	FINE ALONE s. 734	FINE & PROBATION s. 731(1)(b)	PRISON ss. 718.3, 787	PRISON & PROBATION s. 731(1)(b)	PRISON & FINE s. 734	INTERMITTENT s. 732	FINE, PROB. & INTERMIT s. 732	CONDITIONAL SENTENCE s. 742.1	COMMENTS (applicability depends on circumstances of case)
253, 255(1) Operation or having care or control while impaired (not causing bodily harm) or while over .08. (Repealed as of December 21, 2018)	Hyb-Ind.	5 yrs max. Minimums: $1000-1st	×	×	✓	✓	✓	✓	✓	✓	✓	✓	
		30 days-2nd	×	×	×	×	✓	✓	✓	✓	×	×	
		120 days-3rd	×	×	×	×	✓	✓	✓	×	×	×	S. 259(1) mandatory driving prohibition (maximum 3 years plus any period to which offender sentenced to imprisonment, minimum 1 year for first offence; maximum 5 years plus any period to which offender sentenced to imprisonment, minimum 2 years for second offence; for each subsequent offence, minimum 3 years plus any period to which offender sentenced to imprisonment; note: court may authorize offender to operate vehicle with alcohol ignition interlock device during prohibition). Discharge available in some jurisdictions for s. 253 offence, s. 255(5). Higher penalty for second or subsequent offence requires compliance with s. 727. S if by indictment
	Hyb-Sum.	18 mth max. Minimums: $1000-1st	×	×	✓	✓	✓	✓	✓	✓	✓	✓	
		30 days-2nd	×	×	×	×	✓	✓	✓	✓	✓	×	
		120 days-3rd	×	×	×	×	✓	✓	✓	×	×	×	

* $100,000 for organizations for summary conviction offence s. 735.

*** conditional sentence not available if offence involved use of a weapon.

✓ Sentence Option × Illegal Sentence

P = Primary designated offence
S = Secondary designated offence
PC = Primary Compulsory
[see note on p. OG/2]

SECTION	TYPE	MAX/MIN SENTENCE	DISCHARGE s. 730	SUSPENDED SENTENCE s. 731(1)(a)	FINE ALONE s. 734	FINE & PROBATION s. 731(1)(b)	PRISON ss. 718.3, 787	PRISON & PROBATION s. 731(1)(b)	PRISON & FINE s. 734	INTERMITTENT s. 732	FINE, PROB. & INTERMIT s. 732	CONDITIONAL SENTENCE s. 742.1	COMMENTS (applicability depends on circumstances of case)
254(5), 255(1) Refuse to provide breath or blood sample (Repealed as of December 21, 2018)	Hyb-Ind.	5 yrs max. Minimums: $1000-1st	✗	✗	✓	✓	✓	✓	✓	✓	✓	✓	
		30 days-2nd	✗	✗	✗	✗	✓	✓	✓	✓	✓	✗	
		120 days-3rd	✗	✗	✗	✗	✓	✓	✓	✗	✗	✗	S. 259(1) mandatory driving prohibition (maximum 3 years plus any period to which offender sentenced to imprisonment, minimum 1 year for first offence; maximum 5 years plus any period to which offender sentenced to imprisonment, minimum 2 years for second offence; for each subsequent offence, minimum 3 years plus any period to which offender sentenced to imprisonment; note: court may authorize offender to operate vehicle with alcohol ignition interlock device during prohibition). Higher penalty for second or subsequent offence requires compliance with s. 727. S if by indictment
	Hyb-Sum.	18 mth max. Minimums: $1000-1st	✗	✗	✓	✓	✓	✓	✓	✓	✓	✓	
		30 days-2nd	✗	✗	✗	✗	✓	✓	✓	✓	✓	✗	
		120 days-3rd	✗	✗	✗	✗	✓	✓	✓	✓	✗	✗	

* $100,000 for organizations for summary conviction offence s. 735.

*** conditional sentence not available if offence involved use of a weapon.

✓ Sentence Option ✗ Illegal Sentence

P = Primary designated offence
S = Secondary designated offence
PC = Primary Compulsory
[see note on p. OG/2]

SECTION	TYPE	MAX/MIN SENTENCE	DISCHARGE s. 730	SUSPENDED SENTENCE s. 731(1)(a)	FINE ALONE s. 734	FINE & PROBATION s. 731(1)(b)	PRISON ss. 718.3, 787	PRISON & PROBATION s. 731(1)(b)	PRISON & FINE s. 734	INTERMITTENT s. 732	FINE, PROB. & INTERMITT s. 732	CONDITIONAL SENTENCE s. 742.1	COMMENTS (applicability depends on circumstances of case)
253(1), 255(2),(2.1),(2.2) Impaired operation causing bodily harm; "over 80" causing accident resulting in bodily harm; refusing to provide breath or blood sample knowing accident resulted in bodily harm (Repealed as of December 21, 2018)	Indictable	10 yrs max. Minimums: $1000-1st	✗	✗	✓	✓	✓	✓	✓	✓	✓	✗	
		30 days-2nd	✗	✗	✗	✗	✓	✓	✓	✓	✓	✗	
		120 days-3rd	✗	✗	✗	✗	✓	✓	✓	✗	✗	✗	S. 109 mandatory firearms order. S. 259(1) mandatory driving prohibition (maximum 3 years plus any period to which offender sentenced to imprisonment, minimum 1 year for first offence; maximum 5 years plus any period to which offender sentenced to imprisonment, minimum 2 years for second offence; for each subsequent offence, minimum 3 years plus any period to which offender sentenced to imprisonment; note: court may authorize offender to operate vehicle with alcohol ignition interlock device during prohibition). S. 259(2) discretionary driving prohibition up to 10 years (no minimum). Higher penalty for second or subsequent offences requires compliance with s. 727. S
253, 255(3),(3.1),(3.2) Impaired operation causing death; "over 80" causing accident resulting in death; refusing to provide breath or blood sample knowing accident resulted in death or bodily harm leading to death (Repealed as of December 21, 2018)	Indictable	Life max. Minimums: $1000-1st	✗	✗	✓	✓	✓	✓	✓	✓	✓	✗	
		30 days-2nd	✗	✗	✗	✗	✓	✓	✓	✓	✓	✗	
		120 days-3rd	✗	✗	✗	✗	✓	✓	✓	✗	✗	✗	S. 109 mandatory firearms order. S. 259(1) mandatory driving prohibition (maximum 3 years plus any period to which offender sentenced to imprisonment, minimum 1 year for first offence; maximum 5 years plus any period to which offender sentenced to imprisonment, minimum 2 years for second offence; for each subsequent offence, minimum 3 years plus any period to which offender sentenced to imprisonment; note: court may authorize offender to operate vehicle with alcohol ignition interlock device during prohibition). S. 259(2) discretionary driving prohibition up to 10 years (no minimum). Higher penalty for second or subsequent offences requires compliance with s. 727. S

*** $100,000 for organizations for summary conviction offence s. 735.**
***** conditional sentence not available if offence involved use of a weapon.**

✓ Sentence Option ✗ Illegal Sentence

P = Primary designated offence
S = Secondary designated offence
PC = Primary Compulsory
[see note on p. OG/2]

GRID

SECTION	TYPE	MAX/MIN SENTENCE	DISCHARGE s. 730	SUSPENDED SENTENCE s. 731(1)(a)	FINE ALONE s. 734	FINE & PROBATION s. 731(1)(b)	PRISON ss. 718.3, 787	PRISON & PROBATION s. 731(1)(b)	PRISON & FINE s. 734	INTERMITTENT s. 732	FINE, PROB. & INTERMIT s. 732	CONDITIONAL SENTENCE s. 742.1	COMMENTS (applicability depends on circumstances of case)
259(4) Operate vehicle, etc. while disqualified (Repealed as of December 21, 2018)	Hyb-Ind.	5 yrs	✓	✓	✓	✓	✓	✓	✓	✓	✓	✓	S. 259(1) mandatory driving prohibition (maximum 3 years plus any period to which offender sentenced to imprisonment, minimum 1 year for first offence; maximum 5 years plus any period to which offender sentenced to imprisonment, minimum 2 years for second offence; for each subsequent offence, minimum 3 years plus any period to which offender sentenced to imprisonment; note: court may authorize offender to operate vehicle with alcohol ignition interlock device during prohibition). S. 259(2) discretionary driving prohibition up to 10 years (no minimum). Higher penalty for second or subsequent offences requires compliance with s. 727. S if by indictment
	Hyb-Sum.	6 mth/ 5000*	✓	✓	✓	✓	✓	✓	✓	✓	✓	✓	
264 Criminal harassment	Hyb-Ind.	10 yrs	✓	✓	✓	✓	✓	✓	✓	✓	✓	×	Aggravating factors, s. 264(4). S. 109 mandatory firearms prohibition. S
	Hyb-Sum.	6 mth/ 5000*	✓	✓	✓	✓	✓	✓	✓	✓	✓	✓	
264.1(1)(a) Threat to cause death or harm	Hyb-Ind.	5 yrs	✓	✓	✓	✓	✓	✓	✓	✓	✓	✓	S. 110 discretionary firearms order. S. 491 mandatory weapon forfeiture order. S
	Hyb-Sum.	18 mth	✓	✓	✓	✓	✓	✓	✓	✓	✓	✓	
264.1(1)(b) or (c) Threat to damage prop. or harm animal	Hyb-Ind.	2 yrs	✓	✓	✓	✓	✓	✓	✓	✓	✓	✓	S. 110 discretionary firearms order. S. 491 mandatory weapon forfeiture order. S
	Hyb-Sum.	6 mth/ 5000*	✓	✓	✓	✓	✓	✓	✓	✓	✓	✓	
265, 266 Assault	Hyb-Ind.	5 yrs	✓	✓	✓	✓	✓	✓	✓	✓	✓	✓	S. 110 discretionary firearms order. S. 491 mandatory weapon forfeiture order. S
	Hyb-Sum.	6 mth/ 5000*	✓	✓	✓	✓	✓	✓	✓	✓	✓	✓	
267 Assault causing bodily harm or with weapon	Hyb-Ind.	10 yrs	✓	✓	✓	✓	✓	✓	✓	✓	✓	×	Indictable, s. 109 mandatory firearms order. Summary conviction, s. 110 discretionary firearms order. S. 491 mandatory weapon forfeiture order. PC
	Hyb-Sum.	18 mth	✓	✓	✓	✓	✓	✓	✓	✓	✓	✓	

* $100,000 for organizations for summary conviction offence s. 735.
*** conditional sentence not available if offence involved use of a weapon.

✓ Sentence Option   × Illegal Sentence

P = Primary designated offence
S = Secondary designated offence
PC = Primary Compulsory
[see note on p. OG/2]

SECTION	TYPE	MAX/MIN SENTENCE	DISCHARGE s. 730	SUSPENDED SENTENCE s. 731(1)(a)	FINE ALONE s. 734	FINE & PROBATION s. 731(1)(b)	PRISON ss. 718.3, 787	PRISON & PROBATION s. 731(1)(b)	PRISON & FINE s. 734	INTERMITTENT s. 732	FINE, PROB. & INTERMIT s. 732	CONDITIONAL SENTENCE s. 742.1	COMMENTS (applicability depends on circumstances of case)
268 Aggravated assault	Indictable	14 yrs	✗	✓	✓	✓	✓	✓	✓	✓	✓	✗	S. 109 mandatory firearms order. S. 491 mandatory weapon forfeiture order. PC
269 Unlawfully cause bodily harm	Hyb-Ind.	10 yrs	✓	✓	✓	✓	✓	✓	✓	✓	✓	✗	Indictable, s. 109 mandatory firearms order. Summary conviction, s. 110 discretionary firearms order. S. 491 mandatory weapon forfeiture order. May be convicted notwithstanding that charge.
	Hyb-Sum.	18 mth/ 5000*	✓	✓	✓	✓	✓	✓	✓	✓	✓	✓	PC
269.1 Torture	Indictable	14 yrs	✗	✓	✓	✓	✓	✓	✓	✓	✓	✗	S. 109 mandatory firearms order. S. 491 mandatory weapon forfeiture order. S
270 Assault officer, resist arrest, etc.	Hyb-Ind.	5 yrs	✓	✓	✓	✓	✓	✓	✓	✓	✓	✓	S. 110 discretionary firearms order. S. 491 mandatory weapon forfeiture order.
	Hyb-Sum.	6 mth/ 5000*	✓	✓	✓	✓	✓	✓	✓	✓	✓	✓	S
270.01 Assaulting peace officer with weapon or causing bodily harm	Hyb-Ind.	10 yrs	✓	✓	✓	✓	✓	✓	✓	✓	✓	✗	S. 109 mandatory firearms order. S. 491 mandatory weapon forfeiture order. PC
	Hyb-Sum.	18 mth	✓	✓	✓	✓	✓	✓	✓	✓	✓	✓	
270.02 Aggravated assault of peace officer	Indictable	14 yrs	✗	✓	✓	✓	✓	✓	✓	✓	✓	✗	S. 109 mandatory firearms order. PC
270.1 Disarming peace officer	Hyb-Ind.	5 yrs	✓	✓	✓	✓	✓	✓	✓	✓	✓	✓	S. 110 discretionary firearms order. S if by indictment
	Hyb-Sum.	18 mth	✓	✓	✓	✓	✓	✓	✓	✓	✓	✓	

* $100,000 for organizations for summary conviction offence s. 735.

*** conditional sentence not available if offence involved use of a weapon.

✓ Sentence Option ✗ Illegal Sentence

P = Primary designated offence
S = Secondary designated offence
PC = Primary Compulsory
[see note on p. OG/2]

GRID

SECTION	TYPE	MAX/MIN SENTENCE	DISCHARGE s. 730	SUSPENDED SENTENCE s. 731(1)(a)	FINE ALONE s. 734	FINE & PROBATION s. 731(1)(b)	PRISON ss. 718.3, 787	PRISON & PROBATION s. 731(1)(b)	PRISON & FINE s. 734	INTERMITTENT s. 732	FINE, PROB. & INTERMIT s. 732	CONDITIONAL SENTENCE s. 742.1	COMMENTS (applicability depends on circumstances of case)
271 Sexual assault	Hyb-Ind.	10 yrs max/ 14 yrs max, 1 yr min if V under age 16	✓	✓	✓	✓	✓	✓	✓	✓	✓	×	Intermittent sentence illegal if V under age 16 Indictable, s. 109 mandatory firearms order; summary conviction, s. 110 discretionary firearms order. S. 486(2.1) private testimony order. S. 486(3) discretionary publication ban. S. 491 mandatory weapon forfeiture order. S. 161 discretionary order if the complainant is under age 16. PC
	Hyb-Sum.	18 mths max; 2 yrs less a day max., 6 mths min if V under age 16	✓	✓	✓	✓	✓	✓	✓	✓	✓	✓	
272(2)(a) Sexual assault with weapon, threats or causing bodily harm, use of restricted or prohibited firearm, or any firearm, in committing for criminal organization	Indictable	14 yrs Minimum: 5 yrs-1st 7 yrs-2nd	×	×	×	×	✓	×	✓	×	×	×	S. 109 mandatory firearms order. S. 486(2.1) private testimony order. S. 486(3) discretionary publication ban. S. 491 mandatory weapon forfeiture order. S. 161 discretionary order if the complainant is under age 16. PC
272(2)(a.1) Sexual assault with weapon, threats or causing harm, use of firearm (other)	Indictable	14 yrs Min: 4 yrs If V under age 16, 5 yrs min	×	×	×	×	✓	×	✓	×	×	×	S. 109 mandatory firearms order. S. 486(2.1) private testimony order. S. 486(3) discretionary publication ban. S. 491 mandatory weapon forfeiture order. S. 161 discretionary order if the complainant is under age 16. PC
272(2)(a.2) Sexual assault with weapon, victim under age 16	Indictable	Max. life Min: 5 yrs	×	×	×	×	✓	×	✓	×	×	×	S. 109 mandatory firearms order. S. 486(2.1) private testimony order. S. 486(3) discretionary publication ban. S. 491 mandatory weapon forfeiture order. S. 161 discretionary order if the complainant is under age 16. PC
272(2)(b) Sexual assault with weapon, threats or causing harm (other)	Indictable	14 yrs	×	✓	✓	✓	✓	✓	✓	✓	✓	×	S. 109 mandatory firearms order. S. 491 mandatory weapon forfeiture order. S. 161 discretionary order if the complainant is under age 16. PC

* $100,000 for organizations for summary conviction offence s. 735.
*** conditional sentence not available if offence involved use of a weapon.

✓ Sentence Option — × Illegal Sentence

P = Primary designated offence
S = Secondary designated offence
PC = Primary Compulsory
[see note on p. OG/2]

SECTION	TYPE	MAX/MIN SENTENCE	DISCHARGE s. 730	SUSPENDED SENTENCE s. 731(1)(a)	FINE ALONE s. 734	FINE & PROBATION s. 731(1)(b)	PRISON ss. 718.3, 787	PRISON & PROBATION s. 731(1)(b)	PRISON & FINE s. 734	INTERMITTENT s. 732	FINE, PROB. & INTERMIT s. 732	CONDITIONAL SENTENCE s. 742.1	COMMENTS (applicability depends on circumstances of case)
273(2)(a) Aggravated sexual assault, use restricted or prohibited weapon, or any firearm, in committing for criminal organization	Indictable	Life Minimum: 5 yrs-1st 7 yrs-2nd 5 yrs min if V under age 16	×	×	×	×	✓	×	✓	×	×	×	S. 109 mandatory firearms order. S. 491 mandatory weapon forfeiture order. S. 161 discretionary order if the complainant is under age 16. PC
273(2)(a.1) Aggravated sexual assault, use of firearm (other)	Indictable	Life Min: 4 yrs	×	×	×	×	✓	×	✓	×	×	×	S. 109 mandatory firearms order. S. 491 mandatory weapon forfeiture order. S. 161 discretionary order if the complainant is under age 16. PC
273(2)(b) Aggravated sexual assault (other)	Indictable	Life	×	✓	✓	✓	✓	✓	✓	✓	✓	×	S. 109 mandatory firearms order. S. 491 mandatory weapon forfeiture order. S. 161 discretionary order if the complainant is under age 16. PC
273.3(2) Removal of child from Canada	Hyb-Ind.	5 yrs	✓	✓	✓	✓	✓	✓	✓	✓	✓	✓	PC
	Hyb-Sum.	6 mth/ 5000*	✓	✓	✓	✓	✓	✓	✓	✓	✓	✓	
279(1),(1.1)(a) Kidnapping, use restricted or prohibited firearm, or any firearm, in committing for criminal organization	Indictable	Life Minimum: 5 yrs-1st 7 yrs-2nd	×	×	×	×	✓	×	✓	×	×	×	S. 109 mandatory firearms order. S. 491 mandatory weapon forfeiture order. S. 462.37 proceeds of crime forfeiture order on Crown application. PC
279(1),(1.1)(a.1) Kidnapping, use of firearm	Indictable	Life Min: 4 yrs	×	×	×	×	✓	×	✓	×	×	×	S. 109 mandatory firearms order. S. 491 mandatory weapon forfeiture order. S. 462.37 proceeds of crime forfeiture order on Crown application. PC
279(1),(1.1)(a.2) Kidnapping, victim under 16; non-parent accused	Indictable	Life Min: 5 yrs	×	×	×	×	✓	×	✓	×	×	×	S. 109 mandatory firearms order. S. 491 mandatory weapon forfeiture order. S. 462.37 proceeds of crime forfeiture order on Crown application. PC
279(1),(1.1)(b) Kidnapping (other)	Indictable	Life	×	✓	✓	✓	✓	✓	✓	✓	✓	×	S. 109 mandatory firearms order. S. 491 mandatory weapon forfeiture order. PC

*** $100,000 for organizations for summary conviction offence s. 735.**
***** conditional sentence not available if offence involved use of a weapon.**

✓ Sentence Option   × Illegal Sentence

P = Primary designated offence
S = Secondary designated offence
PC = Primary Compulsory
[see note on p. OG/2]

GRID

SECTION	TYPE	MAX/MIN SENTENCE	DISCHARGE s. 730	SUSPENDED SENTENCE s. 731(1)(a)	FINE ALONE s. 734	FINE & PROBATION s. 731(1)(b)	PRISON ss. 718.3, 787	PRISON & PROBATION s. 731(1)(b)	PRISON & FINE s. 734	INTERMITTENT s. 732	FINE, PROB. & INTERMIT s. 732	CONDITIONAL SENTENCE s. 742.1	COMMENTS (applicability depends on circumstances of case)
279(2) Forcible confinement	Hyb-Ind.	10 yrs	✓	✓	✓	✓	✓	✓	✓	✓	✓	×	S. 109 mandatory firearms order. S. 491 mandatory weapon forfeiture order.
	Hyb-Sum.	18 mth/ 5000*	✓	✓	✓	✓	✓	✓	✓	✓	✓	✓	PC Aggravating circumstance, s. 348.1.
279.01(1)(a) Trafficking in persons, aggravating circumstances	Indictable	Life Min: 5 yrs	×	×	×	×	✓	×	✓	×	×	×	S. 109 mandatory firearms prohibition. S. 491 mandatory weapon forfeiture. S. 462.37 proceeds of crime forfeiture order on Crown application. P
279.01(1)(b) Trafficking in persons, other	Indictable	14 yrs Min: 4 yrs	×	×	×	×	✓	×	✓	×	×	×	S. 109 mandatory firearms prohibition. S. 491 mandatory weapon forfeiture. S. 462.37 proceeds of crime forfeiture order on Crown application. P
279.011(1)(a) Trafficking in persons under age of 18 years, kidnapping etc.	Indictable	Life Min: 6 yrs	×	×	×	×	✓	×	✓	×	×	×	S. 109 mandatory firearms prohibition. S. 491 mandatory weapon forfeiture. S. 462.37 proceeds of crime forfeiture order on Crown application. S. 161 discretionary order if the complainant is under age 16. PC
279.011(1)(b) Trafficking in persons under age of 18 years	Indictable	Life Min: 5 yrs	×	×	×	×	✓	×	✓	×	×	×	S. 109 mandatory firearms prohibition. S. 491 mandatory weapon forfeiture. S. 462.37 proceeds of crime forfeiture order on Crown application. S. 161 discretionary order if the complainant is under age 16. PC
279.02(1) Material benefit, trafficking	Indictable	10 yrs	✓	✓	✓	✓	✓	✓	✓	✓	✓	×	S. 109 mandatory firearms prohibition. S. 491 mandatory weapon forfeiture. S. 462.37 proceeds of crime forfeiture order on Crown application. P
279.02(2) Material benefit, trafficking of person under 18 yrs	Indictable	14 yrs Min: 2 yrs	×	×	×	×	✓	×	✓	×	×	×	S. 109 mandatory firearms prohibition. S. 491 mandatory weapon forfeiture. S. 462.37 proceeds of crime forfeiture order on Crown application. S. 161 discretionary order if the complainant is under age 16. PC
279.03(1) Withholding or destroying documents, trafficking	Indictable	5 yrs	✓	✓	✓	✓	✓	✓	✓	✓	✓	✓	P

* $100,000 for organizations for summary conviction offence s. 735.
*** conditional sentence not available if offence involved use of a weapon.

✓ Sentence Option | × Illegal Sentence

P = Primary designated offence
S = Secondary designated offence
PC = Primary Compulsory
[see note on p. OG/2]

SECTION	TYPE	MAX/MIN SENTENCE	DISCHARGE s. 730	SUSPENDED SENTENCE s. 731(1)(a)	FINE ALONE s. 734	FINE & PROBATION s. 731(1)(b)	PRISON ss. 718.3, 787	PRISON & PROBATION s. 731(1)(b)	PRISON & FINE s. 734	INTERMITTENT s. 732	FINE, PROB. & INTERMIT s. 732	CONDITIONAL SENTENCE s. 742.1	COMMENTS (applicability depends on circumstances of case)
279.03(2) Withholding or destroying documents, trafficking of person under 18 yrs	Indictable	10 yrs Min: 1 yr	✗	✗	✗	✗	✓	✗	✓	✗	✗	✗	S. 462.37 proceeds of crime forfeiture order on Crown application. S. 161 discretionary order if the complainant is under age 16. PC
279.1(2)(a) Hostage taking, use restricted or prohibited firearm, or any firearm, in committing for criminal organization	Indictable	Life Minimum: 5 yrs-1st 7 yrs-2nd	✗	✗	✓	✗	✓	✗	✓	✗	✗	✗	S. 109 mandatory firearms order. S. 491 mandatory weapon forfeiture order. P
279.1(2)(a.1) Hostage taking, use of firearm (other)	Indictable	Life Min: 4 yrs	✗	✗	✓	✗	✓	✗	✓	✗	✗	✗	S. 109 mandatory firearms order. S. 491 mandatory weapon forfeiture order. P
279.1(2)(b) Hostage taking (other)	Indictable	Life	✗	✓	✓	✓	✓	✓	✓	✓	✓	✗	S. 109 mandatory firearms order. S. 491 mandatory weapon forfeiture order. P
280 Abduction of person under 16	Indictable	5 yrs	✓	✓	✓	✓	✓	✓	✓	✓	✓	✓	S. 109 mandatory firearms order. S. 161 discretionary order. S
281 Abduction of person under 14	Indictable	10 yrs	✓	✓	✓	✓	✓	✓	✓	✓	✓	✗	S. 109 mandatory firearms order. S. 161 discretionary order. S
282 Abduction contravening custody order	Hyb-Ind.	10 yrs	✓	✓	✓	✓	✓	✓	✓	✓	✓	✓	Indictable, s. 109 mandatory firearms order; summary conviction, s. 110 discretionary firearms order. S. 491 mandatory weapon forfeiture order. S if by indictment
	Hyb-Sum.	6 mth/ 5000*	✓	✓	✓	✓	✓	✓	✓	✓	✓	✓	
283 Abduction where no custody order	Hyb-Ind.	10 yrs	✓	✓	✓	✓	✓	✓	✓	✓	✓	✓	Indictable, s. 109 mandatory firearms order; summary conviction, s. 110 discretionary firearms order. S. 491 mandatory weapon forfeiture order. Needs consent of A.G. or counsel (s. 283(2)). S if by indictment
	Hyb-Sum.	6 mth/ 5000*	✓	✓	✓	✓	✓	✓	✓	✓	✓	✓	

*** $100,000 for organizations for summary conviction offence s. 735.**
***** conditional sentence not available if offence involved use of a weapon.**

✓ Sentence Option ✗ Illegal Sentence

P = Primary designated offence
S = Secondary designated offence
PC = Primary Compulsory
[see note on p. OG/2]

GRID

SECTION	TYPE	MAX/MIN SENTENCE	DISCHARGE s. 730	SUSPENDED SENTENCE s. 731(1)(a)	FINE ALONE s. 734	FINE & PROBATION s. 731(1)(b)	PRISON ss. 718.3, 787	PRISON & PROBATION s. 731(1)(b)	PRISON & FINE s. 734	INTERMITTENT s. 732	FINE, PROB. & INTERMIT s. 732	CONDITIONAL SENTENCE s. 742.1	COMMENTS (applicability depends on circumstances of case)
286.1(1) Obtaining sexual services for consideration	Hyb-Ind.	5 yrs/min fines depending on circumstances	×	×	✓	✓	✓	✓	✓	✓	✓	✓	Indictable, s. 109 mandatory firearms order; summary conviction, s. 110 discretionary firearms order. S. 491 mandatory weapon forfeiture order. Indictable, s. 462.37 proceeds of crime forfeiture order on Crown application. S
	Hyb-Sum.	18 mth/min fines depending on circumstances	×	×	✓	✓	✓	✓	✓	✓	✓	✓	
286.1(2) Obtaining sexual services for consideration from person under 18 yrs	Indictable	10 yrs Min: 6 mths for first offence, 1 yr for second offence and subsequent offences	×	×	×	×	✓	✓	✓	×	×	×	S. 109 mandatory firearms prohibition. S. 491 mandatory weapon forfeiture order. S. 462.37 proceeds of crime forfeiture order on Crown application. S. 161 discretionary order if the complainant is under age 16. PC
286.2(1) Material benefit from sexual services	Indictable	10 yrs	✓	✓	✓	✓	✓	✓	✓	✓	✓	✓	S. 109 mandatory firearms prohibition. S. 491 mandatory weapon forfeiture order. S. 462.37 proceeds of crime forfeiture order on Crown application. P
286.2(2) Material benefit from sexual services provided by person under 18 yrs	Indictable	14 yrs Min: 2 yrs	×	×	×	×	✓	×	✓	×	×	×	S. 109 mandatory firearms prohibition. S. 491 mandatory weapon forfeiture order. S. 462.37 proceeds of crime forfeiture order on Crown application. S. 161 discretionary order if the complainant is under age 16. PC
286.3(1) Procuring	Indictable	14 yrs	×	✓	✓	✓	✓	✓	✓	✓	✓	×	S. 109 mandatory firearms prohibition. S. 491 mandatory weapon forfeiture order. S. 462.37 proceeds of crime forfeiture order on Crown application. S. 161 discretionary order. P
286.3(2) Procuring, person under 18 yrs	Indictable	14 yrs Min: 5 yrs	×	×	×	×	✓	×	✓	×	×	×	S. 109 mandatory firearms prohibition. S. 491 mandatory weapon forfeiture order. S. 462.37 proceeds of crime forfeiture order on Crown application. S. 161 discretionary order if the complainant is under age 16. PC

✓ Sentence Option   × Illegal Sentence

* $100,000 for organizations for summary conviction offence s. 735.
*** conditional sentence not available if offence involved use of a weapon.

P = Primary designated offence
S = Secondary designated offence
PC = Primary Compulsory
[see note on p. OG/2]

SECTION	TYPE	MAX/MIN SENTENCE	DISCHARGE s. 730	SUSPENDED SENTENCE s. 731(1)(a)	FINE ALONE s. 734	FINE & PROBATION s. 731(1)(b)	PRISON ss. 718.3, 787	PRISON & PROBATION s. 731(1)(b)	PRISON & FINE s. 734	INTERMITTENT s. 732	FINE, PROB. & INTERMIT s. 732	CONDITIONAL SENTENCE s. 742.1	COMMENTS (applicability depends on circumstances of case)
286.4 Advertising sexual services	Hyb-Ind.	5 yrs	✓	✓	✓	✓	✓	✓	✓	✓	✓	✓	S if by indictment
	Hyb-Sum.	18 mths	✓	✓	✓	✓	✓	✓	✓	✓	✓	✓	
300 Defamatory libel known to be false	Indictable	5 yrs	✓	✓	✓	✓	✓	✓	✓	✓	✓	✓	S
318 Advocating genocide	Indictable	5 yrs	✓	✓	✓	✓	✓	✓	✓	✓	✓	✓	Attorney General's consent required. S
319(1), (2) Incite or promote hatred	Hyb-Ind.	2 yrs	✓	✓	✓	✓	✓	✓	✓	✓	✓	✓	Attorney General's consent required for s. 319(2) offence.
	Hyb-Sum.	6 mth/ 5000*	✓	✓	✓	✓	✓	✓	✓	✓	✓	✓	
320.13(1) Dangerous operation	Hyb-Ind.	10 yrs	✓	✓	✓	✓	✓	✓	✓	✓	✓	✓	Penalty in s. 320.19(5); Discretionary prohibition order under s. 320.24(4) and (5)(b) for a period of not more than 10 yrs + period of imprisonment. S
	Hyb-Sum.	2 yrs less 1 day	✓	✓	✓	✓	✓	✓	✓	✓	✓	✓	Penalty in s. 320.19(5); Discretionary prohibition order under s. 320.24(4) and (5)(c) for a period of not more than 3 yrs + period of imprisonment.
320.13(2) Dangerous operation causing bodily harm	Hyb-Ind.	14 yrs max. Minimums: 1000 fine-1st; 30 days-2nd; 120 days-3rd and subsequent	×	×	†	†	✓†	†	✓	†	†	×	Penalty in s. 320.2 † Fine alone or fine and probation not possible for 2nd and subsequent offences; intermittent sentence not possible for 3rd and subsequent. S. 109 mandatory firearms order S
	Hyb-Sum.	2 yrs less 1 day max. Minimums: 1000 fine-1st; 30 days-2nd; 120 days-3rd and subsequent	×	×	†	†	†	†	✓	†	†	✓	Penalty in s. 320.2
320.13(3) Dangerous operation causing death	Indictable	Life max.; Minimums: 1000 fine-1st; 30 days-2nd; 120 days-3rd and subsequent	×	×	†	†	†	†	✓	†	†	×	Penalty in s. 320.21 Discretionary prohibition order under s. 320.24(4) and (5)(a) for any duration + period of imprisonment. S. 109 mandatory firearms order S † Fine alone or fine and probation not possible for 2nd and subsequent offences; intermittent sentence not possible for 3rd and subsequent.

GRID

*** $100,000 for organizations for summary conviction offence s. 735.**
***** conditional sentence not available if offence involved use of a weapon.**

✓ Sentence Option | × Illegal Sentence

P = Primary designated offence
S = Secondary designated offence
PC = Primary Compulsory
[see note on p. OG/2]

SECTION	TYPE	MAX/MIN SENTENCE	DISCHARGE s. 730	SUSPENDED SENTENCE s. 731(1)(a)	FINE ALONE s. 734	FINE & PROBATION s. 731(1)(b)	PRISON ss. 718.3, 787	PRISON & PROBATION s. 731(1)(b)	PRISON & FINE s. 734	INTERMITTENT s. 732	FINE, PROB. & INTERMIT s. 732	CONDITIONAL SENTENCE s. 742.1	COMMENTS (applicability depends on circumstances of case)
320.14(1) Operation while impaired	Hyb-Ind.	10 yrs max. Minimums (without high BACor delayed senten-cing): 1000 fine-1st; 30 days-2nd; 120 days-3rd and subsequent	×	×	† **	†	†	†	✓	†	†	††	Penalties in s. 320.19(1) and 320.19(3); Sentencing may be delayed for treatment pursuant to s. 320.23(1), with a prohibition before sentencing (s. 320.24(6) to (9)). If treatment completed, minimums do not apply but discharge still not available (s. 320.23(2)). Mandatory prohibition order unless treatment completed (ss. 320.24 and 320.23(2)) for periods of: 1-3 yrs + imprisonment period-1st; 2-10 yrs + imprisonment period-2nd Not less than 3 yrs + imprisonment period-3rd and subsequent. † Fine alone or fine and probation not possible for 2nd and subsequent offences; intermittent sentence not possible for 3rd and subsequent. †† Conditional sentence not possible for 2nd and subsequent offences. ** Minimum fines higher for convictions under s. 320.14(1)(b) if high blood alcohol concentration: min $1,500 if at or over 120mg/100ml of blood but less than 160mg (s. 320.19(3)(a)); $2,000 if at or over 160mg/100ml of blood (s. 320.19(3)(b)). S
	Hyb-Sum.	2 yrs less 1 day max. Minimums: 1000 fine-1st; 30 days-2nd; 120 days-3rd and subsequent	×	×	✓† **	†	†	†	✓	†	†	††	Penalties in s. 320.19(1) and 320.19(3); Sentencing may be delayed for treatment pursuant to s. 320.23(1), with a prohibition before sentencing (s. 320.24(6) to (9)). If treatment completed, minimums do not apply but discharge still not available (s. 320.23(2)). Mandatory prohibition order unless treatment completed (ss. 320.24 and 320.23(2)) for periods of: 1-3 yrs + imprisonment period-1st; 2-10 yrs + imprisonment period-2nd; Not less than 3 yrs + imprisonment period-3rd and subsequent. † Fine alone or fine and probation not possible for 2nd and subsequent offences; intermittent sentence not possible for 3rd and subsequent. †† Conditional sentence not possible for 2nd and subsequent offences. ** Minimum fines higher for convictions under s. 320.14(1)(b) if high blood alcohol concentration: min $1,500 if at or over 120mg/100ml of blood but less than 160mg (s. 320.19(3)(a)); $2,000 if at or over 160mg/100ml of blood (s. 320.19(3)(b)).

*** $100,000 for organizations for summary conviction offence s. 735.**
***** conditional sentence not available if offence involved use of a weapon.**

✓ Sentence Option **× Illegal Sentence**

P = Primary designated offence
S = Secondary designated offence
PC = Primary Compulsory
[see note on p. OG/2]

SECTION	TYPE	MAX/MIN SENTENCE	DISCHARGE s. 730	SUSPENDED SENTENCE s. 731(1)(a)	FINE ALONE s. 734	FINE & PROBATION s. 731(1)(b)	PRISON ss. 718.3, 787	PRISON & PROBATION s. 731(1)(b)	PRISON & FINE s. 734	INTERMITTENT s. 732	FINE, PROB. & INTERMIT s. 732	CONDITIONAL SENTENCE s. 742.1	COMMENTS (applicability depends on circumstances of case)
320.14(2) Operation while impaired causing bodily harm	Hyb-Ind.	14 yrs max. Minimums: 1000 fine-1st; 30 days-2nd; 120 days-3rd and subsequent	×	×	†	†	†	†	✓	†	†	×	Penalty in s. 320.2; Discretionary prohibition order under s. 320.24(4) and (5)(b) of not more than 10 yrs + period of imprisonment. † Fine alone or fine and probation not possible for 2nd and subsequent offences; intermittent sentence not possible for 3rd and subsequent. Discretionary prohibition order under s. 320.24(4) and (5)(a) for any duration + period of imprisonment. S. 109 mandatory firearms order. S
	Hyb-Sum.	2 yrs less 1 day max. Minimums: 1000 fine-1st; 30 days-2nd; 120 days-3rd and subsequent	×	×	†	†	†	†	✓	†	†	††	Penalty in s. 320.2; Discretionary prohibition order under s. 320.24(4) and (5)(c) of not more than 3 yrs + period of imprisonment. † Fine alone or fine and probation not possible for 2nd and subsequent offences; intermittent sentence not possible for 3rd and subsequent. †† Conditional sentence not possible for 2nd and subsequent offences.
320.14(3) Operation while impaired causing death	Indictable	Life max.; Minimums: 1000 fine-1st; 30 days-2nd; 120 days-3rd and subsequent	×	×	†	†	†	†	✓	†	†	×	Penalty in s. 320.21; Discretionary prohibition order under s. 320.24(4) and (5)(a) for any duration + period of imprisonment. † Fine alone or fine and probation not possible for 2nd and subsequent offences; intermittent sentence not possible for 3rd and subsequent. S. 109 mandatory firearms order. S
320.14(4) Operation - low blood drug concentration	Summary	1000 fine	✓	✓	✓	✓	×	×	×	×	×	×	Penalty in s. 320.19(2). Discretionary prohibition order of not more than 1 year (s. 320.24(3)).

* $100,000 for organizations for summary conviction offence s. 735.
*** conditional sentence not available if offence involved use of a weapon.

✓ Sentence Option × Illegal Sentence

P = Primary designated offence
S = Secondary designated offence
PC = Primary Compulsory
[see note on p. OG/2]

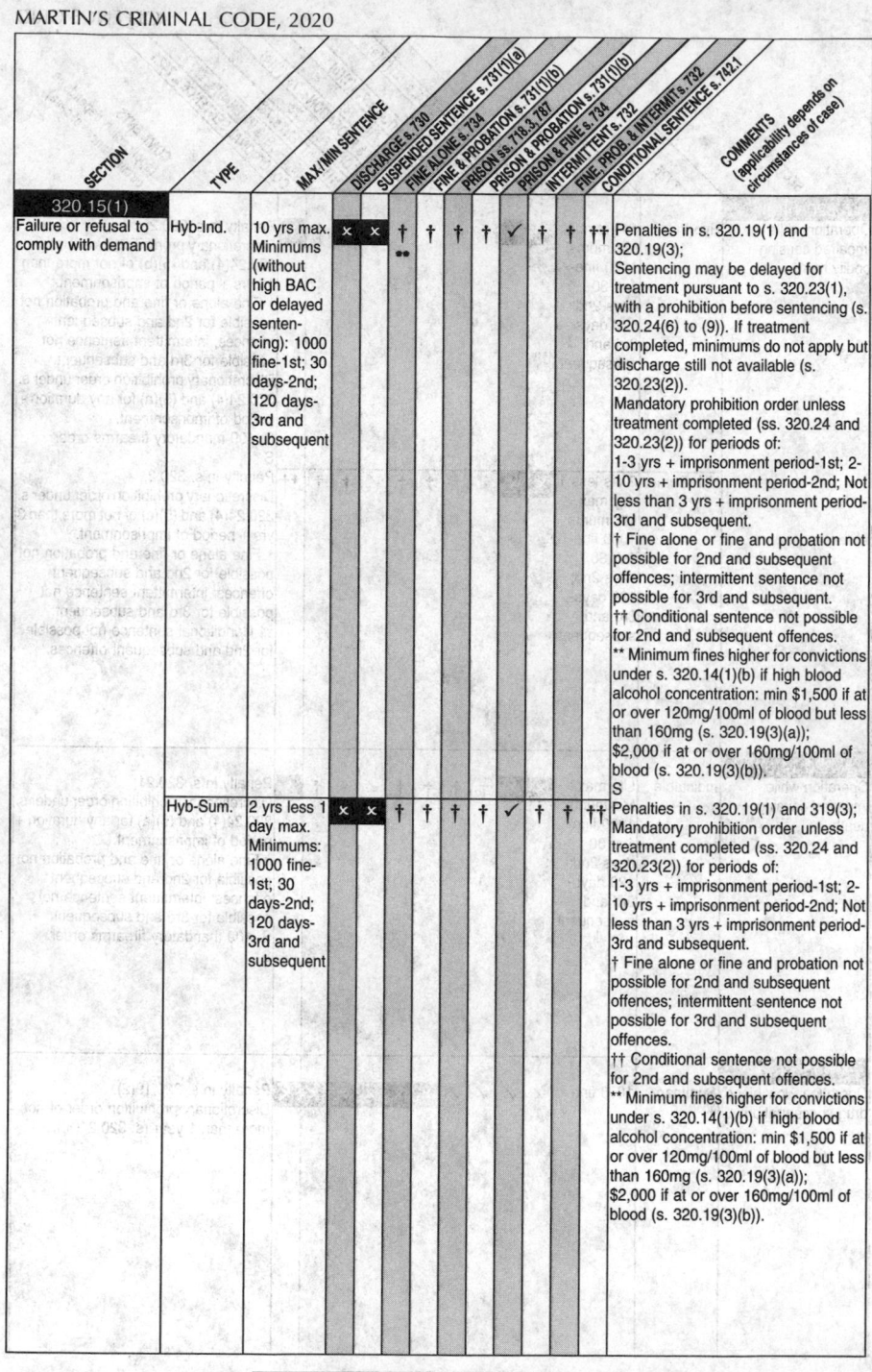

SECTION	TYPE	MAX/MIN SENTENCE	DISCHARGE s. 730	SUSPENDED SENTENCE s. 731(1)(a)	FINE ALONE s. 734	FINE & PROBATION s. 731(1)(b)	PRISON ss. 718.3, 787	PRISON & PROBATION s. 731(1)(b)	PRISON & FINE s. 734	INTERMITTENT s. 732	FINE, PROB. & INTERMIT s. 732	CONDITIONAL SENTENCE s. 742.1	COMMENTS (applicability depends on circumstances of case)
320.15(1) Failure or refusal to comply with demand	Hyb-Ind.	10 yrs max. Minimums (without high BAC or delayed sentencing): 1000 fine-1st; 30 days-2nd; 120 days-3rd and subsequent	×	×	† **	†	†	†	✓	†	†	††	Penalties in s. 320.19(1) and 320.19(3); Sentencing may be delayed for treatment pursuant to s. 320.23(1), with a prohibition before sentencing (s. 320.24(6) to (9)). If treatment completed, minimums do not apply but discharge still not available (s. 320.23(2)). Mandatory prohibition order unless treatment completed (ss. 320.24 and 320.23(2)) for periods of: 1-3 yrs + imprisonment period-1st; 2-10 yrs + imprisonment period-2nd; Not less than 3 yrs + imprisonment period-3rd and subsequent. † Fine alone or fine and probation not possible for 2nd and subsequent offences; intermittent sentence not possible for 3rd and subsequent. †† Conditional sentence not possible for 2nd and subsequent offences. ** Minimum fines higher for convictions under s. 320.14(1)(b) if high blood alcohol concentration: min $1,500 if at or over 120mg/100ml of blood but less than 160mg (s. 320.19(3)(a)); $2,000 if at or over 160mg/100ml of blood (s. 320.19(3)(b)). S
	Hyb-Sum.	2 yrs less 1 day max. Minimums: 1000 fine-1st; 30 days-2nd; 120 days-3rd and subsequent	×	×	†	†	†	†	✓	†	†	††	Penalties in s. 320.19(1) and 319(3); Mandatory prohibition order unless treatment completed (ss. 320.24 and 320.23(2)) for periods of: 1-3 yrs + imprisonment period-1st; 2-10 yrs + imprisonment period-2nd; Not less than 3 yrs + imprisonment period-3rd and subsequent. † Fine alone or fine and probation not possible for 2nd and subsequent offences; intermittent sentence not possible for 3rd and subsequent offences. †† Conditional sentence not possible for 2nd and subsequent offences. ** Minimum fines higher for convictions under s. 320.14(1)(b) if high blood alcohol concentration: min $1,500 if at or over 120mg/100ml of blood but less than 160mg (s. 320.19(3)(a)); $2,000 if at or over 160mg/100ml of blood (s. 320.19(3)(b)).

*** $100,000 for organizations for summary conviction offence s. 735.**
***** conditional sentence not available if offence involved use of a weapon.**

✓ Sentence Option ☒ Illegal Sentence

P = Primary designated offence
S = Secondary designated offence
PC = Primary Compulsory
[see note on p. OG/2]

SECTION	TYPE	MAX/MIN SENTENCE	DISCHARGE s. 730	SUSPENDED SENTENCE s. 731(1)(a)	FINE ALONE s. 734	FINE & PROBATION s. 731(1)(b)	PRISON ss. 718.3, 787	PRISON & PROBATION s. 731(1)(b)	PRISON & FINE s. 734	INTERMITTENT s. 732	FINE, PROB. & INTERMIT s. 732	CONDITIONAL SENTENCE s. 742.1	COMMENTS (applicability depends on circumstances of case)
320.15(2) Failure or refusal to comply with demand after accident resulting in bodily harm	Hyb-Ind.	14 yrs max. Minimums: 1000 fine-1st; 30 days-2nd; 120 days-3rd and subsequent	×	×	†	†	†	†	✓	†	†	×	Penalty in s. 320.2; Discretionary prohibition order under s. 320.24(4) and (5)(b) of not more than 10 yrs + period of imprisonment. † Fine alone or fine and probation not possible for 2nd and subsequent offences; intermittent sentence not possible for 3rd and subsequent offences. S. 109 mandatory firearms order. S
	Hyb-Sum.	2 yrs less 1 day max. Minimums: 1000 fine-1st; 30 days-2nd; 120 days-3rd and subsequent	×	×	†	†	†	†	✓	†	†	††	Penalty in s. 320.2; Discretionary prohibition order under s. 320.24(4) and (5)(c) of not more than 3 yrs + period of imprisonment. † Fine alone or fine and probation not possible for 2nd and subsequent offences; intermittent sentence not possible for 3rd and subsequent offences. †† Conditional sentence not possible for 2nd and subsequent offences.
320.15(3) Failure or refusal to comply with demand after accident resulting in death	Indictable	Life max.; Minimums: 1000 fine-1st; 30 days-2nd; 120 days-3rd and subsequent	×	×	†	†		†	✓	†	†	×	Penalty in s. 320.21; Discretionary prohibition order under s. 320.24(4) and (5)(a) for any duration + period of imprisonment. † Fine alone or fine and probation not possible for 2nd and subsequent offences; intermittent sentence not possible for 3rd and subsequent. S. 109 mandatory firearms order. S
320.16(1) Failure to stop after accident	Hyb-Ind.	10 yrs	✓	✓	✓	✓	✓	✓	✓	✓	✓	✓	Penalty in s. 320.19(5); Discretionary prohibition order under s. 320.24(4) and (5)(b) of not more than 10 yrs + period of imprisonment. S
	Hyb-Sum.	2 yrs less 1 day	✓	✓	✓	✓	✓	✓	✓	✓	✓	✓	Penalty in s. 320.19(5); Discretionary prohibition order under s. 320.24(4) and (5)(c) of not more than 3 yrs + period of imprisonment. S

*** $100,000 for organizations for summary conviction offence s. 735.**
***** conditional sentence not available if offence involved use of a weapon.**

✓ Sentence Option   × Illegal Sentence

P = Primary designated offence
S = Secondary designated offence
PC = Primary Compulsory
[see note on p. OG/2]

GRID

SECTION	TYPE	MAX/MIN SENTENCE	DISCHARGE s. 730	SUSPENDED SENTENCE s. 731(1)(a)	FINE ALONE s. 734	FINE & PROBATION s. 731(1)(b)	PRISON ss. 718.3, 787	PRISON & PROBATION s. 731(1)(b)	PRISON & FINE s. 734	INTERMITTENT s. 732	FINE, PROB. & INTERMIT s. 732	CONDITIONAL SENTENCE s. 742.1	COMMENTS (applicability depends on circumstances of case)
320.16(2) Failure to stop after accident resulting in bodily harm	Hyb-Ind.	14 yrs max. Minimums: 1000 fine-1st; 30 days-2nd; 120 days-3rd and subsequent	×	×	†	†	†	†	✓	†	†	×	Penalty in s. 320.2; Discretionary prohibition order under s. 320.24(4) and (5)(b) of not more than 10 yrs + period of imprisonment. * Fine alone or fine and probation not possible for 2nd and subsequent offences; intermittent sentence not possible for 3rd and subsequent. S. 109 mandatory firearms order. S
	Hyb-Sum.	2 yrs less 1 day max. Minimums: 1000 fine-1st; 30 days-2nd; 120 days-3rd and subsequent	×	×	†	†	†	†	✓	†	†	††	Penalty in s. 320.2; Discretionary prohibition order under s. 320.24(4) and (5)(c) of not more than 3 yrs + period of imprisonment. † Fine alone or fine and probation not possible for 2nd and subsequent offences; intermittent sentence not possible for 3rd and subsequent offences. †† Conditional sentence not possible for 2nd and subsequent offences.
320.16(3) Failure to stop after accident resulting in death	Indictable	Life max.; Minimums: 1000 fine-1st; 30 days-2nd; 120 days-3rd and subsequent	×	×	†	†	†	†	✓	†	†	×	Penalty in s. 320.21; Discretionary prohibition order under s. 320.24(4) and (5)(a) for any duration + period of imprisonment. † Fine alone or fine and probation not possible for 2nd and subsequent offences; intermittent sentence not possible for 3rd and subsequent. S. 109 mandatory firearms order. S
320.17 Flight from peace officer	Hyb-Ind.	10 yrs	✓	✓	✓	✓	✓	✓	✓	✓	✓	✓	Penalty in s. 320.19(5); Discretionary prohibition order under s. 320.24(4) and (5)(b) of not more than 10 yrs + period of imprisonment. S
	Hyb-Sum.	2 yrs less 1 day max.	✓	✓	✓	✓	✓	✓	✓	✓	✓	✓	Penalty in s. 320.19(5); Discretionary prohibition order under s. 320.24(4) and (5)(c) of not more than 3 yrs + period of imprisonment.
320.18(1) Operation while prohibited	Hyb-Ind.	10 yrs	✓	✓	✓	✓	✓	✓	✓	✓	✓	✓	Penalty in s. 320.19(5); Discretionary prohibition order under s. 320.24(4) and (5)(b) of not more than 10 yrs + period of imprisonment. S
	Hyb-Sum.	2 yrs less 1 day max.	✓	✓	✓	✓	✓	✓	✓	✓	✓	✓	Penalty in s. 320.19(5); Discretionary prohibition order under s. 320.24(4) and (5)(c) of not more than 3 yrs + period of imprisonment.
322-332, 334(a) Theft over $5,000	Indictable	10 yrs	✓	✓	✓	✓	✓	✓	✓	✓	✓	×	S. 462.37 proceeds of crime forfeiture order on Crown application. S except s. 372(1)(a)

*** $100,000 for organizations for summary conviction offence s. 735.**
***** conditional sentence not available if offence involved use of a weapon.**

✓ Sentence Option × Illegal Sentence

P = Primary designated offence
S = Secondary designated offence
PC = Primary Compulsory
[see note on p. OG/2]

SECTION	TYPE	MAX/MIN SENTENCE	DISCHARGE s. 730	SUSPENDED SENTENCE s. 731(1)(a)	FINE ALONE s. 734	FINE & PROBATION s. 731(1)(b)	PRISON ss. 718.3, 787	PRISON & PROBATION s. 731(1)(b)	PRISON & FINE s. 734	INTERMITTENT s. 732	FINE, PROB. & INTERMIT s. 732	CONDITIONAL SENTENCE s. 742.1	COMMENTS (applicability depends on circumstances of case)
322-332, 334(b) Theft $5,000 or less	Hyb-Ind. **Absolute PCJ**	2 yrs	✓	✓	✓	✓	✓	✓	✓	✓	✓	✓	S. 462.37 proceeds of crime forfeiture order on Crown application.
	Hyb-Sum.	6 mth/ 5000*	✓	✓	✓	✓	✓	✓	✓	✓	✓	✓	
333.1 Motor vehicle theft	Hyb-Ind.	10 yrs max	✓	✓	✓	✓	✓	✓	✓	✓	✓	×	
		6 mth min on 3rd offence	×	×	×	×	✓	✓	✓	×	×	×	S if by indictment
	Hyb-Sum.	18 mth/ 5000*	✓	✓	✓	✓	✓	✓	✓	✓	✓	✓	
335 Take motor vehicle without consent	Summary	6 mth/ 5000*	✓	✓	✓	✓	✓	✓	✓	✓	✓	✓	
336 Criminal breach of trust	Indictable	14 yrs	×	✓	✓	✓	✓	✓	✓	✓	✓	×	S
338(1) Fraudulently take cattle or deface brand, etc.	Indictable	5 yrs	✓	✓	✓	✓	✓	✓	✓	✓	✓	✓	S
338(2) Cattle theft	Indictable	10 yrs	✓	✓	✓	✓	✓	✓	✓	✓	✓	✓	S
339(1) Take poss'n of drift timber, etc.	Indictable	5 yrs	✓	✓	✓	✓	✓	✓	✓	✓	✓	✓	S
339(2) Dealer in second hand goods	Summary	6 mth/ 5000*	✓	✓	✓	✓	✓	✓	✓	✓	✓	✓	
342 Theft or forgery of credit card	Hyb-Ind.	10 yrs	✓	✓	✓	✓	✓	✓	✓	✓	✓	✓	S if by indictment
	Hyb-Sum.	6 mth/ 5000*	✓	✓	✓	✓	✓	✓	✓	✓	✓	✓	
342.1 Unauthorized use of computer	Hyb-Ind.	10 yrs	✓	✓	✓	✓	✓	✓	✓	✓	✓	✓	S if by indictment
	Hyb-Sum.	6 mth/ 5000*	✓	✓	✓	✓	✓	✓	✓	✓	✓	✓	
342.2 Unlawful possession of device for committing s. 342.1 offence	Hyb-Ind.	2 yrs	✓	✓	✓	✓	✓	✓	✓	✓	✓	✓	Court may also make forfeiture order.
	Hyb-Sum.	6 mth/ 5000*	✓	✓	✓	✓	✓	✓	✓	✓	✓	✓	
343, 344(1)(a) Robbery, use of restricted or prohibited firearm, or any firearm, in committing for criminal organization	Indictable	Life Minimum: 5 yrs-1st 7 yrs-2nd	×	×	×	×	✓	×	✓	×	×	×	S. 109 mandatory firearms order. S. 491 mandatory weapon forfeiture order. S. 462.37 proceeds of crime forfeiture order on Crown application. PC Aggravating circumstance, s. 348.1.

*** $100,000 for organizations for summary conviction offence s. 735.**
***** conditional sentence not available if offence involved use of a weapon.**

✓ Sentence Option | × Illegal Sentence

P = Primary designated offence
S = Secondary designated offence
PC = Primary Compulsory
[see note on p. OG/2]

GRID

SECTION	TYPE	MAX/MIN SENTENCE	DISCHARGE s. 730	SUSPENDED SENTENCE s. 731(1)(a)	FINE ALONE s. 734	FINE & PROBATION s. 731(1)(b)	PRISON ss. 718.3, 787	PRISON & PROBATION s. 731(1)(b)	PRISON & FINE s. 734	INTERMITTENT s. 732	FINE, PROB. & INTERMIT s. 732	CONDITIONAL SENTENCE s. 742.1	COMMENTS (applicability depends on circumstances of case)
343, 344(1)(a.1) Robbery, use of firearm (other)	Indictable	Life Min: 4 yrs	×	×	×	×	✓	×	✓	×	×	×	S. 109 mandatory firearms order. S. 491 mandatory weapon forfeiture order. S. 462.37 proceeds of crime forfeiture order on Crown application. PC Aggravating circumstance, s. 348.1.
343, 344(1)(b) Robbery (other)	Indictable	Life	×	✓	✓	✓	✓	✓	✓	✓	✓	×	S. 109 mandatory firearms order. S. 491 mandatory weapon forfeiture order. S. 462.37 proceeds of crime forfeiture order on Crown application. PC Aggravating circumstance, s. 348.1.
345 Stop mail with intent	Indictable	Life	×	✓	✓	✓	✓	✓	✓	✓	✓	×	S. 109 mandatory firearms order. S. 491 mandatory weapon forfeiture order. S
346(1),(1.1)(a) Extortion, use of restricted or prohibited firearm, or any firearm, in committing for criminal organization	Indictable	Life Minimum: 5 yrs-1st 7 yrs-2nd	×	×	×	×	✓	×	✓	×	×	×	S. 109 mandatory firearms order. S. 491 mandatory weapon forfeiture order. S. 462.37 proceeds of crime forfeiture order on Crown application. Aggravating circumstance, s. 348.1. PC
346(1),(1.1)(a.1) Extortion, use of firearm (other)	Indictable	Life Min: 4 yrs	×	×	×	×	✓	×	✓	×	×	×	S. 109 mandatory firearms order. S. 491 mandatory weapon forfeiture order. S. 462.37 proceeds of crime forfeiture order on Crown application. Aggravating circumstance, s. 348.1. PC
346(1),(1.1)(b) Extortion (other)	Indictable	Life	×	✓	✓	✓	✓	✓	✓	✓	✓	×	S. 109 mandatory firearms order. S. 491 mandatory weapon forfeiture order. S. 462.37 proceeds of crime forfeiture order on Crown application. Aggravating circumstance, s. 348.1. PC
347 Criminal interest rate	Hyb-Ind.	5 yrs	✓	✓	✓	✓	✓	✓	✓	✓	✓	✓	Attorney General's consent required. S. 462.37 proceeds of crime forfeiture order on Crown application. S if by indictment
	Hyb-Sum.	6 mth/ 25,000	✓	✓	✓	✓	✓	✓	✓	✓	✓	✓	

*** $100,000 for organizations for summary conviction offence s. 735.**
***** conditional sentence not available if offence involved use of a weapon.**

✓ Sentence Option **× Illegal Sentence**

P = Primary designated offence
S = Secondary designated offence
PC = Primary Compulsory
[see note on p. OG/2]

SECTION	TYPE	MAX/MIN SENTENCE	DISCHARGE s. 730	SUSPENDED SENTENCE s. 731(1)(a)	FINE ALONE s. 734	FINE & PROBATION s. 731(1)(b)	PRISON ss. 718.3, 787	PRISON & PROBATION s. 731(1)(b)	PRISON & FINE s. 734	INTERMITTENT s. 732	FINE, PROB. & INTERMIT s. 732	CONDITIONAL SENTENCE s. 742.1	COMMENTS (applicability depends on circumstances of case)
348(1)(d) Break & enter with intent, committing indictable offence re: dwelling house	Indictable	Life	×	✓	✓	✓	✓	✓	✓	✓	✓	×	S. 109 mandatory firearms order. S. 491 mandatory weapon forfeiture order. Aggravating circumstance, s. 348.1. P
348(1)(e) Break & enter with intent, committing indictable offence re: non-dwelling house	Hyb-Ind.	10 yrs	✓	✓	✓	✓	✓	✓	✓	✓	✓	×	S Aggravating circumstance, s. 348.1.
	Hyb-Sum.	6 mth/5000	✓	✓	✓	✓	✓	✓	✓	✓	✓	✓	
349 Being unlawfully in dwelling house	Hyb-Ind.	10 yrs	✓	✓	✓	✓	✓	✓	✓	✓	✓	×	Discretionary s. 109 mandatory firearms order. S. 491 mandatory weapon forfeiture order. S
	Hyb-Sum.	6 mth/ 5000*	✓	✓	✓	✓	✓	✓	✓	✓	✓	✓	
351(1) Housebreaking instruments poss'n	Hyb-Ind.	10 yrs	✓	✓	✓	✓	✓	✓	✓	✓	✓	✓	S if by indictment
	Hyb-Sum.	6 mth/ 5000*	✓	✓	✓	✓	✓	✓	✓	✓	✓	✓	
351(2) Disguise with intent	Indictable	10 yrs	✓	✓	✓	✓	✓	✓	✓	✓	✓	✓	S
352 Poss'n, instruments for breaking into coin operated devices, etc.	Indictable	2 yrs	✓	✓	✓	✓	✓	✓	✓	✓	✓	✓	
353 Selling etc. automobile master key	Indictable	2 yrs	✓	✓	✓	✓	✓	✓	✓	✓	✓	✓	
354, 355(a) Poss'n of property over $5,000 obtained by crime	Indictable	10 yrs	✓	✓	✓	✓	✓	✓	✓	✓	✓	✓	S. 462.37 proceeds of crime forfeiture order on Crown application. S
354, 355(b) Poss'n of property under $5,000 obtained by crime	Hyb-Ind. **Absolute PCJ**	2 yrs	✓	✓	✓	✓	✓	✓	✓	✓	✓	✓	S. 462.37 proceeds of crime forfeiture order on Crown application.
	Hyb-Sum.	6 mth/ 5000*	✓	✓	✓	✓	✓	✓	✓	✓	✓	✓	
356 Theft from mail	Indictable	10 yrs	✓	✓	✓	✓	✓	✓	✓	✓	✓	✓	S
357 Bring into Canada property obtained by crime	Indictable	10 yrs	✓	✓	✓	✓	✓	✓	✓	✓	✓	✓	S
362(2)(a) False pretence, property over $5,000	Indictable	10 yrs	✓	✓	✓	✓	✓	✓	✓	✓	✓	✓	S

*** $100,000 for organizations for summary conviction offence s. 735.**
***** conditional sentence not available if offence involved use of a weapon.**

✓ Sentence Option **× Illegal Sentence**

P = Primary designated offence
S = Secondary designated offence
PC = Primary Compulsory
[see note on p. OG/2]

GRID

SECTION	TYPE	MAX/MIN SENTENCE	DISCHARGE s. 730	SUSPENDED SENTENCE s. 731(1)(a)	FINE ALONE s. 734	FINE & PROBATION s. 731(1)(b)	PRISON ss. 718.3, 787	PRISON & PROBATION s. 731(1)(b)	PRISON & FINE s. 734	INTERMITTENT s. 732	FINE, PROB. & INTERMIT s. 732	CONDITIONAL SENTENCE s. 742.1	COMMENTS (applicability depends on circumstances of case)
362(2)(b) False pretence, property $5,000 or less	Hyb-Ind. **Absolute PCJ**	2 yrs	✓	✓	✓	✓	✓	✓	✓	✓	✓	✓	
	Hyb-Sum.	6 mth/ 5000*	✓	✓	✓	✓	✓	✓	✓	✓	✓	✓	
362(3) Obtain credit, etc. by false pretence	Indictable	10 yrs	✓	✓	✓	✓	✓	✓	✓	✓	✓	✓	S
363 Obtain execution of security by fraud	Indictable	5 yrs	✓	✓	✓	✓	✓	✓	✓	✓	✓	✓	S
364 Obtain food or lodging by fraud	Summary	6 mth/ 5000*	✓	✓	✓	✓	✓	✓	✓	✓	✓	✓	
366, 367 Forgery	Hyb-Ind.	10 yrs	✓	✓	✓	✓	✓	✓	✓	✓	✓	✓	S. 462.37 proceeds of crime forfeiture order on Crown application. S if by indictment
	Hyb-Sum.	6 mth/ 5000*	✓	✓	✓	✓	✓	✓	✓	✓	✓	✓	
368 Utter forged document	Hyb-Ind.	10 yrs	✓	✓	✓	✓	✓	✓	✓	✓	✓	✓	S. 462.37 proceeds of crime forfeiture order on Crown application. S if by indictment
	Hyb-Sum.	6 mth/ 5000*	✓	✓	✓	✓	✓	✓	✓	✓	✓	✓	
372(1) False Message	Indictable	2 yrs	✓	✓	✓	✓	✓	✓	✓	✓	✓	✓	S. 110 discretionary firearms order.
372(2) Indecent telephone calls	Summary	6 mth/ 5000*	✓	✓	✓	✓	✓	✓	✓	✓	✓	✓	S. 110 discretionary firearms order.
372(3) Harassing telephone calls	Summary	6 mth/ 5000*	✓	✓	✓	✓	✓	✓	✓	✓	✓	✓	S. 110 discretionary firearms order.
374 Draw document without authority	Indictable	14 yrs	×	✓	✓	✓	✓	✓	✓	✓	✓	×	S
375 Obtaining, etc., based on forged document	Indictable	14 yrs	×	✓	✓	✓	✓	✓	✓	✓	✓	×	S
380(1)(a) Fraud over $5,000 or re: testamentary instrument	Indictable	14 yrs/2 yrs if over $1million (s. 380(1.1))	×	✓	✓	✓	✓	✓	✓	✓	✓	×	S. 462.37 proceeds of crime forfeiture order on Crown application. Aggravating circumstance, s. 380.1. S
380(1)(b) Fraud, $5,000 or less	Hyb-Ind. **Absolute PCJ**	2 yrs	✓	✓	✓	✓	✓	✓	✓	✓	✓	✓	S. 462.37 proceeds of crime forfeiture order on Crown application. Aggravating circumstance, s. 380.1.
	Hyb-Sum.	6 mth/ 5000*	✓	✓	✓	✓	✓	✓	✓	✓	✓	✓	

*** $100,000 for organizations for summary conviction offence s. 735.**
***** conditional sentence not available if offence involved use of a weapon.**

✓ Sentence Option × Illegal Sentence

P = Primary designated offence
S = Secondary designated offence
PC = Primary Compulsory
[see note on p. OG/2]

SECTION	TYPE	MAX/MIN SENTENCE	DISCHARGE s. 730	SUSPENDED SENTENCE s. 731(1)(a)	FINE ALONE s. 734	FINE & PROBATION s. 731(1)(b)	PRISON ss. 718.3, 787	PRISON & PROBATION s. 731(1)(b)	PRISON & FINE s. 734	INTERMITTENT s. 732	FINE, PROB. & INTERMIT s. 732	CONDITIONAL SENTENCE s. 742.1	COMMENTS (applicability depends on circumstances of case)
381 Using mails to defraud	Indictable	2 yrs	✓	✓	✓	✓	✓	✓	✓	✓	✓	✓	
382 Manipulation of stock exchange	Indictable	10 yrs	✓	✓	✓	✓	✓	✓	✓	✓	✓	✓	S. 380.1 aggravating circumstances on sentence. S
382.1 Insider trading	Hyb-Ind.	5 yrs	✓	✓	✓	✓	✓	✓	✓	✓	✓	✓	S. 380.1 aggravating circumstances on sentence. S if by indictment
	Hyb-Sum.	6 mth/ 5000*	✓	✓	✓	✓	✓	✓	✓	✓	✓	✓	
393(1), (2) Fraud in relation to fares	Indictable **Absolute PCJ**	2 yrs	✓	✓	✓	✓	✓	✓	✓	✓	✓	✓	
393(3) Obtain transportation by fraud	Summary	6 mth/ 5000*	✓	✓	✓	✓	✓	✓	✓	✓	✓	✓	
394 Fraud in relation to minerals	Indictable	5 yrs	✓	✓	✓	✓	✓	✓	✓	✓	✓	✓	S. 394(6) discretionary forfeiture order. S
394.1 Possession of stolen minerals	Indictable	5 yrs	✓	✓	✓	✓	✓	✓	✓	✓	✓	✓	S. 394.1(4) discretionary forfeiture order. S
400 False prospectus	Indictable	10 yrs	✓	✓	✓	✓	✓	✓	✓	✓	✓	✓	Aggravating circumstance, s. 380.1. S
402.2 Identity theft	Hyb-Ind.	5 yrs	✓	✓	✓	✓	✓	✓	✓	✓	✓	✓	S if by indictment
	Hyb-Sum.	6 mth/ 5000*	✓	✓	✓	✓	✓	✓	✓	✓	✓	✓	
403 Identity fraud	Hyb-Ind.	10 yrs	✓	✓	✓	✓	✓	✓	✓	✓	✓	✓	S if by indictment
	Hyb-Sum.	6 mth/ 5000*	✓	✓	✓	✓	✓	✓	✓	✓	✓	✓	
423 Intimidation	Hyb-Ind.	5 yrs	✓	✓	✓	✓	✓	✓	✓	✓	✓	✓	S. 110 discretionary firearms order. S. 491 mandatory weapon forfeiture order. S
	Hyb-Sum.	6 mth/ 5000*	✓	✓	✓	✓	✓	✓	✓	✓	✓	✓	
423.1 Intimidation of justice system participant	Indictable	14 yrs	x	✓	✓	✓	✓	✓	✓	✓	✓	x	S. 109 or s. 110 firearms prohibition depending on circumstances. S. 491 mandatory weapon forfeiture. P

*** $100,000 for organizations for summary conviction offence s. 735.**
***** conditional sentence not available if offence involved use of a weapon.**

✓ Sentence Option | **x Illegal Sentence**

P = Primary designated offence
S = Secondary designated offence
PC = Primary Compulsory
[see note on p. OG/2]

GRID

SECTION	TYPE	MAX/MIN SENTENCE	DISCHARGE s. 730	SUSPENDED SENTENCE s. 731(1)(a)	FINE ALONE s. 734	FINE & PROBATION s. 731(1)(b)	PRISON ss. 718.3, 787	PRISON & PROBATION s. 731(1)(b)	PRISON & FINE s. 734	INTERMITTENT s. 732	FINE, PROB. & INTERMIT s. 732	CONDITIONAL SENTENCE s. 742.1	COMMENTS (applicability depends on circumstances of case)
426 Secret commissions	Indictable	5 yrs	✓	✓	✓	✓	✓	✓	✓	✓	✓	✓	S. 462.37 proceeds of crime forfeiture order on Crown application. S
430(2) Wilful mischief endangering life	Indictable	Life	×	✓	✓	✓	✓	✓	✓	✓	✓	×	S. 109 mandatory firearms order. S. 491 mandatory weapon forfeiture order. S
430(3) Wilful mischief, testamentary instrument or property over $5,000	Hyb-Ind.	10 yrs	✓	✓	✓	✓	✓	✓	✓	✓	✓	✓	S if by indictment
	Hyb-Sum.	6 mth/ 5000*	✓	✓	✓	✓	✓	✓	✓	✓	✓	✓	
430(4) Wilful mischief, other property	Hyb-Ind. **Absolute PCJ**	2 yrs	✓	✓	✓	✓	✓	✓	✓	✓	✓	✓	S. 110 discretionary firearms order. S. 491 mandatory weapon forfeiture order. S. 553 absolute PCJ only if $5,000 or less.
	Hyb-Sum.	6 mth/ 5000*	✓	✓	✓	✓	✓	✓	✓	✓	✓	✓	
430(4.1) Mischief relating to religious property	Hyb-Ind.	10 yrs	✓	✓	✓	✓	✓	✓	✓	✓	✓	✓	S if by indictment
	Hyb-Sum.	18 mth/ 5000*	✓	✓	✓	✓	✓	✓	✓	✓	✓	✓	
430(4.11) Mischief relating to war memorials	Hyb-Ind.	10 yrs max/ min $1,000 fine – 1st/ 14 days – 2nd/30 days – 3rd and subsequent	† ††	† ††	✓ ††	✓	✓	✓	✓	✓	✓	✓ ††	† These sentences are not available where the Crown proceeds by Indictment and the offence is a first offence.
	Hyb-Sum.	18 mths max	✓	✓	✓	✓	✓	✓	✓	✓	✓	✓	†† These sentences are not available where the Crown proceeds by Indictment and the offence is a second or subsequent offence.
430(4.2) Mischief relating to cultural property	Hyb-Ind.	10 yrs	✓	✓	✓	✓	✓	✓	✓	✓	✓	✓	S if by indictment
	Hyb-Sum.	6 mth/ 5000*	✓	✓	✓	✓	✓	✓	✓	✓	✓	✓	
430(5) Wilful mischief, data	Hyb-Ind.	10 yrs	✓	✓	✓	✓	✓	✓	✓	✓	✓	✓	S if by indictment
	Hyb-Sum.	6 mth/ 5000*	✓	✓	✓	✓	✓	✓	✓	✓	✓	✓	

*** $100,000 for organizations for summary conviction offence s. 735.**
***** conditional sentence not available if offence involved use of a weapon.**

✓ Sentence Option **× Illegal Sentence**

P = Primary designated offence
S = Secondary designated offence
PC = Primary Compulsory
[see note on p. OG/2]

SECTION	TYPE	MAX/MIN SENTENCE	DISCHARGE s. 730	SUSPENDED SENTENCE s. 731(1)(a)	FINE ALONE s. 734	FINE & PROBATION s. 731(1)(b)	PRISON ss. 718.3, 787	PRISON & PROBATION s. 731(1)(b)	PRISON & FINE s. 734	INTERMITTENT s. 732	FINE, PROB. & INTERMIT s. 732	CONDITIONAL SENTENCE s. 742.1	COMMENTS (applicability depends on circumstances of case)
430(5.1) Wilful act or omission, cause danger to life or mischief to property	Hyb-Ind.	5 yrs	✓	✓	✓	✓	✓	✓	✓	✓	✓	✓	S. 110 discretionary firearms order. S. 491 mandatory weapon forfeiture order. S
	Hyb-Sum.	6 mth/ 5000*	✓	✓	✓	✓	✓	✓	✓	✓	✓	✓	
431 Attack internationally protected premises	Indictable	14 yrs	✗	✓	✓	✓	✓	✓	✓	✓	✓	✗	S. 109 mandatory firearms order. S. 491 mandatory weapon forfeiture order. P
431.1 Attack on U.N. premises	Indictable	14 yrs	✗	✓	✓	✓	✓	✓	✓	✓	✓	✗	S. 109 mandatory firearms order. S. 491 mandatory weapon forfeiture order. P
431.2(2) Delivering explosives	Indictable	Life	✗	✓	✓	✓	✓	✓	✓	✓	✓	✗	S. 109 mandatory firearms order. P
433 Arson, disregard for human life	Indictable	Life	✗	✓	✓	✓	✓	✓	✓	✓	✓	✗	S. 109 mandatory firearms order. S. 491 mandatory weapon forfeiture order. S. 462.37 proceeds of crime forfeiture order on Crown application. S
434 Arson, damage to property of others	Indictable	14 yrs	✗	✓	✓	✓	✓	✓	✓	✓	✓	✗	S. 109 mandatory firearms order. S. 491 mandatory weapon forfeiture order. S
434.1 Arson, damage to own property, threat to safety of others	Indictable	14 yrs	✗	✓	✓	✓	✓	✓	✓	✓	✓	✗	S
435 Arson for fraudulent purpose	Indictable	10 yrs	✓	✓	✓	✓	✓	✓	✓	✓	✓	✗	S
436 Arson by negligence	Indictable	5 yrs	✓	✓	✓	✓	✓	✓	✓	✓	✓	✓	S
436.1 Poss'n incendiary material	Indictable	5 yrs	✓	✓	✓	✓	✓	✓	✓	✓	✓	✓	S
437 False alarm of fire	Hyb-Ind.	2 yrs	✓	✓	✓	✓	✓	✓	✓	✓	✓	✓	
	Hyb-Sum.	6 mth/ 5000*	✓	✓	✓	✓	✓	✓	✓	✓	✓	✓	

* $100,000 for organizations for summary conviction offence s. 735.
*** conditional sentence not available if offence involved use of a weapon.

✓ Sentence Option ✗ Illegal Sentence

P = Primary designated offence
S = Secondary designated offence
PC = Primary Compulsory
[see note on p. OG/2]

SECTION	TYPE	MAX/MIN SENTENCE	DISCHARGE s. 730	SUSPENDED SENTENCE s. 731(1)(a)	FINE ALONE s. 734	FINE & PROBATION s. 731(1)(b)	PRISON ss. 718.3, 787	PRISON & PROBATION s. 731(1)(b)	PRISON & FINE s. 734	INTERMITTENT s. 732	FINE, PROB. & INTERMIT s. 732	CONDITIONAL SENTENCE s. 742.1	COMMENTS (applicability depends on circumstances of case)
445 Injure or endanger other animals	Hyb-Ind.	5 yrs	✓	✓	✓	✓	✓	✓	✓	✓	✓	✓	S. 447.1 discretionary prohibition order. S if by indictment
	Hyb-Sum.	18 mths/ 10,000	✓	✓	✓	✓	✓	✓	✓	✓	✓	✓	
445.01 Killing or injuring a law enforcement animal in the commission of the offence	Hyb-Ind.	5 yrs max/ mins 6 mths of animal dies /consecutive to offence	†	†	†	†	✓	✓	✓	†	†	†	†These sentences not available where the Crown proceeds by indictment and the service animal is killed in the commission of the offence.
	Hyb-Sum.	18 mths consecutive to offence or $10,000 max	✓	✓	✓	✓	✓	✓	✓	✓	✓	✓	
445.1 Cause unnecessary suffering to animals or birds	Hyb-Ind.	5 yrs	✓	✓	✓	✓	✓	✓	✓	✓	✓	✓	S. 447.1 discretionary prohibition order. S if by indictment
	Hyb-Sum.	18 mths/ 10,000	✓	✓	✓	✓	✓	✓	✓	✓	✓	✓	
446 Neglect animal or bird	Hyb-Ind.	2 yrs	✓	✓	✓	✓	✓	✓	✓	✓	✓	✓	S. 447.1 discretionary prohibition order.
	Hyb-Sum.	6 mths/ 5000	✓	✓	✓	✓	✓	✓	✓	✓	✓	✓	
447 Keeping cockpit	Hyb-Ind.	5 yrs	✓	✓	✓	✓	✓	✓	✓	✓	✓	✓	S. 447.1 discretionary prohibition order. S if by indictment
	Hyb-Sum.	18 mths/ 10,000	✓	✓	✓	✓	✓	✓	✓	✓	✓	✓	
449 Make counterfeit money	Indictable	14 yrs	×	✓	✓	✓	✓	✓	✓	✓	✓	×	S. 462.37 proceeds of crime forfeiture order on Crown application. S
450 Possession, etc., of counterfeit money	Indictable	14 yrs	×	✓	✓	✓	✓	✓	✓	✓	✓	×	S. 462.37 proceeds of crime forfeiture order on Crown application. S
452 Uttering, etc., counterfeit money	Indictable	14 yrs	×	✓	✓	✓	✓	✓	✓	✓	✓	×	S. 462.37 proceeds of crime forfeiture order on Crown application. S

*** $100,000 for organizations for summary conviction offence s. 735.**
***** conditional sentence not available if offence involved use of a weapon.**

✓ Sentence Option | **× Illegal Sentence**

P = Primary designated offence
S = Secondary designated offence
PC = Primary Compulsory
[see note on p. OG/2]

SECTION	TYPE	MAX/MIN SENTENCE	DISCHARGE s. 730	SUSPENDED SENTENCE s. 731(1)(a)	FINE ALONE s. 734	FINE & PROBATION s. 731(1)(b)	PRISON ss. 718.3, 787	PRISON & PROBATION s. 731(1)(b)	PRISON & FINE s. 734	INTERMITTENT s. 732	FINE, PROB. & INTERMIT. s. 732	CONDITIONAL SENTENCE s. 742.1	COMMENTS (applicability depends on circumstances of case)
460 Advertising & dealing in counterfeit money	Indictable	5 yrs	✓	✓	✓	✓	✓	✓	✓	✓	✓	✓	S
462.31 Laundering proceeds of crime	Hyb-Ind.	10 yrs	✓	✓	✓	✓	✓	✓	✓	✓	✓	✓	S. 462.37 proceeds of crime forfeiture order on Crown application. S if by indictment
	Hyb-Sum.	6 mth/ 5000*	✓	✓	✓	✓	✓	✓	✓	✓	✓	✓	
463(a) Attempts & accessories, indictable, punishment by life	Indictable	14 yrs	✗	✓	✓	✓	✓	✓	✓	✓	✓	✗	S. 109 mandatory firearms order. S. 462.37 proceeds of crime forfeiture order on Crown application where applicable. S. 491 mandatory weapon forfeiture order. S. 522, release by Superior Court Judge only for offences listed in s. 469. May be designated offence for purpose of forensic DNA analysis; see the substantive offence. S
463(b) Attempts & accessories, indictable, punished by 14 yrs or less	Indictable **Absolute PCJ** if principal offence absolute PCJ S.553	1/2 max. for principal offence	✓	✓	✓	✓	✓	✓	✓	✓	✓	✓	S. 110 discretionary firearms order. S. 462.37 proceeds of crime forfeiture order on Crown application. S. 491 mandatory weapon forfeiture order. May be designated offence for purpose of forensic DNA analysis; see the substantive offence.
463(c) Attempts & accessories, summary conviction	Summary	6 mth/ 5000*	✓	✓	✓	✓	✓	✓	✓	✓	✓	✓	May be designated offence; see s. 487.04.
463(d) Attempts & accessories, hybrid offences	Hyb-Ind. **Absolute PCJ** if principal offence absolute PCJ S.553	1/2 max. for principal offence	✓	✓	✓	✓	✓	✓	✓	✓	✓	✓	S. 110 discretionary firearms order. S. 462.37 proceeds of crime forfeiture order on Crown application where applicable. S. 491 mandatory weapon forfeiture order. For indictable, max. sentence is half of the maximum (indictable) for the principal offence.
	Hyb-Sum.	6 mth/ 5000*	✓	✓	✓	✓	✓	✓	✓	✓	✓	✓	May be designated offence for purpose of forensic DNA analysis; see s. 487.04.
464(a) Counsel indictable offence, offence not committed	Indictable **Absolute PCJ** if princpal offence absolute PCJ S.553	Same as for attempts	✓	✓	✓	✓	✓	✓	✓	✓	✓	✓	S. 462.37 proceeds of crime forfeiture order on Crown application where applicable. Max. sentence is same as for attempt. S, if offence counselled is punishable by 5 yrs or more

*** $100,000 for organizations for summary conviction offence s. 735.**
***** conditional sentence not available if offence involved use of a weapon.**

✓ Sentence Option ✗ **Illegal Sentence**

P = Primary designated offence
S = Secondary designated offence
PC = Primary Compulsory
[see note on p. OG/2]

GRID

SECTION	TYPE	MAX/MIN SENTENCE	DISCHARGE s. 730	SUSPENDED SENTENCE s. 731(1)(a)	FINE ALONE s. 734	FINE & PROBATION s. 731(1)(b)	PRISON ss. 718.3, 787	PRISON & PROBATION s. 731(1)(b)	PRISON & FINE s. 734	INTERMITTENT s. 732	FINE, PROB. & INTERMITS s. 732	CONDITIONAL SENTENCE s. 742.1	COMMENTS (applicability depends on circumstances of case)
464(b) Counsel s/c offence, offence not committed	Summary	6 mth/ 5000*	✓	✓	✓	✓	✓	✓	✓	✓	✓	✓	S. 462.37 proceeds of crime forfeiture order on Crown application where applicable.
465(1)(a) Conspiracy, murder	Indictable	Life	×	✓	✓	✓	✓	✓	✓	✓	✓	×	S. 109 mandatory firearms order. S. 462.37 proceeds of crime forfeiture order on Crown application where applicable. S. 491 mandatory weapon forfeiture order. S. 522, release by Superior Court Judge only. S
465(1)(b)(i) Conspiracy to prosecute, sentence 14 yrs or more	Indictable	10 yrs	✓	✓	✓	✓	✓	✓	✓	✓	✓	×	S
465(1)(b)(ii) Conspiracy to prosecute, sentence under 14 yrs	Indictable	5 yrs	✓	✓	✓	✓	✓	✓	✓	✓	✓	×	S
465(1)(c) Conspiracy to commit other indictable offence	Indictable **Absolute PCJ** if principal offence absolute PCJ S. 553	Same as for principal offence	••	✓	†	†	✓	✓	†	✓	†	† ††	Max. sentence is same as for principal offence. S. 109 mandatory firearms order if punishment for principal offence is 10 yrs or more; otherwise, s. 110 discretionary firearms order. S. 462.37 proceeds of crime forfeiture order on Crown application where applicable. S. 491 mandatory weapon forfeiture order. S. 522, release by Superior Court Judge only for offences listed in s. 469(a). **Discharge only if principal offence is less than 14 yrs. †Fine or conditional sentence only if no minimum imprisonment for principal offence. ††Conditional sentence not available if offence punishable by life imprisonment or 14 years or by 10 years and resulted in bodily harm or involved use of a weapon. May be designated offence for purpose of forensic DNA analysis; see s. 487.04.
465(1)(d) Conspiracy to commit summary conviction offence	Summary	6 mth/ 5000*	✓	✓	✓	✓	✓	✓	✓	✓	✓	✓	
467.11 Participating in criminal organization	Indictable	5 yrs	✓	✓	✓	✓	✓	✓	✓	✓	✓	✓	S. 467.14, sentence to be served consecutive to sentence imposed for offence arising out of same event. P

*** $100,000 for organizations for summary conviction offence s. 735.**
***** conditional sentence not available if offence involved use of a weapon.**

✓ Sentence Option × Illegal Sentence

P = Primary designated offence
S = Secondary designated offence
PC = Primary Compulsory
[see note on p. OG/2]

SECTION	TYPE	MAX/MIN SENTENCE	DISCHARGE s. 730	SUSPENDED SENTENCE s. 731(1)(a)	FINE ALONE s. 734	FINE & PROBATION s. 731(1)(b)	PRISON ss. 718.3, 787	PRISON & PROBATION s. 731(1)(b)	PRISON & FINE s. 734	INTERMITTENT s. 732	FINE, PROB. & INTERMIT s. 732	CONDITIONAL SENTENCE s. 742.1	COMMENTS (applicability depends on circumstances of case)
467.111 Recruitment of members by a criminal organization	Indictable	5 yrs max 6 mth min if V is under age 18	†	†	†	†	✓	✓	✓	†	†	†	S. 110 discretionary order P † These sentences are not available where V is under age 18.
467.12 Commission of offence for criminal organization	Indictable	14 yrs	✗	✓	✓	✓	✓	✓	✓	✓	✓	✗	P
467.13 Instructing offence for criminal organization	Indictable	Life	✗	✓	✓	✓	✓	✓	✓	✓	✓	✗	P
708 Contempt of court witness fail to attend		90 days/ 100	✓	✓	✓	✓	✓	✓	✓	✓	✓	✓	May be ordered to pay costs incident to service and detention: s. 708(2). See s. 605(2) for contempt relating to exhibits. Fine under s. 708(2) not to exceed $100.
733.1 Fail to comply with probation order	Hyb-Ind. **Absolute PCJ**	4 yrs	✓	✓	✓	✓	✓	✓	✓	✓	✓	✓	
	Hyd-Sum.	18 mth/ 5000	✓	✓	✓	✓	✓	✓	✓	✓	✓	✓	
811 Breach of recognizance	Hyb-Ind. **Absolute PCJ**	4 yrs	✓	✓	✓	✓	✓	✓	✓	✓	✓	✓	
	Summary	18 mths	✓	✓	✓	✓	✓	✓	✓	✓	✓	✓	

* $100,000 for organizations for summary conviction offence s. 735.
*** conditional sentence not available if offence involved use of a weapon.

✓ Sentence Option   ✗ Illegal Sentence

P = Primary designated offence
S = Secondary designated offence
PC = Primary Compulsory
[see note on p. OG/2]

GRID

INDEX

NOTE: All references are to sections of the *Criminal Code* unless preceded by the following abbreviations:

CD = Controlled Drugs and Substances Act
CE = Canada Evidence Act
CH = Canadian Charter of Rights and Freedoms
WC = Crimes Against Humanity and War Crimes Act
YC = Youth Criminal Justice Act

NOTE: ***Italicized*** **section numbers in bold type refer to section numbers that were not yet or no longer in effect when this index was published.**

INDEX

INDEX

INDEX

INDEX

INDEX

INDEX

INDEX

INDEX

INDEX

INDEX

INDEX

INDEX

INDEX

INDEX

INDEX

INDEX

INDEX

INDEX

INDEX

INDEX

INDEX

INDEX

INDEX

INDEX

INDEX

INDEX

INDEX

INDEX

INDEX

INDEX

INDEX

INDEX

INDEX

INDEX

INDEX

INDEX

INDEX

INDEX

INDEX

INDEX

INDEX

INDEX

INDEX

INDEX

INDEX

INDEX

INDEX

INDEX

INDEX

INDEX TO FORMS FOR THE CRIMINAL CODE

INDEX

APPENDIX

FORMS OF CHARGES

INTRODUCTORY NOTE

The Appendix contains a collection of suggested forms of charges pursuant to Form 2 of the *Criminal Code* for the offences most commonly encountered by police officers, and suggested forms of charges under the *Controlled Drugs and Substances Act*. It is suggested that the Crown Attorney or appropriate counterpart be consulted in the case of offences not included in these pages, and in all cases where the facts are complicated.

The charges are arranged under the sections of the Code to which they relate, in numerical sequence. If the particular section number is not known, it can be readily found by reference to the Index preceding these pages. The section numbers of the Code and the subject-matter of each charge are printed in bold face type.

The use of square brackets and italic type should be explained. Square brackets are used either to set out editorial instructions, which are in all cases printed in italics, or to indicate alternate words or phrases which are printed in ordinary type. See, for example, the first form of charge for an offence under s. 57(1)(*a*), the opening charge, in which the editorial instruction "specify the forged passport" is printed in italics within square brackets, and the charge under s. 81(1)(*a*) in which the alternate words "was likely to cause serious damage to property" are printed in ordinary type within square brackets preceded by the word "or" which is printed in italics to indicate that it is not part of the charge. Round brackets within square brackets indicate an alternative within the alternative (see, for example, the charge under s. 81(1)(*b*)(ii)).

It will be noted that every charge ends with the word "contrary *etc.*". This phrase has been used to avoid needless repetition, but the actual charge should state the section of the Code under which it is laid, *e.g.*, ". . . contrary to section 81(1)(*a*) of the *Criminal Code*".

FORMS OF CHARGES UNDER THE *CRIMINAL CODE*

57(1)(*a*) Forging a passport

A.B. on .... at .... did forge a passport [*specify the forged passport*] contrary *etc.*

57(1)(*b*) Uttering a forged passport

A.B. on .... at .... did knowingly

(i) use [*or* deal with *or* act on] a forged passport to wit [*specify the forged passport*] as if it were genuine contrary *etc.*

or

(ii) cause [*or* attempt to cause] C.D. to use [*or* deal with *or* act upon] a forged passport to wit [*specify the forged document*] as if it were genuine contrary *etc.*

57(2) False statement for passport

A.B. on .... at .... did for the purpose of procuring a passport for himself [*or* C.D.] make a written [*or* oral] statement to wit [*specify the statement*] that he knew was false [*or* misleading] contrary *etc.*

or

A.B. on .... at .... did for the purpose of procuring a material alteration [*or* addition] to a passport for himself [*or* C.D.] make a written [*or* oral] statement to wit [*specify the statement*] that he knew was false [*or* misleading] contrary *etc.*

57(3) Possession of forged passport

A.B. on .... at .... did without lawful excuse have in his possession a forged passport to wit [*specify the forged passport*] contrary *etc.*

65 Participating in riot

A.B. on .... at .... did take part in a riot [*specify time and place*] contrary *etc.*

66 Unlawful assembly

A.B. on .... at .... was a member of an unlawful assembly [*specify time and place*] contrary *etc.*

72(1) Forcible entry

A.B. on .... at .... did commit forcible entry on the real property of C.D. at [*insert address*] contrary *etc.*

72(2) Forcible detainer

A.B. on .... at .... did commit forcible detainer of the real property known as [*insert address*] against C.D. the person entitled by law to possession of it, contrary *etc.*

76 Hijacking

A.B. on .... at .... did by force [*or* by threat of force *or specify form of intimidation*] seize [*or* exercise control of] an aircraft [*specify*] with intent

(***a***) to cause C.D. on board the said aircraft to be confined [*or* imprisoned] against his will contrary *etc.*

or

(***b***) to cause C.D. on board the said aircraft to be transported against his will to [*specify place*] which place was other than [*specify*], the then next scheduled place of landing of the said aircraft contrary *etc.*

or

(*c*) to hold C.D. on board the said ai rcraft for ransom [*or* to service against his will] contrary, *etc*.

or

(*d*) to cause the said aircraft to deviate in a material respect [*specify*] from its flight plan [*specify*] contrary *etc*.

77(*a*) Assault in aircraft in flight

A.B. on .... on board aircraft [*specify*] was in flight over the Province of .... between [*specify by longitudes and latitudes or geographical locations*] did commit an assault on C.D., which assault was likely to endanger the safety of the said aircraft contrary *etc*.

77(*c*) Damage to aircraft in service

A.B. on .... at .... did cause damage [*specify*] to a [*specify*] aircraft in service that rendered the said aircraft incapable of flight [*or* was likely to endanger the safety of the said aircraft in flight] contrary *etc*.

77(*d*) Placing dangerous substance on an aircraft

A.B. on .... at .... did place [*or* cause to be placed] on board a [*specify*] aircraft in service a [*specify*] that was likely to cause damage to the said aircraft that would render it incapable of flight [*or* that was likely to endanger the safety of the said aircraft in flight] contrary *etc*.

77(*e*) Damaging or interfering with a navigation facility

A.B. on .... at .... did cause damage to [*or* interfere with the operation of] a [*specify*] air navigation facility, which damage [*or* interference] was likely to endanger the safety of aircraft in flight contrary *etc*.

77(*g*) Endangering aircraft by false information

A.B. on .... at .... did endanger the safety of a [*specify*] aircraft in flight between .... and .... in the Province of .... by communicating to C.D. information that [*specify*], which information he knew was false, contrary *etc*.

78(1) Offensive weapon or explosive substance on aircraft

A.B. on .... at .... did take on board a [*specify*] aircraft an offensive weapon [*or* an explosive substance] [*specify*]

(*a*) without the consent of the owner or the operator or any person duly authorized by the owner or the operator to consent thereto contrary *etc*.

or

(*b*) with the consent of the owner [*or* the operator *or* C.D., a person duly authorized by the owner (*or* the operator) to consent thereto] but without complying with the term [*or* condition] [*specify*] on which consent was given contrary *etc*.

78.1(1) Seizing control of ship or fixed platform

A.B. on .... at .... did by force [*or* by threat of force or specify form of intimidation] seize [*or* exercise control of] a ship [*or* fixed platform] [*specify*] contrary *etc*.

78.1(2)(*a*) Violence on ship or fixed platform

A.B. on .... did commit an act of violence against C.D. on board ship [*or* fixed platform] [*specify*] between [*specify by longitudes and latitudes or geographical locations*] which act was likely to endanger the safe navigation of the said ship [*or* safety of the said fixed platform] contrary *etc*.

78.1(2)(*b*) Damage to ship or fixed platform

A.B. on .... did cause damage to ship [*or* the cargo of ship or fixed platform] [*specify*] between [*specify by longitudes and latitudes or geographical locations*] which damage was likely to endanger the safe navigation of the said ship [*or* safety of the said fixed platform] contrary *etc*.

78.1(2)(*c*) Damage to navigational facility

A.B. on .... did destroy [*or* cause serious damage] to a maritime navigational facility between [*specify by longitudes and latitudes or geographical locations*] which destruction [*or* damage] was likely to endanger the safe navigation of a ship [*or* the safety of a fixed platform] contrary *etc.*

78.1(2)(*d*) Placing dangerous substance on a ship or fixed platform

A.B. on .... at .... did place [*or* cause to be placed] on board ship [*or* fixed platform] [*specify*] a [*specify dangerous substance etc.*] that was likely to cause damage to the said ship [*or* the cargo of the said ship or the said fixed platform] and to endanger the safe navigation of the ship [*or* the safety of the fixed platform] contrary *etc.*

78.1(3) Endangering ship by false information

A.B. on .... at .... did endanger the safe navigation of ship [*specify*] between [*specify by longitudes and latitudes or geographical locations*] by communicating to C.D. information that [*specify*], which information he knew was false, contrary *etc.*

78.1(4) Threat to commit offence

A.B. on .... did threaten to commit an act of violence against C.D. on board ship [*or* fixed platform] [*specify*] between [*specify by longitudes and latitudes or geographical locations*] which threat was likely to endanger the safe navigation of the said ship [*or* the safety of the said fixed platform] contrary *etc.*

or

A.B. on .... did threaten to cause damage to the ship [*or* the cargo of the ship or fixed platform] [*specify*] between [*specify by longitudes and latitudes or geographical locations*] which threat was likely to endanger the safe navigation of the said ship [*or* safety of the said fixed platform] contrary *etc.*

or

A.B. on .... did threaten to destroy [*or* cause serious damage] to a maritime navigational facility between [*specify by longitudes and latitudes or geographical locations*] which destruction [*or* damage] was likely to endanger the safe navigation of a ship [*or* the safety of a fixed platform] contrary *etc.*

81(1)(*a*) Explosives: intent to cause explosion

A.B. on .... at .... with intent to cause an explosion of an explosive substance, to wit .... that was likely to cause serious bodily harm or death to persons [*or* was likely to cause serious damage to property] did [*specify act done*] contrary *etc.*

81(1)(*b*) Explosives: intent to cause bodily harm

A.B. on .... at .... with intent to do bodily harm to C.D. did

(i) cause an explosive substance, to wit .... to explode contrary *etc.*

or

(ii) send [*or* deliver] to C.D. [*or* cause C.D. to take (*or* receive)] an explosive substance [*or other dangerous substance or thing*] to wit .... contrary *etc.*

or

(iii) place upon [*or* throw upon *or* throw at] C.D. a corrosive fluid [*or* explosive substance *or* dangerous substance *or* dangerous thing] to wit .... contrary *etc.*

81(1)(*c*) Explosives: intent to cause damage to property

A.B. on .... at .... with intent to destroy or damage the property of C.D. and without lawful excuse did place [*or* throw] an explosive substance, to wit .... upon [*or* at] a [*specify property, e.g., building, motor vehicle, etc.*] of the said C.D. contrary, *etc.*

81(1)(*d*) Explosives: making or possession of substance; intending bodily harm or property damage

A.B. on .... at .... did make [*or* have in his possession *or* have under his care *or* have under his control] an explosive substance to wit .... with intent thereby

(i) to endanger life [*or* to cause serious damage to property] contrary *etc.*

or

(ii) to enable C.D. to endanger life [*or* to cause serious damage to property] contrary *etc.*

82(1) Explosives: making or possession for unlawful purpose

A.B. on .... at .... without lawful excuse did make [*or* have in his possession *or* have under his care or have under his control] an explosive substance to wit .... contrary *etc.*

82(2) Explosives: making or possession for benefit of criminal organization

A.B. on .... at .... without lawful excuse did make [*or* have in his possession *or* have under his care or have under his control] an explosive substance to wit .... for the benefit of [*or* at the direction of or in association with] a criminal organization [*specify*] contrary *etc.*

85(1)(*a*) Firearm: use while committing offence

A.B. on .... at .... did use a firearm to wit .... while committing the indictable offence of [*specify offence, e.g., break and enter with intent to commit an indictable offence*] contrary *etc.*

85(1)(*b*) Firearm: use while attempting to commit offence

A.B. on .... at .... did use a firearm to wit .... while attempting to commit the indictable offence of [*specify offence, e.g., break and enter with intent to commit an indictable offence*] contrary *etc.*

85(1)(*c*) Firearm: use during flight

A.B. on .... at .... did use a firearm to wit .... during his flight after committing [*or* attempting to commit] the indictable offence of [*specify offence, e.g., break and enter with intent to commit an indictable offence*] contrary *etc.*

85(2)(*a*) Imitation firearm: use while committing offence

A.B. on .... at .... did use an imitation firearm to wit .... while committing the indictable offence of [*specify offence, e.g., robbery*] contrary *etc.*

85(2)(*b*) Imitation firearm: use while attempting to commit offence

A.B. on .... at .... did use an imitation firearm to wit .... while attempting to commit the indictable offence of [*specify offence, e.g., robbery*] contrary *etc.*

85(2)(*c*) Imitation firearm: use during flight

A.B. on .... at .... did use an imitation firearm to wit .... during his flight after committing [*or* attempting to commit] the indictable offence of [*specify offence, e.g., robbery*] contrary *etc.*

86(1) Firearm, weapon, ammunition: careless use etc.

A.B. on .... at .... did, without lawful excuse, use [*or* carry, *or* handle, *or* ship *or* transport, *or* store] a firearm [*or* a prohibited weapon, *or* a restricted weapon, *or* a prohibited device *or* ammunition, *or* prohibited ammunition], to wit .... in a careless manner [or without reasonable precaution for the safety of other persons] contrary *etc.*

86(2) Firearm regulations

A.B. on .... at .... did [*specify manner of breach of regulation made under s. 117(h) of the Firearms Act e.g. store a loaded shotgun*] thereby contravening [*specify regulation e.g. s. 5(1)(a) of the Storage, Display, Transportation and Handling of Firearms by Individuals Regulations*] contrary *etc.*

87 Firearm: pointing

A.B. on .... at .... did, without lawful excuse, point a firearm to wit .... at C.D. contrary *etc.*

88 Weapon etc.: possession for dangerous purpose

A.B. on .... at .... did carry [*or* have in his possession] a weapon [*or* an imitation of a weapon *or* a prohibited device *or* ammunition *or* prohibited ammunition], to wit .... , for a purpose dangerous to the public peace [*or* for the purpose of committing an offence] contrary *etc.*

89 Weapon etc.: carrying at public meeting

A.B. on .... at .... did without lawful excuse carry a weapon [*or* a prohibited device *or* ammunition *or* prohibited ammunition], to wit .... while attending [or on his way to attend] a public meeting at [specify meeting place] contrary *etc.*

90 Weapon: carrying concealed weapon

A.B. on .... at .... not being authorized under the *Firearms Act* to carry concealed a weapon [*or* a prohibited device *or* prohibited ammunition], to wit .... did carry it concealed contrary *etc.*

91(1) Firearm: unauthorized possession

A.B. on .... at .... did possess a firearm, to wit .... without being the holder of a licence under which he may possess it [*or* the holder of a registration certificate for the firearm] contrary *etc.*

91(2) Weapon: unauthorized possession

A.B. on .... at .... did have in his possession a prohibited weapon, [*or* a restricted weapon *or* a prohibited device *or* prohibited ammunition] to wit .... without being the holder of a licence under which he may possess it contrary *etc.*

92(1) Firearm: knowledge of unauthorized possession

A.B. on .... at .... did possess a firearm, to wit .... knowing that he was not the holder of a licence under which he may possess it [*or* the holder of a registration certificate for the firearm] contrary *etc.*

92(2) Weapon: knowledge of unauthorized possession

A.B. on .... at .... did have in his possession a prohibited weapon, [*or* a restricted weapon *or* a prohibited device *or* prohibited ammunition] to wit .... knowing that he was not the holder of a licence under which he may possess it contrary *etc.*

93 Firearm etc.: possession at unauthorized place

A.B. being the holder of an authorization [*or* a licence] under which he was entitled to possess a firearm [*or* a prohibited weapon, *or* a restricted weapon, *or* a prohibited device, *or* prohibited ammunition], to wit .... did have it in his possession on .... at ....

(*a*) a place at which he was not entitled to possess it as indicated in the authorization [*or* licence] issued therefore

or

(*b*) being a place other than the place where he was entitled to possess it as indicated in the authorization [*or* licence] therefore

or

(*c*) being a place other than a place where he was entitled to possess it under the *Firearms Act*

contrary *etc.*

94 Firearm etc.: in motor vehicle

A.B. on .... at .... was an occupant of a motor vehicle, to wit .... in which he knew that there was at that time a firearm [*or* prohibited weapon *or* restricted weapon *or* prohibited device *or* prohibited ammunition], to wit .... contrary *etc.*

95 Prohibited or restricted firearm: with ammunition

A.B. on .... at .... did possess

(*a*) a loaded prohibited [*or* restricted] firearm

or

(*b*) a prohibited [*or* restricted] firearm together with readily accessible ammunition capable of being discharged in the said firearm

and was not the holder of an authorization or licence under which he may possess the said firearm in that place [*or* the registration certificate for the said firearm] contrary *etc.*

96 Possession of weapon obtained by crime

A.B. on .... at .... did have in his possession a firearm [*or* a prohibited weapon, *or* a restricted weapon, *or* a prohibited device, *or* prohibited ammunition], to wit .... or knowing that it was obtained

(*a*) by the commission in Canada of an offence

or

(*b*) by an act [*or* omission] in [*specify place e.g. the State of New York*] which act [*or* omission] had it occurred in Canada would have constituted an offence,

contrary *etc.*

98(1)(*a*) Breaking and entering with intent to steal firearm

A.B. on .... at .... did break and enter a certain place to wit [*specify type of place, e.g., a dwelling house or store or factory*] situate at .... with intent to steal a firearm located in it contrary to s. 98 of the *Criminal Code*

98(1)(*b*) Breaking, entering and stealing firearm

A.B. on .... at .... did break and enter a certain place to wit [*specify type of place, e.g., a dwelling house, store, factory etc.*] situate at .... and did steal a firearm located in it contrary to s. 98 of the *Criminal Code*

98(1)(*c*) Breaking out

A.B. on .... at .... did break out of a certain place to wit [*specify type of place, e.g., a dwelling house, store etc.*] situate at .... after stealing a firearm located in it contrary to s. 98 of the *Criminal Code*

or

A.B. on .... at .... did break out of a certain place to wit [*specify type of place*] situate at .... after having entered the said place with intent to steal a firearm located in it contrary to s. 98 of the *Criminal Code*

NOTE: Because of the similarity of this offence to the offence in s. 348, it is suggested that the section number be specified in the information.

98.1 Robbery of firearm

A.B. on .... at .... did steal a firearm from C.D. and at the time thereof did use violence [*or* threats of violence] to C.D. contrary to s. 98.1 of the *Criminal Code*

or

A.B. on .... at .... did steal a firearm from C.D. and at the time thereof [*or* immediately before *or* immediately thereafter] did wound [*or* beat *or* strike *or specify personal violence used*] C.D. contrary to s. 98.1 of the *Criminal Code*

or

A.B. on .... at .... did assault C.D. with intent to steal a firearm from him contrary to s. 98.1 of the *Criminal Code*

or

A.B. on .... at .... did steal from C.D. a firearm while armed with an offensive weapon [*or* imitation of an offensive weapon] to wit [*specify weapon*] contrary to s. 98.1 of the *Criminal Code*

or

(General Charge)

A.B. on .... at .... did rob C.D. of a firearm contrary to s. 98.1 of the *Criminal Code*

Note: Because of the similarity of this offence to the offence in s. 344, it is suggested that the section number be specified in the information.

99 Weapon or firearm: trafficking

A.B. on .... at .... did [*or* did offer to] manufacture [*or* transfer] a firearm [*or* a prohibited weapon, *or* a restricted weapon, *or* a prohibited device *or* ammunition, *or* prohibited ammunition], to wit .... knowing that he was not authorized to do so, contrary *etc.*

99(2) Firearm etc. trafficking

A.B. on .... at .... did [*or* did offer to] manufacture [*or* transfer] a firearm [*or* a prohibited device, *or* ammunition, *or* prohibited ammunition], to wit .... knowing that he was not authorized to do so, contrary *etc.*

99(3) Other weapons

A.B. on .... at .... did [*or* did offer to] manufacture [*or* transfer] a prohibited weapon [*or* a restricted weapon], to wit .... knowing that he was not authorized to do so, contrary *etc.*

100 Weapon or firearm: possession for purpose of trafficking

A.B. on .... at .... did have in his possession a firearm [*or* a prohibited weapon, *or* a restricted weapon, *or* a prohibited device *or* ammunition, *or* prohibited ammunition], to wit .... for the purpose of transferring [*or* offering to transfer] it knowing that he was not authorized to do so, contrary *etc.*

100(2) Firearm etc.: possession for purpose of trafficking

A.B. on .... at .... did have in his possession a firearm [*or* a prohibited device, *or* ammunition, *or* prohibited ammunition], to wit .... for the purpose of transferring [*or* offering to transfer] it knowing that he was not authorized to do so, contrary *etc.*

100(3) Other weapons: possession for the purpose of trafficking

A.B. on .... at .... did have in his possession a prohibited weapon [*or* a restricted weapon], to wit .... for the purpose of transferring [*or* offering to transfer] it knowing that he was not authorized to do so, contrary *etc.*

101 Weapon or firearm: transfer without authority

A.B. on .... at .... did without lawful authority transfer a firearm [*or* a prohibited weapon, *or* a restricted weapon, *or* a prohibited device *or* ammunition, *or* prohibited ammunition], to wit .... to C.D., contrary *etc.*

102 Making automatic firearm

A.B. on .... at .... did without lawful excuse alter [*or* manufacture or assemble] a firearm, to wit .... so that the said firearm is capable of discharging a projectile in rapid succession during one pressure of the trigger contrary *etc.*

103(1) Firearm or weapon: importing etc.

A.B. on .... at .... did import into Canada [*or* export from Canada]:

(*a*) a firearm [*or* a prohibited weapon, *or* a restricted weapon, *or* a prohibited device, *or* prohibited ammunition], to wit ....

or

(*b*) a component [or part] to wit .... designed exclusively for use in the manufacture of [*or* assembly into] an automatic weapon

knowing that he was not authorized to do so, contrary *etc.*

103(2) Firearm etc.: importing etc.

A.B. on .... at .... did import into Canada [*or* export from Canada] a firearm [*or* a prohibited device, *or* prohibited ammunition], to wit .... knowing that he was not authorized to do so, contrary *etc.*

103(2.1) Other weapons: importing etc.

A.B. on .... at .... did import into Canada [*or* export from Canada]

(*a*) a prohibited weapons [*or* a restricted weapon], to wit ....

(*b*) a component [*or* part], to wit .... designed exclusively for use in the manufacture of [*or* assembly into] an automatic firearm

knowing that he was not authorized to do so, contrary *etc.*

104(1) Firearm or weapon: importing etc. without authority

A.B. on .... at .... did without lawful authority import into Canada [*or* export from Canada]:

(*a*) a firearm [*or* a prohibited weapon, *or* a restricted weapon, *or* a prohibited device, *or* prohibited ammunition], to wit ....

or

(*b*) a component [or part] to wit .... designed exclusively for use in the manufacture of [*or* assembly into] an automatic weapon

contrary *etc.*

105(1) Firearm or weapon: losing or finding

(*a*) A.B. having lost [*or* had stolen from his possession] on .... at .... a firearm [*or* a prohibited weapon, *or* a restricted weapon, *or* a prohibited device, *or* prohibited ammunition *or* an authorization *or* a licence *or* a registration certificate], to wit .... failed to report the loss to a peace officer, firearms officer or chief firearms officer with reasonable despatch contrary *etc.*

(*b*) A.B. on .... at .... having found a firearm [*or* a prohibited weapon, *or* a restricted weapon, *or* a prohibited device, *or* prohibited ammunition], to wit .... that he had reasonable grounds to believe had been lost or abandoned failed to deliver it [*or* report its finding] to a peace officer, firearms officer or chief firearms officer with reasonable despatch contrary *etc.*

106(1) Firearm or weapon: destroying

(*a*) A.B. having destroyed on .... at .... a firearm [*or* a prohibited weapon, *or* a restricted weapon, *or* a prohibited device, *or* prohibited ammunition], to wit .... failed to report the destruction to a peace officer, firearms officer or chief firearms officer with reasonable despatch contrary *etc.*

(*b*) A.B. on .... at .... having become aware of the destruction of a firearm [*or* a prohibited weapon, *or* a restricted weapon, *or* a prohibited device, *or* prohibited ammunition], to wit .... failed to report the destruction to a peace officer, firearms officer or chief firearms officer with reasonable despatch contrary *etc.*

107(1) Firearm or weapon: false statements concerning loss etc.

A.B. on .... at .... did knowingly make a false report [*or* statement] concerning the loss [*or* theft *or* destruction] of a firearm [*or* a prohibited weapon, *or* a restricted weapon, *or* a prohibited device, *or* prohibited ammunition *or* an authorization *or* a licence *or* a registration certificate], to wit [*specify statement or report alleged to be false*] to C.D. a peace officer [*or* firearms officer *or* chief firearms officer] contrary *etc.*

108(1) Firearm: tampering with serial number

(*a*) A.B. on .... at .... did without lawful excuse alter [*or* deface *or* remove] a serial number on a firearm to wit .... contrary etc.

(*b*) A.B. on .... at .... was without lawful excuse in possession of a firearm to wit .... knowing that the serial number on it had been altered [*or* defaced *or* removed] contrary etc.

117.01(1) Firearm or weapon: possession contrary to prohibition order

A.B. on .... at .... did have in his possession a firearm [*or* a cross-bow *or* a prohibited weapon, *or* a restricted weapon, *or* a prohibited device, *or* ammunition *or* prohibited ammunition *or* an explosive substance] while he was prohibited from doing so by reason of an order made pursuant to [*here specify basis for prohibition e.g. section 109(1) of the Criminal Code and identify order e.g. at Montreal on January 5, 1999*] contrary *etc.*

120(*a*) Bribery: officers accepting bribes

A.B. on .... at .... being a justice [*or* police comissioner *or* peace officer *or* public officer *or* officer of a juvenile court *or* being employed in the administration of criminal law] to wit [*specify position held*] did corruptly

accept [*or* obtain]

or

agree to accept

or

attempt to obtain

for himself [*or* C.D.] a sum of money [*or* valuable consideration, *or* office, *or* place *or* employment] to wit [*specify item sought*] with intent

(i) to interfere with the administration of justice by [*specify details*] contrary *etc.*

or

(ii) to procure or facilitate the commission of the offence of .... contrary *etc.*

or

(iii) to protect from detection [*or* punishment] E.F. who had committed [*or* who had intended to commit] the offence of .... contrary *etc.*

120(*b*) Bribery of officers

A.B. on .... at .... did corruptly give [*or* offer] C.D., a justice [*or* police commissioner, *or* peace officer *or* public officer *or* officer of a juvenile court *or* a person employed in the administration of criminal law], to wit [*specify position held] a sum of money [or* valuable consideration *or* office *or* place *or* employment] to wit .... with intent that C.D. should

(*a*) interfere with the administration of justice [*specify interference contemplated*] contrary *etc.*

or

(*b*) procure or facilitate the commission of the offence of .... contrary *etc.*

or

(*c*) protect A.B. [*or* E.F.] who had committed [*or* who had intended to commit] the offence of .... from detection or punishment for such offence contrary *etc.*

121(1) Frauds on the government

121(1)(*a*) Giving a benefit to an official/accepting a benefit

(i) A.B. on .... at .... did give [*or* offer *or* agree to give *or* agree to offer] to C.D. [*or* E.F. a member of the family of C.D. *or* G.H. for the benefit of C.D.] an official [*specify nature of office*]

or

(ii) C.D., being an official [*specify nature of office*] on .... at .... did demand [*or* accept *or* offer to accept *or* agree to accept] from A.B. for himself [*or* E.F.]

a loan [*or* reward *or* advantage *or* benefit] to wit [*specify* loan *etc.*] as consideration for cooperation, assistance, exercise of influence or an act or omission in connection with

(iii) the transaction of business with [*or* a matter of business relating to] the government [*specify*] contrary *etc.*

or

(iv) a claim against Her Majesty [*or* a benefit that Her Majesty is authorized or is entitled to bestow] to wit [*specify*] contrary *etc.*

121(1)(*b*) Conferring a benefit by person having dealings with government

A.B. a person having dealings with the government of [*specify*] on .... at .... did, without the consent in writing of the head of the branch of that government, pay a commission to [*or* reward to *or* confer an advantage or benefit on] C.D. [*or* E.F. a member of the family of C.D. *or* G.H. for the benefit of C.D.] an official [*or* employee] of the government of [*specify*] with respect to those dealings contrary *etc.*

121(1)(*c*) Accepting a benefit from person having dealings with government

C.D. being an official [*or* employee] of the government of [*specify*] on .... at .... did, for his benefit and without the consent in writing of the head of the branch of that government of which he is an official [*or* that employs him], demand [*or* accept *or* offer to accept *or* agree to accept] a commission [*or* reward *or* an advantage or benefit] of [*specify*] from A.B. a person having dealings with the government of [*specify*] contrary *etc.*

121(1)(*d*) Influence peddling

C.D. a person having or pretending to have influence with the government [*or* with E.F. a minister of the government] of [*specify*] on .... at .... did demand [*or* accept *or* offer to accept *or* agree to accept] a commission [*or* reward *or* an advantage or benefit] of [*specify*] for himself [*or* G.H.] from A.B. as consideration for cooperation, assistance, exercise of influence or an act or omission [*specify*] in connection with

the transaction of business with [*or* a matter of business relating to] the government [*specify*] contrary *etc.*

or

a claim against Her Majesty [*or* a benefit that Her Majesty is authorized or is entitled to bestow] to wit [*specify*] contrary *etc.*

121(1)(*e*) Offering benefit for exercise of influence

A.B. on .... at .... did give [*or* offer *or* agree to give *or* agree to offer] to C.D. a Minister [*or* official] of the government of [*specify*] as consideration for cooperation, assistance, exercise of influence or an act or omission [*specify*] in connection with

the transaction of business with [*or* a matter of business relating to] the government [*specify*] contrary *etc.*

or

a claim against Her Majesty [*or* a benefit that Her Majesty is authorized or is entitled to bestow] to wit [*specify*] contrary *etc.*

or

his appointment [*or* the appointment of E.F.] to an office to wit [*specify*] contrary *etc.*

121(1)(*f*) Fraud in relation to government tenders

A.B. having made a tender to obtain a contract [*specify*] with the government of [*specify*] on .... at .... did,

(i) give [*or* offer to give] to C.D. [*or* E.F. a member of the family of C.D. *or* G.H. for the benefit of C.D.], a person who has also made a tender to obtain the contract, a reward [*or* an advantage or benefit] of [*specify*] as consideration for C.D. withdrawing his tender contrary *etc.*

or

(ii) demand [*or* accept *or* offer to accept *or* agree to accept] from C.D. a person who has also made a tender to obtain the contract a reward [*or* an advantage or benefit] of [*specify*] as consideration for withdrawing his tender contrary *etc.*

121(2) Contractor subscribing to election fund

A.B. in order to obtain [*or* retain] a contract [*specify*] with the government of [*specify*] on .... at .... did subscribe [*or* give *or* agree to give *or* agree to subscribe] to C.D. the sum of [*specify*]

(*a*) for the purpose of promoting the election of E.F. a candidate [*or, specify class or party*] to Parliament [*or, specify provincial legislature*] contrary *etc.*

or

(*b*) with the intention of influencing or affecting the result of the election held [*or* to be held] on .... for the purpose of electing persons to serve in Parliament [*or, specify provincial legislature*] contrary *etc.*

122 Breach of trust by public officer

A.B. on .... at .... being an official [*specify nature of office*] did commit a fraud [*or* a breach of trust] in connection with the duties of his office by [*specify fraud or breach of trust*] contrary *etc.*

123(1) Municipal corruption
Corruption of municipal official

(*a*) A.B. on .... at .... did give [*or* offer *or* agree to give *or* agree to offer] to C.D. a municipal official to wit [*specify nature of office*]

or

(*b*) C.D., being a municipal official [*specify nature of office*] on .... at .... did demand [*or* accept *or* offer to accept *or* agree to accept] from A.B. a loan [*or* reward *or* advantage *or* benefit] to wit [*specify* loan *etc.*] as consideration for C.D.

or

(*c*) abstaining from voting at a meeting of the municipal council [*or specify committee of council e.g. the committee of adjustment*] in relation to [*specify e.g. severance of the property of A.B. at ....*] contrary *etc.*

or

(*d*) voting in favour of [*or* against] a measure [*or* motion *or* resolution] to wit [*specify the measure, motion or resolution*] contrary *etc.*

or

(*e*) aiding [*or* procuring *or* preventing] the adoption of a measure [*or* motion *or* resolution] to wit [*specify the measure, motion or resolution*] contrary *etc.*

or

(*f*) performing [*or* failing to perform] an official act, to wit, [*specify*] contrary *etc.*

123(2) Influencing municipal official

(*a*) A.B. being under a duty to disclose the truth did on .... at .... suppress the truth in relation to [*specify*]

or

(*b*) A.B. on .... at .... by threats [*or* deceit] [*specify*]

or

(*c*) A.B. on .... at .... by [*specify unlawful means*]

influenced or attempted to influence C.D. a municipal official to wit [*specify nature of office*] to

abstain from voting at a meeting of the municipal council [*or specify committee of council e.g. the committee of adjustment*] in relation to [*specify e.g. severance of the property of A.B. at ....*] contrary *etc.*

or

vote in favour of [*or* against] a measure [*or* motion *or* resolution] to wit [*specify the measure, motion or resolution*] contrary *etc.*

or

aid in [*or* procure *or* prevent] the adoption of a measure [*or* motion *or* resolution] to wit [*specify the measure, motion or resolution*] contrary *etc.*

or

perform [*or* fail to perform] an official act, to wit [*specify*] contrary *etc.*

125 Influencing or negotiating appointments or dealing in offices

(*a*) A.B. on .... at .... did receive from C.D. [*or* agree to receive from C.D. *or* give to C.D. *or* agree to give to C.D. *or* procure to be given to C.D.] a reward [*or* an advantage or benefit] of [*specify*] as consideration for the cooperation [*or* assistance *or* exercise of influence] by [*specify e.g. A.B. or C.D. as the case may be*] to secure the appointment of [*specify person to be appointed*] to the office of [*specify nature of office*] contrary *etc.*

or

(*b*) A.B. on .... at .... did in the expectation of a reward [*or* an advantage or benefit] of [*specify*] solicit [*or* recommend *or* negotiate] the appointment of C.D. to [*or* resignation of C.D. from] the office of [*specify*] contrary *etc.*

or

(*c*) A.B. on .... did without lawful authority keep premises at .... for the purpose of transacting or negotiating business in relation to the filling of vacancies in [*or* the sale of *or* purchase of *or* the appointment to *or* resignation from] offices of [*specify*] contrary *etc.*

127 Disobeying court order
A.B. on .... at .... did without lawful excuse disobey the lawful order made by [*specify judge and court or other body authorized by an act of Parliament or the Legislature*] to [*specify order*] contrary *etc.*

128 Misconduct of officers in executing process
A.B. on .... at .... being a peace officer [*or* coroner] for [*specify police force or as the case may be*] and being entrusted with the execution of a process, to wit [*specify process e.g. execution of a warrant of committal for C.D.*] wilfully

(*a*) misconducted himself in the execution of that process contrary *etc.*

or

(*b*) made a false return to that process contrary *etc.*

129(*a*) Resisting or obstructing public or peace officer
A.B. on .... at .... did resist [*or* wilfully obstruct] C.D. a public [*or* peace] officer to wit [*describe C.D., e.g., a police constable for the City of* ....] engaged in the execution of his duty [*specify act C.D. engaged in*] by [*specify manner of resistance or obstruction*] contrary *etc.*

or

E.F. a person acting in aid of C.D. [a police constable for the City of ....] engaged in the execution of his duty [*specify C.D.'s duty*] by [*specify manner of resistance or obstruction*] contrary *etc.*

129(*b*) Omitting to assist peace officer
A.B. on .... at .... did omit without reasonable excuse, to assist C.D., a public [*or* peace] officer to wit [*describe C.D.*] engaged in the execution of his duty in arresting E.F. [*or* in preserving the peace] after having reasonable notice that he was required to do so contrary *etc.*

129(*c*) Obstructing or resisting bailiff, etc.
A.B. on .... at .... did resist [*or* wilfully obstruct] C.D., a person engaged in the lawful execution of a process issued out of [*specify court*] against the lands [*or* goods] of A.B. [*or* E.F.] contrary *etc.*

or

C.D. a person engaged in the making of a lawful distress [*or* seizure] upon [*specify subject-matter*] contrary *etc.*

130 Personating peace officer

(*a*) A.B. on .... at .... did falsely represent himself to be a peace [*or* public] officer to wit [*specify, e.g., a police constable for the City of* ....] to C.D. contrary *etc.*

or

(*b*) A.B. on .... at .... not being a peace [*or* public] officer did use a badge [*or* article of uniform *or* equipment] to wit .... in a manner that was likely to cause C.D. to believe that A.B. was [*specify, e.g., a police constable for the City of* ....] contrary *etc.*

131(1) Perjury
A.B. on .... at .... did commit perjury at the trial in the [*specify court and place and time of sitting*] between [*state full style of cause of the judicial proceeding*] by swearing falsely and with intent to mislead the court that [*recite evidence verbatim*] contrary *etc.*

or

A.B. on .... at .... being specially permitted [*or* authorized *or* required] by law to make a statement by affidavit [*or* solemn declaration *or* solemn affirmation *or* orally under oath] to wit [*specify, e.g., an affidavit under the Marriage Act*] did make a false statement to wit [*specify false statement, e.g., that he had not been previously married*] knowing that such statement was false contrary *etc.*

134(1) Statements not specially permitted

A.B. on .... at .... not being specially permitted, authorized or required by law to make a statement under oath or solemn affirmation, did make such a statement, by affidavit [*or* solemn declaration *or* disposition *or* orally] to wit [*specify*] before C.D. who was authorized by law to permit it to be made before him, knowing that the statement was false contrary *etc.*

136(1) Witness giving contradictory evidence

A.B. on .... at .... being a witness at [*specify judicial proceeding e.g. the trial of C.D. on a charge of first degree murder before the Honourable Madam Justice Smith in the Court of Queens Bench*] gave evidence that [*specify testimony of matter of fact or knowledge*] which was contrary to the evidence he gave on .... at .... while a witness at [*specify earlier judicial proceeding e.g. the preliminary hearing of C.D. on a charge of first degree murder before His Honour Judge Jones in the Manitoba Provincial Court*] contrary *etc.*

137 Fabricating evidence

A.B. on .... at .... did with intent to mislead fabricate [*specify item fabricated, e.g., a photograph*] with intent that it should be used as evidence in an existing [*or proposed*] judicial proceeding contrary *etc.*

138(*a*) Swearing pretended affidavit

A.B. on .... at .... did sign a writing that purported to be an affidavit [*or* statutory declaration] subscribed to by C.D. and dated the .... day of ...., 19................, and to have been sworn [*or* declared] before him when the writing was not so sworn [*or* declared] contrary *etc.*

or

A.B. on .... at .... did unlawfully sign a writing that purported to be an affidavit [*or* statutory declaration] subscribed to by C.D. and dated the .... day of ...., 19................, when he knew that he had no authority to administer the oath [*or* declaration] contrary *etc.*

138(*b*) Using pretended affidavit

A.B. on .... at .... did [offer for] use a writing that purported to be an affidavit [*or* statutory declaration] dated the .... day of ...., 19................,

> that he knew was not sworn [*or* declared] by C.D. the affiant [*or* declarant] therein contary *etc.*
>
> *or*
>
> that he knew was not sworn [*or* declared] before a person authorized to administer the oath [*or* declaration] contrary *etc.*

138(*c*) Signing pretended affidavit

A.B. on .... at .... did sign a writing that purported to be an affidavit dated the .... day of ...., 19......................, and to have been sworn [*or* declared] before C.D. by him as affiant [*or* declarant] when the writing was not so sworn contrary *etc.*

139(1) Obstructing justice

A.B. on .... at .... did wilfully attempt to obstruct [*or* pervert *or* defeat] the course of justice in a judicial proceeding by [*specify act done*] contrary *etc.*

140(1) Public mischief

A.B. on .... at .... did commit public mischief in that with intent to mislead he caused C.D. a peace officer [*describe C.D., e.g., a police constable for the City of* ....] to enter upon [*or* continue] an investigation by

(*a*) making a false statement to [*specify*] that accused E.F. of having committed the offence of [*specify offence*] contrary *etc.*

or

(*b*) [*specify act done by A.B., e.g., placing counterfeit twenty dollar bills in the seat lining of E.F.'s automobile*], which act was intended to cause E.F. to be suspected of having committed an offence which E.F. had not committed [*or* to divert suspicion from himself] contrary *etc.*

or

(*c*) reporting that the offence .... had been committed when it had not been committed contrary *etc.*

or

(*d*) reporting [*or* making it known] that he had died [*or* that E.F. had died when E.F. had not died] contrary *etc.*

141 Compounding indictable offence

A.B. on .... at .... did ask for [*or* obtain *or* agree to receive or obtain] [*specify valuable consideration, e.g., the sum of fifty dollars*] from C.D. for himself [*or* E.F.] by agreeing to compound [*or* conceal] the indictable offence of .... committed by the said C.D. [*or* X.Y.] contrary *etc.*

142 Corruptly taking reward for recovery of goods

A.B. on .... at .... did corruptly and directly [*or* indirectly] accept a valuable consideration from C.D. to wit [*specify consideration, e.g., the sum of fifty dollars*] under pretence [*or* upon account] of helping C.D. [*or* E.F.] to recover [*specify article*] obtained by the commission of an indictable offence to wit [*specify offence, e.g., robbery*] contrary *etc.*

144 Prison-breach

(*a*) A.B. on .... at .... did by force [*or* violence] break a prison to wit [*specify prison*] with intent to set at liberty himself [*or* C.D. a person confined therein] contrary *etc.*

or

(*b*) A.B. on .... at .... did with intent to escape forcibly break out of [*or* make a breach in] a cell [*or specify other place*] within a prison to wit [*specify prison*] in which he was confined contrary *etc.*

145(1)(*a*) Escape from lawful custody

A.B. on .... at .... did escape from lawful custody at [*specify manner of custody*] contrary *etc.*

145(1)(*b*) Being unlawfully at large

A.B. on .... at .... was, before the expiration of a term of imprisonment to which he was sentenced, at large within Canada without lawful excuse contrary *etc.*

145(2) Failing to attend court when at large on undertaking or recognizance: failing to surrender

A.B. on .... at .... unlawfully

(*a*) did being at large on his undertaking [*or* recognizance] given to [*or* entered into before] a justice [*or* a judge] without lawful excuse fail to attend court [*specify court, e.g., Courtroom 21, 1000 Eagle Street*] in accordance therewith, contrary *etc.*

or

(*b*) [did, fail to surrender himself in accordance with the order of [*here specify Judge*] at [*specify place of surrender*] contrary *etc.*

or

A.B. on .... at .... having appeared before a court [*or* justice *or* judge] to wit [*specify, e.g., Provincial Court Judge C.D.*] on [*specify date of last appearance*] did unlawfully fail to attend court on [*specify date that failed to appear*] at .... as required by the said court [*or* justice *or* judge] contrary *etc.*

145(3) Failing to comply with direction in detention order

A.B. on .... at .... being detained by the order of a justice [*or* judge] made on .... at .... and being bound to comply with a direction of the said justice [*or* judge] did fail without lawful excuse to comply with the direction not to communication with C.D. contrary *etc.*

145(3) Failing to comply with condition of undertaking or recognizance

A.B. on .... at .... did being at large on his undertaking [*or* recognizance] given to [*or* entered into before] a justice [*or* a judge] and being bound to comply with a condition of that undertaking [*or* recognizance] [*here specify condition e.g. that he not communicate with C.D.*] without lawful excuse failed to comply with that condition by [*here specify breach e.g. by telephoning C.D.*] contrary *etc.*

145(4) Failing to appear or to comply with summons

A.B. having been served with a summons did fail without lawful excuse

(*a*) to appear on .... at .... for the purposes of the *Identification of Criminals Act* in accordance therewith, contrary *etc.*

or

(*b*) to attend on .... at [*specify courtroom*] in accordance therewith, contrary *etc.*

145(5) Failing to appear or to comply with appearance notice, promise to appear or recognizance

A.B. on .... at .... unlawfully did having been named in an appearance notice [*or* promise to appear *or* recognizance entered into before an officer in charge] that has been confirmed by a justice under s. 508 of the *Criminal Code* fail without lawful excuse

(*a*) to appear in accordance therewith on .... at .... for the purposes of the *Identification of Criminals Act*, contrary *etc.*

or

(*b*) to attend court in accordance therewith by not appearing in [*specify courtroom*] on .... contrary *etc.*

145(5.1) Failing to comply with condition of undertaking given to officer in charge or peace officer

A.B. on .... at .... did being at large on his undertaking given to an officer in charge [*or* a peace officer] and being bound to comply with a condition of that undertaking directed by the said officer in charge [*or* peace officer] fail without lawful excuse to comply with that condition to wit: [*specify condition, e.g., to abstain from the consumption of alcohol or other intoxicating substances*] contrary *etc.*

146 Escape: permitting, assisting in, or procuring

A.B. on .... at .... did

(*a*) permit C.D. whom he had in lawful custody to escape by failing to perform a legal duty imposed on him to wit [*specify failure of specific legal duty*] contrary *etc.*

or

(*b*) convey [*or* cause to be conveyed by E.F.] [*specify item, e.g., a revolver*] into [*specify prison*] with intent to facilitate the escape of C.D. imprisoned therein contrary *etc.*

or

(*c*) direct [*or* procure] under colour of pretended authority [*specify pretended authority*] the discharge of C.D., a prisoner not entitled to be discharged contrary *etc.*

147(*a*) Escape: rescuing or assisting

A.B. on .... at .... did

rescue C.D. from lawful custody to wit [*specify manner of custody*] contrary *etc.*

or

assist C.D. in escaping [*or* attempting to escape] from lawful custody to wit [*specify manner of custody*] contrary *etc.*

147(*b*) Escape: peace officer permitting

A.B. on .... at .... did

being a peace officer to wit [*describe A.B., e.g., a police officer for the City of ....*,] wilfully permit C.D., a person in his lawful custody, to escape contrary *etc.*

147(*c*) Escape: prison officer permitting

A.B. on .... at .... did

being an officer of [*or* an employee in] a prison to wit [*specify prison*] wilfully permit C.D. to escape from lawful custody therein contrary *etc.*

151 Sexual interference

A.B., on .... at .... did for a sexual purpose touch C.D. a person under the age of sixteen years directly [*or* indirectly]

with a part of his body, to wit [*specify the part of the body*] contrary *etc.*

or

with an object, to wit [*specify the object*] contrary *etc.*

152 Invitation to sexual touching

A.B. on .... at .... did for a sexual purpose invite [*or* counsel *or* incite] C.D. a person under the age of sixteen years to touch directly [*or* indirectly] with a part of his body [*or* with an object] to wit [*specify the part of the body or the object used*] the body of A.B. [*or* the said C.D. *or* E.F. *as the case may be*] contrary *etc.*

153 Sexual exploitation

A.B. on .... at ...., being in a position of trust or authority towards C.D. a young person, [*or* being a person with whom C.D., a young person, was in a relationship of dependency] did

(*a*) for a sexual purpose, touch directly [*or* indirectly] the body of C.D., a young person, with a part of his body [*or* with an object] to wit [*specify the part of the body of A.B. or the object used*] contrary *etc.*

or

(*b*) for a sexual purpose invite [*or* counsel *or* incite] C.D. a young person to touch directly [*or* indirectly] with a part of his body [*or* with an object] to wit [*specify the part of the body or the object used*] the body of A.B. [*or* the said C.D. *or* E.F. *as the case may be*] contrary *etc.*

153.1 Sexual exploitation of person with disability

A.B. on .... at .... , being in a position of trust or authority towards C.D. a person with a mental [*or* physical] disability, [*or* being a person with whom C.D., a person with a mental [*or* physical] disability was in a relationship of dependency,] did without the consent of C.D. for a sexual purpose counsel [*or* incite] C.D. to touch directly [*or* indirectly] with a part of his body [*or* with an object] to wit [specify the part of the body or the object used] the body of A.B. [*or* the said C.D. *or* E.F. as the case may be] contrary etc.

155 Incest

Single charge

A.B. on .... at .... did have sexual intercourse with C.D. while knowing that C.D. was his [*or* her] [*specify blood relationship e.g., daughter*] contrary *etc.*

Joint charge

A.B. and C.D. on .... at .... did have sexual intercourse with each other while knowing that they were related by blood relationship to wit [*specify blood relationship e.g., father and daughter*] contrary *etc.*

160(1) Bestiality

A.B. on .... at .... did commit bestiality with [*specify e.g., an animal e.g. a cow*] contrary *etc.*

160(2) Compelling bestiality

A.B. on .... at .... did compel C.D. to commit bestiality with [*specify e.g., an animal e.g. a cow*] contrary *etc.*

160(3) Bestiality in presence of person under sixteen years etc.

A.B. on .... at .... did commit bestiality with [*specify e.g., an animal e.g. a cow*] in the presence of C.D. a person under the age of sixteen years contrary *etc.*

or

A.B. on .... at .... did incite C.D., a person under the age of sixteen years, to commit bestiality with [*specify e.g., an animal e.g. a cow] contrary etc.*

161(4) Breach of prohibition order in relation to children

A.B. on .... at .... being a person bound by an Order of Prohibition made on .... at .... by [*specify judge who made order*] prohibiting him from [*specify terms of Order eg. attending a public park or public swimming area where persons under the age of 14 are present or can reasonably be expected to be present etc.*] did fail to comply with the said Order by [*specify nature of failure to comply eg. attending the public park at 1000 Eagle Street where persons under the age of 14 were present*] contrary *etc.*

163(1) Obscene matter

Making, etc.

A.B. on .... at .... did make [*or* print *or* publish *or* distribute *or* circulate] obscene matter [*or* an obscene picture *or* model *or* phonograph record *etc.*] to wit [*specify item*] contrary *etc.*

or

Possessing

A.B. on .... at .... unlawfully did have in his possession for the purpose of publication [*or* distribution *or* circulation] obscene written matter [*or* an obscene picture *or* model *or* phonograph record *etc.*] to wit [*specify item*] contrary *etc.*

163(2) Obscene matter: selling, exposing or exhibiting

A.B. on .... at .... knowingly and without lawful justification or excuse did

(*a*) sell [*or* expose to public view *or* have in his possession for the purpose of selling (*or* exposing to public view)] obscene written matter [*or* an obscene picture *or* model *or* phonograph record *etc.*] to wit [*specify item*] contrary *etc.*

or

(*b*) publicly exhibit a disgusting object [*or* an indecent show] to wit [*specify object or show*] contrary *etc.*

163.1(2) Child pornography: printing and publishing

A.B. on .... at .... did make [*or* print *or* publish *or* have in his possession for the purpose of publication] child pornography to wit [*specify item*] contrary *etc.*

163.1(3) Child pornography: importing and distributing

A.B. on .... at .... did import [*or* distribute *or* sell *or* have in his possession for the purpose of distribution *or* sale] child pornography to wit [*specify item*] contrary *etc.*

163.1(4) Child pornography: possession

A.B. on .... at .... did have in his possession child pornography to wit [*specify item*] contrary *etc.*

167 Immoral theatrical performance

A.B. on .... at .... being the lessee [*or* manager *or* agent *or* person in charge] of a theatre to wit [*specify*] did present [*or* give *or* allow to be presented therein] an immoral [*or* indecent *or* obscene] performance [*or* entertainment *or* representation] to wit [*specify*] contrary *etc.*

or

A.B. on .... at .... did unlawfully take part [*or* appear as an actor *or* performer *or* assistant (*state capacity*)] in an immoral [*or* indecent *or* obscene] performance [*or* entertainment *or* representation] to wit [*specify, e.g., a play*] in a theatre to wit [*specify*] contrary *etc.*

168 Obscene matter: mailing

A.B. on .... at .... did make use of the mails for the purpose of transmitting [*or* delivering] obscene [*or* indecent *or* scurrilous] matter to wit [*specify item mailed*] contrary *etc.*

170 Parent or guardian procuring sexual activity

A.B. on .... at .... being the parent [*or* guardian] of C.D., a person under the age of eighteen years, did procure the said C.D. for the purpose of engaging in sexual activity to wit [*specify the prohibited sexual activity e.g. anal intercourse*] prohibited by section [*specify the section number e.g. 159*] of the *Criminal Code*, with E.F. contrary *etc.*

171 Householder permitting sexual activity

A.B. on .... at ....

(*a*) being the owner [*or* occupier *or* manager] of premises to wit [*specify*]

or

(*b*) having control [*or* assisting in the management (*or* control)] of premises to wit [*specify*]

did knowingly permit C.D., a person aged [*specify age under eighteen years*] to resort to [*or* to be in *or* upon] such premises for the purpose of engaging in sexual activity to wit [*specify the prohibited sexual activity e.g. anal intercourse*] prohibited by section [*specify the section number e.g. 159*] of the *Criminal Code*, thereby committing an offence contrary *etc.*

173(1) Indecent acts

A.B. on .... at .... wilfully did an indecent act to wit [*specify act, e.g., expose his private person*]

(*a*) in a public place to wit [*specify*] in the presence of C.D. [*or* of one or more persons] contrary *etc.*

or

(*b*) at [*specify place*] with intent thereby to insult [*or* offend] C.D. contrary *etc.*

173(2) Exposure to person under age of sixteen years

A.B. on .... at .... did for a sexual purpose expose his [*or* her] genital organs to C.D. a person under the age of sixteen years contrary *etc.*

174(1) Nudity

A.B. on .... at ...., without lawful excuse was

(*a*) nude in a public place to wit [*specify the place*] contrary *etc.*

or

(*b*) exposed to public view while nude on private property to wit [*specify the place*] contrary *etc.*

175(1) Causing disturbance; indecent exhibition; loitering

A.B. on .... at ....

(*a*) not being in a dwelling house did cause a disturbance in or near a public place to wit [*specify*]

(i) by fighting [*or* screaming *or* shouting *or* swearing *or* singing *or* using insulting (*or* obscene) language] contrary *etc.*

or

(ii) by being drunk contrary *etc.*

or

(iii) by impeding [*or* molesting] other persons contrary *etc.*

(*b*) did openly expose [*or* exhibit] an indecent exhibition to wit [*specify*] in a public place to wit [*specify*] contrary *etc.*

or

(*c*) did loiter in a public place to wit [*specify*] and obstruct persons who were there contrary *etc.*

or

(*d*) did disturb the peace and quiet of the occupants of a dwelling house to wit [*specify address*] by discharging firearms [*or specify type of disorderly conduct*] in a public place to wit [*specify*] contrary *etc.*

or

not being an occupant thereof did disturb the peace and quiet of the occupants of a dwelling house [*specify address*] comprised in a structure [*specify address*] by discharging firearms [*or specify disorderly conduct*] in a part of the said structure contrary *etc.*

176(1)(*a*) Obstructing officiating clergyman

A.B. on .... at .... did by threats [*or* force] unlawfully obstruct [*or* prevent *or* endeavour to obstruct *or* endeavour to prevent] C.D., a clergyman [*or* minister], from celebrating divine service [*or* performing the function of .... in connection with his calling] contrary *etc.*

176(1)(*b*) Violence to or arrest of officiating clergyman

A.B. on .... at .... did knowing that C.D., a clergyman [*or* minister], was about to perform [*or* on his way to perform *or* returning from performing] a divine service [*or* the function of .... in connection with his calling] assaulted [*or* offered violence to or arrested upon a civil process *or* arrested under the pretense of executing a civil process] the said C.D. contrary *etc.*

177 Trespassing or prowling at night near dwelling

A.B. on .... at .... without lawful excuse did loiter [*or* prowl] at night upon the property of C.D. situate at [*specify address*] near a dwelling house situated thereon contrary *etc.*

179(1)(*a*) Vagrancy: living off gaming or crime

A.B. having no lawful profession or calling by which to maintain himself, did within the period between the .... day of .... 19............... and the .... day of .... 19............... support himself in whole [*or* in part] by gaming [*or* crime] contrary *etc.*

180(1) Common nuisance

(*a*) A.B. on .... at .... did commit a common nuisance by [*specify unlawful act done or legal duty not complied with, e.g., by discharging a tear gas bomb in the .... Theatre on First St.*] and did thereby endanger the lives [*or* safety *or* health *or* property *or* comfort] of the public contrary *etc.*

or

(*b*) A.B. on .... at .... did commit a common nuisance and thereby did cause physical injury to C.D. by [*specify unlawful act or legal duty not complied with*] contrary *etc.*

182(*a*) Dead body: neglect duty

A.B. on .... at .... did neglect, without lawful excuse, to perform a duty imposed upon him by law [*or* that he undertook] with reference to the burial of the human remains of C.D. to wit [*specify legal duty or duty undertaken, e.g., to bury the body of his wife C.D.*] contrary *etc.*

182(*b*) Dead body: indignity to

A.B. on .... at .... did improperly [*or* indecently] interfere with [*or* offer an indignity to] the human remains of C.D. by [*specify interference or indignity*] contrary *etc.*

184(1) Interception of private communication

A.B. on .... at .... by means of an electromagnetic [*or* acoustic *or* mechanical] device to wit [*specify type etc.*] wilfully intercepted a private communication by telephone [*or* radio-telephone *or* orally, etc.] between C.D. and E.F. contrary *etc.*

191(1) Possession of devices for surreptitious interception of private communication

A.B. on .... at .... unlawfully did possess [*or* sell *or* purchase] an electromagnetic device [*or* acoustic device *or* mechanical device, *or* component of an electromagnetic device etc.] knowing that the design thereof rendered it primarily useful for the surreptitious interception of private communications, to wit: [*describe device or component*], contrary *etc.*

193(1) Disclosure of private communication

A.B. on .... at .... without the express consent of C.D. the originator thereof, or of E.F. the person C.D. intended to receive it, wilfully used [*or* disclosed] a private communication between the said C.D. and E.F. contrary *etc.*

201(1) Common gaming or betting house: keeping

A.B. on .... at .... did keep a common gaming [*or* betting] house at [*specify address*] contrary *etc.*

201(2)(*a*) Common gaming or betting house: found in

A.B. on .... at .... was found, without lawful excuse, in a common gaming [*or* betting] house to wit [*specify address*] contrary *etc.*

201(2)(*b*) Common gaming or betting house: owner, etc.

A.B. on .... at .... being the owner [*or* landlord *or* lessor *or* tenant *or* occupier *or* agent] of a place known as [*specify address*] did knowingly permit such place to be let [*or* used] for the purposes of a common gaming [*or* betting] house contrary *etc.*

202(1) Betting, pool-selling, book-making, etc.

A.B. on .... at ....

(*a*) did use [*or* allow to be used] a place under his control to wit [*specify address*] for the purpose of recording [*or* registering] bets [*or* selling a pool] contrary *etc.*

or

(*b*) did import [*or* make *or* buy *or* sell *or* rent *or* lease *or* hire *or* keep *or* exhibit *or* employ *or* knowingly allow to be kept *or* exhibited *or* employed in a place under his control to wit (*specify address*)] a device [*or* apparatus] for the purpose of recording [*or* registering] bets [*or* selling a pool] [*or* a machine *or* device for gambling *or* betting to wit (*specify*)] contrary *etc.*

or

(*c*) did have under his control a sum of money [*or specify other property*] relating to [*specify an offence under s. 202(1), e.g., pool-selling*] contrary *etc.*

or

(*d*) did unlawfully record [*or* register] a bet [*or* sell a pool] to wit (*specify e.g., on the result of a horse race at ....*)] contrary *etc.*

or

(*e*) did engage in pool-selling [*or* book-making *or* the business *or* occupation of betting] [*or* did make an agreement for the purchase (*or* sale) of betting (*or* gaming) privileges *or* for the purchase (*or* sale) of information that was intended to assist in book-making (*or* pool-selling *or* betting) to wit (*specify subject matter of agreement*)] contrary *etc.*

Note: Section 202(1)(*f*) to (*j*) relate to offences as follows:

(*f*) printing or providing book-making, pool-selling or betting information on horse-races, fights, games or sports;

(*g*) importing information or writing to promote gambling, book-making, pool-selling or betting;

(*h*) advertising, printing, publishing, exhibiting or posting up for contests;

(*i*) sending, transmitting or delivering messages by radio, telegraph, telephone, mail or express that convey information relating to these matters;

(*j*) aiding or assisting in anything that is an offence under this section.

203(*a*) Betting: off-track

A.B. on .... at .... did place [*or* offer to place *or* agree to place] a bet on behalf of C.D., to wit .... for a consideration paid [*or* to be paid] by or on behalf of C.D. contrary *etc.*

206(1)(*a*) Lottery scheme: publishing

A.B. on .... at .... did make [*or* print *or* advertise *or* publish *or* cause to be made *or* printed *or* advertised *or* published] a proposal [*or* scheme *or* plan] for advancing [*or* lending *or* giving *or* selling] the disposal of property to wit [*specify property, e.g., an automobile*] by lots [*or* cards *or* tickets (*or specify other mode of chance*)] contrary *etc.*

209 Cheating at play

A.B. on .... at .... did, with intent to defraud C.D., cheat while playing the game of .... [*or* in holding the stakes for a game of .... *or* in betting (*specify, e.g., on a horse-race at etc.*)] contrary *etc.*

210(1) Common bawdy-house: keeping

A.B. on .... at .... did keep a common bawdy-house located at [*specify address*] contrary *etc.*

210(2)(*a*) Common bawdy-house: inmate

A.B. on .... at .... was an inmate of a common bawdy-house at [*specify address*] contrary *etc.*

210(2)(*b*) Common bawdy-house: found in

A.B. on .... at .... was found without lawful excuse in a common bawdy-house at [*specify address*] contrary *etc.*

210(2)(*c*) Common bawdy-house: owner, *etc.*

A.B. on .... at .... being the owner [*or* landlord *or* tenant *or* occupier *or* having charge *or* control] of premises [*specify address*] did knowingly permit [a part of] such premises to be let [*or* used] for the purposes of a common bawdy-house contrary *etc.*

211 Common bawdy-house: transporting person to

A.B. on .... at .... did knowingly take [*or* transport *or* direct *or* offer to take *or* transport *or* direct] C.D. to a common bawdy-house at [*specify address*] contrary *etc.*

212(1) Procuring

A.B. on .... at .... did

(*a*) procure [*or* attempt to procure *or* solicit] C.D. to have illicit sexual intercourse with E.F. at [*specify address*] contrary *etc.*

(*b*) inveigle [*or* entice] C.D., not a prostitute [*or* not of known immoral character], to a common bawdy-house [*or* house of assignation] at [*specify address*] for the purpose of illicit sexual intercourse [*or* prostitution] contrary *etc.*

(*c*) knowingly conceal C.D. in a common bawdy-house [*or* house of assignation] at [*specify address*] contrary *etc.*

(*d*) procure [*or* attempt to procure] C.D. to become a prostitute contrary *etc.*

(*g*) procure C.D. to enter [*or* leave] Canada for the purpose of prostitution contrary *etc.*

(*h*) for the purpose of gain, exercise control [*or* direction *or* influence] over the movements of C.D. in such manner as to show that he was aiding [*or* abetting *or* compelling] C.D. to engage in [*or* carry on] prostitution with E.F. [*or* generally] contrary *etc.*

(*i*) apply [*or* administer] to C.D. [*or* cause C.D. to take] a drug [*or* intoxicating liquor *or specify item*] with intent to stupefy [*or* overpower] him and to enable himself [*or* E.F.] to have illicit sexual intercourse with him contrary *etc.*

212(2.1) Living on avails of juvenile prostitution and using violence

A.B. at .... between the .... day of .... 19 .... , and the .... day of .... 19 .... , did live wholly [*or* partly] on the avails of prostitution of C.D. a person under the age of eighteen years and for the purposes of profit did aid [*or* abet *or* counsel or compel] C.D. to engage in prostitution [*or* carry on prostitution] and used [*or* threatened to use *or* attempt to use] violence [*or* intimidation *or* coercion] in relation to C.D. contrary *etc.*

212(4) Juvenile prostitution

A.B. on .... at .... did obtain [*or* attempt to obtain] for consideration, the sexual services of C.D., a person under the age of eighteen years, contrary *etc.*

213(1) Prostitution offences

A.B. on .... at .... a public place [*or* a place open to public view] did

(*a*) stop [*or* attempt to stop] motor vehicles

or

(*b*) impede the free flow of pedestrian traffic [*or* vehicular traffic *or* ingress to adjacent premises to wit .... *or* egress from adjacent premises to wit ....]

or

for the purpose of engaging in prostitution [*or* of obtaining the sexual services of a prostitute] contrary *etc.*

215(2)(*a*) Necessaries of life: failure to provide to child or spouse

A.B. on .... [*or* between the .... day of .... 19............... and the .... day of .... 19...............] at ...., being the parent of C.D. a child under the age of sixteen years [*or* the spouse of E.F.], did fail without lawful excuse to provide the necessaries of life to C.D. [*or* E.F.]

(i) C.D. [*or* E.F.] then being in destitute [*or* necessitous] circumstances contrary *etc.*

or

(ii) and did thereby endanger the life of C.D. [*or* E.F.] contrary *etc.*

or

thereby causing [*or* being likely to cause] the health of C.D. [*or* E.F.] to be endangered permanently contrary *etc.*

215(2)(*b*) Necessaries of life: failure to provide to person under charge

A.B. on .... [*or* between the .... day of .... 19..............., and the .... day of .... 19...............] at .... did fail without lawful excuse to provide the necessaries of life to C.D., a person under his charge and unable, by reason of detention [*or* age *or* illness *or* insanity *or specify other reason*] to withdraw himself from such charge, and to provide himself with such necessaries and did thereby endanger the life of C.D. [*or* cause *or* likely cause the health of C.D. to be injured permanently] contrary *etc.*

218 Abandoning child

A.B. on .... at .... did unlawfully abandon [*or* expose] C.D., a child under the age of ten years, and did thereby endanger its life [*or* which abandoning *or* exposing was likely to endanger its life] contrary *etc.*

or

A.B. on .... at .... did unlawfully abandon [*or* expose] C.D., a child under the age of ten years, which abandoning [*or* exposing] permanently injured [*or* was likely to permanently injure] its health contrary *etc.*

220(*a*) Criminal negligence causing death by use of firearm

A.B. on .... at .... did use a firearm to wit .... in the commission of the offence of criminal negligence [*specify act done e.g. by discharging the said firearm at C.D.*] thereby causing the death of C.D. contrary *etc.*

220(*b*) Criminal negligence causing death

A.B. on .... at .... did by criminal negligence to wit [*specify act done or duty not complied with, e.g., by operating a motor vehicle at an excessive rate of speed on First St.*] cause the death of C.D. contrary *etc.*

221 Criminal negligence causing bodily harm

A.B. on .... at .... did by criminal negligence to wit [*specify act done or duty not complied with, e.g., by administering drug "A" for drug "B"*] cause bodily harm to C.D. contrary *etc.*

or

A.B. on .... at .... was criminally negligent in the operation of a motor vehicle on [*name of street*] and did thereby cause bodily harm to C.D. contrary *etc.*

233 Infanticide

A.B., a female person, on .... at .... did cause the death of her newly-born child by a wilful act [*or* omission] to wit [*specify act or omission, e.g., by suffocation*] contrary *etc.*

235(1) Murder

A.B. on .... at .... did commit first degree [*or* second degree] murder on the person of C.D. contrary *etc.*

236(*a*) Manslaughter while using firearm

A.B. on .... at .... did unlawfully kill C.D. while using a firearm to wit [*specify*] and thereby commit manslaughter contrary *etc.*

236(*b*) Manslaughter

A.B. on .... at .... did unlawfully kill C.D. and thereby commit manslaughter contrary *etc.*

239(1)(*a*) Attempted murder while using certain firearms etc.

A.B. on .... at .... did attempt to murder C.D.

> while using a restricted firearm [*or* a prohibited firearm] [*specify means used e.g. by discharging the firearm at the said C.D.*] contrary *etc.*
>
> *or*
>
> while using a firearm and did so for the benefit of [*or* at the direction of *or* in association with] a criminal organization to wit .... contrary *etc.*

239(1)(*a.*1) Attempted murder while using other firearms

A.B. on .... at .... did attempt to murder C.D. while using a firearm [*specify means used e.g. by discharging a shotgun at the said C.D.*] contrary *etc.*

239(1)(*b*) Attempted murder

A.B. on .... at .... did attempt to murder C.D. [*specify means used*] contrary *etc.*

240 Accessory after fact to murder

A.B. on .... at .... knowing that C.D. had murdered E.F. did receive [*or* comfort *or* assist] C.D. for the purpose of enabling C.D. to escape contrary *etc.*

241(*a*) Suicide: counselling

A.B. on .... at .... counsel C.D. to commit suicide contrary *etc.*

241(*b*) Suicide: aiding or abetting
A.B. on .... at .... did unlawfully aid [*or* abet] C.D. to commit suicide contrary *etc.*

243 Concealing body of child
A.B. on .... at .... did dispose of the dead body of a child with intent to conceal the fact that she [*or* C.D.] had been delivered of it by [*specify manner of disposal, e.g., secretly burying it*] contrary *etc.*

244 Discharging firearm with intent
A.B. on .... at .... with intent

(*a*) to wound [*or* maim *or* disfigure] C.D.

or

(*b*) to endanger the life of C.D.

or

(*c*) to prevent the arrest [*or* detention] of E.F.
did discharge a firearm [*specify*] at C.D. [*or* any other person] contrary *etc.*

244.1 Discharging air gun or pistol with intent
A.B. on .... at .... with intent

(*a*) to wound [*or* maim or disfigure] C.D.

or

(*b*) to endanger the life of C.D.

or

(*c*) to prevent the arrest [*or* detention] of E.F.
did discharge an air [*or compressed gas*] gun [*or* pistol] at C.D. [*or* any other person] contrary *etc.*

245 Bodily harm: administering noxious thing
A.B. on .... at .... did administer [*or* cause to be administered] to C.D. [*or* cause C.D. to take] poison [*or* a destructive *or* noxious thing] to wit [*specify*] with intent thereby

(*a*) to endanger the life of [*or* cause bodily harm to] C.D. contrary *etc.*

or

(*b*) to aggrieve [*or* annoy] C.D. contrary *etc.*

246 Bodily harm: overcoming resistance to commission of offence
A.B. on .... at .... with intent to enable [*or* assist] himself [*or* C.D.] to commit the indictable offence of .... did

(*a*) attempt to choke [*or* suffocate *or* strangle] C.D. by [*specify means used, e.g., a light cord*] contrary *etc.*

or

attempt to render C.D. insensible [*or* unconscious *or* incapable of resistance] by choking [*or* suffocating *or* strangling] C.D. with [*specify means used*] contrary *etc.*

or

(*b*) administer [*or* cause to be administered *or* attempt to administer] to C.D. [*or* cause *or* attempt to cause C.D. to take] a stupefying [*or* overpowering] drug [*or specify other matter or thing*] contrary *etc.*

247 Setting trap likely to cause death or bodily harm

(1)(*a*) A.B. on .... at .... with intent to cause death [*or* bodily harm] to any person did set [*or* place] a trap [*or* device *or* other thing] to wit [*specify or describe, e.g., a spring gun*] which trap [*or* device] was likely to cause death [*or* bodily harm] to a person contrary *etc.*

(1)(*b*) A.B. on .... at .... being in occupation [*or* possession] of the said premises with intent to cause death [*or* bodily harm] to any person knowingly permitted a trap [*or* device *or* other thing] to wit [*specify or describe, e.g., a spring gun*] which trap [*or* device] was likely to cause death [*or* bodily harm] to a person contrary *etc.*

(2) A.B. on .... at .... with intent to cause death [*or* bodily harm] to any person did set [*or* place] a trap [*or* device *or* other thing] to wit [*specify or describe, e.g., a spring gun*] which trap [*or* device] was likely to cause death [*or* bodily harm] to a person and thereby caused bodily harm to C.D. contrary *etc.*

or

A.B. on .... at .... being in occupation [*or* possession] of the said premises with intent to cause death [*or* bodily harm] to any person knowingly permitted a trap [*or* device *or* other thing] to wit [*specify or describe, e.g., a spring gun*] which trap [*or* device] was likely to cause death [*or* bodily harm] to a person and thereby caused bodily harm to C.D. contrary *etc.*

(3) A.B. on .... at .... which place was kept or used for the purpose of committing another indictable offence [*specify e.g. producing Cannabis marihuana*] with intent to cause death [*or* bodily harm] to any person did set [*or* place] a trap [*or* device *or* other thing] to wit [*specify or describe, e.g., a spring gun*] which trap [*or* device] was likely to cause death [*or* bodily harm] to a person contrary *etc.*

or

A.B. on .... at .... being in occupation [*or* possession] of the said premises which premises were kept or used for the purpose of committing another indictable offence [*specify e.g. producing Cannabis marihuana*] did with intent to cause death [*or* bodily harm] to any person knowingly permit a trap [*or* device *or* other thing] to wit [*specify or describe, e.g., a spring gun*] which trap [*or* device] was likely to cause death [*or* bodily harm] to a person contrary *etc.*

(4) A.B. on .... at .... which place was kept or used for the purpose of committing another indictable offence [*specify e.g. producing Cannabis marihuana*] with intent to cause death [*or* bodily harm] to any person did set [*or* place] a trap [*or* device *or* other thing] to wit [*specify or describe, e.g., a spring gun*] which trap [*or* device] was likely to cause death [*or* bodily harm] to a person and thereby caused bodily harm to C.D. contrary *etc.*

or

A.B. on .... at .... being in occupation [*or* possession] of the said premises which premises were kept or used for the purpose of committing another indictable offence [*specify e.g. producing Cannabis marihuana*] did with intent to cause death [*or* bodily harm] to any person knowingly permit a trap [*or* device *or* other thing] to wit [*specify or describe, e.g., a spring gun*] which trap [*or* device] was likely to cause death [*or* bodily harm] to a person and thereby caused bodily harm to C.D. contrary *etc.*

(5) A.B. on .... at .... with intent to cause death [*or* bodily harm] to any person did set [*or* place] a trap [*or* device *or* other thing] to wit [*specify or describe, e.g., a spring gun*] which trap [*or* device] was likely to cause death [*or* bodily harm] to a person and thereby caused the death of C.D. contrary *etc.*

or

A.B. on .... at .... being in occupation [*or* possession] of the said premises with intent to cause death [*or* bodily harm] to any person knowingly permitted a trap [*or* device *or* other thing] to wit [*specify or describe, e.g., a spring gun*] which trap [*or* device] was likely to cause death [*or* bodily harm] to a person and thereby caused the death of C.D. contrary *etc.*

263(2) Duty to safeguard excavation

A.B. on .... at .... being the owner of [*or* being in charge of *or* being the supervisor of] certain land to wit [*here specify*] on which he left an excavation did fail to guard the excavation in a manner adequate to warn persons that the excavation [*or* to prevent persons from falling in by accident] contrary *etc.*

264(1), (2) Criminal harassment

A.B. on .... [*or* between .... and ....] at .... knowing that C.D. is harassed or being reckless as to whether C.D. is harassed did without lawful authority

(2)(*a*) repeatedly follow C.D. [*or* E.F., a person known to C.D.] from place to place

or

(2)(*b*) repeatedly communicate directly or indirectly with C.D. [*or* E.F., a person known to C.D.]

or

(2)(*c*) beset or watch

(i) the dwelling-house of C.D. [*or* residence of C.D. *or* place of work of C.D. *or* place where C.D. carries on business *or* place where C.D. happens to be] at .... [*here specify the place e.g. by address*]

or

(ii) the dwelling-house of E.F. a person know to C.D. [*or* residence of E.F. a person known to C.D. *or* place of work of E.F. a person known to C.D. *or* place where E.F. a person known to C.D. carries on business *or* place where E.F. a person known to C.D. happens to be] at .... [*here specify the place e.g. by address*]

or

(2)(*d*) engage in threatening conduct directed at C.D. [*or* G.H. a member of the family of C.D.]

thereby causing C.D. to reasonably, in all the circumstances, fear for her safety [*or* the safety of E.F. a person known to C.D.] contrary *etc.*

264.1(1) Uttering threats

A.B. on .... at .... did by [*specify means, e.g., telephone*] knowingly utter a threat to C.D. [*or* convey a threat to C.D. *or* cause C.D. to receive a threat] to

(*a*) cause death [*or* bodily harm] to C.D. [*or* E.F.] contrary *etc.*

or

(*b*) burn [*or* destroy *or* damage] real [*or* personal] property of C.D. [*or* E.F.] to wit [*specify, e.g., his dwelling house or automobile*] contrary *etc.*

or

(*c*) kill [*or* poison *or* injure] an animal [*or* bird] of C.D. to wit [*specify animal or bird, e.g., cattle*] contrary *etc.*

266 Assault

A.B. on .... at .... did commit an assault on C.D. contrary *etc.*

267(*a*) Assault with weapon

A.B. on .... at .... did in committing an assault on C.D. carry [*or* use *or* threaten to use] a weapon [*or* an imitation of a weapon] to wit [*here specify*] contrary *etc.*

267(*b*) Assault causing bodily harm

A.B. on .... at .... did in committing an assault upon C.D. cause bodily harm to him contrary *etc.*

268 Aggravated assault

A.B. on .... at .... did wound [*or* maim *or* disfigure *or* endanger the life of] C.D. thereby committing an aggravated assault contrary *etc.*

269 Unlawfully causing bodily harm

A.B. on .... at .... did unlawfully cause bodily harm to C.D. by [*e.g.*, throwing acid upon the person of C.D.] contrary *etc.*

269.1 Torture

A.B. on .... at ....

being an official to wit [*specify e.g. a peace officer*]

or

acting at the instigation of [*or* with the consent of *or* the acquiescence of] C.D. an official

did inflict torture on C.D. by [*here specify act or omission constituting torture as defined in s. 269.1(2) e.g. beating the said C.D. and thereby intentionally causing him severe pain, for the purpose of obtaining a statement from C.D. as to his alleged involvement in a robbery*] contrary *etc.*

270(1) Assaulting a peace officer

(*a*) **Assaulting peace officer**

A.B. on .... at .... did assault C.D., a public [*or* peace] officer [*describe* C.D.] engaged in the execution of his duty [*or* E.F. a person acting in aid of C.D. a public (*or* peace) officer engaged in the execution of his duty] contrary *etc.*

(*b*) **Assault with intent to resist arrest**

A.B. on .... at .... did assault C.D. with intent to resist [*or* prevent] the lawful arrest [*or* detention] of himself [*or* X.Y.] contrary *etc.*

(*c*) **Assault to prevent execution of process**

A.B. on .... at .... did

(i) assault C.D., a person engaged in the lawful execution of a process against lands [*or* goods] [*or* engaged in making a lawful distress *or* seizure] contrary *etc.*

or

(ii) assault C.D. with intent to rescue property to wit [*specify*] taken under a lawful process [*or* distress *or* seizure] contrary *etc.*

271 Sexual assault

A.B. on .... at .... did commit a sexual assault on C.D. contrary *etc.*

272(2)(*a*) Miscellaneous sexual assaults while using certain firearm

(*a*) Sexual assault with weapon

A.B. on .... at .... did in committing a sexual assault on C.D. carry [*or* use *or* threaten to use] a restricted [*or* prohibited] firearm to wit [*here specify*] contrary *etc.*

(*b*) Sexual assault with threat to third party

A.B. on .... at .... did use a restricted [*or* prohibited] firearm to wit [*here specify*] and threaten to cause bodily harm to E.F. in committing a sexual assault on C.D. contrary *etc.*

(*c*) Sexual assault causing bodily harm

A.B. on .... at .... did use a restricted [*or* prohibited] firearm in committing a sexual assault on C.D. and causing bodily harm to him contrary *etc.*

(*d*) Gang sexual assault

A.B. on .... at .... did use a restricted [*or* prohibited] firearm in committing a sexual assault on C.D. to which sexual assault E.F. was also a party contrary to *etc.*

272(2)(*a*) Miscellaneous sexual assaults while using firearm: criminal organization

(*a*) Sexual assault with weapon

A.B. on .... at .... did in committing a sexual assault on C.D. carry [*or* use *or* threaten to use] a firearm to wit [*here specify*] which offence was committed for the benefit of [*or* at the direction of *or* in association with] a criminal organization to wit .... contrary *etc.*

(*b*) Sexual assault with threat to third party

A.B. on .... at .... did use a firearm to wit [*here specify*] and threaten to cause bodily harm to E.F. in committing a sexual assault on C.D. contrary *etc.*

(*c*) Sexual assault causing bodily harm

A.B. on .... at .... did use a firearm in committing a sexual assault on C.D. and causing bodily harm to him contrary *etc.*

(*d*) Gang sexual assault

A.B. on .... at .... did use a firearm in committing a sexual assault on C.D. to which sexual assault E.F. was also a party contrary to *etc.*

272(2)(*a*.1) Miscellaneous sexual assaults while using firearm

(*a*) Sexual assault with weapon

A.B. on .... at .... did in committing a sexual assault on C.D. carry [*or* use *or* threaten to use] a firearm to wit [*here specify*] contrary *etc.*

(*b*) Sexual assault with threat to third party

A.B. on .... at .... did use a firearm to wit [*here specify*] and threaten to cause bodily harm to E.F. in committing a sexual assault on C.D. contrary *etc.*

(*c*) Sexual assault causing bodily harm

A.B. on .... at .... did use a firearm in committing a sexual assault on C.D. and causing bodily harm to him contrary *etc.*

(*d*) Gang sexual assault

A.B. on .... at .... did use a firearm in committing a sexual assault on C.D. to which sexual assault E.F. was also a party contrary to *etc.*

272(2)(*b*) Miscellaneous sexual assaults

(*a*) Sexual assault with weapon

A.B. on .... at .... did in committing a sexual assault on C.D. carry [*or* use *or* threaten to use] a weapon [*or* an imitation of a weapon] to wit [*here specify*] contrary *etc*.

(*b*) Sexual assault with threat to third party

A.B. on .... at .... did in committing a sexual assault on C.D. threaten to cause bodily harm to E.F. contrary *etc*.

(*c*) Sexual assault causing bodily harm

A.B. on .... at .... did in committing a sexual assault on C.D. cause bodily harm to him contrary *etc*.

(*d*) Gang sexual assault

A.B. on .... at .... did commit a sexual assault on C.D. to which sexual assault E.F. was also a party contrary to *etc*.

NOTE: To ensure that there is no doubt as to which form of sexual assault is charged it is strongly recommended that the particular Code section, subsection and paragraph be specified.

273(2)(*a*) Aggravated sexual assault while using certain firearms

A.B. on .... at .... did use a restricted [*or* prohibited] firearm [*here specify*] in committing a sexual assault on C.D. and wound [*or* maim *or* disfigure or endanger the life of] the said C.D. thereby committing an aggravated sexual assault contrary *etc*.

273(2)(*a*.1) Aggravated sexual assault while using firearm: criminal organization

A.B. on .... at .... did use a firearm [*here specify*] in committing a sexual assault on C.D. and wound [*or* maim *or* disfigure or endanger the life of] the said C.D. thereby committing an aggravated sexual assault which offence was committed for the benefit of [*or* at the direction of *or* in association with] a criminal organization to wit .... contrary *etc*.

273(2)(*b*) Aggravated sexual assault

A.B. on .... at .... did in committing a sexual assault on C.D. wound [*or* maim *or* disfigure or endanger the life of] the said C.D. thereby committing an aggravated sexual assault contrary *etc*.

273.3(1) Removal of child from Canada

(*a*) A.B. on .... at .... with the intention of committing an act outside Canada that if it were committed in Canada would be an offence against section 151 [*or* 152 *or* 160(3) *or* 173(2)] of the *Criminal Code* in respect of C.D. a person ordinarily resident in Canada, and under the age of sixteen years, did [*specify act done e.g. obtain false identification for C.D.*] for the purpose of removing C.D. from Canada contrary *etc*.

(*b*) A.B. on .... at .... with the intention of committing an act outside Canada that if it were committed in Canada would be an offence against section 153 of the *Criminal Code* in respect of C.D. a person ordinarily resident in Canada, and over the age of sixteen years and under the age of eighteen years, did [*specify act done e.g. obtain false identification for C.D.*] for the purpose of removing C.D. from Canada contrary *etc*.

(*c*) A.B. on .... at .... with the intention of committing an act outside Canada that if it were committed in Canada would be an offence against section 155 [*or* 159 *or* 160(2) *or* 170 *or* 171 *or* 267 *or* 268 *or* 269 *or* 271 *or* 272 *or* 273] of the

Criminal Code in respect of C.D. a person ordinarily resident in Canada, and under the age of eighteen years, did [*specify act done e.g. obtain false identification for C.D.*] for the purpose of removing C.D. from Canada contrary *etc.*

276.3(1) Prohibited publication of complainant's sexual activity

A.B. on .... at .... did publish in a newspaper [*or* broadcast] to wit [*here specify*]

(*a*) the contents of an application made under s. 276.1 of the *Criminal Code* at the trial of C.D. to determine the admissibility of evidence of the sexual activity of E.F. to wit [*here specify matter published or broadcast*] contrary *etc.*

or

(*b*) the evidence taken [*or* the information given *or* the representations made] at an application made under s. 276.1 [*or* a hearing under s. 276.2] of the *Criminal Code* at the trial of C.D. to determine the admissibility of evidence of the sexual activity of E.F. to wit [*here specify matter published or broadcast*] contrary *etc.*

or

(*c*) the decision of [*here specify judge, provincial court judge or justice*] made under subsection 276.1(4) of the *Criminal Code* at the trial of C.D. that a hearing be held into the admissibility of evidence of the sexual activity of E.F. to wit [*here specify matter published or broadcast*] contrary *etc.*

or

(*d*) the determination made [*or* the reasons given] by [*here specify judge, provincial court judge or justice*] made under subsection 276.2 of the *Criminal Code* at the trial of C.D. as to the admissibility of the evidence of the sexual activity of E.F. to wit [*here specify matter published or broadcast*] contrary *etc.*

278.9(1) Prohibited publication of personal information records

A.B. on .... at .... did publish in a newspaper [*or* broadcast] to wit [*here specify*]

(*a*) the contents of an application made under s. 278.3 of the *Criminal Code* at the trial of C.D. for production of records containing personal information concerning E.F. to wit [*here specify matter published or broadcast*] contrary *etc.*

or

(*b*) the evidence taken [*or* the information given *or* the submissions made] at a hearing under s. 278.4(1) [*or* s. 278.6(2)] of the *Criminal Code* at the trial of C.D. to determine whether records containing personal information concerning E.F. should be produced to the court [*or* produced to the said C.D.] to wit [*here specify matter published or broadcast*] contrary *etc.*

or

(*c*) the determination made [*or* the reasons given] by [*here specify judge, provincial court judge or justice*] made under subsection 278.5 [*or* subsection 278.7(1) *or* s. 278.8] of the *Criminal Code* at the trial of C.D. as to the production of records containing personal information concerning E.F. to wit [*here specify matter published or broadcast*] contrary *etc.*

279(1.1)(*a*) Kidnapping while using certain firearms

A.B. on .... at .... did use a restricted [*or* prohibited] firearm to wit [*here specify*] in kidnapping C.D. with intent

(*a*) to cause him to be confined [*or* imprisoned] against his will contrary *etc.*

or

(*b*) to cause him to be unlawfully sent [*or* transported] out of Canada against his will contrary *etc.*

or

(*c*) to hold him for ransom [*or* to service against his will] contrary *etc.*

279(1.1)(*a*) Kidnapping while using firearm: criminal organization
A.B. on .... at .... did use a firearm to wit [*here specify*] in kidnapping C.D. with intent

(*a*) to cause him to be confined [*or* imprisoned] against his will which offence was committed for the benefit of [*or* at the direction of *or* in association with] a criminal organization to wit .... contrary *etc.*

or

(*b*) to cause him to be unlawfully sent [*or* transported] out of Canada against his will which offence was committed for the benefit of [*or* at the direction of *or* in association with] a criminal organization to wit .... contrary *etc.*

or

(*c*) to hold him for ransom [*or* to service against his will] which offence was committed for the benefit of [*or* at the direction of *or* in association with] a criminal organization to wit .... contrary *etc.*

279(1.1)(*a*.1) Kidnapping while using firearm
A.B. on .... at .... did use a firearm to wit [*here specify*] in kidnapping C.D. with intent

(*a*) to cause him to be confined [*or* imprisoned] against his will contrary *etc.*

or

(*b*) to cause him to be unlawfully sent [*or* transported] out of Canada against his will contrary *etc.*

or

(*c*) to hold him for ransom [*or* to service against his will] contrary *etc.*

279(1.1)(*b*) Kidnapping
A.B. on .... at .... did kidnap C.D. with intent

(*a*) to cause him to be confined [*or* imprisoned] against his will contrary *etc.*

or

(*b*) to cause him to be unlawfully sent [*or* transported] out of Canada against his will contrary *etc.*

or

(*c*) to hold him for ransom [*or* to service against his will] contrary *etc.*

279(2) Forcible confinement etc.
A.B. on .... at .... did without lawful authority confine [*or* imprison *or* forcibly seize] C.D. contrary *etc.*

279.1(2)(*a*) Hostage taking using certain firearms
A.B. on .... at .... did use a restricted [*or* prohibited] firearm to wit [*specify*] in taking hostage C.D. by confining [*or* imprisoning *or* forcibly seizing *or* detaining] C.D. and uttering [*or* conveying *or* causing any person to receive] a threat to cause the death of C.D. [*or* cause bodily harm to C.D. *or* continue the confinement, imprisonment *or* detention of C.D.] with the intent to induce E.F. [*or* specify the group, state, etc.] to [*specify the demand, e.g., release G.H. from Kingston Penitentiary*] as a condition of the release of C.D. contrary *etc.*

279.1(2)(*a*) Hostage taking using firearm: criminal organization

A.B. for the benefit of [*or* at the direction of *or* in association with] a criminal organization to wit .... on .... at .... did use a firearm to wit [*specify*] in taking hostage C.D. by confining [*or* imprisoning *or* forcibly seizing *or* detaining] C.D. and uttering [*or* conveying *or* causing any person to receive] a threat to cause the death of C.D. [*or* cause bodily harm to C.D. *or* continue the confinement, imprisonment *or* detention of C.D.] with the intent to induce E.F. [*or* specify the group, state, etc.] to [*specify the demand, e.g., release G.H. from Kingston Penitentiary*] as a condition of the release of C.D. contrary *etc.*

279.1(2)(*a*.1) Hostage taking using firearm

A.B. on .... at .... did use a firearm to wit [*specify*] in taking hostage C.D. by confining [*or* imprisoning *or* forcibly seizing *or* detaining] C.D. and uttering [*or* conveying *or* causing any person to receive] a threat to cause the death of C.D. [*or* cause bodily harm to C.D. *or* continue the confinement, imprisonment *or* detention of C.D.] with the intent to induce E.F. [*or* specify the group, state, etc.] to [*specify the demand, e.g., release G.H. from Kingston Penitentiary*] as a condition of the release of C.D. contrary *etc.*

279.1(2)(*b*) Hostage taking

A.B. on .... at .... did take hostage C.D. by confining [*or* imprisoning *or* forcibly seizing *or* detaining] C.D. and uttering [*or* conveying *or* causing any person to receive] a threat to cause the death of C.D. [*or* cause bodily harm to C.D. *or* continue the confinement, imprisonment *or* detention of C.D.] with the intent to induce E.F. [*or* specify the group, state, etc.] to [*specify the demand, e.g., release G.H. from Kingston Penitentiary*] as a condition of the release of C.D. contrary *etc.*

280(1) Abduction of person under sixteen

A.B. on .... at .... without lawful authority did take [*or* cause to be taken] C.D., an unmarried person under the age of sixteen years, out of possession of and against the will of E.F., his parent [*or* guardian *or specify other person*], who had lawful care [*or* charge] of him contrary *etc.*

281 Abduction of person under fourteen

A.B. not being the parent [*or* guardian *or specify other applicable person*] having lawful care [*or* charge] of E.F., a person under the age of fourteen years, on .... at .... with intent to deprive C.D., the parent [*or* guardian *or specify other applicable person*] of the said E.F. of the possession of E.F. did unlawfully

take [*or* entice away *or* detain *or* conceal] the said E.F. contrary *etc.*

or

receive [*or* harbour] the said E.F. contrary *etc.*

282(1) Abduction in contravention of custody order

A.B. being the parent [*or* guardian *or specify other applicable person*] having lawful care [*or* charge] of E.F. a person under the age of fourteen years on .... at .... in contravention of the custody provisions of a custody order in relation to the said E.F. made by [*specify full title of court*] at [*specify place where court order made*] on [*insert date of order*] with intent to deprive C.D. the parent [*or* guardian *or specify other applicable person*] of E.F. of the possession of E.F. did

(*a*) take [*or* entice away *or* detain *or* conceal] the said E.F. contrary *etc.*

or

(*b*) receive [*or* harbour] the said E.F. contrary *etc.*

283(1) Abduction

A.B. being the parent [*or* guardian *or specify other applicable person*] having lawful care [*or* charge] of E.F. a person under the age of fourteen years on .... at .... with intent to deprive C.D. the parent [*or* guardian *or specify other applicable person*] having lawful care [*or* charge] of E.F. of the possession of E.F. did

(*a*) take [*or* entice away *or* detain *or* conceal] the said E.F. contrary *etc.*

or

(*b*) receive [*or* harbour] the said E.F. contrary *etc.*

287(1) Procuring miscarriage of another

A.B. on .... at .... with intent to procure the miscarriage of C.D., did [*specify means used, e.g., use manipulation or an instrument or administer a drug*] for such purpose contrary *etc.*

287(2) Self-procured miscarriage

A.B., a female person being pregnant, on .... at .... with intent to procure her own miscarriage did [*specify means used, e.g., use an instrument or drug or noxious thing or manipulation*] [*or* did permit (*specify means, e.g., an instrument or drug or noxious thing or manipulation*) to be used for such purpose] contrary *etc.*

291 Bigamy

(*a*) A.B. on .... at .... then being married to C.D. [*or* knowing E.F. to be married to G.H.] did go through a form of marriage with E.F. and did thereby commit bigamy contrary *etc.*

or

A.B. on .... at .... did on the same day to wit [*specify date*] [*or* simultaneously] go through a form of marriage with C.D. and E.F. and did thereby commit bigamy contrary *etc.*

(*b*) A.B. on ...., at ...., being then married to C.D. and being a Canadian citizen resident in Canada, did leave Canada with intent to go through a form of marriage with E.F. and did on the .... day of .... 19..............., [at the City of Reno in the State of Nevada, one of the United States of America] go through a form of marriage with E.F. and did thereby commit bigamy contrary *etc.*

NOTE: Charge [b] above may be adapted according to the facts to comply with the provisions of s. 290(1)(*a*)(ii) or (iii)

292 Procuring feigned marriage

A.B. on .... at .... did procure [*or* knowingly aid in procuring] a feigned marriage between himself and C.D. contrary *etc.*

293 Polygamy

A.B., a male person, on .... at .... with C.D., a female person, did practice [*or* enter into *or* agree to practice *or* enter into] a form of polygamy contract *etc.*

294 Pretending to solemnize marriage

(*a*) A.B. on .... at .... without lawful authority did [pretend to] solemnize a marriage between C.D. and E.F. contrary *etc.*

or

(*b*) A.B. on .... at .... did procure C.D. to solemnize a marriage between E.F. and G.H. knowing that C.D. was not lawfully authorized to solemnize the marriage contrary *etc.*

295 Solemnizing marriage contrary to law

A.B. on .... at ...., being lawfully authorized to solemnize a marriage, did knowingly and wilfully solemnize a marriage between C.D. and E.F. in violation of the laws of the Province of .... [*specify violation, e.g., without publication of banns and without any licence*] as required by section .... of the [*specify provincial Act in full*] of the said province contrary *etc.*

300 Defamatory libel known to be false

A.B. on .... at .... did publish a defamatory libel, knowing that it was false, by [*specify means e.g. delivering to C.D. a pamphlet entitled etc.*] contrary *etc.*

301 Defamatory libel

A.B. on .... at .... did publish a defamatory libel by [*specify means e.g. delivering to C.D. a pamphlet entitled etc.*] contrary *etc.*

302(1) Extortion by libel

A.B. on .... at .... with intent

(*a*) to extort money from C.D.

or

(*b*) to induce C.D. to confer on E.F. [*or* procure for E.F.] an appointment [*or* office] of profit [*or* trust] to wit [*specify appointment or office*]

did publish [*or* threaten to publish *or* offer to abstain from publishing *or* offer to prevent the publication of] a defamatory libel, to wit [*specify defamatory libel e.g. a pamphlet entitled etc.*] contrary *etc.*

318(1) Advocating genocide

A.B. on .... at .... did advocate [*or* promote] genocide [*specify means, e.g., by publishing a newsletter entitled "..............." containing a statement "..............."*] contrary *etc.*

319(1) Public incitement of hatred

A.B. on .... at ...., in a public place to wit [*specify*], did by communicating statements [*specify*] incite hatred against an identifiable group to wit [*specify the group*] with a likelihood of leading to a breach of the peace contrary *etc.*

319(2) Wilful promotion of hatred

A.B. on .... at .... did by communicating statements [*specify*] wilfully promote hatred against an identifiable group to wit [*specify the group*] contrary *etc.*

320.13(1) Dangerous operation

A.B. on .... at .... did operate a conveyance in a manner that was dangerous to the public contrary *etc.*

320.13(2) Dangerous operation causing bodily harm

NOTE: Where the dangerous operation has caused bodily harm, prior to the word "contrary" insert "and thereby caused bodily harm to C.D."

320.13(3) Dangerous operation causing death

NOTE: Where the dangerous operation has caused death, prior to the word "contrary" insert "and thereby caused the death of C.D."

320.14(1)(*a*) Operating while impaired

A.B. on .... at .... while his ability to operate a conveyance was impaired by alcohol [*or* a drug *or* a combination of alcohol and a drug] did operate a conveyance contrary *etc.*

320.14(1)(*b*) Operating with over 80 mgs. of alcohol

A.B. on .... at .... did within two hours of ceasing to operate a conveyance have a blood alcohol concentration that was equal to or exceeded eighty milligrams of alcohol in one hundred millilitres of blood contrary *etc.*

320.14(1)(*c*) Operating with excessive blood drug concentration

A.B. on .... at .... did within two hours of ceasing to operate a conveyance have a blood drug concentration that was equal to or exceeded the blood drug concentration prescribed by [*state applicable regulation*] contrary *etc.*

320.14(1)(*d*) Operating with excessive blood alcohol and blood drug concentration

A.B. on .... at .... did within two hours of ceasing to operate a conveyance have a blood alcohol concentration and blood drug concentration that was equal to or exceeded the blood drug concentration prescribed by [*state applicable regulation*] contrary *etc.*

320.14(2) Impaired operation (or operation over legal limit) causing bodily harm

NOTE: Where the impaired operation or operation with excess blood alcohol and/or blood drug concentration has caused bodily harm, prior to the word "contrary" insert "and thereby caused bodily harm to C.D."

320.14(3) Impaired operation (or operation over legal limit) causing death

NOTE: Where the impaired operation or operation with excess blood alcohol and/or blood drug concentration has caused death, prior to the word "contrary" insert "and thereby caused the death of C.D."

320.14(4) Operating with low blood drug concentration (summary conviction offence)

A.B. on .... at .... did within two hours of ceasing to operate a conveyance have a blood drug concentration that was equal to or exceeded the blood drug concentration prescribed by [*specify applicable regulation*] contrary *etc.*

320.15(1) Failure or refusal to comply with breath screening demand

A.B. on .... at .... did without reasonable excuse fail [*or* refuse] to comply with a demand made to him by C.D., a peace officer, under s. 320.27 of the *Criminal Code*

(*a*) to immediately provide the samples of his breath as in the opinion of C.D. was necessary to enable a proper analysis of his breath to be made by means of an approved screening device contrary *etc.*

or

(*b*) to accompany C.D. for the purpose of enabling the samples of his breath as in the opinion of C.D. were necessary to be taken for analysis by means of an approved screening device contrary *etc.*

320.15(1) Failure or refusal to comply with bodily substance screening demand

A.B. on .... at .... did without reasonable excuse fail [*or* refuse] to comply with a demand made to him by C.D., a peace officer, under s. 320.27 of the *Criminal Code*

(*a*) to immediately provide the samples of a bodily substance as in the opinion of C.D. were necessary to enable a proper analysis to be made by means of approved drug screening equipment contrary *etc.*

or

(*b*) to accompany C.D. for the purpose of enabling the samples of a bodily substance as in the opinion of C.D. were necessary to be taken for analysis by means of approved drug screening equipment contrary *etc.*

320.15(1) Failure or refusal to comply with physical coordination test demand

A.B. on .... at .... did without reasonable excuse fail [*or* refuse] to comply with a demand made to him by C.D., a peace officer, under s. 320.27 of the *Criminal Code*

(*a*) to immediately perform the physical coordination tests prescribed by [*specify applicable regulation*] contrary *etc.*

or

(*b*) to accompany C.D. for the purpose of performing physical coordination tests prescribed by [*specify applicable regulation*] contrary *etc.*

320.15(1) Failure or refusal to comply with breath demand

A.B. on .... at .... did without reasonable excuse fail [*or* refuse] to comply with a demand made to him by C.D., a peace officer, under s. 320.28 of the *Criminal Code*

(*a*) to provide then or as soon thereafter as was practicable samples of his breath as in the opinion of a qualified technician were necessary to enable a proper analysis to be made in order to determine the concentration, if any, of alcohol in his blood contrary *etc.*

or

(*b*) to accompany C.D. for the purpose of enabling samples of his breath to be taken contrary *etc.*

320.15(1) Failure or refusal to comply with drug evaluation demand

A.B. on .... at .... did without reasonable excuse fail [*or* refuse] to comply with a demand made to him by C.D., a peace officer, under s. 320.28 of the *Criminal Code*

(*a*) to submit then or as soon thereafter was practicable to an evaluation conducted by an evaluating officer to determine whether his ability to operate a conveyance was impaired by a drug or by a combination of alcohol and a drug contrary *etc.*

or

(*a*) to accompany C.D. for the purpose of enabling an evaluation officer to determine whether his ability to operate a conveyance was impaired by a drug or by a combination of alcohol and a drug contrary *etc.*

320.15(1) Failure or refusal to comply with blood demand

A.B. on .... at .... did without reasonable excuse fail [*or* refuse] to comply with a demand made to him by C.D., a peace officer, under s. 320.28 of the *Criminal Code*

(*a*) to provide then or as soon thereafter as was practicable samples of his blood as in the opinion of a qualified technician [*or* qualified medical practitioner] were necessary to enable a proper analysis to be made in order to determine A.B.'s blood alcohol concentration [*and/or* blood drug concentration] contrary *etc.*

or

(*b*) to accompany C.D. for the purpose of enabling a qualified technician [*or* qualified medical practitioner] to take blood samples contrary *etc.*

320.15(2) Failure to comply with demand after accident resulting in bodily harm

Note: Where the failure or refusal has followed an accident resulting in bodily harm, prior to the words "without reasonable excuse", insert "knowing at the time of the failure [*or* refusal], or being reckless as to whether, he was involved in an accident that resulted in bodily harm to another person . . ."

320.15(3) Failure to comply with demand after accident resulting in death

Note: Where the failure or refusal has followed an accident causing death, prior to the words "without reasonable excuse", insert "knowing at the time of the failure [*or* refusal], or being reckless as to whether, he was involved in an accident that resulted the death of another person . . ."

320.16(1) Failure to stop after accident

A.B. on .... at .... while operating a conveyance and knowing, or being reckless to whether, the conveyance had been involved in an accident with a person or another conveyance, failed without reasonable excuse to stop the conveyance, give their name and address and, if any person has been injured or appeared to require assistance, offer assistance.

320.16(2) Failure to stop after accident resulting in bodily harm

Note: Where the failure to stop followed an accident causing bodily harm, prior to the words "failed without reasonable excuse", insert "and knowing at the time of the failure, or being reckless as to whether, the accident caused bodily harm to another person . . ."

320.16(3) Failure to stop after accident resulting in death

Note: Where the failure to stop followed an accident causing death, prior to the words "failed without reasonable excuse," insert "and knowing at the time of the failure, or being reckless as to whether, the accident caused the death of another person . . ."

320.17 Flight from peace officer

A.B. on .... at .... while operating a motor vehicle [*or* vessel] and being pursued by a peace officer, did fail without reasonable excuse to stop his vehicle [*or* vessel] as soon as was reasonable in the circumstances contrary *etc.*

320.18(1) Operating while prohibited

A.B. on .... at ....did operate a conveyance while prohibited from so doing by reason of

(*a*) an order pursuant to s. 320.24 of the *Criminal Code* contrary *etc.*

or

(*b*) the legal disqualification [*or* restriction] in the Province of .... of his right or privilege to operate a [*specify type of conveyance*] contrary *etc.*

333.1 Motor Vehicle Theft

A.B. on . . . . at . . . . did steal a motor vehicle [*specify the vehicle e.g. by licence plate number*] the property of C.D. and did thereby commit theft contrary to s. 333.1 of the *Criminal Code of Canada.*

Note: We advise specifying the section number so that the accused is aware that he or she is not charged under the general theft section in s. 334.]

334 Theft

A.B. on .... at .... did steal [*specify item*], the property of C.D. of a value [not] exceeding five thousand dollars contrary *etc.*

Note: It is suggested that this general form of charge may be used for the specific forms of theft referred to in ss. 323, 328, 330, 331 and 332. The particular type of theft may be subsequently proved. Two alternate forms for the types of theft referred to in s. 326 follow.

Theft of Electricity or Gas (s. 326(1)(*a*))

A.B. on .... at .... did fraudulently [*or* maliciously *or* without colour of right] consume [*or* abstract *or* use] electricity [*or* gas] the property of .... of a value [not] exceeding five thousand dollars and did thereby commit theft contrary *etc.*

or

Theft of Telecommunications Service (s. 326(1)(*b*))

A.B. on .... at .... did fraudulently [*or* maliciously *or* without colour of right] use a telecommunication wire [*or* cable] the property of .... the value of such use [not] exceeding five thousand dollars and did thereby commit theft contrary *etc.*

335(1) Taking motor vehicle or vessel without consent (joy-riding)

A.B. on .... at .... did take a motor vehicle to wit [*specify vehicle*] without the consent of C.D., the owner thereof, with intent to drive [*or* use] it [*or* cause it to be driven *or* used] contrary *etc.*

or

A.B. on .... at .... did take a vessel to wit [*specify*] without the consent of C.D., the owner thereof, with intent to navigate [*or* operate] it [*or* cause it to be navigated or operated] contrary *etc.*

335(1) Occupant of motor vehicle or vessel without consent

A.B. on .... at .... did occupy a motor vehicle [*or* vessel] to wit [*specify motor vehicle or vessel*] knowing that it was taken without the consent of the owner thereof contrary *etc.*

341 Fraudulent concealment

A.B. on .... at .... did for a fraudulent purpose take [*or* obtain *or* remove *or* conceal] certain property of C.D. to wit [*specify property, e.g., a bicycle*] contrary *etc.*

342(1) Theft, forgery, etc. of credit card

(*a*) A.B. on .... at .... did steal a credit card [*specify credit card, e.g., a Toronto-Dominion VISA card #x*] from C.D. contrary *etc.*

or

(*b*) A.B. on .... at .... did forge [*or* falsify] a credit card [*specify credit card*] by [*specify means, e.g., by altering the numbers on the said card*] contrary *etc.*

or

(*c*)

(i) A.B. on .... at .... did have in his possession [*or* used *or* trafficked in] a credit card [*specify credit card*] knowing that the said card was obtained by the commission in Canada of an offence contrary *etc.*

or

(ii) A.B. on .... at .... did have in his possession [*or* used *or* trafficked in] a credit card [*specify credit card*] knowing that the said card was obtained in [*specify, e.g., the State of New York*] by the commission of an offence which had it occurred in Canada would have constituted an offence contrary *etc.*

or

(*d*) A.B. on .... at .... used a credit card [*specify credit card*] knowing that the said credit card had been revoked [*or* cancelled] contrary *etc.*

342(3) Possess, traffic etc. in credit card data

A.B. on .... at .... did fraudulently and without colour of right have in his [*or* her] possession credit card data that would enable a person to use a credit card [*here specify credit card*] [*or* obtain the services that are provided by the issuer of a credit card [*here specify issuer*] to credit card holders] contrary *etc.*

or

A.B. on .... at .... did fraudulently and without colour of right use credit card data that would enable a person to use a credit card [*here specify credit card*] [*or* obtain the services that are provided by the issuer of a credit card [*here specify issuer*] to credit card holders] contrary *etc.*

or

A.B. on .... at .... did fraudulently and without colour of right traffic in credit card data that would enable a person to use a credit card [*here specify credit card*] [*or* obtain the services that are provided by the issuer of a credit card [*here specify issuer*] to credit card holders] contrary *etc.*

or

A.B. on .... at .... did fraudulently and without colour of right permit C.D. to use credit card data that would enable a person to use a credit card [*here specify credit card*] [*or* obtain the services that are provided by the issuer of a credit card [*here specify issuer*] to credit card holders] contrary *etc.*

342.01 Instrument for use in forging credit card

A.B. on .... at .... did without lawful justification or excuse make [*or* repair *or* buy *or* sell *or* export from Canada *or* import into Canada *or* have in his possession] an instrument [*or* device *or* apparatus *or* material *or* thing] to wit .... that he knew had been used [*or* was adapted for use *or* intended for use] in forging [*or* falsifying] credit cards contrary *etc.*

342.1(1) Unauthorized use of computer

A.B. on .... at .... did fraudulently and without colour of right

(*a*) obtain, directly or indirectly a computer service to wit [*specify computer service e.g., the data processing facility at the University of Toronto*] contrary *etc.*

(*b*) by means of an electromagnetic [*or* acoustic *or* mechanical] device to wit [*specify type etc.*] intercepted [*or* caused to be intercepted], directly or indirectly, a function of a computer system to wit [*specify computer system e.g. the mainframe computer facility of the Public Utilities Commission*] contrary *etc.*

(*c*) used [*or* caused to be used] directly or indirectly, a computer system [*specify computer system*] with intent to

obtain, directly or indirectly a computer service to wit [*specify computer service*] contrary *etc.*

intercept [*or* cause to be intercepted], directly or indirectly a function of a computer system to wit [*specify computer system*] by means of an electromagnetic [*or* acoustic *or* mechanical] device to wit [*specify type etc.*] contrary *etc.*

commit the offence contrary to [*specify offence contrary to s. 430 in relation to data or a computer system e.g. s. 430(1.1)(a) of the Criminal Code*] by wilfully destroying data to wit [*specify data*] contrary *etc.*

(*d*) use [*or* have in his possession *or* traffic in *or* permit C.D. to have access to] a computer password that would enable him [*or* C.D. *or* E.F.] to commit the offence [*here specify offence contrary to paragraph (a), (b) or (c) e.g. contrary to s. 342(1)(a) of the Criminal Code of fraudulently and without colour of right obtaining directly or indirectly the data processing facilty at the University of Toronto*] contrary *etc.*

342.2 Instrument for obtaining authorized use of computer etc.

A.B. on .... at .... did without lawful justification or excuse make an instrument [*or* device *or* component of an instrument *or* component of a device] to wit .... the design of which rendered it primarily useful for committing the offence [*here specify offence under s. 342.1 e.g. contrary to s. 342.1(1)(a) of the Criminal Code of fraudulently and without colour of right obtaining directly or indirectly a computer service*] under circumstances that gave rise to a reasonable inference that the instrument [*or* device *or* component of an instrument *or* component of a device] had been used [*or* is intended for use *or* was intended for use] to commit the said offence contrary *etc.*

344(1)(*a*) Robbery using certain firearms

A.B. on .... at .... did use a restricted [*or* prohibited] firearm to wit [*here specify firearm*] in robbing C.D. of [*specify property taken, e.g., a wallet containing personal papers and the sum of fifty dollars*] contrary *etc.*

344(1)(*a*) Robbery using firearm: criminal organization

A.B. for the benefit of [*or* at the direction of *or* in association with] a criminal organization to wit .... on .... at .... did use a firearm to wit [*here specify firearm*] in robbing C.D. of [*specify property taken, e.g., a wallet containing personal papers and the sum of fifty dollars*] contrary *etc.*

344(1)(*a*.1) Robbery using firearm

A.B. on .... at .... did use a firearm to wit [*here specify firearm*] in robbing C.D. of [*specify property taken, e.g., a wallet containing personal papers and the sum of fifty dollars*] contrary *etc.*

344(1)(*b*) Robbery

A.B. on .... at .... did steal [*specify property stolen, e.g., the sum of fifty dollars*] from C.D. and at the time thereof did use violence [*or* threats of violence] to C.D. contrary *etc.*

or

A.B. on .... at .... did steal [*specify property stolen, e.g., a gold wrist watch*] from C.D. and at the time thereof [*or* immediately before *or* immediately thereafter] did wound [*or* beat *or* strike *or specify personal violence used*] C.D. contrary *etc.*

or

A.B. on .... at .... did assault C.D. with intent to steal from him contrary *etc.*

or

A.B. on .... at .... did steal from C.D. [*specify property stolen, e.g., the sum of fifty dollars*] while armed with an offensive weapon [*or* imitation of an offensive weapon] to wit [*specify weapon*] contrary *etc.*

NOTE: Robbery is defined in s. 343(*a*)-(*d*), with which the above four charges comply.

or

(General Charge)

A.B. on .... at .... did rob C.D. of [*specify property taken, e.g., a wallet containing personal papers and the sum of fifty dollars*] contrary *etc.*

345 Stopping mail with intent

A.B. on .... at .... did stop a mail conveyance to wit [*specify type of conveyance, e.g., truck or train*] with intent to rob [*or* search] it contrary *etc.*

346(1.1)(*a*) Extortion using certain firearms

A.B. on .... at .... without reasonable justification or excuse and with intent to obtain [*specify item requested, e.g., the sum of $1,000*] did use a restricted [*or* prohibited] firearm to wit [*specify firearm*] and induce [*or* attempt to induce] C.D. by threats [*or* accusations *or* menaces *or* violence] to [*specify act done or caused to be done by C.D., e.g., pay the said sum of $1,000 to A.B.*] contrary *etc.*

346(1.1)(*a*) Extortion using firearm: criminal organization

A.B. for the benefit of [*or* at the direction of *or* in association with] a criminal organization to wit .... on .... at .... without reasonable justification or excuse and with intent to obtain [*specify item requested, e.g., the sum of $1,000*] did use a firearm to wit [*specify firearm*] and induce [*or* attempt to induce] C.D. by threats [*or* accusations *or* menaces *or* violence] to [*specify act done or caused to be done by C.D., e.g., pay the said sum of $1,000 to A.B.*] contrary *etc.*

346(1.1)(*a*.1) Extortion using firearm

A.B. on .... at .... without reasonable justification or excuse and with intent to obtain [*specify item requested, e.g., the sum of $1,000*] did use a firearm to wit [*specify firearm*] and induce [*or* attempt to induce] C.D. by threats [*or* accusations *or* menaces *or* violence] to [*specify act done or caused to be done by C.D., e.g., pay the said sum of $1,000 to A.B.*] contrary *etc.*

346(1.1)(*b*) Extortion

A.B. on .... at .... without reasonable justification or excuse and with intent to obtain [*specify item requested, e.g., the sum of $1,000*] did induce [*or* attempt to induce] C.D. by threats [*or* accusations *or* menaces *or* violence] to [*specify act done or caused to be done by C.D., e.g., pay the said sum of $1,000 to A.B.*] contrary *etc.*

or

A.B. on .... at .... without reasonable justification or excuse and with intent to obtain .... dollars from C.D. did [*accuse C.D. of committing the offence of bigamy*] and did receive from C.D. the said sum of .... dollars contrary *etc.*

347(1) Criminal interest rate

(*a*) A.B. on .... at .... entered into an agreement [*or* arrangement] with C.D. to wit [*specify agreement, e.g., for a loan of $1,000 secured by a promissory note dated Aug. 1, 1981*] to receive interest at a criminal rate, namely [*specify rate, e.g., an effective annual rate of interest of 75 per cent on the sum of $1,000 advanced under the agreement*] contrary *etc.*

or

(*b*) A.B. on .... at .... received a payment [*or* partial payment] of interest of [*specify amount, e.g., $750*] from C.D. at a criminal rate to wit, [*specify rate and transaction, e.g., an effective annual rate of interest of 75 per cent on the advance of $1,000 on Aug. 1, 1981*] contrary *etc.*

348(1)(*a*) Breaking and entering with intent

A.B. on .... at .... did break and enter a certain place to wit [*specify type of place, e.g., a dwelling house or store or factory*] situate at .... with intent to commit an indictable offence therein contrary *etc.*

348(1)(*b*) Breaking, entering and committing

A.B. on .... at .... did break and enter a certain place to wit [*specify type of place, e.g., a dwelling house, store, factory etc.*] situate at .... and did commit therein the indictable offence of .... contrary *etc.*

348(1)(*c*) Breaking out

A.B. on .... at .... did break out of a certain place to wit [*specify type of place, e.g., a dwelling house, store etc.*] situate at .... after committing therein the indictable offence of .... contrary *etc.*

or

A.B. on .... at .... did break out of a certain place to wit [*specify type of place*] situate at .... after having entered the said place with intent to commit an indictable offence therein contrary *etc.*

349(1) Being unlawfully in dwelling house

A.B. on .... at .... without lawful excuse did enter [*or* was in] the dwelling house of C.D. situate at .... with intent to commit an indictable offence therein contrary *etc.*

351(1) Possession of break-in instruments

A.B. on .... at .... without lawful excuse did have in his possession [an] instrument[s] suitable for the purpose of breaking into a place [*or* into vehicle *or* vault *or* safe] to wit [*specify instrument(s), e.g., nitro-glycerine etc.*] under circumstances [*specify, e.g., mode of concealment, type of instrument*] that gave rise to a reasonable inference that the said instrument had been used [*or* was intended to be used] for such purpose contrary *etc.*

351(2) Disguise with intent

A.B. on .... at .... with intent to commit an indictable offence did have his face masked [*or* coloured *or specify manner of disguise*] contrary *etc.*

352 Possession of coin-operated device breaking instrument

A.B. on .... at .... did without lawful excuse have in his possession an instrument, to wit .... suitable for breaking into a coin-operated device [*or* a currency exchange device] under circumstances [*specify, e.g., mode of concealment, type of instrument*] that gave rise to a reasonable inference that the said instrument had been used [*or* was intended to be used] for breaking into a coin-operated device [*or* a currency exchange device] contrary *etc.*

353(1)(*a*) Automobile master key: selling or advertising

A.B. on .... at .... did sell [*or* offer for sale *or* advertise] in the Province of .... an automobile master key, to wit .... other than under the authority of a licence issued by the Attorney General of that province contrary *etc.*

353(1)(*b*) Automobile master key: buying or possessing

A.B. on .... at .... did purchase [*or* have in his possession] in the Province of .... an automobile master key, to wit .... other than under the authority of a licence issued by the Attorney General of that province contrary *etc.*

353(4) Automobile master key: record of sale

A.B. on .... at .... did, having sold an automobile master key, to wit .... fail to

(*a*) keep a record of the said transaction showing the name [and address] of the purchaser [and the particulars of the licence issued to the purchaser as described in s. 353(1)(*b*) of the *Criminal Code*] contrary *etc.*

and

(*b*) produce at the request of C.D., a peace officer, the record described in s. 353(3)(*a*) of the *Criminal Code* of the said transaction contrary *etc.*

353.1 Tampering with Vehicle Identification Number

A.B. on . . . . at . . . . did without lawful excuse alter [*or remove or obliterate*] a vehicle identification number on a motor vehicle [*specify the vehicle e.g. by licence plate number*] contrary *etc.*

354(1) Possession of property obtained by crime

(*a*) A.B. on .... at .... did have in his possession property [*or* proceeds of property] [*specify item(s)*] of a value [not] exceeding five thousand dollars knowing that all [*or* part] of the property [*or* proceeds of the property] was obtained [*or* derived directly *or* indirectly] by the commission in Canada of an offence punishable by indictment contrary *etc.*

or

(*b*) A.B. on .... at .... did have in his possession property [*or* proceeds of property] [*specify item(s)*] of a value [not] exceeding five thousand dollars knowing that all [*or* part] of the property [*or* proceeds of the property] was obtained [*or* derived directly *or* indirectly] by the commission of the offence of .... in [the State of New York] [*set out method of obtaining that would constitute an indictable offence in Canada*], which offence had it occurred in Canada would have been punishable by indictment, contrary *etc.*

356(1)(*a*) Theft from mail

A.B. on .... at .... did steal

(i) [*specify item, e.g., a letter or parcel*] sent by post, after it was deposited at a post office and before it was delivered contrary *etc.*

or

(ii) a bag [*or* sack *or* container *or* covering] in which mail is conveyed [*or* containing mail] contrary *etc.*

or

(iii) a key suited to a lock adopted for use by the Canada Post Office contrary *etc.*

356(1)(*b*) Theft from mail: possession of article stolen from mail

A.B. on .... at .... did have in his possession [*specify item set out in* s. 356(1)(*a*)] knowing that an offence under section 356(1)(*a*) of the *Criminal Code* had been committed with respect thereto contrary *etc.*

357 Bringing into Canada property obtained by crime

A.B. on .... at .... did bring into [*or* have in] Canada [*specify item, e.g., an automobile*] that he had obtained outside of Canada by an act that if committed in Canada would have been the offence of theft [*or* an offence under s. 354 of the *Criminal Code*] contrary *etc.*

362(1)(*a*) Obtaining by false pretences

A.B. on .... at .... did by a false pretence [with intent to defraud] [*or* through the medium of a contract obtained by false pretence] obtain from C.D. [*specify item obtained, e.g., a car radio*] of a value [not] exceeding five thousand dollars contrary *etc.*

or

A.B. on .... at .... did by a false pretence [with intent to defraud] [*or* through the medium of a contract obtained by false pretence] cause C.D. to deliver to E.F. [*specify item*] of a value [not] exceeding five thousand dollars contrary *etc.*

362(1)(*b*) Obtaining credit by fraud or false pretence

A.B. on .... at .... did by a false pretence [*or* by fraud] obtain credit from C.D. in the amount of .... dollars contrary *etc.*

362(1)(*c*) False statement in writing

A.B. on .... at .... did knowingly make [*or* cause to be made] directly [*or* indirectly] a false statement in writing with intent that it should be relied upon to wit [*specify type of statement, e.g., a statement of assets and liabilities*] respecting his [*or* E.F.'s] financial position for the purpose of procuring from C.D. for his own benefit [*or* for the benefit of E.F.]

(i) the delivery of personal property to wit [*specify, e.g., an automobile*] contrary *etc.*

or

(ii) the payment of money to wit [*specify sum*] contrary *etc.*

or

(iii) the making of a loan [*specify amount*] contrary *etc.*

or

(iv) the grant [*or* extension] of credit to the value of [*specify amount*] [*or specify item referred to in s. 362(1)(c)(v) and (vi)*] contrary *etc.*

363 Obtaining execution of valuable security by fraud

A.B. on .... at .... with intent to defraud [*or* injure] C.D. did by a false pretence, cause [*or* induce] C.D. [*or* E.F.]

(*a*) to execute [*or* make *or* accept *or* endorse *or* destroy the whole (*or* any part of)] a valuable security to wit [*specify, e.g., a promissory note, bond etc.*] contrary *etc.*

or

(*b*) to write [*or* impress *or* affix] a name [*or* seal] on a paper (*or* parchment) to wit [*specify document*] in order that it might afterwards be made into [*or* converted into *or* used *or* dealt with as] a valuable security contrary *etc.*

364 Fraudulently obtaining food and lodging

A.B. on .... at .... did fraudulently obtain food [*or* lodging *or* other accommodation] from C.D. at [*specify restaurant, hotel etc.*] situate at .... contrary *etc.*

367 Forgery

A.B. on .... at .... did knowingly make a false document to wit [*specify, e.g., a cheque dated .... for $100 payable to C.D. and signed E.F.*] with intent that it be acted upon as genuine and did thereby commit forgery contrary *etc.*

or

A.B. on .... at .... did knowingly make a false document to wit [*specify, e.g., a cheque dated .... for $100 payable to C.D. and signed E.F.*] by forging the endorsement of C.D. thereon with intent that it be acted upon as genuine and did thereby commit forgery contrary *etc.*

368(1) Uttering forged document

A.B. on .... at .... did knowingly

(*a*) use [*or* deal with *or* act upon] a forged document to wit [*specify, e.g., a cheque and give particulars thereof*] as if it were genuine contrary *etc.*

or

(*b*) cause [*or* attempt to cause] C.D. to use [*or* deal with *or* act upon] a forged document to wit [*specify, e.g., a cheque and give particulars thereof*] as if it were genuine contrary *etc.*

or

A.B. on .... at .... knowing a [*specify document, e.g., vacation-with-pay stamp book*] in the name of C.D. to be forged did cause E.F. to act upon such book as if it were genuine contrary *etc.*

369(*a*) Exchequer bill or bank note paper

A.B. on .... at .... did make [*or* use *or* knowingly have in his possession]

(i) exchequer bill paper [*or* revenue paper *or* paper that is used to make bank notes] contrary *etc.*

or

(ii) paper that was intended to resemble exchequer bill paper [*or* revenue paper *or* paper that is used to make bank notes] contrary *etc.*

369(*b*) Instruments for forgery

A.B. on .... at .... did make [*or* offer *or* dispose of *or* knowingly have in his possession] a plate [*or* die *or* machinery *or* instrument *or specify other writing or material*] that was adapted and intended to be used to commit forgery contrary *etc.*

372(1) False message

A.B. on .... at .... did with intent to injure [*or* alarm] C.D. convey [*or* cause *or* procure to be conveyed] by letter [*or* telegram *or* telephone *or* cable *or* radio *or otherwise*] to C.D. information that he knew to be false to wit [*specify information*] contrary *etc.*

372(2) Indecent telephone calls

A.B. on .... at .... did with intent to alarm [*or* annoy] C.D. make an indecent telephone call to C.D. contrary *etc.*

372(3) Harassing telephone calls

A.B. on .... at .... did, without lawful excuse and with intent to harass C.D., make [*or* cause to be made] repeated telephone calls, to wit .... to C.D. contrary *etc.*

374 Drawing document without authority

(*a*) A.B. on .... at .... with intent to defraud and without lawful authority did make [*or* execute *or* draw *or* sign *or* accept *or* endorse] a document to wit [*specify*] in the name [*or* on the account] of C.D. contrary *etc.*

(*b*) A.B. on .... at .... did make use of [*or* utter] a document to wit [*specify*] knowing that it had been made [*or* executed *or* signed *or* accepted *or* endorsed] with intent to defraud and without lawful authority, in the name [*or* on the account] of C.D. contrary *etc.*

375 Obtaining, *etc.*, by instrument based on forged document

A.B. on .... at .... did demand [*or* receive *or* obtain] goods [*or specify*] under [*or* on *or* by virtue of] an instrument issued under the authority of law, knowing that the instrument was based on a forged document to wit [*specify document*] contrary *etc.*

or

A.B. on .... at .... did cause [*or* procure] goods [*or specify*] to be delivered [*or* paid] to C.D. under [*or* on *or* by virtue of] an instrument issued under the authority of law, knowing that the instrument was based on a forged document contrary *etc.*

376(1) Counterfeiting stamp

A.B. on .... at .... did

(*a*) fraudulently use [*or* mutilate *or* affix *or* remove *or* counterfeit] a stamp [*or* part of a stamp] to wit [*specify*] contrary *etc.*

or

(*b*) knowingly and without lawful excuse have in his possession a counterfeit stamp [*or* a stamp that has been fraudulently mutilated *or* a document bearing a stamp of which a part has been fraudulently erased (or removed or concealed) *or* without lawful excuse made *or* knowingly had in his possession a die *or* instrument capable of making the impression of a stamp *or* part of a stamp] contrary *etc.*

or

(*c*) without lawful excuse make [*or* knowingly have in his possession] a die [*or* instrument] capable of making the impression of a stamp [*or* a part of a stamp] to wit [*specify*] contrary *etc.*

377(1)(*b*) False entry in official register

A.B. on .... at .... did unlawfully insert in a register of births [*or* baptisms *or* marriages *or* deaths *or* burials] that was required by law to be kept in Canada, an entry that he knew to be false relating to the birth [*or* baptism *or* marriage *or* death *or* burial] of C.D. to wit [*specify entry made*] contrary *etc.*

380(1) Fraud

A.B. on .... at .... did by deceit, falsehood or other fraudulent means defraud C.D. of [*specify property, money or valuable security or service, e.g., the sum of $1,000*] by [*specify fraud*] contrary *etc.*

380(2) Fraud: affecting public market

A.B. on .... at .... did by deceit, falsehood or other means, with intent to defraud, affect the public market price of stocks [*or* shares, merchandise, securities, articles] by [*specify act done, e.g., publishing false reports of the value of mineral rights leased by United Moose Pastures Limited, whose common stock was then traded on the Toronto Stock Exchange*] contrary *etc.*

381 Using mails to defraud

A.B. on .... at .... did make use of the mails for the purpose of transmitting [*or* delivering] letters [*or* circulars] concerning schemes devised [*or* intended] to defraud [*or* for the purpose of obtaining money under false pretences from] the public by [*e.g.*, posting to divers members of the public letters soliciting subscriptions for the common stock of United Moose Pastures Limited] contrary *etc.*

382 Fraudulent manipulation of stock exchange transactions

A.B. and C.D. on .... at .... did through the facility of a stock exchange [*or* curb market *or* over the counter market] with intent to create a false [*or* misleading] appearance of active public trading in [*specify security*] [*or* with intent to create a false (*or* misleading) appearance with respect to the market price of (*specify security*)],

(*a*) effect a transaction in the said security that involved no change in the beneficial ownership thereof contrary *etc.*

or

(*b*) enter an order for the purchase of [*specify security*] knowing that an order of substantially the same size at substantially the same time and at substantially the same price for the sale of the said security had been [would be] entered by [for] the said A.B. and C.D. [*or* other persons] contrary *etc.*

or

(*c*) enter an order for the sale of [*specify security*] knowing that an order of substantially the same size at substantially the same time and at substantially the same price for the purchase of the said security had been [would be] entered by [for] the said A.B. and C.D. [*or* other persons] contrary *etc.*

390(*a*) Fraudulent receipts under *Bank Act*

A.B. on .... at .... did wilfully make a false statement in a receipt [*or* certificate *or* acknowledgement] for property that may be used for a purpose mentioned in the *Bank Act* contrary *etc.*

392 Defrauding creditors

(*a*) **Disposing of property**
A.B. on .... at .... did with intent to defraud his creditors

(i) make [*or* cause to be made] a gift [*or* conveyance *or* assignment *or* sale *or* transfer *or* delivery] of his property to wit [*specify property transferred*] to C.D. contrary *etc.*

or

(ii) remove [*or* conceal *or* dispose of] his property to wit [*specify property concealed etc.*] contrary *etc.*

(*b*) **Receiving property**
A.B. on .... at .... with intent that C.D. should defraud his creditors did receive from C.D. certain property of C.D. to wit [*specify property received*] by means of [*or* in relation to] which an offence under s. 392(*a*) of the *Criminal Code* had been committed contrary *etc.*

393(1) Fraud in relation to fares etc.
A.B. on .... at .... being under the duty to collect a fare [*or* toll *or* ticket *or* admission] did wilfully

(*a*) fail to collect it from C.D. contrary *etc.*

or

(*b*) collect less than the proper amount payable in respect thereof from C.D. contrary *etc.*

or

(*c*) accept a valuable consideration to wit [*specify consideration received*] for failing to collect such fare [*or* for collecting less than the proper amount payable in respect thereof] from C.D. contrary *etc.*

393(3) Obtaining transportation by fraud
A.B. on .... at .... did by a false pretence [*or* fraud] to wit [*specify false pretence or fraud*] obtain transportation by land [*or* water *or* air] to wit [*specify, e.g., by taxi-cab*] to the value of .... dollars from C.D. contrary *etc.*

396(1) Offences in relation to mines

(*a*) A.B. on .... at .... with the fraudulent intent to affect the result of an assay, [*or* test *or* valuation] that has been made [*or* was to be made] with respect to a mine [*or* prospective mine *or* mining claim *or* oil well] to wit [*specify*] did add [*specify e.g. gold ore*] to [*or* remove (*specify*) from] the mine [*or* mining claim *or* oil well] contrary *etc.*

or

(*b*) A.B. on .... at .... did add [*specify e.g. gold ore*] to [*or* remove (*specify*) from *or* tamper with] a sample [*or* material] that was taken [*or* about to be taken] from a mine [*or* prospective mine *or* mining claim *or* oil well] to wit [*specify*] for the purpose of being assayed [*or* tested *or* otherwise valued] with the fraudulent intent to affect the result of the assay [*or* test *or* valuation] contrary *etc.*

397(1) Falsification of books and documents
A.B. on .... at .... with intent to defraud C.D. did

(*a*) destroy [*or* mutilate *or* alter *or* falsify *or* make a false entry in]

or

(*b*) omit a material particular from [*or* alter a material particular in] to wit [*specify item omitted or altered*]

a book [*or* paper *or* writing *or* valuable security *or* document] to wit [*specify book etc.*] contrary *etc.*

398 Falsifying employment record

A.B. on .... at .... with intent to deceive did falsify an employment record to wit [*specify, e.g., company pay sheet*] by [*specify means used*] contrary *etc.*

400(1) False prospectus

A.B. on .... at .... did make [*or* circulate *or* publish] a prospectus [*or* statement *or* account] which he knew was false in a material particular to wit [*specify false particular*] with intent

(*a*) to induce persons to become shareholders or partners in [*specify company*] contrary *etc.*

or

(*b*) to deceive [*or* defraud] the member [*or* shareholders *or* creditors] of [*specify company*] contrary *etc.*

or

(*c*)(i) to induce C.D. to entrust [*or* advance] a sum of money [*or specify*] to [*specify company*] contrary *etc.*

or

(*c*)(ii) to enter into a security for the benefit of [*specify company*] contrary *etc.*

401(1) Obtaining carriage by false billing

A.B. on .... at .... did knowingly, by means of a false [*or* misleading] representation to wit [*specify*], obtain [*or* attempt to obtain] the carriage of [*specify goods*] by [*specify carrier*] into [*specify province, country or district or other place*], the transportation [*or* importation] of those goods into the said province [*or* country *or* district *or as the case may be*] being unlawful contrary *etc.*

402.2(1) Identity Theft

A.B. on . . . . at . . . . did knowingly obtain [*or* possess] C.D.'s identity information [*specify information e.g. American Express credit card number (see definition in s. 402.1)*] in circumstances giving rise to a reasonable inference that the information was intended to be used to commit the indictable offence of [*specify offence e.g. theft of credit cards*] contrary *etc.*

402.2(2) Trafficking in Identity Information

A.B. on . . . . at . . . . did transmit [*or* make available *or* distribute *or* sell *or* offer for sale] C.D.'s identity information [*specify information e.g. American Express credit card number (see definition in s. 402.1)*] knowing that or being reckless as to whether the information would be used to commit the indictable offence of [*specify offence e.g. theft of credit cards*] contrary *etc.*

or

A.B. on . . . . at . . . . did have in his possession for the purpose of transmitting *or* making available *or* distributing *or* selling *or* offering for sale] C.D.'s identity information [*specify information e.g. American Express credit card number (see definition in s. 402.1)*] knowing that or being reckless as to whether the information would be used to commit the indictable offence of [*specify offence e.g. theft of credit cards*] contrary *etc.*

403 Identity Fraud
A.B. on . . . . at . . . . did fraudulently personate C.D.

(*a*) with intent to gain advantage for himself [*or* E.F.] to wit . . . . contrary *etc.*

or

(*b*) with intent to obtain certain [*or* an interest in] property to wit . . . . contrary *etc.*

or

(*c*) with intent to cause disadvantage to C.D. [*or* E.F.] contrary *etc.*

or

(*d*) with intent to avoid arrest [*or* prosecution *or* obstruct, prevent *or* defeat the course of justice] contrary *etc.*

419 Unlawful use of military uniforms or certificates
A.B. on .... at .... without lawful excuse did

(*a*) wear a uniform of the Canadian [*or name other country, e.g., American*] Forces to wit [*specify uniform worn, e.g., the uniform of a Captain in the Canadian (or American) Army*] contrary *etc.*

[*or* wear a uniform so similar to the uniform of the Canadian [*or name other country*] Forces to wit [*specify*] that it was likely to be mistaken therefor contrary *etc.*]

or

(*b*) wear [an imitation of] a distinctive mark relating to wounds received [*or* a military medal *or* ribbon *or* badge *or* chevron *or* decoration *or* order] to wit [*specify item worn, e.g., the Victoria Cross*] contrary *etc.* [*or* wear a mark [*or* device *or* thing] that was likely to be mistaken for [*specify item imitated*] contrary *etc.*

or

(*c*) have in his possession a certificate of discharge [*or* certificate of release *or* statement of service *or* identity card] from the Canadian Forces [*or specify other country*] that was not issued to and did not belong to him contrary *etc.*

422(1) Criminal breach of contract
A.B. on .... at .... wilfully broke a contract with [*or between (specify)*] knowing or having reasonable cause to believe that the probable consequence of doing so would be

(*a*) to endanger human life contrary *etc.*

or

(*b*) to cause serious bodily injury contrary *etc.*

or

(*c*) to expose valuable property to destruction or serious injury contrary *etc.*

or

(*d*) to deprive the inhabitants of the City of [*or specify*] wholly or to a great extent, of their supply of light [*or* power *or* gas *or* water] contrary *etc.*

or

(*e*) to delay or prevent the running of a locomotive engine [*or* tender *or* freight *or* passenger train *or* car] on the [*specify railway which is common carrier*] contrary *etc.*

423(1) Intimidation

A.B. on .... at .... did wrongfully and without lawful authority for the purpose of compelling C.D. to abstain from [*or* to do] [*specify act, e.g., work at the X.Y.Z. Plant*] which C.D. had a lawful right to do [*or* to abstain from doing]

(*a*) use violence [*or* threats of violence] to the person of C.D. [*or* to the wife *or* husband *or* children of C.D.] [*or* did injure his property to wit (*specify property damaged)*] contrary *etc.*

or

(*c*) persistently follow C.D. about from place to place contrary *etc.*

or

(*e*) with E.F. and G.H. follow C.D. in a disorderly manner, on a highway to wit [*specify highway*] contrary *etc.*

423.1 Intimidation of justice system participant or journalist

(*a*) A.B. on .... at .... did without lawful authority, intending to provoke a state of fear in the general public [*or identify group of persons*] and to impede the administration of criminal justice

or

(*b*) A.B. on .... at .... did without lawful authority, intending to provoke a state of fear in C.D. a justice system participant in order to impede him [*or* her] in the performance of his [*or* her] duties

or

(*c*) A.B. on .... at .... did without lawful authority, intending to provoke a state of fear in C.D. a journalist in order to impede him [*or* her] in the transmission to the public of information in relation to a criminal organization [*specify criminal organization*]

(a) use violence against [*or* destroy the property of *or* cause damage to the property of] C.D. a justice system participant [*or* a journalist] contrary *etc.*

or

use violence against [*or* destroy the property of *or* cause damage to the property of] E.F. a person known to C.D. a justice system participant [*or* a journalist] contrary *etc.*

or

(b) threaten to use violence against [*or* destroy the property of *or* cause damage to the property of] C.D. a justice system participant [*or* a journalist] contrary *etc.*

or

threaten to use violence against [*or* destroy the property of *or* cause damage to the property of] E.F. a person known to C.D. a justice system participant [*or* a journalist] contrary *etc.*

or

(c) persistently [*or* repeatedly] followed C.D. a justice system participant [*or* a journalist] from place to place [*or* in a disorderly manner on a highway to wit *specify highway*] contrary *etc.*

or

persistently [*or* repeatedly] followed E.F. a person known to C.D. a justice system participant [*or* a journalist] from place to place [*or* in a disorderly manner on a highway to wit *specify highway*] contrary *etc.*

or

(d) repeatedly communicated directly or indirectly with C.D. a justice system participant [*or* a journalist] contrary *etc.*

or

repeatedly communicated with E.F. a person known to C.D. a justice system participant [*or* a journalist] contrary *etc.*

or

(e) beset [*or* watched] [*specify place*] where C.D. a justice system participant [*or* a journalist] resides [*or* works *or* attends school *or* carries on business *or* happened to be] contrary *etc.*

or

beset [*or* watched] [*specify place*] where E.F. a person known to C.D. a justice system participant [*or* a journalist] resides [*or* works *or* attends school *or* carries on business *or* happened to be] contrary *etc.*

424 Threat to commit offence against internationally protected person

A.B. on .... at .... did threaten to commit the offence of murder contrary to s. 235 [*or specify offence contrary to s. 266, 267, 268, 269, 269.1, 271, 272, 273, 279 or 279.1*] of the *Criminal Code* against C.D. an internationally protected person contrary *etc.*

or

A.B. on .... at .... did threaten to commit the offence contrary to s. 431 of the Criminal Code by threatening to attack the official premises [*or* private accommodation *or* means of transport] of C.D. an internationally protected person, such attack being likely to endanger the life or liberty of C.D. contrary *etc.*

426(1)(*a*) Bribery of agent

A.B. on .... at .... did corruptly

give [*or* offer *or* agree to give *or* offer] to C.D. an agent for X.Y.

or

being an agent for X.Y. demand [*or* accept *or* offer *or* agree to accept] from C.D.

a reward [*or* advantage *or* benefit] to wit [*specify, e.g., the sum of one hundred dollars*] as consideration for doing [*or* forbearing to do *or* for having done *or* forborne to do] an act relating to the affairs *or* business of X.Y. to wit [*specify act done or to be done or as care may be*] contrary *etc.*

or

a reward [*or* advantage *or* benefit] to wit [*specify, e.g., the sum of one hundred dollars*] for showing [*or* forbearing to show] favour [*or* disfavour] to A.B. [*or* C.D.] with relation to the affairs [*or* business] of X.Y. contrary *etc.*

426(1)(*b*) False account to deceive a principal

A.B. on .... at .... with intent to deceive X.Y. did give to C.D., an agent for X.Y. [*or* A.B., being an agent for X.Y. did use with intent to deceive X.Y.] a receipt [*or* account *or* other writing] to wit [*specify document*] in which X.Y. had an interest that contained a false [*or* erroneous *or* defective] statement in a material particular that was intended to mislead X.Y. to wit [*specify incorrect statement in document*] contrary *etc.*

430(2) Mischief endangering life

A.B. on .... at .... did commit mischief by wilfully damaging without legal justification or excuse and without colour of right the [*specify property damaged, e.g., the dwelling house of C.D. situate at ....*] by [*specify means used, e.g., planting an explosive*] and did thereby endanger the life of C.D. contrary *etc.*

430(3) Mischief over $5,000: to testamentary instrument

A.B. on .... at .... did commit mischief by wilfully .... [*specify act of mischief as described in subsec. (1), e.g., damaging*] without legal justification or excuse and without colour of right property to wit

[*specify property damaged etc., e.g., the automobile*] of C.D. the value of which exceeded five thousand dollars contrary *etc.*

or

[*specify testamentary document, e.g., the codicil dated January 1st, 1986 to the last will and testament*] of C.D.

430(4) Mischief not exceeding $5,000

A.B. on .... at .... did commit mischief by wilfully .... [*specify act of mischief as described in subsec. (1), e.g., damaging*] without legal justification or excuse and without colour of right property to wit [*specify property damaged etc., e.g., the bicycle*] of C.D. the value of which did not exceed five thousand dollars contrary *etc.*

430(4.1) Mischief relating to religious property

A.B. on .... at .... did commit mischief by wilfully .... and for reasons of bias, prejudice or hate based on religion [*or* race *or* colour *or* national *or* ethnic origin] [specify act of mischief as described in subsec. (1), e.g., damaging] without legal justification or excuse and without colour of right property that is primarily used for religious worship to wit [*specify church, mosque, synagogue or temple or object associated with religious worship located in or on the grounds of such building or cemetery*] the value of which did not exceed five thousand dollars contrary etc.

430(5) Mischief to data

A.B. on .... at .... did commit mischief in relation to data by wilfully without legal justification or excuse and without colour of right [*specify act of mischief as described in subsec. (1.1), e.g., destroying or rendering meaningless, useless or ineffective*] data to wit [*specify data*] contrary *etc.*

431 Attack on premises, residence or transport of internationally protected person

A.B. on .... at .... did attack the official premises [*or* private accommodation *or* means of transport] of C.D. an internationally protected person, in manner likely to endanger the life or liberty of C.D. contrary *etc.*

433 Arson: disregard for human life

(*a*) A.B. on .... at .... did intentionally or recklessly cause damage by fire [*or* explosion] to [*specify property damaged, e.g., a dwelling house*] situate at .... knowing that or being reckless with respect whether the said property was inhabited or occupied contrary *etc.*

or

(*b*) A.B. on .... at .... did intentionally or recklessly cause damage by fire [*or* explosion] to [*specify property damaged, e.g., a dwelling house*] situate at .... which fire [*or* explosion] did cause bodily harm to C.D. contrary *etc.*

434 Arson: damage to property

A.B. on .... at .... did intentionally or recklessly cause damage by fire [*or* explosion] to [*specify property damaged, e.g., a dwelling house*] the property of C.D. situate at .... contrary *etc.*

434.1 Arson: damage to own property

A.B. on .... at .... did intentionally or recklessly cause damage by fire [*or* explosion] to [*specify property damaged, e.g., a dwelling house*] owned by the said A.B. situate at .... which fire [*or* explosion] seriously threatened the health [*or* safety, *or* property situate at ....] of C.D. contrary *etc.*

435(1) Arson for fraudulent purpose

A.B. on .... at .... did with intent to defraud C.D. cause damage by fire [*or* explosion] to [*specify property damaged, e.g., a dwelling house*] the property of C.D. situate at .... contrary *etc.*

436(1) Arson by negligence

A.B. on .... at .... did as a result of a marked departure from the standard of care that a reasonably prudent person would use to prevent or control the spread of fires [*or* to prevent explosions] cause a fire [*or* explosion] in [*specify property damaged, e.g., a dwelling house*] owned [*or* controlled] by the said A.B. situate at .... which fire [*or* explosion] did cause bodily harm to [*or* damage the property of] C.D. contrary *etc.*

436.1 Possession of incendiary material

A.B. on .... at .... did possess an incendiary material [*or* incendiary device *or* explosive substance] to wit [*specify material, device or substance*] for the purpose of committing the offence of [*specify an offence contrary to s. 433 to 436, e.g., arson contrary to s. 433(a)*] contrary *etc.*

437 False alarm of fire

A.B. on .... at .... did wilfully without reasonable cause by outcry [*or* ringing bells *or* using a fire alarm *or* telephone *or* telegraph *or specify other means used*] make [*or* circulate *or* cause to be made *or* circulated] an alarm of fire at [*specify premises where fire purported to be*] contrary *etc.*

or

A.B. on .... at .... did wilfully without reasonable cause make an alarm of fire by using a fire alarm signal box on .... Street contrary *etc.*

445 Killing or injuring animals

A.B. on .... at .... did wilfully and without lawful cause

(*a*) kill [*or* maim *or* wound *or* poison *or* injure] [*specify bird or animal, e.g., a dog*] the property of C.D. that was kept for a lawful purpose contrary *etc.*

or

(*b*) place poison in such a position that it might easily be consumed by dogs, birds, or animals that were kept for a lawful purpose to wit [*specify where poison placed, e.g., at the base of a tree on the front lawn of the premises situate at* ....] contrary *etc.*

445.1 Cruelty to animals

A.B. on .... at ....

(*a*) did wilfully cause [*or* being the owner did wilfully permit to be caused] unnecesssary pain [*or* suffering *or* injury] to [*specify animal or bird*] by [*specify means used*] contrary *etc.*

(*b*) did encourage, aid or assist at the fighting [*or* baiting] of [*specify animals or birds*] contrary *etc.*

(*c*) did willfully and without reasonable excuse administer a poisonous [*or* injurious] drug [*or* substance] to wit .... to a domestic animal [*or* bird *or* an animal or bird wild by nature that is kept in captivity] to wit .... contrary *etc.*

or

did being the owner of a domestic animal [*or* bird *or* an animal or bird wild by nature that is kept in captivity] to wit .... willfully permit a poisonous [*or* injurious] drug [*or* substance] to wit .... to be administered to it, contrary *etc.*

(*d*) did promote [*or* arrange, *or* conduct *or* assist in *or* receive money for *or* take part in] a meeting [*or* competition *or* exhibition *or* pastime *or* practice *or* display *or* event] at [*or* in the course of] which captive birds were liberated by [*here specify means e.g. by hand*] for the purpose of being shot when they were liberated contrary *etc.*

(*e*) being the owner [*or* occupier *or* person in charge] of [*specify premises*] permitted those premises to be used for the purpose of promoting [*or* arranging, *or* conducting *or* assisting in *or* receiving money for *or* taking part in] a meeting [*or* competition *or* exhibition *or* pastime *or* practice *or* display *or* event] at [*or* in the course of] which captive bird were liberated by [*herer specify means e.g. by hand*] for the purpose of being shot when they were liberated contrary *etc.*

446 Causing damage or injury to animals or birds

A.B. on .... at ....

(*a*) by willful neglect did cause damage [*or* injury] to [*specify animals or birds*] while they were being driven [*or* conveyed] by A.B. to wit by [*specify neglect, e.g., failure to water them*] contrary *etc.*

(*b*) being the owner [*or* the person having the custody *or* control] of a domestic animal [*or* bird *or* an animal *or* bird wild by nature that was in capativity] to wit [*specify, e.g., a dog*] did willfully neglect [*or* fail] to provide suitable and adequate food [*or* water *or* shelter *or* care] for such [*specify animal or bird*] contrary *etc.*

447.1 Animals: breach of order prohibiting keeping

A.B. on .... at .... did, while prohibited from doing so by an order made under s. 447.1(1)(a) of the *Criminal Code*, own [*or* have the custody of *or* have control of *or* reside in the same premises as] an animal [*or* bird] to wit .... contrary *etc.*

449 Counterfeit money: making

A.B. on .... at .... did [*or* did begin to] make counterfeit money to wit [*specify, e.g., a counterfeit ten dollar Bank of Canada bill*] contrary *etc.*

450 Counterfeit money: buying, receiving, possessing or importing

A.B. on .... at .... without lawful justification or excuse did

(*a*) buy [*or* receive *or* offer to buy *or* receive] from C.D.

or

(*b*) have in his custody [*or* possession]

or

(*c*) introduce into Canada

counterfeit money to wit: [*specify coin or paper*] contrary *etc.*

452 Counterfeit money: uttering, using and exporting

A.B. on .... at .... without lawful justification or excuse did

(*a*) utter [*or* offer to utter *or* use] counterfeit money to wit [*specify, e.g., a counterfeit ten dollar Bank of Canada bill*] as if it were genuine contrary *etc.*

or

(*b*) export [*or* send *or* take] counterfeit money to wit [*specify, e.g., counterfeit ten dollar Bank of Canada bills*] out of Canada contrary *etc.*

453(*a*) Coin not current: uttering

A.B. on .... at .... with intent to defraud C.D. did knowingly utter a coin that was not current contrary *etc.*

453(*b*) Counterfeit coin: uttering

A.B. on .... at .... with intent to defraud C.D. did knowingly utter a piece of metal [*or* mixed metals] that resembled in size, figure and colour a current gold [*or* silver] coin but of less value than the current coin for which it was uttered to wit [*specify, e.g., a current twenty-five cent piece*] contrary *etc.*

454 Fraudulent use of slugs

A.B. on .... at .... did

(*a*) manufacture [*or* produce *or* sell]

or

(*b*) have in his possession

a [*specify article*] that was intended to be fraudulently used in substitution for a coin [*or* token of value] that any coin- [*or* token-] operated device is designed to receive contrary *etc.*

456 Defacing current coin

A.B. on .... at .... did

(*a*) deface [*specify*], a current coin contrary *etc.*

or

(*b*) utter [*specify*], a current coin that had been defaced contrary *etc.*

457 Printing circulars etc. in likeness of notes

(1) A.B. on .... at .... did design [*or* engrave *or* print *or* make *or* execute *or* issue *or* distribute *or* circulate *or* use] a business [*or* professional] card [*or* notice *or* placard *or* circular *or* handbill *or* advertisement] in the likeness [*or* appearance] of [*specify*]

(*a*) a current bank-note [*or* paper money] contrary *etc.*

or

(*b*) an obligation [*or* security] of the Government of [*specify*] [*or the Bank of (specify)*] contrary *etc.*

(2) A.B. on .... at .... did publish [*or* print] [*specify*] in the likeness [*or* appearance] of [*specify*] being

(*a*) a current bank-note [*or* paper money] contrary *etc.*

or

(*b*) an obligation [*or* security] of the Government of [*specify*] [*or the Bank of (specify)*] contrary *etc.*

458 Counterfeiting: instruments for

A.B. on .... at .... without lawful justification or excuse did

(*a*) make [*or* repair]

or

(*b*) begin [*or* proceed] to make [*or* repair]

or

(*c*) buy [*or* sell]

or

(*d*) have in his custody [*or* possession]

a machine [*or* engine *or* tool *or* instrument *or* material *or* thing] that he knew had been used [*or* had been adapted and intended for use] in making counterfeit money [*or* counterfeit tokens of value] contrary *etc.*

462.2 Promoting illicit drug use
A.B. on .... at .... did knowingly

(*a*) import into Canada [*or* export from Canada *or* manufacture *or* promote *or* sell] an instrument to wit [*specify instrument*] which instrument was designed primarily [*or* intended] under the circumstances for consuming [*or* facilitating the consumption of] an illicit drug to wit [*specify illicit drug*] contrary *etc.*

or

(*b*) import into Canada [*or* export from Canada *or* manufacture *or* promote *or* sell] literature to wit [*specify literature*] which literature describes [*or* depicts] the production [*or* preparation *or* consumption] of an illicit drug and is designed primarily [*or* intended] under the circumstances to promote [*or* encourage *or* advocate] the production [*or* preparation *or* consumption of] an illicit drug to wit [*specify illicit drug*] contrary *etc.*

462.31(1) Laundering proceeds of crime
(1) A.B. on .... at .... did use [*or* transfer the possession of *or* transport *or* transmit *or* dispose of *or* otherwise deal with] property [*or* proceeds of any property] to wit [*specify property*] with intent to conceal or convert that property [*or* those proceeds] knowing or believing that all [*or* part] of the property [*or* proceeds of the property] was obtained [*or* derived directly or indirectly] as a result of

(*a*) the commission in Canada of the designated offence of [*specify designated offence*] contrary *etc.*

or

(*b*) an act [*or* omission] in [*specify place e.g. State of New York*] namely [*specify act or omission e.g. uttering counterfeit money which would constitute designated offence if committed in Canada*] which offence had it occurred in Canada would have constituted the designated offence of [*specify designated offence*], contrary *etc.*

or

(2) A.B. on .... at .... did send [*or* deliver] to [*specify person or place*] property [*or* proceeds of any property] to wit [*specify property*] with intent to conceal or convert that property [*or* those proceeds] knowing or believing that all [*or* part] of the property [*or* proceeds of the property] was obtained [*or* derived directly or indirectly] as a result of

(*a*) the commission in Canada of the designated offence of [*specify designated offence*] contrary *etc.*

or

(*b*) an act [*or* omission] in [*specify place e.g. State of New York*] namely [*specify act or omission e.g. uttering counterfeit money which would constitute designated offence if committed in Canada*] which offence had it occurred in Canada would have constituted the designated offence of [*specify designated offence*], contrary *etc.*

464 Counselling offence that is not committed: indictable and summary

(*a*) **Indictable offence**
A.B. on .... at .... did counsel C.D. to commit the indictable offence .... which offence was not committed contrary *etc.*

(*b*) **Summary offence**
A.B. on .... at .... did counsel C.D. to commit an offence punishable on summary conviction to wit [*specify offence, e.g., pretend to use witchcraft*] which offence was not committed contrary *etc.*

465(1)(*a*) Conspiracy to murder
A.B. and C.D. on .... at .... did conspire together to murder E.F. [*or* to cause E.F. to be murdered] contrary *etc.*

465(1)(*c*) Conspiracy to commit indictable offence
A.B. and C.D. on .... at .... did conspire together to commit the indictable offence of .... by [*state sufficient particulars to enable accused to identify the agreement and know nature of charge he has to meet*] contrary *etc.*

465(1)(*d*) Conspiracy to commit summary conviction offence
A.B. and C.D. on .... at .... did conspire together to commit the summary conviction offence of .... by [*state sufficient particulars to enable accused to identify the agreement and know nature of charge they have to meet*] contrary *etc.*

467.11(1) Participation in criminal organization
A.B. on .... at .... did participate in [*or* contribute to] the activities of a criminal organization to wit [*here specify organization*] for the purpose of enhancing the ability of the said organization to facilitate [*or* commit] the indictable offence of [*here specify offence under Criminal Code or other Federal legislation*] contrary *etc.*

467.12(1) Commission of offence for criminal organization
A.B. on .... at .... did commit the indictable offence of [*specify indictable offence*] for the benefit of [*or* at the direction of *or* in association with] a criminal organization to wit [*here specify organization*] [here specify offence] contrary *etc.*

467.13(1) Instructing commission of offence for criminal organization
A.B. being one of the persons constituting the criminal organization of [*here specify organization*] on .... at .... did knowingly directly or indirectly instruct a person [*here specify the person if known*] to commit the indictable offence of [*here specify offence*] for the benefit of [*or* at the direction of *or* in association with] the said criminal organization to wit contrary *etc.*

733.1(1) Probation order: non-compliance
A.B. on [*or* between] .... at .... did, while bound by a probation order made by [*insert full title of the court making the order*] .... on [*insert date of order*]..............., fail [*or* refuse] without reasonable excuse to comply with such order, to wit [*here recite the non-complied with condition of the order*] .... contrary *etc.*

810(1) Fear of injury or damage by another person
A.B. fears that X.Y. will cause personal injury to him [*or* to his spouse *or* to his children] in that X.Y. did on .... at .... utter the words [*specify, e.g., "I will kill you"*] contrary *etc.*

or

A.B. fears that X.Y. will cause personal injury to his property [*specify, e.g., dwelling house situate at 4 Main Street*] in that X.Y. did on .... at .... utter the words [*specify, e.g., "I will burn your house down"*] contrary *etc.*

810.01 Where fear of criminal organization offence
A.B. fears that X.Y. will commit the offence of .... contrary to s. 423.1 [*or specify criminal organization offence or terrorism offence as defined in s. 2*]

810.1 Where fear of sexual offence
A.B. fears that X.Y. will commit an offence under section 151 [*or* 152 *or* 155 *or* 159 *or* 160(2) *or* (3) *or* 170 *or* 171 *or* 173(2) *or* 271 *or* 272 *or* 273] of the *Criminal Code* in respect of C.D. a person under the age of fourteen years in that X.Y. did on .... at .... [*specify grounds for fear*]

FORMS OF CHARGES UNDER THE *CONTROLLED DRUGS AND SUBSTANCES ACT*

4(1) Possession of substance included in Schedule I, II or III

A.B. on .... at .... did unlawfully possess a substance included in Schedule I [*or* II *or* III] to wit . . . . . [*specify substance*] contrary to s. 4 of the *Controlled Drugs and Substances Act.*

4(2) Seeking or obtaining substance or authorization to obtain substance included in Schedule I, II, III or IV from practitioner

A.B. on .... at .... did seek [*or* obtain] a substance [*or* an authorization to obtain a substance] included in Schedule I [*or* II *or* III *or* IV] to wit . . . . . [*specify substance*] from Dr. C.D. a practitioner without disclosing to the said practitioner particulars relating to the acquisition within the preceding thirty days by A.B. from another practitioner Dr. E.F. of a substance in Schedule I, [*or* II, III and IV *or* every authorization to obtain such substances] namely [*here specify particulars not disclosed to practitioner*] contrary to s. 4 of the *Controlled Drugs and Substances Act.*

5(1) Trafficking

A.B. on .... at .... did traffic in a substance

included in Schedule I [*or* II *or* III *or* IV *or* V] to wit .... [*specify substance*] contrary to s. 5 of the *Controlled Drugs and Substances Act.*

or

represented [*or* held out to be] a substance included in Schedule I [*or* II *or* III *or* IV *or* V] to wit .... [*specify substance*] contrary to s. 5 of the *Controlled Drugs and Substances Act.*

5(2) Possession for the purpose of trafficking

A.B. on .... at .... did possess a substance included in Schedule I [*or* II *or* III *or* IV *or* V] to wit .... [*specify substance*] for the purpose of trafficking contrary to s. 5 of the *Controlled Drugs and Substances Act.*

6(1) Importing and exporting

A.B. on .... at .... did unlawfully import into [*or* export from] Canada a substance included in Schedule I [*or* II *or* III *or* IV *or* V *or* VI] to wit .... [*specify substance*] contrary to s. 6 of the *Controlled Drugs and Substances Act.*

6(2) Possession for the purpose of exporting

A.B. on .... at .... did unlawfully possess a substance included in Schedule I [*or* II *or* III *or* IV *or* V *or* VI] to wit .... [*specify substance*] for the purpose of exporting it from Canada contrary to s. 6 of the *Controlled Drugs and Substances Act.*

7 Production of substance

A.B. on .... at .... did unlawfully produce a substance included in Schedule I [*or* II *or* III *or* IV *or* V] to wit .... [*specify substance*] contrary to s. 7 of the *Controlled Drugs and Substances Act.*

NOTES

NOTES

NOTES

NOTES

NOTES

NOTES

NOTES

NOTES